Brian Fleming
Ministry of Education
Ministry of Training, Colleges & Universities
900 Bay St. 13th Floor, Mowat Block
Toronto, ON M7A 1L2

Associations Canada

Associations du Canada

Additional Publications

For more detailed information or to place an order, see the back of the book.

CANADIAN ALMANAC & DIRECTORY 2018
Répetoire et almanach canadien
2,496 pages, 8 ½ x 11, Hardcover
171st edition, December 2017
ISBN 978-1-68217-469-2
ISSN 0068-8193

A combination of textual material, charts, colour photographs and directory listings, the *Canadian Almanac & Directory* provides the most comprehensive picture of Canada, from physical attributes to economic and business summaries to leisure and recreation.

CANADIAN WHO'S WHO 2018
1,184 pages, 8 3/8 x 10 7/8, Hardcover
December 2017
ISBN 978-1-68217-532-3
ISSN 0068-9963

Published for over 100 years, this authoritative annual publication offers access to the top 10,000 notable Canadians in all walks of life, including details such as date and place of birth, education, family details, career information, memberships, creative works, honours, languages, and awards, together with full addresses. Included are outstanding Canadians from business, academia, politics, sports, the arts and sciences, and more, selected because of the positions they hold in Canadian society, or because of the contributions they have made to Canada.

FINANCIAL POST DIRECTORY OF DIRECTORS 2018
Répertoire des administrateurs
1,385 pages, 5 7/8 x 9, Hardcover
71st edition, September 2017
ISBN 978-1-68217-534-7
ISSN 0071-5042

Published biennially and annually since 1931, this comprehensive resource offers readers access to approximately 16,200 executive contacts from Canada's top 1,400 corporations. The directory provides a definitive list of directorships and offices held by noteworthy Canadian business people, as well as details on prominent Canadian companies (both public and private), including company name, contact information and the names of executive officers and directors. Includes all-new front matter and three indexes.

GOVERNMENTS CANADA 2018
Gouvernements du Canada
1,300 pages, 8 ½ x 11, Softcover
11th edition, December 2017
ISBN 978-1-68217-241-4
ISSN 1493-3918

Governments Canada provides a solution to finding the departments and people that you are searching for within our federal and provincial political system.

CANADIAN PARLIAMENTARY GUIDE 2017
Guide parlementaire canadien
1,332 pages, 6 x 9, Hardcover
151st edition, March 2017
ISBN 978-1-68217-524-8
ISSN 0315-6168

Published annually since before Confederation, this indispensable guide to government in Canada provides information on federal and provincial governments, with biographical sketches of government members, descriptions of government institutions, and historical text and charts. With significant bilingual sections, the Guide covers elections from Confederation to the present, including the most recent provincial elections.

FINANCIAL SERVICES CANADA 2017-2018
Services financiers au Canada
1,464 pages, 8 ½ x 11, Softcover
20th edition, April 2017
ISBN 978-1-68217-520-0
ISSN 1484-2408

This directory of Canadian financial institutions and organizations includes banks and depository institutions, non-depository institutions, investment management firms, financial planners, insurance companies, accountants, major law firms, major corporations, associations, and financial technology companies. Fully indexed.

HEALTH GUIDE CANADA 2017-2018
Guide canadien de la santé
1,120 pages, 8 ½ x 11, Softcover
3rd edition, May 2017
ISBN: 978-1-68217-530-9

Health Guide Canada contains thousands of ways to deal with the many aspects of chronic or mental health disorders. It includes associations, government agencies, libraries and resource centres, educational facilities, hospitals and publications, as well as disease descriptions, relevant reports, and statistics.

CANADIAN ENVIRONMENTAL RESOURCE GUIDE 2017-2018
Guide des ressources environnementales canadiennes
946 pages, 8 ½ x 11, Softcover
22nd edition, June 2017
ISBN 978-1-68217-471-5
ISSN 1920-2725

Canada's most complete national listing of environmental organizations, product and service companies and governmental bodies, all indexed and categorized for quick and easy reference. Also included is the Environmental Update, with recent events, maps, rankings, statistics, and trade shows and conferences. The online version features even more content, including associations, special libraries, and federal/provincial government information.

LIBRARIES CANADA 2017-2018
Bibliothèques Canada
894 pages, 8 ½ x 11, Softcover
32nd edition, August 2017
ISBN 978-1-68217-522-4
ISSN 1920-2849

Libraries Canada offers comprehensive information on Canadian libraries, resource centres, business information centres, professional associations, regional library systems, archives, library schools, government libraries, and library technical programs.

MAJOR CANADIAN CITIES: COMPARED & RANKED
Comparaison et classement des principales villes canadiennes
816 pages, 8 ½ x 11, Softcover
1st edition, November 2013
ISBN 978-1-61925-260-8

Major Canadian Cities: Compared & Ranked provides an in-depth comparison and analysis of the 50 most populated cities in Canada. Following the city chapters are ranking tables that compare the demographics, economics, education, religion and infrastructure of the cities listed.

2018
39th Edition

Associations Canada

Associations du Canada

Grey House Publishing Canada
PUBLISHER: Leslie Mackenzie
GENERAL MANAGER: Bryon Moore
MANAGING EDITOR: Stuart Paterson
ASSOCIATE EDITORS: Kathlyn Del Castillo, Laura Lamanna, Samanda Stroud

Grey House Publishing
EDITORIAL DIRECTOR: Laura Mars
MARKETING DIRECTOR: Jessica Moody
PRODUCTION MANAGER & COMPOSITION: Kristen Hayes

Grey House Publishing Canada
555 Richmond Street West, Suite 512
Toronto, ON M5V 3B1
866-433-4739
FAX 416-644-1904
www.greyhouse.ca
e-mail: info@greyhouse.ca

Grey House Publishing Canada is a wholly owned subsidiary of Grey House Publishing, Inc. USA.

While every effort has been made to ensure the reliability of the information presented in this publication, Grey House Publishing Canada, Inc., neither guarantees the accuracy of the data contained herein nor assumes any responsibility for errors, omissions or discrepancies. Grey House Publishing Canada, Inc., accepts no payment for listing; inclusion in the publication of any organization, agency, institution, publication, service or individual does not imply endorsement of the editors or publisher.

Errors brought to the attention of the publisher and verified to the satisfaction of the publisher will be corrected in future editions.

Except by express prior written permission of the Copyright Proprietor no part of this work may be copied by any means of publication or communication now known or developed hereafter including, but not limited to, use in any directory or compilation or other print publication, in any information storage and retrieval system, in any other electronic device, or in any visual or audio-visual device or product.

This publication is an original and creative work, copyrighted by Grey House Publishing Canada, Inc., and is fully protected by all applicable copyright laws, as well as by laws covering misappropriation, trade secrets and unfair competition.

Grey House Publishing Canada, Inc. has added value to the underlying factual material through one or more of the following efforts: unique and original selection; expression; arrangement; coordination; and classification. Grey House Publishing Canada, Inc., will defend its rights in this publication.

Copyright © 2018 Grey House Publishing Canada
All rights reserved

Printed in Canada by Webcom, Inc.

ISSN: 1186-9798

ISBN: 978-1-68217-826-3

Cataloguing in Publication Data is available from Libraries and Archives Canada.

Table of Contents

Introduction — vii
Including how to use the directory, sample entry, abbreviations and translations

Canadian Associations at a Glance — xvi
An outline of the number of associations listed, by type

Associations — xix
The history of associations

Protect Your Organization From Bad Employees — xxiii
Three steps to avoiding 'bad' employees through defining an organization's Core Values

One Step at a Time — xxix
A look at how to successfully merge two associations

The Power of "Old School" Service — xxxvii
Four reasons why associations should maintain engaging, personal service with members

Subject Index — SI1 - 94
Listing of Canadian and foreign association headquarters, alphabetical by subject and keyword

Canadian Associations — 1
Alphabetical listing of all Canadian association entries, including branches, chapters, divisions and offices

Foreign Associations — 1483
Alphabetical listing of foreign associations with affiliations in Canada, Canadian members, or which are of interest to Canadians

Acronym Index — 1611
Alphabetical listing of acronyms and corresponding Canadian and foreign associations, in both official languages

Budget Index — 1657
Listing of Canadian and foreign associations, alphabetical within eight budget categories

Conferences & Conventions Index — 1673
Listing of meetings sponsored by Canadian and foreign associations, alphabetical by conference name for 2018 through 2023

Executive Name Index — 1763
Alphabetical listing of key contacts of Canadian and foreign associations, for both headquarters and branches, including page numbers for corresponding listings in the Canadian and foreign associations sections.

Geographic Index — 1911
Listing of headquarters, branch offices, chapters and divisions of Canadian associations, alphabetical within province and city

Mailing List Index — 1999
Listing of associations that offer mailing lists, alphabetical by subject

Registered Charitable Organizations Index — 2005
Listing of associations that are registered charities, alphabetical by subject

Introduction

This 2018 edition of *Associations Canada* published by Grey House Publishing Canada includes over 20,000 associations, both those that are headquartered in Canada, as well as those headquartered elsewhere with branches in Canada. The Canadian associations are followed by a separate section of Foreign Associations that are of a particular interest to Canadians.

Content

Associations Canada has been a valued reference tool for over three decades, providing the most comprehensive picture of Canada's non-profit sector. This 2018 Grey House Canada edition is no exception. The Canadian organizations and international groups in this edition represent industry, commercial and professional associations, registered charities, and special and common interest organizations. This 39th annual edition includes updates or verification of all major associations, as well as all meetings and conferences. Included are over 12,000 awards and publications, and close to 35,000 executive contacts.

Each listing presents a detailed association profile, including budget, founding date, scope of activity, licensing body, sources of funding, executive information, full address and complete contact information.

Eight indexes offer a variety of ways to search not only for specific associations, but also for specific categories of associations. In addition to association listings, you'll find several valuable articles following this Introduction, including:

- **Associations**, with historical background, types and organization information.
- **Protect Your Organization From Bad Employees**
- **One Step at a Time**
- **The Power of "Old School" Service**

Arrangement

Accessing the factual information contained in the more than 2,000 pages of *Associations Canada* is facilitated by the following organization:

- **Location of Indexes:** The Subject Index in the front of the book is designed to help users quickly find a listing, or group of listings, by subject. The remaining seven indexes are in alphabetical order in the back of the book: *Acronyms; Budget; Conferences & Conventions; Executive Name; Geographic; Mailing List;* and *Registered Charitable Organizations*.
- **Arrangement of Data:** Each profile has boldfaced category headers to help users quickly identify categories of information: *Previous Name; Overview; Chief Officers; Finances; Staff; Membership; Activities; Publications;* and *Mission*.

Available in print, by subscription, and online via Grey House Publishing Canada at www.greyhouse.ca, *Associations Canada* is widely used as a valuable resource of prospects for sales and marketing executives, tourism and convention officials, researchers, government officials—anyone who wants to locate non-profit interest groups and trade associations. To facilitate its use throughout Canada, a significant number of listings appear in French. Some elements, such as select front matter material is offered in both French and English.

We acknowledge the valuable contribution of those individuals and organizations who have responded to our information gathering process throughout the year; your help and timely responses to our questionnaires is greatly appreciated.

Every effort has been made to ensure the accuracy of the information included in this edition of *Associations Canada*. Do not hesitate to contact us if revisions are necessary.

Cette édition 2018 des *Associations du Canada*, publiée par Grey House Publishing Canada, comprend plus de 20 000 associations, dont celles ayant leur siège social au Canada et celles qui, bien qu'ayant leur siège social à l'étranger, ont des succursales ou des divisions au Canada. On y dresse également le profil d'associations étrangères d'un intérêt particulier pour les Canadiens.

Contenu

Associations du Canada, un ouvrage de référence utile et pratique publié depuis plus de trente ans, fournit un tableau complet et actuel du secteur sans but lucratif au Canada. L'édition 2018 de Grey House Canada ne fait pas exception. Les organismes canadiens et internationaux regroupés dans cette édition comprend des associations industrielles, commerciales et professionnelles, des organismes de bienfaisance enregistrés et des organisations d'intérêt public ou particulier. Cette 39e édition annuelle comprend des mises à jour de toutes les associations principales ou la vérification de leurs données, de même que toutes les rencontres et conférences qu'elles offrent. Elle compte plus de 12 000 prix et publications ainsi que les coordonnées de 35 000 dirigeants.

Chaque entrée présente un profil détaillé d'une association avec son budget, sa date de création, ses champs d'activités, l'autorité constituante, ses sources de financement, des renseignements sur ses dirigeants, son adresse et ses coordonnées de contact.

Huit index permettent de rechercher de différentes façons autant une association particulière qu'une catégorie spécifique d'association.

Outre à l'information factuelle des *Associations du Canada*, vous trouverez la présence de quelques articles à la suite de l'Introduction:

- **Associations**, y compris un aperçu historique, les types et l'information relative à l'organisation.
- **Protégez votre organization contre les mauvais employés**
- **Une etape à la fois**
- **La puissance du service « à l'ancienne »**

Présentation

Outre les modifications apportées à l'information factuelle des *Associations du Canada*, nous avons procédé à des changements importants qui faciliteront la recherche de renseignements contenus dans plus de 2 000 pages:

- **Emplacement des index** : L'index sujet situé au début de l'édition a été conçu pour aider l'utilisateur à trouver plus rapidement une entrée ou un groupe d'entrées classées par sujet. Les autres sept index sont maintenant situés à la fin de l'édition et présentés par ordre alphabétique dans cette suite : *Acronyms; Budget; Conferences & Conventions; Executive Name; Geographic; Mailing List;* et *Registered Charitable Organizations*.
- **Agencement des données** : Pour aider les utilisateurs à retrouver rapidement les catégories de renseignement, chaque catégorie est maintenant identifiée à l'aide d'un titre en caractère gras : *Nom précédent; Aperçu; Membre(s) du bureau directeur; Finances; Personnel; Membre; Activités; Publications;* et *Mission*.

Disponible en format imprimée, par souscription, et en ligne sur le site de Grey House Publishing Canada à www.greyhouse.ca, *Associations du Canada* est une ressource pratique de prospection amplement utilisée par les spécialistes de la vente et du marketing, les planificateurs de congrès et d'événements touristiques, les chercheurs, les représentants gouvernementaux et par tous ceux recherchent des groupes oeuvrant dans le secteur sans but lucratif ou des associations commerciales. Pour une consultation pancanadienne, un nombre important d'entrées apparaissent en français.

Nous tenons à souligner la précieuse contribution des personnes et des organismes qui ont collaboré tout au long de l'année à notre procédé de cueillette d'information; votre aide, vos réponses à notre questionnaire dans les délais impartis sont grandement appréciés.

Nous avons mis tous les efforts pour nous assurer de l'exactitude de l'information contenue dans cette édition des *Associations du Canada*. N'hésitez pas à communiquer avec nous si des modifications s'avèrent nécessaires.

Introduction

THE LISTINGS

Associations are listed alphabetically by name. Name changes are reflected in the listings as see references. For example, if you look up the former name *Canadian Petroleum Products Institute*, you will be pointed to their full listing as the *Canadian Fuels Association*. Translated names are also included as see references.

Please refer to the sample entry (page x), which illustrates the kind of information *Associations Canada* provides on each organization.

THE INDEXES

The association listings are indexed in 8 ways to speed your research.

Most prominent of these indexes is the **Subject Index**, which includes words that generically cover a field of interest (i.e., Sports) and also words that occur specifically in the title of a given association (i.e., Fencing).

Acadians
Association acadienne des artistes professionnel.le.s du Nouveau-Brunswick inc., 89
Beaton Institute, 203
Conseil coopératif acadien de la Nouvelle-Écosse, 614

Geographic Index - associations listed by provinces, then cities or towns; includes branches, divisions, chapters, etc.

Québec
Action Patrimoine, 6
Agence municipale de financement et de développement des centres d'urgence 9-1-1 du Québec, 14
AIESEC-Laval, 18

Acronym Index - associations listed alphabetically by acronym:
ABPBC - Association of Book Publishers of British Columbia, 140
ABPNB - Association des bibliothécaires professionnel(le)s du Nouveau-Brunswick, 107
ABPPUM - Association des bibliothécaires, des professeures et professeurs de l'Université de Moncton, 107

Executive Name Index - key contacts listed alphabetically by surnames:
Aalders, Les, *Air Transport Association of Canada*, 19
Aalders, Michelle, *Saskatchewan Registered Music Teachers' Association*, 1273
Aarup, Carolyn, *Miniature Horse Club of Ontario*, 967

Registered Charitable Organizations Index - associations that identify themselves as registered charitable organizations, listed by subject:

Alcoholism
Addictions & Mental Health Ontario, 8
Al-Anon Family Groups (Canada), Inc., 21
Alcoholics Anonymous, 52

Budget Index - organizations by annual budget size, ranging from less than $50,000 to greater than $5 million:

Less than $50,000
Aboriginal Women's Association of Prince Edward Island, 3
Académie de musique du Québec, 3
The Acadian Entomological Society, 4

LES INSCRIPTIONS

Les inscriptions sont classées par ordre alphabétique sous leurs noms officiels. Les changements de nom portent la mention See/Voir. Par exemple, si vous consultez l'ancien nom *Canadian Petroleum Products Institute*, vous serez dirigé vers leur entrée complète *Canadian Fuels Association*. Les noms traduits sont aussi inclus avec la mention voir références.

Veuillez-vous référer à l'exemple d'une inscription (page xi), qui explique le genre de renseignements que vous pouvez obtenir sur les associations inscrites dans *Associations du Canada*.

LES INDEX

Les inscriptions sont indexées de 8 façons différentes afin d'accélérer vos recherches.

Le plus important est **l'index des matières** qui comprend le mot se rapportant au champ d'intérêt générique (ex: Sports) ainsi que les mots spécifiques qui font partie du nom d'une association donnée (ex: Escrime).

Acadians
Association acadienne des artistes professionnel.le.s du Nouveau-Brunswick inc., 89
Beaton Institute, 203
Conseil coopératif acadien de la Nouvelle-Écosse, 614

Index géographique - associations inscrites par provinces, puis par ville ou village; comprend les succursales, divisions, chapitres, etc.

Québec
Action Patrimoine, 6
Agence municipale de financement et de développement des centres d'urgence 9-1-1 du Québec, 14
AIESEC-Laval, 18

Index d'acronymes - associations classées alphabétiquement par acronyme:
ABPBC - Association of Book Publishers of British Columbia, 140
ABPNB - Association des bibliothécaires professionnel(le)s du Nouveau-Brunswick, 107
ABPPUM - Association des bibliothécaires, des professeures et professeurs de l'Université de Moncton, 107

Index des dirigeants - associations classées alphabétiquement par nom de famille:
Aalders, Les, *Air Transport Association of Canada*, 19
Aalders, Michelle, *Saskatchewan Registered Music Teachers' Association*, 1273
Aarup, Carolyn, *Miniature Horse Club of Ontario*, 967

Index des organisations sans buts lucratifs - associations s'identifiant comme ayant le statut d'organisations charitables, sont classées par sujet:

Alcoholism
Addictions & Mental Health Ontario, 8
Al-Anon Family Groups (Canada), Inc., 21
Alcoholics Anonymous, 52

Index du budget annuel - Le budget annuel, affiché par certaines associations, varie entre 50 000$ et 5$ millions:

Moins de 50 000$
Aboriginal Women's Association of Prince Edward Island, 3
Académie de musique du Québec, 3
The Acadian Entomological Society, 4

Introduction

Conferences & Conventions Index - 2018–2023 meetings listed by year, date, and city:

Central Alberta Teachers Convention 2018
Date: February 22-23, 2018
Location: Red Deer College
Red Deer, AB
Sponsor/Contact: Alberta Teachers' Association
Barnett House
11010 - 142 St.
Edmonton, AB T5N 2R1
780-447-9400 *Fax:* 780-455-6481
Toll-Free: 800-232-7208
E-mail: postmaster@ata.ab.ca
URL: www.teachers.ab.ca
Scope: Provincial

Contact Information: Executive Staff Officer: Dan Grassick, E-mail: dan.grassick@ata.ab.ca, Phone: 780-447-9487

Mailing List Index - mailing lists, available for rental from the association, listed by subject:

Architecture
Alberta Association of Architects, 23
Architectural Institute of British Columbia, 79
Manitoba Association of Architects, 929

MAILING LISTS

Our association database can be sorted to provide you with mailing labels by broad category or specific subject interest. Lists are provided in printed or electronic form (see details at the back of the book or call us at 1-866-433-4739).

Index des conventions et congrès - les rencontres pour 2018–2023 sont inscrites par année, date, et ville:

Central Alberta Teachers Convention 2018
Date: February 22-23, 2018
Location: Red Deer College
Red Deer, AB
Sponsor/Contact: Alberta Teachers' Association
Barnett House
11010 - 142 St.
Edmonton, AB T5N 2R1
780-447-9400 *Fax:* 780-455-6481
Toll-Free: 800-232-7208
E-mail: postmaster@ata.ab.ca
URL: www.teachers.ab.ca
Scope: Provincial

Contact Information: Executive Staff Officer: Dan Grassick, E-mail: dan.grassick@ata.ab.ca, Phone: 780-447-9487

Index des listes d'envoi - listes d'envoi à louer, par l'association, sont classées par sujet:

Architecture
Alberta Association of Architects, 23
Architectural Institute of British Columbia, 79
Manitoba Association of Architects, 929

LISTES D'ENVOI

Notre banque de données sur les associations peut être triée par catégorie générale ou par sujet d'intérêt spécifique afin de vous fournir des étiquettes d'envoi. Les listes sont disponibles en format imprimé ou informatisé (voyez les détails à la fin du livre ou téléphonez au 1-866-433-4739).

Introduction

SAMPLE ENTRY

Listings include the following information where available:

- Official name of the association presented in its language of choice (English or French); where a translated name has been provided, that name will appear next to the official association name, and will also appear as a cross-reference in the alphabetical listings (e.g., Société canadienne des directeurs d'association, *See* Canadian Society of Association Executives). The acronym follows the association's name and appears in parantheses. See also the Acronym Index.

- Full address

- Communication numbers, including crisis-lines, info-lines, TTY, toll-free telephone numbers, email & website addresses.

- Social media addresses, including LinkedIn, Facebook, and Twitter links.

- Previous Name: If the name of an association has changed, the previous name appears with a note to see the entry under its new name.

- Also Known As: If an association is better known by a more popular name, this name appears as well.

- Previous Name/ Merged From: If the name of an association has changed, its former name appears as well.

- Overview: This description includes the size (small, medium-sized, large), the jurisdiction (international, national, provincial, local), whether it's a charitable or licensing organization, the year it was founded in and the name of the organization it is overseen by.

- A mission statement

- The organizations of which it is a member or with which it is affiliated.

- Finances: This includes the annual operating budget and the funding sources of the association.

- Staff: Includes both paid and volunteer staff.

- Membership: The number of members, often in specific categories (e.g. individual, corporate, senior, lifetime); fees; the membership criteria; and committees on the board of members.

- Activities: Highlights what the association does, apart from the information contained in its mission statement.

- This includes speakers services and internship programs, awareness events, and whether they have a library or sell mailing lists.

- Chief Officers: Titles may include the following: Executive Director, Director, President, Executive Secretary, Treasurer, Sec.-Treas., General Manager, Coordinator, Chair, Superintendent, Representative, Registrar, Program Head, etc.; eligible for inclusion are both permanent and elected staff. See also the Executive Name Index.

- Awards, Scholarships, Grants: Prizes awarded by the association, along with the amount.

- Publications: Includes details on frequency, author/editor, ISSN or ISBN, language(s) the publication is available in, number of pages, price, advertising, and description of bibliographic contents.

- Meetings: The dates and locations for events to be held in 2018–2023. See also the Conferences and Conventions Index.

- Branches: The association may have various branches, listed at the bottom.

Publishers' Association (PA) / Association des éditeurs (AE)
#1313, 666 King Street East, Toronto, ON, M3Q Z09
Tel: 416-666-6666; *Fax:* 416-666-6667
Toll-Free: 800-666-6666; *TTY:* 416-666-6668
Crisis Hotline: 800-READUS1
Email: info@readus1.com
www.readus1.com
www.linkedin.com/readus
www.facebook.com/readus
twitter.com/readus
www.youtube.com/readus
Previous Name: Read Books Association
Also Known As: Association of Book Lovers
Merged From: BookMakers Association and Editors Association
Overview: A small national charitable licensing organization founded in 2012 overseen by The International Association of Publishers.
Mission: To continue to publish
Member of: North American Publishers Association
Affiliation(s): Association of BookBinders
Finances: *Annual Operating Budget:* $50,000 - $150,000; *Funding Sources:* Membership dues
Staff: 2 staff member(s); 1 volunteer(s)
Membership: 190; *Fees:* $55.50; *Member Profile:* Publishers; *Committees:* Marketing; Finance
Activities: This lists the association's activities; *Awareness Events:* National Book Day, February; *Internships:* Yes; *Speaker Service:* Yes; *Rents Mailing List:* Yes; *Library:* Yes, Publishing Library; Open to public, by appointment.
Chief Officer(s):
Bob Gomez, President, *Tel:* 416-666-6669; *Fax:* 416-666-6670
bgomez@readus1.com

Nancy Gomez, Vice President, *Tel:* 416-666-6671; *Fax:* 416-666-6672
ngomez@readus1.com
Awards:
Best Publisher Award
Here is a description of the award. *Eligibility:* All members of the association; *Location:* Toronto; *Deadline:* 25-Dec; *Amount:* $500; *Contact:* Bob Gomez, President, Tel: 416-666-6667; Fax: 416-666-6668; bgomez@readus1.com
Meetings/Conferences:
International Convention; May 25, 2017, Azteca Inn, Mazatlan, MX
Scope: International
Description: This describes what happens at the convention.
Contact Information: Heather Ramsey, *Tel:* 52-669-44-22-99, hramsey@readus1.com
Publications:
The Annual Publishers' Magazine
Type: Magazine; *Frequency:* a.; *Accepts Advertising; No. of Pages:* 999; *Editor:* Susie Brown; *Author:* Kelly Stewart; *Price:* $150; *ISSN* 9999-9999; *ISBN* 99-999-999-99; *Language:* English, *Contact:* info@readus1.com
Profile: Articles & news

Ontario Division
P.O. Box 666, Hamilton, ON, R1R 1R1
Tel: 613-666-6666; *Fax:* 613-666-6667
Toll-Free: 800-654-3210 ; *TTY:* 613-666-6668
info@readus1.on.ca
www.readus1.on.ca
Chief Officer(s):
Julie Chavez, Director, *Tel:* 613-666-6669; *Fax:* 613-666-6670
jchavez@readus1.on.ca

Introduction

EXEMPLE D'INSCRIPTION

Les inscriptions comprennent les renseignements suivants:

- Nom officiel de l'association, présenté dans la langue choisie (anglais ou français); lorsque la traduction d'un nom est fournie par l'organisme, celui-ci sera à la suite du nom officiel de l'organisme et paraîtra aussi en renvoi par classement alphabétique (Société canadienne des directeurs d'associations, *Voir* Canadian Society of Association Executives). L'acronyme suit le nom de l'organisation et est montré entre parenthèses. Voir aussi l'Index des acronymes.

- Adresse complète.

- Numéros de communication comprenant les téléphones secours, infolignes, ATS, numéros sans frais, courrier électronique, adresses des médias sociaux et adresse URL.

- Nom précédent: Si le nom d'une association a changé, son nom précédent paraît en inscription principale avec renvoi au nouveau nom.

- Aussi connu comme: Certaines associations sont mieux connues par leur appellation plus populaire. Ce nom modifié paraît aussi.

- Date de fondation de l'association.

- Envergure des opérations: Est classée comme suit: internationale, nationale, régionale, provinciale ou locale. Les groupes étrangers ne sont pas définis de cette façon.

- Organisme sans but lucratif: Associations s'identifient comme ayant le statut d'organisations charitables. Voir aussi l'index des organisations à buts non-lucratifs.

- Un énoncé de mission

- Membre de et/ou affiliation à d'autres associations: Associations mères se trouvent sous la rubrique Membre de. Les autres organismes avec lesquels il existe un lien plus distant bien que dynamique se trouvent sous la rubrique Affiliation(s).

- Membres du bureau directeur. Les titres d'emploi peuvent comprendre les suivants: directeur(trice) général(e), président(e), secrétaire ou secrétaire trésorier(ère), gérante(e), coordonnateur(trice), surintendant(e), représentant(e), registraire, chargé(e) de programme, etc. Le nom du personnel permanent ou élu est accepté pour inscription. Voir aussi l'Index par dirigeants.

- Budget annuel d'exploitation/fonctionnement. Voir aussi l'Index du budget annuel.

- Sources de financement: Cite fonds publics et privés et méthode de collecte de fonds.

- Personnel: Salariés et bénévoles.

- Profil des membres et critères d'admission: Qualifications pour membres individuels et corporatifs et les cotisations.

- Nombre de membres, souvent sous différentes catégories spécifiques (corporatifs, individuels, aînés, à vie) et comités et conseils.

- Activités: Énumère les activités qui ne sont pas décrites dans la mission, les buts et objectifs

- Possibilité d'obtenir les services de conférenciers.

- Programme pour stagiaires.

- Bibliothèque: Ouverte au public ou sur rendez-vous.

- Disponibilité de listes d'envoi. Voir aussi l'Index des listes d'envoi.

- Prix décernés, subventions, bourses, avec le montant de ces dernières, si disponible.

- Conventions et congrès: Les dates et endroits où ces réunions auront lieu en 2018–2023.

- Publications: Comprend les renseignements sur la fréquence de publication, les auteurs/rédacteurs, ISSN ou ISBN, la langue (ou langues) dans laquelle la publication est disponible, le nombre de pages, le prix, la publicité et la description du contenu.

- Succursales : L'association peut compter diverses succursales, énumérées au bas.

Association des éditeurs (AE)/Publisher's Association (PA)
#1313, 666 rue King est, Toronto, ON M3Q Z09
Tél: 416-666-6666; *Téléc*: 416-666-6667
Ligne sans frais: 800-666-6666; *ATS*: 416-666-6668
Téléphone secours: 800-READUS1
Courriel: info@readus1.com
www.readus1.com
twitter.com/readus

Nom précédent: Read Books Association
Également appelé: Association of Book Lovers
Fusion de: BookMakers Association et Assocation d'éditeurs
Aperçu: *Dimension*: petite; *Envergure*: national; *Organisme sans but lucratif*; *fondée en 2012*; *surveillé par* The International Association of Publishers.
Mission: Continuer à éditer les livres
Membre de: North American Publishers Association
Affiliation: Association of BookBinders
Finances: *Budget de fonctionnement annuel*: 50000$- 150000$; *Fonds*: Subventions
Personnel: 2 membre(s) du personnel; 1 bénévole(s)
Membre: 190; *Montant de la cotisation*: 55.50$; *Critères d'admissibilité*: Editeurs; *Comités*: Le communications, les finances
Activités: Ceci énumère les activités de l'association. *Evénements de sensibilisation*: National Book Day; *Stagiaires*: Oui; *Service de conférenciers*: Oui; *Listes de destinataire*: Oui; *Bibliothèque*: Oui, Publishing Library; rendez-vous
Membres du bureau directeur:
Bob Gomez, Président, Tél: 416-666-6669; Téléc: 416-666-6670
bgomez@readus1.com

Nancy Gomez, Vice Président, Tél: 416-666-6671; Téléc: 416-666-6672
ngomez@readus1.com

Prix, Bourses:
Best Publisher Award
Ceci décrit le prix. *Critères d'admissibilité*: Tout les membres de l'association. Location: Toronto; Deadline: Dec 25: Amount: 500$; Contact: Bob Gomez, Président, Tél: 416-666-6667; Téléc: 416-666-6668; bgomez@readus1

Conventions et congrès:
International Convention; May 25, 2017, Azteca Inn, Mazatlan, MZ
Scope: International
Description: Ceci décrit ce qui se passe au congrés convention.
Coordonnées: Heather Ramsey, Tél: 52-669-44-22-99, hramsey@readus1.com

Publications:
The Annual Publisher's Magazine
Type: Magazine; *Fréquence*: annuel; Accepte la publicité; No. de pages: 999; Rédacteur: Susie Brown; Auteur: Kelly Stewart; Prix: 150$; ISSN: 9999-9999; ISBN 99-999-999-99; Langue: anglais, Coordonnées: info@readus1.com
Aperçu: Articles et nouvelles

Ontario Division
P.O. Box 666, Hamilton, ON, R1R 1R1
Tél: 613-666-6666; *Téléc*: 613-666-6667
Ligne sans frais: 800-654-3210; *ATP*: 613-666-6668
Membre(s) du bureau directeur:
Julie Chavez, Directrice,
Tél: 613-666-6666; Téléc: 613-666-6667
jchavez@readus1.on.ca

ASSOCIATIONS CANADA 2018

I. ABBREVIATIONS

Academic and other degrees, membership in & degrees conferred by Societies & Institutions, Honours, Labour Union affiliations, Military Titles, etc.

AACI	Accredited Appraiser Canadian Institute
AASA	Associate of the Alberta Society of Artists
AB	Bachelor of Arts (American) (Artium Baccalaureus)
AC	Advanced Certification, Canadian Association of Medical Radiation Technologists
ACA	Associate of the Institute of Chartered Accountants
ACAM	Associate C.A.M.
ACD	Archaeologiae Christianae Doctor
ACIC	Associate of Canadian Institute of Chemistry
ACInstM	- of Institute of Marketing
AIIC	Associate of the Insurance Institute of Canada
ALS	Commissioned Alberta Land Surveyor
AMEIC	Associate Member of the Engineeering Institute of Canada
APR	Accredited Member of the Canadian Public Relations Society
ARDIO	Associate of Registered Interior Designers of Ontario
AScT	Applied Science Technologist
BA	Bachelor of Arts
BAA	- of Applied Arts
B.Acc.	- of Accounting
B.Adm.Pub.	Baccaulauréat spécialisée en administration publique
BAeE(BAeroE)	Bachelor of Aeronautical Engineering
BAS(BASc)	- of Applied Science
BCE	- of Civil Engineering
B.Des.	- of Design
BE(BEng)	- of Engineering
BEE	- of Electrical Engineering (USA)
BES	- of Envrironmental Sciences/Studies
B.ès.A.	Bachelier ès Arts
B.ès.Sc.	- ès Science
B.ès.Sc.App.	- ès Science Appliquée
BEDS	Bachelor of Environmental Design Studies
BFA	- of Fine Arts
BLA	- of Landscape Architecture
BMV	Bachelier en Médicine Vétérinaire
BSA	Bachelor of Science in Agriculture
B.Sc.	- of Science
BSCE	- of Science in Civil Engineering
BSEE	- of Science in Electrical Engineering
BScF(BSF)	- of Science in Forestry
BScFE	- of Science in Forestry Engineering
BTech	- of Technology
CA	Chartered Accountant (Legacy Designation)
CAE	Certified Association Executive
CAE/caé	Chartered Account Executive
CAM	Certified Administrative Manager
Capt.	Captain
CBE	Commander, Order of the British Empire
CBV	Chartered Business Valuator
CC	Companion, Order of Canada
CCU/CSC	Confederation of Canadian Unions/Confédération des syndicats canadiens
CD	Canadian Forces Decoration
Cdr.	Commander
CE	Civil Engineer
CEA	Certified Environmental Auditor
CEQ	Centrale de l'enseignement du Québec/Quebec Teaching Congress
CerE	Ceramic Engineer
CFA	Chartered Financial Analyst
CFP	Chartered Financial Planner
CGA	Certified General Accountant (Legacy Designation)
CHA	Certified Housing Administrator
ChE	Chartered Executive
CHE	- Health Executive
CIF	Canadian Institute of Forestry
CIM	Canadian Investment Manager
CIM	Canadian Investment Manager
CIM	Certificate in Management
CIM	Certified Industrial Manager
CLC/CTC	Canadian Labour Congress/Congrès du travail du Canada
CLM	Certified Industrial Manager
CLS	Canada Land Surveyor
C.M.	Member, Order of Canada
CLU	Chartered Life Underwriter
CMA	Certified Management Accountant (Legacy Designation)
CMC	Certified Management Consultant
C.Mgr.	Chartered Manager
CMM	-Municipal Manager (Ontario)
CMM	Commander, Order of Military Merit
CMOS	Canadian Meteorological and Oceanographic Society Consultant
CNFIU/FCNSI	Canadian National Federation of Independent Unions/Fédération canadienne nationale des syndicats indépendants
Col.	Colonel
CPA	Chartered Professional Accountant
CPPO	Certified Public Purchasing Officer
CRA	Canadian Residential Appraiser
CRSP	Canadian Registered Safety Professional
CSC	Canadian Securities Course
CSD/CDU	Centrale des syndicats démocratiques/Congress of Democratic Unions
CSN	Confédération des syndicats nationaux/Confederation of National Trade Unions
CTC	Certified Travel Counsellor
C.Tech.	-Technician
CWO	Chief Warrant Officer
DDS	Doctor of Dental Surgery
DEng	- of Engineering
D.en Méd.Vét.	Docteur en médicine vétérinaire
D.ès.Sc.App.	- ès science appliquée
Dip.Ing.	Diploma in Engineering
DLS	Dominion Land Surveyor
DMD	Doctor of Dental Medicine
Dr.	Doctor
D.Sc.	Doctor of Science
D.Sc.Nat.	- of Natural Science
D.Th.	- of Theology
DVM(DMV)	- of Veterinary Medicine
D.V.Sc.	- of Veterinary Science
EE	Electrical Engineer
EEE/eee	Expert en évaluation d'entreprises

EM	Mining Engineer	ME	Master of Mechanical Engineering
FAGS	Fellow of the American Geographical Society	MEDS	Master of Environmental Design Studies
FAOU	- of the American Ornithologists Union	MEE	- of Electrical Engineering (USA)
FAPHA	- of the American Public Health Association	MEIC	Member of the Engineering Institute of Canada
FAPS	- of the American Physical Society	M.Eng.	- of Environmental Sciences/Studies
FCA	- of the Institute of Chartered Accountants	MF	- of Forestry
FCIC	- of the Chemical Institute of Canada	MICE	- of the Institution of Civil Engineers (British)
FCMRT	- of the Canadian Association of Medical Radiation Technologists	MIEEE	- of the Institute of Electrical and Electronics Engineers
FCPA	- of the Chartered Professional Accountants of Canada	MIMMM	- of the Institute of Materials, Minerals and Mining (British)
FCSI	- of the Canadian Securities Institute	MLS	Master of Library Science
FE	Forest Engineer	MMM	Member, Order of Military Merit
FEIC	Fellow of the Engineering Institute of Canada	MP	Member of Parliament
FGS	- of the Geological Society (British)	MP	Master of Planning
FGSA	- of the Geological Society of America	M.Ph.(M.Phil.)	- of Philosophy
FICE	- of the Institution of Civil Engineers	MPM	- of Pest Management
FIET	- of the Institution of Engineering and Technology	MRM	- of Resource Management
FIMMM	- of the Institute of Materials, Minerals and Mining (British)	MSA	- of Science in Agriculture
FMSA	- of the Mineralogical Society of America	MSc	- of Science
FRAIC	- of the Royal Architectural Institute of Canada	MScA	- of Applied Science
FRAS	- of the Royal Astronomical Society	MSCE	- of Science in Civil Engineering
FRGS	- of the Royal Geographical Society	MScF	- of Science in Forestry
FRHortS	- of the Royal Horticultural Society	M.Sc.(Med.)	- of Science in Medicine
FRSC	- of the Royal Society of Chemistry	MURP	- of Urban and Rural Planning
FRMS (FRMetS)	- of the Royal Meteorological Society	MUP	- of Urban Planning
IA	Investment Advisor	MVSc	- of Veterinary Science
IC	Investment Counselor	OC	Officer, Order of Canada
IR	Investment Representative	OD	Doctor of Optometry
ISP	Information Systems Professional of Canada	OLS	Ontario Land Surveyor
Jr.	Junior	OMM	Officer, Order of Military Merit
L.ès.Sc.	Licencié ès Sciences	P.Ag.	Professional Agrologist
L.Gen	Lieutenant General	PC	Privy Councillor
LL	License in Civil Law	PE	Professional Engineer
LLB	Bachelor of Laws (Legum Baccalaureus)	PFP	Personal Financial Planner
LLD	Doctor of Laws (usually honorary)	PhD	Doctor of Philosophy
LLL	Licence en droit	Pharm.D.	Doctor of Pharmacology
LLM	Master of Law	P.Mgr.	Professional Manager
LRPS	Licentiate in Royal Photographic Society	Prof.	Professor
LS	Land Surveyor	QAA	Qualified Administrative Assistant
LSA	Licentiate in Agricultural Science	QC	Queen's Counsel
Lt.Col.	Lieutenant Colonel	QLS	Québec Land Surveyor
MA	Master of Arts	Rev.	Reverend
MAeE	Master of Aeronautical Engineering	RFP	Registered Financial Planner
MAIME	- of the American Institute of Mining, Metallurgical, and Petroleum Engineers	RN	Registered Nurse
		R.P.Bio.	Registered Professional Biologist
MAP	Maîtrise en administration publique	RSW	- Specification Writer
MASc(MAS)	Master of Applied Science	ScD	Doctorat ès Sciences
MASCE	Member of the American Society of Civil Engineers	ScL	Licence ès Sciences
MASME	- of the American Society of Mechanical Engineers	SFC	Specialist in Financial Counseling
MBA	Master of Business Administration	SLS	Saskatchewan Land Surveyor
MCE	Member of Civil Engineering	SM	Master of Science
MChE	- of Chemical Engineering (USA)	SPA	Service for Photographic Art
MCIC	- of the Chemical Institute of Canada		
MCIF	- of the Canadian Institute of Forestry		
MCIM	- of the Canadian Institute of Mining, Metallurgy and Petroleum		
MCInstM	Member of the Canadian Institute of Marketing		
MD	Doctor of Medicine		

Introduction

II. GEOGRAPHICAL TERMS

Provinces

Alberta	AB	Alberta
British Columbia	BC	Colombie-Britannique
Manitoba	MB	Manitoba
New Brunswick	NB	Nouveau-Brunswick
Newfoundland & Labrador	NL	Terre-Neuve et Labrador
Northwest Territories	NT	Territoires du Nord-Ouest
Nova Scotia	NS	Nouvelle-Écosse
Nunavut	NU	Nunavut
Ontario	ON	Ontario
Prince Edward Island	PE	Île-du-Prince-Édouard
Québec	QC	Québec
Saskatchewan	SK	Saskatchewan
Yukon	YT	Yukon

The United States

Alabama	AL	Montana	MT	
Alaska	AK	Nebraska	NE	
Arizona	AZ	Nevada	NV	
Arkansas	AR	New Hampshire	NH	
California	CA	New Jersey	NJ	
Colorado	CO	New Mexico	NM	
Connecticut	CT	New York	NY	
Delaware	DE	North Carolina	NC	
District of Columbia	DC	North Dakota	ND	
Florida	FL	Ohio	OH	
Georgia	GA	Oklahoma	OK	
Hawaii	HI	Oregon	OR	
Idaho	ID	Pennsylvania	PA	
Illinois	IL	Rhode Island	RI	
Indiana	IN	South Carolina	SC	
Iowa	IA	South Dakota	SD	
Kansas	KS	Tennessee	TN	
Kentucky	KY	Texas	TX	
Louisiana	LA	Utah	UT	
Maine	ME	Vermont	VT	
Maryland	MD	Virginia	VA	
Massachusetts	MA	Washington	WA	
Michigan	MI	West Virginia	WV	
Minnesota	MN	Wisconsin	WI	
Mississippi	MS	Wyoming	WY	
Missouri	MO			

III. STREET ADDRESSES

Avenue	Ave./av
Boulevard	Blvd./boul
Building	Bldg./Édifice
Care of/au soins de	c/o / a/s
Court	Ct.
Crescent	Cres.
Drive/Promenade	Dr./promenade
Floor/Étage	Fl./étage
Highway/Route	Hwy./Rte
Parkway	Pkwy.
Place/Place	Pl./Place
Post Office Bag	PO Bag
Post Office Box/Caisse postal	PO Box/CP
Postal Sub-Station	Postal Sub-Stn./sous-station
Retail Postal Outlet	RPO
Road/Chemin	Rd./ch
Square/Carré	Sq./carré
Station/Succursale	Stn/Succ
Street/Rue	St./rue

IV. DAYS OF THE WEEK*

Sunday	Sun.	dimanche
Monday	Mon.	lundi
Tuesday	Tues.	mardi
Wednesday	Wed.	mercredi
Thursday	Thu.	jeudi
Friday	Fri.	vendredi
Saturday	Sat.	samedi

*Days of the week expressed in French are presented in full

V. MONTHS OF THE YEAR

January/janvier	Jan./jan.
Februrary/février	Feb./fév.
March/mars	March/mars
April/avril	April/avril
May/mai	May/mai
June/juin	June/juin
July/juillet	July/juillet
August/août	Aug./août
September/septembre	Sept./sept.
October/octobre	Oct./oct.
November/novembre	Nov./nov.
December/décembre	Dec./déc.

VI. TRANSLATIONS

Selected titles, tags & phrases

Acronym	Acronyme
Activities	Activités
Administrator	Administrateur(trice)
Also known as	Également appelé
Amount	Montant
Annual Operating Budget	Budget de fonctionnement annuel
Appointment (Library)	Rendez-vous (Bibliothèque)
Attendees	Participants
Author	Auteur(e)
Awards	Attribution de prix
Awareness Events	Événements de sensiblisation
Chief Officers	Membres du bureau directeur
Commissioner	Commissaire
Committees	Comités
Communications Officer	Agent de communications
Conferences	Conférences
Contact Person	Personne ressource/Responsable
Contents (Publications)	Contenu (Publications)
Conventions	Congrès
Coordinator	Coordonnateur(trice)

Introduction

English	French	English	French
Corresponding Secretary	Secrétaire correspondancier	Merged from	Fusion de
Crisis-Line	Ligne secours	Number of Pages	Nombre de pages
Deadline	Date limite d'inscription	Online Services	Services en ligne
Editor	Rédacteur(trice)	Open to Public	Bibliothèque publique
Eligibility	Admissibilité	Organizational Profile	Description
Email	Courriel	Physical address	Adresse
Executive Assistant	Adjoint(e) de direction	Previous Name	Nom précédant
Executive Director	Directeur(trice) général(e)	President	Président(e)
Executive Manager	Directeur	President-elect	Président(e) désigné(e)
Executive Sec.-Treas.	Sec.-trés. de direction	Recording Secretary	Secrétaire archiviste
Fax (Facsmile Transmission)	Télécopieur	Registered Charity	Organisme sans but lucratif
Fee Schedule	Liste des cotisations	Registrar	Secrétaire
Financial Secretary	Secrétaire financier(ière)	Representative	Représentant(e), Délégué(e)
Founding Date	Date de fondation	Schedule	Barème
Grants	Subventions	Scholarships	Bourses
Info-Line	Infoligne	Scope of Activity	Envergure des opérations
Information Officer	Agent d'information	Secretary	Secrétaire
Interns	Stagiaires	Secretary General	Secrétaire général(e)
ISBN	Numéro ISBN	Secretary-Treasurer (Sec.-Treas.)	Secrétaire-trésorier(ière) (Sec.-trés.)
ISSN	Numéro ISSN	See	Voir
Library	Bibliothèque	See also	Voir aussi
Licensing Body	Organisme de réglementation professionnelle	Speakers Service	Service de conférenciers
Mailing Address	Adresse postale	Sponsors	Commanditaires
Mailing Lists/Labels	Listes de diffusion/étiquettes d'adresses	Staff	Personnel
Manager	Administrateur(trice) ou Gérant(e)	TTY (Text Telephone)	ATS
Meetings	Réunions	Telephone	Téléphone
Member of	Membre de	Toll-free (telephone number)	Ligne sans frais
Membership	Nombre de membres	Treasurer	Trésorier(ière)
Membership criteria	Critères d'admissibilité	URL	Site web
Membership fee	Montant de la cotisation	Volunteers	Bénévoles

ASSOCIATIONS CANADA 2018

Canadian Associations at a Glance

There are approximately 19,272 in-depth, detailed Canadian association profiles in *Associations Canada 2018*, which include the association's various chapters and branch locations. In addition, this resource lists 902 foreign associations — those not headquartered in Canada, but have a Canadian presence, either physically or otherwise. These foreign listings are in their own section, following the extensive Canadian listings. This by-the-numbers summary illustrates the enormous amount of content to be found in the more than 20,000 total listings in this edition.

- **33,708 executives:** This high-powered list includes Chairs, Executive Directors and other crucial association contacts.
- **1,940 Meetings**: Find out who goes where and when, and how many attendees you can expect, for strong, business-building information.
- **5,409 Publications**: With details such as editor names, frequency, and submission information, this data is a valuable, go-to source to research the publications that will best get your message out.
- **6,899 Awards**: This section includes who to contact, deadlines, grants, scholarships, and more, and fills a wide range of research and academic needs, from job hunting to grant money.

Number of Associations in *Associations Canada 2018*, including chapters and branches:

By Province

Ontario	7,127
Québec	3,088
British Columbia	2,387
Alberta	1,938
Manitoba	951
Saskatchewan	915
Nova Scotia	928
New Brunswick	633
Newfoundland and Labrador	415
Prince Edward Island	290
Yukon Territory	156
Northwest Territories	105
Nunavut	41

By Size

Large	1,024
Medium	5,666
Small	13,463

By Type

Professional	2,189
Trade	5,372
Special Interest	12,592

By Budget

Less than $50,000	915
$50,000-$100,000	409
$100,000-$250,000	543
$250,000-$500,000	475
$500,000-$1.5 Million	550
$1.5 Million -$3 Million	250
$3 Million -$5 Million	169
Greater than $5 Million	327

Associations du Canada en un coup d'œil

Associations du Canada 2018 compte environ 19 272 profils détaillés d'associations canadiennes, y compris celles qui ont plusieurs succursales et emplacements. De plus, cette ressource énumère 902 associations étrangères, celles dont les sièges sociaux ne se trouvent pas au Canada, mais qui y sont présents, physiquement ou autrement. Ces entrées se retrouvent dans leur propre section, à la suite des entrées exhaustives canadiennes. Ce résumé en chiffres illustre la quantité impressionnante de contenu qui se trouve dans plus de 20 000 entrées qui composent ce numéro.

- **33 708 dirigeants** : cette liste de hauts dirigeants comprend des présidents, des directeurs généraux et d'autres personnes-ressources d'association essentielles.
- **1 940 rencontres** : découvrez qui va où et quand et combien de participants vous pouvez vous attendre à recevoir afin de consolider de l'information d'affaires solide.
- **5 409 publications** : grâce à des détails comme les noms des maisons d'édition, la fréquence de publication et l'information relative à la soumission de textes, ces données constituent une source précieuse de référence pour effectuer des recherches parmi les publications qui transmettront le mieux votre message.
- **6 899 prix** : cette section comprend les contacts, les échéances, les subventions, les bourses, entre autres, et comblent la vaste gamme de besoins en matière de recherche et d'études universitaires, de la recherche d'emploi aux fonds d'aide gratuite.

Nombre d'associations comprises dans *Associations Canada 2018*, y compris les chapitres et succursales

Par Province

Ontario	7 127
Québec	3 088
British Columbia	2 387
Alberta	1 938
Manitoba	951
Saskatchewan	915
Nova Scotia	928
New Brunswick	633
Newfoundland and Labrador	415
Prince Edward Island	290
Yukon Territory	156
Northwest Territories	105
Nunavut	41

Par taille

Large	1 024
Medium	5 666
Small	13 463

Par Type

Professional	2 189
Trade	5 372
Other	12 592

Par Budget

Less than $50,000	915
$50,000-$100,000	409
$100,000-$250,000	543
$250,000-$500,000	475
$500,000-$1.5 Million	550
$1.5 Million -$3 Million	250
$3 Million -$5 Million	169
Greater than $5 Million	327

Associations

Associations are voluntary, non-governmental, non-profit organizations composed of personal or institutional members, with or without federal or provincial incorporation. Associations are formed for a particular purpose or to advance a common cause, especially of a public nature. Related terms include foundation, society, institute, federation, alliance, club and union.

The freedom of association is one of the fundamental freedoms guaranteed by the Canadian Charter of Rights and Freedoms. It is estimated that individual Canadians on average are associated with at least three associations, such as business, trade and professional associations, chambers of commerce and boards of trade, labour organizations and unions, health and welfare groups, religious organizations, athletic associations, political organizations, learned societies, cultural groups, fraternal organizations and service clubs, charities, and community and neighbourhood groups.

Historical Background

The history of associations in Canada dates from when Samuel de Champlain founded the Ordre de Bon Temps in 1604, for the promotion of recreation and relaxation at Port-Royal. A few Canadian associations still in existence can trace their origins back to the 18th century. For example, the Halifax Board of Trade was founded in 1750, and predates the first recorded association of this type in the United States by approximately 18 years; the Grand Lodge of Upper Canada of the Ancient Free and Accepted Masons was established in 1792; and the Law Society of Upper Canada was organized in 1797. (Most dates given here are formation dates, not incorporation dates.)

Associations formed before Confederation include the Montréal Board of Trade (1822); the Nova Scotia Barristers' Society (1825); the Toronto Board of Trade (1845); the Barristers' Society of New Brunswick (1846); the Collège des médecins et chirurgiens de la province de Québec (1847); the Royal Canadian Institute (1849); the Québec Bar (1849); the Medical Society of Nova Scotia (1854); the Nova Scotia Board of Insurance Underwriters (1857); the Ontario Fruit Growers' Association (1859); the Ontario Educational Association (1861); the Nova Scotian Institute of Natural Science (1862); the Law Society of British Columbia (1863); the Nova Scotia Fruit Growers' Association (1863); the Entomological Society of Canada (1863), the first national association formed in the sciences; the College of Physicians and Surgeons of Ontario (1866); the Canadian Medical Association (1867); and the Ontario Dental Association (1867).

From 1867 to 1900 many new associations were established at both the national and provincial levels. New markets and the growth of factories and manufacturers spawned the expansion of trade associations to ensure fair competition. Examples of national associations formed during this period and still in existence are the Canadian Manufacturers' Association (1871); the Royal Society of Canada (1882); the Canadian Institute of Surveying (1882, as the Association of Dominion Land Surveyors); the Engineering Institute of Canada (1887, as the Canadian Society of Civil Engineers); the Canadian Electrical Association (1889); the Royal Astronomical Society of Canada (1890, as the Astronomical and Physical Society of Toronto); the Canadian Bankers' Association (1891); the Canadian Education Association (1892); and the Canadian Institute of Mining and Metallurgy (1898).

From 1900 to the end of the Second World War, there was a steady increase in the number of associations. The period of greatest growth coincided with the economic prosperity of the 1960s. More than one-third of the 1,500 non-profit corporations incorporated under federal legislation from 1900 to 1970 were incorporated between 1966 and 1970. There are also hundreds of associations operating without federal or provincial incorporation. Many professional associations have developed evaluation standards for their members and their respective industries, and members can be measured using these standards.

Association headquarters are concentrated heavily in Toronto, Ottawa and Montréal. Vancouver, Edmonton, Calgary and Winnipeg and other large urban areas also have significant concentrations.

Origins and Growth

Several Canadian associations owe their origins to foreign parents, particularly American or British. When Canadian membership in foreign associations increased to a significant number, members withdrew from their parent group to form their own associations with headquarters in Canada. There are still scores of foreign associations with Canadian chapters or divisions, such as the American Society of Mechanical Engineers, New York, and the Royal Commonwealth Society, London. In addition, several international associations such as the International Air Transport Association have their headquarters in Canada.

Many Canadian labour unions are affiliated with international unions headquartered in the US; however, the percentage of international union membership in Canada has significantly decreased as membership in national unions has correspondingly increased, continuing a 30-year trend as new national unions and independent local organizations were organized in Canada. By 1995, international union membership had fallen from two-thirds of all union membership in Canada to 29 per cent, and national union representation rose from 21 per cent to 57 per cent. By 2003, more than four million Canadians belonged to a union.

Industry associations provide valuable peer-to-peer support. A 2006 study published by Statistics Canada found that innovative firms refer to industry associations almost 10 times more frequently than federal government research institutes and up to 4.4 times more frequently than universities for information, solutions and business ideas.

The proliferation of associations is partially a result of the growth in population, the expansion and diversification of the economy, and greatly increased government activity, especially in health care and social services, as well as the desire for communication with others who share common interests.

Types

There have been various attempts to classify associations into types according to purpose, function and structure. No classification has been satisfactory because of the diversity in membership, objectives, structure, methods of operation and concerns. One classification makes a distinction between those associations that function primarily for the benefit of the public (charitable organizations) and those that carry on their activities primarily for the benefit of their members (membership organizations). Another distinguishes between corporate-type and federation-type organizations. The latter may bring together associations devoted to the same subject, or to several different subjects. It is also possible to classify associations according to their principal activity.

Incorporation

Incorporation is often advantageous or necessary for non-profit corporations to carry out certain activities. The principal advantages of incorporation as a non-profit corporation without share capital are that it provides greater continuity and permanency for the organization, frees members from liability for the debts and obligations of the corporation, and facilitates certain activities such as the holding of real estate. Such corporations must be conducted without pecuniary gain for the members.

Federal non-profit corporations in Canada include many of the large charitable and membership organizations and virtually all the boards of trade and chambers of commerce incorporated under the *Boards of Trade Act*. For associations whose activities are within a single locality or province, provincial incorporation as a non-profit corporation is sufficient. Each province has its own requirements and procedures for incorporation.

Organization and Operation

The board of directors of an incorporated non-profit corporation manages the corporation's business and affairs. The board is legally responsible for adhering to the corporation constitution and bylaws, for making policy to further the attainment of its stated goals and objectives, and for appointing the chief executive officer. A small group of board members, including the officers, constitutes the executive committee, which sits between board meetings to make decisions on behalf of the board.

The usual officers of an association are the president, vice-president, treasurer and secretary. The officers may be selected by the membership or appointed by the board, and their duties are set out in the bylaws or established by the board. The chief executive officer or executive director (the title may vary) performs duties assigned by the board of directors. This officer executes policies as prescribed by the board, selects employees for the operation of the association office, prepares budgets, approves expenditures and attends all meetings of the board and its executive committee.

The committee structure of an association usually reflects its goals and objectives. Typical committee responsibilities include membership, nominations, education, research, publishing, and public and government relations. Officers and directors are expected to render a periodic account of their stewardship, usually in the form of an annual report. The requirements for membership are usually stated in the bylaws of the association and there may be several classes of membership, such as member, associate, student and honorary member. Some associations admit anyone interested in its activities; others, such as professional associations, have specific requirements for membership. In general, charitable organizations rely on government grants for their income and on donations from business and the general public, whereas membership organizations obtain most of their income from fees and dues.

Contribution to Society

Associations registered federally as charitable organizations are legally obligated to provide services beneficial to the community at large. Although membership associations have the advancement of the interests of their members as their primary aim, they too may respond to changing conditions in society by engaging in programs and activities in the public interest. Associations have an important role in building consensus in society by providing the mechanism for their members to reach agreement on social values, on objectives to be pursued and on the means to achieve objectives. Through interaction with government, associations participate in shaping public policy. National associations, many of which are bilingual, can contribute to the strengthening of national unity by improving communications and understanding among the different peoples and regions of Canada.

Associations have evolved as peer support or mentoring agencies that offer members the experience and resources within their areas of interest. Associations are also important as sources for information about hundreds of specialized activities in our society. By helping those in need, supporting and publishing worthwhile research, educating members of the public, contributing to the personal development of citizens and pressing for just and humanitarian causes, associations are making significant contributions to Canadian society and its citizens.

Extensive information about associations in Canada is available in the publication *Associations Canada*, which is published annually by Grey House Publishing Canada. *Associations Canada* was created by the merger of two annual directories: *Directory of Associations in Canada* and *Associations Canada: An Encyclopedic Directory*. Today, the publication provides details regarding the activities of a variety of associations in Canada including Canadian and foreign associations, professional associations, and non-profit and voluntary organizations. The directory uses more than 1,500 subject classifications ranging from accounting to zoology to describe the activities of more than 18,000 associations listed.

Author R. BRIAN LAND

Source: Courtesy of *The Canadian Encyclopedia*, Historica Canada. www.thecanadianencyclopedia.ca.

Associations

Les associations sont des organisations volontaires, non gouvernementales, sans but lucratif, composées de membres individuels ou institutionnels, constituées ou non en sociétés en vertu d'une loi fédérale ou provinciale, formées dans un but particulier ou pour la défense d'une cause commune, plus particulièrement d'intérêt public. D'autres termes y sont apparentés, comme « fondation », « société », « institut », « fédération », « alliance », « club » et « syndicat ».

La liberté d'association est une des libertés fondamentales garanties par la Charte canadienne des droits et libertés. On estime que, en moyenne, chaque Canadien fait partie d'au moins trois associations telles que des associations de gens d'affaires, de métier ou professionnelles, des chambres et des bureaux de commerce, des organisations ouvrières et des syndicats, des groupes de défense et de promotion de la santé ou du bien commun, des organisations religieuses, des associations sportives, des organisations politiques, des sociétés savantes, des associations culturelles, des sociétés d'aide mutuelle et des organisations philanthropiques, des groupes communautaires et de voisinage.

Historique

L'histoire des associations au Canada remonte à Samuel de Champlain, qui a fondé l'Ordre de Bon Temps en 1604 pour favoriser les loisirs et la détente à Port-Royal. Quelques associations canadiennes nées au XVIIIe siècle sont encore actives : l'Halifax Board of Trade, fondé en 1750, soit environ 18 ans avant la première association de ce genre connue aux États-Unis; la Grand Lodge of Upper Canada of the Ancient Free and Accepted Masons, créée en 1792, et le Barreau du Haut-Canada, formé en 1797 (la plupart des dates mentionnées ici sont celles de la formation des associations et non celles de leur constitution juridique).

Parmi les associations formées avant la Confédération, on compte le Bureau de commerce de Montréal (1822), la Nova Scotia Barristers' Society (1825), le Toronto Board of Trade (1845), le Barreau du Nouveau-Brunswick (1846), le Collège des médecins et chirurgiens de la province de Québec (1847), maintenant l'Ordre des médecins du Québec, le Royal Canadian Institute (1849), le Barreau du Québec (1849), la Medical Society of Nova Scotia (1854), le Nova Scotia Board of Insurance Underwriters (1857), l'Association des fruiticulteurs et des maraîchers de l'Ontario (1859), l'Ontario Educational Association (1861), le Nova Scotian Institute of Natural Science (1862), la Law Society of British Columbia (1863), la Nova Scotia Fruit Growers' Association (1863), la Société entomologique du Canada (1863), la première association nationale dans le domaine des sciences, l'Ordre des médecins et chirurgiens de l'Ontario (1866), l'Association médicale canadienne (1867) et l'Ontario Dental Association (1867).

De 1867 à 1900, de nombreuses nouvelles associations voient le jour tant à l'échelle provinciale que fédérale. Parmi les associations nationales formées au cours de cette période et qui existent toujours, nommons l'Association des manufacturiers canadiens (1871), la Société royale du Canada (1882), l'Association canadienne des sciences géomatiques (1882), anciennement l'Association canadienne des sciences géodésiques, l'Institut canadien des ingénieurs (1887), anciennement la Canadian Society of Civil Engineers, l'Association canadienne de l'électricité (1889), la Société royale d'astronomie du Canada (1890), d'abord l'Astronomical and Physical Society of Toronto, l'Association des banquiers canadiens (1891), l'Association canadienne d'éducation (1892) et l'Institut canadien des mines, de la métallurgie et du pétrole (1898).

De 1900 jusqu'à la fin de la Deuxième Guerre mondiale, le nombre des associations augmente de façon soutenue. Cette période de forte croissance coïncide avec la prospérité économique des années 1960. Plus du tiers des 1 500 sociétés sans but lucratif créées au niveau fédéral de 1900 à 1970 l'ont été entre 1966 et 1970. Il existe aussi des centaines d'associations qui ne sont constituées en personnalité juridique ni au fédéral ni au provincial. Beaucoup d'associations professionnelles ont élaboré des normes régissant les membres et leurs industries respectives et d'après lesquelles ceux-ci peuvent être évalués.

Les sièges sociaux des associations se concentrent fortement à Toronto, Ottawa et Montréal, puis de façon significative à Vancouver, Edmonton, Calgary, Winnipeg et dans d'autres grandes régions urbaines.

Origines et développement

Un certain nombre d'associations canadiennes doivent leur existence à des associations mères de l'étranger, en particulier des États-Unis et de la Grande-Bretagne. Quand les membres canadiens au sein des associations étrangères deviennent suffisamment nombreux, ils se retirent pour former leurs propres associations avec des sièges sociaux au Canada. Toutefois, on trouve encore un bon nombre d'associations étrangères qui comptent des sections ou des filiales au Canada, comme l'American Society of Mechanical Engineers, de New York, et la Royal Commonwealth Society, de Londres. De plus, diverses associations internationales, comme l'Association du Transport aérien international, ont leurs sièges sociaux au Canada.

Plusieurs organisations syndicales canadiennes sont affiliées à des organisations internationales dirigées à partir des États-Unis. Cependant, sur l'ensemble des syndiqués canadiens, la proportion de membres affiliés à des syndicats internationaux diminue pendant qu'augmente la participation à des syndicats nationaux, parallèlement à la tendance, remarquée depuis 30 ans, à fonder de nouveaux syndicats nationaux et des organisations locales indépendantes au Canada. En 1995, l'appartenance à des syndicats internationaux, qui constituait les deux tiers des syndiqués du Canada, est tombée à 29 %. Pendant ce temps, la représentation par un syndicat national passe de 21 % à 57 %. En 2003, plus de quatre millions de Canadiens sont membres d'un syndicat.

Les associations d'industrie apportent un soutien par les pairs fort utile. Une étude de 2006, publiée par Statistique Canada, constate que, lorsqu'il s'agit d'avoir des renseignements, des solutions et des idées commerciales, des entreprises novatrices s'en remettent à des associations de l'industrie environ 10 fois plus souvent qu'aux instituts de recherche du gouvernement fédéral et jusqu'à 4,4 fois plus souvent qu'aux universités.

La prolifération des associations s'explique par la croissance démographique, l'expansion et la diversification de l'économie et l'accroissement important de l'activité gouvernementale, spécialement en matière de soins de santé et de services sociaux, de même que le désir d'échanger avec des personnes qui partagent les mêmes intérêts.

Types

On a essayé, suivant divers critères, de classifier les associations en fonction de leur but, de leur fonction et de leur structure. Aucune classification ne s'est révélée satisfaisante en raison de la diversité de la composition, des objectifs, de la structure, du mode de fonctionnement et des intérêts des associations. Une classification distingue entre les associations qui s'intéressent avant tout à l'intérêt public (associations de bienfaisance) et celles dont les activités visent d'abord l'intérêt de leurs membres (associations de membres). Une autre distingue entre les organisations de type sociétaire et celles de type fédératif. Ces dernières peuvent regrouper des associations actives dans un même domaine ou dans plusieurs domaines différents. Il est aussi possible de classifier les associations selon leur activité principale.

Constitution

Il est souvent avantageux ou nécessaire pour des organisations sans but lucratif de se constituer juridiquement en personnes morales pour mener à bien certaines de leurs activités. Les principaux avantages de la constitution juridique pour une organisation sans but lucratif et sans capital social consistent à lui assurer une plus grande continuité et la permanence, à dégager les membres de toute responsabilité en ce qui concerne les dettes et les obligations de l'organisation et à faciliter certaines activités comme la possession de biens immobiliers. De telles sociétés doivent fonctionner sans avantages pécuniaires pour les membres.

Associations

Au Canada, parmi les sociétés sans but lucratif à charte fédérale se trouvent plusieurs grandes sociétés de bienfaisance et organisations de membres, et pratiquement tous les bureaux et chambres de commerce constitués en vertu de la *Loi sur les chambres de commerce*. Pour les associations qui poursuivent des activités à l'intérieur d'une seule localité ou province, l'obtention d'un acte constitutif provincial comme société à but non lucratif est suffisante. Chaque province a ses propres exigences et procédures en matière de constitution juridique.

Organisation et fonctionnement

Le conseil d'administration d'une société constituée sans but lucratif gère ses activités et ses affaires internes. Il est légalement responsable du respect de la constitution et des règlements, de l'adoption des politiques en vue d'atteindre les buts et objectifs convenus, et de la nomination du directeur général. Un petit groupe de membres du conseil, y compris les dirigeants, forment le comité exécutif, qui se réunit entre les réunions du conseil pour prendre des décisions au nom du conseil.

Habituellement, les dirigeants d'une association sont le président, le vice-président, le trésorier et le secrétaire. Ils peuvent être choisis par les membres ou nommés par le conseil; leurs tâches sont fixées par les règlements ou établis par le conseil. Le directeur général ou chef de la direction (le titre peut varier) assume les tâches que lui confie le conseil d'administration. Il met en oeuvre les politiques définies par le conseil, choisit les employés chargés du fonctionnement du bureau de l'association, prépare les budgets, approuve les dépenses et assiste à toutes les réunions du conseil et de son comité exécutif.

La structure de comités des associations reflète habituellement leurs buts et objectifs. Les responsabilités typiques des comités incluent l'adhésion des membres, les nominations, la formation, la recherche, les publications, les relations publiques et avec le gouvernement. Les dirigeants et les administrateurs sont tenus de rendre compte périodiquement de leur gestion, habituellement sous la forme d'un rapport annuel. Les conditions d'adhésion sont habituellement fixées par les règlements de l'association, et il peut exister plusieurs formes d'adhésion, comme à titre de membres, d'associés, d'étudiants ou de membres honoraires. Certaines associations acceptent toute personne intéressée à leurs activités. D'autres, comme les associations professionnelles, ont des conditions d'admission spécifiques. En général, les organisations de bienfaisance comptent sur des subventions gouvernementales et sur des dons du milieu des affaires ou du grand public pour leur financement, tandis que les associations de membres tirent leurs revenus de droits et de cotisations.

Contribution sociale

Les associations enregistrées au fédéral en tant qu'organisations de bienfaisance sont légalement obligées de fournir des services qui profitent à l'ensemble de la population. Bien que le principal objectif des associations de membres soit la promotion des intérêts de leurs membres, elles peuvent aussi réagir aux conditions sociales changeantes en s'engageant dans des programmes et des activités d'intérêt public. Les associations jouent un rôle important dans l'élaboration d'un consensus au sein de la société, puisqu'elles fournissent les mécanismes permettant à leurs membres de s'entendre sur des valeurs sociales, sur les objectifs à poursuivre et sur les moyens de les atteindre. Par leur interaction avec le gouvernement, les associations contribuent à façonner la politique gouvernementale. Les associations nationales, dont plusieurs sont bilingues, peuvent contribuer au renforcement de l'unité nationale en améliorant la communication et la compréhension entre les différents peuples et régions du Canada.

Les associations ont évolué en tant que groupes d'entraide ou de mentorat offrant à leurs membres l'expérience et les ressources convenant à leur champ d'intérêt. Elles constituent aussi d'importantes sources d'information sur des centaines d'activités spécialisées dans notre société. En aidant ceux qui sont dans le besoin, en soutenant et en publiant des recherches dignes d'intérêt, en faisant de l'éducation auprès du public, en contribuant à l'épanouissement personnel des citoyens et en se portant à la défense de causes justes et humanitaires, les associations fournissent un apport appréciable à la société canadienne et à ses citoyens.

On peut obtenir des renseignements supplémentaires sur les associations au Canada dans la publication annuelle *Associations Canada* de Grey House Publishing Canada. Elle résulte de la fusion de deux répertoires, le *Répertoire des associations du Canada et Associations Canada : un répertoire encyclopédique*. De nos jours, le répertoire donne des détails concernant les activités d'associations diverses du Canada, qu'elles soient canadiennes ou étrangères, d'associations professionnelles et d'organismes sans but lucratif et bénévoles. Le répertoire utilise de plus 1 500 classements par sujet, allant de l'administration à la zoologie, pour décrire les activités de plus de 18 000 associations répertoriées.

Auteur R. BRIAN LAND

Source: *L'Encyclopédie Canadienne*, Historica Canada.
www.thecanadianencyclopedia.ca

PROTECT YOUR ORGANIZATION FROM BAD EMPLOYEES

At the Foundation: Your Core Values

By Mike Campion

How much of a negative impact can the bad apples in your organization have? Are having no bad employees a realistic goal? First things first: What is a bad employee?

- Is it just someone who is bad at their job?
- Takes too much time off?
- Has a penchant for punching other employees?

While none of those are ideal, they all focus on actions and results instead of the root cause. Instead of trying to create a comprehensive list of "do's and don'ts" for your employees to ignore, start at the foundation: your Core Values.

A bad employee is anyone who does not love and live your organization's Core Values.

Discovering your Core Values is an action in-and-of itself, but when you have a set of "rules" to run your organization with, you will find that the people who line up with those rules don't tend to violate the "do's and don'ts" of your organization.

Luckily, you have the keys to the happy employee kingdom. Get ready to discover the Three Steps to protect your organization from the wrong employees:

1. Stop them from showing up
2. Stop them from getting in
3. Stop them from sticking around

Step 1 - Stop Bad Employees from Showing Up

Pre-framing is extremely important when weeding out potential problem employees. How an employee is first exposed to your organization is key. Consider the following two examples:

1. A current employee tells his friend, a prospective employee, "You should apply at my job; the place is so disorganized, we could get away with anything."

2. A prospective employee comes across your website and thinks, "These are my people! I love what they are all about, I wonder if they are hiring..."

When you feature enough of your Core Values on your website, in your hiring ads, phone systems and your current employees become evangelists for your mission, you position your organization as the right place for the right employee. Whenever, however a prospective employee becomes aware of your organization, they feel like they have finally found their tribe. This alone will dramatically increase the quality of your applicant pool. Which brings us to...

Step 2 - Stop the Wrong Employees from Getting In

Once you have laid the foundation in Step One, the job of keeping bad employees from infiltrating your organization is half done. All you have to do is make sure that your organization is actually living and breathing the Core Values that brought prospective employees to you in the first place.

So many employers focus on job history and/or technical ability. Both offer good insight, but are only relevant with employees who have the same Core beliefs as you do. Hire for attitude, train for skill.

If your organization is passionate about outstanding customer service, it is eminently possible to teach an employee how to serve a customer. It is a fool's errand to teach him to be enthusiastic about customer service. Your life will improve exponentially when you are in the business of stoking your employees' passions and values. You are not in the business of convincing people to do something they don't want to do or believe something they don't want to believe.

Craft your interview process around the values that attracted your prospective employees. Once that is a match, job history and ability to do the job at-hand come into play. An unintended consequence of passionately living your organization's Core Values is an extremely attractive community. This can make employees that aren't a good fit work even harder to get in, even when your pre-framing and interview process is Core Values-based. Time for the big guns...

Step 3 - Get 'em Out

Creating a Core Values-driven culture not only naturally repels the wrong employees; it strongly attracts the right employees. They feel "at home," like they have finally found something special. They don't want to leave. They stay longer, work harder and enjoy their jobs more.

The flip side is that people who are not a Core Value fit feel out of place. They don't fit in. They don't understand why everyone acts so differently. They discover that the amazing community that attracted them to your organization isn't for them. More often than not, they wander off into the night on their own free will.

When you do have someone that doesn't get the memo, and needs a little help recognizing they aren't a fit, you will weed them out by systematic recognition and application of your Core Values. Examples of Core

Values being either applied properly or ignored or mishandled are common topics. Decision making conversations regularly start and end with your Core Values.

Those who don't "get" your values will stick out like a sore thumb. When you see that is the case, have a conversation. Refer back to your hiring process. Verify they share your organization's values. If they do, their behavior will follow and all is well. If they don't, it's time to help them transition into an organization that is a better fit.

It can sound like an overwhelming prospect, but integrating your Core Values into your organization is like pushing a flywheel. It takes a lot of energy at the beginning, but when it gets spinning, it creates a tremendous amount of power on its own. Not only will keeping bad employees out of your organization help your bottom line—it will make your life and your employees lives far better.

PROTÉGEZ VOTRE ORGANISATION CONTRE LES MAUVAIS EMPLOYÉS

À la base : vos valeurs clés

Par Mike Campion

Quel impact négatif peuvent avoir les « pommes pourries » dans votre organisation? N'avoir aucun mauvais employé est-il un objectif réaliste? Mais d'abord : qu'est-ce qu'un mauvais employé?

- Est-ce seulement quelqu'un qui fait mal son travail?
- Quelqu'un qui prend trop de congés?
- Quelqu'un qui a tendance à cogner sur d'autres employés?

Bien qu'aucune de ces définitions ne soit idéale, elles sont toutes axées sur les résultats plutôt que la cause fondamentale.

Au lieu de tenter de créer une liste détaillée des choses « à faire » et « à ne pas faire » que vos employés ignoreront, commencez à la base : vos valeurs clés.

Un mauvais employé est quiconque n'admet pas et n'adhère pas aux valeurs clés de votre organisation.

Découvrir vos valeurs clés est une action en elle-même, mais lorsque vous avez établi un ensemble de « règles » avec lesquelles diriger votre organisation, vous constaterez que les gens qui s'adaptent à ces règles n'auront pas tendance à les violer.

Heureusement, vous détenez les clés du royaume de l'employé heureux. Préparez-vous à découvrir les trois étapes pour protéger votre organisation contre les mauvais employés :

1. Les empêcher de se montrer
2. Les empêcher d'entrer
3. Les empêcher de rester

Étape 1 – Empêcher les mauvais employés de se montrer

La pré-formulation est extrêmement importante pour éliminer les possibles employés problèmes. L'exposition initiale de l'employé à votre organisation est la clé. Voyez les deux exemples suivants :

1. Un employé actuel dit à son ami, un employé potentiel : « tu devrais poser ta candidature à mon poste; la place est tellement désorganisée qu'on peut faire n'importe quoi ».

2. Un employé potentiel découvre votre site web et se dit « ce sont mes gens! J'adore ce qu'ils représentent, je me demande s'ils embauchent ... »

Si vous présentez suffisamment de vos valeurs clés sur votre site web, dans vos annonces d'embauche, les systèmes téléphoniques et vos employés actuels deviennent les évangélistes de votre mission, votre position, votre organisation comme étant le bon endroit pour le bon employé. Lorsqu'un employé potentiel découvre votre organisation, il croit avoir enfin trouvé sa tribu. Ce seul phénomène augmentera considérablement la qualité de votre bassin de candidats. Ce qui nous amène à l'étape suivante...

Étape 2 – Empêcher les mauvais employés d'entrer

Une fois que vous avez établi les bases à l'étape un, l'objectif d'empêcher les mauvais employés d'infiltrer votre organisation est à moitié réalisé. Tout ce que vous avez à faire est de vous assurer que votre organisation vie et respire véritablement les valeurs clés qui ont mené vers vous des employés potentiels.

Un grand nombre d'employeurs se concentrent sur les antécédents de travail et/ou les capacités techniques. Ces deux éléments offrent une bonne information, mais ne sont pertinents qu'avec les employés qui ont les mêmes croyances clés que vous. Embauchez pour l'attitude, formez pour les compétences.

Si votre organisation se passionne pour un service à la clientèle exceptionnel, il est parfaitement possible d'enseigner à un employé comment servir un client. Il est inutile de lui enseigner à être enthousiaste au sujet du service à la clientèle. Votre vie s'améliorera exponentiellement si vous œuvrez à attiser les passions et les valeurs de vos employés. Vous ne travaillez pas à convaincre les gens de faire une chose qu'ils ne veulent pas faire ou de croire une chose qu'ils ne veulent pas croire.

Élaborez votre processus d'entrevue autour des valeurs qui ont attiré vos employés potentiels. Une fois cette correspondance établie, les antécédents de travail et la capacité d'effectuer le travail entrent en jeu. Une conséquence involontaire de vivre passionnément les valeurs clés de votre organisation est une communauté extrêmement attrayante. Cela peut amener des employés qui ne correspondent pas au travail à travailler encore plus fort pour entrer dans votre organisation, même lorsque votre pré-formulation et votre processus d'entrevue sont fondés sur les valeurs clés. Le moment est venu de sortir les gros canons...

Étape 3 – Faire sortir les mauvais employés

Créer une culture motivée par les valeurs clés repousse non seulement les mauvais employés, mais attire fortement les bons employés. Ils se sentent « chez eux », comme s'ils avaient enfin trouvé quelque chose de spécial. Ils ne veulent pas quitter. Ils restent plus longtemps, travaillent plus fort et aiment davantage leur travail.

Le revers de la médaille est que les gens qui ne correspondent pas aux valeurs clés ne se sentent pas à leur place. Ils ne sont pas à leur place. Ils ne comprennent pas pourquoi les gens agissent tellement différemment. Ils découvrent que la communauté formidable qui les a attirés vers votre organisation n'est pas pour eux. Plus souvent qu'autrement, ils quittent de leur propre gré.

Si vous avez quelqu'un qui ne saisit pas le message, et a besoin d'un peu d'aide pour reconnaître qu'il n'est pas à sa place, vous l'éliminerez par la reconnaissance systématique et l'application de vos valeurs clés. Les exemples de valeurs clés qui sont appliquées adéquatement, ou ignorées, ou malmenées sont des sujets courants. Les conversations de prise de décision commencent et se terminent régulièrement par vos valeurs clés.

Ceux qui ne saisissent pas vos valeurs ressortiront du lot. Si vous voyez que c'est le cas, ayez une conversation. Reportez-vous à votre processus d'embauche. Vérifiez qu'ils partagent les valeurs de votre organisation. Si c'est le cas, leur comportement suivra et tout va bien. Si ce n'est pas le cas, il est temps de les aider à faire la transition vers une organisation qui leur convient mieux.

Cela peut sembler une dure perspective, mais intégrer vos valeurs clés dans votre organisation est comme faire tourner une toupie. Il faut beaucoup d'énergie au début, mais une fois qu'elle a commencé à tourner, elle crée elle-même une quantité formidable d'énergie. Tenir les mauvais employés à l'écart de votre organisation aidera non seulement vos résultats—mais rendra votre vie et celle de vos employés bien meilleure.

Originally published in *Association*™ *Magazine* (Summer 2017). Reprinted with the permission of the Canadian Society of Association Executives (CSAE), 2017. www.csae.com.

ONE STEP AT A TIME

While there's no official rulebook on merging two associations, there are careful steps that can be taken to optimize success

By Roma Ihnatowycz

For many associations, mergers represent a fabulous window of opportunity, falling under the 'two heads are better than one' axiom. They de facto support the idea that associations coming together to work as one can better service and represent a diverse, often-overlapping membership base, with countless budgetary and administrative benefits.

For others, the mere mention of 'merger' sends shivers down their spine as they envision turf wars, the loss of a voice in their representative body, and an erosion of services catering to their specific needs. They fear they will simply end up a tiny cog in a much larger machine and face a bloody battle fighting for their interests in the amalgamation process.

For Dana Cooper, executive director for Orthotics Prosthetics Canada (OPC) and a consultant with Association Management, Consulting & Evaluation Services (AMCES), this comes as no surprise. Mergers represent change, and human nature is generally averse to change, at least at the beginning.

"Anytime you have significant change you have an immediate apprehension and resistance to that change – sometimes with associations it's even emotional," explains Cooper. "That's the first reaction, and it's something that needs to be overcome. It's about making people at ease with the idea."

Cooper is speaking from personal experience: he was actively involved in the merger of the Canadian Association for Prosthetics and Orthotics and the Canadian Board for Certification of Prosthetists and Orthotists, which resulted in the creation of OPC in January 2015. "It had been talked about for a number of years prior to my arrival," he says, "but it never really got to fruition. They talked about it, but they really didn't know the process to make it happen."

Cooper was brought on as Executive Director of both organizations in early 2014 and oversaw their merger throughout that year. While to the outside eye it appears to have happened swiftly and seamlessly, it was more a question of timing. Cooper says he joined the groups following many years of internal debate and discussion around the topic, so the two organizations were ready for making the change and looking for guidance.

The right time

This speaks to an integral and somewhat uncontrollable part of the merger puzzle: good timing. According to George Lozano, another association management consultant with AMCES who was brought in to manage the OPC merger, the timing needs to be right, with both groups ready to embark on the process.

To help determine this, a third-party consultant can be contracted to assess a group's readiness to take on a merger. "I'm a very big believer in timing – in the case of OPC, the timing was right and they just needed a third-party to bring the two groups together," says Lozano, adding that mistakes tend to happen when associations don't determine their overall preparedness. "They need to assess whether there is readiness for change. Sometimes it means you don't rush; you back off, you work and you prepare."

How long it takes to reach that decision-making point can be anybody's guess. In the case of OPC, the two groups had started talking about merging as early as 2008. So, while some mergers may appear to happen quickly, there are often years of informal discussions laying the foundation. At OPC, the seed had been planted long before the merger was activated, and members therefore had plenty of time to acclimatize to the idea. While not every association may need to ruminate over a possible merger over many years, those that are rushed and poorly timed run a higher risk of failure. With so many stakeholders involved, the fusion of two groups is not something that can be pushed through in an aggressive manner.

Indications that associations may not be ready – or suited – to merge can vary from dissimilar philosophies at the board level, different constituencies among stakeholders, or a mismatch in their financial soundness and size. In the latter case, "it becomes a takeover rather than a merger," says Cooper. "But when it does make sense, when sustainability is enhanced, when there are synergistic benefits like increased efficiencies in delivering services or meeting member needs, then the revitalization that a merger offers an organization is a big benefit."

Even with all these elements in place, amalgamation is not always an easy process, which brings us to the next critical step: calling in expert help. Consolidating two associations into one is not an easy or simple undertaking, and rarely do board members have any experience in this area. "A fatal flaw in associations is when they try to undertake work that they don't have the skills to do," warns Cooper. High on that list is amalgamation.

This can easily be addressed by bringing in an association management consultant to guide the all the players through the process. The added advantage is that an outside expert is a neutral participant, with no leaning or bias to any particular group of stakeholders. This, in turn, helps put everyone at ease. "When you bring in a third party that is neutral, they treat both sides even-handedly in an open and transparent manner. This restores confidence, and confidence in the process is very important," advises Lozano.

First steps

With the OPC merger, Lozano's first steps revolved around facilitating strategic discussions to identify the various pros and cons of amalgamation to figure out if it made sense. Clearly, it did. Both groups were operating out of the same office – one as a certifying body for many members of the other. As such, there was substantial overlap many areas. It was determined it would more economical, efficient and effective for both groups to operate under one umbrella.

An amalgamation task force was established, comprised of executives from the two organizations. It decided on the next steps, and these ranged from settling the disposition of assets and drafting a new set of bylaws compliant with the Not for Profit Corporations Act, to establishing the new association's governance model and membership structure. A formal amalgamation agreement was then drafted, a work plan drawn up, and timeline confirmed. Further along in the process, a transitional board was set up for the new association's first year of operation until a new board could be voted in at its following AGM.

The two associations put significant effort into communicating their strategy and progress with all stakeholders and members. Communication, says Cooper, is the motherlode of any successful amalgamation, and in the case of OPC, this included webinars, town hall meetings, an amalgamation-branded newsletter, as well as a dedicated online micro-site giving members access to amalgamation documents and the chance to comment and ask questions. When it comes to amalgamation, says Cooper, "You really can't under-communicate."

Transparency with all involved parties went a long way to ease any lingering concerns. Soliciting member input was important, as was communicating information to them in a sensitive and appropriate manner. While an outside expert may have provided the two groups with the necessary expertise, Lozano was only there to guide the elected leadership in their decision-making process, not to communicate with or instruct members directly.

"There were lots of little details that had to be communicated very honestly and very openly to the membership of both organizations and this was done in a variety of ways," explains Lozano. "As a consultant, I had to make sure that it was the volunteers who were spearheading this effort and that they were well-informed, so that it wasn't a consultant communicating with members about what to do. It was really their own leadership that was speaking to them."

Given the sensitivities and concerns that members inevitably had, the amalgamation process had to be handled with care. "One wrong move and you upset people who all of a sudden feel betrayed," warns Lozano. "Then you don't have the full confidence of the people in the process, and the next thing you know, it's going south."

Things fortunately went in the opposite direction for OPC, and the new amalgamated association, now in its third year of operation, is running smoothly as planned. While that's not to say there weren't some hiccups in the merger – there always are – the two groups had all the components in place to prime them for success.

Mergers ahead

In all likelihood, there will be more mergers in the not-for-profit sector in the coming years. The decentralization trend of the 1980s is now in reverse, with more organizations moving to a centralized model that works well in today's hi-tech marketplace.

"Because of the various ways of communicating and delivering information and education programs to members, you can still have regional sensitivity, representation and good communication without necessarily having an organization for every single province," says Lozano. "I've even seen associations that are totally virtual."

Cooper agrees, noting that associations need to keep focused on their key objective, which is serving their members and their profession. If merging with another group furthers this aim, it should be considered. "You hold back the profession when you have competing interests and fragmentation among groups," he says.

Certainly, not all groups stand to benefit from a merger. But if they do, it can reap many rewards. So long as they take things one careful step at a time.

UNE ÉTAPE À LA FOIS

Bien qu'il n'existe aucune règle en matière de fusion de deux associations, des mesures de prudence peuvent en optimiser le succès

Par Roma Ihnatowycz

Pour bon nombre d'associations, les fusions représentent une fabuleuse vitrine de possibilités, selon le principe « deux têtes valent mieux qu'une ». Elles soutiennent de fait l'idée que les associations qui s'unissent pour travailler comme une seule entité peuvent mieux servir et représenter un bassin de membres diversifiés et qui se chevauchent, avec d'innombrables avantages budgétaires et administratifs.

Pour d'autres, le seul fait de mentionner le terme « fusion » leur donne des sueurs froides car ils envisagent des guerres de tranchées, la perte d'une voix au sein de l'organe représentatif et une érosion des services répondant à leurs besoins spécifiques. Ils craignent de finir comme un rouage minuscule dans une machine beaucoup plus grosse et de faire face à une bataille sanglante pour leurs intérêts lors du processus de fusion.

Selon Dana Cooper, directeur administratif d'Orthotics Prosthetics Canada (OPC) et expert-conseil chez Association Management, Consulting & Evaluation Services (AMCES), cela n'est pas surprenant. Les fusions représentent un changement, et la nature humaine est en général rébarbative au changement, du moins au début.

« Chaque fois que vous subissez un changement important, vous éprouvez une appréhension et une résistance immédiates à ce changement – et cette réaction est parfois plus émotive avec les associations, » explique M. Cooper. « C'est la première réaction, et c'est une chose à surmonter. Il s'agit de rendre les gens à l'aise avec l'idée. »

M. Cooper parle de sa propre expérience : il a été activement impliqué dans la fusion de l'Association canadienne en prothèses et orthèses et du Conseil canadien de la certification des prothésistes et orthésistes, qui a entraîné la création de l'OPC en janvier 2015. « On en parlait depuis quelques années avant mon arrivé, mais sans jamais que le projet n'aboutisse. Ils en parlaient mais ne savaient réellement pas comment déclencher le processus, » déclare-t-il.

On a recruté M. Cooper comme directeur administratif des deux organisations au début de 2014 et il a supervisé leur fusion pendant l'année. Vue de l'extérieur, la fusion peut sembler s'être déroulée rapidement et sans anicroche, mais c'était une question de moment opportun. M. Cooper affirme avoir joint les groupes après plusieurs années de débats et discussions internes autour du sujet, et les deux organisations étaient donc prêtes à faire le changement et à rechercher des conseils.

Le bon moment

Cela rejoint une partie intégrale et quelque peu incontrôlable du casse-tête de la fusion : le moment opportun. Selon George Lozano, un autre expert-conseil en gestion d'association chez AMCES que l'on a recruté pour diriger la fusion de l'OPC, le moment doit être bien choisi pour que les deux groupes soient prêts à entreprendre le processus.

Afin de déterminer si c'est le cas, on peut engager un expert-conseil externe pour évaluer le degré de préparation d'un groupe à entreprendre une fusion. « Je suis un fervent adepte du moment choisi – dans le cas de l'OPC, le moment était opportun et il ne fallait plus que l'aide d'une tierce partie pour réunir les deux groupes, » déclare M. Lozano, ajoutant que les erreurs tendent à survenir lorsque les associations ne déterminent pas leur état de préparation global. « Elles doivent évaluer si elles sont prêtes au changement. Cela signifie parfois de ne pas se presser, de prendre du recul, de travailler et de se préparer. »

On ne peut prévoir combien de temps il faudra pour atteindre ce point de prise de décision. Dans le cas de l'OPC, les deux groupes avaient commencé dès 2008 à discuter de fusion. Bien que certaines fusions semblent survenir rapidement, il faut souvent plusieurs années de discussions informelles pour établir les fondements. À l'OPC, la graine avait été semée bien longtemps avant que la fusion ne soit activée, et les membres ont par conséquent eu amplement le temps de se faire à l'idée. Les associations n'ont pas toutes à ruminer sur une possible fusion pendant de nombreuses années, mais celles qui sont pressées de fusionner, à un mauvais moment, courent davantage de risques d'échec. Compte tenu du nombre élevé de parties prenantes impliquées, la fusion de deux groupes n'est pas un processus à réaliser de manière agressive.

Les signes que des associations ne sont peut-être pas prêtes– ou convenables – à une fusion peuvent varier de philosophies différentes au conseil d'administration, à une structure de base différente parmi les parties prenantes, ou une incompatibilité dans leur solidité financière et leur taille. Dans ce dernier cas, « cela devient une prise de contrôle plutôt qu'une fusion, » indique M. Cooper. « Mais quand cela fait du sens, lorsque la durabilité en est améliorée, lorsqu'il existe des avantages synergiques tels que des efficacités accrues dans la livraison de services ou la réponse aux besoins des membres, la dynamisation qu'offre la fusion à une organisation est un grand avantage. »

Malgré tous ces éléments en place, la fusion n'est pas toujours un processus aisé, ce qui nous amène à l'étape critique suivante : faire appel à une aide experte. Regrouper deux associations pour n'en faire qu'une n'est pas une entreprise facile ou simple, et les membres du conseil ont rarement de l'expérience en la matière. « Des associations qui tentent d'entreprendre un travail pour lequel elles ne possèdent pas les compétences constitue une faille fatale, » prévient M. Cooper. La fusion se situe très haut sur cette liste.

On peut cependant traiter facilement le problème en recrutant un expert-conseil en gestion d'association pour guider tous les intervenants à travers le processus. L'avantage ajouté est qu'un expert externe est un participant neutre, sans penchant ni parti pris pour un groupe en particulier de parties prenantes. Cela a pour effet de mettre tout le monde à l'aise. « Lorsque vous recrutez une tierce partie neutre, elle traite équitablement les deux parties d'une manière ouverte et transparente. Cela rétablit la confiance, et la confiance envers le processus est très importante, » conseille M. Lozano.

Premières étapes

En ce qui concerne la fusion de l'OPC, les premières étapes de M. Lozano visaient à faciliter les discussions stratégiques afin d'identifier les divers points positifs et négatifs de la fusion et déterminer si elle était logique. C'était de toute évidence le cas. Les deux groupes opéraient depuis le même bureau – l'un comme organe de certification pour de nombreux membres de l'autre groupe. À ce titre, il existait d'importants chevauchements dans de nombreux domaines. On a déterminé qu'il serait plus économique, plus efficient et plus efficace pour les deux groupes d'opérer sous une même enseigne.

On a mis sur pied un groupe de travail sur la fusion, composé de cadres des deux organisations. Ce groupe a décidé des étapes à venir, lesquelles allaient de régler la disposition des actifs et d'ébaucher un nouvel ensemble de règlements administratifs conformes à la nouvelle *Loi sur les organisations à but non lucratif*, à établir le modèle de gouvernance et la structure d'adhésion de la nouvelle association. On a ensuite ébauché un accord officiel de fusion, établi un plan de travail et confirmé un échéancier. Plus tard dans le processus, un conseil d'administration de transition a été formé pour la première année opérationnelle de la nouvelle association, jusqu'à ce qu'un nouveau conseil puisse être élu à son AGA suivante.

Les deux associations ont consacré beaucoup d'efforts à communiquer leur stratégie et leur progression à toutes les parties prenantes et tous les membres. Selon M. Cooper, la communication est le filon principal de toute fusion réussie, et dans le cas de l'OPC, elle incluait des webinaires, des réunions à l'hôtel de ville, un bulletin dédié au thème de la fusion, ainsi qu'un microsite spécial en ligne donnant aux membres accès à des documents sur la fusion et la chance de commenter et de poser des questions. En matière de fusion, indique M. Cooper, « vous ne devez jamais sous-communiquer. »

La transparence avec toutes les parties prenantes a beaucoup contribué à apaiser toute inquiétude persistante. Il était important de demander aux membres leurs suggestions, tout comme de leur communiquer l'information d'une manière sensible et appropriée. Bien qu'un expert externe aurait pu fournir aux deux groupes l'expertise nécessaire, M. Lozano n'était là que pour guider le leadership élu dans son processus décisionnel, et non pour communiquer directement avec les membres ou les informer.

« Beaucoup de petits détails devaient être communiqués très honnêtement et ouvertement aux membres des deux organisations, de diverses manières, » explique M. Lozano. « En tant qu'expert-conseil, je devais m'assurer que les bénévoles soient les fers de lance de cet effort et qu'ils soient bien informés, de façon à ce que ce ne soit pas un expert-conseil qui communique avec les membres à savoir ce qu'il fallait faire. C'était véritablement leur propre leadership qui leur parlait. »

Compte tenu des sensibilités et des inquiétudes qu'exprimaient inévitablement les membres, le processus de fusion devait être traité avec soin. « Un faux mouvement et vous contrariez des gens qui se sentent soudain trahis, » prévient M. Lozano. « Vous n'avez plus la confiance totale des gens faisant partie du processus et avant longtemps, le processus dérive. »

Les choses sont heureusement allées dans la bonne direction pour l'OPC, et la nouvelle association issue de la fusion, maintenant dans sa troisième année d'opération, fonctionne bien, tel que planifié. Nous ne disons pas qu'il n'y a pas eu d'anicroches pendant la fusion – il y en a toujours – mais les deux groupes avaient tous les éléments en place pour les préparer au succès.

Fusions à l'horizon

Selon toute vraisemblance, le secteur sans but lucratif connaîtra davantage de fusions dans les années à venir. La tendance de décentralisation des années 1980 s'est inversée, alors que davantage d'organisations visent un modèle centralisé qui fonctionne bien sur le marché actuel de la haute technologie.

« Étant donné les divers moyens de communiquer et de livrer l'information, et les programmes de formation offerts aux membres, vous pouvez toujours avoir une sensibilité et une représentation régionales, ainsi qu'une bonne communication, sans avoir nécessairement une organisation pour chaque province. J'ai même vu des associations totalement virtuelles, » indique M. Lozano.

M. Cooper est du même avis, soulignant que les associations doivent rester concentrées sur leur objectif clé qui est de servir leurs membres et leur profession. Si une fusion avec un autre groupe favorise cet objectif, il faudrait l'envisager. « Vous freinez la profession lorsque vous avez des intérêts en concurrence et une fragmentation parmi les groupes, » déclare-t-il.

Évidemment, ce ne sont pas tous les groupes qui peuvent tirer profit d'une fusion. Mais si c'est le cas, la fusion peut comporter de nombreux avantages. En autant que l'on suive soigneusement les étapes, une à la fois.

Originally published in *Association™ Magazine* (Fall 2017). Reprinted with the permission of the Canadian Society of Association Executives (CSAE), 2017. www.csae.com.

THE POWER OF "OLD SCHOOL" SERVICE

Four Reasons Your Association Should Bring It Back

By Joseph Michelli

Not-for-profit organizations may be more tech-savvy than ever, but customers (i.e., members) still crave old-fashioned service (albeit with a modern spin). Customer experience thought leader Joseph Michelli says that if you want your organization to thrive, you'd better go retro in your service delivery.

As the tech industry has exploded over the past couple of decades and millennials have risen to power, private, public and not-for-profit organizations have innovated wildly to keep up with relentless customer expectations. *Better, faster, easier!* is the battle cry. *Oh, and make sure there's an app for that!* It's no surprise that sleek, streamlined, lightning-paced organizations abound these days. Yes it *is* what customers wanted—but isn't there something cold and impersonal about many 21st century transactions?
You're not imagining it, says Joseph Michelli. Yes, customers (again, think: members) still demand the speed and efficiency. But what they really *crave* is that feeling of an old school organization that takes the time to really know them, engage them, nurture them.

"No matter how high tech your service becomes, you're still serving human beings," says Michelli, best-selling author of *Driven to Delight: Delivering World-Class Customer Experience the Mercedes-Benz Way* (McGraw-Hill; December 2015; ISBN: 978-0-07-180630-5; $27.00). "Humans don't want to feel like a URL or a Twitter handle or even a consumer. We want to feel like we *matter*. We'll always choose companies and organizations that give us that feeling."

Michelli—who worked with Mercedes-Benz USA to positively and radically transform its customer experience and who has written books on service giants like Zappos and Starbucks—knows how crucial it is to know your customers and show them how much you care.

"It may seem counterintuitive to ask a 2016 dot-com to bring back mom and pop, Main Street values," he says. "But really, it's not a conflict. You *can* provide customized, on-the-spot service and *still* make people feel like they just had an authentic, deeply personal experience."

HOW you create this experience will vary depending on who you are, what you're selling, what your current roadblocks may be. (HINT: You might have culture problems that shape your practices, processes, and priorities in ways that sabotage service.) Yet as you seek to go more "retro" in your service delivery, Michelli suggests you start by knowing the WHYs:

Customers crave a connection to simpler times. Life is so frantic and complicated, due in large part to technology. And people don't want to get rid of technology, because it lets us attain goods and services quickly and efficiently. But when we need to get on the phone with a person, or when we're face to face, we want to know we're talking to a human being who has our interests at heart—not a machine. We long for the days when the shopkeeper would open the store after hours for a customer in need.

"Customers want the organizations that service them to be part Silicon Valley, part Main Street," says Michelli. "There's this tension between our age of incredible technology and the retro, connected, heartwarming, Norman Rockwell-y type of customer service people really want, and I think too many organizations have gone too far in the space-age direction.

"A culture of compassion and empathy still has to come through in your person-to-person interactions," he adds. "There really is something about sharing a smile—sharing a moment together—that becomes increasingly important in the cluttered world. We want people to pause and take a moment with us."

Customers find comfort in "the familiar." No one likes to spend their valuable time dumping less than stellar companies or organizations only to start all over again in the search for better ones. People enjoy predictable organizations they're used to and comfortable with—as long as they deliver great service. An effort to remind valuable stakeholders and members that they are valued goes a long way in ensuring that you retain your customer base.

"I still go to my doctor in Colorado for second opinions—and I live in Florida!" muses Michelli. "I don't have to tell him a huge backstory, because he's known me for years. And the fact that he does great work to serve me, as the customer...that's a big part of it too."

He suggests you find ways to remind your customer how far back you go and that you strive to foster a lasting relationship. Whether that means logging notes about their particular needs in your database so you can follow up or offering "anniversary" discounts honoring their patronage or long term membership, you can earn their loyalty and keep them coming back by treating them like they genuinely matter.

Old school service fits with the burgeoning artisanal movement happening now. For many years there's been a lot of mass-produced junk out there. Customers everywhere are conditioned to expect less thanks to millions of disappointing products coming from across the globe. No wonder we're in the middle of a full-fledged consumer backlash. More and more, shoppers are choosing products and services that are unique, customized labors of love.

"Look at the craft beer craze that's everywhere today," comments Michelli. "For generations, people drank pilsner—they were conditioned to do that. But now, more and more people are falling in love with the amazing craft beers available, because microbrewers have reclaimed the art of beer making.

"Organizations such as associations will delight members when they pride themselves on their craftsmanship and skill level," he adds. "There's something uplifting about watching well-crafted skills and just appreciating that ability. There is an artisanship of service at the Ritz-Carlton. Watching those professionals in action just makes you go, *Wow, that's a lost art!*"

Your service style helps you stand out from the pack. Obviously this is the most compelling reason to adopt an old school approach to service. It will draw customers/members to you and maybe even keep you alive. There's so much competition out there today that the way you treat and relate to your members may be the only thing that makes you *you*.

"You can bring things to market very quickly today," says Michelli. "Speed and global distribution sometimes make for product ubiquity, so it is all the more critical that you differentiate yourself by putting your customers first and really owning a certain style of old-fashioned service."

Here's the bottom line: Even though the times have changed and technology has leapt into the foreground, basic human needs have stayed the same.

"There's **NEVER** going to be a time when people say, *I don't really care if you hurt me. I don't really care if you appreciate me. I don't really care if I belong. You know, as far as I'm concerned, I just want to buy your stuff,*" concludes Michelli. "And I think because of that, we have to anchor ourselves to the timeless truth of humanity, even as we customize the delivery in line with the cultural trends.

"Successful organizations are the ones that really get that," he adds. "They figure out how to integrate technology but still truly connect to the customer face to face or on the phone. They instill it in their training. Team members learn to make sure customers know that they matter—that they are always heard and appreciated."

LA PUISSANCE DU SERVICE « À L'ANCIENNE »

Quatre raisons pour lesquelles votre association devrait les ramener

Par Joseph Michelli

Les organismes sans but lucratif sont peut-être plus technophiles que jamais, mais les clients (c.-à-d. les membres) aspirent encore à un service à l'ancienne (quoique avec une touche moderne). L'expert en réflexion sur l'expérience client Joseph Michelli affirme que si vous souhaitez que votre organisation prospère, vous devriez prendre le virage rétro dans votre livraison de services.

Avec l'explosion de l'industrie technologique au cours des deux dernières décennies, et compte tenu de la montée des milléniaux vers le pouvoir, les organisations privées, publiques et sans but lucratif ont grandement innové pour suivre sans cesse les attentes des clients. *Mieux, plus vite, plus facile!* est un cri de guerre. *Et faites en sorte qu'il y ait une application!* Il n'est pas étonnant que des organisations minimalistes, simplifiées et à la vitesse de l'éclair abondent de nos jours. Oui, c'*est* ce que voulaient les clients—mais n'y a-t-il pas quelque chose de froid et d'impersonnel dans beaucoup de transactions du 21e siècle?

Vous ne rêvez pas, déclare Joseph Michelli. Oui, les clients (pensez de nouveau en termes de membres) exigent toujours vitesse et efficacité. Mais ce à quoi ils *aspirent* vraiment est la sensation d'une organisation à l'ancienne qui prend le temps de vraiment les connaître, les faire participer, les enrichir.

« Peut importe le degré de technologie que votre service atteint, vous servez toujours des êtres humains, » indique Michelli, auteur à succès de *Driven to Delight: Delivering World-Class Customer Experience the Mercedes-Benz Way* (McGraw-Hill; décembre 2015; ISBN: 978-0-07-180630-5; 27 $). « Les humains ne veulent pas se sentir comme un URL, une poignée de messages Twitter ou même un consommateur. Nous voulons sentir que nous *comptons*. Nous choisirons toujours des compagnies et des organisations qui nous donnent ce sentiment. »

Michelli—qui a travaillé chez Mercedes-Benz USA pour transformer positivement et radicalement son expérience client et qui a écrit des livres sur des géants du service tels que Zappos et Starbucks—sait à quel point il est crucial de connaître vos clients et de leur démontrer à quel point vous vous souciez d'eux. « Il peut sembler paradoxal de demander à un point-com 2016 de ramener des valeurs familiales, mais réellement, ce n'est pas un conflit. Vous *pouvez* fournir un service personnalisé sur place, et *continuer* de faire sentir aux gens qu'ils vivent une expérience authentique et profondément personnelle, » explique-t-il. »

Votre FAÇON de créer cette expérience variera selon qui vous êtes, ce que vous vendez, vos obstacles actuels possibles. (INDICE : vous pouvez éprouver des problèmes de culture qui modèlent vos pratiques, vos procédés et vos priorités de manières qui sabotent votre service.) Or, lorsque vous cherchez à adopter une approche plus « rétro » pour votre service, Michelli suggère de commencer par connaître les POURQUOI :

Les clients éprouvent un besoin impérieux d'avoir un lien avec une époque plus simple. La vie est tellement effrénée et compliquée, en grande partie à cause de la technologie. Les gens ne souhaitent certes pas se débarrasser de la technologie, car elle nous permet d'obtenir des biens et des services rapidement et efficacement, mais lorsque nous devons parler avec quelqu'un au téléphone, ou lorsque nous sommes face à face, nous voulons savoir que nous parlons à un être humain qui a nos intérêts à coeur—et non à une machine. L'époque où le tenancier d'une boutique ouvrait ses portes pour un client dans le besoin après les heures d'ouverture nous manque.

« Les clients veulent que les organisations qui les servent représentent à la fois Silicon Valley, et la rue principale, », indique Michelli. « Il existe une tension entre notre ère de technologie incroyable et le service à la clientèle rétro, branché, chaleureux que les gens souhaitent vraiment, et je crois que trop d'organisations sont allées trop loin dans la direction de l'ère spatiale. »

« Une culture de compassion et d'empathie doit passer dans vos interactions de personne à personne, » ajoute-t-il. « Partager un sourire—partager un moment ensemble—a quelque chose de spécial qui devient de plus en plus important dans notre monde encombré. Nous voulons que les gens fassent une pause et prennent un moment avec nous. »

Les clients trouvent du réconfort dans ce qui est « familier ». Personne n'aime perdre son précieux temps à larguer des compagnies ou organisations peu reluisantes pour repartir à zéro et en rechercher de meilleures. Les gens aiment les organisations prévisibles auxquelles ils sont habitués et avec lesquelles ils se sentent à l'aise—en autant qu'elles offrent un excellent service. L'effort de rappeler aux parties prenantes et membres qu'ils sont précieux contribue beaucoup à s'assurer de conserver sa base de clientèle.

« Je consulte encore mon médecin du Colorado pour un deuxième avis—et je vis en Floride! » songe Michelli. « Je n'ai pas à lui décrire longuement mes antécédents puisqu'il me connaît depuis des années. Et le fait qu'il fasse un excellent travail pour me servir, comme client …c'est aussi un facteur très important. »

Il suggère de trouver des façons de rappeler à vos clients depuis combien de temps vous êtes en relation et que vous vous efforcez de favoriser une relation durable. Si cela signifie de consigner des notes au sujet de leurs besoins particuliers dans votre base de données de façon à faire un suivi ou à leur offrir des rabais « anniversaires » pour les remercier de leur clientèle ou de leur adhésion, vous pourrez gagner leur fidélité et faire en sorte qu'ils reviennent en les traitant comme s'ils comptaient véritablement.

Le service à l'ancienne correspond bien au mouvement artisanal en plein essor actuellement. Pendant de nombreuses années, on a vu beaucoup de camelote produite en série. Partout, les clients sont conditionnés à attendre moins, grâce à des millions de produits décevants provenant de partout dans le monde. Il n'est pas étonnant que nous nous retrouvions au centre d'une totale réaction hostile des consommateurs. Les acheteurs choisissent de plus en plus des produits et services uniques et personnalisés, faits avec passion.

« Regardez l'engouement pour la bière artisanale un peu partout » commente Michelli. « Pendant plusieurs générations, les gens buvaient de la bière de type pilsner—ils étaient conditionnés à le faire. Mais maintenant, de plus en plus de gens tombent sous le charme des formidables bières artisanales disponibles, car les microbrasseurs se sont réapproprié l'art du brassage de la bière.

« Les organisations telles que les associations charmeront leurs membres lorsqu'elles se vanteront de leur savoir-faire et leur degré d'habileté, » ajoute-t-il. « Il est réconfortant d'observer des techniques bien maîtrisées et de simplement apprécier cette habileté. Il existe un service artisanal au Ritz-Carlton. Voir ces professionnels à l'œuvre vous fait dire, *Wow, c'est un art perdu!* »

Votre style de service vous aide à vous démarquer. De toute évidence, c'est la raison la plus convaincante d'adopter une approche à l'ancienne en matière de service. Elle vous attirera des clients/membres et vous gardera même peut-être en vie. La concurrence est tellement présente sur le marché que votre manière de traiter vos membres et d'être en relation avec eux pourrait être la seule chose qui fait de vous *ce que vous êtes.*

« Vous pouvez mettre des choses sur le marché très rapidement aujourd'hui, indique Michelli. « La vitesse et la distribution mondiale suscitent parfois l'omniprésence de produits, et il devient donc essentiel de vous différencier en plaçant vos clients au premier plan et de posséder véritablement un certain style de service à l'ancienne. »

En un mot : même si les temps ont changé et que la technologie est apparue au premier plan, les besoins humains fondamentaux sont demeurés les mêmes.

« Il n'arrivera **JAMAIS** que les gens disent, *Ça m'est égal si vous me faites mal. Ça m'est égal si vous m'appréciez. Ça m'est égal si je suis inclus. Vous savez, en ce qui me concerne, je ne veux qu'acheter vos produits,* » conclut Michelli. « Et je crois qu'à cause de cela, nous devons nous ancrer à la vérité humaine intemporelle, même au moment de personnaliser la livraison conformément aux tendances culturelles. »

« Les organisations qui connaissent du succès sont celles qui saisissent vraiment ce principe, » ajoute-t-il. « Elles trouvent comment intégrer la technologie mais établissent vraiment un lien avec les clients, face à face ou au téléphone. Elles l'incorporent à leur formation. Les membres d'équipe apprennent à s'assurer que les clients savent qu'ils comptent—qu'ils sont toujours entendus et appréciés. »

Originally published in *Association™ Magazine* (Spring 2017). Reprinted with the permission of the Canadian Society of Association Executives (CSAE), 2017. www.csae.com.

Subject Index

- Canadian & foreign headquarters listed here by subject
- Subjects are listed alphabetically
- Entries may appear under more than one subject
- Each entry is accompanied by a page number which points you to the corresponding listing in the alphabetical listings of both Canadian and foreign associations

Academic Exchanges
Canadian Institute in Greece, 414
IAESTE Canada (International Association for the Exchange of Students for Technical Experience), 829
Ireland Canada University Foundation, 1567

Acadians
Association acadienne des artistes professionnel.le.s du Nouveau-Brunswick inc., 89
Beaton Institute, 203
Conseil coopératif acadien de la Nouvelle-Écosse, 614
Fédération acadienne de la Nouvelle-Écosse, 707
Fédération culturelle acadienne de la Nouvelle-Écosse, 708
Fédération des caisses populaires acadiennes, 712
Fédération des communautés francophones et acadienne du Canada, 713
Fédération des femmes acadiennes et francophones du Nouveau-Brunswick, 715
Fédération des parents acadiens de la Nouvelle-Écosse, 716
Réseau de développement économique et d'employabilité Ontario, 1219
Société de l'Acadie du Nouveau-Brunswick, 1316
Société des Jeux de l'Acadie inc., 1318
Société nationale de l'Acadie, 1322
La Société Saint-Pierre, 1325
Société Saint-Thomas-d'Aquin, 1325

Accessibility
Accessible Housing Society, 5
Association d'informations en logements et immeubles adaptés, 99
March of Dimes Non-Profit Housing Corporation, 949

Accident Prevention
Association paritaire pour la santé et la sécurité du travail - Administration provinciale, 164
Association paritaire pour la santé et la sécurité du travail - Imprimerie et activités connexes, 164
Association paritaire pour la santé et la sécurité du travail - Secteur Affaires municipales, 165
Association paritaire pour la santé et la sécurité du travail du secteur affaires sociales, 165
Association sectorielle services automobiles, 178
Association sectorielle: Fabrication d'équipement de transport et de machines, 178
Canadian Centre for Occupational Health & Safety, 353
Industrial Accident Victims Group of Ontario, 835
Institut de recherche Robert-Sauvé en santé et en sécurité du travail, 842
International Council on Alcohol, Drugs & Traffic Safety, 1545
MultiPrévention, 980
MultiPrévention ASP: Association paritaire pour la santé et la sécurité au travail des secteurs: métal, électrique, habillement et imprimerie, 980
Ontario Industrial Fire Protection Association, 1087
Via Prévention, 1431
Workplace Safety & Prevention Services, 1464
World Safety Organization, 1607

Accountants, Certified Management
L'Ordre des comptables professionels agréés du Québec, 1120

Accountants, Chartered
Certified General Accountants Association of the Northwest Territories & Nunavut, 538
Chartered Professional Accountants Canada, 552
Chartered Professional Accountants of Alberta, 552
Chartered Professional Accountants of Bermuda, 1516
Chartered Professional Accountants of British Columbia, 553
Chartered Professional Accountants of Manitoba, 553
Chartered Professional Accountants of New Brunswick, 553
Chartered Professional Accountants of Newfoundland & Labrador, 553
Chartered Professional Accountants of Nova Scotia, 553
Chartered Professional Accountants of Ontario, 553
Chartered Professional Accountants of Prince Edward Island, 553
Chartered Professional Accountants of Saskatchewan, 553
Chartered Professional Accountants of the Yukon, 554
CMA Canada - Northwest Territories & Nunavut, 576
Institute of Chartered Accountants of the Northwest Territories & Nunavut, 845
L'Ordre des comptables professionels agréés du Québec, 1120

Accountants, Professional
Association of Filipino Canadian Accountants, 148
Association of Filipino Canadian Accountants in British Columbia, 148
Chartered Institute of Public Finance & Accountancy, 1516
National Council of Philippine American Canadian Accountants, 1575
L'Ordre des comptables professionels agréés du Québec, 1120
The Society of Professional Accountants of Canada, 1330

Accounting
The Association of Professional Accounting & Tax Consultants Inc., 156
Canadian Academic Accounting Association, 285
Canadian Bookkeepers Association, 346
Canadian Insurance Accountants Association, 420
Chartered Accountants' Education Foundation of Alberta, 552
Guild of Industrial, Commercial & Institutional Accountants, 794
International Federation of Accountants, 1547
PBA Society of Alberta, 1146
PBA Society of Atlantic, 1146
PBA Society of Canada, 1146
PBA Society of Ontario, 1146
Petroleum Accountants Society of Canada, 1154
Public Accountants Council for the Province of Ontario, 1192
Receivables Management Assocation of Canada Inc., 1206

Acoustic Neuroma
Acoustic Neuroma Association of Canada, 5

Acoustics
Acoustical Association Ontario, 5
Canadian Acoustical Association, 287

Actors
The Actors' Fund of Canada, 7
American Guild of Variety Artists (AFL-CIO), 1493
Canadian Actors' Equity Association (CLC), 287

Acupuncture
Acupuncture Canada, 7
Alberta College of Acupuncture & Traditional Chinese Medicine, 28
Association des Acupuncteurs du Québec, 105
Canadian Association of Acupuncture & Traditional Chinese Medicine, 307
Canadian Society of Chinese Medicine & Acupuncture, 481
Chinese Medicine & Acupuncture Association of Canada, 565
College of Traditional Chinese Medicine Practitioners & Acupuncturists of British Columbia, 590
Ontario Association of Acupuncture & Traditional Chinese Medicine, 1061
Ordre des acupuncteurs de Québec, 1119

Addiction
Addiction Services of Thames Valley, 8
Addictions & Mental Health Ontario, 8
Addictions Foundation of Manitoba, 8
Association des intervenants en dépendance du Québec, 117
Association of BC First Nations Treatment Programs, 140
Canadian Addiction Counsellors Certification Federation, 288
Canadian Assembly of Narcotics Anonymous, 296
Canadian Society of Addiction Medicine, 479
Caritas School of Life Therapeutic Community, 512
Centre for Addiction & Mental Health, 531
Council on Drug Abuse, 636
F.A.S.T., 706
Lieutenant Governor's Circle on Mental Health & Addiction, 910
Nar-Anon Family Groups of Ontario, 988
National Association of Addiction Treatment Providers, 1573
National Native Addictions Partnership Foundation, 995
Native Addictions Council of Manitoba, 997
Nechi Training, Research & Health Promotions Institute, 1002
Parent Action on Drugs, 1139
Parkdale Focus Community Project, 1140
The Renascent Centres for Alcoholism & Drug Addiction, 1217
Southern Ontario Cocaine Anonymous, 1338

Administrative Assistants
Association of Administrative Professionals, 139
Fédération des secrétaires professionnelles du Québec, 718
Institute of Chartered Secretaries & Administrators - Canadian Division, 845
International Association of Administrative Professionals, 1537
International Virtual Assistants Association, 1566
Office & Professional Employees International Union (AFL-CIO/CLC), 1580

Administrative Sciences
Administrative Sciences Association of Canada, 8
Alberta Educational Facilities Administrators Association, 33
Association canadienne des sciences régionales, 95
Canadian Federation of Business School Deans, 386
Ontario College Administrative Staff Associations, 1072

Adoption
Adoption Council of Canada, 8
Adoption Council of Ontario, 8
Adoption Roots & Rights, 9
Association de parents pour l'adoption québécoise, 103
Children of the World Adoption Society Inc., 560
Children's Resource & Consultation Centre of Ontario, 562
Mouvement Retrouvailles, 978
Ontario Standardbred Adoption Society, 1109
Parent Finders Ottawa, 1139

Adult Education
Adult Basic Education Association of British Columbia, 9
Adult Educators' Provincial Specialist Association, 9
L'Atelier des lettres, 180
British Columbia Career Development Association, 235
Canadian Association for Prior Learning Assesment, 303
Canadian Association for the Study of Adult Education, 306
Canadian Literacy & Learning Network, 427
Centre de documentation sur l'éducation des adultes et la condition féminine, 529
Le Collège du Savoir, 582
L'Écrit Tôt de Saint-Hubert, 674
Institut de coopération pour l'éducation des adultes, 841
Lake of the Woods Adult Learning Line, 896
Learning Centre for Georgina, 903
Learning Enrichment Foundation, 905
Literacy Link South Central, 914
Niagara West Employment & Learning Resource Centres, 1026
Ontario Council for University Lifelong Learning, 1075
People, Words & Change, 1152
Project Adult Literacy Society, 1187
Project READ Literacy Network Waterloo-Wellington, 1188
Simcoe/Muskoka Literacy Network, 1300
Society for Personal Growth, 1326
South Shore Reading Council, 1336
Table des responsables de l'éducation des adultes et de la formation professionnelle des commissions scolaires du Québec, 1366
Vitesse, 1436
West Neighbourhood House, 1446

Advertising
The Advertising & Design Club of Canada, 10
Advertising Association of Winnipeg Inc., 10
The Advertising Club of Toronto, 10
Advertising Standards Canada, 10
Alliance for Audited Media, 56
Association des agences de publicité du Québec, 105
Association of Canadian Advertisers Inc., 140
Broadcast Research Council of Canada, 259
Canadian Marketing Association, 430
Canadian Out-of-Home Measurement Bureau, 448
Concerned Children's Advertisers, 609
Institute of Communication Agencies, 845
Interactive Advertising Bureau of Canada, 851
National Advertising Benevolent Society, 989
Les normes canadiennes de la publicité, 1028
Out-of-Home Marketing Association of Canada, 1133
Promotional Product Professionals of Canada Inc., 1188
Retail Advertising & Marketing Club of Canada, 1228
Trans-Canada Advertising Agency Network, 1395

Aeronautics
Air Force Association of Canada, 19
Canadian Aeronautics & Space Institute, 288
Institute of Air & Space Law, 844
International Federation of Airworthiness, 1547

Aerospace Engineering
Aerospace & Electronic Systems Society, 1485
Aerospace Heritage Foundation of Canada, 11
Centre d'adaptation de la main-d'oeuvre aérospatiale du Québec, 527
University of Toronto Institute for Aerospace Studies, 1420

Subject Index / Aerospace Industries

Aerospace Industries
Aéro Montréal, 11
Aerospace Industries Association of Canada, 11
Aerospace Industry Association of British Columbia, 11
Aviation Alberta, 190
Canadian Air Cushion Technology Society, 290
Centre d'adaptation de la main-d'oeuvre aérospatiale du Québec, 527
International Association of Machinists & Aerospace Workers, 1539
New Brunswick Aerospace & Defence Association, 1004
Ontario Aerospace Council, 1058
UNIFOR, 1405

Aesthetics
Canadian Association of Aesthetic Medicine, 308
Canadian Society for Aesthetics, 473

Afghanistan
Canadian Women for Women in Afghanistan, 504

Afghans in Canada
Afghan Association of Ontario, 12
Afghan Women's Counselling & Integration Community Support Organization, 12

Africa
Africa Inland Mission International (Canada), 12
African Enterprise (Canada), 13
African Medical & Research Foundation Canada, 13
African Students Association of Concordia, 13
Aga Khan Foundation Canada, 14
Canadian Council on Africa, 370
Eritrean Canadian Community Centre of Metropolitan Toronto, 695
Southern African Jewish Association of Canada, 1337
Teamwork Children's Services International, 1368
Vues d'Afriques - Les Journées du cinéma africain et créole, 1439

African Canadians
African & Caribbean Students' Network of Montréal, 12
African Canadian Heritage Association, 12
African Canadian Social Development Council, 12
African Community Health Services, 13
African Nova Scotian Music Association, 13
African Students Association - Univeristy of Alberta, 13
Africans in Partnership Against AIDS, 13
Afro-Caribbean Cultural Association of Saskatchewan Inc., 13
Association of Nigerians in Nova Scotia, 154
Health Association of African Canadians, 806
National African Integration & Families of Ontario, 989

African Studies
African Literature Association, 1486
International African Institute, 1535

Aggregate Industry
British Columbia Stone, Sand & Gravel Association, 255
Ontario Stone, Sand & Gravel Association, 1109

Aging
Active Living Coalition for Older Adults, 7
Alberta Council on Aging, 31
Association québécoise de défense des droits des personnes retraitées et préretraitées, 169
Canadian Academy of Geriatric Psychiatry, 286
Canadian Association on Gerontology, 337
Canadian Society for the Study of the Aging Male, 478
The Council on Aging of Ottawa, 635
Council on Aging, Windsor - Essex County, 636
Golden Age Society, 776
HelpAge Canada, 812
International Council on Active Aging, 856
International Federation on Aging, 857
Mid-Toronto Community Services, 965
Réseau FADOQ, 1223
The Shepherds' Trust, 1295
Yukon Council on Aging, 1478

Agricultural Cooperatives
Canadian Co-operative Wool Growers Ltd., 364
La Coop Fédérée, 627
Prince Edward Island Vegetable Growers Co-op Association, 1178

Agricultural Economics
Agricultural Adaptation Council, 14
Alberta Agricultural Economics Association, 21
Canadian Agricultural Economics Society, 289
Canadian Association of Farm Advisors, 314
International Association of Agricultural Economists, 1537

Agricultural Engineering
Canadian Society for Bioengineering, 473
International Commission of Agricultural & Biosystems Engineering, 1542
Ontario Agri-Food Technologies, 1059

Agricultural Equipment & Machinery
Agricultural Manufacturers of Canada, 15
Association des marchands de machines aratoires de la province de Québec, 119
Association of Equipment Manufacturers - Canada, 148
British Columbia Farm Machinery & Agriculture Museum Association, 240
Canada East Equipment Dealers' Association, 278
International Commission of Agricultural & Biosystems Engineering, 1542
Oldman River Antique Equipment & Threshing Club, 1057
Ontario Agri-Food Technologies, 1059
Prairie Agricultural Machinery Institute, 1169
UNIFOR, 1405

Agricultural Exhibitions
Association des expositions agricoles du Québec, 113
British Columbia Association of Agricultural Fairs & Exhibitions, 231
Canadian Western Agribition Association, 503
Lloydminster Agricultural Exhibition Association, 916
Norfolk County Agricultural Society, 1028
Olds Regional Exhibition, 1057
Ontario Association of Agricultural Societies, 1061
Portage Industrial Exhibition Association, 1166
Royal Agricultural Winter Fair Association, 1237

Agriculture
Aboriginal Agricultural Education Society of British Columbia, 2
Agricultural Alliance of New Brunswick, 14
Agricultural Institute of Canada, 14
Agricultural Institute of Canada Foundation, 15
Agricultural Research & Extension Council of Alberta, 15
Agriculture Union, 15
Alameda Agricultural Society, 21
Alberta Association of Agricultural Societies, 23
Alberta Community & Co-operative Association, 30
Alberta Conservation Tillage Society II, 31
Alberta Institute of Agrologists, 38
Alliance for Sustainability, 1487
American Farmland Trust, 1492
Ashmont & District Agricultural Society, 86
Association des technologues en agroalimentaire, 129
Association of Alberta Agricultural Fieldmen, 139
Barley Council of Canada, 196
Battle River Research Group, 199
Bengough Agricultural Society, 205
Biggar & District Agricultural Society, 210
Binbrook Agricultural Society, 211
British Columbia Institute of Agrologists, 244
British Columbia Investment Agriculture Foundation, 244
Canadian Agricultural Human Resource Council, 289
Canadian Agricultural Safety Association, 289
Canadian Agri-Marketing Association, 290
Canadian Agri-Marketing Association (Alberta), 290
Canadian Agri-Marketing Association (Manitoba), 290
Canadian Agri-Marketing Association (Saskatchewan), 290
Canadian Animal Health Institute, 293
Canadian Faculties of Agriculture & Veterinary Medicine, 383
Canadian Federation of Agriculture, 384
Canadian Forage & Grassland Association, 392
Canadian National Committee for Irrigation & Drainage, 439
Canadian Organic Growers Inc., 446
Canadian Plowing Organization, 456
Canadian Special Crops Association, 489
Carp Agricultural Society, 515
Chinook Applied Research Association, 565
Conseil des entrepreneurs agricoles, 617
Consultative Group on International Agricultural Research, 1519
Creelman Agricultural Society, 641
Demeter Canada, 653
Ecological Agriculture Projects, 672
Egg Farmers of Canada, 681
Essa & District Agricultural Society, 696
Expo agricole de Chicoutimi, 700
Farmers of North America, 705
Farmers of North America Strategic Agriculture Institute, 705
FarmFolk CityFolk, 706
Farming Smarter, 706
Federated Women's Institutes of Canada, 706
Fédération de l'UPA - Abitibi-Témiscamingue, 709
Fédération de l'UPA - Bas-Saint-Laurent, 709
Fédération de l'UPA - Mauricie, 709
Fédération de l'UPA de la Beauce, 709
Fédération de l'UPA de la Montérégie, 709
Fédération de la relève agricole du Québec, 709
Fédération des agriculteurs et agricultrices francophones du Nouveau-Brunswick, 711
Fédérations de l'UPA de Lévis Bellechasse, Rive Nord, Lotbinière-Mégantic, 731
First Nations Agricultural Lending Association, 738
Foothills Forage & Grazing Association, 750
Foreign Agricultural Resource Management Services, 751
Friends of the Greenbelt Foundation, 762
Gateway Research Organization, 767
Grain Farmers of Ontario, 779
Grain Workers' Union, Local 333, 779
Grey Wooded Forage Association, 790
Groupe export agroalimentaire Québec - Canada, 792
Hanley Agricultural Society, 803
Heritage Agricultural Society, 812
Indian Agricultural Program of Ontario, 834
Integrated Vegetation Management Association of British Columbia, 850
International Federation of Organic Agriculture Movements, 1548
International Peat Society - Canadian National Committee, 859
International Plant Propagators Society, Inc., 1555
Keystone Agricultural Producers, 884
Lakeland Agricultural Research Association, 896
Manitoba Forage & Grassland Association, 937
Manitoba Pulse & Soybean Growers Inc., 943
The Marquis Project, Inc., 952
Melfort Agricultural Society, 959
Melville & District Agri-Park Association Inc., 959
Middlesex Federation of Agriculture, 965
Millarville Racing & Agricultural Society, 965
Mushrooms Canada, 983
National Sunflower Association of Canada, 996
New Brunswick Soil & Crop Improvement Association, 1012
Newfoundland & Labrador Federation of Agriculture, 1018
Norfolk County Agricultural Society, 1028
North Peace Applied Research Association, 1032
Nova Scotia Federation of Agriculture, 1044
Olds Regional Exhibition, 1057
Ontario Agri-Food Education Inc., 1059
Ontario Association of Agricultural Societies, 1061
Ontario Farmland Trust, 1078
Ontario Federation of Agriculture, 1079
Ontario Soil & Crop Improvement Association, 1108
Ontario Vegetation Management Association, 1112
Peace Country Beef & Forage Association, 1147
Pesticide Action Network North America, 1583
Prairie Fruit Growers Association, 1169
Prince Edward Island Certified Organic Producers Co-op, 1173
Prince Edward Island Federation of Agriculture, 1174
Ranfurly & District Recreation & Agricultural Society, 1204
Research & Development Institute for the Agri-Environment, 1218
Resource Efficient Agricultural Production, 1227
Richmond Agricultural Society, 1229
The Rocky Mountain Institute, 1586
Saskatchewan Agricultural Graduates' Association Inc., 1255
Saskatchewan Agricultural Hall of Fame, 1255
Saskatchewan Association of Agricultural Societies & Exhibitions, 1256
Saskatchewan Soil Conservation Association, 1275
SeCan Association, 1288
Seed Corn Growers of Ontario, 1288
SHARE Agriculture Foundation, 1294
Smoky Applied Research & Demonstration Association, 1304
Swift Current Agricultural & Exhibition Association, 1358
Syndicat de la relève agricole d'Abitibi-Témiscamingue, 1362
Syndicat des agricultrices de la Beauce, 1362
Syndicat des agricultrices de la Côte-du-Sud, 1362
Syndicat des agricultrices du Centre du Québec, 1362
Syndicat des producteurs en serre du Québec, 1363
Union des producteurs agricoles, 1406
Union Paysanne, 1408
Vanscoy & District Agricultural Society, 1429
Wallace Center, Winrock International, 1601
Weed Science Society of America, 1602
West Central Forage Association, 1444
Western Barley Growers Association, 1447
Weyburn Agricultural Society, 1451
Wild Rose Agricultural Producers, 1454

Agriculture & Youth
AgriVenture Global Ltd, 15
Association des jeunes ruraux du Québec, 117
Canadian 4-H Council, 284
Les Clubs 4-H du Québec, 576
Fédération de la relève agricole du Québec, 709
Junior Farmers' Association of Ontario, 878
Olds Regional Exhibition, 1057

Agrochemicals
Croplife International, 1520
Integrated Vegetation Management Association of British Columbia, 850
Northwest Coalition for Alternatives to Pesticides, 1580
Ontario Vegetation Management Association, 1112
Weed Science Society of America, 1602

Agrologists
Alberta Institute of Agrologists, 38
British Columbia Institute of Agrologists, 244
Manitoba Institute of Agrologists, 939
New Brunswick Institute of Agrologists, 1009
Newfoundland & Labrador Institute of Agrologists, 1019
Nova Scotia Institute of Agrologists, 1046
Ontario Institute of Agrologists, 1087
Ordre des agronomes du Québec, 1120
Prince Edward Island Institute of Agrologists, 1175
Saskatchewan Institute of Agrologists, 1268

Agronomists
Canadian Society of Agronomy, 479
Ordre des agronomes du Québec, 1120

Air Cadets
Air Cadet League of Canada, 19

Air Conditioning
American Society of Heating, Refrigerating & Air Conditioning Engineers, 1499
Heating, Refrigeration & Air Conditioning Institute of Canada, 810
Ontario Refrigeration & Air Conditioning Contractors Association, 1101
Sheet Metal & Air Conditioning Contractors' National Association, 1588
Sheet Metal Contractors Association of Alberta, 1295
Thermal Environmental Comfort Association, 1375

Air Force
Air Force Association of Canada, 19
Army, Navy & Air Force Veterans in Canada, 83

Air Handling
Manitoba Association of Sheet Metal & Air Handling Contractors Inc., 931
Ontario Sheet Metal Contractors Association, 1104

Air Pollution
Air & Waste Management Association, 1486
Association pour la prévention de la contamination de l'air et du sol, 166
Clean Air Strategic Alliance, 572
Scout Environmental, 1286

Air Safety
Canadian Owners & Pilots Association, 448
Canadian Society of Air Safety Investigators, 479

Air Shows
Abbotsford International Air Show Society, 1
Canadian International Air Show, 421

Air Transportation
Air Canada Pilots Association, 19
Air Transport Association of Canada, 19
Association québécoise du transport aérien, 176
Hope Air, 821
International Air Transport Association, 853
International Industry Working Group, 1551
Northern Air Transport Association, 1034

Aircraft
Aerospace Industry Association of British Columbia, 11
Canadian Business Aviation Association, 347
Canadian Federal Pilots Association, 384
Canadian Federation of Aircraft Maintenance Engineers Associations, 384
Canadian Harvard Aircraft Association, 401
Canadian Warplane Heritage, 502
Helicopter Association of Canada, 811
Prince Edward Island Flying Association, 1174
Recreational Aircraft Association, 1208

Airlines
Northern Air Transport Association, 1034

Airports
Airport Management Council of Ontario, 20
Airports Council International - Asia-Pacific Region, 1486
Canadian Airports Council, 291
World Border Organization, 1465

Alcoholic Beverage Industry
Brewery, Winery & Distillery Workers Union - Local 300, 228
Drinks Ontario, 663
Import Vintners & Spirits Association, 831
Ontario Craft Brewers, 1075
Smart Serve Ontario, 1304
Wine Country Ontario, 1457

Alcoholism
Addictions & Mental Health Ontario, 8
Addictions Foundation of Manitoba, 8
Adult Children of Alcoholics, 9
Al-Anon Family Groups (Canada), Inc., 21
Al-Anon Montréal, 21
Alcoholic Beverage Medical Research Foundation, 1486
Alcoholics Anonymous (GTA Intergroup), 52
Alcooliques Anonymes du Québec, 53
Calgary Alpha House Society, 271
Canadian Centre on Substance Use & Addiction, 354

Centre d'intervention et de prévention en toxicomanie de l'Outaouais, 528
Centre de réadaptation et dépendance le virage, 529
Centre for Addiction & Mental Health, 531
Éduc'alcool, 680
Greater Toronto Al-Anon Information Services, 785
Jean Tweed Treatment Centre, 869
Nar-Anon Family Groups of Ontario, 988
Nechi Training, Research & Health Promotions Institute, 1002
Opération Nez rouge, 1116
Parkdale Focus Community Project, 1140
Programme d'aide aux membres du barreau, 1187
The Renascent Centres for Alcoholism & Drug Addiction, 1217

Allergies
AllerGen NCE Inc., 54
Allergy, Asthma & Immunology Society of Ontario, 54
Allergy/Asthma Information Association, 54
Association des Allergologues et Immunologues du Québec, 105
Association québécoise des allergies alimentaires, 171
Asthme et allergies Québec, 179
Canadian Society of Allergy & Clinical Immunology, 479
Environmental Health Association of Nova Scotia, 692
Environmental Health Association of Ontario, 692
Food Allergy Canada, 749

ALS
ALS Society of Alberta, 60
ALS Society of British Columbia, 60
ALS Society of Canada, 60
ALS Society of Manitoba, 60
ALS Society of New Brunswick & Nova Scotia, 60
ALS Society of Newfoundland & Labrador, 60
ALS Society of PEI, 60
ALS Society of Québec, 60
ALS Society of Saskatchewan, 60

Alternative Medicine
Association des herboristes de la province de Québec, 116
Association of Complementary & Integrative Physicians of BC, 145
Association québécoise des phytothérapeutes, 174
Atlantic Therapeutic Touch Network, 186
British Columbia Naturopathic Association, 247
Canadian Association for Integrative & Energy Therapies, 301
Canadian Association of Acupuncture & Traditional Chinese Medicine, 307
Canadian Federation of Aromatherapists, 385
Canadian Holistic Nurses Association, 406
Canadian Institute of Iridology, 416
Canadian Reiki Association, 466
College of Naturopathic Doctors of Alberta, 586
Corporation des praticiens en médecine douce du Canada, 630
Manitoba Naturopathic Association, 941
Natural Health Practitioners of Canada, 998
Ontario Association of Naturopathic Doctors, 1065
Ontario College of Reflexology, 1072
Ontario Herbalists Association, 1084
Ontario Homeopathic Association, 1086
Shiatsu Therapy Association of Ontario, 1296
Trager Canada, 1394

Aluminum
The Aluminum Association, 1487
Syndicat national des employés de l'aluminium d'Alma inc., 1365
Syndicat national des employés de l'aluminium d'Arvida, inc., 1365

Alumni
Association des anciens élèves du collège Sainte-Marie, 105
Canadian Football League Alumni Association, 392
National Hockey League Alumni Association, 994

New College Alumni Association, 1014
Saskatchewan Agricultural Graduates' Association Inc., 1255
UBC Alumni Association, 1401
University of the Philippines Alumni Association of Toronto, 1420

Alzheimer's Disease
Alzheimer Manitoba, 61
Alzheimer Society Canada, 61
Alzheimer Society London & Middlesex, 61
Alzheimer Society of Alberta & Northwest Territories, 61
Alzheimer Society of Belleville/Hastings/Quinte, 62
Alzheimer Society of Brant, 62
Alzheimer Society of British Columbia, 62
Alzheimer Society of Calgary, 62
Alzheimer Society of Chatham-Kent, 62
Alzheimer Society of Cornwall & District, 62
Alzheimer Society of Dufferin County, 62
Alzheimer Society of Durham Region, 62
Alzheimer Society of Grey-Bruce, 62
Alzheimer Society of Haldimand Norfolk, 62
Alzheimer Society of Hamilton Halton, 62
Alzheimer Society of Hastings - Prince Edward, 62
Alzheimer Society of Huron County, 63
Alzheimer Society of Kenora/Rainy River Districts, 63
Alzheimer Society of Kingston, Frontenac, Lennox & Addington, 63
Alzheimer Society of Lanark County, 63
Alzheimer Society of Leeds-Grenville, 63
Alzheimer Society of Miramichi, 63
Alzheimer Society of Moncton, 63
Alzheimer Society of Muskoka, 63
Alzheimer Society of New Brunswick, 63
Alzheimer Society of Newfoundland & Labrador, 63
Alzheimer Society of Niagara Region, 63
Alzheimer Society of North Bay & District, 63
Alzheimer Society of Nova Scotia, 64
Alzheimer Society of Ottawa & Renfrew County, 64
Alzheimer Society of Oxford, 64
Alzheimer Society of Peel, 64
Alzheimer Society of PEI, 64
Alzheimer Society of Perth County, 64
Alzheimer Society of Sarnia-Lambton, 64
Alzheimer Society of Saskatchewan Inc., 64
Alzheimer Society of Sault Ste. Marie & District of Algoma, 64
Alzheimer Society of Simcoe County, 65
Alzheimer Society of Thunder Bay, 65
Alzheimer Society of Timmins/Porcupine District, 65
Alzheimer Society of Toronto, 65
Alzheimer Society of Windsor/Essex County, 65
Alzheimer Society of York Region, 65
Alzheimer Society Ontario, 65
Alzheimer Society Peterborough, Kawartha Lakes, Northumberland, & Haliburton, 65
Alzheimer Society Waterloo Wellington, 65
Fédération québécoise des sociétés Alzheimer, 729
Prince George Alzheimer's Society, 1178
Saint John Alzheimer Society, 1246
Scottish Rite Charitable Foundation of Canada, 1286
Société Alzheimer Society Sudbury-Manitoulin, 1307

Ambulance Service
Corporation des services d'ambulance du Québec, 630
Saskatchewan Emergency Medical Services Association, 1264

American Studies
American Antiquarian Society, 1488
American Studies Association, 1503
Canadian Association for American Studies, 297

Amphibians
Edmonton Reptile & Amphibian Society, 679

Amusement Rides
The Coaster Enthusiasts of Canada, 579

Anatomists
Canadian Association for Anatomy, Neurobiology, & Cell Biology, 297
Human Anatomy & Physiology Society, 1530

Anesthesia
American Society of Regional Anesthesia & Pain Medicine, 1502
Canadian Anesthesiologists' Society, 292
Society of Cardiovascular Anesthesiologists, 1592

Anglicans
The Anglican Church of Canada, 69
Anglican Foundation of Canada, 70
The Christian Episcopal Church of Canada, 567
Integrity Toronto, 850

Anglophones in Québec

Animal Feed Industry
Animal Nutrition Association of Canada, 70
Ontario Agri Business Association, 1059

Animal Rights Movement
Animal Alliance of Canada, 70
Animal Defence & Anti-Vivisection Society of BC, 70
Animal Defence League of Canada, 70
Animal Justice, 70
Animal Protection Party of Canada, 71
Canadian Coalition for Farm Animals, 357
Friends of Animals, 1527
Fur-Bearer Defenders, 765
Humane Society International/Canada, 826
Lifeforce Foundation, 911
People for the Ethical Treatment of Animals, 1583
Sea Shepherd Conservation Society, 1287
Sea Shepherd Conservation Society - USA, 1588
Society for the Prevention of Cruelty to Animals International, 1592
Toronto Pig Save, 1386
Voice for Animals Humane Society, 1436

Animal Science
British Columbia Scientific Cryptozoology Club, 252
Canada Fox Breeders' Association, 279
Canadian Association for Laboratory Animal Science, 302
Canadian Society of Animal Science, 480
International Association for Bear Research & Management, 1535
International Council for Laboratory Animal Science, 1544
National Chinchilla Breeders of Canada, 991
Westgen, 1450

Animal Welfare
Action Volunteers for Animals, 7
Alberta Society for the Prevention of Cruelty to Animals, 47
American Humane Association, 1494
Animal Aid Foundation, 70
Animal Justice, 70
Animal Welfare Foundation of Canada, 71
ARK II, 81
Association des propriétaires canins de Prévost, 126
Atlantic Canadian Anti-Sealing Coalition, 183
Barrhead Animal Rescue Society, 197
Bide Awhile Animal Shelter Society, 208
Brandon Humane Society, 226
British Columbia Society for the Prevention of Cruelty to Animals, 254
Calgary Humane Society, 272
Canadian Association for Humane Trapping, 301
Canadian Association of Swine Veterinarians, 334
Canadian Cat Association, 351
Canadian Chihuahua Rescue & Transport, 355
Canadian Coalition for Farm Animals, 357
Canadian Council on Animal Care, 370
Canadian Farm Animal Care Trust, 384
Canadian Federation of Humane Societies, 386
Canadians for Ethical Treatment of Food Animals, 507
Crowsnest Pass Society for the Prevention of Cruelty to Animals, 645

Edmonton Humane Society for the Prevention of Cruelty to Animals, 677
Education to Spread Compassion, 680
Elsa Wild Animal Appeal of Canada, 685
Etobicoke Humane Society, 697
Exploits Valley Society for the Prevention of Cruelty to Animals, 700
Faro Humane Society, 706
Fort McMurray Society for the Prevention of Cruelty to Animals, 753
Fredericton Society for the Prevention of Cruelty to Animals, 759
Gander & Area Society for the Prevention of Cruelty to Animals, 766
Grande Prairie Society for the Prevention of Cruelty to Animals, 781
Greater Moncton Society for the Prevention of Cruelty to Animals, 784
Guelph Equine Area Rescue Stables, 793
Heaven Can Wait Equine Rescue, 810
Hope for Wildlife Society, 821
Humane Society International/Canada, 826
The Humane Society of the United States, 1530
Humane Society Yukon, 826
International Fund for Animal Welfare Canada, 857
International Primate Protection League, 1556
The Kindness Club, 888
Lethbridge & District Humane Society, 907
Lincoln County Humane Society, 912
Lloydminster Society for the Prevention of Cruelty to Animals, 916
Medicine Hat Society for the Prevention of Cruelty to Animals, 959
Mercy for Animals Canada, 961
Montréal SPCA, 973
Moose Jaw Humane Society Inc., 974
New Brunswick Society for the Prevention of Cruelty to Animals, 1012
Newfoundland & Labrador Society for the Prevention of Cruelty to Animals, 1021
Niagara Action for Animals, 1024
NL West SPCA, 1027
North Bay & District Humane Society, 1030
North Island Wildlife Recovery Association, 1031
Northwest Territories Society for the Prevention of Cruelty to Animals, 1038
Nova Scotia Society for the Prevention of Cruelty to Animals, 1049
Oakville & Milton Humane Society, 1053
Ontario Society for the Prevention of Cruelty to Animals, 1105
Ontario Standardbred Adoption Society, 1109
Oromocto & Area SPCA, 1127
Ottawa Humane Society, 1130
Pincher Creek Humane Society, 1160
Prince Edward Island Humane Society, 1175
Red Deer & District SPCA, 1209
Regina Humane Society Inc., 1211
Registered Veterinary Technologists & Technicians of Canada, 1214
Restigouche County Society for the Prevention of Cruelty to Animals, 1227
Saint John SPCA Animal Rescue, 1247
Sarnia & District Humane Society, 1254
Sasha's Legacy Equine Rescue, 1254
Saskatchewan Society for the Prevention of Cruelty to Animals, 1275
Saskatoon Society for the Prevention of Cruelty to Animals Inc., 1280
Shelter for Helpless Animals in Distress, 1295
Société québécoise pour la défense des animaux, 1324
Society for the Prevention of Cruelty to Animals International, 1592
SPCA of Western Québec, 1339
Standardbred Breeders of Ontario Association, 1347
Toronto Pig Save, 1386
Vancouver Humane Society, 1426
Victoria County Society for the Prevention of Cruelty to Animals, 1432
Wildlife Haven Rehabilitation Centre, 1454
Wildlife Rescue Association of British Columbia, 1455
Winnipeg Humane Society, 1459
World Animal Protection, 1465
Yorkton Society for the Prevention of Cruelty to Animals Inc., 1474
ZOOCHECK Canada Inc., 1482

Animation
Quickdraw Animation Society, 1201
Toronto Animated Image Society, 1381

Anthropology & Ethnology
American Anthropological Association, 1488
Association for the Study of Nationalities, 135
Canadian Anthropology Society, 293
Canadian Sociological Association, 488
International Council for Archaeozoology, 1544
International Union of Anthropological & Ethnological Sciences, 1563
Société québécoise d'ethnologie, 1323

Antibiotics
National Information Program on Antibiotics, 994

Antique Automobiles & Trucks
Alberta Pioneer Auto Club, 42
Antique Automobile Club of America, 1505
Historic Vehicle Society of Ontario, 815
Historical Automobile Society of Canada, Inc., 816
Morgan Sports Car Club of Canada, 974
Ontario Military Vehicle Association, 1091
Voitures anciennes du Québec inc., 1437

Antiques
Canadian Antique Phonograph Society, 293
Canadian Depression Glass Association, 377
Manitoba Antique Association, 928
Muskoka Pioneer Power Association, 985
Oldman River Antique Equipment & Threshing Club, 1057
Ontario Steam & Antique Preservers Association, 1109
Saskatchewan Black Powder Association, 1259
Vancouver Numismatic Society, 1428

Antiquities
Archaeological Institute of America, 1505
Society for the Study of Egyptian Antiquities, 1327

Apartments
British Columbia Apartment Owners & Managers Association, 230
Calgary Residential Rental Association, 274
Canadian Federation of Apartment Associations, 385
The Fair Rental Policy Organization of Ontario, 701
Greater Toronto Apartment Association, 785
Saskatchewan Rental Housing Industry Association, 1274

Aphasia
Aphasie Rive-Sud, 73
Association des personnes intéressées à l'aphasie et à l'accident vasculaire cérébral, 123

Apheresis
Canadian Apheresis Group, 294
Canadian Association of Apheresis Nurses, 308

Aplastic Anemia/Myelodysplasia Synd
Aplastic Anemia & Myelodysplasia Association of Canada, 73

Appraisal
Alberta Assessors' Association, 22
Appraisal Institute of Canada, 74
The Appraisal Institute of Canada - Alberta, 74
The Appraisal Institute of Canada - British Columbia, 74
The Appraisal Institute of Canada - Manitoba, 75
The Appraisal Institute of Canada - Newfoundland & Labrador, 75
The Appraisal Institute of Canada - Ontario, 75
The Appraisal Institute of Canada - Prince Edward Island, 75
The Appraisal Institute of Canada - Saskatchewan, 75
L'Association du Québec de l'Institut canadien des évaluateurs, 131
Canadian Association of Personal Property Appraisers, 325
Canadian General Standards Board, 396
Canadian Institute of Chartered Business Valuators, 414
Institute of Municipal Assessors, 846
National Association of Real Estate Appraisers, 1574
National Association of Review Appraisers & Mortgage Underwriters, 1574
New Brunswick Association of Real Estate Appraisers, 1005
Nova Scotia Real Estate Appraisers Association, 1048
Ontario Association of Property Standards Officers Inc., 1065
Ordre des évaluateurs agréés du Québec, 1121

Aquaculture
Alberta Aquaculture Association, 22
American Fisheries Society, 1493
Aquaculture Association of Canada, 75
Aquaculture Association of Nova Scotia, 75
Association québécoise de commercialisation de poissons et de fruits de mer, 169
Atlantic Canada Fish Farmers Association, 182
British Columbia Salmon Farmers Association, 252
British Columbia Seafood Alliance, 253
Canadian Aquaculture Industry Alliance, 294
Canadian Centre for Fisheries Innovation, 353
Groundfish Enterprise Allocation Council, 790
Gulf of Maine Council on the Marine Environment, 794
Newfoundland Aquaculture Industry Association, 1022
Northern Ontario Aquaculture Association, 1035
Prince Edward Island Aquaculture Alliance, 1171
World Aquaculture Society, 1603

Aquariums
Association of Zoos & Aquariums, 1513
Canada's Accredited Zoos & Aquariums, 281
Canadian Association of Aquarium Clubs, 308
East Coast Aquarium Society, 668

Aquatic Sports
ACUC International, 7
Alberta Underwater Council, 50
Alberta Water Polo Association, 51
Aquatic Federation of Canada, 75
British Columbia Water Polo Association, 258
Canadian Underwater Games Association, 498
Diving Plongeon Canada, 659
Manitoba Underwater Council, 946
Manitoba Water Polo Association Inc., 947
Ontario Underwater Council, 1112
Ontario Water Polo Association Incorporated, 1113
Saskatchewan Underwater Council, 1276
Underwater Council of British Columbia, 1404
Water Polo Canada, 1441
Water Polo Nova Scotia, 1441
Water Polo Saskatchewan Inc., 1441

Arab Canadians
Adala - Canadian Arab Justice Committee, 7
Arab Canadian Association of the Atlantic Provinces, 75
Arab Community Centre of Toronto, 76
Canadian Arab Federation, 294
National Council on Canada-Arab Relations, 992

Arab Countries
Adala - Canadian Arab Justice Committee, 7
Canada-Arab Business Council, 283
Middle East Studies Association of North America, 1571

Arbitration
ADR Institute of Canada, 9
The Association of Maritime Arbitrators of Canada, 151
British Columbia International Commercial Arbitration Centre, 244
Canadian International Institute of Applied Negotiation, 421
Central Ontario Industrial Relations Institute, 525
Centre canadien d'arbitrage commercial, 526
Institut de médiation et d'arbitrage du Québec, 841
Inter-American Commercial Arbitration Commission, 851
Ontario Labour-Management Arbitrators Association, 1088

Arboriculture
Christmas Tree Farmers of Ontario, 568
International Society of Arboriculture, 1560
Manitoba Christmas Tree Growers Association, 934
New Brunswick Christmas Tree Growers Co-op Ltd., 1006
Ontario Urban Forest Council, 1112
Prince Edward Island Forest Improvement Association, 1174
Royal Botanical Gardens, 1239
Société de protection des forêts contre les insectes et maladies, 1317
Western Boreal Growth & Yield Association, 1447
Western Silvicultural Contractors' Association, 1450

Archaeology
Archaeological Institute of America, 1505
Archaeological Society of Alberta, 76
Archaeological Society of British Columbia, 76
Association des archéologues du Québec, 105
Association of Professional Archaeologists, 156
Canadian Archaeological Association, 294
The Canadian Society for Mesopotamian Studies, 476
Cataraqui Archaeological Research Foundation, 517
Explorer's Club (Canadian Chapter), 700
International Council for Archaeozoology, 1544
International Union of Anthropological & Ethnological Sciences, 1563
Nova Scotia Archaeology Society, 1040
The Ontario Archaeological Society, 1059
Saskatchewan Archaeological Society, 1256
Société d'archéologie et de numismatique de Montréal, 1309
Société d'histoire de la Haute Gaspésie, 1310
Society for the Study of Egyptian Antiquities, 1327

Archery
Alberta Bowhunters Association, 26
Alberta Target Archers Association, 49
Archers & Bowhunters Association of Manitoba, 78
Archers Association of Nova Scotia, 78
Archery Association of New Brunswick, 78
Archery Canada Tir à l'Arc, 78
British Columbia Archery Association, 230
Fédération de tir à l'arc du Québec, 710
Ontario Association of Archers Inc., 1061
Saskatchewan Archery Association, 1256
Tir-à-l'arc Moncton Archers Inc., 1380
Toronto Sportsmen's Association, 1387
Traditional Archers Association of Nova Scotia, 1394
World Archery Federation, 1603

Architectural Conservation
Action Patrimoine, 6
Amis et propriétaires de maisons anciennes du Québec, 68
The Architectural Conservancy of Ontario, 78
Architectural Heritage Society of Saskatchewan, 79
Canadian Northern Society, 441
The Friends of Fort York & Garrison Common, 761
ICOMOS Canada, 829
International Council on Monuments & Sites, 1545
Nova Scotia Lighthouse Preservation Society, 1047
Ontario Monument Builders Association, 1091
Weymouth Historical Society, 1451

Architecture
Alberta Association of Architects, 23
Les Amis du centre canadien d'architecture, 67
Architects Association of Prince Edward Island, 78
Architects' Association of New Brunswick, 78
Architectural & Building Technologists Association of Manitoba Inc., 78
Architectural Glass & Metal Contractors Association, 79
Architectural Institute of British Columbia, 79
Architectural Woodwork Manufacturers Association of Canada, 79
The Arts & Letters Club, 85

Subject Index / Arts Councils

Association des Architectes en pratique privée du Québec, 105
Association of Architectural Technologists of Ontario, 139
Canada BIM Council Inc., 278
Canadian Architectural Certification Board, 295
Canadian Centre for Architecture, 353
Glass & Architectural Metals Association, 774
Manitoba Association of Architects, 929
National Trust for Canada, 996
Newfoundland Association of Architects, 1022
Northwest Territories Association of Architects, 1037
Nova Scotia Association of Architects, 1040
Ontario Association of Architects, 1061
Ordre des architectes du Québec, 1120
Royal Architectural Institute of Canada, 1237
Saskatchewan Association of Architects, 1256
Société Logique, 1321
Society for the Study of Architecture in Canada, 1327
Society of Architectural Historians, 1592
Union internationale des architectes, 1598

Archives
Alberni District Historical Society, 21
Archives Association of British Columbia, 80
Archives Association of Ontario, 80
Archives Council of Prince Edward Island, 80
Archives Society of Alberta, 80
Association du Patrimoine d'Aylmer, 131
Association for Manitoba Archives, 133
Association of Canadian Map Libraries & Archives, 142
Association of Newfoundland & Labrador Archives, 154
Campbell River Museum & Archives Society, 276
Canadian Association of Music Libraries, Archives & Documentation Centres, 321
Canadian Council of Archives, 367
Canadian Lesbian & Gay Archives, 426
Council of Archives New Brunswick, 632
Council of Nova Scotia Archives, 634
The Crow's Nest Military Artifacts Association, 644
15th Field Artillery Regiment Museum & Archives Society, 734
The Friends of Library & Archives Canada, 761
International Association of Music Libraries, Archives & Documentation Centres, 1539
King's County Historical Society, 888
Kings Historical Society, 888
Legal Archives Society of Alberta, 906
Margaret M. Allemang Centre for the History of Nursing, 949
Missisquoi Historical Society, 969
Nicola Valley Museum Archives Association, 1026
Northwest Territories Archives Council, 1037
Réseau des services d'archives du Québec, 1222
Saskatchewan Council for Archives & Archivists, 1262
Summerland Museum & Heritage Society, 1354
Touchstones Nelson Museum of Art & History, 1388
Ukrainian Canadian Research & Documentation Centre, 1402
Yukon Council of Archives, 1478

Archivists
Association des archivistes du Québec, 105
Association of Canadian Archivists, 141

Arctic Region
Arctic Council, 81
Arctic Institute of North America, 81
ArcticNet Inc., 81
Association of Canadian Universities for Northern Studies, 144
Canadian Arctic Resources Committee, 295
Canadian Circumpolar Institute, 357
International Arctic Science Committee, 1535
Northwest Territories Tourism, 1039

Armed Forces
Armed Forces Communications & Electronics Association (Canada), 82
Army, Navy & Air Force Veterans in Canada, 83
The Association for the Soldiers of Israel, 135

Armenians & Armenia
Armenian Community Centre of Toronto, 83
Armenian General Benevolent Union, 83
Armenian Holy Apostolic Church - Canadian Diocese, 83
Armenian Relief Society of Canada, Inc., 83
Canadian Armenian Business Council Inc., 295
International Association for Armenian Studies, 1535
Tekeyan Armenian Cultural Association, 1369

Arms Control
Campaign Against Arms Trade, 1515
Canadian Coalition for Nuclear Responsibility, 357

Army Cadets
Army Cadet League of Canada, 83

Art
Artists in Healthcare Manitoba, 85
L'Association des artistes Baltes à Montréal, 106
Association des collections d'entreprises, 109
Bonnyville & District Fine Arts Society, 217
Calgary Aboriginal Arts Awareness Society, 270
The Canadian Art Foundation, 295
Conseil québécois des arts médiatiques, 620
Foundation for the Study of Objective Art, 756
4Cs Foundation, 756
Glass Art Association of Canada, 774
International Association of Art Critics - Canada, 853
Inuit Art Foundation, 862
Oakville Art Society, 1053
Ontario Artist Blacksmith Association, 1060
Oxy-jeunes, 1134
Saint John Gallery Association, 1247
Saskatchewan Filmpool Co-operative, 1265
Storytellers of Canada, 1350
La Trame, 1394
Women's Art Association of Canada, 1461

Art Dealers
Art Dealers Association of Canada Inc., 84

Art Education
Banff Centre for Arts & Creativity, 195
British Columbia Art Teachers' Association, 230
Canadian Society for Education through Art, 474
Centre de formation et de consultation en métiers d'art, 529
Council of Ontario Drama & Dance Educators, 634
Guelph Musicfest, 793
Inner City Angels, 838
Manitoba Association for Art Education, 929
Ontario Art Education Association, 1060
PAVED Arts, 1146
Saskatchewan Society for Education through Art, 1275
Universities Art Association of Canada, 1418

Art Festivals
Algoma Arts Festival Association, 53
Associated Manitoba Arts Festivals, Inc., 89
Réseau indépendant des diffuseurs d'événements artistiques unis, 1224
Société de Promotion et de Diffusion des Arts et de la Culture, 1316
Storytelling Toronto, 1350

Art Galleries
Art Dealers Association of Canada Inc., 84
Association Museums New Brunswick, 138
Atlantic Provinces Art Gallery Association, 184
Bowen Island Arts Council, 219
Foundation for the Study of Objective Art, 756
Kingston Association of Museums, Art Galleries & Historic Sites, 889
Museum London, 983
Museum of Contemporary Canadian Art, 983
Ontario Association of Art Galleries, 1062
Open Space Arts Society, 1114
Touchstones Nelson Museum of Art & History, 1388
Vancouver Art Gallery Association, 1424
Volunteer Circle of the National Gallery of Canada, 1438

Art Therapy
Association des arts thérapeutes du Québec, 106
British Columbia Art Therapy Association, 230
Canadian Art Therapy Association, 295
Canadian Association for Sandplay Therapy, 303
Ontario Art Therapy Association, 1060
Toronto Art Therapy Institute, 1381
The Vancouver Art Therapy Institute, 1425

Arthritis & Rheumatism
Arthritis Health Professions Association, 84
Arthritis Research Foundation, 84
Arthritis Society, 84
Association des médecins rhumatologues du Québec, 120
Canadian Arthritis Network, 295
Canadian Rheumatology Association, 467
Ontario Rheumatology Association, 1102
Ontario Spondylitis Association, 1108

Artisans
The Metal Arts Guild of Canada, 962

Artists
Alberta Society of Artists, 47
Les Amis du vitrail, 67
Artists in Stained Glass, 85
Artscape, 86
Association acadienne des artistes professionnel.le.s du Nouveau-Brunswick inc., 89
Association des artistes en arts visuels de Saint-Jérôme, 106
Association des artistes peintres affiliés de la Rive-Sud, 106
Association des artistes peintres de Longueuil, 106
Bay St. George Folk Arts Council, 200
Black Artists Network of Nova Scotia, 212
Bureau des regroupements des artistes visuels de l'Ontario, 264
Calgary Society of Independent Filmmakers, 274
Canadian Artists Representation, 295
Canadian Artists' Representation British Columbia, 295
Canadian Artists' Representation Manitoba, 296
Canadian Artists' Representation Maritimes, 296
Canadian Artists' Representation Ontario, 296
Canadian Artists' Representation Saskatchewan, 296
Canadian Association for the Advancement of Music & the Arts, 305
Canadian Aviation Artists Assocation, 340
Canadian Mountain Arts Foundation, 437
Canadian Society of Painters in Water Colour, 486
Copyright Visual Arts, 628
English-Language Arts Network, 689
Federation of Canadian Artists, 722
Groupe Brosse Art, 791
Guelph Creative Arts Association, 793
Hispanic Canadian Arts & Culture Association, 815
International Watercolour Society - Canada, 861
KickStart Disability Arts & Culture, 884
Latino Canadian Cultural Association, 900
Manitoba Society of Artists, 944
The Metal Arts Guild of Canada, 962
Rainbow Association of Canadian Artists (Spectra Talent Contest), 1203
Screen Actors Guild - American Federation of Television & Radio Artists, 1588
Society of Canadian Artists, 1327
Vancouver Island Society for Disabled Artists, 1427
Visual Artists Newfoundland & Labrador, 1436

Arts & Crafts
Alberta Craft Council, 32
Association of Latvian Craftsmen in Canada, 150
Canadian Crafts Federation, 372
Canadian Guild of Crafts, 399
Canadian Knifemaker's Guild, 424
Centre de formation et de consultation en métiers d'art, 529
Centre de valorisation du patrimoine vivant, 530
Conseil des métiers d'art du Québec (ind.), 617
Craft & Hobby Association, 1520
Craft Council of British Columbia, 638
Craft Council of Newfoundland & Labrador, 638
Edmonton Weavers' Guild, 679
Embroiderers' Association of Canada, Inc., 685
Georgian Bay Folk Society, 771
Haliburton Highlands Guild of Fine Arts, 798
Lethbridge Handicraft Guild, 908
Manitoba Crafts Council, 934
Medicine Hat Fibre Arts Society, 958
Muskoka Arts & Crafts Inc., 985
New Brunswick Crafts Council, 1007
Nova Scotia Designer Crafts Council, 1044
Nunavut Arts & Crafts Association, 1051
Ontario Crafts Council, 1075
Prince Edward Island Crafts Council, 1173
Rug Hooking Guild of Nova Scotia, 1243
Saskatchewan Craft Council, 1262
Seacoast Trail Arts Association, 1287
Village International Sudbury, 1435
William Morris Society of Canada, 1455

Arts Councils
Abbotsford Arts Council, 1
Algonquin Arts Council, 53
Allied Arts Council of Spruce Grove, 58
Annapolis Region Community Arts Council, 71
Antigonish Culture Alive, 72
Arts Council of Sault Ste Marie & District, 85
Arts Council of Surrey, 85
Arts Council of the Central Okanagan, 85
Arts Council of the North Okanagan, 85
Arts Council Windsor & Region, 85
Arts Etobicoke, 85
Arts Mosaic, 85
Arts Ottawa East-Est, 86
Arts Richmond Hill, 86
ArtsConnect - Tri-Cities Regional Arts Council, 86
Assembly of BC Arts Councils, 88
Assiniboia & District Arts Council, 88
Biggar & District Arts Council, 210
Boundary District Arts Council, 219
Bowen Island Arts Council, 219
Brampton Arts Council, 225
Bulkley Valley Community Arts Council, 264
Burnaby Arts Council, 265
Burrows Trail Arts Council, 266
Canora Arts Council, 509
Carberry Plains Arts Council, 510
Castlegar & District Arts Council, 517
Central Interior Regional Arts Council, 524
Chilliwack Community Arts Council, 563
Cobequid Arts Council, 579
Community Arts Council of Fort St. James, 595
Community Arts Council of Greater Victoria, 595
Community Arts Council of Prince George & District, 595
Community Arts Council of Richmond, 595
Community Arts Council of the Alberni Valley, 595
Comox Valley Community Arts Council, 607
Conseil de la culture de L'Abitibi-Témiscamingue, 615
Conseil de la culture de Lanaudière, 616
Conseil de la culture des Laurentides, 616
Conseil des arts de Hearst, 617
Conseil des arts de Montréal, 617
Conseil montérégien de la culture et des communications, 619
Conseil régional de la culture de l'Outaouais, 620
Conseil régional de la culture et des communications de la Côte-Nord, 621
Conseil régional de la culture Saguenay-Lac-Saint-Jean, 621
Cowichan Valley Arts Council, 637
Cranbrook & District Arts Council, 638
Crowsnest Pass Allied Arts Association, 644
Dauphin & District Allied Arts Council Inc., 651
Delta Arts Council, 653
District of Mission Arts Council, 659
Eagle Valley Arts Council, 666
Eastend Arts Council, 669
Eatonia Arts Council, 671
Edmonton Arts Council, 675
Elora Arts Council, 685
Enderby & District Arts Council, 687
Estevan Arts Council, 697
Eston Arts Council, 697
Fernie & District Arts Council, 732
Folklorama, 742
Golden District Arts Council, 776
Golden Prairie Arts Council, 776

Subject Index / Asbestos Industry

Green Acres Art Centre, 788
Guelph Arts Council, 792
Guelph Creative Arts Association, 793
Haida Gwaii Arts Council, 798
Hamilton Arts Council, 800
Hamilton Folk Arts Heritage Council, 801
Inverness County Centre for the Arts, 862
Island Mountain Arts, 865
Kamsack & District Arts Council, 881
Kimberley Arts Council - Centre 64 Society, 887
Kingston Arts Council, 888
Langham Cultural Society, 898
Langley Arts Council, 899
Logan Lake Arts Council, 917
Mackenzie Community Arts Council, 924
Manitoba Arts Council, 929
Manitoba Arts Network, 929
Maple Ridge Pitt Meadows Arts Council, 948
Melville Arts Council, 959
Mississauga Arts Council, 969
Nelson & District Arts Council, 1003
New Brunswick Arts Board, 1004
Newfoundland & Labrador Arts Council, 1015
Newfoundland & Labrador Folk Arts Society, 1019
Nicola Valley Community Arts Council, 1026
North Vancouver Community Arts Council, 1033
Northwest Territories Arts Council, 1037
Oakville Arts Council, 1053
Oceanside Community Arts Council, 1054
Okotoks Arts Council, 1056
Oliver Community Arts Council, 1057
100 Mile & District Arts Council, 1058
Ontario Arts Council, 1060
Organization of Saskatchewan Arts Councils, 1126
Osoyoos & District Arts Council, 1128
Ottawa Arts Council, 1129
The Pas Arts Council Inc., 1144
Peace-Laird Regional Arts Council, 1147
Penticton & District Community Arts Council, 1150
Pincher Creek Allied Arts Council, 1160
Portage & District Arts Council, 1166
Prince Edward County Arts Council, 1171
Princeton Community Arts Council, 1180
Quesnel & District Arts Council, 1200
Quinte Arts Council, 1201
Red Deer & District Allied Arts Council, 1209
Revelstoke Arts Council, 1228
Scarborough Arts Council, 1282
Seguin Arts Council, 1289
Shaunavon Arts Council, 1294
Sheep Creek Arts Council, 1295
Shuswap District Arts Council, 1297
Société culturelle de la Baie des Chaleurs, 1309
Société culturelle régionale Les Chutes, 1309
Société culturelle Sud-Acadie, 1309
South Peace Community Arts Council, 1335
Southern Kings Arts Council, 1338
Steinbach Arts Council, 1349
Sudbury Arts Council, 1353
Summerland Community Arts Council, 1354
Sunshine Coast Arts Council, 1355
Thunder Bay Regional Arts Council, 1378
Toronto Arts Council, 1381
Toronto Arts Foundation, 1381
Trenton Art Club, 1397
Wallaceburg Arts Council, 1440
Wasagaming Community Arts Inc., 1440
Watrous Area Arts Council, 1442
West Kootenay Regional Arts Council, 1445
West Shore Arts Council, 1446
West Vancouver Community Arts Council, 1446

Asbestos Industry
Chrysotile Institute, 568

Asia
Aga Khan Foundation Canada, 14
Association for the Study of Nationalities, 135
Hautes études internationales, 804
Institute of Asian Research, 844
Pacific Asia Travel Association (Eastern Canada Chapter), 1134
South Asia Partnership Canada, 1334
South Asian Centre of Windsor, 1334
Support Enhance Access Service Centre, 1356

Asian Canadians
Alliance for South Asian AIDS Prevention, 57
Asian Community AIDS Services, 87
Asian Heritage Society of Manitoba, 87
Council of Agencies Serving South Asians, 632
Manitoba Association of Asian Physicians, 929
North American Association of Asian Professionals Vancouver, 1029
South Asian Women's Centre, 1334
University of Alberta South East Asian Students' Association, 1419

Asian Studies
Association for Asian Studies - USA, 1507
Canadian Asian Studies Association, 296

Asphalt Industry
Canadian Technical Asphalt Association, 493
Ontario Asphalt Pavement Council, 1060

Associations
American Society of Association Executives, 1499
Asociación Nacional de Ejecutivos de Organismos Empresariales y Profesionales, A.C., 1506
Australian Society of Association Executives Ltd., 1513
European Society of Association Executives, 1524
Federation of Swiss Association Executives, 1526
Union of International Associations, 1599

Asthma
Allergy, Asthma & Immunology Society of Ontario, 54
Allergy/Asthma Information Association, 54
Asthma Society of Canada, 179
Asthme et allergies Québec, 179
Canadian Network for Respiratory Care, 441
Canadian Society of Allergy & Clinical Immunology, 479
Réseau québécois de l'asthme et de la MPOC, 1225

Astronomy
Canadian Astronomical Society, 337
Fédération des astronomes amateurs du Québec, 712
H.R. MacMillan Space Centre Society, 824
Royal Astronomical Society of Canada, 1238
Thebacha & Wood Buffalo Astronomical Society, 1375

At-Risk Youth
Justice for Girls, 878
Our Place (Peel), 1133

Athletics
Alberta Cheerleading Association, 28
Amateur Athletic Union, 1487
AthletesCAN, 180
Athletics Alberta, 181
Athletics Canada, 181
Athletics Manitoba, 181
Athletics New Brunswick, 181
Athletics Nova Scotia, 181
Athletics Ontario, 181
Athletics PEI, 181
Athletics Yukon, 181
B2ten, 192
BC Cheerleading Association, 201
British Columbia Athletics, 233
Canada DanceSport, 278
Canadian Collegiate Athletic Association, 360
Canadian Rope Skipping Federation, 468
Canadian Trail & Mountain Running Association, 496
Canadian Wheelchair Basketball Association, 503
Cheer Canada, 555
Cheer Nova Scotia, 555
DanceSport Alberta, 650
DanceSport Atlantic, 650
DanceSport Québec, 650
Fédération de cheerleading du Québec, 708
Fédération québécoise d'athlétisme, 727
Greater Montreal Athletic Association, 784
Hamber Foundation, 800
Interior Running Association, 852
International Masters Games Association, 1553
Manitoba Association of Cheerleading, 929
Manitoba Cheer Federation Inc., 933
Manitoba Runners' Association, 943
National Association of Collegiate Directors of Athletics, 1573
Newfoundland & Labrador Athletics Association, 1017
Newfoundland & Labrador Cheerleading Athletics, 1017
Ontario Cheerleading Federation, 1071
Ontario DanceSport, 1076
Pacific Institute for Sport Excellence, 1135
Réseau du sport étudiant du Québec Abitibi-Témiscamingue, 1222
Réseau du sport étudiant du Québec Cantons-de-l'Est, 1222
Réseau du sport étudiant du Québec Chaudière-Appalaches, 1222
Réseau du sport étudiant du Québec Côte-Nord, 1222
Réseau du sport étudiant du Québec Est-du-Québec, 1223
Réseau du sport étudiant du Québec Lac Saint-Louis, 1223
Réseau du sport étudiant du Québec Laurentides-Lanaudière, 1223
Réseau du sport étudiant du Québec Montérégie, 1223
Réseau du sport étudiant du Québec Montréal, 1223
Réseau du sport étudiant du Québec Outaouais, 1223
Réseau du sport étudiant du Québec Saguenay-Lac St-Jean, 1223
Réseau du sport étudiant du Québec, secteur Mauricie, 1223
Sarnia Minor Athletic Association, 1254
Saskatchewan Athletics, 1259
Saskatchewan Cheerleading Association, 1261
Sports Laval, 1346
Trail & Ultra Running Association Of The Yukon, 1394
World Masters Athletics, 1606

Atlantic Provinces
The Acadian Entomological Society, 4
Association of Atlantic Universities, 139
Atlantic Chamber of Commerce, 183
Atlantic Health Promotion Research Centre, 184
Atlantic Mission Society, 184
Council of Atlantic Ministers of Education & Training, 632
Fédération des scouts de l'Atlantique, 718
Gorsebrook Research Institute for Atlantic Canada Studies, 778
L.M. Montgomery Institute, 916
Maritime Fire Chiefs' Association, 950
Québec-Labrador Foundation (Canada) Inc., 1199
Seagull Foundation, 1288
Them Days Inc., 1375

Atmosphere
Association québécoise de lutte contre la pollution atmosphérique, 170
Sierra Club of Canada, 1298

Auctioneers
Auctioneers Association of Alberta, 187
Auctioneers Association of Ontario, 187

Audiology
Association québécoise des orthophonistes et des audiologistes, 173
Canadian Academy of Audiology, 285
College of Audiologists & Speech-Language Pathologists of Ontario, 582
International Association of Physicians in Audiology, 1539
Ordre des audioprothésistes du Québec, 1120

Auditing
Auditing Association of Canada, 187
Canadian Public Accountability Board, 462
The Institute of Internal Auditors, 1533
ISACA, 1567

Auditoriums
International Association of Venue Managers, Inc., 1540

Australians & Australia
Australian Bankers' Association Inc., 1513
Australia-New Zealand Association, 188
Canadian Australian Chamber of Commerce, 1515

Austrians & Austria
Austrian Canadian Edelweiss Club of Regina Inc, 188
Austrian-Canadian Society, 1513

Autism
Aspergers Society of Ontario, 87
Autism Calgary Association, 188
Autism Canada, 188
Autism Nova Scotia, 188
Autism Ontario, 188
Autism Society Alberta, 188
Autism Society Manitoba, 189
Autism Society Newfoundland & Labrador, 189
Autism Society Northwest Territories, 189
Autism Society of British Columbia, 189
Autism Society of PEI, 189
Autism Speaks Canada, 189
Autism Yukon, 189
Canadian National Autism Foundation, 438
Fédération québécoise de l'autisme, 727
Geneva Centre for Autism, 769
Kerry's Place Autism Services, 884
Miriam Foundation, 968
Saskatchewan Families for Effective Autism Treatment, 1265
Society for Treatment of Autism, 1327
Unity for Autism, 1418
Woodview Mental Health & Autism Services, 1464

Autoimmune Diseases
Endometriosis Association, Inc., 1523

Automated Buildings
Continental Automated Buildings Association, 626

Automobile Clubs
Alfa Romeo Club of Canada, 53
Antique Motorcycle Club of Manitoba Inc., 72
Auto Sport Québec, 189
BMW Clubs Canada, 216
Boot'n Bonnet British Car Club, 218
Canadian Automobile Sport Clubs - Ontario Region Inc., 339
Canadian Vintage Motorcycle Group, 501
Citroën Autoclub Canada, 571
Corsa Ontario, 631
Lotus Car Club of Canada, 919
Mazda Sportscar Owners Club, 954
Northern Ramblers Car Club Inc., 1035
Old Chrysler Corporation Auto Club, 1056
Ontario Jaguar Owners Association, 1088
Southern Ontario Thunderbird Club, 1338
Sports Car Club of British Columbia, 1345
Sunbeam Sportscar Owners Club of Canada, 1354

Automobile Dealers
Association des concessionnaires Ford du Québec, 109
Automotive Retailers Association of British Columbia, 190
BCADA - The New Car Dealers of BC, 202
Calgary Motor Dealers Association, 273
Canadian Automobile Dealers' Association, 339
Corporation des concessionnaires d'automobiles du Québec inc., 630
Edmonton Motor Dealers' Association, 678
Halifax-Dartmouth Automobile Dealers' Association, 800
Manitoba Motor Dealers Association, 940
Manitoba Used Car Dealers Association, 946
Motor Dealers' Association of Alberta, 975
Nova Scotia Automobile Dealers' Association, 1041
Prince Edward Island Automobile Dealers Association, 1172
Recreation Vehicle Dealers Association of Canada, 1208
Saskatchewan Automobile Dealers Association, 1259
Trillium Automobile Dealers' Association, 1398
Used Car Dealers Association of Ontario, 1423

Automobile Racing
Motorsport Club of Ottawa, 976
Toronto Autosport Club, 1382

Automobiles
Alberta Motor Association, 40
AUTO21 Network of Centres of Excellence, 189

Automobile Journalists Association of Canada, 189
Automobile Protection Association, 189
Automotive Recyclers Association of Manitoba, 190
CAA British Columbia, 267
CAA Manitoba, 268
CAA Québec, 268
Canadian Automobile Association Atlantic, 339
Canadian Automobile Association Niagara, 339
Canadian Automobile Association North & East Ontario, 339
Canadian Automobile Association Saskatchewan, 339
Canadian Automobile Association South Central Ontario, 339
Dominion Automobile Association Limited, 660
Facility Association, 700
Groupement des assureurs automobiles, 792
Ontario Limousine Owners Association, 1089

Automotive Industry
Alberta Automotive Recyclers & Dismantlers Association, 25
Association des recycleurs de pièces d'autos et de camions, 127
Automotive Industries Association of Canada, 189
Automotive Parts Manufacturers' Association, 190
Automotive Recyclers Association of Atlantic Canada, 190
Automotive Recyclers of Canada, 190
Council for Automotive Human Resources, 632
Global Automakers of Canada, 774
Japan Automobile Manufacturers Association of Canada, 868
National Automotive Trades Association of Canada, 991
Ontario Automotive Recyclers Association, 1067
UNIFOR, 1405

Automotive Services
Automotive Aftermarket Retailers of Ontario, 189
Canadian Automotive Repair & Service Council, 340

Aviation
Aéroclub des cantons de l'est, 11
Aerospace Industries Association of Canada, 11
Aerospace Industry Association of British Columbia, 11
Air Currency Enhancement Society, 19
Air Force Association of Canada, 19
Airports Council International - Asia-Pacific Region, 1486
Alberta Aviation Museum Association, 25
Association québécoise de Vol Libre, 171
British Columbia Aviation Council, 233
Canada's Aviation Hall of Fame, 282
Canadian Aerial Applicators Association, 288
Canadian Aviation Artists Assocation, 340
Canadian Aviation Historical Society, 340
Canadian Business Aviation Association, 347
Canadian Council for Aviation & Aerospace, 366
Canadian Navigation Society, 440
Canadian Owners & Pilots Association, 448
Civil Air Search & Rescue Association, 571
Explorer's Club (Canadian Chapter), 700
International Airborne Geophysics Safety Association, 853
International Civil Aviation Organization: Legal Affairs & External Relations Bureau, 855
International Federation of Airworthiness, 1547
International Flying Farmers, 1549
Mission Aviation Fellowship of Canada, 969
University of Toronto Institute for Aerospace Studies, 1420
Youth Flight Canada, 1475

Awards, Honours, Prizes
Excellence Canada, 699
National Magazine Awards Foundation, 994

Badminton
Badminton Alberta, 193
Badminton BC, 193
Badminton Canada, 193
Badminton New Nouveau Brunswick, 193
Badminton Newfoundland & Labrador Inc., 193
Badminton Ontario, 193
Badminton Québec, 194
Badminton World Federation, 1513
Manitoba Badminton Association, 931
Northwest Territories Badminton Association, 1037
Nova Scotia Badminton Association, 1041
Prince Edward Island Badminton Association, 1172
Saskatchewan Badminton Association, 1259
Yukon Badminton Association, 1477

Bahá'í Faith
Association for Bahá'í Studies, 132
The Bahá'í Community of Canada, 194
Bahá'í Community of Ottawa, 194

Bailiffs
British Columbia Bailiffs Association, 233
Civil Constables Association of Nova Scotia, 571
Ontario Bailiff Association, 1067

Baking Industry
Artisan Bakers' Quality Alliance, 85
Association des Boulangers Artisans du Québec, 107
Bakery, Confectionery, Tobacco Workers & Grain Millers International Union (AFL-CIO/CLC), 1514
Baking Association of Canada, 194
Canadian Pastry Chefs Guild Inc., 451
Canadian Society of Sugar Artistry, 488
Société des chefs, cuisiniers et pâtissiers du Québec, 1317

Ball Hockey
British Columbia Ball Hockey Association, 233
Canadian Ball Hockey Association, 340
Manitoba Ball Hockey Association, 931
New Brunswick Ball Hockey Association, 1006
Newfoundland & Labrador Ball Hockey Association, 1017
Nova Scotia Ball Hockey Association, 1041
Ontario Ball Hockey Association, 1067
Québec Ball Hockey Association, 1196
Wild Rose Ball Hockey Association, 1454

Ballet
Alberta Ballet, 25
Ballet British Columbia, 194
Ballet Jörgen, 194
Ballet West, 195
Les Ballets Jazz de Montréal, 195
Goh Ballet Society, 776
Les Grands Ballets Canadiens de Montréal, 781
National Ballet of Canada, 991
Ontario Ballet Theatre, 1067
Royal Winnipeg Ballet, 1243
Vancouver Ballet Society, 1425
Youth Ballet & Contemporary Dance of Saskatchewan Inc., 1475

Baltic People in Canada
L'Association des artistes Baltes à Montréal, 106
Baltic Federation in Canada, 195

Bands, Musical
Alberta Band Association, 25
Atlantic Canada Pipe Band Association, 182
Calgary Round-Up Band Association, 274
Calgary Stetson Show Band, 274
Canadian Band Association, 340
Fédération des harmonies et des orchestres symphoniques du Québec, 715
Manitoba Band Association, 932
Nova Scotia Band Association, 1041
Ontario Band Association, 1067
Saskatchewan Band Association, 1259

Bangladesh
Canadians of Bangladeshi Origin, 507

Bankruptcy
Alberta Association of Insolvency & Restructuring Professionals, 23
British Columbia Association of Insolvency & Restructuring Professionals, 232
Canadian Association of Insolvency & Restructuring Professionals, 318
Manitoba Association of Insolvency & Restructuring Professionals, 930
New Brunswick Association of Insolvency & Restructuring Professionals, 1005
Newfoundland & Labrador Association of Insolvency & Restructuring Professionals, 1015
Nova Scotia Association of Insolvency & Restructuring Professionals, 1041
Ontario Association of Insolvency & Restructuring Professionals, 1064
Quebec Association of Insolvency & Restructuring Professionals, 1196
Saskatchewan Association of Insolvency & Restructuring Professionals, 1257

Banks
American Bankers Association, 1490
Australian Bankers' Association Inc., 1513
Canadian Bankers Association, 341
Canadian Community Reinvestment Coalition, 361
Canadian Paper Money Society, 449
Environmental Bankers Association, 1523
Interac Association, 851
Ombudsman for Banking Services & Investments, 1057
RBC Foundation, 1204

Baptists
Association d'églises baptistes évangéliques au québec, 99
Baptist General Conference of Canada, 196
Canadian Baptist Ministries, 341
Canadian Baptists of Ontario & Quebec, 341
Canadian Baptists of Western Canada, 341
CNBC, 576
Convention of Atlantic Baptist Churches, 627
Elgin Baptist Association, 684
Fellowship of Evangelical Baptist Churches, 731
Geogrian Bay Association, 769
Middlesex-Lambton-Huron Association of Baptist Churches, 965
Niagara/Hamilton Association of Baptist Churches, 1026
Ottawa Baptist Association, 1129
Oxford-Brant Association of Baptist Churches, 1134
Québec Association of Baptist Churches, 1195
Toronto Baptist Ministries, 1382
Trent Valley Association of Baptist Churches, 1397

Barbados
National Council of Barbadian Associations in Canada, 991

Barbershop Quartets
Barbershop Harmony Society, 1514
Harmony, Inc., 804

Baseball
Alberta Amateur Baseball Council, 22
Aurora King Baseball Association, 188
Baseball Alberta, 198
Baseball BC, 198
Baseball Canada, 198
Baseball New Brunswick, 198
Baseball Nova Scotia, 198
Baseball Ontario, 198
Baseball PEI, 198
Charlottetown Area Baseball Association, 552
Edmonton International Baseball Foundation, 678
Fédération du baseball amateur du Québec, 719
Hamilton Baseball Umpires' Association, 801
Kawartha Baseball Umpires Association, 882
Little League Canada, 915
Major League Baseball Players' Association (Ind.), 1569
Manitoba Baseball Association, 932
Newfoundland Baseball, 1022
Ontario Umpires Association, 1111
Prince Edward Island Baseball Umpires Association, 1172
Saskatchewan Baseball Association, 1259
Windsor & District Baseball Umpires Association, 1456

Basketball
Alberta Northern Lights Wheelchair Basketball Society, 41
Basketball Alberta, 198
Basketball BC, 198
Basketball Manitoba, 198
Basketball New Brunswick, 198
Basketball Nova Scotia, 199
Basketball NWT, 199
Basketball PEI, 199
Basketball Saskatchewan, 199
Basketball Yukon, 199
Canada Basketball, 278
Canadian Wheelchair Basketball Association, 503
Dr. James Naismith Basketball Foundation, 662
Fédération de basketball du Québec, 708
Newfoundland & Labrador Basketball Association, 1017
Ontario Basketball, 1067
Provincial Black Basketball Association, 1190

Baton Twirling
Alberta Baton Twirling Association, 25
Baton New Brunswick, 199
Baton Twirling Association of British Columbia, 199
Canadian Baton Twirling Federation, 342
Canadian National Baton Twirling Association, 438
Manitoba Baton Twirling Sportive Association, 932
Ontario Baton Twirling Association, 1067
Saskatchewan Baton Twirling Association, 1259

Beans
Canadian Soybean Council, 489
Canadian Special Crops Association, 489
Manitoba Pulse & Soybean Growers Inc., 943
Ontario Bean Growers Association, 1067

Beekeeping
Alberta Beekeepers Commission, 26
Beekeepers' Association of Niagara Region, 204
British Columbia Bee Breeders' Association, 233
Canadian Association of Professional Apiculturists, 328
Canadian Honey Council, 408
Capital Region Beekeepers Association, 510
Central Beekeepers' Alliance, 524
Central Ontario Beekeepers' Association, 525
Dufferin County Beekeepers' Association, 664
Durham Region Beekeepers' Association, 665
Eastern Apicultural Society of North America, Inc., 1522
Eastern Ontario Beekeepers' Association, 670
Golden Horseshoe Beekeepers' Association, 776
Grand River Beekeepers' Association, 780
Grey Bruce Beekeepers' Association, 790
Haldimand-Norfolk District Beekeepers' Association, 798
Huronia & District Beekeepers' Association, 828
Huron-Perth Beekeepers' Association, 828
International Federation of Beekeepers' Associations, 1547
Lanark County Beekeepers' Association, 897
Limestone Beekeepers Guild, 912
Manitoba Beekeepers' Association, 932
Middlesex, Oxford, Elgin Beekeepers' Association, 965
Muskoka-Parry Sound Beekeepers' Association, 985
New Brunswick Beekeepers Association, 1006
Nova Scotia Beekeepers' Association, 1042
Ontario Beekeepers' Association, 1067
Prince Edward Island Beekeepers' Cooperative Association, 1172
Quinte Beekeepers' Association, 1201
Rainy River Beekeepers' Association, 1204
Red River Apiarists' Association, 1210
Saskatchewan Beekeepers Association, 1259
Southwestern Ontario Beekeepers' Association, 1338
Sudbury & District Beekeepers' Association, 1353
Thunder Bay Beekeepers' Association, 1377
Toronto District Beekeepers' Association, 1384
United County Beekeepers, 1410
Upper Ottawa Valley Beekeepers' Association, 1422
Wellington County Beekeepers' Association, 1443

Belgo-Canadians
Belgian Canadian Business Chamber, 204
VZW Belgium-Canada, 1601

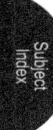

Bereavement
Association des veuves de Montréal inc., 130
Bereaved Families of Ontario, 205
Bereavement Ontario Network, 205
Canadian Hospice Palliative Care Association, 409
Morning Light Ministry, 974

Better Business Bureau
Better Business Bureau of Central & Northern Alberta, 206
Better Business Bureau of Eastern & Northern Ontario & the Outaouais, 206
Better Business Bureau of Mainland BC, 206
Better Business Bureau of Manitoba & Northwest Ontario, 206
Better Business Bureau of Mid-Western & Central Ontario, 206
Better Business Bureau of Saskatchewan, 206
Better Business Bureau of Vancouver Island, 206
Better Business Bureau of Western Ontario, 207
Better Business Bureau Serving Southern Alberta & East Kootenay, 207
Better Business Bureau Serving the Atlantic Provinces, 207
Council of Better Business Bureaus, 1520
IntegrityLink, 850
L'Office de Certification Commerciale du Québec Inc., 1054

Biathlon
Biathlon Alberta, 207
Biathlon BC, 207
Biathlon Canada, 207
Biathlon Manitoba, 207
Biathlon Newfoundland & Labrador, 207
Biathlon Nouveau-New Brunswick, 207
Biathlon Nova Scotia, 207
Biathlon Ontario, 207
Biathlon Prince Edward Island, 207
Biathlon Saskatchewan, 208
Biathlon Yukon, 208
Fédération québécoise de biathlon, 727
Northwest Territories Biathlon Association, 1037

Bible
The Bible Holiness Movement, 208
The Bible League of Canada, 208
Canada's National Bible Hour, 282
Canadian Bible Society, 343
Canadian Society of Biblical Studies, 481
Catholic Biblical Association of Canada, 517
Full Gospel Business Men's Fellowship in Canada, 764
Gideons International in Canada, 773
International Bible Correspondence School, 854
Lutheran Bible Translators of Canada Inc., 922
Olivet New Church, 1057
Société catholique de la Bible, 1309
Wycliffe Bible Translators of Canada, Inc., 1470

Bibliographers
Bibliographical Society of America, 1514
Bibliographical Society of Canada, 208

Bicycling
Alberta Bicycle Association, 26
Bicycle Newfoundland & Labrador, 208
Bicycle Nova Scotia, 208
Bike to Work BC Society, 211
Canadian Independent Bicycle Retailers Association, 410
Centre de plein air du Mont Chalco, 529
Contagious Mountain Bike Club, 626
Cycle Toronto, 647
Cycling Association of the Yukon, 647
Cycling British Columbia, 647
Cycling Canada Cyclisme, 647
Cycling PEI, 647
Edmonton Bicycle & Touring Club, 675
Fédération québécoise des sports cyclistes, 730
Manitoba Cycling Association, 935
Ontario Cycling Association, 1076
Saskatchewan Cycling Association, 1263
Toronto Bicycling Network, 1382
Vélo New Brunswick, 1431
Vélo Québec, 1431
VeloNorth Cycling Club, 1431

Bilingualism
Association québécoise des enseignants de français langue seconde, 172
Canadian Parents for French, 450
Centre interdisciplinaire de recherches sur les activités langagières, 535
Conseil de développement économique des municipalités bilingues du Manitoba, 615
Parents partenaires en éducation, 1140

Billiards
Canadian Billiards & Snooker Association, 343
Canadian Cue Sport Association, 373

Biochemistry
Association des médecins biochimistes du Québec, 119
Canadian Association of Medical Biochemists, 320
Canadian Society for Molecular Biosciences, 476
Controlled Release Society, 1520

Biodiversity
ETC Group, 697
Falls Brook Centre, 701
International Union of Biological Sciences, 1564
Rare Breeds Canada, 1204

Bioethics
Canadian Bioethics Society, 343
Canadian College of Medical Geneticists, 359
Joint Centre for Bioethics, 875
Provincial Health Ethics Network, 1191

Biology
Alberta Society of Professional Biologists, 47
American Society of Plant Biologists, 1502
Association of Professional Biology, 156
Cell Stress Society International, 1516
Coastal Ecosystems Research Foundation, 579
College of Applied Biology British Columbia, 582
Council of Science Editors, 1520
Institut de recherche en biologie végétale, 842
International Federation for Medical & Biological Engineering, 1546
International Union of Biological Sciences, 1564
Society for Conservation Biology, 1590
The Waterbird Society, 1602

Biomedical Engineering
Association des physiciens et ingénieurs biomédicaux du Québec, 123
Canadian Medical & Biological Engineering Society, 433
International Federation for Medical & Biological Engineering, 1546

Biomedical Research
Canadian Association of Medical Biochemists, 320
Institute of Health Economics, 846
Partners in Research, 1144

Biophysics
Biophysical Society of Canada, 211
Canadian College of Physicists in Medicine, 360

Biotechnology
Alberta Biotechnology Association, 26
AllerGen NCE Inc., 54
BioNova, 211
BIOQuébec, 211
BioTalent Canada, 211
BIOTECanada, 212
Canadian Society of Microbiologists, 485
International Society for Evolutionary Protistology, 860
Life Sciences Ontario, 911
LifeSciences British Columbia, 911
Stem Cell Network, 1349

Birds
Alberta Falconry Association, 34
American Birding Association, Inc., 1490
American Ornithological Society, 1496
The Avian Preservation Foundation, 190
Avicultural Advancement Council of Canada, 191
Beaverhill Bird Observatory, 203
Bird Studies Canada, 212
British Columbia Waterfowl Society, 258
Canadian Dove Association, 378
Canadian Racing Pigeon Union Inc., 464
Club d'observateurs d'oiseaux de Laval, 574
Club d'Ornithologie de Longueuil, 574
Club des ornithologues de Québec inc., 575
Durham Avicultural Society of Ontario, 664
Essex-Kent Cage Bird Society, 696
Fondation Les oiseleurs du Québec inc., 747
The Golden Triangle Parrot Club, 776
Grand Manan Whale & Seabird Research Station, 780
Hawk Migration Association of North America, 1529
Jack Miner Migratory Bird Foundation, Inc., 867
National Audubon Society, Inc., 1575
North American Bird Conservation Initiative Canada, 1029
North American Waterfowl Management Plan, 1029
Ontario Field Ornithologists, 1080
Parrot Association of Canada, 1143
Pembroke Area Field Naturalists, 1149
Regroupement QuébecOiseaux, 1216
Society of Canadian Ornithologists, 1327
Toronto Ornithological Club, 1386
The Waterbird Society, 1602
Wild Bird Care Centre, 1453
World Pheasant Association, 1607

Birth Control
Birth Control & Venereal Disease Information Centre, 212
Calgary Sexual Health Centre, 274

Bishops
Assemblée des évêques catholiques du Québec, 88
Assembly of Catholic Bishops of Ontario, 88
Atlantic Episcopal Assembly, 183
Canadian Conference of Catholic Bishops, 362

Black Canadians
Black Academic Scholarship Fund, 212
Black Artists Network of Nova Scotia, 212
Black Business & Professional Association, 213
Black Business Initiative, 213
Black Coalition for AIDS Prevention, 213
Black Community Resource Centre, 213
Black Cultural Society for Nova Scotia, 213
Black Educators Association of Nova Scotia, 213
Black Loyalist Heritage Society, 213
Black Studies Centre, 213
Black Theatre Workshop, 213
Canadian Association of Black Journalists, 308
Canadian Association of Black Lawyers, 308
Central Ontario Network for Black History, 525
Coalition of Black Trade Unionists, 578
Community Enhancement Association, 597
Congress of Black Lawyers & Jurists of Québec, 613
Council for Black Aging, 632
Desta Black Youth Network, 654
Jaku Konbit, 867
Nova Scotia Association of Black Social Workers, 1040
One Full Circle, 1058
Ontario Black History Society, 1068
Provincial Black Basketball Association, 1190
Québec Board of Black Educators, 1196
St. Josephine Bakhita Black Heritage, 1249
West Island Black Community Association, 1445
Windsor & District Black Coalition of Canada, 1456

Blindness
Accessible Media Inc., 5
Alberta Sports & Recreation Association for the Blind, 48
Alliance for Equality of Blind Canadians, 57
Association des sports pour aveugles de Montréal, 128
Association québécoise de joueurs d'échechs handicapeés visuels, 169
Association québécoise des parents d'enfants handicapés visuels, 173
Association sportive des aveugles du Québec inc., 178
BALANCE for Blind Adults, 194
Blind Bowls Association of Canada, 214
Blind Sailing Association of Canada, 214
Blind Sports Nova Scotia, 214
Le Bon Pilote inc., 217
Braille Literacy Canada, 224
British Columbia Blind Sports & Recreation Association, 234
Canadian Blind Sports Association Inc., 344
The Canadian Council of the Blind, 370
Canadian Deafblind Association (National), 376
Canadian National Institute for the Blind, 439
Christian Blind Mission International, 566
Dog Guides Canada, 660
Fondation des aveugles du Québec, 744
Institut Nazareth et Louis-Braille, 843
John Milton Society for the Blind in Canada, 875
Manitoba Blind Sports Association, 932
Montréal Association for the Blind, 972
Ontario Blind Sports Association, 1068
Ontario Foundation for Visually Impaired Children Inc., 1081
Québec Federation of the Blind Inc., 1197
Saskatchewan Blind Sports Association Inc., 1259
Seva Canada Society, 1292
World Blind Union, 1465

Blood Transfusion
Association des bénévoles du don de sang, 107
BloodWatch, 215
Canadian Blood & Marrow Transplant Group, 344
Canadian Blood Services, 344
Canadian Society for Transfusion Medicine, 479

Boards of Education
Association des directeurs généraux des commissions scolaires du Québec, 111
Canadian Association of School System Administrators, 332
Canadian School Boards Association, 468
La Fédération des commissions scolaires du Québec, 713
Fédération des Syndicats de l'Enseignement, 719
Independent Association of Support Staff, 832
Manitoba School Boards Association, 944
Nova Scotia School Boards Association, 1048
Ontario Public School Boards Association, 1099
Québec English School Boards Association, 1197
Saskatchewan School Boards Association, 1274

Boards of Trade
Ajax-Pickering Board of Trade, 20
Annapolis District Board of Trade, 71
Arborfield Board of Trade, 76
Atlin Board of Trade, 187
Aylsham & District Board of Trade, 191
Bear River Board of Trade, 202
Bradford Board of Trade, 224
The Brampton Board of Trade, 225
Carrot River & District Board of Trade, 516
Digby & Area Board of Trade, 656
Dufferin Board of Trade, 664
Edam & District Board of Trade, 674
Fort Vermilion & Area Board of Trade, 754
Greater Corner Brook Board of Trade, 783
The Greater Vancouver Board of Trade, 786
Greenwood Board of Trade, 789
Hellenic Canadian Board of Trade, 811
Kitikmeot Regional Board of Trade, 891
Leader Board of Trade, 903
Lunenburg Board of Trade, 920
Markham Board of Trade, 951
Miramichi Board of Trade, 968
Mississauga Board of Trade, 969
New Hamburg Board of Trade, 1014
North Queens Board of Trade, 1032
Parrsboro & District Board of Trade, 1143
Port Dover Board of Trade, 1165
St. John's Board of Trade, 1249
Stettler Regional Board of Trade & Community Development, 1350
Toronto Region Board of Trade, 1387
Wakaw & District Board of Trade, 1439
Wellesley & District Board of Trade, 1443
West Ottawa Board of Trade, 1446
Zeballos Board of Trade, 1482
Zenon Park Board of Trade, 1482

Boating
Alberta Sailing Association, 45
BC Sailing Association, 202
Boating BC Association, 216

Subject Index / Broadcasting

Boating Ontario, 216
Canadian Boating Federation, 345
Canadian International Dragon Boat Festival Society, 421
Canadian Power & Sail Squadrons (Canadian Headquarters), 459
Canadian Safe Boating Council, 468
Club nautique de Chibougamau inc., 575
Dragon Boat Canada, 662
National Marine Manufacturers Association Canada, 995
New Brunswick Sailing Association, 1011
Ontario Sailing, 1103
PEI Sailing Association, 1149
Sail Canada, 1245
Sail Manitoba, 1246
Sail Nova Scotia, 1246
SailNL, 1246
Saskatchewan Sailing Clubs Association, 1274
Wind Athletes Canada, 1456

Boats
Canadian Ferry Association, 389
CharterAbility, 552
National Marine Manufacturers Association, 1576

Bobsledding & Luge
Alberta Bobsleigh Association, 26
Alberta Luge Association, 39
Bobsleigh Canada Skeleton, 217
Canadian Luge Association, 428
Fédération internationale de bobsleigh et de tobogganing, 1525
Fédération Internationale de Luge de Course, 1525
Ontario Bobsleigh Skeleton Association, 1068
Ontario Luge Association, 1089

Bodybuilding
Alberta Bodybuilding Association, 26
Association des Physiques Québécois, 123
British Columbia Amateur Bodybuilding Association, 230
Canadian Bodybuilding Federation, 345
International Federation of Bodybuilding & Fitness, 1547
Manitoba Amateur Bodybuilding Association, 928
New Brunswick Physique & Figure Association, 1011
Newfoundland & Labrador Amateur Bodybuilding Association, 1015
Nova Scotia Amateur Bodybuilding Association, 1040
Ontario Physique Association, 1096
Saskatchewan Bodybuilding Association, 1260

Book Arts
The Alcuin Society, 53
Canadian Bookbinders & Book Artists Guild, 346

Book Trade
Antiquarian Booksellers' Association of Canada, 72
Association des distributeurs exclusifs de livres en langue française inc., 111
Association des libraires du Québec, 118
Association professionnelle des écrivains de la Sagamie-Côte-Nord, 167
Book & Periodical Council, 218
Canadian Booksellers Association, 346
Canadian Children's Book Centre, 355
Confrérie de la librairie ancienne du Québec, 612
Livres Canada Books, 915

Bosnian Canadians
Bosnian Canadian Relief Association, 218
Bosnian Islamic Association, 218

Botany
American Public Gardens Association, 1497
American Society of Plant Biologists, 1502
Canadian Botanical Association, 346
Canadian Phytopathological Society, 455
Canadian Society of Plant Biologists, 486
Center for Plant Conservation, 1516
Field Botanists of Ontario, 733
International Plant Propagators Society, Inc., 1555
International Society for Plant Pathology, 1559
VanDusen Botanical Garden Association, 1429

Bottled Water
Association des embouteilleurs d'eau du Québec, 111
Canadian Bottled Water Association, 346
International Bottled Water Association, 1541

Bowling
Alberta 5 Pin Bowlers' Association, 21
Bowling Federation of Alberta, 219
Bowling Federation of Canada, 219
Bowling Federation of Saskatchewan, 219
Bowling Proprietors' Association of BC, 219
Bowling Proprietors' Association of Canada, 219
Bowling Proprietors' Association of Ontario, 219
British Columbia Tenpin Bowling Association, 256
Canadian 5 Pin Bowlers' Association, 285
Canadian Tenpin Federation, Inc., 493
Fédération de pétanque du Québec, 710
Manitoba 5 Pin Bowlers' Association, 928
Manitoba Five Pin Bowling Federation, Inc., 936
Manitoba Tenpin Federation, 946
Master Bowlers' Association of Alberta, 953
Master Bowlers' Association of British Columbia, 953
Master Bowlers' Association of Canada, 953
Master Bowlers' Association of Manitoba, 953
Master Bowlers' Association of Ontario, 953
New Brunswick Candlepin Bowlers Association, 1006
Northwest Territories 5 Pin Bowlers' Association, 1037
Ontario 5 Pin Bowlers' Association, 1058
Ontario Tenpin Bowling Association, 1110
Prince Edward Island Five Pin Bowlers Association Inc., 1174
Saskatchewan 5 Pin Bowlers' Association, 1254
Youth Bowling Canada, 1475

Boxing
Boxing Alberta, 220
Boxing BC Association, 220
Boxing Manitoba, 220
Boxing New Brunswick Boxe, 220
Boxing Newfoundland & Labrador, 220
Boxing Nova Scotia, 220
Boxing Ontario, 220
Boxing Saskatchewan, 220
Calgary Combative Sports Commission, 271
Canadian Amateur Boxing Association, 292
Canadian Professional Boxing Council, 460
Edmonton Combative Sports Commission, 676
Fédération Québécoise de Boxe Olympique, 727
Manitoba Combative Sports Commission, 934
Nova Scotia Boxing Authority, 1042
Prince Edward Island Amateur Boxing Association, 1171
Yukon Amateur Boxing Association, 1477

Boys & Girls Clubs
Boys & Girls Clubs of Alberta, 221
Boys & Girls Clubs of British Columbia, 221
Boys & Girls Clubs of Canada, 222
Boys & Girls Clubs of Canada Foundation, 222
Boys & Girls Clubs of Manitoba, 222
Boys & Girls Clubs of New Brunswick, 222
Boys & Girls Clubs of Newfoundland & Labrador, 222
Boys & Girls Clubs of Nova Scotia, 223
Boys & Girls Clubs of Ontario, 223
Boys & Girls Clubs of Prince Edward Island, 224
Boys & Girls Clubs of Québec, 224
Boys & Girls Clubs of Saskatchewan, 224
Boys & Girls Clubs of Yukon, 224

Brain
Brain Tumour Foundation of Canada, 225
Canadian Brain Tumour Consortium, 346
Canadian Brain Tumour Tissue Bank, 346
International Society for Vascular Behavioural & Cognitive Disorders, 1560

Brain Injury
Association des accidentés cérébro-vasculaires et traumatisés crâniens de l'Estrie, 104
Association des handicapés adultes de la Côte-Nord, 116
Association des neurotraumatisés de l'Outaouais, 121
Association des personnes accidentées cérébro-vasculaires, aphasiques et traumatisées crânio-cérébrales du Bas-Saint-Laurent, 122
Association des personnes handicapées physiques et sensorielles du secteur Joliette, 123
Association des TCC (le traumatisme cranio-cérébral) et ACV (un accident vasculaire cérébral) de la Gaspésie et des Îles-de-la-Madeleine Inc., 129
Association des traumatisés crâniens de l'Abitibi-Témiscamingue (Le Pilier), 129
Association des Traumatisés cranio-cérébraux de la Montérégie, 129
Association des traumatisés cranio-cérébraux des deux rives (Québec-Chaudière-Appalaches), 129
Association des traumatisés cranio-cérébraux Mauricie-Centre-du-Québec, 130
Association for the Rehabilitation of the Brain Injured, 135
Association québécoise des traumatisés crâniens, 175
Association québécoise des traumatisés craniens, 175
Association renaissance des personnes traumatisées crâniennes du Saguenay-Lac-Saint-Jean, 178
Brain Care Centre, 225
Brain Injury Association of Alberta, 225
Brain Injury Association of Canada, 225
Brain Injury Association of Nova Scotia, 225
Brain Injury Coalition of Prince Edward Island, 225
British Columbia Brain Injury Association, 234
Centre d'aide personnes traumatisées crâniennes et handicapées physiques Laurentides, 527
Manitoba Brain Injury Association Inc., 932
Newfoundland & Labrador Brain Injury Association, 1017
Ontario Brain Injury Association, 1068
Ontario Neurotrauma Foundation, 1093
Prince George Brain Injured Group, 1179
Regroupement des associations de personnes traumatisées craniocérébrales du Québec, 1214
Saskatchewan Brain Injury Association, 1260
South Okanagan Similkameen Brain Injury Society, 1335
Southern Alberta Brain Injury Society, 1337
Westward Goals Support Services Inc., 1451

Breastfeeding
Canadian Lactation Consultant Association, 425
Infant Feeding Action Coalition, 836
La Leche League Canada, 905
La Leche League International, 1569

Breeding
Alberta Cattle Breeders Association, 27
Alberta Maine-Anjou Association, 39
Alberta Pinzgauer Association, 42
American Galloway Breeders Association, 66
American Saddlebred Horse Association of British Columbia, 66
American Saddlebred Horse Association of Canada, 66
American Saddlebred Horse Association of Ontario, 66
Atlantic Standardbred Breeders Association, 186
Ayrshire Breeders Association of Canada, 191
British Columbia Chicken Growers' Association, 236
British Columbia Sporthorse - Sport Pony Breeders Group, 255
Canada Fox Breeders' Association, 279
Canadian Beef Breeds Council, 342
Canadian Belgian Blue Association, 342
Canadian Cattle Breeders' Association, 351
Canadian Chianina Association, 355
Canadian Hays Converter Association, 401
Canadian Horse Breeders' Association, 408
Canadian Lowline Cattle Association, 428
Canadian Luing Cattle Association, 428
Canadian Maine-Anjou Association, 429
Canadian Meat Goat Association, 432
Canadian Piedmontese Association, 455
Canadian Pinzgauer Association, 455
Canadian Shire Horse Association, 470
Canadian Speckle Park Association, 489
Canine Federation of Canada, 508
Clydesdale Horse Association of Canada, 576
Cypress Hills Registered Horse Breeders' Association, 647
Dominion Rabbit & Cavy Breeders Association, 661
EastGen, 671
Fédération des producteurs de bovins du Québec, 717
Maritime Breeders Association, 950
Miniature Horse Association of Canada, 966
Miniature Horse Club of Ontario, 966
Murray Grey International, Incorporated, 982
National Chinchilla Breeders of Canada, 991
New Brunswick Shorthorn Breeders Association, 1012
North American Lincoln Red Association, 1579
North American Piedmontese Association, 1579
Nova Scotia Mink Breeders' Association, 1047
Ontario Brown Swiss Association, 1069
Ontario Commercial Rabbit Growers' Association, 1073
Ontario Pinzgauer Breeders Association, 1096
Prince Edward Island Sheep Breeders Association, 1177
Prince Edward Island Shorthorn Association, 1177
Prince Edward Island Standardbred Horseowners' Association, 1177
Rare Breeds Canada, 1204
Saskatchewan Cattle Breeders Association, 1260
Saskatchewan Stock Growers Association, 1276
Standardbred Breeders of Ontario Association, 1347
Upper Canada District Canadian Horse Breeders, 1421
Western Ayrshire Club, 1447
Western Canadian Miniature Horse Club, 1448
Westgen, 1450

Brewing Industry
Association des brasseurs du Québec, 108
Brewers Association of Canada, 228
Brewing & Malting Barley Research Institute, 228
Master Brewers Association of The Americas, 1569
The Molson Family Foundation, 971
Ontario Craft Brewers, 1075

Brick Industry
Association des entrepreneurs en maçonnerie du Québec, 112

Bridge (Game of)
Canadian Bridge Federation, 347

British Isles
British Canadian Chamber of Trade & Commerce, 229
British Council - Canada, 259
British Isles Family History Society of Greater Ottawa, 259
Canadian Alliance of British Pensioners, 291
The St. George's Society of Toronto, 1248

British Studies
North American Conference on British Studies, 1578

Broadcasters
Association canadienne des annonceurs inc., 92
British Columbia Association of Broadcasters, 231
Broadcast Educators Association of Canada, 259
Canadian Association of Broadcasters, 309
Canadian Communications Foundation, 361
Canadian Media Guild, 432
National Campus & Community Radio Association, 991
North American Broadcasters Association, 1029
Ontario Association of Broadcasters, 1062
Western Association of Broadcasters, 1447

Broadcasting
Alliance of Canadian Cinema, Television & Radio Artists, 58
Audio Engineering Society, 187
Back to the Bible Canada, 193
British Columbia Association of Broadcasters, 231

Subject Index / Broomball

Broadcast Educators Association of Canada, 259
Broadcast Executives Society, 259
Broadcast Research Council of Canada, 259
Canadian Association of Broadcast Consultants, 309
Canadian Association of Community Television Users & Stations, 311
Canadian Broadcast Standards Council, 347
Canadian Cable Systems Alliance, 348
Canadian Communications Foundation, 361
Canadian Media Production Association, 432
Central Canada Broadcast Engineers, 524
Concerned Children's Advertisers, 609
Friends of Canadian Broadcasting, 760
Interactive Ontario, 851
Legislative Recording & Broadcast Association, 906
Media Smarts, 957
National Campus & Community Radio Association, 991
National Institute of Broadcasting, 994
North American Broadcasters Association, 1029
Ontario Association of Broadcasters, 1062
Radio Advisory Board of Canada, 1202
Radio Television Digital News Association (Canada), 1203
Shaw Rocket Fund, 1295
Western Association of Broadcast Engineers, 1447
Western Association of Broadcasters, 1447
Women in Film & Television - Toronto, 1461
Women in Film & Television Vancouver, 1461
Youth Media Alliance, 1476

Broomball
Alberta Broomball Association, 26
Ballon sur glace Broomball Canada, 195
British Columbia Broomball Society, 234
Broomball Newfoundland & Labrador, 260
Federation of Broomball Associations of Ontario, 722
Fédération québécoise de ballon sur glace, 727
International Federation of Broomball Associations, 857
Manitoba Amateur Broomball Association, 928
Maritime Broomball Association, 950
Northwest Territories Broomball Association, 1037
Saskatchewan Broomball Association, 1260
Yukon Broomball Association, 1477

Buddhism
Buddhist Association of Canada - Cham Shan Temple, 261
Fung Loy Kok Institute of Taoism, 764
Jodo Shinshu Buddhist Temples of Canada, 873
The Palyul Foundation of Canada, 1137
Yasodhara Ashram Society, 1470

Building & Construction Trades Coun
Cape Breton Island Building & Construction Trades Council, 509
Hamilton-Brantford Building & Construction Trades Council, 802
Kamloops, Revelstoke, Okanagan & District Building & Construction Trades Council, 881
London Building & Construction Trades Council, 918
Mainland Nova Scotia Building & Construction Trades Council, 926
Manitoba Building & Construction Trades Council, 933
Northeastern Ontario Building & Construction Trades Council, 1034
Northwestern Ontario Building & Construction Trades Council, 1039
Prince Edward Island Building & Construction Trades Council, 1172
Provincial Building & Construction Trades Council of Ontario, 1190
Quinte - Saint Lawrence Building & Construction Trades Council, 1201
Sarnia Building Trades Council, 1254

Building Inspection
Alberta Building Officials Association, 27
Canadian Association of Home & Property Inspectors, 317
New Brunswick Building Officials Association, 1006
Ontario Building Officials Association Inc., 1070
Saskatchewan Building Officials Association Inc., 1260
World Organization of Building Officials, 1466

Building Maintenance
Building Owners & Managers Association - Canada, 262
Building Owners & Managers Association - Nova Scotia, 263
Manitoba Building Officials Association, 933
World Organization of Building Officials, 1466

Building Materials
Association québécoise de la quincaillerie et des matériaux de construction, 170
Atlantic Building Supply Dealers Association, 182
British Columbia Shake & Shingle Association, 253
Building Materials Reuse Association, 1514
Building Supply Industry Association of British Columbia, 263
Canadian Hardwood Plywood & Veneer Association, 401
Canadian Steel Door Manufacturers Association, 491
Cement Association of Canada, 521
Independent Lumber Dealers Co-operative, 833
Lumber & Building Materials Association of Ontario, 920
Maritime Lumber Bureau, 951
NAIMA Canada, 987
Ontario Lumber Manufacturers' Association, 1089
SPANCAN, 1338
Western Retail Lumber Association, 1450
World Organization of Building Officials, 1466

Building Trades
Architectural & Building Technologists Association of Manitoba Inc., 78
Association canadienne des métiers de la truelle, section locale 100 (CTC), 94
Association provinciale des constructeurs d'habitations du Québec inc., 168
British Columbia Wall & Ceiling Association, 257
Building Energy Management Manitoba, 261
Building Envelope Council of Ottawa Region, 262
Canadian Farm Builders Association, 384
Canadian Home Builders' Association - Northern British Columbia, 407
Concrete Forming Association of Ontario, 610
International Log Builders' Association, 858
International Union of Bricklayers & Allied Craftworkers (AFL-CIO/CFL), 1564
Manitoba Building Envelope Council, 933
Manitoba Wall & Ceiling Association, 947
National Building Envelope Council, 991
Ontario Building Envelope Council, 1069
Sealant & Waterproofing Association, 1288
Waterloo, Wellington, Dufferin & Grey Building & Construction Trades Council, 1442

Burns & Scalds
British Columbia Professional Fire Fighters' Burn Fund, 249
Burn Survivors Association, 265
Calgary Firefighters Burn Treatment Society, 272
Canadian Burn Survivors Community, 347
Firefighters Burn Fund Inc., 738
Fondation des pompiers du Québec pour les grands brûlés, 745
International Society for Burn Injuries, 1557
Mamingwey Burn Survivor Society, 928
Saskatchewan Professional Fire Fighters Burn Unit Fund, 1272

Bus Transport
Bus History Association, Inc., 266
Fédération des transporteurs par autobus, 719
Independent School Bus Operators Association, 833
Motor Carrier Passenger Council of Canada, 975
Motor Coach Canada, 975
Ontario Motor Coach Association, 1091
Ontario School Bus Association, 1103

Business
Abbotsford Downtown Business Association, 1
AIESEC, 18
Alberta Association of Fund Raising Executives, 23
Asia Pacific Foundation of Canada, 86
Associated Senior Executives of Canada Ltd., 89
Association des clubs d'entrepreneurs étudiants du Québec, 109
Association of Accrediting Agencies of Canada, 138
Association of School Business Officials of Alberta, 161
Association of Strategic Alliance Professionals - Toronto Chapter, 162
Belgian Canadian Business Chamber, 204
Black Business & Professional Association, 213
Black Business Initiative, 213
British Columbia Association of Professionals with Disabilities, 232
Business Council of British Columbia, 266
Business Council of Canada, 266
Business Development Centre (Toronto), 267
Business for the Arts, 267
Calgary Danish Businessmen's Association, 271
Canada - Albania Business Council, 277
Canada Bulgaria Business Network, 278
Canada Eurasia Russia Business Association, 279
Canada Korea Business Association, 280
Canada-Arab Business Council, 283
Canada-India Business Council, 283
Canada-Singapore Business Association, 284
Canada-Yukon Business Service Centre, 284
Canadian Armenian Business Council Inc., 295
Canadian Association of Business Incubation, 309
Canadian Association of University Business Officers, 334
Canadian Business for Social Responsibility, 348
Canadian Business Press, 348
Canadian Christian Business Federation, 356
Canadian Columbian Professional Association, 360
Canadian Co-operative Association, 364
Canadian Corporate Counsel Association, 365
Canadian Council for Aboriginal Business, 366
The Canadian Council for Public-Private Partnerships, 366
Canadian Federation of Independent Business, 386
Canadian Institute of Chartered Business Planners, 414
Canadian Institute of Entrepreneurship, 415
Canadian Institute of Management, 416
Canadian Italian Business & Professional Association, 423
Canadian Italian Business & Professional Association of Ottawa, 423
Canadian Management Centre, 429
Canadian Netherlands Business & Professional Association Inc., 440
Canadian Norwegian Business Association, 1515
Canadian Professional Sales Association, 460
Canadian Society of Technical Analysts, 488
Canadian Special Crops Association, 489
The Capital Commission of Prince Edward Island Inc., 510
Centre for Entrepreneurship Education & Development Inc., 532
Centre for Family Business, 532
Chinese Federation of Commerce of Canada, 565
Coalition of BC Businesses, 578
Community Futures Yellowhead East, 599
Conseil du patronat du Québec, 618
Conseil québécois de la franchise, 620
Consumer Protection BC, 626
Co-operatives & Mutuals Canada, 628
Corporation des entrepreneurs généraux du Québec, 630
Downtown Business Association of Edmonton, 661
ESOP Association Canada, 695
Family Enterprise Xchange, 703
Federation of Portuguese Canadian Business & Professionals Inc., 726
Fort Erie Business Success & Loan Centre, 752
Futurpreneur Canada, 765
German Canadian Business Association, 772
German-Canadian Business & Professional Association of Kitchener-Waterloo, 772
Glendon & District Business Alliance, 774
Global Business Travel Association (Canada), 774
Global Network of Director Institutes, 775
Great White North Franchisee Association, 782
The Group Halifax, 790
Hong Kong-Canada Business Association, 820
Independent Contractors & Businesses Association of British Columbia, 832
Industry Training Authority, 835
Innovate Calgary, 839
Innovation Norway, 839
Institute of Corporate Directors, 845
International Association of Business Communicators, 1538
International Virtual Assistants Association, 1566
Junior Chamber International Canada, 877
Korean Business Association, 893
Korean Businessmen's Cooperative Association of British Columbia, 893
Manitoba Association of School Business Officials, 931
Manitoba Pulse & Soybean Growers Inc., 943
Manitoba Quality Network, 943
National Association of Career Colleges, 990
National Crowdfunding Association of Canada, 992
New Brunswick Innovation Foundation, 1009
Northeastern Alberta Aboriginal Business Association, 1034
Ontario Council of Alternative Businesses, 1075
Organisme de développement d'affaires commerciales et économiques, 1125
Pacific Corridor Enterprise Council, 1135
Resource Industry Suppliers Association, 1227
Robson Street Business Association, 1235
Shad Valley International, 1293
Sous-Traitance Industrielle Québec, 1334
Startup Canada, 1348
Strategic Leadership Forum, 1351
Taiwan Entrepreneurs Society Taipei/Toronto, 1366
Toronto Fashion Incubator, 1384
Toronto Japanese Association of Commerce & Industry, 1385
Vancouver Chinatown Business Improvement Area Society, 1425
Vulcan Business Development Society, 1439
Women Expanding Business Network of Lanark County, 1460
Women's Executive Network, 1462
Worldwide Association of Business Coaches, 1468
Young Presidents' Organization, 1608
Yukon Tourism Education Council, 1480

Business Economics
Association of Professional Economists of British Columbia, 157
Atlantic Association of Applied Economists, 182
Canadian Association for Business Economics, 297
Canadians for Clean Prosperity, 506
Manitoba Association for Business Economics, 929
Ottawa Economics Association, 1130
Saskatchewan Economics Association, 1264
Toronto Association for Business Economics Inc., 1382

Business Education
Administrative Sciences Association of Canada, 8
Association des MBA du Québec, 119
Association of MBAs in Canada, 151
Association professionnelle des enseignantes et enseignants en commerce, 167
British Columbia Business Educators Association, 234
The Canadian Institute, 412
Centre d'entrepreneuriat et PME, 528
International Society for Business Education, 1557
Junior Achievement Canada, 877
Les programmes éducatifs JA Québec, 1187
Réseau HEC Montréal, 1224

Business Travel
Association of Corporate Travel Executives Inc. Canada, 146
North West Commercial Travellers' Association, 1033
Society of Incentive & Travel Executives of Canada, 1329

Cabinet Making
Canadian Kitchen Cabinet Association, 424
Kitchen Cabinet Manufacturers Association, 1568

Caisses populaires
L'Alliance des Caisses populaires de l'Ontario limitée, 55
Caisse Groupe Financier, 270
Fédération des caisses populaires acadiennes, 712
Interac Association, 851
Société historique Alphonse-Desjardins, 1319

Call Centres
Canadian Call Management Association, 348
Manitoba Customer Contact Association, Inc., 935

Camping
Alberta Camping Association, 27
Association des camps du Québec inc., 108
British Columbia Camping Association, 234
British Columbia Lodging & Campgrounds Association, 245
Campground Owners Association of Nova Scotia, 277
Camping Association of Nova Scotia & PEI, 277
Camping in Ontario, 277
Camping Québec, 277
Canadian Camping Association, 348
Fédération Internationale de Camping, Caravanning et Autocaravaning, 1525
Fédération québécoise de camping et de caravaning inc., 727
Fédération québécoise du canot et du kayak, 730
Manitoba Camping Association, 933
New Brunswick Camping Association, 1006
Newfoundland & Labrador Camping Association, 1017
Ontario Camps Association, 1070
Saskatchewan Camping Association, 1260

Canada & Canadian Studies
American Council for Québec Studies, 1492
Asociación mexicana de estudios sobre Canadá, 1506
Associaçao Brasileira de Estudos Canadense, 1506
Association for Canadian & Québec Literatures, 132
Association for Canadian Jewish Studies, 132
Association for Canadian Studies, 133
Association for Canadian Studies in Argentina, 1507
Association for Canadian Studies in Australia & New Zealand, 1507
Association for Canadian Studies in China, 1507
Association for Canadian Studies in German-Speaking Countries, 1507
Association for Canadian Studies in Ireland, 1507
Association for Canadian Studies in the Netherlands, 1507
Association for Canadian Studies in the United States, 1507
Association française d'études canadiennes, 1509
British Association for Canadian Studies, 1514
Canada's History, 282
The Canadian Institute, 412
Cátedra de Estudios sobre Canadá, 1515
Central European Association for Canadian Studies, 1516
Centre d'Études Nord-Américaines de l'Université Libre de Bruxelles, 1516
The Council of Canadians, 633
Film Studies Association of Canada, 735
Historica Canada, 815
Indian Association for Canadian Studies, 1531
L'Institut canadien de Québec, 840
International Council for Canadian Studies, 855
Israel Association for Canadian Studies, 1567
Italian Association for Canadian Studies, 1568
Japanese Association for Canadian Studies, 1568
The Laurier Institution, 900
L.M. Montgomery Institute, 916
McGill Institute for the Study of Canada, 955
Nordic Association for Canadian Studies, 1578
Organization of Military Museums of Canada, 1125
Pier 21 Society, 1159
Polish Association for Canadian Studies, 1584
Russian Association of Canadian Studies, 1588
Spanish Association for Canadian Studies, 1595
Venezuelan Association for Canadian Studies, 1431
The Vimy Foundation, 1435

Canada-U.S. Relations
Canada - United States Trade Center, 1515

Cancer
Alberta Cancer Foundation, 27
Alliance of Cancer Consultants, 58
American Society of Pediatric Hematology / Oncology, 1502
Bladder Cancer Canada, 214
Breast Cancer Action, 227
Breast Cancer Action Nova Scotia, 227
Breast Cancer Society of Canada, 228
British Columbia Cancer Foundation, 234
Canadian Association of Provincial Cancer Agencies, 329
Canadian Breast Cancer Network, 347
Canadian Cancer Society, 348
Canadian Cancer Society Research Institute, 349
Canadian Cancer Survivor Network, 349
Canadian Melanoma Foundation, 434
Cancer Advocacy Coalition of Canada, 507
Cancer Care Ontario, 507
Cancer Patient Education Network Canada, 507
Cancer Research Society, 507
CancerCare Manitoba, 508
Candlelighters Simcoe Parents of Children with Cancer, 508
Carcinoid NeuroEndocrine Tumour Society Canada, 510
Childhood Cancer Canada Foundation, 560
Colon Cancer Canada, 591
Colorectal Cancer Association of Canada, 591
Dr. H. Bliss Murphy Cancer Care Foundation, 662
European Society of Gynaecological Oncology, 1524
First Nations Breast Cancer Society, 738
Fondation Centre de cancérologie Charles-Bruneau, 743
Fondation de la greffe de moelle osseuse de l'Est du Québec, 744
Fondation québécoise du cancer, 748
Institut du cancer de Montréal, 842
International Academy of Cytology, 1534
International Union Against Cancer, 1563
Israel Cancer Research Fund, 866
Kidney Cancer Canada Association, 884
Kids Cancer Care Foundation of Alberta, 886
The Leukemia & Lymphoma Society of Canada, 908
Lymphoma Canada, 923
Lymphovenous Association of Ontario, 923
Multinational Association for Supportive Care in Cancer, 1571
Myeloma Canada, 986
Newfoundland Cancer Treatment & Research Foundation, 1023
North American Association of Central Cancer Registries, Inc., 1578
Organisation multiressources pour les personnes atteintes de cancer, 1125
Organisation québécoise des personnes atteintes de cancer, 1125
Ovarian Cancer Canada, 1133
Pancreatic Cancer Canada Foundation, 1138
Procure Alliance, 1181
Prostate Cancer Canada, 1189
Rethink Breast Cancer, 1228
Save Your Skin Foundation, 1282
The Terry Fox Foundation, 1372
The 3C Foundation of Canada, 1377
Wellspring Cancer Support Foundation, 1444
Zane Cohen Centre for Digestive Diseases Familial Gastrointestinal Cancer Registry, 1482

Canoeing & Rafting
Alberta Sprint Racing Canoe Association, 48
Association québécoise de canoë-kayak de vitesse, 169
Atlantic Division, CanoeKayak Canada, 183
Canoe Kayak New Brunswick, 508
Canoe Kayak Nova Scotia, 508
Canoe Kayak Ontario, 509
Canoe Kayak Saskatchewan, 509
CanoeKayak BC, 509
CanoeKayak Canada, 509
CanoeKayak Canada Western Ontario Division, 509
Fédération québécoise de canoë-kayak d'eau vives, 727
Fédération québécoise du canot et du kayak, 730
Ikaluktutiak Paddling Association, 829
Manitoba Paddling Association Inc., 942
Ontario Canoe Kayak Sprint Racing Affiliation, 1070
Ontario Marathon Canoe & Kayak Racing Association, 1090
Ontario Recreational Canoeing & Kayaking Association, 1101
Outward Bound Canada, 1133
Paddle Alberta, 1136
Paddle Canada, 1137
Paddle Manitoba, 1137
Paddle Newfoundland & Labrador, 1137
Prince Edward Island Canoe Kayak Association, 1173
Recreational Canoeing Association BC, 1208
Whitewater Ontario, 1453
Wilderness Canoe Association, 1454
Yukon Canoe & Kayak Club, 1477
Yukon River Marathon Paddlers Association, 1480

Canola
Alberta Canola Producers Commission, 27
Canadian Oilseed Processors Association, 445
Canola Council of Canada, 509
Saskatchewan Canola Development Commission, 1260

Cardiology
American Association for Thoracic Surgery, 1489
American Society of Echocardiography, 1499
Association des cardiologues du Québec, 108
Canadian Association of Cardiovascular Prevention & Rehabilitation, 309
Canadian Association of Interventional Cardiology, 319
Canadian Cardiovascular Society, 350
Canadian Society of Cardiology Technologists Inc., 481
Cardiac Care Network of Ontario, 510
Cardiac Health Foundation of Canada, 510
Cardiac Rehabilitation Network of Ontario, 510
Cardiology Technologists' Association of British Columbia, 511
Children's Heart Association for Support & Education, 561
Institut de cardiologie de Montréal, 841
International Society of Hypertension, 1560
Manitoba Cardiac Institute (Reh-Fit) Inc., 933
New Brunswick Society of Cardiology Techologists, 1012
Society of Cardiovascular Anesthesiologists, 1592

Career Counselling
Association of Career Professionals International, 144
Canadian Education & Research Institute for Counselling, 379
Contact Point, 626

Caribbeans & the Caribbean
African & Caribbean Students' Network of Montréal, 12
Afro-Canadian Caribbean Association of Hamilton & District Inc., 13
Afro-Caribbean Cultural Association of Saskatchewan Inc., 13
Barbados Cultural Association of British Columbia, 196
Barbados Ottawa Association, 196
Canadian Association for Latin American & Caribbean Studies, 302
Canadian Council for the Americas, 367
Canadian Council for the Americas - British Columbia, 367
Canadian-Cuban Friendship Association Toronto, 506
Caribbean Community Council of Calgary, 512
Caribbean Students' Society of McGill University, 512
Centre for Research on Latin America & The Caribbean, 533
Concordia Caribbean Students' Union, 609
Jaku Konbit, 867
Jamaican Canadian Association, 867
National Council of Trinidad & Tobago Organizations in Canada, 992
St. Vincent & the Grenadines Association of Montreal Inc., 1251
Tropicana Community Services Organization, 1399
Turks & Caicos Development Organization of Canada, 1400

Carpentry
Fraternité nationale des forestiers et travailleurs d'usine (CTC), 758
United Brotherhood of Carpenters & Joiners of America (AFL-CIO/CLC), 1599

Carrying Capacity
Carrying Capacity Network, 1515

Carwash
Canadian Carwash Association, 350

Catering Industry
British Columbia Restaurant & Foodservices Association, 251
Canadian College & University Food Service Association, 358
International Caterers Association, 1542
Manitoba Restaurant & Food Services Association, 943

Catholics & Catholicism
Alberta Catholic School Trustees Association, 27
Amma Foundation of Canada, 68
Assemblée des évêques catholiques du Québec, 88
Assembly of Catholic Bishops of Ontario, 88
Association des parents catholiques du Québec, 121
Association of Catholic Retired Administrators, 144
Block Rosary Group of Ontario, 215
Bukas Loob sa Diyos Covenant Community, 264
Calgary Catholic Immigration Society, 271
Canadian Catholic Campus Ministry, 351
Canadian Catholic Historical Association - English Section, 351
Canadian Catholic School Trustees' Association, 351
Canadian Conference of Catholic Bishops, 362
Caritas School of Life Therapeutic Community, 512
Carizon Family & Community Services, 513
Catholic Action Montreal, 517
Catholic Biblical Association of Canada, 517
Catholic Biblical Federation, 1515
Catholic Centre for Immigrants - Ottawa + CIC Foundation, 517
Catholic Charismatic Renewal Council, Toronto, 517
Catholic Charities of The Archdiocese of Toronto, 518
Catholic Children's Aid Society of Hamilton, 518
Catholic Children's Aid Society of Toronto, 518
Catholic Civil Rights League, 518
Catholic Education Foundation of Ontario, 518
Catholic Family Service of Ottawa, 518
Catholic Family Services of Hamilton, 518
Catholic Family Services of Peel Dufferin, 519
Catholic Family Services of Simcoe County, 519
Catholic Family Services of Toronto, 519
The Catholic Foundation of Manitoba, 519
Catholic Health Alliance of Canada, 519
Catholic Health Association of British Columbia, 519
Catholic Health Association of Manitoba, 519

Subject Index / Cats

Catholic Health Association of New Brunswick, 520
Catholic Health Association of Saskatchewan, 520
Catholic Health Sponsors of Ontario, 520
Catholic Missions in Canada, 520
Catholic Near East Welfare Association Canada, 520
The Catholic Principals' Council of Ontario, 520
Catholic Teachers Guild, 520
Catholic Women's League of Canada, 520
Christian Catholic Church Canada, 566
Communion & Liberation Canada, 594
Congregation of Missionaries of the Precious Blood, Atlantic Province, 613
Congregation of St. Basil, 613
Council of Catholic School Superintendents of Alberta, 633
Couples for Christ Canada, 636
Couples For Christ Foundation for Family & Life, 636
Couples For Christ, 636
Covenant Foundation, 637
Covenant Health, 637
Cursillo Movement of the Archdiocese of Toronto, 646
Daughters of Isabella, 651
Development & Peace, 654
Dignity Canada Dignité, 657
Dignity Toronto Dignité, 657
Dignity Vancouver Dignité, 657
Dignity Winnipeg Dignité, 657
Discalced Carmelite Secular Order - Canada, 658
Emmaus Canada, 686
English Speaking Catholic Council, 689
Eucharistic Apostles of the Divine Mercy, 698
Family of the Immaculate Heart of Mary, 704
Family Prayer Mission (Ontario), 704
Federation of North American Explorers, 725
Filipino Canadian Catholic Charismatic Prayer Communities, 735
Foundation of Catholic Community Services Inc., 756
Fountain of Love & Life, 756
Friends of Dismas, 761
Gethsemane Ministries, 773
God, Sex, & the Meaning of Life Ministry, 776
Heralds of the Gospel, 812
HMWN (Holy Mother World Networks) Radio Maria, 817
IMCS Pax Romana, 1531
International Catholic Deaf Association, 854
Jesus Youth Canada, 870
Knights of St. John International - Canada, 892
Kolbe Eucharistic Apostolate, 892
LAUDEM, L'Association des musiciens liturgiques du Canada, 900
Lay Missionaries of Charity - Canada, 902
Légion de Marie - Senatus de Montréal, 906
Madonna House Apostolate, 925
Marguerite Bourgeoys Family Centre Fertility Care Programme, 949
Mary Undoer of Knots, 952
Militia of the Immaculata Canada, 965
Missionary Sisters of The Precious Blood of North America, 969
Morning Light Ministry, 974
Movement for Marriage Enrichment, 978
The Neocatechumenal Way, 1003
Newman Centre Catholic Chaplaincy and Parish, 1024
Ontario Catholic Supervisory Officers' Association, 1070
Ontario English Catholic Teachers' Association (CLC), 1077
Order of Malta - Canadian Association, 1119
L'Ordinariat militaire Catholique Romain du Canada, 1119
Our Lady of Good Health Tamil Parish, 1133
Our Lady of the Rosary of Manaoag Evangelization Group, 1133
Parents as First Educators, 1140
Pontifical Mission Societies, 1164
Regnum Christi Movement, 1214
Rosaries for Canadian Forces Abroad, 1236
The Rosary Apostolate, Inc., 1236
St. John's Cathedral Polish Catholic Church, 1249
St. Josephine Bakhita Black Heritage, 1249
St. Mary's Prayer Group, 1250

Salesian Cooperators, Association of St. Benedict Centre, 1251
ShareLife, 1294
The Shepherds' Trust, 1295
Silent Children's Mission, 1299
Società Unita, 1307
Société canadienne d'histoire de l'Église Catholique - Section française, 1307
Société catholique de la Bible, 1309
Society of St. Vincent de Paul - Toronto Central Council, 1330
Society of the Sacred Heart, 1594
Spiritans, the Congregation of the Holy Ghost, 1344
Theresians International - Canada, 1375
Union mondiale des organisations féminines catholiques, 1599
Vision of Love Ministry - Canada, 1436
Women of the Word - Toronto, 1461
Worldwide Marriage Encounter, 1468

Cats
Toronto Cat Rescue, 1383

Cattle
Alberta Angus Association, 22
Alberta Beef Producers, 25
Alberta Blonde d'Aquitaine Association, 26
Alberta Cattle Breeders Association, 27
Alberta Cattle Feeders' Association, 27
Alberta Galloway Association, 36
Alberta Hereford Association, 37
Alberta Maine-Anjou Association, 39
Alberta Pinzgauer Association, 42
Alberta Salers Association, 45
Alberta Shorthorn Association, 46
Alberta Simmental Association, 46
Alberta Texas Longhorn Association, 50
Algoma Cattlemen's Association, 53
American Association of Bovine Practitioners, 1489
American Galloway Breeders Association, 66
Association Hereford du Québec, 136
Ayrshire Breeders Association of Canada, 191
Beef Farmers of Ontario, 204
Blonde d'Aquitaine du Québec, 215
British Columbia Angus Association, 230
British Columbia Cattlemen's Association, 235
British Columbia Charolais Association, 236
British Columbia Hereford Association, 243
British Columbia Shorthorn Association, 253
Canadian Angus Association, 293
Canadian Beef Breeds Council, 342
Canadian Belgian Blue Association, 342
Canadian Blonde d'Aquitaine Association, 344
Canadian Brown Swiss & Braunvieh Association, 347
Canadian Cattle Breeders' Association, 351
Canadian Cattlemen's Association, 351
Canadian Charolais Association, 355
Canadian Chianina Association, 355
Canadian Dexter Cattle Association, 377
Canadian Galloway Association, 396
Canadian Gelbvieh Association, 396
Canadian Guernsey Association, 399
Canadian Hays Converter Association, 401
Canadian Hereford Association, 404
Canadian Highland Cattle Society, 405
Canadian Limousin Association, 427
Canadian Lowline Cattle Association, 428
Canadian Luing Cattle Association, 428
Canadian Maine-Anjou Association, 429
Canadian Milking Shorthorn Society, 436
Canadian Murray Grey Association, 437
Canadian Piedmontese Association, 455
Canadian Pinzgauer Association, 455
Canadian Red Angus Promotion Society, 465
Canadian Red Poll Cattle Association, 466
Canadian Shorthorn Association, 470
Canadian Simmental Association, 470
Canadian South Devon Association, 489
Canadian Speckle Park Association, 489
Canadian Tarentaise Association, 492
Canadian Welsh Black Cattle Society, 503
Eastern Canadian Galloway Association, 670
Essex County Cattlemen's Association, 696
Fédération des producteurs de bovins du Québec, 717
Gelbvieh Association of Alberta/BC, 768
Holstein Canada, 819
Jersey Canada, 869
Jersey West, 869

Kent County Cattlemen's Association, 884
Manitoba Beef Cattle Performance Association, 932
Manitoba Beef Producers, 932
Manitoba Brown Swiss Association, 933
Manitoba Hereford Association, 938
Manitoba Simmental Association, 944
Maritime Aberdeen Angus Association, 950
Maritime Hereford Association, 950
Maritime Limousin Association, 951
Maritime Shorthorn Association, 951
Murray Grey International, Incorporated, 982
New Brunswick Cattle Producers, 1006
Niagara Cattlemen's Association, 1024
North American Lincoln Red Association, 1579
North American Piedmontese Association, 1579
Nova Scotia Cattle Producers, 1042
Nova Scotia Hereford Club, 1045
Nova Scotia Shorthorn Association, 1048
Ontario Angus Association, 1059
Ontario Blonde d'Aquitaine Association, 1068
Ontario Brown Swiss Association, 1069
Ontario Hereford Association, 1084
Ontario Pinzgauer Breeders Association, 1096
Ontario Shorthorn Association, 1104
Ontario Simmental Association, 1104
Prince Edward Island Cattle Producers, 1173
Québec Angus Association, 1195
Québec Shorthorn Association, 1198
Québec Simmental Association, 1198
Salers Association of Canada, 1251
Saskatchewan Charolais Association, 1260
Saskatchewan Hereford Association, 1267
Saskatchewan Manitoba Galloway Association, 1269
Saskatchewan Shorthorn Association, 1274
Saskatchewan Stock Growers Association, 1276
Saskatchewan/Manitoba Gelbvieh Association, 1279
Shorthorn Breeders of Manitoba Inc., 1297
Simmental Association of British Columbia, 1300
Temiskaming Cattlemen's Association, 1370
Western Ayrshire Club, 1447
The Western Stock Growers' Association, 1450

Celiac Disease
Canadian Celiac Association, 352
Fondation québécoise de la maladie coeliaque, 747

Celtic Culture & Peoples
Antigonish Ceilidh Association, 72
Beaton Institute, 203
Canadian Celtic Arts Association, 353
Irish Dance Teacher's Association of Eastern Canada, 864
Malcolm Scottish Society, 927
Toronto Gaelic Learners Association, 1384
Western Canada Irish Dancing Teachers Association, 1448

Cement
Canadian Ready Mixed Concrete Association, 465
Cement Association of Canada, 521
Concrete Precasters Association of Ontario, 610
Operative Plasterers' & Cement Masons' International Association of the US & Canada (AFL-CIO/CFL) - Canadian Office, 1116

Cemetery & Cremation Services
Écomusée de l'Au-Delà, 672
Ontario Association of Cemetery & Funeral Professionals, 1062

Central America
Canadian Council for the Americas - British Columbia, 367
Friends of the Orphans, Canada, 763

Centres of Excellence (Ontario)
Ontario Centres of Excellence, 1070

Cerebral Palsy
Alberta Cerebral Palsy Sport Association, 27
American Academy for Cerebral Palsy & Developmental Medicine, 1487
Association de paralysie cérébrale du Québec, 103
Association québécoise de sports pour paralytiques cérébraux, 171

British Columbia Centre for Ability Association, 235
Canadian Cerebral Palsy Sports Association, 354
Cerebral Palsy Association in Alberta, 537
Cerebral Palsy Association of British Columbia, 537
Cerebral Palsy Association of Manitoba Inc., 538
Cerebral Palsy Association of Newfoundland & Labrador, 538
Cerebral Palsy Foundation (St. John) Inc., 538
Child Development Centre Society of Fort St. John & District, 558
Halifax Regional Cerebral Palsy Association, 799
Manitoba Cerebral Palsy Sports Association, 933
Ontario Cerebral Palsy Sports Association, 1071
Ontario Federation for Cerebral Palsy, 1079
Prince Edward Island Cerebral Palsy Association Inc., 1173
Quesnel & District Child Development Centre Association, 1200
Saskatchewan Cerebral Palsy Association, 1260
SCOPE for People with Cerebral Palsy, 1588
SportAbility BC, 1345

Chamber Music
Almonte in Concert, 59
Durham Chamber Orchestra, 665
Edmonton Chamber Music Society, 675
Friends of Chamber Music, 760
Kitchener-Waterloo Chamber Music Society, 890
Manitoba Chamber Orchestra, 933
McGill Chamber Orchestra, 955
Oakville Chamber Orchestra, 1053
Scotia Chamber Players, 1285
Soundstreams Canada, 1333
Vetta Chamber Music Society, 1431

Chambers of Commerce
Abbotsford Chamber of Commerce, 1
Aguasabon Chamber of Commerce, 15
Airdrie Chamber of Commerce, 20
Alberni Valley Chamber of Commerce, 21
Albert County Chamber of Commerce, 21
Alberta Beach & District Chamber of Commerce, 25
Alberta Chambers of Commerce, 28
Alexandria & District Chamber of Commerce, 53
Alix Chamber of Commerce, 54
Alliston & District Chamber of Commerce, 59
Altona & District Chamber of Commerce, 61
Amherst & Area Chamber of Commerce, 67
Amherstburg Chamber of Commerce, 67
Annapolis Valley Chamber of Commerce, 71
Antigonish Chamber of Commerce, 72
Arborg Chamber of Commerce, 76
Armstrong-Spallumcheen Chamber of Commerce, 83
Arthur & District Chamber of Commerce, 84
Ashcroft & District Chamber of Commerce, 86
Ashern & District Chamber of Commerce, 86
Assiniboia & District Chamber of Commerce (SK), 88
Assiniboia Chamber of Commerce (MB), 88
Athabasca & District Chamber of Commerce, 180
Atikokan Chamber of Commerce, 181
Atlantic Chamber of Commerce, 183
Aurora Chamber of Commerce, 187
Avon Chamber of Commerce, 191
Baffin Regional Chamber of Commerce, 194
Baie Verte & Area Chamber of Commerce, 194
Bamfield Chamber of Commerce, 195
Bancroft & District Chamber of Commerce, Tourism & Information Centre, 195
Barrhead & District Chamber of Commerce, 197
Barriere & District Chamber of Commerce, 197
Barrington & Area Chamber of Commerce, 197
Bashaw & District Chamber of Commerce, 198
Battlefords Chamber of Commerce, 200
Bay St. George Chamber of Commerce, 200
Bayfield & Area Chamber of Commerce, 200
Beausejour & District Chamber of Commerce, 203
Beaverlodge Chamber of Commerce, 203
Beaverton District Chamber of Commerce, 203

Subject Index / Chambers of Commerce

Beiseker & District Chamber of Commerce, 204
Belleville & District Chamber of Commerce, 204
Berwyn & District Chamber of Commerce, 206
Big River Chamber of Commerce, 210
Biggar & District Chamber of Commerce, 211
Birtle & District Chamber of Commerce, 212
Black River-Matheson Chamber of Commerce, 213
Blackfalds & District Chamber of Commerce, 214
Blaine Lake & District Chamber of Commerce, 214
Blenheim & District Chamber of Commerce, 214
Blind River Chamber of Commerce, 214
Blue Mountains Chamber of Commerce, 215
Blue Water Chamber of Commerce, 215
Bluffton & District Chamber of Commerce, 216
Bobcaygeon & Area Chamber of Commerce, 217
Boissevain & District Chamber of Commerce, 217
Bonavista Area Chamber of Commerce, 217
Bonnyville & District Chamber of Commerce, 217
Bouctouche Chamber of Commerce, 218
Boundary Country Regional Chamber of Commerce, 218
Bow Island / Burdett District Chamber of Commerce, 219
Bowen Island Chamber of Commerce, 219
Boyle & District Chamber of Commerce, 220
Bracebridge Chamber of Commerce, 224
Bragg Creek Chamber of Commerce, 224
Brandon Chamber of Commerce, 226
Breton & District Chamber of Commerce, 228
Bridgetown & Area Chamber of Commerce, 229
Bridgewater & Area Chamber of Commerce, 229
Brier Island Chamber of Commerce, 229
Brighton-Cramahe Chamber of Commerce, 229
British Canadian Chamber of Trade & Commerce, 229
British Columbia Chamber of Commerce, 235
Brockville & District Chamber of Commerce, 260
Brooks & District Chamber of Commerce, 260
Buffalo Narrows Chamber of Commerce, 261
Burin Peninsula Chamber of Commerce, 265
Burlington Chamber of Commerce, 265
Burnaby Board of Trade, 265
Burns Lake & District Chamber of Commerce, 266
Cache Creek Chamber of Commerce, 268
Caledon Chamber of Commerce, 270
Caledonia Regional Chamber of Commerce, 270
Calgary Chamber of Commerce, 271
Cambridge Chamber of Commerce, 275
Campbell River & District Chamber of Commerce, 276
Campbellton Regional Chamber of Commerce, 276
Camrose Chamber of Commerce, 277
Canada China Business Council, 278
Canada Eurasia Russia Business Association, 279
Canada-Finland Chamber of Commerce, 283
Canada-India Business Council, 283
Canada-Poland Chamber of Commerce of Toronto, 284
Canadian Armenian Business Council Inc., 295
Canadian Australian Chamber of Commerce, 1515
The Canadian Chamber of Commerce, 355
Canadian Council for the Americas, 367
Canadian Council for the Americas - British Columbia, 367
Canadian German Chamber of Industry & Commerce Inc., 397
Canadian Slovenian Chamber of Commerce, 472
Canadian Tamils' Chamber of Commerce, 492
Canadian-Croatian Chamber of Commerce, 506
Carberry & District Chamber of Commerce, 510
Cardston & District Chamber of Commerce, 511
Carleton Place & District Chamber of Commerce & Visitor Centre, 513
Carman & Community Chamber of Commerce, 514
Caroline & District Chamber of Commerce, 514
Carstairs Chamber of Commerce, 516

Castlegar & District Chamber of Commerce, 517
Cayuga & District Chamber of Commerce, 521
Central Carleton Chamber of Commerce, 524
Central Coast Chamber of Commerce, 524
Centre Wellington Chamber of Commerce, 536
Centreville Chamber of Commerce, 537
Chamber of Commerce Niagara Falls, Canada, 539
Chamber of Commerce of Brantford & Brant, 539
Chamber of Marine Commerce, 539
Chambre de commerce acadienne et francophone de l'Ile-du-Prince-Édouard, 539
Chambre de commerce au Coeur de la Montérégie, 539
Chambre de commerce Baie-des-Chaleurs, 540
Chambre de commerce Bellechasse-Etchemins, 540
Chambre de Commerce Bois-des-Filion - Lorraine, 540
Chambre de commerce Canada-Pologne, 540
Chambre de commerce Canado-Suisse (Québec) Inc., 540
Chambre de commerce Canado-Tunisienne, 540
Chambre de commerce d'industrie Les Moulins, 540
Chambre de commerce de Beauceville, 540
Chambre de commerce de Brandon, 540
Chambre de Commerce de Cap-des-Rosiers, 540
Chambre de commerce de Carleton, 540
Chambre de commerce de Charlevoix, 540
Chambre de commerce de Chibougamau, 540
Chambre de commerce de Clare, 540
Chambre de commerce de Collette, 540
Chambre de commerce de Cowansville et région, 540
Chambre de commerce de Disraéli, 540
Chambre de commerce de Ferme-Neuve, 541
Chambre de Commerce de Fermont, 541
Chambre de commerce de Forestville, 541
Chambre de commerce de Gatineau, 541
Chambre de commerce de l'Est de la Beauce, 541
Chambre de commerce de l'Est de Montréal, 541
Chambre de commerce de l'Est de Portneuf, 541
Chambre de commerce de l'Ile d'Orléans, 541
Chambre de commerce de l'Ouest-de-l'Ile de Montréal, 541
Chambre de commerce de la grande région de Saint-Hyacinthe, 541
Chambre de commerce de la Haute-Gaspésie, 541
Chambre de commerce de la Haute-Matawinie, 541
Chambre de Commerce de la Jacques-Cartier, 541
Chambre de commerce de la MRC de L'Assomption, 541
Chambre de commerce de la MRC de la Matapédia, 541
Chambre de commerce de la MRC de Rivière-du-Loup, 542
Chambre de commerce de la région d'Acton, 542
Chambre de commerce de la région d'Edmundston, 542
Chambre de commerce de la region de Cap-Pelé, 542
Chambre de commerce de la région de Weedon, 542
Chambre de commerce de Lac-Brome, 542
Chambre de commerce de Lévis, 542
Chambre de commerce de Manicouagan, 542
Chambre de commerce de Mont-Laurier, 542
Chambre de commerce de Montmagny, 542
Chambre de commerce de Mont-Tremblant, 542
Chambre de commerce de Notre Dame, 542
Chambre de commerce de Port-Cartier, 542
Chambre de commerce de Rawdon, 542
Chambre de commerce de Rogersville, 542
Chambre de Commerce de Saint Louis de Kent, 542
Chambre de commerce de Saint-Côme, 542
Chambre de commerce de Sainte-Adèle, 543
Chambre de commerce de Saint-Georges, 543

Chambre de commerce de Ste-Julienne, 543
Chambre de commerce de Ste-Justine, 543
La chambre de commerce de Saint-Malo & District, 543
Chambre de commerce de Saint-Quentin Inc., 543
Chambre de commerce de Sept-Îles, 543
Chambre de commerce de Sherbrooke, 543
Chambre de commerce de Shippagan inc., 543
Chambre de commerce de St-Côme-Linière, 543
Chambre de commerce de St-Donat, 543
Chambre de commerce de St-Frédéric, 543
Chambre de commerce de St-Jean-de-Dieu, 543
Chambre de commerce de St-Jules-de-Beauce, 543
Chambre de commerce de St-Léonard, 543
Chambre de commerce de Tring-Jonction, 543
Chambre de commerce de Valcourt et Région, 543
Chambre de commerce de Val-d'Or, 543
Chambre de commerce des Iles Lamèque et Miscou inc., 544
Chambre de commerce des Jardins de Napierville, 544
Chambre de commerce des Îles-de-la-Madeleine, 544
Chambre de commerce du grand de Châteauguay, 544
Chambre de commerce du Grand Joliette, 544
Chambre de commerce du Grand Tracadie-Sheila, 544
Chambre de commerce du Haut-Richelieu, 544
Chambre de commerce du Haut-Saint-François, 544
Chambre de commerce du Montréal métropolitain, 544
Chambre de commerce du Saguenay-Le Fjord, 544
Chambre de commerce du Témiscouata, 544
Chambre de commerce du Transcontinental, 544
Chambre de commerce Duparquet, 544
Chambre de commerce East Broughton, 544
Chambre de commerce et d'entrepreneuriat des Sources, 544
Chambre de commerce et d'industrie Beauharnois-Valleyfield-Haut Saint-Laurent, 545
Chambre de commerce et d'industrie Berthier-D'Autray, 545
Chambre de commerce et d'industrie d'Abitibi-Ouest, 545
Chambre de commerce et d'industrie d'Argenteuil, 545
Chambre de commerce et d'industrie de Dolbeau-Mistassini, 545
Chambre de commerce et d'industrie de Drummond, 545
Chambre de commerce et d'industrie de la MRC de Maskinongé, 545
Chambre de commerce et d'Industrie de la région de Coaticook, 545
Chambre de commerce et d'industrie de la région de Richmond, 545
Chambre de commerce et d'industrie de la Rive-Sud, 545
Chambre de commerce et d'industrie de la Vallée-du-Richelieu, 545
Chambre de commerce et d'industrie de Laval, 545
Chambre de commerce et d'industrie de Malartic, 545
Chambre de commerce et d'industrie de Maniwaki & Vallée de la Gatineau, 546
Chambre de commerce et d'industrie de Mirabel, 546
Chambre de commerce et d'industrie de Montréal-Nord, 546
Chambre de commerce et d'industrie de Québec, 546
Chambre de commerce et d'industrie de Roberval, 546
Chambre de commerce et d'industrie de Rouyn-Noranda, 546
Chambre de commerce et d'industrie de Shawinigan, 546
Chambre de commerce et d'industrie de Sorel-Tracy, 546

Chambre de commerce et d'industrie de St-Joseph-de-Beauce, 546
Chambre de commerce et d'industrie de St-Laurent-Mont-Royal, 546
Chambre de commerce et d'industrie de Thetford Mines, 546
Chambre de commerce et d'industrie de Varennes, 546
Chambre de commerce et d'industrie des Bois-Francs et de l'Érable, 546
Chambre de commerce et d'industrie du bassin de Chambly, 547
Chambre de Commerce et d'Industrie du Centre-Abitibi, 547
Chambre de commerce et d'industrie du Coeur-du-Québec, 547
Chambre de commerce et d'industrie du Haut St-Maurice, 547
Chambre de commerce et d'industrie du secteur Normandin, 547
Chambre de commerce et d'industrie du Sud-Ouest de Montréal, 547
Chambre de commerce et d'industrie française au canada, 547
Chambre de commerce et d'industrie Lac-Saint-Jean-Est, 547
Chambre de commerce et d'industrie Magog-Orford, 547
Chambre de commerce et d'industrie MRC de Deux-Montagne, 547
Chambre de commerce et d'industrie Nouvelle-Beauce, 547
Chambre de commerce et d'industrie Rimouski-Neigette, 547
Chambre de commerce et d'industrie secteur Saint-Félicien inc., 547
Chambre de commerce et d'industrie St-Jérôme, 548
Chambre de commerce et d'industrie Thérèse-De Blainville, 548
Chambre de commerce et d'industrie Vaudreuil-Soulanges, 548
Chambre de commerce et d'industries de Trois-Rivières, 548
Chambre de commerce et de tourisme de Gaspé, 548
Chambre de commerce et de tourisme de la Vallée de Saint-Sauveur/Piedmont, 548
Chambre de commerce et de tourisme de St-Adolphe-d'Howard, 548
Chambre de commerce et du tourisme du Grand Caraquet, 548
Chambre de commerce et industrie Mont-Joli-Mitis, 548
Chambre de commerce française au Canada - Section Québec, 548
Chambre de commerce francophone de Saint-Boniface, 548
Chambre de commerce francophone de Vancouver, 548
Chambre de commerce Haute-Yamaska et Région, 548
Chambre de commerce Kamouraska-L'Islet, 548
Chambre de commerce Kent-Sud, 549
Chambre de commerce Latino-américaine du Québec, 549
Chambre de commerce LGBT du Québec, 549
Chambre de commerce Mont-Saint-Bruno, 549
Chambre de commerce MRC du Rocher-Percé, 549
Chambre de commerce Notre-Dame-du-Nord, 549
Chambre de commerce région de Matane, 549
Chambre de commerce région de Mégantic, 549
Chambre de commerce régionale de St-Raymond, 549
Chambre de commerce régionale de Windsor, 549
Chambre de commerce Ste-Émélie-de-l'Énergie, 549
Chambre de commerce Saint-Lin-Laurentides, 549
Chambre de commerce secteur ouest de Portneuf, 549
Chambre de commerce St-Félix de Valois, 549
Chambre de commerce St-Jean-de-Matha, 549
Chambre de commerce St-Martin de Beauce, 549
Chambre de commerce Témis-Accord, 549

Subject Index / Chambers of Commerce

Chambre de commerce Témiscaming-Kipawa, 550
Chambre de commerce Vallée de la Missisquoi, 550
Chambre de commerce Vallée de la Petite-Nation, 550
Channel Port Aux Basques & Area Chamber of Commerce, 551
Chase & District Chamber of Commerce, 555
Chatham-Kent Chamber of Commerce, 555
Chemainus & District Chamber of Commerce, 555
Chesley & District Chamber of Commerce, 556
Chester Municipal Chamber of Commerce, 556
Chetwynd & District Chamber of Commerce, 557
Chilliwack Chamber of Commerce, 563
Choiceland & District Chamber of Commerce, 566
Christina Lake Chamber of Commerce, 568
Churchill Chamber of Commerce, 569
Clarenville Area Chamber of Commerce, 572
Claresholm & District Chamber of Commerce, 572
Clearwater & District Chamber of Commerce, 573
Cloverdale & District Chamber of Commerce, 574
Coaldale & District Chamber of Commerce, 577
Cochrane & District Chamber of Commerce, 579
Cold Lake Regional Chamber of Commerce, 580
Collingwood Chamber of Commerce, 591
Columbia Valley Chamber of Commerce, 591
Comox Valley Chamber of Commerce, 607
Conception Bay Area Chamber of Commerce, 609
Consort & District Chamber of Commerce, 623
Cornwall & Area Chamber of Commerce, 629
Coronach Community Chamber of Commerce, 629
Coronation Chamber of Commerce, 629
Cowichan Lake District Chamber of Commerce, 637
Cranbrook & District Chamber of Commerce, 638
Cremona Water Valley & District Chamber of Commerce, 641
Creston Valley Chamber of Commerce, 642
La Crete & Area Chamber of Commerce, 642
Crossfield Chamber of Commerce, 644
Crowsnest Pass Chamber of Commerce, 644
Crystal City & District Chamber of Commerce, 645
Cumberland Chamber of Commerce, 645
Cut Knife Chamber of Commerce, 647
Cypress River Chamber of Commerce, 647
Danish Canadian Chamber of Commerce, 650
Dauphin & District Chamber of Commerce, 651
Dawson City Chamber of Commerce, 652
Dawson Creek & District Chamber of Commerce, 652
Dease Lake & District Chamber of Commerce, 652
Debden & District Chamber of Commerce, 652
Deer Lake Chamber of Commerce, 652
Delburne & District Chamber of Commerce, 653
Deloraine & District Chamber of Commerce, 653
Delta Chamber of Commerce, 653
Devon & District Chamber of Commerce, 655
Diamond Valley Chamber of Commerce, 656
Didsbury Chamber of Commerce, 656
Discovery Islands Chamber of Commerce, 658
Drayton Valley & District Chamber of Commerce, 662
Drumheller & District Chamber of Commerce, 663
Dryden District Chamber of Commerce, 663
Duncan-Cowichan Chamber of Commerce, 664
Dunnville Chamber of Commerce, 664
East Gwillimbury Chamber of Commerce, 668
East Hants & District Chamber of Commerce, 668
Eastend & District Chamber of Commerce, 669
Eastern Charlotte Chamber of Commerce, 670
Eastern Prince Edward Island Chamber of Commerce, 670
Eatonia & District Chamber of Commerce, 671
Eckville & District Chamber of Commerce, 671

Edgerton & District Chamber of Commerce, 674
Edmonton Chamber of Commerce, 675
Edson & District Chamber of Commerce, 680
Elie Chamber of Commerce, 685
Elk Point Chamber of Commerce, 685
Elkford Chamber of Commerce, 685
Elkhorn Chamber of Commerce, 685
Elliot Lake & District Chamber of Commerce, 685
Emo Chamber of Commerce, 686
Enderby & District Chamber of Commerce, 687
Englehart & District Chamber of Commerce, 689
Eriksdale & District Chamber of Commerce, 695
Esquimalt Chamber of Commerce, 696
Esterhazy & District Chamber of Commerce, 696
Estevan Chamber of Commerce, 697
European Union Chamber of Commerce in Toronto, 698
Evansburg & Entwistle Chamber of Commerce, 699
Exploits Regional Chamber of Commerce, 700
Fairview & District Chamber of Commerce, 701
Falcon, West Hawk & Caddy Lakes Chamber of Commerce, 701
Falher Chamber of Commerce, 701
Falkland Chamber of Commerce, 701
Fédération des chambres de commerce du Québec, 713
Fédération des chambres de commerce du Québec, 713
Fenelon Falls & District Chamber of Commerce, 732
Fernie Chamber of Commerce, 732
Fisher Branch & District Chamber of Commerce, 739
Flamborough Chamber of Commerce, 740
Flin Flon & District Chamber of Commerce, 740
Florenceville-Bristol Chamber of Commerce, 741
Foam Lake & District Chamber of Commerce, 741
Foremost & District Chamber of Commerce, 751
Fort Frances Chamber of Commerce, 752
Fort Macleod & District Chamber of Commerce, 752
Fort McMurray Chamber of Commerce, 753
Fort Nelson & District Chamber of Commerce, 753
Fort Qu'Appelle & District Chamber of Commerce, 753
Fort St. James Chamber of Commerce, 753
Fort St. John & District Chamber of Commerce, 753
Fort Saskatchewan Chamber of Commerce, 753
Fort Simpson Chamber of Commerce, 754
Fox Creek Chamber of Commerce, 756
Fox Valley Chamber of Commerce, 756
Fraser Lake Chamber of Commerce, 757
Fredericton Chamber of Commerce, 758
Gabriola Island Chamber of Commerce, 765
Gagetown & Area Chamber of Commerce, 766
Galiano Island Chamber of Commerce, 766
Gander & Area Chamber of Commerce, 766
Georgina Chamber of Commerce, 771
Geraldton Chamber of Commerce, 771
Gibsons & District Chamber of Commerce, 773
Gillam Chamber of Commerce, 773
Gogama Chamber of Commerce, 776
Gold River Chamber of Commerce, 776
Goodsoil & District Chamber of Commerce, 777
Grand Bend & Area Chamber of Commerce, 779
Grand Manan Tourism Association & Chamber of Commerce, 780
Grande Cache Chamber of Commerce, 780
Grande Prairie & District Chamber of Commerce, 781
Grandview & District Chamber of Commerce, 781
Gravelbourg Chamber of Commerce, 782
Gravenhurst Chamber of Commerce/Visitors Bureau, 782
Greater Arnprior Chamber of Commerce, 782
Greater Barrie Chamber of Commerce, 782
Greater Bathurst Chamber of Commerce, 783
Greater Charlottetown & Area Chamber of Commerce, 783

Greater Fort Erie Chamber of Commerce, 783
Greater Innisfil Chamber of Commerce, 783
Greater Kamloops Chamber of Commerce, 783
Greater Kingston Chamber of Commerce, 783
Greater Kitchener & Waterloo Chamber of Commerce, 783
Greater Langley Chamber of Commerce, 784
Greater Moncton Chamber of Commerce, 784
Greater Nanaimo Chamber of Commerce, 784
Greater Niagara Chamber of Commerce, 784
Greater Oshawa Chamber of Commerce, 784
Greater Peterborough Chamber of Commerce, 784
Greater Sackville Chamber of Commerce, 785
Greater Saskatoon Chamber of Commerce, 785
Greater Shediac Chamber of Commerce, 785
Greater Sudbury Chamber of Commerce, 785
Greater Summerside Chamber of Commerce, 785
Greater Vernon Chamber of Commerce, 787
Greater Victoria Chamber of Commerce, 787
Greater Westside Board of Trade, 787
Greater Woodstock Chamber of Commerce, 787
Grey Highlands Chamber of Commerce, 790
Grimsby & District Chamber of Commerce, 790
Grimshaw & District Chamber of Commerce, 790
Grunthal & District Chamber of Commerce, 792
Guelph Chamber of Commerce, 793
Hagersville & District Chamber of Commerce, 798
Haliburton Highlands Chamber of Commerce, 798
Halifax Chamber of Commerce, 798
Halton Hills Chamber of Commerce, 800
Hamilton Chamber of Commerce, 801
Hamiota Chamber of Commerce, 802
Hampton Area Chamber of Commerce, 802
Hanna & District Chamber of Commerce, 803
Hanover Chamber of Commerce, 803
Harrison Agassiz Chamber of Commerce, 804
Harrow & Colchester Chamber of Commerce, 804
Hartney & District Chamber of Commerce, 804
Havelock, Belmont, Methuen & District Chamber of Commerce, 805
Hawkesbury & Region Chamber of Commerce, 805
Hay River Chamber of Commerce, 805
Headingley Chamber of Commerce, 805
Hearst, Mattice - Val Côté & Area Chamber of Commerce, 808
Herbert & District Chamber of Commerce, 812
High Level & District Chamber of Commerce, 814
High Prairie & Area Chamber of Commerce, 814
High River & District Chamber of Commerce, 814
Hinton & District Chamber of Commerce, 815
Hope & District Chamber of Commerce, 820
Houston Chamber of Commerce, 824
Hudson Bay Chamber of Commerce, 824
Humboldt & District Chamber of Commerce, 827
Huntsville, Lake of Bays Chamber of Commerce, 828
Huron Chamber of Commerce - Goderich, Central & North Huron, 828
Huron East Chamber of Commerce, 828
Indo-Canada Chamber of Commerce, 835
Indonesia Canada Chamber of Commerce, 1531
Ingersoll District Chamber of Commerce, 838
Innisfail & District Chamber of Commerce, 839
International Chamber of Commerce, 1542
Inuvik Chamber of Commerce, 862
Iqaluit Chamber of Commerce, 863
Ireland-Canada Chamber of Commerce, 863
Irish Loop Chamber of Commerce, 864
Irma & District Chamber of Commerce, 864
Iroquois Falls & District Chamber of Commerce, 864
Italian Chamber of Commerce of Ontario, 866
Jasper Park Chamber of Commerce, 869
Jeune chambre de commerce de Montréal, 870
Jeune chambre de commerce de Québec, 870
Jewish Chamber of Commerce, 871
Kainai Chamber of Commerce, 880
Kamsack & District Chamber of Commerce, 881

Kapuskasing & District Chamber of Commerce, 881
Kaslo & Area Chamber of Commerce, 882
Kawartha Chamber of Commerce & Tourism, 882
Kelowna Chamber of Commerce, 883
Kenaston & District Chamber of Commerce, 883
Kenora & District Chamber of Commerce, 883
Kensington & Area Chamber of Commerce, 883
Kent Centre Chamber of Commerce, 883
Kerrobert Chamber of Commerce, 884
Kicking Horse Country Chamber of Commerce, 884
Killam & District Chamber of Commerce, 887
Killarney & District Chamber of Commerce, 887
Kimberley & District Chamber of Commerce, 887
Kincardine & District Chamber of Commerce, 888
Kindersley Chamber of Commerce, 888
King Chamber of Commerce, 888
Kinistino & District Chamber of Commerce, 890
Kipling Chamber of Commerce, 890
Kirkland Lake District Chamber of Commerce, 890
Kitimat Chamber of Commerce, 891
Kivalliq Chamber of Commerce, 891
Kootenay Lake Chamber of Commerce, 892
Kugluktuk Chamber of Commerce, 894
Labrador North Chamber of Commerce, 894
Labrador Straits Chamber of Commerce, 894
Labrador West Chamber of Commerce, 894
Lac du Bonnet & District Chamber of Commerce, 894
Lac La Biche & District Chamber of Commerce, 894
LaCloche Foothills Chamber of Commerce, 895
Lacombe & District Chamber of Commerce, 895
Ladysmith Chamber of Commerce, 895
Lake Country Chamber of Commerce, 895
Landis & District Chamber of Commerce, 897
Landmark & Community Chamber of Commerce, 898
Langdon & District Chamber of Commerce, 898
Langenburg & District Chamber of Commerce, 898
Leaf Rapids Chamber of Commerce, 903
Leamington District Chamber of Commerce, 903
Leduc Regional Chamber of Commerce, 906
Legal & District Chamber of Commerce, 906
Lethbridge Chamber of Commerce, 907
Lewisporte & Area Chamber of Commerce, 909
Likely & District Chamber of Commerce, 912
Lillooet & District Chamber of Commerce, 912
Lincoln Chamber of Commerce, 912
Lindsay & District Chamber of Commerce, 912
Lloydminster Chamber of Commerce, 916
London Chamber of Commerce, 918
Longlac Chamber of Commerce, 919
Lucknow & District Chamber of Commerce, 920
Lumby Chamber of Commerce, 920
Lumsden Chamber of Commerce, 920
Lyndhurst Seeleys Bay & District Chamber of Commerce, 923
Lytton & District Chamber of Commerce, 923
MacGregor Chamber of Commerce, 924
Mackenzie Chamber of Commerce, 924
Macklin Chamber of Commerce, 924
Mactaquac Country Chamber of Commerce, 924
Madoc & District Chamber of Commerce, 925
Magrath & District Chamber of Commerce, 925
Mahone Bay & Area Chamber of Commerce, 926
Maidstone & District Chamber of Commerce, 926
Mallaig Chamber of Commerce, 928
The Manitoba Chambers of Commerce, 933
Manning & District Chamber of Commerce, 948
Mannville & District Chamber of Commerce, 948
Maple Creek Chamber of Commerce, 948
Maple Ridge Pitt Meadows Chamber of Commerce, 948
Marathon & District Chamber of Commerce, 949
Marwayne & District Chamber of Commerce, 952
Maxville & District Chamber of Commerce, 954

Subject Index / Chambers of Commerce

Mayne Island Community Chamber of Commerce, 954
McBride & District Chamber of Commerce, 955
McLennan Chamber of Commerce, 955
Meadow Lake & District Chamber of Commerce, 956
Meaford Chamber of Commerce, 956
Medicine Hat & District Chamber of Commerce, 958
Melfort & District Chamber of Commerce, 959
Melita & District Chamber of Commerce, 959
Melville & District Chamber of Commerce, 959
Merritt & District Chamber of Commerce, 962
Millbrook & District Chamber of Commerce, 965
Millet & District Chamber of Commerce, 966
Milton Chamber of Commerce, 966
Minnedosa Chamber of Commerce, 968
Minto Chamber of Commerce, 968
Miramichi Chamber of Commerce, 968
Mission Regional Chamber of Commerce, 969
Mississippi Mills Chamber of Commerce, 970
Moose Jaw & District Chamber of Commerce, 973
Moosomin Chamber of Commerce, 974
Morden & District Chamber of Commerce, 974
Morinville & District Chamber of Commerce, 974
Morris & District Chamber of Commerce, 974
Mount Forest District Chamber of Commerce, 976
Mount Pearl-Paradise Chamber of Commerce, 976
Muskoka Lakes Chamber of Commerce, 985
Nakusp & District Chamber of Commerce, 987
Nanton & District Chamber of Commerce, 988
Napanee & District Chamber of Commerce, 988
Neepawa & District Chamber of Commerce, 1002
Nelson & District Chamber of Commerce, 1003
New Brunswick Chamber of Commerce, 1006
New Clarence-Rockland Chamber of Commerce, 1014
New Westminster Chamber of Commerce, 1015
Newcastle & District Chamber of Commerce, 1015
Newmarket Chamber of Commerce, 1024
Niagara-on-the-Lake Chamber of Commerce, 1026
Nipawin & District Chamber of Commerce, 1027
Niverville Chamber of Commerce, 1027
Norman Wells & District Chamber of Commerce, 1028
Norquay & District Chamber of Commerce, 1028
North Bay & District Chamber of Commerce, 1030
North Grenville Chamber of Commerce, 1031
North Perth Chamber of Commerce, 1032
North Shuswap Chamber of Commerce, 1033
North Vancouver Chamber of Commerce, 1033
Northeast Highlands Chamber of Commerce, 1034
Northumberland Central Chamber of Commerce, 1036
Northwest Territories Chamber of Commerce, 1037
Northwestern Ontario Associated Chambers of Commerce, 1039
Oakville & District Chamber of Commerce, 1053
Oakville Chamber of Commerce, 1053
Okotoks & District Chamber of Commerce, 1056
Olds & District Chamber of Commerce, 1057
1000 Islands Gananoque Chamber of Commerce, 1058
Onoway & District Chamber of Commerce, 1058
Ontario Chamber of Commerce, 1071
Ontario Gay & Lesbian Chamber of Commerce, 1081
Organisme de développement d'affaires commerciales et économiques, 1125
Orillia & District Chamber of Commerce, 1126
Orléans Chamber of Commerce, 1126
Oro-Medonte Chamber of Commerce, 1127
Oromocto & Area Chamber of Commerce, 1127
Ottawa Chamber of Commerce, 1129
Otter Valley Chamber of Commerce, 1132
Outlook & District Chamber of Commerce, 1133
Owen Sound & District Chamber of Commerce, 1134
Oyen & District Chamber of Commerce, 1134
Paradise Hill Chamber of Commerce, 1138
Paris & District Chamber of Commerce, 1140
Parksville & District Chamber of Commerce, 1142
Parry Sound Area Chamber of Commerce, 1143
The Pas & District Chamber of Commerce, 1144
Pasadena Chamber of Commerce, 1145
Peace River & District Chamber of Commerce, 1147
Peachland Chamber of Commerce, 1147
Pemberton & District Chamber of Commerce, 1149
Pender Harbour & District Chamber of Commerce, 1149
Pender Island Chamber of Commerce, 1149
Penticton & Wine Country Chamber of Commerce, 1151
Perth & District Chamber of Commerce, 1152
Pictou County Chamber of Commerce, 1159
Picture Butte & District Chamber of Commerce, 1159
Pigeon Lake Regional Chamber of Commerce, 1159
Pilot Mound & District Chamber of Commerce, 1160
Pinawa Chamber of Commerce, 1160
Pincher Creek & District Chamber of Commerce, 1160
Placentia Area Chamber of Commerce, 1161
Plum Coulee & District Chamber of Commerce, 1163
Pointe-au-Baril Chamber of Commerce, 1163
Ponoka & District Chamber of Commerce, 1164
Pontiac Chamber of Commerce, 1164
Port Colborne-Wainfleet Chamber of Commerce, 1165
Port Hardy & District Chamber of Commerce, 1166
Port Hope & District Chamber of Commerce, 1166
Port McNeill & District Chamber of Commerce, 1166
Port Renfrew Chamber of Commerce, 1166
Port Sydney/Utterson & Area Chamber of Commerce, 1166
Portage la Prairie & District Chamber of Commerce, 1167
Powell River Chamber of Commerce, 1169
Prince Albert & District Chamber of Commerce, 1171
Prince Edward County Chamber of Tourism & Commerce, 1171
Prince George Chamber of Commerce, 1179
Prince Rupert & District Chamber of Commerce, 1179
Princeton & District Chamber of Commerce, 1180
Provost & District Chamber of Commerce, 1191
Pugwash & Area Chamber of Commerce, 1194
Qualicum Beach Chamber of Commerce, 1195
Quesnel & District Chamber of Commerce, 1200
Quinte West Chamber of Commerce, 1202
Radium Hot Springs Chamber of Commerce, 1203
Radville Chamber of Commerce, 1203
Rainy River & District Chamber of Commerce, 1204
Ramara & District Chamber of Commerce, 1204
Raymond Chamber of Commerce, 1204
Red Deer Chamber of Commerce, 1209
Red Lake District Chamber of Commerce, 1210
Redvers Chamber of Commerce, 1210
Redwater & District Chamber of Commerce, 1210
Regina & District Chamber of Commerce, 1211
Regroupement des jeunes chambres de commerce du Québec, 1215
Renfrew & Area Chamber of Commerce, 1217
Revelstoke Chamber of Commerce, 1228
Richmond Chamber of Commerce, 1230
Richmond Hill Chamber of Commerce, 1230
Rideau Chamber of Commerce, 1231
Ridgetown & South East Kent Chamber of Commerce, 1232
Rimbey Chamber of Commerce, 1232
Riverbend District Chamber of Commerce, 1234
Rivers & District Chamber of Commerce, 1234
Riverton & District Chamber of Commerce, 1234
Roblin & District Chamber of Commerce, 1235
Rocky Mountain House & District Chamber of Commerce, 1235
La Ronge & District Chamber of Commerce, 1236
Rosetown & District Chamber of Commerce, 1236
Rossburn & District Chamber of Commerce, 1236
Russell & District Chamber of Commerce, 1244
Saanich Peninsula Chamber of Commerce, 1245
Saint John Region Chamber of Commerce, 1247
St. Albert & District Chamber of Commerce, 1247
St. Andrews Chamber of Commerce, 1248
St Anthony & Area Chamber of Commerce, 1248
St. Elias Chamber of Commerce, 1248
St. Martins & District Chamber of Commerce, 1250
St Paul & District Chamber of Commerce, 1250
St. Pierre Chamber of Commerce, 1251
St. Stephen Area Chamber of Commerce, 1251
St Thomas & District Chamber of Commerce, 1251
St. Walburg Chamber of Commerce, 1251
La Salle & District Chamber of Commerce, 1251
Salmo & District Chamber of Commerce, 1251
Salmon Arm & District Chamber of Commerce, 1252
Salt Spring Island Chamber of Commerce, 1252
Sarnia Lambton Chamber of Commerce, 1254
Saskatchewan Chamber of Commerce, 1260
Sauble Beach Chamber of Commerce, 1280
Saugeen Shores Chamber of Commerce, 1280
Sault Ste Marie Chamber of Commerce, 1281
Scugog Chamber of Commerce, 1287
Sechelt & District Chamber of Commerce, 1288
Selkirk & District Chamber of Commerce, 1289
Seton Portage/Shalalth District Chamber of Commerce, 1292
Sexsmith & District Chamber of Commerce, 1292
Shaunavon Chamber of Commerce, 1294
Sheet Harbour & Area Chamber of Commerce & Civic Affairs, 1295
Shelburne & Area Chamber of Commerce, 1295
Sherwood Park & District Chamber of Commerce, 1296
Shoal Lake & District Chamber of Commerce, 1296
Sicamous & District Chamber of Commerce, 1297
Silver Trail Chamber of Commerce, 1299
Simcoe & District Chamber of Commerce, 1299
Similkameen Chamber of Commerce, 1300
Sioux Lookout Chamber of Commerce, 1300
Slave Lake & District Chamber of Commerce, 1303
Slocan District Chamber of Commerce, 1303
Smithers District Chamber of Commerce, 1304
Smiths Falls & District Chamber of Commerce, 1304
Smoky Lake & District Chamber of Commerce, 1305
Smoky River Regional Chamber of Commerce, 1305
Sooke Chamber of Commerce, 1333
Souris & Glenwood Chamber of Commerce, 1334
South Cariboo Chamber of Commerce, 1334
South Cowichan Chamber of Commerce, 1334
South Dundas Chamber of Commerce, 1334
South Grenville Chamber of Commerce, 1334
South Huron Chamber of Commerce, 1334
South Okanagan Chamber Of Commerce, 1335
South Queens Chamber of Commerce, 1336
South Shore Chamber of Commerce, 1336
South Shuswap Chamber of Commerce, 1336
South Stormont Chamber of Commerce, 1336
South Surrey & White Rock Chamber of Commerce, 1336
Southeast Asia-Canada Business Council, 1337
Southeast Georgian Bay Chamber of Commerce, 1337
Southern Georgian Bay Chamber of Commerce, 1337
Sparwood & District Chamber of Commerce, 1338
Spiritwood Chamber of Commerce, 1344
Springdale & Area Chamber of Commerce, 1346
Springhill & Area Chamber of Commerce, 1346
Spruce Grove & District Chamber of Commerce, 1346
Squamish Chamber of Commerce, 1346
Ste Rose & District Chamber of Commerce, 1349
Steinbach Chamber of Commerce, 1349
Stewart-Hyder International Chamber of Commerce, 1350
Stonewall & District Chamber of Commerce, 1350
Stoney Creek Chamber of Commerce, 1350
Stony Plain & District Chamber of Commerce, 1350
Strait Area Chamber of Commerce, 1351
Straits-St. Barbe Chamber of Commerce, 1351
Stratford & District Chamber of Commerce, 1351
Strathmore & District Chamber of Commerce, 1351
Strathroy & District Chamber of Commerce, 1352
Summerland Chamber of Commerce, 1354
Sundre Chamber of Commerce, 1354
Surrey Board of Trade, 1357
Sussex & District Chamber of Commerce, 1357
Swan Hills Chamber of Commerce, 1358
Swan Valley Chamber of Commerce, 1358
The Swedish-Canadian Chamber of Commerce, 1358
Swift Current & District Chamber of Commerce, 1358
Swiss Canadian Chamber of Commerce (Ontario) Inc., 1359
Sydney & Area Chamber of Commerce, 1359
Sylvan Lake Chamber of Commerce, 1360
Taber & District Chamber of Commerce, 1365
Tahsis Chamber of Commerce, 1366
Tavistock Chamber of Commerce, 1367
Temagami & District Chamber of Commerce, 1370
Temiskaming Shores & Area Chamber of Commerce, 1370
Terrace & District Chamber of Commerce, 1371
Teslin Regional Chamber of Commerce, 1373
Teulon Chamber of Commerce, 1373
Texada Island Chamber of Commerce, 1373
Thebacha Chamber of Commerce, 1375
Thompson Chamber of Commerce, 1376
Thorhild Chamber of Commerce, 1376
Thorsby & District Chamber of Commerce, 1376
Three Hills & District Chamber of Commerce, 1377
Thunder Bay Chamber of Commerce, 1377
Tilbury Chamber of Commerce, 1379
Tillsonburg District Chamber of Commerce, 1379
Timmins Chamber of Commerce, 1380
Tisdale & District Chamber of Commerce, 1380
Tobermory & District Chamber of Commerce, 1380
Tofield & District Chamber of Commerce, 1380
Tofino-Long Beach Chamber of Commerce, 1381
Top of Lake Superior Chamber of Commerce, 1381
Trail & District Chamber of Commerce, 1394
Treherne Chamber of Commerce, 1397
Trent Hills & District Chamber of Commerce, 1397
Tri-Cities Chamber of Commerce Serving Coquitlam, Port Coquitlam & Port Moody, 1398
Trochu Chamber of Commerce, 1399
Truro & Colchester Chamber of Commerce, 1399
Tweed Chamber of Commerce, 1400
Ucluelet Chamber of Commerce, 1402
Unity & District Chamber of Commerce, 1418
Upper Ottawa Valley Chamber of Commerce, 1422
Uxbridge Chamber of Commerce, 1423
Valemount & Area Chamber of Commerce, 1423
Valley Chamber of Commerce, 1424

Valleyview & District Chamber of Commerce, 1424
Vanderhoof Chamber of Commerce, 1429
Vaughan Chamber of Commerce, 1430
Vegreville & District Chamber of Commerce, 1430
Vermilion & District Chamber of Commerce, 1431
Viking Economic Development Committee, 1434
Vilna & District Chamber of Commerce, 1435
Virden Community Chamber of Commerce, 1435
Vonda Chamber of Commerce, 1439
Vulcan & District Chamber of Commerce, 1439
Wabamun District Chamber of Commerce Society, 1439
Wainwright & District Chamber of Commerce, 1439
Walkerton Business Improvement Area, 1440
Wallaceburg & District Chamber of Commerce, 1440
Wasaga Beach Chamber of Commerce, 1440
Wasagaming Chamber of Commerce, 1440
Washademoak Region Chamber of Commerce, 1440
Waskesiu Chamber of Commerce, 1440
Waterton Park Chamber of Commerce & Visitors Association, 1442
Watrous & District Chamber of Commerce, 1442
Watson & District Chamber of Commerce, 1443
Watson Lake Chamber of Commerce, 1443
The Welland/Pelham Chamber of Commerce, 1443
Wells & District Chamber of Commerce, 1444
West Elgin Chamber of Commerce, 1445
West Grey Chamber of Commerce, 1445
West Lincoln Chamber of Commerce, 1445
West Nipissing Chamber of Commerce, 1446
West Shore Chamber of Commerce, 1446
West Vancouver Chamber of Commerce, 1446
Westlock & District Chamber of Commerce, 1451
Westport & Rideau Lakes Chamber of Commerce, 1451
Wetaskiwin Chamber of Commerce, 1451
Weyburn Chamber of Commerce, 1451
Whistler Chamber of Commerce, 1452
Whitby Chamber of Commerce, 1452
Whitchurch-Stouffville Chamber of Commerce, 1452
Whitecourt & District Chamber of Commerce, 1452
Whitehorse Chamber of Commerce, 1452
Wiarton South Bruce Peninsula Chamber of Commerce, 1453
Williams Lake & District Chamber of Commerce, 1455
Windsor-Essex Regional Chamber of Commerce, 1457
Winkler & District Chamber of Commerce, 1458
Winnipeg Chamber of Commerce, 1458
Woodstock District Chamber of Commerce, 1464
World Chambers Federation, 1603
Worsley Chamber of Commerce, 1468
Wynyard & District Chamber of Commerce, 1470
Yarmouth & Area Chamber of Commerce, 1470
Yellowknife Chamber of Commerce, 1471
Yorkton Chamber of Commerce, 1474
Yukon Chamber of Commerce, 1477
Zurich & District Chamber of Commerce, 1482

Chambers of Mines
Alberta Chamber of Resources, 28
Association for Mineral Exploration British Columbia, 134
Chamber of Mines of Eastern British Columbia, 539
East Kootenay Chamber of Mines, 668
Mining Association of Nova Scotia, 967
Northwest Territories & Nunavut Chamber of Mines, 1037
Yukon Chamber of Mines, 1477

Charities
Abundance Canada, 3
Altruvest Charitable Services, 61
Bob Rumball Foundation for the Deaf, 217
Break Open Ticket Program Management Alliance, 227
British Columbia Association for Charitable Gaming, 231
Calgary Chamber of Voluntary Organizations, 271
Calgary Health Trust, 272
Canadian Council of Christian Charities, 368
Canadian Food for Children, 391
Children's Cottage Society, 561
Children's Health Foundations, 561
Children's Hospital Foundation of Manitoba, 562
Children's Hospital Foundation of Saskatchewan, 562
The Counselling Foundation of Canada, 636
Daughters of Isabella, 651
Health Charities Coalition of Canada, 806
HMWN (Holy Mother World Networks) Radio Maria, 817
Humanity First Canada, 827
Imagine Canada, 829
IODE Canada, 863
Lighthouse Mission, 912
Lions Quest Canada - The Centre for Positive Youth Development, 913
The Magic of Christmas, 925
OMID Foundation Canada, 1058
Ontario Nonprofit Network, 1094
The Order of St. Lazarus, 1119
Petits frères des pauvres, 1154
Phoenix Community Works Foundation, 1157
reBOOT Canada, 1206
Sisters of Charity of Halifax, 1300
Yonge Street Mission, 1473

Checkers
Association québécoise des joueurs de dames, 173

Chefs
Canadian Culinary Federation, 373
Société des chefs, cuisiniers et pâtissiers du Québec, 1317

Chemical Engineering
Canadian Society for Chemical Engineering, 473
Chemical Institute of Canada, 556
Controlled Release Society, 1520
Electrochemical Society, 1522

Chemical Industry
Alberta Sulphur Research Ltd., 48
Canadian Association of Agri-Retailers, 308
Canadian Association of Chemical Distributors, 310
Canadian Consumer Specialty Products Association, 363
Canadian Explosives Industry Association, 383
Chemistry Industry Association of Canada, 556
Croplife International, 1520
National Association of the Chemistry Industry, 1574

Chemistry
Association of the Chemical Profession of Alberta, 162
Canadian Institute for Neutron Scattering, 413
Canadian Society for Chemical Technology, 473
Canadian Society for Chemistry, 473
Chemical Institute of Canada, 556
European Photochemistry Association, 1524
International Association of Environmental Analytical Chemistry, 1538
International Confederation for Thermal Analysis & Calorimetry, 1543
International Federation of Clinical Chemistry & Laboratory Medicine, 1547
International Union of Crystallography, 1564
International Union of Pure & Applied Chemistry, 1565
Society of Environmental Toxicology & Chemistry, 1593

Chemists
Association of the Chemical Profession of Ontario, 163
Canadian Society for Chemistry, 473
Canadian Society of Clinical Chemists, 481
Ordre des chimistes du Québec, 1120

Chemotherapy
International Society of Chemotherapy for Infection & Cancer, 1560

Chess
Alberta Chess Association, 28
British Columbia Chess Federation, 236
Canadian Correspondence Chess Association, 366
Chess Federation of Canada, 556
Chess'n Math Association, 556
Fédération québécoise des échecs, 728
International Computer Games Association, 1543
Ontario High School Chess Association, 1084

Child Abuse
Boost Child & Youth Advocacy Centre, 218
Canadian Child Abuse Association, 355
Centre de recherche interdisciplinaire sur la violence familiale et la violence faite aux femmes, 530
Centre de ressources et d'intervention pour hommes abusés sexuellement dans leur enfance, 530
Centre for Research on Violence Against Women & Children, 533
The Child Abuse Survivor Monument Project, 558
Chisholm Services for Children, 566
Comité des orphelins victimes d'abus, 592
Foster Parent Support Services Society, 755
The Freda Centre for Research on Violence Against Women & Children, 758
Metropolitan Action Committee on Violence Against Women & Children, 964
Mouvement contre le viol et l'inceste, 976
Parent Support Services Society of BC, 1139
Parents-Unis Lanaudière, 1140
RESOLVE: Research & Education for Solutions to Violence & Abuse, 1226
Viol-secours inc., 1435

Child Care
Alberta Family Child Care Association, 34
Association of Day Care Operators of Ontario, 146
Association of Early Childhood Educators of Alberta, 147
British Columbia Aboriginal Child Care Society, 229
British Columbia Family Child Care Association, 240
Canadian Child Care Federation, 355
Canadian Disaster Child Care Society, 378
Canadian Pediatric Foundation, 452
Cariboo Chilcotin Child Development Centre Association, 512
Child & Youth Care Association of Alberta, 558
Child & Youth Care Association of Newfoundland & Labrador, 558
Child Care Advocacy Association of Canada, 558
Child Care Connection Nova Scotia, 558
Child Care Providers Resource Network of Ottawa-Carleton, 558
Childcare Resource & Research Unit, 560
CPE du Carrefour, 638
Early Childhood Development Association of Prince Edward Island, 666
Family Day Care Services (Toronto), 703
Fédération des intervenantes en petite enfance du Québec, 715
Kinark Child & Family Services, 888
Manitoba Child Care Association, 933
Nova Scotia Child Care Association, 1042
Ontario Coalition for Better Child Care, 1071
St. Albert Family Resource Centre, 1247
Starbright Children's Development Centre, 1348
Step-By-Step Child Development Society, 1349
Yukon Child Care Association, 1477

Child Psychology
Native Child & Family Services of Toronto, 997
Parents for Children's Mental Health, 1140

Child Welfare
Alva Foundation, 61
Brant Family & Children's Services, 226
Bruce Grey Child & Family Services, 260
Bully B'Ware, 264
Canadian Feed The Children, 389
Canadian Society for the Prevention of Cruelty to Children, 477
C.A.R.E. Jeunesse, 511
Catholic Children's Aid Society of Hamilton, 518
Catholic Children's Aid Society of Toronto, 518
Catholic Family Services of Saskatoon, 519
Le Centre jeunesse de la Montérégie, 536
Child Development Institute, 559
Child Welfare League of Canada, 560
Children of the World Adoption Society Inc., 560
The Children's Aid Foundation of York Region, 560
Children's Aid Society of Algoma, 560
Children's Aid Society of Ottawa, 561
Children's Aid Society of Oxford County, 561
Children's Aid Society of the District of Nipissing & Parry Sound, 561
Children's Aid Society of the Districts of Sudbury & Manitoulin, 561
Children's Aid Society of the Region of Peel, 561
Children's Aid Society of Toronto, 561
Children's Safety Association of Canada, 562
Chisholm Services for Children, 566
Comité des orphelins victimes d'abus, 592
Concerned Children's Advertisers, 609
Family & Children's Services Niagara, 701
Family & Children's Services of Frontenac, Lennox & Addington, 701
Federation of B.C. Youth in Care Networks, 722
Foster Parent Support Services Society, 755
Friends of the Orphans, Canada, 763
Halton Children's Aid Society, 800
Highland Shores Children's Aid, 814
Infant & Toddler Safety Association, 836
Jewish Family & Child, 871
JMJ Children's Fund of Canada Inc, 873
Kawartha-Haliburton Children's Aid Society, 882
Kids Help Phone, 886
London-Middlesex Children's Aid Society, 919
McMan Youth, Family & Community Services Association, 955
Native Child & Family Services of Toronto, 997
New Brunswick Youth in Care Network, 1013
Nova Scotia Council for the Family, 1043
Ontario Association of Children's Aid Societies, 1062
Parent Support Services Society of BC, 1139
Renfrew County Child Poverty Action Network, 1217
Saskatchewan Prevention Institute, 1272
Saskatchewan Youth in Care & Custody Network, 1279
Silent Children's Mission, 1299
Start2Finish, 1348
Sudbury Manitoulin Children's Foundation, 1353
UNICEF Canada, 1404
Voices: Manitoba's Youth in Care Network, 1437
WE Charity, 1443
York Region Children's Aid Society, 1473
Youth in Care in Ontario, 1476
Youth Now on Track Program, 1476

Childbirth
Birthright International, 212
International Confederation of Midwives, 1543
Pacific Post Partum Support Society, 1136

Children
Act To End Violence Against Women, 6
Active Healthy Kids Canada, 7
Air Canada Foundation, 19
Alberta Children's Hospital Foundation, 28
Alberta Council for Exceptional Children, 31
Association de parents d'enfant trisomique-21 de Lanaudière, 103
Association des Grands Frères et Grandes Soeurs du Québec, 115
Association des parents d'enfants handicapés du Témiscamingue inc., 122
Association des parents et amis de la personne atteinte de maladie mentale Rive-Sud, 122
Association du Québec pour enfants avec problèmes auditifs, 131
Association for Childhood Education International, 1508
Big Brothers Big Sisters of Alberta, 209
Big Brothers Big Sisters of British Columbia, 209
Big Brothers Big Sisters of Canada, 209
Big Brothers Big Sisters of Eastern Newfoundland, 209
Big Brothers Big Sisters of Manitoba, 209
Big Brothers Big Sisters of New Brunswick, 209
Big Brothers Big Sisters of Nova Scotia, 210
Big Brothers Big Sisters of Ontario, 210

Subject Index / Choral Music

Big Brothers Big Sisters of Prince Edward Island, 210
Big Brothers Big Sisters of Saskatchewan, 210
Big Brothers Big Sisters of Yukon, 210
Boost Child & Youth Advocacy Centre, 218
Breakfast for Learning, 227
British Columbia Council for Exceptional Children, 237
British Columbia's Children's Hospital Foundation, 259
Calgary Children's Foundation, 271
Canadian Academy of Child & Adolescent Psychiatry, 285
Canadian Association for Child & Play Therapy, 297
Canadian Association for Young Children, 307
Canadian Association of Child Neurology, 310
Canadian Children's Book Centre, 355
Canadian Children's Opera Company, 356
Canadian Coalition for the Rights of Children, 358
Canadian Contemporary Dance Theatre, 364
Canadian Grandparents' Rights Association, 399
Canadian Institute of Child Health, 414
Canadian Paediatric Society, 449
Cariboo Chilcotin Child Development Centre Association, 512
Carl Orff Canada Music for Children, 513
Casa - Pueblito, 516
Centre for Child Development, 531
Les Centres jeunesse de l'Outaouais, 537
Change for Children Association, 551
Chess'n Math Association, 556
Child & Parent Resource Institute, 558
Child Development Centre Society of Fort St. John & District, 558
Child Evangelism Fellowship of Canada, 559
Childhood Cancer Canada Foundation, 560
Children of the World Adoption Society Inc., 560
Children's Arts Umbrella Association, 561
Children's Cottage Society, 561
Children's Health Foundation of Vancouver Island, 561
Children's Health Foundations, 561
Children's Hospital Foundation of Manitoba, 562
Children's Hospital Foundation of Saskatchewan, 562
Children's Hospital of Eastern Ontario Foundation, 562
Children's Mental Health Ontario, 562
Children's Miracle Network, 562
Children's Wish Foundation of Canada, 562
Christian Children's Fund of Canada, 567
Colin B. Glassco Charitable Foundation for Children, 581
Comox Valley Child Development Association, 607
Compassion Canada, 608
Concerned Children's Advertisers, 609
Council for Exceptional Children, 1520
Council of Parent Participation Preschools in British Columbia, 635
Deaf Children's Society of B.C., 652
The Dream Factory, 662
Dreams Take Flight, 662
Early Childhood Educators of British Columbia, 666
Early Childhood Intervention Program (ECIP) Sask. Inc., 667
Ending Violence Association of British Columbia, 687
Enfant-Retour Québec, 688
Firefly, 738
Fondation Centre de cancérologie Charles-Bruneau, 743
Fondation de l'Hôpital de Montréal pour enfants, 744
Fondation pour enfants diabetiques, 747
Forever Chai Foundation of Canada, 752
4Cs Foundation, 756
Green Thumb Theatre for Young People, 789
Gustav Levinschi Foundation, 794
Gymn-eau Laval inc, 795
Help Fill a Dream Foundation of Canada, 812
Hincks-Dellcrest Treatment Centre & Foundation, 815
Inner City Angels, 838
International Pediatric Association, 1555
Justice for Children & Youth, 878
Kids First Parent Association of Canada, 886

Kids Kottage Foundation, 886
Kids Now, 886
Kids Up Front, 886
KidSport Alberta, 886
KidSport British Columbia, 886
KidSport Canada, 886
KidSport Manitoba, 886
KidSport New Brunswick, 886
KidSport Newfoundland & Labrador, 887
KidSport Northwest Territories, 887
KidSport Nova Scotia, 887
KidSport Ontario, 887
KidSport PEI, 887
KidSport Saskatchewan, 887
The Kindness Club, 888
Kitimat Child Development Centre, 891
Lawson Foundation, 902
Let's Talk Science, 907
Make-A-Wish Canada, 927
Maker Kids, 927
Manitoba Council for Exceptional Children, 934
Media Smarts, 957
Merry Go Round Children's Foundation, 962
Moorelands Community Services, 973
Mouvement Retrouvailles, 978
Music for Young Children, 983
National Alliance for Children & Youth, 989
North Eastern Ontario Family & Children's Services, 1030
Ontario Association of Child & Youth Care, 1062
Ontario Association of Children's Rehabilitation Services, 1062
Ontario Council for Exceptional Children, 1075
Ontario Foundation for Visually Impaired Children Inc., 1081
Oxford Child & Youth Centre, 1134
Parachute, 1138
Parents-secours du Québec inc., 1140
Pontifical Mission Societies, 1164
Quesnel & District Child Development Centre Association, 1200
Radius Child & Youth Services, 1203
The Rainbow Society of Alberta, 1203
Ranch Ehrlo Society, 1204
Right to Play, 1232
Romanian Children's Relief, 1235
Ronald McDonald House Charities of Canada, 1235
St. Leonard's Youth & Family Services Society, 1250
Sandbox Project, 1253
Saskatchewan Council for Exceptional Children, 1262
Saskatchewan Early Childhood Association, 1263
Save the Children Canada, 1281
School Lunch Association, 1284
Seasons Centre for Grieving Children, 1288
Shaw Rocket Fund, 1295
Simcoe Muskoka Family Connexions, 1300
Sleeping Children Around the World, 1303
Société pour les enfants handicapés du Québec, 1322
Society for Research in Child Development, 1590
SOS Children's Villages Canada, 1333
SPEC Association for Children & Families, 1339
Sport Jeunesse, 1344
Starlight Children's Foundation Canada, 1348
Sudbury Manitoulin Children's Foundation, 1353
Sunshine Dreams for Kids, 1355
Teamwork Children's Services International, 1368
The Teresa Group, 1371
Théâtres unis enfance jeunesse, 1375
Tim Horton Children's Foundation, 1379
Vancouver International Children's Festival, 1426
Variety - The Children's Charity of Manitoba, Tent 58 Inc., 1430
Victoria Youth Empowerment Society, 1434
Vides Canada, 1434
VOICE for Hearing Impaired Children, 1437
Voices for Children, 1437
Western Canada Children's Wear Markets, 1447
Youth Assisting Youth, 1475
Youth Media Alliance, 1476
Youth Now on Track Program, 1476

Children - Diseases
Ability Online Support Network, 2
American Society of Pediatric Hematology / Oncology, 1502
Association for Vaccine Damaged Children, 135
British Columbia Centre for Ability Association, 235
British Columbia Lions Society for Children with Disabilities, 245
Candlelighters Simcoe Parents of Children with Cancer, 508
CHILD Foundation, 560
Childhood Obesity Foundation, 560
Children's Heart Association for Support & Education, 561
Children's Heart Society, 562
Children's Wish Foundation of Canada, 562
Dreams Take Flight, 662
Fondation des étoiles, 744
Help Fill a Dream Foundation of Canada, 812
Hospital for Sick Children Foundation, 823
International Society for Pediatric & Adolescent Diabetes, 1558
Kids Cancer Care Foundation of Alberta, 886
Make-A-Wish Canada, 927
Ronald McDonald House Toronto, 1235

Children's Literature
Canadian Society of Children's Authors, Illustrators & Performers, 481
International Board on Books for Young People, 1541
International Board on Books for Young People - Canadian Section, 854

China
Calgary Canada-China Friendship Association, 271
Calgary Chinese Cultural Society, 271
Canada China Business Council, 278
Canada-China Bilateral Cooperation Association, 283
Carefirst Seniors & Community Services Association, 511
Centre for Immigrant & Community Services, 532
Chaeo Chow Association of Eastern Canada, 539
China Canada Investment Association, 564
China Council for the Promotion of International Trade - Canadian Office, 564
Chinese Benevolent Association of Vancouver, 564
Chinese Canadian Chiropractic Society, 564
Chinese Canadian National Council, 564
Chinese Cultural Association of Saint John, 564
Chinese Cultural Centre, 564
Chinese Cultural Centre of Greater Toronto, 564
Chinese Family Services of Ontario, 565
Chinese Neighbourhood Society of Montréal, 565
Chinese Professionals Association of Canada, 565
Culture Regeneration Research Society, 645
Federation of Canada-China Friendship Associations, 722
Federation of Canada-China Friendship Associations - Ottawa Chapter, 722
Federation of Chinese Canadian Professionals (Ontario), 723
Federation of Chinese Canadian Professionals (Québec), 723
Greater Moncton Chinese Cultural Association, 784
Hong Kong Trade Development Council, 1530
Hong Kong-Canada Business Association, 820
Hoy Ping Benevolent Association of Canada - Vancouver Branch, 824
Institute of Asian Research, 844
Mon Sheong Foundation, 971
Ottawa Chinese Community Services Centre, 1129
Toronto Association for Democracy in China, 1382
Toronto Canada-China Friendship Association, 1383
Vancouver Chinatown Business Improvement Area Society, 1425
Victoria Canada-China Friendship Association, 1432

Chinese Canadians
BC Chinese Soccer Federation, 201
Calgary Canada-China Friendship Association, 271
Canada Chinese Computer Association, 278
Canadian Fujianese Friendship Association, 396
Chinese Canadian Writers' Association, 564
Chinese Federation of Commerce of Canada, 565
Chinese Real Estate Professionals Association of British Columbia, 565
Chiu Chow Benevolent Association of BC Canada, 566
The Cross-Cultural Community Services Association, 644
Culture Regeneration Research Society, 645
Federation of Canada-China Friendship Associations, 722
Federation of Canada-China Friendship Associations - Ottawa Chapter, 722
Henan Fellowship Association of Canada, 812
Hoy Ping Benevolent Association of Canada - Vancouver Branch, 824
Lee's Benevolent Association of Canada, 906
Richmond Chinese Community Society, 1230
Service à la famille chinoise du Grand Montréal, 1291
Toronto Canada-China Friendship Association, 1383
Victoria Canada-China Friendship Association, 1432
Wong Kung Har Wun Sun Association, 1463

Chiropody
Association des orthésistes et prothésistes du Québec, 121
College of Chiropodists of Ontario, 583
Ontario Society of Chiropodists, 1107

Chiropractic Health Care
Alberta College & Association of Chiropractors, 28
Alliance for Chiropractic, 57
Association des chiropraticiens du Québec, 108
British Columbia Chiropractic Association, 236
Canadian Chiropractic Association, 356
Canadian Chiropractic Examining Board, 356
Canadian Chiropractic Research Foundation, 356
Canadian Federation of Chiropractic Regulatory & Educational Accrediting Boards, 386
Canadian Memorial Chiropractic College, 434
Chinese Canadian Chiropractic Society, 564
Chiropractors' Association of Saskatchewan, 565
College of Chiropractors of British Columbia, 583
College of Chiropractors of Ontario, 583
Manitoba Chiropractors' Association, 933
New Brunswick Chiropractors' Association, 1006
Newfoundland & Labrador Chiropractic Association, 1017
Nova Scotia College of Chiropractors, 1042
Ontario Chiropractic Association, 1071
Ordre des chiropraticiens du Québec, 1120
Prince Edward Island Chiropractic Association, 1173
Saskatchewan Association of Chiropodists, 1257
World Federation of Chiropractic, 1466

Choral Music
Alliance Chorale Manitoba, 55
Alliance des chorales du Québec, 55
Association of Canadian Choral Communities, 141
Bach Elgar Choir, 192
British Columbia Choral Federation, 236
Canadian Children's Opera Company, 356
Choir Alberta, 566
Choirs Ontario, 566
A coeur joie Nouveau-Brunswick Inc., 580
Ensemble vocal Ganymède, 690
Festival Chorus of Calgary, 733
Manitoba Choral Association, 934
Mississauga Choral Society, 970
National Association of Teachers of Singing, 1574
New Brunswick Choral Federation, 1006
Northumberland Orchestra Society, 1036

Subject Index / Christian Education

Nova Scotia Choral Federation, 1042
Prairie Saengerbund Choir Association, 1169
Pro Coro Canada, 1181
Richard Eaton Singers, 1229
Saskatchewan Choral Federation, 1261
Société chorale de Saint-Lambert, 1309
Sweet Adelines International - Westcoast Harmony Chapter, 1358
The Toronto Mendelssohn Choir, 1385
Youth Singers of Calgary, 1476

Christian Education
Accelerated Christian Education Canada, 4
Association of Christian Schools International, 1510
Canadian Catholic Campus Ministry, 351
Catholic Education Foundation of Ontario, 518
Child Evangelism Fellowship of Canada, 559
Manitoba Association of Christian Home Schools, 929
Ontario Alliance of Christian Schools, 1059
Ontario Catholic Supervisory Officers' Association, 1070
Partners International, 1144
Pioneer Clubs Canada Inc., 1160
Sisters of St. Benedict, 1301
Strathcona Christian Academy Society, 1351

Christian Science in Canada
Christian Science, 1517
Creation Science Association of British Columbia, 639
Creation Science of Saskatchewan Inc., 639

Christians & Christianity
Action des Chrétiens pour l'abolition de la torture, 6
Adventist Development & Relief Agency Canada, 10
Adventive Cross Cultural Initiatives, 10
Alberta CGIT Association, 28
Association internationale des études patristiques, 1509
The Bible Holiness Movement, 208
The Bible League of Canada, 208
Bibles & Literature in French Canada, 208
Bibles for Missions Foundation, 208
Brethren in Christ, 228
British Israel World Federation (Canada) Inc., 259
Canadian Bible Society, 343
Canadian Christian Business Federation, 356
Canadian Council of Christian Charities, 368
Canadian Foodgrains Bank, 391
Catholic Health Alliance of Canada, 519
The Christian & Missionary Alliance in Canada, 566
Christian Blind Mission International, 566
Christian Catholic Church Canada, 566
Christian Children's Fund of Canada, 567
The Christian Episcopal Church of Canada, 567
Christian Health Association of Alberta, 567
Christian Labour Association of Canada, 567
Christian Reformed Church in North America, 568
Christian Stewardship Services, 568
Church of the Good Shepherd, 569
Congregational Christian Churches in Canada, 613
CrossTrainers Canada, 644
Direction Chrétienne, 657
L'Église Réformée du Québec, 681
Evangelical Medical Aid Society Canada, 698
Fédération des centres de ressourcement Chrétien, 713
Focus on the Family Canada, 742
Grace Communion International Canada, 779
Indian Métis Christian Fellowship, 834
Institut Séculier Pie X, 843
Institut Voluntas Dei, 843
Intercede International, 851
International Fellowship of Christians & Jews of Canada, 857
Inter-Varsity Christian Fellowship, 862
Jeunes canadiens pour une civilisation chrétienne, 870
Lifewater Canada, 912
Lighthouse Mission, 912
Living Bible Explorers, 915
The Lord's Flock Charismatic Community, 919
M2/W2 Association - Restorative Christian Ministries, 923
Manitoba & Northwestern Ontario CGIT Association, 928
Maritime Regional CGIT Committee, 951
Ontario CGIT Association, 1071
Ontario Christian Music Assembly, 1071
Pacific Life Bible College, 1135
Project Peacemakers, 1187
Provincial CGIT Board of BC, 1190
REHOBOTH Christian Ministries, 1216
Samaritan House Ministries Inc., 1253
Samaritan's Purse Canada, 1253
Saskatchewan CGIT Committee, 1260
Seventh-day Adventist Church in Canada, 1292
Sisters of St. Benedict, 1301
Society of Christian Schools in British Columbia, 1328
Union of Spiritual Communities of Christ, 1408
World Association for Christian Communication, 1465
World Renew, 1467

Christmas
Manitoba Christmas Tree Growers Association, 934

Church of Jesus Christ of Latter-day Saints
Church of Jesus Christ of Latter-day Saints - Canada, 569

Churches
The Apostolic Church in Canada, 73
Apostolic Church of Pentecost of Canada Inc., 73
Armenian Holy Apostolic Church - Canadian Diocese, 83
Associated Gospel Churches, 89
Association of Christian Churches in Manitoba, 145
Association of Regular Baptist Churches (Canada), 161
Association of Unity Churches Canada, 163
The Atlantic District of The Wesleyan Church, 183
The British Methodist Episcopal Church of Canada, 259
Canadian & American Reformed Churches, 284
The Canadian Council of Churches, 368
Canadian Society of Church History, 481
Canadian Society of Patristic Studies, 486
Christian Church (Disciples of Christ) in Canada, 567
Church Council on Justice & Corrections, 569
Church of God of Prophecy in Canada, 569
Congregational Christian Churches in Canada, 613
Edmonton & District Council of Churches, 675
Elgin Baptist Association, 684
Estonian Evangelical Lutheran Church Consistory, 697
General Church of the New Jerusalem in Canada, 768
General Conference of the Canadian Assemblies of God, 768
Georgian Bay Association, 769
Holy Trinity Community - North America, 1530
Middlesex-Lambton-Huron Association of Baptist Churches, 965
New Apostolic Church Canada, 1004
Niagara/Hamilton Association of Baptist Churches, 1026
Ottawa Baptist Association, 1129
Oxford-Brant Association of Baptist Churches, 1134
Québec Association of Baptist Churches, 1195
The Reformed Episcopal Church of Canada - Diocese of Western Canada & Alaska, 1210
Romanian Orthodox Deanery of Canada, 1235
St. John's Cathedral Polish Catholic Church, 1249
Spiritual Science Fellowship/International Institute of Integral Human Sciences, 1344
Toronto Baptist Ministries, 1382
Trent Valley Association of Baptist Churches, 1397
The United Brethren Church in Canada, 1409
Women's Inter-Church Council of Canada, 1462
World Council of Churches, 1604
Yukon Church Heritage Society, 1477

Cinematographers
Canadian Society of Cinematographers, 481

Citizens' Groups
Association des propriétaires de Saint-Bruno, 126
Citizens Concerned About Free Trade, 570
CIVICUS: World Alliance for Citizen Participation, 1517
Environmental Defence, 691
Federation of Saskatchewan Surface Rights Association, 726
Social Justice Cooperative Newfoundland & Labrador, 1305
Table de concertation du faubourg Saint-Laurent, 1365
Toronto Environmental Alliance, 1384

Citizenship
Immigrant Centre Manitoba Inc., 830
Saskatoon Open Door Society Inc., 1279

Civil Engineering
Canadian Society for Civil Engineering, 473

Civil Service Employees
Alberta Municipal Clerks Association, 40
Association des directeurs municipaux du Québec, 111
Association des fonctionnaires issus des communautés culturelles, 114
British Columbia Government & Service Employees' Union, 242
International Federation of Employees in Public Service, 1547
Nova Scotia Government & General Employees Union, 1045
Saskatchewan Government & General Employees' Union, 1266

Classical Studies
Classical Association of Canada, 572
International Association for Neo-Latin Studies, 1537

Climate
Canadian Foundation for Climate & Atmospheric Sciences, 393
Climate Action Network - Canada, 573
Climate Institute, 1517
International Society of Biometeorology, 1560
Manitoba Ozone Protection Industry Association, 941
Tides Canada Foundation, 1379
World Meteorological Organization, 1606

Climate Change
International Emissions Trading Association, 1546
Saskatchewan Environmental Society, 1264

Clocks & Watches
National Association of Watch & Clock Collectors, Inc., 1574

Clothing
Alberta Men's Wear Agents Association, 40
Apparel BC, 73
Apparel Human Resources Council, 74
Apparel Quebec, 74
Canadian Apparel Federation, 294
Canadian Association of Wholesale Sales Representatives, 336
The Canadian Fur Trade Development Institute, 396
The Fur Council of Canada, 765
Groupe CTT Group, 791
MultiPrévention, 980
New Circles Community Services, 1014
Prairie Apparel Market, 1169
UNITE HERE, 1599
Western Canada Children's Wear Markets, 1447

Coaching
Canadian University Football Coaches Association, 499
Coaches Association of Ontario, 576
Coaches Association of PEI, 576
Coaching Association of Canada, 577
Coaching Manitoba, 577
International Coaching Federation, 1542
Worldwide Association of Business Coaches, 1468

Coal
Canadian Carbonization Research Association, 350
Canadian Clean Power Coalition, 357
Coal Association of Canada, 577
World Coal Institute, 1604

Collecting
Association des collections d'entreprises, 109
Canadian Association of Token Collectors, 334
Canadian Depression Glass Association, 377
Canadian Tire Coupon Collectors Club, 495
Canadian Toy Collectors' Society Inc., 496
Club des collectionneurs d'épinglettes Inc., 575
Military Collectors Club of Canada, 965
National Association of Watch & Clock Collectors, Inc., 1574
North York Coin Club, 1033
Ontario Arms Collectors' Association, 1060
Ontario Vintage Radio Association, 1112
Société des collectionneurs d'estampes de Montréal, 1317
South Wellington Coin Society, 1336

Colostomy
Ileostomy & Colostomy Association of Montréal, 829

Commerce
British Columbia International Commercial Arbitration Centre, 244
Canadian Deals & Coupons Association, 376
Canadian Society of Technical Analysts, 488
Chinese Federation of Commerce of Canada, 565
GS1 Canada, 792
The Israel Economic Mission to Canada, 866
Pacific Corridor Enterprise Council, 1135
The Royal Society for the Encouragement of Arts, Manufactures & Commerce, 1587

Commonwealth Games
Commonwealth Games Canada, 593

Commonwealth of Nations
Canadian Association for Commonwealth Literature & Language Studies, 298
Canadian Association for Commonwealth Literature & Language Studies, 298
The Royal Commonwealth Society, 1587
The Royal Commonwealth Society of Canada, 1241

Communications
Armed Forces Communications & Electronics Association (Canada), 82
Association des professionnels de la communication et du marketing, 125
BIOTECanada, 212
Blissymbolics Communication International, 214
Canadian Association of Professional Image Creators, 328
Canadian Call Management Association, 348
Canadian Communication Association, 361
Canadian Interoperability Technology Interest Group, 422
Canadian Women in Communications, 505
Cancer Advocacy Coalition of Canada, 507
Central Coast Communications Society, 524
Ceta-Research Inc., 538
Fédération nationale des communications (CSN), 721
Frequency Co-ordination System Association, 760
Halifax Regional CAP Association, 799
International Association of Business Communicators, 1538
International Electrotechnical Commission - Canadian National Committee, 857
Parlimage CCF, 1143
POWERtalk International, 1584
Radio Advisory Board of Canada, 1202
Société des communicateurs du Québec, 1317
Society for Technical Communication, 1591
TECHNOCompétences, 1369
UniforACL, 1405
Union of Postal Communications Employees, 1408

Communism
Communist Party of Canada, 594
Communist Party of Canada (Marxist-Leninist), 595
Parti communiste du Québec, 1143
Parti communiste révolutionnaire, 1144
Parti marxiste-léniniste du Québec, 1144
Trotskyist League of Canada, 1399

Community Centres
Applegrove Community Complex, 74
Arab Community Centre of Toronto, 76
Association sportive et communautaire du Centre-Sud, 178
Birchmount Bluffs Neighbourhood Centre, 212
Carrefour-Ressources, 516
CDC Centre-Sud, 521
Central Neighbourhood House, 524
Centre Jean-Claude Malépart, 536
Centre Sportif de la Petite Bourgogne, 536
Centre St-Pierre, 536
Christie-Ossington Neighbourhood Centre, 568
Comité Social Centre-Sud, 592
Community Action Resource Centre, 595
Conseil communautaire Beausoleil, 614
Davenport-Perth Neighbourhood & Community Health Centre, 651
Delta Community Living Society, 653
Dixon Hall, 660
Doorsteps Neighbourhood Services, 661
Eastview Neighbourhood Community Centre, 671
Fédération québécoise des centres communautaires de loisir inc., 728
The 519 Church St. Community Centre, 740
Flemingdon Neighbourhood Services, 740
Harbourfront Community Centre, 803
Jane Finch Community & Family Centre, 868
Jewish Federation of Greater Vancouver, 872
Kababayan Multicultural Centre, 879
Kitimat Community Services Society, 891
Lakeshore Area Multi-Service Project, 896
Mosaïque centre d'action bénévole et communautaire, 975
Native Women's Resource Centre of Toronto, 998
North York Community House, 1033
Ottawa South Community Association, 1131
PEERS Victoria Resource Society, 1148
Project Share, 1188
Quest Centre Community Initiatives, 1200
Ralph Thornton Centre, 1204
Ressources Saint-Jean-Vianney, 1227
St. Stephen's Community House, 1251
Scadding Court Community Centre, 1282
Scarborough Centre for Healthy Communities, 1282
La Société Saint-Pierre, 1325
Sudbury Community Service Centre Inc., 1353
Syme-Woolner Neighbourhood & Family Centre, 1360
Toronto Centre for Community Learning & Development, 1383
Tyndale St-Georges Community Centre, 1401
Walkley Centre, 1440
Warden Woods Community Centre, 1440
West Scarborough Neighbourhood Community Centre, 1446
Westhaven-Elmhurst Community Association, 1451
YMCA Canada, 1471

Community Development
Action for Healthy Communities, 6
Agincourt Community Services Association, 14
Applegrove Community Complex, 74
Arusha Centre Society, 86
Association of Neighbourhood Houses BC, 153
Association régionale de la communauté francophone de Saint-Jean inc., 177
Atlantic Association of CBDCs, 182
Atlantic Association of Community Business Development Corporations, 182
Birchmount Bluffs Neighbourhood Centre, 212
Boyle Street Community Services, 221
The Calgary Foundation, 272
Canadian CED Network, 351
Canadian Community Reinvestment Coalition, 361
Canadian Institute of Planners, 418
Centre d'information communautaure et de dépannage Ste-Marie, 528
Community Development Council Durham, 596
Community Development Halton, 596
Community Foundation for Kingston & Area, 597
Community Foundation of Lethbridge & Southwestern Alberta, 597
Community Foundation of Prince Edward Island, 598

Community Futures Development Association of British Columbia, 598
Community Futures Manitoba Inc., 598
Community Futures Network Society of Alberta, 598
Community Futures Saskatchewan, 598
Community Futures West Yellowhead, 598
Community Futures Wild Rose, 598
Community Futures Yellowhead East, 599
Compassion Canada, 608
Cooper Institute, 627
Davenport-Perth Neighbourhood & Community Health Centre, 651
Delta Family Resource Centre, 653
Dixon Hall, 660
Doorsteps Neighbourhood Services, 661
Economic Developers Council of Ontario Inc., 673
Edmonton Community Foundation, 676
Entraide Léo-Théorêt, 690
Family Service Moncton Inc., 704
Federation of Calgary Communities, 722
Federation of Canadian Municipalities, 723
Fondation communautaire du Grand-Québec, 743
Foundation of Greater Montreal, 756
Fred Victor Centre, 758
Frontiers Foundation, 763
Hamilton Community Foundation, 801
Harbourfront Community Centre, 803
Hispanic Development Council, 815
Horizons of Friendship, 821
Jane Finch Community & Family Centre, 868
Jewish Community Foundation of Montréal, 871
The Kitchener & Waterloo Community Foundation, 890
Learning Enrichment Foundation, 905
London Community Foundation, 918
Maisons Adrianna, 927
Markland Homes Association, 952
Mères avec pouvoir, 961
Muskoka Community Futures Development Corporation, 985
Nanaimo Family Life Association, 988
National Association of Towns & Townships, 1574
New Brunswick Association of Community Business Development Corporations, 1004
North York Community House, 1033
Northwest Territories Community Futures Association, 1038
Ontario Association of Community Futures Development Corporations, 1063
The Ontario Trillium Foundation, 1111
Ordre des urbanistes du Québec, 1124
PeerNetBC, 1148
Penticton & District Community Resources Society, 1150
Project Genesis, 1187
Red Deer & District Community Foundation, 1209
Relance jeunes et familles, 1217
SkyWorks Charitable Foundation, 1303
South Lake Community Futures Development Corporation, 1335
Table d'Inter-Action du Quartier Peter-McGill, 1365
United Way/Centraide (Central NB) Inc., 1418
USC Canada, 1423
West Island Black Community Association, 1445
World Renew, 1467
World Society for Ekistics, 1607
Youth Challenge International, 1475

Community Information Services
Access Alliance Multicultural Health & Community Services, 4
Agincourt Community Services Association, 14
Albion Neighbourhood Services, 52
Ancaster Community Services, 68
ASK! Community Information Centre (LAMP), 87
Caledon Community Services, 270
Centre for Immigrant & Community Services, 532
Chinese Neighbourhood Society of Montréal, 565
Community Action Resource Centre, 595
Community Care Peterborough, 596
Community Connection, 596

Community Information Centre of Ottawa, 599
Community Information Fairview, 599
Community Information Hamilton, 599
Community Resource Centre (Killaloe) Inc., 607
Community Support Centre Haldimand-Norfolk, 607
The Cross-Cultural Community Services Association, 644
East Wellington Community Services, 669
Essex Community Services, 696
Findhelp Information Services, 737
Flamborough Information & Community Services, 740
Fraserside Community Services Society, 758
Fredericton Community Services Inc., 759
Haldimand-Norfolk Information Centre, 798
Info Northumberland, 836
Information Barrie, 836
Information Brock, 836
Information Burlington, 836
Information Durham, 837
Information Markham, 837
Information Niagara, 837
Information Oakville, 837
Information Orillia, 837
Information Sarnia Lambton, 837
Information Services Vancouver, 837
Information Tilbury & Help Centre, 837
InformCanada, 838
InformOntario, 838
Jewish Community Centre of Greater Vancouver, 871
Jewish Federation of Greater Vancouver, 872
Jewish Information Referral Service Montréal, 873
Jewish Information Service of Greater Toronto, 873
Lakeshore Community Services, 897
Malton Neighbourhood Services, 928
Neighbourhood Information Post, 1002
Newfoundland & Labrador Sexual Assault Crisis & Prevention Centre Inc., 1021
The Olde Forge Community Resource Centre, 1056
Ottawa Chinese Community Services Centre, 1129
Parkdale Community Information Centre, 1140
Port Colborne Community Association for Research Extension, 1165
Rose & Max Rady Jewish Community Centre, 1236
Social Planning Council of Kitchener-Waterloo, 1306
South Essex Community Centre, 1334
South Simcoe Community Information Centre, 1336
South West Community Care Access Centre, 1336
Telephone Aid Line Kingston, 1369
Thorncliffe Neighbourhood Office, 1376
Tillsonburg & District Multi-Service Centre, 1379
Toronto Entertainment District Residental Association, 1384
Tropicana Community Services Organization, 1399
211 Ontario North, 1401
211 Southwest Ontario, 1401
Unison Health & Community Services, 1408
University Settlement, 1421
Vancouver Community Network, 1425
Volunteer Centre of Guelph/Wellington, 1438
Woodgreen Community Centre, 1463
Woolwich Community Services, 1464

Community Planning
Community Planning Association of Alberta, 607
Community Sector Council, Newfoundland & Labrador, 607
Edmonton Federation of Community Leagues, 677
Institute of Urban Studies, 847
Parkdale Neighbourhood Land Trust, 1141
Saskatchewan Professional Planners Institute, 1272

Commuters
Smart Commute, 1304

Compensation Management
Canadian Payroll Association, 452
World at Work, 1603

Composers
Association of Canadian Women Composers, 144
Canadian League of Composers, 426
Edmonton Composers' Concert Society, 676
Foundation Assisting Canadian Talent on Recordings, 755
Music Canada, 983
Musicaction, 984
Screen Composers Guild of Canada, 1287
Société du droit de reproduction des auteurs, compositeurs et éditeurs au Canada (SODRAC 2003) inc., 1318
Société professionnelle des auteurs et des compositeurs du Québec, 1322
Society of Composers, Authors & Music Publishers of Canada, 1328
Songwriters Association of Canada, 1333

Composting
Compost Council of Canada, 609

Computer Graphics
Eurographics - European Association for Computer Graphics, 1524

Computer Software
Association professionnelle des entreprises en logiciels libres, 167
Association québécoise des technologies, 174
Canadian Association of SAS Users, 331
Digital Nova Scotia, 656
Entertainment Software Association of Canada, 690
Information & Communications Technology Council of Canada, 836
Toronto Association of Systems & Software Quality, 1382

Computer User Groups
Association of Personal Computer Users Groups, 1512
Durham Personal Computer Users' Club, 665
Manitoba UNIX User Group, 946
Personal Computer Club of Toronto, 1152
Toronto Users Group for Power Systems, 1388
T.P.U.G., 1394

Computers
ARMA Canada, 81
ARMA International, 1505
Association for Computing Machinery, 1508
Association of Professional Computer Consultants - Canada, 157
Association pour les applications pédagogiques de l'ordinateur au postsecondaire, 167
Association québécoise des utilisateurs de l'ordinateur au primaire-secondaire, 175
Canada Chinese Computer Association, 278
Canadian Information Processing Society, 411
Centre francophone d'informatisation des organisations, 534
Club informatique de Brossard, 575
Club informatique de Longueuil, 575
Club informatique Mont-Bruno, 575
Computer Modelling Group, 609
Computer-Using Educators of BC, 609
Digital Health Canada, 656
Educational Computing Organization of Ontario, 680
The Instrumentation, Systems & Automation Society of America, 1534
International Game Developers Association, 1549
ISACA, 1567
Municipal Information Systems Association of Canada, 981
National Association of Computer Consulting Business (Canada), 990
reBOOT Canada, 1206
Réseau ACTION TI, 1218
Special Interest Group on Computer Human Interaction, 1339
TechConnex, 1368
Urban & Regional Information Systems Association, 1601
Les Vieux Brachés de Longueuil, 1434

Concrete
Alberta Ready Mixed Concrete Association, 43
American Concrete Institute, 1491
Association Béton Québec, 90
Atlantic Concrete Association, 183

Subject Index / Condominiums

Canadian Concrete Masonry Producers Association, 362
Canadian Concrete Pipe Association, 362
Canadian Precast / Prestressed Concrete Institute, 459
Canadian Ready Mixed Concrete Association, 465
Cement Association of Canada, 521
Concrete B.C., 610
Concrete Forming Association of Ontario, 610
Concrete Manitoba, 610
Concrete Ontario, 610
Concrete Sask, 610
Ontario Concrete Pipe Association, 1074

Condominiums
Association of Condominium Managers of Ontario, 145
Canadian Condominium Institute, 362
Condominium Home Owners' Association of British Columbia, 610

Confectionery Industry
Association nationale des distributeurs aux petites surfaces alimentaires, 138
Bakery, Confectionery, Tobacco Workers & Grain Millers International Union (AFL-CIO/CLC), 1514

Conflict Resolution
Canadian Institute for Conflict Resolution, 412
Peace & Justice Studies Association, 1583
Pragmora, 1169

Conservation of Historic & Artistic
Association for Preservation Technology International, 1508
Cameco Capitol Arts Centre, 276
Canadian Association for Conservation of Cultural Property, 298
Canadian Association of Professional Conservators, 328
Community Heritage Ontario, 599
Costume Society of Ontario, 632
The Friends of Fort York & Garrison Common, 761
Georgian Bay Steam & Antique Association, 771
Heritage Ottawa, 813
International Institute for Conservation of Historic & Artistic Works, 1551
National Trust for Canada, 996
Ontario Heritage Trust, 1084
Ontario Steam & Antique Preservers Association, 1109
Save Ontario Shipwrecks, 1281

Conservation of Natural Resources
African Wildlife Foundation, 1486
Alberta Conservation Association, 31
Alberta Conservation Tillage Society II, 31
Alliance for the Wild Rockies, 1487
Amalgamated Conservation Society, 66
American Cave Conservation Association, 1491
American Rivers, 1497
Ausable Bayfield Conservation Foundation, 188
Barrow Bay & District Sports Fishing Association, 197
Big Rideau Lake Association, 210
British Columbia Conservation Foundation, 237
British Columbia Spaces for Nature, 254
Canadian Aboriginal Minerals Association, 285
Carrying Capacity Network, 1515
Castle-Crown Wilderness Coalition, 516
Clean Annapolis River Project, 573
Clubs 4-H du Québec, 576
Conseil régional de l'environnement de la Gaspésie et des Îles-de-la-Madeleine, 620
Conservation International, 1519
The Cousteau Society, 1520
Earthwatch Institute, 1522
FarmFolk CityFolk, 706
Fondation Les oiseleurs du Québec inc., 747
Foundation for Environmental Conservation, 1526
Friends of Clayoquot Sound, 760
Friends of Ecological Reserves, 761
Friends of the Earth International, 1527
Grand River Conservation Foundation, 780
International Peat Society - Canadian National Committee, 859
International Union for Conservation of Nature, 1563

Jack Miner Migratory Bird Foundation, Inc., 867
Kamloops Wildlife Park Society, 881
The Ladies of the Lake, 895
Lake Simcoe Region Conservation Foundation, 896
Lloydminster & District Fish & Game Association, 915
Manitoba Conservation Districts Association, 934
Meewasin Valley Authority, 959
MiningWatch Canada, 968
Montréal Field Naturalists Club, 972
Muskoka Lakes Association, 985
Muskoka Ratepayers' Association, 985
National Audubon Society, Inc., 1575
National Parks Conservation Association, 1577
National Wildlife Federation, 1577
North American Bird Conservation Initiative Canada, 1029
North American Waterfowl Management Plan, 1029
Nunavut Harvesters Association, 1051
The Ocean Conservancy, 1580
Ontario Federation of Anglers & Hunters, 1079
Ontario Steelheaders, 1109
Ontario Streams, 1109
Ottawa Duck Club, 1130
Partners FOR the Saskatchewan River Basin, 1144
Pollination Guelph, 1164
Prairie Conservation Forum, 1169
Prince George Recycling & Environmental Action Planning Society, 1179
Protected Areas Association of Newfoundland & Labrador, 1190
Rainforest Action Network, 1586
Réseau environnement, 1223
St. Lawrence Valley Natural History Society, 1250
Salmon Arm Bay Nature Enhancement Society, 1252
Salmonid Association of Eastern Newfoundland, 1252
Saskatchewan Soil Conservation Association, 1275
SEEDS Foundation, 1289
Society for Conservation Biology, 1590
Soil & Water Conservation Society, 1594
Soil Conservation Council of Canada, 1332
Sustainable Forestry Initiative Inc., 1597
Toronto Public Spaces Initiative, 1386
UNEP - World Conservation Monitoring Centre, 1598
Upper Thames River Conservation Authority, 1422
USC Canada, 1423
Valhalla Wilderness Society, 1424
Vancouver Island Community Forest Action Network, 1426
Western Boreal Growth & Yield Association, 1447
World Association of Industrial & Technological Research Organizations, 1603
World Blue Chain for the Protection of Animals & Nature, 1603
World Resources Institute, 1607
World Wildlife Fund - USA, 1608
WWF International, 1608

Constitutional Law
Association québécoise de doit constitutionel, 169
Fair Vote Canada, 701
Justice Centre for Constitutional Freedoms, 878

Construction Industry
Alberta Building Envelope Council (South), 26
Alberta Construction Association, 31
Alberta Construction Safety Association, 31
Alberta Construction Trucking Association, 31
Alberta Wall & Ceiling Association, 51
American Concrete Institute, 1491
APCHQ - Montréal Métropolitain, 73
Association de la construction du Québec, 100
Association de la Construction Richelieu Yamaska, 101
Association des constructeurs de routes et grands travaux du Québec, 110
Association des entrepreneurs en construction du Québec, 112
Association des professionnels à l'outillage municipal, 125

Association of Construction Inspectors, 1511
Association patronale des entreprises en construction du Québec, 165
BC Assocation for Crane Safety, 201
BC Construction Safety Alliance, 201
British Columbia Construction Association, 237
British Columbia Saw Filers Association, 252
BuildForce Canada, 261
Building Industry & Land Development Alberta, 262
Building Industry & Land Development Association, 262
Building Industry & Land Development Calgary Region, 262
Canada BIM Council Inc., 278
Canadian Construction Association, 363
Canadian Construction Women, 363
Canadian Disaster Restoration Group, 378
Canadian Fence Industry Association, 389
Canadian Hoisting & Rigging Safety Council, 406
Canadian Home Builders' Association, 406
Canadian Home Builders' Association - British Columbia, 406
Canadian Home Builders' Association - New Brunswick, 407
Canadian Home Builders' Association - Newfoundland Labrador, 407
Canadian Home Builders' Association - Prince Edward Island, 407
Canadian Home Builders' Association - Saskatchewan, 407
Canadian Steel Construction Council, 490
Canadian Wood Truss Association, 505
Conseil de l'enveloppe du bâtiment du Québec, 615
Conseil du bâtiment durable du Canada - Québec, 618
Construction Association of New Brunswick, 623
Construction Association of Nova Scotia, 623
Construction Association of Prince Edward Island, 623
Construction Association of Rural Manitoba Inc., 623
Construction Employers Coordinating Council of Ontario, 624
Construction Labour Relations - An Alberta Association, 624
Construction Labour Relations Association of British Columbia, 624
Construction Labour Relations Association of Newfoundland & Labrador, 624
Construction Maintenance & Allied Workers Canada, 624
Construction Owners Association of Alberta, 624
Construction Resource Initiatives Council, 624
Construction Safety Association of Manitoba, 624
Construction Specifications Canada, 624
Construction Technology Centre Atlantic, 625
Council of Ontario Construction Associations, 634
Crane Rental Association of Canada, 638
Dawson Creek Construction Association, 652
Edmonton Construction Association, 676
Electrical Construction Association of Hamilton, 682
Fédération CSN - Construction (CSN), 708
Fédération des Associations et Corporations en Construction du Québec, 712
Greater Vancouver Home Builders' Association, 786
Independent Contractors & Businesses Association of British Columbia, 832
Infrastructure Health & Safety Association, 838
Insitut canadien des économistes en construction - Québec, 840
Kingston Construction Association, 889
Manitoba Building Envelope Council, 933
Manitoba Home Builders' Association, 938
Merit Canada, 961
Merit Contractors Association of Alberta, 962
Merit Contractors Association of Newfoundland & Labrador, 962
Merit Contractors Association of Nova Scotia, 962
Merit Contractors Association of Saskatchewan, 962

Merit OpenShop Contractors Association of Ontario, 962
National Association of Women in Construction, 1575
National Building Envelope Council, 991
New Brunswick Construction Safety Association, 1007
New Brunswick Merit Contractors Association, 1010
New Brunswick Road Builders & Heavy Construction Association, 1011
Newfoundland & Labrador Construction Association, 1017
Newfoundland & Labrador Construction Safety Association, 1017
Northwest Territories & Nunavut Construction Association, 1037
Nova Scotia Construction Labour Relations Association Limited, 1043
Nova Scotia Construction Safety Association, 1043
Nova Scotia Construction Sector Council - Industrial-Commercial-Institutional, 1043
Nova Scotia Home Builders' Association, 1045
Ontario Construction Secretariat, 1074
Ontario Formwork Association, 1081
Ontario Home Builders' Association, 1085
Ontario Road Builders' Association, 1102
Orillia & District Construction Association, 1126
Ottawa Construction Association, 1130
Pembroke District Construction Association, 1149
Pipe Line Contractors Association of Canada, 1160
Prince George Construction Association, 1179
Quinte Construction Association, 1201
Residential Construction Council of Ontario, 1226
Saskatchewan Construction Association, 1261
Saskatchewan Construction Safety Association Inc., 1262
Southern Interior Construction Association, 1338
Syndicat des travailleurs de la construction du Québec (CSD), 1364
Syndicat québécois de la construction, 1365
Terrazzo, Tile & Marble Guild of Ontario, Inc., 1372
Thermal Insulation Association of Canada, 1376
Vancouver Island Construction Association, 1426
Waterloo, Wellington, Dufferin & Grey Building & Construction Trades Council, 1442
Western Retail Lumber Association, 1450
Winnipeg Construction Association, 1458
World Organization of Building Officials, 1466

Consultants & Consulting
Associated Senior Executives of Canada Ltd., 89
Association des firmes de génie-conseil - Québec, 114
Association of Consulting Engineering Companies - British Columbia, 145
Association of Consulting Engineering Companies - Canada, 145
Association of Consulting Engineering Companies - Manitoba, 146
Association of Consulting Engineering Companies - New Brunswick, 146
Association of Consulting Engineering Companies - Prince Edward Island, 146
Association of Consulting Engineering Companies - Saskatchewan, 146
Association of Independent Consultants, 149
Association of Professional Computer Consultants - Canada, 157
Canadian Association of Broadcast Consultants, 309
Canadian Association of Professional Immigration Consultants, 329
Consulting Engineers of Alberta, 625
Consulting Engineers of Newfoundland & Labrador, 625
Consulting Engineers of Nova Scotia, 625
Consulting Engineers of Ontario, 625
Consulting Engineers of the Northwest Territories, 625
Consulting Engineers of Yukon, 625
Disability Awareness Consultants, 658

Foodservice Consultants Society International - Canadian Chapter, 750
Institute of Certified Management Consultants of British Columbia, 845
LUE-42 Enterprises, 920
Mining Suppliers, Contractors & Consultants Association of BC, 967
National Association of Computer Consulting Business (Canada), 990
Vancouver Consultants, 1425
Western Forestry Contractors Association, 1449

Consumer Protection
Association pour la protection des intérêts des consommateurs de la Côte-Nord, 166
Canadian Community Reinvestment Coalition, 361
Canadian Partnership for Consumer Food Safety Education, 451
Canadian Supply Chain Food Safety Coalition, 491
Centre d'information et de recherche en consommation de Charlevoix-Ouest, 528
Centre de recherche et d'information en consommation de Port-Cartier, 529
Coalition des associations de consommateurs du Québec, 577
Consumer Protection BC, 626
Consumers International, 1519
Consumers' Association of Canada, 626
Financial & Consumer Affairs Authority of Saskatchewan, 736
Service de protection et d'information du consommateur, 1291
Small Investor Protection Association, 1304

Consumers
Centre d'information et de recherche en consommation de Charlevoix-Ouest, 528
Consumers Council of Canada, 626

Containers
Association of Postconsumer Plastic Recyclers, 1513
Canadian Wood Pallet & Container Association, 505
EPS Industry Alliance, 1524
Glass Packaging Institute, 1528
National Association for PET Container Resources, 1573

Contractors
Alberta Roofing Contractors Association, 44
Architectural Glass & Metal Contractors Association, 78
Association des entrepreneurs en maçonnerie du Québec, 112
Association des maîtres couvreurs du Québec, 118
Association of Millwrighting Contractors of Ontario Inc., 152
British Columbia Contract Cleaner's Association, 237
British Columbia Wall & Ceiling Association, 257
Canadian Association of Geophysical Contractors, 317
Canadian Contractors Association, 364
Canadian Electrical Contractors Association, 380
Canadian Masonry Contractors' Association, 431
Canadian Roofing Contractors' Association, 468
Corporation des entrepreneurs spécialisés du Grand Montréal inc., 630
Corporation des maîtres électriciens du Québec, 630
Electrical Association of Manitoba Inc., 682
Electrical Contractors Association of Alberta, 682
Electrical Contractors Association of BC, 682
Electrical Contractors Association of London, 682
Electrical Contractors Association of New Brunswick, Inc., 682
Electrical Contractors Association of Ontario, 682
Electrical Contractors Association of Quinte-St. Lawrence, 683
Electrical Contractors Association of Saskatchewan, 683
Electrical Contractors Association of Thunder Bay, 683
Greater Toronto Electrical Contractors Association, 785
Independent Contractors & Businesses Association of British Columbia, 832
Interior Systems Contractors Association of Ontario, 852
LC Line Contractors' Association of BC, 902
Manitoba Association of Sheet Metal & Air Handling Contractors Inc., 931
Merit Contractors Association of Manitoba, 962
Mining Suppliers, Contractors & Consultants Association of BC, 967
National Trade Contractors Coalition of Canada, 996
New Brunswick Roofing Contractors Association, Inc., 1011
Niagara Peninsula Electrical Contractors Association, 1025
Northwest Wall & Ceiling Bureau, 1580
Ontario General Contractors Association, 1082
Ontario Industrial Roofing Contractors' Association, 1087
Ontario Masonry Contractors' Association, 1090
Ontario Painting Contractors Association, 1094
Resilient Flooring Contractors Association of Ontario, 1226
Roofing Contractors Association of British Columbia, 1236
Roofing Contractors Association of Nova Scotia, 1236
Saskatchewan Wall & Ceiling Bureau Inc., 1277
Sheet Metal & Air Conditioning Contractors' National Association, 1588
Utility Contractors Association of Ontario, Inc., 1423
Western Silvicultural Contractors' Association, 1450
Windsor Electrical Contractors Association, 1456
Yukon Contractors Association, 1478

Cooperative Housing
Association des syndicats de copropriété du Québec, 129
Confédération québécoise des coopératives d'habitation, 611
Confédération québécoise des coopératives d'habitation en Outaouais, 611
Cooperative Housing Federation of British Columbia, 628
Cooperative Housing Federation of Canada, 628
Co-operative Housing Federation of Toronto, 628
Fédération des coopératives d'habitation de l'Estrie, 714
Fédération des coopératives d'habitation de la Mauricie et du Centre-du-Québec, 714
Fédération des coopératives d'habitation du Royaume Saguenay Lac-Saint-Jean, 714
Fédération des coopératives d'habitation intermunicipale du Montréal métropolitain, 714
Fédération des coopératives d'habitation Montérégiennes, 714
Fédération des coopératives de Québec, Chaudière-Appalaches, 714
Golden Horseshoe Co-operative Housing Federation, 776
Office municipal d'habitation de Longueuil, 1055

Cooperative Movement
Arctic Co-operatives Limited, 81
British Columbia Co-operative Association, 237
Canadian Association for Studies in Co-operation, 304
Canadian Co-operative Association, 364
Canadian Worker Co-operative Federation, 505
Conseil canadien de la coopération et de la mutualité, 613
Conseil de coopération de l'Ontario, 615
Conseil de la coopération de L'Ile-du-Prince-Édouard, 615
Conseil de la Coopération de la Saskatchewan, 615
Conseil québécois de la coopération et de la mutualité, 620
Co-operatives & Mutuals Canada, 628
International Cooperative Alliance, 1544
Kensington Cooperative Association Ltd, 883
Manitoba Cooperative Association (MCA) Inc., 934
Newfoundland-Labrador Federation of Cooperatives, 1024
Nova Scotia Co-operative Council, 1043
Ontario Co-operative Association, 1074
Saskatchewan Co-operative Association, 1262
Union of Calgary Co-op Employees, 1407

Copyright
Access Copyright, 4
Association of Research Libraries, 1513
Canadian Coalition for Fair Digital Access, 357
Canadian Copyright Institute, 365
Canadian Literary & Artistic Association, 427
Canadian Musical Reproduction Rights Agency, 438
Canadian Private Copying Collective, 460
Canadian Retransmission Collective, 467
Copyright Visual Arts, 628
Intellectual Property Institute of Canada, 850
Re:Sound Music Licensing Company, 1204
Société du droit de reproduction des auteurs, compositeurs et éditeurs au Canada (SODRAC 2003) inc., 1318
Society of Composers, Authors & Music Publishers of Canada, 1328

Corporate Governance
Canadian Board Diversity Council, 345
Canadian Coalition for Good Governance, 357

Corporate Planning
Association for Corporate Growth, Toronto Chapter, 133
Canadian Centre for Ethics & Corporate Policy, 353
Canadian Society of Professional Event Planners, 487
ESOP Association Canada, 695

Correctional Services
Association internationale de droit pénal, 1509
Canadian Families & Corrections Network, 383
Church Council on Justice & Corrections, 569
M2/W2 Association - Restorative Christian Ministries, 923
Probation Officers Association of Ontario, 1181
St. Leonard's Society of Canada, 1250
Syndicat des Agents Correctionnels du Canada (CSN), 1362
Syndicat des agents de la paix en services correctionnels du Québec, 1362
William W. Creighton Youth Services, 1455

Cosmetics Industry
Canadian Cosmetic, Toiletry & Fragrance Association, 366
Canadian Cosmetics Careers Association Inc., 366
Scented Products Education & Information Association of Canada, 1283

Costumes
Costume Society of Ontario, 632

Cottages
Cecebe Waterways Association, 521
Federation of Ontario Cottagers' Associations, 725
Muskoka Lakes Association, 985

Counselling
A.C.C.E.S. Employment, 4
The Alberta Seventh Step Society, 46
The Barbra Schlifer Commemorative Clinic, 196
British Columbia Association of Clinical Counsellors, 231
British Columbia School Counsellors' Association, 252
British Columbia Society for Male Survivors of Sexual Abuse, 254
Canadian Association of Genetic Counsellors, 316
Canadian Association of School Social Workers & Attendance Counsellors, 332
Canadian Career Development Foundation, 350
Canadian College of Professional Counsellors & Psychotherapists, 360
Canadian Counselling & Psychotherapy Association, 371
Canadian University & College Counselling Association, 499
Catholic Family Services of Saskatoon, 519
Centre d'aide et de lutte contre les agressions à caractère sexuel de Châteauguay, 527
Cornerstone Counselling Society of Edmonton, 628
Counselling Services of Belleville & District, 636
Family Counselling Centre of Cambridge & North Dumfries, 703
Family Service Kent, 704
Family Services Perth-Huron, 705
Family Services Windsor-Essex Counselling & Advocacy Centre, 705
Fondation Diane Hébert Inc, 745
Halton Family Services, 800
International Association for Educational & Vocational Guidance, 853
JVS of Greater Toronto, 879
Maison de Campagne & d'Entraide Communautaire du Lac, 926
Manitoba School Counsellors' Association, 944
McMan Youth, Family & Community Services Association, 955
Nanaimo Family Life Association, 988
Native Counselling Services of Alberta, 997
Native Courtworker & Counselling Association of BC, 997
North Renfrew Family Services Inc., 1032
Nova Scotia School Counsellor Association, 1048
Ontario Association of Child & Youth Care, 1062
Ontario Native Education Counselling Association, 1093
Ontario School Counsellors' Association, 1103
Opportunity For Advancement, 1116
Ordre des conseillers et conseillères d'orientation du Québec, 1121
Signal Hill, 1299
South Peace Community Resources Society, 1335
SPEC Association for Children & Families, 1339
Timmins Family Counselling Centre, Inc., 1380
Women In Crisis (Algoma) Inc., 1460

Country Music
Canadian Country Music Association, 372

Couriers
Canadian Courier & Logistics Association, 372

Courts
British Columbia Shorthand Reporters Association, 253
Canadian Criminal Justice Association, 373
Chambre des huissiers de justice du Québec, 550
Chartered Shorthand Reporters' Association of Ontario, 554
National Court Reporters Association, 1575

Cowboys
Alberta Cowboy Poetry Association, 32

Credit Counselling
Association coopérative d'économie familiale - Abitibi-Témiscamingue, 97
Association coopérative d'économie familiale - Appalaches, Beauce, Etchemins, 97
Association coopérative d'économie familiale - Estrie, 97
Association coopérative d'économie familiale - Lanaudière, 97
Association coopérative d'économie familiale - Montérégie-est, 97
Association coopérative d'économie familiale - Rimouski-Neigette et Mitis, 97
Association coopérative d'économie familiale - Rive-Sud de Montréal, 97
Association coopérative d'économie familiale - Rive-Sud de Québec, 97
Association coopérative d'économie familiale de l'est de Montréal, 97
Association coopérative d'économie familiale de l'Ile-Jésus, 97
Association coopérative d'économie familiale de l'Outaouais, 97
Association coopérative d'économie familiale de la Péninsule, 98
Association coopérative d'économie familiale de Québec, 98
Association coopérative d'économie familiale des Basses Laurentides, 98
Association coopérative d'économie familiale des Bois-Francs, 98
Association coopérative d'économie familiale du Grand-Portage, 98

Subject Index / Credit Unions & Bureaux

Association coopérative d'économie familiale du Haut-Saint-Laurent, 98
Association coopérative d'économie familiale du Nord de Montréal, 98
Association coopérative d'économie familiale du Sud-Ouest de Montréal, 98
Association coopérative d'économie familiale Rimouski-Neigette et Mitis, 98
Association coopérative d'économie familliale de Québec, 98
Canadian Association of Credit Counselling Services, 311
Canadian Association of Independent Credit Counselling Agencies, 318
Canadian Credit Institute Educational Foundation, 372
Carizon Family & Community Services, 513
Carrefour-Ressources, 516
Catholic Family Services of Hamilton, 518
Centre d'intervention budgétaire et sociale de la Mauricie, 528
Coalition des associations de consommateurs du Québec, 577
Community Counselling & Resource Centre, 596
Community Counselling Centre of Nipissing, 596
Community Financial Counselling Services, 597
Consolidated Credit Counseling Services of Canada, Inc., 623
Counselling & Support Services of S.D. & G., 636
Credit Association of Greater Toronto, 639
Credit Canada Debt Solutions, Inc., 639
Credit Counselling Canada, 639
Credit Counselling of Regional Niagara, 639
Credit Counselling Service of Sault Ste. Marie & District, 639
Credit Counselling Services of Atlantic Canada, Inc., 639
Credit Counselling Services of Cochrane District, 640
Credit Counselling Services of Newfoundland & Labrador, 640
Credit Counselling Society, 640
Employment & Education Centre, 687
Family Counselling & Support Services for Guelph-Wellington, 702
Family Counselling Centre of Brant, Inc., 703
Family Service Kent, 704
Family Service Thames Valley, 704
Family Services Perth-Huron, 705
Financial Fitness Centre, 736
Halton Family Services, 800
K3C Community Counselling Centres, 879
Money Mentors, 972
Ontario Association of Credit Counselling Services, 1063
Option consommateurs, 1117
Saskatchewan Provincial Mediation Board, 1272
Service alimentaire et aide budgétaire de Charlevoix-Est, 1291
Service budgétaire communautaire de Jonquière, 1291
Service budgétaire et communautaire de Chicoutimi inc, 1291
Service budgétaire et communautaire de la MRC Maria-Chapdelaine, 1291
Service budgétaire Lac-Saint-Jean-Est, 1291
Service budgétaire populaire de La Baie et du Bas Saguenay, 1291
Service budgétaire populaire de St-Félicien, 1291
Service budgétaire populaire des Sources, 1291
Sudbury Community Service Centre Inc., 1353
Thunder Bay Counselling Centre, 1377
Union des consommateurs, 1406

Credit Unions & Bureaux
Alberta Central, 27
Canadian Co-operative Association, 364
Canadian Credit Union Association, 372
Central 1 Credit Union, 523
Co-operatives & Mutuals Canada, 628
Council of Ukrainian Credit Unions of Canada, 635
Credit Union Central of Manitoba, 641
Credit Unions Atlantic Canada, 641
Fédération des caisses Desjardins du Québec, 712

Interac Association, 851
Newfoundland & Labrador Credit Union, 1018
SaskCentral, 1280
World Council of Credit Unions, Inc., 1604

Cricket
British Columbia Mainland Cricket League, 246
Canada Cricket Umpires Association Inc., 278
Cricket Alberta, 642
Cricket Canada, 642
Cricket Council of Ontario, 642
Cricket New Brunswick, 642
La Fédération Québécoise du Cricket Inc., 730
Manitoba Cricket Association, 935
Newfoundland & Labrador Cricket Association, 1018
Nova Scotia Cricket Association, 1043
PEI Cricket Association, 1148
Saskatchewan Cricket Association, 1262
Scarborough Cricket Association, 1282
Toronto Cricket Umpires' & Scorers' Association, 1383

Crime
The Alberta Community Crime Prevention Association, 30
British Columbia Crime Prevention Association, 238
Canadian Anti-Counterfeiting Network, 293
Canadian Anti-Money Laundering Institute, 293
Centre international pour la prévention de la criminalité, 535
Ending Violence Association of British Columbia, 687
Friends of Dismas, 761
The Mackenzie Institute, 924
Toronto Crime Stoppers, 1383
Victims of Violence, 1432
William W. Creighton Youth Services, 1455

Crime Writers
The Crime Writers of Canada, 642

Criminology
Alberta Criminal Justice Association, 32
Association internationale de droit pénal, 1509
British Columbia Crime Prevention Association, 238
Canadian Training Institute, 496
Cariboo Action Training Society, 512
Centre international de criminologie comparée, 535
Collaborative Centre for Justice & Safety, 581
Manitoba Criminal Justice Association, 935
Newfoundland & Labrador Criminology & Corrections Association, 1018
Nova Scotia Criminal Justice Association, 1043
Ontario Criminal Justice Association, 1076
Société de criminologie du Québec, 1314

Crisis Intervention Services
Battlefords Interval House Society, 200
CAEO Québec, 270
Canadian Association of Sexual Assault Centres, 333
Community Torchlight Guelph/Wellington/Dufferin, 607
Crisis Centre North Bay, 642
Distress Centre Niagara Inc., 659
Distress Centre North Halton, 659
Distress Centre of Durham Region, 659
Distress Centre of Ottawa & Region, 659
Distress Centres of Toronto, 659
Distress Centres Ontario, 659
Distress Line Sarnia, 659
Fédération des maisons d'hébergement pour femmes, 715
Fredericton Sexual Assault Crisis Centre, 759
Gai Écoute inc., 766
Guelph-Wellington Women in Crisis, 793
Kawartha Sexual Assault Centre, 882
Kids Help Phone, 886
Libra House Inc., 909
Manitoba Association of Women's Shelters, 931
New Brunswick Coalition of Transition Houses/Centres for Abused Women, 1007
Niagara Region Sexual Assault Centre, 1025
Oakville Distress Centre, 1053
Ontario Coalition of Rape Crisis Centres, 1072
Oshawa-Durham Rape Crisis Centre, 1128
Ottawa Rape Crisis Centre, 1131
Prince Edward Island Rape & Sexual Assault Centre, 1176

Regroupement provincial des maisons d'hébergement et de transition pour femmes victimes de violence conjugale, 1216
Réseau des femmes du sud de l'Ontario, 1219
Revelstoke Women's Shelter Society, 1228
Saskatoon Crisis Intervention Service, 1279
Sexual Assault Centre Kingston Inc., 1292
Sexual Assault Centre London, 1292
Sexual Assault Crisis Centre of Essex County Inc., 1293
Sexual Assault Support Centre Ottawa, 1293
Sexual Assault Survivors' Centre - Sarnia-Lambton, 1293
South Okanagan Women in Need Society, 1335
Spectra Helpline, 1340
Suicide Action Montréal, 1353
Tel-Aide Outaouais, 1369
Telephone Aid Line Kingston, 1369
Thompson Crisis Centre, 1376
Thunder Bay Sexual Assault / Sexual Abuse Counselling & Crisis Centre, 1378
Timmins & Area Women in Crisis Support & Information Centre on Violence Against Women, 1379
Vancouver Island Crisis Society, 1426
Vancouver Rape Relief & Women's Shelter, 1428
Vernon Women's Transition House Society, 1431
Victoria Cool Aid Society, 1432
Youth Empowerment & Support Services, 1475
YWCA Westman Women's Shelter, 1482

Critical Care
Canadian Association of Critical Care Nurses, 311
Canadian Critical Care Society, 373

Critics
Association internationale de la critique littéraire, 1509
Association québécoise des critiques de cinéma, 172
Canadian Theatre Critics Association, 494

Croatians & Croatia
Canadian Croatian Congress, 373
Canadian-Croatian Chamber of Commerce, 506

Crohn's & Colitis
CHILD Foundation, 560
Crohn's & Colitis Canada, 642
IBD Foundation, 829

Croquet
Croquet Canada, 643
Fédération des clubs de croquet du Québec, 713

Cross-Cultural Communication
Canadian Council for International Co-operation, 366
Canadian International Institute of Applied Negotiation, 421
Coady International Institute, 577
The Comparative & International Education Society of Canada, 608
CUSO International, 646
Global Village Nanaimo, 775
Guelph International Resource Centre, 793
Guyana Ottawa Cultural Association, 794
Guyanese Canadian Cultural Association of BC, 794
International Association for Cross-Cultural Psychology, 1536
International Institute of Integral Human Sciences, 858
Kawartha World Issues Centre, 882
Pier 21 Society, 1159
Queen's University International Centre, 1200
Unisphere Global Resource Centre, 1408

Cryonics
Cryonics Society of Canada, 645

Cubans & Cuba
Canada-Cuba Sports & Cultural Festivals, 283
Canadian-Cuban Friendship Association Toronto, 506

Culinary Arts
British Columbia Culinary Arts Specialist Association, 238

Société des chefs, cuisiniers et pâtissiers du Québec, 1317

Cultural Affairs
Association des diffuseurs culturels de l'Ile de Montréal, 110
Canadian Institute of Cultural Affairs, 415
Société des attractions touristiques du Québec, 1317

Cultural Exchanges
AFS Interculture Canada, 13
Canada-Cuba Sports & Cultural Festivals, 283
The Japan Foundation, Toronto, 868
Saskatchewan Cultural Exchange Society, 1262

Culture
Afro-Caribbean Cultural Association of Saskatchewan Inc., 13
Association of Nigerians in Nova Scotia, 154
Avataq Cultural Institute, 190
BC Alliance for Arts & Culture, 200
Black Cultural Society for Nova Scotia, 213
Canada-Cuba Sports & Cultural Festivals, 283
Canada-Israel Cultural Foundation, 283
Canadian Association for Conservation of Cultural Property, 298
The Canadian Zionist Cultural Association, 506
Centre culturel canadien, 1516
Le Centre culturel francophone de Vancouver, 526
Chinese Cultural Association of Saint John, 564
Chinese Cultural Centre of Greater Toronto, 564
Conseil communautaire Beausoleil, 614
Conseil culturel fransaskois, 614
Conseil de la culture de la Gaspésie, 615
Conseil de la culture des régions de Québec et de Chaudière-Appalaches, 616
Conseil de la culture du Bas-Saint-Laurent, 616
The Cultch, 645
Cultural Human Resources Council, 645
Culture Mauricie, 645
Danish Canadian Club of Calgary, 650
Echange Photographique Franco Canadien, 1522
Echo-Edson Cultural Heritage Organization, 671
Fédération culturelle canadienne-française, 708
Fédération culturelle de L'Ile-du-Prince-Édouard inc., 708
Folklore Canada International, 742
German Canadian Cultural Association, 772
German Canadian Cultural Association of Manitoba Inc., 772
Goethe-Institut (Montréal), 776
Goethe-Institut (Toronto), 776
Heritage Park Society, 813
Icelandic National League of North America, 829
Institut Tshakapesh, 843
Institute of Cultural Affairs International, 846
International Research Institute for Media, Communication & Cultural Development, 1556
Italian Canadian Cultural Association of Nova Scotia, 866
Italian Cultural Centre Society, 866
Italian Cultural Institute (Istituto Italiano di Cultura), 866
Italian Cultural Society of Edmonton, 867
Jaku Konbit, 867
Jamaican Ottawa Community Association, 867
Kanien'kehaka Onkwawen'na Raotitiohkwa Language & Cultural Centre, 881
Kings Historical Society, 888
Lake of the Woods Ojibway Cultural Centre, 896
Latvian Canadian Cultural Centre, 900
The Laurier Institution, 900
La Maison de la culture inc., 926
Mi'kmaq Association for Cultural Studies, 964
Native North American Traveling College, 998
North Peace Cultural Society, 1032
Ojibway & Cree Cultural Centre, 1055
Peretz Centre for Secular Jewish Culture, 1152
Prince of Wales Northern Heritage Centre, 1179
ReelWorld Film Festival, 1210
SaskCulture Inc., 1280
The Scots, 1286
Segal Centre for the Performing Arts at the Saidye, 1289
Sholem Aleichem Community Inc., 1297

Subject Index / Dentistry

Société de conservation de la Baie de l'Isle-Verte, 1314
Société de développement des entreprises culturelles, 1314
Société Saint-Jean-Baptiste de Montréal, 1324
Société Saint-Jean-Baptiste du Centre du Québec, 1324
U'mista Cultural Society, 1401
Victoria Society for Humanistic Judaism, 1433
Viscount Cultural Council Inc., 1435
West Region Tribal Council Cultural Education Centre, 1446
Woodland Cultural Centre, 1464

Curling
Alberta Curling Federation, 32
Canadian Curling Association, 374
Canadian Deaf Curling Association, 375
Club de curling Mont-Bruno, 574
Curl BC, 646
Curling Québec, 646
CurlManitoba Inc., 646
Grand Masters Curling Association Ontario, 780
International Curling Information Network Group, 856
New Brunswick Curling Association, 1007
Newfoundland & Labrador Curling Association, 1018
Northern Alberta Curling Association, 1034
Northern Ontario Curling Association, 1035
Northwest Territories Curling Association, 1038
Nova Scotia Curling Association, 1043
Nunavut Curling Association, 1051
Ontario Curling Association, 1076
Ottawa Valley Curling Association, 1132
Peace Curling Association, 1147
Prince Edward Island Curling Association, 1173
Saskatchewan Curling Association, 1263
Southern Alberta Curling Association, 1337
Toronto Curling Association, 1383
World Curling Federation, 1604
Yukon Curling Association, 1478

Customer Service
British Columbia Contact Centre Association, 237
Contact Centre Canada, 626
Customer Service Professionals Network, 646
Manitoba Customer Contact Association, Inc., 935

Customs & Excise
Customs & Immigration Union, 646

Customs Brokerage
Canadian Society of Customs Brokers, 482

Cybernetics
World Organisation of Systems & Cybernetics, 1606

Cypriot Canadians
Cypriot Federation of Canada, 647

Cystic Fibrosis
Cystic Fibrosis Canada, 647
Fibrose kystique Québec, 733

Cytology
Canadian Society of Cytology, 482
International Academy of Cytology, 1534

Czech Canadians
Czech & Slovak Association of Canada, 648
Edmonton Czech Language Society, 676
Masaryk Memorial Institute Inc., 952

Dairy Industry
Alberta Milk, 40
Atlantic Dairy Council, 183
British Columbia Dairy Association, 238
Canadian Dairy Commission, 375
Canadian Milking Shorthorn Society, 436
Conseil des industriels laitiers du Québec inc., 617
Dairy Farmers of Canada, 648
Dairy Farmers of Newfoundland & Labrador, 648
Dairy Farmers of Nova Scotia, 648
International Dairy Federation, 1545
Manitoba Brown Swiss Association, 933
Manitoba Milk Prices Review Commission, 940
Ontario Creamerymen's Association, 1076
Ontario Dairy Council, 1076
Western Ayrshire Club, 1447

Dams
Canadian Dam Association, 375
Probe International, 1181

Dance
The Actors' Fund of Canada, 7
Alberta Dance Alliance, 32
Antigonish Highland Society, 72
Ballet Creole, 194
BC Alliance for Arts & Culture, 200
Brian Webb Dance Co., 228
British Columbia Dance Educators' Association, 238
Canada Dance Festival Society, 278
Canadian Alliance of Dance Artists, 291
Canadian Contemporary Dance Theatre, 364
Canadian Dance Teachers' Association, 375
Le Carré des Lombes, 515
Casa do Benfica, 516
Cercle d'expression artistique Nyata Nyata, 537
Compagnie de danse Migrations, 608
Compagnie Marie Chouinard, 608
Dance Centre, 648
The Dance Centre, 649
Dance Manitoba Inc., 649
Dance Nova Scotia, 649
Dance Ontario Association, 649
Dance Oremus Danse, 649
Dance Saskatchewan Inc., 649
Dance Umbrella of Ontario, 649
Dancemakers, 649
Dancer Transition Resource Centre, 649
Danse-Cité inc, 650
Decidedly Jazz Danceworks, 652
EDAM Performing Arts Society, 674
Fédération des loisirs-danse du Québec, 715
Footprints Dance Project Society of Alberta, 751
Fortier Danse-Création, 754
Fujiwara Dance Inventions, 764
Gina Lori Riley Dance Enterprises, 773
Harbourfront Centre, 803
Irish Dance Teacher's Association of Eastern Canada, 864
Kinesis Dance Society, 888
Louise Bédard Danse, 919
Lucie Grégoire Danse, 920
Margaret Morris Method (Canada), 949
Margie Gillis Dance Foundation, 949
Mascall Dance, 952
Melville Dance Association, 960
Montréal Danse, 972
O Vertigo Danse, 1052
Opéra Atelier, 1114
Les Productions DansEncorps Inc., 1181
Regroupement québécois de la danse, 1216
Royal Academy of Dance Canada, 1237
Rushnychok Ukrainian Folk Dancing Association, 1244
Saskatchewan Pattern Dance Association, 1271
Springboard Dance, 1346
Sun Ergos, A Company of Theatre & Dance, 1354
Svoboda Dance Festival Association, 1358
Toronto Dance Theatre, 1383
Vancouver Moving Theatre, 1427
Vinok Worldance, 1435
Western Canada Irish Dancing Teachers Association, 1448
Winnipeg's Contemporary Dancers, 1460
World Dance Council Ltd., 1604

Danish Canadians & Denmark
Calgary Danish Businessmen's Association, 271
Dania Home Society, 650
Danish Canadian Chamber of Commerce, 650
Danish Canadian Club of Calgary, 650
Danish Canadian National Museum Society, 650
Danish Canadian Society of Saint John, 650
The Danish Club of Ottawa, 650
Dickson Store Museum Society, 656
Federation of Danish Associations in Canada, 723
New Denmark Historical Society, 1014
Red Deer Danish Canadian Club, 1209
Royal Danish Guards Association of Western Canada, 1242
Vancouver Island Danish-Canadian Club, 1426

Darts
Association de Dards du Québec inc., 100

Darts Alberta, 651
Darts British Columbia Association, 651
Darts Ontario, 651
Darts Prince Edward Island, 651
Ligue de dards Ungava, 912
Manitoba Darts Association Inc., 935
National Darts Federation of Canada, 992
New Brunswick Dart Association, 1007
Newfoundland & Labrador Darts Association, 1018
Northern Ontario Darts Association, 1035
Saskatchewan Darts Association, 1263
World Darts Federation, 1604

Data Base Management
Information Resource Management Association of Canada, 837
North American Association of Central Cancer Registries, Inc., 1578
Professional Petroleum Data Management Association, 1186
Society for Information Management, 1590

Day Care - Adult
Chown Adult Day Care Centre, 566
Crossreach Adult Day Centre, 644

Day Care - Children
Association des garderies privées du Québec, 114
Association of Day Care Operators of Ontario, 146
British Columbia Family Child Care Association, 240
Canadian Child Care Federation, 355
Churchill Park Family Care Society, 569
Early Childhood Care & Education New Brunswick, 666
Home Child Care Association of Ontario, 819
Manitoba Child Care Association, 933

Deans
Canadian Federation of Business School Deans, 386
Conférence des recteurs et des principaux des universités du Québec, 612
Council of Canadian Law Deans, 633
Ontario Association of Deans of Education, 1063

Death & Dying
Canadian Coalition Against the Death Penalty, 357
Canadian Hospice Palliative Care Association, 409
Canadian Integrative Network for Death Education & Alternatives, 420
Dying with Dignity, 665
The Right to Die Society of Canada, 1232

Debating
Alberta Debate & Speech Association, 32
POWERtalk International, 1584
Saskatchewan Elocution & Debate Association, 1264

Defence
Canadian Association of Defence & Security Industries, 312
Conference of Defence Associations, 612
New Brunswick Aerospace & Defence Association, 1004
Union of National Defence Employees, 1407

Democracy
Club de Madrid, 1517
Democracy Watch, 653
Parliamentary Centre, 1142
Toronto Association for Democracy in China, 1382

Dental Assistants
Association des assistant(e)s-dentaires du Québec, 106
Canadian Dental Assistants Association, 376
Certified Dental Assistants of BC, 538
Edmonton Dental Assistants Association, 676
Manitoba Dental Assistants Association, 935
National Dental Assisting Examining Board, 992
New Brunswick Dental Assistants Association, 1007
Newfoundland Dental Assistants Association, 1023

Nova Scotia Dental Assistants' Association, 1044
Ontario Dental Assistants Association, 1077
Saskatchewan Dental Assistants' Association, 1263

Dental Hygienists
Bay of Quinte Dental Society, 200
British Columbia Dental Hygienists' Association, 238
Canadian Dental Hygienists Association, 377
College of Dental Hygienists of British Columbia, 583
College of Dental Hygienists of Nova Scotia, 583
College of Registered Dental Hygienists of Alberta, 589
Manitoba Dental Hygienists Association, 935
National Dental Hygiene Certification Board, 992
Ontario Dental Hygienists' Association, 1077
Ordre des hygiénistes dentaires du Québec, 1121
Saskatchewan Dental Hygienists' Association, 1263

Dental Research
Canadian Association for Dental Research, 299

Dental Surgery
Association des chirurgiens dentistes du Québec, 109
British Columbia Society of Prosthodontists, 254
College of Dental Surgeons of British Columbia, 583
College of Dental Surgeons of Saskatchewan, 583
Royal College of Dental Surgeons of Ontario, 1241

Dentistry
Alberta Dental Association & College, 32
Association des conseils des médecins, dentistes et pharmaciens du Québec, 109
Association of Canadian Faculties of Dentistry, 142
Association of Dental Technologists of Ontario, 146
British Columbia Dental Association, 238
Canadian Academy of Endodontics, 286
Canadian Academy of Periodontology, 286
Canadian Association of Public Health Dentistry, 330
Canadian Dental Association, 376
Canadian Dental Protective Association, 377
Canadian Dental Therapists Association, 377
College of Dental Surgeons of British Columbia, 583
College of Dental Technicians of British Columbia, 583
College of Dental Technologists of Alberta, 583
College of Dental Technologists of Ontario, 583
Dental Association of Prince Edward Island, 653
Dental Council of Prince Edward Island, 653
Dental Technicians Association of Saskatchewan, 653
Fédération des dentistes spécialistes du Québec, 714
Manitoba Dental Association, 935
National Dental Assisting Examining Board, 992
National Dental Examining Board of Canada, 992
New Brunswick Dental Society, 1007
Newfoundland & Labrador Dental Association, 1018
Newfoundland & Labrador Dental Board, 1018
Northwest Territories & Nunavut Dental Association, 1037
Nova Scotia Dental Association, 1044
Ontario Association of Dental Specialists, 1063
Ontario Association of Orthodontists, 1065
Ontario Dental Assistants Association, 1077
Ontario Dental Association, 1077
Ontario Society of Periodontists, 1107
Ordre des dentistes du Québec, 1121
Ordre des techniciens et techniciennes dentaires du Québec, 1124
Provincial Dental Board of Nova Scotia, 1190
Royal College of Dentists of Canada, 1241
Saskatchewan Dental Therapists Association, 1263
Toronto Academy of Dentistry, 1381

Denturism
Association des denturologistes du Québec, 110
College of Alberta Denturists, 582
College of Denturists of British Columbia, 583
College of Denturists of Ontario, 583
Denturist Association of British Columbia, 653
Denturist Association of Canada, 653
Denturist Association of Manitoba, 653
Denturist Association of Newfoundland & Labrador, 653
Denturist Association of Northwest Territories, 654
Denturist Association of Ontario, 654
Denturist Society of Nova Scotia, 654
Denturist Society of Prince Edward Island, 654
New Brunswick Denturists Society, 1007
Ordre des denturologistes du Québec, 1121
Yukon Denturist Association, 1478

Dermatology
Association des dermatologistes du Québec, 110
Canadian Dermatology Association, 377
International League of Dermatological Societies, 1552

DES Exposure
DES Action USA, 1521

Design
The Advertising & Design Club of Canada, 10
Associated Designers of Canada, 89
Association des designers industriels du Québec, 110
Design Exchange, 654
Nova Scotia Designer Crafts Council, 1044
Society of Graphic Designers of Canada, 1329

Desktop Publishing
Xplor Canada Association, 1470

Developing Countries
African Enterprise (Canada), 13
Aga Khan Foundation Canada, 14
Almas Jiwani Foundation, 59
The Belinda Stronach Foundation, 204
Canadian Council for International Co-operation, 366
Canadian Crossroads International, 373
Canadian Food for Children, 391
Canadian Physicians for Aid & Relief, 454
CARE Canada, 511
Carrefour de solidarité internationale inc., 515
Carrefour Tiers-Monde, 516
Change for Children Association, 551
Christian Blind Mission International, 566
CODA International Training, 1518
CODE, 580
Colin B. Glassco Charitable Foundation for Children, 581
Collaboration Santé Internationale, 581
Comité de solidarité/Trois-Rivières, 592
Compassion Canada, 608
CUSO International, 646
Dignitas International, 656
Ethiopiaid, 697
Farm Radio International, 705
Fondation Edward Assh, 746
Foundation for International Training, 755
Friends of the Third World, 763
Horizons of Friendship, 821
Humanity First Canada, 827
The Hunger Project Canada, 827
Ingénieurs Sans Frontières Québec, 838
Inter Pares, 851
International Development Research Centre, 856
The Marquis Project, Inc., 952
MATCH International Women's Fund, 954
Mennonite Central Committee Canada, 960
Nepali Children's Education Project, 1003
Oxfam Canada, 1134
Plan Canada, 1161
The Primate's World Relief & Development Fund, 1170
Probe International, 1181
Project Ploughshares, 1188
Save a Family Plan, 1281
Service universitaire canadien outre-mer, 1291
Sleeping Children Around the World, 1303
SOS Children's Villages Canada, 1333
Terre sans frontières, 1372
Trade Facilitation Office Canada, 1394
United Nations Conference on Trade & Development, 1599
United Nations Research Institute for Social Development, 1600
Village International Sudbury, 1435
WaterCan, 1442
World Accord, 1465
World Vision Canada, 1467
Youth Challenge International, 1475

Development Education
British Columbia Teachers for Peace & Global Education, 256
Canadian Bureau for International Education, 347
Centre canadien d'étude et de coopération internationale, 526
Centre de formation à la coopération interculturelle du Québec, 529
Coady International Institute, 577
CODE, 580
Comité régional d'éducation pour le développement international de Lanaudière, 592
CUSO International, 646
Development & Peace, 654
Global Village Nanaimo, 775
Guelph International Resource Centre, 793
Innovations et réseaux pour le développement, 1532
Kawartha World Issues Centre, 882
MATCH International Women's Fund, 954
One World Arts, 1058
Société de coopération pour le développement international, 1314
Victoria International Development Education Association, 1432

Developmental Disabilities
Action Intégration en Déficience Intellectuelle, 6
Addus, 8
AiMHi, Prince George Association for Community Living, 18
American Association on Intellectual & Developmental Disabilities, 1490
L'Arche Atlantic Region, 76
L'Arche Canada, 77
L'Arche Foundation, 77
L'Arche Ontario, 77
L'Arche Québec, 77
L'Arche Western Region, 77
Association de la déficience intellectuelle de la région de Sorel, 101
Association de la Vallée-du-Richelieu pour la déficience intellectuelle, 102
Association de Montréal pour la déficience intellectuelle, 102
Association de parents d'enfant trisomique-21 de Lanaudière, 103
Association de Sherbrooke pour la déficience intellectuelle, 104
Association des handicapés adultes de la Mauricie, 116
Association du Québec pour l'intégration sociale / Institut québécois de la déficience intellectuelle, 131
Association du syndrome de Down de L'Estrie, 131
Association Jeannoise pour l'intégration sociale inc., 136
Association pour l'intégration communautaire de l'Outaouais, 165
Association pour l'intégration sociale - Région Beauce-Sartigan, 165
Association pour l'intégration sociale (Région de Québec), 166
Association pour l'intégration sociale (Région des Bois-Francs), 166
Association pour l'intégration sociale (Rouyn-Noranda) inc., 166
Association pour l'intégration sociale d'Ottawa, 166
Association pour le développement de la personne handicapée intellectuelle du Saguenay, 167
Association Renaissance de la région de l'Amiante, 177
Barrhead Association for Community Living, 197
BC People First Society, 202
Beehive Support Services Association, 204
Best Buddies Canada, 206
Brampton Caledon Community Living, 226
Bridges Family Programs Association, 228
British Columbia Lions Society for Children with Disabilities, 245
Brockville & District Association for Community Involvement, 260
Bruce Peninsula Association for Community Living, 260
Burnaby Association for Community Inclusion, 265
Calgary Community Living Society, 271
Campbell River & District Association for Community Living, 276
Camrose Association for Community Living, 277
Canadian Association for Community Living, 298
CanLearn Society for Persons with Learning Difficulties, 508
Cedar Crest Society for Community Living, 521
Child & Parent Resource Institute, 558
Chilliwack Society for Community Living, 563
The City of Greater Sudbury Developmental Services, 571
Clay Tree Society for People with Developmental Disabilities, 572
Clements Centre Society, 573
Comité régional des associations pour la déficience intellectuelle, 592
Communitas Supportive Care Society, 595
Community Integration Services Society, 599
Community Living Ajax-Pickering & Whitby, 600
Community Living Algoma, 600
Community Living Alternatives Society, 600
Community Living Association (Lanark County), 600
Community Living Association for South Simcoe, 600
Community Living Atikokan, 600
Community Living Brantford, 600
Community Living Cambridge, 600
Community Living Campbellford/Brighton, 601
Community Living Chatham-Kent, 601
Community Living Dryden-Sioux Lookout, 601
Community Living Dufferin, 601
Community Living Dundas County, 601
Community Living Durham North, 601
Community Living Elgin, 601
Community Living Espanola, 601
Community Living Essex County, 601
Community Living Fort Erie, 602
Community Living Fort Frances & District, 602
Community Living Glengarry, 602
Community Living Greater Sudbury, 602
Community Living Grimsby, Lincoln & West Lincoln, 602
Community Living Guelph Wellington, 602
Community Living Haldimand, 602
Community Living Haliburton County, 602
Community Living Hamilton, 602
Community Living Huntsville, 602
Community Living Huronia, 602
Community Living Kawartha Lakes, 603
Community Living Kincardine & District, 603
Community Living Kingston, 603
Community Living London, 603
Community Living Manitoba, 603
Community Living Manitoulin, 603
Community Living Mississauga, 603
Community Living Newmarket/Aurora District, 603
Community Living North Bay, 603
Community Living North Frontenac, 603
Community Living North Halton, 603
Community Living Oakville, 604
Community Living Ontario, 604
Community Living Oshawa / Clarington, 604
Community Living Owen Sound & District, 604
Community Living Parry Sound, 604
Community Living Peterborough, 604
Community Living Port Colborne-Wainfleet, 604
Community Living Prince Edward (County), 604
Community Living Quinte West, 604
Community Living Renfrew County South, 604
Community Living St. Marys & Area Association, 604
Community Living Sarnia-Lambton, 605
Community Living Society, 605
Community Living South Huron, 605
Community Living South Muskoka, 605
Community Living Stormont County, 605
Community Living Stratford & Area, 605
Community Living Temiskaming South, 605
Community Living Thunder Bay, 605
Community Living Timmins Intégration Communautaire, 605
Community Living Toronto, 605
Community Living Upper Ottawa Valley, 605
Community Living Victoria, 606
Community Living Wallaceburg, 606
Community Living Welland Pelham, 606
Community Living West Nipissing, 606
Community Living West Northumberland, 606
Community Living Windsor, 606
Community Living York South, 606
Corporation l'Espoir, 631
Cranbrook Society for Community Living, 638
Crowsnest Community Support Society, 644
Cypress Hills Ability Centres, Inc., 647
Dawson Creek Society for Community Living, 652
Developmental Disabilities Resource Centre of Calgary, 655
E3 Community Services, 666
Early Childhood Intervention Program (ECIP) Sask. Inc., 667
Families for a Secure Future, 701
La fédération des mouvements personne d'abord du Québec, 716
Fondation québécoise de la déficience intellectuelle, 747
Fort St. John Association for Community Living, 753
Garth Homer Society, 767
Gateway Association, 767
Georgina Association for Community Living, 771
Grande Prairie & District Association for Persons with Developmental Disabilities, 781
Harry E. Foster Foundation, 804
Hearst & Area Association for Community Living, 808
Homestead Christian Care, 820
Inclusion Alberta, 831
Inclusion BC, 831
Inclusion Powell River Soceity, 832
Indefinite Arts Society, 832
Independence Plus Inc., 832
Intégration communautaire Chapleau Community Living, 850
Intégration communautaire Cochrane Association for Community Living, 850
Iroquois Falls Association for Community Living, 864
James Bay Association for Community Living, 868
Kamloops Society for Community Living, 880
Kapuskasing, Cochrane & District Association for Community Living, 881
Kenora Association for Community Living, 883
Kinsight, 890
Kirkland Lake Association for Community Living, 890
Kootenay Society for Community Living, 892
Lambton County Developmental Services, 897
Lennox & Addington Association for Community Living, 907
Lethbridge Association for Community Living, 907
Lo-Se-Ca Foundation, 919
Madawaska Valley Association for Community Living, 924
McMan Youth, Family & Community Services Association, 955
Middlesex Community Living, 965
Mill Woods Society for Community Living, 965
Mission Association for Community Living, 968
MSA Society for Community Living, 978
Nanaimo Association for Community Living, 987
New Brunswick Association for Community Living, 1004
Newfoundland & Labrador Association for Community Living, 1015
Niagara Support Services, 1026
Norfolk Association for Community Living, 1028
North Hastings Community Integration Association, 1031
North Okanagan Neurological Association, 1031
Nova Scotia Association for Community Living, 1040
Ontario Agencies Supporting Individuals with Special Needs, 1059

Subject Index / Diseases

Ontario Association on Developmental Disabilities, 1067
Our Harbour, 1132
Pamiqsaiji Association for Community Living, 1138
Parkland Community Living & Supports Society, 1142
Parksville & District Association for Community Living, 1142
Parrainage civique Montréal, 1143
Pathways Abilities Society, 1145
PEI People First, 1148
Penticton & District Society for Community Living, 1150
People First Nova Scotia, 1151
People First of Canada, 1151
People First of Manitoba, 1151
People First of Newfoundland & Labrador, 1151
People First of Ontario, 1151
People First Society of Yukon, 1151
Port Alberni Association for Community Living, 1165
posAbilities Association of BC, 1167
Prince Edward Island Association for Community Living, 1172
Prince Rupert Association for Community Living, 1179
Quad County Support Services, 1195
Quesnel Community Living Association, 1200
Red Deer Action Group, 1209
Red Lake & District Association for Community Living, 1210
Regroupement de parents de personnes ayant une déficience intellectuelle de Montréal, 1214
Regroupement pour l'intégration dans la communauté de Rivière-des-Prairies, 1216
REHOBOTH Christian Ministries, 1216
Richmond Society for Community Living, 1231
Ridge Meadows Association of Community Living, 1232
St Catharines Association for Community Living, 1248
St. Paul Abilities Network, 1251
The Salvation Army START Program, 1253
Saskatchewan Association for Community Living, 1256
Saskatchewan Association of Rehabilitation Centres, 1258
Semiahmoo Foundation, 1289
Semiahmoo House Society, 1289
Shuswap Association for Community Living, 1297
Skills Unlimited, 1302
Society of St. Vincent de Paul - Toronto Central Council, 1330
Southern Alberta Community Living Association, 1337
Superior Greenstone Association for Community Living, 1355
Supporting Choices of People Edson, 1356
Surrey Association for Community Living, 1357
Terrace & District Community Services Society, 1371
Tillsonburg & District Association for Community Living, 1379
Trail Association for Community Living, 1394
Transitions, 1395
Valoris for Children & Adults of Prescott-Russell, 1424
Vela Microboard Association of British Columbia, 1430
Vera Perlin Society, 1431
Wetaskiwin & District Association for Community Service, 1451
Weyburn Group Home Society Inc, 1451
Wikwemikong Anishinabe Association for Community Living, 1453
Yellowknife Association for Community Living, 1470
Yukon Association for Community Living, 1477

Diabetes
Alberta Diabetes Foundation, 32
Diabète Québec, 655
Diabetes Canada, 655
Fondation pour enfants diabetiques, 747
International Society for Pediatric & Adolescent Diabetes, 1558
Juvenile Diabetes Research Foundation Canada, 878

National Aboriginal Diabetes Association Inc., 988

Diagnostic Medical Sonography
American Association of Neuromuscular & Electrodiagnostic Medicine, 1490
British Columbia Ultrasonographers' Society, 257
International Society for Magnetic Resonance in Medicine, 1558
Sonography Canada, 1333

Dietitians & Nutritionists
College of Dietitians of Alberta, 584
College of Dietitians of British Columbia, 584
College of Dietitians of Manitoba, 584
College of Dietitians of Ontario, 584
Dietitians of Canada, 656
New Brunswick Association of Dietitians, 1005
Newfoundland & Labrador College of Dietitians, 1017
Nova Scotia Dietetic Association, 1044
Ontario Society of Nutrition Professionals in Public Health, 1107
Ordre professionnel des diététistes Québec, 1124
Prince Edward Island Dietetic Association, 1173
Saskatchewan Dietitians Association, 1263
Société des technologues en nutrition, 1318

Diplomatic & Consular Service
Commission internationale de diplomatique, 1518
Professional Association of Foreign Service Officers, 1182

Direct Marketing
Canadian Marketing Association, 430
Data & Marketing Association, 1521
Direct Sellers Association of Canada, 657
Federation of European Direct & Interactive Marketing, 1526

Disabilities
Alberta Association of Rehabilitation Centres, 24
Alberta Cerebral Palsy Sport Association, 27
Alberta Committee of Citizens with Disabilities, 30
Alberta Easter Seals Society, 33
ARCH Disability Law Centre, 76
Assisted Living Southwestern Ontario, 89
Association d'informations en logements et immeubles adaptés, 99
Association de balle des jeunes handicapés de Laval-Laurentides-Lanaudière, 99
Association des alternatives en santé mentale de la Montérégie, 105
Association des goélands de Longueuil, 115
Association des handicapés adultes de la Côte-Nord, 116
Association des handicapés adultes de la Mauricie, 116
Association des parents d'enfants handicapés du Témiscamingue inc., 122
Association des parents et des handicapés de la Rive-Sud métropolitaine, 122
Association des personnes handicapées de Charlevoix inc., 122
Association des personnes handicapées de la Rive-Sud Ouest, 122
Association des personnes handicapées de la Vallée du Richelieu, 123
Association des personnes handicapées physiques et sensorielles du secteur Joliette, 123
Association des personnes handicapés visuels de l'Estrie, inc, 123
Association des usagers du transport adapté de Longueuil, 130
Association multi-ethnique pour l'intégration des personnes handicapées, 137
Association of Service Providers for Employability & Career Training, 162
Association pour la promotion des droits des personnes handicapées, 166
Association québécoise de la dysphasie, 170
Association québécoise de sports pour paralytiques cérébraux, 171
Association québécoise pour le loisir des personnes handicapées, 176
Atelier de Formation Socioprofessionnelle de la Petite-Nation, 179

BC Association for Individualized Technology and Supports, 201
Bridges Family Programs Association, 228
British Columbia Aboriginal Network on Disability Society, 229
British Columbia Association of Professionals with Disabilities, 232
Canadian Abilities Foundation, 285
Canadian Association for Community Living - Antigonish, 298
Canadian Association for Supported Employment, 304
Canadian Association of Physicians with Disabilities, 327
Canadian Association of Professionals with Disabilities, 329
Canadian Centre on Disability Studies, 354
Canadian Cerebral Palsy Sports Association, 354
Canadian Council on Rehabilitation & Work, 371
Canadian Foundation for Physically Disabled Persons, 394
Canadian Society of Professionals in Disability Management, 487
Carefree Society, 511
Carleton Road Industries Association, 513
Centre d'aide personnes traumatisées crâniennes et handicapées physiques Laurentides, 527
Centre de services Guigues, 530
Centre for Child Development, 531
Centre for Independent Living in Toronto, 532
Centre Montérégien de réadaptation, 536
CharterAbility, 552
Colchester Community Workshops Foundation, 580
Community Care for South Hastings, 596
Community Involvement of the Disabled, 599
Confédération des Organismes de Personnes Handicapées du Québec, 611
Corbrook Awakening Abilities, 628
Council of Canadians with Disabilities, 633
Cumberland Equal Rights for the Disabled, 645
DIRECTIONS Council for Vocational Services Society, 657
Disability Alliance British Columbia, 658
Disability Awareness Consultants, 658
Disabled Individuals Alliance, 658
Disabled Peoples' International, 658
DisAbled Women's Network of Canada, 658
Early Childhood Intervention Program (ECIP) Sask. Inc, 667
Easter Seals Canada, 669
Easter Seals New Brunswick, 669
Easter Seals Newfoundland & Labrador, 669
Easter Seals Nova Scotia, 669
Easter Seals Ontario, 669
Elk Valley Society for Community Living, 685
EmployAbility, 686
Entrepreneurs with Disabilities Network, 691
Envol SRT, 693
Falher Friendship Corner Association, 701
FOCUS, 741
Fort McMurray Association for Community Living, 752
Goodwill Industries, 777
Goodwill Industries Essex Kent Lambton, 777
Goodwill Industries of Alberta, 778
Goodwill, The Amity Group, 778
Gustav Levinschi Foundation, 794
Hamilton District Society for Disabled Children, 801
Handicap International Canada, 802
Handicapped Organization Promoting Equality, 803
High Prairie Association for Community Living, 814
Independence Plus Inc., 832
Independent Living Nova Scotia, 833
Kéroul, Tourisme pour personnes à capacité physique restreinte, 884
KickStart Disability Arts & Culture, 884
Kinsmen Foundation of British Columbia & Yukon, 890
Lac La Biche Disability Services, 894
Langley Association for Community Living, 899
Lansdowne Outdoor Recreational Development Association, 899
Lights, Camera, Access!, 912
Manitoba Cerebral Palsy Sports Association, 933

Manitoba League of Persons with Disabilities, 939
March of Dimes Canada, 949
March of Dimes Non-Profit Housing Corporation, 949
National Educational Association of Disabled Students, 993
National Institute of Disability Management & Research, 994
The Neil Squire Foundation, 1002
New Beginnings Association of Southern Alberta, 1004
North Shore ConneXions Society, 1032
North Shore Disability Resource Centre Association, 1032
Nunavummi Disabilities Makinnasuaqtiit Society, 1051
NWT Disabilities Council, 1052
Ontario Brain Injury Association, 1068
Ontario Cerebral Palsy Sports Association, 1071
Ontario Prader-Willi Syndrome Association, 1097
Ontario Track 3 Ski Association for the Disabled, 1110
Open Door Group, 1114
The Order of United Commercial Travelers of America, 1119
Paralympic Sports Association (Alberta), 1138
Planned Lifetime Advocacy Network, 1161
Prince Edward Island Council of People with Disabilities, 1173
Professional Association of Therapeutic Horsemanship International, 1584
Reach Canada, 1204
Reach for the Rainbow, 1205
Red Deer Action Group, 1209
Reena, 1210
Regroupement pour l'intégration sociale de Charlevoix, 1216
Rehabilitation Society of Southwestern Alberta, 1216
Richmond County Disabled Association, 1230
Robin Hood Association for the Handicapped, 1235
Rotary International, 1587
The Salvation Army START Program, 1253
Saskatchewan Abilities Council, 1255
Saskatchewan Voice of People with Disabilities, Inc., 1277
The Shepherds' Trust, 1295
Société Logique, 1321
Société pour les enfants handicapés du Québec, 1322
Society for Manitobans with Disabilities Inc., 1326
Special Needs Planning Group, 1339
Spectrum Society for Community Living, 1340
SportAbility BC, 1345
Step-By-Step Child Development Society, 1349
Sunrise Therapeutic Riding & Learning Centre, 1354
Tetra Society of North America, 1373
Theatre Terrific Society, 1375
Tillicum Centre - Hope Association for Community Living, 1379
VALID Association, 1424
Valoris for Children & Adults of Prescott-Russell, 1424
Vancouver Island Society for Disabled Artists, 1427
The War Amputations of Canada, 1440
Westward Goals Support Services Inc., 1451

Disarmament
ACT for the Earth, 5
Burlington Association for Nuclear Disarmament, 265
Canadian Coalition for Nuclear Responsibility, 357
Coalition to Oppose the Arms Trade, 579
Parliamentarians for Global Action, 1582
Physicians for Global Survival (Canada), 1158
Victoria Peace Coalition, 1433

Disc Jockeys
Canadian Professional DJ Association Inc., 460

Diseases
African & Caribbean Council on HIV/AIDS in Ontario, 12

Subject Index / Disorders

Association of Medical Microbiology & Infectious Disease Canada, 151
Barth Syndrome Foundation of Canada, 197
Batten Disease Support & Research Association - Canadian Chapter, 199
Brain Tumour Foundation of Canada, 225
British Columbia Prader-Willi Syndrome Association, 249
The Canadian Addison Society, 288
Canadian Angelman Syndrome Society, 293
Canadian Fanconi Anemia Research Fund, 384
Canadian Genetic Diseases Network, 397
Canadian Lyme Disease Foundation, 428
Canadian Society for Mucopolysaccharide & Related Diseases Inc., 477
Canadian Syringomyelia Network, 491
CHARGE Syndrome Canada, 552
Confederation of Meningitis Organizations, 1519
Fédération québécoise des laryngectomisés, 729
Foundation for Prader-Willi Research in Canada, 756
Fragile X Research Foundation of Canada, 757
Huntington Society of Canada, 827
International Papillomavirus Society, 1554
Jacob's Ladder - The Canadian Foundation for Control of Neurodegenerative Disease, 867
Meningitis BC, 960
Meningitis Relief Canada, 960
Meningitis Research Foundation of Canada, 960
Ontario Prader-Willi Syndrome Association, 1097
Ontario Spondylitis Association, 1108
Partners in Research, 1144
Prader-Willi Syndrome Association of Alberta, 1169
Promoting Awareness of RSD & CRPS in Canada, 1188
Prostate Cancer Canada, 1189
Regroupement québécois des maladies orphelines, 1216
Société Huntington du Québec, 1321
Thalassemia Foundation of Canada, 1373
Tuberous Sclerosis Canada Sclérose Tubéreuse, 1400
United Mitochondrial Disease Foundation, 1599

Disorders
Alström Syndrome Canada, 60
Anxiety Disorders Association of British Columbia, 72
Association de la fibromyalgie région Ile-De-Montréal, 101
Association des personnes intéressées à l'aphasie et à l'accident vasculaire cérébral, 123
Association du Syndrome de Sjogren, Inc, 131
Association/Troubles de l'Humeur et d'Anxiété au Québec, 179
Barth Syndrome Foundation of Canada, 197
Canadian ADHD Resource Alliance, 288
Canadian Alopecia Areata Foundation, 292
Canadian Association for Clinical Microbiology & Infectious Diseases, 297
Canadian Association for Williams Syndrome, 307
Canadian Hemochromatosis Society, 404
Canadian Organization for Rare Disorders, 447
Canadian Porphyria Foundation Inc., 458
Coffin-Lowry Syndrome Foundation, 1518
Cyclic Vomiting Syndrome Association, 1521
The Facial Pain Association, 1525
Fibromyalgia Association of Saskatchewan, 733
Fibromyalgia Support Group of Winnipeg, Inc., 733
Garrod Association, 767
GI (Gastrointestinal) Society, 773
Guillain-Barré Support Group of Canada, 794
Guillain-Barré Syndrome Foundation of Canada, 794
International Society for Affective Disorders, 1557
International Society for Vascular Behavioural & Cognitive Disorders, 1560
Irritable Bowel Syndrome Self Help & Support Group, 864
Joubert Syndrome & Related Disoarders Foundation, 1568
Kabuki Syndrome Network Inc., 879
Lymphovenous Association of Ontario, 923
MEFM Myalgic Encephalomyelitis & Fibromyalgia Society of British Columbia, 959
National Alopecia Areata Foundation, 1572
National Organization for Rare Disorders, Inc., 1576
Scleroderma Association of British Columbia, 1285
Sickle Cell Association of Ontario, 1297
Sickle Cell Foundation of Alberta, 1298
Sjogren's Syndrome Foundation Inc., 1589
Society for Muscular Dystrophy Information International, 1326
Support Organization for Trisomy 18, 13 & Related Disorders, 1356
Tuberous Sclerosis Canada Sclérose Tubéreuse, 1400
Vasculitis Foundation Canada, 1430

Distance Education
Canadian Network for Innovation in Education, 440
The Commonwealth of Learning, 594
Le Réseau d'enseignement francophone à distance du Canada, 1219

Distilling
Association of Canadian Distillers, 142

Diving
Alberta Diving, 33
Alberta Underwater Council, 50
Association Internationale pour le Développement de l'Apnée Canada, 136
British Columbia Diving, 238
Canadian Association of Freediving & Apnea, 316
Dive Ontario, 659
Diving Plongeon Canada, 659
Fédération du plongeon amateur du Québec, 720
Fédération québécoise des activités subaquatiques, 728
Manitoba Diving Association, 935
Manitoba Underwater Council, 946
Ontario Underwater Council, 1112
Prince Edward Island Underwater Council, 1178
Saskatchewan Diving, 1263
Saskatchewan Underwater Council, 1276
Underwater Council of British Columbia, 1404
Yukon Underwater Diving Association, 1480

Divorce
Family Mediation Canada, 703

Dogs
Association des propriétaires canins de Prévost, 126
Australian Cattle Dog Rescue of Ontario, 188
Boston Terrier Rescue Canada, 218
Canadian Association of Professional Pet Dog Trainers, 329
Canadian Chihuahua Rescue & Transport, 355
Canadian Kennel Club, 424
Canadian Kennel Club Foundation, 424
Canine Federation of Canada, 508
Dog Guides Canada, 660
Doggone Safe, 660
Fundy Trail Beagle Club, 764
Moncton Retriever Club, 972
National Retriever Club of Canada, 996
Responsible Dog Owners of Canada, 1227
The Yellow Dog Project, 1470
Yukon Kennel Club, 1479
Yukon Schutzhund Association, 1480

Domestic Services
West Coast Domestic Workers' Association, 1444

Domestic Violence
Bridges, 228
Crossroads for Women Inc., 644
Metropolitan Action Committee on Violence Against Women & Children, 964
The Shelter Movers of Toronto, 1295
Springtide Resources, 1346
Stop Abuse in Families Society, 1350
Viol-secours inc., 1435

Donkeys & Mules
Canadian Donkey & Mule Association, 378
The Donkey Sanctuary of Canada, 661

Doors & Windows
Association de vitrerie et fenestrations du Québec, 104
Canadian Door Institute of Dealers, Manufacturers & Distributors, 378
Canadian Steel Door Manufacturers Association, 491
Door & Access Systems Manufacturers Association, 1521
Door & Hardware Institute in Canada, 661
Fenestration Association of BC, 732
Fenestration Canada, 732
Siding & Window Dealers Association of Canada, 1298

Doukhobors
The Canadian Doukhobor Society, 378

Down Syndrome
Canadian Down Syndrome Society, 378
Down Syndrome Association of Ontario, 661
Down Syndrome Association of Toronto, 661
Down Syndrome Research Foundation, 661
Manitoba Down Syndrome Society, 935
Regroupement pour la Trisomie 21, 1216
Windsor-Essex Down Syndrome Parent Association, 1457

Drama
Association of BC Drama Educators, 140
British Columbia Drama Association, 239
Canadian Association for Theatre Research, 306
Carousel Players, 514
Centre des auteurs dramatiques, 530
Manitoba Association of Playwrights, 931
The Québec Drama Federation, 1197
Société québécoise des auteurs dramatiques, 1324
Theatre Nova Scotia, 1374

Drilling
Alberta Water Well Drilling Association, 51
Association des enterprises spécialiseés en eau du Québec, 112
British Columbia Ground Water Association, 242
Canadian Association of Drilling Engineers, 312
Canadian Association of Oilwell Drilling Contractors, 324
Canadian Diamond Drilling Association, 377
Nova Scotia Ground Water Association, 1045

Drinking Water
Lifewater Canada, 912

Driver Education
Driving School Association of Ontario, 663

Drug Abuse
Addiction Services of Thames Valley, 8
Addictions & Mental Health Ontario, 8
Addictions Foundation of Manitoba, 8
Calgary Alpha House Society, 271
Canadian Assembly of Narcotics Anonymous, 296
Canadian Centre for Ethics in Sport, 353
Canadian Centre on Substance Use & Addiction, 354
The Canadian Don't Do Drugs Society, 378
Canadian Drug Policy Coalition, 379
Canadian Harm Reduction Network, 401
Centre de réadaptation et dépendance le virage, 529
Centre for Addiction & Mental Health, 531
Council on Drug Abuse, 636
Drug Prevention Network of Canada, 663
L'Écluse des Laurentides, 671
From Grief To Action, 763
International Centre for Science in Drug Policy, 854
Jean Tweed Treatment Centre, 869
Méta d'âme, 962
Nar-Anon Family Groups of Ontario, 988
Nechi Training, Research & Health Promotions Institute, 1002
Parent Action on Drugs, 1139
Parkdale Focus Community Project, 1140
Programme d'aide aux membres du barreau, 1187
The Renascent Centres for Alcoholism & Drug Addiction, 1217
Southern Ontario Cocaine Anonymous, 1338

Drunk Driving
International Council on Alcohol, Drugs & Traffic Safety, 1545
MADD Canada, 925
Ontario Students Against Impaired Driving, 1109

Ducks
Ducks Unlimited Canada, 663
Ducks Unlimited Inc., 1521
Ottawa Duck Club, 1130

Dutch Canadians
Dutch Canadian Association of Greater Toronto Inc., 665
Dutch Canadian Business Club of Calgary, 665
Dutch-Canadian Association Ottawa Valley/Outaouais, 665

Dyslexia
Canadian Dyslexia Association, 379
International Dyslexia Association, 1545

Dystonia
Dystonia Medical Research Foundation Canada, 665

Early Childhood Education
Aboriginal Head Start Association of British Columbia, 2
Association des cadres des centres de la petite enfance, 108
Association francophone à l'éducation des services à l'enfance de l'Ontario, 135
Association of Early Childhood Educators of Newfoundland & Labrador, 147
Association of Early Childhood Educators of Quebec, 147
Association of Early Childhood Educators Ontario, 147
L'Association québécoise des centres de la petite enfance, 172
British Columbia Primary Teachers Association, 249
Certification Council of Early Childhood Educators of Nova Scotia, 538
Concerned Educators Allied for a Safe Environment, 1519
Early Childhood Care & Education New Brunswick, 666
Music for Young Children, 983
Quesnel & District Child Development Centre Association, 1200
Yukon Child Care Association, 1477

East European Studies
Association for Slavic, East European, & Eurasian Studies, 1509
Canadian Association of Slavists, 333
Canadian Institute of Ukrainian Studies, 420
International Council for Central & East European Studies (Canada), 1544

Eastern Europe
Canadian Slovak League, 472
East European Genealogical Society, Inc., 668

Eating Disorders
Bulimia Anorexia Nervosa Association, 264
Eating Disorder Association of Canada, 671
Jessie's Hope Society, 870
National Eating Disorder Information Centre, 992
Sheena's Place, 1295

Ecology
Antarctic & Southern Ocean Coalition, 1505
Bruce Peninsula Environment Group, 261
Canadian Council on Ecological Areas, 371
Coastal Zone Canada Association, 579
Conservation Council of New Brunswick, 621
Conservation Council of Ontario, 622
Conservation Halton Foundation, 622
Credit Valley Conservation Foundation, 641
David Suzuki Foundation, 651
Earthroots, 667
Ecoforestry Institute Society, 671
Ecological Agriculture Projects, 672
Ecological Farmers of Ontario, 672
Ecological Society of America, 1522
Ecology Action Centre, 672
Fédération des sociétés d'horticulture et d'écologie du Québec, 719
Friends of Ecological Reserves, 761

Subject Index / Education

Friends of the Earth Canada, 762
Groupe de recherche en écologie sociale, 791
International Association for Ecology, 1536
International Federation of Organic Agriculture Movements, 1548
International Society for Ecological Economics, 1557
International Society for Ecological Modelling, 1557
International Union for Conservation of Nature, 1563
International Union of Biological Sciences, 1564
John E. Mack Institute, 1568
Lifeforce Foundation, 911
Lynn Canyon Ecology Centre, 923
Meewasin Valley Authority, 959
The Nature Conservancy of Canada, 999
Niagara Peninsula Conservation Authority, 1025
Oakville Community Centre for Peace, Ecology & Human Rights, 1053
Partners FOR the Saskatchewan River Basin, 1144
Québec-Labrador Foundation (Canada) Inc., 1199
Réseau québécois des groupes écologistes, 1225
Sierra Club, 1589
Sierra Club of Canada, 1298
Sierra Youth Coalition, 1298
Society for Ecological Restoration International, 1590
Society Promoting Environmental Conservation, 1331
Stanley Park Ecology Society, 1348
Sustainability Project, 1357
Thames Region Ecological Association, 1373
The Waterbird Society, 1602
World Agroforestry Centre, 1602
World Wildlife Fund - Canada, 1468
Yukon Conservation Society, 1477

Economic Assistance (Domestic)
Armenian Relief Society of Canada, Inc., 83
Canada India Village Aid Association, 280
Canadian Lutheran World Relief, 428
Canadian Ukrainian Immigrant Aid Society, 498
Canadian-Cuban Friendship Association Toronto, 506
Catholic Charities of The Archdiocese of Toronto, 518
Firefighters Burn Fund Inc., 738
Jamaican Self-Help Organization, 867
Jewish Federations of Canada - UIA, 872
Jewish Free Loan Toronto, 872
Oxfam Canada, 1134
The Primate's World Relief & Development Fund, 1170
Richelieu International, 1229
Romanian Children's Relief, 1235
Ronald McDonald House Charities of Canada, 1235
St. Andrew's Society of Montréal, 1248
St. Andrew's Society of Toronto, 1248
Samaritan's Purse Canada, 1253
Saskatoon Open Door Society Inc., 1279
Save the Children Canada, 1281
Service universitaire canadien outre-mer, 1291
Sleeping Children Around the World, 1303
SOS Children's Villages Canada, 1333
SOS Children's Villages Canada, 1333
Victoria Cool Aid Society, 1432
World Vision Canada, 1467

Economic Development
Association canadienne des sciences régionales, 95
Association des professionnels en développement économique du Québec, 126
Atlantic Association of CBDCs, 182
Atlantic Association of Community Business Development Corporations, 182
British Columbia Co-operative Association, 237
British Columbia Economic Development Association, 239
Canadian Aboriginal & Minority Supplier Council, 285
Canadian CED Network, 351
Canadian Council on Africa, 370
Canadian Worker Co-operative Federation, 505
Centre interuniversitaire de recherche en économie quantitative, 535

Centre local de développement Rouyn-Noranda, 536
China Canada Investment Association, 564
Community Futures Development Association of British Columbia, 598
Community Futures Manitoba Inc., 598
Community Futures Network Society of Alberta, 598
Community Futures Saskatchewan, 598
Community Futures West Yellowhead, 598
Community Futures Wild Rose, 598
Conseil canadien de la coopération et de la mutualité, 613
Conseil de coopération de l'Ontario, 615
Conseil de la coopération de L'Ile-du-Prince-Édouard, 615
Conseil de la Coopération de la Saskatchewan, 615
Corporation de développement économique communautaire Centre-Sud/Plateau Mont-Royal, 629
Economic Developers Alberta, 672
Economic Developers Association of Canada, 672
Economic Developers Association of Manitoba, 673
Economic Developers Council of Ontario Inc., 673
Economic Development Brandon, 673
Economic Development Winnipeg Inc., 673
Edmonton Economic Development Corporation, 677
Fondation de l'entrepreneurship, 743
Grahamdale Community Development Corporation, 779
Horizons of Friendship, 821
Institute for Local Self-Reliance, 1532
Institute for Research on Public Policy, 844
Invest Ottawa, 862
KAIROS: Canadian Ecumenical Justice Initiatives, 880
Kingston Economic Development Corporation, 889
Manitouwadge Economic Development Corporation, 948
Martin Prosperity Institute, 952
Mennonite Economic Development Associates Canada, 961
Muskoka Community Futures Development Corporation, 985
Native Investment & Trade Association, 998
New Brunswick Association of Community Business Development Corporations, 1004
Niagara Economic Development, 1025
Northwest Territories Community Futures Association, 1038
Nunavut Economic Developers Association, 1051
Ontario Association of Community Futures Development Corporations, 1063
Organization for Economic Co-operation & Development, 1581
Pacific NorthWest Economic Region, 1582
La Passerelle - Intégration et Développement Économique, 1145
Saskatchewan Economic Development Association, 1264
Sault Ste Marie Economic Development Corporation, 1281
Société de développement économique du Saint-Laurent, 1315
South Lake Community Futures Development Corporation, 1335

Economics
American Economic Association, 1492
Association coopérative d'économie familiale de l'Outaouais, 98
Association des économistes québécois, 111
Atlantic Provinces Economic Council, 185
Canada West Foundation, 281
Canadian Association for Health Services & Policy Research, 300
Canadian Association of Professional Employees, 328
Canadian Centre for Policy Alternatives, 354
Canadian Economics Association, 379
Canadian Foundation for Economic Education, 393
Canadian Law & Economics Association, 425
C.D. Howe Institute, 521

Centre for the Study of Living Standards, 534
CIRANO, 570
The Conference Board of Canada, 611
Connexions Information Sharing Services, 613
Economics Society of Northern Alberta, 673
Enactus Canada, 687
The Fraser Institute, 757
Groupe de recherche en animation et planification économique, 791
Insitut canadien des économistes en construction - Québec, 840
Institute of Health Economics, 846
International Economic History Association, 1546
International Institute for Applied Systems Analysis, 1551
International Institute of Fisheries Economics & Trade, 1551
The North-South Institute, 1036
Responsible Investment Association, 1227
Rotman Institute for International Business, 1236
Société Saint-Thomas-d'Aquin, 1325

Ecumenism
Association of Christian Churches in Manitoba, 145
The Canadian Council of Churches, 368
Forum for Intercultural Leadership & Learning, 754
John Milton Society for the Blind in Canada, 875
KAIROS: Canadian Ecumenical Justice Initiatives, 880
Student Christian Movement of Canada, 1352
VISION TV, 1436
Women's Inter-Church Council of Canada, 1462
World Association for Christian Communication, 1465
World Council of Churches, 1604

Editors
Association nationale des éditeurs de livres, 138
Canadian Ethnic Media Association, 382
Canadian Journalism Foundation, 423
Council of Science Editors, 1520
Editors' Association of Canada, 674

Education
Aboriginal Agricultural Education Society of British Columbia, 2
Académie européenne des sciences, des arts et des lettres, 1485
African Canadian Continuing Education Society, 12
African Enterprise (Canada), 13
AFS Interculture Canada, 13
AIESEC, 18
Alberta Assessment Consortium, 22
Alberta Association of Family School Liaison Workers, 23
Alberta Council for Environmental Education, 31
Alberta Council on Admissions & Transfer, 31
Alberta Home Education Association, 37
Alberta Teachers of English as a Second Language, 49
Alliance of Credential Evaluation Services of Canada, 58
American Academy of Arts & Sciences, 1487
American Academy of Religion, 1488
Associated Medical Services Inc., 89
L'Association des orthopédagogues du Québec inc., 121
Association des parents ayants droit de Yellowknife, 121
Association des Scouts du Canada, 127
Association for Childhood Education International, 1508
Association for Media Literacy, 134
Association francophone internationale des directeurs d'établissements scolaires, 1509
Association of Accrediting Agencies of Canada, 138
Association of Atlantic Universities, 139
Association of Canadian Deans of Education, 141
Association of Educational Researchers of Ontario, 147
Association of Employees Supporting Education Services, 147
Association of New Brunswick Professional Educators, 154

Association of University Forestry Schools of Canada, 163
Association pour la voix études au Québec, 167
Association québécoise d'information scolaire et professionnelle, 168
Association québécoise des cadres scolaires, 171
Association québécoise du personnel de direction des écoles, 176
Atlantic Provinces Special Education Authority, 185
Black Educators Association of Nova Scotia, 213
Black Studies Centre, 213
Boîte à science - Conseil du loisir scientifique du Québec, 217
British Columbia Alternate Education Association, 230
British Columbia Association of School Psychologists, 232
British Columbia School Superintendents Association, 252
Broadcast Educators Association of Canada, 259
Canada BIM Council Inc., 278
Canadian Accredited Independent Schools Advancement Professionals, 287
Canadian Adventist Teachers Network, 288
Canadian Association for Astrological Education, 297
Canadian Association for Curriculum Studies, 299
Canadian Association for Educational Psychology, 300
Canadian Association for Medical Education, 302
Canadian Association for Prior Learning Assesment, 303
Canadian Association for Social Work Education, 304
Canadian Association for Spiritual Care, 304
Canadian Association for Teacher Education, 304
Canadian Association for the Practical Study of Law in Education, 305
Canadian Association for the Study of Educational Administration, 306
Canadian Association for the Study of Indigenous Education, 306
Canadian Association for the Study of Women & Education, 306
Canadian Association for University Continuing Education, 306
Canadian Association of Communicators in Education, 310
Canadian Association of Foundations of Education, 315
Canadian Association of Principals, 328
Canadian Association of Private Language Schools, 328
Canadian Association of Schools of Nursing, 332
Canadian Bureau for International Education, 347
Canadian Committee of Graduate Students in Education, 361
Canadian Conservation Institute, 363
Canadian Council for Aviation & Aerospace, 366
Canadian Council for the Advancement of Education, 367
Canadian Council of Montessori Administrators, 369
Canadian Credit Institute Educational Foundation, 372
Canadian Education & Research Institute for Counselling, 379
Canadian Education & Training Accreditation Commission, 379
Canadian Education Association, 379
Canadian Education Exchange Foundation, 380
Canadian Educational Researchers' Association, 380
Canadian Educational Resources Council, 380
Canadian Engineering Education Association, 381
Canadian Federation of Business School Deans, 386
Canadian Film Centre, 390
Canadian Foundation for Economic Education, 393

Canadian Global Campaign for Education, 398
Canadian Healthcare Engineering Society, 402
Canadian History of Education Association, 405
Canadian Information Centre for International Credentials, 411
Canadian Institute for Child & Adolescent Psychoanalytic Psychotherapy, 412
Canadian Institute for Energy Training, 412
Canadian Institute of Traffic & Transportation, 419
Canadian Memorial Chiropractic College, 434
Canadian Network for Environmental Education & Communication, 440
Canadian Organization for Development through Education, 447
Canadian Philosophy of Education Society, 454
Canadian Post-MD Education Registry, 458
Canadian School Libraries, 468
Canadian Securities Institute, 469
Canadian Securities Institute Research Foundation, 469
Canadian Society for the Study of Education, 478
Canadian Society for the Study of Higher Education, 478
Canadian-Palestinian Education Exchange, 506
Cancer Patient Education Network Canada, 507
CanLearn Society for Persons with Learning Difficulties, 508
Cape Breton University Centre for International Studies, 510
Career Colleges Ontario, 511
Catholic Association of Religious & Family Life Educators of Ontario, 517
Catholic Family Services of Toronto, 519
The Catholic Principals' Council of Ontario, 520
Catholic Teachers Guild, 520
Centrale des syndicats du Québec, 525
Centre canadien de leadership en éducation, 526
Centre d'animation de développement et de recherche en éducation, 528
Centre de documentation sur l'éducation des adultes et la condition féminine, 529
Centre femmes de Rimouski, 531
Centre for Inquiry Canada, 533
Centre for the Study of Learning & Performance, 534
Centre Psycho-Pédagogique de Québec Inc., 536
Chartered Accountants' Education Foundation of Alberta, 552
Chawkers Foundation, 555
Children's Education Funds Inc., 561
Coalition for Music Education in Canada, 578
Colleges and Institutes Canada, 590
Colleges Ontario, 591
The Commonwealth of Learning, 594
The Comparative & International Education Society of Canada, 608
Contact Point, 626
Continuing Legal Education Society of BC, 627
Cooper Institute, 627
Co-operative Education & Work-Integrated Learning Canada, 627
Council of Atlantic Ministers of Education & Training, 632
Council of Canadian Fire Marshals & Fire Commissioners, 633
Council of Ministers of Education, Canada, 634
Council of Ontario Drama & Dance Educators, 634
Council of Ontario Universities, 635
Council of Parent Participation Preschools in British Columbia, 635
The Counselling Foundation of Canada, 636
CPE du Carrefour, 638
Credit Institute of Canada, 640
Curriculum Services Canada, 646
Dance Oremus Danse, 649
Dial-a-Tutor, 656
Disaster Recovery Institute Canada, 658
Dorchester & Westmorland Literacy Council, 661
Dufferin Peel Educational Resource Workers' Association, 664
Earthwatch Institute, 1522
Ecological Farmers of Ontario, 672
Education Assistants Association of the Waterloo Region District School Board, 680
Education International, 1522

Education Support Staff of the Ontario Secondary School Teachers' Federation - District 24 - Waterloo, 680
EduNova, 680
Environmental Careers Organization of Canada, 691
ERS Training & Development Corporation, 695
Evangelical Order of Certified Pastoral Counsellors of America, 699
Fédération des parents francophones de l'Alberta, 717
Fédération des professionnelles et professionnels de l'éducation du Québec, 718
Fédération québécoise des directions d'établissements d'enseignement, 728
First Nations Confederacy of Cultural Education Centres, 738
First Nations Education Council, 738
First Nations SchoolNet, 738
Fondation Richelieu International, 748
Foundation for Education Perth Huron, 755
Hamber Foundation, 800
Hands on Summer Camp Society, 803
Health Law Institute, 806
Holocaust Education Centre, 818
Humanist Canada, 826
Indspire, 835
Institut Tshakapesh, 843
Institute for Performance & Learning, 844
International Arthurian Society - North American Branch, 1535
International Association of Educators for World Peace - USA, 1538
International Council for Canadian Studies, 855
International Council of Associations for Science Education, 1545
International Credential Assessment Service of Canada, 856
International Dyslexia Association, 1545
International Institute of Integral Human Sciences, 858
International Ocean Institute, 1553
International Society for Music Education, 1558
Interpretation Canada - A Professional Association for Heritage Interpretation, 861
Inter-Varsity Christian Fellowship, 862
The Jane Goodall Institute of Canada, 868
Languages Canada, 899
Learning Enrichment Foundation, 905
Legal Education Society of Alberta, 906
Let's Talk Science, 907
Lions Legacy International, 913
Lions Quest Canada - The Centre for Positive Youth Development, 913
The Mackenzie Institute, 924
Manitoba Aboriginal Education Counselling Association Inc., 928
Manitoba Indian Education Association Inc., 939
The Manitoba Tourism Education Council, 946
Media Smarts, 957
Miss G Project, 968
Mouvement d'éducation populaire et d'action communautaire du Québec, 977
NAFSA: Association of International Educators, 1572
National Association of Career Colleges, 990
National Association of Collegiate Directors of Athletics, 1573
National Association of Secondary School Principals, 1574
National Council for Science & the Environment, 1575
National Education Association, 1576
National Educational Association of Disabled Students, 993
National Literacy & Health Program, 994
National Reading Campaign, Inc., 995
Nechi Training, Research & Health Promotions Institute, 1002
Nepali Children's Education Project, 1003
New Beginnings for Youth, 1004
Ontario Agri-Food Education Inc., 1059
Ontario Association For Students At Risk, 1061
Ontario Association of Deans of Education, 1063
Ontario Business Education Partnership, 1070
Ontario College of Teachers, 1072
Ontario Cooperative Education Association, 1074

Ontario Council on Articulation and Transfer, 1075
Ontario Native Education Counselling Association, 1093
Open Learning at Thompson Rivers University, 1114
Ordre des psychoéducateurs et psychoéducatrices du Québec, 1123
ORT Canada, 1127
Outdoor Recreation Council of British Columbia, 1133
Pacific Life Bible College, 1135
Parents as First Educators, 1140
Pathways to Education Canada, 1145
Peace & Justice Studies Association, 1583
PeerNetBC, 1148
People for Education, 1151
Provincial Nurse Educator Interest Group, 1191
Québec Board of Black Educators, 1196
Réseau des cégeps et des collèges francophones du Canada, 1219
Road Scholar, 1586
The Royal Commonwealth Society, 1587
Saskatchewan Association for Multicultural Education, 1256
School Milk Foundation of Newfoundland & Labrador, 1284
SEEDS Foundation, 1289
Shevchenko Scientific Society of Canada, 1296
Skills Canada, 1302
Société des écoles du monde du BI du Québec et de la francophonie, 1317
Société historique Alphonse-Desjardins, 1319
Société Québécoise de Psilogie inc, 1323
Society for Quality Education, 1326
Southeast Asian Ministers of Education Organization, 1595
Start Right Coalition for Financial Literacy, 1348
Sustainability Project, 1357
Teachers of Inclusive Education - British Columbia, 1367
Toronto Montessori Institute, 1386
Union québécoise de réhabilitation des oiseaux de proie, 1408
United World Colleges, 1418
Universal Youth Foundation, 1418
Universities Canada, 1418
Visions of Science Network for Learning, 1436
The W. Garfield Weston Foundation, 1439
Waldorf School Association of Kelowna, 1439
Wikimedia Canada, 1453
The Workers' Educational Association of Canada, 1464
Working Women Community Centre, 1464
World University Roundtable, 1608
Youth Flight Canada, 1475

Educational Media
Association for Canadian Educational Resources, 132
Centre franco-ontarien de ressources pédagogiques, 534
Educational Computing Organization of Ontario, 680
Manitoba Indian Cultural Education Centre, 939
SkyWorks Charitable Foundation, 1303
Youth Media Alliance, 1476

Egg Industry
Alberta Egg Producers' Board, 33
British Columbia Broiler Hatching Egg Producers' Association, 234
British Columbia Egg Marketing Board, 239
Canadian Hatching Egg Producers, 401
Canadian Poultry & Egg Processors Council, 458
Egg Farmers of Canada, 681
Fédération des producteurs d'oeufs de consommation du Québec, 717
Fraser Valley Egg Producers' Association, 757
Manitoba Egg Farmers, 936
New Brunswick Egg Marketing Board, 1007
Nova Scotia Egg Producers, 1044
Ontario Broiler Hatching Egg & Chick Commission, 1069
Ontario Hatcheries Association, 1083
Saskatchewan Egg Producers, 1264

Egypt
The Nile Association of Ontario, 1027
Society for the Study of Egyptian Antiquities, 1327

Eighteenth-Century Studies
Canadian Society for Eighteenth-Century Studies, 474

El Salvador
SalvAide, 1252

Electric Power
Association de l'industrie électrique du Québec, 100
Association of Major Power Consumers in Ontario, 151
CAMPUT, 277
Canadian Electricity Association, 380
Canadian Hydropower Association, 410
Clean Energy British Columbia, 573
Electricity Distributors Association, 683
Electro-Federation Canada, 683
Independent Power Producers Society of Alberta, 833
Power Workers' Union, 1169
The Society of Energy Professionals, 1328
United Utility Workers' Association, 1412

Electrical Engineering
Alberta Electrical League, 33
Electrochemical Society, 1522
Illuminating Engineering Society of North America, 1530
Institute of Electrical & Electronics Engineers Inc., 1532
Institute of Electrical & Electronics Engineers Inc. - Region 7, 846
Maintenance, Engineering & Reliability (MER) Society, 926

Electrical Industry
Association of Power Producers of Ontario, 156
British Columbia Electrical Association, 239
Canadian Electrical Contractors Association, 380
Canadian Electrical Manufacturers Representatives Association, 380
Corporation des maîtres électriciens du Québec, 630
Electrical Association of Manitoba Inc., 682
Electrical Construction Association of Hamilton, 682
Electrical Contractors Association of Alberta, 682
Electrical Contractors Association of BC, 682
Electrical Contractors Association of London, 682
Electrical Contractors Association of New Brunswick, Inc., 682
Electrical Contractors Association of Ontario, 682
Electrical Contractors Association of Quinte-St. Lawrence, 683
Electrical Contractors Association of Saskatchewan, 683
Electrical Contractors Association of Thunder Bay, 683
Electricity Human Resources Canada, 683
Electro-Federation Canada, 683
Fraternité interprovinciale des ouvriers en électricité (CTC), 758
Greater Toronto Electrical Contractors Association, 785
International Brotherhood of Electrical Workers (AFL-CIO/CFL), 1542
MultiPrévention ASP: Association paritaire pour la santé et la sécurité au travail des secteurs: métal, électrique, habillement et imprimerie, 980
National Electricity Roundtable, 993
Niagara Peninsula Electrical Contractors Association, 1025
Ontario Electrical League, 1077
Syndicat des travailleurs énergie électrique nord, 1364
Windsor Electrical Contractors Association, 1456

Electroencephalography
Canadian Association of Electroneurophysiology Technologists Inc., 312
Canadian Board of Registration of Electroencephalograph Technologists Inc., 345

Electrolysis
Association des professionnels en électrolyse et soins esthétiques du Québec, 126
Fédération of Canadian Electrolysis Associations, 723

Electronic Data Interchange
Electronic Frontier Canada Inc., 683
GS1 Canada, 792

Electronic Engineering
Aerospace & Electronic Systems Society, 1485
Institute of Electrical & Electronics Engineers Inc., 1532
Institute of Electrical & Electronics Engineers Inc. - Region 7, 846
International Electrotechnical Commission - Canadian National Committee, 857

Electronic Instruments
The Instrumentation, Systems & Automation Society of America, 1534

Electronic Security Industry
Canadian Security Association, 469
Interac Association, 851
International Council on Global Privacy & Security, By Design, 856

Electronics Industry
Alliance numérique, 58
Armed Forces Communications & Electronics Association (Canada), 82
British Columbia Technology Industries Association, 256
Consumer Electronics Marketers of Canada: A Division of Electro-Federation Canada, 625
Electronics Import Committee, 683
Electronics Product Stewardship Canada, 684
Installation, Maintenance & Repair Sector Council & Trade Association, 840

Electroplating
National Association for Surface Finishing, 1573

Elevators & Escalators
National Elevator & Escalator Association, 993

Embroidery
Embroiderers' Association of Canada, Inc., 685

Emergency Housing
Adsum for Women & Children, 9
Almost Home, 59
Battlefords Interval House Society, 200
Calgary Women's Emergency Shelter Association, 275
Carrefour pour Elle, 516
Chez Doris, 557
Covenant House Toronto, 637
Eva's Initiatives for Homeless Youth, 698
Evangel Hall Mission, 698
Fédération des maisons d'hébergement pour femmes, 715
Halifax Transition House Association - Bryony House, 799
Hébergement la casa Bernard-Hubert, 811
Inn From the Cold Society, 838
Kenora Fellowship Centre, 883
Lloydminster Interval Home Society, 916
Lookout Emergency Aid Society, 919
Mission Bon Accueil, 969
Nellie's Shelter, 1003
New Brunswick Coalition of Transition Houses/Centres for Abused Women, 1007
Pavillon Marguerite de Champlain, 1146
Regina Transition Women's Society, 1212
Regroupement provincial des maisons d'hébergement et de transition pour femmes victimes de violence conjugale, 1216
Revelstoke Women's Shelter Society, 1228
La rue des femmes, 1243
Sanctuary, 1253
Shuswap Area Family Emergency Society, 1297
South Okanagan Women in Need Society, 1335
Women In Crisis (Algoma) Inc., 1460
Yellowhead Emergency Shelter for Women Society, 1470

Emergency Services
Alberta College of Paramedics, 29
Ambulance Paramedics of British Columbia, 66
Association des spécialistes en médecine d'urgence du Québec, 128
Bon Accord/Gibbons Food Bank, 217
Canadian Avalanche Association, 340
Canadian College of Emergency Medical Services, 358
Canadian Interoperability Technology Interest Group, 422
Centre for Excellence in Emergency Preparedness, 532
Civil Air Search & Rescue Association, 571
Corporation des services d'ambulance du Québec, 630
Disaster Recovery Institute Canada, 658
Fédération des employés du préhospitaliers du Québec, 714
Focus Humanitarian Assistance Canada, 741
Hampton Food Basket & Clothing Centre Inc., 802
Hatzoloh Toronto, 804
National Emergency Nurses Association, 993
New Brunswick Association of Food Banks, 1005
Occupational First Aid Attendants Association of British Columbia, 1054
Ontario Association of Emergency Managers, 1063
Ontario Paramedic Association, 1094
Oromocto & Surrounding Area Food & Clothing Bank, 1127
Paramedic Association of Canada, 1138
Paramedic Association of Manitoba, 1138
Paramedic Association of New Brunswick, 1138
Paramedic Association of Newfoundland & Labrador, 1138
St. John Ambulance, 1248
Saskatchewan College of Paramedics, 1261
Saskatchewan Emergency Medical Services Association, 1264
Shock Trauma Air Rescue Society, 1296
The Tema Conter Memorial Trust, 1370
Toronto Paramedic Association, 1386

Employee Benefits
Canadian Pension & Benefits Institute, 453
International Foundation of Employee Benefit Plans, 1549

Employee Counselling
Unemployed Help Centre, 1404

Employees
Alberta Association of Recreation Facility Personnel, 24
Alberta Union of Provincial Employees, 50
Association of Employees Supporting Education Services, 147
Canadian Employee Assistance Program Association, 380
Canadian LabourWatch Association, 425
Manitoba Association of Non-Teaching Employees, 930
Masonry Industry Employers Council of Ontario, 952
National Seafood Sector Council, 996
Ontario Municipal Human Resources Association, 1092
Professional Employees Association (Ind.), 1183

Employment
A.C.C.E.S. Employment, 4
The Ark/Lunenburg County Association for the Specially Challenged, 81
Association of Canadian Search, Employment & Staffing Services, 143
Association of Service Providers for Employability & Career Training, 162
Atelier de Formation Socioprofessionnelle de la Petite-Nation, 179
Beehive Adult Service Centre, Inc., 204
Bridge Adult Service Society, 228
Building Futures Employment Society, 262
Canada Employment & Immigration Union, 278
Canadian Association for Community Living - Clare Branch, 298
Canadian Association for Supported Employment, 304
Canadian Association of Career Educators & Employers, 309
Canadian Steel Trade & Employment Congress, 491
Carrefour jeunesse emploi de l'Outaouais, 515
Carrefour jeunesse emploi du Pontiac, 515
Carrefour Jeunesse Emploi Vallée-de-la-Gatineau, 516
Carrefour jeunesse-emploi Papineau, 516
Centre de recherche et d'intervention interuniversitaire sur l'éducation et la vie au travail, 530
Centre for Adults in Progressive Employment Society, 531
Centre intégré d'employabilité locale des Collines-de-l'Outaouais, 535
Cheticamp Association for Community Living, 557
Conseil d'intervention pour l'accès des femmes au travail, 615
Les Conseillers en développement de l'employabilité, 621
Conway Workshop Association, 627
Corbrook Awakening Abilities, 628
Corridor Community Options for Adults, 631
Dartmouth Adult Services Centre, 650
DIRECTIONS Council for Vocational Services Society, 657
Dress for Success, 662
EmployAbilities, 686
Envol SRT, 693
Flowercart, 741
Gerald Hardy Memorial Society, 771
Golden Opportunities Vocational Rehabilitation Centre Workshop, 776
Good Jobs for All Coalition, 777
Goodwill Industries, 777
Goodwill Industries Essex Kent Lambton, 777
Goodwill Industries of Alberta, 778
Goodwill, The Amity Group, 778
Haley Street Adult Services Centre Society, 798
Heatherton Activity Centre, 810
Horizon Achievement Centre, 821
International Credential Assessment Service of Canada, 856
Inter-Provincial Association on Native Employment, 861
Inverness Cottage Workshop, 862
Jobs Unlimited, 873
Kaye Nickerson Adult Service Centre, 883
LakeCity Employment Services Association, 896
Maison internationale de la Rive-Sud, 927
Mouvement action chômage de Longueuil, 976
The Neil Squire Foundation, 1002
New Boundaries, 1004
New Leaf Enterprises, 1014
Ontario Network of Employment Skills Training Projects, 1093
Open Door Group, 1114
Port Colborne Community Association for Research Extension, 1165
Prescott Group, 1170
Prospect Human Services, 1189
Queens Association for Supported Living, 1200
Regional Occupation Centre Foundation, 1212
Regional Occupation Centre Society, 1213
Regroupement québécois des organismes pour le développement de l'employabilité, 1216
Réseau de développement économique et d'employabilité Ontario, 1219
Service Intégration Travail Outaouais, 1291
Shelburne Association Supporting Inclusion, 1295
Summer Street, 1354
Thunder Bay Counselling Centre, 1377
Times Change Women's Employment Service, 1379
Toronto Community Employment Services, 1383
Yukon Mine Training Association, 1479

Endocrinology
Association des médecins endocrinologues du Québec, 119
Canadian Pediatric Endocrine Group, 452
Canadian Society of Endocrinology & Metabolism, 482
Pediatric Endocrine Society, 1583

Endometriosis
Endometriosis Association, Inc., 1523
The Endometriosis Network, 687

Energy
Ag Energy Co-operative, 13
Association of Major Power Consumers in Ontario, 151
Association of Manitoba Hydro Staff & Supervisory Employees, 151
Association of Power Producers of Ontario, 156
Association québécoise de la production d'énergie renouvelable, 170
Association québécoise pour la maîtrise de l'énergie, 176
British Columbia Sustainable Energy Association, 255
Canadian Clean Power Coalition, 357
Canadian Electricity Association, 380
Canadian Energy Efficiency Alliance, 381
Canadian Energy Research Institute, 381
Canadian Energy Workers' Association, 381
Canadian GeoExchange Coalition, 397
Canadian Institute for Energy Training, 412
Canadian Institute of Energy (British Columbia), 415
Clean Energy British Columbia, 573
Community Energy Association, 597
Earth Energy Society of Canada, 667
Energy Action Council of Toronto, 688
Energy Council of Canada, 688
Energy Probe Research Foundation, 688
Independent Power Producers Society of Alberta, 833
Institut de la Francophonie pour le développement durable, 841
International Academy of Energy, Minerals & Materials, 852
International Association for Hydrogen Energy, 1536
The Maritimes Energy Association, 951
NAIMA Canada, 987
Offshore Energy Research Association of Nova Scotia, 1055
Ontario Energy Association, 1077
Ontario Geothermal Association, 1082
Ontario Sustainable Energy Association, 1109
Ontario Waterpower Association, 1113
Planetary Association for Clean Energy, Inc., 1161
Resource Industry Suppliers Association, 1227
The Rocky Mountain Institute, 1586
SEEDS Foundation, 1289
Toronto Renewable Energy Co-operative, 1387
World Coal Institute, 1604
World Energy Council, 1604
World Nuclear Association, 1606

Energy Conservation
American Council for an Energy-Efficient Economy, 1492
British Columbia Sustainable Energy Association, 255
Building Energy Management Manitoba, 261
Earth Energy Society of Canada, 667
Elora Environment Centre, 685
Energy Action Council of Toronto, 688
Energy Probe Research Foundation, 688
Foundation for Environmental Conservation, 1526
International Institute for Energy Conservation, 1551
Toronto Renewable Energy Co-operative, 1387
Windfall Ecology Centre, 1456
World Energy Council, 1604

Engineering
American Association for the Advancement of Science, 1489
American Society of Heating, Refrigerating & Air Conditioning Engineers, 1499
American Society of Mining & Reclamation, 1501
Applied Science Technologists & Technicians of British Columbia, 74
Association des Diplômés de Polytechnique, 110
Association des firmes de génie-conseil - Québec, 114
Association des ingénieurs municipaux du Québec, 116
Association des ingénieurs-professeurs des sciences appliquées, 116
Association for Facilities Engineering, 1508
Association of Consulting Engineering Companies - British Columbia, 145
Association of Consulting Engineering Companies - Canada, 145
Association of Consulting Engineering Companies - Manitoba, 146

Subject Index / English as a Second Language

Association of Consulting Engineering Companies - New Brunswick, 146
Association of Consulting Engineering Companies - Prince Edward Island, 146
Association of Consulting Engineering Companies - Saskatchewan, 146
Association of Engineering Technicians & Technologists of Newfoundland & Labrador, 147
Association of Environmental Engineering & Science Professors, 1511
Association of Korean Canadian Scientists & Engineers, 150
Association of Polish Engineers in Canada, 155
Association of Professional Engineers & Geoscientists of Alberta, 157
Association of Professional Engineers & Geoscientists of British Columbia, 157
Association of Professional Engineers & Geoscientists of Manitoba, 158
Association of Professional Engineers & Geoscientists of New Brunswick, 158
Association of Professional Engineers & Geoscientists of Saskatchewan, 158
Association of Professional Engineers of Prince Edward Island, 159
Association of Professional Engineers of Yukon, 159
Association of Science & Engineering Technology Professionals of Alberta, 162
Association professionnelle des ingénieurs du gouvernement du Québec (ind.), 167
Canada BIM Council Inc., 278
The Canadian Academy of Engineering, 286
Canadian Associated Air Balance Council, 297
Canadian Association of Drilling Engineers, 312
Canadian Biomaterials Society, 344
Canadian Engineering Education Association, 381
Canadian Federation of Aircraft Maintenance Engineers Associations, 384
Canadian Federation of Engineering Students, 386
Canadian Healthcare Engineering Society, 402
Canadian Institute of Transportation Engineers, 420
Canadian Society for Engineering Management, 474
Central Canada Broadcast Engineers, 524
Centre for Transportation Engineering & Planning, 534
Certified Technicians & Technologists Association of Manitoba, 538
Consulting Engineers of Alberta, 625
Consulting Engineers of Newfoundland & Labrador, 625
Consulting Engineers of Nova Scotia, 625
Consulting Engineers of Ontario, 625
Consulting Engineers of the Northwest Territories, 625
Consulting Engineers of Yukon, 625
Electrical & Mechanical Engineering Association, 682
The Engineering Institute of Canada, 688
Engineers Canada, 689
Engineers Canada, 689
Engineers Nova Scotia, 689
Engineers Without Borders, 689
Hungarian Canadian Engineers' Association, 827
Ingénieurs Sans Frontières Québec, 838
L'Institut de développement de produits, 841
Institute of Power Engineers, 846
Institute of Transportation Engineers, 1534
International Association for Earthquake Engineering, 1536
International Federation of Professional & Technical Engineers (AFL-CIO/CLC), 1549
International Society for Rock Mechanics, 1559
International Society for Soil Mechanics & Geotechnical Engineering, 1559
International Union of Operating Engineers (AFL-CIO/CFL), 1565
International Union of Societies for Biomaterials Science & Engineering, 1565
Island Technology Professionals, 865
Maintenance, Engineering & Reliability (MER) Society, 926
Municipal Engineers Association, 980
NACE International, 1571

Natural Sciences & Engineering Research Council of Canada, 999
New Brunswick Society of Certified Engineering Technicians & Technologists, 1012
Northwest Territories & Nunavut Association of Professional Engineers & Geoscientists, 1036
NSERC Chair for Women in Science & Engineering, 1050
Ontario Association of Certified Engineering Technicians & Technologists, 1062
Ontario Society of Professional Engineers, 1107
Ordre des ingénieurs du Québec, 1122
Ordre des ingénieurs forestiers du Québec, 1123
Professional Engineers & Geoscientists Newfoundland & Labrador, 1183
Professional Engineers for Public Safety Association, 1183
Professional Engineers Government of Ontario, 1183
Professional Engineers Ontario, 1183
Refrigeration Service Engineers Society (Canada), 1211
Saskatchewan Applied Science Technologists & Technicians, 1255
Society of Fire Protection Engineers, 1593
Society of Manufacturing Engineers - Canada Office, 1330
Society of Motion Picture & Television Engineers, 1593
Society of Petroleum Engineers, 1593
Society of Professional Engineers & Associates, 1330
Society of Tribologists & Lubrication Engineers, 1594
Society of Women Engineers, 1594
Structural Innovation & Monitoring Technologies Resources Centre, 1352
Syndicat professionnel des scientifiques à pratique exclusive de Montréal, 1365
TechNova, 1369
Tunnelling Association of Canada, 1400
Visions of Science Network for Learning, 1436
Western Association of Broadcast Engineers, 1447
The Western Canada Group of Chartered Engineers, 1448
World Federation of Ukrainian Engineering Societies, 1466

English as a Second Language
Alberta Teachers of English as a Second Language, 49
Association of British Columbia Teachers of English as an Additional Language, 140
English Additional Language Learners Provincial Specialist Association, 689
Folk Arts Council of St Catharines, 742
Haldimand-Norfolk Literacy Council, 798
Project Adult Literacy Society, 1187
Saskatchewan Council for Educators of Non-English Speakers, 1262
Society for the Promotion of the Teaching of English as a Second Language in Quebec, 1326
South Okanagan Immigrant & Community Services, 1335
Teachers of English to Speakers of Other Languages, Inc., 1597
TEAL Manitoba, 1368
TESL Canada Federation, 1372
TESL New Brunswick, 1372
TESL Newfoundland & Labrador, 1372
TESL Nova Scotia, 1372
TESL Ontario, 1373
TESL Prince Edward Island, 1373
TESL Yukon, 1373
Victoria READ Society, 1433

English Language
American Dialect Society, 1492
Association of Canadian College & University Teachers of English, 141
Association of Teachers of English in Quebec, 162
British Columbia Teachers of English Language Arts, 256
Canadian Council of Teachers of English Language Arts, 370
Catholic Action Montreal, 517
English Speaking Catholic Council, 689

English-Language Arts Network, 689
International Association of University Professors of English, 1540
Newcomer Women's Services Toronto, 1015
Québec Community Newspaper Association, 1196
Québec Writers' Federation, 1199
Teachers of English to Speakers of Other Languages, Inc., 1597
Townshippers' Association, 1393

Enterostomy
Ostomy Canada Society, 1129
Winnipeg Ostomy Association, 1459

Entertainment
Association des juristes pour l'avancement de la vie artistique, 118
Association québécoise de l'industrie du disque, du spectacle et de la vidéo, 170
Canadian Film Centre, 390
Canadian Professional DJ Association Inc., 460
Canadians Concerned About Violence in Entertainment, 506
Casting Directors Society of Canada, 516
George Street Association, 771
Talent Agents & Managers Association of Canada, 1366

Entomology
The Acadian Entomological Society, 4
Association des entomologistes amateurs du Québec inc., 112
Entomological Society of Alberta, 690
Entomological Society of British Columbia, 690
Entomological Society of Canada, 690
Entomological Society of Manitoba Inc., 690
Entomological Society of Ontario, 690
Entomological Society of Saskatchewan, 690
North American Butterfly Association, 1578
Société d'entomologie du Québec, 1309
Toronto Entomologists Association, 1384

Environment
Acadia Environmental Society, 4
Agricultural Research & Extension Council of Alberta, 15
Alberta Council for Environmental Education, 31
Alberta Ecotrust Foundation, 33
Alberta Environmental Network, 33
Alberta Institute of Agrologists, 38
Algoma Manitoulin Environmental Awareness, 53
Alternative Land Use Services Canada, 60
American Society for Environmental History, 1498
American Society of Mining & Reclamation, 1501
Les AmiEs de la Terre de Québec, 67
Arctic Council, 81
Association for Literature, Environment, & Culture in Canada, 133
Atlantic Canada Centre for Environmental Science, 182
Ausable Bayfield Conservation Foundation, 188
Battle River Research Group, 199
Bedeque Bay Environmental Management Association, 203
Big Rideau Lake Association, 210
Bike to Work BC Society, 211
British Columbia Environmental Network, 240
British Columbia Institute of Agrologists, 244
British Columbia Spaces for Nature, 254
Bruce Peninsula Environment Group, 261
BurlingtonGreen Environmental Association, 265
Canada's Oil Sands Innovation Alliance, 282
Canadian Association of Physicians for the Environment, 327
Canadian Council of Forest Ministers, 368
Canadian Council of Ministers of the Environment, 368
Canadian Environmental Grantmakers' Network, 382
Canadian Environmental Network, 382
Canadian Network for Environmental Education & Communication, 440
Canadian Society for the Protection of Nature in Israel, 477
Canadian Standards Association, 490
Canadians for Clean Prosperity, 506

Cape Breton University Centre for International Studies, 510
Carolinian Canada Coalition, 514
Carthy Foundation, 516
Castle-Crown Wilderness Coalition, 516
Centre for Indigenous Environmental Resources, Inc., 532
Chawkers Foundation, 555
Chinook Applied Research Association, 565
Citizens for a Safe Environment, 570
Citizens Opposed to Paving the Escarpment, 570
Citizens' Environment Watch, 570
Clubs 4-H du Québec, 576
Coalition on the Niagara Escarpment, 578
Coast Waste Management Association, 579
Coastal First Nations, 579
Commission for Environmental Cooperation, 593
Community Enhancement & Economic Development Society, 597
Concerned Educators Allied for a Safe Environment, 1519
Conference of New England Governors & Eastern Canadian Premiers, 612
Connexions Information Sharing Services, 613
Conseil du bâtiment durable du Canada - Québec, 618
Conseil régional de l'environnement de la Gaspésie et des Îles-de-la-Madeleine, 620
Conservation Council of Ontario, 622
Conservation Foundation of Greater Toronto, 622
Conserver Society of Hamilton & District Inc., 623
Council of Atlantic Premiers, 633
Cumulative Environmental Management Association, 646
CUSO International, 646
David Suzuki Foundation, 651
Division of Sustainable Development, 1521
Earth Day Canada, 667
Earth Island Institute, 1521
Earthsave Canada, 667
Earthwise Society, 668
East Coast Trail Association, 668
Ecology Action Centre, 672
Ecology North, 672
EcoPerth, 673
Éco-Quartier Sainte-Marie, 673
EcoSource Mississauga, 673
Ecotrust Canada, 673
Electric Vehicle Council of Ottawa, 682
Electric Vehicle Society, 682
Elora Environment Centre, 685
Enviro-Accès Inc., 691
EnviroLink, 1523
Environmental Action Barrie - Living Green, 691
Environmental Careers Organization of Canada, 691
Environmental Coalition of Prince Edward Island, 691
Environmental Defence, 691
Environmental Defense, 1523
Environmental Information Association, 1523
Environmental Studies Association of Canada, 692
Environmental Youth Alliance, 692
Environnement jeunesse, 693
FarmFolk CityFolk, 706
Farming Smarter, 706
First Nations Environmental Network, 738
Fondation Hydro-Québec pour l'environnement, 746
Fondation québécoise en environnement, 748
Foothills Forage & Grazing Association, 750
Fraser Basin Council, 757
Friends of Clayoquot Sound, 760
Friends of Red Hill Valley, 762
Friends of the Central Experimental Farm, 762
Friends of the Earth Canada, 762
Friends of the Earth International, 1527
Friends of the Greenbelt Foundation, 762
Front commun québécois pour une gestion écologique des déchets, 763
Gateway Research Organization, 767
Grand River Conservation Foundation, 780
Great Lakes Institute for Environmental Research, 782
Greenpeace Canada, 789
Greenpeace International, 1528

Greenpeace USA, 1529
Greenspace Alliance of Canada's Capital, 789
Grey Wooded Forage Association, 790
Groupe de recherche appliquée en macroécologie, 791
Groupe de recherche en écologie sociale, 791
Habitat Acquisition Trust, 795
Harmony Foundation of Canada, 803
Heartwood Centre for Community Youth Development, 810
Institute for Local Self-Reliance, 1532
International Association for Impact Assessment, 1537
International Council for Local Environmental Initiatives, 1544
International Society for Environmental Ethics, 1557
International Society of Indoor Air Quality & Climate, 1560
Island Nature Trust, 865
Jasper Environmental Association, 869
Kamloops Wildlife Park Society, 881
The Kindness Club, 888
Lakeland Agricultural Research Association, 896
Lakeland Industry & Community Association, 896
Lambton Wildlife Inc., 897
Land Trust Alliance, 1569
London Regional Resource Centre for Heritage & the Environment, 919
Macleod Institute, 924
Manitoba Eco-Network Inc., 936
Manitoba Environment Officers Association Inc., 936
Marine Renewables Canada, 950
The Marquis Project, Inc., 952
Montréal Field Naturalists Club, 972
Muniscope, 982
NACE International, 1571
National Council for Science & the Environment, 1575
National Parks Conservation Association, 1577
The Nature Conservancy of Canada, 999
Nature Trust of New Brunswick, 1001
New Brunswick Environmental Network, 1007
Newfoundland & Labrador Environment Network, 1018
Niagara Peninsula Conservation Authority, 1025
Nipissing Environmental Watch, 1027
North American Bird Conservation Initiative Canada, 1029
North Peace Applied Research Association, 1032
Northwatch, 1036
Nova Scotia Nature Trust, 1047
Oak Ridges Moraine Foundation, 1053
Ontario Environmental Network, 1078
Ontario Public Health Association, 1098
Ontario Steelheaders, 1109
Ontario Streams, 1109
Ottawa Riverkeeper, 1131
Outdoor Recreation Council of British Columbia, 1133
Pacific States-British Columbia Oil Spill Task Force, 1136
Peace & Environment Resource Centre, 1146
Peace Country Beef & Forage Association, 1147
Peace Valley Environment Association, 1147
The Pembina Institute, 1149
Petroleum Tank Management Association of Alberta, 1154
Pickering & Ajax Citizens Together for the Environment, 1159
The Pollution Probe Foundation, 1164
Prince Edward Island Eco-Net, 1173
Prince George Recycling & Environmental Action Planning Society, 1179
Protected Areas Association of Newfoundland & Labrador, 1190
Rainforest Action Network, 1586
Réseau environnement, 1223
Réseau québécois des groupes écologistes, 1225
Rideau Environmental Action League, 1231
Rideau Valley Conservation Authority, 1231
Ruiter Valley Land Trust, 1244
St. John's Clean & Beautiful, 1249
Salmon Arm Bay Nature Enhancement Society, 1252

Sarnia-Lambton Environmental Association, 1254
Saskatchewan Eco-Network, 1264
Saskatchewan Environmental Society, 1264
Sentier Urbain, 1290
Severn Sound Environmental Association, 1292
Sierra Club, 1589
Sierra Club of Canada, 1298
Smoky Applied Research & Demonstration Association, 1304
Society of Environmental Toxicology & Chemistry, 1593
Society Promoting Environmental Conservation, 1331
Spruce City Wildlife Association, 1346
Stockholm Environment Institute, 1597
TD Friends of the Environment Foundation, 1367
Tellus Institute, 1597
Temiskaming Environmental Action Committee, 1370
Thousand Islands Watershed Land Trust, 1376
Tides Canada Foundation, 1379
Toronto Environmental Alliance, 1384
Union québécoise de réhabilitation des oiseaux de proie, 1408
Upper Thames River Conservation Authority, 1422
USC Canada, 1423
Valhalla Wilderness Society, 1424
Vertes boisées du fjord, 1431
Vrac environnement group d'action et de recherche en développement durable, 1439
The W. Garfield Weston Foundation, 1439
Waterfront Regeneration Trust, 1442
West Central Forage Association, 1444
World Resources Institute, 1607
Worldwatch Institute, 1608
Yukon Territory Environmental Network, 1480

Environment Industry
Associated Environmental Site Assessors of Canada Inc., 89
Association of Environmental Engineering & Science Professors, 1511
Association of Postconsumer Plastic Recyclers, 1513
British Columbia Environment Industry Association, 239
Canadian Association of Recycling Industries, 330
Canadian Environment Industry Association, 381
Canadian Environmental Technology Advancement Corporation - West, 382
Canadian Hydrogen & Fuel Cell Association, 409
Conseil patronal de l'environnement du Québec, 619
Environmental Abatement Council of Ontario, 691
Environmental Bankers Association, 1523
Environmental Services Association of Alberta, 692
Environmental Services Association of Nova Scotia, 692
EPS Industry Alliance, 1524
Fuse Collective, 765
GLOBE Foundation, 775
Green Roofs for Healthy Cities, 789
Hamilton Industrial Environmental Association, 801
Hamilton Technology Centre, 802
Institute of Scrap Recycling Industries, Inc., 1533
International Geosynthetics Society, 1550
Manitoba Environmental Industries Association Inc., 936
National Association of Environmental Professionals, 1573
National Waste & Recycling Association, 1577
Newfoundland & Labrador Environmental Industry Association, 1018
North American Recycled Rubber Association, 1029
Ontario Environment Industry Association, 1078
Ontario Pollution Control Equipment Association, 1096
Product Care Association, 1181
Saskatchewan Environmental Industry & Managers' Association, 1264

The Vinyl Institute, 1601

Environmental & Outdoor Education
Alberta Council for Environmental Education, 31
Australian Association for Environmental Education, 1513
Boundless Adventures Association, 219
Citizen Scientists, 570
Clubs 4-H du Québec, 576
Coalition for Education in the Outdoors, 1517
Council of Outdoor Educators of Ontario, 635
Environmental Educators' Provincial Specialist Association, 691
Evergreen, 699
Falls Brook Centre, 701
FortWhyte Alive, 754
Global, Environmental & Outdoor Education Council, 775
Green Communities Canada, 788
Green Kids Inc., 788
Greenest City, 789
Inside Education, 839
LEAD Canada Inc., 902
National Association for Environmental Education (UK), 1572
North American Association for Environmental Education, 1578
Northwest Wildlife Preservation Society, 1039
Ontario Association for Geographic & Environmental Education, 1061
Ontario Society for Environmental Education, 1105
Peterborough Field Naturalists, 1153
Saskatchewan Outdoor & Environmental Education Association, 1271
Seagull Foundation, 1288
Strathcona Park Lodge & Outdoor Education Centre, 1351
VanDusen Botanical Garden Association, 1429
Whole Village, 1453

Environmental Biology
Canadian Society of Environmental Biologists, 482

Environmental Databases
Atlantic Canada Centre for Environmental Science, 182

Environmental Design
Canada Green Building Council, 279
Society for Environmental Graphic Design, 1590
U.S. Green Building Council, 1601

Environmental Health
American Industrial Hygiene Association, 1494
Environmental Health Association of British Columbia, 691
Environmental Health Association of Nova Scotia, 692
Environmental Health Association of Ontario, 692
Environmental Health Foundation of Canada, 692
Green Roofs for Healthy Cities, 789
International Institute of Concern for Public Health, 858
International Society for Environmental Epidemiology, 1557
National Environmental Health Association, 1576
Offshore Energy Research Association of Nova Scotia, 1055
Pacific States-British Columbia Oil Spill Task Force, 1136
Sarnia-Lambton Environmental Association, 1254

Environmental Law
Asia-Pacific Centre for Environmental Law, 1506
Canadian Environmental Law Association, 382
Canadian Institute of Resources Law, 419
Centre québécois du droit de l'environnement, 536
Ecojustice Canada Society, 672
The Environmental Law Centre (Alberta) Society, 692
Environmental Law Institute, 1523
Foundation for International Environmental Law & Development, 1527
International Council of Environmental Law, 1545

International Society for Environmental Ethics, 1557
West Coast Environmental Law, 1444

Environmental Management
Alberta Lake Management Society, 39
Canadian Association of Environmental Management, 313
Environmental Managers Association of British Columbia, 692
Environmental Services Association of Alberta, 692
Green Communities Canada, 788
Gulf of Maine Council on the Marine Environment, 794
International Network for Environmental Management, 1553
National Association for Environmental Management, 1572
Ontario Society for Environmental Management, 1105
Ontario Sustainable Energy Association, 1109
Research & Development Institute for the Agri-Environment, 1218
Saskatchewan Environmental Industry & Managers' Association, 1264

Environmental Policy
Canadian Environmental Certification Approvals Board, 381
Consumer Policy Institute, 626
Council on Hemispheric Affairs, 1520
The Fraser Institute, 757
Greenest City, 789
International Institute for Applied Systems Analysis, 1551
Nova Scotia Public Interest Research Group, 1047
Ontario Public Interest Research Group, 1099
Paper & Paperboard Packaging Environmental Council, 1138
Peace Valley Environment Association, 1147
Québec Public Interest Research Group - McGill, 1198
Simon Fraser Public Interest Research Group, 1300
United Nations Environment Programme, 1600
Vancouver Island Public Interest Research Group, 1426

Ephemera
Ephemera Society of Canada, 693

Epilepsy & Related Disorders
Association québécoise de l'épilepsie, 169
British Columbia Epilepsy Society, 240
Canadian Epilepsy Alliance, 382
Canadian League Against Epilepsy, 426
Edmonton Epilepsy Association, 677
Epilepsy & Seizure Association of Manitoba, 693
Epilepsy Association of Calgary, 693
Epilepsy Association of Nova Scotia, 693
Epilepsy Canada, 693
Epilepsy Foundation of America, 1524
Epilepsy Ontario, 693
Epilepsy Saskatoon, 694
Victoria Epilepsy & Parkinson's Centre Society, 1432

Equal Opportunity Employment
Black Business & Professional Association, 213
Nova Scotia League for Equal Opportunities, 1046

Equestrian Sports & Activities
Alberta Equestrian Federation, 34
Alberta Horse Trials Association, 37
Association Trot & Amble du Québec, 179
Atlantic Canada Trail Riding Association, 182
British Columbia Competitive Trail Riders Association, 236
Canadian Dressage Owners & Riders Association, 378
Canadian Pony Club, 457
Canadian Sport Horse Association, 489
Distance Riders of Manitoba Association, 658
Endurance Riders Association of British Columbia, 687
Endurance Riders of Alberta, 687
Equestrian Association for the Disabled, 694
Equestrian Canada, 694
Equine Association of Yukon, 694

Subject Index / Equipment & Machinery

Fédération équestre du Québec inc., 720
Horse Council British Columbia, 822
Horse Trials New Brunswick, 822
Horse Trials Nova Scotia, 822
Island Horse Council, 865
Manitoba Horse Council Inc., 938
Manitoba Trail Riding Club Inc., 946
New Brunswick Equestrian Association, 1008
Newfoundland Equestrian Association, 1023
Nova Scotia Equestrian Federation, 1044
Ontario Competitive Trail Riding Association Inc., 1073
Ontario Equestrian Federation, 1078
Ontario Horse Trials Association, 1086
Ontario Trail Riders Association, 1111
Professional Association of Therapeutic Horsemanship International, 1584
Saskatchewan Horse Federation, 1267
Trail Riding Alberta Conference, 1394
Yukon Horse & Rider Association, 1479

Equipment & Machinery
Association des propriétaires de machinerie lourde du Québec inc., 126
Association of Equipment Manufacturers - Canada, 148
Association sectorielle: Fabrication d'équipement de transport et de machines, 178
Canada West Equipment Dealers Association, 281
Canadian Machinery Vibration Association, 429
Canadian Rental Association, 467
Heavy Equipment & Aggregate Truckers Association of Manitoba, 810
International Association of Machinists & Aerospace Workers, 1539
Mining Suppliers Trade Association Canada, 967
Municipal Equipment & Operations Association (Ontario) Inc., 981
Muskoka Pioneer Power Association, 985
Ontario Pollution Control Equipment Association, 1096
Printing Equipment & Supply Dealers' Association of Canada, 1180

Ergonomics
Association of Canadian Ergonomists, 142
Commonwealth Human Ecology Council, 1518
International Ergonomics Association, 1546

Esperanto
Esperanto Association of Canada, 695
Esperanto Rondo de Otavo, 695
Esperanto-Toronto, 695
International Society of Friendship & Good Will, 1560
Société québécoise d'espéranto, 1323
Universala Esperanto-Asocio, 1600

Estonian Canadians
Estonian Central Council in Canada, 697
Estonian Evangelical Lutheran Church Consistory, 697

Ethics
Canadian Centre for Ethics & Corporate Policy, 353
Canadian Centre for Ethics in Sport, 353
Canadian Society for the Study of Practical Ethics, 478
Ethics Practitioners' Association of Canada, 697
Institute for Global Ethics (Canada), 843
International Humanist & Ethical Union, 1550
International Society for Environmental Ethics, 1557
McGill Centre for Medicine, Ethics & Law, 955
National Council on Ethics in Human Research, 992
Provincial Health Ethics Network, 1191
W. Maurice Young Centre for Applied Ethics, 1439

Ethiopian Canadians
Ethiopian Association in the Greater Toronto Area & Surrounding Regions, 697

Ethiopian Jewish People

Europe
Association for the Study of Nationalities, 135
European Union Chamber of Commerce in Toronto, 698

Evangelism
African Enterprise (Canada), 13
Billy Graham Evangelistic Association of Canada, 211
Catholic Charismatic Renewal Council, Toronto, 517
Child Evangelism Fellowship of Canada, 559
Community of Christ - Canada East Mission, 606
Community of Christ - Canada West Mission, 607
Emmanuel International Canada, 686
Evangelical Covenant Church of Canada, 698
Evangelical Fellowship of Canada, 698
Evangelical Mennonite Conference, 699
Evangelical Order of Certified Pastoral Counsellors of America, 699
Evangelical Tract Distributors, 699
Fellowship of Evangelical Baptist Churches, 731
Foursquare Gospel Church of Canada, 756
Global Outreach Mission, 775
Gospel Tract & Bible Society, 778
Independent Assemblies of God International - Canada, 832
MB Mission, 954
Solbrekken Evangelistic Association of Canada, 1332
TEAM of Canada Inc., 1368
Threshold Ministries, 1377

Executives
Academy of Canadian Executive Nurses, 4
American Society of Association Executives, 1499
Asociación Nacional de Ejecutivos de Organismos Empresariales y Profesionales, A.C., 1506
Associated Senior Executives of Canada Ltd., 89
Association of Corporate Travel Executives Inc. Canada, 146
Association of Fundraising Professionals, 1511
Association of Professional Executives of the Public Service of Canada, 159
Australian Society of Association Executives Ltd., 1513
Broadcast Executives Society, 259
Canadian Association of Foodservice Professionals, 315
Canadian Association of Women Executives & Entrepreneurs, 336
Canadian Executive Service Organization, 383
Canadian Hotel Marketing & Sales Executives, 409
CIO Association of Canada, 570
Edmonton Executives Association, 677
European Society of Association Executives, 1524
Federation of Swiss Association Executives, 1526
Financial Executives International Canada, 736
Global Network of Director Institutes, 775
Institute of Corporate Directors, 845
Sales & Marketing Executives of Vancouver, 1251
Society of Incentive & Travel Executives of Canada, 1329
Vancouver Executives Association, 1425
Winnipeg Executives Association, 1458
World Presidents' Organization, 1607
Young Presidents' Organization, 1608

Exhibitions & Fairs
Association des professionnels en exposition du Québec, 126
Battlefords Agricultural Society, 200
British Columbia Association of Agricultural Fairs & Exhibitions, 231
Calgary Exhibition & Stampede, 271
Canadian Association of Exposition Management, 313
Canadian Association of Fairs & Exhibitions, 314
Canadian National Exhibition Association, 439
Canadian Western Agribition Association, 503
The Coaster Enthusiasts of Canada, 579
Estevan Exhibition Association, 697
Exhibitions Association of Nova Scotia, 699
Festivals et Événements Québec, 733
German-Canadian Mardi Gras Association Inc., 772
International Live Events Association Canada, 858
Moose Jaw Exhibition Company Ltd., 974
Nipawin Exhibition Association Inc., 1027
Pacific National Exhibition, 1135
Prince Albert Exhibition Association, 1171
Prince Edward Island Association of Exhibitions, 1172
Provincial Exhibition of Manitoba, 1190
Red River Exhibition Association, 1210
Regina Exhibition Association Ltd., 1211
Richmond Agricultural Society, 1229
Royal Agricultural Winter Fair Association, 1237
UFI - The Global Association of the Exhibition Industry, 1598
Vancouver Jewish Film Centre Society, 1427
Western Fair Association, 1449
Westerner Park, 1450

Export Trade
Association des maisons de commerce extérieur du Québec, 118
Canada Pork International, 280
Canadian Association of Film Distributors & Exporters, 314
Canadian Food Exporters Association, 391
Canadian Manufacturers & Exporters, 429
Canadian Swine Exporters Association, 491
Groupe export agroalimentaire Québec - Canada, 792
The Israel Economic Mission to Canada, 866
Livres Canada Books, 915
Mining Suppliers Trade Association Canada, 967
Ontario Association of Trading Houses, 1066
Saskatchewan Trade & Export Partnership, 1276
Trade Facilitation Office Canada, 1394

Eye Banks
Banque d'yeux nationale, inc., 196
Eye Bank of BC, 700
Eye Bank of Canada - Ontario Division, 700
Fondation de la banque d'yeux du Québec inc., 744
Lions Eye Bank of Manitoba & Northwest Ontario, Incorporated, 913
Saskatchewan Lions Eye Bank, 1269

Eye Diseases & Disorders
The Foundation Fighting Blindness, 755
Glaucoma Research Society of Canada, 774
International Society for Eye Research, 1557
Ontario Foundation for Visually Impaired Children Inc., 1081
Operation Eyesight Universal, 1115
Regroupement des aveugles et amblyopes du Montréal métropolitain, 1215
Vision Institute of Canada, 1435

Facial Disfigurement
AboutFace, 3

Facility Management
Alberta Educational Facilities Administrators Association, 33
International Facility Management Association, 1546

Faculty & Staff Associations
Acadia University Faculty Association, 4
Administrative & Professional Staff Association, 8
Association des employés de l'Université de Moncton, 112
Association des professeur(e)s à temps partiel de l'Université d'Ottawa, 124
Association des professeurs de Campus Notre-Dame-de-Foy, 124
Association des professeurs de l'université d'Ottawa, 125
Association du personnel administratif et professionnel de l'Université de Moncton, 131
Association of Academic Staff - University of Alberta, 138
Association of Administrative & Professional Staff - University of British Columbia, 138
Association of Canadian Faculties of Dentistry, 142
Association of Professors of Bishop's University, 160
Association of University of New Brunswick Teachers, 163
Athabasca University Faculty Association, 180
Brandon University Faculty Association, 226
British Columbia Institute of Technology Faculty & Staff Association, 244
Brock University Faculty Association, 259
Camosun College Faculty Association, 276
Canadian Association of University Teachers, 335
Canadian Military Colleges Faculty Association, 436
Cape Breton University Faculty Association, 510
Capilano University Faculty Association, 510
Carleton University Academic Staff Association, 513
College of the Rockies Faculty Association, 590
Concordia University Faculty Association, 609
Concordia University Part-time Faculty Association, 610
Confederation of Alberta Faculty Associations, 611
Confederation of Ontario University Staff Associations & Unions, 611
Confederation of University Faculty Associations of British Columbia, 611
Dalhousie Faculty Association, 648
Douglas College Faculty Association, 661
Emily Carr University of Art & Design Faculty Association, 686
Faculty Association of Medicine Hat College, 700
Faculty Association of Red Deer College, 700
Faculty Association of the College of New Caledonia, 701
Faculty Association of University of Saint Thomas, 701
Fédération du personnel professionnel des collèges, 720
Fédération du personnel professionnel des universités et de la recherche, 720
Federation of New Brunswick Faculty Associations, 725
Grande Prairie Regional College Academic Staff Association, 781
Grant MacEwan College Faculty Association, 782
Keyano College Faculty Association, 884
Kwantlen Faculty Association, 894
Lakehead University Faculty Association, 896
Lakeland College Faculty Association, 896
Langara Faculty Association, 898
Laurentian University Faculty Association, 900
Lethbridge Community College Faculty Association, 908
MacEwan Staff Association, 924
McGill University Non Academic Certified Association, 955
McMaster University Faculty Association, 956
McMaster University Staff Association, 956
Mount Allison Faculty Association, 976
Mount Saint Vincent University Faculty Association, 976
Non-Academic Staff Association for the University of Alberta, 1028
North Island College Faculty Association, 1031
Northern Alberta Institute of Technology Academic Staff Association, 1034
Olds College Faculty Association, 1057
Ontario Confederation of University Faculty Associations, 1074
Queen's University Faculty Association, 1199
Ryerson Faculty Association, 1244
Saint Mary's University Faculty Union, 1247
SAIT Academic Faculty Association, 1251
Simon Fraser University Faculty Association, 1300
Syndicat des employées de soutien de l'Université de Sherbrooke, 1362
Syndicat des professeures et professeurs de l'Université de Sherbrooke, 1363
Syndicat des professeures et professeurs de l'Université du Québec à Chicoutimi, 1363
Syndicat des professeures et professeurs de l'Université du Québec à Rimouski, 1363
Syndicat des professeures et professeurs de l'Université du Québec en Outaouais, 1363
Syndicat des professeurs de l'Université Laval, 1364

Subject Index / Fibromyalgia Syndrome

Syndicat des professeurs et des professeures de l'Université du Québec à Trois-Rivières, 1364
Syndicat des professeurs et professeures de l'Université du Québec à Montréal, 1364
Thompson Rivers University Faculty Association, 1376
Thompson Rivers University Open Learning Faculty Association, 1376
Trent University Faculty Association, 1397
University of British Columbia Faculty Association, 1419
University of Calgary Faculty Association, 1419
University of Guelph Professional Staff Association, 1419
University of Lethbridge Faculty Association, 1419
University of Manitoba Faculty Association, 1419
University of Prince Edward Island Faculty Association, 1420
University of Regina Faculty Association, 1420
University of Saskatchewan Faculty Association, 1420
University of the Fraser Valley Faculty & Staff Association, 1420
University of Toronto Faculty Association, 1420
University of Victoria Faculty Association, 1421
University of Waterloo Staff Association, 1421
University of Western Ontario Staff Association, 1421
University of Winnipeg Faculty Association, 1421
Vancouver Community College Faculty Association, 1425
Vancouver Island University Faculty Association, 1427
Wilfrid Laurier University Faculty Association, 1455
Windsor University Faculty Association, 1457
York University Faculty Association, 1474

Family
Association coopérative d'économie familiale de l'Outaouais, 98
Association coopérative d'économie familliale de Québec, 98
Association de médiation familiale du Québec, 102
Association of Saskatchewan Home Economists, 161
The Atlantic Alliance of Family Resource Centres, 182
Awo Taan Healing Lodge Society, 191
British Columbia Association of Family Resource Programs, 231
British Columbia Council for Families, 237
Calgary Community Living Society, 271
Canadian Association of Family Resource Programs, 314
Canadian Caregiver Coalition, 350
Canadian Coalition for the Rights of Children, 358
Canadian Families & Corrections Network, 383
Carrefour-Ressources, 516
Catholic Family Services of Saskatoon, 519
Centre d'entraide et de ralliement familial, 528
Centre for Family Business, 532
Children's Aid Society of the Region of Peel, 561
Coalition des familles LGBT, 577
Confédération des organismes familiaux du Québec, 611
Couples for Christ Canada, 636
Dufferin Child & Family Services, 664
Elizabeth House, 685
Family & Children's Services of Guelph & Wellington County, 702
Family Enterprise Xchange, 703
Family Service Moncton Inc., 704
Family Services of Greater Vancouver, 704
Family Supports Institute Ontario, 705
Fédération nationale des services de préparation au mariage, 722
La Fédération québécoise des organismes communautaires Famille, 729
4Korners Family Resource Center, 756
GRAND Society, 780
Jewish Family & Child, 871
Jewish Family Services - Calgary, 871
Jewish Family Services Edmonton, 871
Jewish Family Services of Ottawa-Carleton, 872
Kids First Parent Association of Canada, 886
Kinark Child & Family Services, 888
Maison de la famille de la Vallée du Richelieu, 926
Manitoba Association of Home Economists, 930
Metro (Toronto) Association of Family Resource Programs, 963
Mouvement québécois des vacances familiales inc., 978
New Brunswick Association of Family Resource Centres, 1005
Newfoundland & Labrador Provincial Association of Family Resource Centres, 1021
Nova Scotia Council for the Family, 1043
Parenting Education Saskatchewan, 1140
Prince Edward Island Association of Family Resource Programs, 1172
Provincial Council of Women of Manitoba Inc., 1190
REAL Women of Canada, 1206
Ressources Saint-Jean-Vianney, 1227
St. Leonard's Youth & Family Services Society, 1250
Save a Family Plan, 1281
Settlement Assistance & Family Support Services, 1292
South Peace Community Resources Society, 1335
SPEC Association for Children & Families, 1339
Valley Family Resource Centre Inc., 1424
Vanier Institute of The Family, 1429
Wong Kung Har Wun Sun Association, 1463

Family Planning
Action Canada for Sexual Health & Rights, 6
Cape Breton Centre for Sexual Health, 509
Compass Centre for Sexual Wellness, 608
Fédération du Québec pour le planning des naissances, 720
Halifax Sexual Health Centre, 799
Health Initiatives for Youth Hamilton, 806
Jessie's - The June Callwood Centre for Young Women, 870
Marguerite Bourgeoys Family Centre Fertility Care Programme, 949
Natural Family Planning Association, 998
Options for Sexual Health, 1117
Pictou County Centre for Sexual Health, 1159
Planned Parenthood - Newfoundland & Labrador Sexual Health Centre, 1161
Planned Parenthood of Toronto, 1161
Planned Parenthood Ottawa, 1161
Planned Parenthood Regina, 1162
Planned Parenthood Waterloo Region, 1162
Serena Canada, 1290
Sexual Health Centre for Cumberland County, 1293
Sexual Health Centre Lunenburg County, 1293
Sexual Health Network of Québec Inc., 1293
Sexuality Education Resource Centre Manitoba, 1293
World Organization Ovulation Method Billings Inc., 1466
YWCA of Banff Programs & Services, 1482

Family Therapy
Alberta Association of Marriage & Family Therapy, 24
British Columbia Association for Marriage & Family Therapy, 231
Carizon Family & Community Services, 513
Catholic Family Service of Ottawa, 518
Catholic Family Services of Hamilton, 518
Catholic Family Services of Simcoe County, 519
Catholic Family Services of Toronto, 519
Child & Family Services of Western Manitoba, 558
Community Counselling Centre of Nipissing, 596
Counselling & Support Services of S.D. & G., 636
Family & Children's Services of Lanark, Leeds & Grenville, 702
Family & Community Support Services Association of Alberta, 702
Family Counselling & Support Services for Guelph-Wellington, 702
Family Counselling Centre of Brant, Inc., 703
Family Mediation Canada, 703
Family Service Canada, 704
Family Service Centre of Ottawa-Carleton, 704
Family Service Thames Valley, 704
Family Service Toronto, 704
Family Services York Region (Georgina), 705
Native Child & Family Services of Toronto, 997
Ontario Association for Marriage & Family Therapy, 1061
Peel Family Services, 1147
Québec Association of Marriage & Family Therapy, 1196
Service familial de Sudbury, 1291
Stop Abuse in Families Society, 1350
Thunder Bay Counselling Centre, 1377

Farms & Farming
Alberta Barley Commission, 25
Alberta Conservation Tillage Society II, 31
Alberta Farm Fresh Producers Association, 34
Alberta Farmers' Market Association, 34
American Farmland Trust, 1492
Asparagus Farmers of Ontario, 87
Association des fermières de l'Ontario, 114
Association des jeunes ruraux du Québec, 117
Association québécoise des industries de nutrition animale et céréalière, 173
Canadian Association of Farm Advisors, 314
Canadian Canola Growers Association, 349
Canadian Farm Builders Association, 384
Canadian Farm Writers' Federation, 384
Canadian Forage & Grassland Association, 392
Cercles de fermières du Québec, 537
Christian Farmers Federation of Ontario, 567
Ecological Farmers of Ontario, 672
Egg Farmers of Canada, 681
Farm & Food Care Canada, 705
Farm & Ranch Safety & Health Association, 705
Farm Management Canada, 705
Farm Radio International, 705
Farmers of North America, 705
Farmers of North America Strategic Agriculture Institute, 705
Farmers' Markets of Nova Scotia Cooperative Ltd., 706
Farmers' Markets Ontario, 706
Fédération de l'UPA - Abitibi-Témiscamingue, 709
Fédération de l'UPA de la Beauce, 709
Fédération de l'UPA de la Montérégie, 709
Fédérations de l'UPA de Lévis Bellechasse, Rive Nord, Lotbinière-Mégantic, 731
Foreign Agricultural Resource Management Services, 751
Friends of the Central Experimental Farm, 762
Grain Growers of Canada, 779
Inland Terminal Association of Canada, 838
International Federation of Organic Agriculture Movements, 1548
International Flying Farmers, 1549
Junior Farmers' Association of Ontario, 878
National Farmers Foundation, 993
National Farmers Union, 993
North American Farmers' Direct Marketing Association, Inc., 1579
Ontario Farmland Trust, 1078
Ontario Ginseng Growers Association, 1082
Ontario Greenhouse Vegetable Growers, 1083
Ontario Processing Vegetable Growers, 1097
Provincial Farm Women's Association, 1190
Québec Farmers' Association, 1197
Saskatoon Farmers' Markets, 1265
Union des cultivateurs franco-ontariens, 1406
USC Canada, 1423
Western Canadian Wheat Growers, 1449
Western Grain Elevator Association, 1449
World Ploughing Organization, 1607

Fashion Design
Association of Image Consultants International Canada, 149
Canadian Apparel Federation, 294
Costume Society of Ontario, 632
Ontario Fashion Exhibitors, 1078
Toronto Fashion Incubator, 1384

Fathers
Association des pères gais de Montréal inc., 122
Dads Can, 648
Gay Fathers of Toronto, 768

Fencing
Alberta Fencing Association, 35
British Columbia Fencing Association, 241
Canadian Fencing Federation, 389
Fédération d'escrime du Québec, 708
Fencing - Escrime New Brunswick, 732
Fencing Association of Nova Scotia, 732
Manitoba Fencing Association, 936
Newfoundland & Labrador Fencing Association, 1019
Ontario Fencing Association, 1080
Prince Edward Island Fencing Association, 1174
Saskatchewan Fencing Association, 1265

Fertility & Infertility (Human)
Canadian Fertility & Andrology Society, 389
Infertility Awareness Association of Canada, 836
Infertility Network, 836
Serena Canada, 1290

Fertilizer Industry
Canadian Association of Agri-Retailers, 308
Fertilizer Canada, 732
Fertilizer Safety & Security Council, 733
International Plant Nutrition Institute, 1555

Festivals
Associated Manitoba Arts Festivals, Inc., 89
Bard on the Beach Theatre Society, 196
The Battlefords Music Festival, 200
Caribbean Community Council of Calgary, 512
Carnaval de Québec, 514
Edmonton Heritage Festival Association, 677
Edmonton International Film Festival Society, 678
Edmonton Kiwanis Music Festival, 678
Fédération culturelle acadienne de la Nouvelle-Écosse, 708
Festival d'été de Québec, 733
Festivals & Events Ontario, 733
Festivals et Événements Québec, 733
First Vancouver Theatre Space Society, 739
Folk Arts Council of St Catharines, 742
Greater Vancouver International Film Festival Society, 786
Grey County Kiwanis Festival of Music, 790
Guelph Musicfest, 793
Harbourfront Centre, 803
Inside Out Toronto LGBT Film & Video Festival, 839
Intrepid Theatre Co. Society, 862
Kingston Kiwanis Music Festival, 889
Kitchener-Waterloo Kiwanis Music Festival, 890
Kiwanis Music Festival of Windsor/Essex County, 892
Lakes District Festival Association, 896
Moose Jaw Music Festival, 974
New Westminster Hyack Festival Association, 1015
Oshawa-Whitby Kiwanis Music & Theatre Festival, 1128
Parkland Music Festival, 1142
Peel Music Festival, 1148
Pembroke Kiwanis Music Festival, 1149
Performing Arts BC, 1152
St. John's Kiwanis Music Festival, 1249
Salon du livre de Toronto et Festival des écrivains, 1252
Sault Ste. Marie Music Festival, 1281
Société St-Jean-Baptiste Richelieu-Yamaska, 1325
Svoboda Dance Festival Association, 1358
Toronto International Film Festival Inc., 1385
Vancouver Jewish Film Centre Society, 1427
Vues d'Afriques - Les Journées du cinéma africain et créole, 1439
Yorkton Film Festival, 1474
Yukon Sourdough Rendezvous Society, 1480

Fibromyalgia Syndrome
Association de la fibromyalgie de la Montérégie, 101
Association de la Fibromyalgie des Laurentides, 101
Association de la fibromyalgie région Ile-De-Montréal, 101
Association québécoise de la fibromyalgie, 170
Fibromyalgia Association of Saskatchewan, 733
Fibromyalgia Support Group of Winnipeg, Inc., 733

Subject Index / Field Hockey

MEFM Myalgic Encephalomyelitis & Fibromyalgia Society of British Columbia, 959
National ME/FM Action Network, 995

Field Hockey
Field Hockey Alberta, 734
Field Hockey BC, 734
Field Hockey Canada, 734
Field Hockey Manitoba, 734
Field Hockey Nova Scotia, 734
Field Hockey Ontario, 734
PEI Field Hockey Association, 1148
Saskatchewan Field Hockey Association, 1265

Field Service
Technology Services Industry Association, 1597

Filipino Canadians & the Philippine
Association of Filipino Canadian Accountants, 148
Association of Filipino Canadian Accountants in British Columbia, 148
Canadian-Filipino Association of Yukon, 506
Filipino Association of Nova Scotia, 735
Filipino Canadian Association of London & District, 735
Filipino Canadian Association of Vaughan, 735
Filipino Canadian Catholic Charismatic Prayer Communities, 735
Filipino Canadian Technical Professionals Association of Manitoba, Inc., 735
Filipino Students' Association of Toronto, 735
Forever Young Seniors Society, 752
Markham Federation of Filipino Canadians, 952
Movement for Marriage Enrichment, 978
National Council of Canadian Filipino Associations, 991
National Council of Philippine American Canadian Accountants, 1575
Philippine Association of Manitoba, Inc., 1157
University of the Philippines Alumni Association of Toronto, 1420

Film
Academy of Canadian Cinema & Television, 3
The Actors' Fund of Canada, 7
ACTRA Fraternal Benefit Society, 7
Ajjiit Nunavut Media Association, 20
Alberta Media Production Industries Association, 39
Alliance of Canadian Cinema, Television & Radio Artists, 58
Alliance québécoise des techniciens de l'image et du son, 58
Association des cinémas parallèles du Québec, 109
Association des propriétaires de cinémas du Québec, 126
Association des réalisateurs et réalisatrices du Québec, 127
Association of Canadian Film Craftspeople, 142
Association québécoise de la production médiatique, 170
Association québécoise des critiques de cinéma, 172
The Atlantic Film Festival Association, 184
Atlantic Filmmakers Cooperative, 184
Atlantic Motion Picture Exhibitors Association, 184
Calgary Society of Independent Filmmakers, 274
Canadian Association of Film Distributors & Exporters, 314
Canadian Film Centre, 390
Canadian Film Institute, 390
Canadian Filmmakers Distribution Centre, 390
Canadian Labour International Film Festival, 425
Canadian Media Production Association, 432
Canadian Picture Pioneers, 455
La cinémathèque québécoise, 569
Conseil québécois des arts médiatiques, 620
Creative BC, 639
Cultural Industries Ontario North, 645
Directors Guild of Canada, 657
Documentary Organization of Canada, 660
Edmonton International Film Festival Society, 678
The Factory: Hamilton Media Arts Centre, 700
Fédération internationale des associations de producteurs de films, 1525

Film & Video Arts Society Alberta, 735
Film Studies Association of Canada, 735
FilmOntario, 735
Greater Vancouver International Film Festival Society, 786
The Harold Greenberg Fund, 804
Independent Filmmakers' Co-operative of Ottawa, 832
Independent Media Arts Alliance, 833
Inside Out Toronto LGBT Film & Video Festival, 839
Island Media Arts Co-op, 865
Liaison of Independent Filmmakers of Toronto, 909
Motion Picture Association - Canada, 975
Motion Picture Theatre Association of Alberta, 975
Motion Picture Theatre Association of British Columbia, 975
Motion Picture Theatre Association of Central Canada, 975
Moving Images Distribution, 978
NABET 700 CEP, 987
National Screen Institute - Canada, 996
New Brunswick Filmmakers' Co-op, 1008
North of Superior Film Association, 1031
On Screen Manitoba, 1058
Pacific Cinémathèque Pacifique, 1135
Parlimage CCF, 1143
PAVED Arts, 1146
ReelWorld Film Festival, 1210
St. John's International Women's Film Festival, 1249
Saskatchewan Filmpool Co-operative, 1265
Saskatchewan Motion Picture Industry Association, 1270
Screen Composers Guild of Canada, 1287
Shaw Rocket Fund, 1295
Society of Canadian Cine Amateurs, 1327
Society of Motion Picture & Television Engineers, 1593
Toronto Film Society, 1384
Toronto International Film Festival Inc., 1385
Toronto Jewish Film Society, 1385
Vues d'Afriques - Les Journées du cinéma africain et créole, 1439
Winnipeg Film Group, 1458
Women in Film & Television - Toronto, 1461
Women in Film & Television Alberta, 1461
Women in Film & Television Vancouver, 1461
Writers Guild of Canada, 1468
Yorkton Film Festival, 1474
Yukon Film Society, 1478

Finance
AFOA Canada, 12
Association de planification fiscale et financière, 103
Association des cadres municipaux de Montréal, 108
Association of Women in Finance, 164
Canada Media Fund, 280
Canadian Anti-Money Laundering Institute, 293
Canadian Co-operative Association, 364
Canadian Credit Institute Educational Foundation, 372
Canadian ETF Association, 382
Canadian Finance & Leasing Association, 390
Canadian Institute of Bookkeeping, 414
Canadian Payments Association, 452
Canadian Securities Institute, 469
Canadian Tax Foundation, 492
Canadian Taxpayers Federation, 492
Cercle de la finance internationale de Montréal, 537
Children's Education Funds Inc., 561
Christian Stewardship Services, 568
Co-operatives & Mutuals Canada, 628
Finance Montréal, 735
Financial Executives International Canada, 736
Financial Planning Standards Council, 737
Government Finance Officers Association, 1528
Government Finance Officers Association of British Columbia, 778
International Fiscal Association Canada, 857
Invest Ottawa, 862
National Aboriginal Capital Corporations Association, 988
Northern Finance Association, 1035
Ontario Aboriginal Lands Association, 1058
Responsible Investment Association, 1227

Society of Trust & Estate Practitioners, 1331
Startup Canada, 1348
Western Finance Association, 1602
Women in Capital Markets, 1460

Financial Services Industry
Advocis, 11
Association CFA Montréal, 96
Association for Financial Professionals, 1508
Association for Financial Professionals - Calgary, 133
Association for Financial Professionals - Edmonton, 133
Association for Financial Professionals - Ottawa, 133
Association for Financial Professionals - Vancouver, 133
Association of Canadian Compliance Professionals, 141
ATM Industry Association Canada Region, 187
Buy-Side Investment Management Association, 267
Canadian Acquirer's Association, 287
Canadian Association of Financial Institutions in Insurance, 314
Canadian Association of Income Trusts Investors, 318
Canadian Association of Student Financial Aid Administrators, 334
Canadian Bond Investors' Association, 345
Canadian Capital Markets Association, 349
Canadian ETF Association, 382
Canadian Institute of Financial Planners, 415
Canadian Paper Money Society, 449
Canadian Payday Loan Association, 452
CFA Society Calgary, 538
CFA Society Toronto, 538
CFA Society Vancouver, 539
CFA Society Winnipeg, 539
Chartered Institute of Public Finance & Accountancy, 1516
Consolidated Credit Counseling Services of Canada, Inc., 623
Credit Institute of Canada, 640
Edmonton CFA Society, 675
Federation of Mutual Fund Dealers, 725
Financial Management Institute of Canada, 737
Financial Markets Association of Canada, 737
Financial Planning Association, 737
Financial Planning Standards Council, 737
GAMA International Canada, 766
Institut québécois de planification financière, 843
Institute of Professional Bookkeepers of Canada, 847
International Financial Centre of Montréal, 857
Investment Funds Institute of Canada, 862
Joint Forum of Financial Market Regulators, 875
Mutual Fund Dealers Association of Canada, 986
Northern Finance Association, 1035
Ontario Association of Credit Counselling Services, 1063
Ontario Association of Student Financial Aid Administrators, 1066
Portfolio Management Association of Canada, 1167
Private Capital Markets Association of Canada, 1180
Registered Deposit Brokers Association, 1213
Service budgétaire et communautaire de Chicoutimi inc, 1291
Society of Actuaries, 1592
Toronto Financial Services Alliance, 1384
Treasury Management Association of Canada - Toronto, 1396

Finnish Canadians
Canada-Finland Chamber of Commerce, 283
Finnish Canadian Cultural Federation, 737
Finnish Canadian Rest Home Association, 738
Toronto Finnish-Canadian Seniors Centre, 1384

Fire Fighting
Aboriginal Firefighters Association of Canada, 2
Alberta Fire Chiefs Association, 35
Association des chefs en sécurité incendie du Québec, 108
Association des pompiers de Laval, 124
Association des Pompiers de Montréal inc., 124
Canadian Association of Fire Chiefs, 315
Canadian Fallen Firefighters Foundation, 383

Edmonton Fire Fighters Union, 677
Fédération Québécoise des Intervenants en Sécurité Incendie, 728
Fire Fighters Historical Society of Winnipeg, Inc., 738
Firefighters Burn Fund Inc., 738
Halifax Professional Fire Fighters Association, 799
International Association of Fire Fighters (AFL-CIO/CLC), 1538
Manitoba Association of Fire Chiefs, 929
Maritime Fire Chiefs' Association, 950
Ontario Association of Fire Chiefs, 1063
Ontario Fire Buff Associates, 1080
Ontario Professional Fire Fighters Association, 1097
Prince Rupert Fire Museum Society, 1179
Saskatchewan Professional Fire Fighters Burn Unit Fund, 1272
Toronto Professional Fire Fighters Association, 1386

Fire Prevention Equipment Industry
Canadian Automatic Sprinkler Association, 338
Canadian Fire Alarm Association, 390

Fire Protection & Prevention
Canadian Fire Safety Association, 390
Council of Canadian Fire Marshals & Fire Commissioners, 633
Fire Prevention Canada, 738
Ontario Industrial Fire Protection Association, 1087
Society of Fire Protection Engineers, 1593
Underwriters' Laboratories of Canada, 1404
World Safety Organization, 1607

Firearms
British Columbia Rifle Association, 251
British Columbia Target Sports Association, 255
Buckskinners Muzzleloading Association, Limited, 261
Canada's National Firearms Association, 282
Coalition for Gun Control, 578
Dominion of Canada Rifle Association, 660
Fédération québécoise de tir, 728
Lloydminster & District Fish & Game Association, 915
Ontario Arms Collectors' Association, 1060
Ontario Muzzle Loading Association, 1093
Prince Edward Island Rifle Association, 1176
Shooting Federation of Canada, 1297

First Aid
Advanced Coronary Treatment (ACT) Foundation of Canada, 10
Care Institute of Safety & Health Inc., 511
Corporation des services d'ambulance du Québec, 630
Occupational First Aid Attendants Association of British Columbia, 1054
St. John Ambulance, 1248

Fish
Association of Fish & Wildlife Agencies, 1511
Canadian Sablefish Association, 468
East Coast Aquarium Society, 668
Eskasoni Fish & Wildlife Commission, 695
Groundfish Enterprise Allocation Council, 790
North Pacific Anadromous Fish Commission, 1031
Ontario Commercial Fisheries' Association, 1073

Fish & Game
Aiviq Hunters & Trappers Organization, 20
Alberta Fish & Game Association, 35
Association chasse et pêche du Lac Brébeuf, 96
Association de chasse et pêche nordique, inc., 100
Castor Fish & Game Association, 517
Eskasoni Fish & Wildlife Commission, 695
Fort Saskatchewan Fish & Game Association, 754
Fredericton Fish & Game Association, 759
Hussar Fish & Game Association, 828
Irma Fish & Game Association, 864
Lethbridge Fish & Game Association, 908
Lloydminster & District Fish & Game Association, 915
Medicine Hat Fish & Game Association, 958

Mittimatalik Hunters' & Trappers' Organization, 970
Newfoundland & Labrador Outfitters Association, 1020
Nova Scotia Swordfish Association, 1049
Rimbey Fish & Game Association, 1232
St. Albert Fish & Game Association, 1248
Salmon Preservation Association for the Waters of Newfoundland, 1252
Saskatchewan Outfitters Association, 1271
Sherwood Park Fish & Game Association, 1296
Vulcan & District Fish & Game Club, 1439
Whitecourt Fish & Game Association, 1452
Yukon Fish & Game Association, 1478

Fisheries
American Fisheries Society, 1493
Association coopérative des pêcheurs de l'île Itée, 98
Association des capitaines propriétaires de Gaspésie inc, 108
Association québécoise de l'industrie de la pêche, 170
Atlantic Fishing Industry Alliance, 184
Atlantic Salmon Federation, 186
British Columbia Seafood Alliance, 241
Canadian Association of Prawn Producers, 328
Canadian Council of Professional Fish Harvesters, 369
Council of the Haida Nation - Haida Fisheries Program, 635
Fish Harvesters Resource Centres, 739
Fisheries Council of Canada, 739
Freshwater Fisheries Society of British Columbia, 760
International Coalition of Fisheries Associations, 1542
International Commission for the Conservation of Atlantic Tunas, 1542
International Institute of Fisheries Economics & Trade, 1551
North Pacific Cannery - National Historic Site, 1032
Northwest Atlantic Fisheries Organization, 1036
Nova Scotia Fish Packers Association, 1044
Nova Scotia Mackerel Fishermen's Association, 1047
Nova Scotia Salmon Association, 1048
Nova Scotia Swordfish Association, 1049
Oceana Canada, 1054
Pacific Urchin Harvesters Association, 1136
Snow Crab Fishermans Inc., 1305

Fisheries Science
Alberta Aquaculture Association, 22
American Fisheries Society, 1493
Aquaculture Association of Nova Scotia, 75
Canadian Centre for Fisheries Innovation, 353
Fédération québécoise pour le saumon atlantique, 731
Fishermen & Scientists Research Society, 740
Guysborough County Inshore Fishermen's Association, 795
World Aquaculture Society, 1603

Fishermen
Association coopérative des pêcheurs de l'île Itée, 98
Association des capitaines propriétaires de Gaspésie inc, 108
Eastern Fishermen's Federation, 670
Eastern Shore Fisherman's Protective Association, 670
Eskasoni Fish & Wildlife Commission, 695
Fish, Food & Allied Workers, 739
Fishermen & Scientists Research Society, 740
Grand Manan Fishermen's Association, 779
Maritime Fishermen's Union (CLC), 950
Native Fishing Association, 998
Northern Native Fishing Corporation, 1035
PEI Shellfish Association, 1149
Prince Edward Island Fishermen's Association Ltd., 1174
Scotia Fundy Mobile Gear Fishermen's Association, 1286
Snow Crab Fishermans Inc., 1305

Fishing & Angling
Association de la Rivière Ste-Marguerite Inc., 102
Association des Pêcheurs de Longueuil, 122

Barrow Bay & District Sports Fishing Association, 197
Big Salmon River Anglers Association, 210
British Columbia Fishing Resorts & Outfitters Association, 241
Canadian Association of Smallmouth Anglers, 333
Canadian Casting Federation, 350
Cape Breton Island Wildlife Association, 509
Edmonton Trout Fishing Club, 679
Galiano Rod & Gun Club, 766
Guide Outfitters Association of British Columbia, 793
Guysborough County Inshore Fishermen's Association, 795
Lunenburg County Wildlife Association, 921
New Brunswick Outfitters Association Inc., 1011
New Brunswick Sportfishing Association, 1013
Ontario Federation of Anglers & Hunters, 1079
Ontario Fly & Bait Casting Association, 1080
Ontario Sportfishing Guides' Association, 1108
Toronto Sportsmen's Association, 1387
Women That Hunt, 1461

Flags
Canadian Flag Association, 391

Flax
Flax Council of Canada, 740

Floor Covering Industry
Alberta Floor Covering Association, 35
Atlantic Floor Covering Association, 184
British Columbia Floor Covering Association, 241
Canadian Carpet Institute, 350
Canadian Flooring, Cleaning & Restoration Association, 391
Fédération québécoise des revêtements de sol, 729
Fédération québécoise des revêtements de sol, 729
National Floor Covering Association, 993
Resilient Flooring Contractors Association of Ontario, 1226
Terrazzo Tile & Marble Association of Canada, 1371

Flowers
African Violet Society of Canada, 13
Aldergrove Daylily Society, 53
American Rhododendron Society, 1497
British Columbia Fuchsia & Begonia Society, 242
Canadian Hemerocallis Society, 404
Canadian Iris Society, 422
Canadian Peony Society, 453
Canadian Rose Society, 468
Central Ontario Orchid Society, 525
Eastern Canada Orchid Society, 670
Fédération interdisciplinaire de l'horticulture ornementale du Québec, 721
FloraQuebeca, 741
Flowers Canada, 741
Flowers Canada Growers, 741
The Garden Clubs of Ontario, 766
Greater Toronto Rose & Garden Horticultural Society, 786
International Lilac Society, 1552
Manitoba Regional Lily Society, 943
North American Native Plant Society, 1029
Nova Scotia Daylily Society, 1043
Nova Scotia Wild Flora Society, 1050
Ontario Daylily Society, 1076
Ontario Delphinium Club, 1076
The Ontario Greenhouse Alliance, 1083
Ottawa Orchid Society, 1131
Société québécoise des hostas et des hémérocalles, 1324
Société québécoise du dahlia, 1324
Southern Ontario Orchid Society, 1338
Victoria Orchid Society, 1433

Folk Arts
Association of Latvian Craftsmen in Canada, 150
Canadian Celtic Arts Association, 353
Canadian Quilters' Association, 464
Casa do Benfica, 516
Community Folk Art Council of Toronto, 597
Fogo Island Folk Alliance, 742
Folk Arts Council of St Catharines, 742
Folklorama, 742

Georgian Bay Folk Society, 771
Newfoundland & Labrador Folk Arts Society, 1019

Folk Dancing
Alberta Square & Round Dance Federation, 48
Alberta Ukrainian Dance Association, 50
Amethyst Scottish Dancers of Nova Scotia, 67
Antigonish Highland Society, 72
Border Boosters Square & Round Dance Association, 218
British Columbia Square & Round Dance Federation, 255
Canadian Square & Round Dance Society, 490
Federation of Dance Clubs of New Brunswick, 723
Federation of Newfoundland & Labrador Square Dance, 725
Fraser Valley Square & Round Dance Association, 758
Manitoba Square & Round Dance Federation, 945
Ontario Folk Dance Association, 1080
Ontario Square & Round Dance Federation, 1108
Polanie-Polish Song & Dance Association, 1163
Prince Edward Island Square & Round Dance Clubs, 1177
The Royal Scottish Country Dance Society, 1587
Saskatchewan Square & Round Dance Federation, 1276
Square & Round Dance Federation of Nova Scotia, 1346
Toronto & District Square & Round Dance Association, 1381

Folk Music
Alberta Ukrainian Dance Association, 50
Calgary Folk Club, 272
Canadian Society for Traditional Music, 479
Canmore Folk & Blues Club, 508
Edmonton Folk Music Festival, 677
Folk Festival Society of Calgary, 742
Georgian Bay Folk Society, 771
Mariposa Folk Foundation, 950
Polanie-Polish Song & Dance Association, 1163

Folklore
Association Québécoise des Loisirs Folkloriques, 173
British Columbia Folklore Society, 241
Canadian Nautical Research Society, 440
Centre franco-ontarien de folklore, 534
Folklore Canada International, 742
Folklore Studies Association of Canada, 742
Institute for Folklore Studies in Britain & Canada, 1532
The Pennsylvania German Folklore Society of Ontario, 1149
Saskatchewan History & Folklore Society Inc., 1267

Food Banks
Abbotsford Food Bank & Christmas Bureau, 1
Agape Food Bank, 14
Agassiz-Harrison Community Services, 14
Airdrie Food Bank, 20
Ashcroft & Area Food Bank, 86
Atelier RADO Inc., 180
Banff Food Bank Association, 195
Les banques alimentaires du Québec, 196
Barriere & District Food Bank Society, 197
Beaverlodge Food Bank, 203
Berwick Food Bank, 206
Bon Accord/Gibbons Food Bank, 217
Bouffe pour tous/Moisson Longueuil, 218
Bow Valley Food Bank, 219
Boyle Food Bank Association, 221
Calgary Food Bank, 272
Cambridge Self-Help Food Bank, 275
Campbell River & District Food Bank, 276
Camrose & District Food Bank, 277
Central Okanagan Community Food Bank, 524
Chemainus Harvest House Society Food Bank, 555
Clearwater & District Food Bank Society, 573
Comité de bénévolat de Rogersville, 591
Community Food Sharing Association, 597
Community Kitchen Program of Calgary, 599
Comox Valley Food Bank Society, 608
Cowichan Valley Basket Society, 637

Cranbrook Food Bank Society, 638
Daily Bread Food Bank, 648
East Wellington Community Services, 669
Eastern Shore Volunteer Food Bank, 671
Eden Community Food Bank, 674
Edmonton's Food Bank, 680
Feed Nova Scotia, 731
Food Bank of Waterloo Region, 749
Food Banks Alberta Association, 749
Food Banks Canada, 749
Food Depot Alimentaire, Inc., 749
Food for Life Canada, 749
Foodshare Toronto, 750
Fort York Food Bank, 754
Gananoque Food Bank, 766
Glace Bay Food Bank Society, 774
Gleaners Food Bank, 774
Golden Food Bank, 776
Goldstream Food Bank Society, 777
Grande Prairie Food Bank, 781
Greater Vancouver Food Bank Society, 786
Greniers de Joseph, 789
Guelph Food Bank, 793
Hamilton Food Share, 801
Hampton Food Basket & Clothing Centre Inc., 802
Hope Food Bank, 821
Hornby Island Food Bank, 821
Humanity First Canada, 827
Inner City Home of Sudbury, 839
Interfaith Food Bank Society of Lethbridge, 852
Kamloops Foodbank & Outreach Society, 880
Kent County Community Volunteer Action Organization, 884
Kimberley Helping Hands Food Bank, 887
Kitimat Food Bank, 891
Ladysmith Food Bank, 895
Lake Country Food Assistance Society, 895
Lanark County Food Bank, 897
Langley & Aldergrove Food Bank, 898
Langley District Help Network, 899
Leduc & District Food Bank Association, 906
Lethbridge Soup Kitchen Association, 908
Lighthouse Food Bank Society, 912
Lillooet Food Bank, 912
Loaves & Fishes Community Food Bank, 916
London Food Bank, 918
Lytton Community Food Bank, 923
Medicine Hat & District Food Bank, 958
Mission Community Services Food Centre, 969
Mississauga Food Bank, 970
Moisson Laurentides, 971
Moisson Mauricie/Centre-du-Québec, 971
Moisson Québec, 971
Moose Jaw & District Food Bank, 973
Mustard Seed Food Bank, 986
New Brunswick Association of Food Banks, 1005
Nicola Valley & District Food Bank, 1026
North Bay Food Bank, 1030
North York Harvest Food Bank, 1033
Oliver Food Bank, 1057
100 Mile House Food Bank Society, 1058
Ontario Association of Food Banks, 1064
Operation Harvest Sharing, 1115
Oromocto & Surrounding Area Food & Clothing Bank, 1127
Osoyoos Food Bank, 1128
Ottawa Food Bank, 1130
Parkland Food Bank, 1142
Peachland Food Bank, 1147
PEDVAC Foundation, 1147
Picton United Church County Food Bank, 1159
Ponoka Food Bank, 1164
Port Hardy Harvest Food Bank, 1166
Project Chance, 1187
Project Share, 1188
Quadra Island Food Bank, 1195
Red Deer Food Bank Society, 1209
Regina & District Food Bank Inc., 1211
Renfrew & District Food Bank, 1217
Revelstoke Community Connections Food Bank, 1228
Richmond Food Bank Society, 1230
Saint John Community Food Basket, 1246
Saint John East Food Bank Inc., 1246
Salmo Community Resource Society, 1251
Salmon Arm - Salvation Army Food Bank, 1252
Salt Spring Community Centre Food Bank, 1252

Subject Index / Food Industry

Salvation Army Mt. Arrowsmith Community Ministries - Food Bank, 1253
Saskatoon Food Bank & Learning Centre, 1279
School Lunch Association, 1284
Second Harvest, 1288
The Sharing Place - Orillia & District Food Bank, 1294
Sidney Lions Food Bank, 1298
Sooke Food Bank Society, 1333
South Delta Food Bank, 1334
Southern Kings & Queens Food Bank Inc., 1338
Squamish Food Bank, 1346
The Stop Community Food Centre, 1350
Strathcona Food Bank, 1351
Summerland Food Bank & Resource Centre, 1354
Surrey Food Bank, 1357
Sussex Sharing Club, 1357
Trenton Care & Share Food Bank, 1397
Vernon BC Food Bank, 1431
Whistler Food Bank, 1452
Winnipeg Harvest Inc., 1459
Wood Buffalo Food Bank, 1463
Yarmouth Food Bank Society, 1470

Food Industry
Alberta Food Processors Association, 35
Association des détaillants en alimentation du Québec, 110
Atlantic Food & Beverage Processors Association, 184
Breakfast Cereals Canada, 227
British Columbia Restaurant & Foodservices Association, 251
CanadaGAP, 283
Canadian Association for Food Studies, 300
Canadian Association of Foodservice Professionals, 315
Canadian Food Exporters Association, 391
Canadian Pasta Manufacturers Association, 451
Canadian Snack Food Association, 472
Conseil de la transformation agroalimentaire et des produits de consommation, 616
Farm & Food Care Canada, 705
Flavour Manufacturers Association of Canada, 740
Food & Consumer Products of Canada, 749
Food Beverage Canada, 749
Food Processors of Canada, 750
Foodservice & Packaging Institute, 1526
Foodservice Consultants Society International - Canadian Chapter, 750
International Alliance of Dietary/Food Supplement Associations, 1535
Manitoba Food Processors Association, 936
Manitoba Restaurant & Food Services Association, 943
Ontario Agri-Food Education Inc., 1059
Ontario Food Protection Association, 1080
Provision Coalition, 1191
Raspberry Industry Development Council, 1204
Restaurants Canada, 1227
Saskatchewan Food Processors Association, 1265
Taste of Nova Scotia, 1367
United Food & Commercial Workers' International Union, 1599
Women in Food Industry Management, 1461

Food Science
British Columbia Food Technolgists, 241
Canadian Foundation for Dietetic Research, 393
Canadian Institute of Food Science & Technology, 415
Canadian Meat Science Association, 432
Canadian Partnership for Consumer Food Safety Education, 451
Canadian Supply Chain Food Safety Coalition, 491
Fondation Initia, 746
Institute of Food Technologists, 1532
International Commission of Agricultural & Biosystems Engineering, 1542
International Union of Food Science & Technology, 861

Football
Alberta Amateur Football Association, 22
Association régionale de football Laurentides Lanaudière, 177

Canadian Football Hall of Fame & Museum, 391
Canadian Football League, 392
Canadian Football League Alumni Association, 392
Canadian Football League Players' Association, 392
Canadian Football Officials Association, 392
Canadian Junior Football League, 423
Canadian University Football Coaches Association, 499
Football BC, 750
Football Canada, 750
Football Nova Scotia Association, 750
Football PEI, 750
Football Québec, 750
Ontario Football Alliance, 1080
Thunder Bay Minor Football Association, 1378
Touch Football Ontario, 1388

Footwear
Shoe Manufacturers' Association of Canada, 1296
Two/Ten Charity Trust of Canada Inc., 1401

Foreign Aid
Adventist Development & Relief Agency Canada, 10
Armenian Relief Society of Canada, Inc., 83
Canadian Lutheran World Relief, 428
Hope for the Nations, 821
Intercede International, 851
International Relief Agency Inc., 859
Save the Children Canada, 1281
Vides Canada, 1434

Forensic Science
Canadian Society of Forensic Science, 483

Forest Industries
Alberta Forest Products Association, 35
American Forest & Paper Association, 1493
Canadian Council of Forest Ministers, 368
The Canadian Woodlands Forum, 505
Central British Columbia Railway & Forest Industry Museum Society, 524
Conseil de l'industrie forestière du Québec, 615
Council of Forest Industries, 633
Fédération des producteurs forestiers du Québec, 717
Forest Nova Scotia, 751
Forest Products Association of Canada, 751
New Brunswick Forest Products Association Inc., 1008
Ontario Forest Industries Association, 1081

Forestry
Alberta Forest Products Association, 35
Association forestières du sud du Québec, 135
Association of British Columbia Forest Professionals, 140
Association of Registered Professional Foresters of New Brunswick, 161
Association of Saskatchewan Forestry Professionals, 161
Association of University Forestry Schools of Canada, 163
Canadian Council of Forest Ministers, 368
Canadian Forestry Accreditation Board, 392
Canadian Forestry Association, 392
Canadian Forestry Association of New Brunswick, 392
Canadian Institute of Forestry, 416
Canadian Institute of Forestry, Newfoundland & Labrador, 416
Carleton-Victoria Forest Products Marketing Board & Wood Producers Association, 513
College of Alberta Professional Foresters, 582
Commonwealth Forestry Association - Canadian Chapter, 593
Earthroots, 667
Eastern Ontario Model Forest, 670
Ecoforestry Institute Society, 671
Fédération québécoise des coopératives forestières, 728
Foothills Research Institute, 751
Forest Nova Scotia, 751
Forests Ontario, 751
FPInnovations, 756
Friends of the Forestry Farm House Inc., 762
Fundy Model Forest Network, 764
International Union of Forest Research Organizations, 1564
Lake Abitibi Model Forest, 895

Madawaska Forest Products Marketing Board, 924
Manitoba Forestry Association Inc., 937
Manitoba Model Forest, 940
McGregor Model Forest, 955
Model Forest of Newfoundland & Labrador, 971
National Aboriginal Forestry Association, 988
North Shore Forest Products Marketing Board, 1032
Nova Forest Alliance, 1040
Nova Scotia Forest Technicians Association, 1045
Nova Scotia Forestry Association, 1045
Ontario Professional Foresters Association, 1097
Ordre des ingénieurs forestiers du Québec, 1123
Poplar Council of Canada, 1165
Prince Albert Model Forest Association Inc., 1171
Prince Edward Island Forest Improvement Association, 1174
Prince Edward Island Forestry Training Corp., 1174
Rainforest Action Network, 1586
Registered Professional Foresters Association of Nova Scotia, 1214
Resource Industry Suppliers Association, 1227
Saskatchewan Forestry Association, 1265
Sustainable Forestry Initiative Inc., 1597
Trees Winnipeg, 1397
Waswanipi Cree Model Forest, 1440
Western Boreal Growth & Yield Association, 1447
Western Forestry Contractors Association, 1449
World Agroforestry Centre, 1602

Foster Parents
Alberta Foster Parent Association, 35
British Columbia Federation of Foster Parent Associations, 240
British Columbia Federation of Foster Parent Associations, 240
Federation of Aboriginal Foster Parents, 722
Federation of Foster Families of Nova Scotia, 724
Foster Parents Association of Ottawa, 755
International Foster Care Organisation, 1549
Plan Canada, 1161
Prince Edward Island Federation of Foster Families, 1174

Foundations
ABC Life Literacy Canada, 1
Active Healthy Kids Canada, 7
Acupuncture Canada, 7
Adam Mickiewicz Foundation of Canada, 7
Addictions Foundation of Manitoba, 8
ADR Institute of Canada, 9
Advanced Coronary Treatment (ACT) Foundation of Canada, 10
Aerospace Heritage Foundation of Canada, 11
African Medical & Research Foundation Canada, 13
African Wildlife Foundation, 1486
Aga Khan Foundation Canada, 14
Agricultural Institute of Canada Foundation, 15
The AIDS Foundation of Canada, 17
Air Canada Foundation, 19
Alberta Cancer Foundation, 27
Alberta Children's Hospital Foundation, 28
Alberta Diabetes Foundation, 32
Alberta Ecotrust Foundation, 33
Alberta Foundation for the Arts, 35
Alberta Historical Resources Foundation, 37
Alberta Innovates, 38
Alberta Law Foundation, 39
Alcoholic Beverage Medical Research Foundation, 1486
Allen & Milli Gould Family Foundation, 54
Allstate Foundation of Canada, 59
Almas Jiwani Foundation, 59
Alva Foundation, 61
Amma Foundation of Canada, 68
Anglican Foundation of Canada, 70
Animal Aid Foundation, 70
Animal Welfare Foundation of Canada, 71
Arthritis Research Foundation, 84
Asper Foundation, 87
Atkinson Charitable Foundation, 182
Au Coup de pouce Centre-Sud inc., 187
Ausable Bayfield Conservation Foundation, 188

The Avian Preservation Foundation, 190
Azrieli Foundation, 191
Baby's Breath, 192
Banff World Television Festival Foundation, 196
The Barnard-Boecker Centre Foundation, 196
Baycrest Foundation, 200
Bechtel Foundation of Canada, 203
The Belinda Stronach Foundation, 204
Bibles for Missions Foundation, 208
Birks Family Foundation, 212
Blue Mountain Foundation for the Arts, 215
Bonavista Historic Townscape Foundation, 217
Boys & Girls Clubs of Canada Foundation, 222
Brain Tumour Foundation of Canada, 225
Branscombe Family Foundation, 226
Brantwood Foundation, 227
Breakfast for Learning, 227
Brian Bronfman Family Foundation, 228
British Columbia Cancer Foundation, 234
British Columbia Conservation Foundation, 237
British Columbia Neurofibromatosis Foundation, 247
British Columbia's Children's Hospital Foundation, 259
Burgess Shale Geoscience Foundation, 265
Butler Family Foundation, 267
Calgary Children's Foundation, 271
The Calgary Foundation, 272
Cameco Capitol Arts Centre, 276
CAMH Foundation, 276
Canada Foundation for Innovation, 279
Canada West Foundation, 281
Canada-Israel Cultural Foundation, 283
Canadian Alopecia Areata Foundation, 292
The Canadian Art Foundation, 295
Canadian Association of Foundations of Education, 315
Canadian Athletes Now Fund, 337
Canadian Battlefields Foundation, 342
Canadian Children's Optimist Foundation, 356
Canadian Chiropractic Research Foundation, 356
The Canadian Continence Foundation, 364
Canadian Credit Institute Educational Foundation, 372
Canadian Digestive Health Foundation, 378
Canadian Fallen Firefighters Foundation, 383
Canadian Foundation for AIDS Research, 392
Canadian Foundation for Climate & Atmospheric Sciences, 393
Canadian Foundation for Masorti Judaism, 393
Canadian Foundation for Pharmacy, 393
Canadian Foundation for Ukrainian Studies, 394
Canadian Group Psychotherapy Association, 399
Canadian Institute for the Relief of Pain & Disability, 413
Canadian Kennel Club Foundation, 424
Canadian Liver Foundation, 427
Canadian Lyme Disease Foundation, 428
Canadian Medical Foundation, 434
Canadian MedicAlert Foundation, 434
Canadian Melanoma Foundation, 434
Canadian National Autism Foundation, 438
Canadian Nurses Foundation, 443
Canadian Occupational Therapy Foundation, 444
Canadian Ornamental Plant Foundation, 448
Canadian Orthopaedic Foundation, 448
Canadian Polish Foundation, 457
Canadian Porphyria Foundation Inc., 458
Canadian Progress Charitable Foundation, 460
Canadian Race Relations Foundation, 464
Canadian Scholarship Trust Foundation, 468
Canadian Securities Institute Research Foundation, 469
Canadian Social Work Foundation, 472
Canadian Women's Foundation, 505
Canadian Writers' Foundation Inc., 506
Canadian-Scandinavian Foundation, 507
Cape Breton Regional Hospital Foundation, 509
Carthy Foundation, 516
Catherine Donnelly Foundation, 517
Catholic Centre for Immigrants - Ottawa + CIC Foundation, 517
Catholic Education Foundation of Ontario, 518
The Catholic Foundation of Manitoba, 519
Central Okanagan Foundation, 525
Cerebral Palsy Foundation (St. John) Inc., 538
C.G. Jung Foundation of Ontario, 539
Chai-Tikvah The Life & Hope Foundation, 539

Subject Index / Foundations

Chartered Accountants' Education Foundation of Alberta, 552
Chawkers Foundation, 555
CHILD Foundation, 560
The Children's Aid Foundation of York Region, 560
Children's Health Foundations, 561
Children's Hospital Foundation of Manitoba, 562
Children's Hospital Foundation of Saskatchewan, 562
Children's Hospital of Eastern Ontario Foundation, 562
Children's Tumor Foundation, 1516
Children's Wish Foundation of Canada, 562
Chinook Regional Hospital Foundation, 565
Chris Spencer Foundation, 566
Clean Nova Scotia Foundation, 573
Coast Foundation Society, 579
Coastal Ecosystems Research Foundation, 579
Coffin-Lowry Syndrome Foundation, 1518
Colchester Community Workshops Foundation, 580
Colchester-East Hants Public Library Foundation, 580
Cole Foundation, 581
Colin B. Glassco Charitable Foundation for Children, 581
Community Foundation for Kingston & Area, 597
The Community Foundation of Durham Region, 597
Community Foundation of Lethbridge & Southwestern Alberta, 597
Community Foundation of Nova Scotia, 597
Community Foundation of Ottawa, 597
Community Foundation of Prince Edward Island, 598
Community Foundations of Canada, 598
Conservation Foundation of Greater Toronto, 622
Conservation Halton Foundation, 622
CP24 CHUM Christmas Wish, 638
Cranbrook Archives, Museum & Landmark Foundation, 638
Credit Valley Conservation Foundation, 641
Crohn's & Colitis Canada, 642
Cystic Fibrosis Canada, 647
Dalhousie Medical Research Foundation, 648
David Foster Foundation, 651
David Suzuki Foundation, 651
Donner Canadian Foundation, 661
Down Syndrome Research Foundation, 661
Dr. H. Bliss Murphy Cancer Care Foundation, 662
Dr. James Naismith Basketball Foundation, 662
Dreams Take Flight, 662
Drummond Foundation, 663
Dystonia Medical Research Foundation Canada, 665
East Georgian Bay Historical Foundation, 668
Easter Seals Nova Scotia, 669
Eastern Kings Health Research Foundation Inc., 670
The Eckhardt-Gramatté Foundation, 671
Ecotrust Canada, 673
Edith Lando Charitable Foundation, 674
Edmonton Community Foundation, 676
Edmonton Space & Science Foundation, 679
The EJLB Foundation, 681
Eldee Foundation, 685
Energy Probe Research Foundation, 688
Epilepsy Foundation of America, 1524
Equitas - International Centre for Human Rights Education, 695
Ernest C. Manning Awards Foundation, 695
Evergreen, 699
The Farha Foundation, 705
Farm & Food Care Canada, 705
Fondation Alfred Dallaire, 742
Fondation Caritas-Sherbrooke inc., 743
Fondation Centre de cancérologie Charles-Bruneau, 743
Fondation CHU de Québec, 743
Fondation CHU Dumont Foundation, 743
Fondation CHU Sainte-Justine, 743
Fondation de l'Hôpital de Montréal pour enfants, 744
Fondation de l'Hôpital du Sacré-Coeur de Montréal, 744
Fondation de l'Hôpital Général de Montréal, 744
Fondation de l'Hôpital Maisonneuve-Rosemont, 744

Fondation de la banque d'yeux du Québec inc., 744
Fondation des aveugles du Québec, 744
Fondation des étoiles, 744
Fondation des maladies du coeur du Québec, 745
Fondation des maladies mentales, 745
Fondation des pompiers du Québec pour les grands brûlés, 745
Fondation Desjardins, 745
Fondation Diane Hébert Inc, 745
Fondation du barreau du Québec, 745
Fondation du CHUM, 745
Fondation Dufresne et Gauthier, 746
Fondation Edward Assh, 746
Fondation franco-ontarienne, 746
Fondation Hôpital Charles-LeMoyne, 746
Fondation Hydro-Québec pour l'environnement, 746
Fondation Initia, 746
Fondation Institut de Cardiologie de Montréal, 746
Fondation Jeanne-Crevier, 746
Fondation Lionel-Groulx, 747
Fondation Lucie et André Chagnon, 747
Fondation Marie-Ève Saulnier, 747
Fondation Père-Ménard, 747
Fondation québécoise de la déficience intellectuelle, 747
Fondation québécoise de la maladie coeliaque, 747
Fondation québécoise en environnement, 748
Fondation Ressources-Jeunesse, 748
Fondation Richelieu International, 748
Fondation Santé Gatineau, 748
Fondation Tourisme Jeunesse, 748
Fort Edmonton Foundation, 752
Foundation Assisting Canadian Talent on Recordings, 755
The Foundation Fighting Blindness, 755
Foundation for Advancing Family Medicine of the College of Family Physicians of Canada, 755
Foundation for Education Perth Huron, 755
Foundation for Educational Exchange Between Canada & the United States of America, 755
Foundation for International Environmental Law & Development, 1527
Foundation for Legal Research, 755
Foundation for Prader-Willi Research in Canada, 756
Foundation for the Study of Objective Art, 756
Foundation of Greater Montreal, 756
4Cs Foundation, 756
Francofonds inc., 757
Friends of The Moncton Hospital Foundation, 763
Frontiers Foundation, 763
Futurpreneur Canada, 765
Gainey Foundation, 766
The Gairdner Foundation, 766
Genesis Research Foundation, 769
George Cedric Metcalf Charitable Foundation, 770
The Gershon Iskowitz Foundation, 772
GLOBE Foundation, 775
Golf Canada Foundation, 777
Good Foundation Inc., 777
Gordon Foundation, 778
Governor General's Performing Arts Awards Foundation, 778
Graham Boeckh Foundation, 779
Grand River Conservation Foundation, 780
The Great Lakes Marine Heritage Foundation, 782
Gustav Levinschi Foundation, 794
Hal Jackman Foundation, 798
Halifax Foundation, 799
Hamber Foundation, 800
Hamilton Community Foundation, 801
Harmony Foundation of Canada, 803
Harold Crabtree Foundation, 804
The Harold Greenberg Fund, 804
Harry & Martha Cohen Foundation, 804
Harry A. Newman Memorial Foundation, 804
Harry E. Foster Foundation, 804
Health Sciences Centre Foundation, 807
Hearing Foundation of Canada, 808
Heart & Stroke Foundation of British Columbia & Yukon, 808
Heart & Stroke Foundation of Canada, 808

Heart & Stroke Foundation of Manitoba, 808
Heart & Stroke Foundation of New Brunswick, 808
Heart & Stroke Foundation of Newfoundland & Labrador, 809
Heart & Stroke Foundation of Nova Scotia, 809
Heart & Stroke Foundation of Ontario, 809
Heart & Stroke Foundation of Prince Edward Island Inc., 809
Heart & Stroke Foundation of Saskatchewan, 809
Helderleigh Foundation, 811
Help Fill a Dream Foundation of Canada, 812
The Henry White Kinnear Foundation, 812
Heritage Foundation of Newfoundland & Labrador, 813
Hillfield-Strathallan College Foundation, 815
Hockey Canada Foundation, 817
Hospital for Sick Children Foundation, 823
Housing Inspection Foundation, 1530
Hunter Family Foundation, 827
IBD Foundation, 829
I.C.C. Foundation, 829
Independent Production Fund, 833
Indspire, 835
Inspirit Foundation, 840
International Development & Relief Foundation, 856
International Foundation of Employee Benefit Plans, 1549
Inuit Art Foundation, 862
Is Five Foundation, 864
Islamic Foundation of Toronto, 864
Islamic Information Foundation, 864
IWK Health Centre Foundation, 867
J. Armand Bombardier Foundation, 867
J. Douglas Ferguson Historical Research Foundation, 867
Jack Miner Migratory Bird Foundation, Inc., 867
Janeway Children's Hospital Foundation, 868
The Japan Foundation, Toronto, 868
Jerusalem Foundation of Canada Inc, 869
Jewish Community Foundation of Montréal, 871
Jewish Foundation of Manitoba, 872
Jewish General Hospital Foundation, 872
The Joe Brain Foundation, 873
Joubert Syndrome & Related Disoarders Foundation, 1568
Juvenile Diabetes Research Foundation Canada, 878
The J.W. McConnell Family Foundation, 879
Kenneth M Molson Foundation, 883
Kensington Foundation, 883
Kidney Foundation of Canada, 885
Kids Cancer Care Foundation of Alberta, 886
Kids Kottage Foundation, 886
Kin Canada Foundation, 887
Kinsmen Foundation of British Columbia & Yukon, 890
The Kitchener & Waterloo Community Foundation, 890
Laidlaw Foundation, 895
Lake Simcoe Region Conservation Foundation, 896
Law Foundation of British Columbia, 900
Law Foundation of Newfoundland & Labrador, 900
Law Foundation of Nova Scotia, 901
Law Foundation of Ontario, 901
Law Foundation of Prince Edward Island, 901
Law Foundation of Saskatchewan, 901
Lawson Foundation, 902
Learning Enrichment Foundation, 905
The Leon & Thea Koerner Foundation, 907
Lifeforce Foundation, 911
Lions Foundation of Canada, 913
Lions Gate Hospital Foundation, 913
Lithuanian-Canadian Foundation, 915
Lloydminster Region Health Foundation, 916
London Community Foundation, 918
London Health Sciences Foundation, 918
Lo-Se-Ca Foundation, 919
Lupus Foundation of Ontario, 921
Mahatma Gandhi Canadian Foundation for World Peace, 925
Make-A-Wish Canada, 927
The Manitoba Law Foundation, 939
Manitoba Medical Service Foundation Inc., 940
Manitoba Paraplegia Foundation Inc., 942
Margie Gillis Dance Foundation, 949
Mariposa Folk Foundation, 950

Markham Stouffville Hospital Foundation, 952
Marmot Recovery Foundation, 952
Masonic Foundation of Manitoba Inc., 952
Masonic Foundation of Ontario, 952
Max Bell Foundation, 954
Maytree Foundation, 954
McGill University Health Centre Foundation, 955
The McLean Foundation, 955
Meningitis Research Foundation of Canada, 960
Michael Smith Foundation for Health Research, 964
Michaëlle Jean Foundation, 964
MindFuel, 966
Mississauga Heritage Foundation Inc., 970
The Molson Family Foundation, 971
Mon Sheong Foundation, 971
Mount Sinai Hospital Foundation, 976
Mr. & Mrs. P.A. Woodward's Foundation, 978
The M.S.I. Foundation, 978
MuchFACT, 978
Mulgrave Road Theatre Foundation, 978
The Muttart Foundation, 986
Nanaimo Community Foundation, 987
National Alopecia Areata Foundation, 1572
National Arts Centre Foundation, 989
National Farmers Foundation, 993
National Magazine Awards Foundation, 994
National Native Addictions Partnership Foundation, 995
National Press Club of Canada Foundation, 995
National Psoriasis Foundation - USA, 1577
National Trust for Canada, 996
The Neil Squire Foundation, 1002
Neptune Theatre Foundation, 1003
New Brunswick Law Foundation, 1010
Newfoundland Cancer Treatment & Research Foundation, 1023
Newman Centre Catholic Chaplaincy and Parish, 1024
Niagara Peninsula Conservation Authority, 1025
Northwest Territories Law Foundation, 1038
Old Strathcona Foundation, 1056
Ontario Foundation for Visually Impaired Children Inc., 1081
Ontario Mental Health Foundation, 1090
Ontario Neurotrauma Foundation, 1093
The Ontario Trillium Foundation, 1111
The Order of St. Lazarus, 1119
Our Lady of The Prairies Foundation, 1133
Pacific Salmon Foundation, 1136
The Palyul Foundation of Canada, 1137
Pancreatic Cancer Canada Foundation, 1138
Parkinson Society Saskatchewan, 1141
The Paterson Foundation, 1145
PEDVAC Foundation, 1147
Peter Gilgan Foundation, 1153
Phoenix Community Works Foundation, 1157
Physicians Services Inc. Foundation, 1158
Polish-Jewish Heritage Foundation of Canada, 1164
The Pollution Probe Foundation, 1164
Portuguese Canadian Seniors Foundation, 1167
Prairieaction Foundation, 1170
Prince County Hospital Foundation, 1171
Prince Edward Island Museum & Heritage Foundation, 1175
Princess Margaret Cancer Foundation, 1180
Prostate Cancer Canada, 1189
Québec-Labrador Foundation (Canada) Inc., 1199
Queen Elizabeth Hospital Foundation, 1199
Quetico Foundation, 1201
Quidi Vidi Rennie's River Development Foundation, 1201
RBC Foundation, 1204
Red Deer & District Community Foundation, 1209
Reena, 1210
Regional Occupation Centre Foundation, 1212
Richard Ivey Foundation, 1229
Rick Hansen Foundation, 1231
Robert L. Conconi Foundation, 1234
Rocky Mountain Elk Foundation Canada, 1586
Rotary Club of Stratford Charitable Foundation, 1236
Royal University Hospital Foundation, 1243
Saint John Jeux Canada Games Foundation Inc., 1247
St. Andrew's Society of Toronto, 1248

Subject Index / Founding

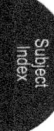

St. Joseph's Healthcare Foundation, 1249
The Sam Sorbara Charitable Foundation, 1253
Sandford Fleming Foundation, 1253
Saskatoon Community Foundation, 1279
Savoy Foundation Inc., 1282
School Milk Foundation of Newfoundland & Labrador, 1284
Scottish Rite Charitable Foundation of Canada, 1286
Scottish Studies Foundation Inc., 1286
Seagull Foundation, 1288
SEEDS Foundation, 1289
Semiahmoo Foundation, 1289
Seva Foundation, 1588
SHARE Agriculture Foundation, 1294
Sikh Foundation of Canada, 1299
Sjogren's Syndrome Foundation Inc., 1589
SkyWorks Charitable Foundation, 1303
Smoking & Health Action Foundation, 1304
Société internationale du réseau ÉCONOMUSÉE et Société ÉCONOMUSÉE du Québec, 1321
Soroptimist Foundation of Canada, 1333
South Saskatchewan Community Foundation Inc., 1336
The Speech & Stuttering Institute, 1340
Starlight Children's Foundation Canada, 1348
Steel Structures Education Foundation, 1349
Sunshine Dreams for Kids, 1355
SUS Foundation of Canada, 1357
The T. R. Meighen Foundation, 1365
Taras H. Shevchenko Museum & Memorial Park Foundation, 1367
TD Friends of the Environment Foundation, 1367
Telemiracle/Kinsmen Foundation Inc., 1369
The Terry Fox Foundation, 1372
Thomas Sill Foundation Inc., 1376
Thunder Bay Community Foundation, 1377
Thyroid Foundation of Canada, 1378
Tides Canada Foundation, 1379
Tim Horton Children's Foundation, 1379
Toronto Arts Foundation, 1381
Toronto Community Foundation, 1383
Toronto General & Western Hospital Foundation, 1385
Toronto Public Library Foundation, 1386
Toronto PWA Foundation, 1386
The Toronto-Calcutta Foundation, 1388
Trans Canada Trail Foundation, 1394
Tree Canada Foundation, 1397
T.R.E.E. Foundation for Youth Development, 1397
The Trident Mediation Counselling & Support Foundation, 1398
Trillium Health Partners Foundation, 1398
True Sport Foundation, 1399
Ukrainian Canadian Foundation of Taras Shevchenko, 1402
United Church of Canada Foundation, 1409
United Mitochondrial Disease Foundation, 1599
United Way of Canada - Centraide Canada, 1413
Vancity Community Foundation, 1424
Vancouver Foundation, 1425
Vernon Jubilee Hospital Foundation, 1431
Victoria Hospitals Foundation, 1432
The W. Garfield Weston Foundation, 1439
Walker Lynch Foundation, 1439
Waterloo Regional Heritage Foundation, 1442
Wellspring Cancer Support Foundation, 1444
West Coast Environmental Law, 1444
West Vancouver Community Foundation, 1447
Western Magazine Awards Foundation, 1450
Winnipeg Foundation, 1459
World Citizen Foundation, 1604
Youth Science Canada, 1476
Yukon Foundation, 1478
Yukon Law Foundation, 1479

Founding
American Foundry Society, 1493
Canadian Foundry Association, 394
Glass, Molders, Pottery, Plastic & Allied Workers International Union (AFL-CIO/CLC), 1528

France
Association France-Québec, 1509
Réseau Québec-France, 1225

Franchises
Canadian Franchise Association, 394
Conseil québécois de la franchise, 620
Great White North Franchisee Association, 782

Francophones in Canada
Alliance des femmes de la francophonie canadienne, 55
Alliance Française, 57
Alliance Française d'Edmonton, 57
Alliance Française d'Ottawa, 57
Alliance Française de Calgary, 57
Alliance Française du Manitoba, 57
Alliance Française Halifax, 57
Assemblée communautaire fransaskoise, 87
Assemblée de la francophonie de l'Ontario, 87
Assemblée parlementaire de la Francophonie, 88
Association canadienne-française de l'Alberta, 96
Association canadienne-française de l'Ontario, Mille-Îles, 96
Association canadienne-française de Régina, 96
L'Association communautaire francophone de St-Jean, 97
Association de parents pour l'adoption québécoise, 103
Association des enseignantes et des enseignants francophones du Nouveau-Brunswick, 112
Association des francophones de Fort Smith, 114
Association des francophones du delta du Mackenzie, 114
Association des francophones du nord-ouest de l'Ontario, 114
Association des francophones du Nunavut, 114
Association des parents ayants droit de Yellowknife, 121
Association des parents fransaskois, 122
Association des professionnels de la chanson et de la musique, 125
Association des théâtres francophones du Canada, 129
Association des universités de la francophonie canadienne, 130
L'Association française des municipalités de l'Ontario, 135
Association franco-culturelle de Hay River, 135
Association franco-culturelle de Yellowknife, 135
Association francophone des parents du Nouveau-Brunswick, 135
Association francophone internationale des directeurs d'établissements scolaires, 1509
Association francophone pour le savoir, 135
Association franco-yukonnaise, 136
Association internationale des maires francophones - Bureau à Québec, 136
Association jeunesse fransaskoise, 137
Association ontarienne des Sourd(e)s francophones, 164
Bureau des regroupements des artistes visuels de l'Ontario, 264
Centre culturel franco-manitobain, 526
Le Centre culturel francophone de Vancouver, 526
Centre franco-ontarien de folklore, 534
Centre franco-ontarien de ressources pédagogiques, 534
Centre francophone de Toronto, 535
Chambre de commerce francophone de Vancouver, 548
Chez les français de L'Anse-à-Canards inc., 557
La Clé d'la Baie en Huronie - Association culturelle francophone, 572
Club canadien de Toronto, 574
Coalition des femmes de l'Alberta, 577
Le Collège du Savoir, 582
Commission nationale des parents francophones, 593
Conseil communautaire en santé du Manitoba, 614
Conseil culturel fransaskois, 614
Conseil des organismes francophones de la région de Durham, 617
Conseil jeunesse francophone de la Colombie-Britannique, 618
Conseil jeunesse provincial (Manitoba), 619
Les EssentiElles, 696
Fédération acadienne de la Nouvelle-Écosse, 707
Fédération culturelle acadienne de la Nouvelle-Écosse, 708
Fédération culturelle canadienne-française, 708
Fédération culturelle de L'Ile-du-Prince-Édouard inc., 708
Fédération de la jeunesse canadienne-française inc., 709
Fédération de la jeunesse franco-ontarienne, 709
Fédération des agriculteurs et agricultrices francophones du Nouveau-Brunswick, 711
Fédération des aînées et aînés francophones du Canada, 711
Fédération des aînés et des retraités francophones de l'Ontario, 711
Fédération des aînés Franco-Albertains, 711
Fédération des aînés franco-manitobains inc., 711
Fédération des aînés fransaskois, 711
Fédération des associations de juristes d'expression française de common law, 712
Fédération des communautés francophones et acadienne du Canada, 713
La Fédération des francophones de la Colombie-Britannique, 715
La Fédération des francophones de Terre-Neuve et du Labrador, 715
Fédération des jeunes francophones du Nouveau-Brunswick Inc., 715
Fédération des parents de l'Ile-du-Prince-Édouard, 716
Fédération des parents francophones de Colombie-Britannique, 716
Fédération des parents francophones de l'Alberta, 717
Fédération des parents francophones de Terre-Neuve et du Labrador, 717
Fédération des scouts de l'Atlantique, 718
Fédération franco-ténoise, 721
Fondation franco-ontarienne, 746
Fondation fransaskoise, 746
Fondation Lionel-Groulx, 747
Franco-Jeunes de Terre-Neuve et du Labrador, 757
Francophonie jeunesse de l'Alberta, 757
French Institute, 1527
Hebdos Québec, 810
L'Institut canadien de Québec, 840
Institut d'histoire de l'Amérique française, 841
Institut féminin francophone du Nouveau-Brunswick, 842
Jeunesse Acadienne et Francophone de l'Île-du-prince-Édouard, 870
Médecins francophones du Canada, 957
Mouvement national des québécoises et québécois, 977
Oasis Centre des femmes, 1054
Partenariat communauté en santé, 1143
La Passerelle - Intégration et Développement Économique, 1145
Reflet Salvéo, 1210
Réseau de développement économique et d'employabilité Ontario, 1219
Réseau de Santé en Français au Nunavut, 1219
Réseau des services de santé en français de l'Est de l'Ontario, 1222
Réseau du mieux-être francophone du Nord de l'Ontario, 1222
Réseau du patrimoine franco-ontarien, 1222
Réseau franco-santé du Sud de l'Ontario, 1224
Réseau Santé - Nouvelle-Écosse, 1225
Réseau santé albertain, 1225
Réseau santé en français de la Saskatchewan, 1225
Réseau Santé en français I.-P.-É., 1226
Réseau santé en français Terre-Neuve-et-Labrador, 1226
Réseau TNO Santé en français, 1226
Réso Santé Colombie Britannique, 1226
Société de l'Acadie du Nouveau-Brunswick, 1316
Société de la francophonie manitobaine, 1316
Société francophone de Victoria, 1319
Société généalogique canadienne-française, 1319
Société Santé en français, 1325
Société Santé et Mieux-être en français du Nouveau-Brunswick, 1325
L'Union culturelle des Franco-Ontariennes, 1406
Union des cultivateurs franco-ontariens, 1406

Fraternal Organizations
Ancient, Free & Accepted Masons of Canada - Grand Lodge in the Province of Ontario, 68
Ancient, Free & Accepted Masons of Canada - Grand Lodge of Alberta, 68
Ancient, Free & Accepted Masons of Canada - Grand Lodge of British Columbia & Yukon, 68
Ancient, Free & Accepted Masons of Canada - Grand Lodge of New Brunswick, 69
Ancient, Free & Accepted Masons of Canada - Grand Lodge of Nova Scotia, 69
Ancient, Free & Accepted Masons of Canada - Grand Lodge of Prince Edward Island, 69
Benevolent & Protective Order of Elks of Canada, 204
The Canadian Club of Toronto, 357
Canadian Fraternal Association, 394
Canadian Progress Club, 460
Les Chevaliers de Colomb du Québec, 557
Empire Club of Canada, 686
Grand Chapter, R.A.M. of Nova Scotia, 779
Grand Chapter, Royal Arch Masons of Québec, 779
Grand Lodge of Québec - Ancient, Free & Accepted Masons, 779
Grand Orange Lodge of Canada, 780
International Association of Rebekah Assemblies, 1540
International Order of the King's Daughters & Sons, 1554
Kin Canada, 887
Kin Canada Foundation, 887
Knights Hospitallers, Sovereign Order of St. John of Jerusalem, Knights of Malta, Grand Priory of Canada, 892
Knights of Columbus, 1568
Knights of Pythias - Domain of British Columbia, 892
Ladies' Orange Benevolent Association of Canada, 895
Mission Aviation Fellowship of Canada, 969
Order of Malta - Canadian Association, 1119
The Order of United Commercial Travelers of America, 1119
Rotary International, 1587
Royal Arch Masons of Canada, 1237
Royal Danish Guards Association of Western Canada, 1242
Sons of Scotland Benevolent Association, 1333
Ukrainian Fraternal Society of Canada, 1403
United Jewish Peoples' Order, 1411
Yukon Order of Pioneers, 1479

Fraud Investigation
Association of Certified Forensic Investigators of Canada, 145
Canadian Anti-Counterfeiting Network, 293

Free Trade
Canadian Council for the Americas, 367
Canadian Council for the Americas - British Columbia, 367
Citizens Concerned About Free Trade, 570
KAIROS: Canadian Ecumenical Justice Initiatives, 880

Free-Nets
Chebucto Community Net, 555
Edmonton Community Networks, 676
National Capital FreeNet, 991
Sea to Sky Free-Net Association, 1287
Toronto Free-Net, 1384
Vancouver Community Network, 1425

Freedom of Information
British Columbia Freedom of Information & Privacy Association, 241
International Federation of Library Associations & Institutions, 1548

Freight Services
Canadian International Freight Forwarders Association, 421
Coalition of Rail Shippers, 578
Freight Carriers Association of Canada, 759
Freight Management Association of Canada, 759
Intermodal Association of North America, 1534

National Transportation Brokers Association, 996
Teamsters Canada Rail Conference, 1368

French Immersion Programs
Association Provinciale des Professeurs d'Immersion et du Programme Francophone, 168
Parents partenaires en éducation, 1140

French Language
Agence universitaire de la Francophonie, 14
Alliance canadienne des responsables et enseignants en français (langue maternelle), 55
Alliance Française, 57
Alliance Française d'Edmonton, 57
Alliance Française d'Ottawa, 57
Alliance Française de Calgary, 57
Alliance Française du Manitoba, 57
Alliance Française Halifax, 57
Assemblée parlementaire de la Francophonie, 88
Assemblée parlementaire de la Francophonie (Section canadienne), 88
Association canadienne d'éducation de langue française, 90
Association des auteurs et des auteurs de l'Ontario français, 106
Association des conseils en gestion linguistique Inc., 109
Association des distributeurs exclusifs de livres en langue française inc., 111
Association des juristes d'expression française de l'Ontario, 117
Association des juristes d'expression française de la Saskatchewan, 118
Association des juristes d'expression française du Manitoba inc., 118
Association des juristes d'expression française du Nouveau-Brunswick, 118
Association des professeurs de français des universités et collèges canadiens, 124
Association internationale des sociologues de langue française, 1510
Association nationale des éditeurs de livres, 138
Association québécoise des écoles de français langue étrangère, 172
Association québécoise des enseignants de français langue seconde, 172
Association québécoise des professeurs de français, 174
Canadian Parents for French, 450
Centre canadien de leadership en éducation, 526
Centre international de documentation et d'échanges de la francophonie, 535
Conseil communautaire Beausoleil, 614
Conseil francophone de la chanson, 618
Conseil pour le développement de l'alphabétisme et des compétences des adultes du Nouveau-Brunswick, 619
École internationale de français, 672
Fédération internationale des professeurs de français, 1525
Forum francophone des affaires, 754
Institut de la Francophonie pour le développement durable, 841
Organisation internationale de la Francophonie, 1581
Parents partenaires en éducation, 1140
Regroupement des éditeurs canadiens-français, 1215
Le Réseau d'enseignement francophone à distance du Canada, 1219
Réseau des cégeps et des collèges francophones du Canada, 1219
Réseau pour le développement de l'alphabétisme et des compétences, 1225
Salon du livre de Toronto et Festival des écrivains, 1252
Société de développement des périodiques culturels québécois, 1314
Société Louis-Napoléon Dugal/Société Grande-Rivière, 1321
Société Saint-Jean-Baptiste du Centre du Québec, 1324
Société St-Jean-Baptiste Richelieu-Yamaska, 1325
Society for Existential & Phenomenological Theory & Culture, 1326

Théâtre français de Toronto, 1374
Union internationale de la presse francophone, 1598

French Media
Association de la presse francophone, 101
Vidéographe, 1434
Vues d'Afriques - Les Journées du cinéma africain et créole, 1439

Friedreich's Ataxia
Association canadienne des ataxies familiales, 92

Friends of Groups
Les Amis du centre canadien d'architecture, 67
The Friends of Algonquin Park, 760
Friends of Animals, 1527
The Friends of Awenda Park, 760
The Friends of Bon Echo Park, 760
The Friends of Bonnechere Parks, 760
The Friends of Charleston Lake Park, 760
Friends of Clayoquot Sound, 760
Friends of Devonian Botanic Garden, 761
Friends of Ecological Reserves, 761
Friends of Ferris Provincial Park, 761
The Friends of Frontenac Park, 761
The Friends of Killarney Park, 761
The Friends of MacGregor Point, 761
Friends of Mashkinonje Park, 761
The Friends of Nancy Island Historic Site & Wasaga Beach Park, 761
Friends of Nature Conservation Society, 761
The Friends of Pinery Park, 761
The Friends of Presqu'ile Park, 761
The Friends of Rondeau Park, 762
The Friends of Sandbanks Park, 762
Friends of Short Hills Park, 762
The Friends of Sleeping Giant, 762
Friends of the Archibald, 762
Friends of the Coves Subwatershed Inc., 762
Friends of the Earth Canada, 762
Friends of the Earth International, 1527
Friends of the Forestry Farm House Inc., 762
Friends of the Greater Sudbury Public Library, 762
Friends of the Oldman River, 763
Friends of the Ukrainian Village Society, 763
The Friends of West Kootenay Parks Society, 763
Niijkiwenhwag - Friends of Lake Superior Park, 1027

Fruit & Vegetables
Alberta Greenhouse Growers Association, 37
Apple Growers of New Brunswick, 74
Association québécoise de la distribution de fruits et légumes, 170
British Columbia Blueberry Council, 234
British Columbia Cranberry Marketing Commission, 238
British Columbia Fruit Growers' Association, 242
CanadaGAP, 283
Canadian Produce Marketing Association, 460
Horticulture Nova Scotia, 822
International Society of Citriculture, 1560
New Brunswick Fruit Growers Association Inc., 1008
Not Far From The Tree, 1040
Nova Scotia Fruit Growers' Association, 1045
Ontario Berry Growers' Association, 1068
Ontario Farm Fresh Marketing Association, 1078
Ontario Fruit & Vegetable Growers' Association, 1081
The Ontario Greenhouse Alliance, 1083
Ontario Tender Fruit Producers Marketing Board, 1110
Prairie Fruit Growers Association, 1169
Prince Edward Island Vegetable Growers Co-op Association, 1178
Raspberry Industry Development Council, 1204
Vegetable Growers' Association of Manitoba, 1430
Wild Blueberry Association of North America, 1453
Wild Blueberry Producers Association of Nova Scotia, 1454

Fundraising
Alberta Association of Fund Raising Executives, 23

Association for Healthcare Philanthropy, 1508
Association of Fundraising Professionals, 1511
Association of Professional Researchers for Advancement - Canada, 160
Break Open Ticket Program Management Alliance, 227
British Columbia's Children's Hospital Foundation, 259
Canadian Association of Gift Planners, 317
Children's Miracle Network, 562
Covenant Foundation, 637
Imagine Canada, 829
The International Grenfell Association, 857
National Crowdfunding Association of Canada, 992
UNICEF Canada, 1404
WinSport Canada, 1460

Funeral Planning
Alberta Funeral Service Association, 36
Alberta Funeral Services Regulatory Board, 36
Bereavement Authority of Ontario, 205
British Columbia Funeral Association, 242
Calgary Co-operative Memorial Society, 271
Corporation des thanatologues du Québec, 630
Federation of Ontario Memorial Societies - Funeral Consumers Alliance, 726
Funeral & Cremation Services Council of Saskatchewan, 764
Funeral Advisory & Memorial Society of BC, 764
Funeral Advisory & Memorial Society of Saskatchewan, 764
Funeral Consumers Advocacy of London & Windsor, 764
Funeral Information & Memorial Society of Guelph, 764
Funeral Planning & Memorial Society of Manitoba, 764
Funeral Service Association of Canada, 764
Guaranteed Funeral Deposits of Canada, 792
Last Post Fund, 899
Manitoba Funeral Service Association, 937
Memorial Society of British Columbia, 960
Memorial Society of Edmonton & District, 960
Memorial Society of Kitchener-Waterloo & Area, 960
Memorial Society of Northern Ontario, 960
Memorial Society of Red Deer & District, 960
Mount Pleasant Group, 976
New Brunswick Funeral Directors & Embalmers Association, 1008
Newfoundland & Labrador Funeral Services Association, 1019
Ontario Association of Cemetery & Funeral Professionals, 1062
Ontario Funeral Service Association, 1081
People's Memorial Society of BC & Vancouver Island Memorial Society, 1152
Prince Edward Island Funeral Directors & Embalmers Association, 1174

Fur Trade
Aiviq Hunters & Trappers Organization, 20
Alberta Trappers' Association, 50
BC Trappers' Association, 202
Canadian Association for Humane Trapping, 301
The Canadian Fur Trade Development Institute, 396
Fédération des trappeurs gestionnaires du Québec, 719
The Fur Council of Canada, 765
Fur Institute of Canada, 765
Fur-Bearer Defenders, 765
Mittimatalik Hunters' & Trappers' Organization, 970
Newfoundland & Labrador Fur Breeders Association, 1019
North American Wild Fur Shippers Council, 1030
Nova Scotia Mink Breeders' Association, 1047
Trappers Association of Nova Scotia, 1396
Yukon Trappers Association, 1480

Furniture Industry
Association des fabricants de meubles du Québec inc., 113
Business & Institutional Furniture Manufacturer's Association, 1515
Canadian Home Furnishings Alliance, 408
Conseil national du meuble, 619

Futurism
World Future Society, 1605
World Futures Studies Federation, 1605

Gambling
Addiction Services of Thames Valley, 8
Addictions Foundation of Manitoba, 8
Canadian Centre on Substance Use & Addiction, 354
Canadian Gaming Association, 396
Interactive Gaming Council, 851
Responsible Gambling Council (Ontario), 1227

Games
Association québécoise des joueurs de dames, 173
Canadian Bridge Federation, 347
Colchester Highland Games & Gathering Society, 580
International Game Developers Association, 1549

Gas
L'association québécoise des fournisseurs de services pétroliers et gaziers du Québec, 172
Canada - Newfoundland & Labrador Offshore Petroleum Board, 277
Canada - Nova Scotia Offshore Petroleum Board, 278
Canadian Association of Drilling Engineers, 312
Canadian Association of Petroleum Land Administration, 325
Canadian Association of Petroleum Producers, 326
Canadian Biogas Association, 343
Canadian Energy Law Foundation, 381
Canadian Fuels Association, 395
Canadian Propane Association, 461
Compressed Gas Association, Inc., 1518
Enform, 688
Explorers & Producers Association of Canada, 700
Gas Processing Association Canada, 767
Industrial Gas Users Association, 835
Noia, 1027
Ontario Petroleum Institute Inc., 1095
Orphan Well Association, 1127
Petroleum Tank Management Association of Alberta, 1154
Petroleum Technology Alliance Canada, 1154
Society of Petroleum Engineers, 1593
World Petroleum Council, 1607

Gastroenterology
Association des gastro-entérologues du Québec, 114
Canadian Association of Gastroenterology, 316
Canadian Digestive Health Foundation, 378
Canadian Society of Gastroenterology Nurses & Associates, 483
Ontario Association of Gastroenterology, 1064

Gems
Alberni Valley Rock & Gem Club, 21
Alberta Federation of Rock Clubs, 35
Bancroft Gem & Mineral Club, 195
Barrhead Gem Seekers, 197
Barrie Gem & Mineral Society Inc., 197
Brantford Lapidary & Mineral Society Inc., 227
Burnaby Laphounds Club, 266
Calgary Rock & Lapidary Club, 274
Canadian Gemmological Association, 396
Canadian Institute of Gemmology, 416
Courtenay Gem & Mineral Club, 637
Creative Jewellers Guild of BC, 639
Creston Valley Prospectors & Lapidary Club, 642
Delta Rockhound Gem & Mineral Club, 653
Dunbar Lapidary Club, 664
Edmonton Tumblewood Lapidary Club, 679
Fraser Valley Rock & Gem Club, 758
Gem & Mineral Club of Scarborough, 768
Gem & Mineral Federation of Canada, 768
Golden Rock & Fossil Club, 776
Hastings Centre Rockhounds, 804
Kingston Lapidary & Mineral Club, 889
Lacombe Handicraft & Lapidary Guild, 895
Lapidary Club of West Vancouver, 899
Maple Ridge Lapidary Club, 948
Medicine Hat Rock & Lapidary Club, 958
Mid-Pro Rock & Gem Society, 965
Montréal Gem & Mineral Club, 972
The Nova Scotia Mineral & Gem Society, 1047

Subject Index / Genealogy

Oxford County Geological Society, 1134
Parksville & District Rock & Gem Club, 1142
Port Moody Rock & Gem Club, 1166
Powell River Lapidary Club, 1169
Prairie Rock & Gem Society, 1169
Richmond Gem & Mineral Society, 1230
Ripple Rock Gem & Mineral Club, 1233
Saskatoon Lapidary & Mineral Club, 1279
Shuswap Rock Club, 1297
Sudbury Rock & Lapidary Society, 1353
Thompson Valley Rock Club, 1376
Vernon Lapidary & Mineral Club, 1431
Victoria Lapidary & Mineral Society, 1433
Walker Mineralogical Club, 1439

Genealogy
Alberta Family History Society, 34
Alberta Genealogical Society, 36
Association des familles Gosselin, Inc., 113
Association des familles Rioux d'Amérique inc., 113
British Columbia Genealogical Society, 242
British Isles Family History Society of Greater Ottawa, 259
Canadian Society of Mayflower Descendants, 484
Clan Donald Canada, 571
Clan Farquharson Association of Canada, 571
Clan Fraser Society of Canada, 571
Clan Gunn Society of North America - Eastern Canada Branch, 571
Clan Lamont Society of Canada, 571
Clan Mackenzie Society of Canada, 571
Clan MacLeod Society of Canada, 572
Clan Matheson Society of Nova Scotia, 572
Clans & Scottish Societies of Canada, 572
Cumberland County Genealogical Society, 645
Dartmouth N.S. Family History Centre, 651
East European Genealogical Society, Inc., 668
Family History Society of Newfoundland & Labrador, 703
Fédération des associations de familles du Québec, 711
Fédération québécoise des sociétés de généalogie, 730
La Fondation des Amis de la généalogie, 744
Gatineau Valley Historical Society, 768
Genealogical Association of Nova Scotia, 768
Genealogical Institute of The Maritimes, 768
Généalogie Abitibi-Témiscamingue, 768
Harrow Early Immigrant Research Society, 804
Historic Restoration Society of Annapolis County, 815
Jewish Genealogical Institute of British Columbia, 872
Jewish Genealogical Society of Toronto, 872
Kings Historical Society, 888
Manitoba Genealogical Society Inc., 937
Miramichi Historical Society, Inc., 968
New Brunswick Genealogical Society Inc., 1008
Norfolk Historical Society, 1028
The Nova Scotia Genealogy Network Association, 1045
Ontario Genealogical Society, 1081
Prince Edward Island Genealogical Society Inc., 1174
Québec Family History Society, 1197
Queens County Historical Society, 1200
The Royal Nova Scotia Historical Society, 1242
Saskatchewan Genealogical Society, 1265
Shelburne County Genealogical Society, 1295
Société d'histoire et de généalogie de l'Île Jésus, 1312
Société d'histoire et de généalogie de la Matapédia, 1312
Société d'histoire et de généalogie de Matane, 1312
Société d'histoire et de généalogie de Rivière-du-Loup, 1312
Société d'histoire et de généalogie de Saint-Casimir, 1312
Société d'histoire et de généalogie de Salaberry, 1313
Société d'histoire et de généalogie de Verdun, 1313
Société d'histoire et de généalogie Maria-Chapdelaine, 1313
Société d'histoire et généalogie du granit, 1313
Société de généalogie de l'Outaouais, 1315
Société de généalogie de la Beauce, 1315
Société de généalogie de la Jemmerais, 1315
Société de généalogie de la Mauricie et des Bois-Francs, 1315
Société de généalogie de Lanaudière, 1315
Société de généalogie de Longueuil, 1315
Société de généalogie de Québec, 1315
Société de généalogie de Saint-Eustache, 1315
Société de généalogie des Cantons de l'Est, 1315
Société de généalogie des Laurentides, 1316
Société de généalogie du Saguenay, inc., 1316
Société de généalogie et d'archives de Rimouski, 1316
Société de généalogie et d'histoire de la région de Thetford-Mines, 1316
Société de généalogie Gaspésie-Les Îles, 1316
Société de généalogie Saint-Hubert, 1316
Société généalogique canadienne-française, 1319
Société généalogique de Châteauguay, 1319
Société historique du Saguenay, 1321
Société historique et généalogique de Trois-Pistoles, inc., 1321
South Shore Genealogical Society, 1336
Sunbury West Historical Society, 1354
Tweed & Area Historical Society, 1400
Ukrainian Genealogical & Historical Society of Canada, 1403
United Empire Loyalists' Association of Canada, 1410
West Elgin Historical & Genealogical Society, 1445

Genetic Diseases & Disorders
Canadian Coalition for Genetic Fairness, 357
Huntington Society of Canada, 827
Shwachman-Diamond Syndrome Canada, 1297
Société Huntington du Québec, 1321

Genetics
AllerGen NCE Inc., 54
Association des médecins généticiens du Québec, 119
Canadian Association of Genetic Counsellors, 316
Canadian Genetic Diseases Network, 397
International Federation of Human Genetics Societies, 1548
International Genetics Federation, 1549

Genomics
Genome Canada, 769

Geochemistry
Association of Applied Geochemists, 139
Geochemical Society, 1527
Geological Association of Canada, 769

Geography
Association of American Geographers, 1510
Canadian Association of Geographers, 316
Canadian Cartographic Association, 350
Commonwealth Geographical Bureau, 1518
International Geographic Union, 1550
International Geographical Union - Canadian Committee, 857
Ontario Association for Geographic & Environmental Education, 1061
The Royal Canadian Geographical Society, 1239

Geology
The American Association of Petroleum Geologists, 1490
Burgess Shale Geoscience Foundation, 265
Canadian Quaternary Association, 464
Canadian Rock Mechanics Association, 467
Canadian Society of Petroleum Geologists, 486
Explorer's Club (Canadian Chapter), 700
Geological Association of Canada, 769
International Association for Earthquake Engineering, 1536
International Association of Sedimentologists, 1540
International Permafrost Association, 1555
International Society for Rock Mechanics, 1559
International Society for Soil Mechanics & Geotechnical Engineering, 1559
Mineralogical Association of Canada, 966
Niagara Peninsula Geological Society, 1025
The Nova Scotia Mineral & Gem Society, 1047
Ordre des Géologues du Québec, 1121
Oxford County Geological Society, 1134
Penticton Geology & Lapidary Club, 1151
Sarnia Rock & Fossil Club, 1254

Geomatics
Canadian Institute of Geomatics, 416
Canadian Remote Sensing Society, 466
GEOIDE Network, 769
Geomatics Industry Association of Canada, 770

Geophysics
Canadian Association of Geophysical Contractors, 317
Canadian Federation of Earth Sciences, 386
Canadian Geophysical Union, 397
Canadian Society of Exploration Geophysicists, 483
European Association of Geoscientists & Engineers, 1524
European Geosciences Union, 1524
Geological Association of Canada, 769
International Airborne Geophysics Safety Association, 853
International Permafrost Association, 1555
International Union of Geodesy & Geophysics, 1564

Geoscience
Association of Professional Engineers & Geoscientists of Alberta, 157
Association of Professional Engineers & Geoscientists of British Columbia, 157
Association of Professional Engineers & Geoscientists of Manitoba, 158
Association of Professional Engineers & Geoscientists of New Brunswick, 158
Association of Professional Engineers & Geoscientists of Saskatchewan, 158
Association of Professional Geoscientists of Nova Scotia, 159
Association of Professional Geoscientists of Ontario, 159
Canadian Federation of Earth Sciences, 386
Engineers Nova Scotia, 689
Geological Association of Canada, 769
Northwest Territories & Nunavut Association of Professional Engineers & Geoscientists, 1036
Ontario Geothermal Association, 1082
Professional Engineers & Geoscientists Newfoundland & Labrador, 1183

Geotechnics
Canadian Geotechnical Society, 397
Geotechnical Society of Edmonton, 771
International Geosynthetics Society, 1550

German Canadians
Association for German Education in Calgary, 133
German Canadian Association of Nova Scotia, 771
German Canadian Cultural Association, 772
German Society of Winnipeg, 772
German-Canadian Association of Alberta, 772
Prairie Saengerbund Choir Association, 1169

German Language
Canadian Association of University Teachers of German, 335
Goethe-Institut (Montréal), 776
Goethe-Institut (Toronto), 776

Germany
Canadian German Chamber of Industry & Commerce Inc., 397
German Canadian Business Association, 772
German Canadian Cultural Association of Manitoba Inc., 772
German-Canadian Association of Alberta, 772
German-Canadian Business & Professional Association of Kitchener-Waterloo, 772
German-Canadian Congress (Manitoba) Inc., 772
German-Canadian Congress (Ontario), 772
German-Canadian Historical Association Inc., 772
German-Canadian Mardi Gras Association Inc., 772
Goethe-Institut (Montréal), 776
Goethe-Institut (Toronto), 776
Lloydminster German Heritage Society Inc., 916
The Pennsylvania German Folklore Society of Ontario, 1149
Saskatchewan German Council Inc., 1266

Gerontology
Alberta Association on Gerontology, 25
Alberta Gerontological Nurses Association, 37
Association québécoise de gérontologie, 169
Canadian Association on Gerontology, 337
Canadian Geriatrics Society, 397
Canadian Gerontological Nursing Association, 397
Gerontological Nursing Association of British Columbia, 772
Gerontological Nursing Association of Ontario, 772
Gustav Levinschi Foundation, 794
Manitoba Gerontological Nurses' Association, 937
Nova Scotia Gerontological Nurses Association, 1045
Ontario Gerontology Association, 1082
Prince Edward Island Gerontological Nurses Association, 1174
Société québécoise de gériatrie, 1323
Yukon Council on Aging, 1478

Gifted Children
Alberta Associations for Bright Children, 25
Association for Bright Children (Ontario), 132
Association of Educators of Gifted, Talented & Creative Children in BC, 147

Glass
Architectural Glass & Metal Contractors Association, 78
Canadian Depression Glass Association, 377
Glass & Architectural Metals Association, 774
Glass Art Association of Canada, 774
Glass Packaging Institute, 1528
Glass, Molders, Pottery, Plastic & Allied Workers International Union (AFL-CIO/CLC), 1528

Global Governance
Forum of Federations, 755
Global Village Nanaimo, 775
Institute for Planetary Synthesis, 1532
World Citizen Foundation, 1604
World Federalist Movement, 1605
World Federalist Movement - Canada, 1465
Worldwatch Institute, 1608

Global Warming
Climate Institute, 1517

Goats
Canadian Goat Society, 398
Canadian Meat Goat Association, 432
Ontario Goat Breeders Association, 1083
Syndicat des producteurs de chèvres du Québec, 1363

Golf
Alberta Golf Association, 37
Association des golfeurs professionnels du Québec, 115
Association des surintendants de golf du Québec, 129
Atlantic Turfgrass Research Foundation, 186
British Columbia Golf Association, 242
British Columbia Golf Superintendents Association, 242
Canadian Amputee Golf Association, 292
Canadian Caribbean Amateur Golfers Association, 350
Canadian Deaf Golf Association, 376
Canadian Golf Hall of Fame & Museum, 398
Canadian Golf Superintendents Association, 398
Canadian Junior Golf Association, 423
Canadian Society of Club Managers, 482
Club de golf Chibougamau-Chapais inc., 574
Fédération de golf du Québec, 708
Golf Association of Ontario, 777
Golf Canada, 777
Golf Canada Foundation, 777
Golf Manitoba Inc., 777
Golf Newfoundland & Labrador, 777
Ladies' Golf Union, 1569
National Golf Course Owners Association Canada, 993
New Brunswick Golf Association, 1009
Nova Scotia Golf Association, 1045
Ontario Golf Superintendents' Association, 1083
Prince Edward Island Golf Association, 1174

Professional Golfers' Association of British Columbia, 1185
Professional Golfers' Association of Canada, 1185
Saskatchewan Golf Association Inc., 1266
Yukon Golf Association, 1478

Government
Alberta Development Officers Association, 32
Alliance des cadres de l'État, 55
Association des employées et employés du gouvernement du Québec, 112
Association of Kootenay & Boundary Local Governments, 150
Association of Vancouver Island Coastal Communities, 163
Association professionnelle des ingénieurs du gouvernement du Québec (ind.), 167
British Columbia Government & Service Employees' Union, 242
Canada-Yukon Business Service Centre, 284
Canadian Association for Security & Intelligence Studies, 303
Canadian Association of Crown Counsel, 312
The Canadian Council for Public-Private Partnerships, 366
Canadian Council of Forest Ministers, 368
Canadian Council of Ministers of the Environment, 368
Canadian Intergovernmental Conference Secretariat, 420
Commonwealth Parliamentary Association, 1518
Confederation des peuples autochtones du Québec, 611
Conference of New England Governors & Eastern Canadian Premiers, 612
Council of Atlantic Premiers, 633
Democracy Watch, 653
Federation of Calgary Communities, 722
Government Finance Officers Association, 1528
Government Finance Officers Association of British Columbia, 778
House of Commons Security Services Employees Association, 824
Inter-Parliamentary Union, 1567
Legislative Recording & Broadcast Association, 906
Lower Mainland Local Government Association, 920
National Institute of Governmental Purchasing, Inc., 1576
North Central Local Government Association, 1030
The Public Affairs Association of Canada, 1192
Southern Interior Local Government Association, 1338

Government Libraries
Association of Parliamentary Libraries in Canada, 155
Federal Libraries Coordination Secretariat, 706

Graduate Studies
Canadian Association for Graduate Studies, 300
Ontario Council on Graduate Studies, 1075

Grains
Animal Nutrition Association of Canada, 70
Canada Grains Council, 279
Canadian International Grains Institute, 421
Grain Elevator & Processing Society, 1528
Grain Services Union (CLC), 779
Ontario Agri Business Association, 1059
Saskatchewan Pulse Growers, 1273
Vancouver Grain Exchange, 1425
Western Barley Growers Association, 1447
Western Grain Elevator Association, 1449

Grandparents
Association des grands-parents du Québec, 115
Association G.R.A.N.D., 136
CANGRANDS Kinship Support, 508
Helping Unite Grandparents & Grandchildren, 812

Grants
Canadian Environmental Grantmakers' Network, 382
The Counselling Foundation of Canada, 636

Grape Industry
British Columbia Grapegrowers' Association, 242
Grape Growers of Ontario, 782

Graphic Arts & Design
Association of Registered Graphic Designers of Ontario, 160
British Columbia Printing & Imaging Association, 249
Canadian Society of Children's Authors, Illustrators & Performers, 481
Eurographics - European Association for Computer Graphics, 1524
International Council of Design, 855
Manitoba Printmakers Association, 942
Ontario Printing & Imaging Association, 1097
Printing & Graphics Industries Association of Alberta, 1180
Saskatchewan Graphic Arts Industries Association, 1266
Société des collectionneurs d'estampes de Montréal, 1317
Société des designers graphiques du Québec, 1317
Society for Environmental Graphic Design, 1590
Society of Graphic Designers of Canada, 1329
Specialty Graphic Imaging Association, 1596

Great Lakes
Association of Great Lakes Outdoor Writers, 1512
Citizens' Environment Alliance, 570
Conference of Great Lakes & St. Lawrence Governors & Premiers, 1519
Great Lakes Institute for Environmental Research, 782
The Great Lakes Marine Heritage Foundation, 782
The Great Lakes Research Consortium, 1528
International Association for Great Lakes Research, 1536

Greek Canadians
Greek Community of Toronto, 787
Greek Orthodox Community of East Vancouver, 787
Greek Orthodox Metropolis of Toronto (Canada), 788
Greek-Canadian Cultural Centre, 788
Hellenic Canadian Board of Trade, 811
Hellenic Canadian Congress of BC, 811
Hellenic Community of Vancouver, 811

Grocery Trade
Breakfast Cereals Canada, 227
Canadian Federation of Independent Grocers, 387
Food & Consumer Products of Canada, 749

Guide Dogs
Canadian Guide Dogs for the Blind, 399

Guides
Association des guides touristiques de Québec, 116
Association des Scouts du Canada, 127
Canadian Tour Guide Association of British Columbia, 495
Girl Guides of Canada, 773
Nova Scotia Guides Association, 1045

Guitar
Edmonton Classical Guitar Society, 676
Guitar Society of Toronto, 794

Gymnastics
Alberta Gymnastics Federation, 37
British Columbia Rhythmic Sportive Gymnastics Federation, 251
Fédération de gymnastique du Québec, 708
Gymnastics B.C., 795
Gymnastics Canada Gymnastique, 795
Gymnastics Newfoundland & Labrador Inc., 795
Gymnastics Nova Scotia, 795
Gymnastics PEI, 795
Gymnastics Saskatchewan, 795
Manitoba Gymnastics Association, 937
New Brunswick Gymnastics Association, 1009
Ontario Gymnastic Federation, 1083
Polarettes Gymnastics Club, 1163
Rhythmic Gymnastics Alberta, 1229
Rhythmic Gymnastics Manitoba Inc., 1229
Yukon Gymnastics Association, 1478

Hairdressing
Allied Beauty Association, 58
BeautyCouncil, 203
Cosmetology Association of Nova Scotia, 631
Manitoba Hairstylists' Association, 937

Haitian Canadians & Haiti
Friends of the Orphans, Canada, 763
Maison D'Haiti, 926

Halls of Fame
Alberta Sports Hall of Fame & Museum, 48
British Columbia Sports Hall of Fame & Museum, 255
Canada's Aviation Hall of Fame, 282
Canada's Sports Hall of Fame, 283
Canadian Football Hall of Fame & Museum, 391
Canadian Golf Hall of Fame & Museum, 398
Canadian Lacrosse Hall of Fame, 425
Canadian Olympic Hall of Fame, 446
Manitoba Sports Hall of Fame & Museum, 945
New Brunswick Sports Hall of Fame, 1013
North America Railway Hall of Fame, 1029
Northwestern Ontario Sports Hall of Fame & Museum, 1039
Novia Scotia Sports Hall of Fame, 1050
Original Hockey Hall of Fame & Museum, 1126
Ottawa Sports Hall of Fame Inc., 1131
Prince Edward Island Sports Hall of Fame & Museum Inc., 1177
Saskatchewan Agricultural Hall of Fame, 1255
Saskatchewan Sports Hall of Fame & Museum, 1275

Handball
Alberta Handball Association, 37
Alberta Team Handball Federation, 49
Balle au mur Québec, 194
British Columbia Team Handball Federation, 256
Canadian Handball Association, 400
Canadian Team Handball Federation, 493
Fédération québécoise de handball olympique, 727
Handball Association of Newfoundland & Labrador, 802
Handball Association of Nova Scotia, 802
Manitoba Team Handball Federation, 946
New Brunswick Team Handball Federation, 1013
Ontario Handball Association, 1083
Saskatchewan Handball Association, 1267
Team Handball Ontario, 1368

Hang Gliding
British Columbia Hang Gliding & Paragliding Association, 243
Great Lakes Gliding Club, 782
Hang Gliding & Paragliding Association of Atlantic Canada, 803
Hang Gliding & Paragliding Association of Canada, 803
Manitoba Hang Gliding Association, 937
Southwestern Ontario Gliding Association, 1338

Harbours & Ports
Association of Canadian Port Authorities, 143
International Association of Ports & Harbours, 1539

Hard of Hearing
Audition Québec, 187
Canadian Hard of Hearing Association, 400
Canadian Hearing Society, 403
Hearing Foundation of Canada, 808
Island Deaf & Hard of Hearing Centre, 865
Réseau québécois pour l'inclusion social des personnnes sourdes et malentendantes, 1225
Saskatchewan Deaf & Hard of Hearing Services Inc., 1263
Speech & Hearing Association of Nova Scotia, 1340
Western Institute for the Deaf & Hard of Hearing, 1450
World Federation of the Deaf, 1605

Hardware Industry
Canadian Hardware & Housewares Manufacturers' Association, 401
Door & Hardware Institute in Canada, 661

Harness Racing
Central Ontario Standardbred Association, 525
Prince Edward Island Colt Stakes Association, 1173
Prince Edward Island Harness Racing Industry Association, 1174

Hawks
Hawk Migration Association of North America, 1529

Hazardous Wastes
Air & Waste Management Association, 1486
Center for Health, Environment & Justice, 1516
Dangerous Goods Advisory Council, 1521
Ontario Waste Management Association, 1112
Toxics Watch Society of Alberta, 1394

Head Injury
Association québécoise des traumatisés craniens, 175

Health
Action Canada for Sexual Health & Rights, 6
Action on Smoking & Health, 6
Active Healthy Kids Canada, 7
African & Caribbean Council on HIV/AIDS in Ontario, 12
Alberta Association of Travel Health Professionals, 25
Alzheimer Manitoba, 61
Les Amis de la déficience intellectuelle Rive-Nord, 67
Association des cadres supérieurs de la santé et des services sociaux du Québec, 108
Association des intervenantes et des intervenants en soins spirituels du Québec, 117
Association des Perfusionnistes du Québec Inc., 122
Association générale des insuffisants rénaux, 136
Association of Local Public Health Agencies, 150
Atlantic Health Promotion Research Centre, 184
Barth Syndrome Foundation of Canada, 197
BC Lymphedema Association, 201
Canada Health Infoway, 280
Canadian Agency for Drugs & Technologies in Health, 289
Canadian Association for Enterostomal Therapy, 300
Canadian Association for Health Services & Policy Research, 300
Canadian Association for School Health, 303
Canadian Association of Wound Care, 337
Canadian Centre for Wellbeing, 354
Canadian Council for Tobacco Control, 367
Canadian Dupuytren Society, 379
Canadian Federation of Medical Students, 388
Canadian Health Coalition, 401
Canadian Horticultural Therapy Association, 408
Canadian Hypnosis Association, 410
Canadian Institute of Child Health, 414
Canadian Lymphedema Framework, 429
Canadian Natural Health Association, 440
Canadian Nurse Continence Advisors Association, 442
Canadian Pediatric Foundation, 452
Canadian Red Cross, 465
Canadian Society for International Health, 475
Canadian Society for Medical Laboratory Science, 476
Canadians for Health Research, 507
The Change Foundation, 551
CHARGE Syndrome Canada, 552
Children's Health Foundation of Vancouver Island, 561
Christian Children's Fund of Canada, 567
Coalition for a Smoke-Free Nova Scotia, 578
Collaboration Santé Internationale, 581
Consumer Health Organization of Canada, 625
Digital Health Canada, 656
Eli Bay Relaxation Response Institute, 684
Entre-amis Lavallois inc, 691
Fédération des syndicats de la santé et des services sociaux, 719
Fondation Lucie et André Chagnon, 747
Groupe d'entraide à l'intention des personnes séropositives, itinérantes et toxicomanes, 791
Gymn-eau Laval inc, 795
Hamber Foundation, 800

Subject Index / Health Care

Health & Safety Conference Society of Alberta, 805
Health Action Network Society, 805
Health Association Nova Scotia, 805
Health Association of African Canadians, 806
Health Charities Coalition of Canada, 806
Health Employers Association of British Columbia, 806
Health Law Institute, 806
Health Sciences Association of Alberta, 807
Health Sciences Association of Saskatchewan, 807
Health Sciences Centre Foundation, 807
HealthBridge Foundation of Canada, 807
Healthy Indoors Partnership, 807
Hepatitis Outreach Society of Nova Scotia, 812
Infant Feeding Action Coalition, 836
Institut de réadaptation en déficience physique de Québec, 841
Institute for Optimizing Health Outcomes, 843
Island Fitness Council, 865
Kidney Cancer Canada Association, 884
LAMP Community Health Centre, 897
Manitoba Tobacco Reduction Alliance, 946
McCreary Centre Society, 955
Michael Smith Foundation for Health Research, 964
National Literacy & Health Program, 994
Ontario Health Libraries Association, 1084
Ontario Healthy Communities Coalition, 1084
Ontario Physical & Health Education Association, 1095
Partage Humanitaire, 1143
Patients Canada, 1145
Physical & Health Education Canada, 1158
Physicians for Global Survival (Canada), 1158
Quintiles IMS Canada, 1202
The Recreation Association, 1207
The Regional Health Authorities of Manitoba, 1212
Sandbox Project, 1253
Saskatchewan Coalition for Tobacco Reduction, 1261
SIGMA Canadian Menopause Society, 1298
Simcoe Women's Wellness Centre Corporation, 1300
Syndicat des professionnels et des techniciens de la santé du Québec, 1364
Temporomandibular Joint Society of Canada, 1370
The 3C Foundation of Canada, 1377
Union of Canadian Transportation Employees, 1407
World Health Organization, 1605

Health Care
Advanced Coronary Treatment (ACT) Foundation of Canada, 10
African Community Health Services, 13
African Medical & Research Foundation Canada, 13
Artists in Healthcare Manitoba, 85
Association des fondations d'établissements de santé du Québec, 114
Association des Perfusionnistes du Québec Inc., 122
Association of Electromyography Technologists of Canada, 147
Association of Family Health Teams of Ontario, 148
British Columbia Association of Healthcare Auxiliaries, 231
Canadian Agency for Drugs & Technologies in Health, 289
Canadian Association of Community Health Centres, 311
Canadian Association of Medical Teams Abroad, 321
Canadian Association of Music Therapists, 321
Canadian Federation of Podiatric Medicine, 388
Canadian Foundation for Healthcare Improvement, 393
Canadian MedicAlert Foundation, 434
Canadian Midwifery Regulators Consortium, 436
Canadian Network for Improved Outcomes in Systemic Lupus Erythematosus, 440
Canadian Nurse Continence Advisors Association, 442
Canadian Professional Association for Transgender Health, 460

Cancer Patient Education Network Canada, 507
Carefirst Seniors & Community Services Association, 511
Catholic Health Alliance of Canada, 519
Catholic Health Association of British Columbia, 519
Catholic Health Association of Manitoba, 519
Catholic Health Association of New Brunswick, 520
Catholic Health Association of Saskatchewan, 520
Catholic Health Sponsors of Ontario, 520
Centre for Effective Practice Inc., 532
Christian Health Association of Alberta, 567
Conseil communauté en santé du Manitoba, 614
Dignitas International, 656
East Wellington Community Services, 669
Eastern Kings Health Foundation Inc., 670
Evangelical Medical Aid Society Canada, 698
Federation of Health Regulatory Colleges of Ontario, 724
Greater Vancouver Community Services Society, 786
Hamilton Niagara Haldimand Brant Community Care Access Centre, 801
Health Association of PEI, 806
Health Care Public Relations Association, 806
Healthcare Information & Management Systems Society, 1529
Infectious Diseases Society of America, 1531
Institute for Safe Medication Practices Canada, 844
Life Science Association of Manitoba, 910
Manitoba Association of Personal Care Home Social Workers, 931
Medical Device Reprocessing Association of Ontario, 958
Mr. & Mrs. P.A. Woodward's Foundation, 978
Nova Scotia Recreation Professionals in Health, 1048
Ontario Association of Community Care Access Centres, 1063
Ontario Association of Naturopathic Doctors, 1065
Partenariat communauté en santé, 1143
Patients Canada, 1145
Reflet Salvéo, 1210
Réseau de Santé en Français au Nunavut, 1219
Réseau des services de santé en français de l'Est de l'Ontario, 1222
Réseau du mieux-être francophone du Nord de l'Ontario, 1222
Réseau franco-santé du Sud de l'Ontario, 1224
Réseau Santé - Nouvelle-Écosse, 1225
Réseau santé albertain, 1225
Réseau Santé en français de la Saskatchewan, 1225
Réseau Santé en français I.-P.-É, 1226
Réseau santé en français Terre-Neuve-et-Labrador, 1226
Réseau TNO Santé en français, 1226
Réso Santé Colombie Britannique, 1226
Saint Elizabeth Health Care, 1246
Saskatchewan Association of Health Organizations, 1257
Société Santé en français, 1325
Société Santé et Mieux-être en français du Nouveau-Brunswick, 1325
The 3C Foundation of Canada, 1377
Toronto Community Care Access Centre, 1383
VHA Home HealthCare, 1431

Health Care Facilities
Accreditation Canada, 5
Alberta Association of Clinic Managers, 23
Association des établissements privés conventionnés - santé services sociaux, 113
Association des gestionnaires des établissements de santé et des services sociaux, 115
Association of Ontario Health Centres, 154
Baycrest Foundation, 200
Children's Mental Health Ontario, 562
Dr. H. Bliss Murphy Cancer Care Foundation, 662
Fondation Santé Gatineau, 748
HealthCareCAN, 807
Immigrant Women's Health Centre, 831
Infection & Prevention Control Canada, 836

Lions Gate Hospital Foundation, 913
Lloydminster Region Health Foundation, 916
Medical Group Management Association of Canada, 958
Ontario Association of Children's Rehabilitation Services, 1062
Ontario Coalition for Abortion Clinics, 1071
The Renascent Centres for Alcoholism & Drug Addiction, 1217

Health Care Workers
Alberta College of Combined Laboratory & X-Ray Technologists, 29
Association of New Brunswick Licensed Practical Nurses, 153
Canadian Association of Physician Assistants, 327
Canadian Nurse Continence Advisors Association, 442
College of Licensed Practical Nurses of Manitoba, 585
Employees' Union of St. Mary's of the Lake Hospital - CNFIU Local 3001, 687
Hospital Employees' Union, 823
National Health Union, 994
Ontario Healthcare Housekeepers' Association Inc., 1084
Ontario Home Care Association, 1086

Health Professionals
Alliance du personnel professionnel et technique de la santé et des services sociaux, 56
Armenian Canadian Medical Association of Ontario, 82
Association of Allied Health Professionals: Newfoundland & Labrador (Ind.), 139
Association of Complementary & Integrative Physicians of BC, 145
Association of Electromyography Technologists of Canada, 147
Canadian Association of Professional Regulatory Affairs, 329
Canadian College of Health Leaders, 358
Canadian Nurse Continence Advisors Association, 442
Canadian Register of Health Service Psychologists, 466
Canadian Tamil Medical Association, 492
Federation of Health Regulatory Colleges of Ontario, 724
Health Sciences Association of British Columbia, 807
Manitoba Association of Health Care Professionals, 929
New Brunswick Society of Cardiology Techologists, 1012
SIGMA Canadian Menopause Society, 1298

Health Records
Association des Gestionnaires de l'information de la santé du Québec, 115
Canadian Health Information Management Association, 402
Canadian Institute for Health Information, 412
Health Record Association of British Columbia, 807
Healthcare Information & Management Systems Society, 1529
International Federation of Health Information Management Associations, 1548

Hearing
Association du Québec pour enfants avec problèmes auditifs, 131
BC Hands & Voices, 201
Canadian Hard of Hearing Association, 400
Canadian Hearing Instrument Practitioners Society, 403
Canadian Hearing Society, 403
Canadian Tinnitus Foundation, 495
College of Audiologists and Speech-Language Pathologists of Manitoba, 582
College of Hearing Aid Practitioners of Alberta, 585
Connect Society - D.E.A.F. Services, 613
Interpreting Services of Newfoundland & Labrador Inc., 861
Nova Scotia Hearing & Speech Foundation, 1045
Prince Edward Island Speech & Hearing Association, 1177

Saskatchewan Deaf & Hard of Hearing Services Inc., 1263
Society of Deaf & Hard of Hearing Nova Scotians, 1328
Speech & Hearing Association of Nova Scotia, 1340
Speech-Language & Audiology Canada, 1341
VOICE for Hearing Impaired Children, 1437

Hearing Aid Industry
Association des implantés cochléaires du Québec, 116
Association of Hearing Instrument Practitioners of Ontario, 148
College of Hearing Aid Practitioners of Alberta, 585
Ordre des audioprothésistes du Québec, 1120

Hearing Impaired
Accessible Media Inc., 5
Alberta Association of the Deaf, 25
Alberta Cultural Society of the Deaf, 32
Association des Gais et Lesbiennes Sourds, 114
Association des malentendants Québécois, 118
Association des Sourds de l'Estrie Inc., 128
Association des Sourds de Lanaudière, 128
Association des Sourds de Québec inc., 128
Association montérégienne de la surdité inc., 137
Association of Hearing Instrument Practitioners of Ontario, 148
Association ontarienne des Sourd(e)s francophones, 164
Association sportive des sourds du Québec inc., 178
Audition Québec, 187
BC Hands & Voices, 201
BC Rainbow Alliance of the Deaf, 202
The Bob Rumball Centre for the Deaf, 216
Bob Rumball Foundation for the Deaf, 217
British Columbia Deaf Sports Federation, 238
British Columbia Video Relay Services Committee, 257
Calgary Association of the Deaf, 271
Canadian Association of the Deaf, 334
Canadian Cultural Society of The Deaf, Inc., 374
Canadian Deaf Curling Association, 375
Canadian Deaf Golf Association, 376
Canadian Deaf Ice Hockey Federation, 376
Canadian Deaf Sports Association, 376
Canadian Deafblind Association (National), 376
Canadian Hearing Instrument Practitioners Society, 403
Canadian Hearing Society, 403
Centre de la Communauté sourde du Montréal métropolitain, 529
College of Hearing Aid Practitioners of Alberta, 585
Connect Society - D.E.A.F. Services, 613
Deaf Children's Society of B.C., 652
Deafness Advocacy Association Nova Scotia, 652
Dog Guides Canada, 660
Durham Deaf Services, 665
Edmonton Association of the Deaf, 675
Fondation des sourds du Québec inc., 745
Greater Vancouver Association of the Deaf, 786
Hands on Summer Camp Society, 803
Hearing Foundation of Canada, 808
International Catholic Deaf Association, 854
International Committee of Sports for the Deaf, 1543
Island Deaf & Hard of Hearing Centre, 865
Manitoba Cultural Society of the Deaf, 935
Manitoba Deaf Sports Association Inc., 935
Newfoundland & Labrador Association of the Deaf, 1016
Newfoundland & Labrador Deaf Sports Association, 1018
Nova Scotia Deaf Sports Association, 1043
Ontario Deaf Sports Association, 1076
Ontario Rainbow Alliance of the Deaf, 1100
Pax Natura Society for Rehabilitation of the Deaf, 1146
Regroupement des Sourds de Chaudière-Appalaches, 1215
Saint John Deaf & Hard of Hearing Services, Inc, 1246
Saskatchewan Cultural Society of the Deaf, 1263

Subject Index / History

Saskatchewan Deaf & Hard of Hearing Services Inc., 1263
Saskatchewan Deaf Sports Association, 1263
Silent Voice Canada Inc., 1299
Society of Deaf & Hard of Hearing Nova Scotians, 1328
Western Institute for the Deaf & Hard of Hearing, 1450
Windsor Association for the Deaf, 1456
World Federation of the Deaf, 1605
Yukon Speech-Language Pathology & Audiology Association, 1480

Heart Diseases
Canadian Adult Congenital Heart Network, 288
Canadian Association of Cardio-Pulmonary Technologists, 309
Canadian Council of Cardiovascular Nurses, 367
Canadian Society of Atherosclerosis, Thrombosis & Vascular Biology, 480
Children's Heart Association for Support & Education, 561
Children's Heart Society, 562
Fondation des maladies du coeur du Québec, 745
Fondation Institut de Cardiologie de Montréal, 746
Heart & Stroke Foundation of Alberta, NWT & Nunavut, 808
Heart & Stroke Foundation of British Columbia & Yukon, 808
Heart & Stroke Foundation of Canada, 808
Heart & Stroke Foundation of Manitoba, 808
Heart & Stroke Foundation of New Brunswick, 808
Heart & Stroke Foundation of Newfoundland & Labrador, 809
Heart & Stroke Foundation of Nova Scotia, 809
Heart & Stroke Foundation of Ontario, 809
Heart & Stroke Foundation of Prince Edward Island Inc., 809
Heart & Stroke Foundation of Saskatchewan, 809

Heating
American Society of Heating, Refrigerating & Air Conditioning Engineers, 1499
Association des professionnels du chauffage, 125
Association québécoise du chauffage au mazout, 175
Canadian Institute of Plumbing & Heating, 418
Canadian Oil Heat Association, 445
Heating, Refrigeration & Air Conditioning Institute of Canada, 810
Thermal Environmental Comfort Association, 1375

Heavy Construction
Alberta Roadbuilders & Heavy Construction Association, 44
British Columbia Road Builders & Heavy Construction Association, 251
Heavy Civil Association of Newfoundland & Labrador, Inc., 810
Manitoba Heavy Construction Association, 937
Nova Scotia Road Builders Association, 1048
Prince Edward Island Road Builders & Heavy Construction Association, 1177
Saskatchewan Heavy Construction Association, 1267
Western Canada Roadbuilders & Heavy Construction Association, 1448

Heavy Equipment Industry
Association des propriétaires de machinerie lourde du Québec inc., 126
Heavy Equipment & Aggregate Truckers Association of Manitoba, 810

Hebrew Language
Federation of Teachers of Jewish Schools, 726

Height
Association québécoise des personnes de petite taille, 174
Little People of Manitoba, 915
Little People of Ontario, 915

Hematology
American Society of Pediatric Hematology / Oncology, 1502
Association des médecins hématologistes-oncologistes du Québec, 119
Canadian Hematology Society, 404

Hemophilia
Association of Hemophilia Clinic Directors of Canada, 149
Canadian Hemophilia Society, 404
World Federation of Hemophilia, 1466

Hepatitis
Canadian AIDS Treatment Information Exchange, 290
Hepatitis Outreach Society of Nova Scotia, 812
Living Positive Resource Centre, Okanagan, 915
P.E.E.R.S. Alliance, 1148

Heraldry
Royal Heraldry Society of Canada, 1242

Herbal Medicine
Canadian Society of Chinese Medicine & Acupuncture, 481

Herbs
British Columbia Herb Growers Association, 243
Herb Society of Manitoba, 812
Saskatchewan Herb & Spice Association, 1267

Heritage
Action Patrimoine, 6
Aerospace Heritage Foundation of Canada, 11
African Canadian Heritage Association, 12
American Antiquarian Society, 1488
Architectural Heritage Society of Saskatchewan, 79
Asian Heritage Society of Manitoba, 87
Association du Patrimoine d'Aylmer, 131
Association of Nova Scotia Museums, 154
Association québécoise des interprètes du patrimoine, 173
Black Loyalist Heritage Society, 213
Campbellford/Seymour Heritage Society, 276
Canada's Aviation Hall of Fame, 282
Canadian Association of Heritage Professionals, 317
Canadian Association of Professional Conservators, 328
Canadian Heritage Information Network, 405
Canadian Horse Heritage & Preservation Society, 408
Canadian Italian Heritage Foundation, 423
Canadian Northern Society, 441
Canadian Society of Mayflower Descendants, 484
Canadian Warplane Heritage, 502
The Capital Commission of Prince Edward Island Inc., 510
The Celtic Way, 521
Centre de valorisation du patrimoine vivant, 530
Chester Municipal Heritage Society, 557
Cole Harbour Rural Heritage Society, 581
Comité du patrimoine paysager estrien, 592
Community Heritage Ontario, 599
Community Museums Association of Prince Edward Island, 606
Conservation Foundation of Greater Toronto, 622
Cumberland County Genealogical Society, 645
Dickson Store Museum Society, 656
Echo-Edson Cultural Heritage Organization, 671
Edmonton Heritage Festival Association, 677
Edmonton Radial Railway Society, 679
Fortress Louisbourg Association, 754
The Friends of Fort York & Garrison Common, 761
Friends of the Haileybury Heritage Museum, 762
Genealogical Institute of The Maritimes, 768
Grande Prairie Museum, 781
The Great Lakes Marine Heritage Foundation, 782
Halifax Citadel Regimental Association, 799
Hamilton Folk Arts Heritage Council, 801
Harrow Early Immigrant Research Society, 804
Heritage Association of Antigonish, 812
Heritage Belleville, 812
L'Héritage canadien du Québec, 813
L'Héritage de L'Ile Rouge, 813
Heritage Foundation of Newfoundland & Labrador, 813
Héritage Kinnear's Mills, 813
Héritage Montréal, 813
Heritage Ottawa, 813
Heritage Society of British Columbia, 813
Heritage Toronto, 813
Heritage Trust of Nova Scotia, 813
Heritage Winnipeg Corp., 813
Heritage York, 814
Historic Sites Association of Newfoundland & Labrador, 815
Huntsville & Lake of Bays Railway Society, 828
Icelandic National League of North America, 829
Interpretation Canada - A Professional Association for Heritage Interpretation, 861
J. Douglas Ferguson Historical Research Foundation, 867
Jewish Historical Society of BC, 872
Langley Heritage Society, 899
Lethbridge & District Japanese Garden Society, 907
London Regional Resource Centre for Heritage & the Environment, 919
Lunenburg Heritage Society, 921
Mainland South Heritage Society, 926
Manitoba Indian Cultural Education Centre, 939
Marsh Collection Society, 952
Mississauga Heritage Foundation Inc., 970
Mossley Post Heritage & Citizenship Society, 975
National Trust for Canada, 996
Nova Scotia Lighthouse Preservation Society, 1047
Old Strathcona Foundation, 1056
Old Sydney Society, 1056
Ontario Heritage Trust, 1084
Ontario Monument Builders Association, 1091
Ontario Steam & Antique Preservers Association, 1109
Organization of Military Museums of Canada, 1125
Patrimoine Huntingville, 1145
Pier 21 Society, 1159
Port Moody Heritage Society, 1166
Prince Edward Island Museum & Heritage Foundation, 1175
Regroupement Pour-Valorisation, 1216
Réseau du patrimoine de Gatineau et de l'Outaouais, 1222
Réseau du patrimoine franco-ontarien, 1222
Saanich Native Heritage Society, 1245
St. Patrick's Society of Richmond & Vicinity, 1250
Saskatchewan Black Powder Association, 1259
Saskatchewan History & Folklore Society Inc., 1267
Saskatoon Heritage Society, 1279
SaskCulture Inc., 1280
Sault Ste Marie & 49th Field Regt. RCA Historical Society, 1281
Save Ontario Shipwrecks, 1281
Save Our Heritage Organization, 1281
Scandinavian Home Society of Northwestern Ontario, 1282
Sherbrooke Snow Shoe Club, 1296
La Société d'histoire de la Rivière-du-Nord, 1310
Société de Conservation du Patrimoine de Saint-François-de-la-Rivière-du-Sud inc., 1314
Société du patrimoine de Boucherville, 1319
Society for the Preservation of Old Mills - Canadian Chapter, 1326
Stephan G. Stephansson Icelandic Society, 1349
Them Days Inc., 1375
Ukrainian Canadian Research & Documentation Centre, 1402
United Empire Loyalists' Association of Canada, 1410
Walpole Island Heritage Centre, 1440
Waterloo Regional Heritage Foundation, 1442
Westmount Historical Association, 1451
Wilno Heritage Society, 1456
York Pioneer & Historical Society, 1473
Yukon Church Heritage Society, 1477

Heritage Language Programs
Manitoba Indian Cultural Education Centre, 939
Multilingual Association of Regina, Inc., 979
Saskatchewan Organization for Heritage Languages Inc., 1270
Toronto Gaelic Learners Association, 1384

High Technology
AdvaMed, 1485
Canadian Association for Composite Structures & Materials, 298
Continental Automated Buildings Association, 626
Hamilton Technology Centre, 802
Mathematics of Information Technology & Complex Systems, 954
Technology Services Industry Association, 1597
Vancouver Island Advanced Technology Centre, 1426
Vitesse, 1436

Hiking
American Hiking Society, 1494
The Avon Trail, 191
The Bruce Trail Conservancy, 261
East Coast Trail Association, 668
Federation of Mountain Clubs of British Columbia, 725
Fédération québécoise de la marche, 727
Ganaraska Hiking Trail Association, 766
Grand Valley Trails Association, 780
Great Divide Trails Association, 782
Guelph Hiking Trail Club, 793
Halifax North West Trails Association, 799
Hike Ontario, 814
International Orienteering Federation, 1554
The Maitland Trail Association, 927
Musquodoboit Trailways Association, 986
Nova Scotia Trails Federation, 1050
Oak Ridges Trail Association, 1053
Ontario Trails Council, 1111
Rideau Trail Association, 1231
Thames Valley Trail Association Inc., 1373
Trans Canada Trail Foundation, 1394
Voyageur Trail Association, 1439
Yukon Outfitters' Association, 1479

Hinduism
Hindu Society of Alberta, 815

History
Alberni District Historical Society, 21
Alberta Historical Resources Foundation, 37
American Antiquarian Society, 1488
American Historical Association, 1494
American Society for Environmental History, 1498
American Society for Legal History, 1498
Amherstburg Historic Sites Association, 67
Annapolis Valley Historical Society, 71
Antique Motorcycle Club of Manitoba Inc., 72
Archelaus Smith Historical Society, 78
Archives du Centre acadien, 80
Arkona & Area Historical Society, 81
Arrow Lakes Historical Society, 84
Associated Medical Services Inc., 89
Association des études du Proche-Orient ancien, 113
Association Gaspé-Jersey & Guernesey, 136
Atelier d'histoire Hochelaga-Maisonneuve, 179
Aurora Historical Society, Inc., 187
Battle River Historical Society, 199
Beachville District Historical Society, 202
Bear River Historical Society, 202
Beaverton Thorah Eldon Historical Society, 203
Le Berceau de Kamouraska inc., 205
Bertie Historical Society, 206
Bonavista Historic Townscape Foundation, 217
Bothwell-Zone & District Historical Society, 218
Bowden Historical Society, 219
Bracebridge Historical Society, 224
Brant Historical Society, 226
Breton & District Historical Society, 228
Bridgetown & Area Historical Society, 229
British Columbia Historical Federation, 243
British Columbia Railway Historical Association, 250
Brome County Historical Society, 260
Bruce County Historical Society, 260
Burford Township Historical Society, 265
Burlington Historical Society, 265
Bus History Association, Inc., 266
Bytown Railway Society, 267
Cabbagetown Preservation Association, 268

Subject Index / History

Subject Index

Caledon East & District Historical Society, 270
Canada's History, 282
Canadian Academy of the History of Pharmacy, 287
Canadian Association for the History of Nursing, 305
Canadian Aviation Historical Society, 340
Canadian Catholic Historical Association - English Section, 351
Canadian Committee of Byzantinists, 360
Canadian Committee on Labour History, 361
Canadian Conservation Institute, 363
Canadian Historical Association, 405
Canadian Nautical Research Society, 440
Canadian Oral History Association, 446
Canadian Paper Money Society, 449
Canadian Railroad Historical Association, 465
Canadian Science & Technology Historical Association, 468
Canadian Society for the History & Philosophy of Science, 477
Canadian Society for the History of Medicine, 477
Canadian Society of Church History, 481
Canadian Society of Mayflower Descendants, 484
Canadian Society of Presbyterian History, 487
Canadian Titanic Society, 495
Canadian Vintage Motorcycle Group, 501
Canadiana, 506
Cannington & Area Historical Society, 508
Canso Historical Society, 509
Cape Sable Historical Society, 510
Cardston Historical Society, 511
Carleton County Historical Society, Inc., 513
Carleton Place & Beckwith Historical Society, 513
Carstairs & District Historical Society, 516
Central Ontario Network for Black History, 525
Centre d'Histoire de Saint-Hyacinthe, 528
Centre historique de St-Armand, 535
The Champlain Society, 551
Chapel Hill Historical Society, 552
Chatham Railroad Museum Society, 555
Chezzetcook Historical Society, 557
Cobourg & District Historical Society, 579
Colchester Historical Society, 580
Collingwood & District Historical Society, 591
Commission canadienne d'histoire militaire, 592
Commission internationale de diplomatique, 1518
Community Heritage Ontario, 599
Compton County Historical Museum Society, 609
Compton Historical Society, 609
Cornwall Township Historical Society, 629
Corporation des Chemins Craig et Gosford, 629
Courtenay & District Historical Society, 637
Cranbrook Archives, Museum & Landmark Foundation, 638
Creston & District Historical & Museum Society, 641
Cumberland Museum Society, 645
Dartmouth Historical Association, 651
Didsbury & District Historical Society, 656
Dundalk Historical Society, 664
East Georgian Bay Historical Foundation, 668
East Hants Historical Society, 668
East York Historical Society, 669
Edgerton & District Historical Society, 674
Edmonton Radial Railway Society, 679
Essa Historical Society, 696
Etobicoke Historical Society, 697
Fédération des sociétés d'histoire du Québec, 719
Fernie & District Historical Society, 732
Fire Fighters Historical Society of Winnipeg, Inc., 738
Fondation Lionel-Groulx, 747
Fort Edmonton Foundation, 752
Fort Macleod Historical Association, 752
Fort McMurray Historical Society, 753
Fort Saskatchewan Historical Society, 754
Fort Whoop-up Interpretive Society, 754
Friends Historical Association, 1527
Friends Historical Society - London, 1527
The Friends of Fort York & Garrison Common, 761
Friends of the Forestry Farm House Inc., 762
Gatineau Valley Historical Society, 768
Genealogical Institute of The Maritimes, 768
Georgeville Historical Society, 771
German-Canadian Historical Association Inc., 772
Glanbrook Heritage Society, 774
Gloucester Historical Society, 775
Grand Manan Museum Inc., 780
Grenville County Historical Society, 789
Guelph Historical Society, 793
Guysborough Historical Society, 795
Halifax Citadel Regimental Association, 799
Hanna Museum & Pioneer Village, 803
Hantsport & Area Historical Society, 803
Harrow Early Immigrant Research Society, 804
Hastings County Historical Society, 804
Head-of-the-Lake Historical Society, 805
L'Héritage canadien du Québec, 813
Heritage Toronto, 813
Historic Restoration Society of Annapolis County, 815
Historical Association of Annapolis Royal, 815
Historical Society of Alberta, 816
Historical Society of Ottawa, 816
Historical Society of St. Boniface & Maryhill Community, 816
Historical Society of St. Catharines, 816
Hudson's Hope Museum, 824
Huntley Township Historical Society, 828
Huntsville & Lake of Bays Railway Society, 828
Institut d'histoire de l'Amérique française, 841
International Arthurian Society - North American Branch, 1535
International Economic History Association, 1546
International Federation for Research in Women's History, 1547
International Napoleonic Society, 858
International Society for the History of Medicine - Canadian Section, 860
Iroquois Falls Historical Society, 864
Islands Historical Society, 866
J. Douglas Ferguson Historical Research Foundation, 867
Jewish Heritage Centre of Western Canada Inc., 872
Jewish Historical Society of BC, 872
Jewish Historical Society of Southern Alberta, 872
King's County Historical Society, 888
Kings Historical Society, 888
Kingston Association of Museums, Art Galleries & Historic Sites, 889
Kingston Historical Society, 889
Kneehill Historical Society, 892
Lambton County Historical Society, 897
Legal Archives Society of Alberta, 906
Lennox & Addington Historical Society, 907
Lennoxville-Ascot Historical & Museum Society, 907
Literary & Historical Society of Québec, 914
London & Middlesex Historical Society, 917
The Lord Selkirk Association of Rupert's Land, 919
Lost Villages Historical Society, 919
Lundy's Lane Historical Society, 920
Lunenburg County Historical Society, 921
Manitoba Historical Society, 938
Manitoba Mennonite Historical Society, 940
Maple Ridge Museum & Community Archives, 948
Margaret M. Allemang Centre for the History of Nursing, 949
Markham District Historical Society, 952
Marsh Collection Society, 952
Matsqui Sumas Abbotsford Museum Society, 954
Meanskinisht Village Historical Association, 956
Megantic County Historical Society, 959
Mennonite Historical Society of Canada, 961
Middle River & Area Historical Society, 964
Millbrook & Cavan Historical Society, 965
Millet & District Historical Society, 966
Milton Historical Society, 966
Miramichi Historical Society, Inc., 968
Mission Heritage Association, 969
Missisquoi Historical Society, 969
Multicultural History Society of Ontario, 979
Municipality of Port Hope Historical Society, 982
Museum London, 983
Muskoka Steamship & Historical Society, *985*
Nanaimo *Historical Society, 988*
National Trust for Canada, 996
Naval Museum of Alberta Society, 1001
New Brunswick Historical Society, 1009
New Denmark Historical Society, 1014
New Westminster Historical Society, 1015
Newcastle Village & District Historical Society, 1015
Newfoundland Historical Society, 1023
Norfolk Historical Society, 1028
Norman Wells Historical Society, 1028
North American Society for Oceanic History, 1579
The North Cumberland Historical Society, 1030
North Grenville Historical Society, 1031
North Lanark Historical Society, 1031
North Pacific Cannery - National Historic Site, 1032
North Peace Historical Society, 1032
North Sydney Historical Society, 1033
Oakville Historical Society, 1053
Okanagan Historical Society, 1055
Old Strathcona Foundation, 1056
Old Sydney Society, 1056
On to Ottawa Historical Society, 1058
Ontario Black History Society, 1068
Ontario Electric Railway Historical Association, 1077
Ontario Historical Society, 1084
Ontario Military Vehicle Association, 1091
Organization of American Historians, 1581
Osgoode Twp. Historical Society, 1127
Oshawa Historical Society, 1128
Ottawa Valley Historical Society, 1132
Parrsborough Shore Historical Society, 1143
Patrimoine et Culture du Portage, 1145
Pelham Historical Society, 1149
Peterborough Historical Society, 1153
Petrolia Discovery, 1155
Photographic Historical Society of Canada, 1157
Pictou County Historical Society, 1159
Pier 21 Society, 1159
Pittsburgh Historical Society, 1160
Port Clements Historical Society, 1165
Port Hastings Historical Society, 1166
Postal History Society of Canada, 1168
Pouce Coupe & District Museum & Historical Society, 1168
Prairie West Historical Society Inc., 1170
Prince Edward Historical Society, 1171
Queens County Historical Society, 1200
Rainy Hills Historical Society, 1204
Renfrew & District Historical Society, 1217
Richard III Society of Canada, 1229
Richmond County Historical Society, 1230
Rimbey Historical Society, 1232
The Royal Nova Scotia Historical Society, 1242
Saanich Historical Artifacts Society, 1245
Saint John Jewish Historical Society, 1247
St. Albert Historical Society, 1248
Saskatchewan History & Folklore Society Inc., 1267
Sault Ste Marie & 49th Field Regt. RCA Historical Society, 1281
Scarborough Historical Society, 1282
Scottish Settlers Historical Society, 1286
Shelburne Historical Society, 1295
Simcoe County Historical Association, 1299
Smith-Ennismore Historical Society, 1304
Smiths Falls & District Historical Society, 1304
Société canadienne d'histoire de l'Église Catholique - Section française, 1307
Société d'histoire d'Amos, 1310
Société d'histoire d'Asbestos, 1310
Société d'histoire Danville-Shipton, 1310
Société d'histoire de Beloeil - Mont-Saint-Hilaire, 1310
Société d'histoire de Coaticook, 1310
Société d'histoire de Greenfield Park, 1310
Société d'histoire de l'Outaouais inc., 1310
Société d'histoire de la Côte-des-Neiges, 1310
Société d'histoire de la Haute Gaspésie, 1310
Société d'histoire de la Haute-Yamaska, 1310
Société d'histoire de la MRC de l'Assomption, 1310
Société d'histoire de La Prairie-de-la-Magdeleine, 1310
Société d'histoire de la Rivière du Nord inc., 1310
Société d'histoire de la Rivière Saint-Jean incorporée, 1310
La Société d'histoire de la Rivière-du-Nord, 1310
Société d'histoire de la Seigneurie de Chambly, 1311
Société d'histoire de la Seigneurie de Monnoir, 1311
Société d'histoire de Lachine, 1311
Société d'histoire de Longueuil, 1311
Société d'histoire de Louiseville inc., 1311
Société d'histoire de Magog, 1311
Société d'histoire de Montarville, 1311
Société d'histoire de Rouyn-Noranda, 1311
Société d'histoire de Sainte-Foy, 1311
Société d'histoire de Saint-Hubert, 1311
Société d'histoire de Saint-Tite, 1311
Société d'histoire de Sherbrooke, 1311
Société d'histoire de Sillery, 1311
La Société d'histoire de Toronto, 1311
Société d'histoire de Warwick, 1312
Société d'histoire de Weedon, 1312
Société d'histoire des Iles-Percées, 1312
Société d'histoire des Six Cantons, 1312
Société d'histoire du Haut-Richelieu, 1312
Société d'histoire du Lac-St-Jean/Maison des Bâtisseurs, 1312
Société d'histoire du Témiscamingue, 1312
Société d'histoire et d'archéologie du Témiscouata, 1312
Société d'histoire et de généalogie de l'Ile Jésus, 1312
Société d'histoire et de généalogie de la Matapédia, 1312
Société d'histoire et de généalogie de Matane, 1312
Société d'histoire et de généalogie de Rivière-du-Loup, 1312
Société d'histoire et de généalogie de Saint-Casimir, 1312
Société d'histoire et de généalogie de Salaberry, 1313
Société d'histoire et de généalogie de Shawinigan-sud, 1313
Société d'histoire et de généalogie de Val-d'Or, 1313
Société d'histoire et de généalogie de Verdun, 1313
Société d'histoire et de généalogie des Mille-Iles, 1313
Société d'histoire et de généalogie des Pays-d'en-Haut, inc., 1313
Société d'histoire et de généalogie des Quatre Lieux, 1313
Société d'histoire et de généalogie Maria-Chapdelaine, 1313
Société d'histoire et généalogie du granit, 1313
Société d'histoire régionale de Lévis, 1313
Société d'histoire régionale Deux-Montagnes, 1313
Société d'histoire St-Stanislas inc., 1314
Société de conservation de la Baie de l'Isle-Verte, 1314
Société de généalogie de Drummondville, 1315
Société de généalogie et d'histoire de la région de Thetford-Mines, 1316
Société des archives historiques de la région de l'Amiante, 1317
Société des professeurs d'histoire du Québec inc., 1318
Société du patrimoine de Boucherville, 1319
Société histoire de Mouillepied, 1319
Société historique acadienne de la Baie Sainte-Marie, 1319
Société historique Alphonse-Desjardins, 1319
Société historique Cavelier-de-LaSalle, 1319
Société historique de Bellechasse, 1319
Société historique de Charlesbourg, 1319
Société historique de Dorval, 1319
Société historique de Joliette-De Lanaudière, 1319
Société historique de la Côte-du-Sud, 1320
Société historique de la Côte-Nord, 1320
Société historique de la région de Mont-Laurier, 1320
Société historique de la Vallée de la Châteauguay, 1320
La Société historique de Nouvelle-Beauce, 1320
Société historique de Pubnico-Ouest, 1320
Société historique de Québec, 1320
Société historique de Rivière-des-Prairies, 1320
Société historique de Saint-Boniface, 1320

SI - 44

ASSOCIATIONS DU CANADA 2018

Société historique de Saint-Henri, 1320
Société historique de Saint-Romuald, 1320
La Société historique du Cap-Rouge, 1320
Société historique du Saguenay, 1321
Société historique et culturelle du Marigot inc., 1321
Société historique et généalogique de Trois-Pistoles, inc., 1321
Société historique Machault, 1321
Société historique Pierre-de-Saurel inc., 1321
Société Louis-Napoléon Dugal/Société Grande-Rivière, 1321
Society for the History of Technology, 1591
Society of Architectural Historians, 1592
South Norwich Historical Society, 1335
Stanstead Historical Society, 1348
Stewart Historical Society, 1350
Stoney Creek Historical Society, 1350
Stormont, Dundas & Glengarry Historical Society, 1350
Streetsville Historical Society, 1352
Strome & District Historical Society, 1352
Sunbury West Historical Society, 1354
Sydney & Louisburg Railway Historical Society, 1360
Tecumseth & West Gwillimbury Historical Society, 1369
Telephone Historical Centre, 1369
Them Days Inc., 1375
Thunder Bay Historical Museum Society, 1378
Tofield Historical Society, 1381
Toronto Railway Historical Association, 1386
Touchstones Nelson Museum of Art & History, 1388
Town of York Historical Society, 1393
Trent Port Historical Society, 1397
Trinity Historical Society Inc., 1399
Tweed & Area Historical Society, 1400
United Empire Loyalists' Association of Canada, 1410
Uxbridge Historical Centre, 1423
Victoria County Historical Society, 1432
Victorian Studies Association of Western Canada, 1434
The Vimy Foundation, 1435
Vintage Locomotive Society Inc., 1435
Wallaceburg & District Historical Society, Inc., 1440
Waterford & Townsend Historical Society, 1442
Waterloo Historical Society, 1442
Wellington County Historical Society, 1443
West Coast Railway Association, 1445
West Elgin Historical & Genealogical Society, 1445
West Hants Historical Society, 1445
West Lincoln Historical Society & Archives, 1446
West Toronto Junction Historical Society, 1446
Westmorland Historical Society, 1451
Westmount Historical Association, 1451
Weston Historical Society, 1451
Weymouth Historical Society, 1451
White River District Historical Society, 1452
Whitewater Historical Society, 1453
Windermere District Historical Society, 1456
Wolfville Historical Society, 1460
Yarmouth County Historical Society, 1470
York Pioneer & Historical Society, 1473
York-Grand River Historical Society, 1474
Yukon Historical & Museums Association, 1478

HIV/AIDS
African & Caribbean Council on HIV/AIDS in Ontario, 12
Africans in Partnership Against AIDS, 13
AIDS Action Now, 15
AIDS Coalition of Cape Breton, 15
AIDS Committee of Cambridge, Kitchener/Waterloo & Area, 16
AIDS Committee of Durham Region, 16
AIDS Committee of Newfoundland & Labrador, 16
AIDS Committee of North Bay & Area, 16
AIDS Committee of Ottawa, 16
AIDS Committee of Simcoe County, 16
AIDS Committee of Toronto, 16
AIDS Committee of Windsor, 16
AIDS Committee of York Region, 17
The AIDS Foundation of Canada, 17
AIDS Moncton, 17
AIDS New Brunswick, 17
AIDS Niagara, 17
AIDS Programs South Saskatchewan, 17
AIDS Saint John, 17
AIDS Saskatoon, 17
AIDS Vancouver Island, 17
Alberta Reappraising AIDS Society, 43
Alliance for South Asian AIDS Prevention, 57
ANKORS, 71
Asian Community AIDS Services, 87
Black Coalition for AIDS Prevention, 213
Blood Ties Four Directions Centre, 215
Bruce House, 260
Bureau local d'intervention traitant du SIDA, 264
Bureau régional d'action sida (Outaouais), 264
Canadian Aboriginal AIDS Network, 285
Canadian AIDS Society, 290
Canadian AIDS Treatment Information Exchange, 290
Canadian Association of Nurses in HIV/AIDS Care, 323
Canadian Foundation for AIDS Research, 392
Canadian HIV Trials Network, 405
Canadian HIV/AIDS Legal Network, 405
Casey House Hospice Inc., 516
Centre d'action sida Montréal (Femmes), 527
Centre sida amitié, 536
Coalition des organismes communautaires québécois de lutte contre le sida, 578
Coalition sida des sourds du Québec, 578
Comité des personnes atteintes du VIH du Québec, 592
CUSO International, 646
Dignitas International, 656
Elevate NWO, 684
The Farha Foundation, 705
Fife House, 734
HALCO, 798
Hamilton AIDS Network, 800
Healing Our Nations, 805
Healing Our Spirit BC Aboriginal HIV/AIDS Society, 805
Hébergements de l'envol, 811
HIV Community Link, 816
HIV Network of Edmonton Society, 816
HIV/AIDS Regional Services, 817
HIV/AIDS Resources and Community Health, 817
International Council of AIDS Service Organizations, 855
Intervention régionale et information sur le sida en Estrie, 862
John Gordon Home, 873
Kali-Shiva AIDS Services, 880
Living Positive, 915
Living Positive Resource Centre, Okanagan, 915
Maggie's: The Toronto Sex Workers Action Project, 925
Maison Amaryllis, 926
Maison du Parc, 927
Maison Plein Coeur, 927
Mouvement d'information et d'entraide dans la lutte contre le sida à Québec, 977
Mouvement d'information, d'éducation et d'entraide dans la lutte contre le sida, 977
The Northern AIDS Connection Society, 1034
Ontario HIV Treatment Network, 1084
Peel HIV/AIDS Network, 1148
P.E.E.R.S. Alliance, 1148
Positive Living BC, 1167
Positive Living North: No kheyoh t'sih'en t'sehena Society, 1168
Positive Women's Network, 1168
Positive Youth Outreach, 1168
Prisoners' HIV/AIDS Support Action Network, 1180
Red Road HIV/AIDS Network, 1210
Regional HIV/AIDS Connection, 1212
Regroupement des personnes vivant avec le VIH-sida de Québec et la région, 1215
Réseau ACCESS Network, 1218
Sidaction Mauricie, 1298
SIDALYS, 1298
The Teresa Group, 1371
Toronto PWA Foundation, 1386
2-Spirited People of the First Nations, 1401

Hobbies
Antique Motorcycle Club of Manitoba Inc., 72
Canadian Vintage Motorcycle Group, 501
Craft & Hobby Association, 1520
East Coast Aquarium Society, 668
Halifax Amateur Radio Club, 798

Hockey
Abbotsford Female Hockey Association, 1
British Columbia Amateur Hockey Association, 230
British Columbia Floorball Federation, 241
Calgary Sledge Hockey Association, 274
Canadian Adult Recreational Hockey Association, 288
Canadian Deaf Ice Hockey Federation, 376
Canadian Electric Wheelchair Hockey Association, 380
Canadian Hockey League, 406
Cape Breton County Minor Hockey Association, 509
Fédération internationale de hockey, 1525
Floorball Alberta, 741
Floorball Canada, 741
Floorball Nova Scotia, 741
Floorball Québec, 741
George Bray Sports Association, 770
Hockey Alberta, 817
Hockey Canada, 817
Hockey Canada Foundation, 817
Hockey Development Centre for Ontario, 817
Hockey Eastern Ontario, 817
Hockey Manitoba, 818
Hockey New Brunswick, 818
Hockey Newfoundland & Labrador, 818
Hockey North, 818
Hockey Northwestern Ontario, 818
Hockey Nova Scotia, 818
Hockey PEI, 818
Hockey Québec, 818
Hockey Yukon, 818
International Ice Hockey Federation, 1550
Lethbridge Oldtimers Sports Association, 908
Minor Hockey Alliance of Ontario, 968
National Hockey League Alumni Association, 994
National Hockey League Players' Association, 994
Northern Ontario Hockey Association, 1035
Nova Scotia Minor Hockey Council, 1047
Ontario Floorball Association, 1080
Ontario Hockey Federation, 1084
Ontario Minor Hockey Association, 1091
Ontario Sledge Hockey Association, 1105
Ontario Women's Hockey Association, 1113
Original Hockey Hall of Fame & Museum, 1126
Ottawa District Minor Hockey Association, 1130
Pan American Hockey Federation, 1138
Prince Edward Island Hockey Referees Association, 1174
Professional Hockey Players' Association, 1185
Saskatchewan Hockey Association, 1267
Sledge Hockey of Canada, 1303
Summerside & Area Minor Hockey Association, 1354
Thunder Bay Minor Hockey Association, 1378
Township of Clarence Minor Hockey Association, 1393
Western Hockey League, 1449
Whitehorse Minor Hockey Association, 1453
Whitehorse Women's Hockey Association, 1453
Yukon Indian Hockey Association, 1479

Holocaust & Holocaust Studies
Association of Holocaust Organizations, 1512
Canadian Society for Yad Vashem, 479
Center for Holocaust & Genocide Studies, 1516
Friends of Simon Wiesenthal Centre for Holocaust Studies - Canada, 762
Holocaust Education Centre, 818
Holocaust Memorial Foundation of Illinois, 1529
The Montréal Holocaust Memorial Centre, 972
Rosenthal Institute for Holocaust Studies, 1587
Vancouver Holocaust Centre Society - A Museum for Education & Remembrance, 1425

Home & School Associations
Alberta School Councils' Association, 45
British Columbia Confederation of Parent Advisory Councils, 236
Canadian Home & School Federation, 406
Manitoba Association of Parent Councils, 930
New Brunswick Federation of Home & School Associations, Inc., 1008
Nova Scotia Federation of Home & School Associations, 1044
Ontario Federation of Home & School Associations Inc., 1079
Prince Edward Island Home & School Federation Inc., 1175
Québec Federation of Home & School Associations Inc., 1197
Saskatchewan Association of School Councils, 1258

Home Care
L'Appui pour les proches aidants d'aînés, 75
Canadian Home Care Association, 408
Carefirst Seniors & Community Services Association, 511
Caregivers Alberta, 512
Caregivers Nova Scotia, 512
Carers ARK, 512
Centre de soutien entr'Aidants, 530
Community Care for South Hastings, 596
Family Caregivers of British Columbia, 702
Greater Vancouver Community Services Society, 786
Home Child Care Association of Ontario, 819
Manitoba Association of Personal Care Home Social Workers, 931
Ontario Community Support Association, 1073
Ontario Home Care Association, 1086
Saint Elizabeth Health Care, 1246
Toronto Community Care Access Centre, 1383
VHA Home HealthCare, 1431
Victorian Order of Nurses for Canada, 1434

Home Economics
Association coopérative d'économie familliale de Québec, 98
Association of Saskatchewan Home Economists, 161
International Federation for Home Economics, 1546
Manitoba Association of Home Economists, 930
Ontario Home Economics Association, 1086
Saskatchewan Home Economics Teachers Association, 1267
Teachers of Home Economics Specialist Association, 1367

Home Inspection
Alberta Professional Home Inspectors Society, 43
Canadian Association of Home & Property Inspectors, 317
Home Inspectors Association BC, 819

Home Schooling
Alberta Home Education Association, 37
Educators for Distributed Learning PSA (British Columbia), 680
Home School Legal Defence Association of Canada, 819
Manitoba Association of Christian Home Schools, 929
Ontario Federation of Teaching Parents, 1080
Saskatchewan Home Based Educators, 1267

Homeopathy
Homeopathic College of Canada, 819
Homeopathic Medical Association Of Canada, 820
National United Professional Association of Trained Homeopaths, 996
Ontario Homeopathic Association, 1086
Syndicat professionnel des homéopathes du Québec, 1365

Honey
Alberta Beekeepers Commission, 26
Beekeepers' Association of Niagara Region, 204
British Columbia Honey Producers Association, 243
Canadian Association of Professional Apiculturists, 328
Canadian Honey Council, 408
Capital Region Beekeepers Association, 510
Central Beekeepers' Alliance, 524
Central Ontario Beekeepers' Association, 525
Dufferin County Beekeepers' Association, 664
Durham Region Beekeepers' Association, 665
Eastern Apicultural Society of North America, Inc., 1522
Eastern Ontario Beekeepers' Association, 670

Subject Index / Horse Racing

Fédération des apiculteurs du Québec, 711
Golden Horseshoe Beekeepers' Association, 776
Grand River Beekeepers' Association, 780
Grey Bruce Beekeepers' Association, 790
Haldimand-Norfolk District Beekeepers' Association, 798
Huronia & District Beekeepers' Association, 828
Huron-Perth Beekeepers' Association, 828
Lanark County Beekeepers' Association, 897
Limestone Beekeepers Guild, 912
Manitoba Beekeepers' Association, 932
Manitoba Cooperative Honey Producers Ltd., 934
Middlesex, Oxford, Elgin Beekeepers' Association, 965
Muskoka-Parry Sound Beekeepers' Association, 985
Nova Scotia Beekeepers' Association, 1042
Prince Edward Island Beekeepers' Cooperative Association, 1172
Quinte Beekeepers' Association, 1201
Rainy River Beekeepers' Association, 1204
Southwestern Ontario Beekeepers' Association, 1338
Sudbury & District Beekeepers' Association, 1353
Thunder Bay Beekeepers' Association, 1377
Toronto District Beekeepers' Association, 1384
United County Beekeepers, 1410
Upper Ottawa Valley Beekeepers' Association, 1422
Wellington County Beekeepers' Association, 1443

Horse Racing
Atlantic Standardbred Breeders Association, 186
Central Ontario Standardbred Association, 525
Equine Association of Yukon, 694
Jockey Club of Canada, 873
Jockeys Benefit Association of Canada, 873
Ontario Horse Racing Industry Association, 1086
Ontario Standardbred Adoption Society, 1109
Standardbred Breeders of Ontario Association, 1347

Horses
Alberta Carriage Driving Association, 27
Alberta Clydesdale & Shire Association, 28
Alberta Dressage Association, 33
Alberta Equestrian Federation, 34
Alberta Percheron Club, 42
Alberta Reined Cow Horse Association, 44
Alberta Walking Horse Association, 51
American Saddlebred Horse Association of Alberta, 66
American Saddlebred Horse Association of British Columbia, 66
American Saddlebred Horse Association of Canada, 66
American Saddlebred Horse Association of Ontario, 66
Appaloosa Horse Club of Canada, 73
Arabian Horse Association of Eastern Canada, 76
Association des éleveurs de chevaux Belge du Québec, 111
Association des Poneys Welsh & Cob au Québec, 124
Association québécoise pour le tourisme équestre et l'équitation de loisir du Québec, 177
Atlantic Standardbred Breeders Association, 186
Back Country Horsemen of British Columbia, 192
British Columbia Miniature Horse Club, 246
British Columbia Sporthorse - Sport Pony Breeders Group, 255
British Columbia Welsh Pony & Cob Association, 258
CADORA British Columbia, 268
CADORA Ontario Association Inc., 269
Canadian Arabian Horse Registry, 294
Canadian Belgian Horse Association, 342
Canadian Connemara Pony Society, 363
Canadian Cutting Horse Association, 375
Canadian Dressage Owners & Riders Association, 378
Canadian Fjord Horse Association, 391

Canadian Haflinger Association, 400
Canadian Horse Breeders' Association, 408
Canadian Horse Heritage & Preservation Society, 408
Canadian Icelandic Horse Federation, 410
Canadian Morgan Horse Association, 437
Canadian Palomino Horse Association, 449
Canadian Percheron Association, 453
Canadian Pony Club, 457
Canadian Pony Society, 458
Canadian Quarter Horse Association, 464
Canadian Registry of Tennessee Walking Horse, 466
Canadian Shire Horse Association, 470
Canadian Thoroughbred Horse Society, 494
Canadian Trakehner Horse Society, 496
Canadian Warmblood Horse Breeders Association, 502
Clydesdale Horse Association of Canada, 576
Cypress Hills Registered Horse Breeders' Association, 647
Equestrian Canada, 694
Equine Association of Yukon, 694
Equine Guelph, 694
Fédération équestre du Québec inc., 720
Guelph Equine Area Rescue Stables, 793
Heaven Can Wait Equine Rescue, 810
Horse Council British Columbia, 822
Horse Industry Association of Alberta, 822
Island Horse Council, 865
Jump Alberta, 877
Manitoba Horse Council Inc., 938
Manitoba Percheron & Belgian Club, 942
Manitoba Welsh Pony & Cob Association, 947
Maritime Breeders Association, 950
Miniature Horse Association of Canada, 966
Miniature Horse Association of Nova Scotia, 966
Miniature Horse Club of Ontario, 966
New Brunswick Equestrian Association, 1008
Nova Scotia Equestrian Federation, 1044
Okanagan Miniature Horse Club, 1055
Ontario Association of Equine Practitioners, 1063
Ontario Equestrian Federation, 1078
Ontario Percheron Horse Association Inc., 1095
Ontario Standardbred Adoption Society, 1109
Peruvian Horse Association of Canada, 1152
Prince Edward Island Draft Horse Association, 1173
Prince Edward Island Standardbred Horseowners' Association, 1177
Sasha's Legacy Equine Rescue, 1254
Saskatchewan Horse Breeders Association, 1267
Saskatchewan Horse Federation, 1267
Standardbred Breeders of Ontario Association, 1347
Standardbred Canada, 1347
Tennessee Walking Horse Association of Western Canada, 1370
Upper Canada District Canadian Horse Breeders, 1421
Vancouver Island Miniature Horse Club, 1426
Welsh Pony & Cob Association of Ontario, 1444
Welsh Pony & Cob Society of Canada, 1444
Welsh Pony & Cob Society of Saskatchewan, 1444
Western Canadian Miniature Horse Club, 1448
Wild Rose Draft Horse Association, 1454
World Arabian Horse Organization, 1603

Horseshoe Pitching
Alberta Horseshoe Pitchers Association, 38
B.C. Horseshoe Association, 201
Fédération des clubs de fers du Québec, 713
Horseshoe Canada, 822
Horseshoe New Brunswick, 822
Horseshoe Ontario, 822
Horseshoe Saskatchewan Inc., 822
Nova Scotia Horseshoe Players Association, 1046
Nova Scotia Horseshoe Players Association, 1046

Horticulture
Alpine Garden Club of BC, 59
American Public Gardens Association, 1497
Les Amis du Jardin botanique de Montréal, 67
Brampton Horticultural Society, 226
Calgary Horticultural Society, 272
Canadian Botanical Conservation Network, 346

Canadian Horticultural Council, 408
Canadian Horticultural Therapy Association, 408
Canadian Nursery Landscape Association, 442
Canadian Ornamental Plant Foundation, 448
Canadian Society for Horticultural Science, 475
Center for Plant Conservation, 1516
City Farmer - Canada's Office of Urban Agriculture, 571
Club violettes Longueuil, 576
Conserver Society of Hamilton & District Inc., 623
Expo agricole de Chicoutimi, 700
Fédération des sociétés d'horticulture et d'écologie du Québec, 719
Fédération interdisciplinaire de l'horticulture ornementale du Québec, 721
Friends of Devonian Botanic Garden, 761
The Garden Clubs of Ontario, 766
Greater Toronto Water Garden & Horticultural Society, 786
Integrated Vegetation Management Association of British Columbia, 850
International Plant Propagators Society, Inc., 1555
Landscape Alberta Nursery Trades Association, 898
Landscape New Brunswick Horticultural Trades Association, 898
Lethbridge & District Japanese Garden Society, 907
Manitoba Regional Lily Society, 943
Newfoundland Horticultural Society, 1023
Newfoundland Rock Garden Society, 1023
North American Native Plant Society, 1029
Ontario Horticultural Association, 1086
Ontario Rock Garden Society, 1102
Ontario Vegetation Management Association, 1112
Ottawa Valley Rock Garden & Horticultural Society, 1132
Royal Botanical Gardens, 1239
Seeds of Diversity Canada, 1289
Société d'horticulture de Saint-Lambert, 1314
Société d'horticulture et d'écologie de Boucherville, 1314
Société d'Horticulture et d'Écologie de Brossard, 1314
Société d'horticulture et d'Écologie de Longueuil, 1314
Société de protection des plantes du Québec, 1317
Tottenham & District Horticultural Association, 1388
Vancouver Island Rock & Alpine Garden Society, 1427
Vancouver Japanese Gardeners Association, 1427
VanDusen Botanical Garden Association, 1429
Weed Science Society of America, 1602

Hospice Care
British Columbia Hospice Palliative Care Association, 243
Casey House Hospice Inc., 516
Hospice Niagara, 822
Hospice of Waterloo Region, 822
Hospice Palliative Care Association of Prince Edward Island, 823
John Gordon Home, 873
Nelson & District Hospice Society, 1003
North Shore Hospice Society, 1032
Palliative Manitoba, 1137

Hospital Auxiliaries
Hospital Auxiliaries Association of Ontario, 823

Hospitality Industry
British Columbia Bed & Breakfast Innkeepers Guild, 233
Federation of Ontario Bed & Breakfast Accommodation, 725
Niagara-on-the-Lake Bed & Breakfast Association Inc., 1026
Ontario Farm & Country Accommodations Association, 1078
Saskatchewan Bed & Breakfast Association, 1259
University of Guelph Food Service Employees Association, 1419

Hospitals
Academy of Canadian Executive Nurses, 4
Accreditation Canada, 5
Alberta Children's Hospital Foundation, 28
Association des pharmaciens des établissements de santé du Québec, 123
CAMH Foundation, 276
Canadian Association of Paediatric Health Centres, 325
Canadian Friends of Bikur Cholim Hospital, 394
Canadian Healthcare Engineering Society, 402
Canadian Society of Hospital Pharmacists, 483
Cape Breton Regional Hospital Foundation, 509
Children's Hospital Foundation of Manitoba, 562
Children's Hospital Foundation of Saskatchewan, 562
Children's Hospital of Eastern Ontario Foundation, 562
Children's Miracle Network, 562
Chinook Regional Hospital Foundation, 565
Covenant Foundation, 637
Covenant Health, 637
Fondation CHU de Québec, 743
Fondation CHU Dumont Foundation, 743
Fondation CHU Sainte-Justine, 743
Fondation de l'Hôpital de Montréal pour enfants, 744
Fondation de l'Hôpital du Sacré-Coeur de Montréal, 744
Fondation de l'Hôpital Général de Montréal, 744
Fondation de l'Hôpital Maisonneuve-Rosemont, 744
Fondation du CHUM, 745
Friends of The Moncton Hospital Foundation, 763
Gustav Levinschi Foundation, 794
Health Employers Association of British Columbia, 806
HealthCareCAN, 807
Hospital for Sick Children Foundation, 823
Infection & Prevention Control Canada, 836
International Hospital Federation, 1550
IWK Health Centre Foundation, 867
Janeway Children's Hospital Foundation, 868
Jewish General Hospital Foundation, 872
Lions Gate Hospital Foundation, 913
Lloydminster Region Health Foundation, 916
London Health Sciences Foundation, 918
Markham Stouffville Hospital Foundation, 952
McGill University Health Centre Foundation, 955
Mount Sinai Hospital Foundation, 976
Ontario Hospital Association, 1086
Prince County Hospital Foundation, 1171
Queen Elizabeth Hospital Foundation, 1199
Royal University Hospital Foundation, 1243
St. Joseph's Healthcare Foundation, 1249
Saskatchewan Association of Health Organizations, 1257
Toronto General & Western Hospital Foundation, 1385
Trillium Health Partners Foundation, 1398
Vernon Jubilee Hospital Foundation, 1431
Victoria Hospitals Foundation, 1432

Hostelling
Fondation Tourisme Jeunesse, 748

Hotels & Motels
Alberta Hotel & Lodging Association, 38
American Hotel & Lodging Association, 1494
Association Hôtellerie Québec, 136
British Columbia Hotel Association, 243
British Columbia Lodging & Campgrounds Association, 245
Canadian Hotel Marketing & Sales Executives, 409
Les Clefs d'Or Canada, 573
Greater Toronto Hotel Association, 786
Hotel Association of Canada Inc., 823
Hotel Association of Nova Scotia, 824
Hotel Association of Prince Edward Island, 824
Hotel Association of Vancouver, 824
Innkeepers Guild of Nova Scotia, 839
Institut de tourisme et d'hôtellerie du Québec, 842
International Hotel & Restaurant Association, 1550
Manitoba Hotel Association, 938
Ontario Restaurant, Hotel & Motel Association, 1101

Ontario's Finest Inns & Spas, 1114
Saskatchewan Hotel & Hospitality Association, 1267

Housewares Industry
Association of Home Appliance Manufacturers Canada Council, 149
Canadian Gift Association, 398
Canadian Hardware & Housewares Manufacturers' Association, 401
Hearth, Patio & Barbecue Association of Canada, 809
Installation, Maintenance & Repair Sector Council & Trade Association, 840
SPANCAN, 1338

Housing
Abbeyfield Houses Society of Canada, 1
Alberta Senior Citizens' Housing Association, 46
Arctic Bay Housing Association, 81
Artscape, 86
Association d'entraide Le Chaînon inc., 99
Atelier habitation Montréal, 180
Bruce House, 260
Canadian Association for Studies in Co-operation, 304
Canadian Association of Home & Property Inspectors, 317
Canadian Housing & Renewal Association, 409
Canadian Manufactured Housing Institute, 429
Centre for Equality Rights in Accommodation, 532
Edmonton Inner City Housing Society, 677
Entre Nous Femmes Housing Society, 690
Fédération des OSBL d'habitation de Montréal, 716
Fife House, 734
Groupe CDH, 791
Habitat for Humanity Canada, 796
H.O.M.E. Society, 819
Hong Fook Mental Health Association, 820
Housing Inspection Foundation, 1530
Institute of Housing Management, 846
Inter-loge, 852
International Federation for Housing & Planning, 1546
LandlordBC, 898
Lookout Emergency Aid Society, 919
Lu'ma Native Housing Society, 920
Manitoba Non-Profit Housing Association, 941
Modular Housing Association Prairie Provinces, 971
Muniscope, 982
Ontario Coalition Against Poverty, 1071
Regroupement des offices d'habitation du Québec, 1215

Human Resources
Administrators of Volunteer Resources BC, 8
Apparel Human Resources Council, 74
Association des gestionnaires de ressources bénévoles du Québec, 115
Association of Canadian Search, Employment & Staffing Services, 143
Association of Career Professionals Internatinal, 144
Association of Professional Recruiters of Canada, 159
BioTalent Canada, 211
BIOTECanada, 212
BuildForce Canada, 261
Canadian Agricultural Human Resource Council, 289
Canadian Apprenticeship Forum, 294
Canadian Association of Career Educators & Employers, 309
Canadian Automotive Repair & Service Council, 340
Canadian Council of Professional Fish Harvesters, 369
Canadian Payroll Association, 452
Canadian Steel Trade & Employment Congress, 491
Canadian Technology Human Resources Board, 493
Canadian Tourism Human Resource Council, 495
Chartered Professionals in Human Resources, 554
Chartered Professionals in Human Resources Manitoba, 554
Chartered Professionals in Human Resources of Alberta, 554
Chartered Professionals in Human Resources of British Columbia & Yukon, 554
Chartered Professionals in Human Resources Saskatchewan, 554
Contact Centre Canada, 626
Council for Automotive Human Resources, 632
Cultural Human Resources Council, 645
Electricity Human Resources Canada, 683
Environmental Careers Organization of Canada, 691
Forum for International Trade Training, 754
Foundation for International Training, 755
HRMS Professionals Association, 824
Human Resources Association of New Brunswick, 825
Human Resources Association of Nova Scotia, 825
Human Resources Professionals Association, 825
Human Resources Professionals of Durham, 826
Human Resources Professionals of Newfoundland & Labrador, 826
Indigenous Works, 835
Information & Communications Technology Council of Canada, 836
Installation, Maintenance & Repair Sector Council & Trade Association, 840
International Association for Human Resource Information Management, 1536
International Labour & Employment Relations Association, 1551
International Personnel Management Association - Canada, 859
International Society for Performance Improvement, 1558
Manitoba Association for Volunteer Administration, 929
Mining Industry Human Resources Council, 967
Motor Carrier Passenger Council of Canada, 975
National Seafood Sector Council, 996
Ordre des conseillers en ressources humaines agréés, 1120
Police Sector Council, 1163
Trucking Human Resources Canada, 1399
Wood Manufacturing Council, 1463
Yukon Tourism Education Council, 1480

Human Rights
Alberta Civil Liberties Research Centre, 28
Amnesty International, 1504
Amnesty International - Canadian Section (English Speaking), 68
Amnistie internationale, Section canadienne (Francophone), 68
ARCH Disability Law Centre, 76
Association pour la promotion des droits des personnes handicapées, 166
B'nai Brith Canada, 192
B'nai Brith Canada Institute for International Affairs, 192
British Columbia Civil Liberties Association, 236
British Columbia Freedom of Information & Privacy Association, 241
Canadian Association for Free Expression, 300
Canadian Association of Statutory Human Rights Agencies, 333
The Canadian Centre/International P.E.N., 354
Canadian Civil Liberties Association, 357
Canadian Coalition Against the Death Penalty, 357
Canadian Committee of Lawyers & Jurists for World Jewry, 361
Canadian Council for International Co-operation, 366
Canadian Journalists for Free Expression, 423
Canadian Lawyers Association for International Human Rights, 426
Canadian Tribute to Human Rights, 497
Cape Breton University Centre for International Studies, 510
Centre for Equality Rights in Accommodation, 532
Centre for Inquiry Canada, 533
Centre international pour la prévention de la criminalité, 535
CPJ Corp., 638
CUSO International, 646
Disabled Individuals Alliance, 658
Disabled Peoples' International, 658
Egale Canada, 681
Electronic Frontier Canada Inc., 683
Equitas - International Centre for Human Rights Education, 695
Fair Vote Canada, 701
Handicap International Canada, 802
Human Rights Internet, 826
Human Rights Research & Education Centre, 826
International Commission of Jurists (Canadian Section), 855
International Council of Voluntary Agencies, 1545
International Humanist & Ethical Union, 1550
International Society for Human Rights, 1558
League for Human Rights of B'nai Brith Canada, 903
Macedonian Human Rights Movement International, 923
Nova Scotia League for Equal Opportunities, 1046
Nova Scotia Public Interest Research Group, 1047
Oakville Community Centre for Peace, Ecology & Human Rights, 1053
One Sky, 1058
PEN International, 1583
Quakers Fostering Justice, 1195
Québec Public Interest Research Group - McGill, 1198
Simon Fraser Public Interest Research Group, 1300
Social Justice Committee, 1305
Toronto Association for Democracy in China, 1382
Treaty & Aboriginal Rights Research Centre of Manitoba Inc., 1397
Vancouver Island Public Interest Research Group, 1426
World Sikh Organization of Canada, 1467

Humanism
Humanist Canada, 826
International Humanist & Ethical Union, 1550
The Royal Society of Canada, 1242

Humanities
American Society for Environmental History, 1498
Association for Canadian Studies, 133
Association of Canadian College & University Teachers of English, 141
Canadian Association for American Studies, 297
Canadian Association for Commonwealth Literature & Language Studies, 298
Canadian Association for Commonwealth Literature & Language Studies, 298
Canadian Comparative Literature Association, 361
Canadian Ethnic Studies Association, 382
Canadian Historical Association, 405
Classical Association of Canada, 572
Emil Skarin Fund, 686
Union académique internationale, 1598

Hungarian Canadians
Hungarian Canadian Cultural Centre, 827
Hungarian Canadian Engineers' Association, 827

Hungary
Hungarian Studies Association of Canada, 827

Hunger
Canadian Food for the Hungry International, 391
Canadian Foodgrains Bank, 391
Chatham Outreach for Hunger, 555
Foodshare Toronto, 750
The Hunger Project Canada, 827

Hunting
Aiviq Hunters & Trappers Organization, 20
Alberta Bowhunters Association, 26
Alberta Professional Outfitters Society, 43
Archers & Bowhunters Association of Manitoba, 78
Association chasse & pêche de Chibougamau, 96
Bowhunters Association of Nova Scotia, 219
Cape Breton Island Wildlife Association, 509
Galiano Rod & Gun Club, 766
Guide Outfitters Association of British Columbia, 793
Lloydminster & District Fish & Game Association, 915
Lunenburg County Wildlife Association, 921
Mittimatalik Hunters' & Trappers' Organization, 970
New Brunswick Outfitters Association Inc., 1011
Nova Scotia Federation of Anglers & Hunters, 1044
Ontario Federation of Anglers & Hunters, 1079
Toronto Sportsmen's Association, 1387
Women That Hunt, 1461
Yukon Outfitters' Association, 1479

Huntington's Disease
Huntington Society of Canada, 827
Société Huntington du Québec, 1321

Hydrocephalus
L'Association de spina-bifida et d'hydrocéphalie du Québec, 104
Spina Bifida & Hydrocephalus Association of British Columbia, 1341
Spina Bifida & Hydrocephalus Association of New Brunswick, 1342
Spina Bifida & Hydrocephalus Association of Northern Alberta, 1342
Spina Bifida & Hydrocephalus Association of Nova Scotia, 1342
Spina Bifida & Hydrocephalus Association of Ontario, 1342
Spina Bifida & Hydrocephalus Association of Prince Edward Island, 1342

Hydrogen
Canadian Hydrogen & Fuel Cell Association, 409
International Association for Hydrogen Energy, 1536

Hydrogeology
International Association of Hydrogeologists, 1538
International Association of Hydrogeologists - Canadian National Chapter, 854

Hydrography
Canadian Hydrographic Association, 409
Canadian Institute of Geomatics, 416
International Federation of Hydrographic Societies, 1548

Hydrology
World Meteorological Organization, 1606

Hypertension
Hypertension Canada, 829
International Society of Hypertension, 1560
World Hypertension League, 1466

Hypnotism
Association des hypnologues du Québec, 116
Canadian Hypnosis Association, 410

Ice
Canadian Ice Carvers' Society, 410
Salt Institute, 1588

Icelanders & Iceland
Icelandic National League of North America, 829
Stephan G. Stephansson Icelandic Society, 1349
Vatnabyggd Icelandic Club of Saskatchewan Inc., 1430

Ileitis
Crohn's & Colitis Canada, 642

Ileostomy
Ileostomy & Colostomy Association of Montréal, 829

Illustrators & Illustration
Association des Illustrateurs et Illustratrices du Québec, 116
Canadian Association of Professional Image Creators, 328
Canadian Society of Children's Authors, Illustrators & Performers, 481

Image Processing
Association for Image & Information Management International - 1st Canadian Chapter, 133
Canadian Image Processing & Pattern Recognition Society, 410
Canadian Imaging Trade Association, 410

Immigrants
A.C.C.E.S. Employment, 4
Afghan Women's Counselling & Integration Community Support Organization, 12
Association for New Canadians, 134
Association of Americans & Canadians in Israel, 1510
The Barbra Schlifer Commemorative Clinic, 196
Calgary Immigrant Women's Association, 272
Canadian Ukrainian Immigrant Aid Society, 498
Centre for Immigrant & Community Services, 532
Centre for Newcomers Society of Calgary, 533
Collectif des femmes immigrantes du Québec, 581
COSTI Immigrant Services, 631
Cowichan Intercultural Society, 637
DIVERSEcity Community Resources Society, 659
Edmonton Immigrant Services Association, 677
Eritrean Canadian Community Centre of Metropolitan Toronto, 695
Ethiopian Association in the Greater Toronto Area & Surrounding Regions, 697
Focus for Ethnic Women, 741
Folk Arts Council of St Catharines, 742
Harrow Early Immigrant Research Society, 804
Hong Fook Mental Health Association, 820
Immigrant & Multicultural Services Society, 830
Immigrant Services Association of Nova Scotia, 830
Immigrant Services Calgary, 830
Immigrant Services Society of BC, 830
Immigrant Women Services Ottawa, 831
Immigrant Women's Health Centre, 831
Inter-Cultural Association of Greater Victoria, 851
Jewish Immigrant Aid Services of Canada, 873
Kababayan Multicultural Centre, 879
Kamloops Immigrant Services, 880
Maison D'Haiti, 926
Maison internationale de la Rive-Sud, 927
Malton Neighbourhood Services, 928
Manitoba Interfaith Welcome Place, 939
Multilingual Orientation Service Association for Immigrant Communities, 979
National Organization of Immigrant & Visible Minority Women of Canada, 995
New Canadians Centre Peterborough Immigrant Services, 1013
Ontario Council of Agencies Serving Immigrants, 1075
Ottawa Community Immigrant Services Organization, 1130
Pacific Immigrant Resources Society, 1135
La Passerelle - Intégration et Développement Économique, 1145
Prince Edward Island Association for Newcomers to Canada, 1172
Quinte Immigrant Services, 1201
Richmond Multicultural Community Services, 1231
Riverdale Immigrant Women's Centre, 1234
Saskatoon Open Door Society Inc., 1279
Service Intégration Travail Outaouais, 1291
Somali Immigrant Women's Association, 1332
Tamil Eelam Society of Canada, 1366
Toronto Community Employment Services, 1383
Vancouver Society of Immigrant & Visible Minority Women, 1428
WIL Employment Connections, 1453
Windsor Women Working with Immigrant Women, 1457
Working Women Community Centre, 1464

Immigration
Affiliation of Multicultural Societies & Service Agencies of BC, 11
American Immigration Lawyers Association - Canadian Chapter, 66
Association québécoise des avocats et avocates en droit de l'immigration, 171
Calgary Catholic Immigration Society, 271
Canada Employment & Immigration Union, 278
Canadian Association of Professional Immigration Consultants, 329
Catholic Centre for Immigrants - Ottawa + CIC Foundation, 517
Catholic Cross Cultural Services, 518
Corporation culturelle Latino-Américaine de l'Amitié, 629
International Social Service Canada, 860
Korean Canadian Women's Association, 893
Lesbian & Gay Immigration Task Force, 907
Maison internationale de la Rive-Sud, 927
National African Integration & Families of Ontario, 989
Pier 21 Society, 1159
Regina Immigrant Women Centre, 1211
World Border Organization, 1465

Immunology
Allergy, Asthma & Immunology Society of Ontario, 54
Association des Allergologues et Immunologues du Québec, 105
Canadian Association for Immunization Research & Evaluation, 301
Canadian Society for Immunology, 475
Canadian Society of Allergy & Clinical Immunology, 479
Centre for Immunization & Respiratory Infectious Diseases, 532

Impact Assessment
Association québécoise pour l'évaluation d'impacts, 176
International Association for Impact Assessment, 1537
International Association for Impact Assessment - Western & Northern Canada, 853
Ontario Association for Impact Assessment, 1061

Import Trade
Canadian Association of Importers & Exporters, 318
Canadian Association of Regulated Importers, 331
Electronics Import Committee, 683
Global Automakers of Canada, 774
International Cheese Council of Canada, 855
Ontario Association of Trading Houses, 1066
Trade Facilitation Office Canada, 1394

Incontinence
The Canadian Continence Foundation, 364
Canadian Nurse Continence Advisors Association, 442
International Continence Society, 1544

Independent Schools
Association of Christian Schools International, 1510
Association of Independent Schools & Colleges in Alberta, 149
Atlantic Conference of Independent Schools, 183
Canadian Accredited Independent Schools, 287
Canadian Council of Montessori Administrators, 369
Centre for Jewish Education, 533
Conference of Independent Schools (Ontario), 612
Federation of Independent School Associations of BC, 724
Manitoba Federation of Independent Schools Inc., 936
Ontario Alliance of Christian Schools, 1059
Ontario Federation of Independent Schools, 1079
Québec Association of Independent Schools, 1196
Youth Ballet & Contemporary Dance of Saskatchewan Inc., 1475

Indexing & Abstracting
Indexing Society of Canada, 834

India
AWIC Community & Social Services, 191
Canada-India Business Council, 283
Canadian Association of Physicians of Indian Heritage, 327
India Rainbow Community Services of Peel, 834
Institute of Asian Research, 844
National Association of Canadians of Origins in India, 990
The Toronto-Calcutta Foundation, 1388

Indonesia
Indonesia Canada Chamber of Commerce, 1531

Indoor Air Quality
Healthy Indoors Partnership, 807
International Society of Indoor Air Quality & Climate, 1560

Industrial Design
Association de la recherche industrielle du Québec, 102
Association des designers industriels du Québec, 110
Association of Canadian Industrial Designers, 142
Association of Chartered Industrial Designers of Ontario, 145
British Columbia Industrial Designer Association, 244

Industrial Development
Aluminium Association of Canada, 61
Association industrielle de l'est de Montréal, 136
Canadian Innovation Centre, 411
United Nations Industrial Development Organization, 1600

Industrial Engineering
Association de la recherche industrielle du Québec, 102
Association for Facilities Engineering, 1508
Institute of Industrial & Systems Engineers, 1533
Plant Engineering & Maintenance Association of Canada, 1162

Industrial Equipment
Association des propriétaires de machinerie lourde du Québec inc., 126
Canadian Process Control Association, 460
Heavy Equipment & Aggregate Truckers Association of Manitoba, 810
Printing Equipment & Supply Dealers' Association of Canada, 1180

Industrial Materials, Advanced
ASM International, 1506
ASM International - Calgary Chapter, 87
Canadian Advanced Technology Alliance, 288
Industrial Fabrics Association International, 1531
Industrial Fabrics Association International Canada, 835

Industrial Waste
Air & Waste Management Association, 1486
American Industrial Hygiene Association, 1494
Center for Health, Environment & Justice, 1516
Ontario Waste Management Association, 1112

Infant Mortality
Baby's Breath, 192

Infants
Baby's Breath, 192
Les Centres jeunesse de l'Outaouais, 537
Early Childhood Intervention Program (ECIP) Sask. Inc., 667
Infant & Toddler Safety Association, 836
Infant Feeding Action Coalition, 836
International Association of Infant Massage Canada, 854

Infection Control
Canadian Association of Wound Care, 337
Centre for Immunization & Respiratory Infectious Diseases, 532
Infection & Prevention Control Canada, 836
Infectious Diseases Society of America, 1531

Information Science
American Society for Information Science & Technology, 1498
Association québécoise des troubles d'apprentissage - section Outaouais, 175
Canadian Association for Information Science, 301
Canadian Information Processing Society, 411
Centre femmes de Rimouski, 531
Dalhousie University School of Information Management Associated Alumni, 648
Healthcare Information & Management Systems Society, 1529
University of Toronto, Faculty of Information Alumni Association, 1421
Urban & Regional Information Systems Association, 1601

Information Technology
Armed Forces Communications & Electronics Association (Canada), 82
Association de la sécurité de l'information du Québec, 102
Association for Image & Information Management International - 1st Canadian Chapter, 133
Association of Research Libraries, 1513
Association québécoise des informaticiennes et informaticiens indépendants, 173
British Columbia Technology Industries Association, 256
Canada's Advanced Internet Development Organization, 281
Canadian Information Processing Society, 411
Canadian IT Law Association, 422
CIO Association of Canada, 570
Digital Health Canada, 656
Digital Nova Scotia, 656
Electronic Frontier Canada Inc., 683
GS1 Canada, 792
Information & Communication Technologies Association of Manitoba, 836
Information Systems Security Association, 1532
Information Technology Association of Canada, 837
International Association of Business Communicators, 1538
Newfoundland & Labrador Association of Technology Industries, 1016
Ontario Library & Information Technology Association, 1088
TECHNOCompétences, 1369
Toronto Association of Systems & Software Quality, 1382
Xplor Canada Association, 1470

Infrastructure
Canada Foundation for Innovation, 279
Canadian Common Ground Alliance, 361
Ontario Regional Common Ground Alliance, 1101

Injured Workers
Canadian Injured Workers Alliance, 411
Cape Breton Injured Workers' Association, 509
Fondation pour l'aide aux travailleuses et travailleurs accidentés, 747
Industrial Accident Victims Group of Ontario, 835
Injured Workers Association of Manitoba Inc., 838
Union of Injured Workers of Ontario, 1407

Insulation
Association d'isolation du Québec, 99
Canadian Urethane Foam Contractors Association, 500
Master Insulators' Association of Ontario Inc., 953
North American Insulation Manufacturers Association, 1579
Thermal Insulation Association of Alberta, 1375

Insurance Brokers
Canadian Association of Independent Life Brokerage Agencies, 318
Chambre de l'assurance de dommages, 550
Independent Financial Brokers of Canada, 832
Insurance Brokers Association of Canada, 848
Surety Association of Canada, 1357
Toronto Insurance Conference, 1385

Insurance Industry
Alberta Insurance Council, 38
Association des actuaires I.A.R.D., 105
Association des experts en sinistre indépendants du Québec inc, 113
Association des femmes d'assurance de Montréal, 114
Association of Certified Fraud Examiners - Toronto Chapter, 145

Canadian Association of Direct Response Insurers, 312
Canadian Association of Financial Institutions in Insurance, 314
Canadian Association of Independent Life Brokerage Agencies, 318
Canadian Association of Insurance Women, 318
Canadian Association of Mutual Insurance Companies, 322
Canadian Automobile Insurance Rate Regulators Association, 339
Canadian Bar Insurance Association, 342
Canadian Board of Marine Underwriters, 345
Canadian Captive Insurance Association, 349
Canadian Council of Insurance Regulators, 368
Canadian Crop Hail Association, 373
Canadian Independent Adjusters' Association, 410
Canadian Institute of Actuaries, 414
Canadian Institute of Underwriters, 420
Canadian Insurance Accountants Association, 420
Canadian Insurance Claims Managers Association, 420
Canadian Lawyers Insurance Association, 426
Centre for Study of Insurance Operations, 534
Chambre de l'assurance de dommages, 550
Corporations des assureurs directs de dommage, 631
Edmonton Insurance Association, 678
Facility Association, 700
Fédération de sociétés mutuelles d'assurance générale (Groupe promutuel), 710
Financial Services Commission of Ontario, 737
General Insurance OmbudService, 769
The Geneva Association, 1527
Global Commercial Insurers' Association, 774
Groupement des assureurs automobiles, 792
L'Institut d'assurance de dommages du Québec, 841
Institute for Catastrophic Loss Reduction, 843
Insurance Bureau of Canada, 848
Insurance Council of British Columbia, 849
Insurance Council of Manitoba, 849
Insurance Councils of Saskatchewan, 849
Insurance Institute of British Columbia, 849
Insurance Institute of Canada, 849
Insurance Institute of Manitoba, 849
Insurance Institute of New Brunswick, 849
Insurance Institute of Newfoundland & Labrador Inc., 849
Insurance Institute of Northern Alberta, 849
Insurance Institute of Nova Scotia, 849
Insurance Institute of Ontario, 849
Insurance Institute of Prince Edward Island, 850
Insurance Institute of Saskatchewan, 850
Insurance Institute of Southern Alberta, 850
Insurance Professionals of Calgary, 850
Insurance Women's Association of Western Manitoba, 850
London Insurance Professionals Association, 918
Manitoba Association of Insurance Professionals, 930
Manitoba Independent Insurance Adjusters' Association, 939
Marine Insurance Association of British Columbia, 949
New Brunswick & Prince Edward Island Independent Adjusters' Association, 1004
Newfoundland & Labrador Independent Adjusters' Association, 1019
Northwestern Ontario Insurance Professionals, 1039
Nova Scotia Independent Adjusters' Association, 1046
Nova Scotia Insurance Women's Association, 1046
Nuclear Insurance Association of Canada, 1050
Ontario Independent Insurance Adjusters' Association, 1087
Ontario Insurance Adjusters Association, 1088
Ontario Mutual Insurance Association, 1093
Pacific Independent Insurance Adjusters' Association, 1135
Receivables Insurance Association of Canada, 1206
Registered Insurance Brokers of Ontario, 1213
Regroupement des assureurs de personnes à charte du Québec, 1215
Reinsurance Research Council, 1217
Risk & Insurance Management Society Inc., 1233
Saskatchewan Independent Insurance Adjusters' Association, 1268
Saskatchewan Municipal Hail Insurance Association, 1270
Society of Public Insurance Administrators of Ontario, 1330
Title Insurance Industry Association of Canada, 1380
Toronto Insurance Women's Association, 1385
Travel Health Insurance Association of Canada, 1396
Western Independent Adjusters' Association, 1450

Insurance, Health
Canadian Association of Blue Cross Plans, 309
Canadian Association of Independent Life Brokerage Agencies, 318
Canadian Life & Health Insurance Association Inc., 426
OmbudService for Life & Health Insurance, 1057

Insurance, Life
Advocis, 11
Canadian Association of Independent Life Brokerage Agencies, 318
Canadian Life & Health Insurance Association Inc., 426
Canadian Life Insurance Medical Officers Association, 426
Chambre de la sécurité financière, 550
Independent Financial Brokers of Canada, 832
LOMA Canada, 917
OmbudService for Life & Health Insurance, 1057

Intellect
Mensa Canada Society, 961

Interior Design
Association des entrepreneurs de systèmes intérieurs du Québec, 112
Association of Interior Designers of Nova Scotia, 149
Association of Registered Interior Designers of New Brunswick, 161
Association of Registered Interior Designers of Ontario, 161
Association professionnelle des designers d'intérieur du Québec, 167
Canadian Decorators' Association, 376
Interior Designers Association of Saskatchewan, 852
Interior Designers Institute of British Columbia, 852
Interior Designers of Alberta, 852
Interior Designers of Canada, 852
Interior Designers of Newfoundland & Labrador, 852
Paint & Decorating Retailers Association, 1582
Professional Interior Designers Institute of Manitoba, 1185

International Cooperation
Association québécoise des organismes de coopération internationale, 173
Canadian Association for the Study of International Development, 306
Canadian Council for International Co-operation, 366
Cape Breton University Centre for International Studies, 510
CARE Canada, 511
Carrefour de solidarité internationale inc., 515
Carrefour Tiers-Monde, 516
Casa - Pueblito, 516
Centre canadien d'étude et de coopération internationale, 526
Change for Children Association, 551
Children's International Summer Villages (Canada) Inc., 562
CoDevelopment Canada, 580
CUSO International, 646
Development & Peace, 654
Earthwatch Institute, 1522
European Solidarity Towards Equal Participation of People, 1524
Foundation for International Environmental Law & Development, 1527
Global Village Nanaimo, 775
HOPE International Development Agency, 821
Horizons of Friendship, 821
Innovations et réseaux pour le développement, 1532
Institute of Cultural Affairs International, 846
Inter Pares, 851
International Organization of Securities Commissions, 1554
International Peace Bureau, 1555
International Society of Friendship & Good Will, 1560
International Student Pugwash, 1562
Jamaican Self-Help Organization, 867
Jeunesse du Monde, 870
Manitoba Council for International Cooperation, 934
The Marquis Project, Inc., 952
The North-South Institute, 1036
Ontario Council for International Cooperation, 1075
Oxfam Canada, 1134
Parliamentarians for Global Action, 1582
Partners International, 1144
SalvAide, 1252
Saskatchewan Council for International Co-operation, 1262
Scarboro Foreign Mission Society, 1282
Seva Canada Society, 1292
Social Justice Committee, 1305
Société de coopération pour le développement international, 1314
South Asia Partnership Canada, 1334
Trans-Himalayan Aid Society, 1395
United Nations Environment Programme, 1600
World Federalist Movement, 1605
World Vision Canada, 1467

International Law
American Society of International Law, 1500
Amnesty International, 1504
Avocats sans frontières Canada, 191
Canadian Council on International Law, 371
Hautes études internationales, 804
International Law Association, 1552
International Law Association - Canadian Branch, 858
Société Québécoise de droit international, 1323

International Relations
Association Canado-Américaine, 1507
Canada-Sri Lanka Business Council, 284
Canadian Association for the Study of International Development, 306
Canadian Bureau for International Education, 347
Canadian Commission for UNESCO, 360
Canadian Friends of Burma, 395
Canadian Friends of Ukraine, 395
Canadian International Council, 421
Cape Breton University Centre for International Studies, 510
Centre canadien d'étude et de coopération internationale, 526
Connexions Information Sharing Services, 613
Conseil des relations internationales de Montréal, 617
Council on Hemispheric Affairs, 1520
Hautes études internationales, 804
Institut de la Francophonie pour le développement durable, 841
Institute of Cultural Affairs International, 846
International Labour Organization, 1552
KAIROS: Canadian Ecumenical Justice Initiatives, 880
Parliamentary Centre, 1142
Professional Association of Foreign Service Officers, 1182
Project Ploughshares, 1188
Réseau Québec-France, 1225
SOS Children's Villages Canada, 1333
Syrian Canadian Council, 1365
United Nations Association in Canada, 1411
World Federalist Movement - Canada, 1465

International Relief
Adventist Development & Relief Agency Canada, 10
Armenian Relief Society of Canada, Inc., 83
Canadian Association for Mine & Explosive Ordnance Security, 302
Canadian Feed The Children, 389
Canadian Foodgrains Bank, 391
Canadian Global Campaign for Education, 398
Canadian Lutheran World Relief, 428
Canadian Organization for Development through Education, 447
CARE Canada, 511
Doctors without Borders Canada, 660
Engineers Without Borders, 689
Global Outreach Mission, 775
HelpAge International, 1529
Hope for the Nations, 821
Human Concern International, 824
International Community for Relief of Suffering & Starvation Canada, 855
International Relief Agency Inc., 859
Islamic Relief Canada, 865
Librarians Without Borders, 910
Lifewater Canada, 912
Mouvement ATD Quart Monde Canada, 976
Nepali Children's Education Project, 1003
Operation Eyesight Universal, 1115
Probe International, 1181
Save the Children Canada, 1281
Seva Canada Society, 1292
SHARE Agriculture Foundation, 1294
Teachers Without Borders, 1597
Vides Canada, 1434
The World Job & Food Bank Inc., 1466
World Renew, 1467

International Standard Book Number
Canadian ISBN Agency, 422
International ISBN Agency, 1551

International Trade
Asia Pacific Foundation of Canada, 86
Association des maisons de commerce extérieur du Québec, 118
British Canadian Chamber of Trade & Commerce, 229
Business Council of Canada, 266
Canada - United States Trade Center, 1515
Canada China Business Council, 278
Canada Eurasia Russia Business Association, 279
Canada-China Bilateral Cooperation Association, 283
Canada-Finland Chamber of Commerce, 283
Canada-India Business Council, 283
Canada-Singapore Business Association, 284
Canada-Sri Lanka Business Council, 284
Canadian Association of Importers & Exporters, 318
Canadian Australian Chamber of Commerce, 1515
Canadian Council on Africa, 370
Canadian German Chamber of Industry & Commerce Inc., 397
Canadian Society of Customs Brokers, 482
Canadian-Croatian Chamber of Commerce, 506
Can-Am Border Trade Alliance, 1515
Centre for International Business Studies, 533
China Council for the Promotion of International Trade - Canadian Office, 564
Council on Hemispheric Affairs, 1520
European Union Chamber of Commerce in Toronto, 698
Forum for International Trade Training, 754
Hong Kong-Canada Business Association, 820
Innovation Norway, 839
The Israel Economic Mission to Canada, 866
Pacific Corridor Enterprise Council, 1135
Taiwan Trade Center, Vancouver, 1366
United Nations Conference on Trade & Development, 1599
World Trade Centre Atlantic Canada, 1467
World Trade Centre Montréal, 1467
World Trade Centres Association, 1608

Internet
Ability Online Support Network, 2
Alliance numérique, 58
Association of Internet Marketing & Sales, 149
British Columbia Broadband Association, 234
Canada's Advanced Internet Development Organization, 281
Canadian Association for Renewable Energies, 303
Canadian Association of Wireless Internet Service Providers, 336
Canadian Internet Registration Authority, 422
Central Coast Communications Society, 524

Subject Index / Interpreters

Chebucto Community Net, 555
East Shore Internet Society, 668
Edmonton Community Networks, 676
Entertainment Software Association of Canada, 690
EnviroLink, 1523
First Nations SchoolNet, 738
Halifax Regional CAP Association, 799
Interactive Advertising Bureau of Canada, 851
OpenMedia Engagement Network, 1114
Peace Region Internet Society, 1147
Society of Internet Professionals, 1329
Telecommunities Canada Inc., 1369
Vancouver Community Network, 1425
Webgrrls Canada, 1443
Wireless Toronto, 1460
ZAP Montérégie, 1482

Interpreters
Association canadienne des interprètes de conférence, 90
Association of Legal Court Interpreters & Translators, 150
Association of Sign Language Interpreters of Alberta, 162
Association of Translators & Interpreters of Alberta, 163
Association of Translators & Interpreters of Ontario, 163
Association of Translators & Interpreters of Saskatchewan, 163
Association of Translators, Terminologists & Interpreters of Manitoba, 163
Association of Visual Language Interpreters of Canada, 164
Association of Visual Language Interpreters of New Brunswick, 164
Canadian Translators, Terminologists & Interpreters Council, 496
Corporation des traducteurs, traductrices, terminologues et interprètes du Nouveau-Brunswick, 631
Manitoba Association of Visual Language Interpreters, 931
Maritime Association of Professional Sign Language Interpreters, 950
Ontario Association of Sign Language Interpreters, 1066
Sign Language Interpreters of the National Capital, 1299
Society of Translators & Interpreters of British Columbia, 1331
Westcoast Association of Visual Language Interpreters, 1447

Inuit
Aiviq Hunters & Trappers Organization, 20
Avataq Cultural Institute, 190
I.C.C. Foundation, 829
Inuit Art Foundation, 862
Inuit Tapiriit Kanatami, 862
Kivalliq Inuit Association, 891
Makivik Corporation, 927
Mittimatalik Hunters' & Trappers' Organization, 970
National Inuit Youth Council, 994
Northern Youth Abroad Program, 1035
Nunavut Tourism, 1051
Pauktuutit Inuit Women of Canada, 1146
Qikiqtani Inuit Association, 1194

Inventions
Inventors Association of Ottawa, 862

Inventory Control
AIM Global, 1486

Investment
British Columbia Investment Agriculture Foundation, 244
Buy-Side Investment Management Association, 267
Canada's Venture Capital & Private Equity Association, 283
Canadian Association of Income Trusts Investors, 318
Canadian Bond Investors' Association, 345
Canadian Capital Markets Association, 349
Canadian Investor Protection Fund, 422
Canadian Investor Relations Institute, 422
Canadian Securities Administrators, 469
Canadian Securities Institute, 469
Canadian Securities Institute Research Foundation, 469
Canadian Security Traders Association, Inc., 469
Federation of Mutual Fund Dealers, 725
Institutional Limited Partners Association, 848
Investment Industry Association of Canada, 863
Investment Industry Regulatory Organization of Canada, 863
Investment Property Owners Association of Cape Breton, 863
Investment Property Owners Association of Nova Scotia Ltd., 863
Mortgage Investment Association of British Columbia, 975
Mouvement d'éducation et de défense des actionnaires, 977
National Aboriginal Trust Officers Association, 989
National Angel Capital Organization, 989
Native Investment & Trade Association, 998
Pension Investment Association of Canada, 1150
Portfolio Management Association of Canada, 1167
Private Capital Markets Association of Canada, 1180
Réseau des SADC et CAE, 1219
Responsible Investment Association, 1227
Richmond Club of Toronto, 1230
Shareholder Association for Research & Education, 1294
ShareOwner Education Inc., 1294
Small Investor Protection Association, 1304

Iran & Iranian Canadians
Iranian Community Association of Ontario, 863

Iraquis in Canada
Iraqi Canadian Society of Ontario, 863
Iraqi Jewish Association of Ontario, 863

Ireland
Ireland Canada University Foundation, 1567
The Ireland Funds, Canada, 863
Ireland-Canada Chamber of Commerce, 863

Iris
Canadian Iris Society, 422

Irish Canadians
An Cumann/The Irish Association of Nova Scotia, 68
Benevolent Irish Society of Prince Edward Island, 205
Ireland Canada University Foundation, 1567
Irish Canadian Cultural Association of New Brunswick, 864
St. Patrick's Society of Richmond & Vicinity, 1250

Irish Studies
Canadian Association for Irish Studies, 301

Iron
American Iron & Steel Institute, 1494
International Association of Bridge, Structural, Ornamental & Reinforcing Iron Workers (AFL-CIO), 1538
Ontario Artist Blacksmith Association, 1060

Irrigation
Alberta Irrigation Projects Association, 38
Canadian National Committee for Irrigation & Drainage, 439
International Commission on Irrigation & Drainage, 1543

Islam
Ahmadiyya Muslim Jama'at Canada, 15
ANNISAA Organization of Canada, 71
Association of Islamic Charitable Projects, 149
Bosnian Islamic Association, 218
Canadian Council of Muslim Theologians, 369
Canadian Council of Muslim Women, 369
Hilal Committee of Metropolitan Toronto & Vicinity, 814
International Development & Relief Foundation, 856
Islamic Association of Nova Scotia, 864
Islamic Association of Saskatchewan, 864
Islamic Care Centre, 864
Islamic Foundation of Toronto, 864
Islamic Information Foundation, 864
Islamic Propagation Centre of Ontario, 865
The Jerrahi Sufi Order of Canada, 869
Manitoba Islamic Association, 939
Muslim Association of New Brunswick, 985
Muslim Council of Montréal, 985
National Council of Canadian Muslims, 991
Windsor Islamic Association, 1456

Israel
The Association for the Soldiers of Israel, 135
Association of Americans & Canadians in Israel, 1510
Canada Israel Experience Centre, 280
Canada-Israel Cultural Foundation, 283
Canadian Associates of Ben-Gurion University of the Negev, 297
Canadian Association for Israel Philately, 301
Canadian Foundation for Masorti Judaism, 393
Canadian Friends of Bar-Ilan University, 394
Canadian Friends of Beth Hatefutsoth, 394
Canadian Friends of Bikur Cholim Hospital, 394
Canadian Friends of Peace Now (Shalom Achshav), 395
Canadian Friends of the Hebrew University, 395
Canadian Friends of Yeshiva University, 395
Canadian Institute for Jewish Research, 412
Canadian Magen David Adom for Israel, 429
Canadian Society for the Protection of Nature in Israel, 477
The Canadian Society for the Weizmann Institute of Science, 478
Canadian Young Judaea, 506
The Canadian Zionist Cultural Association, 506
Canadian Zionist Federation, 506
Forever Chai Foundation of Canada, 752
Israel Aliyah Center, 866
Israel Cancer Research Fund, 866
The Israel Economic Mission to Canada, 866
Jerusalem Foundation of Canada Inc, 869
Jewish Federations of Canada - UIA, 872
Mizrachi Organization of Canada, 970
Sar-El Canada, 1253
Technion Canada, 1368

Italian Canadians & Italy
Association of Italian Canadian Writers, 150
Canadian Italian Business & Professional Association, 423
Canadian Italian Business & Professional Association of Ottawa, 423
Canadian Italian Heritage Foundation, 423
Canadian Society for Italian Studies, 476
Conseil régional des personnes âgées italo-canadiennes de Montréal, 621
50 & Piu Enasco, 734
Fogolârs Federation of Canada, 742
Italian Canadian Cultural Association of Nova Scotia, 866
Italian Chamber of Commerce of Ontario, 866
Italian Cultural Centre Society, 866
Italian Cultural Institute (Istituto Italiano di Cultura), 866
Italian Cultural Society of Edmonton, 867
National Congress of Italian-Canadians, 991
Order of Sons of Italy in Canada, 1119
Patronato INAS (Canada), 1145
Villa Charities Inc. (Toronto District), 1434

Jamaican Canadians
Jamaican Canadian Association, 867
Jamaican Ottawa Community Association, 867
Jamaican Self-Help Organization, 867
National Council of Jamaicans & Supportive Organizations in Canada, 991

Japan
Institute of Asian Research, 844
Japan Automobile Manufacturers Association of Canada, 868
Japan External Trade Organization (Toronto), 868
The Japan Foundation, Toronto, 868
Toronto Japanese Association of Commerce & Industry, 1385

Japanese Canadians
Calgary Japanese Community Association, 273
The Canada-Japan Society of British Columbia, 283
Canada-Japan Society of Toronto, 283
Canadian Association for Japanese Language Education, 301
Edmonton Japanese Community Association, 678
Greater Vancouver Japanese Canadian Citizens' Association, 787
The Japan Society Canada, 869
Japanese Canadian Association of Yukon, 869
Japanese Canadian Cultural Centre, 869
Japanese Cultural Association of Manitoba, 869
Lakehead Japanese Cultural Association, 896
National Association of Japanese Canadians, 990
Ottawa Japanese Community Association Inc., 1131
Société Canada-Japon de Montréal, 1307
Vancouver Japanese Gardeners Association, 1427
Vernon Japanese Cultural Society, 1431

Jazz
Les Ballets Jazz de Montréal, 195
Coastal Jazz & Blues Society, 579
Decidedly Jazz Danceworks, 652
The Duke Ellington Society - Toronto Chapter #40, 664
Edmonton Jazz Society, 678
Jazz Yukon, 869
Toronto Downtown Jazz Society, 1384
Victoria Jazz Society, 1432

Jehovah's Witnesses
Watch Tower Bible & Tract Society of Canada, 1441

Jesuits
Canadian Jesuits International, 423
Jesuit Development Office, 870

Jewellery
Calgary Faceter's Guild, 272
Canadian Jewellers Association, 423
Corporation des bijoutiers du Québec, 629
Jewellers Vigilance Canada Inc., 871
Society of Bead Researchers, 1592

Jewish People
Act To End Violence Against Women, 6
Antisemitism Must End Now, 72
Asper Foundation, 87
Association of Jewish Day Schools, 150
Association of Jewish Libraries (Montréal), 150
Association of Jewish Libraries (Toronto), 150
Association of Jewish Seniors, 150
The Atlantic Jewish Council, 184
Azrieli Foundation, 191
Bernard Betel Centre for Creative Living, 205
Canadian Hadassah WIZO, 399
Canadian Young Judaea, 506
The Centre for Israel & Jewish Affairs, 533
Chabad Lubavitch Youth Organization, 539
Hamilton Jewish Federation, 801
Hashomer Hatzair Canada, 804
Hatzoloh Toronto, 804
Hillel of Greater Toronto, 814
International Fellowship of Christians & Jews of Canada, 857
Iraqi Jewish Association of Ontario, 863
Jewish Chamber of Commerce, 871
Jewish Child & Family Services, 871
Jewish Community Centre of Greater Vancouver, 871
Jewish Community Foundation of Montréal, 871
Jewish Family & Child, 871
Jewish Family Services - Calgary, 871
Jewish Family Services Edmonton, 871
Jewish Family Services of Ottawa-Carleton, 872
Jewish Federation of Greater Vancouver, 872
Jewish Free Loan Toronto, 872
Jewish Genealogical Institute of British Columbia, 872
Jewish Genealogical Society of Toronto, 872
Jewish Heritage Centre of Western Canada Inc., 872
Jewish Historical Society of BC, 872
Jewish Historical Society of Southern Alberta, 872
Jewish Immigrant Aid Services of Canada, 873
Jewish Information Referral Service Montréal, 873
Jewish Information Service of Greater Toronto, 873
Jews for Judaism, 873
JVS of Greater Toronto, 879
Kashruth Council of Canada, 882

London Jewish Federation, 918
Lord Reading Law Society, 919
Maccabi Canada, 923
Na'amat Canada Inc., 987
National Council of Jewish Women of Canada, 992
Peretz Centre for Secular Jewish Culture, 1152
Polish-Jewish Heritage Foundation of Canada, 1164
Pride of Israel, 1170
Prosserman Jewish Community Centre, 1189
Reena, 1210
Rose & Max Rady Jewish Community Centre, 1236
Saint John Jewish Historical Society, 1247
Segal Centre for the Performing Arts at the Saidye, 1289
Sholem Aleichem Community Inc., 1297
Southern African Jewish Association of Canada, 1337
Toronto Hebrew Benevolent Society, 1385
Toronto Jewish Film Society, 1385
UJA Federation of Greater Toronto, 1402
Vancouver Jewish Film Centre Society, 1427
Victoria Society for Humanistic Judaism, 1433

Jewish Studies
Aish Thornhill Community Shul & Learning Centre, 20
Association for Jewish Studies - USA, 1508
Canadian Friends of Bar-Ilan University, 394
Canadian Friends of the Hebrew University, 395
Canadian Institute for Jewish Research, 412
Canadian Society for Jewish Studies, 476
Canadian Young Judaea, 506
Federation of Teachers of Jewish Schools, 726
Pride of Israel, 1170

Journalism
Association de la presse francophone, 101
Association des journalistes indépendants du Québec, 117
Automobile Journalists Association of Canada, 189
Canadian Association of Black Journalists, 308
Canadian Association of Journalists, 319
Canadian Committee for World Press Freedom, 360
Canadian Farm Writers' Federation, 384
Canadian Journalism Foundation, 423
Canadian Journalists for Free Expression, 423
Canadian Media Guild, 432
The Canadian Press, 459
Canadian University Press, 499
Conseil de presse du Québec, 616
Fédération professionnelle des journalistes du Québec, 726
Hebdos Québec, 810
Human Rights & Race Relations Centre, 826
International Association for Literary Journalism Studies, 853
National Press Club of Canada Foundation, 995
Professional Writers Association of Canada, 1187
Radio Television Digital News Association (Canada), 1203
Toronto Press & Media Club, 1386
Union internationale de la presse francophone, 1598

Judaism
Aish Thornhill Community Shul & Learning Centre, 20
Am Shalom, 66
Association for Canadian Jewish Studies, 132
Association of Jewish Chaplains of Ontario, 150
B'nai Brith Canada, 192
B'nai Brith Canada Institute for International Affairs, 192
B'nai Brith Youth Organization, 192
Beach Hebrew Institute, 202
Canadian Committee of Lawyers & Jurists for World Jewry, 361
Canadian Council for Reform Judaism, 367
Canadian Foundation for Masorti Judaism, 393
Canadian Friends of Bar-Ilan University, 394
Canadian Friends of Boys Town Jerusalem, 395
Canadian Friends of the Hebrew University, 395
The Centre for Israel & Jewish Affairs, 533
Chosen People Ministries (Canada), 566
Congregation Beth Israel - British Columbia, 612

Emunah Women of Canada, 687
Jewish Foundation of Manitoba, 872
Jews for Jesus, 873
Jews for Judaism, 873
Kosher Check, 894
League for Human Rights of B'nai Brith Canada, 903
Mercaz-Canada, 961
Mizrachi Organization of Canada, 970
Oraynu Congregation for Humanistic Judaism, 1117
ORT Canada, 1127
Peretz Centre for Secular Jewish Culture, 1152
Shaare Zion Congregation, 1293
Shaarei Tefillah, 1293
Sholem Aleichem Community Inc., 1297
Toronto Association of Synagogue & Temple Administrators, 1382
Toronto Council of Hazzanim (Cantors), 1383
United Jewish Peoples' Order, 1411
United Synagogue of Conservative Judaism, Canadian Region, 1412
United Synagogue Youth, 1412
Victoria Society for Humanistic Judaism, 1433
World ORT Union, 1607

Judges
Canadian Association of Provincial Court Judges, 329
International Association of Judges, 1539
Northwest Territories Association of Provincial Court Judges, 1037

Kayaking
Alberta Whitewater Association, 52
Association québécoise de canoë-kayak de vitesse, 169
Atlantic Division, CanoeKayak Canada, 183
Canoe Kayak New Brunswick, 508
Canoe Kayak Saskatchewan, 509
CanoeKayak BC, 509
CanoeKayak Canada, 509
CanoeKayak Canada Western Ontario Division, 509
Fédération québécoise de canoë-kayak d'eau vives, 727
Ikalukutiak Paddling Association, 829
Ontario Canoe Kayak Sprint Racing Affiliation, 1070
Ontario Marathon Canoe & Kayak Racing Association, 1090
Ontario Recreational Canoeing & Kayaking Association, 1101
Paddle Alberta, 1136
Paddle Canada, 1137
Paddle Newfoundland & Labrador, 1137
Prince Edward Island Canoe Kayak Association, 1173
Wilderness Canoe Association, 1454
Yukon Canoe & Kayak Club, 1477
Yukon River Marathon Paddlers Association, 1480

Kidney Disorders & Diseases
Association générale des insuffisants rénaux, 136
British Columbia Provincial Renal Agency, 249
Kidney Cancer Canada Association, 884
Kidney Foundation of Canada, 885

Kinesiology
British Columbia Association of Kinesiologists, 232
Canadian Association of Specialized Kinesiology, 333
Canadian Federation of Orthotherapists, 388
Ontario Kinesiology Association, 1088

Korean Canadians & Korea
Association of Korean Canadian Scientists & Engineers, 150
Canada Korea Business Association, 280
Federation of Korean Canadian Associations, 724
Institute of Asian Research, 844
Korea Veterans Association of Canada Inc., Heritage Unit, 893
Korean Association of Newfoundland & Labrador, 893
Korean Business Association, 893
Korean Businessmen's Cooperative Association of British Columbia, 893
Korean Canadian Association of Ottawa, 893

Korean Canadian Association of Waterloo & Wellington, 893
Korean Canadian Cultural Association of the Greater Toronto Area, 893
Korean Canadian Society of London, 893
Korean Canadian Women's Association, 893
Korean Community of Greater Montréal, 893
Korean Senior Citizens Society of Toronto, 893
Korean Society of British Columbia for Fraternity & Culture, 893
Korean Society of Manitoba, 893
Korean Students' Association of Canada, 893

Kosher Food
Baron de Hirsch Hebrew Benevolent Society, 196
Jewish Community Council of Montreal, 871
Kashruth Council of Canada, 882
Kosher Check, 894
Pride of Israel, 1170

Kurdistan
Kurdish Community & Information Centre of Toronto, 894

Laboratories
Canadian Association for Laboratory Accreditation Inc., 301
Canadian Council of Independent Laboratories, 368
Canadian Laboratory Suppliers Association, 424
Canadian Society for Medical Laboratory Science, 476
Manitoba Association for Medical Laboratory Science, 929
New Brunswick Society of Medical Laboratory Technologists, 1012
Ontario Association of Medical Laboratories, 1064

Laboratory Medicine
British Columbia Association of Laboratory Physicians, 232
College of Medical Laboratory Technologists of Alberta, 586
International Council for Laboratory Animal Science, 1544
Nova Scotia College of Medical Laboratory Technologists, 1042
Ontario Association of Medical Laboratories, 1064
Saskatchewan Society of Medical Laboratory Technologists, 1275
World Association of Societies of Pathology and Laboratory Medicine, 1465

Labour
Association des jeunes travailleurs et travailleuses de Montréal inc, 117
Canadian Association of Labour Media, 319
Canadian Committee on Labour History, 361
Canadian Labour International Film Festival, 425
Centrale des syndicats du Québec, 525
Centre for the Study of Living Standards, 534
Centre international de solidarité ouvrière, 535
House of Commons Security Services Employees Association, 824
International Labour Organization, 1552
International Trade Union Confederation, 1563
North Bay Police Association, 1030
Peel Regional Police Association, 1148

Labour Councils
Algoma-Manitoulin & District Labour Council, 53
Bathurst & District Labour Council, 199
Brantford & District Labour Council, 227
Calgary & District Labour Council, 270
Campbell River & Courtenay District Labour Council, 276
Chatham-Kent Labour Council, 555
Conseil central de l'Estrie (CSN), 614
Conseil économique du Nouveau-Brunswick inc., 618
Conseil FTQ Drummondville, 618
Conseil régional de Baie Comeau (Manicouagan) - Bureau régional FTQ Côte Nord, 620
Conseil régional FTQ Abitibi-Témiscamingue - Nord-du-Québec, 621
Conseil régional FTQ Bas St-Laurent - Gaspésie-Îles-de-la-Madeleine, 621

Conseil régional FTQ de la Haute-Yamaska - Bureau régional FTQ - Montérégie, 621
Conseil régional FTQ de la Mauricie et du Centre-du-Québec - Bureau régional FTQ - Maurice et Centre du Québec, 621
Conseil régional FTQ du Richelieu - Bureau régional FTQ - Montérégie, 621
Conseil régional FTQ du Suroît - Bureau régional FTQ - Montérégie, 621
Conseil régional FTQ Estrie, 621
Conseil régional FTQ Montréal Métropolitain, 621
Conseil régional FTQ Québec et Chaudière-Appalaches, 621
Conseil régional FTQ Saguenay-Lac-St-Jean-Chibougamau-Chapais, 621
Conseil régional FTQ Sept-Îles et Côte-Nord - Bureau régional FTQ Côte Nord, 621
Corner Brook & District Labour Council, 628
Cornwall & District Labour Council, 629
Durham Regional Labour Council, 665
East Kootenay District Labour Council, 668
Edmonton & District Labour Council, 675
Estevan & District Labour Committee, 696
Fort Frances & District Labour Council, 752
Fraser Valley Labour Council, 757
Guelph & District Labour Council, 792
Humboldt & District Labour Council, 827
Kamloops & District Labour Council, 880
Kenora District Labour Council, 883
Kingston & District Labour Council, 888
Kitimat, Terrace & District Labour Council, 891
London & District Labour Council, 917
Moose Jaw & District Labour Council, 973
Nanaimo, Duncan & District Labour Council, 988
New Westminster & District Labour Council, 1015
Niagara Regional Labour Council, 1025
North Battleford & District Labour Council, 1030
North Central Labour Council of British Columbia, 1030
North Okanagan Labour Council, 1031
Ottawa & District Labour Council, 1129
Oxford Regional Labour Council, 1134
Peel Regional Labour Council, 1148
Peterborough & District Labour Council, 1153
Port Alberni & District Labour Council, 1165
Powell River & District Labour Council, 1168
Prince Albert & District Labour Council, 1171
Prince Rupert Labour Council, 1180
Quesnel & District Labour Council, 1200
Quinte Labour Council, 1201
Regina & District Labour Council, 1211
Saint John & District Labour Council, 1246
St Catharines & District Labour Council, 1248
Sarnia & District Labour Council, 1254
Saskatoon & District Labour Council, 1279
Shuswap Columbia District Labour Council, 1297
South Coast District Labour Council, 1334
South Okanagan Boundary Labour Council, 1335
Squamish & District Labour Committee, 1346
Stratford & District Labour Council, 1351
Sudbury & District Labour Council, 1353
Sunshine Coast Labour Council, 1355
Thunder Bay & District Labour Council, 1377
Toronto & York Region Labour Council, 1381
Vancouver & District Labour Council, 1424
Victoria Labour Council, 1433
Waterloo Regional Labour Council, 1442
West Kootenay District Labour Council, 1445
Weyburn & District Labour Council, 1451
Windsor & District Labour Council, 1456
Winnipeg Labour Council, 1459
Yorkton & District Labour Council, 1474

Labour Legislation
Canadian Association of Administrators of Labour Legislation, 307
International Labour & Employment Relations Association, 1551
International Society for Labour & Social Security Law - Canadian Chapter, 860

Labour Relations
Association canadienne des relations industrielles, 94
British Columbia Maritime Employers Association, 246

Subject Index / Labour Unions

Central Ontario Industrial Relations Institute, 525
Construction Employers Coordinating Council of Ontario, 624
Construction Labour Relations - An Alberta Association, 624
Construction Labour Relations Association of British Columbia, 624
Construction Labour Relations Association of Newfoundland & Labrador, 624
Good Jobs for All Coalition, 777
Halifax Employers Association, 799
Health Employers Association of British Columbia, 806
International Labour & Employment Relations Association, 1551
Ontario Labour-Management Arbitrators Association, 1088
Ordre des conseillers en ressources humaines agréés, 1120
Pipe Line Contractors Association of Canada, 1160
Public Services International, 1585
Syndicat des conseillères et conseillers de la CSQ, 1362
Utility Contractors Association of Ontario, Inc., 1423

Labour Unions

Administrative & Professional Staff Association, 8
Administrative & Supervisory Personnel Association, 8
Agriculture Union, 15
Air Canada Pilots Association, 19
Air Line Pilots Association, International - Canada, 19
Alberta Federation of Labour, 34
Alberta Teachers' Association, 49
Alberta Union of Provincial Employees, 50
Alliance des professeures et professeurs de Montréal, 56
Alliance des professionels et des professionnelles de la Ville de Québec, 56
Alliance du personnel professionnel et technique de la santé et des services sociaux, 56
Alliance internationale des employé(e)s de scène, de théâtre et de cinéma, 57
Alliance of Canadian Cinema, Television & Radio Artists, 58
Amalgamated Transit Union (AFL-CIO/CLC), 1487
American Federation of Labor & Congress of Industrial Organizations (AFL-CIO), 1493
American Federation of Musicians of the United States & Canada (AFL-CIO/CLC), 1493
American Guild of Variety Artists (AFL-CIO), 1493
Association canadienne des métiers de la truelle, section locale 100 (CTC), 94
Association des policières et policiers provinciaux du Québec, 123
Association des pompiers de Laval, 124
Association des professeurs de Campus Notre-Dame-de-Foy, 124
Association des professionnels et superviseurs de Radio-Canada, 126
Association des réalisateurs et réalisatrices de Télé-Québec, 127
Association des réalisateurs et réalisatrices du Québec, 127
Association nationale des peintres - locale 99, 138
Association of Administrative & Professional Staff - University of British Columbia, 138
Association of Allied Health Professionals: Newfoundland & Labrador (Ind.), 139
Association of Canadian Film Craftspeople, 142
Association of Canadian Financial Officers, 142
Association of Management, Administrative & Professional Crown Employees of Ontario, 151
Association of Manitoba Hydro Staff & Supervisory Employees, 151
Association of New Brunswick Professional Educators, 154
Association professionnelle des ingénieurs du gouvernement du Québec (ind.), 167
Association provinciale des enseignantes et enseignants du Québec, 168

Association québécoise des auteurs dramatiques, 171
Association syndicale des employées de production et de service, 178
Atlantic Federation of Musicians, Local 571, 184
Bakery, Confectionery, Tobacco Workers & Grain Millers International Union (AFL-CIO/CLC), 1514
Belleville Police Association, 204
Brandon Police Association, 226
Brantford Police Association, 227
Brewery, Winery & Distillery Workers Union - Local 300, 228
Bricklayers, Masons Independent Union of Canada (CLC), 228
British Columbia Federation of Labour, 240
British Columbia Ferry & Marine Workers' Union (CLC), 241
British Columbia Government & Service Employees' Union, 242
British Columbia Nurses' Union, 248
British Columbia Police Association, 249
British Columbia Principals & Vice-Principals Association, 249
Brotherhood of Maintenance of Way Employes (AFL-CIO/CLC), 1514
Calgary Police Association, 274
Canada Employment & Immigration Union, 278
Canadian Actors' Equity Association (CLC), 287
Canadian Association of Professional Employees, 328
Canadian Federal Pilots Association, 384
Canadian Federation of Nurses Unions, 388
Canadian Football League Players' Association, 392
Canadian Labour Congress, 424
Canadian LabourWatch Association, 425
Canadian Media Guild, 432
Canadian Merchant Service Guild, 435
Canadian Military Colleges Faculty Association, 436
Canadian National Federation of Independent Unions, 439
Canadian Office & Professional Employees Union, 444
Canadian Overseas Telecommunications Union, 448
Canadian Postmasters & Assistants Association, 458
Canadian Union of Postal Workers, 498
Canadian Union of Public Employees, 498
Centrale des syndicats démocratiques, 525
Centrale des syndicats du Québec, 525
City of Waterloo Staff Association, 571
Civic Institute of Professional Personnel, 571
Compensation Employees' Union (Ind.), 608
Concordia University Part-time Faculty Association, 610
Confédération des syndicats nationaux, 611
Confederation of Ontario University Staff Associations & Unions, 611
Congress of Union Retirees Canada, 613
Conseil des métiers d'art du Québec (ind.), 617
Conseil régional FTQ de l'Ouatouais, 621
Construction Maintenance & Allied Workers Canada, 624
Cornwall Police Association, 629
Customs & Immigration Union, 646
Directors Guild of Canada, 657
Dufferin Peel Educational Resource Workers' Association, 664
Durham Regional Police Association, 665
Eastern Shores Independent Association for Support Personnel, 671
Education Assistants Association of the Waterloo Region District School Board, 680
Education Support Staff of the Ontario Secondary School Teachers' Federation - District 24 - Waterloo, 680
Elementary Teachers' Federation of Ontario, 684
Emily Carr University of Art & Design Faculty Association, 686
Employees Association of Milltronics - CNFIU Local 3005, 686
Employees' Association Hammond Manufacturing Company Ltd., 687
Employees' Union of St. Mary's of the Lake Hospital - CNFIU Local 3001, 687
Faculty Association of University of Saint Thomas, 701

Fédération autonome du collégial (ind.), 707
Fédération CSN - Construction (CSN), 708
Fédération de l'industrie manufacturière (FIM-CSN), 708
Fédération de la santé et des services sociaux, 710
Fédération des employées et employés de services publics inc. (CSN), 714
Fédération des enseignants de cégeps, 714
Fédération des intervenantes en petite enfance du Québec, 715
Fédération des médecins résidents du Québec inc. (ind.), 716
Fédération des policiers et policières municipaux du Québec (ind.), 717
Fédération des professionnèles, 717
Fédération des professionnelles et professionnels de l'éducation du Québec, 718
Fédération des syndicats de l'action collective, 719
Fédération des Syndicats de l'Enseignement, 719
Fédération des syndicats de la santé et des services sociaux, 719
Fédération des travailleurs et travailleises du Québec, 719
Fédération des travailleurs et travailleuses du Québec - Construction, 719
Fédération du personnel de l'enseignement privé, 720
Fédération du personnel de soutien scolaire (CSQ), 720
Fédération du personnel professionnel des collèges, 720
Fédération du personnel professionnel des universités et de la recherche, 720
Fédération indépendante des syndicats autonomes, 721
Fédération interprofessionnelle de la santé du Québec, 721
Fédération nationale des communications (CSN), 721
Fish, Food & Allied Workers, 739
Fraternité interprovinciale des ouvriers en électricité (CTC), 758
Fraternité nationale des forestiers et travailleurs d'usine (CTC), 758
FTQ Laurentides-Lanaudière, 764
Glass, Molders, Pottery, Plastic & Allied Workers International Union (AFL-CIO/CLC), 1528
Government Services Union, 778
Grain Services Union (CLC), 779
Grain Workers' Union, Local 333, 779
Greater Vancouver Regional District Employees' Union, 787
Guelph Police Association Inc., 793
Halifax Regional Police Association, 799
Halton District Educational Assistants Association, 800
Health Sciences Association of Alberta, 807
Health Sciences Association of British Columbia, 807
Health Sciences Association of Saskatchewan, 807
Hospital Employees' Union, 823
IAMAW District 78, 829
Independent Association of Support Staff, 832
Independent Canadian Extrusion Workers Union, 832
International Alliance of Theatrical Stage Employees, Moving Picture Technicians, Artists & Allied Crafts of the U.S., Its Territories & Canada, 1535
International Allied Printing Trades Association, 1535
International Association of Bridge, Structural, Ornamental & Reinforcing Iron Workers (AFL-CIO), 1538
International Association of Fire Fighters (AFL-CIO/CLC), 1538
International Association of Machinists & Aerospace Workers, 1539
International Brotherhood of Boilermakers, Iron Ship Builders, Blacksmiths, Forgers & Helpers (AFL-CIO), 1541
International Brotherhood of Electrical Workers (AFL-CFL), 1542
International Brotherhood of Teamsters (AFL-CIO/CLC), 1542

International Federation of Employees in Public Service, 1547
International Federation of Professional & Technical Engineers (AFL-CIO/CLC), 1549
International Longshore & Warehouse Union (CLC), 1553
International Longshoremen's Association (AFL-CIO/CLC), 1553
International Police Association - Canada, 859
International Union of Bricklayers & Allied Craftworkers (AFL-CIO/CFL), 1564
International Union of Elevator Constructors, 1564
International Union of Operating Engineers (AFL-CIO/CFL), 1565
International Union of Painters & Allied Trades, 1565
International Union, United Automobile, Aerospace & Agricultural Implement Workers of America, 1565
Kingston Independent Nylon Workers Union, 889
Kingston Police Association, 889
Laborers' International Union of North America (AFL-CIO/CLC), 1568
Laurentian University Staff Union, 900
Lethbridge Community College Faculty Association, 908
MacEwan Staff Association, 924
Major League Baseball Players' Association (Ind.), 1569
Manitoba Association of Health Care Professionals, 929
Manitoba Federation of Labour, 936
Manitoba Government & General Employees' Union, 937
Manitoba Nurses' Union, 941
Maritime Fishermen's Union (CLC), 950
McGill University Non Academic Certified Association, 955
McMaster University Staff Association, 956
Medicine Hat Police Association, 958
Merit Canada, 961
Mount Allison Faculty Association, 976
Mount Royal Staff Association, 976
Musicians' Association of Victoria & the Islands, Local 247, AFM, 984
National Conferences of Firemen & Oilers (SEIU), 1575
National Health Union, 994
National Union of Public & General Employees, 996
Natural Gas Employees' Association, 998
Natural Resources Union, 999
New Brunswick Federation of Labour, 1008
New Brunswick Nurses Union, 1010
New Brunswick Union, 1013
Newfoundland & Labrador Association of Public & Private Employees, 1016
Newfoundland & Labrador Federation of Labour, 1018
Newfoundland & Labrador Nurses' Union, 1020
The Newspaper Guild (AFL-CIO/CLC), 1577
Niagara Region Police Association, 1025
North Island College Faculty Association, 1031
Northern Territories Federation of Labour, 1035
Nova Scotia Federation of Labour, 1044
Nova Scotia Government & General Employees Union, 1045
Nova Scotia Nurses' Union, 1047
Nova Scotia Teachers Union, 1049
Nova Scotia Union of Public & Private Employees (CCU), 1050
Nunavut Employees Union, 1051
Nunavut Teachers' Association, 1051
Office & Professional Employees International Union (AFL-CIO/CLC), 1580
Ontario Construction Secretariat, 1074
Ontario English Catholic Teachers' Association (CLC), 1077
Ontario Federation of Labour, 1079
Ontario Nurses' Association, 1094
Ontario Professional Fire Fighters Association, 1097
Ontario Provincial Police Association, 1098
Ontario Public Service Employees Union, 1099
Ontario Secondary School Teachers' Federation, 1103
Operative Plasterers' & Cement Masons' International Association of the US & Canada (AFL-CIO/CFL) - Canadian Office, 1116

Ordre professionnel des diététistes Québec, 1124
Peterborough Police Association, 1154
Police Association of Nova Scotia, 1163
Power Workers' Union, 1169
Prince Edward Island Federation of Labour, 1174
Prince Edward Island Police Association, 1176
Prince Edward Island Union of Public Sector Employees, 1178
Professional Association of Foreign Service Officers, 1182
Professional Association of Internes & Residents of Newfoundland, 1182
Professional Association of Residents & Interns of Manitoba, 1182
Professional Association of Residents in the Maritime Provinces, 1182
Professional Association of Residents of Alberta, 1182
Professional Association of Residents of Ontario, 1182
Professional Employees Association (Ind.), 1183
Professional Engineers for Public Safety Association, 1183
Professional Engineers Government of Ontario, 1183
Professional Hockey Players' Association, 1185
The Professional Institute of the Public Service of Canada, 1185
Professional Student Services Personnel, 1186
Professional Writers Association of Canada, 1187
Public Service Alliance of Canada, 1193
Public Services International, 1585
Pulp, Paper & Woodworkers of Canada, 1194
Registered Practical Nurses Association of Ontario, 1213
Regroupement des artistes en arts visuels du Québec (ind.), 1214
Research Council Employees' Association (Ind.), 1218
Réseau de la coopération du travail du Québec, 1219
Resident Doctors of British Columbia, 1226
Retail, Wholesale & Department Store Union (AFL-CIO/CLC), 1586
Royal Newfoundland Constabulary Association, 1242
Saint Mary's University Faculty Union, 1247
St. Albert Firefighters - Union Local 2130, 1247
Saskatchewan Federation of Labour, 1265
Saskatchewan Government & General Employees' Union, 1266
Saskatchewan Joint Board Retail, Wholesale & Department Store Union, 1268
Saskatchewan Teachers' Federation, 1276
Saskatchewan Union of Nurses, 1277
Saskatoon Civic Middle Management Association, 1279
Sault Ste Marie Police Association, 1281
Schneider Office Employees' Association, 1284
Screen Actors Guild - American Federation of Television & Radio Artists, 1588
Seafarers' International Union of Canada (AFL-CIO/CLC), 1287
Senate Protective Service Employees Association, 1290
Service Employees International Union (AFL-CIO/CLC), 1588
Sheet Metal Workers' International Association (AFL-CIO/CFL), 1588
Shipyard General Workers' Federation of British Columbia, 1296
Société des Auteurs de Radio, Télévision et Cinéma, 1317
Société des technologues en nutrition, 1318
Société professionnelle des auteurs et des compositeurs du Québec, 1322
The Society of Energy Professionals, 1328
Syndicat de la fonction publique du Québec inc. (ind.), 1361
Syndicat de professionnelles et professionnels du gouvernement du Québec, 1362
Syndicat des Agents Correctionnels du Canada (CSN), 1362
Syndicat des agents de la paix en services correctionnels du Québec, 1362
Syndicat des agents de maîtrise de TELUS (ind.), 1362

Syndicat des employé(e)s de magasins et de bureau de la Société des alcools du Québec (ind.), 1362
Syndicat des employés en radio-télédiffusion de Télé-Québec (CSQ), 1363
Syndicat des employés et employées des syndicats et des organismes collectifs du Québec, 1363
Syndicat des pompiers et pompières du Québec (CTC), 1363
Syndicat des professeurs et professeurs de l'Université de Sherbrooke, 1363
Syndicat des professeurs et professeurs de l'Université du Québec à Chicoutimi, 1363
Syndicat des professeurs de l'État du Québec (ind.), 1363
Syndicat des professionnelles et professionnels municipaux de Montréal, 1364
Syndicat des professionnels et des techniciens de la santé du Québec, 1364
Syndicat des technicien(ne)s et artisan(e)s du réseau français de Radio-Canada (ind.), 1364
Syndicat des technologues en radiologie du Québec, 1364
Syndicat des travaileurs énergie électrique nord, 1364
Syndicat des travailleurs de la construction du Québec (CSD), 1364
Syndicat du personnel technique et professionnel de la Société des alcools du Québec (ind.), 1364
Syndicat interprovincial des ferblantiers et couvreurs, la section locale 2016 à la FTQ-Construction, 1364
Syndicat national des employés de l'aluminium d'Arvida, inc., 1365
Syndicat professionnel des homéopathes du Québec, 1365
Syndicat professionnel des ingénieurs d'Hydro-Québec, 1365
Syndicat professionnel des médecins du gouvernement du Québec (ind.), 1365
Syndicat professionnel des scientifiques à pratique exclusive de Montréal, 1365
Syndicat professionnel des scientifiques de l'IREQ, 1365
Syndicat québécois de la construction, 1365
Teaching Support Staff Union, 1367
Teamsters Canada (CLC), 1368
Teamsters Canada Rail Conference, 1368
Telecommunications Employees Association of Manitoba, 1369
Thompson Rivers University Open Learning Faculty Association, 1376
Thunder Bay Police Association, 1378
Toronto Musicians' Association, 1386
UNIFOR, 1405
UniforACL, 1405
Union des écrivaines et écrivains québécois, 1406
Union of Calgary Co-op Employees, 1407
Union of National Defence Employees, 1407
Union of Northern Workers, 1407
Union of Postal Communications Employees, 1408
Union of Solicitor General Employees, 1408
Union of Taxation Employees, 1408
Union of Veterans' Affairs Employees, 1408
UNITE HERE, 1599
UNITE HERE Canada, 1408
United Association of Journeymen & Apprentices of the Plumbing & Pipe Fitting Industry of the United States & Canada, 1599
United Brotherhood of Carpenters & Joiners of America (AFL-CIO/CLC), 1599
United Food & Commercial Workers Canada, 1410
United Food & Commercial Workers' International Union, 1599
United Mine Workers of America (CLC), 1599
United Nurses of Alberta, 1412
United Steelworkers of America (AFL-CIO/CLC), 1600
United Transportation Union (AFL-CIO/CLC), 1600
United Utility Workers' Association, 1412
University of Guelph Food Service Employees Association, 1419
University of Waterloo Staff Association, 1421

University of Western Ontario Staff Association, 1421
West Vancouver Municipal Employees Association, 1447
Windsor Police Association, 1457
Winnipeg Association of Non-Teaching Employees, 1458
Winnipeg Clinic Employees Association, 1458
York University Staff Association, 1474
Yukon Employees Union, 1478
Yukon Federation of Labour, 1478
Yukon Teachers' Association, 1480

Lacrosse
Alberta Lacrosse Association, 38
BC Lacrosse Association, 201
Canadian Lacrosse Association, 425
Canadian Lacrosse Hall of Fame, 425
Fédération de crosse du Québec, 708
Lacrosse New Brunswick, 895
Lacrosse Nova Scotia, 895
Lethbridge Lacrosse Association, 908
Manitoba Lacrosse Association, 939
Newfoundland & Labrador Lacrosse Association, 1019
Ontario Lacrosse Association, 1088
Saskatchewan Lacrosse Association, 1268

Land Mines
Canadian Association for Mine & Explosive Ordnance Security, 302

Land Reclamation
American Society of Mining & Reclamation, 1501
Canadian Land Reclamation Association, 425
Canadian Society of Soil Science, 488
Federation of Saskatchewan Surface Rights Association, 726
International Soil Reference & Information Centre, 1561

Land Surveying
Alberta Land Surveyors' Association, 39
Association of British Columbia Land Surveyors, 140
Association of Canada Lands Surveyors, 140
Association of Manitoba Land Surveyors, 151
Association of New Brunswick Land Surveyors, 153
Association of Newfoundland Land Surveyors, 154
Association of Nova Scotia Land Surveyors, 154
Association of Ontario Land Surveyors, 155
Association of Prince Edward Island Land Surveyors, 156
Canadian Board of Examiners for Professional Surveyors, 345
Canadian Institute of Geomatics, 416
Commonwealth Association of Surveying & Land Economy, 1518
International Federation of Surveyors, 1549
Ordre des arpenteurs-géomètres du Québec, 1120
Professional Surveyors Canada, 1186
Saskatchewan Land Surveyors' Association, 1268

Land Use
American Farmland Trust, 1492
American Society of Mining & Reclamation, 1501
Association of Ontario Land Economists, 155
Canadian Land Reclamation Association, 425
Canadian Society of Soil Science, 488
Commonwealth Association of Surveying & Land Economy, 1518
International Soil Reference & Information Centre, 1561
Land Improvement Contractors of Ontario, 897
Land Trust Alliance, 1569
National Aboriginal Lands Managers Association, 989
Urban Development Institute Greater Edmonton Chapter, 1422
Urban Development Institute of Canada, 1422
Urban Development Institute of Nova Scotia, 1422
World Agroforestry Centre, 1602

Landlords
Association des propriétaires du Québec inc., 126
British Columbia Apartment Owners & Managers Association, 230
Canadian Federation of Apartment Associations, 385
Corporation des propriétaires immobiliers du Québec, 630
Landlord's Self-Help Centre, 898
Ligue des propriétaires de Montréal, 912

Landscape Architecture
Alberta Association of Landscape Architects, 23
Association des architectes paysagistes du Québec, 105
Atlantic Provinces Association of Landscape Architects, 185
British Columbia Society of Landscape Architects, 254
Canadian Society of Landscape Architects, 484
International Federation of Landscape Architects, 1548
Manitoba Association of Landscape Architects, 930
Northwest Territories Association of Landscape Architects, 1037
Nunavut Association of Landscape Architects, 1051
Ontario Association of Landscape Architects, 1064
Saskatchewan Association of Landscape Architects, 1257
Saskatchewan Nursery Landscape Association, 1270

Language Disorders
International Society for Augmentative & Alternative Communication, 860
Prince Edward Island Speech & Hearing Association, 1177
Speech & Hearing Association of Nova Scotia, 1340
The Speech & Stuttering Institute, 1340

Language Teaching
Alliance Française, 57
Alliance Française d'Edmonton, 57
Alliance Française d'Ottawa, 57
Alliance Française du Manitoba, 57
Alliance Française Halifax, 57
Association canadienne d'éducation de langue française, 90
Association canadienne des professeurs d'immersion, 94
Association québécoise des enseignants de français langue seconde, 172
Canadian Association for Japanese Language Education, 301
Canadian Association of Private Language Schools, 328
Canadian Association of Second Language Teachers, 332
Canadian Association of University Teachers of German, 335
Canadian Council of Teachers of English Language Arts, 370
Centre for Canadian Language Benchmarks, 531
English Additional Language Learners Provincial Specialist Association, 689
Fédération internationale des professeurs de français, 1525
Federation of Teachers of Jewish Schools, 726
International Association of University Professors of English, 1540
Languages Canada, 899
Mon Sheong Foundation, 971
Parents partenaires en éducation, 1140
Teachers of English to Speakers of Other Languages, Inc., 1597

Languages
American Dialect Society, 1492
British Columbia Association of Teachers of Modern Languages, 233
Canadian Association for Commonwealth Literature & Language Studies, 298
Canadian Association for Commonwealth Literature & Language Studies, 298
Canadian Comparative Literature Association, 361

Canadian Linguistic Association, 427
Centre interdisciplinaire de recherches sur les activités langagières, 535
Esperanto Association of Canada, 695
Language Industry Association, 899
Languages Canada, 899
Modern Language Association of America, 1571
Northeast Modern Language Association, 1579
Ontario Modern Language Teachers Association, 1091
Parents partenaires en éducation, 1140
Société québécoise d'espéranto, 1323
Teachers of English to Speakers of Other Languages, Inc., 1597
Universala Esperanto-Asocio, 1600

Lao Canadians
Communauté Laotienne du Québec, 594
Lao Association of Ontario, 899

Latin America
Canadian Association for Latin American & Caribbean Studies, 302
Canadian Council for the Americas, 367
Canadian Council for the Americas - British Columbia, 367
Centre for Research on Latin America & The Caribbean, 533
Latin American Mission Program, 899
Latin American Studies Association, 1569

Latin American Canadians
Canadian Columbian Professional Association, 360
Chambre de commerce Latino-américaine du Québec, 549
Corporation culturelle Latino-Américaine de l'Amitié, 629
Hispanic Canadian Heritage Council, 815
Hola, 818
New Brunswick Latino Association, 1010

Latvian Canadians & Latvia
Association of Latvian Craftsmen in Canada, 150
Latvian Canadian Cultural Centre, 900
Latvian National Federation in Canada, 900
The Latvian Relief Society of Canada, 900
Toronto Latvian Concert Association, 1385

Law
Alberta Association of Professional Paralegals, 24
Alberta Law Foundation, 39
Alberta Law Reform Institute, 39
Alberta Restorative Justice Association, 44
Algoma District Law Association, 53
American Association for Justice, 1488
American Immigration Lawyers Association - Canadian Chapter, 66
American Society for Legal History, 1498
ARCH Disability Law Centre, 76
Association canadienne des juristes-traducteurs, 93
Association d'entraide Le Chaînon inc., 99
Association des avocats en droit de la jeunesse, 106
Association internationale de droit pénal, 1509
Association québécoise de doit comparé, 169
British Columbia Criminal Justice Association, 238
British Columbia Law Institute, 244
Canadian Academy of Psychiatry & the Law, 286
Canadian Association for the Practical Study of Law in Education, 305
Canadian Association of Elizabeth Fry Societies, 312
Canadian Association of Paralegals, 325
Canadian Corporate Counsel Association, 365
Canadian Council on International Law, 371
Canadian Criminal Justice Association, 373
Canadian Grandparents' Rights Association, 399
Canadian HIV/AIDS Legal Network, 405
Canadian Institute for the Administration of Justice, 413
Canadian Law & Economics Association, 425
Canadian Law & Society Association, 425
Carleton County Law Association, 513
Church Council on Justice & Corrections, 569
Coalition for International Criminal Court, 1517
Community Legal Information Association of Prince Edward Island, 600
Council of Canadian Law Deans, 633
County of Perth Law Association, 636
Durham Region Law Association, 665
Essex Law Association, 696
Federation of Law Reform Agencies of Canada, 724
Federation of Ontario Law Associations, 725
Fondation du barreau du Québec, 745
Foundation for Legal Research, 755
Frontenac Law Association, 763
Grey County Law Association, 790
Groupe de droit collaboratif du Québec, 791
Hamilton Law Association, 801
Hastings County Law Association, 804
Health Law Institute, 806
Indigenous Bar Association, 834
Institute of Air & Space Law, 844
Institute of Law Clerks of Ontario, 846
International Bar Association, 1540
International Centre for Criminal Law Reform & Criminal Justice Policy, 854
International Commission of Jurists (Canadian Section), 855
Justice Centre for Constitutional Freedoms, 878
Justice for Children & Youth, 878
Justice Institute of British Columbia, 878
Law Foundation of British Columbia, 900
Law Foundation of Newfoundland & Labrador, 900
Law Foundation of Nova Scotia, 901
Law Foundation of Ontario, 901
Law Foundation of Prince Edward Island, 901
Law Foundation of Saskatchewan, 901
Law Union of Ontario, 902
Legal Archives Society of Alberta, 906
Legal Education Society of Alberta, 906
Legal Services Society, 906
Lennox & Addington County Law Association, 907
Licensed Paralegals Association (Ontario), 910
Lincoln County Law Association, 912
Lord Reading Law Society, 919
Manitoba Bar Association, 932
The Manitoba Law Foundation, 939
McGill Centre for Medicine, Ethics & Law, 955
Medico-Legal Society of Toronto, 959
Middlesex Law Association, 965
National Association of Women & the Law, 990
National Judicial Institute, 994
New Brunswick Law Foundation, 1010
Nipissing Law Association, 1027
Northwest Territories Law Foundation, 1038
Ontario Community Justice Association, 1073
Ontario Criminal Justice Association, 1076
Oxford County Law Association, 1134
Peel Law Association, 1148
Peterborough Law Association, 1153
Pivot Legal Society, 1161
The Public Interest Advocacy Centre, 1192
Renfrew County Law Association, 1217
Simcoe County Law Association, 1299
Society of Ontario Adjudicators & Regulators, 1330
Society of Trust & Estate Practitioners, 1331
Stormont, Dundas & Glengarry Law Association, 1350
Surety Association of Canada, 1357
Temiskaming Law Association, 1370
Thunder Bay Law Association, 1378
Uniform Law Conference of Canada, 1405
Welland County Law Association, 1443
Wellington Law Association, 1443
York Region Law Association, 1473
Yukon Law Foundation, 1479

Law Libraries
Association des bibliothèques de droit de Montréal, 107
British Columbia Courthouse Library Society, 238
Calgary Law Library Group, 273
Canadian Association of Law Libraries, 319
Edmonton Law Libraries Association, 678
Toronto Association of Law Libraries, 1382
Vancouver Association of Law Libraries, 1425

Lawn Bowling
Blind Bowls Association of Canada, 214
Bowls British Columbia, 220
Bowls Canada Boulingrin, 220
Bowls Manitoba, 220
Bowls Saskatchewan Inc., 220
Lawn Bowls Association of Alberta, 902
Ontario Lawn Bowls Association, 1088
Prince Edward Island Lawn Bowling Association, 1175
Québec Lawn Bowling Federation, 1198

Lawyers
The Advocates' Society, 11
Alberta Civil Trial Lawyers' Association, 28
American Association for Justice, 1488
Association d'entraide des avocats de Montréal, 99
Association des avocats de la défense de Montréal, 106
Association des avocats et avocates de province, 106
Association des avocats et avocates représentant les bénéficiaires des régimes d'indemnisation publics, 107
Association des avocats et avocates en droit familial du Québec, 107
Association des familialistes de Québec, 113
Association des jeunes Barreaux du Québec, 117
Association des juristes d'expression française de l'Ontario, 117
Association des juristes d'expression française de la Saskatchewan, 118
Association des juristes d'expression française du Manitoba inc., 118
Association des juristes d'expression française du Nouveau-Brunswick, 118
Association des juristes pour l'avancement de la vie artistique, 118
Association des procureurs de cours municipales du Québec, 124
Association du jeune barreau de Montréal, 130
Association québécoise de doit constitutionel, 169
Association québécoise des avocats et avocates de la défense, 171
Association québécoise des avocats et avocates en droit de l'immigration, 171
Atlantic Provinces Trial Lawyers Association, 185
Avocats Hors Québec, 191
Avocats sans frontières Canada, 191
Barreau de Montréal, 197
Canadian Association of Black Lawyers, 308
Canadian Association of Crown Counsel, 312
Canadian Association of Refugee Lawyers, 330
Canadian Bar Association, 341
Canadian Bar Insurance Association, 342
Canadian Committee of Lawyers & Jurists for World Jewry, 361
Canadian IT Law Association, 422
Canadian Lawyers Association for International Human Rights, 426
Canadian Lawyers Insurance Association, 426
Canadian Transport Lawyers Association, 497
Chambre des notaires du Québec, 550
Congress of Black Lawyers & Jurists of Québec, 613
Criminal Lawyers' Association, 642
Fédération des associations de juristes d'expression française de common law, 712
Federation of Law Societies of Canada, 724
Groupe de droit collaboratif du Québec, 791
International Pension & Employee Benefits Lawyers Association, 859
Jeune Barreau de Québec, 870
Law Society of Alberta, 901
Law Society of British Columbia, 901
Law Society of Manitoba, 901
Law Society of New Brunswick, 901
Law Society of Newfoundland & Labrador, 901
Law Society of Nunavut, 901
Law Society of Prince Edward Island, 902
Law Society of Saskatchewan, 902
Law Society of the Northwest Territories, 902
Law Society of Upper Canada, 902
Law Society of Yukon, 902
Moncton Area Lawyers' Association, 972
Nova Scotia Barristers' Society, 1042
Ontario Crown Attorneys Association, 1076
Ontario Trial Lawyers Association, 1111
Pro Bono Québec, 1181
Programme d'aide aux membres du barreau, 1187
Saint John Law Society, 1247
Société Québécoise de droit international, 1323
Toronto Lawyers Association, 1385
Trial Lawyers Association of British Columbia, 1397
West Coast Domestic Workers' Association, 1444

Learned Societies
American Anthropological Association, 1488
American Antiquarian Society, 1488
American Council of Learned Societies, 1492
American Musicological Society, 1495
American Political Science Association, 1496
American Sociological Association, 1503
American Studies Association, 1503
Anthroposophical Society in Canada, 72
Archaeological Institute of America, 1505
Associação Brasileira de Estudos Canadense, 1506
Association des professeurs de français des universités et collèges canadiens, 124
Association for Bahá'í Studies, 132
Association for Canadian & Québec Literatures, 132
Association for Canadian Studies in China, 1507
Association for Canadian Studies in German-Speaking Countries, 1507
Association for Canadian Studies in Ireland, 1507
Association for Slavic, East European, & Eurasian Studies, 1509
Association internationale des études patristiques, 1509
Association of Canadian College & University Teachers of English, 141
Bibliographical Society of America, 1514
Bibliographical Society of Canada, 208
Canadian Asian Studies Association, 296
Canadian Association for Irish Studies, 301
Canadian Association for Studies in Co-operation, 304
Canadian Association for the Advancement of Netherlandic Studies, 305
Canadian Association of Learned Journals, 319
Canadian Association of Professional Employees, 328
Canadian Association of Slavists, 333
Canadian Association of University Teachers of German, 335
Canadian Catholic Historical Association - English Section, 351
Canadian Committee of Byzantinists, 360
Canadian Economics Association, 379
Canadian Education Association, 379
Canadian Historical Association, 405
Canadian Institute for Mediterranean Studies, 412
Canadian Linguistic Association, 427
Canadian Philosophical Association, 454
Canadian Political Science Association, 457
Canadian Psychological Association, 462
Canadian Science & Technology Historical Association, 468
Canadian Society for Aesthetics, 473
Canadian Society for Continental Philosophy, 474
The Canadian Society for Mesopotamian Studies, 476
Canadian Society for the History & Philosophy of Science, 477
Canadian Society for the Study of Education, 478
Canadian Society for the Study of Higher Education, 478
Canadian Society for the Study of Names, 478
Canadian Society for the Study of Religion, 478
Canadian Society of Patristic Studies, 486
Canadian Sociological Association, 488
Canadian Theological Society, 494
Dictionary Society of North America, 1521
Film Studies Association of Canada, 735
Hungarian Studies Association of Canada, 827
International Association for Armenian Studies, 1535
International Council for Central & East European Studies (Canada), 1544
International Husserl & Phenomenological Research Society, 1550
International Political Science Association, 859

International Union of Anthropological & Ethnological Sciences, 1563
Medieval Academy of America, 1570
The Ontario Archaeological Society, 1059
Organization of American Historians, 1581
Renaissance Society of America, 1586
Royal Astronomical Society of Canada, 1238
Royal Canadian Institute, 1240
The Royal Society of Canada, 1242
Société internationale pour l'étude de la philosophie médiévale, 1589
Société québécoise d'ethnologie, 1323
Society for Classical Studies, 1589
Society for Socialist Studies, 1326
Society for the Study of Egyptian Antiquities, 1327
Women's & Gender Studies et Recherches Féminstes, 1461

Learning Disabilities
Adult Learning Development Association, 9
Alberta Council for Exceptional Children, 31
American Association on Intellectual & Developmental Disabilities, 1490
Association de Montréal pour la déficience intellectuelle, 102
Association québécoise des troubles d'apprentissage, 175
British Columbia Council for Exceptional Children, 237
Canadian Dyslexia Association, 379
Centre for ADHD Awareness, Canada, 531
Learning Assistance Teachers' Association, 903
Learning Disabilities Association of Alberta, 903
Learning Disabilities Association of British Columbia, 904
Learning Disabilities Association of Canada, 904
Learning Disabilities Association of Manitoba, 904
Learning Disabilities Association of New Brunswick, 904
Learning Disabilities Association of Newfoundland & Labrador Inc., 904
Learning Disabilities Association of Ontario, 904
Learning Disabilities Association of Prince Edward Island, 905
Learning Disabilities Association of Saskatchewan, 905
Learning Disabilities Association of The Northwest Territories, 905
Learning Disabilities Association of Yukon Territory, 905
Manitoba Council for Exceptional Children, 934
Ontario Council for Exceptional Children, 1075
Saskatchewan Council for Exceptional Children, 1262
Teachers of Inclusive Education - British Columbia, 1367
Victoria READ Society, 1433

Leather Industry
Luggage, Leathergoods, Handbags & Accessories Association of Canada, 920
Two/Ten Charity Trust of Canada Inc., 1401

Lebanese Canadians & Lebanon
Canadian Lebanon Society of Halifax, 426
Diman Association Canada (Lebanese), 657
Lebanese Canadian Heritage Association, 905
Lebanese Syrian Canadian Ladies Aid Society, 905

Legal Assistants
British Columbia Paralegal Association, 248

Legal Clinics
Aboriginal Legal Services of Toronto, 2
Advocacy Centre for the Elderly, 10
ARCH Disability Law Centre, 76
Au bas de l'échelle, 187
The Barbra Schlifer Commemorative Clinic, 196
British Columbia Public Interest Advocacy Centre, 250
Community Legal Assistance Society, 599
Community Legal Education Ontario, 600
Downtown Legal Services, 661
East Toronto Community Legal Services, 668
Edmonton Community Legal Centre, 676
Flemingdon Community Legal Services, 740
HALCO, 798
Landlord's Self-Help Centre, 898
Legal Aid New Brunswick, 906

Legal Aid Ontario, 906
Legal Services Society, 906
Metro Toronto Chinese & Southeast Asian Legal Clinic, 963
Parkdale Community Legal Services, 1140
Pro Bono Law Ontario, 1180
Rexdale Community Legal Services, 1229
South Etobicoke Community Legal Services, 1334
Student Legal Services of Edmonton, 1352
Willowdale Community Legal Services, 1455

Legal Education
Advocacy Centre for the Elderly, 10
Community Legal Education Association (Manitoba) Inc., 600
Community Legal Education Ontario, 600
Legal Information Society of Nova Scotia, 906
New Brunswick Continuing Legal Education, 1007
People's Law School, 1151
Public Legal Education Association of Canada, 1192
Public Legal Education Association of Saskatchewan, Inc., 1192
Public Legal Information Association of Newfoundland, 1192
Women's Legal Education & Action Fund, 1462
Yukon Public Legal Education Association, 1479

Legal Services
Legal Aid Ontario, 906
Legal Aid Society of Alberta, 906

Leprosy
effect:hope, 680
Heiser Program for Research in Leprosy & Tuberculosis, 1529
Secours aux lépreux (Canada) inc., 1288

Leukemia
Leucan - Association pour les enfants atteints de cancer, 908
The Leukemia & Lymphoma Society of Canada, 908

LGBTQ
Affirm United, 11
Association des Gais et Lesbiennes Sourds, 114
Association des lesbiennes et des gais sur Internet, 118
Association des pères gais de Montréal inc., 122
BC Rainbow Alliance of the Deaf, 202
Bi Unité Montréal, 207
Buddies in Bad Times Theatre, 261
CAEO Québec, 270
Canadian Lesbian & Gay Archives, 426
Canadian Professional Association for Transgender Health, 460
Centre communautaire des gais et lesbiennes de Montréal, 526
Centre de solidarité lesbienne, 530
Chambre de commerce LGBT du Québec, 549
Coalition des familles LGBT, 577
Community One Foundation, 607
Conseil québécois des gais et lesbiennes du Québec, 620
Dignity Canada Dignité, 657
Dignity Toronto Dignité, 657
Dignity Vancouver Dignité, 657
Dignity Winnipeg Dignité, 657
Egale Canada, 681
Ensemble vocal Ganymède, 690
The 519 Church St. Community Centre, 740
Fondation Émergence inc., 746
Gai Écoute inc., 766
Gay Fathers of Toronto, 768
Groupe gai de l'Outaouais, 792
Groupe gai de l'Université Laval, 792
Hola, 818
Hominum, 820
Inside Out Toronto LGBT Film & Video Festival, 839
Integrity Toronto, 850
Kind Space, 888
Lace Up Your Cleats, 895
Lesbian & Gay Immigration Task Force, 907
Metropolitan Community Church of Toronto, 964
Ontario Gay & Lesbian Chamber of Commerce, 1081

Ontario Rainbow Alliance of the Deaf, 1100
Out on the Shelf, 1133
Parents, Families & Friends of Lesbians & Gays, 1582
PFLAG Canada Inc., 1155
Pride Centre of Edmonton, 1170
Projet 10, 1188
Queer Ontario, 1200
The Rainbow Alliance, 1203
Rainbow Association of Canadian Artists (Spectra Talent Contest), 1203
Rainbow Resource Centre, 1203
RÉZO, 1229
Toronto Area Gays & Lesbians Phoneline & Crisis Counselling, 1381
La Trame, 1394
2-Spirited People of the First Nations, 1401
Welcome Friend Association, 1443
Women for Recreation, Information & Business, 1460

Librarians
Association des bibliothécaires professionnel(le)s du Nouveau-Brunswick, 107
Association des bibliothécaires, des professeures et professeurs de l'Université de Moncton, 107
Association of Parliamentary Libraries in Canada, 155
Association of Professional Librarians of New Brunswick, 159
British Columbia Teacher-Librarians' Association, 255
Canadian Association of Professional Academic Librarians, 328
Corporation des bibliothécaires professionnels du Québec, 629
Ex Libris Association, 699
Librarians Without Borders, 910
PEI Teacher-Librarians' Association, 1149
Québec Library Association, 1198

Libraries
American Library Association, 1494
Amis de la Bibliothèque de Brossard Georgette-Lepage, 67
Art Libraries Society of North America, 1506
Association des bibliothèques de l'Ontario-Franco, 107
Association des bibliothèques publiques de la Montérégie, 107
Association des bibliothèques publiques du Québec, 107
Association of College & Research Libraries, 1511
Association of Jewish Libraries (Montréal), 150
Association of Jewish Libraries (Toronto), 150
Association of Prince Edward Island Libraries, 156
Association of Research Libraries, 1513
Association pour la promotion des services documentaires scolaires, 166
Atlantic Provinces Library Association, 185
Bibliographical Society of Canada, 208
British Columbia Library Association, 244
Calgary Law Library Group, 273
Canadian Association of Professional Academic Librarians, 328
Canadian Association of Research Libraries, 331
Canadian Committee on Cataloguing, 361
Canadian Committee on MARC, 361
Canadian Federation of Library Associations, 387
Canadian School Libraries, 468
Canadian Urban Libraries Council, 500
Colchester-East Hants Public Library Foundation, 580
Commission de la Médiathèque Père-Louis-Lamontagne, 593
Ex Libris Association, 699
Federation of Ontario Public Libraries, 726
Foothills Library Association, 750
The Friends of Library & Archives Canada, 761
Friends of the Archibald, 762
Friends of the Greater Sudbury Public Library, 762
Greater Edmonton Library Association, 783
Halifax Library Association, 799
International Federation of Library Associations & Institutions, 1548

Library Association of Alberta, 910
Manitoba Library Association, 939
Manitoba Library Consortium Inc., 940
Manitoba School Libraries Association, 944
National Reading Campaign, Inc., 995
Newfoundland & Labrador Library Association, 1019
North Central Library Federation, 1030
North West Library Federation, 1033
Northwest Territories Library Association, 1038
Nova Scotia Government Libraries Council, 1045
Nova Scotia Library Association, 1046
Nunavut Library Association, 1051
Ontario College & University Library Association, 1072
Ontario Health Libraries Association, 1084
Ontario Library & Information Technology Association, 1088
Ontario Library Association, 1088
Ontario Public Library Association, 1099
Ontario School Library Association, 1103
Pacific Northwest Library Association, 1135
Provincial & Territorial Public Library Council, 1190
Réseau BIBLIO du Québec, 1218
Saskatchewan Library Association, 1269
Special Libraries Association, 1595
Toronto Public Library Foundation, 1386
University of Alberta Library & Information Studies Alumni Association, 1419
University of Toronto, Faculty of Information Alumni Association, 1421
Woodland Cultural Centre, 1464

Library Administrators
Council of Post Secondary Library Directors, British Columbia, 635
Dalhousie University School of Information Management Associated Alumni, 648
Library Boards Association of Nova Scotia, 910

Library Science
Canadiana, 506

Library Technicians
Alberta Association of Library Technicians, 23
Association professionnelle des techniciennes et techniciens en documentation du Québec, 167
British Columbia Library Association Library Technicians' & Assistants' Section, 245
Manitoba Association of Library Technicians, 930
Ontario Association of Library Technicians, 1064
Saskatchewan Association of Library Technicians, Inc., 1257

Library Trustees
Alberta Library Trustees Association, 39
British Columbia Library Trustees' Association, 245
Manitoba Library Trustees Association, 940
New Brunswick Library Trustees' Association, 1010
Ontario Library Boards' Association, 1089
Saskatchewan Library Trustees' Association, 1269

Lifesaving
Lifesaving Society, 911

Lifestyle
Commonwealth Human Ecology Council, 1518
Hub for Active School Travel, 824
Island Fitness Council, 865
Society of Bastet, 1327

Lighting
Illuminating Engineering Society of North America, 1530
International Commission on Illumination, 1542

Limnology
International Society of Limnology, 1561

Linguistics
American Dialect Society, 1492
Association des conseils en gestion linguistique Inc., 109
Association of Translators & Interpreters of Nova Scotia, 163
Atlantic Provinces Linguistic Association, 185

Subject Index / Literacy

Canadian Linguistic Association, 427
Canadian Society for the Study of Names, 478
Centre interdisciplinaire de recherches sur les activités langagières, 535
International Union of Anthropological & Ethnological Sciences, 1563
Linguistic Society of America, 1569
Teachers of English to Speakers of Other Languages, Inc., 1597

Literacy
ABC Life Literacy Canada, 1
Adult Literacy Council of Greater Fort Erie, 9
L'Atelier des lettres, 180
Barrie Literacy Council, 197
Braille Literacy Canada, 224
Brant Skills Centre, 226
Canadian Council of Teachers of English Language Arts, 370
Canadian Literacy & Learning Network, 427
Carleton Literacy Council, 513
Centre for Community Learning & Development, 531
CODE, 580
Conseil pour le développement de l'alphabétisme et des compétences des adultes du Nouveau-Brunswick, 619
Copian, 628
Dorchester & Westmorland Literacy Council, 661
East York Learning Experience, 669
Essential Skills Ontario, 696
Fondation québécoise pour l'alphabétisation, 748
GATEWAY Centre For Learning, 767
Glace Bay Literacy Council, 774
Haldimand-Norfolk Literacy Council, 798
Houston Link to Learning, 824
International Literacy Association, 1552
Kitimat Community Services Society, 891
Labrador Literacy Information & Action Network, 894
Learning Enrichment Foundation, 905
Learning for Living South Muskoka, 905
Literacy Alberta, 913
Literacy Alliance of West Nipissing, 913
Literacy Central Vancouver Island, 913
Literacy Coalition of New Brunswick, 913
The Literacy Council of Burlington, 913
Literacy Council of Durham Region, 913
Literacy Council York-Simcoe, 913
The Literacy Group of Waterloo Region, 914
Literacy Link South Central, 914
Literacy Nova Scotia, 914
Literacy Ontario Central South, 914
Metro Toronto Movement for Literacy, 963
National Literacy & Health Program, 994
Niagara West Employment & Learning Resource Centres, 1026
North Algoma Literacy Coalition, 1028
Nova Scotia Teachers Association of Literacy & Learning, 1049
People, Words & Change, 1152
Prince Edward Island Literacy Alliance Inc., 1175
Project Adult Literacy Society, 1187
Project READ Literacy Network Waterloo-Wellington, 1188
Quality in Lifelong Learning Network, 1195
Quebec English Literacy Alliance, 1197
Reading Council for Literacy Advance in Montréal, 1205
Réseau pour le développement de l'alphabétisme et des compétences, 1225
Saskatchewan Literacy Network, 1269
Simcoe/Muskoka Literacy Network, 1300
South Shore Reading Council, 1336
Start Right Coalition for Financial Literacy, 1348
Toronto Centre for Community Learning & Development, 1383
Victoria READ Society, 1433
West Neighbourhood House, 1446
Western Québec Literacy Council, 1450
Windsor Public Library Adult Literacy Program, 1457
World Literacy of Canada, 1466
Wycliffe Bible Translators of Canada, Inc., 1470
Yamaska Literacy Council, 1470
Young Alberta Book Society, 1474
Yukon Learn Society, 1479

Literary Appreciation
Bard on the Beach Theatre Society, 196
The Bimetallic Question, 211
The Bronte Historical Society, 260
The Brontë Society, 1514
The CPR Stockholder's Society, 638
The Great Herd of Bisons of the Fertile Plains, 782
Jane Austen Society of North America, 868

Literature
African Literature Association, 1486
The Arts & Letters Club, 85
Association for Canadian & Québec Literatures, 132
Association for Literature, Environment, & Culture in Canada, 133
Association professionnelle des écrivains de la Sagamie-Côte-Nord, 167
BC Alliance for Arts & Culture, 200
The Bronte Historical Society, 260
The Brontë Society, 1514
Canadian Association for Commonwealth Literature & Language Studies, 298
Canadian Association for Commonwealth Literature & Language Studies, 298
Canadian Committee of Byzantinists, 360
Canadian Comparative Literature Association, 361
Centre for Comparative Literature, 531
Fédération québécoise du loisir littéraire, 731
La Fondation Émile-Nelligan, 746
The G.K. Chesterton Institute for Faith & Culture, 1528
Indigenous Literary Studies Association, 835
International Arthurian Society - North American Branch, 1535
International Association for Literary Journalism Studies, 853
International Board on Books for Young People, 1541
International Board on Books for Young People - Canadian Section, 854
Jane Austen Society of North America, 868
Literary & Historical Society of Québec, 914
L.M. Montgomery Institute, 916
Québec Writers' Federation, 1199
Science Writers & Communicators of Canada, 1285
Society for Existential & Phenomenological Theory & Culture, 1326
Young Alberta Book Society, 1474

Lithuanian Canadians
The Lithuanian Canadian Community, 914
Lithuanian Community Association of Toronto, 914
The Lithuanian Society of Edmonton, 915
Lithuanian-Canadian Foundation, 915

Liver & Biliary Tract Diseases
Canadian Association for the Study of the Liver, 306
Canadian Liver Foundation, 427
International Liver Cancer Association, 1552

Livestock
Alberta Bison Association, 26
Alpaca Livestock Producers & Cooperators Association, 59
Beef Farmers of Ontario, 204
British Columbia Bison Association, 233
Canadian Animal Health Institute, 293
Canadian Bison Association, 344
Canadian Council on Animal Care, 370
Canadian Goat Society, 398
Canadian Guernsey Association, 399
Canadian Hackney Society, 399
Canadian Livestock Records Corporation, 428
Canadian Llama & Alpaca Association, 428
Canadians for Ethical Treatment of Food Animals, 507
Farm & Food Care Ontario, 705
Manitoba Forage & Grassland Association, 937
National Bison Association, 1575
Nipawin Exhibition Association Inc., 1027
Ontario Camelids Association, 1070
Rare Breeds Canada, 1204
Saskatchewan Livestock Association, 1269
Saskatchewan Stock Growers Association, 1276
Vaccine & Infectious Disease Organization, 1423
The Western Stock Growers' Association, 1450

Locks & Keys
The Association of Ontario Locksmiths, 155
Professional Locksmith Association of Alberta, 1186

Logging
Association de la santé et de la sécurité des pâtes et papiers et des industries de la forêt du Québec, 102
Canadian Well Logging Society, 503

Logistics
Canadian Institute of Traffic & Transportation, 419
The Chartered Institute of Logistics & Transport in North America, 552
International Warehouse Logistics Association, 1566
The Logistics Institute, 917

Long Term Care Facilities
AdvantAge Ontario, 10
Alberta Continuing Care Association, 31
British Columbia Care Providers Association, 234
Canadian Alliance for Long Term Care, 291
Canadian Hospice Palliative Care Association, 409
Concerned Friends of Ontario Citizens in Care Facilities, 609
Continuing Care Association of Nova Scotia, 626
La coopérative de Solidarité de Répit et d'Etraide, 627
HealthCareCAN, 807
Kensington Foundation, 883
Long Term & Continuing Care Association of Manitoba, 919
New Brunswick Association of Nursing Homes, Inc., 1005
New Brunswick Special Care Home Association Inc., 1012
Ontario Association of Community Care Access Centres, 1063
Ontario Association of Residents' Councils, 1066
Ontario Long Term Care Association, 1089

Longshoremen
International Longshore & Warehouse Union (CLC), 1553
International Longshoremen's Association (AFL-CIO/CLC), 1553
Shipyard General Workers' Federation of British Columbia, 1296

Lotteries
World Lottery Association, 1606

Lumber Industry
Association de la santé et de la sécurité des pâtes et papiers et des industries de la forêt du Québec, 102
Canadian Lumber Standards Accreditation Board, 428
Coast Forest Products Association, 579
Conseil de l'industrie forestière du Québec, 615
Independent Lumber Dealers Co-operative, 833
Lumber & Building Materials Association of Ontario, 920
Maritime Lumber Bureau, 951
New Brunswick Federation of Woodlot Owners Inc., 1008
Ontario Lumber Manufacturers' Association, 1089
Ontario Woodlot Association, 1114
Syndicat des producteurs de bois du Saguenay-Lac-Saint-Jean, 1363
Truck Loggers Association, 1399
Western Red Cedar Lumber Association, 1450
Western Retail Lumber Association, 1450
Wood Manufacturing Council, 1463

Lung Disorders & Diseases
Alberta & Northwest Territories Lung Association, 21
American Lung Association, 1495
Association des pneumologues de la province de Québec, 123
British Columbia Lung Association, 245
Canadian Association of Cardio-Pulmonary Technologists, 309
Canadian Association of Thoracic Surgeons, 334
Canadian Lung Association, 428
Canadian Respiratory Health Professionals, 467
Canadian Thoracic Society, 494
The Lung Association of Nova Scotia, 921
Manitoba Lung Association, 940
New Brunswick Lung Association, 1010
Newfoundland & Labrador Lung Association, 1020
Ontario Lung Association, 1089
Ontario Respiratory Care Society, 1101
Ontario Thoracic Society, 1110
Prince Edward Island Lung Association, 1175
Québec Lung Association, 1198
Saskatchewan Lung Association, 1269

Lupus Erythematosus
British Columbia Lupus Society, 245
Canadian Network for Improved Outcomes in Systemic Lupus Erythematosus, 440
Lupus Canada, 921
Lupus Foundation of Ontario, 921
Lupus New Brunswick, 921
Lupus Newfoundland & Labrador, 921
Lupus Ontario, 921
Lupus PEI, 922
Lupus SK Society, 922
Lupus Society of Alberta, 922
Lupus Society of Manitoba, 922

Lutheran Church
Canadian Lutheran World Relief, 428
Evangelical Lutheran Church in Canada, 698
Lutheran Association of Missionaries & Pilots, 922
Lutheran Church - Canada, 922
Lutheran Laymen's League of Canada, 922

Macedonian Canadians
Macedonian Human Rights Movement International, 923
United Macedonians Organization of Canada, 1411

Machine Tools
Canadian Tooling & Machining Association, 495

Maltese in Canada
Malta Band Club, Inc., 928
Maltese Veterans Association of Canada, 928
Maltese-Canadian Federation Inc., 928
Maltese-Canadian Society of Toronto, Inc., 928

Management
Academy of Management, 1485
Administrators of Volunteer Resources BC, 8
Alberta Association of Clinic Managers, 23
American Management Association, 1495
American Society of Association Executives, 1499
Asociación Nacional de Ejecutivos de Organismos Empresariales y Profesionales, A.C., 1506
Association des Aménagistes Régionaux du Québec, 105
Association des cadres supérieurs de la santé et des services sociaux du Québec, 108
Association des gestionnaires de ressources bénévoles du Québec, 115
Association des MBA du Québec, 119
Association of Administrative Professionals, 139
Australian Society of Association Executives Ltd., 1513
Canadian Association of Exposition Management, 313
Canadian Association of University Business Officers, 334
Canadian Council of Professional Certification, 369
Canadian Federation of Business School Deans, 386
Canadian Institute of Management, 416
Canadian Management Centre, 429
Canadian Society of Association Executives, 480
Canadian Society of Physician Executives, 486
Canadian Urban Libraries Council, 500
Commonwealth Association for Public Administration & Management, 593
The Conference Board of Canada, 611

Conseil du patronat du Québec, 618
European Society of Association Executives, 1524
Farm Management Canada, 705
Federation of Swiss Association Executives, 1526
Global Network of Director Institutes, 775
Governance Professionals of Canada, 778
Institute of Certified Management Consultants of British Columbia, 845
Institute of Chartered Secretaries & Administrators - Canadian Division, 845
Institute of Corporate Directors, 845
Institute of Housing Management, 846
The Institute of Internal Auditors, 1533
Institute of Professional Management, 847
International Association of Venue Managers, Inc., 1540
Manitoba Association for Volunteer Administration, 929
Medical Group Management Association of Canada, 958
Music Managers Forum Canada, 984
Music/Musique NB, 984
Ontario Association of Emergency Managers, 1063
Ordre des administrateurs agréés du Québec, 1119
POWERtalk International, 1584
Strategic Leadership Forum, 1351
Supply Chain Management Association - Alberta, 1355
Technology Services Industry Association, 1597
Toronto Law Office Management Association, 1385
Volunteer Management Professionals of Canada, 1439
Winnipeg Executives Association, 1458

Management Consultants
Canadian Association of Management Consultants, 320
Institute of Certified Management Consultants of Alberta, 845
Institute of Certified Management Consultants of Atlantic Canada, 845
Institute of Certified Management Consultants of Manitoba, 845
Institute of Certified Management Consultants of Saskatchewan, 845

Manual Therapy
Canadian Orthopractic Manual Therapy Association, 448

Manufacturing
Agricultural Manufacturers of Canada, 15
Association for Operations Management, 134
Association industrielle de l'est de Montréal, 136
British Columbia Paint Manufacturers' Association, 248
Canadian Explosives Industry Association, 383
Canadian Generic Pharmaceutical Association, 397
Canadian Hardware & Housewares Manufacturers' Association, 401
Canadian Home Furnishings Alliance, 408
Canadian Manufacturers & Exporters, 429
Canadian MedTech Manufacturers' Alliance, 434
Canadian Pasta Manufacturers Association, 451
Canadian Printing Ink Manufacturers' Association, 460
Canadian Supply Chain Sector Council, 491
Canadian Tooling & Machining Association, 495
Canadian Toy Association / Canadian Toy & Hobby Fair, 496
Canadian Vehicle Manufacturers' Association, 501
Council for Continuing Pharmaceutical Education, 632
Door & Access Systems Manufacturers Association, 1521
Fédération de l'industrie manufacturière (FIM-CSN), 708
Flavour Manufacturers Association of Canada, 740
Global Automakers of Canada, 774
International Snowmobile Manufacturers Association, 1557
National Marine Manufacturers Association, 1576
Polyurethane Manufacturers Association, 1584
Poplar Council of Canada, 1165
The Royal Society for the Encouragement of Arts, Manufactures & Commerce, 1587
Society of Manufacturing Engineers - Canada Office, 1330
Sous-Traitance Industrielle Québec, 1334

Maple Syrup
Fédération des producteurs acéricoles du Québec, 717
New Brunswick Maple Syrup Association, 1010
Ontario Maple Syrup Producers' Association, 1090

Maps
Antiquarian Booksellers' Association of Canada, 72
Canadian Cartographic Association, 350
Canadian Institute of Geomatics, 416

Marfan Syndrome
Canadian Marfan Association, 430

Marine Biology
Bamfield Marine Sciences Centre, 195
Canadian Meteorological & Oceanographic Society, 435
Coastal Ecosystems Research Foundation, 579
Explorer's Club (Canadian Chapter), 700
Grand Manan Whale & Seabird Research Station, 780
International Ocean Institute, 1553

Marine Engineering
Marine Renewables Canada, 950

Marine Mammals
Antarctic & Southern Ocean Coalition, 1505
Ceta-Research Inc., 538
Grand Manan Whale & Seabird Research Station, 780
International Whaling Commission, 1566
Marmot Recovery Foundation, 952
Sea Shepherd Conservation Society, 1287
Sea Shepherd Conservation Society - USA, 1588

Marine Trades
Boating BC Association, 216
British Columbia Ferry & Marine Workers' Union (CLC), 241
The Canadian Marine Industries and Shipbuilding Association, 430
Canadian Marine Pilots' Association, 430
Chamber of Marine Commerce, 539
Comité maritime international, 1518
Council of Marine Carriers, 634
Fish, Food & Allied Workers, 739
International Association of Ports & Harbours, 1539
International Maritime Organization, 1553
Marine Insurance Association of British Columbia, 949
Master Mariners of Canada, 953
National Marine Manufacturers Association, 1576
National Marine Manufacturers Association Canada, 995
Vancouver Maritime Museum, 1427

Mariners
Mariners' House of Montréal, 950
Master Mariners of Canada, 953
Seafarers' International Union of Canada (AFL-CIO/CLC), 1287

Maritime Law
The Association of Maritime Arbitrators of Canada, 151
The Canadian Maritime Law Association, 430
Canadian Nautical Research Society, 440

Marketing
Alliance for Audited Media, 56
American Marketing Association, 1495
Association des professionnels de la communication et du marketing, 125
Association of Internet Marketing & Sales, 149
Canadian Agencies Practicing Marketing Activation, 289
Canadian Agri-Marketing Association, 290
Canadian Agri-Marketing Association (Alberta), 290
Canadian Agri-Marketing Association (Manitoba), 290
Canadian Agri-Marketing Association (Saskatchewan), 290
Canadian Automatic Merchandising Association, 338
Canadian Hotel Marketing & Sales Executives, 409
Canadian Institute of Marketing, 417
Canadian Marketing Association, 430
Canadian Out-of-Home Measurement Bureau, 448
Canadian Produce Marketing Association, 460
Greater Toronto Marketing Alliance, 786
Marketing Research & Intelligence Association, 951
Multicultural Marketing Society of Canada, 979
Periodical Marketers of Canada, 1152
Photo Marketing Association International - Canada, 1157
Sales & Marketing Executives of Vancouver, 1251
Tourism Prince George, 1390
Trans-Canada Advertising Agency Network, 1395
Vividata, 1436

Marketing Boards & Commissions
Alberta Chicken Producers, 28
Alberta Turkey Producers, 50
Asparagus Farmers of Ontario, 87
British Columbia Farm Industry Review Board, 240
British Columbia Hog Marketing Commission, 243
British Columbia Turkey Farms, 257
Canadian Pork Council, 458
Carleton-Victoria Forest Products Marketing Board & Wood Producers Association, 513
Chicken Farmers of Canada, 557
Chicken Farmers of New Brunswick, 557
Chicken Farmers of Newfoundland & Labrador, 557
Chicken Farmers of Nova Scotia, 557
Chicken Farmers of Prince Edward Island, 557
Chicken Farmers of Saskatchewan, 557
Dairy Farmers of Manitoba, 648
Dairy Farmers of New Brunswick, 648
Fédération des producteurs d'agneaux et moutons du Québec, 717
Fédération des producteurs de pommes de terre du Québec, 717
Grape Growers of Ontario, 782
Madawaska Forest Products Marketing Board, 924
Manitoba Chicken Producers, 933
Manitoba Egg Farmers, 936
Manitoba Milk Prices Review Commission, 940
Manitoba Pork Council, 942
Natural Products Marketing Council, 999
New Brunswick Cattle Producers, 1006
New Brunswick Egg Marketing Board, 1007
Nova Scotia Egg Producers, 1044
Ontario Flue-Cured Tobacco Growers' Marketing Board, 1080
Ontario Pork Producers' Marketing Board, 1097
Ontario Potato Board, 1097
Ontario Sheep Marketing Agency, 1104
Porc NB Pork, 1165
Pork Nova Scotia, 1165
Potato Growers of Alberta, 1168
Potatoes New Brunswick, 1168
Prince Edward Island Hog Commodity Marketing Board, 1174
Prince Edward Island Marketing Council, 1175
Sask Pork, 1254
Saskatchewan Egg Producers, 1264
Saskatchewan Turkey Producers' Marketing Board, 1276
Seed Corn Growers of Ontario, 1288
Turkey Farmers of Canada, 1400
Turkey Farmers of New Brunswick, 1400

Martial Arts
Aikido Yukon Association, 18
Alberta Taekwondo Association, 49
Association de taekwondo du Québec, 104
BC Taekwondo Association, 202
Canadian Chito-Ryu Karate-Do Association, 356
Canadian Jiu-jitsu Council, 423
Canadian Kendo Federation, 424
Club de karaté Shotokan Chibougamau, 574
International Judo Federation, 1551
Judo Alberta, 875
Judo BC, 876
Judo Manitoba, 876
Judo New Brunswick, 876
Judo Nova Scotia, 876
Judo Nunavut, 876
Judo Ontario, 876
Judo Prince Edward Island, 876
Judo Saskatchewan, 876
Judo Yukon, 876
Judo-Québec inc, 876
Karate Alberta Association, 881
Karate BC, 881
Karate Canada, 881
Karate Manitoba, 881
Karate New Brunswick, 881
Karate Newfoundland & Labrador, 882
Karate Nova Scotia, 882
Karate Ontario, 882
Karaté Québec, 882
National Taekwon-Do Federation, 996
Newfoundland & Labrador Judo Association, 1019
Ontario Jiu-Jitsu Association, 1088
Ontario Taekwondo Association, 1109
Police Martial Arts Association Inc., 1163
Prince Edward Island Karate Association, 1175
Sask Taekwondo, 1254
Saskatchewan Karate Association, 1268
Saskatchewan Martial Arts Association, 1269
Taekwondo Canada, 1366
Taekwondo Manitoba, 1366
World Amateur Muay Thai Association of Canada, 1465
WTF Taekwondo Federation of British Columbia, 1469
WushuCanada, 1469
WushuOntario, 1469

Masonry
Association des entrepreneurs en maçonnerie du Québec, 112
Canadian Concrete Masonry Producers Association, 362
Canadian Masonry Contractors' Association, 431
International Union of Bricklayers & Allied Craftworkers (AFL-CIO/CFL), 1564
Masonry Industry Employers Council of Ontario, 952
MasonryWorx, 952
Ontario Masonry Contractors' Association, 1090

Massage Therapy
Alliance des massothérapeutes du Québec, 56
Association des massologues et techniciens en massage du Canada - Association des massothérapeutes professionnels du Québec, 119
Association of New Brunswick Massage Therapists, 154
Canadian Federation of Orthotherapists, 388
Canadian Massage Therapist Alliance, 431
Canadian Sport Massage Therapists Association, 490
College of Massage Therapists of British Columbia, 585
College of Massage Therapists of Ontario, 585
Fédération québécoise des massothérapeutes, 729
International Association of Infant Massage Canada, 854
Massage Therapist Association of Alberta, 953
Massage Therapist Association of Saskatchewan, 953
Massage Therapists' Association of Nova Scotia, 953
Massage Therapy Association of Manitoba Inc., 953
Mon Réseau Plus, Association professionnelle des massothérapeutes spécialisés du Québec inc., 971
Natural Health Practitioners of Canada, 998
New Brunswick Massotherapy Association, 1010
Newfoundland & Labrador Massage Therapists' Association, 1020

Subject Index / Materials Management

Prince Edward Island Massage Therapy Association, 1175
Registered Massage Therapists' Association of British Columbia, 1213
Registered Massage Therapists' Association of Ontario, 1213

Materials Management
AIM Global, 1486
International Warehouse Logistics Association, 1566
The Logistics Institute, 917
National Institute of Governmental Purchasing, Inc., 1576

Mathematics
Association mathématique du Québec, 137
British Columbia Association of Mathematics Teachers, 232
Canadian Applied & Industrial Mathematics Society, 294
Canadian Mathematical Society, 431
Mathematics of Information Technology & Complex Systems, 954
Pacific Institute for the Mathematical Sciences, 1135
Visions of Science Network for Learning, 1436

Measuring Instruments
The Instrumentation, Systems & Automation Society of America, 1534

Meat
Alberta Bison Association, 26
Beef Cattle Research Council, 203
Beef Improvement Ontario, 204
British Columbia Bison Association, 233
Canadian Beef, 342
Canadian Bison Association, 344
Canadian Meat Council, 432
Fédération des producteurs de bovins du Québec, 717
Manitoba Beef Cattle Performance Association, 932
National Bison Association, 1575
Ontario Independent Meat Processors, 1087
Ontario Veal Association, 1112
Saskatchewan Meat Processors' Association, 1270

Mechanical Contractors
Association of Commercial & Industrial Contractors of PEI, 145
Mechanical Contractors Association of Alberta, 956
Mechanical Contractors Association of British Columbia, 956
Mechanical Contractors Association of Canada, 956
Mechanical Contractors Association of Manitoba, 957
Mechanical Contractors Association of New Brunswick, 957
Mechanical Contractors Association of Newfoundland & Labrador, 957
Mechanical Contractors Association of Nova Scotia, 957
Mechanical Contractors Association of Ontario, 957
Mechanical Contractors Association of Ottawa, 957
Mechanical Contractors Association of Saskatchewan Inc., 957
Mechanical Service Contractors of Canada, 957

Mechanical Engineering
American Society of Mechanical Engineers, 1500
AUTO21 Network of Centres of Excellence, 189
Canadian Society for Mechanical Engineering, 476
Corporation des maîtres mécaniciens en tuyauterie du Québec, 630
Institution of Mechanical Engineers, 1534
International Union of Theoretical & Applied Mechanics, 1565
Maintenance, Engineering & Reliability (MER) Society, 926
Ontario Plumbing Inspectors Association, 1096

Medals & Insignia
Military Collectors Club of Canada, 965

Media
Accessible Media Inc., 5
Ajjiit Nunavut Media Association, 20
Alliance québécoise des techniciens de l'image et du son, 58
Association for Media Literacy, 134
British Columbia Association of Broadcasters, 231
Broadcast Educators Association of Canada, 259
Canada Media Fund, 280
Canadian Association of Community Television Users & Stations, 311
Canadian Association of Labour Media, 319
Canadian Committee for World Press Freedom, 360
Canadian Communications Foundation, 361
Canadian Journalism Foundation, 423
Canadian Media Directors' Council, 432
Conseil des directeurs médias du Québec, 617
Conseil québécois des arts médiatiques, 620
Cultural Industries Ontario North, 645
Health Care Public Relations Association, 806
Interactive Advertising Bureau of Canada, 851
Interactive Ontario, 851
International Research Institute for Media, Communication & Cultural Development, 1556
Lights, Camera, Access!, 912
Media Access Canada, 957
Media Smarts, 957
Radio Television Digital News Association (Canada), 1203
Rumble Productions Society, 1244
Saskatchewan Filmpool Co-operative, 1265
Travel Media Association of Canada, 1396
Vividata, 1436
Western Association of Broadcasters, 1447
Wikimedia Canada, 1453
Yukon Film Society, 1478

Mediation
ADR Institute of Canada, 9
Alberta Family Mediation Society, 34
Alternative Dispute Resolution Atlantic Institute, 60
Association de médiation familiale du Québec, 102
Canadian International Institute of Applied Negotiation, 421
Central Ontario Industrial Relations Institute, 525
Centre canadien d'arbitrage commercial, 526
Conflict Resolution Saskatchewan, 612
Elder Mediation Canada, 681
Family Mediation Manitoba, 704
Institut de médiation et d'arbitrage du Québec, 841
Inter-American Commercial Arbitration Commission, 851
Mediate BC Society, 957
Mediation Yukon Society, 957
Ontario Association for Family Mediation, 1061
Ontario Labour-Management Arbitrators Association, 1088
Sport Dispute Resolution Centre of Canada, 1344

Medical Assistance
Canadian Association of MAiD Assessors & Providers, 320
Canadian Physicians for Aid & Relief, 454
International Association for Medical Assistance to Travellers, 853
Operation Eyesight Universal, 1115
Saskatchewan Professional Fire Fighters Burn Unit Fund, 1272
Secours aux lépreux (Canada) inc., 1288
Telemiracle/Kinsmen Foundation Inc., 1369
Union of Canadian Transportation Employees, 1407

Medical Care
Hope Air, 821
Institute for Safe Medication Practices Canada, 844

Medical Devices
Association des implantés cochléaires du Québec, 116
Canadian Association of Medical Device Reprocessing, 320

Medical Engineering
International Federation for Medical & Biological Engineering, 1546

Medical Ethics
Christian Medical & Dental Society of Canada, 568
National Council on Ethics in Human Research, 992
Provincial Health Ethics Network, 1191

Medical Genetics
Canadian College of Medical Geneticists, 359

Medical Libraries
Association des bibliothèques de la santé affiliées à l'Université de Montréal, 107
Association pour l'avancement des sciences et des techniques de la documentation, 165
Canadian Health Libraries Association, 402
Hamilton & District Health Library Network, 800
Health Libraries Association of British Columbia, 806
International Federation of Health Information Management Associations, 1548
Manitoba Association of Health Information Providers, 930
Maritimes Health Libraries Association, 951
Medical Library Association, 1570
Newfoundland & Labrador Health Libraries Association, 1019
Northern Alberta Health Libraries Association, 1034
Ottawa Valley Health Libraries Association, 1132
Saskatchewan Health Libraries Association, 1267
Southern Alberta Health Libraries Association, 1337
Southwestern Ontario Health Libraries & Information Network, 1338
Toronto Health Libraries Association, 1385
Wellington Waterloo Dufferin Health Library Network, 1444

Medical Mycology
International Society for Human & Animal Mycology, 1558

Medical Radiation
Alberta College of Medical Diagnostic & Therapeutic Technologists, 29
British Columbia Association of Medical Radiation Technologists, 232
Canadian Association of Medical Radiation Technologists, 320
Canadian Association of Nuclear Medicine, 323
Canadian Association of Radiation Oncology, 330
Canadian Organization of Medical Physicists, 447
Manitoba Association of Medical Radiation Technologists, 930
New Brunswick Association of Medical Radiation Technologists, 1005
Newfoundland & Labrador Association of Medical Radiation Technologists, 1016
Nova Scotia Association of Medical Radiation Technologists, 1041
Ontario Association of Medical Radiation Sciences, 1064
Ordre des technologues en imagerie médicale, en radio-oncologie et en élétrophysiologie médicale du Québec, 1124
Prince Edward Island Association of Medical Radiation Technologists, 1172
Saskatchewan Association of Medical Radiation Technologists, 1257

Medical Research
Academic Pediatric Association, 1485
Canadian Association for Dental Research, 299
Canadian Association for Population Therapeutics, 303
Canadian Chiropractic Research Foundation, 356
Canadian Foundation for AIDS Research, 392
Canadian Foundation on Fetal Alcohol Research, 394
Canadian Genetic Diseases Network, 397
Canadian HIV Trials Network, 405
Canadian Institute for the Relief of Pain & Disability, 413
Canadian Society for Clinical Investigation, 474
Canadian Society for Epidemiology & Biostatistics, 474
Canadian Society for Pharmaceutical Sciences, 477
Canadian Urologic Oncology Group, 500
Canadians for Health Research, 507
CancerCare Manitoba, 508
Dalhousie Medical Research Foundation, 648
Dystonia Medical Research Foundation Canada, 665
Fondation de l'Ordre des infirmières et infirmiers du Québec, 744
Fondation des étoiles, 744
Fondation Initia, 746
The Foundation Fighting Blindness, 755
Institut de recherches cliniques de Montréal, 842
Institute for Clinical Evaluative Sciences, 843
Institute for the Study & Treatment of Pain, 844
International Pediatric Association, 1555
International Society for Cellular Therapy, 860
Israel Cancer Research Fund, 866
The Leukemia & Lymphoma Society of Canada, 908
Lunenfeld-Tanenbaum Research Institute, 921
The M.S.I. Foundation, 978
National Council on Ethics in Human Research, 992
Victoria Medical Society, 1433

Medical Schools
Alberta College of Acupuncture & Traditional Chinese Medicine, 28
Association des professeures et professeurs de la Faculté de médecine de l'Université de Sherbrooke, 124
Association of Faculties of Medicine of Canada, 148
Canadian Association for Medical Education, 302
College of Traditional Chinese Medicine Practitioners & Acupuncturists of British Columbia, 590
International College of Traditional Chinese Medicine of Vancouver, 855
The Michener Institute for Applied Health Sciences, 964

Medical Specialists
Academic Pediatric Association, 1485
American Society of Echocardiography, 1499
Association d'oto-rhino-laryngologie et de chirurgie cervico-faciale du Québec, 99
Association de neurochirurgie du Québec, 103
Association des Allergologues et Immunologues du Québec, 105
Association des cardiologues du Québec, 108
Association des denturologistes du Québec, 110
Association des dermatologistes du Québec, 110
Association des gastro-entérologues du Québec, 114
Association des médecins biochimistes du Québec, 119
Association des médecins endocrinologues du Québec, 119
Association des médecins gériatres du Québec, 119
Association des médecins hématologistes-oncologistes du Québec, 119
Association des médecins microbiologistes-infectiologues du Québec, 119
Association des médecins ophtalmologistes du Québec, 120
Association des médecins rhumatologues du Québec, 120
Association des médecins spécialistes en médecine nucléaire du Québec, 120
Association des néphrologues du Québec, 120
Association des neurologues du Québec, 120
Association des obstétriciens et gynécologues du Québec, 121
Association des optométristes du Québec, 121
Association des pathologistes du Québec, 122
Association des pédiatres du Québec, 122
Association des physiatres du Québec, 123
Association des pneumologues de la province de Québec, 123

Subject Index / Mental Health

Association des radio-oncologues du Québec, 127
Association des spécialistes en chirurgie plastique et esthétique du Québec, 128
Association des spécialistes en médecine interne du Québec, 128
Association des urologues du Québec, 130
British Columbia Society of Electroneurophysiology Technologists, 254
Canadian Psychiatric Association, 461
Canadian Society of Clinical Perfusion, 482
Canadian Society of Internal Medicine, 484
Canadian Society of Medical Evaluators, 484
Fédération des médecins spécialistes du Québec, 716
GI (Gastrointestinal) Society, 773
International Pediatric Association, 1555
Ontario Association of Pathologists, 1065
Ordre des denturologistes du Québec, 1121
The Royal College of Physicians & Surgeons of Canada, 1241
Société canadienne-française de radiologie, 1309
Society of Gynecologic Oncologists of Canada, 1329

Medical Supplies
Canada's Medical Technology Companies, 282
Canadian MedTech Manufacturers' Alliance, 434

Medical Technology
AdvaMed, 1485
Alberta College of Combined Laboratory & X-Ray Technologists, 29
British Columbia Society of Laboratory Science, 254
College of Medical Laboratory Technologists of Alberta, 586
Manitoba Association for Medical Laboratory Science, 929
Medical Device Reprocessing Association of Ontario, 958
New Brunswick Society of Cardiology Techologists, 1012
New Brunswick Society of Medical Laboratory Technologists, 1012
Newfoundland & Labrador Society for Medical Laboratory Science, 1021
Nova Scotia College of Medical Laboratory Technologists, 1042
Ontario Society of Medical Technologists, 1107
Ordre professionnel des technologistes médicaux du Québec, 1124
Prince Edward Island Society for Medical Laboratory Science, 1177
Saskatchewan Society of Medical Laboratory Technologists, 1275

Medicine
Alberta College of Acupuncture & Traditional Chinese Medicine, 28
Alberta Innovates, 38
Alberta Medical Association, 40
American Academy for Cerebral Palsy & Developmental Medicine, 1487
American Medical Association, 1495
American Society for Bone & Mineral Research, 1497
Associated Medical Services Inc., 89
Association des conseils des médecins, dentistes et pharmaciens du Québec, 109
Association des médecins cliniciens enseignants de Laval, 119
Association des médecins omnipraticiens de Montréal, 119
Association des médecins spécialistes en santé communautaire du Québec, 120
Association for Healthcare Philanthropy, 1508
Association médicale du Québec, 137
Canadian Association of Medical Cannabis Dispensaries, 320
Canadian Association of Pharmacy Students & Interns, 326
Canadian Association of Physical Medicine & Rehabilitation, 327
Canadian Biomaterials Society, 344
Canadian College of Physicists in Medicine, 360
Canadian Federation of Medical Students, 388
Canadian Medical Association, 433
Canadian Medical Foundation, 434

The Canadian Medical Protective Association, 434
Canadian MedicAlert Foundation, 434
Canadian Organization of Medical Physicists, 447
Canadian Orthopaedic Residents Association, 448
Canadian Resident Matching Service, 467
Canadian Safe Cannabis Society, 468
Canadian Society for the History of Medicine, 477
Canadian Society for Transfusion Medicine, 479
Canadian Society of Addiction Medicine, 479
Canadian Society of Transplantation, 488
Cannabis Canada Association, 508
College of Physicians & Surgeons of Nova Scotia, 588
Doctors Manitoba, 660
Doctors Nova Scotia, 660
Doctors of BC, 660
Fédération des médecins résidents du Québec inc. (ind.), 716
Federation of Medical Regulatory Authorities of Canada, 724
Federation of Medical Regulatory Authorities of Canada, 724
Institute for Safe Medication Practices Canada, 844
International College of Traditional Chinese Medicine of Vancouver, 855
International Federation of Medical Students' Associations, 1548
International Medical Informatics Association, 1553
International Society for Magnetic Resonance in Medicine, 1558
International Society for the History of Medicine - Canadian Section, 860
International Society of Physical & Rehabilitation Medicine, 1561
International Union of Societies for Biomaterials Science & Engineering, 1565
Manitoba Association for Medical Laboratory Science, 929
Manitoba Medical Service Foundation Inc., 940
Manitoba Medical Students' Association, 940
McGill Centre for Medicine, Ethics & Law, 955
Medical Council of Canada, 958
Medical Marijuana Association, 958
Medical Society of Prince Edward Island, 958
Medico-Legal Society of Toronto, 959
The M.S.I. Foundation, 978
National Institute for Cannabis Health & Education, 994
National Organization for the Reform of Marijuana Laws Canada, 995
Natural Health Practitioners of Canada Association, 999
New Brunswick Medical Society, 1010
Newfoundland & Labrador Medical Association, 1020
Northwest Territories Medical Association, 1038
Occupational & Environmental Medical Association of Canada, 1054
Ontario Medical Association, 1090
Ontario Medical Students Association, 1090
Québec Black Medical Association, 1196
Resident Doctors of Canada, 1226
Saskatchewan Medical Association, 1270
Society for Adolescent Health & Medicine, 1589
The Transplantation Society, 1395
Victoria Medical Society, 1433
World Association of Sleep Medicine, 1603
World Health Organization Partnership for Health in the Criminal Justice Sytem, 1606
Yukon Medical Association, 1479

Medieval Studies
Canadian Society of Medievalists, 484
International Arthurian Society - North American Branch, 1535
Medieval Academy of America, 1570
Société internationale pour l'étude de la philosophie médiévale, 1589

Meditation
Falun Dafa Canada, 701
Réseau Tara Canada (Québec), 1226
Sivananda Ashram Yoga Camp, 1301
The Supreme Master Ching Hai Meditation Association of Ontario, 1357
Tara Canada Network Association, 1367

Yasodhara Ashram Society, 1470

Mediterranean
Canadian Institute for Mediterranean Studies, 412

Meetings & Conventions
Canadian Intergovernmental Conference Secretariat, 420
Canadian University & College Conference Organizers Association, 499
Destination Halifax, 654
GLOBE Foundation, 775
International Association of Professional Congress Organizers, 1539
Meeting Professionals International, 1570
Meetings & Conventions Prince Edward Island, 959
Professional Convention Management Association - Canada West Chapter, 1183
Stratford Tourism Alliance, 1351
Tourism London, 1390
Tourism Yorkton, 1392
Westerner Park, 1450

Men
British Columbia Society for Male Survivors of Sexual Abuse, 254
Men for Change, 960
Réseau Hommes Québec, 1224

Men's Health
Canadian Society for the Study of the Aging Male, 478
Prostate Cancer Canada, 1189

Mennonites
Alberta Conference of Mennonite Brethren Churches, 30
Association des Églises des frères mennonites du Québec, 111
British Columbia Conference of MB Churches, 237
Canadian Conference of Mennonite Brethren Churches, 363
Centre for Newcomers Society of Calgary, 533
Communitas Supportive Care Society, 595
Evangelical Mennonite Conference, 699
International Mennonite Health Association Inc., 858
Manitoba Mennonite Historical Society, 940
MB Mission, 954
Mennonite Brethren Church of Manitoba, 960
Mennonite Central Committee Canada, 960
Mennonite Church Canada, 961
Mennonite Economic Development Associates Canada, 961
Mennonite Historical Society of Canada, 961
Northwest Mennonite Conference, 1036
Ontario Conference of Mennonite Brethren Churches, 1074
Saskatchewan Conference of Mennonite Brethren Churches, 1261

Mental Health
Action Autonomie, 6
AiMHi, Prince George Association for Community Living, 18
Alberta Alliance on Mental Illness & Mental Health, 21
American Association on Intellectual & Developmental Disabilities, 1490
American Psychological Association, 1497
Anxiety Disorders Association of British Columbia, 72
Anxiety Disorders Association of Canada, 72
Anxiety Disorders Association of Manitoba, 72
Anxiety Disorders Association of Ontario, 72
The Ark/Lunenburg County Association for the Specially Challenged, 81
Aspergers Society of Ontario, 87
Association de Laval pour la déficience intellectuelle, 102
Association de loisirs pour personnes handicapées psychiques de Laval, 102
Association des alternatives en santé mentale de la Montérégie, 105
Association des groupes d'intervention en défense de droits en santé mentale du Québec, 116
Association des parents et amis de la personne atteinte de maladie mentale Rive-Sud, 122
Association Et si c'était moi, 132

Association Québécoise pour la Santé Mentale des Nourrisson, 176
Association/Troubles de l'Humeur et d'Anxiété au Québec, 179
Beehive Adult Service Centre, Inc., 204
Bridge Adult Service Society, 228
British Columbia Psychogeriatric Association, 249
Building Futures Employment Society, 262
Calgary Association of Self Help, 271
CAMH Foundation, 276
Canadian Alliance on Mental Illness & Mental Health, 291
Canadian Art Therapy Association, 295
Canadian Association for Community Living - Clare Branch, 298
Canadian Association for Integrative & Energy Therapies, 301
Canadian Coalition for Seniors Mental Health, 358
Canadian Depression Research & Intervention Network, 377
Canadian Federation of Mental Health Nurses, 388
Canadian Mental Health Association, 434
Caritas School of Life Therapeutic Community, 512
Le Centre de soutien en santé mentale - Montérégie, 530
Centre for Addiction & Mental Health, 531
Centre for Adults in Progressive Employment Society, 531
C.G. Jung Foundation of Ontario, 539
Chai-Tikvah The Life & Hope Foundation, 539
Cheticamp Association for Community Living, 557
Child & Parent Resource Institute, 558
Child Development Institute, 559
Children and Youth in Challenging Contexts Network, 560
Children's Mental Health Ontario, 562
Conway Workshop Association, 627
Corridor Community Options for Adults, 631
Dartmouth Adult Services Centre, 650
L'Écluse des Laurentides, 671
Envol SRT, 693
Fédération des familles et amis de la personne atteinte de maladie mentale, 715
Flowercart, 741
Fondation des maladies mentales, 745
Gerald Hardy Memorial Society, 771
Golden Opportunities Vocational Rehabilitation Centre Workshop, 776
Graham Boeckh Foundation, 779
Groupe d'entraide G.E.M.E., 791
Haley Street Adult Services Centre Society, 798
Healthy Minds Canada, 807
Heatherton Activity Centre, 810
Hincks-Dellcrest Treatment Centre & Foundation, 815
Hong Fook Mental Health Association, 820
Horizon Achievement Centre, 821
Inner Peace Movement of Canada, 839
International Academy of Law & Mental Health, 853
International PhotoTherapy Association, 859
International Society for the Study of Trauma & Dissociation, 1559
Inverness Cottage Workshop, 862
Jack.org, 867
Kaye Nickerson Adult Service Centre, 883
Kenora Association for Community Living, 883
Kinark Child & Family Services, 888
LakeCity Employment Services Association, 896
Lieutenant Governor's Circle on Mental Health & Addiction, 910
Mood Disorders Association of British Columbia, 973
Mood Disorders Association of Manitoba, 973
Mood Disorders Association of Ontario, 973
Mood Disorders Society of Canada, 973
National Network for Mental Health, 995
New Boundaries, 1004
New Leaf Enterprises, 1014
Ontario Association of Consultants, Counsellors, Psychometrists & Psychotherapists, 1063
Ontario Mental Health Foundation, 1090
The Organization for Bipolar Affective Disorder, 1125

Subject Index / Mesopotamian Studies

Pacific Post Partum Support Society, 1136
Parents for Children's Mental Health, 1140
Phobies-Zéro, 1157
A Post Psychiatric Leisure Experience, 1167
Post Traumatic Stress Disorder Association, 1167
Postpartum Depression Association of Manitoba, 1168
Prescott Group, 1170
Queens Association for Supported Living, 1200
Regional Occupation Centre Foundation, 1212
Regional Occupation Centre Society, 1213
Rehtaeh Parsons Society, 1217
Responsible Gambling Council (Ontario), 1227
Revivre, 1228
Revivre - Association Québécoise de soutien aux personnes souffrant de troubles anxieux, dépressifs ou bipolaires, 1228
Scottish Rite Charitable Foundation of Canada, 1286
Shelburne Association Supporting Inclusion, 1295
Society of St. Vincent de Paul - Toronto Central Council, 1330
STRIDE, 1352
Summer Street, 1354
Toronto Art Therapy Institute, 1381
Waypoint Centre for Mental Health Care, 1443
World Federation for Mental Health, 1605
York Region Family Services (Markham), 1473

Mesopotamian Studies
The Canadian Society for Mesopotamian Studies, 476

Metabolic Diseases
American Society for Bone & Mineral Research, 1497
Canadian Fabry Association, 383
Canadian PKU and Allied Disorders Inc., 455
Canadian Society of Endocrinology & Metabolism, 482
Garrod Association, 767
Pediatric Endocrine Society, 1583
Québec Society of Lipidology, Nutrition & Metabolism Inc., 1199

Metal Arts
The Metal Arts Guild of Canada, 962

Metal Industries
Aluminium Association of Canada, 61
American Foundry Society, 1493
American Galvanizers Association, 1493
Architectural Glass & Metal Contractors Association, 78
Canadian Copper & Brass Development Association, 364
Glass & Architectural Metals Association, 774
International Titanium Association, 1563
The Metal Working Association of New Brunswick, 962
MultiPrévention ASP: Association paritaire pour la santé et la sécurité au travail des secteurs: métal, électrique, habillement et imprimerie, 980
Nickel Institute, 1026
Syndicat interprovincial des ferblantiers et couvreurs, la section locale 2016 à la FTQ-Construction, 1364
United Steelworkers of America (AFL-CIO/CLC), 1600
Western Employers Labour Relations Association, 1449

Metallurgy
Canadian Institute of Mining, Metallurgy & Petroleum, 417
International Titanium Association, 1563
Metallurgy & Materials Society of the Canadian Institute of Mining, Metallurgy & Petroleum, 962

Metaphysics
Canadian Society of Questers, 487

Meteorology
Canadian Meteorological & Oceanographic Society, 435
Climate Institute, 1517
International Society of Biometeorology, 1560
World Meteorological Organization, 1606

Methodists
The Bible Holiness Movement, 208
Free Methodist Church in Canada, 759

Mexico
Friends of the Orphans, Canada, 763

Microbiology
Association des médecins microbiologistes-infectiologues du Québec, 119
Association des microbiologistes du Québec, 120
Canadian Association for Clinical Microbiology & Infectious Diseases, 297
Canadian Society of Microbiologists, 485
International Federation for Cell Biology, 1546
International Society for Cellular Therapy, 860
International Society for Human & Animal Mycology, 1558
International Union of Microbiological Societies, 1564

Microcomputers
Urban & Regional Information Systems Association, 1601

Microreproduction
Canadiana, 506

Midwives
Alberta Association of Midwives, 24
Association of Midwives of Newfoundland & Labrador, 152
Association of Ontario Midwives, 155
Canadian Association of Midwives, 321
Canadian Midwifery Regulators Consortium, 436
College of Midwives of British Columbia, 586
College of Midwives of Manitoba, 586
College of Midwives of Ontario, 586
International Confederation of Midwives, 1543
Midwives Association of British Columbia, 965
Midwives Association of Saskatchewan, 965
Midwives Collective of Toronto, 965
Ordre des sages-femmes du Québec, 1123

Migraine
Headache Network Canada, 805
Help for Headaches, 812

Military
Armed Forces Pensioners'/Annuitants' Association of Canada, 82
Canadian Corps Association, 365
Canadian Forces Logistics Association - Montréal, 392
Commission canadienne d'histoire militaire, 592
Conference of Defence Associations, 612
The Crow's Nest Military Artifacts Association, 644
Electrical & Mechanical Engineering Association, 682
15th Field Artillery Regiment Museum & Archives Society, 734
New Brunswick Signallers Association, 1012
Ontario Military Vehicle Association, 1091
L'Ordinariat militaire Catholique Romain du Canada, 1119
Organization of Military Museums of Canada, 1125
Princess Patricia's Canadian Light Infantry Association, 1180
Rosaries for Canadian Forces Abroad, 1236
Royal Alberta United Services Institute, 1237
Royal Canadian Armoured Corps Association, 1239
Royal Canadian Army Service Corps Association-(Atlantic Region), 1239
Royal Canadian Artillery Association, 1239
Royal Canadian Military Institute, 1240
The Royal Canadian Regiment Association, 1241
Royal United Services Institute - Vancouver Society, 1243
Royal United Services Institute of Regina, 1243
Royal United Services Institute of Vancouver Island, 1243
The Vimy Foundation, 1435

Military Memorabilia
Canadian Militaria Preservation Society, 436
Military Collectors Club of Canada, 965

Military Weapons
Canadian Association for Mine & Explosive Ordnance Security, 302
International Committee of Museums & Collections of Arms & Military History, 1543

Milk
British Columbia Milk Marketing Board, 246
Dairy Farmers of Manitoba, 648
Dairy Farmers of New Brunswick, 648
Dairy Farmers of Ontario, 648
Ontario Milk Transport Association, 1091
Les producteurs de lait du Québec, 1181

Millers
Canadian National Millers Association, 440

Millwork
Architectural Woodwork Manufacturers Association of Canada, 79
Association of Millwrighting Contractors of Ontario Inc., 152

Mineralogy
Alberta Federation of Rock Clubs, 35
Bancroft Gem & Mineral Club, 195
Canadian Micro-Mineral Association, 436
Canadian Mineral Processors Society, 437
Canadian Rock Mechanics Association, 467
Central Canadian Federation of Mineralogical Societies, 524
Gem & Mineral Federation of Canada, 768
Geological Association of Canada, 769
International Academy of Energy, Minerals & Materials, 852
International Council for Applied Mineralogy, 1544
International Titanium Association, 1563
International Union of Crystallography, 1564
Kingston Lapidary & Mineral Club, 889
Mineral Society of Manitoba, 966
Mineralogical Association of Canada, 966
Musée minéralogique et minier de Thetford Mines, 982
Niagara Peninsula Geological Society, 1025
The Nova Scotia Mineral & Gem Society, 1047
Oxford County Geological Society, 1134
Parksville & District Rock & Gem Club, 1142
Richmond Gem & Mineral Society, 1230
Ripple Rock Gem & Mineral Club, 1233
Sarnia Rock & Fossil Club, 1254
Saskatoon Lapidary & Mineral Club, 1279
Sudbury Rock & Lapidary Society, 1353
Vernon Lapidary & Mineral Club, 1431
Victoria Lapidary & Mineral Society, 1433
Walker Mineralogical Club, 1439

Mining
Alberta Chamber of Resources, 28
Aluminium Association of Canada, 61
American Society of Mining & Reclamation, 1501
Association de l'exploration minière de Québec, 100
Association minière du Québec, 137
Association of Applied Geochemists, 139
Association paritaire pour la santé et la sécurité du travail - Secteur Affaires municipales, 165
Canadian Institute of Mining, Metallurgy & Petroleum, 417
Canadian Land Reclamation Association, 425
Canadian Mineral Analysts, 436
Canadian Mineral Processors Society, 437
Canadian Mining Industry Research Organization, 437
European Association of Geoscientists & Engineers, 1524
Kamloops Exploration Group, 880
Klondike Placer Miners' Association, 892
Maintenance, Engineering & Reliability (MER) Society, 926
Minalliance, 966
Mineralogical Association of Canada, 966
Mining Association of British Columbia, 967
Mining Association of Canada, 967
Mining Association of Manitoba Inc., 967
Mining Industry Human Resources Council, 967
Mining Industry NL, 967
Mining Society of Nova Scotia, 967
Mining Suppliers Trade Association Canada, 967
Mining Suppliers, Contractors & Consultants Association of BC, 967
MiningWatch Canada, 968
Musée minéralogique et minier de Thetford Mines, 982
Ontario Mining Association, 1091
Resource Industry Suppliers Association, 1227
Saskatchewan Mining Association, 1270
Table jamésienne de concertation minière, 1366
United Mine Workers of America (CLC), 1599
Women's Association of the Mining Industry of Canada, 1461
Yukon Mine Training Association, 1479

Mink
Nova Scotia Mink Breeders' Association, 1047

Minorities
Immigrant Women Services Ottawa, 831
National Organization of Immigrant & Visible Minority Women of Canada, 995
Vancouver & Lower Mainland Multicultural Family Support Services Society, 1424
Vancouver Society of Immigrant & Visible Minority Women, 1428

Missing Children
Child Find British Columbia, 559
Child Find Canada Inc., 559
Child Find Newfoundland & Labrador, 559
Child Find Nova Scotia, 559
Child Find Ontario, 559
Child Find PEI Inc., 559
Child Find Saskatchewan Inc., 559
Missing Children Society of Canada, 968

Missions & Missionaries
Adventive Cross Cultural Initiatives, 10
Africa Inland Mission International (Canada), 12
The Bible Holiness Movement, 208
Canada's National Bible Hour, 282
Canadian Baptist Ministries, 341
Canadian Jesuits International, 423
The Christian & Missionary Alliance in Canada, 566
Christian Blind Mission International, 566
L'Église Réformée du Québec, 681
Fondation Père-Ménard, 747
Institut Voluntas Dei, 843
Intercede International, 851
International Mennonite Health Association Inc., 858
Latin American Mission Program, 899
Lutheran Association of Missionaries & Pilots, 922
MB Mission, 954
Missionary Sisters of The Precious Blood of North America, 969
Les Missions des Soeurs Missionnaires du Christ-Roi, 969
Les Oblates Missionnaires de Marie Immaculée, 1054
OMF International - Canada, 1057
Operation Mobilization Canada, 1116
Pentecostal Assemblies of Canada, 1150
Pontifical Mission Societies, 1164
The Secular Institute of Missionaries of the Kingship of Christ, 1288
SIM Canada, 1299
Soeurs missionnaires de Notre-Dame des Anges, 1331
Women's Missionary Society, 1463
Wycliffe Bible Translators of Canada, Inc., 1470
Yonge Street Mission, 1473

Model Airplanes
Model Aeronautics Association of Canada Inc., 970

Models & Modelmaking
Group 25 Model Car Builders' Club, 790
Maritime Model Horse Collectors & Showers Association, 951
Toronto Society of Model Engineers, 1387

Molding (Founding)
American Foundry Society, 1493
Canadian Association of Moldmakers, 321
Glass, Molders, Pottery, Plastic & Allied Workers International Union (AFL-CIO/CLC), 1528

Molecular Biology
Canadian Society for Molecular Biosciences, 476

Monarchy
Monarchist League of Canada, 971
Richard III Society of Canada, 1229

Monuments
Canadian Tribute to Human Rights, 497

Mopeds
Motorcycle & Moped Industry Council, 975

Mortgages
Canadian Mortgage Brokers Association, 437
Mortgage Investment Association of British Columbia, 975
Mortgage Professionals Canada, 975
National Association of Review Appraisers & Mortgage Underwriters, 1574

Mothers
Forever Chai Foundation of Canada, 752
International Confederation of Midwives, 1543

Motor Vehicles
Association des commerçants de véhicules récréatifs du Québec, 109
Association des véhicules électriques du Québec, 130
Canadian Parking Association, 450
Canadian Vehicle Manufacturers' Association, 501
Ontario Motor Vehicle Industry Council, 1091
Ontario Recovery Group Inc., 1100
Vancouver Electric Vehicle Association, 1425
Vintage Road Racing Association, 1435

Motorcycles
Association des motocyclistes gais du Québec, 120
Canadian Motorcycle Association, 437
Fédération motocycliste du Québec, 721
Motorcycle & Moped Industry Council, 975
Vintage Road Racing Association, 1435

Mountaineering
Alpine Club of Canada, 59
Association of Canadian Mountain Guides, 142
British Columbia Mountaineering Club, 246
Federation of Mountain Clubs of British Columbia, 725
Fédération québécoise de la montagne et de l'escalade, 727

Moving Trade
Canadian Association of Movers, 321
Canadian Employee Relocation Council, 380

Multi-Media
Aboriginal Multi-Media Society, 2
Alliance numérique, 58
Entertainment Software Association of Canada, 690
Le groupe multimédia du Canada, 792

Multiculturalism
Affiliation of Multicultural Societies & Service Agencies of BC, 11
Albanian Canadian Community Association, 21
Alianza Hispano-Canadiense Ontario, 54
Associaça Portuguesa de LaSalle, 89
Associaça Portuguesa de Ste-Thérèse, 89
Associaça Portuguesa Do Canadà, 89
Associaça Portuguesa do West Island, 89
Associaça Portuguesa Espirito Santo, 89
Associaçao dos Pais, 89
Athmajothi Tamils Association, 181
Beaton Institute, 203
Brockville & District Multicultural Council Inc., 260
Burnaby Multicultural Society, 266
Canada - Albania Business Council, 277
Canadian Colombian Professional Association, 360
Canadian Ethnic Studies Association, 382
Canadian Ethnocultural Council, 382
Canadian Race Relations Foundation, 464
Canadian Tamil Congress, 492
Canadian Tamil Youth Development Centre, 492
Carrefour de ressources en interculturel, 515
Casa Cultural Peruana, 516
Casa do Ribatejo, 516
Central Vancouver Island Multicultural Society, 525
Centre multiethnique de Québec, 536
Centro Comunitàrio Divino Espirito Santo, 537
Clube Oriental Português de Montreal, 576
Clube Portugal de Montreal, 576
Community Folk Art Council of Toronto, 597
Cowichan Intercultural Society, 637
Eaglesland Albanian Society of BC, 666
Esperanto Rondo de Otavo, 695
Focus for Ethnic Women, 741
Halton Multicultural Council, 800
Halton Peel Hispanic Association, 800
Hispanic Canadian Arts & Culture Association, 815
Immigrant & Multicultural Services Society, 830
Immigrant Services - Guelph Wellington, 830
Immigrant Welcome Centre, 831
Inspirit Foundation, 840
Institute of Cultural Affairs International, 846
Inter-Cultural Association of Greater Victoria, 851
Intercultural Heritage Association, 852
International Network for Cultural Diversity, 858
Kamloops Multicultural Society, 880
Kashmiri Canadian Council, 882
Kitchener-Waterloo Multicultural Centre, 891
Latino Canadian Cultural Association, 900
Little Faces of Panama Association, 915
La Maison des Açores du Québec, 926
Moose Jaw Multicultural Council, 974
Moroccan Association of Toronto, 974
Multicultural Association of Carleton County Inc., 978
Multicultural Association of Fredericton, 978
Multicultural Association of Kenora & District, 978
Multicultural Association of Northwestern Ontario, 979
Multicultural Association of Nova Scotia, 979
Multicultural Association of Saint John Inc., 979
Multicultural Association of the Greater Moncton Area, 979
Multicultural Council of Windsor & Essex County, 979
Multicultural History Society of Ontario, 979
Multicultural Marketing Society of Canada, 979
Multilingual Association of Regina, Inc., 979
National Association of Canadians of Origins in India, 990
National Council of Jamaicans & Supportive Organizations in Canada, 991
New Brunswick Multicultural Council, 1010
Newfoundland & Labrador Multicultural Council Inc., 1020
North Shore Multicultural Society, 1033
Ottawa Tamil Seniors Association, 1132
Parkdale Intercultural Association, 1140
Peel Multicultural Council, 1148
Regina Multicultural Council, 1212
Richmond Multicultural Community Services, 1231
Saskatchewan Association for Multicultural Education, 1256
Saskatchewan Intercultural Association Inc., 1268
SaskCulture Inc., 1280
Serbian National Shield Society of Canada, 1290
South Okanagan Immigrant & Community Services, 1335
Tamil Eelam Society of Canada, 1366
Tamil Writers' Association of Canada, 1366
Thunder Bay Multicultural Association, 1378
Vancouver Multicultural Society, 1427
Welfare Committee for the Assyrian Community in Canada, 1443
YMCA Immigrant & Community Services, 1473

Multifaith
Manitoba Interfaith Welcome Place, 939
Multifaith Action Society, 979

Multiple Births
Association de Parents de Jumeaux et de Triplés de la région de Montréal, 103
Chatham-Kent Multiple Birth Association, 555
Durham Parents of Multiples, 665
Edmonton Twin & Triplet Club, 679
Fredericton Area Moms of Multiples, 758
Kitchener-Waterloo Parents of Multiple Births Association, 891
London Multiple Births Association, 918
Multiple Birth Families Association, 979
Multiple Births Canada, 979
Multiple Births Guelph-Wellington, 980
Newmarket Parents of Multiple Births Association, 1024
Prince George Parents of Twins & Triplets Association, 1179
Saskatoon Parents of Twins & Triplets Organization, 1280
Simcoe County Parents of Multiples, 1299
Temiskaming Multiple Births, 1370
Toronto Parents of Multiple Births Association, 1386
Twins Plus Association of Brampton, 1400
Windsor/Essex County Parents of Multiple Births Association, 1457

Multiple Sclerosis
Association Sclérose en Plaques Rive-Sud, 178
Consortium of Multiple Sclerosis Centers, 1519
Multiple Sclerosis International Federation, 1571
Multiple Sclerosis Society of Canada, 980
Société canadienne de la sclérose en plaques (Division du Québec), 1308

Municipal Government
Alberta Association of Municipal Districts & Counties, 24
Alberta Development Officers Association, 32
Alberta Rural Municipal Administrators Association, 45
Alberta Urban Municipalities Association, 50
Association des Aménagistes Régionaux du Québec, 105
Association des cadres municipaux de Montréal, 108
Association des directeurs généraux des municipalités du Québec, 111
Association des ingénieurs municipaux du Québec, 116
L'Association française des municipalités de l'Ontario, 135
Association francophone des municipalités du Nouveau-Brunswick Inc., 135
Association internationale des maires francophones - Bureau à Québec, 136
Association of Manitoba Municipalities, 151
Association of Municipal Administrators of New Brunswick, 152
Association of Municipal Administrators, Nova Scotia, 152
Association of Municipal Managers, Clerks & Treasurers of Ontario, 152
Association of Municipalities of Ontario, 152
Association of Yukon Communities, 164
British Columbia Municipal Safety Association, 246
Canadian Association of Municipal Administrators, 321
Cities of New Brunswick Association, 570
City of Waterloo Staff Association, 571
Conseil de développement économique des municipalités bilingues du Manitoba, 615
Corporation des officiers municipaux agréés du Québec, 633
Downtown Truro Partnership, 662
Downtown Vancouver Association, 662
Drainage Superintendents Association of Ontario, 662
Federation of Canadian Municipalities, 723
Federation of Northern Ontario Municipalities, 725
Federation of Prince Edward Island Municipalities Inc., 726
Fédération Québécoise des Municipalités, 729
Greater Vancouver Regional District Employees' Union, 787
Halifax Partnership, 799
Local Government Administrators of the Northwest Territories, 916
Local Government Management Association of British Columbia, 916
Manitoba Municipal Administrators' Association Inc., 941
Municipal Finance Officers' Association of Ontario, 981
Municipal Law Departments Association of Ontario, 981
Municipal Pension Retirees Association, 981
Municipalities Newfoundland & Labrador, 982
National Association of Towns & Townships, 1574
Northwest Territories Association of Communities, 1037
Northwestern Ontario Municipal Association, 1039
Ontario Municipal Administrators' Association, 1092
Ontario Municipal Human Resources Association, 1092
Ontario Municipal Management Institute, 1092
Ontario Municipal Social Services Association, 1092
Ontario Municipal Tax & Revenue Association, 1092
Ontario Small Urban Municipalities, 1105
Rainy River District Municipal Association, 1204
Rural Municipal Administrators' Association of Saskatchewan, 1244
Saskatchewan Association of Rural Municipalities, 1258
Saskatchewan Urban Municipalities Association, 1277
Society of Local Government Managers of Alberta, 1329
Syndicat des professionnelles et professionnels municipaux de Montréal, 1364
Thunder Bay District Municipal League, 1377
Union des municipalités du Québec, 1406
Union of British Columbia Municipalities, 1407
Union of Municipalities of New Brunswick, 1407
Union of Nova Scotia Municipalities, 1407
Urban & Regional Information Systems Association, 1601
Urban Municipal Administrators' Association of Saskatchewan, 1422
West Vancouver Municipal Employees Association, 1447

Muscular Dystrophy
Muscular Dystrophy Canada, 982
Society for Muscular Dystrophy Information International, 1326

Museums
Alberta Aviation Museum Association, 25
Alberta Museums Association, 40
Alberta Pioneer Railway Association, 42
Alberta Sports Hall of Fame & Museum, 48
Association Museums New Brunswick, 138
Association of Manitoba Museums, 151
Association of Nova Scotia Museums, 154
Badlands Historical Centre, 193
Brant Historical Society, 226
British Columbia Farm Machinery & Agriculture Museum Association, 240
British Columbia Museums Association, 246
British Columbia Sports Hall of Fame & Museum, 255
Campbell River Museum & Archives Society, 276
Canadian Association of Science Centres, 332
Canadian Centre for Architecture, 353
Canadian Federation of Friends of Museums, 386
Canadian Football Hall of Fame & Museum, 391
Canadian Golf Hall of Fame & Museum, 398
Canadian Heritage Information Network, 405
Canadian Museums Association, 437
Canadian Railroad Historical Association, 465
Cardston Historical Society, 511
Central British Columbia Railway & Forest Industry Museum Society, 524
Commonwealth Association of Museums, 593
Community Museums Association of Prince Edward Island, 606
Compton County Historical Museum Society, 609
Creston & District Historical & Museum Society, 641
Danish Canadian National Museum Society, 650
DeBolt & District Pioneer Museum Society, 652
Design Exchange, 654
Enderby & District Museum Society, 687
15th Field Artillery Regiment Museum & Archives Society, 734
Fort Calgary Society, 752
Friends of The Canadian War Museum, 762
Friends of the Haileybury Heritage Museum, 762
Frontenac County Schools Museum Association, 763
Grand Manan Museum Inc., 780
Grande Prairie Museum, 781
Historical Society of Ottawa, 816

Subject Index / Music

ICOM Museums Canada, 829
International Committee for Documentation of the International Council of Museums, 1543
International Committee of Museums & Collections of Arms & Military History, 1543
International Council of Museums, 1545
Kingston Association of Museums, Art Galleries & Historic Sites, 889
LaHave Islands Marine Museum Society, 895
The Lanark County Museums Network, 897
Lennoxville-Ascot Historical & Museum Society, 907
Lunenburg Marine Museum Society, 921
Mackenzie & District Museum Society, 924
Manitoba Sports Hall of Fame & Museum, 945
Maple Ridge Museum & Community Archives, 948
Margaret Laurence Home, Inc., 949
McCord Museum of Canadian History, 955
Meanskinisht Village Historical Association, 956
Mirror & District Museum Association, 968
Missisquoi Historical Society, 969
Musée minéralogique et minier de Thetford Mines, 982
Museum Association of Newfoundland & Labrador, 982
Museum London, 983
Museum of Contemporary Canadian Art, 983
Museums Association of Saskatchewan, 983
Museums of Niagara Association, 983
Nanaimo District Museum, 987
Nicola Valley Museum Archives Association, 1026
North Peace Historical Society, 1032
Northwestern Ontario Sports Hall of Fame & Museum, 1039
Nose Creek Valley Museum Society, 1040
Novia Scotia Sports Hall of Fame, 1050
O'Keefe Ranch & Interior Heritage Society, 1053
Old Sydney Society, 1056
Ontario Museum Association, 1092
Organization of Military Museums of Canada, 1125
Original Hockey Hall of Fame & Museum, 1126
Petrolia Discovery, 1155
Port Clements Historical Society, 1165
Pouce Coupe & District Museum & Historical Society, 1168
Prince Edward Island Museum & Heritage Foundation, 1175
Prince Edward Island Sports Hall of Fame & Museum Inc., 1177
Prince of Wales Northern Heritage Centre, 1179
Prince Rupert Fire Museum Society, 1179
Rocanville & District Museum Society Inc., 1235
Saskatchewan Sports Hall of Fame & Museum, 1275
Save Our Heritage Organization, 1281
Shag Harbour Incident Society, 1294
Société des musées québécois, 1318
Société historique Alphonse-Desjardins, 1319
Société internationale du réseau ÉCONOMUSÉE et Société ÉCONOMUSÉE du Québec, 1321
La Société Saint-Pierre, 1325
Stephan G. Stephansson Icelandic Society, 1349
Summerland Museum & Heritage Society, 1354
Sydney & Louisburg Railway Historical Society, 1360
Taras H. Shevchenko Museum & Memorial Park Foundation, 1367
Touchstones Nelson Museum of Art & History, 1388
U'mista Cultural Society, 1401
Vancouver Maritime Museum, 1427
Vancouver Museum Society, 1427
Yukon Historical & Museums Association, 1478

Music
Académie de musique du Québec, 3
African Nova Scotian Music Association, 13
Alberta Music Industry Association, 41
Alliance for Canadian New Music Projects, 56
The Arts & Letters Club, 85
Association québécoise de l'industrie du disque, du spectacle et de la vidéo, 170
Atlantic Canada Pipe Band Association, 182
Banda de nossa Senhora dos Milagres, 195
Banff International String Quartet Competition, 195
The Battlefords Music Festival, 200
BC Chinese Music Association, 201
British Columbia Registered Music Teachers' Association, 250
Calgary Marching Showband Association, 273
Calgary Society of Organists, 274
Calgary Stetson Show Band, 274
Calypso Association of Manitoba, 275
Canadian Academy of Recording Arts & Sciences, 286
Canadian Association for the Advancement of Music & the Arts, 305
Canadian Bureau for the Advancement of Music, 347
Canadian Music Centre, 438
Canadian Music Week Inc., 438
Canadian Musical Reproduction Rights Agency, 438
Canadian New Music Network, 441
Canadian Society for Traditional Music, 479
Canadian University Music Society, 499
Canadian Viola Society, 501
Canmore Folk & Blues Club, 508
Carl Orff Canada Music for Children, 513
Chinook Musical Society, 565
Classical Accordion Society of Canada, 572
Coalition for Music Education in British Columbia, 578
Coalition for Music Education in Canada, 578
Concours de musique du Canada inc., 610
Conseil francophone de la chanson, 618
Conseil québécois de la musique, 620
Conservatory Canada, 622
Cosmopolitan Music Society, 631
Creative BC, 639
Deep Roots Music Cooperative, 652
Early Music Vancouver, 667
East Coast Music Association, 668
Edmonton Composers' Concert Society, 676
Edmonton Kiwanis Music Festival, 678
Fédération des Associations de Musiciens-Éducateurs du Québec, 712
Fédération des harmonies et des orchestres symphoniques du Québec, 715
Fédération mondiale des concours internationaux de musique, 1526
Filarmónica Portuguesa de Montreal, 735
The Galpin Society, 1527
Grey County Kiwanis Festival of Music, 790
Guelph Musicfest, 793
International Music Council, 1553
International Society for Music Education, 1558
Jeunesses Musicales du Canada, 871
Kitchener-Waterloo Kiwanis Music Festival, 890
Kiwanis Music Festival of Windsor/Essex County, 892
Ladies' Morning Musical Club, 895
Manitoba Blues Society Inc., 932
Metronome Canada, 963
Moose Jaw Music Festival, 974
MuchFACT, 978
Music BC Industry Association, 983
Music Canada, 983
Music for Young Children, 983
Music Managers Forum Canada, 984
Music Nova Scotia, 984
Music NWT, 984
Music PEI, 984
Music Yukon, 984
Music/Musique NB, 984
Musicaction, 984
MusicNL, 984
National Shevchenko Musical Ensemble Guild of Canada, 996
New Music USA, 1577
Nova Scotia Music Educators' Association, 1047
Ontario Christian Music Assembly, 1071
Oshawa-Whitby Kiwanis Music & Theatre Festival, 1128
Ottawa Flute Association, 1130
Pacific Bluegrass Heritage Society, 1135
Parkland Music Festival, 1142
Peel Music Festival, 1148
Pembroke Kiwanis Music Festival, 1149
Pro Coro Canada, 1181
Radio Starmaker Fund, 1202
Re:Sound Music Licensing Company, 1204
Royal Canadian College of Organists, 1239
St. John's Kiwanis Music Festival, 1249
Sarnia Concert Association, 1254
Saskatchewan Recording Industry Association, 1273
Saskatchewan Registered Music Teachers' Association, 1273
Sault Ste. Marie Music Festival, 1281
Société Pro Musica Inc., 1322
Society of Composers, Authors & Music Publishers of Canada, 1328
Toronto Blues Society, 1382
The Toronto Consort, 1383
Toronto Latvian Concert Association, 1385
Toronto Musicians' Association, 1386
Urban Music Association of Canada, 1422
Vancouver Moving Theatre, 1427
Vancouver New Music, 1427
Vancouver Pro Musica Society, 1428
Vision of Love Ministry - Canada, 1436
Women's Musical Club of Toronto, 1463

Music Festivals
Alberta Music Festival Association, 41
Associated Manitoba Arts Festivals, Inc., 89
Canadian Music Festival Adjudicators' Association, 438
Canadian Music Week Inc., 438
Deep Roots Music Cooperative, 652
Edmonton Folk Music Festival, 677
Federation of Canadian Music Festivals, 723
Federation of Music Festivals of Nova Scotia, 725
Kiwanis Music Festival Association of Greater Toronto, 892
New Brunswick Competitive Festival of Music Inc., 1007
New Brunswick Federation of Music Festivals Inc., 1008
Newfoundland Federation of Music Festivals, 1023
Ontario Music Festivals Association, 1093
Performing Arts BC, 1152
Prince Edward Island Kiwanis Music Festival Association, 1175
Québec Competitive Festival of Music, 1196
Saskatchewan Music Festival Association Inc., 1270
Saskatchewan Recording Industry Association, 1273

Music Libraries
Canadian Association of Music Libraries, Archives & Documentation Centres, 321
International Association of Music Libraries, Archives & Documentation Centres, 1539

Music Teachers
Alberta Registered Music Teachers' Association, 44
British Columbia Music Educators' Association, 246
Canadian Federation of Music Teachers' Associations, 388
Canadian Music Educators' Association, 438
International Society for Music Education, 1558
Music for Young Children, 983
Ontario Music Educators' Association, 1093
Ontario Registered Music Teachers' Association, 1101
Saskatchewan Music Educators Association, 1270

Music Therapy
Canadian Association of Music Therapists, 321
Friends of Music Therapy, 761

Musical Theatre
Vinok Worldance, 1435

Musicians
American Federation of Musicians of the United States & Canada (AFL-CIO/CLC), 1493
Atlantic Federation of Musicians, Local 571, 184
Brantford Musicians' Association, 227
Calgary Musicians Association, 273
Canadian Amateur Musicians, 292
Canadian Association for the Advancement of Music & the Arts, 305
Cape Breton Professional Musicians Association, AFM Local 355, 509
Central Ontario Musicians' Association, 525
Edmonton Musicians' Association, 678
La Guilde des Musiciens/Musiciennes du Québec, 794
London Musicians' Association, 918
Manitoba Music, 941
Music Managers Forum Canada, 984
Music NWT, 984
Music PEI, 984
Music Yukon, 984
Music/Musique NB, 984
Musicians' Association of Victoria & the Islands, Local 247, AFM, 984
MusicNL, 984
New Brunswick Musicians' Association, Local 815 of the American Federation of Musicians, 1010
Radio Starmaker Fund, 1202
Regina Musicians' Association, 1212
Saskatchewan Recording Industry Association, 1273
Saskatoon Musicians' Association, 1279
Sault Ste Marie Musicians' Association, 1281
Society of Composers, Authors & Music Publishers of Canada, 1328
Stratford Musicians' Association, Local 418 of the American Federation of Musicians, 1351
Thunder Bay Musicians' Association, 1378
Toronto Musicians' Association, 1386
Vancouver Musicians' Association, 1427
West Coast Amateur Musicians' Society, 1444
Windsor Federation of Musicians, 1456
Winnipeg Musicians' Association, 1459

Musicology
American Musicological Society, 1495
Society for Ethnomusicology, 1590

Muslims
Ahmadiyya Muslim Jama'at Canada, 15
ANNISAA Organization of Canada, 71
Association of Islamic Charitable Projects, 149
British Columbia Muslim Association, 246
Canadian Council of Muslim Women, 369
Islamic Association of Nova Scotia, 864
Islamic Association of Saskatchewan, 864
Islamic Foundation of Toronto, 864
Islamic Information Foundation, 864
Islamic Propagation Centre of Ontario, 865
Manitoba Islamic Association, 939
Muslim Association of Canada, 985
Muslim Association of New Brunswick, 985
Muslim Community of Québec, 985
Muslim Council of Montréal, 985
Muslim World League - Canada, 985
National Council of Canadian Muslims, 991
Ottawa Muslim Association, 1131
Regroupement des Marocains au Canada, 1215
Scarborough Muslim Association, 1282
Windsor Islamic Association, 1456

Muteness
Association québécoise de la dysphasie, 170

Mutual Funds
Association of Canadian Compliance Professionals, 141
Federation of Mutual Fund Dealers, 725
Hedge Fund Association Canada, 1529
Mutual Fund Dealers Association of Canada, 986

Myalgic Encephalomyelitis
MEFM Myalgic Encephalomyelitis & Fibromyalgia Society of British Columbia, 959
Myalgic Encephalomyelitis Association of Halton/Hamilton-Wentworth, 986
Myalgic Encephalomyelitis Association of Ontario, 986
National ME/FM Action Network, 995

Myasthenia Gravis
Myasthenia Gravis Association of British Columbia, 986

Mycology
Mycological Society of Toronto, 986

Names
Canadian Society for the Study of Names, 478

Native Communications
Native Communications Society of the Northwest Territories, 997

Société de communication
  Atikamekw-Montagnais, 1314
Wawatay Native Communications Society, 1443

Native Development Corporations
Apeetogosan (Metis) Development Inc., 73
Council for Advancement of Native
  Development Officers, 632
Denesoline Corporation Ltd., 653
Enokhok Development Corporation Ltd., 689
Makivik Corporation, 927
Native Investment & Trade Association, 998
Nunasi Corporation, 1051
Tecumseh Community Development
  Corporation, 1369

Native Friendship Centres
Aboriginal Friendship Centre of Calgary, 2
Aboriginal Friendship Centres of Saskatchewan, 2
Alberta Native Friendship Centres Association, 41
Athabasca Native Friendship Centre Society, 180
Atikokan Native Friendship Centre, 181
Barrie Native Friendship Centre, 197
Battlefords Indian & Métis Friendship Centre, 200
Bonnyville Canadian Native Friendship Centre, 217
Brandon Friendship Centre, 226
British Columbia Association of Aboriginal
  Friendship Centres, 231
Buffalo Narrows Friendship Centre, 261
Canadian Native Friendship Centre, 440
CanAm Indian Friendship Centre of Windsor, 507
Cariboo Friendship Society, 512
Centre d'amitié autochtone de Val-d'Or, 527
Centre d'amitié autochtone du Québec, 527
Cold Lake Native Friendship Centre, 580
Conayt Friendship Society, 609
Dauphin Friendship Centre, 651
Dryden Native Friendship Centre, 663
Dze L K'ant Friendship Centre Society, 666
Edson Friendship Centre, 680
Elbert Chartrand Friendship Centre, 681
First Nations Friendship Centre, 738
Flin Flon Aboriginal Friendship Association Inc., 741
Fort Erie Native Friendship Centre, 752
Fort Nelson Aboriginal Friendship Society, 753
Friendship House Association of Prince Rupert, 763
Georgian Bay Native Friendship Centre, 771
Grande Prairie Friendship Centre, 781
Hamilton Regional Indian Centre, 802
High Level Native Friendship Centre, 814
High Prairie Native Friendship Centre, 814
Hiiye'yu Lelum Society House of Friendship, 814
Hinton Friendship Centre, 815
Ile-a-la-Crosse Friendship Centre Inc., 829
Indian & Metis Friendship Centre of Prince
  Albert, 834
Indian & Metis Friendship Centre of Winnipeg
  Inc., 834
Indian Friendship Centre in Sault Ste Marie, 834
Ininew Friendship Centre, 838
Interior Indian Friendship Society, 852
Inuit Community Centre, 862
Kapuskasing Friendship Centre, 881
Kermode Friendship Society, 884
Kikinahk Friendship Centre, 887
Ki-Low-Na Friendship Society, 887
Labrador Friendship Centre, 894
Lac La Biche Canadian Native Friendship
  Centre, 894
Lloydminster Native Friendship Centre, 916
Lynn Lake Friendship Centre, 923
Ma-Mow-We-Tak Friendship Centre Inc., 928
Manitoba Association of Friendship Centres, 929
Mannawanis Native Friendship Centre, 948
Mi'kmaq Native Friendship Centre, 964
Mission Indian Friendship Centre, 969
Moose Mountain Friendship Centre, 974
N'Amerind (London) Friendship Centre, 986
N'swakamok Native Friendship Centre, 986
Napi Friendship Association, 988
National Association of Friendship Centres, 990
Native Canadian Centre of Toronto, 997

Native Friendship Centre of Montréal Inc., 998
Nawican Friendship Centre, 1002
Ne'Chee Friendship Centre, 1002
Niagara Regional Native Centre, 1026
Nishnawbe - Gamik Friendship Centre, 1027
Nistawoyou Association Friendship Centre, 1027
North Bay Indian Friendship Centre, 1030
Northwest Territories/Nunavut Council of
  Friendship Centres, 1039
Odawa Native Friendship Centre, 1054
Ontario Federation of Indian Friendship
  Centres, 1079
Parry Sound Friendship Centre, 1143
The Pas Friendship Centre Inc., 1145
Port Alberni Friendship Center, 1165
Portage Friendship Centre Inc., 1166
Prince George Native Friendship Centre, 1179
Pulaarvik Kablu Friendship Centre, 1194
Qu'Appelle Valley Friendship Centre, 1195
Quesnel Tillicum Society Friendship Centre, 1200
Red Deer Native Friendship Society, 1209
Red Lake Indian Friendship Centre, 1210
Regroupement des centres d'amitié autochtone
  du Québec, 1215
Riverton & District Friendship Centre, 1234
Rocky Native Friendship Society, 1235
Sagitawa Friendship Centre, 1245
St. John's Native Friendship Centre, 1249
Saskatoon Indian & Métis Friendship Centre, 1279
Selkirk Friendship Centre, 1289
Sik-ooh-kotoki Friendship Society, 1299
Skookum Jim Friendship Centre, 1303
Slave Lake Native Friendship Centre, 1303
Soaring Eagle Friendship Centre, 1305
Tansi Friendship Centre Society, 1366
Thunder Bay Indian Friendship Centre, 1378
Thunderbird Friendship Centre, 1378
Tillicum Lelum Aboriginal Friendship Centre, 1379
Timmins Native Friendship Centre, 1380
Toronto Council Fire Native Cultural Centre, 1383
United Native Friendship Centre, 1412
Vancouver Aboriginal Friendship Centre
  Society, 1424
Victoria Native Friendship Centre, 1433
Yorkton Friendship Centre, 1474
Zhahti Koe Friendship Centre, 1482

Native Peoples
Aboriginal Agricultural Education Society of
  British Columbia, 2
Aboriginal Firefighters Association of Canada, 2
Aboriginal Head Start Association of British
  Columbia, 2
Aboriginal Legal Services of Toronto, 2
Aboriginal Multi-Media Society, 2
Aboriginal Sport & Wellness Council of Ontario, 2
Aboriginal Tourism Association of British
  Columbia, 2
Aboriginal Tourism Association of Southern
  Ontario, 2
AFOA Canada, 12
Alliance autochtone du Québec, 54
Assemblée des premières nations du Québec et
  du Labrador, 88
Assembly of First Nations, 88
Assembly of Manitoba Chiefs, 88
Association for Native Development in the
  Performing & Visual Arts, 134
Association of BC First Nations Treatment
  Programs, 140
Association of Iroquois & Allied Indians, 149
Awo Taan Healing Lodge Society, 191
British Columbia Aboriginal Network on
  Disability Society, 229
Calgary Aboriginal Arts Awareness Society, 270
Canadian Aboriginal & Minority Supplier
  Council, 285
Canadian Aboriginal AIDS Network, 285
Canadian Aboriginal Minerals Association, 285
Canadian Aboriginal Veterans & Serving
  Members Association, 285
Canadian Association for the Study of
  Indigenous Education, 306
Canadian Council for Aboriginal Business, 366
Canadian Indigenous Nurses Association, 411

Centre for Indigenous Environmental
  Resources, Inc., 532
Centre for Indigenous Sovereignty, 532
Chiefs of Ontario, 558
Circle of Eagles Lodge, 570
Coastal First Nations, 579
Confederacy of Mainland Mi'kmaq, 610
Confederation des peuples autochtones du
  Québec, 611
Congress of Aboriginal Peoples, 613
Council of the Haida Nation - Haida Fisheries
  Program, 635
Cree-Naskapi Commission, 641
Edmonton Aboriginal Senior Centre, 675
Federation of Saskatchewan Indian Nations, 726
Femmes autochtones du Québec inc., 731
First Nations Agricultural Lending Association, 738
First Nations Chiefs of Police Association, 738
First Nations Child & Family Caring Society of
  Canada, 738
First Nations Confederacy of Cultural Education
  Centres, 738
First Nations Education Council, 738
Gitxsan Treaty Office, 774
Indian Agricultural Program of Ontario, 834
Indigenous Bar Association, 834
Indigenous Literary Studies Association, 835
Indigenous Physicians Association of Canada, 835
Indigenous Works, 835
Indspire, 835
Institut Tshakapesh, 843
Institute for the Advancement of Aboriginal
  Women, 844
Inter-Provincial Association on Native
  Employment, 861
Jake Thomas Learning Centre, 867
James Bay Association for Community Living, 868
Kanien'kehaka Onkwawen'na Raotitiohkwa
  Language & Cultural Centre, 881
Kivalliq Inuit Association, 891
Lake of the Woods Ojibway Cultural Centre, 896
Lu'ma Native Housing Society, 920
Manitoba Aboriginal Education Counselling
  Association Inc., 928
Manitoba Association of Friendship Centres, 929
Manitoba Indian Cultural Education Centre, 939
Manitoba Indian Education Association Inc., 939
Manitoba Métis Federation, 940
Maritime Aboriginal Peoples Council, 950
Meanskinisht Village Historical Association, 956
Métis Child & Family Services Society
  (Edmonton), 962
Métis National Council, 963
Mi'kmaq Association for Cultural Studies, 964
National Aboriginal Capital Corporations
  Association, 988
National Aboriginal Circle Against Family
  Violence, 988
National Aboriginal Diabetes Association Inc., 988
National Aboriginal Forestry Association, 988
National Aboriginal Lands Managers
  Association, 989
National Aboriginal Trust Officers Association, 989
National Native Addictions Partnership
  Foundation, 995
Native Addictions Council of Manitoba, 997
Native Brotherhood of British Columbia, 997
Native Canadian Centre of Toronto, 997
Native Child & Family Services of Toronto, 997
Native Clan Organization Inc., 997
Native Coordinating Council, 997
Native Council of Nova Scotia, 997
Native Council of Prince Edward Island, 997
Native Counselling Services of Alberta, 997
Native Courtworker & Counselling Association
  of BC, 997
Native Earth Performing Arts Inc., 998
Native Fishing Association, 998
Native Investment & Trade Association, 998
Native North American Traveling College, 998
Naut'sa mawt Resource Group, 1001
NEC Native Education College Society, 1002

New Brunswick Aboriginal Peoples Council, 1004
Niagara Regional Native Centre, 1026
Northeastern Alberta Aboriginal Business
  Association, 1034
Northern Native Fishing Corporation, 1035
Northern Ontario Native Tourism Association, 1035
Nova Scotia Native Women's Society, 1047
Nunavut Tourism, 1051
Ojibway & Cree Cultural Centre, 1055
Ontario Aboriginal Lands Association, 1058
Ontario Coalition of Aboriginal Peoples, 1071
Ontario Federation of Indian Friendship
  Centres, 1079
Ontario Native Education Counselling
  Association, 1093
Oshki Anishnawbeg Student Association, 1128
Qalipu Mi'kmaq First Nations Band, 1194
Quaker Aboriginal Affairs Committee, 1195
Recherches amérindiennes au Québec, 1207
Red Road HIV/AIDS Network, 1210
Regroupement des centres d'amitié autochtone
  du Québec, 1215
Rocky Native Friendship Society, 1235
Saanich Native Heritage Society, 1245
Société touristique des Autochtones du
  Québec, 1325
Treaty & Aboriginal Rights Research Centre of
  Manitoba Inc., 1397
2-Spirited People of the First Nations, 1401
U'mista Cultural Society, 1401
Union of British Columbia Indian Chiefs, 1406
Union of Nova Scotia Indians, 1407
Union of Ontario Indians, 1408
United Native Nations Society, 1412
University of Toronto Native Students
  Association, 1421
Walpole Island Heritage Centre, 1440
West Region Tribal Council Cultural Education
  Centre, 1446
Woodland Cultural Centre, 1464
Yukon Aboriginal Sport Circle, 1476
Yukon Aboriginal Women's Council, 1477
Yukon First Nations Culture & Tourism
  Association, 1478
Yukon Indian Hockey Association, 1479

Native Women
Aboriginal Women's Association of Prince
  Edward Island, 3
Alberta Aboriginal Women's Society, 21
British Columbia Native Women's Association, 247
Femmes autochtones du Québec inc., 731
First Nations Breast Cancer Society, 738
Helping Spirit Lodge Society, 812
Institute for the Advancement of Aboriginal
  Women, 844
Labrador Native Women's Association, 894
Mamawehetowin Crisis Centre, 928
Métis National Council of Women, 963
Mother of Red Nations Women's Council of
  Manitoba, 975
Native Women's Association of Canada, 998
Native Women's Resource Centre of Toronto, 998
Native Women's Transition Centre Inc., 998
New Brunswick Aboriginal Women's Council, 1004
Newfoundland Native Women's Association, 1023
Nova Scotia Native Women's Society, 1047
Ontario Native Women's Association, 1093
Pacific Association of First Nations' Women, 1134
Pauktuutit Inuit Women of Canada, 1146
Saskatchewan Aboriginal Women's Circle
  Corporation, 1255
Yukon Aboriginal Women's Council, 1477

NATO
Atlantic Council of Canada, 183

Natural Gas
Association pétrolière et gazière du Québec, 165
Canadian Gas Association, 396
Natural Gas Employees' Association, 998

Subject Index / Natural History

Natural History
Natural History Society of Newfoundland & Labrador, 999
Nature Saskatchewan, 1000
Nature Vancouver, 1001
St. Lawrence Valley Natural History Society, 1250
Société Provancher d'histoire naturelle du Canada, 1322
Victoria Natural History Society, 1433
Waterton Natural History Association, 1442

Natural Products Industry
Canadian Health Food Association, 401
Canadian Organic Growers Inc., 446
International Federation of Organic Agriculture Movements, 1548
International Organic Inspectors Association, 1554
Natural Products Marketing Council, 999
Slow Food, 1589
Slow Food Canada, 1304

Naturalists
Abbotsford-Mission Nature Club, 1
Alberni Valley Outdoor Club, 21
Alouette Field Naturalists, 59
Arrowsmith Naturalists, 84
Blomidon Naturalists Society, 215
Bowen Nature Club, 219
Brereton Field Naturalists' Club Inc., 228
British Columbia Nature (Federation of British Columbia Naturalists), 247
Buffalo Lake Naturalists Club, 261
Bulkley Valley Naturalists, 264
Burke Mountain Naturalists, 265
Calgary Field Naturalists' Society, 272
Central Okanagan Naturalists Club, 525
Cercles des jeunes naturalistes, 537
Chilliwack Field Naturalists, 563
Cole Harbour Rural Heritage Society, 581
Cowichan Valley Naturalists' Society, 637
Explorer's Club (Canadian Chapter), 700
Field Botanists of Ontario, 733
Grasslands Naturalists, 782
Halifax Field Naturalists, 799
Hamilton Naturalists' Club, 801
Ingersoll District Nature Club, 838
Kamloops Naturalist Club, 880
Kennebecasis Naturalists' Society, 883
Kingston Field Naturalists, 889
Kitchener-Waterloo Field Naturalists, 890
Kitimat Valley Naturalists, 891
Langley Field Naturalists Society, 899
Lethbridge Naturalists' Society, 908
McIlwraith Field Naturalists, 955
Montréal Field Naturalists Club, 972
National Audubon Society, Inc., 1575
Nature Alberta, 999
Nature Canada, 999
Nature Manitoba, 1000
Nature NB, 1000
Nature Nova Scotia (Federation of Nova Scotia Naturalists), 1000
Nature Québec, 1000
Niagara Falls Nature Club, 1025
Norfolk Field Naturalists, 1028
North Okanagan Naturalists Club, 1031
Nova Scotia Wild Flora Society, 1050
Oliver-Osoyoos Naturalists, 1057
Ontario Field Ornithologists, 1080
Ontario Nature, 1093
Osoyoos Desert Society, 1128
Ottawa Field-Naturalists' Club, 1130
Peace Parkland Naturalists, 1147
Pembroke Area Field Naturalists, 1149
Pender Island Field Naturalists, 1149
Peninsula Field Naturalists, 1149
Peterborough Field Naturalists, 1153
Pickering Naturalists, 1159
Prince George Backcountry Recreation Society, 1179
Prince George Naturalists Club, 1179
Quesnel Naturalists, 1200
Red Deer River Naturalists, 1209
Richmond Hill Naturalists, 1230
Rideau Valley Field Naturalists, 1231
Rocky Mountain Naturalists, 1235
Royal Botanical Gardens, 1239
Royal City Field Naturalists, 1241
Saint John Naturalists' Club, 1247
Sargeant Bay Society, 1253
Sault Naturalists, 1281
Seniors for Nature Canoe Club, 1290
Shuswap Naturalists, 1297
Skeena Valley Naturalists, 1302
Somenos Marsh Wildlife Society, 1333
South Lake Simcoe Naturalists, 1335
South Peel Naturalists' Club, 1336
Sydenham Field Naturalists, 1359
Thunder Bay Field Naturalists, 1377
Timberline Trail & Nature Club, 1379
Toronto Entomologists Association, 1384
Toronto Field Naturalists, 1384
Toronto Ornithological Club, 1386
Vermilion Forks Field Naturalists, 1431
West Elgin Nature Club, 1445
West Kootenay Naturalists Association, 1445
White Rock & Surrey Naturalists, 1452
Williams Lake Field Naturalists, 1455
Willow Beach Field Naturalists, 1455
Woodstock Field Naturalists, 1464

Naturism
Federation of Canadian Naturists, 723
Fédération québécoise de naturisme, 727
Helios Nudist Association, 811

Naturopathy
American Association of Naturopathic Physicians, 1489
Association des naturopathes professionnels du Québec, 120
British Columbia Naturopathic Association, 247
The Canadian Association of Naturopathic Doctors, 322
The Canadian College of Naturopathic Medicine, 360
College of Naturopathic Doctors of Alberta, 586
College of Naturopathic Physicians of British Columbia, 586
The College of Naturopaths of Ontario, 586
Corporation des praticiens en médecine douce du Canada, 630
Manitoba Naturopathic Association, 941
Natural Health Practitioners of Canada Association, 999
New Brunswick Association of Naturopathic Doctors, 1005
Nova Scotia Association of Naturopathic Doctors, 1041
Ontario Association of Naturopathic Doctors, 1065
Québec Association of Naturopathic Medicine, 1196
Saskatchewan Association of Naturopathic Practitioners, 1257

Naval Art & Science
Canadian Nautical Research Society, 440

Navigation
Association internationale permanente des congrès de navigation, 1510
Canadian Marine Pilots' Association, 430
Canadian Navigation Society, 440
International Association of Marine Aids to Navigation & Lighthouse Authorities, 1539

Navy
Army, Navy & Air Force Veterans in Canada, 83
Canadian Merchant Navy Veterans Association Inc., 435
Naval Club of Toronto, 1001
The Naval Officers' Association of Canada, 1001
Navy League of Canada, 1001
Royal Canadian Naval Benevolent Fund, 1240

Needlework
Canadian Quilters' Association, 464
Embroiderers' Association of Canada, Inc., 685

Nephrology
Association des néphrologues du Québec, 120
British Columbia Provincial Renal Agency, 249
Canadian Association of Nephrology Nurses & Technologists, 322
Canadian Society of Nephrology, 485

Netball
British Columbia Netball Association, 247
Fédération de Netball du Québec, 710
Netball Alberta, 1003
Netball Canada, 1003
Netball Ontario, 1003

Netherlandic Studies
Canadian Association for the Advancement of Netherlandic Studies, 305

Networks of Centres of Excellence
ArcticNet Inc., 81
AUTO21 Network of Centres of Excellence, 189
Canadian Arthritis Network, 295
Canadian Genetic Diseases Network, 397
Canadian Water Network, 502
Mathematics of Information Technology & Complex Systems, 954
Stem Cell Network, 1349
Sustainable Forestry Initiative Inc., 1597

Neurofibromatosis
AboutFace, 3
L'Association de la Neurofibromatose du Québec, 101
British Columbia Neurofibromatosis Foundation, 247
Children's Tumor Foundation, 1516
Neurofibromatosis Association of Saskatchewan, 1003
Neurofibromatosis Society of Ontario, 1003

Neurology
American Academy for Cerebral Palsy & Developmental Medicine, 1487
American Academy of Neurology, 1487
American Association of Neuromuscular & Electrodiagnostic Medicine, 1490
Association des neurologues du Québec, 120
British Columbia Centre for Ability, 235
British Columbia Society of Electroneurophysiology Technologists, 254
Canadian Association of Child Neurology, 310
Canadian Neurological Sciences Federation, 441
Canadian Neurological Society, 441
Canadian Transverse Myelitis Association, 497
Fondation de l'Ataxie Charlevoix-Saguenay, 743
Neurological Health Charities Canada, 1004
North Okanagan Neurological Association, 1031

Neuropathology
Canadian Association of Neuropathologists, 322
Edmonton (Alberta) Nerve Pain Association, 675

Neurophysiology
Canadian Society of Clinical Neurophysiologists, 482

Neuroscience
American Society of Neuroradiology, 1501
Canadian Association for Neuroscience, 302
Canadian Association of Neuroscience Nurses, 322
Canadian College of Neuropsychopharmacology, 360
Canadian Society for Brain, Behaviour & Cognitive Science, 473
Headache Network Canada, 805
International Society for Neurochemistry, 1558

Neurosurgery
Alberta Neurosurgical Society, 41
Association de neurochirurgie du Québec, 103

New Zealand
Australia-New Zealand Association, 188
Canada New Zealand Business Council, 1515

Newspapers
Alberta Weekly Newspapers Association, 51
Association des médias écrits communautaires du Québec, 120
British Columbia & Yukon Community Newspapers Association, 229
Canadian Community Newspapers Association, 361
The Canadian Press, 459
Circulation Management Association of Canada, 570
Hebdos Québec, 810
Manitoba Community Newspapers Association, 934
National NewsMedia Council, 995
The Newspaper Guild (AFL-CIO/CLC), 1577
Newspapers Atlantic, 1024
Newspapers Canada, 1024
Ontario Community Newspapers Association, 1073
Québec Community Newspaper Association, 1196
Saskatchewan Weekly Newspapers Association, 1278
Unifor87-M, 1405

Noise Pollution
Right to Quiet Society, 1232

Northern Canada
Arctic Institute of North America, 81
Association of Canadian Universities for Northern Studies, 144
Canadian Circumpolar Institute, 357
Prince of Wales Northern Heritage Centre, 1179
Union of Northern Workers, 1407

Norway
Canadian Norwegian Business Association, 1515
Innovation Norway, 839

Notaries
The Society of Notaries Public of British Columbia, 1330

Nuclear Energy
Canadian Coalition for Nuclear Responsibility, 357
Canadian National Energy Alliance, 439
Canadian Nuclear Association, 442
Canadian Nuclear Society, 442
CANDU Owners Group Inc., 508
International Atomic Energy Agency, 1540
Nuclear Information & Resource Service, 1580
Nuclear Insurance Association of Canada, 1050
Organization of Canadian Nuclear Industries, 1125
World Nuclear Association, 1606

Nuclear Law
International Nuclear Law Association, 1553

Nuclear Medicine
Association des médecins spécialistes en médecine nucléaire du Québec, 120
Canadian Association of Nuclear Medicine, 323

Nuclear Weapons
Canadian Coalition for Nuclear Responsibility, 357
Canadian Network to Abolish Nuclear Weapons, 441
Physicians for Global Survival (Canada), 1158

Numismatics
Alberni Valley Coin Club, 21
American Numismatic Society, 1496
Apprenp'tits Numismates, 75
Association des Numismates et des Philatélistes de Boucherville, 121
Atlantic Provinces Numismatic Association, 185
Beaumont Coin Discovery Group, 203
Brantford Numismatic Society, 227
Calgary Numismatic Society, 273
Canadian Association of Numismatic Dealers, 323
Canadian Association of Token Collectors, 334
Canadian Association of Wooden Money Collectors, 336
Canadian Numismatic Research Society, 442
Canadian Paper Money Society, 449
Canadian Tire Coupon Collectors Club, 495
Champlain Coin Club, 551
Chedoke Numismatic Society, 555
Classical & Medieval Numismatic Society, 572
Club de Numismates du Bas St-Laurent, 575
Edmonton Numismatic Society, 678
Fredericton Numismatic Society, 759
Halifax Regional Coin Club, 799
Ingersoll Coin Club, 838
Kent Coin Club, 883
Lake Superior Coin Club, 896
Lakeshore Coin Club, 897
London Numismatic Society, 918
Manitoba Coin Club, 934
Medicine Hat Coin & Stamp Club, 958
Mid-Island Coin Club, 965
Mississauga-Etobicoke Coin Stamp & Collectibles Club, 970
Moncton Coin Club, 972
Montreal Numismatic Society, 973

Niagara Falls Coin Club, 1025
Nickel Belt Coin Club, 1026
Nipissing Coin Club, 1027
North Shore Numismatic Society, 1033
North York Coin Club, 1033
Ontario Numismatic Association, 1094
Oshawa & District Coin Club, 1127
Ottawa Numismatic Society, 1131
Peterborough Numismatic Club, 1153
Prince Edward Island Numismatic Association, 1176
Regina Coin Club, 1211
Royal Canadian Numismatic Association, 1241
Saint John Coin Club, 1246
St. Catharines Coin Club, 1248
Saskatoon Coin Club, 1279
Scarborough Coin Club, 1282
Société d'archéologie et de numismatique de Montréal, 1309
La Société Numismatique de Québec, 1322
Sou'wester Coin Club, 1333
South Wellington Coin Society, 1336
Stratford Coin Club, 1351
Strathcona Coin Discovery Group, 1351
Timmins Coin Club, 1380
Toronto Coin Club, 1383
Vancouver Numismatic Society, 1428
Victoria Numismatic Society, 1433
Waterloo Coin Society, 1442
Windsor Coin Club, 1456
Woodstock Coin Club, 1464

Nursery Trades
British Columbia Landscape & Nursery Association, 244
Canadian Nursery Landscape Association, 442
Flowers Canada, 741
Flowers Canada Growers, 741
Landscape Alberta Nursery Trades Association, 898
Landscape Newfoundland & Labrador, 898
Landscape Nova Scotia, 898
Landscape Ontario Horticultural Trades Association, 898
Nursery Sod Growers' Association of Ontario, 1052
Saskatchewan Nursery Landscape Association, 1270

Nurses
Academy of Canadian Executive Nurses, 4
Alberta Gerontological Nurses Association, 37
Association des professionnels en santé du travail, 126
Association of New Brunswick Licensed Practical Nurses, 153
Association of Occupational Health Nurses of Newfoundland & Labrador, 154
Association of Registered Nurses of Prince Edward Island, 161
Association québécoise des infirmières et intervenants en recherche clinique, 173
British Columbia Nurse Practitioner Association, 248
British Columbia Nurses' Union, 248
Canadian Association for Nursing Research, 302
Canadian Association for the History of Nursing, 305
Canadian Association of Apheresis Nurses, 308
Canadian Association of Critical Care Nurses, 311
Canadian Association of Foot Care Nurses, 315
Canadian Association of Hepatology Nurses, 317
Canadian Association of Nephrology Nurses & Technologists, 322
Canadian Association of Neuroscience Nurses, 322
Canadian Association of Nurses in HIV/AIDS Care, 323
Canadian Association of Nurses in Oncology, 323
Canadian Association of Perinatal & Women's Health Nurses, 325
Canadian Association of Schools of Nursing, 332
Canadian Council of Cardiovascular Nurses, 367
Canadian Council of Practical Nurse Regulators, 369

Canadian Federation of Mental Health Nurses, 388
Canadian Federation of Nurses Unions, 388
Canadian Gerontological Nursing Association, 397
Canadian Holistic Nurses Association, 406
Canadian Indigenous Nurses Association, 411
Canadian Nurse Continence Advisors Association, 442
Canadian Nurses Association, 442
Canadian Nurses Foundation, 443
Canadian Nurses Protective Society, 443
Canadian Nursing Informatics Association, 443
Canadian Nursing Students' Association, 443
Canadian Occupational Health Nurses Association, 444
Canadian Orthopaedic Nurses Association, 448
Canadian Society of Gastroenterology Nurses & Associates, 483
Canadian Society of Ophthalmic Registered Nurses, 485
Canadian Vascular Access Association, 501
Clinical Nurse Specialist Association of Ontario, 574
The College & Association of Registered Nurses of Alberta, 581
College of Licensed Practical Nurses of BC, 585
College of Licensed Practical Nurses of Manitoba, 585
College of Licensed Practical Nurses of PEI, 585
College of Nurses of Ontario, 586
College of Registered Nurses of British Columbia, 589
College of Registered Nurses of Manitoba, 589
College of Registered Nurses of Nova Scotia, 589
Community Health Nurses of Canada, 599
Corporation des infirmières et infirmiers de salle d'opération du Québec, 630
Fédération de la santé du Québec - CSQ, 709
Fédération interprofessionnelle de la santé du Québec, 721
Fondation de l'Ordre des infirmières et infirmiers du Québec, 744
Gerontological Nursing Association of British Columbia, 772
Gerontological Nursing Association of Ontario, 772
Independent Practice Nurses Interest Group, 833
Licensed Practical Nurses Association of British Columbia, 910
Manitoba Gerontological Nurses' Association, 937
Manitoba Nurses' Union, 941
Manitoba Operating Room Nurses Association, 941
Margaret M. Allemang Centre for the History of Nursing, 949
National Association of PeriAnesthesia Nurses of Canada, 990
National Emergency Nurses Association, 993
New Brunswick Nurses Union, 1010
New Brunswick Operating Room Nurses, 1010
Newfoundland & Labrador Nurse Practitioner Association, 1020
Newfoundland & Labrador Nurses' Union, 1020
Newfoundland & Labrador Operating Room Nurses Association, 1020
Nova Scotia Gerontological Nurses Association, 1045
Nova Scotia Nurses' Union, 1047
Nurse Practitioner Association of Canada, 1051
Nurse Practitioners Association of Alberta, 1052
Nurse Practitioners of Saskatchewan, 1052
Nurse Practitioners' Association of Nova Scotia, 1052
Nurse Practitioners' Association of Ontario, 1052
Nurses Association of New Brunswick, 1052
Ontario Nurses' Association, 1094
Operating Room Nurses Association of Canada, 1115
Operating Room Nurses Association of Nova Scotia, 1115
Operating Room Nurses Association of Ontario, 1115
Operating Room Nurses of Alberta Association, 1115

Ordre des infirmières et infirmiers auxiliaires du Québec, 1121
Ordre des infirmières et infirmiers du Québec, 1121
Perioperative Registered Nurses Association of British Columbia, 1152
Prince Edward Island Gerontological Nurses Association, 1174
Prince Edward Island Nurses' Union, 1176
Provincial Nurse Educator Interest Group, 1191
The Registered Nurses Association of the Northwest Territories & Nunavut, 1213
Registered Nurses' Association of Ontario, 1213
Saskatchewan PeriOperative Registered Nurses' Group, 1271
Saskatchewan Registered Nurses' Association, 1273
Saskatchewan Union of Nurses, 1277
Secrétariat international des infirmières et infirmiers de l'espace francophone, 1288
United Nurses of Alberta, 1412
Urology Nurses of Canada, 1422
Victorian Order of Nurses for Canada, 1434
Yukon Registered Nurses Association, 1480

Nursing Homes
AdvantAge Ontario, 10
New Brunswick Association of Nursing Homes, Inc., 1005
Ontario Long Term Care Association, 1089

Nutrition
Alberta Milk, 40
American Society for Parenteral & Enteral Nutrition, 1498
American Vegan Society, 1504
Canadian Foundation for Dietetic Research, 393
Canadian Nutrition Society, 443
Canadian Society of Nutrition Management, 485
Dietitians of Canada, 656
Helderleigh Foundation, 811
Infant Feeding Action Coalition, 836
International Union of Nutritional Sciences, 1565
International Vegetarian Union, 1565
New Brunswick Association of Dietitians, 1005
Newfoundland & Labrador College of Dietitians, 1017
Nova Scotia Dietetic Association, 1044
Ontario Society of Nutrition Professionals in Public Health, 1107
Pacific Society for Nutrition Management, 1136
Prince Edward Island Dietetic Association, 1173
Saskatchewan Dietitians Association, 1263
School Milk Foundation of Newfoundland & Labrador, 1284

Nuts
Society of Ontario Nut Growers, 1330

Obesity
Active Healthy Kids Canada, 7
Canadian Association of Bariatric Physicians & Surgeons, 308
Canadian Obesity Network, 444
Childhood Obesity Foundation, 560
ÉquiLibre - Groupe d'action sur le poids, 694
Fondation Lucie et André Chagnon, 747
TOPS Club, Inc., 1598

Obstetrics & Gynecology
Association des obstétriciens et gynécologues du Québec, 121
Canadian Association of Perinatal & Women's Health Nurses, 325
European Society of Gynaecological Oncology, 1524
Society of Gynecologic Oncologists of Canada, 1329
Society of Obstetricians & Gynaecologists of Canada, 1330

Occupational Health & Safety
Alberta Construction Safety Association, 31
Alberta Occupational Health Nurses Association, 41
Association de la santé et de la sécurité des pâtes et papiers et des industries de la forêt du Québec, 102
Association des professionnels en santé du travail, 126

Association paritaire pour la santé et la sécurité du travail - Administration provinciale, 164
Association paritaire pour la santé et la sécurité du travail - Imprimerie et activités connexes, 164
Association paritaire pour la santé et la sécurité du travail - Secteur Affaires municipales, 165
Association paritaire pour la santé et la sécurité du travail du secteur affaires sociales, 165
Association québécoise pour l'hygiène, la santé et la sécurité du travail, 176
Association sectorielle services automobiles, 178
Association sectorielle: Fabrication d'équipement de transport et de machines, 178
BC Assocation for Crane Safety, 201
BC Construction Safety Alliance, 201
Board of Canadian Registered Safety Professionals, 216
Canadian Agricultural Safety Association, 289
Canadian Assessment, Vocational Evaluation & Work Adjustment Society, 297
Canadian Centre for Occupational Health & Safety, 353
Canadian Council on Rehabilitation & Work, 371
Canadian Hoisting & Rigging Safety Council, 406
Canadian Occupational Health Nurses Association, 444
Canadian Society of Safety Engineering, Inc., 487
Centre patronal de santé et sécurité du travail du Québec, 536
Construction Safety Association of Manitoba, 624
Industrial Accident Victims Group of Ontario, 835
Institut de recherche Robert-Sauvé en santé et en sécurité du travail, 842
Institute for Work & Health, 844
International Commission on Occupational Health, 1543
International Occupational Safety & Health Information Network, 1553
MultiPrévention, 980
MultiPrévention ASP: Association paritaire pour la santé et la sécurité au travail des secteurs: métal, électrique, habillement et imprimerie, 980
National Institute of Disability Management & Research, 994
New Brunswick Construction Safety Association, 1007
Newfoundland & Labrador Construction Safety Association, 1017
Nova Scotia Construction Safety Association, 1043
Occupational & Environmental Medical Association of Canada, 1054
Occupational First Aid Attendants Association of British Columbia, 1054
Occupational Health Clinics for Ontario Workers, 1054
Occupational Hygiene Association of Ontario, 1054
Occupational Nurses' Specialty Association of British Columbia, 1054
Ontario Occupational Health Nurses Association, 1094
Saskatchewan Construction Safety Association Inc., 1262
Via Prévention, 1431
Workplace Safety & Prevention Services, 1464
World Safety Organization, 1607

Occupational Therapy
Alberta College of Occupational Therapists, 29
Canadian Association of Occupational Therapists, 323
Canadian Association of Occupational Therapists - British Columbia, 324
Canadian Association of Physical Medicine & Rehabilitation, 327
Canadian Occupational Therapy Foundation, 444
Canadian Society of Hand Therapists, 483
College of Occupational Therapists of British Columbia, 586
College of Occupational Therapists of Manitoba, 586

Subject Index / Oceanography

College of Occupational Therapists of Nova Scotia, 587
College of Occupational Therapists of Ontario, 587
Manitoba Society of Occupational Therapists, 945
New Brunswick Association of Occupational Therapists, 1005
Newfoundland & Labrador Association of Occupational Therapists, 1016
Newfoundland & Labrador Occupational Therapy Board, 1020
Nova Scotia Society of Occupational Therapists, 1049
Ontario Society of Occupational Therapists, 1107
Ordre des ergothérapeutes du Québec, 1121
Prince Edward Island Occupational Therapy Society, 1176
Saskatchewan Society of Occupational Therapists, 1275
World Federation of Occupational Therapists, 1605

Oceanography
Canadian Meteorological & Oceanographic Society, 435
The Oceanography Society, 1580

Oceans
Antarctic & Southern Ocean Coalition, 1505
International Council for the Exploration of the Sea, 1544
International Ocean Institute, 1553
International Oceans Institute of Canada, 858
The Ocean Conservancy, 1580
Oceana Canada, 1054

Offenders (Criminal) & Ex-Offenders
The Alberta Seventh Step Society, 46
Atlantic Halfway House Association, 184
British Columbia-Yukon Halfway House Association, 259
Canadian Association of Elizabeth Fry Societies, 312
Canadian Coalition Against the Death Penalty, 357
Canadian Training Institute, 496
Circle of Eagles Lodge, 570
John Howard Society of Alberta, 874
The John Howard Society of British Columbia, 874
The John Howard Society of Canada, 874
The John Howard Society of Manitoba, 874
The John Howard Society of New Brunswick, Inc., 874
The John Howard Society of Newfoundland & Labrador, 874
The John Howard Society of Northwest Territories, 874
The John Howard Society of Nova Scotia, 874
The John Howard Society of Ontario, 874
The John Howard Society of Prince Edward Island, 875
The John Howard Society of Saskatchewan, 875
M2/W2 Association - Restorative Christian Ministries, 923
Ontario Halfway House Association, 1083
Operation Springboard, 1116
Prairie Region Halfway House Association, 1169
Prison Fellowship Canada, 1180
Prisoners' HIV/AIDS Support Action Network, 1180
Regional Halfway House Association, 1212
St. Leonard's Society of Canada, 1250
Seventh Step Society of Canada, 1292
William W. Creighton Youth Services, 1455

Office Employees
International Association of Administrative Professionals, 1537
Office & Professional Employees International Union (AFL-CIO/CLC), 1580

Oil
The American Association of Petroleum Geologists, 1490
Association pétrolière et gazière du Québec, 165
L'association québécoise des fournisseurs de services pétroliers et gaziers du Québec, 172
Association québécoise du chauffage au mazout, 175
Canada - Newfoundland & Labrador Offshore Petroleum Board, 277
Canada - Nova Scotia Offshore Petroleum Board, 278
Canada's Oil Sands Innovation Alliance, 282
Canadian Association of Drilling Engineers, 312
Canadian Association of Oilwell Drilling Contractors, 324
Canadian Association of Petroleum Land Administration, 325
Canadian Association of Petroleum Landmen, 326
Canadian Association of Petroleum Producers, 326
Canadian Energy Law Foundation, 381
Canadian Fuels Association, 395
Canadian Heavy Oil Association, 403
Canadian Institute of Mining, Metallurgy & Petroleum, 417
Canadian Oil Heat Association, 445
Canadian Society of Petroleum Geologists, 486
Enform, 688
Explorers & Producers Association of Canada, 700
Noia, 1027
NORA, An Association of Responsible Recyclers, 1578
Ontario Petroleum Institute Inc., 1095
Orphan Well Association, 1127
Petroleum Accountants Society of Canada, 1154
Petroleum Research Newfoundland & Labrador, 1154
Petroleum Services Association of Canada, 1154
Petroleum Tank Management Association of Alberta, 1154
Petroleum Technology Alliance Canada, 1154
Petrolia Discovery, 1155
Professional Petroleum Data Management Association, 1186
Society of Petroleum Engineers, 1593
World Petroleum Council, 1607

Olympic Games
B2ten, 192
Canadian Olympic Committee, 445
Pan American Sports Organization, 1582
WinSport Canada, 1460

Ombudsman
General Insurance OmbudService, 769
International Ombudsman Institute, 1554
OmbudService for Life & Health Insurance, 1057
Ombudsman for Banking Services & Investments, 1057

Oncology
American Society of Pediatric Hematology / Oncology, 1502
Association des radio-oncologues du Québec, 127
Canadian Association of Medical Oncologists, 320
Canadian Association of Nurses in Oncology, 323
Canadian Association of Pharmacy in Oncology, 326
Canadian Association of Psychosocial Oncology, 330
Canadian Association of Radiation Oncology, 330
Canadian Oncology Societies, 446
Canadian Society for Surgical Oncology, 477
Canadian Urologic Oncology Group, 500
European Society of Gynaecological Oncology, 1524
Society of Gynecologic Oncologists of Canada, 1329

Opera
Calgary Opera Association, 273
Canadian Children's Opera Company, 356
Canadian Opera Company, 446
Chants Libres, compagnie lyrique de création, 551
Edmonton Opera Association, 678
Manitoba Opera Association Inc., 941
Modern Baroque Opera Society, 971
Opera America Inc., 1580
Opéra Atelier, 1114
L'Opéra de Montréal, 1114
Opéra de Québec, 1115
Opera.ca, 1115
Pacific Opera Victoria, 1135
The Queen of Puddings Music Theatre Company, 1199
Soundstreams Canada, 1333
Vancouver Opera, 1428
Western Canadian Opera Society, 1449

Ophthalmology
Association des médecins ophtalmologistes du Québec, 120
Canadian Ophthalmological Society, 446
Canadian Retina Society, 467
Canadian Society of Ophthalmic Registered Nurses, 485
International Council of Ophthalmology, 1545
Saskatchewan College of Opticians, 1261

Opticians
College of Opticians of Alberta, 587
College of Opticians of British Columbia, 587
College of Opticians of Ontario, 587
Ontario Opticians Association, 1094
Opticians Association of Canada, 1116
Opticians Association of New Brunswick, 1116
Opticians of Manitoba, 1116
Ordre des opticiens d'ordonnances du Québec, 1123

Optics
Institut national d'optique, 843
Structural Innovation & Monitoring Technologies Resources Centre, 1352

Optometry
Alberta Association of Optometrists, 24
Alberta College of Optometrists, 29
American Optometric Association, 1496
Association des optométristes du Québec, 121
British Columbia Doctors of Optometry, 239
Canadian Association of Optometrists, 324
Canadian Examiners in Optometry, 383
College of Optometrists of BC, 587
College of Optometrists of Ontario, 587
Manitoba Association of Optometrists, 930
National Association of Canadian Optician Regulators, 989
New Brunswick Association of Optometrists, 1005
Newfoundland & Labrador Association of Optometrists, 1016
Nova Scotia Association of Optometrists, 1041
Ontario Association of Optometrists, 1065
Opticians of Manitoba, 1116
Ordre des optométristes du Québec, 1123
Prince Edward Island Association of Optometrists, 1172
Saskatchewan Association of Optometrists, 1257

Oral Surgeons
Canadian Association of Oral & Maxillofacial Surgeons, 324
College of Dental Surgeons of British Columbia, 583
College of Dental Surgeons of Saskatchewan, 583
Ontario Association of Dental Specialists, 1063
Royal College of Dental Surgeons of Ontario, 1241

Orchestras
Association des orchestres de jeunes de la Montérégie, 121
Association des orchestres de jeunes du Québec inc., 121
Banda de nossa Senhora dos Milagres, 195
Brandon University School of Music, 226
Brantford Symphony Orchestra Association Inc., 227
Calgary Philharmonic Society, 273
Calgary Youth Orchestra, 275
Canadian Sinfonietta Youth Orchestra, 470
Cathedral Bluffs Symphony Orchestra, 517
Chebucto Symphony Orchestra, 555
Chilliwack Symphony Orchestra & Chorus, 563
Counterpoint Community Orchestra, 636
Crowsnest Pass Symphony, 645
Deep River Symphony Orchestra, 652
Dundas Valley Orchestra, 664
Durham Chamber Orchestra, 665
Durham Youth Orchestra, 665
Edmonton Symphony Orchestra, 679
Edmonton Youth Orchestra Association, 679
Ensemble contemporain de Montréal, 690
Esprit Orchestra, 695
Etobicoke Philharmonic Orchestra, 697
Filarmónica Portuguesa de Montreal, 735
Fraser Valley Symphony Society, 758
Georgian Bay Symphony, 771
Greater Victoria Youth Orchestra, 787
Guelph Symphony Orchestra, 793
Halton Mississauga Youth Orchestra, 800
Hamilton Philharmonic Orchestra, 801
Hamilton Philharmonic Youth Orchestra, 801
Hart House Orchestra, 804
Huronia Symphony Orchestra, 828
International Symphony Orchestra of Sarnia, Ontario & Port Huron, Michigan, 861
International Symphony Orchestra Youth String Ensemble, 861
La Jeunesse Youth Orchestra, 870
Kamloops Symphony, 880
Kingston Symphony Association, 889
Kingston Youth Orchestra, 890
Kitchener-Waterloo Chamber Orchestra, 890
Kitchener-Waterloo Symphony Orchestra Association Inc., 891
Kitchener-Waterloo Symphony Youth Orchestra, 891
Korean-Canadian Symphony Orchestra, 894
Lethbridge Symphony Orchestra, 908
London Community Orchestra, 918
London Youth Symphony, 919
Mooredale Youth Concert Orchestra, 973
National Academy Orchestra, 989
National Arts Centre Orchestra of Canada, 989
National Youth Orchestra Canada, 997
Newfoundland Symphony Orchestra Association, 1023
Newfoundland Symphony Youth Orchestra, 1023
Niagara Youth Orchestra Association, 1026
Northumberland Orchestra Society, 1036
Nova Scotia Youth Orchestra, 1050
Oakville Symphony Orchestra, 1053
Okanagan Symphony Society, 1056
Ontario Philharmonic, 1095
Orchestra Toronto, 1117
Orchestras Canada, 1117
Orchestras Mississauga, 1117
Orchestre de chambre de Montréal, 1117
Orchestre Métropolitain, 1118
Orchestre symphonique de Laval, 1118
Orchestre symphonique de Longueuil, 1118
Orchestre symphonique de Montréal, 1118
Orchestre symphonique de Québec, 1118
Orchestre symphonique de Sherbrooke, 1118
Orchestre symphonique de Trois-Rivières, 1118
Orchestre symphonique des jeunes de Montréal, 1118
Orchestre symphonique des jeunes de Sherbrooke, 1118
Orchestre symphonique des jeunes du West Island, 1118
Orchestre symphonique des jeunes Philippe-Filion, 1118
Orchestre symphonique du Saguenay-Lac-St-Jean, 1119
Orchestre symphonique régional Abitibi-Témiscamingue, 1119
Orillia Youth Symphony Orchestra, 1126
Ottawa Chamber Orchestra, 1129
Ottawa Symphony Orchestra Inc., 1132
Ottawa Youth Orchestra Academy, 1132
Pembroke Symphony Orchestra, 1149
Peterborough Symphony Orchestra, 1154
Prince Edward Island Symphony Society, 1178
Prince George Symphony Orchestra Society, 1179
Quinte Symphony, 1201
Red Deer Symphony Orchestra, 1209
Regina Symphony Orchestra, 1212
Richmond Delta Youth Orchestra, 1230
Richmond Orchestra & Chorus Association, 1231
Royal Conservatory Orchestra, 1242
Saskatchewan Orchestral Association, Inc., 1270
Saskatoon Symphony Society, 1280

Subject Index / Parents

Saskatoon Youth Orchestra, 1280
Sault Symphony Association, 1281
Scarborough Philharmonic Orchestra, 1282
Sooke Philharmonic Society, 1333
Soundstreams Canada, 1333
South Saskatchewan Youth Orchestra, 1336
Sudbury Symphony Orchestra Association Inc., 1353
Sudbury Youth Orchestra Inc., 1353
Surrey Symphony Society, 1357
Symphony New Brunswick, 1360
Symphony Nova Scotia, 1360
Symphony on the Bay, 1360
Tafelmusik Baroque Orchestra & Chamber Choir, 1366
Thunder Bay Symphony Orchestra Association, 1378
Timmins Symphony Orchestra, 1380
Toronto Sinfonietta, 1387
Toronto Symphony Orchestra, 1387
Toronto Symphony Youth Orchestra, 1387
University of British Columbia Symphony Orchestra, 1419
University of Toronto Symphony Orchestra, 1421
University of Western Ontario Symphony Orchestra, 1421
Vancouver Island Symphony, 1427
Vancouver Philharmonic Orchestra, 1428
Vancouver Symphony Society, 1429
Vancouver Youth Symphony Orchestra Society, 1429
Victoria Symphony Society, 1433
Wilfrid Laurier University Symphony Orchestra, 1455
Windsor Symphony Orchestra, 1457
Winnipeg Symphony Orchestra Inc., 1459
Winnipeg Youth Orchestras, 1459
York Symphony Orchestra Inc., 1474

Orchids
Central Ontario Orchid Society, 525
Central Vancouver Island Orchid Society, 525
Eastern Canada Orchid Society, 670
Essex County Orchid Society, 696
Foothills Orchid Society, 751
Frasier Valley Orchid Society, 758
Kingston Orchid Society, 889
London Orchid Society, 918
Manitoba Orchid Society, 941
Native Orchid Conservation Inc., 998
Niagara Region Orchid Society, 1025
Okanagan Orchid Society, 1056
Orchid Society of Alberta, 1119
Orchid Society of Nova Scotia, 1119
Orchid Society of Royal Botanical Gardens, 1119
Orchidophiles de Québec, 1119
Ottawa Orchid Society, 1131
Regina Orchid Society, 1212
Richmond Orchid Club, 1231
Saskatchewan Orchid Society, 1270
Société des orchidophiles de Montréal, 1318
Southern Ontario Orchid Society, 1338
Victoria Orchid Society, 1433
Windsor Orchid Society, 1457

Organ Retrieval & Donation
British Columbia Transplant Society, 257
Canadian Association of Transplantation, 334
Canadian Blood & Marrow Transplant Group, 344
Canadian Liver Foundation, 427
Canadian Transplant Association, 496
David Foster Foundation, 651
Fondation Diane Hébert Inc, 745
Trillium Gift of Life Network, 1398

Organic Farming & Gardening
Alberta Organic Producers Association, 41
Atlantic Canadian Organic Regional Network, 183
Bio-dynamic Agricultural Society of British Columbia, 211
Boundary Organic Producers Association, 219
British Columbia Association for Regenerative Agriculture, 231
Canada Organic Trade Association, 280
Canadian Organic Growers Inc., 446
Certified Organic Associations of British Columbia, 538
Ecological Agriculture Projects, 672

Ecological Farmers of Ontario, 672
International Federation of Organic Agriculture Movements, 1548
International Organic Inspectors Association, 1554
International WWOOF Association, 1567
Islands Organic Producers Association, 866
North Okanagan Organic Association, 1031
Northeast Organic Farming Association, 1580
Organic Crop Improvement Association - New Brunswick, 1125
Organic Crop Improvement Association (International), 1580
Organic Producers Association of Manitoba Co-operative Inc., 1125
Organic Trade Association, 1581
Prince Edward Island Certified Organic Producers Co-op, 1173
Similkameen Okanagan Organic Producers Association, 1300
Society for Organic Urban Land Care, 1326
Table de développement de la production biologique, 1365
Wallace Center, Winrock International, 1601
WWOOF Canada, 1469

Organists
LAUDEM, L'Association des musiciens liturgiques du Canada, 900

Organizers
Professional Organizers in Canada, 1186

Orienteering
Alberta Orienteering Association, 41
Canadian Orienteering Federation, 447
International Orienteering Federation, 1554
Manitoba Orienteering Association Inc., 941
Orienteering Association of British Columbia, 1126
Orienteering Association of Nova Scotia, 1126
Orienteering New Brunswick, 1126
Orienteering Ontario Inc., 1126
Orienteering Québec, 1126
Yukon Orienteering Association, 1479

Orthodox Church
The Antiochan Orthodox Christian Archdiocese of North America, 1505
British Israel World Federation (Canada) Inc., 259
The Coptic Orthodox Church (Canada), 628
Greek Orthodox Metropolis of Toronto (Canada), 788
Orthodox Church in America Archdiocese of Canada, 1127
Romanian Orthodox Deanery of Canada, 1235
Russian Orthodox Church in Canada, 1244
Serbian Orthodox Church - Orthodox Diocese of Canada, 1290
Ukrainian Orthodox Church of Canada, 1403
Ukrainian Self-Reliance League of Canada, 1403
Ukrainian Women's Association of Canada, 1403
World Fellowship of Orthodox Youth, 1605

Orthopaedics
Association d'orthopédie du Québec, 99
Association of Children's Prosthetic-Orthotic Clinics, 1510
Canadian Orthopaedic Association, 448
Canadian Orthopaedic Foundation, 448
Canadian Orthopaedic Nurses Association, 448
Canadian Orthopaedic Residents Association, 448
Canadian Society of Orthopaedic Technologists, 485
Orthotics Prosthetics Canada, 1127

Orthoptics
Canadian Federation of Orthotherapists, 388
Canadian Orthoptic Council, 448
International Orthoptic Association, 1554

Osteopathy
Prairie Osteopathic Association, 1169

Osteoporosis
Osteoporosis Canada, 1128

Otolaryngology
Canadian Society of Otolaryngology - Head & Neck Surgery, 485

Ozone Layer Depletion
Climate Institute, 1517

Pacific Islands
Pacific Peoples' Partnership, 1135

Packaging
Association of Independent Corrugated Converters, 149
Association of Postconsumer Plastic Recyclers, 1513
Canadian Corrugated Containerboard Association, 366
EPS Industry Alliance, 1524
Foodservice & Packaging Institute, 1526
Institute of Packaging Professionals, 1533
Packaging Association of Canada, 1136
Paper & Paperboard Packaging Environmental Council, 1138
Paperboard Packaging Council, 1582
Plastics Foodservice Packaging Group, 1584
World Packaging Organization, 1607

Pain
American Society of Regional Anesthesia & Pain Medicine, 1502
Association de la fibromyalgie région Ile-De-Montréal, 101
Canadian Institute for the Relief of Pain & Disability, 413
Canadian Pain Society, 449
Chronic Pain Association of Canada, 568
Institute for the Study & Treatment of Pain, 844
International Association for the Study of Pain, 1537
Pain Society of Alberta, 1137

Paint
British Columbia Paint Manufacturers' Association, 248
Canadian Paint & Coatings Association, 449

Painting & Decorating
Association nationale des peintres - locale 99, 138
Association québécoise de l'industrie de la peinture, 170
International Union of Painters & Allied Trades, 1565
International Watercolour Society - Canada, 861
Manitoba Professional Painting Contractors Association, 942
Master Painters & Decorators Association, 954
Ontario Painting Contractors Association, 1094

Pakistani Canadians
Canada-Pakistan Association of the National Capital Region, 283
Pakistan Canada Association of Calgary, 1137
Pakistan Canada Association of Edmonton, 1137
Pakistani Canadian Cultural Association of British Columbia, 1137

Paleontology
British Columbia Paleontological Alliance, 248
Burgess Shale Geoscience Foundation, 265
Niagara Peninsula Geological Society, 1025
Oxford County Geological Society, 1134
Vancouver Paleontological Society, 1428

Palliative Care
Alberta Hospice Palliative Care Association, 38
Association québécoise de soins palliatifs, 171
Canadian Hospice Palliative Care Association, 409
Canadian Society of Palliative Care Physicians, 486
Council on Palliative Care, 636
Hospice of Waterloo Region, 822
Hospice Palliative Care Association of Prince Edward Island, 823
Hospice Palliative Care Ontario, 823
New Brunswick Hospice Palliative Care Association, 1009
Newfoundland & Labrador Palliative Care Association, 1020
North Shore Hospice Society, 1032
Nova Scotia Hospice Palliative Care Association, 1046
Saskatchewan Palliative Care Association, 1271

Palmistry
International Society for Research in Palmistry Inc., 860

Palynology
Canadian Association of Palynologists, 325

Parachuting
Alberta Sport Parachuting Association, 48
Canadian Sport Parachuting Association, 490
Manitoba Sport Parachute Association, 945
Sport Parachute Association of Saskatchewan, 1345

Paralysis
Association canadienne des ataxies familiales, 92
Canadian Spinal Research Organization, 489
Fondation de l'Ataxie Charlevoix-Saguenay, 743

Paraplegia
Ability New Brunswick, 1
Canadian Paraplegic Association (Manitoba), 449
Canadian Paraplegic Association (Nova Scotia), 450
Manitoba Paraplegia Foundation Inc., 942
Moelle Épinière et Motricité Québec, 971
Spinal Cord Injury (Prince Edward Island), 1342
Spinal Cord Injury Alberta, 1342
Spinal Cord Injury British Columbia, 1343
Spinal Cord Injury Canada, 1343
Spinal Cord Injury Newfoundland & Labrador, 1343
Spinal Cord Injury Ontario, 1343
Spinal Cord Injury Saskatchewan, 1344

Parents
Active Parenting Canada, 7
Association Carrefour Famille Montcalm, 96
Association de Parents de Jumeaux et de Triplés de la région de Montréal, 103
Association des familles monoparentales et recomposées de l'Outaouais, 113
Association des parents ayants droit de Yellowknife, 121
Association des parents catholiques du Québec, 121
Association des parents d'enfants handicapés du Témiscamingue inc., 122
Association des parents et amis de la personne atteinte de maladie mentale Rive-Sud, 122
Association des parents fransaskois, 122
Association francophone des parents du Nouveau-Brunswick, 135
Association of Parent Support Groups in Ontario Inc., 155
Association québécoise des parents d'enfants handicapés visuels, 173
Block Parent Program of Canada, 214
Block Watch Society of British Columbia, 215
Bridges Family Programs Association, 228
British Columbia Federation of Foster Parent Associations, 240
Canadian Parents for French, 450
Commission nationale des parents francophones, 593
Council of Parent Participation Preschools in British Columbia, 635
Fédération des comités de parents du Québec inc., 713
Fédération des parents acadiens de la Nouvelle-Écosse, 716
Fédération des parents de l'Ile-du-Prince-Édouard, 716
Fédération des parents du Manitoba, 716
Fédération des parents francophones de Colombie-Britannique, 716
Fédération des parents francophones de l'Alberta, 717
Fédération des parents francophones de Terre-Neuve et du Labrador, 717
Foster Parent Support Services Society, 755
Helping Other Parents Everywhere Inc., 812
Kids First Parent Association of Canada, 886
Maison de la famille de la Vallée du Richelieu, 926
Mouvement Retrouvailles, 978
Multiple Birth Families Association, 979
Ontario Federation of Teaching Parents, 1080
Parent Action on Drugs, 1139
Parent Finders Ottawa, 1139
Parent Support Services Society of BC, 1139

Subject Index / Parkinson's

Parents as First Educators, 1140
Parents for Children's Mental Health, 1140
Parents Without Partners Inc., 1582
Parents, Families & Friends of Lesbians & Gays, 1582
Parents-secours du Québec inc., 1140
People for Education, 1151
Pilot Parents, 1160
Regroupement de parents de personnes ayant une déficience intellectuelle de Montréal, 1214
St. Albert Family Resource Centre, 1247
Toronto Parents of Multiple Births Association, 1386
Twins, Triplets & More Association of Calgary, 1400

Parkinson's
Parkinson Alberta Society, 1141
Parkinson Canada, 1141
Parkinson Society British Columbia, 1141
Parkinson Society Central & Northern Ontario, 1141
Parkinson Society Manitoba, 1141
Parkinson Society Maritime Region, 1141
Parkinson Society Newfoundland & Labrador, 1141
Parkinson Society of Eastern Ontario, 1141
Parkinson Society Saskatchewan, 1141
Parkinson Society Southwestern Ontario, 1142
Société Parkinson du Québec, 1322
Victoria Epilepsy & Parkinson's Centre Society, 1432

Parks
Alberta Recreation & Parks Association, 44
Association des jardins du Québec, 117
Association for Mountain Parks Protection & Enjoyment, 134
British Columbia Recreation & Parks Association, 250
Canada's Accredited Zoos & Aquariums, 281
Canadian Parks & Recreation Association, 450
Canadian Parks & Wilderness Society, 450
Conservation Ontario, 622
The Friends of Algonquin Park, 760
The Friends of Awenda Park, 760
The Friends of Bon Echo Park, 760
The Friends of Bonnechere Parks, 760
The Friends of Charleston Lake Park, 760
Friends of Ferris Provincial Park, 761
The Friends of Frontenac Park, 761
The Friends of Killarney Park, 761
The Friends of MacGregor Point, 761
Friends of Mashkinonje Park, 761
The Friends of Nancy Island Historic Site & Wasaga Beach Park, 761
The Friends of Pinery Park, 761
The Friends of Presqu'ile Park, 761
The Friends of Rondeau Park, 762
The Friends of Sandbanks Park, 762
Friends of Short Hills Park, 762
The Friends of Sleeping Giant, 762
Jasper Environmental Association, 869
National Parks Conservation Association, 1577
Niijkiwenhwag - Friends of Lake Superior Park, 1027
Okanagan Similkameen Parks Society, 1056
Ontario Parks Association, 1095
Park People, 1140
Parks & Recreation Ontario, 1142
Protected Areas Association of Newfoundland & Labrador, 1190
Quetico Foundation, 1201
Recreation & Parks Association of the Yukon, 1207
Recreation New Brunswick, 1207
Recreation Newfoundland & Labrador, 1207
Saskatchewan Parks & Recreation Association, 1271
Sheridan Park Association, 1296

Parliament
Assemblée parlementaire de la Francophonie (Section canadienne), 88
Canadian Association of Former Parliamentarians, 315
Commonwealth Parliamentary Association, 1518
House of Commons Security Services Employees Association, 824
Inter-Parliamentary Union, 1567

Ontario Association of Former Parliamentarians, 1064
Parliamentary Centre, 1142

Pastoral Counselling
Association des psychothérapeutes pastoraux du Canada, 126

Patents
Intellectual Property Institute of Canada, 850
International Trademark Association, 1563

Pathology
Association des pathologistes du Québec, 122
Canadian Association of Pathologists, 325
Ontario Association of Pathologists, 1065
World Association of Societies of Pathology and Laboratory Medicine, 1465

Patient Care
Canadian Association of Ambulatory Care, 308
Kidney Cancer Canada Association, 884
Patients Canada, 1145

Patient Safety
Canadian Patient Safety Institute, 452
Kidney Cancer Canada Association, 884
Patients Canada, 1145

Patients' Rights
Concerned Friends of Ontario Citizens in Care Facilities, 609
Kidney Cancer Canada Association, 884
Patients Canada, 1145

Pay Equity
Nova Scotia League for Equal Opportunities, 1046

Peace
ACT for the Earth, 5
The Barnard-Boecker Centre Foundation, 196
British Columbia Teachers for Peace & Global Education, 256
Burlington Association for Nuclear Disarmament, 265
Canadian Friends of Peace Now (Shalom Achshav), 395
Canadian Peace Alliance, 452
Canadian Peacekeeping Veterans Association, 452
Christian Peace Conference, 1517
Coalition to Oppose the Arms Trade, 579
Concerned Educators Allied for a Safe Environment, 1519
Development & Peace, 654
Fellowship of Reconciliation, 1526
Group of 78, 791
Institute for Planetary Synthesis, 1532
International Association of Educators for World Peace - USA, 1538
International Peace Bureau, 1555
Mahatma Gandhi Canadian Foundation for World Peace, 925
The Marquis Project, Inc., 952
Mosaic Institute, 975
Oakville Community Centre for Peace, Ecology & Human Rights, 1053
Parliamentarians for Global Action, 1582
Peace & Environment Resource Centre, 1146
Peace & Justice Studies Association, 1583
Peace Brigades International (Canada), 1146
Peacebuild: The Canadian Peacebuilding Network, 1147
Physicians for Global Survival (Canada), 1158
Pragmora, 1169
Project Peacemakers, 1187
Project Ploughshares, 1188
Regina Peace Council, 1212
Religions for Peace, 1586
Science for Peace, 1285
Victoria Peace Coalition, 1433
Women's International League for Peace & Freedom, 1462
World Federalist Movement, 1605
World Federalist Movement - Canada, 1465

Peat
Canadian Sphagnum Peat Moss Association, 489
International Peat Society, 1555
International Peat Society - Canadian National Committee, 859

Pelvic Inflammatory Disease
Endometriosis Association, Inc., 1523

Pensions & Benefits
Armed Forces Pensioners'/Annuitants' Association of Canada, 82
Association des avocats et avocates représentant les bénéficiaires des régimes d'indemnisation publics, 107
Association of Canadian Pension Management, 143
Athletes International, 180
Canadian Alliance of British Pensioners, 291
Canadian Association of Pension Supervisory Authorities, 325
Canadian Federation of Pensioners, 388
Canadian Institute of Actuaries, 414
Canadian Pension & Benefits Institute, 453
Congress of Union Retirees Canada, 613
International Pension & Employee Benefits Lawyers Association, 859
Municipal Pension Retirees Association, 981
National Association of Federal Retirees, 990
National Pensioners Federation, 995
Patronato INAS (Canada), 1145
Pension Investment Association of Canada, 1150

Pentathlon
Ontario Modern Pentathalon Association, 1091
Pentathlon Alberta, 1150
Pentathlon Canada, 1150

Pentecostal Assemblies
Independent Assemblies of God International - Canada, 832
Pentecostal Assemblies of Canada, 1150
The Pentecostal Assemblies of Newfoundland & Labrador, 1150

Performing Arts
ACTRA Fraternal Benefit Society, 7
Alberta Music Festival Association, 41
Alliance of Canadian Cinema, Television & Radio Artists, 58
American Society for Theatre Research, 1499
Associated Designers of Canada, 89
Associated Manitoba Arts Festivals, Inc., 89
Association for Native Development in the Performing & Visual Arts, 134
Association québécoise des marionnettistes, 173
Banff Centre for Arts & Creativity, 195
BC Alliance for Arts & Culture, 200
Bowen Island Arts Council, 219
British Columbia Drama Association, 239
Calgary Stetson Show Band, 274
Canadian Arts Presenting Association, 296
Canadian Association for the Advancement of Music & the Arts, 305
Canadian Society of Children's Authors, Illustrators & Performers, 481
Canadians Concerned About Violence in Entertainment, 506
Centre culturel canadien, 1516
Children's Arts Umbrella Association, 561
Community Folk Art Council of Toronto, 597
Dance Manitoba Inc., 649
Dance Nova Scotia, 649
Dance Ontario Association, 649
Dancemakers, 649
EDAM Performing Arts Society, 674
Fédération des loisirs-danse du Québec, 715
Federation of Music Festivals of Nova Scotia, 725
Footprints Dance Project Society of Alberta, 751
Governor General's Performing Arts Awards Foundation, 778
Guelph Musicfest, 793
The Guild Society, 794
Intrepid Theatre Co. Society, 862
Kingston Kiwanis Music Festival, 889
Melville Dance Association, 960
National Arts Centre Foundation, 989
New Brunswick Arts Board, 1004
New Brunswick Federation of Music Festivals Inc., 1008
Newfoundland Federation of Music Festivals, 1023
O Vertigo Danse, 1052
Ontario Music Festivals Association, 1093
Open Space Arts Society, 1114

Palais Montcalm, 1137
Performing Arts BC, 1152
Prologue to the Performing Arts, 1188
Québec Competitive Festival of Music, 1196
Saskatchewan Music Festival Association Inc., 1270
Theatre Nova Scotia, 1374
Theatre Saskatchewan, 1375
Toronto Alliance for the Performing Arts, 1381
Union des artistes, 1406
Yukon Arts Centre, 1477

Perfumes
Canadian Cosmetic, Toiletry & Fragrance Association, 366

Periodicals & Magazines
Alberta Magazine Publishers Association, 39
Association québécoise des éditeurs de magazines, 172
Book & Periodical Council, 218
Magazines Canada, 925
National Magazine Awards Foundation, 994
Periodical Marketers of Canada, 1152
Société de développement des périodiques culturels québécois, 1314
Unifor87-M, 1405

Permafrost
International Permafrost Association, 1555

Personal Development
Heartwood Centre for Community Youth Development, 810
Open Learning at Thompson Rivers University, 1114
Society for Personal Growth, 1326

Pest Management
Association québécoise de la gestion parasitaire, 170
Atlantic Pest Management Association, 184
Beyond Pesticides, 1514
Canadian Pest Management Association, 453
CropLife Canada, 643
Croplife International, 1520
Integrated Vegetation Management Association of British Columbia, 850
Manitoba Pest Management Association, 942
Northwest Coalition for Alternatives to Pesticides, 1580
Ontario Vegetation Management Association, 1112
Pest Management Association of Alberta, 1152
Pesticide Action Network North America, 1583
Pesticide Education Network, 1153
Société de protection des forêts contre les insectes et maladies, 1317
Structural Pest Management Association of British Columbia, 1352
Structural Pest Management Association of Ontario, 1352
Weed Science Society of America, 1602

Pet Industry
Pet Food Association of Canada, 1153
PIJAC Canada, 1159

Petroleum Law
Canadian Energy Law Foundation, 381

Pets
Animal Aid Foundation, 70
Greyhound Pets of Atlantic Canada Society, 790
Ontario Cavy Club, 1070
Pet Industry Joint Advisory Council, 1153
Pet Therapy Society of Northern Alberta, 1153
Responsible Dog Owners of Canada, 1227

Pharmaceuticals
Canada's Medical Technology Companies, 282
Canadian Association for Pharmacy Distribution Management, 303
Canadian Association of Professional Regulatory Affairs, 329
Canadian Foundation for Drug Policy, 393
Canadian Generic Pharmaceutical Association, 397
Canadian Harm Reduction Network, 401
Canadian Society for Pharmaceutical Sciences, 477
College of Pharmacists of Manitoba, 587
Commonwealth Pharmacists Association, 1518

Consumer Health Products Canada, 626
Council for Continuing Pharmaceutical Education, 632
Innovative Medicines Canada, 839
New Brunswick Pharmaceutical Society, 1011
Pharmaceutical Advertising Advisory Board, 1156
Saskatchewan College of Pharmacists, 1261

Pharmacists
Alberta College of Pharmacists, 30
Alberta Pharmacists' Association (RxA), 42
Association des pharmaciens des établissements de santé du Québec, 123
Association professionnelle des pharmaciens salariés du Québec, 167
British Columbia Pharmacy Association, 248
Canadian Society of Consultant Pharmacists, 482
Canadian Society of Hospital Pharmacists, 483
College of Pharmacists of British Columbia, 587
New Brunswick Pharmacists' Association, 1011
Newfoundland & Labrador Pharmacy Board, 1021
Nova Scotia College of Pharmacists, 1042
Ontario College of Pharmacists, 1072
Ontario Pharmacists' Association, 1095
Ordre des pharmaciens du Québec, 1123
Pharmacists' Association of Newfoundland & Labrador, 1156
Pharmacists' Association of Saskatchewan, Inc., 1156
Pharmacy Association of Nova Scotia, 1157
Prince Edward Island Pharmacists Association, 1176

Pharmacology
Canadian College of Neuropsychopharmacology, 360
Canadian Society of Pharmacology & Therapeutics, 486
Institute of Health Economics, 846
International Union of Basic & Clinical Pharmacology, 1564

Pharmacy
Alberta Pharmacists' Association (RxA), 42
Association des conseils des médecins, dentistes et pharmaciens du Québec, 109
Association of Faculties of Pharmacy of Canada, 148
Association québécoise des pharmaciens propriétaires, 174
Canadian Academy of the History of Pharmacy, 287
Canadian Association of Pharmacy in Oncology, 326
Canadian Association of Pharmacy Students & Interns, 326
Canadian Association of Pharmacy Technicians, 326
The Canadian Council for Accreditation of Pharmacy Programs, 366
The Canadian Council on Continuing Education in Pharmacy, 371
Canadian Foundation for Pharmacy, 393
Canadian Pharmacists Association, 453
Manitoba Society of Pharmacists Inc., 945
National Association of Pharmacy Regulatory Authorities, 990
Neighbourhood Pharmacy Association of Canada, 1002
Newfoundland & Labrador Pharmacy Board, 1021
Pharmacists' Association of Newfoundland & Labrador, 1156
Pharmacists' Association of Saskatchewan, Inc., 1156
Pharmacy Association of Nova Scotia, 1157
The Pharmacy Examining Board of Canada, 1157
Pharmacy Technician Society of Alberta, 1157
Prince Edward Island Pharmacists Association, 1176
Prince Edward Island Pharmacy Board, 1176

Philanthropy
Asper Foundation, 87
Association des professionnels en gestion philanthropique, 126
Association for Healthcare Philanthropy, 1508
Azrieli Foundation, 191

Canadian Association of Gift Planners, 317
Imagine Canada, 829
Toronto Community Foundation, 1383
Uncles & Aunts at Large, 1404

Philately
Association des Numismates et des Philatélistes de Boucherville, 121
Bramalea Stamp Club, 225
Brantford Stamp Club, 227
British Columbia Philatelic Society, 248
British North America Philatelic Society Ltd., 259
Calgary Philatelic Society, 273
Canadian Aerophilatelic Society, 289
Canadian Association for Israel Philately, 301
Canadian Meter Study Group, 436
The Canadian Philatelic Society of Great Britain, 1515
Canadian Stamp Dealers' Association, 490
Club timbres et monnaies de Sorel inc., 576
Edmonton Stamp Club, 679
Essex County Stamp Club (Windsor), 696
Fédération québécoise de philatélie, 728
Fenelon Falls Stamp Club, 732
Fundy Stamp Collectors Club, 764
Greater Victoria Philatelic Society, 787
Grey, Bruce, Dufferin, & Simcoe Postal History Study Group, 790
Hamilton Stamp Club, 802
International Machine Cancel Research Society of Canada, 858
Kelowna & District Stamp Club, 883
Kent County Stamp Club, 884
Kingston Stamp Club, 889
Kitchener-Waterloo Philatelic Society, 891
Lakehead Stamp Club, 896
Lakeshore Stamp Club Inc., 897
London Philatelic Society, 918
Mississauga-Etobicoke Coin Stamp & Collectibles Club, 970
North Bay & District Stamp Club, 1030
North Shore Stamp Club, 1033
Northern Canada Study Group, 1034
Nova Scotia Stamp Club, 1049
Ottawa Philatelic Society, 1131
Oxford Philatelic Society, 1134
Postal History Society of Canada, 1168
RA Stamp Club, 1202
Regina Philatelic Club, 1212
The Royal Philatelic Society of Canada, 1242
St Catharines Stamp Club, 1248
St. John's Philatelic Society, 1249
Société Philatelique de Québec, 1322
Sudbury Stamp Club, 1353
Union des philatélistes de Montréal, 1406
West Toronto Stamp Club, 1446
Winnipeg Philatelic Society, 1459

Philosophy
Association for Science & Reason, 134
Canadian Philosophical Association, 454
Canadian Philosophy of Education Society, 454
Canadian Society for the History & Philosophy of Science, 477
Canadian Society of Questers, 487
Canadian Theosophical Association, 494
La Compagnie des philosophes, 608
International Husserl & Phenomenological Research Society, 1550
Société de philosophie du Québec, 1316
Société internationale pour l'étude de la philosophie médiévale, 1589
Society for Classical Studies, 1589
Society for Existential & Phenomenological Theory & Culture, 1326
Society of Kabalarians of Canada, 1329

Photography
L'Association des artistes Baltes à Montréal, 106
Association longueuilloise des photographes amateurs, 137
Canadian Association for Photographic Art, 303
Canadian Association of Professional Image Creators, 328
Canadian Imaging Trade Association, 410
Club de photo de Boucherville, 575
Club de photographie L'Oeil qui voit de Saint-Hubert, 575
Club photo Évasion, 576

Echange Photographique Franco Canadien, 1522
Fédération Internationale de l'Art Photographique, 1525
International PhotoTherapy Association, 859
News Photographers Association of Canada, 1024
PAVED Arts, 1146
Photo Marketing Association International - Canada, 1157
Photographic Historical Society of Canada, 1157
Professional Photographers of Canada, 1186

Photonics
Canadian Photonic Industry Consortium, 454

Physical Education & Training
Canadian Association for the Advancement of Women & Sport & Physical Activity, 305
Canadian Council of University Physical Education & Kinesiology Administrators, 370
Fédération des éducateurs et éducatrices physiques enseignants du Québec, 714
Ontario Physical & Health Education Association, 1095
Physical & Health Education Canada, 1158
Physical & Health Educators of Manitoba, 1158
Physical Education in British Columbia, 1158
Provincial Fitness Unit of Alberta, 1191
Saskatchewan Physical Education Association, 1271

Physical Fitness
Active Healthy Kids Canada, 7
The Canadian Association of Fitness Professionals, 315
Canadian Fitness & Lifestyle Research Institute, 390
Canadian Society for Exercise Physiology, 475
Certified Professional Trainers Network, 538
Club cycliste de la Montérégie, 574
Club de marche de Québec, 574
Club de marche de Rimouski, 574
Club de marche moi mes souliers, 575
Club de plein air Les Aventuriers, 575
Coalition for Active Living, 578
Coop kayak des îles, 627
Cyclo-Nature, 647
Fitness New Brunswick, 740
Island Fitness Council, 865
Les Kilomaîtres de LaSalle, 887
Margaret Morris Method (Canada), 949
National Association of Physical Activity & Health, 990
Nordic Walking Nova Scotia, 1028
Oxygène, 1134
Physical & Health Education Canada, 1158
Physical Culture Association of Alberta, 1158
Provincial Fitness Unit of Alberta, 1191
Randonnées plein air du Québec, 1204
Randonneurs du Saguenay, 1204
The Recreation Association, 1207
Sentiers de l'estrie, 1290
Vert l'Aventure Plein Air, 1431
Vertes boisées du fjord, 1431

Physical Therapy
Canadian Alliance of Physiotherapy Regulators, 291
Canadian Physiotherapy Association, 454
Canadian Society of Hand Therapists, 483
College of Physical Therapists of British Columbia, 587
College of Physiotherapists of Manitoba, 588
College of Physiotherapists of Ontario, 589
Newfoundland & Labrador College of Physiotherapists, 1017
Northwest Territories & Nunavut Council of the Canadian Physiotherapy Association, 1037
Nova Scotia College of Physiotherapists, 1042
Ontario Physiotherapy Association, 1096
Ordre professionnel de la physiothérapie du Québec, 1124
Physiotherapy Alberta - College + Association, 1158
Physiotherapy Association of British Columbia, 1158
Physiotherapy Association of Yukon, 1159
Physiotherapy Education Accreditation Canada, 1159

Prince Edward Island College of Physiotherapists, 1173
Saskatchewan College of Physical Therapists, 1261
Saskatchewan Physiotherapy Association, 1272
World Confederation for Physical Therapy, 1604

Physicians
American College of Chest Physicians, 1491
Association des médecins cliniciens enseignants de Montréal, 119
Association des médecins omnipraticiens de Montréal, 119
Association of International Physicians & Surgeons of Ontario, 149
British Columbia Association of Laboratory Physicians, 232
British Columbia Naturopathic Association, 247
Calgary & Area Medical Staff Society, 270
Canadian Association of Bariatric Physicians & Surgeons, 308
Canadian Association of Physicians for the Environment, 327
Canadian Association of Physicians of Indian Heritage, 327
Canadian Association of Physicians with Disabilities, 327
Canadian Association of Staff Physician Recruiters, 333
Canadian Physicians for Life, 454
Canadian Post-MD Education Registry, 458
Canadian Society of Palliative Care Physicians, 486
Canadian Society of Physician Executives, 486
Collège des médecins du Québec, 582
College of Family Physicians of Canada, 584
College of Physicians & Surgeons of Alberta, 588
College of Physicians & Surgeons of British Columbia, 588
College of Physicians & Surgeons of Manitoba, 588
College of Physicians & Surgeons of New Brunswick, 588
College of Physicians & Surgeons of Newfoundland & Labrador, 588
College of Physicians & Surgeons of Ontario, 588
College of Physicians & Surgeons of Prince Edward Island, 588
College of Physicians & Surgeons of Saskatchewan, 588
Doctors of BC, 660
Doctors without Borders Canada, 660
Edmonton Zone Medical Staff Association, 680
Fédération des médecins omnipraticiens du Québec, 716
Foundation for Advancing Family Medicine of the College of Family Physicians of Canada, 755
Indigenous Physicians Association of Canada, 835
International Association of Physicians in Audiology, 1539
Israel Medical Association-Canadian Chapter, 866
Manitoba Association of Asian Physicians, 929
Médecins francophones du Canada, 957
Medical Women's International Association, 958
Ontario Medical Association, 1090
Physicians for a Smoke-Free Canada, 1158
Physicians Services Inc. Foundation, 1158
Professional Association of Internes & Residents of Newfoundland, 1182
Professional Association of Residents & Interns of Manitoba, 1182
Professional Association of Residents in the Maritime Provinces, 1182
Professional Association of Residents of Alberta, 1182
Professional Association of Residents of Ontario, 1182
Resident Doctors of British Columbia, 1226
The Royal College of Physicians & Surgeons of Canada, 1241
Society of Rural Physicians of Canada, 1330

Physics
Canadian Association of Physicists, 327
Canadian Organization of Medical Physicists, 447

Subject Index / Physiology

Ontario Association of Physics Teachers, 1065

Physiology
Canadian Association for Anatomy, Neurobiology, & Cell Biology, 297
Canadian Physiological Society, 454
Canadian Society for Exercise Physiology, 475
Human Anatomy & Physiology Society, 1530
Society of Toxicology of Canada, 1331

Piano Tuners
Piano Technicians Guild Inc., 1583

Pilots
Air Canada Pilots Association, 19
Air Line Pilots Association, International - Canada, 19
Association des Aviateurs et Pilotes de Brousse du Québec, 106
Canadian Owners & Pilots Association, 448
Lutheran Association of Missionaries & Pilots, 922
The Ninety-Nines Inc., 1578
Ontario Seaplane Association, 1103
Prince Edward Island Flying Association, 1174
Ultralight Pilots Association of Canada, 1404

Pipelines
Canadian Energy Pipeline Association, 381
Orphan Well Association, 1127
Pipe Line Contractors Association of Canada, 1160

Pipes
Canadian Concrete Pipe Association, 362
Corporation des maîtres mécaniciens en tuyauterie du Québec, 630
Corrugated Steel Pipe Institute, 631
Ontario Concrete Pipe Association, 1074
Ontario Pipe Trades Council, 1096
United Association of Journeymen & Apprentices of the Plumbing & Pipe Fitting Industry of the United States & Canada, 1599

Planetariums
H.R. MacMillan Space Centre Society, 824

Planning
Alberta Professional Planners Institute, 43
American Planning Association, 1496
Atlantic Planners Institute, 184
Canadian Association for Studies in Co-operation, 304
Canadian Association of Certified Planning Technicians, 310
Canadian Institute of Chartered Business Planners, 414
Canadian Institute of Planners, 418
Canadian Institutional Research & Planning Association, 420
Centre for Transportation Engineering & Planning, 534
Manitoba Professional Planners Institute, 942
Ontario Professional Planners Institute, 1098
Planning Institute of British Columbia, 1162
Retirement Planning Association of Canada, 1228
Strategic Leadership Forum, 1351

Plasterers
Operative Plasterers' & Cement Masons' International Association of the US & Canada (AFL-CIO/CFL) - Canadian Office, 1116

Plastic & Reconstructive Surgery
American Society for Aesthetic Plastic Surgery, 1497
American Society of Plastic Surgeons, 1502
Association des spécialistes en chirurgie plastique et esthétique du Québec, 128
Canadian Academy of Facial Plastic & Reconstructive Surgery, 286
The Canadian Laser and Aesthetic Specialists Society, 425
Canadian Society for Aesthetic Plastic Surgery, 472
Canadian Society of Plastic Surgeons, 487
International Confederation for Plastic Reconstructive & Aesthetic Surgery, 1543

Plastics
Alberta Plastics Recycling Association, 42
American Chemistry Council, 1491
Association of Postconsumer Plastic Recyclers, 1513
Bureau of International Recycling, 1515
Canadian Plastics Industry Association, 455
Kingston Independent Nylon Workers Union, 889
National Association for PET Container Resources, 1573
Plastic Loose Fill Council, 1584
Plastics Foodservice Packaging Group, 1584
Society of Plastics Engineers, 1593
SPI: The Plastics Industry Trade Association, 1596

Playwriting
Alberta Playwrights' Network, 42
Association québécoise des auteurs dramatiques, 171
Centre des auteurs dramatiques, 530
Manitoba Association of Playwrights, 931
Playwrights Guild of Canada, 1162
Playwrights Theatre Centre, 1162
Saskatchewan Playwrights Centre, 1272

Plowing
Canadian Plowing Organization, 456
Ontario Plowmen's Association, 1096
World Ploughing Organization, 1607

Plumbing
American Society of Plumbing Engineers, 1502
Canadian Institute of Plumbing & Heating, 418
Corporation des maîtres mécaniciens en tuyauterie du Québec, 630
Ontario Plumbing Inspectors Association, 1096
Plumbing Officials' Association of British Columbia, 1163
United Association of Journeymen & Apprentices of the Plumbing & Pipe Fitting Industry of the United States & Canada, 1599

Podiatry
British Columbia Podiatric Medical Association, 249
Canadian Association of Foot Care Nurses, 315
Canadian Federation of Podiatric Medicine, 388
Canadian Podiatric Medical Association, 456
College of Chiropodists of Ontario, 583
College of Podiatric Physicians of Alberta, 589
College of Podiatrists of Manitoba, 589
Ontario Podiatric Medical Association, 1096
Ordre des Podiatres du Québec, 1123
Saskatchewan Association of Chiropodists, 1257
Saskatchewan College of Podiatrists, 1261

Poetry
Adam Mickiewicz Foundation of Canada, 7
Alberta Cowboy Poetry Association, 32
Canadian Poetry Association, 456
La Fondation Émile-Nelligan, 746
The League of Canadian Poets, 903
The Ontario Poetry Society, 1096
The Saskatchewan Poetry Society, 1272
Stroll of Poets Society, 1352

Poison
British Columbia Drug & Poison Information Centre, 239
Centre Anti-Poison du Québec, 526
Manitoba Poison Control Centre, 942
Ontario Regional Poison Information Centre, 1101
Poison & Drug Information Service, 1163

Police
Alberta Association of Police Governance, 24
Alberta Federation of Police Associations, 34
Association de bienfaisance et de retraite des policiers et policières de la ville de Montréal, 99
Association des policières et policiers provinciaux du Québec, 123
Belleville Police Association, 204
Blue Line Racing Association, 215
Brandon Police Association, 226
Brantford Police Association, 227
British Columbia Police Association, 249
Calgary Police Association, 274
Canadian American Law Enforcement Organization, 1515
Canadian Association of Chiefs of Police, 310
Canadian Association of Police Educators, 327
Canadian Association of Police Governance, 327
Canadian Police Association, 456
Canadian Search Dog Association, 469
Cornwall Police Association, 629
Durham Regional Police Association, 665
Edmonton Police Association, 678
Fédération des policiers et policières municipaux du Québec (ind.), 717
First Nations Chiefs of Police Association, 738
Fraternité des Policiers et Policières de la Ville de Québec, 758
Fredericton Police Association, 759
Guelph Police Association Inc., 793
Halifax Regional Police Association, 799
Halton Regional Police Association, 800
Hamilton Police Association, 802
International Association of Chiefs of Police, 1538
International Police Association - Canada, 859
Kingston Police Association, 889
London Police Association, 919
Medicine Hat Police Association, 958
Merry Go Round Children's Foundation, 962
Municipal Law Enforcement Officers' Association, 981
Niagara Region Police Association, 1025
North Bay Police Association, 1030
Ontario Association of Chiefs of Police, 1062
Ontario Association of Police Services Boards, 1065
Ontario Gang Investigators Association, 1081
Ontario Provincial Police Association, 1098
Ontario Special Constable Association, 1108
Ottawa Police Association, 1131
Peel Regional Police Association, 1148
Peterborough Police Association, 1154
Police Association of Nova Scotia, 1163
Police Association of Ontario, 1163
Police Martial Arts Association Inc., 1163
Police Sector Council, 1163
Prince Edward Island Police Association, 1176
Regina Policemen Association Inc., 1212
Royal Newfoundland Constabulary Association, 1242
Saskatchewan Federation of Police Officers, 1265
Saskatoon City Police Association, 1279
Sault Ste Marie Police Association, 1281
Thunder Bay Police Association, 1378
Toronto Police Accountability Coalition, 1386
Toronto Police Association, 1386
Waterloo Regional Police Association, 1442
Windsor Police Association, 1457
Winnipeg Police Association, 1459
York Regional Police Association, 1473

Poliomyelitis
Barrie Post Polio Association, 197
Polio Québec, 1163
Polio Regina, 1163
Post-Polio Awareness & Support Society of BC, 1168
Post-Polio Network Manitoba Inc., 1168
Southern Alberta Post Polio Support Society, 1337
Wildrose Polio Support Society, 1455

Polish Canadians
Adam Mickiewicz Foundation of Canada, 7
Association of Polish Engineers in Canada, 155
Canada-Poland Chamber of Commerce of Toronto, 284
Canadian Polish Congress, 456
Canadian Polish Foundation, 457
Canadian Polish Society, 457
Chambre de commerce Canada-Pologne, 540
Polanie-Polish Song & Dance Association, 1163
Polish Alliance of Canada, 1163
Polish Army Veterans Association of America, 1163
Polish Canadian Women's Federation, 1163
Polish Combatants Association, 1164
Polish Combatants Association - Winnipeg, 1164
Polish National Union of Canada, 1164
Polish North American Trucking Association, 1164
Polish Teachers Association in Canada, 1164
Polish-Jewish Heritage Foundation of Canada, 1164
St. John's Cathedral Polish Catholic Church, 1249
Toronto Sinfonietta, 1387
Wilno Heritage Society, 1456

Political Organizations
Alberta Liberal Party, 39
Alberta Party, 42
Alberta Social Credit Party, 47
Animal Protection Party of Canada, 71
BC First Party, 201
Beaver Party of Canada, 203
Bloc québécois, 214
British Columbia Conservative Party, 237
British Columbia Liberal Party, 244
British Columbia Libertarian Party, 244
British Columbia Marijuana Party, 246
British Columbia Party, 248
British Columbia Refederation Party, 250
Canadians' Choice Party, 507
Christian Heritage Party of British Columbia, 567
Christian Heritage Party of Canada, 567
Coalition Avenir Québec, 577
Communist Party of BC, 594
Communist Party of Canada, 594
Communist Party of Canada (Alberta), 594
Communist Party of Canada (Manitoba), 594
Communist Party of Canada (Marxist-Leninist), 595
Communist Party of Canada (Ontario), 595
Conservative Party of Canada, 622
Federal Liberal Association of Nunavut, 706
Freedom Party of Ontario, 759
The Green Party of Alberta, 788
Green Party of Canada, 788
The Green Party of Manitoba, 788
Green Party of New Brunswick, 788
Green Party of Nova Scotia, 789
The Green Party of Ontario, 789
Green Party of Prince Edward Island, 789
Green Party Political Association of British Columbia, 789
The Island Party of Prince Edward Island, 865
The Liberal Party of Canada, 909
The Liberal Party of Canada (British Columbia), 909
The Liberal Party of Canada (Manitoba), 909
Liberal Party of Canada (Ontario), 909
Liberal Party of Canada in Alberta, 909
Liberal Party of Newfoundland & Labrador, 909
Liberal Party of Nova Scotia, 909
Liberal Party of Prince Edward Island, 909
The Libertarian Party of Canada, 909
Manitoba Liberal Party, 939
Marijuana Party, 949
The National Citizens Coalition, 991
New Brunswick Liberal Association, 1010
New Democratic Party, 1014
Northwest Territories Federal Liberal Association, 1038
Nova Scotia Progressive Conservative Association, 1047
Ontario Liberal Party, 1088
Ontario Progressive Conservative Party, 1098
Parti communiste du Québec, 1143
Parti communiste révolutionnaire, 1144
Parti libéral du Québec, 1144
Parti marxiste-léniniste du Québec, 1144
Parti québécois, 1144
Parti Vert du Québec, 1144
People's Alliance of New Brunswick, 1151
The Platinum Party of Employers Who Think & Act to Increase Awareness, 1162
Progressive Canadian Party, 1187
Progressive Conservative Association of Prince Edward Island, 1187
Progressive Conservative Party of Manitoba, 1187
Progressive Conservative Party of New Brunswick, 1187
Progressive Conservative Party of Saskatchewan, 1187
Rhinoceros Party, 1229
Saskatchewan Liberal Association, 1268
Saskatchewan Party, 1271
Socialist Party of Canada, 1307
Trillium Party of Ontario, 1398
United Conservative Association, 1410
Unparty: The Consensus-Building Party, 1421

Subject Index / Professional Development

Western Independence Party of Saskatchewan, 1450
Your Political Party of BC, 1475
Yukon Green Party, 1478
Yukon Liberal Party, 1479
Yukon Party, 1479

Political Prisoners
Amnesty International, 1504
Amnesty International - Canadian Section (English Speaking), 68
Amnistie internationale, Section canadienne (Francophone), 68
The Canadian Centre/International P.E.N., 354
PEN International, 1583

Political Science
American Political Science Association, 1496
Canadian Political Science Association, 457
Canadian Political Science Students' Association, 457
International Political Science Association, 859
The Mackenzie Institute, 924
Société québécoise de science politique, 1324

Pollution
Association québécoise de lutte contre la pollution atmosphérique, 170
Beyond Pesticides, 1514
Canadians for Clean Prosperity, 506
Clean North, 573
Community Enhancement & Economic Development Society, 597
Friends of the Earth International, 1527
Green Calgary, 788
Ontario Clean Air Alliance, 1071
Ontario Pollution Control Equipment Association, 1096
Pacific States-British Columbia Oil Spill Task Force, 1136
The Pollution Probe Foundation, 1164

Polo
Canadian Polo Association, 457

Pool
Canadian Poolplayers Association, 458

Populations
Association des démographes du Québec, 110
Canadian Population Society, 458
Carrying Capacity Network, 1515
Foundation for Environmental Conservation, 1526
Population Connection, 1584

Pork
Alberta Pork, 42
British Columbia Hog Marketing Commission, 243
Canada Pork International, 280
Canadian Pork Council, 458
Éleveurs de porcs du Québec, 684
Manitoba Pork Council, 942
Ontario Pork Producers' Marketing Board, 1097
Porc NB Pork, 1165
Pork Nova Scotia, 1165
Pork Producers Association of Newfoundland & Labrador, 1165
Prince Edward Island Hog Commodity Marketing Board, 1174
Sask Pork, 1254

Portuguese Canadians
Associaça Portuguesa de LaSalle, 89
Associaça Portuguesa de Ste-Thérèse, 89
Associaça Portuguesa Do Canadà, 89
Associaça Portuguesa do West Island, 89
Associaça Portuguesa Espirito Santo, 89
Associaçao dos Pais, 89
Casa do Benfica, 516
Casa do Ribatejo, 516
Casa dos Acores do Ontário, 516
Centro Comunitário Divino Espirito Santo, 537
Clube Oriental Português de Montreal, 576
Clube Portugal de Montreal, 576
Federation of Portuguese Canadian Business & Professionals, 726
First Portuguese Canadian Cultural Centre, 739
La Maison des Açores du Québec, 926
Portuguese Canadian Seniors Foundation, 1167
Portuguese Club of London, 1167
Portuguese Interagency Network, 1167

Postal Service
Canadian Meter Study Group, 436
Canadian Postmasters & Assistants Association, 458
Canadian Union of Postal Workers, 498
Grey, Bruce, Dufferin, & Simcoe Postal History Study Group, 790
International Machine Cancel Research Society of Canada, 858
National Association of Major Mail Users, Inc., 990
Northern Canada Study Group, 1034
Postal History Society of Canada, 1168
Union of Postal Communications Employees, 1408

Potash
International Plant Nutrition Institute, 1555

Potatoes
Fédération des producteurs de pommes de terre du Québec, 717
Horticulture Nova Scotia, 822
Ontario Potato Board, 1097
Potato Growers of Alberta, 1168
Potatoes New Brunswick, 1168
World Potato Congress, 1466

Pottery
Glass, Molders, Pottery, Plastic & Allied Workers International Union (AFL-CIO/CLC), 1528
Pine Tree Potters Guild, 1160

Poultry
Alberta Chicken Producers, 28
Alberta Turkey Producers, 50
British Columbia Broiler Hatching Egg Producers' Association, 234
British Columbia Chicken Growers' Association, 236
British Columbia Turkey Farms, 257
Canadian Hatching Egg Producers, 401
Canadian Poultry & Egg Processors Council, 458
Chicken Farmers of Canada, 557
Chicken Farmers of New Brunswick, 557
Chicken Farmers of Newfoundland & Labrador, 557
Chicken Farmers of Nova Scotia, 557
Chicken Farmers of Prince Edward Island, 557
Chicken Farmers of Saskatchewan, 557
Éleveurs de volailles du Québec, 684
Farm & Food Care Ontario, 705
Further Poultry Processors Association of Canada, 765
Manitoba Chicken Producers, 933
Nova Scotia Egg Producers, 1044
Ontario Broiler Hatching Egg & Chick Commission, 1069
Ontario Independent Meat Processors, 1087
Poultry Industry Council, 1168
Saskatchewan Turkey Producers' Marketing Board, 1276
Turkey Farmers of Canada, 1400
Turkey Farmers of New Brunswick, 1400

Poultry Science
Rare Breeds Canada, 1204
Vaccine & Infectious Disease Organization, 1423
World Veterinary Poultry Association, 1608
World's Poultry Science Association, 1608
World's Poultry Science Association - Canadian Branch, 1468

Poverty
Active Support Against Poverty, 7
Blankets for Canada Society Inc., 214
The Bloom Group, 215
Boyle Street Community Services, 221
Canada Without Poverty, 281
Canadian Physicians for Aid & Relief, 454
Candora Society of Edmonton, 508
Change for Children Association, 551
Collectif pour un Québec sans pauvreté, 581
L'Écluse des Laurentides, 671
Emmanuel International Canada, 686
End Legislated Poverty, 687
Evangel Hall Mission, 698
Fredericton Anti-Poverty Association, 758
Frontiers Foundation, 763
HelpAge Canada, 812
Humanity First Canada, 827
KAIROS: Canadian Ecumenical Justice Initiatives, 880
Lookout Emergency Aid Society, 919
Moorelands Community Services, 973
Mouvement ATD Quart Monde Canada, 976
Ontario Coalition Against Poverty, 1071
Port Colborne Community Association for Research Extension, 1165
Renfrew County Child Poverty Action Network, 1217
Réseau d'action et de communication pour le développement international, 1218
La rue des femmes, 1243
Society of St. Vincent de Paul - Toronto Central Council, 1330
The World Job & Food Bank Inc., 1466
World Vision Canada, 1467
Youth Empowerment & Support Services, 1475

Powerlifting
Alberta Powerlifting Union, 42
British Columbia Powerlifting Association, 249
Canadian Powerlifting Federation, 459
Canadian Powerlifting Union, 459
Fédération Québécoise de Dynamophilie, 727
Manitoba Powerlifting Association, 942
Newfoundland & Labrador Powerlifting Association, 1021
Nova Scotia Powerlifting Association, 1047
Ontario Powerlifting Association, 1097
PEI Powerlifting Association, 1148
Saskatchewan Powerlifting Association, 1272

Practical Nurses
Canadian Council of Practical Nurse Regulators, 369
College of Licensed Practical Nurses of Alberta, 585
College of Licensed Practical Nurses of Newfoundland & Labrador, 585
College of Licensed Practical Nurses of Nova Scotia, 585
Licensed Practical Nurses Association of British Columbia, 910
Ordre des infirmières et infirmiers auxiliaires du Québec, 1121
Registered Practical Nurses Association of Ontario, 1213
Saskatchewan Association of Licensed Practical Nurses, 1257

Pregnancy
Birthright International, 212
Canadian Association of Pregnancy Support Services, 328
Canadian Lactation Consultant Association, 425
International Confederation of Midwives, 1543
Society for the Study of Pathophysiology of Pregnancy, 1592
World Organization Ovulation Method Billings Inc., 1466

Presbyterians
Atlantic Mission Society, 184
Canadian Society of Presbyterian History, 487
Presbyterian Church in Canada, 1170
Women's Missionary Society, 1463

Preschools
Association d'éducation préscolaire du Québec, 99
Council of Parent Participation Preschools in British Columbia, 635
Parent Cooperative Preschools International, 1139

Primates
International Primate Protection League, 1556
The Jane Goodall Institute for Wildlife Research, Education & Conservation, 1568
The Jane Goodall Institute of Canada, 868

Principals & Vice-Principals
British Columbia Principals & Vice-Principals Association, 249
Canadian Association of Principals, 328
The Catholic Principals' Council of Ontario, 520
Conférence des recteurs et des principaux des universités du Québec, 612
International Confederation of Principals, 1544
National Association of Secondary School Principals, 1574
Ontario Principals' Council, 1097

Printing Industries
Association des enseignants en infographie et en imprimerie du Québec, 112
Association paritaire pour la santé et la sécurité du travail - Imprimerie et activités connexes, 164
British Columbia Printing & Imaging Association, 249
Canadian Printable Electronics Industry Association, 459
Canadian Printing Industries Association, 459
Canadian Printing Industries Scholarship Trust Fund, 460
Canadian Printing Ink Manufacturers' Association, 460
Digital Imaging Association, 656
International Allied Printing Trades Association, 1535
Ontario Association of Quick Printers, 1065
Ontario Printing & Imaging Association, 1097
Printing & Graphics Industries Association of Alberta, 1180
Printing Equipment & Supply Dealers' Association of Canada, 1180
Pulp & Paper Products Council, 1194
Saskatchewan Graphic Arts Industries Association, 1266
Specialty Graphic Imaging Association, 1596
Toronto Chapter of the International Association of Printing House Craftsmen, 1383
Xplor Canada Association, 1470

Prisons
Association internationale de droit pénal, 1509
Canadian Families & Corrections Network, 383
Church Council on Justice & Corrections, 569
Quakers Fostering Justice, 1195
Syndicat des agents de la paix en services correctionnels du Québec, 1362
World Health Organization Partnership for Health in the Criminal Justice Sytem, 1606

Private Investigators
Council of Private Investigators - Ontario, 635

Private Schools
Canadian Accredited Independent Schools Advancement Professionals, 287
Centre d'animation de développement et de recherche en éducation, 528
Fédération des établissements d'enseignement privés, 714
Fédération du personnel de l'enseignement privé, 720
Waldorf School Association of Kelowna, 1439

Pro-Choice Movement
Ontario Coalition for Abortion Clinics, 1071

Pro-Life Movement
Action Life (Ottawa) Inc., 6
Campaign Life Coalition, 276
Canadian Physicians for Life, 454
Hamilton Right to Life, 802
Human Life International, 1530
Lethbridge & District Pro-Life Association, 907
Life's Vision, 911
LifeCanada, 911
Newfoundland & Labrador Right to Life Association, 1021
Prince Edward Island Right to Life Association, 1176
The Right to Life Association of Toronto & Area, 1232
Saskatchewan Pro Life Association, 1272
Wilberforce Project, 1453

Production Control
Association for Operations Management, 134
Canadian Supply Chain Sector Council, 491

Professional Development
Business Professional Association of Canada, 267
Canadian Accredited Independent Schools Advancement Professionals, 287
Canadian Council of Professional Certification, 369
Canadian Tamil Professionals Association, 492
Continuing Legal Education Society of BC, 627
Council of Canadian Fire Marshals & Fire Commissioners, 633
Institute for Performance & Learning, 844

Subject Index / Professions

International Coaching Federation, 1542
International Society for Performance Improvement, 1558
North American Association of Asian Professionals Vancouver, 1029

Professions
Alliance of Credential Evaluation Services of Canada, 58
Canadian Association of Paralegals, 325
Canadian Cosmetics Careers Association Inc., 366
Canadian Italian Business & Professional Association of Ottawa, 423
Canadian Network of National Associations of Regulators, 441
Chinese Professionals Association of Canada, 565
Conseil interprofessionnel du Québec, 618
Qualifications Evaluation Council of Ontario, 1195
Women in Capital Markets, 1460

Professors
Alliance des professeures et professeurs de Montréal, 56
Association des bibliothécaires, des professeures et professeurs de l'Université de Moncton, 107
Association des professeures et professeurs de la Faculté de médecine de l'Université de Sherbrooke, 124
Association pour l'enseignement de la science et de la technologie au Québec, 165
Fédération québécoise des professeures et professeurs d'université, 729

Project Management
Project Management Institute, 1585

Propane
Canadian Propane Association, 461

Property Management
Association of Condominium Managers of Ontario, 145
BOMA Québec, 217
Building Officials' Association of British Columbia, 262
Building Owners & Managers Association - Canada, 262
Building Owners & Managers Association - Nova Scotia, 263
Building Owners & Managers Association International, 1514
Building Owners & Managers Association of British Columbia, 263
Building Owners & Managers Association of Edmonton, 263
Building Owners & Managers Association of Manitoba, 263
Building Owners & Managers Association of Ottawa, 263
Building Owners & Managers Association Toronto, 263
Building Owners & Managers Institute of Canada, 263
Canadian Association of Rent to Own Professionals, 331
Canadian Condominium Institute, 362
International Right of Way Association, 1556
Investment Property Owners Association of Cape Breton, 863
Investment Property Owners Association of Nova Scotia Ltd., 863
Professional Property Managers Association Inc., 1186
Real Estate Institute of Canada, 1205

Prospecting
Alberta Chamber of Resources, 28
Association de l'exploration minière de Québec, 100
Association of Applied Geochemists, 139
European Association of Geoscientists & Engineers, 1524
Manitoba-Saskatchewan Prospectors & Developers Association, 948
Mineralogical Association of Canada, 966
Newfoundland & Labrador Prospectors Association, 1021
Northern Prospectors Association, 1035

Northwestern Ontario Prospectors Association, 1039
Nova Scotia Prospectors Association, 1047
Ontario Prospectors Association, 1098
Porcupine Prospectors & Developers Association, 1165
Prospectors & Developers Association of Canada, 1189

Prosthetics
Alberta Association of Prosthetists & Orthotists, 24
Association of Children's Prosthetic-Orthotic Clinics, 1510
Atlantic Association of Prosthetists & Orthotists, 182
Manitoba Association of Prosthetists & Orthotists, 931
Ontario Association of Prosthetists & Orthotists, 1065
Orthotics Prosthetics Canada, 1127
Prosthetics & Orthotics Association of British Columbia, 1190
Saskatchewan Association of Prosthetists & Orthotists, 1257
The War Amputations of Canada, 1440

Prostitution
Maggie's: The Toronto Sex Workers Action Project, 925

Protestants
Grand Orange Lodge of Canada, 780
Ladies' Orange Benevolent Association of Canada, 895
Operation Mobilization Canada, 1116
The Wesleyan Church of Canada - Central Canada District, 1447

Psoriasis
National Psoriasis Foundation - USA, 1577
Psoriasis Society of Canada, 1191

Psychiatric Nurses
College of Registered Psychiatric Nurses of Alberta, 589
College of Registered Psychiatric Nurses of B.C., 590
College of Registered Psychiatric Nurses of British Columbia, 590
College of Registered Psychiatric Nurses of Manitoba, 590
Registered Psychiatric Nurses Association of Saskatchewan, 1214

Psychiatric Patients
Psychosocial Rehabilitation Canada, 1192

Psychiatry
Alberta Psychiatric Association, 43
Association des médecins-psychiatres du Québec, 120
Canadian Academy of Child & Adolescent Psychiatry, 285
Canadian Academy of Geriatric Psychiatry, 286
Canadian Academy of Psychiatry & the Law, 286
Canadian Psychiatric Association, 461
Child & Parent Resource Institute, 558
College of Registered Psychiatric Nurses of B.C., 590
Ontario Psychiatric Association, 1098
Saskatchewan Psychiatric Association, 1272

Psychoanalysis
Association des psychothérapeutes psychanalytiques du Québec, 127
Canadian Institute for Child & Adolescent Psychoanalytic Psychotherapy, 412
Canadian Psychoanalytic Society, 461

Psychology
Adlerian Psychology Association of British Columbia, 8
American Psychological Association, 1497
Association of Psychologists of Nova Scotia, 160
Association of Psychologists of the Northwest Territories, 160
Association of Psychology Newfoundland & Labrador, 160
British Columbia Association for Behaviour Analysis, 231

British Columbia Association of School Psychologists, 232
British Columbia Psychological Association, 249
Canadian Association for Educational Psychology, 300
Canadian Association for Integrative & Energy Therapies, 301
Canadian Centre for Wellbeing, 354
Canadian Positive Psychology Association, 458
Canadian Psychological Association, 462
Canadian Register of Health Service Psychologists, 466
Canadian Society for Brain, Behaviour & Cognitive Science, 473
Canadian Society of Questers, 487
Centre Psycho-Pédagogique de Québec Inc., 536
C.G. Jung Foundation of Ontario, 539
College of Alberta Psychologists, 582
College of Psychologists of British Columbia, 589
College of Psychologists of New Brunswick, 589
The College of Psychologists of Ontario, 589
International Association for Cross-Cultural Psychology, 1536
International Society for Affective Disorders, 1557
John E. Mack Institute, 1568
Manitoba Association for Behaviour Analysis, 929
Manitoba Association of School Psychologists Inc., 931
North American Society of Adlerian Psychology, 1579
Ontario Association for Behaviour Analysis, 1061
Ontario Psychological Association, 1098
Ordre des psychoéducateurs et psychoéducatrices du Québec, 1123
L'Ordre des psychologues du Québec, 1123
Psychological Association of Manitoba, 1191
Psychological Association of Prince Edward Island, 1192
Psychologists Association of Alberta, 1192
Psychology Association of Saskatchewan, 1192
Saskatchewan College of Psychologists, 1261
Société québécoise de psychologie du travail, 1323

Psychotherapy
Association des psychothérapeutes pastoraux du Canada, 126
Association des psychothérapeutes psychanalytiques du Québec, 127
Canadian College of Professional Counsellors & Psychotherapists, 360
Canadian Group Psychotherapy Association, 399
College of Registered Psychotherapists of Ontario, 590
General Practice Psychotherapy Association, 769
Ontario Association of Consultants, Counsellors, Psychometrists & Psychotherapists, 1063
Ontario Society of Psychotherapists, 1108
Société québécoise des psychothérapeutes professionnels, 1324

Public Administration
Alberta Rural Municipal Administrators Association, 45
Canadian Association of Programs in Public Administration, 329
Commonwealth Association for Public Administration & Management, 593
CPJ Corp., 638
Institute of Public Administration of Canada, 847
Muniscope, 982
Ontario Association of Committees of Adjustment & Consent Authorities, 1063
Ontario Public Supervisory Officers' Association, 1100
The Public Affairs Association of Canada, 1192

Public Health
Alberta Public Health Association, 43
Association des directeurs généraux des services de santé et des services sociaux du Québec, 111
Association des médecins spécialistes en santé communautaire du Québec, 120

Association pour la santé publique du Québec, 166
Canadian Association of Medical Teams Abroad, 321
Canadian Association of Public Health Dentistry, 330
Canadian Drug Policy Coalition, 379
Canadian Foundation for Drug Policy, 393
Canadian Institute of Public Health Inspectors, 419
Canadian Public Health Association, 462
Canadian Public Health Association - NB/PEI Branch, 462
Canadian Public Health Association - NWT/Nunavut Branch, 462
Environmental Health Foundation of Canada, 692
International Institute of Concern for Public Health, 858
Manitoba Public Health Association, 942
Newfoundland & Labrador Public Health Association, 1021
Ontario Public Health Association, 1098
Ontario Society of Nutrition Professionals in Public Health, 1107
Public Health Association of British Columbia, 1192
Public Health Association of Nova Scotia, 1192
Saskatchewan Public Health Association Inc., 1272
World Safety Organization, 1607

Public Libraries
Association des bibliothèques publiques de l'Estrie, 107
Les bibliothèques publiques des régions de la Capitale-Nationale et Chaudière-Appalaches, 208
Canadian Urban Libraries Council, 500
Church Library Association of British Columbia, 569
Federation of Ontario Public Libraries, 726
Ontario Public Library Association, 1099
Reseau Biblio de l'Abitibi-Témiscamingue Nord-du-Québec, 1218
Réseau BIBLIO de la Côte-Nord, 1218
Réseau BIBLIO du Saguenay-Lac-Saint-Jean, 1218

Public Participation
International Association for Public Participation, 1537
International Association for Public Participation Canada, 853

Public Policy
Atlantic Institute for Market Studies, 184
Business Council of Canada, 266
Caledon Institute of Social Policy, 270
Canada West Foundation, 281
Canada's Public Policy Forum, 282
Canadian Centre for Policy Alternatives, 354
Cardus Institute, 511
C.D. Howe Institute, 521
CIRANO, 570
The Conference Board of Canada, 611
Couchiching Institute on Public Affairs, 632
CPJ Corp., 638
Downtown Vancouver Association, 662
The Fraser Institute, 757
George Grant Society, 770
Institute for Research on Public Policy, 844
Institute On Governance, 848
International Centre for Science in Drug Policy, 854
Pacific NorthWest Economic Region, 1582
Rotman Institute for International Business, 1236

Public Relations
Canadian Public Relations Society Inc., 462
Health Care Public Relations Association, 806

Public Service Employees
Alberta Municipal Clerks Association, 40
Association of Canadian Financial Officers, 142
Association of Management, Administrative & Professional Crown Employees of Ontario, 151
Association of Professional Executives of the Public Service of Canada, 159
Canadian National Railways Police Association (Ind.), 440

Canadian Union of Public Employees, 498
International Federation of Employees in Public Service, 1547
Newfoundland & Labrador Association of Public & Private Employees, 1016
Nova Scotia Union of Public & Private Employees (CCU), 1050
Ontario Public Service Employees Union, 1099
Prince Edward Island Union of Public Sector Employees, 1178
The Professional Institute of the Public Service of Canada, 1185
Public Service Alliance of Canada, 1193
The Recreation Association, 1207
Syndicat de la fonction publique du Québec inc. (ind.), 1361
Winnipeg Association of Public Service Officers, 1458

Public Utilities
American Public Works Association, 1497
CAMPUT, 277
Canadian Energy Workers' Association, 381
Canadian Public Works Association, 464
Electricity Distributors Association, 683
Municipal Equipment & Operations Association (Ontario) Inc., 981
Ontario Municipal Water Association, 1092
Utility Contractors Association of Ontario, Inc., 1423

Public Works
American Public Works Association, 1497
Association of Ontario Road Supervisors, 155
Canadian Public Works Association, 464
Ontario Public Works Association, 1100
Public Works Association of British Columbia, 1193

Publishing
Association of American Publishers, 1510
Association of Book Publishers of British Columbia, 140
Association of Canadian Publishers, 143
Association of Canadian University Presses, 144
Association of English Language Publishers of Québec, 148
Association of Manitoba Book Publishers, 151
Association québécoise des éditeurs de magazines, 172
Association québécoise des salons du livre, 174
Atlantic Publishers Marketing Association, 186
Book Publishers Association of Alberta, 218
Canadian Association of Learned Journals, 319
Canadian Book Professionals Association, 346
Canadian Business Press, 348
Canadian Centre for Studies in Publishing, 354
Canadian Church Press, 356
Canadian Circulations Audit Board Inc., 357
Canadian Publishers' Council, 464
The Champlain Society, 551
Creative BC, 639
The Literary Press Group of Canada, 914
Manitoba Magazine Publishers Association, 940
Newspapers Canada, 1024
Ontario Book Publishers Organization, 1068
Playwrights Guild of Canada, 1162
The Publishers Association, 1585
Regroupement des éditeurs canadiens-français, 1215
Salon du livre de Toronto et Festival des écrivains, 1252
Saskatchewan Publishers Group, 1272
Small Publishers Association of North America, 1589
Société du droit de reproduction des auteurs, compositeurs et éditeurs au Canada (SODRAC 2003) inc., 1318
Specialized Information Publishers Association, 1596
Unifor87-M, 1405
Women of the Word - Toronto, 1461

Pulp & Paper Industry
Bureau of International Recycling, 1515
Forest Nova Scotia, 751
Forest Products Association of Canada, 751
Pulp & Paper Centre, 1194
Pulp & Paper Employee Relations Forum, 1194
Pulp & Paper Products Council, 1194

Pulp & Paper Technical Association of Canada, 1194
Pulp, Paper & Woodworkers of Canada, 1194

Puppetry
Association québécoise des marionnettistes, 173
Ontario Puppetry Association, 1100

Purchasing
Corporation des approvisionneurs du Québec, 629
National Institute of Governmental Purchasing, Inc., 1576
Ontario Public Buyers Association, 1098
Supply Chain Management Association, 1355
Supply Chain Management Association - Alberta, 1355
Supply Chain Management Association - British Columbia, 1355
Supply Chain Management Association - Manitoba, 1356
Supply Chain Management Association - New Brunswick, 1356
Supply Chain Management Association - Newfoundland & Labrador, 1356
Supply Chain Management Association - Northwest Territories, 1356
Supply Chain Management Association - Nova Scotia, 1356
Supply Chain Management Association - Ontario, 1356
Supply Chain Management Association - Saskatchewan, 1356

Quality Management
American Society for Quality, 1498
Canadian Society for Quality, 477
Excellence Canada, 699
Mouvement québécois de la qualité, 978
QMI - SAI Global, 1194

Quantity Surveying
Association of Quantity Surveyors of Alberta, 160
Canadian Institute of Quantity Surveyors, 419
Canadian Institute of Quantity Surveyors - British Columbia, 419
Canadian Institute of Quantity Surveyors - Maritimes, 419
Canadian Institute of Quantity Surveyors - Ontario, 419
Insitut canadien des économistes en construction - Québec, 840

Quilting
Canadian Quilters' Association, 464

Rabbis
Kosher Check, 894

Rabbits
Dominion Rabbit & Cavy Breeders Association, 661
Ontario Commercial Rabbit Growers' Association, 1073

Race Relations
Affiliation of Multicultural Societies & Service Agencies of BC, 11
Arusha Centre Society, 86
B'nai Brith Canada, 192
B'nai Brith Canada Institute for International Affairs, 192
Center for Research-Action on Race Relations, 522
Coalition of Black Trade Unionists, 578
FAST (Fighting Antisemitism Together), 706
Kamloops Immigrant Services, 880
League for Human Rights of B'nai Brith Canada, 903
Urban Alliance on Race Relations, 1422

Racing
Canadian International Dragon Boat Festival Society, 421
Canadian Race Communications Association, 464
Canadian Trail & Mountain Running Association, 496
Dragon Boat Canada, 662
Interior Running Association, 852
Manitoba Runners' Association, 943
Toronto Autosport Club, 1382

VeloNorth Cycling Club, 1431
Vintage Road Racing Association, 1435
Yukon River Marathon Paddlers Association, 1480

Racquetball
Alberta Racquetball Association, 43
Association québécoise de racquetball, 171
British Columbia Racquetball Association, 250
New Brunswick Racquetball Association, 1011
Newfoundland Racquetball Association, 1023
Racquetball Canada, 1202
Racquetball Manitoba Inc., 1202
Racquetball Ontario, 1202
Racquetball PEI, 1202
Saskatchewan Racquetball Association, 1273

Radiation
Canadian Radiation Protection Association, 464
International Commission on Radiological Protection, 855
Radiation Safety Institute of Canada, 1202

Radio Broadcasting
ACTRA Fraternal Benefit Society, 7
Alliance des radios communautaires du Canada, 56
Alliance of Canadian Cinema, Television & Radio Artists, 58
Association des professionnels et superviseurs de Radio-Canada, 126
Association des radiodiffuseurs communautaires du Québec, 127
Association des réalisateurs et réalisatrices de Télé-Québec, 127
British Columbia Association of Broadcasters, 231
Broadcast Educators Association of Canada, 259
Canada's National Bible Hour, 282
Canadian Communications Foundation, 361
Canadian International DX Club, 421
Canadian Women in Communications, 505
Catholic Youth Studio - KSM Inc., 521
Central Canada Broadcast Engineers, 524
Farm Radio International, 705
Fondation fransaskoise, 746
Foundation Assisting Canadian Talent on Recordings, 755
HMWN (Holy Mother World Networks) Radio Maria, 817
IEEE Microwave Theory & Techniques Society, 1530
National Campus & Community Radio Association, 991
North American Broadcasters Association, 1029
Numeris, 1050
Ontario Association of Broadcasters, 1062
Ontario Campus Radio Organization, 1070
Ontario Vintage Radio Association, 1112
Parlimage CCF, 1143
Radio Advisory Board of Canada, 1202
Radio Television Digital News Association (Canada), 1203
Screen Actors Guild - American Federation of Television & Radio Artists, 1588
Western Association of Broadcasters, 1447

Radio, Amateur
Canadian International DX Club, 421
Halifax Amateur Radio Club, 798
Ontario DX Association, 1077
Radio Amateur Québec inc., 1202
Radio Amateurs of Canada Inc., 1202
Yukon Amateur Radio Association, 1477

Radiography
International Society of Radiographers & Radiological Technologists, 1561

Radiology
Alberta Society of Radiologists, 47
American Society of Neuroradiology, 1501
Association des radiologistes du Québec, 127
Canadian Association of Radiologists, 330
College of Medical Radiation Technologists of Ontario, 586
International Society of Radiographers & Radiological Technologists, 1561
Ontario Association of Radiology Managers, 1065
Société canadienne-française de radiologie, 1309

Syndicat des technologues en radiologie du Québec, 1364

Railroads & Railways
Alberta Pioneer Railway Association, 42
British Columbia Railway Historical Association, 250
Bytown Railway Society, 267
Canadian Association of Railway Suppliers, 330
Canadian Heartland Training Railway, 403
Canadian National Railways Police Association (Ind.), 440
Canadian Northern Society, 441
Canadian Railroad Historical Association, 465
Canadian Railway Club, 465
Central British Columbia Railway & Forest Industry Museum Society, 524
Chatham Railroad Museum Society, 555
Coalition of Rail Shippers, 578
Edmonton Radial Railway Society, 679
Huntsville & Lake of Bays Railway Society, 828
International Heavy Haul Association, 1550
Maple Ridge Museum & Community Archives, 948
National Association of Railroad Passengers, 1573
North America Railway Hall of Fame, 1029
Operation Lifesaver, 1115
Railway Association of Canada, 1203
Sydney & Louisburg Railway Historical Society, 1360
Teamsters Canada Rail Conference, 1368
Toronto Railway Historical Association, 1386
Vintage Locomotive Society Inc., 1435
West Coast Railway Association, 1445

Rainforests
Conservation International, 1519
Friends of Clayoquot Sound, 760
Rainforest Action Network, 1586
Rainforest Alliance, 1586

Rape
Canadian Association of Sexual Assault Centres, 333
Libra House Inc., 909
Newfoundland & Labrador Sexual Assault Crisis & Prevention Centre Inc., 1021
Ontario Coalition of Rape Crisis Centres, 1072
Oshawa-Durham Rape Crisis Centre, 1128
Ottawa Rape Crisis Centre, 1131
Prince Edward Island Rape & Sexual Assault Centre, 1176
Timmins & Area Women in Crisis Support & Information Centre on Violence Against Women, 1379
Vancouver Rape Relief & Women's Shelter, 1428

Reading
Canadian Council of Teachers of English Language Arts, 370
East York - Scarborough Reading Association, 669
International Board on Books for Young People, 1541
International Board on Books for Young People - Canadian Section, 854
International Literacy Association, 1552
Reading Council for Literacy Advance in Montréal, 1205
Réseau pour le développement de l'alphabétisme et des compétences, 1225
Saskatchewan Reading Council, 1273

Real Estate
Alberta Real Estate Association, 43
Association of Regina Realtors, 160
Association of Saskatchewan Realtors, 161
BC Northern Real Estate Association, 201
Brantford Regional Real Estate Association Inc., 227
British Columbia Real Estate Association, 250
Building Owners & Managers Association Toronto, 263
Canadian Association of Rent to Own Professionals, 331
Canadian National Association of Real Estate Appraisers, 438
The Canadian Real Estate Association, 465
Chambre immobilière Centre du Québec Inc., 550
Chambre immobilière de l'Estrie inc., 550

Subject Index / Real Estate Boards

Chambre immobilière de l'Outaouais, 550
Chambre immobilière de la Haute Yamaska Inc., 550
Chambre immobilière de la Mauricie Inc., 550
Chambre immobilière de Lanaudière Inc., 551
Chambre immobilière de Québec, 551
Chambre immobilière de Saint-Hyacinthe Inc., 551
Chambre immobilière des Laurentides, 551
Chambre immobilière du Grand Montréal, 551
Chambre immobilière du Saguenay-Lac St-Jean Inc., 551
Chinese Real Estate Professionals Association of British Columbia, 565
Fédération des Chambres immobilières du Québec, 713
Fédération internationale des professions immobilières, 1526
International Real Estate Institute, 1556
Investment Property Owners Association of Nova Scotia Ltd., 863
Kamloops & District Real Estate Association, 880
Kingston & Area Real Estate Association, 888
Manitoba Real Estate Association, 943
NAIOP Greater Toronto, 987
National Association of Real Estate Appraisers, 1574
New Brunswick Real Estate Association, 1011
Newfoundland & Labrador Association of Realtors, 1016
Nova Scotia Association of REALTORS, 1041
Nova Scotia Real Estate Commission, 1048
Ontario Real Estate Association, 1100
Organisme d'autoréglementation du courtage immobilier du Québec, 1125
Prince Edward Island Real Estate Association, 1176
Real Estate Council of Alberta, 1205
Real Estate Council of British Columbia, 1205
Real Estate Council of Ontario, 1205
Real Estate Institute of British Columbia, 1205
Real Estate Institute of Canada, 1205
Real Property Association of Canada, 1206
Yukon Real Estate Association, 1480

Real Estate Boards
Alberta Real Estate Association, 43
Alberta West Realtors' Association, 51
Annapolis Valley Real Estate Board, 71
Association of Battlefords Realtors, 139
Association of Saskatchewan Realtors, 161
Bancroft District Real Estate Board, 195
Barrie & District Association of REALTORS Inc., 197
Brampton Real Estate Board, 226
Brandon Real Estate Board, 226
British Columbia Northern Real Estate Board, 248
British Columbia Real Estate Association, 250
Calgary Real Estate Board Cooperative Limited, 274
Cambridge Association of Realtors Inc., 275
Central Alberta Realtors Association, 523
Chambre immobilière de l'Abitibi-Témiscamingue Inc., 550
Chatham-Kent Real Estate Board, 555
Chilliwack & District Real Estate Board, 563
Cornwall & District Real Estate Board, 629
Durham Region Association of REALTORS, 665
Fédération des Chambres immobilières du Québec, 713
Fort McMurray Realtors Association, 753
Fraser Valley Real Estate Board, 758
Grande Prairie & Area Association of Realtors, 781
Greater Moncton Real Estate Board Inc., 784
Guelph & District Real Estate Board, 792
Hamilton-Burlington & District Real Estate Board, 802
Huron Perth Association of Realtors, 828
Kawartha Lakes Real Estate Association, 882
Kootenay Real Estate Board, 892
Lakelands Association of Realtors, 896
Lethbridge & District Association of Realtors, 907
London & St. Thomas Association of Realtors, 918
Manitoba Real Estate Association, 943
Medicine Hat Real Estate Board Co-operative Ltd., 958
Melfort Real Estate Board, 959
Mississauga Real Estate Board, 970
Moose Jaw Real Estate Board, 974
New Brunswick Real Estate Association, 1011
Newfoundland & Labrador Association of Realtors, 1016
Niagara Association of REALTORS, 1024
North Bay Real Estate Board, 1030
Northumberland Hills Association of Realtors, 1036
The Oakville, Milton & District Real Estate Board, 1054
Okanagan Mainline Real Estate Board, 1055
Orangeville & District Real Estate Board, 1117
Organisme d'autoréglementation du courtage immobilier du Québec, 1125
Ottawa Real Estate Board, 1131
Parry Sound & Area Association of REALTORS, 1143
Peterborough & the Kawarthas Association of Realtors Inc., 1153
Portage La Prairie Real Estate Board, 1167
Powell River Sunshine Coast Real Estate Board, 1169
Prince Albert & District Association of Realtors, 1171
Prince Edward Island Real Estate Association, 1176
Quinte & District Association of REALTORS Inc., 1201
Real Estate Board of Greater Vancouver, 1205
Real Estate Board of the Fredericton Area Inc., 1205
Realtors Association of Edmonton, 1206
REALTORS Association of Grey Bruce Owen Sound, 1206
Realtors Association of Lloydminster & District, 1206
Realtors Association of South Central Alberta, 1206
Renfrew County Real Estate Board, 1217
Rideau-St. Lawrence Real Estate Board, 1232
Saint John Real Estate Board Inc., 1247
Sarnia-Lambton Real Estate Board, 1254
Saskatoon Region Association of REALTORS, 1280
Sault Ste Marie Real Estate Board, 1281
Simcoe & District Real Estate Board, 1299
South Okanagan Real Estate Board, 1335
Southern Georgian Bay Association of REALTORS, 1337
Sudbury Real Estate Board, 1353
Thunder Bay Real Estate Board, 1378
Tillsonburg District Real Estate Board, 1379
Timmins, Cochrane & Timiskaming District Association of REALTORS, 1380
Toronto Real Estate Board, 1386
Vancouver Island Real Estate Board, 1426
Victoria Real Estate Board, 1433
Windsor-Essex County Real Estate Board, 1457
Winnipeg Real Estate Board, 1459
Woodstock-Ingersoll & District Real Estate Board, 1464
Yellowknife Real Estate Board, 1471
Yorkton Real Estate Association Inc., 1474

Real Estate Development
Urban Development Institute Greater Edmonton Chapter, 1422
Urban Development Institute of Canada, 1422
Urban Development Institute of Nova Scotia, 1422

Recording Industry
Alberta Music Industry Association, 41
Association québécoise de l'industrie du disque, du spectacle et de la vidéo, 170
Canadian Academy of Recording Arts & Sciences, 286
Canadian Antique Phonograph Society, 293
Canadian Independent Music Association, 410
East Coast Music Association, 668
Foundation Assisting Canadian Talent on Recordings, 755
Manitoba Music, 941
Music Canada, 983
Music Managers Forum Canada, 984
Music Yukon, 984
Music/Musique NB, 984
Musicaction, 984
MusicNL, 984
Radio Starmaker Fund, 1202
Saskatchewan Recording Industry Association, 1273
Society of Composers, Authors & Music Publishers of Canada, 1328
Toronto Musicians' Association, 1386
Western Canadian Music Alliance, 1449

Records Management
AIM Global, 1486
ARMA Canada, 81
ARMA International, 1505

Recovery Vehicles
Ontario Recovery Group Inc., 1100

Recreation
Abbotsford Social Activity Association, 1
Active Living Coalition for Older Adults, 7
Alberta Association of Recreation Facility Personnel, 24
Alberta Recreation & Parks Association, 44
Alberta Senior Citizens Sport & Recreation Association, 46
Alberta Sport Connection, 48
Alberta Therapeutic Recreation Association, 50
Association de joueurs de bridge de Boucherville, 100
Association québécoise de joueurs d'échecs handicapeés visuels, 169
Association québécoise du loisir municipal, 175
Association québécoise pour le loisir des personnes handicapées, 176
Boating BC Association, 216
British Columbia Fishing Resorts & Outfitters Association, 241
British Columbia Play Therapy Association, 249
British Columbia Recreation & Parks Association, 250
British Columbia Therapeutic Recreation Association, 256
Canada-Cuba Sports & Cultural Festivals, 283
Canadian Association for Leisure Studies, 302
Canadian Owners & Pilots Association, 448
Canadian Parks & Recreation Association, 450
Canadian Recreation Facilities Council, 465
Canadian Rope Skipping Federation, 468
Canadian Volkssport Federation, 501
Centre Sportif de la Petite Bourgogne, 536
Club d'Ornithologie de Longueuil, 574
Club de curling Mont-Bruno, 574
Coalition for Active Living, 578
The Coaster Enthusiasts of Canada, 579
Fédération des syndicats de l'action collective, 719
Fédération Internationale de Camping, Caravanning et Autocaravaning, 1525
Fédération québécoise de la marche, 727
Fédération québécoise de la montagne et de l'escalade, 727
Fédération québécoise des centres communautaires de loisir inc., 728
Fédération québécoise des jeux récréatifs, 729
Fitness New Brunswick, 740
Girl Guides of Canada, 773
Golden Age Society, 776
Halifax Sport & Social Club, 799
International Curling Information Network Group, 856
International Orienteering Federation, 1554
Kids Up Front, 886
Lansdowne Outdoor Recreational Development Association, 899
Manitoba Runners' Association, 943
National Marine Manufacturers Association Canada, 995
Northwest Territories Recreation & Parks Association, 1038
Nova Scotia Recreation Professionals in Health, 1048
Nova Scotia Trails Federation, 1050
Ontario Recreation Facilities Association, 1100
Ontario Research Council on Leisure, 1101
Ontario Trails Council, 1111
Orienteering New Brunswick, 1126
Outdoor Recreation Council of British Columbia, 1133
Outward Bound Canada, 1133
ParaSport & Recreation PEI, 1138
Parks & Recreation Ontario, 1142
Physical & Health Education Canada, 1158
Ranfurly & District Recreation & Agricultural Society, 1204
Recreation & Parks Association of the Yukon, 1207
The Recreation Association, 1207
Recreation Facilities Association of British Columbia, 1207
Recreation New Brunswick, 1207
Recreation Newfoundland & Labrador, 1207
Recreation Nova Scotia, 1207
Recreation Prince Edward Island, 1207
Recreational Aircraft Association, 1208
Regina Therapeutic Recreation Association, 1212
Right to Play, 1232
Road Scholar, 1586
Saskatchewan Association of Recreation Professionals, 1258
Saskatchewan Camping Association, 1260
Saskatchewan Parks & Recreation Association, 1271
Scouts Canada, 1286
Strathcona Park Lodge & Outdoor Education Centre, 1351
Sunrise Therapeutic Riding & Learning Centre, 1354
Trail & Ultra Running Association Of The Yukon, 1394
Trail Riders of the Canadian Rockies, 1394
Trans Canada Trail Foundation, 1394
Vecova Centre for Disability Services & Research, 1430
VeloNorth Cycling Club, 1431
World Leisure & Recreation Association, 1606
YMCA Canada, 1471
YWCA Canada, 1481

Recreational Vehicles
Bikes Without Borders, 211
Canadian Recreational Vehicle Association, 465
Recreation Vehicle Dealers Association of Canada, 1208

Recycling
Alberta Automotive Recyclers & Dismantlers Association, 25
Alberta Bottle Depot Association, 26
Alberta Plastics Recycling Association, 42
The Aluminum Association, 1487
Association des recycleurs de pièces d'autos et de camions, 127
Association of Alberta Coordinated Action for Recycling Enterprises, 139
Association of Postconsumer Plastic Recyclers, 1513
Automotive Recyclers Association of Atlantic Canada, 190
Automotive Recyclers Association of Manitoba, 190
Automotive Recyclers of Canada, 190
Bluewater Recycling Association, 215
British Columbia Bottle & Recycling Depot Association, 234
Bureau of International Recycling, 1515
Call2Recycle Canada, Inc., 275
Canadian Association of Recycling Industries, 330
Center for Health, Environment & Justice, 1516
Centre de formation en entreprise et récupération Normand-Maurice, 529
Clean Nova Scotia Foundation, 573
Conserver Society of Hamilton & District Inc., 623
Éco Entreprises Québec, 671
Electronics Product Stewardship Canada, 684
Environmental Education Ontario, 691
EPS Industry Alliance, 1524
Front commun québécois pour une gestion écologique des déchets, 763
Green Action Centre, 788
Institute for Local Self-Reliance, 1532
Institute of Scrap Recycling Industries, Inc., 1533
Municipal Waste Association, 981
NAID Canada, 987
National Association for Information Destruction, 1573
National Association for PET Container Resources, 1573
National Recycling Coalition, Inc., 1577
New Brunswick Solid Waste Association, 1012
NORA, An Association of Responsible Recyclers, 1578

Subject Index / Research

North American Recycled Rubber Association, 1029
Ontario Automotive Recyclers Association, 1067
Pitch-In Canada, 1160
Prince George Recycling & Environmental Action Planning Society, 1179
Recycling Council of Alberta, 1208
Recycling Council of British Columbia, 1208
Recycling Council of Ontario, 1208
Resource Recycling Inc., 1586
Rubber Manufacturers Association, 1587
Saskatchewan Waste Reduction Council, 1277
Société québécoise de récupération et de recyclage, 1323
Steel Recycling Institute, 1597
Thames Region Ecological Association, 1373
The Vinyl Institute, 1601

Red Cross
Canadian Red Cross, 465
International Federation of Red Cross & Red Crescent Societies, 1549

Reflexology
Académie de Réflexologie du Québec, 3
Ontario College of Reflexology, 1072
Reflexology Association of Canada, 1210

Reforestation
Tree Canada Foundation, 1397

Refrigeration
American Society of Heating, Refrigerating & Air Conditioning Engineers, 1499
Corporation des entreprises de traitement de l'air et du froid, 630
Heating, Refrigeration & Air Conditioning Institute of Canada, 810
Ontario Refrigeration & Air Conditioning Contractors Association, 1101
Refrigeration Service Engineers Society (Canada), 1211

Refugees
Association for New Canadians, 134
Canadian Association of Refugee Lawyers, 330
Canadian-Palestinian Education Exchange, 506
Corporation culturelle Latino-Américaine de l'Amitié, 629
Dejinta Beesha Multi-Service Centre, 652
Eritrean Canadian Community Centre of Metropolitan Toronto, 695
Folk Arts Council of St Catharines, 742
Inland Refugee Society of BC, 838
International Council of Voluntary Agencies, 1545
International Development & Relief Foundation, 856
Micah House, 964
Multicultural Association of the Greater Moncton Area, 979
Newcomer Women's Services Toronto, 1015
Open Harbour Refugee Association, 1114
Programme Action Réfugiés Montréal, 1187
Reception House Waterloo Region, 1206
Refugee Research Network, 1211
Saskatoon Open Door Society Inc., 1279
Sojourn House, 1332
U.S. Committee for Refugees & Immigrants, 1601
World Vision Canada, 1467

Regional Development
Association canadienne des sciences régionales, 95
Réseau des SADC et CAE, 1219

Regional Planning
Association des Aménagistes Régionaux du Québec, 105
International Federation for Housing & Planning, 1546

Rehabilitation
Ability Society of Alberta, 2
Association des services de réhabilitation sociale du Québec inc., 128
British Columbia Centre for Ability Association, 235
Calgary Association of Self Help, 271
Canadian Association of Elizabeth Fry Societies, 312
Canadian Association of Physical Medicine & Rehabilitation, 327
Canadian Council on Rehabilitation & Work, 371
Cardiac Rehabilitation Network of Ontario, 510
Centre de réadaptation Constance-Lethbridge, 529
Centre de réadaptation et dépendance le virage, 529
Centre Montérégien de réadaptation, 536
Easter Seals Canada, 669
Easter Seals New Brunswick, 669
Hébergement la casa Bernard-Hubert, 811
Institut Nazareth et Louis-Braille, 843
International Society of Physical & Rehabilitation Medicine, 1561
John Howard Society of Alberta, 874
The John Howard Society of British Columbia, 874
The John Howard Society of Canada, 874
The John Howard Society of Manitoba, 874
The John Howard Society of New Brunswick, Inc., 874
The John Howard Society of Newfoundland & Labrador, 874
The John Howard Society of Northwest Territories, 874
The John Howard Society of Nova Scotia, 874
The John Howard Society of Ontario, 874
The John Howard Society of Prince Edward Island, 875
The John Howard Society of Saskatchewan, 875
Marigold Enterprises Rehabilitation Services Society, 949
Méta d'âme, 962
National Association of Addiction Treatment Providers, 1573
National Institute of Disability Management & Research, 994
Ontario Association of Children's Rehabilitation Services, 1062
Operation Springboard, 1116
The Renascent Centres for Alcoholism & Drug Addiction, 1217
Saskatchewan Abilities Council, 1255
Saskatchewan Association of Rehabilitation Centres, 1258
Seventh Step Society of Canada, 1292
Starbright Children's Development Centre, 1348
Vecova Centre for Disability Services & Research, 1430
Vocational Rehabilitation Association of Canada, 1436

Religion
Affirm United, 11
Africa Inland Mission International (Canada), 12
American Academy of Religion, 1488
Amma Foundation of Canada, 68
Association des intervenantes et des intervenants en soins spirituels du Québec, 117
L'Association Zoroastrianne du Québec, 179
Back to the Bible Canada, 193
The Bible Holiness Movement, 208
Block Rosary Group of Ontario, 215
Bukas Loob sa Diyos Covenant Community, 264
Canadian & American Reformed Churches, 284
Canadian Adventist Teachers Network, 288
Canadian Association for Spiritual Care, 304
Canadian Christian Relief & Development Association, 356
Canadian Church Press, 356
Canadian Committee of Byzantinists, 360
Canadian Society for the Study of Religion, 478
Canadian Society of Presbyterian History, 487
Canadian Unitarians for Social Justice, 499
Catholic Association of Religious & Family Life Educators of Ontario, 517
Catholic Civil Rights League, 518
Catholic Youth Studio - KSM Inc., 521
Christian Medical & Dental Society of Canada, 568
The Church Lads' Brigade, 569
Church of Scientology of Toronto, 569
Communion & Liberation Canada, 594
Congregation of Missionaries of the Precious Blood, Atlantic Province, 613
Couples For Christ Foundation for Family & Life, 636
Couples For Christ, 636
Cursillo Movement of the Archdiocese of Toronto, 646
Daughters of Isabella, 651
Discalced Carmelite Secular Order - Canada, 658
Edmonton & District Council of Churches, 675
Fédération des centres de ressourcement Chrétien, 713
Focolare Movement - Canada, 741
God, Sex, & the Meaning of Life Ministry, 776
Gospel Tract & Bible Society, 778
Heralds of the Gospel, 812
HMWN (Holy Mother World Networks) Radio Maria, 817
Holy Face Association, 819
International Community for Relief of Suffering & Starvation Canada, 855
International Institute of Integral Human Sciences, 858
Jesus Youth Canada, 870
Jews for Jesus, 873
Kolbe Eucharistic Apostolate, 892
Légion de Marie - Senatus de Montréal, 906
Madonna House Apostolate, 925
Marguerite Bourgeoys Family Centre Fertility Care Programme, 949
Maritime Sikh Society, 951
Mary Undoer of Knots, 952
Metropolitan Community Church of Toronto, 964
Militia of the Immaculata Canada, 965
Morning Light Ministry, 974
Multifaith Action Society, 979
The Neocatechumenal Way, 1003
Ontario Consultants on Religious Tolerance, 1074
Our Lady of the Rosary of Manaoag Evangelization Group, 1133
Pagan Federation International - Canada, 1137
Prison Fellowship Canada, 1180
Regnum Christi Movement, 1214
Religions for Peace, 1586
Rosaries for Canadian Forces Abroad, 1236
The Rosary Apostolate, Inc., 1236
St. Mary's Prayer Group, 1250
Salesian Cooperators, Association of St. Benedict Centre, 1251
Seicho-No-Ie Toronto Centre, 1289
Sisters of Charity of Halifax, 1300
Società Unita, 1307
Société internationale de sociologie des religions, 1589
Société québécoise pour l'étude de la religion, 1324
Society of St. Vincent de Paul - Toronto Central Council, 1330
Toronto's Hare Krishna Centre, 1388
Vision of Love Ministry - Canada, 1436
VISION TV, 1436
Wiccan Church of Canada, 1453
Worldwide Marriage Encounter, 1468
Yasodhara Ashram Society, 1470
Youth for Christ Canada, 1475
Zoroastrian Society of Ontario, 1482

Religious Orders of Brothers
Augustines de la Miséricorde de Jésus, 187
The Brothers of the Good Shepherd, 260
Congrégation de Sainte-Croix - Les Frères de Sainte-Croix, 612
Congregation des Soeurs de Saint-Joseph de Saint-Vallier, 612
Congregation of St. Basil, 613
Frères de Notre-Dame de la Miséricorde, 760
Messagères de Notre-Dame de l'Assomption, 962
Sisters Adorers of the Precious Blood, 1300
Sisters of Saint Joseph of Pembroke, 1301
Sisters of Saint Joseph of Peterborough, 1301
Sisters of Saint Joseph of Sault Ste Marie, 1301
Sisters of the Child Jesus, 1301
Sisters of the Sacred Heart of Ragusa, 1301
Soeurs de Sainte-Marie de Namur, 1331

Religious Society of Friends
Canadian Friends Service Committee, 395
Friends Historical Association, 1527
Friends Historical Society - London, 1527
Quakers Fostering Justice, 1195

Remote Sensing
Canadian Institute of Geomatics, 416
Canadian Remote Sensing Society, 466

Renaissance Studies
International Association for Neo-Latin Studies, 1537
Renaissance Society of America, 1586
Toronto Renaissance & Reformation Colloquium, 1387

Renewable Energy Resources
Canadian Association for Renewable Energies, 303
Canadian Wind Energy Association, 504
Clean Energy British Columbia, 573
Energy Action Council of Toronto, 688
Fédération des producteurs de cultures commerciales du Québec, 717
Grain Farmers of Ontario, 779
Groupe de recherche appliquée en macroécologie, 791
International Solar Energy Society, 1561
Marine Renewables Canada, 950
Renewable Industries Canada, 1217
Renewable Natural Resources Foundation, 1586
Toronto Renewable Energy Co-operative, 1387
Windfall Ecology Centre, 1456

Reptiles
Edmonton Reptile & Amphibian Society, 679

Research
Addictions Foundation of Manitoba, 8
Agricultural Research & Extension Council of Alberta, 15
Alberta Innovates, 38
Alberta Research Council Inc., 44
Alberta Sulphur Research Ltd., 48
American Society for Theatre Research, 1499
ArcticNet Inc., 81
Association de la recherche industrielle du Québec, 102
Association des chercheurs et chercheures étudiants en médecine, 108
Association of Canadian Deans of Education, 141
Association of College & Research Libraries, 1511
Association of Educational Researchers of Ontario, 147
Association of Professional Researchers for Advancement - Canada, 160
Association of Research Libraries, 1513
Association pour la recherche au collégial, 166
Atlantic Turfgrass Research Foundation, 186
AUTO21 Network of Centres of Excellence, 189
Battle River Research Group, 199
Beef Cattle Research Council, 203
Brewing & Malting Barley Research Institute, 228
Broadcast Research Council of Canada, 259
Canada Foundation for Innovation, 279
Canada Media Fund, 280
Canadian Association for Food Studies, 300
Canadian Association for Health Services & Policy Research, 300
The Canadian Association for HIV Research, 301
Canadian Association for Immunization Research & Evaluation, 301
Canadian Association for Leisure Studies, 302
Canadian Association for Nursing Research, 302
Canadian Association of Research Administrators, 331
Canadian Association of Research Libraries, 331
Canadian Association on Water Quality, 337
Canadian Carbonization Research Association, 350
Canadian Centre for Fisheries Innovation, 353
Canadian Centre for Policy Alternatives, 354
Canadian Centre on Disability Studies, 354
Canadian Circumpolar Institute, 357
Canadian Education & Research Institute for Counselling, 379
Canadian Educational Researchers' Association, 380
Canadian Energy Research Institute, 381
Canadian Federation for the Humanities & Social Sciences, 384

Subject Index / Residents & Ratepayers

Canadian Fitness & Lifestyle Research Institute, 390
Canadian Foundation for Healthcare Improvement, 393
Canadian Information Centre for International Credentials, 411
Canadian Institute for Advanced Research, 412
Canadian Institute for Jewish Research, 412
Canadian Institute for Research in Nondestructive Examination, 413
Canadian Institutional Research & Planning Association, 420
Canadian Mining Industry Research Organization, 437
Canadian Nautical Research Society, 440
Canadian Numismatic Research Society, 442
Canadian Operational Research Society, 446
Canadian Photonic Industry Consortium, 454
Canadian Research Institute for the Advancement of Women, 467
Canadian Tourism Research Institute, 495
Canadian Transportation Research Forum, 497
Canadian Water Network, 502
C.D. Howe Institute, 521
Cell Stress Society International, 1516
Centre d'animation de développement et de recherche en éducation, 528
Centre d'entrepreneuriat et PME, 528
Centre for Addiction & Mental Health, 531
Centre for Community Based Research, 531
Centre for International Business Studies, 533
Centre for Research on Latin America & The Caribbean, 533
Child & Parent Resource Institute, 558
Chinook Applied Research Association, 565
CIRANO, 570
Coastal Ecosystems Research Foundation, 579
Commission canadienne pour la théorie des machines et des mécanismes, 593
Communication & Natural Logic International Society, 594
Consultative Group on International Agricultural Research, 1519
Earthwatch Institute, 1522
Eastern Townships Resource Centre, 671
Farming Smarter, 706
Fishermen & Scientists Research Society, 740
Fondation Les oiseleurs du Québec inc., 747
Foothills Forage & Grazing Association, 750
Foundation for Legal Research, 755
FPInnovations, 756
Gateway Research Organization, 767
Genesis Research Foundation, 769
GEOIDE Network, 769
George Morris Centre, 770
Gorsebrook Research Institute for Atlantic Canada Studies, 778
Grand Manan Whale & Seabird Research Station, 780
Great Lakes Institute for Environmental Research, 782
The Great Lakes Research Consortium, 1528
Grey Wooded Forage Association, 790
Groupe de recherche en écologie sociale, 791
Harrow Early Immigrant Research Society, 804
Health Law Institute, 806
Heiser Program for Research in Leprosy & Tuberculosis, 1529
Hope Studies Central, 821
Human Rights Research & Education Centre, 826
Institut de recherche Robert-Sauvé en santé et en sécurité du travail, 842
Institute for Risk Research, 844
Institute of Air & Space Law, 844
Institute of Asian Research, 844
International Association for Bear Research & Management, 1535
International Association for Great Lakes Research, 1536
International Council for the Exploration of the Sea, 1544
International Development Research Centre, 856
International Federation for Research in Women's History, 1547
International Institute for Applied Systems Analysis, 1551
International Papillomavirus Society, 1554
International Research Group on Wood Protection, 1556

International Society for Evolutionary Protistology, 860
International Society for Eye Research, 1557
International Society for Research in Palmistry Inc., 860
International Society for Sexually Transmitted Diseases Research, 1559
International Telecommunications Society, 1562
International Union of Forest Research Organizations, 1564
Invest Ottawa, 862
The Jane Goodall Institute for Wildlife Research, Education & Conservation, 1568
The Jane Goodall Institute of Canada, 868
Lakeland Agricultural Research Association, 896
Macleod Institute, 924
Marketing Research & Intelligence Association, 951
Mathematics of Information Technology & Complex Systems, 954
Muniscope, 982
National Council for Science & the Environment, 1575
Natural Sciences & Engineering Research Council of Canada, 999
North Peace Applied Research Association, 1032
The North-South Institute, 1036
Nova Scotia Public Interest Research Group, 1047
Numeris, 1050
Offshore Energy Research Association of Nova Scotia, 1055
Ontario Public Interest Research Group, 1099
Ontario Research Council on Leisure, 1101
Peace & Justice Studies Association, 1583
Peace Country Beef & Forage Association, 1147
Petroleum Research Newfoundland & Labrador, 1154
Pulp & Paper Centre, 1194
Québec Public Interest Research Group - McGill, 1198
Quesnel & District Child Development Centre Association, 1200
Recherches amérindiennes au Québec, 1207
Reinsurance Research Council, 1217
Research Council Employees' Association (Ind.), 1218
Shevchenko Scientific Society of Canada, 1296
Simon Fraser Public Interest Research Group, 1300
Smoky Applied Research & Demonstration Association, 1304
Société des Auteurs de Radio, Télévision et Cinéma, 1317
Société historique Alphonse-Desjardins, 1319
Society for Research in Child Development, 1590
Society for Research on Nicotine & Tobacco, 1591
Society of Bead Researchers, 1592
Stem Cell Network, 1349
Stockholm Environment Institute, 1597
TechnoCentre éolien, 1368
Tellus Institute, 1597
The Terry Fox Foundation, 1372
Traffic Injury Research Foundation, 1394
Travel and Tourism Research Association (Canada Chapter), 1396
Ukrainian Canadian Research & Documentation Centre, 1402
Vancouver Island Public Interest Research Group, 1426
Vecova Centre for Disability Services & Research, 1430
West Central Forage Association, 1444
Western Finance Association, 1602
World Agroforestry Centre, 1602
World Association of Industrial & Technological Research Organizations, 1603

Residents & Ratepayers
Association des résidents du Lac Écho, 127
Association des résidents du Lac Renaud, 127
Charlottetown Downtown Residents Association, 552
Confederation of Resident & Ratepayer Associations, 611
Muskoka Ratepayers' Association, 985

Roncesvalles Macdonell Residents' Association, 1235
The West Bend Community Association, 1444

Resorts
British Columbia Lodging & Campgrounds Association, 245
Canadian Resort Development Association, 467
Provincial Association of Resort Communities of Saskatchewan, 1190
Resorts Ontario, 1226
Whistler Resort Association, 1452

Respiratory Disorders
Association des handicapés respiratoires de Québec, 116
Canadian Association of Thoracic Surgeons, 334
Canadian Network for Respiratory Care, 441
Canadian Respiratory Health Professionals, 467
Canadian Thoracic Society, 494
Centre for Immunization & Respiratory Infectious Diseases, 532
International Primary Care Respiratory Group, 1555
Ontario Lung Association, 1089
Ontario Respiratory Care Society, 1101
TB Vets, 1367

Respiratory Therapy
British Columbia Society of Respiratory Therapists, 254
Canadian Board for Respiratory Care Inc., 345
Canadian Society of Respiratory Therapists, 487
College & Association of Respiratory Therapists of Alberta, 581
College of Respiratory Therapists of Ontario, 590
International Primary Care Respiratory Group, 1555
Manitoba Association of Registered Respiratory Therapists, Inc., 931
The New Brunswick Association of Respiratory Therapists Inc., 1005
Newfoundland & Labrador Association of Respiratory Therapists, 1016
Nova Scotia College of Respiratory Therapists, 1043
Ontario Home Respiratory Services Association, 1086
Ontario Lung Association, 1089
Ontario Respiratory Care Society, 1101
Ordre professionnel des inhalothérapeutes du Québec, 1124
Respiratory Therapy Society of Ontario, 1227

Restaurants
Association des restaurateurs du Québec, 127
British Columbia Restaurant & Foodservices Association, 251
International Hotel & Restaurant Association, 1550
Manitoba Restaurant & Food Services Association, 943
Ontario Restaurant, Hotel & Motel Association, 1101
Restaurants Canada, 1227

Retail Trade
Association des marchands dépanneurs et épiciers du Québec, 119
Association québécoise de la quincaillerie et des matériaux de construction, 170
Association Québécoise des dépanneurs en alimentation, 172
Atlantic Convenience Store Association, 183
Canada East Equipment Dealers' Association, 278
Canadian Convenience Stores Association, 364
Canadian Deals & Coupons Association, 376
Canadian Professional Sales Association, 460
Canadian Tire Dealers Association, 495
Conseil québécois du commerce de détail, 620
The Fur Council of Canada, 765
International Federation of Hardware & Housewares Association, 1548
International Right of Way Association, 1556
Neighbourhood Pharmacy Association of Canada, 1002
Ontario Convenience Store Association, 1074
Retail Advertising & Marketing Club of Canada, 1228

Retail Council of Canada, 1228
Retail, Wholesale & Department Store Union (AFL-CIO/CLC), 1586
Saskatchewan Joint Board Retail, Wholesale & Department Store Union, 1268
Western Convenience Store Association, 1449
Western Retail Lumber Association, 1450

Retinitis Pigmentosa
The Foundation Fighting Blindness, 755

Retirement
Association of Catholic Retired Administrators, 144
Association québécoise de défense des droits des personnes retraitées et préretraitées, 169
Association québécoise des directeurs et directrices d'établissement d'enseignement retraités, 172
Canadian Association of Retired Teachers, 331
CARP, 514
College & University Retiree Associations of Canada, 581
Congress of Union Retirees Canada, 613
McMaster University Retirees Association, 956
Retirement Planning Association of Canada, 1228
Seniors Association of Greater Edmonton, 1290
The Shepherds' Trust, 1295
Steelworkers Organization of Active Retirees, 1349

Retirement Communities
Finnish Canadian Rest Home Association, 738
Ontario Retirement Communities Association, 1102

Rett Syndrome
Ontario Rett Syndrome Association, 1102

Rifles
Alberta Provincial Rifle Association, 43
British Columbia Rifle Association, 251
British Columbia Target Sports Association, 255
Dominion of Canada Rifle Association, 660
Fédération québécoise de tir, 728
Manitoba Provincial Rifle Association Inc., 942
Nova Scotia Rifle Association, 1048
Ontario Muzzle Loading Association, 1093
Prince Edward Island Rifle Association, 1176
Province of Québec Rifle Association, 1190
Royal New Brunswick Rifle Association Inc., 1242
Shooting Federation of Canada, 1297

Ringette
Association de Ringuette de Longueuil, 103
Association de ringuette de Lotbinière, 103
Association de Ringuette de Sainte-Marie, 103
Association de Ringuette de Ste-Julie, 103
Association de Ringuette de Sept-Îles, 103
Association de Ringuette de Thetford, 103
Association de Ringuette de Vallée-du-Richelieu, 103
Association de Ringuette des Moulins, 104
Association de Ringuette Lévis, 104
Association de Ringuette Repentigny, 104
Association de ringuette Roussillon, 104
Association régionale de ringuette Laval, 177
Association Régionale de Ringuette Richelieu Yamaska, 177
Association Sportive de Ringuette Brossard, 178
Berwick & District Ringette Association, 206
British Columbia Ringette Association, 251
Cole Harbour Ringette Association, 581
Dartmouth Ringette Association, 651
Eastern Shore Ringette Association, 671
Fédération sportive de ringuette du Québec, 731
Halifax Hurricanes Ringette Association, 799
International Ringette Federation - Canada, 859
Manitoba Ringette Association, 943
Nova Central Ringette Association, 1040
Ontario Ringette Association, 1102
Régionale Ringuette Rive-Sud, 1213
Ringette Alberta, 1232
Ringette Association of Saskatchewan, 1232
Ringette Canada, 1232
Ringette New Brunswick, 1233
Ringette Nova Scotia, 1233
Ringette PEI, 1233

Ringuette 96 Montréal-Nord-Est, 1233
Ringuette Boucherville, 1233
Ringuette Bourrassa-Laval-Lanaudière, 1233
Ringuette de la Capitale, 1233
Ringuette St-Hubert, 1233
Ringuette St-Hyacinthe, 1233
Ringuette-Québec, 1233

Rivers & Streams
American Rivers, 1497
Black Creek Conservation Project, 213
Friends of the Oldman River, 763
Grand River Conservation Foundation, 780
Meewasin Valley Authority, 959
Ottawa Riverkeeper, 1131
Partners FOR the Saskatchewan River Basin, 1144
Quidi Vidi Rennie's River Development Foundation, 1201
Sackville Rivers Association, 1245
St Mary's River Association, 1250

Roads & Roadbuilding
Alberta Roadbuilders & Heavy Construction Association, 44
Association des constructeurs de routes et grands travaux du Québec, 110
Association of Ontario Road Supervisors, 155
British Columbia Road Builders & Heavy Construction Association, 251
Canadian Association of Road Safety Professionals, 331
Heavy Civil Association of Newfoundland & Labrador, Inc., 810
New Brunswick Road Builders & Heavy Construction Association, 1011
Nova Scotia Road Builders Association, 1048
Ontario Good Roads Association, 1083
Prince Edward Island Road Builders & Heavy Construction Association, 1177
Salt Institute, 1588
Saskatchewan Heavy Construction Association, 1267
Trans Canada Yellowhead Highway Association, 1394
Western Canada Roadbuilders & Heavy Construction Association, 1448

Robotics
FIRST Robotics Canada, 739

Rodeos
Canadian Cowboys' Association, 372
Canadian Girls Rodeo Association, 398
Canadian Senior Pro Rodeo Association, 470
Ontario Rodeo Association, 1102
Professional Bull Riders Inc, 1585

Roller Skating
Roller Sports Canada, 1235

Romanian Canadians & Romania
Fondation roumaine de Montréal, 748

Roofing Trade
Alberta Roofing Contractors Association, 44
Association des maîtres couvreurs du Québec, 118
Canadian Roofing Contractors' Association, 468
Green Roofs for Healthy Cities, 789
New Brunswick Roofing Contractors Association, Inc., 1011
Ontario Industrial Roofing Contractors' Association, 1087
Roofing Contractors Association of British Columbia, 1236
Roofing Contractors Association of Manitoba Inc., 1236
Roofing Contractors Association of Nova Scotia, 1236

Rope
Cordage Institute, 1520

Roses
Canadian Rose Society, 468
Greater Toronto Rose & Garden Horticultural Society, 786

Rowing
Alberta Rowing Association, 45
Aviron Québec, 191
Manitoba Rowing Association, 943
Ontario Rowing Association, 1102
Row Nova Scotia, 1237
Rowing British Columbia, 1237
Rowing Canada Aviron, 1237
Rowing New Brunswick Aviron, 1237
Rowing Newfoundland, 1237
Rowing PEI, 1237
Saskatchewan Rowing Association, 1274

Royal Canadian Mounted Police
Mounted Police Professional Association of Canada, 976
Royal Canadian Mounted Police Veterans' Association, 1240

Rubber
North American Recycled Rubber Association, 1029
Tire and Rubber Association of Canada, 1380

Rugby
Alberta Rugby Football Union, 45
British Columbia Rugby Union, 252
Fédération de rugby du Québec, 710
New Brunswick Rugby Union, 1011
Newfoundland & Labrador Rugby Union, 1021
Nova Scotia Rugby Football Union, 1048
Prince Edward Island Rugby Union, 1177
Rugby Canada, 1244
Rugby Manitoba, 1244
Rugby Ontario, 1244
Saskatchewan Rugby Union, 1274

Rural Living
Alberta Community & Co-operative Association, 30
Alberta Rural Municipal Administrators Association, 45
Associated Country Women of the World, 1506
BC Rural & Multigrade Teachers' Association, 202
British Columbia Women's Institutes, 258
Cole Harbour Rural Heritage Society, 581
Federated Women's Institutes of Canada, 706
Federated Women's Institutes of Ontario, 706
Fédération des agricultrices du Québec, 711
Manitoba Rural Tourism Association Inc., 943
Manitoba Women's Institutes, 947
National Farmers Foundation, 993
National Farmers Union, 993
New Brunswick Women's Institute, 1013
Newfoundland & Labrador Women's Institutes, 1022
Prince Edward Island Women's Institute, 1178
Québec Women's Institutes, 1199
Saskatchewan Association of Rural Municipalities, 1258
Saskatchewan Women's Institute, 1278
Society of Rural Physicians of Canada, 1330
Women's Institutes of Nova Scotia, 1462

Russian Canadians & Russia
Canada Eurasia Russia Business Association, 279

Safety
Alberta Boilers Safety Association, 26
Alberta Motor Transport Association, 40
Alberta Safety Council, 45
American Industrial Hygiene Association, 1494
Association de la santé et de la sécurité des pâtes et papiers et des industries de la forêt du Québec, 102
Block Parent Program of Canada, 214
Block Watch Society of British Columbia, 215
Board of Canadian Registered Safety Professionals, 216
British Columbia Municipal Safety Association, 246
British Columbia Safety Authority, 252
Canada Safety Council, 280
CanadaGAP, 283
Canadian Centre for Occupational Health & Safety, 353
Canadian Dam Association, 375
Canadian Fire Safety Association, 390
Canadian National Railways Police Association (Ind.), 440
Canadian Safe Boating Council, 468
Canadian Ski Patrol, 471
Children's Safety Association of Canada, 562
Doggone Safe, 660
Enform, 688
Farm & Ranch Safety & Health Association, 705
Federal Association of Security Officials, 706
Fire Prevention Canada, 738
Health & Safety Conference Society of Alberta, 805
Incident Prevention Association of Manitoba, 831
Infant & Toddler Safety Association, 836
Infrastructure Health & Safety Association, 838
Institut de recherche Robert-Sauvé en santé et en sécurité du travail, 842
International Council on Global Privacy & Security, By Design, 856
International Federation of Airworthiness, 1547
Ontario Food Protection Association, 1080
Ontario Industrial Fire Protection Association, 1087
Ontario Safety League, 1103
Ontario Traffic Council, 1110
Operation Lifesaver, 1115
Ottawa Safety Council, 1131
Parachute, 1138
Parents-secours du Québec inc., 1140
Public Services Health & Safety Association, 1193
Radiation Safety Institute of Canada, 1202
Safe Schools Manitoba, 1245
Safety Services Manitoba, 1245
Safety Services New Brunswick, 1245
Safety Services Newfoundland & Labrador, 1245
Safety Services Nova Scotia, 1245
Saskatchewan Prevention Institute, 1272
Saskatchewan Safety Council, 1274
The Society for Safe & Caring Schools & Communities, 1326
World Border Organization, 1465
World Safety Organization, 1607

Safety Engineering
American Society of Safety Engineers, 1502
Canadian Association of Road Safety Professionals, 331
Canadian Society of Safety Engineering, Inc., 487

Sailing
Alberta Sailing Association, 45
Association maritime du Québec, 137
BC Sailing Association, 202
Blind Sailing Association of Canada, 214
Canadian Albacore Association, 291
Canadian Power & Sail Squadrons (Canadian Headquarters), 459
Canadian Safe Boating Council, 468
Disabled Sailing Association of B.C., 658
Fédération de voile du Québec, 710
New Brunswick Sailing Association, 1011
Ontario Sailing, 1103
PEI Sailing Association, 1149
Sail Canada, 1245
Sail Manitoba, 1246
Sail Nova Scotia, 1246
SailNL, 1246
S.A.L.T.S. Sail & Life Training Society, 1252
Saskatchewan Sailing Clubs Association, 1274
Wind Athletes Canada, 1456

Salmon
Atlantic Canada Fish Farmers Association, 182
Atlantic Salmon Federation, 186
British Columbia Salmon Farmers Association, 252
Fédération québécoise pour le saumon atlantique, 731
Margaree Salmon Association, 949
Miramichi Salmon Association, 968
Nepisiguit Salmon Association, 1003
New Brunswick Salmon Council, 1011
Northumberland Salmon Protection Association, 1036
Nova Scotia Salmon Association, 1048
Pacific Salmon Foundation, 1136
Salmon Preservation Association for the Waters of Newfoundland, 1252

Salt
Salt Institute, 1588

Salvation Army
The Salvation Army in Canada, 1252

Sanitation Supply Industry
International Sanitary Supply Association Canada, 859
International Sanitary Supply Association, Inc., 1556

Scandinavian Canadians
Association for the Advancement of Scandinavian Studies in Canada, 134
Canadian-Scandinavian Foundation, 507
Scandinavian Home Society of Northwestern Ontario, 1282

Schizophrenia
British Columbia Schizophrenia Society, 252
Le Centre de soutien en santé mentale - Montérégie, 530
Hamilton Program for Schizophrenia, 802
International Schizophrenia Foundation, 860
Manitoba Schizophrenia Society, Inc., 943
Schizophrenia Society of Alberta, 1283
Schizophrenia Society of Canada, 1283
Schizophrenia Society of New Brunswick, 1283
Schizophrenia Society of Newfoundland & Labrador, 1284
Schizophrenia Society of Nova Scotia, 1284
Schizophrenia Society of Ontario, 1284
Schizophrenia Society of Prince Edward Island, 1284
Schizophrenia Society of Saskatchewan, 1284
Société québécoise de la schizophrénie, 1323

Scholarships & Bursaries
Black Academic Scholarship Fund, 212
Canadian Association of Rhodes Scholars, 331
Canadian Scholarship Trust Foundation, 468
Horatio Alger Association of Canada, 821
The Latvian Relief Society of Canada, 900

School Libraries
Alberta Association of Academic Libraries, 23
Alberta School Learning Commons Council, 45
Canadian Association of Professional Academic Librarians, 328
Manitoba School Library Association, 944
Ontario School Library Association, 1103
Saskatchewan School Library Association, 1274

Schools
Alberta Schools' Athletic Association, 46
Association montréalaise des directions d'établissement scolaire, 137
Association of Administrators of English Schools of Québec, 139
Association of Catholic Retired Administrators, 144
Association of Jewish Day Schools, 150
Association of School Business Officials of Alberta, 161
The Association of School Transportation Services of British Columbia, 162
Association québécoise des écoles de français langue étrangère, 172
Association québécoise du personnel de direction des écoles, 176
BC School Sports, 202
British Columbia Association of School Business Officials, 232
British Columbia School Counsellors' Association, 252
British Columbia School Superintendents Association, 252
Canadian Association for School Health, 303
Canadian Association of School System Administrators, 332
Canadian Association of Schools of Nursing, 332
Conseil communautaire Beausoleil, 614
École internationale de français, 672
Fédération québécoise des coopératives en milieu scolaire, 728
Fédération québécoise des directions d'établissements d'enseignement, 728
Hillfield-Strathallan College Foundation, 815
Interprovincial School Development Association, 861
Manitoba Association of School Business Officials, 931
Manitoba Association of School Superintendents, 931
Manitoba School Counsellors' Association, 944
New Brunswick Interscholastic Athletic Association, 1009
Newfoundland & Labrador Federation of School Councils, 1019
Nova Scotia School Athletic Federation, 1048

Subject Index / Science

Nova Scotia School Counsellor Association, 1048
NWT School Athletic Federation, 1052
Ontario Association of School Business Officials, 1066
Ontario Federation of School Athletic Associations, 1079
Ontario School Counsellors' Association, 1103
Prince Edward Island School Athletic Association, 1177
Public School Boards' Association of Alberta, 1193
Safe Schools Manitoba, 1245
Saskatchewan High Schools Athletic Association, 1267
School Sport Canada, 1284
Société des écoles du monde du BI du Québec et de la francophonie, 1317
The Society for Safe & Caring Schools & Communities, 1326
Winnipeg Association of Non-Teaching Employees, 1458
Yukon Schools' Athletic Association, 1480

Science
American Association for the Advancement of Science, 1489
Association francophone pour le savoir, 135
Association of Professional Geoscientists of Nova Scotia, 159
Association pour l'enseignement de la science et de la technologie au Québec, 165
Boîte à science - Conseil du loisir scientifique du Québec, 217
British Columbia Science Teachers' Association, 252
The Canadian Association for HIV Research, 301
Canadian Association of Palynologists, 325
Canadian Association of Science Centres, 332
Canadian Council of Professional Geoscientists, 370
Canadian Institute for Neutron Scattering, 413
Canadian Science & Technology Historical Association, 468
Canadian Society for Chemical Technology, 473
Canadian Society for the History & Philosophy of Science, 477
The Canadian Society for the Weizmann Institute of Science, 478
Centre de caractérisation microscopique des matériaux, 528
Centre for Inquiry Canada, 533
Club des débrouillards, 575
Council of Canadian Academies, 633
Earthwatch Institute, 1522
Fondation Cardio-Montérégienne, 743
International Association of Hydrogeologists, 1538
International Association of Science & Technology for Development, 854
International Council of Associations for Science Education, 1545
International Student Pugwash, 1562
International Union of Biological Sciences, 1564
International Union of Crystallography, 1564
Let's Talk Science, 907
Microscopical Society of Canada, 964
MindFuel, 966
Montréal Science Fiction & Fantasy Association, 973
Natural Sciences & Engineering Research Council of Canada, 999
Nova Scotian Institute of Science, 1050
NSERC Chair for Women in Science & Engineering, 1050
Réseau Technoscience, 1226
Science Atlantic, 1285
Science for Peace, 1285
Science Teachers' Association of Ontario, 1285
Science Writers & Communicators of Canada, 1285
Société Québécoise de Psilogie inc, 1323
Society for Canadian Women in Science & Technology, 1325
Technoscience Estrie, 1369
Union québécoise de réhabilitation des oiseaux de proie, 1408
Visions of Science Network for Learning, 1436
Youth Science Canada, 1476

Scientists
Association of Korean Canadian Scientists & Engineers, 150
Association of Professional Geoscientists of Nova Scotia, 159
Canadian Council of Professional Geoscientists, 370
Syndicat professionnel des scientifiques de l'IREQ, 1365

Scleroderma
Scleroderma Association of British Columbia, 1285
Scleroderma Canada, 1285
The Scleroderma Society of Ontario, 1285

Scottish Canadians
Amethyst Scottish Dancers of Nova Scotia, 67
Clans & Scottish Societies of Canada, 572
New Brunswick Scottish Cultural Association Inc., 1012
Québec Thistle Council Inc., 1199
St. Andrew's Society of Montréal, 1248
St. Andrew's Society of Toronto, 1248
The Scots, 1286
The Scots Society of Colchester, 1286
Scottish Settlers Historical Society, 1286

Scottish Clans
Clan Donald Canada, 571
Clan Farquharson Association of Canada, 571
Clan Fraser Society of Canada, 571
Clan Gunn Society of North America - Eastern Canada Branch, 571
Clan Lamont Society of Canada, 571
Clan Mackenzie Society of Canada, 571
Clan MacLeod Society of Canada, 572
Clan Matheson Society of Nova Scotia, 572
Clans & Scottish Societies of Canada, 572
Federation for Scottish Culture in Nova Scotia, 720

Scottish Studies
Canadian Association for Scottish Studies, 303
Scottish Studies Foundation Inc., 1286

Scouts
Association des Scouts du Canada, 127
Fédération des scouts de l'Atlantique, 718
Fédération des scouts de l'ouest, 718
Scouts Canada, 1286
World Organization of the Scout Movement, 1606

Sculpture
Sculptors Society of Canada, 1287
Sculptors' Association of Alberta, 1287

Seafood
Association of Seafood Producers, 162
Charlotte Seafood Employees Association, 552
Fisheries Council of Canada, 739
International Institute of Fisheries Economics & Trade, 1551
National Seafood Sector Council, 996
Seafood Producers Association of Nova Scotia, 1288

Search & Rescue
Canadian Avalanche Association, 340
Canadian Lifeboat Institution, 427
Canadian Search Dog Association, 469
Civil Air Search & Rescue Association, 571
International Cospas-Sarsat Programme, 855
New Brunswick Ground Search & Rescue Association, 1009
Northwestern Ontario Air Search & Rescue Association, 1039
Search & Rescue Volunteer Association of Canada, 1288
Shock Trauma Air Rescue Society, 1296

Securities
Alberta Securities Commission, 46
Autorité des marchés financiers, 190
British Columbia Securities Commission, 253
Canadian Investor Protection Fund, 422
Canadian Securities Administrators, 469
Canadian Securities Institute, 469
Canadian Securities Institute Research Foundation, 469
Chambre de la sécurité financière, 550
Financial & Consumer Affairs Authority of Saskatchewan, 736
Financial & Consumer Services Commission, 736
International Organization of Securities Commissions, 1554
Manitoba Securities Commission, 944
Nova Scotia Securities Commission, 1048
Nunavut Securities Office, 1051
Office of the Superintendent of Securities of Newfoundland & Labrador, 1055
Office of the Superintendent of Securities of the Northwest Territories, 1055
Office of the Yukon Superintendent of Securities, 1055
Ontario Securities Commission, 1104
Prince Edward Island Office of the Superintendent of Securities, 1176

Security Services
The Canadian Corps of Commissionaires, 365
Council of Private Investigators - Ontario, 635
Federal Association of Security Officials, 706
House of Commons Security Services Employees Association, 824
Information Systems Security Association, 1532

Seeds
Canadian Seed Growers' Association, 469
Canadian Seed Trade Association, 470
Commercial Seed Analysts Association of Canada Inc., 592
International Seed Federation, 1556
National Sunflower Association of Canada, 996
Ontario Seed Growers Association, 1104
Saskatchewan Pulse Growers, 1273
SeCan Association, 1288
Seeds of Diversity Canada, 1289

Senior Citizens
Abbeyfield Houses Society of Canada, 1
Abbotsford Social Activity Association, 1
AdvantAge Ontario, 10
Advocacy Centre for the Elderly, 10
Age & Opportunity Inc., 14
Alberta Council on Aging, 31
Alberta Senior Citizens Sport & Recreation Association, 46
Alberta Senior Citizens' Housing Association, 46
ARC - Aînés et retraités de la communauté, 76
Association of Jewish Seniors, 150
Association of Mature Canadians, 151
Association pour aînés résidant à Laval, 165
Association québécoise de défense des droits des personnes retraitées et préretraitées, 169
British Columbia Care Providers Association, 234
British Columbia Coalition to Eliminate Abuse of Seniors, 236
British Columbia Psychogeriatric Association, 249
British Columbia Seniors Living Association, 253
Calgary Meals on Wheels, 273
Calgary Seniors' Resource Society, 274
Canadian Alliance for Long Term Care, 291
Canadian Coalition for Seniors Mental Health, 358
Canadian Frailty Network, 394
Canadian Snowbird Association, 472
Carefirst Seniors & Community Services Association, 511
CARP, 514
Centre d'écoute Montérégie, 528
LA Centre for Active Living, 531
Community Care for South Hastings, 596
Conseil du troisième âge de Saint-Lambert, 618
Conseil régional des personnes âgées italo-canadiennes de Montréal, 621
Council for Black Aging, 632
The Council of Senior Citizens Organization of British Columbia, 635
The Council on Aging of Ottawa, 635
Council on Aging, Windsor - Essex County, 636
Crossreach Adult Day Centre, 644
Drummond Foundation, 663
Elder Abuse Ontario, 681
Elder Active Recreation Association, 681
Fédération des aînées et aînés francophones du Canada, 711
Fédération des aînés et des retraités francophones de l'Ontario, 711
Fédération des aînés Franco-Albertains, 711
Fédération des aînés franco-manitobains inc., 711
Fédération des aînés fransaskois, 711
Federation of Senior Citizens & Pensioners of Nova Scotia, 726
Forever Young Seniors Society, 752
Grand Masters Curling Association Ontario, 780
GRAND Society, 780
Grands-Parents Tendresse, 781
HelpAge Canada, 812
HelpAge International, 1529
Kerby Centre for the 55 Plus, 884
Korean Senior Citizens Society of Toronto, 893
Lansdowne Outdoor Recreational Development Association, 899
Long Term & Continuing Care Association of Manitoba, 919
Mid-Toronto Community Services, 965
Mon Sheong Foundation, 971
National Initiative for the Care of the Elderly, 994
National Pensioners Federation, 995
New Brunswick Senior Citizens Federation Inc., 1012
NWT Seniors' Society, 1052
Older Adult Centres' Association of Ontario, 1056
The Older Women's Network, 1056
Ontario Association of Residents' Councils, 1066
Ontario Senior Games Association, 1104
Ontario Society of Senior Citizens' Organizations, 1108
Ottawa Tamil Seniors Association, 1132
Parents-secours du Québec inc., 1140
Petits frères des pauvres, 1154
Portuguese Canadian Seniors Foundation, 1167
Prince Edward Island Senior Citizens Federation Inc., 1177
Réseau FADOQ, 1223
Road Scholar, 1586
Saskatoon Senior Citizens Action Now Inc., 1280
Senior Link, 1290
Seniors in Need, 1290
Seniors Peer Helping Program, 1290
Seniors Resource Centre Association of Newfoundland & Labrador Inc., 1290
SPRINT Senior Care, 1346
Toronto Finnish-Canadian Seniors Centre, 1384
United Generations Ontario, 1411
United Senior Citizens of Ontario Inc., 1412
Vancouver Second Mile Society, 1428
Les Vieux Brachés de Longueuil, 1434

Seniors Centres
Action Centre-Ville, 6
Bernard Betel Centre for Creative Living, 205
Carrefour 50+ du Québec, 515
Centre de services Guigues, 530
Council for Black Aging, 632
Edmonton Aboriginal Senior Centre, 675
The Olde Forge Community Resource Centre, 1056
Place Vermeil, 1161

Separate Schools
The Catholic Principals' Council of Ontario, 520
Council of Catholic School Superintendents of Alberta, 633
Federation of Teachers of Jewish Schools, 726
Ontario Catholic School Trustees' Association, 1070
Québec English School Boards Association, 1197
Society of Christian Schools in British Columbia, 1328

Separatism
Bloc québécois, 214
Conseil de la souveraineté du Québec, 616
Parti québécois, 1144

Sephardic Jews
Communauté sépharade unifiée du Québec, 594

Serbian Canadians
Serbian National Shield Society of Canada, 1290
Serbian Orthodox Church - Orthodox Diocese of Canada, 1290

Service Industries
National Association of College Auxiliary Services, 1573
Service Employees International Union (AFL-CIO/CLC), 1588

Service Organizations
Association des Grands Frères et Grandes Soeurs du Québec, 115
Benevolent Irish Society of Prince Edward Island, 205
Big Brothers Big Sisters of Alberta, 209
Big Brothers Big Sisters of British Columbia, 209
Big Brothers Big Sisters of Canada, 209
Big Brothers Big Sisters of Eastern Newfoundland, 209
Big Brothers Big Sisters of Manitoba, 209
Big Brothers Big Sisters of New Brunswick, 209
Big Brothers Big Sisters of Nova Scotia, 210
Big Brothers Big Sisters of Ontario, 210
Big Brothers Big Sisters of Prince Edward Island, 210
Big Brothers Big Sisters of Saskatchewan, 210
Big Brothers Big Sisters of Yukon, 210
Canadian Children's Optimist Foundation, 356
Canadian Federation of Junior Leagues, 387
Canadian Progress Club, 460
Foresters, 751
IODE Canada, 863
Junior Chamber International, 1568
Junior League of Calgary, 878
Junior League of Edmonton, 878
Junior League of Halifax, 878
Junior League of Hamilton-Burlington, Inc., 878
Junior League of Toronto, 878
Katimavik, 882
Kin Canada, 887
Kin Canada Foundation, 887
Kiwanis International (Eastern Canada & the Caribbean District), 891
Kiwanis International (Western Canada District), 892
Lions Clubs International, 1569
Lions Foundation of Canada, 913
The Municipal Chapter of Toronto IODE, 980
One Full Circle, 1058
Optimist International, 1580
Optimist International Canada, 1116
Rotary Club of Stratford Charitable Foundation, 1236
The Rotary Club of Toronto, 1236
Rotary International, 1587
Sons of Scotland Benevolent Association, 1333
Soroptimist Foundation of Canada, 1333
Soroptimist International of the Americas, 1595
Variety - The Children's Charity (Ontario), 1429
Variety - The Children's Charity of BC, 1429
Variety - The Children's Charity of Manitoba, Tent 58 Inc., 1430
Variety Club of Northern Alberta, Tent 63, 1430
Variety Club of Southern Alberta, 1430
Western Regional Advocacy Group Society, 1450
World ORT Union, 1607

Sewing
Embroiderers' Association of Canada, Inc., 685

Sex Education
Action Canada for Sexual Health & Rights, 6
Groupe d'entraide à l'intention des personnes séropositives, itinérantes et toxicomanes, 791
Health Initiatives for Youth Hamilton, 806
P.E.E.R.S. Alliance, 1148
Planned Parenthood Ottawa, 1161
RÉZO, 1229
Sex Information & Education Council of Canada, 1292
Sexual Health Centre Lunenburg County, 1293
Sexual Health Centre Saskatoon, 1293

Sex Therapy
Association des sexologues du Québec, 128
Ordre professionnel des sexologues du Québec, 1124

Sexism
Miss G Project, 968

Sexual Abuse
Amelia Rising Sexual Assault Centre of Nipissing, 66
British Columbia Society for Male Survivors of Sexual Abuse, 254
Centre d'aide et de lutte contre les agressions à caractère sexuel de Châteauguay, 527
Centre d'aide et de lutte contre les agressions à caractère sexuel de Granby, 527
EMPHASE Mauricie-Centre-du-Québec, 686
Fredericton Sexual Assault Crisis Centre, 759
Groupe d'aide et d'information sur le harcèlement sexuel au travail de la province de Québec, 791
Mouvement contre le viol et l'inceste, 976
Niagara Region Sexual Assault Centre, 1025
Ontario Coalition of Rape Crisis Centres, 1072
Oshawa-Durham Rape Crisis Centre, 1128
Ottawa Rape Crisis Centre, 1131
Parents-Unis Lanaudière, 1140
Point d'appui, centre d'aide et de prévention des agressions à caractère sexuel de Rouyn-Noranda, 1163
Sexual Assault Centre Kingston Inc., 1292
Sexual Assault Centre London, 1292
Sexual Assault Centre of Edmonton, 1292
Sexual Assault Crisis Centre of Essex County Inc., 1293
Sexual Assault Support Centre Ottawa, 1293
Sexual Assault Survivors' Centre - Sarnia-Lambton, 1293
Survivors of Abuse Recovering, 1357
Thompson Crisis Centre, 1376
Thunder Bay Sexual Assault / Sexual Abuse Counselling & Crisis Centre, 1378
Timmins & Area Women in Crisis Support & Information Centre on Violence Against Women, 1379
Vancouver Rape Relief & Women's Shelter, 1428
Women's Support Network of York Region, 1463

Sexual Harassment
Canadian Association for the Prevention of Discrimination & Harassment in Higher Education, 305
Rehtaeh Parsons Society, 1217

Sexually Transmitted Infections
International Society for Sexually Transmitted Diseases Research, 1559
Sexual Health Centre for Cumberland County, 1293

Shakespeare, William
Bard on the Beach Theatre Society, 196

Sheep
Alberta Katahdin Sheep Association, 38
Alberta Sheep Breeders Association, 46
British Columbia Katahdin Sheep Association, 244
British Columbia Purebred Sheep Breeders' Association, 250
Canadian Finnsheep Breeders' Association, 390
Canadian Katahdin Sheep Association Inc., 423
Canadian Sheep Breeders' Association, 470
Canadian Sheep Federation, 470
Fédération des producteurs d'agneaux et moutons du Québec, 717
Ontario Katahdin Sheep Association Inc., 1088
Ontario Sheep Marketing Agency, 1104
Prince Edward Island Sheep Breeders Association, 1177
Purebred Sheep Breeders Association of Nova Scotia, 1194
Saskatchewan Katahdin Sheep Association Inc., 1268
Saskatchewan Sheep Breeders' Association, 1274

Sheet Metal
British Columbia Sheet Metal Association, 253
Bureau of International Recycling, 1515
Manitoba Association of Sheet Metal & Air Handling Contractors Inc., 931
Ontario Sheet Metal Contractors Association, 1104
Sheet Metal & Air Conditioning Contractors' National Association, 1588
Sheet Metal Contractors Association of Alberta, 1295
Toronto Sheet Metal Contractors Association, 1387

Shellfish
British Columbia Shellfish Growers Association, 253
Canadian Association of Prawn Producers, 328

Sherlock Holmes
The Bimetallic Question, 211
The CPR Stockholder's Society, 638
The Great Herd of Bisons of the Fertile Plains, 782

Shiatsu
Canadian Shiatsu Society of British Columbia, 470
Shiatsu Therapy Association of Ontario, 1296

Shipbuilding
The Canadian Marine Industries and Shipbuilding Association, 430

Shipping
Association of Canadian Port Authorities, 143
British Columbia Supercargoes' Association, 255
Canadian International Freight Forwarders Association, 421
Coalition of Rail Shippers, 578
Freight Management Association of Canada, 759
International Maritime Organization, 1553
Ontario Milk Transport Association, 1091
Shipping Federation of Canada, 1296
Shipyard General Workers' Federation of British Columbia, 1296
Western Canadian Shippers' Coalition, 1449

Ships
Armateurs du Saint-Laurent, 82
Canadian Titanic Society, 495
Master Mariners of Canada, 953

Shooting Sports
Alberta Federation of Shooting Sports, 35
Alberta Metallic Silhouette Association, 40
Atlantic Marksmen Association, 184
Biathlon Canada, 207
British Columbia Rifle Association, 251
British Columbia Target Sports Association, 255
Buckskinners Muzzleloading Association, Limited, 261
Calgary & District Target Shooters Association, 270
Canadian Shooting Sports Association, 470
Canadian Trapshooting Association, 497
Dominion of Canada Rifle Association, 660
Fédération québécoise de tir, 728
Manitoba Provincial Handgun Association, 942
Manitoba Provincial Rifle Association Inc., 942
Nova Scotia Rifle Association, 1048
Ontario Muzzle Loading Association, 1093
Ontario Provincial Trapshooting Association, 1098
Ontario Rifle Association, 1102
Ontario Skeet Shooting Association, 1104
Province of Québec Rifle Association, 1190
Saskatchewan Black Powder Association, 1259
Saskatchewan Provincial Rifle Association Inc., 1272
Shooting Federation of Canada, 1297
Shooting Federation of Nova Scotia, 1297
Yellowknife Shooting Club, 1471
Yukon Shooting Federation, 1480

Shorthand Reporters
Alberta Shorthand Reporters Association, 46
British Columbia Shorthand Reporters Association, 253
Chartered Shorthand Reporters' Association of Ontario, 554
National Court Reporters Association, 1575

Sickle Cell Anemia
Sickle Cell Association of Ontario, 1297
Sickle Cell Foundation of Alberta, 1298

Sign Language
Association of Sign Language Interpreters of Alberta, 162
Association of Visual Language Interpreters of Canada, 164
Association of Visual Language Interpreters of New Brunswick, 164
Manitoba Association of Visual Language Interpreters, 931
Maritime Association of Professional Sign Language Interpreters, 950
Ontario Association of Sign Language Interpreters, 1066
Sign Language Interpreters of the National Capital, 1299
Westcoast Association of Visual Language Interpreters, 1447

Signs
Alberta Sign Association, 46
Manitoba Sign Association, 944
Sign Association of Canada, 1298

Sikhs
Khalsa Diwan Society, 884
Maritime Sikh Society, 951
Ontario Sikh & Gurudwara Council, 1104
Sikh Foundation of Canada, 1299
World Sikh Organization of Canada, 1467

Singapore
Canada-Singapore Business Association, 284

Single Parent Families
Association des familles monoparentales et recomposées de l'Outaouais, 113
Entre Nous Femmes Housing Society, 690
Fédération des associations de familles monoparentales et recomposées du Québec, 711
Massey Centre for Women, 953
One Parent Families Association of Canada, 1058
Parents Without Partners Inc., 1582
Single Parent Association of Newfoundland, 1300
Single Persons Association of Montréal, 1300

Skating
Alberta Amateur Speed Skating Association, 22
British Columbia Speed Skating Association, 254
Club de patinage artistique Les lames givrées inc., 575
Fédération de Patinage de Vitesse du Québec, 710
International Skating Union, 1556
Manitoba Speed Skating Association, 945
Newfoundland & Labrador Speed Skating Association, 1022
Northwest Territories Amateur Speed Skating Association, 1037
Nunavut Speed Skating Association, 1051
Ontario Speed Skating Association, 1108
Patinage Québec, 1145
Saskatchewan Amateur Speed Skating Association, 1255
Skate Canada, 1301
Skate Ontario, 1302
Speed Skate New Brunswick, 1341
Speed Skate Nova Scotia, 1341
Speed Skate PEI, 1341
Speed Skating Canada, 1341
Yukon Amateur Speed Skating Association, 1477

Skiing
Alberta Alpine Ski Association, 22
Alberta Freestyle Ski Association, 36
Alberta Ski Jumping & Nordic Combined, 46
Alpine Canada Alpin, 59
Alpine Ontario Alpin, 59
Alpine Saskatchewan, 59
Association des stations de ski du Québec, 128
BC Adaptive Snowsports, 200
BC Freestyle Ski Association, 201
Biathlon Canada, 207
British Columbia Alpine Ski Association, 229
Canadian Association for Disabled Skiing, 299
Canadian Association for Disabled Skiing - Alberta, 299
Canadian Association for Disabled Skiing - National Capital Division, 299
Canadian Association for Disabled Skiing - New Brunswick, 299
Canadian Association for Disabled Skiing - Newfoundland & Labrador Division, 299
Canadian Association for Disabled Skiing - Nova Scotia, 299

Subject Index / Skills Education

Canadian Association for Disabled Skiing - Ontario, 300
Canadian Association of Nordic Ski Instructors, 322
Canadian Freestyle Ski Association, 394
Canadian Masters Cross-Country Ski Association, 431
Canadian Ski Council, 471
Canadian Ski Instructors' Alliance, 471
Canadian Ski Marathon, 471
Canadian Ski Patrol, 471
Canadian Snowsports Association, 472
Centre de plein air du Mont Chalco, 529
Commission de Ski pour Personnes Handicapées du Québec, 593
Cross Country Alberta, 643
Cross Country British Columbia, 643
Cross Country Canada, 643
Cross Country New Brunswick, 643
Cross Country Newfoundland & Labrador, 643
Cross Country Nova Scotia, 643
Cross Country PEI, 643
Cross Country Saskatchewan, 643
Cross Country Ski Association of Manitoba, 644
Cross Country Ski Ontario, 644
Cross Country Yukon, 644
Freestyle Ski Nova Scotia, 759
Freestyle Skiing Ontario, 759
HeliCat Canada, 811
Manitoba Freestyle Ski Association, 937
Nakiska Alpine Ski Association, 987
National Winter Sports Association, 997
Nordic Combined Ski Canada, 1028
Northwest Territories Ski Division, 1038
Ontario Track 3 Ski Association for the Disabled, 1110
Patrouille de ski St-Jean, 1146
Prince Edward Island Alpine Ski Association, 1171
Saskatchewan Freestyle Ski Incorporated, 1265
Saskatchewan Ski Association - Skiing for Disabled, 1274
Ski de fond Québec, 1302
Ski Hawks Ottawa, 1302
Ski Jumping Canada, 1302
Ski Québec alpin, 1302
Union internationale des associations d'alpinisme, 1598
Whitehorse Cross Country Ski Club, 1453
Yukon Freestyle Ski Association, 1478

Skills Education
Le Collège du Savoir, 582
Community Microskills Development Centre, 606
Essential Skills Ontario, 696
Niagara West Employment & Learning Resource Centres, 1026
Ontario Network of Employment Skills Training Projects, 1093
Skills Canada, 1302
Skills for Change, 1302
Skills/Compétences Canada, 1302

Skin, Diseases & Disorders
Alliance Québécoise du Psoriasis, 58
Association Québécoise du Lymphoedème, 176
Canadian Burn Survivors Community, 347
Canadian Dermatology Association, 377
Canadian Melanoma Foundation, 434
Canadian Skin Patient Alliance, 471
DEBRA Canada, 652
Eczema Society of Canada, 674
effect:hope, 680
Heiser Program for Research in Leprosy & Tuberculosis, 1529
Save Your Skin Foundation, 1282
The Scleroderma Society of Ontario, 1285
Secours aux lépreux (Canada) inc., 1288

Sleep Disorders
Canadian Sleep Society, 472
Fondation Sommeil: Association de personnes atteintes de déficiences reliées au sommeil, 748
World Association of Sleep Medicine, 1603

Small Business
Acadia Entrepreneurship Centre, 4
Canadian Council for Small Business & Entrepreneurship, 367

Canadian Federation of Independent Business, 386
Centre d'entrepreneuriat et PME, 528
Centre for Entrepreneurship Education & Development Inc., 532
Entrepreneurs with Disabilities Network, 691
Fondation de l'entrepreneurship, 743
Gardiner Centre, 767
Hamilton Technology Centre, 802
Small Business Association, 1304
Small Business Centre, 1304
Small Publishers Association of North America, 1589
SOHO Business Group, 1332

Smoking
Action on Smoking & Health, 6
Airspace Action on Smoking & Health, 20
Canadian Council for Tobacco Control, 367
Canadian Vaping Association, 500
Coalition for a Smoke-Free Nova Scotia, 578
Coalition québécoise pour le contrôle du tabac, 578
Conseil québécois sur le tabac et la santé, 620
Manitoba Tobacco Reduction Alliance, 946
Non-Smokers' Rights Association, 1028
The Ontario Campaign for Action on Tobacco, 1070
Physicians for a Smoke-Free Canada, 1158
Saskatchewan Coalition for Tobacco Reduction, 1261
Smoking & Health Action Foundation, 1304
Union des tenanciers de bars du Québec, 1406

Snack Food Industry
Snack Food Association, 1589

Snowboarding
Alberta Snowboard Association, 47
Association of Ontario Snowboarders, 155
Association Québec Snowboard, 168
British Columbia Snowboard Association, 253
Canadian Association for Disabled Skiing, 299
Canadian Association of Snowboard Instructors, 333
Canadian Ski Council, 471
Canadian Snowboard Federation, 472
Canadian Snowsports Association, 472
HeliCat Canada, 811
Manitoba Snowboard Association, 944
Newfoundland & Labrador Snowboard Association, 1021
Prince Edward Island Snowboard Association, 1177
Saskatchewan Snowboard Association, 1275
Snowboard Nova Scotia, 1305
Snowboard Yukon, 1305

Snowmobiles
Alberta Snowmobile Association, 47
British Columbia Snowmobile Federation, 253
Canadian Council of Snowmobile Organizations, 370
Club d'auto-neige Chibougamau inc., 574
Fédération des clubs de motoneigistes du Québec, 713
Great Slave Snowmobile Association, 782
International Snowmobile Manufacturers Association, 1557
Klondike Snowmobile Association, 892
Ontario Federation of Snowmobile Clubs, 1080
Saskatchewan Snowmobile Association, 1275
Snowmobilers Association of Nova Scotia, 1305
Snowmobilers of Manitoba Inc., 1305
Thunder Bay Adventure Trails, 1377

Snowshoeing
Centre de plein air du Mont Chalco, 529
Sherbrooke Snow Shoe Club, 1296

Soaring
Alberni Valley Soaring Association, 21
Alberta Soaring Council, 47
Association de vol à voile Champlain, 104
Base Borden Soaring, 197
Bonnechere Soaring Club, 217
Central Alberta Gliding Club, 523
Club de vol à voile de Québec, 575
Cu Nim Gliding Club, 645
Edmonton Soaring Club, 679
Erin Soaring Society, 695
Gatineau Gliding Club, 768
Grande Prairie Soaring Society, 781

London Soaring Club, 919
Manitoba Soaring Council, 944
Montréal Soaring Council, 973
Prince Albert Gliding & Soaring Club, 1171
Regina Gliding & Soaring Club, 1211
Rideau Valley Soaring, 1232
Saskatoon Soaring Club, 1280
Soaring Association of Canada, 1305
SOSA Gliding Club, 1333
Toronto Soaring Club, 1387
Vancouver Soaring Association, 1428
Winnipeg Gliding Club, 1459
York Soaring Association, 1473

Soccer
Airdrie & District Soccer Association, 20
Alberta Soccer Association, 47
Association de soccer du Sud-Ouest de Montréal, 104
Australian Football League Ontario, 188
Battle River Soccer Association, 200
BC Chinese Soccer Federation, 201
British Columbia Soccer Association, 253
Calgary Minor Soccer Association, 273
Calgary Soccer Federation, 274
Calgary United Soccer Association, 275
Calgary Women's Soccer Association, 275
Canadian Soccer Association, 472
Central Alberta Soccer Association, 523
Edmonton District Soccer Association, 677
Edmonton Interdistrict Youth Soccer Association, 678
Edmonton Minor Soccer Association, 678
Fédération de soccer du Québec, 710
Fort McMurray Youth Soccer Association, 753
Halifax County United Soccer Club, 799
International Federation of Corporate Football, 857
Lace Up Your Cleats, 895
Lakeland District Soccer Association, 896
Lethbridge Soccer Association, 908
Medicine Hat Soccer Association, 959
Newfoundland & Labrador Soccer Association, 1021
Northwest Peace Soccer Association, 1036
Northwest Territories Soccer Association, 1038
Ontario Soccer Association, 1105
Prince Edward Island Soccer Association, 1177
Red Deer City Soccer Association, 1209
St. Albert Soccer Association, 1248
Saskatchewan Soccer Association Inc., 1275
Sherwood Park District Soccer Association, 1296
Soccer New Brunswick, 1305
Soccer Nova Scotia, 1305
Sunny South District Soccer Association, 1354
Tournoi de Soccer de Victoriaville, 1393
Tri-County Soccer Association, 1398
Whitehorse Minor Soccer Association, 1453
Women's Soccer Assocation of Lethbridge, 1463
Yukon Soccer Association, 1480

Social Assistance (International)
Catholic Near East Welfare Association Canada, 520
CAUSE Canada, 521
Fondation Jules et Paul-Émile Léger, 746
Oxfam Canada, 1134
Save the Children Canada, 1281
Sleeping Children Around the World, 1303
World University Service of Canada, 1467

Social Development
Action-Gardien, la table de concertation communautaire de Pointe-Saint-Charles, 7
Bikes Without Borders, 211
Canadian Business for Social Responsibility, 348
Canadian Council on Social Development, 371
Cooper Institute, 627
Global Youth Volunteer Network, 775
The Ontario Trillium Foundation, 1111
Relance jeunes et familles, 1217
Réseau d'action et de communication pour le développement international, 1218
United Nations Research Institute for Social Development, 1600

Social Housing
Active Support Against Poverty, 7

Alberta Public Housing Administrators' Association, 43
BC Society of Transition Houses, 202
British Columbia Non-Profit Housing Association, 247
Christie-Ossington Neighbourhood Centre, 568
La Fondation des Auberges du coeur, 744
LOFT Community Services, 917
Micah House, 964
Nellie's Shelter, 1003
Ontario Association of Interval & Transition Houses, 1064
Ontario Non-Profit Housing Association, 1093
Our Harbour, 1132
Progressive Housing Society, 1187
Réseau québécois des OSBL d'habitation, 1225

Social Planning Councils
Amherstburg Community Services, 67
Brant Community Social Planning Council, 226
Community Development Council Durham, 596
Community Development Council of Quinte, 596
Community Development Halton, 596
Edmonton Social Planning Council, 679
Lakehead Social Planning Council, 896
North Durham Social Development Council, 1030
Opportunity For Advancement, 1116
Penticton & District Community Resources Society, 1150
Peterborough Social Planning Council, 1154
Social Planning & Research Council of BC, 1306
Social Planning & Research Council of Hamilton, 1306
Social Planning Council for the North Okanagan, 1306
Social Planning Council of Cambridge & North Dumfries, 1306
Social Planning Council of Kitchener-Waterloo, 1306
Social Planning Council of Ottawa, 1306
Social Planning Council of Peel, 1306
Social Planning Council of Sudbury Region, 1306
Social Planning Council of Winnipeg, 1306
Social Planning Toronto, 1306
United Way of Guelph, Wellington & Dufferin, 1414

Social Policy
Caledon Institute of Social Policy, 270
Canada West Foundation, 281
Catherine Donnelly Foundation, 517
CIRANO, 570
Community Sector Council, Newfoundland & Labrador, 607
The Fraser Institute, 757
Institute for Change Leaders, 843
Maytree Foundation, 954
Ontario Public Interest Research Group, 1099
Social Justice Committee, 1305
Social Justice Cooperative Newfoundland & Labrador, 1305
Social Planning Council of Kitchener-Waterloo, 1306
Toronto Action for Social Change, 1381
Vancouver Island Public Interest Research Group, 1426

Social Science
Canadian Communication Association, 361
Canadian Ethnic Studies Association, 382
Canadian Federation for the Humanities & Social Sciences, 384
International Network for Social Network Analysis, 1553

Social Services
Abbotsford Community Services, 1
Access Counselling & Family Services, 5
Acclaim Health, 5
Action Nouvelle Vie, 6
Agincourt Community Services Association, 14
Alberta Association of Marriage & Family Therapy, 24
ALIGN Association of Community Services, 54
Alliance des communautés culturelles pour l'égalité dans la santé et les services sociaux, 55
Ami-e du Quartier, 67

Subject Index / Social Services

Les Amis de la déficience intellectuelle Rive-Nord, 67
APER Santé et services sociaux, 73
Association des cadres supérieurs de la santé et des services sociaux du Québec, 108
Association des directeurs généraux des services de santé et des services sociaux du Québec, 111
Association des fondations d'établissements de santé du Québec, 114
Association des services de réhabilitation sociale du Québec inc., 128
Association of Neighbourhood Houses BC, 153
Atelier habitation Montréal, 180
Atlantic Halfway House Association, 184
AWIC Community & Social Services, 191
Batshaw Youth & Family Centres, 199
Battlefords United Way Inc., 200
The Bloom Group, 215
Bouffe pour tous/Moisson Longueuil, 218
Brant Family & Children's Services, 226
Brant United Way, 226
British Columbia-Yukon Halfway House Association, 259
BullyingCanada Inc., 264
Burns Lake Christian Supportive Society, 266
Calgary Urban Project Society, 275
Campbell River & District United Way, 276
Canadian Training Institute, 496
Carefirst Seniors & Community Services Association, 511
Carrefour d'Actions Populaires, 515
Carrefour d'entraide de Drummond, 515
Catholic Children's Aid Society of Hamilton, 518
Catholic Children's Aid Society of Toronto, 518
Catholic Family Services of Peel Dufferin, 519
Catholic Family Services of Saskatoon, 519
Centraide Abitibi Témiscamingue et Nord-du-Québec, 522
Centraide Bas St-Laurent, 522
Centraide Centre du Québec, 522
Centraide du Grand Montréal, 522
Centraide Duplessis, 522
Centraide Estrie, 522
Centraide Gaspésie Îles-de-la-Madeleine, 522
Centraide Gatineau-Labelle-Hautes-Laurentides, 522
Centraide Haute-Côte-Nord/Manicouagan, 522
Centraide KRTB-Côte-du-Sud, 522
Centraide Lanaudière, 522
Centraide Laurentides, 522
Centraide Mauricie, 522
Centraide Outaouais, 523
Centraide Québec, 523
Centraide Richelieu-Yamaska, 523
Centraide Saguenay-Lac St-Jean, 523
Centraide sud-ouest du Québec, 523
Centre d'organisation mauricien de services et d'éducation populaire, 528
Centre de protection de l'enfance et de la jeunesse, 529
Centre for Community Based Research, 531
Centre for Newcomers Society of Calgary, 533
Le Centre jeunesse de la Montérégie, 536
Le centre jeunesse de Québec, 536
Les Centres jeunesse de l'Outaouais, 537
Les Centres jeunesse de la Mauricie et du Centre de Québec, 537
Chemins du soleil, 556
Chez Doris, 557
Child & Family Services of Western Manitoba, 558
Children's Aid Society of Algoma, 560
Children's Aid Society of Ottawa, 561
Children's Aid Society of Oxford County, 561
Children's Aid Society of the District of Nipissing & Parry Sound, 561
Children's Aid Society of the Districts of Sudbury & Manitoulin, 561
Children's Aid Society of Toronto, 561
Children's Health Foundation of Vancouver Island, 561
Chinese Family Services of Ontario, 565
Chipman Community Care Inc., 565
Community Action Resource Centre, 595
Community Care for South Hastings, 596
Community Counselling Centre of Nipissing, 596
Community Living Walkerton & District, 606
Community Social Services Employers' Association, 607

Comox Valley United Way, 608
Conseil national Société de Saint-Vincent de Paul, 619
Corporation de développement économique communautaire Centre-Sud/Plateau Mont-Royal, 629
Counselling & Support Services of S.D. & G., 636
Counselling Services of Belleville & District, 636
Covenant House Toronto, 637
Cowichan United Way, 637
East Wellington Community Services, 669
Employment & Education Centre, 687
Entraide familiale de l'Outaouais inc., 690
Evangel Hall Mission, 698
Family & Children's Services Niagara, 701
Family & Children's Services of Frontenac, Lennox & Addington, 701
Family & Children's Services of Guelph & Wellington County, 702
Family & Children's Services of Lanark, Leeds & Grenville, 702
Family & Children's Services of Renfrew County, 702
Family & Children's Services of the District of Rainy River, 702
Family & Community Support Services Association of Alberta, 702
Family Counselling & Support Services for Guelph-Wellington, 702
Family Counselling Centre of Brant, Inc., 703
Family Counselling Centre of Cambridge & North Dumfries, 703
Family Day Care Services (Toronto), 703
Family Mediation Canada, 703
Family Service Canada, 704
Family Service Centre of Ottawa-Carleton, 704
Family Service Kent, 704
Family Service Ontario, 704
Family Service Thames Valley, 704
Family Service Toronto, 704
Family Services of Greater Vancouver, 704
Family Services Perth-Huron, 705
Family Services Windsor-Essex Counselling & Advocacy Centre, 705
Family Services York Region (Georgina), 705
Fédération des OSBL d'habitation de Montréal, 716
Fédération des syndicats de la santé et des services sociaux, 719
50 & Piu Enasco, 734
First Nations Child & Family Caring Society of Canada, 738
Foundation of Catholic Community Services Inc., 756
Fraserside Community Services Society, 758
Fredericton Community Services Inc., 759
Front commun des personnes assistées sociales du Québec, 763
Frontiers Foundation, 763
Good Jobs for All Coalition, 777
Good Shepherd Refuge Social Ministries, 777
Grande Prairie & Region United Way, 781
Greniers de Joseph, 789
Groupe CDH, 791
Habitat for Humanity Canada, 796
Halton Children's Aid Society, 800
Halton Family Services, 800
Hébergement la casa Bernard-Hubert, 811
HelpAge Canada, 812
Highland Shores Children's Aid, 814
The Identification Clinic, 829
Independent Living Canada, 833
India Rainbow Community Services of Peel, 834
Inn From the Cold Society, 838
Inner City Home of Sudbury, 839
Inter-loge, 852
International Social Service, 1557
International Social Service Canada, 860
International Society for Labour & Social Security Law - Canadian Chapter, 860
Jessie's - The June Callwood Centre for Young Women, 870
Jewish Child & Family Services, 871
Jewish Family Services - Calgary, 871
Jewish Family Services of Ottawa-Carleton, 872
Kawartha-Haliburton Children's Aid Society, 882
Kenora Fellowship Centre, 883
Kids Now, 886

Kiwassa Neighbourhood Services Association, 892
Lakeland United Way, 896
Lloydminster & District United Way, 916
London-Middlesex Children's Aid Society, 919
La Maison Benoit Labre, 926
Many Rivers Counselling & Support Services, 948
Mid-Toronto Community Services, 965
Mission Bon Accueil, 969
Mission Old Brewery, 969
Mouvement action chômage de Longueuil, 976
Native Clan Organization Inc., 997
Neepawa & District United Way, 1002
New Circles Community Services, 1014
North Renfrew Family Services Inc., 1032
Northumberland United Way, 1036
Northwood Neighbourhood Services, 1040
Ontario Association for Marriage & Family Therapy, 1061
Ontario Association of Credit Counselling Services, 1063
Ontario Association of Residences Treating Youth, 1065
Ontario Halfway House Association, 1083
Ontario Municipal Social Services Association, 1092
Ontario Personal Support Worker Association, 1095
Ontario Society of Senior Citizens' Organizations, 1108
Operation Come Home, 1115
Opération Nez rouge, 1116
Options: Services to Communities Society, 1117
Oxy-jeunes, 1134
Pas de la rue, 1144
PEDVAC Foundation, 1147
Peel Family Services, 1147
Pivot Legal Society, 1161
PLEA Community Services Society of BC, 1162
Portage Plains United Way, 1167
Powell River & District United Way, 1168
Prairie Region Halfway House Association, 1169
Pro Bono Québec, 1181
Projet T.R.I.P., 1188
Québec Association of Marriage & Family Therapy, 1196
Regional Halfway House Association, 1212
Regroupement des Aidantes et Aidants Naturel(le)s de Montréal, 1214
Regroupement québécois des organismes pour le développement de l'employabilité, 1216
Renfrew County United Way, 1217
Réseau d'aide aux personnes seiles et itinérantes de Montréal, 1218
Rexdale Women's Centre, 1229
St. Christopher House, 1248
The Scott Mission, 1286
Second Harvest, 1288
Second Story Women's Centre, 1288
Service à la famille chinoise du Grand Montréal, 1291
Service alimentaire et aide budgétaire de Charlevoix-Est, 1291
Service alimentaire et aide budgétaire de Charlevoix-Est, 1291
Service budgétaire communautaire de Jonquière, 1291
Service budgétaire et communautaire de la MRC Maria-Chapdelaine, 1291
Service budgétaire populaire de La Baie et du Bas Saguenay, 1291
Service budgétaire populaire de St-Félicien, 1291
Service budgétaire populaire des Sources, 1291
Service familial de Sudbury, 1291
Share Family & Community Services Society, 1294
ShareLife, 1294
Simcoe Muskoka Family Connexions, 1300
Smithers Community Services Association, 1304
Sources Foundation, 1333
South Peace Community Resources Society, 1335
South-East Grey Support Services, 1337
SPEC Association for Children & Families, 1339
Sudbury Community Service Centre Inc., 1353
Sunshine Coast Community Services Society, 1355

Support Enhance Access Service Centre, 1356
Swift Current United Way, 1358
Thompson, Nicola, Cariboo United Way, 1376
Tikinagan Child & Family Services, 1379
Timmins Family Counselling Centre, Inc., 1380
Toronto Community Care Access Centre, 1383
Tri-County Women's Centre, 1398
Ukrainian Canadian Social Services (Toronto) Inc, 1403
United Way Alberta Northwest, 1412
United Way Central & Northern Vancouver Island, 1413
United Way Elgin-St. Thomas, 1413
United Way for the City of Kawartha Lakes, 1413
United Way of Brandon & District Inc., 1413
United Way of Burlington & Greater Hamilton, 1413
United Way of Calgary & Area, 1413
United Way of Cambridge & North Dumfries, 1413
United Way of Canada - Centraide Canada, 1413
United Way of Cape Breton, 1413
United Way of Central Alberta, 1413
United Way of Chatham-Kent County, 1413
United Way of Cochrane-Timiskaming, 1413
United Way of Cumberland County, 1414
United Way of Durham Region, 1414
United Way of East Kootenay, 1414
United Way of Estevan, 1414
United Way of Fort McMurray, 1414
United Way of Greater Moncton & Southeastern New Brunswick, 1414
United Way of Greater Saint John Inc., 1414
United Way of Greater Simcoe County, 1414
United Way of Guelph, Wellington & Dufferin, 1414
United Way of Haldimand-Norfolk, 1414
United Way of Halifax Region, 1414
United Way of Halton Hills, 1414
United Way of Kingston, Frontenac, Lennox & Addington, 1414
United Way of Kitchener-Waterloo & Area, 1415
United Way of Lanark County, 1415
United Way of Leeds & Grenville, 1415
United Way of Lethbridge & South Western Alberta, 1415
United Way of London & Middlesex, 1415
United Way of Milton, 1415
United Way of Morden & District Inc., 1415
United Way of Niagara Falls & Greater Fort Erie, 1415
United Way of North Okanagan Columbia Shuswap, 1415
United Way of Northern BC, 1415
United Way of Oakville, 1415
United Way of Oxford, 1415
United Way of Peel Region, 1416
United Way of Perth-Huron, 1416
United Way of Peterborough & District, 1416
United Way of Pictou County, 1416
United Way of Prince Edward Island, 1416
United Way of Quinte, 1416
United Way of Regina, 1416
United Way of St Catharines & District, 1416
United Way of Sarnia-Lambton, 1416
United Way of Saskatoon & Area, 1416
United Way of Sault Ste Marie & District, 1417
United Way of South Eastern Alberta, 1417
United Way of Stormont, Dundas & Glengarry, 1417
United Way of the Alberta Capital Region, 1417
United Way of the Central Okanagan & South Okanagan/Similkameen, 1417
United Way of the Fraser Valley, 1417
United Way of the Lower Mainland, 1417
United Way of Trail & District, 1417
United Way of Windsor-Essex County, 1417
United Way of Winnipeg, 1417
United Way South Niagara, 1417
United Way Toronto & York Region, 1417
United Way Worldwide, 1600
United Way/Centraide (Central NB) Inc., 1418
United Way/Centraide Ottawa, 1418
United Way/Centraide Sudbury & District, 1418
Victoria Youth Empowerment Society, 1434
Wellspring Cancer Support Foundation, 1444
Weyburn & District United Way, 1451
Windsor-Essex Children's Aid Society, 1457
Winkler & District United Way, 1458

Subject Index / Social Work

Woodstock & District Developmental Services, 1464
YMCA Canada, 1471
York Region Children's Aid Society, 1473
York Region Family Services (Markham), 1473
Yorkton & District United Way Inc., 1474
Youth Assisting Youth, 1475
Youth in Care Canada, 1475
YOUTHLINK, 1476
YWCA Canada, 1481

Social Work
Alberta College of Social Workers, 30
The Association of Social Workers of Northern Canada, 162
British Columbia Association of Social Workers, 232
British Columbia College of Social Workers, 236
Canadian Association for Social Work Education, 304
Canadian Association of School Social Workers & Attendance Counsellors, 332
Canadian Association of Social Workers, 333
Canadian Social Work Foundation, 472
Kinark Child & Family Services, 888
Maison de Campagne & d'Entraide Communautaire du Lac, 926
Manitoba Association of Personal Care Home Social Workers, 931
Manitoba College of Registered Social Workers, 934
New Brunswick Association of Social Workers, 1006
Newfoundland & Labrador Association of Social Workers, 1016
Nova Scotia Association of Black Social Workers, 1040
Nova Scotia Association of Social Workers, 1041
Ontario Association of Social Workers, 1066
Ontario College of Social Workers & Social Service Workers, 1072
Ordre professionnel des travailleurs sociaux du Québec, 1125
Prince Edward Island Association of Social Workers, 1172
Saskatchewan Association of Social Workers, 1258

Socialism
Socialist Party of Canada, 1307
Society for Socialist Studies, 1326

Sociology
American Sociological Association, 1503
Association internationale des sociologues de langue française, 1510
Canadian Association of Professional Employees, 328
Canadian Sociological Association, 488
International Sociological Association, 1561
International Union of Anthropological & Ethnological Sciences, 1563
Société internationale de sociologie des religions, 1589

Soft Drinks Industry
Canadian Beverage Association, 342
Food Beverage Canada, 749

Softball
Alberta Amateur Softball Association, 22
British Columbia Amateur Softball Association, 230
Canadian Amateur Softball Association, 292
Northwest Territories Softball, 1038
Ontario Amateur Softball Association, 1059
Ontario Rural Softball Association, 1103
Provincial Women's Softball Association of Ontario, 1191
Slo-Pitch Ontario Association, 1303
Softball Manitoba, 1331
Softball NB Inc., 1331
Softball Newfoundland & Labrador, 1332
Softball Nova Scotia, 1332
Softball Ontario, 1332
Softball Prince Edward Island, 1332
Softball Québec, 1332
Softball Saskatchewan, 1332
Softball Yukon, 1332

Soil Science
Alberta Conservation Tillage Society II, 31
Bedeque Bay Environmental Management Association, 203
Canadian Society of Soil Science, 488
International Erosion Control Association, 1546
International Society for Soil Mechanics & Geotechnical Engineering, 1559
International Soil Reference & Information Centre, 1561
International Union of Soil Sciences, 1565
New Brunswick Soil & Crop Improvement Association, 1012
Ontario Soil & Crop Improvement Association, 1108
Saskatchewan Soil Conservation Association, 1275
Soil & Water Conservation Society, 1594
Soil Conservation Council of Canada, 1332
Weed Science Society of America, 1602

Solar Energy
Canadian Solar Industries Association, 489
Énergie Solaire Québec, 688
International Solar Energy Society, 1561

Somalis & Somalia
Dejinta Beesha Multi-Service Centre, 652
Somali Immigrant Women's Association, 1332

South America
Alianza Hispano-Canadiense Ontario, 54
Canadian Colombian Professional Association, 360
Canadian Council for the Americas - British Columbia, 367
Casa Cultural Peruana, 516
Guyana Ottawa Cultural Association, 794
Guyanese Canadian Cultural Association of BC, 794
Halton Peel Hispanic Association, 800
Hispanic Canadian Arts & Culture Association, 815
Latino Canadian Cultural Association, 900
Little Faces of Panama Association, 915

South Asia
AWIC Community & Social Services, 191
Settlement Assistance & Family Support Services, 1292
South Asia Partnership Canada, 1334
South Asian Women's Centre, 1334

Southeast Asia
Alliance for South Asian AIDS Prevention, 57
Canadian Friends of Burma, 395
Institute of Asian Research, 844
Southeast Asia-Canada Business Council, 1337
University of Alberta South East Asian Students' Association, 1419

Spa Pools
Pool & Hot Tub Council of Canada, 1164

Space Sciences
The American Astronautical Society, 1490
Canadian Aeronautics & Space Institute, 288
Canadian Space Society, 489
Edmonton Space & Science Foundation, 679
European Geosciences Union, 1524
European Space Agency, 1524
H.R. MacMillan Space Centre Society, 824
Institute of Space & Atmospheric Studies, 847
National Space Society, 1577
The Planetary Society, 1584
SEDS - USA, 1588

Spanish Language
Centre for Spanish Speaking Peoples, 533
Hispanic Development Council, 815

Speakers
Canadian Association of Professional Speakers, 329

Special Libraries
Art Libraries Society of North America, 1506
Association of Canadian Map Libraries & Archives, 142
Church Library Association of Ontario, 569
Special Libraries Association, 1595

Special Olympics
Jeux Olympiques Spéciaux du Québec Inc., 871
Special Olympics Alberta, 1339
Special Olympics BC, 1339
Special Olympics Canada, 1339
Special Olympics International, 1596
Special Olympics Manitoba, 1339
Special Olympics New Brunswick, 1339
Special Olympics Newfoundland & Labrador, 1340
Special Olympics Northwest Territories, 1340
Special Olympics Nova Scotia, 1340
Special Olympics Ontario, 1340
Special Olympics Prince Edward Island, 1340
Special Olympics Saskatchewan, 1340
Special Olympics Yukon, 1340

Spectroscopy
Canadian Society for Analytical Sciences & Spectroscopy, 473

Speech Disorders
Association des jeunes bègues de Québec, 117
British Columbia Association of People Who Stutter, 232
Canadian Stuttering Association, 491
College of Audiologists and Speech-Language Pathologists of Manitoba, 582
Communicative Disorders Assistant Association of Canada, 594
The Hanen Centre, 803
International Society for Augmentative & Alternative Communication, 860
Ottawa Association of People Who Stutter, 1129
Prince Edward Island Speech & Hearing Association, 1177
Speech & Hearing Association of Nova Scotia, 1340
The Speech & Stuttering Institute, 1340

Speech Therapy
Institute for Stuttering Treatment & Research & the Communication Improvement Program, 844

Speech-Language Pathologists & Audiologists
Alberta College of Speech-Language Pathologists & Audiologists, 30
Association of Northwest Territories Speech Language Pathologists & Audiologists, 154
British Columbia Association of Speech-Language Pathologists & Audiologists, 233
College of Audiologists & Speech-Language Pathologists of Ontario, 582
New Brunswick Association of Speech-Language Pathologists & Audiologists, 1006
Newfoundland & Labrador Association of Speech-Language Pathologists & Audiologists, 1016
Nova Scotia Hearing & Speech Foundation, 1045
Ontario Association of Speech-Language Pathologists & Audiologists, 1066
Ordre des orthophonistes et audiologistes du Québec, 1123
Saskatchewan Association of Speech-Language Pathologists & Audiologists, 1258
Speech-Language & Audiology Canada, 1341
Yukon Speech-Language Pathology & Audiology Association, 1480

Speleology
Alberta Speleological Society, 48
American Cave Conservation Association, 1491
Société québécoise de spéléologie, 1324

Spices
Canadian Spice Association, 489
Saskatchewan Herb & Spice Association, 1267

Spina Bifida
L'Association de spina-bifida et d'hydrocéphalie du Québec, 104
Spina Bifida & Hydrocephalus Association of British Columbia, 1341
Spina Bifida & Hydrocephalus Association of Canada, 1341
Spina Bifida & Hydrocephalus Association of New Brunswick, 1342
Spina Bifida & Hydrocephalus Association of Northern Alberta, 1342
Spina Bifida & Hydrocephalus Association of Nova Scotia, 1342
Spina Bifida & Hydrocephalus Association of Ontario, 1342
Spina Bifida & Hydrocephalus Association of Prince Edward Island, 1342
Spina Bifida & Hydrocephalus Association of South Saskatchewan, 1342
Spina Bifida & Hydrocephalus Association of Southern Alberta, 1342
Spina Bifida Association of Manitoba, 1342

Spinal Cord
Ability New Brunswick, 1
Canadian Paraplegic Association (Manitoba), 449
Canadian Paraplegic Association (Nova Scotia), 450
Canadian Spinal Research Organization, 489
Fondation pour la recherche sur la moelle épinière, 747
International Society for the Study of the Lumbar Spine, 1559
Manitoba Paraplegia Foundation Inc., 942
Moelle Épinière et Motricité Québec, 971
Rick Hansen Foundation, 1231
Spinal Cord Injury (Prince Edward Island), 1342
Spinal Cord Injury Alberta, 1342
Spinal Cord Injury British Columbia, 1343
Spinal Cord Injury Canada, 1343
Spinal Cord Injury Newfoundland & Labrador, 1343
Spinal Cord Injury Ontario, 1343
Spinal Cord Injury Saskatchewan, 1344

Sport Medicine
Alberta Athletic Therapists Association, 25
Athletic Therapy Association of British Columbia, 180
Atlantic Provinces Athletic Therapists Association, 185
Canadian Academy of Sport Medicine, 287
Canadian Athletic Therapists Association, 337
Canadian Sport Massage Therapists Association, 490
Corporation des thérapeutes du sport du Québec, 631
Manitoba Athletic Therapists Association Inc., 931
Ontario Athletic Therapists Association, 1067
Saskatchewan Athletic Therapists Association, 1258
Sport Medicine & Science Council of Manitoba Inc., 1344
Sport Medicine Council of Alberta, 1344
Sport Physiotherapy Canada, 1345
SportMedBC, 1345

Sport Sciences
Canadian Society for Psychomotor Learning & Sport Psychology, 477

Sporting Goods Industry
Canadian Sporting Goods Association, 490

Sports
Aboriginal Sport & Wellness Council of Ontario, 2
Alberta Colleges Athletic Conference, 30
Alberta Schools' Athletic Association, 46
Alberta Senior Citizens Sport & Recreation Association, 46
Alberta Sport Connection, 48
Alberta Sports Hall of Fame & Museum, 48
Amateur Athletic Union, 1487
Arctic Winter Games International Committee, 81
Association sportive et communautaire du Centre-Sud, 178
Athletes International, 180
AthletesCAN, 180
Atlantic Collegiate Athletic Association, 183
Atlantic University Sport Association, 186
B2ten, 192
BC Games Society, 201
BC School Sports, 202
BC Soccer Referees Association, 202
British Columbia Disc Sports, 238
British Columbia Floorball Federation, 241
British Columbia Sports Hall of Fame & Museum, 255
Canada Bandy, 278
Canada Games Council, 279
Canada West Universities Athletic Association, 281

Subject Index / Standards

Canada's Sports Hall of Fame, 283
Canada-Cuba Sports & Cultural Festivals, 283
Canadian Centre for Ethics in Sport, 353
Canadian Collegiate Athletic Association, 360
Canadian Football League Alumni Association, 392
Canadian International Dragon Boat Festival Society, 421
Canadian Interuniversity Sport, 422
Canadian Junior Golf Association, 423
Canadian Olympic Hall of Fame, 446
Canadian Paralympic Committee, 449
Canadian Sport Tourism Alliance, 490
Canadian Volkssport Federation, 501
Commonwealth Games Canada, 593
Dragon Boat Canada, 662
Fédération québécoise des sports cyclistes, 730
Floorball Alberta, 741
Floorball Canada, 741
Floorball Nova Scotia, 741
Floorball Québec, 741
Fort Saskatchewan Minor Sports Association, 754
FunTeam Alberta, 765
International Curling Information Network Group, 856
International Masters Games Association, 1553
Island Fitness Council, 865
Judo Canada, 876
Kitchener Sports Association, 890
Lower Mainland Independent Secondary School Athletic Association, 920
Manitoba High Schools Athletic Association, 938
Manitoba Organization of Disc Sports, 941
Manitoba Sports Hall of Fame & Museum, 945
Napanee Sports Association, 988
New Brunswick Interscholastic Athletic Association, 1009
New Brunswick Sports Hall of Fame, 1013
Northwestern Ontario Sports Hall of Fame & Museum, 1039
Nova Scotia School Athletic Federation, 1048
Novia Scotia Sports Hall of Fame, 1050
NWT School Athletic Federation, 1052
Ontario Colleges Athletic Association, 1073
Ontario Disc Sports Association, 1077
Ontario Federation of School Athletic Associations, 1079
Ontario Floorball Association, 1080
Ontario Shuffleboard Association, 1104
Ontario University Athletics, 1112
Orienteering New Brunswick, 1126
Ottawa Carleton Ultimate Association, 1129
Ottawa Sports Hall of Fame Inc., 1131
Pacific Institute for Sport Excellence, 1135
Pacific Western Athletic Association, 1136
Pan American Sports Organization, 1582
Parksville Golden Oldies Sports Association, 1142
Prince Edward Island School Athletic Association, 1177
Prince Edward Island Sports Hall of Fame & Museum Inc., 1177
The Recreation Association, 1207
Réseau du sport étudiant du Québec, 1222
Réseau du sport étudiant du Québec Est-du-Québec, 1223
Réseau du sport étudiant du Québec Montréal, 1223
Sask Sport Inc., 1254
Saskatchewan High Schools Athletic Association, 1267
Saskatchewan Sports Hall of Fame & Museum, 1275
School Sport Canada, 1284
School Sports Newfoundland & Labrador, 1284
Société des Jeux de l'Acadie inc., 1318
Sport BC, 1344
Sport Dispute Resolution Centre of Canada, 1344
Sport Manitoba, 1344
Sport New Brunswick, 1344
Sport Newfoundland & Labrador, 1345
Sport North Federation, 1345
Sport Nova Scotia, 1345
Sport PEI Inc., 1345
Sport Yukon, 1345
Sports-Québec, 1346
Toronto Ukraina Sports Association, 1388
Tournoi de Soccer de Victoriaville, 1393
True Sport Foundation, 1399
Ultimate Canada, 1404
ViaSport, 1432
Vintage Road Racing Association, 1435
WinSport Canada, 1460
York Region Athletic Association, 1473
Yukon Aboriginal Sport Circle, 1476
Yukon Schools' Athletic Association, 1480

Sports Cars
Sports Car Club of British Columbia, 1345
Sunbeam Sportscar Owners Club of Canada, 1354

Sports Facilities
Association québécoise des arénas et des installations récréatives et sportives, 171

Sports for People with Disabilities
Achilles Canada, 5
Alberta Amputee Sports & Recreation Association, 22
Alberta Cerebral Palsy Sport Association, 27
Alberta Deaf Sports Association, 32
Alberta Northern Lights Wheelchair Basketball Society, 41
Association québécoise de sports pour paralytiques cérébraux, 171
Association sportive des sourds du Québec inc., 178
BC Adaptive Snowsports, 200
Blind Sailing Association of Canada, 214
Blind Sports Nova Scotia, 214
British Columbia Blind Sports & Recreation Association, 234
British Columbia Deaf Sports Federation, 238
British Columbia Wheelchair Sports Association, 258
Calgary Sledge Hockey Association, 274
Canadian Amputee Golf Association, 292
Canadian Amputee Sports Association, 292
Canadian Association for Disabled Skiing, 299
Canadian Association for Disabled Skiing - Alberta, 299
Canadian Association for Disabled Skiing - National Capital Division, 299
Canadian Association for Disabled Skiing - New Brunswick, 299
Canadian Association for Disabled Skiing - Newfoundland & Labrador Division, 299
Canadian Association for Disabled Skiing - Nova Scotia, 299
Canadian Association for Disabled Skiing - Ontario, 300
Canadian Blind Sports Association Inc., 344
Canadian Cerebral Palsy Sports Association, 354
Canadian Deaf Ice Hockey Federation, 376
Canadian Electric Wheelchair Hockey Association, 380
Canadian Paralympic Committee, 449
Canadian Wheelchair Basketball Association, 503
Canadian Wheelchair Sports Association, 503
Commission de Ski pour Personnes Handicapées du Québec, 593
Disabled Sailing Association of B.C., 658
George Bray Sports Association, 770
Manitoba Blind Sports Association, 932
Manitoba Cerebral Palsy Sports Association, 933
Manitoba Wheelchair Sports Association, 947
Nova Scotia Deaf Sports Association, 1043
Ontario Amputee & Les Autres Sports Association, 1059
Ontario Blind Sports Association, 1068
Ontario Cerebral Palsy Sports Association, 1071
Ontario Deaf Sports Association, 1076
Ontario Sledge Hockey Association, 1105
Ontario Wheelchair Sports Association, 1113
Paralympic Sports Association (Alberta), 1138
ParaSport & Recreation PEI, 1138
ParaSport Ontario, 1139
Parasports Québec, 1139
Saskatchewan Deaf Sports Association, 1263
Saskatchewan Ski Association - Skiing for Disabled, 1274
Saskatchewan Wheelchair Sports Association, 1278
Ski Hawks Ottawa, 1302
Special Olympics BC, 1339
Special Olympics Yukon, 1340
SportAbility BC, 1345
Wheelchair Sports Alberta, 1452
Wheelchair Sports Association of Newfoundland & Labrador, 1452
Wolverines Wheelchair Sports Association, 1460

Sports, Amateur
Alberta Amateur Baseball Council, 22
Alberta Amateur Softball Association, 22
Alberta Amateur Speed Skating Association, 22
Alberta Amateur Wrestling Association, 22
Alberta Bodybuilding Association, 26
Baseball Alberta, 198
Baseball BC, 198
Baseball New Brunswick, 198
Baseball Nova Scotia, 198
Baseball Ontario, 198
Baseball PEI, 198
Basketball Manitoba, 198
Basketball Yukon, 199
Biathlon Yukon, 208
Boxing Alberta, 220
Boxing BC Association, 220
Boxing Manitoba, 220
Boxing New Brunswick Boxe, 220
Boxing Newfoundland & Labrador, 220
Boxing Nova Scotia, 220
Boxing Ontario, 220
Boxing Saskatchewan, 220
British Columbia Amateur Bodybuilding Association, 230
British Columbia Amateur Hockey Association, 230
British Columbia Amateur Softball Association, 230
British Columbia Netball Association, 247
British Columbia Speed Skating Association, 254
British Columbia Weightlifting Association, 258
British Columbia Wrestling Association, 258
Canadian Amateur Boxing Association, 292
Canadian Amateur Softball Association, 292
Canadian Amateur Wrestling Association, 292
Canadian Association of Freediving & Apnea, 316
Canadian Athletes Now Fund, 337
Charlottetown Area Baseball Association, 552
Diving Plongeon Canada, 659
Edmonton International Baseball Foundation, 678
Fédération de Netball du Québec, 710
Fédération de Patinage de Vitesse du Québec, 710
Fédération du baseball amateur du Québec, 719
Fédération Québécoise de Boxe Olympique, 727
Football BC, 750
Football PEI, 750
Halifax County United Soccer Club, 799
Halifax Sport & Social Club, 799
Hamilton Baseball Umpires' Association, 801
Hockey Alberta, 817
Hockey Canada, 817
Hockey Canada Foundation, 817
Hockey Manitoba, 818
Hockey New Brunswick, 818
Hockey Newfoundland & Labrador, 818
Hockey North, 818
Hockey Northwestern Ontario, 818
Hockey Nova Scotia, 818
Hockey PEI, 818
Hockey Québec, 818
Hockey Yukon, 818
Kawartha Baseball Umpires Association, 882
KidSport Alberta, 886
KidSport British Columbia, 886
KidSport Canada, 886
KidSport Manitoba, 886
KidSport New Brunswick, 886
KidSport Newfoundland & Labrador, 887
KidSport Northwest Territories, 887
KidSport Nova Scotia, 887
KidSport Ontario, 887
KidSport PEI, 887
KidSport Saskatchewan, 887
Manitoba Amateur Bodybuilding Association, 928
Manitoba Baseball Association, 932
Manitoba Speed Skating Association, 945
Netball Alberta, 1003
Netball Canada, 1003
Netball Ontario, 1003
Newfoundland & Labrador Amateur Bodybuilding Association, 1015
Newfoundland & Labrador Speed Skating Association, 1022
Newfoundland Baseball, 1022
Northern Ontario Hockey Association, 1035
Northwest Territories Amateur Speed Skating Association, 1037
Nova Scotia Amateur Bodybuilding Association, 1040
Nunavut Speed Skating Association, 1051
Ontario Amateur Softball Association, 1059
Ontario Amateur Wrestling Association, 1059
Ontario Hockey Federation, 1084
Ontario Physique Association, 1096
Ontario Speed Skating Association, 1108
Ontario Umpires Association, 1111
Prince Edward Island Amateur Boxing Association, 1171
Prince Edward Island Baseball Umpires Association, 1172
Prince Edward Island Hockey Referees Association, 1174
Rowing Canada Aviron, 1237
Saint John Jeux Canada Games Foundation Inc., 1247
Saskatchewan Amateur Speed Skating Association, 1255
Saskatchewan Amateur Wrestling Association, 1255
Saskatchewan Baseball Association, 1259
Saskatchewan Bodybuilding Association, 1260
Saskatchewan Hockey Association, 1267
Speed Skate New Brunswick, 1341
Speed Skate Nova Scotia, 1341
Speed Skate PEI, 1341
Speed Skating Canada, 1341
Sport Jeunesse, 1344
Thunder Bay Minor Hockey Association, 1378
Vintage Road Racing Association, 1435
Whitehorse Minor Soccer Association, 1453
Windsor & District Baseball Umpires Association, 1456
Wrestling Nova Scotia, 1468
Yukon Amateur Boxing Association, 1477
Yukon Amateur Speed Skating Association, 1477
Yukon Golf Association, 1478
Yukon Schools' Athletic Association, 1480
Yukon Weightlifting Association, 1480

Squash
NWT Squash, 1052
Saskatchewan Squash, 1276
Squash Alberta, 1347
Squash British Columbia, 1347
Squash Canada, 1347
Squash Manitoba, 1347
Squash Newfoundland & Labrador Inc., 1347
Squash Nova Scotia, 1347
Squash Ontario, 1347
Squash PEI, 1347
Squash Québec, 1347
Squash Yukon, 1347

Staff Training & Development
Association of Service Providers for Employability & Career Training, 162
British Columbia Career Development Association, 235
Canadian Heartland Training Railway, 403
Ontario Municipal Management Institute, 1092
Open Door Group, 1114
Prospect Human Services, 1189
Toronto Workforce Innovation Group, 1388

Stained Glass
Artists in Stained Glass, 85

Standards
Advertising Standards Canada, 10
Alliance of Credential Evaluation Services of Canada, 58
Association pour la protection des intérêts des consommateurs de la Côte-Nord, 166
Canadian Agency for Drugs & Technologies in Health, 289
Canadian Circulations Audit Board Inc., 357

Subject Index / Statistics

Canadian Evaluation Society, 383
Canadian General Standards Board, 396
Canadian Lumber Standards Accreditation Board, 428
Canadian Standards Association, 490
Consumers International, 1519
Consumers' Association of Canada, 626
International Organization for Standardization, 1554
Ontario Association of Property Standards Officers Inc., 1065
Qualifications Evaluation Council of Ontario, 1195
Vividata, 1436

Statistics
Alberta Society of Surveying & Mapping Technologies, 48
Association des statisticiennes et statisticiens du Québec, 128
Canadian Association of Professional Employees, 328
Canadian Institute for Health Information, 412
Canadian Society for Epidemiology & Biostatistics, 474
Council of Canadian Fire Marshals & Fire Commissioners, 633
International Statistical Institute, 1562
Statistical Society of Canada, 1348

Steel Industry
American Iron & Steel Institute, 1494
American Wire Producers Association, 1504
Canadian Institute of Steel Construction, 419
Canadian Sheet Steel Building Institute, 470
Canadian Steel Construction Council, 490
Canadian Steel Door Manufacturers Association, 491
Canadian Steel Producers Association, 491
Canadian Steel Trade & Employment Congress, 491
Reinforcing Steel Institute of Ontario, 1217
Steel Recycling Institute, 1597
Steel Structures Education Foundation, 1349
United Steelworkers of America (AFL-CIO/CLC), 1600

Stem Cells
Stem Cell Network, 1349

Storytelling
Canadian Oral History Association, 446
Storytellers of Canada, 1350

Streetcars
Ontario Electric Railway Historical Association, 1077

Stress
Canadian Centre for Wellbeing, 354
Canadian Institute of Stress, 419
Cell Stress Society International, 1516

Stroke
Association des neurotraumatisés de l'Outaouais, 121
Fondation des maladies du coeur du Québec, 745
Heart & Stroke Foundation of Alberta, NWT & Nunavut, 808
Heart & Stroke Foundation of British Columbia & Yukon, 808
Heart & Stroke Foundation of Canada, 808
Heart & Stroke Foundation of Manitoba, 808
Heart & Stroke Foundation of New Brunswick, 808
Heart & Stroke Foundation of Newfoundland & Labrador, 809
Heart & Stroke Foundation of Nova Scotia, 809
Heart & Stroke Foundation of Ontario, 809
Heart & Stroke Foundation of Prince Edward Island Inc., 809
Heart & Stroke Foundation of Saskatchewan, 809
Stroke Recovery Association of BC, 1352
Stroke Recovery Association of Manitoba Inc., 1352

Student Exchanges
AFS Interculture Canada, 13
Canadian Education Exchange Foundation, 380
Experiences Canada, 699
Foundation for Educational Exchange Between Canada & the United States of America, 755
IAESTE Canada (International Association for the Exchange of Students for Technical Experience), 829
Queen's University International Centre, 1200

Students
African & Caribbean Students' Network of Montréal, 12
African Students Association - Univeristy of Alberta, 13
African Students Association of Concordia, 13
Alberta Council on Admissions & Transfer, 31
Association pour la voix études au Québec, 167
Athabasca University Students' Union, 180
Canadian Alliance of Student Associations, 291
Canadian Association of College & University Student Services, 310
Canadian Association of Pharmacy Students & Interns, 326
Canadian Association of Student Financial Aid Administrators, 334
Canadian Catholic Campus Ministry, 351
Canadian Committee of Graduate Students in Education, 361
Canadian Federation of Engineering Students, 386
Canadian Federation of Students, 388
Canadian Friends of Yeshiva University, 395
Canadian Nursing Students' Association, 443
Canadian Organization of Campus Activities, 447
Canadian Political Science Students' Association, 457
Canadian Student Leadership Association, 491
Caribbean Students' Society of McGill University, 512
Concordia Caribbean Students' Union, 609
Confédération des associations d'étudiants et étudiantes de l'Université Laval, 610
Fédération des associations étudiantes du campus de l'université de Montréal, 712
Fédération étudiante universitaire du Québec, 720
Filipino Students' Association of Toronto, 735
FIRST Robotics Canada, 741
Greater Montreal Athletic Association, 784
Groupe gai de l'Université Laval, 792
Hillel of Greater Toronto, 814
IMCS Pax Romana, 1531
International Federation of Medical Students' Associations, 1548
International Student Pugwash, 1562
Korean Students' Association of Canada, 893
Manitoba Medical Students' Association, 940
National Educational Association of Disabled Students, 993
Ontario Association of Student Financial Aid Administrators, 1066
Ontario Medical Students Association, 1090
Ontario Undergraduate Student Alliance, 1111
Oshki Anishnawbeg Student Association, 1128
Professional Student Services Personnel, 1186
Réseau du sport étudiant du Québec Abitibi-Témiscamingue, 1222
Réseau du sport étudiant du Québec Cantons-de-l'Est, 1222
Réseau du sport étudiant du Québec Chaudière-Appalaches, 1222
Réseau du sport étudiant du Québec Côte-Nord, 1222
Réseau du sport étudiant du Québec Lac Saint-Louis, 1223
Réseau du sport étudiant du Québec Laurentides-Lanaudière, 1223
Réseau du sport étudiant du Québec Montérégie, 1223
Réseau du sport étudiant du Québec Outaouais, 1223
Réseau du sport étudiant du Québec Saguenay-Lac St-Jean, 1223
Réseau du sport étudiant du Québec, secteur Mauricie, 1223
SEDS - USA, 1588
Sports Laval, 1346
Student Christian Movement of Canada, 1352
University of Alberta Library & Information Studies Alumni Association, 1419
University of Alberta South East Asian Students' Association, 1419
University of Alberta Students' Union, 1419
University of Toronto Native Students Association, 1421

Stuttering
Association des jeunes bègues de Québec, 117
British Columbia Association of People Who Stutter, 232
Canadian Stuttering Association, 491
Institute for Stuttering Treatment & Research & the Communication Improvement Program, 844

Sugar
Canadian Society of Sugar Artistry, 488
Canadian Sugar Institute, 491

Suicide Prevention
Association québécoise de prévention du suicide, 171
Canadian Association for Suicide Prevention, 304
Centre for Suicide Prevention, 534
Suicide Action Montréal, 1353
Vancouver Island Crisis Society, 1426
Your Life Counts, 1475

Sulphur
Alberta Sulphur Research Ltd., 48

Support Groups
Affected Families of Police Homicide, 11
Al-Anon Montréal, 21
Alcoholics Anonymous (GTA Intergroup), 52
Alcooliques Anonymes du Québec, 53
Association of Parent Support Groups in Ontario Inc., 155
Association québécoise des troubles d'apprentissage - section Outaouais, 175
BC Hands & Voices, 201
Burn Survivors Association, 265
Calgary Alpha House Society, 271
Canadian Assembly of Narcotics Anonymous, 296
Canadian Association of Pregnancy Support Services, 328
Canadian Cancer Survivor Network, 349
Childhood Cancer Canada Foundation, 560
Chronic Pain Association of Canada, 568
Co-Dependents Recovery Society, 580
Emotions Anonymous, 1523
From Grief To Action, 763
Greater Toronto Al-Anon Information Services, 785
Hamilton Program for Schizophrenia, 802
Helping Other Parents Everywhere Inc., 812
Hominum, 820
Inner Peace Movement of Canada, 839
Mamingwey Burn Survivor Society, 928
MEFM Myalgic Encephalomyelitis & Fibromyalgia Society of British Columbia, 959
Mood Disorders Association of Ontario, 973
Mood Disorders Society of Canada, 973
Outremangeurs Anonymes, 1133
Parents Without Partners Inc., 1582
Parents, Families & Friends of Lesbians & Gays, 1582
PeerNetBC, 1148
PFLAG Canada Inc., 1155
Phobies-Zéro, 1157
Projet d'Intervention auprès des mineurs-res prostitués-ées, 1188
Self-Help Connection Clearinghouse Association, 1289
Self-Help Resource Centre, 1289
Seniors Peer Helping Program, 1290
Southern Ontario Cocaine Anonymous, 1338
Suicide Action Montréal, 1353
Support Organization for Trisomy 18, 13 & Related Disorders, 1356
Survivors of Abuse Recovering, 1357
Vasculitis Foundation Canada, 1430
Westward Goals Support Services Inc., 1451

Surgeons
Association des Perfusionnistes du Québec Inc., 122
Association of International Physicians & Surgeons of Ontario, 149
Association Québécoise de chirurgie, 169
British Columbia Surgical Society, 255
Canadian Association of General Surgeons, 316
Canadian Association of Paediatric Surgeons, 325
Canadian Association of Thoracic Surgeons, 334
Canadian Society of Cardiac Surgeons, 481
Canadian Society of Clinical Perfusion, 482
College of Physicians & Surgeons of Alberta, 588
College of Physicians & Surgeons of British Columbia, 588
College of Physicians & Surgeons of Manitoba, 588
College of Physicians & Surgeons of New Brunswick, 588
College of Physicians & Surgeons of Newfoundland & Labrador, 588
College of Physicians & Surgeons of Ontario, 588
College of Physicians & Surgeons of Prince Edward Island, 588
College of Physicians & Surgeons of Saskatchewan, 588
The Royal College of Physicians & Surgeons of Canada, 1241
Society of Urologic Surgeons of Ontario, 1331

Surgery
American Association for Thoracic Surgery, 1489
American Society of Colon & Rectal Surgeons, 1499
Association d'oto-rhino-laryngologie et de chirurgie cervico-faciale du Québec, 99
Canadian Society for Surgical Oncology, 477
Canadian Society for Vascular Surgery, 479
Canadian Society of Otolaryngology - Head & Neck Surgery, 485
International Society of Surgery, 1561
Operating Room Nurses Association of Canada, 1115
Ostomy Canada Society, 1129

Sustainable Cities
BurlingtonGreen Environmental Association, 265
EcoPerth, 673
EcoSource Mississauga, 673
FutureWatch Environment & Development Education Partners, 765
International Centre for Sustainable Cities, 855
Rideau Environmental Action League, 1231
Severn Sound Environmental Association, 1292
Sustainable Kingston, 1358
Sustainable Urban Development Association, 1358
Sustainable Urban Development Association, 1358
Toronto Environmental Alliance, 1384
Urban Development Institute Greater Edmonton Chapter, 1422
Urban Development Institute of Canada, 1422
Urban Development Institute of Nova Scotia, 1422
World Council on City Data, 1465

Sustainable Development
African Wildlife Foundation, 1486
Alliance for Sustainability, 1487
American Farmland Trust, 1492
American Fisheries Society, 1493
The Barnard-Boecker Centre Foundation, 196
Battle River Research Group, 199
Canada's Oil Sands Innovation Alliance, 282
Canadian Arctic Resources Committee, 295
Citizens Opposed to Paving the Escarpment, 570
Community Energy Association, 597
Construction Resource Initiatives Council, 624
David Suzuki Foundation, 651
Division of Sustainable Development, 1521
Eastern Ontario Model Forest, 670
Ecological Agriculture Projects, 672
EnviroLink, 1523
Evergreen, 699
Foothills Research Institute, 751
Fraser Basin Council, 757
Friends of the Earth Canada, 762
Fundy Model Forest Network, 764
Greenspace Alliance of Canada's Capital, 789
Groupe de recherche appliquée en macroécologie, 791
Groupe de recherche en écologie sociale, 791

Gulf of Maine Council on the Marine Environment, 794
Ingénieurs Sans Frontières Québec, 838
Institute of Urban Studies, 847
International Commission of Agricultural & Biosystems Engineering, 1542
International Institute for Applied Systems Analysis, 1551
International Institute for Sustainable Development, 858
International Institute of Fisheries Economics & Trade, 1551
International Society for Ecological Economics, 1557
International Union for Conservation of Nature, 1563
Lake Abitibi Model Forest, 895
LEAD Canada Inc., 902
Manitoba Model Forest, 940
Marine Renewables Canada, 950
McGregor Model Forest, 955
Model Forest of Newfoundland & Labrador, 971
Muniscope, 982
The Natural Step Canada, 999
New Brunswick Soil & Crop Improvement Association, 1012
Nunavut Harvesters Association, 1051
Ontario Farmland Trust, 1078
Ontario Sustainable Energy Association, 1109
Pacific Peoples' Partnership, 1135
The Pembina Institute, 1149
Physicians for Global Survival (Canada), 1158
Prince Albert Model Forest Association Inc., 1171
Resource Efficient Agricultural Production, 1227
The Rocky Mountain Institute, 1586
Saskatchewan Soil Conservation Association, 1275
Society for Ecological Restoration International, 1590
Sustainable Buildings Canada, 1357
Sustainable Development Technology Canada, 1357
Sustainable Kingston, 1358
UNEP - World Conservation Monitoring Centre, 1598
United Nations Development Programme, 1599
United Nations Environment Programme, 1600
United Nations Human Settlements Programme (Habitat), 1600
USC Canada, 1423
Vrac environnement groupe d'action et de recherche en développement durable, 1439
Wallace Center, Winrock International, 1601
Waswanipi Cree Model Forest, 1440
Whole Village, 1453
Wildlife Habitat Canada, 1454
World Business Council for Sustainable Development, 1603

Swimming
Alberta Summer Swimming Association, 48
British Columbia Summer Swimming Association, 255
Club de natation Natchib inc., 575
Fédération de natation du Québec, 710
International Amateur Swimming Federation, 1535
Solo Swims of Ontario Inc., 1332
Swim Alberta, 1358
Swim BC, 1358
Swim Nova Scotia, 1358
Swim Ontario, 1359
Swim Saskatchewan, 1359
Swim Yukon, 1359
Swimming Canada, 1359
Swimming New Brunswick, 1359
Swimming Newfoundland & Labrador, 1359
Swimming Prince Edward Island, 1359
Swim-Natation Manitoba, 1359
Synchro Alberta, 1360
Synchro BC, 1360
Synchro Canada, 1360
Synchro Manitoba, 1360
Synchro Newfoundland & Labrador, 1360
Synchro Nova Scotia, 1361
Synchro PEI, 1361
Synchro Saskatchewan, 1361
Synchro Swim Ontario, 1361
Synchro Yukon Association, 1361
Synchro-Québec, 1361

Whitehorse Glacier Bears Swim Club, 1453

Swine
Canadian Association of Swine Veterinarians, 334
Canadian Swine Breeders' Association, 491
Canadian Swine Exporters Association, 491
Saskatchewan Swine Breeders' Association, 1276

Swiss Canadians & Switzerland
Canadian Swiss Cultural Association, 491
Chambre de commerce Canado-Suisse (Québec) Inc., 540
Swiss Canadian Chamber of Commerce (Ontario) Inc., 1359
Swiss Club Saskatoon, 1359

Synagogues
Canadian Council of Conservative Synagogues, 368
Congregation Beth Israel - British Columbia, 612
Shaare Zion Congregation, 1293
Toronto Association of Synagogue & Temple Administrators, 1382

Systems Management
AFCOM, 1485

Table Soccer
Canadian Table Soccer Federation, 492
Foosball Québec, 750
Ontario Table Soccer Association, 1109

Table Tennis
Alberta Table Tennis Association, 48
British Columbia Table Tennis Association, 255
Chinese Canadian Table Tennis Federation, 564
Fédération de tennis de table du Québec, 710
Manitoba Table Tennis Association, 945
Newfoundland & Labrador Table Tennis Association, 1022
Nova Scotia Table Tennis Association, 1049
Ontario Table Tennis Association, 1109
Prince Edward Island Table Tennis Association, 1178
Saskatchewan Table Tennis Association Inc., 1276
Table Tennis Canada, 1366
Table Tennis Yukon, 1366

Tai Chi
Taoist Tai Chi Society of Canada, 1366

Taiwanese Canadians & Taiwan
Canada Taiwan Trade Association, 280
Greater Vancouver Taiwanese Canadian Association, 787
Taiwan Entrepreneurs Society Taipei/Toronto, 1366
Taiwan Trade Center, Vancouver, 1366
Taiwanese Canadian Cultural Society, 1366

Taoism
Fung Loy Kok Institute of Taoism, 764
Taoist Tai Chi Society of Canada, 1366

Taxation
The Association of Professional Accounting & Tax Consultants Inc., 156
Canadian Property Tax Association, Inc., 461
Canadian Tax Foundation, 492
Canadian Taxpayers Federation, 492
EFILE Association of Canada, 681
Ontario Municipal Tax & Revenue Association, 1092
Union of Taxation Employees, 1408

Tea Industry
Tea Association of Canada, 1367

Teaching
Adult Educators' Provincial Specialist Association, 9
Alberta Teachers' Association, 49
Alliance canadienne des responsables et enseignants en français (langue maternelle), 55
Alliance des professeures et professeurs de Montréal, 56
Alliance Française de Calgary, 57
Appalachian Teachers' Association, 73
Association canadienne des professeurs d'immersion, 94

Association des enseignantes et des enseignants franco-ontariens, 112
Association des enseignantes et des enseignants francophones du Nouveau-Brunswick, 112
Association des enseignants en infographie et en imprimerie du Québec, 112
Association des ingénieurs-professeurs des sciences appliquées, 116
Association des médecins cliniciens enseignants de Montréal, 119
Association des professeurs de français des universités et collèges canadiens, 124
Association des professeurs de l'École Polytechnique de Montréal, 124
Association of BC Drama Educators, 140
Association of British Columbia Teachers of English as an Additional Language, 140
Association of Canadian College & University Teachers of English, 141
Association of Educators of Gifted, Talented & Creative Children in BC, 147
Association of Teachers of English in Quebec, 162
Association pour les applications pédagogiques de l'ordinateur au postsecondaire, 167
Association provinciale des enseignantes et enseignants du Québec, 168
Association Provinciale des Professeurs d'Immersion et du Programme Francophone, 168
Association québécoise de pédagogie collégiale, 170
Association québécoise des éducatrices et éducateurs spécialisés en arts plastiques, 172
Association québécoise des enseignantes et des enseignants du primaire, 172
Association québécoise des professeurs de français, 174
Association québécoise des utilisateurs de l'ordinateur au primaire-secondaire, 175
BC Rural & Multigrade Teachers' Association, 202
Black Educators Association of Nova Scotia, 213
British Columbia Art Teachers' Association, 230
British Columbia Association of Mathematics Teachers, 232
British Columbia Association of Teachers of Modern Languages, 233
British Columbia Cooperative Learning Provincial Specialist Association, 237
British Columbia Culinary Arts Specialist Association, 238
British Columbia Dance Educators' Association, 238
British Columbia Primary Teachers Association, 249
British Columbia Registered Music Teachers' Association, 250
British Columbia Science Teachers' Association, 252
British Columbia Social Studies Teachers Association, 253
British Columbia Teacher Regulation Branch, 255
British Columbia Teacher-Librarians' Association, 255
British Columbia Teachers for Peace & Global Education, 256
British Columbia Teachers of English Language Arts, 256
British Columbia Teachers' Federation, 256
British Columbia Technology Education Association, 256
Canadian Association for the Study of Discourse & Writing, 306
Canadian Association of Montessori Teachers, 321
Canadian Association of Retired Teachers, 331
Canadian Association of University Teachers, 335
Canadian Council of Teachers of English Language Arts, 370
Canadian Dance Teachers' Association, 375
Canadian Society of Teachers of the Alexander Technique, 488
Canadian Teachers' Federation, 493
Computer-Using Educators of BC, 609

Conseil pédagogique interdisciplinaire du Québec, 619
Curriculum Services Canada, 646
Early Childhood Educators of British Columbia, 666
École internationale de français, 672
Education International, 1522
Educators for Distributed Learning PSA (British Columbia), 680
Elementary Teachers' Federation of Ontario, 684
English Additional Language Learners Provincial Specialist Association, 689
Environmental Educators' Provincial Specialist Association, 691
Fédération des Associations de Musiciens-Éducateurs du Québec, 712
Fédération des enseignants de cégeps, 714
Fédération des professionnelles et professionnels de l'éducation du Québec, 718
Fédération des Syndicats de l'Enseignement, 719
Fédération nationale des enseignants et des enseignantes du Québec, 721
Federation of Teachers of Jewish Schools, 726
Fédération québécoise des professeures et professeurs d'université, 729
Halton District Educational Assistants Association, 800
Irish Dance Teacher's Association of Eastern Canada, 864
Laurier Teachers Union, 900
Learning Assistance Teachers' Association, 903
Manitoba Teachers' Society, 946
National Association of Teachers of Singing, 1574
New Brunswick Teachers' Association, 1013
Newfoundland & Labrador Teachers' Association, 1022
Northwest Territories Teachers' Association, 1038
Nova Scotia Music Educators' Association, 1047
Nova Scotia Teachers Union, 1049
Nunavut Teachers' Association, 1051
Ontario Association of Physics Teachers, 1065
Ontario College of Teachers, 1072
Ontario English Catholic Teachers' Association (CLC), 1077
Ontario Federation of Teaching Parents, 1080
Ontario Modern Language Teachers Association, 1091
Ontario Secondary School Teachers' Federation, 1103
Ontario Teachers' Federation, 1110
Physical & Health Educators of Manitoba, 1158
Physical Education in British Columbia, 1158
Polish Teachers Association in Canada, 1164
Prince Edward Island Teachers' Federation, 1178
Provincial Intermediate Teachers' Association, 1191
Québec Board of Black Educators, 1196
The Retired Teachers of Ontario, 1228
Saint Francis Xavier Association of University Teachers, 1246
Saskatchewan Council for Educators of Non-English Speakers, 1262
Saskatchewan Home Economics Teachers Association, 1267
Saskatchewan Registered Music Teachers' Association, 1273
Saskatchewan Teachers' Federation, 1276
Science Teachers' Association of Ontario, 1285
Société des professeurs d'histoire du Québec inc., 1318
South Western Alberta Teachers' Convention Association, 1336
Teachers of English to Speakers of Other Languages, Inc., 1597
Teachers of Home Economics Specialist Association, 1367
Teachers of Inclusive Education - British Columbia, 1367
Teachers Without Borders, 1597
TEAL Manitoba, 1368
TESL Canada Federation, 1372
TESL Ontario, 1373
TESL Prince Edward Island, 1373
Toronto Gaelic Learners Association, 1384

Subject Index / Technicians & Technologists

Vancouver Elementary School Teachers' Association, 1425
Western Canada Irish Dancing Teachers Association, 1448
Yukon Teachers' Association, 1480

Technicians & Technologists
Alberta College of Medical Diagnostic & Therapeutic Technologists, 29
Applied Science Technologists & Technicians of British Columbia, 74
Architectural & Building Technologists Association of Manitoba Inc., 78
Association des technologues en agroalimentaire, 129
Association of Architectural Technologists of Ontario, 139
Association of Engineering Technicians & Technologists of Newfoundland & Labrador, 147
Association of Science & Engineering Technology Professionals of Alberta, 162
British Columbia Association of Medical Radiation Technologists, 232
British Columbia Food Technolgists, 241
Canadian Association of Cardio-Pulmonary Technologists, 309
Canadian Association of Electroneurophysiology Technologists Inc., 312
Canadian Association of Medical Radiation Technologists, 320
Canadian Association of Pharmacy Technicians, 326
Canadian Board of Registration of Electroencephalograph Technologists Inc., 345
Canadian Council of Technicians & Technologists, 370
Canadian Explosive Technicians' Association, 383
Canadian Society for Medical Laboratory Science, 476
Canadian Society of Cardiology Technologists Inc., 481
Canadian Society of Orthopaedic Technologists, 485
Cardiology Technologists' Association of British Columbia, 511
Certified Technicians & Technologists Association of Manitoba, 538
College of Dental Technicians of British Columbia, 583
College of Dental Technologists of Alberta, 583
College of Dental Technologists of Ontario, 583
Dental Technicians Association of Saskatchewan, 653
Filipino Canadian Technical Professionals Association of Manitoba, Inc., 735
Institute of Food Technologists, 1532
International Society of Radiographers & Radiological Technologists, 1561
Island Technology Professionals, 865
Manitoba Association of Medical Radiation Technologists, 930
New Brunswick Society of Certified Engineering Technicians & Technologists, 1012
Newfoundland & Labrador Association of Medical Radiation Technologists, 1016
Newfoundland & Labrador Society for Medical Laboratory Science, 1021
Nova Scotia Association of Medical Radiation Technologists, 1041
Ontario Association of Certified Engineering Technicians & Technologists, 1062
Ontario Association of Medical Radiation Sciences, 1064
Ordre des technologues en imagerie médicale, en radio-oncologie et en élétrophysiologie médicale du Québec, 1124
Ordre des technologues professionnels du Québec, 1124
Pharmacy Technician Society of Alberta, 1157
Prince Edward Island Association of Medical Radiation Technologists, 1172
Prince Edward Island Society for Medical Laboratory Science, 1177
Saskatchewan Applied Science Technologists & Technicians, 1255
Saskatchewan Association of Medical Radiation Technologists, 1257

Société des technologues en nutrition, 1318
TechNova, 1369

Technology
Ability Society of Alberta, 2
Advanced Card Technology Association of Canada, 9
Alberta Sulphur Research Ltd., 48
American Association for the Advancement of Science, 1489
ASM International, 1506
ASM International - Calgary Chapter, 87
BC Association for Individualized Technology and Supports, 201
British Columbia Technology Education Association, 256
British Columbia Technology Industries Association, 256
Canada BIM Council Inc., 278
Canadian Advanced Technology Alliance, 288
Canadian Agency for Drugs & Technologies in Health, 289
Canadian Environmental Technology Advancement Corporation - West, 382
Canadian Innovation Centre, 411
Canadian Institute of Food Science & Technology, 415
Canadian Printable Electronics Industry Association, 459
Canadian Science & Technology Historical Association, 468
Canadian Society for Chemical Technology, 473
Canadian Technology Human Resources Board, 493
Centre for the Study of Learning & Performance, 534
College of Medical Laboratory Technologists of Alberta, 586
Commission canadienne pour la théorie des machines et des mécanismes, 593
Communitech, 595
Construction Technology Centre Atlantic, 625
HealthBridge Foundation of Canada, 807
IEEE Microwave Theory & Techniques Society, 1530
Information Technology Association of Canada, 837
Innovate Calgary, 839
Innovation & Technology Association of Ontario, 839
Interactive Ontario, 851
International Association of Science & Technology for Development, 854
International Council on Global Privacy & Security, By Design, 856
International Student Pugwash, 1562
International Union of Food Science & Technology, 861
Merry Go Round Children's Foundation, 962
The Neil Squire Foundation, 1002
New Brunswick Society of Medical Laboratory Technologists, 1012
Newfoundland & Labrador Association of Technology Industries, 1016
Northwestern Ontario Technology Association, 1040
Nova Scotia College of Medical Laboratory Technologists, 1042
Shad Valley International, 1293
Society for Canadian Women in Science & Technology, 1325
Society for the History of Technology, 1591
TechConnex, 1368
Technion Canada, 1368
Visions of Science Network for Learning, 1436

Telecommunications
Bell Aliant Pioneers, 204
British Columbia Association of Broadcasters, 231
British Columbia Broadband Association, 234
Broadcast Educators Association of Canada, 259
Canadian Communications Foundation, 361
Canadian Overseas Telecommunications Union, 448
Canadian Wireless Telecommunications Association, 504
Independent Telecommunications Providers Association, 833
Information & Communication Technologies Association of Manitoba, 836

International Telecommunications Society, 1562
Ontario Pioneers, 1096
Radio Advisory Board of Canada, 1202
SaskTel Pioneers, 1280
Telecommunications Employees Association of Manitoba, 1369
Telecommunities Canada Inc., 1369
TelecomPioneers, 1597
TelecomPioneers of Alberta, 1369
TelecomPioneers of Canada, 1369

Telehealth
Association of Telehealth Service Providers, 1513
Canada Health Infoway, 280
International Society for Telemedicine & eHealth, 1559
MBTelehealth Network, 955

Telephones
Canadian Independent Telephone Association, 411
Syndicat des agents de maîtrise de TELUS (ind.), 1362
Telephone Historical Centre, 1369
UniforACL, 1405

Television Broadcasting
Academy of Canadian Cinema & Television, 3
The Actors' Fund of Canada, 7
ACTRA Fraternal Benefit Society, 7
Ajjiit Nunavut Media Association, 20
Alliance of Canadian Cinema, Television & Radio Artists, 58
Alliance québécoise des techniciens de l'image et du son, 58
Association des réalisateurs et réalisatrices du Québec, 127
Association québécoise de la production médiatique, 170
The Atlantic Film Festival Association, 184
Banff World Television Festival Foundation, 196
British Columbia Association of Broadcasters, 231
Broadcast Educators Association of Canada, 259
Canada Media Fund, 280
Canadian Association of Community Television Users & Stations, 311
Canadian Association of Film Distributors & Exporters, 314
Canadian Communications Foundation, 361
Canadian Media Production Association, 432
Canadian Women in Communications, 505
Central Canada Broadcast Engineers, 524
Directors Guild of Canada, 657
FilmOntario, 735
The Harold Greenberg Fund, 804
Independent Production Fund, 833
Interactive Ontario, 851
Motion Picture Association - Canada, 975
NABET 700 CEP, 987
National Association of Television Program Executives, 1574
National Screen Institute - Canada, 996
North American Broadcasters Association, 1029
Numeris, 1050
Ontario Association of Broadcasters, 1062
Parlimage CCF, 1143
Radio Television Digital News Association (Canada), 1203
Screen Actors Guild - American Federation of Television & Radio Artists, 1588
Society of Motion Picture & Television Engineers, 1593
Television Bureau of Canada, Inc., 1370
VISION TV, 1436
Western Association of Broadcasters, 1447
Women in Film & Television - Toronto, 1461
Women in Film & Television Alberta, 1461
Women in Film & Television Vancouver, 1461
Writers Guild of Canada, 1468

Telework
Women in a Home Office, 1460

Tenants
Federation of Metro Tenants' Associations, 725

Tennis
Alberta Tennis Association, 49
Club 'Les Pongistes d'Ungava', 574
International Tennis Federation, 1562

Northwest Territories Tennis Association, 1038
Nova Scotia Tennis Association, 1049
Ontario Tennis Association, 1110
Prince Edward Island Tennis Association, 1178
Tennis BC, 1370
Tennis Canada, 1370
Tennis Manitoba, 1371
Tennis New Brunswick, 1371
Tennis Newfoundland & Labrador, 1371
Tennis Québec, 1371
Tennis Saskatchewan, 1371
Tennis Yukon Association, 1371

Testing
Association des consultants et laboratoires experts, 110
Canadian Associated Air Balance Council, 297
Canadian Institute for NDE, 413
Canadian Standards Association, 490
Canadian Test Centre Inc., 494
Canadian Toy Testing Council, 496
Underwriters' Laboratories of Canada, 1404

Textiles
Canadian Textile Association, 494
Costume Society of Ontario, 632
Groupe CTT Group, 791
Industrial Fabrics Association International, 1531
Industrial Fabrics Association International Canada, 835
Institute of Textile Science, 847
International Textile Manufacturers Federation, 1562
Préventex - Association paritaire du textile, 1170
Syndicat des ouvriers du textile de Magog, 1363
UNITE HERE Canada, 1408
William Morris Society of Canada, 1455

Thalidomide
Thalidomide Victims Association of Canada, 1373

The Arts
Alberta Foundation for the Arts, 35
Algoma Arts Festival Association, 53
BC Alliance for Arts & Culture, 200
Blue Mountain Foundation for the Arts, 215
Business for the Arts, 267
Camrose Arts Society, 277
Canadian Arts Presenting Association, 296
Canadian Conference of the Arts, 363
Carleton-Victoria Arts Council, 513
Centre culturel canadien, 1516
Children's Arts Umbrella Association, 561
Conseil des arts et des lettres du Québec, 617
Dufferin Arts Council, 664
The Eckhardt-Gramatté Foundation, 671
Emil Skarin Fund, 686
Fort St. John Community Arts Council, 753
Hamber Foundation, 800
International Research Institute for Media, Communication & Cultural Development, 1556
Manitoba Holiday Festival of the Arts Inc., 938
Ontario Society of Artists, 1107
Royal Canadian Academy of Arts, 1239
The Royal Society for the Encouragement of Arts, Manufactures & Commerce, 1587
Saskatchewan Arts Board, 1256
Segal Centre for the Performing Arts at the Saidye, 1289
Station Arts Centre Cooperative, 1348
Tiger Hills Arts Association Inc., 1379
Truro Art Society, 1400
University of Saskatchewan Arts Council, 1420
Vancouver International Children's Festival, 1426
Volunteer Circle of the National Gallery of Canada, 1438
Western Front Society, 1449
X Changes Artists' Gallery & Studios Society, 1470
Yukon Art Society, 1477
Yukon Arts Centre, 1477

The Middle East
Canadian Friends of Peace Now (Shalom Achshav), 395
Middle East Studies Association of North America, 1571

Theatre
The Actors' Fund of Canada, 7
American Society for Theatre Research, 1499
The Arts & Letters Club, 85
Associated Designers of Canada, 89
Association des compagnies de théâtre, 109
Association des professionnels des arts de la scène du Québec, 125
Bard on the Beach Theatre Society, 196
BC Alliance for Arts & Culture, 200
Black Theatre Workshop, 213
British Columbia Drama Association, 239
Buddies in Bad Times Theatre, 261
Canadian Association for Theatre Research, 306
Canadian Institute for Theatre Technology, 413
The Canadian Stage Company, 490
Canadian Theatre Critics Association, 494
Carousel Players, 514
Catalyst Theatre Society of Alberta, 517
Centre des auteurs dramatiques, 530
Le Cercle Molière, 537
Compagnie vox théâtre, 608
Conseil québécois du théâtre, 620
Evergreen Theatre Society, 699
Fédération québécoise du théâtre amateur, 731
First Pacific Theatre Society, 739
First Vancouver Theatre Space Society, 739
Globe Theatre Society, 775
Greater Vancouver Professional Theatre Alliance, 787
Green Kids Inc., 788
Green Thumb Theatre for Young People, 789
The Guild Society, 794
Harbourfront Centre, 803
International Amateur Theatre Association, 1535
International Organization of Scenographers, Theatre Architects & Technicians, 1554
Intrepid Theatre Co. Society, 862
Kaleidoscope Theatre Productions Society, 880
Kitsilano Showboat Society, 891
Mulgrave Road Theatre Foundation, 978
Native Earth Performing Arts Inc., 998
Neptune Theatre Foundation, 1003
New West Theatre Society, 1014
Newfoundland & Labrador Drama Society, 1018
Ontario Ballet Theatre, 1067
Ontario Summer Theatre Association, 1109
Opéra Atelier, 1114
Playwrights Theatre Centre, 1162
Playwrights' Workshop Montréal, 1162
Prairie Theatre Exchange, 1170
Pumphouse Theatres Society, 1194
Royal Manitoba Theatre Centre, 1242
Rumble Productions Society, 1244
Segal Centre for the Performing Arts at the Saidye, 1289
Shaw Festival, 1294
Sun Ergos, A Company of Theatre & Dance, 1354
Tarragon Theatre, 1367
Théâtre Action, 1373
Theatre Alberta Society, 1373
Theatre Calgary, 1374
Théâtre de la Vieille 17, 1374
Théâtre des épinettes, 1374
Théâtre du Nouvel-Ontario, 1374
Théâtre du Trillium, 1374
Théâtre français de Toronto, 1374
Théâtre l'Escaouette, 1374
Théâtre la Catapulte, 1374
Théâtre la Seizième, 1374
Theatre Network (1975) Society, 1374
Theatre New Brunswick, 1374
Theatre Newfoundland Labrador, 1374
Theatre Ontario, 1374
Théâtre populaire d'Acadie, 1375
Theatre Saskatchewan, 1375
Theatre Terrific Society, 1375
Théâtres unis enfance jeunesse, 1375
Toronto Alliance for the Performing Arts, 1381
Toronto Association of Acting Studios, 1382
La Troupe du Jour, 1399
Two Planks & a Passion Theatre Company, 1401
Vancouver Moving Theatre, 1427
Vancouver TheatreSports League, 1429
Western Canada Theatre Company Society, 1448
Young People's Theatre, 1474

Theatres
Association des théâtres francophones du Canada, 129
Atlantic Motion Picture Exhibitors Association, 184
Cameco Capitol Arts Centre, 276
Motion Picture Theatre Association of Alberta, 975
Motion Picture Theatre Association of British Columbia, 975
Motion Picture Theatre Association of Central Canada, 975
Professional Association of Canadian Theatres, 1181
Théâtres associés inc., 1375

Theology
Canadian Council of Muslim Theologians, 369
Canadian Society for the Study of Religion, 478
Canadian Theological Society, 494
International Association of Patristic Studies, 1539
Student Christian Movement of Canada, 1352

Therapeutic Riding
Antigonish Therapeutic Riding Association, 72
British Columbia Therapeutic Riding Association, 257
Canadian Therapeutic Riding Association, 494
Cavalier Riding Club Ltd., 521
Central Ontario Developmental Riding Program, 525
Community Association for Riding for the Disabled, 596
Comox Valley Therapeutic Riding Society, 608
Cowichan Therapeutic Riding Association, 637
Equestrian Association for the Disabled, 694
Errington Therapeutic Riding Association, 695
Halifax Area Leisure & Therapeutic Riding Association, 798
Lanark County Therapeutic Riding Program, 897
Lethbridge Therapeutic Riding Association, 908
Little Bits Therapeutic Riding Association, 915
Manitoba Riding for the Disabled Association Inc., 943
Mirabel Morgan Special Riding Centre, 968
Mount View Special Riding Association, 976
Ontario Therapeutic Riding Association, 1110
Pacific Riding for Developing Abilities, 1136
PARD Therapeutic Riding, 1139
Peace Area Riding for the Disabled, 1146
Quest Support Services Inc., 1200
Quinte Therapeutic Riding Association, 1202
Regina Therapeutic Riding Association, 1212
SARI Therapeutic Riding, 1254
Sunrise Therapeutic Riding & Learning Centre, 1354
Therapeutic Ride Algoma, 1375
Victoria Therapeutic Riding Association, 1434
Windsor-Essex Therapeutic Riding Association, 1457

Therapeutic Touch
Atlantic Therapeutic Touch Network, 186

Therapy
British Columbia Play Therapy Association, 249
British Columbia Therapeutic Recreation Association, 256
Canadian Association for Child & Play Therapy, 297
Canadian Association for Population Therapeutics, 303
Canadian Association for Sandplay Therapy, 303
Canadian College of Professional Counsellors & Psychotherapists, 360
Canadian Counselling & Psychotherapy Association, 371
Canadian Horticultural Therapy Association, 408
Canadian Institute for Child & Adolescent Psychoanalytic Psychotherapy, 412
Catholic Family Services of Toronto, 519
International Society for Emotion Focused Therapy, 860
Pet Therapy Society of Northern Alberta, 1153
Regina Therapeutic Recreation Association, 1212
The Therapeutic Touch Network of Ontario, 1375
The Trident Mediation Counselling & Support Foundation, 1398

Thyroid Diseases
American Thyroid Association, 1503
Thyroid Foundation of Canada, 1378

Tibetans & Tibet
Canadian Tibetan Association of Ontario, 495

Tires
Association des spécialistes du pneus et Mécanique du Québec, 128
Atlantic Tire Dealers Association, 186
Ontario Tire Dealers Association, 1110
Rubber Manufacturers Association, 1587
Tire Stewardship BC Association, 1380
Western Canada Tire Dealers Association, 1448

Tobacco Industry
Association nationale des distributeurs aux petites surfaces alimentaires, 138
Bakery, Confectionery, Tobacco Workers & Grain Millers International Union (AFL-CIO/CLC), 1514
Ontario Flue-Cured Tobacco Growers' Marketing Board, 1080
Society for Research on Nicotine & Tobacco, 1591

Toiletries Industry
Canadian Cosmetic, Toiletry & Fragrance Association, 366

Tool & Die Industry
Canadian Die Casters Association, 378
North American Die Casting Association, 1579

Torture
Action des Chrétiens pour l'abolition de la torture, 6
Amnesty International, 1504
Amnesty International - Canadian Section (English Speaking), 68
Amnistie internationale, Section canadienne (Francophone), 68
Canadian Centre for Victims of Torture, 354
Vancouver Association for the Survivors of Torture, 1425

Tourette Syndrome
Tourette Syndrome Foundation of Canada, 1388

Tourism
Abbotsford Downtown Business Association, 1
Aboriginal Tourism Association of British Columbia, 2
Aboriginal Tourism Association of Southern Ontario, 2
Alliance internationale de tourisme, 1487
Association for Mountain Parks Protection & Enjoyment, 134
Association québécoise de promotion du tourisme socioculturel, 171
Association touristique régionale de Charlevoix, 178
Association touristique régionale du Saguenay-Lac-Saint-Jean, 179
Associations touristiques régionales associées du Québec, 179
Atlantic Canada Cruise Association, 182
Attractions Ontario, 187
Banff & Lake Louise Tourism, 195
Cambridge Tourism, 275
Canadian Resort Development Association, 467
Canadian Sport Tourism Alliance, 490
Canadian Tourism Human Resource Council, 495
Canadian Tourism Research Institute, 495
Cariboo Chilcotin Coast Tourism Association, 512
Central Nova Tourist Association, 524
Destination Eastern & Northumberland Shores, 654
Destination Sherbrooke, 654
East Coast Trail Association, 668
Economic Development Winnipeg Inc., 673
Fondation Tourisme Jeunesse, 748
Fredericton Tourism, 759
Georgian Bay Country Tourism Association, 771
The Georgian Triangle Tourist Association & Tourist Information Centre, 771
Hospitality Newfoundland & Labrador, 823
Hostelling International - Canada, 823
Institut de tourisme et d'hôtellerie du Québec, 842
Kensington & Area Tourist Association, 883
Kéroul, Tourisme pour personnes à capacité physique restreinte, 884
Kingston Economic Development Corporation, 889
Klondike Visitors Association, 892
Kootenay Rockies Tourism, 892
The Manitoba Tourism Education Council, 946
Muskoka Tourism, 985
Niagara Economic Development, 1025
Niagara Falls Tourism, 1025
North of Superior Tourism Association, 1031
Northeastern Ontario Tourism, 1034
Northern British Columbia Tourism Association, 1034
Northern Frontier Visitors Association, 1035
Northern Ontario Native Tourism Association, 1035
Northern Rockies Alaska Highway Tourism Association, 1035
Northwest Territories Tourism, 1039
Nunavut Tourism, 1051
Office de Tourisme du Rocher-Percé, 1055
Office du tourisme et des congrès de Québec, 1055
Ontario Farm & Country Accommodations Association, 1078
Ottawa Tourism, 1132
Ottawa Valley Tourist Association, 1132
Peterborough & the Kawarthas Tourism, 1153
Prince Edward County Chamber of Tourism & Commerce, 1171
Regina Regional Opportunities Commission, 1212
Société touristique des Autochtones du Québec, 1325
Stratford Tourism Alliance, 1351
Sudbury Tourism, 1353
Thompson Okanagan Tourism Association, 1376
Tourism Burlington, 1389
Tourism Calgary, 1389
Tourism Canmore Kananaskis, 1389
Tourism Cape Breton, 1389
Tourism Goderich, 1389
Tourism Hamilton, 1389
Tourism Industry Association of British Columbia, 1389
Tourism Industry Association of Canada, 1389
Tourism Industry Association of New Brunswick Inc., 1390
Tourism Industry Association of Nova Scotia, 1390
Tourism Industry Association of PEI, 1390
Tourism Industry Association of the Yukon, 1390
Tourism Kelowna, 1390
Tourism Moncton, 1390
Tourism Nanaimo, 1390
Tourism Prince Albert, 1390
Tourism Red Deer, 1390
Tourism Saint John, 1391
Tourism Sarnia Lambton, 1391
Tourism Saskatoon, 1391
Tourism Simcoe County, 1391
Tourism Thunder Bay, 1391
Tourism Toronto, 1391
Tourism Vancouver/Greater Vancouver Convention & Visitors Bureau, 1391
Tourism Vernon, 1391
Tourism Victoria/Greater Victoria Visitors & Convention Bureau, 1391
Tourism Windsor Essex Pelee Island, 1392
Tourisme Abitibi-Témiscamingue, 1392
Tourisme Baie-James, 1392
Tourisme Bas-Saint-Laurent, 1392
Tourisme Cantons-de-l'Est, 1392
Tourisme Centre-du-Québec, 1392
Tourisme Chaudière-Appalaches, 1392
Tourisme Côte-Nord, 1392
Tourisme Gaspésie, 1392
Tourisme Lanaudière, 1392
Tourisme Laurentides, 1392
Tourisme Laval, 1393
Tourisme Mauricie, 1393
Tourisme Montérégie, 1393
Tourisme Montréal/Office des congrès et du tourisme du Grand Montréal, 1393
Tourisme Outaouais, 1393

Subject Index / Toxicology

Tourisme Îles-de-la-Madeleine, 1393
Travel and Tourism Research Association (Canada Chapter), 1396
Travel Manitoba, 1396
Vancouver, Coast & Mountains Tourism Region, 1429
Whistler Resort Association, 1452
Wilderness Tourism Association, 1454
World Leisure & Recreation Association, 1606
World Tourism Organization, 1607
Yukon First Nations Culture & Tourism Association, 1478
Yukon Tourism Education Council, 1480

Toxicology
Association des intervenants en toxicomanie du Québec inc., 117
British Columbia Drug & Poison Information Centre, 239
Canadian Network of Toxicology Centres, 441
Centre Anti-Poison du Québec, 526
Manitoba Poison Control Centre, 942
Ontario Regional Poison Information Centre, 1101
Poison & Drug Information Service, 1163
Society of Environmental Toxicology & Chemistry, 1593
Society of Toxicology, 1594
Society of Toxicology of Canada, 1331

Toys
Canadian Toy Association / Canadian Toy & Hobby Fair, 496
Canadian Toy Collectors' Society Inc., 496
Canadian Toy Testing Council, 496

Track & Field Sports
Achilles Canada, 5
Athletics Canada, 181
Canadian Masters Athletic Association, 431
Ontario Masters Athletics, 1090
Prince Edward Island Roadrunners Club, 1177

Trade
British Canadian Chamber of Trade & Commerce, 229
Business Council of Canada, 266
Canada - Albania Business Council, 277
Canada Korea Business Association, 280
Canada Organic Trade Association, 280
Canada Taiwan Trade Association, 280
Canadian German Chamber of Industry & Commerce Inc., 397
Canadian Security Traders Association, Inc., 469
Can-Am Border Trade Alliance, 1515
China Canada Investment Association, 564
Frontier Duty Free Association, 763
Hong Kong Trade Development Council, 1530
International Institute of Fisheries Economics & Trade, 1551
International Trade Centre, 1563
The Israel Economic Mission to Canada, 866
Japan External Trade Organization (Toronto), 868
Ontario Association of Trading Houses, 1066
Pacific Corridor Enterprise Council, 1135
Poplar Council of Canada, 1165
Saskatchewan Trade & Export Partnership, 1276
Trade Facilitation Office Canada, 1394
Turks & Caicos Development Organization of Canada, 1400
United Nations Conference on Trade & Development, 1599
World Trade Centre Atlantic Canada, 1467
World Trade Centres Association, 1608

Trade Marks
Intellectual Property Institute of Canada, 850

Traffic Injury
Traffic Injury Research Foundation, 1394

Trail Riding
Back Country Horsemen of British Columbia, 192
Trail Riders of the Canadian Rockies, 1394

Translation
Association camadienne des interprètes de conférence, 90
Association canadienne de traductologie, 92

Association canadienne des juristes-traducteurs, 93
Association of Canadian Corporations in Translation & Interpretation, 141
Association of Legal Court Interpreters & Translators, 150
Association of Translators & Interpreters of Alberta, 163
Association of Translators & Interpreters of Nova Scotia, 163
Association of Translators & Interpreters of Ontario, 163
Association of Translators & Interpreters of Saskatchewan, 163
Association of Translators, Terminologists & Interpreters of Manitoba, 163
Canadian Translators, Terminologists & Interpreters Council, 496
Corporation des traducteurs, traductrices, terminologues et interprètes du Nouveau-Brunswick, 631
Fédération Internationale des Traducteurs, 1526
Language Industry Association, 899
Literary Translators' Association of Canada, 914
Lutheran Bible Translators of Canada Inc., 922
Ordre des traducteurs, terminologues et interprètes agréés du Québec, 1124
Société québécoise de la rédaction professionnelle, 1323
Society of Translators & Interpreters of British Columbia, 1331
Wycliffe Bible Translators of Canada, Inc., 1470

Transportation
Air Transport Association of Canada, 19
Alberta Motor Transport Association, 40
Amalgamated Transit Union (AFL-CIO/CLC), 1487
Association des usagers du transport adapté de Longueuil, 130
Association des véhicules électriques du Québec, 130
Association du camionnage du Québec inc., 130
Association du transport urbain du Québec, 132
The Association of School Transportation Services of British Columbia, 162
Association québécoise des transports, 175
Atlantic Provinces Trucking Association, 185
Bike to Work BC Society, 211
British Columbia Ferry & Marine Workers' Union (CLC), 241
Canadian Association of Railway Suppliers, 330
Canadian Automobile Association, 339
Canadian Council of Motor Transport Administrators, 369
Canadian Ferry Association, 389
Canadian Fuels Association, 395
Canadian Institute of Traffic & Transportation, 419
Canadian Institute of Transportation Engineers, 420
Canadian Marine Pilots' Association, 430
Canadian Parking Association, 450
Canadian Transport Lawyers Association, 497
Canadian Transportation Equipment Association, 497
Canadian Transportation Research Forum, 497
Canadian Trucking Alliance, 497
Canadian Urban Transit Association, 500
Carefree Society, 511
Centre for Transportation Engineering & Planning, 534
Chamber of Marine Commerce, 539
The Chartered Institute of Logistics & Transport in North America, 552
Club de trafic de Québec, 575
Downtown Vancouver Association, 662
Electric Vehicle Council of Ottawa, 682
Electric Vehicle Society, 682
Freight Carriers Association of Canada, 759
Freight Management Association of Canada, 759
Hub for Active School Travel, 824
Industrial Truck Association, 1531
Institute of Transportation Engineers, 1534
International Heavy Haul Association, 1550
The Logistics Institute, 917
Manitoba Trucking Association, 946
National Association of Railroad Passengers, 1573

National Transportation Brokers Association, 996
Ontario Good Roads Association, 1083
Ontario Public Transit Association, 1100
Ontario Traffic Council, 1110
Ontario Trucking Association, 1111
Prince Edward Island Trucking Sector Council, 1178
Private Motor Truck Council of Canada, 1180
Railway Association of Canada, 1203
Recreational Aircraft Association, 1208
Saskatchewan Trucking Association, 1276
Shipping Federation of Canada, 1296
Société des traversiers du Québec, 1318
Teamsters Canada (CLC), 1368
Toronto Transportation Society, 1388
Transport Action Canada, 1395
Transportation Association of Canada, 1395
Truck Training Schools Association of Ontario Inc., 1399
UNIFOR, 1405
Union of Canadian Transportation Employees, 1407
The Van Horne Institute for International Transportation & Regulatory Affairs, 1424
Via Prévention, 1431
Vintage Locomotive Society Inc., 1435
West Coast Railway Association, 1445
Western Transportation Advisory Council, 1450

Transportation Sustainability
Canadian Fuels Association, 395
Electric Mobility Canada, 681

Trauma
International Society for the Study of Trauma & Dissociation, 1559
Radius Child & Youth Services, 1203
Trauma Association of Canada, 1396

Travel Industry
Alberta Association of Travel Health Professionals, 25
Algoma Kinniwabi Travel Association, 53
Alliance internationale de tourisme, 1487
Almaguin-Nipissing Travel Association, 59
American Society of Travel Agents, 1503
Association de l'Agricotourism et du Tourisme Gourmand, 100
Association of Canadian Travel Agencies, 143
Association of Canadian Travel Agencies - Atlantic, 144
Association of Canadian Travel Agents - Alberta & NWT, 144
Association of Canadian Travel Agents - British Columbia & Yukon, 144
Association of Canadian Travel Agents - Manitoba & Nunavut, 144
Association of Canadian Travel Agents - Ontario, 144
Association of Canadian Travel Agents - Québec, 144
Association of Retail Travel Agents, 1513
Association québécoise pour le tourisme équestre et l'équitation de loisir du Québec, 177
Canadian Association of Tour Operators, 334
Canadian Automobile Association, 339
Canadian Resort Development Association, 467
Canadian Snowbird Association, 472
Cruise Lines International Association, Inc., 1520
Destination Eastern & Northumberland Shores, 654
Global Business Travel Association (Canada), 774
Hostelling International - Canada, 823
International Association for Medical Assistance to Travellers, 853
Kootenay Rockies Tourism, 892
Maison du Tourisme, 927
Northwest Ontario Sunset Country Travel Association, 1036
Ontario East Tourism Association, 1077
Pacific Asia Travel Association (Eastern Canada Chapter), 1134
Shuswap Tourism, 1297
Tourism Prince George, 1390
Tourism Yorkton, 1392
Travel Industry Council of Ontario, 1396
Travel Media Association of Canada, 1396
Travellers' Aid Society of Toronto, 1396

Whistler Resort Association, 1452
World Tourism Organization, 1607

Treasury Management
Association for Financial Professionals, 1508
Association for Financial Professionals - Calgary, 133
Association for Financial Professionals - Edmonton, 133
Association for Financial Professionals - Ottawa, 133
Association for Financial Professionals - Vancouver, 133
Association of Municipal Managers, Clerks & Treasurers of Ontario, 152
Treasury Management Association of Canada - Toronto, 1396

Triathlon
Alberta Triathlon Association, 50
Ontario Association of Triathletes, 1066
Saskatchewan Triathlon Association Corporation, 1276
Triathlon British Columbia, 1397
Triathlon Canada, 1397
Triathlon Manitoba, 1398
Triathlon New Brunswick, 1398
Triathlon Newfoundland & Labrador, 1398
Triathlon Nova Scotia, 1398
Triathlon Price Edward Island, 1398
Triathlon Québec, 1398

Tribal Councils
Bimose Tribal Council, 211
Grand Council of the Crees, 779
Heiltsuk Tribal Council, 811
Independent First Nations' Alliance, 832
Island Lake Tribal Council, 865
Keewatin Tribal Council, 883
Kwakiutl District Council, 894
Lesser Slave Lake Indian Regional Council, 907
Lillooet Tribal Council, 912
Meadow Lake Tribal Council, 956
Mohawk Council of Akwesasne, 971
Musgamagw Tsawataineuk Tribal Council, 983
Nisga'a Lisims Government, 1027
Ogemawahj Tribal Council, 1055
Shibogama First Nations Council, 1296
Southern First Nations Secretariat, 1337
Swampy Cree Tribal Council, 1358
Windigo First Nations' Council, 1456
Wolastoqey Tribal Council Inc., 1460

Tribology & Lubrication
Society of Tribologists & Lubrication Engineers, 1594

Trout
Trout Unlimited Canada, 1399

Trucks & Trucking
Alberta Construction Trucking Association, 31
Alberta Motor Transport Association, 40
Association du camionnage du Québec inc., 130
Association nationale des camionneurs artisans inc., 138
Atlantic Provinces Trucking Association, 185
British Columbia Trucking Association, 257
Canadian Trucking Alliance, 497
Industrial Truck Association, 1531
Manitoba Trucking Association, 946
Ontario Trucking Association, 1111
Polish North American Trucking Association, 1164
Prince Edward Island Trucking Sector Council, 1178
Private Motor Truck Council of Canada, 1180
Provincial Towing Association (Ontario), 1191
Saskatchewan Trucking Association, 1276
Truck Training Schools Association of Ontario Inc., 1399
Truckers Association of Nova Scotia, 1399
Trucking Human Resources Canada, 1399

Trust Companies
Interac Association, 851
National Aboriginal Trust Officers Association, 989

Trustees, School
Alberta Catholic School Trustees Association, 27
Alberta School Boards Association, 45

British Columbia School Trustees Association, 252
Canadian Catholic School Trustees' Association, 351
Manitoba School Boards Association, 944
Newfoundland & Labrador School Boards Association, 1021
Nova Scotia School Boards Association, 1048
Ontario Catholic School Trustees' Association, 1070
Saskatchewan School Boards Association, 1274

Tuberculosis
Heiser Program for Research in Leprosy & Tuberculosis, 1529
TB Vets, 1367

Tunnelling
Tunnelling Association of Canada, 1400

Turkish Canadians
Federation of Canadian Turkish Associations, 723
Turkish Community Heritage Centre of Canada, 1400

Turner's Syndrome
Association du Syndrome de Turner du Québec, 132
Turner's Syndrome Society, 1400

Ukrainian Canadians
Canadian Foundation for Ukrainian Studies, 394
Canadian Friends of Ukraine, 395
Canadian Ukrainian Immigrant Aid Society, 498
Council of Ukrainian Credit Unions of Canada, 635
Friends of the Ukrainian Village Society, 763
League of Ukrainian Canadian Women, 903
League of Ukrainian Canadians, 903
Plast Ukrainian Youth Association of Canada, 1162
SUS Foundation of Canada, 1357
Ukrainian Canadian Civil Liberties Association, 1402
Ukrainian Canadian Congress, 1402
Ukrainian Canadian Foundation of Taras Shevchenko, 1402
Ukrainian Canadian Research & Documentation Centre, 1402
Ukrainian Canadian Social Services (Toronto) Inc, 1403
Ukrainian Democratic Youth Association, 1403
Ukrainian Fraternal Society of Canada, 1403
Ukrainian Genealogical & Historical Society of Canada, 1403
Ukrainian National Federation of Canada, 1403
Ukrainian Orthodox Church of Canada, 1403
Ukrainian Self-Reliance League of Canada, 1403
Ukrainian War Veterans Association of Canada, 1403
Ukrainian Women's Association of Canada, 1403
Ukrainian World Congress, 1403
Ukrainian Youth Association of Canada, 1404
United Ukrainian Charitable Trust, 1412
World Federation of Ukrainian Women's Organizations, 1466

Ukrainian Studies
Shevchenko Scientific Society of Canada, 1296
Ukrainian National Federation of Canada, 1403
Ukrainian Self-Reliance League of Canada, 1403
Ukrainian Women's Association of Canada, 1403
Ukrainian Youth Association of Canada, 1404

Underwater Archaeology
Save Ontario Shipwrecks, 1281
Underwater Archaeological Society of British Columbia, 1404

Unitarians
Canadian Unitarian Council, 499
Canadian Unitarians for Social Justice, 499
First Unitarian Congregation of Toronto, 739

United Church of Canada
Alberta CGIT Association, 28
Manitoba & Northwestern Ontario CGIT Association, 928
Maritime Regional CGIT Committee, 951
Ontario CGIT Association, 1071
Provincial CGIT Board of BC, 1190
Saskatchewan CGIT Committee, 1260
United Church of Canada, 1409
United Church of Canada Foundation, 1409

United Empire Loyalists
Missisquoi Historical Society, 969
United Empire Loyalists' Association of Canada, 1410

United Nations
Canadian Commission for UNESCO, 360
United Nations Association in Canada, 1411
United Nations Conference on Trade & Development, 1599
United Nations Development Programme, 1599
United Nations Environment Programme, 1600
United Nations Industrial Development Organization, 1600
United Nations Research Institute for Social Development, 1600
World Federalist Movement - Canada, 1465

United States of America
American Antiquarian Society, 1488
Association Canado-Américaine, 1507

Universities & Colleges
Agence universitaire de la Francophonie, 14
AIESEC, 18
Alberta Colleges Athletic Conference, 30
Association des collèges privés du Québec, 109
Association des professeurs de français des universités et collèges canadiens, 124
Association des universités de la francophonie canadienne, 130
Association of Atlantic Universities, 139
Association of Canadian College & University Teachers of English, 141
Association of Canadian Universities for Northern Studies, 144
Association of Canadian University Presses, 144
Association of Faculties of Medicine of Canada, 148
Association of Faculties of Pharmacy of Canada, 148
Association of Registrars of the Universities & Colleges of Canada, 161
Association of University Forestry Schools of Canada, 163
Association pour la recherche au collégial, 166
Association québécoise de pédagogie collégiale, 170
Athabasca University Students' Union, 180
Atlantic Collegiate Athletic Association, 183
Atlantic University Sport Association, 186
British Columbia Career College Association, 235
Canadian Associates of Ben-Gurion University of the Negev, 297
Canadian Association for the Prevention of Discrimination & Harassment in Higher Education, 305
Canadian Association for University Continuing Education, 306
Canadian Association of College & University Student Services, 310
Canadian Association of Learned Journals, 319
Canadian Association of Research Administrators, 331
Canadian Association of Schools of Nursing, 332
Canadian Association of University Business Officers, 334
Canadian Association of University Teachers, 335
Canadian Association of University Teachers of German, 335
Canadian College & University Food Service Association, 358
Canadian College of Emergency Medical Services, 358
Canadian Collegiate Athletic Association, 360
Canadian Council of University Physical Education & Kinesiology Administrators, 370
Canadian Education & Training Accreditation Commission, 379
Canadian Federation for the Humanities & Social Sciences, 384
Canadian Federation of Students, 388
Canadian Federation of University Women, 388
Canadian Forestry Accreditation Board, 392
Canadian Friends of Beth Hatefutsoth, 394
Canadian Institutional Research & Planning Association, 420
Canadian Interuniversity Sport, 422
Canadian Society for the Study of Higher Education, 478
Canadian University & College Conference Organizers Association, 499
Canadian University & College Counselling Association, 499
Canadian University Football Coaches Association, 499
Canadian University Music Society, 499
Canadian University Press, 499
College & University Retiree Associations of Canada, 581
College of Midwives of Manitoba, 586
Conférence des recteurs et des principaux des universités du Québec, 612
Conseil provincial du soutien scolaire, 619
Council of Ontario Universities, 635
Fédération des cégeps, 712
Fédération des enseignants de cégeps, 714
Fédération du personnel professionnel des collèges, 720
Fédération du personnel professionnel des universités et de la recherche, 720
International Association of University Professors of English, 1540
Laurentian University Staff Union, 900
McMaster University Retirees Association, 956
Mount Royal Staff Association, 976
National Association of College Auxiliary Services, 1573
National Educational Association of Disabled Students, 993
Ontario Campus Radio Organization, 1070
Ontario Colleges Athletic Association, 1073
Ontario Council on Articulation and Transfer, 1075
Ontario Undergraduate Student Alliance, 1111
Ontario University Athletics, 1112
Pacific Institute for the Mathematical Sciences, 1135
Pacific Western Athletic Association, 1136
Physiotherapy Education Accreditation Canada, 1159
Saint Francis Xavier Association of University Teachers, 1246
Teaching Support Staff Union, 1367
United World Colleges, 1418
University of the Philippines Alumni Association of Toronto, 1420
World University Roundtable, 1608
World University Service of Canada, 1467
York University Staff Association, 1474

University & College Libraries
Association des bibliothèques de la santé affiliées à l'Université de Montréal, 107
Council of Prairie & Pacific University Libraries, 635
Ontario College & University Library Association, 1072
Ontario Council of University Libraries, 1075

Uranium
World Nuclear Association, 1606

Urban Planning
Associated Research Centres for the Urban Underground Space, 89
Association québécoise d'urbanisme, 168
Canadian Institute of Planners, 418
Downtown Vancouver Association, 662
Groupe de recherche appliquée en macroécologie, 791
Institute of Urban Studies, 847
International Centre for Sustainable Cities, 855
International Federation for Housing & Planning, 1546
International Society of City & Regional Planners, 1560
Muniscope, 982
Ordre des urbanistes du Québec, 1124
Urban Development Institute Greater Edmonton Chapter, 1422
Urban Development Institute of Canada, 1422
Urban Development Institute of Nova Scotia, 1422
World Society for Ekistics, 1607

Urethane
Polyurethane Manufacturers Association, 1584

Urology
Association des urologues du Québec, 130
The Canadian Continence Foundation, 364
Canadian Urologic Oncology Group, 500
Canadian Urological Association, 500
Society of Urologic Surgeons of Ontario, 1331
Urology Nurses of Canada, 1422

Vacation Industry
Alberta Country Vacations Association, 32
British Columbia Lodging & Campgrounds Association, 245
Cruise Lines International Association, Inc., 1520
Manitoba Rural Tourism Association Inc., 943
Mouvement québécois des vacances familiales inc., 978
Ontario Farm & Country Accommodations Association, 1078
Whistler Resort Association, 1452

Vaccine
Association for Vaccine Damaged Children, 135
Immunize Canada, 831
Vaccination Risk Awareness Network Inc., 1423

Vegans
American Vegan Society, 1504
Vancouver Island Vegan Association, 1427

Vegetables
Association québécoise de la distribution de fruits et légumes, 170
British Columbia Vegetable Marketing Commission, 257
Ontario Farm Fresh Marketing Association, 1078

Vegetarians
Earthsave Canada, 667
Halifax Association of Vegetarians, 798
International Vegetarian Union, 1565
Mercy for Animals Canada, 961
Toronto Vegetarian Association, 1388
Vegetarians of Alberta Association, 1430
Winnipeg Vegetarian Association, 1459

Vending Industry
Canadian Automatic Merchandising Association, 338

Venture Capital
Canada's Venture Capital & Private Equity Association, 283
National Angel Capital Organization, 989

Veterans
AirCrew Association - Western Canada Region, 20
Army, Navy & Air Force Veterans in Canada, 83
Association of Veterans & Friends of the Mackenzie-Papineau Battalion, International Brigades in Spain, 164
British Exservicemen's Association, 259
Canadian Aboriginal Veterans & Serving Members Association, 285
Canadian Association of Veterans in United Nations Peacekeeping, 335
Canadian Battlefields Foundation, 342
The Canadian Corps of Commissionaires, 365
Canadian Merchant Navy Veterans Association Inc., 435
Canadian Peacekeeping Veterans Association, 452
Korea Veterans Association of Canada Inc., Heritage Unit, 893
Last Post Fund, 899
Maltese Veterans Association of Canada, 928
Monte Cassino Society, 1571
National Council of Veteran Associations, 992
Naval Club of Toronto, 1001
New Brunswick Signallers Association, 1012
Polish Army Veterans Association of America, 1163
Polish Combatants Association, 1164
Polish Combatants Association - Winnipeg, 1164
The Royal Canadian Legion, 1240

Subject Index / Veterinary Medicine

Royal Canadian Naval Benevolent Fund, 1240
Ukrainian War Veterans Association of Canada, 1403
Union of Veterans' Affairs Employees, 1408
The War Amputations of Canada, 1440
Yukon RCMP Veteran's Association, 1479

Veterinary Medicine
Alberta Veterinary Medical Association, 50
Alberta Veterinary Technologist Association, 50
American Association of Bovine Practitioners, 1489
Association des médecins vétérinaires praticiens du Québec, 120
Association des techniciens en santé animale du Québec, 129
British Columbia Veterinary Technologists Association, 257
Canadian Animal Health Institute, 293
Canadian Association of Swine Veterinarians, 334
Canadian Chihuahua Rescue & Transport, 355
Canadian Faculties of Agriculture & Veterinary Medicine, 383
Canadian Veterinary Medical Association, 501
College of Veterinarians of British Columbia, 590
College of Veterinarians of Ontario, 590
Eastern Veterinary Technician Association, 671
International Council for Laboratory Animal Science, 1544
Manitoba Animal Health Technologists Association, 928
Manitoba Veterinary Medical Association, 946
New Brunswick Veterinary Medical Association, 1013
Newfoundland & Labrador Veterinary Medical Association, 1022
Nova Scotia Veterinary Medical Association, 1050
Ontario Association of Bovine Practitioners, 1062
Ontario Association of Equine Practitioners, 1063
Ontario Association of Veterinary Technicians, 1066
Ontario Veterinary Medical Association, 1112
Ordre des médecins vétérinaires du Québec, 1123
Prince Edward Island Veterinary Medical Association, 1178
Registered Veterinary Technologists & Technicians of Canada, 1214
Saskatchewan Association of Veterinary Technologists, Inc., 1258
Saskatchewan Veterinary Medical Association, 1277
Union québécoise de réhabilitation des oiseaux de proie, 1408
Vaccine & Infectious Disease Organization, 1423
Western Canadian Association of Bovine Practitioners, 1448
World Small Animal Veterinary Association, 1467
World Veterinary Poultry Association, 1608

Video
Association québécoise de l'industrie du disque, du spectacle et de la vidéo, 170
Entertainment Merchants Association - International Head Office, 1523
Fédération internationale des associations de producteurs de films, 1525
Film & Video Arts Society Alberta, 735
Foundation Assisting Canadian Talent on Recordings, 755
Groupe intervention vidéo, 792
Independent Media Arts Alliance, 833
Island Media Arts Co-op, 865
Motion Picture Association - Canada, 975
MuchFACT, 978
NABET 700 CEP, 987
Parlimage CCF, 1143
Society of Canadian Cine Amateurs, 1327
Vidéographe, 1434
Yorkton Film Festival, 1474

Vietnamese Canadians
Association des vietnamiens de Sherbrooke, 130
Calgary Vietnamese Canadian Association, 275
Communauté vietnamienne au Canada, région de Montréal, 594
Free Vietnamese Association of Manitoba, 759
Vietnamese Association, Toronto, 1434
Vietnamese Canadian Federation, 1434

Vinyl
The Vinyl Institute, 1601

Violence
Affected Families of Police Homicide, 11
Association québécoise Plaidoyer-Victimes, 176
Awo Taan Healing Lodge Society, 191
Canadian Safe School Network, 468
Canadians Concerned About Violence in Entertainment, 506
Centre de prévention de la radicalisation menant à la violence, 529
Centre des ressources sur la non-violence inc, 530
A Coeur d'Homme, 580
EMPHASE Mauricie-Centre-du-Québec, 686
Ending Violence Association of British Columbia, 687
Leave Out Violence Everywhere, 905
The Mackenzie Institute, 924
Metropolitan Action Committee on Violence Against Women & Children, 964
National Aboriginal Circle Against Family Violence, 988
Ontario Association of Interval & Transition Houses, 1064
Ontario Gang Investigators Association, 1081
Prairieaction Foundation, 1170
Radius Child & Youth Services, 1203
Sexual Assault Centre of Edmonton, 1292
Victims of Violence, 1432
Viol-secours inc., 1435
YWCA December 6 Fund of Toronto, 1482

Violence Against the Elderly
British Columbia Coalition to Eliminate Abuse of Seniors, 236
Elder Abuse Ontario, 681
Montréal Council of Women, 972
Stop Abuse in Families Society, 1350

Violence Against Women
Amnesty International, 1504
The Barbra Schlifer Commemorative Clinic, 196
Canadian Association of Sexual Assault Centres, 333
Centre de recherche interdisciplinaire sur la violence familiale et la violence faite aux femmes, 530
Centre for Research on Violence Against Women & Children, 533
The Freda Centre for Research on Violence Against Women & Children, 758
Fredericton Sexual Assault Crisis Centre, 759
Guelph-Wellington Women in Crisis, 793
Immigrant Women Services Ottawa, 831
Kawartha Sexual Assault Centre, 882
Libra House Inc., 909
Metropolitan Action Committee on Violence Against Women & Children, 964
Niagara Region Sexual Assault Centre, 1025
Ontario Coalition of Rape Crisis Centres, 1072
Ontario Women's Justice Network, 1113
Oshawa-Durham Rape Crisis Centre, 1128
Ottawa Rape Crisis Centre, 1131
Peel Committee Against Woman Abuse, 1147
Prince Edward Island Rape & Sexual Assault Centre, 1176
Rehtaeh Parsons Society, 1217
RESOLVE: Research & Education for Solutions to Violence & Abuse, 1226
Sexual Assault Centre Kingston Inc., 1292
Springtide Resources, 1346
Stop Abuse in Families Society, 1350
Thompson Crisis Centre, 1376
Thunder Bay Sexual Assault / Sexual Abuse Counselling & Crisis Centre, 1378
Timmins & Area Women in Crisis Support & Information Centre on Violence Against Women, 1379
Vancouver & Lower Mainland Multicultural Family Support Services Society, 1424
Vancouver Rape Relief & Women's Shelter, 1428
Viol-secours inc., 1435
The White Ribbon Campaign, 1452
Women Educating in Self-Defense Training, 1460

Violin
Canadian Grand Masters Fiddling Association, 398

Visual Arts
Art Dealers Association of Canada Inc., 84
The Arts & Letters Club, 85
Association des artistes en arts visuels de Saint-Jérôme, 106
Association des artistes peintres affiliés de la Rive-Sud, 106
Association des artistes peintres de Longueuil, 106
Association Et si c'était moi, 132
Association for Native Development in the Performing & Visual Arts, 134
Association longueilloise des photographes amateurs, 137
Association québécoise des éducatrices et éducateurs spécialisés en arts plastiques, 172
BC Alliance for Arts & Culture, 200
Canadian Artists Representation, 295
Canadian Artists' Representation British Columbia, 295
Canadian Artists' Representation Maritimes, 296
Canadian Artists' Representation Ontario, 296
Canadian Association for Photographic Art, 303
Canadian Aviation Artists Assocation, 340
Canadian Society of Painters in Water Colour, 486
Centre culturel canadien, 1516
Club de photo de Boucherville, 575
Club de photographie L'Oeil qui voit de Saint-Hubert, 575
Club photo Évasion, 576
La Fondation Émile-Nelligan, 746
Fusion: The Ontario Clay & Glass Association, 765
Haliburton Highlands Guild of Fine Arts, 798
Harbourfront Centre, 803
Malaspina Printmakers Society, 927
Manitoba Printmakers Association, 942
Open Space Arts Society, 1114
Pastel Artists Canada, 1145
Regroupement des artistes en arts visuels du Québec (ind.), 1214
Universities Art Association of Canada, 1418
Visual Artists Newfoundland & Labrador, 1436
Visual Arts Nova Scotia, 1436
Yukon Arts Centre, 1477

Vocational & Technical Education
Alberta Council on Admissions & Transfer, 31
British Columbia Cooperative Learning Provincial Specialist Association, 237
Canadian Apprenticeship Forum, 294
Canadian College of Emergency Medical Services, 358
Canadian Training Institute, 496
Canadian Vocational Association, 501
Excellence Canada, 699
JVS of Greater Toronto, 879
Niagara West Employment & Learning Resource Centres, 1026
Skills for Change, 1302
Skills Unlimited, 1302
Skills/Compétences Canada, 1302
Truck Training Schools Association of Ontario Inc., 1399

Vocational Rehabilitation
The Ark/Lunenburg County Association for the Specially Challenged, 81
Beehive Adult Service Centre, Inc., 204
Bridge Adult Service Society, 228
Building Futures Employment Society, 262
Canadian Association for Community Living - Clare Branch, 298
Canadian Council on Rehabilitation & Work, 371
Centre for Adults in Progressive Employment Society, 531
Cheticamp Association for Community Living, 557
Conway Workshop Association, 627
Corridor Community Options for Adults, 631
Dartmouth Adult Services Centre, 650
Flowercart, 741
Gerald Hardy Memorial Society, 771
Golden Opportunities Vocational Rehabilitation Centre Workshop, 776
Goodwill Industries of Alberta, 778
Goodwill, The Amity Group, 778
Haley Street Adult Services Centre Society, 798
Heatherton Activity Centre, 810
Horizon Achievement Centre, 821
Inverness Cottage Workshop, 862
Kaye Nickerson Adult Service Centre, 883
LakeCity Employment Services Association, 896
National Institute of Disability Management & Research, 994
New Boundaries, 1004
New Leaf Enterprises, 1014
Prescott Group, 1170
Queens Association for Supported Living, 1200
Regional Occupation Centre Foundation, 1212
Regional Occupation Centre Society, 1213
Saskatchewan Abilities Council, 1255
Shelburne Association Supporting Inclusion, 1295
Summer Street, 1354
Vecova Centre for Disability Services & Research, 1430
The War Amputations of Canada, 1440

Volleyball
Fédération de volleyball du Québec, 710
International Volleyball Association, 1566
Manitoba Volleyball Association, 946
Newfoundland & Labrador Volleyball Association, 1022
Northwest Territories Volleyball Association, 1039
Ontario Volleyball Association, 1112
Saskatchewan Volleyball Association, 1277
Volleyball Alberta, 1437
Volleyball BC, 1437
Volleyball Canada, 1437
Volleyball New Brunswick, 1438
Volleyball Nova Scotia, 1438
Volleyball Nunavut, 1438
Volleyball Prince Edward Island, 1438
Volleyball Yukon, 1438

Volunteers
Administrators of Volunteer Resources BC, 8
Association des bénévoles du don de sang, 107
Association des gestionnaires de ressources bénévoles du Québec, 115
Associés bénévoles qualifiés au service des jeunes, 179
Bathurst Volunteer Centre de Bénévolat Inc., 199
Bell Aliant Pioneers, 204
British Columbia Association of Healthcare Auxiliaries, 231
Burnaby Volunteer Centre Society, 266
Calgary Chamber of Voluntary Organizations, 271
Canadian Children's Optimist Foundation, 356
Canadian Crossroads International, 373
Cape Breton Chamber of Voluntary Organizations, 509
Centre d'action bénévole de Montréal, 527
Centre de Bénévolat de la Péninsule Acadienne Inc., 528
CODA International Training, 1518
Edmonton Chamber of Voluntary Organizations, 676
Fédération des centres d'action bénévole du Québec, 712
Health Association of PEI, 806
International Council of Voluntary Agencies, 1545
Junior League of Edmonton, 878
Manitoba Association for Volunteer Administration, 929
Nanaimo Volunteer and Information Centre Society, 988
Newcomer Women's Services Toronto, 1015
Ontario Pioneers, 1096
Optimist International, 1580
Optimist International Canada, 1116
Pillar Nonprofit Network, 1160
Professional Association of Volunteer Leaders Ontario, 1183
Restigouche County Volunteer Action Association Inc., 1228
Sar-El Canada, 1253

Subject Index / Wine

SaskTel Pioneers, 1280
Search & Rescue Volunteer Association of Canada, 1288
TelecomPioneers, 1597
TelecomPioneers of Alberta, 1369
TelecomPioneers of Canada, 1369
Volunteer Alberta, 1438
Volunteer BC, 1438
Volunteer Canada, 1438
Volunteer Central Society, 1438
Volunteer Centre of Charlotte County Inc., 1438
Volunteer Grandparents, 1438
Volunteer Management Professionals of Canada, 1439
Volunteer Red Deer, 1439
Waypoint Centre for Mental Health Care, 1443

Walking
Volkssport Association of Alberta, 1437
Volkssport Association of British Columbia, 1437

Waste Management
Air & Waste Management Association, 1486
Alberta Plastics Recycling Association, 42
Association of Alberta Coordinated Action for Recycling Enterprises, 139
Atlantic Canada Water & Wastewater Association, 182
Center for Health, Environment & Justice, 1516
Centre de formation en entreprise et récupération Normand-Maurice, 529
Citizens for a Safe Environment, 570
Clean Nova Scotia Foundation, 573
Coast Waste Management Association, 579
Construction Resource Initiatives Council, 624
Ecology Action Centre, 672
Electronic Recycling Association, 683
Electronics Product Stewardship Canada, 684
Environmental Action Barrie - Living Green, 691
Environmental Education Ontario, 691
Front commun québécois pour une gestion écologique des déchets, 763
Green Action Centre, 788
International Solid Waste Association, 1562
Municipal Waste Association, 981
National Waste & Recycling Association, 1577
Newfoundland & Labrador Environment Network, 1018
Ontario Waste Management Association, 1112
Pitch-In Canada, 1160
Recycling Council of Alberta, 1208
Recycling Council of British Columbia, 1208
Société québécoise de récupération et de recyclage, 1323
Solid Waste Association of North America, 1595

Water & Wastewater
Alberta Water & Wastewater Operators Association, 51
Atlantic Canada Water & Wastewater Association, 182
British Columbia Water & Waste Association, 257
Canadian Water & Wastewater Association, 502
Canadian Water Network, 502
Canadian Water Quality Association, 502
Gordon Foundation, 778
International Solid Waste Association, 1562
IRC International Water & Sanitation Centre, 1567
Manitoba Water & Wastewater Association, 947
New Brunswick Ground Water Association, 1009
Ontario Sewer & Watermain Construction Association, 1104
Regroupement des organismes de bassins versants du Québec, 1215
Saskatchewan Water & Wastewater Association, 1277
Water Environment Association of Ontario, 1441
Water Environment Federation, 1601
Western Canada Water, 1448

Water Pollution
American Water Works Association, 1504
Bonn Agreement, 1514
Canadian Association on Water Quality, 337
Clean Water Action, 1517
International Water Association, 1566
Ontario Water Works Association, 1113

OSPAR Commission, 1582
Water Environment Association of Ontario, 1441
Water Environment Federation, 1601
WaterCan, 1442

Water Polo
Alberta Water Polo Association, 51
British Columbia Water Polo Association, 258
Fédération de Water-Polo du Québec, 711
Manitoba Water Polo Association Inc., 947
Ontario Water Polo Association Incorporated, 1113
Water Polo Canada, 1441
Water Polo New Brunswick, 1441
Water Polo Newfoundland, 1441
Water Polo Nova Scotia, 1441
Water Polo Saskatchewan Inc., 1441

Water Resources
Alberta Irrigation Projects Association, 38
Alberta Lake Management Society, 39
Alberta Water Council, 51
Alberta Water Well Drilling Association, 51
American Water Resources Association, 1504
Canadian Water Network, 502
Canadian Water Resources Association, 503
Elora Environment Centre, 685
FogQuest, 742
International Association for Environmental Hydrology, 1536
International Water Association, 1566
IRC International Water & Sanitation Centre, 1567
Manitoba Conservation Districts Association, 934
National Ground Water Association, 1576
North Saskatchewan Watershed Alliance, 1032
Northeast Avalon ACAP, Inc., 1034
Ontario Ground Water Association, 1083
Ontario Water Works Association, 1113
Ontario Waterpower Association, 1113
Soil & Water Conservation Society, 1594
Swift Current Creek Watershed Stewards, 1358
Water Environment Federation, 1601
WaterCan, 1442
World Association of Industrial & Technological Research Organizations, 1603

Water Safety
Canadian Lifeboat Institution, 427

Water Skiing
Fédération ski nautique et planche Québec, 731
Ontario Water Ski Association, 1113
Water Ski & Wakeboard Manitoba, 1441
Water Ski & Wakeboard Alberta, 1441
Water Ski & Wakeboard British Columbia, 1441
Water Ski & Wakeboard Canada, 1441
Water Ski & Wakeboard Saskatchewan, 1442
Water Ski & Wakeboard Nova Scotia, 1442
Water Ski & Wakeboard New Brunswick, 1442

Water Supply
American Water Works Association, 1504
Atlantic Canada Water & Wastewater Association, 182
Bedeque Bay Environmental Management Association, 203
Christian Children's Fund of Canada, 567
FogQuest, 742
IRC International Water & Sanitation Centre, 1567
Manitoba Water Well Association, 947
Newfoundland & Labrador Ground Water Association, 1019
Ontario Ground Water Association, 1083
Ontario Municipal Water Association, 1092
Ontario Water Works Association, 1113
Prince Edward Island Ground Water Association, 1174
Saskatchewan Ground Water Association, 1266
Water Environment Federation, 1601

Watercolour
Canadian Society of Painters in Water Colour, 486

Weightlifting
British Columbia Weightlifting Association, 258
Ontario Weightlifting Association, 1113
Yukon Weightlifting Association, 1480

Weights & Measures
Bureau international des poids et mesures, 1515

Welding
Canadian Welding Bureau, 503
United Association of Journeymen & Apprentices of the Plumbing & Pipe Fitting Industry of the United States & Canada, 1599

Wells
Association des enterprises spécialiseés en eau du Québec, 112
British Columbia Ground Water Association, 242
Manitoba Water Well Association, 947
National Ground Water Association, 1576
New Brunswick Ground Water Association, 1009
Newfoundland & Labrador Ground Water Association, 1019
Nova Scotia Ground Water Association, 1045
Ontario Ground Water Association, 1083
Prince Edward Island Ground Water Association, 1174
Saskatchewan Ground Water Association, 1266

Wheat
Western Canadian Wheat Growers, 1449
Western Grains Research Foundation, 1449

Wholesale Trade
Canadian Association for Pharmacy Distribution Management, 303
Canadian Association of Wholesale Sales Representatives, 336
Prairie Apparel Market, 1169
Retail, Wholesale & Department Store Union (AFL-CIO/CLC), 1586
Saskatchewan Joint Board Retail, Wholesale & Department Store Union, 1268

Wilderness
Alberta Native Plant Council, 41
Alberta Wilderness Association, 52
Canadian Parks & Wilderness Society, 450
Conservation International, 1519
Earthroots, 667
Guide Outfitters Association of British Columbia, 793
Outward Bound Canada, 1133
Quetico Foundation, 1201
Sierra Club, 1589
Sierra Club of Canada, 1298
Sierra Youth Coalition, 1298
Valhalla Wilderness Society, 1424
Wilderness Committee, 1454
Wilderness Tourism Association, 1454

Wildlife
African Wildlife Foundation, 1486
Association of Fish & Wildlife Agencies, 1511
British Columbia Waterfowl Society, 258
Calgary Wildlife Rehabilitation Society, 275
Canadian Association for Humane Trapping, 301
Canadian Wild Turkey Federation, 504
Canadian Wildlife Federation, 504
Cape Breton Island Wildlife Association, 509
Ducks Unlimited Canada, 663
East African Wild Life Society, 1522
Eskasoni Fish & Wildlife Commission, 695
Fédération québécoise des chasseurs et pêcheurs, 728
Fondation de la faune du Québec, 744
Fur-Bearer Defenders, 765
Halifax Wildlife Association, 799
Hope for Wildlife Society, 821
Lambton Wildlife Inc., 897
Lunenburg County Wildlife Association, 921
Manitoba Wildlife Federation, 947
National Wildlife Federation, 1577
New Brunswick Wildlife Federation, 1013
Newfoundland & Labrador Wildlife Federation, 1022
North American Bird Conservation Initiative Canada, 1029
North American Waterfowl Management Plan, 1029
North Island Wildlife Recovery Association, 1031
Prince Edward Island Wildlife Federation, 1178

Saskatchewan Outfitters Association, 1271
Saskatchewan Wildlife Federation, 1278
Trappers Association of Nova Scotia, 1396
Wildlife Habitat Canada, 1454
Wildlife Rescue Association of British Columbia, 1455

Wildlife Conservation
Animal Alliance of Canada, 70
Animal Defence League of Canada, 70
Association of Fish & Wildlife Agencies, 1511
Association of Zoos & Aquariums, 1513
Atlantic Wildlife Institute, 186
Big Game Society of Nova Scotia, 210
Calgary Wildlife Rehabilitation Society, 275
Canadian Peregrine Foundation, 453
Canadian Wild Turkey Federation, 504
Conservation Enforcement Officers Association of Nova Scotia, 622
Ducks Unlimited Canada, 663
Earthroots, 667
East African Wild Life Society, 1522
Elsa Wild Animal Appeal of Canada, 685
Eskasoni Fish & Wildlife Commission, 695
Foundation for Environmental Conservation, 1526
Friends of Ecological Reserves, 761
Friends of Nature Conservation Society, 761
Friends of the Earth International, 1527
Hope for Wildlife Society, 821
International Association for Bear Research & Management, 1535
International Primate Protection League, 1556
International Union for Conservation of Nature, 1563
International Whaling Commission, 1566
International Wildlife Rehabilitation Council, 1566
The Jane Goodall Institute for Wildlife Research, Education & Conservation, 1568
The Jane Goodall Institute of Canada, 868
Kings County Wildlife Association, 888
Northwest Wildlife Preservation Society, 1039
Nova Scotia Federation of Anglers & Hunters, 1044
Nunavut Harvesters Association, 1051
Ottawa Duck Club, 1130
Port Morien Wildlife Association, 1166
Queens County Fish & Game Association, 1200
Rocky Mountain Elk Foundation Canada, 1586
Sea Shepherd Conservation Society, 1287
Sea Shepherd Conservation Society - USA, 1588
Sierra Club, 1589
Sierra Club of Canada, 1298
Sierra Youth Coalition, 1298
Société québécoise pour la défense des animaux, 1324
South Shore Wildlife Association, 1336
Spruce City Wildlife Association, 1346
Sunshine Coast Natural History Society, 1355
Toronto Zoo, 1388
Valhalla Wilderness Society, 1424
Wild Bird Care Centre, 1453
Wildlife Preservation Canada, 1455
Wildlife Rescue Association of British Columbia, 1455
World Animal Protection, 1465
World Blue Chain for the Protection of Animals & Nature, 1603
World Wildlife Fund - Canada, 1468
World Wildlife Fund - USA, 1608
WWF International, 1608
ZOOCHECK Canada Inc., 1482
Zoological Society of Montréal, 1482

Wind Engineering
Canadian Wind Energy Association, 504
TechnoCentre éolien, 1368

Wine
Amicale des Sommeliers du Québec, 67
Amici dell'Enotria Toronto, 67
Australian Wine Society of Toronto, 188
British Columbia Wine Institute, 258
Canadian Vintners Association, 501
Drinks Ontario, 663
International Wine & Food Society, 1567
Opimian Society, 1116
Vintners Quality Alliance, 1435
Wine Country Ontario, 1457
Wine Writers' Circle of Canada, 1458

Subject Index / Women

Women
Act To End Violence Against Women, 6
Afghan Women's Counselling & Integration Community Support Organization, 12
Alberta Women's Institutes, 52
Alliance des femmes de la francophonie canadienne, 55
Almas Jiwani Foundation, 59
Associated Country Women of the World, 1506
Association des fermières de l'Ontario, 114
Association féminine d'éducation et d'action sociale, 132
Au Coup de pouce Centre-Sud inc., 187
Awo Taan Healing Lodge Society, 191
Breast Cancer Action, 227
Calgary Immigrant Women's Association, 272
Canadian Association for the Study of Women & Education, 306
Canadian Association of Elizabeth Fry Societies, 312
Canadian Council of Muslim Women, 369
Canadian Federation of University Women, 388
Canadian Hadassah WIZO, 399
Canadian Research Institute for the Advancement of Women, 467
Canadian Women Voters Congress, 505
Canadian Women's Foundation, 505
Catholic Women's League of Canada, 520
Central Alberta Women's Outreach Society, 524
Central Nova Women's Resource Centre, 524
Centre d'éducation et d'action des femmes de Montréal, 528
Centre de documentation sur l'éducation des adultes et la condition féminine, 529
Centre des femmes de Montréal, 530
Cercles de fermières du Québec, 537
Coalition des femmes de l'Alberta, 577
Collectif des femmes immigrantes du Québec, 581
Comité condition féminine Baie-James, 591
Comité québécois femmes et développement, 592
Coverdale Centre for Women Inc., 637
DisAbled Women's Network of Canada, 658
Dress for Success, 662
Emunah Women of Canada, 687
Ending Violence Association of British Columbia, 687
Les EssentiElles, 696
Federated Women's Institutes of Canada, 706
Fédération des agricultrices du Québec, 711
La Fédération des femmes acadiennes de la Nouvelle-Écosse, 715
Fédération des femmes acadiennes et francophones du Nouveau-Brunswick, 715
Fédération des femmes du Québec, 715
Feminist Alliance for International Action, 731
Girl Guides of Canada, 773
Golden Women's Resource Centre Society, 776
Groupe intervention vidéo, 792
Immigrant Women Services Ottawa, 831
Immigrant Women's Health Centre, 831
Institut féminin francophone du Nouveau-Brunswick, 842
Inter Pares, 851
International Federation for Research in Women's History, 1547
International Women's Forum, 1567
Jean Tweed Treatment Centre, 869
Junior League of Edmonton, 878
Lace Up Your Cleats, 895
Ladies' Morning Musical Club, 895
Ladies' Orange Benevolent Association of Canada, 895
League of Ukrainian Canadian Women, 903
Malton Neighbourhood Services, 928
Massey Centre for Women, 953
MATCH International Women's Fund, 954
Miss G Project, 968
Montréal Council of Women, 972
Na'amat Canada Inc., 987
National Action Committee on the Status of Women, 989
National Association of Women & the Law, 990
The National Council of Women of Canada, 992
National Organization of Immigrant & Visible Minority Women of Canada, 995
Newcomer Women's Services Toronto, 1015
Nova Scotia Advisory Council on the Status of Women, 1040
The Older Women's Network, 1056
OMID Foundation Canada, 1058
Planned Parenthood Ottawa, 1161
Polish Canadian Women's Federation, 1163
Positive Women's Network, 1168
Provincial Council of Women of Manitoba Inc., 1190
Red Hat Society Inc., 1586
Regina Immigrant Women Centre, 1211
Regroupement des femmes de la Côte-de-Gaspé, 1215
Réseau Femmes Québec, 1224
Rexdale Women's Centre, 1229
Riverdale Immigrant Women's Centre, 1234
Scarborough Women's Centre, 1283
Second Story Women's Centre, 1288
Soroptimist Foundation of Canada, 1333
South Asian Women's Centre, 1334
Status of Women Council of the Northwest Territories, 1349
Syndicat des agricultrices de la Beauce, 1362
Syndicat des agricultrices de la Côte-du-Sud, 1362
Syndicat des agricultrices du Centre du Québec, 1362
Toronto Community Employment Services, 1383
Tri-County Women's Centre, 1398
L'Union culturelle des Franco-Ontariennes, 1406
Vancouver Society of Immigrant & Visible Minority Women, 1428
Vancouver Status of Women, 1428
Webgrrls Canada, 1443
West Kootenay Women's Association, 1445
WIL Employment Connections, 1453
Windsor Women Working with Immigrant Women, 1457
Women's & Gender Studies et Recherches Féministes, 1461
Women's Centre of Montréal, 1462
Women's International League for Peace & Freedom, 1462
Women's Missionary Society, 1463
Women's Network PEI, 1463
Working Women Community Centre, 1464
World Federation of Ukrainian Women's Organizations, 1466
YWCA Canada, 1481
YWCA December 6 Fund of Toronto, 1482

Women & Health
Advanced Coronary Treatment (ACT) Foundation of Canada, 10
British Columbia Centre of Excellence for Women's Health, 235
Canadian Association for Size Acceptance, 304
Centre d'action sida Montréal (Femmes), 527
Endometriosis Association, Inc., 1523
Federation of Medical Women of Canada, 724
Genesis Research Foundation, 769
Marguerite Bourgeoys Family Centre Fertility Care Programme, 949
Medical Women's International Association, 958
Ontario Women's Health Network, 1113
Options for Sexual Health, 1117
Ovarian Cancer Canada, 1133
SIGMA Canadian Menopause Society, 1298
Simcoe Women's Wellness Centre Corporation, 1300
Vancouver Women's Health Collective, 1429

Women & Religion
Congrégation des Soeurs de Sainte-Anne, 612
Mouvement des femmes Chrétiennes, 977
National Council of Jewish Women of Canada, 992
Theresians International - Canada, 1375
Union mondiale des organisations féminines catholiques, 1599
Women of the Word - Toronto, 1461
Women's Inter-Church Council of Canada, 1462

Women & the Arts
Association of Canadian Women Composers, 144
First Vancouver Theatre Space Society, 739
Women's Art Association of Canada, 1461
Women's Musical Club of Toronto, 1463

Women & the Environment
British Columbia Women's Institutes, 258
Federated Women's Institutes of Ontario, 706
The Ladies of the Lake, 895
Manitoba Women's Institutes, 947
New Brunswick Women's Institute, 1013
Newfoundland & Labrador Women's Institutes, 1022
Prince Edward Island Women's Institute, 1178
Québec Women's Institutes, 1199
Saskatchewan Women's Institute, 1278
Women's Environment & Development Organization, 1602
Women's Healthy Environments Network, 1462
Women's Institutes of Nova Scotia, 1462

Women in Business, Industry & Trade
Alberta Women Entrepreneurs, 52
Association of Women in Finance, 164
Business Women's Networking Association, 267
Canadian Association of Women Executives & Entrepreneurs, 336
Canadian Board Diversity Council, 345
Canadian Construction Women, 363
The Canadian Federation of Business & Professional Women's Clubs, 385
Centre de documentation sur l'éducation des adultes et la condition féminine, 529
Centre for Women in Business, 534
Company of Women, 608
Conseil d'intervention pour l'accès des femmes au travail, 615
International Federation of Business & Professional Women, 1547
National Association of Women in Construction, 1575
Newfoundland & Labrador Organization of Women Entrepreneurs, 1020
Prince Edward Island Business Women's Association, 1172
Réseau des femmes d'affaires du Québec inc., 1219
Soroptimist International of the Americas, 1595
Wings & Heros, 1458
Women Business Owners of Manitoba, 1460
Women Entrepreneurs of Saskatchewan Inc., 1460
Women Expanding Business Network of Lanark County, 1460
Women in a Home Office, 1460
Women in Capital Markets, 1460
Women Who Excel Inc., 1461
Women's Association of the Mining Industry of Canada, 1461
Women's Business Network of Ottawa, 1462
Women's Enterprise Centre of Manitoba, 1462
Women's Executive Network, 1462

Women in Crisis
Act To End Violence Against Women, 6
Adsum for Women & Children, 9
Assaulted Women's Helpline, 87
Association d'entraide Le Chaînon inc., 99
Aurora House, 187
Awo Taan Healing Lodge Society, 191
The Barbra Schlifer Commemorative Clinic, 196
Battlefords Interval House Society, 200
Calgary Women's Emergency Shelter Association, 275
Canadian Association of Sexual Assault Centres, 333
Canadian Women for Women in Afghanistan, 504
Carrefour pour Elle, 516
Centre d'aide et de lutte contre les agressions à caractère sexuel de la Rive-Sud, 527
Centre de recherche interdisciplinaire sur la violence familiale et la violence faite aux femmes, 530
Centre des Femmes de Longueuil, 530
Centre for Research on Violence Against Women & Children, 533
Centre for Spanish Speaking Peoples, 533
Chez Doris, 557
Crossroads for Women Inc., 644
Fédération de maisons d'hébergement pour femmes, 715
The Freda Centre for Research on Violence Against Women & Children, 758
Fredericton Sexual Assault Crisis Centre, 759
Guelph-Wellington Women in Crisis, 793
Halifax Transition House Association - Bryony House, 799
Helping Spirit Lodge Society, 812
Interval House, 861
Lloydminster Interval Home Society, 916
Maison des femmes de Québec inc., 926
Mamawehetowin Crisis Centre, 928
Manitoba Association of Women's Shelters, 931
Nellie's Shelter, 1003
New Brunswick Coalition of Transition Houses/Centres for Abused Women, 1007
Newfoundland & Labrador Sexual Assault Crisis & Prevention Centre Inc., 1021
Oasis Centre des femmes, 1054
Ontario Association of Interval & Transition Houses, 1064
Ontario Women's Justice Network, 1113
Opportunity For Advancement, 1116
Parkland Crisis Centre & Women's Shelter, 1142
Pavillion Marguerite de Champlain, 1146
Peel Committee Against Woman Abuse, 1147
Regina Transition Women's Society, 1212
Regroupement provincial des maisons d'hébergement et de transition pour femmes victimes de violence conjugale, 1216
RESOLVE: Research & Education for Solutions to Violence & Abuse, 1226
Revelstoke Women's Shelter Society, 1228
La rue des femmes, 1243
Sexual Assault Centre Kingston Inc., 1292
Sexual Assault Centre London, 1292
Sexual Assault Crisis Centre of Essex County Inc., 1293
Sexual Assault Support Centre Ottawa, 1293
Sexual Assault Survivors' Centre - Sarnia-Lambton, 1293
Shamattawa Crisis Centre, 1294
Shuswap Area Family Emergency Society, 1297
Sistering - A Woman's Place, 1300
Society of St. Vincent de Paul - Toronto Central Council, 1330
South Central Committee on Family Violence, Inc., 1334
South Okanagan Women in Need Society, 1335
Springtide Resources, 1346
Street Haven at the Crossroads, 1352
Thompson Crisis Centre, 1376
Thunder Bay Sexual Assault / Sexual Abuse Counselling & Crisis Centre, 1378
Timmins & Area Women in Crisis Support & Information Centre on Violence Against Women, 1379
Transition House Association of Nova Scotia, 1395
Vancouver Rape Relief & Women's Shelter, 1428
Vernon Women's Transition House Society, 1431
West Niagara Second Stage Housing & Counselling, 1446
Women In Crisis (Algoma) Inc., 1460
The Women's Centre, 1462
Yellowhead Emergency Shelter for Women Society, 1470

Women in Insurance
Association des femmes d'assurance de Montréal, 114
Canadian Association of Insurance Women, 318
Edmonton Insurance Association, 678
Insurance Professionals of Calgary, 850
Insurance Women's Association of Western Manitoba, 850
London Insurance Professionals Association, 918
Manitoba Association of Insurance Professionals, 930
Northwestern Ontario Insurance Professionals, 1039
Nova Scotia Insurance Women's Association, 1046
Toronto Insurance Women's Association, 1385

Women in Professions
Canadian Association of Women Executives & Entrepreneurs, 336
The Canadian Federation of Business & Professional Women's Clubs, 385
Canadian Indigenous Nurses Association, 411

Subject Index / Youth

International Federation of Business & Professional Women, 1547
The Ninety-Nines Inc., 1578
NSERC Chair for Women in Science & Engineering, 1050
Pacific Association of First Nations' Women, 1134
Society for Canadian Women in Science & Technology, 1325
Society of Women Engineers, 1594
Soroptimist International of the Americas, 1595
Women's Legal Education & Action Fund, 1462

Women in Sports
Abbotsford Female Hockey Association, 1
Canadian Association for the Advancement of Women & Sport & Physical Activity, 305
Ladies' Golf Union, 1569
Nova Scotia Curling Association, 1043
ProMOTION Plus, 1188
Whitehorse Women's Hockey Association, 1453

Women in the Mass Media
Canadian Women in Communications, 505
Centre femmes de Rimouski, 531
Women in Film & Television - Toronto, 1461
Women in Film & Television Alberta, 1461
Women in Film & Television Vancouver, 1461

Wood
American Forest & Paper Association, 1493
British Columbia Wood Specialities Group Association, 258
Canadian Hardwood Plywood & Veneer Association, 401
Canadian Plywood Association, 456
Canadian Wood Council, 505
International Research Group on Wood Protection, 1556
Wood Pellet Association of Canada, 1463
Wood Preservation Canada, 1463

Wood Energy
Wood Energy Technology Transfer Inc., 1463

Woodworking
Architectural Woodwork Manufacturers Association of British Columbia, 79
Architectural Woodwork Manufacturers Association of Canada, 79
Architectural Woodwork Manufacturers Association of Canada - Atlantic, 79
Architectural Woodwork Manufacturers Association of Canada - Manitoba, 79
Architectural Woodwork Manufacturers Association of Canada - Northern Alberta, 79
Architectural Woodwork Manufacturers Association of Canada - Ontario Chapter, 79
Architectural Woodwork Manufacturers Association of Canada - Québec, 80
Architectural Woodwork Manufacturers Association of Canada - Saskatchewan, 80
Architectural Woodwork Manufacturers Association of Canada - Southern Alberta, 80
United Steelworkers Local 1-424, 1412

Wool
Canadian Co-operative Wool Growers Ltd., 364
Nova Scotia Wool Marketing Board, 1050

Workers' Compensation
Association of Workers' Compensation Boards of Canada, 164
Cape Breton Injured Workers' Association, 509
Industrial Accident Victims Group of Ontario, 835
Institute for Work & Health, 844

World Wars
Canadian Battlefields Foundation, 342
Commonwealth War Graves Commission - Canadian Agency, 594
Monte Cassino Society, 1571
The Royal Canadian Legion, 1240

Wrestling
Alberta Amateur Wrestling Association, 22
British Columbia Wrestling Association, 258
Calgary Combative Sports Commission, 271
Canadian Amateur Wrestling Association, 292
Canadian Arm Wrestling Federation, 295
Edmonton Combative Sports Commission, 676
Fédération de lutte olympique du Québec, 710
Lutte NB Wrestling, 922
Manitoba Amateur Wrestling Association, 928
Manitoba Arm Wrestling Association, 928
Newfoundland & Labrador Amateur Wrestling Association, 1015
Nova Scotia Arm Wrestling Association, 1040
Ontario Amateur Wrestling Association, 1059
Saskatchewan Amateur Wrestling Association, 1255
World Armwrestling Federation, 1603
Wrestling Nova Scotia, 1468
Wrestling PEI, 1468

Writers
Académie des lettres du Québec, 3
Access Copyright, 4
Alexandra Writers' Centre Society, 53
Association des auteures et des auteurs de l'Ontario français, 106
Association of Great Lakes Outdoor Writers, 1512
Association of Italian Canadian Writers, 150
Association professionnelle des écrivains de la Sagamie-Côte-Nord, 167
Burnaby Writers' Society, 266
Canadian Association for the Study of Discourse & Writing, 306
Canadian Authors Association, 338
The Canadian Centre/International P.E.N., 354
Canadian Ethnic Media Association, 382
Canadian Farm Writers' Federation, 384
Canadian Journalism Foundation, 423
Canadian Society of Children's Authors, Illustrators & Performers, 481
Canadian Writers' Foundation Inc., 506
Children's Writers & Illustrators of British Columbia Society, 563
Chinese Canadian Writers' Association, 564
Écrivains Francophones d'Amérique, 674
Federation of British Columbia Writers, 722
The G.K. Chesterton Institute for Faith & Culture, 1528
The Harold Greenberg Fund, 804
InScribe Christian Writers' Fellowship, 839
Island Writers' Association (P.E.I.), 866
Manitoba Writers' Guild Inc., 947
Ottawa Independent Writers, 1130
Outdoor Writers of Canada, 1133
PEN International, 1583
Professional Writers Association of Canada, 1187
The Saskatchewan Poetry Society, 1272
Saskatchewan Writers Guild, 1278
Science Writers & Communicators of Canada, 1285
SF Canada, 1293
Société des Auteurs de Radio, Télévision et Cinéma, 1317
Société du droit de reproduction des auteurs, compositeurs et éditeurs au Canada (SODRAC 2003) inc., 1318
Société professionnelle des auteurs et des compositeurs du Québec, 1322
Society of Composers, Authors & Music Publishers of Canada, 1328
Tamil Writers' Association of Canada, 1366
Union des écrivaines et écrivains québécois, 1406
Wine Writers' Circle of Canada, 1458
Writers Guild of Canada, 1468
Writers' Alliance of Newfoundland & Labrador, 1468
Writers' Federation of New Brunswick, 1468
Writers' Federation of Nova Scotia, 1468
The Writers' Guild of Alberta, 1469
The Writers' Trust of Canada, 1469
The Writers' Union of Canada, 1469

Yoga
Iyengar Yoga Association of Canada, 867
Sivananda Ashram Yoga Camp, 1301
Yasodhara Ashram Society, 1470
Yoga Association of Alberta, 1473

Young Men's Christian Association
YMCA Canada, 1471

Young Offenders
The John Howard Society of Ontario, 874
St. Leonard's Society of Canada, 1250
Saskatchewan Youth in Care & Custody Network, 1279

Young Women's Christian Association
YWCA Canada, 1481

Youth
Active Healthy Kids Canada, 7
Alberta CGIT Association, 28
Association des avocats en droit de la jeunesse, 106
Association des centres jeunesse du Québec, 108
Association des Grands Frères et Grandes Soeurs du Québec, 115
Association des jeunes bègues de Québec, 117
Association des jeunes travailleurs et travailleuses de Montréal inc, 117
Association des orchestres de jeunes de la Montérégie, 121
Association des orchestres de jeunes du Québec inc., 121
Association jeunesse fransaskoise, 137
Associés bénévoles qualifiés au service des jeunes, 179
The Atlantic Film Festival Association, 184
B'nai Brith Youth Organization, 192
Big Brothers Big Sisters of Alberta, 209
Big Brothers Big Sisters of British Columbia, 209
Big Brothers Big Sisters of Canada, 209
Big Brothers Big Sisters of Eastern Newfoundland, 209
Big Brothers Big Sisters of Manitoba, 209
Big Brothers Big Sisters of New Brunswick, 209
Big Brothers Big Sisters of Nova Scotia, 210
Big Brothers Big Sisters of Ontario, 210
Big Brothers Big Sisters of Prince Edward Island, 210
Big Brothers Big Sisters of Saskatchewan, 210
Big Brothers Big Sisters of Yukon, 210
Black Community Resource Centre, 213
Boost Child & Youth Advocacy Centre, 218
Boundless Adventures Association, 219
Calgary Youth Orchestra, 275
Canada Israel Experience Centre, 280
Canada World Youth, 281
Canadian 4-H Council, 284
Canadian Children's Optimist Foundation, 356
Canadian Safe School Network, 468
Canadian Sinfonietta Youth Orchestra, 470
Canadian Tamil Youth Development Centre, 492
Canadian Young Judaea, 506
C.A.R.E. Jeunesse, 511
Cariboo Action Training Society, 512
Carrefour jeunesse emploi de l'Outaouais, 515
Carrefour jeunesse emploi du Pontiac, 515
Carrefour Jeunesse Emploi Vallée-de-la-Gatineau, 516
Carrefour jeunesse-emploi Papineau, 516
Carthy Foundation, 516
Catholic Youth Studio - KSM Inc., 521
Centre de protection de l'enfance et de la jeunesse, 529
Centre for Entrepreneurship Education & Development Inc., 532
Centre intégré d'employabilité locale des Collines-de-l'Outaouais, 535
Le Centre jeunesse de la Montérégie, 536
Le centre jeunesse de Québec, 536
Cercles des jeunes naturalistes, 537
Chabad Lubavitch Youth Organization, 539
Chantiers jeunesse, 551
Chemins du soleil, 556
Child & Youth Care Association of Newfoundland & Labrador, 558
The Church Lads' Brigade, 569
Conseil jeunesse francophone de la Colombie-Britannique, 618
Conseil jeunesse provincial (Manitoba), 619
Covenant House Toronto, 637
Desta Black Youth Network, 654
Durham Youth Orchestra, 665
East Prince Youth Development Centre, 668
Edmonton Youth Orchestra Association, 679
Enactus Canada, 687
Environmental Youth Alliance, 692
Environnement jeunesse, 693
Envol SRT, 693
ERS Training & Development Corporation, 695
Eva's Initiatives for Homeless Youth, 698
Fédération de la jeunesse canadienne-française inc., 709
Fédération de la jeunesse franco-ontarienne, 709
Fédération des jeunes francophones du Nouveau-Brunswick Inc., 715
Federation of B.C. Youth in Care Networks, 722
Federation of North American Explorers, 725
La Fondation des Auberges du coeur, 744
Fondation Dufresne et Gauthier, 746
Fondation maman Dion, 747
Fondation Ressources-Jeunesse, 748
Fondation Tourisme Jeunesse, 748
Force Jeunesse, 751
4Cs Foundation, 756
Franco-Jeunes de Terre-Neuve et du Labrador, 757
Francophonie jeunesse de l'Alberta, 757
Futurpreneur Canada, 765
Gainey Foundation, 766
Girl Guides of Canada, 773
Girls Action Foundation, 774
Global Youth Volunteer Network, 775
Greater Victoria Youth Orchestra, 787
Guid'amies franco-manitobaines, 793
Halton Mississauga Youth Orchestra, 800
Hamilton Philharmonic Youth Orchestra, 801
Hashomer Hatzair Canada, 804
Heartwood Centre for Community Youth Development, 810
Horatio Alger Association of Canada, 821
Hostelling International - Canada, 823
Impact Society, 831
Inner City Angels, 838
International Symphony Orchestra Youth String Ensemble, 861
Jesus Youth Canada, 870
Jeune chambre de commerce de Montréal, 870
Jeunes canadiens pour une civilisation chrétienne, 870
Jeunesse Acadienne et Francophone de l'Île-du-prince-Édouard, 870
Jeunesse du Monde, 870
La Jeunesse Youth Orchestra, 870
Jeunesses Musicales du Canada, 871
Junior Achievement Canada, 877
Junior Chamber International Canada, 877
Justice for Children & Youth, 878
Kids Help Phone, 886
Kingston Youth Orchestra, 890
Kitchener-Waterloo Symphony Youth Orchestra, 891
Lions Quest Canada - The Centre for Positive Youth Development, 913
Living Bible Explorers, 915
London Youth Symphony, 919
Maison Kekpart, 927
Malton Neighbourhood Services, 928
Manitoba & Northwestern Ontario CGIT Association, 928
Maritime Regional CGIT Committee, 951
The Marquis Project, Inc., 952
McCreary Centre Society, 955
McMan Youth, Family & Community Services Association, 955
Mon Sheong Foundation, 971
Moorelands Community Services, 973
National African Integration & Families of Ontario, 989
National Inuit Youth Council, 994
National Youth Orchestra Canada, 997
New Beginnings for Youth, 1004
New Brunswick Youth in Care Network, 1013
Newfoundland Symphony Youth Orchestra, 1023
Niagara Youth Orchestra Association, 1026
Northern Youth Abroad Program, 1035
Nova Scotia Youth Orchestra, 1050
One Full Circle, 1058
Ontario Association For Students At Risk, 1061
Ontario Association of Child & Youth Care, 1062
Ontario Association of Residences Treating Youth, 1065
Ontario CGIT Association, 1071
Operation Come Home, 1115
Optimist International, 1580
Optimist International Canada, 1116
Orchestre symphonique des jeunes de Montréal, 1118
Orchestre symphonique des jeunes de Sherbrooke, 1118
Orchestre symphonique des jeunes du West Island, 1118

Orchestre symphonique des jeunes Philippe-Filion, 1118
Orillia Youth Symphony Orchestra, 1126
Ottawa Youth Orchestra Academy, 1132
Our Place (Peel), 1133
Oxford Child & Youth Centre, 1134
Oxy-jeunes, 1134
Partners for Youth, 1144
Pathways to Education Canada, 1145
Pioneer Clubs Canada Inc., 1160
Planned Parenthood Ottawa, 1161
Plast Ukrainian Youth Association of Canada, 1162
Projet T.R.I.P., 1188
Provincial CGIT Board of BC, 1190
Ranch Ehrlo Society, 1204
Rehtaeh Parsons Society, 1217
Réseau Technoscience, 1226
Richmond Delta Youth Orchestra, 1230
St. Leonard's Youth & Family Services Society, 1250
Saskatchewan CGIT Committee, 1260
Saskatchewan Youth in Care & Custody Network, 1279
Saskatoon Youth Orchestra, 1280
Scouts Canada, 1286
Sierra Youth Coalition, 1298
Société d'investissement jeunesse, 1314
Society for Adolescent Health & Medicine, 1589
South Saskatchewan Youth Orchestra, 1336
Sudbury Youth Orchestra Inc., 1353
Théâtres unis enfance jeunesse, 1375
Toronto Symphony Youth Orchestra, 1387
T.R.E.E. Foundation for Youth Development, 1397
Ukrainian Democratic Youth Association, 1403
Ukrainian Youth Association of Canada, 1404
United Generations Ontario, 1411
United Synagogue Youth, 1412
Universal Youth Foundation, 1418
Vancouver Youth Symphony Orchestra Society, 1429
Victoria Youth Empowerment Society, 1434
Visions of Science Network for Learning, 1436
Voices for Children, 1437
Voices: Manitoba's Youth in Care Network, 1437
Winnipeg Youth Orchestras, 1459
World Assembly of Youth, 1603
World Fellowship of Orthodox Youth, 1605
Young Alberta Book Society, 1474
Young People's Theatre, 1474
Youth Assisting Youth, 1475
Youth Ballet & Contemporary Dance of Saskatchewan Inc., 1475
Youth Bowling Canada, 1475
Youth Challenge International, 1475
Youth Empowerment & Support Services, 1475
Youth Flight Canada, 1475
Youth for Christ Canada, 1475
Youth in Care Canada, 1475
Youth in Care in Ontario, 1476
Youth Now on Track Program, 1476
Youth Science Canada, 1476
YOUTHLINK, 1476

Zionism
ARZA-Canada: The Zionist Voice of the Canadian Reform Movement, 86
Canadian Young Judaea, 506
Canadian Zionist Federation, 506
Hashomer Hatzair Canada, 804
Mercaz-Canada, 961
Mizrachi Organization of Canada, 970

Zoology
Canadian Society of Zoologists, 488
International Council for Archaeozoology, 1544
Société des établissements de plein air du Québec, 1318

Zoos
Assiniboine Park Conservancy, 88
Association of Zoos & Aquariums, 1513
Calgary Zoological Society, 275
Canada's Accredited Zoos & Aquariums, 281
Toronto Zoo, 1388
ZOOCHECK Canada Inc., 1482
Zoological Society of Montréal, 1482

Zoroastrianism
L'Association Zoroastrianne du Québec, 179
Ontario Zoroastrian Community Foundation, 1114
Zoroastrian Society of Ontario, 1482

Abbeyfield Houses Society of Canada
PO Box 1, 427 Bloor St. West, Toronto ON M5S 1X7
Tel: 416-920-7483; *Fax:* 416-920-6956
info@abbeyfield.ca
www.abbeyfield.ca
Overview: A small national charitable organization founded in 1984
Mission: To provide accommodation and companionship for lonely older people within their own community.
Affiliation(s): Abbeyfield International, U.K.
Activities: *Speaker Service:* Yes
Awards:
• Queen's Jubilee Medals

Abbotsford Arts Council (AAC)
PO Box 336, 2387 Ware St., Abbotsford BC V2T 6Z6
Tel: 604-852-9358
www.abbotsfordartscouncil.org
www.linkedin.com/company/abbotsford-arts-council
www.facebook.com/AbbotsfordArtsCouncil
twitter.com/AbbyArtsCouncil
www.pinterest.com/abbyartscouncil
Overview: A small local charitable organization founded in 1972
Mission: To promote the vision, creativity & energy of the community through the arts; To develop & enhance all of the arts & culture in the Abbotsford community; To encourage & support arts organizations & individuals including professional & emerging artists & hobbyists by coordinating projects & events; To provide education opportunities that stimulate & promote excellence in the arts
Member of: Assembly of BC Arts Councils
Affiliation(s): BC Touring Council; Festivals BC
Finances: *Annual Operating Budget:* $50,000-$100,000; *Funding Sources:* Government; corporate; private
Staff Member(s): 2; 50 volunteer(s)
Membership: 400; *Fees:* $15 Individual; $35 Group
Activities: Christmas Craft Fair; For the Love of the Arts Studio Tour; Art Walk; unity statue project; Artisans Fair; Art Benches; Arty Awards; *Awareness Events:* Envision Coffee House Concert Series; Snowflake Christmas Market; Art of Marketing; *Library:* Not open to public
Chief Officer(s):
Gail Gromaski, Executive Director
gail@abbotsfordartscouncil.com
Awards:
• Arty Awards

Abbotsford Chamber of Commerce (ACOC)
207 - 32900 South Fraser Way, Abbotsford BC V2S 5A1
Tel: 604-859-9651; *Fax:* 604-850-6880
www.abbotsfordchamber.com
twitter.com/acoc
Overview: A small local charitable organization founded in 1913
Mission: To represent, serve & connect our members to build & sustain a thriving business community
Member of: British Columbia Chamber of Commerce; Canadian Chamber of Commerce
Finances: *Annual Operating Budget:* $250,000-$500,000; *Funding Sources:* Membership fees; fundraising
Staff Member(s): 4; 150 volunteer(s)
Membership: 700+; *Fees:* Schedule available; *Member Profile:* Business & non-profit organizations; *Committees:* Agriculture; Business Excellence Awards; Government & Industry Relations; Membership Services; Public Policy
Activities: Operating business information centre; Organizing business luncheons, training & skills seminars & workshops, awards ceremonies, & networking & fundraising events; Lobbying; *Library:* Resource Centre; Open to public
Chief Officer(s):
Allan Asaph, Executive Director
allan@abbotsfordchamber.com
Awards:
• Business Excellence Awards

Abbotsford Community Services
2420 Montrose St., Abbotsford BC V2S 3S9
Tel: 604-859-7681; *Fax:* 604-859-6334
info@abbotsfordcommunityservices.com
abbotsfordcommunityservices.com
www.facebook.com/abbotsfordcommunityservices\
www.twitter.com/abbcommservs
www.youtube.com/channel/UC3R4UpwNYqQyk8ojejUnJGg
Overview: A medium-sized local charitable organization founded in 1969
Mission: To provide supportive community social services in partnership with government ministries & the local community
Member of: British Columbia Association for Community Living; Federation of Family & Children Services
Affiliation(s): Social Planning & Research Council of BC; Community Social Services Employers' Association
Finances: *Annual Operating Budget:* Greater than $5 Million; *Funding Sources:* Government; community donors; foundations; sales; membership fees
Staff Member(s): 300; 1000 volunteer(s)
Membership: 75 individual; *Fees:* $2; *Committees:* Board Development; Community Relations; Finance; Health & Safety; Multicultural; Nominations; Fund Development
Activities: Family services; recycling operation; multi-cultural services; senior services; employment services; food bank; services for developmentally disabled; legal services intake; *Awareness Events:* Multi-cultural Week; Substance Abuse Awareness Week; Volunteer Appreciation Day; *Internships:* Yes; *Library:* Not open to public
Chief Officer(s):
Serge Blanchette, President
Rod Santiago, Executive Director
Rod.santiago@abbotsfordcommunityservices.com
Awards:
• Cultural Diversity

Abbotsford Downtown Business Association
2615A Montrose Ave., Abbotsford BC V2S 3T5
Tel: 604-850-6547; *Fax:* 604-859-6507
hello@downtownabbotsford.com
www.downtownabbotsford.com
www.facebook.com/AbbotsfordDowntown
twitter.com/downtownabbybc
Overview: A small local organization
Mission: To attract patrons to Historic Downtown Abbotsford

Abbotsford Female Hockey Association (AFHA)
#476, 33771 George Ferguson Way, Abbotsford BC V2S 2M5
afharegistrar@gmail.com
www.abbotsfordfemalehockey.com
www.facebook.com/AbbotsfordFemaleHockeyAssociation
twitter.com/AbbyIceGirls
Overview: A small local organization
Mission: The Abbotsford Female Hockey Association seeks to provide an opportunity for females of all ages & all skill levels to play hockey in Abbotsford in an all-female league.
Member of: BC Hockey

Abbotsford Food Bank & Christmas Bureau (AFB)
33914 Essendene Ave., Abbotsford BC V2S 2H8
Tel: 604-859-5749; *Fax:* 604-859-2717
Toll-Free: 877-859-5749
afb@abbotsfordcommunityservices.com
www.abbotsfordfoodbank.com
www.facebook.com/AbbyFoodbank
twitter.com/AbbyFoodBank
www.instagram.com/abbotsfordfoodbank
Previous Name: Matsqui-Abbotsford Food Bank
Overview: A small local organization founded in 1979
Mission: To serve the community in Abbotsford through the provision of supplemental food assistance & supportive programs
Member of: Canadian Food Bank Association
Finances: *Annual Operating Budget:* $100,000-$250,000; *Funding Sources:* Donations
Activities: Christmas Bureau; Food distribution; Free dental clinic; Mentoring; Garden box; Comedy tours; Kids sports; School breakfast programs; *Speaker Service:* Yes
Chief Officer(s):
Dave Murray, Manager
dave.murray@abbotsfordcommunityservices.com

Abbotsford International Air Show Society (AIAS) / Spectacle aérienne d'Abbotsford
1464 Tower Rd., Abbotsford BC V2T 6H5
Tel: 604-852-8511; *Fax:* 604-852-6093
info@abbotsfordairshow.com
www.abbotsfordairshow.com
www.facebook.com/360068150851
twitter.com/AbbyAirshow
Overview: A small local organization founded in 1966
Mission: To produce & orchestrate an international flying events show
Member of: Abbotsford Chamber of Commerce; International Council of Airshows
Staff Member(s): 3; 1000 volunteer(s)
Activities: The Abbotsford International Airshow, August; *Speaker Service:* Yes
Chief Officer(s):
Ron Price, President & CEO

Abbotsford Social Activity Association
33889 Essendene Ave., Abbotsford BC V2S 2H6
Tel: 604-853-4014; *Fax:* 604-853-4031
abbysocialactivityassoc@gmail.com
www.abbysocialactivityassoc.com
Overview: A small local charitable organization founded in 1972
Mission: To provide recreational facilities & activities for seniors in the Abbotsford area of British Columbia
Membership: *Fees:* $10 / year
Activities: Dancing; Classes; Crafts; Exercise
Chief Officer(s):
Jim Curran, Acting President, 604-859-6531

Abbotsford-Mission Nature Club
PO Box 612, Abbotsford BC V2T 6Z8
Tel: 604-853-4283
info@abbymissionnatureclub.org
www.centralvalleynaturalists.org
Previous Name: Central Valley Naturalists
Overview: A small local organization
Affiliation(s): Federation of BC Naturalists
Membership: 120; *Fees:* $30 individual; $35 family
Chief Officer(s):
Hank Roos, President

ABC CANADA Literacy Foundation *See* ABC Life Literacy Canada

ABC Life Literacy Canada
#604, 110 Eglinton Ave. East, Toronto ON M4P 2Y1
Tel: 416-218-0010; *Fax:* 416-218-0457
Toll-Free: 800-303-1004
info@abclifeliteracy.ca
abclifeliteracy.ca
www.facebook.com/abclifeliteracy
twitter.com/abclifeliteracy
Previous Name: ABC CANADA Literacy Foundation
Overview: A medium-sized national charitable organization founded in 1990
Mission: To inspire Canadians to increase their literacy skills
Finances: *Annual Operating Budget:* $1.5 Million-$3 Million; *Funding Sources:* Federal government; Private sector
Staff Member(s): 11
Membership: 1-99; *Committees:* Audit; Communications; Executive; Research; Board; Finance
Activities: Connecting businesses, communities, & individuals to literacy program opportunities; *Awareness Events:* PGI Golf Tournaments for Literacy; Family Literacy Day; Financial Literacy Month, November *Library:* ABC CANADA Collection at Alpha Plus Centre; Open to public by appointment
Chief Officer(s):
Gillian Mason, President, 416-218-0010 Ext. 120
gmason@abclifeliteracy.ca
Stephanie Wells, Manager, Communications, 416-218-0010 Ext. 122
swells@abclifeliteracy.ca
Awards:
• Great-West Life, London Life & Canada Life Literacy Innovation Award
Honours innovation in the creation & delivery of adult literacy programs delivered by a Canadian community organization; *Amount:* $20,000 + 4 honourable mention awards of $5,000 each *Contact:* Mack Rogers, Director, Community Programs, E-mail: mrogers@abclifeliteracy.ca, Phone: 416-218-0010, ext. 132
• Dr. Alan Middleton Workplace Literacy and Learning Award
Contact: Mack Rogers, Director, Community Programs, E-mail: mrogers@abclifeliteracy.ca, Phone: 416-218-0010, ext. 132

Abilities Foundation of Nova Scotia *See* Easter Seals Nova Scotia

Ability New Brunswick / Capacité Nouveau-Brunswick
#102, 440 Wilsey Rd., Fredericton NB E2B 7G5
Tel: 506-462-9555; *Fax:* 506-458-9134
Toll-Free: 866-462-9555
info@abilitynb.ca
www.abilitynb.ca
www.facebook.com/abilitynb
twitter.com/AbilityNB
www.youtube.com/user/abilitynb
Previous Name: Canadian Paraplegic Association (New Brunswick) Inc.

Overview: A medium-sized provincial organization overseen by Spinal Cord Injury Canada
Mission: To respond to the needs of people with spinal cord injuries & their families in New Brunswick
Staff Member(s): 9
Activities: Offering information & support services
Chief Officer(s):
Bill Leonard, President
Haley Flaro, Executive Director
haley.flaro@abilitynb.ca
Publications:
• Ability Now! [a publication of Ability New Brunswick]
Type: Newsletter
  Moncton
  #407, 236 St. George St., Moncton NB E1C 1W1
  Tel: 506-858-0311; *Fax:* 506-858-8290
  info@abilitynb.ca

Ability Online Support Network / En ligne directe
PO Box 18515, 250 Wincott Dr., Toronto ON M9R 4C8
Tel: 416-650-6207; *Fax:* 866-829-6780
Toll-Free: 866-650-6207
information@abilityonline.org
www.abilityonline.org
www.facebook.com/AbilityOnline
twitter.com/Ability_Online
Also Known As: Ability Online
Overview: A small national charitable organization founded in 1992
Mission: To enhance the lives of children with disabilities or illness by providing an online community for friendship, support & skill development
Finances: *Annual Operating Budget:* $250,000-$500,000; *Funding Sources:* Corporations; private foundations; special events; private donations
Staff Member(s): 5; 70 volunteer(s)
Membership: 6,300; *Member Profile:* Children, youth, young adults with disabilities or illness, parents & caregivers; *Committees:* Fundraising, Program/Volunteers; Audit; Executive
Activities: Golf tournament; *Awareness Events:* People in Motion, 1st weekend in June; *Internships:* Yes
Chief Officer(s):
Michelle McClure, Executive Director
Michael Teixeira, Chair
miket@abilityonline.org
George Kyriakis, Vice-Chair

Ability Society of Alberta (ASA)
#302, 327 - 41 Ave. NE, Calgary AB T2E 2N4
Tel: 403-262-9445; *Fax:* 403-262-4539
www.abilitysociety.org
www.linkedin.com/in/abilitysociety
www.facebook.com/AbilitySociety
twitter.com/AbilitySociety
plus.google.com/114873957698483644364
Previous Name: Society for Technology & Rehabilitation
Overview: A medium-sized provincial charitable organization founded in 1984
Mission: To build a caring community; to provide innovative, appropriate, & needed technical aids to individuals with any type of disability, seniors, their families, & support systems; to provide access to technology that is used as a tool by a person with a disability to live with dignity
Staff Member(s): 17
Activities: *Library:* Resource Centre; Open to public by appointment
Chief Officer(s):
Adrian Bohach, President/CEO
adrian@abilitysociety.org

Aboriginal Agricultural Education Society of British Columbia (AAESBC)
PO Box 1186, Stn. Main, 7410 Dallas Dr., Kamloops BC V2C 6H3
Tel: 778-469-5040; *Fax:* 778-469-5030
info@aaesbc.ca
www.aaesbc.ca
Overview: A small provincial organization founded in 2005
Mission: To provide culturally appropriate & respectful training for First Nations agricultural businesses
Affiliation(s): First Nations Agricultural Association; First Nations Agricultural Lending Association
Finances: *Funding Sources:* Government; Corporate sponsors

Aboriginal Financial Officers Association *See* AFOA Canada

Aboriginal Firefighters Association of Canada (AFAC) / Association des pompiers autochtones de Canada
12411 Dawson Pl., Maple Ridge BC V4R 2L6
Tel: 250-267-2579
info@afac-acpi.ca
www.afac-acpi.ca
www.facebook.com/AFAC.ACPI
Overview: A small national organization
Mission: A united body of regional First Nations Fire Protection Associations from across Canada.
Chief Officer(s):
William Moffat, President

Aboriginal Friendship Centre of Calgary
#101, 427 - 51 Ave. SE, Calgary AB T2H 0M8
Tel: 403-270-7379
info@afccalgary.org
www.afccalgary.org
www.facebook.com/AboriginalFriendshipCentreOfCalgary
www.twitter.com/AbYouthCouncil
Overview: A small local organization overseen by Alberta Native Friendship Centres Association
Member of: Alberta Native Friendship Centres Association
Membership: *Fees:* $2 Singles; $10 Families
Chief Officer(s):
Sandra Sutter, President

Aboriginal Friendship Centres of Saskatchewan
115 Wall St., Saskatoon SK S7K 6C2
Tel: 306-955-0762; *Fax:* 306-955-0972
www.afcs.ca
www.facebook.com/192129454182112
twitter.com/afcsk
www.youtube.com/user/theAFCS
Overview: A medium-sized provincial organization founded in 1963 overseen by National Association of Friendship Centres
Mission: The objectives of the Aboriginal Friendship Centres (AFC) of Sask. are: the promotion of the goals and objectives of its member Friendship Centres; the facilitation of communication and cooperation amongst all Centres w/in SK,,.; the providing of information regarding the operation and dvlp. of AFCs to the public; negotiation with all tiers of gov't on matters of concern to the member Centres; assistance in Program Dvlp.; and assistance to all members in terms of funding information, debt recovery plans, financial negotiation, and networking.
Staff Member(s): 6
Membership: 11 friendship centres
Chief Officer(s):
Gwen Bear, Executive Director

Aboriginal Head Start Association of British Columbia (AHSABC)
PO Box 21058, Duncan BC V9L 0C2
Tel: 250-858-4543; *Fax:* 250-743-2478
www.ahsabc.com
www.facebook.com/681649201857689
Overview: A medium-sized provincial organization founded in 1998
Mission: To promote excellence in Aboriginal early childhood learning programs across British Columbia
Finances: *Funding Sources:* Federal government
Membership: 12 urban Aboriginal Head Start preschool sites
Activities: Training & workshops; Leadership administration & management programs; Quality assessment of early childhood programs; Conference planning & facilitation
Chief Officer(s):
Joan Gignac, Executive Director
executivedirector@ahsabc.com

Aboriginal Human Resources Council *See* Indigenous Works

Aboriginal Legal Services of Toronto (ALST)
#803, 415 Yonge St., Toronto ON M5B 2E7
Tel: 416-408-3967; *Fax:* 416-408-1568
www.aboriginallegal.ca
Overview: A small local organization founded in 1990
Mission: To strengthen the capacity of the Aboriginal community and its citizens to deals with justice issues and provide Aboriginal controlled and culturally based justice alternatives.
Staff Member(s): 3
Chief Officer(s):
Jonathan Rudin, Program Director

Aboriginal Multi-Media Society (AMMSA)
13245 - 146th St., Edmonton AB T5L 4S8
Tel: 780-455-2700; *Fax:* 780-455-7639
www.ammsa.com
www.facebook.com/windspeakernews
twitter.com/windspeakernews
Previous Name: Aboriginal Multi-Media Society of Alberta
Overview: A small provincial organization founded in 1983
Mission: Committed to facilitating the exchange of information reflecting Aboriginal culture to a growing & diverse audience; dedicated to providing objective, mature & balanced coverage of news, information & entertainment relevant to Aboriginal issues & peoples while maintaining profound respect for the values, principles & traditions of Aboriginal people
Staff Member(s): 21
Chief Officer(s):
Bert Crowfoot, CEO
Paul Macedo, Director, Publishing Operations

Aboriginal Multi-Media Society of Alberta *See* Aboriginal Multi-Media Society

Aboriginal Nurses Association of Canada; Indian & Inuit Nurses of Canada *See* Canadian Indigenous Nurses Association

Aboriginal Sport & Wellness Council of Ontario (ASWCO)
2425 Matheson Blvd. East, 7th Fl., Mississauga ON L4W 5K4
Tel: 416-479-0928; *Fax:* 905-412-0325
aswco@shaw.ca
www.aswco.ca
www.facebook.com/aswco
twitter.com/aswco
www.instagram.com/aswco
Overview: A medium-sized provincial organization founded in 2011
Mission: To organize sporting events for Aboriginal athletes throughout Ontario; To promote active & healthy Aboriginal individuals & communities in Ontario
Activities: Offering sporting programs & leadership development opportunities
Chief Officer(s):
Marc Laliberté, President
marclaliberte@shaw.ca
Publications:
• Aboriginal Sport & Wellness Council of Ontario Newsletter
Type: Newsletter
Profile: Provides information & updates for athletes, coaches, & supporters

Aboriginal Tourism Association of British Columbia
#600 - 100 Park Royal South, West Vancouver BC V7T 1A2
Tel: 604-921-1070; *Fax:* 604-921-1072
Toll-Free: 877-266-2822
info@aboriginalbc.com
www.aboriginalbc.com
www.facebook.com/AboriginalBC
twitter.com/AboriginalBC
www.youtube.com/user/aboriginalbc
Overview: A small provincial organization
Chief Officer(s):
Paula Amos, Executive Director, 604-921-1070 Ext. 223
paula@aboriginalbc.com
Awards:
• Coast Hotels & Resorts Ambassador Award
• Inspirational Leadership Award
• Young Adult Achievement Award
• Power of Education Award
• Cultural Authenticity Award
• Strength in Marketing Award
• Tourism Conservation Award
• Excellence in Customer Service Award
• Industry Partner Award

Aboriginal Tourism Association of Southern Ontario (ATASO)
34 Merton St., Ottawa ON K1Y 1V5
Tel: 613-722-0315; *Fax:* 613-722-2344
Toll-Free: 877-746-5658
info@ataso.ca
www.ataso.ca
Overview: A small provincial organization founded in 1998
Chief Officer(s):
Mae Maracle, President
Kim Porter, Sec.-Treas.

Aboriginal Women of Manitoba *See* Mother of Red Nations Women's Council of Manitoba

Aboriginal Women's Association of Prince Edward Island
PO Box 145, 312 Sweetgrass Trail, Lennox Island PE C0B 1P0
Tel: 902-831-3059; *Fax:* 902-831-3027
info@awapei.org
www.awapei.org
www.facebook.com/193334154037222
twitter.com/awapei1
Overview: A small provincial organization founded in 1975 overseen by Native Women's Association of Canada
Mission: To address issues of concern to off-reserve Aboriginal women; To improve the educational, social & economic conditions surrounding Aboriginal women
Finances: *Annual Operating Budget:* Less than $50,000
Activities: Outreach; Maowmi; drop-in play; traditional parenting; a community kitchen
Chief Officer(s):
Judith Clark, President

AboutFace
51 Wolseley St., Toronto ON M5T 1A4
Tel: 416-597-2229; *Fax:* 416-597-8494
Toll-Free: 800-665-3223
info@aboutface.ca
www.aboutface.ca
www.facebook.com/AboutFaceInternational
twitter.com/AboutFace
www.youtube.com/user/AboutFaceEvents
Overview: A small international charitable organization founded in 1985
Mission: To provide emotional support & information to, & on behalf of, individuals who have a facial difference & their families
Staff Member(s): 4
Membership: 5,000-14,999; *Fees:* $35
Activities: Public education; hospital visits; school programs; volunteer training; *Speaker Service:* Yes
Chief Officer(s):
Danielle Griffin, Executive Director
danielle@aboutface.ca
Emily Rivers, Manager, Communications & Database
emily@aboutface.ca
Amanda Lizon, Manager, Client Programs & Outreach
amanda@aboutface.ca

Abundance Canada
#12, 1325 Markham Rd., Winnipeg MB R3T 4J6
Tel: 204-488-1985; *Fax:* 204-488-1986
Toll-Free: 800-772-3257
winnipeg@abundance.ca
www.abundance.ca
www.linkedin.com/company/abundance-canada
www.facebook.com/AbundanceCan
twitter.com/abundancecan
Previous Name: Mennonite Foundation of Canada
Overview: A medium-sized national charitable organization founded in 1974
Mission: To provide gift planning services for Canadians interested in faithful charitable giving
Affiliation(s): Mennonite Church Canada; Evangelical Mennonite Mission Conference; Mennonite Church Eastern Canada; Northwest Mennonite Conference; Evangelical Mennonite Conference; Chortitzer Mennonite Conference; Evangelical Missionary Church of Canada
Staff Member(s): 21
Membership: 24; *Member Profile:* Representatives of 7 conferences
Activities: *Speaker Service:* Yes; *Library:* Open to public
Chief Officer(s):
Darren Pries-Klassen, Executive Director, 519-745-7821 Ext. 209
dpklassen@abundance.ca
Rick Braun-Janzen, Director, Finance, 204-488-1985 Ext. 108
rbjanzen@abundance.ca
Jesse Huxman, Director, Communications, 519-745-7821 Ext. 203
jhuxman@abundance.ca
Pamela Miles, Director, Gift Planning, 519-745-7821 Ext. 212
pmiles@abundance.ca
Awards:
• MFC Spirit of Generosity Award
Awarded to students from Mennonite secondary & post-secondary schools to recognize generosity; *Amount:* $700

Abbotsford Office
#102, 2825 Clearbrook Rd., Abbotsford BC V2T 6S3
Tel: 604-850-9613; *Fax:* 604-859-5574
Toll-Free: 888-212-8608
abbotsford@abundance.ca
Chief Officer(s):
Irm Nickel, Administrative Assistant
inickel@abundance.ca

Calgary Office
#220, 2946 - 32 St. NE, Calgary AB T1Y 6J7
Tel: 403-717-0331; *Fax:* 403-717-0335
Toll-Free: 877-717-0708
calgary@abundance.ca
Chief Officer(s):
Kevin Davidson, Consultant, Gift Planning
kdavidson@abundance.ca

Kitchener Office
#207, 50 Kent Ave., Kitchener ON N2G 3R1
Tel: 519-745-7821; *Fax:* 519-745-8940
Toll-Free: 888-212-7759
kitchener@abundance.ca
Chief Officer(s):
Denise Mazik, Office Administrator
dmazik@abundance.ca
Mike Strathdee, Consultant, Gift Planning
mstrathdee@abundance.ca

Saskatoon Office
600 - 45 St. West, Saskatoon SK S7L 5W9
Toll-Free: 800-772-3257
Chief Officer(s):
Harold Penner, Consultant, Gift Planning
hpenner@abundance.ca

Académie canadienne d'audiologie *See* Canadian Academy of Audiology

L'Académie canadienne d'endodontie *See* Canadian Academy of Endodontics

Académie canadienne d'histoire de la pharmacie *See* Canadian Academy of the History of Pharmacy

Académie canadienne de médecine du sport *See* Canadian Academy of Sport Medicine

Académie canadienne de parodontologie *See* Canadian Academy of Periodontology

Académie canadienne de psychiatrie de l'enfant et de l'adolescent *See* Canadian Academy of Child & Adolescent Psychiatry

L'Académie canadienne de psychiatrie et droit *See* Canadian Academy of Psychiatry & the Law

L'Académie canadienne de psychiatrie gériatrique *See* Canadian Academy of Geriatric Psychiatry

Académie canadienne des arts et des sciences de l'enregistrement *See* Canadian Academy of Recording Arts & Sciences

Académie canadienne du cinéma et de la télévision *See* Academy of Canadian Cinema & Television

L'Académie canadienne du génie *See* The Canadian Academy of Engineering

Académie de musique du Québec (AMQ)
CP 818, Succ. C, Montréal QC H2X 4L6
Tél: 514-528-1961
prixdeurope@videotron.ca
www.prixdeurope.ca/lacademie.html
www.facebook.com/prixdeurope
Aperçu: *Dimension:* moyenne; *Envergure:* provinciale; Organisme sans but lucratif; fondée en 1870
Mission: Promouvoir le goût et l'avancement de la musique au Québec, aux professeurs oeuvrant dans le secteur privé et soucieux à la fois d'autonomie et d'encadrement, aux élèves qui désirent une reconnaissance officielle de leur travail
Finances: *Budget de fonctionnement annuel:* Moins de $50,000;
Fonds: Ministère de la Culture et des communications du Québec
Membre(s) du personnel: 1; 5 bénévole(s)
Membre: 120; *Montant de la cotisation:* 30$; *Critères d'admissibilite:* Répondre aux besoins de l'AMQ selon les régions et les disciplines; être disponible pour juger des examens, rédiger des épreuves d'examens et/ou des programmes; posséder des talents de communicateur; être parrainé par un membre de l'AMQ
Activités: Gestion d'un concours de musique depuis 1911; sessions d'examens annuels depuis 1870; le concours "Prix d'Europe"
Membre(s) du bureau directeur:
Frédéric Bednarz, Conseiller artistique
Prix, Bourses:
• Prix Fernand-Lindsay
; *Amount:* 10 000$
• Prix d'Europe
; *Amount:* 25 000$

Académie de Réflexologie du Québec
1285, rue de la Visitation, Sainte-Foy QC G1W 3K5
Tél: 418-651-8575
Ligne sans frais: 800-701-8575
www.academiereflexologie.ca
Aperçu: *Dimension:* petite; *Envergure:* provinciale; fondée en 1984
Mission: Faire connaître la remarquable efficacité des thérapies réflexes pour améliorer rapidement de beaucoup la santé; grâce à de meilleures connaissances en biochimie cellulaire et en neurobiologie, l'Académie de Réflexologie du Québec a développé depuis de nombreuses années des nouvelles techniques très performantes (massage articulaire ou massage intégral) qui agissent simultanément pour détecter (prévenir), détendre (relaxer) et qui ont un effet thérapeutique profond pour résoudre d'innombrables problèmes de santé; de ses recherches est née la carrière de Thérapeute Réflexe; toute personne certifiée est assujettie à un code de déontologie et appartient à son regroupement professionnel de même formation; le maître massothérapeute travaille avec les bases majeures du corps humain, dont les réflexes des différents mécanismes du système nerveux autonome
Membre de: Association des maîtres massothérapeutes
Membre(s) du personnel: 3; 4 bénévole(s)
Membre: 1-99; *Montant de la cotisation:* 60-100; *Critères d'admissibilite:* Etre diplomé de l'A.R.Q. en podoreflexologie et maître massotherapeute
Activités: *Evénements de sensibilisation:* Porte Ouverte, mai et sept.; *Stagiaires:* Oui; *Service de conférenciers:* Oui; *Bibliothèque:* Propre à l'École; Not open to public

Académie des lettres du Québec
2275, rue Holt, #R-75, Montréal QC H2G 3H1
Tél: 514-873-4496; *Téléc:* 514-873-4612
secretariat@academiedeslettresduquebec.ca
www.academiedeslettresduquebec.ca
Aperçu: *Dimension:* moyenne; *Envergure:* provinciale; fondée en 1944
Membre(s) du bureau directeur:
Émile Martel, Président
Laurier Lacroix, Secrétaire général

Académie internationale de droit et de santé mentale *See* International Academy of Law & Mental Health

Académie royale des arts du Canada *See* Royal Canadian Academy of Arts

Academy of Canadian Cinema & Television (ACCT) / Académie canadienne du cinéma et de la télévision
#501, 49 Ontario St., Toronto ON M5A 2V1
Tel: 416-366-2227; *Fax:* 416-366-8454
Toll-Free: 800-644-5194
communications@academy.ca
www.academy.ca
Overview: A medium-sized national charitable organization founded in 1979
Mission: To promote & celebrate exceptional creative achievement in the Canadian film & television industries; To heighten public awareness & increase audience appreciation of Canadian film & television productions through its national Award program
Finances: *Funding Sources:* Government; industry & corporate sponsors; membership dues; award show revenue
Staff Member(s): 24
Membership: 4,000; *Fees:* Schedule available; *Member Profile:* Professionals working in Canadian film & television industry; *Committees:* Film Governance; Television Governance; Digital Media Governance; News & Sports Governance
Activities: National Apprenticeship Training Program; Academy Speaker Series; Academy Screening Series; *Internships:* Yes; *Speaker Service:* Yes
Chief Officer(s):
Beth Janson, Chief Executive Officer, 416-366-2227 Ext. 240
beth@academy.ca

Canadian Associations / Academy of Canadian Executive Nurses (ACEN)

Awards:
- Canadian Screen Awards

The nationally telecast awards for excellence & achievement in Canadian English-language television, film & digital media production are awarded annually & presented to winners in more than 100 categories covering Best Motion Pictre, Best Dramatic Series & Best Cross-Platform Project, as well as special awards following nomination & voting by a peer group *Eligibility:* Achievement in Canadian film, digital media & English television production

> **Montréal Office**
> #106, 225, rue Roy est, Montréal QC H2W 1M5
> *Tél:* 514-849-7448; *Téléc:* 514-849-5069
> academie@acct.ca
> www.acct.ca
> www.facebook.com/acct.quebec
> twitter.com/acctquebec
> **Chief Officer(s):**
> Patrice Lachance, Directrice
> plachance@acct.ca

Academy of Canadian Executive Nurses (ACEN)
#400, 331 Cooper St., Ottawa ON K2P 0G5
Tel: 613-235-3033
www.acen.ca
Overview: A small national organization founded in 1982
Mission: To advance nursing practice, education, research, & leadership; To work in partnership with other national organizations to influence health policy & set direction of healthcare in Canada to assure quality of care to Canadians
Finances: *Funding Sources:* Membership dues
Membership: *Fees:* $400 full/emerging nurse/leader; $100 retired; *Member Profile:* Canadian executive nurses in academic health care organizations associated with university schools / faculties of nursing, who are accountable for strategic, operational practice; Membership is by invitation of the Academy; *Committees:* Leadership/Policy; Finance; The CJNL Editorial Advisory Board; Professional Development
Chief Officer(s):
Lori Lamont, President
Awards:
- Leadership Award

Acadia Entrepreneurship Centre (AEC)
c/o Acadia University, PO Box 142, 21 University Ave., Wolfville NS B4P 2R6
Tel: 902-585-1180
Toll-Free: 866-654-4499
entrepreneurship@acadiau.ca
www.acadiaentrepreneurshipcentre.com
www.linkedin.com/company/acadia-entrepreneurship-centre
www.facebook.com/acadiaEcentre
twitter.com/AcadiaECentre
Overview: A small local organization
Mission: To foster an entrepreneurial culture through specialized programming
Affiliation(s): Acadia University; Centre for Entrepreneurship Education & Development Inc.
Membership: *Member Profile:* Individuals, businesses, non-profits & business development professionals
Chief Officer(s):
Findlay Macrae, Executive Director
findlay.macrae@acadiau.ca

> **Wolfville - Innovation & Incubation Services**
> c/o Acadia University, PO Box 20, 24 University Ave., Wolfville NS B4P 2R6
> *Tel:* 902-585-1835
>
> **Bridgewater**
> 373 King St., Bridgewater NS B4V 1B1
> *Tel:* 902-543-1067
> *Toll-Free:* 877-232-2723

Acadia Environmental Society
c/o Acadia Students' Union, PO Box 6002, Wolfville NS B4P 2R5
Tel: 902-585-2110
aes@acadiau.ca
Overview: A small local organization founded in 1989
Mission: To provide an information resource on environmental issues; to encourage & help the Acadia community to adopt & maintain environmentally sound & sustainable practices
Finances: *Funding Sources:* Acadia Students' Union

Acadia University Faculty Association (AUFA) / Association des professeurs de l'Université Acadia
Acadia University, Huggins Science Hall, #211, 12 University Ave., Wolfville NS B4P 2R6
Tel: 902-585-1422; *Fax:* 902-585-1153
aufa@acadiau.ca
www.acadiafaculty.ca
Overview: A small local organization
Mission: To promote the interests of faculty at Acadia University; To encourage academic discussion among the members; To provide full support for all activities; To maintain & improve the quality & stature of members
Member of: Canadian Association of University Teachers
Staff Member(s): 1; 9 volunteer(s)
Membership: 272; *Committees:* Appointments, Renewal, Tenure & Promotion; Association Grievance; Communications (Media) & The Communicator; Financial Benefits; Investment; Job Action; Negotiating; Nominating; Proposal Review; Women's; Working Conditions
Chief Officer(s):
Stephen Ahern, President
stephen.ahern@acadiau.ca
Awards:
- Lois Vallely-Fischer Award for Democratic Student Citizenship
Eligibility: Students in final year of undergraduate study at Acadia University
- CAUT Dedicated Service Award

The Acadian Entomological Society (AES)
PO Box 4000, Atlantic Forestry Centre, 1350 Regent St., Fredericton NB E3B 597
Drew.Carleton@gnb.ca
www.acadianes.org
twitter.com/AcadianESCanada
Overview: A small local organization founded in 1915
Mission: To bring about a close association of entomologists & those interested in entomology in the four Atlantic provinces & the neighbouring New England States; To cooperate with, & to support the Entomological Society of Canada
Affiliation(s): Entomological Society of Canada
Finances: *Annual Operating Budget:* Less than $50,000; *Funding Sources:* Membership dues; Entomological Society of Canada
5 volunteer(s)
Membership: 50; *Fees:* Regular: $20; Student: $10; *Committees:* Archives; Memberships; Pest Management; Public Education
Chief Officer(s):
Drew Carleton, President
Drew.Carleton@gnb.ca
Kirk Hillier, Vice-President, 902-585-1314
vice-president@acadianes.ca
Andrew Morrison, Secretary & Teasurer, 506-452-3239
treasurer@acadianes.ca
Meetings/Conferences:
- The Acadian Entomological Society 77th Annual Meeting, 2018
Publications:
- The Journal of the Acadian Entomological Society
Editor: Don Ostaff; *ISSN:* 1710-4033

Accelerated Christian Education Canada
PO Box 1360, Portage la Prairie MB R1N 3N9
Tel: 204-428-5332; *Fax:* 204-428-5386
Toll-Free: 800-976-7226
info@acecanada.net
www.acecanada.net
Also Known As: School of Tomorrow Canada
Previous Name: Canadian National Accelerated Christian Education Association
Overview: A small national organization founded in 1974
Mission: To continue to assure Canadians of the freedom to choose alternative Christian education
Affiliation(s): Federation of Independent Schools in Canada
Finances: *Annual Operating Budget:* Less than $50,000; *Funding Sources:* Provincial dues
24 volunteer(s)
Membership: 100-499
Chief Officer(s):
Alfred MacLaren, Manager, 204-428-5332 Ext. 211
amaclaren@acecanada.net

A.C.C.E.S. Employment
#100, 489 College St., Toronto ON M6G 1A5
Tel: 416-921-1800; *Fax:* 416-921-3055
www.accesemployment.ca
www.linkedin.com/company/acces-employment
twitter.com/ACCESEmployment
Also Known As: Accessible Community Counselling & Employment Services
Overview: A small local charitable organization founded in 1986
Mission: To assist job seekers from diverse backgrounds who are facing barriers to employment, to integrate into the Canadian job market; to provide employment services, linking employers to skilled people & building strong networks in collaboration with community partners
Affiliation(s): Ontario Coalition of Agencies Serving Immigrants
Finances: *Annual Operating Budget:* $500,000-$1.5 Million; *Funding Sources:* Provincial government
Staff Member(s): 45; 25 volunteer(s)
Membership: 1-99
Activities: Job Connect Program; information & referral services; job search workshop; resume clinic; computer training; *Library:* Resource Centre
Chief Officer(s):
Allison Pond, President & CEO
Irene Sihvonen, Vice-President, Services & Organizational Development
Manjeet Dhiman, Vice-President, Services & Business Development

> **Brampton**
> #201, 44 Peel Centre Dr., Brampton ON L6T 4B5
> *Tel:* 905-454-2316
>
> **Mississauga**
> #600, 151 City Centre Dr., Mississauga ON L5B 1M7
> *Tel:* 905-361-2522
>
> **North York**
> #201, 2001 Sheppard Ave. East, Toronto ON M2J 4Z8
> *Tel:* 416-443-9008
>
> **Scarborough**
> #250, 2100 Ellesmere Rd., Toronto ON M1H 3B7
> *Tel:* 416-431-5326; *Fax:* 416-431-5286

Access Alliance Multicultural Health & Community Services
#500, 340 College St., Toronto ON M5T 3A9
Tel: 416-324-8677; *Fax:* 416-324-9074
Other Communication: Confidential Fax: 416-324-9490
mail@accessalliance.ca
accessalliance.ca
Overview: A small local charitable organization founded in 2001
Mission: To improve health outcomes for vulnerable immigrants, refugees & their communities through services & addressing system inequalities
Member of: United Way
Finances: *Funding Sources:* Government funding
Chief Officer(s):
Erik Landriault, Chair
Yatti Tjipto, Executive Assistant
ytjipto@accessalliance.ca
Publications:
- Access Alliance E-News
Type: Newsletter

> **AccessPoint on Danforth**
> 3079 Danforth Ave., Toronto ON M1L 1A8
> *Tel:* 416-324-8677; *Fax:* 416-693-1330
>
> **AccessPoint on Jane**
> 761 Jane St., 2nd Fl., Toronto ON M6N 4B4
> *Tel:* 416-324-8677; *Fax:* 416-760-8670
>
> **Neighbourhood Centre**
> 91 Barrington Ave., Toronto ON M4C 4Y9
> *Tel:* 416-698-1626

Access Copyright
#320, 56 Wellesley St. West, Toronto ON M5S 2S3
Tel: 416-868-1620; *Fax:* 416-868-1621
Toll-Free: 800-893-5777
info@accesscopyright.ca
www.accesscopyright.ca
Also Known As: Canadian Copyright Licensing Agency
Previous Name: Canadian Reprography Collective
Overview: A medium-sized national licensing organization founded in 1988
Mission: To licence copyright users who wish to reproduce copyright-protected works; To collect a fee for this service & to distribute royalties to the copyright owners whose works have been copied; To provide protection for copyright owners as well as legal access to published works for copyright users
Member of: Book & Periodical Council
Affiliation(s): International Federation of Reproduction Rights Organization

Finances: *Annual Operating Budget:* $3 Million-$5 Million; *Funding Sources:* Licensing revenue
Staff Member(s): 40
Membership: 37 voting members + 8,000 rightsholders; *Member Profile:* Rightsholders - publishers & creators whose work has been published; voting - associations representing Canadian publishers & creators; *Committees:* Executive; Finance; Distribution; Licensing; Nomination; Communications; Membership; Systems
Activities: *Internships:* Yes; *Speaker Service:* Yes; *Library:* Open to public
Chief Officer(s):
Roanie Levy, Executive Director
Eden Dhaliwal, Director, Innovation & Strategic Partnership
Claire Gillis, Director, Business Affairs

Access Counselling & Family Services
#200, 460 Brant St., Burlington ON L7R 4B6
Tel: 905-637-5256; *Fax:* 905-637-8221
Toll-Free: 866-457-0234
info@accesscounselling.ca
www.accesscounselling.ca
Overview: A small local charitable organization founded in 1968 overseen by Family Service Ontario
Mission: To serve members of the community in times of crisis, assisting people to cope with conflict, grief, loss, violence, abuse.
Member of: United Way Burlington
Finances: *Funding Sources:* Ministry of Community & Social Services; Ministry of the Attorney General; United Way; donations
Activities: Counselling services; Violence Against Women program; Caring Dads program; Employee Assistance program; Family Life Education program; *Internships:* Yes
Chief Officer(s):
Susan Jewett, Executive Director

Accessible Housing Society
Deerfoot Junction III, #215, 1212 - 31st Ave. NE, Calgary AB T2E 7S8
Tel: 403-282-1872; *Fax:* 403-284-0304
info@accessiblehousing.ca
www.accessiblehousing.ca
www.facebook.com/AccessibleHousing
twitter.com/AccessibleYYC
Overview: A small local charitable organization founded in 1974
Mission: To create opportunities for safe, affordable, barrier-free housing for people experiencing mobility problems
Staff Member(s): 4
Activities: Provides housing & coordinated personal care at 3 sites in Calgary; acts as a resource to the community on barrier-free design & modification for accessibility through a residential assessment & design service; library resources; maintains a housing registry; facilitates opportunities for wheelchair accessible housing; *Library:* ACT Library; Open to public
Chief Officer(s):
Jeff Dyer, Executive Director
jeff@accessiblehousing.ca
Awards:
• Yes In My Backyard Award
• Legacy Award
• Kent Hehr Leadership Award
Publications:
• Accessible Housing Society Newsletter
Type: Newsletter

Accessible Media Inc. (AMI)
#200, 1090 Don Mills Rd., Toronto ON M3C 3R6
Tel: 416-422-4222; *Fax:* 416-422-1633
Toll-Free: 800-567-6755
info@ami.ca
www.ami.ca
www.linkedin.com/company/accessible-media-inc
www.facebook.com/AccessibleMediaInc
twitter.com/AccessibleMedia
www.youtube.com/user/accessiblemedia
Overview: A medium-sized national charitable organization
Mission: To bring media in an alternate form to those not able to follow in traditional ways
Affiliation(s): Achilles Canada; Canadian Council of the Blind; CNIB; Courage Canada; Sight Night; Foundation Fighting Blindness
Activities: Operating two broadcast services, AMI-audio & AMI-tv, & a multi-functional website
Chief Officer(s):

David Errington, President & CEO
John Melville, Vice-President, Programming & Production
Line Gendreau, Vice-President, Finance
Terry Reid, Vice-President, Human Resources
Peter Burke, Vice-President, Marketing & Communications
Darrel Sauerlender, Vice-President, Technology Services
Chris O'Brien, Accessibility Officer
Awards:
• Accessible Media Inc. Scholarship
Created to further strengthen AMI's commitment to making media accessible to all Canadians. *Eligibility:* Canadian citizens or permanent residents of Canada planning to enrol or continuing to be enrolled in full-time studies in a diploma or degree program at a Canadian post-secondary school.; *Amount:* $5,000 (2)

ACCIS - The Graduate Workforce Professionals *See* Canadian Association of Career Educators & Employers

Acclaim Health
2370 Speers Rd., Oakville ON L6L 5M2
Tel: 905-827-8800; *Fax:* 905-827-3390
Toll-Free: 800-387-7127
www.acclaimhealth.ca
ca.linkedin.com/company/acclaim-health
www.facebook.com/acclaimhealth
twitter.com/AcclaimHealth
Overview: A small local charitable organization founded in 1971
Mission: To provide elderly patients with home health care solutions; to help improve their patients' quality of life through volunteer visitors
Staff Member(s): 400; 600 volunteer(s)
Chief Officer(s):
Angelia Brewer, RN, MBA, CEO
abrewer@acclaimhealth.ca

Burlington
2180 Itabashi Way, Burlington ON L7R 4B8
Tel: 905-632-8168

Accreditation Canada / Agrément Canada
1150 Cyrville Rd., Ottawa ON K1J 7S9
Tel: 613-738-3800; *Fax:* 613-738-7755
Toll-Free: 800-814-7769
www.accreditation.ca
www.linkedin.com/company/accreditation-canada
twitter.com/AccredCanada
Previous Name: Canadian Council on Health Services Accreditation; Canadian Council on Health Facilities Accreditation
Overview: A large national licensing charitable organization founded in 1958
Mission: To improve quality in health services through accreditation; To provide health care organizations with a voluntary, external peer review to assess the quality of their services
Finances: *Funding Sources:* Membership fees
Membership: *Fees:* Schedule available (based on budget)
Activities: Qmentum Accreditation Program, which focuses on quality improvement & patient safety
Chief Officer(s):
George Weber, Chair
Leslee Thompson, President & CEO
Meetings/Conferences:
• Accreditation Canada Quality Conference 2018, 2018
Scope: National
Publications:
• Accreditation Canada Annual Report
Type: Yearbook; *Frequency:* Annually
• Accreditation Standard
Type: Newsletter; *Frequency:* Semiannually; *ISBN:* 978-1-55149-086-1
Profile: Updates & information about accreditation for Accreditation Canada's client organizations
• Canadian Health Accreditation Report
Frequency: Annually; *ISBN:* 978-1-55149-073-1
Profile: Findings from accreditation surveys, highlights of challenges & successes in health care, & leading practices by health organizations across Canada
• In Touch: A Newsletter for Surveyors
Type: Newsletter
Profile: Information for surveyors
• Leadership in the Journey to Quality Heath Care: The History of Accreditation
Type: Book
Profile: Evolution of Accreditation Canada over the past fifty years

• Leading Practices
Frequency: Annually
Profile: Companion report to the annual Canadian Health Accreditation Report which presents a compilation of practices identified by surveyors
• Qmentum Quarterly
Type: Journal; *Frequency:* Quarterly; *Accepts Advertising*
Profile: Educational information for health & social services organizations to improve quality & patient safety
• The Value & Impact of Accreditation in Health Care: A Review of the Literature
Author: Wendy Nicklin; Sarah Dickson
• Within Our Grasp: A Healthy Workplace Action Strategy for Success & Sustainability in Canada's Healthcare System

Accreditation Council for Canadian Physiotherapy Academic Programs *See* Physiotherapy Education Accreditation Canada

Accueil Grossesse *See* Birthright International

Achilles Canada
119 Snowden Ave., Toronto ON M4N 2A8
Tel: 416-485-6451; *Fax:* 416-485-0823
www.achillescanada.ca
Previous Name: Achilles Track Club Canada
Overview: A medium-sized national charitable organization founded in 1999
Mission: To encourage & assist all persons with disabilities (visual disability, cerebral palsy, paraplegia, arthritis, epilepsy, multiple sclerosis, amputation, cystic fibrosis, stroke, cancer, traumatic head injury, & many others) to enjoy running for health in a social environment
Membership: *Fees:* $25 donation encouraged
Activities: Providing support, training, & technical expertise to runners at all levels; *Awareness Events:* Achilles St. Patrick's Day 5K Run/Walk, March
Chief Officer(s):
Brian McLean, Contact
bmclean@achillescanada.ca

Achilles Track Club Canada *See* Achilles Canada

Acoustic Neuroma Association of Canada (ANAC) / Association pour les neurinomes acoustiques du Canada
PO Box 1005, 7B Pleasant Blvd., Toronto ON M4T 1K2
Tel: 416-546-6426
Toll-Free: 800-561-2622
www.anac.ca
Overview: A medium-sized national charitable organization founded in 1984
Mission: To provide support & information for those who have experienced acoustic neuromas or other tumors affecting the cranial nerves; To furnish information on patient rehabilitation to physicians & health care personnel; To promote & support research; To educate the public regarding symptoms suggestive of acoustic neuromas, thus promoting early diagnosis & consequent successful treatment
Finances: *Funding Sources:* Private; corporate; federal government grant
Staff Member(s): 1
Activities: *Awareness Events:* A-Wear-Ness Day, June 24
Chief Officer(s):
Carole Humphries, Executive Director

Acoustical Association Ontario (AAO)
32 Vancho Cres., Toronto ON M9A 4Z2
Tel: 416-605-6417; *Fax:* 416-246-1993
info@aao-online.ca
www.aao-online.ca
Overview: A small provincial organization founded in 1963
Mission: The Acoustical Association Ontario (AAO) is an association representing unionized employers engaged in Acoustic and Drywall construction in the Industrial, Commercial and Institutional sector of the construction industry in the Province of Ontario.
Membership: 42; *Member Profile:* Unionized contractors engaged in interior finishing construction
Chief Officer(s):
Joseph De Caria, Executive Secretary

ACT for Disarmament Coalition *See* ACT for the Earth

ACT for the Earth
238 Queen St. West, Toronto ON M5V 1Z7
Tel: 647-436-6398
Previous Name: ACT for Disarmament Coalition

Canadian Associations / Act To End Violence Against Women

Overview: A small national organization founded in 1982
Mission: To make Canadians aware of the dangers of the arms race & to mobilize them against Canada's involvement in the arms race; To help build international non-aligned peace movement; To oppose nuclear fuel cycle in Canada; To work on issues related to ecology, the environment, human rights
Affiliation(s): International Peace Bureau; Ontario Environment Network; War Resisters International
Finances: *Annual Operating Budget:* Less than $50,000
200 volunteer(s)
Membership: 200; *Fees:* $20
Activities: *Internships:* Yes; *Speaker Service:* Yes; *Library:* Open to public
Chief Officer(s):
Dylan Penner, Executive Director

Act To End Violence Against Women
#209, 390 Steeles Ave. West, Thornhill ON L4J 6X2
Tel: 905-695-5372; *Fax:* 905-695-5375
Toll-Free: 866-333-5942
info@acttoendvaw.org
www.acttoendvaw.org
www.facebook.com/acttoendvaw
Previous Name: B'nai Brith Women of Eastern Canada; Jewish Women International of Canada
Overview: A medium-sized national organization
Mission: Works locally, nationally & internationally to strengthen the effectiveness of women in the Jewish community & society; to foster the emotional well-being of children; to perpetuate Jewish values & secure world Jewry. Programs include ending violence towards women, sexual assault awareness, emergency housing for women & children, & advocacy to end child poverty in Canada. Offices in Toronto & Montréal, & chapters in Toronto, Montréal, B.C., Windsor & Winnipeg.
Affiliation(s): Jewish Women International
Finances: *Funding Sources:* Fundraising; membership fees
Staff Member(s): 3
Membership: 3,000; *Fees:* $36+
Activities: Education; advocacy; shelters for abused women; homes for emotionally abused children
Chief Officer(s):
Penny Krowitz, Executive Director

Action Autonomie
3958, rue Dandurand, Montréal QC H1X 1P7
Tél: 514-525-5060; *Téléc:* 514-525-5580
lecollectif@actionautonomie.qc.ca
www.actionautonomie.qc.ca
Aperçu: *Dimension:* petite; *Envergure:* locale
Mission: Protéger les droits des personnes vivant des problèmes de santé mentale par une approche d'éducation
Activités: Information; aide & accompagnement; information & orientation; conscience publique; atelier de formation

Action Budget Denis Riverin Inc. *Voir* Carrefour-Ressources

Action by Christians for the Abolition of Torture *Voir* Action des Chrétiens pour l'abolition de la torture

Action Canada for Sexual Health & Rights / Action Canada pour la santé et les droits sexuels
251 Bank St., 2nd Fl., Ottawa ON K2P 1X3
Tel: 613-241-4474
Toll-Free: 888-642-2725
Other Communication: Donor inquiries ext 8; Media inquiries ext 7
info@sexualhealthandrights.ca
www.sexualhealthandrights.ca
www.facebook.com/actioncanadaSHR
twitter.com/action_canada
Merged from: Canadians for Choice; Canadian Federation for Sexual Health; Action Canada for Population
Overview: A large national charitable organization founded in 2014
Mission: To advance sexual & reproductive health & rights in Canada & abroad through Public education & awareness; Support for the delivery of programs & services in Canada.
Member of: International Planned Parenthood Federation
Finances: *Funding Sources:* Donations; project grants
Staff Member(s): 10
Membership: *Member Profile:* Provincial, territorial or local sexual & reproductive health organizations in Canada with similar objectives & policies; associate - other organizations in sympathy with objectives of the Federation
Activities: Sexuality education & fair access to contraception & abortion services; sexual & reproductive health policy; works toward reaching high risk & hard-to-reach populations of youth & adults; extension of services to visible minority populations; encourages the development of new & safer forms of contraception; monitors the developments of new reproductive technologies; advocacy
Chief Officer(s):
Sandeep Prasad, Executive Director
Frédérique Chabot, Health Information Officer
Awards:
• The Helen & Fred Bentley Awards for Excellence of Achievement
Publications:
• Beyond the Basics: A Sourcebook on Sexual & Reproductive Health Education
Type: Book
Profile: Resource used in schools, public health offices, & community-based health organizations

Action Canada pour la santé et les droits sexuels *See* Action Canada for Sexual Health & Rights

Action Catholique Montréal *See* Catholic Action Montreal

Action Centre-Ville
#210, 105, rue Ontario est, Montréal QC H2X 1G9
Tél: 514-878-0847; *Téléc:* 214-878-0452
info@acv-montreal.com
www.acv-montreal.com
Aperçu: *Dimension:* petite; *Envergure:* locale
Mission: Fournit des personnes âgées avec services remisé tels que les repas et les cours d'impôt, ainsi que l'activité physique et de activité récréative
Membre: *Montant de la cotisation:* 10$; *Critères d'admissibilite:* Toute gens qui a 50 ans ou plus
Activités: Activité récréative; activité phsyical; voyages

Action des Chrétiens pour l'abolition de la torture (ACAT) / Action by Christians for the Abolition of Torture
2715, ch de la Côte-Sainte-Catherine, Montréal QC H3T 1B6
Tél: 514-890-6169; *Téléc:* 514-890-6484
acat@acatcanada.org
www.acatcanada.org
www.facebook.com/acatcanada
Également appelé: ACAT Canada
Aperçu: *Dimension:* moyenne; *Envergure:* nationale; Organisme sans but lucratif; fondée en 1984
Mission: Dans un but d'engagement évangélique, encourager les différentes communautés Chrétiennes du Canada à porter ensemble, par la prière, les souffrances des victimes de la torture; dans un but éducatif, sensibiliser particulièrement les Chrétiens au scandale de la torture (par l'information et la formation aux droits de la personne); dans un but de soulager la misère des victimes de la torture, apporter une aide concrète par l'envoi de lettres et pétitions aux responsables de torture et des lettres d'encouragement aux victimes
Affiliation(s): Fédération internationale de l'action des Chrétiens pour l'abolition de la torture (FIACAT)
Finances: *Budget de fonctionnement annuel:* $50,000-$100,000; *Fonds:* Organisations philanthropiques et particuliers.
Membre(s) du personnel: 2; 20 bénévole(s)
Membre: 150; *Montant de la cotisation:* 35 $; *Comités:* Commission des interventions; Financement; Relations publiques; Ressourcement
Activités: Campagne annuelle; Bulletins; Appels à l'action; *Stagiaires:* Oui; *Service de conférenciers:* Oui; *Listes de destinataires:* Oui
Membre(s) du bureau directeur:
Raoul Lincourt, Président
François Poulin, Coordonnateur

Action Dignité de Saint-Léonard
9089A, boul Viau, Saint-Léonard QC H1R 2V6
Tél: 514-251-2874
Aperçu: *Dimension:* petite; *Envergure:* locale
Mission: Groupe de défense des droits des locataires

Action Emploi Papineau Inc. *Voir* Carrefour jeunesse-emploi Papineau

Action for Healthy Communities (AHC)
#101, 10554 - 110 St., Edmonton AB T5H 3C5
Tel: 780-944-4687; *Fax:* 780-423-4193
a4hc.ca
www.facebook.com/217084201652707
Previous Name: Edmonton Health Care Citizenship Society
Overview: A small local charitable organization founded in 1995
Mission: Works with individuals, families and groups to build community through the provision of public education and other initiatives to enable individuals to enhance their own lives.
Finances: *Funding Sources:* Fundraising projects
Chief Officer(s):
Idalia Ivon Pereira, Executive Director

Action Intégration Brossard *Voir* Action Intégration en Déficience Intellectuelle

Action Intégration en Déficience Intellectuelle (AIDI)
6180, rue Agathe, Brossard QC J4Z 1E1
Tél: 450-676-5058; *Téléc:* 450-676-5686
secretariat@actionintegration.org
actionintegration.org
Nom précédent: Action Intégration Brossard
Aperçu: *Dimension:* petite; *Envergure:* locale; Organisme sans but lucratif; fondée en 1978
Mission: Promouvoir les intérêts et défendre les droits des personnes ayant une déficience intellectuelle; favoriser leur intégration sociale; soutenir leur famille
Affiliation(s): Association du Québec pour l'intégration sociale
Membre(s) du personnel: 31
Membre: 300
Activités: Répits; loisirs; soutien
Membre(s) du bureau directeur:
Yves Gougeon, Président
Sylvie Léger, Directrice générale

Action Life (Ottawa) Inc. / Action pour la vie
#40, 100 Brookfield Rd., Ottawa ON K1V 6J1
Tel: 613-798-4494; *Fax:* 613-798-4496
info@actionlife.org
www.actionlife.org
www.facebook.com/ActionLifeOttawa
Overview: A small local charitable organization founded in 1976
Mission: To promote respect for human life from conception to natural death through public education
Finances: *Annual Operating Budget:* $100,000-$250,000
Staff Member(s): 2
Membership: 4,000; *Fees:* $25 general; $15 senior/student
Activities: Pro-life education; *Speaker Service:* Yes; *Library:* Open to public
Chief Officer(s):
Louise Harbour, Executive Director

Action Nouvelle Vie
740, rue Saint-Charles est, Longueuil QC J4H 1C2
Tél: 450-646-5815; *Téléc:* 450-646-3509
info@actionnouvellevie.com
actionnouvellevie.com
Aperçu: *Dimension:* petite; *Envergure:* locale; fondée en 1993
Mission: Pour aider les familles défavorisées, les personnes et les enfants ont accès à la nourriture et à l'éducation
Membre(s) du personnel: 8
Membre(s) du bureau directeur:
Suzanne Fournier, Directrice générale
Jérémie Olivier, Communications

Action on Smoking & Health (ASH)
PO Box 4500, Stn. South, Edmonton AB T6E 6K2
Tel: 780-426-7867; *Fax:* 780-488-7195
info@ash.ca
www.ash.ca
twitter.com/actiononsmoking
Overview: A small national charitable organization founded in 1979
Mission: To act as a tobacco control agency in western Canada
Finances: *Funding Sources:* Donations; Membership fees
Membership: *Fees:* $25 household; $100 corporate
Activities: Reducing tobacco use through advocacy, policy development, & public education
Publications:
• Action on Smoking & Health Newsletter
Type: Newsletter; *Price:* Free, with membership in Action on Smoking & Health
Profile: News & events from Action on Smoking & Health

Action Patrimoine
82, Grande-Allée ouest, Québec QC G1R 2G6
Tél: 418-647-4347; *Téléc:* 418-647-6483
Ligne sans frais: 800-494-4347
info@actionpatrimoine.ca
actionpatrimoine.ca
www.facebook.com/Actionpatrimoine
Aperçu: *Dimension:* petite; *Envergure:* provinciale; fondée en 1975

Mission: Afin de préserver et de promouvoir repères culturels au Québec
Affiliation(s): Continuité; Fonation Québécoise du patriomoine
Membre(s) du personnel: 4
Membre: *Critères d'admissibilite:* Ouvert à toute personne intéressée par la sauvegarde et la mise en valeur du patrimoine du Québec
Activités: *Listes de destinataires:* Oui; *Bibliothèque*
Membre(s) du bureau directeur:
Émilie Vézina-Doré, Directrice générale
direction@actionpatrimoine.ca

Action pour la vie *See* Action Life (Ottawa) Inc.

Action Séro Zéro *Voir* RÉZO

Action Volunteers for Animals (AVA)
PO Box 64578, Unionville ON L3R 0M9
Tel: 416-439-8770
ava2009@actionvolunteersforanimals.com
www.actionvolunteersforanimals.com
www.facebook.com/ActionVolunteersforAnimals
Overview: A medium-sized local charitable organization founded in 1972
Mission: To abolish all cruelty against & suffering of non-human animals
Finances: *Annual Operating Budget:* $50,000-$100,000
20 volunteer(s)
Membership: 600; *Fees:* $25; *Committees:* Stray Animals; Vet Fund; Anti-Fur; Fundraising
Activities: Meetings, demonstrations, membership parties, lectures, fundraising events; *Library:* AVA Library; Open to public
Chief Officer(s):
Josephine Polk
Shana Mortimer-Gibson
Carol Lawson

Action-Gardien, la table de concertation communautaire de Pointe-Saint-Charles
Centre Lorne, #203, 2390, rue de Ryde, Montréal QC H3K 1R6
Tél: 514-509-0795
info@actiongardien.org
www.actiongardien.org
Aperçu: *Dimension:* petite; *Envergure:* locale; fondée en 1981
Mission: Promouvoir un développement du quartier
Membre: 26 organismes; *Comités:* Aménagement; Artères solidaires; Attribution de fonds; Défense des droits; Jeunesse; Santé mentale; Sécurité alimentaire
Membre(s) du bureau directeur:
Karine Triollet, Coordonnatrice

Active Healthy Kids Canada / Jeunes en forme Canada
#1205, 77 Bloor St. West, Toronto ON M5S 1M2
Tel: 416-913-0238; *Fax:* 416-913-1541
info@activehealthykids.ca
www.activehealthykids.ca
www.facebook.com/ActiveHealthyKidsCanada
twitter.com/ActiveHealthyKi
www.youtube.com/user/ActiveHealthyKids
Previous Name: The Foundation for Active Healthy Kids
Overview: A small national charitable organization founded in 1994
Mission: To advocate the importance of quality, accessible & enjoyable physical activity participation experiences for children & youth; To provide expertise & direction to decision makers at all levels, from policy-makers to parents, in order to increase the attention given to, investment in, & effective implementation of physical activity opportunities for all Canadian children & youth
Finances: *Annual Operating Budget:* $500,000-$1.5 Million; *Funding Sources:* Corporate sponsorship
Activities: *Awareness Events:* Active Healthy Kids' Day, last Thur. in May; *Speaker Service:* Yes
Chief Officer(s):
Jennifer Cowie Bonne, Chief Executive Officer

Active Living Coalition for Older Adults (ALCOA) / Coalition d'une vie active pour les ainé(e)s
PO Box 143, Stn. Main, Shelburne ON L9V 3L8
Tel: 519-925-1676
Toll-Free: 800-549-9799
Other Communication: Other URL: www.silvertimes.ca
alcoa@uniserve.com
www.alcoa.ca
www.facebook.com/726682140748841
Overview: A medium-sized national organization founded in 1993
Mission: To encourage older Canadians to maintain & enhance their well-being & independence through a lifestyle that embraces daily physical activities
Finances: *Annual Operating Budget:* $100,000-$250,000
Membership: *Committees:* Silver Times Editorial; Nominating
Chief Officer(s):
Patricia Clark, Executive Director

Active Parenting Canada
5409 - 50 Ave., Red Deer AB T4N 4B7
Tel: 403-877-8395; *Fax:* 403-358-7801
Toll-Free: 800-668-5131
apcanada@fsca.ca
www.activeparentingcanada.com
www.facebook.com/ActiveParentingCanada
twitter.com/activeparentcan
Overview: A small national organization founded in 1992
Mission: To provide video-based materials & leader training workshops in the area of parenting, teacher-in-service, self-esteem, loss education & parent involvement in schools
Member of: North American Association of Adlerian Psychologists; College of Alberta Psychologists

Active Support Against Poverty (ASAP)
1188 - 6 Ave., Prince George BC V2L 3M6
Tel: 250-563-6112; *Fax:* 250-563-1612
Toll-Free: 877-563-6112
asap@princegeorge.com
www.princegeorge.com
Overview: A small local charitable organization founded in 1987
Mission: To act as a guide for the empowerment, education & self-determination of the financially poor; To act as an agent of change for an inclusive community
Affiliation(s): Federated Anti-Poverty Groups of BC
Finances: *Annual Operating Budget:* $500,000-$1.5 Million; *Funding Sources:* Regional & provincial government; Law Fdn. of BC
Staff Member(s): 20; 10 volunteer(s)
Activities: *Speaker Service:* Yes
Chief Officer(s):
Audrey Schwartz, Executive Director

The Actors' Fund of Canada / La Caisse des acteurs du Canada inc.
#301, 1000 Yonge St., Toronto ON M4W 2K2
Tel: 416-975-0304; *Fax:* 416-975-0306
Toll-Free: 877-399-8392
Other Communication: Toll-Free Fax: 1-866-372-0985
contact@afchelps.ca
www.afchelps.ca
www.facebook.com/AFChelps
twitter.com/AFC_helps
www.youtube.com/channel/UCL0JtQXEEkamb1-cMw-OcFw
Overview: A small national charitable organization founded in 1958
Mission: The Actors' Fund of Canada promotes artistic excellence for performers, creators, technicians & other members of creative & production teams in all entertainment industry sectors. The Fund carries out this mission by providing encouragement & short-term financial aid to help entertainment industry workers maintain their health, housing & ability to work after an illness, injury or sudden unemployment.
Finances: *Annual Operating Budget:* $500,000-$1.5 Million; *Funding Sources:* Benefits; donations
Staff Member(s): 1
Membership: 1,000; *Fees:* Schedule available
Chief Officer(s):
David Hope, Executive Director
david@afchelps.ca
Fiona Reid, President
Publications:
• The Actors' Fund of Canada Newsletter
Type: Newsletter
Profile: News & updates for members

ACTRA Fraternal Benefit Society
1000 Yonge St., Toronto ON M4W 2K2
Tel: 416-967-6600; *Fax:* 416-967-4744
Toll-Free: 800-387-8897
info@afbs.ca
www.afbs.ca
www.facebook.com/enrichingcreativelives
twitter.com/AFBSCanada
Overview: A large national organization founded in 1975
Mission: To act as a member-owned insurance, financial, & fraternal benefits collective
Membership: 15,000
Chief Officer(s):
David Ferry, Chair

ACUC International
PO Box 1179, #3, 101 Nelson St. East, Port Dover ON N0A 1N0
Tel: 519-583-9798; *Fax:* 519-583-3247
acuchq@acuc.ca
www.acuc.es
www.facebook.com/acucinternational
Also Known As: American & Canadian Underwater Certification Inc.
Overview: A medium-sized international licensing organization founded in 1968
Mission: To supply quality training for sport scuba divers & instructors; To teach the highest standards in safety, sport, & marine conservation
Affiliation(s): World Diving Federation; Undersea Hyperbaric Medical Society
Activities: *Internships:* Yes; *Speaker Service:* Yes
Chief Officer(s):
Juan Rodriguez, President & Chief Executive Officer
jra@acuc.es
Nancy Cronkwright, Vice-President & Officer Manager,
519-750-5767, Fax: 519-750-5769
acuchq@acuc.ca
Patricia Molina, Vice-President & Manager, Clinet Service
comercial@acuc.es

Acupuncture Canada
Tower II, #109, 895 Don Mills Rd., Toronto ON M3C 1W3
Tel: 416-752-3988; *Fax:* 416-752-4398
www.acupuncturecanada.org
Previous Name: Acupuncture Foundation of Canada Institute
Overview: A medium-sized national organization founded in 1995
Mission: To define & maintain the highest professional standards for the use of acupuncture; To gain recognition of acupuncture's legitimate place in western medicine as a safe, efficient complement to conventional medical treatment; To design educational training programs for physicians, physiotherapists, RNs, dentists, chiropractors & naturopaths in the methodology & practice of acupuncture
Affiliation(s): World Federation of Acupuncture Societies; Pan Pacific Medical Acupuncture Forum
Finances: *Annual Operating Budget:* $500,000-$1.5 Million
Staff Member(s): 5
Membership: 1,200; *Fees:* $255; *Member Profile:* Physicians, physiotherapists, dentists, chiropractors, naturopaths & licensed acupuncturists, RNs (baccalaurate); *Committees:* Education; Executive; Nominating
Chief Officer(s):
Jacek Brachaniec, President
Cathy Donald, Treasurer
Ronda Kellington, Executive Director
rkellington@acupuncturecanada.org
Ann Eldemire, Administrative Coordinator
aeldemire@acupuncturecanada.org
Sheila Williams, Director, Education Administration
Christina Rogoza, Director, Education Curriculum

Acupuncture Foundation of Canada Institute *See* Acupuncture Canada

Adala - Canadian Arab Justice Committee
PO Box 56530, Burnaby BC V3J 7W2
Tel: 604-506-5155; *Fax:* 604-941-5627
info@adala.ca
www.adala.ca
Overview: A small national organization founded in 2002
Mission: To increase the collective understanding on issues of importance to Arab Canadians, such as the Palestine question & the war in Iraq
Membership: *Fees:* $25 basic

Adam Mickiewicz Foundation of Canada
#2102, 61 Richview Rd., Toronto ON M9A 4M8
Tel: 416-243-8984
arpaudyn@rogers.com
polishcanadians.ca/Adam_Mickiewicz_foundation_EN.html
www.facebook.com/1341946082541080
Overview: A small local organization founded in 1963
Mission: The oldest Polish cultural foundation in Canada; to provide grants & financial support for students of Polish origin studying at Canadian universities; To help various libraries & printing houses; To assist in the development of contacts between universities in Poland & in Canada; To organize lectures in Polish & English

Canadian Associations / Addiction Services of Thames Valley

Addiction Research Foundation *See* Centre for Addiction & Mental Health

Addiction Services of Thames Valley
#260, 200 Queens Ave., London ON N6A 1J3
Tel: 519-673-3242; *Fax:* 519-673-1022
intake@adstv.on.ca
www.adstv.on.ca
Overview: A small local organization
Mission: Addiction remedial services in the Thames Valley area of Southwestern Ontario
Activities: Service in Middlesex, Elgin & Oxford counties, London, Strathroy, St. Thomas & Woodstock, Ingersoll & Tillsonburg; Substance Abuse; Problem Gambling; Back on Track; Heartspace; Youth Services

Addictions & Mental Health Ontario
#104, 970 Lawrence Ave. West, Toronto ON M6A 2B6
Tel: 416-490-8900; *Fax:* 866-295-6394
info@addictionsandmentalhealthontario.ca
www.addictionsandmentalhealthontario.ca
twitter.com/AMHont
Previous Name: Alcohol and Drug Recovery Association of Ontario
Merged from: Addictions Ontario; Ontario Federation of Community Mental Health & Addiction Programs
Overview: A small provincial charitable organization founded in 1968
Mission: To ensure that the best possible addictions treatment & recovery services are available to people throughout Ontario
Finances: *Funding Sources:* Membership fees; donations
Staff Member(s): 5
Membership: *Fees:* Schedule available based on budget
Chief Officer(s):
Gail Czukar, Chief Executive Officer
gail.czukar@addictionsandmentalhealthontario.ca

Addictions Foundation of Manitoba (AFM) / Fondation manitobaine de lutte contre les dépendances
1031 Portage Ave., Winnipeg MB R3G 0R8
Tel: 204-944-6236; *Fax:* 204-944-7082
Toll-Free: 866-638-2561
execoff@afm.mb.ca
afm.mb.ca
Overview: A medium-sized provincial organization founded in 1956
Mission: To be a sensitive, caring, learning organization dedicated to continuously improving our services related to addiction & to collaborate with community members in providing a holistic approach, resulting in an improved quality of life for Manitobans; provides prevention, education & treatment programs related to addictions to individuals & communities; conducts research into the negative effects of addictions
Finances: *Annual Operating Budget:* Greater than $5 Million; *Funding Sources:* Dept. of Health, Manitoba Government
Staff Member(s): 400
Membership: *Committees:* Executive Policy; Audit
Activities: *Awareness Events:* Manitoba Addiction Awareness Week, Nov.; *Speaker Service:* Yes; *Library:* William Potoroka Memorial Library; Open to public
Chief Officer(s):
Don McCaskill, Chair
Yvonne Block, CEO

   Northern Region Office
   Polaris Place, 90 Princeton Dr., Thompson MB R8N 0L3
   Tel: 204-677-7300; *Fax:* 204-677-7328
   Toll-Free: 866-291-7774
   northreg@afm.mb.ca
   Western Region Office
   Parkwood Centre, 510 Frederick St., Brandon MB R7A 6Z4
   Tel: 204-729-3838; *Fax:* 204-729-3844
   Toll-Free: 866-767-3838
   parkwood@afm.mb.ca
   Winnipeg Region Office
   1031 Portage Ave., Winnipeg MB R3G 0R8
   Tel: 204-944-6200; *Fax:* 204-786-7768
   Toll-Free: 866-638-2561
   wpgreg@afm.mb.ca

Addus
#213, 40 Orchard View Blvd., Toronto ON M4R 1B9
Tel: 416-544-8847; *Fax:* 416-544-0951
www.addus.org
Overview: A small local organization founded in 1997
Mission: To create & promote opportunities for adults with developmental disabilities; To increase accessibility & inclusion
Finances: *Funding Sources:* Donations; fundraising
Activities: Creating & providing programs
Chief Officer(s):
Mary Vieni, Executive Director
mary@addus.org
Lorne Weinreb, Office Manager
lorne@addus.org

Adlerian Psychological Association of British Columbia *See* Adlerian Psychology Association of British Columbia

Adlerian Psychology Association of British Columbia (APABC)
#440, 2184 West Broadway, Vancouver BC V6K 2E1
Tel: 604-742-1818; *Fax:* 604-742-1811
apabc@adler.bc.ca
www.adlercentre.ca
www.facebook.com/Adler-Centre-1401879176699468
twitter.com/AdlerCentre
Also Known As: Adler School of Professional Psychology
Previous Name: Adlerian Psychological Association of British Columbia
Overview: A small provincial charitable organization founded in 1973 overseen by North American Society of Adlerian Psychology
Member of: North American Society of Adlerian Psychologists; Canadian Guidance & Counselling Association
Staff Member(s): 2
Membership: *Fees:* Schedule available
Activities: Graduate programs; lectures; parenting groups; bookstore; *Library:* Not open to public
Chief Officer(s):
James Skinner, Executive Director, 204-742-1818
Publications:
• Canadian Journal of Adlerian Psychology [a publication of the Adlerian Psychology Association of British Columbia]

Administrative & Professional Staff Association (APSA)
Simon Fraser University, #AQ 5133, 8888 University Dr., Vancouver BC V5A 1S6
Tel: 778-782-4319; *Fax:* 778-782-4245
apsa@sfu.ca
apsa.sfu.ca
Overview: A small local organization founded in 1981
Staff Member(s): 2
Membership: 587; *Fees:* Monthly fees; *Member Profile:* Administrative & professional staff at Simon Fraser University; *Committees:* Advocacy; Salaries & Benefits; APIN; Nominating; University Affairs; Liaison; Pension
Activities: Participates in deliberations for salaries & benefits; plays a role in forming & revising university policies & procedures that govern the working environment
Chief Officer(s):
Neal Baldwin, President
baldwin@sfu.ca
Anne Mason, Director, Association

Administrative & Supervisory Personnel Association (ASPA)
Kirk Hall, #304, 117 Science Place, Saskatoon SK S7N 5C8
Tel: 306-966-2471; *Fax:* 306-966-2962
aspa@usask.ca
www.aspasask.ca
Overview: A small local organization founded in 1978
Finances: *Annual Operating Budget:* $50,000-$100,000
Staff Member(s): 2
Membership: 849; *Fees:* % of monthly salary; *Member Profile:* Administrative, supervisory, professional, instructional personnel of the University of Saskatchewan

Administrative Sciences Association of Canada (ASAC) / Association des sciences administratives du Canada
c/o Thompson Rivers University, 900 McGill Rd., Kamloops BC V2C 0C8
Tel: 250-828-5000
www.asac.ca
Overview: A medium-sized national organization founded in 1957
Mission: To develop teaching & research in management studies at Canadian universities
Finances: *Annual Operating Budget:* $100,000-$250,000; *Funding Sources:* Membership fees
Membership: 100 student + 700 individual; *Fees:* $75-$260; *Member Profile:* Students, academics & business professionals interested in management scholarship, teaching & practice
Chief Officer(s):
Mike Henry, President
mihenry@tru.ca
Patricia Genoe McLaren, Secretary
pmclaren@wlu.ca
Meetings/Conferences:
• Administrative Sciences Association of Canada 2018 Conference, May, 2018, Ryerson University, Toronto, ON
Scope: National
Publications:
• ASAC [Administrative Sciences Association of Canada] Newsletter
Type: Newsletter
Profile: Discusses events & ASAC updates

Administrators of Volunteer Resources BC (AVRBC)
PO Box 2259, Vancouver BC V6B 3W2
info@avrbc.com
www.avrbc.com
www.facebook.com/avrbc
twitter.com/avrbc
Overview: A small provincial organization founded in 1975
Mission: To promote leadership in the management of volunteer resources & to provide a supportive network for all its members
Member of: Canadian Administrators of Volunteer Resources
Membership: 130+; *Fees:* $110-$140; *Committees:* External Communications; Internal Communications; Membership; Professional Development; Regional Representation; Website
Chief Officer(s):
Heidi Jakop, President
president@avrbc.com

Adoption Council of Canada (ACC) / Conseil d'Adoption du Canada
#416, 2249 Carling Ave., Ottawa ON K2B 7E9
Toll-Free: 888-542-3678
info@adoption.ca
www.adoption.ca
www.facebook.com/acc.cac
twitter.com/adoptioncanada
Overview: A medium-sized national charitable organization founded in 1991
Mission: To inform & educate Canadians on all aspects of adoption; to promote the placement of waiting children in permanent homes; to promote openness & honesty in adoption; to work toward legislative reform
Member of: North American Council of Adoptable Children
Affiliation(s): Child & Family Canada; Canadian Coalition for Rights of the Child
Finances: *Annual Operating Budget:* $100,000-$250,000
Staff Member(s): 1; 3 volunteer(s)
Membership: 200+
Activities: Operates Canada's waiting children program to make Canadians aware of Canadian children in need of families; *Awareness Events:* National Adoption Awareness Month, Nov.; *Speaker Service:* Yes; *Library:* by appointment
Chief Officer(s):
Laura Eggertson, Interm Executive Director

Adoption Council of Ontario (ACO)
#503, 36 Eglinton Ave. West, Toronto ON M4R 1A1
Tel: 416-482-0021; *Fax:* 416-482-1586
Toll-Free: 877-236-7820
info@adoptontario.ca
www.adoption.on.ca
www.facebook.com/adoptioncouncilontario
twitter.com/ontarioadopts
Overview: A medium-sized provincial charitable organization founded in 1987
Mission: To education, support & advocate on behalf of those touched by adoption in Ontario
Member of: Adoption Council of Canada; North American Council on Adoptable Children
Finances: *Annual Operating Budget:* $100,000-$250,000; *Funding Sources:* Membership dues; donations; programs
Staff Member(s): 4; 20 volunteer(s)
Membership: 15; *Fees:* $50/year; $130/3 years; *Member Profile:* Adoptees; birth parents; adoptive & pre-adoptive parents; professionals
Activities: Workshops; seminars; helpline; advocacy; *Awareness Events:* Adoption Awareness Month, Nov.; *Internships:* Yes; *Speaker Service:* Yes; *Library:* Adoption Resource Centre; Open to public

Adoption Roots & Rights (ARR)
ON
Tel: 519-268-3674
Overview: A small local organization founded in 1994
Mission: To help people separated by adoption to reconnect with birth family members; To offer search assistance; To help people be informed of their rights
Affiliation(s): Parent Finders
Finances: *Annual Operating Budget:* Less than $50,000
Staff Member(s): 1; 1 volunteer(s)
Membership: 200; *Fees:* $20 individual; *Member Profile:* Adult adoptees; birth relatives; adoptive parents & adult foster persons

ADR Institute of Canada (ADRIC) / Institut d'arbitrage et de médiation du Canada
#405, 234 Eglinton Ave. East, Toronto ON M4P 1K5
Tel: 416-487-4733; *Fax:* 416-487-4429
Toll-Free: 877-475-4353
admin@adrcanada.ca
www.adrcanada.ca
www.linkedin.com/groups?gid=3303518
www.facebook.com/ADRInstituteOfCanadaADRIC.IAMC
twitter.com/adrcanada
Previous Name: Arbitration & Mediation Institute of Canada Inc.; Canadian Foundation for Dispute Resolution
Overview: A medium-sized national charitable organization founded in 1974
Mission: To promote the use of arbitration & mediation (ADR - alternative dispute resolution) to settle disputes; to provide information & education on ADR to practitioners, parties, the public, & the business, professional & government communities; to assist those wishing to use ADR through the provision of Arbitration & Mediation Rules, administrative services, & information about the process & member arbitrators & mediators
Affiliation(s): British Columbia Arbitration & Mediation Institute; ADR Institute of Alberta; ADR Institute of Saskatchewan Inc.; ADR Institute of Ontario, Inc.; Institut de médiation d'arbitrage du Québec; ADR Atlantic Institute
Finances: *Funding Sources:* Membership fees
Staff Member(s): 5
Membership: 2,000 individuals; *Fees:* Schedule available; *Member Profile:* ADR professionals & corporate users
Activities: ADR Connect; chartered mediators (C.Med.) & chartered arbitrators (C.Arb.) designations
Chief Officer(s):
Janet McKay, Executive Director
Awards:
• Lionel J. McGowan Award of Excellence

ADR Atlantic Institute
PO Box 123, Halifax NS B3J 2M4
Tel: 709-437-2359
admin@adratlantic.ca
www.adratlantic.ca
Chief Officer(s):
Andrew Butt, President

ADR Institute of Alberta (ADRIA)
Ralph King Athletic Centre, Concordia University, 7128 Ada Blvd., #CE223A, Edmonton AB T5B 4E4
Tel: 780-433-4881; *Fax:* 780-433-9024
Toll-Free: 800-232-7214
info@adralberta.com
www.adralberta.com
www.linkedin.com/company/adr-institute-of-alberta
www.facebook.com/ADRAlberta
twitter.com/ADRAlberta
www.youtube.com/user/AAMS2010
Chief Officer(s):
Paul Conway, Executive Director
paul@adralberta.com

ADR Institute of Ontario, Inc.
#405, 234 Eglinton Ave. East, Toronto ON M4P 1K5
Tel: 416-487-4447; *Fax:* 416-487-4429
admin@adrontario.ca
www.adrontario.ca
www.linkedin.com/groups?gid=2754057
www.facebook.com/ADRInstituteOfOntario
Chief Officer(s):
Susette Clunis, Executive Director

ADR Institute of Saskatchewan Inc.
PO Box 22015, RPO Wildwood, Saskatoon SK S7H GP1
Fax: 855-487-4429
Toll-Free: 866-596-7275
info@adrsaskatchewan.ca
www.adrsaskatchewan.ca
Chief Officer(s):
Scott Siemens, President, 306-780-6755
scott.siemens@cra-arc.gc.ca

British Columbia Arbitration & Mediation Institute
#510, 700 West Pender St., Vancouver BC V6C 1G8
Tel: 604-736-6614; *Fax:* 604-736-6614
Toll-Free: 877-332-2264
info@bcami.com
www.bcami.com
Chief Officer(s):
Michael Welsh, President
mwelsh@mwelshlaw.com

Adsum for Women & Children
2421 Brunswick St., Halifax NS B3K 2Z4
Tel: 902-423-5049; *Fax:* 902-423-9336; *Crisis Hot-Line:* 902-423-4443
adsum@adsumforwomen.org
www.adsumforwomen.org
www.facebook.com/111571128907431
twitter.com/AdsumForWomen
www.youtube.com/user/adsumforwomen
Previous Name: Association for Women's Residential Facilities
Overview: A medium-sized local charitable organization founded in 1983
Mission: To administer Adsum House; To provide emergency shelter for homeless women & children
Finances: *Funding Sources:* Government; private & corporate donations; fundraising
Staff Member(s): 14
Activities: *Speaker Service:* Yes; *Rents Mailing List:* Yes
Chief Officer(s):
Sheri Lecker, Executive Director
sheri.lecker@adsumforwomen.org

Adult Basic Education Association of British Columbia (ABEABC)
5476 - 45th Ave., Delta BC V4K 1L4
Tel: 604-296-6901
www.abeabc.ca
Overview: A small provincial organization
Mission: Fosters and promotes excellence in adult basic education instruction and programming.
Membership: *Fees:* $40 non-profit community group/individual; $50 individual outside Canada; $75 Organization (no bursary); *Committees:* Membership; Groundwork; Fundraising & Conference
Chief Officer(s):
Yvonne Chard, President, 604-594-6100
ychard@deltasd.bc.ca
John Cowan, Treasurer, 604-594-6100
jcowan@deltasd.bc.ca
Meetings/Conferences:
• Adult Basic Education Association of British Columbia Conference 2018, April, 2018, Harrison Hot Springs Resort and Spa, Harrison Hot Springs, BC
Scope: Provincial
Contact Information: abeabcnews@gmail.com

Adult Children of Alcoholics (ACA)
#505, 5863 Leslie St., Toronto ON M2H 1J8
Tel: 416-631-3614
acatoronto@hotmail.com
www.acatoronto.org
Overview: A small national organization
Mission: To improve members' lives through the 12 step program
Activities: Weekly meetings; annual workshops; *Speaker Service:* Yes

Adult Educators' Provincial Specialist Association (AEPSA)
c/o British Columbia Teachers' Federation, #100, 550 West 6th Ave., Vancouver BC V5Z 4P2
Tel: 604-871-2283; *Fax:* 604-871-2286
adultedpsa.org
twitter.com/AEPSAEditor
Overview: A small provincial organization
Mission: The aims of AEPSA include facilitating communication between adult educators, exchanging ideas & advocating on behalf of them and their students. Most members work in adult education programs, such as Adult Basic Education (ABE), Adult Literacy, Adult Foundations, General Education Development (GED), Grade 10 Completion, English as a Second Language (ESL) or English Language Services for Adults (ELSA), High School Completion (HSC) or Adult Secondary School Completion (ASSC), and Adult Special Education (ASE).
Member of: BC Teachers' Federation
Finances: *Funding Sources:* BCTF union membership dues; membership fees
Membership: *Fees:* $20 BCTF members; $10 students & TAs

Adult Learning Development Association (ALDA)
#608, 409 Granville St., Vancouver BC V6C 1T2
Tel: 604-683-5554
Previous Name: Association of Learning Disabled Adults
Overview: A small local charitable organization founded in 1988
Mission: ALDA exclusively represents and works with adults and older youth who have suspected or diagnosed learning disabilities; Provides a compregensive range of services and programs that are adapted and designed to meet the needs of their clients and members and that are accessible to all.
Member of: Affiliation of Multicultural Societies & Service Agencies of BC; SUCCESS; Learning Disabilities Association of Canada; BC Coalition of People with Disabilities; ENET Educational Society
Finances: *Funding Sources:* Service Canada, City of Vancouver Community Services Grant, Province of British Columbia, memberships and donations
Membership: *Member Profile:* Adults & older youth who have learning disabilities/difficulties; professionals
Activities: Information & referrals; assessment; advocacy; employment services; career exploration; transition to work skill; individual counselling & research; videos & DVDs; *Speaker Service:* Yes; *Library:* "I-Improve" Learning Disability Resource Centre; by appointment
Publications:
• ALDA Update Express

Adult Literacy Council of Greater Fort Erie (ALC)
PO Box 86, Fort Erie ON L2A 5M6
Tel: 905-871-6626
info@literacyforterie.ca
www.literacyforterie.ca
Overview: A small local charitable organization founded in 1978
Mission: To promote literacy to adults in the Greater Fort Erie area in order to enhance the lives of individuals & of the community through individual literacy programs & community events
Member of: Laubach Literacy of Canada - Ontario
Affiliation(s): United Way
Finances: *Funding Sources:* Donations; bingo; events; membership fee; United Way; Trillium Fondation; foundations
Staff Member(s): 2
Activities: Provision of literacy services for adults; "Each One, Teach One"; Sponsor-a-Student Learner Group; *Library:* by appointment
Chief Officer(s):
Jessica Grimes, Chair
Salvati Maria, Program Coordinator
maria@literacyforterie.ca

Advanced Card Technology Association of Canada / Association canadienne de la technologie des cartes à mémoire
85 Mullen Dr., Ajax ON L1T 2B3
Tel: 905-426-6360; *Fax:* 905-619-3275
info@actcda.com
www.actcda.com
Also Known As: ACT Canada
Overview: A small national organization founded in 1989
Mission: To promote the understanding & use of all advanced card technologies across a wide range of applications; to connect users & suppliers; to work with governments, financial institutions & users to advance standards, develop card related policies & prepare the marketplace for a broad based acceptance of advanced cards
Affiliation(s): AFPC; European Experts in Electronic Transactions; Eurosmart; GlobalPlatform; International Card Manufacturers Association; Information Security Media Group; National Association of Campus Card Users; Smart Card Alliance; Smart Card Forum of India
Finances: *Annual Operating Budget:* $100,000-$250,000; *Funding Sources:* Membership dues; seminars; consulting
Staff Member(s): 4; 15 volunteer(s)
Membership: 80+; *Fees:* Based on membership level; *Member Profile:* Users, suppliers & parties interested in smart, optical & other advanced card technologies; *Committees:* Membership; Education; Conference; Communication; Marketing
Activities: Teaching; advocacy; consulting; market research; setting international standards; *Speaker Service:* Yes; *Rents Mailing List:* Yes; *Library:* by appointment

Chief Officer(s):
Catherine Johnston, President & CEO
Michelle Weir, Contact, 905-426-6360 Ext. 125
michelle@actcda.com
Publications:
• ACTion Newsletter [a publication of the Advanced Card Technology Association of Canada]
Type: Newsletter; *Frequency:* Monthly

Advanced Coronary Treatment (ACT) Foundation of Canada / La fondation des soins avancés en urgence coronarienne du Canada
379 Holland Ave., Ottawa ON K1Y 0Y9
Tel: 613-729-3455
Toll-Free: 800-465-9111
Other Communication: www.flickr.com/photos/actfoundation
act@actfoundation.ca
www.actfoundation.ca
www.facebook.com/theactfoundation
twitter.com/actfoundation
www.youtube.com/theactfoundation
Also Known As: ACT Foundation
Overview: A small national charitable organization founded in 1985
Mission: To work with health professionals, governments, & the community in educating the public about the prevention, management, & treatment of illnesses that can lead to prehospital health emergencies
Finances: *Annual Operating Budget:* $250,000-$500,000
Staff Member(s): 5; 300 volunteer(s)
Membership: 50 individual; *Committees:* Medical Advisory; Media/Communications Advisory; Education Advisory; Community Advisory
Activities: Helping establish high school CPR across Canada
Chief Officer(s):
Sandra Clarke, Executive Director

Advancing Canadian Entrepreneurship Inc.; Canada's Future Entrepreneurial Leaders *See* Enactus Canada

AdvantAge Ontario
#700, 7050 Weston Rd., Woodbridge ON L4L 8G7
Tel: 905-851-8821; *Fax:* 905-851-0744
www.advantageontario.ca
Previous Name: Ontario Association of Non-Profit Homes & Services for Seniors; Ontario Association of Homes for the Aged
Overview: A medium-sized provincial charitable organization founded in 1919 overseen by Canadian Alliance for Long Term Care
Mission: To support members in the provision of quality non-profit long term care, seniors' community services, & housing
Finances: *Funding Sources:* Membership fees; Revenue from programs & services
Membership: 580+; *Member Profile:* Non-profit providers of long term care, services, & housing for seniors; Commercial suppliers; Associate & personal members
Activities: Engaging in political advocacy activities; Providing educational opportunities & certification programs
Chief Officer(s):
Althea Whyte, Manager, Finance & Administration
awhyte@advantageontario.ca
Chris Noone, Manager, Communications & Member Services
cnoone@advantageontario.ca
Awards:
• AdvantAge Ontario Leadership Award
To recognize a senior executive who has demonstrated exemplary leadership
• Community Connections Award
To recognize initiatives that enhance community relations
• Innovation & Excellence Supporting Seniors Award
To recognize innovative programs in the provision of care & services for seniors
Meetings/Conferences:
• AdvantAge Ontario 2018 Annual General Meeting & Convention, April, 2018, Westin Harbour Castle, Toronto, ON
Scope: Provincial
Description: A professional development event & trade show, featuring expert speakers, for senior staff from the long term care, seniors' housing, & community services sectors

Adventist Development & Relief Agency Canada (ADRA)
20 Robert St. West, Newcastle ON L1B 1C6
Tel: 905-446-2372; *Fax:* 905-446-2372
Toll-Free: 888-274-2372
Other Communication: donor-relations@adra.ca
info@adra.ca
www.adra.ca
www.facebook.com/adracanada
twitter.com/adracanada
www.youtube.com/adracanada
Also Known As: ADRA Canada
Overview: A medium-sized international charitable organization founded in 1985
Mission: To provide community development & disaster relief without regard to political or religious association, age, or ethnicity
Member of: Canadian Council of Christian Charities, Canadian Churches in Action, Canadian Council for International Cooperation, Canadian Christian Relief and Development Association
Affiliation(s): Canadian Council of Christian Charities
Finances: *Annual Operating Budget:* $1.5 Million-$3 Million; *Funding Sources:* Resources & donations received from the public & the Canadian government.
Staff Member(s): 14; 1500 volunteer(s)
Membership: 7,000
Activities: Emegency relief in the areas of: refugee assistance, improving health, hunger, safe drinking water, raising income, education & international development
Chief Officer(s):
James Astleford, Executive Director
Publications:
• Global Impact
Type: Newsletter; *Frequency:* Quarterly

Adventive Cross Cultural Initiatives (ACCI)
89 Auriga Dr., Nepean ON K2E 7Z2
Tel: 613-298-1546; *Fax:* 613-225-7455
lauren@adventive.ca
www.adventive.ca
www.facebook.com/AdventiveCCI
Previous Name: New Life League
Overview: A small national charitable organization founded in 1986
Mission: To operate as an international, interdenominational Christian missionary organization; To minister through printing & literature, children's homes, national workers, evangelism & church planting
Member of: Canadian Council of Christian Charities
Finances: *Annual Operating Budget:* Less than $50,000; *Funding Sources:* Donations
Staff Member(s): 4; 1 volunteer(s)
Activities: *Internships:* Yes
Chief Officer(s):
John Haley, Executive Director
johnhaley@adventive.ca
Lauren Roth, Canadian National Director
lauren@adventive.ca

The Advertising & Design Club of Canada (ADCC)
#235, 401 Richmond St. West, Toronto ON M5V 3A8
Tel: 416-423-4113; *Fax:* 416-423-3362
info@theadcc.ca
www.theadcc.ca
www.facebook.com/TheADCC
twitter.com/TheADCC
Previous Name: Art Directors' Club of Toronto
Overview: A small national organization founded in 1948
Mission: To recognize, support & promote creative excellence in the Canadian advertising, publishing & design community
Finances: *Funding Sources:* Memberships; entry fees
Membership: *Fees:* $150 professional; $35 student
Chief Officer(s):
Fidel Peña, President
Dawn Wickstrom, Executive Director
Awards:
• The Advertising & Design Club of Canada Awards
Main categories of awards are: Advertising Print, Advertising Broadcast, Advertising Multiple Media, Graphic Design, Editorial Design & Interactive Design; winners receive gold, silver or merit awards

Advertising Association of Winnipeg Inc. (AAW)
PO Box 2278, 950 Borebank St., Winnipeg MB R3C 4B3
Tel: 204-831-1077; *Fax:* 204-885-6265
www.adwinnipeg.ca
www.linkedin.com/groups/Advertising-Association-Winnipeg-3100170
www.facebook.com/AdWinnipeg
twitter.com/AdWinnipeg
www.youtube.com/AdWinnipeg
Overview: A small local licensing organization founded in 1944
Mission: To encourage professional development among its members & those involved in advertisement
Membership: 92 individuals; 64 companies; *Fees:* $50 student; $100 single; $285 corporate
Activities: Monthly luncheons with speakers; workshops
Chief Officer(s):
Matt Cohen, President

The Advertising Club of Toronto
Toronto ON
www.adclub.ca
www.linkedin.com/company/330264
www.facebook.com/AdClubToronto
twitter.com/Adclubtoronto
www.youtube.com/user/AdClubToronto
Overview: A small local organization
Mission: To organize meetings & seminars for ACT members & guests that will present the newest ideas & developments in the advertising industry; create social & business events which will give ACT members opportunities to interact with colleagues in the advertising industry; to establish & maintain an informal structure within the club to promote a sense of accessibility between all members & directors
Activities: *Rents Mailing List:* Yes
Chief Officer(s):
Mladen Raickovic, President

Advertising Standards Canada *Voir* Les normes canadiennes de la publicité

Advertising Standards Canada (ASC) / Les normes canadiennes de la publicité
South Tower, #1801, 175 Bloor St. East, Toronto ON M4W 3R8
Tel: 416-961-6311; *Fax:* 416-961-7904
www.adstandards.com
Previous Name: Advertising Standards Council
Overview: A medium-sized national organization founded in 1957
Mission: To ensure the integrity & viability of advertising through industry self-regulation.
Staff Member(s): 16
Membership: 167; *Fees:* Schedule available; *Member Profile:* Advertisers; advertising agencies; media organizations; suppliers
Activities: Standards Division administers the industry's principal self-regulatory code, the Canadian Code of Advertising Standards; handles complaints from consumers regarding advertising & coordinates the Council on Diversity in Advertising; Advertising Clearance Division previews advertisement in six industry categories, helping advertisers adhere to applicable legislation, regulatory codes & industry standards
Chief Officer(s):
Linda J. Nagel, President/CEO Ext. 222
   Québec
   #915, 2015, rue Peel, Montréal QC H3A 1T8
   Tél: 514-931-8060; *Téléc:* 877-956-8646
   www.normespub.com
   Chief Officer(s):
   Danielle Lefrançois, Directrice, Communications,
   514-931-8060 Ext. 260

Advertising Standards Council *See* Advertising Standards Canada

Advocacy Centre for the Elderly (ACE)
#701, 2 Carlton St., Toronto ON M5B 1J3
Tel: 416-598-2656; *Fax:* 416-598-7924
www.acelaw.ca
Also Known As: Holly Street Advocacy Centre for the Elderly Inc.
Overview: A small provincial charitable organization founded in 1984
Mission: To provide legal services to low income senior citizens
Finances: *Funding Sources:* Membership fees; Donations; Legal Aid Ontario
Staff Member(s): 8
Membership: *Fees:* $10 individuals; $25 corporations
Activities: Providing individual & group client advice & representation; Offering public legal education, such as community presentations & workshops; Engaging in law reform activities of importance to the senior population; *Speaker Service:* Yes
Chief Officer(s):
Judith Wahl, Executive Director
Publications:
• ACE [Advocacy Centre for the Elderly] Newsletter
Type: Newsletter; *Frequency:* Semiannually; *Price:* Free with

membership in the Advocacy Centre for the Elderly
Profile: Articles on legal issues related to seniors
• ACE [Advocacy Centre for the Elderly] Library Reports
Type: Report; *Price:* Free with membership in the Advocacy Centre for the Elderly
Profile: A series of articles on legal issues related to seniors

The Advocates' Society
#2700, 250 Yonge St., Toronto ON M5B 2L7
Tel: 416-597-0243; *Fax:* 416-597-1588
mail@advocates.ca
www.advocates.ca
www.linkedin.com/company-beta/1311912
www.facebook.com/TheAdvocatesSociety
twitter.com/Advocates_Soc
Overview: A large provincial organization founded in 1963
Mission: To teach the skills & ethics of advocacy through information sharing, educational programs, seminars, conferences & workshops; To speak out on behalf of advocates; To protect the right to representation by an independent bar; To initiate appropriate reforms to the legal system
Finances: *Annual Operating Budget:* $1.5 Million-$3 Million; *Funding Sources:* Membership fees
Staff Member(s): 16
Membership: 5,000+; *Fees:* Schedule available; *Member Profile:* Lawyers; *Committees:* Advocacy & Practice; Collegiality, Mentoring & Membership; Education; National; Finance & Audit; Young Advocates Standing
Chief Officer(s):
Alexandra Chyczij, Executive Director, 888-597-0243 Ext. 103
alex@advocates.ca

Advocis
#209, 390 Queens Quay West, Toronto ON M5V 3A2
Tel: 416-444-5251; *Fax:* 416-444-8031
Toll-Free: 800-563-5822
info@advocis.ca
www.advocis.ca
www.linkedin.com/company/advocis
www.facebook.com/advocis
twitter.com/Advocis
www.youtube.com/user/AdvocisTFAAC
Also Known As: The Financial Advisors Association of Canada
Previous Name: Life Underwriters Association of Canada
Merged from: Canadian Association of Insurance & Financial Advisors; Canadian Association of Financial Planners
Overview: A medium-sized national organization founded in 1906
Mission: To represent Advice & Advocacy; to carry on the tradition of effectively representing members' interests with all levels of government, regulators, & industry, always with the intention of putting the interests of consumers first
Member of: Financial Planners Standards Council
Affiliation(s): Advocis Protective Association; The Institute for Advanced Financial Education; GAMA International Canada; Conference for Advanced Life Underwriting
Membership: 11,000 in 40 chapters; *Committees:* Governance; Law & Regulatory
Activities: Advocacy; professional development courses towards the CFP & CLU designations; *Library:* Not open to public
Chief Officer(s):
David Juvet, Chair
chair@advocis.ca
Greg Pollock, President & CEO
president@advocis.ca

AEAQ Inc. *See* Association of English Language Publishers of Québec

Aéro Montréal
#8000, 380, rue Saint-Antoine ouest, Montréal QC H2Y 3X7
Tél: 514-987-9330; *Téléc:* 514-987-1948
info@aeromontreal.ca
www.aeromontreal.ca
www.linkedin.com/company/a-ro-montr-al
twitter.com/AeroMontreal
Aperçu: Dimension: petite; *Envergure:* provinciale; fondée en 2006
Mission: Regrouper les professionnels de l'industrie aérospatiale afin de faire progresser la concurrence au Québec
Finances: *Fonds:* Gouvernement
Membre(s) du personnel: 12
Membre: *Montant de la cotisation:* 825$ industriel/institutionnelle; $1,130 partenaire
Membre(s) du bureau directeur:
Suzanne M. Benoît, Présidente-directrice générale
Meetings/Conferences:
• Assemblée générale annuelle d'Aéro Montréal 2018, 2018, QC
Scope: Local

Aéroclub des cantons de l'est
Aéroport Roland-Désourdy, 101, rue du Ciel, Bromont QC V6B 3X9
Tél: 514-862-1216
www.facebook.com/AeroclubDesCantonsDeLEst
Aperçu: Dimension: petite; *Envergure:* locale
Membre de: Soaring Association of Canada
Membre(s) du bureau directeur:
Marc Arsenault, Contact
marcarsenault@sympatico.ca

Aerospace Heritage Foundation of Canada (AHFC)
PO Box 246, Stn. Etobicoke D, Toronto ON M9A 4X2
Tel: 416-410-3350
www.ahfc.org
Overview: A small national charitable organization founded in 1989
Mission: Current emphasis of AHFC is on Avro & Orenda.
Finances: *Annual Operating Budget:* Less than $50,000
12 volunteer(s)
Membership: 248; *Fees:* $35 new; $25 renewal; $10 student; *Committees:* Shows; Speakers; Executive; Editorial
Activities: Meetings; displays; heritage retrival; *Speaker Service:* Yes
Chief Officer(s):
Frank Harvey, President
fwbd.harvey@sympatico.ca
Nick Doran, Membership Secretary
dorans@idirect.com
Al Sablatnig, Treasurer

Aerospace Industries Association of Canada (AIAC) / Association des industries aérospatiales du Canada
#703, 255 Albert St., Ottawa ON K1P 6A9
Tel: 613-232-4297; *Fax:* 613-232-1142
info@aiac.ca
www.aiac.ca
ca.linkedin.com/company/aerospace-industries-association-of-canada
twitter.com/AIAC_News
Previous Name: Air Industries Association of Canada
Overview: A large national organization founded in 1962
Mission: To promote & facilitate the continued success & growth of this strategic industry; To establish & maintain a public policy environment that enables sustained aerospace industry growth; To strengthen the international competitiveness of all aerospace firms in Canada; To strengthen Canadian aerospace SME capabilities & position them as "suppliers of choice"; To represent & involve the full range of aerospace companies that operate in Canada
Staff Member(s): 7
Membership: 400; *Fees:* Based on a company's Canadian 'Aerospace and Defence' related revenue and are $1,100+ annually; *Member Profile:* Individuals associated with the aerospace and space industries in Canada; *Committees:* Civil Aviation; Public Procurement & Defence; Labour Market; Small Business; Market Access (Ad-Hoc); Space; Technology & Innovation
Activities: *Library:* Aerospace Industries Association of Canada Library
Chief Officer(s):
Jim Quick, President & CEO, 613-232-4297
Barry Kohler, Chair
Awards:
• Dave Caddey Memorial Scholarship (DCMS)
Supports students in their choice of a career in aerospace, space and the defence sector *Eligibility:* Any individual enrolled full-time or part-time at a Canadian college or university; pursuing an aerospace/space, engineering or business/marketing-related program; have current or past expereince working within the aerospace/space industry *Deadline:* August 1
• James C. Floyd Award
Acknowledges an individual or a team that has made an outstanding contribution to the Canadian aerospace industry *Eligibility:* Any individual or team from an AIAC member company, Canadian university, college or research institution, or government department may be nominated for this award. Nominees of all ages and experience levels will be considered.

Meetings/Conferences:
• 2018 Aerospace, Defence & Security Expo, August, 2018, Abbotsford, BC
Scope: National
Description: Promotes the Western Canadian aerospace industry; takes place at the same time as the Abbotsford International Airshow
• 2018 Canadian Aerospace Summit, November, 2018
Scope: National
Description: Visionaries and practitioners will speak on the new evolution and expectations in aerospace, meet leading industry decision-makers, and gain first-hand intelligence on key business opportunities.
Publications:
• AIAC Guide to Canada's Aerospace Industry
Type: Guide; *Frequency:* Annually
Profile: Resource for aerospace industry statistics, companies, products and services.

Aerospace Industry Association of British Columbia (AIABC)
#102, 211 Columbia St., Vancouver BC V6A 2R5
Tel: 604-638-1477
info@aiabc.com
www.aiabc.com
Overview: A small provincial organization founded in 1994
Mission: To enhance the growth of the provincial aerospace industry by acting as a watchdog, advocate & facilitator for BC companies seeking Canadian & international business opportunities
Member of: Aerospace Industry Association of Canada
Finances: *Funding Sources:* Membership dues

Affairs pour les arts *See* Business for the Arts

Affected Families of Police Homicide (AFPH)
Tel: 289-880-9950
grief2action@gmail.com
www.facebook.com/groups/BFRJC
Overview: A small provincial organization
Mission: To promote change in the methods that police officers utilize to deal with mental illness & use of force in Ontario
Staff Member(s): 1
Activities: Lobbying for change in policy; Meeting with authorities to discuss issues
Chief Officer(s):
Karyn Greenwood-Graham, Contact

Affiliation of Multicultural Societies & Service Agencies of BC (AMSSA)
#205, 2929 Commercial Dr., Vancouver BC V5N 4C8
Tel: 604-718-2780; *Fax:* 604-298-0747
Toll-Free: 888-355-5560
amssa@amssa.org
www.amssa.org
www.facebook.com/amssabc
twitter.com/amssabc
Overview: A medium-sized provincial organization founded in 1977
Mission: To provide leadership in advocacy & education in British Columbia for anti-racism, human rights & social justice; To support members in serving immigrants, refugees & culturally diverse communities
Member of: Canadian Immigrant Settlement Sector Alliance
Finances: *Annual Operating Budget:* $500,000-$1.5 Million; *Funding Sources:* Provincial & federal governments; foundations; donations
Staff Member(s): 11
Membership: 70+ organizations; *Fees:* $75 associate; *Member Profile:* Agencies providing immigrant settlement & multicultural services; *Committees:* Cultures West; Immigrant Integration Coordinating
Activities: Providing informational services for settlement, integration & diversity agencies; Organizing Safe Harbour program to bring diversity & inclusion education into workplaces; *Awareness Events:* Safe Harbour Champions Breakfast *Library:* AMSSA Resource Database; Open to public
Chief Officer(s):
Katie Rosenberger, Executive Director
Tracy Wideman, Program Director
Publications:
• AMSSA [Affiliation of Multicultural Societies & Service Agencies of BC] Annual Report
Type: Report; *Frequency:* Annually

Affirm United / S'affirmer Ensemble
PO Box 57057, Stn. Somerset, Ottawa ON K1R 1A1

Canadian Associations / Afghan Association of Ontario

affirmunited@affirmunited.ca
www.affirmunited.ca
Overview: A medium-sized national organization founded in 1982
Mission: To affirm gay, lesbian, bisexual & transgender people & their friends, within The United Church of Canada; to provide a network of supports among affirming ministries & regional groups; to act as a point of contact for individuals; to speak to the church in a united fashion encouraging it to act prophetically & pastorally both within & beyond the church structure.
Affiliation(s): United Church of Canada
Finances: *Annual Operating Budget:* Less than $50,000
20 volunteer(s)
Membership: 200 ministries; *Fees:* $40 individual/household; $100 institutional
Activities: *Speaker Service:* Yes
Chief Officer(s):
Linda Hutchinson, Coordinator, Affirming Ministry
Brian Mitchell-Walker, Coordinator, Affirming Ministry

Afghan Association of Ontario
29 Pemican Ct., Toronto ON M9M 2Z3
Tel: 416-744-9289; *Fax:* 416-744-6671
info@aaocanada.ca
www.aaocanada.ca
Overview: A small provincial organization founded in 1982
Mission: To provide services to newly immigrated Afghans in order to help settle in Canada
Member of: Ontario Council of Agencies Serving Immigrants
Membership: *Committees:* Membership; Sponsorship; Cultrual; Youth; Women; Finance; Social; Religous
Chief Officer(s):
Mahmood Baher Formuli, President
fformuli@gmail.com

Afghan Women's Counselling & Integration Community Support Organization
#203, 150 Consumers Rd., Toronto ON M2J 1P9
Tel: 416-588-3585; *Fax:* 416-588-4552
www.afghanwomen.org
www.facebook.com/afghanwomengreatertoronto
Also Known As: Afghan Women's Organization (AWO)
Overview: A small local charitable organization
Mission: To assist Afghan women in their integration & adaptation to Canadian life; To encourage & motivate Afghan women to participate & contribute to life in Canada; To develop a community support network for Afghan women; To emphasize the acquisition of English language in Afghan women; To organize & implement social programs which will educate children/youth about their current social issues; To encourage & promote the development of skills in Afghan women
Activities: Language Instruction for Newcomers to Canada (LINC) program; Immigration Settlement & Adaptation Program (ISAP); homework club; job search workshop; family support; Senior Afghan Women's Circle; youth programs; sponsorship; itinerant services
Chief Officer(s):
Adeena Niazi, Executive Director
aniazi@afghanwomen.org
Eglantina Resulaj, Manager, Finance

Mississauga
#302, 3050 Confederation Pkwy., Mississauga ON L5B 3Z6
Tel: 905-279-3679; *Fax:* 905-279-4691

North York
#212, 747 Don Mills Rd., Toronto ON M3C 1T2
Tel: 416-422-2225

Scarborough
#211, 2555 Eglinton Ave. East, Toronto ON M1K 5J1
Tel: 416-266-1777; *Fax:* 416-266-8145

AFOA Canada
#301, 1066 Somerset St. West, Ottawa ON K1Y 4T3
Tel: 613-722-5543; *Fax:* 613-722-3467
Toll-Free: 866-722-2362
info@afoa.ca
www.afoa.ca
www.linkedin.com/company/afoa-canada
www.facebook.com/aboriginalfinancialofficersassociation
twitter.com/afoa_canada
Previous Name: Aboriginal Financial Officers Association
Overview: A medium-sized national organization founded in 1999
Mission: To provide leadership in Aboriginal financial management by developing & promoting quality standards, practices, research, certification, & professional development to members & Aboriginal organizations.
Finances: *Annual Operating Budget:* $500,000-$1.5 Million
Staff Member(s): 8
Membership: 500-999; *Fees:* Schedule available
Activities: *Awareness Events:* Annual National Conference
Chief Officer(s):
Terry Goodtrack, President & CEO
tgoodtrack@afoa.ca
Simon Brascoupé, Vice-President, Education & Training
sbrascoupe@afoa.ca
Awards:
• AFOA-Xerox Excellence in Leadership Awards
• AFOA-PotashCorp Aboriginal Youth Financial Management Awards
• Norman Taylor Memorial Scholarships & Bursaries
Meetings/Conferences:
• 2018 AFOA Canada National Conference, October, 2018, Shaw Centre, Ottawa, ON
Scope: National
Publications:
• JAM: The Journal of Aboriginal Management [a publication of AFOA Canada]
Type: Journal; *Frequency:* Semiannually; *Accepts Advertising*

AFOA Alberta
PO Box 1010, Siksika AB T0J 3W0
Tel: 403-734-5446; *Fax:* 403-734-5342
administration@afoaab.ca
www.afoaab.ca
Chief Officer(s):
Robert Andrews, Executive Director
robert.andrews@afoaab.com

AFOA Atlantic
R15, 150 Cliffe Street, Fredericton NB E3A 0A1
Chief Officer(s):
Debbie Christmas, Chair

AFOA British Columbia
#1010, 100 Park Royal, West Vancouver BC V7T 1A2
Tel: 604-925-6370; *Fax:* 604-925-6390
exec@afoabc.org
www.afoabc.org
www.facebook.com/afoabc
twitter.com/afoabc
Chief Officer(s):
Michael Mearns, General Manager
mmearns@afoabc.org

AFOA Manitoba
PO Box 137, Scanterbury MB R0E 1W0
info@afoamb.ca
www.afoamb.ca
Chief Officer(s):
Allan Munroe, President, 204-623-3423, Fax: 204-623-2882
amunroe@swampycree.com

AFOA Northwest Territories
PO Box 1698, Inuvik NT X0E 0T0
Tel: 867-777-2004
okpik@northwestel.net
Chief Officer(s):
Gloria Allen, President
gloria.allen@servicecanada.gc.ca

AFOA Ontario
313 Railway St., Timmins ON P4N 2P4
Tel: 705-268-9066
finance@wabun.on.ca
Chief Officer(s):
Darlene Lafontaine, President

AFOA Québec
221 Pitobig Mikan, Maniwaki QC J9E 3B1
Tel: 819-449-3460
AAFA-AFOA-QC@hotmail.com
Chief Officer(s):
Andre Richer, President

AFOA Saskatchewan
#117, 335 Packham Ave., Saskatoon SK S7N 4S1
Tel: 306-477-1066; *Fax:* 306-665-7577
afoa.sask@sasktel.net
www.afoask.ca
Chief Officer(s):
Eugene McKay, Executive Director

Africa Inland Mission International (Canada) (AIM) / Mission à l'intérieur de l'Afrique (Canada)
1641 Victoria Park Ave., Toronto ON M1R 1P8
Tel: 416-751-6077; *Fax:* 416-751-3467
Toll-Free: 877-407-6077
ca.aimint.org
www.facebook.com/aimcanada
twitter.com/aimcan
Also Known As: AIM Canada
Overview: A medium-sized international charitable organization founded in 1895
Mission: To evangelize within Eastern & Central Africa & Islands around India Ocean; To establish churches; To provide training leadership for those churches; To provide medical, educational, & agricultural services
Member of: Africa Inland Mission International, Bristol, England; Interdenominational Foreign Mission Association
Finances: *Annual Operating Budget:* $1.5 Million-$3 Million;
Funding Sources: Donations from churches & individuals
Staff Member(s): 8; 3 volunteer(s)
Membership: 135; *Committees:* Finance; Personnel; Projects

African & Caribbean Council on HIV/AIDS in Ontario (ACCHO)
20 Victoria St., 4th Fl., Toronto ON M5C 2N8
Tel: 416-977-9955; *Fax:* 416-977-7664
administration@accho.ca
www.accho.ca
www.facebook.com/ACCHOntario
twitter.com/ACCHOntario
www.youtube.com/ACCHOntario
Overview: A medium-sized provincial organization
Mission: To provide support & resources to members of the African, Caribbean & Black communities in Ontario who are affected by HIV/AIDS
Chief Officer(s):
Valérie Pierre-Pierre, Director, 416-977-9955 Ext. 292
v.pierrepierre@accho.ca

African & Caribbean Students' Network of Montréal
c/o Concordia Student Union, #H-711, 1455, boul de Maisonneuve ouest, Montréal QC H3G 1M8
Tel: 514-613-0125
acsion@acsionmontreal.org
www.acsmontreal.org
www.facebook.com/acsionnetwork
twitter.com/ACSioNNetwork
Also Known As: ACSioN Network; Réseau ACSioN
Overview: A small local organization
Mission: To form a more interconnected and self-determined union of Black student organizations, which collaborate to elevate the entire Black community beyond the highest standards of academic, economic, political, and cultural excellence.
Membership: *Member Profile:* Black student associations in Montréal Universities and Colleges.
Chief Officer(s):
Dwight Best, Chief Executive Coordinator

African Canadian Continuing Education Society (ACCES)
PO Box 44986, RPO Ocean Park, Surrey BC V4A 9L1
Tel: 604-688-4880
info@acceskenya.org
www.acceskenya.org
www.facebook.com/138185519562017
twitter.com/acceskenya
Overview: A medium-sized national organization founded in 1993
Mission: To help young Africans obtain the skills & education needed to benefit themselves & their society.
Finances: *Funding Sources:* Private & corporate donations
Chief Officer(s):
Donna Van Sant, President

African Canadian Heritage Association (ACHA)
PO Box 99576, 1095 O'Connor Dr., Toronto ON M4B 3M9
Tel: 416-208-3149
acha@achaonline.org
www.achaonline.org
Overview: A small local organization founded in 1969
Mission: African Heritage and language program for families with children aged 5-16; provides history lessons about African people in Canada; special events include Black History Challenge, Entrepreneurs' Day, Kwanzaa Open House.
Member of: African Canadian Social Development Council
Activities: Parent Committee seminars & workshops
Chief Officer(s):
Cushnie Carole, President

African Canadian Social Development Council (ACSDC)
#107B, 2238 Dundas St. West, Toronto ON M6R 3A9

Tel: 647-352-5775
www.acsdc.net
www.facebook.com/AfricanCanadianSDC
twitter.com/acsdc_1
Overview: A small national organization
Mission: To promote social, economic & cultural development within the continental African community in Canada
Member of: Alternative Planning Group
Membership: 74 member organizations; *Fees:* Free; *Committees:* Executive; Finance; Seniors' Group; Management & Administration
Activities: Collaboration with community members & stakeholders; developing programs to support member agencies; research & advocacy
Chief Officer(s):
Kayode (Kay) Alabi, Executive Director/CEO
kayalabi@acsdc.net

African Community Health Services
#207, 110 Spadina Ave., Toronto ON M5V 2K4
Tel: 416-591-7600
Overview: A small local organization
Mission: To offer health & social support services to African immigrants & African Canadians
Activities: Providing services in Amharic, Ibo, Somali, Trigrinya, & Twi, as well as English and French, & will attempt to arrange translators for other African languages

African Enterprise (Canada) (AE)
4509 West 11th Ave., Vancouver BC V6R 2M5
Tel: 604-228-0930
admin@africanenterprise.ca
www.africanenterprise.com/en/canada
www.facebook.com/AEMissions
twitter.com/AEinternational
www.youtube.com/user/AfricanEnterprise62
Also Known As: AE Canada
Overview: A small national charitable organization founded in 1965
Mission: To service & expand an active partnership among Canadian Christians to raise prayer, financial, material & human resources to enable AE to achieve its mission: to evangelise the cities of Africa through word & deed in partnership with the church
Affiliation(s): AE International
Staff Member(s): 2
Activities: *Internships:* Yes; *Speaker Service:* Yes
Chief Officer(s):
David Richardson, Executive Director & CEO

African Legacy
Dawson College, 3040, rue Sherbrooke ouest, Montréal QC H3Z 1A4
Tel: 514-931-8731; *Fax:* 514-931-1864
african.legacy@mydsu.ca
Overview: A small local organization
Mission: To serve the social, cultural, & educational needs of the African diaspora both within the Canadian mosaic & in the larger global context

African Medical & Research Foundation Canada (AMREF Canada)
#403, 489 College St., Toronto ON M6G 1A5
Tel: 416-961-6981; *Fax:* 416-961-6984
Toll-Free: 888-318-4442
info@amrefcanada.org
www.amrefcanada.org
www.facebook.com/amrefcanada
twitter.com/amrefcanada
www.youtube.com/amrefcanada
Also Known As: Flying Doctors
Overview: A medium-sized international charitable organization founded in 1957
Mission: Development agency working to enhance community health in East & Southern Africa; headquartered in Nairobi, Kenya; eleven national offices in both Europe & America; acts as support office in raising private & public funds for overseas health programs & also plays active role in maintaining working relations with Canadian International Development Agency (CIDA)
Member of: Canadian Council for International Cooperation
Affiliation(s): African Medical & Research Foundations Nairobi; Canadian Centre for Philanthropy; Ontario Council for International Cooperation; Canadian Council for International Cooperation; Canadian Society of International Health
Finances: *Funding Sources:* CIDA; private donations; foundations
Activities: Runs variety of innovative projects which emphasize effective, low-cost health care for rural communities; East African Flying Doctors' Service airlifts medical supplies & services to isolated communities; fundraising & awareness events in Canada to support AMREF projects in Africa; *Awareness Events:* Annual African Marketplace; *Rents Mailing List:* Yes; *Library:* Open to public by appointment
Chief Officer(s):
Anne-Marie Kamanye, Executive Director

African Nova Scotian Music Association (ANSMA)
10 Cherry Brook Rd., Halifax NS B2Z 1A6
Tel: 902-404-3036; *Fax:* 902-434-0462
ansma@eastlink.ca
www.ansma.com
www.facebook.com/AfricanNovaScotianMusicAssociationANSMA
twitter.com/ANSMA1
Overview: A medium-sized provincial organization founded in 1997
Mission: To develop, promote & enhance African Nova Scotia music locally, nationally & internationally
Membership: 131 artist, 10 industry
Chief Officer(s):
Louis (Lou) Gannon Jr., President

African Students Association - Univeristy of Alberta (AFSA)
c/o Student Group Services Office, Students' Union Bldg., Univ. of Alb, #040A, 8900 - 114 St. NW, Edmonton AB
Tel: 780-915-8151
Afsa09@ualberta.ca
sites.ualberta.ca/~afsu
www.facebook.com/AfricanStudentsAssociationUOfA
twitter.com/AFSAUAlberta
Overview: A small local organization
Mission: A student group that provides an engaging forum for all students of African descent and all those interested in issues of African concern in Edmonton.
Chief Officer(s):
Isaac Odoom, President
Meetings/Conferences:
• University of Alberta African Students' Association 2018 Conference, 2018
Scope: Local

African Students Association of Concordia (ASAC)
K Annex, Concordia University, #K-201, 2150, rue Bishop, Montréal QC H3G 2E9
Tel: 514-848-2424
asac@asac.concordia.ca
asac.concordia.ca
www.facebook.com/asacconcordia
twitter.com/asacconcordia
instagram.com/asacconcordia
Overview: A small local organization
Mission: To represent the students of African descent at Concordia University; To facilitate the social networking of African students; To promote African culture & awareness at Concordia University & in the greater Montreal community
Member of: African & Caribbean Students' Network of Montreal
Chief Officer(s):
Sokhna Fatim Niang, President

African Violet Society of Canada
c/o 349 Hyman Dr., Dollard-des-Ormeaux QC H9B 1L5
other@avsc.ca
www.avsc.ca
Overview: A small national organization
Membership: 400+; *Fees:* $15 annual
Chief Officer(s):
Paul F. Kroll, President
Publications:
• Chatter
Type: Magazine; *Frequency:* Quarterly

Africans in Partnership Against AIDS (APAA)
526 Richmond St. East, 2nd Fl, Toronto ON M5A 1R3
Tel: 416-924-5256; *Fax:* 416-924-6575
info@apaa.ca
www.apaa.ca
www.facebook.com/162063662030
Overview: A small international charitable organization founded in 1993 overseen by Canadian AIDS Society
Mission: To create a stable organization & community response to the impact of HIV/AIDS through capacity development, partnership, growth, & community development & involvement.
Member of: Ontario AIDS Network; Canadian AIDS Society; African Canadian Social Development Council
Finances: *Funding Sources:* City of Toronto Department of Public Health, donations
Staff Member(s): 10
Membership: *Member Profile:* Community-based organization to respond to the increased need for linguistically & culturally appropriate services & support for Africans living with HIV/AIDS.
Activities: Emotional support, counselling & advice on testing, treatment, nutrition; advice & help arranging palliative care; *Library:* Open to public
Chief Officer(s):
Fanta Ongoiba, Executive Director
Publications:
• Kibaru
Type: Newsletter; *Frequency:* Quarterly

Afro-Canadian Caribbean Association of Hamilton & District Inc. (ACCA)
423 King St. East, Hamilton ON L8N 1C5
Tel: 905-385-0925; *Fax:* 905-385-4914
acca@cogeco.net
accahamilton.ca
Overview: A small local organization founded in 1979
Mission: To provide a vehicle for bringing together the Afro-Canadian Caribbean people residing in Hamilton & District
100 volunteer(s)
Membership: 500 individual; *Fees:* $25 individual; $35 family; $12.50 student/senior; *Committees:* Youth; Education; Cultural Arts; *Membership:* Social; Finance; Walkathon; Spelling Bee
Chief Officer(s):
Elvis Foster, President

Afro-Caribbean Cultural Association of Saskatchewan Inc.
307 Ave. H North, Saskatoon SK S7K 4J1
Overview: A small provincial organization

AFS Interculture Canada (AFSIC)
#1100, 1425, boul René-Lévesque ouest, Montréal QC H3G 1T7
Tel: 514-282-2224; *Fax:* 514-843-9119
Toll-Free: 800-361-7248
info-canada@afs.org
www.afscanada.org
www.facebook.com/afsinterculturecanada
twitter.com/afscanada
www.pinterest.com/afscanada
Also Known As: Interculture Canada
Previous Name: AFS Programs Canada
Overview: A large international charitable organization founded in 1978
Mission: To promote global education & international development through intercultural exchange programs for both young people & adults; To offer international internships; To work as part of the largest network of international exchange programs in the world
Member of: AFS Intercultural Programs
Affiliation(s): United Nations
Finances: *Annual Operating Budget:* $3 Million-$5 Million; *Funding Sources:* Parents; Participants; Sponsors
Staff Member(s): 5; 500 volunteer(s)
Membership: 30,000 individuals in over 50 countries
Activities: Providing intercultural learning opportunities through high school & adult programs; *Internships:* Yes
Chief Officer(s):
Anisara Creary, National Director
anisara.creary@afs.org
Awards:
• Intercultural Program Grants
Offered to help students participate in intercultural programs; *Amount:* $1,500 - $5,000

AFS Programs Canada See AFS Interculture Canada

Ag Energy Co-operative
#2, 45 Speedvale Ave. East, Guelph ON N1H 1J2
Tel: 519-763-3026; *Fax:* 519-763-5231
Toll-Free: 866-818-8828
www.fireflyenergy.ca
Overview: A small local organization founded in 1988
Mission: To offer energy products & services to its members
Membership: *Fees:* $100; *Member Profile:* Agricultural producers & processors
Chief Officer(s):
Rose Gage, Chief Executive Officer

Aga Khan Foundation Canada (AKFC)
The Delegation of the Ismaili Imamat, 199 Sussex Dr., Ottawa ON K1N 1K6
Tel: 613-237-2532; *Fax:* 613-567-2532
Toll-Free: 800-267-2532
info@akfc.ca
www.akfc.ca
Overview: A medium-sized international charitable organization founded in 1980
Mission: To support cost-effective development projects in Asia & Africa in the fields of primary health care, education & rural development, with special attention paid to the needs of women. Major initiatives include: The Pakistan-Canada Social Institutions Development Program; the Tajikistan Institutional Support Program and the Non-Formal Education Program of the Bangladesh Rural Advancement Committee.
Staff Member(s): 65
Chief Officer(s):
Khalil Z. Shariff, CEO
Awards:
• Fellowship in International Development Management Program Postgraduate studies in the area of International Development
Deadline: February; *Amount:* Dependent on application

Agape Food Bank
c/o Agape Centre, 40 - 5th St., Cornwall ON K6J 2T4
Tel: 613-938-9297
info@agapecentre.ca
www.agapecentre.ca
Overview: A small local charitable organization founded in 1971
Mission: To collect & distribute surplus & donated food for the needy
Member of: Ontario Association of Food Banks
Finances: *Funding Sources:* Donations from events (concerts, marathons, food drives)
Staff Member(s): 2; 20 volunteer(s)
Activities: Food bank; soup kitchen; thrift shop
Chief Officer(s):
Johanne Gauthier, Operations Manager

Agassiz-Harrison Community Services
#7, 7086 Pioneer Ave., Agassiz BC V0M 1A0
Tel: 604-796-2585; *Fax:* 604-796-2517
Overview: A small local organization overseen by Food Banks British Columbia
Mission: A registered, non-profit, multi-service agency that provides over 20 different services and programs to the community, including: Food Bank, Thrift Store, Big Brothers & Big Sisters, Youth Centre, English as a Second Language Settlement Assistance Program.
Member of: Food Banks British Columbia; Food Banks Canada

Age & Opportunity Inc.
#200, 280 Smith St., Winnipeg MB R3C 1K2
Tel: 204-956-6440; *Fax:* 204-946-5667
info@ageopportunity.mb.ca
www.ageopportunity.mb.ca
Overview: A small provincial organization founded in 1957
Mission: Age & Opportunity Inc. is a not-for-profit, social service agency that offers services and programs to adults aged 55+, living in Manitoba. Services include: legal counselling, housing consultation, therapy dog pairing, crime preventation, settlement & orientation sessions for older immigrants. Programs are numerous, including: language lessons, fitness sessions, arts & crafts, social events.
Chief Officer(s):
Macrae Amanda, CEO

Agence canadienne de l'ISBN *See* Canadian ISBN Agency

Agence canadienne des droits de production musicaux limitée *See* Canadian Musical Reproduction Rights Agency

Agence canadienne des médicaments et des technologies de la santé *See* Canadian Agency for Drugs & Technologies in Health

Agence municipale de financement et de développement des centres d'urgence 9-1-1 du Québec / Municipal finance & development agency for emergency 9-1-1 call centres in Quebec
#300, 2954, boul Laurier, Québec QC G1V 4T2
Tél: 418-653-3911; *Téléc:* 418-653-6198
Ligne sans frais: 888-653-3911
info@agence911.org
www.agence911.org
Aperçu: *Dimension:* moyenne; *Envergure:* provinciale; fondée en 2009
Mission: Pour collecter les recettes fiscales et les répartir entre les centres d'urgence 9-1-1
Membre de: Nena; ACUQ
Affiliation(s): Fédération Québécoise des Municipalités; Union des municipalités du Québec; Ville de Montréal; Ministère des affaires municipales, des régions et de l'occupation du territoire
Membre: 3
Activités: *Service de conférenciers:* Oui
Membre(s) du bureau directeur:
Jean-Marc Gibeau, Président
president@agence911.org
Serge Allen, Directeur général
sallen@agence911.org

Agence universitaire de la Francophonie (AUF)
CP 49714, Succ. Musée, 3034, boul Edouard-Montpetit, Montréal QC H3T 1J7
Tél: 514-343-6630; *Téléc:* 514-343-5783
recorat@auf.org
www.auf.org
www.facebook.com/profile.php?id=1691871982
twitter.com/planeteauf
www.youtube.com/planeteauf
Nom précédent: Association des universités partiellement ou entièrement de langue française
Aperçu: *Dimension:* moyenne; *Envergure:* internationale; Organisme sans but lucratif; fondée en 1961
Mission: Le développement, au sein de l'espace francophone, d'une coopération internationale pour assurer à la fois le dialogue permanent des cultures et la circulation des personnes, des idées, des expériences entre institutions universitaires, dans l'intérêt de l'éducation et du progrès de la science
Finances: *Budget de fonctionnement annuel:* Plus de $5 Million
Membre(s) du personnel: 454
Membre: 710 institutionnel; *Critères d'admissibilite:* Universités; centres de recherche; écoles supérieures
Activités: *Evénements de sensibilisation:* Semaine de la francophonie
Membre(s) du bureau directeur:
Bernard Cerquiglini, Recteur

Aggregate Producers Association of BC *See* British Columbia Stone, Sand & Gravel Association

Aggregate Producers' Association of Ontario *See* Ontario Stone, Sand & Gravel Association

Agincourt Community Services Association (ACSA)
#100, 4155 Sheppard Ave. East, Toronto ON M1S 1T4
Tel: 416-321-6912; *Fax:* 416-321-6922
info@agincourtcommunityservices.com
www.agincourtcommunityservices.com
www.linkedin.com/company/agincourt-community-services-association
www.facebook.com/AgincourtCommunityServices
twitter.com/AginComServices
Previous Name: Information Agincourt; Information Scarborough
Overview: A small local charitable organization founded in 1970 overseen by InformOntario
Mission: A charitable, multi-service neighbourhood agency that exists to identify & provide services, information & programs in response to the diverse needs & interest of the multicultural community; strives to improve the quality of life for individuals & families by mobilizing volunteers, providing links & partnerships between those who wish to help & those who need services
1324 volunteer(s)
Membership: *Fees:* $5
Activities: Information & referral; emergency food; free income tax clinic; free legal counselling; parent & child program; agency luncheons; job bank; Metro Voice Mail Project; Homeless Drop-In; Housing Connections Access Centre; C.A.P.; shower & laundry facilites; babysitting registry; doctor & dentist listing; volunteer drivers for seniors to medical appointments; food security program; lockers; good food box; cooking clubs; community gardens; *Speaker Service:* Yes
Chief Officer(s):
Vinitha Gengatharan, Chairperson

Agincourt Community Services Association (ACSA)
#100, 4155 Sheppard Ave. East, Toronto ON M1S 1T4
Tel: 416-321-6912; *Fax:* 416-321-6922
info@agincourtcommunityservices.com
www.agincourtcommunityservices.com
www.linkedin.com/company/agincourt-community-services-association
www.facebook.com/AgincourtCommunityServices
twitter.com/AginComServices
Overview: A medium-sized local organization founded in 1970
Mission: To address a variety of issues including systemic poverty, hunger, housing, homelessness, unemployment, accessibility and social isolation in the Scarborough community.
Finances: *Funding Sources:* United Way, Government, Donations
1324 volunteer(s)
Membership: *Fees:* $5
Chief Officer(s):
Lee Soda, Executive Director
Vinitha Gengatharan, Chair

Agrément Canada *See* Accreditation Canada

Agrément de l'enseignement de la physiothérapie au Canada *See* Physiotherapy Education Accreditation Canada

Agricultural Adaptation Council (AAC)
Ontario ArgriCentre, #103, 100 Stone Rd. West, Guelph ON N1G 5L3
Tel: 519-822-7554; *Fax:* 519-822-6248
info@adaptcouncil.org
www.adaptcouncil.org
twitter.com/adaptcouncil
www.youtube.com/user/adaptcouncil
Overview: A small provincial organization founded in 1995
Mission: To provide funding to its members so that they may grow their business
Staff Member(s): 11
Membership: 67; *Fees:* $150; *Member Profile:* Agricultural, agri-food & rural organizations
Chief Officer(s):
Terry Thompson, Executive Director
tthompson@adaptcouncil.org

Agricultural Alliance of New Brunswick (AANB) / Alliance agricole du Nouveau-Brunswick
#303, 259 Brunswick St., Fredericton NB E3B 1G8
Tel: 506-452-8101; *Fax:* 506-452-1085
alliance@fermenbfarm.ca
www.fermenbfarm.ca
Previous Name: New Brunswick Federation of Agriculture
Overview: A medium-sized provincial charitable organization founded in 1876 overseen by Canadian Federation of Agriculture
Mission: To promote & advance the social & economic conditions of those engaged in agricultural pursuits; to formulate & promote agricultural policies to meet changing economic conditions
Member of: Atlantic Farmers Council
Finances: *Annual Operating Budget:* $100,000-$250,000; *Funding Sources:* Membership fees
Staff Member(s): 3; 12 volunteer(s)
Membership: 1,200 individual; *Fees:* $150-500; *Member Profile:* Farmers maintaining specified level of specific commodity; *Committees:* Training; Sustainable Agriculture; Farm Safety; Farm Finance
Activities: *Speaker Service:* Yes; *Library*
Chief Officer(s):
Nicole Arseneau, Office Manager
Mélanie Godin, Coordinator, Environmental Farm Plan

Agricultural Institute of Canada (AIC) / Institut agricole du Canada
#320, 176 Gloucester St., Ottawa ON K2P 0A6
Tel: 613-232-9459; *Fax:* 613-594-5190
office@aic.ca
www.aic.ca
twitter.com/aginstitute
Overview: A large national organization founded in 1920
Mission: To provide the voice for national knowledge & expertise; To promote the creation, production, & delivery of safe foods & sustainable use of related national resources in Canada & beyond
Affiliation(s): Canadian Agricultural Economics; Canadian Consulting Agrologists' Association; Canadian Society of Agronomy; Canadian Society of Animal Science; Canadian Society for Horticultural Science; Canadian Society of Soil Science; Canadian Society of Agrometeorology; British Columbia Institute of Agrologists; Alberta Institute of Agrologists; Saskatchewan Institute of Agrologists; Manitoba Institute of Agrologists; Ontario Institute of Agrologists; New Brunswick Institute of Agrologists; Nova Scotia Institute of Agrologists; PEI Institute of Agrologists; Newfoundland/Labrador Institute of Agrologists

Finances: *Annual Operating Budget:* $100,000-$250,000; *Funding Sources:* Membership fees
Staff Member(s): 5
Membership: 14; *Fees:* Schedule available
Chief Officer(s):
Serge Buy, Chief Executive Officer
sbuy@aic.ca
Gabriele Leguerrier, Manager, Finance, 613-232-9459 Ext. 306
gleguerrier@aic.ca
Awards:
• International Recognition Award, Individual
• International Recognition Award, Organization
• AIC Fellowship
• Sustainable Futures Award
Meetings/Conferences:
• Agricultural Institute of Canada 2018 Conference, April, 2018, Guelph, ON
Scope: National
Description: Theme: "Education in Agricultural Sciences & Technology - Ready for the Future?"
Publications:
• AIC [Agricultural Institute of Canada] Monthly Report
Type: Newsletter; *Frequency:* Monthly
• GEM (Gender Equality Mainstreaming) Digest [a publication of the Agricultural Institute of Canada]
Type: Newsletter; *Frequency:* Monthly

Agricultural Institute of Canada Foundation (AICF)
#233, 300 Earl Grey Dr., Ottawa ON K2T 1C1
www.aicfoundation.ca
Overview: A large national charitable organization founded in 1987
Mission: To enhance agriculture & the role it plays in providing Canadians with a safe, affordable, nutritious food supply
Affiliation(s): Agricultural Institute of Canada
Finances: *Annual Operating Budget:* Less than $50,000; *Funding Sources:* Personal donations; Corporate sponsorship
Staff Member(s): 1
Chief Officer(s):
Frances Rodenburg, General Manager
manager@aicfoundation.ca
Publications:
• Agricultural Institute of Canada Foundation Annual Report
Type: Report; *Frequency:* Annually

Agricultural Manufacturers of Canada (AMC)
Evraz Place, Stockman's Arena, PO Box 636, Stn. Main, Regina SK S4P 3A3
Tel: 306-522-2710; *Fax:* 306-781-7293
admin@a-m-c.ca
www.a-m-c.ca
Previous Name: Prairie Implement Manufacturers Association; PIMA - Agricultural Manufacturers of Canada
Overview: A medium-sized local licensing charitable organization founded in 1970
Mission: To foster & promote the growth & development of the agricultural equipment manufacturing industry in Canada; To encourage governments to enact legislation & offer programs that enhance the growth potential of the industry; To provide a forum for members to exchange ideas & discuss their industry as it relates to the national & international economy
Finances: *Annual Operating Budget:* $250,000-$500,000; *Funding Sources:* Membership fees; special projects
Staff Member(s): 9
Membership: 200 regular + 5 affiliate + 300 associate; *Fees:* Schedule available; *Member Profile:* Regular - manufacturer of farm & ranch equipment; associate - supplier of goods & services; *Committees:* Alberta Provincial; Saskatchewan Provincial; Manitoba Provincial; Ontario Provincial
Chief Officer(s):
Leah Olson, President
Ty Hamil, Executive Assistant
April Jackman, Manager, Marketing & Communications
Meetings/Conferences:
• 48th Annual Agricultural Manufacturers of Canada Convention & Trade Show, 2018

Agricultural Research & Extension Council of Alberta (ARECA)
#2, 5304 - 50 St., Ludec AB T9E 6Z6
Tel: 780-612-9712; *Fax:* 780-612-9711
www.areca.ab.ca
www.facebook.com/132819060066672
twitter.com/ARECAresearch
Overview: A medium-sized provincial organization

Mission: To provide agricultural producers with access to field research & new technology, in order to enhance & improve their operations
Finances: *Funding Sources:* Government; Sponsors
Membership: 9 associations
Chief Officer(s):
Janette McDonald, Executive Director
Publications:
• ARECA [Agricultural Research & Extension Council of Alberta] E-Newsletter
Type: Newsletter; *Frequency:* Monthly

Agricultural Technologists Association Inc. *Voir* Association des technologues en agroalimentaire

Agriculture Union / Syndicat Agriculture
#1000, 233 Gilmour St., Ottawa ON K2P 0P2
Tel: 613-560-4306; *Fax:* 613-235-0517
agrunion@psac-afpc.com
www.agrunion.com
Overview: A medium-sized national organization overseen by Public Service Alliance of Canada
Mission: To advance the workplace interests of its membership; To fight for a society that recognizes the value of the important public services provided by Agriculture Union members
Membership: 8,000+; *Member Profile:* Members of the public health, sustainable agriculture & secure food chain industries; *Committees:* Bylaws & Education; Collective Bargaining & Health & Safety; Finance & Communications; General; Agriculture Union Social Justice Fund
Chief Officer(s):
Bob Kingston, National President, 613-560-4306, Fax: 613-235-0517
kingstb@psac-afpc.com

Agrienergy Producers' Association of Ontario *See* Canadian Biogas Association

Agri-Food Export Group Québec - Canada *Voir* Groupe export agroalimentaire Québec - Canada

AgriVenture Global Ltd
Lake Lenore SK S0K 2J0
Tel: 306-598-4415; *Fax:* 306-598-4416
canada@agriventure.com
www.facebook.com/agriventureglobal
Previous Name: AgriVenture International Rural Placements; International Agricultural Exchange Association
Overview: A small international organization
Mission: To administer agricultural exchange for young people
Staff Member(s): 250
Membership: 5,000 in 14 countries

AgriVenture International Rural Placements; International Agricultural Exchange Association *See* AgriVenture Global Ltd

Aguasabon Chamber of Commerce
PO Box 40, 1 Selkirk Ave., Terrace Bay ON P0T 2W0
Tel: 807-825-3315
bdi@terracebay.ca
www.asuperiorchamber.com
www.facebook.com/aguasabonchamber
Overview: A small local organization
Mission: To represent businesses in the community
Member of: Northwestern Ontario Associated Chambers of Commerce
Finances: *Annual Operating Budget:* Less than $50,000; *Funding Sources:* Membership fees
13 volunteer(s)
Membership: 35; *Committees:* Tourism
Activities: Organizing & promoting events, including Curling Bonspeil, golf tournaments, & regional trade shows; *Library:* Open to public by appointment
Chief Officer(s):
Sylvie LeBlanc, President

Ahmadiyya Muslim Jama'at Canada
10610 Jane St., Maple ON L6A 3A2
Tel: 905-303-4000; *Fax:* 905-832-3220
info@ahmadiyya.ca
www.ahmadiyya.ca
www.facebook.com/AhmadiyyaMuslim
twitter.com/@AhmadiyyaCanada
www.youtube.com/channel/UCXxEbBjwR1CZE8ir4po34Rw
Also Known As: Ahmadiyya Muslim Community Canada
Overview: A medium-sized national charitable organization

Mission: To promote interfaith understanding
Affiliation(s): The Ahmadiyya Muslim Medical Association of Canada (AMMAC)
Finances: *Annual Operating Budget:* Greater than $5 Million
Staff Member(s): 30; 1,00 volunteer(s)
Activities: Offering religious education; Muslim TV (www.mta.tv); *Internships:* Yes; *Speaker Service:* Yes; *Library:* Ahmadiyya Muslim Jamaat Canada Library; Open to public by appointment
Chief Officer(s):
Lal Khan Malik, President
Abdul Aziz Khalifa, Vice-President
Aslam Daud, Secretary
Khalid Naeem, Treasurer
Rana Manzoor Ahmed, Librarian, 905-832-2669 Ext. 2245
Awards:
• Sir Muhammad Zafrulla Khan Award
Meetings/Conferences:
• Ahmadiyya Muslim Jama'at Canada 2018 42nd Annual Convention, July, 2018, International Center, Mississauga, ON
Scope: National
Description: A Muslim convention, featuring religious addresses & the presentation of awards
Publications:
• Ahmadiyya Gazette Canada
Type: Magazine; *Frequency:* Monthly; *Accepts Advertising*; *Editor:* Chaudhary Hadi Ali sahib; *Price:* Free
Profile: Educational material about Islam, summaries of sermons or addresses, announcements & news about the organization

Aide à l'enfance - Canada *See* Save the Children Canada

Aide aux aînés Canada *See* HelpAge Canada

Aide aux personnes âgées en résidence à Laval inc *Voir* Association pour aînés résidant à Laval

Aide juridique Ontario *See* Legal Aid Ontario

AIDS Action Now / Le groupe d'action sida
Toronto ON
aidsactionnowtoronto@gmail.com
www.aidsactionnow.org
www.facebook.com/AidsActionNow
twitter.com/AIDSActionNow
vimeo.com/channels/152729
Overview: A small local organization founded in 1989 overseen by Canadian AIDS Society
Mission: To fight for improved treatment, care & support for people living with AIDS & HIV infection
Finances: *Funding Sources:* Donations
Activities: Advocacy programme, consultation services

AIDS Calgary Awareness Association *See* HIV Community Link

AIDS Coalition of Cape Breton (ACCB)
150 Bentinck St., Sydney NS B1P 4W4
Tel: 902-567-1766
accb.ns.ca
www.facebook.com/CB.4.harmreduction
Overview: A small local organization founded in 1991 overseen by Canadian AIDS Society
Staff Member(s): 9
Activities: Anonymous testing; drop-in centre; PHA support; public education; safer sex supplies; needle exchange; Queer Youth Matter; Trans Support Group; *Library:* AIDS Coalition of Cape Breton Resource Centre; Open to public
Chief Officer(s):
Christine Porter, Executive Director
christine.porter@bellaliant.com
Frances Macleod, SANE Project Coordinator
frances.macleod@bellaliant.com

AIDS Coalition of Nova Scotia (ACNS)
#200, 5516 Spring Garden Rd., Halifax NS B3J 1G6
Tel: 902-429-7922; *Fax:* 902-422-6200
Toll-Free: 800-566-2437
Other Communication: Alternate Phone: 902-425-4882
acns.ns.ca
www.facebook.com/AIDSNS
twitter.com/AIDS_NS
Previous Name: Nova Scotia PWA Coalition
Overview: A small provincial charitable organization founded in 1995 overseen by Canadian AIDS Society
Mission: To empower persons living with & affected by HIV/AIDS & those at risk through health promotion & mutual support & to reduce the spread of HIV in Nova Scotia

Canadian Associations / AIDS Committee of Cambridge, Kitchener/Waterloo & Area (ACCKWA)

Member of: Canadian AIDS Society; Canadian HIV/AIDS Legal Network
Finances: *Annual Operating Budget:* $250,000-$500,000
Staff Member(s): 4; 120 volunteer(s)
Membership: 200; *Member Profile:* Full - HIV positive or living with AIDS; associate - supportive of aims & objectives of organization
Activities: Advocacy; anonymous HIV testing clinic; Complimentary & Alternative Therapies (CATS) Program; Haircuts for Health; health fund; hospital tv/telephone services; PHA drop-in; referrals; treatment information; Positive Connections Project; *Awareness Events:* AIDS Awareness Week; World AIDS Day; *Library:* Open to public
Chief Officer(s):
Michelle Johnson, Coordinator, Programs, 902-425-4882 Ext. 226
pc@acns.ns.ca

AIDS Committee of Cambridge, Kitchener/Waterloo & Area (ACCKWA)
#203, 639 King St. West, Kitchener ON N2G 1C7
Tel: 519-570-3687; *Fax:* 519-570-4034
Toll-Free: 877-770-3687
www.acckwa.com
www.facebook.com/ACCKWA
twitter.com/AIDSCKW
Overview: A small local charitable organization founded in 1987
Mission: To provide support & education services for people affected by & infected with HIV/AIDS; To mobilize community to respond effectively & with compassion to individuals affected by HIV/AIDS; To advocate on behalf of people infected or affected by HIV
Member of: Canadian Public Health Association
Affiliation(s): Ontario AIDS Network; Canadian AIDS Society
Finances: *Funding Sources:* Ontario Ministry of Health; United Way; fundraising
Activities: Providing counselling either in person or by phone for people living with HIV/AIDS; Giving referrals to housing, medical, nutrition, financial & treatment services; Offering buddy & practical care services for the partners, families & friends of people living with HIV/AIDS; Providing speakers, presentations, & displays; *Awareness Events:* AIDS Awareness Week, Nov.; World AIDS Day, Dec. 1; *Speaker Service:* Yes; *Library:* Open to public
Chief Officer(s):
Ruth Cameron, Executive Director
director@acckwa.com

AIDS Committee of Durham Region (ACDR)
#202, 22 King St. West, Oshawa ON L1H 1A3
Tel: 905-576-1445; *Fax:* 905-576-4610
Toll-Free: 877-361-8750
info@aidsdurham.com
www.aidsdurham.com
www.facebook.com/AIDSDurham
twitter.com/AIDSDurham
Overview: A small local charitable organization founded in 1992 overseen by Canadian AIDS Society
Mission: To provide HIV/AIDS related services to the infected, affected & general community in the Region of Durham
Member of: Ontario AIDS Network
Affiliation(s): Interagency Coalition on AIDS & Development; Canadian AIDS Treatment Information Exchange; Canadian HIV/AIDS Legal Network; Community Networks; Community Advisory Committee; Local Planning & Coordinating Group; Feed The Need in Durham; African & Caribbean Council on HIV/AIDS in Ontario
Finances: *Funding Sources:* Ministry of Health; Health Canada; private
Staff Member(s): 10
Membership: *Fees:* $5 current; $10 new
Activities: Support groups; workshops; individual counselling; prevention education; street program; *Awareness Events:* AIDS Walk; *Speaker Service:* Yes; *Library:* Open to public
Chief Officer(s):
Margaret McCormack, President
Adrian Betts, Executive Director, 905-576-1445 Ext. 11
director@aidsdurham.com

AIDS Committee of Guelph & Wellington County *See* HIV/AIDS Resources and Community Health

AIDS Committee of London *See* Regional HIV/AIDS Connection

AIDS Committee of Newfoundland & Labrador (ACNL)
47 Janeway Pl., St. John's NL A1A 1R7
Tel: 709-579-8656; *Fax:* 709-579-0559
Toll-Free: 800-563-1575
www.acnl.net
www.facebook.com/AIDSCommitteeNL
twitter.com/aidscommitteenl
Previous Name: Newfoundland & Labrador AIDS Committee
Overview: A medium-sized provincial charitable organization founded in 1988 overseen by Canadian AIDS Society
Mission: To prevent new HIV infections through education; to provide support to persons living with HIV/AIDS & their families, friends & partners
Member of: Atlantic AIDS Network
Staff Member(s): 6
Membership: *Member Profile:* Volunteers
Activities: *Awareness Events:* Aids Awareness Week; World Aids Day; AIDS Walk; *Library:* Open to public
Chief Officer(s):
Gerard Yetman, Executive Director

AIDS Committee of North Bay & Area (ACNBA) / Comité du sida de North Bay et de la région
#201, 269 Main St. West, North Bay ON P1B 2T8
Tel: 705-497-3560; *Fax:* 705-497-7850
Toll-Free: 800-387-3701
oaacnba@gmail.com
www.aidsnorthbay.com
www.facebook.com/aidscommitteenorthbay
twitter.com/ACNBA
Overview: A small local organization founded in 1990 overseen by Canadian AIDS Society
Mission: To assist & support all those affected & infected by HIV/AIDS; To limit the spread of the virus through education & awareness strategies
Member of: Ontario AIDS Network
Affiliation(s): Chamber of Commerce Downtown Inprovement Area
Finances: *Funding Sources:* Ontario Ministry of Health; Health Canada
Staff Member(s): 11
Membership: *Committees:* Nipissing District Homelessness; Community Abuse Advisory; Northern Points Advisory; ACNBA Party Planner; Women on the Inside; Provincial Harm Reduction Advisory; Mattawa Cares
Activities: Support groups; one-on-one counselling; safer sex & info phone line; needle exchange; prevention services; bingo nights; *Awareness Events:* AIDS Awareness Week; Krispy Kreme Doughnuts Day, June; Paint the Town Red Gala, Nov.; *Speaker Service:* Yes; *Library*
Chief Officer(s):
Stacey L. Mayhill, Executive Director
acnbaed@gmail.com

AIDS Committee of Ottawa (ACO) / Comité du SIDA d'Ottawa
19 Main St., Ottawa ON K1S 1A9
Tel: 613-238-5014; *Fax:* 613-238-3425
info@aco-cso.ca
www.aco-cso.ca
www.linkedin.com/company/1098145
www.facebook.com/acocso
twitter.com/ACOttawa
Overview: A small local charitable organization founded in 1985 overseen by Canadian AIDS Society
Mission: To fight AIDS & HIV infection through advocacy, education & support services
Member of: Ontario AIDS Network
Finances: *Funding Sources:* Provincial, federal & regional government; private; corporate
Staff Member(s): 16
Activities: Support Services; Drop In Centre; Education; *Awareness Events:* AIDS Walk Ottawa; *Speaker Service:* Yes; *Library:* Open to public
Chief Officer(s):
Khaled Salam, Executive Director, 613-238-5014 Ext. 234
ed@aco-cso.ca

AIDS Committee of Simcoe County (ACSC)
#555, 80 Bradford St., Barrie ON L4N 6S7
Tel: 705-722-6778; *Fax:* 705-722-6560
Toll-Free: 800-372-2272
www.acsc.ca
www.facebook.com/AIDSCommitteeofSimcoeCounty
twitter.com/acsc

Overview: A small local charitable organization overseen by Canadian AIDS Society
Mission: To provide support, education & advocacy to people infected & affected by HIV/AIDS in Simcoe County
Member of: The Canadian AIDS Society; The Ontario AIDS Network; The Greater Barrie Chamber of Commerce
Finances: *Funding Sources:* Ontario Ministry of Health; Health Canada; community; fundraising
Staff Member(s): 6
Membership: *Fees:* $20
Activities: *Speaker Service:* Yes
Chief Officer(s):
Gerry L. Croteau, Executive Director
ed@acsc.ca

AIDS Committee of Sudbury; Access AIDS Committee *See* Réseau ACCESS Network

AIDS Committee of Toronto (ACT)
399 Church St., 4th Fl., Toronto ON M5B 2J6
Tel: 416-340-2437; *Fax:* 416-340-8224
ask@actoronto.org
www.actoronto.org
www.facebook.com/ACToronto
twitter.com/ACToronto
www.youtube.com/user/AIDSCommitteeToronto
Overview: A medium-sized local charitable organization founded in 1983 overseen by Canadian AIDS Society
Mission: To provide health promotion, support, education & advocacy for people living with HIV/AIDS & those affected by HIV/AIDS
Member of: Ontario AIDS Network
Finances: *Funding Sources:* Private; Corporate; Government
Staff Member(s): 40
Membership: *Fees:* $5
Activities: Providing education & outreach to gay & bisexual men & at-risk women & youth; *Awareness Events:* AIDS Walk for Life Toronto; *Library:* Open to public
Chief Officer(s):
John Maxwell, Executive Director, 416-340-2437 Ext. 245
jmaxwell@actoronto.org
Winston Husbands, Director, Research, 416-340-2437 Ext. 454
Jason Patterson, Director, Development, 416-340-2437 Ext. 268
Don Phaneuf, Director, Employment Services, 416-340-2437 Ext. 262
Publications:
• Being Well: The PWA/ACT Wellness Newsletter

AIDS Committee of Windsor (ACW)
511 Pelissier St., Windsor ON N9A 4L2
Tel: 519-973-0222; *Fax:* 519-973-7389
Toll-Free: 800-265-4858
www.aidswindsor.org
www.facebook.com/aidswindsor
Overview: A small local charitable organization founded in 1985 overseen by Canadian AIDS Society
Mission: To mobilize communities to help people affected by HIV/AIDS in the Windsor-Essex & Chatham-Kent areas through advocacy, education & support
Member of: Ontario AIDS Network
Affiliation(s): AIDS Support Chatham Kent; Drouillard Road Clinic
Finances: *Funding Sources:* Federal, provincial, private
Staff Member(s): 14
Membership: *Committees:* Executive; Fund Development; Governance; Finance; Nominating & AGM; PHA Advisory; Gay Men's Sexual Health Program Advisory; Women & HIV Program Advisory; African Caribbean Black Strategy Program Advisory
Activities: Youth project; needle exchange program; safer sex outreach; support services; speakers' bureau; women's project; phoneline; methadone program; *Awareness Events:* AIDS Walk for Life, Sept.; *Speaker Service:* Yes; *Library:* Resource Library; Open to public
Chief Officer(s):
Michael Brennan, Executive Director
mbrennan@aidswindsor.org

> **AIDS Support Chatham-Kent**
> Adelaide Place, 67 Adelaide St. South, Chatham ON N7M 4R1
> *Tel:* 519-352-2121; *Fax:* 519-351-7067
> *Toll-Free:* 800-265-4858
> **Chief Officer(s):**
> Karyn O'Neil, Associate Director, Development
> koneil@aidswindsor.org

AIDS Committee of York Region
#203, 10909 Yonge St., Richmond Hill ON L4C 3E3
Tel: 905-884-0613; *Fax:* 905-884-7215
Toll-Free: 800-243-7717
info@acyr.org
www.acyr.org
www.facebook.com/AIDSCommitteeOfYorkRegion
twitter.com/outreachacyr
Overview: A small local organization
Mission: To provide support & education; To promote access to dignified care for people living with HIV/AIDS & those affected by HIV/AIDS
Chief Officer(s):
Vibhuti Mehra, Executive Director

The AIDS Foundation of Canada
#505, 744 West Hastings St., Vancouver BC V6C 1A5
Tel: 604-688-7294
www.aidsfoundationofcanada.ca
Overview: A medium-sized national organization founded in 1986
Mission: To address the growing problem of HIV disease in Canada; to fund new & innovative ways of assisting infected/affected people with HIV; to support new ways to heighten awareness of HIV disease among the general population
Finances: *Funding Sources:* Casinos; donations
Activities: AIDS/HIV educational services; *Speaker Service:* Yes

AIDS Jasper Society *See* HIV West Yellowhead Society

AIDS Moncton / SIDA Moncton
80 Weldon St., Moncton NB E1C 5V8
Tel: 506-859-9616; *Fax:* 506-855-4726
sidaidsm@nb.aibn.com
www.sida-aidsmoncton.com
twitter.com/AIDSMoncton
Overview: A small local charitable organization founded in 1989 overseen by Canadian AIDS Society
Mission: To improve the quality of life for persons infected & affected by HIV / AIDS; To reduce HIV & other sexually transmitted infections
Finances: *Funding Sources:* Fundraising; Donations
Staff Member(s): 4
Activities: Providing subsidized housing; Delivering a needle distribution service; Offering information & referrals about health promotion & treatment; Presenting prevention education sessions at local schools & other community organizations; Organizing informational displays; Accessing workshops; Training for peer education; Engaging in awareness campaigns; *Library:* AIDS Moncton Resource Library
Chief Officer(s):
Deborah Warren, Executive Director

AIDS Network of Edmonton Society *See* HIV Network of Edmonton Society

AIDS Network, Outreach & Support Society *See* ANKORS

AIDS New Brunswick / Sida Nouveau Brunswick
#G17, 65 Brunswick St., Fredericton NB E3B 1G5
Fax: 888-501-6301
Toll-Free: 800-561-4009
info@aidsnb.com
www.aidsnb.com
www.linkedin.com/company/aids-nb
www.facebook.com/aidsnb
twitter.com/aidsnb
www.youtube.com/aidsnb
Overview: A small provincial charitable organization founded in 1987
Mission: To facilitate community-based responses to the issue of HIV/AIDS
Member of: Canadian AIDS Society
Affiliation(s): Atlantic AIDS Network
Finances: *Annual Operating Budget:* $250,000-$500,000; *Funding Sources:* Federal government; private donations
Staff Member(s): 5
Activities: *Awareness Events:* AIDS Awareness Week; World AIDS Day; Candlelight Memorial; *Speaker Service:* Yes; *Library:* Resource Centre/Centre des ressources; Open to public by appointment
Chief Officer(s):
Karen Tanner, President
Stephen Alexander, Executive Director, 800-561-4009 Ext. 105
stephen@aidsnb.com

AIDS Niagara
120 Queenston St., St Catharines ON L2R 2Z3
Tel: 905-984-8684; *Fax:* 905-988-1921
Toll-Free: 800-773-9843
info@aidsniagara.com
www.aidsniagara.com
www.facebook.com/AIDSNiagara
twitter.com/aidsniagara
Overview: A small local charitable organization founded in 1987
Mission: To improve quality of life for those infected &/or affected by HIV/AIDS & to reduce the spread of HIV
Member of: United Way
Affiliation(s): Ontario AIDS Network; Canadian AIDS Society
Finances: *Funding Sources:* Ontario Ministry of Health, Public Health Agency of Canada
Staff Member(s): 34
Membership: *Fees:* $10
Activities: StreetWorks program; support services; supportive housing; community development & education; women's community development; *Awareness Events:* World AIDS Day, Dec. 1; *Speaker Service:* Yes; *Library*
Chief Officer(s):
Francis Gregotski, Chair
Glen Walker, Executive Director, 905-984-8684 Ext. 112
gwalker@aidsniagara.com

AIDS PEI *See* P.E.E.R.S. Alliance

AIDS Programs South Saskatchewan (APSS)
2911 - 5th Ave., Regina SK S4T 0L4
Tel: 306-924-8420; *Fax:* 306-525-0904
Toll-Free: 877-210-7623
aidsprograms@sasktel.net
www.aidsprogramssouthsask.com
www.facebook.com/aidsprogramssouthsask
twitter.com/aidsprograms
Previous Name: AIDS Regina, Inc.
Overview: A small local charitable organization founded in 1985 overseen by Canadian AIDS Society
Mission: To meet the needs of people living with AIDS & HIV positive persons; To educate society about HIV & AIDS; To address issues in society which may arise as a result of HIV & AIDS
Member of: Canadian AIDS Society
Finances: *Funding Sources:* Government; fundraising
Staff Member(s): 10
Membership: *Fees:* Schedule available
Activities: Community development, advocacy; harm reduction; *Awareness Events:* AIDS Walk for Life, Sept.; *Speaker Service:* Yes; *Library:* AIDS Resource Centre
Chief Officer(s):
Stephanie Milla, Executive Director

AIDS Regina, Inc. *See* AIDS Programs South Saskatchewan

AIDS Saint John (ASJ)
62 Waterloo St., Saint John NB E2L 3P3
Tel: 506-652-2437; *Fax:* 506-652-2438
info@aidssaintjohn.com
www.aidssaintjohn.com
Overview: A small local charitable organization founded in 1987
Mission: To confront HIV & AIDS through providing education, support, prevention & awareness initiatives; to create supportive social environments to people living with & affected with HIV/AIDS; to share our resources & build partnerships to promote the collaborative development of a community-based response to AIDS locally, provincially & regionally
Finances: *Funding Sources:* AIDS Community Action Program (ACAP)
Activities: *Speaker Service:* Yes; *Rents Mailing List:* Yes; *Library:* Open to public
Chief Officer(s):
Leslie Jeffrey, President

AIDS Saskatoon
PO Box 4062, Saskatoon SK S7K 4E3
Tel: 306-242-5005; *Fax:* 306-665-9976
Toll-Free: 800-667-6876
admin@aidssaskatoon.ca
www.aidssaskatoon.ca
www.facebook.com/aidssaskatoon
Overview: A small local charitable organization founded in 1986 overseen by Canadian AIDS Society
Mission: To provide support to those affected by AIDS & HIV; to educate & inform the community; to have the community embrace the issues addressed by AIDS Saskatoon
Staff Member(s): 33; 191 volunteer(s)
Activities: Drop-in programming; *Awareness Events:* Red Ribbon Tag Day; AIDS Walk; AIDS Awareness Week; *Speaker Service:* Yes; *Library:* Open to public
Chief Officer(s):
Dave Moors, President
Danielle Genest, Executive Director

AIDS Thunder Bay *See* Elevate NWO

AIDS Vancouver (AV)
803 East Hastings St., Vancouver BC V6A 1R8
Tel: 604-893-2201; *Fax:* 604-893-2205; *Crisis Hot-Line:* 604-696-4666
contact@aidsvancouver.org
www.aidsvancouver.org
www.facebook.com/aidsvancouver
twitter.com/AIDSVancouver
Also Known As: Vancouver AIDS Society
Overview: A small local charitable organization founded in 1983 overseen by Canadian AIDS Society
Mission: To alleviate individual & collective vulnerability to HIV & AIDS, through care, support, education, advocacy, & research
Member of: Canadian Public Health Association
Finances: *Annual Operating Budget:* $1.5 Million-$3 Million; *Funding Sources:* Federal, provincial & municipal grants; private Donations; Fundraising
Staff Member(s): 28; 200 volunteer(s)
Membership: 350
Activities: *Awareness Events:* AIDS Awareness Week, Nov.; World AIDS Day, Dec. 1 *Library:* Pacific AIDS Resource Centre Library; Open to public
Chief Officer(s):
Brian Chittock, Executive Director, 604-696-4655
brian@aidsvancouver.org

AIDS Vancouver Island (AVI)
Access Health Centre, 713 Johnson St., 3rd Fl., Victoria BC V8W 1M8
Tel: 250-384-2366; *Fax:* 250-380-9411
Toll-Free: 800-665-2437
info@avi.org
www.avi.org
www.facebook.com/aidsvancouverisland?ref=ts
twitter.com/AIDSVanIsle
Overview: A small local charitable organization founded in 1986 overseen by Canadian AIDS Society
Mission: To serve people infected & affected by HIV & Hepatitis C on Vancouver Island & the Gulf Islands, British Columbia; To provide support & combat stigma; To prevent infection
Finances: *Funding Sources:* Donations; Government funders; Foundations; Businesses; Special event sponsors
Staff Member(s): 31
Activities: Engaging in research in partnership with university & community-based researchers; Providing prevention information
Chief Officer(s):
Katrina Jensen, Executive Director
James Boxshall, Manager, Fund Development & Volunteer Services
Heidi Exner, Manager, Health Promotion & Community Development
George Pine, Manager, Operations
Bryson Hawkins, Director, Finance
Kristen Kvakic, Director, Programs
Publications:
• AVI [AIDS Vancouver Island] Newsletter
Type: Newsletter

Campbell River Office
1371 c. Cedar St., Campbell River BC V9W 2W6
Tel: 250-830-0787; *Fax:* 250-830-0784
Toll-Free: 877-650-8787
Chief Officer(s):
Leanne Cunningham, Contact

Courtenay/Comox Office
355 - 6th St., Courtenay BC V9N 1M2
Tel: 250-338-7400; *Fax:* 250-334-8224
Toll-Free: 877-311-7400
Chief Officer(s):
Sarah Sullivan, Contact

Nanaimo Office
#216, 55 Victoria Rd., Nanaimo BC V9R 5N9
Tel: 250-754-9111; *Fax:* 250-754-9888
health.centre@avi.org
avihealthcentre.org
Chief Officer(s):
Dana Becker, Manager

Canadian Associations / AIESEC

Port Hardy Office
PO Box 52, Port Hardy BC V0N 2P0
Tel: 250-902-2238; *Fax:* 250-949-9953
Chief Officer(s):
Shane Thomas, Manager

AIDS Yukon Alliance *See* Blood Ties Four Directions Centre

AIESEC
#208m 164 Eglinton Ave. East, Toronto ON M4P 1G4
Tel: 416-368-1001; *Fax:* 416-368-4490
info@aiesec.ca
www.aiesec.ca
www.facebook.com/AIESECCanada
twitter.com/aieseccanada
Overview: A large international charitable organization founded in 1958
Mission: To provide an international platform for young people to discover & develop their potential to have a positive impact on society by providing leadership opportunities for students
Finances: *Annual Operating Budget:* $500,000-$1.5 Million; *Funding Sources:* Donations; Membership fees
Membership: 60,000; *Member Profile:* Post-secondary students, or indivduals who have graduated from a post-secondary institution in the past two years
Activities: Facilitating leadership opportunities for students through their Global Internship Program (internships are offered in the areas of management, technology, education, & development); Hosting 470 annual conferences, including local, regional, national, & international, which provide members with soft skill & training sessions; *Internships:* Yes
Chief Officer(s):
Danial Mazhar Shafi, President
danialms@aiesec.ca
Mitch Donnelly, Vice-President, Business Development
mitchd@aiesec.ca
Vicky Gordiano, Vice-President, Marketing & Communications
vickyg@aiesec.ca
Publications:
• AIESEC Annual Report
Type: Yearbook; *Frequency:* Annually
Profile: Financial statements plus highlights of the organization's activities during the year

Calgary
University of Calgary, Scurfield Hall, #199C, 2500 University Dr. NW, Calgary AB
Tel: 403-220-6454; *Fax:* 403-220-9001
aiesec@ucalgary.ca
www.facebook.com/AIESECCalgary

Carleton
Carleton University, Sprott School of Business, Dunton Tower, #710, 1125 Colonel By Dr., Ottawa ON
Tel: 613-520-2600; *Fax:* 613-520-4427
info@aiesecarleton.ca
www.facebook.com/aiesecarleton

Chicoutimi
Université du Québec à Chicoutimi, #P0-4105, 555, boul de L'Universite, Chicoutimi QC G7H 2B1
Tél: 418-545-5011; *Téléc:* 418-545-5012
aiesec@uqac.ca
twitter.com/AIESECUQAC

Concordia
Concordia University, Loyola Campus, #SC 3-07, 7141 rue Sherbrooke ouest, Montréal QC H3G 1M8
Tél: 514-848-7466; *Téléc:* 514-848-7450
concordia@aiesec.ca
www.facebook.com/AIESECCanada
twitter.com/AIESECConcordia

École des Hautes Études Commerciales (HEC)
Local RJ.870, 3000, ch de la Côte-Sainte-Catherine, Montréal QC H3T 2A7
Tél: 514-340-6228; *Téléc:* 514-340-6978
aiesec@hec.ca
www.facebook.com/aiesechecmontreal

Edmonton
University of Alberta, School of Business, #2-04H, Edmonton AB T6G 2R6
Tel: 780-492-2453; *Fax:* 780-492-9450
aiesec@ualberta.ca
www.linkedin.com/groups/AIESEC-Edmonton-3643877
www.facebook.com/aiesecedmonton
twitter.com/AIESECEdmonton
www.youtube.com/user/AIESECedmonton

Guelph
University of Guelph, University Centre, #234, Guelph ON N1G 2W1
Tel: 519-834-4120; *Fax:* 519-763-9603
vpcomm.aiesecguelph@gmail.com
www.linkedin.com/groups/AIESEC-Guelph-3852109
twitter.com/aiesecguelph

Halifax
St. Mary's University, Loyola Bldg., Halifax NS B3H 3C3
Tel: 902-491-8673; *Fax:* 902-491-8673
aiesechalifax@gmail.com
ca.linkedin.com/pub/aiesec-halifax/38/ab7/692

Kwantlen
Kwantlen Polytechnic University, 12666 - 72nd Ave., Surrey BC V3W 2M8
Tel: 778-991-3717
aiesec.kwantlen@gmail.com
www.linkedin.com/groups/AIESEC-KWANTLEN-4089203

Laurier
Wilfrid Laurier University, SBE 1250, 75 University Ave. West, Waterloo ON N2L 3C5
aieseclaurier@gmail.com
www.linkedin.com/company/2266780?trk=tyah
www.facebook.com/AIESECLaurier
• Explore AIESEC
Type: Magazine

Laval
Université Laval, Pavillon Palasis-Prince, Local 0325-A, 2325, rue de la Terrasse, Québec QC G1V 0A6
Tél: 418-656-7810
aiesec.laval@gmail.com
www.facebook.com/AIESECLaval

Manitoba
University of Manitoba, Drake Centre, #127, 181 Freedman Cres., Winnipeg MB R3T 5V4
Tel: 204-275-5539; *Fax:* 204-474-7545
aiesec@cc.umanitoba.ca
www.facebook.com/AIESECmanitoba

McGill
McGill University, #407, 3600, rue McTavish, Montréal QC H3A 0G3
Tel: 514-398-3001
general@aiesecmcgill.ca
www.facebook.com/AIESECMcGill
twitter.com/aiesecmcgill

McMaster
McMaster University, Degroote School of Business, #132, 1280 Main St. West, Hamilton ON L8S 4L8
Tel: 905-525-9140
mcmaster@aiesec.ca
www.linkedin.com/groups/AIESEC-McMaster-3827920
www.facebook.com/aiesecmcmaster

Ottawa
University of Ottawa, 638 King Edward Ave., Ottawa ON K1N 6N5
Tel: 613-562-5800; *Fax:* 613-562-5164
info@aiesecottawa.com
www.aiesecottawa.org
www.facebook.com/AIESECOttawa
twitter.com/aiesecottawa
Chief Officer(s):
Ibby Abouelenein, Local Chapter President

Queen's
Queen's University, Athletics & Recreation Centre, 284 Earl Street, #A605, Kingston ON K7L 2H8
Tel: 613-533-6000
vpcomm.queens@gmail.com
www.facebook.com/aiequeens
twitter.com/AIESECQueensU

Ryerson
Ryerson University, TRS 1-053, 55 Dundas St. West, Toronto ON M5G 2C3
Tel: 416-979-5000; *Fax:* 416-979-5266
aiesec@ryerson.ca
www.facebook.com/aiesecryerson
twitter.com/aiesec_ryerson

Saskatoon
University of Saskatchewan, Place Riel Student Centre, #80, 1 Campus Dr., Saskatoon SK S7N 5A3
Tel: 306-966-7767; *Fax:* 306-966-7769
aiesec.saskatoon@gmail.com
www.facebook.com/AIESEC.Saskatoon
twitter.com/AIESECSaskatoon

Sherbrooke
Université de Sherbrooke, faculté d'administration, 2500, boul de l'Université, #K1-1011, Sherbrooke QC J1K 2R1
Tél: 819-542-1349
lcp.aiesec.sherbrooke@gmail.com
www.facebook.com/AIESECCanada
twitter.com/AIESEC

Simon Fraser University (SFU)
Beedie School of Business Administration, Simon Fraser University, 8888 University Dr., Burnaby BC V5A 1S6
Tel: 778-782-4187; *Fax:* 778-782-5571
aiesec@sfu.ca
www.linkedin.com/company/aiesec-simon-fraser-university
www.facebook.com/AIESECsfu
twitter.com/aiesecsfu
flickr.com/aiesecsfu

Toronto
University of Toronto, #412, 21 Sussex Ave., Toronto ON M5S 1J6
Tel: 416-978-3335; *Fax:* 416-978-5433
info@aiesectoronto.com
aiesectoronto.com
www.facebook.com/AIESECtoronto
twitter.com/AIESECToronto

Université du Québec à Montréal (UQAM)
315, rue Sainte-Catherine est, #R-M213, Montréal QC H2X 3X2
Tél: 514-987-3288; *Téléc:* 514-987-6534
vpcomm.aiesec.uqam@gmail.com
www.facebook.com/aiesecesguqam
twitter.com/AIESECESGUQAM

University of British Columbia (UBC)
6133 University Blvd., AMS Student Nest, Vancouver BC V6T 1Z1
Tel: 604-822-6256; *Fax:* 604-822-8187
info@aiesecubc.ca
www.linkedin.com/company/aiesec-ubc
www.facebook.com/AIESECUBC
twitter.com/aiesecubc

Victoria
University of Victoria, Student Union Bldg., 3800 Finnerty Rd., Victoria BC VC8 5C2
aiesec@uvic.ca
www.facebook.com/aiesecvictoria
twitter.com/aiesecvictoria

Western
University of Western Ontario, University Community Centre, #340, London ON N6A 3K7
western.ca@aiesec.net
www.facebook.com/aiesecwestern
twitter.com/AIESECWestern

Windsor
University of Windsor, Odette School of Business, 401 Sunset Ave., Windsor ON N9B 3P4
aiesec.windsor@gmail.com
www.linkedin.com/groups/AIESEC-Windsor-4390569
www.facebook.com/269861425400
twitter.com/AIESEC_Windsor

York
York University, Schulich School of Business, #W036C, 4700 Keele St., Toronto ON M3J 1P3
aiesecyork.hr@gmail.com
www.facebook.com/aiesecyork

Aikido Yukon Association
c/o Sport Yukon, 4061 - 4th Ave., Whitehorse YT Y1A 1H1
Tel: 867-667-4690; *Fax:* 867-667-4237
info@aikidoyukon.ca
www.aikidoyukon.ca
www.facebook.com/aikidoyukon
Overview: A small provincial organization
Mission: To teach the martial art of Aikido in the Yukon.
Chief Officer(s):
Gaël Marchanfd, President

AiMHi, Prince George Association for Community Living
950 Kerry St., Prince George BC V2M 5A3
Tel: 250-564-6408; *Fax:* 250-564-6801
Other Communication: Room Booking e-mail: bookings@aimhi.ca
aimhi@aimhi.ca
www.aimhi.ca
www.facebook.com/AiMHibc
twitter.com/AiMHiBC

Also Known As: AiMHi
Overview: A medium-sized local charitable organization founded in 1957
Mission: To advocate for adults who have developmental disabilities & children who have special needs; to promote opportunities for community access, education, health care, relationships, freedom from discrimination & equality for all; to encourage choices, respect diversity, & acknowledge each person's rights & contributions to our community
Member of: British Columbia Association for Community Living
Finances: *Annual Operating Budget:* Greater than $5 Million
Staff Member(s): 440
Membership: *Fees:* Schedule available; *Committees:* Executive; Finance; Aging
Activities: Programs & services include: Community Options; Family Support; Home Sharing; Infant Development Program; Infinite Employment Solutions; Kitchen Program; Life Skills; Residential services; Skill Building Library; *Library:* Skill Building Library; Open to public
Chief Officer(s):
Melinda P. Heidsma, Executive Director
Wendy Brophy, Assistant Executive Director

Air Cadet League of Canada / Ligue des cadets de l'air du Canada
#201, 1505 Laperriere Ave., Ottawa ON K1Z 7T1
Tel: 613-941-3739; *Fax:* 613-941-3744
Toll-Free: 877-422-6359
leaguehq@aircadetleague.com
www.aircadetleague.com
www.facebook.com/Air.Cadet.League.of.Canada
twitter.com/AirCadetLeague
www.youtube.com/user/AirCadetLeague
Overview: A large national charitable organization founded in 1941
Mission: To promote & encourage a practical interest in aeronautics among young people; To assist those intending to pursue a career in aviation
Finances: *Annual Operating Budget:* $250,000-$500,000
Staff Member(s): 4; 7400 volunteer(s)
Membership: 55 corporate + 3,322 associate + 28,000 student + 458 sponsor + 1,935 officers; *Committees:* Executive; National Honours & Awards; National Fund Raising; National Finance; National Flying; Policies & Procedures; Effective Speaking Contest; National Selections
Activities: *Speaker Service:* Yes; *Rents Mailing List:* Yes
Chief Officer(s):
Donald A. Berrill, CD, President
Pierre Forgues, Executive Director
Publications:
• Air Cadet League of Canada Newsletter
Type: Newsletter

Air Canada Foundation
Montréal QC
foundation-fondation@aircanada.ca
www.aircanada.com/en/about/community/foundation
Overview: A medium-sized national charitable organization founded in 2012
Mission: To help connect sick children to the medical care they need; to help alleviate child poverty
Activities: Hospital Transportation; Every Bit Counts program; Wings of Courage Program; Volunteer Involvement Program; golf tournament

Air Canada Pilots Association (ACPA) / L'Association des pilotes d'Air Canada
#205, 6299 Airport Rd., Mississauga ON L4V 1N3
Tel: 905-678-9008; *Fax:* 905-678-9016
Toll-Free: 800-634-0944
info@acpa.ca
www.acpa.ca
Overview: A medium-sized national organization founded in 1995
Mission: To provide advocacy on critical industry and aviation issues on behalf of Air Canada pilots
Affiliation(s): Association of Star Alliance Pilots
50 volunteer(s)
Membership: 3,100; *Member Profile:* Air Canada pilots
Chief Officer(s):
Kevin Vaillant, Master Elected Council
Milt Isaacs, CEO
Paul Strachan, Chair, Master Executive Council

Air Currency Enhancement Society (ACES)
c/o Bud Bernston, 13 Casavechia Ct., Dartmouth NS B2X 3G7
www.soaraces.ca
www.facebook.com/AirCurrencyEnhancementSociety
twitter.com/soaraces
www.youtube.com/user/soaraces
Overview: A small local organization founded in 1991
Mission: To promote & improve standards in aviation
Member of: Soaring Association of Canada
Membership: *Fees:* $50 youth/junior/air cadet; $150 affiliate
Chief Officer(s):
Robert Francis, Chairman
robert.francis@soaraces.ca
Patrick Dalton, Contact, Communications
patrick.dalton@soaraces.ca

Air Force Association of Canada (AFAC) / L'Association des forces aériennes du Canada
PO Box 2460, Stn. D, Ottawa ON K1P 5W6
Tel: 613-232-2303; *Fax:* 613-232-2156
Toll-Free: 866-351-2322
rcafassociation.ca
www.facebook.com/RCAFAssociationARC
twitter.com/RCAFAssociation
Previous Name: Royal Canadian Air Force Association
Overview: A large national organization founded in 1948
Mission: To promote a viable well-equipped air force & a strong Canadian aerospace industry
Member of: National Council of Veteran Associations
Affiliation(s): Air Force Association of United States; Royal Air Forces Association
Finances: *Annual Operating Budget:* $500,000-$1.5 Million; *Funding Sources:* Membership dues; magazine subscriptions
Staff Member(s): 5
Membership: 200 senior/lifetime + 16,000 individual; *Fees:* $35; *Member Profile:* Wartime & peacetime air force veterans; *Committees:* Airpower Advocacy
Activities: Operates 67 wings in Canada; *Awareness Events:* Battle of Britain Sunday, mid-Sept.; *Speaker Service:* Yes; *Library:* AFAC Library; Not open to public
Chief Officer(s):
Terry Chester, National President
Dean Black, National Executive Director
director@airforce.ca
Awards:
• Air Marshal William Avery "Billy" Bishop Memorial Trophy
• Air Marshal Charles Roy Slemon Memorial Award
• John Alexander Douglas McCurdy Memorial Trophy
• Douglas Marshall "Bitsy" Grant Memorial Award
• Gordon Roy McGregor Memorial Trophy
• Andrew Charles "Andy" Mynarski Memorial Trophy
• NORAD Commemorative Trophy
• RCAF Association Trophy
• Ordre de la Tuque
Publications:
• Airforce Magazine [a publication of the Air Force Association of Canada]
Type: Magazine; *Frequency:* Quarterly; *ISSN:* 0704-6804

Air Industries Association of Canada *See* Aerospace Industries Association of Canada

Air Line Pilots Association, International - Canada (ALPA)
#1715, 360 Albert St., Ottawa ON K1R 7X7
Tel: 613-569-5668
www.alpa.org
www.linkedin.com/companies/air-line-pilots-association
www.facebook.com/WeAreALPA
twitter.com/WeAreALPA
www.youtube.com/user/WeAreALPA;
www.instagram.com/we_are_alpa
Previous Name: Canadian Air Line Pilots Association
Overview: A large national organization founded in 1931
Mission: To promote & represent the interests of the airline pilot profession; To safeguard the rights of individual members; To promote & maintain the highest standards of flight safety; To function as a trade union & professional association
Affiliation(s): International Federation of Air Line Pilots' Associations; Canadian Labour Congress
Finances: *Funding Sources:* Membership dues
Staff Member(s): 10; 360 volunteer(s)
Membership: 2,200 + 19 locals in Canada; *Member Profile:* Active airline pilots employed by airlines in Canada; *Committees:* Air Safety; Aeromedical; Insurance; Membership
Chief Officer(s):
Tim Canoll, President
Joe DePete, First Vice-President
Rick Dominguez, Executive Administrator
Publications:
• Air Line Pilot [a publication of the Air Line Pilots Association, International]
Type: Magazine
Toronto Contract Office
#200, 180 Atwell Dr., Toronto ON M9W 6A9
Tel: 416-679-8210
Vancouver Regional Office
#62, 16655 - 64th Ave., Cloverdale BC V3S 3V1
Tel: 604-575-2572; *Fax:* 604-575-2571
Toll-Free: 866-293-2572

Air Transport Association of Canada (ATAC) / Association du transport aérien du Canada
#700, 255 Albert St., Ottawa ON K1P 6A9
Tel: 613-233-7727; *Fax:* 613-230-8648
atac@atac.ca
www.atac.ca
twitter.com/atac_canada
Overview: A medium-sized national organization founded in 1934
Mission: To advance the issues that affect members from the commercial aviation & flight training industries as well as aviaition industry suppliers
Staff Member(s): 7
Membership: 200; *Fees:* Schedule available; *Member Profile:* Any Canadian person, partnership or corporation engaged in the commerical operation of aircraft, or engaged in aviation or education; Industry partners; Any trade association or other related not-for-profit organizations associated with the aviation industry; *Committees:* Cabin Operations; Environmental Affairs; Flight Operations; Maintenance, Repair and Overheaul; Safety Advisory; Technical Operations; Accessible Transportation; Cargo; Facilitation; Industry and Monetary Affairs; Legal; Security; Tax; UAV; Airports; Dangerous Goods; Flight Training; Vocational Training Regulation; International Marketing of Flight Training; Special Projects; Industry Monetary Affairs
Activities: Engaging in lobbying activities; *Speaker Service:* Yes
Chief Officer(s):
John McKenna, President & Chief Executive Officer, 613-233-7727 Ext. 313
jmckenna@atac.ca
Les Aalders, Executive Vice President, 613-233-7727 Ext. 314
laalders@atac.ca
Wayne Gouveia, Senior Vice President, 613-233-7727 Ext. 309
wgouveia@atac.ca
Bernard Champagne, Vice President
bchampagne@atac.ca
François Roquet, Manager, Communications, 613-407-4816
froquet@atac.ca
Debbie Simpson, Corporate Secretary & Executive Assistant, 613-233-7727 Ext. 312
dsimpson@atac.ca
Awards:
• ATAC Lifetime Honoree Award
Recognizes individuals as having contributed significantly to the development of the association and the industry *Eligibility:* Individuals who have been engaged in the Canadian air transport industry for 25+ years; shall have participated actively in the affairs of the ATAC
• ATAC Outstanding Achievement Award
Recognizes companies that demonstrate incorporated best practices for increasing safety & increased product quality or strategy that is so innovative it will serve as an example for others to follow & learn from *Eligibility:* Individuals who have been engaged in the Canadian air transport industry for 25+ years; shall have participated actively in the affairs of the ATAC *Deadline:* Nominations Close June 30
• Jim Glass Humanitarian Award
Eligibility: Any ATAC member, or other member of the Canadian aviation community, that has demonstrated strong business acumen and serious community involvement *Deadline:* May *Contact:* Danielle Lavoie, dlavoie@atac.ca
• Paul Mulrooney Memorial Award of Excellence
Eligibility: Given every other year to an employee of an operator member company who has demonstrated progressive advancement to & within a management position; must be sponsored by employer *Deadline:* May 13
Meetings/Conferences:
• ATAC 84th Canadian Aviation Conference & Tradeshow, November, 2018, Westin Bayshore Hotel, Vancouver, BC
Scope: National
Description: National gathering for operators, suppliers to the industry & government stakeholders involved in commerical

Canadian Associations / AirCrew Association - Western Canada Region (ACA Canada)

aviation and flight training in Canada
Contact Information: Debbie Simpson; dsimpson@atac.ca; 613-233-7727 ext. 312
• ATAC 85th Canadian Aviation Conference & Tradeshow, November, 2019, Fairmont Queen Elizabeth Hotel, Montreal, QC
Scope: National
Description: National gathering for operators, suppliers to the industry & government stakeholders involved in commerical aviation and flight training in Canada
Contact Information: Debbie Simpson; dsimpson@atac.ca; 613-233-7727 ext. 312
• ATAC 86th Canadian Aviation Conference & Tradeshow, November, 2020, Westin Bayshore Hotel, Vancouver, BC
Scope: National
Description: National gathering for operators, suppliers to the industry & government stakeholders involved in commerical aviation and flight training in Canada
Contact Information: Debbie Simpson; dsimpson@atac.ca; 613-233-7727 ext. 312
• ATAC 87th Canadian Aviation Conference & Tradeshow, November, 2021, Fairmont Queen Elizabeth Hotel, Montreal, QC
Scope: National
Description: National gathering for operators, suppliers to the industry & government stakeholders involved in commerical aviation and flight training in Canada
Contact Information: Debbie Simpson; dsimpson@atac.ca; 613-233-7727 ext. 312
• ATAC 88th Canadian Aviation Conference & Tradeshow, November, 2022, Westin Bayshore Hotel, Vancouver, BC
Scope: National
Description: National gathering for operators, suppliers to the industry & government stakeholders involved in commerical aviation and flight training in Canada
Contact Information: Debbie Simpson; dsimpson@atac.ca; 613-233-7727 ext. 312
• ATAC 89th Canadian Aviation Conference & Tradeshow, November, 2023, Fairmont Queen Elizabeth Hotel, Montreal, QC
Scope: National
Description: National gathering for operators, suppliers to the industry & government stakeholders involved in commerical aviation and flight training in Canada
Contact Information: Debbie Simpson; dsimpson@atac.ca; 613-233-7727 ext. 312
Publications:
• @ATAC [Air Transport Association of Canada] Newsletter
Type: Newsletter
Profile: Association activities, such as events, awards, & membership information
• Air Transport Association of Canada Annual Report
Type: Magazine; *Frequency:* Annually
• Flightplan
Type: Magazine; *Price:* Free with Air Transport Association of Canada membership

Air Waste Management Association - Québec Section *Voir* Association pour la prévention de la contamination de l'air et du sol

Aircraft Operations Group Association (Ind.) *See* Canadian Federal Pilots Association

AirCrew Association - Western Canada Region (ACA Canada)
PO Box 153, Saanichton BC V8M 2C3
Tel: 250-655-6325
avder@pacificcoast.net
www.aircrew.ca
Also Known As: Vancouver Island Aircrew Association
Overview: A small local organization founded in 1953
Mission: To foster comradeship among those who, having been awarded an official flying badge, have qualified to operate military aircraft & are serving or have served as military aircrew in the armed forces of Canada & its Allies
Finances: *Funding Sources:* Membership dues
Membership: *Fees:* $40 regular; $25 associate
Activities: Branches in Victoria, Sidney, West Vancouver & Calgary
Chief Officer(s):
Scott Eichel, President, 250-360-0939

Airdrie & District Soccer Association
Genesis Pl., 800 East Lake Blvd., Airdrie AB T4A 0H6
Tel: 403-948-6260; *Fax:* 403-948-6290
admin@airdriesoccer.com
airdriesoccer.com
www.facebook.com/airdriesoccerassociation

Overview: A small local organization overseen by Alberta Soccer Association
Member of: Alberta Soccer Association
Membership: *Fees:* Schedule available
Chief Officer(s):
Steve Thomas, Technical Director
td@airdriesoccer.com
Juliet Smith, Office Manager/Registrar
manager@airdriesoccer.com

Airdrie Chamber of Commerce
#102, 150 Edwards Way NW, Airdrie AB T4B 4B9
Tel: 403-948-4412; *Fax:* 403-948-3141
info@airdriechamber.ab.ca
www.airdriechamber.ab.ca
www.linkedin.com/company/1862330
www.facebook.com/AirdrieChamber
twitter.com/airdriechamber
Overview: A small local charitable organization founded in 1973
Mission: To promote, represent, & enhance the interests of Airdrie Alberta's business community
Member of: Alberta Chamber of Commerce
Staff Member(s): 2
Membership: *Fees:* Schedule available based on number of employees; *Committees:* Signs; Home & Garden Fair; Special Events; Policy/Issues; Strategic Plan
Chief Officer(s):
Hunt Lorna, Executive Director

Airdrie Food Bank (AFB)
20 East Lake Way NE, Airdrie AB T4A 2J2
Tel: 403-948-0063; *Fax:* 403-948-9332
info@airdriefoodbank.com
www.airdriefoodbank.com
www.facebook.com/airdriefoodbank
twitter.com/airdriefoodbank
www.youtube.com/playlist?list=FLhMDx5mkeznB3FeSW8LCDOw
Overview: A small local charitable organization founded in 1984 overseen by Food Banks Alberta Association
Mission: To collect and distribute food to those in need and educate the community on hunger-related issues
Member of: Food Banks Canada; Alberta Food Bank Network Association; Food Banks Alberta
Finances: *Funding Sources:* Donations; grants/government funding
Staff Member(s): 6; 150+ volunteer(s)
Chief Officer(s):
Lori McRitchie, Executive Director

Airport Management Council of Ontario (AMCO)
#5, 50 Terminal St., North Bay ON P1B 8G2
Tel: 705-474-1080; *Fax:* 705-474-4073
Toll-Free: 877-636-2626
amco@amco.on.ca
www.amco.on.ca
Overview: A small provincial organization founded in 1985
Mission: To provide advocacy for and education to Ontario's airports and aerodromes
Membership: 58 airports + 56 businesses; *Fees:* Schedule available; *Member Profile:* Individuals associated with Transport Canada, Nav Canada, educational facilities and business men and women
Activities: Training; Annual networking events; Communication & advocacy; *Speaker Service:* Yes; *Library:* Airport Management Council of Ontario Resource Centre
Chief Officer(s):
Steve McKeown, President
Meetings/Conferences:
• AMCO Workshop 2018, May, 2018, Niagara District Airport, Niagara-on-the-Lake, ON
Description: Informative speakers, round table discussions, tours, demonstrations & a half-day live emergency exercise
• AMCO's 33rd Annual Convention & Trade Show, October, 2018, Kenora, ON
Description: Informative speakers & exhibitors
Publications:
• The Airport and You [AMCO Newsletter]
Type: E-Newsletter; *Frequency:* 4 pa; *Accepts Advertising*; *Number of Pages:* 13; *Author:* Laura McNeice; *Editor:* Laura McNeice
Profile: Newsletter concerning imformation important to invidiuals involved in the Ontario airport industry

Airspace Action on Smoking & Health
PO Box 18004, 1215C - 56th St., Delta BC V4L 2M4

Tel: 778-899-4832
airspace.bc.ca
www.facebook.com/234024210003649
twitter.com/airspace_bc
Previous Name: AIRSPACE Non-Smokers' Rights Society
Overview: A medium-sized provincial organization founded in 1981
Mission: To educate non-smokers on the effects that smoking has on them & of their legal right to smoke-free air; to help establish laws to protect the comfort, safety & health of non-smokers; to help reduce the number of future smokers
Affiliation(s): Non-Smokers' Rights Association; Canadian Council on Smoking & Health
Finances: *Funding Sources:* Membership dues
Membership: *Fees:* $25 individual; $30 family; $50 institution; $100 Sworn Enemy of the Tobacco Industry
Activities: *Internships:* Yes; *Speaker Service:* Yes; *Library:* Open to public

AIRSPACE Non-Smokers' Rights Society *See* Airspace Action on Smoking & Health

Aish HaTorah Learning Centre *See* Aish Thornhill Community Shul & Learning Centre

Aish Thornhill Community Shul & Learning Centre
949 Clark Ave. West, Thornhill ON L4J 8G6
Tel: 905-764-1891; *Fax:* 905-764-1606
theshul@aish.com
www.thornhillshul.com
Previous Name: Aish HaTorah Learning Centre
Overview: A small local charitable organization founded in 1981
Mission: To provide Jewish educational programs
Finances: *Annual Operating Budget:* $1.5 Million-$3 Million
Staff Member(s): 15
Activities: *Speaker Service:* Yes; *Rents Mailing List:* Yes; *Library*
Chief Officer(s):
Avram Rothman
arothman@aish.edu

Aiviq Hunters & Trappers Organization
PO Box 300, Cape Dorset NU X0A 0C0
Tel: 867-897-8214
aiviq_hunters@qiniq.com
Overview: A small local organization
Chief Officer(s):
Quvianatiliaq Tapaungai, Chair

Ajax, Pickering & Whitby Association for Community Living *See* Community Living Ajax-Pickering & Whitby

Ajax-Pickering Board of Trade (APBOT)
#3, 144 Old Kingston Rd., Ajax ON L1T 2Z9
Tel: 905-686-0883; *Fax:* 905-686-1057
admin@apboardoftrade.com
www.apboardoftrade.com
www.facebook.com/APBOT
twitter.com/APBoardofTrade
Overview: A medium-sized local organization founded in 1955
Mission: To represent Ajax & Pickering businesses across a range of sectors; To engage in advocacy and policy initiatives relating to issues in economic, community & social development
Member of: Canadian Chamber of Commerce
Finances: *Annual Operating Budget:* $100,000-$250,000; *Funding Sources:* Membership fees
Staff Member(s): 5; 37 volunteer(s)
Membership: 360; *Fees:* Based on number of employees
Activities: Organizing networking & educational events; Providing access to business presentations, directories & information; *Awareness Events:* Business Links Golf Tournament, May; Trade Show, September; Business Excellence Awards, October; *Speaker Service:* Yes
Chief Officer(s):
Chrystine Langille, Executive Director, 905-686-0883 Ext. 223
clangille@apboardoftrade.com
Iris Nicolaison, Manager, Business Development, 905-686-0883 Ext. 224
inicolaison@apboardoftrade.com
Brooke Pollard, Specialist, Policy & Communications, 905-686-0883 Ext. 229
bpollard@apboardoftrade.com

Ajax-Pickering Chamber Orchestra *See* Durham Chamber Orchestra

Ajjiit Nunavut Media Association
PO Box 6011, Iqaluit NU X0A 0H0

alethea@unikkaat.com
www.ajjiit.ca
Overview: A small provincial organization
Mission: To advocate for film, television, & new media in Nunavut; To promote Nunavut's film, television, & new media industry; To act as a point of contact for outside organizations & the Government of Nunavut
Finances: *Funding Sources:* Memberships; Sponsorships
Membership: *Fees:* $15 Nunavut elders & youth under 18; $50 individuals, businesses, supporters, & providers of services to the industry; $100 persons outside Nunavut; *Member Profile:* Persons engaged in film, television, & new media occupations in Nunavut; Non-Nunavut based producers who collaborate on northern media projects
Activities: Consulting with the territorial government & Nunavut Film on issues which affect the industry; Hosting workshops; Presenting awards
Chief Officer(s):
Alethea Arnaquq-Baril, President

Alameda Agricultural Society
PO Box 181, Alameda SK S0C 0A0
Overview: A small local charitable organization
Finances: *Funding Sources:* Donations
Activities: Hosting a summer fair, 4-H show, & flower show

Al-Anon Family Groups (Canada), Inc. / Groupe familiaux Al-Anon
#900, 275 Slater St., Ottawa ON K1P 5H9
Tel: 613-723-8484
afgwso@al-anon.org
www.al-anon.org
www.facebook.com/AlAnonFamilyGroupsWSO
twitter.com/AlAnon_WSO
Also Known As: AL-ANON/ALATEEN
Overview: A medium-sized national charitable organization founded in 1951
Mission: To provide support for friends & family members of alcoholics
Finances: *Funding Sources:* Literature sales; contributions from members & groups
Membership: *Fees:* Voluntary contributions
Activities: Support groups for families, friends & relatives of alcoholics; Alateen - support groups for youth aged 12 - 20 with alcoholic parents; *Speaker Service:* Yes; *Library*

Al-Anon Montréal
CP 37322, Succ. Marquette, Montréal QC H2E 3B5
Tél: 514-866-9803
information@al-anon-montreal.org
al-anon-montreal.org
Aperçu: *Dimension:* petite; *Envergure:* locale
Mission: Pour aider les personnes souffrant d'alcoolisme et de leurs familles, et les enfants d'aide qui sont touchés par l'alcoolisme

Albanian Canadian Community Association
85 Ingram Dr., Toronto ON M6M 2L7
Tel: 416-503-4704; *Fax:* 416-503-4704
info@albcan.ca
albcan.ca
www.facebook.com/shoqata.shqiptarokanadeze
Also Known As: Shoqata Bashkesia Shqiptaro Kanadeze; Albcan
Overview: A small national organization founded in 1990
Mission: To develop the culture, art and heritage of Albanians in Ontario
Membership: *Fees:* Students: $20; Adults: $30; Families: $50
Chief Officer(s):
Ruki Kondaj, President, Board of Directors, 416-876-7665
r.kondaj@albcan.ca

Alberni District Historical Society
Alberni Valley Museum, 4255 Wallace St., Port Alberni BC V9Y 3Y6
Tel: 250-723-2181
aadhs1@gmail.com
Overview: A small local charitable organization founded in 1965
Mission: To preserve & make available local history, to collect, arrange & maintain community archives with a concentration on "paper treasures."
Member of: BC Historical Federation; Archives Association of BC
Finances: *Funding Sources:* Membership fees; donations
Membership: *Member Profile:* Community residents
Activities: Public education; special speakers; *Library:* Archives; Open to public

Alberni Valley Chamber of Commerce
2533 Port Alberni Hwy., Port Alberni BC V9Y 8P2
Tel: 250-724-6535; *Fax:* 250-724-6560
office@avcoc.com
www.avcoc.com
Overview: A small local organization
Mission: To improve our community through the promotion of business & removal of barriers to business development
Member of: BC Chamber of Commerce
Staff Member(s): 4
Membership: 332
Chief Officer(s):
Neil Malbon, President
neil@alberniheritage.com
Mike Carter, Executive Director

Alberni Valley Coin Club
4689 - 10th Ave, Port Alberni BC V9Y 4Y1
Overview: A small local organization
Member of: Royal Canadian Numismatic Association

Alberni Valley Outdoor Club
Port Alberni BC
Tel: 250-724-4535
albernivalleyoutdoorclub.wordpress.com
Overview: A small local organization
Member of: Federation of Mountain Clubs of British Columbia
Membership: *Fees:* $25 single; $45 family; $7.50 associate
Chief Officer(s):
Judy Carlson, President

Alberni Valley Rock & Gem Club
PO Box 1291, Stn. A, Port Alberni BC V9Y 7M2
Tel: 250-723-0281
compudoc@telus.net
Overview: A small local organization founded in 1958
Member of: British Columbia Lapidary Society
Activities: Meetings are held 1st Sun. of every month in Cherry Creek Community Hall, Moore Rd., Port Alberni.
Chief Officer(s):
Dave West, Contact

Alberni Valley Soaring Association
8064 Richards Trail, Duncan BC V9L 6B2
Toll-Free: 866-590-7627
info@avsa.ca
www.avsa.ca
www.facebook.com/AlberniValleySoaringAssociation
Overview: A small local organization
Mission: To offer opportunities to fly to its members & guests
Member of: Soaring Association of Canada
Affiliation(s): Vancouver Island Soaring Centre; Vancouver Soaring Association
Membership: *Fees:* Schedule available

Albert County Chamber of Commerce
PO Box 3051, Hillsborough NB E4H 4W5
accofc@gmail.com
www.albertcountychamber.com
Overview: A small local organization
Mission: To encourage economic growth & prosperity in Albert County
Membership: *Fees:* $75
Chief Officer(s):
David Briggs, President
Janine Underhill, Secretary

Alberta & Northwest Territories Lung Association
PO Box 4500, Stn. South, #208, 17420 Stony Plain Rd., Edmonton AB T6E 6K2
Tel: 780-488-6819; *Fax:* 780-488-7195
Toll-Free: 888-566-5864
info@ab.lung.ca
www.ab.lung.ca
www.facebook.com/lungassociationabnwt
twitter.com/lungabnwt
Overview: A medium-sized provincial charitable organization founded in 1939 overseen by Canadian Lung Association
Mission: To educate the public & medical professionals about lung health
Finances: *Funding Sources:* Donations; Fundraising; Sponsorships
Membership: *Fees:* $25
Activities: Providing indepth information about asthma, COPD, sleep apnea, tuberculosis, & other lung conditions, as well as smoking & clean air; Organizing & promoting events about lung health to support the association; Funding medical research; *Awareness Events:* Radon Awareness Campaign; Northwest Territories Asthma & Allergies Door-to-Door Campaign, May
Chief Officer(s):
Paul Borrett, Chair
Evangeline Berube, Vice-Chair & Treasurer
Kate Hurlburt, Secretary
Publications:
• Alberta & Northwest Territories Lung Association Annual Report
Type: Yearbook; *Frequency:* Annually
Profile: Highlights of fundraising activities, advocacy activities, & patient support programs

Alberta 5 Pin Bowlers' Association (A5-PBA)
Bowling Headquarters, 432 - 14 St. South, Lethbridge AB T1J 2X7
Tel: 403-320-2695; *Fax:* 403-320-2676
Toll-Free: 800-762-3075
generalenquires@centralalberta5pin.com
www.alberta5pin.com
www.facebook.com/a5pba
Overview: A medium-sized provincial charitable organization founded in 1979 overseen by Canadian 5 Pin Bowlers' Association
Chief Officer(s):
Annette Bruneau, President
Julie Kind, Secretary
Don MacIver, Treasurer
Brian Sudbury, Director, Technical

Alberta Aboriginal Women's Society
PO Box 5168, Stn. Main, Peace River AB T8S 1R8
Tel: 780-624-3416; *Fax:* 780-624-3409
aaws@telusplanet.net
Overview: A medium-sized provincial organization overseen by Native Women's Association of Canada
Chief Officer(s):
Ruth Kidder, President

Alberta Aerospace Association *See* Aviation Alberta

Alberta Agricultural Economics Association (AAEA)
Dept. of Resource Economics & Environmental Sociology, U of Alberta, 515 General Services Bldg., Edmonton AB T6G 2H1
Tel: 780-422-3122
info@aaea.ab.ca
aaea.ualberta.ca
Overview: A small provincial charitable organization founded in 1984
Mission: To provide an opportunity for communication among those interested in the agricultural & rural social sciences; To provide a forum for the discussion of issues affecting the rural economy; To encourage research & dissemination of research results & other information relating to Alberta's rural economy; To provide avenues for continuing education & professional upgrading
Finances: *Annual Operating Budget:* Less than $50,000
Membership: 100-499; *Fees:* $30
Activities: Annual 'Visions' Conference in May; regional seminars & luncheon speakers; newsletter; undergraduate & graduate scholarships in agricultural economics at University of Alberta
Chief Officer(s):
Lukas Matejovsky, President, 780-422-2887
lukas.matejovsky@gov.ab.ca
Vitor Dias, Secretary, 780-644-8702
vitor.dias@gov.ab.ca
Awards:
• AAEA Undergraduate Scholarship
• AAEA Masters Scholarship

Alberta Alliance on Mental Illness & Mental Health
Capital Place, #320, 9707 - 110 St., Edmonton AB T5K 2L9
Tel: 780-482-4993; *Fax:* 780-482-6348
www.aamimh.ca
Overview: A small provincial organization
Mission: To act as a voice for the mental health & mental illness community; To ensure mental health & mental illness issues are prominent on health & social policy agendas in Alberta
Membership: 12; *Member Profile:* Mental health organizations in Alberta
Chief Officer(s):
Orrin Lyseng, Executive Director
executivedirector@aamimh.ca

Canadian Associations / Alberta Alpine Ski Association (AASA)

Alberta Alpine Ski Association (AASA)
Bill Warren Training Centre, #100, 1995 Olympic Way, Canmore AB T1W 2T6
Tel: 403-609-4730; *Fax:* 403-678-3644
memberservices@albertaalpine.ca
www.albertaalpine.ca
www.facebook.com/AlbertaAlpine
twitter.com/AlbertaAlpine
www.youtube.com/user/AlbertaAlpine
Also Known As: Alberta Alpine
Overview: A small provincial organization
Mission: To be the provincial governing body for the sport of alpine skiing in Alberta
Chief Officer(s):
Nigel Loring, President & CEO, 403-609-4731
nigel@albertaalpine.ca
Alied Ten Broek, Vice President, Corporate Services, 403-609-4733
alied@albertaalpine.ca
Erin Gellhaus, Member Services, 403-609-4730
memberservices@albertaalpine.ca

Alberta Amateur Baseball Council (AABC)
Building 140, #106, 88 Canada Olympic Road SW, Calgary AB T3B 5R5
Tel: 403-247-5480; *Fax:* 403-320-2053
aabc@albertabaseball.org
www.albertabaseball.org
www.facebook.com/1008463665926674
twitter.com/AABC_2017
Overview: A medium-sized provincial organization founded in 1998
Mission: To be the provincial governing body for baseball associations throughout Alberta
Finances: *Funding Sources:* Alberta Sport Connection
Membership: 5 leagues + 31,000 individuals
Chief Officer(s):
Ron Van Keulen, President
Kim Brigitzer, Manager, Administration & Communications
k.brigitzer@albertabaseball.org
Aaron Lavorato, Coordinator, High Performance
a.lavorato@albertabaseball.org

Alberta Amateur Boxing Association *See* Boxing Alberta

Alberta Amateur Football Association (AAFA)
Percy Page Centre, 11759 Groat Rd., Edmonton AB T5M 3K6
Tel: 780-427-8108; *Fax:* 780-422-2663
admin@footballalberta.ab.ca
www.footballalberta.ab.ca
www.facebook.com/FootballAlberta
twitter.com/FootballAlberta
Also Known As: Football Alberta
Overview: A medium-sized provincial organization founded in 1973
Mission: To provide a consistent representative voice for football of all levels throughout the province of Alberta
Member of: Football Canada
Staff Member(s): 3
Membership: *Fees:* Schedule available
Chief Officer(s):
Jay Hetherington, President
jhetherington@rdpsd.ab.ca
Brian Fryer, Executive Director
bfryer@telus.net

Alberta Amateur Softball Association (AASA)
9860 - 33 Ave., Edmonton AB T6N 1C6
Tel: 780-461-7735; *Fax:* 780-461-7757
info@softballalberta.ca
www.softballalberta.ca
www.facebook.com/238456432957672
Also Known As: Softball Alberta
Overview: A large provincial organization founded in 1971 overseen by Canadian Amateur Softball Association
Mission: To foster & promote the playing of amateur softball; To regulate play in all classifications of the game as may be deemed in its best interests
Member of: Canadian Amateur Softball Association
Affiliation(s): Western Canada Softball Association
Finances: *Funding Sources:* Alberta Sport, Recreation & Parks; Wildlife Foundation
Staff Member(s): 4
Activities: *Internships:* Yes; *Speaker Service:* Yes; *Library:* Open to public
Chief Officer(s):
Michele Patry, Executive Director
michele@softballalberta.ca
Awards:
- Softball Alberta Scholarships
 Deadline: September 1
- Umpire Recognition Award
- Minor Player of the Year (Male and Female)
- Adult Slo-Pitch Player of the Year (Male and Female)
- Adult Fast-Pitch Player of the Year (Male and Female)
- Coach of the Year (Minor, Adult Slo-Pitch, Adult Fast-Pitch)

Alberta Amateur Speed Skating Association (AASSA)
2500 University Dr. NW, Calgary AB T2N 1N4
Tel: 403-220-7911; *Fax:* 403-220-9226
info@aassa.ca
www.albertaspeedskating.ca
www.facebook.com/albertaspeedskating
twitter.com/AB_SpeedSkating
instagram.com/albertaspeedskating
Also Known As: Alberta Speed Skating
Overview: A small provincial organization overseen by Speed Skating Canada
Member of: Speed Skating Canada
Chief Officer(s):
Nicole Cooney, President
Wendy Walker, Program Coordinator
Mike Marshall, Technical Director
Awards:
- Kevin Sirois Memorial Award
- Bruce Jones Memorial Award
- Mike Heitman Memorial Award

Alberta Amateur Wrestling Association (AAWA)
Percy Page Centre, 11759 Groat Rd., Edmonton AB T5M 3K6
Tel: 780-415-0140; *Fax:* 780-427-0524
aawa@ocii.com
www.albertaamateurwrestling.ca
www.facebook.com/AlbertaWrestling
twitter.com/AlbertaWrestlin
Overview: A small provincial organization founded in 1974 overseen by Canadian Amateur Wrestling Association
Mission: The AAWA is the governing body for amateur wrestling & grappling in Alberta.
Member of: Canadian Amateur Wrestling Association
Finances: *Annual Operating Budget:* $100,000-$250,000; *Funding Sources:* Government grants; fundraising
Staff Member(s): 2
Membership: 2,000; *Fees:* Schedule available; *Member Profile:* Male & female ages 13+
Activities: Training camps; officials & coaches clinics; school clinics; major games; coordinate provincial program
Chief Officer(s):
Tammie Bradley, Executive Director
Michael Drought, Technical Director, 780-643-0799
aawatechnical@gmail.com
Awards:
- Coach of the Year Award
- Outstanding School Coach of the Year Award
- Outstanding Official Award

Alberta Amputee Sports & Recreation Association (AASRA)
PO Box 86093, Stn. Marda Loop, Calgary AB T2T 6B7
Tel: 403-201-0507
info@aasra.ab.ca
www.aasra.ab.ca
www.facebook.com/495810413773520
Overview: A small provincial charitable organization founded in 1977
Mission: To support & provide opportunities for amputees in recreational & sporting activities, in events for both the disabled & able-bodied; To provide moral support to new amputees & family
Finances: *Funding Sources:* Donations; corporate & government support
Membership: *Fees:* $50 Annual; $150 Lifetime; *Member Profile:* People who have lost a limb(s) at a major joint; *Committees:* Volunteer
Activities: Annual Pro/Amp Golf Tournament; cycling clinic, golf clinic; support group meetings; *Speaker Service:* Yes; *Library*
Chief Officer(s):
Rachael Pasay, President

Alberta Angus Association
PO Box 3725, Olds AB T4H 1P5
Tel: 403-556-9057
Toll-Free: 888-556-9057
office@albertaangus.ca
www.albertaangus.ca
Overview: A medium-sized provincial organization founded in 1917
Mission: To protect the interests of Angus cattle in Alberta; To promote cooperation between breeders & others interested in Angus cattle
Member of: Canadian Angus Association
Finances: *Annual Operating Budget:* $50,000-$100,000
Staff Member(s): 1
Membership: 100-499; *Fees:* $25 + GST; *Committees:* Executive; Commercial Development; 4-H/Youth; Member Programs; Shows
Chief Officer(s):
Tiffany Richmond, Vice-President
tiffany@richmondranch.com
Awards:
- Purebred Breeder of the Year
- Commercial Breeder of the Year
- Spirit of Angus Award
Publications:
- The Angus Angle
Type: Newsletter

Alberta Aquaculture Association
c/o Dan Menard, Treasurer, PO Box 26, Site 3, RR#1, Red Deer AB T4N 5E1
Tel: 403-342-5206; *Fax:* 403-342-2646
info@smokytroutfarm.com
www.affa.ab.ca
Previous Name: Alberta Fish Farmers Association
Overview: A small local organization
Mission: To support the pursuit of aquaculture promotion & education
Member of: Canadian Aquaculture Producers' Council
Membership: *Fees:* $10 associate; $100 full; $250 corporate & educational institution
Chief Officer(s):
Dan Menard, Treasurer
dan@smokytroutfarm.com

Alberta Assessment Consortium (AAC)
#700, 11010 - 142 St., Edmonton AB T5N 2R1
Tel: 780-761-0530; *Fax:* 780-761-0533
info@aac.ab.ca
www.aac.ab.ca
twitter.com/AACinfo
Overview: A medium-sized provincial organization
Mission: Develops a broad range of classroom assessment materials, directly aligned to Alberta curriculum, that address both formative and summative processes.
Membership: 100-499; *Fees:* $5,500 regular; $1,100 associate; *Member Profile:* School authorities and other educational organizations having a central role in the education of children.
Activities: Classroom assessment materials
Chief Officer(s):
Sherry Bennett, Executive Director

Alberta Assessors' Association (AAA)
10555 - 172 St., Edmonton AB T5S 1P1
Tel: 780-483-4222
membership@assessor.ab.ca
www.assessor.ab.ca
twitter.com/AlbertaAssessor
Overview: A small provincial licensing organization founded in 1962
Mission: To promote assessment as a profession, & to ensure the professional integrity & skill of assessors through, for example, the advancement of educational programming.
Affiliation(s): International Association of Assessing Officers
Finances: *Funding Sources:* Membership fees; seminars
Staff Member(s): 2
Membership: *Fees:* $425 Accredited; $350 Associate/Candidate; $75 Retired; $0 Student; *Committees:* Executive; Registration; Practice Review; Discipline; Legislative Policy; Marketing; Editorial
Chief Officer(s):
Laurie Hodge, Executive Administrator/Registrar
registrar@assessor.ab.ca
Meetings/Conferences:
- Alberta Assessors' Association 2018 Conference, April, 2018, Sheraton Cavalier Calgary, Calgary, AB
Scope: Provincial

Alberta Association for Community Living; Alberta Association for the Mentally Handicapped See Inclusion Alberta

Alberta Association of Academic Libraries (AAAL)
c/o Genevieve Luthy, SAIT, 1301 - 16 Ave. NW, Calgary AB T2M 0L4
aaal.ca
www.facebook.com/AlbertaAssociationofAcademicLIbraries
twitter.com/AlbertaAAL
Overview: A medium-sized provincial organization founded in 1973
Mission: To facilitate planning, cooperation, & communication among Alberta's academic libraries; To promote continuing education
Finances: *Funding Sources:* Membership dues
Membership: 32; *Fees:* $100; *Member Profile:* All academic libraries in Alberta
Activities: Facilitating professional development oppprtunities for members; Encouraging greater participation & collaboration between members; Communicating with members through listserv & Round Tables; Providing mentorship opportunities
Chief Officer(s):
Sonya Betz, Co-Chair
sonya.betz@ualberta.ca
Robyn Hall, Co-Chair
hallr27@macewan.ca
Genevieve Luthy, Secretary-Treasurer
genevieve.luthy@sait.ca
Meetings/Conferences:
• Alberta Association of Academic Libraries Spring Meeting 2018, April, 2018, Calgary, AB
Scope: Provincial
• Alberta Association of Academic Libraries Fall Meeting 2018, November, 2018, Edmonton, AB
Scope: Provincial

Alberta Association of Agricultural Societies (AAAS)
J.G. O'Donoghue Building, #200, 7000 - 113 St., Edmonton AB T6H 5T6
Tel: 780-427-2174; *Fax:* 780-422-7755
aaas@gov.ab.ca
www.albertaagsocieties.ca
Overview: A medium-sized provincial organization founded in 1947
Mission: To preserve & enhance the viability of agricultural societies in Alberta
Membership: 294+; *Fees:* $150 service membership; $200 agricultural societies; *Member Profile:* Agricultural societies & communities in Alberta
Activities: Presenting education programs; Lobbying government; Providing information; Facilitating networking
Chief Officer(s):
Tim Carson, Chief Executive Officer
tim.carson@xplornet.com
Lisa Hardy, Executive Director
lisa.hardy@gov.ab.ca
Monica Bradley, Treasurer
monica.bradley@shaw.ca
Meetings/Conferences:
• Alberta Association of Agricultural Societies 2018 Annual Meeting & Convention, 2018, AB
Scope: Provincial
Description: An event attended by members of the Alberta Association of Agricultural Societies, where agricultural societies can submit resolutions to the annual general meeting & vote
Contact Information: E-mail: aaas@gov.ab.ca
Publications:
• Across the Fence [a publication of the Alberta Association of Agricultural Societies]
Type: Newsletter; *Frequency:* Quarterly; *Accepts Advertising*;
Price: Free with Alberta Association of Agricultural Societies membership
Profile: Contents include the chief executive officer's message, industry topics, conventions, awards, grant opportunities, & regionalissues
• Alberta Association of Agricultural Societies Membership Directory
Type: Directory; *Price:* Free access on request, with Alberta Association of Agricultural Societies membership

The Alberta Association of Animal Health Technologists See Alberta Veterinary Technologist Association

Alberta Association of Architects (AAA)
Duggan House, 10515 Saskatchewan Dr. NW, Edmonton AB T6E 4S1
Tel: 780-432-0224; *Fax:* 780-439-1431
info@aaa.ab.ca
www.aaa.ab.ca
www.linkedin.com/company/the-alberta-association-of-architects
www.facebook.com/AlbertaAssociationOfArchitects
twitter.com/theABarchitects
www.instagram.com/theabarchitects
Overview: A medium-sized provincial licensing organization founded in 1906
Mission: To regulate the practice of architecture & interior design in Alberta for the protection of the public & the administration of the profession; To bring together architects & support commitment to superior architecture
Member of: Royal Architectural Institute of Canada; Committee of Canadian Architectural Councils
Finances: *Annual Operating Budget:* $250,000-$500,000
Staff Member(s): 10; 160 volunteer(s)
Membership: 2,400+; *Fees:* Schedule available; *Member Profile:* Registered architects; Intern architects; Licensed interior designers; Intern interior designers; *Committees:* Communications Advisory; Complaints Review; Practice Review; Professional Development Advisory; Registration; Reinstatement
Activities: *Awareness Events:* Professional Development Day, October; *Internships:* Yes; *Rents Mailing List:* Yes; *Library*
Chief Officer(s):
Barbara Bruce, Executive Director
execdir@aaa.ab.ca
Awards:
• Prairie Design Awards

Alberta Association of Clinic Managers (AACM)
c/o Jennifer Hendricks, Treasurer, 30 Prestwick Row SE, Calgary AB T2Z 3L7
info@aacm.ca
aacm.ca
www.facebook.com/AACM.ca
Overview: A small provincial organization founded in 1957
Membership: *Fees:* $150
Chief Officer(s):
Renee Puchailo, President
Meetings/Conferences:
• Alberta Association of Clinic Managers 2018 Conference, June, 2018, Coast Hotel, Canmore, AB
Scope: Provincial
Description: Joint conference with the Medical Group Management Association of Canada (MGMAC)

Alberta Association of Family School Liaison Workers (AAFSLW)
c/o Tonia Koversky, St. Albert Family & Community Support Services, #10, 50 Bellerose Dr., St. Albert AB T8N 3L5
Tel: 780-459-1749; *Fax:* 780-458-1260
www.aafslw.ca
www.linkedin.com/groups/AAFSLW-6609871
www.facebook.com/AAFSLW
Overview: A small provincial organization founded in 1991
Mission: AAFSLW provides an opportunity for networking among professionals through conferences, regional meetings, newsletters, resource sharing, and case conferencing.
Membership: *Fees:* $40-$50; *Member Profile:* Family School Liaison Workers across the Province of Alberta
Chief Officer(s):
Christine Payne, President, 403-253-9257 Ext. 218
Meetings/Conferences:
• 27th Alberta Association of Family School Liaison Workers 2018 Conference, 2018
Scope: Provincial

Alberta Association of Fund Raising Executives (AAFRE)
11704 - 44 Ave., Edmonton AB T6J 0Z6
Tel: 780-761-1840; *Fax:* 888-423-5976
info@aafre.org
www.aafre.org
twitter.com/aafreorg
Overview: A small provincial organization founded in 1988
Mission: To foster the use of ethical standards in fund raising programs by providing educational and networking opportunities for fund raisers and to enhance the understanding of the benefits to society accomplished through fund raising.
Membership: *Fees:* $200 Charities, Foundations, Not-for-Profit Organizations, Businesses; $150 Individuals; $50 Associate Members
Chief Officer(s):
Carmen Boyko, President
Publications:
• AAFRE [Alberta Association of Fund Raising Executives] News
Type: Newsletter; *Frequency:* 4 pa

Alberta Association of Insolvency & Restructuring Professionals (AAIRP)
c/o MNP Ltd., #500, 10104 - 103 Ave., Edmonton AB T5J 0H8
Tel: 780-969-1491; *Fax:* 780-409-5415
www.aairp.com
Previous Name: Alberta Insolvency Practitioners Association
Overview: A small provincial organization overseen by Canadian Association of Insolvency & Restructuring Professionals
Mission: Non-profit organization that exists to attract, develop and support its members who provide insolvency and restructuring services
Member of: Canadian Association of Insolvency & Restructuring Professionals
Membership: *Member Profile:* Trustees in bankruptcy, receivers, consultants, agents for secured creditors
Chief Officer(s):
Eric Sirrs, President
eric.sirrs@mnp.com

Alberta Association of Landscape Architects (AALA)
PO Box 21052, Edmonton AB T6R 2V4
Tel: 780-435-9902; *Fax:* 780-413-0076
aala@aala.ab.ca
www.aala.ab.ca
Overview: A medium-sized provincial organization founded in 1970 overseen by Canadian Society of Landscape Architects
Mission: To advance the quality of the professional practice of landscape architecture in Alberta
Member of: Canadian Society of Landscape Architects
Finances: *Funding Sources:* Membership dues; Sponsorships
Membership: *Fees:* $50; *Committees:* Registration; Discipline & Practice Review; Website; Grievance; Promotions; Continuing Education; Examining Board; Calgary; Edmonton
Activities: Offering a continuing education program; *Internships:* Yes *Library:* Alberta Association of Landscape Architects Resource Library
Chief Officer(s):
Jill Lane, Manager
Mark Nolan, Registrar, 780-428-4000
mnolan7@hotmail.com
Brian Charanduk, Treasurer, 780-917-7219
brian.charanduk@stantec.com
Michelle Lefebre, Secretary
Meetings/Conferences:
• Alberta Association of Landscape Architects 2018 Annual General Meeting, 2018, AB
Scope: Provincial
Publications:
• Alberta Association of Landscape Architects Newsletter
Type: Newsletter
Profile: Association activities & forthcoming events

Alberta Association of Library Technicians (AALT)
PO Box 700, Edmonton AB T5J 2L4
Toll-Free: 866-350-2258
president@aalt.org
www.aalt.org
www.linkedin.com/in/librarytechnicians
twitter.com/AALTLibraryTech
Overview: A medium-sized provincial organization founded in 1974
Mission: To foster & enhance the professional image of library technicians in Alberta; To support library technicians throughout the province
Membership: *Fees:* $20 student membership; $35 affiliate membership; $40 personal & associate membership; $55 institutional membership; *Member Profile:* Library technicians from all types of libraries throughout Alberta; *Committees:* Awards; Conference; Journal; Marketing; Membership; Membership Survey; Mentoring; Nomination; Salary Survey; Web Site
Activities: Providing information to library technicians; Promoting the profession; Offering educational opportunities
Chief Officer(s):
Karen Hildebrandt, President
president@aalt.org
Christy Nichols, Director, Online Services
Lynda Shurko, Director, Administrative Services
secretary@aalt.org

Canadian Associations / Alberta Association of Marriage & Family Therapy (AAMFT)

Awards:
- AALT Advocacy Award
Deadline: December 31
- AALT Library Technician Award of Excellence
Deadline: December 31
- Bernice Neufeld Special Service Award
Deadline: December 31
- Merle Harris Achievement Award
Deadline: December 31
- AALT Student Awards
Deadline: December 31
- AALT Conference Bursary
To provide financial assistance to an AALT member who otherwise would be unable to attend the AALT annual conference *Deadline:* December 31
- AALT Professional Development Bursary
To provide financial assistance to an AALT member who is enrolled in the Library and Information Technology or Library Operations Assistant distance education programs, or a graduate of a recognized Library Technician program, for their professional development endeavors *Deadline:* December 31

Publications:
- The AALT [Alberta Association of Library Technicians] Technician
Type: Journal; *Frequency:* Quarterly; *Accepts Advertising;*
Editor: Amy Southgate
Profile: Association highlights & business, feature articles, & calendar of events
- AALT [Alberta Association of Library Technicians] Membership Directory
Type: Directory
Profile: Contact information for current association members

Alberta Association of Marriage & Family Therapy (AAMFT)
907 - 25 Ave NW, Calgary AB T2M 2B5
Tel: 403-519-2198
info@aamft.ab.ca
www.aamft.ab.ca
Overview: A small provincial organization founded in 1995
Mission: To provide individual marriage & family therapy; to provide educational seminars for therapists
Affiliation(s): American Association for Marriage & Family Therapy; Registry of Marriage & Family Therapists in Canada
Finances: *Funding Sources:* Membership fees; workshops
Membership: *Member Profile:* Must first become a member of the American Association for Marriage and Family Theraphy (AAMFT) and membership is then drawn from the membership of the national organization.
Activities: *Speaker Service:* Yes; *Rents Mailing List:* Yes
Chief Officer(s):
Lori Limacher, Interim President
drlori@shaw.ca

Alberta Association of Medical Radiation Technologists *See* Alberta College of Medical Diagnostic & Therapeutic Technologists

Alberta Association of Midwives (AAM)
#166, 63 - 4307-130 Ave. SE, Calgary AB T2Z 3V8
Tel: 403-214-1882; *Fax:* 888-859-5228
info@alberta-midwives.com
www.alberta-midwives.com
Overview: A small provincial organization founded in 1986
Mission: To promote awareness of the profession of midwifery, supports midwifery-centered research, participates in a provincial education program.
Member of: Canadian Association of Midwives
Affiliation(s): International Confederation of Midwives
Finances: *Funding Sources:* Membership dues
Membership: *Fees:* $500 full/restricted; $350 inactive; $100 associate/student
Activities: *Awareness Events:* International Day of Midwife, May 5; *Speaker Service:* Yes
Chief Officer(s):
Joan Margaret Laine, President
jmlaine@alberta-midwives.com
Alex Andrews, Excutive Director
exec.director@alberta-midwives.com

Alberta Association of Municipal Districts & Counties (AAMDC)
2510 Sparrow Dr., Nisku AB T9E 8N5
Tel: 780-955-3639; *Fax:* 780-955-3615
Toll-Free: 855-548-7233
aamdc@aamdc.com
www.aamdc.com
twitter.com/aamdc
www.flickr.com/photos/45829734@N03
Overview: A medium-sized provincial organization founded in 1909
Member of: Federation of Canadian Municipalities
Finances: *Annual Operating Budget:* $500,000-$1.5 Million
Staff Member(s): 13
Membership: 69 regular; 650 associate; *Member Profile:* Rural municipalities, counties & municipal districts in Alberta
Chief Officer(s):
Bob Barss, President, 780-842-7309
bbarss@aamdc.com
Gerald Rhodes, Executive Director, 780-955-4076
Meetings/Conferences:
- Alberta Association of Municipal Districts & Counties Spring 2018 Convention, March, 2018, Shaw Conference Centre, Edmonton, AB
- Alberta Association of Municipal Districts & Counties Fall 2018 Convention, November, 2018, Shaw Conference Centre, Edmonton, AB

Alberta Association of Naturopathic Practitioners *See* College of Naturopathic Doctors of Alberta

Alberta Association of Optometrists (AAD)
#100, 8407 Argyll Rd., Edmonton AB T6C 4B2
Tel: 780-451-6824; *Fax:* 780-452-9918
Toll-Free: 800-272-8843
www.optometrists.ab.ca
www.facebook.com/AskaDoctorofOptometry
twitter.com/AAOOptometrists
www.youtube.com/DoctorsofOptometry
Overview: A medium-sized provincial organization overseen by Canadian Association of Optometrists
Mission: To promote excellence in the practice of Optometry, to enhance public recognition of Optometry as the primary vision care provider in Alberta, and to advance the interests of the profession.
Finances: *Annual Operating Budget:* $500,000-$1.5 Million
Staff Member(s): 7
Membership: *Member Profile:* Optometrists, optometry students & optometric staff
Chief Officer(s):
Brian Wik, Executive Director
Meetings/Conferences:
- Alberta Association of Optometrists 2018 Conference, October, 2018, Sheraton, Red Deer, AB
Scope: Provincial

Alberta Association of Police Governance (AAPG)
PO Box 36098, Stn. Lakeview Post Office, Calgary AB T3E 7C6
Tel: 587-892-7874
admin@aapg.ca
www.aapg.ca
Overview: A medium-sized provincial organization founded in 2003
Mission: The AAPG is an association of police commissions and RCMP policing committees created pursuant to Alberta's Police Act.
Finances: *Funding Sources:* Membership dues; Conference
Chief Officer(s):
Terry Noble, Chair
Meetings/Conferences:
- Alberta Association of Police Governance 2018 Conference and Annual General Meeting, April, 2018, Best Western Plus Lacombe Inn & Suites, Lacombe, AB
Scope: Provincial

Alberta Association of Professional Paralegals (AAPP)
PO Box 47211, Stn. Edmonton Centre, Edmonton AB T5J 4N1
alberta-paralegal.com
twitter.com/ABProfParalegal
Overview: A small provincial organization founded in 1981 overseen by Canadian Association of Legal Assistants
Mission: To promote professional unity and mutual assistance among paralegals; to enhance knowledge & expertise for the benefit of members & the practice of law, in general; to support & advance status & interests of all legal assistants.
Finances: *Funding Sources:* Membership dues
Membership: *Fees:* $100 regular; $0 student; *Member Profile:* Full: employed as paralegal & employed for 5 years or successfully graduated from course approved by association, presently employed as paralegal & employed for 3 years; Associate: employed as paralegal & employed in legal field for 3 years or graduated from course approved by association, presently employed as paralegal; Affiliate: graduate from approved paralegal program or approved evening course certificate program, employed by lawyer or law firm but not as paralegal, or person working for lawyer or law firm performing at least 50% paralegal duties
Activities: *Library:*
Chief Officer(s):
Lorretta Klein, President
aapppresident@gmail.com

Alberta Association of Prosthetists & Orthotists
c/o Orthotics Prosthetics Canada, #202, 300 March Rd., Ottawa ON K2K 2E2
secretary@albertaoandp.com
www.albertaoandp.com
Overview: A small provincial organization overseen by Orthotics Prosthetics Canada
Mission: To represent members in Alberta's prosthetic & orthotic field; To promote high standards of patient care & professionalism
Membership: *Member Profile:* Prosthetic & orthotic practitioners, registered technicians, allied health professionals, students, & retired persons across Alberta
Activities: Providing continuing education opportunities
Chief Officer(s):
Jon Allen, President
Nolan Hayday, Vice-President
Ryan Cochrane, Secretary

Alberta Association of Recreation Facility Personnel
PO Box 100, 312 - 3rd St. West, #B, Cochrane AB T4C 1A4
Tel: 403-851-7626; *Fax:* 403-851-9181
Toll-Free: 888-253-7544
office@aarfp.com
www.aarfp.com
www.linkedin.com/company/recreation-facility-personnel
www.facebook.com/aarfp
Also Known As: Recreation Facility Personnel (RFP)
Overview: A medium-sized provincial organization founded in 1978
Mission: To provide education, consultation, & advocacy for people involved in recreation & facility operations
Member of: Alberta Recreation & Parks Association; Alberta Urban Municipalities Association
Finances: *Annual Operating Budget:* $500,000-$1.5 Million; *Funding Sources:* Self-generated funds; Membership dues; Course fees; Foundation grant
Staff Member(s): 3; 75 volunteer(s)
Membership: 900; *Fees:* $95 individual; $310 associate; $400 facility; *Member Profile:* People who work in recreation facilities; *Committees:* Education; Conference
Activities: Providing hands-on training courses, technical advice, consultation, & advocacy; *Internships:* Yes; *Speaker Service:* Yes; *Library:* Not open to public
Chief Officer(s):
Stuart Ray, Executive Director, 403-851-7626
stuart@aarfp.com
Awards:
- Don Moore Scholarship
; *Amount:* $1,500
- William Metcalfe Award
- Bruce Fowlow Memorial Facility Operator of the Year Award
Eligibility: An individual currently operating or managing a recreational facility
- Charles Mousseau Associates Award
- Student Achievement Awards Program
Presented to honour the top marks in each certification course (Swimming Pool Operator, Arena Operator, Parks & Sports Field Operator, Building Maintenance); *Amount:* $250
Meetings/Conferences:
- Alberta Association of Recreation Facility Personnel 2018 Conference, April, 2018, Banff, AB
Scope: Provincial

Alberta Association of Registered Nurses *See* The College & Association of Registered Nurses of Alberta

Alberta Association of Registered Occupational Therapists *See* Alberta College of Occupational Therapists

Alberta Association of Rehabilitation Centres (AARC)
#19, 3220 - 5 Ave. NE, Calgary AB T2A 5N1
Tel: 403-250-9495; *Fax:* 403-291-9864
acds@acds.ca
www.acds.ca
Overview: A medium-sized provincial organization founded in 1972

Mission: To support organizations that provide services & supports to people with disabilities; To act as a voice for the field of community rehabilitation to the political & administrative arms of government; To focus on human resource initiatives for the services sector; To provide in-service training opportunities for people employed in the field; To accredit & certify service in Alberta
Membership: *Fees:* Schedule available; *Member Profile:* Organizations serving persons with disabilities
Chief Officer(s):
Ann Nicol, CEO, 403-250-9495 Ext. 238
Helen Ficocelli, President
Bob Diewold, Vice-President

Alberta Association of Services for Children & Families; Alberta Association of Child Care Centres See ALIGN Association of Community Services

Alberta Association of Social Workers; Alberta Association of Registered Social Workers See Alberta College of Social Workers

Alberta Association of the Appraisal Institute of Canada See The Appraisal Institute of Canada - Alberta

Alberta Association of the Deaf (AAD)
#204, 11404 - 142 St., Edmonton AB T5M 1V1
www.aadnews.ca
www.facebook.com/deaf.alberta
twitter.com/deafalberta
www.youtube.com/deafalberta
Overview: A small provincial charitable organization
Mission: To promote equal rights for deaf people in Alberta; To improve the quality of life for deaf people in general
Affiliation(s): Calgary Association of the Deaf; Edmonton Association for the Deaf; Edmonton Fellowship of the Deaf Blind; Alberta Cultural Society of the Deaf; Alberta Deaf Sports Association; Association of Sign Language Interpreters of Alberta
Membership: *Fees:* $15 senior/student; $25 individual
Chief Officer(s):
Amber Schultz, Secretary

Alberta Association of Travel Health Professionals (AATHP)
North Tower, #440, 10030-107 St., Edmonton AB T5J 3E4
www.aathp.com
Overview: A medium-sized provincial organization founded in 1997
Membership: *Fees:* $40
Chief Officer(s):
Catherine Shepherd, President
Meetings/Conferences:
• Alberta Association of Travel Health Professionals 2018 Conference, June, 2018, Coast Canmore Hotel, Canmore, AB
Scope: Provincial

Alberta Association on Gerontology (AAG)
PO Box 47022, Stn. Edmonton Centre, Edmonton AB T5J 4N1
info@albertaaging.ca
www.albertaaging.ca
Overview: A medium-sized provincial charitable organization founded in 1980
Mission: To support persons involved in & concerned with gerontology in their efforts to enhance the lives of the aging population
Member of: Canadian Association on Gerontology
Finances: *Funding Sources:* Membership dues
Membership: *Fees:* $15 student; $20 senior; $50 individual; $75 organization; *Member Profile:* Professionals working with seniors/seniors issues
Chief Officer(s):
Vivien Lai, President
Brenda Hannah, Vice-President
Awards:
• AAG Student Bursary
• Mary Morrison Davis Award of Excellence

Alberta Associations for Bright Children (AABC)
c/o Edmonton Association for Bright Children, 1644 Tompkins Place, Edmonton AB T6R 2Y6
www.edmontonabc.org/aabc
Overview: A medium-sized provincial charitable organization founded in 1981
Mission: To inform & support professionals & parents who are facing the challenge of dealing with bright, gifted, talented children; to advocate at the school board & government levels to ensure that resources & expertise are allocated in a manner that serves the children best
Affiliation(s): Action for Bright Children Calgary Society; Edmonton Association for Bright Children; Cold Lake Network Group
Finances: *Annual Operating Budget:* Less than $50,000; *Funding Sources:* Donations; government grants
Activities: *Speaker Service:* Yes; *Library:* Bright Site

Alberta Athletic Therapists Association
PO Box 61115, Kengsington RPO, Calgary AB T2N 4S6
Tel: 403-220-8957
www.aata.ca
www.facebook.com/452665388145479?ref=ts&fref=ts
twitter.com/AATA_therapy
Overview: A small provincial organization
Member of: Canadian Athletic Therapists Association
Chief Officer(s):
Breda Lau, President
president@aata.ca
Danielle Larsen, Secretary
secretary@aata.ca

Alberta Automotive Recyclers & Dismantlers Association (AARDA)
20 Oakmount Dr., St. Albert AB T8N 6K6
Tel: 780-478-5820; *Fax:* 780-628-6463
admin@aarda.com
www.aarda.com
Overview: A medium-sized provincial organization
Mission: To conserve the valuable resources involved in producing and operating the vehicles driven by Albertans today when they become damaged or inoperable, by recycling the parts.
Member of: Automotive Recyclers of Canada
Membership: 50; *Member Profile:* Automotive recyclers (wholesale and retail recycled auto parts dealers); Suppliers of end-of-life vehicles to provincial shredding facilities
Chief Officer(s):
Ian Hope, Executive Director
Meetings/Conferences:
• Alberta Automotive Recyclers & Dismantlers Association AGM & Conference 2018, September, 2018, Drumheller, AB
Scope: Provincial

Alberta Aviation Museum Association
11410 Kingsway Ave., Edmonton AB T5G 0X4
Tel: 780-451-1175; *Fax:* 780-451-1607
aama@live.ca
www.albertaaviationmuseum.com
Overview: A small provincial organization
Mission: To collect, preserve, restore, research & display the history of aviation in Alberta & the city of Edmonton
Member of: Edmonton Aviation Heritage Society
Activities: Aircraft restoration workshops

Alberta Badminton Association See Badminton Alberta

Alberta Ballet
141 - 18 Ave. SW, Calgary AB T2S 0B8
Tel: 403-245-4222; *Fax:* 403-245-6573
info@albertaballet.com
www.albertaballet.com
www.facebook.com/AlbertaBalletCanada
twitter.com/albertaballet
Overview: A medium-sized provincial charitable organization founded in 1966
Mission: To enrich & bring beauty to people's lives through creating, performing & teaching ballet
Finances: *Annual Operating Budget:* $3 Million-$5 Million; *Funding Sources:* Earned income; Fundraising; Government grants; Corporate, individual, and subscription donations; Corporate sponsorship
Staff Member(s): 50; 300 volunteer(s)
Membership: 32; *Fees:* Schedule available
Activities: Presenting live performances in Calgary & Edmonton; Touring nationally & internationally; *Internships:* Yes; *Speaker Service:* Yes
Chief Officer(s):
Chris George, Executive Director
Jean Grand-Maître, Artistic Director
Peter Dala, Music Director

Alberta Band Association (ABA)
#104, 4818 - 50 Ave., Red Deer AB T4N 4A3
Tel: 403-347-2237; *Fax:* 403-347-2241
Toll-Free: 877-687-4239
www.albertabandassociation.com
Overview: A medium-sized provincial charitable organization overseen by Canadian Band Association
Mission: To promote & develop the musical, educational & cultural values of bands & band music in Alberta
Member of: Music Alberta; Canadian Band Association
Finances: *Funding Sources:* Alberta Foundation for the Arts
Staff Member(s): 2
Membership: 500-999; *Fees:* $75 regular; $125 institutional; $150 commercial; $25 student; *Member Profile:* School, community and military band directors; Professional composers; Students, Parents
Activities: *Speaker Service:* Yes; *Library:* R. Bruce Marsh Memorial Library
Chief Officer(s):
Darwin Krips, President

Alberta Barley Commission
#200, 6815 - 8 St. NE, Calgary AB T2E 7H7
Tel: 403-291-9111; *Fax:* 403-291-0190
Toll-Free: 800-265-9111
barleyinfo@albertabarley.com
www.albertabarley.com
www.facebook.com/209980095717832
twitter.com/AlbertaBarley
www.youtube.com/user/GoBarleyTV
Also Known As: Alberta Barley
Overview: A large provincial organization founded in 1991
Mission: To supprt barley farmers & help advance the industry
Member of: Barley Council of Canada; Canadian Agri-food Trade Alliance; Grain Growers of Canada
Affiliation(s): Alberta Wheat Commission; Feed Coalition; Gainswest Magazine; Growing Forward 2; Western Canadian Deduction
Staff Member(s): 5
Membership: 11,000; *Fees:* Schedule available; *Member Profile:* Barley farmers in Alberta; *Committees:* Audit & Finance; Communications; Governance; Market Development Group; Policy; Research; Resolutions
Chief Officer(s):
Rob Davies, General Manager, 403-219-6262
rdavies@albertabarley.com

Alberta Baton Twirling Association (ABTA)
Percy Page Centre, 11759 Groat Rd., Edmonton AB T5M 3K6
Tel: 780-415-1440; *Fax:* 780-415-0170
abta@telusplanet.net
www.albertabaton.com
www.facebook.com/106834729351227
Overview: A small provincial organization founded in 1971 overseen by Canadian Baton Twirling Federation
Mission: To be the voice of baton twirling in the province; To promote the values & development of the sport; To unite the province in interest of baton twirling; To provide exposure; To manage the business of baton, inform members, provide opportunity & demonstration/competition
Member of: Canadian Baton Twirling Federation
Affiliation(s): Alberta Sport, Recreation, Parks, Wildlife Foundation
Activities: *Library:* Open to public
Chief Officer(s):
Bonnie Brinker, Chair
Shari Foster, Executive Director

Alberta Beach & District Chamber of Commerce
PO Box 280, Alberta Beach AB T0E 0A0
Tel: 780-924-3255; *Fax:* 780-924-3257
www.albertabeachchamber.com
www.facebook.com/albertabeach
twitter.com/ouralbertabeach
Overview: A small local organization founded in 1965
Mission: To support & promote local businesses
Membership: 71; *Fees:* $45
Chief Officer(s):
Bert Pyper, President

Alberta Beef Producers (ABP)
#165, 6815 - 8th St. NE, Calgary AB T2E 7H7
Tel: 403-275-4400; *Fax:* 403-274-0007
abpfeedback@albertabeef.org
www.albertabeef.org
twitter.com/albertabeef
Previous Name: Alberta Cattle Commission
Overview: A medium-sized provincial organization founded in 1969
Mission: To strengthen the sustainability & competitiveness of the beef industry; To produce beef in an environmentally sustainable manner; To support responsible animal care &

handling
Member of: Canadian Cattlemen's Association (CCA)
Membership: 15,000-49,999
Activities: Influencing government policy; Improving the beef industry's public image; Engaging in research activities; Providing landowners with information on rangeland health
Chief Officer(s):
Rich Smith, Executive Director, 403-451-1183
RichS@albertabeef.org
Katelyn Laverdure, Manager, Communications, 403-451-1176
katelynl@albertabeef.org
Fred Hays, Policy Analyst, 403-451-1181
fredh@albertabeef.org
Awards:
• Environmental Stewardship Award
Presented annually to the beef producer who best exemplifies environmentally sustainable cattle production
Meetings/Conferences:
• Alberta Beef Industry Conference, 2018, AB
Scope: Provincial
Contact Information: www.abiconference.ca
Publications:
• Beneficial Management Practices: Envrionmental Manual for Alberta Cow/Calf Producers
Price: Free to all Alberta cattleproducers
Profile: Developed in partnership with Alberta Beef Producers (ABP) & Alberta Agriculture, Food, & Rural Development
• Recommended Code of Practice for the Care & Handling of Farm Animals: Beef Cattle Edition
Type: Booklet; *Price:* Free

Alberta Beekeepers Association *See* Alberta Beekeepers Commission

Alberta Beekeepers Commission
#102, 11434 - 168 St., Edmonton AB T5M 3T9
Tel: 780-489-6949; *Fax:* 780-487-8640
www.albertabeekeepers.org
Previous Name: Alberta Beekeepers Association
Overview: A small provincial organization founded in 2006
Mission: To work as a refundable commission, under the Marketing of Agriculture Products Act of the Province of Alberta
Membership: *Fees:* $50 producers + $0.75 per colony, if 100 or more live colonies; $100 affiliate members; $50 keep in touch members; *Member Profile:* Producers in Alberta; Industry related businesses or affiliate members; Beekeepers outside Alberta, or any other individuals, who want to "keep in touch" with Alberta beekeepers; *Committees:* Research; Bee Health; CHC; Crop Spraying - Pollination; Food Safety; Importation; PMRA; AFSC - Crop Insurance; Alberta - BC Liason; Convention; GPRC - Fairview Campus; Labour; Legislative; Marketing Council; Website
Activities: Offering liability insurance to eligible producers & hobby members
Chief Officer(s):
Grant Hicks, President, 780-324-3688
grhicks77@gmail.com
Jon Zwiers, Vice-President, 403-701-2804
jon.zwiers@gmail.com
Gertie Adair, General Manager, 780-489-6949, Fax: 780-487-8640
Gertie.Adair@AlbertaBeekeepers.org
Publications:
• Alberta Bee News
Type: Magazine; *Frequency:* Monthly; *Price:* Free with membership in the Alberta Beekeepers Commission

Alberta Bicycle Association (ABA)
11759 Groat Rd., Edmonton AB T5M 3K6
Tel: 780-427-6352; *Fax:* 780-427-6438
Toll-Free: 877-646-2453
www.albertabicycle.ab.ca
Overview: A small provincial licensing organization overseen by Cycling Canada Cyclisme
Mission: To promote all aspects of cycling in Alberta
Affiliation(s): Canadian Cycling Association; Union Cycliste International
Staff Member(s): 6
Membership: *Fees:* Schedule available; *Member Profile:* Cyclists; *Committees:* BMX; Racing; Recreation & Transportation
Activities: *Internships:* Yes
Chief Officer(s):
Heather Lothian, Executive Director
heather@albertabicycle.ab.ca

Alberta Biotechnology Association
Ledgeview Business Centre, #314, 9707 - 110 St., Edmonton AB T5K 2L9
Tel: 780-425-3804; *Fax:* 780-409-9263
admin@bioalberta.com
www.bioalberta.com
www.linkedin.com/company/bioalberta-alberta-biotechnology-association
www.facebook.com/BioAlberta
twitter.com/Bioalberta
Also Known As: BioAlberta
Overview: A small provincial organization founded in 1998
Mission: To act as the central voice & organizing hub for life science industries in Alberta
Staff Member(s): 5
Membership: *Fees:* Schedule available; *Committees:* Policy; BIO; Partnering
Activities: Representing Alberta's life sciences sector; Providing services & programs to member organizations, such as educational sessions, in order to expand the companies' dollars & reach
Chief Officer(s):
Paul Stinson, President & CEO

Alberta Bison Association
501 - 11 Ave., Nisku AB T9E 7N5
Tel: 780-955-1995; *Fax:* 780-955-1990
info@bisoncentre.com
www.bisoncentre.com
www.facebook.com/199914170156327
Overview: A small provincial organization
Mission: To represent bison producers in Alberta & to conduct research aimed towards increasing productivit & profitability as well as solving issues that surround the industry
Member of: Canadian Bison Association
Membership: *Fees:* $236.25
Chief Officer(s):
Thomas Achermann, Chair
Linda Sautner, Office Manager

Alberta Blonde d'Aquitaine Association
PO Box 5959, Westlock AB T7P 2P7
Tel: 780-348-5308
aba@clearwave.ca
www.albertablondecattle.com
Overview: A small provincial organization
Mission: To represent breeders of Blonde d'Aquitaine cattle in Alberta
Membership: *Member Profile:* Breeders of Blonde d'Aquitaine cattle from Alberta
Activities: Providing information for breeders of Blonde d'Aquitaine cattle; Organizing field days
Chief Officer(s):
Reed Rigney, President
Publications:
• Blonde Bullet [a publication of the Alberta & Manitoba / Saskatchewan Blonde d'Aquitaine Associations]
Type: Newsletter; *Accepts Advertising*

Alberta Bobsleigh Association (ABA)
Bob Niven Training Centre, #205, 88 Canada Olympic Rd. SW, Calgary AB T3B 5R5
Tel: 403-297-2721; *Fax:* 403-286-7213
slide@albertabobsleigh.com
www.albertabobsleigh.com
www.facebook.com/albertabobsleigh
Overview: A small provincial charitable organization founded in 1983
Mission: To develop a broad interest in bobsleigh in Alberta; to provide opportunities for all Albertans to participate in bobsleigh; to provide opportunities for Albertans to progress to national & international levels
Member of: Bobsleigh Canada
Finances: *Annual Operating Budget:* $100,000-$250,000
Staff Member(s): 1; 70 volunteer(s)
Membership: 560; *Fees:* Schedule available
Activities: Summer training programs; *Library:* Not open to public
Chief Officer(s):
Sarah Monk, Technical Director
Dennis Marineau, Head Coach
Awards:
• Pat Stopa Memorial Award
• Service Award

Alberta Bodybuilding Association (ABBA)
Edmonton Centre, PO Box 47248, Edmonton AB T5J 4N1
Tel: 780-709-5309
www.abba.ab.ca
www.facebook.com/Albertabodybuildingassociation
twitter.com/AlbertaBBAssoc
Overview: A small provincial organization overseen by Canadian Bodybuilding Federation
Mission: To be the provincial governing body for the sport of amateur bodybuilding in Alberta
Member of: Canadian Bodybuilding Federation; International Federation of Bodybuilding
Chief Officer(s):
Brenda Rose, President
president@abba.ab.ca
Tara Ostafichuk, Vice President
vp@abba.ab.ca
Melissa Lefebvre, Secretary-Treasurer
treasurer@abba.ab.ca

Alberta Boilers Safety Association (ABSA)
9410 - 20th Ave. NW, Edmonton AB T6N 0A4
Tel: 780-437-9100; *Fax:* 780-437-7787
hr@absa.ca
www.absa.ca
Overview: A small provincial organization
Mission: To serve as the pressure equipment regulatory authority for Alberta; To review & register pressure equipment designs & equipment; To certify & register pressure welders, power engineers, & equipment inspectors; To investigate accidents that involve pressure equipment
Activities: Conducting safety education & training
Chief Officer(s):
Mike Poehlmann, General Manager

Alberta Bottle Depot Association (ABDA)
#202, 17850 - 105 Ave., Edmonton AB T5S 2H5
Tel: 780-454-0400; *Fax:* 780-454-0464
Toll-Free: 877-787-2232
info@abda.ca
www.abda.ca
www.facebook.com/albertadepot
twitter.com/AlbertaDepot
www.instagram.com/albertadepot
Overview: A small provincial organization
Mission: To educate about industry & to standardize the practices for depot operation
Finances: *Funding Sources:* Membership dues
Staff Member(s): 2; 14 volunteer(s)
Membership: 184
Activities: *Library:* Not open to public
Chief Officer(s):
Laura Nelson, Coordinator, Member Services

Alberta Bowhunters & Archers Association *See* Alberta Bowhunters Association

Alberta Bowhunters Association (ABA)
202 Copperfield Grove SE, Calgary AB T2Z 4L7
www.bowhunters.ca
Previous Name: Alberta Bowhunters & Archers Association
Overview: A medium-sized provincial organization
Mission: To promote bowhunting in Alberta
Member of: Federation of Canadian Archers
Membership: *Fees:* $35 Adult; $25 Youth; $70 Family; $500 Life
Chief Officer(s):
Brent Watson, President
brent@albertabowhunters.com

Alberta Broomball Association (ABA)
11759 Groat Rd., Edmonton AB T5M 3K6
www.albertabroomball.ca
Overview: A small provincial organization overseen by Ballon sur glace Broomball Canada
Member of: Ballon sur glace Broomball Canada
Chief Officer(s):
Greg Mastervick, President
gregma@telusplanet.net
Wayne Neigel, Secretary-Treasurer
neigel@shaw.ca
Meetings/Conferences:
• Alberta Broomball Association Annual General Meeting 2018, 2018, AB
Scope: Provincial

Alberta Building Envelope Council (South) (ABEC)
PO Box 61152, Stn. Kensington, Calgary AB T2N 4S6

Tel: 403-246-4500
webmaster@abecsouth.org
www.abecsouth.org
Overview: A small provincial organization founded in 1983
Mission: To promote the understanding of the building envelope
Member of: National Building Envelope Council
Finances: *Funding Sources:* Membership dues
Membership: 163; *Fees:* Individual: $48; Corporate: $65; Student: $10
Activities: The link between architects, building owners, engineers & contractors; *Speaker Service:* Yes
Chief Officer(s):
Mike Dietrich, President
mdietrich@morrisonhershfield.com
Bob Passmore, Secretary, 403-703-7535
bpassmore@bsaa.ca
Anton Vlooswyk, Treasurer, 403-651-1514
anton@beei.ca

Alberta Building Officials Association
12010 - 111 Avenue, Edmonton AB T5G 0E6
www.aboa.ab.ca
Also Known As: ABOA
Overview: A small local organization founded in 1959
Mission: To improve standards of building inspection; To be a discussion forum for shared issues and concerns; To assist in education of building inspectors in various fields
Membership: *Fees:* $125 regular; $150 associate
Chief Officer(s):
Ryan Nixon, President, 780-454-5048
rnixon@inspectionsgroup.com
Brian Boddez, Director, Membership, 780-459-1655
bboddez@st-albert.net

Alberta CA Profession's Non-Profit Foundation *See* Chartered Accountants' Education Foundation of Alberta

Alberta Camping Association (ACA)
Percy Page Centre, 11759 Groat Rd., Edmonton AB T5M 3K6
Tel: 403-477-5443
info@albertacamping.com
www.albertacamping.com
www.facebook.com/AlbertaCampingAssociation
twitter.com/Alberta_Camping
Overview: A medium-sized provincial charitable organization founded in 1949 overseen by Canadian Camping Association
Mission: To promote & coordinate organized camping in Alberta by providing camp information & leadership direction as well as promoting high standards of camp programs & activities for all populations; to take a leading role in the recognition & promotion of professional standards for organized camps in Alberta
Member of: Canadian Camping Association
Finances: *Annual Operating Budget:* $50,000-$100,000; *Funding Sources:* Lotteries; community development; recreation; Parks & Wildlife Foundation
Staff Member(s): 1; 18 volunteer(s)
Membership: 20 corporate + 400 individual + 100 camps; *Fees:* $15 student; $35 general; $150 camps; $100 commercial; *Committees:* Conference & Education; Marketing & Fundraising; Standards; Research & Development; Newsletter
Activities: *Speaker Service:* Yes; *Rents Mailing List:* Yes; *Library:* ACA Resource Centre; Open to public
Chief Officer(s):
Gerrit Leewes, President
gerrit@campwarwa.org
Gwen Dell'Anno, Executive Director
gdellanno@albertacamping.com
Meetings/Conferences:
• Alberta Camping Association Annual Conference 2018, March, 2018, Camp Kindle, Water Valley, AB
Scope: Provincial

Alberta Cancer Foundation (ACF)
#710, 10123 - 99 St. NW, Edmonton AB T5J 3H1
Tel: 780-643-4400; *Fax:* 780-643-4398
Toll-Free: 866-412-4222
acfonline@albertacancer.ca
albertacancer.ca
www.facebook.com/albertacancerfoundation
twitter.com/albertacancer
www.youtube.com/user/ABCancerFoundation
Overview: A small provincial charitable organization founded in 1984
Mission: To raise funds to support & enhance the programs & treatment facilities of the Alberta Cancer Board
Member of: Alberta Cancer Board
Finances: *Funding Sources:* Individual & corporate donors
Activities: Fundraising for the Alberta Cancer Board which operates two tertiary care facilities: the Cross Cancer Institute, Edmonton, the Tom Baker Cancer Centre, Calgary & 15 other cancer centres throughout Alberta; cancer research, treatment, prevention & education
Chief Officer(s):
Myka Osinchuk, CEO

Alberta Canola Producers Commission (ACPC)
Vantage Business Park, 14560 - 116 Ave. NW, Edmonton AB T5M 3E9
Tel: 780-454-0844; *Fax:* 780-451-6933
web@albertacanola.com
www.albertacanola.com
www.facebook.com/albertacanola
twitter.com/albertacanola
www.youtube.com/albertacanola
Overview: A medium-sized provincial organization founded in 1989
Mission: To provide leadership in a vibrant canola industry for the benefit of Alberta canola producers; to strive to improve the long-term profitability of Alberta canola producers
Member of: Canola Council of Canada
Affiliation(s): Canadian Canola Growers Association
Finances: *Annual Operating Budget:* $500,000-$1.5 Million
Staff Member(s): 8
Membership: 26,000; *Fees:* Schedule available, based on canola seed sales; *Committees:* Administration & Finance; Market Development; Member Relation & Extension; Research
Activities: *Speaker Service:* Yes
Chief Officer(s):
Ward Toma, General Manager, 780-454-0844
ward.toma@canola.ab.ca

Alberta Carriage Driving Association (ACDA)
c/o Steve Remus, PO Box 575, Redwater AB T0A 2W0
Tel: 780-942-3452
www.albertadriving-acda.ca
Overview: A small provincial organization founded in 1987
Mission: To promote carriage driving & combined driving; to host events that allow drivers with different levels of experience to interact
Membership: *Fees:* $35 individual; $45 family; *Member Profile:* Members are required to join the Alberta Equestrian Federation.
Chief Officer(s):
Patty Carley, President
Denise MacDonald, Secretary, 780-853-0305
dennynordin@gmail.com

Alberta Catholic School Trustees Association (ACSTA)
#205, 9940 - 106 St., Edmonton AB T5K 2N2
Tel: 780-484-6209; *Fax:* 780-484-6248
admin@acsta.ab.ca
www.acsta.ab.ca
twitter.com/acstanews
Overview: A medium-sized provincial organization
Mission: To promote, preserve, celebrate & enhance Catholic education in Alberta, Northwest Territories & Yukon
Member of: Canadian Catholic School Trustees Association
Chief Officer(s):
Adrianna LaGrange, President
John Tomkinson, Vice President

Alberta Cattle Breeders Association
PO Box 1060, Stn. M, Calgary AB T2P 2K8
Tel: 403-261-9316; *Fax:* 403-262-3067
albertacattlebreeders.com
Overview: A medium-sized provincial organization
Membership: *Member Profile:* Ranchers; farmers
Activities: Annual bull sale
Chief Officer(s):
Doug Finseth, President

Alberta Cattle Commission *See* Alberta Beef Producers

Alberta Cattle Feeders' Association (ACFA)
#6, 11010 - 46th St. SE, Calgary AB T2C 1G4
Tel: 403-250-2509; *Fax:* 403-209-3255
Toll-Free: 800-363-8598
info@cattlefeeders.ca
www.cattlefeeders.ca
www.linkedin.com/company/cattlefeedersab
www.facebook.com/CattleFeedersAB
twitter.com/CattleFeedersAB
Overview: A medium-sized provincial organization
Mission: To represent the cattle feeding industry in Alberta, in areas such as market development & access, taxation, water & air quality, & manure management
Finances: *Funding Sources:* Membership fees; Membership service activities
Membership: *Member Profile:* Cattle producers in Alberta
Activities: Implementing research; Developing new management practices & technology; Liaising with partners to develop new opportunities
Chief Officer(s):
Bryan Walton, CEO
bwalton@cattlefeeders.ca
Jennifer Brunette, Manager, Events & Member Services
jbrunette@cattlefeeders.ca
Shannon Lyons, Manager, Communications
slyons@cattlefeeders.ca
Joe Novecosky, Manager, Financial
jnovecosky@cattlefeeders.ca
Casey Vander Ploeg, Manager, Policy & Research
cvanderploeg@cattlefeeders.ca
Kimberli Nummi, Coordinator
knummi@cattlefeeders.ca
Publications:
• Business Directory
Type: Directory
Profile: Listings of companies & organizations which offer specialized services to the cattle feeding industry in Alberta

Alberta Central
#350N, 8500 Macleod Trail South, Calgary AB T2H 2N1
Tel: 403-258-5900; *Fax:* 403-253-7720
email@albertacentral.com
www.albertacentral.com
www.linkedin.com/company/536834
www.facebook.com/346088465461276
twitter.com/ABCreditUnions
www.youtube.com/user/AlbertaCreditUnions
Also Known As: Credit Unions of Alberta
Previous Name: Credit Union Central of Alberta
Overview: A small provincial organization overseen by Canadian Credit Union Association
Mission: To act as the central banking facility, trade association, & service bureau for the credit union system of Alberta; To safeguard the financial stability of the province's credit union system by maintaining liquidity; To provide leadership & support to Alberta's credit unions
Member of: Canadian Credit Union Association
Affiliation(s): Alberta Community and Co-operative Association (ACCA); Canadian Co-operative Association; Credit Union Deposit Guarantee Corporation; Credit Union Electronic Transaction Services (CUETS); World Council of Credit Unions; CUPS Payment Services (CUPS); CUSOURCE
Staff Member(s): 230
Membership: 45 credit unions; *Member Profile:* Independent credit unions across Alberta
Activities: Offering financial & technological products & services, as well as corporate & strategic planning & legal counsel to credit unions in Alberta; Facilitating credit union system development; Raising the profile of credit unions in Alberta
Chief Officer(s):
Alison Starke, Chair
Graham Wetter, President & CEO
Publications:
• Credit Union Central of Alberta Annual Report
Type: Yearbook; *Frequency:* Annually

Alberta Cerebral Palsy Sport Association (ACPSA)
Percy Page Centre, 11759 Groat Rd., Edmonton AB T5M 3K6
Tel: 780-422-2904; *Fax:* 780-422-2663
contact@acpsa.ca
www.acpsa.ca
www.facebook.com/165504436855126
twitter.com/AlbertaCPSports
instagram.com/powerchair_sports
Also Known As: Sportability Alberta
Overview: A small provincial charitable organization founded in 1984 overseen by Canadian Cerebral Palsy Sports Association
Mission: To promote recreational & competitive sporting opportunities for persons with cerebral palsy, brain injury & related conditions
Member of: Canadian Cerebral Palsy Sports Association
Finances: *Annual Operating Budget:* Less than $50,000
Staff Member(s): 2; 40 volunteer(s)
Membership: 220; *Fees:* $15 individual; $25 family; travelling athletes add $65 to membership fees; *Member Profile:*

Individuals with cerebral palsy, brain injury & other related conditions
Activities: Track & field; boccia; cycling; swimming; pre-school children's program; *Speaker Service:* Yes

Alberta CGIT Association
c/o 5720 Lodge Cres. SW, Calgary AB T3E 5Y7
Tel: 780-532-2947
cgit@telus.net
www.albertacgit.ca
Also Known As: Canadian Girls in Training - Alberta
Overview: A small provincial organization
Chief Officer(s):
Valerie Jenner, President

Alberta Chamber of Commerce *See* Alberta Chambers of Commerce

Alberta Chamber of Resources
Sun Life Place, 800, 10123 - 99 St. NW, Edmonton AB T5J 3H1
Tel: 780-420-1030; *Fax:* 780-425-4623
admin@acr-alberta.com
www.acr-alberta.com
twitter.com/orderlyRESCdev
Overview: A medium-sized provincial organization
Mission: Alberta Chamber of Resources provides leadership for the orderly and responsible development of our natural resources.
Membership: *Committees:* Mining Industry Advisory Committee; Social License to Operate and Grow; Aboriginal Participation; Workforce Working Group; Innovating Towards Alberta's Triple Future; Transportation; Responsible Development; Dam Integrity Advisory Committee; Positioning Alberta for Growth & Recovery; Resource Development + The Economy
Chief Officer(s):
Leon Zupan, President
Brad Anderson, Executive Director
Awards:
- Resource Person of the Year
- Environmental Award
- Major Reclamation Award
- Aboriginal Rewarding Partnerships
- MIAC Scholarships

Alberta Chambers of Commerce (ACC)
#1808, 10025 - 102A Ave., Edmonton AB T5J 2Z2
Tel: 780-425-4180; *Fax:* 780-429-1061
Toll-Free: 800-272-8854
tacom@abchamber.ca
www.abchamber.ca
www.facebook.com/ABChambersofCommerce
twitter.com/albertachambers
Previous Name: Alberta Chamber of Commerce
Overview: A large provincial organization founded in 1937
Mission: To enhance private enterprise in Alberta
Affiliation(s): Canadian Chamber of Commerce
Finances: *Annual Operating Budget:* $100,000-$250,000; *Funding Sources:* Membership dues; programs; events
Staff Member(s): 5
Membership: 126 chambers representing 23,000 businesses; *Fees:* Schedule available; *Committees:* Executive
Activities: *Speaker Service:* Yes
Chief Officer(s):
Sean Ballard, Chair
sballard@abchamber.ca
Chris J. Dugan, Chair-Elect
cdugan@abchamber.ca
Ken Kobly, President & CEO
kkobly@abchamber.ca
Awards:
- Business Awards of Distinction
Meetings/Conferences:
- Alberta Chambers of Commerce 2018 AGM & Policy Plenary Session, May, 2018, Grande Prairie, AB
Scope: Provincial

Alberta Chapter of the Registry of Interpreters for the Deaf, Inc. *See* Association of Sign Language Interpreters of Alberta

Alberta Cheerleading Association (ACA)
PO Box 31006, Edmonton AB T5Z 3P3
Tel: 780-417-0050; *Fax:* 780-417-0093
Toll-Free: 888-756-9220
info@albertacheerleading.ca
www.albertacheerleading.ca
www.facebook.com/115045571883130
Overview: A small provincial organization overseen by Cheer Canada
Mission: To be the provincial regulator of cheerleading in Alberta.
Member of: Cheer Canada
Chief Officer(s):
Jennifer Guiney, President
jennifer@albertacheerleading.ca
Denise Fisher, Executive Director
executivedirector@albertacheerleading.ca

Alberta Chess Association (ACA)
PO Box 11839, Stn. Main, Edmonton AB T5J 3K9
Tel: 403-970-8032
www.albertachess.org
Overview: A small provincial organization founded in 1975
Mission: To promote activity in Alberta through chess playing
Member of: Chess Federation of Canada
Membership: 400; 19 clubs; *Fees:* $28 juniors; $43 adults
Chief Officer(s):
Vlad Rekhson, Executive Director
vrekhson@yahoo.ca

Alberta Chicken Producers
2518 Ellwood Dr. SW, Edmonton AB T6X 0A9
Tel: 780-488-2125; *Fax:* 780-488-3570
Toll-Free: 877-822-4425
www.chicken.ab.ca
Overview: A medium-sized provincial organization founded in 1966 overseen by Chicken Farmers of Canada
Mission: To offer an environment for profitable chicken production; To promote a competitive & consumer-focused industry, with safe, high quality chicken products
Membership: *Member Profile:* Marketing board representing over 230 chicken producers in Alberta
Activities: Liaising with government; Funding research projects to benefit the industry
Chief Officer(s):
Karen Kirkwood, Executive Director
kkirkwood@chicken.ab.ca
Meetings/Conferences:
- Alberta Chicken Producers 2018 Annual General Meeting, February, 2018, Sheraton Red Deer, Red Deer, AB
Scope: Provincial
Description: An interactive educational event focussing upon biosecurity & emergency preparedness, plus a business meeting, & a keynote speaker
Publications:
- Alberta Chicken Producers Annual Report
Type: Yearbook; *Frequency:* Annually
Profile: Organization reports, upcoming events, market conditions, recipes & industry information
- Alberta Chicken Producers Newsletter
Type: Newsletter; *Frequency:* Bimonthly

Alberta Children's Hospital Foundation
2888 Shaganappi Trail NW, Calgary AB T3B 6A8
Tel: 403-955-8818; *Fax:* 403-955-8840
Toll-Free: 877-715-5437
kids@achf.com
www.childrenshospital.ab.ca
www.facebook.com/AlbertaChildrensHospitalFoundation
www.youtube.com/user/ACHF1
Overview: A small provincial charitable organization founded in 1957
Mission: To raise money on behalf of the Alberta Children's Hospital in order to improve the services provided to patients & to fund research
Chief Officer(s):
Saifa Koonar, President & CEO

Alberta Choir Federation *See* Choir Alberta

Alberta Civil Liberties Research Centre (ACLRC)
c/o Murray Fraser Hall, Faculty of Law, University of Calgary, #2350, 2500 University Dr. NW, Calgary AB T2N 1N4
Tel: 403-220-2505; *Fax:* 403-284-0945
aclrc@ucalgary.ca
www.aclrc.com
Previous Name: Calgary Civil Liberties Association
Overview: A small provincial charitable organization founded in 1982
Mission: To promote awareness among Albertans about civil liberties & human rights through research & education
Affiliation(s): University of Calgary
Activities: *Speaker Service:* Yes; *Library:* Open to public
Chief Officer(s):
Linda McKay-Panos, Executive Director
lmmckayp@ucalgary.ca

Alberta Civil Trial Lawyers' Association (ACTLA)
#550, 10055 - 106 St., Edmonton AB T5J 2Y2
Tel: 780-429-1133; *Fax:* 780-429-1199
Toll-Free: 800-665-7248
admin@actla.com
www.actla.com
Overview: A medium-sized provincial organization founded in 1986
Mission: To advocate for a strong civil justice system that protects the rights of all Albertans
Affiliation(s): Association of Trial Lawyers of America
Finances: *Funding Sources:* Membership dues; seminar revenue; advertising
Staff Member(s): 2
Membership: 600; *Fees:* Schedule available; *Member Profile:* Members of Law Society of Alberta; Students enrolled in law school
Activities: Offering educational seminars & events; *Library:* Expert Witness Bank Database; Not open to public
Chief Officer(s):
Sandy Leske, Executive Director
Maureen McCartney-Cameron, President

Alberta Clydesdale & Shire Association
PO Box 33, Fawcett AB T0G 0Y0
Tel: 780-954-3810
www.albertaclydesdalesandshires.com
Previous Name: Alberta Clydesdale Association
Overview: A small provincial organization
Membership: 20; *Fees:* $40 individual; $50 family
Chief Officer(s):
Fay Campbell, Sec.-Treas.
fcampbell@mcsnet.ca

Alberta Clydesdale Association *See* Alberta Clydesdale & Shire Association

Alberta College & Association of Chiropractors (ACAC)
Manulife Place, 11203 - 70 St. NW, Edmonton AB T5B 1T1
Tel: 780-420-0932; *Fax:* 780-425-6583
Other Communication: Blog: www.everydaychiropractic.com
office@albertachiro.com
www.albertachiro.com
www.facebook.com/AlbertaChiropractors
twitter.com/AlbertaChiro
www.youtube.com/user/albertachiro
Previous Name: College of Chiropractors of Alberta; Alberta Chiropractic Association
Overview: A medium-sized provincial licensing organization founded in 1986 overseen by Canadian Chiropractic Association
Mission: To ensure quality chiropractic care that enhances the well-being & protects the rights of the people of Alberta; To promote the art, science, & philosophy of chiropractic & its value in the health care community
Membership: 1000+ individual
Activities: *Library:* Not open to public
Chief Officer(s):
Deb Manz, Chief Executive Officer
dmanz@albertachiro.com

Alberta College & Association of Respiratory Therapy *See* College & Association of Respiratory Therapists of Alberta

Alberta College of Acupuncture & Traditional Chinese Medicine (ACATCM)
Main Lobby, 4935 - 40 Ave. NW, Calgary AB T3A 2N1
Tel: 403-286-8788
Toll-Free: 888-789-9984
info@acatcm.com
www.acatcm.com
Overview: A medium-sized provincial organization founded in 1997
Mission: To maintain & strengthen leadership in Acupuncture & Traditional Chinese Medical education; To provide quality education in Acupuncture & TCM; To provide continuing education programs to health care professionals seeking to enhance their skills; To help graduates achieve success as primary health care providers using the principles of Traditional Chinese Medicine
Affiliation(s): Beijing University of Chinese Medicine
Chief Officer(s):
Dennis Lee, Co-President
Colton Oswald, Co-President

Alberta College of Combined Laboratory & X-Ray Technologists (ACCLXT)
2004 Sherwood Dr., Sherwood Park AB T8A 0Z1
Tel: 780-438-3323; *Fax:* 855-299-0829
info@acclxt.ca
www.acclxt.ca
Overview: A medium-sized provincial organization founded in 1969
Mission: To be responsible for the registration, discipline & competency of all registered Combined Laboratory & X-Ray Technicians / Technologists currently practicing in the province of Alberta; To strive to provide excellence in the combined fields of laboratory, radiography, & electrocardiography medicine
Membership: 550; *Member Profile:* Active Membership is granted upon completion of a 2 year diploma program in Laboratory & X-Ray Sciences or substantial equivalence & successfully challenging the ACCLXT Provincial Registration Examination. Graduates from the NAIT CLXT program or a program deemed as substantially equivalent, who have not yet challenged the ACCLXT Provincial Registration Examination, may apply for a Temporary Membership, which allows them to register with the ACCLXT and work in AB, while waiting to challenge the exam. This membership extends from the date of application until the exam results are received. Honorary Membership may be conferred upon any person who has rendered notable service in the College, for its members or the field of Laboratory, X-Ray or Cardiology testing. Associate Membership may be granted to any individual who has been a registered as a CLXT and who no longer wishes to practice as a CLXT.
Chief Officer(s):
Nichol Roy, President
Terry Schlitter, Vice-President
Lyndsay Arndt, Executive Director & Registrar
Sandi Toepfer, Director, Education & Competency
Susan Battle, Coordinator, Administration
Publications:
• Alberta College of Combined Laboratory & X-Ray Technologists By-laws
Number of Pages: 20
Profile: Information about items such as meetings, committees, fees, ethics, & standards of practice
• Alberta College of Combined Laboratory & X-Ray Technologists Annual Report
Type: Yearbook; *Frequency:* Annually
Profile: Information about governance, membership, programs, examinations, & finances
• Competency Profile for Alberta Combined Laboratory & X-Ray Technologists
Number of Pages: 80
Profile: Prepared by the Alberta College of Combined Laboratory & X-Ray Technologists & the Alberta Health & Wellness Health Workforce Policy & Planning Branch
• Wavelengths [a publication of the Alberta College of Combined Laboratory & X-Ray Technologists]
Type: Newsletter
Profile: Information about the college's activities

Alberta College of Medical Diagnostic & Therapeutic Technologists
#800, 4445 Calgary Trail NW, Edmonton AB T6H 5R7
Tel: 780-487-6130; *Fax:* 780-432-9106
Toll-Free: 800-282-2165
info@acmdtt.com
acmdtt.com
twitter.com/acmdtt
Also Known As: ACMDTT
Previous Name: Alberta Association of Medical Radiation Technologists
Overview: A medium-sized provincial organization founded in 2004 overseen by Canadian Association of Medical Radiation Technologists
Mission: To act in accordance with the Province of Alberta Health Professions Act, Medical Diagnostic & Therapeutic Technologists Profession Regulation, & by the ACMDTT Bylaws; To abide by & promote ethical practice as described in the ACMDTT Code of Ethics for diagnostic & therapeutic professionals; To promote standards of practice within the discipline; To advance the profession in Alberta; To ensure that the public receives safe & ethical diagnostic & therapeutic care
Member of: Alliance of Medical Radiation Technologists Regulators of Canada; Alberta Federation of Regulated Health Professions; Canadian National Network of the Profession of Medical Radiological Technology; Canadian Association of Medical Radiation Technologists
Finances: *Annual Operating Budget:* $500,000-$1.5 Million; *Funding Sources:* Membership dues
Staff Member(s): 7; 40 volunteer(s)
Membership: 2,400; *Fees:* $450; *Member Profile:* Alberta professionals in the disciplines of radiological technology (RTR), radiation therapy (RTT), nuclear medicine technology (RTNM), magnetic resonance imaging (RTMR), & electroneurophysiology (ENP); *Committees:* Awards; Conference; Continuing Competence; Nominating; Registration
Activities: Offering an extensive continuing education course program; Distributing current professional information; Providing networking opportunities; Increasing awareness of the profession; *Speaker Service:* Yes
Chief Officer(s):
Karen Stone, Chief Executive Officer & Registrar
kstone@acmdtt.com
Pree Tyagi, Deputy Registrar
ptyagi@acmdtt.com
Awards:
• Dr. Marshall Mallett Scholastic Award in Radiological Technology
• Scholastic Award in Nuclear Medicine Technology
• Scholastic Award in Magnetic Resonance Technology
• Scholastic Award in Radiation Therapy
• Scholastic Award in Electroneurophysiology Technology
• Student Leadership Award in Radiological Technology
• Student Leadership Award in Nuclear Medicine Technology
• Student Leadership Award in Magnetic Resonance Technology
• Student Leadership Award in Radiation Therapy
• Student Leadership Award in Electroneurophysiology Technology
• CAMRT Leadership Development Institute Award
• Excellence in Professional Collaboration Award
• Professional Excellence in Leadership Award
• Professional Excellence in Patient Care Award
• Herbert M. Welch Memorial Award
• Joan Graham Award
• ACMDTT Honorary Lifetime Membership
• Carol Van Velzer Memorial Award
Meetings/Conferences:
• Alberta College of Medical Diagnostic & Therapeutic Technologists 2018 Annual General Conference, 2018, AB
Scope: Provincial
• Alberta College of Medical Diagnostic & Therapeutic Technologists 2018 Annual General Meeting, 2018, AB
Scope: Provincial
Publications:
• Alberta College of Medical Diagnostic & Therapeutic Technologists Annual Report
Type: Yearbook; *Frequency:* Annually
Profile: A yearly report on the activities of the College, including complaints, hearings, & appeals, & audited financial information
• Alberta College of Medical Diagnostic & Therapeutic Technologists Member Directory
Type: Directory
• Internal Matters [a publication of the Alberta College of Medical Diagnostic & Therapeutic Technologists]
Type: Newsletter; *Frequency:* Quarterly
Profile: Updates from the College, including branch, education, & awards information

Alberta College of Medical Laboratory Technologists *See* College of Medical Laboratory Technologists of Alberta

Alberta College of Occupational Therapists (ACOT)
#300, 10436 - 81 Ave., Edmonton AB T6E 1X6
Tel: 780-436-8381; *Fax:* 780-434-0658
Toll-Free: 800-561-5429
info@acot.ca
www.acot.ca
Previous Name: Alberta Association of Registered Occupational Therapists
Overview: A medium-sized provincial licensing organization founded in 1952 overseen by Canadian Association of Occupational Therapists
Mission: To operate as the regulatory body in Alberta for the profession of occupational therapists; to ensure competent & ethical occupational therapy services for the public of the province; to uphold the Code of Ethics & the Standards of Practice for occupational therapists in Alberta
Staff Member(s): 4
Membership: *Fees:* $150; *Member Profile:* Regulated members practising occupational therapy in Alberta
Activities: Investigating complaints about occupational therapists practising in Alberta; Reviewing professional conduct; Disciplining members for unprofessional conduct to protect the public
Chief Officer(s):
Ryan Sommer, President
council@acot.ca
Gina Kroetsch, Vice-President
council@acot.ca
Maggie Fulford, Registrar
registrar@acot.ca
Awards:
• ACOT Centenary PhD Scholarship, in the Faculty of Rehabilitation Medicine at the University of Alberta
; *Amount:* $5,000 per annum, for graduate student funding in occupational therapy
• President's Awards
In recognition of individuals who have shown an exemplary level of service & commitment to the profession of occupational therapy
Publications:
• ACOT News
Type: Newsletter; *Frequency:* 3 pa
Profile: College reports, activities, upcoming events, & articles on the profession
• Alberta College of Occupational Therapists Code of Ethics
Number of Pages: 29
• Alberta College Of Occupational Therapists Standards of Practice
Number of Pages: 15
• Alberta College of Occupational Therapists Annual Report
Type: Yearbook; *Frequency:* Annually
• Alberta OT register
Type: Directory
Profile: Listings of regulated members registered with the Alberta College of Occupational Therapists

Alberta College of Optometrists (ACO)
#102, 8407 Argyll Rd. NW, Edmonton AB T6C 4B2
Tel: 780-466-5999; *Fax:* 780-466-5969
Toll-Free: 800-668-2694
admin@collegeofoptometrists.ab.ca
www.collegeofoptometrists.ab.ca
Overview: A small provincial licensing organization founded in 1993
Mission: To act as the regulatory body for the profession of optometry in Alberta
Staff Member(s): 5
Membership: *Member Profile:* Optometrists; *Committees:* Nominating; Competence; Registration; Legislation; Complaint Review
Chief Officer(s):
Gordon Hensel, Registrar & CEO
registrar@collegeofoptometrists.ab.ca

Alberta College of Paramedics (ACP)
#220, 2755 Broadmoor Blvd., Sherwood Park AB T8H 2W7
Tel: 780-449-3114; *Fax:* 780-417-6911
Toll-Free: 877-351-2267
acp@collegeofparamedics.org
www.collegeofparamedics.org
Overview: A small provincial licensing organization
Mission: To carry out operations in accordance with the Health Disciplines Act; to govern & regulate the practice of paramedicine in Alberta; to maintain & enforce the Code of Ethics, to ensure safe & ethical care for Alberta's citizens; to establish & enforce standards of practice for the profession, to ensure competent care for the protection of the public interest
Membership: *Fees:* Schedule available; *Member Profile:* Individuals in Alberta who are registered emergency medical responders (EMR), emergency medical technicians (EMT), & emergency medical technologist-paramedics (EMT-P); *Committees:* Registration; Registration / Examination Advisory; Professional Conduct; Continuing Competence; Communications; Complaint Review; Practical Exam Appeal Review Working Subcommittee; Educational Institutions Program Approval / Audit Working Subcommittee; Substantial Equivalency Review Working Subcommittee
Activities: Overseeing the resolution of complaints involving alleged professional misconduct by registered practitioners
Chief Officer(s):
Sheldon Thunstrom, President
Tim Essington, Registrar/Executive Director
tim.essington@collegeofparamedics.org
Becky Donelon, Deputy Registrar
becky.donelon@collegeofparamedics.org
Carl Damour, Manager, Education & Equivalency
carl.damour@collegeofparamedics.org

Canadian Associations / Alberta College of Pharmacists (ACP)

Becky Donelon, Manager, Continuing Education & Standards
becky.donelon@collegeofparamedics.org
Heather Verbaas, Manager, Communications
heather.verbaas@collegeofparamedics.org
Bill Carstairs, Manager, Finance, 780-410-4138
bill.carstairs@collegeofparamedics.org
Publications:
• Alberta College of Paramedics Annual Report
Type: Yearbook; *Frequency:* Annually
• Alberta College of Paramedics Continuing Competency Program Handbook
Type: Handbook
• Emergency Medical Dialogue (EMD)
Frequency: 3 pa
Profile: Alberta College of Paramedics updates from the pre-hospital field, for practitioners
• The Pulse: News from the Alberta College of Paramedics
Type: Newsletter; *Frequency:* Monthly
Profile: Updates & announcements for the Emergency Medical Services profession

Alberta College of Pharmacists (ACP)
#1100, 8215 - 112 St. NW, Edmonton AB T6G 2C8
Tel: 780-990-0321; *Fax:* 780-990-0328
Toll-Free: 877-227-3838
acpinfo@pharmacists.ab.ca
www.pharmacists.ab.ca
www.linkedin.com/company/alberta-college-of-pharmacists
www.facebook.com/ACPharmacists
twitter.com/ACPharmacists
Overview: A medium-sized provincial organization overseen by National Association of Pharmacy Regulatory Authorities
Member of: Canadian Council on Continuing Education in Pharmacy
Staff Member(s): 30
Membership: *Committees:* Competence; Executive; Hearing Tribunal/Complaint Review; Nominating; Resolutions
Chief Officer(s):
Greg Eberhart, Registrar

Alberta College of Social Workers (ACSW) / Association des travailleurs sociaux de l'Alberta
#550, 10707 - 100 Ave. NW, Edmonton AB T5J 3M1
Tel: 780-421-1167; *Fax:* 780-421-1168
Toll-Free: 800-661-3089
www.acsw.ab.ca
Previous Name: Alberta Association of Social Workers; Alberta Association of Registered Social Workers
Overview: A medium-sized provincial organization founded in 1969
Mission: To promote, regulate & govern the profession of social work in the Province of Alberta; To advocate for skilled & ethical social work practices & for policies, programs & services that promote the profession & protect the best interests of the public
Member of: Canadian Association of Social Workers
Affiliation(s): International Federation of Social Workers
Staff Member(s): 16
Membership: *Member Profile:* Registered social workers; *Committees:* Registration; Competence; Clinical Social Work; Professional Social Work Education
Activities: *Awareness Events:* Social Work Week
Chief Officer(s):
Lynn Labrecque King, Executive Director/Registrar
acswexd@acsw.ab.ca
Awards:
• AARSW Award for Excellence in Social Work Practice
Recognizes Registered Social Workers who have exhibited exemplary skills & commitment to the Code of Ethics & mission of the AARSW while engage in providing direct service to clients
• Honourary Memberships
Awarded to a person or group that has made a significant contribution to the values & ideals inherent in the profession of social work & who have advanced the goals of the AARSW
• John Hutton Memorial Award for Social Action/Policy
Recognizes members in good standing who have made an outstanding contribution to the profession of social work & the community through advocacy, social action, policy development/analysis, program development or political action aimed at enhancing social functioning, service delivery systems & the environments in which we work with our clients

Alberta College of Speech-Language Pathologists & Audiologists (ACSLPA)
#209, 3132 Parsons Rd., Edmonton AB T6N 1L6
Tel: 780-944-1609; *Fax:* 780-408-3925
Toll-Free: 800-537-0589
admin@acslpa.ab.ca
www.acslpa.ab.ca
Previous Name: Speech Language Hearing Association of Alberta
Overview: A small provincial licensing charitable organization founded in 1965
Mission: To provide leadership & coordination among speech-language pathologists & audiologists & the public in order to promote speech, language, & hearing health for Albertans
Affiliation(s): Canadian Association of Speech-Language Pathologists & Audiologists
Membership: *Fees:* $650 general; $175 inactive; $125 out of province renewal; *Member Profile:* Speech-language pathologists & audiologists
Activities: *Rents Mailing List:* Yes
Chief Officer(s):
Harpreet Chaggar, President
president@acslpa.ab.ca
Michael Neth, CEO & Registrar
registrar@acslpa.ab.ca
Leanne Kisilevich, Coordinator, Communications & Office

Alberta Colleges Athletic Conference (ACAC)
Percy Page Centre, 11759 Groat Rd., Edmonton AB T5M 3K6
www.acac.ab.ca
www.facebook.com/AlbertaCollegesAthleticConference
twitter.com/ACAC_Sport
Previous Name: Western Inter-College Conference (WICC)
Overview: A small provincial charitable organization founded in 1964
Mission: To act as the governing body for intercollegiate athletics in Alberta; To develop student athletes
Member of: Canadian Colleges Athletic Association
Finances: *Funding Sources:* Membership; Government of Alberta, through the Alberta Sport, Recreation, Parks, & Wildlife Foundation
Membership: 17 schools; *Member Profile:* Colleges & universities in Saskatchewan & Alberta
Activities: Administering intercollegiate athletics
Chief Officer(s):
Mark Kosak, Chief Executive Officer, 403-875-7329, Fax: 780-427-9289
markk@acac.ab.ca
Anthony Wong, Manager, Operations, 780-644-1143
anthonyw@acac.ab.ca
Publications:
• ACAC By-laws
• ACAC Operating Code
• Alberta Colleges Athletic Conference Annual Report
Type: Yearbook; *Frequency:* Annually
• Official's Handbooks
Type: Handbook
Profile: Handbooks include Basketball Off-Court Officials Handbook, Hockey Off-Ice Officials Handbook, & Volleyball Off-Court Officials Handbook
• Outlook: The Newsletter of the ACAC
Type: Newsletter
Profile: Previews & reviews of championships & seasons, sport reports & awards

Alberta Committee of Citizens with Disabilities (ACCD)
#106, 10423 - 178 St. NW, Edmonton AB T5S 1R5
Tel: 780-488-9088; *Fax:* 780-488-3757
Toll-Free: 800-387-2514
accd@accd.net
www.accd.net
www.facebook.com/accdisabilities
twitter.com/accdisabilities
Overview: A medium-sized provincial charitable organization founded in 1973
Mission: To promote full participation in society for Albertans with disabilities
Member of: Alberta Disability Forum
Affiliation(s): Council of Canadians with Disabilities
Finances: *Annual Operating Budget:* $500,000-$1.5 Million; *Funding Sources:* Donations; government; fundraising
Membership: *Fees:* $10 individual; $25 organization; *Member Profile:* Individuals with disabilities & organizations of people with disabilities
Activities: Information sharing & disability awareness; *Speaker Service:* Yes; *Library:* ACCD Resource Centre; by appointment
Chief Officer(s):
Beverley D. Matthiessen, Executive Director
Awards:
• Education for Life Bursary

Alberta Community & Co-operative Association (ACCA)
#202, 5013 - 48 St., Stony Plain AB T7Z 1L8
Tel: 780-963-3766; *Fax:* 780-968-6733
info@acca.coop
www.acca.coop
www.facebook.com/CoopAlberta
twitter.com/CoopAlberta
Previous Name: Rural Education & Development Association
Overview: A small local organization founded in 2005
Mission: To strengthen communities in Alberta, through cooperative & agricultural awareness & development
Member of: Canadian Co-operative Association (CCA)
Finances: *Annual Operating Budget:* $500,000-$1.5 Million; *Funding Sources:* Member dues; Service fees
Staff Member(s): 5; 60 volunteer(s)
Membership: 38 organizations; *Fees:* Schedule available; *Member Profile:* Organizations & individuals registered or incorporated to carry out business in Alberta on a co-operative basis; Persons & organizations who support ACCA goals & objectives
Activities: Promoting the co-operative model; Launching the Rural Co-operative Outreach & Development Project; Providing training opportunities; Offering networking opportunities amongst co-operatives; Disseminating co-op development resources for agricultural organizations, co-operatives & credit unions; *Internships:* Yes; *Speaker Service:* Yes
Chief Officer(s):
Michele Aasgard, Executive Director
maasgard@acca.coop
Cindy Dixon, Director, Operations
cdixon@acca.coop
Awards:
• ACCA Co-operative Merit Award, ACCA Co-operative Leadership Awards
Awarded to individuals who grant outstanding and continuous service to co-operatives & credit unions *Deadline:* October
• ACCA Co-operative Visionary Leadership Award, ACCA Co-operative Leadership Awards
Awarded to recognize inspiring leadership in a co-operative or credit union *Deadline:* October
• ACCA Co-operative Innovation Award, ACCA Co-operative Leadership Awards
Awarded to recognize innovation in the field of co-operatives and credit unions *Deadline:* October
• ACCA Inspiring Young Co-operator Award, ACCA Co-operative Leadership Awards
Presented to demonstrate leadership that responds to the needs & values of younger co-operative members *Deadline:* October
• ACCA Young Co-operative Leaders Award, ACCA Co-operative Leadership Awards
Awarded to individuals 30 years of age or younger in co-operatives or credit inions who demonstrate leadership *Deadline:* October
• ACCA Global Co-operator Award
Awarded to recognize members of ACCA who demonstrate participation & support to the Association through volunteering, fundraising, & advocacy *Deadline:* October

The Alberta Community Crime Prevention Association (ACCPA)
1609 - 14 St. SW, Calgary AB T3C 1E4
Tel: 403-313-2566; *Fax:* 403-313-2569
connect@albertacrimeprevention.com
www.albertacrimeprevention.com
www.youtube.com/user/ACCPAconnection
Overview: A medium-sized provincial organization founded in 1989
Mission: To involve Albertans as active partners in crime prevention
Finances: *Funding Sources:* Government of Alberta
Membership: *Fees:* $60 individual; $30 student; $125 non-profit/government; $250 corporate
Activities: Organizing membership meetings; *Awareness Events:* Alberta Crime Prevention Week
Chief Officer(s):
Jean Bota, President

Alberta Conference of Mennonite Brethren Churches (ABMB)
MB Ministry Centre, #60, 340 Midpark Way SE, Calgary AB T2X 1P1

Chief Officer(s):
Lynn Hamilton, Chair
Gillian Clarke, Vice-Chair
Carla Woodward, Treasurer
Brad Fournier, Executive Director
Hardik Patel, Manager, Finance & Human Resources
Twyla McGann, Coordinator, Communications & Events
Publications:
• inFocus: Working towards a Cure
Type: Newsletter
Profile: Articles about diabetics, research, & giving options, plus recipes & upcoming events

Alberta Diving
AB
www.albertadiving.ca
Overview: A small provincial organization
Mission: To act as the governing body in Alberta for the Olympic sport of amateur diving; to strive for personal & organizational excellence in all areas of diving
Finances: Funding Sources: Fundraising; Sponsorships
Activities: Promoting sportsmanship & respect for rules; Encouraging community involvement; Promoting both the physical & mental well being of members
Awards:
• Misette Lahey Award

Alberta Dressage Association (ADA)
c/o Rita Behan, PO Box 1032, Black Diamond AB T0L 0H0
ada@albertadressage.com
www.albertadressage.com
Also Known As: Canadian Dressage Owners & Riders Association, Western Chapter
Overview: A small provincial organization founded in 1978 overseen by Canadian Dressage Owners & Riders Association
Mission: To promote dressage in Alberta
Member of: Alberta Equestrian Federation
Finances: Funding Sources: Fundraising; Membership fee; Sponsorships
Membership: Member Profile: Senior & junior dressage riders from throughout Alberta
Activities: Liaising with the Alberta Equestrian Federation; Presenting shows; Coordinating dressage clinics for athletes & coaches; Arranging lectures about dressage; Presenting awards
Chief Officer(s):
Lorraine Hill, President
lohill@shockware.com
Rita Behan, Secretary
ritabehan@telus.net
Jennifer Peers, Treasurer
peersj@telus.net

   Calgary Area Chapter (CA / ADA)
   c/o Karen Mercier, 28 Cimarron Estates Way, Okotoks AB T1S 2P3
   Tel: 403-982-5700
   www.ca-ada.com
   Chief Officer(s):
   Sue Hewton-Waters, President, 403-251-1504
   suehw@me.com
   Karen Mercier, Vice-President, 403-540-5732
   kmercier7@gmail.com
   Kathy Ogryzlo, Treasurer
   ogryzlok@shaw.ca
   • CA / ADA [Calgary Area, Alberta Dressage Association] Extensions Newsletter
   Type: Newsletter; Price: Free with membership in the Alberta Dressage Association CalgaryArea Chapter
   Profile: Chapter announcements, such as upcoming events & executive reports

   Chinook Country Chapter (CC / ADA)
   c/o Dinah Sailer, 96 Canyoncrest Pt. West, Lethbridge AB T1K 0B4
   Tel: 403-381-2664
   lohill@shockware.com
   Chief Officer(s):
   Lorraine Hill, Chair, 403-328-3617
   lohill@shockware.com
   Barb Edgecombe-Green, Vice-Chair
   edgecombegreen@shaw.ca
   Audrey Kokesch, Secretary
   akokesch@shaw.ca
   Lynn Dennis, Treausrer
   dlde@telus.net
   Doug Orr, Director, Communication
   lohill@shockware.com

   Hope Olsen, Coordinator, Membership, 403-642-2146
   eholsen@telusplanet.net
   • Chinook Country Alberta Dressage Association Newsletter
   Type: Newsletter; Price: Free with Alberta Dressage Association Chinook Country Chapter membership
   Profile: Chapter notices, such as upcoming events, meeting summaries, & show reports

   Cold Lake Area Chapter (CL / ADA)
   PO Box 1147, Cold Lake AB T9M 1P3
   Tel: 780-594-2035
   carol.porteous@worldpost.ca
   www.albertadressage.com
   Chief Officer(s):
   Carol Porteous, President, 780-594-2035
   carol.porteous@worldpost.ca
   Nancy Gauthier, Vice-President
   hooves_paws@worldpost.ca
   Chris Gingell, Secretary, 780-639-2164
   caruaidd@worldpost.ca
   Shannon Reid Burlinguette, Treasurer
   shannonreid@royallepage.com
   • Cold Lake Area Alberta Dressage Association Newsletter
   Type: Newsletter; Editor: Niki Elash
   Profile: Chapter information, such as upcoming events, as well as articles about dressage

   Edmonton Area Chapter (EA / ADA)
   c/o Caroline Litke, 4536 - 33 Ave., Edmonton AB T6L 4X7
   Tel: 780-886-7419
   Member of: United States Dressage Federation
   Chief Officer(s):
   Gillian Sutherland, President
   gillians@rogers.com
   Alex Evans, Vice-President
   aeevans@ualberta.ca
   Brittany Kroening, Secretary
   brittdkroening@gmail.com
   Susan Hughes, Treasurer
   susanhughes1@hotmail.com
   • Bits & Pieces - EAADA
   Type: Newsletter; Accepts Advertising; Price: Free with membership in the Edmonton Area Alberta Dressage Association
   Profile: Chapter information, including upcoming clinics & shows

   Parkland Area Chapter (PA / ADA)
   c/o Lix Fletcher, PO Box 614, Alix AB T0C 0B0
   Chief Officer(s):
   Diane Luxen, Secretary
   dluxen@telusplanet.net

Alberta Easter Seals Society
#103, 811 Manning Rd. NE, Calgary AB T2E 7L4
Tel: 403-235-5662; Fax: 403-248-1716
Toll-Free: 877-732-7837
calgary@easterseals.ab.ca
www.easterseals.ab.ca
www.facebook.com/EasterSealsAlberta
twitter.com/eastersealsAB
pinterest.com/clienttell
Previous Name: Alberta Rehabilitation Council for the Disabled
Overview: A medium-sized provincial charitable organization founded in 1951 overseen by Easter Seals Canada
Mission: To represent interests of all people with disabilities in Alberta; to promote change at all policy-making levels through public awareness campaigns, projects, seminars; to provide mobility equipment; to conduct public awareness programs; to provide recreational activities through summer camp - Camp Horizon; to provide a residential home program - Easter Seals McQueen Residence
Membership: Fees: $20
Chief Officer(s):
Susan Boivin, Chief Executive Officer, 403-325-5662 Ext. 212
susan@easterseals.ab.ca

Alberta Ecotrust Foundation
#1020, 105 - 12 Ave. SE, Calgary AB T5G 1A1
Tel: 403-209-2245
Toll-Free: 800-465-2147
info@albertaecotrust.com
albertaecotrust.com
twitter.com/AlbertaEcotrust
Overview: A medium-sized provincial charitable organization founded in 1991
Mission: To provide grants to environmental groups that work towards improving Alberta's eco health
Staff Member(s): 7

Membership: Committees: Grant Review
Chief Officer(s):
Pat Letizia, Executive Director
pat.letizia@albertaecotrust.com

Alberta Educational Facilities Administrators Association (AEFAA)
7 White Pelican Way, Lake Newell Resort AB T1R 0X5
Tel: 403-376-0461
www.aefaa.ca
twitter.com/AlanKloepper
Overview: A small provincial organization founded in 1971
Membership: Member Profile: Employees employed by school jurisdictions, colleges, universities, trade schools and the provincial government.
Chief Officer(s):
Alan Kloepper, Executive Director
alan.kloepper@grasslands.ab.ca
Meetings/Conferences:
• Alberta Educational Facilities Administrators Association 2018 Conference, 2018, AB
Scope: Provincial

Alberta Egg Producers' Board (EFA)
#101, 90 Freeport Blvd. NE, Calgary AB T3J 5J9
Tel: 403-250-1197; Fax: 403-291-9216
Toll-Free: 877-302-2344
info@eggs.ab.ca
eggs.ab.ca
www.facebook.com/EggFarmersAlberta
twitter.com/EFA_AB_eggs
Also Known As: Egg Farmers of Alberta
Overview: A medium-sized provincial organization founded in 1968
Mission: To provide effective promotion, control & regulation of the marketing of eggs in Alberta
Affiliation(s): Egg Farmers of Canada (EFC); Alberta Agriculture & Rural Development (ARD); Alberta Farm Animal Care (AFAC); Canada Food Inspection Agency (CFIA)
Staff Member(s): 10
Membership: 170 egg producers in Alberta; Committees: Grader Advisory; Production Management; Research
Chief Officer(s):
Susan Gal, General Manager
susan.gal@eggs.ab.ca
David Webb, Manager, Marketing & Communications
david.web@eggs.ab.ca

Alberta Electrical League (AEL)
PO Box 80091, Stn. Towerlane, Airdrie AB T4B 2V8
Tel: 403-514-3085; Fax: 403-514-6169
Toll-Free: 800-642-5508
info@elecleague.ab.ca
albertaelectricalleague.com
ca.linkedin.com/pub/tara-ternes/12/735/b06
twitter.com/AELtweets
Overview: A small provincial licensing organization founded in 1994
Mission: To promote the electric industry in Alberta; To develop business opportunities for league members
Membership: 150+; Member Profile: Practitioners & companies from the electrical industry in Alberta, such as engineers, manufacturers, distributors, contractors, inspectors, utilities, & colleges & universities
Activities: Hosting electrical trade shows; Providing educational programs; Offering networking opportunities
Chief Officer(s):
Ron Stocks, President
ronald.stocks@rdc.ab.ca
Tara Ternes, Executive Director
Publications:
• Power UP E-News
Type: Newsletter; Frequency: Monthly
Profile: Current events in the electrical industry in Alberta
• Power UP Newsletter
Type: Newsletter; Frequency: Quarterly
Profile: Information distributed to 5,000 individuals involved in Alberta's electrical industry

Alberta Environmental Network (AEN)
PO Box 4541, Edmonton AB T6E 5G4
Tel: 780-757-4872
Other Communication: events@aenweb.ca
admin@aenweb.ca
www.aenweb.ca
twitter.com/ABEnvNet

Canadian Associations / Alberta Equestrian Federation (AEF)

Overview: A medium-sized provincial organization founded in 1980 overseen by Canadian Environmental Network
Mission: To facilitate communication & cooperation among environmental groups in Alberta in order to contribute to the enhancement & protection of the environment
Membership: 287; *Member Profile:* Alberta Environmental NGOs; *Committees:* Clean Air/Energy; Forest; Waste Avoidance/Toxics
Activities: *Rents Mailing List:* Yes
Chief Officer(s):
Melissa Gorrie, Co-Chair
Nikki Way, Co-Chair

Alberta Equestrian Federation (AEF)
#100, 251 Midpark Blvd. SE, Calgary AB T2X 1S3
Tel: 403-253-4411; *Fax:* 403-252-5260
Toll-Free: 877-463-6233
info@albertaequestrian.com
www.albertaequestrian.com
www.facebook.com/AlbertaEquestrian
twitter.com/ab_equestrian
www.instagram.com/alberta_equestrian
Overview: A small provincial organization founded in 1978
Member of: Equine Canada
Finances: *Annual Operating Budget:* $100,000-$250,000; *Funding Sources:* Alberta Sport, Recreation, Parks & Wildlife Foundation
Staff Member(s): 6
Membership: 12,000+; *Fees:* $50 individual; $110 family; $75 club; $120 business; *Committees:* Executive; Rec. & Trails; Competitions; Officials; Trail Ride
Activities: Administering equestrian NCCP Level I & II for Western, English & Driving Coaching; Coordinating, sanctioning & administering body for equestrian sport & recreation in Alberta; Providing assistance & expertise in areas such as competitions, coaching, officials, games & sporting events, recreation & travel insurance, awards, human & equine medication control; *Awareness Events:* Annual Trail Ride
Chief Officer(s):
Les Oakes, President
lesoakes@gmail.com
Sonia Dantu, Executive Director
execdir@albertaequestrian.com
Meetings/Conferences:
• Alberta Equestrian Federation Annual General Meeting 2018, 2018
Scope: Provincial
Publications:
• Alberta Bits [a publication of the Alberta Equestrian Federation]
Type: Magazine; *Frequency:* Quarterly; *Editor:* Jennifer Webster
Profile: News & updates for members

Alberta Falconry Association
22 Chilcotin Way West, Lethbridge AB T1K 7L8
info@albertafalconry.com
www.albertafalconry.com
Overview: A small local organization founded in 1965
Mission: In addition to providing guidance for any Alberta resident who is interested in falconry & the care of falcons, the aims of the association are to promote the conservation of raptors and their prey, & to perpetuate the highest standards of the practice.
Membership: 35; *Fees:* $70; $35 renewal
Chief Officer(s):
Alex Stokes, Contact

Alberta Family Child Care Association (AFCCA)
Gail Blixt, Calgary & Region Family Dayhomes, 3224 - 28 St. SW, Calgary AB T3E 2J6
Tel: 403-217-5394; *Fax:* 403-240-2668
www.afcca.ca
Overview: A medium-sized provincial organization founded in 1989
Mission: To promote a high standard of well being for children & the child care industry
Member of: Canadian Child Care Federation
Membership: 67; *Fees:* $125; *Member Profile:* Family day home agencies
Chief Officer(s):
Gail Blixt, Contact
gail@calgaryfamilydayhomes.com

Alberta Family History Society (AFHS)
712 - 16 Ave. NW, Calgary AB T2M 0J8
Tel: 403-214-1447
www.afhs.ab.ca
www.facebook.com/AlbertaFHS

Overview: A medium-sized provincial charitable organization founded in 1980
Mission: To encourage accuracy & thoroughness in family histories & genealogical research
Member of: Federation of Family History Societies (England); Federation of Genealogical Societies
Finances: *Annual Operating Budget:* Less than $50,000; *Funding Sources:* Membership dues; Grants
10 volunteer(s)
Membership: 300; *Fees:* $40 individual; $50 family; $60 institutional; *Member Profile:* Open to anyone interested in genealogy; *Committees:* Publications; Projects; Seminar; Publicity; Education; Program; Library
Activities: Seminars, workshops, classes; Database of births, marriages & deaths; Cemetery database; *Library:* Not open to public
Chief Officer(s):
Irene Oickle, Membership Chair
membership@afhs.ab.ca
Lorna Loughton, President
president@afhs.ab.ca

Alberta Family Mediation Society (AFMS)
#1650, 246 Stewart Green SW, Calgary AB T3H 3C8
Tel: 403-233-0143
Toll-Free: 877-233-0143
info@afms.ca
www.afms.ca
Overview: A small provincial organization
Mission: To advocate for the resolution of family conflict through mediation by qualified professionals
Affiliation(s): Family Mediation Canada
Membership: *Fees:* Schedule available
Chief Officer(s):
Gordon Andreiuk, Chair
Awards:
• Dr. John Haynes Memorial Award
Meetings/Conferences:
• Alberta Family Mediation Society Conference 2018, 2018
Scope: Provincial

Alberta Farm Fresh Producers Association (AFFPA)
PO Box 56, Kelsey AB T0B 2K0
Tel: 780-373-2503; *Fax:* 780-373-2297
Toll-Free: 800-661-2642
info@albertafarmfresh.com
www.albertafarmfresh.com
www.facebook.com/475524020289
twitter.com/AB_Farm_Fresh
Overview: A small provincial organization
Mission: To develop a sustainable & profitable farm direct marketing industry; To support the production of farm direct market vegetable, berry, & fruit crops, perennials, herbs, flowers, & bedding plants, meat, poulty, & eggs, & other specialty items; To contribute to the health & economic well-being of Albertans
Membership: 162; *Fees:* $145; *Member Profile:* Agri-preneuers in Alberta
Activities: Promoting the farm direct market industry; Providing educational opportunities, such as courses & workshops; Supporting horticultural research; Collaborating with industry partners & government; Arranging insurance; Branding Alberta products from members; Offering networking opportunities with growers acrossAlberta
Chief Officer(s):
Ron Erdmann, President, 780-961-3912
erdmannsgardens@mcsnet.ca
Blaine Staples, Vice-President, 403-227-4231
info@thejunglefarm.com
Tim Vrieselaar, Treasurer, 403-393-2059
nblgardens@gmail.com
Publications:
• Come To Our Farm Guide
Type: Guide; *Price:* Free
Profile: Contact & product information about Alberta Farm Fresh Producers Association members
• Direct Currents [a publication of the Alberta Farm Fresh Producers Association]
Type: Newsletter; *Frequency:* Quarterly; *Accepts Advertising*;
Price: Free with Alberta Farm Fresh Producers Association membership
Profile: Association updates

Alberta Farmers' Market Association (AFMA)
PO Box 69071, 13040 - 137 Ave., Edmonton AB T5L 5E3
Tel: 780-265-2362; *Fax:* 866-754-2362
Toll-Free: 866-754-2362

info@albertafarmersmarket.com
www.albertafarmersmarket.com
www.facebook.com/albertafarmersmarket
Overview: A small provincial organization founded in 1994
Mission: To provide direction & support to members; To assist Alberta Approved Farmers' Markets in playing a major role in the establishment of vibrant communities; To advocate for farmers' markets in Alberta
Member of: Alberta Farm Fresh Producers Association; Growing Alberta; Dine Alberta; Alberta Association of Agricultural Societies; GO Organic
Affiliation(s): Alberta Farmers' Market Program; Alberta Agriculture & Rural Development; RBC Agencies/The Cooperators; Times Two Gifts & Promotions; Whytespace
Membership: *Member Profile:* Alberta Approved Farmers' Markets in Alberta; Vendors; Managers; Boards; Sponsors; Persons who support the principles by which farmers' markets operate
Activities: Promoting Alberta's farmers' markets; Providing education for members, such as regional workshops & market manager training; Offering networking opportunities; Funding & establishing surveys; Advising government organizations regarding guidelines for markets; Arranging market & vendor group liability insurance; *Awareness Events:* Alberta Farmers' Market Awareness Week
Chief Officer(s):
Johwanna Alleyne, President
Awards:
• Wanda Klimke Memorial Award for Distinguished Long-Term Service
• Outstanding Perennial Vendor Award
• Outstanding New Vendor Award
• Outstanding Market Manager of the Year Award
Publications:
• Market Express [a publication of Alberta Farmers' Market Association]
Type: Newsletter; *Frequency:* Quarterly
Profile: Feature articles, recipes, & reports from executive members, committes, & regional directors

Alberta Fashion Market *See* Alberta Men's Wear Agents Association

Alberta Federation of Labour (AFL) / Fédération du travail de l'Alberta
#300, 10408 - 124 St., Edmonton AB T5N 1R5
Tel: 780-483-3021; *Fax:* 780-484-5928
Toll-Free: 800-661-3995
afl@afl.org
www.afl.org
twitter.com/abfedlabour
Overview: A large provincial organization founded in 1912 overseen by Canadian Labour Congress
Mission: To act as a central labour body, representing Alberta's organized workers & their families; To improve conditions for Alberta's workers, their families & communities
Staff Member(s): 8
Membership: 145,000; *Member Profile:* Alberta workers & their families from twenty-nine unions & employee organizations of both the public & private sectors; *Committees:* Education; Political Action
Activities: Publishing research, reports, submissions to government, policy papers, & speeches; Hosting an AFL Kids Camp for children & youth of AFL affiliates; Speaking out on social issues, such as public health care
Chief Officer(s):
Gil McGowan, President
Susan Cake, Director, Policy Analysis
Cam Dykstra, Director, Research
Chris Gallaway, Director, Government Relations & Political Action
Glynnis Lieb, Director, Outreach
Janelle Morin, Director, Communications
Meetings/Conferences:
• Alberta Federation of Labour Convention 2019, May, 2019, Calgary Telus Convention Centre, Calgary, AB
Scope: Provincial
Contact Information: Administrator: Maureen Werlin, E-mail: afl@afl.org

Alberta Federation of Police Associations (AFPA)
10150 - 97 Ave. NW, Edmonton AB T5K 2T5
Tel: 780-496-8600; *Fax:* 780-428-0374
www.albertapolice.ca
Overview: A medium-sized provincial organization

Mission: To represent the interests of members; To address the issues affecting local, provincial & national police associations
Member of: Canadian Police Association
Membership: 8 associations
Chief Officer(s):
Michael Elliot, President
michael.elliott@edmontonpolice.ca
Publications:
• Alberta Police Beat [a publication of Alberta Federation of Police Associations]
Frequency: Biannually
Profile: Information, updates & perspectives on the policing profession, as well as federal & provincial legislation

Alberta Federation of Rock Clubs (AFRC)
#13, 3650 - 19th St. NE, Calgary AB T2E 6V2
Tel: 780-430-6694
www.afrc.ca
Overview: A small provincial organization founded in 1963
Mission: To assist member clubs by providing information & expertise; To promote the study of the Earth Sciences
Affiliation(s): Gem & Mineral Federation of Canada
Membership: 6 clubs
Activities: Awareness Events: May Daze
Chief Officer(s):
Valerie Harty, Secretary, 403-850-7528
vharty@live.ca

Alberta Federation of Shooting Sports (AFSS)
Percy Page Centre, 11759 Groat Rd., Edmonton AB T5M 3K6
Tel: 780-415-1775; Fax: 780-422-2663
afss@abshooters.org
www.abshooters.org
Overview: A small provincial organization
Mission: The AFSS provides funding & support to 11 shooting organizations throughout the province.
Affiliation(s): Alberta Handgun Association; Alberta Smallbore Rifle Association; Alberta Provincial Rifle Association; International Practical Shooting Confederation Alberta; Alberta Sporting Clays Association; Alberta Skeet Shooting Association; Alberta International Skeetshooting Association; Alberta International Style Trapshooting Association; Alberta Metallic Silhouette Association; Alberta Black Powder Association; Alberta Frontier Shootists Society
Membership: 11 associations; Member Profile: Shooting associations in Alberta
Chief Officer(s):
Kyla Clark, Office Manager

Alberta Fencing Association (AFA)
Percy Page Centre, 11759 Groat Rd., Edmonton AB T5M 3K6
Tel: 780-427-9474
info@fencing.ab.ca
www.fencing.ab.ca
Overview: A small provincial organization founded in 1976 overseen by Canadian Fencing Federation
Mission: To promote the sport of fencing in Alberta
Member of: Canadian Fencing Federation
Finances: Annual Operating Budget: $250,000-$500,000
Staff Member(s): 1; 16 volunteer(s)
Membership: 800+; Fees: $30 associate; $65 competitive
Chief Officer(s):
Sean Rathwell, Executive Director
ed@fencing.ab.ca

Alberta Fire Chiefs Association (AFCA)
AB
Tel: 780-719-7939; Fax: 780-892-3333
www.afca.ab.ca
Overview: A small provincial organization
Membership: Member Profile: Assistant Chiefs; Deputy Chiefs; Platoon Chiefs; Battalion Chiefs; District Chiefs; Division Chiefs; Directors of fire departments in Alberta.
Chief Officer(s):
William Purdy, Executive Director, 780-892-2125
bpurdy@xplornet.com
Meetings/Conferences:
• Alberta Fire Chiefs Association 71st Annual Conference & Trade Show 2018, May, 2018, Edmonton EXPO Centre, Edmonton, AB
Scope: Provincial

Alberta Fish & Game Association (AFGA)
6924 - 104 St., Edmonton AB T6H 2L7
Tel: 780-437-2342; Fax: 780-438-6872
office@afga.org
www.afga.org
www.facebook.com/120693761350755
twitter.com/AlbertaFishGame
Overview: A medium-sized provincial organization overseen by Canadian Wildlife Federation
Mission: To ensure fish & wildlife habitat & resources in Alberta
Finances: Funding Sources: Membership fees; Donations
Membership: 20,000 members in 100+ clubs; Fees: $35 individuals; $55 families; Committees: Finance; Environment; Fishing; Hunting; Programs
Activities: Providing educational programs; Liaising with government, industry, & other organizations
Chief Officer(s):
Martin Sharren, Executive Vice-President
Awards:
• Wildlife Awards
Meetings/Conferences:
• Alberta Fish & Game Association 2018 Annual Conference, 2018, AB
Scope: Provincial

Alberta Fish Farmers Association See Alberta Aquaculture Association

Alberta Fitness Leadership Certification Association See Provincial Fitness Unit of Alberta

Alberta Flatwater Canoe Association See Alberta Sprint Racing Canoe Association

Alberta Floor Covering Association (AFCA)
60 Martindale Close NE, Calgary AB T3J 2V1
Tel: 403-280-6006; Fax: 403-280-6056
Toll-Free: 800-292-9712
afca@shaw.ca
www.albertafloors.com
Overview: A small provincial organization founded in 1979 overseen by National Floor Covering Association
Mission: To ensure professionalism in Alberta's floor covering industry; To promote high standards within the industry, by upholding the Code of Ethics & the Code of Trade & Practice; To represent members on issues related to the construction industry
Affiliation(s): National Floor Covering Association
40 volunteer(s)
Membership: Fees: $1,000 manufacturers, distributors & retailers; $500 multi branch dealers; $450 associates & affiliates; $100 installers; $50 apprentice installers; Member Profile: Floor covering manufacturers, distributors, retailers, installers, & associates in Alberta
Activities: Liaising between all sectors of the floor covering industry in Alberta; Providing seminars & training; Offering technical support; Conducting an inspection program, approved by the Alberta New Home Warranty & the National Home Warranty Programs Ltd., for association members & consumers; Improving apprenticeship training, by working with the Alberta Provincial Apprenticeship Committee
Chief Officer(s):
Peggy Alkenbrack, Executive Director
Publications:
• Alberta Floor Covering Association Inspection Services Policy Manual
Type: Manual
Profile: A guide to the inspection process, disclosure policy, fees, & resolution
• Alberta Floor Covering Association Newsletter
Type: Newsletter; Frequency: Quarterly
• Jobsite Preparation Standards Manual
Type: Manual

Alberta Food Bank Network Association See Food Banks Alberta Association

Alberta Food Processors Association (AFPA)
#100W, 4760 - 72 Ave. SE, Calgary AB T2C 3Z2
Tel: 403-201-3657; Fax: 403-201-2513
info@afpa.com
www.afpa.com
www.facebook.com/AFPAfood
twitter.com/AFPA_food
Overview: A medium-sized provincial organization
Mission: To help Alberta food & beverage companies compete successfully in the marketplace
Membership: 300+ organizations
Chief Officer(s):
Marilynn Boehm, President
marilynn@afpa.com

Alberta Forest Products Association (AFPA)
#900, 10707 - 100 Ave., Edmonton AB T5J 3M1
Tel: 780-452-2841; Fax: 780-455-0505
www.albertaforestproducts.ca
Overview: A medium-sized provincial licensing organization founded in 1942
Mission: To represent companies that manufacture forest products throughout Alberta
Finances: Funding Sources: Membership fees; Sponsorships
Membership: Member Profile: Manufacturers of pulp & paper, lumber, panelboard, & secondary manufactured wood products in Alberta
Chief Officer(s):
Neil Shelly, Executive Director
Brady Whittaker, President & Chief Executive Officer
Norm Dupuis, Director, Grade Bureau, 780-452-2841 Ext. 235
Brock Mulligan, Director, Communications, 780-452-2841 Ext. 229
Keith Murray, Director, Policy & Regulation, 780-452-2841 Ext. 227
Carola von Sass, Director, Health & Safety, 780-452-2841 Ext. 237
Meetings/Conferences:
• Alberta Forest Products Association 76th Annual General Meeting & Conference 2018, 2018, AB
Scope: Provincial
Description: A business meeting, sessions on topics relevant to the industry, networking opportunities, & a recognition dinner

Alberta Foster Parent Association (AFPA)
9750 - 35th Ave., Edmonton AB T6E 6J6
Tel: 780-429-9923; Fax: 780-426-7151
Toll-Free: 800-667-2372
reception@afpaonline.com
www.afpaonline.com
Overview: A small local charitable organization founded in 1974
Finances: Funding Sources: Donations
Membership: Fees: $50 household; Member Profile: Department foster homes, where children are placed through the department; Agency foster homes, where children are placed through an agency; Associate members (staff members from the Department of Family & Social Services or a partnering agency); Support members (friends of foster care who are not foster parents); Honorary members (appointed lifetime members)
Activities: Offering a support line (1-800-667-2372 or 780-906-3890); Providing supportive materials for adoptive families; Offering financial assistance for legal issues; Providing a conflict resolution program; Facilitating networking opportunities for foster parents & social workers
Chief Officer(s):
Norm Brownell, President
Sylvia Thompson, Vice-President
Katherine Jones, Executive Director, 780-701-4089
katherinejones@afpaonline.com
Awards:
• Foster Family of the Year Award
• Bursary Fund
• Citation Awards
Meetings/Conferences:
• 2018 Alberta Foster Parent Association It's All About Kids Annual Conference, 2018
Scope: Provincial
Publications:
• The Bridge
Type: Newsletter; Frequency: Quarterly
Profile: Association reports & information for foster families

Alberta Foundation for the Arts (AFA)
10708 - 105 Ave., Edmonton AB T5H 0A1
Tel: 780-427-9968
Toll-Free: -310-0000
afacontact@gov.ab.ca
www.affta.ab.ca
www.facebook.com/AlbertaFoundationfortheArts
twitter.com/AFA1991
www.instagram.com/afa.1991
Overview: A large provincial organization founded in 1991
Mission: To create the best possible climate for the arts in Alberta
Finances: Annual Operating Budget: Greater than $5 Million; Funding Sources: Alberta Lotteries
Staff Member(s): 3
Membership: 11; Member Profile: Appointment by order in council; Committees: Art Collection; Communications; Executive; Grants

Canadian Associations / Alberta Freestyle Ski Association (AFSA)

Activities: Provides grant funding to artists, art organizations & cultural industries; manages an extensive art collection featuring Alberta artists
Chief Officer(s):
Jeff Brinton, Executive Director, 780-415-0283
jeff.brinton@gov.ab.ca
Awards:
• Arts Organizations Operational Grants
• Arts Organizations Project Grants
• Individual Artists Project Grants
• Dr. MacEwan Literary Arts Scholarship
; *Amount:* $5,000
• Queen's Golden Jubilee Scholarship for Performing Arts
; *Amount:* $5,000
• Queen's Golden Jubilee Scholarship for Visual Arts
; *Amount:* $5,000
• Film & Video Arts Scholarship
; *Amount:* $5,000

Alberta Freestyle Ski Association (AFSA)
88 Canada Olympic Rd., Calgary AB T3B 5R5
Tel: 403-297-2718; *Fax:* 403-202-2522
info@abfreestyle.com
www.abfreestyle.com
www.facebook.com/AlbertaFreestyleSkiingAssociation
twitter.com/ABFreestyleSki
Overview: A small provincial charitable organization founded in 1990 overseen by Canadian Freestyle Ski Association
Mission: To develop & coordinate the sport of freestyle skiing in Alberta
Member of: Canadian Freestyle Ski Association
Finances: *Funding Sources:* Sponsorships
Activities: Promoting freestyle skiing at all levels in Alberta; Supporting the high performance Alberta Mogul Team & the Alberta Park & Pipe Team; Offering judges' clinics
Chief Officer(s):
Dan Bowman, Chair
DBowman@shaw.ca
Paulo Kapronczai, Vice-Chair
deekorber@shaw.ca
Dan Jefferies, Treasurer
djefferies@bdo.ca
Maureen Calder, Executive Director
Publications:
• Alberta Freestyle Skiing Association Newsletter
Type: Newsletter
Profile: Upcoming events, association updates, & club news

Alberta Friends of Schizophrenics *See* Schizophrenia Society of Alberta

Alberta Funeral Service Association (AFSA)
3030 - 55 St., Red Deer AB T4P 3S6
Tel: 403-342-2460; *Fax:* 403-342-2495
Toll-Free: 800-803-8809
inquiry@afsa.ca
www.afsa.ca
Overview: A medium-sized provincial licensing organization founded in 1928
Mission: To promote & improve funeral service in Alberta
Affiliation(s): Funeral Service Association of Canada
Finances: *Annual Operating Budget:* $50,000-$100,000; *Funding Sources:* Membership fees
Staff Member(s): 1; 8 volunteer(s)
Membership: 95 corporate + 21 associate + 23 senior/lifetime + 225 individual; *Fees:* Schedule available; *Committees:* Consumer Relations; National; Legal; Education; Peacetime Emergency Response
Activities: *Library:* by appointment
Chief Officer(s):
Deanna Schroeder, Executive Administrator
deanna@afsa.ca

Alberta Funeral Services Regulatory Board (AFSRB)
11810 Kingsway Ave., Edmonton AB T5G 0X5
Tel: 780-452-6130; *Fax:* 780-452-6085
Toll-Free: 800-563-4652
office@afsrb.ab.ca
www.afsrb.ab.ca
Overview: A small provincial organization founded in 1992
Mission: To establish educational standards for the provision of funeral services in Alberta; To set & maintain ethical standards for the funeral services business in the province; To license pre-need salespeople, funeral directors, funeral businesses, embalmers, & crematories in Alberta; To act in accordance with the Alberta Funeral Services Act
Membership: *Committees:* Education; Complaints

Activities: Monitoring the performance of funeral services in Alberta; Investigating consumer complaints
Chief Officer(s):
Marilyn McPherson, Administrator
Marion Wombold, Chair
Peter Portlock, Vice-Chair
Kathy Bruce-Kavanagh, Treasurer
Publications:
• Alberta Funeral Services Regulatory Board Annual Report
Type: Yearbook; *Frequency:* Annually
• Alberta Funeral Services Regulatory Board Newsletter
Type: Newsletter

Alberta Galloway Association
RR#1, Red Deer AB T4N 5E1
Tel: 403-227-3428; *Fax:* 406-227-3423
www.albertagalloway.ca
Overview: A small provincial organization
Mission: To promote Galloway, White Galloway & Belted Galloway cattle in the use of sustainable agriculture; to encourage improvements in the performance of the Galloway family of cattle
Member of: Canadian Galloway Association
Membership: 27; *Fees:* $60 regular; $30 associate; $10 junior; *Member Profile:* Farmers, ranchers & other Galloway breeders; *Committees:* Advertising & Promotion; 4H - Shows - Sales; Finance
Activities: Promotion of Galloways, White Galloways & Belted Galloways
Chief Officer(s):
Bonnie Schweer, Secretary
schweer@xplornet.com

Alberta Genealogical Society (AGS)
#162, 14315 - 118 Ave., Edmonton AB T5L 4S6
Tel: 780-424-4429; *Fax:* 780-423-8980
agsoffice@abgensoc.ca
abgensoc.ca
www.facebook.com/122764957754850
Overview: A medium-sized provincial organization founded in 1973
Mission: To promote the study of genealogy in Alberta
Member of: The Federation of Family History Societies
Finances: *Funding Sources:* Grants; Fundraising
Membership: *Fees:* $50 individual & family; $45 senior individual & family; *Committees:* Finance; Nominations; Archives; Bylaws, Policies, & Procedures; Communications & Public Relations; Conference; Grants & Fundraising; History; Inventory & Property; Library; Master Surname Database; Membership; Publications; Relatively Speaking; Research; Translations; Treasury; Website; Facilities; Gaming; Policies & Procedures
Activities: Encouraging genealogical research in Alberta; Organizing workshops; Facilitating networking opportunities; Conducting research in response to queries; Recording cemeteries; Indexing; Enabling access to databases, such as Index to Alberta Homestead Records - 1870 to 1930 & Index to Alberta Homestead Records - post 1930, through the AGS website; *Library:* Alberta Genealogical Society Library
Chief Officer(s):
Les Campbell, President
Susan Haga, 1st Vice-President
Maxine Maxwell, 2nd Vice-President
Jock Howard, Vice-President, Finance
Mary Ann Legris, Secretary
Linda Winski, Office Coordinator
Publications:
• Alberta Index to Registrations of Birth, Marriages, & Deaths 1870 - 1905
Number of Pages: 648; *Price:* $48
Profile: Registrations in the years before Alberta became a province
• Alberta Sources
Profile: Listings of Alberta cemeteries
• Relatively Speaking
Type: Newsletter; *Frequency:* Quarterly; *Editor:* Marilyn Hindmarch; Peter Staveley; *Price:* Free with Alberta Genealogical Society membership
Profile: Genealogical research in Canada, sources, research methods, library news, book reviews, & personal experiences
  Brooks & District Branch
  PO Box 1538, Brooks AB T1R 1C4
  Tel: 403-362-8642
  info@agsbrooks.com
  www.agsbrooks.com
  Chief Officer(s):

  Robert Franz, President
  Eileen French, Vice-President
  Karyn Norden, Treasurer
  Carol Anderson, Secretary
• B & D Heir Lines
Type: Newsletter; *Frequency:* Semiannually; *Price:* $2.50
  Camrose Branch
  4310 - 50 Ave., Camrose AB T4V 0R3
  Tel: 780-608-6243
  camrose@abgenealogy.ca
  camrose.abgensoc.ca
  Chief Officer(s):
  Janine Carroll, President
  Adele Goa, Secretary
  Sharon Olsen, Treasurer
• Roots 'N Shoots
Type: Newsletter; *Frequency:* Semiannually; *Editor:* Norm Prestage & Jack Cunningham
Profile: Branch happenings
  Drayton Valley Branch
  PO Box 115, Rocky Rapids AB T0E 1Z0
  Tel: 780-542-2787
  ags.dvbranch@gmail.com
  www.abgenealogy.ca
  www.facebook.com/DraytonValleyBranchAlbertaGenealogicalSociety
  Chief Officer(s):
  Connie Stuhl, President
• Past Finder
Type: Newsletter; *Frequency:* Quarterly
  Edmonton Branch
  #162, 14315 - 118 Ave., Edmonton AB T5L 4S6
  Tel: 780-424-4429; *Fax:* 780-423-8980
  edmontonbranchags@gmail.com
  www.agsedm.edmonton.ab.ca
  Chief Officer(s):
  Lynne Duigou, President
• Clandigger
Type: Newsletter; *Frequency:* 9 pa
  Fort McMurray Branch
  10011 Franklin Ave., Fort McMurray AB T9H 2K7
  Tel: 780-791-5663
  ftmacgen@telus.net
  www.rootsweb.ancestry.com/~abfmags
  Chief Officer(s):
  Tammy Grantham, President
  tgrant@shaw.ca
  Laverne Cormier, Vice-President
  blcormier@shaw.ca
  Bobbie Driscoll, Secretary
  BobbieD@shaw.ca
  Cathy Marriott, Treasurer
  we4rher@shaw.ca
• Lines of Descent
Type: Newsletter; *Frequency:* Quarterly; *Price:* Free with Fort McMurray Branch membership
  Grande Prairie & District Branch
  PO Box 1257, Grande Prairie AB T8V 2Z1
  gp@abgenealogy.ca
  www.gp.abgensoc.ca
  Chief Officer(s):
  Jean Gray, President
  Carol Thomson, Treasurer
• Heritage Seekers
Type: Newsletter; *Frequency:* Quarterly; *ISSN:* 0707-0708
Profile: Information from historical sources in the Peace Country, genealogical articles, & member news
  Lethbridge & District Branch
  #128, 909 - 3rd Ave. North, Lethbridge AB T1H 0H5
  Tel: 403-328-9564
  lethags@theboss.net
  lethbridgeags.theboss.net
  Mission: To promote genealogy in the Lethbridge area; to maintain standards in genealogy
  Chief Officer(s):
  Doug McLeod, President
  Susan Haga, Vice-President
  Alma Berridge, Secretary
  Pat Barry, Treasurer
• Yesterday's Footprints
Type: Newsletter; *Frequency:* 3 pa
  Medicine Hat & District Branch
  Hillside Monumental Bldg., 974 - 13th Ave. SW, Medicine Hat AB T1A 7G8

Tel: 403-526-1163
mhgs@telus.net
mhdgs.ca
Mission: To promote the search for family history in the Medicine Hat area
Chief Officer(s):
Doreen Schank, President
Leanne Balfour, Secretary
Kathy Gleisner, Treasurer
• The Saamis Seeker
Type: Newsletter; *Frequency:* 3 pa; *Editor:* Barb Dewald; *Price:* Free with Medicine Hat & District Branch membership

Peace River & District Branch
9807 - 97 Ave., Peace River AB T8S 1H6
Tel: 780-624-3269
www.rootsweb.ancestry.com/~abprdgs
Chief Officer(s):
Joan Wahl, President
Linda Chmielewski, Secretary-Treasurer
• Echoes of the Past
Type: Newsletter

Red Deer & District Branch
PO Box 922, Red Deer AB T4N 5H3
Tel: 403-347-1826
www.rdgensoc.ab.ca
Chief Officer(s):
Diane Lehr, President
Joan Shortt, Secretary
Vic Willouby, Treasurer
• The Tree Climber
Type: Newsletter; *Frequency:* Quarterly; *Editor:* Jim Coutts; *Price:* Free with Red Deer & District Branch membership

Wetaskiwin Branch
RR#3, Wetaskiwin AB T9A 1X1
Tel: 780-352-2150
wetaskiwin@abgenealogy.ca
www.abgenealogy.ca/wetaskiwin-branch
Mission: To promote family history searches in the Wetaskiwin area
Chief Officer(s):
Alice Hoyle, Secretary
alihoy@xplornet.com
• Roots & Branches
Type: Newsletter; *Frequency:* 3 pa; *Editor:* Claudia Malloch

Alberta Gerontological Nurses Association (AGNA)
PO Box 67040, Stn. Meadowlark, Edmonton AB T5R 5Y3
info@agna.ca
www.agna.ca
twitter.com/AGNAtweets
Overview: A medium-sized provincial organization founded in 1981 overseen by Canadian Gerontological Nursing Association
Mission: To promote a high standard of nursing care & related health services for older adults; To enhance professionalism in the practice of gerontological nursing
Membership: *Fees:* $35 associate; $45 student; $67.50 RPN/LPN; $75 RN/NP; *Member Profile:* Nurses interested in gerontology; *Committees:* Advocacy & Political Action
Activities: Offering professional networking opportunities; Providing professional development; Advocating for comprehensive services for older adults; Supporting research related to gerontological nursing; Promoting gerontological nursing to the public
Chief Officer(s):
Lynne Moulton, President
president@agna.ca
Meetings/Conferences:
• Alberta Gerontological Nurses Association 37th AGM & Conference 2018, 2018, AB
Scope: Provincial
Publications:
• AGNA [Alberta Gerontological Nurses Association] Newsletter
Type: Newsletter; *Frequency:* Quarterly; *Editor:* Debbie Lee

Alberta Golf Association (AGA)
#22, 11410 - 27 St. SE, Calgary AB T2Z 3R6
Tel: 403-236-4616; *Fax:* 403-236-2915
Toll-Free: 888-414-4849
info@albertagolf.org
www.albertagolf.org
www.facebook.com/144026188016
twitter.com/Alberta_Golf
www.instagram.com/alberta_golf
Overview: A medium-sized provincial organization founded in 1912 overseen by Golf Canada

Mission: To promote the positive impacts of golf on both individuals & communities across Alberta; To improve the quality of life for Albertans through sport
Finances: *Funding Sources:* Membership fees; Fundraising; Sponsorships
Staff Member(s): 7
Membership: 57,000 individual + 225 clubs; *Fees:* Schedule available; *Member Profile:* Organized golf clubs in Alberta & member golfers
Activities: *Speaker Service:* Yes; *Library:* Open to public by appointment
Chief Officer(s):
Matt Rollins, Executive Director, 403-613-3034
matt@albertagolf.org
Jack Lane, Chief Operating Officer, 403-698-4631
jack@albertagolf.org

Alberta Gravel Truckers Association *See* Alberta Construction Trucking Association

Alberta Greenhouse Growers Association (AGGA)
18051 - 107 Ave. NW, Edmonton AB T5S 1K5
Tel: 780-489-1991; *Fax:* 780-444-2152
www.agga.ca
Overview: A small provincial organization
Mission: To strengthen the greenhouse growing industry in Alberta; To act as the voice of the industry, in areas such as taxation, natural gas rebates, disaster relief, & electricity costs
Membership: *Fees:* Schedule available; *Member Profile:* Growers; Allied trades people; Educators; Students; Individuals with an interest in horticulture
Activities: Promoting the greenhouse growing industry in Alberta; Providing workshops & seminars; Conducting research; Liaising with related organizations, such as the Canadian Horticultural Council & the Alberta Professional Horticultural Growers Congress Foundation; Increasing cooperation; Assisting members in marketing
Chief Officer(s):
Albert Cramer, Vice-President, 403-526-3059
Awards:
• Alberta Greenhouse Growers Association Scholarship
Eligibility: Awarded to the child of an AGGA grower member; *Amount:* $500
• Herb Knodel Award
Eligibility: Awarded to a grower who has made a major contribution to the industry
• Meritorious Service Award
Eligibility: Awarded to people who are not growers, but who have contributed to the industry, mainly in terms of research
• Grower of the Year Award
Publications:
• Alberta Greenhouse Growers Association Newsletter
Type: Newsletter; *Frequency:* Quarterly
Profile: Association activities, & greenhouse growing industry research, developments, & policy
• Regional Crop Reports

Alberta Gymnastics Federation (AGF)
#207, 5800 - 2 St. SW, Calgary AB T2H 0H2
Tel: 403-259-5500; *Fax:* 403-259-5588
Toll-Free: 800-665-1010
www.abgym.ab.ca
www.facebook.com/AlbertaGymnastics
twitter.com/agf_comm
www.youtube.com/albertagymnastics
flickr.com/photos/albertagymnastics
Overview: A medium-sized provincial organization founded in 1971
Mission: To operate as the governing body of gymnastics in Alberta; To provide administrative support in the development & delivery of programs & competitions in recreational gymnastics, national coaching certification programs, women's artistic gymnastics, trampoline & tumbling, men's artistic gymnastics, & special events
Staff Member(s): 10
Membership: 75 member clubs; *Committees:* Women's Program; Women's Program Judging; Trampoline & Tumbling Technical; Men's Technical; Recreational Development
Chief Officer(s):
Scott Hayes, President & CEO
shayes@abgym.ab.ca

Alberta Handball Association (AHA)
AB
www.albertahandball.com
www.facebook.com/Albertateamhandball
Overview: A small provincial organization

Mission: To promote & develop the sport of handball in Alberta
Activities: Operates three clubs: Calgary, Edmonton & Sherwood Park

Alberta Hereford Association (AHA)
PO Box 570, Hardisty AB T0B 1V0
Tel: 780-888-2813
abherefords@xplornet.ca
www.albertaherefords.com
www.facebook.com/AlbertaHerefords
Overview: A medium-sized provincial licensing organization founded in 1971
Mission: To promote the benefits of Hereford genetics commercial ranchers & farmers, feedlots, & auction markets; To gather feedback on Hereford cattle
Member of: Canadian Hereford Association
Affiliation(s): Calgary District Hereford Club; Central Alberta Hereford Club; East Central Hereford Club; Northern Alberta Hereford Club; Peace River Hereford Club; Southern Alberta Hereford Club
Membership: 650; *Member Profile:* Alberta seedstock producers who raise purebred Hereford cattle for the commercial industry
Chief Officer(s):
Blair Fenton, President, 780-754-2891
blair.fenton@hotmail.com
Brad Doenz, Executive Director, 403-642-3894
vdoenz@gmail.com

Alberta Heritage Foundation for Medical Research *See* Alberta Innovates

Alberta Historical Resources Foundation (AHRF)
Old St. Stephen's College, 8820 - 112 St., Edmonton AB T6G 2P8
Tel: 780-431-2300; *Fax:* 780-427-5598
Overview: A medium-sized provincial organization founded in 1976
Mission: To assist in the preservation of Alberta's historic sites, buildings & objects; To encourage & promote public awareness of the province's past
Finances: *Annual Operating Budget:* $3 Million-$5 Million; *Funding Sources:* Alberta Lotteries
Staff Member(s): 3
Activities: Heritage Preservation Partnership Program; Provincial Heritage Markers Program; Geographical Names Program; Heritage Awards
Chief Officer(s):
Laurel Halladay, Chair
Aimee Benoit, Vice Chair
Awards:
• Heritage Awards
Established in 1981 to stimulate awareness & recognize outstanding contributions to the preservation of Alberta's past
• Roger Soderstrom Scholarship in Historical Preservation
Encourages professional development & advanced studies in the field of heritage conservation in Alberta; for university students at the graduate level in disciplines relating to heritage preservation & research, focussing on Alberta; includes studies in architectural restoration; area conservation & research preservation planning &/or interpretive development of archaeological, historical or palaeontological sites in the province, as well as related thematic work. *Eligibility:* Canadian citizen or landed immigrant & a resident of Alberta for at least six months prior to applying *Deadline:* February & September; *Amount:* up to $3,000 *Contact:* Community Resources Officer

Alberta Home Education Association (AHEA)
AB
www.aheaonline.com
Overview: A small provincial organization
Mission: AHEA serves home schooling parents as needs arise, to support local groups of parents and individuals, and to interact with various levels of government to protect the responsibilities of parents.
Chief Officer(s):
Paul van den Bosch, President
president@aheaonline.com
Meetings/Conferences:
• Alberta Home Education Association Convention 2018, April, 2018, Red Deer, AB
Scope: Provincial

Alberta Horse Trials Association (AHTA)
c/o Aislyn Havell, Membership Secretary, #23, 38440 Range Rd. 284, Red Deer County AB T4S 2E2

Canadian Associations / Alberta Horseshoe Pitchers Association (AHPA)

albertahorsetrials@gmail.com
www.albertahorsetrials.com
Overview: A small provincial organization
Mission: To promote & develop 3-day eventing in Alberta & Canada & assist in producing Olympic athletes
Affiliation(s): Canadian Equestrian Federation
Finances: *Annual Operating Budget:* Less than $50,000; *Funding Sources:* National Government, Provincial Government 13 volunteer(s)
Membership: 170 student; 240 individual; 20 associate; *Fees:* $30 associate; $50 junior; $60 senior; $120 family; *Committees:* Membership; Competitions; Special Events; Communications; Athlete Development; Clinics; Marketing
Chief Officer(s):
Kristine Haut, President
ahtapresident@gmail.com
Awards:
• AHTA Bursary
Eligibility: Full members of AHTA enrolled in post-secondary education who show commitment to the sport of eventing; special consideration is given to applicants who "give back" through volunteerism & mentorship *Deadline:* September 30; *Amount:* $750
• High Point Awards
• Championship Awards
• Dressage Bonus Award
• Preliminary Upgrading Award
• Out of Province Competition Subsidies
• Top Rider Award
• Coach of the Year Award
• Canadian Warmblood of the Year Award
• Thoroughbred of the Year Award
• Canadian Sport Hose of the Year Award
• President's Award
Meetings/Conferences:
• Alberta Horse Trials Association Annual General Meeting & Awards Banquet, 2018, AB
Scope: Provincial
Contact Information: Coordinator, Special Events: Carly Moore, E-mail: ahtaspecialevents@gmail.com
Publications:
• AHTA [Alberta Horse Trials Association] Newsbites
Type: Newsletter
Profile: News & updates for members

Alberta Horseshoe Pitchers Association (AHPA)
AB
Tel: 403-946-4109
abhorseshoepitchers.com
Overview: A small provincial organization founded in 1977 overseen by Horseshoe Canada
Mission: To promote the sport of horseshoe pitching in Alberta.
Member of: Horseshoe Canada
Chief Officer(s):
Bruce Grandel, President
brucegrandel@hotmail.com

Alberta Hospice Palliative Care Association (AHPCA)
#1245, 70 Ave. SE, Calgary AB T2H 2X8
Tel: 403-206-9938; *Fax:* 403-206-9958
director@ahpca.ca
www.ahpca.ca
www.facebook.com/AlbertaHospicePalliativeCare
twitter.com/AHPCA
www.youtube.com/watch?v=6Z3044hPlrl
Previous Name: Palliative Care Association of Alberta
Overview: A medium-sized provincial charitable organization
Mission: To engage in actions & strategies that result in comprehensive, equitable & quality end of life care for Albertans
Member of: Canadian Palliative Care Association
Finances: *Annual Operating Budget:* $100,000-$250,000; *Funding Sources:* Donations; 50/50 Draw; Silent Auction
Staff Member(s): 4; 50 volunteer(s)
Membership: 300; *Fees:* $45
Activities: Raising provincial awareness of palliative care within Alberta
Chief Officer(s):
Pansy Angevine, Chair
Leslie Penny, Treasurer
Jennifer Elliott, Executive Director
Theresa Bellows, Road Show Coordinator
Reilly Bellows, Social Media
Meetings/Conferences:
• Alberta Hospice Palliative Care Association 2018 Imagine Conference, 2018, AB
Scope: Provincial
Publications:
• Alberta Hospice Palliative Care Association Newsletter
Type: Newsletter
Profile: Association highlights, including membership information & courses
• Alberta Hospice Palliative Care Association Volunteer Training Manual
Type: Manual
Profile: Information based upon the CHPCA Norms of Practice

Alberta Hotel & Lodging Association
2707 Ellwood Dr. SW, Edmonton AB T6X 0P7
Tel: 780-436-6112; *Fax:* 780-436-5404
Toll-Free: 888-436-6112
www.ahla.ca
www.linkedin.com/company/alberta-hotel-&-lodging-association
www.facebook.com/171333316227097
twitter.com/ABHotelAssoc
Overview: A medium-sized provincial organization founded in 1919 overseen by Hotel Association of Canada Inc.
Mission: To enhance the image, the quality & efficiency of the hotel industry in Alberta
Chief Officer(s):
Dave Kaiser, President & CEO
dkaiser@ahla.ca
Meetings/Conferences:
• Alberta Hotel and Lodging Association 98th Annual Convention and Trade Show 2018, April, 2018, Fairmont Jasper Park Lodge, Jasper, AB
Scope: Provincial
Contact Information: Administrator: Gayle Day, E-mail: gday@ahla.ca, Phone: 780-436-6112, ext. 220

Alberta Innovates
#1500, 10104 - 103 Ave., Edmonton AB T5J 4A7
Tel: 780-423-5727; *Fax:* 780-429-3509
Toll-Free: 877-423-5727
health@aihealthsolutions.ca
www.aihealthsolutions.ca
www.facebook.com/179968058752241
twitter.com/_AIHS_
www.youtube.com/user/AIHSChannel
Previous Name: Alberta Heritage Foundation for Medical Research
Overview: A small provincial organization founded in 1980
Mission: To support basic biomedical, clinical & health research in Alberta; To contribute funds to scientific community to carry out research
Finances: *Annual Operating Budget:* Greater than $5 Million
Staff Member(s): 35
Activities: *Library:* Not open to public
Chief Officer(s):
Pamela Valentine, PhD, Interim CEO
pamela.valentine@albertainnovates.ca
Anne Thomas, Executive Director, Operations
anne.thomas@albertainnovates.ca
Denise Guevara, Administrator
denise.guevara@albertainnovates.ca

Alberta Insolvency Practitioners Association *See* Alberta Association of Insolvency & Restructuring Professionals

Alberta Institute of Agrologists
#1430, 5555 Calgary Trail NW, Edmonton AB T6H 5P9
Tel: 780-435-0606; *Fax:* 780-464-2155
Toll-Free: 855-435-0606
www.albertaagrologists.ca
www.linkedin.com/company/alberta-institute-of-agrologists
twitter.com/ABagrologists
Overview: A small provincial licensing organization founded in 1947 overseen by Agricultural Institute of Canada
Mission: To serve as a regulatory body within the province for matters related to agrology
Finances: *Funding Sources:* Membership fees
Membership: 2,500+; *Member Profile:* Professional Agrologists (P.Ag.); Articling Agrologists (A.Ag.)
Chief Officer(s):
David Lloyd, CEO & Registrar
Awards:
• Distinguished Agrologist Award
$1000/year to a University of Saskatchewan agrology student
• Outstanding Young Agrologist Award
• Professional Recognition Award
• Honorary Member Award
• Distinguished Registered Technologist in Agrology Award
• Outstanding Young Registered Technologist in Agrology Award
• Lifetime Member Award
Meetings/Conferences:
• Alberta Institute of Agrologists 14th Annual Banff Conference 2018, April, 2018, Banff, AB
Scope: Provincial
Description: Theme: "Governments & People"
• Alberta Institute of Agrologists Annual General Meeting 2018, 2018, AB
Scope: Provincial
Publications:
• AIA [Alberta Institute of Agrologists] Bulletin
Profile: Events of interest to Agrologists
• News Update [a publication of the Alberta Institute of Agrologists]
Type: Newsletter
Profile: Update on Institute issues

Alberta Institute Purchasing Management Association of Canada *See* Supply Chain Management Association - Alberta

Alberta Insurance Council (AIC)
Bell Tower, #600, 10104 - 103rd Ave., Edmonton AB T5J 0H8
Tel: 780-421-4148; *Fax:* 780-425-5745
www.abcouncil.ab.ca
twitter.com/AbCouncil
Overview: A small provincial organization
Mission: Regulatory body responsible for licensing and discipline of insurance agents, brokers and adjusters in the Province of Alberta
Membership: *Fees:* Schedule available
Chief Officer(s):
Joanne Abram, Chief Executive Officer
Carolyn Janz, Chief Financial Officer

Calgary Office
#500, 222 - 58th Ave. SW, Calgary AB T2H 2S3
Tel: 403-233-2929; *Fax:* 403-233-2990
Chief Officer(s):
Anthoney Maramieri, Chief Operating Officer

Alberta Irrigation Projects Association (AIPA)
2825 - 18 Ave. North, Lethbridge AB T1H 6T5
Tel: 403-328-3063
www.aipa.ca
Overview: A medium-sized provincial organization founded in 1946
Mission: To advance understanding of the value of irrigation to Alberta; To promote progressive water management practices
Affiliation(s): Canadian Water Resources Association
Membership: *Member Profile:* Incorporated Irrigation Districts in Alberta; Associate members; Honorary members
Activities: Participating in education & outreach activities; Developing policy; Researching; Providing information to federal, provincial, & local government officials, departments & agencies, water management stakeholders, members, the public, & the media; Promoting the benefits of Alberta's irrigations infrastructure; Developing partnerships
Chief Officer(s):
Margo Redelback, Executive Director
Vicky Kress, Administrator
vicky.kress@aipa.org

Alberta Katahdin Sheep Association
c/o Val Sebree, PO Box 43, Vegreville AB T9C 1R1
Tel: 780-658-2415
www.katahdinsheep.com
Overview: A small provincial organization overseen by Canadian Katahdin Sheep Association Inc.
Mission: To promote the Katahdin sheep breed in Alberta
Membership: *Member Profile:* Owners of Canadian registered Katahdin sheep in Alberta
Activities: Showing Katahdin sheep at various events; Providing information about the breed to members & the public
Chief Officer(s):
Lynette Kreddig, President, 780-786-4754, Fax: 780-786-4754
lynette.kreddig@franklynfarm.ca
Michael King, Vice-President, 403-860-2289
michaelj.king@shaw.ca
Val Sebree, Secretary-Treasurer, 780-658-2415

Alberta Lacrosse Association (ALA)
#4, 9 Chippewa Rd., Sherwood Park AB T8A 6J7
Tel: 780-464-1861
www.albertalacrosse.com
www.facebook.com/257864104242295
twitter.com/AlbertaLacrosse

Overview: A small provincial organization overseen by Canadian Lacrosse Association
Mission: To be the provincial governing body for the sport of lacrosse in Alberta
Member of: Canadian Lacrosse Association
Chief Officer(s):
Rob Matsuoka, President
president@albertalacrosse.com
Lisa Grant, Executive Director
lisa@albertalacrosse.com
Andrew McBride, Technical Director
Awards:
• James McFall Award
• Ekke Loo Memorial Award

Alberta Lake Management Society (ALMS)
PO Box 4283, Edmonton AB T6E 4T3
Tel: 780-702-2567; *Fax:* 780-468-2494
programs@alms.ca
www.alms.ca
www.facebook.com/AlbertaLakeManagement
twitter.com/AlbertaLake
Also Known As: Lakewatch
Overview: A small provincial charitable organization founded in 1991
Mission: To promote understanding & comprehensive management of lakes & reservoirs & their watersheds
Member of: North American Lake Management Society
Finances: *Annual Operating Budget:* Less than $50,000; *Funding Sources:* Government; workshops
16 volunteer(s)
Membership: 100+; *Fees:* $50 associations; $25 individual; $15 student; *Member Profile:* Private citizens; municipalities; government organizations
Activities: Water sampling; conservation & lake management; *Speaker Service:* Yes; *Library:* ALMS Library; by appointment
Chief Officer(s):
Bradley Peter, Executive Director
Awards:
• Alberta Lake Management Society Scholarship
Eligibility: Graduate Student with Alberta research project relevant to managing lakes.; *Amount:* $2000

Alberta Land Surveyors' Association (ALSA)
#1000, 10020 - 101A Ave., Edmonton AB T5J 3G2
Tel: 780-429-8805; *Fax:* 888-459-1664
Toll-Free: 800-665-2572
info@alsa.ab.ca
www.alsa.ab.ca
Overview: A medium-sized provincial organization founded in 1910 overseen by Professional Surveyors Canada
Mission: To regulate the practice of land surveying.
Finances: *Funding Sources:* Membership fees; products
Staff Member(s): 9
Membership: *Fees:* $200 affiliate/articled pupil; $100 associate; *Committees:* Articling Process; Association Finances; Boundary Pane; Discipline; External Relations; Historical and Biographical; Legislation; Practice Review Board; Professional Development; Registration; RST Implementation; Safety; Standards
Activities: *Library:*
Chief Officer(s):
Brian Munday, Executive Director
munday@alsa.ab.ca
David McWilliam, Registrar
alsaregistrar@shaw.ca
Robert Scott, President
Bruce Clark, Secretary-Treasurer
Meetings/Conferences:
• Alberta Land Surveyors' Association 2018 Annual General Meeting, 2018, AB
Scope: Provincial

Alberta Law Foundation (ALF)
#980, 105 - 12 Ave. SE, Calgary AB T2G 1A1
Tel: 403-264-4701; *Fax:* 403-294-9238
info@albertalawfoundation.org
www.albertalawfoundation.org
Overview: A medium-sized provincial charitable organization founded in 1973
Mission: To conduct research into & recommend reform of law & administration of justice in Alberta; To establish, maintain & operate law libraries; To contribute to legal education & knowledge of people of Alberta; To provide assistance to Native people's legal & student programs
Affiliation(s): Association of Canadian Law Foundations
Finances: *Annual Operating Budget:* $100,000-$250,000
Staff Member(s): 2; 7 volunteer(s)
Chief Officer(s):
Deborah Duncan, Executive Director
dduncan@albertalawfoundation.org
Diana M. Porter, Administrative Assistant
dporter@albertalawfoundation.org

Alberta Law Reform Institute (ALRI)
402 Law Centre, University of Alberta, Edmonton AB T6G 2H5
Tel: 780-492-5291; *Fax:* 780-492-1790
lawreform@ualberta.ca
www.alri.ualberta.ca
Overview: A small provincial organization founded in 1967
Mission: To advance just & effective laws through independent legal research, consultation, & analysis
Staff Member(s): 10
Chief Officer(s):
Sandra Petersson, Executive Director

Alberta Liberal Party
10247 - 124 St. NW, Edmonton AB T5N 1P8
Tel: 780-414-1124
www.albertaliberal.com
www.facebook.com/ablib
twitter.com/abliberal
www.youtube.com/albertaliberalcaucus
Overview: A medium-sized provincial organization overseen by The Liberal Party of Canada
Mission: To elect Liberals to the Legislative Assembly of Alberta; To enunciate & promote liberal principles & policies; To initiate & maintain effective electoral constituencies
Finances: *Funding Sources:* Donations
Staff Member(s): 5
Membership: Over 50,000; *Fees:* $10
Chief Officer(s):
David Khan, Party Leader
Karen Sevcik, President

Alberta Library Association *See* Library Association of Alberta

Alberta Library Trustees Association (ALTA)
4024 - 37A Ave., Edmonton AB T6L 7A1
Tel: 780-761-2582; *Fax:* 866-419-1451
www.librarytrustees.ab.ca
www.linkedin.com/company/alberta-library-trustees-association
www.facebook.com/librarytrustees
twitter.com/librarytrustees
Overview: A small provincial organization founded in 1971
Mission: To act as the collective voice for library trustees in Alberta; To develop effective trustees
Finances: *Funding Sources:* Alberta Ministry of Municipal Affairs, Public Library Services
Membership: *Fees:* Schedule available, based upon population served; *Member Profile:* Library trustees, past & present; in the following areas & urban districts of Alberta: Peace, Yellowhead, Parkland, Marigold, Chinook, Shortgrass, Metro Edmonton, Northern Lights, Edmonton, & Calgary; Public library supporters; *Committees:* Advocacy & Engagement; Executive; Operations; Trustee Education & Resources; Trustee Recognition
Activities: Providing education, including online modules, to members; Promoting effective library service; Engaging in advocacy activities; Presenting awards, such as the Lois Hole Award & the ALTA Award of Excellence
Chief Officer(s):
Heather Coulson, Executive Director
Awards:
• Lois Hole Lifetime Achievement Award
• Award of Excellence
• Lorne MacRae Intellectual Freedom Fund Award
Meetings/Conferences:
• Alberta Library Trustees Association 2018 Alberta Library Conference, 2018, AB
Scope: Provincial
Description: Hosted annually in conjunction with the Library Association of Alberta (LAA); Provides attendees with professional development & networking opportunities
• Alberta Library Trustees Association 2018 Annual General Meeting, 2018, AB
Scope: Provincial
Description: Financial statements, a proposed budget, nominations report, & special resolutions
Publications:
• Trustee Voice [a publication of the Alberta Library Trustees Association]
Type: Newsletter; *Frequency:* q.
Profile: An information resource featuring association news & updates; also features submissions from members

Alberta Luge Association (ALA)
#201, BNTC, 88 Canada Olympic Rd. SW, Calgary AB T3B 5R5
Tel: 403-202-6570
admin@albertaluge.com
www.albertaluge.com
Overview: A small provincial organization founded in 1983
Mission: To ensure the continued successful growth of the sport of luge in Alberta through the development of its athletes, coaches & volunteers at the recreational & elite levels
Affiliation(s): Canadian Luge Association
Finances: *Annual Operating Budget:* $100,000-$250,000
Staff Member(s): 2; 150 volunteer(s)
Membership: 700; *Fees:* Schedule available

Alberta Magazine Publishers Association (AMPA)
#304, 1240 Kensington Rd. NW, Calgary AB T2N 3P7
Tel: 403-262-0081; *Fax:* 403-670-0492
ampa@albertamagazines.com
www.albertamagazines.com
www.facebook.com/AlbertaMagazines
twitter.com/albertamags
pinterest.com/albertamagazine
Overview: A medium-sized provincial organization
Mission: To sustain a healthy magazine industry in Alberta; to act as a voice for the province's magazine publishers
Staff Member(s): 2
Membership: *Fees:* Schedule available; *Member Profile:* Creators, publishers, printers, & distributors of Alberta magazines
Activities: Promoting the magazine industry in Alberta; Engaging in advocacy activities; Providing professional assistance; Disseminating professional development resources; Offering bursaries to members to upgrade skills; Providing a subsidized intern program; Facilitating networking opportunities; Offering a one-on-one training program (Pros on the Road) & seminars; *Internships:* Yes
Chief Officer(s):
Suzanne Trudel, Executive Director
director@albertamagazines.com
Joyce Byrne, President
Chris Welner, Vice-President
Allan Lacey, Treasurer
Meetings/Conferences:
• Alberta Magazines Conference 2018, March, 2018, Calgary, AB
Scope: Provincial
Publications:
• Currents
Type: Newsletter; *Frequency:* 3 pa
Profile: Alberta Magazine Publishers Association updates
• MagaScene
Type: Newsletter; *Frequency:* Monthly; *Price:* Free
Profile: Magazine publishing industry news & events, plus profiles of member magazines

Alberta Maine-Anjou Association
PO Box 129, Derwent AB T0B 1C0
Tel: 780-741-2188
albertamaineanjou@hotmail.com
www.albertamaine-anjou.com
Overview: A small provincial organization
Affiliation(s): Canadian Maine-Anjou Association
Finances: *Funding Sources:* Sponsorships
Membership: 1-99; *Fees:* $50
Chief Officer(s):
Kevin Shuckburgh, President, 403-742-6475
kshuck@telus.net
Robert Stenberg, Vice-President, 780-388-2182
rcstenb@gmail.com
Doug Roxburgh, Secretary, 403-748-4030
dunriteag@telus.net
Jean Renton, Treasurer, 780-789-3770
jeanr@jkrconcepts.com
Awards:
• Jack Lee Memorial Booster
• Commercial Cattleman Of The Year
Publications:
• The Maine Connection
Type: Newsletter; *Frequency:* Semiannually; *Accepts Advertising;* Editor: Ashley Shannon

Alberta Media Production Industries Association (AMPIA)
#200, 7316 - 101 Ave., Edmonton AB T6A 0J2
Tel: 780-944-0707
action@ampia.org

Canadian Associations / Alberta Party

Overview: A small provincial organization founded in 1974
Mission: To promote, encourage, co-ordinate and administer orienteering as sport and recreation in Alberta which includes providing orienteering opportunities for all levels of ability.
Member of: Canadian Orienteering Federation
Staff Member(s): 1
Membership: *Fees:* $30 individual; $45 group
Activities: Sport orienteering; amateur sport; navigation; map reading; *Library:* Open to public
Chief Officer(s):
Kim Kasperski, President
Kitty Jones, Treasurer
Pascale Levesque, Executive Director
pascale@orienteeringalberta.ca
Publications:
• The Reentrant
Type: Newsletter

Alberta Party
PO Box 1045, Stn. Main, Edmonton AB T5J 2M1
Toll-Free: 844-453-5505
info@albertaparty.ca
www.albertaparty.ca
www.facebook.com/albertaparty
twitter.com/AlbertaParty
www.youtube.com/user/TheAlbertaParty
Overview: A medium-sized provincial organization
Finances: *Funding Sources:* Membership purchases; Donations
Chief Officer(s):
 Vacant, Party Leader

Alberta Percheron Club
c/o Julie Roy, RR#1, Markerville AB T0M 1M0
Tel: 403-728-3127
sanlan@platinum.ca
www.albertapercherons.com
Overview: A small provincial organization
Mission: To promote the Alberta Percheron horse in Alberta, throughout Canada, & internationally
Membership: 1-99; *Fees:* $15 youth & associate members; $25 single members; $35 families; *Member Profile:* Persons in Alberta with an interest in the Percheron horse
Activities: Hosting & participating in various shows, such as the annual Provincial Percheron Show & the annual Percheron Club Draft Horse Foal Show; Offering the Alberta Percheron Club Youth Program
Chief Officer(s):
John Ruzicka, President, 780-336-2011
Brian Coleman, Vice-President, 403-637-3700
Julie Roy, Secretary, 403-728-3127
sanlan@platinum.ca
Karen Ruzicka, Treasurer, 780-336-2011
Awards:
• Alberta Percheron Club Yearly Scholarship
Eligibility: Junior members of the Alberta Percheron Club, from ages 16 to 21; *Amount:* $500
Meetings/Conferences:
• Alberta Percheron Club 2018 AGM, February, 2018, Westerner Park, Red Deer, AB
Scope: Provincial
Contact Information: Lisa Evans, E-mail: albertapercheronclub@yahoo.ca, Phone: 403-809-4930
Publications:
• Alberta Percheron Club Breed Directory
Type: Directory; *Frequency:* Annually; *Accepts Advertising*;
Editor: Cam Roy
Profile: Listings of Alberta Percheron Club members their farms, & their horses

Alberta Pharmacists' Association (RxA)
Canadian Western Bank Building, #1725, 10303 Jasper Ave., Edmonton AB T5J 3N6
Tel: 780-990-0326; *Fax:* 780-990-1236
rxa@rxa.ca
www.rxa.ca
Overview: A small provincial organization
Mission: To represent the interests of pharmacists & pharmacies in Alberta to enhance enhance the health of Albertans
Staff Member(s): 8
Membership: *Fees:* $425 pharmacist; $0 student; *Member Profile:* Pharmacies & pharmacists across Alberta
Activities: Providing continuing education; Offering information to members; Promoting the role of pharmacists; Engaging in advocacy activities
Chief Officer(s):

Margaret Wing, Chief Executive Officer
margaret.wing@rxa.ca
Rose Dehod, Manager, Professional Development
rose.dehod@rxa.ca
Jody Johnson, Manager, Member Services
jody.johnson@rxa.ca
Meghan Cooper, Communications Coordinator
meghan.cooper@rxa.ca
Jeff Whissell, Director, Pharmacy Practice
jeff.whissell@rxa.ca
Meetings/Conferences:
• Alberta Pharmacists' Association 2018 Spring Professional Development Conference, March, 2018, DoubleTree by Hilton Hotel West Edmonton, Edmonton, AB
Scope: Provincial
Publications:
• The Capsule
Type: Newsletter; *Frequency:* Weekly; *Accepts Advertising*
Profile: Updates sent to approximately 900 pharmacies throughout Alberta
• RxPress
Type: Magazine; *Frequency:* Quarterly; *Accepts Advertising*
Profile: Recent developments in the industry, of interest to pharmacists & stakeholders

Alberta Pinzgauer Association (APA)
c/o Donna Smith, RR#2, Olds AB T4H 1P3
Tel: 403-556-2290; *Fax:* 403-506-8583
diamondt@airenet.com
www.pinzgauer.ca
Overview: A small provincial organization
Mission: To facilitate the exhibition & sale of Pinzgauer cattle in Alberta
Membership: *Member Profile:* Breeders of Pinzgauer cattle in Alberta
Activities: Promoting interest in Pinzgauer cattle; Recognizing youth involvement
Chief Officer(s):
Donna Smith, Secretary-Treasurer

Alberta Pioneer Auto Club
PO Box 111, Stn. M, Calgary AB T2P 2G9
apac.calgary@gmail.com
www.apaccalgary.ca
Overview: A small provincial organization founded in 1959
Mission: To encourage the preservation & restoration of all classic, antique & special interest automobiles
Finances: *Funding Sources:* Membership fees
Membership: 180; *Fees:* $40; *Member Profile:* Owners of cars more than 25 years old
Activities: Meetings held 2nd Tues. of each month

Alberta Pioneer Railway Association (APRA)
24215 - 34 St., Edmonton AB T5Y 6B4
Tel: 780-472-6229; *Fax:* 780-968-0167
www.albertarailwaymuseum.com
Also Known As: Alberta Railway Museum
Overview: A small provincial charitable organization founded in 1968
Mission: To collect, preserve, restore, exhibit & interpret artifacts that represent the history & social impact of the railways in Western Canada, with emphasis on Canadian National Railways & Northern Alberta Railways & their predecessors in northern & central Alberta
Member of: Alberta Museums Association; Museums Canada
Affiliation(s): Heritage Canada
Finances: *Funding Sources:* Grants; donations
Membership: *Fees:* $34 regular; $45 family; $20 senior/associate; *Member Profile:* Railway enthusiasts; retired railway workers
Activities: Operates Alberta Railway Museum; *Library:* John Rechner Memorial Library; Open to public by appointment
Chief Officer(s):
Stephen Wakimets, President

Alberta Plastics Recycling Association (APRA)
PO Box 56092, Stn. Airways, Calgary AB T2E 8K5
Toll-Free: 855-939-2386
info@albertaplasticsrecycling.com
www.albertaplasticsrecycling.com
Overview: A medium-sized provincial organization founded in 1991
Mission: To minimize plastic waste to landfill in Alberta
Affiliation(s): Canadian Plastics Industry Association (CPIA)
Membership: *Member Profile:* Plastics resin producers; Plastic manufacturers, fabricators, & converters; Packagers & fillers of plastic products; Wholesalers & retailers of plastic products &

products in plastics packaging; Plastics recyclers & the recycling community; Industry associations; Interested members of the public
Activities: Collaborating with industry, environmental interest groups, & all levels of government; Providing resources to companies, groups, & individuals
Chief Officer(s):
Tammy Schwass, Executive Director
tammy@albertaplasticsrecycling.com
Dave Schwass, President
JY Vanier, Vice-President
Kevin Kernaghan, Secretary-Treasurer
Publications:
• Alberta Plastics Recycling Association News
Type: Newsletter
Profile: Highlights & accomplishments of the Alberta Plastics Recycling Association
• Alberta Post-Consumer Plastics Recycling Strategy, Recycled Plastic Audit
Number of Pages: 36
Profile: An initiative of the Alberta Plastics Recycling Association in partnership with Alberta Environment

Alberta Playwrights' Network (APN)
#208, 331 41 Ave. NE, Calgary AB T2E 2N4
Tel: 403-269-8564; *Fax:* 403-265-6773
Toll-Free: 800-268-8564
www.albertaplaywrights.com
www.linkedin.com/company/3775416
www.facebook.com/Albertaplaywrights
twitter.com/APNPlaywrights
Overview: A small provincial charitable organization founded in 1985
Mission: To foster playwriting in Alberta
Member of: Theatre Alberta
Finances: *Funding Sources:* Grants; member & program fees
Staff Member(s): 5
Membership: *Fees:* $35 student; $55 individual; $65 organization; *Member Profile:* Playwrights & members of the theatre community resident or formerly resident of Alberta
Activities: Offering programs for playwrights, including Playwright Cabaret Readings, Alberta Playwriting Competition, playwriting retreats, workshops, script reading services & fundraising events; *Internships:* Yes *Library:* Script Library/Reading Room; Open to public
Chief Officer(s):
Trevor Rueger, Executive Director
trevor@albertaplaywrights.com

Alberta Poison Centre *See* Poison & Drug Information Service

Alberta Pork
4828 89 St., Edmonton AB T6E 5K1
Tel: 780-474-8288; *Fax:* 780-479-5128
Toll-Free: 877-247-7675
info@albertapork.com
www.albertapork.com
Overview: A small provincial organization
Mission: To maintain safety, animal care, & environmental standards within Alberta's hog industry
Member of: Canadian Pork Council
Membership: *Member Profile:* Pork producers
Activities: Offering market information, hog price listings, & risk management programs
Chief Officer(s):
Darcy Fitzgerald, Executive Director
darcy.fitzgerald@albertapork.com

Alberta Potato Marketing Board *See* Potato Growers of Alberta

Alberta Powerlifting Union (APU)
c/o James Bartlett, 4805 Vandyke Rd. NW, Calgary AB T3A 0J6
Tel: 403-471-4754
www.powerliftingab.com
www.youtube.com/user/AlbertaPL
Overview: A small provincial organization founded in 1983 overseen by Canadian Powerlifting Union
Mission: To promote powerlifting in Alberta
Affiliation(s): Canadian Powerlifting Union; International Powerlifting Federation
Membership: *Fees:* $60 open; $50 junior; $40 special
Chief Officer(s):
Shane Martin, Interim President
mr.shane.c.martin@gmail.com
James Bartlett, Chair, Registration
bartlettJ@bennettjones.com

Alberta Pro Life Alliance Association *See* Wilberforce Project

Alberta Professional Home Inspectors Society (APHIS)
PO Box 27039, Stn. Tuscany, Calgary AB T3L 2Y1
Tel: 403-248-6893; *Fax:* 888-812-4249
Toll-Free: 800-351-9993
admin@aphis.ca
www.aphis.ca
Overview: A small provincial organization
Mission: To support & regulate the home inspection profession in Alberta
Chief Officer(s):
Alan Fisher, President

Alberta Professional Outfitters Society (APOS)
#100, 3802 - 49 Ave., Stony Plain AB T7Z 2J7
Tel: 780-414-0249; *Fax:* 780-465-6801
info@apos.ab.ca
www.apos.ab.ca
Previous Name: Professional Outfitters Association of Alberta
Overview: A small provincial organization founded in 1997
Mission: To provide leadership & direction in the continuing development of Alberta's outfitter-hunting industry; To strive for long term sustainability in its approach to wildlife management, business opportunities & global competitiveness
Affiliation(s): Safari Club International; Foundation for North American Wild Sheep; Rocky Mountain Elk Foundation
Finances: *Annual Operating Budget:* $500,000-$1.5 Million
Staff Member(s): 3; 30 volunteer(s)
Membership: 450; *Fees:* OG permit $107
Activities: Providing all administrative services to the industry; government liaison; cooperative marketing; disciplinary function
Chief Officer(s):
Carla Rhyant Mal, Managing Director, 780-414-0249 Ext. 225
carla@apos.ab.ca
Fiona Nelson, Manager, Accounts, 780-414-0249 Ext. 224
fiona@apos.ab.ca
Cathy Wiltsie, Senior Coordinator, Member Services, 780-414-0249 Ext. 222
cathy@apos.ab.ca

Alberta Professional Planners Institute (APPI)
PO Box 596, Edmonton AB T5J 2K8
Tel: 780-435-8716; *Fax:* 780-452-7718
Toll-Free: 888-286-8716
admin@albertaplanners.com
www.albertaplanners.com
Overview: A medium-sized provincial organization founded in 1963 overseen by Canadian Institute of Planners
Mission: To expand the depth & enhance the credibility of the association; To promote professional growth of practicing planners throughout Alberta, the Northwest Territories, & Nunavut; To maximize membership potential; To provide an effective level of service to the membership
Finances: *Funding Sources:* Membership dues; Application fees
40 volunteer(s)
Membership: 400; *Member Profile:* Public & private sector professional planners & academics, practicing in Alberta, the Northwest Territories, or Nunavut, who have met all the membership requirements for education & responsible professional planning experience
Activities: *Rents Mailing List:* Yes
Chief Officer(s):
Eleanor Mohammed, RPP, MCIP, President
president@albertaplanners.com
MaryJane Alanko, Executive Director
execdir@albertaplanners.com
Meetings/Conferences:
• Alberta Professional Planners Institute 2018 Conference, September, 2018, Kananaskis Lodge, Kananaskis, AB
Scope: National

Alberta Provincial Council
c/o Edmonton Public School Board, Centre for Education, 1 Kingsway, Edmonton AB T5H 4G9
Tel: 780-429-8000; *Fax:* 780-429-8318
Also Known As: Council No: CE995
Overview: A small provincial organization overseen by International Reading Association
Chief Officer(s):
Su Kerslake, Coordinator, 780-498-8772
su.kerslake@epsb.ca

Alberta Provincial Rifle Association
PO Box 1015, Stn. M, Calgary AB T2P 2K4
www.albertarifle.com
Overview: A medium-sized provincial organization
Mission: To promote in every lawful way the interests of small arms marksmanship in the province of Alberta; To create public interest for the encouragement of small arms shooting, both as a sport & as a necessary means of national defense
Member of: Dominion of Canada Rifle Association; Shooting Federation of Canada
Chief Officer(s):
Bob Richards, President

Alberta Psychiatric Association (APA)
#400, 1040 - 7 Ave. SW, Calgary AB T2P 3G9
Tel: 403-244-4487; *Fax:* 403-244-2340
info@albertapsych.org
www.albertapsych.org
Overview: A small provincial organization
Affiliation(s): Canadian Psychiatric Association
Finances: *Funding Sources:* Membership fees; Donations; Grants
Membership: *Member Profile:* Psychiatrists in Alberta
Chief Officer(s):
Thomas Raedler, President
Meetings/Conferences:
• Alberta Psychiatric Association Scientific Conference and AGM 2018, March, 2018, Rimrock Resort Hotel, Banff, AB
Scope: Provincial
Attendance: 300+

Alberta Public Health Association (APHA)
c/o Injury Prevention Centre, University of Alberta, #4075 RTF, 8308 - 114 St., Edmonton AB T6G 2E1
apha.comm@gmail.com
www.apha.ab.ca
Overview: A medium-sized provincial charitable organization founded in 1943 overseen by Canadian Public Health Association
Mission: To protect public health through advocacy, partnerships, & education
Finances: *Annual Operating Budget:* $100,000-$250,000; *Funding Sources:* Membership dues; conferences; charitable donations; grants
15 volunteer(s)
Membership: 300; *Fees:* $50 regular; $22 student/retired; *Member Profile:* Public health practitioners; professionals from NGOs; educators, government & citizens interested in advocating for, promoting & protecting the health of the public; *Committees:* Governance; Membership & Communications; Partnerships & Funding; Public Health Issues; Student
Chief Officer(s):
Lindsay McLaren, President
Awards:
• Dr. John Waters Memorial Public Health Award
• Dr. John Waters Memorial Fund

Alberta Public Housing Administrators' Association (APHAA)
14220 - 109 Ave. NW, Edmonton AB T5N 4B3
Tel: 780-498-1971; *Fax:* 780-464-7039
www.aphaa.org
twitter.com/AphaaInfo
Overview: A medium-sized provincial organization
Mission: Works with the Province of Alberta in the publicly-funded housing industry to promote excellence in publicly funded housing administration through education, information and networking
Membership: *Member Profile:* Chief Administrative Officers for Management Bodies; *Committees:* Communications; Conference Planning; Education; Membership Selection; Nominations
Chief Officer(s):
Raymond Swonek, President
Meetings/Conferences:
• Alberta Public Housing Administrators' Association Spring AGM & Education Sessions 2018, May, 2018
Scope: Provincial
• Alberta Public Housing Administrators' Association Fall Conference 2018, 2018
Scope: Provincial

Alberta Publishers Association *See* Book Publishers Association of Alberta

Alberta Racquetball Association (ARA)
47 Walden Cres., St Albert AB T8N 3N5
Tel: 780-918-5332
albertaracquetball@shaw.ca
www.albertaracquetball.com
www.facebook.com/Alberta-Racquetball-Association-81312018623
www.youtube.com/channel/UCdxaKwlmilNEEnGN5dDpNig
Overview: A small provincial organization founded in 1971 overseen by Racquetball Canada
Mission: To develop the sport of racquetball in Alberta.
Member of: Racquetball Canada
Membership: *Fees:* $10
Chief Officer(s):
Barbara May, Executive Director

Alberta Ready Mixed Concrete Association (ARMCA)
4944 Roped Rd. NW, Edmonton AB T6B 3T7
Tel: 780-436-5645; *Fax:* 780-436-6503
info@concretealberta.ca
www.concretealberta.ca
www.facebook.com/concretealberta
twitter.com/concretealberta
Also Known As: Concrete Alberta
Overview: A medium-sized provincial organization founded in 1963 overseen by Canadian Ready Mixed Concrete Association
Mission: To provide industry representation for the advancement of quality concrete in Alberta
Member of: Canadian Ready Mixed Concrete Association; Alberta Chamber of Commerce
Finances: *Annual Operating Budget:* $100,000-$250,000; *Funding Sources:* Membership fees
Staff Member(s): 3; 40 volunteer(s)
Membership: 270 companies; *Member Profile:* Producer members consist of producers & sellers of ready-mixed concrete; Associate members consist of product or service suppliers; Affiliate members consist of companies that serve as a sub-trade or user of concrete; *Committees:* Technical; Residential; Transportation; Pumping; Membership; & Convention
Activities: *Speaker Service:* Yes; *Library:* ARMCA Technical Information; Open to public by appointment
Chief Officer(s):
Dan Hansen, Executive Director
dan.hanson@concretealberta.ca
Paul Masson, Director, Technical Services & Training
paul.masson@concretealberta.ca
Meetings/Conferences:
• Alberta Ready Mixed Concrete Association 2018 Annual General Meeting & Convention, 2018, AB
Scope: Provincial
Description: Featuring speakers, meetings, & networking opportunities

Alberta Real Estate Association (AREA)
#217, 3332 - 20 St. SW, Calgary AB T2T 6T9
Tel: 403-228-6845; *Fax:* 780-228-4360
Toll-Free: 800-661-0231
communications@areahub.ca
www.areahub.ca
Overview: A medium-sized provincial organization founded in 1947
Mission: To protect the interests of realtors & real estate boards in Alberta
Member of: The Canadian Real Estate Association
Membership: 6,750; *Committees:* Finance & Audit; Governance & Board Development; Provincial Forms & Practice; Provincial Government Relations; Provincial Professional Development
Chief Officer(s):
Ian Burns, CEO

Alberta Reappraising AIDS Society (ARAS)
PO Box 61037, Stn. Kensington, Calgary AB T2N 4S6
Tel: 403-220-0129
aras@aras.ab.ca
www.aras.ab.ca
Overview: A small provincial organization founded in 1999
Mission: To provide a science-based alternative information on HIV/AIDS & other infectious diseases; does not provide treatment recommendations
Finances: *Annual Operating Budget:* Less than $50,000
2 volunteer(s)
Membership: 135; *Member Profile:* People interested in questioning the dominant HIV/AIDS paradigm
Activities: Offering education & information; *Speaker Service:* Yes; *Library:* by appointment
Chief Officer(s):
David Crowe, President, 403-289-6609, Fax: 403-206-7717
david.crowe@aras.ab.ca
Roger Swan, Treasurer

Canadian Associations / Alberta Recreation & Parks Association (ARPA)

Awards:
- Healer
- Administrator

Awards to the bravest rethinking administrator, bureaucrat, lawyer, NGO employee or politician in the previous year
- Scribe

Awarded to journalist, writer or film-maker for rethinking AIDS article in the previous year
- Activist

Awards to activist, who was most hard working & effective in the previous year
- Researcher

Awarded to researcher, scientist or academic who effectively challeneds HIV/AIDS dogma in the previous year, through their research or scientific publications

Alberta Recreation & Parks Association (ARPA)
11759 Groat Rd., Edmonton AB T5M 3K6
Tel: 780-415-1745; *Fax:* 780-451-7915
Toll-Free: 877-544-1747
arpa@arpaonline.ca
arpaonline.ca
www.linkedin.com/company/alberta-recreation-and-parks-association
www.facebook.com/arpaonline
twitter.com/arpaonline
www.youtube.com/channel/UCWpGvr7VoeGnxXeivhcuETQ
Overview: A medium-sized provincial charitable organization overseen by Canadian Parks & Recreation Association
Mission: To promote accessibility to recreation & parks & their benefits to Albertans; To work toward economic sustainability, natural resource protection, & conservation within provincial parks & natural environments
Membership: 1,300+; *Member Profile:* Students; Municipal elected officials, staff, volunteers & stakeholders; Business staff, suppliers & clients; Eductional institution staff; Non-profit association & government agency elected officials, staff, volunteers & stakeholders; Individuals interested in or working in areas of recreation, parks, leisure, & tourism
Activities: Providing leadership to Alberta's recreation & parks industry; Facilitating communication & information networking; Maximizing human & financial resources for recreation & parks services; Establishing relations with the provincial government; Advocating recreational safety, fair play & gender equity; Increasing public awareness of recreation & active lifestyles; Monitoring development of formal post-secondary educational opportunities for recreation & parks; Research & preparing position papers on various issues; *Awareness Events:* Recreation & Parks Month, June; Communities in Bloom; Community Choosewell Challenge
Chief Officer(s):
Bill Wells, Chief Executive Officer, 780-415-1745
wwells@arpaonline.ca
Steve Allan, Director, Finance & Operations, 780-644-4799
sallan@arpaonline.ca
Anna Holtby, Coordinator, Communications, 780-644-6976
aholtby@arpaonline.ca
Awards:
- Alberta Recreation & Parks Association Merit Award
- Wild Rose Award
- A.V. Pettigrew Award
- Excellence in Youth Development Award
- Parks Excellence Award
- Halladay Memorial Scholarship
- Lieutenant Governor's Leadership for Active Communities Award
- Alberta Advisory Board on Recreation for the Disabled (AABRD) Legacy Award
- Alberta Advisory Board on Recreation for the Disabled (AABRD) Undergraduate & Graduate Scholarships
; *Amount:* $3,000 graduate; $1,000 undergraduate
- Rick Curtis HIGH FIVE Award

Meetings/Conferences:
- Alberta Recreation & Parks Association 2018 Youth Development Through Recreation Services Symposium, March, 2018, Radisson Hotel, Red Deer, AB
Scope: Provincial
Contact Information: Coordinator, Administration: Lori Simmonds, E-mail: lsimmonds@arpaonline.ca, Phone: 780-415-1745
Publications:
- Alberta Recreation & Parks Association Recreation Buyers Guide
Type: Booklet; *Accepts Advertising*
Profile: Advertisements with contact information

- Alberta Recreation & Parks Association Annual Report
Type: Report

Alberta Registered Music Teachers' Association (ARMTA)
PO Box 247, Stn. Main, Edmonton AB T5J 2J1
Tel: 780-554-7682
www.armtaedmonton.ab.ca
Overview: A medium-sized provincial organization founded in 1982
Mission: To enhance quality of life by promoting the love & knowledge of music through professional music teaching & studies in the community & through providing cultural events of a high standard for the community
Member of: Canadian Federation of Music Teachers Associations
Affiliation(s): Alberta Music Education Foundation
Finances: *Annual Operating Budget:* $50,000-$100,000
Staff Member(s): 1; 50 volunteer(s)
Membership: 400; *Fees:* Schedule available; *Member Profile:* Accredited music educators & performers
Activities: *Internships:* Yes; *Speaker Service:* Yes; *Rents Mailing List:* Yes
Chief Officer(s):
Vicki Martin, Provincial Administrator
admin@armta.ca

Alberta Registered Professional Foresters Association See College of Alberta Professional Foresters

Alberta Rehabilitation Council for the Disabled See Alberta Easter Seals Society

Alberta Reined Cow Horse Association (ARCHA)
PO Box 18, RR#2, Site 13, Olds AB T4H 1P3
Tel: 403-556-2640; *Fax:* 403-556-8766
info@cowhorse.ca
www.cowhorse.ca
Overview: A small provincial organization founded in 1981
Mission: To improve the quality of the western reined stock horse; To perpetuate the early Spanish traditions of highly trained & well reined working cow horse events & contests in expositions & shows; To promote the training of reined cow horses & reining horses among the younger horsemen of the West; To use & encourage the use of standard rules for holding & judging contests of the working cow horse
Affiliation(s): NRCHA
Finances: *Annual Operating Budget:* Less than $50,000
Staff Member(s): 1; 12 volunteer(s)
Membership: 400 individual; *Fees:* $25 youth; $50 individual; $90 family
Chief Officer(s):
Mel Mabbott, President, 403-558-0135, Fax: 403-558-2390
greenpine@xplornet.com
Terri Loree, Office Manager

Alberta Research Council Inc. (ARC)
250 Karl Clark Rd., Edmonton AB T6N 1E4
Tel: 780-450-5111; *Fax:* 780-450-5333
referral@albertainnovates.ca
www.albertatechfutures.ca
www.linkedin.com/company/alberta-innovates---technology-futures
www.facebook.com/AlbertaInnovates
twitter.com/TechFuturesAB
www.youtube.com/user/TechFutures
Overview: A medium-sized provincial organization founded in 1921
Mission: To operate as an applied research & development corporation; To develop & commercialize technology to grow innovative enterprises; To specialize in converting early stage ideas into marketable technology products & services
Finances: *Annual Operating Budget:* Greater than $5 Million;
Funding Sources: Provincial grants; Fees; Revenue
Activities: *Library:* Information Centre; Open to public
Chief Officer(s):
Stephen Lougheed, President/CEO
Sandra Scott, Executive Vice-President

Calgary Office
3608 - 33 St. NW, Calgary AB T2L 2A6
Tel: 403-210-5222; *Fax:* 403-210-5380
www.arc.ab.ca

Devon Branch
1 Oil Patch Dr., Devon AB T9G 1A8
Chief Officer(s):
John McDougall, President/CEO

Vegreville Branch
PO Box 4000, Hwy 16A & 75 St., Vegreville AB T9C 1T4
Tel: 780-632-8211; *Fax:* 780-632-8385
Chief Officer(s):
John McDougall, President/CEO

Alberta Restorative Justice Association (ARJA)
PO Box 1053, Stn. Main, Edmonton AB T5J 2M1
Tel: 780-628-6801
Toll-Free: 800-601-7310
info@arja.ca
www.arja.ca
www.facebook.com/RJAlberta
twitter.com/RJAlberta
Overview: A small provincial organization founded in 2005
Mission: To be a collective voice to strengthen Restorative Justice in Alberta communities by establishing and providing information, education, and awareness towards best practices in Restorative Justice.
Chief Officer(s):
Barb Barclay, Chair
Awards:
- George Brertton Award
Recognizes individuals' contributions to advancement of restorative justice in their communities

Alberta Rhythmic Sportive Gymnastics Federation See Rhythmic Gymnastics Alberta

Alberta Roadbuilders & Heavy Construction Association (ARHCA)
#201, 9333 - 45 Ave., Edmonton AB T6E 5Z7
Tel: 780-436-9860; *Fax:* 780-436-4910
Toll-Free: 866-436-9860
administration@arhca.ab.ca
www.arhca.ab.ca
twitter.com/AB_Roadbuilders
Overview: A medium-sized provincial organization founded in 1954 overseen by Canadian Construction Association
Mission: To represent contractors, suppliers & consulting engineers who work in the heavy construction industry; To support long-term investment in transportation infrastructure
Affiliation(s): Western Canada Roadbuilders Association; Alberta Construction Safety Association; Roads & Transportation Association Canada
Finances: *Annual Operating Budget:* $500,000-$1.5 Million
Staff Member(s): 7
Membership: 500+; *Fees:* Schedule available; *Member Profile:* Regular members consist of individuals, firms or corporations that work in heavy construction; Associate members consist of individuals, firms or corporations that serve as suppliers to the industry; Consultant members consist of individuals, firms or corporations that engage in civil consulting engineering for heavy construction projects
Activities: Providing industry resources to members
Chief Officer(s):
Ron Glen, Chief Executive Officer
ron.glen@arhca.ab.ca
Vacant, Director, Government & External Relations
Paul Cashman, Manager, Communications & Media Relations
paul.cashman@arhca.ab.ca
Jenna Klynstra, Manager, Environment, Safety & Education
jenna@arhca.ab.ca
Publications:
- ARHCA [Alberta Roadbuilders & Heavy Construction Association] Newsletter
Type: Newsletter
Profile: Information about ARHCA activities & events; news & updates
- Equipment Rental Rates Guide & Member Listings [a publication of the Alberta Roadbuilders & Heavy Construction Association]
Type: Guide; *Price:* $80

Alberta Roofing Contractors Association (ARCA)
2380 Pegasus Rd. NE, Calgary AB T2E 8G8
Tel: 403-250-7055; *Fax:* 403-250-1702
Toll-Free: 800-382-8515
info@arcaonline.ca
www.arcaonline.ca
Overview: A medium-sized provincial organization founded in 1961 overseen by Canadian Roofing Contractors' Association
Mission: To provide continuing education for roofing contractors, their personnel & interested others; to represent the roofing contracting industry in its relationships with legislative & regulating bodies; to work closely with affiliate organizations & liaison groups in advancing professionalism of roofing

contracting; to provide a forum for interaction of members; to encourage high standards of professional conduct among roofing contractors; to develop a comprehensive body of knowledge about roofing management & technology, & disseminate ideas & knowledge to members & others; to monitor new products & systems; to work for cooperation & greater understanding between contracting, inspection, manufacturing & supply segments of the roofing industry
Member of: Canadian Roofing Contractors' Association
Affiliation(s): National Roofing Contractors Association USA
Finances: *Annual Operating Budget:* $250,000-$500,000
Staff Member(s): 4
Membership: 70; *Fees:* Schedule available; *Member Profile:* Roofing contractors, suppliers & manufacturers
Activities: *Library:* by appointment

Alberta Rowing Association (ARA)
11759 Groat Rd., Edmonton AB T5M 3K6
Tel: 780-427-8154
office@albertarowing.ca
www.albertarowing.ca
www.facebook.com/131265308366
twitter.com/AlbertaRowing
Overview: A medium-sized provincial organization overseen by Rowing Canada Aviron
Mission: To govern the sport of rowing in Alberta
Member of: Rowing Canada Aviron
Finances: *Funding Sources:* Membership fees; Fundraising; Government support
Membership: 7 regional clubs + 2 university clubs
Chief Officer(s):
Peter Walsh, President
p.walsh@albertarowing.ca

Alberta Rugby Football Union
Percy Page Centre, 11759 Groat Rd., Edmonton AB T5M 3K6
Tel: 780-415-1773; *Fax:* 780-422-5558
info@rugbyalberta.com
www.rugbyalberta.com
twitter.com/AlbertaRugby
Overview: A medium-sized provincial organization founded in 1961 overseen by Rugby Canada
Mission: To develop & promote an interest in rugby in Alberta
Member of: Rugby Canada
Finances: *Funding Sources:* Alberta Sport, Recreation, Parks and Wildlife Foundation
Staff Member(s): 3
Activities: *Library:* Open to public
Chief Officer(s):
Sandy Nesbitt, President
Simon Chi, Vice-President
Debby Ashmore, Executive Director, 780-638-4547
Rick Melia, Director, Finance & Administration

Alberta Rural Municipal Administrators Association
6027 - 4th St. NE, Calgary AB T2K 4Z5
Tel: 403-275-0622; *Fax:* 403-275-8179
www.armaa.ca
Overview: A medium-sized provincial organization founded in 1922
Mission: To represent administrators in Alberta municipal governments
Finances: *Funding Sources:* Membership dues; grant
Membership: *Member Profile:* Rural municipal administrator
Chief Officer(s):
Valerie Schmaltz, Executive Director
d_vschmaltz@shaw.ca
Sheila Kitz, President
skitz@county.stpaul.ab.ca
Meetings/Conferences:
• Alberta Rural Municipal Administrators' Association 2018 Conference, 2018
Scope: Provincial

Alberta Safety Council
4831 - 93 Ave., Edmonton AB T6B 3A2
Tel: 780-462-7300; *Fax:* 780-462-7318
Toll-Free: 800-301-6407
info@safetycouncil.ab.ca
www.safetycouncil.ab.ca
www.facebook.com/189043441145255
twitter.com/ABSafetycouncil
Overview: A medium-sized provincial organization founded in 1946
Mission: To create awareness & provide educational & training programs to citizens of Alberta on how to maintain a safe environment at home, in traffic, at work & at play

Affiliation(s): Canada Safety Council; National Safety Council; Safety Services Canada
Membership: 209; *Member Profile:* Companies, organizations, agencies which promote safety
Activities: *Speaker Service:* Yes; *Library:* Open to public
Chief Officer(s):
Laurie Billings, Executive Director

Alberta Sailing Association (ASA)
PO Box 52058, Stn. Edmonton Trail, Calgary AB T2E 8K9
info@albertasailing.com
www.albertasailing.com
Overview: A small provincial organization founded in 1973 overseen by Sail Canada
Mission: Alberta Sailing Association in partnership with its member clubs, sailing schools & Sail Canada addresses the needs of sailors; encourages improved access to water & sailing facilities; sail training & safety programs & opportunities to compete at the club, provincial & international levels
Member of: Sail Canada
Finances: *Annual Operating Budget:* $50,000-$100,000
Staff Member(s): 1
Membership: 1,500; *Fees:* $20
Chief Officer(s):
Ron Hewitt, President
president@albertasailing.com
Fie Hulsker, Executive Director, 403-827-5578

Alberta Salers Association
5160 Skyline Way NE, Calgary AB T2E 6V1
Tel: 403-264-5850; *Fax:* 403-264-5895
info@salerscanada.com
www.salerscanada.com
Overview: A small provincial organization founded in 1973
Mission: To promote salers cattle in Alberta
Member of: Salers Association of Canada
Finances: *Annual Operating Budget:* Less than $50,000
11 volunteer(s)
Membership: 60; *Fees:* $25; *Member Profile:* Purebred cattle breeders
Activities: Raising awareness of salers cattle in Alberta
Chief Officer(s):
Heidi Voegeli-Bleiker, Office Manager

Alberta School Boards Association (ASBA)
#1200, 9925 - 109 St., Edmonton AB T5K 2J8
Tel: 780-482-7311
reception@asba.ab.ca
www.asba.ab.ca
twitter.com/ABSchoolBoards
Previous Name: Alberta School Trustees' Association
Overview: A medium-sized provincial organization founded in 1907 overseen by Canadian School Boards Association
Mission: To promote the availability of high quality schooling for all; To assist member boards in fulfilling their mission of achieving excellence in education
Finances: *Annual Operating Budget:* Greater than $5 Million; *Funding Sources:* Membership fees; Government grants; Fee for service
Staff Member(s): 24
Membership: 1-99; *Fees:* Schedule available; *Member Profile:* All school boards in Alberta
Activities: Providing professional development opportunities
Chief Officer(s):
Scott McCormack, Executive Director, 780-451-7132
smccormack@asba.ab.ca
Heather Massel, Director, Communications
hmassel@asba.ab.ca
Heather Rogers, Director, Finance & Corporate Services
hrogers@asba.ab.ca
Awards:
• Indigenous Shining Student Award
Eligibility: A grade 10 to 12 student of First Nations, Métis or Inuit heritage
• Edwin Parr Teacher Award
Awarded to honour outstanding first-year teachers
• Friends of Education Award
Awarded to recognize individuals or institutions who are committed to improving education for Alberta students & who demonstrate this through service & contributions
• Honourary Life Membership Award
Presented to an Alberta trustee who has provided distinguished service towards the work of the association
• Long Service Awards
Awarded to recognize significant milestone years of service for trustees *Eligibility:* Any trustee serving a minimum of two terms

• Premier's Award for School Board Excellence and Innovation
Awarded in conjunction with Xerox Canada; recognizes a school board's unique contributions to the improvement of students' learning experiences
• Public Engagement Award
Awarded to a school board that has engaged its community throughout the previous school year
• Zone Appreciation Award
Awarded to a trustee, superintendent, or secretary-treasurer who has displayed outstanding service to trusteeship in their zone
Meetings/Conferences:
• Alberta School Boards Association 2018 Spring General Meeting, 2018, AB
Scope: Provincial
Description: An Alberta School Boards Association professional development event
Contact Information: Contact, Meetings: Noreen Pownall, E-mail: npownall@asba.ab.ca
• Alberta School Boards Association 2018 Fall General Meeting, 2018, AB
Scope: Provincial
Description: An Alberta School Boards Association professional development event
Contact Information: Contact, Meetings: Noreen Pownall, E-mail: npownall@asba.ab.ca
Publications:
• Alberta School Boards Association Annual Report
Type: Yearbook; *Frequency:* Annually
Profile: A review of the year's activities

Alberta School Councils' Association (ASCA)
#1200, 9925 - 109 St., Edmonton AB T5K 2J8
Tel: 780-454-9867; *Fax:* 780-455-0167
Toll-Free: 800-661-3470
www.albertaschoolcouncils.ca
www.linkedin.com/company-beta/3862745
www.facebook.com/ABschoolcouncil
twitter.com/ABschoolcouncil
Overview: A medium-sized provincial organization overseen by Canadian Home & School Federation
Mission: To be the voice of parents/families committed to the best possible education for Alberta children, so that they may reach their potential to participate in society in a meaningful & responsible way
Finances: *Annual Operating Budget:* $50,000-$100,000
Staff Member(s): 5; 20 volunteer(s)
Membership: 500; *Fees:* $25 individual parent; $60 school council; $50 associate; *Member Profile:* School council
Activities: *Speaker Service:* Yes; *Library:* Resource Centre; by appointment
Chief Officer(s):
Allison Pike, President
president@albertaschoolcouncils.ca
Wendy Keiver, Acting Executive Director, 780-451-7148
wendyk@albertaschoolcouncils.ca
Jolaine Kochisarli, Manager, Communications, 780-451-7149
jolainek@albertaschoolcouncils.ca
Meetings/Conferences:
• Alberta School Councils' Association School Councils Conference & Annual General Meeting 2018, April, 2018, Delta Edmonton South, Edmonton, AB
Scope: Provincial
Description: Features school council delegates & a discussion of issues concerning Alberta school councils

Alberta School Learning Commons Council (ASLC)
c/o Alberta Teachers' Association, Barnett House, 11010 - 142 St. NW, Edmonton AB T5N 2R1
www.aslc.ca
Previous Name: Alberta School Library Council
Overview: A small provincial organization
Mission: To advance teaching & learning excellence through effective school library practices; To cultivate & enhance effective school library operation through leadership, information, & professional development
Affiliation(s): Alberta Teachers' Association (ALA)
Membership: *Fees:* Schedule available; *Member Profile:* Alberta Teachers' Association members wishing to join a specialized council
Activities: Organizing professional development opportunities; Disseminating information to members through various platforms
Chief Officer(s):
Karen Belter, President
kebelter@gmail.com
Meetings/Conferences:
• Alberta School Learning Commons Council Annual General

Canadian Associations / Alberta Schools' Athletic Association (ASAA)

Meeting 2018, 2018, AB
Scope: Provincial

Alberta School Library Council *See* Alberta School Learning Commons Council

Alberta School Trustees' Association *See* Alberta School Boards Association

Alberta Schools' Athletic Association (ASAA)
Percy Page Centre, 11759 Groat Rd., Edmonton AB T5M 3K6
Tel: 780-427-8182; *Fax:* 780-415-1833
info@asaa.ca
www.asaa.ca
twitter.com/ASAA
Overview: A medium-sized provincial organization founded in 1956 overseen by School Sport Canada
Mission: To provide leadership in the promotion of high school sport; to regulate sports competition & promote the belief that education includes development of the whole person
Member of: School Sport Canada
Affiliation(s): National Federation of State High School Associations
Finances: *Funding Sources:* Lotteries; membership dues; fundraising; corporate sponsors
Staff Member(s): 5
Membership: 371 schools + 8,000 student athletes
Chief Officer(s):
John F. Paton, Executive Director
john@asaa.ca
Garret Doll, President
gdoll@gsacrd.ab.ca

Alberta Securities Commission (ASC)
#600, 250 - 5th St. SW, Calgary AB T2P 0R4
Tel: 403-297-6454; *Fax:* 403-297-6156
Toll-Free: 877-355-0585
Other Communication: Records & File Requests, E-mail: records.requests@asc.ca
inquiries@asc.ca
www.albertasecurities.com
www.linkedin.com/company/alberta-securities-commission_2
www.facebook.com/ASCUpdates
twitter.com/ASCUpdates
Overview: A medium-sized provincial organization overseen by Canadian Securities Administrators
Mission: To regulate securities trading in Alberta, through the administration of the Securities Act (Alberta); To report to the Legislature, through the minister responsible for the administration of the Securities Act; To foster a fair & competitive securities market; To protect investors & market integrity
Member of: Canadian Securities Administrators
Finances: *Funding Sources:* Fees collected from market participants under the legislation
Activities: Regulating in Alberta the Investment Industry Regulatory Organization of Canada (IIROC), the Mutual Fund Dealers Association of Canada (MFDA), the Natural Gas Exchange Inc., the Alberta Watt Exchange Limited & the TSX Venture Exchange (TSXV) (with the British Columbia Securities Commission)
Chief Officer(s):
Stan Magidson, Chair & Chief Executive Officer
David Linder, Executive Director
Lara Gaede, CFO & Chief Accountant
Publications:
• The Alberta Capital Market: A Comparative Overview [a publication of the Alberta Securities Commission]
Type: Report; *Frequency:* Annually
• Alberta Securities Commission Annual Report
Type: Report; *Frequency:* Annually
• Alberta Women on Boards Index [a publication of the Alberta Securities Commission]
Type: Report; *Frequency:* Annually
• Enforcement Report [a publication of the Alberta Securities Commission]
Type: Report; *Frequency:* Annually
• Oil & Gas Review Report [a publication of the Alberta Securities Commission]
Type: Report; *Frequency:* Annually

Alberta Senior Citizens Sport & Recreation Association (ASCSRA)
#400, 7015 Macleod Trail., Calgary AB T2H 2K6
Tel: 403-803-9852; *Fax:* 403-800-5599
info@alberta55plus.ca
www.alberta55plus.ca
Also Known As: Alberta 55 Plus
Overview: A medium-sized provincial organization founded in 1980
Mission: To promote sport & recreation development for seniors (55+) across Alberta; to act as a provincial voice to ensure input by age categories for seniors in Alberta Winter & Summer Games; to promote future Alberta Seniors' Games
Affiliation(s): Alberta Sport, Recreation, Parks & Wildlife Foundation
Finances: *Annual Operating Budget:* $100,000-$250,000; *Funding Sources:* Government & private sector sponsorhip
Staff Member(s): 2; 100 volunteer(s)
Membership: 4,000; *Fees:* $15/1yr, $25/2yrs individual; $50 association; $25-$50 club
Activities: Workshops & instructional clinics; *Speaker Service:* Yes
Chief Officer(s):
Vern Hafso, President, 780-336-2270, Fax: 780-336-3525
tollarav@mscnet.ca

Alberta Senior Citizens' Housing Association (ASCHA)
9711 - 47 Ave., Edmonton AB T6E 5M7
Tel: 780-439-6473; *Fax:* 780-433-3717
ascha@ascha.com
www.ascha.com
www.facebook.com/ascha.team
twitter.com/ABSeniorsLiving
Overview: A small provincial organization founded in 1967
Mission: To support the providers of seniors housing & act as a vehicle that provides & promotes leadership, an exchange of ideas, resources, communication & education to the members
Affiliation(s): Red Deer College Certificate Programs: Site Manager & Activity Coordinator
Staff Member(s): 6
Membership: 139 organizations + 1 individual; *Fees:* Schedule available; *Member Profile:* Operators of seniors' housing (regular & associate members); product & service providers (corporate members) & individual members (mainly students in ASCHA Certificate Program)
Activities: Information & support services; advocacy; standards; educational services; housing registry; *Library:* Not open to public
Chief Officer(s):
Irene Martin-Lindsay, Executive Director
irene@ascha.com
Meetings/Conferences:
• Alberta Seniors Communities & Housing Association 2018 Convention & Tradeshow, April, 2018, Sheraton Red Deer, Red Deer, AB
Scope: Provincial

The Alberta Seventh Step Society
1820 - 27th Ave. SW, Calgary AB T2T 1H1
Tel: 403-228-7778; *Fax:* 403-228-7773
info@albertaseventhstep.com
www.albertaseventhstep.com
Also Known As: 7th Step Society of Alberta
Overview: A medium-sized provincial organization founded in 1971
Mission: To prevent crime & reduce recidivism through the provision of services & programs to persons in conflict with the law
Affiliation(s): The 7th Step Society of Canada
Finances: *Annual Operating Budget:* $500,000-$1.5 Million
Staff Member(s): 22; 467 volunteer(s)
Membership: 48; *Fees:* $10 individual; $100 corporate; *Committees:* Audit; Finance; Governance & Strategy; Policy & Program
Chief Officer(s):
Bob Alexander, Executive Director, 403-228-7778 Ext. 103
execdirector@albertaseventhstep.com

Alberta Sheep Breeders Association (ASBA)
PO Box 7, St Albert AB T8N 1N2
Fax: 403-443-7221
Toll-Free: 866-967-4337
office@albertasheepbreeders.ca
www.albertasheepbreeders.ca
Overview: A small provincial organization overseen by Canadian Sheep Breeders' Association
Mission: To promote the purebred sheep industry within Alberta
Finances: *Annual Operating Budget:* Less than $50,000
Staff Member(s): 1; 13 volunteer(s)
Membership: 80; *Fees:* $36.75; *Member Profile:* Producers of purebred sheep in Alberta; *Committees:* Newsletter; Recognition Awards & Memorial Scholarships; Symposium; Website
Activities: Sheep sale; Alberta sheep symposium; produces promotional material; developing website
Chief Officer(s):
Linda Brandes, Contact, Office
Awards:
• Shepherds Past Memorial Award
• Good Shepherd Award
• ASBA Memorial Scholarship

Alberta Shorthand Reporters Association (ASRA)
64 Desmarais Cres., St. Albert AB T8N 6A9
Tel: 780-913-8740
asra@asraonline.com
www.asraonline.com
Overview: A small provincial organization founded in 1958
Mission: To advance the court reporting profession by promoting court reporters as experts in the field of verbatim shorthand reporting; To provide continuing education to its members; To advocate quality service, high ethical standards & state-of-the-art technology
Affiliation(s): National Court Reporters Association
Finances: *Annual Operating Budget:* $50,000-$100,000
8 volunteer(s)
Membership: 350; *Fees:* $125 reporters; $10 associates & students; *Committees:* Practice Review; Communications
Activities: Annual convention; seminars; training programs
Chief Officer(s):
Sandra Burns, President
sandraburns@asraonline.com

Alberta Shorthorn Association
c/o Albert and Susan Oram, PO Box 939, Castor AB T0C 0X0
Fax: 800-387-6909
Toll-Free: 800-387-6909
albertashorthorn@gmail.com
www.albertashorthorn.com
www.facebook.com/abshorthornassoc
Overview: A small provincial organization
Mission: To produce & promote the Shorthorn breed of cattle
Member of: Canadian Shorthorn Association
Finances: *Annual Operating Budget:* Less than $50,000
Membership: 87
Chief Officer(s):
Dennis Wishnowski, Executive Director

Alberta Sign Association
PO Box 3362, Sherwood Park AB T8H 2T3
Tel: 587-336-8283; *Fax:* 780-464-3137
info@albertasigns.com
www.albertasigns.com
Overview: A small provincial charitable organization founded in 1992
Mission: To promote the growth & professionalism of the Sign Industry through communication & education
Member of: Sign Association of Canada
Affiliation(s): Northwest Sign Council

Alberta Simmental Association (ASA)
131 Stonegate Cres., Airdrie AB T4B 2S8
Tel: 403-861-6352; *Fax:* 403-948-2059
info@albertasimmental.com
www.albertasimmental.com
Overview: A small provincial organization founded in 1971
Mission: To promote Simmental as a highly sought after, productive & efficient breed; To recognize the value of both purebred Simmental & Simmental influenced cattle; through continuous public awareness, strive for increased acceptance by the producer & consumer markets resulting in a greater share of the beef production industry
Member of: Canadian Simmental Association
Staff Member(s): 1; 9 volunteer(s)
Membership: 16; *Committees:* Show and Sale; 4H/YC3; Feeder Sale; Promotions; Advertising; Website
Activities: Financial prudence, fair & equal representation, support of the provincial 4-H program, encouragement & endorsement of the Alberta Young Canadian Simmentalers
Chief Officer(s):
Ashley Anderson, President
ashleyandblair@gmail.com
Healther Saucier, Office Administrator
Awards:
• Simmental Double Crown
• Wild Rose Classic

Alberta Ski Jumping & Nordic Combined (ASJNC)
PO Box 96022, RPO West Springs, Calgary AB T3H 0L3

Tel: 403-703-7157
mikebodnarchuk@shaw.ca
skijumpingalberta.com
www.facebook.com/ASJNC
Also Known As: Ski Jumping Alberta
Overview: A small provincial organization founded in 1991
Mission: To be the provincial governing body of ski jumping & nordic combined programs in Alberta
Chief Officer(s):
Mike Bodnarchuk, Chair
Jeremy Hamming, Vice Chair

Alberta Snowboard Association (ASA)
Bob Niven Training Centre, Bldg. 140, #108, 88 Canada Olympic Rd. SW, Calgary AB T3B 5R5
Tel: 403-247-5609
admin@albertasnowboarding.com
www.albertasnowboarding.com
www.facebook.com/albertaSnowboardingAssociation
twitter.com/AB_Snowboard
instagram.com/albertasnowboard
Overview: A small provincial organization overseen by Canadian Snowboard Federation
Mission: To be the provincial governing body of competitive snowboarding in Alberta
Member of: Canadian Snowboard Federation
Membership: *Fees:* $25 associate; $35-$50 athlete; $50-$120 coach; $25 judge/official
Chief Officer(s):
Chris Blain, President
Wes Miskiman, Vice President
Jeff Jarvis, Treasurer
Ryan Rausch, Secretary

Alberta Snowmobile Association (ASA)
11759 Groat Rd., Edmonton AB T5M 3K6
Tel: 780-427-2695; *Fax:* 780-415-1779
www.altasnowmobile.ab.ca
www.facebook.com/103977149653938
twitter.com/Altasnowmobile
Overview: A medium-sized provincial organization founded in 1971
Mission: To promote safe recreational snowmobiling in the province of Alberta
Affiliation(s): Canadian Council of Snowmobile Organizations
Membership: *Fees:* $60-$70
Chief Officer(s):
Lyle Birnie, President
ljbirnie@telus.net
Denise England, Vice-President
plasticandpowder@hotmail.com
Meetings/Conferences:
• Alberta Snowmobile & Powersports Show 2018, 2018, AB
Scope: Provincial
Contact Information: www.albertasnowmobileshow.com

Alberta Soaring Council
PO Box 13, Black Diamond AB T0L 0H0
Tel: 403-813-6658
asc@stade.ca
www.soaring.ab.ca
www.facebook.com/AlbertaSoaringCouncil
Overview: A medium-sized provincial organization founded in 1966 overseen by Soaring Association of Canada
Mission: To promote soaring sports provincially in all aspects; To plan & support local & provincial events & national competitions
Member of: Aero Club of Canada
Membership: 5 member associations
Activities: *Library:*
Chief Officer(s):
Phil Stade, Executive Director
asc@stade.ca

Alberta Soccer Association (ASA)
9023 - 111 Ave., Edmonton AB T5B 0C3
Tel: 780-474-2200; *Fax:* 780-474-6300
Toll-Free: 866-250-2200
office@albertasoccer.com
www.albertasoccer.com
www.linkedin.com/company/alberta-soccer-association
twitter.com/AlbertaSoccer
www.youtube.com/SoccerAlberta
Overview: A large provincial organization founded in 1909 overseen by Canadian Soccer Association
Mission: To govern & promote the sport of soccer in Alberta
Member of: Canadian Soccer Association

Staff Member(s): 16
Membership: 90,000; *Committees:* Constitution & By-Laws; Technical; Competitions; Referee Development; Appeals & Discipline; Development of Women in Soccer
Chief Officer(s):
Shaun Lowther, Executive Director
execdir@albertasoccer.com
Darron Bunt, Coordinator, Competitions, 780-378-8107
competitions@albertasoccer.com
Carmen Charron, Coordinator, Programs, 780-378-8104
programs@albertasoccer.com
Tiana Squire, Coordinator, Communications, 780-378-8100
Rachel Appels, Coordinator, Office, 780-378-8101
Awards:
• Golden Shoe
• Shield of Merit
• Golden Whistle
• President's Award
• Award of Merit
• Life Membership
• Silver Badge Award
• Woman of Distinction
Publications:
• ASA [Alberta Soccer Association] Newsletter
Type: Newsletter

Alberta Social Credit Party
12 Spruce Ctr. SW, Calgary AB T3C 3B3
Toll-Free: 855-398-8486
communicate@socialcredit.com
www.socialcredit.com
Overview: A large provincial organization
Chief Officer(s):
Jeremy Fraser, Party Leader

Alberta Society for the Prevention of Cruelty to Animals
17904 - 118 Ave. NW, Edmonton AB T5S 2W3
Tel: 780-447-3600; *Fax:* 780-447-4748
info@albertaspca.org
www.albertaspca.org
www.linkedin.com/company/alberta-spca
www.facebook.com/AlbertaSPCA
twitter.com/AlbertaSPCA
www.youtube.com/user/AlbertaSPCA
Also Known As: Alberta SPCA
Overview: A medium-sized provincial charitable organization founded in 1959
Mission: To promote education of public about welfare of domestic animals & livestock; To deal with wildlife issues; To work on improving legislation; To concentrate on enforcement & education; To have every animal in Alberta humanely treated
Member of: Canadian Federation of Humane Societies
Finances: *Annual Operating Budget:* $500,000-$1.5 Million; *Funding Sources:* Public fundraising
Staff Member(s): 16; 600 volunteer(s)
Membership: 2,000; *Fees:* $20 single; $35 family; $150 corporate; $15 student/senior
Activities: *Library:* Open to public by appointment
Chief Officer(s):
Terra Johnston, Executive Director
Meetings/Conferences:
• Alberta Society for the Prevention of Cruelty to Animals 2018 Annual General Meeting, 2018, AB
Scope: Provincial
Publications:
• AnimalKind [a publication of the Alberta Society for the Prevention of Cruelty to Animals]
Type: Newsletter

Alberta Society of Artists (ASA)
Crossroads Art Centre, #305, 1235 - 26th Ave. SE, Calgary AB T2G 1R7
Tel: 403-265-0012
coordinator@albertasocietyofartists.com
albertasocietyofartists.com
www.facebook.com/AlbertaSocietyofArtists
twitter.com/asa_artists
Overview: A small provincial charitable organization founded in 1931
Mission: To promote & foster visual arts in Alberta; To represent & endorse the recognition of Alberta artists; To support public engagement in arts programs; To contribute to the appreciation of the arts community as a whole in the province of Alberta, in Canada, & abroad

Finances: *Annual Operating Budget:* $50,000-$100,000; *Funding Sources:* Membership dues, Donations, Government
53 volunteer(s)
Membership: 200; *Fees:* $80 full member; $30 supporting member; $25 student member; *Member Profile:* Professional visual artists in Alberta
Activities: Organizing exhibitions, including Travelling Exhibition Program (TREX); Advocating for its membership; Offering education programs
Chief Officer(s):
Dennis Envolden, Coordinator, Programs
coordinator@albertasocietyofartists.com
Awards:
• ASA Post-Secondary Scholarship Awards
Eligibility: Alberta residents enrolled as a full-time student in a Fine Arts program at a post-secondary institution in Alberta; students must be taking predominantly 2nd and 3rd year courses; *Amount:* 2 at $1,000 *Contact:* Alberta Society of Artists, E-mail: scholarships@albertasocietyofartists.com
TREX Southwest Office
Crossroads Art Centre, #305, 1235 - 26th Ave. SE, Calgary AB T2G 1R7
Tel: 403-262-4669; *Fax:* 403-263-4610
trex@albertasocietyofartists.com
albertasocietyofartists.com/trex-sw
Chief Officer(s):
Shannon Bingeman, Manager/Curator

Alberta Society of Engineering Technologists See Association of Science & Engineering Technology Professionals of Alberta

Alberta Society of Petroleum Geologists See Canadian Society of Petroleum Geologists

Alberta Society of Professional Biologists (ASPB)
#370, 105 - 12 Ave. East, Calgary AB T2G 1A1
Tel: 403-264-1273
pbiol@aspb.ab.ca
www.aspb.ab.ca
www.linkedin.com/company/alberta-society-of-professional-biologists
twitter.com/albertabiology
Overview: A medium-sized provincial organization founded in 1975
Mission: To promote excellence in the practice of biology; To provide a voice for professional biologists in Alberta
Membership: *Fees:* $325 professional; $225 registered; $75 biologists in training; $25 student; *Member Profile:* Persons from all disciplines of biology, such as aquatic biology, botany, ecology, genetics, biotechnology, entomology, physiology, & zoology; Student biologists
Activities: Organizing seminars for practitioners; Offering a mentorship program
Chief Officer(s):
Jennifer Sipkens, Executive Director, 403-264-2504
jsipkens@aspb.ab.ca
Awards:
• Peggy Thompson Publication Awards
• Dr. J.D. Soper Award
• Distinguished Service Award
• Volunteer Of The Year Award
• ASPB Graduate Scholarship - University of Alberta
• D. Alan Birdsall Memorial Scholarship - University of Alberta
• ASPB Scholarship - University of Lethbridge
• ASPB Graduate Scholarship - University of Calgary
• Lakeland College at Vermillion Scholarship
• Northern Alberta Institute of Technology Scholarship
• Science Fair Awards
Meetings/Conferences:
• Alberta Society of Professional Biologists 2018 Conference, March, 2018, Calgary Zoo, Calgary, AB
Scope: Provincial
Attendance: 200+
Description: Theme: "Keeping Pace with a Changing Landscape: Technology, Regulations & Policy Navigation"
Publications:
• BIOS [a publication of the Alberta Society of Professional Biologists]
Type: Newsletter; *Frequency:* q.; *Editor:* Peter Kingsmill; *ISSN:* 1188-8423
Profile: Articles to inform & educate members of the society & the public

Alberta Society of Radiologists (ASR)
#220, 10339 - 124th St., Edmonton AB T5N 3W1

Tel: 780-443-2615
www.radiologists.ab.ca
Overview: A small provincial organization founded in 1957
Mission: To represent radiologists & radiology residents in Alberta
Staff Member(s): 1; 6 volunteer(s)
Membership: 249; *Committees:* Imaging Advisory Committee
Chief Officer(s):
Chris Hayduk, Executive Director
execdir@radiologists.ab.ca
Meetings/Conferences:
• Alberta Society of Radiologists 19th Annual Continuing Medical Education Conference, April, 2018, Banff Springs Hotel, Banff, AB
Scope: Provincial
Description: Theme: "Grey is the New Black"

Alberta Society of Surveying & Mapping Technologies (ASSMT)
PO Box 68168, 28 Crowfoot Terrace NW, Calgary AB T3G 3N8
Tel: 403-214-7504
Toll-Free: 855-462-7768
www.assmt.ca
Overview: A medium-sized provincial organization founded in 1970
Mission: To promote the knowledge, skill & proficiency of technicians & technologists involved in the field of surveying & mapping in Alberta
Affiliation(s): Alberta Land Surveyors' Association
Finances: *Annual Operating Budget:* Less than $50,000
Staff Member(s): 1; 15 volunteer(s)
Membership: 30 student; 250 individual; 10 associate; *Fees:* $75 individual; $50 associate; students free; *Committees:* AGM; Education; Legislative; Membership; Nomination; Public Relations
Activities: Regional meetings; Annual general meeting; certification
Chief Officer(s):
Lilly Wong, Executive Assistant
executive.assistant@assmt.ca
Awards:
• Annual Bursary
Eligibility: Student members in qualifying programs at Lethbridge College, Olds College, NAIT, & SAIT

Alberta Special Olympics Inc. *See* Special Olympics Alberta

Alberta Special Waste Services Association *See* Environmental Services Association of Alberta

Alberta Speleological Society (ASS)
c/o Andrea Corlett, #1606 924 - 14 Ave. SW, Calgary AB T2R 0N7
info@caving.ab.ca
www.caving.ab.ca
Overview: A medium-sized provincial organization founded in 1968
Mission: To promote cave conservation; To facilitate cave explorations, primarily in the Canadian Rockies, with some activities throughout Western Canada & internationally
Member of: Federation of Alberta Naturalists
Finances: *Funding Sources:* Membership fees
Activities: *Library:* by appointment Not open to public
Chief Officer(s):
Jeremy Burns, President
Meetings/Conferences:
• Alberta Speleological Society 2018 Annual General Meeting, 2018, AB
Scope: Provincial
Description: A meeting of cavers, featuring the election of executive members, the presentation of awards
Contact Information: info@caving.ab.ca
Publications:
• Journal of Subterranean Metaphysics
Type: Newsletter; *Frequency:* Quarterly
Profile: A publication in both paper & digital formats, with articles about exploration, as well as society administrative information & event announcements

Alberta Sport Connection
HSBC Bldg., #500, 10055 - 106 St., Edmonton AB T5J 1G3
Tel: 780-415-1167; *Fax:* 780-415-0308
Other Communication: Calgary Phone: 403-297-2909; Fax: 403-297-6669
albertasport.ca
Previous Name: Alberta Sport, Recreation, Parks & Wildlife Foundation

Overview: A medium-sized provincial organization founded in 1976
Mission: To facilitate & enhance activities, lifestyles & legacies through the development of active partnerships in sport
Finances: *Annual Operating Budget:* Greater than $5 Million; *Funding Sources:* Private & corporate sector donations; Lottery Board grant, Alberta Gaming
Staff Member(s): 41
Activities: *Library:* by appointment
Chief Officer(s):
John Short, Chair
Lloyd Bentz, Chief Executive Officer

Alberta Sport Parachuting Association (ASPA)
c/o Tina Connolly, #301, 7708 - 106 Ave., Edmonton AB T6A 1H5
Tel: 780-996-5266
admin@aspa.ca
www.aspa.ca
www.facebook.com/groups/5261851254/
Overview: A small provincial organization overseen by Canadian Sport Parachuting Association
Mission: To promote & facilitate the development of the sport of skydiving in Alberta
Member of: Canadian Sport Parachuting Association
Finances: *Annual Operating Budget:* $50,000-$100,000
Staff Member(s): 2
Membership: 1,400; *Fees:* $20
Activities: *Awareness Events:* Provincial Championships, early July; *Speaker Service:* Yes
Chief Officer(s):
Dan Stith, President

Alberta Sport, Recreation, Parks & Wildlife Foundation *See* Alberta Sport Connection

Alberta Sports & Recreation Association for the Blind (ASRAB)
#007, 15 Colonel Baker Pl. NE, Calgary AB T2E 4Z3
Tel: 403-262-5332; *Fax:* 403-265-7221
Toll-Free: 888-882-7722
info@asrab.ab.ca
www.asrab.ab.ca
Overview: A small provincial charitable organization founded in 1975 overseen by Canadian Blind Sports Association Inc.
Mission: To provide recreation & sports opportunities for Albertans who are blind & partially sighted
Member of: CBSA
Staff Member(s): 4
Membership: *Fees:* $15 individual; $30 family
Activities: Swimming; Lawn Bowling; Powerlifting; Goalball Athletics; Tandem Cycling; *Awareness Events:* Sight Night, Nov.; *Speaker Service:* Yes
Chief Officer(s):
Linda MacPhail, Executive Director
execdirector@asrab.ab.ca

Alberta Sports Hall of Fame & Museum (ASHFM)
#102 - 4200 Hwy 2, Red Deer AB T4N 1E3
Tel: 403-341-8614; *Fax:* 403-341-8619
info@ashfm.ca
www.ashfm.ca
www.facebook.com/ashfm.ca
twitter.com/ashfm1
www.youtube.com/user/ABSportsHallOfFame/videos
Overview: A medium-sized provincial charitable organization founded in 1957
Mission: To honour Albertans who have distinguished themselves in sport & to operate a facility to house artifacts that are significant in Alberta's sports history
Member of: Museums Alberta; Canadian Museums Association; Canadian Association for Sport Heritage; International Sport Heritage Association
Finances: *Annual Operating Budget:* $250,000-$500,000
Staff Member(s): 5; 40 volunteer(s)
Membership: 950
Activities: Induction into Sports Hall of Fame; Museum; fundraising; *Awareness Events:* Induction Banquet; Annual Golf Tournament *Library:* Alberta Sport History Library; Open to public
Chief Officer(s):
Dennis Allan, Chair
Donna Hateley, Managing Director

Alberta Sprint Racing Canoe Association
11759 Groat Rd., Edmonton AB T5M 3K6

Tel: 780-203-3987
www.asrca.com
Previous Name: Alberta Flatwater Canoe Association
Overview: A small provincial organization overseen by CanoeKayak Canada
Member of: CanoeKayak Canada
Chief Officer(s):
Jeffrey Baker, President
president@asrca.com

Alberta Square & Round Dance Federation
PO Box 114, Holden AB T0B 2C0
Tel: 780-688-2380
www.squaredance.ab.ca
Overview: A medium-sized provincial organization overseen by Canadian Square & Round Dance Society
Mission: To promote square dancing, round dancing, & clogging in Alberta
Chief Officer(s):
Wayne Lowther, Co-President
waylow@telusplanet.net
Helen Lowther, Co-President

Alberta Squash Racquets Association *See* Squash Alberta

Alberta Sulphur Research Ltd. (ASRL)
Center for Applied Catalysts & Industrial Sulfur Chemistry, #6, 3535 Research Rd. NW, Calgary AB T2L 2K8
Tel: 403-220-5346; *Fax:* 403-284-2054
asrinfo@ucalgary.ca
www.chem.ucalgary.ca/asr
Overview: A small international organization founded in 1964
Mission: Provides technological support for producers & users of sulfur; research & technology training through seminars & courses; provides contact between industry & academia for applied catalysis & industrial sulfur chemistry; examination of the chemistry & technology of sulfur & its compunds; emphasis on research relevant to sour gas, sulfur & refining industries
Affiliation(s): Chemistry Dept., Univ. of Calgary
Finances: *Annual Operating Budget:* $500,000-$1.5 Million; *Funding Sources:* Membership research contributions
Staff Member(s): 21
Membership: 62; *Member Profile:* Sulphur producers & users; *Committees:* Technical Advisory; Finance; Executive
Activities: *Library:* by appointment Not open to public
Chief Officer(s):
Richard Surprenant, President & Chair
Jon Gorrie, 1st Vice-President & Treasurer
Publications:
• ASRL [Alberta Sulphur Research Ltd.] Board Newsletter
Type: Newsletter

Alberta Summer Swimming Association (ASSA)
c/o Swim Alberta, 11759 Groat Rd., Edmonton AB T5M 3K6
Tel: 780-415-1780; *Fax:* 780-415-1788
assa@swimalberta.ca
www.assa.ca
Overview: A medium-sized provincial organization
Mission: To provide a summer swimming program for swimmers of all ages in Alberta
Membership: 59 clubs + 3,323 individuals
Chief Officer(s):
Paige Park, President
Lynnette Thoresen, Vice President

Alberta Table Tennis Association (ATTA)
Percy Page Centre, 11759 Groat Rd., Edmonton AB T5M 3K6
Tel: 780-427-8588
Other Communication: Toll-Free Fax: 1-866-427-0524
atta@abtabletennis.com
www.abtabletennis.com
Overview: A small provincial organization founded in 1970 overseen by Table Tennis Canada
Mission: To foster & promote the play of table tennis in a sportsmanlike manner; to award, sanction &, when necessary, supervise or manage all championship matches & tournaments; to interpret & enforce the laws & rules of table tennis; to provide & keep a permanent & official record of all championships established under its jurisdiction; generally to govern the sport in Alberta
Member of: Table Tennis Canada
Affiliation(s): International Table Tennis Federation
Finances: *Annual Operating Budget:* $100,000-$250,000; *Funding Sources:* Fundraising; Alberta Sport, Park & Wildlife Foundation; Alberta Gaming
Staff Member(s): 2; 100 volunteer(s)

Membership: 1,200; Fees: Schedule available; Committees: Communication; Tournaments; Ratings; Officials; Membership/Marketing; Regional/Junior Developments; Schools
Activities: Coaching & officials development; club assistance; sport outreach; summer camps; high performance athletic training; provincial tournament hosting; preparation & sending of athletes to events; Rents Mailing List: Yes
Chief Officer(s):
Lei Jiang, Program Coordinator

Alberta Taekwondo Association (ATA)
#1589, 5328 Calgary Trail NW, Edmonton AB T6H 4JB
Tel: 780-446-0246
admin@taekwondoalberta.com
www.taekwondoalberta.com
www.facebook.com/13172614788
twitter.com/TKD_Alberta
Overview: A small provincial organization
Mission: To be the provincial governing body for the sport of taekwondo in Alberta
Affiliation(s): Taekwondo Canada; World Taekwondo Federation
Membership: Fees: $20-$30 individual; $150-$300 club
Chief Officer(s):
Su Hwan Chung, Chairman
gmsuchung@gmail.com
Linda Kwan, Secretary General
lindakwan888@yahoo.ca

Alberta Target Archers Association (ATAA)
AB
Tel: 780-717-2597
membership@ataa-org.ca
www.ataa-org.ca
Overview: A small provincial organization
Mission: To be the provincial governing body for the sport of archery in Alberta
Affiliation(s): Alberta Sport, Recreation, Parks & Wildlife Foundation
Membership: Fees: $28-$103
Chief Officer(s):
Rene Schaub, President, 780-689-8488
president@ataa-org.ca
David Middlebrough, Vice President, 780-997-6411
vice-president@ataa-org.ca

Alberta Teachers of English as a Second Language (ATESL)
c/o University of Alberta, #6, 102 Education North, Edmonton AB T6G 2G5
Tel: 780-455-7649
ask@atesl.ca
www.atesl.ca
www.linkedin.com/pub/atesl-alberta-teachers-of-esl/61/8a6/314
www.facebook.com/170856763052757
twitter.com/ATESLnews
plus.google.com/105900523013702188458
Also Known As: Association of Alberta Teachers of English as a Second Language
Overview: A small provincial organization founded in 1974 overseen by TESL Canada Federation
Mission: To promote the highest standards of teaching & English language program provision for all learners in Alberta whose first language is other than English
Membership: Committees: Accreditation
Activities: Professional development; accreditation; advocacy
Chief Officer(s):
Sheri Rhodes, President

Alberta Teachers' Association (ATA)
Barnett House, 11010 - 142 St. NW, Edmonton AB T5N 2R1
Tel: 780-447-9400; Fax: 780-455-6481
Toll-Free: 800-232-7208
postmaster@ata.ab.ca
www.teachers.ab.ca
www.linkedin.com/company/the-alberta-teachers'-association
www.facebook.com/ABteachers
twitter.com/albertateachers
Overview: A large provincial organization founded in 1918 overseen by Canadian Teachers' Federation
Mission: To advance the cause of education in Alberta; To improve the teaching profession; To increase public interest in & support for education; To cooperate with other bodies having similar objectives
Finances: Annual Operating Budget: $3 Million-$5 Million; Funding Sources: Membership dues
Staff Member(s): 105
Membership: 43,460; Fees: $1,242 active; schedule for teachers on leave, substitutes, & interns; $1 students; Member Profile: All teachers employed by a school board in Alberta
Activities: Library: Open to public
Chief Officer(s):
Janice Sledz, Treasurer/Chief Financial Officer
Brian Andrais, Coordinator, Member Services
ms@ata.ab.ca
Mark Yurick, Coordinator, Professional Development
pd@ata.ab.ca
Awards:
• Educational Research Award, ATA Grants
Awarded annually to a faculty of education member or sessional lecturer at an Alberta post-secondary institution who has undertaken high quality research on classroom learning & teaching Deadline: May; Amount: $5,000 Contact: J-C Couture, Officer, Research Award, E-mail: jc.couture@ata.ab.ca
• ATA Doctoral Fellowships in Education, ATA Grants
Eligibility: ATA members who have been accepted into, or have already embarked upon, full-time study in a doctoral program in education at an Alberta post-secondary institution Deadline: February; Amount: $15,000 Contact: Mardi Veinot, Officer, Scholarship Committee, E-mail: mardi.veinot@ata.ab.ca
• Grants Supporting Diversity, Equity & Human Rights, ATA Grants
Awarded to help fund innovative projects designed to build inclusive learning environments based on principles of diversity, equity, & human rights Deadline: April; Amount: $2,000
• Local Community Relations Grants, ATA Grants
Awarded to locals undertaking activities that profile public education Deadline: April; Amount: $250 + $1 per member Contact: Shelley Magnusson, Executive Officer, E-mail: shelley.magnusson@ata.ab.ca
• Political Engagement Grant, ATA Grants
Awarded to locals that develop a political engagement plan; Amount: $600 Contact: Jonathan Teghtmeyer, Coordinator, E-mail: jonathan.teghtmeyer@ata.ab.ca
• Strategic Planning Grant Program, ATA Grants
Awarded to locals, specialist councils, or convention associations to offset the costs of strategic planning retreats Deadline: September 30; Amount: $2,000 Contact: J-C Couture, Officer, Planning Grant, E-mail: jc.couture@ata.ab.ca
• John Mazurek Memorial-Morgex Insurance Scholarship, ATA Grants
Awarded to an individual to be used for a professional development course or part of an organized program of study in the field of business education or computer technology in education Deadline: September 30; Amount: $2,500 Contact: Mardi Veinot, Officer, Scholarship Committee, E-mail: mardi.veinot@ata.ab.ca
• Nadene M Thomas Graduate Research Bursary, ATA Grants
Awarded to an individual who is enrolled in a graduate program in a specialty in education at a recognized Canadian post-secondary institution Deadline: February; Amount: $5,000 Contact: Mardi Veinot, Officer, Scholarship Committee, E-mail: mardi.veinot@ata.ab.ca
• Local Association Diversity, Equity and Human Rights Award, ATA Awards
Awarded to recognize projects, programs, or events organized by a local association to promote diversity & equity Deadline: May Contact: Robert Mazzotta, Officer, Development, E-mail: robert.mazzotta@ata.ab.ca
• Gold Medals in Education, ATA Awards
Awarded to the student at each of the four faculties of education who attains the highest general proficiency in the final two years of a Bachelor of Education program; faculties include University of Alberta, University of Calgary, University of Lethbridge, & Faculté Saint-Jean at the University of Alberta
• Local Political Engagement Awards, ATA Awards
Awarded to recognize excellence in political engagement among local associations Deadline: June Contact: Jonathan Teghtmeyer, Coordinator, E-mail: jonathan.teghtmeyer@ata.ab.ca
• Local Public Relations Awards, ATA Awards
Awarded to recognize excellence in public relations among local associations Deadline: June Contact: Shelley Magnusson, Executive Officer, E-mail: shelley.magnusson@ata.ab.ca
Meetings/Conferences:
• North Central Teachers Convention 2018, February, 2018, Edmonton, AB
Scope: Provincial
Contact Information: Executive Staff Officer: Dan Grassick, E-mail: dan.grassick@ata.ab.ca, Phone: 780-447-9487
• Calgary City Teachers Convention 2018, February, 2018, Telus Convention Centre, Calgary, AB
Scope: Provincial
Contact Information: Executive Staff Officer, Dan Grassick, E-mail: dan.grassick@ata.ab.ca, Phone: 780-447-9487
• North East Teachers Convention 2018, February, 2018, Doubletree by Hilton Hotel, Edmonton, AB
Scope: Provincial
Contact Information: Executive Staff Officer: Dan Grassick, E-mail: dan.grassick@ata.ab.ca, Phone: 780-447-9487
• Central Alberta Teachers Convention 2018, February, 2018, Red Deer College, Red Deer, AB
Scope: Provincial
Contact Information: Executive Staff Officer: Dan Grassick, E-mail: dan.grassick@ata.ab.ca, Phone: 780-447-9487
• Central East Alberta Teachers Convention 2018, March, 2018, Shaw Conference Centre, Edmonton, AB
Scope: Provincial
Contact Information: Executive Staff Officer: Dan Grassick, E-mail: dan.grassick@ata.ab.ca, Phone: 780-447-9487
• Alberta Teachers' Association Summer Conference 2018, 2018
Scope: Provincial
• Alberta Teachers' Association Annual Representative Assembly 2018, 2018
Scope: Provincial
Publications:
• Alberta Teachers' Association Annual Report
Type: Yearbook; Frequency: a.
• Alberta Teachers' Association Members' Handbook
Type: Yearbook; Frequency: a.; Price: $10 with ATA membership; $15 withoutmembership
Profile: Contains ATA officer directory, an explanation of ATA services, & a compilation of its bylaws & policies
• ATA [Alberta Teachers' Association] Magazine
Type: Magazine; Frequency: 4 pa; Accepts Advertising; Editor: Gordon Thomas; ISSN: 0380-9102; Price: Free with ATA membership; Schedule for non-membersin Canada & internationally
Profile: Features association & industry news; welcomes article submissions from readers
• The Learning Team [a publication of the Alberta Teachers' Association]
Type: Magazine; Frequency: 4 pa; Editor: Phil McRae; ISSN: 1480-7688
Profile: Distributed to all public & separate school councils in Alberta; contains industry & association news;welcomes article submissions from readers

Alberta Team Handball Federation (ATHF)
Percy Page Centre, 11749 Groat Rd., Edmonton AB T5M 3K6
Tel: 780-415-2666; Fax: 780-422-2663
Handballalberta@gmail.com
www.teamhandball.ab.ca
www.facebook.com/Albertateamhandball
twitter.com/handballalberta
www.youtube.com/user/HandballAlberta1;
vimeo.com/channels/123390
Overview: A medium-sized provincial organization founded in 1960
Mission: To govern the promotion of team handball throughout Alberta, by encouraging the development of athletes, coaches, referees, & administrators of all ages & abilities
Member of: Canadian Team Handball Federation
Finances: Funding Sources: Membership & course fees; fundraising; donations; Alberta Sport, Recreation, Parks & Wildlife Foundation
Activities: Organizing provincial championships, regional leagues, coaching courses; programs for 8 years of age to adults, sport outreach clinics, & the City of Champions Tournament
Chief Officer(s):
Dan Stetic, CEO
Surroosh Ghofrani, Chief Financial Officer

Alberta Tennis Association (ATA)
11759 Groat Rd., Edmonton AB T5M 3K6
Tel: 780-415-1661; Fax: 780-415-1693
info@tennisalberta.com
www.tennisalberta.com
www.facebook.com/tennisalberta
twitter.com/tennisalberta
Also Known As: Tennis Alberta
Overview: A medium-sized provincial charitable organization founded in 1973 overseen by Tennis Canada
Mission: To facilitate participation, development, & visibility of tennis throughout Alberta
Member of: International Tennis Federation; Tennis Canada

Canadian Associations / Alberta Texas Longhorn Association (ATLA)

Finances: Funding Sources: ASRPW Foundation; Tennis Canada; Sponsors; Self-generated revenue
Staff Member(s): 3
Activities: Coaching; Officiating; *Library:* Tennis Resource Centre
Chief Officer(s):
Jill Richard, Executive Director, 780-644-0440
jill.richard@tennisalberta.com
Brendan Smith, Coordinator, Tournament & Programs

Alberta Texas Longhorn Association (ATLA)
RR#1, Leduc AB T9E 2X1
Tel: 780-387-4874
www.albertatexaslonghorn.com
Overview: A small provincial organization founded in 1982
Mission: To provide new & existing breeders with the opportunity to purchase top quality longhorn cattle for herd improvement; to increase public awareness about longhorn cattle; to provide clinics for judging & evaluating the Texas Longhorn
Affiliation(s): Texas Longhorn Breeders Association of America
Membership: 35; *Fees:* $40 Active; $20 Associate
Chief Officer(s):
Ron Walker, President, 403-548-6684

Alberta Therapeutic Recreation Association (ATRA)
8038 Fairmount Dr. SE, Calgary AB T2H 0Y1
Tel: 403-258-2520; *Fax:* 403-255-2234
Toll-Free: 888-258-2520
atra@alberta-tr.org
www.alberta-tr.org
Overview: A small provincial organization founded in 1985
Mission: To offer mentorships, continuing education, bursaries, & awards
Membership: Fees: $300; $50 student/supporting; *Member Profile:* Professionals who work in the field of therapeutic recreation in Alberta
Chief Officer(s):
Kari Medd, President
president@alberta-tr.org

Alberta Track & Field Association *See* Athletics Alberta

Alberta Trappers' Association
Industrial Park Lot 14, PO Box 6020, Stn. Main, Hwy. 44 South, Westlock AB T7P 2P7
Tel: 780-349-6626; *Fax:* 888-362-4679
info@albertatrappers.com
www.albertatrappers.com
Overview: A small provincial organization
Mission: To represent registered & resident trappers in Alberta; To promote the harvesting of wild furbearers in a humane & sustainable manner
Membership: 2,000+; *Fees:* $35; *Member Profile:* Licensed trappers in Alberta
Activities: Supporting the protection of threatened & endangered species; Operating a fur depot for tanning & shipping; Providing trapper & public education
Chief Officer(s):
Marcie Mazurenko, Executive Director
ataexec@albertatrappers.com
Donna Moore, Office Manager
atafinance@albertatrappers.com
Ross Hinter, Coordinator, Education
ross@albertatrappers.com
Publications:
• Alberta Trapper Magazine
Type: Magazine; *Frequency:* Quarterly; *Accepts Advertising*; *Price:* Free with membership in the Alberta Trappers' Association
Profile: Issues encountered by trappers, plus anecdotes about trapping experiences
• Alberta Trappers' Association Newsletter
Type: Newsletter; *Frequency:* Monthly
Profile: Updates from the association, including upcoming courses

Alberta Triathlon Association (ATA)
Percy Page Centre, 11759 Groat Rd., Edmonton AB T5M 3K6
Tel: 780-427-8616; *Fax:* 780-427-8628
Toll-Free: 866-888-7448
info@triathlon.ab.ca
www.triathlon.ab.ca
www.facebook.com/160835077267482
twitter.com/TriAlberta
Overview: A small provincial organization founded in 1984 overseen by Triathlon Canada
Mission: ATA is the official, non-profit governing body for, & has a mandate to develop, the sports of triathlon, duathlon, aquathlon & other related multi-endurance sports in Alberta.
Member of: Triathlon Canada
Finances: Annual Operating Budget: $100,000-$250,000
Staff Member(s): 1; 16 volunteer(s)
Membership: 1,000+; *Fees:* $15 youth (19 & under); $50 adult/coach
Activities: Speaker Service: Yes
Chief Officer(s):
Calli Stromner, General Manager
general.manager@triathlon.ab.ca
Sebastian Porten, Manager, Programs
coordinator@triathlon.ab.ca

Alberta Turkey Producers
#101, 2520 Ellwood Dr. SW, Edmonton AB T6X 0A9
Tel: 780-465-5755; *Fax:* 780-465-5528
info@albertaturkey.com
ab.canadianturkey.ca
www.facebook.com/AlbertaTurkey
twitter.com/AlbertaTurkey
www.instagram.com/CanadianTurkey
Overview: A small provincial organization
Finances: Annual Operating Budget: $250,000-$500,000
Staff Member(s): 2
Membership: 1-99; *Member Profile:* To provide an environment that will enhance the overall growth of the Alberta turkey industry
Chief Officer(s):
Cara Prout, Executive Director
cara@albertaturkey.com

Alberta Ukrainian Dance Association
Percy Page Centre, 11759 Groat Rd., Edmonton AB T5M 3K6
Tel: 780-422-9700; *Fax:* 780-422-2663
info@abuda.ca
www.abuda.ca
Overview: A medium-sized provincial organization founded in 1983
Mission: To help serve the needs of the Ukrainian dance community; To promote Ukranian heritage through dance; To provide information about Ukranian dancing; To assist dance groups & instructors in Alberta
Membership: 86 dance groups + 4,000 dancers; *Fees:* $15 individual; $25 group
Activities: Ukrainian dance workshops held throughout the year; intensive program offers classes in technique & history seminars; *Library*
Chief Officer(s):
Andrew Wujcik, Executive Director
Gordon Gordey, President

Alberta Underwater Council (AUC)
Percy Page Building, 11759 Groat Rd., 2nd Fl., Edmonton AB T5M 3K6
Tel: 780-427-9125; *Fax:* 780-427-8139
Toll-Free: 888-307-8566
info@albertaunderwatercouncil.com
www.albertaunderwatercouncil.com
Overview: A medium-sized local organization founded in 1962
Mission: To represent responsible participation in & awareness of underwater activities
Affiliation(s): Canadian Underwater Games Association
Finances: Funding Sources: Alberta Gaming; Alberta Sport Recreation Parks & Wildlife Foundation
Membership: 600 individual; *Fees:* Schedule available
Activities: Awareness Events: Divescapes
Chief Officer(s):
Cathie McCuaig, Executive Director, 780-427-9125, Fax: 780-427-8139

Alberta Union of Provincial Employees / Syndicat de la fonction publique de l'Alberta
10451 - 170 St., Edmonton AB T5P 4S7
Tel: 780-930-3300; *Fax:* 780-930-3392
Toll-Free: 800-232-7284
www.aupe.org
www.facebook.com/yourAUPE
twitter.com/_AUPE_
www.youtube.com/user/AlbertaUnion
Overview: A medium-sized provincial organization
Staff Member(s): 95
Membership: 60,000
Chief Officer(s):
Carl Soderstrom, Executive Director, 780-930-3340
Tim Gough, Director, Labour Relations, 780-930-5217
Jim Petrie, Director, Labour Relations, 780-930-3335

Alberta Urban Municipalities Association (AUMA)
#300, 8616 51 Ave., Edmonton AB T6E 6E6
Tel: 780-433-4431; *Fax:* 780-433-4454
Toll-Free: 877-421-6644
main@auma.ca
www.auma.ca
www.linkedin.com/company/alberta-urban-municipalities-association
www.facebook.com/theauma
twitter.com/theauma
www.youtube.com/channel/UC_HJ3RFfvOwFpdVDcLifGLw/feed
Overview: A medium-sized provincial organization founded in 1905
Mission: To provide leadership in advocating local government interests to the provincial government & other organizations, & to provide services that address the needs of its membership
Affiliation(s): The Alberta Municipal Services Corporation
Finances: Funding Sources: Membership dues
Staff Member(s): 44
Membership: 284 municipalities; *Fees:* $1205 Government Organization (Provincial, Federal, Municipal); $55 Not-for-profit Organization; $875 For-profit Organization; *Committees:* 15 Committees & Task Forces
Activities: Rents Mailing List: Yes; *Library*
Chief Officer(s):
Sue Bohaichuk, FCPA (CMA); ICD, Chief Executive Officer, 780-409-4312
jmcgowan@auma.ca
Meetings/Conferences:
• Alberta Urban Municipalities Association Convention & AMSC Trade Show 2018, 2018, AB
Scope: Provincial

Alberta Veterinary Medical Association (AVMA)
Weber Centre, #950, 5555 Calgary Trail NW, Edmonton AB T6H 5P9
Tel: 780-489-5007
Toll-Free: 800-404-2862
www.avma.ca
www.linkedin.com/company/alberta-veterinary-medical-association
www.facebook.com/ABVMA
twitter.com/abvma
www.youtube.com/abvma
Overview: A medium-sized provincial licensing organization founded in 1905 overseen by Canadian Veterinary Medical Association
Mission: To represent Alberta veterinarians in small animal, large animal & mixed practice as well as those employed in government, industry or other institutions
Finances: Funding Sources: Membership fees
Staff Member(s): 10
Membership: 3,037; *Member Profile:* Veterinarians & animal health technologists; *Committees:* Discipline Hearing Tribunal & Complaint Review; Practice Inspection & Practice Standards; Practice Review Board; Registration; Alternate Livestock & Wildlife; Animal Welfare; Companion Animal; Equine; Food Animal; Vet Med 21
Chief Officer(s):
Duane Landals, Senior Advisor
duane.landals@avma.ab.ca

Alberta Veterinary Technologist Association (ABVTA)
#104, 9452 51 Ave. NW, Edmonton AB T6E 5A6
Tel: 587-525-6566
admin.aaaht@abvma.ca
www.abvta.ca
www.facebook.com/ABVTA.official
www.instagram.com/abvta.official
Previous Name: The Alberta Association of Animal Health Technologists
Overview: A small provincial organization founded in 1978
Mission: To promote professional & educational advancement of the Animal Health Technologist; To enhance the knowledge & skills of the Animal Health Technologist through continuing education programs; To promote positive legislation & to speak for the Animal Health Technologist in regard to legislative action; To develop & maintain a code of ethics & high professional standards of the Animal Health Technologist; To develop & maintain communication & cooperation among Animal Health Technologists, the veterinary medical profession, government & industry; To promote progressive & humane medical care for all animals
Member of: Canadian Association of Animal Health Technologists & Technicians

Finances: *Annual Operating Budget:* $100,000-$250,000; *Funding Sources:* Membership dues
10 volunteer(s)
Membership: 800+; *Member Profile:* 2-year CVMA accredited AHT program & veterinary technician national examination; *Committees:* Continuing Education; Communications
Activities: *Awareness Events:* Animal Health Technologist Week
Chief Officer(s):
Vanessa George, Executive Director
Awards:
• ABVTA Appreciation Award
Awarded to an active member who has contributed to the ABVTA through activities as a board member, affiliated position, or committee member
• ABVTA Meritorious Service Award
Awarded to an active member who has provided outstanding service to the ABVTA

Alberta Walking Horse Association (AWHA)
c/o Shirley Wesslen, RR#1, Blackfalds AB T0M 0J0
Tel: 403-885-5290
albertawalkinghorse@gmail.com
www.walkinghorse.ca
Overview: A small provincial organization
Mission: To promote the Tennessee Walking Horse in Alberta
Membership: *Fees:* $30 single members; $50 families; $20 youth; *Member Profile:* Tennessee Walking Horse owners & riders in Alberta
Activities: Participating in horse shows & events; Creating networking opportunities; Presenting awards
Chief Officer(s):
Blair Dyberg, President, 780-352-3531
seedsandsteeds@aol.com
Shirley Wesslen, Secretary, 403-885-5290
swesslen@aol.com
Rhonda Lemmon, Chair, Alberta Celebration Show, 403-782-3118
yonafeda@gmail.com
Publications:
• Alberta Walking Horse Association Newsletter
Type: Newsletter; *Frequency:* Monthly

Alberta Wall & Ceiling Association (AWCA)
PO Box 21016, Edmonton AB T6R 2V4
Tel: 780-757-9277; *Fax:* 888-280-1172
Toll-Free: 888-240-7045
awca.ed@shaw.ca
www.albertawallandceiling.com
Previous Name: Alberta Wall & Ceiling Bureau
Overview: A small provincial organization overseen by Northwest Wall & Ceiling Bureau
Mission: To act as the provincial voice for the industry, providing & promoting technical information & training to its members, the construction industry & consumers at large.

Alberta Wall & Ceiling Bureau *See* Alberta Wall & Ceiling Association

Alberta Water & Wastewater Operators Association (AWWOA)
10806 - 119 St., Edmonton AB T5H 3P2
Tel: 780-454-7745; *Fax:* 780-454-7748
Toll-Free: 877-454-7745
www.awwoa.ab.ca
www.facebook.com/157981630910194
twitter.com/awwoa
Overview: A small provincial organization founded in 1976
Mission: To contribute to the training & upgrading of persons employed in the water & wastewater field in Alberta; To encourage the best possible operation of water & wastewater facilities
Affiliation(s): Western Canada Water & Wastewater Association
Membership: *Fees:* $60
Activities: Providing manuals to operators; *Awareness Events:* Water Week
Chief Officer(s):
Ryan Ropcean, Chair
Awards:
• Alberta Water & Wastewater Operators Association Outreach Student Applicant Bursaries
Available to students entering the Water & Wastewater Technician program at the Northern Alberta Institute of Technology *Eligibility:* Applicant must provide a copy of the Alberta Environment approved course completion certificate; *Amount:* $500 *Contact:* AWWOA Outreach Student Bursaries, *Address:* 10806 - 229 St., Edmonton, AB T5H 3P2
• Alberta Water & Wastewater Operators Association Steve Blonsky Honorary Life Membership Award
For persons retired from the water or sewage field *Deadline:* October
• Alberta Water & Wastewater Operators Association NAIT Achievement Award
Eligibility: The student enrolled in the Northern Alberta Institute of Technology's full time Water & Wastewater Technician Program, who achieves the highest marks; *Amount:* $500
• Alberta Water & Wastewater Operators Association Operator of the Year Award
Eligibility: A member in good standing of the Alberta Water & Wastewater Operators Association who has provided exemplary service to the water or wastewater operations field over an extended period of time *Deadline:* January
• Alberta Water & Wastewater Operators Association Ron Bayne Service Award
To recognize outstanding service to the Alberta Water & Wastewater Operators Association & contribution to the water & wastewater operartions field *Deadline:* January
• Alberta Water & Wastewater Operators Association NAIT North Scholarship
To honour academically outstanding individuals who have made significant contributions in extracurricular or community activities *Eligibility:* Registration in the full-time Water & Wastewater Technician program at the Edmonton Campus of the Northern Alberta Institute of Technology; *Amount:* 2 at $1,500 *Contact:* Alberta Water & Wastewater Operators Assn, *Address:* 10806 - 229 St., Edmonton, AB T5H 3P2
• Alberta Water & Wastewater Operators Association NAIT South Scholarship
To recognize academic credentials, personal leadership activities, excellence in extracurricular activities, & notable contributions to the community *Eligibility:* Registration in the full-time Water & Wastewater Technician program at the Calgary Campus of the Northern Alberta Institute of Technology; *Amount:* 2 at $1,500 *Contact:* Alberta Water & Wastewater Operators Assn, *Address:* 10806 - 229 St., Edmonton, AB T5H 3P2
Meetings/Conferences:
• Alberta Water & Wastewater Operators Association 2018 43rd Annual Operators Seminar, 2018, AB
Scope: Provincial
Description: Speakers, including operators, supervisors, technical industry representatives, & other experts in their fields, bring operators up-to-date on numerous topics in the water & wastewater field
Publications:
• Alberta Utility Operator Newsletter [a publication of the Alberta Water & Wastewater Operators Association]
Type: Newsletter; *Frequency:* 3 pa
Profile: Information about Alberta's water & wastewater operations, outstanding service, new technologies, research, regulatory changes, & training opportunities

Alberta Water Council
Petroleum Plaza, South Tower, #1400, 9915 - 108 St., Edmonton AB T5K 2G8
Tel: 780-644-7380
info@awchome.ca
www.albertawatercouncil.ca
Overview: A medium-sized provincial organization
Mission: The Alberta Water Council is a stakeholder partnership that provides leadership, expertise and advocacy, to engage and empower individuals, organizations, business and governments to achieve the outcomes of the Water for Life strategy.
Membership: 24 institutional
Chief Officer(s):
Gord Edwards, Executive Director, 780-644-7373
g.edwards@awchome.ca
Meetings/Conferences:
• 2018 Alberta Water Council Symposium, 2018
Scope: Provincial

Alberta Water Polo Association (AWPA)
PO Box 54, 2225 Macleod Trail SE, Calgary AB T2G 5B6
Tel: 403-281-7797; *Fax:* 403-281-7798
office@albertawaterpolo.ca
www.albertawaterpolo.ca
www.facebook.com/143394719017308
Overview: A medium-sized provincial organization founded in 1974 overseen by Water Polo Canada
Mission: To provide a safe & positive environment for the ongoing development & growth of water polo in Alberta for the recreational to the elite athlete
Member of: Water Polo Canada
Chief Officer(s):
Cori Paul, President
cpaul@gss.org
Dayna Christmas, Executive Director
office@albertawaterpolo.ca
Nicolas Youngblud, Treasurer
Blud_1@hotmail.com

Alberta Water Well Drilling Association (AWWDA)
PO Box 130, Lougheed AB T0B 2V0
Tel: 780-386-2335; *Fax:* 780-386-2344
awwda@xplornet.com
www.awwda.com
Overview: A medium-sized provincial organization founded in 1958
Mission: To assist, promote, encourage, & support the interest and welfare of the water well industry in all of its phases; To foster aid and promote scientific education, standard research, and technique in order to improve methods of well construction: To advance the science of groundwater in Alberta
Chief Officer(s):
Michael Schmidt, Secretary Manager, 403-938-2220, Fax: 403-783-8828
m.schmidt@darcysdrilling.com

Alberta Weekly Newspapers Association (AWNA)
3228 Parsons Rd., Edmonton AB T6H 5R7
Tel: 780-434-8746; *Fax:* 780-438-8356
Toll-Free: 800-282-6903
info@awna.com
www.awna.com
releases@awna.com
Overview: A medium-sized provincial organization overseen by Canadian Community Newspapers Association
Mission: To assist members to publish high quality community newspapers; To serve advertisers by providing information about the markets of community newspapers in Alberta
Membership: 118 newspapers; *Member Profile:* Community newspapers throughout Alberta & the Northwest Territories; *Committees:* Advertising; AdWest Representatives; Membership; AWSOM Archive / Technology; Community Education / VCOY; Government Relations; Newspaper Symposium; Convention; Better Newspapers Competition; Audit; Nominating; Industry Education; Bing Crosby Golf Tournament
Activities: Providing workshops; Assisting with marketing; Recognizing excellence; Presenting bursaries & scholarships; Offering networking opportunities
Chief Officer(s):
Dennis Merrell, Executive Director
dennis@awna.com
Ossie Sheddy, President, 403-823-2580
editor@drumhellermail.com
Murray Elliott, Vice-President, 403-556-7510
melliott@olds.greatwest.ca
Chrissie Hamblin, Controller
chrissie@awna.com
Maurizia Hinse, Coordinator, Professional Development & Communication
maurizia@awna.com
Fred Gorman, Corporate Secretary, 403-314-4311
fgorman@reddeeradvocate.com
Meetings/Conferences:
• Alberta Weekly Newspapers Association 97th Annual General Meeting & Convention 2018, 2018, AB
Scope: Provincial
Publications:
• Alberta Weekly Newspapers Association Membership Directory
Type: Directory

Alberta West Realtors' Association
162 Athabasca Ave., Hinton AB T7V 2A5
Tel: 780-865-7511; *Fax:* 780-865-7517
admin.awra@shaw.ca
www.abwra.com
Previous Name: Hinton-Edson & District Real Estate Board
Overview: A small local organization founded in 1978 overseen by Alberta Real Estate Association
Mission: To provide its members with quality structure and services
Member of: Alberta Real Estate Association; The Canadian Real Estate Association
Staff Member(s): 1
Membership: 110
Chief Officer(s):

Canadian Associations / Alberta Whitewater Association (AWA)

Karen Spencer-Miller, President

Alberta Whitewater Association (AWA)
Percy Page Centre, 11759 Groat Rd., Edmonton AB T5M 3K6
Tel: 403-628-2336
admin@albertawhitewater.ca
www.albertawhitewater.ca
www.facebook.com/alberta.whitewater
Overview: A small provincial organization founded in 1972 overseen by CanoeKayak Canada
Mission: To encourage whitewater paddlesport activities
Member of: CanoeKayak Canada
Affiliation(s): International Canoe Federation
Finances: *Annual Operating Budget:* $50,000-$100,000
Staff Member(s): 2
Membership: 500-999; *Fees:* Individual: $15; Club: $120
Activities: Canoe polo; slalom; wild water races; recreational river trips; freestyle events
Chief Officer(s):
Chuck Lee, Executive Director

Alberta Wilderness Association (AWA)
455 - 12 St. NW, Calgary AB T2N 1Y9
Tel: 403-283-2025; *Fax:* 403-270-2743
Toll-Free: 866-313-0713
awa@abwild.ca
albertawilderness.ca
www.facebook.com/AlbertaWilderness
twitter.com/ABWilderness
www.youtube.com/AlbertaWilderness
Overview: A large provincial charitable organization founded in 1965
Mission: To promote the protection of Alberta's rivers & wildlands areas; To restore the natural ecosystems of Alberta; To educate Albertans on wilderness conservation & sustainable use of natural lands & waters
Member of: Alberta Environment Network; Environmental Law Centre; Calgary & Area Outdoor Council; Volunteer Centre of Calgary
Affiliation(s): Environmental Resource Centre
Finances: *Annual Operating Budget:* $250,000-$500,000; *Funding Sources:* Provincial grants; Fundraising events; Membership fees; Donations
Staff Member(s): 4; 250 volunteer(s)
Membership: 2,500 individual + 110 organizations; *Fees:* $25 single; $30 family
Activities: Researching wilderness issues; *Awareness Events:* Climb & Run for Wilderness, April; *Speaker Service:* Yes; *Library:* Wilderness Resource Centre; Open to public
Chief Officer(s):
Owen McGoldrick, President
Christyann Olson, Executive Director
colson@abwild.ca
Awards:
• Great Gray Owl Award
For individuals who meet a high standard of volunteerism, dedication & commitment
• Alberta Wilderness Defenders Awards
To recognize individuals' efforts & achievements for conservation
Publications:
• Bighorn Wildland [a publication of the Alberta Wilderness Association]
Type: Book; *ISBN:* 0-920074-20-0
• Elbow Sheep Wilderness [a publication of the Alberta Wilderness Association]
Type: Book
• Recall of the Wild [a publication of the Alberta Wilderness Association]
Profile: A supplement to the Wild Lands Advocate
• Rivers on Borrowed Time [a publication of the Alberta Wilderness Association]
Type: Book
• The Western Swan Hills [a publication of the Alberta Wilderness Association]
Type: Book
• Wild Lands Advocate [a publication of the Alberta Wilderness Association]
Type: Journal; *Frequency:* 6 pa.; *Editor:* Ian Urquhart
• Willmore Wilderness Park [a publication of the Alberta Wilderness Association]
Type: Book

Alberta Women Entrepreneurs
Melton Building, #308, 10310 Jasper Ave., Edmonton AB T5J 2W4
Fax: 780-422-0756
Toll-Free: 800-713-3558
info@awebusiness.com
www.awebusiness.com
www.linkedin.com/company/alberta-women-entrepreneurs
www.facebook.com/awebusiness
twitter.com/AWEbusiness
Overview: A medium-sized provincial organization founded in 1995
Mission: AWE is a not-for-profit organization that helps women in Alberta succeed in business through business advice, business skills development, financing & networking.
Member of: Western Canada Business Service Network
Finances: *Funding Sources:* Western Economic Diversification Canada
Staff Member(s): 8
Activities: Annual conference
Chief Officer(s):
Marie C. Robidoux, Chair
Tracey Scarlett, CEO

Calgary Office
#370, 105 - 12 Ave. SE, Calgary AB T2G 1A1
Fax: 403-777-4258
Toll-Free: 800-713-3558

Alberta Women's Institutes (AWI)
AB
awi.athabascau.ca
Overview: A medium-sized provincial organization founded in 1909 overseen by Federated Women's Institutes of Canada
Mission: To help discover, stimulate & develop leadership among women
Affiliation(s): Associated Country Women of the World; Federated Women's Institutes of Canada
Chief Officer(s):
Evelyn Ellerman, Contact
evelyne@athabascau.ca

Albion Neighbourhood Services
#14, 21 Panorama Ct., Toronto ON M9V 4E3
Tel: 416-740-3704; *Fax:* 416-740-7124
ans@albionservices.ca
www.albionneighbourhoodservices.ca
Previous Name: Etobicoke North Community Information Centre
Overview: A small local organization founded in 1971 overseen by InformOntario
Mission: To provide accessible programs that educate & enable individuals & families to achieve self-sufficiency & social wellbeing
Activities: Information & referral; language resource bank, interpreting & translating; income tax clinic; immigrant settlement services; advocacy; housing counselling, child & youth recreational activities; child breakfast clubs, after school programs, camps
Chief Officer(s):
Lisa Kostakis, Executive Director

Alcohol and Drug Recovery Association of Ontario *See* Addictions & Mental Health Ontario

Alcoholics Anonymous (GTA Intergroup) (AA)
#202, 234 Eglinton Ave. East, Toronto ON M4P 1K5
Tel: 416-487-5591; *Fax:* 416-928-2521
Toll-Free: 877-404-5591; *TTY:* 866-831-4657
office@aatoronto.org
www.aatoronto.org
Overview: A large national charitable organization founded in 1947
Mission: Fellowship of men & women who share their experience, strength & hope with each other so that they may solve their common problem & help others recover from alcoholism; the primary purpose is to stay sober & help other alcoholics to achieve sobriety
Finances: *Funding Sources:* Donations; literature sales; conferences
Membership: *Member Profile:* Must have a desire to stop drinking; *Committees:* Accessibility; Archives; Communications; Correctional; Cooperation with the Professional Community; Finance; Information A.A. Day; Ontario Regional Conference; Executive; Public Information; Treatment; Twelfth Step; Winter Season Open House
Activities: Annual Ontario Regional Conference; Christmas Day Open House & Dinner; Archives Breakfast, Nov.; Information AA Day, May; AA Picnic, summer; *Library:* Toronto Intergroup Literature Library; Open to public

Publications:
• Better Times [a publication of Alcoholics Anonymous (GTA Intergroup)]
Type: Newsletter; *Frequency:* Monthly

Abbotsford - Intergroup Committee
#17, 1961 Eagle St., Abbotsford BC V2S 3A7
Crisis Hot-Line: 604-850-0811
abbotsfordintrgrp@hotmail.com
www.theabbotsfordintergroup-aa.org

Barrie - Barrie & Area Intergroup
#622, 80 Bradford St., Barrie ON L4N 6S7
Tel: 705-725-8682
barrieaa@barrieaa.com
www.barrieaa.com

Calgary - Central Service Office
#2, 4015 - 1st St. SE, Calgary AB T2G 4X7
Tel: 403-777-1212; *Fax:* 403-287-6540
centraloffice@telus.net
www.calgaryaa.org

Edmonton - AA Central Office
#205, 10544 - 114 St. NW, Edmonton AB T5H 3J7
Tel: 780-424-5900
www.edmontonaa.org

Guelph - Central West District 3
PO Box 210, #17A, 218 Silvercreek Pkwy. North, Guelph ON N1H 8E8
Tel: 519-836-1522
www.centralwest2district3aa.org

Halifax Central Office
PO Box 31338, Halifax NS B3K 5Z1
Tel: 902-461-1119
help.aahalifax@gmail.com
www.aahalifax.org

Hamilton - Central Office
#205, 627 Main St. East, Hamilton ON L8M 1J5
Tel: 905-522-8399; *Fax:* 905-522-1946
info@aahamilton.org
www.aahamilton.org

London - London Area Intergroup
201 Consortium Crt., London ON
Tel: 519-438-9006
www.aalondon.org

Montréal - Intergroupe de Montréal
3920, rue Rachel est, Montréal QC H1X 1Z3
Tel: 514-374-3688; *Fax:* 514-374-2250
region87@aa-quebec.org
aa87.org

Oshawa - Lakeshore Intergroup
200 Thornton Rd. North, Oshawa ON L1J 6T8
Tel: 905-728-1020
aa.oshawa@live.com
www.aaoshawa.org

Ottawa - Ottawa Area Intergroup
#108, 211 Bronson Ave., Ottawa ON K1R 6H5
Tel: 613-237-6000
www.ottawaaa.org

Peterborough - Kawartha District Intergroup
625 Cameron St., Peterborough ON K9J 3Z9
Tel: 705-745-6111
district86aa@hotmail.com
www.peterboroughaa.org

Prince Edward Island - Green Acres Intergroup
5 Summer St., Summerside PE C1N 3H3
Tel: 902-436-7721

Québec - Northeast Area of Québec Central Office
14, rue St-Amand, Québec QC G2A 2K9
Tel: 418-915-2929; *Fax:* 418-915-4959
region89@aa-quebec.org
aa-quebec.org/region89

Québec - Northwest Area of Québec Central Office
PO Box 361, Saint-Jérôme QC J7Z 5V2
Tel: 450-560-3902; *Fax:* 450-560-3903
region@aa90.org
www.aa90.org

Regina - Central Office
#107, 845 Broad St., Regina SK S4R 8G9
Tel: 306-545-9300
a.a@sasktel.net
www.aaregina.com

St Catharines - Niagara District Intergroup
Tel: 905-682-2140
Toll-Free: 866-311-9042

info@aaniagara.org
www.aaniagara.org
St. John's - Central Office
#117, 183 Kenmount Rd., St. John's NL A1B 3P9
Tel: 709-579-6091
Toll-Free: 888-579-5215
sjintergroup@nl.rogers.com
www.aastjohns.nf.net
Saskatoon - Saskatoon Central Office
#515, 245 - 3rd Ave. South, Saskatoon SK S7K 1M4
Tel: 306-665-6727; *Fax:* 306-665-6753
aasaskatoon@sasktel.net
www.aasaskatoon.org
Trenton - District 30 Quinte West
Toll-Free: 866-951-3711
www.quintewestaa.org
Vancouver - Greater Vancouver Intergroup Society
3457 Kingsway, Vancouver BC V5R 5L5
Tel: 604-434-3933; *Fax:* 604-434-2553
staff@vancouveraa.ca
www.vancouveraa.ca
Victoria - AA Central Office
#8, 2020 Douglas St., Victoria BC V8T 4L1
Tel: 250-383-0415; *Fax:* 250-383-0417; *Crisis Hot-Line:* 250-383-7744
vicintgpco@shaw.ca
www.aavictoria.ca
Whitehorse - Whitehorse Intergroup
c/o BC/Yukon Area 79, PO Box 42114, Vancouver BC V5S 4R5
Tel: 604-435-2181
info@bcyukonaa.org
www.bcyukonaa.org
Winnipeg - Manitoba Central Office
1856 Portage Ave., Winnipeg MB R3J 0G9
Tel: 204-942-0126
Toll-Free: 877-942-0126
aambco@mts.net
www.aamanitoba.org

Alcooliques Anonymes du Québec
Bureau des services de la Région 87, 3920, rue Rachel est, Montréal QC H1X 1Z3
Tél: 514-374-3688; *Téléc:* 514-374-2250
www.aa-quebec.org
Aperçu: *Dimension:* petite; *Envergure:* provinciale; fondée en 1935
Mission: Demeurer abstinent et aider d'autres alcooliques à le devenir
Membre: Over 50,000
Membre(s) du bureau directeur:
Marco L., Président
president@aa87.org

Alcooliques Anonymes Groupe La Vallée du Cuivre
CP 21, Chibougamau QC G8P 2K5
Ligne sans frais: 866-376-6279
Aperçu: *Dimension:* petite; *Envergure:* locale

The Alcuin Society
PO Box 3216, Vancouver BC V6B 3X8
info@alcuinsociety.com
www.alcuinsociety.com
www.facebook.com/alcuinsociety
twitter.com/alcuin
www.flickr.com/photos/alcuinsociety
Overview: A small provincial charitable organization founded in 1965
Mission: To sponsor educational programs; Yo publish a journal; To offer awards & citations for excellence in book arts
Member of: Fellowship of American Bibliophilic Societies
Finances: *Annual Operating Budget:* Less than $50,000; *Funding Sources:* Membership dues; donations; BC Gaming Commission
Staff Member(s): 1; 10 volunteer(s)
Membership: 370; *Fees:* Annual - Student: $25; Individual: $50; Institutional: $75; Patron: $125; *Member Profile:* Anyone interested in book arts, fine printing, typography, reading; *Committees:* Publishing; Citation Awards
Activities: Book Fair, March
Chief Officer(s):
Howard Greaves, Chair
Awards:
• Alcuin Society Citation Awards for Excellence in Book Design in Canada

Aldergrove Daylily Society
24642 - 51 Ave., Langley BC V2Z 1H9
Tel: 604-856-5758
www.distinctly.on.ca/chs/aldergrove.html
Overview: A small local organization founded in 1991
Membership: *Fees:* $10 individual; $15 family
Chief Officer(s):
Pam Erikson, President
pamela1@istar.ca

Alexandra Writers' Centre Society (AWCS)
922 - 9th Ave. SE., Calgary AB T2G 0S4
Tel: 403-264-4730
awcs@telusplanet.net
www.alexandrawriters.org
www.facebook.com/alexandra.writers
twitter.com/alexwriters
Overview: A small local charitable organization founded in 1981
Mission: To encourage the voices of new, emerging, & experienced writers & provide a platform for their work
Member of: Alberta Magazine Publishers Association
Finances: *Annual Operating Budget:* Less than $50,000
Staff Member(s): 1; 16 volunteer(s)
Membership: 135 individual; *Fees:* $60; *Member Profile:* Writers of all ages & experience; *Committees:* Registration; Publicity; Library; Free Fall Magazine; Events; Volunteer; Writer in Residence
Activities: Writing courses; public readings; Alexandra Café; magazine launches; discussion groups; FreeFall Fiction & Poetry Contest; *Library:* AWCS Library; by appointment Not open to public
Chief Officer(s):
Bob Laws, President
awcsboard@alexandrawriters.org
Awards:
• Writer in Residence
• FreeFall Fiction & Poetry Contest Award
Publications:
• FreeFall Magazine
Editor: Lynn Fraser

Alexandria & District Chamber of Commerce
PO Box 1058, Alexandria ON K0C 1A0
Tel: 613-525-0588
alexandriachamber.ca
www.facebook.com/AlexOnChamber
twitter.com/AlexOnChamber
Overview: A small local organization
Mission: To support local businesses
Membership: *Committees:* Craft Show; Finance; Golf Tournament; Membership; Trade Show; Website & Promotions
Chief Officer(s):
Michael Madden, President

Alfa Romeo Club of Canada (ARCC)
PO Box 62, Stn. Q, Toronto ON M4T 2L7
admin@alfaclub.ca
www.alfaclub.ca
www.facebook.com/alfaclub.ca
Overview: A medium-sized national organization founded in 1977
Mission: To share common interest in use, preservation & appreciation of Alfa Romeo automobiles
Finances: *Annual Operating Budget:* Less than $50,000; *Funding Sources:* Membership fees
12 volunteer(s)
Membership: 500; *Fees:* $55
Activities: *Library:* by appointment
Chief Officer(s):
Alex Csank, President
Christine Pickering, Secretary

Algoma Arts Festival Association (AAFA)
680 Albert St. East, Sault Ste Marie ON P6A 2K6
Tel: 705-949-0822
fallfestival@algomafallfestival.com
www.algomafallfestival.com
www.facebook.com/AlgomaFestival
twitter.com/AlgomaFallFest
Also Known As: Algoma Fall Festival
Overview: A small local organization founded in 1972
Mission: To promote the arts; To encourage interest in & the study of the performing & visual arts & their traditions through presentation of performances & exhibitions; To provide opportunity to Sault Ste Marie and district students to learn the performing, literary & visual arts; To provide improved opportunities for Canadian artistic talent
Finances: *Annual Operating Budget:* $100,000-$250,000
Staff Member(s): 2; 200 volunteer(s)
Membership: 300; *Fees:* $25
Activities: *Awareness Events:* Annual Algoma Fall Festival, Sept./Oct.; Festival of Learning

Algoma Cattlemen's Association
Algoma ON
Tel: 705-843-2208
Overview: A small local organization
Affiliation(s): Ontario Cattlemen's Association
Chief Officer(s):
Cleave O'Malley, President

Algoma District Law Association (ADLA)
444 Queen St. East, Sault Ste Marie ON P6A 1Z7
Tel: 705-946-5691; *Fax:* 705-946-5630
Toll-Free: 866-840-2540
algomalaw@shaw.ca
Overview: A small local organization founded in 1922
Finances: *Annual Operating Budget:* Less than $50,000
Staff Member(s): 1
Membership: 65 individual
Activities: *Library:* Not open to public
Chief Officer(s):
Amanda Ward-Pereira, Contact

Algoma Kinniwabi Travel Association (AKTA)
334 Bay St., Sault Ste Marie ON P6A 1X1
Tel: 705-254-4293; *Fax:* 705-254-4892
Toll-Free: 800-263-2546
info@algomacountry.com
www.algomacountry.com
www.facebook.com/algomacountry
twitter.com/AlgomaCountry
www.youtube.com/user/OntarioAlgomaCountry
Also Known As: Algoma Country
Overview: A small local organization founded in 1974
Mission: To promote the Algoma Country region to the travelling public
Member of: Ontario Tourism Marketing Partnership Corp.; Tourism Federation of Ontario
Finances: *Funding Sources:* Public & private donations
Membership: *Member Profile:* Tourism industry
Chief Officer(s):
Lori Johnson, President

Algoma Manitoulin Environmental Awareness (AMEA)
RR#1, Kagawong ON P0P 1J0
Tel: 705-282-2886
Overview: A small local organization
Mission: To encourage participation in envionmental matters in the Algoma Manitoulin region of Ontario
Member of: Ontario Clean Air Alliance

Algoma-Manitoulin & District Labour Council
20 Alberta Rd., Elliot Lake ON P5A 1Z6
Tel: 705-848-2226
Overview: A small local organization founded in 1983 overseen by Ontario Federation of Labour
Mission: Tp provides free services to non-unionized injured workers and their survivors in workplace insurance matters (formerly called workers' compensation)

Algonquin Arts Council (AAC)
A Place For The Arts, 23E Bridge St. West, Bancroft ON K0L 1C0
Tel: 613-630-0063
info@algonquinarts.ca
www.algonquinarts.ca
www.facebook.com/algonquinartscouncil
Overview: A small local charitable organization founded in 1978
Mission: To promote & foster cultural activities in the the 12 northern townships of Hastings County & surrounding areas
Member of: Community Arts Ontario
Affiliation(s): Ontario Association of Art Galleries
Finances: *Annual Operating Budget:* Less than $50,000; *Funding Sources:* Village of Bancroft; Donations; Membership; Used book sales; Craftshop
25 volunteer(s)
Membership: 120; *Fees:* $20; *Member Profile:* Individuals with an interest in the arts; *Committees:* Bancroft Art Gallery; Performing Arts; School Arts; The Village Playhouse; Theatrics; Rainbow Man Theatre
Activities: Facilitating the Art Gallery of Bancroft; Offering concert series & studio tours

Chief Officer(s):
Kim Crawford, President, 613-474-3309
myc6@xplornet.com
Teena Surma, Secretary, 613-332-2090
t.surma@nhcia.ca
Avis Price, Treasurer, 613-332-4171
avisprice@xplornet.com

Alianza Hispano-Canadiense Ontario / Hispanic-Canadian Alliance of Ontario
PO Box 14, Pickering ON L1V 2R2
info@alianzahispano.org
www.alianzahispano.org
Overview: A small local organization
Mission: To help the Hispanic community living in Durham region
Membership: *Fees:* $15 Indvidual; $25 Families
Activities: Parties; BBQs; Trips
Chief Officer(s):
Karen Kannon, President, Board of Directors

ALIGN Association of Community Services
Bonnie Doon Mall, #255, 8330 - 82nd Ave., Edmonton AB T6C 4E3
Tel: 780-428-3660; *Fax:* 780-428-3844
info@alignab.ca
www.alignab.ca
twitter.com/alignalberta
Previous Name: Alberta Association of Services for Children & Families; Alberta Association of Child Care Centres
Overview: A medium-sized provincial organization founded in 1967
Mission: To strengthen & represent the interests of member agencies; To develop & advocate for conditions & practices that improve quality of services for vulnerable children & families
Member of: Child Welfare League of Canada; Canadian Council on Social Development
Finances: *Annual Operating Budget:* $250,000-$500,000; *Funding Sources:* Fee for service
Staff Member(s): 5; 100 volunteer(s)
Membership: 143 institutional, associate & corporate; *Fees:* Schedule available; *Member Profile:* Members consist of organizations that provide services directly to children & families; Associate members consist of individuals or organizations that are interested in child & family welfare but do not provide direct service; Corporate members consist of corporations or organizations that support child & family welfare initiatives but do not provide direct service; Life members consist of individuals or organizations that are conferred as such by Board of Directors; *Committees:* Executive; Nominating
Activities: Advocating, developing policies & providing information for service providers
Chief Officer(s):
Rhonda Barraclough, Executive Director
rhondab@alignab.ca
Meetings/Conferences:
• ALIGN Association of Community Services 2018 Annual Conference, January, 2018, Fantasyland Hotel, West Edmonton Mall, Edmonton, AB
Scope: Provincial
Description: Theme: "Strengthening Today, Building Tomorrow"

Alix Chamber of Commerce
c/o Village of Alix, PO Box 87, 4849 50th St., Alix AB T0C 0B0
Tel: 403-747-2444
www.villageofalix.com
Overview: A small local organization
Member of: Alberta Chamber of Commerce
Finances: *Annual Operating Budget:* Less than $50,000
Membership: 20 individual
Chief Officer(s):
Catherine Hepburn, President

All Terrain Vehicle Association of Nova Scotia (ATVANS)
PO Box 46020, Stn. Novalea, Halifax NS B3K 5V8
Tel: 902-241-3200
Toll-Free: 877-288-4244
admin@atvans.org
www.atvans.org
Overview: A medium-sized provincial organization founded in 1997
Mission: To represent the interest of ATV'ers to Government, Land owners, other recreation user groups and the general public and educate, inform and organize ATV'ers to preserve and expand ATV recreational opportunities to promote safe family activities.

Chief Officer(s):
Vince Sawler, President
president@atvans.org
Barry Barnet, Executive Director
execdirector@atvans.org

All-Canada Committee of the Christian Church (Disciples of Christ) *See* Christian Church (Disciples of Christ) in Canada

Allen & Milli Gould Family Foundation
310 Main St. West, Hamilton ON L8P 1J8
Tel: 905-527-1531
beng@milli.ca
Overview: A small national charitable organization founded in 1985
Mission: To operate as a foundation whose philanthropic interests are local Jewish charities centred in Hamilton & Toronto, with primary focus on Shalom Village, St Joseph's Hospital, McMaster University, & the National Academy Orchestra
Staff Member(s): 1
Chief Officer(s):
Ben Gould, Contact
Awards:
• The Allen and Milli Gould Family Foundation Bursaries
Eligibility: McMaster students enrolled in the Faculty of Business who demonstrate financial need.

AllerGen NCE Inc.
Michael DeGroote Centre for Learning & Discovery, McMaster University, #3120, 1280 Main St. West, Hamilton ON L8S 4K1
Tel: 905-525-9140; *Fax:* 905-524-0611
info@allergen-nce.ca
www.allergen-nce.ca
Overview: A medium-sized national organization founded in 2004
Mission: To support research, capacity building activities, & networking regarding allergic disease in Canada; To reduce the mortality & socio-economic impacts of allergy, asthma, & related immune diseases
Finances: *Funding Sources:* Government of Canada, through the Networks of Centres of Excellence (NCE) Program
Chief Officer(s):
Judah Denburg, CEO & Scientific Director
Diana Royce, COO & Managing Director
Kim Wright, Director, Communications & Knowledge Mobilization
April O'Connell, Administrator, Research
Kelly McNagny, Associate Scientific Director
Meetings/Conferences:
• AllerGen 2018 Research Conference, 2018
Scope: National
Publications:
• Agenda [a publication of AllerGen NCE Inc.]
Type: Newsletter
Profile: An overview of research, training, partnerships, & networking
• AirWays [a publication of AllerGen NCE Inc.]
Type: Newsletter
Profile: News about training & professional development opportunities
• AllerGen NCE Inc. Annual Report
Type: Yearbook; *Frequency:* Annually
Profile: Highlights of the year & a financial overview
• AllerGen Network Newsletter
Type: Newsletter; *Frequency:* Quarterly
Profile: Information about the management of the network for board & committee members & investigators
• ReAction [a publication of AllerGen NCE Inc.]
Type: Newsletter
Profile: Partnership, training, & networking opportunities

Allergie/Asthme association d'information *See* Allergy/Asthma Information Association

Allergy & Environmental Health Association *See* Environmental Health Association of Ontario

Allergy, Asthma & Immunology Society of Ontario
2 Demaris Ave., Toronto ON M3N 1M1
Tel: 416-633-2215
www.allergyasthma.on.ca
Previous Name: Ontario Allergy Society
Overview: A small provincial organization founded in 1958
Mission: To strive to provide high quality medical services to the public, through consultation by referral from other physicians, as well as through public service education
Membership: *Member Profile:* Practicing physicians

Activities: *Speaker Service:* Yes

Allergy/Asthma Information Association (AAIA) / Allergie/Asthme association d'information
#200, 17 Four Season Place, Toronto ON M9B 6E6
Tel: 416-621-4571; *Fax:* 416-621-5034
Toll-Free: 800-611-7011
admin@aaia.ca
www.aaia.ca
www.facebook.com/AllergyAsthmaInformationAssociation
Overview: A large national charitable organization founded in 1964
Mission: To create a safer environment for Canadians with allergies, asthma, & anaphylaxis; To assist persons coping with allergies; To act as a national voice for individuals affected by allergy, asthma, & anaphylaxis
Affiliation(s): Canadian Society of Allergy & Immunology
Finances: *Funding Sources:* Donations; Corporate partnerships
Membership: *Fees:* $35/one year; $60/two years
Activities: Providing education; Raising money for research; Working with related organizations, government, & the food industry; Engaging in advocacy activities; Offering food allergy summer camps; *Awareness Events:* Walk to Axe Anaphylaxis
Chief Officer(s):
Sharon Van Gyzen, Chair
Sharon Lee, Executive Director
slee@aaia.ca
Louis Isabella, C.A., Treasurer
Publications:
• Allergy Asthma Information Association Newsletter
Type: Newsletter; *Frequency:* Quarterly
Profile: Information for persons affected by allergy, asthma, & anaphylaxis

AAIA BC/Yukon
4730 Redridge Rd., Kelowna BC V1W 3A6
Tel: 250-764-7507; *Fax:* 250-764-7587
Toll-Free: 877-500-2242
bc@aaia.ca
Chief Officer(s):
Yvonne Rousseau, Regional Coordinator

AAIA Ontario/Québec/Atlantic
#200, 17 Four Season Pl., Toronto ON M6B 6E6
Tel: 416-621-4571; *Fax:* 416-621-5034
Toll-Free: 800-611-7011

AAIA Prairies/NWT/Nunavut
16531 - 114 St. NW, Edmonton AB T5X 3V6
Tel: 780-456-6651; *Fax:* 780-456-6651
Toll-Free: 866-456-6651
prairies@aaia.ca
Chief Officer(s):
Lilly Byrtus, Regional Coordinator

Alliance agricole du Nouveau-Brunswick *See* Agricultural Alliance of New Brunswick

Alliance animale du Canada *See* Animal Alliance of Canada

Alliance autochtone du Québec / Native Alliance of Québec
21, rue Brodeur, Gatineau QC J8Y 2P6
Tél: 819-770-7763; *Téléc:* 819-770-6070
info@aaqnaq.com
www.aaqnaq.com
Aperçu: *Dimension:* moyenne; *Envergure:* provinciale surveillé par Congress of Aboriginal Peoples
Mission: Promouvoir et représenter les intérêts des Autochtones (Indiens, Inuits et Métis) qui vivent à l'extérieur des réserves au Québec
Membre: 26,000 members
Membre(s) du bureau directeur:
Robert Bertrand, Président Grand Chef

Région 1 (Abitibi - Témiscamingue)
QC
Tél: 819-797-8503
jnault@tlb.sympatico.ca
www.aaqnaq.com
Mission: Provides assistance and solidarity to citizens of Quebec who are Metis or off-reserve natives whose Native status is not recognized by the Indian Act of the Government of Canada. It promotes recreational activities for the Metis and off-reserve Indians, to assist them in the development of a social fraternity, a dignified and human understanding to contribute to help our members better understand their history, their accomplishments and their contribution to the Canadian society.
Membre(s) du bureau directeur:

Johanne Nault, Directrice générale
Région 2 (Outaouais - Pontiac - Gatineau - Labelle)
QC
Tél: 819-438-2158
allianceautochtone080@hotmail.com
www.aaqnaq.com
Mission: Provides assistance and solidarity to citizens of Quebec who are Metis or off-reserve natives whose Native status is not recognized by the Indian Act of the Government of Canada. It promotes recreational activities for the Metis and off-reserve Indians, to assist them in the development of a social fraternity, a dignified and human understanding to contribute to help our people better understand their history, their accomplishments and their contribution to the Canadian society.
Membre(s) du bureau directeur:
Carole Romain, Directrice générale, 819-683-3757
cromain@waskahegen.com
Région 3 (Montréal - Trois-Rivières - Estrie - Gaspésie)
Trois-Rivières QC
Tél: 819-846-3962; *Téléc:* 819-846-1162
bouliane.denis@hotmail.ca
www.aaqnaq.com
Mission: Provides assistance and solidarity to citizens of Quebec who are Metis or off-reserve natives whose Native status is not recognized by the Indian Act of the Government of Canada. It promotes recreational activities for the Metis and off-reserve Indians, to assist them in the development of a social fraternity, a dignified and human understanding to contribute to help our people better understand their history, their accomplishments and their contribution to the Canadian society.
Membre(s) du bureau directeur:
Denis Bouliane, Directeur général
Région 4 (Saguenay - Lac-St-Jean - La Tuque - Québec)
QC
Tél: 418-679-1237; *Téléc:* 418-679-1237
castonguay.roger@videotron.ca
www.aaqnaq.com
Mission: Provides assistance and solidarity to citizens of Quebec who are Metis or off-reserve natives whose Native status is not recognized by the Indian Act of the Government of Canada. It promotes recreational activities for the Metis and off-reserve Indians, to assist them in the development of a social fraternity, a dignified and human understanding to contribute to help our people better understand their history, their accomplishments and their contribution to the Canadian society.
Membre(s) du bureau directeur:
Roger Castonguay, Directeur général
Région 5 (Côte-Nord - Basse-Côte-Nord)
Chute-aux-Outardes QC
Tél: 418-233-2273; *Téléc:* 418-233-2273
gtremblay13@hotmail.com
www.aaqnaq.com
Mission: Provides assistance and solidarity to citizens of Quebec who are Metis or off-reserve natives whose Native status is not recognized by the Indian Act of the Government of Canada. It promotes recreational activities for the Metis and off-reserve Indians, to assist them in the development of a social fraternity, a dignified and human understanding to contribute to help our people better understand their history, their accomplishments and their contribution to the Canadian society.
Membre(s) du bureau directeur:
Ginette Tremblay, Directrice générale

L'Alliance canadienne de l'épilepsie *See* Canadian Epilepsy Alliance

Alliance Canadienne de Massothérapeutes *See* Canadian Massage Therapist Alliance

Alliance canadienne des associations étudiantes *See* Canadian Alliance of Student Associations

Alliance canadienne des organismes de réglementation de la physiothérapie *See* Canadian Alliance of Physiotherapy Regulators

Alliance canadienne des responsables et enseignants en français (langue maternelle) (ACREF) / Canadian Association for the Teachers of French as a First Language
Place de la Francophonie, Succ. A, #401, 450, rue Reideau, Ottawa ON K1N 5Z4
Tél: 613-744-3192; *Téléc:* 613-744-0154
acref@franco.ca
Aperçu: *Dimension:* moyenne; *Envergure:* nationale; Organisme sans but lucratif; fondée en 1989
Mission: Développer un réseau d'identification nationale des professeurs de français langue maternelle; favoriser le développement et l'épanouissement des associations provinciales vouées à l'enseignement du français langue maternelle; promouvoir la diffusion de l'information en matière de théories pédagogiques, de formation à l'approche communicative, et de pratiques scolaires et d'idéologie visant l'identité des francophones, l'égalité en tant que groupe national et le contrôle des structures éducatives; appuyer les organismes provinciaux lors de leur rencontre annuelle; développer des instruments de diffusion de l'information à l'intention de ses membres; favoriser le développement d'une politique nationale en ce qui a trait à la gestion des institutions d'enseignement et voir à ce qu'elle respecte l'autonomie des francophones
Membre de: Fédération internationale des professeurs de français
Activités: *Stagiaires:* Oui; *Bibliothèque:* rendez-vous Not open to public

Alliance canadienne des services d'évaluation de diplômes *See* Alliance of Credential Evaluation Services of Canada

L'Alliance canadienne des victimes d'accidents et de maladies du travail *See* Canadian Injured Workers Alliance

L'Alliance canadienne du camionnage *See* Canadian Trucking Alliance

Alliance canadienne pour la paix *See* Canadian Peace Alliance

Alliance canadiennes des artistes de danse *See* Canadian Alliance of Dance Artists

Alliance catholique canadienne de la santé *See* Catholic Health Alliance of Canada

Alliance Champlain *Voir* Québec dans le monde

Alliance Chorale Manitoba
340, boul Provencher, Winnipeg MB R2H 0G7
Tél: 204-233-7423; *Téléc:* 204-233-8972
Aperçu: *Dimension:* petite; *Envergure:* provinciale; fondée en 1971
Mission: De promouvoir le chant choral en français et de favoriser ainsi l'épanouissement de la culture francophone du Manitoba
Affiliation(s): Centre culturel franco-manitobain
Membre(s) du bureau directeur:
Louise Dupont, Directrice générale

L'Alliance chrétienne et missionnaire au Canada *See* The Christian & Missionary Alliance in Canada

Alliance de l'industrie canadienne de l'aquiculture *See* Canadian Aquaculture Industry Alliance

Alliance de la Fonction publique du Canada *See* Public Service Alliance of Canada

Alliance des artistes canadiens du cinéma, de la télévision et de la radio *See* Alliance of Canadian Cinema, Television & Radio Artists

Alliance des arts médiatiques indépendants *See* Independent Media Arts Alliance

Alliance des cadres de l'État
#306, 1305, ch Ste-Foy, Québec QC G1S 4N5
Tél: 418-681-2028
info@alliancedescadres.com
www.alliancedescadres.com
Aperçu: *Dimension:* moyenne; *Envergure:* provinciale
Mission: Pour protéger et défendre les droits des personnes qui travaillent comme cadres dans les organisations gouvernementales
Membre: 3,871
Membre(s) du bureau directeur:
Carole Roberage, Présidente-directrice générale

L'Alliance des Caisses populaires de l'Ontario limitée (ACPOL)
CP 3500, 1870 Bond St., North Bay ON P1B 4V6
Tél: 705-474-5634; *Téléc:* 705-474-5326
support@acpol.com
www.caissealliance.com
www.linkedin.com/company/l'alliance-des-caisses-populaires-de-l'ontario-limit-e
www.facebook.com/174831179214242
Aperçu: *Dimension:* moyenne; *Envergure:* provinciale; fondée en 1979 surveillé par Canadian Credit Union Association
Membre de: Canadian Credit Union Association
Activités: *Bibliothèque:* Not open to public
Membre(s) du bureau directeur:
Pierre Dorval, Directeur général

Alliance des chorales du Québec (ACQ)
CP 1000, Succ. M, 4545, av Pierre de Coubertin, Montréal QC H1V 0B2
Tél: 514-252-3020; *Téléc:* 514-252-3222
Ligne sans frais: 888-924-6387
information@chorale.qc.ca
www.chorale.qc.ca
www.facebook.com/95274112113
twitter.com/AcqChorale
Aperçu: *Dimension:* moyenne; *Envergure:* provinciale; Organisme sans but lucratif
Mission: Regrouper des chorales de tous styles et de tous niveaux; donner des moyens de mieux chanter; promouvoir et développer le chant choral au Québec
Finances: *Budget de fonctionnement annuel:* $100,000-$250,000
Membre(s) du personnel: 3
Membre: 235 chorales + 15 organismes régionaux; *Montant de la cotisation:* 250$
Activités: *Stagiaires:* Oui; *Bibliothèque:* Service de ventes de partitions de l'ACQ; rendez-vous
Membre(s) du bureau directeur:
Decroix Charles, Directeur général
Publications:
• Chanter [a publication of the Alliance des chorales du Québec] *Type:* Newsletter; *Frequency:* irregular

Alliance des communautés culturelles pour l'égalité dans la santé et les services sociaux (ACCÉSSS)
#408, 7000, av Du Parc, Montréal QC H3N 1X1
Tél: 514-287-1106; *Téléc:* 514-287-7443
Ligne sans frais: 866-744-1106
accesss@accesss.net
accesss.net
www.facebook.com/pages/ACCÉSSS/273142908412
Aperçu: *Dimension:* petite; *Envergure:* provinciale; fondée en 1984
Mission: Offre des services facilitant l'intégration et l'adaptation des services sociaux et de santé aux personnes issues des communautés ethnoculturelles; représente les intérêts des communautés ethnoculturelles auprès des instances décisionnelles en matières de santé et services sociaux; mène des recherches sur les besoins d'adaptation et d'adéquation des services sociaux et de santé en vue de leur pleine utilisation par les personnes issues des communautés ethnoculturelles
Finances: *Fonds:* Ministère de la Santé et des services sociaux
Membre(s) du personnel: 6
Membre: *Montant de la cotisation:* 25$ actif; 50$ associé
Membre(s) du bureau directeur:
Carmen Gonzalez, Présidente
Jérôme Di Giovanni, Directeur général
jerome.digiovanni@accesss.net

Alliance des femmes de la francophonie canadienne (AFFC)
Place de la francophonie, #302, 450, rue Rideau, Ottawa ON K1N 5Z4
Tél: 613-241-3500; *Téléc:* 613-241-6679
Ligne sans frais: 866-535-9422
info@affc.ca
www.affc.ca
www.facebook.com/229810340365531
twitter.com/AFFCfemmes
Nom précédent: Fédération nationale des femmes canadiennes-françaises; Fédération des femmes canadiennes-françaises
Aperçu: *Dimension:* moyenne; *Envergure:* nationale; Organisme sans but lucratif; fondée en 1914
Mission: Favorise l'autonomie des femmes canadiennes-françaises sur tous les plans; assure le respect des droits des femmes francophones vivant en milieu minoritaire; soutien le développement de l'action collective et politique des femmes au Canada français; souligne la spécificité des femmes francophones auprès des instances gouvernementales, des diverses associations et du grand public
Membre de: Gropues Femmes, Politiques et Démocratie

Canadian Associations / Alliance des gais et lesbiennes Laval-Laurentides (AGLLL Inc.)

Affiliation(s): Fédération des communautés francophones et acadienne du Canada
Membre(s) du personnel: 3; 13 bénévole(s)
Membre: 11 groupes; 7 000 individus; *Montant de la cotisation:* Barème; *Critères d'admissibilite:* Etre un groupe et s'intéresser à la condition féminine, à l'avancement des droits des femmes dans la société; *Comités:* Comité d'études et d'action politique; Comité des statuts et règlements
Activités: Bourses d'études; *Service de conférenciers:* Oui; *Bibliothèque:* rendez-vous
Membre(s) du bureau directeur:
Manon Beaulieu, Directrice générale
direction@affc.ca
Lepage Maria, Présidente
lepagemariea@hotmail.com
Prix, Bourses:
• Bourse d'étude Almanda-Walker-Marchand
• Une femme remarquable

Alliance des gais et lesbiennes Laval-Laurentides (AGLLL Inc.)
CP 98030, 95, boul Labelle, Sainte-Thérèse QC J7E 5R4
Courriel: aglll@hotmail.com
www.algi.qc.ca/asso/aglll/
Aperçu: *Dimension:* petite; *Envergure:* locale
Mission: Groupe de discussion; activités
Membre de: Association des lesbiennes et des gais sur Internet (ALGI)

Alliance des massothérapeutes du Québec (AMQ)
147, boul Laurier, Saint-Basile-le-Grand QC J3N 1A9
Tél: 450-441-1117; *Téléc:* 450-441-1157
Ligne sans frais: 888-687-1786
info@massotherapeutes.qc.ca
www.massotherapeutes.qc.ca
www.facebook.com/147162382012847
twitter.com/AllianceMasso
Aperçu: *Dimension:* petite; *Envergure:* provinciale; Organisme sans but lucratif; fondée en 1999
Mission: Vérifier les qualifications des massothérapeutes et offrir un service de formation afin que membres demeurent à l'avant-garde de la profession et des besoins du public
Finances: *Budget de fonctionnement annuel:* Moins de $50,000
Membre: 165; *Montant de la cotisation:* 200$/an; *Critères d'admissibilité:* Massothérapeutes; kinésithérapeutes
Activités: Association; formation; *Stagiaires:* Oui
Membre(s) du bureau directeur:
Marie-Josée Poisson, Présidente

Alliance des moniteurs de ski du Canada *See* Canadian Ski Instructors' Alliance

Alliance des professeures et professeurs de Montréal (APPM)
8225, boul Saint-Laurent, Montréal QC H2P 2M1
Tél: 514-383-4880; *Téléc:* 514-384-5756
presidence@alliancedesprofs.qc.ca
www.alliancedesprofs.qc.ca
Aperçu: *Dimension:* moyenne; *Envergure:* locale; fondée en 1919 surveillé par Centrale des syndicats du Québec
Membre de: Fédération des syndicats de l'enseignements (FSE)
Finances: *Budget de fonctionnement annuel:* $1.5 Million-$3 Million
Membre(s) du personnel: 20; 500 bénévole(s)
Membre: 8 000
Activités: Services aux membres; Défense de leurs droits; *Bibliothèque:* Centre de documentation - APPM; rendez-vous
Membre(s) du bureau directeur:
Alain Marois, Président
alain.marois@alliancedesprofs.qc.ca

Alliance des professionels et des professionnelles de la Ville de Québec (ALLPPVQ)
www.allppvq.ca
Aperçu: *Dimension:* petite; *Envergure:* locale; fondée en 2001
Membre: 500; *Critères d'admissibilite:* Professionnels et professionnelles travaillant dans des sphères d'activités requérant un diplôme universitaire; *Comités:* Comité d'évaluation et de classification des emplois; Comité de retraite; Comité des relations professionnelles; Comité santé et sécurité
Membre(s) du bureau directeur:
Sylvie Dolbec, Présidente
sylvie.dolbec@allppvq.ca
Louise Ouellet, 2e Vice-Présidente
louise-e.ouellet@ville.quebec.qc.ca

Alliance des radios communautaires du Canada
#1206, 1, rue Nicholas, Ottawa ON K1N 7B7
Tél: 613-562-0000; *Téléc:* 613-562-2182
radiorfa.com
www.facebook.com/arcducanada
twitter.com/arcducanada
www.youtube.com/arcducanada
Également appelé: ARC du Canada
Aperçu: *Dimension:* moyenne; *Envergure:* nationale
Membre(s) du bureau directeur:
François Coté, Secrétaire général
f.cote@radiorfa.com

Alliance du personnel professionel et administratif de Ville de Laval (APPAVL)
Tél: 450-629-0453; *Téléc:* 450-629-9307
appavl@qc.aira.com
www.appavl.ca
Aperçu: *Dimension:* petite; *Envergure:* locale; fondée en 2005
Membre: *Critères d'admissibilite:* Personnel professionnel ou administratif travaillant en Laval
Membre(s) du bureau directeur:
Philippe Dutin, Président Ext. 5127
Nathalie Sampaio, 1re Vice-Président Ext. 6256
Mireille Fournier, 2e Vice-Président Ext. 8793

Alliance du personnel professionnel et technique de la santé et des services sociaux (APTS)
#1050, 1111, rue Saint-Charles ouest, Longueuil QC J4K 5G4
Tél: 450-670-2411; *Téléc:* 450-679-0107
Ligne sans frais: 866-521-2411
info@aptsq.com
www.aptsq.com
www.facebook.com/SyndicatAPTS
twitter.com/APTSQ
Nom précédent: Centrale des professionnelles et professionnels de la santé
Aperçu: *Dimension:* grande; *Envergure:* provinciale; Organisme sans but lucratif; fondée en 2004
Mission: Regrouper les organisations syndicales représentant toutes les catégories des personnes salariées professionnelles ou paramédicales travaillant dans le domaine de la santé; défendre, promouvoir et sauvegarder les intérêts collectifs des membres
Membre: 31 000; *Critères d'admissibilite:* Personnel professionnel et technique du réseau québécois de la santé.; *Comités:* Action féministe; Action sociopolitique; Santé et sécurité du travail - Développement durable; Sécurité sociale
Membre(s) du bureau directeur:
Carolle Dubé, Présidente

Alliance évangélique du Canada *See* Evangelical Fellowship of Canada

Alliance féministe pour l'action internationale *See* Feminist Alliance for International Action

Alliance for Audited Media
Canadian Member Service Office, #850, 151 Bloor St. West, Toronto ON M5S 1S4
Tel: 416-962-5840; *Fax:* 416-962-5844
www.accessabc.com
www.linkedin.com/groups?about=&gid=2975919
www.facebook.com/auditedmedia
twitter.com/auditedmedia
www.youtube.com/auditedmedia
Previous Name: Audit Bureau of Circulations
Overview: A medium-sized national organization founded in 1914
Mission: To be the pre-eminent self-regulatory auditing organization, responsible to advertisers, advertising agencies, & the media they use, for the verification & dissemination of members' circulation data & other information for the benefit of the advertising marketplace in the United States & Canada
Membership: *Committees:* Newspaper Buyers' Advisory; NAA/AAM Liaison; NAA/AAM Circulation; Magazine Buyers' Advisory; Magazine Directors' Advisory; Business Publication Buyers' Advisory; Business Publication Industry; Digital Advisory
Activities: *Library:* by appointment
Chief Officer(s):
Michael J. Lavery, President & Managing Director

Alliance for Canadian New Music Projects (ACNMP) / Alliance pour des projets de musique canadienne nouvelle
20 St. Joseph St., Toronto ON M4Y 1J9
Tel: 416-963-5937; *Fax:* 416-961-7198
info@acnmp.ca
www.acnmp.ca
Also Known As: Contemporary Showcase
Overview: A medium-sized national charitable organization founded in 1978
Mission: To provide young musicians with an opportunity to celebrate & enjoy the music of their own time & country through the organization's syllabus & its festival, Contemporary Showcase
Finances: *Funding Sources:* Donations; Foundations; Government
Membership: *Fees:* $25
Activities: Contemporary Showcase Centres across Canada; *Library:* by appointment
Chief Officer(s):
Elizabeth Groskorth, General Manager

Contemporary Showcase - Calgary
37 Hollyburn Rd. SW, Calgary AB T2V 3H2
Tel: 403-454-8859
Chief Officer(s):
Katrina Thompson Frost, Contact
kthompson11@hotmail.com

Contemporary Showcase - Chatham
34 Gladstone Ave., Chatham ON N7L 2C1
Tel: 519-436-0775
Chief Officer(s):
Alice Van Stempvoort, Contact
vanstemp@gmail.com

Contemporary Showcase - East Central Alberta
PO Box 295, Castor AB T0C 0X0
Tel: 403-882-4545
Chief Officer(s):
Doreen Renschler, Contact
drrenschler@gmail.com

Contemporary Showcase - Edmonton
10 Spruce Cres., St. Albert AB T8N 0H4
Tel: 780-489-4191
Chief Officer(s):
Marlaine Osgood, Coordinator
jamesosgoode@interbaun.com

Contemporary Showcase - London
#29, 70 Chapman Ct., London ON N6G 4Z4
Tel: 519-472-1402
Chief Officer(s):
Grace Yip, Coordinator
graceyip49@hotmail.com

Contemporary Showcase - Mississauga
3132 Folkway Dr., Mississauga ON L5L 2A2
Tel: 905-820-8529; *Fax:* 905-820-2960
Chief Officer(s):
Jill Kelman, Coordinator
jillkl@eol.ca

Contemporary Showcase - North Bay
North Bay ON
Tel: 705-476-0776
Chief Officer(s):
Beth Chartrand, Contact
bemachartrand@hotmail.com

Contemporary Showcase - Ottawa/Carleton
89 Switch Grass Cres., Nepean ON K2J 5Z3
Tel: 613-447-2618
Chief Officer(s):
Tania Granata, Coordinator
taniag5@sympatico.ca

Contemporary Showcase - Parry Sound
2 Brenda Ave., Parry Sound ON P2A 2Z3
Tel: 705-773-2049
Chief Officer(s):
Judy Freeman, Coordinator
tojudyfreeman@yahoo.ca

Contemporary Showcase - Red Deer
3204 - 57th Ave., Red Deer AB T4N 5V4
Tel: 403-588-3258

Contemporary Showcase - Regina
4166 Elphinstone St., Regina SK S4S 3L2
Tel: 306-584-1274
Chief Officer(s):
Corinne Goff, Coordinator
musiclessons@sasktel.net

Contemporary Showcase - St. John/Kennebecasis Valley
1 Earles' Crt., Quispamsis NB E2E 1C3
Tel: 506-849-3917
Chief Officer(s):

Rita Raymond-Millett, Coordinator
jrmilray@nb.sympatico.ca
Contemporary Showcase - Saskatoon
Saskatoon SK
Tel: 306-934-4566
Chief Officer(s):
Bernadette Fanner, Contact

Contemporary Showcase - Toronto
395 Kingswood Rd., Toronto ON M4E 3P2
Tel: 416-694-4205
Chief Officer(s):
Wendy Potter, Coordinator
potterwa@lycos.com
Janet Fothergill, Contact, 416-481-8802
janetlfothergill@gmail.com

Contemporary Showcase - West Central Saskatchewan
PO Box 727, Biggar SK S0K 0M0
Tel: 306-948-5231
Chief Officer(s):
Peggy L'Hoir, Contact
rplhoir@sasktel.net

Alliance for Chiropractic (AFC)
#126, 17A - 218 Silvercreek Pkwy. North, Guelph ON N1H 8E8
Tel: 519-822-1879; *Fax:* 519-822-1239
Toll-Free: 877-997-9927
www.allianceforchiropractic.com
Previous Name: Chiropractic Awareness Council
Overview: A small national organization founded in 1998
Mission: To promote public awareness of chiropractic life principles by promoting an awareness of the devastating effects of vertebral subluxation complex on the expression of human health potential; To educate the public with the conviction that chiropractic care is an integral aspect of health for people of all ages & to society in general
Member of: Chiropractic Coalition
Finances: *Annual Operating Budget:* $100,000-$250,000; *Funding Sources:* Membership fees
Staff Member(s): 1; 8 volunteer(s)
Membership: 350; *Fees:* $295; *Member Profile:* Chiropractors, staff, students, corporations; *Committees:* CCO; Convention; Public Awareness; Student Affairs
Activities: *Speaker Service:* Yes
Chief Officer(s):
Craig Hazel, Chair

Alliance for Equality of Blind Canadians / Alliance pour l'Égalité des Personnes Aveugles du Canada
PO Box 20262, Stn. RPO Town Centre, Kelowna BC V1Y 9H2
Toll-Free: 800-561-4774
www.blindcanadians.ca
twitter.com/blindcanadians
Previous Name: National Federation of the Blind: Advocates for Equality
Overview: A medium-sized national charitable organization
Mission: To promote the inclusion of blind, deaf-blind & partially-sighted Canadians in all aspects of social life, from employment to participation in elections
Membership: *Fees:* $5 Annual, $50 Lifetime; *Committees:* Accessibility in Procurement; CRTC; Education and Employment; Library; Point of Sale Devices and Household Products; Strategic Planning; Town Hall; Web Accessibility
Chief Officer(s):
Dar Wournell, President

Alliance for South Asian AIDS Prevention (ASAAP)
#315, 120 Carlton st., Toronto ON M5A 4K3
Tel: 416-599-2727; *Fax:* 416-599-6011
info@asaap.ca
www.asaap.ca
www.facebook.com/asaaptoronto
twitter.com/ASAAP
www.youtube.com/user/ASAAPTV
Overview: A small local charitable organization founded in 1989 overseen by Canadian AIDS Society
Mission: To prevent the spread of HIV & to promote the health of South Asians infected with & affected by HIV/AIDS.
Member of: Ontario AIDS Network; Council of Agencies Serving South Asians; Interagency Coalition on AIDS & Development
Finances: *Funding Sources:* Federal & provincial government; City of Toronto: Community Partners of ACT
Staff Member(s): 13
Membership: *Committees:* Board Development & Recruitment; Fund Development; Policies and Bylaw
Activities: HIV/AIDS education & prevention to South Asians; PHA support services; work with other South Asian & AIDS service organizations; information & referral services; materials in South Asian languages; *Library:* ASAAP Resource Centre; Open to public
Chief Officer(s):
Rupal Shah, Chair
Vihaya Chikermane, Executive Director
ed@asaap.ca

Alliance Française (AF)
352 rue MacLaren, Ottawa ON K2P 0M6
Tél: 613-234-9470; *Téléc:* 613-233-1559
www.af.ca
Aperçu: *Dimension:* moyenne; *Envergure:* nationale; Organisme sans but lucratif; fondée en 1903
Mission: Promotion de la langue et de la culture française
Affiliation(s): Alliance Française réseau international
Membre: 9 alliances
Activités: Enseignement du français; Activités culturelles et sociales; *Bibliothèque:* rendez-vous
Membre(s) du bureau directeur:
Komlanvi Dodjro, Responsable des communications, com@af.ca, 613-234-9470 Ext. 226

Alliance Française d'Edmonton
Maison de la France, 10424, 123 rue Nord Ouest, Edmonton AB T5N 1N7
Tél: 780-469-0399; *Téléc:* 780-488-0396
info@afedmonton.ca
www.af.ca/edmonton
www.facebook.com/145880992114853
twitter.com/afedmonton
Aperçu: *Dimension:* petite; *Envergure:* locale; fondée en 1947
Mission: Promouvoir la langue et la culture française
Affiliation(s): Alliance Française réseau international
Membre(s) du personnel: 11
Membre: *Montant de la cotisation:* 35$ individu; 50$ famille; 100$ organisation; *Critères d'admissibilité:* Francophone et allophone désireux d'entretenir la culture et de la langue française
Activités: culturelles variées et École de langue française
Membre(s) du bureau directeur:
Todd Babiak, Président
Anthony Bertrand, Directeur général

Alliance Française d'Ottawa
340, rue MacLaren, Ottawa ON K2P 0M6
Tél: 613-234-9470; *Téléc:* 613-233-1559
info@af.ca
www.af.ca/ottawa
www.facebook.com/AFOttawa
Aperçu: *Dimension:* petite; *Envergure:* locale; Organisme sans but lucratif; fondée en 1905
Mission: Propagation de la langue et de la culture française; dialogue des cultures; formation
Affiliation(s): Alliance Française réseau international
Activités: Cours de français et activités culturelles; *Bibliothèque:* Centre de ressources; Bibliothèque publique rendez-vous
Membre(s) du bureau directeur:
Michel Tremblay, Président
Julie Desbien, Directrice des cours, 613-234-9470 Ext. 224
french@af.ca

Alliance Française de Calgary (AFC)
#350, 1721 - 29e av sud, Calgary AB T2T 6T7
Tél: 403-245-5662
info@afcalgary.ca
www.afcalgary.ca
www.facebook.com/AllianceFrancaiseCalgary
twitter.com/AFCalgary
Également appelé: École de langue et centre culturel français
Aperçu: *Dimension:* petite; *Envergure:* locale; Organisme sans but lucratif; fondée en 1947 surveillé par Alliance Française
Mission: Promotion de la langue et de la culture française
Membre de: Alliance Française réseau international
Membre(s) du personnel: 22; 50 bénévole(s)
Membre: *Montant de la cotisation:* Barème
Activités: Cours de langue; Ateliers; Centre culturel; Événements culturels; Ccentre de ressources
Membre(s) du bureau directeur:
Jean-Baptiste Roux, Directrice, 403-245-5662
director@afcalgary.ca
Hélène Girardot, Coordinator, Culture & Communications, 403-245-5662
communication@afcalgary.ca
Lyne Laquerre, Office Manager, 403-245-5662
admin@afcalgary.ca
Julie Pouderoux, Courses Coordinator, 403-245-5662
courses@afcalgary.ca

Alliance Française de Winnipeg *Voir* Alliance Française du Manitoba

Alliance Française du Manitoba
934, av Corydon, Winnipeg MB R3M 0Y5
Tél: 204-477-1515
info@afmanitoba.ca
www.afmanitoba.ca
www.facebook.com/AFManitoba
twitter.com/AFManitoba
Nom précédent: Alliance Française de Winnipeg
Aperçu: *Dimension:* petite; *Envergure:* locale; Organisme sans but lucratif; fondée en 1915
Mission: Promouvoir la langue et la culture française; oeuvrer au rapprochement et à l'amitié des peuples français et canadiens
Affiliation(s): Alliance Française réseau international
Finances: *Fonds:* Gouvernement provincial et national
Membre(s) du personnel: 10
Membre: *Critères d'admissibilité:* Étudiant anglophone, francophone non-étudiant
Activités: Conférences; Théâtre; Musique; Danse; Promotion des auteurs français; Arts visuels; *Bibliothèque:* Bibliothèque publique rendez-vous
Membre(s) du bureau directeur:
Agnès Champagne, Présidente
Alan Nobili, Directeur général
direction@afmanitoba.ca

Alliance Française Halifax (AFH)
5509, rue Young, Halifax NS B3K 1Z7
Tél: 902-455-4411; *Téléc:* 902-455-4149
info@afhalifax.ca
www.afhalifax.ca
www.facebook.com/AF.Halifax
twitter.com/AFHalifax
Aperçu: *Dimension:* petite; *Envergure:* locale; Organisme sans but lucratif; fondée en 1903
Mission: Promotion de la langue et de la culture française
Affiliation(s): Alliance Française réseau international; Fédération des alliances françaises du Canada
Membre(s) du personnel: 14
Activités: Enseignement du français; activités culturelles et sociales; *Bibliothèque:* rendez-vous
Membre(s) du bureau directeur:
Diane Kenny, Présidente
Isabelle Pédot, Directrice générale

Alliance internationale des employé(e)s de scène, de théâtre et de cinéma (AIESTC) / International Alliance of Theatrical Stage Employees, Moving Picture Technicians, Artists & Allied Crafts of the U.S. (IATSE)
#160, 1945, rue Mullin, Montréal QC H3K 1N9
Tél: 514-937-6855; *Téléc:* 514-272-5163
Ligne sans frais: 866-331-4095
admin@iatselocal262.com
www.iatselocal262.com
www.facebook.com/iatselocal262
Nom précédent: Alliance internationale des opérateurs de machines à vues
Aperçu: *Dimension:* petite; *Envergure:* internationale; fondée en 1912
Mission: Représentation des travailleurs/travailleuses sur les lieux de travail afin de faire respecter leurs droits par l'application de leur convention collective
Membre de: Montréal FTQ Labour Council
Affiliation(s): Fédération des travailleurs et travailleuses du Québec
Finances: *Budget de fonctionnement annuel:* $250,000-$500,000; *Fonds:* Union dues
Membre(s) du personnel: 3; 51 bénévole(s)
Membre: 850
Membre(s) du bureau directeur:
Sylvain Bisaillon, Président/Administrateur, 514-814-0750
s.bisaillon@iatselocal262.com
Stéphane Ross, Business Agent, 514-814-4694
s.ross@iatselocal262.com

Alliance internationale des opérateurs de machines à vues *Voir* Alliance internationale des employé(e)s de scène, de théâtre et de cinéma

Alliance Médias Jeunesse *See* Youth Media Alliance

Canadian Associations / Alliance numérique

Alliance nationale pour l'enfance et la jeunesse *See* National Alliance for Children & Youth

Alliance numérique
380, rue Saint-Antoine ouest, 8e étage, Montréal QC H2Y 3X7
Tél: 514-987-9340
www.alliancenumerique.com
www.linkedin.com/company/alliance-numerique
www.facebook.com/alliancenumerique
twitter.com/anumerique
Également appelé: Réseau de l'industrie numérique du Québec
Aperçu: *Dimension:* moyenne; *Envergure:* provinciale
Mission: Vise à soutenir et à accélérer la croissance et la compétitivité de son industrie dans le respect de tous ses intervenants
Membre: 100+
Membre(s) du bureau directeur:
Catherine Émond, Directrice générale

Alliance of Canadian Cinema, Television & Radio Artists (ACTRA) / Alliance des artistes canadiens du cinéma, de la télévision et de la radio
625 Church St., 3rd Fl., Toronto ON M4Y 2G1
Tel: 416-489-1311; *Fax:* 416-489-8076
Toll-Free: 800-387-3516
Other Communication: media@actra.ca
national@actra.ca
www.actra.ca
www.facebook.com/ACTRANational
twitter.com/ACTRAnat
www.youtube.com/user/ACTRANational
Previous Name: Association of Canadian Television & Radio Artists
Overview: A large national organization founded in 1943
Mission: To represent performers in recorded media; To negotiate & administer collective agreements which set minimum rates & basic conditions governing work; To advocate public policies designed to create strong Canadian broadcasting & film industries in order to provide work opportunities for members in their own country
Member of: Canadian Conference of the Arts; Fédération internationale d'acteurs
Affiliation(s): Canadian Labour Congress
Finances: *Annual Operating Budget:* $3 Million-$5 Million
Staff Member(s): 110
Membership: 23,000; *Fees:* Schedule available; *Member Profile:* Performers; full - performer with 6 professional engagements in ACTRA's jurisdiction; alternatively, a performer may apply on basis of professional reputation, or may qualify as a member of a guild associated with ACTRA as a member of Canadian Actors' Equity Association or as member of Screen Actors Guild or AFTRA; *Committees:* Communications; Constitution & Bylaws; Disipline; Diversity; Finance; Stunt Performers; Women's
Activities: ACTRA Performers' Rights Society; Face to Face Online, ACTRA's online talent catalog
Chief Officer(s):
Stephen Waddell, National Executive Director
Daintry Dalton, Regional Executive Director
Elliott Anderson, Director, Public Policy & Communications
Cathia Badiere, Director, Research
Anna Bucci, Director, Finance & Administration
Manny Kandola, Director, Information Services
Awards:
• ACTRA's John Drainie Award
Presented to a performer who has made a distinguished contribution to Canadian broadcasting.
Publications:
• ACTRA [a publication of the Alliance of Canadian Cinema, Television & Radio Artists]
Type: Magazine; *Frequency:* Quarterly

ACTRA Alberta
#602, 7015 MacLeod Trail SW, Calgary AB T2H 2K6
Tel: 403-228-3123; *Fax:* 403-228-3299
Toll-Free: 866-913-3123
alberta@actra.ca
www.actraalberta.com
Chief Officer(s):
Duval Lang, President
dlang@actraalberta.com

ACTRA BC Branch - Union of B.C. Performers
#400, 1155 West Pender St., Vancouver BC V6E 2P4
Tel: 604-689-0727; *Fax:* 604-689-1145
Toll-Free: 866-689-0727
info@ubcp.com
www.ubcp.com
www.facebook.com/UBCP.ACTRA
twitter.com/UBCP_ACTRA
Chief Officer(s):
Alvin Sanders, President
alvin.sanders@ubcp.com

ACTRA Manitoba
#203, 245 McDermot Ave., Winnipeg MB R3B 0S6
Tel: 204-339-9750; *Fax:* 204-947-5664
manitoba@actra.ca
actramanitoba.ca
Chief Officer(s):
Talia Pura, President

ACTRA Maritimes
#103, 1660 Hollis St., Halifax NS B3J 1V7
Tel: 902-420-1404; *Fax:* 902-422-0589
Toll-Free: 877-272-2872
maritimes@actra.ca
www.actramaritimes.ca
Chief Officer(s):
Jamie Bradley, President
jbradley@actramaritimes.ca

ACTRA Montréal
#530, 1450, rue City Councillors, Montréal QC H3A 2E6
Tel: 514-844-3318; *Fax:* 514-844-2068
montreal@actra.ca
www.actramontreal.ca
Chief Officer(s):
Don Jordan, President
djordan@actra.ca

ACTRA Newfoundland
#202, 245 Duckworth St., St. John's NL A1C 1G8
Tel: 709-722-0430; *Fax:* 709-722-2113
newfoundland@actra.ca
www.actranewfoundland.ca
Chief Officer(s):
Amy House, President

ACTRA Ottawa
The Arts Court, #170, 2 Daly Ave., Ottawa ON K1N 6E2
Tel: 613-565-2168; *Fax:* 613-565-4367
ottawa@actra.ca
www.actraottawa.ca
Chief Officer(s):
Sally Clelford, President

ACTRA Saskatchewan
#212, 1808 Smith St., Regina SK S4P 2N4
Tel: 306-757-0885; *Fax:* 306-359-0044
Toll-Free: 800-615-5041
saskatchewan@actra.ca
www.actrasask.com
Chief Officer(s):
Alan Bratt, President

ACTRA Toronto
625 Church St., 1st Fl., Toronto ON M4Y 2G1
Tel: 416-928-2278; *Fax:* 416-928-2852
Toll-Free: 877-913-2278
info@actratoronto.com
www.actratoronto.com
www.facebook.com/ACTRAToronto
twitter.com/ACTRAToronto
www.youtube.com/user/ACTRAToronto
Chief Officer(s):
Karen Ritson, Director of Finance and Administration, 416-642-6722

Alliance of Cancer Consultants
#206, 2571 Shaughnessy St., Port Coquitlam BC V3C 3G3
Previous Name: International Alliance of Breast Cancer Organizations
Overview: A small local organization
Chief Officer(s):
Tadeusz Slubowski, Director

Alliance of Credential Evaluation Services of Canada (ACESC) / Alliance canadienne des services d'évaluation de diplômes (ACSED)
c/o The Canadian Information Centre for International Credentials, #1106, St. Clair Ave. West, Toronto ON M4V 1N6
Tel: 416-962-9725; *Fax:* 416-962-2800
www.canalliance.org
Overview: A small national organization
Mission: To offer standardized assessment of foreign credentials for education, employment, & professional membership
Finances: *Funding Sources:* Human Resources & Skills Development Canada; Citizenship & Immigration Canada; Canadian Heritage
Membership: *Member Profile:* Public or private credential assessment services from across Canada that comply with & maintain standards
Activities: Recommending & implementing policies & standards to develop & maintain quality assurance; Raising awareness of the Alliance
Chief Officer(s):
Yves E. Beaudin, National Coordinator, Canadian Information Centre for International Credentials, 416-962-8100 Ext. 242

Alliance of Manufacturers & Exporters Canada *See* Canadian Manufacturers & Exporters

Alliance pour des projets de musique canadienne nouvelle *See* Alliance for Canadian New Music Projects

Alliance pour l'Égalité des Personnes Aveugles du Canada *See* Alliance for Equality of Blind Canadians

Alliance québécoise des techniciens de l'image et du son (AQTIS)
#300, 533, rue Ontario est, Montréal QC H2L 1N8
Tél: 514-844-2113; *Téléc:* 514-844-3540
Ligne sans frais: 888-647-0681
info@aqtis.qc.ca
www.aqtis.qc.ca
Aperçu: *Dimension:* moyenne; *Envergure:* provinciale
Membre(s) du bureau directeur:
Bernard Arseneau, Président
barseneau@aqtis.qc.ca
Jean-Claude Rocheleau, Directeur général
jcrocheleau@aqtis.qc.ca

Alliance Québécoise du Psoriasis / Quebec Psoriasis Alliance
#200, 5700, rue J.-B.-Michaud, Lévis QC G6V 0B1
Tel: 418-838-9779
info@psoriasisquebec.org
www.facebook.com/211449008933190
twitter.com/psoriasisquebec
www.youtube.com/PsoriasisQuebec
Overview: A small provincial organization founded in 2008
Mission: Pour représenter les patients atteints de psoriasis et de sensibiliser le public sur le psoriasis
Membership: *Fees:* Gratuit; *Member Profile:* Patients atteints de psoriasis et de leurs familles, les professionnels de soins de santé; tous ceux qui veulent soutenir la cause

Allied Arts Council of Spruce Grove
Melcor Cultural Centre, 35 - 5th Ave., Spruce Grove AB T7X 2C5
Tel: 780-962-0664
alliedac@shaw.ca
www.alliedartscouncil.com
www.facebook.com/193509347393424
Overview: A small local charitable organization founded in 1980
Mission: To encourage, foster & sponsor cultural activites in the region
Affiliation(s): Visual Arts Alberta Association
Finances: *Funding Sources:* Art sales & classes; city grant; Alberta Foundation for the Arts
Membership: *Fees:* $40; *Member Profile:* Artist or arts supporter
Activities: Art classes; *Awareness Events:* Open Art Competition, 3rd week in Aug.; *Speaker Service:* Yes
Chief Officer(s):
Bonnie Halliday, President

Allied Beauty Association (ABA)
#26-27, 145 Traders Blvd. East, Mississauga ON L4Z 3L3
Tel: 905-568-0158; *Fax:* 905-568-1581
abashows@abacanada.com
www.abacanada.com
www.facebook.com/ABACanada
twitter.com/abacanada
www.youtube.com/user/TheABACanada
Overview: A small national organization founded in 1934
Mission: To encourage & create a greater understanding & knowledge of the professional beauty industry to the salons, the public, the federal & provincial governments, & to members
Finances: *Annual Operating Budget:* $500,000-$1.5 Million; *Funding Sources:* Trade shows; membership dues
Staff Member(s): 4
Membership: 265; *Fees:* $700
Activities: *Speaker Service:* Yes; *Rents Mailing List:* Yes

Chief Officer(s):
Marc Speir, Executive Director
Meetings/Conferences:
• Allied Beauty Association Trade Show - Montréal 2018, March, 2018, Montréal, QC
Scope: National
Description: A trade show for beauty professionals to learn about new happenings in the beauty industry
• Allied Beauty Association Trade Show - Toronto 2018, March, 2018, Metro Toronto Convention Centre, Toronto, ON
Scope: National
Description: A trade show for beauty professionals to learn about new happenings in the beauty industry
• Allied Beauty Association 2018 Annual General Meeting, 2018
Scope: National

Alliston & District Chamber of Commerce
PO Box 32, 60B Victoria St. West, Alliston ON L9R 1T9
Tel: 705-435-7921; *Fax:* 705-435-0289
www.adcc.ca
www.facebook.com/allistonchamber
twitter.com/allistonchamber
www.youtube.com/user/AllistonChamber
Overview: A medium-sized local organization founded in 1981
Member of: Ontario Chamber of Commerce
Membership: 200; *Fees:* Schedule available
Chief Officer(s):
Crystal Kellard, Executive Director

Allstate Foundation of Canada
#100, 27 Allstate Pkwy., Markham ON L3R 5P8
Tel: 905-477-6900; *Fax:* 905-513-4018
foundation@allstate.ca
www.allstate.ca
Overview: A small national charitable organization founded in 1977
Awards:
• Allstate Foundation Grant
Eligibility: Registered not-for-profit charities that require funding for educational initiatives in crime prevention, road safety, or home safety, as well as projects or funds

Almaguin-Nipissing Travel Association
PO Box 351, Stn. Regional Information Centre, North Bay ON P1B 8H5
Tel: 705-474-6634
Toll-Free: 800-387-0516
Also Known As: Ontario's Near North
Overview: A medium-sized local organization founded in 1974
Mission: To market Ontario's Near North as a four-seasons family-oriented outdoor vacation destination on behalf of the organized tourist industry
Member of: Tourism Industry Association of Canada
Activities: *Library:* Photo; Open to public

Almas Jiwani Foundation
#502, 331 Cooper St., Ottawa ON K2P 0G5
Tel: 613-234-8252
info@almasjiwanifoundation.org
www.almasjiwanifoundation.org
www.facebook.com/AlmasJiwaniFoundation
twitter.com/AlmasJiwaniFdn
Overview: A medium-sized international charitable organization
Mission: To empower & improve the status of women & girls; To eliminate inequality by identifying & addressing disparities in the areas of education, entrepreneurship, equality, entertainment, & energy rights; To develop projects that provide gender conscious solutions for marginalized communities; To serve as a platform for discourse & action on major global issues; To improve societal & economic conditions in developing countries
Finances: *Funding Sources:* Donations
Membership: *Fees:* $25 student; $50 individual; $1,000 corporate; *Committees:* International Executive
Activities: Projects designed to provide sustainable energy, gender equality, better education, & improved living conditions to communities in need
Chief Officer(s):
Almas Jiwani, President & CEO
Myriam Amato, Vice-President, Outreach & Philanthropy
Jason Dupuis, Vice-President, Communications & Philanthropy
Naline Rampersad, Vice-President, Public Relations
Kevin West, Vice-President, International Operations
kwest@almasjiwanifoundation.org
Michelle Young, Vice-President, Communications

Almonte & District Arts Council *See* Almonte in Concert

Almonte in Concert
PO Box 1199, 14 Bridge St., Almonte ON K0A 1A0
Tel: 613-253-3353
info@almonteinconcert.com
www.almonteinconcert.com
www.facebook.com/AlmonteinConcert
Previous Name: Almonte & District Arts Council
Overview: A small local organization
Membership: *Fees:* $10-$500
Chief Officer(s):
Maureen Nevins, Artistic Director

Almost Home
PO Box 2204, 118 William St., Kingston ON K7L 5J9
Tel: 613-548-8255; *Fax:* 613-547-6948
www.almosthome.on.ca
Overview: A small local charitable organization
Mission: To provide a place where families of children hospitalized in Kingston can stay while their child is in the hospital
Finances: *Funding Sources:* Donations
Chief Officer(s):
Laurie Morgan, Executive Director
LaurieM@almosthome.on.ca

Alouette Field Naturalists (AFN)
12554 Grace St., Maple Ridge BC V2X 5N2
Tel: 604-463-8743
www.facebook.com/337236449737753
Overview: A small local organization founded in 1973
Mission: To promote the enjoyment of nature through environmental appreciation & conservation; To encourage wise use & conservation of natural resources & environmental protection
Member of: Federation of BC Naturalists
Membership: 30-35; *Fees:* $22 individual; $32 family; *Committees:* Pitt Polder Preservation Society; Blue Mountain-Kanata Creek Conservation Committee
Activities: Rivers Day, Nature Day, with displays; hiking, camping, birding, botanizing, mycologizing; *Awareness Events:* Earth Day, April; Annual Christmas Bird Count, December
Chief Officer(s):
Joan Domer, Contact, 604-460-6415
jdomer@shaw.ca

Alpaca Livestock Producers & Cooperators Association (ALPACA)
PO Box 78098, Stn. Callingwood, Edmonton AB T5T 6A1
info@alpaca.ca
www.alpaca.ca
Overview: A small national organization
Mission: To create an environment for small &/or large producers with equal opportunities in today's ever changing market; To create & to maintain a central comprehensive database on Alpacas & Alpaca related industries; To provide members with easy access to the database information resulting in an efficient network of cooperative Alpaca producers, buyers & related businesses; To promote the importance of a strong & united society as it relates to information gathering, information access, national & international affairs concerning purity, integrity & the financial security of the Canadian Alpaca industry
Membership: *Fees:* $74

Alphabétisation mondiale Canada *See* World Literacy of Canada

Alpine Canada Alpin
Canada Olympic Park, #302, 151 Canada Olympic Rd. SW, Calgary AB T3B 6B7
Tel: 403-777-3200; *Fax:* 403-777-3213
info@alpinecanada.org
alpinecanada.org
www.facebook.com/AlpineCanada
twitter.com/Alpine_Canada
www.youtube.com/user/AlpineCanadaAlpin;
instagram.com/alpinecanada
Overview: A medium-sized national organization
Mission: The ACA is the governing body for ski racing in Canada. Founded in 1920 & accounting for close to 200,000 supporting members, ACA represents coaches, officials, supporters & athletes, including elite racers of the Canadian Alpine Ski Team & the Canadian Disabled Alpine Ski Team.
Chief Officer(s):
Mark Rubinstein, President & CEO, 403-777-4246
mrubinstein@alpinecanada.org
Nicholas Bass, Chief Operating Officer, 403-777-3218
nbass@alpinecanada.org
Linsey Ferguson, Vice-President, Partnerships, 416-967-9339
lferguson@alpinecanada.org

Alpine Club of Canada (ACC) / Club alpin du Canada (CAC)
PO Box 8040, Stn. Main, 201 Indian Flats Rd., Canmore AB T1W 2T8
Tel: 403-678-3200; *Fax:* 403-678-3224
info@alpineclubofcanada.ca
www.alpineclubofcanada.ca
www.facebook.com/alpineclubofcanada
twitter.com/alpineclubcan
Overview: A large national charitable organization founded in 1906
Mission: To encourage & promote mountaineering & mountain crafts; To educate Canadians in the appreciation of mountain heritage; To explore alpine & glacial regions primarily in Canada; To preserve the natural beauty of mountains & their fauna & flora; To promote mountain art & literature; To disseminate scientific & educational knowledge concerning mountains & mountaineering through meetings & publications; To conduct summer & ski mountaineering camps
Affiliation(s): International Union of Alpinist Associations
Finances: *Funding Sources:* Donations; Grants; Corporate
Staff Member(s): 11
Membership: *Fees:* $38 individual; $58 family; $26 youth
Activities: Providing financial support necessary to advocate protection & preservation of mountain & climbing environments; Enhancing constitutional objective of ACC to work towards preservation of alpine environment & flora & fauna in their natural habitat; *Library:* Open to public
Chief Officer(s):
Lawrence White, Executive Director
lwhite@alpineclubofcanada.ca
Chris Petrauskas, Director, Programs
cpetrauskas@alpineclubofcanada.ca
Kish Stephenson, Director, Finance
kstephenson@alpineclubofcanada.ca

Alpine Garden Club of BC
43212 Honeysuckle Dr., Chilliwack BC V2R 4A4
Tel: 604-580-3219
info@agc-bc.ca
www.agc-bc.ca
Overview: A small local organization
Mission: To promote the propagation & display of plants suitable for the alpine garden & alpine house, rare & unusual species of hardy plants, trees, shrubs & ferns, plants suitable for the art of bonsai; to promote an interest in the native plants of British Columbia & their preservation
Member of: North American Rock Garden Society
Membership: 500; *Fees:* $30
Activities: Seed exchange; open gardens; field trips; plants sales; *Library:* Not open to public
Chief Officer(s):
Linda Verbeek, President, 604-526-6656
Publications:
• The Bulletin
Type: Newsletter; *Frequency:* Quarterly

Alpine Ontario Alpin (AOA)
#10, 191 Hurontario St., Collingwood ON L9Y 2M1
Tel: 705-444-5111; *Fax:* 705-444-5116
admin@alpineontario.ca
www.alpineontario.ca
Overview: A medium-sized provincial organization
Mission: To provide skiing opportunities for competitive & recreational athletes
Staff Member(s): 5
Membership: 30,000+ in 44 clubs; *Fees:* Schedule available
Chief Officer(s):
Scott Barrett, Acting Executive Director
sbarrett@alpineontario.ca

Alpine Saskatchewan
1860 Lorne St., Regina SK S4P 2L7
Tel: 306-780-9236; *Fax:* 306-780-9462
office@saskalpine.com
www.saskalpine1.com
www.instagram.com/saskalpine
Also Known As: Sask Alpine
Overview: A small provincial organization
Mission: To be the provincial governing body for noncompetitive & competitive alpine skiing in Saskatchewan
Affiliation(s): BC Alpine; Alberta Alpine; Manitoba Alpine; Alpine Canada; Alpine Canada-Live Timing; National Points; Snow Stars

Canadian Associations / ALS Society of Alberta

Chief Officer(s):
Karen Musgrave, President
president@saskalpine.com
Alana Ottenbreit, Office Manager

ALS Society of Alberta
#250, 4723 - 1 St. SW, Calgary AB T2G 4Y8
Tel: 403-228-3857; *Fax:* 403-228-7752
Toll-Free: 888-309-1111
info@alsab.ca
www.alsab.ca
www.facebook.com/ALSALBERTA
twitter.com/ALS_AB
Overview: A small provincial charitable organization overseen by ALS Society of Canada
Staff Member(s): 12
Chief Officer(s):
Karen Caughey, Executive Director, 403-228-3857 Ext. 103

Edmonton Chapter
5418 - 97 St. NW, Edmonton AB T6E 5C1
Tel: 780-487-0754; *Fax:* 780-486-3604
Toll-Free: 866-447-0754
societynorth@alsab.ca
Chief Officer(s):
Sarah Quinton, Coordinator, Administration & Volunteer Services

ALS Society of British Columbia
1233-133351 Commerce Pkwy., Richmond BC V6V 2X7
Tel: 604-278-2257; *Fax:* 604-278-4257
Toll-Free: 800-708-3228
info@alsbc.ca
www.alsbc.ca
www.facebook.com/ALSBC
twitter.com/ALS_BC
Overview: A medium-sized provincial charitable organization overseen by ALS Society Of Canada
Mission: The ALS Society of BC is dedicated to providing direct support to ALS patients, along with their families and caregivers
Activities: *Awareness Events:* Annual ALS Memorial Golf Tournament, June; Peoples Drug Mart Walks for ALS, January; Cycle of Hope
Chief Officer(s):
Wendy Toyer, Executive Director, 604-278-2257 Ext. 222
w.toyer@alsbc.ca

North Central Island Chapter
1233 - 13351 Commerce Parkway, Richmond BC V6V 2X7
ncic@alsbc.ca
Chief Officer(s):
Sheldon Cleaves, President, 250-748-8072

Victoria Chapter
PO Box 48038, 3511 Blanshard St., Victoria BC V8Z 7H5
victoria@alsbc.ca
Chief Officer(s):
Joyanne Plewes, President

ALS Society of Canada (ALS) / La Société canadienne de la SLA (SLA)
#200, 3000 Steeles Ave. East, Markham ON L3R 4T9
Tel: 905-248-2052; *Fax:* 905-248-2019
Toll-Free: 800-267-4257
www.als.ca
www.linkedin.com/company/als-society-of-canada
www.facebook.com/ALSCanada1
twitter.com/alscanada
Also Known As: Amyotrophic Lateral Sclerosis Society of Canada
Overview: A large national charitable organization founded in 1977
Mission: To support research towards a cure for ALS; To support ALS partners in their provision of quality care for persons affected by ALS
Member of: Canadian Society of Gift Planners; National Society of Fundraising Executives; International Alliance of ALS/MND Associations; Canadian Centre for Philanthropy; Neuromuscular Research Partnership; Canadian Coalition for Genetic Fairness
Affiliation(s): Health Charities Council of Canada
Finances: *Annual Operating Budget:* $3 Million-$5 Million; *Funding Sources:* Direct mail campaign; Corporate & foundation support; ALS Canada Golf Outing
Staff Member(s): 9; 45 volunteer(s)
Membership: 1,000-4,999; *Member Profile:* 10 provincial societies
Activities: Offering information & referral services; Raising public awareness; Fundraising for research; *Awareness Events:* Walk for ALS, June-Sept.; ALS Charity Golf Classic, Sept.; Hike for ALS, Sept.; *Internships:* Yes; *Speaker Service:* Yes; *Library:* ALS Canada Library; by appointment
Chief Officer(s):
Tammy Moore, Chief Executive Officer
tm@als.ca
Awards:
• ALS Canada Awards Program
Publications:
• Manual for People Living with ALS [a publication of the ALS Society of Canada]
Type: Manual; *Editor:* Jane McCarthy
• Research News [a publication of the ALS Society of Canada]
Type: Newsletter

ALS Society of Manitoba / La societe Manitobaine de la SLA
#2A, 1717 Dublin Ave., Winnipeg MB R3H 0H2
Tel: 204-831-1510; *Fax:* 204-837-9023
Toll-Free: 866-718-1642
HOPE@alsmb.ca
www.alsmb.ca
www.facebook.com/ALSmanitoba
twitter.com/ALSmanitoba
Overview: A small provincial charitable organization founded in 1980 overseen by ALS Society Of Canada
Mission: To improve the quality of life for people with ALS/MND; To invest in research & offer client services
Activities: *Library:* Resource Library
Chief Officer(s):
Diana Rasmussen, Executive Director, 204-837-1291
drasmussen@alsmb.ca

ALS Society of New Brunswick & Nova Scotia
#113, 900 Windmill Rd., Dartmouth NS B3B 1P7
Tel: 902-454-3636; *Fax:* 902-453-3646
Toll-Free: 866-625-7257
CareandHope@alsnbns.ca
alsnbns.ca
www.facebook.com/ALSNBNS
twitter.com/careandhope
Previous Name: ALS Society of New Brunswick; ALS Society of Nova Scotia
Overview: A small provincial charitable organization overseen by ALS Society Of Canada
Mission: To support people living with ALS
Chief Officer(s):
Kimberly Carter, President & CEO

ALS Society of New Brunswick; ALS Society of Nova Scotia
See ALS Society of New Brunswick & Nova Scotia

ALS Society of Newfoundland & Labrador
Downtown Health Centre, Upper Level, Suite 3, PO Box 844, Corner Brook NL A2H 6H6
Tel: 709-634-9499; *Fax:* 709-634-9499
Toll-Free: 888-364-9499
alssocietyofnfld@nf.aibn.com
www.envision.ca/webs/alsnl
Overview: A small provincial charitable organization overseen by ALS Society Of Canada
Activities: *Awareness Events:* Walk for ALS, June
Chief Officer(s):
Cheryl Power, Executive Director

ALS Society of PEI
PO Box 1643, Summerside PE C1N 2V5
Tel: 902-439-1600
als_society_pei@hotmail.com
www.alspei.ca
www.facebook.com/AlsSocietyOfPei
Overview: A small provincial charitable organization founded in 1984 overseen by ALS Society Of Canada
Mission: To act as a fund-raising and awareness building group for ALS

ALS Society of Québec / Société de la SLA du Québec
#200, 5415, rue Paré, Montréal QC H4P 1P7
Tél: 514-725-2653; *Téléc:* 514-725-6184
Ligne sans frais: 877-725-7725
info@sla-quebec.ca
www.sla-quebec.ca
www.facebook.ca/slaquebec
twitter.com/SLA_ALS_Quebec
www.flickr.com/photos/slaquebec/collections
Aperçu: Dimension: petite; *Envergure:* provinciale; Organisme sans but lucratif; fondée en 1983 surveillé par ALS Society Of Canada
Finances: *Budget de fonctionnement annuel:* $500,000-$1.5 Million
Membre(s) du personnel: 10; 300 bénévole(s)
Activités: *Evénements de sensibilisation:* ALS Awareness Month, June; National Caregiver Week, November; *Stagiaires:* Oui; *Service de conférenciers:* Oui
Membre(s) du bureau directeur:
Claudine Cook, Executive Director, 514-725-2653 Ext. 101
ccook@sla-quebec.ca

ALS Society of Saskatchewan
90C Cavendish St., Regina SK S4N 5G7
Tel: 306-949-4100; *Fax:* 306-949-4020
alssask@gmail.com
alssask.ca
www.facebook.com/474047055603
Overview: A small provincial charitable organization overseen by ALS Society Of Canada
Activities: *Library:* Resource Library

Alström Syndrome Canada
PO Box 204, RR#2, Finch ON K0C 1K0
Overview: A small national organization
Mission: To raise awareness within the medical community about the existence of Alström Syndrome & its symptoms; To raise money for research; To support the children & families living with Alström Syndrome
Affiliation(s): Alström Syndrome International
Chief Officer(s):
Randy Douglas, Director
randydouglas@sympatico.ca

AlterHéros
CP 56073, Succ. Alexis-Nihon, Montréal QC H3Z 1X5
Tél: 514-360-1320
info@alterheros.com
www.alterheros.com
www.facebook.com/alterheros
twitter.com/alterheros
Aperçu: Dimension: petite; *Envergure:* provinciale; fondée en 2003
Mission: Organisme communautaire bénévole à but non lucratif qui favorise l'insertion sociale des personnes d'orientation homosexuelle, bisexuelle et d'identité transsexuelle
Membre(s) du personnel: 6
Membre(s) du bureau directeur:
Véronique Daneau, Directrice générale

Alternative Dispute Resolution Atlantic Institute / Institut de médiation et d'arbitrage de l'Atlantique
PO Box 123, Halifax NS B3J 2M4
admin@adratlantic.ca
adratlantic.wildapricot.org
www.facebook.com/adratlantic
Also Known As: ADR Atlantic Institute
Overview: A small provincial organization
Mission: To assist ADR users in using alternative dispute resolution strategies
Activities: Provide training standards & accreditation procedures
Chief Officer(s):
Wendy Scott, President, 506-450-3710
wmscott@nbnet.nb.ca
Ron Pizzo, Vice President, 902-209-6661
rpizzo@pinklarkin.com

Alternative Land Use Services Canada
#555, 2938 Dundas St. West, Toronto ON M6P 4E7
Tel: 416-999-7985
www.alus.ca
www.linkedin.com/company/alus-canada
www.facebook.com/ALUSCanada
twitter.com/ALUSCanada
Also Known As: ALUS Canada
Overview: A medium-sized national organization
Mission: To sustain agriculture, wildlife, & natural spaces in Canada
Activities: Funding local ecological projects on Canadian farms & ranches
Chief Officer(s):
Bryan Gilvesy, Executive Director
Bridget Wayland, Director, Communications
bwayland@alus.ca

Lynn Bishop, Director, Operations
lbishop@alus.ca
Michelle Primus, Director, Grants & Funding
mprimus@alus.ca

Alternatives Action & Communication Network for International Development *Voir* Réseau d'action et de communication pour le développement international

Altona & District Chamber of Commerce
Golden West Building, PO Box 329, 125 Centre Ave. East, Altona MB R0G 0B0
Tel: 204-324-8793; *Fax:* 204-324-1314
chamber@shopaltona.com
www.shopaltona.com
www.facebook.com/207573636007862
twitter.com/altonabusiness
Overview: A small local organization
Mission: To strengthen the business climate of Altona & district
Member of: Manitoba Chamber of Commerce; Canadian Chamber of Commerce
Finances: *Annual Operating Budget:* $50,000-$100,000
Staff Member(s): 1; 8 volunteer(s)
Membership: 147 institutional; *Fees:* $52.50-$492.37
Activities: *Awareness Events:* Canada Day in the Park; Manitoba Sunflower Festival, July
Chief Officer(s):
Stephanie Harris, General Manager

Altruvest Charitable Services
#600, 2 Carlton St., Toronto ON M5B 1J3
Tel: 416-597-2293; *Fax:* 416-597-2294
information@altruvest.org
www.altruvest.org
Overview: A small local charitable organization founded in 1994
Mission: To help improve the charitable sector in Canada by strengthening its employment base, creating volunteer interest & improving charitable leaders through training.
Activities: BoardMatch and BoardWorx programs; *Speaker Service:* Yes
Chief Officer(s):
Robert C. Follows, Chair
Susan Dunne, Executive Director

Aluminium Association of Canada (AAC) / Association de l'aluminium du Canada
#1600, 1010, rue Sherbrooke ouest, Montréal QC H3A 2R7
Tél: 514-288-4842; *Téléc:* 514-288-0944
www.thealuminiumdialog.com
twitter.com/AAC_aluminium
Aperçu: *Dimension:* moyenne; *Envergure:* nationale
Mission: To be a representative for the Canadian aluminium industry & to enhance its presence in industrial sectors, especially road & mass transit infrastructure & the automotive industry.
Membre(s) du bureau directeur:
Jean Simard, President & General Manager

Alva Foundation
c/o Graham Hallward, 199 Albertus Ave., Toronto ON M4R 1J6
info@alva.ca
www.alva.ca
Previous Name: Southam Foundation
Overview: A medium-sized local charitable organization founded in 1965
Mission: To fund research into risk factors in early childhood development (pre-natal to 3 years of age); To fund pilot programs on demonstrations of new therapies serving the constituency described above
Finances: *Funding Sources:* Investment portfolio
Membership: *Committees:* Donations
Chief Officer(s):
Christopher Kerrigan, President
Graham F. Hallward, Chair, Donations Committee

Alzheimer Manitoba
#10, 120 Donald St., Winnipeg MB R3C 4G2
Tel: 204-943-6622; *Fax:* 204-942-5408
Toll-Free: 800-378-6699
alzmb@alzheimer.mb.ca
www.alzheimer.mb.ca
www.facebook.com/AlzheimerSocietyManitoba
twitter.com/AlzheimerMB
www.youtube.com/AlzheimerMB
Also Known As: Alzheimer Society of Manitoba
Overview: A medium-sized provincial charitable organization founded in 1982 overseen by Alzheimer Society of Canada
Mission: To allieviate the individual, family & social consequences of Alzheimer type dementia while supporting the search for a cure
Finances: *Annual Operating Budget:* $1.5 Million-$3 Million; *Funding Sources:* Donations; events
Staff Member(s): 30; 3476 volunteer(s)
Activities: Helpline; support groups; education; *Awareness Events:* Alzheimer Awareness Month, Jan.; *Speaker Service:* Yes
Chief Officer(s):
Wendy Schettler, CEO
wschettler@alzheimer.mb.ca
Meetings/Conferences:
• Alzheimer Society Manitoba: A Night in Tuscany Gala 2018, February, 2018, RBC Convention Centre, Winnipeg, MB
Scope: Provincial

Alzheimer Society Canada (ASC) / Société Alzheimer Canada
20 Eglinton Ave. West, 16th Fl., Toronto ON M4R 1K8
Tel: 416-488-8772; *Fax:* 416-322-6656
Toll-Free: 800-616-8816
info@alzheimer.ca
www.alzheimer.ca
www.facebook.com/AlzheimerCanada
twitter.com/AlzCanada
www.youtube.com/alzheimercanada
Overview: A large national charitable organization founded in 1978
Mission: To identify, develop, & facilitate national priorities that enable members to alleviate personal & social consequences of Alzheimer's disease & related disorders; To promote research & lead the search for a cure
Member of: Alzheimer Disease International; Canadian Coalition for Genetic Fairness
Affiliation(s): HealthPartners
Finances: *Annual Operating Budget:* Greater than $5 Million; *Funding Sources:* Public support, including bequests & in memoria; corporations, foundations & event sponsorships; grants
Membership: 1-99; *Member Profile:* 10 provincial organizations make up the membership; active in over 150 local communities; *Committees:* Peer Review Panel; Research Policy; Community Representatives
Activities: Provides support, information & education to people with Alzheimer's disease, families, physicians & health-care providers; funds researchers in the search for a cause & a cure; *Awareness Events:* World Alzheimer's Month, Sept.
Chief Officer(s):
Marjorie Sullivan, Chair
Awards:
• Regular Grants, Alzheimer Society Research Program
• Young Investigator Grants, Alzheimer Society Research Program
• Doctoral Awards, Alzheimer Society Research Program
• Post-Doctoral Awards, Alzheimer Society Research Program

Alzheimer Society London & Middlesex (ASLM)
435 Windermere Rd., London ON N5X 2T1
Tel: 519-680-2404; *Fax:* 519-680-2864
Toll-Free: 888-495-5855
info@alzheimerlondon.ca
www.alzheimerlondon.ca
www.facebook.com/alzheimerlondon
twitter.com/alzheimerldn
www.youtube.com/user/evokemediasolutions
Overview: A small local charitable organization founded in 1979
Mission: To provide support services & education for persons affected by Alzheimer's Disease & related dementias in Ontario's London & Middlesex region
Finances: *Funding Sources:* Donations; Fundraising; Sponsorships
Activities: Advocating on behalf of persons affected by Alzheimer's Disease & related dementias; Promoting research; Providing memory screening for persons experiencing memory concerns; Offering community resource information, sensory stimulation games & activities, plus journals & periodicals; *Awareness Events:* Walk for Memories *Library:* Weldon Family Welcome & Resource Centre; Open to public
Chief Officer(s):
Betsy Little, CEO
blittle@alzheimerlondon.ca
Rose Brochu, Manager, Accounting & Operations
rbrochu@alzheimerlondon.ca
Leslie Rand, Manager, Fund Development
lrand@alzheimerlondon.ca
Bruce Wray, Manager, Communications
bwray@alzheimerlondon.ca
Publications:
• Connections [a publication of Alzheimer Society London & Middlesex]
Type: Newsletter; *Frequency:* Quarterly
Profile: New developments plus volunteer news, fundraising activities, & upcoming events from the Alzheimer Society of London & Middlesex

Alzheimer Society of Alberta & Northwest Territories
High Park Corner, #308, 14925 - 111 Ave. NW, Edmonton AB T5M 2P6
Tel: 780-761-0030; *Fax:* 780-761-0031
Toll-Free: 866-950-5465
reception@alzheimer.ab.ca
www.alzheimer.ca/ab
Overview: A medium-sized provincial charitable organization founded in 1988 overseen by Alzheimer Society of Canada
Mission: To alleviate the personal & social consequences of Alzheimer's disease through the development, support & coordination of local societies & chapters; To promote the search for a cure through education & research; Registered charity, BN: 129690343RR0001
Affiliation(s): Canadian Association on Gerontology; Alberta Association on Gerontology; Canadian Centre for Philanthropy
Finances: *Annual Operating Budget:* $500,000-$1.5 Million; *Funding Sources:* Public donations
Staff Member(s): 20; 140 volunteer(s)
Membership: 1-99; *Committees:* Education/Support Services; Advocacy; Fund Development; Research
Activities: *Awareness Events:* National Alzheimer Awareness Month, Jan. *Library:* Resource Centre; Open to public
Chief Officer(s):
Michele Mulder, Chief Executive Officer
mmulder@alzheimer.ab.ca
Christene Gordon, Director, Client Services & Programs
cgordon@alzheimer.ab.ca
Monique Trudelle, Director, Communications
mtrudelle@alzheimer.ab.ca
Edmonton & Area Chapter
10531 Kingsway Ave., Edmonton AB T5H 4K1
Tel: 780-488-2266; *Fax:* 780-488-3055
Chief Officer(s):
Arlene Huhn, Manager, Client Services & Programs
ahuhn@alzheimer.ab.ca
Fort McMurray - Wood Buffalo Chapter
#200, 10010 Franklin Ave., Fort McMurray AB T9H 2K6
Tel: 780-743-6175; *Fax:* 780-791-0088
Chief Officer(s):
Jennifer Kennedy, Community Relations Coordinator
jkennedy@alzheimer.ab.ca
Grande Prairie Chapter
#205, 8712 - 116 Ave., Grande Prairie AB T8V 4B4
Tel: 780-882-8870; *Fax:* 780-882-8780
Chief Officer(s):
Cindy McLeod, Coordinator, First Link/Intake
cmcleod@alzheimer.ab.ca
Lethbridge & Area Chapter
#402, 740 - 4th Ave. South, Lethbridge AB T1J 0N9
Tel: 403-329-3766; *Fax:* 403-327-3711
Chief Officer(s):
Brenda Hill, Manager, Client Services & Programs
hill@alzheimer.ab.ca
Medicine Hat & Area - Palliser Chapter
Hammond Bldg., #401D - 3rd St. SE, Medicine Hat AB T1A 0G8
Tel: 403-528-2700; *Fax:* 403-526-4994
Chief Officer(s):
Alariss Schmid, Community Relations Coordinator
aschmid@alzheimer.ab.ca
Northwest Territories - Yellowknife Chapter
Yellowknife NT
Tel: 867-669-9390
Red Deer & Central Alberta Chapter
#1, 5550 - 45 St., Red Deer AB T4N 1L1
Tel: 403-342-0448; *Fax:* 403-986-3693
Chief Officer(s):
Laurie Grande, Manager, Client Services & Programs
firstlinkreddeer@alzheimer.ab.ca

Alzheimer Society of Barrie & District, Alzheimer Society of Greater Simcoe County *See* Alzheimer Society of Simcoe County

Alzheimer Society of Belleville/Hastings/Quinte
Bay View Mall, #63, 470 Dundas St. East, Belleville ON K8N 1G1
Tel: 613-962-0892; Fax: 613-962-1225
Toll-Free: 800-361-8036
www.alzheimer.ca/bhq
www.facebook.com/AlzheimerBHQ
twitter.com/AlzBHQ
www.youtube.com/AlzBHQ
Overview: A small local organization founded in 1987
Mission: To alleviate the personal & social consequences of Alzheimer disease & to promote research
Affiliation(s): Alzheimer Society of Ontario
Finances: *Funding Sources:* Memorials; donations; memberships; fundraisers; government
Staff Member(s): 7
Activities: Support groups; Wandering Person Registry; education; fairs; tag days; in-services; workshops; *Awareness Events:* Awareness Month, Jan. *Library:* Alzheimer Resource Centre
Chief Officer(s):
Jon Leavens, President
Laura Hare, Executive Director
laura.hare@alzheimerhpe.ca

North Hastings
PO Box 1786, 1 Manor Lane, Bancroft ON K0K 1C0
Tel: 613-332-4614; Fax: 613-332-0432
www.alzheimer.ca/en/chapters-on/bhq
Mission: To alleviate the personal & social consequences of Alzheimer's Disease & related disorders; To promote research
Chief Officer(s):
Sarah Krieger, Coordinator, Education & Support

Alzheimer Society of Brant
#701, 6 Bell Lane, Brantford ON N3T 0C3
Tel: 519-759-7692; Fax: 519-759-8353
www.alzbrant.ca
www.facebook.com/alzhbrant
Overview: A small local organization
Mission: To alleviate the personal & social consequences of Alzheimer Disease and related disorders and to promote research.
Member of: Alzheimer Association of Ontario
Chief Officer(s):
Mary Burnett, CEO

Alzheimer Society of British Columbia
#300, 828 West 8th Ave., Vancouver BC V5Z 1E1
Tel: 604-681-6530; Fax: 604-669-6907
Toll-Free: 800-667-3742
info@alzheimerbc.org
www.alzheimerbc.org
www.linkedin.com/company/alzheimer-society-of-b.c.
www.facebook.com/AlzheimerBC
twitter.com/AlzheimerBC
www.youtube.com/AlzheimerBC
Previous Name: Alzheimer Support Association of BC
Overview: A medium-sized provincial charitable organization founded in 1981 overseen by Alzheimer Society of Canada
Mission: To alleviate the personal & social consequences of Alzheimer disease & related dementias; to promote public awareness & to search for the causes & the cures
Finances: *Annual Operating Budget:* Greater than $5 Million; *Funding Sources:* Donations; membership dues; grants; special events
Staff Member(s): 58; 500 volunteer(s)
Activities: Support groups, Dementia Helpline, education, information resources, advocacy, research funding, fundraising, marketing & communications; *Awareness Events:* Investors Group Walk for Memories, Jan.; A Breakfast to Remember; Forget Me Not Golf Tournament, May; Ascent for Alzheimer's, Sept.; Mt. Kilimanjaro Grouse Grind for Alzheimer's, Sept.; Coffee Break, Sept.; *Speaker Service:* Yes; *Library:* Open to public
Chief Officer(s):
Maria Howard, CEO, 604-742-4901
mhoward@alzheimerbc.org

Alzheimer Society of Calgary
#201, 222 - 58 Ave. SW, Calgary AB T2H 2S3
Tel: 403-290-0110
Toll-Free: 877-569-4357
info@alzheimercalgary.com
www.alzheimercalgary.com
www.facebook.com/116306041728999
twitter.com/alzcalgary
Overview: A medium-sized local charitable organization founded in 1981
Mission: To offer educational & support services to individuals & families in the Calgary region experiencing Alzheimer Disease & related disorders (dementia), as well as to professionals in the field; to support research
Affiliation(s): Alzheimer Society of Canada; Alzheimer Society of Alberta
Finances: *Annual Operating Budget:* $500,000-$1.5 Million
Staff Member(s): 21; 258 volunteer(s)
Activities: *Internships:* Yes; *Speaker Service:* Yes; *Library:* Resource Centre; Open to public
Chief Officer(s):
Barb Ferguson, Executive Director

Alzheimer Society of Chatham-Kent
36 Memory Lane, Chatham ON N7L 5M8
Tel: 519-352-1043; Fax: 519-352-3680
info@alzheimerchathamkent.ca
www.alzheimer.ca/chathamkent
www.facebook.com/321344923495
www.youtube.com/thealzheimersociety
Overview: A small local charitable organization founded in 1983
Mission: To alleviate the personal and social consequences of Alzheimer Disease and related disorders and to promote research.
Member of: Alzheimer Soceity of Canada
Staff Member(s): 15
Chief Officer(s):
Mary Ellen Parker, CEO

Alzheimer Society of Cornwall & District
106B - 2 St. West, Cornwall ON K6H 6N6
Tel: 613-932-4914; Fax: 613-932-6154
Toll-Free: 888-222-1445
alzheimer.info@one-mail.on.ca
www.alzheimer.ca/cornwall
Overview: A small local charitable organization
Mission: To alleviate the personal & social consequences of Alzheimer Disease and related disorders and to promote research.

Alzheimer Society of Dufferin County
#1, 25 Centennial Rd., Orangeville ON L9W 1R1
Tel: 519-941-1221; Fax: 519-941-1730
info@alzheimerdufferin.org
www.alzheimerdufferin.org
www.facebook.com/Alzheimerdufferin
Overview: A small local charitable organization founded in 1999
Mission: To alleviate the personal & social consequences of Alzheimer Disease and related disorders and to promote research.
Member of: Alzheimer Society of Ontario
Staff Member(s): 8
Activities: Coffee Break; Physician lunch support groups; Education & awarenss
Chief Officer(s):
Diane Cowen, Interim Executive Director
dianecowen@alzheimerdufferin.org

Alzheimer Society of Durham Region (ASDR)
Oshawa Executive Centre, Oshawa Centre, #207, 419 King St. West, Oshawa ON L1J 2K5
Tel: 905-576-2567; Fax: 905-576-2033
Toll-Free: 888-301-1106
information@alzheimerdurham.com
www.alzheimerdurham.com
www.facebook.com/alzheimer.durham
twitter.com/AlzheimerDurham
www.youtube.com/thealzheimersociety
Also Known As: Alzheimer Durham
Overview: A small local charitable organization founded in 1979
Mission: To improve the quality of life of persons with Alzheimer's Disease, or related dementias, & their caregivers in Ontario's Durham Region
Member of: Alzheimer Society of Ontario
Finances: *Funding Sources:* Donations; Fundraising; Sponsorships; Membership fees
Staff Member(s): 10
Activities: Offering support & education programs; Engaging in advocacy activities; Raising public awareness; *Awareness Events:* Walk for Memories
Chief Officer(s):
Denyse Newton, Executive Director
dnewton@alzheimerdurham.com
Michelle Pepin, Director, Family Support
mpepin@alzheimerdurham.com
Loretta Tanner, Director, Public Education
ltanner@alzheimerdurham.com
Brenda Davie, Coordinator, Family Support & Education
bdavie@alzheimerdurham.com
Karen Morley, Coordinator, Caregiver
kmorley@alzheimerdurham.com
Publications:
• Staying Connected: A Newsletter from Alzheimer Society of Durham Region
Type: Newsletter; *Frequency:* Quarterly; *Price:* Free with membership in the Alzheimer Society of Durham Region
Profile: Notices about forthcoming events, education, & support groups

Alzheimer Society of Grey-Bruce
753 - 2nd Ave. East, Owen Sound ON N4K 2G9
Tel: 519-376-7230; Fax: 519-376-2428
Toll-Free: 800-265-9013
info@alzheimergreybruce.com
www.alzheimer.ca/greybruce
www.facebook.com/AlzheimerSocietyofGreyBruce
twitter.com/AlzheimerSGB
Overview: A small local charitable organization founded in 1986
Mission: To alleviate the personal & social consequences of Alzheimer's Disease & related disorders & to promote research
Member of: Alzheimer Association of Ontario
Staff Member(s): 13
Activities: *Library:* Open to public
Chief Officer(s):
Stephen Musehl, Executive Director
smusehl@alzheimergreybruce.com

Alzheimer Society of Haldimand Norfolk
645 Norfolk St. North, Simcoe ON N3Y 3R2
Tel: 519-428-7771; Fax: 519-428-2968
Toll-Free: 800-565-4614
www.alzhn.ca
www.facebook.com/alzhbrant
Overview: A small local charitable organization founded in 1993
Mission: To help people as they deal with the consequences of Alzheimer's Disease & related disorders
Finances: *Funding Sources:* Donations
Activities: Establishing a Wandering Person Registry; Increasing public awareness; Promoting education; Offering supportive counselling; Providing consultation services to community organization & health care agencies; Engaging in advocacy activities; *Awareness Events:* Walk for Memories
Library: Alzheimer Resource Library; Open to public
Chief Officer(s):
Mary Burnett, Chief Executive Officer
mary.burnett@alzda.ca

Alzheimer Society of Hamilton Halton
#700, 1575 Upper Ottawa St., Hamilton ON L8W 3E2
Tel: 905-529-7030; Fax: 905-529-3787
Toll-Free: 888-343-1017
www.alzheimerhamiltonhalton.org
www.facebook.com/alzhbrant
Overview: A small local charitable organization founded in 1982
Mission: To provide programs & services to help caregivers handle the challenges associated with caring for people with Alzheimer's Disease & related disorders in the communities of Ancaster, Dundas, Flamborough, Glanbrook, Hamilton, & Stoney Creek within the City of Hamilton, & the the communities of Burlington, Halton Hills, Milton & Oakville within Halton Region
Finances: *Annual Operating Budget:* $100,000-$250,000; *Funding Sources:* Donations; Fundraising
Activities: Establishing the Wandering Person Registries in Hamilton & Halton; Offering education services to professionals who work in dementia related areas & to families affected by Alzheimer's Disease; *Awareness Events:* Walk for Memories
Library: Hamilton Resource Centre; Open to public
Chief Officer(s):
Mary Burnett, Chief Executive Officer
mary.burnett@alzda.ca
JoAnne Chalifour, Regional Director, Operations
joanne.chalifour@alzda.ca
Trevor Clark, Regional Director, Development
trevor.clark@alzda.ca

Alzheimer Society of Hastings - Prince Edward
Bay View Mall, #63, 470 Dundas St. East, Belleville ON K8N 1G1
Tel: 613-962-0892; Fax: 613-962-1225
Toll-Free: 800-361-8036

www.alzheimer.ca/hpe
www.facebook.com/AlzheimerHPE
Overview: A small local charitable organization founded in 1985
Mission: To help people diagnosed with Alzheimer's Disease or a related dementia in Prince Edward County of southeastern Ontario
Member of: South East Local Health Integration Network (LHIN)
Finances: *Funding Sources:* Donations; Fundraising
Activities: Offering education programs; Advocating for families of people with Alzheimer's Disease & related dementias; Promoting research
Chief Officer(s):
Maureen Corrigan, Executive Director, 613-962-0892 Ext. 7012
maureen.corrigan@alzheimerhpe.ca

Alzheimer Society of Huron County
PO Box 639, 317 Huron Rd., Clinton ON N0M 1L0
Tel: 519-482-1482; *Fax:* 519-482-8692
Toll-Free: 800-561-5012
admin@alzheimerhuron.on.ca
www.alzheimerhuron.on.ca
www.facebook.com/AlzheimerSocietyHuron
twitter.com/AlzSociety
www.youtube.com/user/AlzheimerSouthwest
Overview: A small local organization
Mission: To alleviate the personal and social consequences of Alzheimer Disease and related disorders and to promote research.
Staff Member(s): 8
Chief Officer(s):
Cathy Ritsema, Executive Director
cathy@alzheimerhuron.on.ca

Alzheimer Society of Kenora/Rainy River Districts
618 - 9th St. North, Kenora ON P9N 2S9
Tel: 807-468-1516; *Fax:* 807-468-9013
Toll-Free: 800-682-0245
info@alzheimerkrr.com
www.alzheimer.ca/krr
www.facebook.com/Alzheimerkrr
Overview: A small local charitable organization founded in 1991
Mission: To alleviate the personal and social consequences of Alzheimer Disease and related disorders and to promote research.
Staff Member(s): 5
Activities: Education sessions & support; fundraising events; lending library
Chief Officer(s):
Lynn Moffatt, Executive Director
lynn@alzheimerkrr.com

Alzheimer Society of Kingston, Frontenac, Lennox & Addington
#4, 400 Elliot Ave., Kingston ON K7K 6M9
Tel: 613-544-3078; *Fax:* 613-544-6320
Toll-Free: 800-266-7516
reception@alzking.com
www.alzheimer.ca/kfla
www.facebook.com/AlzheimerKingston
twitter.com/AlzSocKing
www.youtube.com/thealzheimersociety
Overview: A small local charitable organization founded in 1986
Mission: To improve the quality of life of people with Alzheimer disease & other dementias & their caregivers
Member of: Alzheimer Association of Ontario
Staff Member(s): 6
Activities: *Awareness Events:* Walk for Memories; *Speaker Service:* Yes; *Library:* Open to public
Chief Officer(s):
Jan White, President
Vicki Poffley, Executive Director

Alzheimer Society of Lanark County
115 Christie Lake Rd., Perth ON K7H 3C6
Tel: 613-264-0307
Toll-Free: 800-511-1911
alz@storm.ca
www.alzheimer.ca/lanark
www.facebook.com/AlzheimerSocietyLanarkCounty
twitter.com/1ASLC
Overview: A small local organization
Mission: To alleviate the personal and social consequences of Alzheimer Disease and related disorders and to promote research.
Member of: Alzheimer Association of Ontario
Staff Member(s): 12
Chief Officer(s):

Don McDiarmid, President
Louise Noble, Executive Director
alzlnoble@storm.ca

Alzheimer Society of Leeds-Grenville
c/o Garden Street Site, Brockville General Hospital, 42 Garden St., Brockville ON K6V 2C3
Tel: 613-345-7392; *Fax:* 613-345-3186
Toll-Free: 866-576-8556
administrator@alzheimerleedsgrenville.ca
www.alzheimer.ca/en/lg
www.facebook.com/alzheimerleedsgrenville
Overview: A small local charitable organization founded in 1987
Mission: To help persons diagnosed with Alzheimer's Disease or a related dementia in the Leeds-Grenville region of Ontario
Finances: *Funding Sources:* Donations; Fundraising
Staff Member(s): 4
Activities: Providing support groups, such as caregiver support groups, early stage support groups for individuals with dementia, & "Just for You" groups for persons living with Alzheimer's Disease or a related dementia for some time; Offering education for professionals & the public; Advocating on behalf of families of people with Alzheimer's Disease or related dementias; Promoting research to find a cause & cure; Increasing public awareness, through campaigns such as Heads Up for Healthier Brains; *Library:* Resources Centre & Loaning Library; Open to public
Chief Officer(s):
Louise Noble, Interim Executive Director
administrator@alzheimerleedsgrenville.ca
Sean McFadden, Coordinator, Education & Support
education@alzheimerleedsgrenville.ca
Publications:
• Alzheimer Society of Leeds-Grenville Newsletter
Type: Newsletter; *Frequency:* 3 pa; *Price:* Free with membership in the Alzheimer Society of Leeds-Grenville
Profile: Updates about the society's activities, plus educational information, caregiver tips, & research reports
• Alzheimer Update
Type: Newsletter
Profile: Medical information & resources for physicians in the Leeds-Grenville region

Alzheimer Society of Miramichi
PO Box 205, Miramichi NB E1N 3A6
Tel: 506-773-7093; *Fax:* 506-773-7093
Toll-Free: 800-664-8411
alzmir@nb.aibn.com
www.alzheimernb.ca
Overview: A small local organization
Mission: To alleviate the personal and social consequences of Alzheimer Disease and related disorders and to promote research.

Alzheimer Society of Moncton
960 St. George Blvd., Moncton NB E1E 3Y3
Tel: 506-858-8380; *Fax:* 506-855-7697
Toll-Free: 800-664-8411
moncton@alzheimernb.ca
www.alzheimernb.ca
Overview: A small local charitable organization founded in 1986
Mission: To alleviate the personal & social consequencs of Alzheimer's Disease & related diseases in the Moncton New Brunswick region
Member of: Société Alzheimer Society New Brunswick / Nouveau-Brunswick
Finances: *Funding Sources:* Donations; Fundraising
Activities: Arranging support groups; Providing information & education; Increasing public awareness
Chief Officer(s):
Joanne Sonier, Regional Coordinator

Alzheimer Society of Muskoka
#205, 230 Manitoba St., Bracebridge ON P1L 2E1
Tel: 705-645-5621; *Fax:* 705-645-4397
Toll-Free: 800-605-2076
alzmusk@muskoka.com
www.alzheimer.ca/en/muskoka
www.facebook.com/alzheimersocietyofmuskoka
twitter.com/alz_muskoka
Overview: A small local charitable organization founded in 1995
Mission: To assist persons living with Alzheimer's Disease & other dementias in the Muskoka region of Ontario; To provide education programs; To promote research
Member of: Alzheimer Society of Ontario
Finances: *Funding Sources:* Donations; Sponsorships

Activities: Providing referral services; Offering counselling & support groups; Advocating for individuals, families, & caregivers; Visiting; *Library:* Alzheimer Society of Muskoka Lending Library & Resource Centre; Open to public
Chief Officer(s):
Karen Quernby, Executive Director

Alzheimer Society of New Brunswick / Société alzheimer du nouveau brunswick
PO Box 1553, Stn. A, Fredericton NB E3B 5G2
Tel: 506-459-4280; *Fax:* 506-452-0313
Toll-Free: 800-664-8411
info@alzheimernb.ca
www.alzheimernb.ca
www.facebook.com/127071537361985
twitter.com/AlzheimerNB
Overview: A medium-sized provincial organization founded in 1987 overseen by Alzheimer Society of Canada
Mission: To alleviate the personal & social consequences of Alzheimer disease; to promote the search for a cause & cure
Activities: *Speaker Service:* Yes; Library

Alzheimer Society of Newfoundland & Labrador
#107, 835 Topsail Rd., Mount Pearl NL A1N 3J6
Tel: 709-576-0608; *Fax:* 709-576-0798
Toll-Free: 877-776-0608
alzheimersociety@nf.aibn.com
www.alzheimernl.org
www.facebook.com/ASNL2
twitter.com/asnl2
Overview: A small provincial charitable organization founded in 1988 overseen by Alzheimer Society of Canada
Mission: To support the search for the cause & cure of Alzheimer Disease; To raise public awareness of the personal & social impact of the disease; To promote the provision of support to families & caregivers in Newfoundland
Finances: *Funding Sources:* Fundraising; donations; sponsorship
Staff Member(s): 4
Activities: *Awareness Events:* Awareness Month, Jan.; *Library:* Open to public
Chief Officer(s):
Shirley Lucas, Executive Director
slucas@alzheimernl.ca

Alzheimer Society of Niagara Region
#1, 403 Ontario St., St Catharines ON L2N 1L5
Tel: 905-687-3914; *Fax:* 905-687-9952
Toll-Free: 877-818-3202
niagara@alzheimerniagara.ca
www.alzheimer.ca/niagara
www.facebook.com/106624255247
twitter.com/alzheimerniagar
www.youtube.com/user/alzheimerniagara
Overview: A small local charitable organization founded in 1984
Mission: To ensure quality services for individuals with Alzheimer disease & related dementias; to support & advocate for individuals, families, caregivers & community through counselling, education & the promotion of research to compassionately respond to the very special needs of those experiencing dementia
Finances: *Annual Operating Budget:* $1.5 Million-$3 Million; *Funding Sources:* Ministry of Health; fundraising; donations
Staff Member(s): 27; 174 volunteer(s)
Activities: Support groups; visiting & driving program; wandering registry; caregiver education series; *Awareness Events:* International Alzheimer Day, Sept. 21; Coffee Break, Sept.; Walk for Memories, Jan.; *Internships:* Yes; *Speaker Service:* Yes; *Library:* Open to public
Chief Officer(s):
Judy Willems, President
Teena Kindt, CEO

Alzheimer Society of North Bay & District
1180 Cassells St., North Bay ON P1B 4B6
Tel: 705-495-4342; *Fax:* 705-495-0329
www.alzheimer.ca/northbay
www.facebook.com/alzheimersmnbd
Overview: A small local charitable organization founded in 1978
Mission: To alleviate the personal & social consequences of Alzheimer Disease & related disorders & to promote research
Member of: Alzheimer Society of Ontario
Staff Member(s): 4
Activities: *Awareness Events:* Walk for Memories; *Library:* Open to public
Chief Officer(s):

Canadian Associations / Alzheimer Society of Nova Scotia

Linda Brown, Family Counsellor & Site Supervisor
lbrown@alzheimernorthbay.com

Alzheimer Society of Nova Scotia
#112, 2719 Gladstone St., Halifax NS B3K 4W6
Tel: 902-422-7961; *Fax:* 902-422-7971
Toll-Free: 800-611-6345
alzheimer@asns.ca
www.alzheimer.ca/ns
www.facebook.com/alzheimersocietyns
twitter.com/alzheimerns
www.youtube.com/user/alzheimerns
Overview: A medium-sized provincial charitable organization founded in 1983 overseen by Alzheimer Society of Canada
Mission: To enhance the quality of life of people with Alzheimer disease through providing & promoting public education & family support; to engage in advocacy on behalf of people with Alzheimer disease & their families; to promote research at the provincial & national levels
Finances: *Annual Operating Budget:* $500,000-$1.5 Million
Activities: *Awareness Events:* Alzheimer Awareness Month, Jan.; *Speaker Service:* Yes; *Library:* Alzheimer Resource Centre; Open to public
Chief Officer(s):
Lloyd O. Brown, Executive Director
Chris Wilson, President

Alzheimer Society of Ottawa *See* Alzheimer Society of Ottawa & Renfrew County

Alzheimer Society of Ottawa & Renfrew County / Société Alzheimer d'Ottawa et Renfrew County
#1742, 1750 Russell Rd., Ottawa ON K1G 5Z6
Tel: 613-523-4004
info@asorc.org
www.alzheimerottawa.ca
www.linkedin.com/company/alzheimer-society-of-ottawa-and-renfrew-county
www.facebook.com/alzheimerottawa
twitter.com/AlzheimerOttawa
www.youtube.com/user/ASOttawa
Previous Name: Alzheimer Society of Ottawa
Overview: A medium-sized local charitable organization founded in 1980
Mission: To increase the understanding of, & to alleviate the personal & social consequences of Alzheimer disease through patient & family support, information & education & promotion of research
Member of: Alzheimer Society of Ontario; Alzheimer Society of Canada
Affiliation(s): Perley & Rideau Veterans' Health Centre; Care for Health & Community Services; Champlain Dementia Network
Finances: *Annual Operating Budget:* $1.5 Million-$3 Million; *Funding Sources:* Donations; Memberships; Bequests; Fundraising events; Government (approximately 30%)
Staff Member(s): 25; 300 volunteer(s)
Activities: Family support & education services; specialized family support groups (wives, daughters, husbands, sons, Early Alzheimer Group); workshops for families & professional caregivers; Safely Home Program; Alzheimer Info Line; Enhancing Care Program; resource centre; speakers' bureau; Alzheimer website; Renfrew County Satellite Office; *Awareness Events:* National Alzheimer Awareness Month, Jan. *Library:* Resource Centre; Open to public
Chief Officer(s):
Kathy Wright, Executive Director, 613-369-5628
Debbie Seto, Manager, 613-369-5634
Publications:
• Société Alzheimer Society Ottawa & Renfrew County Annual Report
Type: Yearbook; *Frequency:* Annually
Profile: A review of the year's events
• Société Alzheimer Society Ottawa & Renfrew County Newsletter
Type: Newsletter
Profile: Information about programs & services provided by the society, plus research & education updates

Alzheimer Society of Oxford (ASO)
575 Peel St., Woodstock ON N4S 1K6
Tel: 519-421-2466; *Fax:* 519-421-3098
info@alzheimer.oxford.on.ca
www.alzheimer.ca/oxford
www.facebook.com/alzoxford
twitter.com/AlzSociety
www.youtube.com/thealzheimersociety
Overview: A small local charitable organization founded in 1989

Mission: To improve the quality of life for people with Alzheimer disease or related dementias & their caregivers
Member of: Alzheimer Society of Ontario
Finances: *Funding Sources:* Donations; provincial government; Nevada ticket sales; bingo; fundraising
Activities: Support Groups; Volunteer Companion; Sensory Stimulation Resource Centre; Children's Information Series; Caring with Respect course; Information Support; advocacy; "Walk for Memories"; Tag Day; "Cuddle Bear" Program; Teen Education Series; Information & support group for individuals in the early stages of the disease; *Library:* Open to public
Chief Officer(s):
Andrew Szasz, President

Alzheimer Society of Peel
60 Briarwood Ave., Mississauga ON L5G 3N6
Tel: 905-278-3667; *Fax:* 905-278-3964
www.alzheimerpeel.com
www.facebook.com/112857568321
twitter.com/AlzPeel
Overview: A small local charitable organization founded in 1983
Mission: To alleviate the personal and social consequences of Alzheimer Disease and related disorders and to promote research.
Member of: Alzheimer Association of Ontario
Finances: *Annual Operating Budget:* Greater than $5 Million
Membership: *Member Profile:* Caregivers; professionals in community health area
Activities: Counselling; day programs; family support; education
Chief Officer(s):
Mary-Lynn Peters, President

Alzheimer Society of PEI
166 Fitzroy St., Charlottetown PE C1A 1S1
Tel: 902-628-2257; *Fax:* 902-368-2715
Toll-Free: 866-628-2257
society@alzpei.ca
www.alzheimer.ca/pei
www.facebook.com/AlzheimerPEI
twitter.com/AlzheimerPEI
www.youtube.com/user/Alzpei
Overview: A small provincial charitable organization founded in 1989 overseen by Alzheimer Society of Canada
Mission: To support & assist Islanders affected by Alzheimer Disease; To raise the level of awareness & educate the public at large about the disease
Finances: *Annual Operating Budget:* Greater than $5 Million; *Funding Sources:* Fee for services; fundraising
Staff Member(s): 4
Activities: Counselling; mediation; Day Respite support groups; advocacy; Wandering Person Registry - Safely Home; Enhancing care program; music therapy; *Awareness Events:* Alzheimer Awareness Month, Jan.; *Speaker Service:* Yes; *Library:* Open to public
Chief Officer(s):
Corrine Hendricken-Eldershaw, CEO
Awards:
• Leadership Award

Alzheimer Society of Perth County
#5, 1020 Ontario St., Stratford ON N5A 6Z3
Tel: 519-271-1910; *Fax:* 519-271-1231
Toll-Free: 888-797-1882
info@alzheimerperthcounty.com
www.alzheimerperthcounty.com
www.facebook.com/AlzheimerSocietyPerth
twitter.com/Alzperth
Overview: A small local charitable organization founded in 1988
Mission: To assist those affected by Alzheimer's Disease & other types of dementia
Finances: *Annual Operating Budget:* $500,000-$1.5 Million; *Funding Sources:* Donations; Fundraising; Sponsorships
Staff Member(s): 7; 350 volunteer(s)
Membership: 65
Activities: Providing support services; Offering a learning series; Promoting research; *Awareness Events:* Walk for Memories; Alzheimer Awareness Month
Chief Officer(s):
Debbie Deichert, Executive Director
debdeichert@wightman.ca
Publications:
• The Helping Hand
Type: Newsletter; *Price:* Free with Alzheimer Society of Perth County membership
Profile: Articles to help caregivers & upcoming events

Alzheimer Society of Sarnia-Lambton
420 East St. North, Sarnia ON N7T 6Y5
Tel: 519-332-4444; *Fax:* 519-332-6673
info@alzheimersarnia.ca
alzheimer.sarnia.com
www.facebook.com/alzheimersarnialambton
twitter.com/AlzheimerSociet
Overview: A small local charitable organization founded in 1986
Mission: To improve the quality of live of people with Alzheimer disease or related dementia, & their caregivers
Member of: Alzheimer Society of Ontario
Affiliation(s): Ministry of Health, Long-Term Care; Ontario Trillium Foundation
Staff Member(s): 7
Membership: *Member Profile:* Caregivers, medical personnel, organizations, general public
Activities: Support meetings; library; educational training; fundraising; public & staff education; Caregiver Series, Oct.; information series; Remember Me: Children's Education; cadaver transportation; counselling & referral; wandering registry; mobility monitors; *Awareness Events:* Walk for Memories, Jan.; *Speaker Service:* Yes; *Library:* Resource Library; Open to public
Chief Officer(s):
Bill Seymour, Chair
Judy Doan, CEO

Alzheimer Society of Saskatchewan Inc. (ASOS)
#301, 2550 - 12 Ave., Regina SK S4P 3X1
Tel: 306-949-4141
Toll-Free: 800-263-3367
info@alzheimer.sk.ca
www.alzheimer.sk.ca
www.facebook.com/217901721605861
twitter.com/AlzheimerSK
www.youtube.com/thealzheimersociety
Previous Name: Saskatchewan Alzheimer & Related Diseases Association
Overview: A medium-sized provincial charitable organization founded in 1982 overseen by Alzheimer Society of Canada
Mission: To alleviate the personal & social consequences of Alzheimer's disease & related disorders & to promote the search for a cause & a cure
Finances: *Annual Operating Budget:* $1.5 Million-$3 Million; *Funding Sources:* Donations; Fundraising; Education; Government; Interest; Major gifts; National revenue sharing; Planned giving; Sponsorship
Staff Member(s): 21; 100+ volunteer(s)
Membership: *Member Profile:* Family; Professional care providers; Interested members of the public; Health care organizations; Regional health authorities
Activities: Offering practical information and strategies to help people living with dementia and their caregivers; Providing education programs; Providing access to community resources; Funding research for cures and treatments for Alzheimer's disease; *Awareness Events:* Alzheimer Awareness Month, Jan.; Alzheimer Coffee Break, Sept.; Alzheimer Fall Gala, Oct.; *Internships:* Yes; *Speaker Service:* Yes; *Library:* Open to public
Chief Officer(s):
Joanne Bracken, CEO
ceo@alzheimer.sk.ca
Publications:
• Prairie View [a publication of the Alzheimer Society of Saskatchewan]
Frequency: 3 pa; *Price:* Free with online subscription
Profile: A publication with important updates about the ASC

Alzheimer Society of Sault Ste. Marie & District of Algoma
341 Trunk Rd., Sault Ste Marie ON P6A 3S9
Tel: 705-942-2195; *Fax:* 705-256-6777
Toll-Free: 877-396-7888
info@alzheimeralgoma.org
www.alzheimeralgoma.org
Overview: A small local charitable organization founded in 1987
Mission: To improve the quality of life for people with Alzheimer disease & related disorders & to provide support for their caregivers
Member of: Alzheimer Association of Ontario
Staff Member(s): 17
Activities: Door-to-door campaign; coffee break; Walk for Memories; *Speaker Service:* Yes; *Library:* Kay L. Punch Resource Centre; Open to public
Chief Officer(s):
Graham Clark, President
Terry Caporossi, Executive Director

Alzheimer Society of Simcoe County
PO Box 1414, Barrie ON L4M 5R4
Tel: 705-722-1066; *Fax:* 705-722-9392
Toll-Free: 800-265-5391
simcoecounty@alzheimersociety.ca
www.alzheimersociety.ca
www.facebook.com/AlzheimerSocietySimcoeCounty
twitter.com/AlzheimerSimcoe
Previous Name: Alzheimer Society of Barrie & District, Alzheimer Society of Greater Simcoe County
Merged from: Alzheimer Society of Greater Simcoe County & Alzheimer Society of North East Simcoe County
Overview: A small local charitable organization founded in 1985
Mission: To improve the quality of life of persons who are directly affected by Alzheimer's diseases or related dementias
Finances: *Funding Sources:* Membership dues; Donations; Fundraising programs/events; Provincial government
Staff Member(s): 13; 350 volunteer(s)
Membership: 136; *Fees:* $15 regular; $10 seniors; $50 organizations/corporate; *Member Profile:* Family caregivers; Professional caregivers; Volunteers; Organizations
Activities: *Awareness Events:* Alzheimer Awareness Month, Jan.; *Internships:* Yes; *Speaker Service:* Yes; *Library:* Open to public
Chief Officer(s):
Debbie Islam, Executive Director
dislam@alzheimersociety.ca

Alzheimer Society of Thunder Bay (ASTB)
#310, 180 Park Ave., Thunder Bay ON P7B 6J4
Tel: 807-345-9556; *Fax:* 807-345-1518
Toll-Free: 800-879-4226; *TTY:* 888-887-5140
info@alzheimerthunderbay.ca
www.alzheimer.ca/thunderbay
www.facebook.com/ASTBAY
Overview: A small local charitable organization founded in 1986
Mission: To improve the quality of life of persons with Alzheimer disease or related dementia & their caregivers; to promote the rights & well-being of persons with the disease & their caregivers; to support the delivery of programmes for individuals affected by the disease; to provide funds for research
Finances: *Annual Operating Budget:* $100,000-$250,000; *Funding Sources:* Fundraising; Donations
Staff Member(s): 6; 100 volunteer(s)
Membership: *Committees:* Board Task Forces; Special Events
Activities: Providing individual & family counselling, Raising public awareness through education & outreach; Operating a resource library; Advocating for patients & their families; *Awareness Events:* Walk for Memories; Alzheimer Coffee Break Campaign; Alzheimer Rendez-vous; *Speaker Service:* Yes; *Library:* Resource Centre; Open to public
Chief Officer(s):
Randy Moore, Executive Director
ramoore@alzheimerthunderbay.ca
Jaclyn Woods, Coordinator, Marketing & Events
awareness@alzheimerthunderbay.ca

Alzheimer Society of Timmins/Porcupine District
70 Cedar St. South, Timmins ON P4N 2G6
Tel: 705-268-4554; *Fax:* 705-360-4492
ww.alzheimer.ca/en/timmins
www.facebook.com/AlzheimerSocietyTimmins
Overview: A small local charitable organization founded in 1986
Mission: To alleviate the personal & social consequences of Alzheimer disease; To promote the search for the causes & cure of the disease
Member of: Alzheimer Association of Ontario
Staff Member(s): 7
Activities: *Speaker Service:* Yes; *Library*
Chief Officer(s):
Tracy Koskamp-Bergeron, Executive Director
director@alzheimertimmins.com

Alzheimer Society of Toronto
20 Eglinton Ave. West, 16th Fl., Toronto ON M4R 1K8
Tel: 416-322-6560; *Fax:* 416-322-6656
write@alzheimertoronto.org
www.alzheimertoronto.org
www.linkedin.com/company/alzheimer-society-of-toronto
www.facebook.com/AlzheimerToronto
twitter.com/alztoronto
www.youtube.com/user/alzheimertoronto
Overview: A medium-sized local charitable organization founded in 1982
Mission: To enhance the lives of persons with Alzheimer Disease & their caregivers by providing family support, raising awareness & advocating for services & research
Member of: Alzheimer Society of Ontario
Staff Member(s): 39
Activities: *Speaker Service:* Yes; *Library:* Alzheimer Resource Centre; Open to public
Chief Officer(s):
Cathy Barrick, Chief Ececutive Officer
cbarrick@alzheimertoronto.org
Neil Jacoby, Chair

Alzheimer Society of Windsor/Essex County
2135 Richmond St., Windsor ON N8Y 0A1
Tel: 519-974-2220; *Fax:* 519-974-9727
generalinformation@aswecare.com
www.alzheimerwindsor.com
www.facebook.com/AlzheimerSocietyOfWindsorEssexCounty
twitter.com/ASWE_Care
Overview: A small local charitable organization founded in 1981
Mission: To improve the quality of life of those affected by Alzheimer disease or other dementia
Member of: Alzheimer Association of Ontario
Affiliation(s): Windsor & District Chamber of Commerce, Alzheimer Association of Canada
Finances: *Annual Operating Budget:* $1.5 Million-$3 Million
Staff Member(s): 44
Membership: *Member Profile:* Windsor businesses, local Alzheimer chapters, public; *Committees:* Executive; Finance/Services; Nominating & Governance; Community Advisory Council
Activities: Day Away; caregiver & client support groups; in-home respite care; public education; volunteer opportunities; one to one caregiver support; *Awareness Events:* Awareness Month, Jan.; National Coffee Break, Sept.; *Library:* Open to public
Chief Officer(s):
Gaston Franklyn, Chair
Sally Bennett Olczak, CEO

Alzheimer Society of York Region
#2, 240 Edward St., Aurora ON L4G 3S9
Tel: 905-726-3477; *Fax:* 905-726-1917
Toll-Free: 888-414-5550
info@alzheimer-york.com
www.alzheimer-york.com
www.facebook.com/AlzheimerSocietyYork
twitter.com/AlzheimerYork
Overview: A small local charitable organization founded in 1985
Mission: To support individuals & families, in Ontario's York Region, who cope with Alzheimer's Disease & related disorders; To promote research
Finances: *Annual Operating Budget:* $1.5 Million-$3 Million; *Funding Sources:* Donations; Central Local Health Integration Network; Ontario Trillium Foundation; United Way of York Region
Staff Member(s): 48
Activities: Providing dementia specific day program services; Offering education programs & support groups for caregivers; Working in partnership with other agencies in the Region of York to offer services; Providing a Wandering Person Registry; *Awareness Events:* Walk for Memories; Annual Alzheimer Awareness Breakfast; Alzheimer Awareness Month *Library:* Alzheimer Society of York Region Resource Library; Open to public
Chief Officer(s):
Loren Freid, Chief Executive Officer
Janice Clarke, Manager, Finance & Support Services
Publications:
• Alzheimer Society York Region Newsletter
Type: Newsletter
Profile: Articles about Alzheimer's Disease & dementia, plus information about support groups & workshops for caregivers & forthcoming events in the area

Alzheimer Society Ontario / Société Alzheimer Ontario
20 Eglinton Ave. West, 16th Fl., Toronto ON M4R 1K8
Tel: 416-967-5900; *Fax:* 416-967-3826
Toll-Free: 800-879-4226
staff@alzheimeront.org
www.alzheimer.ca
www.facebook.com/AlzheimerSocietyofOntario
twitter.com/Alzheimeront
www.youtube.com/alzheimersocietyont
Also Known As: Alzheimer Ontario
Overview: A large provincial charitable organization founded in 1983 overseen by Alzheimer Society of Canada
Mission: To improve the quality of life for persons with Alzheimer disease & their families; To inform & educate the public & health care professionals about Alzheimer disease; To coordinate a chapter network & liaison in order to present a united voice to the Government of Ontario & other provincial groups on matters relating to legal concerns, health care, research, & community needs; To raise funds for research
Finances: *Annual Operating Budget:* Greater than $5 Million; *Funding Sources:* Private donations
Staff Member(s): 25
Membership: 32 chapters
Activities: Research; education & training; advocacy; member support services; *Awareness Events:* Alzheimer Awareness Month, Jan.; *Speaker Service:* Yes; *Rents Mailing List:* Yes; *Library:* Resource Library; Open to public by appointment
Chief Officer(s):
Pamela Waeland, Chair

Alzheimer Society Peterborough, Kawartha Lakes, Northumberland, & Haliburton (ASPKLNH)
183 Simcoe St., Peterborough ON K9H 2H6
Tel: 705-748-5131; *Fax:* 705-748-6174
Toll-Free: 800-561-2588
info@alzheimerjourney.ca
www.alzheimer.ca/pklnha
www.facebook.com/AlzheimerPKLNH
twitter.com/Alzheimerpklnh
www.youtube.com/thealzheimersociety
Overview: A small local charitable organization founded in 1981
Mission: To improve the quality of life of persons affected by Alzheimer's Disease & related dementias in the Peterborough, Kawartha Lakes, Northumberland & Haliburton regions of Ontario
Finances: *Annual Operating Budget:* $500,000-$1.5 Million; *Funding Sources:* Donations; Fundraising; Ontario Ministry of Health
Staff Member(s): 13; 250 volunteer(s)
Activities: Providing information & support services; Offering a learning series; *Internships:* Yes; *Speaker Service:* Yes; *Library:* Alzheimer Society Lending Library; Open to public
Chief Officer(s):
Carolyn Hemminger, Interim Executive Director
carolyn@alzeimerjourney.ca
Publications:
• Alzheimer Society Peterborough, Kawartha Lakes, Northumberland, & Haliburton eNewsletter
Type: Newsletter
Profile: Reports & forthcoming events in the region

Kawartha Lakes & Haliburton Office
#201, 55 Mary St., Lindsay ON K9V 5Z6
Tel: 705-878-0126; *Fax:* 705-878-0127
Toll-Free: 800-765-0515
admin@alzheimerjourney.ca
www.alzheimer.ca/pklnh
Chief Officer(s):
Pat Finkle, Client Support Coordinator
pat@alzheimerjourney.ca

Lindsay Office
#201, 55 Mary St., Lindsay ON K9V 5Z6
Tel: 705-878-0126; *Fax:* 705-878-0127
Toll-Free: 800-765-0515
info@alzheimerjourney.ca
Chief Officer(s):
Carolyn Hemminger, Coordinator, Public Education
carolyn@alzheimerjourney.ca

Alzheimer Society Waterloo Wellington
1145 Concession Rd., Cambridge ON N3H 4L6
Tel: 519-650-1628; *Fax:* 519-742-1862
asww@alzheimerww.ca
www.alzheimer.ca/ww
www.facebook.com/alzsocww
twitter.com/alzsocww
www.pinterest.com/alzsocietyww
Merged from: Alzheimer Societies of Cambridge, Guelph-Wellington & Kitchener-Waterloo
Overview: A small local charitable organization founded in 2014
Mission: To enhance the lives of persons with Alzheimer disease or related dementias & their care-givers by providing support, information, education, public awareness, advocacy & promotion of research
Member of: Alzheimer Society of Ontario
Affiliation(s): Alzheimer Society of Canada
Finances: *Funding Sources:* Memorial & general donations; fundraising; Ministry of Health
Staff Member(s): 13; 200 volunteer(s)

Canadian Associations / Am Shalom

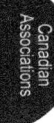

Activities: Walk for Memories; Coffee Break; Caregiver Education Day; *Awareness Events:* Walk for Memories, January; *Speaker Service:* Yes; *Library:* Open to public
Chief Officer(s):
Nancy Kauffman-Lambert, Chair
Jennifer Gillies, Executive Director
jgillies@alzheimerww.ca
   Guelph Office
   #207, 255 Woodlawn Rd. West, Guelph ON N1H 8J1
   Tel: 519-836-7672; *Fax:* 519-742-1862
   Kitchener Office
   831 Frederick St., Kitchener ON N2B 2B4
   Tel: 519-742-1422; *Fax:* 519-742-1862

Alzheimer Support Association of BC *See* Alzheimer Society of British Columbia

Am Shalom
767 Huronia Rd., Barrie ON L4N 9H2
Tel: 705-792-3949; *Fax:* 705-792-3982
amshalomcongregation@bellnet.ca
www.amshalom.ca
www.facebook.com/amshalombarrie
Previous Name: Simcoe County Jewish Association (SCJA)
Overview: A small local charitable organization founded in 1974
Mission: To serve the spiritual & cultural needs of the Jewish population of Barrie & Simcoe County, Ontario; To encourage the observance & study of Jewish religion & culture; To support the Jewish values of social responsibility & knowledge
Membership: *Member Profile:* A Reform Jewish congregation
Activities: Providing weekly services; Offering a children's religious school & adult education programs; Maintaining a Judaica collecion of books that may be borrowed by Am Shalom members; *Library:* Am Shalom's Library
Chief Officer(s):
Audrey Kaufman, Spiritual Leader

Amalgamated Conservation Society (ACS)
PO Box 8741, Victoria BC V8W 3S3
Tel: 250-382-8502
governor@shaw.ca
acsbc.ca
Previous Name: Amalgamated Lower Islands Sportsmen's Association
Overview: A small local organization founded in 1963
Mission: To promote the conservation of fish, game & natural resources; To provide the machinery necessary to put up a united front to combat any program by which the democratic rights of individuals may be threatened; To provide a permanent council through which such joint action may be directed
Finances: *Annual Operating Budget:* Less than $50,000; *Funding Sources:* Donations; government grants
3 volunteer(s)
Membership: 10 organizations representing 3,000 individuals; *Fees:* $30; *Member Profile:* Membership restricted to associations with similar objectives; *Committees:* Projects
Activities: Salmonid Enhancement Projects; *Speaker Service:* Yes
Chief Officer(s):
Thomass Cole, CPO, President, 250-478-1306
Wayne Zaccarelli, Secretary-Treasurer, 250-391-1844

Amalgamated Construction Association of British Columbia *See* British Columbia Construction Association

Amalgamated Lower Islands Sportsmen's Association *See* Amalgamated Conservation Society

Amazones des grands espaces
Montréal QC
Tél: 514-525-3663
info@plein-air-amazones.org
www.plein-air-amazones.org
Aperçu: *Dimension:* petite; *Envergure:* locale; fondée en 1993
Mission: Club de plein air pour lesbiennes
Membre: *Montant de la cotisation:* 20$

Ambulance Paramedics of British Columbia
#105, 21900 Westminster Hwy., Richmond BC V6V 0A8
Tel: 604-273-5722; *Fax:* 604-273-5762
Toll-Free: 866-273-5766
info@apbc.ca
www.paramedicsofbc.com
www.facebook.com/APBC873
twitter.com/apbc873
www.youtube.com/user/APBCCUPE873
Overview: A small provincial organization

Mission: To provide emergency medical care to the sick & injured in British Columbia
Member of: Paramedic Association of Canada
Membership: 3600+
Activities: Offering the following six levels of services: Emergency Medical Dispatching; Medical Air Evacuations (CCT); Infant Transport (ITT); Advanced Care Paramedics (ACP); Primary Care Paramedics (PCP); & Emergency Medical Responder (EMR)

Ambulance Saint-Jean *See* St. John Ambulance

Amelia Rising Sexual Assault Centre of Nipissing / Amelia Rising: Centre d'agressions sexuelles de Nippissing
#11, 101 Worthington St. East, North Bay ON P1B 1G5
Tel: 705-840-2403; *Fax:* 705-840-5050; *Crisis Hot-Line:* 705-476-3355
info@ameliarising.ca
www.ameliarising.ca
www.facebook.com/AmeliaRising
Overview: A small local charitable organization founded in 1994
Mission: To empower & provide a voice for women & the communities in which they live to eliminate violence against women & children; To create social change with respect to issues of equality & justice; to develop, apply & increase awareness of feminist approaches (with an emphasis on action & healing)
Finances: *Annual Operating Budget:* $250,000-$500,000
Staff Member(s): 6; 50 volunteer(s)
Membership: 50
Activities: *Awareness Events:* No One Asks for It!, May; Sexual Assault Awareness Month, May; Take Back the Night, Oct; *Library:* Open to public by appointment
Chief Officer(s):
Brenda Quenneville, Executive Director
executive.director@ameliarising.ca

Amelia Rising: Centre d'agressions sexuelles de Nippissing *See* Amelia Rising Sexual Assault Centre of Nipissing

American Association of Critical Care Nurses - Toronto Chapter; National Society of Critical Care Nurses *See* Canadian Association of Critical Care Nurses

American Connemara Association - Western Canada *See* Canadian Connemara Pony Society

American Council of Co-operative Preschools *See* Parent Cooperative Preschools International

American Galloway Breeders Association (AGBA)
c/o Canadian Livestock Records Corporation, 2417 Holly Lane, Ottawa ON K1V 0M7
Tel: 613-731-7110; *Fax:* 613-731-0704
clrc@clrc.ca
www.americangalloway.com
Overview: A small international organization
Mission: To support the Galloway breed
Affiliation(s): Canadian Livestock Records Corporation (guardians of the American Galloway Breeder's Association herdbook)
Membership: *Fees:* $80 active; $40 junior; $25 associate; *Member Profile:* Galloway breeders
Activities: Offering networking opportunities through shows & events
Chief Officer(s):
Harley Blegen, President
Deb Vance, Vice-President
Joyce Jones, Secretary-Treasurer
Publications:
• AGBA Breeders Directory
Type: Directory; *Price:* Free with American Galloway Breeders Association membership
• The Galloway Dispatch
Type: Newsletter; *Frequency:* Quarterly; *Accepts Advertising*; *Price:* Free with membership in the American Galloway Breeders' Association
Profile: Information about meetings, shows & association happenings

American Immigration Lawyers Association - Canadian Chapter (AILA)
c/o Green & Spiegel LLP, #2800, 390 Bay St., Toronto ON M5H 2Y2
Tel: 416-365-5957; *Fax:* 416-865-9042
Overview: A small international organization
Chief Officer(s):
Evan Green, Chapter Chair

American Saddlebred Horse Association of Alberta (ASHA AB)
10 Lowe Ave., Fort Saskatchewan AB T4N 5E1
Tel: 780-998-4513
rmcwade@xplornet.com
www.saddlebredsofalberta.com
Overview: A small provincial organization founded in 1960
Mission: To foster good sportsmanship, a healthy lifestyle, a sense of responsibility in all age groups through the involvement in the care, training & breeding of the American Saddlebred Horse for both recreation & participation in all disciplines in the sport of horses
Member of: Alberta Equestrian Federation; ASHA Inc.
Affiliation(s): ASHA of Canada
Finances: *Annual Operating Budget:* Less than $50,000
10 volunteer(s)
Membership: 137 individual; *Fees:* $50 family; $30 individual senior; $15 individual junior
Activities: Horse shows; clinics; newsletter; breed promotions
Chief Officer(s):
Suzanne Keglowitsch, President
suekeg@gmail.com

American Saddlebred Horse Association of British Columbia (ASHA of BC)
c/o Carol Court, 7011 Lefeuvre Rd., Abbotsford BC V4X 2C1
Tel: 604-856-4542
courtfarms@telus.net
www.facebook.com/375386385825352
Overview: A small provincial organization overseen by American Saddlebred Horse Association of Canada
Mission: To promote purebred American Saddlebred horses & amateur sport in British Columbia
Membership: *Member Profile:* Individuals, partnerships, & companies in British Columbia interested in the American Saddlebred horse breed for show or for pleasure; Members do not need to own an American Saddlebred horse
Activities: Hosting events, clinics, & shows to showcase American Saddlebred horses in British Columbia; Organizing monthly general meetings in Abbotsford
Chief Officer(s):
Carol Court, Contact

American Saddlebred Horse Association of Canada (ASHAC)
c/o Ellen Murray, PO Box Site 170 Box 27 RR#1, Brandon MB R7A 5Y1
Tel: 204-728-2076
info@saddlebredcanada.com
www.saddlebredcanada.com
Overview: A small national organization founded in 1948
Mission: To develop & regulate the breeding of purebred American Saddlebred horses in Canada; To carry out a system of registration under the Canadian Livestock Records Corporation; To establish breeding standards
Affiliation(s): Canadian Livestock Records Corporation
Membership: *Fees:* $50 / year; *Member Profile:* Individuals, partnerships, & companies in Canada; *Committees:* Executive; Versatility; Fundraising; International Affairs; Promotion; Pedigree
Activities: Encouraging the breeding of purebred American Saddlebred horses in Canada; Supervising breeders; Promoting the breed; Keeping records; Compiling statistics about the industry; Publishing documents
Chief Officer(s):
Melodie Schwieger, President, 403-843-0076
fschwieg@albertahighspeed.net
Publications:
• American Saddlebred Horse Association of Canada Membership Directory
Type: Directory; *Frequency:* Annually; *Price:* Free with membership in the American Saddlebred Horse Association of Canada
Profile: A reference guide with member contact information

American Saddlebred Horse Association of Ontario
c/o Nancy MacDonald, 2792 Concession 9 Drummond, Balderson ON K0G 1A0
www.ashaontario.com
Overview: A small provincial organization overseen by American Saddlebred Horse Association of Canada
Mission: To promote purebred American Saddlebred horses in Ontario
Membership: *Fees:* $25 youth; $35 adult/associate; $50 family; $150 stable/farm; *Member Profile:* Individuals, partnerships, & companies in Ontario

Activities: Hosting events, clinics, & horse shows to showcase American Saddlebred horses in Ontario
Chief Officer(s):
Nancy MacDonald, Contact

American Society of Insurance Management *See* Risk & Insurance Management Society Inc.

American/Canadian Log Builders' Association *See* International Log Builders' Association

Amethyst Scottish Dancers of Nova Scotia
c/o #103, 87 Pebblecreek Cres., Dartmouth NS B2W 0J9
amethystdancersns@gmail.com
www.amethystscottishdancersns.ca
www.facebook.com/1652014618410076
twitter.com/amesthystdancers
Overview: A small provincial organization
Mission: To enrich Nova Scotia's Scottish culture through traditional & modern dance performances
Membership: *Member Profile:* Trained highland & step dancers aged 9-25
Chief Officer(s):
Elizabeth McCorkell, Artistic Director

Amherst & Area Chamber of Commerce
PO Box 283, Amherst NS B4H 3Z4
Tel: 902-667-8186; *Fax:* 902-667-1452
info@amherstchamber.ca
amherstchamberns.ca
www.facebook.com/amherstchamber
twitter.com/amherstchamber
Overview: A small local organization
Membership: *Fees:* Schedule available
Chief Officer(s):
Wayne Bishop, Acting Chair

Amherst Township Historical Society *See* Cumberland Museum Society

Amherstburg Anderdon & Malden Chamber of Commerce *See* Amherstburg Chamber of Commerce

Amherstburg Chamber of Commerce
PO Box 101, 268 Dalhousie St., Amherstburg ON N9V 2Z3
Tel: 519-736-2001; *Fax:* 519-736-9721
amherstburgchamber@gmail.com
www.amherstburgchamber.com
Previous Name: Amherstburg Anderdon & Malden Chamber of Commerce
Overview: A small local organization
Mission: To stimulate economic development in Amherstburg; To improve quality of life for the community
Member of: Ontario Chamber of Commerce
Staff Member(s): 2
Membership: 100-499
Chief Officer(s):
Monica Bunde, General Manager

Amherstburg Community Services
179 Victoria St., Amherstburg ON N9V 3N5
Tel: 519-736-5471; *Fax:* 519-736-1391
staffacs@bellnet.ca
www.amherstburg-cs.com
Overview: A small local organization founded in 1973 overseen by InforOntario
Mission: To study the social, health, educational, recreational and other human needs of the Amherstburg area, and services available to satisfy those needs; To promote the orderly development of well-balanced community services.
Activities: Meals on Wheels; Care A Van Senior Transportation; Security Reassurance Calls; Friendly Visiting; Information and Referral; Coats for Kids; Keep the Heat; NCBS Children's Recreation Program; Jumpstart; Job Bank Computer and Internet Access; Photocopying and Faxing; Free Income Tax Clinic
Chief Officer(s):
Kathy DiBartolomeo, Executive Director
edacs@bellnet.ca

Amherstburg Historic Sites Association
Kings Navy Yard, 214 Dalhousie St., Amherstburg ON N9V 1W4
Tel: 519-736-2511; *Fax:* 519-736-2511
parkhousemuseum@bellnet.ca
www.parkhousemuseum.com
Overview: A small local charitable organization founded in 1973
Mission: To collect, preserve, & exhibit the heritage of Amherstburg, Ontario
Finances: *Funding Sources:* Donations; Grants
Activities: Operating the Park House Museum
Chief Officer(s):
Stephanie L. Pouget, Curator
curator@parkhousemuseum.com
Awards:
• O.H.F. Heritage Community Recognition Award/Cultural Heritage

Les Ami(e)s de la Terre Canada *See* Friends of the Earth Canada

Amicale des Sommeliers du Québec (ASQ)
5310, boul de L'Assomption, Montréal QC H1T 2M2
Tél: 514-729-9537; *Téléc:* 514-729-0366
secretaire@amicaledessommeliers.com
www.amicaledessommeliers.com
Aperçu: *Dimension:* petite; *Envergure:* provinciale; fondée en 1962
Mission: Propager l'amour et la connaissance du vin
Membre: 800; *Montant de la cotisation:* 60$ couple
Activités: Dégustations de vins et des repas gastronomiques; cours sur la connaissance des vins; ateliers sur l'accord des mets et des vins
Membre(s) du bureau directeur:
Lyne Pelletier, Présidente

Amici dell'Enotria Toronto / Friends of the Land of the Wine
31 Shaver Ave. North, Toronto ON M9B 4N5
Tel: 416-234-0079
www.amicidellenotria.com
Also Known As: The Italian Wine Club
Overview: A small international organization founded in 1977
Mission: To promote the appreciation of Italian wines; To organize wine tastings & social events
Finances: *Annual Operating Budget:* Less than $50,000; *Funding Sources:* Membership dues
6 volunteer(s)
Membership: 150; *Fees:* $45 (plus $20 initiation fee)
Activities: *Speaker Service:* Yes
Chief Officer(s):
Vico Paloschi, Chapter Master
vico@amicidellenotria.com

Ami-e du Quartier
655, rue Filion, Saint-Jérôme QC J7Z 1J6
Tél: 450-431-1424
www.facebook.com/lamie.duquartier
Aperçu: *Dimension:* petite; *Envergure:* locale
Mission: Apporter aide et soutien aux personnes et aux familles moins fortunées
Membre: *Montant de la cotisation:* 3$
Membre(s) du bureau directeur:
Sophie Desmarais, Responsable

Les AmiEs de la Terre de Québec (ATQ)
Centre culture et environnement Frédéric Back, #210, 870, rue Salaberry, Québec QC G1R 2T9
Tél: 418-524-2744
info@atquebec.org
www.atquebec.org
Aperçu: *Dimension:* petite; *Envergure:* locale; Organisme sans but lucratif; fondée en 1978
Mission: Conscientiser la population à la crise écologique mondiale versus le droit de tous à un environnement sain; éduquer les gens à leur propre prise en charge personnelle et collective face à cette crise; améliorer les communications entre écologistes aussi bien qu'entre ceux-ci et la population qu'ils desservent; renforcer la qualité de la vie associative chez-nous aussi bien qu'ailleurs dans la région et au Québec
Membre de: Réseau Québécois des Groupes Écologistes (RQGE); Regroupement d'éducation populaire en action communautaire (Répac)
Finances: *Budget de fonctionnement annuel:* Moins de $50,000
Membre(s) du personnel: 9
Membre: 1 857; *Montant de la cotisation:* 10$ travailleur; 5$ non-travailleur; *Comités:* Paix; Environnement et mondialisation; Écologie et santé; Eau; Forêt
Activités: RadioTerre; émission hebdomadaire d'écologie politique diffusée sur les ondes de CKIA FM (Québec); une conférence par mois sur des thèmes reliés à l'écologie; *Service de conférenciers:* Oui; *Bibliothèque:* Centre de documentation des ATQ
Membre(s) du bureau directeur:
Joanie Beaumont, Co-Présidente
Mathieu Goulet, Co-Président

Les amis canadiens de la Birmanie *See* Canadian Friends of Burma

Les Amis de Bibliothèque et archives Canada *See* The Friends of Library & Archives Canada

Amis de la Bibliothèque de Brossard Georgette-Lepage
7855, av San-Francisco, Brossard QC J4X 2A4
Tél: 450-923-6350; *Téléc:* 450-923-7042
lesamis_bibliotheque@brossard.ca
biblio.brossard.ca/amis-de-la-bibliotheque
Aperçu: *Dimension:* petite; *Envergure:* locale; fondée en 2004
Mission: Soutenir l'action et le rayonnement de la Bibliothèque de Brossard; faire la promotion de la Bibliothèque auprès de la population
Membre(s) du bureau directeur:
Jacques-André Chartrand, Président

Les Amis de la déficience intellectuelle Rive-Nord
#213, 50, rue Thouin, Repentigny QC J6A 4J4
Tél: 450-585-3632; *Téléc:* 450-585-3633
lesamis@deficienceintellectuel.org
www.lesamisdirn.org
Aperçu: *Dimension:* petite; *Envergure:* locale; Organisme sans but lucratif; fondée en 1979
Mission: L'organisme vise à sensibiliser la communauté et promouvoir la compréhension des besoins de la personne; offrir l'opportunité et les moyens pour bénéficier au maximum des services et ressources disponibles de la région; donner un support technique pour répondre aux besoins individuels de ses membres et promouvoir une plus grande intégration sociale
Finances: *Fonds:* Gouvernement national; Autofinancement
Membre(s) du personnel: 4
Membre: *Critères d'admissibilite:* Personnes vivant avec une déficience intellectuelle, leurs parents et leurs proches.
Activités: Promotion et défense des droits de nos membres; Activités de loisirs et et de formations
Membre(s) du bureau directeur:
Paulette Goulet, Présidente
Stéphanie-Claude Leclerc, Coordonnatrice

Les Amis du centre canadien d'architecture / Friends of the Canadian Centre for Architecture
1920, rue Baile, Montréal QC H3H 2S6
Tel: 514-939-7026
info@cca.qc.ca
www.cca.qc.ca
www.facebook.com/cca.conversation
twitter.com/ccawire
www.youtube.com/user/CCAchannel
Overview: A medium-sized local organization
Membership: *Fees:* $25 student; $45 adult/architect; $35 senior; $70 family

Les Amis du Jardin botanique de Montréal / Friends of the Montréal Botanical Garden
#206A, 4101, rue Sherbrooke est, Montréal QC H1X 2B2
Tél: 514-872-1493; *Téléc:* 514-872-3765
amisjardin@ville.montreal.qc.ca
www.amisjardin.qc.ca
www.facebook.com/LesAmisduJardinbotaniquedeMontreal
Nom précédent: Société d'animation du Jardin et de l'Institut botanique
Aperçu: *Dimension:* moyenne; *Envergure:* locale; Organisme sans but lucratif; fondée en 1975
Membre de: Fédération des sociétés d'horticulture et d'écologie du Québec (FSHEQ); Flora Québéca
Membre(s) du personnel: 6; 70 bénévole(s)
Membre: 28 000; *Montant de la cotisation:* 30$ étudiant/aîné; 45$ individu; 60$ familial; $180 corporatif
Activités: Cours et ateliers donnés par des spécialistes; Conférences; Visites guidées et excursions; Voyages
Membre(s) du bureau directeur:
Maud Fillion, Contact
maud-ext.fillion@ville.montreal.qc.ca
Paule Lamontagne, Présidente

Les Amis du Musée canadien de la guerre *See* Friends of The Canadian War Museum

Les Amis du Parc Awenda *See* The Friends of Awenda Park

Les Amis du vitrail
Centre Boisvert, 6005, boul Payer, Saint-Hubert QC J3Y 8A6
Tél: 450-812-3799
lesamisduvitrail@hotmail.com
www.lesamisduvitrail.org

Canadian Associations / Amis et propriétaires de maisons anciennes du Québec (APMAQ)

Aperçu: *Dimension:* petite; *Envergure:* locale; fondée en 1980
Mission: De rassembler les gens qui aiment la fabrication de vitraux afin de les encourager et de faire des projets ensemble
Activités: Ateliers; Cours de vitrail; Séminaires
Membre(s) du bureau directeur:
Normand Carrière, Président, Conseil d'administraion

Amis et propriétaires de maisons anciennes du Québec (APMAQ)
2050, rue Amherst, Montréal QC H2L 3L8
Tél: 514-528-8444; *Téléc:* 514-528-8686
apmaq@globetrotter.net
www.maisons-anciennes.qc.ca
Aperçu: *Dimension:* petite; *Envergure:* provinciale; Organisme sans but lucratif; fondée en 1980
Prix, Bourses:
- Prix Robert-Lionel-Séguin
- Prix régional
- Prix de mérite

Amitié Chinoise de Montréal *See* Chinese Neighbourhood Society of Montréal

Amity Goodwill Industries *See* Goodwill, The Amity Group

Amma Foundation of Canada
PO Box 21037, RPO Meadowvale, Mississauga ON L5N 6A2
Tel: 905-785-8175
info@ammacanada.ca
www.ammacanada.ca
Overview: A small national organization
Mission: To help the poor & destitute by seeking out & participating in programs; to follow the example of Amma, who instucts, "compassion to the poor is our duty to God"
Membership: *Member Profile:* Individuals who are inspired by the love & compassion of Amma & wish to work to help the less fortunate
Activities: Donating money, food, clothing, & education to the less fortunate; Offering assistance to those in need through Amma's Kitchen, Amma's Closet, food banks, garage sales, penny money collection, & empty pop can collectin
Chief Officer(s):
Raman Nair, Contact
toronto@ammacanada.ca

Amnesty International - Canadian Section (English Speaking)
312 Laurier Ave. East, Ottawa ON K1N 1H9
Tel: 613-744-7667; *Fax:* 613-746-2411
Toll-Free: 800-266-3789
info@amnesty.ca
www.amnesty.ca
www.facebook.com/amnestycanada
twitter.com/AmnestyNow
Also Known As: Amnesty Canada
Overview: A medium-sized international charitable organization founded in 1973
Mission: AI Canada is part of a worldwide movement which is independent of any government, political grouping, ideology, economic interest or religious creed. It's primary aim is to bring public attention to abuses of human rights standards, particularly cases where people are imprisoned for their beliefs, or "prisoners of conscience." It holds that mass public pressure, expressed through effective forms of action, is critical to preventing & ending human rights violations. It also works to abolish the death penalty, torture, & other cruel treatment of prisoners, to end political killings & "disappearances."
Affiliation(s): Formal relations with United Nations Economic & Social Council (ECOSOC), UNESCO, Council of Europe; Organization of American States, Organization of African Unity & Inter-Parliamentary Union
Finances: *Annual Operating Budget:* Greater than $5 Million; *Funding Sources:* Individuals
Staff Member(s): 47
Membership: 58,000; *Fees:* $35; *Member Profile:* All cultures & walks of life; human rights activists & financial supporters
Activities: Film festivals; Meetings; Yoga fundraisers
Chief Officer(s):
David Smith, Chair
dsmith@amnesty.ca
Sharmila Setaram, President
ssetaram@amnesty.ca
Robert Goodfellow, Executive Director
Toronto Office
1992 Yonge St., 3rd Fl., Toronto ON M4S 1Z7
Tel: 416-363-9933; *Fax:* 416-363-3103
www.aito.ca
www.facebook.com/AmnestyToronto
twitter.com/AmnestyToronto
www.youtube.com/user/AmnestyIntlToronto
Mission: To help fight human rights injustices by raising awareness about them through events
Member of: Amenstry International
Chief Officer(s):
Ted Wood, Chair
Vancouver Regional Office
#430, 319 West Pender St., Vancouver BC V6B 1T4
Tel: 604-294-5160; *Fax:* 604-294-5130
vancouver.intern@amnesty.ca
www.amnesty.ca
www.facebook.com/128797077188904

Amnesty International, Canadian Section (Francophone)
Voir Amnistie internationale, Section canadienne (Francophone)

Amnistie internationale, Section canadienne (Francophone) / Amnesty International, Canadian Section (Francophone)
#500, 50, rue Sainte-Catherine ouest, Montréal QC H2X 3V4
Tél: 514-766-9766; *Téléc:* 514-766-2088
Ligne sans frais: 800-565-9766
accueil@amnistie.ca
www.amnistie.ca
www.facebook.com/Amnistie.internationale.Canada.francophone
twitter.com/AmnistieCa
Aperçu: *Dimension:* moyenne; *Envergure:* internationale; fondée en 1973
Mission: Mouvement d'intervention directe formé de bénévoles qui visent à la libération des prisonniers d'opinion, la tenue de procès équitables pour les prisonniers politiques, l'abolition de la torture et la cessation des "disparitions" et assassinats politiques
Membre(s) du personnel: 14
Membre: 20 000
Activités: *Evénements de sensibilisation:* Congrès des jeunes d'Amnistie; *Service de conférenciers:* Oui; *Bibliothèque:* Bibliothèque publique rendez-vous
Membre(s) du bureau directeur:
Béatrice Vaugrante, Directrice générale
direction@amnistie.ca

Among Equals *See* Inter Pares

Amputee Society of Ottawa & District
#1404, 505 Smyth Rd., Ottawa ON K1H 8M2
Tel: 613-737-7350; *Fax:* 613-737-7056
Overview: A small local organization
Mission: Provides support to new amputees from trained amputee visitors, information on community services available to amputees and ongoing contact with amputees via a visitor program
Chief Officer(s):
Betty Lanigan, President
bblanigan@hotmail.com

Les Amputés de guerre du Canada *See* The War Amputations of Canada

An Cumann/The Irish Association of Nova Scotia
PO Box 27153, Halifax NS B3H 4M8
info@ancumann.org
www.ancumann.org
Overview: A small provincial organization founded in 1990
Mission: To foster knowledge & enjoyment of Irish customs, culture & heritage throughout Nova Scotia
Membership: *Fees:* $15 individual; $20 family
Activities: Irish heritage evenings; workshops; *Speaker Service:* Yes
Chief Officer(s):
David Moriarity, President
Pat Curran, Secretary

Analystes des minéraux canadiens *See* Canadian Mineral Analysts

Anaphylaxis Canada *See* Food Allergy Canada

Ancaster Community Services (ACS)
300 Wilson St. East, Ancaster ON L9G 2B9
Tel: 905-648-6675
www.ancastercommunityservices.ca
www.facebook.com/AncasterCommunityServices.ca
Previous Name: Ancaster Information Centre & Community Services Inc.
Overview: A small local charitable organization founded in 1969 overseen by InformOntario
Finances: *Annual Operating Budget:* $100,000-$250,000
Membership: *Committees:* Personnel; Public Awareness
Activities: Meals on Wheels; assisted driving; community outreach and counselling; home support; Christmas outreach; senior services; food vouchers; youth empowerment services
Chief Officer(s):
Melanie Barlow, Interim Executive Director

Ancaster Information Centre & Community Services Inc.
See Ancaster Community Services

Anchor Industries Society *See* Building Futures Employment Society

Les Anciens combattants de l'armée, de la marine et des forces aériennes au Canada *See* Army, Navy & Air Force Veterans in Canada

Ancient, Free & Accepted Masons of Canada - Grand Lodge in the Province of Ontario (AF & AM)
363 King St. West, Hamilton ON L8P 1B4
Tel: 905-528-8644; *Fax:* 905-528-6979
office@grandlodge.on.ca
www.grandlodge.on.ca
Overview: A medium-sized provincial organization
Mission: To promote Freemasonry in Ontario
Publications:
- The Ontario Mason Magazine

Type: Magazine; *Accepts Advertising; Editor:* V.W. Bro. Bruce Miller
Profile: Articles about charitable work, events, & local activities

Ancient, Free & Accepted Masons of Canada - Grand Lodge of Alberta (AF & AM)
330 - 12 Ave. SW, Calgary AB T2R 0H2
Tel: 403-262-1149; *Fax:* 403-290-0671
grandsecretary@freemasons.ab.ca
www.freemasons.ab.ca
twitter.com/albertamasons
Overview: A medium-sized provincial organization founded in 1905
Staff Member(s): 4
Activities: *Library:* by appointment
Chief Officer(s):
Peter Dunlop, Grand Master
Jerry Kopp, Grand Secretary, 403-262-1149, Fax: 403-290-0671
Awards:
- Masonic Higher Education Bursaries

Awarded to worthy students across Alberta & the Northwest Territories *Eligibility:* Students in Alberta & the Northwest Territories who are in financial need & are trying to pursue post-secondary education; *Amount:* $2,000
Meetings/Conferences:
- Ancient, Free & Accepted Masons of the Grand Lodge of Alberta 2018 Annual Communication, June, 2018, Grande Prairie, AB

Scope: Provincial
Publications:
- The Alberta Freemason

Type: Magazine; *Frequency:* 10 pa; *Editor:* RW Bro. George Tapley; *Price:* $10 plus mailing costs, non-members
Profile: Updates about programs, activities & events, provided to Freemason of Alberta & the Northwest Territories west of the 4th Meridian who are members of The Grand Lodge of Alberta,A.F. & A.M.

Ancient, Free & Accepted Masons of Canada - Grand Lodge of British Columbia *See* Ancient, Free & Accepted Masons of Canada - Grand Lodge of British Columbia & Yukon

Ancient, Free & Accepted Masons of Canada - Grand Lodge of British Columbia & Yukon
1495 West 8th Ave., Vancouver BC V6H 1C9
Tel: 604-736-8941; *Fax:* 604-736-5097
grand_secretary@freemasonry.bcy.ca
freemasonry.bcy.ca
Previous Name: Ancient, Free & Accepted Masons of Canada - Grand Lodge of British Columbia
Overview: A medium-sized provincial organization founded in 1871
Staff Member(s): 4
Membership: 13,000
Chief Officer(s):
William R. Cave, Grand Master
Meetings/Conferences:
- Ancient, Free & Accepted Masons of the Grand Lodge of British Columbia & Yukon 2018 Masonic Leadership & Ladies Conference, 2018

Scope: Provincial
Description: Discussions of leadership skills, best practices in lodge leadership, & information about the Grand Lodge
Publications:
• The Freemasons & the Masonic Family of British Columbia & Yukon Information Booklet
Type: Booklet
Profile: Contents include an introductions to Freemasonry, historical highlights of Freemasonry, the organization of the Grand Lodge of BritishColumbia, charity, religion, & Grand Masters of the jurisdiction
• Masonic Bulletin
Type: Newsletter; *Frequency:* Monthly; *Editor:* VW Bro. Trevor W. McKeown
Profile: Distributed though the lodge secretaries to every member of the jurisdiction

Ancient, Free & Accepted Masons of Canada - Grand Lodge of New Brunswick
PO Box 6430, Stn. A, Saint John NB E2L 4R6
masonic@nbnet.nb.ca
www.nbmf.org/othrpage/blue0001.htm
Overview: A medium-sized provincial organization founded in 1867
Mission: To improve life by improving the men who live it while never losing sight of the need to preserve the past, serve the present & prepare for the future
Activities: *Library:*

Ancient, Free & Accepted Masons of Canada - Grand Lodge of Nova Scotia
167 Coronation Ave., Halifax NS B3N 2N2
Tel: 902-423-6149; *Fax:* 902-423-6254
www.grandlodgens.org
Overview: A medium-sized international charitable organization founded in 1866
Membership: *Member Profile:* Male, 21 years old & over; belief in God; *Committees:* Public Relations
Activities: *Library:* Open to public by appointment
Chief Officer(s):
Robert Northup, Grand Secretary
Publications:
• The Nova Scotia Freemason: The Official Bulletin of the Grand Lodge of Nova Scotia
Type: Newsletter
Profile: Articles & information from the lodges & districts

Ancient, Free & Accepted Masons of Canada - Grand Lodge of Prince Edward Island
PO Box 337, Charlottetown PE C1A 7K7
Tel: 902-964-2925
www.peifreemasonry.com
Also Known As: Grand Lodge of PEI
Overview: A medium-sized provincial organization founded in 1875
Finances: *Annual Operating Budget:* Less than $50,000; *Funding Sources:* Membership fees
Membership: 845
Activities: *Library:* by appointment
Chief Officer(s):
Donald Rodd, Grand Secretary
grandsecretary@freemasonry.pe.ca

Ancient, Free & Accepted Masons of Canada - Grand Lodge of Québec *See* Grand Lodge of Québec - Ancient, Free & Accepted Masons

Anemia Institute for Research & Education *See* Institute for Optimizing Health Outcomes

The Anglican Church of Canada (ACC) / L'Église anglicane du Canada
80 Hayden St., Toronto ON M4Y 3G2
Tel: 416-924-9192; *Fax:* 416-968-7983
information@national.anglican.ca
www.anglican.ca
www.facebook.com/canadiananglican
twitter.com/generalsynod
www.youtube.com/generalsynod
Previous Name: Church of England in Canada
Overview: A large national charitable organization founded in 1893
Mission: To proclaim & celebrate the gospel of Jesus Christ in worship & action, as a partner in the world-wide Anglican Communion & the universal church; To value heritage of faith, reason, liturgy, tradition, bishops & synods, & the rich variety of life in community; To acknowledge that God calls His followers to greater diversity of membership, wider participation in ministry & leadership, better stewardship in God's creation & a strong resolve in challenging attitudes & structures which cause injustice
Member of: Canadian Council of Churches
Membership: 500,000+ members; 1,700 churches;
Committees: Communications & Information Resources; Faith, Worship & Ministry; Financial Management; Partners in Missions & Ecojustice; Philanthropy
Activities: Operates four incorporated bodies: the Anglican Foundation of Canada, Anglican Journal, Primate's World Relief & Development Fund, & Pension Office Corporation.; *Library:* Anglican Church of Canada Library; by appointment
Chief Officer(s):
Fred Hiltz, Primate, Anglican Church of Canada
primate@national.anglican.ca
Michael Thompson, General Secretary
mthompson@national.anglican.ca
Publications:
• Anglican Journal [a publication of the Anglican Church of Canada]
Type: Newspaper; *Frequency:* 10x/yr.; *Editor:* Marites (Tess) N. Sison; *ISSN:* 0847-978X
Profile: The national newspaper of the Anglican Church of Canada, with a circulation of 160,000

Diocese of Algoma
PO Box 1168, 619 Wellington St. East, Sault Ste Marie ON P6A 5N7
Tel: 702-256-5061; *Fax:* 702-946-1860
secretary@dioceseofalgoma.com
www.dioceseofalgoma.com
Chief Officer(s):
Stephen Andrews, Bishop
bishop@dioceseofalgoma.com

Diocese of the Arctic
PO Box 190, Yellowknife NT X1A 2N2
Tel: 867-873-5432; *Fax:* 867-873-8478
dota@arcticnet.org
www.arcticnet.org
Chief Officer(s):
Doug Doak, Executive Officer
doug@arcticnet.org

Diocese of Athabasca
PO Box 6868, Peace River AB T8S 1S6
Tel: 780-624-2767; *Fax:* 780-624-2365
www.dioath.ca
www.facebook.com/TheDioceseOfAthabasca
twitter.com/AthabascaDioces
Chief Officer(s):
Fraser Lawton, Bishop

Diocese of Brandon
341 13th St., Brandon MB R7A 4P8
Tel: 204-727-7550; *Fax:* 204-727-4135
office@dioceseb.com
www.dioceseofbrandon.org
Chief Officer(s):
William Grant Cliff, BA, MDiv, MA, D, Bishop

Diocese of British Columbia
900 Vancouver St., Victoria BC V8V 3V7
Tel: 250-386-7781; *Fax:* 250-386-4013
Toll-Free: 800-582-8627
synod@bc.anglican.ca
www.bc.anglican.ca
www.facebook.com/BCAnglican
twitter.com/BCAnglican
Chief Officer(s):
Logan McMenamie, Bishop
bishop@bc.anglican.ca

Diocese of Caledonia
#201, 4716 Lazelle Ave., Terrace BC V8G 1T2
Tel: 250-635-6016; *Fax:* 250-635-6026
caledonia@telus.net
www.caledoniaanglican.ca
Chief Officer(s):
William Anderson, Bishop
bishopbill@telus.net

Diocese of Calgary
#180, 1209 - 59th Ave. SE, Calgary AB T2H 2P6
Tel: 403-243-3673; *Fax:* 403-243-2182
diocese@calgary.anglican.ca
www.calgary.anglican.ca
www.facebook.com/calgary.anglican
twitter.com/@CalgaryAnglican
Chief Officer(s):
Barry Foster, Executive Officer & Archdeacon, 403-243-3673 Ext. 112, *Fax:* 403-243-2182
bfoster@calgary.anglican.ca

Diocese of Central Newfoundland
34 Fraser Rd., Gander NL A1V 2E8
Tel: 709-256-2372; *Fax:* 709-256-2396
Chief Officer(s):
David Torraville, Bishop
bishopcentral@nfld.net

Diocese of Eastern Newfoundland & Labrador
19 King's Bridge Rd., St. John's NL A1C 3K4
Tel: 709-576-6697; *Fax:* 709-576-7122
anglicanenl.net
Chief Officer(s):
Geoff Peddle, BA, MA, PhD, Bishop, 709-576-6697
geoffpeddle48@gmail.com

Diocese of Edmonton
#10035, 103 St., Edmonton AB T5J 0X5
Tel: 780-439-7344; *Fax:* 780-439-6549
Toll-Free: 877-494-8890
churched@edmonton.anglican.ca
edmonton.anglican.org
Chief Officer(s):
Jane Alexander, Bishop
bishop@edmonton.anglican.ca

Diocese of Fredericton
115 Church St., Fredericton NB E3B 4C8
Tel: 506-459-1801; *Fax:* 506-460-0520
diocese@anglican.nb.ca
www.anglican.nb.ca
Chief Officer(s):
David Edwards, Bishop, 506-459-1801 Ext. 223

Diocese of Huron
190 Queens Ave., London ON N6A 6H7
Tel: 519-434-6893; *Fax:* 519-673-4151
huron@huron.anglican.ca
www.diohuron.org
Chief Officer(s):
Robert F. Bennett, BA, MDiv, DD, Bishop

Diocese of Keewatin
915 Ottawa St., Keewatin ON P0X 1C0
Tel: 807-547-3353; *Fax:* 807-547-3356
dioceseofkeewatin@shaw.ca
www.dioceseofkeewatin.ca
Chief Officer(s):
David Ashdown, Bishop
keewatinbishop@shaw.ca

Diocese of Kootenay
#201, 380 Leathead Rd., Kelowna BC V1X 2H8
Tel: 778-478-8310; *Fax:* 778-478-8314
admin@kootenay.info
www.kootenayanglican.ca
Chief Officer(s):
John Privett, Bishop

Diocese of Montréal
1444, av Union, Montréal QC H3A 2B8
Tel: 514-843-6577
Toll-Free: 800-355-3788
info@montreal.anglican.ca
www.montreal.anglican.ca
www.facebook.com/AnglicanMtl
twitter.com/AnglicanMtl
www.instagram.com/anglicanmtl
Chief Officer(s):
Mary Irwin Gisbon, Bishop
bishops.office@montreal.anglican.ca

Diocese of Moosonee
PO Box 735, 113 Third St., Cochrane ON P0L 1C0
Tel: 705-272-4310; *Fax:* 705-272-4932
administrator@moosoneeanglican.ca
www.moosoneeanglican.ca
Chief Officer(s):
Colin Johnson, Bishop

Diocese of New Westminster
1410 Nanton Ave., Vancouver BC V6H 2E2
Tel: 604-684-6306; *Fax:* 604-684-7017
info@vancouver.anglican.ca
www.vancouver.anglican.ca
www.facebook.com/130319853684475
twitter.com/dofnwcomm
www.instagram.com/bishop_melissa
Chief Officer(s):
Melissa M. Skelton, Bishop
bishop@vancouver.anglican.ca

Canadian Associations / Anglican Foundation of Canada

Diocese of Niagara
Cathedral Place, 252 James St. North, Hamilton ON L8R 2L3
Tel: 905-527-1316
www.niagara.anglican.ca
www.facebook.com/niagaraanglican
twitter.com/NiagaraAnglican
Chief Officer(s):
Michael A. Bird, Bishop, 905-527-1316 Ext. 310

Diocese of Nova Scotia & Prince Edward Island
1340 Cathedral Ln, Halifax NS B3H 2Z1
Tel: 902-420-0717; *Fax:* 902-425-0717
office@nspeidiocese.ca
www.nspeidiocese.ca
Chief Officer(s):
Ron Cutler, Bishop, 902-420-0717 Ext. 1168, Fax: 902-425-0717
rcutler@nspeidiocese.ca

Diocese of Ontario
90 Johnson St., Kingston ON K7L 1X7
Tel: 613-544-4774; *Fax:* 613-547-3745
Toll-Free: 866-524-4774
www.ontario.anglican.ca
Chief Officer(s):
Michael D Oulton, Bishop
moulton@ontario.anglican.ca

Diocese of Ottawa
71 Bronson Ave., Ottawa ON K1R 6G6
Tel: 613-232-7124; *Fax:* 613-232-7088
admin@ottawa.anglican.ca
ottawa.anglican.ca
www.facebook.com/OttawaAnglican
twitter.com/OttawaAnglican
Chief Officer(s):
John H Chapman, BA, MDiv, DMin, Bishop, 613-233-7741
bishopsoffice@ottawa.anglican.ca

Diocese of Qu'Appelle
Regina SK
Tel: 360-522-1608
hello@quappelle.anglican.ca
quappelle.anglican.ca
www.linkedin.com/company/diocese-of-qu%27appelle
www.facebook.com/dioceseofquappelle
twitter.com/dioquappelle
www.youtube.com/user/dioceseofquappelle
Chief Officer(s):
Robert Hardwick, Bishop, 306-522-1608
bishop.rob@sasktel.net

Diocese of Québec
31, rue des Jardins, Québec QC G1R 4L6
Tel: 418-692-3858
synodoffice@quebec.anglican.ca
www.quebec.anglican.org
www.facebook.com/174486834962
twitter.com/quebecdiocese
Chief Officer(s):
Dennis Paul Drainville, Bishop
bishop@quebec.anglican.ca

Diocese of Rupert's Land
935 Nesbitt Bay, Winnipeg MB R3T 1W6
Tel: 204-992-4200; *Fax:* 204-992-4219
general@rupertsland.ca
www.rupertsland.ca
Chief Officer(s):
Donald Phillips, PhD, Bishop, 204-992-4212
bishop@rupertsland.ca

Diocese of Saskatchewan
1308 - Fifth Ave. East, Prince Albert SK S6V 2H7
Tel: 306-763-2455; *Fax:* 306-764-5172
synod@sasktel.net
www.skdiocese.com
Chief Officer(s):
Michael W. Hawkins, Bishop
bishopmichael@sasktel.net

Diocese of Saskatoon
1403 9th Ave. North, Saskatoon SK S7K 2Z6
Tel: 306-244-5651; *Fax:* 306-933-4606
anglicansynod@sasktel.net
www.anglicandiocesesaskatoon.com
Chief Officer(s):
David M. Irving, Bishop
bishopdavid@sasktel.net

Diocese of Toronto
135 Adelaide St. East, Toronto ON M5C 1L8
Tel: 416-363-6021; *Fax:* 416-363-7678
Toll-Free: 800-668-8932
www.toronto.anglican.ca
Chief Officer(s):
Colin R. Johnson, Bishop, 416-363-6021 Ext. 250
cjohnson@toronto.anglican.ca

Diocese of Western Newfoundland
25 Main St., Corner Brook NL A2H 1C2
Tel: 709-639-8712; *Fax:* 709-639-1636
dsown@nf.aibn.com
www.westernnewfoundland.anglican.org
Chief Officer(s):
Percy D. Coffin, Bishop, 709-632-7868
bishop_dsown@nf.aibn.com

Diocese of the Yukon
PO Box 31136, Whitehorse YT Y1A 5P7
Tel: 867-667-7746; *Fax:* 867-667-6125
anglican.yukon.net
www.facebook.com/Diocese-of-Yukon-169969219696045
Chief Officer(s):
Larry Robertson, Bishop
synodoffice@klondiker.com

Anglican Foundation of Canada
Anglican Church House, 80 Hayden St., Toronto ON M4V 3G2
Tel: 416-924-9199
Toll-Free: 866-924-9192
foundation@anglicanfoundation.org
www.anglicanfoundation.org
www.youtube.com/user/AnglicanFoundation
Overview: A small national charitable organization founded in 1957
Mission: To assist parishes, dioceses & programs of Anglican Church of Canada with low interest loans &/or grants
Affiliation(s): World Council of Churches
Activities: *Speaker Service:* Yes
Chief Officer(s):
Judy Rois, Executive Director, 416-924-9199 Ext. 234
Emily Wall, Project Manager, 416-924-9199 Ext. 322

Anglican Houses *See* LOFT Community Services

Anglophones for Québec Independence (AQI)
info@aqi.quebec
aqi.quebec
twitter.com/AnglosQCindepen
Overview: A small provincial organization
Mission: To promote Québec sovereignty
Chief Officer(s):
Jennifer Drouin, Founder

Animal Aid Foundation
PO Box 6, #114, 2400 Dundas St. West, Mississauga ON L5K 2R8
Tel: 647-558-7387
info@animalaidfoundation.ca
www.animalaidfoundation.ca
www.facebook.com/animalaidfoundationcanada
Overview: A medium-sized national charitable organization
Mission: To reduce animal overpopulation; To provide support for spay/neuter programs of local animal charities
Finances: *Funding Sources:* Donations; Corporations
Activities: Fundraising; Funding local spay/neuter programs & projects

Animal Alliance Environment Voters Party of Canada *See* Animal Protection Party of Canada

Animal Alliance of Canada (AAC) / Alliance animale du Canada
#101, 221 Broadview Ave., Toronto ON M4M 2G3
Tel: 416-462-9541; *Fax:* 416-462-9647
contact@animalalliance.ca
www.animalalliance.ca
www.facebook.com/132125293547127
twitter.com/Animal_Alliance
www.youtube.com/user/AACoffice
Overview: A medium-sized national organization founded in 1990
Mission: To preserve & protect all animals; to promote harmonious relationship between people, animals & the environment; to address issues including pound seizure, cosmetic & product testing, puppy mills, pet overpopulation, exotic pet trade, the fur trade, sport hunting, factory farming, animals as "entertainment"
Finances: *Funding Sources:* Private donations; garage sales; merchandise; information & displays
Staff Member(s): 5; 130 volunteer(s)
Membership: 20,000
Activities: Promoting cruelty-free, environmentally friendly biodegradable products; currently involved in working to ban pound seizure; information displays; National Wolf Campaign; Endangered Species Campaign; working to end the destruction of over 1,000,000 companion animals (abandoned & unwanted pets) in Canada each year through legislation, spay/neuter programs & public education; working to ban the keeping of exotic animals as pets; *Awareness Events:* "Literary Lions" annual literary benefit; "Animal Magnetism" annual music benefit
Library: Animal Alliance Resource Centre
Chief Officer(s):
Liz White, Coordinator, Fundraising, 416-462-9541 Ext. 23
liz@animalalliance.ca
Lia Laskaris, Coordinator, Donor Relations
lia@animalalliance.ca

Animal Defence & Anti-Vivisection Society of BC (ADAV)
PO Box 34553, 1268 Marine Dr., North Vancouver BC V7P 1T0
adavsociety@gmail.com
vivisectionresearch.ca
Overview: A small provincial organization
Finances: *Funding Sources:* Private
Staff Member(s): 6
Membership: 200; *Fees:* $5 student/senior; $10 individual; $50 lifetime
Chief Officer(s):
Anne Birthistle, Director
shamrockstudio@shaw.ca
John Pranger, Director, 604-564-1432
prangerjohn@yahoo.ca

Animal Defence League of Canada (ADLC)
PO Box 3880, Stn. C, Ottawa ON K1Y 4M5
Tel: 613-233-6117; *Fax:* 613-233-6117
animal-defence.ncf.ca
Overview: A medium-sized national organization founded in 1958
Mission: To promote animal welfare/rights; To disseminate information; To encourage spaying & neutering of cats & dogs; To increase public awareness of oppression of animals & how to prevent or alleviate animal exploitation, cruelty & suffering
Member of: World Society for the Protection of Animals
Finances: *Funding Sources:* Donations; Membership fees
Membership: *Fees:* $50 lifetime; $10 individual; $5 senior/student
Activities: *Speaker Service:* Yes; *Library:* Open to public

Animal Health Technologists Association of BC *See* British Columbia Veterinary Technologists Association

Animal Justice
#5700, 100 King St. West, Toronto ON M5X 1C7
info@animaljustice.ca
www.animaljustice.ca
www.facebook.com/animaljusticecanada
twitter.com/AnimalJustice
www.instagram.com/animaljustice_
Overview: A medium-sized national organization
Mission: To advocate for animal protection in Canada; To pass progressive animal protection legislation; To enforce existing animal laws; To ensure the prosecution of animal abusers; To fight on behalf of animals in court
Chief Officer(s):
Camille Labchuk, Executive Director

Animal Nutrition Association of Canada (ANAC) / Association de nutrition animale du Canada
#1301, 150 Metcalfe St., Ottawa ON K2P 1P1
Tel: 613-241-6421; *Fax:* 613-241-7970
info@anacan.org
www.anacan.org
Previous Name: Canadian Feed Industry Association
Overview: A large national organization founded in 1929
Mission: ANAC advocates on behalf of the livestock & poultry feed industry with government regulators & policy-makers, & works to maintain high standards of feed & food safety.
Member of: International Feed Industry Federation (IFIF)
Affiliation(s): Canola Council of Canada; Canada Grains Council; Canadian Egg Marketing Agency; Canadian Chicken Marketing Agency; Canadian Turkey Marketing Agency
Finances: *Funding Sources:* Membership fees
Staff Member(s): 4
Membership: 170 organizations; *Fees:* Variable; *Member Profile:* Manufacturers & suppliers of animal nutrition products to

Canada's livestock & poultry industries; *Committees:* Executive; Nutrition
Activities: FeedAssure program; ISO 22000 Certification; webinars; promotion of environment & animal care issues, & regulations & legislation pertaining to feed products, manufacturing, food safety & salmonella control; monitors regulations pertaining to agricultural trade & international & interprovincial import & export
Chief Officer(s):
Des Gelz, Chair
Graham Cooper, Executive Director
Awards:
• ANAC Graduate Scholarship
Eligibility: Must be enrolled in Animal Science or a related field of study, with an interest in animal nutrition; *Amount:* $2,000
Meetings/Conferences:
• Animal Nutrition Association of Canada 2018 Animal Nutrition Conference of Canada, May, 2018, Chateau Lacombe Hotel, Edmonton, AB
Scope: National
Publications:
• Directory of Members [a publication of the Animal Nutrition Association of Canada]
Type: Directory
Alberta Division
PO Box 1095, Brooks AB T1R 1B9
Tel: 403-362-2905; *Fax:* 403-501-5456
anac-ab.ca
Chief Officer(s):
Glenn Ravnsborg, Division Manager
Atlantic Division
53 Elliott Dr., Sussex NB E4E 2K5
Tel: 506-433-5917
anacatla@rogers.com
Chief Officer(s):
Dave Colpitts, Executive Manager & Secretary-Treasurer
British Columbia Division
44370 Simpson Rd., Chilliwack BC V2R 4B7
Tel: 604-866-2378; *Fax:* 604-794-3697
Chief Officer(s):
Robert Dornan, Secretary-Treasurer
rjdornan@telus.net
Manitoba Division
55 River Heights Dr., La Salle MB R0G 0A2
Tel: 204-736-4833; *Fax:* 204-736-3583
Chief Officer(s):
John Enns, Business Manager
jenns.anac@gmail.com
Ontario Agri Business Association (OABA)
#104, 160 Research Lane, Guelph ON N1G 5B2
Tel: 519-822-3004; *Fax:* 519-822-8862
info@oaba.on.ca
www.oaba.on.ca
Chief Officer(s):
Dave Buttenham, Chief Executive Officer
dave@oaba.on.ca
Québec Division
#200, 4790, rue Martineau, Saint-Hyacinthe QC J2S 7B4
Tél: 450-799-2440; *Téléc:* 450-799-2445
info@aqinac.com
www.aqinac.com
Chief Officer(s):
Yves Lacroix, Président-directeur général
yvan.lacroix@aqinac.com
Saskatchewan Division
c/o Hood Packaging Corp., 339 Poth Cres., Saskatoon SK S7M 4T7
Tel: 306-978-4720; *Fax:* 306-978-4745
Allen Doherty, Secretary-Treasurer
adoherty@hoodpkg.com

Animal Protection Party of Canada
#101, 221 Broadview Ave., Toronto ON M4M 2G3
Tel: 416-462-9541; *Fax:* 416-462-9647
www.animalprotectionparty.ca
www.facebook.com/AnimalProtectionParty
twitter.com/AnimalProtectCA
Previous Name: Animal Alliance Environment Voters Party of Canada
Overview: A medium-sized national organization founded in 2005
Mission: To promote a principle of just & equitable human progress that respects, protects, & enhances the environment & the lives of the animals.
Affiliation(s): Animal Alliance of Canada
Finances: *Funding Sources:* Private donations
Chief Officer(s):
Liz White, Leader
liz@animalprotectionparty.ca
Stephen Best, Chief Agent
stephen@animalprotectionparty.ca

Animal Welfare Foundation of Canada (AWF) / Fondation du bien-être animal du Canada
#343, 300 Earl Grey Dr., Ottawa ON K2T 1C1
info@awfc.ca
www.awfc.ca
Overview: A small national charitable organization founded in 1965
Mission: The Animal Welfare Foundation of Canada is a registered charity, supported by donors and administered by a volunteer Board of Directors. The Foundation seeks to improve the quality of life for animals in this country. Since the 1960s the Foundation, an independent watchdog organization, has been at the forefront of issues of humane care of animals in Canada.
Affiliation(s): World Society for the Protection of Animals
Finances: *Annual Operating Budget:* $100,000-$250,000
14 volunteer(s)
Activities: *Speaker Service:* Yes
Chief Officer(s):
Alice Crook, President & Chair
Frances Rodenberg, Secretary

ANKORS
West Kootenay Regional Office, 101 Baker St., Nelson BC V1L 4H1
Tel: 250-505-5506; *Fax:* 250-505-5507
information@ankors.bc.ca
www.ankors.bc.ca
www.facebook.com/ankors.west
twitter.com/ankorswest
Also Known As: AIDS Network Kootenay Outreach & Support Society
Previous Name: AIDS Network, Outreach & Support Society
Overview: A small local charitable organization founded in 1992
Mission: To provide support, care, outreach & harm reduction services to individuals living with & affected by HIV, AIDS & HepC
Member of: Pacific AIDS Network; Kootenay Pride; Canadian Aids Society; CATIE; Canadian Treatment Action Council; Positive Living BC; Canadian HIV/AIDS Legal Network; HepC BC; Positive Women's Network; Canadian Aboriginial AIDS Network
Affiliation(s): West Kootenay Women's Association; Advocacy Centre; Nelson CARES Society; Nelson Committee on Homelessness
Finances: *Funding Sources:* Donations; Health Canada; HRAC; Columbia Basin Trust; Interior Health Authority
Staff Member(s): 9
Membership: *Fees:* Free; *Member Profile:* Those infected or affected by HIV, AIDS or HepC
Activities: Education, prevention, awareness, & advocacy for persons with HCV, HIV/AIDS; *Awareness Events:* Red Ribbon Campaign; AIDS Walk for Life, Sept.; AIDS Memorial, Dec.; *Speaker Service:* Yes; *Library:* Open to public by appointment
Chief Officer(s):
Cheryl Dowden, Executive Director
cheryl@ankors.bc.ca
East Kootenay Regional Office
46 - 17th Ave. South, Cranbrook BC V1C 5A8
Tel: 250-426-3383; *Fax:* 250-426-3221
gary@ankors.bc.ca

Annapolis District Board of Trade (ADBOT)
PO Box 2, Annapolis Royal NS B0S 1A0
Tel: 902-532-5454
info@tradeannapolis.com
www.tradeannapolis.com
www.facebook.com/AnnapolisBoardofTrade
Overview: A small local organization founded in 1946
Member of: APCC, NSCC
Membership: 70; *Fees:* $25-150
Chief Officer(s):
Jane Nicholson, President

Annapolis Region Community Arts Council (ARCAC)
PO Box 534, 396 St. George St., Annapolis Royal NS B0S 1A0
Tel: 902-532-7069; *Fax:* 902-532-7357
Toll-Free: 800-228-4492
arcac@ns.aliantzinc.ca
rcac-artsplace.weebly.com
Overview: A small local charitable organization founded in 1982
Mission: To foster an understanding & appreciation of the arts in the Annapolis region; to provide creative opportunities for professional artists in all media in the community
Finances: *Annual Operating Budget:* $100,000-$250,000; *Funding Sources:* Private; corporate; fundraising
Staff Member(s): 1; 50 volunteer(s)
Membership: 220; *Fees:* $5 student; $20 individual; $35 family; $100 patron; *Committees:* Festival; Fundraising; Programs; Scholarship; Exhibitions
Activities: Workshops in all media; exhibits; advocacy; arts resource for community; annual arts festival; monthly board meetings; *Library:* Art Gallery; Open to public
Chief Officer(s):
Gene Lane, Executive Director

Annapolis Valley Chamber of Commerce (EKCC)
PO Box 314, 66 Cornwallis St., Kentville NS B4N 3X1
Tel: 902-678-4634
coordinator@annapolisvalleychamber.ca
annapolisvalleychamber.ca
www.facebook.com/avcc1
twitter.com/avccommerce
Previous Name: Kentville & Area Board of Trade; Eastern Kings Chamber of Commerce
Overview: A small local organization founded in 1893
Mission: To proactively promote & support the interests of business in Eastern Kings County
Member of: Nova Scotia Chamber of Commerce; Atlantic Provinces Chamber of Commerce
Finances: *Funding Sources:* Membership fees
Staff Member(s): 2
Membership: *Fees:* Schedule available based on number of employees; *Committees:* Professional Development; Tourism; Advocacy; Agriculture & Agri-Food
Chief Officer(s):
Sue Hayes, President
Judy Rafuse, Executive Director
Awards:
• Business Awards
• Young Entrepreneur Scholarship

Annapolis Valley Historical Society (AVHS)
PO Box 925, 21 School St., Middleton NS B0S 1P0
Tel: 902-825-6116; *Fax:* 902-825-0531
contact@macdonaldmuseum.ca
www.macdonaldmuseum.ca
Overview: A small local organization founded in 1978
Mission: To act as the governing body for the Macdonald (Consolidated School) Museum; To collect, preserve, & exhibit the historical artifacts of Nova Scotia's Annapolis Valley; To provide genealogical resources, such as vital statistics for Annapolis, Kings, Digby, & Lunenburg Counties, local newspapers, family files, school records, church registers, obituaries, & cemetery inscriptions
Finances: *Funding Sources:* Donations; Fundraising
Membership: *Fees:* $11.50 individual; $17.25 couple; $20.75 family
Activities: Operating a gallery with the works of local artists; *Library:* Annapolis Valley Historical Society Research Library; Open to public by appointment
Publications:
• Annapolis Valley Historical Society Newsletter
Type: Newsletter; *Frequency:* Quarterly; *Price:* Free with membership in the Annapolis Valley Historical Society
Profile: Information about society activities

Annapolis Valley Real Estate Board
1 Hwy. 1, Aylesford NS B0P 1C0
Tel: 902-847-9336; *Fax:* 902-847-9869
avreb@eastlink.ca
Overview: A small local organization overseen by Nova Scotia Association of REALTORS
Member of: The Canadian Real Estate Association
Chief Officer(s):
Cathy Simpson, Executive Officer

ANNISAA Organization of Canada
#111, 7 St. Dennis Dr., Toronto ON M3C 1E4
Tel: 647-761-0745
info@annisaa.org
annisaa.org
www.facebook.com/ANNISAAORG
twitter.com/ANNISAAORG
www.instagram.com/annisaaorg

Overview: A medium-sized national organization founded in 2012
Mission: To create inspirational programs that bring women together in developing their leadership skills; To promote an interest in education, research, sports & recreation, social development, Islamic spiritual advancement & moral values
Membership: *Fees:* $50 individual; $200 corporate; *Member Profile:* Practising Muslim women
Activities: Sponsoring literary, art & other educational & cultural events, festivals & conventions for the promotion of Islam and Muslims; *Awareness Events:* World Hijab Day; Women in Health Care Week; Sports Day
Meetings/Conferences:
• ANNISSA Organization of Canada Women's Health Conference, 2018
Publications:
• ANNISAA Magazine
Type: Magazine; *Frequency:* Quarterly
Profile: Magazine presents various aspects of morality, and of Islamic religion, to be useful both in this life and the Hereafter.

Anthroposophical Society in Canada (ASC) / Société anthroposophique au Canada
#130A, 1 Hesperus Rd., Thornhill ON L4J 0G9
Tel: 416-892-3656
Toll-Free: 877-892-3656
info@anthroposophy.ca
www.anthroposophy.ca
Overview: A medium-sized national charitable organization founded in 1953
Mission: To nurture the soul & to make artistic, scientific & cultural contributions through the work of Rudolf Steiner (1861-1925)
Affiliation(s): General Anthroposophical Society, Dornach, Switzerland
Finances: *Annual Operating Budget:* $50,000-$100,000
Staff Member(s): 2; 10 volunteer(s)
Membership: 500+; *Fees:* $275 annual contribution; *Member Profile:* Adults of all ages & professions
Activities: Offering information about anthroposophy; Organizing lectures, workshops & conferences; Engaging in education, arts & science initiatives; *Library:* National Library of the Anthroposophical Society in Canada; Open to public
Chief Officer(s):
Jeffrey Saunders, Administrator, Membership & Communication

Anti-Defamation League of B'nai Brith *See* League for Human Rights of B'nai Brith Canada

Antigonish Ceilidh Association
31 Arbor Dr., Antigonish NS B2G 1S8
Tel: 902-735-2014
Overview: A small provincial organization
Mission: To promote Celtic culture
Activities: Showcasing Celtic performers
Chief Officer(s):
Shelley Anderson, Contact
shelley_anderson76@yahoo.com

Antigonish Chamber of Commerce
#6, 188 Main St., Antigonish NS B2G 2B9
Tel: 902-863-6308; *Fax:* 902-863-2656
contact@antigonishchamber.com
www.antigonishchamber.com
www.facebook.com/AntigonishChamberofCommerce
twitter.com/AntigonishChmbr
Overview: A small local charitable organization founded in 1904
Mission: To represent businesses in Antigonish
Member of: Nova Scotia Chambers of Commerce; Atlantic Chamber of Commerce; Canadian Chamber of Commerce
Finances: *Funding Sources:* Membership dues; Special projects
Membership: *Fees:* $66.13 student/senior; $138.86 1-4 employees; $198.38 5-20 employees; $330.63 20+ employees; *Committees:* Member Services & Communications; Events; Finance; Governance & Human Resources
Activities: Networking; Advocating; Providing marketing opportunities
Chief Officer(s):
Dan Fougere, President
Awards:
• Ian Spencer Award
• Outstanding Customer Service Award

Antigonish Culture Alive
PO Box 1175, Antigonish NS B2G 2L6
Tel: 902-783-2948
info@antigonishculturealive.ca
www.antigonishculturealive.ca
Previous Name: Guysborough Antigonish Pictou Arts & Culture Council
Overview: A small local organization
Mission: To promote excellence in art practice; To raise awareness of the arts in our region
Membership: *Fees:* $20 individual; $35 associate
Activities: Annual Gathering of the Arts, travelling juried exhibition & workshops, July; special events; concerts & readings
Chief Officer(s):
Sarah O'Toole, Coordinator

Antigonish Highland Society (AHS)
20 East Main St., Antigonish NS B2G 2E9
Tel: 902-863-4275; *Fax:* 902-863-0466
info@antigonishhighlandgames.ca
www.antigonishhighlandsociety.ca
www.facebook.com/antigonishgames
twitter.com/AntigonishGames
Overview: A small local organization
Finances: *Annual Operating Budget:* $100,000-$250,000
Staff Member(s): 1; 50 volunteer(s)
Membership: 50; *Fees:* $10 individual; $15 family
Activities: Antigonish Highland Games

Antigonish Therapeutic Riding Association
1216 Ohio East Rd., Antigonish NS B2G 2K8
Tel: 902-863-4853
www.facebook.com/399942843470547
Overview: A small local charitable organization founded in 1987
Mission: To provide a therapeutic and recreational horseback riding program for physically, mentally, and emotionally handicapped people, and to promote public awareness of such a program
Activities: Two six-week sessions per year; weekly horseback riding lessons for handicapped children & adults

The Antiquarian & Numismatic Society of Montréal *Voir* Société d'archéologie et de numismatique de Montréal

Antiquarian Booksellers' Association of Canada (ABAC) / Association de la librairie ancienne du Canada (ALAC)
c/o Michael Park, Greenfield Books, 217 Academy Rd., Winnipeg MB R3M 0E3
Tel: 204-488-2023
info@abac.org
www.abac.org
www.facebook.com/210124119032896
twitter.com/A_B_A_C
Overview: A small national organization founded in 1966
Mission: To maintain high standards in the antiquarian book trade; To promote interest in rare books & manuscripts
Member of: International League of Antiquarian Booksellers
Finances: *Annual Operating Budget:* Less than $50,000; *Funding Sources:* Membership dues
Membership: 60; *Fees:* $400 (plus $200 initiation fee); *Member Profile:* Booksellers with minimum of 3 years experience & able to provide four recommendations from members in good standing who can vouch for applicant's expertise & integrity
Activities: Insurance & donation appraisals; stolen book registry; international prize for bibliography (in conjunction with ILAB); *Awareness Events:* Annual Toronto Bookfair, May; *Rents Mailing List:* Yes
Chief Officer(s):
Michael Park, President

Antique Motorcycle Club of Manitoba Inc. (AMCM)
1377 Niakwa Rd. East, Winnipeg MB R2J 3T3
www.amcm.ca
www.facebook.com/groups/862177597223304
Overview: A small provincial organization
Chief Officer(s):
Rick Poirier, President
Dan Catte, Librarian

Antisemitism Must End Now (AMEN)
#300, 1370 Don Mills Rd., Toronto ON M3B 3N7
Tel: 416-424-6613
amen613@yahoo.com
Overview: A small national charitable organization
Mission: To combat & prevent intolerance & discrimination against Jewish people in Canada
Activities: Advocating for Jewish people; Offering education, lectures & workshops

Anti-Tuberculosis Society *See* British Columbia Lung Association

Anxiety Disorders Association of British Columbia
#103, 237 Columbia St. East, New Westminster BC V3L 3W4
Tel: 604-525-7566; *Fax:* 604-525-7586
info@anxietybc.com
www.anxietybc.com
www.facebook.com/AnxietyBC
twitter.com/AnxietyBC
www.youtube.com/user/AnxietyBC/
Also Known As: AnxietyBC
Overview: A small provincial organization founded in 1999 overseen by Anxiety Disorders Association of Canada
Mission: To increase awareness of anxiety disorders, including panic disorder, phobias, obsessive-compulsive disorder, and post-traumatic stress disorder; To provide information and resources for individuals wanting to manage their own anxiety
Member of: BC Partners for Mental Health and Addictions Information
Affiliation(s): Anxiety BC
Finances: *Funding Sources:* Provincial Health Services Authority, the Ministry for Children and Family Development; donations; membership fees
Membership: *Committees:* Scientific; Executive
Chief Officer(s):
Amir Rasheed, President
Judith Law, Executive Director

Anxiety Disorders Association of Canada (ADAC) / Association Canadienne des Troubles Anxieux (ACTA)
PO Box 117, Stn. Cote-St-Luc, Montréal QC H4V 2Y3
Tel: 514-484-0504
Toll-Free: 888-223-2252
contactus@anxietycanada.ca
www.anxietycanada.ca
twitter.com/anxietycanada
Overview: A medium-sized national charitable organization founded in 2002
Mission: To promote the prevention, treatment & management of anxiety disorders, & to improve the lives of people who suffer from them
Membership: *Fees:* $25 professional; $10 general; *Committees:* Scientific Advisory; Consumer Advisory
Chief Officer(s):
Lynn Miller, President

Anxiety Disorders Association of Manitoba (ADAM)
#100, 4 Fort St., Winnipeg MB R3C 1C4
Tel: 204-925-0600; *Fax:* 204-925-0609
Toll-Free: 800-805-8885
adam@adam.mb.ca
www.adam.mb.ca
www.facebook.com/anxietydisordersassociationofmanitoba
Overview: A small provincial charitable organization founded in 1986 overseen by Anxiety Disorders Association of Canada
Mission: A peer-led organization for the support of people with anxiety, and to share knowledge and hope with others.
Activities: Education and Public Awareness; Information and Referral Service; Cognitive Behavioural Groups & Support Groups
Chief Officer(s):
Richard Shore, Chair

Anxiety Disorders Association of Ontario (ADAO)
Heartwood House, 404 McArthur Ave., Ottawa ON K1K 1G5
Tel: 613-729-6761
Toll-Free: 877-308-3843
info@anxietydisordersontario.ca
www.anxietydisordersontario.ca
www.facebook.com/anxietyottawa
twitter.com/AnxietyOttawa
www.youtube.com/user/anxietyottawa
Overview: A small provincial charitable organization founded in 1997 overseen by Anxiety Disorders Association of Canada
Mission: ADAO's mission is to empower, in an holistic way, the lives of those affected by anxiety through advocacy, education, research support and community programming.
Membership: *Committees:* 14-Week Program; Finance; Communications
Chief Officer(s):
Joan Riggs, BA, B.S.W., M.S, President

APCHQ - Montréal Métropolitain
5800, boul Louis H. Lafontaine, Anjou QC H1M 1S7
Tél: 514-354-8722; *Téléc:* 514-355-7777
info@apchqmontreal.ca
www.apchqmontreal.ca
Aperçu: Dimension: petite; *Envergure:* provinciale; Organisme sans but lucratif; fondée en 1950
Mission: Représente plus de 3 300 membres oeuvrant dans l'industrie de la construction et de la rénovation résidentielle
Finances: Budget de fonctionnement annuel: $1.5 Million-$3 Million
Membre(s) du personnel: 9
Membre: 3,300; *Montant de la cotisation:* 500$; *Critères d'admissibilite:* Entrepreneurs en construction
Activités: Service de conférenciers: Oui
Membre(s) du bureau directeur:
Ivan Roger, Président
Marc Savard, Directeur général

Apeetogosan (Metis) Development Inc.
#302, 12308 - 111 Ave., Edmonton AB T5M 2N4
Tel: 780-452-7951
Toll-Free: 800-252-7963
www.apeetogosan.com
www.facebook.com/apeetogosan
twitter.com/Apeetogosan
Overview: A small local organization founded in 1984
Mission: To provide assistance with developing and commercializing community members' business ideas
Member of: Metis Nation of Alberta Association; National Aboriginal Capital Corporation Association
Affiliation(s): The Métis Nation of Alberta
Staff Member(s): 11
Membership: Committees: Audit; HR; Loans
Activities: Louis Riel Week Festivities; Aboriginal Day
Chief Officer(s):
Michael Ivy, General Manager

APER Santé et services sociaux (APERSSS)
#5104, 1751, rue Richardson, Montréal QC H3K 1G6
Tél: 514-933-4118; *Téléc:* 514-933-2397
association@aper.qc.ca
www.aper.qc.ca
Nom précédent: Association des cadres de la santé et des services sociaux du Québec
Aperçu: Dimension: moyenne; *Envergure:* provinciale; fondée en 1974
Membre(s) du personnel: 4
Membre: 900; *Critères d'admissibilite:* Cadres réseau santé et services sociaux
Membre(s) du bureau directeur:
Franceen Alovisi, Directrice générale

Aphasie Rive-Sud
170, rue de Gaulle, Saint-Hubert QC J4T 1M9
Tél: 450-550-4466
info@aphasierivesud.org
www.aphasierivesud.org
Aperçu: Dimension: petite; *Envergure:* locale
Mission: Pour amener les gens souffrant d'aphasie ensemble des activités sociales et pour aider à leur réhabilitation
Membre de: Regrouper les associations de personnes aphasiques de Québec
Activités: Sport; Artisanat; Chant et musique
Membre(s) du bureau directeur:
Natalie Taupier, Coordonnatrice

Aplastic Anemia & Myelodysplasia Association of Canada (AAMAC)
#321, 11181 Yonge St., Richmond Hill ON L4S 1L2
Tel: 905-780-0698; *Fax:* 905-780-1648
Toll-Free: 888-840-0039
info@aamac.ca
www.aamac.ca
Previous Name: Aplastic Anemia Association of Canada
Overview: A small national charitable organization founded in 1987
Mission: To disseminate information concerning the disease; To form a nation-wide support network for patients, families & medical professionals; To support Canadian Blood Services & their programs; To raise funds for research
Member of: Health Charities Council of Canada
Affiliation(s): Network of Rare Blood Disorders
Finances: Funding Sources: Private donors
Activities: Research; Support; Awareness; *Speaker Service:* Yes
Chief Officer(s):
Pam Wishart, President
Michelle Joseph, Secretary
Janice Cook, Coordinator, British Columbia
Bob Ross, Coordinator, Ontario

Aplastic Anemia Association of Canada *See* Aplastic Anemia & Myelodysplasia Association of Canada

The Apostolic Church in Canada
220 Adelaide St. North, London ON N6B 3H4
Tel: 519-438-7036
cheryl@apostolic.ca
www.apostolic.ca
www.facebook.com/117271988314359
twitter.com/ACCnat
Overview: A small national organization founded in 1934
Mission: A Trinitarian, Pentecostal denomination with a strong commitment to mission.
Finances: Annual Operating Budget: $500,000-$1.5 Million
Staff Member(s): 15
Membership: 500-999
Activities: Internships: Yes
Chief Officer(s):
D. Karl Thomas, National Leader

Apostolic Church of Pentecost of Canada Inc. (ACOP) / Église apostolique de Pentecôte du Canada inc.
International Office, #119, 2340 Pegasus Way NE, Calgary AB T2E 8M5
Tel: 403-273-5777; *Fax:* 403-273-8102
www.acop.ca
www.facebook.com/ACOPcanada
twitter.com/ACOPcanada
google.com/+AcopCa
Overview: A small national licensing charitable organization founded in 1921
Mission: To provide fellowship, encouragement & accountability in the proclamation of the Gospel of Jesus Christ by the Power of the Holy Spirit
Affiliation(s): Evangelical Fellowship of Canada
Finances: Annual Operating Budget: $1.5 Million-$3 Million; *Funding Sources:* Donations
Staff Member(s): 30
Membership: 155 affiliated churches + 436 members; *Fees:* Varies
Activities: Internships: Yes; *Speaker Service:* Yes; *Library:* by appointment
Chief Officer(s):
Wes Mills, President & National Director

Appalachian Teachers' Association (ATA) / Association des enseignant(e)s des Appalaches (AEA)
#104, 155, rue Principale, Magog QC J1X 2A7
Tel: 819-843-2630; *Fax:* 819-843-6297
Toll-Free: 855-443-2630
ataunion@hotmail.com
www.ataunion.org
www.facebook.com/ataunion
Previous Name: Eastern Townships Association of Teachers
Overview: A small local organization founded in 1999
Mission: To protect & advance the professional, economic, & social welfare of members
Affiliation(s): Québec Provincial Association of Teachers
Finances: Annual Operating Budget: $50,000-$100,000
Staff Member(s): 1
Membership: 500 individual; *Fees:* $260 individual; *Committees:* Central Professional Improvement; Executive; Health & Safety; Labour Relations; Negotiations; New Teachers; Nominations; Special Education Board Parity; Special Education Advisory
Chief Officer(s):
Megan Seline, President

Appaloosa Horse Club of Canada (ApHCC)
PO Box 940, Claresholm AB T0L 0T0
Tel: 403-625-3326; *Fax:* 403-625-2274
registry@appaloosa.ca
www.appaloosa.ca
www.facebook.com/255499284509
Overview: A medium-sized national organization founded in 1954
Mission: To collect records & historical data relating to origin of the Appaloosa; to file records & issue certificates of registration; to preserve, improve & standardize the breed
Membership: Committees: Executive; Nomination; Personnel; National Show; Rules; Judges & Judging; Shows & Showing; Handbook; Breed Improvement; Racing; Activity & Disciplines; Trail, Sports & Recreation;'Discipline; Promotion & Publicity; Booth; Membership; Museum Liasion; Recognition & Awards; Youth; Law Review; International Liasion; Inspectors & Inspections
Activities: Library: APHCC Museum & Archives; Open to public
Chief Officer(s):
Sharon Duncan, Executive Secretary

Appaloosa Horse Club of Nova Scotia
c/o Bill Milligan, 1595 Corkum Burns Rd., RR#2, Wolfville NS B4P 2R2
www.aphcns.com
Member of: Appaloosa Horse Club of Canada
Chief Officer(s):
Bill Milligan, President & Treasurer
bill@aphcns.ca
Jim Rafferty, Vice-President
jim@aphcns.ca

Calgary Regional Appaloosa Club (CRAC)
c/o 3438 Cedarville Dr. SW, Calgary AB T2W 5A9
calgaryappaloosa.wildapricot.org
Brian Miles, President
brianmiles@hotmail.com
Pat Hyndman, Vice-President
pat@rprappaloosa.com
Patti Parslow, Treasurer
pattiparslow@shaw.ca

Kawartha Regional Appaloosa Horse Club (KRAHC)
RR#21, Port Perry ON L9L 1B5
Tel: 705-696-3469
kawartha.appaloosa@gmail.com
www.kawarthaappaloosa.com
www.facebook.com/groups/KRAHC/
www.twitter.com/kawartha_apps
Chief Officer(s):
Doug Mileham, President
milehamshowhorses216@hotmail.com

Manitoba Appaloosa Club
Site 510, Box 4, RR#5, Brandon MB R7A 5Y5
mbappaloosaclub.yolasite.com
Chief Officer(s):
Cheryle McClure, President
cmcclure@mymts.net
Jocelyn Kish, Vice-President
horseaddict@yahoo.com
Carol Rea, Sec.-Treas.
sonrea_ranch@yahoo.ca

Mighty Peace Appaloosa Club
PO Box 92, Manning AB T0H 2M0
Tel: 780-836-2793
jimcreekranch@yahoo.com
Chief Officer(s):
Barb Whillans, Contact

New Brunswick Appaloosa Horse Club
c/o Roberta Gorham, 16 Cedar Wharf Rd., Long Reach NB E5S 1Y3
newbrunswickappaloosahorseclub.com
Chief Officer(s):
Roberta Gorham, Contact
appaloosalady@hotmail.com

Saskatchewan Appaloosa Club
c/o Eleanor Porth, RR#2, Box 26B, Regina SK S4P 2Z2
Tel: 306-868-4526
www.saskapp.ca
Chief Officer(s):
Karen Bedford, President

Thunder Bay Appaloosa Club
226 Hinton Ave., Thunder Bay ON P7A 7E4
Tel: 807-767-3541
tbapphor@nwconx.net

Apparel BC (ABC)
1859 Franklin St., Vancouver BC V5V 1P9
Tel: 604-986-2003; *Fax:* 604-986-2097
Also Known As: BC Apparel Manufacturers Association
Overview: A small provincial licensing organization founded in 1994
Mission: To enhance & strengthen the viability of the BC apparel industry in a competitive & global environment through advocacy, marketing, education, mentorships, liaison & the setting of ethical standards
Member of: Canadian Apparel Federation

Canadian Associations / Apparel Human Resources Council (AHRC) / Conseil des ressources humaines de l'industrie du vêtement

Finances: *Annual Operating Budget:* $250,000-$500,000
Staff Member(s): 1
Membership: 100-499; *Member Profile:* BC manufacturers, contractors, designers & suppliers to the industry
Activities: Industry networking events; lobbyist for tariff & trade issues; training seminars; marketing support; *Library:* Not open to public
Chief Officer(s):
Jacqueline Kirby, Executive Director

Apparel Human Resources Council (AHRC) / Conseil des ressources humaines de l'industrie du vêtement
#360, 6750, av de l'Esplanade, Montréal QC H2V 4M1
Tel: 514-388-7779; *Fax:* 888-738-7854
info@apparelconnexion.ca
www.apparelconnexion.com
www.linkedin.com/groups/Apparel-Human-Resources-4801586
www.facebook.com/ApparelConnexionConnexionVetement
twitter.com/Apparel_HR
Also Known As: Apparel Connexion
Overview: A small national organization founded in 1998
Mission: To serve human resources development & adjustment needs of managers & employees in the apparel manufacturing industry; To help apparel manufacturers recruit & maintain a strong workforce through the development of tools & services; To create business opportunities for the industry
Staff Member(s): 4
Membership: *Fees:* $25 partner; $75 members; $100 associate; $300 schools; *Committees:* Apparel Affinity Group; Executive
Activities: Providing human resources training, tools & networking opportunities; Disseminating up-to-date data on the apparel industry; Strategic planning for apparel companies; Offering a Job Sources Centre; Organizing events, including job fairs, technology fairs, workshops, seminars & webinars; *Internships:* Yes; *Speaker Service:* Yes
Chief Officer(s):
Adrian Bussoli, President
Patrick Thomas, General Manager, 514-388-7779 Ext. 101
patrick@apparelconnexion.ca
Awards:
• Apparel Career Focus Program
Eligibility: Post-secondary graduates between 15 & 30 years of age, out of school & working in their field of study, a Canadian citizen or permanent resident or granted refugee status, & legally entitled to work in Canada; *Amount:* $15,000

Apparel Quebec (AMIQ) / Vêtement Québec
#1270, 1435, rue Saint-Alexandre, Montréal QC H3A 2G4
Tel: 514-382-3846; *Fax:* 514-940-5336
cs@apparelquebec.com
www.vetementquebec.com
Overview: A medium-sized provincial organization
Mission: To advance the exchange of best practices & technological innovations in such areas as sourcing, design & fashion
Affiliation(s): Canadian Apparel Federation (CAF); Apparel Human Reousrces Council (AHRC); Fashion Bureau of Montreal; Ministry of Economic Development, Innovation & Export Trade; Groupe Sensation Mode; Men's Clothing Manufacturers Association; Quebec Council of Odd Pants Employers; Montreal Clothing Contractors Association Inc.; Rainwear & Sportswear Manufacturers Association; The Canadian Trimmings Manufacturers Association
Staff Member(s): 1
Membership: *Member Profile:* Apparel producers, importers, marketers & suppliers
Activities: Labour negotiations & government relations
Chief Officer(s):
Oxana Sushilnikova, Project Coordinator

Apple Growers of New Brunswick / Producteurs de pommes du Nouveau-Brunswick
#2, 150 Woodside Lane, Fredericton NB E3C 2R9
Tel: 506-440-5257
nbapples@applesnb.ca
www.applesnb.ca
Overview: A small provincial organization
Mission: To represent apple growers in New Brunswick
Activities: Providing information about apple orchards & the purchase of apples in New Brunswick

Applegrove Community Complex
60 Woodfield Rd., Toronto ON M4L 2W6
Tel: 416-461-8143; *Fax:* 416-461-5513
applegrove@applegrovecc.ca
www.applegrovecc.ca
www.facebook.com/pages/Applegrove-Community-Complex/99742456574
Also Known As: Applegrove
Overview: A medium-sized local charitable organization founded in 1979
Mission: To provide social service programs for infants, children, teens, adults and seniors living in the Queen-Greenwood area of Toronto.
Finances: *Annual Operating Budget:* $500,000-$1.5 Million; *Funding Sources:* City of Toronto, Government, Donations
Membership: *Committees:* Finance & Fundraising; Personnel
Chief Officer(s):
Susan Fletcher, Executive Director
Ann McKechnie, Chair

AppleRoute Country Chamber of Commerce *See*
Brighton-Cramahe Chamber of Commerce

Applied Science Technologists & Technicians of British Columbia (ASTTBC)
10767 - 148 St., Surrey BC V3R 0S4
Tel: 604-585-2788; *Fax:* 604-585-2790
info@asttbc.org
www.asttbc.org
www.linkedin.com/company/asttbc
www.facebook.com/ASTTBC
twitter.com/asttbc
www.youtube.com/user/ASTTBC
Previous Name: Society of Engineering Technologists of BC
Overview: A large provincial organization founded in 1958 overseen by Canadian Council of Technicians & Technologists
Mission: To advance the profession of applied science technology & the professional recognition of applied science technologists, certified technician, & other members in a manner that serves & protects the public interest
Member of: Canadian Council of Technicians & Technologists
Finances: *Funding Sources:* Membership dues; Accreditation; Member services; Advertising; Education
Membership: *Committees:* Construction Safety Certification Board; Fire Protection Certification Board; Public Works Inspection Certification Board
Activities: *Internships:* Yes; *Rents Mailing List:* Yes
Chief Officer(s):
John Leech, AScT, CAE, Chief Executive Officer
jleech@asttbc.org
Cindy Aitken, Manager, Governance & Events
caitken@asttbc.org
Anne Sharp, Manager, Marketing
asharp@asttbc.org
Jason Jung, Manager, Professional Practice & Development
jjung@asttbc.org
Nicky Malli, Manager, Finance
nmalli@asttbc.org
Geoff Sale, AScT, Manager, Internationally Trained Professionals
gsale@asttbc.org
Jacqueline de Raadt, Manager, Executive Initiatives
jderaadt@asttbc.org
Karen Taylor, Manager, Member Services & Operations
ktaylor@asttbc.org
Awards:
• Peter Allan AScT Leadership Award
• Advanced Technology Award
• Certificate of Appreciation
• Life Membership
• Professional Achievement
• R. Littledale Memorial Award
• Service Award
• Special Award
• Honorary Membership
• Employer Award For Career Enhancement & Success of Technology Professionals
• Professional Leadership Award For Women in Technology
• Top in Technology
• TechGREEN
Publications:
• Member Compensation Survey [a publication of Applied Science Technologists & Technicians of British Columbia]
Type: Report
• Member Satisfaction Survey [a publication of Applied Science Technologists & Technicians of British Columbia]
Type: Report

Appraisal Institute of Canada (AIC) / Institut canadien des évaluateurs (ICE)
#403, 200 Catherine St., Ottawa ON K2P 2K9
Tel: 613-234-6533; *Fax:* 613-234-7197
Toll-Free: 888-551-5521
info@aicanada.ca
www.aicanada.ca
www.linkedin.com/company/appraisal-institute-of-canada
www.facebook.com/AppraisalInstitute.Canada
twitter.com/aic_canada
Overview: A large national licensing organization founded in 1938
Mission: To grant professional designations in real estate appraisal (Accredited Appraiser Canadian Institute (AACI) & Canadian Residential Appraiser (CRA)); To strive to maintain high standards in real estate appraisal to protect the public interest
Affiliation(s): Appraisal Institute of Canada - Alberta, British Columbia, Manitoba, New Brunswick, Newfoundland & Labrador, Nova Scotia, Ontario, Prince Edward Island, Québec, Saskatchewan
Membership: 5,000+; *Member Profile:* Professional real estate appraisers; Valuation consultants; *Committees:* Executive; Professional Practice; Communications; Conference; Audit & Finance; Nominating; Bylaws, Regulations & Procedures; Admissions & Accreditation; Research & Development
Activities: Career awareness & promotion; Professional standards & designation; Research; Education; Career development & continuing education; Communications; Professional & member services
Chief Officer(s):
Keith Lancastle, Chief Executive Officer
keithl@aicanada.ca
Glenda Cardinal, Director, Finance & Administration
glendac@aicanada.ca
Sheila Roy, Director, Marketing & Communications
sheilar@aicanada.ca
Nathalie Roy-Patenaude, Director, Professional Practice
nathalier@aicanada.ca
Meetings/Conferences:
• Appraisal Institute of Canada / Institut canadien des évaluateurs 2018 Conference, June, 2018, Québec, QC
Scope: National

The Appraisal Institute of Canada - Alberta (AIC-AB)
#245, 495 - 36 St. NE, Calgary AB T2A 6K3
Tel: 403-207-7892; *Fax:* 403-207-7857
aic.alberta@shawlink.ca
www.aicanada.ca/province-alberta/alberta
Previous Name: Alberta Association of the Appraisal Institute of Canada
Overview: A small provincial licensing organization founded in 1979 overseen by Appraisal Institute of Canada
Mission: To maintain professional ethics & standards in real estate valuation; to qualify real estate appraisers in Alberta, Nunavut & the Northwest Territories
Finances: *Funding Sources:* Membership dues; fees for services
Staff Member(s): 2
Membership: 700; *Fees:* Schedule available
Activities: Training, certification & membership services
Chief Officer(s):
Sanjit Singh, President
sanjitsingh@shaw.ca
Christine Vandelinder, Executive Director

The Appraisal Institute of Canada - British Columbia (AIC-BC)
#210, 10451 Shellbridge Way, Richmond BC V6X 2W8
Tel: 604-284-5515; *Fax:* 604-284-5514
Toll-Free: 888-707-8287
info@appraisal.bc.ca
www.aicanada.ca/province-british-columbia/british-columbia
Previous Name: British Columbia Association of the Appraisal Institute of Canada
Overview: A medium-sized provincial licensing organization founded in 1973 overseen by Appraisal Institute of Canada
Mission: To represent, promote & support members as leaders in the counselling, analysis & evaluation of real property.
Chapters: Fraser Valley, Nanaimo, Okanagan, Vancouver, Kamloops, The North, Victoria, & Kootenay.
Finances: *Annual Operating Budget:* $100,000-$250,000; *Funding Sources:* Membership dues
Staff Member(s): 2
Membership: 1,100; *Fees:* Schedule available
Activities: *Speaker Service:* Yes
Chief Officer(s):
Steve Blacklock, President

Christina Dhesi, Executive Director
christina@appraisal.bc.ca

The Appraisal Institute of Canada - Manitoba (AIC-MB)
5 Donwood Dr., Winnipeg MB R2G 0V9
Tel: 204-771-2982; Fax: 204-654-9583
mbaic@mts.net
www.aicanada.ca
Previous Name: Manitoba Association of the Appraisal Institute of Canada
Overview: A small provincial licensing organization founded in 1978 overseen by Appraisal Institute of Canada
Mission: To maintain professional ethics & standards in real estate valuation; to qualify real estate appraisers in the province
Member of: Winnipeg Real Estate Board (Business Partner)
Finances: Annual Operating Budget: $50,000-$100,000; Funding Sources: Membership dues; courses & seminars
Staff Member(s): 1; 9 volunteer(s)
Membership: 200; Fees: Schedule available; Member Profile: Residential & commercial real estate appraisers
Activities: Winnipeg Free Press home section articles; annual fall meeting
Chief Officer(s):
Dan Diachun, President
dandwpg@gmail.com
Pamela Wylie, Executive Director

The Appraisal Institute of Canada - Newfoundland & Labrador (AIC-NL)
PO Box 1571, Stn. C, St. John's NL A1C 5P3
Tel: 709-759-5769
Other Communication: Alt. E-mail: naaic.nl@gmail.com
naaic@nf.aibn.com
www.aicanada.ca/province-newfoundland-labrador
Previous Name: Newfoundland & Labrador Association of the Appraisal Institute of Canada
Overview: A small provincial licensing organization overseen by Appraisal Institute of Canada
Mission: To promote the appraisal profession throughout Newfoundland & Labrador.
Membership: 90
Activities: Administering the designation process; Providing workshops & seminars
Chief Officer(s):
Greg Bennett, President
Sherry House, Executive Director

The Appraisal Institute of Canada - Ontario (AIC-ON)
#108, 16 Four Seasons Place, Toronto ON M9B 6E5
Tel: 416-695-9333; Fax: 877-413-4081
info@oaaic.on.ca
www.aicanada.ca/ontario
Previous Name: Ontario Association of the Appraisal Institute of Canada
Overview: A medium-sized provincial licensing organization founded in 1960 overseen by Appraisal Institute of Canada
Mission: To serve the public interest by advancing high standards in the analysis & valuation of real property matters by enhancing the professional competence of its members.
Chapters: Credit Valley, Hamilton-Niagara, Huronia, Kingston, London, North Bay, Oshawa/Durham, Ottawa, Peterborough/Lindsay, Sudbury & Sault Ste. Marie, Thunder Bay, Toronto, Waterloo/Wellington, Windsor, York.
Finances: Annual Operating Budget: $250,000-$500,000; Funding Sources: Membership fees
Staff Member(s): 4
Membership: 1,800 in 15 chapters; Committees: Finance; Leadership Development & Nominations; Public & Government Relations; Professional Development; By-Law Task Force; Chapter Task Force
Activities: Internships: Yes
Chief Officer(s):
Robin Jones, President
Bonnie Prior, Executive Director, 416-695-9333 Ext. 224
bprior@aicontario.ca

The Appraisal Institute of Canada - Prince Edward Island (AIC-PEI)
PO Box 1796, Charlottetown PE C1A 7N4
Tel: 902-368-3355; Fax: 902-368-3582
peiaic@bellaliant.net
www.aicanada.ca/province-prince-edward-island
Previous Name: Prince Edward Island Association of the Appraisal Institute of Canada
Overview: A small provincial licensing organization overseen by Appraisal Institute of Canada

Mission: To promote the appraisal profession throughout Prince Edward Island; to assist members, those wishing to become members & the public
Membership: 50
Chief Officer(s):
Boyce Costello, President
bdcostello@gov.pe.ca
Suzanne Pater, Executive Director

The Appraisal Institute of Canada - Québec Voir
L'Association du Québec de l'Institut canadien des évaluateurs

The Appraisal Institute of Canada - Saskatchewan (AIC-SK)
#505, 2300 Broad St., Regina SK S4P 1Y8
Tel: 306-352-4195
skaic@sasktel.net
sk.aicanada.ca
Previous Name: Saskatchewan Association of the Appraisal Institute of Canada
Overview: A small provincial licensing organization overseen by Appraisal Institute of Canada
Mission: To assist members, those hoping to become appraisers & the public
Membership: 175
Chief Officer(s):
Wanda Styre, President
Marilyn Sterdnica, Executive Director

Apprenp'tits Numismates
CP 81183, Québec QC G2B 3W7
Aperçu: Dimension: petite; Envergure: locale; Organisme sans but lucratif
Mission: Promouvoir la numismatique auprès de la jeunesse francophone au Canada et partout dans le monde
Membre: Montant de la cotisation: 10$
Membre(s) du bureau directeur:
Claude Bernard, Contact

L'Appui pour les proches aidants d'aînés
#720, 400, boul de Maisonneuve ouest, Montréal QC H3A 1L4
Tél: 514-789-2460
Ligne sans frais: 855-852-7784
info@lappui.org
www.lappui.org
Aperçu: Dimension: moyenne; Envergure: provinciale
Mission: De soutenir le développement d'une offre de services d'information, de formation, de soutien psychosocial et de répit, offerts par des organismes du milieu
Membre(s) du bureau directeur:
Monique Nadeau, Directrice générale
nadeaum@lappui.org

Aquaculture Association of Canada (AAC) / Association Aquacole du Canada
16 Lobster Lane, St Andrews NB E5B 3T6
Tel: 506-529-4766; Fax: 506-529-4609
aac@dfo-mpo.gc.ca
www.aquacultureassociation.ca
Overview: A medium-sized national charitable organization founded in 1984
Mission: To foster an aquaculture industry in Canada; To encourage & support the educational, technological, & scientific advancement of aquaculture
Finances: Funding Sources: Donations
Membership: 900+; Member Profile: Students; Educators; Producers; Suppliers; Scientists; Government representatives; Committees: Election; Finance; Rules; Time & Place; Arrangements; Program; Publications; Awards; Student Affairs; Membership; Business Development
Activities: Promoting the study of aquaculture & related sciences; Providing scientific & technical information related to aquaculture; Increasing public awareness & understanding of aquaculture; Liaising with goverment & industry; Providing networking opportunities; Conducting seminars
Chief Officer(s):
Susan Waddy, Manager, Association Office, 506-529-4766
Susan.Waddy@dfo-mpo.gc.ca
Tim Jackson, President, 506-636-3728, Fax: 506-636-3479
timothy.jackson@nrc-cnrc.gc.ca
Tim DeJager, Vice-President, 250-751-0634
dejagert@co3.ca
Joy Wade, Vice-President, 250-754-6884
joy2004wade@yahoo.ca
Shelley King, Secretary, 902-421-5646, Fax: 902-421-2733
sking@genomeatlantic.ca

Caroline Graham, Treasurer
cpgraham@rogers.com
Meetings/Conferences:
• Aquaculture Canada 2018, 2018
Scope: National
Description: Featuring presentations, special sessions, workshops, & posters
Publications:
• Aquaculture Canada Abstracts
Profile: Conference program guides, featuring conference sessions
• Aquaculture Canada Proceedings of Contributed Papers
Profile: Proceedings of the contributed papers of the annual meetings of the Aquaculture Association of Canada
• Bulletin of the Aquaculture Association of Canada
Type: Newsletter
Profile: Topics have included sea-urchin aquaculture, application of genome science to sustainable aquaculture, proceedings of the scallop aquaculture session, fish health,aquaculture public awareness & education, water movement & aquatic animal health, aquaculture biotechnology, & progress in cod farming
• The Watermark [a publication of the Aquaculture Association of Canada]
Type: Newsletter; Frequency: 3 pa; Editor: Gregor Reid; Candace Durston
Profile: Aquaculture Association of Canada updates, such as donations, awards, & meetings

Aquaculture Association of Nova Scotia (AANS)
2960 Oxford St., Halifax NS B3L 2W4
Tel: 902-422-6234; Fax: 902-422-6248
outreach@seafarmers.ca
www.aansonline.ca
twitter.com/AANSOnline
www.youtube.com/user/aansonline
Overview: A small provincial organization founded in 1977
Member of: Canadian Aquaculture Industry Alliance
Finances: Funding Sources: Membership fees
Staff Member(s): 3
Membership: 40; Fees: Producers $500-10,000; Suppliers/Processors $375-10,000; Friends $150; Students $25; Member Profile: Not-for-profit association of growers, suppliers & industry supporters; Committees: Nova Scotia Aquaculture Environmental Coordinating Committee
Chief Officer(s):
Angela Bishop, Executive Director
abishop@seafarmers.ca
Awards:
• Cathy Enright Scholarship
To recognize and help advance students who are demonstrating outstanding research work related to aquaculture. Eligibility: Honours & masters students studying in NS who are conducting research projects related to aquaculture (any field); Amount: $1000 Contact: Danielle Goodfellow, R&D Coordinator, dgoodfellowaans@eastlink.ca

Aquariums et zoos accrédités du Canada See Canada's Accredited Zoos & Aquariums

Aquatic Federation of Canada (AFC) / Fédération aquatique du Canada
c/o Martin Richard, Director, Communications, Swimming Canada, #B140, 2445 St-Laurent Blvd., Ottawa ON K1G 6C3
Tel: 613-260-1348
www.aquaticfederation.ca
Overview: A medium-sized national organization founded in 1968
Mission: To promote olympic aquatic sports in Canada
Affiliation(s): Synchro Canada; Canadian Amateur Diving Association Inc.; Water Polo Canada; Swimming Canada
Chief Officer(s):
Bill Hogan, President

Arab Canadian Association of the Atlantic Provinces (ACAAP)
PO Box 1024, Halifax NS B3J 2X1
Tel: 902-429-9100
Overview: A small provincial charitable organization founded in 1978
Mission: To promote friendship between Arab & Canadian people
Member of: Multicultural Association of Nova Scotia
Finances: Funding Sources: Donations & investments
Membership: Member Profile: Persons of Arabic-speaking descent & their spouses
Activities: Social & cultural activities; assist new immigrants to integrate in community; struggle against racism & sterotyping

Chief Officer(s):
Ismail Zayid, President, 902-429-9100
izayid@hfx.eastlink.ca

Arab Community Centre of Toronto
#209, 555 Burnhamthorpe Rd., Toronto ON M9C 2Y3
Tel: 416-231-7746; Fax: 416-231-4770
info@arabnewcomers.org
arabcommunitycentre.com
Overview: A small local organization founded in 1972 overseen by Ontario Council of Agencies Serving Immigrants
Mission: To help integrate Arab immigrants into Canada
Member of: African Canadian Social Development Council
Staff Member(s): 18
Membership: Fees: $6 student; $12 individual; $24 family
Chief Officer(s):
Naglaa Raouf, Executive Director
nraouf@arabnewcomers.org

Arabian Horse Association of Eastern Canada (AHAEC)
c/o Allan Ehrlick, 8259 Walkers Line, Campbellville ON L0P 1B0
Tel: 905-854-0762; Fax: 905-854-1386
aoc@milestoneac.ca
www.ahaec.on.ca
Overview: A small local organization founded in 1955
Mission: To promote multi-discipline Arabian & Half-Arabian horses; To coordinate the activities of horse owners
Member of: Ontario Equestrian Federation
Affiliation(s): Arabian Horse Association
Finances: Funding Sources: Membership fees; Fundraising
Membership: Member Profile: Arabian & Half-Arabian horse owners, breeders, & enthusiasts in eastern Canada
Activities: Providing networking opportunities for members; Coordinating, sponsoring, & participating in horse shows & competitive trail rides; Offering learning experiences about the Arabian horse breed
Chief Officer(s):
Allan Ehrlick, President
Jane Whitwell, Vice-President, 905-887-9303
jane.lee.whitwell@sympatico.ca
Jill Barton, Treasurer, 613-386-3195
jill.barton613@gmail.com
Awards:
• Freda Currie Scholarship Awards
Eligibility: AHAEC members who are a minimum of 18 years of age at a certain date, & who will be attending a post-secondary institution; Amount: $300 Contact: Janet Wojcik, wojcik@simcoe.net
• AHAEC Special Youth Award
To recognize a young Arabian enthusiasts for hard work in the association & the community; Amount: $250; $150 Contact: Janet Wojcik, wojcik@simcoe.net
Publications:
• Arabian Horse Association of Eastern Canada Newsletter
Type: Newsletter; Editor: Jill Barton; Price: Free with membership in the Arabian Horse Association of Eastern Canada
Profile: Associaton information

Arbitration & Mediation Institute of Canada Inc.; Canadian Foundation for Dispute Resolution See ADR Institute of Canada

Arbitration & Mediation Institute of Nova Scotia See ADR Institute of Canada

Les Arbitres Maritimes Associés du Canada See The Association of Maritime Arbitrators of Canada

Arborfield Board of Trade
PO Box 236, Arborfield SK S0E 0A0
Tel: 306-769-8627
Overview: A small local organization
Finances: Annual Operating Budget: Less than $50,000
30 volunteer(s)
Membership: 30; Fees: $10

Arborg Chamber of Commerce
c/o Town of Arborg, PO Box 159, Arborg MB R0C 0A0
www.townofarborg.com
Overview: A small local organization
Chief Officer(s):
Owen Eyolfson, Chair, 204-376-5453
owen@arborghotel.com

Arbres Canada See Tree Canada Foundation

Arbutus Vocational Society; THEO BC See Open Door Group

ARC - Aînés et retraités de la communauté
#110, 2075, rue Plessis, Montréal QC H2L 2Y4
Tél: 514-730-8870
arcssc2@gmail.com
www.arc.algi.qc.ca
www.facebook.com/arc.montreal
Aperçu: Dimension: petite; Envergure: locale; fondée en 2001
Mission: Regroupement d'hommes gais aînés retraités ou préretraités, visant à briser l'isolement et à demeurer actifs dans la communauté
Finances: Budget de fonctionnement annuel: Moins de $50,000;
Fonds: Membership
60 bénévole(s)
Membre: 250; Montant de la cotisation: 25$
Activités: Activités communautaires, sociales, sportives, culturelles et récréatives pour ses membres visant à favoriser leur bien-être physique et psychologique; 25 activités hebdomadaires, mensuelles ou annuelles - 250 sessions - 4 000 présences

ARC, AIDS Resource Centre, Okanagan & Region See Living Positive Resource Centre, Okanagan

L'arc-en-ciel littéraire
CP 180, Succ. C, Montréal QC H2L 4K1
Courriel: arcenciellitteraire@yahoo.ca
arcenciellitteraire.site.voila.fr
Aperçu: Dimension: petite; Envergure: provinciale
Mission: Le seul regroupement d'écrivains GLBT au Québec; promouvoit la littérature gaie et des auteurs gais
Membre(s) du bureau directeur:
Réjean Roy, Président fondateur

ARCH Disability Law Centre
#110, 425 Bloor St. East, Toronto ON M4W 3R5
Tel: 416-482-8255; Fax: 416-482-2981
Toll-Free: 866-482-2724; TTY: 416-482-1254
archlib@lao.on.ca
www.archdisabilitylaw.ca
www.facebook.com/ARCHDisabilityLawCentre
twitter.com/ARCHDisability
www.youtube.com/channel/UCZl_6YpK8XB7LJ_dQxdonlg
Previous Name: A Legal Resource Centre for Persons with Disabilities
Overview: A medium-sized provincial charitable organization founded in 1980
Mission: To defend & advance the equality rights of persons with disabilities; assisting individuals with disabilities to understand their rights & how to enforce them; working with groups representing people with disabilities throughout Ontario; representing in precedent setting cases where client cannot be represented appropriately by other legal services; summary advice & referral - lawyers who specialize in areas of law as they relate to disability provide free, confidential, basic legal advice & referral to other sources of assistance
Finances: Funding Sources: Major source of funding is the Clinic Funding Program of Legal Aid Ontario
Staff Member(s): 10
Activities: Speaker Service: Yes; Library: Open to public
Chief Officer(s):
Ivana Petricone, Executive Director

Archaeological Society of Alberta (ASA)
c/o Colleen Haukaas, 190 Tudor Lane, Edmonton AB T6J 3T5
Tel: 780-862-5220
arkysocietyalberta@gmail.com
www.arkyalberta.com
Overview: A medium-sized provincial charitable organization founded in 1975 overseen by Canadian Archaeological Association
Mission: To promote the regulations of the Alberta Historical Act & to disseminate archaeological information by means of publications & seminars
Finances: Annual Operating Budget: Less than $50,000;
Funding Sources: Dept. of Culture & Multiculturalism grants; government of Alberta
2 volunteer(s)
Membership: 300+; Fees: Schedule available
Activities: Annual seminar; publications; monitors archaeological sites
Chief Officer(s):
Colleen Haukaas, Executive Secretary-Treasurer
Robyn Crook, Provincial Coordinator
Publications:
• The Alberta Archaeological Review [a publication of the Archaeological Society of Alberta]
Editor: Dan Meyer
Bodo Archaeological Society
PO Box 1781, Provost AB T0B 3S0
Tel: 780-753-6353; Fax: 780-753-6352
bodo@bodoarchaeology.com
www.bodoarchaeology.com
Chief Officer(s):
Courtney Lakevold, President
Calgary Centre
PO Box 65123, Stn. North Hill, Calgary AB T2N 4T6
info@arkycalgary.com
www.arkycalgary.com
Chief Officer(s):
Janet Blakey, President
Lethbridge Centre
97 Eton Rd. West, Lethbridge AB T1K 4T9
Tel: 403-381-2655
Chief Officer(s):
Jim McMurchy, Contact
jnemc@telus.net
Red Deer Centre
Chief Officer(s):
Larry Steinbrenner, President
Doug Shaw, Provincial Representative
Southeastern Centre
Tel: 403-527-5440
Chief Officer(s):
Bruce Shepard, President
Strathcona Centre
Edmonton AB
arkyedmonton@gmail.com
www.arkyedmonton.ca
twitter.com/arkyedmonton
arkyedmonton.tumblr.com
Chief Officer(s):
Kurtis Blaikie-Birkigt, President

Archaeological Society of British Columbia (ASBC)
c/o Archaeology Unit/G.Hill, Royal BC Museum, 675 Belleville St., Victoria BC V8W 9W2
asbcvictoria@gmail.com
www.asbc.bc.ca
Overview: A small provincial organization founded in 1966 overseen by Canadian Archaeological Association
Mission: To protect the archaeological heritage of British Columbia; To promote public understanding of the scientific approach to archaeology; To encourage government to preserve archaeological & pre-historic sites
Member of: Heritage Council of British Columbia
Affiliation(s): Canadian Archaeological Association
Finances: Funding Sources: Membership fees
Membership: Fees: $25 individual; $35 family; $18 student/senior
Activities: Library: by appointment
Chief Officer(s):
Jacob Earnshaw, President
Publications:
• The Midden [a publication of the Archaeological Society of British Columbia]
Type: Journal; Frequency: Quarterly

L'Arche Atlantic Region
1381 Orangedale Rd., Orangedale NS B0E 2K0
Tel: 902-295-0050; Fax: 902-895-6349
office@larcheatlantic.ca
www.larcheatlantic.ca
www.facebook.com/larcheatlantic
Overview: A medium-sized provincial charitable organization founded in 1983 overseen by L'Arche Canada
Mission: Regional office contact information for the Atlantic Canada communities of L'Arche
Member of: L'Arche International
Membership: 5 communities
Chief Officer(s):
Jenn Power, Regional Leader
L'Arche Antigonish
4 West St., Antigonish NS B2G 1R8
Tel: 902-863-5000; Fax: 902-863-8224
www.larcheantigonish.ca
www.facebook.com/larcheantigonish
Affiliation(s): St. Francis Xavier University
Chief Officer(s):
Beth Wolters, Community Leader

L'Arche Cape Breton
3 L'Arche Lane, Whycocomagh NS B0E 3M0
Tel: 902-756-3162; *Fax:* 902-756-3381
office@larchecapebreton.org
www.larchecapebreton.org
www.facebook.com/pages/LArche-Cape-Breton-Community/128981923841453
www.youtube.com/user/larchecapebreton
Chief Officer(s):
Lisa Poirier-Sinclair, Community Leader

L'Arche Halifax
5512 Sullivan St., Halifax NS B3K 1X7
Tel: 902-407-5512; *Fax:* 902-405-9755
office@larchehalifax.org
www.larchehalifax.org
Chief Officer(s):
Rosaire Geddes-Pfaff, Community Leader

L'Arche Homefires
10 Gaspereau Ave., Wolfville NS B4P 2C2
Tel: 902-542-3520; *Fax:* 902-542-7686
office@larchehomefires.org
www.larchehomefires.org
Chief Officer(s):
Ingrid Blais, Director
director@larchehomefires.org

L'Arche Saint-John
623 Lancaster Ave., Saint John NB E2M 2M3
Tel: 506-672-6504
larchesaintjohn@nb.aibn.com
www.larchesaintjohn.org
Chief Officer(s):
Jocelyn Worster, Community Leader

L'Arche Canada
1280, av Bernard ouest, Outremont QC H1H 1H1
Tel: 514-844-1661; *Fax:* 514-844-1960
office@larche.ca
www.larche.ca
Overview: A medium-sized national charitable organization founded in 1969
Mission: To provide care & a sense of belonging for people who have developmental disabilities
Member of: L'Arche International
Finances: *Funding Sources:* Donations
Membership: 200 homes & day settings across Canada
Activities: Offering programs & publications to schools, professionals & the general public

L'Arche Foundation
#300, 10271 Yonge St., Richmond Hill ON L4C 3B5
Tel: 905-770-7696; *Fax:* 905-884-4819
Toll-Free: 800-571-0212
info@larchefoundation.ca
www.larchefoundation.ca
www.facebook.com/larchecanadafoundation
www.twitter.com/LArcheCanadaF1
Overview: A medium-sized national charitable organization overseen by L'Arche Canada
Mission: To raise money to support the activities of L'Arche Canada
Member of: L'Arche International
Finances: *Annual Operating Budget:* $1.5 Million-$3 Million; *Funding Sources:* Donations
Chief Officer(s):
Gary Sim, President & CEO

L'Arche Ontario
186 Floyd Ave., Toronto ON M4J 2J1
Tel: 416-406-2869
larcheontario.org
www.facebook.com/larcheontario
Overview: A medium-sized provincial charitable organization overseen by L'Arche Canada
Mission: Regional office contact information for the Ontario communities of L'Arche
Member of: L'Arche International
Membership: 9 communities
Chief Officer(s):
John Guido, Regional Coordinator
johnguido@larche.ca

L'Arche Arnprior
#103, 16 Edward St., Arnprior ON K7S 3W4
Tel: 613-623-7323
office@larchearnprior.org
www.larche.ca/en/communities/arnprior
Chief Officer(s):
Jeanette Fraser, Community Leader

L'Arche Daybreak
11339 Yonge St., Richmond Hill ON L4S 1L1
Tel: 905-884-3454; *Fax:* 905-884-0584
office@larchedaybreak.com
www.larchedaybreak.com
www.facebook.com/larchedaybreak
Mission: L'Arche Daybreak is a non-denominational, inter-faith community of people with different intellectual capacity, social origin & culture. It is located on a 13-acre property & includes 8 homes, 5 vocational programs & a spiritual centre. Live-in assistants join the core members (people with intellectual disabilities) in performing tasks of daily living.
Member of: L'Arche International

L'Arche Hamilton
664 Main St. East, Hamilton ON L8M 1K2
Tel: 905-312-0162; *Fax:* 905-312-0165
office@larcheham.com
www.larche.ca/en/communities/hamilton
Chief Officer(s):
Lynn Godfrey, Community Leader

L'Arche London
#121, 4056 Meadowbrook Dr., London ON N6L 1E3
office@larchelondon.org
larchelondon.org
www.facebook.com/larchelondon
Chief Officer(s):
Marietta Drost, Community Leader

L'Arche North Bay
102 - 1st Ave. East, North Bay ON P1B 1J6
Tel: 705-474-0081; *Fax:* 705-497-3447
www.larchenorthbay.ca
www.facebook.com/LArcheNorthBay
Chief Officer(s):
Martina Getz, Community Leader

L'Arche Ottawa
11 Rossland Ave., Ottawa ON K2G 2K2
Tel: 613-228-7136; *Fax:* 613-228-8829
office@larcheottawa.org
www.larche.ca/en/communities/ottawa
Chief Officer(s):
Raphael Amato, Community Leader

L'Arche Stratford
PO Box 522, Stn. Main, Stratford ON N5A 6T7
Tel: 519-271-9751; *Fax:* 519-271-1861
info@larche.stratford.on.ca
www.larchestratford.ca
Chief Officer(s):
Stephanie Calma, Community Leader
commleader@larche.stratford.on.ca

L'Arche Sudbury
1173 Rideau St., Sudbury ON P3A 3A5
Tel: 705-525-1015; *Fax:* 705-525-4448
larchesudbury@larchesudbury.org
www.larchesudbury.org
Chief Officer(s):
Jennifer McCauley, Community Leader
jennifer.mccauley@larchesudbury.org

L'Arche Toronto
186 Floyd Ave., Toronto ON M4J 2J1
Tel: 416-406-2869
office@larchetoronto.org
www.larchetoronto.org
www.facebook.com/larchetoronto
twitter.com/larchetoronto
www.youtube.com/larchetoronto
Chief Officer(s):
Raphael Arens, Community Leader
raphael@larchetoronto.org

L'Arche Québec
1280, rue Bernard ouest, Outremont QC H2V 1V9
Tél: 514-849-0110
aaq@larche.ca
archequebec.ca
www.facebook.com/arche.quebec
twitter.com/archequebec
plus.google.com/+ArchequebecCa
Aperçu: *Dimension:* moyenne; *Envergure:* provinciale; Organisme sans but lucratif surveillé par L'Arche Canada
Mission: Régional d'information contacter le bureau pour les collectivités du Québec de L'Arche
Membre de: L'Arche International
Membre: 8 communities
Membre(s) du bureau directeur:
Sylvie Morin, Directrice régionale
smorin-aaq@larche.ca

L'Arche Abitibi-Témiscamingue
42, rue Principale sud, Amos QC J9T 3A5
Tél: 819-732-1265
courrier@larcheamos.org
www.larcheamos.org
Membre(s) du bureau directeur:
Perrine Forgeot D'Arc, Responsable de communauté

L'Arche Agapè
19, rue Hanson, Gatineau QC J8Y 3M4
Tél: 819-770-2000; *Téléc:* 819-770-3907
arche.agape@bellnet.ca
www.larcheagape.org
www.facebook.com/larche.agape
Membre(s) du bureau directeur:
Nancy Lamothe, Responsable de communauté

L'Arche Beloeil
221, rue Bernard-Pilon, Beloeil QC J3G 1V2
Tél: 450-446-1061; *Téléc:* 450-446-2396
archebelo@qc.aira.com
www.larche.ca/en/communities/beloeil
www.facebook.com/larchebeloeil
Membre(s) du bureau directeur:
Marie Fréchette, Responsable de communauté

L'Arche Joliette
#3-21, 144, rue St-Joseph, Beloeil QC J6E 5C4
Tél: 450-759-0408; *Téléc:* 450-759-8266
larchejoliette@bellnet.ca
www.larche.ca/en/communities/joliette
Membre(s) du bureau directeur:
Elisabeth Richard, Responsable de communauté

L'Arche l'Étoile
218, rue St-Sauveur, Québec QC G1N 4S1
Tél: 418-527-8839; *Téléc:* 418-527-8738
larcheletoile@videotron.ca
arche-quebec.ca
www.facebook.com/cdjetoile
Membre(s) du bureau directeur:
Lynda St-Pierre, Responsable de communauté

L'Arche Le Printemps
1375, rue Principale, Saint-Malachie QC G0R 3N0
Tél: 418-642-5785
archeleprintemps@globetrotter.net
www.larche.ca/en/communities/le_printemps
Membre(s) du bureau directeur:
Geneviève Moutquin, Responsable de communauté

L'Arche Mauricie
570, rue St-Paul, Trois-Rivières QC G9A 1H8
Tél: 819-373-8781
archemauricie@qc.aira.com
www.larchemauricie.org
www.facebook.com/LARCHEMAURICIE
Membre(s) du bureau directeur:
Patrice Paradis, Responsable de communauté

L'Arche Montréal
6105, rue Jogues, Montréal QC H4E 2W2
Tél: 514-761-7307
info@larche-montreal.org
www.larche-montreal.org
Mission: Faire connaître le don des personnes présentant une déficience intellectuelle qui se révèle à travers des relations mutuelles, sources de transformation; Développer un environnement communautaire qui réponde aux besoins changeants de nos membres, en demeurant fidèle aux valeurs essentielles de notre histoire fondatrice; S'engager dans les cultures respectives et travailler ensemble à construire une société plus humaine
Membre de: L'Arche internationale
Membre(s) du bureau directeur:
Alain Ouedraogo, Directeur
direction@larche-montreal.org

L'Arche Western Region
307 - 57 Ave. SW, Calgary AB T2H 2T6
Tél: 403-571-0155; *Téléc:* 403-255-1354
Aperçu: *Dimension:* moyenne; *Envergure:* provinciale; Organisme sans but lucratif surveillé par L'Arche Canada
Mission: Regional office contact information for the communities of L'Arche in Western Canada
Membre de: L'Arche International
Membre: 7 communities

Membre(s) du bureau directeur:
Pat Favaro, Regional Coordinator
pfavaro@larchecalgary.org

L'Arche Calgary
307 - 57th Ave. SW, Calgary AB T2H 2T6
Tel: 403-571-0155; *Fax:* 403-255-1354
office@larchecalgary.org
www.larchecalgary.org
www.facebook.com/larchecalgary
twitter.com/larchecalgary
www.pinterest.com/larchecalgary
Membre(s) du bureau directeur:
Garth Reesor, Community Leader
GReesor@larchecalgary.org

L'Arche Comox Valley
1225C England Ave., Courtenay BC V9N 2P1
Tel: 250-334-8320; *Fax:* 250-334-8321
office@larchecomoxvalley.org
www.larchecomoxvalley.org
www.facebook.com/pages/LArche-Comox-Valley/491779427541959
Membre(s) du bureau directeur:
Christine Monier, Community Leader

L'Arche Edmonton
Fulton Place, 10310 - 56 St. NW, Edmonton AB T6A 2J2
Tel: 780-465-0618; *Fax:* 780-465-8091
edmoffice@larcheedmonton.org
www.larcheedmonton.org
www.facebook.com/pages/LArche-Edmonton/174434082672376
twitter.com/larcheedmonton
Membre(s) du bureau directeur:
Pat Desnoyers, Executive Director & Community Leader Ext. 205
pdesnoyers@larcheedmonton.org

L'Arche Greater Vancouver
7401 Sussex Ave., Burnaby BC V5J 3V6
Tel: 604-435-9544
office@larchevancouver.org
www.larchevancouver.org
www.facebook.com/LArcheV
Member of: British Columbia Association for Community Living
Membre(s) du bureau directeur:
Denise Haskett, Executive Diretor & Community Leader, 604-435-9544 Ext. 27
dhaskett@larchevancouver.org

L'Arche Lethbridge
240 - 12C St. North, Lethbridge AB T1H 2M7
Tel: 403-328-3735; *Fax:* 403-320-6737
office@larchelethbridge.org
www.larchelethbridge.org
Membre(s) du bureau directeur:
Tim Wiebe, Community Leader

L'Arche Saskatoon
PO Box 23006, Saskatoon SK S7J 5H3
Tel: 306-262-7243; *Fax:* 306-373-5746
www.larchesaskatoon.org
www.facebook.com/larchesaskatoon
Membre(s) du bureau directeur:
Wyndham Thiessen, Community Leader
wthiessen@larchesaskatoon.org

L'Arche Winnipeg
118 Regent Ave. East, Winnipeg MB R2C 0C1
Tel: 204-237-0300; *Fax:* 204-237-0316
office@larchewinnipeg.org
www.larchewinnipeg.org
Membre(s) du bureau directeur:
Jim Lapp, Community Leader Ext. 6
jimlapp@larchewinnipeg.org

Archelaus Smith Historical Society
PO Box 190, Clarks Harbour NS B0W 1P0
Tel: 902-745-2642
www.archelaus.org
Overview: A small local charitable organization founded in 1970
Mission: To collect & display artifacts pertaining to the history of Cape Sable Island
Member of: Federation of the Nova Scotian Heritage
Finances: *Annual Operating Budget:* Less than $50,000
Staff Member(s): 3; 7 volunteer(s)
Membership: 20 individual; *Fees:* $10; *Member Profile:* Interest in local history
Activities: Operates a small museum; *Library:* Open to public
Chief Officer(s):
Blanche O'Connell, President
blancherossoconnell@hotmail.com

Archers & Bowhunters Association of Manitoba (ABAM)
145 Pacific Ave., Winnipeg MB R3B 2Z6
Tel: 204-925-5697; *Fax:* 204-925-5792
info@abam.ca
www.abam.ca
facebook.com/archersandbowhuntersassociationofmanitoba
Overview: A small provincial organization
Mission: To oversee the sports of archery & bowhunting in Manitoba
Member of: Sport Manitoba
Membership: *Committees:* Athletic Development; Officials
Activities: Offering archery development program & olympic program
Chief Officer(s):
Ryan Van Berkel, Executive Director

Archers Association of Nova Scotia (AANS)
c/o Sport Nova Scotia, 5516 Spring Garden Rd., 4th Fl., Halifax NS B3J 1G6
www.aans.ca
Overview: A medium-sized provincial organization founded in 1967 overseen by Archery Canada Tir à l'Arc
Mission: To govern archery in Nova Scotia
Member of: Archery Canada Tir à l'Arc
Finances: *Annual Operating Budget:* Less than $50,000
Membership: 22 clubs; 450 individuals; *Fees:* $35 individuals; $60 family; includes membership with the Federation of Canadian Archers (FCA)
Chief Officer(s):
William Currie, President, 902-852-4393
wcurrie@dal.ca

Archery Association of New Brunswick (AANB)
141 Isington St., Moncton NB E1A 1Y7
Tel: 506-855-6169
archerynb.ca
Overview: A small provincial organization founded in 1969 overseen by Archery Canada Tir à l'Arc
Mission: To promote & encourage archery in New Brunswick
Member of: Archery Canada Tir à l'Arc
Membership: 19 clubs; *Committees:* Executive
Chief Officer(s):
Julie Murphy, President
akt@nbnet.nb.ca
Maurice Levesque, Executive Director
mlevesqu@nbnet.nb.ca

Archery Canada Tir à l'Arc
#108, 2255 St. Laurent Blvd., Ottawa ON K1G 4K3
Tel: 613-260-2113; *Fax:* 613-260-2114
information@archerycanada.ca
www.archerycanada.ca
www.facebook.com/ArcheryCanada
twitter.com/ArcheryCanada
Previous Name: Federation of Canadian Archers Inc.
Overview: A medium-sized national charitable organization founded in 1927
Mission: To promote & develop the sport of archery in a safe & ethical manner; To act as the official representative for archery to the federal government, & national & international sport organizations
Affiliation(s): World Archery Federation
Finances: *Funding Sources:* Government support
Membership: *Member Profile:* Archers
Activities: Promoting archery participation across Canada; Supporting high performance excellence in archery; Presenting awards; Providing a vehicle for communication across Canada; Registering competitions; Maintaining Canadian records; Selecting archers to represent Canada at international events; Coordinating research; Training coaches & officials across Canada; Obtaining support for paralympic programs; *Library*
Chief Officer(s):
Scott Ogilvie, Executive Director
Publications:
• Archery Canada Annual Report
Type: Yearbook; *Frequency:* Annually
Profile: Featuring the financial statements of the association

Architects Association of Prince Edward Island (AAPEI)
PO Box 1766, 92 Queen St., Charlottetown PE C1A 7N4
Tel: 902-566-3699
www.aapei.com
www.facebook.com/architectsassociationpei
Overview: A small provincial organization
Mission: To increase awareness & understanding of architecture & its professional services.
Finances: *Funding Sources:* Membership dues
Membership: 1-99; *Fees:* Schedule available; *Committees:* Continuing Education; Scholarship; Sustainable Architecture; Architectural Outreach; Nominating; Disciplinary
Activities: *Internships:* Yes
Chief Officer(s):
Scott Stewart, Executive Director
director@aapei.com
David Lopes, Registrar, 902-626-8253
david@coastdesign.ca

Architects' Association of New Brunswick (AANB) / Association des architectes du Nouveau-Brunswick
PO Box 5093, 36 Maple Ave., Sussex NB E4E 2N5
Tel: 506-433-5811; *Fax:* 506-432-1122
aanb@nb.aibn.com
www.aanb.org
Overview: A small provincial licensing organization founded in 1933
Mission: To govern & regulate persons in New Brunswick who offer architectural services; To advance & maintain the standards of architecture in New Brunswick
Finances: *Funding Sources:* Membership fees; Sponsorship
Membership: *Fees:* $56.50 students; $118.65 interns; $717.55 registered & reciprocal memberships; *Member Profile:* Students; Persons with a certificate of practice, or a temporary licence; Intern members; Registered members from New Brunswick; Reciprocal membership for persons outside New Brunswick; Retired members, who have left the practice of architecture
Activities: Offering a continuing education program to ensure a safe environment for the public
Chief Officer(s):
Christian Hébert, President
Fernand Daigie, Treasurer
John Leroux, Registrar
Publications:
• Intern Architect Program
Type: Manual; *Price:* Free with intern membership in the Architects' Association of New Brunswick

Architectural & Building Technologists Association of Manitoba Inc. (ABTAM)
1447 Waverley St., Winnipeg MB R3T 0P7
Tel: 204-956-4727
abtam.info@gmail.com
www.abtam.ca
Overview: A small provincial organization
Membership: *Fees:* $80 general; $120 certified
Chief Officer(s):
Leighton Klassen, President

The Architectural Conservancy of Ontario (ACO)
#403, 10 Adelaide St. East, Toronto ON M5C 1J3
Tel: 416-367-8075; *Fax:* 416-367-8630
Toll-Free: 877-264-8937
manager@arconserv.ca
www.arconserv.ca
www.facebook.com/119712261437141
twitter.com/arconserve
Overview: A medium-sized provincial charitable organization founded in 1933
Mission: To preserve buildings & structures of architectural merit & places of natural beauty or interest
Affiliation(s): Ontario Heritage Alliance
Finances: *Funding Sources:* Donations; government grants; membership dues; fundraising activities
Staff Member(s): 2
Activities: Technical consulting service for property owners, groups & municipalities; neighbourhood & garden tours; conferences & workshops; capital fundraising for repair & restoration work; architectural research; property acquisition
Chief Officer(s):
Susan Ratcliffe, President
Rollo Myers, Manager

Architectural Glass & Metal Contractors Association (AGMCA)
619 Liverpool Rd., Pickering ON L1W 1R1
Tel: 905-420-7272; *Fax:* 905-420-7288
info@agmca.ca
www.agmca.ca

Overview: A small provincial licensing organization founded in 1979
Membership: *Member Profile:* Contractors (Ontario) industrial; commercial; institutional
Chief Officer(s):
Kline Holland, Director, Labour Relations

Architectural Heritage Society of Saskatchewan (AHSS)
202 - 1275 Broad St., Regina SK S4R 1Y2
Tel: 306-359-0933; *Fax:* 306-359-3899
sahs@sasktel.net
www.ahsk.ca
Overview: A small provincial organization founded in 1987
Mission: To promote, support & facilitate the preservation, conservation, restoration & reuse of distinct architectural & historical heritage properties (designated or potential) throughout the province, ensuring that our built heritage is maintained for present & future citizens to appreciate the contributions & craftsmanship of past generations; to enhance the current social, economic & environmental quality of life
Member of: Saskatchewan Council of Cultural Organizations; Canadian Heritage Network; National Preservation Trust
Finances: *Annual Operating Budget:* $50,000-$100,000; *Funding Sources:* Private & public sector funding
Staff Member(s): 1
Membership: 230; *Fees:* $20; *Committees:* Membership; Finance; Administration; Policy

Architectural Institute of British Columbia (AIBC)
#100, 440 Cambie St., Vancouver BC V6B 2N5
Tel: 604-683-8588; *Fax:* 604-683-8568
Toll-Free: 800-667-0753
Other Communication: Toll Free Fax: 1-800-661-2955
info@aibc.ca
www.aibc.ca
twitter.com/AIBConnected
Overview: A medium-sized provincial licensing organization founded in 1914
Mission: To regulate the profession of architecture in accordance with the Architects Act; to promote & increase the knowledge, skill & proficiency of its members in all things relating to the practice of architecture; to advance & maintain high standards of qualification & professional ethics; to promote public appreciation of architecture, allied arts, sciences & the professions
Member of: Committee of Canadian Architectural Councils
Affiliation(s): Royal Architectural Institute of Canada
Finances: *Annual Operating Budget:* $1.5 Million-$3 Million; *Funding Sources:* Membership dues; Document sales; Sponsorship
Staff Member(s): 17; 200 volunteer(s)
Membership: 1,310; *Fees:* $760; *Member Profile:* Architects registered to practice in BC; architectural technologists & interns; *Committees:* Act & Bylaw Review Task Force; Advisory Service; Architects in the Community; Architects in Schools; Architectural Technologist Admissions; Building Envelope Education Program; Building Envelope; Communications Board; Design Panel; Educational Facilities; Energy & Environment; Experience Review; Fees & Services; Health Care Facilities; Intern-Architect; Practice Board; Professional Conduct; Professional Development; Registration Board; Regulatory Coordination
Activities: Providing free architectural advisory & architectural summer walking tours; Determining the education, experience, & examinations requirements for those seeking entry to the architectural profession; Working with national counterparts & agencies to evaluate post-secondary education standards; Offering internship programs; Providing a continuing education system; *Internships:* Yes; *Rents Mailing List:* Yes; *Library:* Architecture Centre; Open to public by appointment
Chief Officer(s):
Mark Vernon, Chief Executive Officer, 604-683-8588 Ext. 304
mvernon@aibc.ca
Grace Battiston, Director, Communications, 604-683-8588 Ext. 308
gbattiston@aibc.ca
Paul Becker, Director, Professional Services, 604-683-8588 Ext. 307
pbecker@aibc.ca
Awards:
• Lieutenant Governor of British Columbia Awards
• AIBC Innovation Awards
• AIBC Special Jury Award
• AIBC Emerging Firm Award
• AIBC Lifetime Achievement Award

• AIBC Special Certificate of Recognition
• The Barbara Dalrymple Memorial Award for Community Service
Meetings/Conferences:
• Architectural Institute of British Columbia Annual Conference 2018, May, 2018, Vancouver Convention Centre West, Vancouver, BC
Scope: Provincial
Description: Theme: "Spaces Between"
Contact Information: www.conference.aibc.ca
Publications:
• AIBC [Architectural Institute of British Columbia] Regulatory Review
Profile: A series of short articles for members, associates, & the public; Contains topical updates on professional practice & conduct
• AIBS [Architectural Institute of British Columbia] eNews
Type: Journal; *Frequency:* weekly
Profile: Weekly updates for members
• architectureBC [a publication of the Architectural Institute of British Columbia]
Type: Journal; *Editor:* Grace Battiston
Profile: Featuring industry & association news & member profiles

Architectural Millworkers of Ontario *See* Architectural Woodwork Manufacturers Association of Canada - Ontario Chapter

Architectural Woodwork Manufacturers Association of British Columbia (AWMA-BC)
#101, 4238 Lozells Ave., Burnaby BC V5A 0C4
Tel: 604-298-3555; *Fax:* 604-298-3558
info.bc@awmac.com
bc.awmac.com
Previous Name: Architectural Woodwork Manufacturers Association of Canada - British Columbia
Overview: A medium-sized provincial charitable organization founded in 1926 overseen by Architectural Woodwork Manufacturers Association of Canada
Mission: To advance the highest standards of education, quality workmanship, warranties & business practices in architectural woodwork manufacturing in British Columbia
Member of: Construction Specifications Canada
Finances: *Annual Operating Budget:* $250,000-$500,000; *Funding Sources:* Membership dues; inspections
Staff Member(s): 2; 12 volunteer(s)
Membership: 70; *Fees:* Schedule available, please contact; *Member Profile:* Architectural woodworkers; Suppliers; Advisory; Life members; *Committees:* Apprenticeship; Finance; GIS; Membership Services; Social Affairs
Activities: Organizing lunch & learn for architectural & design firms, seminars, & retreats; Offering guarantee & inspection service program
Chief Officer(s):
Martin Berryman, President
Awards:
• Awards of Excellence in Quality & Service

Architectural Woodwork Manufacturers Association of Canada (AWMAC) / Association des manufacturiers de menuiserie architecturale du Canada
PO Box 36525, Stn. MacTaggart, Edmonton AB T6R 0T4
Tel: 403-981-7300
info@awmac.com
www.awmac.com
Overview: A medium-sized national organization founded in 1970
Mission: To develop & promote the use of AWMAC's quality standards for the manufacturing & installation of architectural woodwork; To promote assurance of adherence to those quality standards & sustainable practices in the woodworking industry
Finances: *Funding Sources:* Association chapters
Staff Member(s): 3
Membership: 400+; *Member Profile:* Professionals & associations that design, engineer, manufacture, & install architectural woodwork
Activities: Offering programs & services to members
Chief Officer(s):
Michelle Morrell, Association Manager
Awards:
• Outstanding Service Award
Meetings/Conferences:
• Architectural Woodwork Manufacturers Association of Canada 2018 Convention & Annual General Meeting, May, 2018,

Fairmont Hotel Macdonald, Edmonton, AB
Scope: National
Publications:
• The Sounding Board [a publication of The Architectural Woodwork Manufacturers Association of Canada]

Architectural Woodwork Manufacturers Association of Canada - Atlantic
PO Box 38136, Dartmouth NS B3B 1X2
Tel: 902-483-4213
atlantic@awmac.com
atl.awmac.com
Also Known As: AWMAC-Atlantic
Overview: A medium-sized provincial organization overseen by Architectural Woodwork Manufacturers Association of Canada
Mission: To promote the interests of individuals & organizations in the architectural wood manufacturing, supply & installation industry
Finances: *Annual Operating Budget:* Less than $50,000
Membership: 40
Chief Officer(s):
Tim Pedersen, President

Architectural Woodwork Manufacturers Association of Canada - British Columbia *See* Architectural Woodwork Manufacturers Association of British Columbia

Architectural Woodwork Manufacturers Association of Canada - Manitoba
1447 Waverly St., Winnipeg MB R3T 0P7
manitoba@awmac.com
mb.awmac.com
Also Known As: AWMAC-Manitoba
Overview: A medium-sized provincial organization overseen by Architectural Woodwork Manufacturers Association of Canada
Mission: To foster & advance the interests of those who are engaged in or who are directly or indirectly connected with or affected by the production & installation of architectural woodwork; To endeavor to achieve a closer relationship & a better understanding among the various branches of the industry
Finances: *Annual Operating Budget:* Less than $50,000
Membership: 25; *Fees:* $850 Contractors; $350 Associates
Chief Officer(s):
Dave Hudon, President
Curtis Popel, Vice-President
Greg Barre, Secretary
Trevor Parks, Treasurer

Architectural Woodwork Manufacturers Association of Canada - Northern Alberta
c/o Margo Love, 12816 - 89 St. NW, Edmonton AB T5E 3J9
Tel: 780-937-8572
northernalberta@awmac.com
nab.awmac.com
Also Known As: AWMAC-Northern Alberta
Overview: A small local organization overseen by Architectural Woodwork Manufacturers Association of Canada
Mission: To promote the architectural woodwork field in Northern Alberta
Membership: 50+
Chief Officer(s):
Kevin Balicki, President

Architectural Woodwork Manufacturers Association of Canada - Ontario Chapter (AWMAC-ON)
70 Leek Cres., Richmond Hill ON L4B 1H1
Tel: 416-499-4000; *Fax:* 416-499-8752
gis@awmacontario.com
on.awmac.com
Also Known As: AWMAC-Ontario
Previous Name: Architectural Millworkers of Ontario
Overview: A small provincial organization founded in 1966 overseen by Architectural Woodwork Manufacturers Association of Canada
Mission: To foster & advance the interests of those engaged in the production & installation of architectural woodwork in Ontario
Finances: *Annual Operating Budget:* Less than $50,000
Staff Member(s): 10; 35 volunteer(s)
Membership: 100+; *Member Profile:* Manufacturers & suppliers in the architectural millwork industry; *Committees:* Convention; GIS; Membership
Chief Officer(s):
Peter Gallagher, President
Robert Antonel, Secretary-Treasurer

Canadian Associations / Architectural Woodwork Manufacturers Association of Canada - Québec

Architectural Woodwork Manufacturers Association of Canada - Québec
89, av Godfrey, Saint-Sauveur QC J0R 1R5
Tel: 450-227-4048
info@awmacquebec.com
qc.awmac.com
Also Known As: AWMAC-Québec
Overview: A medium-sized provincial organization founded in 2009 overseen by Architectural Woodwork Manufacturers Association of Canada
Mission: To promote the interests of the architectural woodwork industry in Québec
Finances: Annual Operating Budget: Less than $50,000
Membership: 50+; Fees: Schedule available
Chief Officer(s):
Gaëtan Lauzon, Executive Director
glauzon@awmacquebec.com

Architectural Woodwork Manufacturers Association of Canada - Saskatchewan
PO Box 26032, Stn. Lawson Heights, Saskatoon SK S7K 8C1
Tel: 306-652-2704; Fax: 306-664-2552
saskatchewan@awmac.com
sk.awmac.com
Also Known As: AWMAC-Saskatchewan
Overview: A medium-sized provincial organization overseen by Architectural Woodwork Manufacturers Association of Canada
Mission: To foster & advance the interests of those who are engaged in or who are directly or indirectly connected with or affected by the production & installation of architectural woodwork
Membership: 20+
Chief Officer(s):
Kasia Robinson, President

Architectural Woodwork Manufacturers Association of Canada - Southern Alberta
#2A, 4803 Centre St. NW, Calgary AB T2E 2Z6
Tel: 403-264-5979; Fax: 403-286-9400
southernalberta@awmac.com
sab.awmac.com
Also Known As: AWMAC-Southern Alberta Chapter
Overview: A small local organization overseen by Architectural Woodwork Manufacturers Association of Canada
Mission: To advance the interests of those related to the production & installation of architectural woodwork; To foster a closer relationship among the various branches of the industry
Membership: 70+; Fees: $150 design authority; $1000 associate; $1450 manufacturer
Activities: Providing awards for excellence in design
Chief Officer(s):
Rob Hodgins, President
Sarah Cantrill, Secretary
Chris Weening, AWNAC Director

Archives Association of British Columbia (AABC)
#249, 34A-2755 Lougheed Hwy., Port Coquitlam BC V3B 5Y9
info@aabc.ca
www.aabc.ca
www.facebook.com/ArchivesAssociationBC
Merged from: Association of British Columbia Archivists; British Columbia Archives Council
Overview: A small provincial charitable organization founded in 1990 overseen by Canadian Council of Archives
Mission: To act as the voice of archivists & archival institutions in British Columbia; To undertake projects that strengthen the archival network in the province; To preserve & promote access to British Columbia's documentary heritage
Finances: Funding Sources: Membership dues; National Archival Development Program; Donations
Membership: Fees: $30 retired/volunteer/student; $72 associate institutional/individual; $96 sustaining; $120-$480 institutional (based on operating budget); Member Profile: Institutions approved by the AABC executive; Individuals who support the association's objectives; Students who are registered full-time in a community college or university program; Committees: Constitution & By-laws; Grants; Membership; Nominations & Elections; Programs; Finance; Communications
Activities: Providing educational opportunities & advisory services; Coordinating grant programs; Offering a job board; Building & maintaining the provincial catalogue; Providing networking opportunities for members; Offering access to a range of free conservation services for members; Developing & maintaining web resources created by the AABC; Awareness Events: Archive Week
Chief Officer(s):
Cindy McLellan, President
aabc.president@aabc.ca
Sarah Jensen, Secretary
sarah.jensen@gov.bc.ca
Sarah Romkey, Treasurer
treasurer@aabc.ca
Meetings/Conferences:
• Archives Association of British Columbia 2018 Conference, 2018
Scope: Provincial
• Archives Association of British Columbia 2018 Annual General Meeting, 2018
Scope: Provincial

Archives Association of Ontario (AAO) / L'Association des archives de l'Ontario
#200, 411 Richmond St. East, Toronto ON M5A 3S5
Tel: 647-343-3334
aao@aao-archivists.ca
aao-archivists.ca
www.linkedin.com/company/archives-association-of-ontario
www.facebook.com/ArchivesAssociationOfOntario
twitter.com/AAO_tweet
Merged from: Ontario Association of Archivists; Ontario Council of Archives
Overview: A medium-sized provincial organization founded in 1993
Mission: To encourage, through the establishment of networks, the public knowledge & appreciation of archives & their function; To promote the advancement of general education in the preservation of the cultural heritage & identity of the various regions of the province; To represent the interests of the archival community before the government of Ontario, local government, & other provincial institutions of a public or private nature; To provide professional guidance & leadership through communication & cooperation with all persons, groups, & associations interested in the preservation & use of records of the human experience in Ontario
Affiliation(s): Ontario Heritage Trust
Finances: Funding Sources: Ministry of Tourism, Culture & Sport; Archives of Ontario
Membership: 300; Fees: Schedule available based on budget for institutions; $95 individual; $35 friend of AAO/retired; $30 student; Member Profile: Open to any person &/or organization interested in the preservation & use of historical records & the heritage of the province of Ontario, & to those who are sympathetic to the aims of the association & who wish to further its work; Committees: Archeion; Awards; Communications & Advocacy; Fundraising; Institutional Development; Preservation; Professional Development
Activities: Advocating on behalf of Ontario's archival community to local & provincial government; Facilitating communication among member institutions; Offering educational & networking oppportunities; Operating & maintaining a Listserv; Awareness Events: Archives Awareness Week, April
Chief Officer(s):
Dana Thorne, President
president@aao-archivists.ca
Jodi Aoki, Secretary & Treasurer
secretary.treasurer@aao-archivists.ca
Awards:
• Alexander Fraser Award
Awarded to an individual who has contributed in a significant way to the advancement of the archival community in Ontario
• James J. Talman Award
Awarded to an individual who has demonstrated an exemplary level of imagination & innovation in contribution to their institution or the profession as a whole
• Institutional Award
Awarded to an institution that has contributed significantly to the advancement of the archival field or community, or has shown innovation & creativity in the establishment of programs & services
• Corporate Award
Awarded to an organization, agency, or corporation that has shown significant support to the archival community
• Shirley Spragge Bursary
Assists an individual in attending the annual AAO Conference
Eligibility: AAO student members enrolled in a recognized archival program, AAO members who are recent (1-3 years) gradutes of an archival program & AAO members who are practicing (or volunteer) archivists in financial need; Amount: Free conference registration + $650 in travel reimbursement
Meetings/Conferences:
• Archives Association of Ontario Conference 2018, 2018, Waterloo, ON
Scope: Provincial
Publications:
• Off the Record [a publication of the Archives Association of Ontario]
Type: Newsletter; Frequency: Quarterly; Editor: Grant Hurley; ISSN: 2370-1099
Profile: Activities of the AAO & its chapters; News relating to archives in Ontario; Technical & professionaladvice; Educational & employment opportunities; Information about grants

Durham Region Area Archives (DRAAG)
www.durhamregionarchivesgroup.com
www.facebook.com/DurhamRegionAreaArchivesGroup
twitter.com/durhamarchives
Chief Officer(s):
Sarah Ferencz, Chair
Jennifer Weymark, Vice-Chair

Eastern Ontario Chapter
ON
aaoeast@gmail.com
aao-archivists.ca/eoc
www.facebook.com/209300655827038
aaoeast.blogspot.ca
Chief Officer(s):
John D. Lund, President

Northwestern Ontario Archivists' Association (NOAA)
ON
aao-archivists.ca/noaa
Chief Officer(s):
Christina Wakefield, Chair

Southwestern Ontario Chapter (SWOC)
ON
aao-archivists.ca/swoc
Chief Officer(s):
Jessica Blackwell, President

Toronto Area Archivists' Group (TAAG)
Toronto ON
taag.chapter@gmail.com
aao-archivists.ca/taag
www.facebook.com/torontoarchivists
Chief Officer(s):
James Roussain, President

Archives Council of Prince Edward Island
PO Box 1000, Charlottetown PE C1A 7M4
acpei@gov.pe.ca
www.archives.pe.ca
Overview: A small provincial organization founded in 1987 overseen by Canadian Council of Archives
Mission: To facilitate the development of the archival system in PEI; To make recommendations about the system's operation & financing; To develop & facilitate the implementation & management of programs to assist the archival community; To communicate archival needs & concerns to decision-makers, researchers, & the general public
Membership: 12 institutions
Chief Officer(s):
Simon Lloyd, President, 902-566-0536, Fax: 902-628-4305
slloyd@upei.ca

Archives du Centre acadien (ACA)
Université Sainte-Anne, 1695, Rte. 1, Pointe-de-l'Église NS B0W 1M0
Tél: 902-769-2114; Téléc: 902-769-0063
centre.acadien@usainteanne.ca
www.usainteanne.ca/centre-acadien
Aperçu: Dimension: petite; Envergure: locale; Organisme sans but lucratif; fondée en 1972
Mission: Faire connaître et rayonner l'histoire et la culture des Acadiens de la Nouvelle-Écosse, et ce, premièrement au sein des provinces Maritimes et deuxièmement, auprès des autres collectivités et regroupements du Canada, des États-Unis et de l'Europe
Membre de: Council of Nova Scotia Archives
Finances: Budget de fonctionnement annuel: $100,000-$250,000
Membre(s) du personnel: 5
Activités:; Bibliothèque: Bibliothèque du Centre acadien
Membre(s) du bureau directeur:
Carmen d'Entremont, Coordonatrice
carmen.dentremont@usainteanne.ca

Archives Society of Alberta (ASA)
#407, 10408 - 124 St. NW, Edmonton AB T5N 1R5

Tel: 780-424-2697; Fax: 780-425-1679
info@archivesalberta.org
www.archivesalberta.org
Merged from: Alberta Archives Council; Alberta Society of Archivists
Overview: A medium-sized provincial organization founded in 1993 overseen by Canadian Council of Archives
Mission: To provide professional leadership among persons engaged in practice of archival science; To promote development of archives & archivists in Alberta; To encourage cooperation of archivists & archives with all those interested in preservation & use of documents of human experience
Finances: Funding Sources: Membership dues; Alberta Historical Resources Foundation
Membership: 102 individual; 44 institutional; 16 honorary; 11 associate institutional; Fees: $25 student/senior/volunteer/archives supporter; $50 individual; institutional: schedule based on operating budget; Committees: Alberta on Record; Communications; Conference Program; Education; Financial Review; Fonds D'Archives; Grants; Nominations & Awards
Activities: Awareness Events: Archives Week, September; Internships: Yes
Chief Officer(s):
Shamin Malmas, President
smalmas@nurses.ab.ca
Sara King, Secretary
sara.king@gov.ab.ca
Rene Georgopalis, Executive Director & Advisor, Archives
reneg@archivesalberta.org
Awards:
• Alan D. Ridge Publications Award
Honours excellence in the form of research, opinion & analysis on some aspect of archives studies, records management, the use of records, archival institutions, or the archival profession
Meetings/Conferences:
• Archives Society of Alberta 2018 Annual General Meeting, 2018, AB
Scope: Provincial
• Archives Society of Alberta 2018 Biennial Conference, 2018, AB
Scope: Provincial

Arctic Bay Housing Association
PO Box 59, Arctic Bay NU X0A 0A0
Tel: 867-439-8833; Fax: 867-439-8245
Overview: A small local organization

Arctic Co-operatives Limited
1645 Inkster Blvd., Winnipeg MB R2X 2W7
Tel: 204-697-1625; Fax: 204-697-1880
info@ArcticCo-op.com
www.arcticco-op.com
Overview: A small provincial organization founded in 1972
Mission: To provide service to, & foster cooperation among the multi-purpose Cooperative businesses in Canada's North; to provide leadership & expertise; to develop & safeguard the ownership participation of Member Owners
Membership: 31 Co-ops
Chief Officer(s):
Andy Morrison, Chief Executive Officer
AMorrison@Arctic.Coop
Rod Wilson, Vice-President, Member Management Services
Nunavut Regional Office
PO Box 697, 1121 Mivvik St., Iqaluit NU X0A 0H0
Tel: 867-979-2448; Fax: 867-979-2535

Arctic Council
Global Affairs Canada, 125 Sussex Dr., Ottawa ON K1A 0G2
Tel: 613-995-1874
Other Communication: Canada Media E-mail:
media@international.gc.ca
acs@arctic-council.org
www.arctic-council.org
www.facebook.com/arcticcouncil
twitter.com/arcticcouncil
vimeo.com/arcticcouncil; www.instagram.com/arcticcouncil
Mission: To operate as an intergovernmental forum; To address common concerns & challenges by the member states; To address environmental, social & economic issues; To carry out scientific work in six expert working groups, focusing on such issues as monitoring, assessing & preventing pollution in the Arctic, climate change, biodiversity conservation & sustainable use, emergency preparedness, & prevention; To meet every two years, with the secretariat rotating among the member states

Membership: Member Profile: Member states include Canada, Denmark (including Greenland & the Faroe Islands), Finland, Iceland, Norway, the Russian Federation, Sweden & the United States; Permananent participants are the Arctic Athabascan Council, the Aleut International Association, the Gwich'in Council International, the Inuit Circumpolar Council, the Russian Association of Indigenous Peoples of the North, & the Saami Council
Activities: Six working groups are as follows: Sustainable Development Working Group; Arctic Monitoring & Assessment Programme; Protection of the Marine Environment; Conservation of Arctic Flora & Fauna; Emergency, Prevention, Preparedness & Response; & Arctic Contaminants Action Program
Chief Officer(s):
Nina Buvang Vaaja, Director of the Secretariat
Nina@arctic-council.org
Alison LeClaire, Senior Arctic Official, Canada
Alison.LeClaire@international.gc.ca

Arctic Institute of North America (AINA)
University of Calgary, 2500 University Dr. NW, Calgary AB T2N 1N4
Tel: 403-220-7515; Fax: 403-282-4609
arctic@ucalgary.ca
www.arctic.ucalgary.ca
www.facebook.com/ArcticInstituteofNorthAmerica
twitter.com/ASTISdatabase
Overview: A medium-sized local organization founded in 1945
Mission: To encourage & support scientific research pertaining to the polar regions
Member of: University of the Arctic; Canadian Heritage Information Network
Affiliation(s): The University of Alaska
Finances: Annual Operating Budget: $500,000-$1.5 Million
Staff Member(s): 10; 5 volunteer(s)
Membership: 1,000+; Fees: $65 online; $90 print; $100 print & online
Activities: Speaker Service: Yes; Library
Chief Officer(s):
Marybeth Murray, Executive Director, 403-220-7516
Mary Li, Institute Manager, 403-220-8373
mmli@ucalgary.ca
Awards:
• Jennifer Robinson Memorial Scholarship
For Master's or Ph.D. students; must submit a brief statement of research objectives Deadline: December 1; Amount: $5,000
• Grant-in-Aid
Aimed at young investigators, to provide funding to support research. Deadline: February 1; Amount: $1,000
• Lorraine Allison Scholarship
Granted on the basis of academic standing, commitment to northern Canadian research & benefit to Northerners; Master's or Ph.D. students from the Yukon & NWT are encouraged to apply Deadline: May 1; Amount: $2,000
Publications:
• Arctic
Type: Journal; Editor: Karen McCullough
Profile: A peer-reviewed journal about northern research (polar & subpolar regions)

Arctic Winter Games International Committee (AWGIC)
www.awg.ca
Overview: A medium-sized local organization founded in 1968
Mission: To provide common ground for developing Northern athletes; to promote cultural & social exchanges among Northern regions of the continent
Finances: Annual Operating Budget: $100,000-$250,000
9 volunteer(s)
Membership: 1-99
Activities: To invite & review bids from communities wanting to host the Games; to select sports for each set of Games & prepare the technical package of rules, categories, events, team composition, medals to be awarded, competition format; to oversee the preparations of a Host Society for the Games; Library: Arctic Winter Games Archives; by appointment
Chief Officer(s):
Jens Brinch, President
Ian Legaree, Technical Director

ArcticNet Inc.
Pavillon Alexandre-Vachon, Université Laval, #4081, 1045, av de la Médecine, Québec QC G1V 0A6
Tel: 418-656-5830; Fax: 418-656-2334
arcticnet@arcticnet.ulaval.ca

www.arcticnet.ulaval.ca
twitter.com/arcticnet
Overview: A medium-sized national organization founded in 2003
Mission: To study the impacts of climate change in the coastal Canadian Arctic; To engage Inuit organizations, northern communities, universities, research institutes, industry, government, & international agencies as partners in the scientific process
Member of: Network of Centres of Excellence of Canada
Finances: Funding Sources: Government of Canada, through the Networks of Centres of Excellence programs
Membership: 1-99; Member Profile: Educational institutions; Committees: Executive; Communications; Audit & Finance; Environmental Review; Industrial Partnership; Inuit Partnership; Research Management; Inuit Advisory
Activities: Conducting Integrated Regional Impact Studies on marine & terrestrial coastal ecosystems & societies in the Eastern Canadian Arctic, the Canadian High Arctic & in Hudson Bay; Disseminating knowledge; Facilitating networking opportunities
Chief Officer(s):
Martin Fortier, Executive Director, 418-656-5233
martin.fortier@arcticnet.ulaval.ca
Louis Fortier, Scientific Director, 418-656-5646
louis.fortier@bio.ulaval.ca
Meetings/Conferences:
• ArcticNet Annual Scientific Meeting 2018, 2018
Scope: National
Publications:
• ArcticNet Inc. Annual Report
Type: Yearbook; Frequency: Annually
• ArcticNet Newsletter
Type: Newsletter

Argentia Area Chamber of Commerce See Placentia Area Chamber of Commerce

ARK II
PO Box 687, Stn. Q, Toronto ON M4T 2N5
Tel: 416-536-2308
info@ark-ii.com
www.ark-ii.com
www.facebook.com/AnimalRightsKollective
twitter.com/ARKII_TO
Also Known As: Animal Rights Kollective
Overview: A small local charitable organization
Mission: To promote & protect the rights of all animals & foster their individual liberties through direct action, political action, & public awareness campaigns
Membership: Fees: Annual: $10; Lifetime: $50
Activities: Anti-fur campaigns, Veganism/Vegetarianism promotion, Anti-animal experimentation campaigns

The Ark/Lunenburg County Association for the Specially Challenged
655 King St., Bridgewater NS B4V 1B5
Tel: 902-543-1189; Fax: 902-543-6041
theark@ns.sympatico.ca
www.thearkns.org
Also Known As: The Ark/LCASC
Overview: A small local organization founded in 1963
Mission: To provide disabled adults with programs suited to their needs; to foster happiness through the creation of an environment that focusses on wellness & integration with the larger community
Member of: DIRECTIONS Council for Vocational Services Society
Activities: Services such as antique refurbishment & furniture repair, document shredding, woodcrafts & hand-made braided rugs
Chief Officer(s):
Richard Greek, President

Arkona & Area Historical Society
PO Box 83, Arkona ON N0M 1B0
Overview: A small local organization founded in 1976
Mission: To stimulate genealogical & historical research; to record the results of current research & all ongoing events of historical significance in our community; to preserve books, documents & records
Finances: Funding Sources: Membership fees
Membership: 23; Fees: $2

ARMA Canada
6, rue Viateur Gauvreau, Chambly QC J3L 6V3

www.armacanada.org
www.linkedin.com/groups/6629965/profile
twitter.com/armacanada
Also Known As: Association for Information Management Professionals
Previous Name: Association of Records Managers & Administrators
Overview: A large national organization founded in 1955
Mission: To work to advance records & information management as a discipline & a profession; To organize programs of research, education, training & networking
Membership: 10,000; *Fees:* US$175 Professional; US$95 Associate; *Member Profile:* Records & information managers
Activities: *Speaker Service:* Yes; *Rents Mailing List:* Yes
Chief Officer(s):
Stephane Bourbonniere, Region Director
sbourbonniere@kpmg.ca
Awards:
• International Speaker Grant, ARMA International Grants
Awarded to assist a chapter in acquiring high-quality speakers for their chapter educational offerings; *Amount:* $500
• Leadership Training Grant, ARMA International Grants
Awarded to a chapter to assist them in sending chapter leaders to their region leadership training; *Amount:* $400
• Leadership Grant, ARMA Canada Grants
To assist a chapter in sending a representative from its Board of Directors to the annual Leadership Meeting; *Amount:* up to $1,000
• CRM Grant, ARMA Canada Grants
Awarded to assist a chapter member in obtaining their Certified Records Manager designation; *Amount:* up to $250
• Publishing Grant, ARMA Canada Grants
Awarded to encourage members to share their knowledge & raise awareness of the Records & Information Management profession; *Amount:* $250
• Chapter Speaker Grant, ARMA Canada Grants
Awarded to assist a chapter in acquiring a high-quality speaker for their membership at an event; *Amount:* $500
• Special Project Grant, ARMA Canada Grants
Awarded to assist a chapter or region to undertake new projects to promote the Records and Information Management Profession/ARMA in the community; *Amount:* up to $5,000
• Distinguished Member Award, ARMA Canada Awards
To recognize the contributions of an ARMA member
• Member Recognition Award, ARMA Canada Awards
To recognize the contributions of ARMA members
• Region Member of the Year Award, ARMA Canada Awards
To recognize an ARMA Canada member for their significant volunteer contributions to the Association
• Chapter of the Year Award, ARMA Canada Awards
Awarded to honour two chapters for their consistent efforts in pursuing excellence through its membership & activities; *Amount:* $1,000
Meetings/Conferences:
• Association for Information Management Professionals Canada Conference 2018, 2018
Scope: National
Description: Brings together delegates & exhibitors & provides professional development opportunities
Contact Information: Director, Conference Program: Christy Walters, Email: armacanadaprogramdirector@gmail.com; Phone: 604-926-9903
Publications:
• Canadian RIM [a publication of ARMA Canada]
Type: Guide; *Frequency:* Annually
Profile: Showcases practical & theoretical articles, publications & scholarly research relating to records & information management in Canada

Calgary Chapter
PO Box 6624, Stn. D, Calgary AB T2P 2E4
www.armacalgary.org
twitter.com/ARMACalgary
Chief Officer(s):
Rob McLauchlin, President
president@armacalgary.org

Edmonton Chapter
PO Box 345, #21, 10405 Jasper Ave., Edmonton AB T5J 3S2
communications@armaedmonton.org
edmonton.arma.org
Chief Officer(s):
Nina Leonardis, President
president@armaedmonton.org

Montréal Chapter
PO Box 337, Stn. B, Montréal QC H3B 3J7
www.armamontreal.org
www.linkedin.com/groups?gid=2368275
Chief Officer(s):
Catherine Nadeau, President

New Brunswick Chapter
PO Box 382, Stn. A, Fredericton NB E3B 4Z9
www.nbarma.org
www.facebook.com/554376717925865
Chief Officer(s):
Patrick Jeune, President, 506-453-8488
president@nbarma.org

Newfoundland Chapter
PO Box 23061, RPO Churchill Square, St. John's NL A1B 4J9
secretary@armaterranova.org
www.armaterranova.org
Chief Officer(s):
Rhonda Guay, President
president@armaterranova.org

Nova Scotia Chapter
24 Greenly Ct., Dartmouth NS B2W 4Y1
info@armahalifax.org
www.armanovascotia.org
www.facebook.com/145838402163975

Ottawa
PO Box 600, Stn. B, Ottawa ON K1P 5P7
www.armancr.ca
www.facebook.com/ARMANCROttawaChapter
twitter.com/ARMA_NCR
Chief Officer(s):
Jennifer Woods, President
president@armancr.ca

Prince Edward Island Chapter
PO Box 22055, Stn. Charlottetown-Parkdale, Charlottetown PE C1A 9J2
armapeichapter@gmail.com
www.armapei.org

Saskatchewan Chapter
SK
info@armasask.org
www.armasask.org
www.facebook.com/523397911057961
twitter.com/armaskchapter
Chief Officer(s):
Denise Harry, President
denise.harry@armasask.org

Southwestern Ontario Chapter
ON
armaswo@gmail.com
armaswo.com
www.linkedin.com/groups?home=&gid=8172598
twitter.com/ARMASWO
Chief Officer(s):
Anne Hepplewhite, President

Toronto Chapter
Toronto ON
www.armatoronto.on.ca
twitter.com/ARMAToronto
Chief Officer(s):
Jen Ford, President

Vancouver Chapter
#413, 280 Nelson St., Vancouver BC V6B 2E2
info@armavancouver.org
vancouver.arma.org
www.linkedin.com/groups/ARMA-Vancouver-2018278
Chief Officer(s):
Ellie Kim, President

Vancouver Island Chapter
PO Box 8005, Victoria BC V8W 3R7
www.armavi.org
www.linkedin.com/groups/ARMA-Vancouver-Island-5091338
twitter.com/arma_VI
Chief Officer(s):
David Young, President
president@armavi.org

Winnipeg Chapter
PO Box 1908, Stn. Main, Winnipeg MB R3C 3R2
info@armawinnipeg.org
www.armawinnipeg.org
www.linkedin.com/company/arma-winnipeg-chapter-inc-
twitter.com/armawinnipeg
Chief Officer(s):
Shelly Smith, President
president@armawinnipeg.org

Armateurs du Saint-Laurent (ASL) / St. Lawrence Shipoperators
#101, 271, rue de l'Estuaire, Québec QC G1K 8S8
Tél: 418-648-4378; *Téléc:* 418-649-6495
info@asl-sls.org
www.armateurs-du-st-laurent.org
Nom précédent: Association des armateurs du Saint-Laurent inc.; Association des opérateurs de navires du Saint-Laurent
Aperçu: *Dimension:* petite; *Envergure:* nationale; Organisme sans but lucratif; fondée en 1936
Mission: Voir à la défense et à la promotion des intérêts des armateurs canadiens actifs sur le fleuve Saint-Laurent, les Grands Lacs et dans l'Arctique canadien
Finances: *Budget de fonctionnement annuel:* $100,000-$250,000
Membre(s) du personnel: 2
Membre: 14 actifs; 85 associés; *Critères d'admissibilite:* Posséder ou opérer un navire canadien
Membre(s) du bureau directeur:
Martin Fournier, Directeur général
martin.fournier@asl-sls.org
Ariane Charette, Agente de communication et coordonnatrice
ariane.charette@asl-sls.org

Armed Forces Communications & Electronics Association (Canada)
Ottawa Chapter, Ottawa ON
Tel: 613-721-6031
ottawa.afceachapters.org
Also Known As: AFCEA Canada
Overview: A medium-sized national charitable organization founded in 1985
Mission: To provide a forum for information exchange & ethical government-industry dialogue with the Canadian communications, electronics, intelligence & information technology community in support of national security
Finances: *Annual Operating Budget:* $100,000-$250,000; *Funding Sources:* Membership fees; proceeds of shows & seminars
Staff Member(s): 1; 50 volunteer(s)
Membership: 639; *Fees:* $35
Activities: Information exchange; professional development; education fund
Chief Officer(s):
Kelly Stewart-Belisle, President
Dave Johnson, Vice-President, Communications
Sara Pike, Vice-President, Membership
Bernadette Terry, Vice-President, Programs
Wayne Teeple, Treasurer
Publications:
• Signal Magazine
Profile: Intelligence/technology news magazine

Armed Forces Pensioners'/Annuitants' Association of Canada (AFP/AAC) / Association canadienne des pensionnés et rentiers militaires (ACPRM)
PO Box 370, #3, 247 Barr St., Renfrew ON K7V 4A6
Tel: 613-432-9491; *Fax:* 613-432-6840
www.afpaac.ca
www.facebook.com/AFPAAC
twitter.com/AFPAAC
Overview: A small national organization
Mission: To promote & protect the rights & interests of members
Membership: *Fees:* $15; *Member Profile:* Canadian Forces retirees & their survivors
Chief Officer(s):
Anthony E. Huntley, National Chair
Bonnie James, Executive Director
executivedirector@afpaac.ca

Armenian Canadian Medical Association of Ontario (ACMAO)
2030 Victoria Park Ave., Toronto ON M1R 1V2
Tel: 416-443-9971; *Fax:* 416-443-8865
acmaoexecutive@gmail.com
www.acmao.ca
Overview: A small provincial charitable organization founded in 1988
Mission: The Armenian Canadian Medical Association of Ontario (ACMAO) is a multidisciplinary organization of health care professionals in Ontario
Activities: Health education, humanitarian projects and academic endeavors.
Chief Officer(s):
Avedis Bogosyan, President

Armenian Community Centre See Armenian Community Centre of Toronto

Armenian Community Centre of Toronto
45 Hallcrown Pl., Toronto ON M2J 4Y4
Tel: 416-491-2900; *Fax:* 416-491-2211
accmanager@armenian.ca
www.armenian.ca
Previous Name: Armenian Community Centre
Overview: A small local organization

Armenian General Benevolent Union (AGBU)
Toronto Chapter, 930 Progress Ave., Toronto ON M1G 3T5
Tel: 416-431-2428; *Fax:* 416-431-2510
agbutoronto@bellnet.ca
www.agbutoronto.ca
Overview: A small local charitable organization
Finances: *Annual Operating Budget:* Less than $50,000
Activities: *Library:* Open to public
Chief Officer(s):
Salpi Der Ghazarian, Executive Director

Armenian Holy Apostolic Church - Canadian Diocese (AHAC)
615, av Stuart, Outremont QC H2V 3H2
Tel: 514-276-9479; *Fax:* 514-276-9960
Other Communication: Alt. E-mail: adiocese@aol.com
contact@armenianchurch.ca
www.armenianchurch.ca
www.facebook.com/239802236057531
www.youtube.com/user/CanArmChurch
Overview: A medium-sized national charitable organization founded in 1984
Mission: To preserve & promote Christian & national heritage; humanitarian aid to Armenia
Affiliation(s): Canadian Council of Churches
Finances: *Annual Operating Budget:* $250,000-$500,000; *Funding Sources:* Donations; parish dues
Staff Member(s): 6
Membership: Over 50,000; *Member Profile:* Baptized in the Armenian faith; *Committees:* Endowment Fund
Activities: Humanitarian Aid to Armenia; *Library:* by appointment Not open to public
Chief Officer(s):
Abgar Hovakimian, Primate

Armenian Relief Society of Canada, Inc. (ARS Canada)
3401, rue Olivar-Asselin, Montréal QC H4J 1L5
Tel: 514-333-1616
ars-canada@bellnet.ca
www.ars-canada.ca
Overview: A medium-sized international organization founded in 1990
Mission: To serve the humanitarian needs of the Armenian people everywhere, & preserves the cultural heritage & identity of the Armenian nation.
Affiliation(s): Armenian Relief Society, Inc.
Finances: *Funding Sources:* Membership fees; donations
Membership: 1,250
Activities: Emergency relief & reconstruction; humanitarian assistance; education; social services; health care services; cultural support; summer camp; orphanage project
Chief Officer(s):
Seta Malkhassian, President
Annie Tachejian, Secretary

Cambridge Chapter: "Meghri"
15 International Village Dr., Cambridge ON N1R 7M5
Tel: 519-623-4812
Chief Officer(s):
Connie Titizian, Chair

Hamilton Chapter: "Arev"
191 Barton St., Stoney Creek ON L8E 2K3
Tel: 905-662-3370
Chief Officer(s):
Nathalie Manoukian, Chair

Laval Chapter: "Shoushi"
397, boul des Prairies, Laval QC H7N 2W6
Tel: 450-688-7270
arsshoushi@yahoo.com
Chief Officer(s):
Nelly Hamalian Barsemian, Chair

Mississauga Chapter: "Arakasd"
3230 Ridgeleigh Hills, Mississauga ON L5M 6S6
Tel: 905-542-9621
Chief Officer(s):
Lilian Sarian, Chair

Montréal Chapter: "Sosse"
3401, rue Olivar-Asselin, Montréal QC H4J 1L5
Tel: 514-335-2222
sosse-montreal@hotmail.com
Chief Officer(s):
Lucy Manguian Chahinian, Chair

St. Catharines Chapter: "Araz"
156 Martindale Rd., St Catharines ON L2S 2X9
Tel: 905-682-6178
Chief Officer(s):
Angel Derderian, Chair

Toronto Chapter: "Roubina"
45 Hallcrown Pl., Toronto ON M2J 4Y4
Tel: 416-491-2900
arstorontoroubinachapter@yahoo.com
Chief Officer(s):
Varsenig Sarkissian, Chair

Vancouver Chapter: "Araz"
13780 Westminster Hwy., Richmond BC V6V 1A2
Tel: 604-276-9627
Chief Officer(s):
Clara Hagopian, Chair

Windsor Chapter: "Roubina"
702 Pierre St., Windsor ON N9A 2K5
Tel: 519-256-1082
Chief Officer(s):
Ferida Ashekian, Chair

Armstrong-Spallumcheen Chamber of Commerce
PO Box 118, 3550 Bridge St., Armstrong BC V0E 1B0
Tel: 250-546-8155
manager@aschamber.com
aschamber.com
www.facebook.com/ASChamberofCommerce
pinterest.com/asvisitorcentre
Overview: A small local organization founded in 1951
Mission: To stimulate prosperity by promoting business & tourism in our community; to facilitate & enhance the region's quality of life, through the support of the people & business by working together
Member of: British Columbia Chamber of Commerce
Finances: *Funding Sources:* City/municipality grants; membership dues; government grant; fundraising
Staff Member(s): 1
Membership: 204; *Member Profile:* Interest in the community well-being, success & promotion
Activities: *Library:* Resource Centre; Open to public
Chief Officer(s):
Fran Stecyk, President

Army Cadet League of Canada (ACLC) / Ligue des cadets de l'armée du Canada
#201, 1505 Laperriere Ave., Ottawa ON K1Z 7T1
Fax: 613-941-3744
Toll-Free: 877-276-9223
national@armycadetleague.ca
www.armycadetleague.ca
www.facebook.com/armycadetleague
twitter.com/ArmyCadetLeague
Overview: A medium-sized international charitable organization founded in 1971
Mission: To provide accommodation, transportation, & financial support for the army cadets; To promote the corps & assists in recruitment
Affiliation(s): Army Cadet Force Association, UK; Deutscher-Bundeswehr-Verband
Finances: *Funding Sources:* Government grant; donations
Staff Member(s): 3
Activities: *Library:* Open to public
Chief Officer(s):
Robert Gill, Executive Director
executivedirector@armycadetleague.ca

Alberta Branch
c/o 8705 - 96 St., Grande Prairie AB T8V 3E1
Fax: 780-532-1887
Toll-Free: 866-230-2769
secretary@armycadetleagueab.ca
www.armycadetleagueab.ca
www.facebook.com/ArmyCadetLeague.Alberta
Chief Officer(s):
Joanne Nilsson, Executive Director

British Columbia Branch
#21, 724 Vanalman Ave., Victoria BC V8Z 3B5
Tel: 250-708-0281; *Fax:* 250-708-0284
Toll-Free: 877-733-1980
www.armycadetleague.bc.ca
Chief Officer(s):
Richard J. Finley, Executive Director
execdir@armycadetleague.bc.ca

Ligue des cadets de l'armée du Canada (Québec)
CP 1000, Succ. Forces, Courcelette QC G0A 4Z0
Ligne sans frais: 800-463-1584
info@lcac.qc.ca
www.lcac.qc.ca

Manitoba Branch
MB
Tel: 204-391-6700
www.armycadetsmb.ca
Chief Officer(s):
Patrick Douglass, President

New Brunswick Branch
939, ch St André, St André Leblanc NB E4P 6E1

Nova Scotia Branch
NS
www.armycadetleaguens.ca
Chief Officer(s):
Marie Leloup, President

Ontario Branch
#527, 1200 Markham Rd., Toronto ON M1H 3C3
Fax: 416-431-2022
Toll-Free: 800-561-4786
www.armycadetleague.on.ca
Chief Officer(s):
Marian MacDonald, Executive Director

Saskatchewan Branch
811 McCarthy Blvd. North, Regina SK S4X 2Y1
Tel: 306-543-8809; *Fax:* 306-949-6534
nonprofits.accesscomm.ca/aclofcsk
Chief Officer(s):
Eddie Mathew, Executive Director
ematthew@accesscomm.ca

Yukon Branch
YT

Army, Navy & Air Force Veterans in Canada (ANAVETS) / Les Anciens combattants de l'armée, de la marine et des forces aériennes au Canada
#2, 6 Beechwood Ave., Ottawa ON K1L 8B4
Tel: 613-744-0222; *Fax:* 613-744-0208
anavets@storm.ca
www.anavets.ca
Overview: A medium-sized national organization founded in 1917
Mission: To unite veterans & their supporters to maintain entitlements & benefits; To provide a fraternal milieu for members by acquiring & operating clubs & homes; To strive to promote patriotism in Canada, & nurture cooperation & unity within the British Commonwealth
Finances: *Annual Operating Budget:* $100,000-$250,000; *Funding Sources:* Membership dues
Staff Member(s): 2
Membership: 7 provincial commands + 85 units + 74 ladies auxiliaries + 40,000 individuals; *Member Profile:* Service in the Armed Forces; *Committees:* Finance; Publicity; Sports; Constitution; Awards; Resolutions; Membership
Activities: Service to the community & to the nation; *Awareness Events:* Remembrance Day; Veterans' Week
Chief Officer(s):
Deanna Fimrite, Secretary-Treasurer
Laila Saikaley, Administrative Assistant
Publications:
• ANAVETS [Army, Navy & Air Force Veterans in Canada] Shoulder to Shoulder
Type: Magazine; *Frequency:* Quarterly; *Accepts Advertising*; *Editor:* Derek Walter

Alberta Provincial Command
c/o Command Secretary, 8106 - 168 St., Edmonton AB T5R 2V4

British Columbia Provincial Command
#200, 951 - 8th Ave. East, Vancouver BC V5T 4L2
Tel: 604-874-8105; *Fax:* 604-874-0633
bcanavets@telus.net

Manitoba & Northwestern Ontario Provincial Command
3584 Portage Ave., Winnipeg MB R2Y 0V5
Tel: 204-896-9897; *Fax:* 204-896-8837
anavets@mts.net

Canadian Associations / Arrow Lakes Historical Society

Nova Scotia Provincial Command
422 Heelen St., New Waterford NS B1H 3C7
anavetsnscommand@gmail.com

Ontario Provincial Command
1655 Weston Rd., Toronto ON M9N 1V2
Tel: 416-259-4145; *Fax:* 416-259-1677
anaf_opc@bellnet.ca

Québec Provincial Command
18, rue Massawippi, Sherbrooke QC J1M 1L2

Saskatchewan Provincial Command
c/o Stephanie Minion, 254 Langevin Cres., Saskatoon SK S7L 5R3
Tel: 306-384-0106; *Fax:* 306-653-4760
aands2@shaw.ca

Arrow Lakes Historical Society
PO Box 819, 92 - 6th Ave. NW, Nakusp BC V0G 1R0
Tel: 250-265-0110
Other Communication: 250-265-3323
alhs1234@telus.net
www.alhs-archives.com
www.facebook.com/arrowlakeshistoricalsociety
Overview: A small local charitable organization founded in 1984
Mission: To record the history of the area; To keep archives open & staffed; To provide archival information, school tours & educational information
Member of: British Columbia Historical Federation; British Columbia Archives & Records Service; Cultural Community of Nakusp & Area; Heritage Federation of South Eastern BC
Finances: *Annual Operating Budget:* Less than $50,000; *Funding Sources:* BC Gaming; book sales; research donor 20 volunteer(s)
Membership: 38; *Fees:* $5 annual; $50 lifetime; *Committees:* Archives; Publication
Activities: Centennial series (five) of history books, 9x12 hard-cover; History of Halcyon Hot Springs, "Halcyon, the Captains Paradise"; *Library:* Arrow Lakes Historical Society Archives
Chief Officer(s):
Marilyn Taylor, President
Publications:
• Caulkboot Riverdance
Type: Book; *Price:* $25
Profile: The history of logging & mills in the Arrow Lakes region
• Halcyon - The Captain's Paradise
Type: Book; *Price:* $25
Profile: Book on the history of the Halcyon Hot Springs

Arrowsmith Natural History Society *See* Arrowsmith Naturalists

---

Arrowsmith Naturalists
PO Box 1542, Parksville BC V9P 2H4
Tel: 250-752-0445
arrowsmithnats@gmail.com
www.arrowsmithnats.org
Previous Name: Arrowsmith Natural History Society
Overview: A small local organization founded in 1970
Mission: To further the understanding & conservation of nature
Member of: Federation of BC Naturalists
Affiliation(s): B.C. Nature; Nature Canada
Finances: *Annual Operating Budget:* Less than $50,000
Membership: 94; *Fees:* $25 individual; $35 family; $12 junior (up to 18); *Member Profile:* Parksville community members who are interested in nature & who enjoy monthly meetings & field trips; *Committees:* Botany; Birds; Outings
Chief Officer(s):
Sandra Gray, Contact, saninerrshaw.ca, 250-248-5565

Art Dealers Association of Canada Inc. (ADAC) / Association des marchands d'art du Canada
#393, 401 Richmond St. West, Toronto ON M5V 3A8
Tel: 416-934-1583; *Fax:* 866-280-9432
Toll-Free: 866-435-2322
info@ad-ac.ca
www.ad-ac.ca
www.facebook.com/ArtDealersAssociationofCanada
twitter.com/ADAC_AMAC
Overview: A small international organization founded in 1966
Mission: To promote & encourage public awareness of visual arts in Canada & abroad
Member of: CINOA
Affiliation(s): AGAC; CMA
Staff Member(s): 2
Membership: 80 art dealers; *Member Profile:* Commercial gallery must be operating bona fide exhibition space for minimum of 5 years & deal in original fine art
Activities: Provides qualified appraisals to public & cultural institutions for donation purposes; *Internships:* Yes; *Speaker Service:* Yes
Chief Officer(s):
Elizabeth Edwards, Executive Director
Jeanette Langmann, President

Art Directors' Club of Toronto *See* The Advertising & Design Club of Canada

---

Art Gallery of North York *See* Museum of Contemporary Canadian Art

---

Arthritis Health Professions Association (AHPA)
#244, 12-16715 Yonge St., Newmarket ON L3X 1X4
chardv@yahoo.com
www.ahpa.ca
Overview: A small national charitable organization founded in 1982
Mission: To improve health care standards for people with rheumatic diseases through the promotion of education & support of research among members
Affiliation(s): The Arthritis Society
Membership: *Fees:* $75; $40 students; *Member Profile:* Health professionals who work in the field of rheumatology
Chief Officer(s):
Leslie Soever, President
Awards:
• Best Occupational Therapy Abstract
• Research Grant
; *Amount:* $5,000
• Best Scientific Abstract
; *Amount:* $100
• Best Educational/Special Interest Abstract
; *Amount:* $100

Arthritis Research Foundation
R. Fraser Elliott Bldg., 190 Elizabeth St., 5th Fl, Toronto ON M5G 2C4
Tel: 416-340-4975; *Fax:* 416-340-3496
info@beatarthritis.ca
www.beatarthritis.ca
Overview: A small local organization
Activities: *Awareness Events:* Day at the Races, September
Chief Officer(s):
Joy Davidson, Director, Development
Joy.Davidson@beatarthritis.ca

Arthritis Society / Société de l'arthrite
#1700, 393 University Ave., Toronto ON M5G 1E6
Tel: 416-979-7228; *Fax:* 416-979-8366
Toll-Free: 800-321-1433
info@arthritis.ca
www.arthritis.ca
www.facebook.com/arthritissociety
twitter.com/arthritissoc
Previous Name: Canadian Arthritis & Rheumatism Society
Overview: A large national licensing charitable organization founded in 1948
Mission: To fund & promote arthritis research, programs & patient care. There are division offices in each province & nearly 1,000 community branches throughout Canada
Member of: Canadian Centre for Philanthropy; Coalition of National Voluntary Organizations
Affiliation(s): The Bone & Joint Decade
Membership: *Committees:* Executive; Nominating & Governance; Audit & Finance; Scientific Advisory; Medical Advisory
Activities: Joints in Motion, Arthritis Self-Management Program; *Awareness Events:* Walk to Fight Arthritis; *Speaker Service:* Yes
Chief Officer(s):
Janet Yale, President & CEO
Cheryl McClellan, Chief Operating Officer
Publications:
• Impact eNewsletter [a publication of the Arthritis Society]
Type: Newsletter

Alberta/NWT Division
#300, 1301 - 8th St. SW, Calgary AB T2R 1B7
Tel: 403-228-2571; *Fax:* 403-229-4232
Toll-Free: 800-321-1433
info@ab.arthritis.ca
www.arthritis.ca/ab
www.facebook.com/TheArthritisSocietyAlberta
Chief Officer(s):
Shirley Philips, Executive Director

British Columbia / Yukon Division
895 West 10 Ave., Vancouver BC V5Z 1L7
Tel: 604-714-5550; *Fax:* 604-714-5555
Toll-Free: 866-414-7766
info@bc.arthritis.ca
www.arthritis.ca/bc
Chief Officer(s):
Christine Basque, Executive Director

Manitoba / Nunavut Division
#100A, 1485 Buffalo Pl., Winnipeg MB R3T 1L8
Tel: 204-942-4892; *Fax:* 204-942-4894
Toll-Free: 800-321-1433
info@mb.arthritis.ca
www.arthritis.ca/mb
Chief Officer(s):
Donna Wills, Regional Manager

New Brunswick Division
2 - 1010 Hanwell Rd., Fredericton NB E3B 6A4
Tel: 506-452-7191
Toll-Free: 800-321-1433
info@nb.arthritis.ca
www.arthritis.ca/nb
Chief Officer(s):
Susan Tilley-Russell, Executive Director, Atlantic Region
stilley-russell@ns.arthritis.ca

Newfoundland & Labrador Division
#220, 31 Peet St., St. John's NL A1B 3W8
Tel: 709-579-8190
Toll-Free: 800-321-1433
info@nl.arthritis.ca
www.arthritis.ca/nl
Chief Officer(s):
Susan Tilley-Russell, Executive Director, Atlantic Region
stilley-russell@ns.arthritis.ca

Nova Scotia Division
#210, 3770 Kempt Rd., Halifax NS B3K 4X8
Tel: 902-429-7025; *Fax:* 902-423-6479
Toll-Free: 800-321-1433
info@ns.arthritis.ca
www.arthritis.ca/ns
Chief Officer(s):
Susan Tilley-Russell, Executive Director, Atlantic Region
stilley-russell@ns.arthritis.ca

Ontario Division
#1700, 393 University Ave., Toronto ON M5G 1E6
Tel: 416-979-7228; *Fax:* 416-979-8366
Toll-Free: 800-321-1433
info@on.arthritis.ca
arthritis.ca/on
www.facebook.com/ArthritisSocietyON
twitter.com/arthritissocON
Chief Officer(s):
Ahmad Zbib, Executive Director

Prince Edward Island Division
Leisure World Bldg., 95 Capital Dr., Charlottetown PE C1E 1E8
Tel: 902-628-2288
Toll-Free: 800-321-1433
info@pe.arthritis.ca
www.arthritis.ca/pei
Chief Officer(s):
Susan Tilley-Russell, Executive Director, Atlantic Region
stilley-russell@ns.arthritis.ca

Québec Division
#3120, 380, rue Saint-Antoine ouest, Montréal QC H2Y 3X7
Tél: 514-846-8840; *Téléc:* 514-846-8999
Ligne sans frais: 800-321-1433
info@qc.arthrite.ca
www.arthritis.ca/qc
Chief Officer(s):
Eric Amar, Directeur général
eamar@qc.arthritis.ca

Saskatchewan Division
#2, 706 Duchess St., Saskatoon SK S7K 0R3
Tel: 306-244-0045
Toll-Free: 800-321-1433
info@sk.arthritis.ca
www.arthritis.ca/sk

Arthur & District Chamber of Commerce
PO Box 519, 146 George St., Arthur ON N0G 1A0
Tel: 519-848-5603; *Fax:* 519-848-4030
achamber@wightman.ca

www.arthurchamber.ca
www.facebook.com/154989094563799
Overview: A small local organization founded in 1993
Mission: To promote & improve trade, commerce & the economic, civic & social welfare of the Village of Arthur & the surrounding area
Member of: Ontario Chamber of Commerce
Finances: *Annual Operating Budget:* Less than $50,000; *Funding Sources:* Membership dues; Flowerbag campaign
Staff Member(s): 1; 8 volunteer(s)
Membership: 65; *Fees:* $125
Activities: *Internships:* Yes
Chief Officer(s):
Corey Bilton, President

Artisan Bakers' Quality Alliance (ABQA)
20 Plastics Ave., Toronto ON M8Z 4B7
Overview: A small provincial organization founded in 2002
Membership: 34
Chief Officer(s):
Shasha (Shaun) Navazesh, President

Artists in Healthcare Manitoba (AHM)
#2, 1325 Markham Rd., Winnipeg MB R3T 4J6
Tel: 204-999-0057
info@artistsinhealthcare.com
www.artistsinhealthcare.com
Overview: A small provincial charitable organization
Mission: To integrate the creative arts into health care as a way of introducing the healing effects of creative expression to help relieve depression
Membership: 100-499; *Fees:* $20

Artists in Stained Glass (AISG)
c/o Elizabeth Steinebach, PO Box 302, Parry Sound ON P2A 2X4
www.aisg.on.ca
Overview: A small local organization founded in 1975
Mission: To encourage the development of stained glass as a contemporary art form, in Ontario & throughout Canada.
Affiliation(s): Ontario Crafts Council
Membership: *Fees:* $40; *Member Profile:* glass crafters, architects, hobbyists, galleries, & anyone with an interest
Activities: Gallery shows; workshops; conferences
Chief Officer(s):
Elizabeth Steinebach, Contact
Robert Brown, President
robert@robertbrown.com

Artists' Union *Voir* Union des artistes

Arts & Crafts Training & Consultation Center *Voir* Centre de formation et de consultation en métiers d'art

The Arts & Letters Club (ALC)
14 Elm St., Toronto ON M5G 1G7
Tel: 416-597-0223; *Fax:* 416-597-9544
info@artsandlettersclub.ca
www.artsandlettersclub.ca
Also Known As: Arts & Letters Club of Toronto
Overview: A small local organization founded in 1908
Mission: To provide a milieu for the free & vigorous interchange of ideas & opinions
Membership: *Fees:* Schedule available; *Committees:* Executive
Activities: New Year's Eve Gala; Robbie Burn's Night; Spring Show; *Library:* Archives; by appointment
Chief Officer(s):
Fiona McKeown, Club Manager
manager@artsandlettersclub.ca
Scott James, Archivist
archives@artsandlettersclub.ca

Arts Council of Sault Ste Marie & District
#104A, 369 Queen St. East, Sault Ste Marie ON P6A 1Z4
Tel: 705-945-9756; *Fax:* 705-945-8665
artscouncilssm@gmail.com
www.ssmarts.org
Overview: A medium-sized local charitable organization founded in 1978
Mission: To enhance quality of life in the community by promoting & fostering the arts; To encourage education in & appreciation of all aspects of the arts
Member of: Ontario Crafts Council; Ontario Chamber of Commerce; Community Arts Ontario
Affiliation(s): Canadian Conference of the Arts; Ontario Arts Council; Theatre Ontario; Visual Arts Ontario

Finances: *Annual Operating Budget:* Less than $50,000; *Funding Sources:* Ontario Arts Council; Ministry of Culture & Communications; City of Sault Ste Marie; JP Bickell Foundation
Staff Member(s): 2; 50 volunteer(s)
Membership: 50 organizations; 200 individuals; *Fees:* $45 group; $20-$25 individual; *Member Profile:* Artists; *Committees:* Publicity; Membership; Information/Technology; Archives; Strategic Planning
Activities: *Awareness Events:* Art in the Park, Aug.; *Speaker Service:* Yes; *Library:* Open to public
Chief Officer(s):
Sandra Houston, Executive Director
Chris Rous, President

Arts Council of Surrey
13530 - 72 Ave., Surrey BC V3W 2P1
Tel: 604-594-2700; *Fax:* 604-585-2777
info@artscouncilofsurrey.ca
www.artscouncilofsurrey.ca
www.facebook.com/ArtsCouncilofSurrey
twitter.com/SurreyArts
Overview: A small local organization founded in 1964
Mission: To promote & foster performing, visual, literary arts in Surrey
Member of: Assembly of BC Arts Councils
Finances: *Annual Operating Budget:* $50,000-$100,000; *Funding Sources:* Provincial government; City of Surrey; BC Gaming Commission; membership fees; activity fees; general donations
Staff Member(s): 1; 25 volunteer(s)
Membership: 36 group + 79 individual + 20 honorary + 2 patrons; *Fees:* $50 group; $25 individual; $35 business; *Committees:* Juried Art Exhibition; Grants; Scholarship; Choral Festival
Activities: Arts Forum; Annual Juried Art Exhibition; Air Canada Championship Art Exhibition; Choral Festival; Craft Markets; Literary Fair; Fraser Downs Art Competition; Parade of Lights; Surrey Festival of Dance
Chief Officer(s):
Carol Girardi, President
Maxine Howchin, Vice-President
Awards:
• Outstanding Service to the Arts Award
• Scholarships
Surrey youth aged 12-18 years of age participating in the creative, performing or visual arts
• Business & the Arts Award

Arts Council of the Central Okanagan
#203, 1905 Evergreen Ct., Kelowna BC V1Y 9L4
Tel: 250-861-4123
info@artsco.ca
www.artsco.ca
www.facebook.com/artsokanagan
Previous Name: Kelowna & District Arts Council
Overview: A small local charitable organization founded in 1966
Mission: To increase & broaden the opportunities for public enjoyment of & participation in cultural activities; To stimulate & encourage the development of cultural projects & activities; To render service to all participating groups; to act as a clearinghouse for information on cultural projects & activities; To foster interest & pride in the cultural heritage of the community; To interpret the work of cultural groups to the community, enlist public interest & promote public understanding
Member of: Assembly of BC Arts Councils
Affiliation(s): Kelowna Chamber of Commerce; Okanagan Mainline Region Arts Council; Canadian Conference of the Arts
Finances: *Funding Sources:* Provincial & municipal governments
Staff Member(s): 2
Membership: 300; *Fees:* $15 youth; $25 individual; $30 family; $50 group; $75 commercial; $100 patron
Activities: Artist registry; Honour in the Arts Program; courses in arts & cultural studies; Artscape Program; grants & fundraising; *Library:* Open to public
Chief Officer(s):
Elke Lange, Executive Director
Cheryl Miller, President

Arts Council of the North Okanagan (ACNO)
2704A Hwy. 6, Vernon BC V1T 5G5
Tel: 250-542-6243
vcacinfo@shaw.ca
www.acno.ca
twitter.com/artscouncilno
Previous Name: Vernon Community Arts Council

Overview: A small local organization
Mission: To stimulate, encourage, & develop arts & culture in the Greater Vernon Area of BC; To foster an awareness & appreciation of the value of the arts in the community at large
Finances: *Funding Sources:* Membership dues; Donations
Membership: 28 groups + 600 individuals; *Fees:* $21 individual; $10.50 student/senior; $10 youth; $31.50 family; $52.50 group; *Member Profile:* Not-for-profit arts groups; Individuals & families
Chief Officer(s):
Mary Jo O'Keefe, President
David Woodhouse, Treasurer

Arts Council Windsor & Region (ACWR)
1942 Wyandotte St. East, Windsor ON N8Y 1E4
Tel: 519-252-6855; *Fax:* 519-252-6553
info@acwr.net
www.acwr.net
www.facebook.com/ArtsCouncilWindsorRegion
twitter.com/theACWR
Overview: A medium-sized local organization founded in 1977
Mission: To enrich the quality of life for all by strengthening the arts & the community through leadership, education & promotion
Member of: Community Arts Ontario; Convention & Visitors Bureau of Windsor, Essex County & Pelee Island; Canadian Conference of the Arts; Visual Arts Ontario; Ontario Crafts Council
Finances: *Annual Operating Budget:* $100,000-$250,000; *Funding Sources:* Government; foundation; membership fees; fundraising initiatives
Staff Member(s): 2; 50 volunteer(s)
Membership: 350 individuals/organizations; *Fees:* $125 business; $45 non-profit organizations; $30 individual
Activities: "Articpate" ongoing campaign; "Chair-ity"; "Arts Vote"; "Arthouse"; Awards of Excellence in the Arts; *Library:* Not open to public
Chief Officer(s):
Nadja Pelkey, Executive Director
ed@acwr.net

Arts Etobicoke
4893A Dundas St. West, Toronto ON M9A 1B2
Tel: 416-622-8731; *Fax:* 416-622-5782
info@artsetobicoke.com
www.artsetobicoke.com
www.facebook.com/123257461082590
twitter.com/artsetobicoke
Overview: A medium-sized local charitable organization founded in 1973
Mission: To engage all people in West Toronto with the arts & artists in their own community
Member of: Community Arts Ontario; Toronto Community Arts Alliance
Affiliation(s): Partner & support groups & organizations such as MABELLEarts; Lakeshorte Arts; Expect Theatre; Milkweed Collective; Toronto District School Board; University of Toronto Centre for Community Partnerships; Art Gallery of Ontario; Humber River Shakespeare Company; City of Toronto; Ontario Trillium Foundation; TD Canada Trust; Ontario Arts Council
Staff Member(s): 6
Membership: 55 groups + 200 individuals; *Fees:* $45 individuals; $65 groups
Activities: Arts Discovery Program; Art Rental/Sales Program; Student Art Show; Annual Juried Art Show; Presidents' Legacy Scholarship Fund; *Library:* Resource Centre; by appointment
Chief Officer(s):
Dominique Sanguinetti, Co-Chair
Karl Sprogin, Co-Chair
Louise Garfield, Executive Director
Ruth Cumberbatch, Manager, Fundraising & Communications
Chantelle Grant, Office Manager
Shira Spector, Coordinator, Program & Outreach
Graham Curry, Director, Gallery

Arts Mosaic
425 - 6th Ave. South, Virden MB R0M 2C0
Tel: 204-748-3014; *Fax:* 204-748-6985
artsmosaic@outlook.com
www.artsmosaic.ca
www.facebook.com/mbartsmosaic
www.pinterest.com/artsmosaic
Previous Name: Virden Community Arts Council
Overview: A small local charitable organization founded in 1981
Mission: To encourage the development of an interest in & appreciation for the visual, literary, performing & functional arts by providing appropriate programming & facilities within the Fort

la Bosse School Division
Member of: Manitoba Arts Network; Dance Manitoba
Finances: *Annual Operating Budget:* $100,000-$250,000; *Funding Sources:* Manitoba Culture, Heritage & Tourism; Enbridge Pipelines; municipal; private donations
65 volunteer(s)
Membership: 130; *Fees:* $5 individual; $10 organizations/commercial enterprises; *Member Profile:* Keen interest in the arts with some desire to actively participate; *Committees:* Costume Closet; Exhibitions; Fundraising/Membership; Publicity; Scholarship; Performing Arts
Activities: Performances; travelling exhibitions; workshops & classes; films; *Library:* Costume Closet; by appointment
Chief Officer(s):
Tina Williams, President
Awards:
• High School Scholarship, General Scholarship, Peace Garden Scholarship

Arts Ottawa East-Est (AOE) / Conseil de arts AOE
Shenkman Arts Centre, #260, 245 Centrum Blvd., Ottawa ON K1E 0A1
Tel: 613-580-2767; *Fax:* 613-580-2767
info@artsoe.ca
www.artsoe.ca
www.facebook.com/313002426106
twitter.com/AOEOttawa
Previous Name: Gloucester Arts Council
Overview: A medium-sized local charitable organization founded in 1987
Mission: To encourage & support the practice & appreciation of the arts in Ottawa
Member of: Community Arts Ontario; Gloucester Chamber of Commerce; Canadian Conference of the Arts
Affiliation(s): Volunteer Ottawa
Finances: *Annual Operating Budget:* $100,000-$250,000; *Funding Sources:* Fundraising; corporate; government; earned revenue
Staff Member(s): 4; 450 volunteer(s)
Membership: 6,500; *Fees:* $25 individual; $15 student; $30 family; $75 not-for-profit organizartion; up to $50 individual patrons; *Committees:* Planning; Advocacy; Membership; Volunteer Development & Fundraising; Nominations
Activities: FestivArts; Arts Party; Luncheon for the Arts; Write-on-Workshop; professional development workshops; *Library:* Open to public
Chief Officer(s):
Victoria Steele, Executive Director, 613-580-2767 Ext. 4
victoria@artsoe.ca

Arts Richmond Hill
PO Box 139, 10520 Yonge St., Richmond Hill ON L4C 3C7
Tel: 905-508-0789; *Fax:* 888-380-2268
info@artsrichmondhill.org
artsrichmondhill.org
www.facebook.com/ARTSRH
Also Known As: Art Council of Richmond Hill
Previous Name: Richmond Hill Arts Council
Overview: A small local organization founded in 1986
Mission: To foster & coordinate activities of groups, organizations & individuals engaged in the arts; to encourage education & appreciation for the arts; to provide an information service for the public; to provide forum for exchange of information; to act as liaison between cultural & other art organizations & government organizations
Affiliation(s): Community Arts Ontario
Finances: *Annual Operating Budget:* Less than $50,000; *Funding Sources:* Membership; fundraising; grants
Staff Member(s): 1; 30 volunteer(s)
Membership: 1 institutional + 2 honorary + 30 individual + 30 arts groups; *Fees:* Schedule available; *Member Profile:* Interest/participation in any of the arts; *Committees:* Events; Publicity; Executive; Membership; Nomination
Activities: Music Festival; Heritage Day; Festival of Lights Concert; Workshops; *Rents Mailing List:* Yes
Chief Officer(s):
Emmanuel Abara, President

Arts Scarborough *See* Scarborough Arts Council

Artscape
#224, 171 East Liberty St., Toronto ON M6K 3P6
Tel: 416-392-1038; *Fax:* 416-535-6260
info@artscape.ca
www.torontoartscape.org
www.facebook.com/TorontoArtscape
twitter.com/Artscape
www.youtube.com/torontoartscape;
www.flickr.com/photos/artscape
Also Known As: Artscape Non-Profit Homes Inc.
Overview: A medium-sized local organization founded in 1986
Mission: To provide affordable living &/or working space for artists for the relief of poverty & the advancement of education, culture, art & other purposes beneficial to the community
Member of: Parkdale/Liberty Economic Development Corp.; Liberty Village Business Improvement Area; Queen West Gallery District; Ontario Non-Profit Housing Association
Finances: *Annual Operating Budget:* Less than $50,000; *Funding Sources:* City of Toronto; Ministry of Municipal Affairs & Housing; Laidlaw Foundation; Toronto Arts Council
Staff Member(s): 8; 1,08 volunteer(s)
Activities: Acquisition, funding, development & management of property; liaison, information & outreach services; consulting services; provision of programs & services for artists & the non-profit, charitable, education & government sectors; *Awareness Events:* Inside Artscape; Art for Art's Sake Fundraising Event
Chief Officer(s):
Tim Jones, Chief Executive Officer, 416-392-1038 Ext. 24
tjones@artscape.ca
LoriAnn Girvan, Chief Operating Officer, 416-392-1038 Ext. 37
lgirvan@artscape.ca
Carol Davies, Director, Communications
cdavies@artscape.ca
Jane Hopgood, Director, Fund Development, 416-392-1038 Ext. 36
jhopgood@artscape.ca
Alec Stevenson, Director, Finance & Administration, 416-392-1038 Ext. 22
astevenson@artscape.ca

ArtsConnect - Tri-Cities Regional Arts Council
Fernwood Lodge, #158, 2601 Lougheed Hwy., Coquitlam BC V3C 4J2
Tel: 604-931-8255; *Fax:* 604-524-4666
info@artsconnect.tv
artsconnect.tv
www.facebook.com/ArtsConnectBC
twitter.com/artsconnectbc
www.youtube.com/user/ArtsConnectBC
Also Known As: ArtsConnect
Previous Name: Coquitlam Area Fine Arts Council; ARC Arts Council
Overview: A small local charitable organization founded in 1969
Mission: To promote & advance the development of the arts & culture in school district #43 Anmore, Belcarra, Coquitlam, Port Coquitlam & Port Moody; To improve arts literacy; To advocate for the arts at municipal & provincial levels; To identify cultural needs & issues & to provide support services, resources & related activities
Member of: Assembly of BC Arts Councils; Alliance for Arts & Culture; Arts in Education Council
Affiliation(s): Canadian Conference of the Arts
Finances: *Annual Operating Budget:* $100,000-$250,000; *Funding Sources:* Provincial & municipal government; private; corporate sponsorship; membership dues
Staff Member(s): 2; 100 volunteer(s)
Membership: 2,000; *Fees:* $5 for 2 years; *Member Profile:* Artists & art groups; general public; municipalities; libraries; educational institutions; arts facilities; *Committees:* Executive; Marketing & Communication; Member Services; Finance; Fundraising; Programs
Activities: *Library:* Open to public
Chief Officer(s):
Craig Townsend, President
Roger Loubert, Vice-President
Gabriela Caranfil, Director

Arusha Centre Society
The Old "Y" Bldg., #106, 223 - 12 Ave. SW, Calgary AB T2R 0G6
Tel: 403-270-3200; *Fax:* 403-270-8832
arusha@arusha.org
www.arusha.org
www.facebook.com/ArushaCentre
twitter.com/ArushaCentre
www.youtube.com/user/calgaryd
Overview: A small local charitable organization founded in 1972
Mission: To provide opportunities for, & remove barriers to, individual & community participation, self-determination & empowerment, especially for those who have been marginalized; To acknowledge, respect & actively value diversity, based on the belief in inherent human dignity; To challenge unjust internal & external assumptions & structures & work toward socially just alternatives; To connect social, economic & ecological issues, both locally & globally; to create a meaningful partnership that fosters social justice internally & externally
Member of: Volunteer Centre of Calgary; Parklands Institute
Finances: *Annual Operating Budget:* $250,000-$500,000; *Funding Sources:* Federal & provincial government; donations; United Way
Staff Member(s): 7; 75 volunteer(s)
Membership: 225; *Fees:* $10; *Member Profile:* Calgary community; *Committees:* Finance; Fundraising; Membership; Programming; Marketing
Activities: *Library:* Resource Centre; Open to public
Chief Officer(s):
Sharon Stevens, Info-activee Coordinator

ARZA-Canada: The Zionist Voice of the Canadian Reform Movement
#301, 3845 Bathurst St., Toronto ON M3H 3N2
info@arzacanada.org
www.arzacanada.org
Also Known As: AZRA-Canada
Overview: A medium-sized national organization
Mission: To help foster a better understanding of Israel & to support the Reform Movement in Israel
Member of: ARZA-World Union-North America
Affiliation(s): Canadian Zionist Federation
Finances: *Funding Sources:* Membership dues; Donations
Membership: 6,000 individual; *Fees:* $36 Household; $18 Adult; $5 Student
Chief Officer(s):
Miriam Pearlman, President
Glenn Coehn, Vice-President
Jeff Denaburg, Vice-President
Cheryl Englander, Vice-President
Dorothy Millman, Vice-President
Valerie Whitefield, Treasurer

ASEAN-Canada Business Council *See* Southeast Asia-Canada Business Council

Ashcroft & Area Food Bank
PO Box 603, 601 Bancroft St., Ashcroft BC V0K 1A0
Tel: 250-453-9656; *Fax:* 250-453-2034
Overview: A small local organization overseen by Food Banks British Columbia
Member of: Food Banks British Columbia
Chief Officer(s):
Denise Fiddick, Contact
scelizfry@telus.net

Ashcroft & District Chamber of Commerce
PO Box 741, Ashcroft BC V0K 1A0
www.ashcroftbc.ca
Overview: A small local organization
Finances: *Funding Sources:* Membership dues

Ashern & District Chamber of Commerce
PO Box 582, Ashern MB R0C 0E0
info@ashern.ca
www.ashern.ca
www.facebook.com/asherncchamberofcommerce
Overview: A small local organization
Mission: To encourage business growth & economic development; To promote Ashern outside the local area
Member of: Manitoba Chamber of Commerce
Membership: *Member Profile:* Small, independent business
Activities: Country Trade Fest; Midnight Madness; Ashem Welcome Wagon; Chamber Golf Tournament

Ashmont & District Agricultural Society
PO Box 23, Ashmont AB T0A 0C0
Tel: 780-726-3897
Overview: A small local organization founded in 1984
Finances: *Funding Sources:* Fundraising; donations
30 volunteer(s)
Membership: 60; *Fees:* $1; *Committees:* Economic Development; Agricultural Services; Aspen Grove Seniors Lodge; Agri-Plex Management; Heritage Day; Minor Sports; Continuing Education; Government Liaison
Chief Officer(s):
Jenny Bespalko, Contact
jbsbespalko@yahoo.com

Asia Pacific Foundation of Canada (APFC) / Fondation Asie Pacifique du Canada
#900, 675 Hastings St. West, Vancouver BC V6B 1N2

Tel: 604-684-5986; *Fax:* 604-681-1370
info@asiapacific.ca
www.asiapacific.ca
www.linkedin.com/company-beta/522469
www.facebook.com/asiapacificfoundationofcanada
twitter.com/AsiaPacificFdn
Also Known As: APF Canada
Overview: A medium-sized international organization founded in 1984
Mission: To bring together people & knowledge to provide the most current & comprehensive research, analysis & information on Canada's transpacific relations; To promote dialogue on economic, security, political & social issues, helping to influence public policy & foster informed decision-making in the Canadian public, private & non-governmental sectors
Finances: *Annual Operating Budget:* $1.5 Million-$3 Million; *Funding Sources:* Federal & provincial government
Staff Member(s): 30
Activities: Business; Media; Education; Public policy; Research; *Internships:* Yes; *Library*
Chief Officer(s):
Stewart Beck, President & CEO

Asian Community AIDS Services (ACAS)
#410, 260 Spadina Ave., Toronto ON M5T 2E4
Tel: 416-963-4300; *Fax:* 416-963-4371
Toll-Free: 877-630-2227
info@acas.org
www.acas.org
www.facebook.com/AsianCommunityAIDSServices
twitter.com/ACAStoronto
www.youtube.com/user/acasorg
Merged from: Gay Asians Toronto's Gay Asian AIDS Project; Vietnamese AIDS Project; AIDS Alert Project
Overview: A small local charitable organization founded in 1994 overseen by Canadian AIDS Society
Mission: To provide education, prevention & support services on HIV/AIDS to the East & Southeast Asian communities; programs are based on a proactive & holistic approach to HIV/AIDS & are provided in a collaborative, empowering & non-discriminatory manner
Member of: Ontario AIDS Network
Finances: *Funding Sources:* City of Toronto; Ontario Ministry of Health; Health Canada
Staff Member(s): 15
Membership: *Member Profile:* People living with HIV/AIDS & program volunteers
Activities: Programs for men, women, & youth; Support Program; Asian Migrant Farmworkers' Research Project; *Awareness Events:* Scotiabank Toronto Waterfront Marathon, Oct.; *Library:* Open to public
Chief Officer(s):
Giovanni Temansja, Chair
Noulmook Sutdhibhasilp, Executive Director, 416-963-4300 Ext. 227
ed@acas.org

Asian Heritage Society of Manitoba
MB
Tel: 204-488-8059
www.asianheritagemanitoba.ca
Overview: A small provincial organization
Mission: To bring together members of the Asian Canadian communities in Manitoba; To share the arts, culture, traditions, cuisine, & faiths of Asian Canadians with Manitobans; To reduce racism towards Asian Canadians
Membership: *Member Profile:* Representatives from Chinese, Japanese, Korean, Indian, Vietnamese, Filipino, & Indo-Chinese communities in Manitoba
Activities: Creating partnerships with Asian Canadian groups; Raising public awareness & fostering understanding of Asian cultures; Sharing knowledge of Asian medicinal & meditative traditions; Highlighting the contributions of Asian Canadians in Manitoba; Planning member meeetings; Facilitating networking opportunities; Encouraging participation by Asian Canadian youth; Organizing events, such as the young Asian entrepreneur forum, Asian writers showcase, Asian storytelling, & the Asian Canadian Festival of the Forks; *Awareness Events:* Asian Heritage Month, May
Chief Officer(s):
Art Miki, President

ASK! Community Information Centre (LAMP)
185 - 5th St., Toronto ON M8V 2Z5
Tel: 416-252-6471; *Fax:* 416-252-4474
www.lampchc.org
www.facebook.com/LAMPCHEALTHC
Previous Name: YMCA ASK! & YMCA ASCC
Overview: A small local organization founded in 1969 overseen by InformOntario
Mission: To offer a range of programs & services to support residents & workers of southern Etobicoke (South/West Toronto); To offer community information, referral, legal advice, immigrant program, & refugee support
Member of: Federation of Community Information Centres of Toronto; Lakeshore Area Multi-Servcies Program
Finances: *Funding Sources:* Municipal, Federal & Regional governments; United Way of Greater Toronto
Staff Member(s): 6
Membership: *Fees:* $3
Activities: Medical and dental services; children and youth programs; family programs; community support services
Chief Officer(s):
Russ Ford, Executive Director

ASM International - Calgary Chapter
PO Box 40411, Stn. Highfield, Calgary AB T2G 5G7
www.asminternational.org/portal/site/calgary
www.facebook.com/AsmInternationalCalgaryChapter
Overview: A small local organization founded in 1999
Chief Officer(s):
Sammy Tang, Vice Chair & Co-Treasurer
smtang@telus.net
Awards:
- M. Brian Ives Lectureship Award
- Best Student Paper
- 5 Star Quality Performance Award

Asociación Venezolana de Estudios Canadienses *See* Venezuelan Association for Canadian Studies

Asparagus Farmers of Ontario (AFO)
PO Box 587, 1283 Blueline Rd., Simcoe ON N3Y 4N5
Tel: 519-426-7529; *Fax:* 519-426-9087
info@asparagus.on.ca
asparagus.on.ca
twitter.com/onasparagus
Previous Name: Ontario Asparagus Growers' Marketing Board
Overview: A large provincial organization
Chief Officer(s):
Bernie Solymar, Executive Director
bernie.solymar@asparagus.on.ca

Asper Foundation
#2810, 201 Portage Ave., Winnipeg MB R3B 3K6
Tel: 204-989-5537; *Fax:* 204-989-5536
www.asperfoundation.com
twitter.com/AsperFoundation
www.youtube.com/user/asperfoundation2
Overview: A medium-sized international charitable organization
Mission: To drive positive change by undertaking & supporting philanthropic initiatives involving Jewish causes, culture, education, community development, & human rights
Activities: Supporting projects & charitable initiatives in Canada & Israel
Chief Officer(s):
David Asper, Chair
Gail Asper, President
Moses Levy, Executive Director

Aspergers Society of Ontario
#231, 3219 Yonge St., Toronto ON M4N 3S1
Tel: 416-651-4037
info@aspergers.ca
www.aspergers.ca
www.facebook.com/AspergerOntario
twitter.com/aspergerontario
Overview: A small provincial charitable organization founded in 2000
Mission: To improve public & professional awareness & understanding of Aspergers Syndrome; To promote & support research & the development of diagnoses, treatment, & education programs for those with Aspergers Syndrome; To provide information & referrals for those interested in Aspergers Syndrome; To initiate programs & services which respond to the needs of those affected by Aspergers Syndrome
Finances: *Funding Sources:* Donations; Membership dues; SickKids Foundation; Centre for Addiction & Mental Health
Activities: Infoline; Adult social group
Chief Officer(s):
Alexandra Prefasi, Executive Director

ASPHME *Voir* MultiPrévention

Assaulted Women's Helpline (AWH)
PO Box 369, Stn. B, Toronto ON M5T 2E2
Tel: 416-364-4144; *Fax:* 416-364-0563
Toll-Free: 888-364-1210; *TTY:* 866-863-7868; *Crisis Hot-Line:* 866-863-0511
admin@awhl.org
www.awhl.org
www.facebook.com/AssaultedWomensHelpline
twitter.com/awhl
Overview: A medium-sized local charitable organization founded in 1985
Mission: To provide 24-hour crisis counselling, referral, & an information telephone line, province-wide
Affiliation(s): Ontario Association of Interval & Transition Houses; Ontario Network of Sexual Assault/Domestic Treatment Centres; Community Legal Education Ontario; Metropolitan Action Committee on Violence Against Women & Children; Family Law Education for Women; Challenge Sexual Violence; Springtide Resources; Ontario Coalition of Rape Crisis Centres; Women Abuse Council of Toronto
Finances: *Annual Operating Budget:* $1.5 Million-$3 Million; *Funding Sources:* Provincial government
Staff Member(s): 22; 20 volunteer(s)
Membership: 30 institutional; *Fees:* $15 institutional
Activities: *Awareness Events:* Gala, annual (April); *Library*
Chief Officer(s):
Huong Pham, Executive Director
Beth Jordan, Director, Programs & Services

Assemblée communautaire fransaskoise (ACF)
#215, 1440, 9 av Nord, Regina SK S4R 8B1
Tél: 306-569-1912; *Téléc:* 306-781-7916
Ligne sans frais: 800-991-1912
acf@fransaskois.sk.ca
www.fransaskois.sk.ca
www.facebook.com/assembleecommunautairefransaskoise.acf
Nom précédent: Association catholique franco-canadienne de la Saskatchewan; Association culturelle franco-canadienne de la Saskatchewan
Aperçu: *Dimension:* moyenne; *Envergure:* provinciale; Organisme sans but lucratif; fondée en 1912 surveillé par Fédération des communautés francophones et acadienne du Canada
Mission: Travaille au développement, à l'épanouissement et au rayonnement de tous ses membres; est l'entité gouvernante de la communauté fransaskoise
Membre(s) du personnel: 24
Activités: Réunions publiques; *Bibliothèque:* Archives; rendez-vous
Membre(s) du bureau directeur:
Dominique Sarny, Directeur général
dominique.sarny@fransaskois.sk.ca
Marc Masson, Directeur des communications
marc.masson@fransaskois.sk.ca
   Bureau de Gravelbourg
   CP 176, Gravelbourg SK S0H 1X0
   Tél: 306-648-3103; *Téléc:* 306-648-3258
   acfg1@sasktel.net
   Bureau de St-Isidore de Bellevue, Domrémy et St Louis
   CP 127, St-Isidor-de-Bellevue SK S0K 3Y0
   Tél: 306-423-5303; *Téléc:* 306-423-5606
   info@cfbds.ca

Assemblée de la francophonie de l'Ontario (AFO)
1490, ch Star Top, Ottawa ON K1B 3W6
Tél: 613-744-6649; *Téléc:* 416-744-8861
Ligne sans frais: 866-596-4692
ad@monassemblee.ca
www.monassemblee.ca
www.facebook.com/monassemblee.ca
twitter.com/MonAssemblee
www.youtube.com/monassemblee
Également appelé: L'Assemblée
Aperçu: *Dimension:* moyenne; *Envergure:* provinciale; fondée en 2005 surveillé par Fédération des communautés francophones et acadienne du Canada
Mission: Pour représenter la voix politique des francophones en Ontario
Membre de: Fédération des communautés francophones et acadienne du Canada
Finances: *Budget de fonctionnement annuel:* $500,000-$1.5 Million; *Fonds:* Patrimoine canadien; Industrie Canada; Fondation Trillium; Office des Affaires francophones
Membre(s) du personnel: 5; 11 bénévole(s)

Membre: 400; *Montant de la cotisation:* Barème; *Comités:* Finances; Gouvernance; Travail
Activités: Promotion de la langue française; *Stagiaires:* Oui; *Service de conférenciers:* Oui
Membre(s) du bureau directeur:
Peter Hominuk, Directeur général, 613-744-6649 Ext. 111
phominuk@monassemblee.ca
Publications:
• Prises de Position: Dossiers Prioritaires pour la Communauté Francophone de L'Ontario
Type: Bulletin; *Frequency:* annuel
• Rapport annuel de L'Assemblée de la francophonie de l'Ontario
Type: Rapport; *Frequency:* annuel

L'Assemblée des aînées et aînés francophones du Canada
Voir Fédération des aînées et aînés francophones du Canada

Assemblée des évêques catholiques de l'Ontario *See* Assembly of Catholic Bishops of Ontario

Assemblée des évêques catholiques du Québec (AEQ) / Assembly of Québec Catholic Bishops
3331, rue Sherbrooke est, Montréal QC H1W 1C5
Tél: 514-274-4323; *Téléc:* 514-274-4383
aeq@eveques.qc.ca
www.eveques.qc.ca
twitter.com/evequesQuebec
Nom précédent: Assemblée des Évêques du Québec
Aperçu: *Dimension:* petite; *Envergure:* provinciale; Organisme sans but lucratif; fondée en 1871 surveillé par Canadian Conference of Catholic Bishops
Mission: Être un lieu d'échange et de concertation où ses membres s'entraident dans la recherche d'actions à entreprendre pour rendre l'Église au Québec toujours plus vivante et engagée dans la société et la culture contemporaines
Affiliation(s): Conférence des évêques catholiques du Canada
Finances: *Budget de fonctionnement annuel:* $500,000-$1.5 Million
Membre(s) du personnel: 8
Membre: 37; *Critères d'admissibilité:* Évêque diocésain; Évêque auxiliaire; *Comités:* Éducation; Laicat; Ministères; Missions; Affaires sociales; Théologie; Communications; Prospective; Législation; Administration; Relations interculturelles; Pastorale des Autochtones
Membre(s) du bureau directeur:
Bertrand Ouellet, Secrétaire général

Assemblée des évêques de l'Atlantique *See* Atlantic Episcopal Assembly

Assemblée des Évêques du Québec *Voir* Assemblée des évêques catholiques du Québec

Assemblée des Premières Nations *See* Assembly of First Nations

Assemblée des premières nations du Québec et du Labrador
#201, 250, Place Chef Michel-Laveau, Wendake QC G0A 4V0
Tél: 418-842-5020; *Téléc:* 418-842-2660
www.apnql.com
Aperçu: *Dimension:* moyenne; *Envergure:* provinciale
Membre: 43
Membre(s) du bureau directeur:
Ghislain Picard, Chef

Assemblée internationale des parlementaires de langue française *Voir* Assemblée parlementaire de la Francophonie

Assemblée internationale des parlementaires de langue française (Section canadienne) *Voir* Assemblée parlementaire de la Francophonie (Section canadienne)

Assemblée parlementaire de la Francophonie (APF)
Région Amérique, Assemblée nationale, 1050, rue des Parlementaires, 4e étage, Québec QC G1A 1A3
Tél: 418-643-7391; *Téléc:* 418-643-1865
www.regionamerique-apf.org
Nom précédent: Assemblée internationale des parlementaires de langue française
Aperçu: *Dimension:* moyenne; *Envergure:* internationale; fondée en 1992
Mission: Promouvoir la langue et la culture francaise; Promouvoir les droits de l'homme et la démocratie
Finances: *Budget de fonctionnement annuel:* Moins de $50,000
Membre: 1-99
Activités: *Service de conférenciers:* Oui
Membre(s) du bureau directeur:
André Lavoie, Secrétaire administrative régionale

Assemblée parlementaire de la Francophonie (Section canadienne) (APF)
Parliament of Canada, 131 Queen St., 5th Fl., Ottawa ON K1A 0A6
Tél: 613-995-9560; *Téléc:* 613-995-0212
assem.franco@parl.gc.ca
Nom précédent: Assemblée internationale des parlementaires de langue française (Section canadienne)
Aperçu: *Dimension:* petite; *Envergure:* provinciale; fondée en 1967
Mission: L'Assemblée parlementaire de la Francophonie est un lieu de débats, de propositions et d'échanges d'informations sur tous les sujets d'intérêt commun à ses membres. Par ses avis et recommandations à la Conférence ministérielle de la Francophonie et au Conseil permanent de la Francophonie, elle participe à la vie institutionnelle de la Francophonie; elle intervient devant les chefs d'État lors des Sommets de la Francophonie. En étroite collaboration avec l'Agence de la Francophonie, elle engage et met en oeuvre des actions dans les domaines de la coopération interparlementaire et du développement de la démocratie. Ses actions visent à renforcer la solidarité entre institutions parlementaires et à promouvoir la démocratie et l'État de droit, plus particulièrement au sein de la communauté francophone
Membre(s) du bureau directeur:
Jean-François Lafleur, Secrétaire

Assemblées de la Pentecôte du Canada *See* Pentecostal Assemblies of Canada

Assembly of BC Arts Councils
PO Box 28533, Stn. Willingdon, Burnaby BC V5C 2H9
Tel: 604-291-0046; *Fax:* 604-648-9454
Toll-Free: 888-315-2288
info@artsbc.org
www.artsbc.org
twitter.com/artsbcdotorg
Also Known As: ArtsBC
Overview: A medium-sized provincial charitable organization founded in 1979
Mission: To promote & advance the role of arts & culture in building community; to work with community based organizations in furthering the impact & contribution of the arts locally, regionally & province-wide
Finances: *Funding Sources:* Public, private & earned revenues
Membership: 300; *Member Profile:* Arts councils & other local arts agencies
Activities: *Library:* by appointment
Chief Officer(s):
Stephen Parsons, President

Assembly of Catholic Bishops of Ontario (ACBO) / Assemblée des évêques catholiques de l'Ontario
#810, 90 Eglinton Ave. East, Toronto ON M4P 2Y3
Tel: 416-923-1423; *Fax:* 416-923-1509
acbo@acbo.on.ca
www.acbo.on.ca
Overview: A small provincial organization overseen by Canadian Conference of Catholic Bishops
Mission: To enable Ontario Catholic Bishops to collaborate on projects to proclaim, celebrate & live the Good News of Jesus Christ
Membership: *Committees:* Commission for Priests; Education Commission; Social Affairs Commission; Executive; Institutional Chaplaincy; Ontario Diocesan Insurance
Chief Officer(s):
Ronald P. Fabbro, c.s.b., President, 519-433-0658, Fax: 519-433-0011
Thomas Collins, Vice President, 416-934-0606, Fax: 416-934-3452

Assembly of First Nations (AFN) / Assemblée des Premières Nations (APN)
#1600, 55 Metcalfe St., Ottawa ON K1P 6L5
Tel: 613-241-6789; *Fax:* 613-241-5808
Toll-Free: 866-869-6789
www.afn.ca
www.facebook.com/AssemblyofFirstNations
twitter.com/AFN_Updates
www.youtube.com/user/afnposter
Previous Name: National Indian Brotherhood
Overview: A large national organization
Mission: To act as an advocate for First Nations on many issues, including Aboriginal & Treaty Rights, economic development, education, languages & literacy, health, housing, social development, justice, land claims, & the environment
Finances: *Funding Sources:* Federal grants
Membership: 634 First Nations in Canada
Chief Officer(s):
Perry Bellegarde, National Chief

Assembly of Manitoba Chiefs
#200, 275 Portage Ave., Winnipeg MB R3B 2B3
Tel: 204-956-0610; *Fax:* 204-956-2109
Toll-Free: 888-324-5483
info@manitobachiefs.com
www.manitobachiefs.com
Overview: A medium-sized provincial organization
Mission: To promote & preserve Aboriginal and treaty rights while striving to improve the quality of life of the First Nation citizens in Manitoba.
Affiliation(s): Assembly of First Nations
Membership: 58 member communities
Chief Officer(s):
Derek Nepinak, Grand Chief

Assembly of Québec Catholic Bishops *Voir* Assemblée des évêques catholiques du Québec

Assiniboia & District Arts Council
PO Box 1596, 122 - 3rd Ave. West, Assiniboia SK S0H 0B0
Tel: 306-642-5294; *Fax:* 306-642-5441
assiniboia.artscouncil@sasktel.net
www.facebook.com/AssiniboiaArtsCouncil
Overview: A small local charitable organization founded in 1981
Mission: To increase & broaden the opportunities for public enjoyment of & participation in cultural activities; To stimulate & encourage the development of cultural projects & activities; To act as a clearinghouse for information on cultural projects & activities
Member of: Organization of Saskatchewan Arts Councils
Finances: *Annual Operating Budget:* Less than $50,000
15 volunteer(s)
Membership: 20; *Fees:* $35; *Member Profile:* All ages & walks of life; *Committees:* Visual Arts; Performing Arts; Art & Craft Sale
Chief Officer(s):
Joanne Weiss, Executive Director
Darlene Kowalchuk, President

Assiniboia & District Chamber of Commerce (SK)
PO Box 1803, Assiniboia SK S0H 0B0
Tel: 306-642-5553; *Fax:* 306-642-3529
www.assiniboia.net/business/chamber_of_commerce.html
Overview: A small local organization
Mission: To stimulate economic growth in the area
Activities: *Awareness Events:* First Responders Day, Sept.; Career Fair, Sept.; Light Parade, Dec.
Chief Officer(s):
Glen Hall, Chief Administration Officer

Assiniboia Chamber of Commerce (MB) (ACC)
PO Box 42122, Stn. Ferry Road, 1867 Portage Ave., Winnipeg MB R3J 3X7
Tel: 204-774-4154; *Fax:* 204-774-4201
info@assiniboiacc.mb.ca
www.assiniboiacc.mb.ca
twitter.com/assiniboiacc
Overview: A medium-sized local organization founded in 1930
Mission: To promote entrepreneurship & competitive enterprise in West Winnipeg
Member of: Canadian Chamber of Commerce; Manitoba Chamber of Commerce
Finances: *Annual Operating Budget:* $100,000-$250,000; *Funding Sources:* Membership fees; Corporate sponsorship
Staff Member(s): 1; 14 volunteer(s)
Membership: 425; *Fees:* $175 businesses with up to 150 employees; $295 businesses with 150+ employees; $35 retired/student; *Member Profile:* Small to medium size businesses & community groups; *Committees:* Communications/Public Relations; Government Relations; Membership; Programs & Services
Activities: Offering monthly lunches & programs; *Awareness Events:* Golf Tournament, June; Lobster Fest Dinner, October; *Speaker Service:* Yes; *Rents Mailing List:* Yes
Chief Officer(s):
Ernie Nairn, Executive Director, 204-774-4154, Fax: 204-774-4201

Assiniboine Park Conservancy
55 Pavilion Cres., Winnipeg MB R3P 2N7
Tel: 204-927-6001
Other Communication: comments@assiniboinepark.ca
info@assiniboinepark.ca
www.zoosociety.com

www.facebook.com/assiniboineparkzoo
twitter.com/assiniboinepark
www.instagram.com/assiniboineparkzoo
Previous Name: Zoological Society of Manitoba
Overview: A small provincial charitable organization founded in 1956
Mission: To redevelop & manage the Park's operations & ongoing financial viability
Finances: *Annual Operating Budget:* $1.5 Million-$3 Million
Membership: *Fees:* $10-$95
Activities: School & group programs; Workshops & classes; Outreach & sleepovers; Day camps; Guided tours
Chief Officer(s):
Hartley Richardson, Chair
Margaret Redmond, President & CEO

Assisted Living Southwestern Ontario (ALSO)
3141 Sandwich St., Windsor ON N9C 1A7
Tel: 519-969-8188; *Fax:* 519-969-0390
info@alsogroup.org
www.appdgroup.org
Previous Name: Association for Persons with Physical Disabilities of Windsor & Essex County
Overview: A small local organization founded in 1985
Mission: Provides personal care, homemaking services and assistance with tasks of daily living to adults with permanent physical disabilities.
Membership: *Committees:* Executive; Finance; Social Recreation; Personnel; Facility Pl; Integration
Chief Officer(s):
Lyn Calder, Executive Director

Associaça Portuguesa de LaSalle / Association Culturelle Récréative Portugaise de Lasalle
2136A, rue Pigeon, LaSalle QC H8N 1A6
Tél: 514-366-6305
Également appelé: LaSalle Portuguese Association
Aperçu: *Dimension:* petite; *Envergure:* locale

Associaça Portuguesa de Ste-Thérèse / Association Portugaise De Sainte-Thérèse
103B, rue Turgeon, Sainte-Thérèse QC J7E 3H8
Tél: 450-435-0301
Également appelé: Saint Therese Portuguese Association
Aperçu: *Dimension:* petite; *Envergure:* locale

Associaça Portuguesa Do Canadà (APC) / Portuguese Assocation of Canada
4170, rue Saint-Urbain, Montréal QC H1W 3Y3
Tel: 514-844-2269
apc4170@hotmail.com
www.facebook.com/151731518227684
Overview: A small national organization founded in 1956
Mission: To promote & preserve Portuguese culture; reuinte people of Portuguese origin; to help integrate amd participate in the community

Associaça Portuguesa do West Island / Association Portugaise De L'Ile De L'Ouest
4789, boul des Sources, Pierrefonds QC H8Y 3C6
Tél: 514-684-0857
Également appelé: West Island Portuguese Association
Aperçu: *Dimension:* petite; *Envergure:* locale

Associaça Portuguesa Espirito Santo / Association Portugaise du Saint-Esprit
6024, rue Hochelaga, Montréal QC H1N 1X6
Tél: 514-254-4647
Également appelé: Saint Esprit Portuguese Association
Aperçu: *Dimension:* petite; *Envergure:* locale

Associaçao dos Pais
333, rue Castelnau est, Montréal QC H2R 1P8
Tél: 514-495-3284
Également appelé: Montreal Association of Parents
Aperçu: *Dimension:* petite; *Envergure:* locale

Associated Boards of Trade of Ontario *See* Ontario Chamber of Commerce

Associated Business Executives of Canada *See* Associated Senior Executives of Canada Ltd.

Associated Designers of Canada (ADC)
#434 Queen St. East, 2nd Fl., Toronto ON M5A 1T4
Tel: 416-907-5829
associateddesignerscanada@gmail.com
www.designers.ca
www.linkedin.com/groups?gid=1846687
www.facebook.com/634308563283161
twitter.com/AssocDesignCda
Overview: A small national organization founded in 1965
Mission: To promote, pursue & protect the interests & needs of theatrical designers working in Canada
Member of: Theatre Ontario; Toronto Theatre Alliance
Finances: *Annual Operating Budget:* $50,000-$100,000; *Funding Sources:* Membership dues; government
Staff Member(s): 2
Membership: 160; *Fees:* $260; *Member Profile:* Set, costume, lighting, projection, & sound designers working in Canada's live performing arts industry
Activities: *Library:* Virtual Resource Centre
Chief Officer(s):
April Viczko, President
Michael Walsh, Secretary-Treasurer
Sheila Sky, Executive Director

Associated Environmental Site Assessors of Canada Inc. (AESAC)
PO Box 490, Fenelon Falls ON K0M 1N0
Toll-Free: 877-512-3722
info@aesac.ca
www.aesac.ca
Overview: A small national organization founded in 1992
Mission: To provide services to assist site assessors in meeting the needs of potential clients such as lenders & major property owners; To assist practitioners from many different professional backgrounds in identifying & maintaining appropriate standards for conducting site assessments

Associated Gospel Churches (AGC) / Association des églises évangéliques (AEE)
1500 Kerns Rd., Burlington ON L7P 3A7
Tel: 905-634-8184; *Fax:* 905-634-6283
admin@agcofcanada.com
www.agcofcanada.com
www.facebook.com/associatedgospelchurches
www.youtube.com/user/donnaagc
Overview: A medium-sized national charitable organization founded in 1925
Mission: To glorify God by partnering together in obedience to the Great Commandment & the Great Commission; to become a movement of healthy, reproducing churches
Affiliation(s): World Relief; World Team; UFM International; Evangelical Fellowship of Canada
Finances: *Annual Operating Budget:* $250,000-$500,000
Staff Member(s): 5
Membership: 21,400 members; 140+ churches; *Fees:* 4% of revenue minus missions support; *Committees:* Doctrine & Credentials; Church Planting; Church Health & Leadership
Chief Officer(s):
Bill Fietje, President
bill@agcofcanada.com
Susan Page, Coordinator, Church Relations
sue@agcofcanada.com

Canada West Office
#138, 445 Yates Rd., Kelowna BC V1V 1Y4
Tel: 306-260-4411
Chief Officer(s):
Russ Wilson, Superintendent
russ@agcofcanada.com

Quebec Office
c/o Rev. Del Gibbons, Eglise Evangelique Associee de Verdun, 350, av Woodland, Verdun QC H4H 1V6
Tél: 514-768-8446
Chief Officer(s):
Del Gibbons, Director
del@agcofcanada.com

Associated Manitoba Arts Festivals, Inc. (AMAF)
#2, 88 St. Anne's Rd., Winnipeg MB R2M 2Y7
Tel: 204-231-4507; *Fax:* 204-231-4510
www.amaf.mb.ca
Overview: A medium-sized provincial charitable organization founded in 1977 overseen by Federation of Canadian Music Festivals
Mission: To promote & encourage participation in growth & development of & appreciation for creative & performing arts in partnership with local festivals
Finances: *Annual Operating Budget:* $100,000-$250,000; *Funding Sources:* Government; fundraising; program revenue
Staff Member(s): 3; 4000 volunteer(s)
Membership: 120 individual + 28 festivals + 10 affiliate; *Fees:* $30 individual; *Committees:* Program; Finance; Fundraising; Public Relations; Syllabus; Board of Directors
Activities: Provincial Music & Speech Finals Competition; Provincial Syllabus Annual Conference; Rising Stars program; *Awareness Events:* Festival Awareness Week *Library:* Arts Resource Library
Chief Officer(s):
William Gordon, President
gordonw@brandonu.ca
Judith Oatway, Secretary
oatway.judith@gmail.com
Tannie Lam, Treasurer
tanlam9@gmail.com

Associated Medical Services Inc. (AMS)
#228, 162 Cumberland St., Toronto ON M5R 3N5
Tel: 416-924-3368; *Fax:* 416-323-3338
info@ams-inc.on.ca
php.ams-inc.on.ca
Overview: A small local charitable organization founded in 1937
Mission: To sponsor programs in the history of medicine, medical education & bioethics; to facilitate education, research & other initiatives which promote the development & understanding of those human & social values that are fundamental to health
Affiliation(s): Thomas Fisher Rare Book Library, University of Toronto; Association of Faculties of Medicine of Canada; Canadian Association for the History of Nursing; Canadian Institutes of Health Research; Canadian Society for the History of Medicine; College of Family Physicians of Canada; McGill University Faculty of Medicine; McGill-Queen's University Press; McMaster University; Queen's University; Royal Society of Canada; University of Calgary; University of Ottawa; University of Toronto; University of Western Ontario
Activities: Hannah Institute for the History of Medicine Program; Bioethics Program; Education Program; Special Awards
Chief Officer(s):
Gail Paech, CEO
Dorothy Pringle, Chair/President

Associated Research Centres for the Urban Underground Space (ACUUS) / Association des Centres de recherche sur l'Utilisation Urbaine du Sous-sol (ACLUS)
ACUUS Secrétariat, 34, rue Seville, Montréal QC H9B 2S5
info@acuus.qc.ca
www.acuus.qc.ca
www.linkedin.com/groups/4204639/profile
Overview: A small international organization founded in 1996
Mission: To enhance the international co-operation & exchange amongst the world community of planners, researchers, builders, investors, decision-makers & other parties involved in the use & development of the urban underground space
Finances: *Annual Operating Budget:* Less than $50,000; *Funding Sources:* Public & private
Staff Member(s): 1
Membership: 10; *Member Profile:* Organizations & individuals interested in furthering the objectives of the ACUUS in regard to urban underground space
Activities: Co-ordination of international events; creation of international directory of urban underground planning data; promotion of strategies & actions for the integrated planning & management of urban underground spaces; *Library:* by appointment Not open to public
Chief Officer(s):
Ray Sterling, President
Jacques Besner, General Manager

Associated Senior Executives of Canada Ltd. (ASE)
450 The West Mall, Toronto ON M9C 1E9
Tel: 416-695-2435
contactus@a-s-e.ca
www.a-s-e.ca
Previous Name: Associated Business Executives of Canada
Overview: A small national organization founded in 1963
Mission: To offer practical business advice
Membership: *Member Profile:* Retired executives with experience in a wide variety of corporate areas

Association acadienne des artistes professionnel.le.s du Nouveau-Brunswick inc. (AAAPNB)
#29, 140, rue Botsford, Moncton NB E1C 4X5
Tél: 506-852-3313
info@aaapnb.ca
www.aaapnb.ca
www.facebook.com/aaapnb
twitter.com/AAAPNB
www.youtube.com/AAAPNB

Canadian Associations / Association Béton Québec (ABQ)

Aperçu: *Dimension:* petite; *Envergure:* provinciale; Organisme sans but lucratif; fondée en 1990
Mission: Promouvoir et défendre les droits et les intérêts des artistes. A titre de porte-parole officiel, représente ses membres auprès des instances gouvernementales, travaille au développement des secteurs artistiques et offre des services d'information, de publication et de promotion
Membre de: Fédération culturelle canadienne-française (FCCF); Conférence canadienne des arts
Membre(s) du personnel: 10
Membre: *Montant de la cotisation:* 50$ artiste professionnel; 25$ artiste stagiaire/ami des arts; *Critères d'admissibilite:* Artistes acadiens et acadiennes de profession
Activités:; *Bibliothèque:* Centre de ressources des arts et de la culture
Membre(s) du bureau directeur:
Carmen Gibbs, Directrice générale
carmen.gibbs@aaapnb.ca

Association accréditée du personnel non enseignant de l'université McGill *See* McGill University Non Academic Certified Association

Association albertaine des parents francophones *Voir* Fédération des parents francophones de l'Alberta

Association amateur des sports des sourds du Québec; Fédération sportive des sourds du Québec inc. *Voir* Association sportive des sourds du Québec inc.

Association Aquacole du Canada *See* Aquaculture Association of Canada

Association Atlantique du Sport Collegial *See* Atlantic Collegiate Athletic Association

Association béton Atlantique *See* Atlantic Concrete Association

Association Béton Québec (ABQ)
#2200, 520 rue D'Avaugour, Boucherville QC J4B 0G6
Tel: 450-650-0930; *Fax:* 450-650-0935
Toll-Free: 855-650-0930
info@betonabq.org
betonabq.org
twitter.com/BetonQc
Overview: A medium-sized provincial organization overseen by Canadian Ready Mixed Concrete Association
Mission: Promouvoir l'utilisation du béton prêt à l'emploi dans le respect des bonnes pratiques de l'industrie, mobiliser nos membres et partenaires envers l'amélioration continue des connaissances et des pratiques
Staff Member(s): 3
Membership: 50; *Member Profile:* Producteurs de béton
Chief Officer(s):
Luc Bédard, Directeur général
lbedard@betonabq.org

Association botanique du Canada *See* Canadian Botanical Association

Association camadienne des interprètes de conférence (AIIC Canada) / Canadian Association of Conference Interpreters (CACI)
c/o Susan Asselin, 11 Woodbrook Rd. SW, Calgary AB T2W 4M5
www.aiic.ca
Aperçu: *Dimension:* petite; *Envergure:* internationale; fondée en 1953
Mission: Fournir des conseils aux organisateurs de conférences en ce qui concerne les services d'interprétation; l'AIIC est la seule association internationale professionnelle d'interprètes de conférence
Affiliation(s): Centre du Commerce Mondial
Membre: 100-499; *Montant de la cotisation:* Barème; *Critères d'admissibilite:* Diplôme post-universitaire; expérience; parrainage par les pairs; *Comités:* Technique; Santé; Formation; Associations internationales; Secteur privé; Relations publiques; Interprètes permanénts
Activités: *Service de conférenciers:* Oui
Membre(s) du bureau directeur:
Susan Asselin, Membre du conseil, 403-698-2012, Fax: 403-454-5500
s.asselin@aiic.net
Gabriela Rangel, Secrétaire régional, 613-863-2843, Fax: 613-821-3134
g.rangel@aiic.net

Aisbel Guerrero, Trésorier régional, 613-841-4934, Fax: 613-818-3957
aisbelguerrero@rogers.com
Linda Ballantyne, Membre du Bureau régional, 514-286-4310, Fax: 514-281-5551
linda.ballantyne@sympatico.ca
Wendy Greene, Membre du Bureau régional, 416-545-1470, Fax: 416-545-0581
wgreene@dialogueinterpreters.ca

L'Association canadienne Angus *See* Canadian Angus Association

Association canadienne d'Accès Vasculaire *See* Canadian Vascular Access Association

Association canadienne d'acoustique *See* Canadian Acoustical Association

Association canadienne d'anatomie, de neurobiologie et de biologie cellulaire *See* Canadian Association for Anatomy, Neurobiology, & Cell Biology

Association canadienne d'archéologie *See* Canadian Archaeological Association

L'Association canadienne d'art photographique *See* Canadian Association for Photographic Art

L'association canadienne d'art thérapie *See* Canadian Art Therapy Association

Association canadienne d'articles de sport *See* Canadian Sporting Goods Association

Association canadienne d'assurance nucléaire *See* Nuclear Insurance Association of Canada

L'Association canadienne d'auto-distribution *See* Canadian Automatic Merchandising Association

Association Canadienne d'Aviron Amateur *See* Rowing Canada Aviron

Association canadienne d'économique *See* Canadian Economics Association

Association canadienne d'éducation *See* Canadian Education Association

Association canadienne d'éducation de langue française (ACELF)
#303, 265, rue de la Couronne, Québec QC G1K 6E1
Tél: 418-681-4661; *Téléc:* 418-681-3389
info@acelf.ca
www.acelf.ca
www.linkedin.com/company/association-canadienne-d%27education-de-langue-francaise
www.facebook.com/acelf.ca
twitter.com/_ACELF
www.youtube.com/acelfcanada
Aperçu: *Dimension:* grande; *Envergure:* nationale; Organisme sans but lucratif; fondée en 1947
Mission: Inspire et soutient le développement et l'action des institutions éducatives francophones du Canada; renforcer la vitalité des communautés francophones
Affiliation(s): UNESCO
Finances: *Budget de fonctionnement annuel:* $500,000-$1.5 Million
Membre(s) du personnel: 9
Membre: 385; *Montant de la cotisation:* 63,24$ individu; 172,46$ taxes incluses collectif; *Critères d'admissibilite:* Doit être une personne, un organisme, une institution ou une association de langue française qui souscrit aux objectifs généraux de l'ACELF et reconnu comme tel par le conseil d'administration; *Comités:* Stages de perfectionnement; thématique du congrès; Semaine nationale de la francophonie; Échanges francophones; Outils d'intervention
Activités: Élaborer des ressources en construction identitaire francophone; Stages de perfectionnement en construction identitaire; Échanges francophones; Congrès annuel pancanadien; Semaine nationale de la francophonie; revue Éducation et francophonie; *Evénements de sensibilisation:* Semaine nationale de la francophonie, mars; *Listes de destinataires:* Oui
Membre(s) du bureau directeur:
Anne Vinet-Roy, Président
Richard Lacombe, Directeur général
lacombe@acelf.ca

Meetings/Conferences:
• Association canadienne d'éducation de langue française 2018 Congrès pancanadien, September, 2018, Moncton, NB
Scope: National
Publications:
• L'ACELF en action [publication de Association canadienne d'éducation de langue française]
Type: Newsletter

Association canadienne d'énergie éolienne *See* Canadian Wind Energy Association

Association canadienne d'énergie fluide *See* Canadian Fluid Power Association

Association canadienne d'équitation thérapeutique *See* Canadian Therapeutic Riding Association

L'Association canadienne d'ergonomie *See* Association of Canadian Ergonomists

Association canadienne d'esperanto *See* Esperanto Association of Canada

Association canadienne d'ethnologie et de folklore *See* Folklore Studies Association of Canada

L'Association canadienne d'études du développement international *See* Canadian Association for the Study of International Development

Association canadienne d'études en loisir *See* Canadian Association for Leisure Studies

Association canadienne d'études environnementales *See* Environmental Studies Association of Canada

Association canadienne d'experts-conseils en patrimoine *See* Canadian Association of Heritage Professionals

Association canadienne d'habitation et de rénovation urbaine *See* Canadian Housing & Renewal Association

L'Association canadienne d'histoire de l'éducation *See* Canadian History of Education Association

Association canadienne d'histoire ferroviaire *See* Canadian Railroad Historical Association

Association canadienne d'hydrographie *See* Canadian Hydrographic Association

Association canadienne d'investissement dans des fiducies de revenu *See* Canadian Association of Income Trusts Investors

Association Canadienne d'oncologie psychosociale *See* Canadian Association of Psychosocial Oncology

Association canadienne d'orthopédie *See* Canadian Orthopaedic Association

Association canadienne de basketball en fauteuil roulant *See* Canadian Wheelchair Basketball Association

Association canadienne de boxe amateur *See* Canadian Amateur Boxing Association

Association canadienne de cadeaux *See* Canadian Gift Association

Association canadienne de cardiologie d'intervention *See* Canadian Association of Interventional Cardiology

Association canadienne de cartographie *See* Canadian Cartographic Association

Association canadienne de caution *See* Surety Association of Canada

Association canadienne de communication *See* Canadian Communication Association

Association canadienne de compagnies de traductions et d'interpretation *See* Association of Canadian Corporations in Translation & Interpretation

L'Association canadienne de counseling et de psychothérapie *See* Canadian Counselling & Psychotherapy Association

Association canadienne de counseling universitaire et collégial *See* Canadian University & College Counselling Association

Association canadienne des constructeurs d'habitations *See* Canadian Home Builders' Association

Association canadienne des constructeurs d'habitations - Nouveau-Brunswick *See* Canadian Home Builders' Association - New Brunswick

Association canadienne des constructeurs de véhicules *See* Canadian Vehicle Manufacturers' Association

Association canadienne des consultantes en lactation *See* Canadian Lactation Consultant Association

Association Canadienne des Consultants en Radio-télédiffusion *See* Canadian Association of Broadcast Consultants

Association canadienne des coopératives financières *See* Canadian Credit Union Association

Association canadienne des cosmétiques, produit de toilette et parfums *See* Canadian Cosmetic, Toiletry & Fragrance Association

Association canadienne des courtiers de fonds mutuels *See* Mutual Fund Dealers Association of Canada

Association Canadienne des Croix Bleue *See* Canadian Association of Blue Cross Plans

Association canadienne des déménageurs *See* Canadian Association of Movers

Association Canadienne des dépanneurs en alimentation *See* Canadian Convenience Stores Association

Association canadienne des détaillants de vélos isdépendants *See* Canadian Independent Bicycle Retailers Association

Association canadienne des directeurs d'école *See* Canadian Association of Principals

Association canadienne des directeurs d'expositions *See* Canadian Association of Exposition Management

Association canadienne des directeurs de l'information en radio-télévision *See* Radio Television Digital News Association (Canada)

Association Canadienne des Directeurs Médicaux en Assurance-Vie *See* Canadian Life Insurance Medical Officers Association

Association canadienne des distributeurs de produits chimiques *See* Canadian Association of Chemical Distributors

Association canadienne des distributeurs et exportateurs de films *See* Canadian Association of Film Distributors & Exporters

Association canadienne des docteurs en naturopathie *See* The Canadian Association of Naturopathic Doctors

Association Canadienne des Doyens et Doyennes d'Éducation *See* Association of Canadian Deans of Education

Association canadienne des eaux potables et usées *See* Canadian Water & Wastewater Association

L'Association canadienne des échecs par correspondance *See* Canadian Correspondence Chess Association

Association canadienne des écoles de sciences infirmières *See* Canadian Association of Schools of Nursing

Association canadienne des éducateurs de musique *See* Canadian Music Educators' Association

L'Association canadienne des éleveurs de porcs *See* Canadian Swine Breeders' Association

Association canadienne des embouteilleurs d'eau *See* Canadian Bottled Water Association

Association canadienne des employés professionnels *See* Canadian Association of Professional Employees

Association Canadienne des Enseignantes et des Enseignants Retraités *See* Canadian Association of Retired Teachers

Association canadienne des entraîneurs *See* Coaching Association of Canada

Association canadienne des entrepreneurs électriciens *See* Canadian Electrical Contractors Association

Association canadienne des entrepreneurs en couverture *See* Canadian Roofing Contractors' Association

Association canadienne des entrepreneurs en mousse de polyuréthane *See* Canadian Urethane Foam Contractors Association

Association canadienne des entreprises de géomatique *See* Geomatics Industry Association of Canada

Association canadienne des épices *See* Canadian Spice Association

Association canadienne des ergothérapeutes *See* Canadian Association of Occupational Therapists

Association canadienne des études asiatiques *See* Canadian Asian Studies Association

Association canadienne des études cinématographiques *See* Film Studies Association of Canada

Association canadienne des études hongroises *See* Hungarian Studies Association of Canada

Association canadienne des études latino-américaines et caraïbes *See* Canadian Association for Latin American & Caribbean Studies

Association canadienne des études patristiques *See* Canadian Society of Patristic Studies

L'Association canadienne des études sur l'alimentation *See* Canadian Association for Food Studies

Association canadienne des étudiants et internes en pharmacie *See* Canadian Association of Pharmacy Students & Interns

Association canadienne des évaluateurs de capacités de travail société *See* Canadian Assessment, Vocational Evaluation & Work Adjustment Society

L'Association canadienne des ex-parlementaires *See* Canadian Association of Former Parliamentarians

Association canadienne des experts indépendants *See* Canadian Independent Adjusters' Association

Association canadienne des exportateurs à l'alimentation *See* Canadian Food Exporters Association

Association canadienne des fabricants de fermes de bois *See* Canadian Wood Truss Association

Association canadienne des fabricants de produits de quincaillerie et d'articles ménagers *See* Canadian Hardware & Housewares Manufacturers' Association

Association canadienne des fabricants de tuyaux de béton *See* Canadian Concrete Pipe Association

Association canadienne des fabricants des grignotines *See* Canadian Snack Food Association

Association canadienne des femmes cadres et entrepreneurs *See* Canadian Association of Women Executives & Entrepreneurs

Association canadienne des femmes d'assurance *See* Canadian Association of Insurance Women

Association canadienne des femmes en communication *See* Canadian Women in Communications

Association canadienne des foires et expositions *See* Canadian Association of Fairs & Exhibitions

Association canadienne des fondements de l'éducation *See* Canadian Association of Foundations of Education

Association canadienne des fournisseurs de chemins de fer *See* Canadian Association of Railway Suppliers

Association canadienne des géographes *See* Canadian Association of Geographers

Association canadienne des gestionnaires de fonds de retraite *See* Pension Investment Association of Canada

Association canadienne des greffes *See* Canadian Transplant Association

Association canadienne des harmonies *See* Canadian Band Association

Association canadienne des hygiènistes dentaires *See* Canadian Dental Hygienists Association

Association canadienne des importateurs & exportateurs *See* Canadian Association of Importers & Exporters

Association canadienne des importateurs règlementés *See* Canadian Association of Regulated Importers

Association canadienne des industries du recyclage *See* Canadian Association of Recycling Industries

Association canadienne des infirmières en oncologie *See* Canadian Association of Nurses in Oncology

Association canadienne des infirmières en soins holistiques *See* Canadian Holistic Nurses Association

Association canadienne des infirmières et infirmiers en gérontologie *See* Canadian Gerontological Nursing Association

Association canadienne des infirmières et infirmiers en hépatologie *See* Canadian Association of Hepatology Nurses

Association canadienne des infirmières et infirmiers en orthopédie *See* Canadian Orthopaedic Nurses Association

Association canadienne des infirmières et infirmiers en périnatalité et en santé des femmes *See* Canadian Association of Perinatal & Women's Health Nurses

Association canadienne des infirmières et infirmiers en santé du travail *See* Canadian Occupational Health Nurses Association

Association canadienne des infirmières et infirmiers en sidologie *See* Canadian Association of Nurses in HIV/AIDS Care

Association canadienne des infirmières et infirmiers en soins intensifs *See* Canadian Association of Critical Care Nurses

Association canadienne des infirmières et infirmiers et technologues de néphrologie *See* Canadian Association of Nephrology Nurses & Technologists

Association Canadienne des Infirmiers et Infirmieres d'Apheresis *See* Canadian Association of Apheresis Nurses

Association canadienne des infirmiers et infirmières en sciences neurologiques *See* Canadian Association of Neuroscience Nurses

Association canadienne des inspecteur(e)s en bâtiments du Québec *Voir* Canadian Association of Home & Property Inspectors

Association canadienne des inspecteurs de biens immobiliers *See* Canadian Association of Home & Property Inspectors

Association canadienne des institutions financières en assurance *See* Canadian Association of Financial Institutions in Insurance

Association canadienne des intervenants en formation policière *See* Canadian Association of Police Educators

Association canadienne des investisseurs obligataires *See* Canadian Bond Investors' Association

L'Association canadienne des journalistes *See* Canadian Association of Journalists

L'Association canadienne des juges de cours provinciales *See* Canadian Association of Provincial Court Judges

Association canadienne des juristes de l'État *See* Canadian Association of Crown Counsel

Association canadienne des juristes-traducteurs (ACJT) / Canadian Association of Legal Translators (CALT)

a/s OOTTIAQ, #1108, 2021, av Union, Montréal QC H3A 2S9
Courriel: info@acjt.ca
www.acjt.ca
Aperçu: *Dimension:* petite; *Envergure:* nationale; fondée en 1988
Mission: Pour promouvoir le double qualification comme avocat (ou juriste) et comme traducteur pour la traduction de documents juridiques.

Canadian Associations / Association canadienne des métiers de la truelle, section locale 100 (CTC) / Trowel Trades Canadian Association, Local 100 (CLC)

Membre: 156
Membre(s) du bureau directeur:
Louis Fortier, President

Association canadienne des laboratoires d'essais *Voir* Association des consultants et laboratoires experts

Association canadienne des lésés cérébraux *See* Brain Injury Association of Canada

Association canadienne des libertés civiles *See* Canadian Civil Liberties Association

Association canadienne des maîtres de poste et adjoints *See* Canadian Postmasters & Assistants Association

Association canadienne des maîtres en ski de fond *See* Canadian Masters Cross-Country Ski Association

Association canadienne des manufacturiers de palettes et contenants *See* Canadian Wood Pallet & Container Association

Association canadienne des marchands numismatiques *See* Canadian Association of Numismatic Dealers

Association canadienne des marchés des capitaux *See* Canadian Capital Markets Association

Association canadienne des massothérapeutes du sport *See* Canadian Sport Massage Therapists Association

L'Association canadienne des medecins et chirurgiens bariatrique *See* Canadian Association of Bariatric Physicians & Surgeons

Association canadienne des médecins vétérinaires *See* Canadian Veterinary Medical Association

Association canadienne des métiers de la truelle, section locale 100 (CTC) / Trowel Trades Canadian Association, Local 100 (CLC)
#2000, 565, rue Crémazie est, Montréal QC H2M 2V6
Tél: 514-326-3691; Téléc: 514-326-5562
Ligne sans frais: 888-326-3691
acmt@qc.aira.com
truellelocal100.org
www.facebook.com/ACMTLOCAL100
Aperçu: Dimension: moyenne; *Envergure:* nationale
Mission: La FTQ-Construction a, bien entendu, de manière très précise le mandat de négocier les conventions collectives applicables dans les sous secteurs d'activités (industriel, commercial et institutionnel, génie civil et voirie, résidentiel) et de voir à leur application. Mais bien au-delà de ce mandat traditionnel, la FTQ-Construction veut s'assurer d'être présent dans l'ensemble des débats représentant un intérêt pour les travailleurs et les travailleuses qu'il représente.
Membre: 2 000 en 4 régions
Membre(s) du bureau directeur:
Roger Poirier, Directeur-général

Association canadienne des moniteurs de ski nordique *See* Canadian Association of Nordic Ski Instructors

Association canadienne des moniteurs de surf des neiges *See* Canadian Association of Snowboard Instructors

Association canadienne des mouleurs sous pression *See* Canadian Die Casters Association

Association canadienne des musicothérapeutes *See* Canadian Association of Music Therapists

Association canadienne des négociants en timbres-poste *See* Canadian Stamp Dealers' Association

Association Canadienne des Officiels de Football *See* Canadian Football Officials Association

Association canadienne des oncologues médicaux *See* Canadian Association of Medical Oncologists

Association canadienne des optométristes *See* Canadian Association of Optometrists

Association canadienne des organismes artistiques *See* Canadian Arts Presenting Association

Association canadienne des organismes de contrôle des régimes de retraite *See* Canadian Association of Pension Supervisory Authorities

Association canadienne des orthodontists *See* Canadian Association of Orthodontists

Association canadienne des paiements *See* Canadian Payments Association

Association canadienne des palynologues *See* Canadian Association of Palynologists

Association canadienne des parajuristes *See* Canadian Association of Paralegals

Association canadienne des parcs et loisirs *See* Canadian Parks & Recreation Association

Association canadienne des pathologistes *See* Canadian Association of Pathologists

Association canadienne des pensionnés et rentiers militaires *See* Armed Forces Pensioners'/Annuitants' Association of Canada

Association canadienne des physiciens et physiciennes *See* Canadian Association of Physicists

Association canadienne des pilotes d'avions ultra-légers *See* Ultralight Pilots Association of Canada

Association canadienne des policiers *See* Canadian Police Association

Association canadienne des prêteurs sur salaire *See* Canadian Payday Loan Association

Association canadienne des producteurs d'acier *See* Canadian Steel Producers Association

Association canadienne des producteurs de semences *See* Canadian Seed Growers' Association

Association canadienne des producteurs pétroliers *See* Canadian Association of Petroleum Producers

Association canadienne des professeures et professeurs d'université *See* Canadian Association of University Teachers

Association canadienne des professeurs d'immersion (ACPI) / Canadian Association of Immersion Teachers (CAIT)
#1104, 170, rue Gloucester, Ottawa ON K15 5V5
Tél: 613-230-9111; Téléc: 613-230-5940
bureau@acpi.ca
www.acpi.ca
www.facebook.com/acpimmersion
twitter.com/acpi_
Aperçu: Dimension: moyenne; *Envergure:* nationale; Organisme sans but lucratif; fondée en 1977
Finances: Budget de fonctionnement annuel: $50,000-$100,000
Membre(s) du personnel: 4
Membre: 1 400; *Montant de la cotisation:* 45$
Membre(s) du bureau directeur:
Chantal Bourbonnais, Directrice générale
cbourbonnais@acpi.ca

Association canadienne des professeurs de comptabilité *See* Canadian Academic Accounting Association

Association canadienne des professeurs de danse *See* Canadian Dance Teachers' Association

Association canadienne des professeurs de langues secondes *See* Canadian Association of Second Language Teachers

Association Canadienne des Professionels de l'Apiculture *See* Canadian Association of Professional Apiculturists

Association canadienne des professionnels de l'insolvabilité et de la réorganisation *See* Canadian Association of Insolvency & Restructuring Professionals

Association canadienne des professionnels de la sécurité routière *See* Canadian Association of Road Safety Professionals

Association canadienne des professionnels de la vente *See* Canadian Professional Sales Association

Association canadienne des professionnels des services alimentaires *See* Canadian Association of Foodservice Professionals

Association canadienne des professionnels en conditionnement physique *See* The Canadian Association of Fitness Professionals

Association canadienne des professionnels en conformité *See* Association of Canadian Compliance Professionals

Association canadienne des professionnels en dons planifiés *See* Canadian Association of Gift Planners

Association canadienne des professionnels en réglementation *See* Canadian Association of Professional Regulatory Affairs

Association canadienne des programmes d'aide aux employés *See* Canadian Employee Assistance Program Association

Association canadienne des programmes de ressources pour la famille *See* Canadian Association of Family Resource Programs

Association canadienne des prospecteurs & entrepreneurs *See* Prospectors & Developers Association of Canada

Association canadienne des radiodiffuseurs *See* Canadian Association of Broadcasters

L'Association canadienne des radiologistes *See* Canadian Association of Radiologists

Association canadienne des relations industrielles (ACRI) / Canadian Industrial Relations Association (CIRA)
Département des relations industrielles, Université Laval, #3129, 1025, av des Sciences-Humaines, Québec QC G1V 0A6
Courriel: acri-cira@rlt.ulaval.ca
www.cira-acri.ca
Aperçu: Dimension: moyenne; *Envergure:* nationale; Organisme sans but lucratif; fondée en 1963
Mission: Promouvoir la discussion, la recherche, et la formation dans le domaine des relations industrielles
Affiliation(s): International Industrial Relations Association; Industrial Relations Research Association; La Fédération canadienne des sciences sociales
Finances: Budget de fonctionnement annuel: Moins de $50,000
Membre(s) du personnel: 1
Membre: 400; *Montant de la cotisation:* 120$ régulier; 60$ étudiant/retraité; 160$ institutionnel; *Critères d'admissibilité:* Ouverte à toute personne ou organisation qui s'intéresse aux relations industrielles, par exemple aux relations patronales-syndicales, au droit du travail, aux problèmes de main-d'oeuvre et à la gestion des ressources humaines; parmi les membres actuels de l'Association, on retrouve des avocats, des économistes, des sociologues, des syndicalistes, des gestionnaires; quatre catégories de membres - régulier, institutionnel, étudiant, à la retraite
Activités: Congrès annuel; *Listes de destinataires:* Oui
Membre(s) du bureau directeur:
Kelly Williams Whitt, Président
kelly.williams@uleth.ca
Étienne Cantin, Secrétaire
etienne.cantin@rlt.ulaval.ca
Prix, Bourses:
• Le prix Allen Ponak
Eligibility: Étudiant aux études supérieures; *Amount:* 500$
• Prix Gérard Dion
Eligibility: Personne our organisation qui s'est démarquée dans sa discipline
• Prix H.D. Woods
Eligibility: Praticien ou praticienne ou une personne du milieu académique du domaine des relations industrielles
Meetings/Conferences:
• Canadian Industrial Relations Association 2018 Conference, May, 2018, Montréal, QC
Scope: National

Association canadienne des représentants de ventes en gros *See* Canadian Association of Wholesale Sales Representatives

L'Association Canadienne des Residents en Orthopédie *See* Canadian Orthopaedic Residents Association

Association canadienne des ressources hydriques *See* Canadian Water Resources Association

Association canadienne des restaurateurs professionnels *See* Canadian Association of Professional Conservators

Association canadienne des réviseurs *See* Editors' Association of Canada

Association canadienne des revues savantes *See* Canadian Association of Learned Journals

L'Association canadienne des sages-femmes *See* Canadian Association of Midwives

Association canadienne des sciences de l'information *See* Canadian Association for Information Science

Association canadienne des sciences géomatiques *See* Canadian Institute of Geomatics

Association canadienne des sciences régionales (ACSR) / Canadian Regional Science Association (CRSA)
3359 Mississauga Rd. North, Mississauga ON L5L 1C6
geog.utm.utoronto.ca/crsa-acsr
Aperçu: *Dimension:* petite; *Envergure:* nationale; fondée en 1977
Mission: Favoriser la circulation des idées et promouvoir les études canadiennes portant sur les régions en se servant d'instruments, de méthodes et de cadres théoriques; propos aux sciences régionales comme ceux mis en avant par les diverses sciences, sociales ou autres
Membre de: Humanities & Social Sciences Federation of Canada
Finances: *Budget de fonctionnement annuel:* Moins de $50,000
Membre: 245; *Montant de la cotisation:* 60$ individuel; 25$ étudiant/sans emploi
Activités: *Listes de destinataires:* Oui
Membre(s) du bureau directeur:
Pierre Desrochers, Secrétaire-trésorier
Publications:
• Revue canadienne des sciences régionales [publication d'Association canadienne des sciences régionales]

Association canadienne des slavistes *See* Canadian Association of Slavists

Association canadienne des Snowbirds *See* Canadian Snowbird Association

Association canadienne des sociétés Elizabeth Fry *See* Canadian Association of Elizabeth Fry Societies

Association canadienne des sociétés fraternelles *See* Canadian Fraternal Association

Association canadienne des spécialistes en emploi et des employeurs *See* Canadian Association of Career Educators & Employers

L'Association canadienne des sports d'hiver *See* Canadian Snowsports Association

Association canadienne des sports en fauteuil roulant *See* Canadian Wheelchair Sports Association

Association canadienne des sports pour amputés *See* Canadian Amputee Sports Association

Association canadienne des sports pour aveugles inc. *See* Canadian Blind Sports Association Inc.

Association canadienne des stomathérapeutes *See* Canadian Association for Enterostomal Therapy

Association canadienne des surintendants de golf *See* Canadian Golf Superintendents Association

Association canadienne des techniciens en explosif *See* Canadian Explosive Technicians' Association

Association canadienne des technologues en electroneurophysiologie inc. *See* Canadian Association of Electroneurophysiology Technologists Inc.

Association canadienne des technologues en radiation médicale *See* Canadian Association of Medical Radiation Technologists

Association canadienne des télécommunications sans fil *See* Canadian Wireless Telecommunications Association

Association canadienne des thérapeutes du sport *See* Canadian Athletic Therapists Association

Association canadienne des travailleurs sociaux *See* Canadian Association of Social Workers

Association canadienne des travaux publics *See* Canadian Public Works Association

Association canadienne des traversiers *See* Canadian Ferry Association

Association Canadienne des Troubles Anxieux *See* Anxiety Disorders Association of Canada

L'association Canadienne des troubles d'apprentissage *See* Learning Disabilities Association of Canada

Association canadienne des tunnels *See* Tunnelling Association of Canada

Association canadienne des utilisateurs SAS *See* Canadian Association of SAS Users

Association canadienne des vétérans de la Corée *See* Korea Veterans Association of Canada Inc., Heritage Unit

Association Canadienne des Vétérans des Forces de la Paix pour les Nations Unies *See* Canadian Association of Veterans in United Nations Peacekeeping

Association Canadienne des Vétérinaires Porcins *See* Canadian Association of Swine Veterinarians

Association canadienne des victimes de la thalidomide *See* Thalidomide Victims Association of Canada

Association canadienne droit et société *See* Canadian Law & Society Association

Association canadienne du bison *See* Canadian Bison Association

Association canadienne du camionnage d'entreprise *See* Private Motor Truck Council of Canada

Association canadienne du capital de risque et d'investissement *See* Canada's Venture Capital & Private Equity Association

Association canadienne du cartonnage ondulé et du carton-caisse *See* Canadian Corrugated Containerboard Association

Association canadienne du cheval Percheron *See* Canadian Percheron Association

Association canadienne du ciment *See* Cement Association of Canada

Association canadienne du commerce des semences *See* Canadian Seed Trade Association

Association canadienne du commerce des valeurs mobilières *See* Investment Industry Association of Canada

Association canadienne du Contreplaqué et de Placages de bois dur *See* Canadian Hardwood Plywood & Veneer Association

Association canadienne du contrôle du trafic aérien *See* Canadian Air Traffic Control Association

Association canadienne du couvre-plancher, nettoyage et restauration *See* Canadian Flooring, Cleaning & Restoration Association

Association canadienne du diabète *See* Diabetes Canada

Association canadienne du droit de l'environnement *See* Canadian Environmental Law Association

Association canadienne du droit des technologies de l'information *See* Canadian IT Law Association

Association canadienne du gaz *See* Canadian Gas Association

L'Association canadienne du Jouet *See* Canadian Toy Association / Canadian Toy & Hobby Fair

Association canadienne du marketing *See* Canadian Marketing Association

L'Association canadienne du médicament générique *See* Canadian Generic Pharmaceutical Association

Association canadienne du parachutisme sportif *See* Canadian Sport Parachuting Association

Association canadienne du personnel administratif universitaire *See* Canadian Association of University Business Officers

Association canadienne du plongeon amateur Inc. *See* Diving Plongeon Canada

L'Association canadienne du pneu et du caoutchouc *See* Tire and Rubber Association of Canada

Association canadienne du propane *See* Canadian Propane Association

Association canadienne du soin des plaies *See* Canadian Association of Wound Care

Association canadienne du sport collégial *See* Canadian Collegiate Athletic Association

Association canadienne du téléphone indépendant *See* Canadian Independent Telephone Association

Association canadienne du transport urbain *See* Canadian Urban Transit Association

Association canadienne du véhicule récréatif *See* Canadian Recreational Vehicle Association

L'association Canadienne en psychopedagogie *See* Canadian Association for Educational Psychology

Association canadienne en vibrations de machines *See* Canadian Machinery Vibration Association

Association canadienne française pour l'avancement des sciences *Voir* Association francophone pour le savoir

Association canadienne Hereford *See* Canadian Hereford Association

Association canadienne pour l'avancement des études néerlandaises *See* Canadian Association for the Advancement of Netherlandic Studies

Association canadienne pour l'avancement des femmes du sport et de l'activité physique *See* Canadian Association for the Advancement of Women & Sport & Physical Activity

Association canadienne pour l'éducation médicale *See* Canadian Association for Medical Education

Association canadienne pour l'étude de l'administration scolaire *See* Canadian Association for the Study of Educational Administration

Association canadienne pour l'étude de l'éducation des adultes *See* Canadian Association for the Study of Adult Education

Association canadienne pour l'etude de l'éducation des autochtones *See* Canadian Association for the Study of Indigenous Education

Association canadienne pour l'étude des langues et de la littérature du Commonwealth *See* Canadian Association for Commonwealth Literature & Language Studies

Association canadienne pour l'étude du foie *See* Canadian Association for the Study of the Liver

Association canadienne pour l'étude du Quaternaire *See* Canadian Quaternary Association

Association canadienne pour l'étude sur les femmes et l'éducation *See* Canadian Association for the Study of Women & Education

Association canadienne pour l'histoire du nursing *See* Canadian Association for the History of Nursing

Association canadienne pour l'intégration communautaire *See* Canadian Association for Community Living

Association canadienne pour l'obtention des services aux personnes autistiques *See* Society for Treatment of Autism

Association canadienne pour la conservation et la restauration des biens culturels *See* Canadian Association for Conservation of Cultural Property

Association canadienne pour la formation des enseignants *See* Canadian Association for Teacher Education

Association canadienne pour la formation en travail social *See* Canadian Association for Social Work Education

L'association canadienne pour la prévention de la discrimination et du harcèlement en milieu d'enseignement supérieur *See* Canadian Association for the Prevention of Discrimination & Harassment in Higher Education

L'Association canadienne pour la prévention du suicide *See* Canadian Association for Suicide Prevention

Association canadienne pour la promotion des services de garde à l'enfance See Child Care Advocacy Association of Canada

Association canadienne pour la recherche infirmière See Canadian Association for Nursing Research

Association canadienne pour la recherche sur les services et les politiques de la santé See Canadian Association for Health Services & Policy Research

L'Association canadienne pour la reconnaissance des acquis See Canadian Association for Prior Learning Assesment

Association canadienne pour la santé mentale See Canadian Mental Health Association

Association canadienne pour la science des animaux de laboratoire See Canadian Association for Laboratory Animal Science

Association canadienne pour les énergies renouvelables See Canadian Association for Renewable Energies

Association canadienne pour les études de renseignement et de sécurité See Canadian Association for Security & Intelligence Studies

L'Association canadienne pour les études irlandaises See Canadian Association for Irish Studies

Association canadienne pour les études supérieures See Canadian Association for Graduate Studies

Association canadienne pour les études sur la coopération See Canadian Association for Studies in Co-operation

Association canadienne pour les jeunes enfants See Canadian Association for Young Children

Association canadienne pour les Nations Unies See United Nations Association in Canada

Association Canadienne pour les Plantes Fourragères See Canadian Forage & Grassland Association

Association canadienne pour les skieurs handicapés See Canadian Association for Disabled Skiing

Association canadienne pour les structures et matériaux composites See Canadian Association for Composite Structures & Materials

Association canadienne pour une étude pratique de la loi dans le système éducatif See Canadian Association for the Practical Study of Law in Education

Association canadienne sur la qualité de l'eau See Canadian Association on Water Quality

Association canadienne Tourbe de Sphaigne See Canadian Sphagnum Peat Moss Association

Association canadienne-française de l'Alberta (ACFA)
#303, Pav. II, 8627, rue Marie-Anne-Gaboury, Edmonton AB T6C 3N1
Tél: 780-466-1680; *Téléc:* 780-465-6773
acfa@acfa.ab.ca
www.acfa.ab.ca
www.facebook.com/acfaab
www.youtube.com/user/acfaab
Aperçu: Dimension: moyenne; *Envergure:* provinciale; Organisme sans but lucratif; fondée en 1926 surveillé par Fédération des communautés francophones et acadienne du Canada
Mission: Représenter la population francophone de l'Alberta; promouvoir le bien-être intellectuel, culturel et social des francophones de l'Alberta; encourager, faciliter et développer l'enseignement en français; entretenir des relations amicales avec les groupes de différentes origines ethniques et anglophones dans la province
Membre de: Association canadienne d'éducation de langue française
Affiliation(s): Fédération culturelle canadienne-française
Membre(s) du personnel: 9
Membre: 13 associations régionales
Activités: Service de conférenciers: Oui; *Bibliothèque:* rendez-vous
Membre(s) du bureau directeur:
Isabelle Laurin, Directrice générale
i.laurin@acfa.ab.ca

Association canadienne-française de l'Ontario (ACFO) *Voir* Association canadienne-française de l'Ontario, Mille-îles

Association canadienne-française de l'Ontario, Mille-îles (ACFOMI)
Barriefield Centre, 760, Hwy. 15, Kingston ON K7L 0C3
Tél: 613-546-7863; *Téléc:* 613-546-7918
Ligne sans frais: 800-561-4695
info@acfomi.org
www.acfomi.org/acfo
Nom précédent: Association canadienne-française de l'Ontario (ACFO)
Aperçu: Dimension: moyenne; *Envergure:* provinciale surveillé par Fédération des communautés francophones et acadienne du Canada
Mission: Appuyer le développement communautaire; rassembler les forces vives de la communauté franco-ontarienne; faire des représentations politiques
Membre: 1-99; *Critères d'admissibilite:* Quiconque de langue ou de culture française résident en Ontario
Membre(s) du bureau directeur:
Lucie Mercier, Directrice générale

Association canadienne-française de Régina (ACFR)
#100, 3850, rue Hillsdale, Regina SK S4S 7J5
Tél: 306-545-4533
www.acfr.ca
www.facebook.com/acfr.deregina
twitter.com/communautairea1
Aperçu: Dimension: petite; *Envergure:* locale; fondée en 1965 surveillé par Fédération des communautéS francophones et acadienne du Canada
Mission: Assurer une concertation entre les associations francophones de Régina; assurer la visibilité des francophones de Régina; promouvoir l'épanouissement de la langue française dans les secteurs ci-haut mentionnés; assurer l'accès à des services répondant aux besoins de la communauté francophone de Régina; défendre et promouvoir les droits et les intérêts des francophones de Régina; offrir aux associations communautaires des services d'information
Membre de: Association culturelle franco-canadienne de la Saskatchewan
Affiliation(s): Commission culturelle fransaskoise; Regina Multicultural Council
Membre(s) du personnel: 3
Membre: Critères d'admissibilite: Francophones et francophiles; *Comités:* Comité culturel
Activités: Activités sociales, culturelles, éducatives et sportives; vente de produits français
Membre(s) du bureau directeur:
Jessica Chartier, Directrice générale
direction.acfr@gmail.com
Siriki Diabagaté, Président
Jean-Marie Allard, Vice-président
Isabelle Nkapnang, Trésorière

Association Carrefour Famille Montcalm (ACFM)
197, rue Industrielle, Saint-Lin-Laurentides QC J5M 2S9
Tél: 450-439-2669; *Téléc:* 450-439-8763
Ligne sans frais: 877-439-2669
info@acfm-qc.org
www.acfmqc.org
www.facebook.com/293704847321436
Également appelé: Maison de la Famille Montcalm
Nom précédent: Association des familles monoparentales et recomposées de Montcalm
Aperçu: Dimension: petite; *Envergure:* locale; Organisme sans but lucratif; fondée en 1986
Mission: Le but premier de l'association est d'améliorer la qualité de vie de toutes les familles qui résident dans le comté de Montcalm en leur apportant les ressources et les outils nécessaires
Membre de: Familles de Montcalm
Affiliation(s): Fédération des associations de familles monoparentales du Québec; Fédération québécoise des organismes communautaires Famille; Carrefour Jeunesse Emploi; Les Filandières; Centre Jeunesse; Le Tremplin; Régie régionale de la Santé et des Services sociaux des Laurentides; Centraide; Santé Canada; Le Réseau; Centre local de services communautaires
Finances: Fonds: Gouvernement régional
Membre(s) du personnel: 20
Membre: Montant de la cotisation: Gratuite; *Critères d'admissibilite:* Familles
Activités: Accueil, écoute et références; journal mensuel; ateliers; relation d'aide; sorties familiales; rencontres avec intervenants; alphabétisation; café; rencontres; toxicomanie; transport accompagnement; Halte-garderie; conferences; location sieges d'auto; Programme d'Aide Personnelle, Familiale, et Communautaire; Programme d'action communautaire pour les enfants; *Stagiaires:* Oui; *Service de conférenciers:* Oui
Membre(s) du bureau directeur:
Henri Thibodeau, Directeur général
henri.thibodeau@acfm-qc.org
Nathalie Tessier, Présidente
Jennifer Mojor, Vice-présidente par intérim

L'Association catholique de la santé du Nouveau-Brunswick See Catholic Health Association of New Brunswick

Association catholique franco-canadienne de la Saskatchewan; Association culturelle franco-canadienne de la Saskatchewan *Voir* Assemblée communautaire fransaskoise

Association catholique manitobaine de la santé See Catholic Health Association of Manitoba

Association CFA Montréal / Montreal CFA Society
CP 49644, Succ. Musée, Montréal QC H3T 2A5
Tél: 514-990-4720
Autres numéros: Alt. courriel: activity@cfamontreal.org
info@cfamontreal.org
www.cfamontreal.org
www.linkedin.com/company/2400033
www.facebook.com/cfamontreal
twitter.com/cfamontreal
Également appelé: Association des analystes financiers de Montréal
Aperçu: Dimension: petite; *Envergure:* locale; fondée en 1950
Mission: Faire respecter le code de déontologie et les règles de comportement professionel élaboré par le CFA Institute à l'intention des professionnels de l'industrie de l'analyse financière de manière à assurer la qualité et la perception de notre profession auprès du public. Appuyer ses membres dans leurs efforts de perfectionnement et de formation par le biais de: conférences avec un grand contenu formatif, de nature pratique ou théorique; cours de préparation à l'examen du CFA Institute; la promotion du programme d'accréditation du CFA Institute pour les membres possédant déjà le titre de CFA
Membre: 2 500; *Comités:* Programme; adhésion; communications; relations universitaires; gouvernance; relations avec les employeurs et autres associations; développement carrière; réeseaux sociaux et avantages aux membres
Activités: Evénements de sensibilisation: Soirée bénéfice annuelle
Membre(s) du bureau directeur:
Frederick Chenel, Président
Caroline Soulas, Directrice générale
caroline.soulas@cfamontreal.org

Association chasse & pêche de Chibougamau
CP 171, Chibougamau QC G8P 2K6
Tél: 418-748-2021
info@acpcchibougamau.org
www.acpcchibougamau.com
Aperçu: Dimension: petite; *Envergure:* locale
Mission: Favoriser et développer parmi les membres l'esprit sportif en préservant la conservation des richesses naturelles
Membre(s) du bureau directeur:
Serge Picard, Président

Association chasse et pêche du Lac Brébeuf
247, ch du Lac Brébeuf, Saint-Félix-d'Otis QC G0V 1M0
Tél: 418-544-4884; *Téléc:* 418-544-7456
Aperçu: Dimension: petite; *Envergure:* locale
Mission: S'occupe de ce territoire protégé et contrôlé de chasse, de pêche et de villégiature
Affiliation(s): Regroupement régional de gestionnaires de Zec
Finances: Fonds: Gouvernement provincial

Association chiropratique canadienne See Canadian Chiropractic Association

Association chiropratique de l'Ontario See Ontario Chiropractic Association

Association chrétienne du travail du Canada See Christian Labour Association of Canada

Association Cinématographique - Canada See Motion Picture Association - Canada

L'Association commerciale Hong Kong-Canada *See* Hong Kong-Canada Business Association

L'Association communautaire francophone de St-Jean (ACFSJ) / St. John's Francophone Community Association
#245, 65, rue Ridge, St. John's NL A1B 4P5
Tél: 709-726-4900
bonjour@acfsj.ca
www.acfsj.ca
Également appelé: Association francophone de St-Jean
Aperçu: *Dimension:* petite; *Envergure:* locale; fondée en 2003
Mission: Inspirer et soutenir le développement et l'action de la communauté francophone de St-Jean par le biais du centre scolaire et communautaire des Grands-Vents
Membre de: Le Fédération des francophones de Terre-Neuve et du Labrador
Membre(s) du personnel: 4
Membre: *Montant de la cotisation:* 20$ individu; 40$ famille; 15$ étudiant
Activités: Programmation socio-culturelle; *Bibliothèque:* Centre de ressources Centre scolaire et communautaire des Grands-; Bibliothèque publique
Membre(s) du bureau directeur:
Adrienne Pratt, Directrice générale

Association continentale pour l'automatisation des bâtiments *See* Continental Automated Buildings Association

Association coopérative d'économie familiale - Abitibi-Témiscamingue
CP 514, Rouyn-Noranda QC J9X 3C6
Tél: 819-279-5721
acef.at@gmail.com
Également appelé: ACEF - Abitibi-Témiscamingue
Aperçu: *Dimension:* petite; *Envergure:* locale; Organisme sans but lucratif
Mission: Défendre les droits des consommateurs; éducation et prévention en matière de budget, crédit, endettement
Membre de: Fédération des ACEF du Québec
Activités: Consultation budgétaire, cours sur le budget - service aux consommateurs

Association coopérative d'économie familiale - Amiante, Beauce, Etchemins; Association coopérative d'économie familiale - Thetford Mines *Voir* Association coopérative d'économie familiale - Appalaches, Beauce, Etchemins

Association coopérative d'économie familiale - Appalaches, Beauce, Etchemins
1176, rue Notre-Dame est, Thetford Mines QC G6G 1J1
Tél: 418-338-4755; *Téléc:* 418-338-6234
Ligne sans frais: 888-338-4755
info@acef-abe.org
www.acef-abe.org
www.facebook.com/ACEF.ABE
twitter.com/AcefAbe
Également appelé: ACEF - Appalaches-Beauce-Etchemins
Nom précédent: Association coopérative d'économie familiale - Amiante, Beauce, Etchemins; Association coopérative d'économie familiale - Thetford Mines
Aperçu: *Dimension:* petite; *Envergure:* locale; Organisme sans but lucratif; fondée en 1967 surveillé par Union des consommateurs
Mission: Intervenir dans les domaines du budget, du crédit, de l'endettement et de la protection des consommateurs; défendre les droits des personnes assistées sociales
Membre de: Union des consommateurs

Association coopérative d'économie familiale - Estrie
#202, 187, rue Laurier, Sherbrooke QC J1H 4Z4
Tél: 819-563-8144
acefestrie@consommateur.qc.ca
www.acefestrie.ca
Également appelé: ACEF - Estrie
Aperçu: *Dimension:* petite; *Envergure:* locale; Organisme sans but lucratif; fondée en 1972 surveillé par Union des consommateurs
Mission: De défendre et de promouvoir des droits des consommatrices et consommateurs
Membre de: Union des consommateurs
Affiliation(s): Table d'action contre l'appauvrissement Estrie; Solidarité populaire Estrie
Finances: *Fonds:* Agence de l'efficacité énergétique; Secrétariat à l'action communautaire autonome du Québec (SACA)

Membre: *Montant de la cotisation:* 10$ individuel; 5$ personne à faible revenu; 25$ organisme; 100$ syndicat; *Critères d'admissibilite:* Individus; organismes; syndicats; caisses populaires
Activités: Rencontre d'information; service aux consommateurs; *Bibliothèque:* Centre de documentation

Association coopérative d'économie familiale - Granby *Voir* Association coopérative d'économie familiale - Montérégie-est

Association coopérative d'économie familiale - Lanaudière
#124, 200, rue de Salaberry, Joliette QC J6E 4G1
Tél: 450-756-1333; *Téléc:* 450-759-8749
Ligne sans frais: 866-414-1333
www.consommateur.qc.ca/acef-lan
www.facebook.com/314361095272708
Également appelé: ACEF - Lanaudière
Aperçu: *Dimension:* petite; *Envergure:* locale; Organisme sans but lucratif; fondée en 1974 surveillé par Union des consommateurs
Membre de: Union des consommateurs
Finances: *Budget de fonctionnement annuel:* $100,000-$250,000
Membre(s) du personnel: 7
Membre: 100-499; *Critères d'admissibilite:* Individus, coopératives, OSBL
Activités: Consultation budgétaire; cours en budget et consommation; ateliers thématiques; conseils en crédit, budget familial, endettement et consommation
Membre(s) du bureau directeur:
Lise Dalpé, Coordonnatrice

Association coopérative d'économie familiale - Mauricie *Voir* Centre d'intervention budgétaire et sociale de la Mauricie

Association coopérative d'économie familiale - Montérégie-est
162, rue St-Charles sud, Granby QC J2G 7A4
Tél: 450-375-1443; *Téléc:* 450-776-1364
Ligne sans frais: 888-375-1443
acefme@videotron.ca
www.acefmonteregie-est.com
Également appelé: ACEF - Montérégie-est
Nom précédent: Association coopérative d'économie familiale - Granby
Aperçu: *Dimension:* petite; *Envergure:* locale; Organisme sans but lucratif; fondée en 1974 surveillé par Union des consommateurs
Mission: Promouvoir et à défendre les intérêts des consommateurs à faibles et moyens revenus.
Membre de: Union des consommateurs
Membre(s) du personnel: 7
Membre: *Critères d'admissibilité:* Individus et syndicats
Activités: Consultations budgétaires; rencontres éducatives sur le budget et sur la loi de la protection du consommateur; cours sur le budget; service de référence et d'aide en consommation; *Stagiaires:* Oui; *Service de conférenciers:* Oui
Membre(s) du bureau directeur:
Roger Lafrance, Coordinateur
coordo.acefme@videotron.ca
Prix, Bourses:
• Office de la protection du consommateur

Association coopérative d'économie familiale - Montréal (Centre) *Voir* Option consommateurs

Association coopérative d'économie familiale - Rimouski-Neigette et Mitis
CP 504, #303A, 161, rue Rouleau, Rimouski QC G5L 7C5
Tél: 418-723-0744
notracef@globetrotter.net
www.consommateur.qc.ca/acef-rn
Également appelé: ACEF - Rimouski-Neigette et Mitis
Aperçu: *Dimension:* petite; *Envergure:* locale surveillé par Coalition des associations de consommateurs du Québec
Membre de: Coalition des associations de consommateurs du Québec (CACQ)

Association coopérative d'économie familiale - Rive-Sud de Montréal
2010, ch de Chambly, Longueuil QC J4J 3Y2
Tél: 450-677-6394; *Téléc:* 450-677-0101
Ligne sans frais: 877-677-6394
acefrsm@consommateur.qc.ca
www.acefrsm.com
www.facebook.com/1535938029951065
Également appelé: ACEF - Rive-Sud de Montréal

Aperçu: *Dimension:* petite; *Envergure:* locale; fondée en 1973 surveillé par Coalition des associations de consommateurs du Québec
Mission: Pour fournir des conseils financiers aux gens pour qu'ils puissent devenir stable financière
Membre de: Coalition des associations de consommateurs du Québec (CACQ)
Membre: *Montant de la cotisation:* Barème
Membre(s) du bureau directeur:
Marie-Edith Trudel, Coordonnatrice

Association coopérative d'économie familiale - Rive-Sud de Québec
33, rue Carrier, Lévis QC G6V 5N5
Tél: 418-835-6633; *Téléc:* 418-835-5818
Ligne sans frais: 877-835-6633
acef@acefrsq.com
www.acefrsq.com
www.facebook.com/218767461471174
twitter.com/acefrsq
www.youtube.com/user/acefrsq
Également appelé: ACEF de la Rive Sud de Québec
Aperçu: *Dimension:* petite; *Envergure:* locale; Organisme sans but lucratif; fondée en 1987 surveillé par Union des consommateurs
Mission: L'Association coopérative d'économie familiale (ACEF) Rive-Sud est un organisme à but non lucratif d'aide, d'éducation et d'intervention dans les domaines du budget, de l'endettement et de la consommation. L'ACEF travaille à défendre les droits des consommatrices et consommateurs
Membre de: Union des Consommateurs
Finances: *Budget de fonctionnement annuel:* $100,000-$250,000
Membre(s) du personnel: 87; 20 bénévole(s)
Membre: 40; *Montant de la cotisation:* 20$ individuel; 30$ organisme à but non lucratif; 65$ autres types d'organismes
Activités: *Stagiaires:* Oui; *Service de conférenciers:* Oui; *Bibliothèque:* Bibliothèque publique
Membre(s) du bureau directeur:
Denise Lavallée, Présidente
Édith St-Hilaire, Coordonnatrice

Association coopérative d'économie familiale de l'est de Montréal
5955, rue de Marseille, Montréal QC H1N 1K6
Tél: 514-257-6622; *Téléc:* 514-257-7998
accueil@acefest.ca
www.acefest.ca
www.facebook.com/acefestmtl
Également appelé: ACEF de l'Est de Montréal
Aperçu: *Dimension:* petite; *Envergure:* locale; Organisme sans but lucratif; fondée en 1983 surveillé par Union des consommateurs
Mission: Informer le consommateur pour le réhabiliter dans son fonctionnement budgétaire, économique et social; travailler à l'émancipation économique du consommateur, dans l'intérêt de la famille
Membre de: Union des consommateurs
Membre(s) du personnel: 6
Activités: Conférences publiques sur la consommation; consultations budgétaires; *Service de conférenciers:* Oui
Membre(s) du bureau directeur:
Maryse Bouchard, Coordonnatrice
coordination@acefest.ca

Association coopérative d'économie familiale de l'Ile-Jésus
#103, 1686, boul des Laurentides, Vimont QC H7M 2P4
Tél: 450-662-9428
info@aceflaval.com
www.aceflaval.com
www.facebook.com/1612384305678522
Également appelé: ACEF de l'Ile-Jésus
Aperçu: *Dimension:* petite; *Envergure:* locale; fondée en 1997 surveillé par Union des consommateurs
Mission: D'offrir des services facilitant l'atteinte de l'équilibre du budget familial ou personnel.
Membre de: Union des consommateurs
Membre(s) du bureau directeur:
Lyne Lavoie, Présidente

Association coopérative d'économie familiale de l'Outaouais
109, rue Wright, Gatineau QC J8X 2G7
Tél: 819-770-4911
Ligne sans frais: 866-770-4911
acefoutaouais@videotron.ca

Canadian Associations / Association coopérative d'économie familiale de l'Outaouais (ACEF)

acefo.com
www.facebook.com/acefoutaouais
soundcloud.com/acefo
Également appelé: ACEF de l'Outaouais
Aperçu: Dimension: petite; *Envergure:* locale surveillé par Coalition des associations de consommateurs du Québec
Membre de: Coalition des associations de consommateurs du Québec (CACQ)
Membre(s) du personnel: 5
Membre(s) du bureau directeur:
René Coignaud, Directeur, 819-770-4911 Ext. 23
direction.acefoutaouais@gmail.com

Association coopérative d'économie familiale de l'Outaouais (ACEF)
109, rue Wright, Gatineau QC J8X 2G7
Tél: 819-770-4911
Ligne sans frais: 866-770-4911
acefoutaouais@videotron.ca
acefo.com
Aperçu: Dimension: petite; *Envergure:* locale; fondée en 1966
Mission: Association de défense des consommateurs et consommatrices; offre des services de consultation budgétaire, cours sur le budget, informations téléphoniques et aide aux consommateurs. Champs d'activités: endettement et consommation
Affiliation(s): Coalition des associations consommateurs du Québec
Finances: Fonds: Gouvernement provincial
Membre(s) du personnel: 3; 20 bénévole(s)
Membre: 30 institutionnel; 200 individu; *Montant de la cotisation:* 10$

Association coopérative d'économie familiale de la Péninsule
#302, 159, rue St-Pierre, Matane QC G4W 2B8
Tél: 418-562-7645; *Téléc:* 418-562-7645
Ligne sans frais: 866-566-7645
info@acefpeninsule.ca
www.acefpeninsule.ca
www.facebook.com/239804772752205
Également appelé: ACEF de la Péninsule
Aperçu: Dimension: petite; *Envergure:* locale surveillé par Coalition des associations de consommateurs du Québec
Membre de: Coalition des associations de consommateurs du Québec (CACQ)
Membre(s) du bureau directeur:
Jean-Mathieu Fortin, Directeur

Centre de services de Bonaventure
114-B, av de Grand-Pré, Bonaventure QC G0C 1E0
Tél: 581-362-0034

Centre de services de Gaspé
37, rue Chrétien, Local Z-38, Gaspé QC G4X 1E1
Tél: 418-368-8123; *Téléc:* 418-368-5174

Association coopérative d'économie familiale de Québec
#210, 265, rue de la Couronne, Québec QC G1K 6E1
Tél: 418-522-1568
acefque@mediom.qc.ca
Également appelé: ACEF de Québec
Aperçu: Dimension: petite; *Envergure:* locale surveillé par Coalition des associations de consommateurs du Québec
Membre de: Coalition des associations de consommateurs du Québec (CACQ)

Association coopérative d'économie familiale des Basses Laurentides
42B, rue Turgeon, Sainte-Thérèse QC J7E 3H4
Tél: 450-430-2228
acefbl@consommateur.qc.ca
acefbl.org
Également appelé: ACEF des Basses Laurentides
Aperçu: Dimension: petite; *Envergure:* locale; Organisme sans but lucratif surveillé par Coalition des associations de consommateurs du Québec
Mission: Viser la protection, la défense et la représentation des consommateurs et consommatrices de la région des Basses-Laurentides
Membre de: Coalition des associations de consommateurs du Québec (CACQ)
Affiliation(s): Ligue des droits et libertés; Regroupement des organismes communautaires des Laurentides (ROCL)
Membre(s) du personnel: 4
Membre: Montant de la cotisation: 10$
Activités: Consultations budgétaires; ateliers d'éducation populaire
Membre(s) du bureau directeur:
Sylvie Perron, Coordonnatrice
coordination-acefbl@b2b2c.ca

Association coopérative d'économie familiale des Bois-Francs
#230, 59, rue Monfette, Victoriaville QC G6P 1J8
Tél: 819-752-5855; *Téléc:* 819-752-6426
acefbf@cdcbf.qc.ca
Également appelé: ACEF des Bois-Francs
Aperçu: Dimension: petite; *Envergure:* locale; Organisme sans but lucratif surveillé par Coalition des associations de consommateurs du Québec
Membre de: Coalition des associations de consommateurs du Québec (CACQ)

Association coopérative d'économie familiale du Grand-Portage
5, rue Iberville, Rivière-du-Loup QC G5R 1G5
Tél: 418-867-8545; *Téléc:* 418-867-8546
Ligne sans frais: 866-762-0269
acefgp@videotron.ca
www.acefgp.ca
www.facebook.com/110965225714446
Également appelé: ACEF du Grand-Portage
Aperçu: Dimension: petite; *Envergure:* locale; fondée en 1990 surveillé par Union des consommateurs
Membre de: Union des consommateurs
Finances: Budget de fonctionnement annuel: Moins de $50,000
Membre(s) du bureau directeur:
Jean-Philippe Nadeau, Président
Sonia St-Pierre, Coordonnatrice

Association coopérative d'économie familiale du Haut-Saint-Laurent
#203, 340, boul du Havre, Salaberry-de-Valleyfield QC J6S 1S6
Tél: 450-371-3470
acefhsl@hotmail.com
www.acefhsl.org
Également appelé: ACEF du Haut-Saint-Laurent
Aperçu: Dimension: petite; *Envergure:* locale surveillé par Coalition des associations de consommateurs du Québec
Membre de: Coalition des associations de consommateurs du Québec (CACQ)
Membre: 78
Membre(s) du bureau directeur:
Carole Gadoua, Coordonnatrice

Association coopérative d'économie familiale du Nord de Montréal
7500, av Chateaubriand, Montréal QC H2R 2M1
Tél: 514-277-7959; *Téléc:* 514-277-7730
info@acefnord.org
acefnord.org
www.facebook.com/497617063658798
Également appelé: ACEF du Nord de Montréal
Aperçu: Dimension: petite; *Envergure:* locale; fondée en 1974 surveillé par Union des consommateurs
Mission: Offrir des services de consultation budgétaire, d'aide aux consommateurs, des cours sur le budget, des sessions sur le budget, crédit, endettement
Membre de: Union des consommateurs
Finances: Budget de fonctionnement annuel: $100,000-$250,000
Membre: 100-499
Activités: Consultations budgétairee; cours sur le budget; soirées de l'ACEF; rencontres d'information; service d'aide aux consommateurs; *Service de conférenciers:* Oui; *Bibliothèque:* Centre de documentation; Bibliothèque publique rendez-vous
Publications:
• Consomm'action
Type: Newsletter

Association coopérative d'économie familiale du Sud-Ouest de Montréal
6734, boul Monk, 2e étage, Montréal QC H4E 3J1
Tél: 514-362-1771; *Téléc:* 514-362-0660
acefsom@consommateur.qc.ca
consommateur.qc.ca/acef-som
www.facebook.com/538226086193985
Également appelé: ACEF du Sud-Ouest de Montréal
Aperçu: Dimension: petite; *Envergure:* locale; Organisme sans but lucratif; fondée en 1984
Mission: Défendre des droits des consommateurs, individuels et collectifs dans le domaine de la consommation, de la formation en gestion des finances personnelles, de la prévention de l'endettement aux solutions du surendettement
Membre de: Coalition des associations de consommateurs du Québec
Membre(s) du personnel: 6
Membre: Montant de la cotisation: 10$ régulier; 2$ personne à faible revenu
Activités: Cours sur le budget; ateliers sur finances personnelles et solutions à l'endettement; projets d'animation de milieu; *Bibliothèque:* rendez-vous
Membre(s) du bureau directeur:
Marie-Claude Desjardins, Coordonnatrice

Association coopérative d'économie familiale Rimouski-Neigette et Mitis (ACEF)
CP 504, #306, 124, rue Sainte-Marie, Rimouski QC G5L 7C5
Tél: 418-723-0744; *Téléc:* 418-723-7972
acefriki@globetrotter.net
www.consommateur.qc.ca/acef-rn
Aperçu: Dimension: petite; *Envergure:* locale; Organisme sans but lucratif; fondée en 1993
Mission: Aider les personnes à moyens et faibles revenus, qui éprouvent des difficultés dans les domaines du budget et de la consommation; travailler à la défense des intérêts des consommateurs dans le but de promouvoir une plus grande justice sociale
Membre de: Coalition des associations de consommateurs du Québec
Finances: Budget de fonctionnement annuel: $50,000-$100,000
Membre(s) du personnel: 2; 13 bénévole(s)
Membre: 101; *Montant de la cotisation:* 10$ individu; *Critères d'admissibilite:* Consommateurs et organismes qui souscrivent aux objectifs de l'organisme; *Comités:* Logement; Promotion
Activités: Consultation budgétaire; rencontres de groupes; cours sur budget; aide en consommation; *Evénements de sensibilisation:* Concours Endettement: Prudence!; *Service de conférenciers:* Oui; *Bibliothèque:* Centre de documentation

Association coopérative d'économie famililiale de Québec (ACEF)
570, rue du Roi, Québec QC G1K 2X2
Tél: 418-522-1568; *Téléc:* 418-522-7023
acefque@mediom.qc.ca
www.acefdequebec.org
Également appelé: Association Coopérative d'économie sociale de Québec
Nom précédent: Association d'économie familiale du Québec; Association québécoise d'économie familiale
Aperçu: Dimension: moyenne; *Envergure:* provinciale
Membre(s) du bureau directeur:
Réjeanne Cyr-Reid, Coordonnatrice
Ulla Gunst, Secrétaire
Publications:
• L'Intercom

Association coopérative des pêcheurs de l'île ltée (ACPI) / Island Fishermen Cooperative Association Ltd. (IFCA)
90, rue principale, Lamèque NB E8T 1M8
Tél: 506-344-2204; *Téléc:* 506-344-0413
www.acpi-ifca.com
Aperçu: Dimension: petite; *Envergure:* locale; fondée en 1943
Membre(s) du bureau directeur:
Brian Bezeau, Directeur général
brian@acpi-ifca.com

Association Culturelle Latino Canadienne *See* Latino Canadian Cultural Association

Association Culturelle Récréative Portugaise de Lasalle *Voir* Associaça Portuguesa de LaSalle

Association cycliste ontarienne *See* Ontario Cycling Association

L'Association d'Action Communautaire Bénévole du Restigouche *See* Restigouche County Volunteer Action Association Inc.

Association d'Acupuncture du Québec *Voir* Association des Acupuncteurs du Québec

Association d'art des universités du Canada *See* Universities Art Association of Canada

Association d'assurances des juristes canadiens *See* Canadian Lawyers Insurance Association

Association d'économie familiale du Québec; Association québécoise d'économie familiale Voir Association coopérative d'économie familliale de Québec

Association d'éducation juridique communautaire (Manitoba) inc. See Community Legal Education Association (Manitoba) Inc.

Association d'éducation préscolaire du Québec (AÉPQ)
CP 99039, Succ. CSP Du Tremblay, Longueuil QC J4N 0A5
Tél: 514-343-6111
aepq@aepq.ca
www.aepq.ca
www.pinterest.com/aepq
Aperçu: *Dimension:* moyenne; *Envergure:* provinciale; Organisme sans but lucratif; fondée en 1976
Mission: Défendre la qualité de vie des enfants d'éducation préscolaire
Membre de: Conseil pédagogique interdisciplinaire du Québec (CPIQ)
Membre: 1,000+; *Critères d'admissibilite:* Personnes intéressées à l'éducation préscolaire (enseignantes, éducatrices, cadres, conseillers pédagogiques, parents, chercheurs, professeurs)
Activités: Congrès; formation; *Service de conférenciers:* Oui
Membre(s) du bureau directeur:
Maryse Rondeau, Présidente
Raymonde Hébert, Vice-Présidente
Véronique Chaloux, Trésorière
Prix, Bourses:
• Prix Monique-Vaillancourt-Antippa
Avoir contribué à la promotion et à l'amélioration de la qualité de l'éducation préscolaire par un projet original et pertinent ayant un impact dans le milieu préscolaire

Association d'églises baptistes évangéliques au québec
9780, rue Sherbrooke est, Montréal QC H1L 6N6
Tél: 514-337-2555; Téléc: 514-337-8892
www.aebeq.qc.ca
www.facebook.com/aebeq.qc
Aperçu: *Dimension:* moyenne; *Envergure:* nationale; fondée en 1971 surveillé par Canadian Baptist Ministries
Mission: Aider les églises à communiquer l'évangile de Jésus-Christ à tous les Québécois; former des disciples et des leaders; devenir plus solides et se reproduire
Membre de: Fellowship of Evangelical Baptist Churches in Canada
Affiliation(s): Camp des Bouleaux, Camp Patmos, Aujourd'hui l'Espoir, Organisme Renaissance Autochtone
Membre: 65 000
Activités: Camps de jeunes; retraites; congrès; cohortes; *Stagiaires:* Oui; *Service de conférenciers:* Oui
Membre(s) du bureau directeur:
Michel M. Habbib, Secrétaire général
Gilles Lapierre, Directeur général

Association d'élocution et des débats de la Saskatchewan See Saskatchewan Elocution & Debate Association

Association d'entraide des avocats de Montréal / Montreal Advocates' Mutual Assistance Assocation
#980, 1, rue Notre-Dame est, Montréal QC H2Y 1B6
Tél: 514-866-9392; Téléc: 514-866-1488
aeam@barreaudemontreal.qc.ca
www.barreaudemontreal.qc.ca
Nom précédent: Association de bienfaisance des avocats de Montréal
Aperçu: *Dimension:* petite; *Envergure:* locale; fondée en 1938
Mission: Pour aider financièrement les membres du Barreau de Montréal dans leurs moments de besoin
10 bénévole(s)
Membre: *Montant de la cotisation:* 25$
Membre(s) du bureau directeur:
Jeffrey Boro, Président, Conseil d'administration

Association d'entraide Le Chaînon inc.
4373, rue de l'Esplanade, Montréal QC H2W 1T2
Tél: 514-845-0151; Téléc: 514-844-4180
info@lechainon.org
www.lechainon.org
www.facebook.com/lechainonmontreal
twitter.com/LeChainonMTL
Également appelé: Le Chaînon
Aperçu: *Dimension:* petite; *Envergure:* provinciale; Organisme sans but lucratif; fondée en 1932
Mission: Quatre programmes d'hébergement: A des femmes, momentanément sans logement et sans moyen financier/l'unité accueil de nuit (18 ans et plus) (16 places) et l'unité court terme (18 ans et plus) (20 places) offre un chez-soi temporaire avec présence attentionnée, support, consultation et orientation; A des femmes de 18 ans et plus en besoin d'un milieu de vie et en difficulté d'autonomie, l'unité transition (16 places) offre un chez-soi à moyen terme (durée maximale d'un an) avec accompagnement intensif. A des femmes d'un âge avancé et en perte d'autonomie, la maison Yvonne-Maisonneuve (maison de chambres supervisée avec services) (15 places) offre un chez-soi autonome à long terme
Affiliation(s): Fédération de ressources d'hébergement pour femmes violentées et en difficulté du Québec
300 bénévole(s)
Membre(s) du bureau directeur:
Marcèle Lamarche, Directeur général

Association d'épilepsie de Calgary See Epilepsy Association of Calgary

Association d'équipement de transport du canada See Canadian Transportation Equipment Association

Association d'équitation thérapeutique Windsor-Essex See Windsor-Essex Therapeutic Riding Association

Association d'escrime de l'Ontario See Ontario Fencing Association

Association d'escrime de la Nouvelle-Écosse See Fencing Association of Nova Scotia

Association d'études américaines au Canada See Canadian Association for American Studies

Association d'études Baha'is See Association for Bahá'í Studies

Association d'études canadiennes See Association for Canadian Studies

Association d'études juives canadiennes See Association for Canadian Jewish Studies

Association d'hospitalisation Canassurance See Canadian Association of Blue Cross Plans

Association d'iléostomie et colostomie de Montréal See Ileostomy & Colostomy Association of Montreal

Association d'informations en logements et immeubles adaptés (AILIA)
#213, 150, rue Grant, Longueuil QC J4H 3H6
Tél: 450-646-4343; Téléc: 450-646-6446
ailia@qc.aira.com
ailia.info
Aperçu: *Dimension:* petite; *Envergure:* locale; fondée en 1986
Mission: Encourager les personnes handicapées à vivre de façon autonome et à réformer les normes de construction résidentielle ainsi que tous les bâtiments sont accessibles aux personnes handicapées
Membre de: Groupement des personnes handicapées de la rive-sud de Montréal; Confédération des organismes de personnes handicapées du Québec; Habitations communautaires Longueuil; Logis des Aulniers
Membre: *Comités:* Ville de Longueuil sur le Plan d'intervention des personnes handicapées; Bâtiments de la Ville de Longueuil sur le Plan d'intervention des personnes handicapées; Coordination de la Table des personnes handicapées de la Rive-Sud; Ressources résidentielles de la TPHRS; Environnement bâti et aménagement public
Activités: Rencontres; Conférences
Membre(s) du bureau directeur:
Lloyd Feeney, Président, Conseil d'administration

Association d'isolation du Québec (AIQ)
#102, 4099, boul St-Jean-Baptiste, Montréal QC H1B 5V3
Tél: 514-354-9877; Téléc: 514-354-7401
Ligne sans frais: 800-711-2381
info@isolation-aiq.ca
www.isolation-aiq.ca
Nom précédent: Association des entrepreneurs en isolation de la Province de Québec
Aperçu: *Dimension:* petite; *Envergure:* provinciale; fondée en 1959
Mission: L'AIQ fait la promotion du respect des règles de l'art du métier et de l'utilisation de l'isolation dans les secteurs commerciaux, industriels et institutionnels.
Membre: *Montant de la cotisation:* 700 $ - 1 073.24 $; *Critères d'admissibilite:* Entrepreneurs; fabricants; distributeurs
Membre(s) du bureau directeur:
Linda Wilson, Directrice générale
linda.wilson@isolation-aiq.ca

Association d'orthopédie du Québec
Tour de L'Est, CP 216, Succ. Desjardins, 2, Complexe Desjardins, 30e étage, Montréal QC H5B 1G8
Tél: 514-844-0803; Téléc: 514-844-6786
aoq@fmsq.org
www.orthoquebec.ca
Aperçu: *Dimension:* moyenne; *Envergure:* provinciale surveillé par Fédération des médecins spécialistes du Québec
Mission: Valoriser le statut professionnel de ses membres; promouvoir leurs intérêts économiques; contribuer au développement de la chirurgie orthopédique et de la traumatologie par le biais d'activités de formation médicale continue
Membre: 354; *Comités:* Exécutif; Développement professionnel continu; Affaires économiques; Exercice Professionnel et normes de pratique
Membre(s) du bureau directeur:
Robert Turcotte, Président
Jean-François Joncas, Secrétaire-trésorier

Association d'oto-rhino-laryngologie et de chirurgie cervico-faciale du Québec
CP 216, #3000, 2, Complexe Desjardins, Montréal QC H5B 1G8
Tél: 514-350-5125; Téléc: 514-350-5165
assorl@fmsq.org
www.orlquebec.ca
Aperçu: *Dimension:* petite; *Envergure:* provinciale; Organisme sans but lucratif; fondée en 1959 surveillé par Fédération des médecins spécialistes du Québec
Mission: Valoriser le statut professionnel de ses membres, promouvoir leurs intérêts scientifiques, économiques et professionnels, et contribuer au développement de l'oto-rhino-laryngologie
Membre: 200
Membre(s) du bureau directeur:
Janik Sarrazin, Président
Jocelyne Fortin, Directrice, Administration

Association de balle des jeunes handicapés de Laval-Laurentides-Lanaudière (ABJHLLL)
2020, av Laplante, Laval QC H7S 1E7
Tél: 450-689-4668
Également appelé: Association de balle des jeunes handicapés de Laval/ABJHL
Aperçu: *Dimension:* petite; *Envergure:* locale; Organisme sans but lucratif; fondée en 1995
Mission: Etablir et opérer des équipes de balle pour la détente de l'esprit et du corps de jeunes handicapés physiques et/ou intellectuels, garçons et filles, principalement des régions de Laval, Laurentides et Lanaudière. Organiser et maintenir toute autre activités social, sportive et culturelle connexe pour promouvoir les buts de la corporations
Membre de: La petite ligue de baseball du Québec (Division Challenger)
Membre: *Critères d'admissibilite:* Fille ou garçon 6 à 18 ans, déficient physique et/ou intellectuel et ses père et mère
Activités: *Stagiaires:* Oui; *Service de conférenciers:* Oui
Membre(s) du bureau directeur:
Tony Condello, Responsable
tcondello@videotron.ca

Association de bienfaisance des avocats de Montréal Voir Association d'entraide des avocats de Montréal

Association de bienfaisance et de retraite des policiers de la communauté urbaine de Montréal Voir Association de bienfaisance et de retraite des policiers et policières de la ville de Montréal

Association de bienfaisance et de retraite des policiers et policières de la ville de Montréal
#200, 480, rue Gilford, Montréal QC H2J 1N3
Tél: 514-527-8061; Téléc: 514-522-7736
info@caisse-abr.com
caisse-abr.com
Nom précédent: Association de bienfaisance et de retraite des policiers de la communauté urbaine de Montréal
Aperçu: *Dimension:* petite; *Envergure:* locale
Membre(s) du bureau directeur:
Louis Monette, Président/Directeur général

Canadian Associations / Association de chasse et pêche nordique, inc.

Association de chasse et pêche nordique, inc.
148, rue St-Marcellin ouest, Les Escoumins QC G0T 1K0
Tél: 418-233-3062; *Téléc:* 418-233-3083
Aperçu: *Dimension:* petite; *Envergure:* locale; fondée en 1978
Affiliation(s): Fédération québécoise des gestionnaires de Zec
Finances: *Budget de fonctionnement annuel:*
$100,000-$250,000; *Fonds:* Gouvernement régional
Membre: 600; *Montant de la cotisation:* 12$
Membre(s) du bureau directeur:
Donald Tremblay, Responsable

Association de Curling des Sourdes du Canada *See* Canadian Deaf Curling Association

Association de Curling du Nouveau-Brunswick *See* New Brunswick Curling Association

Association de Dards du Québec inc. (ADQDA) / Québec Dart Association Inc.
#3, 3177, rue Notre-Dame, Lachine QC H8S 2H4
Tél: 514-637-2858
www.adqda.com
www.facebook.com/groups/ADQDA
Aperçu: *Dimension:* moyenne; *Envergure:* provinciale; Organisme sans but lucratif; fondée en 1978 surveillé par National Darts Federation of Canada
Mission: L'A.D.Q. est la seule et unique Association de dards qui représente la Fédération de dards du Canada et aussi la seule qui est reconnue par la Fédération de Dards mondiale (World Darts Federation)
Membre de: National Darts Federation of Canada
Membre: 700; *Montant de la cotisation:* $25
Membre(s) du bureau directeur:
Maggie LeBlanc, Présidente
maggieleblanc417@hotmail.com

Association de droit Lord Reading *See* Lord Reading Law Society

Association de golf du nouveau brunswick *See* New Brunswick Golf Association

Association de golf du Québec *Voir* Fédération de golf du Québec

Association de Hearst et de la région pour l'intégration communautaire *See* Hearst & Area Association for Community Living

Association de hockey amateur de la Colombie-Britannique *See* British Columbia Amateur Hockey Association

Association de hockey de la Saskatchewan *See* Saskatchewan Hockey Association

Association de hockey de Terre-Neuve et Labrador *See* Hockey Newfoundland & Labrador

Association de hockey féminin de l'Ontario *See* Ontario Women's Hockey Association

Association de Hockey-Balle du Québec *See* Québec Ball Hockey Association

Association de joueurs de bridge de Boucherville
780, rue Pierre Viger, Boucherville QC J4B 3V5
ajbb2009.tripod.com
Aperçu: *Dimension:* petite; *Envergure:* locale
Activités: Bridge
Membre(s) du bureau directeur:
Mary Ann Shtym, Contact, 450-465-7476
mash2810@hotmail.com

Association de l'Agricotourism et du Tourisme Gourmand
4545, av Pierre-de-Coubertin, Montréal QC H1V 0B2
Tél: 514-252-3138; *Téléc:* 514-252-3173
info@terroiretsaveurs.com
www.terroiretsaveurs.com
www.facebook.com/terroiretsaveurs
twitter.com/terroirsaveurs
www.youtube.com/user/terroiretsaveurs
Nom précédent: Fédération des Agricotours du Québec
Aperçu: *Dimension:* moyenne; *Envergure:* provinciale; fondée en 1976
Mission: La Fédération développe et fait la promotion du tourisme au Québec en maison privée de style Bed & Breakfast
Membre(s) du bureau directeur:
Odette Chaput, Directrice générale

Association de l'aluminium du Canada *Voir* Aluminium Association of Canada

Association de l'éducation coopérative de l'Ontario *See* Ontario Cooperative Education Association

L'Association de l'efficacité énergétique du Canada *See* Canadian Energy Efficiency Alliance

Association de l'exploration minière de Québec (AEMQ) / Quebec Mineral Exploration Assocation (QMEA)
#203, 132, av du Lac, Rouyn-Noranda QC J9X 4N5
Tél: 819-762-1599; *Téléc:* 819-762-1522
info@aemq.org
www.aemq.org
www.linkedin.com/company/association-de-l%27exploration-mini-re-du-qu-bec-aemq-
www.facebook.com/AEMQ1975
twitter.com/AEMQ_
Nom précédent: Association des prospecteurs du Québec
Aperçu: *Dimension:* moyenne; *Envergure:* provinciale; fondée en 1975
Mission: Développer, défendre et promouvoir l'exploration minière au Québec
Finances: *Budget de fonctionnement annuel:*
$100,000-$250,000
Membre(s) du personnel: 5; 20 bénévole(s)
Membre: 2000 membres individuels; plus de 250 corporatifs; *Montant de la cotisation:* 20$ étudiant - 2 000$ entreprises; *Critères d'admissibilite:* Oeuvrer en exploration minière
Activités: *Evénements de sensibilisation:* Événements Explo-Abiti; *Service de conférenciers:* Oui
Membre(s) du bureau directeur:
Philippe Cloutier, Président
Valerie Fillion, Directrice générale, 819-762-1599 Ext. 224
dg@aemq.org
Meetings/Conferences:
• Quebec Mineral Exploration Association Explo Abitibi 2018, 2018

Association de l'industrie alimentaire de l'Atlantique *See* Atlantic Food & Beverage Processors Association

Association de l'industrie de la langue *See* Language Industry Association

Association de l'industrie des technologies de la santé *See* Canada's Medical Technology Companies

Association de l'industrie électrique du Québec (AIEQ)
#1470, 1155, rue Metcalfe, Montréal QC H3B 2V6
Tél: 514-281-0615; *Téléc:* 514-281-7965
info@aieq.net
www.aieq.net
www.linkedin.com/groups/4314122/profile
www.facebook.com/AIEQuebec
twitter.com/_AIEQ
www.youtube.com/user/aiequebec
Nom précédent: Club d'électricité du Québec inc.
Aperçu: *Dimension:* moyenne; *Envergure:* provinciale; Organisme sans but lucratif; fondée en 1916
Mission: Etre porte parole de l'industrie 'électrique au Québec; favoriser la circulation de toute information et intérêt pour les membres et l'industrie électrique en général; contribuer au développement de nos membres et à la promotion de leurs intérêts par des initiatives de concertation et de représentation; encourager l'utilisation rationnelle des ressources dans une perspective de développement
Affiliation(s): ABB; AECOM; ALSTOM; DESSAU; SNC-LAVALIN; VOITH; BPR; Brookfield; Mitsubishi Electric Power Products, Inc.; Qualitas
Finances: *Budget de fonctionnement annuel:* $500,000-$1.5 Million
Membre(s) du personnel: 7
Membre: 121; *Montant de la cotisation:* Barème, selon le nombre d'employés au Québec; *Critères d'admissibilité:* Membres industriels; *Comités:* Consultatif; Finances; Services aux membres; Promotion; Débats projects
Activités: Déjeuners; conférences; activités sociales; *Service de conférenciers:* Oui
Membre(s) du bureau directeur:
Denis Tremblay, Président et directeur général, 514-281-0615 Ext. 122
dtremblay@aieq.net

Association de l'industrie touristique du Canada *See* Tourism Industry Association of Canada

Association de l'industrie touristique du Nouveau-Brunswick inc. *See* Tourism Industry Association of New Brunswick Inc.

Association de l'Ontario des officers en bâtiment inc. *See* Ontario Building Officials Association Inc.

Association de l'opéra de vancouver *See* Vancouver Opera

Association de la boulimie et d'anorexie mentale *See* Bulimia Anorexia Nervosa Association

Association de la chirurgie infantile canadienne *See* Canadian Association of Paediatric Surgeons

L'Association de la construction d'Ottawa *See* Ottawa Construction Association

Association de la construction du nouveau-brunswick *See* Construction Association of New Brunswick

Association de la construction du Québec (ACQ) / Construction Association of Québec
9200, boul Métropolitain est, Anjou QC H1K 4L2
Tél: 514-354-0609; *Téléc:* 514-354-8292
Ligne sans frais: 888-868-3424
info@prov.acq.org
www.acq.org
www.linkedin.com/company/association-de-la-construction-du-qu-bec
www.facebook.com/ACQprovinciale
twitter.com/ACQprovinciale
www.youtube.com/user/ACQprovinciale
Aperçu: *Dimension:* grande; *Envergure:* provinciale; fondée en 1989 surveillé par Canadian Construction Association
Mission: Promotion et défense des intérêts des entreprises de construction, de gestionnaire de plans de garantie des bâtiments résidentiels neufs (Qualité Habitation) et d'agent patronal négociateur pour tous les employeurs des secteurs institutionnel/commercial et industriel (IC/I)
Membre: 17 000 entreprises; 11 associations affiliées; *Critères d'admissibilite:* Entrepreneur en construction; *Comités:* Exécutif; Finances; Mises en nomination et élection; Déontologie; Relations du travail
Activités: Qualification professionnelle des entreprises; Lobbying gouvernemental; Services professionnels aux entrepreneurs; Relations de travail pour les secteurs institutionnel-commercial et industriel; Olans de garantie, salles de plans; *Bibliothèque:* Centre de documentation; Bibliothèque publique
Membre(s) du bureau directeur:
Francis Roy, Président
Jean-François Arbour, Vice-président, Finances
René Hamel, Vice-président, Habitation
Éric Fraser, Vice-président, Régions
Meetings/Conferences:
• Association de la construction du Québec 2018 congrès annuel, 2018, QC
Scope: Provincial

Région Bas-St-Laurent - Gaspésie - Les Iles
424, 2e rue est, 2e étage, Rimouski QC G5M 1S6
Tél: 418-724-4044; *Téléc:* 418-724-0673
info@acqbsl.org
Membre(s) du bureau directeur:
Christine Bujold, Directrice général

Région de l'Outaouais / Abitibi / Nord-Ouest du Québec (ACQ)
170, boul Maisonneuve, Gatineau QC J8X 3N4
Tél: 819-770-1818; *Téléc:* 819-770-8272
Ligne sans frais: 844-770-1818
acq-outaouais@acqouestqc.org
www.acq.org/outaouais
Membre(s) du bureau directeur:
Sylvie Leblond, Directrice générale
leblonds@acq.org

Région de la Mauricie - Bois-Francs - Lanaudière - Centre-du-Québec
#100, 2575, rue de l'Industrie, Trois-Rivières QC G8Z 4T1
Tél: 819-374-1465; *Téléc:* 819-374-5757
Ligne sans frais: 800-785-7519
acq-mbfl@acq.org
www.acq.org/region-mauricie.html
Membre(s) du bureau directeur:
André Trudel, Directeur général

Région de Québec
#100, 375, rue de Verdun, Québec QC G1N 3N8
Tél: 418-687-4121; *Téléc:* 418-687-3026
acq@acqquebec.org
www.acq.org/region-quebec.html
Membre(s) du bureau directeur:
Véronique Mercier, Directrice générale
mercierv@acqquebec.org

Région Estrie
2925, rue Hertel, Sherbrooke QC J1L 1Y3
Tél: 819-566-7077; *Téléc:* 819-566-2440
Ligne sans frais: 866-893-7077
info@acqestrie.org
www.acq.org/region-estrie.html
www.linkedin.com/company/acq-estrie
Membre(s) du bureau directeur:
Conia Boutin, Directrice générale

Région Laval / Laurentides (ACQ LL)
#113, 50, rue Sicard, Sainte-Thérèse QC J7E R51
Tél: 450-420-9240; *Téléc:* 450-420-9242
Ligne sans frais: 855-420-9240
info@acqlavallaurentides.org
Membre(s) du bureau directeur:
Marie Claude Fournier, Directrice générale
fourniermc@acqlavallaurentides.org

Région Métropolitaine
8245, boul du Golf, Anjou QC H1J 0B2
Tél: 514-355-3245; *Téléc:* 514-351-7490
acq-metro@acqmetropolitaine.org
www.acq.org/region-metropolitaine.html
www.facebook.com/ACQmetropolitaine
twitter.com/ACQprovinciale
Membre(s) du bureau directeur:
Gregoria Modolo, Directrice générale

Région Montérégie
1060, rue Bernier, Saint-Jean-sur-Richelieu QC J2W 1X4
Tél: 450-348-6114; *Téléc:* 450-348-0057
acq-monteregie@acqmonteregie.org
www.acq.org/region-monteregie.html
Membre(s) du bureau directeur:
Suzie Bessette, Directrice générale

Région Montérégie - Bureau de Ste-Julie
#206, 2141, rue Nobel, Sainte-Julie QC J3E 1Z9
Tél: 450-649-3004; *Téléc:* 450-649-0087
stejulie@acqmonteregie.org

Région Nord-Est du Québec
#257, 350, rue Smith, Sept-Iles QC G4R 3X2
Tél: 418-968-9302; *Téléc:* 418-968-9310
acq.nordest@globetrotter.net
www.acq.org/region-nord-est-du-quebec.html

Région Saguenay / Lac St-Jean
2496, rue Dubose, Jonquière QC G7S 1B4
Tél: 418-548-4678; *Téléc:* 418-548-9218
info@acqsaguenay.com
www.acq.org/region-saguenay-lac-saint-jean.html
Membre(s) du bureau directeur:
Jean-François Simard, Directeur général

Association de la construction navale du Canada *See* The Canadian Marine Industries and Shipbuilding Association

Association de la Construction Richelieu Yamaska (ACRY)
1190, rue Dessaules, Saint-Hyacinthe QC J2S 7X8
Tél: 450-773-0166; *Téléc:* 450-773-9148
Ligne sans frais: 877-743-0166
info@acry.qc.ca
acry.qc.ca
Nom précédent: Regroupement des professionnels de la construction Richelieu Yamaska
Aperçu: *Dimension:* petite; *Envergure:* locale; Organisme sans but lucratif; fondée en 1957
Mission: Promotion et défense des droits et intérêts des entrepreneurs en construction
Membre de: Fédération des Associations et Corporations en Construction du Québec
Affiliation(s): Fédération des Associations et Corporations en Construction du Québec (FACCQ)
Finances: *Budget de fonctionnement annuel:* $100,000-$250,000
Membre(s) du personnel: 3
Membre: 260; *Montant de la cotisation:* 430$; *Critères d'admissibilité:* Entrepreneur de construction; *Comités:* Activités sociales
Membre(s) du bureau directeur:

Marco Gaudette, Président
mgaudette@ntic.qc.ca
Bruno Bazinet, Vice-président
bruno2012@cgocable.ca
Jacqueline Rainville, Directrice générale

Association de la déficience intellectuelle de la région de Sorel (ADIRS)
#210, 189, rue Prince, Sorel-Tracy QC J3P 4K6
Tél: 450-743-0664; *Téléc:* 450-743-1769
adirs@videotron.ca
adirs.e-monsite.com
www.facebook.com/adirs.sorel
Aperçu: *Dimension:* petite; *Envergure:* locale
Affiliation(s): Association du Québec pour l'intégration sociale
Membre(s) du personnel: 8
Membre(s) du bureau directeur:
Julie Trudeau, Directrice générale

Association de la fibromyalgie de la Montérégie
#205, 570, boul Roland-Therrien, Longueuil QC J4H 3V7
Tél: 450-928-1261
Ligne sans frais: 888-928-1261
info@fibromyalgiemonteregie.ca
www.fibromyalgiemonteregie.ca
Aperçu: *Dimension:* petite; *Envergure:* locale
Mission: Fournir des informations et des soutien pour des personnes atteintes de fibromyalgie
Membre(s) du bureau directeur:
Zina Manoka, Coordonnatrice, Services aux membres

Association de la Fibromyalgie des Laurentides
366, rue Laviolette, Saint-Jérôme QC J7Y 2S9
Tél: 450-569-7766; *Téléc:* 450-569-7769
Ligne sans frais: 877-705-7766
afl@videotron.ca
www.fibromyalgie-des-laurentides.ca
www.facebook.com/376578422426237
twitter.com/FibromyaLaurent
Aperçu: *Dimension:* moyenne; *Envergure:* locale; Organisme sans but lucratif; fondée en 1995
Membre de: Fédération québécoise de la fibromyalgie; Regroupement des Organismes communautaires des Laurentides; Réseau de concertation pour les personnes handicapées des Laurentides
Membre(s) du personnel: 2
Membre: *Montant de la cotisation:* 20$ membre fibromyalgique; 20$ membres accompagnateur; *Critères d'admissibilite:* Personnes des Laurentides atteintes de fibromyalgie et des gens qui assistent les personnes atteintes de fibromyalgie
Membre(s) du bureau directeur:
Lise Cloutier, Directrice générale

Association de la fibromyalgie du Québec *Voir* Association québécoise de la fibromyalgie

Association de la fibromyalgie région Ile-De-Montréal
CP 48681, Succ. Outremont, Montréal QC H2V 4T9
Tél: 438-496-7448
info@afim.qc.ca
www.afim.qc.ca
www.facebook.com/fibromyalgie.montreal
www.youtube.com/channel/UCCJ__R9NjtU_1-XBrYEOuCA
Aperçu: *Dimension:* petite; *Envergure:* locale; fondée en 1995
Mission: Défendre les intérêts des personnes atteintes de fibromyalgie dans la région de l'Ile-de-Montréal
Membre de: Société québécoise de la fibromyalgie
Membre: *Montant de la cotisation:* 25$
Activités: Les renseignant sur les ressources disponibles
Membre(s) du bureau directeur:
Alain Lariviere, Président

Association de la gendarmerie royale de Terre-Neuve *See* Royal Newfoundland Constabulary Association

Association de la gestion de la chaîne d'approvisionnement *See* Supply Chain Management Association

Association de la librairie ancienne du Canada *See* Antiquarian Booksellers' Association of Canada

Association de la musique country canadienne *See* Canadian Country Music Association

Association de la musique de la côte est *See* East Coast Music Association

L'Association de la Neurofibromatose du Québec (ANFQ)
CP 150, Succ. St-Michel, Montréal QC H2A 3B0
Tél: 514-385-6702; *Téléc:* 514-385-1420
Ligne sans frais: 888-385-6702
www.anfq.org
Aperçu: *Dimension:* petite; *Envergure:* provinciale; Organisme sans but lucratif; fondée en 1989
Mission: Regrouper les membres et leurs familles; diffuser l'information sur la NF auprès des membres et des professionnels de la santé et de l'éducation; favoriser la recherche
Membre de: Confédération des organismes de personnes handicapées; National Neurofibromatosis Foundation; Association québécoise pour les troubles d'apprentissage; NF Canada
Finances: *Fonds:* Provincial
12 bénévole(s)
Membre: 200; *Montant de la cotisation:* 20$; *Critères d'admissibilité:* Personne atteinte de la NF et leur famille ou ami; intervenants en santé et en éducation
Activités: Rencontres; conférences de professionnels; informations; soutien téléphonique; levées de fonds (concert-bénéfice); sensibilisation; *Evénements de sensibilisation:* Journée mondiale de la Neurofibromatose mai
Membre(s) du bureau directeur:
Louise L'Africain, Chair

Association de la police d'Edmonton *See* Edmonton Police Association

Association de la police de Belleville *See* Belleville Police Association

Association de la police de Cornwall *See* Cornwall Police Association

Association de la police de Guelph inc. *See* Guelph Police Association Inc.

Association de la police de Hamilton *See* Hamilton Police Association

Association de la police de Kingston *See* Kingston Police Association

Association de la police de la région de Niagara *See* Niagara Region Police Association

Association de la police de la ville de Brandon *See* Brandon Police Association

Association de la police de la ville de Saskatoon *See* Saskatoon City Police Association

Association de la police de London *See* London Police Association

Association de la police de Peterborough *See* Peterborough Police Association

Association de la police de Sault-Ste-Marie *See* Sault Ste Marie Police Association

Association de la police de Thunder Bay *See* Thunder Bay Police Association

Association de la police de Toronto *See* Toronto Police Association

Association de la police de Waterloo *See* Waterloo Regional Police Association

Association de la police de Windsor *See* Windsor Police Association

Association de la police de Winnipeg *See* Winnipeg Police Association

Association de la presse francophone (APF) / Association of Francophone Newspapers
267, rue Dalhousie, Ottawa ON K1N 7E3
Tél: 613-241-1017; *Téléc:* 613-241-6313
admin@apf.ca
www.apf.ca
www.facebook.com/Associationdelapressefrancophone
twitter.com/apf_journaux
Aperçu: *Dimension:* moyenne; *Envergure:* nationale; Organisme sans but lucratif; fondée en 1976
Mission: Promouvoir l'existence d'une presse communautaire écrite en langue française aussi vigoureuse et aussi répandue que possible dans les communautés de langue française à

Canadian Associations / Association de la recherche industrielle du Québec (ADRIQ)

l'extérieur du Québec; Contribuer à l'amélioration de sa qualité et de son rayonnement; défendre énergiquement les principes de la liberté de parole et de la presse écrite
Membre de: Fédération des communautés francophones et acadienne
Finances: *Budget de fonctionnement annuel:* $250,000-$500,000; *Fonds:* Patrimoine Canada
Membre(s) du personnel: 3
Membre: 22
Activités: *Stagiaires:* Oui
Membre(s) du bureau directeur:
Jean-Patrice Meunier, Directeur général
dg@apf.ca
Sophie Bègue, Chargée, Des communications et projets spéciaux
projets@apf.ca
Prix, Bourses:
• Prix d'excellence de l'APF
Eligibility: Les journalistes, photographes, graphistes et autres artistes employés par un membre journal APF *Deadline:* 11 janvier
Meetings/Conferences:
• Association de la presse francophone Congrès annuel, 2018
Scope: National
Description: Les éditeurs de journaux de langue française du Canada se réunissent pour discuter de nouvelles de l'industrie et de participer à des occasions de perfectionnement professionnel

L'Association de la recherche et de l'intelligence marketing *See* Marketing Research & Intelligence Association

Association de la recherche industrielle du Québec (ADRIQ)
#1120, 555, boul René-Lévesque ouest, Montréal QC H2Z 1B1
Tél: 514-337-3001; *Téléc:* 514-337-2229
adriq@adriq.com
www.adriq.com
www.linkedin.com/groups?gid=2999463
twitter.com/ADRIQ_RCTi
Nom précédent: Association des directeurs de recherche industrielle du Québec
Aperçu: *Dimension:* moyenne; *Envergure:* provinciale; Organisme sans but lucratif; fondée en 1978
Mission: De promouvoir les nouvelles technologies afin d'accroître le commerce concurrentiel au Québec et à l'étranger
Membre(s) du bureau directeur:
Pascal Monette, Président-directeur général

Association de la Rivière Ste-Marguerite Inc. (ARSM)
160, rue Principale, Sacré-Coeur QC G0T 1Y0
Tél: 418-236-4604
Ligne sans frais: 877-236-4604
info@rivieresainte-marguerite.com
www.rivieresainte-marguerite.com
www.facebook.com/rivieresaintemarguerite
www.youtube.com/user/RivSainteMarguerite
Aperçu: *Dimension:* petite; *Envergure:* locale; Organisme sans but lucratif; fondée en 1980
Finances: *Budget de fonctionnement annuel:* $100,000-$250,000
Membre: 100-499; *Montant de la cotisation:* 23$
Activités: Pêche au saumon; pêche à la truite de mer; fête vallée du Saumon; cours d'initiation à la pêche à la morue; interprétation saumon atlantique
Membre(s) du bureau directeur:
Valérie Maltais, Directrice générale

Association de la Sainte Face *See* Holy Face Association

Association de la santé et de la sécurité des pâtes et papiers et des industries de la forêt du Québec (ASSIFQ-ASSPPQ)
Place Iberville II, #210, 1175, av Lavigerie, Québec QC G1V 4P1
Tél: 418-657-2267; *Téléc:* 418-651-4622
Ligne sans frais: 888-632-9326
info@santesecurite.org
www.santesecurite.org
Aperçu: *Dimension:* moyenne; *Envergure:* provinciale; fondée en 2010
Mission: De soutenir et d'accompagner les entreprises dans l'amélioration continue de la santé et de la sécurité du travail
Affiliation(s): Association des entrepreneurs en travaux sylvicoles du Québec; Association des fabricants des meubles du Québec; Association des manufacturiers de palettes et contenants du Québec; Conseil de l'industrie forestière du Québec; Fédération québécoise des coopératives forestières;

Regroupement des sociétés d'aménagement du Québec; Commission de la santé et de la sécurité du travail
Membre(s) du personnel: 27
Membre: 600 entreprises; *Montant de la cotisation:* Barème; *Critères d'admissibilite:* Oeuvrer dans le domaine des industries de la forêt ou des pâtes ou papiers
Activités: Information; formation; expertise-conseil et impartition; mutuelles de prévention; activités régionales; *Stagiaires:* Oui; *Bibliothèque*
Membre(s) du bureau directeur:
Jacques Laroche, Président-directeur général
jlaroche@santesecurite.org
Suzanne Lavoie, Adjointe administrative
slavoie@santesecurite.org

Association de la sécurité de l'information du Québec (ASIQ)
CP 9772, Succ. Ste-Foy, Québec QC G1V 4C3
Tél: 418-621-0464; *Téléc:* 418-621-0464
administration@asiq.org
www.asiq.org
www.linkedin.com/groups?gid=1934860
www.facebook.com/AssociationASIQ
twitter.com/ASIQCQSI
www.youtube.com/asiqvideos
Nom précédent: Association de sécurité de l'information de la région de Québec
Aperçu: *Dimension:* petite; *Envergure:* provinciale; Organisme sans but lucratif; fondée en 1983
Mission: Promouvoir la sécurité de l'information; regouper les personnes qui s'intéressent à la sécurité; favoriser les échanges entre les membres; diffuser de l'information pour permettre aux membres de suivre l'évolution dans le domaine de la sécurité de l'information
Finances: *Budget de fonctionnement annuel:* Moins de $50,000
10 bénévole(s)
Membre: 200+; *Montant de la cotisation:* 85$ étudiant; 170$ individuel; 250$ corporatif (de base - 1 membre), 125$ membres supplémentaires; *Comités:* Travail (pour répartir les tâches à réaliser)
Activités: Conférences, colloque annuel, ateliers
Membre(s) du bureau directeur:
Alex Bédard, Président

Association de la Vallée-du-Richelieu pour la déficience intellectuelle (AVRDI)
625, rue Lechasseur, Beloeil QC J3G 2L3
Tél: 450-467-8644
infos@avrdi.org
www.avrdi.org
Nom précédent: Association de la Vallée-du-Richelieu pour les déficients mentaux
Aperçu: *Dimension:* petite; *Envergure:* locale
Mission: D'aider les familles à l'intégration des personnes vivant avec une déficience intellectuelle. L'organisme offre des activités pour stimuler talents et intérêts, et informe et dirige les familles vers les différents recours disponible dans la région
Affiliation(s): Association du Québec pour l'intégration sociale
Membre(s) du personnel: 10
Membre(s) du bureau directeur:
Jocelyn Chauveau, Président
Joelichauveau@yahoo.ca

Association de la Vallée-du-Richelieu pour les déficients mentaux *Voir* Association de la Vallée-du-Richelieu pour la déficience intellectuelle

Association de Laval pour la déficience intellectuelle (ALDI)
73, boul Saint-Elzéar ouest, Laval QC H7W 1E7
Tél: 450-972-1010; *Téléc:* 450-972-1515
secretariat@aldi1959.com
www.aldi1959.com
www.facebook.com/381062655279547
Aperçu: *Dimension:* petite; *Envergure:* locale; fondée en 1959
Mission: L'association a pour mission de permettre aux personnes ayant une déficience intellectuelle de vivre de la façon la plus normale possible en sus itant le développement de conditions facilitantes favorisant l'intégration et l'adaptation sociale
Affiliation(s): Association du Québec pour l'intégration sociale
Membre: *Montant de la cotisation:* 10$ personne vivant avec une déficience; 20$ membre de la famille élargie; 25$ les tuteurs et responsable de résidence; 50$ organismes et associés
Membre(s) du bureau directeur:
France Locas, Présidente
Claude Bonneville, Vice-Président

Johanne Lefebvre, Trésorière

Association de le communauté noire de Côte-des-Neiges inc. / Côte-des-Neiges Black Community Association Inc.
#30, 6999, Côte-des-Neiges, Montréal QC H3S 2B6
Tél: 514-737-8321; *Téléc:* 514-737-6893
www.cdnbca.org
www.facebook.com/245257718844085
Aperçu: *Dimension:* petite; *Envergure:* locale
Mission: Cultural, recreational & social activities for youth & adults; after-school tutorials; summer camp; Teen Leadership Program; adult classes & sports activities
Membre(s) du bureau directeur:
John Cruickshank, Chairperson

Association de linguistique des provinces atlantiques *See* Atlantic Provinces Linguistic Association

Association de location du Canada *See* Canadian Rental Association

Association de loisirs pour personnes handicapées psychiques de Laval (ALPHPL)
6600, 29e av, Laval QC H7R 3M3
Tél: 450-627-4525; *Téléc:* 450-627-4370
alphpl@videotron.ca
www.alphpl.org
Aperçu: *Dimension:* petite; *Envergure:* locale; Organisme sans but lucratif; fondée en 1983
Mission: Promouvoir l'évolution sociale des personnes handicapées psychiques en stimulant leurs intérêts pour des activités physiques, socio-culturelles et des loisirs; les soutenir dans leur apprentissage, l'entraînement et l'utilisation des ressources et équipements socio-communautaires; créer un sentiment d'appartenance du participant dans son milieu
Membre de: Association régionale pour personnes handicapées des Laurentides; Association québécoise pour la réadaptation psychosociale; Regroupement des ressources alternatives en santé mentale du Québec; l'Association canadienne pour la santé mentale
Activités: Expositions des travaux des bénéficiaires
Membre(s) du bureau directeur:
François Bullock, Directeur général

Association de maison de transition atlantique *See* Atlantic Halfway House Association

Association de medecine naturapathique du Québec *See* Québec Association of Naturopathic Medicine

Association de médiation familiale du Québec (AMFQ)
4800, ch Queen Mary, Montréal QC H3W 1W9
Tél: 514-990-4011; *Téléc:* 514-733-9081
Ligne sans frais: 800-667-7559
info@mediationquebec.ca
www.mediationquebec.ca
www.facebook.com/669501183095454
twitter.com/Amfqinfo
Aperçu: *Dimension:* petite; *Envergure:* provinciale; fondée en 1985
Mission: L'Association de médiation familiale du Québec a pour mission de développer et promouvoir la médiation familiale et les médiateurs familiaux accrédités, au Québec et à l'étranger.
Affiliation(s): Family Mediation Canada
Membre: 244+
Activités: Formation; colloque annuel; distribution de publications; écoute et soutien
Membre(s) du bureau directeur:
Jean-François Chabot, Présidente
Gerald Schoel, Trésorier
José Mongeau, Secrétaire

Association de Montréal pour la déficience intellectuelle (AMDI) / Montreal Association for the Intellectually Handicapped (MAIH)
#100, 633, boul Crémazie est, Montréal QC H2M 1L9
Tél: 514-381-2300; *Téléc:* 514-381-0454
info@amdi.info
www.amdi.info
www.facebook.com/181368175217004
Aperçu: *Dimension:* moyenne; *Envergure:* locale; Organisme sans but lucratif; fondée en 1935
Mission: De promouvoir et défendre les droits et intérêts des personnes présentant une déficience intellectuelle et ceux de leur famille

Membre de: Centraide
Affiliation(s): Association du Québec pour l'intégration sociale
Finances: Budget de fonctionnement annuel: $500,000-$1.5 Million; Fonds: Gouvernement provincial et municipaux
Membre(s) du personnel: 8; 60 bénévole(s)
Membre: 1 244; Critères d'admissibilité: Parents; personnes présentant une déficience intellectuelle
Activités: Service de références; fin de semaine de plein air; camps familiaux; voyages organisés; accompagnements; gardiennage; Bibliothèque: Centre Allen Hanley; rendez-vous
Membre(s) du bureau directeur:
Patricia Tonelli, Présidente
Stéphane Dupupet, Directeur général
direction.generale@amdi.info

Association de Musicothérapie du Canada See Friends of Music Therapy

Association de neurochirurgie du Québec (ANCQ)
CP 216, Succ. Desjardins, #3000, 2, Complexe Desjardins, Montréal QC H5B 1G8
Tél: 514-350-5120; *Téléc:* 514-350-5100
ancq@fmsq.org
www.ancq.net
Aperçu: Dimension: petite; Envergure: provinciale; fondée en 1965 surveillé par Fédération des médecins spécialistes du Québec
Mission: Pour représenter les médecins spécialistes et de promouvoir leurs intérêts
Membre de: Fédération des Médecins Spécialistes de Québec (FMSQ)
Membre(s) du bureau directeur:
David Mathieu, Président
Manon Gaudry, Directrice, Administration
Publications:
• Interneurone
Type: Newsletter

Association de nutrition animale du Canada See Animal Nutrition Association of Canada

Association de paralysie cérébrale du Québec (APCQ) / Québec Cerebral Palsy Association
CP 1781, Sherbrooke QC J1H 5N8
Tél: 819-829-1144; *Téléc:* 819-829-1144
Ligne sans frais: 800-311-3770
info@paralysiecerebrale.com
www.paralysiecerebrale.com
Aperçu: Dimension: petite; Envergure: provinciale; fondée en 1949
Mission: Favoriser l'amélioration de la qualité de vie et l'intégration sociale des personnes vivant avec une paralysie cérébrale ou toutes autres déficiences; défendre leurs droits; sensibiliser et informer la population, les organismes et les gouvernements; encourager la recherche et découverte de nouvelles thérapies
Activités: Orientation; information; prêt d'équipements spécialisés; aide financière
Membre(s) du bureau directeur:
Joseph Khoury, Président
Michel Larochelle, Directeur général
m.larochelle@paralysiecerebrale.com
  Bureau de Granby
  170, rue St-Antoine nord, Granby QC J2G 5G8
  Tél: 450-777-2907
  Membre(s) du bureau directeur:
  Denise Arès, Responsable
  d.ares@paralysiecerebrale.com
  Bureau de Montréal
  2000, boul St-Joseph est, Montréal QC H2M 1E4
  Tél: 514-253-9444
  Membre(s) du bureau directeur:
  Katia Heise-Jensen, Responsable
  k.heise-jensen@paralysiecerebrale.com
  Bureau de Saint-Jean-sur-Richelieu
  870, rue Curé St-Georges, St-Jean-sur-Richelieu QC J2X 2Z8
  Tél: 450-357-2740
  Ligne sans frais: 866-849-2740
  Membre(s) du bureau directeur:
  Monique Laberge, Responsable
  m.laberge@paralysiecerebrale.com

Association de parents d'enfant trisomique-21 de Lanaudière
245, ch des Anglais, Mascouche QC J7L 3P3
Tél: 450-477-4116; *Téléc:* 560-477-3534
www.apetl.org
www.facebook.com/199268050113168
Aperçu: Dimension: petite; Envergure: locale; fondée en 1990
Affiliation(s): Association du Québec pour l'intégration sociale
Membre(s) du personnel: 6; 50 bénévole(s)
Membre: Montant de la cotisation: 20$ actif; 15$ souscripteurs; 35$ associé
Membre(s) du bureau directeur:
Chantal Lamarre, Directrice générale

Association de Parents de Jumeaux et de Triplés de la région de Montréal (APJTM)
CP 52, Succ. Du Parc, Montréal QC H2S 3K6
Tél: 514-990-6165
apjtm@apjtm.com
www.apjtm.com
Aperçu: Dimension: petite; Envergure: locale; Organisme sans but lucratif; fondée en 1961
Mission: Support et informations aux familles ayant des jumeaux, triplés, quadruplés ou en attentes de naissances multiples
Membre: Critères d'admissibilite: Parents d'enfants de naissances multiples
Activités: Réunions mensuelles avec conférenciers; pique-Nique; cabane à sucre; fête de Noël; bazar; marraines d'allaitemen; parrainage; casting; téléphones du mois; bibliothèque, joujouthèque, vidéothèque; Bibliothèque: BJV

Association de parents pour l'adoption québécoise (APAQ)
#112, 921, boul du Séminaire nord, Saint-Jean-sur-Richelieu QC J3A 1B6
Tél: 514-990-9144
apaq@quebecadoption.net
apaq.quebecadoption.net
Aperçu: Dimension: petite; Envergure: provinciale; fondée en 1996
Mission: Promouvoir l'adoption d'enfants québécois; en faisant connaître les réalités particulières des enfants du Québec adoptés ou en voie de l'être; en faisant connaître la situation de l'adoption des enfants du Québec et ses principaux enjeux actuels; favoriser l'entraide, le partage et le soutien mutuel entre les parents qui vivent l'adoption; vous faire profiter de rabais de 25-30% sur des ouvrages de références et livres d'enfants
Membre: Montant de la cotisation: 35$ famille
Membre(s) du bureau directeur:
Kathleen Neault, Présidente

Association de planification fiscale et financière (APFF) / Fiscal & Financial Planning Association
#660, 1100, boul René-Lévesque ouest, Montréal QC H3B 4N4
Tél: 514-866-2733; *Téléc:* 514-866-0113
Ligne sans frais: 877-866-0113
Autres numéros: Télécopier sans frais: 877-866-0113
apff@apff.org
www.apff.org
www.linkedin.com/groups/Association-planification-fiscale-financière-APFF-3958598
Aperçu: Dimension: moyenne; Envergure: provinciale; Organisme sans but lucratif; fondée en 1976
Mission: Regrouper les personnes intéressées à la planification fiscale successorale et financière; publier et diffuser l'information dans ces domaines; favoriser la recherche
Membre(s) du personnel: 15
Membre: 2,500+; Critères d'admissibilite: Avocats, notaires, comptables agréés, comptables en management accrédités, comptables généraux accrédités, conseillers en sécurité financière, planificateurs financiers, gestionnaires de patrimoines, actuaires, conseillers en placements, économistes, chercheurs universitaires, enseignants et étudiants.; Comités: Activités régionales; colloques; Congrès; Flash Fiscal; planification financière; Revue de planification fiscale et financière; stratège; symposiums; communications et du développement; affaires gouvernementales; liaison; cours en fiscalité; La relève
Activités: 5 à 8 colloques d'une journée par année sur des thèmes spécifiques avec publication intégrale des textes de conférences; Evénements de sensibilisation: Congrès annuel; Tournoi de golf annuel; Bibliothèque: Centre d'information
Membre(s) du bureau directeur:
Maurice Mongrain, Président et directeur général
mongrainm@apff.org

Association de protection des épargnants et investisseurs du Québec Voir Mouvement d'éducation et de défense des actionnaires

Association de Ringuette Chutes Chaudière Voir Association de Ringuette Lévis

Association de ringuette de Colombie-Britannique See British Columbia Ringette Association

Association de ringuette de l'Ontario See Ontario Ringette Association

Association de Ringuette de Longueuil
2258, rue Papineau, Longueuil QC J4K 3M1
Tél: 450-442-0808
www.ringuettelongueuil.com
Aperçu: Dimension: petite; Envergure: provinciale surveillé par Ringuette-Québec
Membre de: Ringuette-Québec
Membre: Montant de la cotisation: Barème
Membre(s) du bureau directeur:
Marie-Lyne Fortin Thibault, Président
marielynefortin87@outlook.com

Association de ringuette de Lotbinière
c/o Marie-Noël Duclos, 412, rue Belanger, Saint-Narcisse-de-Beaurivage QC G0S 1W0
Tél: 418-475-4125
Aperçu: Dimension: petite; Envergure: provinciale surveillé par Ringuette-Québec
Mission: Site Internet: kreezee.com/sport/association/association-de-ringuette-de-lotbiniere/7671
Membre de: Ringuette-Québec
Membre: 7 équipes; Montant de la cotisation: Barème
Membre(s) du bureau directeur:
Marie-Noel Duclos, Présidente
robertetmarie@axion.ca

Association de Ringuette de Sainte-Marie
QC
www.ringuettestemarie.com
www.facebook.com/181771528541007
Aperçu: Dimension: petite; Envergure: provinciale; fondée en 1983 surveillé par Ringuette-Québec
Membre de: Ringuette-Québec
Membre(s) du bureau directeur:
Tony Fecteau, Président, 418-387-8847
presidence@ringuettestemarie.com

Association de Ringuette de Ste-Julie
QC
Aperçu: Dimension: petite; Envergure: provinciale surveillé par Ringuette-Québec
Membre de: Ringuette-Québec

Association de ringuette de Saskatchewan See Ringette Association of Saskatchewan

Association de Ringuette de Sept-Îles
QC
www.ringuettesept-iles.org
fr.facebook.com/228073003907401
Aperçu: Dimension: petite; Envergure: provinciale surveillé par Ringuette-Québec
Membre de: Ringuette-Québec
Membre: 7 équipes
Membre(s) du bureau directeur:
Frédéric Lesage, Président, 418-968-2036
fred.lesage@icloud.com

Association de Ringuette de Thetford
555, rue St-Alphonse nord, Thetford Mines QC G6G 3X1
Tél: 418-338-3729
www.ringuettethetford.com
Aperçu: Dimension: petite; Envergure: provinciale surveillé par Ringuette-Québec
Membre de: Ringuette-Québec
Membre: 5 équipes
Membre(s) du bureau directeur:
Dany Harvey, Président
dharvey27@hotmail.ca

Association de Ringuette de Vallée-du-Richelieu
CP 85113, 345, boul Sir-Wilfrid-Laurier, Mont-Saint-Hilaire QC J3H 5W1
Courriel: vdrringuette@hotmail.com
www.ringuettevdr.com
www.facebook.com/145272202165165
twitter.com/ringuettevdr
www.youtube.com/user/VDRringuette

Canadian Associations / Association de Ringuette des Moulins

Aperçu: *Dimension:* petite; *Envergure:* provinciale surveillé par Ringuette-Québec
Membre de: Ringuette-Québec
Membre(s) du bureau directeur:
Patrick Beauchemin, Président

Association de Ringuette des Moulins
840, rue Brien, Mascouche QC J7K 2X3
Tél: 450-961-9295
admin@ringuettedesmoulins.com
www.ringuettedesmoulins.com
Aperçu: *Dimension:* petite; *Envergure:* provinciale surveillé par Ringuette-Québec
Membre de: Ringuette-Québec
Membre(s) du bureau directeur:
Daniel Gagné, Président
president@ringuettedesmoulins.com

Association de ringuette du Manitoba *See* Manitoba Ringuette Association

Association de Ringuette Lévis
CP 1807, Saint-Rédempteur QC G6K 1N6
Courriel: communications.arl@gmail.com
www.ringuettearl.com
www.facebook.com/ringuettelevis/
Nom précédent: Association de Ringuette Chutes Chaudière
Aperçu: *Dimension:* petite; *Envergure:* provinciale surveillé par Ringuette-Québec
Membre de: Ringuette-Québec
Membre: 14 équipes
Membre(s) du bureau directeur:
Tanya Moore, Présidente

Association de Ringuette Repentigny
QC
www.ringuetterepentigny.com
www.facebook.com/Ringuette-Repentigny-1773415112879301
Aperçu: *Dimension:* petite; *Envergure:* provinciale surveillé par Ringuette-Québec
Membre de: Ringuette-Québec
Membre: 10 équipes
Membre(s) du bureau directeur:
Gordon Britton, Président
gordon.britton@ringuetterepentigny.com

Association de ringuette Roussillon
CP 164, Saint-Constant QC J5A 2G2
Courriel: communications@ringuetteroussillon.ca
www.ringuetteroussillon.ca
www.facebook.com/ARRoussillon
twitter.com/ARRoussillon
www.youtube.com/playlist?list=PLjva740E_gw1xyVGbSm6XtpLcR-HOjbYD
Aperçu: *Dimension:* petite; *Envergure:* provinciale surveillé par Ringuette-Québec
Membre de: Ringuette-Québec

Association de sécurité de l'information de la région de Québec *Voir* Association de la sécurité de l'information du Québec

Association de Sherbrooke pour la déficience intellectuelle (ASDI)
2065, rue Belvédère sud, Sherbrooke QC J1H 5R8
Tél: 819-346-2227; Téléc: 819-346-8752
info@asdi-org.qc.ca
asdi-org.qc.ca
Aperçu: *Dimension:* petite; *Envergure:* locale; Organisme sans but lucratif; fondée en 1965
Mission: Promouvoir l'intégration sociale; favoriser le bien-être; défendre les droits des personnes ayant une déficience intellectuelle
Affiliation(s): Association du Québec pour l'intégration sociale
Membre(s) du personnel: 6
Membre: *Montant de la cotisation:* 20$
Activités: *Stagiaires:* Oui; *Bibliothèque:* Bibliothèque publique rendez-vous
Membre(s) du bureau directeur:
Denis Crête, Directeur général
Chantal Charland, Présidente

Association de soccer du Sud-Ouest de Montréal (ASSOM)
5485, ch de la Côte-Saint-Paul, Montréal QC H4C 1X3
Tél: 514-931-7778
www.soccerassom.com
Aperçu: *Dimension:* petite; *Envergure:* locale; fondée en 1999
Membre(s) du bureau directeur:
Azzeddine Baghdadi, President

Association de spina-bifida et d'hydrocephalie du Canada *See* Spina Bifida & Hydrocephalus Association of Canada

L'Association de spina-bifida et d'hydrocéphalie du Québec (ASBHQ)
#303, 55, av Mont-Royal ouest, Montréal QC H2T 2S6
Tél: 514-340-9019
Ligne sans frais: 800-567-1788
info@spina.qc.ca
www.spina.qc.ca
www.facebook.com/asbhq
twitter.com/ASBHQ
Aperçu: *Dimension:* moyenne; *Envergure:* provinciale; Organisme sans but lucratif; fondée en 1975 surveillé par Spina Bifida & Hydrocephalus Association of Canada
Mission: Promouvoir et défendre les droits, les intérêts et le bien-être des personnes ayant le spina-bifida et l'hydrocéphalie; sensibiliser le public à la nature du spina-bifida et de l'hydrocéphalie ainsi qu'aux besoins des personnes ayant ces malformations; favoriser et soutenir la recherche sur les causes, les nouveaux traitements et les techniques de prévention du spina-bifida et de l'hydrocéphalie
Membre de: Confédération des organismes provinciaux de personnes handicappées du Québec
Affiliation(s): Institut de réadaptation en déficience physique de Québec; Hôpital Shriners, Centre de réadaptation Constance-Lethbridge, Centre de réadaptation en déficience physique Chaudière-Appalaches
Finances: *Fonds:* MSSS; diverses activités de levées de fonds; individuels et corporatifs
Activités: Organiser des colloques permettant aux membres une mise à jour avec des professionnels de la santé, de l'éducation et des services sociaux; recueillir, traduire, réorganiser et distribuer la documentation; une attention particulière est portée aux personnes qui habitent dans les régions éloignées des grands centres médicaux afin de leur prêter un appui moral et technique nécessaire à leur intégration et à leur épanouissement; *Evénements de sensibilisation:* Campagne de prévention du spina-bifida; *Service de conférenciers:* Oui; *Bibliothèque:* rendez-vous Not open to public
Membre(s) du bureau directeur:
Marc Picard, Président

A.S.B.H. Région Estrie
928, rue Fédéral, Sherbrooke QC J1H 5A7
Tél: 819-822-3772; Téléc: 819-822-4529
asbhestrie@hotmail.com
www.spina.qc.ca/estrie
Membre(s) du bureau directeur:
René Labonté, Président
Aline Nault, Coordonnatrice

A.S.B.H. Région Montréal
#448, 14115, Prince-Arthur, Montréal QC H1A 1A8
Tél: 514-739-5515; Téléc: 514-739-5505
asbhrm@mainbourg.org
www.spina.qc.ca
www.facebook.com/asbhq.quebec
twitter.com/ASBHQ
Membre(s) du bureau directeur:
André Bougie, Président

Association de taekwondo du Québec
4545, av Pierre-de Coubertin, Montréal QC H1V 3R2
Tél: 514-252-3198; Téléc: 514-254-7075
Ligne sans frais: 800-762-9565
info@taekwondo-quebec.ca
www.taekwondo-quebec.ca
www.facebook.com/115348592723
Également appelé: Taekwondo Québec
Aperçu: *Dimension:* moyenne; *Envergure:* provinciale
Mission: Favoriser le développement du taekwondo québécois
Membre(s) du bureau directeur:
Jean Faucher, Président
jfaucher@taekwondo-quebec.ca
Martin Desjardins, Vice-président
mdesjardins@taekwondo-quebec.ca
Abdel Ilah Es Sabbar, Directeur exécutif
essabbar@taekwondo-quebec.ca

Association de TED du Canada *See* EFILE Association of Canada

Association de tir de la province de Québec *See* Province of Québec Rifle Association

L'Association de tir dominion du canada *See* Dominion of Canada Rifle Association

Association de ventes directes du Canada *See* Direct Sellers Association of Canada

Association de vitrerie et fenestrations du Québec (AVFQ)
#216, 2065, rue Frank-Carrel, Québec QC G1N 2G1
Tél: 418-688-1256; Téléc: 418-688-2460
Ligne sans frais: 800-263-4032
info@avfq.ca
www.avfq.ca
www.linkedin.com/groups?home=&gid=5142613
www.facebook.com/1383936025162152
Nom précédent: L'Association des industries de produits verriers et de fenestration du Québec; L'Association des industries de portes et fenêtres du Québec
Aperçu: *Dimension:* moyenne; *Envergure:* provinciale; Organisme sans but lucratif; fondée en 1964
Mission: Promouvoir et défendre les intérêts des membres; regrouper et représenter toutes les entreprises de produits verriers, de portes et fenêtres du Québec
Affiliation(s): Association canadienne des manufacturiers de portes et fenêtres du Canada
Membre(s) du personnel: 3
Membre: 200+; *Critères d'admissibilite:* Fournisseurs de composants et manufacturiers; *Comités:* Bourses d'Études; Commercial; Congrès; Contrats; Développement; Formation; Gala; Golf; Hydro-Québec; Innovation Bois; Technique
Activités: Séminaires; congrès; salon; *Service de conférenciers:* Oui
Membre(s) du bureau directeur:
Gilbert Lemay, Vice-président à la direction
glemay@avfq.ca
Marc Bilodeau, Président, 450-681-0483, Fax: 450-681-8432
marcbilodeau@vitreco.ca

Association de voile de l'Ontario *See* Ontario Sailing

Association de vol à voile Champlain
#10, 745 de Martigny, Montréal QC H2B 2N1
Tél: 450-771-0500
info@avvc.qc.ca
www.avvc.qc.ca
Aperçu: *Dimension:* petite; *Envergure:* locale; Organisme sans but lucratif
Mission: Former des pilotes de planeur et les amener au niveau du vol voyage; répondre aux attentes de ses membres actifs
Membre de: Soaring Association of Canada
Membre: *Montant de la cotisation:* 620$

L'Association de water polo d'Ontario *See* Ontario Water Polo Association Incorporated

L'Association dentaire canadienne *See* Canadian Dental Association

Association des accidentés cérébro-vasculaires et traumatisés crâniens de l'Estrie (ACTE)
68, boul Jacques-Cartier nord, Sherbrooke QC J1J 2Z8
Tél: 819-821-2799; Téléc: 819-821-4599
info@acteestrie.com
www.acteestrie.com
www.facebook.com/ACTEEstrie
Aperçu: *Dimension:* petite; *Envergure:* locale; fondée en 1984
Mission: Pour aider les personnes de la région de l'Estrie du Québec qui ont subi un accident vasculaire cérébral ou un traumatisme crânien; regrouper et soutenir les personnes victimes d'AVC et de traumatisme craniocérébral
Membre de: Regroupement des associations de personnes traumatisées craniocérébrales du Québec / Coalition of Associations of Craniocerebral Trauma in Quebec; Regroupement des associations de personnes aphasiques du Québec
Finances: *Budget de fonctionnement annuel:* $250,000-$500,000
Membre(s) du personnel: 8; 12 bénévole(s)
Membre: 204; *Montant de la cotisation:* 10$ par année; *Critères d'admissibilite:* Personnes de la région de l'Estrie, Québec qui ont survécu à un accident vasculaire cérébral (AVC) ou à un traumatisme crânien; Membres de la famille des personnes qui ont survécu à un accident vasculaire cérébral
Activités: La sensibilisation du public et la diffusion d'informations sur les accidents cérébraux ou un traumatisme crânien; Défendre les droits et intérêts des personnes qui ont survécu à un accident vasculaire cérébral; Aider les personnes à maintenir leurs capacités et développer

les intérêts, en organisant des ateliers sur des sujets tels que l'art et loisirs de plein air; Offrir un soutien psychosocial, à travers des réunions de groupe de soutien aux victimes, aux familles, et amis; *Stagiaires:* Oui; *Service de conférenciers:* Oui
Membre(s) du bureau directeur:
Peter Nieman, Directeur général, 819-821-2799
peter.nieman@acteestrie.com
Publications:
• L'Actif [publication de Association des accidentés cérébro-vasculaires et traumatisés crâniens de l'Estrie]
Type: Journal; *ISSN:* 1488-4453
Profile: Journal inspiré par les membres de l'ACTE

Association des actuaires I.A.R.D.
QC
Autres numéros: Alt. courriel: babillard@aaiard.com
commentaire@aaiard.com
www.aaiard.com
Aperçu: Dimension: petite; *Envergure:* provinciale
Mission: Promouvoir la connaissance de la science actuarielle appliquée aux situations d'assurance I.A.R.D. et domaines connexes
Membre(s) du bureau directeur:
Sébastien Vachon, Président
president@aaiard.com
Frédérick Guillot, Vice-président
vicepresident@aaiard.com

Association des Acupuncteurs du Québec (L'AAQ)
#203, 1453, rue Beaubien est, Montréal QC H2G 3C6
Tél: 514-564-5115
Ligne sans frais: 844-564-5115
info@acupuncture-quebec.com
www.acupuncture-quebec.com
fr-ca.facebook.com/128162563939912
Nom précédent: Association d'Acupuncture du Québec
Aperçu: Dimension: petite; *Envergure:* provinciale; Organisme sans but lucratif; fondée en 2000
Mission: Promouvoir la médecine traditionnelle chinoise et l'acupuncture; défendre les intérets de ses membres
Affiliation(s): Ordre des acupuncteurs du Québec; Département d'acupuncture: Collège de Rosemont; Distributeurs de l'AAQ
8 bénévole(s)
Membre: *Montant de la cotisation:* 200$ actif; 150$ nouveau gradué; 100$ congé parental; 75$ retraité ou inactif; 50$ sympathisant
Activités: Échanges professionnels; séminaires; symposiums; recherches; matériel promotionnel
Membre(s) du bureau directeur:
Mélanie Lévesque, Présidente

Association des administrateurs des écoles anglaises du Québec *See* Association of Administrators of English Schools of Québec

Association des administrateurs municipaux du Nouveau-Brunswick *See* Association of Municipal Administrators of New Brunswick

Association des affaires publiques du Canada *See* The Public Affairs Association of Canada

Association des agences d'agrément du Canada *See* Association of Accrediting Agencies of Canada

Association des agences de publicité du Québec (AAPQ) / Association of Québec Advertising Agencies
#925, 2015, rue Peel, Montréal QC H3A 1T8
Tél: 514-848-1732; *Téléc:* 514-848-1950
Ligne sans frais: 877-878-1732
aapq@aapq.ca
www.aapq.ca
Aperçu: Dimension: moyenne; *Envergure:* provinciale; Organisme sans but lucratif; fondée en 1988
Mission: Promouvoir et défendre les intérêts des agences membres
Membre(s) du personnel: 5
Membre: 70 agences membres; *Montant de la cotisation:* Barème
Membre(s) du bureau directeur:
Dominique Villeneuve, Directrice générale
d.villeneuve@aapq.ca

Association des agents de police de la ville de Regina *See* Regina Policemen Association Inc.

Association des agents de services au public de Winnipeg *See* Winnipeg Association of Public Service Officers

Association des agents de voyages du Québec *Voir* Association of Canadian Travel Agents - Québec

L'Association des agents des immobiliers du Nouveau-Brunswick *See* New Brunswick Real Estate Association

Association des Allergologues et Immunologues du Québec
CP 216, Succ. Desjardins, #3000, 2, Complexe Desjardins, Montréal QC H5B 1G8
Tél: 514-350-5101
aaiq@fmsq.org
www.allerg.qc.ca
Aperçu: Dimension: moyenne; *Envergure:* provinciale surveillé par Fédération des médecins spécialistes du Québec
Membre de: Fédération des medecins spéialistes du Québec
Membre(s) du bureau directeur:
Sylvie Pelletier, Directrice, Administration

Association des alternatives en santé mentale de la Montérégie (AASMM)
#309, 170, rue Saint-Antoine nord, Granby QC J2G 5G8
Tél: 450-375-5868; *Téléc:* 450-375-5319
info@aasmm.com
www.aasmm.com
Aperçu: Dimension: petite; *Envergure:* locale; Organisme sans but lucratif; fondée en 1986
Mission: Promouvoir la vie associative par des action concrètes; promouvoir les expertises de ses ressources membres; soutenir et défendre les intérêts de ses ressources membres; promouvoir l'idéologie alternative en santé mentale auprès de ses ressources membres et auprès des communautés
Membre(s) du bureau directeur:
André Leduc, Président
Joseph-Anne St-Hilaire, Vice-Présidente

Association des Aménagistes Régionaux du Québec (AARQ)
#204, 870, av de Salaberry, Québec QC G1R 2T9
Tél: 418-524-4666
administration@aarq.qc.ca
www.aarq.qc.ca
www.facebook.com/160531930681615
Aperçu: Dimension: petite; *Envergure:* provinciale; Organisme sans but lucratif; fondée en 1984
Membre: *Critères d'admissibilité:* Aménagiste travaillant au sein d'une M.R.C.; *Comités:* Vigie; représentation; évaluation; opérations
Activités: Lieu d'échange entre les professionnels de l'aménagement du territoire oeuvrant au sein des municipalités régionales de comté (M.R.C.)
Membre(s) du bureau directeur:
François Lestage, Président

Association des amis canadiens de l'Université Hébraïque *See* Canadian Friends of the Hebrew University

Association des Amis d'ATD Quart-Monde *Voir* Mouvement ATD Quart Monde Canada

L'Association des Anciens Combattants de la marine marchande canadienne Inc. *See* Canadian Merchant Navy Veterans Association Inc.

Association des anciens de la Gendarmerie royale du Canada *See* Royal Canadian Mounted Police Veterans' Association

Association des anciens élèves du collège Sainte-Marie
www.saintemarie.ca
Aperçu: Dimension: petite; *Envergure:* locale; fondée en 1882
Membre: *Montant de la cotisation:* 35$
Membre(s) du bureau directeur:
Richard L'Heureux, Président, 514-482-0095
richard.lheureux@videotron.ca
Jacques D. Girard, Contact, 514-485-8114
jacques.girard@saintemarie.ca

Association des archéologues du Québec (AAQ)
CP 322, Succ. Haute-Ville, Québec QC G1R 4P8
Courriel: info@archeologie.qc.ca
www.archeologie.qc.ca
Également appelé: AAQ
Aperçu: Dimension: moyenne; *Envergure:* provinciale; Organisme sans but lucratif; fondée en 1979 surveillé par Canadian Archaeological Association
Mission: Définir les standards de la profession; veiller à la saine gestion et la mise en valeur du patrimoine archéologique à cause d'une éthique exemplaire et de la qualité de ses membres; agir comme interlocuteur privilégié pour tout ce qui regarde la question archéologique auprès des gouvernements et des organismes, privés ou publics, qui ont à coeur la préservation de notre patrimoine collectif
Membre de: 'éseau-Archéo; Fédération des sociétés d'histoire du Québec
Finances: *Fonds:* Ministère de la Culture et des communications du Québec
Membre: *Montant de la cotisation:* 125$ régulier; 60$ associé; 30$ étudiant; *Critères d'admissibilite:* Archéologue professionel
Activités: Colloque annuel; publications; prises de position

Association des architectes du Nouveau-Brunswick *See* Architects' Association of New Brunswick

Association des Architectes en pratique privée du Québec (AAPPQ) / Association of Architects in Private Practice of Québec
#302, 420, rue McGill, Montréal QC H2Y 2G1
Tél: 514-937-4140; *Téléc:* 514-937-2329
aappq@aappq.qc.ca
www.aappq.qc.ca
Aperçu: Dimension: moyenne; *Envergure:* provinciale; fondée en 1977
Mission: Représente et défend les intérêts de firmes d'architecture
Membre(s) du personnel: 2; 20 bénévole(s)
Membre: 400 sociétés; *Montant de la cotisation:* Barème; *Critères d'admissibilite:* Il faut être architecte et avoir un bureau d'architecte à son compte; *Comités:* Comité de formation continue et de recherche; Comité honoraires, conditions d'engagement et de pratique; Comité de liaisons; Comité de relations publiques
Activités: Formation; Marketing; Médiation; Qualité-totale
Membre(s) du bureau directeur:
Sylvie Perrault, Présidente
Publications:
• InfoMembres [a publication of Association des Architectes en pratique privée du Québec]
Type: Newsletter; *Frequency:* Mensuel
Profile: Des derniers travaux de l'Association, des services proposés, ainsi que les formations et actualités de l'indutrie

Association des architectes paysagistes du Canada *See* Canadian Society of Landscape Architects

Association des architectes paysagistes du Québec (AAPQ)
#406, 420, rue McGill, Montréal QC H2Y 2G1
Tél: 514-526-6385; *Téléc:* 514-526-6385
info@aapq.org
www.aapq.org
www.facebook.com/pageaapq
twitter.com/AAPQ_paysages
Aperçu: Dimension: petite; *Envergure:* provinciale; fondée en 1965
Mission: Promouvoir la création et la valorisation du paysage en milieu naturel et construit dans le but de constituer un cadre de vie sain, fonctionnel, esthétique, axé sur les besoins de la population et répondant aux exigences écologiques
Affiliation(s): Association des Architectes Paysagistes du Canada
Membre: *Montant de la cotisation:* Barème
Membre(s) du bureau directeur:
Édith Normandeau, Directrice générale par intérim
dg@aapq.org

L'Association des archives de l'Ontario *See* Archives Association of Ontario

Association des archivistes du Québec (AAQ)
CP 9768, Succ. Sainte-Foy, Québec QC G1V 4C3
Tél: 418-652-2357; *Téléc:* 418-646-0868
infoaaq@archivistes.qc.ca
www.archivistes.qc.ca
www.linkedin.com/groups/2311475/profile
www.facebook.com/ArchivistesQc
twitter.com/archivistesQc
Aperçu: Dimension: moyenne; *Envergure:* nationale; Organisme sans but lucratif; fondée en 1967

Canadian Associations / L'Association des artistes Baltes à Montréal (AAB) / Baltic Artists' Association - Montréal

Mission: Regrouper les personnes qui offrent aux organisations et à leurs clientèles des services liés à la gestion de leur information organique et consignée; offrir à ses membres des services en français et propres à assurer le développement, l'enrichissement et la promotion de leur profession et de leur discipline; assurer aux membres les services susceptibles de favoriser et d'accroître les échanges et la communication internes et externes des idées et des connaissances; promouvoir le développement professionnel des membres en s'impliquant activement au plan de la formation et du perfectionnement, en favorisant la recherche et le développement et en assurant une représentation adéquate de la profession au sein de la société et auprès des corps politiques
Membre de: Conseil canadien des archives
Finances: *Fonds:* Cotisation, Congrès
Membre: *Montant de la cotisation:* Barème; *Critères d'admissibilite:* Professionnel ou technicien; *Comités:* Revue Archives; Congrès annuel; Certification et perfectionnement; Affaire professionnelles; Communications
Activités: Formation; banque de consultants; congrès; *Service de conférenciers:* Oui
Membre(s) du bureau directeur:
Carole Saulnier, Présidente
Anne Dumont, Directrice générale
anne.dumont@archivistes.qc.ca
Prix, Bourses:
• Prix du président
• Prix Jacques-Grimard
• Prix Jacques-Ducharme
• Prix Robert-Garon
• Prix du meilleur article de la revue Archives
Meetings/Conferences:
• 47e Congrès de l'Association des archivistes du Québec, 2018, QC
Scope: Provincial
Publications:
• Archives: La revue de l'Association des archivistes du Québec
Type: Revue; *Number of Pages:* 175; *ISSN:* 0044-9423
Profile: Présente des articles sur la gestion des archives, traditionnelle et électronique des archives
• Archiviste d'aujourd'hui: guide pratique [publication de l'Association des archivistes du Québec]
Type: Guide
• Infolettre AAQ [publication de l'Association des archivistes du Québec]
Type: Bulletin
Profile: Les dernières nouvelles concernant l'Association

Association des Arénas du Québec Voir Association québécoise des arénas et des installations récréatives et sportives

Association des armateurs du Saint-Laurent inc.; Association des opérateurs de navires du Saint-Laurent Voir Armateurs du Saint-Laurent

Association des arpenteurs des terres du Canada See Association of Canada Lands Surveyors

Association des arpenteurs-géomètres du Nouveau-Brunswick See Association of New Brunswick Land Surveyors

L'Association des artistes Baltes à Montréal (AAB) / Baltic Artists' Association - Montréal
Overview: A small local organization
Mission: To support Baltic artists in the Montréal area
Finances: *Annual Operating Budget:* Less than $50,000
6 volunteer(s)
Membership: *Member Profile:* Visual artists, photographers & makers of handcrafts
Activities: Meetings; workshops; annual exhibitions
Chief Officer(s):
Ann Kallaste-Kruzelecky, President
Mara Rudzitis, Vice-President
Dzintra Palejs, Secretary
Aleksandras Piesena, Treasurer
John Vazalinskas, Contact, Newsletter/Membership

Association des artistes en arts visuels de Saint-Jérôme (AAAV)
101, pl du Curé Labelle, Saint-Jérôme QC J7Z 1X6
Courriel: courrier@aaavsj.com
aaavsj.com
Aperçu: *Dimension:* petite; *Envergure:* locale; Organisme sans but lucratif; fondée en 1990

Mission: Promouvoir l'art dans la région; aider chacun des membres dans son cheminement personnel; demeurer accessible à tous; créer une dynamique de groupe pour favoriser l'émulation et les échanges
Affiliation(s): Conseil québécois de l'Estampe; Conseil de la sculpture du Québec; Conseil des arts textiles du Québec; Conseil des artistes peintres du Québec; Association des illustrateurs et illustratrices du Québec
Finances: *Budget de fonctionnement annuel:* Moins de $50,000
20 bénévole(s)
Membre: 140 à 180 chaque année; *Montant de la cotisation:* 25$ membres; 20$ amis de l'Art; *Critères d'admissibilite:* Artistes peintre-sculpteur (reliés aux arts)
Activités: Réunions mensuelles; expositions; ateliers; *Événements de sensibilisation:* Exposition annuelle nov. Galeries Laurentides
Membre(s) du bureau directeur:
Lorraine Bergeron, Présidente

Association des artistes peintres affiliés de la Rive-Sud (AAPARS)
PO Box 261, Saint-Bruno-de-Montarville QC J3V 4P9
aapars.com
Overview: A small local organization
Mission: Promouvoir de nouveaux artistes avec l'aide d'artistes établis
Chief Officer(s):
Jacques Landry, Président, Conseil d'administration, 450-461-3796
famille_landry00@sympatico.ca

Association des artistes peintres de Longueuil
CP 55083, Succ. Vieux Longueuil, Longueuil QC J4H 0A2
Tél: 450-646-8450
laapl@hotmail.com
laapl.blogspot.ca
Aperçu: *Dimension:* petite; *Envergure:* locale; fondée en 1989
Mission: Pour encourager les gens à développer leurs compétences artistiques
Activités: Des expositions; des ateliers
Membre(s) du bureau directeur:
Claude Charter, Présidente, Conseil d'administration

Association des arts thérapeutes du Québec (AATQ)
#307B, 911, rue Jean-Talon est, Montréal QC H2R 1V5
Tél: 514-990-5415
info@aatq.org
aatq.org
Aperçu: *Dimension:* petite; *Envergure:* provinciale; fondée en 1981
Membre: *Montant de la cotisation:* 100$ professionnels/alliés; 45$ étudiants; 80$ affiliés spéciaux; 95$ affiliés étrangers/bienfaiteurs affilié; 45$ étudiants affiliés
Membre(s) du bureau directeur:
Sylvie Goyette, Président

Association des assistant(e)s-dentaires du Québec (CDAA/AADQ)
#403, 2030, boul Pie-IX, Montréal QC H1V 2C8
Tél: 514-722-9900; Téléc: 514-355-4159
aadq@spg.qc.ca
www.aadq.ca
www.facebook.com/199089516940427
Aperçu: *Dimension:* petite; *Envergure:* provinciale; fondée en 1973 surveillé par Canadian Dental Assistants Association
Mission: Aider ses membres à parfaire leurs connaissances par des cours pratiques et théoriques; moderniser le domaine dentaire; règlementer les assistants-dentaires
Membre: *Montant de la cotisation:* Barème; *Critères d'admissibilite:* Hygiénistes dentaires, des étudiants et des professeurs

Association des Assistantes Dentaires du Nouveau-Brunswick See New Brunswick Dental Assistants Association

Association des auteures et des auteurs de l'Ontario français (AAOF)
335B, rue Cumberland, Ottawa ON K1N 7J3
Tél: 613-744-0902; Téléc: 613-744-6915
dg@aaof.ca
www.aaof.ca
Aperçu: *Dimension:* moyenne; *Envergure:* provinciale; Organisme sans but lucratif; fondée en 1988
Mission: Promotion et diffusion de la littérature d'expression française en Ontario; Promotion des auteurs/es membres et de leurs oeuvres; Services professionnels aux membres; Représentation des intérêts des membres auprès d'intervenants publics
Affiliation(s): Alliance culturelle de l'Ontario; Assemblée de la francophonie de l'Ontario
Membre(s) du personnel: 15; 8 bénévole(s)
Membre: 125; *Montant de la cotisation:* 85$ Membre agréé; 45$ Membre affilié; *Critères d'admissibilite:* Écrivaines et écrivains; *Comités:* Bulletin
Activités: *Evénements de sensibilisation:* Journée mondiale du livre et du droit d'auteur, 23 avril; *Bibliothèque:* Centre de ressources pour écrivains/es en herbe et professionnels/; Bibliothèque publique
Membre(s) du bureau directeur:
Yves Turbide, Directeur général, dg@aaof.ca, 613-744-0902, Fax: 613-744-6915

Association des auteurs-compositeurs canadiens See Songwriters Association of Canada

L'Association des autocaristes Canadiens See Motor Coach Canada

Association des Aviateurs et Pilotes de Brousse du Québec (APBQ)
#207, 3509, boul de la Concorde est, Laval QC H7E 2C6
Tél: 514-255-9998; Téléc: 450-436-4411
Ligne sans frais: 877-317-2727
secretariat@apbq.com
www.apbq.com
Nom précédent: Association des pilotes de brousse du Québec
Aperçu: *Dimension:* moyenne; *Envergure:* provinciale; Organisme sans but lucratif; fondée en 1979
Mission: Regrouper et représenter les aviateurs du Québec; promouvoir l'aviation récréative et le vol de brousse; protéger le droit de voler; favoriser l'accessibilité et la sécurité du vol; faciliter l'échange entre les membres; donner accès à des ressources d'aide, de formation et d'information
Finances: *Fonds:* Cotisations; vente de publicité sur le web; ristournes; petites annonces
Membre: *Montant de la cotisation:* Barème
Activités: Assemblée générale; soirées techniques; programme de formation
Membre(s) du bureau directeur:
Bernard Gervais, Président

Association des avocats de la défense de Montréal (AADM)
#300, 402, rue Notre-Dame est, Montréal QC H2Y 1C8
Tél: 514-687-4924; Téléc: 514-687-4923
info@aadm.ca
aadm.ca
twitter.com/aadm_expo
Aperçu: *Dimension:* petite; *Envergure:* locale
Mission: Association d'avocats de la défense en droit criminel et pénal pratiquant essentiellement à Montréal. Sa mission comporte deux volets principaux: la défense des intérêts de ses membres et la promotion des droits et libertés individuels au sein du système judiciaire
Membre: 475; *Montant de la cotisation:* Basé sur le statut d'avocat
Activités: Journée d'étude; Symposium; Formation
Membre(s) du bureau directeur:
Richard F. Prihoda, Président
rprihoda@yourdefence.ca
Alexandre Bergevin, Vice-présidente
abergevin@aadm.ca

Association des avocats en droit de la jeunesse
410, rue de Bellechasse, Montréal QC H2S 1X3
Tél: 514-278-1738
Aperçu: *Dimension:* petite; *Envergure:* provinciale

Association des avocats et avocates de la région de Moncton See Moncton Area Lawyers' Association

Association des avocats et avocates de province (AAP)
2097, rue Casson, Trois-Rivières QC G8Y 7E8
Tél: 450-516-4800
secretaire@avocatsdeprovince.qc.ca
www.avocatsdeprovince.qc.ca
Aperçu: *Dimension:* moyenne; *Envergure:* provinciale
Mission: Pour réunir des juristes qui partagent des expériences et conseils avec l'autre
Membre(s) du bureau directeur:
Daniel Kimpton, Directeur général et secrétaire
secretaire@avocatsdeprovince.qc.ca

Caroline Blache, Présidente
cblache@cjll.qc.ca

Association des avocats et avocates représentant les bénéficiaires des régimes d'indemnisation publics (AAARBRIP)
445, boul Saint-Laurent, Montréal QC H2Y 3T8
Tél: 514-954-3471; *Téléc:* 517-954-3451
Ligne sans frais: 800-361-8495
www.aaarbrip.com
Aperçu: Dimension: petite; *Envergure:* locale
Mission: Protéger ceux qui reçoivent des prestations du Régime des rentes du Québec et de créer une communauté de juristes qui défendent leurs droits
Membre: Montant de la cotisation: 75$
Membre(s) du bureau directeur:
André Laporte, Président, Conseil d'administration

Association des avocats et avovates en droit familial du Québec (AAADFQ)
445, boul St-Laurent, 5e étage, Montréal QC H2Y 3T8
Tél: 514-954-3471
Ligne sans frais: 800-361-8495
info@aaadfq.ca
www.aaadfq.ca
Aperçu: Dimension: petite; *Envergure:* locale; fondée en 1985
Mission: Pour aider à rendre la pratique du droit de la famille plus pratique et plus efficace et de créer une communauté parmi ses membres
Membre: Montant de la cotisation: 45$ Avocat stagiaire; 70$ Moins de 5 ans de pratique; 90$ 5 ans et plus de pratique
Membre(s) du bureau directeur:
Marie Annik Walsh, Présidente, Conseil d'administration

L'Association des Avocats Noirs du Canada *See* Canadian Association of Black Lawyers

Association des banques alimentaires du Nouveau-Brunswick *See* New Brunswick Association of Food Banks

Association des banquiers canadiens *See* Canadian Bankers Association

Association des bénévoles du don de sang (ABDS) / Association of Blood Donation Volunteers (ABDV)
4045, boul Côte-Vertu, Montréal QC H4R 2W7
Tél: 514-832-5000; *Téléc:* 514-832-0872
Ligne sans frais: 888-666-4362
abdsdondesang@gmail.com
www.abdsdondesang.com
www.linkedin.com/in/abdsdondesang
www.facebook.com/ABDS-333369506845428
Aperçu: Dimension: petite; *Envergure:* provinciale; Organisme sans but lucratif; fondée en 1998
Mission: Soutenir le recrutement de nouveaux donneurs en partenariat avec Héma-Québec; Promouvoir le don de sang
Finances: Fonds: Des dons
Membre: 500 membres dans 13 sections régionales
Activités: La promotion du don de sang à des kiosques d'information; Utiliser un don kiosque de sang mobile; Offrant kits pédagogiques aux enseignants pour éduquer les élèves sur le don de sang
Membre(s) du bureau directeur:
Florentina Costache, Directrice des opérations

Association des bibliotechniciens de l'Ontario *See* Ontario Association of Library Technicians

Association des bibliothécaires du Québec *See* Québec Library Association

Association des bibliothécaires professionnel(le)s de Nouveau-Brunswick *See* Association of Professional Librarians of New Brunswick

Association des bibliothécaires professionnel(le)s du Nouveau-Brunswick (ABPNB) / Association of Professional Librarians of New Brunswick (APLNB)
PO Box 423, Fredericton NB E3B 4Z9
info@aplnb-abpnb.ca
www.aplnb-abpnb.ca
Overview: A medium-sized provincial organization founded in 1992
Mission: Promouvoir les bibliothécaires et les services de bibliothèques au Nouveau-Brunswick
Membership: Committees: Adhésion; Hackmatack; Information et de publicité; Bulletin de nouvelles; Bibliothèques scolaires; Alphabétisation
Activities: *Rents Mailing List:* Yes
Awards:
• Prix de reconnaissance

Association des bibliothécaires, des professeurs et professeurs de l'Université de Moncton (ABPPUM)
Université de Moncton, Pavillon Pierre-A.-Landry, #234, Moncton NB E1A 3E9
Tél: 506-858-4509; *Téléc:* 506-858-4559
abppum@umoncton.ca
www.caut.ca/abppum
Aperçu: Dimension: petite; *Envergure:* locale; fondée en 1976
Mission: Prendre toutes mesures susceptibles de sauvegarder et promouvoir le bien-être et les intérêts de l'association et de ses membres; se livrer aux activités d'enseignement et de recherche jugées utiles et nécessaires; agir de façon à promouvoir les meilleurs intérêts de l'Université de Moncton
Affiliation(s): Association canadienne des professeures et professeurs d'université; Fédération des associations des professeures et professeurs d'université du Nouveau-Brunswick
Membre(s) du personnel: 2
Membre: 300; *Montant de la cotisation:* Barème; *Critères d'admissibilité:* Ouvert à toute personne employée à plein temps par le campus de Moncton de l'Université de Moncton à titre de professeur ou professeur ou de bibliothécaire
Activités: Stagiaires: Oui
Membre(s) du bureau directeur:
Michel Cardin, Présidente

Association des bibliothèques de droit de Montréal (ABDM) / Montréal Association of Law Libraries (MALL)
CP 482, 800, carré Victoria, Montréal QC H4Z 1J7
Courriel: abdmmall@yahoo.ca
www.abdm-mall.org
Aperçu: Dimension: petite; *Envergure:* locale; Organisme sans but lucratif; fondée en 1987
Mission: Vise à permettre aux gens qui travaillent dans les bibliothèques de droit et qui exercent des fonctions connexes de communiquer et d'échanger des idées; d'encourager l'avancement de la profession; de maintenir et d'accroître l'utilité des bibliothèques de droit; promouvoir la coopération
Membre: Montant de la cotisation: 20$ étudiant; 45$ membre actif; 100$ membre associé
Activités: Réunions mensuelles sous forme de conférence avec conférencier et table ronde des membres; *Stagiaires:* Oui
Membre(s) du bureau directeur:
Sophie Lecoq, Présidente
sophie.lecoq@cnq.org

Association des bibliothèques de l'Ontario-Franco
a/s Association des bibliothèques de l'Ontario, 2, rue Toronto, 3e étage, Toronto ON M5C 2B6
Tél: 416-363-3388; *Téléc:* 416-941-9581
Ligne sans frais: 866-873-9867
www.accessola.org
twitter.com/ABO_FRANCO
Également appelé: ABO-Franco
Aperçu: Dimension: moyenne; *Envergure:* provinciale
Membre(s) du bureau directeur:
Maryse Laflamme, Présidente
maryse.laflamme@uottawa.ca
Prix, Bourses:
• Prix Micheline-Persaud
Honorer une personne, un groupe ou une institution qui s'est distinguée dans le développement des services de bibliothèque en français en Ontario
Meetings/Conferences:
• Association des bibliothèques de l'Ontario-Franco (ABO-Franco) Assemblée générale annuelle 2018, 2018, QC
Scope: Provincial

Association des bibliothèques de la santé affiliées à l'Université de Montréal (ABSAUM)
a/s Bibliothèque de la santé, Université de Montréal, CP 6128, Succ. Centre-Ville, Montréal QC H3C 3J7
Tél: 514-343-7664; *Téléc:* 514-343-6457
www.bib.umontreal.ca/absaum
Aperçu: Dimension: petite; *Envergure:* locale; fondée en 1978
Mission: Favoriser les rencontres entre les membres et promouvoir l'étude des problèmes communs; mettre de l'avant des projets d'intérêt commun; faire des recommandations auprès des autorités ou organismes concernés
Affiliation(s): Université de Montréal
Finances: Budget de fonctionnement annuel: Moins de $50,000
Membre: 15; *Montant de la cotisation:* 50$; *Critères d'admissibilite:* Bibliothécaire

Activités: 3 réunions par an
Membre(s) du bureau directeur:
Audrey Attia

Association des bibliothèques de la santé des Maritimes *See* Maritimes Health Libraries Association

Association des bibliothèques de la santé du Canada *See* Canadian Health Libraries Association

Association des bibliothèques de recherche du Canada *See* Canadian Association of Research Libraries

Association des bibliothèques de santé de la Vallée d'Outaouais *See* Ottawa Valley Health Libraries Association

Association des bibliothèques parlementaires au Canada *See* Association of Parliamentary Libraries in Canada

Association des bibliothèques publiques de l'Estrie (ABIPE)
1002, av J.-A.-Bombardier, Valcourt QC J0E 2L0
Tél: 450-532-1532; *Téléc:* 450-532-5807
www.bpq-estrie.qc.ca
Aperçu: Dimension: petite; *Envergure:* locale; fondée en 1990
Mission: Regrouper les bibliothèques publiques d'Estrie pour en favoriser le développement; informer les membres et échanger sur toute question pertinente au dossier des bibliothèques; représenter les intérêts des bibliothèques membres de la région 05 en étant leur porte-parole officiel auprès des instances gouvernementales et autres; organiser et réaliser des activités d'animation culturelle; sensibiliser le milieu au rôle et à l'importance de la bibliothèque publique dans la communauté
Membre: 11 bibliothèques
Membre(s) du bureau directeur:
Karine Corbeil, Présidente
k.corbeil@fjab.qc.ca

Association des bibliothèques publiques de la Montérégie
c/o Bibliothèque de Brossard, 7855, av San-Francisco, Brossard QC J4X 2A4
Tél: 450-923-6350; *Téléc:* 450-923-7042
www.abpq.ca/fr/monteregie
Aperçu: Dimension: petite; *Envergure:* locale
Membre(s) du bureau directeur:
Julie Desautels, Présidente
julie.desautels@brossard.ca

Association des bibliothèques publiques du Québec (ABPQ)
#215, 1453, rue Beaubien est, Montréal QC H2G 3C6
Tél: 514-279-0550; *Téléc:* 514-845-1618
info@abpq.ca
www.abpq.ca
www.facebook.com/ABPQc
Nom précédent: Les bibliothèques publiques du Québec; Association des directeurs de bibliothèques publiques du Québec
Aperçu: Dimension: moyenne; *Envergure:* provinciale; Organisme sans but lucratif; fondée en 1984
Mission: Agit à titre de représentant officiel des bibliothèques publiques du Québec
Membre(s) du personnel: 3
Activités: Evénements de sensibilisation: Semaine des Bibliothèques publiques du Québec
Membre(s) du bureau directeur:
Eve Lagacé, Directrice générale
eve.lagace@abpq.ca
Meetings/Conferences:
• Association des bibliotheques publiques du Quebec Rendez-vous des bibliotheques publiques du Quebec, 2018, QC
Scope: Provincial

Association des bleuets sauvages de l'Amérique du Nord *See* Wild Blueberry Association of North America

Association des Boulangers Artisans du Québec (ABAQC)
2180, av Aird, Montréal QC H1V 2W2
Courriel: info@abaqc.com
abaqc.com
www.linkedin.com/company/association-des-boulangers-artisans-du-qu-bec
www.facebook.com/ABAQc
twitter.com/BoulangersArtis
Aperçu: Dimension: petite; *Envergure:* provinciale
Mission: De promouvoir la cuisson comme une profession; pour créer camaraderie entre ses membres

Canadian Associations / Association des brasseurs du Québec (ABQ) / Québec Brewers Association

Membre: *Montant de la cotisation:* Barème
Membre(s) du bureau directeur:
Guy Bonraisin, Président

L'association des brasseurs du Canada *See* Brewers Association of Canada

Association des brasseurs du Québec (ABQ) / Québec Brewers Association
#888, 2000, rue Peel, Montréal QC H3A 2W5
Tél: 514-284-9199; *Téléc:* 514-284-0817
Ligne sans frais: 800-854-9199
asbq@brasseurs.qc.ca
brasseurs.qc.ca
Aperçu: Dimension: moyenne; *Envergure:* provinciale; fondée en 1943
Mission: De représenter les intérêts de ses membres à des organismes et des intervenants govenment
Membre de: Brewers Association of Canada
Membre(s) du personnel: 3
Membre: 3; *Critères d'admissibilite:* Brasseurs en Québec et participants en l'industrie; *Comités:* Communications
Membre(s) du bureau directeur:
Philippe Batani, Directeur général
p.batani@brasseurs.qc.ca

Association des cadres de la santé et des services sociaux du Québec *Voir* APER Santé et services sociaux

Association des cadres des centres de la petite enfance (ACCPE) / Association of Managers of Childcare Centers (AMCC)
CP 4042, Succ. D, Montréal QC
Tél: 514-933-3954
info@associationdescadres.ca
www.associationdescadres.ca
Aperçu: Dimension: petite; *Envergure:* provinciale
Mission: Réunir les cadres de centres de la petite enfance; Travailler en collaboration avec le Ministère de la Famille
Membre(s) du personnel: 3
Membre: *Montant de la cotisation:* 375$ générale; $350 adjointe; *Critères d'admissibilite:* Les cadres de centres d'éducation de la petite enfance; *Comités:* Rémunération et les conditions de travail des cadres; Paritaire d'assurance collective et du congé de maternité; Retraite du personnel des CPE et des gardieries privées subventionnées du Québec; Colloque; Financement, la gouvernance, la pérennité et l'optimisation des CPE; Formation et développement professionnel des cadres
Activités: Développement professionnel; Offrant un coaching personnalisé et soutien; Communiquer avec les membres; Organiser une conférence biennale
Membre(s) du bureau directeur:
Isabelle Palardy, Directrice générale
Meetings/Conferences:
• Association des cadres des centres de la petite enfance Conference 2018, 2018
Scope: Provincial
Publications:
• Définir la structure organisationnelle d'un centre de la petite enfance et d'un bureau coordonnateur [publication ACCPE]
Type: Rapport; *Author:* Claude Tremblay; *Price:* 35$ avec adhésion; 50$ sans adhésion
• La politique de gestion et le contrat d'emploi du personnel d'encadrement d'un CPE [publication ACCPE]
Type: Rapport; *Author:* Claude Tremblay; *Price:* 30$ avec adhésion; 60$ sans adhésion
• Pour bien se comprendre: la directrice générale et le conseil d'administration d'un centre de la petite enfance
Type: Rapport; *Author:* Claude Tremblay; *Price:* 60$ avec adhésion; 85$ sans adhésion

Association des cadres municipaux de Montréal (ACMM)
#305, 7245, rue Clark, Montréal QC H2R 2Y4
Tél: 514-499-1130; *Téléc:* 514-499-1737
acmm@acmm.qc.ca
www.acmm.qc.ca
Aperçu: Dimension: petite; *Envergure:* provinciale
Mission: A pour objet l'établissement de relations ordonnées entre l'employeur et les membres ainsi que l'étude, la défense et le développement des intérêts économiques sociaux, moraux et professionnels de ces derniers
Membre(s) du bureau directeur:
Pascale Tremblay, Présidente

Association des cadres scolaires du Québec *Voir* Association québécoise des cadres scolaires

Association des cadres supérieurs de la santé et des services sociaux du Québec (ACSSSS)
#1494, rue Victoria, Greenfield Park QC J4V 1M2
Tél: 450-465-0360; *Téléc:* 450-465-0444
cadres.superieurs@acssss.qc.ca
www.acssss.qc.ca
www.linkedin.com/company/association-des-cadres-superieurs-de-la-santé-et-des-services-sociaux-acssss-
www.facebook.com/1438926259719098
www.youtube.com/user/ACSSSSQC
Aperçu: Dimension: petite; *Envergure:* provinciale; fondée en 1959
Affiliation(s): La Coalition de l'encadrement en matière de retraite d'assurance; Commission administrative des régimes de retraite et d'assurances; Commission administrative des régimes de retraite et d'assurances Québec
Membre(s) du bureau directeur:
Carole Trempe, Directrice générale
carole.trempe.acssss@ssss.gouv.qc.ca

Association des camps du Canada *See* Canadian Camping Association

Association des camps du Québec inc. (ACQ) / Québec Camping Association
CP 1000, Succ. M, 4545, av Pierre-de Coubertin, Montréal QC H1V 3R2
Tél: 514-252-3113; *Téléc:* 514-252-1650
Ligne sans frais: 800-361-3586
info@camps.qc.ca
www.camps.qc.ca
www.facebook.com/130062375961
www.instagram.com/campsduquebec
Aperçu: Dimension: moyenne; *Envergure:* provinciale; Organisme sans but lucratif; fondée en 1950 surveillé par Canadian Camping Association
Mission: Assurer le développement, la promotion et la qualité des camps de vacances; s'assurer de la formation du personnel des camps
Affiliation(s): Regroupement loisir Québec; Association des camps du Canada
Finances: Budget de fonctionnement annuel: $250,000-$500,000; *Fonds:* Secrétariat au loisir et au sport du Québec
Membre(s) du personnel: 6; 25 bénévole(s)
Membre: 120 camp; 60 individu; *Montant de la cotisation:* Barème; *Critères d'admissibilite:* Camp de vacances accredité par l'ACQ ou membre individuel; *Comités:* Ressources Humaines; Communications; Membership
Activités: Stagiaires: Oui; *Listes de destinataires:* Oui
Membre(s) du bureau directeur:
Eric Beauchemin, Directeur
ericbeauchemin@camps.qc.ca

Association des capitaines propriétaires de Gaspésie inc (ACPG)
CP 9, 1, rue de la Langevin, Gaspé QC G4X 5G4
Tél: 418-269-7701; *Téléc:* 418-269-3278
www.acpgaspesie.com
Aperçu: Dimension: petite; *Envergure:* locale; fondée en 1983
Membre(s) du bureau directeur:
Jean-Pierre Couillard, Directeur général

Association des cardiologues du Québec (ACQ)
CP 216, Succ. Desjardins, #3000, 2, Complexe Desjardins, Montréal QC H5B 1G8
Tél: 514-350-5106; *Téléc:* 514-350-5156
acq@fmsq.org
Aperçu: Dimension: petite; *Envergure:* provinciale surveillé par Fédération des médecins spécialistes du Québec
Membre: 448
Membre(s) du bureau directeur:
Gilles O'Hara, Président
Louise Girard, Directrice

Association des cartothèques et archives cartographiques du Canada *See* Association of Canadian Map Libraries & Archives

L'Association des CBDC du Nouveau-Brunswick *See* New Brunswick Association of Community Business Development Corporations

Association des centres de réadaptation en dépendance du Québec *Voir* Association des intervenants en dépendance du Québec

Association des Centres de recherche sur l'Utilisation Urbaine du Sous-sol *See* Associated Research Centres for the Urban Underground Space

Association des centres de santé de l'Ontario *See* Association of Ontario Health Centres

Association des centres hospitaliers et centres d'accueil privés du Québec *Voir* Association des établissements privés conventionnés - santé services sociaux

Association des centres jeunesse du Québec (ACJQ)
#410, 1001, boul de Maisonneuve ouest, Montréal QC H3A 3C8
Tél: 514-842-5181; *Téléc:* 514-842-4834
info.acjq@ssss.gouv.qc.ca
www.acjq.qc.ca
Aperçu: Dimension: moyenne; *Envergure:* provinciale; fondée en 1992
Mission: Concertation, coordination et représentation des Centres Jeunesse du Québec
Finances: Fonds: Fundraising; donations
Membre(s) du bureau directeur:
Alain St-Pierre, Directeur général par intérim

Association des centres pour aînés de l'Ontario *See* Older Adult Centres' Association of Ontario

Association des chefs de services d'incendie du Québec *Voir* Association des chefs en sécurité incendie du Québec

Association des chefs en sécurité incendie du Québec (ACSIQ) / Québec Association of Fire Chiefs
5, rue Dupré, Beloeil QC J3G 3J7
Tél: 450-464-6413; *Téléc:* 450-467-6297
Ligne sans frais: 888-464-6413
administration@acsiq.qc.ca
www.acsiq.qc.ca
Nom précédent: Association des chefs de services d'incendie du Québec
Aperçu: Dimension: moyenne; *Envergure:* provinciale; Organisme sans but lucratif; fondée en 1968
Mission: Regrouper les personnes détanant un poste de commande dans le domaine de la prévention et de la lutte contre les incendies
Membre: *Montant de la cotisation:* 230$; *Critères d'admissibilite:* Chefs de service incendie de municipalités ou de brigade en industries; *Comités:* Mise en candidature; Vérification des politiques; Évaluation du rendement du directeur général; Finances; Consultatif; Reconnaissances; Développement et de stratégie de l'ACSIQ; Stratégique avec le MSP; Stratégique MSP; Prévention de l'ACSIQ; Réduction des alarmes non-fondées; Consultatif sur la législation du gaz propane; Guide de prévention; Certification des résidences pour personnes âgées; Consultatif sur l'Éducation du public; Consultatif provincial sur le code de construction du Québec; Les foyers à l'éthanol; Le code de sécurité; Les résidences pour personnes âgées autonomes
Membre(s) du bureau directeur:
Daniel Brazeau, Président

Association des chemins de fer du Canada *See* Railway Association of Canada

Association des chercheurs et chercheures étudiants en médecine (ACCEM)
Pavillon Ferdinand-Vandry, Faculté de médecine, Université Laval, #4645, 1050, av de la Médecine, Québec QC G1V 0A6
Courriel: accem@asso.ulaval.ca
www.fmed.ulaval.ca/ACCEM
www.facebook.com/accemulaval
twitter.com/ACCEMulaval
Aperçu: Dimension: petite; *Envergure:* locale
Membre: *Critères d'admissibilite:* Chercheurs étudiant à la faculté de médecine de l'Université Laval
Membre(s) du bureau directeur:
Jean-Philippe Pialasse, Président

Association des chevaux Morgan canadien inc. *See* Canadian Morgan Horse Association

Association des chiropraticiens du Nouveau-Brunswick *See* New Brunswick Chiropractors' Association

Association des chiropraticiens du Québec
7960, boul Métropolitain est, Montréal QC H1K 1A1
Tél: 514-355-0557; *Téléc:* 514-355-0070
Ligne sans frais: 866-292-4476
acq@chiropratique.com

www.chiropratique.com
www.facebook.com/AssoDesChirosQc
twitter.com/AssoChiroQc
www.youtube.com/user/AssoDesChirosQc
Aperçu: Dimension: moyenne; *Envergure:* provinciale; fondée en 1967 surveillé par Canadian Chiropractic Association
Mission: Défendre les intérêts professionnels, sociaux et économiques de ses membres

Association des chirurgiens dentistes du Québec (ACDQ)
#1425, 425, boul de Maisonneuve ouest, Montréal QC H3A 3G5
Tél: 514-282-1425; *Téléc:* 514-282-0255
Ligne sans frais: 800-361-3794
info@acdq.qc.ca
www.acdq.qc.ca
www.linkedin.com/company/3085144
www.facebook.com/acdqquebec
twitter.com/AcdqQuebec
Aperçu: Dimension: moyenne; *Envergure:* provinciale; Organisme de réglementation; fondée en 1966 surveillé par Canadian Dental Association
Mission: L'Association a pour objet l'étude, la défense et le développement des intérêts économiques, sociaux et moraux de ses membres.
Membre(s) du bureau directeur:
Serge Langlois, DDS, Président

Association des chirurgiens généraux du Québec *Voir* Association Québécoise de chirurgie

Association des cinémas parallèles du Québec (ACPQ)
4545, av Pierre-de Coubertin, Montréal QC H1V 0B2
Tél: 514-252-3021; *Téléc:* 514-252-3063
www.cinemasparalleles.qc.ca
www.facebook.com/CinemasParalleles
Également appelé: L'oeil cinéma réseau plus
Aperçu: Dimension: petite; *Envergure:* provinciale; fondée en 1979
Mission: Regrouper les organisations du cinéma non commercial du Québec dans le but de promouvoir auprès des Québécois la culture cinématographique et de développer une activité de loisir cinématographique diversifiée et de qualité.
Membre de: SODEP; CQL; RLSQ; CQRHC
Finances: *Budget de fonctionnement annuel:* $500,000-$1.5 Million; *Fonds:* Financement du gouvernement; Financement privé; Vente de services
Membre(s) du personnel: 5
Membre: 57; *Montant de la cotisation:* 80$
Activités: Conférences; Ateliers; *Stagiaires:* Oui; *Service de conférenciers:* Oui
Membre(s) du bureau directeur:
Martine Mauroy, Directrice générale
m.mauroy@cinemasparalleles.qc.ca

Association des citoyennes averties Alma *Voir* Maison de Campagne & d'Entraide Communautaire du Lac

Association des clubs d'entrepreneurs étudiants du Québec
1510, rue Jean-Berchmans-Michaud, Drummondville QC J2C 7V3
Tél: 819-850-7573
info@acee.qc.ca
www.acee.qc.ca
Également appelé: ACEE du Québec
Aperçu: Dimension: petite; *Envergure:* provinciale; Organisme sans but lucratif; fondée en 1991
Mission: Organisme de dépistage du profil entrepreneurial à travers la francophonie et de mise en réseautage
Finances: *Budget de fonctionnement annuel:* $500,000-$1.5 Million
Membre(s) du personnel: 6; 60 bénévole(s)
Membre: 2 500; *Montant de la cotisation:* 50$; *Critères d'admissibilité:* Étudiant de tout champ d'études
Activités: Colloque annuel
Membre(s) du bureau directeur:
Nicolas Duval-Mace, Président
Pierre Touzel, Directeur général
touzelp@acee.qc.ca

Association des clubs de biathlon du Québec *Voir* Fédération québécoise de biathlon

Association des collections d'entreprises (ACE) / Corporate Art Collectors Association
QC
Courriel: info@ace-cca.ca
ace-cca.ca
Aperçu: Dimension: moyenne; *Envergure:* nationale; Organisme sans but lucratif; fondée en 1985
Mission: Réunir les conservateurs et les propriétaires de collections corporatives; favoriser l'échange d'information, d'idées, d'expériences, d'expertise, de systèmes ou de services; représenter de façon générale les intérêts de ses membres; favoriser la diffusion de l'art au Québec
3 bénévole(s)
Membre: 20 sociétés; *Critères d'admissibilite:* Sociétés ayant des collections d'art ou désirant devenir collectionneurs
Activités: Réunions; séminaires; attribution de subventions occasionnelles à des organismes artistiques
Membre(s) du bureau directeur:
Jo-Ann Kane, Présidente et secrétaire
jkane@ace-cca.ca
François Rochon, Trésorier
Kimberlee Clarke, Responsable, Logistique
kclarke@ace-cca.ca

Association des collèges communautaires du Canada *See* Colleges and Institutes Canada

Association des collèges privés du Québec (ACPQ)
1940, boul Henri-Bourassa est, Montréal QC H2B 1S2
Tél: 514-381-8891; *Téléc:* 514-381-4086
Ligne sans frais: 888-381-8891
acpq@acpq.net
www.acpq.net
www.facebook.com/campleadershipacpq
twitter.com/acpq_net
Aperçu: Dimension: moyenne; *Envergure:* provinciale; Organisme sans but lucratif; fondée en 1968
Mission: Défendre les intérêts de ses collèges membres et contribuer au développement de l'enseignement collégial privé au Québec
Membre de: Conseil du Patronat du Québec
Finances: *Budget de fonctionnement annuel:* $250,000-$500,000
Membre(s) du personnel: 2
Membre: 24 institutions d'enseignement; *Montant de la cotisation:* Barème
Membre(s) du bureau directeur:
Pierre L'Heureux, Directeur général
Marili B.-Desrochers, Chargée de projets, 514-833-8891

Association des commerçants de véhicules récréatifs du Canada *See* Recreation Vehicle Dealers Association of Canada

Association des commerçants de véhicules récréatifs du Québec (ACVRQ) / RVDA of Québec
#100, 4360, av Pierre-de Coubertin, Montréal QC H1V 1A6
Tél: 514-338-1471; *Téléc:* 514-335-6250
Ligne sans frais: 866-338-1471
info@acvrq.org
www.acvrq.com
Aperçu: Dimension: petite; *Envergure:* provinciale; fondée en 1988
Mission: L'Association des Commerçants de Véhicules Récréatifs du Québec représente les principales entreprises ouvrant dans l'industrie du Véhicule Récréatif. L'A.C.V.R.Q. est une compagnie sans but lucratif constituée en vertu de la Partie III de la Loi sur les Compagnies du Québec, aux fins de venir en aide à ses membres relativement à la promotion et au développement de l'industrie des véhicules récréatifs et à l'harmonisation des relations entre les consommateurs et les commerçants
Finances: *Budget de fonctionnement annuel:* $500,000-$1.5 Million
Membre(s) du personnel: 2
Membre: 119; *Montant de la cotisation:* Barème
Activités: Participation aux salons des véhicules récréatifs; *Événements de sensibilisation:* Salons des VR, mars/avril
Membre(s) du bureau directeur:
Danielle Godbout, Directrice générale
dgodbout@acvrq.org
Jean-François Lussier, Président

Association des commissaires d'écoles de Colombie-Britannique *See* British Columbia School Trustees Association

Association des commissaires de bibliothèque du Nouveau-Brunswick, inc. *See* New Brunswick Library Trustees' Association

Association des commissaires industriels du Québec (ACIQ) *Voir* Association des professionnels en développement économique du Québec

Association des commissions des accidents du travail du Canada *See* Association of Workers' Compensation Boards of Canada

Association des commissions scolaires anglophones du Québec *See* Québec English School Boards Association

Association des communautés chorales canadiennes *See* Association of Canadian Choral Communities

Association des compagnies de théâtre (ACT)
605, rue Prospect, Sherbrooke QC J1H 1B1
Téléc: 866-499-5587
Ligne sans frais: 866-348-8960
info@act-theatre.ca
www.act-theatre.ca
www.facebook.com/118684904872068
Aperçu: Dimension: petite; *Envergure:* provinciale; fondée en 1989
Membre: *Montant de la cotisation:* 20$ l'ouverture de dossier; 25$ nouveaux membres; 200$ membre actif; 100$ par production & 50$ par une première production; 200$ corporation
Membre(s) du bureau directeur:
Jacques Jobin, Coordonnateur
Mélanie St-Laurent, Présidente
info@petittheatredunord.com
Étienne Langlois, Vice-président
elanglois@theatresdf.com

L'association des compositeurs d'Edmonton *See* Edmonton Composers' Concert Society

Association des concessionnaires Ford du Québec
16, rue Marguerite-Bourgeoys, Boucherville QC J4B 2H3
Tél: 450-655-2090
Aperçu: Dimension: petite; *Envergure:* provinciale; Organisme sans but lucratif

Association des conseils des médecins, dentistes et pharmaciens du Québec (ACMDP) / Association of Councils of Physicians, Dentists & Pharmacists of Québec
#212, 560, boul Henri-Bourassa ouest, Montréal QC H3L 1P4
Tél: 514-858-5885; *Téléc:* 514-858-6767
acmdp@acmdp.qc.ca
www.acmdp.qc.ca
Aperçu: Dimension: moyenne; *Envergure:* provinciale; Organisme sans but lucratif; fondée en 1946
Mission: Offrir l'information, la motivation, et la formation médico-administrative nécessaire aux Conseils des médecins, dentistes, et pharmaciens membres afin qu'ils accomplissent adéquatement leurs tâches
Membre(s) du personnel: 4
Membre: 154; *Montant de la cotisation:* Barème; *Critères d'admissibilité:* Conseils de médecins, dentistes et pharmaciens des établiseements de santé du Québec
Activités: *Bibliothèque:* Not open to public
Membre(s) du bureau directeur:
Martin Arata, Président-Directeur général
Meetings/Conferences:
• Association des conseils des médecins, dentistes et pharmaciens du Québec Colloque 2018, 2018
Scope: Provincial
Publications:
• Conseiller express [publication de l'Association des conseils des médecins, dentistes et pharmaciens du Québec]
Type: Infolettre
• Guides de formation [publication de l'Association des conseils des médecins, dentistes et pharmaciens du Québec]
• Mémoire [publication de l'Association des conseils des médecins, dentistes et pharmaciens du Québec]

Association des conseils en gestion linguistique Inc. (ACGL) / Association of Linguistic Services Managerse (ALSM)
#403, 2030, boul Pie-IX, Montréal QC H1V 2C8
Tél: 514-355-8001; *Téléc:* 514-355-4159
acgl@spg.qc.ca
www.lacgl.org
Aperçu: Dimension: petite; *Envergure:* provinciale
Mission: Apporter une aide concrète et efficace aux responsables de services linguistiques; Permettre aux membres d'échanger des expériences pratiques; Informer ses membres des nouvelles techniques en usage dans les professions

Canadian Associations / Association des constructeurs de routes et grands travaux du Québec (ACRGTQ) / Québec Road Builders & Heavy Construction Association

langagières; Offrir à ses membres des possibilités de perfectionnement; Favoriser la concertation entre les universités et les employeurs.
Finances: *Fonds:* individual and corporate members
Membre: *Montant de la cotisation:* 350$ individuel; 525$ enterprise
Activités: Organization has seminars, committees, publications and training and development
Membre(s) du bureau directeur:
François Chartrand, Président
francois.chartrand@textualis.com

Association des conseils scolaires de la Nouvelle-Écosse *See* Nova Scotia School Boards Association

Association des consommateurs du Canada *See* Consumers' Association of Canada

L'association des consommateurs industriels de gaz *See* Industrial Gas Users Association

Association des constructeurs de routes et grands travaux du Québec (ACRGTQ) / Québec Road Builders & Heavy Construction Association
435, av Grande-Allée est, Québec QC G1R 2J5
Tél: 418-529-2949; *Téléc:* 418-529-5139
Ligne sans frais: 800-463-4672
acrgtq@acrgtq.qc.ca
www.acrgtq.qc.ca
Aperçu: *Dimension:* grande; *Envergure:* provinciale; Organisme sans but lucratif; fondée en 1944 surveillé par Canadian Construction Association
Mission: Défendre les intérêts des entrepreneurs en génie civil et voirie du Québec
Membre(s) du personnel: 32
Membre: 596; *Montant de la cotisation:* Barème; *Critères d'admissibilite:* Entrepreneurs génie civil et voirie et fournisseurs de services; *Comités:* Camionnage; Événements spéciaux; Chaussées en béton, ouvrages d'art et matériaux de béton; Entrepreneurs en transport d'énergie; Professionnel des exploitants de centrales d'enrobage; Professionnel des producteurs de granulat; Négociation; Patronal en santé et sécurité du travail; Relations du travail; Environnment; Cahier des charges; Travaux municipaux, terrassement, drainage, fondations et granulats; Déneigement
Membre(s) du bureau directeur:
Roger Arsenault, Président
Gisèle Bourque, Directrice générale
Publications:
• CONSTAS [a publication of the Association des constructeurs de routes et grands travaux du Québec]
Type: Magazine; *Frequency:* q.
  Bureau à la Romaine
  Tél: 418-538-7676
  Membre(s) du bureau directeur:
  Denis Houle, Contact, 418-538-0708
  Bureau de Montréal
  #100, 7905, boul Louis-Hippolyte-Lafontaine, Montréal QC H1K 4E4
  Tél: 514-354-1362; *Téléc:* 514-354-1301
  Ligne sans frais: 800-463-4672

Association des consultants et conseillers en santé mentale, psychométriciens, et psychothérapeutes de l'Ontario *See* Ontario Association of Consultants, Counsellors, Psychometrists & Psychotherapists

Association des consultants et laboratoires experts (ACLE)
#211, 6360, rue Jean-Talon est, Saint-Léonard QC H1S 1M8
Tél: 514-253-2878; *Téléc:* 514-253-6825
info@acle.qc.ca
www.acle.qc.ca
Nom précédent: Association canadienne des laboratoires d'essais
Aperçu: *Dimension:* moyenne; *Envergure:* nationale; Organisme sans but lucratif; fondée en 1959
Mission: Développer, promouvoir et sauvegarder les intérêts techniques et commerciaux communs des membres et de leurs clients.
Membre(s) du personnel: 1
Membre: 100; *Critères d'admissibilite:* Entreprises indépendantes réparties en trois divisions - Ingénierie des Sols et Matériaux; Services Analytiques et Environnement; Toiture et Étanchéité
Membre(s) du bureau directeur:
Ghislain Houde, Président
ghoude@groupesm.com

Association des coopératives du Canada *See* Canadian Co-operative Association

Association des coordonnateurs de congrès des universités et des collèges du Canada *See* Canadian University & College Conference Organizers Association

Association des cordes de la Rive-Sud *Voir* Association des orchestres de jeunes de la Montérégie

Association des courtiers d'assurances de la Province de Québec *Voir* Chambre de l'assurance de dommages

Association des courtiers d'assurances du Canada *See* Insurance Brokers Association of Canada

Association des courtiers d'assurances du Nouveau-Brunswick *See* Insurance Brokers Association of Canada

Association des critiques de théâtre du Canada *See* Canadian Theatre Critics Association

l'Association des déchets solides du Nouveau-Brunswick *See* New Brunswick Solid Waste Association

Association des démographes du Québec (ADQ)
CP 49532, Succ. du Musée, Montréal QC H3T 2A5
www.demographesqc.org
Aperçu: *Dimension:* petite; *Envergure:* provinciale; fondée en 1971
Mission: Resserrer les liens entre les démographes; faire connaître la démographie sur le marché du travail; diffuser les connaissances d'ordre démographique
Membre: 160; *Montant de la cotisation:* Barème
Activités: Colloque annuel de démographie dans le cadre du colloque de l'Association canadienne française pour l'avancement des sciences
Membre(s) du bureau directeur:
Marc Tremblay, Président
marc_tremblay@uqac.ca
Julien Bérard-Chagnon, Vice-président
Julien.Berard-Chagnon@statcan.gc.ca
Rufteen Shumanty, Trésorière
rufteen.shumanty@stat.gouv.qc.ca

Association des denturologistes du Canada *See* Denturist Association of Canada

Association des denturologistes du Québec (ADQ)
#230, 8150, boul Métropolitain est, Anjou QC H1K 1A1
Tél: 514-252-0270; *Téléc:* 514-252-0392
Ligne sans frais: 800-563-6273
denturo@adq-qc.com
www.adq-qc.com
www.facebook.com/denturo
Aperçu: *Dimension:* moyenne; *Envergure:* provinciale; fondée en 1971
Mission: Protéger et développer les intérêts professionnels, moraux, sociaux et économiques de ses membres
Membre de: Association des denturologistes du Canada; Fédération internationale de denturologie
Membre(s) du personnel: 4
Membre: *Montant de la cotisation:* 528,89$; *Comités:* Exécutif
Membre(s) du bureau directeur:
Marie-France Brisson, Directrice générale
marie-france.brisson@adq-qc.com

Association des dermatologistes du Québec (ADQ) / Association of Dermatologists of Québec
CP 216, Succ. Desjardins, #3000, 2, Complexe Desjardins, Montréal QC H5B 1G8
Tél: 514-350-5111; *Téléc:* 514-350-5161
www.adq.org
Aperçu: *Dimension:* moyenne; *Envergure:* provinciale; Organisme sans but lucratif; fondée en 1950 surveillé par Fédération des médecins spécialistes du Québec
Mission: Syndicat professionnel: assure la défense des intérêts économiques, professionnels et scientifiques de ses membres
Affiliation(s): Fédération des médecins spécialistes du Québec
Membre(s) du bureau directeur:
Dominique Hanna, Présidente

Association des designers d'intérieur immatriculés du Nouveau-Brunswick *See* Association of Registered Interior Designers of New Brunswick

Association des designers industriels du Canada *See* Association of Canadian Industrial Designers

Association des designers industriels du Québec (ADIQ)
#406, 420, rue McGill, Montréal QC H2Y 2G1
Tél: 514-287-6531; *Téléc:* 514-278-3049
info@adiq.ca
www.adiq.ca
www.facebook.com/adiquebec
Aperçu: *Dimension:* moyenne; *Envergure:* provinciale; fondée en 1984 surveillé par Association of Canadian Industrial Designers
Mission: De soutenir, de représenter et de promouvoir les membres professionels et de mettre en valeur la profession.
Membre de: Forum Design Montréal
Membre: 398; *Comités:* Services; Communication
Activités: Forum annuel; séminaires techniques/juridiques
Membre(s) du bureau directeur:
Mario Gagnon, Président

Association des détaillants de matériaux de construction du Québec *Voir* Association québécoise de la quincaillerie et des matériaux de construction

Association des détaillants en alimentation du Québec (ADA) / Québec Food Retailers' Association
#900, 2120, rue Sherbrooke est, Montréal QC H2K 1C3
Tél: 514-982-0104; *Téléc:* 514-849-3021
Ligne sans frais: 800-363-3923
info@adaq.qc.ca
www.adaq.qc.ca
www.facebook.com/ADAQuebec
twitter.com/ADAquebec
vimeo.com/adaquebec
Aperçu: *Dimension:* moyenne; *Envergure:* provinciale; fondée en 1955
Mission: Représenter et défendre les intérêts professionnels, socio-politiques et économiques de tous les détaillants du Québec, et ce, quels que soient leur bannière et le type de surface qu'ils opèrent
Membre de: Centre de promotion de l'industrie alimentaire du Québec; Éco Entreprises Québec
Membre(s) du personnel: 7
Membre: *Montant de la cotisation:* Barème; *Critères d'admissibilite:* Propriétaire-détaillants en alimentation
Activités: *Stagiaires:* Oui; *Listes de destinataires:* Oui
Membre(s) du bureau directeur:
Daniel Choquette, Président
Florent Gravel, Président-directeur général

Association des devenus sourds et des malentendants du Québec *Voir* Audition Québec

Association des diététistes du Nouveau-Brunswick *See* New Brunswick Association of Dietitians

Association des diffuseurs culturels de l'Ile de Montréal (ADICIM)
176, ch du Bord-du-Lac, Pointe-Claire QC H9S 4J7
Tél: 514-630-1220; *Téléc:* 514-630-1259
info@adicim.ca
www.adicim.ca
Nom précédent: Association des diffuseurs culturels des arrondissements de Montréal; Association des diffuseurs culturels des banlieues de Montréal
Aperçu: *Dimension:* petite; *Envergure:* locale
Mission: De promouvoir et développer des activités artistiques sur l'île de Montréal
Membre de: Réseau indépendant des diffuseurs d'événements artistiques unis
10 bénévole(s)
Membre: 10
Membre(s) du bureau directeur:
Micheline Bélanger, Présidente, 514-630-1220 Ext. 1773
belangerm@ville.pointe-claire.qc.ca
Virginia Elliot, Vice-présidente, 514-989-5265

Association des diffuseurs culturels des arrondissements de Montréal; Association des diffuseurs culturels des banlieues de Montréal *Voir* Association des diffuseurs culturels de l'Ile de Montréal

Association des diplômés de l'École des hautes Études commerciales *Voir* Réseau HEC Montréal

Association des Diplômés de Polytechnique
CP 6079, Succ. Centre-Ville, Montréal QC H3C 3A7

Tél: 514-340-4764; *Téléc:* 514-340-4472
Ligne sans frais: 866-452-3296
adp@polymtl.ca
www.adp.polymtl.ca
www.linkedin.com/groups/Association-Diplômés-Polytechnique-Montréal-Groupe-130121
Aperçu: Dimension: moyenne; *Envergure:* provinciale; fondée en 1910
Mission: Établir des relations amicales entre les membres; défendre et promouvoir leurs intérêts
Affiliation(s): Roche, Gestion Férique, TD, Hydro Québec, Banque Nationale Group Financier, Rio Tinto Alcan
Membre(s) du personnel: 5
Membre: 29,000+; *Comités:* Communications; Jeunes Diplômés; Relations avec les étudiants; Prix Mérite; Matins ADP; Soirée Retrouvailles; Golf; Technologie; Partie d'huîtres; Sections; Activité familiale; Ambassadeurs; Événements spéciaux
Membre(s) du bureau directeur:
Martin Choinière, Président
Diane de Champlain, Directrice générale, 514-340-3225, Fax: 514-340-4472
Stéphanie Oscarson, Directrice, des opérations

Association des directeurs d'école de Montréal *Voir* Association montréalaise des directions d'établissement scolaire

Association des directeurs de recherche industrielle du Québec *Voir* Association de la recherche industrielle du Québec

Association des directeurs généraux des commissions scolaires du Québec (ADIGECS)
a/s Directeur exécutif, #212, 195, ch de Chambly, Longueuil QC J4H 3L3
Tél: 450-674-6700; *Téléc:* 450-674-7337
adigecs.qc.ca
Aperçu: Dimension: petite; *Envergure:* provinciale; fondée en 1972
Mission: Contribuer à l'avancement de l'éducation au Québec; protéger les intérêts de ses membres notamment au chapitre des conditions de travail
Affiliation(s): Ministère de l'éducation, loisir et sport; Fédération des commissions scolaires du Québec
Membre: 163
Activités: Programmes d'aide; bourses d'études; *Evénements de sensibilisation:* Colloque ADIGECS (novembre); Congrès ADIGECS (mai); *Service de conférenciers:* Oui
Membre(s) du bureau directeur:
Raynald Thibeault, Président
Serge Lefebvre, Directeur exécutif

Association des directeurs généraux des municipalités du Québec
#470, 43, rue de Buade, Québec QC G1R 4A2
Tél: 418-660-7591; *Téléc:* 418-660-0848
adgmq@adgmq.qc.ca
adgmq.qc.ca
Aperçu: Dimension: moyenne; *Envergure:* provinciale; fondée en 1973
Mission: Permettre l'amélioration des connaissances et du statut de ses membres et la promotion de la formule de gestion conseil/directeur général
Membre(s) du personnel: 3
Membre: 200; *Montant de la cotisation:* 365$; *Critères d'admissibilité:* Directeur général d'une municipalité gérée par la loi des cités et villes
Membre(s) du bureau directeur:
Jack Benzaquen, Président
Martine Lévesque, Directrice génerale
martine.levesque@adgmq.qc.ca

Association des directeurs généraux des services de santé et des services sociaux du Québec (ADGSSSQ) / Association of Executive Directors of Québec Health & Social Services
425, boul de Maisonneuve ouest, #B-10, Montréal QC H3A 3G5
Tél: 514-281-1896; *Téléc:* 514-281-5054
www.adgsssq.qc.ca
Aperçu: Dimension: moyenne; *Envergure:* provinciale; Organisme de réglementation; fondée en 1973
Mission: L'Association des directeurs généraux des services de santé et des services sociaux du Québec est une société dont l'objet premier est ® l'étude, la défense et le développement des intérêts économiques, sociaux et moraux de ses membres
Membre: 350; *Comités:* Défense professionnelle; Communications; Travail
Membre(s) du bureau directeur:

André Côté, Président-directeur général
Michel Lapointe, Président

Association des directeurs généraux, secrétaires et trésoriers municipaux de l'Ontario *See* Association of Municipal Managers, Clerks & Treasurers of Ontario

Association des directeurs municipaux du Québec (ADMQ)
Hall Est, #535, 400, boul Jean-Lesage, Québec QC G1K 8W1
Tél: 418-647-4518; *Téléc:* 418-647-4115
admq@admq.qc.ca
admq.qc.ca
Aperçu: Dimension: moyenne; *Envergure:* provinciale; Organisme sans but lucratif; fondée en 1939
Mission: De voir à la promotion et à la défense des membres en plus d'offrir un soutien professionnel constant au niveau des outils de formation et de communication
Membre(s) du personnel: 7
Membre: 1 100; *Montant de la cotisation:* 395$; *Comités:* Internes; Direction
Membre(s) du bureau directeur:
Charles Ricard, Président
Marc Laflamme, Directeur général
mlaflamme@admq.qc.ca

Association des distillateurs canadiens *See* Association of Canadian Distillers

Association des distributeurs exclusifs de livres en langue française inc. (ADELF)
47, av Wicksteed, Mont-Royal QC H3P 1P9
Tél: 514-739-2220; *Téléc:* 514-739-8307
adelf@videotron.ca
www.adelf.qc.ca
Aperçu: Dimension: petite; *Envergure:* locale; Organisme sans but lucratif; fondée en 1978
Mission: Promotion et défense des intérêts des diffuseurs d'éditeurs de langue française; soutenir la diffusion et la distribution de livres en français et leurs produits dérivés; établir entre ses membres des rapports de confraternité; promouvoir la lecture
Affiliation(s): Société de développement du livre et du périodique
Finances: Fonds: Ministère du Patrimoine canadien; Société de développement des entreprises culturelles
Membre(s) du personnel: 1
Membre: 24
Activités: Listes de destinataires: Oui
Membre(s) du bureau directeur:
Pascal Chamaillard, Président
Benoit Prieur, Directeur général

Association des eaux souterraines du Québec *Voir* Association des enterprises spécialiseés en eau du Québec

Association des écoles forestières universitaires du Canada *See* Association of University Forestry Schools of Canada

Association des écoles juives *See* Association of Jewish Day Schools

Association des écoles privées du Québec *See* Québec Association of Independent Schools

Association des économistes québécois (ASDÉQ)
#7118, 385, rue Sherbrooke est, Montréal QC H2X 1E3
Tél: 514-342-7537; *Téléc:* 514-342-3967
Ligne sans frais: 866-342-7537
info@economistesquebecois.com
www.economistesquebecois.com
www.linkedin.com/groups/3809359
www.facebook.com/127117010671812
twitter.com/EconomistesQc
Aperçu: Dimension: moyenne; *Envergure:* provinciale; Organisme sans but lucratif; fondée en 1975
Mission: Assurer la promotion professionnelle des économistes
Membre(s) du personnel: 4
Membre: Critères d'admissibilité: Économistes; tout intervenant intéressé par les questions économiques; *Comités:* Développement
Activités: Congrès; colloques; prix de journalisme; ateliers de formation; déjeuners causeries; *Service de conférenciers:* Oui
Membre(s) du bureau directeur:
Bernard Barrucco, Directeur général
bernardbarrucco@economistesquebecois.com
Meetings/Conferences:
• Congrès de l'association des économistes québécois 2018, 2018, QC
Scope: Provincial

Association des éditeurs canadiens *See* Association of Canadian Publishers

Association des éditeurs de langue anglaise du Québec *See* Association of English Language Publishers of Québec

Association des Éditeurs de périodiques culturels québécois *Voir* Société de développement des périodiques culturels québécois

Association des éducateurs professionnels du Nouveau-Brunswick *See* Association of New Brunswick Professional Educators

Association des églises chrétiennes du Manitoba *See* Association of Christian Churches in Manitoba

Association des Églises des frères mennonites du Québec (AEFMQ) / Québec Association of Mennonite Brethren Churches
#100, 4824, ch de la Côte-des-neiges, Montréal QC H3V 1G4
Tél: 514-331-0878
info@aefmq.org
aefmq.org
Aperçu: Dimension: petite; *Envergure:* provinciale surveillé par Canadian Conference of Mennonite Brethren Churches
Mission: Contribuer à la croissance des églises mennonites dans la grande région de Montréal; Pour augmenter la force et l'influence de l'église
Membre(s) du personnel: 12
Membre(s) du bureau directeur:
Gilles Dextraze, Directeur général, 514-893-0442
g.dextraze@aefmq.org

Association des églises évangéliques *See* Associated Gospel Churches

Association des électrolystes et esthéticiennes du Québec; Association des électrolystes du Québec *Voir* Association des professionnels en électrolyse et soins esthétiques du Québec

Association des éleveurs de chevaux Belge du Québec / Breeders of Belgian Horses Association of Québec
611, ch Léon-Gérin, Compton QC J0B 1L0
Tél: 819-570-5626
www.belgequebec.com
www.facebook.com/201986326506407
Aperçu: Dimension: moyenne; *Envergure:* provinciale; Organisme sans but lucratif; fondée en 1905
Mission: Promouvoir l'élevage de chevaux de race pure de grande qualité et aider les éleveurs à améliorer leur cheptel chevalin à travers la province au moyen de concours et d'expositions
Finances: Budget de fonctionnement annuel: Moins de $50,000
Membre: 88; *Montant de la cotisation:* Barème; *Critères d'admissibilité:* Avoir un intérêt aux choses agricoles et spécialement en ce qui regarde la production chevaline et une race en particulier et se conformer au règlement général de l'association
Membre(s) du bureau directeur:
Johanne Fréchette, Secrétaire
secretaire@belgequebec.com

Association des embouteilleurs d'eau du Québec (AEEQ) / Québec Water Bottlers' Association
a/s CTAC, #102, 200, rue MacDonald, Saint-Jean-sur-Richelieu QC J3B 8J6
Tél: 450-349-1521; *Téléc:* 450-349-6923
info@conseiltac.com
www.aeeq.org
Aperçu: Dimension: moyenne; *Envergure:* provinciale; fondée en 1975
Mission: L'association des embouteilleurs d'eau du Québec (AEEQ) est le porte-parole de l'industrie québécoise de l'embouteillage de l'eau de source et de l'eau minérale
Membre de: Canadian Bottled Water Federation
Membre: Critères d'admissibilité: Entreprises spécialisées dans le commerce de l'eau embouteillée; fournisseurs de services et d'équipments
Membre(s) du bureau directeur:
Benoit Grégoire, Président
Nicole Lelièvre, Vice-présidente

Association des employées et employés du gouvernement du Québec (AEGQ)
700, boul René-Lévesque est, 2e étage, Québec QC G1R 5H1
Tél: 418-643-4020; *Téléc:* 418-643-4064
association@aegq.qc.ca
www.aegq.qc.ca
Aperçu: Dimension: grande; *Envergure:* provinciale; Organisme sans but lucratif; fondée en 1925
Mission: Défendre les intérêts professionnels des employés de la fonction publique; club social
Finances: Budget de fonctionnement annuel: $100,000-$250,000
Membre(s) du personnel: 3; 6 bénévole(s)
Membre: 500; *Montant de la cotisation:* 52$; *Critères d'admissibilite:* Fonctionnaires provinciaux
Publications:
• Le Journal [a publication of the Association des employées et employés du gouvernement du Québec]
Type: Newspaper

Association des employés de bureau de Schneider (FCNSI) *See* Schneider Office Employees' Association

Association des employés de Charlotte Seafood *See* Charlotte Seafood Employees Association

Association des employés de l'Université de Moncton (AEUM) / Moncton University Employees Association
Université de Moncton, Moncton NB E1A 3E9
Tél: 506-858-4574; *Téléc:* 506-858-4166
Ligne sans frais: 800-363-8336
Également appelé: Local 120
Aperçu: Dimension: petite; *Envergure:* locale; Organisme de réglementation; fondée en 1969
Mission: Négocier la convention collective des membres et organiser les relations ouvrières entre les employés et l'Université de Moncton; améliorer les conditions de vie et de travail des employés
Membre(s) du personnel: 5
Membre: 182
Membre(s) du bureau directeur:
Éric Maltais, Président
eric.maltais@umoncton.ca

Association des employés de Milltronics (FCNSI) *See* Employees Association of Milltronics - CNFIU Local 3005

Association des employés du conseil de recherches (ind.) *See* Research Council Employees' Association (Ind.)

Association des employés du Service de sécurité de la Chambre des communes *See* House of Commons Security Services Employees Association

Association des employés du Service de sécurité du Sénate *See* Senate Protective Service Employees Association

Association des employés et employées gestionnaires, administratifs et professionnels de la Couronne de l'Ontario *See* Association of Management, Administrative & Professional Crown Employees of Ontario

Association des employés municipaux de Vancouver-Ouest *See* West Vancouver Municipal Employees Association

Association des employés non enseignants de Winnipeg *See* Winnipeg Association of Non-Teaching Employees

Association des employés non enseignants du Manitoba *See* Manitoba Association of Non-Teaching Employees

Association des employés professionnels (ind.) *See* Professional Employees Association (Ind.)

Association des employés, l'Hôpital Saint Mary's of the Lake (FCNSI) *See* Employees' Union of St. Mary's of the Lake Hospital - CNFIU Local 3001

Association des enseignant(e)s des Appalaches *See* Appalachian Teachers' Association

Association des enseignantes et des enseignants du Yukon *See* Yukon Teachers' Association

Association des enseignantes et des enseignants franco-ontariens (AEFO) / Franco-Ontarian Teachers' Association
#801, 1420, place Blair, Ottawa ON K1J 9L8
Tél: 613-244-2336; *Téléc:* 613-563-7718
Ligne sans frais: 800-267-4217
aefo@aefo.on.ca
www.aefo.on.ca
www.facebook.com/155281931200167
twitter.com/AEFO_ON_CA
Aperçu: Dimension: moyenne; *Envergure:* provinciale; Organisme sans but lucratif; fondée en 1939
Mission: De regrouper les travailleuses et les travailleurs au service des établissements publics et privés francophones en Ontario
Membre de: Fédération canadienne des enseignantes et des enseignants
Affiliation(s): Ontario Teachers' Federation
Membre: 7,855
Activités: Bibliothèque: Not open to public
Membre(s) du bureau directeur:
Pierre Léonard, Directeur général
pleonard@aefo.on.ca
Nicole Beauchamp, Responsable des communications
nbeauchamp@aefo.on.ca

Association des enseignantes et des enseignants francophones du Nouveau-Brunswick (AEFNB)
CP 712, 650, rue Montgomery, Fredericton NB E3B 5B4
Tél: 506-452-8921; *Téléc:* 506-452-1838
www.aefnb.ca
www.facebook.com/aefnb/
twitter.com/aefnb
www.youtube.com/channel/UCjZukUoeNt4styGTFsrxF0A
Aperçu: Dimension: moyenne; *Envergure:* provinciale; fondée en 1970 surveillé par Canadian Teachers' Federation
Mission: Représenter les intérêts des enseignantes et des enseignants francophones de la province; favoriser et maintenir au Nouveau-Brunswick des services éducatifs de langue française de première qualité
Finances: Budget de fonctionnement annuel: $500,000-$1.5 Million
Membre(s) du personnel: 8
Membre: 2 500; *Montant de la cotisation:* 58$ associé; *Critères d'admissibilite:* Enseignant ou enseignante
Activités: Stagiaires: Oui; *Bibliothèque:* Centre d'information; Not open to public
Membre(s) du bureau directeur:
Marc Arseneau, Président

Association des enseignants de l'Université du Nouveau-Brunswick *See* Association of University of New Brunswick Teachers

Association des enseignants de Terre-Neuve *See* Newfoundland & Labrador Teachers' Association

Association des enseignants du collège régional de Grande Prairie *See* Grande Prairie Regional College Academic Staff Association

Association des enseignants en infographie et en imprimerie du Québec (AEIQ)
QC
Courriel: aeiqinfo@gmail.com
aeiq.wordpress.com
Aperçu: Dimension: petite; *Envergure:* provinciale; Organisme sans but lucratif; fondée en 1982
Mission: De regrouper les enseignants, les industriels ainsi que toutes les personnes qui ont un intérêt dans l'enseignement et l'industrie des arts graphiques au Québec
Membre de: Conseil pédagogique interdisciplinaire du Québec
Finances: Budget de fonctionnement annuel: Moins de $50,000
Membre(s) du personnel: 7; 7 bénévole(s)
Membre: 70
Activités: Listes de destinataires: Oui
Membre(s) du bureau directeur:
Martin Cabana, Président

Association des enterprises spécialiseés en eau du Québec
5930, boul Louis-H. Lafontaine, Montréal QC H1M 1S7
Tél: 514-353-9960; *Téléc:* 514-352-5259
Ligne sans frais: 800-468-8160
contact@aeseq.com
www.aeseq.com
Nom précédent: Association des eaux souterraines du Québec
Aperçu: Dimension: moyenne; *Envergure:* provinciale
Mission: Regrouper les entrepreneurs de construction oeuvrant dans tous les secteurs du cycle de l'eau décentralisé au Québec
Membre(s) du personnel: 3
Membre: Critères d'admissibilite: Entrepreneurs puisatiers; entrepreneurs en installation de pompe, ou en assainissement autonome, ou en traitement d'eau potable; fournisseurs d'équipement et de matériaux; consultants; organismes publics et parapublics
Membre(s) du bureau directeur:
Daniel Schanck, Directeur général

Association des entomologistes amateurs du Québec inc. (AEAQ)
302, rue Gabrielle Roy, Varennes QC J3X 1L8
Courriel: info@aeaq.ca
www.aeaq.ca
www.facebook.com/114179175276983
Aperçu: Dimension: petite; *Envergure:* provinciale; Organisme sans but lucratif; fondée en 1973
Mission: Promouvoir l'entomologie comme loisir scientifique; favoriser l'échange d'informations entre les membres lors des réunions; publier les travaux et les observations entomologiques des membres; veiller à la protection et à la conservation de l'entomofaune et du patrimoine entomologique du Québec; initier les nouveaux membres à l'étude des insectes à l'aide de séances d'identification, d'excursions et de rencontres avec des spécialistes
Affiliation(s): Société d'entomologie du Québec; Corporation Entomofaune du Québec; Amis de l'Insectarium de Montréal
Membre: Montant de la cotisation: 30$ régulière; 35$ familiale; 50$ de soutien; 35$ institutions Canadien
Membre(s) du bureau directeur:
Claude Chantal, Président

Association des entrepreneurs de systèmes intérieurs du Québec
#227, 3221, Autoroute 440 ouest, Laval QC H7P 5P2
Tél: 450-978-2666; *Téléc:* 450-978-1833
www.aesiq.org
Aperçu: Dimension: petite; *Envergure:* provinciale
Mission: Promouvoir et défendre les intérêts de nos membres et de l'industrie des systèmes intérieurs au Québec

Association des entrepreneurs en construction du Québec (AECQ) / Association of Building Contractors of Québec (ABCQ)
#101, 7905, boul Louis-H. Lafontaine, Anjou QC H1K 4E4
Tél: 514-353-5151; *Téléc:* 514-353-6689
Ligne sans frais: 800-361-4304
info@aecq.org
www.aecq.org
Aperçu: Dimension: grande; *Envergure:* provinciale; fondée en 1976
Mission: Étudier, promouvoir, protéger et défendre les intérêts des employeurs en matière de relations de travail; négocier les clauses du tronc commun à chacune des quatre conventions collectives sectorielles
Affiliation(s): Canadian Construction Association
Finances: Budget de fonctionnement annuel: $500,000-$1.5 Million
Membre(s) du personnel: 4
Membre: 25 000
Activités: Service de conférenciers: Oui
Membre(s) du bureau directeur:
Pierre Dion, Directeur général

Association des entrepreneurs en couverture du Nouveau-Brunswick *See* New Brunswick Roofing Contractors Association, Inc.

Association des entrepreneurs en isolation de la Province de Québec *Voir* Association d'isolation du Québec

Association des entrepreneurs en maçonnerie du Québec (AEMQ)
#101, 4097 boul St-Jean-Baptiste, Montréal QC H1B 5V3
Tél: 514-645-1113; *Téléc:* 514-645-1114
Ligne sans frais: 866-645-1113
aemq@aemq.com
www.aemq.com
www.facebook.com/171902572902949
Aperçu: Dimension: petite; *Envergure:* provinciale; fondée en 1984
Mission: Faire la promotion du métier de maçon et s'assurer que tous travaillent à promouvoir davantage le marché de la maçonnerie
Membre de: Institut de la maçonnerie
Affiliation(s): Association des entrepreneurs en construction du Québec; Association de la construction du Québec
Finances: Budget de fonctionnement annuel: Moins de $50,000
Membre: 225; *Montant de la cotisation:* 688,85$ corporatif et affilié; 344,93$ professionnel

Activités: Offre des produits et services à tous les entrepreneurs ou organismes dont les activités commerciales sont reliées à l'industrie de la maçonnerie
Membre(s) du bureau directeur:
Martin Cormier, Directeur général

Association des entrepreneurs en mécanique d'Ottawa *See* Mechanical Contractors Association of Ottawa

Association des entrepreneurs en mécanique du Canada *See* Mechanical Contractors Association of Canada

Association des entreprises métallurgiques du Nouveau-Brunswick *See* The Metal Working Association of New Brunswick

Association des ergothérapeutes du Nouveau-Brunswick *See* New Brunswick Association of Occupational Therapists

Association des Estimateurs et Économistes en Construction du Québec *Voir* Insitut canadien des économistes en construction - Québec

Association des établissements privés conventionnés - santé services sociaux (AEPC)
#200, 1076, rue de Bleury, Montréal QC H2Z 1N2
Tél: 514-499-3630; *Téléc:* 514-873-7063
info@aepc.qc.ca
www.aepc.qc.ca
www.facebook.com/416653585019212
twitter.com/AEPC_SSS
Nom précédent: Association des centres hospitaliers et centres d'accueil privés du Québec
Aperçu: *Dimension:* moyenne; *Envergure:* nationale; Organisme sans but lucratif; fondée en 1979
Mission: Promouvoir l'amélioration continue de la qualité des soins et des services donnés au sein des entreprises membres; protéger et promouvoir l'entreprise privée dans le domaine de la santé et du bien-être
Membre(s) du personnel: 7
Membre: *Critères d'admissibilité:* Détenir un permis d'établissement privé conventionnel du Ministère de la santé et des services sociaux du Québec
Membre(s) du bureau directeur:
Danny Macdonald, Directeur général par intérim

Association des études du Proche-Orient ancien
Pavillon Hubert-Aquin, 400, rue Sainte-Catherine est, Montréal QC H2L 2C5
Tél: 514-343-2109; *Téléc:* 514-343-5738
aepoa@uqam.ca
www.aepoa.uqam.ca
Aperçu: *Dimension:* moyenne; *Envergure:* locale
Mission: La promotion des études du Proche-Orient ancien
Membre: *Critères d'admissibilité:* Des chercheurs, des professeurs, des étudiants et tous ceux qui s'intéressent à l'histoire et les civilisations du Proche-Orient ancien
Membre(s) du bureau directeur:
Jean Revez, Président
Publications:
• La Revue RECAPO [a publication of Association des études du Proche-Orient ancien]
Price: 15$ non-membre

Association des étudiantes infirmières du Canada *See* Canadian Nursing Students' Association

Association des Étudiants de Science Politique du Canada *See* Canadian Political Science Students' Association

L'Association des etudiants noirs en droit du Canada *See* Black Law Students' Association of Canada

Association des évaluateurs immobiliers du Nouveau-Brunswick *See* New Brunswick Association of Real Estate Appraisers

Association des experts en sinistre indépendants du Québec inc (AESIQ)
a/s Denis Duchesne, Cunningham Lindsey Canada Claims Services Ltd., #1000, 1250, rue Guy, Montréal QC H3H 2T4
Tél: 514-938-5400; *Téléc:* 514-938-5445
www.ciaa-adjusters.ca
Aperçu: *Dimension:* petite; *Envergure:* provinciale; fondée en 1942 surveillé par Canadian Independent Adjusters' Association
Affiliation(s): Association canadienne des experts indépendants/Canadian Independent Adjusters' Association
Membre: *Critères d'admissibilité:* Détenteur d'un certificat d'expert en sinistre du B.S.F.
Membre(s) du bureau directeur:
Denis Duchesne, Président
dduchesne@cl-na.com

Association des expositions agricoles du Québec (AEAQ)
#223, 1173, boul Charest ouest, Québec QC G1N 2C9
Tél: 418-527-1196; *Téléc:* 418-527-6954
info@expoduquebec.com
expoduquebec.com
www.facebook.com/203811642990737
Aperçu: *Dimension:* petite; *Envergure:* provinciale; fondée en 1955
Mission: D'offrir aux agriculteurs et aux éleveurs des événements professionnels spécialisés et bien organisés; et de présenter au grand public des événements populaires, éducatifs, divertissants et sécuritaires.
Finances: *Budget de fonctionnement annuel:* $250,000-$500,000
Membre(s) du personnel: 1
Membre: 39
Membre(s) du bureau directeur:
André Labonté, Presidente, 418-882-5649
deuxl@videotron.ca
Publications:
• Quoi de neuf? [une publication de l'Association des expositions agricoles du Québec]
Type: Bulletin; *Frequency:* 4 fois par an; *Price:* Gratuit
Profile: Fournit des informations importantes et des mises à jour pour les membres de l'Association des expositions agricoles du Québec

Association des fabricants d'aliments pour animaux familiers du Canada *See* Pet Food Association of Canada

Association des fabricants de meubles du Québec inc. (AFMQ) / Québec Furniture Manufacturers Association Inc.
#101, 1111, rue St-Urbain, Montréal QC H2Z 1Y6
Tél: 514-866-3631; *Téléc:* 514-871-9900
Ligne sans frais: 800-363-6681
info@afmq.com
www.afmq.com
Aperçu: *Dimension:* moyenne; *Envergure:* provinciale; Organisme sans but lucratif; fondée en 1942
Mission: Participer activement au développement de l'industrie du meuble du Québec
Membre de: Canadian Council of Furniture Manufacturers
Membre(s) du personnel: 9
Membre: 150; *Critères d'admissibilite:* Fabricants de meubles, de composantes et fournisseurs de l'industrie
Membre(s) du bureau directeur:
Pierre Richard, Président/Directeur général
prichard@afmq.com
Anne Marie Byrnes, Coordonnatrice, Communications et marketing
abyrnes@afmq.com

Association des fabricants et détaillants de l'industrie de la cuisine du Québec (AFDICQ)
841, rue des Oeillets, Saint-Jean-Chrysostome QC G6Z 3B7
Tél: 418-834-0200; *Téléc:* 418-834-7924
info@afdicq.ca
www.afdicq.ca
www.facebook.com/Afdicq
Aperçu: *Dimension:* moyenne; *Envergure:* provinciale; fondée en 1981
Mission: L'AFDICQ regroupe des fabricants et des distributeurs d'armoires de cuisine et de salle de bains, de meubles sur mesure et d'ébénisterie architecturale. Services: programme hors-série, la licence RBQ, mutuelles de prévention, assurance collective, représentation auprès du gouvernement, opportunité d'établir des contacts d'affaires, sécurité et main d'oeuvre, et le Bulletin.
Membre: 157; *Critères d'admissibilite:* Manufacturiers et distributeurs d'armoires de cuisine et de salle de bains, de meubles sur mesure et d'ébénisterie architecturale
Membre(s) du bureau directeur:
Simon Bouchard, Président

L'Association des facultés de médecine du Canada *See* Association of Faculties of Medicine of Canada

Association des facultés de pharmacie du Canada *See* Association of Faculties of Pharmacy of Canada

Association des facultés dentaires du Canada *See* Association of Canadian Faculties of Dentistry

Association des faculty du universitaire du Cap-Breton *See* Cape Breton University Faculty Association

Association des familialistes de Québec
300, boul Jean Lesage, #RC-21, Québec QC G1K 8K6
Tél: 418-529-0301
www.barreaudequebec.ca
Aperçu: *Dimension:* moyenne; *Envergure:* provinciale; fondée en 1994
Mission: Pour représenter les intérêts de ses membres avec les différents organismes et à assurer la formation de ses membres
Membre: *Montant de la cotisation:* 50$ Membre du Barreau depuis moins de 5 ans; 65$ Membre du Barreau depius plus de 5 ans
Activités: Les conférences; Activités sociales
Membre(s) du bureau directeur:
Isabelle Perreault, Présidente, Conseil d'administration, 418-627-2442, Fax: 418-627-6656

Association des familles Gosselin, Inc.
1647, ch Royal, Montréal QC G0A 3Z0
Tél: 418-828-2896; *Téléc:* 418-828-0149
associationfamillesgosselin@hotmail.com
www.genealogie.org/famille/gosselin
Aperçu: *Dimension:* petite; *Envergure:* locale; fondée en 1979
Mission: Informer et guider les recherches en généalogie sur le patronyme Gosselin; faire connaître le résultat des recherches sur tout ce qui touche le patronyme Gosselin; faciliter la communication et les échanges entre les cousins Gosselin
7 bénévole(s)
Membre: 200; *Montant de la cotisation:* 20$
Activités: Assemblemt annuel des familles Gosselin; recherches en généalogie; basse de données
Membre(s) du bureau directeur:
Jacques Gosselin, Président
lac-gosselin@hotmail.com
William Gosselin, Vice-président

Association des familles monoparentales et recomposées de l'Outaouais (AFMRO)
584, rue Guizot est, Montréal QC H2P 1N3
Tél: 514-729-6666; *Téléc:* 514-729-6746
fafmrq.info@videotron.ca
www.fafmrq.org
www.facebook.com/215273325165435
twitter.com/FAFMRQ
Aperçu: *Dimension:* petite; *Envergure:* locale
Mission: Aider les chefs de famille monoparentale démunis à acquérir l'autonomie financière, sociale, personnelle et familiale. Etre un centre de consultation, de support, d'évaluation, de formation et d'éducation en matière de rupture et de réorganisation familiale.
Affiliation(s): Fédération des associations de familles monoparentales et recomposées du Québec
Finances: *Fonds:* Gouvernement régional
Membre(s) du personnel: 3
Membre: *Montant de la cotisation:* 45$ individuelle; 150$ associé; 50$ actif moins de 50 000$/année; 100$ actif entre 50 000$ et 99 999$/année; 150$ actif 100 000$ et plus/année
Membre(s) du bureau directeur:
Sylvie Lévesque, Directrice générale
fafmrq.sylvie@videotron.ca

Association des familles monoparentales et recomposées de Montcalm *Voir* Association Carrefour Famille Montcalm

Association des familles Rioux d'Amérique inc. (AFRA)
CP 7141, Trois-Pistoles QC G0L 4K0
www.famillesriou-x.com
Aperçu: *Dimension:* petite; *Envergure:* nationale; Organisme sans but lucratif; fondée en 1984
Mission: Regrouper dans une même grande famille tous les Riou-x d'Amérique et d'ailleurs issus de Jean Riou et de Catherine Leblond; faire connaître l'histoire des ancêtres et de leurs descendants
Membre de: Fédération des familles-souches québécoises inc.
Finances: *Budget de fonctionnement annuel:* Moins de $50,000
10 bénévole(s)
Membre: 450; *Montant de la cotisation:* 25$; *Critères d'admissibilite:* Agé de 50 ans et plus
Activités: Assemblée générale; organiser des rencontres des familles Rioux
Membre(s) du bureau directeur:
Raynald Rioux, Président

Association des familles unies de la rue Walkley *See* Walkley Centre

Association des familles uniparentales du Canada *See* One Parent Families Association of Canada

Association des femmes acadiennes en marche de la région de Richmond *Voir* La Fédération des femmes acadiennes de la Nouvelle-Écosse

L'Association des femmes autochtones du Canada *See* Native Women's Association of Canada

L'Association des femmes compositeurs canadiennes *See* Association of Canadian Women Composers

Association des femmes d'assurance de Montréal (AFAM) / Montréal Association of Insurance Women
Montréal QC
Courriel: info@afam-maiw.com
www.afam-maiw.com
Aperçu: Dimension: petite; *Envergure:* locale; fondée en 1963
Mission: Promouvoir et coordonner des programmes pratiques et éducatifs afin d'encourager ses membres à rechercher le plus haut niveau de connaissances en matière d'assurance ainsi que dans la conduite des affaires; Encourager une franche loyauté et entretenir des relations amicales entre membres; Sensibiliser ses membres aux besoins et nécessités de leurs collègues.
Membre de: Canadian Association of Insurance Women
Membre: 300+; *Montant de la cotisation:* 60$/adhésion; *Comités:* Exécutif; Programme et éducation; Bulletin; Accueil; Adhésion et recrutement; Archiviste; Communication; Législation; Constitution et règlement; Levée de fonds; Prix réalisations première générale; Prix éducation encan d'auto impact; Golf; Site internet; Traduction; Projets spéciaux; Vérificateurs externes; Relais pour la vie
Membre(s) du bureau directeur:
Josée Loyer, Présidente, 450-452-4043, Fax: 450-452-2310
jloyer@impactauto.ca
Prix, Bourses:
• Mildred Jones Award - Insurance Woman of the Year

Association des fermières de l'Ontario (AFO)
CP 190, Saint-Eugène ON K0B 1P0
Tél: 613-674-2035; *Téléc:* 613-674-1176
fermieres@cacseo.ca
Aperçu: Dimension: moyenne; *Envergure:* provinciale; Organisme sans but lucratif; fondée en 1969
Mission: Travailler aux intérêts des femmes et jeunes filles dans les paroisses, en artisanat, au progrès spirituel, social, culturel, économique et technique
Affiliation(s): Association canadienne-française de l'Ontario
Membre: Critères d'admissibilité: Femme de 20 ans (en moyenne) et plus, intéressée à sa santé, bien-être, culture (artisanat), connaissances générales, économie, loi etc.
Activités: Exposition artisanale annuelle; *Service de conférenciers:* Oui
Membre(s) du bureau directeur:
Rachèle St-Denis-Lachaîne, Présidente
Louise Myler, Sec.-trés.

L'Association des firmes d'ingénieurs-conseils - Canada *See* Association of Consulting Engineering Companies - Canada

Association des firmes d'ingénieurs-conseils - Nouveau-Brunswick *See* Association of Consulting Engineering Companies - New Brunswick

Association des firmes de génie-conseil - Québec (AFG) / Association of Consulting Engineering Companies - Quebec
#930, 1440, rue Sainte-Catherine ouest, Montréal QC H3G 1R8
Tél: 514-871-2229; *Téléc:* 514-871-9903
info@afg.quebec
afg.quebec
www.youtube.com/aicqtv
Nom précédent: Association des ingénieurs-conseils du Québec
Aperçu: Dimension: grande; *Envergure:* provinciale; fondée en 1974 surveillé par Association of Consulting Engineering Companies - Canada
Mission: Promouvoir et développer l'industrie du génie-conseil en regroupant des membres qui offrent des services de qualité
Membre(s) du personnel: 5; 100 bénévole(s)
Membre: 280 bureaux; *Comités:* Bâtiment; Énergie; Environnement; Industrie; Municipal; Télécommunications et nouvelles technologies; Transport

Activités: Listes de destinataires: Oui; *Bibliothèque:* rendez-vous
Membre(s) du bureau directeur:
Isabelle Jodoin, Président du Conseil
André Rainville, Président-directeur général, 514-871-2229 Ext. 23
arainville@afg.quebec
Pierre Nadeau, Directeur, Communications, 514-871-0589 Ext. 28
pnadeau@afg.quebec

Association des flûtistes d'Ottawa *See* Ottawa Flute Association

Association des fonctionnaires issus des communautés culturelles (AFICC)
1308, rue des Grandes-Marées, Québec QC G1Y 2T1
Aperçu: Dimension: petite; *Envergure:* locale
Membre(s) du bureau directeur:
Othman Mzoughi, President

Association des fondations d'établissements de santé du Québec (AFÉSAQ)
455, boul Base-de-Roc, #A301, Joliette QC J6E 5P3
Tél: 450-760-2325; *Téléc:* 450-760-2326
Ligne sans frais: 888-760-2325
www.afesaq.qc.ca
Aperçu: Dimension: petite; *Envergure:* provinciale
Mission: Pour représenter les intérêts des associations de soins de santé et les associations de services sociaux
Membre: 100+; *Critères d'admissibilité:* Fondations provenant du réseau de la santé; *Comités:* Directeurs généraux; Gouvernance; Nomination et des ressources humaines; Relations établissement/fondation; Consultatif colloque
Membre(s) du bureau directeur:
Roland Granger, Président-directeur général
rgranger@afesaq.qc.ca

Association des fonderies canadiennes *See* Canadian Foundry Association

L'Association des forces aériennes du Canada *See* Air Force Association of Canada

Association des forestiers agréés du Nouveau-Brunswick *See* Association of Registered Professional Foresters of New Brunswick

Association des fournisseurs de service internet sans fil *See* Canadian Association of Wireless Internet Service Providers

Association des foyers de soins du Nouveau-Brunswick, inc. *See* New Brunswick Association of Nursing Homes, Inc.

L'Association des franchisés Great White North *See* Great White North Franchisee Association

Association des francophones de Fort Smith (AFFS)
212, ch McDougal, Fort Smith NT X0E OPO
Tél: 867-872-2338; *Téléc:* 867-872-5710
affs@northwestel.net
www.associationfrancophonesfortsmith.ca
Aperçu: Dimension: petite; *Envergure:* locale; fondée en 1984 surveillé par Fédération franco-ténoise
Mission: Afin de préserver et de développer la communauté francophone de Fort Smith
Membre(s) du bureau directeur:
Marie-Christine Aubrey, Présidente

Association des francophones du delta du Mackenzie (AFDM)
CP 2845, Inuvik NT X0E OTO
Tél: 867-678-2661; *Téléc:* 867-777-2799
afdm@hotmail.ca
www.afdm.ca
Aperçu: Dimension: petite; *Envergure:* locale surveillé par Fédération franco-ténoise
Mission: Pour représenter les intérêts et les droits de la communauté francophone de delta du Mackenzie
Membre(s) du bureau directeur:
André Church, Président

Association des francophones du nord-ouest de l'Ontario (AFNOO)
#200, 234, rue Van Norman, Thunder Bay ON P7A 4B8
Ligne sans frais: 888-248-1712
www.afnoo.org
Aperçu: Dimension: moyenne; *Envergure:* locale; Organisme sans but lucratif; fondée en 1977

Mission: Vise la promotion et la valorisation de la communauté francophone dans le Nord-Ouest de l'Ontario afin de célébrer la richesse et la valeur ajoutée qu'elle représente pour les communautés, la région, la société ontarienne, et pour l'ensemble du pays
Membre de: La Coopérative du regroupement des organismes francophones de Thunder Bay Inc.
Affiliation(s): Assemblée de la Francophonie de l'Ontario 35 bénévole(s)
Membre: 28 groupes; *Montant de la cotisation:* 85$; *Critères d'admissibilité:* Agences et groupes francophones du Nord-Ouest de l'Ontario
Activités:; Bibliothèque: rendez-vous
Membre(s) du bureau directeur:
Élodie Grunerud, Directrice générale
dg@afnoo.org

Association des francophones du Nunavut (AFN)
CP 880, Iqaluit NU X0A 0H0
Tél: 867-979-4606; *Téléc:* 867-979-0800
cuerrier@nunafranc.ca
www.afnunavut.ca
Aperçu: Dimension: petite; *Envergure:* provinciale; fondée en 1981 surveillé par Fédération des communautés francophones et acadienne du Canada
Mission: Pour représenter la communauté française et l'aider à développer
Affiliation(s): Coopérative de tourisme Odyssée limitée; Conseil de coopération du Nunavut; Société immobilière Franco-Nunavut; CFRT; la Nunavoix; Commission scolaire francophone du Nunavut; Défi Nunavut; Réseau de développement économique et d'employabilité Nunavut; SAFRAN; Toit du monde
Membre(s) du bureau directeur:
Mylène Chartrand, Présidente

L'Association des fruiticulteurs et des maraîchers de l'Ontario *See* Ontario Fruit & Vegetable Growers' Association

Association des Gais et Lesbiennes Sourds (AGLS)
Montréal QC
Courriel: agls@live.ca
www.agls.ca
www.facebook.com/214130285283518
Aperçu: Dimension: petite; *Envergure:* provinciale; fondée en 2003
Mission: L'Association des Gais et Lesbiennes Sourds est un organisme provincial à but non lucratif qui offre des activités sociales et des ateliers sur l'homophobie auprès de la communauté sourde et malentendante du Québec et du Grand Montréal.

L'Association des gais, lesbiennes et bisexuel(le)s du Québec *Voir* GRIS-Mauricie/Centre-du-Québec

Association des galeries d'art des provinces de l'Atlantique *See* Atlantic Provinces Art Gallery Association

Association des garderies privées du Québec (AGPQ)
#230, 5115, av Trans Island, Montréal QC H3W 2Z9
Tél: 514-485-2221
Ligne sans frais: 888-655-6060
correspondance@agpq.ca
www.agpq.ca
www.facebook.com/agpq.quebec
Aperçu: Dimension: petite; *Envergure:* provinciale; fondée en 1973
Mission: Promouvoir, favoriser, développer et améliorer la qualité des services de garde éducatifs pour les enfants et les familles; assurer le libre choix des parents et la pérennité du réseau; protéger, défendre et représenter les droits des membres; informer les membres, formuler des recommandations et les promouvoir auprès des instances gouvernementales et organismes partenaires; valoriser le perfectionnement et le développement du personnel en milieu de garde
5 bénévole(s)
Activités: Événements de sensibilisation: Semaine des services de garde du Québec
Membre(s) du bureau directeur:
Sylvain Lévesque, Président
Samir Alahmad, Vice-Président

Association des gastro-entérologues du Québec (AGEQ)
CP 216, Succ. Desjardins, 2, Complexe Desjardins, Montréal QC H5B 1G8

Tél: 514-350-5112; Téléc: 514-350-5146
www.ageq.net
Aperçu: *Dimension:* petite; *Envergure:* !E!; fondée en 1965 surveillé par Fédération des médecins spécialistes du Québec
Mission: D'informer et de formations aux médecins de première ligne, aux patients souffrant de pathologies gastro-intestinales et aux autres médecins intéressés par la gastro-entérologie; de créer des liens avec la communauté médicale internationale
Membre(s) du bureau directeur:
Josée Parent, Présidente
Sylvie Bergeron, Directrice, Administration
sbergeron@fmsq.org

Association des gens d'affaires & professionnels italo-canadiens *See* Canadian Italian Business & Professional Association

Association des Gestionnaires de l'information de la santé du Québec (AGISQ)
#104, 5104, boul Bourque, Sherbrooke QC J1N 2K7
Tél: 819-823-6670; Téléc: 819-823-0799
Ligne sans frais: 800-793-6935
info@agisq.ca
www.agisq.ca
www.facebook.com/392680864114521
Nom précédent: Association québécoise des archivistes médicales; Association des archivistes médicales de la province de Québec
Aperçu: *Dimension:* moyenne; *Envergure:* provinciale; Organisme sans but lucratif; fondée en 1960
Mission: Promouvoir les connaissances scientifiques, techniques, professionnelles, morales, sociales et légales se rattachant directement ou indirectement à la profession d'archiviste médicale; promouvoir la formation et le perfectionnement des membres; promouvoir la profession dans les différents établissements de santé, organismes gouvernementaux, paragouvernementaux et privés; favoriser les échanges et les communications entre les membres; offrir des services-conseils; accomplir toute activité qui peut être nécessaire à l'atteinte des objectifs fixés
Membre: 1000; *Montant de la cotisation:* 227,30$ régulier ou affilié; 102,33$ retraité; 45,64$ étudiant; *Critères d'admissibilite:* Avant complété ses études en archives médicales dans une école reconnue par le ministère de l'Éducation du Québec et posséder son diplôme d'études collégiales ou être certifié de la CHIMA; *Comités:* Archivistes médicaux en milieu psychiatrique; Éducation; Gestion de l'information; Information; Organisation; Promotion de la confidentialité; Régionaux; Registraires en oncologie; Registraires en traumatologie; Site Internet et forum de discussion
Activités: Journée de perfectionnement; formation continue; *Evénements de sensibilisation:* Semaine de sensibilisation à la confidentialité aux 2 ans (nov); *Stagiaires:* Oui
Membre(s) du bureau directeur:
Alexandre Allard, Président
Monica Ouellet, Vice-Présidente
Charles Saulnier, Trésorier
Prix, Bourses:
• Prix Jean-Guy-Fréchette

Association des gestionnaires de ressources bénévoles du Québec (AGRBQ)
#1608, 6, rue McMahon, Québec QC G1R 3S1
Tél: 418-525-4444
www.agrbq.com
Aperçu: *Dimension:* petite; *Envergure:* provinciale; fondée en 1958
Mission: L'Association permet la mise en commun d'idées, d'expériences et de recherches afin d'avoir une vision plus contemporaine et plus globale de l'action bénévole
Membre de: Canadian Administrators of Volunteer Resources
Membre: *Montant de la cotisation:* 135$
Membre(s) du bureau directeur:
Chantal Ouellet, Présidente

Association des Gestionnaires de Risques et d'Assurance du Québec *Voir* Risk & Insurance Management Society Inc.

Association des gestionnaires des établissements de santé et des services sociaux (AGESSS) / Association for Manager of Health Facilities & Social Services
#101, 601, rue Adoncour, Longueuil QC J4G 2M6
Tél: 450-651-6000; Téléc: 450-651-9750
Ligne sans frais: 800-361-6526
reception@agesss.qc.ca
www.agesss.qc.ca

Aperçu: *Dimension:* moyenne; *Envergure:* provinciale; fondée en 1969
Mission: Représenter ses membres; promouvoir et défendre l'intérêt de ses membres; tenir ses membres informés; gérer ses biens pour assurer sa survie et l'efficacité de son action
Affiliation(s): Desjardins Sécurité financière; laPersonelle; RACAR; La Capitale; Le Point
Finances: *Budget de fonctionnement annuel:* $1.5 Million-$3 Million
Membre(s) du personnel: 18
Membre: 5 000+; *Critères d'admissibilite:* Cadre intermédiaire d'établissements de santé et de services sociaux; *Comités:* Comité des conditions de travail; comité de rénumération et fonctions types; comité sur l'équité salariale; comité sur l'assurance et la retraite; comité de développement professionnel; comité des finances; comité de coordination des communications; comité des retraités
Membre(s) du bureau directeur:
Yves Bolduc, Président-directeur général
Chantal Marchand, Vice-Président
Johanne Simard, Trésorière
Prix, Bourses:
• Prix d'excellence du réseau de la santé et des services sociaux

Association des goélands de Longueuil
#203, 425, rue Leblanc ouest, Longueuil QC J4J 1L2
Tél: 450-674-3490
Aperçu: *Dimension:* petite; *Envergure:* locale
Mission: Pour réunir des personnes ayant des handicaps physiques et de leur fournir des services de loisirs et de l'information

Association des golfeurs professionnels du Canada *See* Professional Golfers' Association of Canada

Association des golfeurs professionnels du Québec (AGP)
435, boul Saint-Luc, Saint-Jean-sur-Richelieu QC J2W 1E7
Tél: 450-349-5525; Téléc: 450-349-6640
agpinfo@agp.qc.ca
www.agp.qc.ca
www.facebook.com/384893361542645
twitter.com/AGPduQuebec
/www.youtube.com/user/AGPduQuebec
Aperçu: *Dimension:* petite; *Envergure:* provinciale; fondée en 1927
Mission: Vouée à la promotion et à l'évolution du golf
Membre(s) du personnel: 21
Membre: 500; *Comités:* Finance-vérification; Formation/éducation; Discipline et administrateur; Gouvernance; Ressources humaines; Assistance aux membres; Discipline
Membre(s) du bureau directeur:
Jean Châtelain, Président
Jean Trudeau, Directeur général
jtrudeau@agp.qc.ca

Association des Grands Frères et Grandes Soeurs du Québec (GFGS) / Big Brothers & Big Sisters of Québec
QC
Aperçu: *Dimension:* moyenne; *Envergure:* provinciale; Organisme sans but lucratif; fondée en 1981 surveillé par Big Brothers Big Sisters of Canada
Membre de: Big Brothers Big Sisters of Canada
Membre(s) du bureau directeur:
Francine Vandal, Secrétaire administrative

Grands Frères Grandes Soeurs d'Abitibi Ouest (GFGS-AO)
CP 460, 10, 7e av est, La Sarre QC J9Z 1M4
Tél: 819-333-9132
abitibi.ouest@grandsfreresgrandessoeurs.ca
www.bigbrothersbigsisters.ca/abitibi
Membre(s) du bureau directeur:
Claudia Lambert, Présidente

Grands Frères Grandes Soeurs du Domaine du Roy
CP 182, 869, rue Arthur, Roberval QC G8H 2N6
Tél: 418-275-0483; Téléc: 418-275-0483
www.gfgsddr.ca
Membre(s) du bureau directeur:
Véronique Potvin, Coordonnatrice
veronique.potvin@grandsfreresgrandessoeurs.ca

Grands Frères Grandes Soeurs de l'Estrie
1265, rue Belvedere sud, Sherbrooke QC J1H 4E2
Tél: 819-822-3243; Téléc: 819-652-9352
Ligne sans frais: 866-922-3243
information.estrie@grandsfreresgrandessoeurs.ca

www.gfgsestrie.ca
www.facebook.com/GFGSEstrie
Membre(s) du bureau directeur:
Josée Boisvert, Présidente

Grands Frères Grandes Soeurs du Lac St-Jean Nord
1420, boul Wallberg, Dolbeau-Mistassini QC G8L 1H4
Tél: 418-276-8297; Téléc: 418-276-8297
gfgslsjn@bellnet.ca
www.gfgslsjn.ca
Membre(s) du bureau directeur:
Audrey Paquin, Présidente
Membre(s) du bureau directeur:
Annie Lamothe, Directrice générale

Grands Frères Grandes Soeurs du Grand Montréal
10871, av Salk, #A100, Montréal-Nord QC H1G 6M7
Tél: 514-842-9715; Téléc: 514-842-2454
www.gfgsmtl.qc.ca
www.facebook.com/GFGSmontreal
Membre(s) du bureau directeur:
Julie Gaudreault-Martel, Présidente

Grands Frères Grandes Soeurs de l'Ouest de l'île
16711 Rte Transcanadienne, Kirkland QC H9H 3L1
Tél: 514-538-6100
www.bbbsofwi.org
Membre(s) du bureau directeur:
Francesca Corso, Directrice générale, 514-538-6100 Ext. 3331
francesca.corso@bigbrothersbigsisters.ca

Grands Frères Grandes Soeurs de l'Outaouais
195, rue Deveault, Gatineau QC J8Z 1S7
Tél: 819-778-0101; Téléc: 819-778-3750
www.gfgso.com
Membre(s) du bureau directeur:
Yvonne Dubé, Directrice Générale
dons@gfgso.com

Grands Frères Grandes Soeurs de La Porte du Nord
770, rue Labelle, Saint-Jérôme QC J7Z 5M3
Tél: 450-565-4562; Téléc: 450-436-9735
info.portedunord@grandsfreresgrandessoeurs.ca
www.gfgsportedunord.ca
Membre(s) du bureau directeur:
Carole Dionne
carole.dionne@grandsfreresgrandessoeurs.ca

Grands Frères Grandes Soeurs de Québec
#201, 2380 av du Mont-Thabor, Québec QC G1J 3W7
Tél: 418-624-3304; Téléc: 418-624-4013
gfgsquebec@videotron.ca
www.bigbrothersbigsisters.ca/quebec
Membre(s) du bureau directeur:
Guillaume de Montigny, Président

Grands Frères Grandes Soeurs des Appalaches
#202, 733, boul Frontenac ouest, Thetford Mines QC G6G 7X9
Tél: 418-335-7404; Téléc: 418-335-0937
caroline.gagne@gfgsamiante.com
www.gfgsamiante.com
Membre(s) du bureau directeur:
Caroline Gagné, Directrice
caroline.gagne@gfgsappalaches.com

Grands Frères Grandes Soeurs de Rouyn-Noranda
#225, 380, av Richard, Rouyn-Noranda QC J9X 4L3
Tél: 819-762-0167; Téléc: 819-762-9967
rouyn.noranda@grandsfreresgrandessoeurs.ca
www.bigbrothersbigsisters.ca/rouynnoranda
Membre(s) du bureau directeur:
Kevin Séguin, Directeur Général

Grands Frères Grandes Soeurs de la Montérégie
#204, 1195, rue Saint-Antoine, Saint-Hyacinthe QC J2S 3K6
Tél: 450-774-8723; Téléc: 450-261-0983
Ligne sans frais: 866-464-6188
info.monteregie@grandsfreresgrandessoeurs.ca
www.gfgsm.org
Membre(s) du bureau directeur:
Martin Fredette, Président
Michel Dion, Directeur général, 866-464-6188 Ext. 5
michel.dion@grandsfreresgrandessoeurs.ca

Association des Grands Frères Grands Soeurs du Québec *Voir* Association des Grands Frères Grandes Soeurs du Québec

Association des grands-parents du Québec
3, rue Fatima, Beaupré QC G0A 1E0
Tél: 514-745-6110; Téléc: 514-745-6110
Ligne sans frais: 866-745-6110
Autres numéros: Téléphone de Québec: 418-529-2355;

Canadian Associations / Association des groupes d'intervention en défense de droits en santé mentale du Québec (AGIDD-SMQ)

Télécopier: 418-529-2355
agp@grands-parents.qc.ca
www.grands-parents.qc.ca
twitter.com/grandsparents
Aperçu: *Dimension:* petite; *Envergure:* provinciale
Mission: Aider des grands-parents et des petits-enfants préserver leur lien et lutter contre la maltraitance des personnes âgées
Activités: *Evénements de sensibilisation:* Journée des grands-parents (septembre)

Association des groupes d'intervention en défense de droits en santé mentale du Québec (AGIDD-SMQ)
#210, 4837, rue Boyer, Montréal QC H2J 3E6
Tél: 514-523-3443; *Téléc:* 514-523-0797
Ligne sans frais: 866-523-3443
info@agidd.org
www.agidd.org
Aperçu: *Dimension:* moyenne; *Envergure:* provinciale; fondée en 1990
Mission: Au service des personnes qui ont des problèmes et qui ont besoin d'aide et de soutien pour exercer et faire valoir leurs droits
Membre(s) du personnel: 4
Membre(s) du bureau directeur:
Doris Provencher, Directrice générale

Association des guides de montagne canadiens *See* Association of Canadian Mountain Guides

Association des guides touristiques de Québec (AGTQ)
CP 17, 755, ch St-Louis, Québec QC G1S 1C1
Tél: 418-683-2104; *Téléc:* 418-624-0450
Aperçu: *Dimension:* petite; *Envergure:* provinciale; fondée en 1993
Mission: L'Association des guides touristiques de Québec (AGTQ) vise à assurer une formation continue à ses membres, à protéger leurs droits, à valoriser cette fonction auprès des intervenants et, d'une manière générale, à contribuer au développement touristique dans la région de Québec
Membre: 170

Association des handicapées de Charlevoix *Voir* Association des personnes handicapées de Charlevoix inc.

Association des handicapés adultes de la Côte-Nord / Association of Disabled Adults on the North Shore (AHACNI)
#103, 859, rue Bossé, Baie-Comeau QC G5C 3P8
Tél: 418-589-2393; *Téléc:* 418-589-2953
www.ahacn.org
Aperçu: *Dimension:* petite; *Envergure:* locale; fondée en 1978
Mission: Pour répondre aux besoins des personnes handicapées et une lésion cérébrale traumatique, et leurs familles sur la Rive-Nord de Québec
Membre de: Regroupement des associations de personnes traumatisées craniocérébrales du Québec / Coalition of Associations of Craniocerebral Trauma in Quebec
Membre(s) du personnel: 3
Membre: *Critères d'admissibilité:* Les personnes handicapées et les lésions cérébrales traumatiques de Tadoussac à Blanc-Sablon et sur l'île d'Anticosti au Québec
Activités: Promouvoir et protéger les droits des personnes ayant une lésion traumatique du cerveau et handicapées; L'organisation de groupes de soutien; Offrir un soutien psychosocial; Offrant des activités de loisirs, pour éviter l'isolement; Offrant des services d'accompagnement
Membre(s) du bureau directeur:
Stéphanie Jourdain, Directrice générale

Association des handicapés adultes de la Mauricie (AHAM)
1322, rue Ste-Julie, Trois-Rivières QC G9A 1Y6
Tél: 819-374-9566; *Téléc:* 819-374-2230
aham1322@yahoo.com
www.ahamauricie.org
Aperçu: *Dimension:* petite; *Envergure:* locale; fondée en 1951
Mission: Promouvoir et sauvegarder les droits et privilèges des personnes handicapées; offrir également des services de prêt de fauteuils roulants, de béquilles, et de marchettes
Finances: *Fonds:* Agence de santé et des services sociaux de la Mauricie et Centre-du-Québec
Membre(s) du personnel: 2
Membre: 196; *Critères d'admissibilité:* Personnes adultes vivant avec un handicap permanent, et limitations physiques

Activités: Activités culturelles et récréatives; voyages; visites guidées; soirées; rencontres d'informations
Membre(s) du bureau directeur:
Francois Dubois, Président
Stephane Drolet, Vice-Président

Association des handicapés respiratoires de Québec
#204, 1001, rte de l'Église, Québec QC G1V 3V7
Tél: 418-657-2477; *Téléc:* 418-657-4823
ahrq@videotron.ca
pages.videotron.com/ahrq1984
Aperçu: *Dimension:* petite; *Envergure:* provinciale
Mission: D'améliorer la qualité de vie des personnes aux prises avec une maladie respiratoire

Association des herboristes de la province de Québec
CP 80, 7, 70e av ouest, Blainville QC J7C 1R7
Tél: 450-435-2979
herbesunivers@bellnet.ca
Aperçu: *Dimension:* petite; *Envergure:* provinciale
Membre: 100-499

Association des hôteliers du Québec *Voir* Association Hôtellerie Québec

Association des hôtels du Canada *See* Hotel Association of Canada Inc.

Association des hypnologues du Québec
8206, rue Berri, Montréal QC H2P 2E9
Tél: 514-939-3780; *Téléc:* 514-846-1601
info@hypno-quebec.com
www.hypno-quebec.com
Aperçu: *Dimension:* petite; *Envergure:* provinciale; fondée en 1977
Mission: Promouvoir les bienfaits de l'hypnose auprès des utilisateurs et de faire respecter les règles de conduite définies par le code de déontologie
Membre de: Ordre canadien des practiciens de naturopathie et des naturothérapies
Membre(s) du personnel: 1; 5 bénévole(s)
Membre: *Montant de la cotisation:* 200$; *Critères d'admissibilité:* Hypnologue clinicien; *Comités:* Discipline
Activités: Conférences; groupes de discussion

Association des Illustrateurs et Illustratrices du Québec (AIIQ)
#123, 372, Sainte-Catherine ouest, Montréal QC H3B 1A2
Tél: 514-522-2040; *Téléc:* 514-521-0297
Ligne sans frais: 888-522-2040
info@illustrationquebec.com
www.illustrationquebec.com
Aperçu: *Dimension:* petite; *Envergure:* provinciale; Organisme sans but lucratif; fondée en 1983
Mission: Promouvoir l'art de l'illustration et faire en sorte que la profession se pratique dans les meilleures conditions possibles
Finances: *Budget de fonctionnement annuel:* $50,000-$100,000; *Fonds:* Gouvernement provincial
Membre(s) du personnel: 1
Membre: 100-499; *Montant de la cotisation:* Barème
Activités: Répertoire annuel destiné aux clients des communications graphiques autant au Canada, aux Etats-Unis et au niveau international; exposition annuelle intitulée 'Salon de l'illustration québécoise'; soirées; portefeuilles; bulletin; cours d'infographie; participation à divers salons du livre ou congrès touchant de près ou de loin le domaine de l'illustration
Membre(s) du bureau directeur:
Yves Dumont, Président, 514-799-4573
yvesushi@gmail.com

Association des implantés cochléaires du Québec (AICQ)
#130, 5100, rue des Tournelles, Québec QC G2J 1E4
Tél: 418-623-7417; *Téléc:* 418-623-7462
aicq@bellnet.ca
www.aicq-implant.org
Aperçu: *Dimension:* petite; *Envergure:* provinciale; Organisme sans but lucratif; fondée en 1995
Mission: Promouvoir l'implant cochléaire; supporter le patient et sa famille; offrir des activités
Membre(s) du personnel: 1; 30 bénévole(s)
Membre: 100-499; *Montant de la cotisation:* 25$; *Comités:* Acceuil et hébergement; Comité de Montréal; Comité de Québec; Promotion et sollicitation; Comité du journal
Activités: *Evénements de sensibilisation:* Journée nationale de l'implant cochléaire - 17 mai

Membre(s) du bureau directeur:
Cécile Viel, Présidente

Association des industries aérospatiales du Canada *See* Aerospace Industries Association of Canada

Association des industries canadiennes de défense et de sécurité *See* Canadian Association of Defence & Security Industries

Association des industries de l'automobile du Canada *See* Automotive Industries Association of Canada

L'Association des industries de produits verriers et de fenestration du Québec; L'Association des industries de portes et fenêtres du Québec *Voir* Association de vitrerie et fenestrations du Québec

L'Association des Infirmier(ère)s Auxiliaires Autorisé(e)s du Nouveau-Brunswick *See* Association of New Brunswick Licensed Practical Nurses

L'Association des infirmières et infirmiers autorisés de l'Ontario *See* Registered Nurses' Association of Ontario

Association des infirmières et infirmiers d'urgence *See* National Emergency Nurses Association

Association des infirmières et infirmiers de l'Ontario *See* Ontario Nurses' Association

Association des infirmières et infirmiers de salles d'opération du Canada *See* Operating Room Nurses Association of Canada

Association des infirmières et infirmiers du Canada *See* Canadian Nurses Association

Association des infirmières et infirmiers du Nouveau-Brunswick *See* Nurses Association of New Brunswick

Association des infirmières et infirmiers en santé du travail du Québec *Voir* Association des professionnels en santé du travail

Association des infirmières et infirmiers practiciens du Canada *See* Nurse Practitioner Association of Canada

Association des ingénieurs et géoscientifiques du Nouveau-Brunswick *See* Association of Professional Engineers & Geoscientists of New Brunswick

Association des ingénieurs municipaux du Québec (AIMQ) / Association of Québec Municipal Engineers
CP 792, Succ. B, Montréal QC H3B 3K5
Tél: 514-845-5303
www.aimq.net
Aperçu: *Dimension:* moyenne; *Envergure:* provinciale; fondée en 1963
Mission: Améliorer les connaissances et le statut de l'ingénieur municipal par l'échange d'information, la coopération entre ingénieurs municipaux et avec d'autres associations professionnelles et la promotion des intérêts communs des membres de l'Association
Finances: *Budget de fonctionnement annuel:* $100,000-$250,000
Membre(s) du personnel: 3; 15 bénévole(s)
Membre: 200; *Montant de la cotisation:* 315$; *Critères d'admissibilité:* Membre de l'Ordre des ingénieurs du Québec; employé d'une administration municipale ou régionale; *Comités:* Externes; Internes
Activités: Séminaire de formation annuel; *Listes de destinataires:* Oui
Membre(s) du bureau directeur:
Robert Millette, Directeur général
dg@aimq.net

Association des ingénieurs-conseils du Québec *Voir* Association des firmes de génie-conseil - Québec

Association des ingénieurs-professeurs des sciences appliquées (AIPSA)
c/o Université de Sherbrooke, Faculté de génie, 2500, boul Université, #C1-5105, Sherbrooke QC J1K 2R1
Tél: 819-821-7929; *Téléc:* 819-821-7955
www.aipsa.ca
Aperçu: *Dimension:* petite; *Envergure:* locale; Organisme sans but lucratif; fondée en 1970
Mission: Négocier la convention collective des ingénieur-professeurs; représenter les ingénieur-professeurs au sens du code du travail

Finances: *Budget de fonctionnement annuel:* Moins de $50,000
Membre(s) du personnel: 6
Membre: 95; *Montant de la cotisation:* 0.75% du salaire régulier annuel; *Critères d'admissibilite:* Membre de l'ordre des ingénieurs du QC; salarié affecté à une tâche d'enseignement ou de recherche à l'Université de Sherbrooke
Membre(s) du bureau directeur:
Radhouane Masmoudi, Président
Suzanne Hébert, Secrétariat de l'AIPSA
suzanne.hebert@usherbrooke.ca

Association des institutions d'enseignement secondaire; Association québécoise des Écoles secondaires privées
Voir Fédération des établissements d'enseignement privés

Association des intermédiaires en assurance de personnes du Québec
Voir Chambre de la sécurité financière

Association des interprètes en langage visuel du Canada
See Association of Visual Language Interpreters of Canada

Association des intervenantes et des intervenants en soins spirituels du Québec (AIISSQ)
#402, 8815, av du Parc, Montréal QC H2N 1Y7
Tél: 514-259-9229; *Téléc:* 514-259-3741
secretariat@aiissq.org
www.aiissq.org
Nom précédent: Association québécoise de la pastorale de la santé
Aperçu: *Dimension:* petite; *Envergure:* provinciale; Organisme sans but lucratif; fondée en 2005
Mission: Formation professionnelle des membres et promotion de leurs intérêts spirituels et professionnels; représentation des membres auprès d'instances civiles et religieuses reconnues
Membre de: Association canadienne des périodiques catholiques
Affiliation(s): Association canadienne pour la pratique et l'éducation pastorale; Association catholique canadienne de la santé; Carrefour Humanisation - Santé
Finances: *Budget de fonctionnement annuel:* $50,000-$100,000
Membre(s) du personnel: 1
Membre: 200; *Montant de la cotisation:* 275$; 70$ par jour; *Critères d'admissibilite:* Animateur(trice) de pastorale dans un établissement de santé; *Comités:* Pastorale pratique; pastorale en santé mentale
Activités: Congrès annuel; colloques; sessions de formation; *Stagiaires:* Oui; *Listes de destinataires:* Oui
Membre(s) du bureau directeur:
Lorraine Rooke, Présidente
presidence@aiissq.org
Fernand Patry, Vice-président
vice-presidence@aiissq.org

Association des intervenants en dépendance du Québec (AIDQ)
#420, 1001, boul de Maisonneuve ouest, Montréal QC H3A 3C8
Tél: 514-287-9625; *Téléc:* 514-287-9649
Ligne sans frais: 877-566-9625
info@aidq.org
www.aidq.org
Nom précédent: Association des centres de réadaptation en dépendance du Québec
Aperçu: *Dimension:* petite; *Envergure:* provinciale
Mission: Soutenir l'intervention dans le traitement des personnes aux prises avec une dépendance
Membre(s) du bureau directeur:
Lisa Massicotte, Directrice générale
lmassicotte@aidq.org

Association des intervenants en toxicomanie du Québec inc. (AITQ)
505, rue Ste-Hélène, 2e étage, Longueuil QC J4K 3R5
Tél: 450-646-3271; *Téléc:* 450-646-3275
info@aitq.com
www.aitq.com
www.facebook.com/480553332024591
Aperçu: *Dimension:* moyenne; *Envergure:* provinciale; Organisme sans but lucratif; fondée en 1977
Mission: Regrouper les intervenants professionnels et bénévoles oeuvrant dans le domaine de la toxicomanie et du jeu excessif
Membre(s) du personnel: 3
Membre: 240 individus; *Montant de la cotisation:* 40$ étudiant; 75$ individu; 295$ corporatif
Activités: Journées de formation; colloque annuel
Membre(s) du bureau directeur:
Carmen Trottier, Directrice générale
ctrottier@aitq.com
Prix, Bourses:
• Rose des Sables

Association des jardins du Québec / Québec Gardens Association
82, Grande-Allée ouest, Québec QC G1R 2G6
Tél: 418-692-0886
www.jardinsduquebec.com
www.facebook.com/9180555411
Aperçu: *Dimension:* petite; *Envergure:* provinciale
Mission: L'Association des jardins du Québec a comme mission de regrouper en corporation les jardins du Québec ouverts au public afin d'aider à leur développement et à leur promotion et de souligner leur apport à la culture et au patrimoine québécois
Membre: 20
Membre(s) du bureau directeur:
Geneviève David, Chargée de projet en communication
gdavid@tapagecreation.com

Association des jeunes Barreaux du Québec (AJBQ)
445, boul St-Laurent, Montréal QC H2Y 3T8
Tél: 514-954-3471; *Téléc:* 514-954-3451
Ligne sans frais: 800-361-8495
Autres numéros: AJBQ.Info@gmail.com
info@votreavocate.com
ajbq.net
www.facebook.com/553959894636970
twitter.com/AJBQInfo
Aperçu: *Dimension:* moyenne; *Envergure:* provinciale
Mission: Pour représenter les intérêts des avocats qui ont moins de dix ans d'expérience et de créer un réseau d'avocats à travers le Québec
Membre: *Comités:* Législation; Communications; Financement
Membre(s) du bureau directeur:
Marie-Eve Landreville, Présidente, Conseil d'administration

Association des jeunes bègues de Québec (AJBQ)
CP 79044, Succ. Bird, Laval QC H7L 5J1
Tél: 514-388-8455
www.ajbq.qc.ca
www.linkedin.com/company/association-des-jeunes-bègues-du-québec
www.facebook.com/assjeunesbeguesquebec
twitter.com/AJBQ_1993
Aperçu: *Dimension:* petite; *Envergure:* provinciale; Organisme sans but lucratif; fondée en 1993
Mission: Contrer la méconnaissance de la société à l'égard du bégaiement; offrir du soutien aux jeunes bègues de 2 à 25 ans; promouvoir les services qui leur sont accessibles ainsi qu'à leurs parents
Finances: *Budget de fonctionnement annuel:* $50,000-$100,000
Membre(s) du personnel: 1; 60 bénévole(s)
Membre: 250; *Montant de la cotisation:* 30$; *Critères d'admissibilite:* Parents, professionnels; jeunes adultes
Activités: Soutien, information, conseils aux jeunes bègues et leurs familles; activités de regroupement; thérapies; programmes de sensibilisation dans les écoles et auprès du grand public; *Événements de sensibilisation:* Journée mondiale du bégaiement 22 oct.; *Bibliothèque:* AJBQ; rendez-vous
Membre(s) du bureau directeur:
Julie Tanguy, Présidente
Chantale Baillargeon, Directrice générale

Association des jeunes femmes chrétiennes du Canada
See YWCA Canada

Association des jeunes ruraux du Québec (AJRQ)
65, rang 3 est, Princeville QC G6L 4B9
Tél: 819-364-5606; *Téléc:* 819-364-5006
info@ajrq.qc.ca
www.ajrq.qc.ca
Aperçu: *Dimension:* moyenne; *Envergure:* provinciale; fondée en 1974
Mission: Promouvoir la formation auprès de nos membres; soutenir leur sentiment d'appartenance au milieu rural
Membre de: Regroupement Loisir Québec
Affiliation(s): Conseil des 4-H du Canada
Activités: *Stagiaires:* Oui; *Listes de destinataires:* Oui
Membre(s) du bureau directeur:
Cindy Jaton, Présidente
cindyjaton15@hotmail.com
Annie Chabot, Directrice générale

Association des jeunes travailleurs et travailleuses de Montréal inc
3565, ch du Lac Legault, Sainte-Lucie-des-Laurentides QC J0T 2J0
Tél: 819-326-4069; *Téléc:* 819-326-0837
info@interval.qc.ca
interval.qc.ca
Également appelé: L'Interval base de plein-air
Aperçu: *Dimension:* petite; *Envergure:* locale; Organisme sans but lucratif; fondée en 1971
Mission: Accès aux vacances dans la nature
Membre de: Association touristique des Laurentides
Affiliation(s): Mouvement Québécois des camps familiaux; Éducation, Loisir et Sport Québec; Patrouille canadienne de ski; Tourisme Laurentides; Bonjour Quebec
Finances: *Budget de fonctionnement annuel:* $500,000-$1.5 Million; *Fonds:* Provincial government
Membre(s) du personnel: 26; 80 bénévole(s)
Membre: 1-99; *Montant de la cotisation:* 6$
Activités: Séjours en milieu naturel
Membre(s) du bureau directeur:
Cloée La Rocque, Directrice générale
dg@interval.qc.ca

Association des joueurs de la ligue de football canadienne
See Canadian Football League Players' Association

Association des journalistes automobile du Canada
See Automobile Journalists Association of Canada

Association des journalistes indépendants du Québec (AJIQ) / Québec Association of Independent Journalists
#12, 1124, rue Marie-Anne est, Montréal QC H2J 2B7
Tél: 514-529-3105
info@ajiq.qc.ca
www.ajiq.qc.ca
www.facebook.com/lajiq
twitter.com/ajiq
Aperçu: *Dimension:* moyenne; *Envergure:* provinciale; fondée en 1988
Mission: Défendre les droits des journalistes à statut précaire: les pigistes, les contractuels et les surnuméraires
Affiliation(s): Fédération nationale des communications(FNC); Confédération des syndicats nationaux(CSN)
Membre: *Montant de la cotisation:* 130$ régulier; 95$ associé; 90$ bénévole; 65$ étudiant; 100$ sympathisant; *Comités:* Recrutement
Activités: *Service de conférenciers:* Oui
Membre(s) du bureau directeur:
Simon Van Vliet, Vice-président
Sara-Emmanuelle Dichesne, Vice-présidente
Marie-Eve Cloutier, Vice-présidente
Prix, Bourses:
• Bourse AJIQ-Le Devoir
Gagnant du concours passera un stage de 4 mois au quotidien le Devoir

Association des journaux régionaux du Québec
See Québec Community Newspaper Association

Association des juristes d'expression française de l'Ontario (AJEFO)
#201, 214 ch Montréal, Ottawa ON K1L 8L8
Tél: 613-842-7462; *Téléc:* 613-842-8389
bureau@ajefo.ca
www.ajefo.ca
www.facebook.com/ajefo?fref=nf
Aperçu: *Dimension:* petite; *Envergure:* provinciale; Organisme sans but lucratif; fondée en 1980
Mission: Représenter les intérêts des avocates, des avocats, des juges, des fonctionnaires de la justice, des notaires, des professeurs, des étudiantes et des étudiants en droit, et des autres participants et participantes du monde juridique, qui travaillent à la promotion des services juridiques en français sur le territoire de l'Ontario; viser à donner un accès égal à la justice, sans pénalité, délai, obstacle ou hésitation à l'utilisation du français par l'appareil judiciaire, les membres du Barreau ou la population francophone de notre province
Finances: *Budget de fonctionnement annuel:* $50,000-$100,000
Membre(s) du personnel: 1
Membre: 650; *Montant de la cotisation:* 30-125; *Critères d'admissibilite:* Étudiants en droit, avocats, juges, professeurs, et autres juristes
Membre(s) du bureau directeur:
Paul Le Vay, Président
Danielle Manton, Directrice générale

Association des juristes d'expression française de la Saskatchewan (AJEFS) / French Jurists Association of Saskatchewan
#219, 1440, 9e av Nord, Regina SK S4R 8B1
Tél: 306-924-8543; *Téléc:* 306-781-7916
Ligne sans frais: 800-991-1912
ajefs@sasktel.net
www.ajefs.ca
www.facebook.com/ajefs.saskatchewan
twitter.com/AJEFS1
Aperçu: *Dimension:* petite; *Envergure:* provinciale; Organisme sans but lucratif; fondée en 1989
Mission: Développer et promouvoir les droits et services en français auprès des instances juridiques et gouvernementales; informer et sensibiliser la population fransaskoise sur la vulgarisation des lois et l'utilisation des services juridiques en français
Membre: *Critères d'admissibilité:* Avocats, juges, traducteurs, greffiers; professeurs; étudiants en droit
Activités: Services d'information légale en français; documentation légale en français; ateliers; conférences; cours de perfectionnement; *Service de conférenciers:* Oui; *Listes de destinataires:* Oui; *Bibliothèque*
Membre(s) du bureau directeur:
Francis Poulin, Président
fpoulin@millerthomson.com
Prix, Bourses:
• Prix Turgeon
Décerné à un juriste francophone qui a contribué à l'avancement des droits des francophones

Association des juristes d'expression française du Manitoba inc. (AJEFM)
177-B, rue Eugénie, Winnipeg MB R2H 0X9
Tél: 204-415-7526; *Téléc:* 204-415-4482
reception@ajefm.ca
www.mondroitmonchoix.com
Aperçu: *Dimension:* petite; *Envergure:* provinciale; Organisme sans but lucratif; fondée en 1988
Mission: Promouvoir et protéger les droits linguistiques des membres de la communauté francophone du Manitoba; assurer une plus grande offre de services en français dans l'administration de la justice au Manitoba
Membre de: Fédération des associations de juristes d'expression française de common law inc.
Finances: *Budget de fonctionnement annuel:* $50,000-$100,000
Membre(s) du personnel: 2
Membre: 99; *Montant de la cotisation:* 35$; *Critères d'admissibilité:* Juristes d'expression française du Manitoba; *Comités:* Groupe de travail sur l'amélioration des services en langue française au sein du système judiciaire au Manitoba; Table ronde - Gendarmerie royale au Canada
Activités: Comités; suivis de rapports; interventions visés vers l'accès à la justice en français; ateliers; activités de sensibilisation; *Service de conférenciers:* Oui
Membre(s) du bureau directeur:
Robert Tétrault, Président
Philippe Richer, Directeur général
dg@ajefm.ca
Paulette Desaulniers, Directrice adjointe
direction@ajefm.ca

Association des juristes d'expression française du Nouveau-Brunswick (AJEFNB)
Pavillon A.-J. Cormier, Université de Moncton, 18, av Antonine-Maillet, Moncton NB E1A 3E9
Tél: 506-853-4151; *Téléc:* 506-853-4152
association@ajefnb.nb.ca
www.ajefnb.nb.ca
Aperçu: *Dimension:* petite; *Envergure:* provinciale; Organisme sans but lucratif; fondée en 1987
Mission: Continue à oeuvrer pour l'avancement des droits linguistiques dans la province du Nouveau-Brunswick; travaille avec ténacité à accroître l'exercice de la pratique du droit en français et à concrétiser et faciliter l'accès aux tribunaux néo-brunswickois, dans toutes ses facettes, dans les deux langues officielles
Membre de: Fédération des associations de juristes d'expression française de common law
Finances: *Budget de fonctionnement annuel:* $50,000-$100,000
Membre(s) du personnel: 2; 20 bénévole(s)
Membre: 260; *Montant de la cotisation:* 50-80
Membre(s) du bureau directeur:
Philippe Morin, Contact
  Chaleur
  NB

  Restigouche
  NB
  Victoria-Carleton
  265, boul Broadway, Grand-Sault NB E3Z 2K1
  Tél: 506-473-7620
  Membre(s) du bureau directeur:
  Brigitte Ouellette, Contact
  bmouellette@nb.aibn.com
  Madawaska
  103, rue St-François, Edmundston NB E3V 1E5
  Tél: 506-735-6865; *Téléc:* 506-739-1994
  Membre(s) du bureau directeur:
  Nadia Michaud, Contact
  nadia.michaud@nb.aibn.com
  Fredericton
  Miramichi-Kent
  NB
  Westmorland
  Stewart McKelvey, #601, 644, rue Main, Moncton NB E1C 9N4
  Tél: 506-853-1970; *Téléc:* 506-858-8454
  Membre(s) du bureau directeur:
  Alexis Couture, Contact
  acouture@stewartmckelvey.com
  Péninsule acadienne
  CP 5729, Caraquet NB E1W 1B7
  Tél: 506-720-0908; *Téléc:* 506-726-6286
  Membre(s) du bureau directeur:
  Harold Michaud, Contact

Association des juristes pour l'avancement de la vie artistique (AJAVA)
445, boul Saint-Laurent, Montréal QC H2Y 3T8
Tél: 514-954-3471; *Téléc:* 514-954-3451
Ligne sans frais: 800-361-8495
lajava@barreau.qc.ca
www.lajava.org
Aperçu: *Dimension:* petite; *Envergure:* locale; fondée en 1997
Mission: Pour sensibiliser les membres sur le droit du divertissement et de créer un réseau de professionnels qui travaillent dans l'industrie du divertissement
Membre: *Montant de la cotisation:* 50$; *Critères d'admissibilité:* Les avocats qui se droit de divertissement pratique; les personnes qui travaillent dans l'industrie du divertissement
Membre(s) du bureau directeur:
Martin Lavallée, Président, Conseil d'administration

Association des laryngectomisés de Montréal *Voir*
Fédération québécoise des laryngectomisés

Association des lesbiennes et des gais sur Internet (ALGI)
CP 476, Succ. C, Montréal QC H2L 4K4
Tél: 514-528-8424
info@algi.qc.ca
www.algi.qc.ca
www.facebook.com/algi.qc.ca
Aperçu: *Dimension:* petite; *Envergure:* provinciale
Mission: Favoriser l'expression des lesbiennes et des gais au moyen de l'Internet; favoriser l'échange entre les individus et les organismes de la communauté gaie et lesbienne dans un esprit d'entraide
Membre: *Montant de la cotisation:* 20$

Association des libraires du Québec (ALQ)
483, boul St-Joseph est, Montréal QC H2J 1J8
Tél: 514-526-3349; *Téléc:* 514-526-3340
info@alq.qc.ca
www.alq.qc.ca
Aperçu: *Dimension:* moyenne; *Envergure:* provinciale; Organisme sans but lucratif; fondée en 1969
Mission: Regrouper, pour leur bénéfice mutuel, les libraires engagées dans la vente au détail au Québec et celles engagées dans la vente du livre en langue française au Canada; fournir des services, faire des études, fournir de l'information, tenir des réunions et des rencontres et contribuer à des programmes pour le bénéfice et l'amélioration de ses membres; encourager la vente au détail du livre au Québec; encourager la communication et la collaboration entre les éditeurs, les distributeurs et les autres participants de l'industrie du livre; aider les libraires à encourager la lecture; lutter contre toute forme de censure
Membre(s) du personnel: 7
Membre: 125 libraires; *Comités:* Prix des libraires (Roman); Prix des libraires (Jeunesse); Prix des libraires (Poésie québécoise); Pratiques commerciales; Orientations stratégiques; Formation

Activités: Gestion des programmes de subventions accessibles aux libraires; protocole d'entente avec les fournisseurs; service de recherche; participation, gestion, élaboration et promotion de la Banque de données (BTLF); rencontres, colloques, ateliers; *Bibliothèque*
Membre(s) du bureau directeur:
Katherine Fafard, Directrice générale, 514-526-3349 Ext. 21
kfafard@alq.qc.ca

L'Association des littératures canadiennes et québécoise *See* Association for Canadian & Québec Literatures

Association des locataires de l'Ile-des-Soeurs (ALIS/NITA) / Nuns' Island Tenants Association
CP 63008, 40, Place du Commerce, Verdun QC H3E 1V6
Tél: 514-767-1003
Aperçu: *Dimension:* petite; *Envergure:* locale; fondée en 1993
Mission: Défense des droits des locataires

Association des maisons de commerce extérieur du Québec (AMCEQ) / Québec Association of Export Trading Houses (QAETH)
643, av Grosvenor, Westmount QC H3Y 2S9
Tél: 514-486-5308
www.amceq.org
Aperçu: *Dimension:* petite; *Envergure:* internationale; fondée en 1985
Mission: Développer des maisons de commerce, la promotion des intérêts, du rôle et de l'importance des Maisons de commerce, l'augmentation des exportations par l'intégration systématique de maisons de commerce dans la stratégie de marketing international de l'industrie Québécoise, le rapprochement entre maisons de commerce et PME manufacturières; la reconnaissance et la valorisation de la profession de trader; la formation de traders qualifiés
Membre de: Alliance of Manufacturers & Exporters Canada; Forum Francophone des Affaires
Affiliation(s): Manufacturiers et Exportateurs du Québec
Membre: *Montant de la cotisation:* 225$ membre associé; 400$ membre affilié ou accrédité
Activités: Formation; *Stagiaires:* Oui; *Service de conférenciers:* Oui
Membre(s) du bureau directeur:
Claude Tardif, Administrateur
claude@interunion.ca

Association des maîtres couvreurs du Québec (AMCQ) / Québec Master Roofers Association
3001, boul Tessier, Laval QC H7S 2M1
Tél: 450-973-2322; *Téléc:* 450-973-2321
Ligne sans frais: 888-973-2322
amcq@amcq.qc.ca
www.amcq.qc.ca
Aperçu: *Dimension:* petite; *Envergure:* provinciale; Organisme sans but lucratif; fondée en 1967 surveillé par Canadian Roofing Contractors' Association
Mission: Promouvoir les intérêts généraux des entreprises de couvertures et ceux de diverses entreprises des secteurs connexes dans la province de Québec; promouvoir la hausse de la qualité des travaux de couvertures
Membre de: Canadian Roofing Contractors' Association
Finances: *Fonds:* Comm. santé, sécurité du travail du Québec, promotion sécurité
Membre: 163; *Comités:* Gouvernance et éthique; présidentiel; marketing et services aux membres; garantie; formation et santé-sécurité; technique; membres associés; bureaux de contrôle; relève et mentorat
Activités:; *Bibliothèque:* Centre de documentation; Bibliothèque publique rendez-vous
Membre(s) du bureau directeur:
Marc Savard, Directeur général

Association des malentendants canadiens *See* Canadian Hard of Hearing Association

Association des malentendants Québécois (AMQ)
7260, boul Cloutier, Charlesbourg QC G1H 3E8
Tél: 418-623-5080; *Téléc:* 418-623-8936
Aperçu: *Dimension:* moyenne; *Envergure:* locale; Organisme sans but lucratif; fondée en 1985
Mission: Offrir un service d'accueil, d'écoute, d'informations, de références aux personnes vivant avec la surdité afin d'améliorer leur réalité quotidienne, et de développer un réseau d'entraide et de support
Membre de: Centre québécois de la déficience auditive, Centre d'action bénévole de Québec; Regroupement des organismes de promotion region D3

Finances: *Budget de fonctionnement annuel:* $50,000-$100,000
Membre(s) du personnel: 2; 20 bénévole(s)
Membre: 130; *Montant de la cotisation:* 10$ étudiants; 25$ adultes; 35$ organisme; *Critères d'admissibilite:* Personnes sourdes congénitale, devenues sourdes ou malentendantes
Activités: Information, formation, sensibisation, défense des droits, entraide, écoute, support et activités sociales

Association des manufacturiers de bois de sciage de l'Ontario *See* Ontario Lumber Manufacturers' Association

Association des manufacturiers de bois de sciage du Québec *Voir* Conseil de l'industrie forestière du Québec

Association des manufacturiers de chaussures du Canada *See* Shoe Manufacturers' Association of Canada

Association des manufacturiers de menuiserie architecturale du Canada *See* Architectural Woodwork Manufacturers Association of Canada

Association des manufacturiers de produits alimentaires de Saskatchewan *See* Saskatchewan Food Processors Association

Association des manufacturiers de produits alimentaires du Québec *Voir* Conseil de la transformation agroalimentaire et des produits de consommation

Association des marchands d'art du Canada *See* Art Dealers Association of Canada Inc.

Association des marchands de machines aratoires de la province de Québec (AMMAQ)
7, rue Bernier, Bedford QC J0J 1A0
Tél: 450-248-7946; *Téléc:* 450-248-3264
info@ammaq.ca
www.ammaq.ca
Aperçu: *Dimension:* petite; *Envergure:* provinciale; Organisme sans but lucratif; fondée en 1949
Mission: Aider et regrouper tous les concessionnaires de machineries agricoles de toute la province; compiler des statistiques et des renseignements sur la vente de machines aratoires dans la province du Québec; obtenir une plus grande coopération entre les marchands de machines aratoires des diverses régions de la province; promouvoir la vente et l'utilisation des machines aratoires
Activités: Congrès annuel; tournoi de golf annuel; rencontre régionale; matériel de support
Membre(s) du bureau directeur:
Peter Maurice, Directeur général, 450-248-7946

Association des marchands dépanneurs et épiciers du Québec (AMDEQ)
#229, 3075, boul W-Hamel, Québec QC G1P 4C6
Tél: 418-654-3232; *Téléc:* 418-654-3222
Ligne sans frais: 877-227-6045
info@amdeq.ca
www.amdeq.ca
www.facebook.com/205891622815182
Nom précédent: Association des marchands détaillants de l'est du Québec
Aperçu: *Dimension:* moyenne; *Envergure:* provinciale
Mission: Représenter et défendre les intérêts socio-économiques des membres; négocier des ristournes supplémentaires, des rabais ou de meilleurs prix auprès des fournisseurs; informer les détaillants-membres sur les sujets pertinents à la bonne gestion de leur commerce
Affiliation(s): RDEI
Membre(s) du personnel: 9
Membre: 1,000-4,999
Activités: Congrès annuel; cours de formation; rencontres régionales; *Événements de sensibilisation:* Conférence de Presse - Lutte contre la contrebande du tabac; Tournée sur la contrebande - Réduire a 10%
Membre(s) du bureau directeur:
Yves Servais, Directeur général

Association des marchands détaillants de l'est du Québec *Voir* Association des marchands dépanneurs et épiciers du Québec

Association des marchés financiers du Canada *See* Financial Markets Association of Canada

Association des massologues et techniciens en massage du Canada - Association des massothérapeutes professionnels du Québec
#200, 5967, rue Jean-Talon est, Saint-Léonard QC H1S 1M5
Téléc: 514-727-6555
Ligne sans frais: 888-434-6914
Aperçu: *Dimension:* moyenne; *Envergure:* provinciale; Organisme sans but lucratif; fondée en 1984
Membre: *Critères d'admissibilite:* Technicien ou étudiant en massage; Massothérapeute

Association des massothérapeutes du Nouveau-Brunswick *See* New Brunswick Massotherapy Association

Association des MBA du Québec (AMBAQ)
1970, rue Notre-Dame ouest, Montréal QC H3C 1K8
Tél: 514-323-8480; *Téléc:* 514-282-4292
info@ambaq.com
www.ambaq.com
www.linkedin.com/groups/Association-MBA-Québec-78306
www.facebook.com/ambaq
twitter.com/AMBAQ
Aperçu: *Dimension:* moyenne; *Envergure:* provinciale; fondée en 1974
Mission: Ôtre le porte-parole des MBA du Québec; constituer un réseau actif de diplômés et étudiants MBA; favoriser le développement personnel et professionnel des membres; valoriser et promouvoir le diplôme MBA
Membre: 1,300; *Montant de la cotisation:* Barème; *Critères d'admissibilité:* Diplômé de maîtrise en administration des affaires; *Comités:* Gala MBA; Classique de golf; Midis-conférences; Échanges et découvertes; Cercles d'échange; Publications; Région de Québec; Membership et fidélisation; Région de Gatineau-Ottawa; Région de Sherbrooke; Webinaires; Relations universitaires; Activités du 40e anniversaire; Réseaux sociaux
Activités: Ateliers, conférences; tournois de golf; déjeuners-rencontres
Membre(s) du bureau directeur:
Ivan Roy, Directeur général, 514-282-2731
iroy@ambaq.com

Association des médecins biochimistes du Canada *See* Canadian Association of Medical Biochemists

Association des médecins biochimistes du Québec (AMBQ)
CP 216, Succ. Desjardins, #3000, 2, Complexe Desjardins, Montréal QC H5B 1G8
Tél: 514-350-5105
ambq@fmsq.org
www.ambq.med.usherbrooke.ca
Aperçu: *Dimension:* petite; *Envergure:* provinciale surveillé par Fédération des médecins spécialistes du Québec
Mission: Promouvoir l'utilisation optimale des tests de laboratoire au Québec en offrant, au professionnel de la santé et au patient, les meilleurs services de diagnostic et de dépistage de maladies grâce à des techniques biochimiques et immunologiques
Membre(s) du bureau directeur:
Jean Dubé, Président

Association des médecins cliniciens enseignants de Laval (AMCEL)
c/o Hôpital Laval, 2360, ch Ste-Foy, Québec QC G1V 4H2
Tél: 418-656-4810; *Téléc:* 418-656-4825
amcel@criucpq.ulaval.ca
Aperçu: *Dimension:* petite; *Envergure:* locale; fondée en 1975
Mission: Défense des intérêts de ses membres (médecins-professeurs à l'Université Laval)
Finances: *Budget de fonctionnement annuel:* Moins de $50,000
Membre: 130; *Montant de la cotisation:* 0.40%

Association des médecins cliniciens enseignants de Montréal (AMCEM)
a/s Dr. Jean-Luc Senécal, 1255, boul du Mont-Royal, Montréal QC H2V 2H7
Aperçu: *Dimension:* petite; *Envergure:* locale; fondée en 1969
Membre: 167; *Critères d'admissibilite:* Médicins professeurs à la Faculté de Médecine Université de Montréal
Membre(s) du bureau directeur:
Jean-Luc Senécal, Président

Association des médecins de langue française du Canada *Voir* Médecins francophones du Canada

Association des médecins endocrinologues du Québec
CP 216, Succ. Desjardins, #3000, 2, Complexe Desjardins, Montréal QC H5B 1G8
Tél: 514-350-5135; *Téléc:* 514-350-5049
Ligne sans frais: 800-561-0703
ameq@fmsq.org
www.ameq.qc.ca
Aperçu: *Dimension:* petite; *Envergure:* provinciale surveillé par Fédération des médecins spécialistes du Québec
Mission: L'Association est un porte-parole des endocrinologues; elle favorise les intérêts scientifiques de ses membres et organise plusieurs réunions afin de permettre une formation médicale continue des endocrinologues
Activités: Programmation éducative, expositions

Association des médecins généticiens du Québec
#3000, 2, Complexe Desjardins, Montréal QC H5B 1G8
Tél: 514-350-5141; *Téléc:* 514-350-5116
www.medecingeneticien.ca
Aperçu: *Dimension:* petite; *Envergure:* provinciale surveillé par Fédération des médecins spécialistes du Québec
Membre: 28
Membre(s) du bureau directeur:
Bruno Maranda, M.D., Président
Sandrine Guillot, Directrice
sguillot@fmsq.org

Association des médecins gériatres du Québec
CP 216, Succ. Desjardins, #3000, 2, Complexe Desjardins, Montréal QC H5B 1G8
Tél: 514-350-5145; *Téléc:* 514-350-5151
info@amgq.ca
www.amgq.ca
Aperçu: *Dimension:* petite; *Envergure:* provinciale surveillé par Fédération des médecins spécialistes du Québec
Affiliation(s): Fédération des médecins spécialistes du Québec
Membre: 60+
Membre(s) du bureau directeur:
Maurice St-Laurent, Président
Lillian Plasse, Directrice, Administration
amgq@fmsq.org

Association des médecins hématologistes-oncologistes du Québec (AMHOQ)
CP 216, Succ. Desjardins, 2, Complexe Desjardins, Montréal QC H5B 1G8
Tél: 514-350-5121; *Téléc:* 514-350-5126
info@amhoc.org
amhoq.org
www.facebook.com/311775155609901
Aperçu: *Dimension:* petite; *Envergure:* provinciale; Organisme sans but lucratif; fondée en 1976 surveillé par Fédération des médecins spécialistes du Québec
Membre: *Comités:* OPTILAB; Développement professionnel continu
Membre(s) du bureau directeur:
Daniel Bélanger, Président
Nathalie Latendresse, Directrice administrative

Association des médecins microbiologistes-infectiologues du Québec (AMMIQ)
#3000, 2, Complexe Desjardins, Montréal QC H5B 1G8
Tél: 514-350-5104; *Téléc:* 514-350-5144
info@ammiq.org
www.ammiq.org
Aperçu: *Dimension:* petite; *Envergure:* provinciale surveillé par Fédération des médecins spécialistes du Québec
Mission: L'Association regroupe des médecins (de laboratoire et dans le diagnostic clinique) spécialisés dans l'épidémiologie, le traitement et la prévention des maladies infectieuses
Membre: 210
Activités: Formation; réunions
Membre(s) du bureau directeur:
Karl Weiss, Président

Association des médecins omnipraticiens de Montréal (AMOM)
2 Place Alexis Nihon, #2000, 3550, boul de Maisonneuve ouest, Westmount QC H3Z 3C1
Tél: 514-878-1911; *Téléc:* 514-878-2608
Autres numéros: 514-878-9219
contact@amom.net
www.amom.net
www.facebook.com/1592356060980998
twitter.com/AMOMTL
www.youtube.com/channel/UCeavcJVodU-j6Cdq7eRuAWA
Aperçu: *Dimension:* petite; *Envergure:* locale; fondée en 1961
Mission: L'AMOM représente plus de 1900 médecins généralistes oeuvrant dans les différentes sphères de l'omnipratique, de l'urgentologie à la gériatrie en passant par la médecine familiale

Affiliation(s): Fédération des médecins omnipraticiens du Québec
Membre: 1,938; *Critères d'admissibilite:* Médecins généralistes
Membre(s) du bureau directeur:
Michel Vachon, Président, 514-376-7702, Fax: 514-376-2639
mvachon@amom.net

Association des médecins ophtalmologistes du Québec (AMOQ)
CP 216, Succ. Desjardins, 2, Complexe Desjardins, Montréal QC H5B 1G8
Tél: 514-350-5124; Téléc: 514-350-5174
amoq@fmsq.org
www.amoq.org
Aperçu: *Dimension:* petite; *Envergure:* provinciale; Organisme sans but lucratif; fondée en 1955 surveillé par Fédération des médecins spécialistes du Québec
Mission: Promouvoir les intérêts professionnels et économiques de ses membres; se préoccuper du maintien de la compétence; susciter et appuyer des activités scientifiques susceptibles de favoriser l'avancement de l'ophtalmologie; se préoccuper de l'accessibilité aux soins ophtalmologiques
Membre: *Critères d'admissibilite:* Médecins ophtalmologistes
Membre(s) du bureau directeur:
Côme Fortin, Président
Sylvie Gariépy, Directrice, Administration

Association des médecins rhumatologues du Québec (AMRQ)
CP 216, Succ. Desjardins, Montréal QC H5B 1G8
Tél: 514-350-5136; Téléc: 514-350-5029
Ligne sans frais: 800-561-0703
info@rhumatologie.org
www.rhumatologie.org
Aperçu: *Dimension:* petite; *Envergure:* provinciale surveillé par Fédération des médecins spécialistes du Québec
Mission: La rhumatologie se consacre au diagnostic et au traitement des pathologies qui touchent les articulations, les os, les muscles et tendons et parfois tout organe dans le cadre de maladies systémiques. Ceci regroupe au-delà de 100 conditions pouvant aller de l'arthrite rhumatoïde au lupus érythémateux disséminé en passant par l'arthrose, les vasculites et l'ostéoporose.
Membre de: Fédération des Médecins Spécialistes de Québec (FMSQ)
Membre(s) du bureau directeur:
Frédéric Morin, Président

Association des médecins spécialistes en médecine nucléaire du Québec (AMSMNQ)
CP 216, Succ. Desjardins, #3000, 2, Complexe Desjardins, Montréal QC H5B 1G8
Tél: 514-350-5133; Téléc: 514-350-5151
Ligne sans frais: 800-561-0703
amsmnq@fmsq.org
www.medecinenucleaire.com
Aperçu: *Dimension:* petite; *Envergure:* provinciale surveillé par Fédération des médecins spécialistes du Québec
Mission: Pour former ses membres et maintenir un haut niveau de professionnalisme
Membre: *Comités:* Développement Professionnel Continu; Exercice professionnel; Radioprotection; Tarification; Site Internet
Membre(s) du bureau directeur:
François Lamoureux, Président
Jean Guimond, Vice-président
Michelle Laviolette, Directrice administrative

Association des médecins spécialistes en santé communautaire du Québec (AMSSCQ)
CP 216, #3000, 2, Complexe Desjardins, Montréal QC H5B 1G8
Tél: 514-350-5138; Téléc: 514-350-5151
asmpq@fmsq.org
www.amscq.org
Aperçu: *Dimension:* petite; *Envergure:* provinciale; fondée en 1982 surveillé par Fédération des médecins spécialistes du Québec
Mission: De promouvoir les intérêts professionnels et économiques de ses membres
Membre: 173
Membre(s) du bureau directeur:
Isabelle Samson, Présidente
Valery Gasse, Coordonnatrice

Association des médecins vétérinaires du Nouveau-Brunswick *See* New Brunswick Veterinary Medical Association

Association des médecins vétérinaires praticiens du Québec (AMVPQ)
#4500, 2336, ch Ste-Foy, Québec QC G1V 1S5
Tél: 418-651-0477; Téléc: 450-261-9435
amvpq@amvpq.org
www.amvpq.org
www.facebook.com/amvpq
Aperçu: *Dimension:* petite; *Envergure:* provinciale; Organisme sans but lucratif; fondée en 1969
Membre de: Canadian Veterinary Medical Association
Finances: *Fonds:* Cotisations syndicales
Membre(s) du personnel: 2
Membre: 480+; *Critères d'admissibilite:* Médecins vétérinaires praticiens
Activités: Formation continue; étude et défense des membres; promotion; développement
Membre(s) du bureau directeur:
Michel Savard, Directeur général
Meetings/Conferences:
• Congrès Association des médecins vétérinaires praticiens du Québec 2018, 2018, QC
Scope: Provincial

Association des médecins-psychiatres du Québec (AMPQ) / Québec Psychiatrists' Association
CP 216, Succ. Desjardins, Montréal QC H5B 1G8
Tél: 514-350-5128; Téléc: 514-350-5198
www.ampq.org
Aperçu: *Dimension:* moyenne; *Envergure:* provinciale; fondée en 1953
Mission: Promouvoir les intérêts professionnels et économiques de ses membres
Membre: *Critères d'admissibilite:* Médecins-psychiatres
Membre(s) du bureau directeur:
Karine J. Igartua, Présidente
Guillaume Dumont, Secrétaire

Association des médias écrits communautaires du Québec (AMECQ)
#206, 86 boul des Entreprises, Boisbriand QC J7G 2T3
Tél: 514-383-8533; Téléc: 514-383-8976
Ligne sans frais: 800-867-8533
medias@amecq.ca
www.amecq.ca
www.facebook.com/JournauxAmecq
twitter.com/AmecqMedias
Aperçu: *Dimension:* moyenne; *Envergure:* provinciale; Organisme sans but lucratif; fondée en 1981
Mission: Fournir des services de soutien et de formation à ses journaux communautaires membres; les regrouper et les représenter pour que ceux-ci puissent remplir leur rôle et leur mission fondamentale.
Finances: *Budget de fonctionnement annuel:* $100,000-$250,000
Membre(s) du personnel: 2
Membre: 90; *Montant de la cotisation:* 75$; *Critères d'admissibilite:* Journaux communautaires
Activités: *Evénements de sensibilisation:* Mois de la presse communautaire, avril; Le Congrès annuel de L'AMECQ; *Bibliothèque:* Centre de documentation et d'archives; rendez-vous
Membre(s) du bureau directeur:
Yvan Noé Girouard, Directeur général
medias@amecq.ca

Association des microbiologistes du Québec (AMQ)
5094A, av Charlemagne, Montréal QC H1X 3P3
Tél: 514-728-1087; Téléc: 514-374-3988
amq@microbiologistes.ca
www.microbiologistes.ca
www.facebook.com/AssociationDesMicrobiologistesDuQuebec
Aperçu: *Dimension:* moyenne; *Envergure:* provinciale; fondée en 1975
Mission: De regrouper les microbiologistes du Québec oeuvrant principalement en environnement, en alimentaire et en pharmaceutique; d'étudier, de protéger et de développer les intérêts économiques, sociaux et professionnels des microbiologistes et de promouvoir l'essor de la microbiologie en général
Membre: *Montant de la cotisation:* Barème; *Critères d'admissibilite:* 30 crédits universitaires en microbiologie; *Comités:* Statut professionnel; Inspection professionnelle; Risques biologiques; Sélection; Affaires académiques; Communications
Membre(s) du bureau directeur:
Patrick D. Paquette, Président
patrick.d.paquette@microbiologistes.ca

Association des mines de métaux du Québec inc. *Voir* Association minière du Québec

Association des motocyclistes gais du Québec (AMGQ)
CP 36, Succ. C, Montréal QC H2L 4J7
Courriel: info.amgq@gmail.com
www.amgq.org
Aperçu: *Dimension:* petite; *Envergure:* provinciale; Organisme sans but lucratif; fondée en 1989
Mission: L'AMGQ est une association apolitique qui répond aux intérêts, aux goûts et aux besoins de ses membres par des activités et des services dans le domaine du motocyclisme.
Membre de: Alliance Motocycliste Métropolitaine; Fédération Motocycliste du Québec; Association des lesbiennes et des gais sur Internet; Table de concertation des lesbiennes et des gais du Québec; Égale Canada
Membre: *Montant de la cotisation:* 65$; *Critères d'admissibilite:* Gai (homme) et propriétaire de moto
Activités: Balades, soupers mensuels, brunchs; *Bibliothèque* Not open to public
Membre(s) du bureau directeur:
Coquille St-Jacques, Président
James Connolly, Vice-président
Dan Grondin, Trésorier

Association des municipalités bilingues du Manitoba *Voir* Conseil de développement économique des municipalités bilingues du Manitoba

Association des municipalités du Nouveau-Brunswick *Voir* Association francophone des municipalités du Nouveau-Brunswick Inc.

Association des musées canadiens *See* Canadian Museums Association

Association des musées de l'Ontario *See* Ontario Museum Association

Association des musées de la province de Québec (1973) *Voir* Société des musées québécois

Association des musées du Nouveau-Brunswick *See* Association Museums New Brunswick

Association des naturopathes professionnels du Québec (ANPQ)
192, rue Saint-Joseph, Terrebonne QC J6W 2Y7
Tél: 450-824-3550; Téléc: 450-824-1887
Ligne sans frais: 888-268-2516
anm.anpq@videotron.ca
www.anpq.qc.ca
Aperçu: *Dimension:* petite; *Envergure:* provinciale; fondée en 1971
Mission: Association à but non lucratif et à charte provinciale qui regroupe des praticiens en naturopathie dûment qualifiés
Membre: 500+; *Montant de la cotisation:* 180$
Membre(s) du bureau directeur:
Yves Dussault, Président

Association des néphrologues du Québec
CP 216, Succ. Desjardins, #3000, 2, Complexe Desjardins, Montréal QC H5B 1G8
Tél: 514-350-5134; Téléc: 514-350-5151
nephrologie@fmsq.org
Aperçu: *Dimension:* petite; *Envergure:* provinciale surveillé par Fédération des médecins spécialistes du Québec
Membre(s) du bureau directeur:
Robert Charbonneau, Président
Lillian Plasse, Directrice, Administration

Association des neurologues du Québec (ANQ)
CP 216, Succ. Desjardins, #3000, 2, Complexe Desjardins, Montréal QC H5B 1G8
Tél: 514-350-5122; Téléc: 514-350-5172
anq@fmsq.org
www.anq.qc.ca
www.facebook.com/109136899239391
twitter.com/assneuroquebec
Aperçu: *Dimension:* petite; *Envergure:* provinciale surveillé par Fédération des médecins spécialistes du Québec
Mission: Représenter des médecins spécialistes qui diagnostique et traite les maladies affectant le système nerveux central ainsi que le système nerveux périphérique

Membre: *Comités:* Développement professional continu; Effectifs médicaux; Neurophysiologie clinique; Rémunération; Relations avec les médias
Membre(s) du bureau directeur:
Sylvain Chouinard, Président
Anne Lortie, Secrétaire
Ginette Guilbault, Directrice, Administration

Association des neurotraumatisés de l'Outaouais (ANO)
#1, 115 boul Sacré-Coeur, Gatineau QC J8X 1C5
Tél: 819-770-8804; *Téléc:* 819-770-5863
ano@ano.ca
www.ano.ca
www.facebook.com/ano.ca
Aperçu: *Dimension:* petite; *Envergure:* locale; fondée en 1990
Mission: Pour aider les personnes dans la région québécoise de l'Outaouais qui ont subi un traumatisme crânien ou un AVC
Membre de: Regroupement des associations de personnes traumatisées craniocérébrals du Québec; Regroupement des associations de personnes handicapées de l'Outaouais; CDC Rond Point
Finances: *Budget de fonctionnement annuel:* $100,000-$250,000; *Fonds:* Agence de la santé; agence des services sociaux; SAAQ; LSO
Membre(s) du personnel: 3; 40 bénévole(s)
Membre: 140; *Montant de la cotisation:* 10$; *Critères d'admissibilite:* Les survivants de lésions cérébrales et accidents vasculaires cérébraux, et leurs familles, dans la région de l'Outaouais au Québec
Activités: Fournir des informations sur les blessures et accidents vasculaires cérébraux traumatiques au cerveau; Offrir un soutien psychosocial aux membres; Offrant des activités pour favoriser la réinsertion sociale des victimes de la blessure et accident vasculaire cérébral traumatique
Membre(s) du bureau directeur:
Julie Larochelle, Présidente
Georgette Lachance, Vice-présidente
Servane Chesnais, Secrétaire
Raphaëlle Robidoux, Trésorière
Publications:
• Le Mieux Etre [publication d'Association des neurotraumatisés de l'Outaouais]
Type: Newsletter; *Frequency:* 3 pa
Profile: Information sur les services de santé et services sociaux et loisirs pour les membres de l'Association des neurotraumatisés de l'Outaouais

L'association des nouveaux Canadiens *See* Association for New Canadians

Association des Numismates et des Philatélistes de Boucherville
CP 111, Boucherville QC J4B 5E6
Tél: 450-655-4433
anpb.net
Aperçu: *Dimension:* petite; *Envergure:* locale; fondée en 1967
Mission: Promouvoir l'activité de collecte de pièces et les timbres

Association des obstétriciens et gynécologues du Québec (AOGQ)
#3000, 2, Complexe Desjardins, Montréal QC H5B 1G8
Tél: 514-849-4969; *Téléc:* 514-849-5011
info@gynecoquebec.com
www.gynecoquebec.com
Aperçu: *Dimension:* petite; *Envergure:* provinciale; fondée en 1966 surveillé par Fédération des médecins spécialistes du Québec
Mission: Promouvoir l'intérêt professionnel scientifique et économique de ses membres
Membre de: Fédération des médecins spécialistes du Québec
Membre: *Critères d'admissibilite:* Obstétriciens, gynécologues certifiés
Membre(s) du bureau directeur:
Sylvie Bouvet, Présidente
Marie-Eve Lefebvre, Directrice, Administration

Association des offices municipaux d'habitation du Québec *Voir* Regroupement des offices d'habitation du Québec

L'Association des officiels de la construction du Nouveau-Brunswick *See* New Brunswick Building Officials Association

L'Association des officiers de la marine du Canada *See* The Naval Officers' Association of Canada

Association des optométristes du Nouveau-Brunswick *See* New Brunswick Association of Optometrists

Association des optométristes du Québec (AOQ) / Québec Optometric Association
#217, 1255, boul Robert-Bourassa, Montréal QC H3B 3B2
Tél: 514-288-6272; *Téléc:* 514-288-7071
aoq@aoqnet.qc.ca
www.aoqnet.qc.ca
www.linkedin.com/company/association-des-optom-tristes-du-qu-bec
www.facebook.com/109631962406806
Aperçu: *Dimension:* moyenne; *Envergure:* provinciale; fondée en 1973 surveillé par Canadian Association of Optometrists
Mission: De développer meilleures conditions de pratique économiques et professionnelles pour les optométristes du Québec
Membre(s) du personnel: 10
Membre: 1 447; *Critères d'admissibilite:* Optométriste en pratique privée; *Comités:* Gouvernance; Réflexion sur l'avenir de la pratique optométrique; Négociation; Services aux membres; Relations publiques; AOQnet, le portail Internet; Réglementation et formation professionnelles; A.C.O. et affaires fédérales; Relations gouvernementales; Assurances et Placements A.O.Q.; C.P.R.O.; Guide des lentilles ophtalmiques progressives; Vision des enfants; Information-communication; Optométrie sportive
Activités: Service aux membres; information au public; relation gouvernementale; *Service de conférenciers:* Oui
Membre(s) du bureau directeur:
Steven Carrier, Président
Maryse Nolin, Directrice générale

Association des orchestres de jeunes de la Montérégie (AOJM)
CP 36573, 58, rue Victoria, Saint-Lambert QC J4P 3S8
Tél: 450-923-3733
courrier@aojm.org
www.aojm.org
www.facebook.com/349656105067547
Également appelé: Orchestre symphonique des jeunes de la Montérégie
Nom précédent: Association des cordes de la Rive-Sud
Aperçu: *Dimension:* petite; *Envergure:* locale; fondée en 1974 surveillé par Orchestras Canada
Mission: De promouvoir le développement et la formation de jeunes musiciens
Membre de: Association des orchestres de jeunes de Québec; Orchestres Canada
Membre(s) du personnel: 11
Membre: 75
Membre(s) du bureau directeur:
Sophie Roberge, Présidente

Association des orchestres de jeunes du Québec inc. (AOJQ)
901, rue Saint-Louis, Terrebonne QC J6W 1K1
Tél: 514-899-1150; *Téléc:* 514-658-1603
info@aojq.qc.ca
www.aojq.qc.ca
www.facebook.com/AOJQuebec
www.youtube.com/user/AOJQuebec
Aperçu: *Dimension:* petite; *Envergure:* provinciale; fondée en 1979
Mission: De regrouper les orchestres de jeunes dûment incorporés pour offrir aux cadres bénévoles un soutien administratif et aux jeunes musiciens en formation des activités de perfectionnement
Membre: 8; *Critères d'admissibilite:* Orchestre de jeunes de 14-25 ans
Activités: Concerts
Membre(s) du bureau directeur:
Louise Richard, Présidente
lrichard@aojq.qc.ca

L'Association des organistes liturgiques du Canada *Voir* LAUDEM, L'Association des musiciens liturgiques du Canada

Association des orthésistes et prothésistes du Québec (AOPQ)
715-A, ch des Pères, Magog QC J1X 5R9
Tél: 514-396-9303; *Téléc:* 514-396-9304
Ligne sans frais: 888-323-8834
info@aopq.ca
www.aopq.ca
Nom précédent: Association nationale des orthésistes du pied
Aperçu: *Dimension:* petite; *Envergure:* provinciale

Mission: Protéger et à développer des intérêts professionnels, moraux, sociaux et économiques des membres

L'Association des orthopédagogues du Québec inc. (ADOQ)
#410, 7400, bcul les Galeries d'Anjou, Montréal QC H1M 3M2
Tél: 514-374-5883; *Téléc:* 514-355-4159
Ligne sans frais: 888-444-0222
info@ladoq.ca
www.adoq.ca
Aperçu: *Dimension:* petite; *Envergure:* provinciale; Organisme sans but lucratif; fondée en 1988
Mission: Promouvoir les services d'orthopédagogie, assurer un programme de formation continue de grande qualité
Finances: *Budget de fonctionnement annuel:* $50,000-$100,000 8 bénévole(s)
Membre: 760; *Montant de la cotisation:* 100$ membre actif; 50$ étudiant; *Comités:* Conseil d'administration; Comités de section (situés dans différentes régions au Québec); Visibilité et Publicité; Formation continue; Site web; Revue
Activités: Colloque annuel; programme de formation continue comprenant de nombreuses activités; café-rencontre; code de déontologie et revue semestrielle remis gratuitement aux membres; publicité; annuaire offert aux membres; références pour la pratique privée; service de secrétariat; *Bibliothèque:* Centre de ressources didactiques; rendez-vous
Membre(s) du bureau directeur:
Christine Pruneau, Présidente
Jacynthe Turgeon, Vice-présidente

Association des orthophonistes et des audiologistes du Manitoba *See* College of Audiologists and Speech-Language Pathologists of Manitoba

Association des orthophonistes et des audiologistes du Nouveau-Brunswick *See* New Brunswick Association of Speech-Language Pathologists & Audiologists

Association des otpiciens du Nouveau-Brunswick *See* Opticians Association of New Brunswick

L'Association des paramédics du Nouveau-Brunswick *See* Paramedic Association of New Brunswick

Association des parents ayants droit de Yellowknife (APADY)
CP 2103, Yellowknife NT X1A 2P5
Tél: 867-446-6821
apady@franco-nord.com
apady.ca
Nom précédent: Association des parents francophones de Yellowknife
Aperçu: *Dimension:* petite; *Envergure:* locale surveillé par Fédération franco-ténoise
Mission: Les parents ayants droit de Yellowknife interviennent pour mettre en place toutes les conditions indispensables à la prestation de services d'éducation de qualité en français favorisant l'épanouissement de leurs enfants et la transmission de l'identité canadienne-française
Affiliation(s): Commission nationale des parents francophones
Membre: *Montant de la cotisation:* 5$
Membre(s) du bureau directeur:
Jacques Lamarche, Président

Association des parents catholiques du Québec (APCQ)
CP 55038, Succ. Maisonneuve, Montréal QC H1W 0A1
Tél: 514-276-8068; *Téléc:* 514-948-2595
info@parentscatholiques.org
parentscatholiques.org
www.facebook.com/parentscatholiques
Aperçu: *Dimension:* moyenne; *Envergure:* provinciale; Organisme sans but lucratif; fondée en 1966
Mission: Regroupe des parents catholiques pour promouvoir et défendre leurs droits et leurs intérêts selon les valeurs catholiques en matière d'éducation, de famille, et de culture par l'information et la représentation de ses membres auprès de la population et des autorités civiles et religieuses
Membre de: Regroupement Inter-Organismes pour une politique familiale au Québec
Affiliation(s): Organisation internationale de l'enseignement catholique (OIEC)
Finances: *Budget de fonctionnement annuel:* $50,000-$100,000 25 bénévole(s)
Membre: 4 000; *Montant de la cotisation:* 12$; *Critères d'admissibilite:* Familles; *Comités:* Éducation de la foi; Comité provincial d'enseignement privé; Carrefour famille-Québec

Canadian Associations / Association des parents d'enfants handicapés du Témiscamingue inc.

Activités: Secrétariat permanent; Périodique; Colloques; Conférences; Cours; Congrès parents-jeunes; Pétitions; Rédactions de mémoires; *Service de conférenciers:* Oui
Membre(s) du bureau directeur:
Georges Buscemi, Présidente
Publications:
• Famille Québec [a publication of the Association des parents catholiques du Québec]
Type: Journal

Association des parents d'enfants handicapés du Témiscamingue inc.
#1, 3, rue Industrielle, Ville-Marie QC JV9 1S3
Tél: 819-622-1126; *Téléc:* 819-622-0021
apeht@cablevision.qc.ca
Aperçu: Dimension: petite; *Envergure:* locale
Mission: Offrir des services d'aide aux personnes vivant avec un handicap physique et intellectuel ainsi qu'à leurs familles.
Affiliation(s): Association du Québec pour l'intégration sociale

Association des parents et amis de la personne atteinte de maladie mentale Rive-Sud (APAMM-RS)
#206, 10, boul Churchill, Greenfield Park QC J4V 2L7
Tél: 450-766-0524; *Crisis Hot-Line:* 450-679-8689
www.apammrs.org
www.facebook.com/apammrs
Aperçu: Dimension: petite; *Envergure:* locale; Organisme sans but lucratif
Mission: Aide des familles qui sont touchées par la maladie mentale et soutient des recherches sur les maladies mentales
Membre(s) du personnel: 5
Membre: *Montant de la cotisation:* 20$ par membres; 35$ par famille
Membre(s) du bureau directeur:
Guy Savoie, Président
Patricia Arnaud, Directrice générale

Association des parents et des handicapés de la Rive-Sud métropolitaine (APHRSM)
#200, 2545, rue de Lorimier, Longueuil QC J4K 3P7
Tél: 450-674-5224; *Téléc:* 450-674-8594
aphrsm@hotmail.com
www.aphrsm.org
Aperçu: Dimension: petite; *Envergure:* locale
Mission: Pour offrir aux personnes souffrant de handicaps mentaux et physiques à des activités récréatives et d'éviter l'isolement
Membre: *Critères d'admissibilite:* Toutes personne qui a un handicap physique ou mental
Activités: Sports; Chorale; Vacances; Ateliers; *Evénements de sensibilisation:* Semaine québécoise de la déficience intellectuelle (mars)
Membre(s) du bureau directeur:
Stephanie Coutellier, Directrice générale

Association des parents francophones de la Colombie-Britannique *Voir* Fédération des parents francophones de Colombie-Britannique

Association des parents francophones de Yellowknife *Voir* Association des parents ayants droit de Yellowknife

Association des parents fransaskois (APF) / Fransaskois Parents Association
910, 5, rue est, Saskatoon SK S7N 2C6
Tél: 306-653-7444; *Téléc:* 306-653-7001
Ligne sans frais: 855-653-7444
apf.direction@sasktel.net
www.parentsfransaskois.ca
www.facebook.com/148583571881687
Nom précédent: Association provinciale des parents fransaskois
Aperçu: Dimension: moyenne; *Envergure:* provinciale; fondée en 1982
Mission: Assurer la mise sur pied et le développement d'un système scolaire complet de qualité, conforme au Projet éducatif de la communauté des familles fransaskoises
Membre de: Commission nationale des parents francophones
Finances: *Budget de fonctionnement annuel:* $250,000-$500,000
Membre(s) du personnel: 5; 50 bénévole(s)
Membre: 1200; *Montant de la cotisation:* 5 $ par famille; *Critères d'admissibilite:* Parents francophones d'enfants d'âge préscolaire & scolaire
Activités: Projet éducatif fransaskois; intégration culturelle; *Bibliothèque:* Centre de ressources éducatives à la petite enfance (CREPE); Bibliothèque publique

Membre(s) du bureau directeur:
Danielle Raymond, Directrice générale
Brigitte Chassé, Agente à la petite enfance
apf.info@sasktel.net

Association des pathologistes du Québec (APQ)
CP 216, Succ. Desjardins, #3000, 2, Complexe Desjardins, Montréal QC H5B 1G8
Tél: 514-350-5102; *Téléc:* 514-350-5152
Ligne sans frais: 800-561-0703
patho@fmsq.org
www.apq.qc.ca
Aperçu: Dimension: petite; *Envergure:* provinciale surveillé par Fédération des médecins spécialistes du Québec
Mission: Promouvoir les intérêts professionnels et économiques de ses membres
Membre de: Fédération des médecins spécialistes du Québec
Activités: Le Prix Pierre-Masson
Membre(s) du bureau directeur:
Christian Lussier, Président
Danielle Joncas, Directrice, Administration
Prix, Bourses:
• Prix Pierre-Masson

Association des Pêcheurs de Longueuil
1895, rue Adoncour, Longueuil QC J4J 5G8
Tél: 514-726-1786
info@assopechelongueuil.ca
assopechelongueuil.ca
Aperçu: Dimension: petite; *Envergure:* locale; fondée en 2004
Mission: De promouvoir la pêche dans Longueuil
Membre: *Montant de la cotisation:* 15$
Activités: Tournois de pêche
Membre(s) du bureau directeur:
Théo Gionet, Président

Association des pédiatres du Québec
CP 216, Succ. Desjardins, #3000, 2, Complexe Desjardins, Montréal QC H5B 1G8
Tél: 514-350-5127; *Téléc:* 514-350-5177
pediatrie@fmsq.org
www.pediatres.ca
Aperçu: Dimension: moyenne; *Envergure:* provinciale surveillé par Fédération des médecins spécialistes du Québec
Membre de: Fédération des Médcins Spécialistes du Québec (FMSQ)
Affiliation(s): Association des allergologues et immunologues du Québec; Association des anesthésiologistes du Québec; Association des médecins biochimistes du Québec; Association des cardiologues du Québec; Association des chirurgiens cardio-vasculaires et thoraciques du Québec; Association québécoise de chirurgie; Association des chirurgiens vasculaires du Québec; Association des spécialistes en chirurgie plastique et esthétique du Québec; Association des dermatologistes du Québec; Association des médecins endocrinologues du Québec; Association des gastro-entérologues du Québec
Membre: 35 associations
Membre(s) du bureau directeur:
May Dagher, Directrice, Administration

Association des pères gais de Montréal inc. (APGM) / Gay Fathers of Montréal Inc.
4245, rue Laval, Montréal QC H2W 2J6
Tél: 514-528-8424; *Téléc:* 514-528-9708
peresgais@gmail.com
www.algi.qc.ca/asso/apgm/
Aperçu: Dimension: petite; *Envergure:* locale; Organisme sans but lucratif; fondée en 1984
Mission: Regrouper les hommes qui sont à la fois pères et gais; offrir support et aide aux hommes gais soucieux d'éduquer leurs enfants; permettre au père gai de se situer face à la condition de vie au moyen d'échanges, de discussion et d'information; promouvoir la condition des pères gais et la défense de leurs intérêts communs
Membre: *Montant de la cotisation:* 20$; *Critères d'admissibilite:* Etre père d'enfant naturel ou adoptif; se reconnaissant gai
Activités: Rencontres hebdomadaires

Association des Perfusionnistes du Québec Inc. (APQI)
CP 32172, Succ. Saint-André, Montréal QC H2L 4Y5
www.apqi.com
Aperçu: Dimension: petite; *Envergure:* provinciale
Membre(s) du bureau directeur:
Alina Parapuf, Présidente, 514-415-7622
Audrey Chapman, Vice-Présidente, 514-406-2186
Catherine André-Guimont, Trésorière

Thierry Lamarre-Renaud, Secrétaire, 514-406-4676

Association des personnes accidentées cérébro-vasculaires, aphasiques et traumatisées crânio-cérébrales du Bas-Saint-Laurent (ACVA-TCC du BSL)
391, boul Jessop, Rimouski QC G5L 1M9
Tél: 418-723-2345
Ligne sans frais: 888-302-2282
acvatcc@globetrotter.net
www.acvatcc.com
www.facebook.com/pages/ACVA-TCC-du-Bas-Saint-Laurent/614417028571908
Aperçu: Dimension: petite; *Envergure:* locale; fondée en 1991
Mission: Pour soutenir les personnes dans la région du Bas-Saint-Laurent qui ont été touchées par une lésion cérébrale, accident vasculaire cérébral, ou d'aphasie.
Membre de: Regroupement des associations de personnes traumatisées craniocérébrales du Québec / Coalition of Associations of Craniocerebral Trauma in Quebec
Membre: *Critères d'admissibilite:* Personnes dans la région Bas-Saint-Laurent du Québec qui ont subi une lésion cérébrale traumatique, un accident vasculaire cérébral ou qui sont aphasique; Membres de la famille de la personne vivant avec une lésion cérébrale, accident vasculaire cérébral, ou d'aphasie.
Activités: Informer le public sur une lésion cérébrale, accident vasculaire cérébral, et l'aphasie; Plaidoyer en faveur des personnes touchées par une lésion cérébrale, accident vasculaire cérébral, et l'aphasie; Offrant des groupes de soutien; Se engager dans des activités de plaidoyer.
Membre(s) du bureau directeur:
Mathieu Lajoie, Directeur

Association des personnes en perte d'autonomie de Chibougamau inc. & Jardin des aînés
101, av du Parc, Chibougamau QC G8P 3A5
Tél: 418-748-4411
jardindesaines@tlb.sympatico.ca
Aperçu: Dimension: petite; *Envergure:* locale
Membre(s) du bureau directeur:
Chantal Lessard, Directrice générale

Association des personnes handicapées de Charlevoix inc. (APHC)
#428, 367, rue St-Étienne, La Malbaie QC G5A 1M3
Tél: 418-665-0015; *Téléc:* 418-665-6787
www.aphcharlevoix.com
www.facebook.com/aphcharlevoix
Nom précédent: Association des handicapées de Charlevoix
Aperçu: Dimension: petite; *Envergure:* locale; fondée en 1978
Mission: Regrouper régionalement les personnes handicapées du Comté de Charlevoix afin de permettre leur intégration pleine et entière à la collectivité dans toutes les sphères d'activités du milieu, et à tous les niveaux
Finances: *Budget de fonctionnement annuel:* $50,000-$100,000
Membre(s) du personnel: 2; 50 bénévole(s)
Membre: 215; *Montant de la cotisation:* 5$ pour 1 an; 12$ pour 3 ans; *Critères d'admissibilite:* Personnes handicapées physiques
Membre(s) du bureau directeur:
Yves Lavoie, Président
Sylvie Breton, Coordonnatrice

Association des personnes handicapées de la Rive-Sud Ouest (APHRSO)
100, rue Ste-Marie, La Prairie QC J5R 1E8
Tél: 450-659-6519; *Téléc:* 450-659-6510
info@aphrso.org
www.aphrso.org
www.facebook.com/aphrso
Aperçu: Dimension: petite; *Envergure:* locale; Organisme sans but lucratif; fondée en 1980
Mission: Promotion, intégration et défense des droits des personnes handicapées
Affiliation(s): Groupement des Associations personnes handicapées Rive-Sud Montréal
Finances: *Fonds:* ASSM; Centraide; EEC (emploi été); revenue des membres; SQPH; Municipalités; Autres
Membre: 219; *Critères d'admissibilite:* Personnes handicapées
Activités: Loisirs pour personnes handicapées; *Bibliothèque:* rendez-vous
Membre(s) du bureau directeur:
Priscille Arel, Présidente
Nancy Côté, Directrice

Association des personnes handicapées de la Vallée du Richelieu (APHVR)
308, rue Montsabré, #D209, Beloeil QC J3G 2H5
Tél: 450-464-7445; *Téléc:* 450-464-6049
informations@aphvr.org
www.aphvr.org
Aperçu: *Dimension:* petite; *Envergure:* locale; fondée en 1981
Mission: Aider ses membres à accroître leur qualité de vie et informer le public sur les problèmes rencontrés par les personnes handicapées
Membre(s) du bureau directeur:
Louis McDuff, Président

Association des personnes handicapées physiques et sensorielles du secteur Joliette (APHPSSJ)
200, rue de Salaberry, Joliette QC J6E 4G1
Tel: 450-759-3322; *Fax:* 450-759-8749
Toll-Free: 888-756-3322
aphpssj@cepap.ca
www.aphpssj.com
Previous Name: Association of Physically Disabled Joliette - L'Assomption; Association of People with Physical Disabilities Joliette
Overview: A small local organization founded in 1977
Mission: To promote the rights of people with physical & sensory disabilities in the Joliette region; To encourage social integration of disabled people
Member of: Regroupement des associations de personnes traumatisées craniocérébrales du Québec / Coalition of Associations of Craniocerebral Trauma in Quebec
Finances: *Funding Sources:* Membership fees; Grants; Fundraising
Staff Member(s): 6; 60 volunteer(s)
Membership: 300; *Member Profile:* People with physical & sensory disabilities in Joliette, St-Felix-de-Valois, St. Ligouri, Saint-Esprit, St-Jacques, St-Alexis Ste-Marie-Salome, & Lanaudière, Québec
Activities: Advocating on behalf of persons with physical & sensory disabilities; Offering home support services; Organizing recreational activities; Providing psychosocial services; Offering information services; Providing accompaniment for disabled persons to various activities; Coordinating support groups, for persons with aphasia, Parkinson's disease, & brian injury
Chief Officer(s):
Jocelyn Picard, Président
Jacynthe Arseneau, 1ère Vice-président
Michel Lacourse, 2e Vice-président
François Gagnon, Secretaire
Murielle Desrosiers, Trésorière
Publications:
• Dynamic Player
Type: Newsletter
Profile: Association updates, announcements, & forthcoming activities

Association des personnes handicapés visuels de l'Estrie, inc (AHVEI)
838, rue St-Charles, Sherbrooke QC J1H 4Z2
Tél: 819-566-4848; *Téléc:* 819-566-5913
aphve@cooptel.qc.ca
www.aphve.com
Aperçu: *Dimension:* petite; *Envergure:* locale; Organisme sans but lucratif; fondée en 1991
Mission: Favoriser l'intégration sociale des personnes handicapées visuelles; promouvoir les droits et intérêts des personnes handicapées visuelles; sensibiliser la population à la problématique du handicap visuel
Affiliation(s): Regroupement des aveugles et amblyopes du Québec
Finances: *Budget de fonctionnement annuel:* Moins de $50,000; *Fonds:* Gouvernement provincial
Membre(s) du personnel: 1; 10 bénévole(s)
Membre: 115; *Montant de la cotisation:* $5; *Critères d'admissibilite:* Personnes hanicapées visuelles
Activités: conférences; entrevues; émissions de radio et télévision; animation de groupes de personnes âgées handicapées visuelles; rencontres d'information; *Bibliothèque*
Membre(s) du bureau directeur:
Denis Barrette, Président
Publications:
• Journal Nouveau Regard
Type: Newsletter; *Frequency:* Quarterly; *Editor:* Marie Claude Guay, Hélène Dubois

Association des personnes intéressées à l'aphasie *Voir*
Association des personnes intéressées à l'aphasie et à l'accident vasculaire cérébral

Association des personnes intéressées à l'aphasie et à l'accident vasculaire cérébral (APIA)
525, boul Wilfrid-Hamel, #A07, Québec QC G1M 2S8
Tél: 418-647-3684; *Téléc:* 418-647-1925
apia-avc@bellnet.ca
www.apia-avc.org
Nom précédent: Association des personnes intéressées à l'aphasie
Aperçu: *Dimension:* petite; *Envergure:* provinciale; Organisme sans but lucratif; fondée en 1985
Mission: Répondre à toute demande d'information sur l'aphasie; sensibiliser le public à la problématique de l'aphasie; promouvoir et défendre les droits des personnes aphasiques; améliorer la qualité de vie des personnes aphasiques et de leurs proches
Membre(s) du personnel: 2
Activités: *Service de conférenciers:* Oui
Membre(s) du bureau directeur:
Claude Hébert, Co-Présidente
Claudia-Lynn Pelletier, Co-Présidente

L'Association des Personnes Seules de Montréal *See* Single Persons Association of Montréal

Association des personnes traumatisées cranio-cérébrales de la Gaspésie et des Iles-de-la-Madeleine inc. *Voir*
Association des TCC (le traumatisme cranio-cérébral) et ACV (un accident vasculaire cérébral) de la Gaspésie et des Îles-de-la-Madeleine Inc.

Association des pharmaciens des établissements de santé du Québec (APES)
#320, 4050, rue Molson, Montréal QC H1Y 3N1
Tél: 514-286-0776; *Téléc:* 514-286-1081
info@apesquebec.org
www.apesquebec.org
Aperçu: *Dimension:* moyenne; *Envergure:* provinciale; fondée en 1963
Membre: 1 300; *Comités:* Évaluation du directeur général; Gouvernance et éthique; Négociation et relations professionnelles; Planification stratégique; Vérification
Membre(s) du bureau directeur:
Linda Vaillant, Directrice générale
France Boucher, Directrice générale adjointe

L'Association des pharmaciens des établissements du Québec *See* Canadian Society of Hospital Pharmacists

Association des pharmaciens du Canada *See* Canadian Pharmacists Association

Association des pharmaciens du Nouveau-Brunswick *See* New Brunswick Pharmacists' Association

Association des photographes de presse du Canada *See* News Photographers Association of Canada

Association des physiatres du Québec (APQ)
CP 216, Succ. Desjardins, #3000, 2, Complexe Desjardins, Montréal QC H5B 1G8
Tél: 514-350-5119; *Téléc:* 514-350-5147
apq@fmsq.org
www.fmsq.org
Aperçu: *Dimension:* petite; *Envergure:* provinciale surveillé par Fédération des médecins spécialistes du Québec
Mission: Pour ouvrer à la prévention, au diagnostic et au traitement médical des douleurs et des troubles de l'appareil locomoteur (la colonne vertébrale, les os, les muscles, les tendons, les articulations, les vaisseaux et le cerveau)
Membre de: Féderation des Médecins Spéecialistes du Québec (FMSQ)
Membre: 66
Membre(s) du bureau directeur:
Marc Filiatrault, Président
Elsa Fournier, Directrice, Administration

Association des physiciens et ingénieurs biomédicaux du Québec (APIBQ)
1817, boul des Laurentides, Laval QC H7M 2P7
www.apibq.ca
Aperçu: *Dimension:* petite; *Envergure:* provinciale; fondée en 1971
Mission: Promouvoir la production et la diffusion de connaissances en lien avec la technologie médicale; assurer l'utilisation sécuritaire de celle-ci pour le bénéfice de la population; favoriser la synergie entre ses membres
Membre: *Critères d'admissibilite:* Ingénieurs, physiciens et autres professionnels oeuvrant dans le domaine de la santé; *Comités:* Étudiant; Radioprotection; Sécurité électrique; Terminologie; Bonnes pratiques en génie biomédical; Certification; Formation continue; Mentorat
Membre(s) du bureau directeur:
Claude Pérusse, Président
claude.perusse.agence16@ssss.gouv.qc.ca

Association des Physiques Québécois (APQ)
96, rue Principale, Granby QC J2G 2T4
Tél: 450-991-1174; *Téléc:* 450-991-1184
apquebec.informations@gmail.com
www.apquebec.com
Aperçu: *Dimension:* petite; *Envergure:* provinciale surveillé par Canadian Bodybuilding Federation
Membre de: Canadian Bodybuilding Federation; International Federation of Bodybuilding
Membre(s) du bureau directeur:
Yves Desbiens, Director technique
photoyd@videotron.ca
Joe Spinello, Directeur des juges
spinellojoe@hotmail.com

L'Association des pilotes d'Air Canada *See* Air Canada Pilots Association

Association des pilotes de brousse du Québec *Voir* Association des Aviateurs et Pilotes de Brousse du Québec

Association des pilotes fédéraux du Canada *See* Canadian Federal Pilots Association

Association des pilotes maritimes du Canada *See* Canadian Marine Pilots' Association

Association des planificateurs de retraite du Canada *See* Retirement Planning Association of Canada

Association des pneumologues de la province de Québec (APPQ)
CP 216, #3000, 2, Complexe Desjardins, Montréal QC H5B 1G8
Tél: 514-350-5117; *Téléc:* 514-350-5153
appq@fmsq.org
www.fmsq.org
Aperçu: *Dimension:* petite; *Envergure:* provinciale surveillé par Fédération des médecins spécialistes du Québec
Mission: Promouvoir les intérêts professionnels et économiques de ses membres; se préoccuper du maintien de leur compétence; se prononcer sur les problématiques de la pneumologie dans les meilleurs intérêts de la population
Membre de: Fédération des médecins spécialistes du Québec
Membre: 240
Membre(s) du bureau directeur:
Pierre Mayer, Président
Elsa Fournier, Directrice, Administration

Association des policières et policiers provinciaux du Québec (APPQ) / Québec Provincial Police Association
1981, rue Léonard-De Vinci, Sainte-Julie QC J3E 1Y9
Tél: 450-922-5414; *Téléc:* 450-922-5417
info@appq-sq.qc.ca
www.appq-sq.qc.ca
Aperçu: *Dimension:* moyenne; *Envergure:* provinciale; Organisme sans but lucratif; fondée en 1966
Mission: Promouvoir le bien-être de ses membres et voir à leurs intérêts sociaux, moraux et culturels
Finances: *Budget de fonctionnement annuel:* $1.5 Million-$3 Million
Membre(s) du personnel: 18
Membre: 4,812; *Montant de la cotisation:* 746.20$
Activités: *Bibliothèque:* Not open to public
Membre(s) du bureau directeur:
Pierre Veilleux, Président
Jocelyn Boucher, Vice-président, Ressources humaines
Luc Fournier, Vice-président, Finances
Jacques Painchaud, Vice-président, Discipline et déontologie
Pierre Lemay, Vice-président, Griefs et formation
Daniel Rolland, Vice-président, Ress. matérielles et santé et sécurité du travail

Association des policiers de Fredericton *See* Fredericton Police Association

Association des policiers de l'Ontario *See* Police Association of Ontario

Association des policiers de la Nouvelle-Écosse *See* Police Association of Nova Scotia

Association des policiers de la région de Peel *See* Peel Regional Police Association

Association des policiers de Medicine Hat *See* Medicine Hat Police Association

Association des policiers des chemins de fer nationaux du Canada (ind.) *See* Canadian National Railways Police Association (Ind.)

Association des pompiers autochtones de Canada *See* Aboriginal Firefighters Association of Canada

Association des pompiers de Laval
374, boul Cartier ouest, Laval QC H7N 2K2
Tél: 450-663-3025; *Téléc:* 450-663-3037
info@pompierslaval.org
www.apl.tel
Aperçu: *Dimension:* petite; *Envergure:* locale; fondée en 1979
Mission: Rassembler les membres en un groupement qui les représente et parle en leur nom; revaloriser les membres sur le plan physique, moral et intellectuel; promouvoir et défendre les intérêts économiques, sociaux et moraux des membres.
Membre(s) du bureau directeur:
Richard Carpentier, Président
r.carpentier@pompierslaval.org
Luc Gauthier, Vice-Président, Santé Sécurité
l.gauthier@pompierslaval.org
Hugo Lamarche, Vice-Président, Griefs et Secrétariat
h.lamarche@pompierslaval.org
Claude Gagné, Vice-Président, Finances et Activités Sociales
c.gagne@pompierslaval.org

Association des Pompiers de Montréal inc. (APM) / Montréal Firefighters' Association Inc.
2655, place Chassé, 2e étage, Montréal QC H1Y 2C3
Tél: 514-527-9691; *Téléc:* 514-527-8119
info@adpm.qc.ca
www.adpm.qc.ca
Aperçu: *Dimension:* moyenne; *Envergure:* locale; Organisme sans but lucratif; fondée en 1920
Finances: *Budget de fonctionnement annuel:* $1.5 Million-$3 Million
Membre: 2 290; *Montant de la cotisation:* 754$; *Comités:* Aide aux employés; Caisse de retraite; Encadrement des délégués; Griefs; Négociations; Placements et assurances collectives; Répartition; Publicité et portelance; Relations professionnelles; Santé et sécurité au travail; Social; Stratégie et orientation; Promotions; Uniformes
Activités: Syndicats; *Stagiaires:* Oui
Membre(s) du bureau directeur:
Ronald Martin, Président
rmartin@adpm.qc.ca
Chris Ross, Vice-président
cross@adpm.qc.ca

Association des pompiers professionnels de l'Ontario (ind.) *See* Ontario Professional Fire Fighters Association

Association des Poneys Welsh & Cob au Québec / Québec Welsh Pony & Cob Association
a/s Diane Belhumeur, 354, rang 3, Kingsey Falls QC J0A 1B0
Tel: 819-358-5495; *Fax:* 819-358-5435
welshquebec@hotmail.com
www.apwcq.com
www.facebook.com/APWCQ
Overview: A small provincial organization overseen by Welsh Pony & Cob Society of Canada
Mission: Pour promouvoir et développer la race de poney Welsh au Québec
Membership: 31; *Member Profile:* Personnes impliquées dans la race de poney Welsh au Québec
Chief Officer(s):
Michel Bougie, Président
boogie@telwarwick.net
Diane Belhumeur, Secrétaire

Association des Praticiens de la santé naturelle du Canada *See* Natural Health Practitioners of Canada Association

Association des praticiens en éthique du Canada *See* Ethics Practitioners' Association of Canada

Association des presses universitaires canadiennes *See* Association of Canadian University Presses

Association des procureurs de cours municipales du Québec (APCMQ)
700, av Hôtel-de-ville, Saint-Hyacinthe QC J2S 5B2
Tél: 450-778-8316; *Téléc:* 450-778-2514
www.apcmq.com
Aperçu: *Dimension:* moyenne; *Envergure:* provinciale; fondée en 1998
Mission: Pour défendre les intérêts des avocats qui travaillent dans les tribunaux municipaux
Membre: 68; *Montant de la cotisation:* 85$ Membre officiel; 60$ Membre honoraire; *Critères d'admissibilité:* Tout procureur agissant en poursuite devant une cour municipale
Activités: Réunions; Formations
Membre(s) du bureau directeur:
Normand Sauvageau, Président, Conseil d'administration
n.sauvageau@ville.laval.qc.ca

Association des procureurs de la couronne de l'Ontario *See* Ontario Crown Attorneys Association

Association des producteurs de films et de télévision du Québec *Voir* Association québécoise de la production médiatique

Association des producteurs maraîchers du Québec (APMQ) / Québec Produce Growers Association (QPGA)
905, rue du Marché-Central, Montréal QC H4N 1K2
Tél: 514-387-8319
Autres numéros: www.mangezquebec.com
apmq@apmquebec.com
www.apmquebec.com
Aperçu: *Dimension:* petite; *Envergure:* provinciale
Mission: Favorise le développement du secteur horticole québécois et veille à la promotion des fruits et légumes cultivés au Québec, sur le marché local et sur les marchés extérieurs.
Membre: 450

Association des produits forestiers du Canada *See* Forest Products Association of Canada

L'Association des produits forestiers du Nouveau-Brunswick *See* New Brunswick Forest Products Association Inc.

Association des professeur(e)s à temps partiel de l'Université d'Ottawa (APTPUO) / Association of Part-Time Professors of the University of Ottawa
#124, 85 University St., Ottawa ON K1N 6N5
Tél: 613-562-5800; *Téléc:* 613-562-5153
info@aptpuo.ca
www.aptpuo.ca
twitter.com/APTPUO
Aperçu: *Dimension:* petite; *Envergure:* locale; fondée en 1986
Mission: Promouvoir et protéger les droits et privilèges des professeurs à temps partiel travaillant sur le campus de l'Université d'Ottawa
Membre(s) du personnel: 1
Membre: 2,500; *Comités:* Employeur-Employé; Harcèlement sexuel; Régime de retraite; Santé et sécurité au travail; Sécurité sur le campus; Services alimentaires; Stationnement; Fonds de développement académique et professionnel
Membre(s) du bureau directeur:
Robert Johnson, Président
Prix, Bourses:
• Prix d'excellence
Décerné à un professeur à temps partiel pour l'excellence en enseignement, les activités de recherche et la participation à la vie universitaire.

Association des professeures et professeurs à temps partiel de l'Université Concordia *See* Concordia University Part-time Faculty Association

Association des professeures et professeurs de la Faculté de médecine de l'Université de Sherbrooke (APPFMUS)
Faculté de médecine, 3001, 12e av nord, Sherbrooke QC J1H 5N4
Tél: 819-564-5257; *Téléc:* 819-564-5394
appfmus-med@USherbrooke.ca
www.usherbrooke.ca/appfmus/
Aperçu: *Dimension:* petite; *Envergure:* locale; fondée en 1974
Mission: Représente plus de 300 professeures et professeurs oeuvrant en Médecine, en Sciences fondamentales ou en Sciences infirmières à la Faculté de médecine de l'Université de Sherbrooke
Membre de: Fédération québécoise des professeures et professeurs des universités du Québec
Affiliation(s): Association canadienne des professeurs et professeures d'universités
Finances: *Budget de fonctionnement annuel:* $50,000-$100,000
Membre(s) du personnel: 1
Membre: 300
Activités: Voir à l'application du protocole d'entente et défendre les intérêts des membres
Membre(s) du bureau directeur:
Yves Patenaude, Président

L'Association des professeurs d'allemand des universités canadiennes *See* Canadian Association of University Teachers of German

Association des professeurs d'anglais du Québec *See* Association of Teachers of English in Quebec

Association des professeurs de Campus Notre-Dame-de-Foy
5000, rue Clément-Lockquell, Saint-Augustin-de-Desmaures QC G3A 1B3
Tél: 418-877-3217; *Téléc:* 418-872-3448
Aperçu: *Dimension:* petite; *Envergure:* locale
Membre de: Fédération autonome du collégial
Finances: *Budget de fonctionnement annuel:* Moins de $50,000
Membre: 400; *Montant de la cotisation:* .95% du salaire brut; *Critères d'admissibilité:* Professeurs au cégep

Association des professeurs de Collège Communautaire de Vancouver *See* Vancouver Community College Faculty Association

Association des professeurs de Dalhousie *See* Dalhousie Faculty Association

Association des professeurs de français des universités et collèges canadiens (APFUCC) / Canadian Association of University & College Teachers of French (CAUCTF)
Département de Françaises, Université de Simon Fraser, 8888 University Dr., Burnaby BC V5A 1S6
www.apfucc.net
Aperçu: *Dimension:* moyenne; *Envergure:* nationale; fondée en 1958
Mission: Constitue sur le plan national un lieu de recontre destiné à présentation de recherches individuelles ou collectives portant sur la langue français, les littératures et les civilisations de la francophonie; collabore avec des organismes ayant des objectifs similaires
Membre de: La Fédération canadienne des études humaines; La Fédération internationale des professeurs de français
Membre: *Montant de la cotisation:* 55$ professeur à plein temps; 25$ étudiant ou autre/professeur à la retraite
Membre(s) du bureau directeur:
Jorge Calderon, Président
calderon@sfu.ca
Prix, Bourses:
• Le Prix de l'APFUCC
Décerné chaque année au meilleur ouvrage et au meilleur article publiés au cours de l'année précédente par les membres de l'APFUCC
Meetings/Conferences:
• Congrès 2018 de l'Association des professeurs de français des universités et collèges canadiens, 2018

Association des professeurs de Kwantlen *See* Kwantlen Faculty Association

Association des professeurs de l'École Polytechnique de Montréal (APEP)
CP 6079, Succ. Centre-Ville, Montréal QC H3C 3A7
Tél: 514-340-4979; *Téléc:* 514-340-5215
apep@polymtl.ca
www.apep.polymtl.ca
Aperçu: *Dimension:* petite; *Envergure:* locale
Membre(s) du bureau directeur:
Christian Mascle, Président

Association des professeurs de l'Université Acadia *See* Acadia University Faculty Association

Association des professeurs de l'Université Bishop *See* Association of Professors of Bishop's University

Association des professeurs de l'Université Brock *See* Brock University Faculty Association

Association des professeurs de l'Université Concordia *See* Concordia University Faculty Association

Association des professeurs de l'Université d'Athabasca *See* Athabasca University Faculty Association

Association des professeurs de l'université d'Ottawa (APUO) / Association of Professors of the University of Ottawa
170 Waller St., Ottawa ON K1N 9B9
Tél: 613-230-3659
apuo@uottawa.ca
www.apuo.ca
Aperçu: Dimension: moyenne; *Envergure:* locale; fondée en 1976
Mission: L'association est l'agent négociateur exclusif de tous les 1250 employés qui font partie de l'unité de négociation qu'elle représente. L'unité comprend les professeurs (autres que les professeurs invités), les professeurs de langue, les conseillers, les bibliothécaires et certains chercheurs boursiers
Membre: 1 250
Membre(s) du bureau directeur:
Jennifer Dekker, Président

Association des professeurs de l'Université de Brandon *See* Brandon University Faculty Association

Association des professeurs de l'Université de Calgary *See* University of Calgary Faculty Association

Association des professeurs de l'Université de l'Ile-du-Prince-Edouard *See* University of Prince Edward Island Faculty Association

Association des professeurs de l'Université de la Colombie-Britannique *See* University of British Columbia Faculty Association

Association des professeurs de l'Université de la Saskatchewan *See* University of Saskatchewan Faculty Association

Association des professeurs de l'Université de Lethbridge *See* University of Lethbridge Faculty Association

Association des professeurs de l'Université de Regina *See* University of Regina Faculty Association

Association des professeurs de l'Université de Toronto *See* University of Toronto Faculty Association

Association des professeurs de l'Université de Victoria *See* University of Victoria Faculty Association

Association des professeurs de l'Université de Winnipeg *See* University of Winnipeg Faculty Association

Association des professeurs de l'Université du Manitoba *See* University of Manitoba Faculty Association

Association des professeurs de l'Université Lakehead *See* Lakehead University Faculty Association

Association des professeurs de l'Université Laurentienne *See* Laurentian University Faculty Association

Association des professeurs de l'Université McMaster *See* McMaster University Faculty Association

Association des professeurs de l'Université Mount Saint Vincent *See* Mount Saint Vincent University Faculty Association

Association des professeurs de l'Université Queen's *See* Queen's University Faculty Association

Association des professeurs de l'Université Saint-François-Xavier *See* Saint Francis Xavier Association of University Teachers

Association des professeurs de l'Université Saint-Thomas *See* Faculty Association of University of Saint Thomas

Association des professeurs de l'Université Simon Fraser *See* Simon Fraser University Faculty Association

Association des professeurs de l'Université Trent *See* Trent University Faculty Association

Association des professeurs de l'Université Wilfrid-Laurier *See* Wilfrid Laurier University Faculty Association

Association des professeurs de l'Université Windsor *See* Windsor University Faculty Association

Association des professeurs de l'Université York *See* York University Faculty Association

Association des professeurs de Langara *See* Langara Faculty Association

Association des professeurs de Mount Allison *See* Mount Allison Faculty Association

Association des professeurs de musique enregistrés de l'Ontario *See* Ontario Registered Music Teachers' Association

Association des professeurs de Ryerson *See* Ryerson Faculty Association

Association des professeurs de sciences de l'Ontario *See* Science Teachers' Association of Ontario

Association des professeurs de sciences de Québec *Voir* Association pour l'enseignement de la science et de la technologie au Québec

Association des professeurs du Collège Camosun *See* Camosun College Faculty Association

Association des professeurs du Collège de Lakeland *See* Lakeland College Faculty Association

Association des professeurs du Collège de Medicine Hat *See* Faculty Association of Medicine Hat College

Association des professeurs du Collège de New Caledonia *See* Faculty Association of the College of New Caledonia

Association des professeurs du Collège Douglas *See* Douglas College Faculty Association

Association des professeurs du Collège Grant MacEwan *See* Grant MacEwan College Faculty Association

Association des professeurs du Collège Keyano *See* Keyano College Faculty Association

Association des professeurs du Collège Olds *See* Olds College Faculty Association

Association des professeurs du Collège Red Deer *See* Faculty Association of Red Deer College

Association des professeurs du SAIT *See* SAIT Academic Faculty Association

Association des professeurs(es) des collèges militaires du Canada *See* Canadian Military Colleges Faculty Association

Association des professionnels à l'outillage municipal (APOM)
11, av du Ruisseau, Montréal QC H4K 2C8
Téléc: 866-334-1264
Ligne sans frais: 866-337-5136
info@apom-quebec.ca
www.apom-quebec.ca
www.facebook.com/apomquebec
Aperçu: Dimension: petite; *Envergure:* locale; fondée en 1970
Mission: Répondre aux besoins créés par l'achat, l'entretien et la réparation de l'outillage utilisé dans l'exécution des travaux publics municipaux; Encourager la coopération entre ses organisations membres
Membre: 1,100; *Montant de la cotisation:* $105 régulier; $275 collaborateur; 25$ retraité; *Critères d'admissibilite:* Directeurs, surintendants, contremaîtres, chefs mécaniques, employés municipaux, fournisseurs
Membre(s) du bureau directeur:
Eric Landry, President, 819-474-8860, Fax: 819-478-8531
elandry@ville.drummondville.qc.ca
Meetings/Conferences:
• Association des professionnels à l'outillage municipal rencontre annuelle 2018, June, 2018, Victoriaville, QC
Scope: Local

Association des professionnels de l'administration *See* Association of Administrative Professionals

Association des professionnels de la chanson et de la musique (APCM)
#401, 450 rue Rideau, Ottawa ON K1N 5Z4
Tél: 613-745-5642; *Téléc:* 613-745-9715
Ligne sans frais: 800-465-2726
communications@apcm.ca
www.apcm.ca
www.facebook.com/MusiqueAPCM
Aperçu: Dimension: petite; *Envergure:* provinciale; Organisme sans but lucratif; fondée en 1990
Mission: Afin de promouvoir et distribuer de la musique et des artistes francophones de l'Ontario et ailleurs au Canada
Membre de: Alliance Nationale de l'industrie musicale
Affiliation(s): Alliance culturelle de l'Ontario
Membre(s) du personnel: 7
Membre: Montant de la cotisation: 50$ amis/associés; 75$ renouvellement; 100$ toute nouvelle adhésion; 150$ groupe; *Critères d'admissibilite:* Auteurs, compositeurs et chanteurs francophones
Activités: Gala de la chanson et et la musique franco-ontariennes, semestriellement; Vendredis de la chanson francophone, chaque année; *Service de conférenciers:* Oui; *Bibliothèque:* Bibliothèque; Bibliothèque publique rendez-vous
Membre(s) du bureau directeur:
Daniel Sauvé, Président
Anique Granger, Vice-Présidente

Association des professionnels de la communication et du marketing (APM)
#925, 2015, rue Peel, Montréal QC H3A 1T8
Tél: 514-842-5681; *Téléc:* 514-842-8836
info@apcm.biz
www.communicationmarketing.org
www.linkedin.com/groups?gid=100675
www.facebook.com/apcm.biz
Aperçu: Dimension: petite; *Envergure:* locale
Membre: Montant de la cotisation: 225$ régulier; 50$ étudiant; *Comités:* Membership; Think Tank; Communications; Concours STRAT et exSTRAT; Relève publicitaire; Défi Marketing TD Assurance; 5 à 8 réseautage; Conférences B2B et B2C; Classique estivale
Membre(s) du bureau directeur:
Nathalie Dupont, Présidente

Association des professionnels de la santé du Manitoba *See* Manitoba Association of Health Care Professionals

Association des professionnels des arts de la scène du Québec (APASQ)
#014, 2065, rue Pathenais, Montréal QC H2K 3T1
Tél: 514-523-4221; *Téléc:* 514-523-4418
Ligne sans frais: 877-523-4221
info@apasq.org
www.apasq.org
Aperçu: Dimension: petite; *Envergure:* provinciale; Organisme sans but lucratif; fondée en 1984
Mission: A pour mandat l'étude, la défense et le développement des intérêts économiques, sociaux, moraux et professionnels de ses membres; négocie des ententes avec les associations de producteurs; promeut et difffuse la scènographie québécoise. Incorporée sous la loi des syndicats professionnels et reconnue en vertu de la loi sur le statut professionnel et des conditions d'engagement des artistes de la scène, du disque et du cinéma
Membre de: L'Académie québécoise du théâtre
Affiliation(s): Fédération nationale des communications (FNC)
Finances: Fonds: Emploi-Québec; Conseil des arts et des lettres du Québec; Conseil des arts du Canada
Membre(s) du personnel: 5
Membre: Montant de la cotisation: 25$ membre associé; 50$ membre adhérent; 100$ membre actif; *Critères d'admissibilite:* Artiste concepteur de tous les aspects des arts de la scène
Activités: Expositions; colloques; tables rondes; *Service de conférenciers:* Oui
Membre(s) du bureau directeur:
Michel Beauchemin, Directeur général
mbeauchemin@apasq.org
Claude Accolas, Président
Mathieu Marcil, Vice-président

Association des professionnels du chauffage (APC)
1376, boul Roland-Therrien, Longueuil QC J4J 4M1
Tél: 450-748-6937; *Téléc:* 450-748-6938
Ligne sans frais: 855-748-6937
apc@poelesfoyers.ca
www.poelesfoyers.ca
Aperçu: Dimension: moyenne; *Envergure:* provinciale; fondée en 1983
Mission: Représenter l'industrie du chauffage d'appoint auprès des diverses instances et servir de centre d'informations aux consommateurs
Membre: Montant de la cotisation: Barème
Activités: Cours de formation
Membre(s) du bureau directeur:
Chantal Demers, Directrice générale
chantal.demers@poelesfoyers.ca

Canadian Associations / Association des professionnels en développement économique du Québec (APDEQ) / Economic Development Professionals Association of Québec

Association des professionnels en développement économique du Québec (APDEQ) / Economic Development Professionals Association of Québec
CP 297, Magog QC J1X 3W8
Tél: 819-868-9778; *Téléc:* 819-868-9907
Ligne sans frais: 800-361-8470
info@apdeq.qc.ca
www.apdeq.qc.ca
www.linkedin.com/companies/111964
twitter.com/apdeq
Nom précédent: Association des commissaires industriels du Québec (ACIQ)
Aperçu: *Dimension:* moyenne; *Envergure:* provinciale; fondée en 1959
Mission: Pour aider les artisans du Développement économique à acquérir des compétences et de la formation afin de les aider à réussir
Membre(s) du personnel: 3
Membre: 695; *Montant de la cotisation:* 450$ individuelle; 795$ multimembres; *Comités:* Formation; Communication; Services aux membres; Congrès; Activité printanière
Activités: *Stagiaires:* Oui
Membre(s) du bureau directeur:
Patrice Gagnon, Directeur général
pgagnon@apdeq.qc.ca

Association des professionnels en électrolyse et soins esthétiques du Québec
3381, rue des Récollets, Québec QC G2A 2S7
Tél: 418-407-4454; *Téléc:* 418-407-4452
Ligne sans frais: 800-363-9009
www.apeseq.ca
Nom précédent: Association des électrolystes et esthéticiennes du Québec; Association des électrolystes du Québec
Aperçu: *Dimension:* petite; *Envergure:* provinciale; Organisme sans but lucratif; fondée en 1976
Mission: Valoriser la profession des soins esthétiques
Finances: *Budget de fonctionnement annuel:* $50,000-$100,000
Membre(s) du personnel: 1; 15 bénévole(s)
Membre(s) du bureau directeur:
Édith Pilote, Directrice générale

Association des professionnels en exposition du Québec (APEQ)
Succ. 89022, l'Ile-Bizard QC H9C 2Z3
Tél: 514-315-1794
Ligne sans frais: 888-276-1633
info@apeq.org
www.apeq.org
Aperçu: *Dimension:* moyenne; *Envergure:* provinciale; fondée en 1991
Mission: Faire reconnaître le rôle vital de l'industrie des expositions dans la vie économique, industrielle, culturelle et sociale au Québec; Promouvoir, auprès du monde des affaires, l'efficacité des expositions comme moyen de promotion, de commercialisation et de communication; Favoriser l'éducation de ses membres
Finances: *Budget de fonctionnement annuel:* $50,000-$100,000
Membre: 130; *Montant de la cotisation:* 395$; *Critères d'admissibilité:* Membres directeurs - directeurs, promoteurs d'expositions commerciales, professionnelles, industrielles ou publiques; membres fournisseurs - fournisseurs d'équipements et services; halls d'expositions, hôtels et autres sites de réunion; décorateurs et accessoiristes; fabricants de signalisation; spécialistes en logistique et services techniques; communicateurs; spécialistes en douanes et transport; service de personnel; autres services reliés à l'industrie; *Comités:* Activités; Congrès
Activités: *Listes de destinataires:* Oui
Membre(s) du bureau directeur:
Jacques Perreault, Directeur général, 514-990-0224
info@apeq.org

Association des professionnels en gestion philanthropique (APGP)
CP 22124, Succ. Iberville, 2505, boul Rosemont, Montréal QC H1Y 3K8
Tél: 514-529-6865; *Téléc:* 800-217-1562
Ligne sans frais: 866-545-2747
apgp@apgp.com
www.apgp.com
www.facebook.com/apgpqc
twitter.com/APGP_
www.youtube.com/APGPphilanthropie
Aperçu: *Dimension:* petite; *Envergure:* locale; Organisme sans but lucratif; fondée en 1988
Mission: Promouvoir et développer la profession de gestionnaire en philanthropie
Finances: *Budget de fonctionnement annuel:* $100,000-$250,000
Membre: 380; *Montant de la cotisation:* 100$ étudiant; 150$ membre certifié; 300$ corporatif; *Critères d'admissibilite:* Professionnel en gestion philanthropique; consultant
Activités: Déjeuners-causeries
Membre(s) du bureau directeur:
Isabelle Morin, Présidente
France Locas, Vice-présidente
Maryse Beaulieu, Directrice générale

Association des professionnels en ressources humaines du Québec *Voir* Ordre des conseillers en ressources humaines agréés

Association des professionnels en santé du travail (APST)
1370, rue Notre-Dame ouest, Montréal QC H3C 1K8
Tél: 514-282-4231; *Téléc:* 514-282-4292
admin@santedutravail.ca
www.santedutravail.ca
Nom précédent: Association des infirmières et infirmiers en santé du travail du Québec
Aperçu: *Dimension:* moyenne; *Envergure:* provinciale; Organisme sans but lucratif; fondée en 1978
Mission: Assurer la protection du statut; consolider l'autonomie professionnelle et définir les besoins de ses membres; promouvoir et maintenir la qualité des services professionnels dispensés; favoriser l'actualisation des connaissances dans un contexte de constante évolution; intensifier le lien entre ses membres et la santé et sécurité au travail
Membre de: Association canadienne des infirmiers et infirmières en santé du travail
Activités: Déjeuners causerie; sessions de formation et de perfectionnement; congrès; colloque; *Service de conférenciers:* Oui
Membre(s) du bureau directeur:
Carl Brouillette, Président
Bruno-Gil Breton, Vice-président
Benoît Blossier, Administrateur

Association des professionnels en SGRH *See* HRMS Professionals Association

Association des professionnels et superviseurs de Radio-Canada (APS SRC) / Association of Professionals & Supervisors of the Canadian Broadcasting Corporation (APS CBC)
1212, rue Panet, Montréal QC H2L 2Y7
Tél: 514-845-0411; *Téléc:* 450-575-0572
aps@apscbcsrc.org
www.apscbcsrc.org
Aperçu: *Dimension:* moyenne; *Envergure:* nationale
Membre: 6700; *Montant de la cotisation:* 5$; *Critères d'admissibilité:* Toutes les personnes de supervision de la Société Radio-Canada dont les tâches principales comportent la surveillance d'autres employés; *Comités:* Mixte national; négociation
Membre(s) du bureau directeur:
Mario Poudrier, Président, 514-597-7214
Maria Gaglione, Administratrice

Association des professionnels unis de la santé: Terre-Neuve et Labrador (ind.) *See* Association of Allied Health Professionals: Newfoundland & Labrador (Ind.)

Association des Projets charitables Islamiques *See* Association of Islamic Charitable Projects

Association des propriétaires canins de Prévost (APCP)
CP 604, Prévost QC J0R 1T0
Tél: 450-335-1140
info@wouflaurentides.org
www.wouflaurentides.org
Aperçu: *Dimension:* petite; *Envergure:* locale
Membre: *Montant de la cotisation:* Cotisation annuelle de 5$
Membre(s) du bureau directeur:
Michel Fuller, Président

Association des propriétaires de cinémas du Québec (APCQ)
5744, rue De Contrecoeur, Montréal QC H1K 0E2
Tél: 514-493-9898; *Téléc:* 514-493-4848
Ligne sans frais: 877-540-1900
info@apcq.ca
www.apcq.com
www.linkedin.com/groups?gid=4416873
www.youtube.com/channel/UC7-iriaaDjcuw7i7fqlxiLg
Aperçu: *Dimension:* petite; *Envergure:* provinciale; Organisme sans but lucratif; fondée en 1932
Mission: Promouvoir et protéger les intérêts des propriétaires de cinémas au Québec
Membre de: Association cinématographique - Canada
Finances: *Budget de fonctionnement annuel:* $50,000-$100,000; *Fonds:* Cotisations des membres
Membre(s) du personnel: 1
Membre: 1-99; *Montant de la cotisation:* Barème
Membre(s) du bureau directeur:
Carole Boudreault, Directrice générale
Vincent Guzzo, Président

Association des propriétaires de machinerie lourde du Québec inc. (APMLQ)
Plaza Laval, #259, 2750, ch Ste-Foy, Sainte-Foy QC G1V 1V6
Tél: 418-650-1877; *Téléc:* 418-650-3361
Ligne sans frais: 800-268-7318
info@apmlq.com
www.apmlq.com
Aperçu: *Dimension:* moyenne; *Envergure:* provinciale; fondée en 1966
Mission: Informer et instruire ses membres au moyen de publications; maintenir un secrétariat permanent dans un but de liaison entre les membres et de contact avec différentes autorités; négocier avec les autorités publiques toutes ententes susceptibles de promouvoir les buts de l'Association et ceux de ses membres
Membre de: Conseil du Patronat du Québec
Affiliation(s): Association des entrepreneurs en forage du Québec; Association des propriétaires de grues du Québec; Association des propriétaires de pompes à béton du Québec; Association des transporteurs épandeurs de pierre à chaux agricole du Québec; Regroupement des loueurs de véhicules du Québec
Membre(s) du personnel: 3
Membre: 500 individu; 108 associé; *Montant de la cotisation:* Barème
Membre(s) du bureau directeur:
Jacques Guimond, Président
Yvan Grenier, Directeur général

Association des propriétaires de Saint-Bruno
CP 81, Saint-Bruno-de-Richelieu QC J3V 4P8
Tél: 450-461-0445
info@apsb.ca
apsb.ca
Aperçu: *Dimension:* petite; *Envergure:* locale
Mission: Fournir une voix pour les habitants de Saint-Bruno
Membre(s) du bureau directeur:
Claude Lamarre, Président, Conseil d'administration, 450-461-0445

Association des propriétaires du Québec inc. (APQ) / Quebec Landlords Association (QLA)
10720, boul St-Laurent, Montréal QC H3L 2P7
Tél: 514-382-9670; *Téléc:* 514-382-9676
Ligne sans frais: 888-382-9670
www.apq.org
www.facebook.com/141154527095
twitter.com/apquebec
www.youtube.com/user/assopropriétaires
Aperçu: *Dimension:* moyenne; *Envergure:* provinciale; fondée en 1984
Mission: Défendre les droits et les intérêts des propriétaires de logements locatifs du Québec
Membre: 8,000; *Montant de la cotisation:* Barème

Association des propriétaires et administrateurs d'immeubles du Québec *Voir* BOMA Québec

Association des prospecteurs du Québec *Voir* Association de l'exploration minière de Québec

Association des psychiatres du Canada *See* Canadian Psychiatric Association

Association des psychologues du Manitoba *See* Psychological Association of Manitoba

Association des psychothérapeutes pastoraux du Canada (APPC) / Association of Pastoral Psychotherapists of Canada
892, rue Bernard Pilon, McMasterville QC J3G 5W8
Tél: 450-446-9058; *Téléc:* 450-446-9058

Aperçu: Dimension: petite; *Envergure:* nationale; fondée en 1985
Mission: Regrouper tous les psychothérapeutes pastoraux qui s'intéressent à la dimension pastorale en relation d'aide; assurer la spécificité de la psychothérapie pastorale afin d'empêcher tout empiètement dans les domaines connexes, et de sauvegarder ainsi l'autonomie de chaque profession concernée par la relation d'aide; veiller de manière efficace à la compétence vérifiée des psychothérapeutes pastoraux membres de l'Association pour éviter les dangers du charlatanisme; promouvoir la psychothérapie pastorale étant donnée son importance pour assurer le respect réel de la personne totale dans la relation d'aide
Activités: *Service de conférenciers:* Oui

Association des psychothérapeutes psychanalytiques du Québec
#310, 911, rue Jean-Talon est, Montréal QC H2R 1V5
Tél: 514-383-1240
info@appq.com
www.appq.com
Aperçu: Dimension: petite; *Envergure:* provinciale; fondée en 1985
Mission: Développer chez ses membres un sentiment d'appartenance à un groupe partageant des vues théoriques et thérapeutiques communes basées sur la pensée psychanalytique
Membre: 140; *Montant de la cotisation:* 55$; *Critères d'admissibilite:* Détenir un diplôme de premier cycle en sciences humaines ou de la santé, posséder une solide culture psychanalytique
Activités: Journées cliniques; séminaires; colloques; soirées cinéma
Membre(s) du bureau directeur:
Thérèse Nadeau, Présidente
Marie Gauthier, Trésorière

Association des radiodiffuseurs communautaires du Québec (ARCQ)
#202, 2, rue Sainte-Catherine est, Montréal QC H2X 1K4
Tél: 514-287-9094; *Téléc:* 514-285-2814
radiovision.ca/arq/
Aperçu: Dimension: petite; *Envergure:* provinciale; Organisme sans but lucratif; fondée en 1979
Mission: Contribuer au progrès et à la renomée de la radiophonie communautaire
Membre(s) du bureau directeur:
Martin Bougie, Directeur général

Association des radiologistes du Québec
CP 216, Succ. Desjardins, #3000, 2, Complexe Desjardins, Montréal QC H5B 1G8
Tél: 514-350-5129; *Téléc:* 514-350-5179
bureau@arq.qc.ca
www.arq.qc.ca
twitter.com/SCFRQuebec
Aperçu: Dimension: petite; *Envergure:* provinciale surveillé par Fédération des médecins spécialistes du Québec
Mission: Regrouper les médecins spécialisés en radiologie; défendre leurs intérêts et promouvoir leur spécialité
Membre: 592
Membre(s) du bureau directeur:
Vincent Oliva, Président
Lisette Pipon, Directrice, Administration

Association des radio-oncologues du Québec (AROQ)
CP 216, Succ. Desjardins, #3000, 2, Complexe Desjardins, Montréal QC H5B 1G8
Tél: 514-350-5130; *Téléc:* 514-350-5126
aroq@fmsq.org
www.aroq.ca
Aperçu: Dimension: petite; *Envergure:* provinciale surveillé par Fédération des médecins spécialistes du Québec
Mission: De fournir un forum où ses membres peuvent échanger des idées afin d'aider à améliorer leurs méthodes de traitement
Membre: 121
Membre(s) du bureau directeur:
Khalil Sultanem, Président

Association des réalisateurs et réalisatrices de Télé-Québec (ARRTQ)
1000, rue Fullum, Montréal QC H2K 3L7
Tél: 514-521-2424
Aperçu: Dimension: petite; *Envergure:* provinciale surveillé par Centrale des syndicats du Québec
Affiliation(s): Centrale des syndicats du Québec
Membre: *Critères d'admissibilité:* Tout réalisateur ayant signé un contrat avec la Société Télé-Québec
Membre(s) du bureau directeur:
Rachel Archambault, Coordonnatrice
rarchambault@sympatico.ca

Association des réalisateurs et réalisatrices du Québec (ARRQ)
5154, rue St-Hubert, Montréal QC H2J 2Y3
Tél: 514-842-7373; *Téléc:* 514-842-6789
realiser@arrq.qc.ca
www.arrq.qc.ca
Nom précédent: Association québécoise des réalisateurs et réalisatrices de cinéma et de télévision
Aperçu: Dimension: petite; *Envergure:* provinciale; fondée en 1973
Mission: Défendre les intérêts et les droits professionnels, économiques, culturels, sociaux et moraux des réalisateurs pigistes membres, travaillant principalement dans les domaines du cinéma et de la télévision
Membre de: Fédération professionnelle des réalisateurs et réalisatrices de cinéma et de télévision du Québec
Affiliation(s): Coalition des créateurs et titulaires de droits d'auteur; Association littéraire et artistique internationale
Membre(s) du personnel: 4
Membre: 670 réalisateurs/réalisatrices pigistes; *Montant de la cotisation:* 150$ professionnel; 75$ stagiaire; *Critères d'admissibilite:* Réalisateurs de longs, courts moyens métrages, téléfilms, vidéoclips, films publicitaires
Activités: Programmes d'aide financière, droits d'auteur, politiques de diffusion, promotion du statut professionnel, etc.; *Service de conférenciers:* Oui; *Listes de destinataires:* Oui
Membre(s) du bureau directeur:
Caroline Fortier, Directrice générale
cfortier@arrq.qc.ca
Prix, Bourses:
• Prix lumières

Association des recycleurs de pièces d'autos et de camions (ARPAC) / Association of Auto Part Recyclers
#101, 37, rue de la Gare, Saint-Jérôme QC J7Z 2B7
Tél: 450-504-8315; *Téléc:* 450-504-8313
Ligne sans frais: 855-504-8315
info@arpac.org
arpac.org
www.facebook.com/106847846016208
www.youtube.com/user/ARPACpiecesvertes
Aperçu: Dimension: moyenne; *Envergure:* provinciale
Membre de: Automotive Recyclers of Canada
Membre: 88; *Comités:* Environnement; Communications informatiques; Achats regroupés et congrès; Standardisation des normes; Formation; Publicité
Membre(s) du bureau directeur:
Simon Matte, Président-directeur général
Meetings/Conferences:
• 2018 Association des recycleurs de pièces d'autos et de camions Congrès, 2018
Scope: Provincial

Association des registraires des universités et collèges du Canada *See* Association of Registrars of the Universities & Colleges of Canada

Association des relations publiques des organismes de la santé *See* Health Care Public Relations Association

Association des résidents du Lac Écho
CP 343, Saint-Hippolyte QC J8A 3P6
Tél: 450-224-4338
Aperçu: Dimension: petite; *Envergure:* locale
Membre(s) du bureau directeur:
Michel Lamontagne, Contact

Association des résidents du Lac Renaud
Prévost QC J0R 1T0
www.lac-renaud.ca
www.facebook.com/1504982449798839
Aperçu: Dimension: petite; *Envergure:* locale
Membre: *Montant de la cotisation:* 35$
Membre(s) du bureau directeur:
Jean-René Bureau, Président

Association des ressources humaines du Nouveau-Brunswick *See* Human Resources Association of New Brunswick

Association des ressources intervenant auprès des hommes ayant des comportement violent *Voir* A Coeur d'Homme

Association des restaurateurs du Québec (ARQ) / Québec Restaurant Association
5880, boul Louis-H. Lafontaine, Montréal QC H1M 2T2
Tél: 514-527-9801; *Téléc:* 514-527-3066
Ligne sans frais: 800-463-4237
arq@arq.qc.ca
www.restaurateurs.ca
www.facebook.com/167396323369138
twitter.com/ARQ_resto
Aperçu: Dimension: petite; *Envergure:* provinciale; Organisme sans but lucratif; fondée en 1938
Mission: Fournir à l'ensemble des restaurateurs du Québec des services complets d'information, de formation, d'escomptes, d'assurances et de représentation gouvernementale
Membre de: Conseil du Patronat; Conseil québécois des ressources humaines en tourisme
Membre(s) du personnel: 26
Membre: 4 500; *Montant de la cotisation:* 385$ restaurant/hôtel/brasserie; 235$ saisonnier; 185$ service; *Critères d'admissibilite:* Restaurateurs, fournisseurs
Activités: Volet économique - rabais sur frais d'administration de cartes de crédit, d'achat d'essence et d'approvisionnements; réduction de la cotisation à la Commission de la santé et de la sécurité du travail; assurances; volet politique - représentation gouvernementale; information (règlementation et statistiques); programmes de formation - séminaires de perfectionnement, santé et sécurité au travail; conférences; programme d'ateliers de formation accréditée
Membre(s) du bureau directeur:
Alain Mailhot, Président directeur général
Prix, Bourses:
• Prix Coup de Chapeau
Remis annuellement à des restaurateurs pour leur contribution au rayonnement de l'industrie de la restauration

Association des sages-femmes de l'Ontario *See* Association of Ontario Midwives

Association des sciences administratives du Canada *See* Administrative Sciences Association of Canada

Association des sciences de la santé de l'Alberta (ind.) *See* Health Sciences Association of Alberta

Association des sciences de la santé de la Saskatchewan (ind.) *See* Health Sciences Association of Saskatchewan

Association des Scouts du Canada
7331, rue Saint-Denis, Montréal QC H2R 2E5
Tél: 514-252-3011; *Téléc:* 514-254-1946
Ligne sans frais: 866-297-2688
infoscout@scoutsducanada.ca
www.scoutsducanada.ca
www.facebook.com/scoutsducanada
Également appelé: Les Scouts du Québec
Nom précédent: Fédération québécoise du scoutisme
Aperçu: Dimension: moyenne; *Envergure:* internationale; Organisme sans but lucratif; fondée en 1980
Mission: Assurer la qualité, la permanence et la croissance du scoutisme francophone au Canada; elle détermine les orientations, objectifs, moyens et politiques pour répondre aux besoins de ses membres; elle développe aussi les processus de planification stratégique, réalise, anime des recherches, des scénarios de l'environnement; elle agit comme porte parole du scoutisme au Québec
Membre de: Association des scouts du Canada
Affiliation(s): Organisation Mondiale du Mouvement Scout
Finances: *Budget de fonctionnement annuel:* $1.5 Million-$3 Million
Membre(s) du personnel: 8; 30 bénévole(s)
Membre: 35 000; *Montant de la cotisation:* 22$; *Critères d'admissibilité:* Jeune (7-21 ans); adulte (18 ans et plus)
Activités: *Stagiaires:* Oui; *Service de conférenciers:* Oui; *Bibliothèque:* La Référence; rendez-vous
Membre(s) du bureau directeur:
Sylvain Fredette, Commissaire national/Chef de la direction
commissaire.national@scoutsducanada.ca
Mark Chalouhi, Président
president@scoutsducanada.ca

Association des services aux étudiants des universités et collèges du Canada *See* Canadian Association of College & University Student Services

Canadian Associations / Association des services de réhabilitation sociale du Québec inc. (ASRSQ) / Association of Social Rehabilitation Agencies of Québec Inc.

Association des services de garde à l'enfance de la Nouvelle-Écosse See Nova Scotia Child Care Association

Association des services de réhabilitation sociale du Québec inc. (ASRSQ) / Association of Social Rehabilitation Agencies of Québec Inc.
2000, boul St-Joseph est, Montréal QC H2H 1E4
Tél: 514-521-3733; *Téléc:* 514-521-3753
info@asrsq.ca
www.asrsq.ca
www.facebook.com/asrsq
Aperçu: *Dimension:* moyenne; *Envergure:* provinciale; Organisme sans but lucratif; fondée en 1962
Mission: Promouvoir la participation des citoyens dans l'administration de la justice, la prévention du crime et la réhabilitation des délinquants adultes
12 bénévole(s)
Membre: 50 corporations; 109 points de services
Activités: Semaine de la justice réparatrice; *Service de conférenciers:* Oui
Membre(s) du bureau directeur:
Nicole Quesnel, Présidente
Solange Bastille, Vice-présidente
Guy Pellerin, Secrétaire
Sylvie Brunet-Lusignan, Trésorier
Prix, Bourses:
• Prix Reneault-Tremblay
Décerné tous les deux ans à une personne ou un organisme communautaire en reconnaissance de son apport unique et exceptionnel à l'action communautaire en justice pénale, à la prévention du crime et à la réhabilitation sociale des personnes contrevenantes adultes

L'Association des services funéraires du Canada See Funeral Service Association of Canada

Association des services sociaux des municipalités de l'Ontario See Ontario Municipal Social Services Association

Association des sexologues du Québec (ASQ)
CP 22147, Succ. Iberville, Montréal QC H1Y 3K8
Tél: 514-270-9289
www.associationdessexologues.com
www.facebook.com/144131012376823
twitter.com/Asso_Sexologues
Aperçu: *Dimension:* petite; *Envergure:* provinciale; fondée en 1978
Mission: Susciter auprès du public une meilleure connaissance de la sexologie et du rôle du sexologue, en favorisant et en maintenant les normes scientifiques et professionnelles les plus élevées dans l'exercice de la sexologie et dans la formation des sexologues
Membre de: Sex Information & Education Council of Canada; World Association of Sexology
Membre: 200+; *Montant de la cotisation:* 150$ régulier; 45$ étudiant; 75$ membre retraité; *Critères d'admissibilite:* Maîtrise ou étudiant à la maîtrise en sexologie clinique
Activités: *Service de conférenciers:* Oui; *Listes de destinataires:* Oui; *Bibliothèque:* rendez-vous

Association des Sociétés d'aide au développement des collectivités de l'Ontario See Ontario Association of Community Futures Development Corporations

Association des Sourds de Beauce Voir Regroupement des Sourds de Chaudière-Appalaches

Association des Sourds de l'Estrie Inc. (ASE)
#100, 359, rue King est, Sherbrooke QC J1G 1B3
Tél: 819-563-1186; *Téléc:* 819-563-3476; *TTY:* 819-563-1186
sourdestrie@videotron.ca
www.sourdestrie.com
www.facebook.com/sourdestrie
Aperçu: *Dimension:* petite; *Envergure:* locale; Organisme sans but lucratif; fondée en 1968
Mission: Briser l'isolement des sourds; sensibilisation des intervenants et de la population en général sur la surdité
Membre de: Centre québécois de la déficience auditive; Regroupement québécois pour le sous-titrage inc.
Affiliation(s): Coalition Sida des sourds de Québec; Regroupement Canadien des Enseignants et Enseignantes Sourds en Langue des Signes Québécois
Finances: *Budget de fonctionnement annuel:* $100,000-$250,000; *Fonds:* Agence de la Santé et services sociaux de l'Estrie, Centraide, Emploi été Canada, Communautique, dons
Membre(s) du personnel: 1; 15 bénévole(s)
Membre: 120; *Montant de la cotisation:* 20$ individuel; 25$ couple/organisme; *Critères d'admissibilité:* Sourd, malentendant, entendant connaissant la langue des signes québécois;
Comités: Comité de poches baseball, 50e anniversaire, histoire
Activités: Activités de loisirs; conférences; information; accueil; St-Valentin; Noël; fêtes pour enfants; café internet; cours de Langue des Signes Québécois; journal d'information;
Evénements de sensibilisation: Journée Mondiale des Sourds;
Stagiaires: Oui; *Service de conférenciers:* Oui; *Bibliothèque:* Not open to public
Membre(s) du bureau directeur:
Céline Martineau, Directrice
Alain Ouellette, Adjoint administratif
Publications:
• Nouvellestrie [a publication of Association des Sourds de l'Estrie inc.]
Type: Journal; *Frequency:* Trimestriel

Association des Sourds de Lanaudière
200, rue de Salaberry, local 312, Joliette QC J6E 4G1
Tél: 450-752-1426; *TTY:* 450-752-1426
asl@cepap.ca
www.asljoliette.org
www.facebook.com/ASLanaudiere
Aperçu: *Dimension:* petite; *Envergure:* locale
Membre(s) du bureau directeur:
Richard Geoffroy, Président

Association des Sourds de Québec inc.
4100, 3e av ouest, Québec QC G1H 6E1
Tél: 418-614-0652; *Téléc:* 418-614-0672
asq1964@hotmail.com
sourdsquebec.com
Aperçu: *Dimension:* petite; *Envergure:* provinciale; Organisme sans but lucratif; fondée en 1964
Membre(s) du bureau directeur:
Richard Dagenault, Président

Association des sourds du Canada See Canadian Association of the Deaf

Association des Sourds du Haut-Richelieu Voir Association montérégienne de la surdité inc.

Association des spécialistes du pneus et Mécanique du Québec (ASPMQ)
CP 51017, Laval QC H7T 2Z3
Ligne sans frais: 866-454-0477
info@aspmq.ca
www.aspmq.ca
www.linkedin.com/company/aspmq---association-des-specialistes-pneu-et-mécanique-du-québec
Aperçu: *Dimension:* moyenne; *Envergure:* provinciale; fondée en 1969
Membre: 150
Membre(s) du bureau directeur:
Cynthia Fredette, Présidente

Association des spécialistes en chirurgie plastique et esthétique du Québec (ASCPEQ)
CP 216, Succ. Desjardins, 2, Complexe Desjardins, Montréal QC H5B 1G8
Tél: 514-350-5109; *Téléc:* 514-350-5246
ascpeq@fmsq.org
www.ascpeq.org
Aperçu: *Dimension:* petite; *Envergure:* provinciale surveillé par Fédération des médecins spécialistes du Québec
Mission: L'Association entend se consacrer essentiellement au développement continu de l'art et de la science de la chirurgie plastique et esthétique, entre autres par la diffusion de renseignements pertinents auprès du public, par la promotion d'une relation médecin-patient fondée sur la communication, la compréhension et le respect mutuel, ainsi que par une contribution active aux programmes d'éducation et de formation continue et par une participation critique aux débats relatifs au rôle et à la place des professionnels de la santé au sein de la société québécoise
Affiliation(s): La Société canadienne des chirurgiens plasticiens, The Toronto Aesthetic Meeting, The Toronto Breast Symposium, La Société canadienne de chirurgie plastique esthétique, The Canadian Association for Accreditation of Ambulatory Surgical Facilities
Membre(s) du bureau directeur:
Éric Bensimon, Président

Association des spécialistes en extermination du Québec Voir Association québécoise de la gestion parasitaire

Association des spécialistes en médecine d'urgence du Québec
Tour de l'Est, #3000, 2, Complexe Desjardins, Montréal QC H5B 1G8
Tél: 514-350-5115; *Téléc:* 514-350-5116
www.asmuq.org
Aperçu: *Dimension:* moyenne; *Envergure:* provinciale surveillé par Fédération des médecins spécialistes du Québec
Membre: *Comités:* Exécutif; Négociations; Développement Professionnel Continu; Effectifs et déploiement de la spécialité; Scientifique
Membre(s) du bureau directeur:
François Dufresne, Président

Association des spécialistes en médecine interne du Québec
Tour Est, 2, Complexe Desjardins, 30e étage, Montréal QC H5B 1G8
Tél: 514-350-5118; *Téléc:* 514-350-5168
asmiq.org
Aperçu: *Dimension:* moyenne; *Envergure:* provinciale; Organisme sans but lucratif
Membre de: Fédération des médecins spécialistes du Québec
Membre: 512; *Comités:* Éducation médicale continue; Communications; Formation en médecine interne
Membre(s) du bureau directeur:
Mario Dallaire, Président

Association des sports des sourds du Canada See Canadian Deaf Sports Association

Association des sports pour aveugles de Montréal (ASAM)
4545, av Pierre-de Coubertin, Montréal QC H1V 0B2
Tél: 514-252-3178
infoasaq@sportsaveugles.qc.ca
www.sportsaveugles.qc.ca/asam
www.facebook.com/ASAMONTREAL
Aperçu: *Dimension:* petite; *Envergure:* locale; Organisme sans but lucratif; fondée en 1983
Mission: Promouvoir l'accessibilité et la pratique des sports et loisirs aux personnes handicapées visuelles; organiser et structurer les différentes activités sportives; recruter et former des bénévoles accompagnateurs
Affiliation(s): Association sportive des aveugles du Québec
Finances: *Budget de fonctionnement annuel:* $50,000-$100,000
Membre(s) du personnel: 1; 75 bénévole(s)
Membre: 175 individu; 2 associées; *Critères d'admissibilite:* Personne ayant un handicap visuel
Activités: Goalball; conditionnement physique; aqua forme; tandem; ski alpin et ski de fond; tai-chi; activités ponctuelles: équitation, escalade, canot, randonnée pédestre; *Evénements de sensibilisation:* Tournoi de golf, sept.
Membre(s) du bureau directeur:
Nathalie Chartrand, Directrice générale
nchartrand@sportsaveugles.qc.ca

Association des stations de ski du Québec (ASSQ)
1347, rue Nationale, Terrebonne QC J6W 6H8
Tél: 450-765-2012; *Téléc:* 450-765-2025
www.maneige.ski
www.facebook.com/skiqc
twitter.com/assq_maneige
Aperçu: *Dimension:* moyenne; *Envergure:* provinciale; Organisme sans but lucratif
Mission: Représenter et défendre les intérêts des membres; favoriser la pratique du ski alpin; améliorer la qualité du produit ainsi que la performance des stations
Membre(s) du personnel: 16
Membre: 75 stations de ski
Activités: *Listes de destinataires:* Oui
Membre(s) du bureau directeur:
Yves Juneau, Président-directeur général

Association des statisticiennes et statisticiens du Québec (ASSQ)
3340, rue de La Pérade, 3e étage, Québec QC G1X 2L7
Courriel: assq@association-assq.qc.ca
www.association-assq.qc.ca
Aperçu: *Dimension:* petite; *Envergure:* provinciale
Mission: Regrouper les statisticiennes et statisticiens en vue de promouvoir la statistique et d'en favoriser la bonne utilisation
Membre: *Montant de la cotisation:* $10
Membre(s) du bureau directeur:
Christian Genest, President

Association des surintendants de golf du Québec (ASGQ) / Québec Golf Superintendents Association (QSGA)
1370, rue Notre-Dame ouest, Montréal QC H3C 1K8
Tél: 514-285-4874; *Téléc:* 514-282-4292
info@asgq.org
www.asgq.org
Aperçu: Dimension: petite; *Envergure:* provinciale; Organisme sans but lucratif; fondée en 1964
Mission: Dédiée à la promotion des intérêts des surintendants; offre à ses membres des avantages, informations et défense des intérêts des surintendants
Finances: *Budget de fonctionnement annuel:* $50,000-$100,000
Membre(s) du personnel: 1; 12 bénévole(s)
Membre: 400; *Critères d'admissibilite:* Surintendant; adjoint; aspirant
Activités: Tournois de golf; salon exposition; *Service de conférenciers:* Oui
Membre(s) du bureau directeur:
John Scott, Président
john.scott@summerlea.com

Association des syndicalistes retraités du Canada See Congress of Union Retirees Canada

Association des syndicats de copropriété du Québec (ASCQ) / Syndicates of Co-Ownership Association of Québec
#1800, 1010, rue Sherbrooke ouest, Montréal QC H3A 2R7
Tél: 514-866-3557; *Téléc:* 514-866-4149
Ligne sans frais: 800-568-5512
ascq@ascq.qc.ca
www.ascq.qc.ca
Aperçu: Dimension: grande; *Envergure:* provinciale; Organisme sans but lucratif; fondée en 1976
Mission: Former, informer, aider à la gestion les syndicats de copropriété membres
Membre de: Centre patronal santé sécurité au travail
Membre(s) du personnel: 4
Membre: *Critères d'admissibilite:* Syndicat de copropriété
Activités: Sessions formation colloques, séminaires; *Stagiaires:* Oui
Membre(s) du bureau directeur:
Michel G. Charlebois, Président
Publications:
• Bulletin de la Copropriété Plus [publication d'Association des syndicats de copropriété du Québec]
Type: Bulletin

Association des TCC (le traumatisme cranio-cérébral) et ACV (un accident vasculaire cérébral) de la Gaspésie et des Îles-de-la-Madeleine Inc.
CP 308, Maria QC G0C 1Y0
Tél: 418-759-5120; *Téléc:* 418-759-8188
Ligne sans frais: 888-278-2280
tccacv@globetrotter.net
www.tccacvgim.org
Nom précédent: Association des personnes traumatisées cranio-cérébrales de la Gaspésie et des Iles-de-la-Madeleine inc.
Aperçu: Dimension: petite; *Envergure:* locale; fondée en 1993
Mission: Pour informer et aider les personnes cranio-cérébral, traumatisme et leurs familles, en Gaspésie et les Iles de la Madeleine
Membre de: Regroupement des associations de personnes traumatisées craniocérébrales du Québec / Coalition of Associations of Craniocerebral Trauma in Quebec
Membre: *Critères d'admissibilite:* Les survivants de traumatisme crânien cérébral-des Iles de la Madeleine et Gaspésie
Activités: S'engager dans des activités de plaidoyer; Fournir un soutien psychosocial; Se référant victimes et les familles vers les ressources appropriées; Organiser des réunions et des groupes de discussion
Publications:
• La Bulle
Type: Newsletter; *Frequency:* Quarterly
Profile: Association activities

Association des techniciennes et techniciens en diététique du Québec *Voir* Société des technologues en nutrition

Association des techniciens en santé animale du Québec (ATSAQ)
#240, 2300 - 54e av, Montréal QC H8T 3R2
Tél: 514-324-5202
Ligne sans frais: 800-463-8555
atsaq@atsaq.org
www.atsaq.org
Aperçu: Dimension: petite; *Envergure:* provinciale; fondée en 1979
Membre de: Canadian Association of Animal Health Technologists & Technicians
Membre(s) du bureau directeur:
Élisabeth Lebeau, Directrice générale
atsaq@atsaq.org
Danny Ménard, Président
Laurence Santerre-Bélec, Vice-Président
Brigitte Couturier, Trésorière

Association des technologistes agro-alimentaires inc. *Voir* Association des technologues en agroalimentaire

Association des technologistes de laboratoire médical du Nouveau-Brunswick *See* New Brunswick Society of Medical Laboratory Technologists

Association des technologues en agroalimentaire (ATA) / Agricultural Technologists Association Inc.
a/s Ordre des technologues professionnels du Québec, #720, 1265, rue Berri, Montréal QC H2L 4X4
Tél: 514-845-3247; *Téléc:* 514-845-3643
Ligne sans frais: 800-561-3459
www.otpq.qc.ca
Nom précédent: Association des technologistes agro-alimentaires inc.
Aperçu: Dimension: moyenne; *Envergure:* provinciale; Organisme sans but lucratif; fondée en 1964
Mission: Défendre des intérêts professionnels; promouvoir la profession et le perfectionnement des membres
Membre de: Ordre des technologues professionnels du Québec
Membre(s) du personnel: 8
Membre: 4,000; *Montant de la cotisation:* 25,23$ étudiante/affilié; 75$ régulier
Membre(s) du bureau directeur:
Alain Bernier, Président
alain.bernier@collegeahuntsic.qc.ca
Denis Beauchamp, Directeur général
dbeauchamp@otpq.qc.ca

Association des théâtres francophones du Canada (ATFC)
#405, 450, rue Rideau, Ottawa ON K1N 5Z4
Tél: 613-562-2233; *Téléc:* 613-241-6064
Ligne sans frais: 866-821-2233
info@atfc.ca
www.atfc.ca
www.facebook.com/ATFC.officielle
Aperçu: Dimension: petite; *Envergure:* nationale; fondée en 1984
Mission: Défendre les intérêts et à assurer le développement et la promotion des théâtres francophones professionnels oeuvrant dans les régions canadiennes où les francophones sont minoritaires
Membre: *Critères d'admissibilite:* 14 compagnies de théâtre francophones professionnelles; *Comités:* Programmation; Politiques; Formation; Mises en nomination
Membre(s) du bureau directeur:
Geneviève Pineault, Directrice générale
dg@atfc.ca

Association des Therapeuets de Sport des Provinces Altantique *See* Atlantic Provinces Athletic Therapists Association

L'Association des thérapeutes respiratoires du Manitoba, inc. *See* Manitoba Association of Registered Respiratory Therapists, Inc.

L'Association des thérapeutes respiratoires du Nouveau-Brunswick inc. *See* The New Brunswick Association of Respiratory Therapists Inc.

Association des Townshippers *See* Townshippers' Association

Association des traducteurs et interprètes de l'Alberta *See* Association of Translators & Interpreters of Alberta

Association des traducteurs et interprètes de l'Ontario *See* Association of Translators & Interpreters of Ontario

Association des traducteurs et interprètes de la nouvelle-écosse *See* Association of Translators & Interpreters of Nova Scotia

Association des traducteurs et interprètes de la Saskatchewan *See* Association of Translators & Interpreters of Saskatchewan

Association des traducteurs et interprètes judiciares *See* Association of Legal Court Interpreters & Translators

Association des traducteurs et traductrices littéraires du Canada *See* Literary Translators' Association of Canada

Association des traducteurs, terminologues et des interprètes du Manitoba *See* Association of Translators, Terminologists & Interpreters of Manitoba

Association des transitaires internationaux canadiens *See* Canadian International Freight Forwarders Association

Association des transports du Canada *See* Transportation Association of Canada

Association des traumatisés crâniens de l'Abitibi-Témiscamingue (Le Pilier)
3, 9e rue, Rouyn-Noranda QC J9X 2A9
Tél: 819-762-7478; *Téléc:* 819-797-8313
pilieratcat@cablevision.qc.ca
www.pilieratcat.qc.ca
Aperçu: Dimension: petite; *Envergure:* locale
Mission: Pour fournir des services de soutien aux personnes qui ont subi une lésion cérébrale acquise, et leurs familles, dans la région de l'Abitibi-Témiscamingue du Québec
Membre de: Regroupement des associations de personnes traumatisées craniocérébrales du Québec / Coalition of Associations of Craniocerebral Trauma in Quebec
Finances: *Fonds:* Les frais d'adhésion; Collecte de fonds
Membre(s) du personnel: 5
Membre: *Montant de la cotisation:* $10
Activités: Offrir des programmes de soutien psychosocial aux personnes de la région de l'Abitibi-Témiscamingue qui ont subi un traumatisme cranio-cérébral; Fournir des activités sociales, culturelles, et de loisirs; Plaidoyer en faveur des victimes de traumatisme crânien
Membre(s) du bureau directeur:
Francine Chalifoux, Directrice générale et responsable clinique, 819-762-7478 Ext. 47421

Association des Traumatisés cranio-cérébraux de la Montérégie (ATCCM)
#D-131, 308, rue Montsabré, Beloeil QC J3G 2H5
Tél: 450-446-1111; *Téléc:* 450-446-6405
Ligne sans frais: 877-661-2822
atcc@atccmonteregie.qc.ca
www.atccmonteregie.qc.ca
Aperçu: Dimension: petite; *Envergure:* locale; fondée en 1994
Mission: Pour fournir des services de soutien aux personnes de la région de la Montérégie du Québec qui ont subi une lésion cérébrale traumatique ou un accident vasculaire cérébral; Pour favoriser la réinsertion et les expériences d'apprentissage
Membre de: Regroupement des associations de personnes traumatisées craniocérébrales du Québec / Coalition of Associations of Craniocerebral Trauma in Quebec
Membre(s) du personnel: 6
Membre: *Critères d'admissibilite:* Les survivants de traumatisme crânien ou accident vasculaire cérébral, et leurs familles, dans la région de la Montérégie au Québec
Activités: Création d'opportunités de partager des expériences avec d'autres personnes qui ont subi une lésion cérébrale traumatique dans la région de la Montérégie; L'animation de groupes de soutien; Offrant des services psychosociaux; Offrir une éducation; Promouvoir la prévention des lésions cérébrales
Membre(s) du bureau directeur:
Chantal Bourguignon, Directrice générale
c.bourguignon@atccmonteregie.qc.ca

Association des traumatisés cranio-cérébraux des deux rives (Québec-Chaudière-Appalaches)
Territoire de Québec et de Chaudiere-Appalaches, 14, rue Saint-Amand, Loretteville QC G2A 2K9
Tél: 418-842-8421; *Téléc:* 418-842-9616
Ligne sans frais: 866-844-8421
tcc2rives@oricom.ca
www.tcc2rives.qc.ca
Aperçu: Dimension: petite; *Envergure:* locale; fondée en 1989
Mission: Pour aider les victimes, les parents, les amis, et les professionnels touchés par une lésion cérébrale traumatique dans la région Chaudière-Appalaches du Québec.
Membre de: Regroupement des associations de personnes traumatisées craniocérébrales du Québec / Coalition of Associations of Craniocerebral Trauma in Quebec

sjogren.montreal@qc.aira.com
www.sjogrens.ca
Overview: A small national charitable organization
Mission: To work to draw the attention of medical world to Sjogren's Syndrome & the urgent need to discover a cause & cure; to provide support & education to patients & information to the medical community
Finances: *Funding Sources:* Donations

Association du Syndrome de Turner du Québec
1484, Montée Gagnon, Val-David QC J0T 2N0
Tél: 819-320-0409
turnerquebec@gmail.com
www.syndrometurnerquebec.com
Aperçu: *Dimension:* petite; *Envergure:* provinciale; Organisme sans but lucratif; fondée en 1984
Mission: Faire connaître les personnes atteintes du S.T.; faire circuler l'information médicale; créer des nouveaux contacts
Membre: *Montant de la cotisation:* 25$ (personne atteinte); 30$ famille; 50$ professionnel(le) de la santé
Activités: Écoute téléphonique; information de base; Info Cassette; articles médicaux
Membre(s) du bureau directeur:
Marie-Claude Doire, Présidente
Jocelyne Jeanneau, Coordonnatrice

Association du thé du Canada *See* Tea Association of Canada

Association du transport aérien du Canada *See* Air Transport Association of Canada

Association du transport aérien international *See* International Air Transport Association

Association du transport urbain du Québec (ATUQ) / Quebec Urban Transit Association
#8090, 800, rue de la Gauchetière, Montréal QC H5A 1J6
Tél: 514-280-4640; Téléc: 514-280-7053
info@atuq.com
www.atuq.ca
www.linkedin.com/company/association-du-transport-urbain-du-quebec-atuq
twitter.com/atuq3
Aperçu: *Dimension:* moyenne; *Envergure:* provinciale; fondée en 1983
Mission: Organisme de concertation et de représentation politique qui a pour mandat d'assurer la promotion du transport en commun et la défense des intérêts de ses membres auprès des partenaires de l'industrie et des différentes instances gouvernementales
Membre(s) du personnel: 6
Membre: 9; *Critères d'admissibilite:* Sociétés de transport en commun du Québec; *Comités:* Comité des approvisionneurs; Comité benchmarking; Comité transport adapté; Comité développement durable; Comité entretien; Comité planification/exploitation; Comité marketing et commercialisation; Comité ressources humaines; Comité systèmes de transport intelligents (STI); Comité des secrétaires; Comité sécurité; Comité des trésoriers
Membre(s) du bureau directeur:
Philippe Schnobb, Président
France Vézina, Directrice générale
Valérie Leclerc, Responsable de communications, 514-280-8167
valerie.leclerc@atuq.com
Meetings/Conferences:
• Colloque annuel de l'Association du transport urbain du Québec 2018, 2018

Association du verre d'art du Canada *See* Glass Art Association of Canada

Association échecs et maths *See* Chess'n Math Association

Association Et si c'était moi
#106, 386, rue De Gentilly ouest, Longueuil QC J4H 2A2
Tél: 450-651-2006
Aperçu: *Dimension:* petite; *Envergure:* locale
Mission: Aider les gens à surmonter les angoisses sociales avec l'art

Association fédérale des représentants de la sécurité *See* Federal Association of Security Officials

Association féline Canadienne *See* Canadian Cat Association

Association féminine d'éducation et d'action sociale (AFEAS) / Feminine Association for Education & Social Action
5999, rue de Marseille, Montréal QC H1N 1K6
Tél: 514-251-1636; Téléc: 514-251-9023
info@afeas.qc.ca
www.afeas.qc.ca
twitter.com/afeas1966
Aperçu: *Dimension:* moyenne; *Envergure:* provinciale; fondée en 1966
Mission: Avec ses Activités femmes d'ici organisées sur tout le territoire québécois, l'Afeas informe ses membres, suscite des échanges et des débats et les incite à participer davantage aux différentes structures de la société
Affiliation(s): Union mondiale des organisations féminines catholiques (UMOFC)
Membre: 14 000; *Montant de la cotisation:* 35$
Activités: *Bibliothèque*

Saguenay-Lac-St-Jean-Chibougamau
208, rue Dequen, Saint-Gédéon QC G0W 2P0
Tél: 418-345-8324; Téléc: 418-345-8289
afeas02@hotmail.com
www.afeas.qc.ca
Membre(s) du bureau directeur:
France Morissette, Responsable

Association for Awareness & Networking around Disordered Eating *See* Jessie's Hope Society

Association for Bahá'í Studies (ABS) / Association d'études Baha'is
34 Copernicus St., Ottawa ON K1N 7K4
Tel: 613-233-1903; Fax: 613-233-3644
abs-na@bahai-studies.ca
www.bahai-studies.ca
www.facebook.com/331784303733
vimeo.com/absna
Previous Name: Canadian Association for Studies in the Bahá'í Faith
Overview: A medium-sized international charitable organization founded in 1975
Mission: To foster Bahá'í scholarship & to demonstrate the value of this scholarly approach; To promote courses of study of the Bahá'í faith; To foster relationships with various leaders of thought & persons of capacity; To publish scholarly materials examining the Bahá'í faith, especially on its application to the concerns & needs of humanity
Finances: *Annual Operating Budget:* $100,000-$250,000; *Funding Sources:* Grants; Conference & Literature revenue; Membership fees
Staff Member(s): 2
Membership: 2,000; *Fees:* $50 adult; $60 couple; $25 student/senior; $60 institution; $999 individual life
Activities: Publications; Conferences; Webinars; Working Groups; *Library:* Association for Bahá'í Studies Library; Open to public by appointment
Awards:
• Awards for Distinguished Scholarship
Eligibility: Scholarship advancing our collective understanding of Baha'i teachings; two awards: 1) published research study; 2) graduate thesis
Meetings/Conferences:
• Association for Bahá'í Studies 2018 42nd Annual Conference, August, 2018, Sheraton Atlanta Hotel, Atlanta, GA
Publications:
• The Journal of Bahá'í Studies
Frequency: irregular; *Number of Pages:* 110; *Editor:* John S. Hatcher

Association for Bright Children (Ontario) (ABC Ontario) / Société pour enfants doués et surdoués (Ontario)
c/o 135 Brant St., Oakville ON L6K 2Z8
Tel: 416-925-6136
abcinfo@abcontario.ca
www.abcontario.ca
Overview: A small provincial charitable organization founded in 1975
Mission: To provide information & support to parents of bright & gifted children; To increase the understanding & acceptance of bright & gifted children/youth at home, at school & in the community
Finances: *Funding Sources:* Membership fees; Donations
Membership: *Fees:* $40; *Member Profile:* Anyone interested in special needs of bright & gifted children; *Committees:* Finance; Advocacy; Research & Support; Business Development

Chief Officer(s):
Kathleen Keane, President
president@abcontario.ca
Meetings/Conferences:
• Association for Bright Children Ontario 2018 Annual Conference, 2018, ON
Scope: Provincial
Contact Information: E-mail: president@abcontario.ca

Association for Canadian & Québec Literatures (ACQL) / L'Association des littératures canadiennes et québécoise (ALCQ)
c/o Steven Urquhart, Dept. Modern Languages, University of Lethbridge, 4401 University Dr., Lethbridge AB T1K 3M4
www.alcq-acql.ca
Overview: A small national organization founded in 1975
Mission: To promote research, theory, & literary criticism about the literature of Canada & Québec
Membership: *Fees:* $25 students; $50 regular membership; $350 lifetime membership
Activities: Encouraging scholarly conversation among persons studying & researching the literature of Canada & Québec in English & French
Chief Officer(s):
Steven Urquhart, Treasurer
steven.urquhart@uleth.ca
Awards:
• Priz Gabrielle Roy Prize
To honour the best works of Canadian literary criticism in English & French
• Barbara Godard Emerging Scholar Prize
To honour the best paper by an emerging scholar

Association for Canadian Educational Resources (ACER)
#202, 92 Lakeshore Rd. East, Mississauga ON L5G 4S2
Tel: 905-891-6004
office@acer-acre.ca
www.acer-acre.ca
www.linkedin.com/groups/3962684
www.facebook.com/climatesake
twitter.com/AcerAcre
Overview: A small national organization founded in 1991
Mission: To promote & to help create Canadian materials for classroom life early learners
Finances: *Annual Operating Budget:* Less than $50,000; *Funding Sources:* Membership fees; donations; grants
Staff Member(s): 1; 30 volunteer(s)
Membership: 50; *Fees:* $30 adult; $20 retired person; $10 student; *Member Profile:* Volunteers from all sectors especially retired educators
Activities: Schools, community groups volunteer as part of Environment Canada delivery of mentoring system; community outreach; training workshops; displays at conferences
Chief Officer(s):
Alice Casselman, President
Nimesha Basnayaka, Program Manager

Association for Canadian Jewish Studies (ACJS) / Association d'études juives canadiennes (AEJC)
c/o Institute for Canadian Jewish Studies, Concordia University, 1455, boul de Maisonneuve ouest, #SB215, Montréal QC H3G 1M8
Tel: 514-848-2424; Fax: 514-848-4541
acjs-aejc.ca
twitter.com/ACJSaejc
Overview: A small national charitable organization founded in 1974
Mission: To encourage interdisciplinary study of the Canadian Jewish experience
Member of: Canadian Jewish Congress
Finances: *Annual Operating Budget:* Less than $50,000; *Funding Sources:* Foundations
Staff Member(s): 1; 38 volunteer(s)
Membership: 28 institutional; 20 student; 150 individual; *Fees:* $180 institutional; $60 individual, libraries, archives; $25 seniors, unemployed, students; *Member Profile:* Academics, students, professionals, individuals interested in the study of Jewish life
Activities: Hosting an annual conference; Publishing a bulletin & journal; Sponsoring local workshops & activities; Facilitating an online discussion group
Chief Officer(s):
Barry Stiefel, President
Awards:
• Louis Rosenberg Canadian Jewish Studies Distinguished Service Award

Awarded to recognize significant contribution by an individual or institution to Canadian Jewish studies
• Marcia Koven Award for Best Student Paper
Awarded to recognize significant contribution by an individual or institution to Canadian Jewish studies
Meetings/Conferences:
• Association for Canadian Jewish Studies Annual Conference 2018, May, 2018, Montréal, QC
Scope: National
Description: Allows members to share scholarly research on Canadian Jewish life, culture, & history
Publications:
• ACJS [Association for Canadian Jewish Studies] Bulletin
Type: Newsletter; *Frequency:* s-a.; *Editor:* Rebecca Margolis
Profile: Contains association news, reviews, & photos
• Canadian Jewish Studies/Études juives canadiennes [a publication of the Association for Canadian Jewish Studies]
Type: Journal; *Frequency:* Annually; *Editor:* David Koffman & Stephanie Schwartz; *ISSN:* 1198-3493
Profile: Publishes scholarly work on all facets ofthe Canadian Jewish experience

Association for Canadian Registered Safety Professionals
See Board of Canadian Registered Safety Professionals

Association for Canadian Studies (ACS) / Association d'études canadiennes (AEC)
1822A, rue Sherbooke ouest, Montréal QC H3H 1E4
Tel: 514-925-3097; *Fax:* 514-925-3095
general@acs-aec.ca
acs-aec.ca
www.facebook.com/acs.aec.canadianstudies
twitter.com/Canadianstudies
Overview: A large national charitable organization founded in 1973
Mission: To initiate & support activities in the areas of research, teaching, communications & the training of students in Canadian studies, especially in interdisciplinary & multidisciplinary perspectives; To strive to raise public awareness of Canadian issues
Member of: International Council for Canadian Studies; Humanities & Social Sciences Federation of Canada
Finances: *Annual Operating Budget:* $500,000-$1.5 Million; *Funding Sources:* Federal government; Membership dues
Staff Member(s): 5; 25 volunteer(s)
Membership: 130 institutional + 350 individual; *Fees:* $55-$125 regular; $90-$160 institutional; $25-$95 student/retired
Activities: Publications; National programs for students (graduate scholarship; aid for conferences); International programs (Chinese faculty meet & greet program; foreign speakers program); Annual meeting of Canadian Studies program administrators; *Rents Mailing List:* Yes; *Library:* Documentation Centre
Chief Officer(s):
Jack Jedwab, Executive Vice President
jack.jedwab@acs-aec.ca
James Ondrick, Director, Programs & Administration, 514-925-3097
james.ondrick@acs.aec.ca
Awards:
• Award of Merit
Meetings/Conferences:
• 20th National Metropolis Conference, March, 2018, Westin Calgary, Calgary, AB
Scope: National
Description: Theme: "Immigration Futures: Marking 20 Years of the National Metropolis Conference"

Association for Canadian Theatre History *See* Canadian Association for Theatre Research

Association for Community Living - Manitoba *See* Community Living Manitoba

Association for Corporate Growth, Toronto Chapter (ACG)
#202, 720 Spadina Ave, Toronto ON M5S 2T9
Tel: 416-868-1881; *Fax:* 416-292-5256
acgtoronto@managingmatters.com
www.acg.org/toronto
Also Known As: ACG Toronto
Previous Name: Canadian Association for Corporate Growth
Overview: A medium-sized national organization founded in 1973
Mission: To foster sound corporate growth by providing its members with an opportunity to gain new ideas from speakers, seminars & discussions with people working in the field of corporate growth; to develop additional skills & techniques which will contribute to the growth of their respective organizations; to meet other corporate growth professionals who can provide counsel & valuable contacts
Member of: Association for Corporate Growth, Chicago USA
Finances: *Annual Operating Budget:* Less than $50,000; *Funding Sources:* Membership dues; events
Staff Member(s): 1
Membership: 14,000 worldwide; *Fees:* $406.80; $960 corporate; *Member Profile:* Granted on an individual basis only to those involved in corporate growth; approximately 2/3 membership drawn from the industrial & consumer product fields, & the balance from accounting firms, financial intermediaries, & related service businesses; *Committees:* Nominations; Programming; Membership; Social
Chief Officer(s):
Stephen B. Smith, President

Association for Democracy in Romania *See* Romanian Children's Relief

Association for Financial Professionals - Calgary (AFPC)
PO Box 20177, Stn. Bow Valley, Calgary AB T2P 4L2
admin@afpcalgary.org
afpcalgary.org
Also Known As: AFP - Calgary
Overview: A small local organization overseen by Association for Financial Professionals
Mission: To enhance members' expertise in the field of treasury management
Member of: Association for Financial Professionals
Membership: *Fees:* $65 individual; $395 corporate; $495 affiliate; *Member Profile:* Local treasury professionals
Activities: Networking & career development opportunities
Chief Officer(s):
President Morrison, President

Association for Financial Professionals - Edmonton
PO Box 559-21, 10405 Jasper Ave., Edmonton AB T5J 3S2
afpcedmonton.shuttlepod.org
Also Known As: AFP - Edmonton
Previous Name: Treasury Management Association of Canada - Edmonton
Overview: A small local organization founded in 1982 overseen by Association for Financial Professionals
Mission: To serve the needs of treasury & finance professionals from private & public sector companies in Edmonton & surrounding communities.
Member of: Association for Financial Professionals
Membership: *Fees:* $200 corporate
Activities: Monthly luncheons & other networking opportunities
Chief Officer(s):
Dustin Meyer, President
dustinmeyer@shaw.ca
Amanda Popik, Membership Contact, 780-412-8864
apopik@epcor.com

Association for Financial Professionals - Ottawa
PO Box 889, Stn. B, Ottawa ON K1P 5P9
www.afpc-ottawa.ca
Also Known As: AFP - Ottawa
Overview: A small local organization overseen by Association for Financial Professionals
Mission: To exchange knowledge, ideas & solutions for challenges facing the industry
Member of: Association for Financial Professionals
Membership: *Fees:* $125 individual; $325 corporate; $600 large corporate; *Member Profile:* Treasury, risk & financial professionals in Ottawa; *Committees:* Program; Event; Membership; Publicity/Sponsorship; Nominating
Activities: Networking & speaker events
Chief Officer(s):
Anju Malhotra, President, 613-564-5138
anju.malhotra@scotiabank.com

Association for Financial Professionals - Vancouver
Vancouver BC
Other Communication: Technical Support:
support@afpvancouver.com
info@afpvancouver.com
www.afpvancouver.com
Also Known As: AFP - Vancouver
Previous Name: Treasury Management Association of Canada - British Columbia
Overview: A small local organization founded in 2010 overseen by Association for Financial Professionals
Mission: To promote & facilitate high standards of professional development & conduct in treasury management
Member of: Association for Financial Professionals
Membership: *Fees:* $50-$150 regular & associate; $50 student; *Member Profile:* Treasury professionals from mid-market corporations, crown corporations, banks, investment dealers, finance & trust companies, software vendors, management consultants & government organizations
Activities: Networking & career development opportunities
Chief Officer(s):
Paula Merrier, President
Donald Weylie, Director, Membership

Association for German Education in Calgary (AGEC)
3940 - 73 St. NW, Calgary AB T3B 2L9
germaneducationcalgary@gmail.com
www.germaneducationcalgary.ca
www.facebook.com/AssociationForGermanEducationInCalgary
Overview: A small local charitable organization founded in 2001
Mission: To promote bilingual German-English education from kindergarten to grade 6 in Calgary
Membership: *Fees:* $20 individual; $40 couple/family
Chief Officer(s):
Beatrix Downton, President

Association for Image & Information Management International - 1st Canadian Chapter (AIIM Canada)
Toronto ON
www.aiim.org/Community/Chapters/First-Canadian
Previous Name: Canadian Micrographic Society; Canadian Information & Image Management Society
Overview: A medium-sized international organization founded in 2000
Mission: To connect users & suppliers of e-business technologies & services
Affiliation(s): Association for Information & Image Management
Finances: *Funding Sources:* Membership fees; conference
Chief Officer(s):
Winnie Tsang, President
winnie.tsang@teranet.ca

Association for Literature, Environment, & Culture in Canada (ALECC) / Association pour la littérature, l'environnement et la culture au Canada
c/o Department of English, University of Calgary, 2500 University Dr. NW, 11th Fl., Calgary AB T2N 1N4
contactus@alecc.ca
www.alecc.ca
Overview: A small national organization founded in 2005
Mission: To promote and support artistic, critical and cultural studies work on a wide range of environmental issues.
Membership: *Fees:* $25-$40
Chief Officer(s):
Robert Boschman, President
rboschman@mtroyal.ca
Meetings/Conferences:
• Association for Literature, Environment, & Culture in Canada 2018 Biennial Conference, 2018
Scope: National

Association for Manager of Health Facilities & Social Services *Voir* Association des gestionnaires des établissements de santé et des services sociaux

Association for Manitoba Archives (AMA)
600 Shaftesbury Blvd., Winnipeg MB R3P 0M4
Tel: 204-942-3491
ama1@mts.net
mbarchives.ca
Previous Name: Manitoba Council of Archives
Overview: A medium-sized provincial organization founded in 1992 overseen by Canadian Council of Archives
Mission: To promote understanding & awareness of the role & use of archives; To promote standards, procedures, & practices in the management of archives; To provide assistance & education to persons seeking to improve their skills in the development, management, or operation of archives
Affiliation(s): Association of Canadian Archivists
Finances: *Annual Operating Budget:* $100,000-$250,000; *Funding Sources:* Government grants; membership fees
Staff Member(s): 1
Membership: 36 institutions + 100 individual; *Committees:* Advisory Services; Education; Finance & Grants; Information & Outreach; Management; Membership/Accreditation
Chief Officer(s):
Heather Bidzinski, Chair

Association for Media Literacy (AML)
Toronto ON
associationformedialiteracy@gmail.com
www.aml.ca
twitter.com/A_M_L_
www.youtube.com/user/AssociationMediaLit
Overview: A medium-sized international organization founded in 1978
Mission: Made up of teachers, librarians, consultants, parents, cultural workers, and media professionals concerned about the impact of the mass media on contemporary culture.
Chief Officer(s):
Neil Anderson, President

Association for Mineral Exploration British Columbia (AMEBC)
#800, 889 West Pender St., Vancouver BC V6C 3B2
Tel: 604-689-5271; *Fax:* 604-681-2363
info@amebc.ca
www.amebc.ca
www.linkedin.com/company/association-for-mineral-exploration-bc
www.facebook.com/Association.for.Mineral.Exploration.BC
twitter.com/ame_bc
Previous Name: British Columbia & Yukon Chamber of Mines
Overview: A medium-sized provincial organization founded in 1912
Mission: To promote & assist development & growth of mining of mineral exploration in BC
Affiliation(s): Mining Association of Canada; Mining Association of BC
Finances: *Annual Operating Budget:* $250,000-$500,000; *Funding Sources:* Membership dues
Staff Member(s): 13
Membership: 3,605 individual + 179 corporate; *Fees:* $84 individual; Schedule for organizations; *Member Profile:* Geoscientists, prospectors, engineers, exploration companies, suppliers, mineral producers; *Committees:* Aboriginal Relations; Awards; Communications & Marketing; Environment, Health & Safety; Finance; Integrated Social Responsibility; Land Access & Use; Membership; Mineral Exploration Editorial; Roundup Organizing; Taxation, Securities & Investment; Transboundary Relations
Activities: *Library:* Charles S. Ney Library; Open to public
Chief Officer(s):
Edie Thome, President & CEO, 604-630-3920
ethome@amebc.ca
Jonathan Buchanan, Director, Communications & Public Affairs, 604-630-3923
jbuchanan@amebc.ca
Simone Hill, Director, Member Relations & Events, 604-630-3921
shill@amebc.ca
Awards:
• H.H. "Spud" Huestis Award, AMEBC Annual Awards
To honour a member who has made a significant contribution to enhance the mineral resources of B.C. through the application of prospecting techniques or other technology
• E.A. Scholz Award, AMEBC Annual Awards
Awarded to a member who has made a notable contribution towards the development of a mining operation in B.C. or the Yukon Territory
• Murray Pezim Award, AMEBC Annual Awards
Awarded to a mineral industry financier who has provided a significant contribution to the B.C or Yukon mineral exploration industry *Eligibility:* Individuals engaged in the financing of mineral exploration
• Hugo Dummett Diamond Award, AMEBC Annual Awards
Awarded to an individual who has made a significant contribution towards diamond exploration
• Colin Spence Award, AMEBC Annual Awards
Awarded to an individual who has made a significant contribution to enhance the mineral resources within Canada (exclusive of B.C. or Yukon) or in foreign countries *Eligibility:* Individuals engaged in any phase of mineral exploration within Cnada or in foreign countries
• Robert R. Hedley Award, AMEBC Annual Awards
Awarded to an individual who has made a significant contribution to enhance environmental responsibility in the mineral exploration industry
• David Barr Award, AMEBC Annual Awards
Awarded to honour an individual who has demonstrated leadership, innovation, excellence in mineral exploration safety, or compassionate behaviour in dealing with an unfortunate accident
• Outreach Education Fund, AMEBC Annual Awards
A fund available for distribution in the form of scholarships per proposed projects *Eligibility:* All B.C.-focused projects relating to mineral exploration; *Amount:* $20,000 available
• Gold Pan Award, AMEBC Annual Awards
Awarded to individuals who have contributed exceptional service to the mineral exploration industry through the Association
• Frank Woodside Award, AMEBC Annual Awards
Awarded to recognize outstanding service to the Association
Meetings/Conferences:
• Association for Mineral Exploration British Columbia 2018 Mineral Exploration Roundup, January, 2018, Vancouver Convention Centre, Vancouver, BC
Scope: Provincial
Contact Information: Phone: 604-630-3930, Email: roundup@amebc.ca
Publications:
• Aboriginal Engagement Guidebook [a publication of the Association for Mineral Exploration British Columbia]
Type: Report
• Mineral Exploration [a publication of the Association for Mineral Exploration British Columbia]
Type: Magazine; *Accepts Advertising*; *Editor:* Jonathan Buchanan
Profile: Features industry news & updates
• Mineral Exploration Life Cycle [a publication of the Association for Mineral Exploration British Columbia]
Type: Report
Profile: An overview of the major steps in mineral exploration
• Safety Guidelines for Mineral Exploration in Western Canada [a publication of the AMEBC]
Type: Booklet; *Price:* Free with AMEBC membership; $15.95 without membership
Profile: A safety guide for mineral exploration
• Women: An Unmined Resource [a publication of the Association for Mineral Exploration British Columbia]
Type: Report
Profile: A summary on female participation in the BC mining industry

Association for Mountain Parks Protection & Enjoyment (AMPPE)
PO Box 2999, 209 - 220 Bear St., Banff AB T1L 1C7
Tel: 403-762-3800
admin@amppe.org
www.amppe.org
www.facebook.com/AMPPE.ORG
twitter.com/amppe
Overview: A small provincial organization founded in 1994
Mission: To champion & promote sustainable tourism, a vibrant mountain economy, & responsible human use in mountain parks
Membership: *Fees:* Schedule available
Chief Officer(s):
Casey Peirce, Executive Director

Association for Native Development in the Performing & Visual Arts (ANDPVA)
#10, 610 Baldwin St., Toronto ON M5T 3K7
Tel: 416-535-4567; *Fax:* 416-535-9331
info@andpva.com
www.andpva.com
Overview: A medium-sized national organization founded in 1974
Mission: To coordinate & develop programs that will encourage Indigenous peoples & communities to become more actively involved in the arts; to act as liaison for Native groups & individuals who are seeking funds for specific arts projects
Finances: *Funding Sources:* Government
Staff Member(s): 3
Membership: 300; *Fees:* $25 - $75; *Committees:* Music Advisory; Writers & Storytellers; Visual Arts
Activities: *Internships:* Yes; *Speaker Service:* Yes; *Rents Mailing List:* Yes
Chief Officer(s):
Millie Knapp, Executive Director
millie.andpva@gmail.com

Association for New Canadians (ANC) / L'association des nouveaux Canadiens (ANC)
Head Office & Settlement Services, PO Box 2031, Stn. C, 144 Military Rd., St. John's NL A1C 5R6
Tel: 709-722-9680; *Fax:* 709-754-4407
settlement@nfld.net
www.ancnl.ca
Overview: A small provincial organization founded in 1979
Mission: To provide full service immigrant settlement programs & services to the newcomer community in Newfoundland & Labrador; To support integration, & cross cultural understanding
Finances: *Funding Sources:* Citizenship & Immigration Canada; HRSDC; Service Canada; Canadian Hertiage; ACOA; Government of Newfoundland & Labrador; United Way
100 volunteer(s)
Activities: Providing ESL adult training, career services, life skills training, diversity & organizational change training, an immigrant settlement adaptation program, integration programs, a resettlement assistance program, a settlement workers in the schools program, programming for children, youth, & women, & public education activities

Association for Operations Management (APICS)
#300, 1370 Don Mills Rd., Toronto ON M3B 3N7
Tel: 416-366-5388; *Fax:* 416-381-4054
info@apics.ca
www.apics.ca
Previous Name: Canadian Association for Production & Inventory Control; American Production & Inventory Control Society
Overview: A medium-sized national licensing organization founded in 1962
Mission: To offer programs & materials on business management techniques; To promotes education in resource management
9 volunteer(s)
Membership: 3,000; *Fees:* Schedule available; *Member Profile:* Professional operations managers; *Committees:* Specific Interest Groups: Aerospace & Defence; Process Industry; Remanufacturing; Repetitive Manufacturing Group; Small Manufacturing; Textile & Apparel
Activities: Administering courses for CPIM (Certified in Production & Inventory Management) & CIRM (Certified in Integrated Resource Management) certifications; *Speaker Service:* Yes; *Rents Mailing List:* Yes
Chief Officer(s):
Shari Bricks, Executive Director
shari.bricks@apics.ca
Lina DeMatteo, Manager, Events
events@apics.ca
Anthony Nijmeh, Manager, Technical Support
anthony.nijmeh@apics.ca
Greg Mulroney, Coordinator, Membership Support
info@apics.ca

Association for Persons with Physical Disabilities of Windsor & Essex County *See* Assisted Living Southwestern Ontario

Association for Science & Reason (ASR)
Toronto ON
www.scienceandreason.ca
Previous Name: Skeptics Canada
Overview: A small national organization
Mission: To promote the understanding and application of critical thinking skills and scientific methodology in the explanation of human experience - from the seemingly mundane to the alleged paranormal.

Association for the Advancement of Scandinavian Studies in Canada (AASSC) / L'association pour l'avancement des études scandinaves au Canada
3270 Albert St., Regina SK S4S 3N9
aassc.com
Overview: A small national organization founded in 1982
Mission: AASSC is an association for research in Canada on all aspects of life in the Scandinavian societies. It provides a multi-disciplinary forum for the presentation of papers on all matters relevant to Scandinavia.
Member of: Canadian Federation for the Humanities & Social Sciences
Finances: *Annual Operating Budget:* Less than $50,000; *Funding Sources:* Membership fees, donations, Canadian Institute of Nordic Studies
Membership: 150; *Fees:* $50 regular; $50 institutional; $30 retired; $25 student; *Member Profile:* Academics; students; interested members of the community
Activities: Scholarly research of Scandinavian topics & dissemination of its results
Chief Officer(s):
Natalie van Deusen, President
vandeuse@ualberta.ca
Publications:
• Association for the Advancement of Scandanavian Studies in Canada

Type: Newsletter; *Editor:* Erin McGuire; *Price:* Free for members
Profile: Eighteen volumes, available in digital format from vol. 15 on, in a searchable database
- Scandinavian-Canandian Studies
Type: Journal; *Price:* Free for members
Profile: Eighteen volumes, available in digital format from vol. 15 on, in a searchable database

Association for the Export of Canadian Books *See* Livres Canada Books

Association for the Hearing Handicapped *See* Connect Society - D.E.A.F. Services

Association for the Rehabilitation of the Brain Injured (ARBI)
3412 Spruce Dr. SW, Calgary AB T3C 3A4
Tel: 403-242-7116; *Fax:* 403-242-7478
info@arbi.ca
arbi.ca
twitter.com/arbi_ca
Overview: A medium-sized provincial charitable organization founded in 1972
Mission: To improve the quality of life of individuals with severe acquired brain injury through long-term personalized rehabilitation
Finances: *Funding Sources:* United Way; Calgary Health Region; service clubs; foundations; individual donations
Activities: Volleyball tournament; golf tournament; *Awareness Events:* Brain Injury Awareness Week, June; *Speaker Service:* Yes
Chief Officer(s):
Mary Ellen Neilson, Executive Director
Bruce Murray, President

The Association for the Soldiers of Israel (ASI)
#201, 788 Marlee Ave., Toronto ON M6B 3K1
Tel: 416-783-3053; *Fax:* 416-787-7496
Toll-Free: 800-433-6226
info@asicanada.org
asicanada.org
Also Known As: ASI Canada
Overview: A small international organization founded in 1971
Mission: To support the well-being of Israeli soldiers on active duty; to fund social, spiritual & recreational programs & facilities to ease the burden faced by young soldiers defending the Jewish homeland
Membership: 500-999
Activities: Mobile clubrooms; fitness rooms; synagogues on IDF bases; Spirit Program; Dignity Program; Lone Soliders program; Soliders in Transit program
Chief Officer(s):
Talia Klein Leighton, Administrator
talia.klein@asicanada.org

Association for the Study of Nationalities (ASN)
c/o Harriman Institute, Columbia University, 420 West 118th St., 12th Fl., New York NY 10027 USA
www.nationalities.org
www.facebook.com/Nationalities
twitter.com/ASN_Org
Overview: A small international organization
Mission: The Association for the Study of Nationalities (ASN) is the only scholarly association devoted to the study of ethnicity and nationalism from Europe to Eurasia.
Membership: *Fees:* US$70 individual; US$40 student; *Committees:* Program
Chief Officer(s):
Zsuzsa Csergo, President
csergo@queensu.ca
Ryan Kreider, Executive Director
rk2780@columbia.edu

Association for the Voice of Education in Quebec *Voir* Association pour la voix études au Québec

Association for Vaccine Damaged Children
67 Shier Dr., Winnipeg MB R3R 2H2
Overview: A small national organization founded in 1986
Mission: To inform parents of the risks of immunization; To support parents in any challenging situation with public health authorities
Chief Officer(s):
Mary James, Co-Founder
tjames4@shaw.ca

Association for Women's Residential Facilities *See* Adsum for Women & Children

Association forestière canadienne *See* Canadian Forestry Association

Association forestière canadienne du Nouveau-Brunswick *See* Canadian Forestry Association of New Brunswick

Association forestières du sud du Québec (ASFQ)
#100, 138, rue Wellington nord, Sherbrooke QC J1H 5C5
Tél: 819-562-3388
info@afsq.org
www.afsq.org
www.facebook.com/AssFCE
twitter.com/AFSudQuebec
Nom précédent: Regroupement des associations forestières régionales du Québec
Aperçu: *Dimension:* moyenne; *Envergure:* provinciale surveillé par Canadian Forestry Association
Membre(s) du bureau directeur:
Amélie Normand, Directrice générale, 819-562-3388 Ext. 28
amelie@afsq.org

L'Association française des municipalités de l'Ontario / Francophone Association of Municipalities of Ontario
#310, 1173, rue Cyrville, Ottawa ON K1J 7S6
Tél: 613-746-7707; *Téléc:* 613-746-8187
admin@afmo.on.ca
www.afmo.on.ca
Aperçu: *Dimension:* petite; *Envergure:* provinciale; fondée en 1989
Mission: De revendiquer le maintien et l'amélioration de la gouvernance et de la prestation des services municipaux en français et en anglais dans les régions de l'Ontario désignées en vertu de la Loi sur les services en français de l'Ontario.
Membre(s) du personnel: 2
Membre: 35 corporations, 47 membres associés
Membre(s) du bureau directeur:
Jacqueline Noiseux, Directrice générale
dg@afmo.on.ca

Association franco-culturelle de Hay River
CP 4482, 77A, rue Woodland, Hay River NT X0E 1G2
Tél: 867-674-3171
afchr.ca
www.facebook.com/AssociationFrancoCulturelleDeHayRiver
Aperçu: *Dimension:* petite; *Envergure:* locale; fondée en 1987 surveillé par Fédération franco-ténoise
Mission: Pour représenter la communauté francophone de Hay River et de défendre leurs droits
Membre(s) du bureau directeur:
Christian Girard, Président

Association franco-culturelle de Yellowknife (AFCY)
CP 1586, Succ. Principale, 5016, 48 rue, Yellowknife NT X1A 2P2
Tél: 867-873-3292; *Téléc:* 867-873-2158
dgafcy@franco-nord.com
afcy.info
www.facebook.com/afcy.yellowknife
twitter.com/AFCYTNO
Aperçu: *Dimension:* petite; *Envergure:* locale; fondée en 1985 surveillé par Fédération franco-ténoise
Membre(s) du personnel: 2
Membre: *Montant de la cotisation:* 20$ individuel; 30$ famille
Activités: Musique; théâtre; arts visuels; événements communautaires
Membre(s) du bureau directeur:
Pascaline Gréau, Direction générale

Association francophone à l'éducation des services à l'enfance de l'Ontario (AFÉSEO)
#222. 135, rue Alice, Ottawa ON K1L 7X5
Tél: 613-741-5107; *Téléc:* 613-746-6140
communications@afeseo.ca
afeseo.ca
www.facebook.com/245498925585517
Aperçu: *Dimension:* moyenne; *Envergure:* provinciale; fondée en 1991
Mission: Pour aider les personnes en Ontario qui ont un intérêt dans l'éducation de la petite enfance
Membre de: Canadian Child Care Federation
Membre: *Montant de la cotisation:* $25 étudiant; $75 individuel; $175 corporatif
Membre(s) du bureau directeur:
Martine St-Engo, Directrice générale
Bianca Nugent, Agente en communications

Association francophone des municipalités du Nouveau-Brunswick Inc. (AFMNB)
#322, 702, rue Principale, Petit-Rocher NB E8J 1V1
Tél: 506-542-2622; *Téléc:* 506-542-2618
Ligne sans frais: 888-236-2622
afmnb@afmnb.org
www.afmnb.org
www.facebook.com/afmnb
www.twitter.com/AFMNB
Nom précédent: Association des municipalités du Nouveau-Brunswick
Aperçu: *Dimension:* moyenne; *Envergure:* provinciale; fondée en 1989
Mission: Promouvoir le développement des municipalités francophones du Nouveau-Brunswick
Affiliation(s): Association internationale des maires et responsables des capitales et métropoles partiellement ou entièrement francophones; Fédération canadienne des municipalités; Union des municipalités régionales de comté et des municipalités locales du Québec
Finances: *Budget de fonctionnement annuel:* $50,000-$100,000
Membre(s) du personnel: 3
Membre: 48 municipalités; *Montant de la cotisation:* 750$ - 3,500$; *Comités:* Formation et spéciaux
Activités: Relations gouvernementales; Porteur de dossiers contribuant au développement des municipalités francophones du Nouveau-Brunswick; *Stagiaires:* Oui; *Listes de destinataires:* Oui; *Bibliothèque:* Centre de documentation; Bibliothèque publique
Membre(s) du bureau directeur:
Frédérick Dion, Directeur général
direction@afmnb.org
Roger Doiron, Président

Association francophone des parents du Nouveau-Brunswick (AFPNB)
#201C, 835, rue Champlain, Dieppe NB E1A 1P6
Tél: 506-859-8107; *Téléc:* 506-859-7191
Ligne sans frais: 888-369-9955
www.facebook.com/AFPNB1
Nom précédent: Comité de parents du Nouveau-Brunswick
Aperçu: *Dimension:* petite; *Envergure:* provinciale; Organisme sans but lucratif; fondée en 1988
Mission: Est l'organisme porte-parole des parents acadiens et francophones du NB sur toutes les questions concernant le mieux-être de ses enfants et de la jeunesse
Membre de: Commission nationale des parents francophones
Affiliation(s): Forum de concertation des organismes acadiens
Finances: *Budget de fonctionnement annuel:* $250,000-$500,000; *Fonds:* Min. de l'Éducation; Patrimoine canadien; Min. des Affaires intergouvernementales
Membre(s) du personnel: 3; 15 bénévole(s)
Membre: 1 000; *Critères d'admissibilite:* Parents et autres personnes intéressés par l'éducation et la petite enfance
Activités: *Événements de sensibilisation:* Semaine d'appréciation de l'éducation fév.
Prix, Bourses:
- Prix des Parents
Décerné à une personne ou un groupe de personnes qui par leurs actions quotidiennes perpétuent une meilleure qualité de vie en milieu francophone
- Prix de la Commission nationale des parents francophones
Reconnaît une personne qui a oeuvré au sein des comit,s de parents; pour encourager et renforcer l'engagement et la solidarité des parents et de la communauté; pour permettre l'épanouissement de l'enfant et de sa famille; pour promouvoir la langue et la culture française

Association francophone pour le savoir (ACFAS)
425, rue de la Gauchetière, Montréal QC H2L 2M7
Tél: 514-849-0045; *Téléc:* 514-849-5558
www.acfas.ca
linkedin.com/company/acfas---association-francophone-pour-le-savoir
www.facebook.com/Acfas/
twitter.com/_Acfas
Nom précédent: Association canadienne française pour l'avancement des sciences
Aperçu: *Dimension:* moyenne; *Envergure:* nationale; fondée en 1923
Mission: Promouvoir et soutenir la science et la technologie pour encourager le développement culturel et économique de la société
Finances: *Budget de fonctionnement annuel:* $500,000-$1.5 Million; *Fonds:* Fonds de recherche du Québec, Partenariats, Autofinancement

Canadian Associations / Association franco-yukonnaise (AFY)

Membre(s) du personnel: 12
Membre: 2900+; *Montant de la cotisation:* 50$, 25$ pour étudiants; *Comités:* Le bénévolat; la recherche au collégial comité de réflexion sur l'avenir du congrès; d'orientation des journées de la relève en recherche; des prix de l'ACFAS
Activités: *Stagiaires:* Oui
Membre(s) du bureau directeur:
Esther Gaudreault, Directrice générale, 514-849-0045 Ext. 232
esther.gaudreault@acfas.ca
Isabelle Gandilhon, Conseillère principale, 514-849-0045 Ext. 222
isabelle.gandilhon@acfas.ca
Prix, Bourses:
• Prix J.-Armand-Bombardier
Award for technological innovation; *Amount:* $2,500
• Prix Léo-Pariseau
Award for biological or health sciences; *Amount:* $2,500
• Prix Marcel-Vincent
Award for social sciences; sponsored by Bell Canada; *Amount:* $2,500
• Prix Urgel-Archambault
Award for physics, mathematics or engineering; sponsored by Alcan; *Amount:* $2,500
• Prix Desjardins d'excellence étudiants-chercheurs
For master's or doctoral students; sponsored by the Fondation Desjardins; *Amount:* Three awards of $2,500
• Prix Bernard-Belleau
Award for doctoral student in health or pharmaceuticals; *Amount:* $2,500
• Prix Michel-Jurdant
Award recognizes research in environmental sciences; sponsored by Hydro-Québec; *Amount:* $2,500
Publications:
• Avis et mémoires
Type: Magazine; *Frequency:* irrégulier; *Price:* Gratuit
Profile: Contient opinions et des informations sur les questions concernant l'avenir de la recherche dans l'enseignement supérieur au Québec et au Canada
• Consultations
Type: Bulletin; *Frequency:* irrégulier; *Price:* Gratuit
Profile: Permet aux membres de l'ACFAS et toute personne intéressée par l'ACFAS à envoyer leurs opinions sur la politique du gouvernement envers recherche et l'innovation
• Découvrir
Type: Magazine; *Frequency:* irrégulier; *Price:* Gratuit
Profile: Un forum accessible pour les chercheurs de présenter leurs travaux
• Savoirs
Type: Bulletin; *Frequency:* mensuel; *Price:* Gratuit
Profile: Une source d'association nouvelles et des informations pour les membres

Association franco-yukonnaise (AFY)
302, rue Strickland, Whitehorse YT Y1A 2K1
Tél: 867-668-2663; *Téléc:* 867-663-3511
afy@afy.yk.ca
www.afy.yk.ca
www.facebook.com/AFY.Yukon
Aperçu: *Dimension:* petite; *Envergure:* provinciale; Organisme sans but lucratif; fondée en 1982 surveillé par Fédération des communautés francophones et acadienne du Canada
Mission: D'offrir plusieurs activités sociales, culturelles et artistiques
Membre de: Fédération culturelle canadienne-française; Fédération canadienne pour l'alphabétisation en français; Fédération de la jeunesse canadienne-française
Affiliation(s): Chambre de commerce du Yukon et de Whitehorse
Finances: *Fonds:* Bureau des services en français; Développement des ressources humaines du Canada; sports et récréati
Membre(s) du personnel: 22
Activités: *Service de conférenciers:* Oui
Membre(s) du bureau directeur:
Isabelle Salesse, Directrice générale, 867-668-2663 Ext. 328
isalesse@afy.yk.ca

Association Frontière Hors Taxes *See* Frontier Duty Free Association

Association Gaspé-Jersey & Guernesey
CP 6004, Gaspé QC G4X 1A0
Courriel: gaspejga@gogaspe.com
www.gogaspe.com/gcis
Aperçu: *Dimension:* petite; *Envergure:* locale; fondée en 2002
Membre: *Montant de la cotisation:* 15$

Membre(s) du bureau directeur:
Suzanne Mauger, Présidente
Publications:
• L'Anglo-Normand
Type: Newsletter

Association généalogique de la Nouvelle-Écosse *See* Genealogical Association of Nova Scotia

Association générale des insuffisants rénaux (AGIR)
4865, boul Gouin est, Montréal QC H1G 1A1
Tél: 514-852-9297; *Téléc:* 514-323-1231
Ligne sans frais: 888-852-9297
reins@agir.ca
www.agir.ca
www.facebook.com/groups/assoagir
Aperçu: *Dimension:* moyenne; *Envergure:* provinciale; fondée en 1979
Mission: Pour soutenir les personnes atteintes de maladies rénales et qui ont eu des greffes de rein et pour aider à améliorer leur vie
Membre de: Office des personnes handicapées du Québec
Membre: *Critères d'admissibilité:* Professionels de la santé, insuffisant rénal, sympathisants; *Comités:* Bien-être des patients; Levées de fonds; Activités sociales; Bon d'organes
Membre(s) du bureau directeur:
Berthe Martin, Directrice générale

Association géologique du Canada *See* Geological Association of Canada

Association G.R.A.N.D.
#1, 12, Place du Parc, Westmount QC H3Z 2K5
Tél: 514-846-0574
Aperçu: *Dimension:* petite; *Envergure:* locale
Mission: Aider des grands-parents et des petits-enfants créent et se maintiennenet un lien

Association gymnastique du Nouveau-Brunswick *See* New Brunswick Gymnastics Association

Association Hereford du Québec
162, rue des Érables, Ste-Catharine-de-la-Jacques-Cartier QC G3N 1A7
Tél: 418-875-2343
CCRBQ@hotmail.com
www.herefordquebec.ca
Aperçu: *Dimension:* petite; *Envergure:* provinciale; fondée en 1950
Membre de: Canadian Hereford Association
Membre: 250; *Montant de la cotisation:* 85$
Membre(s) du bureau directeur:
André Beaumont, Secrétaire

Association historique de Westmount *See* Westmount Historical Association

Association Horatio Alger du Canada *See* Horatio Alger Association of Canada

Association Hôtellerie Québec (AHQ)
#100, 450, ch de Chambly, Longueuil QC J4H 3L7
Tél: 579-721-6215; *Téléc:* 579-721-3663
Ligne sans frais: 877-769-9776
info@hotelleriequebec.org
www.hotelleriequebec.com
www.facebook.com/HoteliersQuebecAHQ
Nom précédent: Association des hôteliers du Québec
Aperçu: *Dimension:* moyenne; *Envergure:* provinciale; Organisme sans but lucratif; fondée en 1949 surveillé par Hotel Association of Canada Inc.
Mission: Regrouper les établissements hôteliers pour les représenter, défendre leurs intérêts et leurs fournir des services et ce, tout en collaborant au développement de la qualité de la profession hôtelière et de l'industrie touristique en général
Membre de: Chambre de commerce du Québec; Hotel Association of Canada
Finances: *Budget de fonctionnement annuel:* $250,000-$500,000
Membre(s) du personnel: 3
Membre: 540; *Critères d'admissibilité:* Hôtelier/associés
Membre(s) du bureau directeur:
Benoit Sirard, Président

Association indépendante des employés de soutien *See* Independent Association of Support Staff

Association industrielle de l'est de Montréal
#412, 11370, rue Notre-Dame est, Montréal QC H1B 2W6

Tél: 514-645-8111
www.aiem.qc.ca
Aperçu: *Dimension:* petite; *Envergure:* locale; fondée en 1960
Mission: Contribuer à l'harmonisation des activités industrielles de ses membres avec leur environnement physique et communautaire
Membre: 13; *Critères d'admissibilité:* Entreprises de l'est de l'Ile de Montréal qui sont actives dans les secteurs industriels du raffinage de pétrole, de la pétrochimie et de la métallurgie

L'Association Interac *See* Interac Association

Association internationale d'orientation scolaire et professionnelle *See* International Association for Educational & Vocational Guidance

Association internationale de communicateurs professionels *See* International Association of Business Communicators

Association internationale de science politique *See* International Political Science Association

Association internationale des Critiques d'art - Canada *See* International Association of Art Critics - Canada

Association internationale des études québécoises
#830, 900, boul René-Lévesque est, Québec QC G1R 2B5
Tél: 418-528-7560
accueil@aieq.qc.ca
www.aieq.qc.ca
www.facebook.com/aieq.qc.ca
Aperçu: *Dimension:* moyenne; *Envergure:* internationale; fondée en 1997
Mission: Soutient les activités sur la recherche québécoise partout dans le monde
Membre: *Montant de la cotisation:* 70$ membre régulier Québec; 50$ membre régulier hors Québec; 35$ membre étudiant Québec; 25$ membre étudiant hors Québec
Membre(s) du bureau directeur:
Miléna Santoro, Présidente

L'Association internationale des machinistes et des travailleurs et travailleuses de l'aérospatiale *See* International Association of Machinists & Aerospace Workers

Association internationale des maires francophones - Bureau à Québec (AIMF)
CP 700, Succ. Haute-Ville, #312, 2, rue des Jardins, Québec QC G1R 4S9
Tél: 418-641-6188; *Téléc:* 418-641-6437
Aperçu: *Dimension:* moyenne; *Envergure:* internationale; Organisme sans but lucratif
Mission: Favoriser les échanges et la coopérations entre les villes membres
Finances: *Budget de fonctionnement annuel:* $3 Million-$5 Million
Membre: 1-99
Membre(s) du bureau directeur:
Régis Labeaume

Association Internationale pour le Développement de l'Apnée Canada
967, av Rockland, Outremont QC H2V 3A3
Tel: 780-399-4998
www.aidacanada.org
www.facebook.com/AidaCanada
twitter.com/aidacanada
Also Known As: AIDA Canada
Overview: A large national organization founded in 2009
Mission: To develop the sport of freediving in Canada as both a pastime & an athletic pursuit
Affiliation(s): AIDA International
Finances: *Funding Sources:* Membership dues; Donations
Membership: *Fees:* $25; *Member Profile:* Freedivers; *Committees:* Competition; Social Media; Website
Activities: Supporting freediving clubs across Canada; Offering information & resources for members; Organizing competitions
Chief Officer(s):
Roberta Cenedese, President

Association Jeannoise pour l'intégration sociale inc. (AJIS)
CP 53, Roberval QC G8H 2N4
Tél: 418-275-1360
ajis53@hotmail.com
Aperçu: *Dimension:* petite; *Envergure:* locale
Affiliation(s): Association du Québec pour l'intégration sociale
Membre(s) du bureau directeur:

Marie-Claude Dallaire, Responsable

Association jeunesse fransaskoise (AJF) / Saskatchewan Francophone Youth Association
2320 av Louise, Saskatoon SK S7J 3M7
Tél: 306-653-7447; *Téléc:* 306-653-7448
Ligne sans frais: 855-253-1225
info@ajf.ca
www.ajf.ca
www.facebook.com/AJFransaskoise
twitter.com/AJFransaskoise
www.flickr.com/photos/ajfhardis/collections
Aperçu: *Dimension:* petite; *Envergure:* nationale; Organisme sans but lucratif; fondée en 1977
Mission: L'Association jeunesse fransaskoise est l'organisme voué à l'épanouissement de la jeunesse, au développement du leadership et de l'identité fransaskois
Membre de: Fédération de la jeunesse canadienne-française inc.
Finances: *Budget de fonctionnement annuel:* $250,000-$500,000
Membre(s) du personnel: 8; 40 bénévole(s)
Membre: 400; *Critères d'admissibilite:* Jeunes fransaskois(es) entre 14 et 25 ans; *Comités:* Conseil d'administration
Activités: Parlement jeunesse fransaskois; parlement franco-canadien du Nord et de l'Ouest; équipe Saskatchewan; jeux fransaskois; sports et loisirs
Membre(s) du bureau directeur:
Julien Gaudet, Directeur général
direction@ajf.ca

Association littéraire et artistique canadienne inc. *See* Canadian Literary & Artistic Association

Association longueuilloise des photographes amateurs (ALPA)
Centre Culturel Jacques-Ferron, 100, boul St-Laurent ouest, Longueuil QC J4H 1M1
Tél: 450-463-9699
info@alpaphoto.ca
alpaphoto.ca
www.facebook.com/alpaphoto
twitter.com/alpaphoto
Aperçu: *Dimension:* petite; *Envergure:* locale
Mission: D'inspirer de nouveaux artistes et de partager leur travail avec les personnes ainsi que d'accroître les connaissances de la photographie
Membre: *Montant de la cotisation:* 80$
Activités: Conférences de photographes; concours de photo; ateliers
Membre(s) du bureau directeur:
Mario Paquet, Président, Conseil d'administration
president@alpaphoto.ca

Association manitobaine des conseillers d'Orientation *See* Manitoba School Counsellors' Association

Association Marie-Reine de Chibougamau
CP 295, Chibougamau QC G8P 2K7
Tél: 418-748-4760
Aperçu: *Dimension:* petite; *Envergure:* locale
Mission: Aider les femmes & les enfants victimes de violence
Membre(s) du bureau directeur:
Marie-Paule Lévesque, Présidente

Association maritime du Québec (AMQ)
#200, 621, rue Stravinski, Brossard QC J4X 1Y7
Tél: 450-466-1777; *Téléc:* 450-768-5433
Ligne sans frais: 877-560-1777
info@nautismequebec.com
www.nautismequebec.com
www.linkedin.com/groups/4019040
www.facebook.com/associationmaritimeduquebec
twitter.com/AMQ_nautismeQc
www.flickr.com/photos/nautismequebec
Aperçu: *Dimension:* moyenne; *Envergure:* provinciale; Organisme sans but lucratif; fondée en 1996
Mission: Promouvoir la sécurité nautique; organiser des représentations et des séances d'information auprès des instances gouvernementales et de différents regroupements canadiens et américains
Finances: *Budget de fonctionnement annuel:* $250,000-$500,000
Membre(s) du personnel: 6; 7 bénévole(s)
Membre: 3 500; *Montant de la cotisation:* 30$ plaisanciers; 300$ corporatif; *Critères d'admissibilite:* Propriétaires de bateaux de plaisance et industrie nautique
Activités: Salon du bateau
Membre(s) du bureau directeur:
Alain Roy, Directeur général
aroy@nautismequebec.com

Association marketing canadienne de l'affichage *See* Out-of-Home Marketing Association of Canada

Association Marocaine de Toronto *See* Moroccan Association of Toronto

Association mathématique du Québec (AMQ)
a/s Département de didactique, Université de Montréal, CP 6128, Succ. Centre-ville, Montréal QC H3C 3J7
Tél: 514-278-4263; *Téléc:* 514-343-7286
info@amq.math.ca
archimede.mat.ulaval.ca/amq
Aperçu: *Dimension:* moyenne; *Envergure:* internationale; Organisme sans but lucratif; fondée en 1958
Membre: *Montant de la cotisation:* 68,99$ régulier; 40,24$ étudiant; 40,24$ retraité; 229,95$ institutoin; 86,23$ domiciliés à l'étranger; *Critères d'admissibilite:* Professeurs de mathématiques
Membre(s) du bureau directeur:
France Caron, Présidente
france.caron@umontreal.ca

Association médicale canadienne *See* Canadian Medical Association

Association médicale du Québec (AMQ) / Québec Medical Association (QMA)
#3200, 380, rue Saint-Antoine ouest, Montréal QC H2Y 3X7
Tél: 514-866-0660; *Téléc:* 514-866-0670
Ligne sans frais: 800-363-3932
admin@amq.ca
www.amq.ca
www.facebook.com/Association.medicale.du.Quebec
twitter.com/amquebec
Aperçu: *Dimension:* moyenne; *Envergure:* provinciale; Organisme sans but lucratif; fondée en 1922 surveillé par Canadian Medical Association
Mission: Rassembler et soutenir les médecins du Québec afin de garantir à la population québécoise des conditions et des soins de santé de qualité
Membre(s) du personnel: 12
Membre: 9 700; *Critères d'admissibilite:* Òtre médecin et être membre de la Corporation professionnelle des médecins du Québec; *Comités:* Affaires professionnelles; Formation; Regroupement des étudiants en médecine; Bureau des gouverneurs
Membre(s) du bureau directeur:
Normand Laberge, Directeur général
normand.laberge@amq.ca

Association médicale podiatrique canadienne *See* Canadian Podiatric Medical Association

Association minéralogique du Canada *See* Mineralogical Association of Canada

Association minière du Canada *See* Mining Association of Canada

Association minière du Québec (AMQ) / Québec Mining Association (QMA)
Place de la Cité - Tour Belle Cour, #720, 2590, boul Laurier, Québec QC G1V 4M6
Tél: 418-657-2016; *Téléc:* 418-657-2154
amq@amq-inc.com
www.amq-inc.com
Nom précédent: Association des mines de métaux du Québec inc.
Aperçu: *Dimension:* grande; *Envergure:* provinciale; Organisme sans but lucratif; fondée en 1936 surveillé par Mining Association of Canada
Mission: Promouvoir le développement de l'industrie des mines, de la métallurgie et des industries connexes; défendre les intérêts généraux de ses membres; soutenir les efforts de ses membres quant au bien-être, à la sécurité et à la prévention des accidents au travail
Finances: *Budget de fonctionnement annuel:* $500,000-$1.5 Million
Membre(s) du personnel: 9
Membre: 1-99; *Critères d'admissibilite:* Toutes les compagnies opérant dans le secteur minier ou dans un secteur connexe; *Comités:* Environnement; Prévention des accidents; Santé; Relations publiques; Fiscalité; Contrôle de terrain; Sauvetage minier (catamine); Entretien
Membre(s) du bureau directeur:
Claude Bélanger, Directeur générale
Prix, Bourses:
• Bourses d'études de l'industrie minière
• Bourses d'études supérieures Claude-Drouin pour la recherche
Meetings/Conferences:
• Association minière du Québec congrès annuel 2018, June, 2018, Fairmont Tremblant, Mont-Tremblant, QC
Scope: Provincial

Association mondiale pour la communication *See* World Association for Christian Communication

Association montérégienne de la surdité inc. (AMS)
#11, 125, rue Jacques-Cartier nord, Saint-Jean-sur-Richelieu QC J3B 6Z4
Tél: 450-346-6029; *Téléc:* 450-895-1010
amsinc2@hotmail.com
amsweb.ca
Nom précédent: Association des Sourds du Haut-Richelieu
Aperçu: *Dimension:* petite; *Envergure:* locale; Organisme sans but lucratif
Mission: Aider les personnes, de Montérégie, vivant avec une surdité et leurs proches; offrir des services pour briser l'isolement; promouvoir les droits de ces personnes; sensibiliser la population
Finances: *Budget de fonctionnement annuel:* Moins de $50,000
Membre: 1-99
Activités: Rencontres mensuelles sociales
Membre(s) du bureau directeur:
Esther Paradis, Présidente

Association montréalaise de science-fiction et de fantastique *See* Montréal Science Fiction & Fantasy Association

Association montréalaise des directions d'établissement scolaire (AMDES)
3751, rue Fleury est, Montréal QC H1H 2T2
Tél: 514-328-6990; *Téléc:* 514-328-9324
amdes@amdes.qc.ca
www.amdes.qc.ca
Nom précédent: Association des directeurs d'école de Montréal
Aperçu: *Dimension:* petite; *Envergure:* locale; fondée en 1942
Mission: Promouvoir et défendre les droits et les intérêts des membres; assurer le développement professionnel des membres; apporter une contribution significative à l'éducation
Membre(s) du personnel: 4
Membre(s) du bureau directeur:
Hélène Bourdages, Présidente

Association montréalaise pour les aveugles *See* Montréal Association for the Blind

Association motocycliste canadienne *See* Canadian Motorcycle Association

Association mototocycliste Chibougamau Chapais
CP 580, Chibougamau QC G8P 2Y8
Tél: 418-745-3765
amcc.e-monsite.com
Aperçu: *Dimension:* petite; *Envergure:* locale
Membre(s) du bureau directeur:
Jean-Paul Mercier, President
jpomercier@hotmail.com

Association multiculturelle de Fredericton Inc. *See* Multicultural Association of Fredericton

Association multiculturelle de la Nouvelle-Écosse *See* Multicultural Association of Nova Scotia

Association multiculturelle, Grand Moncton *See* Multicultural Association of the Greater Moncton Area

Association multi-ethnique pour l'intégration des personnes handicapées (AMEIPH) / Multi-Ethnic Association for the Integration of Persons with Disabilities
6462, boul St-Laurent, Montréal QC H2S 3C4
Tél: 514-272-0680; *Téléc:* 514-272-8530
ameiph@ameiph.com
www.ameiph.com
Aperçu: *Dimension:* moyenne; *Envergure:* provinciale; Organisme sans but lucratif; fondée en 1981
Mission: Intervenir pour faciliter l'intégration et l'amélioration de la qualité de vie des personnes handicapées issues de

Canadian Associations / Association Museums New Brunswick (AMNB) / Association des musées du Nouveau-Brunswick

l'immigration et des communautés ethnoculturelles, ainsi que les membres de leur famille, à travers l'intervention directe, la promotion des droits et la défense des intérêts et la concertation avec les différents organismes partenaires
Finances: *Budget de fonctionnement annuel:* $250,000-$500,000
Membre(s) du personnel: 10; 50+ bénévole(s)
Membre: 450; *Montant de la cotisation:* 5$ personnes handicapées et famille; 7$ associé; 25$ corporatif; 50$ de soutien; *Critères d'admissibilite:* Personnes handicapées d'origine ethnoculturelle
Activités: Journée Minorité inVISIBLE; *Evénements de sensibilisation:* Journée 'Minorité inVISIBLE'; *Stagiaires:* Oui; *Service de conférenciers:* Oui
Membre(s) du bureau directeur:
Luciana Soave, Directrice générale
Caddeo Caddeo, Director of Services
icaddeo@ameiph.com

Association Museums New Brunswick (AMNB) / Association des musées du Nouveau-Brunswick
668 Brunswick St., Fredericton NB E3B 1H6
Tel: 506-454-3561; *Fax:* 506-462-7687
info@amnb.ca
www.amnb.ca
www.facebook.com/AMNB2012
Overview: A medium-sized provincial charitable organization founded in 1974
Mission: To preserve New Brunswick's heritage by uniting, promoting & advancing our heritage workers, supporters & organizations
Member of: Canadian Museums Association
Affiliation(s): Canadian Heritage Information Network
Finances: *Annual Operating Budget:* $100,000-$250,000; *Funding Sources:* Provincial & federal governments; membership dues; donations & foundations
Staff Member(s): 2; 16 volunteer(s)
Membership: 126 individual + 70 corporate + 11 honorary + 84 museums; *Fees:* $35 institution; $25 individual; $20 associate; *Committees:* Advocacy; Awards; Membership; Professional Development
Activities: *Awareness Events:* New Brunswick Day Initiative; Heritage Week *Library:* Resource Centre/Centre de documentation; by appointment Not open to public
Chief Officer(s):
David Desjardins, President
Chantal Brideau, Administrative Officer
Awards:
- Certificate of Distinction
- Recognition of Achievement
- Award of Merit

Association nationale de la femme et du droit *See* National Association of Women & the Law

Association nationale des camionneurs artisans inc. (ANCAI)
#235, 670, rue Bouvier, Québec QC G2J 1A7
Tél: 418-623-7923; *Téléc:* 418-623-0448
infos@ancai.com
www.ancai.com
www.facebook.com/1134322149952494
Aperçu: *Dimension:* moyenne; *Envergure:* provinciale; fondée en 1966
Mission: Défendre les intérêts des transporteurs en vrac (gravier et forêts) auprès des gouvernements, organismes patronaux et entreprises privées
Membre(s) du personnel: 16
Membre: 5,000; *Montant de la cotisation:* $205; *Critères d'admissibilite:* Camionneur propriétaire de son véhicule; *Comités:* Négociations
Activités: Congrès annuel; Tirage camion
Membre(s) du bureau directeur:
Jean-Pierre Garand, Président
jp.garand@ancai.com
Gaétan Légaré, Directeur général
g.legare@ancai.com

Association nationale des Canadiens d'origine indienne *See* National Association of Canadians of Origins in India

Association nationale des centres d'amitié *See* National Association of Friendship Centres

Association nationale des collèges de carrières *See* National Association of Career Colleges

Association nationale des distributeurs aux petites surfaces alimentaires (ANDPSA) / National Convenience Stores Distributors Association (NACDA)
#410, 1695, boul Laval, Laval QC H7S 2M2
Toll-Free: 800-686-2823
nacda@nacda.ca
www.nacda.ca
Previous Name: Association nationale des distributeurs de tabac et de confiserie
Overview: A medium-sized national charitable organization founded in 1955
Mission: Promouvoir le bien-être et les intérêts de nos membres distributeurs-grossistes ainsi que de l'industrie
Finances: *Annual Operating Budget:* $500,000-$1.5 Million
Staff Member(s): 6
Membership: 1-99; *Fees:* 550$ - 1 650$; *Member Profile:* Grossistes-distributeurs et manufacturiers; *Committees:* Exécutif; Developpement des Affaires
Chief Officer(s):
Raymond Bouchard, Président du conseil d'administration
raymond.bouchard@metro.ca

Association nationale des distributeurs de tabac et de confiserie *See* Association nationale des distributeurs aux petites surfaces alimentaires

Association nationale des éditeurs de livres (ANEL)
2514, boul Rosemont, Montréal QC H1Y 1K4
Tél: 514-273-8130; *Téléc:* 514-273-9657
Ligne sans frais: 866-900-2635
info@anel.qc.ca
anel.qc.ca
www.facebook.com/61084204798
twitter.com/ANEL_QE
anel.qc.ca/blogue
Aperçu: *Dimension:* moyenne; *Envergure:* nationale; fondée en 1992
Mission: Soutenir le développement d'une industrie nationale de l'édition québécoise et canadienne de langue française; établir entre ses membres des rapports de bonne confraternité; étudier et défendre les intérêts tant généraux que politiques et économiques de ses membres; étudier toute question relative à la profession et diffuser l'information auprès de ses membres; constituer une représentation réelle et efficace de la profession à toute les instances pertinentes
Membre de: Union internationale des éditeurs (UIE)
Finances: *Budget de fonctionnement annuel:* $250,000-$500,000
Membre(s) du personnel: 9
Membre: 125 maisons d'éditions; *Montant de la cotisation:* 412,50$ - 4 290$; *Critères d'admissibilite:* 10 titres au catalogue minimum; propriété 100% canadienne; *Comités:* Finances; médiation; formation et services aux membres; promotion du livre; édition scolaire; Québec Édition
Activités: *Stagiaires:* Oui; *Service de conférenciers:* Oui; *Bibliothèque:* rendez-vous
Membre(s) du bureau directeur:
Jean-François Bouchard, Président
Richard Prieur, Directeur général

Association nationale des entreprises en recrutement et placement de personnel *See* Association of Canadian Search, Employment & Staffing Services

Association nationale des étudiant(e)s handicapé(e)s au niveau postsecondaire *See* National Educational Association of Disabled Students

Association nationale des ferblantiers et couvreurs, section locale 2020 *Voir* Syndicat interprovincial des ferblantiers et couvreurs, la section locale 2016

Association nationale des ferblantiers et couvreurs, section locale 2020 (CTC) *Voir* Syndicat interprovincial des ferblantiers et couvreurs, la section locale 2016 à la FTQ-Construction

Association nationale des gestionnaires des terres autochones *See* National Aboriginal Lands Managers Association

Association nationale des grands usagers postaux inc. *See* National Association of Major Mail Users, Inc.

Association nationale des organismes de réglementation de la pharmacie *See* National Association of Pharmacy Regulatory Authorities

Association nationale des orthésistes du pied *Voir* Association des orthésistes et prothésistes du Québec

Association nationale des peintres - locale 99 / National Association of Painters - Local 99
#202, 8300, boul Métropolitain est, Anjou QC H1K 1A2
Tél: 438-382-9990; *Téléc:* 438-383-9991
Ligne sans frais: 855-382-9990
www.local99.ca
www.facebook.com/ftqlocal99
twitter.com/ftqlocal99
Aperçu: *Dimension:* moyenne; *Envergure:* provinciale; Organisme sans but lucratif; fondée en 1984
Mission: Aider nos membres dans leur métier; faire respecter les conventions collectives sur les chantiers
Affiliation(s): Fédération des travailleuses et travailleurs du Québec - Construction
Membre(s) du personnel: 3
Membre: 1 756; *Critères d'admissibilite:* Peintre en bâtiment

L'Association nationale des propriétaires de terrains de golf du Canada *See* National Golf Course Owners Association Canada

Association nationale des radio étudiantes et communautaires *See* National Campus & Community Radio Association

Association nationale des retraités fédéraux *See* National Association of Federal Retirees

Association nationale des revêtements de sol *See* National Floor Covering Association

L'association néo-brunswickoise de massothérapeutes *See* Association of New Brunswick Massage Therapists

Association nucléaire canadienne *See* Canadian Nuclear Association

Association of Academic Staff - University of Alberta (AAS-UA) / Association du personnel enseignant de l'Université de l'Alberta
University of Alberta, 1600 College Plaza, 8215 - 112 St., Edmonton AB T6G 2C8
Tel: 780-492-5321; *Fax:* 780-492-7449
reception@ualberta.ca
www.aasua.ca
Overview: A small local organization founded in 1950
Mission: To act as the negotiating & administering body for contract agreements between its members & the university governors
Affiliation(s): Canadian Association of University Teachers
Finances: *Funding Sources:* Membership dues
Staff Member(s): 8
Membership: 4,429 individual; *Committees:* Economic Benefits; Equity; Finance; Governance; Members' Advisory; Personnel; Research & Scholarly Activity; Salary; Teaching & Learning; Academic Faculty; Academic Librarians; Administrative & Professional Officers; Contract Academic Staff: Teaching; Faculty Service Officers; Sessionals & Other Temporary Staff; Trust/Research Academic Staff; Copyright; Other Intellectual Property; Nominating; Renaissance
Chief Officer(s):
Kevin Kane, President
kevin.kane@ualberta.ca
Brygeda Renke, Executive Director
brygeda.renke@aasua.ca

Association of Accrediting Agencies of Canada (AAAC) / Association des agences d'agrément du Canada (AAAC)
PO Box 370, #3, 247 Barr St., Renfrew ON K7V 1J6
Tel: 613-432-9491; *Fax:* 613-432-6840
info@aaac.ca
www.aaac.ca
Overview: A small national organization
Mission: Pursues excellence in standards and processes of accreditation to foster the highest quality of professional education.
Membership: *Fees:* $750 for all member agencies
Chief Officer(s):
Bob Cross, Executive Director
bobcross@aaac.ca

Association of Administrative & Professional Staff - University of British Columbia (AAPS-UBC)
Tef III Building, #208, 6190 Agronomy Rd., Vancouver BC V6T 1Z3

Tel: 604-822-9025; Fax: 604-822-4699
aaps.office@ubc.ca
www.aaps.ubc.ca
Overview: A small local organization founded in 1977
Mission: To negotiate terms & conditions of employment on behalf of its members with the university administration
Staff Member(s): 5
Membership: 3,700+; *Member Profile:* Administrative & professional staff at UBC; *Committees:* Advocacy; Communications; Professional Development; Bargaining; Finance; Member Engangement
Chief Officer(s):
Joey Hansen, Executive Director, 604-822-8230
joey.hansen@ubc.ca

Association of Administrative Assistants *See* Association of Administrative Professionals

Association of Administrative Professionals (AAP) / Association des professionnels de l'administration
PO Box 114, 5589 Rd. 38, Hartington ON K0H 1W0
Tel: 905-580-7855
contact@aaa.ca
www.aaa.ca
www.linkedin.com/in/association-of-administrative-assistants-41a3563a
www.facebook.com/AAACanada
twitter.com/canada_aaa
Previous Name: Association of Administrative Assistants
Overview: A medium-sized national organization founded in 1951
Mission: To promote the professional growth & advancement of members; To assist members in the continuing development of administrative skills
Finances: *Annual Operating Budget:* Less than $50,000; *Funding Sources:* Membership fees; branch-level fundraising 45 volunteer(s)
Membership: 200+; *Fees:* $156 per annum; *Member Profile:* Persons with appropriate experience & education as administrative assistants, coordinators, office administrators, board liaisons, office managers, & senior secretaries
Activities: Q.A.A. (Qualified Administrative Assistant) Program offered at colleges & universities across Canada
Chief Officer(s):
Katherine Vaillancourt, National Director-President
aap.national.president@gmail.com
Jackie Pontin, National Director-Past President
aap.national.pastpresident@gmail.com
Bridget Cochrane, National Director-Registrar
aap.national.registrar@gmail.com

Association of Administrators of English Schools of Québec (AAESQ) / Association des administrateurs des écoles anglaises du Québec
#5, 17035, boul Brunswick, Montréal QC H9H 5G6
Tel: 514-426-5110; Fax: 514-426-5109
www.aaesq.ca
Overview: A small provincial charitable organization founded in 1998
Mission: To act as the negotiating body, on behalf of its members, with educational authorities regarding salary, working conditions & fringe benefits. It also a regluating body, maintaining adequate qualifications & training in educational administration.
Affiliation(s): Canadian Association of Principals; Canadian Association of School Administrators
Staff Member(s): 5
Membership: 475; *Member Profile:* Board-level administrators; in-school administrators
Activities: *Internships:* Yes
Chief Officer(s):
Jim Jordan, President
Ron Silverstone, Executive Director

Association of Alberta Agricultural Fieldmen (AAAF)
c/o Municipal District of Rocky View, 911 - 32nd Ave. NE, Calgary AB T2E 6X6
Tel: 403-230-1401
info@aaaf.ab.ca
www.aaaf.ab.ca
www.facebook.com/175905085771203
twitter.com/aaafieldmen
Overview: A small provincial organization
Mission: Committed to the enhancement, promotion & protection of the agricultural resources of Alberta
Finances: *Annual Operating Budget:* Less than $50,000

Membership: 107; *Fees:* $125; *Member Profile:* Agricultural fieldmen develop, implement, and control programs that adhere to the priorities and policies set by the Agricultural Service Board across the province; *Committees:* Education; Policy; Soils; Weed Control
Chief Officer(s):
Jason Storch, President, 403-526-2888
Stephen Majek, Secretary-Treasurer, 780-352-3321

Association of Alberta Coordinated Action for Recycling Enterprises
5212 - 49 St., Leduc AB T9E 7H5
Tel: 780-980-0035; Fax: 780-980-0232
Toll-Free: 866-818-2273
www.albertacare.org
Also Known As: Alberta CARE
Overview: A medium-sized provincial organization founded in 2010
Mission: To support waste management & recycling activities at the community level in Alberta
Membership: *Fees:* $52.50 associate, non-voting membership; $105 non-profit; $262.50 corporate; $272 goverment; $105-$525 municipality, based on population; *Member Profile:* Non-profit organizations; Governments; Municipalities; Businesses
Activities: Organizing partnerships; Establishing & operating programs such as Electronic Waste Recycling, Regional Concrete & Asphalt Crushing, Regional Scrap Metals Recycling, Alberta CARE Ink Recycle, Paper Fibre Recycling, Fluorescent Tube Recycling, Wood Waste Grinding
Chief Officer(s):
Linda McDonald, Executive Director
executivedirector@albertacare.org
Publications:
- Reuse / Recycle Directory
Type: Directory; *Number of Pages:* 122
Profile: A list of organizations & companies that offer alternatives to throwing garbage in landfills

Association of Allied Health Professionals: Newfoundland & Labrador (Ind.) (AAHP) / Association des professionnels unis de la santé: Terre-Neuve et Labrador (ind.)
6 Mount Carson Ave., Mount Pearl NL A1N 3K4
Tel: 709-722-3353; Fax: 709-722-0987
Toll-Free: 800-728-2247
info@aahp.nf.ca
www.aahp.nf.ca
Overview: A small provincial organization founded in 1975

Association of Applied Geochemists (AEG)
PO Box 26099, 72 Robertson Rd., Nepean ON K2H 9R0
Tel: 613-828-0199; Fax: 613-828-9288
office@appliedgeochemists.org
www.appliedgeochemists.org
Previous Name: Association of Exploration Geochemists
Overview: A medium-sized international organization founded in 1970
Mission: To promote interest in the applications of geochemistry to mineral & petroleum exploration, resource evaluation & related fields
Affiliation(s): International Union of Geological Sciences (IUGS)
Finances: *Annual Operating Budget:* $50,000-$100,000; *Funding Sources:* Membership dues; publisher rebates
Staff Member(s): 2; 70 volunteer(s)
Membership: 650; *Fees:* US$100; *Committees:* New Membership; Admissions; Awards and Medals; Education; Symposia
Activities: *Speaker Service:* Yes
Chief Officer(s):
David R. Cohen, President
Betty Arseneault, Business Manager

Association of Architects in Private Practice of Québec *Voir* Association des Architectes en pratique privée du Québec

Association of Architectural Technologists of Ontario (AATO)
#38, 2355 Derry Rd. East, Mississauga ON L5S 1V6
Tel: 905-405-0840; Fax: 905-405-9882
Toll-Free: 866-805-2286
aato@bellnet.ca
aato.on.ca
Overview: A medium-sized provincial organization founded in 1969
Mission: To maintain the standard of professional conduct of its members, as well as advocates to all levels of government on behalf of them & the industry.

Finances: *Funding Sources:* Membership fees; advertisements
Membership: *Fees:* $220 accredited; $190 interns; $35 students; *Member Profile:* Architectural technologists & technicians; building technologists & technicians in Ontario; *Committees:* Annual General Meeting; Board of Examiners; By-law Review, Ethics & Professional Practice; Certification Board; Education; External Affiliations; Membership Services; Newsletter; Private Practice; Student Membership; Web Site
Activities: Chapter meetings; accreditation exams; information seminars; networking; referral services; professional recognition; advocacy; *Internships:* Yes; *Speaker Service:* Yes
Chief Officer(s):
Sharon Creasor, President
Awards:
- Recognition Awards
- Chapter Chair Awards
- AATO Student Awards Program

  Hamilton-Niagara Chapter
  Hamilton ON
  Mission: The chapter is not active at this time.

  London Chapter
  London ON
  London@aato.ca
  Chief Officer(s):
  Jim Dodge, Chair
  jkjdodge@hotmail.com

  Ottawa Chapter
  Ottawa ON
  aato.ottawa@gmail.com
  www.aato-ottawa.ca
  www.facebook.com/aatoottawachapter
  Chief Officer(s):
  Greg Leese, Chair

  Sudbury Chapter
  Sudbury ON
  Sudbury@aato.ca
  Mission: This chapter is not active at this time.

  Thousand Islands Chapter
  Kingston ON
  Mission: Chapter is not active at this time.

  Toronto Central Chapter
  Toronto ON
  TorontoCentral@aato.ca
  Chief Officer(s):
  Denis Heroux, Interim Secretary

  Toronto East Chapter
  Toronto ON
  TorontoEast@aato.ca
  Chief Officer(s):
  Ron Bourdon, Chair

  Toronto West Chapter
  Toronto ON
  TorontoWest@aato.ca
  Chief Officer(s):
  Alonzo Jones, Chair

Association of Atlantic Universities (AAU) / Association des universités de l'Atlantique
#403, 5657 Spring Garden Rd., Halifax NS B3J 3R4
Tel: 902-425-4230; Fax: 902-425-4233
info@atlanticuniversities.ca
www.atlanticuniversities.ca
twitter.com/aau_aua
Overview: A medium-sized provincial organization founded in 1964 overseen by Universities Canada
Mission: To assist in assuring the quality & coordination of higher education in Atlantic Provinces; to provide a forum for university administrators to discuss & coordinate their views, interests & concerns in support of higher education in the Atlantic provinces
Member of: Universities Canada
Finances: *Funding Sources:* Membership fees
Staff Member(s): 3
Membership: 16 universities; *Member Profile:* Universities & colleges
Chief Officer(s):
Peter Halpin, Executive Director, 902-425-4238

Association of Auto Part Recyclers *Voir* Association des recycleurs de pièces d'autos et de camions

Association of Battlefords Realtors
8916 - 19th Ave., North Battleford SK S9A 2V9
Tel: 306-445-6300; Fax: 306-445-9020
bfords.realestate@sasktel.net

Overview: A small local organization overseen by Saskatchewan Real Estate Association
Mission: To advance & promote interest of those engaged in real estate as brokers, agents, valuators, examiners & experts; To increase public confidence in & respect for those engaged in real estate
Member of: The Canadian Real Estate Association
Finances: Annual Operating Budget: $50,000-$100,000
Membership: 33 individuals
Chief Officer(s):
Rick Cann, Executive Officer

Association of BC Drama Educators (ABCDE)
c/o BC Teachers' Federation, #100, #550 West 6 Ave., Vancouver BC V5Z 4P2
Tel: 604-871-2283; Fax: 604-871-2286
Toll-Free: 800-663-9163
www.bcdramateachers.com
twitter.com/BCDRAMATEACHERS
Overview: A small provincial organization
Mission: To provide help drama teachers with guidance, resources & communication
Member of: BC Teachers' Federation
Chief Officer(s):
Lana O'Brien, President
lobrien@sd22.bc.ca
Christine Knight, Director, Communications
christine.knight@sd72.bc.ca
Meetings/Conferences:
• Association of BC Drama Educators 2018 Fall Conference, 2018, BC
Scope: Provincial

Association of BC First Nations Treatment Programs
PO Box 325, Invermere BC V0A 1K0
Tel: 778-526-2501; Fax: 778-526-2505
Overview: A small provincial organization
Mission: To provide a forum that promotes culturally relevant practices to enhance & advance the continuum of care in addressing addictions among First Nations peoples

Association of Blood Donation Volunteers Voir Association des bénévoles du don de sang

Association of Book Publishers of British Columbia (ABPBC)
#600, 402 West Pender St., Vancouver BC V6B 1T6
Tel: 604-684-0228; Fax: 604-684-5788
admin@books.bc.ca
books.bc.ca
Overview: A medium-sized provincial organization founded in 1974
Mission: To encourage writing, publishing, distribution & promotion of books written by BC & Canadian authors; to cooperate with other associations & organizations to further the reading & studying of books; to work for the development & maintenance of strong competitive book publishing houses owned & controlled in BC & Canada; to further professional training for individuals engaged in book publishing
Affiliation(s): Association of Canadian Publishers
Finances: Annual Operating Budget: $100,000-$250,000; Funding Sources: Canada Council; Dept. of Canadian Heritage
Staff Member(s): 2
Membership: 26 active + 2 associate + 6 supporting; Fees: $350 Active, Associates & Supporting; Member Profile: Active - 7 titles in print, 2 per year; associate - 2 titles in print, published in previous 3 years; supporting - 1 title published in previous 3 years
Activities: Awareness Events: BC Book & Magazine Week, April; Rents Mailing List: Yes; Library: by appointment
Chief Officer(s):
Ruth Linka, President
Margaret Reynolds, Executive Director

Association of British Columbia Forest Professionals (ABCFP)
#602 - 1281 West Georgia St., Vancouver BC V6E 3J7
Tel: 604-687-8027; Fax: 604-687-3264
info@abcfp.ca
www.abcfp.ca
www.facebook.com/ABCFP
twitter.com/abcfp
www.youtube.com/user/TheABCFP
Previous Name: Association of British Columbia Professional Foresters
Overview: A medium-sized provincial licensing organization founded in 1947
Mission: To protect the public interest in the practice of professional forestry by ensuring the competence, independence & integrity of its members; to ensure that every person practising professional forestry is accountable to the association & to the public
Member of: Canadian Federation of Professional Foresters Association
Finances: Annual Operating Budget: $500,000-$1.5 Million; Funding Sources: Membership dues
Staff Member(s): 12; 300 volunteer(s)
Membership: 5,300; Fees: $300-330 + GST; Member Profile: Individual - membership is mandatory for all who practise professional forestry in the province of British Columbia; Committees: ABCFP Forestrust
Activities: Policy review seminars; Professional Foresters' Network; Forest Capital of BC; Awareness Events: National Forest Week, September
Chief Officer(s):
Christine Gelowitz, Chief Executive Officer, 250-298-2562
cgelowitz@abcfp.ca
Mike Larock, Director, Professional Practice & Forest Stewardship, 604-331-2324
mlarock@abcfp.ca
Dean Pelkey, Director, Communications, 604-331-2321
dpelkey@abcfp.ca
Awards:
• Honorary Membership
Non-members, nominated by the membership
• Distinguished Forest Professional Award
Eligibility: BC registered professional foresters, nominated by their peers
• Forester of the Year Award
Eligibility: BC registered professional foresters, nominated by their peers
Meetings/Conferences:
• Association of BC Forest Professionals 70th Annual Forestry Conference and Anuual General Meeting 2018, 2018, BC
Scope: Provincial
Publications:
• BC Forest Professional Magazine
Type: Magazine; Frequency: 6 pa

Association of British Columbia Grape Growers See British Columbia Grapegrowers' Association

Association of British Columbia Land Surveyors (ABCLS)
#301, 2400 Bevan Ave., Sidney BC V8L 1W1
Tel: 250-655-7222; Fax: 250-655-7223
Toll-Free: 800-332-1193
office@abcls.ca
www.abcls.ca
Also Known As: Association of BC Land Surveyors
Previous Name: Corporation of BC Land Surveyors
Overview: A medium-sized provincial licensing organization founded in 1905 overseen by Professional Surveyors Canada
Mission: To protect the public interest & the integrity of the survey system in British Columbia by regulating & governing the practice of land surveying in the province.
Member of: Professional Surveyors Canada
Affiliation(s): Canadian Society of Association Executives
Finances: Annual Operating Budget: $500,000-$1.5 Million; Funding Sources: Membership dues; Electronic Checklist Registry
Staff Member(s): 7
Membership: 600; Fees: Various; Member Profile: Land Surveyors
Activities: Conducting examining for admission; Performing legal surveys in British Columbia; Providing professional development opportunities; Internships: Yes Library: BC Land Surveyors Foundation Anna Papove Memorial; Open to public by appointment
Chief Officer(s):
R. Chad Rintoul, Chief Administrative Officer
crintoul@abcls.ca
Ian Lloyd, President
Chuck Salmon, Secretary & Treasurer
csalmon@abcls.ca
Meetings/Conferences:
• Association of British Columbia Land Surveyors 2018 113th Annual General Meeting, 2018, BC
Scope: Provincial
Contact Information: Board & Administrative Coordinator: Bev Renny, E-mail: office@abcls.ca

Publications:
• The Land Surveyor
Type: Newsletter; Editor: Janice Henshaw
Profile: Articles about land surveying in British Columbia
• The Link
Type: Magazine; Frequency: 3 pa; Accepts Advertising; Editor: Dave Morton, BCLS
Profile: Articles & news relevant to British Columbia land surveyors

Association of British Columbia Professional Foresters See Association of British Columbia Forest Professionals

Association of British Columbia Teachers of English as an Additional Language (BC TEAL)
#206, 640 West Broadway, Vancouver BC V5Z 1G4
Tel: 604-736-6330; Fax: 604-736-6306
admin@bcteal.org
www.bcteal.org
Overview: A medium-sized provincial charitable organization founded in 1967
Mission: To foster & promote effective instruction in English as a second language in BC; to raise the professional status of BC ESL teachers; to promote communication among BC ESL professionals
Member of: TESL Canada; TESOL International
Affiliation(s): Affiliation of Multicultural Societies & Service Agencies of B.C., TESL Canada, TESOL, and ELSA Net
Finances: Funding Sources: Membership dues; conferences
Staff Member(s): 1
Membership: 800; Fees: Schedule available; Member Profile: ESL teacher; Committees: Awards; Action; Policy; Certification; Newsletter
Activities: Rents Mailing List: Yes
Chief Officer(s):
Shawna Williams, President

Association of Building Contractors of Québec Voir Association des entrepreneurs en construction du Québec

Association of Canada Lands Surveyors / Association des arpenteurs des terres du Canada
100E, 900 Dynes Rd., Ottawa ON K2C 3L6
Tel: 613-723-9200; Fax: 613-723-5558
www.acls-aatc.ca
Previous Name: Canadian Institute of Surveying
Overview: A medium-sized national organization
Mission: To establish & maintain standards of qualification for Canada Lands Surveyors; to regulate Canada Lands Surveyors; To establish & maintain standards of conduct, knowledge & skill among members of the Association & permit holders; to govern the activities of members of the Association & permit holders; To cooperate with other organizations for the advancement of surveying; To perform the duties & exercise the powers that are imposed or conferred on the Association by the Act
Chief Officer(s):
Jean-Claude Tétreault, Executive Director
jctetreault@acls-aatc.ca
Meetings/Conferences:
• Association of Canada Lands Surveyors 2018 National Surveyors'/Canadian Hydrographic Conference, March, 2018, Empress Hotel & Victoria Conference Center, Victoria, BC
Scope: National

Association of Canadian Advertisers Inc. (ACA) / Association canadienne des annonceurs
#1103, 95 St. Clair Ave. West, Toronto ON M4V 1N6
Tel: 416-964-3805; Fax: 416-964-0771
Toll-Free: 800-565-0109
www.acaweb.ca
www.linkedin.com/company/2553878
twitter.com/aca_tweets
Overview: A medium-sized national organization founded in 1914
Mission: To promote the common interests of advertisers & to provide expertise, education & information
Member of: The World Federation of Advertisers
Staff Member(s): 8
Membership: 200 corporate; Member Profile: Advertiser of a product or service in Canada; Committees: Media; Marcom Financial Management & Procurement; Digital Marketing
Chief Officer(s):
Ronald S. Lund, President & CEO
rlund@ACAweb.ca
Susan Charles, Vice President, Member Services
scharles@ACAweb.ca

Awards:
• ACA Gold Medal
Established in 1941 to encourage high standards of personal achievement in advertising - for introducing new concepts or techniques, for significantly improving existing practices, or for enhancing the stature of advertising

Association of Canadian Archivists (ACA) / Association canadienne des archivistes
PO Box 2596, Stn. D, #911, 75 Albert St., Ottawa ON K1P 5W6
Tel: 613-234-6977; *Fax:* 613-234-8500
www.archivists.ca
www.linkedin.com/company/2154820
www.facebook.com/AssociationofCanadianArchivists
twitter.com/archivistsdotca
www.youtube.com/user/archivistsdotca
Previous Name: Canadian Historical Association, Archives Section
Overview: A medium-sized national organization founded in 1975
Mission: To ensure the preservation & accessibility of Canada's documentary heritage; To provide professional leadership among persons engaged in the discipline & practice of archival science; To promote the development of archives & archivists in Canada; To encourage cooperation of archivists with all those interested in the preservation & use of documents of human experience
Finances: *Funding Sources:* Membership fees
Membership: 600+; *Fees:* Schedule available; *Member Profile:* Practising archivists; Institutions with archival collections; Archival students; Individuals with an interest in archival activities; *Committees:* Communications; Outreach; Professional Learning; Membership Development; Governance; Ethics
Activities: Organizing professional development events; Engaging in advocacy activities; Increasing appreciation for Canada's archival heritage; Offering networking opportunities
Meetings/Conferences:
• Association of Canadian Archivists 2018 43rd Annual Conference, June, 2018, Chateau Lacombe Hotel, Edmonton, AB
Scope: National
Description: A meeting occurring in May or June each year, for archivists from across Canada, featuring educational presentations, trade show exhibits, networking opportunities, as well as workshops immediately prior or following conference sessions
• Association of Canadian Archivists 2019 44th Annual Conference, 2019
Scope: National
Description: A meeting occurring in May or June each year, for archivists from across Canada, featuring educational presentations, trade show exhibits, networking opportunities, as well as workshops immediately prior or following conference sessions
Publications:
• The ACA [Association of Canadian Archivists] Bulletin
Type: Newsletter; *Frequency:* Quarterly; *Accepts Advertising*; *Editor:* Leah Sander; *ISSN:* 0709-4604
Profile: Association activities & professional news, such as conferences, workshops, archival developments, & publications
• The Archival Imagination: Essays in Honour of Hugh Taylor
Type: Book; *Number of Pages:* 263; *Editor:* Barbara L. Craig; *ISBN:* 1-895382-06-8
Profile: A collection of eleven essays
• Archivaria: The Journal of the Association of Canadian Archivists
Type: Journal; *Frequency:* Semiannually; *Accepts Advertising*; *ISSN:* 0318-6954
Profile: A scholarly journal, with feature articles, book & exhibition reviews, & material related to the archival community in Canada & internationally
• Association of Canadian Archivists Membership Directory
Type: Directory; *Frequency:* Annually; *Accepts Advertising*
Profile: An annual spring publication for more than 600 individual & institutional members, containing contact information as well as key association documents
• Association of Canadian Archivists Conference Program
Frequency: Annually; *Accepts Advertising*
Profile: A detailed description of the annual conference's sessions & social events
• Canadian Archival Studies & the Rediscovery of Provenance
Editor: Tom Nesmith
Profile: A joint publication with the Society of American Archivists
• Imagining Archives: Essays & Reflections by Hugh A. Taylor
Type: Book; *Number of Pages:* 254; *Editor:* Terry Cook; Gordon Dodds; *ISBN:* 0-8108-4771-X
Profile: A collection of fifteen essays
• The Monetary Appraisal of Archival Documents in Canada
Type: Book; *Number of Pages:* 21; *Author:* S.D. Hanson; *ISBN:* 1-895382-04-1
Profile: Information about establishing the fair market value of archival documents
• The Power and Passion of Archives: A Festschrift in Honour of Kent Haworth
Type: Book; *Number of Pages:* 269; *Editor:* R. Ware; M. Beyea; C. Avery; *ISBN:* 1-895382-26-2; *Price:* $20 members; $25 non-members
Profile: A collection of fifteen essays
• Preparing for Monetary Appraisals: A Guide for Canadian Archival Institutions
Type: Book; *Number of Pages:* 18; *Author:* Brock Silversides; *ISBN:* 1-895382-22-X
Profile: A practical guide featuring a bibliography & a information checklist
• Promoting Archives: A Handbook
Type: Handbook; *Number of Pages:* 26; *Author:* Anne ten Cate; *ISBN:* 1-895382-08-4

Association of Canadian Choral Communities (ACCC) / Association des communautés chorales canadiennes
A-1422 Bayview Ave., Toronto ON M4G 3A7
Tel: 647-606-2467
info@choralcanada.org
www.choralcanada.org
www.facebook.com/111037998913858
twitter.com/choralcanada
choralbytes.blogspot.ca
Overview: A small national organization founded in 1980
Mission: To promote choral music, particularly Canadian works, in schools, post-secondary institutions, churches & communities throughout Canada; to support and encourage participation in all levels of choral music through training and resources
Affiliation(s): Canadian Conference of the Arts; International Federation for Choral Music
Finances: *Annual Operating Budget:* Less than $50,000; *Funding Sources:* Membership fees; donations; advertising
Staff Member(s): 6; 25 volunteer(s)
Membership: 500; *Fees:* $100 individual/institutional/choir; $175 industry; $35 student; *Committees:* Advocacy; Communications; Professional Development; Financial
Activities: National Youth Choir of Canada; Podium (biennial National Conference) choral composition competition; National Choral Awards; NYC Conducting Apprenticeship Program; Canadian Choral Foundation; *Awareness Events:* National Competition for Canadian Amateur Choirs; Choralscapes Podium; Competition for Choral Writing
Chief Officer(s):
Marta McCarthy, President
John Wiebe, President Elect
Denise Gress, Treasurer
Awards:
• National Choral Awards / Prix nationaux de chant choral
Publications:
• Anacrusis [a publication of the Association of Canadian Choral Communities]
Type: Journal; *Frequency:* 3 pa; *Accepts Advertising*; *Editor:* Dean Jobin-Bevans; *Price:* Freewith membership in the Assocation of Canadian Choral Communities
Profile: Articles on subjects relating to the art of choral music, including choral history, performance practice, and technique.

Association of Canadian College & University Teachers of English (ACCUTE)
c/o Department of English & Writing Studies, Western University, 1151 Richmond St., London ON N6A 3K7
Tel: 519-661-2111; *Fax:* 519-661-3776
info.accute@gmail.com
www.accute.ca
twitter.com/ACCUTEnglish
Overview: A small national organization founded in 1957
Mission: To represent faculty teaching English in Canadian universities & colleges, & students studying English at the graduate level; To act as the lobbying body at the provincial & federal levels; To encourage the dissemination & exchange of research
Member of: Canadian Federation for the Humanities & Social Sciences
Affiliation(s): Congress of Learned Societies
Finances: *Funding Sources:* Membership fees
Membership: *Fees:* Schedule available dependent on yearly earnings of the member
Activities: *Rents Mailing List:* Yes
Chief Officer(s):
Manina Jones, President
mjones@uwo.ca
Awards:
• F.E.L. Priestley Prize
Awarded annually for an outstanding essay published in English Studies in Canada & service to ACCUTE

Association of Canadian Compliance Professionals / Association canadienne des professionnels en conformité
c/o Hub Capital Inc., #1001, 3700 Steeles Ave. West, Woodbridge ON L4L 8M9
info@complianceprofessionals.ca
www.complianceprofessionals.ca
Also Known As: Association of Compliance Professionals
Overview: A small national organization founded in 2000
Mission: To represent individuals in the field of compliance, who are dedicated to improving compliance operations within the mutual fund & exempt market dealer communities
Membership: 100+; *Fees:* $300 individual; $150 per subsequent person (corporate); *Member Profile:* Compliance professionals working with the following: mutual fund dealers, exempt market dealers, mutual fund companies, insurance companies & MGAs, as well as industry service providers including legal, technology & independent consultants
Activities: Job center; events; educational programs
Chief Officer(s):
Manny DaSilva, Chair
Cheryl Hamilton, Treasurer, 905-264-1634 Ext. 2075
Kathleen Black, Executive Director, 403-796-8298

Association of Canadian Corporations in Translation & Interpretation (ACCTI) / Association canadienne de compagnies de traductions et d'interpretation
#306, 421 Bloor St. East, Toronto ON M4W 3T1
Tel: 416-975-5000; *Fax:* 416-975-0505
Other Communication: info_francais@accti.org
english_info@accti.org
www.accti.org
Overview: A medium-sized national organization founded in 2003
Mission: To unite the Canadian translation industry, providing a quality standard to protect the public & service providers alike; to arrange for arbitration in the event of a dispute; to operate in the best interest of members
Member of: American Translator's Association, Translation Companies; Association of Hungarian Translation Companies; Association of Language Companies; Association of Translation Companies; European Union Association of Translation Companies
Finances: *Funding Sources:* Membership fees, sponsors
Staff Member(s): 3
Membership: *Fees:* Non-voting $500; Associate $1,000; Voting $1,500; Cost per specialty $2,000; *Member Profile:* Non-voting, all parties interested in being involved with Canadian corporations providing translation & interpreting services; Voting, Canadian corporations whose core business is in traditional translation &/or interpretation services, which adhere to the ACCTI Code of Professional Conduct, Ethics & Business Practices.; *Committees:* Executive; Membership; R&D
Activities: Keeps members abreast of developments, new technologies & opportunities within the industry through website postings, newsletters & annual conferences; arranges for preferred pricing from interested vendors
Chief Officer(s):
Paul Penzo, President
Maryse M. Benhoff, Vice-President, 514-376-7919, Fax: 514-376-4486

Association of Canadian Deans of Education (ACDE) / Association Canadienne des Doyens et Doyennes d'Éducation
c/o ACDE Secretariat, 1144 Skana Dr., Delta BC V4M 2L4
Tel: 604-943-6374
acde@telus.net
csse-scee.ca/associations/acde
Overview: A medium-sized national organization overseen by Canadian Society for the Study of Education
Mission: To advance knowledge & inform practice in educational settings
Member of: Canadian Society for the Study of Education

Canadian Associations / Association of Canadian Distillers (ACD) / Association des distillateurs canadiens

Finances: *Funding Sources:* Primarily by the fees of individual & institutional members & a small subsidy from the Social Sciences & Humanities Research Council of Canada
Chief Officer(s):
Sal Badali, President
sal.badali@msvu.ca
Katy Ellsworth, Executive Director

Association of Canadian Distillers (ACD) / Association des distillateurs canadiens
#2-B, 219 Dufferin St., Toronto ON M6K 1Y9
Tel: 416-626-0100
info@spiritscanada.ca
www.spiritscanada.ca
www.facebook.com/1422057448099551
twitter.com/SpiritsCanada
Also Known As: Spirits Canada
Overview: A large national organization founded in 1947
Mission: To protect & advance the interests of its members; To promote & protect, both nationally & internationally, the well-being & viability of the Canadian distilling industry; To foster responsible attitudes toward the consumption of distilled spirits (gin, vodka, rum, Canadian Whisky) in Canada; To aggressively pursue & enhance the recognition of the name & positive reputation of Canadian Whisky as Canada's unique appellation distilled spirits product; To preserve & protect the integrity & standards of all distilled products
Membership: *Member Profile:* Canadian licensed manufacturers & marketers of distilled spirits products
Activities: *Library:* Not open to public

Association of Canadian Ergonomists (ACE) / L'Association canadienne d'ergonomie
#200, 411 Richmond St. East, Toronto ON M5A 3S5
Tel: 416-477-0914; *Fax:* 416-929-5256
Toll-Free: 888-432-2223
info@ace-ergocanada.ca
www.ace-ergocanada.ca
Previous Name: Human Factors Association of Canada
Overview: A small national organization founded in 1968
Mission: To advance human factors/ergonomics through encouraging a high quality of practice, education & research; To facilitate communication among members; To represent the discipline; To increase awareness of human factors/ergonomics; To identify resources
Member of: International Ergonomics Association
Finances: *Annual Operating Budget:* $100,000-$250,000; *Funding Sources:* Membership dues; annual conference
Staff Member(s): 2
Membership: 600 individuals; *Fees:* $173 full; $87 affiliate; $40 student; *Member Profile:* Engineers; medical practitioners; safety specialists; research scientists; architects; designers; educators; managers; consultants; kinesiologists; psychologists; ergonomists
Activities: *Speaker Service:* Yes
Chief Officer(s):
Karen Hoodless, President
acepresident1@gmail.com
Kristen Lépine dos Santos, Executive Director
Awards:
• Student Paper Awards
; *Amount:* $250
Meetings/Conferences:
• Association of Canadian Ergonomists Conference 2018, October, 2018, Sudbury, ON
Scope: National

Association of Canadian Faculties of Dentistry (ACFD) / Association des facultés dentaires du Canada (AFDC)
#350, 2194 Health Sciences Mall, Vancouver BC V6T 1Z3
Tel: 604-827-1083; *Fax:* 604-822-4532
admin@acfd.ca
www.acfd.ca
Overview: A medium-sized national organization founded in 1968 overseen by Universities Canada
Mission: To assure the quality of dental education & research in Canada; To keep members informed of issues regarding University-based dental education & promote communication between its members
Member of: Universities Canada; Canadian Dental Association; Canadian Dental Hygienist Association; Canadian Dental Assistants Association; National Dental Examining Board of Canada; Royal College of Dentists of Canada; American Association of Dental Schools; American Dental Education Association

Finances: *Annual Operating Budget:* $50,000-$100,000
Staff Member(s): 1
Membership: 400; *Member Profile:* Canadian University-based Faculty, School, or other entity that offers an undergraduate dental program leading to the DDS/DMD degree; *Committees:* Deans Committee; Academic Affairs; Clinical Affairs; Research Affairs
Chief Officer(s):
Paul Allison, President
paul.allison@mcgill.ca
Andrea Esteves, Vice-President & Treasurer
aesteves@dentistry.ubc.ca
Awards:
• ACFD Distinguished Service Award
Recognizes individuals or groups who have made significant contributions to dental education in Canada.
• Bisco National Dental Teaching Award
Recognizes a faculty member who has displayed the qualities of an outstanding dental educator.; *Amount:* $2,500

Association of Canadian Film Craftspeople
Local 2020 Communications, Energy & Paperworkers Union of Canada, #108, 3993 Henning Dr., Burnaby BC V5C 6P7
Tel: 604-299-2232; *Fax:* 604-299-2243
info@acfcwest.com
www.acfcwest.com
Also Known As: ACFC West, Local 2020 Unifor
Overview: A medium-sized national organization
Mission: To create the best working conditions for members of the technical film industry in British Columbia
Chief Officer(s):
Perm Marimuthu, President
president@acfcwest.com
Ken Frost, Ssecretary/Treasurer
secretarytreasurer@acfcwest.com
Greg Chambers, Business Manager
businessagent@acfcwest.com

Association of Canadian Financial Officers (ACFO) / Association canadienne des agents financiers (ACAF)
#400, 2725 Queensview Dr., Ottawa ON K2B 0A1
Tel: 613-728-0695; *Fax:* 613-761-9568
Toll-Free: 877-728-0695
information@acfo-acaf.com
www.acfo-acaf.com
www.linkedin.com/company/401947
twitter.com/acfoacaf
Previous Name: Association of Public Service Financial Administrators (Ind.)/Association des gestionnaires financiers de la fonction publique (Ind.)
Overview: A medium-sized national organization founded in 1989
Mission: To unite in a democratic organization all public service financial administrators for which the association becomes or applies to become a bargaining agent; to serve the welfare of its members through effective collective bargaining with their employers; to obtain for members best levels of compensation for services rendered to their employers & the best terms & conditions of employment; to protect the rights & interests of all members in all matters upon their employment or upon their relationship with their employers; to seek to maintain high professional standards & promote their professional development; to affiliate as appropriate with other associations, unions or labour organizations for the purpose of enhancing the interests of members in the attainment of their professional & bargaining goals
Staff Member(s): 14
Membership: *Member Profile:* Financial Administrators
Activities: *Library:*
Chief Officer(s):
Milt Isaacs, President
misaacs@acfo-acaf.com

Association of Canadian Franchisors *See* Canadian Franchise Association

Association of Canadian Industrial Designers (ACID) / Association des designers industriels du Canada
#251, 157 Adelaide St. West, Toronto ON M5H 4E7
info@designcanada.org
www.designcanada.org
Overview: A medium-sized national organization founded in 1948
Mission: To represent Canadian industrial designers throughout world. The ACID represents the collective interests of designers and is dedicated to increasing the knowledge, skill and proficiency of its members through networking, discussion forums, seminars and trade events
Affiliation(s): International Council of Societies of Industrial Design - Helsinki, Finland
Finances: *Annual Operating Budget:* Less than $50,000
Membership: 3 corporate, & members-at-large; *Fees:* $50 annually; *Member Profile:* Graduate of recognized design institution; minimum of 2 years experience in design field; portfolio of work to be presented
Activities: *Speaker Service:* Yes; *Rents Mailing List:* Yes

Association of Canadian Knights of the Sovereign Military Order of Malta *See* Order of Malta - Canadian Association

Association of Canadian Map Libraries & Archives (ACMLA) / Association des cartothèques et archives cartographiques du Canada (ACACC)
c/o Deena Yanofsky, Humanities & Social Sciences Library, McGill U, 3459, rue McTavish, Montréal QC H3A 0C9
Tel: 514-398-1087
www.acmla-acacc.ca
Overview: A medium-sized national organization founded in 1967
Mission: To represent Canadian map librarians & cartographic archivists, as well as others who are interested in geographic information; To develop professional standards & international cataloguing rules for the management & access to geographic information; To promote the contributions of map libraries & cartographic archives
Membership: *Fees:* $20 students; $65 individuals/institutions; *Member Profile:* Individuals, libraries, archives, & other organizations with an interest in maps & geographic data; *Committees:* Awards; Bibliographic Control; Copyright; Geospatial Data Access; Historical Maps; Membership; Nominating; Web; Conference
Activities: Offering a mentoring program; Disseminating information to members; Facilitating the exchange of ideas through the member ACMLA- ACACC-L Listserv; Organizing professional development activities; Publishing maps, including the ACMLA Facsimile Map Series & historical maps of Canada
Chief Officer(s):
Deena Yanofsky, President
president@acmla-acacc.ca
Awards:
• Cathy Moulder Paper Award
Awarded to the best paper published in the ACMLA Bulletin; *Amount:* $200
• Student Paper Award
Eligibility: Student currently enrolled in a post-secondary institution in Canada; *Amount:* $250 + free ACMLA membership for one year
Meetings/Conferences:
• Association of Canadian Map Libraries & Archives 2018 Annual Conference, 2018
Scope: National
Description: A yearly gathering of map librarians & archivists & other individuals with an interest in maps & geographic data who support the objectives of the association
Publications:
• ACMLA [Association of Canadian Map Libraries & Archives] Bulletin
Type: Journal; *Frequency:* 3 pa; *Editor:* Eva Dodsworth; *ISSN:* 0840-9331; *Price:* Free with membership in the Association of Canadian Map Libraries & Archives
Profile: Content reflecting the goals, interests, & values of the Association of Canadian Map Libraries & Archives of interest to the Canadiancartographic & geographic communities

Association of Canadian Medical Colleges *See* Association of Faculties of Medicine of Canada

Association of Canadian Mountain Guides (ACMG) / Association des guides de montagne canadiens
PO Box 8341, Canmore AB T1W 2V1
Tel: 403-678-2885; *Fax:* 403-609-0070
acmg@acmg.ca
www.acmg.ca
www.facebook.com/ACMG.ca
twitter.com/ACMGca
Overview: A small national organization founded in 1963
Mission: To represent mountain guides in dealing with both public & private official bodies; to maintain standards of guiding & acts as a public relations body to promote the sport in a safe & educational manner.
Member of: International Federation of Mountain Guides Associations
Finances: *Funding Sources:* Membership fees

Membership: 904; Fees: Schedule available; Member Profile: Personal membership is open exclusively to trained/certified professional guides & instructors.
Activities: Training & Certification Program
Chief Officer(s):
Marc Ledwidge, President, 403-762-4129
pres@acmg.ca
Peter Tucker, Executive Director, 403-949-3587
ed@acmg.ca

Association of Canadian Pension Management (ACPM) / Association canadienne des administrateurs de régimes de retraite
#304, 1255 Bay St., Toronto ON M5R 2A9
Tel: 416-964-1260; Fax: 416-964-0567
info@acpm.com
www.acpm.com
www.linkedin.com/company/the-association-of-canadian-pension-management
Overview: A medium-sized national organization founded in 1976
Mission: To act as the voice of Canada's pension industry; To foster the growth of the the national retirement income system
Membership: Fees: Free students; $75 retired persons; $575 individuals engaged in the industry; Member Profile: Individuals in the pension & benefit industry from across Canada; Retired persons; Students; Committees: Audit & Finance; Governance & Nominating; Human Resources; National Policy; Strategic Initiatives; National Conference Planning; Executive Member Engagement; Editorial
Activities: Liaising with govenments; Advocating for an effective & sustainable retirement income system
Chief Officer(s):
Michel Jalbert, Chair
Ric Marrero, Interim Chief Executive Officer, 416-964-1260 Ext. 223
Ric.Marrero@acpm.com
Judy Lei, Manager, 416-964-1260 Ext. 224
Judy.Lei@acpm.com
Meetings/Conferences:
• 2018 Association of Canadian Pension Management National Conference, September, 2018, Fairmont Le Château Frontenac, Québec, QC
Scope: National
Publications:
• ACPM [Association of Canadian Pension Management] Education Initiative Report
Type: Booklet; Number of Pages: 35
Profile: Roundtable discussions, case studies, & resources
• Association of Canadian Pension Management Newsletter
Type: Newsletter
Profile: Information for members only
• Association of Canadian Pension Management Member Directory
Type: Directory
Profile: Contact information for members
• Back from the Brink: Securing the Future of Defined Benefit Pension Plan
Type: Report; Number of Pages: 40
Profile: Issues related to the funding of defined benefit pension plans
• Delivering the Potential of DC Retirement Savings Plans [Association of Canadian Pension Management]
Type: Booklet; Number of Pages: 33
Profile: Information about improving the retirement saving plan system
• Dependence or Self-reliance: Which way for Canada's Retirement Income System?
Type: Booklet; Number of Pages: 36
Profile: Overview & recommendations
• Improving Retirement Income Coverage in Canada: The ACPM [Association of Canadian Pension Management] Five-Point Plan
Type: Booklet; Number of Pages: 9
• Retirement Income Strategy for Canada: Creating the Best Retirement Income System in the World
Type: Booklet; Number of Pages: 39
Profile: Overview & recommendations

Association of Canadian Port Authorities (ACPA)
#1006, 75 Albert St., Ottawa ON K1P 5E7
Tel: 613-232-2036; Fax: 613-232-9554
info@acpa-ports.net
www.acpa-ports.net
twitter.com/ACPA_AAPC
Previous Name: Canadian Port & Harbour Association
Overview: A medium-sized national organization founded in 1958
Mission: To encourage, mentor & stimulate the development of excellence within Canadian ports
Member of: National Marine Advisory Board; Canadian Marine Advisory Council; Transport Canada/National Port Security Committee (NPSC); Critical Infrastructure Multi-sector Network
Affiliation(s): American Association of Port Authorities
Finances: Funding Sources: Membership fees; seminars
Staff Member(s): 2
Membership: 18 corporate + 37 supporters; Fees: $795 businesses; $100 individual; Committees: Law & Governance; Operations; Finance; Environment; Port Security Sub-Committee
Activities: Annual conferences where papers are given by experts in the field of port operations & where members inspect the host port's dock & industrial facilities; port-related research; special seminars; Speaker Service: Yes
Chief Officer(s):
Wendy Zatylny, Executive Director, 613-232-2036 Ext. 201
wzatylny@acpa-ports.net
Francine Paulin, Executive Assistant/Office Manager, 613-232-2036 Ext. 200
fpaulin@acpa-ports.net
Debbie Murray, Director, Policy & Regulatory Affairs, 613-407-0114
dmurray@acpa-ports.net
Meetings/Conferences:
• 60th Association of Canadian Port Authorities Annual Conference & General Meeting, September, 2018, Saint John, NB
Description: Brings together Canadian professionals and key decision makers to discuss port trade topics and issues; speaker series
Publications:
• RePORTage [publication of the Association of Canadian Port Authorities]
Type: Magazine; Frequency: a.; Accepts Advertising; Number of Pages: 44; Author: Don Cummer; Editor: Mike Ircha, Ph.D.; Price: Free download
Profile: Information concerning the ACPA, including a list of board members, a directory of Canada's port authorities and ahost profile on a notable Canadian port

Association of Canadian Publishers (ACP) / Association des éditeurs canadiens
#306, 174 Spadina Ave., Toronto ON M5T 2C2
Tel: 416-487-6116; Fax: 416-487-8815
admin@canbook.org
www.publishers.ca
twitter.com/CdnPublishers
Overview: A large national organization founded in 1976
Mission: To encourage writing, publishing, distribution & promotion of books written by Canadian authors in particular, & reading & study of books in general; To represent the members at international book fairs; To facilitate the exchange of information & professional expertise among members; To promote Canadian books; To expand Canadian-owned publishers' domestic & international market share
Affiliation(s): Association of Book Publishers of British Columbia; Book Publishers Association of Alberta; Saskatchewan Publishers Group; Association of Manitoba Book Publishers; Ontario Publishers Group; Association des editeurs anglophones du Québec; Atlantic Publishers Association; The Literary Press Group of Canada
Staff Member(s): 3
Membership: 135 corporate members; Fees: Sliding scale; Member Profile: Canadian-owned & controlled firms which engage in every major type of book publishing - educational, scholarly, & the full range of trade publications; Committees: Canada Council; Copyright; Export; Supply Chain; Children's Publishers; Education
Activities: Book fairs; conferences; seminars; professional development programs; workshops; Top Grade: CanLit for the Classroom; eBOUND Canada; National reading Campaign; The 49th Shelf; BNC Buying Groups; Writers' Coalition Benefits Program; Rents Mailing List: Yes
Chief Officer(s):
Matt Williams, President
matt@anansi.ca
Kate Edwards, Executive Director, 416-487-6116 Ext. 234
kate_edwards@canbook.org
Emily Kellogg, Manager, Programs, 416-487-6116 Ext. 222
emily_kellogg@canbook.org
Meetings/Conferences:
• Association of Canadian Publishers 2018 Mid-Winter Meeting, January, 2018
Scope: National
• Association of Canadian Publishers 2018 Annual General Meeting, June, 2018
Scope: National
Description: An event featuring plenary sessions, professional development seminars, presentations, as well as committee meetings & reports
Publications:
• ACP [Association of Canadian Publishers] Update
Type: Newsletter

Association of Canadian Search, Employment & Staffing Services (ACSESS) / Association nationale des entreprises en recrutement et placement de personnel
#100, 2233 Argentia Rd., Mississauga ON L5N 2X7
Tel: 905-826-6869; Fax: 905-826-4873
Toll-Free: 888-232-4962
acsess@acsess.org
www.acsess.org
www.linkedin.com/company/281336
twitter.com/ACSESS_
www.youtube.com/user/acsess123
Previous Name: Federation of Temporary Help Services
Merged from: Association of Professional Placement Agencies & Consultants; Employment & Staffing Services Associa
Overview: A medium-sized national organization founded in 1998
Mission: To promote the advancement & growth of the employment & staffing services industry in Canada
Finances: Funding Sources: Membership dues; member services
Staff Member(s): 3
Membership: Committees: Executive; Nominating; Ethics; Government Relations; Public Relations & Communications; Certification & Education; Awards; National Conference; Chapter Presidents' Committee Mandate
Chief Officer(s):
Neil Smith, National President
neil.smith@ctsna.ca
Amanda Curtis, Executive Director
acurtis@acsess.org
Meetings/Conferences:
• Association of Canadian Search, Employment & Staffing Services Conference 2018, May, 2018, Fallsview Casino Resort, Niagara Falls, ON
Scope: National
Description: Theme: "Leading Canada to Work"

Association of Canadian Television & Radio Artists See Alliance of Canadian Cinema, Television & Radio Artists

Association of Canadian Travel Agencies (ACTA) / Association canadienne des agences de voyages
#226, 2560 Matheson Blvd. East, Mississauga ON L4W 4Y9
Tel: 905-282-9294; Fax: 905-282-9826
Toll-Free: 866-725-2282
actacan@acta.ca
www.acta.ca
www.linkedin.com/company/association-of-canadian-travel-agencies-acta
www.facebook.com/ACTACanada
twitter.com/actacanada
Previous Name: Association of Canadian Travel Agents; Alliance of Canadian Travel Associations
Overview: A large national organization founded in 1977
Mission: To provide leadership for the retail travel professional
Affiliation(s): Universal Federation of Travel Agency Associations
Finances: Annual Operating Budget: $1.5 Million-$3 Million
Staff Member(s): 9; 20 volunteer(s)
Membership: 3,000 corporate; Fees: Schedule available; Member Profile: Travel agencies, tour operators, travel wholesalers, national & international travel service suppliers such as airlines, hotels, tourist boards, cruise lines, railways, car rental companies & other members of the travel industry; Committees: Board of Directors
Activities: Offering education, training & certification courses; Advocating for its membership
Chief Officer(s):
Heather Craig-Peddie, Vice-President, 905-282-9294 Ext. 122
hcraig-peddie@acta.ca

Marco Pozzobon, Director, Digital & Communications, 905-282-9294 Ext. 123
mpozzobon@acta.ca
Deanne Osborne, Office Coordinator, 905-282-9294 Ext. 125
dosborne@acta.ca

Association of Canadian Travel Agencies - Atlantic
PO Box 21007, Quispamsis NB E2E 4Z4
Tel: 888-257-2282; *Fax:* 855-349-0658
actaatlantic@acta.ca
www.acta.ca
Also Known As: ACTA - Atlantic
Overview: A medium-sized provincial organization founded in 1976 overseen by Association of Canadian Travel Agencies
Mission: To represent & defend the interests of the retail travel services industry; To serve as the focal point for the retail travel services industry; To support initiatives designed to create & maintain a healthy business & legislative environment
Membership: *Fees:* Schedule available
Activities: *Rents Mailing List:* Yes
Chief Officer(s):
Lorie Cohen Hackett, Regional Manager

Association of Canadian Travel Agents - Alberta & NWT
PO Box 21058, Stn. Terwilligar, 584 Riverbend SW NW, Edmonton AB T6R 2V4
Tel: 780-437-2555; *Fax:* 855-349-0658
Toll-Free: 888-257-2282
www.acta.ca
Also Known As: ACTA - Alberta & NWT
Overview: A medium-sized provincial organization founded in 1977 overseen by Association of Canadian Travel Agencies
Mission: To represent the retail travel sector of Canada's tourism industy, with a focus on travel agents in Alberta & the Northwest Territories
Membership: *Fees:* Schedule available; *Member Profile:* Travel agencies
Chief Officer(s):
Anthony Tonkinson, Regional Chair
Barbara Sutherland, Regional Manager
bsutherland@acta.ca

Association of Canadian Travel Agents - British Columbia & Yukon
c/o Association of Canadian Travel Agencies, #226, 2560 Matheson Blvd. East, Mississauga ON L4W 4Y9
Toll-Free: 888-257-2282
www.acta.ca
Also Known As: ACTA - BC/Yukon
Previous Name: Association of Travel Agents of British Columbia
Overview: A medium-sized provincial organization overseen by Association of Canadian Travel Agencies
Mission: To promote the interests of the retail travel sector in British Columbia & Yukon
Membership: *Fees:* $190-$2,850
Chief Officer(s):
Liz Fleming, Regional Chair

Association of Canadian Travel Agents - Manitoba & Nunavut
c/o Association of Canadian Travel Agencies, #226, 2560 Matheson Blvd. East, Mississauga ON L4W 4Y9
Toll-Free: 888-257-2282
actambsk@acta.ca
www.acta.ca
Also Known As: ACTA - Manitoba & Nunavut
Overview: A medium-sized provincial charitable organization founded in 1978 overseen by Association of Canadian Travel Agencies
Mission: To promote & represent the retail travel field in Manitoba & Nunavut
Finances: *Annual Operating Budget:* $50,000-$100,000
Staff Member(s): 1; 20 volunteer(s)
Membership: 155; *Fees:* $195-$295; *Committees:* Trade Show; Golf; Executive
Activities: Organizing Manitoba Travel Marketplace
Chief Officer(s):
Mary Jane Hiebert, Regional Chair

Association of Canadian Travel Agents - Ontario
#226, 2560 Matheson Blvd. East, Mississauga ON L4W 4Y9
Tel: 905-282-9294; *Fax:* 855-349-0658
Toll-Free: 888-257-2282
www.acta.ca
Also Known As: ACTA - Ontario

Overview: A medium-sized provincial organization founded in 1974 overseen by Association of Canadian Travel Agencies
Mission: To represent the retail travel sector of Canada's tourism industry, with a focus on Ontario travel agents
Finances: *Funding Sources:* Membership dues; fundraising
Membership: *Fees:* Schedule available; *Member Profile:* Travel agency owners; Tour operators; Travel suppliers
Chief Officer(s):
Fiona Bowen, Regional Manager
fbowen@acta.ca
Mike Foster, Regional Chair

Association of Canadian Travel Agents - Québec / Association des agents de voyages du Québec
CP 76063, Mascouche QC J7K 3N9
Tél: 514-357-0890; *Téléc:* 855-349-0658
Ligne sans frais: 888-257-2282
www.acta.ca
Également appelé: ACTA - Québec
Aperçu: *Dimension:* moyenne; *Envergure:* provinciale; fondée en 1972 surveillé par Association of Canadian Travel Agencies
Mission: Défense des droits et intérêts de l'industrie du voyage
Finances: *Budget de fonctionnement annuel:* $100,000-$250,000
Membre(s) du personnel: 5; 100 bénévole(s)
Membre: 500
Activités: *Stagiaires:* Oui; *Listes de destinataires:* Oui; *Bibliothèque:* Bibliothèque publique
Membre(s) du bureau directeur:
Manon Martel, Directeur régional
mmartel@acta.ca

Association of Canadian Travel Agents; Alliance of Canadian Travel Associations See Association of Canadian Travel Agencies

Association of Canadian Universities for Northern Studies (ACUNS) / Association universitaire canadienne d'études nordiques
PO Box 321, Stn. A, Ottawa ON K1N 8V3
Tel: 613-669-8162
office@acuns.ca
www.acuns.ca
www.facebook.com/110949402264676
twitter.com/acunsaucen
Overview: A small national charitable organization founded in 1977 overseen by Universities Canada
Mission: To encourage the government & private sector to support polar scholarship, which fosters programs to increase public awareness of polar sciences & research; to represent its member universities & colleges, encouraging the establishment of funds & resources to ensure a network of trained researchers, regional managers & educators.
Member of: Universities Canada
Finances: *Funding Sources:* University dues
Membership: 45 universities/colleges
Activities: Maintaining a network of circumpolar contacts; providing education & public awareness programs; triennial Student Conference on Northern Studies
Chief Officer(s):
Peter Geller, President
Monique Bernier, Vice-President
Gary Wilson, Secretary-Treasurer
Heather Cayouette, Program Manager
Awards:
• Caribou Research Award
Awarded to students enrolled in a recognized Canadian community college or university pursuing studies that will contribute to the understanding of the Beverly & Qamanirjuaq Barren Ground Caribou (& their habitat) in Canada *Deadline:* January 31; *Amount:* Up to $1,500
• Studentships in Northern Studies
Research culminating in a thesis or similar document involving direct northern experience; for students enrolled in graduate & undergraduate degree programs or other courses of study recognized at a Canadian university with special relevance to Canada's northern territories & adjacent regions *Deadline:* January 31; *Amount:* $10,000
• Cooperative Award
Awarded to a student whose studies will contribute to the understanding & development of cooperatives in NWT; applicants who are not northern residents must be full-time students at the Cooperative College of Canada, a recognized Canadian community college, or a Canadian university *Deadline:* January 31; *Amount:* $2,000

• Research Support Opportunity in Arctic Environmental Studies
Preference is given to environmental research proposals in the physical &/or biological sciences for which location at the High Arctic Weather Stations would be advantageous; graduate level studies *Deadline:* January 31; *Amount:* Logistical support
• Canadian Northern Studies Polar Commission Scholarship

Association of Canadian University Presses (ACUP) / Association des presses universitaires canadiennes (APUC)
#700, 10 St. Mary St., Toronto ON M4Y 2W8
Tel: 416-978-2239; *Fax:* 416-978-4738
www.acup.ca
Overview: A medium-sized national organization founded in 1972
Mission: To support scholarly publishing by university presses in Canada
Finances: *Annual Operating Budget:* Less than $50,000; *Funding Sources:* Membership dues
Staff Member(s): 1
Membership: 15; *Fees:* Schedule available
Activities: Offering publishing advice & assistance to scholarly bodies & institutions of higher learning; Acting as a major voice of the scholarly publishing community to government, media & the public; *Rents Mailing List:* Yes
Chief Officer(s):
John Yates, President
jyates@utpress.utoronto.ca

Association of Canadian Women Composers (ACWC) / L'Association des femmes compositeurs canadiennes (AFCC)
c/o Canadian Music Centre, 20 St. Joseph St., Toronto ON M4Y 1J9
acwcafcc@gmail.com
www.acwc.ca
www.facebook.com/215231155239835
Overview: A small national organization founded in 1980
Mission: To build on the achievements of & further encourage Canadian women & women-identified composers; To develop & provide a body of well-researched, catalogued & preserved arcival material to be accesible to students, researchs & performers
Affiliation(s): Fondezione Adkins Chiti: Donne in Musica, Italy; Women in Music Foundation
Finances: *Funding Sources:* Membership fees; Canada Council; SOCAN
Membership: 40; *Fees:* $25 student; $35 associate/affiliate; $40 individual; *Member Profile:* Women only; professional composer active - Canadian citizen/landed immigrant; professional composer affiliate - other nationality; associate - performer, teacher, non-composer; student composer
Activities: *Library:* Archives
Chief Officer(s):
Carol Ann Weaver, Chair
caweaver@waterloo.ca

Association of Career Professionals Internatinal (ACPI)
PO Box 38179, Toronto ON M5N 3A8
Tel: 416-233-4440; *Fax:* 866-605-0657
info@acpinternational.org
www.acpinternational.org
twitter.com/ACPIntl
Previous Name: International Association of Outplacement Professionals
Overview: A medium-sized international organization founded in 1989
Mission: A global organization dedicated to advancing public awareness of the career management profession, as well as in promoting the international profile and credibility of its varied membership.
Membership: *Fees:* $120 professional; $40 student
Activities: Professional development tools and events; Research; Networking opportunities; Certification; Ethical practice standards

Association of Catholic Retired Administrators (ACRA)
Tel: 514-626-1060
www.acracan.org
Overview: A small local organization founded in 1998
Mission: To represent retired administrators & professionals from English-language Catholic educational boards & schools
Chief Officer(s):
Maria Di Perna, President
mcdiperna@gmail.com

Publications:
• ACRA [Association of Catholic Retired Administrators] Newsletter
Type: Newsletter; *Editor:* Charles Jeannotte

Association of Certified Engineering Technicians & Technologists of PEI; Prince Edward Island Society of Certified Engineering Technologists *See* Island Technology Professionals

Association of Certified Forensic Investigators of Canada (ACFI)
4 Iris St., Huntsville ON P1H 1L8
Tel: 416-226-3018
Toll-Free: 877-552-5585
info@acfi.ca
www.acfi.ca
Overview: A small national organization founded in 1998
Mission: To act as a governing body for professionals who provide forensic investivations for governments, the public, & employers; To promote high standards in the field for the benefit of the public
Membership: *Fees:* $245 regular members; $100 associate members; *Member Profile:* Individuals with expertise in fraud prevention, detection, & investigation; Candidates for membership must demonstrate their competency through education, examination, & experience
Activities: Accrediting forensic investigators; Promoting the Certified Forensic Investigator (CFI) designation; Providing continuing education opportunities
Chief Officer(s):
Alan M. Langley, Executive Director & Officer, Information

Association of Certified Fraud Examiners - Toronto Chapter
PO Box 1408, 3230 Yonge St., Toronto ON M4N 3P6
Tel: 416-480-9475; *Fax:* 416-480-1813
acfe.toronto@sympatico.ca
ca.linkedin.com/pub/acfe-toronto-chapter/25/971/329
facebook.com/acfeto
twitter.com/ACFETO
Also Known As: ACFE Toronto
Overview: A small national organization
Membership: *Fees:* $85 individuals; $22 students; *Member Profile:* Individuals who offer investigative, forensic, & security services to the public; *Committees:* Canada Chapter Development; Conference; Educational Outreach; Membership; Newsletter; Training
Activities: Education, training, seminars, conferences, networking, & outreach presentations; *Library:* Association of Certified Fraud Examiner Library
Chief Officer(s):
Toby Bishop, CFE, CPA, FCA, President
Astra Williamson, CPA, CGA, CFE, Vice-President
Tom Eby, MBA, CPA, CA, Secretary
William Vasiliou, CGA, CFE, CCRA, Treasurer
Penny Hill, Administrator
Publications:
• ACFE [Association of Certified Fraud Examiners] Toronto Newsletter
Type: Newsletter; *Editor:* Eric Bettencourt

Association of Chartered Industrial Designers of Ontario (ACIDO)
998 Bloor St. West, Toronto ON M6H 1L0
Tel: 416-940-3080
www.acido.info
www.facebook.com/ACIDOntario
Also Known As: Ontario Industrial Design Organization
Overview: A small provincial organization founded in 1948 overseen by Association of Canadian Industrial Designers
Mission: To develop & promote the industrial design profession in Ontario; To act as the voice of Ontario's industrial design profession; To foster interaction between the industrial design community & other industries
Affiliation(s): International Council of Societies of Industrial Design (ICSID)
Finances: *Annual Operating Budget:* Less than $50,000; *Funding Sources:* Membership fees
10 volunteer(s)
Membership: 300+; *Fees:* $150-$300; students free; *Member Profile:* Accredited Ontario industrial designers; *Committees:* Education; Mentorship; Rocket Design Show
Activities: Promoting common standards throughout Ontario; Providing networking opportunities; Increasing public awareness of the profession's benefit to society; Offering continuing education opportunities; Organizing annual student thesis design show, monthly get-togethers & learning sessions; Developing industry outreach efforts; *Awareness Events:* Rocket: ACIDO's Annual Industrial Design Graduation Show & Competition; *Internships:* Yes
Chief Officer(s):
Jonathan Loudon, President, 416-564-9780
jonathan@swavestudios.com
David Green, Director, Public Relations, 416-940-3080
acido.pr@gmail.com
Publications:
• Association of Chartered Industrial Designers of Ontario Membership Directory
Type: Directory
Profile: Names, addresses, telephone numbers, & membership status of all ACIDO members

Association of Christian Churches in Manitoba (ACCM) / Association des églises chrétiennes du Manitoba
151 de la Cathedrale Ave., Winnipeg MB R2H 0H6
Tel: 204-237-9851
Previous Name: Ecumenical Committee of Manitoba
Overview: A medium-sized provincial organization founded in 1990
Mission: To bring Christian churches into living encounter with one another; to provide a network of news & events which can help member churches act together in all matters except those in which deep differences compel us to act separately; to act as common Christian voice & media contact on issues of spiritual & social concern in the Province
Finances: *Annual Operating Budget:* Less than $50,000

Association of Colleges of Applied Arts & Technology of Ontario *See* Colleges Ontario

Association of Commercial & Industrial Contractors of PEI
PO Box 1685, Charlottetown PE C1A 7N4
Tel: 902-566-3456; *Fax:* 902-368-2754
wmm@wmm93.pe.ca
Overview: A small provincial organization overseen by Mechanical Contractors Association of Canada
Chief Officer(s):
Mary MacDonald, Contact

Association of Complementary & Integrative Physicians of BC (ACIPBC)
PO Box 526, #185, 911 Yates St., Victoria BC V8V 4Y9
www.acpbc.org
Overview: A small provincial organization founded in 1995
Mission: To ensure the delivery of quality holistic patient care through education, information, research, & the professional development of physicians
Affiliation(s): Canadian Complementary Medical Association
Membership: *Fees:* $100; $30 student/resident/retired; *Committees:* Education
Chief Officer(s):
Bill Code, President
Publications:
• ACIPBC [Association of Complementary & Integrative Physicians of BC] Newsletter
Type: Newsletter; *Frequency:* Quarterly

Association of Condominium Managers of Ontario (ACMO)
#100, 2233 Argentia Rd., Mississauga ON L5N 2X7
Tel: 905-826-6890; *Fax:* 905-826-4873
Toll-Free: 800-265-3263
www.acmo.org
www.linkedin.com/groups/ACMOnews-3782859
www.facebook.com/ACMO.org1977
twitter.com/ACMOnews
Overview: A medium-sized provincial organization founded in 1977
Mission: To enhance the quality performance of condominium property managers & management companies in Ontario
Finances: *Annual Operating Budget:* $250,000-$500,000; *Funding Sources:* Membership dues; advertising
10 volunteer(s)
Membership: 534 R.C.M.s + 132 candidates + 47 corporate + 14 affiliate + 331 associate; *Fees:* 106.00 individual; $270 general; $450-550 corporate; *Member Profile:* Any person in a full-time capacity in the managment of condominiums in Ontario may become a member of the Association and must agree to meet all of the criteria to be elgible to write and pass the R.C.M. examiniation with a further six months. A Candidate Membership shall not be renewed after the fourth year.
Activities: Educational certification designation - Registered Condominium Manager RCM; *Speaker Service:* Yes; *Library:* by appointment Not open to public
Chief Officer(s):
Steven Christodoulou, R.C.M., President

Association of Consulting Engineering Companies - British Columbia (ACEC-BC)
#1258, 409 Granville St., Vancouver BC V6C 1T2
Tel: 604-687-2811; *Fax:* 604-688-7110
info@acec-bc.ca
www.acec-bc.ca
Previous Name: Consulting Engineers of British Columbia
Overview: A medium-sized provincial organization founded in 1976 overseen by Association of Consulting Engineering Companies - Canada
Mission: To improve the commercial environment for consulting engineering firms
Membership: *Member Profile:* Consulting engineering firms across British Columbia that provide services to the built & natural environment; *Committees:* Building Engineering; Municipal Engineering; Resource & Energy; Transportation; Business Practice; Membership Affairs; Professional Development; Young Professsionals' Group; Okanagan/Thompson Liaison; Vancouver Island Liaison
Activities: Lobbying to policymakers in districts, provincial & municipal governments, & private sector clients; Coordinating a common industry approach to issues; Promoting members' consulting services; Providing networking, educational, & professional development opportunities
Chief Officer(s):
Catherine Fritter, Chair
Keith Sashaw, President & CEO
Alla Samusevich, Coordinator, Accounting & Events
Awards:
• Awards for Engineering Excellence
To honour outstanding achievements in engineering
Meetings/Conferences:
• Association of Consulting Engineering Companies British Columbia 2018 AGM, 2018, BC
Scope: Provincial
• Association of Consulting Engineering Companies British Columbia 2018 Annual Transportation Conference, 2018, BC
Scope: Provincial
• Association of Consulting Engineering Companies British Columbia 2018 Awards Gala, 2018, BC
Scope: Provincial
Description: The presentation of the Awards for Engineering Excellence in categories such as buildings, municipal, transportation, natural resources, energy & industry, & soft engineering
Publications:
• Association of Consulting Engineering Companies - British Columbia Annual Report
Type: Yearbook; *Frequency:* Annually
Profile: The association's profile, reports from the president, executive director, treasurer, & the committees, the minutes from the annual generalmeeting, awards, & events
• Directory of ACEC-BC [Association of Consulting Engineering Companies - British Columbia] Member Firms
Type: Directory
Profile: Listings of Consulting Engineers of British Columbia members, available for the public online

Association of Consulting Engineering Companies - Canada (ACEC) / L'Association des firmes d'ingénieurs-conseils - Canada (AFIC)
#420, 130 Albert St., Ottawa ON K1P 5G4
Tel: 613-236-0569; *Fax:* 613-236-6193
Toll-Free: 800-565-0569
info@acec.ca
www.acec.ca
www.linkedin.com/groups/7450101
twitter.com/ACECCanada
www.youtube.com/ACECAFIC
Previous Name: Association of Consulting Engineers of Canada
Overview: A large national organization founded in 1925
Mission: To assist in promoting satisfactory business relations between its Member Firms & their clients; To promote cordial relations among the various consulting engineering firms in Canada & to foster the interchange of professional, management & business experience & information among them; To safeguard the interest of the consulting engineer; To further the maintenance of high professional standards in the consulting

engineering profession
Member of: International Federation of Consulting Engineers
35 volunteer(s)
Membership: 500; *Fees:* Based on annual revenue; *Member Profile:* Firms which have passed a thorough membership screening process: proven technical capability, necessary experience as consultants, adherence to rules of ethical practice & professional responsibility; membership is voluntary & is limited to those firms primarily engaged in providing independent consulting engineering services to the public; *Committees:* Budget & Finance; Business Integrity & Transparency Task Force; Business Practices Advisory Group; Federal/Industry Real Property Advisory Council; DND/DCC Liaison; General Reserve Investment; International Advisory Group; Governance; Student Outreach Advisory Group
Activities: Federal government lobbying on major public policy issues; Negotiations with government departments re: contracting-out of public work, selection of consultants & remuneration; Negotiations with other industry organizations re: establishment of guidelines for contracts; International market development; *Awareness Events:* National Engineering Month; *Speaker Service:* Yes; *Rents Mailing List:* Yes; *Library:* Open to public
Chief Officer(s):
John D. Gamble, CET, P.Eng., President
jgamble@acec.ca
Jean-Marc Carrière, Vice-President, Finance & Administration, 613-236-0569 Ext. 209
jmcarriere@acec.ca
Martine Proulx, Director, Programs & Member Services, 613-236-0569 Ext. 203
mproulx@acec.ca
Mark Buzan, Director, Business Development & Corporate Partnerships, 613-236-0569 Ext. 214
mbuzan@acec.ca
Awards:
• Public Service Awards, Canadian Consulting Engineering Awards
• Shreyer Award, Canadian Consulting Engineering Awards
• Awards of Excellence & Merit, Canadian Consulting Engineering Awards
• Allen D. Williams Scholarship
Meetings/Conferences:
• Association of Consulting Engineering Companies Leadership Conference 2018, October, 2018, Ottawa, ON
Scope: National
Publications:
• Concept [a publication of the Association of Consulting Engineering Companies - Canada]
Number of Pages: 4
• Source [a publication of the Association of Consulting Engineering Companies - Canada]
Type: Newsletter; *Frequency:* Monthly
• Source Express [a publication of the Association of Consulting Engineering Companies - Canada]
Type: Newsletter

Association of Consulting Engineering Companies - Manitoba (ACEC-MB)
PO Box 1547, Stn. Main, Winnipeg MB R3C 2Z4
Tel: 204-774-5258; *Fax:* 204-779-0788
acec-mb.ca
twitter.com/acec_manitoba
Previous Name: Consulting Engineers of Manitoba Inc.
Overview: A medium-sized provincial organization founded in 1978 overseen by Association of Consulting Engineering Companies - Canada
Mission: To promote & enhance the business interests of the consulting engineers of Manitoba; to lead in the application of technology for the benefit of society
Affiliation(s): Association of Professional Engineers of Manitoba; International Federation of Consulting Engineers; Manitoba Association of Architects
Finances: *Annual Operating Budget:* $50,000-$100,000; *Funding Sources:* Membership dues
Membership: 31 firms; *Member Profile:* Offer primarily consulting engineering services to public; *Committees:* Awards; Business Practices Conference; Contracts; Energy, Science & Technology; First Nations; Golf; Government Affairs; Image; Institutional; Private Sector; Professional Development; Transportation; TWICE; Water & Environment; Young Professionals
Activities: *Speaker Service:* Yes
Chief Officer(s):
Cameron Dyck, P.Eng., P.E., President

Shirley E. Tillett, Executive Director
shirley@acec-mb.ca

Association of Consulting Engineering Companies - New Brunswick (ACEC-NB) / Association des firmes d'ingénieurs-conseils - Nouveau-Brunswick
PO Box 415, Moncton NB E1C 8L4
Tel: 506-380-5776
info@acec-nb.ca
www.acec-nb.ca
Overview: A medium-sized provincial organization founded in 1983 overseen by Association of Consulting Engineering Companies - Canada
Mission: To develop & support member firms; To improve the business environment for member firms & their clients; To further the professional standards of the consulting engineering profession
Membership: 30
Activities: Advocating for consulting engineering companies in New Brunswick; Providing training opportunities
Chief Officer(s):
Nadine Boudreau, Executive Director
nboudreau@acec-nb.ca
Awards:
• CENB Showcase Awards
Includes the following awards: Benefit to Society Award, Innovation Award, Technical Excellence Award, & Sustainability Award
Publications:
• CE [Consulting Engineers] News
Type: Newsletter; *Frequency:* Bimonthly
Profile: Information for Association of Consulting Engineering Companies - New Brunswick members

Association of Consulting Engineering Companies - Prince Edward Island (ACEC-PEI)
c/o James C Johnson Associates Inc., #2, Pickard Bldg., Harbourside II, Charlottetown PE C1A 8R4
Tel: 902-629-5895; *Fax:* 902-368-2196
Overview: A small provincial organization overseen by Association of Consulting Engineering Companies - Canada
Chief Officer(s):
Hal Brothers, Acting Executive Director
hal@jcjinc.com

Association of Consulting Engineering Companies - Quebec *Voir* Association des firmes de génie-conseil - Québec

Association of Consulting Engineering Companies - Saskatchewan (ACEC-SK)
#12, 2010 - 7 Ave., Regina SK S4R 1C2
Tel: 306-359-3338; *Fax:* 306-522-5325
info@acec-sk.ca
www.acec-sk.ca
Previous Name: Consulting Engineers of Saskatchewan; Association of Consulting Engineers of Saskatchewan
Overview: A small provincial organization founded in 1977 overseen by Association of Consulting Engineering Companies - Canada
Mission: To further the maintenance of high professional standards in consulting engineering profession; To promote cordial relations among various consulting firms in Saskatchewan; To foster interchange of professional management & business experience & information among consulting engineers; To develop regional representation & participation in affairs of the association
Finances: *Annual Operating Budget:* $50,000-$100,000
Staff Member(s): 3; 100+ volunteer(s)
Membership: 49 firms + 9 associates; *Committees:* Building; Communications; Environment/Water Resources; Human Resources; Industry Resources; Transportation; Young Professionals Group (YPG); Awards; Risk Mitigation; Consultant Selection Working Group Government Relations
Chief Officer(s):
Jason Gasmo, P.Eng, Chair
jason_gasmo@clifton.ca
Beverly MacLeod, Executive Director
bmacleod@acec-sk.ca
Awards:
• CES Brian Eckel Award
To promote the consulting engineering industry. *Eligibility:* CES member firms
• CES Young Professional Award
Eligibility: Young professionals who demonstrates excellence in: his/her field of expertise; the business of consulting engineering/geoscience; dedication to his/her consulting engineering/geoscience association and community; as well as increasing awareness of the value of young professionals in the Saskatchewan consulting engineering/geoscience industry.

Association of Consulting Engineers of Canada *See* Association of Consulting Engineering Companies - Canada

Association of Corporate Travel Executives Inc. Canada
PO Box 85020, Stittsville ON K2S 1X6
Tel: 613-831-6568
canada@acte.org
www.acte.org
www.linkedin.com/company/1278017
www.facebook.com/acteglobal
twitter.com/ACTEtweets
www.instagram.com/actephotos
Also Known As: ACTE Canada
Overview: A medium-sized national organization
Mission: To promote dialogue through education, advocacy & research for the global corporate travel community
Membership: *Member Profile:* Travel management companies; Corporate buyers; Suppliers; Students
Activities: Offering educational events; Providing professional networking opportunities
Chief Officer(s):
Maria Stevens, Senior Regional Manager, Canada
mstevens@acte.org

Association of Councils of Physicians, Dentists & Pharmacists of Québec *Voir* Association des conseils des médecins, dentistes et pharmaciens du Québec

Association of Day Care Operators of Ontario (ADCO)
6 Davidson St., St Catharines ON L2R 2V4
Fax: 705-733-2154
www.adco-o.on.ca
Overview: A medium-sized provincial organization founded in 1977
Mission: To promote the growth of private & independent (non-profit) licensed child care programs & safeguard the interests of the providers of this service in Ontario through public education, advocacy, professional (management) development & advisory activities locally & provincially
Finances: *Annual Operating Budget:* $100,000-$250,000; *Funding Sources:* Membership dues
Staff Member(s): 3
Membership: 350+; *Fees:* Schedule available
Activities: Centre of the Year Competition; conferences; luncheons; management training seminars; extensive insurance program; *Awareness Events:* Kids Helping Kids Walkathon, May; *Speaker Service:* Yes; *Library:* Resource Centre; by appointment

Association of Dental Technologists of Ontario (ADTO)
#235, 7181 Woodbine Ave., Markham ON L3R 1A3
Tel: 416-742-2386; *Fax:* 416-742-2386
Toll-Free: 877-788-2386
info@adto.ca
www.adto.ca
Overview: A small provincial organization
Mission: To advance the dental technologist profession through education, communication among members & liaison with external agencies; To promote quality delivery of dental technology services
Finances: *Funding Sources:* Membership dues & events revenue
Staff Member(s): 1
Membership: 500-999; *Fees:* $670; *Member Profile:* Registered dental technologists practicing in Ontario
Activities: Continuing education; social events
Chief Officer(s):
Franklin Parada, President
Chris Ji, Vice-President
Duy Cuong Banh, Secretary
Shabana Mirza, Treasurer
Publications:
• The Benchmark [a publication of the Association of Dental Technologists of Ontario]
Type: Newsletter; *Frequency:* Quarterly
Profile: Keeps members informed of the activities of the ADTO

Association of Dermatologists of Québec *Voir* Association des dermatologistes du Québec

Association of Disabled Adults on the North Shore *Voir* Association des handicapés adultes de la Côte-Nord

Association of Early Childhood Educators of Alberta (AECEA)
#54, 9912 - 106 St., Edmonton AB T5K 1C5
Tel: 780-421-7544; *Fax:* 780-428-0080
Toll-Free: 877-421-9937
info@aecea.ca
www.aecea.ca
twitter.com/AECEA_
Merged from: Alberta Child Care Network Association; Early Childhood Professional Association of Alberta
Overview: A medium-sized provincial organization
Mission: To strengthen & advance the early learning & child care profession in Alberta
Affiliation(s): Canadian Child Care Federation; Provincial Ministry of Children and Youth Services; FRP Canada
Membership: *Fees:* $50 student; $125 associate/individual; *Member Profile:* ELCC educators, staff, students, academics, operators, & other interested individuals & groups
Chief Officer(s):
Manna Middleton, Chair

Association of Early Childhood Educators of Newfoundland & Labrador (AECENL)
PO Box 8657, #19, 50 Pippy Pl., St. John's NL A1B 3T1
Tel: 709-579-3028; *Fax:* 709-579-0217
Toll-Free: 877-579-3028
Other Communication: aecenlpd@nfld.net
aecenl@nfld.net
www.aecenl.ca
www.facebook.com/AECENL
twitter.com/aecenl
Overview: A small provincial organization founded in 1989
Mission: To promote professionalism in the field of early childhood education; To improve working conditions for early childhood educators in Newfoundland & Labrador; To ensure quality child care & education for young children in the province
Affiliation(s): Canadian Child Care Federation (CCCF)
Staff Member(s): 3; 12 volunteer(s)
Membership: *Fees:* $50 individual/associate; $85 organization; *Member Profile:* Early childhood educators; Students; Associate member, such as associations or agencies
Activities: Providing the Child Care Services Certification service; Supporting orientation courses to achieve certification; Offering professional development workshops; Advocating for early childhood educators in Newfoundland & Labrador; Liaising with the Government of Newfoundland & Labrador & related organizations; Promoting awareness of quality child care; *Awareness Events:* NL Early Childhood Educators Week, last week of May; National Child Day, November 20th
Chief Officer(s):
Skye Crawford Taylor, Director, Professional Development
Mojca Bas, Registrar, Child Care Services Certification
Roisin Cowley, Office Administrator
Publications:
• Association of Early Childhood Educators of Newfoundland & Labrador Newsletter
Type: Newsletter; *Price:* Free with Assn. of Early Childhood Educators of Newfoundland & Labrador membership

Association of Early Childhood Educators of Quebec (AECEQ)
1001, rue Lenoir, #A2-10, Montréal QC H4C 2Z6
membership@aeceq.ca
www.aeceq.ca
Previous Name: Nursery School Teachers Association
Overview: A medium-sized provincial organization founded in 1946
Mission: To improve the quality of early childhood education in Quebec
Member of: Canadian Child Care Federation
Membership: *Fees:* $35; *Member Profile:* Early childhood educators
Chief Officer(s):
Julie Butler, Contact

Association of Early Childhood Educators Ontario (AECEO)
#211, 40 Orchard View Blvd., Toronto ON M4R 1B9
Tel: 416-487-3157; *Fax:* 416-487-3758
Toll-Free: 866-932-3236
info@aeceo.ca
www.aeceo.ca
www.facebook.com/189978994376068
twitter.com/AECEO
Overview: A medium-sized provincial charitable organization founded in 1950
Mission: To support early childhood educators throughout Ontario
Affiliation(s): Canadian Child Care Federation
Finances: *Funding Sources:* Membership fees; Advertising; Sponsorships
Membership: *Fees:* $60-$125; *Member Profile:* Early childhood educators in Ontario; Students enrolled in an Ontario College of Applied Arts & Technology or an Ontario university leading to a diploma or degree in early childhood education; Individuals interested in the field of early childhood education
Activities: Advocating on behalf of early childhood educators across Ontario; Disseminating research; Providing professional development opportunities; Offering networking events for persons interested in early childhood education & care; Educating the public about the quality of early childhood education; *Awareness Events:* Week of the Child, October
Chief Officer(s):
Rachel Langford, President
Eduarda Sousa, Executive Director
esousa@aeceo.ca
Lena DaCosta, Coordinator, Professional Development, Marketing & Advertising
ldacosta@aeceo.ca
Sue Parker, Coordinator, Membership Services & Office Manager
membership@aeceo.ca
Goranka Vukelich, Secretary
Gaby Chauvet, Treasurer
Awards:
• Children's Service Award
An annual award to recognize two persons who have made significant contributions toward young people
Meetings/Conferences:
• Association of Early Childhood Educators Ontario 2018 68th Annual Provincial Conference, 2018, ON
Scope: Provincial
Description: A conference & exhibits for delegates from across Ontario
Publications:
• Association of Early Childhood Educators Ontario Annual Report
Type: Yearbook; *Frequency:* Annually
• Association of Early Childhood Educators Ontario e-Bulletin
Type: Newsletter; *Frequency:* Weekly
Profile: Current events of the association & child care updates
• eceLINK
Type: Newsletter; *Frequency:* Quarterly; *Accepts Advertising*
Profile: A publication for members of the Association of Early Childhood Educators Ontario, affiliate organizations, & ministry contacts

Association of Educational Research Officers of Ontario
See Association of Educational Researchers of Ontario

Association of Educational Researchers of Ontario (AERO) / Association ontarienne des chercheurs et chercheuse en éducation
c/o Research & Information Services, Toronto District School Board, 1 Civic Centre Court, Lower Level, Toronto ON M9C 2B3
Tel: 416-394-4929; *Fax:* 416-394-4946
info@aero-aoce.org
www.aero-aoce.org
Previous Name: Association of Educational Research Officers of Ontario
Overview: A small provincial organization founded in 1972
Mission: To promote & improve research, education, planning & development pertaining to education in the Ontario school system
Affiliation(s): American Educational Research Association
Finances: *Funding Sources:* Membership fees
Membership: *Fees:* $40; *Member Profile:* Active - based on current employment & training in research, supervisory responsibility, past employment or interest in goals of the Association; *Committees:* Fall & Spring Professional Learning; Communications & Partnerships; Research & Resources
Activities: *Speaker Service:* Yes
Chief Officer(s):
Terry Spencer, President
tspencer@office.ldcsb.on.ca

Association of Educators of Gifted, Talented & Creative Children in BC
c/o British Columbia Teachers' Federation, #100, 550 West 6th Ave., Vancouver BC V5Z 4P2
Tel: 604-871-2283
Toll-Free: 800-663-9163
psac63@bctf.ca
aegtccbc.ca
Overview: A small provincial organization founded in 1979
Mission: To advocate the special needs of gifted children in the province.
Affiliation(s): Council for Exceptional Children
Membership: *Member Profile:* Member of British Columbia Teachers' Federation
Activities: *Speaker Service:* Yes; *Rents Mailing List:* Yes; *Library:* by appointment
Chief Officer(s):
Elizabeth Ensing, Contact
conference@aegtccbc.ca

Association of Electromyography Technologists of Canada (AETC)
info@aetc.ca
www.aetc.ca
Overview: A small national organization founded in 1976
Mission: To enhance the standards & education of individuals involved in the electromyography (EMG) technology field
Chief Officer(s):
Jodi Beswick, President
jodi.beswick@aetc.ca
Angela Scott, Vice-President
angela.scott@aetc.ca
Nancy Verreault, Secretary-Treasurer
nancy.verreault@aetc.ca

Association of Employees Supporting Education Services (AESES)
#102, 900 Harrow St. East, Winnipeg MB R3M 3Y7
Tel: 204-949-5200; *Fax:* 204-949-5215
aeses@aeses.ca
www.aeses.ca
Overview: A small local organization founded in 1972
Mission: To act as the certified bargaining agent for the support staff at the University of Manitoba, the University of Winnipeg, & St. Andrew's College, as well as the University of Manitoba's security services staff; To represent the interests of members; To maintain the welfare of members; To foster & maintain communication & goodwill between employers & employees
Membership: 2,000+; *Member Profile:* Support staff & security services employees at the University of Manitoba; Support staff at the University of Winnipeg & St. Andrew's College
Activities: Securing appropriate working conditions for the support staff employees of the University of Manitoba, St. Andrew's College, & the University of Winnipeg, plus the University of Manitoba's security services staff; Educating members about collective bargaining; Providing fellowship opportunities
Chief Officer(s):
Lisa McKendry, Office Manager
lmckendry@aeses.ca
Alice Foster, Secretary
Publications:
• Inside AESES
Type: Newsletter; *Frequency:* 5 pa
Profile: Association happenings

Association of Engineering Technicians & Technologists of Newfoundland & Labrador (AETTNL)
Donovan's Industrial Park, PO Box 790, 22 Sagona Ave., Mount Pearl NL A1N 2Y2
Tel: 709-747-2868; *Fax:* 709-747-2869
Toll-Free: 888-238-8600
aettnl@aettnl.com
www.aettnl.com
Overview: A small provincial organization founded in 1968 overseen by Canadian Council of Technicians & Technologists
Mission: To advance the profession of Applied Science/Engineering Technology & the professional recognition of Certified Technicians & Technologists.
Membership: 1279; *Fees:* $165 certified; $110 associate; $50 student; $82.20 retired/unemployed; *Committees:* Certification/Registration Board; Act; Public Relations; Consitution By-laws; Accreditation; AETTNL/PEGNL; AETTNL/ALBNL-NLAA; Ethics-Disciplinary; Nominations; Professional Ethics Exam
Chief Officer(s):
Newton Pritchett, President
Donna Parsons, Registrar

Association of English Language Publishers of Québec (AELAQ) / Association des éditeurs de langue anglaise du Québec
#3, 1200, av Atwater, Montréal QC H3Z 1X4
Tel: 514-932-5633
admin@aelaq.org
www.aelaq.org
Previous Name: AEAQ Inc.
Overview: A small provincial organization founded in 1990 overseen by Association of Canadian Publishers
Mission: To raise the profile of English-language books published in Québec
Finances: Funding Sources: Canada Council for the ARts; Dept. of Canadian Heritage; SODEC; Conseil des arts de Montréal
Membership: 21 publishers; Member Profile: Membership is open to any firm, partnership, indivdual proprietorships or institutions which; has its chief office of business in Québec; Is at least 80 % owned by persons who are Canadian citizens or landed immigrants; Is effectively controlled by persons who are residents in Quebec and are Canadian citizens or landed immigrants; Publishes original Canadian books as an important and substantial part of its business; Has in print not less than five original Canadian titles and an on-going publishing program of not less than one title a year, and has been in operation for at least two years from the date of publication of its first title; Has no more than 25 % of its books written by its principals; Is a member of ACP or other national organization.
Activities: Professional development; public awareness; promotion of English-language literature from Québec; book of the month
Chief Officer(s):
Julia Kater, Executive Director

Association of Equipment Manufacturers - Canada (AEM-Canada)
World Exchange Plaza, PO Box 81067, #880, 111 Albert St., Ottawa ON K1P 1B1
Tel: 613-566-4568; Fax: 613-566-2026
www.aem.org
Previous Name: Canadian Farm & Industrial Equipment Institute
Overview: A small national organization founded in 1966
Mission: To act as a voice for its members to the public & on a governmental level. It is also a regulatory body setting standars for safety, offering a variety of educational programs & seminars.
Membership: Member Profile: Manufacturers & distributors of equipment, & those who offer services, in the agriculture, construction, forestry, mining & utility industries.
Chief Officer(s):
Dennis Slater, President, 414-298-4140
dslater@aem.org
Howard Mains, Canada Consultant, Public Policy
hmains@aem.org

Association of Executive Directors of Québec Health & Social Services
Voir Association des directeurs généraux des services de santé et des services sociaux du Québec

Association of Exploration Geochemists
See Association of Applied Geochemists

Association of Faculties of Medicine of Canada (AFMC) / L'Association des facultés de médecine du Canada (AFMC)
#800, 265 Carling Ave., Ottawa ON K1S 2E1
Tel: 613-730-0687; Fax: 613-730-1196
username@afmc.ca
www.afmc.ca
twitter.com/afmc_e
Previous Name: Association of Canadian Medical Colleges
Overview: A medium-sized national charitable organization founded in 1943
Mission: To represent the interests of members in medical research policy formulation; to promote & advance academic medicine through the review & development of standards for medical education, through the development of national policies appropriate to the aims & purposes of Canadian faculties of medicine, through the fostering of research, & through representation of Canadian faculties of medicine to professional associations & governments
Affiliation(s): Canadian Medical Association; Association of Universities & Colleges of Canada
Finances: Funding Sources: Membership fees; annual meeting; research contracts; sale of publications
Staff Member(s): 35
Membership: 17 Canadian Faculties of Medicine; Fees: Fixed fee per school & a capitation fee based on first-time undergraduate enrollment; Member Profile: Accredited Canadian Faculties of Medicine; Committees: Admissions; Undergraduate Medical Education; Postgraduate Medical Education; Research & Graduate Studies; Continuing Professional Development; Faculty Development; Student Affairs; Senior Administration
Chief Officer(s):
Genevieve Moineau, President & CEO

Association of Faculties of Pharmacy of Canada (AFPC) / Association des facultés de pharmacie du Canada
PO Box 59025, Stn. Alta Vista, Ottawa ON K1G 5T7
admin@afpc.info
www.afpc.info
Previous Name: Canadian Conference of Pharmaceutical Faculties
Overview: A medium-sized national charitable organization founded in 1945
Mission: To develop & implement policies & programs which will provide a forum for exchange of ideas, ensure a liaison with other organizations; To foster & promote excellence in pharmaceutical education & research in Canada
Member of: Canadian Council on Continuing Education in Pharmacy
Affiliation(s): Canadian Pharmacists Association
Membership: Member Profile: Full - member of teaching faculty of Canadian Faculty of Pharmacy; associate - interested in goals of the association; Committees: Awards; Communications; Education; PEP Canada; Research
Chief Officer(s):
Janet Cooper, Executive Director
executivedirector@afpc.info

Association of Faculties of Veterinary Medicine in Canada
See Canadian Faculties of Agriculture & Veterinary Medicine

Association of Family Health Teams of Ontario (AFHTO)
#800, 60 St. Clair Ave. East, Toronto ON M4T 1N5
Tel: 647-234-8605
info@afhto.ca
www.afhto.ca
www.facebook.com/afhto
twitter.com/afhto
Overview: A medium-sized provincial organization
Mission: To promote the expansion of high-quality, comprehensive, well-integrated interprofessional primary care for the benefit of all Ontarians
Membership: Fees: Schedule available
Chief Officer(s):
Kavita Mehta, Chief Executive Officer
kavita.mehta@afhto.ca
Sombo Saviye, Office Manager
sombo.saviye@afhto.ca
Paula Myers, Coordinator, Membership, Communications & Conference
paula.myers@afhto.ca
Meetings/Conferences:
• Association of Family Health Teams of Ontario 2018 Conference, October, 2018
Scope: Provincial
• Association of Family Health Teams of Ontario 2019 Conference, October, 2019
Scope: Provincial

Association of Filipino Canadian Accountants (AFCA)
PO Box 55554, Stn. Cedar Heights, Toronto ON M1H 3G7
www.afcatoronto.org
Overview: A small national organization founded in 1978 overseen by National Council of Philippine American Canadian Accountants
Mission: To promote the continuing education of Filipino Canadian accountants; To promote high professional standards; To liaise with other international organizations
Member of: National Council of Philippine American Canadian Accountants (NCPACA)
Finances: Funding Sources: Membership fees; Sponsorships; Fundraising
Membership: 400; Fees: $30 individuals; $50 couples; Member Profile: Filipino designated accounting professionals; Filipino students, who are pursuing a career in accounting; Committees: Scholarship
Activities: Presenting professional development activities, such as career options seminars, tax preparation training, & accounting software training; Helping new immigrant members evaluate their credentials & qualifications with Canadian accounting bodies; Facilitating members' assimilation in Canada; Assisting with job placements; Organizing an AFCA toastmasters club; Arranging social & recreational activities; Engaging in community services, such as the free income tax preparation program
Chief Officer(s):
Mercedita Gonzales, President
president@afcatoronto.com
Ramon Guanzon, Executive Vice-President
Imelda Bautista, Vice-President, External Affairs
Rodel Acoba, Vice-President, Internal Affairs
Nimfa Santos, Secretary
Leonora Salvador, Treasurer
Nechane Vitales, Officer, Public Relations
Awards:
• AFCA Scholarship
To provide financial assistance to Filipino Canadian students in Ontario who are pursuing a career in accounting
Publications:
• Association of Filipino Canadian Accountants Members' Directory
Type: Directory
• Spreadsheet [a publication of the Association of Filipino Canadian Accountants]
Type: Newsletter; Frequency: Quarterly; Editor: Ramon Guanzon
Profile: Association of Filipino Canadian Accountants' achievements & activities, plus important events

Association of Filipino Canadian Accountants in British Columbia (AFCA-BC)
BC
Other Communication: Library E-mail: library@afca-bc.org
information@afca-bc.org
www.afca-bc.org
twitter.com/AFCABC
Overview: A small provincial organization founded in 2008 overseen by National Council of Philippine American Canadian Accountants
Member of: National Council of Philippine American Canadian Accountants (NCPACA)
Finances: Funding Sources: Membership fees; Sponsorships; Fundraising
Membership: Member Profile: Filipino designated accounting professionals; Filipino students, who are pursuing a career in accounting; Committees: Finance & Fundraising; Membership & Recruitment; Mentorship Program Coordinator; Nomination & Election; Professional Development & Education; Public Relations & Communications; Social & Community Relations; Values & Ethics; Web Development Team
Activities: Workshops; professional development activities; Library: AFCA-BC Library
Chief Officer(s):
Eloisa Peralta, President
Mary Anthonette Tecson, Vice-President
Marilyn Aceja-Uy, Secretary
Paolo Sanchez, Treasurer
Awards:
• AFCA-BC Scholarship

Association of First Nations' Women; West Coast Professional Native Women's Association
See Pacific Association of First Nations' Women

Association of Food Banks & CVAs for New Brunswick
See New Brunswick Association of Food Banks

Association of Francophone Newspapers
Voir Association de la presse francophone

Association of Hearing Instrument Practitioners of Ontario (AHIP)
#211, 55 Mary St. West, Lindsay ON K9V 5Z6
Tel: 705-328-0907; Fax: 705-878-4110
Toll-Free: 888-745-2447
office@ahip.ca
www.helpmehear.ca
Overview: A small provincial organization
Mission: AHIP is a non-profit organization that serves as a regulatory & lobbying body for it membership of hearing healthcare professoinals. It ensures education requirements, a code of ethics, & ultimately an improvement of services by its members to the public.
Staff Member(s): 3
Membership: Fees: $790 full; $60 student
Activities: Symposiums; Internships: Yes
Chief Officer(s):

B. Maggie Arzani, President
Joanne Sproule, Executive Director

Association of Hemophilia Clinic Directors of Canada (AHCDC)
70 Bond St., Toronto ON M5B 1X3
Tel: 416-864-5042; Fax: 416-864-5251
ahcdc@smh.ca
www.ahcdc.ca
Overview: A small national organization founded in 1994
Mission: To improve the treatment of people with hemophilia
Affiliation(s): Canadian Hemophilia Society
Membership: 83; Member Profile: Directors of Hemophilia Clinics; Committees: Executive; Membership & Nominating; CHR & CHARMS; Research; Inhibitor; Privacy; FIX
Chief Officer(s):
Annie Kaplan, Contact

Association of Heritage Consultants See Canadian Association of Heritage Professionals

Association of Home Appliance Manufacturers Canada Council (AHAM)
#1200, 130 Albert St., Ottawa ON K1P 5G4
Tel: 613-236-8428
info@aham.org
www.aham.org/AHAM/AuxAHAMCanada
twitter.com/AHAM_Voice
Merged from: The Canadian Appliance Manufacturers Association
Overview: A small national organization
Mission: To represent member interests in the establishment of product standards & in environmental legislation; To advocate the safe removal of mercury & other ozone depleting substances from older appliances; To support the development of energy efficient products
Membership: 61; Member Profile: Canadian manufacturers of major, portable, & floor care appliances
Activities: Conducting industry research projects; Identifying & communicating issues of members; Providing information required to operate in the Canadian market
Chief Officer(s):
Bruce Rebel, General Manager & Vice-President
brebel@ahamcanada.ca
Kevin Girdharry, Manager, Policy & Data Analysis, 613-236-8428 Ext. 452
kgirdharry@ahamcanada.ca
Lisa Sattler, Manager, Regulatory Affairs, 613-236-8428 Ext. 451
lsattler@ahamcanada.ca

Association of Image Consultants International Canada (AICI Canada)
c/o Mihaela Ciocan, ImagePro International Institute, PO Box 16079, 1199 Lynn Valley Rd., North Vancouver BC V7J 3H2
www.aicicanada.com
Overview: A small local organization founded in 1994
Mission: To advance professionalism within the field of image consultants
Membership: 110+; Member Profile: Image professionals who specialize in visual appearance, & verbal & non-verbal communication, such as media trainers, career coaches, cosmetic & skin care specialists, colour & wardrobe consultants, & etiquette experts
Activities: Providing networking opportunities; Offering certification levels for members; Upgrading technical knowledge through continuing professional development; Liaising with related organizations
Chief Officer(s):
Mihaela Ciocan, President, 778-861-5776
mihaela.ciocan@image-pro.ca
Carol Robichaud, Treasurer, 905-278-1472
kcrimage@eol.ca
Mirella Zanatta, Vice-President, Communications, 519-473-2396
mz@firstimpressionsimageconsulting.com
Publications:
• Association of Image Consultants International Membership Directory
Type: Directory
• Image Insights
Type: Newsletter; Frequency: Quarterly; Editor: Porcia Blake, AICI FLC; Price: Free with AICI Canada membership

Association of Independent Consultants (AIC)
145 Thornway Ave., Thornhill ON L4J 7Z3
Tel: 416-410-8163; Fax: 905-669-5233
info1@aiconsult.ca
www.aiconsult.ca
Overview: A small national charitable organization founded in 1989
Affiliation(s): Society of Internet Professionals (SIP); Canadian Association of Professional Speakers (CAPS); XL Results Canada Inc.; The Mississauga Technology Association (MTA)
Finances: Funding Sources: Sponsorships
Membership: Fees: $149 full membership; $55 remote membership; Member Profile: Canadian individuals who run their own consulting businesses
Activities: Providing networking opportunities; Offering professional development activities; Assisting people to hire a consultant in many fields; Speaker Service: Yes
Chief Officer(s):
Lawrence Fox, President
president1@aiconsult.ca
Paul Marcus, Vice-President, Membership Services
membership1@aiconsult.ca
Publications:
• Association of Independent Consultants Newsletter
Type: Newsletter; Frequency: Monthly
• Marketing Tip of the Month [a publication of the Association of Independent Consultants]
Frequency: Monthly; Price: Free with Association of Independent Consultants membership
Profile: Information for Canadian consultants & entrepreneurs

Association of Independent Corrugated Converters
PO Box 73063, Stn. White Shields, 2300 Lawrence Ave. East, Toronto ON M1P 4Z5
Tel: 905-727-9405; Fax: 905-727-1061
info@aiccbox.ca
www.aiccbox.ca
www.linkedin.com/company/aicc-canada
Also Known As: AICC Canada
Overview: A small national organization founded in 1975
Mission: To provide a forum for independent corrugated converters on legitimate matters of mutual interest; To enhance the level of professionalism of the independent converter in the operation of his/her business; To implement democratically determined goals on matters civil & governmental that have a positive effect on all independent corrugated converters
Member of: AICC International
Finances: Funding Sources: Membership fees
Membership: Fees: Levels based on gross sales or total number of staff; Member Profile: Sheet plant owners & associated members; Committees: Golf; Christmas
Chief Officer(s):
Jana Marmei, Executive Administrator

Association of Independent Schools & Colleges in Alberta (AISCA)
#201, 11830 - 111 Ave., Edmonton AB T5X 5Y3
Tel: 780-469-9868; Fax: 780-469-9880
office@aisca.ab.ca
www.aisca.ab.ca
Overview: A medium-sized provincial organization founded in 1958 overseen by Canadian Accredited Independent Schools
Mission: To defend & promote the right of parents to determine the context for their children's education; to create a positive social, fiscal & political environment in which independent schools are free to maintain their identity as they serve the public interest; to support & encourage independent schools in providing significant educational choices for parents & their children; to foster public understanding & appreciation of independent schools & their services
Finances: Annual Operating Budget: $100,000-$250,000; Funding Sources: Membership fees; grants
Staff Member(s): 5
Membership: 200 schools & private ECS operators; Member Profile: Independent schools in Alberta
Chief Officer(s):
Duane Plantinga, Executive Director

Association of Interior Designers of Nova Scotia (IDNS)
PO Box 2042, Halifax NS B3J 3B4
Tel: 902-425-4367
idns.ca
Overview: A small provincial charitable organization founded in 1975 overseen by Interior Designers of Canada
Mission: To promote the profession; to serve both the interests of public and the interior design industry.
Affiliation(s): Interior Designers of Canada
Membership: 37; Member Profile: Registered; Intern; Inactive; Allied; Non-Resident Registered; Sutdent; Retired; Honorary; Fellow.
Chief Officer(s):
Fran Underwood, President

Association of International Automobile Manufacturers of Canada; Automobile Importers of Canada See Global Automakers of Canada

Association of International Physicians & Surgeons of Ontario (AIPSO)
#850, 36 Toronto St., Toronto ON M5C 2C5
imdontario@yahoo.ca
aipso.webs.com
Overview: A small provincial organization founded in 1998
Mission: To assist internationally trained physicians & surgeons by facilitating access to the licensing process in Canada; To ensure the integration of internationally-trained physicians & surgeons into the Canadian health care system
Membership: 2,000+ registered physicians from 105 countries in AIPSO & its local affiliates; Fees: Free; Member Profile: Physicians & surgeons trained & licensed in jurisdictions outside Canada
Activities: Developing orientation, upgrading & integration programs, plus assessment, for internationally trained physicians; Providing information to members; Offering networking opportunities; Liaising with regulatory & government bodies; Engaging in advocacy activities
Chief Officer(s):
Amin Lakhani, President
aylakhani@hotmail.com
Publications:
• Association of International Physicians & Surgeons of Ontario Members Directory
Type: Directory

Association of Internet Marketing & Sales (AIMS)
#650, 99 Spadina Ave., Toronto ON M5V 3P8
admin@aimscanada.com
www.aimscanada.com
www.linkedin.com/groups/2239/profile
www.facebook.com/153321404762068
twitter.com/AIMS_Canada
Overview: A medium-sized national organization founded in 1996
Mission: To assist business professionals to leverage the internet in their daily business
Finances: Funding Sources: Sponsorships
Membership: 5,000+; Fees: $195 premium members; $95 virtual members; free for basic members; Member Profile: Business professionals, including developers, designers, salespeople, marketers & executives
Activities: Providing networking opportunities; Offering learning activities
Chief Officer(s):
Bruce Powell, Member, Executive Board
Publications:
• AIMS Newsletter
Type: Newsletter; Price: Free with Association of Internet Marketing & Sales membership
• Association of Internet Marketing & Sales Member Directory
Type: Directory

Association of Investigators & Guard Agencies of Ontario Inc. See Council of Private Investigators - Ontario

Association of Iroquois & Allied Indians
387 Princess Ave., London ON N6B 2A7
Tel: 519-434-2761; Fax: 519-675-1053
Toll-Free: 888-269-9593
www.aiai.on.ca
Overview: A medium-sized local organization founded in 1969
Mission: To advocate for the political interests of eight member nations in Ontario
Staff Member(s): 17
Membership: 20,000+; Member Profile: Member of Batchewana First Nation, Caldwell First Nation, Delaware Nation, Hiawatha First Nation, Oneida Nation of the Thames, Mississaugas of the New Credit, Mohawks of the Bay of Quinte, or Wahta Mohawks
Chief Officer(s):
Geoff Stonefish, Office Manager
gstonefish@aiai.on.ca

Association of Islamic Charitable Projects (AICP) / Association des Projets charitables Islamiques
6691, av du Parc, Montréal QC H2V 4J1

Tel: 514-274-6194; Fax: 514-274-0011
www.aicp.ca
www.facebook.com/AicpCanada
twitter.com/AICP_CANADA
www.youtube.com/user/aicpmultimediamtl
Overview: A medium-sized international organization
Mission: To denounce all acts of terrorism & promote support for the Muslim community
Activities: Yearly pilgrimage trip; Madih group; Marriage contracts & funerary services

Association of Islamic Community Gazi Husrev-Beg *See* Bosnian Islamic Association

Association of Italian Canadian Writers (AICW)
c/o Delia De Santis, 2961 Delia Cres., Bright's Grove ON N0N 1C0
info@aicw.ca
www.aicw.ca
www.facebook.com/AICWCanada
twitter.com/aicwcanada
www.youtube.com/user/AICWCanada
Overview: A small international organization founded in 1986
Mission: To promote Italian Canadian literature & culture; To implement education toward the understanding of heritage in a diversified society
Membership: 100+; *Member Profile:* Writers; Critics; Academics; Artists
Chief Officer(s):
Maria Cristina Seccia, President
Publications:
• Association of Italian Canadian Writers Newsletter / Bollettino dell'ASSIC / Bulletin d' AEIC
Type: Newsletter; *Frequency:* 4 pa
Profile: Information about AICW readings, author updates, book launches, contest winners, & conferences

Association of Jewish Chaplains of Ontario
c/o Beth Emeth Bais Yehuda Synagogue, 100 Elder St., Toronto ON M3H 5G7
Tel: 416-633-3838; *Fax:* 416-633-3153
info@beby.org
www.beby.org
www.facebook.com/BEBY.Toronto
twitter.com/BethEmeth
Overview: A small local organization
Mission: To draw together those who are active in pastoral care of Jewish people & their families, for fellowship, mutual support & education; to facilitate the understanding of the role & function that a professional performs in the pastoral care of Jewish people in hospitals, seniors' homes, correctional institutions, synagogues & schools; to develop & define standards for Jewish pastoral care providers; to develop & provide training & ensure the availability of competent pastor care where needed
Affiliation(s): Toronto Board of Rabbis
Finances: *Funding Sources:* Membership fees; donations
Membership: *Committees:* Cantor Edwards Mentoring; Greening; Golf; Investment; Nomination; Rabbi Lipson Advisory
Activities: Public lectures; *Speaker Service:* Yes
Chief Officer(s):
Bernard Schwartz, President
Pearl Grundland, Executive Director

Association of Jewish Day Schools (AJDS) / Association des écoles juives
1, carré Cummings, Montréal QC H3W 1M6
Tel: 514-345-2615; *Fax:* 514-345-6415
Overview: A small provincial organization founded in 1976
Mission: To act as the central body for Montreal's Jewish day schools; to represent the interests and educational needs of its members to governments and outside public and private bodies.
Activities: Liason with the Québec Ministry of Education & schools' associations

Association of Jewish Libraries (Montréal) (AJL - Montréal)
c/o Sol Katz, 5770, av McAlear, Montréal QC H4W 2H1
katzsol@videotron.ca
Overview: A small local organization founded in 1986
Mission: To support the production, collection, organization & dissemination of Jewish resources & library services in the Montréal area; To promote professional standards in the field of Judaica librarianship
Member of: Association of Jewish Libraries (USA based)
Membership: *Fees:* Schedule available; *Member Profile:* Interested librarians, researchers, & educators from Montréal & the surrounding area

Activities: Providing information about general & specific local resources for Jewish libraries in Montréal & the surrounding area; Promoting the growth of Judaic library collections; Updating members about recent technological developments & offering technical assistance; Facilitating the exchange of information & experience

Association of Jewish Libraries (Toronto) (AJL - Toronto)
73 Richvalley Cres., Richmond Hill ON L4E 4C8
Tel: 416-781-5658
ajl-ontario@yahoo.com
Overview: A medium-sized provincial organization founded in 1994
Mission: To support Jewish library services in Toronto & the surrounding region
Member of: Association of Jewish Libraries (USA based)
Membership: *Member Profile:* Interested librarians, researchers, & educators from Toronto & the surrounding area
Activities: Participating in the Association of Jewish Libraries annual conventions
Chief Officer(s):
Etti Stubbs, President
ettistubbs@yahoo.ca

Association of Jewish Seniors (AJS)
4211 Yonge St., 4th Fl., Toronto ON M2P 2A9
Tel: 416-635-2860; *Fax:* 416-635-1692
info@circleofcare.com
www.circleofcare.com
Overview: A medium-sized local organization
Mission: To act as a collective voice for affiliated organizations & members-at-large; To support individual independence among seniors & sustain quality of life in the community
Member of: Circle of Care
Membership: *Fees:* $15 individual; $25 couple
Chief Officer(s):
Michael F. Scheinert, President & Chief Executive Officer

Association of Kootenay & Boundary Local Governments (AKBLG)
c/o Arlene Parkinson, 790 Shakespeare St., Trail BC V1R 2B4
Tel: 250-368-8650
akblg@shaw.ca
www.akblg.ca
Overview: A small local organization
Mission: To serve communities by ensuring effective local government that engages citizens & helps communities
Membership: *Member Profile:* Community leaders from regional governments of the Kootenay & Boundary area
Activities: Liaising with municipal, provincial, & federal governments
Chief Officer(s):
Andy Shadrack, President
Christina Benty, Vice-President
Arlene Parkinson, Secretary-Treasurer
Meetings/Conferences:
• Association of Kootenay & Boundary Local Governments AGM 2018, April, 2018, Fernie, BC
Scope: Local

Association of Korean Canadian Scientists & Engineers (AKCSE)
#206, 1133 Leslie St., Toronto ON M3C 2J6
Tel: 416-449-5204; *Fax:* 416-449-2875
info@akcse.org
www.akcse.org
Overview: A small national organization founded in 1986
Mission: To contribute to the advancement of science & technology
Affiliation(s): Korean Federation of Science & Technology Societies (KOFST)
Membership: *Fees:* $10 undergraduate student; $20 graduate student; $30 regular; $100 foreign; *Member Profile:* Korean Canadian scientists & engineers; Science & engineering university undergraduate & graduate students
Activities: Organizing seminars; Facilitating cooperative networking opportunities; Participating in the Young Generation Forum
Chief Officer(s):
Chi-Guhn Lee, President
Gap Soo Chang, Vice-President, External
Sun Hee Cho, Vice-President, Internal
Youn Young Shim, Secretary General
Haloo Choi, Treasurer
Awards:
• AKCSE Annual Service Award

• AKCSE Annual Best Chapter Award
• AKCSE Annual Student Award
Publications:
• AKCSE Newsletter
Type: Newsletter
Profile: Information about upcoming events, reviews of past events, & scholarship & award application information

Association of Large School Boards of Ontario *See* Ontario Public School Boards Association

Association of Latvian Craftsmen in Canada / Latviesu Dailamatnieku Savieniba
Latvian Canadian Cultural Centre, 4 Credit Union Dr., Toronto ON M4A 2N8
Tel: 416-759-4900; *Fax:* 416-759-9311
Overview: A small national organization founded in 1953
Affiliation(s): Canadian-Latvian Cultural Centre
30 volunteer(s)
Membership: 1-99; *Committees:* Display; Sales; Research; Heritage

Association of Learning Disabled Adults *See* Adult Learning Development Association

Association of Legal Court Interpreters & Translators (ALCIT) / Association des traducteurs et interprètes judiciares (ATIJ)
483, rue St-Antoine est, Montréal QC H2Y 1A5
Tel: 514-845-3113; *Fax:* 514-845-3006
admin@atij.ca
www.atij.ca
Overview: A medium-sized national organization founded in 1972
Mission: To provide translation & interpretation services, mainly for the Municipal Court of Montréal and the City of Montréal Police Department
Staff Member(s): 15
Membership: 1,300 individual

Association of Licensed Nursing Homes (ALNH); Associated Homes for Special Care (AHSC) *See* Continuing Care Association of Nova Scotia

Association of Linguistic Services Managerse *Voir* Association des conseils en gestion linguistique Inc.

Association of Little People of Quebec *Voir* Association québécoise des personnes de petite taille

Association of Local Official Health Agencies (ALOHA) *See* Association of Local Public Health Agencies

Association of Local Public Health Agencies (ALPHA)
#1306, 2 Carlton St., Toronto ON M5B 1J3
Tel: 416-595-0006; *Fax:* 416-595-0030
info@alphaweb.org
www.alphaweb.org
Previous Name: Association of Local Official Health Agencies (ALOHA)
Overview: A medium-sized provincial organization founded in 1986
Mission: To provide leadership in public health management to health units in Ontario; To assist local public health units in the provision of efficient & effective services
Affiliation(s): ANDSOOHA - Public Health Nursing Management; Association of Ontario Public Health Business Administrators; Association of Public Health Epidemiologists in Ontario; Association of Supervisors of Public Health Inspectors of Ontario; Health Promotion Ontario; Ontario Association of Public Health Dentistry; Ontario Society of Nutrition Professionals in Public Health
Membership: 36 public health units; *Member Profile:* Board of health members of health units in Ontario; Medical & associate medical officers of health; *Committees:* Advocacy; AlPha Executive; Boards of Health Section Executive; Council of Ontario Medical Officers of Health Executive; Professional Development Steering
Activities: Advocating for public health policies, programs, & services
Chief Officer(s):
Loretta Ryan, Executive Director
loretta@alphaweb.org
Gordon Fleming, Manager, Public Health Issues
gordon@alphaweb.org
Susan Lee, Manager, Administrative & Association Services
susan@alphaweb.org

Canadian Associations / Association of Medical Microbiology & Infectious Disease Canada (AMMI Canada) / Association pour la microbiologie médicale et l'infectiologie Canada

Meetings/Conferences:
- Association of Local Public Health Agencies 2018 Annual General Meeting & Conference, June, 2018, Toronto, ON
Scope: Provincial

Association of Major Power Consumers in Ontario (AMPCO)
Thomson Bldg., #1510, 65 Queen St. West, Toronto ON M5H 2M5
Tel: 416-260-0280; *Fax:* 416-260-0442
info@ampco.org
www.ampco.org
Overview: A medium-sized provincial organization founded in 1975
Mission: To represent Ontario's electricity-intensive companies; To ensure reliability of power supply to support the economy of Ontario; To advocate a fair & equitable pricing system for electricity; To present views on energy matters to such groups as the Ontario Energy Board, the Ontario Government, Ontario Hydro, the news media & the general public; To provide decision makers with recommendations on resolving issues
Finances: *Funding Sources:* Membership fees
Membership: 44; *Fees:* Based on electrical energy usage; *Member Profile:* Companies that are major manufacturers, employers & power consumers (represents key industries - mining, pulp & paper, automobile manufacturing, petro-chemicals, metals, consumer products, steel, etc.)
Chief Officer(s):
Colin Anderson, President
Fareeda Heeralal, Executive Assistant
Publications:
- AMPCO [Association of Major Power Consumers in Ontario] Bulletins
Type: Newsletter

Association of Management, Administrative & Professional Crown Employees of Ontario (AMAPCEO) / Association des employés et employées gestionnaires, administratifs et professionnels de la Couronne de l'Ontario
PO Box 72, #2310, 1 Dundas St. West, Toronto ON M5G 1Z3
Tel: 416-595-9000; *Fax:* 416-340-6461
Toll-Free: 888-262-7326
amapceo@amapceo.on.ca
www.amapceo.on.ca
twitter.com/AMAPCEONews
Overview: A medium-sized provincial organization founded in 1992
Mission: To represent the interests of Ontario Public Service employees
Affiliation(s): Professional Employees Network
Staff Member(s): 41
Membership: 12,000; *Member Profile:* Middle managers & professional employees of the Ontario public service
Activities: Collective bargaining; workplace advocacy
Chief Officer(s):
Gary Gannage, President & CEO
gannage@amapceo.on.ca

Association of Managers of Childcare Centers *Voir*
Association des cadres des centres de la petite enfance

Association of Manitoba Book Publishers (AMBP)
#404, 100 Arthur St., Winnipeg MB R3B 1H3
Tel: 204-947-3335; *Fax:* 204-956-4689
Overview: A medium-sized provincial organization founded in 1979 overseen by Association of Canadian Publishers
Mission: To promote Manitoba publishing industry
Activities: *Awareness Events:* Manitoba Book Week (April)
Chief Officer(s):
Michelle Peters, Executive Director
Awards:
- Manitoba Book Awards

Association of Manitoba Hydro Staff & Supervisory Employees (AMHSSE)
820 Taylor Ave., Winnipeg MB R3C 2Z1
Tel: 204-474-3950; *Fax:* 204-474-4972
Overview: A small provincial organization
Membership: 900

Association of Manitoba Land Surveyors
#202, 83 Gary St., Winnipeg MB R3C 4J9
Tel: 204-943-6972; *Fax:* 204-957-7602
www.amls.ca
Overview: A medium-sized provincial licensing organization founded in 1881 overseen by Professional Surveyors Canada
Mission: To license qualified persons becoming commissioned land surveyors; To protect public interests concerning land boundary matters
Affiliation(s): Canadian Institute of Surveying & Mapping; Western Canadian Board of Examiners for Land Surveyors
Finances: *Funding Sources:* Membership fees
Membership: *Fees:* Schedule available; *Member Profile:* Commissioned land surveyor in Manitoba; *Committees:* Professional Association Liaison; Annual General Mtg Planning; AMLS Annual Golf Tournament; Nominating; Red River College Advisory; Canadian Board of Examiners for Professional Surveyors; Bylaw Rewrite; Public Awareness/Website; Professional Standards & Ethics; Unauthorized Practice; Manual of Good Practice; Professional Practice Review; Professional Development; Complaint/Discipline Investigation
Activities: *Internships:* Yes; *Speaker Service:* Yes; *Rents Mailing List:* Yes; *Library:* Open to public by appointment
Chief Officer(s):
Lori McKietiuk, Executive Director

Association of Manitoba Municipalities (AMM)
1910 Saskatchewan Ave. West, Portage la Prairie MB R1N 0P1
Tel: 204-857-8666; *Fax:* 204-856-2370
amm@amm.mb.ca
www.amm.mb.ca
www.facebook.com/124665930946719
twitter.com/AMMManitoba
Merged from: Union of Manitoba Municipalities; Manitoba Association of Urban Municipalities
Overview: A medium-sized provincial organization founded in 1905
Mission: To provide communications link between municipalities; to lobby for municipal governments with senior levels of government
Member of: Federation of Canadian Municipalities
Finances: *Annual Operating Budget:* $500,000-$1.5 Million; *Funding Sources:* Membership fees
Staff Member(s): 6
Membership: 165 municipalities
Activities: *Library:* Not open to public
Chief Officer(s):
Joe Masi, Executive Director, 204-856-2360
Doug Dobrowolski, President
Meetings/Conferences:
- Association of Manitoba Municipalities 20th Annual Convention, November, 2018, RBC Convention Centre, Winnipeg, MB
- Association of Manitoba Municipalities 21st Annual Convention, November, 2019, Keystone Centre, Brandon, MB

Association of Manitoba Museums (AMM)
#1040, 555 Main St., Winnipeg MB R3B 1C3
Tel: 204-947-1782; *Fax:* 204-942-3749
www.museumsmanitoba.com
Overview: A medium-sized provincial charitable organization founded in 1972
Mission: To strengthen the museum community by promoting excellence in preserving & presenting Manitoba's heritage; To improve the AMM's ability to communicate with its members; To continue a training program
Member of: Canadian Museums Association; American Museums Association
Finances: *Annual Operating Budget:* $100,000-$250,000; *Funding Sources:* Federal & provincial government; membership fees; registration fees
Staff Member(s): 3
Membership: 248; *Fees:* $30 individual; $40 family; $20 student; $40 associate; institutional based on organization's budget; *Member Profile:* Museums; heritage organizations; families; students; individuals; *Committees:* Advocacy; Exhibits; Membership Services; Publications; Standards; Training
Activities: *Library:* AMM Resource Library; Not open to public
Chief Officer(s):
Monique Brandt, Executive Director
director@museumsmanitoba.com
Beryth Strong, Coordinator, Training
training@museumsmanitoba.com
Jame Dalley, Conservator, Cultural Stewardship Program
conservator@museumsmanitoba.com
Meetings/Conferences:
- Association of Manitoba Museums Annual Conference 2018, 2018, MB
Scope: Provincial

Association of Marine Underwriters of British Columbia *See*
Marine Insurance Association of British Columbia

The Association of Maritime Arbitrators of Canada (AMAC) / Les Arbitres Maritimes Associés du Canada
c/o Fednav Limitée, #3500, 1000, rue de la Gauchetière ouest, Montréal QC H3B 4W5
Tel: 514-878-6439; *Fax:* 514-878-7670
Overview: A small national organization founded in 1986
Mission: To promote & provide arbitration facilities for all types of maritime disputes whether in or outside Canada
Finances: *Annual Operating Budget:* Less than $50,000
Membership: 100-499; *Fees:* $50; *Member Profile:* Shipping, transport & maritime corporations; law firms, surveyors, adjusters & insurers
Chief Officer(s):
Donald Pinkerton, Secretary-Treasurer
dpinkerton@fednav.com
John Weale, President, 514-878-6676, Fax: 514-878-6508
j.weale@fednav.com

Association of Massage Therapists & Wholistic Practitioners *See* Natural Health Practitioners of Canada

Association of Mature Canadians (AMC)
366 Bay St., 7th Fl., Toronto ON M5H 4B2
Tel: 416-601-0429
Toll-Free: 800-667-0429
service@maturecanadians.ca
www.maturecanadians.ca
Overview: A medium-sized national organization
Membership: *Fees:* $15
Chief Officer(s):
Robert Bruce, Executive Director
rbruce@maturecanadians.ca

Association of MBAs in Canada (AMBA)
admin@ambac.ca
ambac.ca
www.linkedin.com/company/the-association-of-mbas-in-canada
Overview: A medium-sized national organization founded in 2013
Mission: The prominent body in Canada representing and supporting those who have invested in an MBA.
Membership: 1700+; *Fees:* Free; *Member Profile:* Canadians who have obtained a Master's in Business Administration (MBA).
Chief Officer(s):
Muradali Amir, President

Association of Medical Microbiology & Infectious Disease Canada (AMMI Canada) / Association pour la microbiologie médicale et l'infectiologie Canada
192 Bank St., Ottawa ON K2P 1W8
Tel: 613-260-3233; *Fax:* 613-260-3235
communications@ammi.ca
www.ammi.ca
Previous Name: Canadian Infectious Disease Society
Overview: A small national charitable organization founded in 1978
Mission: To represent the broad interests of researchers & physicians who specialize in the fields of infectious diseases & medical microbiology in Canada; To contribute to the health of people at risk of, or affected by, infectious diseases; To promote & facilitate research; To develop policies for the prevention, diagnosis, & management of infectious diseases
Membership: *Fees:* $43.38 + applicable taxes in province of residence for associates; $191.30 + applicable taxes for active members; $1,695.65 for sustaining members; *Member Profile:* Professionals dealing with human microbiology & infectious disease in Canada; Infectious disease or medical microbiology trainees in accredited training programs; Post-graduate trainees in related disciplines; Organizations & corporations interested in the objectives of Association of Medical Microbiology & Infectious Disease Canada; *Committees:* Associate; Guidelines; Canadian Hospital Epidemiology; Nominations; Education / Continuing Professional Development; Grants & Awards; Program Planning; Communications & Public Relations; Finance; Nominations
Activities: Offering opportunities for communication among members; Engaging in advocacy activities; Communicating with other organizations with common interests; Encouraging excellence in infectious disease & medical microbiology professional training; Providing professional development opportunities; Protecting & educating the public; Communicating issues to the medical community & the public; Promoting ethical behaviour of members; Providing access to information about research grants, awards, & career opportunities; *Awareness Events:* Antibiotic Awareness Week, Nov.
Chief Officer(s):

Riccarda Galioto, Chief Operating Officer
manager@ammi.ca
Paul Glover, Coordinator, Meetings & Membership
info@ammi.ca
Tamara Nahal, Coordinator, Communications
communications@ammi.ca
Awards:
• Association of Medical Microbiology & Infectious Disease Canada / Pfizer Post Residency Fellowship
Contact: Tamara Nahal, Coordinator, Communications, E-mail: communications@ammi.ca
• Canadian Journal of Infectious Diseases & Medical Microbiology Trainee Review Article Award
Contact: Tamara Nahal, Coordinator, Communications, E-mail: communications@ammi.ca
• Association of Medical Microbiology & Infectious Disease Canada Distinguished Service Award
Contact: Tamara Nahal, Coordinator, Communications, E-mail: communications@ammi.ca
• Association of Medical Microbiology & Infectious Disease Canada Lifetime Achievement Award
Contact: Tamara Nahal, Coordinator, Communications, E-mail: communications@ammi.ca
• Association of Medical Microbiology & Infectious Disease Canada Honorary Membership
Contact: Tamara Nahal, Coordinator, Communications, E-mail: communications@ammi.ca
• Association of Medical Microbiology & Infectious Disease Canada / Astellas Post Residency Fellowship
Contact: Tamara Nahal, Coordinator, Communications, E-mail: communications@ammi.ca
• Association of Medical Microbiology & Infectious Disease Canada Trainee Research Award
Contact: Tamara Nahal, Coordinator, Communications, E-mail: communications@ammi.ca
• Association of Medical Microbiology & Infectious Disease Canada Young Investigator Award
Contact: Tamara Nahal, Coordinator, Communications, E-mail: communications@ammi.ca
Meetings/Conferences:
• Association of Medical Microbiology & Infectious Disease Canada 2018 Annual Conference, May, 2018, Sheraton Vancouver Wall Centre, Vancouver, BC
Scope: National
Description: A yearly professional development event for AMMI members; features workshops on a variety of topics
Contact Information: Coordinator, Meetings: Paul Glover, E-mail: paul@ammi.ca
• Association of Medical Microbiology & Infectious Disease Canada 2019 Annual Conference, April, 2019, The Westin Ottawa, Ottawa, ON
Scope: National
Description: A yearly professional development event for AMMI members; features workshops on a variety of topics
Contact Information: Coordinator, Meetings: Paul Glover, E-mail: paul@ammi.ca
• Association of Medical Microbiology & Infectious Disease Canada 2020 Annual Conference, April, 2020, Sheraton Vancouver Wall Centre, Vancouver, BC
Scope: National
Description: A yearly professional development event for AMMI members; features workshops on a variety of topics
Contact Information: Coordinator, Meetings: Paul Glover, E-mail: paul@ammi.ca
Publications:
• Association of Medical Microbiology & Infectious Disease Canada Annual Report
Type: Yearbook; *Frequency:* Annually
• Association of Medical Microbiology & Infectious Disease Canada Membership Directory
Type: Directory
• Canadian Journal of Infectious Disease & Medical Microbiology
Type: Journal; *Editor:* Dr. John M. Conly; *Price:* Free with membership in the Association of Medical Microbiology & Infectious Disease
• Members Connect [a publication of the Association of Medical Microbiology & Infectious Disease Canada]
Type: Newsletter; *Price:* Free with membership in theAssociation of Medical Microbiology & Infectious Disease
Profile: The newsletter of the Association of Medical Microbiology & Infectious Disease Canada

Association of Midwives of Newfoundland & Labrador (AMNL)
Southcott Hall, Centre for Nursing Studies, #1017, 100 Forest Rd., St. John's NL A1A 1E5
Tel: 709-777-8140
www.ucs.mun.ca/~pherbert
Overview: A small provincial organization founded in 1983
Mission: To promote midwifery in Newfoundland & Labrador
Membership: *Member Profile:* Midwives in Newfoundland & Labrador
Activities: Creating information sharing opportunities for midwives; Advocating for the practice of midwives; Offering continuing education through workshops & publications; Liaising with other professional & special interest groups; Establishing & maintaining a code of ethics for midwives in the province

Association of Millwrighting Contractors of Ontario Inc. (AMCO)
#218, 290 North Queen St., Toronto ON M9C 5L2
Tel: 416-620-8558; *Fax:* 416-620-1293
amco@amcontario.ca
www.amcontario.ca
Overview: A small provincial organization founded in 1959
Mission: Established to further the aims and objectives of its members with particular reference to Labour Relations and related activities including Collective Bargaining & Administration
Affiliation(s): Council of Ontario Construction Association; Construction Employers Coordinating Council of Ontario; Construction Safety Associan of Ontario; Provincial Labour Management Health & Safety Committee; Ontario Construction Secretariat
Staff Member(s): 1; 20 volunteer(s)
Membership: 51; *Fees:* $262.50; *Member Profile:* Millwrighting contractors; *Committees:* Finance; Apprenticeship; Millwright Trust Fund; Labour/Management Health & Safetty; Commuting Trust Fund; Construction Millwright Apprenticeship Provincial Advisory; Labour Management Relations; Scholarship; Negotiation; Nominating
Chief Officer(s):
R.H. LeChien, General Manager

Association of Municipal Administrators of New Brunswick (AMANB) / Association des administrateurs municipaux du Nouveau-Brunswick (AAMNB)
20 Courtney St., Douglas NB E3G 8A1
Tel: 506-453-4229; *Fax:* 506-444-5452
amanb@nb.aibn.com
www.amanb-aamnb.ca
Overview: A medium-sized provincial organization founded in 1977
Mission: To promote & advance status of persons employed in field of municipal administration; to advance quality of administration of municipal services; to encourage closer official & personal relationship among members to facilitate interchange of ideas & experience; to establish & maintain standards of performance for members; to assist in provision of formal training & educational facilities
Finances: *Annual Operating Budget:* Less than $50,000
Staff Member(s): 1
Membership: 105 municipal + 18 associate; *Committees:* Legislation; Education; Membership
Chief Officer(s):
Melanie MacDonald, President, 506-460-2160, Fax: 506-460-2905
Danielle Charron, Executive Director
Meetings/Conferences:
• Association of Municipal Administrators of New Brunswick 2018 Annual Conference, June, 2018, K.C. Irving Regional Centre, Bathurst, NB
Scope: Provincial

Association of Municipal Administrators, Nova Scotia (AMANS)
CIBC Building, #1106, 1809 Barrington St., Halifax NS B3J 3K8
Tel: 902-423-2215; *Fax:* 902-425-5592
info@amans.ca
www.amans.ca
Overview: A medium-sized provincial organization founded in 1970
Mission: To improve the quality of local government in Nova Scotia through the development of educational programs; To provide a forum for the exchange of ideas; to provide a resource to municipal officials; To provide service to members to improve their professional capabilities
Finances: *Funding Sources:* Membership dues; Conference surplus
Membership: 165; *Fees:* $175
Chief Officer(s):
Janice Wentzell, Executive Director, 902-423-8323, Fax: 902-425-5592
jwentzell@amans.ca
Kristy Hardie, Event Coordinator/ Financial Officer, 902-423-2215, Fax: 902-425-5592
khardie@amans.ca

Association of Municipal Clerks & Treasurers of Ontario
See Association of Municipal Managers, Clerks & Treasurers of Ontario

Association of Municipal Managers, Clerks & Treasurers of Ontario (AMCTO) / Association des directeurs généraux, secrétaires et trésoriers municipaux de l'Ontario (ASTMO)
#610, 2680 Skymark Ave., Mississauga ON L4W 5L6
Tel: 905-602-4294; *Fax:* 905-602-4295
amcto@amcto.com
www.amcto.com
Previous Name: Association of Municipal Clerks & Treasurers of Ontario
Overview: A medium-sized provincial organization founded in 1938
Mission: To foster administrative excellence in local government; to identify & meet training & education needs in local government; to be an influential voice for local government; to provide an effective communication forum for local government; to promote public awareness of & confidence in local government; to facilitate change within AMCTO
Affiliation(s): Association of Municipalities of Ontario; International Institute of Municipal Clerks; Municipal Information Systems Association
Finances: *Funding Sources:* Membership fees; program fees; products
Staff Member(s): 13
Membership: 2,200; *Fees:* Schedule available; *Member Profile:* Accreditation program in Canada for those involved in municipal government.; *Committees:* Annual Conference Coordinating; CMO (Certified Municipal Officer) Review; Legislative and Policy Advisory
Activities: Education & training; software; reference surveys
Chief Officer(s):
Andy Koopmans, Executive Director
akoopmans@amcto.com
Roger Ramkissoon, Manager, Finance & Administration
rramkissoon@amcto.com
Awards:
• E.A. Danby Award
Meetings/Conferences:
• 2018 Association of Municipal Managers, Clerks & Treasurers of Ontario Annual Conference, June, 2018, Blue Mountain Resort, The Blue Mountains, ON
Scope: Provincial

Association of Municipal Recycling Coordinators
See Municipal Waste Association

Association of Municipal Tax Collectors of Ontario
See Ontario Municipal Tax & Revenue Association

Association of Municipalities of Ontario (AMO)
#801, 200 University Ave., Toronto ON M5H 3C6
Tel: 416-971-9856; *Fax:* 416-971-6191
Toll-Free: 877-426-6527
amo@amo.on.ca
www.amo.on.ca
Overview: A medium-sized provincial organization founded in 1899
Mission: To support & enhance strong & effective municipal government in Ontario; To represent almost all of Ontario's 444 municipal governments
Member of: Federation of Canadian Municipalities
Finances: *Funding Sources:* Membership fees; Sales of services & products; Sponsorships
Membership: 100-499; *Member Profile:* Ontario municipalities; Related non-profit organizations & private corporations
Activities: Developing policy positions; Reporting on issues; Liaising with the Ontario provincial government; Informing & educating the media & the public; Marketing services to the municipal sector
Chief Officer(s):
Pat Vanini, Executive Director, 416-971-9856 Ext. 316
pvanini@amo.on.ca

Nancy Plumridge, Director, Administration & Business Development
NPlumridge@amo.on.ca
Monika Turner, Director, Policy
MTurner@amo.on.ca
Meetings/Conferences:
• 2018 Association of Municipalities of Ontario AGM & Annual Conference, August, 2018, Shaw Centre, Ottawa, ON
Scope: Provincial
Description: A yearly gathering of municipal government officials to discuss current issues.
• 2019 Association of Municipalities of Ontario AGM & Annual Conference, August, 2019, Shaw Centre, Ottawa, ON
Scope: Provincial
Description: A yearly gathering of municipal government officials to discuss current issues.
• 2020 Association of Municipalities of Ontario AGM & Annual Conference, August, 2020, Shaw Centre, Ottawa, ON
Scope: Provincial
Description: A yearly gathering of municipal government officials to discuss current issues.
Publications:
• AMO Watch File e-Newstter
Type: Newsletter
• Association of Municipalities of Ontario Annual Report
Type: Yearbook; *Frequency:* Annually

Association of Naturopathic Physicians of British Columbia
See College of Naturopathic Physicians of British Columbia

Association of Neighbourhood Houses BC (ANH)
#203, 3102 Main St., Vancouver BC V5T 3G7
Tel: 604-875-9111; *Fax:* 604-875-1256
central@anhbc.org
www.anhbc.org
www.facebook.com/148894038481998
twitter.com/anhbc
Previous Name: Association of Neighbourhood Houses of Greater Vancouver; Alexandra Neighbourhood House
Overview: A small local charitable organization founded in 1894 overseen by United Way of the Lower Mainland
Mission: To enhance neighbourhoods; To enable people to enhance their lives & strengthen their communities; To work with communities to develop innovative programs & services that meet the changing needs of a diverse population
Member of: International Federation of Settlement & Neighbourhood Centres
Affiliation(s): Multicultural Societies
Finances: *Annual Operating Budget:* $1.5 Million-$3 Million; *Funding Sources:* 3 levels of government; United Way; fundraising; endowment funds
Staff Member(s): 400; 2000 volunteer(s)
Membership: 1-99; *Committees:* Finance; Personnel; Executive; Board Development
Activities: Good Neighbour Award, Nov.; *Awareness Events:* Celebration of Good Neighbour, 3rd Thu. in Nov.; *Library:* Not open to public
Chief Officer(s):
Deb Bryant, CEO
dbryant@anhbc.org
Awards:
• Good Neighbour Award - House/Unit
• Good Neighbour Award - Youth
• Good Neighbour Award - Lower Mainland
• Good Neighbour Award - Corporate

Alexandra
2916 McBride Ave., Surrey BC V4A 3G2
Tel: 604-535-0015; *Fax:* 604-535-2720
info@alexhouse.net
www.alexhouse.net
www.facebook.com/AlexHousebc
twitter.com/AlexHouseBC
Chief Officer(s):
Penny Bradley, Executive Director
pbradley@alexhouse.net

Cedar Cottage
4065 Victoria Dr., Vancouver BC V5N 4M9
Tel: 604-874-4231; *Fax:* 604-874-7169
ccnh@cedarcottage.org
www.cedarcottage.org
www.facebook.com/CedarCottageNeighbourhoodHouse
twitter.com/ccnhbc
Chief Officer(s):
Donna Chang, Executive Director
dchang@cedarcottage.org
Anjani Singh, Director, Operations
asingh@cedarcottage.org
Kelly Woods, Director, Community Development & Special Projects
kwoods@cedarcottage.org

Frog Hollow
2131 Renfrew St., Vancouver BC V5M 4M5
Tel: 604-251-1225; *Fax:* 604-254-3764
contact@froghollow.bc.ca
www.froghollow.bc.ca
www.facebook.com/FrogHollowNeighbourhoodHouse
Chief Officer(s):
Gary Dobbin, Executive Director
Gladis Rivera, Office Manager
Julia Woo, Office Administrator

Gordon House
1019 Broughton St., Vancouver BC V6G 2A7
Tel: 604-683-2554; *Fax:* 604-683-4486
welcome@gordonhouse.org
www.gordonhouse.org
www.facebook.com/GordonNeighbourhoodHouse
twitter.com/GordonNHouse
www.instagram.com/gordonnhouse

Kitsilano House
2305 West 7th Ave., Vancouver BC V6K 1Y4
Tel: 604-736-3588
frontdesk@kitshouse.org
www.kitshouse.org
www.facebook.com/KitsilanoNeighbourhoodHouse
twitter.com/kitshouse
www.youtube.com/user/KitsHouseCommunity
Chief Officer(s):
Allen Smith, Executive Director
allens@kitshouse.org
Christa Wang, Manager, Operations
christaw@kitshouse.org

Mount Pleasant
800 East Broadway Ave., Vancouver BC V5T 1Y1
Tel: 604-879-8208; *Fax:* 604-879-4136
info@mpnh.org
www.mpnh.org
www.facebook.com/mountpleasantneighbourhoodhouse
twitter.com/mountpleasantnh
Chief Officer(s):
Jocelyne Hamel, Executive Director
execdir@mpnh.org

Sasamat Outdoor Centre
3302 Senkler Rd., Belcarra BC V3H 4S3
Tel: 604-939-2268; *Fax:* 604-939-8522
info@sasamat.org
www.sasamat.org
www.facebook.com/SasamatOutdoorCentreOfficial
Chief Officer(s):
Bronco Cathcart, Executive Director
bronco@sasamat.org
Ben Quinn, Office Manager
ben@sasamat.org

South Vancouver
6470 Victoria Dr., Vancouver BC V5P 3X7
Tel: 604-324-6212; *Fax:* 604-324-6116
svnh@southvan.org
www.southvan.org
www.facebook.com/southvanNH
twitter.com/southvanNH
Chief Officer(s):
Zahra Esmail, Executive Director
zahra@southvan.org
Paul Riley, Director, Operations
paul@southvan.org
Roberta Kihn, Office Manager
roberta@southvan.org

Association of Neighbourhood Houses of Greater Vancouver; Alexandra Neighbourhood House *See* Association of Neighbourhood Houses BC

Association of New Brunswick Land Surveyors (ANBLS) / Association des arpenteurs-géomètres du Nouveau-Brunswick (AA-GN-B)
#312, 212, Queen St., Fredericton NB E3B 1A8
Tel: 506-458-8266; *Fax:* 506-458-8267
anbls@nb.aibn.com
www.anbls.nb.ca
Overview: A small provincial licensing organization founded in 1954 overseen by Professional Surveyors Canada
Mission: To regulate & govern the practice of land surveying in New Brunswick; To develop & maintain standards of knowledge, skill, & professional ethics
Staff Member(s): 2
Membership: 140; *Member Profile:* Individuals who comply with the requirements as specified in the New Brunswick Land Surveyors Act, 1986, & By-Laws
Activities: Increasing public awareness of the role of the association; Liaising with other professional organizations
Chief Officer(s):
Doug Morgan, Executive Director
dmorgan@nb.aibn.com
Meetings/Conferences:
• Association of New Brunswick Land Surveyors 2018 Annual General Meeting, 2018, NB
Scope: Provincial
Publications:
• Surveyor-In-Training Manual
Type: Manual

Association of New Brunswick Licensed Practical Nurses (ANBLPN) / L'Association des Infirmier(ère)s Auxiliares Autorisé(e)s du Nouveau-Brunswick (AIAANB)
384 Smythe St., Fredericton NB E3B 3E4
Tel: 506-453-0747; *Fax:* 506-459-0503
Toll-Free: 800-942-0222
www.anblpn.ca
Overview: A medium-sized provincial organization founded in 1965
Mission: To ensure the public's right to quality ethical care by regulating & enhancing the profession of practical nursing
Chief Officer(s):
JoAnne Graham, Executive Director & Registrar
Awards:
• LPN Bursary
Eligibility: Students enrolled in continuing education programs
• Audrey D. Galbraith Excellence in Practice Award
To honour those who demonstrate excellence in nursing practice
• The Foster Greenlaw Scholarship
Eligibility: A person enrolled in the Practical Nurse program who is he child, grandchild or someone in the guardianship of a Licensed Practical Nurse
• The Inez Smith Scholarship
Eligibility: A person enrolled in any post-secondary education program who is the child, grandchild, or someone in the guardianship of an LPN
Meetings/Conferences:
• Association of New Brunswick Licensed Practical Nurses 2018 Annual General Meeting, 2018
Scope: Provincial
Publications:
• The Blue Band [a publication of the Association of New Brunswick Licensed Practical Nurses]
Type: Newsletter; *Frequency:* Semiannually; *Editor:* JoAnne Graham
Profile: Messages from the president & executive director, educational articles, meeting reviews, & upcoming events
• Care of the Patient Receiving IV Therapy Manual
Type: Manual; *Price:* $15
Profile: A manual used for the Association of New Brunswick Licensed Practical Nurses' workshop
• Catheterization Manual
Type: Manual; *Price:* $10
Profile: A manual used for the Association of New Brunswick Licensed Practical Nurses' catheterization workshop
• Dressings Manual
Type: Manual; *Price:* $40
Profile: A manual used for the Association of New Brunswick Licensed Practical Nurses' self-learning module
• Feeding Tubes & Medication Administration by the Enteral Route for Licensed Practical Nurses Manual
Type: Manual; *Price:* $15
Profile: A manual used for the Association of New Brunswick Licensed Practical Nurses' workshop
• Insulin Administration for Licensed Practical Nurses Manual
Type: Manual; *Price:* $25
Profile: A manual used for the Association of New Brunswick Licensed Practical Nurses' course
• Intramuscular Injection Manual
Type: Manual; *Price:* $15
Profile: A manual used for the Association of New Brunswick Licensed Practical Nurses' self-learning module

Association of New Brunswick Massage Therapists (ANBMT) / L'association néo-brunswickoise de massothérapeutes (ANBMT)
PO Box 323, Stn. A, Fredericton NB E3B 4Y9
Tel: 506-452-6972; Fax: 506-451-8173
anbmt@anbmt.ca
www.anbmt.ca
www.facebook.com/443659605703364
Overview: A small provincial organization founded in 1994
Mission: To represent massage therapists in New Brunswick; To ensure members provide safe & effective massage therapy
Membership: Fees: Schedule available; Member Profile: Massage therapists in New Brunswick, with training accepted by the CMTO; Members must graduate from a school with a provincially accepted curriculum & with provincially legislated standards for practice; All active members must carry Professional Liability Insurance
Activities: Encouraging high standards of practice in massage therapy; Upholding a code of ethics; Promoting massage therapy; Representing members before governmental & regulatory bodies; Offering a mentoring program
Chief Officer(s):
Coralie Hopkins, Executive Director
Publications:
• ANBMT [Association of New Brunswick Massage Therapists] Newsletter
Type: Newsletter; Frequency: Quarterly; Price: Free with ANBMT membership

Association of New Brunswick Professional Educators (ANBPE) / Association des éducateurs professionnels du Nouveau-Brunswick
Overview: A small provincial organization
Mission: To operate as a bargaining unit of the New Brunswick Union of Public & Private Employees (NBUPPE / NUPGE)
Membership: 99; Member Profile: Members of the New Brunswick Community College system

Association of Newfoundland & Labrador Archives (ANLA)
PO Box 23155, St. John's NL A1B 4J9
Tel: 709-726-2867; Fax: 709-722-9035
anla@nf.aibn.com
www.anla.nf.ca
Merged from: Newfoundland & Labrador Council of Archives
Overview: A medium-sized provincial charitable organization founded in 1982 overseen by Canadian Council of Archives
Mission: To provide professional leadership among persons engaged in practice of archival science; To promote development of archives & archivists in Newfoundland & Labrador; To encourage cooperation of archivists with all those interested in preservation & use of documents of human experience
Finances: Funding Sources: Dept. of Canadian Heritage; Province of Newfoundland & Labrador; membership fees
Staff Member(s): 1
Membership: 90+ institutional members; Fees: $25 individuals; $50 institutions; Committees: Education; Grants; Information Technology; Outreach; Publications
Activities: Speaker Service: Yes; Library: by appointment
Chief Officer(s):
Emily Gushue, President
Meetings/Conferences:
• Association of Newfoundland & Labrador Archives Annual General Meeting 2018, 2018, NL
Scope: Provincial

Association of Newfoundland Land Surveyors
#203, 62-64 Pippy Pl., St. John's NL A1B 4H7
Tel: 709-722-2031; Fax: 709-722-4104
www.surveyors.nf.ca
Overview: A small provincial licensing organization founded in 1953 overseen by Professional Surveyors Canada
Mission: To establish & maintain standards of knowledge, skill, & professional conduct in the practice of land surveying, in order to serve & protect the public interest in Newfoundland; to regulate & govern the practice of land surveying in the province
Staff Member(s): 2
Membership: 100; Committees: Archives; Board of Examiners; Discipline; Liaison; Nominating; Continuing Professional Development; Executive; Act & Manual of Practice; AGM; By-laws & Regulations; Quality Assurance; Finance
Activities: Advancing & protecting the interests of members; Improving the knowledge & skill of members; Liaising with other professional organizations

Chief Officer(s):
Robert Way, President
r.way@nf.sympatico.ca
Paula Baggs, Executive Director
paulabaggs@anls.ca

Association of Nigerians in Nova Scotia (ANNS)
PO Box 883, Halifax NS B3J 2V9
Tel: 902-233-3524
info@nigeriansinnovascotia.org
www.nigeriansinnovascotia.org
www.facebook.com/nigeriansinnovascotia
twitter.com/Nigerians_NS
Previous Name: Nigerian Students Association
Overview: A small provincial organization founded in 1983
Mission: To foster Canadians' awareness of Nigeria; To encourage Nigerians to participate in economic & social activities in Canada
Membership: Member Profile: Nigerians who have immigrated to Canada
Activities: Liaising with similar organizations

Association of Northwest Territories Speech Language Pathologists & Audiologists (ANTSLPA)
PO Box 982, Yellowknife NT X1A 2N7
Overview: A small provincial organization
Mission: Supports and represents the professional needs of speech-language pathologists, audiologists and supportive personnel inclusively within one organization.

Association of Nova Scotia Land Surveyors (ANSLS)
325A Prince Albert Rd., Dartmouth NS B2Y 1N5
Tel: 902-469-7962; Fax: 902-469-7963
ansls@accesswave.ca
www.ansls.ca
Overview: A medium-sized provincial licensing organization founded in 1951 overseen by Professional Surveyors Canada
Mission: To establish & maintain standards of professional ethics among its members, student members & holders of a certificate of authorization, in order that the public interest may be served & protected; & knowledge & skills among its members, student members & holders of a certificate of authorization; to regulate the practice of professional land surveying & govern the profession in accordance with the Act, the regulations & the by-laws; & to communicate & cooperate with other professional organizations for the advancement of the best interests of the surveying profession
Finances: Funding Sources: Membership dues
Membership: 174 regular + 17 student; Member Profile: Examinations & apprenticeship; licensed professionals; Committees: Legislative Review; Life & Honourary Membership; MCE Evaluation Group; Administrative Review; AGM; PSC; Nominating; NS Board of Examiners; Continuing Education; Public Awareness; Discipline; SRD Advisory; Strategic Planning; Governance; Unauthorized Practice; Wetlands
Activities: Internships: Yes; Speaker Service: Yes; Library: Not open to public
Chief Officer(s):
Fred Hutchinson, Executive Director
Awards:
• J.E.R. March Prize
• J.A.H. Church Prize
• G.T. Bates Scholarship

Association of Nova Scotia Museums (ANSM)
1113 Marginal Rd., Halifax NS B3H 4P7
Tel: 902-423-4677; Fax: 902-422-0881
Toll-Free: 800-355-6873
admin@ansm.ns.ca
ansm.ns.ca
www.facebook.com/113166268748419
Previous Name: Federation of Nova Scotian Heritage
Overview: A medium-sized provincial organization founded in 1976
Mission: The Association of Nova Scotia Museums, using a consultative regional representative model, proactively champions museums through education, outreach, networking and advocacy to achieve excellence.
Affiliation(s): Heritage Canada; Canadian Museums Association; Association for State & Local History
Membership: 50 organizational + 25 individual + 1 student + 2 lifetime; Fees: $50 organizational; $25 individual; $15 student
Activities: Training & Education Program; Heritage Studies Certificate; applied learning workshops; seminars
Chief Officer(s):

Anita Price, Managing Director
director@ansm.ns.ca
Awards:
• President's Award
• Dr. Phyllis R. Blakeley Lifetime Achievement Award
• Outstanding Exhibit Award/Outstanding Promotion Award

Association of Nurses of Prince Edward Island See
Association of Registered Nurses of Prince Edward Island

Association of Occupational Health Nurses of Newfoundland & Labrador (AOHNNL)
c/o ARNNL, 55 Military Rd., St. John's NL A1C 2C5
www.aohnnl.net63.net
Overview: A small provincial organization founded in 1981
Mission: To promote and maintain the physical, social and psychological well-being of all individuals in working as Occupational Health Nurses.
Affiliation(s): Association of Registered Nurses of Newfoundland & Labrador
Membership: Fees: $25
Chief Officer(s):
Pamela Wells, President
pamela.wells@easternhealth.ca

Association of Occupational Therapists of Manitoba See
College of Occupational Therapists of Manitoba

Association of Ontario Health Centres (AOHC) / Association des centres de santé de l'Ontario (ACSO)
#500, 970 Lawrence Ave. West, Toronto ON M6A 3B6
Tel: 416-236-2539; Fax: 416-236-0431
mail@aohc.org
www.aohc.org
www.facebook.com/AOHC.ACSO
twitter.com/aohc_acso
Overview: A medium-sized provincial charitable organization founded in 1982
Mission: To promote community based primary care, health promotion, & illness prevention services, focusing on the broader determinants of health such as education, employment, poverty, isolation, & housing
Member of: Canadian Alliance of Community Health Centre Associations; Ontario Health Providers Alliance; Ontario Public Health Association
Affiliation(s): Healthy Communities; Ontario Rural Council; Health Determinants Partnership; Canadian Health Network
Finances: Funding Sources: Membership fees; Grants; Fundraising
100 volunteer(s)
Membership: 86 institutional; Fees: Schedule available; Member Profile: Community Health Centres (CHC); Aboriginal Health Access Centres (AHAC) & Community Health Service Organizations (CHSO); associates; Committees: Conference Planning; Executive; Information Systems Coordinating; Membership Secretariat; Nominations; Public Relations; Resolutions
Activities: Awareness Events: Community Health Day, April; Speaker Service: Yes; Library: Resource Centre
Chief Officer(s):
Adrianna Tetley, Chief Executive Officer, 416-236-2539 Ext. 222
adrianna@aohc.org
Leah Stephenson, Director, Special Projects, 416-236-2539 Ext. 244
leah.stephenson@aohc.org
Sandra Wong, Manager, Corporate Services, 416-236-2539 Ext. 241
sandra@aohc.org
Awards:
• Community Health Champion Award
Awards significant contributions to the community health field in the legislative or administrative branch of an agency
• Media Award
Awarded to a story that explicitly calls for the need for policy change in the health field in Ontario
• Joe Leonard Award
Awarded to an individual who has made a significant contribution to community health through leadership
• Health Equity Award
Awarded to recognize excellence in advancing health equity through the delivery of innovative services & programs
• Community Engagement Award
Awarded to recognize excellence in engaging community members & therefore improving the overall health of the community

- Innovator of the Year Award
Honours excellence in developing a new innovation with respect to primary care or health promotion that improves the overall health of the community
- Emerging Leader Award
Awarded to recognize an individual who shows promise & potential in advancing health & wellbeing in their organization
Meetings/Conferences:
- Association of Ontario Health Centres 2018 Annual Conference & General Meeting, June, 2018, Sheraton Parkway Toronto North, Richmond Hill, ON
Scope: Provincial
Description: Theme: "Health Equity Action & Transformation"
Publications:
- Bridging the Gap [a publication of the Association of Ontario Health Centres]
Type: Report
Profile: 2014 report released in conjunction with the Coalition of Community Health & Resource Centres of Ottawa (CHRC) to evaluate the wellbeing of Ottawa using the Canadian Index of Wellbeing framework
- Leading Transformative Change: [a publication of the Association of Ontario Health Centres]
Type: Report
Profile: A report on the 2012-2015 AOHC strategic plan
- Measuring What Matters [a publication of the Association of Ontario Health Centres]
Type: Report
Profile: A report on how the Canadian Index of Wellbeing can improve the quality of life in Ontario

Association of Ontario Land Economists
#205, 555 St. Clair Ave. West, Toronto ON M4V 2Y7
Tel: 416-283-0440; *Fax:* 866-401-3665
admin@aole.org
www.aole.org
Overview: A medium-sized provincial organization founded in 1962
Mission: To continue attracting membership-quality professionals engaged in land economics pursuits; To broaden & enrich the professional development of members; To promote & maintain high ethical work standards throughout our membership; To make submissions to government for improvements in law & public administration bearing on land economics
Membership: *Fees:* $197; *Member Profile:* Architects; Certified Property Managers; Economists; Land Use Planners; Management Consultants; Mortgage Brokers; Municipal Assessors; Ontario Land Surveyors; Engineers; Property Tax Agents; Quantity Surveyors; Real Estate Brokers; Real Property Appraisers
Chief Officer(s):
Andrea Calla, President, 416-736-2610
acalla@tridel.com
John Blackburn, Vice-President & Secretary, 416-948-6969
johnblackburn@brightstarcorp.ca
Naomi Irizawa, Treasurer, 416-283-0440
naomiiriz@yahoo.ca

Association of Ontario Land Surveyors (AOLS)
1043 McNicoll Ave., Toronto ON M1W 3W6
Tel: 416-491-9020; *Fax:* 416-491-2576
Toll-Free: 800-268-0718
info@aols.org
www.aols.org
www.linkedin.com/groups/Association-Ontario-Land-Surveyors-AOLS-4083207
www.facebook.com/288456831275733
twitter.com/_AOLS
www.youtube.com/user/AOLSTUBE
Overview: A medium-sized provincial licensing organization founded in 1892 overseen by Professional Surveyors Canada
Mission: To be responsible for the licensing and governance of professional land surveyors, in accordance with the Surveyors Act.
Finances: *Funding Sources:* Membership fees
Staff Member(s): 12
Membership: 245; *Fees:* $155 associate; *Member Profile:* Individuals with a degree in Geomatics from an accredited university program, followed bu a term of articles & professional examinations
Activities: Providing continuing education; *Speaker Service:* Yes
Chief Officer(s):
Blain W. Martin, Executive Director
blain@aols.org
William D. Buck, Registrar
bill@aols.org
Meetings/Conferences:
- Association of Ontario Land Surveyors 2018 Annual General Meeting, February, 2018, Sheraton On The Falls Hotel, Niagara Falls, ON
Scope: Provincial
Contact Information: Lena Kassabian; Email: lena@aols.org; Phone: 416-491-9020 ext. 25

The Association of Ontario Locksmiths (TAOL)
#106, 2220 Midland Ave., Toronto ON M1P 3E6
Tel: 416-321-2219; *Fax:* 416-321-5115
office@taol.net
www.taol.net
Overview: A medium-sized provincial organization founded in 1973
Mission: To promote the exchange of information & ideas among members; To advance the positions of individuals who install and service security & access control hardware; To develop training programs for locksmiths; To cooperate with security organizations
Finances: *Funding Sources:* Membership dues
14 volunteer(s)
Membership: 400; *Fees:* $160; *Member Profile:* Locksmiths; Security-related personnel; Manufacturers; Suppliers; *Committees:* Building; Education; Ethics; Membership; Professional Standards; Public Relations
Activities: *Speaker Service:* Yes
Chief Officer(s):
Alvin Dorder, President
president@taol.net
Steve Kischak, Treasurer
treasurer@taol.net

Association of Ontario Midwives (AOM) / Association des sages-femmes de l'Ontario
#301, 365 Bloor St. E., Toronto ON M3W 3L4
Tel: 416-425-9974; *Fax:* 416-425-6905
Toll-Free: 866-418-3773
admin@aom.on.ca
www.aom.on.ca
Previous Name: Ontario Association of Midwives
Overview: A small provincial organization founded in 1985
Mission: To represent midwives & the practice of midwifery in Ontario
Finances: *Annual Operating Budget:* $250,000-$500,000; *Funding Sources:* Membership fees
Staff Member(s): 3
Membership: 500; *Member Profile:* Midwives, student midwives & supporting members
Activities: *Library:* AOM Resource Centre; by appointment
Chief Officer(s):
Kelly Stadelbauer, Executive Director
executivedirector@aom.on.ca
Meetings/Conferences:
- Association of Ontario Midwives 2018 Annual General Meeting & Conference, 2018
Scope: Provincial

Association of Ontario Road Supervisors (AORS)
PO Box 129, 160 King St., Thorndale ON N0M 2P0
Tel: 519-461-1271; *Fax:* 519-461-1343
admin@aors.on.ca
www.aors.on.ca
www.linkedin.com/company-beta/10805233
www.facebook.com/aorsofficial
twitter.com/AORS_Official
Overview: A medium-sized provincial organization founded in 1961
Mission: To promote the exchange of ideas & information concerning public works among municipalities
Finances: *Annual Operating Budget:* $250,000-$500,000; *Funding Sources:* Membership dues; certification; publication; trade show
Staff Member(s): 2; 30 volunteer(s)
Membership: 1,719 municipal, supplier, honouray & individual members; *Fees:* $40; *Committees:* Booth & Promotions; Certification Board; Education; Constitution; Finance; Personnel; Strategic Planning; Trade Show
Activities: Certification; Educational programs; Group interactions
Chief Officer(s):
John Maheu, Executive Director, 519-461-1271, Fax: 519-461-1343
johnmaheu@aors.on.ca

Association of Ontario Snowboarders (AOS)
#203, 4 - 115 First St., Collingwood ON L9Y 4W3
Tel: 705-446-1488
aos@ontariosnowboarders.ca
www.ontariosnowboarders.ca
Also Known As: Snowboard Ontario (SO)
Overview: A small provincial organization founded in 1998 overseen by Canadian Snowboard Federation
Mission: To be the governing body for the sport of competitive snowboarding in Ontario
Member of: Canadian Snowboard Federation
Affiliation(s): Women's Snowboard Federation
Membership: *Committees:* Events; Sponsorship; Communications
Chief Officer(s):
Janet Richter, Executive Director, 705-446-1488
janetrichter@ontariosnowboarders.ca

Association of Parent Support Groups in Ontario Inc. (APSGO)
PO Box 27581, Stn. Yorkdale, Toronto ON M6A 3B8
Toll-Free: 800-488-5666
mail@apsgo.ca
www.apsgo.ca
twitter.com/APSGOca
Overview: A small provincial charitable organization founded in 1985
Mission: To enable parents to develop strategies to deal with their children's disruptive behaviour
Finances: *Funding Sources:* Donations; Fundraising
Membership: *Member Profile:* Parents of disruptive youth; *Committees:* Group Development; Public Relations; Nominations; Fundraising; Ad Hoc; Support Services; Financial
Activities: Supporting parents to deal with their disruptive youth; Offering weekly meetings; Providing seminars & workshops; Disseminating resources to parents & professionals; Operating an information line; *Speaker Service:* Yes
Chief Officer(s):
Maureen MacNeil, President
Publications:
- Parent to Parent
Type: Newsletter; *Editor:* Sue Kranz

Association of Parliamentary Libraries in Canada (APLIC) / Association des bibliothèques parlementaires au Canada (ABPAC)
c/o Valerie Footz, Alberta Legislature Library, 216 Legislature Bldg., 10800 - 97th Ave., Edmonton AB T5K 2B6
Tel: 780-427-0202; *Fax:* 780-427-6016
www.aplic-abpac.ca
Overview: A small national organization founded in 1975
Mission: To improve parliamentary library service in Canada; To encourage cooperation with related officials & organizations
Membership: 13; *Member Profile:* Parliamentary / legislature libraries in Canada; Chief executive officers of the library of each jurisdiction are the voting members in the association
Activities: Identifying research areas; Facilitating communication among members; Highlighting best practices to support members' work
Chief Officer(s):
Valerie Footz, President
val.footz@assembly.ab.ca
Publications:
- Library Directory [a publication of the Association of Parliamentary Libraries in Canada]
Type: Directory
Profile: Contact information for Canada's parliamentary libraries

Association of Part-Time Professors of the University of Ottawa *Voir* Association des professeur(e)s à temps partiel de l'Université d'Ottawa

Association of Pastoral Psychotherapists of Canada *Voir* Association des psychothérapeutes pastoraux du Canada

Association of Physically Disabled Joliette - L'Assomption; Association of People with Physical Disabilities Joliette *See* Association des personnes handicapées physiques et sensorielles du secteur Joliette

Association of Polish Engineers in Canada
206 Beverly St., Toronto ON M5T 1Z3
Tel: 416-977-7723; *Fax:* 416-977-3996
webmaster@polisheng.ca
www.polisheng.ca
www.facebook.com/polisheng

Canadian Associations / Association of Power Producers of Ontario (APPrO)

Overview: A medium-sized national organization founded in 1941
Mission: To represent the Polish Canadian engineering community; to provide assistance & contribute to social life
Member of: Canadian Polish Congress
Finances: *Funding Sources:* Membership fees
Membership: *Member Profile:* Engineers
Activities: Monthly meetings; lectures; annual ball; help with immigration; advice regarding Canadian life & its engineering aspects; submissions to federal & provincial governments
Chief Officer(s):
Jerome Teresinski, President, 416-497-9810
hieronim@interlog.com

Edmonton Branch
1332 - 116 St. NW, Edmonton AB T6J 7B3
Tel: 780-450-9367
ajedrych@shaw.ca
edmonton.polisheng.ca
Chief Officer(s):
Andrzej Jedrych, Contact

Hamilton Branch
263 Wellington St., Brantford ON N3S 3Z8
Tel: 905-578-6584
andrzej.felinczak@sympatico.ca
www.hamilton.polisheng.ca
Chief Officer(s):
Ryszard Murynowicz, Contact

Kitchener Branch
#2, 285 Sandowne Dr., Kitchener ON N2K 2C1
Tel: 519-747-1402
bulik@sympatico.ca
kitchener.polisheng.ca
Chief Officer(s):
Jerzy Bulik, Contact

London Branch
80 Ann St., London ON N6A 1G9
sip.london.ca@gmail.com
london.polisheng.ca
Chief Officer(s):
Bartek Froncisz, President

Mississauga Branch
c/o Cyclone MFG. Inc., 7300 Rapistan Crt., Mississauga ON L5N 5S1
Tel: 905-578-6584
slawomir.basiukiewicz@polisheng.ca
mississauga.polisheng.ca
Chief Officer(s):
Slawomir Basiukiewicz, Contact

Montréal Branch
63, rue Prince Arthur est, Montréal QC H2X 1B4
Tel: 514-996-9723
bella97@videotron.ca
montreal.polisheng.ca
Chief Officer(s):
Lech Bilinski, Contact
Lech Bilinski, President

Ottawa Branch
1945 South Lavant Rd., Poland ON K0G 1K0
Tel: 613-259-5015
sip@kpk-ottawa.org
www.kpk-ottawa.org/sip
Chief Officer(s):
Bogdan Gajewski, Contact

Toronto Branch
206 Beverley St., Toronto ON M5T 1Z3
Tel: 416-486-7346
toronto.polisheng.ca
Chief Officer(s):
Krystyna Sroczynska, Contact

Association of Power Producers of Ontario (APPrO)
#1602, 25 Adelaide St. East, Toronto ON M5C 3A1
Tel: 416-322-6549; *Fax:* 416-481-5785
appro@appro.org
www.appro.org
www.linkedin.com/company/association-of-power-producers-of-ontario-appro-
www.facebook.com/APPrOPowerMemoryProject
twitter.com/APPrOntario
www.youtube.com/channel/UCAwW194Kmge1AcvSuAV2ihg
Previous Name: Independent Power Producers Society of Ontario (IPPSO)
Overview: A medium-sized *provincial* organization founded in 1986
Mission: To act as the voice of electricity generators in Ontario; To support a reliable & secure electricity supply in Ontario
Membership: 100+; *Member Profile:* Companies involved in the generation of electricity in Ontario, including suppliers of services & consulting services
Activities: Advocating for generators; Offering resources to assist business, government, utilities & researchers; Organizing educational programs
Chief Officer(s):
Jake Brooks, Executive Director
jake.brooks@appro.org
David Butters, President, 416-322-6549 Ext. 231
david.butters@appro.org
Soraya Rivera, Manager, Registration & Data, 416-322-6549 Ext. 223
soraya.rivera@appro.org
Meetings/Conferences:
• Association of Power Producers of Ontario 2018: 30th Annual Canadian Power Conference & Networking Centre, November, 2018, ON
Scope: Provincial
Publications:
• APPrO [Association of Power Producers of Ontario] Conference Proceedings
Type: Yearbook; *Frequency:* Annually; *Price:* $40
• Canadian Power Directory
Type: Directory
Profile: Contact information for organizations involved in all aspects of electricity generation in Canada, such as developers, equipment & service suppliers, utilities, & resource groups
• IPPSO FACTO: Magazine of the Association of Power Producers of Ontario
Type: Magazine; *Frequency:* Bimonthly; *Accepts Advertising*;
Price: Free with Association of Power Producers of Ontario membership
Profile: Ontario, national, international, & regulatory news

Association of Prince Edward Island Land Surveyors (APEILS)
PO Box 20100, Charlottetown PE C1A 9E3
Tel: 902-394-3121
info@apeils.ca
www.apeils.ca
Overview: A small provincial licensing organization overseen by Professional Surveyors Canada
Mission: To regulate the practice of land surveying in PEI
Membership: 27
Chief Officer(s):
Serge Bernard, Secretary-Treasurer
bernardsurvey@gmail.com
John Mantha, President

Association of Prince Edward Island Libraries (APEIL)
c/o Trina O'Brien Leggott, 187 North River Rd., Charlottetown PE C1A 3L4
apeilibraries@gmail.com
www.apeilibraries.wordpress.com
www.facebook.com/peilibraries
Previous Name: Prince Edward Island Professional Librarians Association
Overview: A small provincial organization founded in 1982
Mission: To represent the interests of individuals working or interested in library services; To promote library & information services in Prince Edward Island
Finances: *Funding Sources:* Membership fees
Membership: *Fees:* $20; *Member Profile:* Librarians; Library technicians & support staff; Students; Individuals & organizations with an interest in libraries
Chief Officer(s):
Trina O'Brien Leggott, President
Jennie Thompson, Vice-President
Ray MacLeod, Secretary & Treasurer

The Association of Professional Accounting & Tax Consultants Inc. (APATC)
#310, 4025 Dorchester Rd., Niagara Falls ON L2E 7K8
Tel: 905-354-1856; *Fax:* 905-374-0600
Toll-Free: 888-621-1005
www.apatcinc.com
www.linkedin.com/groups?gid=2112088
Overview: A small national organization founded in 1981
Mission: To represent professionals involved in accounting, bookkeeping & tax
Membership: *Fees:* $386.25 affiliated; $283.25 associate; $35 application fee
Activities: Continuing education; seminars; Group Errors & Omissions Insurance Plan for members

Association of Professional Archaeologists (APAA)
#600, 3250 Bloor St. West, Toronto ON M8X 2X9
Tel: 647-775-1674
info@apaontario.ca
www.facebook.com/APAOntario
Overview: A medium-sized provincial organization founded in 1988
Mission: To integrate the concerns of archaeologists in Ontario for all avenues of employment; To maintain commonly recognized standards for dealing with issues affecting archaeological resources
Finances: *Funding Sources:* Membership dues
Membership: *Fees:* $75 professional; $50 field director/associate; $20 student; *Member Profile:* Practicing professional archaeologists in the Province of Ontario and across North America
Activities: Representing archaeologists in Ontario; Offering resources & professional development opportunities; Liaisoning with First Nations communities
Chief Officer(s):
Margie Kenedy, President, 416-677-5186
Publications:
• Association of Professional Archaeologists Newsletter
Type: Newsletter; *Frequency:* 3 pa
Profile: An information resource including industry-related news, association events, & member-written articles

Association of Professional Biology (APB)
#300, 1095 McKenzie Ave., Victoria BC V8P 2L5
Tel: 250-483-4283; *Fax:* 250-483-3439
info@professionalbiology.com
professionalbiology.com
www.linkedin.com/in/probio
twitter.com/BIOLOGYAPBWORLD
Overview: A medium-sized provincial organization founded in 1980
Mission: To represent biology professionals who are practicing in Western Canada; To promote the professional practice of applied biology
Staff Member(s): 2
Membership: *Fees:* First year free; $85 regular renewal; $50 retired renewal; $25 student renewal; *Member Profile:* Biology professionals, trainees, students; *Committees:* Budget & Finance; Practice Advisory; Advocacy; Regulatory Policy; Communications & Liaison; Internal Policy Maintenance; Member Interests & Benefits; Conference; AGM Resolutions; Awards & Scholarships; Mentorship; Nominations; Fellows
Activities: Providing continuing education opportunities; Advocating for advancements & development in the practice of biological sciences
Chief Officer(s):
Marie Vander Heiden, Executive Director
executivedirector@professionalbiology.com
Awards:
• Ian McTaggart-Cowan Award for Excellence in Biology
To recognize significant contribution to the biological sciences in British Columbia
• W. Young Award for Integrated Resource Management
Sponsored jointly with the Association of BC Forest Professionals
• Biology Professional of the Year Award
To honour contributions to biological science & the application of biology in a local or regional area
• President's Award
Awarded in special circumstances to honour exemplary service to the APB *Contact:* Domenico Iannidinardo, Contact
• Fellowship in Association of Professional Biology
A designation reserved for members who bring distinction to the profession through inspiration & mentorship to others *Contact:* Domenico Iannidinardo, Contact, FAPB Award
• Association of Professional Biology Scholarships
; *Amount:* $1,500
Meetings/Conferences:
• Association of Professional Biology 2018 Conference & Annual General Meeting, April, 2018, Westin Wall Conference Centre, Richmond, BC
Scope: Provincial
Contact Information: Director, Operations: Isabelle Houde, E-mail: registrar@professionalbiology.com
Publications:
• Advisory Practice Bulletins [publications of the Association of Professional Biology]

Profile: Topics include principles of stewardship, professional behaviour, & the code of ethics interpretive notes
• Association of Professional Biology Annual Report
Type: Report; *Frequency:* Annually
• BioNews [a publication of the Association of Professional Biology]
Type: Newsletter; *Frequency:* Quarterly
Profile: Featuring a summary of the meetings of the association's board of directors & other information of interest to members
• Professional Conduct & Guidance Documents [a publication of the Association of Professional Biology]
Profile: A series of guides concerning professional conduct; includes advice on common professional conduct issues

Association of Professional Community Planners of Saskatchewan *See* Saskatchewan Professional Planners Institute

Association of Professional Computer Consultants - Canada (APCC)
#700, 2200 Yonge St., Toronto ON M4S 2C6
Tel: 416-545-5275
Toll-Free: 800-487-2722
information@apcconline.com
www.apcconline.com
www.linkedin.com/groups?home=&gid=3768080
www.facebook.com/APCCOnline
twitter.com/APCC_Canada
Overview: A medium-sized provincial organization founded in 1997
Mission: To promote the interests of independent computer consultants; to provide cost-saving services to members; to provide members with a forum for interaction & exchange
Finances: *Funding Sources:* Membership fees
Membership: *Fees:* $22.60 general; $90.40 gold; *Member Profile:* Independent computer consultant
Chief Officer(s):
Frank McCrea, President

Association of Professional Economists of British Columbia (APEBC)
#102, 211 Columbia St., Vancouver BC V6A 2R5
Tel: 604-689-1455; *Fax:* 604-681-4545
info@apebc.ca
www.apebc.ca
Overview: A small provincial organization founded in 1967 overseen by Canadian Association for Business Economics
Member of: Canadian Association for Business Economics
Chief Officer(s):
Jacob Helliwell, President

Association of Professional Engineers & Geoscientists of Alberta (APEGA)
Scotia One, #1500, 10060 Jasper Ave. NW, Edmonton AB T5J 4A2
Tel: 780-426-3990; *Fax:* 780-426-1877
Toll-Free: 800-661-7020
email@apega.ca
www.apega.ca
twitter.com/APEGA_AB
Overview: A large provincial licensing organization founded in 1920 overseen by Engineers Canada
Mission: To register & set practice standards & codes of professional conduct & ethics for professional engineers, geologists, & geophysicists in Alberta, according to The Engineering, Geological & Geophysical Professions Act
Member of: Engineers Canada
Affiliation(s): Association of Science & Engineering Technology Professionals of Alberta
Staff Member(s): 5
Membership: 58,000+; *Committees:* Council: Audit; Executive; Governance; Nominating. Statutory Committes & Board: Discipline; Enforcement; Environment; Investigative; Practice Standards; Appeal Board; Board of Examiners; Practice Review Board
Activities: Determining disciplinary actions, when necessary, for members; Providing continuing professional development activities; Offering networking opportunities; *Raising awareness* of achievements in engineering & geoscience, as well as science, math, & technology, during National Engineering & Geoscience Week; Conducting salary surveys
Chief Officer(s):
Jay Nagendran, P.Eng., FEC, QE, Registrar & Chief Executive Officer
Matthew Oliver, CD, P.Eng., Deputy Registrar & Chief Regulatory Officer

Sharilee Fossum, MBA, CPA, CMA, Chief Financial & Administrative Officer
Heidi Yang, P.Eng., FEC, Chief Operating Officer
Gisela Hippolt-Squair, Acting Director, Communications
Awards:
• Teacher Awards Program
Recognizing excellence in the teaching of science & math
• Awards & Scholarships Program
Funding Alberta engineering & geoscience education
• Summit Awards
Recognizing personal & professional contributions
• Service Awards
Recognizes members for their outstanding accomplishments; awarded to those retiring from positions on council, the branches, boards, & committees
Meetings/Conferences:
• Association of Professional Engineers, Geologists & Geophysicists of Alberta 2018 Annual Conference & Annual General Meeting, 2018, AB
Scope: Provincial
Description: An annual gathering in Calgary or Edmonton, featuring professional development activities & other conference events
Publications:
• Association of Professional Engineers, Geologists & Geophysicists of Alberta Annual Report
Type: Yearbook; *Frequency:* Annually
Profile: A review of activities, plus financial information
• e-PEG [a publication of the Association of Professional Engineers & Geoscientists of Alberta]
Type: Newsletter
Profile: A review of APEGA activities & industry news
• The PEG [a publication of the Association of Professional Engineers & Geoscientists of Alberta]
Type: Magazine; *Accepts Advertising*
Profile: A review of APEGA activities & industry news
  Calgary Branch
  Scotia Centre, #2200, 700 - 2 St. SW, Calgary AB T2P 2W1
  Tel: 403-262-7714; *Fax:* 403-269-2787
  calgarybranch@apega.ca
  Chief Officer(s):
  Gobind Khiani, P.Eng., Chair
  Samantha Oler, P.Eng., Vice-Chair
  Central Alberta Branch
  AB
  centralalbertabranch@apega.ca
  Chief Officer(s):
  Genesh Chariyil, P.Eng., Chair
  Travis Fillier, P.Eng., Vice-Chair
  Edmonton Branch
  AB
  edmontonbranch@apega.ca
  Chief Officer(s):
  Bob Rundle, P.Eng., Chair
  Kyle Fodchuk, P.Eng., Vice-Chair
  Fort McMurray Branch
  AB
  fortmcmurraybranch@apega.ca
  Chief Officer(s):
  Roya Iranitalab, P.Eng., Chair
  Anuradha (Ajay) Ghosh, P.Eng., Vice-Chair
  Lakeland Branch
  AB
  lakelandbranch@apega.ca
  Chief Officer(s):
  Azam Khan, P.Eng., Chair
  Andrew Francis, EIT, Vice-Chair
  Lethbridge Branch
  AB
  lethbridgebranch@apega.ca
  Chief Officer(s):
  Albert Tagoe, P.Eng., Chair
  Jonathan Assels, P.Eng., Vice-Chair
  Medicine Hat Branch
  AB
  medicinehatbranch@apega.ca
  Chief Officer(s):
  James Johansen, P.Eng., Chair
  Clayton Bos, P.Eng., Vice-Chair
  Peace Region Branch
  AB
  peaceregionbranch@apega.ca
  Chief Officer(s):
  Youssef Iskandar, EIT, Chair

  Kari Anderson, P.Eng., Vice-Chair
  Vermilion River Branch
  AB
  vermilionriverbranch@apega.ca
  Chief Officer(s):
  Dustin Wiltermuth, P.Eng., Chair
  Blake McCord, P.Eng., Vice-Chair
  Yellowhead Branch
  AB
  yellowheadbranch@apega.ca
  Chief Officer(s):
  Colleen Mireau, P.Eng., Chair
  Sharlene Frisen, P.Eng., Vice-Chair

Association of Professional Engineers & Geoscientists of British Columbia (EGBC)
#200, 4010 Regent St., Burnaby BC V5C 6N2
Tel: 604-430-8035; *Fax:* 604-430-8085
Toll-Free: 888-430-8035
info@egbc.ca
www.egbc.ca
twitter.com/EngGeoBC
Also Known As: Engineers & Geoscientists British Columbia
Overview: A large provincial licensing organization founded in 1920 overseen by Engineers Canada
Mission: To protect the public interest in matters related to geoscience & engineering; To regulate & govern the professions of professional engineers & geoscientists in British Columbia, according to the Engineers & Geoscientists Act; To strive for professional excellence, by establishing academic, experience, & professional practice standards
Member of: Engineers Canada
Staff Member(s): 13
Membership: 34,000
Activities: Maintaining practice standards; Upholding the code of ethics; Publishing brochures, position papers, & other association documents; Promoting the professions; Protecting members' interests; Establishing the Engineers Benevolent Fund to assist members; Setting up Foundation Trustees to support education through scholarships & bursaries & to promote professional development opportunities
Chief Officer(s):
Ann English, P.Eng., Chief Executive Officer & Registrar
aenglish@egbc.ca
Tony Chong, P.Eng., Chief Regulatory Officer & Deputy Registrar
tchong@egbc.ca
Jennifer Cho, Chief Financial & Administration Officer
jcho@egbc.ca
Awards:
• President's Awards
• Environmental Award
• Sustainability Award
• Mentor of the Year Award
• Forest Engineering Award of Excellence
Meetings/Conferences:
• Association of Professional Engineers & Geoscientists of British Columbia 2018 Conference & 99th Annual General Meeting, October, 2018, Vancouver, BC
Scope: Provincial
Attendance: 750+
Description: A chance to learn & network with colleagues & suppliers during business & technical sessions, a trade exhibition, & social events
Contact Information: Director, Member Services: Deesh Olychick, E-mail: dolychick@apeg.bc.ca
Publications:
• APEGBC [Association of Professional Engineers & Geoscientists of British Columbia] Membership Directory
Type: Directory
Profile: Rosters of professional engineers & professional geoscientists with contact information & scope of practice
• APEGBC [Association of Professional Engineers & Geoscientists of British Columbia] Professional Practice Guidelines
Type: Guides
Profile: Examples of guidelines are as follows: APEGBC/CEBC Budget Guidelines for Engineering Services; Guidelinesfor Terrain Stability Assessments in the Forest Sector; & Guidelines for Legislated Landslide Assessments for Proposed Residential Development in British Columbia
• Association of Professional Engineers & Geoscientists of British Columbia Compensation Survey
Profile: Information on APEGBC members' compensation & benefits

Canadian Associations / Association of Professional Engineers & Geoscientists of Manitoba (APEGM)

- Association of Professional Engineers & Geoscientists of British Columbia Annual Report
Type: Yearbook; *Frequency:* Annually
Profile: A yearly review, featuring reports from the association's executive director & president, as well as the auditor
- Association of Professional Engineers & Geoscientists of British Columbia Technical Bulletins
Type: Bulletins
Profile: Examples of technical bulletins are as follows: Assessment of Seismic Slope Stability; Engineering Modifications to FireTested & Listed Assemblies; & Addressing Smoke & CO Control in Elevator Machine Rooms
- Bylaws of the Association [a publication of the Association of Professional Engineers & Geoscientists of British Columbia]
Type: Booklet
Profile: Information about items such as conduct of meetings, election of council, finances, & membership
- Innovation [a publication of the Association of Professional Engineers & Geoscientists of British Columbia]
Type: Magazine; *Frequency:* Bimonthly; *Accepts Advertising;*
Editor: Melinda Lau
Profile: Information circulated to more than 26,000 British Columbia registered professionalengineers & geoscientists, industry & government reporesentatives, educational institutions, as well as the general public

Burnaby/New West Branch
bn@apeg.bc.ca
Chief Officer(s):
Alireza Talaee, P.Eng, Chair
Lien Tran, EIT, Vice-Chair

Central Interior Branch
ci@apeg.bc.ca
Chief Officer(s):
Mike Mason, EIT, Chair
Lee Peltz, P.Eng., Vice-Chair

East Kootenay Branch
ek@apeg.bc.ca
Chief Officer(s):
Jeremy Zandbergen, P.Eng., Chair
Jay Armstrong, P.Eng., Vice-Chair

Fraser Valley Branch
fv@apeg.bc.ca
Chief Officer(s):
Ria Bhagnari, EIT, Chair
Saeed Mehdipour, P.Eng., Vice-Chair

Northern Branch
no@apeg.bc.ca
Chief Officer(s):
Rhonda Mellafont, P.Geo., Chair
Kevin Ilott, EIT, Vice-Chair

Okanagan Branch
ok@apeg.bc.ca
Chief Officer(s):
James Barr, P.Geo., Chair
Keith Recsky, P.Eng., Vice-Chair

Peace River Branch
pr@apeg.bc.ca
Chief Officer(s):
Chris Flury, P.Eng., Chair
Abbad Shah, P.Eng., Vice-Chair

Richmond/Delta Branch
rd@apeg.bc.ca
Chief Officer(s):
Abbas Nikbakht, EIT, Chair
Vacant, Vice-Chair

Sea-to-Sky Branch
ss@apeg.bc.ca
Chief Officer(s):
Brent Lyon, P.Eng., Chair
Vadim Airiants, P.Eng., Vice-Chair

South Central Branch
sc@apeg.bc.ca
Chief Officer(s):
Jessica Steeves, EIT, Chair
Deanna Erickson, EIT, Vice-Chair

Tri-City Branch
tc@apeg.bc.ca
Chief Officer(s):
Michael Qiu, P.Eng., Chair
Allison Westin, GIT, Vice-Chair

Vancouver Branch
van@apeg.bc.ca
Chief Officer(s):
Keith Martin, P.Eng., Chair
Travis Nguyen, EIT, Vice-Chair

Vancouver Island Branch
vi@apeg.bc.ca
Chief Officer(s):
Maya Charnell, P.Eng., Chair
Craig Work, P.Eng., Vice-Chair

Victoria Branch
vic@apeg.bc.ca
Chief Officer(s):
Faisal Hamood, P.Eng., Chair
Ed Lyons, P.Geo., Vice-Chair

West Kootenay Branch
wk@apeg.bc.ca
Chief Officer(s):
Mark Stephens, P.Eng, Chair
Alison MacLeod, P.Eng, Vice-Chair

Association of Professional Engineers & Geoscientists of Manitoba (APEGM)
870 Pembina Hwy., Winnipeg MB R3M 2M7
Tel: 204-474-2736; *Fax:* 204-474-5960
Toll-Free: 866-227-9600
info@enggeomb.ca
www.enggeomb.ca
Also Known As: Engineers Geoscientists Manitoba
Overview: A large provincial organization founded in 1920 overseen by Engineers Canada
Mission: To serve & protect public interest by governing & advancing the practice of engineering in accordance with the Engineering Profession Act of Manitoba
Member of: Engineers Canada
Finances: *Annual Operating Budget:* $500,000-$1.5 Million
Membership: 3,500; *Committees:* Academic Review; Continuing Competency; Executive; Experience Review; Registration; Discipline; Investigation; Keystone Professional; Heritage; Indigenous Professionals Initiative (IPIC); Public Awareness; Public Interest Review; Women in Engineering (CIPWIE); Awards; Engineering & Geoscience Week; Ingenium; Salaray Research; Sports & Social
Chief Officer(s):
Grant Koropatnick, P.Eng., FEC, Chief Executive Officer & Registrar, 204-474-2736 Ext. 234
gkoropatnick@enggeomb.ca
Michael Gregoire, P.Eng., FEC, Director, Professional Standards, 204-474-2736 Ext. 225
mgregoire@enggeomb.ca
Sharon E. Sankar, P.Eng., FEC, Director, Admissions, 204-474-2736 Ext. 229
ssankar@enggeomb.ca
C. Scott Sarna, Director, Government Relations
ssarna@enggeomb.ca

Association of Professional Engineers & Geoscientists of New Brunswick (APEGNB) / Association des ingénieurs et géoscientifiques du Nouveau-Brunswick (AINB)
183 Hanwell Rd., Fredericton NB E3B 2R2
Tel: 506-458-8083; *Fax:* 506-451-9629
Toll-Free: 888-458-8083
info@apegnb.com
www.apegnb.com
twitter.com/APEGNB
Also Known As: Engineers & Geoscientists New Brunswick
Overview: A large provincial licensing organization founded in 1920 overseen by Engineers Canada
Mission: To establish, maintain & develop standards of knowledge & skill, qualification & practice, & professional ethics; To promote public awareness of the role of the association
Member of: Engineers Canada
Finances: *Funding Sources:* Membership fees
200+ volunteer(s)
Membership: 5,500; *Fees:* Schedule available; *Committees:* Executive; Councillors; Board of Admissions; Examination; Experience Review; Discipline; Scrutineers; Internship; Legislation; Nominating; Complaints; Awards & Sub-Committee; Climate Change; Continued Competency; Public Representative Appointment; Public Interest Action; Diversity & Inclusion; Audit; Representatives
Chief Officer(s):
Matt Hayes, P.Eng., President
Jeffrey Underhill, P.Eng., Vice-President
Andrew McLeod, Chief Executive Officer
mcleod@apegnb.com
Awards:
- C.C. Kirby Award
- L.W. Bailey Award
- Individual Award for Technical Excellence
- Corporate Award of Excellence
- Community Leadership Award
- Honorary Membership
- APEGNB PResident's Award
- Support of Women in Engineering Award
- Outstanding Educator Award
- Outstanding Student Award
- Young Professional Achievement Award
- Volunteer Award
- Inspirational STEM Teacher Award

Meetings/Conferences:
- 2018 Association of Professional Engineers & Geoscientists of New Brunswick Annual Meeting, 2018, NB
Scope: Provincial
Publications:
- APEGNB [Association of Professional Engineers & Geoscientists of New Brunswick] Annual Meeting Magazine
Type: Magazine; *Frequency:* Annual; *Editor:* Melissa Mertz
- Association of Professional Engineers & Geoscientists of New Brunswick Annual Report
Type: Yearbook; *Frequency:* Annual
- Engenuity [a publication of the Association of Professional Engineers & Geoscientists of New Brunswick]
Type: Newsletter; *Frequency:* 3 pa; *Editor:* Melissa Mertz
- Member Salary Survey [Association of Professional Engineers & Geoscientists of New Brunswick]
Type: Report; *Frequency:* Annual

Fredericton Branch
NB
engineersfredericton.ca
www.facebook.com/265016493527114
twitter.com/apegnbf
Chief Officer(s):
Maikel Bonilla-Rodriguez, P.Eng., Chair
Diana Loomer, P.Geo., Vice-Chair

Moncton Branch
NB
Chief Officer(s):
Serge Dupuis, P.Eng., Chair
Shawn Amberman, P.Eng., Vice-Chair

Northeastern Branch
c/o Kevin Gallant, 1907 Water St., Miramichi NB E1N 1B2
Tel: 506-773-7873; *Fax:* 506-778-6001
Chief Officer(s):
Ray Ritchie, P.Eng., Chair, 506-622-5654
rritchie@scie.ca
Brian Lavallee, P.Eng., Vice-Chair, 506-826-6390

Northwestern Branch
NB
Chief Officer(s):
Marc Steeves, MIT, Chair
Thomas Chenard, MIT, Co-Chair

Saint John Branch
NB
saintjohn.apegnb@gmail.com
www.engineerssaintjohn.com
twitter.com/APEGNBSJ
Chief Officer(s):
Lauren Boulanger, P.Eng., Chair
Sean James, P.Eng., Vice-Chair

Association of Professional Engineers & Geoscientists of Newfoundland *See* Professional Engineers & Geoscientists Newfoundland & Labrador

Association of Professional Engineers & Geoscientists of Saskatchewan (APEGS)
#300 - 4581 Parliament Ave., Regina SK S4W 0G3
Tel: 306-525-9547; *Fax:* 306-525-0851
Toll-Free: 800-500-9547
apegs@apegs.ca
www.apegs.ca
Overview: A large provincial licensing organization founded in 1930 overseen by Engineers Canada
Mission: To achieve a safe & prosperous future through engineering & geoscience in Saskatchewan; to regulate the practice of engineering & geoscience at a business level
Member of: Engineers Canada; Geoscientists Canada
Finances: *Funding Sources:* Membership dues
Staff Member(s): 18; 200 volunteer(s)
Membership: 14,000; *Fees:* Schedule available; *Committees:* Education Board (Professional Development, Student Development, K-12, Environment & Sustainability); Governance

Board (Academic Review, Experience Review, Professional Practice Exam, Licensee Admissions, Registrar's Advisory, Legislative Liaison); Image & Identity Board (Awards, Communications & Public Relations, Connection & Involvement, Professional Edge, Equality & Diversity); Discipline; Investigation; Executive
Activities: *Internships:* Yes; *Speaker Service:* Yes
Chief Officer(s):
Ernie M. Barber, P.Eng., P.Ag., President
Bob McDonald, P.Eng., MBA, LL, Executive Director & Registrar
rhmcdonald@apegs.ca
Shawna Argue, P.Eng., FEC, FC, Director, Education & Compliance
sargue@apegs.ca
Ferguson Earnshaw, P.Eng., Director, Corporate Practice & Compliance
fearnshaw@apegs.ca
Kate MacLachlan, Ph.D., P.Geo., Director, Academic Review
katem@apegs.ca
Tina Maki, P.Eng., FEC, FG, Director, Registration
tmaki@apegs.ca
Chris Wimmer, P.Eng., FEC, Director, Professional Standards
cwimmer@apegs.ca
Awards:
• Outstanding Achievement Award
• Promising Member Award
• McCannel Award
• Brian Eckel Distinguished Service Award
• Environmental Excellence Award
• Exceptional Engineering/Geoscience Project Award
• Friend of the Professions Award
Publications:
• APEGS [Association of Professional Engineers & Geoscientists of Saskatchewan] Salary Survey
Type: Report
• Association of Professional Engineers & Geoscientists of Saskatchewan Annual Report
Type: Report; *Frequency:* Annually
• The Professional Edge [a publication of the Association of Professional Engineers & Geoscientists of Saskatchewan]
Type: Magazine; *Accepts Advertising*; *Editor:* Lyle Hewitt

Association of Professional Engineers of Ontario See Professional Engineers Ontario

Association of Professional Engineers of Prince Edward Island (APEPEI)
135 Water St., Charlottetown PE C1A 1A8
Tel: 902-566-1268; *Fax:* 902-566-5551
info@engineerspei.com
www.engineerspei.com
www.facebook.com/259153067491096
twitter.com/EngineersPEI
Also Known As: Engineers PEI
Overview: A small provincial licensing charitable organization founded in 1955 overseen by Engineers Canada
Mission: To regulate the practice of professional engineering in P.E.I., with authority over members, licensees, engineers-in-training, & holders of certificates of authorization
Member of: Engineers Canada
Finances: *Funding Sources:* Membership dues
Staff Member(s): 2
Membership: *Fees:* $300; *Committees:* Act Enforcement; Act Review; Advocacy; Annual General Meeting; Awards; Construction & Consulting; Discipline; EIT Committee & Experience Review Board; Engineering Qualifications; Environment; Finance; Nominating; Professional Development & Continuing Education; Social; Student Outreach; Women in Engineering
Activities: Bridge Building Contest for students, grades 5-12; *Awareness Events:* National Engineering Month, March; *Internships:* Yes
Chief Officer(s):
Jason Lindsay, P.Eng., President
Jim Landrigan, P.Eng., Executive Director, Registrar & Treasurer
Awards:
• Engineering Award for Excellence
• Lieutenant Governor's Award for Engineering Achievement
• Award for the Advancement of Diversity in the Engineering Profession
• Young Engineer Achievement Award
• Community Service Award
• Environment Award
• The Ralph L. Woodside Memorial Award for Service to the Profession
• Friend of the Profession Award

• Honorary Life Members
• Engineers Canada Fellowship
Meetings/Conferences:
• 2018 Engineers PEI Annual General Meeting, 2018

Association of Professional Engineers of the Government of Québec (Ind.) *Voir* Association professionnelle des ingénieurs du gouvernement du Québec (ind.)

Association of Professional Engineers of Yukon (APEY)
312B Hanson St., Whitehorse YT Y1A 1Y6
Tel: 867-667-6727; *Fax:* 867-668-2142
staff@apey.yk.ca
www.apey.yk.ca
Overview: A medium-sized provincial licensing organization founded in 1955 overseen by Engineers Canada
Mission: To establish, maintain & develop standards of knowledge & skil; qualification & practice; & professional ethics; To promote public awareness of the role of the association
Member of: Engineers Canada
Finances: *Funding Sources:* Membership fees
Membership: *Fees:* $10.50-$278.25 individual; $278.25 corporate; *Member Profile:* Persons with a degree in engineering from an accredited university & with 4 years of experience
Activities: Annual Bridge Building Competition; Professional development; National Secondary Professional Liability Insurance Program; *Awareness Events:* Engineering Week
Awards:
• APEY Educational Award
• APEY Excellence Award
Meetings/Conferences:
• Engineers Yukon 2018 Annual General Meeting, February, 2018
Publications:
• Association of Professional Engineers of Yukon Newsletter
Type: Newsletter; *Frequency:* 3 pa

Association of Professional Executives of the Public Service of Canada (APEX) / L'Association professionnelle des cadres de la fonction publique du Canada
#508, 75 Albert St., Ottawa ON K1P 5E7
Tel: 613-995-6252; *Fax:* 613-943-8919
info@apex.gc.ca
www.apex.gc.ca
Overview: A medium-sized national organization founded in 1984
Mission: The association focuses on issues such as compensation, the work environment and public service management reform.
Finances: *Annual Operating Budget:* $250,000-$500,000
Staff Member(s): 4; 120 volunteer(s)
Membership: 1,000+; *Fees:* $95
Chief Officer(s):
Nadir Patel, Chair
Nadir.Patel@international.gc.ca
Lisanne Lacroix, Chief Executive Officer, 613-995-6252
lisannel@apex.gc.ca

Association of Professional Geoscientists of Nova Scotia (APGNS)
PO Box 232, 53 Queen St., Dartmouth NS B2Y 1C2
Tel: 902-420-9928; *Fax:* 902-463-1419
info@geoscientistsns.ca
www.apgns.ns.ca
Overview: A small provincial organization
Mission: To ensure high standards of practice within the geoscience community; To promote & advance the profession; To work with associated organizations across Canada to facilitate the registration of APGNS members in other provinces
Membership: *Fees:* $200 Member-in-Training; $400 License to Practice; $450 Member
Chief Officer(s):
David C. Carter, Executive Director & Registrar
exec.director@geoscientistsns.ca

Association of Professional Geoscientists of Ontario (APGO)
#1100, 25 Adelaide St. East, Toronto ON M5C 3A1
Tel: 416-203-2746; *Fax:* 416-203-6181
Toll-Free: 877-557-2746
info@apgo.net
www.apgo.net
www.linkedin.com/groups?gid=4495029
www.facebook.com/489636501070336
Overview: A small provincial organization founded in 2000

Mission: To govern the practice of professional geoscience in Ontario, in accordance with The Professional Geoscientists Act, 2000, in order to protect the public & investors; To develop standards of knowledge & skills for association members
Affiliation(s): Canadian Council of Professional Geoscientists; Canadian Geoscience Standards Board; National Professional Practice & Ethics Exam Advisory Committee; CCPG Licensure Compliance Committee
Finances: *Funding Sources:* Sponsorships
Membership: 1,389 practising members + 12 temporary members + 10 limited members + 12 non-practising members + 60 geoscientists in training + 24 student members; *Committees:* Discipline; Complaints; Registration; Executive; Finance; Nomination; Non-Member Appointment; Insurance Advisory; Governance; Professional Practice; Enforcement & Compliance; Communications & Public Awareness
Activities: Reporting to Ontario's Minister of Northern Development & Mines; Accepting registration for the licensure to practice professional geoscience in Ontario; Disciplining members for professional misconduct; Organizing continuing professional development programs
Chief Officer(s):
Gord White, CEO
gwhite@apgo.net
Ian Macdonald, President
imac@wesa.ca
Andrew Cheatle, Vice-President
amcheatle@mac.com
Publications:
• Association of Professional Geoscientists of Ontario Annual Report
Type: Yearbook; *Frequency:* Annually
• Field Notes: Association of Professional Geoscientists of Ontario Newsletter
Type: Newsletter; *Frequency:* Bimonthly; *Editor:* Wendy Diaz, M.Sc., P.Geo.
Profile: Association reports, meetings, awards, & news for all APGO members

Association of Professional Librarians of New Brunswick (APLNB) / Association des bibliothécaires professionnel(le)s de Nouveau-Brunswick (ABPNB)
c/o Tyler Griffin, Fredericton Public Library, 12 Carleton St., Fredericton NB E3B 5P4
www.aplnb-abpnb.ca
twitter.com/APLNB
Overview: A small provincial organization founded in 1992
Mission: To promote librarians & libraries in New Brunswick
Membership: *Fees:* $30
Activities: Organizing professional development activities; Lobbying on behalf of librarians; Fostering & encouraging networking among membership
Chief Officer(s):
Tyler Griffin, President
tyler.griffin@gnb.ca
Awards:
• Recognition Award
Awarded to recognize support of librarians, literacy, and information access

Association of Professional Librarians of New Brunswick See Association des bibliothécaires professionnel(le)s du Nouveau-Brunswick

Association of Professional Recruiters of Canada
#2210, 1081 Ambleside Dr., Ottawa ON K2B 8C8
Tel: 613-721-5957; *Fax:* 613-721-5850
Toll-Free: 888-421-0000
www.workplace.ca/resources/aprc_assoc.html
www.facebook.com/InstituteofProfessionalManagement
Previous Name: Canadian Recruiters Guild
Overview: A medium-sized national licensing organization founded in 1984
Mission: To establish standards & practices for the recruitment & selection of human resources in Canada & to provide members with the tools to practice at the highest professional levels
Member of: Institute of Professional Management
30 volunteer(s)
Membership: 800; *Fees:* $175; *Member Profile:* Senior human resources & management professionals
Activities: Chapter meetings; regional & national conferences; *Speaker Service:* Yes; *Library:* Online Workplace Library

Association of Professional Researchers for Advancement - Canada
c/o Sheila Larin, Trillium Health Partners Foundation, #800, 89 Queensway West, Mississauga ON L5B 2V2
www.apracanada.ca
Also Known As: APRA Canada
Overview: A medium-sized national organization
Membership: *Fees:* $42-$46 depending on province; *Member Profile:* Canadian researchers; Front-line fundraisers; Individuals interested in advancement research
Activities: Providing networking opportunities; Offering professional development days; Mentoring activities
Chief Officer(s):
Selene Hur, President
selene.hur@ymcagta.org
John Hermans, Vice-President
john.hermans@utoronto.ca
Corinne Hynes, Director, Membership
corinne.hynes@dal.ca
Sheila Larin, Director, Communications
sheila.larin@thp.ca
Meetings/Conferences:
• APRA Canada Conference 2018, October, 2018, DoubleTree by Hilton, Toronto, ON
Scope: National
Contact Information: Co-Chair: Katherine Scott, E-mail: katherine.scott@redcross.ca; Co-Chair: Crystal Leochko Johnston, E-mail: crystal@eclipseresearchgroup.com
Publications:
• Association of Professional Researchers for Advancement - Canada Membership Directory
Type: Directory; *Price:* Free with APRA-Canada membership

Association of Professionals & Supervisors of the Canadian Broadcasting Corporation *Voir* Association des professionnels et superviseurs de Radio-Canada

Association of Professors of Bishop's University (APBU) / Association des professeurs de l'Université Bishop
McGreer Hall, Bishop's University, #304, 2600, rue College, Sherbrooke QC J1M 1Z7
Tel: 819-822-9600; *Fax:* 819-822-9727
apbuoffice@ubishops.ca
apbu.ca
Overview: A small local organization founded in 1975
Mission: To promote their members' interests in negotiations with the university regarding employment
Member of: Fédération québécoise des professeures et professeurs d'université; Canadian Association of University Teachers
Membership: *Member Profile:* University professors; professional librarians; contract academic staff; non-academic staff; *Committees:* Faculty Joint; Staff Joint; Staff Council Executive; Staff Stewards
Activities: Bursaries & scholarships made available to Bishop's students contributes to crisis fund for students in dire financial need
Chief Officer(s):
Virginia Stroeher, President
virginia.stroeher@ubishops.ca

Association of Professors of the University of Ottawa *Voir* Association des professeurs de l'université d'Ottawa

Association of Psychologists of Nova Scotia (APNS)
#435, 5991 Spring Garden Rd., Halifax NS B3H 1Y6
Tel: 902-422-9183; *Fax:* 902-462-9801
apns@apns.ca
www.apns.ca
www.facebook.com/AssociationofPsychologistsofNovaScotia
twitter.com/apnsPsych
Overview: A small provincial organization founded in 1965
Mission: To represent psychology in Nova Scotia; to establish professional guidelines; to promote psychology as a science & a profession for human welfare
Affiliation(s): Council of Provincial Associations of Psychology; Canadian Psychological Association (CPAP); Canadian Register of Health Service Providers in Psychology (CRHSPP); American Psychological Association (APA).
Membership: *Fees:* Schedule available; *Member Profile:* Psychology professionals in Nova Scotia; *Committees:* Advocacy; Continuing Education; Convention; Elections; Membership; Private Practice, ad hoc; Post Trauma Services; Psychology Month Advisory; Publications; Archivist
Activities: Providing professional development activities; Engaging in advocacy activities; Liaising with government; Presenting awards; *Awareness Events:* Psychology Month, Feb.
Chief Officer(s):
Shelley Goodwin, President
Awards:
• Gerald Gordon Memorial Prize for Undergrad Psychology Students
; *Amount:* $500
• Brian Dufton Memorial Prize for Grad Psychology Students
; *Amount:* $1,000
• APNS Award
Publications:
• The APNS Private Practice Directory
Type: Directory

Association of Psychologists of the Northwest Territories
PO Box 1320, Yellowknife NT X1A 2L9
Tel: 867-920-8058
psych@theedge.ca
Overview: A small provincial organization
Affiliation(s): Canadian Provincial Association of Psychologists (CPAP)
Chief Officer(s):
Robert O'Rourke, President

Association of Psychology in Newfoundland & Labrador; Association of Newfoundland Psychologists (ANP) *See* Association of Psychology Newfoundland & Labrador

Association of Psychology Newfoundland & Labrador (APNL)
PO Box 26061, Stn. LeMarchant Rd., St. John's NL A1E 0A5
Tel: 709-739-5405
info@apnl.ca
www.apnl.ca
www.facebook.com/479381738747827
twitter.com/apnladvocacy
Previous Name: Association of Psychology in Newfoundland & Labrador; Association of Newfoundland Psychologists (ANP)
Overview: A small provincial organization founded in 1976
Mission: To promote all areas of professional psychology in Newfoundland & Labrador
Member of: Canadian Psychological Association
Membership: 200; *Fees:* Schedule available; *Member Profile:* Registered psychologists, working in healthcare, education, or in private practice in Newfoundland & Labrador; Psychology graduate students; *Committees:* Archives; Constitution; Continuing Education; Finance; Membership; Information Technology; Advocacy
Activities: Upholding the Canadian Psychological Association's Code of Ethics & Practice Guidelines, & the Newfoundland & Labrador Psychology Board's Standards of Professional Conduct for psychologists; Supporting the profession of psychology; Promoting continuing education of psychologists; Engaging in advocacy activities; Providing information to the public; *Awareness Events:* Psychology Month, Feb.
Chief Officer(s):
Janine Hubbard, President
janine@janinehubbard.com

Association of Public Service Financial Administrators (Ind.)/Association des gestionnaires financiers de la fonction publique (Ind.) *See* Association of Canadian Financial Officers

Association of Quantity Surveyors of Alberta (AQSA)
Kingsway Mall, PO Box 34062, Edmonton AB T5G 3G4
Tel: 780-628-7324
info@aqsa.ca
www.aqsa.ca
Overview: A small provincial organization founded in 1979
Mission: To promote & advance the professional status of quantity surveyors & certified cost estimators; To establish & maintain high standards of professional competence
Member of: International Cost Engineering Council; Pacific Association of Quantity Surveyors
Affiliation(s): Canadian Institute of Quantity Surveyors (CIQS); Australian Institute of Quantity Surveyors (Reciprocal Agreement); Canadian Construction Association (Reciprocal Agreement); Appraisal Institute of Canada (Memoranda of Understanding); Royal Institution of Chartered Surveyors - Canada (Memoranda of Understanding)
Membership: *Member Profile:* Professional Quantity Surveyors (PQS) & Construction Estimator Certifieds (CEC), from areas such as construction companies, private practice, & government organizations, in the provinces of Alberta, Saskatchewan, & Manitoba, as well as the Northwest Territories & Nunavut
Activities: Offering continuing professional development programs; Facilitating networking opportunities & the exchange of knowledge; Providing professional costing, value, & estimating advice; Disciplining members; Collaborating with other organizations
Chief Officer(s):
Norman Lux, PQS, President
president@aqsa.ca
Chris Reinert, Vice-President
vicepresident@aqsa.ca
Doug Eastwell, Registrar
registrar@aqsa.ca
Publications:
• Association of Quantity Surveyors of Alberta Newsletter
Type: Newsletter; *Price:* Free with association membership
Profile: Association reports, chapter news, forthcoming events, & Canadian Institute of Quantity Surveyors (CIQS) updates
• Consultants Directory [a publication of the Association of Quantity Surveyors of Alberta]
Type: Directory
Profile: Listing of firms, with one or more principals who are Professional Quantity Surveyors (PQS) &, which are operating in privatepractice in Alberta, Saskatchewan, Manitoba, the Northwest Territories, or Nunavut

Association of Québec Advertising Agencies *Voir* Association des agences de publicité du Québec

Association of Québec Municipal Engineers *Voir* Association des ingénieurs municipaux du Québec

Association of Québec Regional English Media *See* Québec Community Newspaper Association

Association of Records Managers & Administrators *See* ARMA Canada

Association of Regina Realtors
1854 McIntyre St., Regina SK S4P 2P9
Tel: 306-791-2700; *Fax:* 306-781-7940
www.reginarealtors.com
www.facebook.com/ReginaREALTORS
twitter.com/ReginaREALTORS
Overview: A small local organization founded in 1912 overseen by Saskatchewan Real Estate Association
Mission: To serve Regina through professional real estate services & community involvement
Member of: The Canadian Real Estate Association
Finances: *Annual Operating Budget:* $500,000-$1.5 Million
Staff Member(s): 7
Membership: 400+; *Member Profile:* Registered realtors in Regina & Southern Saskatchewan
Chief Officer(s):
Gord Archibald, CEO

Association of Registered Graphic Designers of Ontario
#210, 96 Spadina Ave., Toronto ON M5V 2J6
Tel: 416-367-8819
Toll-Free: 888-274-3668
info@rgdontario.com
www.rgdontario.com
www.linkedin.com/groups/RGD-Association-Registered-Graphic-Designers-1847385
www.facebook.com/RGDhub
twitter.com/rgdontario
instagram.com/rgdhub
Also Known As: RGD Ontario
Overview: A small provincial organization founded in 1996
Mission: To act as the voice of graphic design in Ontario; to improve standards of education in the industry; to establish standards of knowledge, skills, & ethics for the profession
Member of: International Council of Graphic Design Associations (ICOGRADA)
Finances: *Funding Sources:* Advertising; Sponsorships
Staff Member(s): 8
Membership: *Member Profile:* Professional graphic designers, managers, educators, & students in Ontario; *Committees:* Communications; Education; Ethics; Membership; PR; Provisional; Student
Activities: Granting those who qualify the right to use the designation Registered Graphic Designer (R.G.D.); Organizing professional development events; Facilitating the exchange of ideas & information; Disseminating information about the

industry; Increasing public recognition of the R.G.D. designation; Promoting the value of graphic design in business; Lobbying government & business; Presenting student awards; Mentoring; *Speaker Service:* Yes
Chief Officer(s):
Hilary Ashworth, Executive Director, 416-367-8819 Ext. 23
execdir@rgd.ca
Heidi Veri, Chief Operating Officer & Director, Membership, 416-367-8819 Ext. 22
Publications:
• E-Flash: Email Newsletter of the Association of Registered Graphic Designers of Ontario
Type: Newsletter; *Frequency:* Biweekly; *Accepts Advertising*
Profile: Announcements, upcoming RGD & design-related events, member news, industry updates, & employment opportunities
• RGD Ontario Membership Directory
Type: Directory
Profile: Listing of RGD Ontario members distributed to more than 1,000 marketing & adverising executives
• RGD Review
Type: Newsletter; *Frequency:* Bimonthly
Profile: Articles, RGD presentations, members news, & book reviews

Association of Registered Interior Designers of New Brunswick (ARIDNB) / Association des designers d'intérieur immatriculés du Nouveau-Brunswick (ADIINB)
PO Box 1541, Fredericton NB E3B 5G2
Tel: 506-459-3014
info@aridnb.ca
www.aridnb.ca
Previous Name: Interior Designers of New Brunswick
Overview: A small provincial licensing organization founded in 1987 overseen by Interior Designers of Canada
Mission: To establish & maintain standards of knowledge, skill, & professional ethics among association members; To serve the public interest by governing the practice of interior design in New Brunswick
Member of: Interior Designers of Canada (IDC)
Membership: *Member Profile:* Registered interior design practitioners in New Brunswick; Interns; Students; Trade affiliates
Activities: Increasing public awareness of quality interior design; Disciplining members of the association
Chief Officer(s):
Rachel Mitton, President
Lyn Van Tassel, Vice-President
Chrystalla Wilde, Treasurer & Registrar
Ginette Fougère, Secretary

Association of Registered Interior Designers of Ontario (ARIDO)
43 Hanna Ave., #C536, Toronto ON M6K 1X1
Tel: 416-921-2127; *Fax:* 416-921-3660
Toll-Free: 800-334-1180
adminoffice@arido.ca
www.arido.ca
Previous Name: Interior Designers of Ontario (IDO)
Overview: A medium-sized provincial organization founded in 1984 overseen by Interior Designers of Canada
Mission: To govern the conduct & professional standards of members; To increase awareness of the profession & ensure rights of interior designers & the public they serve
Affiliation(s): Interior Designers Educators Council; National Council for Interior Design Education; American Society of Interior Designers; Foundation for Interior Design Education; International Federation of Interior Designers
Finances: *Funding Sources:* Membership dues
Staff Member(s): 4
Membership: 3,300+; *Fees:* $25 student; $280 educator; $295.50 intern; $654.50 registered; *Member Profile:* Registered - fully accredited members who are interior designers; intern - graduate interior designers with recognized interior design degree/diploma working towards registered member status; resource alliance - manufacturers &/or suppliers of goods & services for interior design industry; affiliate - allied professionals, media, educators & individuals interested in the advancement of interior design; student - students presently enrolled in recognized interior design program
Activities: *Internships:* Yes
Chief Officer(s):
Sharon Portelli, Registrar
sportelli@arido.ca

Association of Registered Nurses of Prince Edward Island (ARNPEI)
#6, 161 Maypoint Rd., Charlottetown PE C1A 1K8
Tel: 902-368-3764; *Fax:* 902-628-1430
Toll-Free: 844-843-3933
info@arnpei.ca
www.arnpei.ca
Previous Name: Association of Nurses of Prince Edward Island
Overview: A medium-sized provincial licensing organization founded in 1922 overseen by Canadian Nurses Association
Mission: To represent the nursing profession
Finances: *Annual Operating Budget:* $500,000-$1.5 Million
Staff Member(s): 4
Membership: 1,700; *Fees:* $450; *Member Profile:* Registered nurses practicing in Prince Edward Island
Chief Officer(s):
Sheila Marchant-Short, Executive Director
sjmshort@arnpei.ca

Association of Registered Professional Foresters of New Brunswick (ARPFNB) / Association des forestiers agréés du Nouveau-Brunswick (AFANB)
#221, 1350 Regent St., Fredericton NB E3C 2G6
Tel: 506-452-6933; *Fax:* 506-450-3128
info@arpfnb.ca
www.arpfnb.ca
www.facebook.com/arpfnb
Overview: A small provincial organization founded in 1937
Mission: To manage the forest resources of New Brunswick for the sustained development of these resources; To assure the proficiency & competency of Registered Professional Foresters in New Brunswick
Affiliation(s): Canadian Federation of Professional Foresters Association (CFPFA)
Membership: 300; *Fees:* Schedule available; *Member Profile:* Registered Professional Foresters eligible to practice Forestry in New Brunswick, including forestry consultants, & federal & provincial public servants
Activities: Improving forestry practice in New Brunswick; Increasing understanding of forestry issues; Promoting the knowledge & skill of association members
Chief Officer(s):
Edward Czerwinski, Executive Director, 506-452-6933
ed.czerwinski@arpfnb.ca
Jody Jenkins, President
Jasen Golding, Secretary-Treasurer
Meetings/Conferences:
• Association of Registered Professional Foresters of New Brunswick Annual General Meeting 2018, 2018, NB
Scope: Provincial

Association of Registrars of the Universities & Colleges of Canada (ARUCC) / Association des registraires des universités et collèges du Canada
c/o Angelique Saweczko, Thompson Rivers University, 900 McGill Rd., Kamloops BC V2C 0C8
Tel: 250-828-5019
www.arucc.ca
Overview: A medium-sized national organization founded in 1964 overseen by Universities Canada
Mission: ARUCC was developed in response to the professional needs of student administrative services personnel in universities.
Member of: Universities Canada
Finances: *Annual Operating Budget:* Less than $50,000; *Funding Sources:* Membership fees
Staff Member(s): 4; 4 volunteer(s)
Membership: 139 institutional + 23 associate + 6 corporate + 718 individual; *Fees:* Based on budget of each institution; *Member Profile:* Member of AUCC & Association of Canadian Community Colleges
Activities: *Rents Mailing List:* Yes
Chief Officer(s):
Hans Rouleau, President, 819-822-9600 Ext. 2217
hrouleau@ubishops.ca
Meetings/Conferences:
• Association of Registrars of the Universities and Colleges of Canada 2018 Conference, June, 2018
Scope: National

Association of Regular Baptist Churches (Canada) (ARBC)
130 Gerrard St. East, Toronto ON M5A 3T4
Tel: 416-925-3261; *Fax:* 416-925-8305
Overview: A small national organization founded in 1957
Membership: 10 churches, 1500 members

Association of Saskatchewan Forestry Professionals (ASFP)
#102C, 1061 Central Ave., Prince Albert SK S6V 4V4
Tel: 306-922-4655; *Fax:* 306-764-7461
registrar@asfp.ca
www.asfp.ca
Overview: A small provincial organization founded in 2006
Mission: To promote the profession of forestry & its members; to satisfy the public demand for competent & ethical management of the province's forests
Finances: *Annual Operating Budget:* Less than $50,000; *Funding Sources:* Membership dues
Membership: 166; *Member Profile:* Registered Professional Foresters & Forest Technologists; Foresters-in-training & forest technologists-in-training; *Committees:* Admissions; Finance; Continuing Competence; Professional Conduct; Discipline
Chief Officer(s):
Roman Ornyik, Registrar
David Stevenson, Vice-President

Association of Saskatchewan Home Economists (ASHE)
c/o Gayleen Turner, President, 270 Battleford Trail, Swift Current SK S9H 4J5
Tel: 306-773-2574
www.homefamily.info
Overview: A small provincial organization founded in 1958
Mission: To provide professional support to members & persons in allied professions in managing personal & public resources to meet the needs of individuals & families as they strive to achieve a desirable quality of life
Membership: *Member Profile:* Home economists
Chief Officer(s):
Gayleen Turner, President
Beverley Dinnell, Registrar
beverley.dinnell@spiritsd.ca

Association of Saskatchewan Realtors (ASR)
2811 Estey Dr., Saskatoon SK S7J 2V8
Tel: 306-373-3350; *Fax:* 306-373-5377
Toll-Free: 877-306-7732
info@saskatchewanrealestate.com
www.saskatchewanrealestate.com
www.linkedin.com/company/854852
www.facebook.com/69418510914
twitter.com/saskREALTORS
Previous Name: Saskatchewan Real Estate Association
Overview: A medium-sized provincial organization founded in 1949
Mission: To represent real estate boards & their realtor members on government affairs & provincial issues; To develop standards of professional practice; To administer training; To provide information to members, governments & the public; To provide support services to members; To register brokers & salespeople; To develop special projects for the educational benefit of all registrants in Saskatchewan
Member of: The Canadian Real Estate Association
Staff Member(s): 7
Membership: 1,300; *Committees:* Audit & Finance; Buyer Brokerage Task Force; Education; Energy Awareness Task Force; Government Relations; Non-Registrants Trading in Real Estate; Professional Standards/Trademarks; Quality of Life; REALTOR Marketing; Saskatchewan REALTOR Technology Council; Standard Forms; Young Professionals Network
Activities: *Library:* Not open to public
Chief Officer(s):
Bill Madder, Chief Executive Officer
bmadder@saskatchewanrealestate.com
Patty Kalytuk, Director, Executive Communications
patty@saskatchewanrealestate.com
Jacqueline Zabolotney, Director, Learning
jzabolotney@saskatchewanrealestate.com
Sharon Hiebert, Coordinator, Member Services
sharon@saskatchewanrealestate.com

Association of Saskatchewan Taxpayers; Resolution One Association of Alberta *See* Canadian Taxpayers Federation

Association of School Business Officials of Alberta (ASBOA)
#1200, 9925 - 109 St., Edmonton AB T5K 2J8
Tel: 780-451-7103; *Fax:* 780-482-5659
www.asboa.ab.ca
www.linkedin.com/company/association-of-school-business-officials-of-alberta-asboa-
www.facebook.com/220709328072097
twitter.com/ASBOA_

Overview: A small provincial organization founded in 1939
Mission: To promote the highest standards of school business management in all aspects & the status, competency, leadership qualities & ethical standards of school business officials at all levels
Affiliation(s): Association of School Business Officials International
Finances: *Funding Sources:* Membership fees
Staff Member(s): 1
Membership: *Committees:* Communications; Discipline; Information Reporting; Leadership Development; Legislative; Practice Review; Professional Development; Registration
Chief Officer(s):
Susan Lang, Executive Director
Meetings/Conferences:
• Association of School Business Officials of Alberta Conference 2018, May, 2018, AB
Scope: Provincial

The Association of School Transportation Services of British Columbia (ASTSBC)
BC
Tel: 250-804-7892; *Fax:* 250-832-2584
info@astsbc.org
www.astsbc.org
Overview: A small provincial organization
Mission: To be dedicated to the promotion of safe transportation
Membership: *Fees:* $85 associate; $175 full
Chief Officer(s):
Robyn Stephenson, President
Tracey Syrota, Treasurer
Meetings/Conferences:
• 53rd Annual Association of School Transportation Services of British Columbia Convention and Trade Show, 2018, BC
Scope: Provincial
Contact Information: info@astsbc.org

Association of Science & Engineering Technology Professionals of Alberta (ASET)
#1600, 9888 Jasper Ave., Edmonton AB T5J 5C6
Tel: 780-425-0626; *Fax:* 780-424-5053
Toll-Free: 800-272-5619
asetadmin@aset.ab.ca
www.aset.ab.ca
www.linkedin.com/company/asetmembers
www.facebook.com/ASETmembers
twitter.com/asetmembers
Previous Name: Alberta Society of Engineering Technologists
Overview: A large provincial organization founded in 1963 overseen by Canadian Council of Technicians & Technologists
Mission: To benefit the public & the profession by regulating & promoting safe, high quality, professional technology practice; To focus on the engineering technology, applied science, & information technology fields; To issue credentials to qualified individuals; To accredit training programs. There are 9 chapters across the province
Member of: Canadian Council of Technicians & Technologists
Membership: 18,000
Activities: Awarding Engineering Technology Scholarship Foundation of Alberta (ETSFA) scholarships; *Speaker Service:* Yes
Chief Officer(s):
Barry Cavanaugh, CEO & General Counsel
barryc@aset.ab.ca
Mat Steppan, Director, Programs & Services
mats@aset.ab.ca
Norman Viegas, Privacy Officer & Director, Finance & Administration
normv@aset.ab.ca
Jennifer Bertrand, Director, Registration & Practice
jenniferb@aset.ab.ca
Awards:
• Tech of the Year Award
• Tech Employer of the Year
• Technical Excellence
• Technical Instruction
• Volunteer of the Year
• Certificate of Achievement
• Certificate of Appreciation
• Certificate of Recognition
• Award of Merit
• Honourary Membership
• Honourary Life Membership
• Years of Membership Pins
• College & Institute Scholarships & Bursaries
• Dale Tufts Memorial Scholarship
• Don Stirling Memorial Bursary
• TD Insurance Meloche Monnex Technology Scholarship
• Women in Technology Scholarship
Publications:
• Salary Survey [a publication of the Association of Science & Engineering Technology Professionals of Alberta]
• Technology Alberta [a publication of the Association of Science & Engineering Technology Professionals of Alberta]
Frequency: 4 pa

Association of Seafood Producers
#103, 10 Fort William Pl., St. John's NL A1C 1K4
Tel: 709-726-3730; *Fax:* 709-726-3731
info@seafoodproducers.org
www.seafoodproducers.org
Overview: A small provincial organization
Mission: To represent the interests of seafood producers in Newfoundland & Labrador
Membership: *Member Profile:* Seafood producers in the Newfoundland & Labrador
Activities: Liaising with government at all levels; Promoting the industry
Chief Officer(s):
Derek Butler, Executive Director
dbutler@seafoodproducers.org
Sherry Day, Executive Secretary
sday@seafoodproducers.org
Roger Hollahan, Coordinator, Programs
rhollahan@seafoodproducers.org

Association of Service Providers for Employability & Career Training (ASPECT)
977 Alston St., Victoria BC V9A 3S5
Tel: 250-382-9675; *Fax:* 250-382-9677
Toll-Free: 888-287-4957
info@aspect.bc.ca
www.aspect.bc.ca
www.linkedin.com/company/aspect-bc
www.facebook.com/aspect.bc.ca
twitter.com/aspectbc
Overview: A small provincial organization
Mission: To represent & promote the interests & activities of members; To strengthen members' capacity to provide services to people with barriers to employment
Affiliation(s): Canadian Coalition for Community Based Employability Training; Canada Career Consortium; National Headquarters for Human Resources & Skills Development Canada; Canadian Counselling Association; Career Management Association; Canadian Community Economic Development Network; BC Career Information Partnership; BC Workinfonet
Staff Member(s): 5
Membership: 175 agencies; *Fees:* $100 satellite; $200 associate; $300 voting
Chief Officer(s):
Janet Morris-Reade, CEO
Publications:
• Association of Service Providers for Employability & Career Training Newsletter
Type: Newsletter; *Accepts Advertising*

Association of Sign Language Interpreters of Alberta (ASLIA)
6240 - 113 St., Edmonton AB T6H 3L2
Tel: 780-438-2319
aslia@aslia.ca
www.aslia.ca
Previous Name: Alberta Chapter of the Registry of Interpreters for the Deaf, Inc.
Overview: A small provincial organization founded in 1978 overseen by Association of Visual Language Interpreters of Canada
Mission: To uphold the Code of Ethics for professional conduct within the profession; To maintain national standards; To ensure the provision of quality services
Finances: *Funding Sources:* Donations; Fundraising
Membership: *Fees:* Schedule available; *Member Profile:* Professional sign language interpreters; Deaf & hard of hearing persons; Interested individuals who support the goals of the organization
Activities: Providing professional development opportunities
Chief Officer(s):
Deb Flaig, President
president@aslia.ca
Robyn Sauks, Treasurer
treasurer@alisa.ca
Awards:
• Donna Korpiniski Mentorship Award
• Greg Douglas Bursary
; *Amount:* $500
• Community Spirit Award
• Volunteer Award
• President's Award
Publications:
• ACRID Express
Type: Newsletter; *Frequency:* 3 pa; *Editor:* Karen Sheets
Profile: ACRID activities, meeting minute summaries, upcoming events, & awards
• Alberta Chapter of the Registry of Interpreters for the Deaf Directory
Type: Directory
Profile: Listings of interpreters & services

Association of Social Rehabilitation Agencies of Québec Inc. *Voir* Association des services de réhabilitation sociale du Québec inc.

The Association of Social Workers of Northern Canada (ASWNC) / L'Association des travailleurs sociaux du Nord canadien (ATSNC)
PO Box 2963, Yellowknife NT X1A 2R2
Tel: 867-699-7964
ed@socialworknorth.com
www.socialworknorth.com
Overview: A small provincial organization founded in 1974
Mission: The ASWNC represents social workers practicing in Canada's three Territories in the far north - Nunavut, the Northwest Territories, and the Yukon Territory.
Member of: Canadian Association of Social Workers
Chief Officer(s):
Dana Jennejohn, President

Association of Strategic Alliance Professionals - Toronto Chapter
Also Known As: ASAP Toronto Chapter
Overview: A medium-sized local organization
Activities: Networking; professional development; member programs; *Awareness Events:* Seminar & Golf Event, June; Global Alliance Summit
Chief Officer(s):
T. Scott Sheard, President

Association of Teachers of English in Quebec (ATEQ) / Association des professeurs d'anglais du Québec
PO Box 46547, Stn. Comptoire Newman, LaSalle QC H8N 3G3
info@ateq.org
www.ateq.org
www.linkedin.com/groups?gid=6543092
www.facebook.com/ateqorg
twitter.com/ATEQc
pinterest.com/quebecteach
Overview: A small provincial organization
Mission: To provide leadership in the development of teaching theory, practice & resources; to strengthen communicaion between English language educators through a sharing of resources & language arts conferences.
Affiliation(s): Canadian Council of Teachers of English Language Arts; Conseil pédagogique interdisciplinaire du Québec; National Council of Teachers of English
Membership: *Fees:* $25
Activities: Springboards, an annual conference; workshops; site-based project grants
Chief Officer(s):
Anne Beamish, President
Judy Brebner, Administrative Assistant

Association of the Chemical Profession of Alberta (ACPA)
PO Box 21017, Edmonton AB T6R 2V4
Tel: 780-413-0004; *Fax:* 780-413-0076
www.pchem.ca
www.linkedin.com/groups/Association-Chemical-Profession-Alberta-4151513
www.facebook.com/396279680466303
Overview: A small provincial organization founded in 1992
Mission: To provides a legal definition of chemistry; To promote & increase the knowledge, skills, & proficiency of members in all things relating to chemistry
Membership: *Fees:* $150 Professional Chemist; $75 Chemist-in-Training; $50 Retired Member. Associate Member; Student Members free; *Committees:* Awards; Discipline; Legislative; Practice Review; Registration; Technical Seminar

Chief Officer(s):
Maurice Shevalier, President
Kathy Janzen, Executive Director
Awards:
• Frank W. Bachelor Award
This award recognizes outstanding volunteer contributions to the chemical profession in Alberta.
• ACPA Undergraduate Scholarship in Chemistry
Awarded annually to a student who is registered in a full-time undergraduate chemistry program at a university in the province of Alberta. *Eligibility:* Applicant must be registered in a program accredited by the Canadian Society for Chemistry (CSC); *Amount:* $1000
• Arthur Bollo-Kamara Graduate Scholarship
Awarded annually to a student registered in a graduate chemistry program at a university in the province of Alberta. *Deadline:* March 31; *Amount:* $1000
Meetings/Conferences:
• Association of the Chemical Profession of Alberta 2018 Annual General Meeting, 2018
Scope: Provincial
Publications:
• Association of the Chemical Profession of Alberta Newsletter
Type: Newsletter; *Frequency:* Irregular

Association of the Chemical Profession of Ontario (ACPO)
#1801, 1 Yonge St., Toronto ON M5E 1W7
Tel: 416-364-4609; *Fax:* 416-369-0515
Toll-Free: 800-260-0992
Other Communication: executivedirector@acpo.on.ca
info@acpo.on.ca
www.acpo.on.ca
Overview: A medium-sized provincial organization founded in 1958
Mission: To promote & increase the knowledge, skills & proficiency of its members in all things relating to chemistry & to establish standards of chemical practice for its members; provides a legal definition of chemistry & of those practising chemistry in Ontario
Finances: *Annual Operating Budget:* Less than $50,000
Membership: 1,200; *Fees:* $40-$140; *Member Profile:* Honours degree with work experience deemed acceptable by the association; 3-year chemistry degree with 5 years experience; 6 years experience & written examinations set by the association; *Committees:* Professional Affairs; Membership; Environmental
Activities: *Speaker Service:* Yes
Chief Officer(s):
T. Obal, President

Association of Trade & Consumer Exhibitions *See* Canadian Association of Exposition Management

Association of Translators & Interpreters of Alberta (ATIA) / Association des traducteurs et interprètes de l'Alberta
PO Box 546, Stn. Main, Edmonton AB T5J 2K8
Tel: 780-434-8384
www.atia.ab.ca
Overview: A small provincial organization founded in 1979 overseen by Canadian Translators, Terminologists & Interpreters Council
Mission: To protect the interests of their members
Member of: International Federation of Translators
Finances: *Funding Sources:* Membership dues; exam revenues
Membership: 151; *Fees:* $150 associate; $200 certified
Activities: *Speaker Service:* Yes
Chief Officer(s):
Hellen Martinez, President
info@etstranslations.com

Association of Translators & Interpreters of Nova Scotia (ATINS) / Association des traducteurs et interprètes de la nouvelle-écosse
PO Box 372, Halifax NS B3J 2P8
info@atins.org
www.atins.org
Overview: A small provincial organization founded in 1990 overseen by Canadian Translators, Terminologists & Interpreters Council
Mission: To ensure that clients have access to a body of qualified professionals; to promote the profession & the development of its members
Affiliation(s): Fédération internationale des traducteurs (FIT)
Membership: *Fees:* $110 associate; $140 certified
Chief Officer(s):
Bassima Jurdak O'Brien, President

Association of Translators & Interpreters of Ontario (ATIO) / Association des traducteurs et interprètes de l'Ontario
#1202, 1 Nicholas St., Ottawa ON K1N 7B7
Tel: 613-241-2846; *Fax:* 613-241-4098
Toll-Free: 800-234-5030
info@atio.on.ca
www.atio.on.ca
Overview: A medium-sized provincial licensing organization founded in 1921 overseen by Canadian Translators, Terminologists & Interpreters Council
Mission: To promote a high degree of professionalism & to protect the interest of those who use the language services provided by its members; to organize professional development activities & to encourage exchanges among its members
Member of: Fédération internationale des traducteurs (FiT)
Finances: *Funding Sources:* Membership dues; services
Staff Member(s): 3
Membership: 859; *Fees:* $378.55 certified; $189.27 senior; $62.15 retired; $124.30 special circumstances; $343.52 candidate for certification; $0 student; *Member Profile:* Associate; translator; interpreter & terminologist
Activities: *Speaker Service:* Yes
Chief Officer(s):
Catherine Bertholet-Schweizer, Executive Director
cbertholet@atio.on.ca
Barbara Collishaw, President
bcollishaw@rogers.com

Association of Translators & Interpreters of Saskatchewan (ATIS) / Association des traducteurs et interprètes de la Saskatchewan
50 Harvard Cres., Regina SK S7H 3R1
www.atis-sk.ca
www.facebook.com/ATIS.SK.CA
Overview: A medium-sized provincial organization founded in 1980 overseen by Canadian Translators, Terminologists & Interpreters Council
Mission: To provide a collective voice for members; to ensure that members exercise the profession in accordance with their code of ethics; to administer admission procedures of national certification examination; to provide a list of current certified members
Affiliation(s): Canadian Translators & Interpreters Council, Regional Center for North America (USA, Canada, Mexico); Fédération internationale des traducteurs
Finances: *Funding Sources:* Membership fees
Membership: 70; *Fees:* $125 certified; $85 associate/affiliate; *Member Profile:* Must pass national certification examination
Chief Officer(s):
Robert Jerrett, President
Estelle Bonetto, Vice-President

Association of Translators, Terminologists & Interpreters of Manitoba (ATIM) / Association des traducteurs, terminologues et des interprètes du Manitoba
PO Box 83, 200 Cathédrale Ave., Winnipeg MB R2H 0H7
Tel: 204-797-3247
info@atim.mb.ca
www.atim.mb.ca
Overview: A small provincial organization founded in 1980 overseen by Canadian Translators, Terminologists & Interpreters Council
Mission: To provide a collective voice for its members, ensure that members exercise their profession in accordance with its Code of Ethics, & protect the public interest by ensuring the quality of the services rendered by its members.
Affiliation(s): Canadian Translators & Interpreters Council (CTIC)
Membership: 49 individuals

Association of Travel Agents of British Columbia *See* Association of Canadian Travel Agents - British Columbia & Yukon

Association of Treatment Centres of Ontario *See* Ontario Association of Children's Rehabilitation Services

Association of Unity Churches Canada
2631 Kingsway Dr., Kitchener ON N2C 1A7
Tel: 519-894-0810
Other Communication: Alt. E-mail: UnityCanadaOffice@gmail.com
info@unitycanada.org
www.unitycanada.org
www.facebook.com/592422397477914

Also Known As: Unity Canada
Overview: A small national charitable organization founded in 1978
Mission: Unity is a Christian association asserting that reunion with God in mind brings certain fulfillment in life. It is a registered charity, BN: 118794544RR0001.
Affiliation(s): Association of Unity Churches USA
Finances: *Annual Operating Budget:* $50,000-$100,000
Membership: 20 churches
Activities: *Internships:* Yes; *Speaker Service:* Yes
Chief Officer(s):
Dagmar Mikkila, President
president@unitycanada.org
Pat Bell, Judicatory Representative
ucjr@unitycanada.org

Association of Universities & Colleges of Canada *See* Universities Canada

Association of University Forestry Schools of Canada (AUFSC) / Association des écoles forestières universitaires du Canada
c/o Faculty of Agric., Life & Environ. Sciences, University of Alberta, 751 General Services Building, Edmonton AB T6G 1H1
Tel: 780-492-6722
www.aefuc-aufsc.ca
Overview: A medium-sized national organization overseen by Universities Canada
Member of: Universities Canada
Membership: 8 organizations; *Member Profile:* Forest education and research organizations in Canada.
Chief Officer(s):
Vic Lieffers, Chair
Victor.Lieffers@ualberta.ca

Association of University of New Brunswick Teachers (AUNBT) / Association des enseignants de l'Université du Nouveau-Brunswick
University Of New Brunswick, PO Box 4400, Fredericton NB E3B 5A3
Tel: 506-453-4661; *Fax:* 506-453-3514
aunbt@aunbt.ca
aunbtweb.wordpress.com
www.linkedin.com/company/association-of-university-of-new-brunswick-teachers-aunbt-
www.facebook.com/211900002197182
twitter.com/AUNBTweeter
www.youtube.com/AUNBT
Overview: A medium-sized local organization founded in 1956
Mission: To stimulate research, instruction, cooperative relations; to promote professional interests of instructors, faculty & librarians; to protect freedom of expression, thought & research within the university; to act as a bargaining agent; to cooperate with like-minded organizations; to seek full representation of all members in academic operations of the University
Member of: Canadian Association of University Teachers; Federation of New Brunswick Faculty Associations
Staff Member(s): 2
Membership: 1000+; *Committees:* Collective Bargaining; Grievance; Negotiating; Status of Women; Investment; Pension; Personnel; Accessibility & Accommodation; Adjustment; Economic Adjustment; Employment Equity; Fringe Benefits; Impact of Technology; Joint Health & Safety; Joint Liaison; Assessment of Teaching Competence; Credit in Rank Anomalies; External Partners; Graduate Training & Supervision; Harassment Policy; Pre-Retirement Benefit; Teaching Apprenticeships
Chief Officer(s):
Miriam Jones, President, 506-453-4661, Fax: 506-453-3514
miriamjones@aunbt.ca
Juan Carretero, Secretary
jcarrete@unb.ca

Association of Vancouver Island Coastal Communities (AVICC)
Local Government House, 525 Government St., Victoria BC V8W 0A8
Tel: 250-356-5122; *Fax:* 250-356-5119
www.avicc.ca
Overview: A small local organization
Mission: To represent & provide a unified voice for the coastal communities of Vancouver Island
Membership: *Member Profile:* Municipalities & regional districts of Vancouver Island

Canadian Associations / Association of Veterans & Friends of the Mackenzie-Papineau Battalion, International Brigades in Spain / Association des vétérans et amis du bataillon Mackenzie-Papineau, Brigades internationales en Espagne

Activities: Providing information to its member municipalities & regional districts; Liaising with the provincial & federal governments
Chief Officer(s):
Joe Stanhope, President
Larry Cross, First Vice-President
Cindy Solda, Second Vice-President
Iris Hesketh-Boles, Contact
iheskethboles@ubcm.ca
Meetings/Conferences:
• Association of Vancouver Island Coastal Communities 2018 Annual General Meeting & Convention, April, 2018, Fairmont Empress & Victoria Conference Centre, Victoria, BC
Scope: Local
Publications:
• Association of Vancouver Island Coastal Communities Annual Report
Type: Yearbook; *Frequency:* Annually
• AVICC Newsletter
Type: Newsletter

Association of Veterans & Friends of the Mackenzie-Papineau Battalion, International Brigades in Spain / Association des vétérans et amis du bataillon Mackenzie-Papineau, Brigades internationales en Espagne
c/o S. Skup, 56 Riverwood Terrace, Bolton ON L7E 1S4
Tel: 905-951-8499; *Fax:* 905-951-7629
www.macpapbattalion.ca
Also Known As: Mac-Paps
Overview: A small national charitable organization founded in 1990
Mission: To promote programs & activities to inform the public on the role of the Mackenzie-Papineau Battalion of the International Brigades in Spain in 1936-1939
Affiliation(s): Canadian Peace Alliance
Activities: Mackenzie-Papineau Memorial Fund; *Speaker Service:* Yes

Association of Visual Language Interpreters of Canada (AVLIC) / Association des interprètes en langage visuel du Canada
#562, 125-A - 1030 Denman St., Vancouver BC V6G 2M6
Tel: 778-874-3165
avlic@avlic.ca
www.avlic.ca
www.facebook.com/AVLIC
www.youtube.com/user/TheAVLIC
Overview: A small national organization founded in 1979
Mission: To represent interpreters whose working languages are English & American Sign Language (ASL); To promote high standards & uniformity within the profession of interpreting
Membership: *Member Profile:* Providers of visual language interpreting services; Students; Organizations of visual language interpreters; *Committees:* Awards; Board & Committee Development; Dispute Resolution; Educational Interpreting Issues; Evaluations; Health & Safety; Member Services; Public Relations; Publications; Website; Interpreting in Legal Settings Document Review; Use of the Term "Certified Interpreter"; 2012 & 2014 Biennial Conference Planning
Activities: Implementing accreditation of visual language interpreters; Providing professional development opportunities
Chief Officer(s):
Christie Reaume, President
president@avlic.ca
Caroline Tetreault, Secretary
secretary@avlic.ca
Cindy Haner, Treasurer
treasurer@avlic.ca
Jane Pannell, Administrative Manager
Meetings/Conferences:
• Association of Visual Language Interpreters of Canada Summer 2018 Biennial Conference, July, 2018, Niagara Falls, ON
Scope: National
Publications:
• AVLIC Directory
Type: Directory
Profile: Interpreters in Canada & the United States
• AVLIC News
Type: Newsletter; *Frequency:* 3 pa; *Accepts Advertising*; *Editor:* Miriam West; *Price:* Free with Association of Visual Language Interpreters of Canada membership
Profile: Articles & information about interpreting, plus association activities

Association of Visual Language Interpreters of New Brunswick (AVLI-NB)
324 Duke St. West, Saint John NB E2M 1V2
avli_nb@hotmail.com
Overview: A small provincial organization founded in 1998 overseen by Association of Visual Language Interpreters of Canada
Mission: To ensure confidentiality, impartiality, & integrity of visual language interpreters in New Brunswick
Member of: Association of Visual Language Interpreters of Canada (AVLIC)
Affiliation(s): Maritime Association of Professional Sign Language Interpreters (MAPSLI)
Membership: *Member Profile:* Visual language interpreters in New Brunswick

Association of Women in Finance (AWF)
#142, 757 West Hastings St., Vancouver BC V6C 1A1
Tel: 604-765-2850
admin@womeninfinance.ca
womeninfinance.ca
www.linkedin.com/company/association-of-women-in-finance
twitter.com/AWFbc
Overview: A small provincial organization founded in 1996
Mission: To promote women in finance-related industries by encouraging their advancement, development & involvement in the business community; to acknowledge accomplished women who have achieved excellence in their field
Membership: *Member Profile:* Women in finance industry in B.C.; *Committees:* PEAK Nominations; PEAK Judging
Activities: Monthly networking events; Aug. & Dec. social; Annual PEAK Awards Gala
Chief Officer(s):
Danielle Slavin, President
Rikki Senghera, Treasurer
Awards:
• Lifetime Achievement Award, PEAK Awards
• Performance & Excellence Award, PEAK Awards
• Knowledge & Leadership Award, PEAK Awards

Association of Women of India in Canada *See* AWIC Community & Social Services

Association of Women's Health, Obstetric & Neonatal Nurses Canada *See* Canadian Association of Perinatal & Women's Health Nurses

Association of Workers' Compensation Boards of Canada (AWCBC) / Association des commissions des accidents du travail du Canada
6551B Mississauga Rd., Mississauga ON L5N 1A6
Tel: 905-542-3633; *Fax:* 905-542-0039
Toll-Free: 855-282-9222
contact@awcbc.org
www.awcbc.org
Overview: A medium-sized national organization founded in 1919
Mission: To facilitate cooperation among Canadian Boards & Commissions; To foster greater public understanding or dialogue about workplace health & safety & workers' compensation
Member of: Canadian Society of Association Executives
Membership: 12 provincial & territorial workers' compensation jurisdictions; *Fees:* $400 associate; *Member Profile:* Full - restricted to the 12 Canadian Workers' Compensation Boards & Commissions; associate - offered to any regional, national or international organization having adjudicative or policy-making responsibilities in administration of workers' compensation laws; *Committees:* Financial Comparability; College Advisory; Research; Communications
Chief Officer(s):
Cheryl Tucker, Executive Director

Association of Yukon Communities (AYC)
#140, 2237 2nd Ave., Whitehorse YT Y1A 0K7
Tel: 867-668-4388; *Fax:* 867-668-7574
www.ayc-yk.ca
Previous Name: Association of Yukon Municipalities
Overview: A medium-sized provincial organization founded in 1974
Mission: To further the establishment of responsible government at the community level; To provide a united approach to issues affecting local governments; To advance ambitions & goals of member communities by developing a shared common vision of the future; To represent members in matters affecting them & the welfare of their communities; To provide programs & services of common interest & benefit to members
Affiliation(s): Federation of Canadian Municipalities
Finances: *Funding Sources:* Membership dues; Government
Membership: 78; *Fees:* Schedule available; *Member Profile:* Yukon communities & elected officials; *Committees:* Energy; Municipal Act Review
Chief Officer(s):
Bev Buckway, Executive Director
ayced@northwestel.net

Association of Yukon Municipalities *See* Association of Yukon Communities

Association ontarienne d'équitation thérapeutique *See* Ontario Therapeutic Riding Association

Association ontarienne de gérontologie *See* Ontario Gerontology Association

Association ontarienne de soutien communautaire *See* Ontario Community Support Association

Association ontarienne des chercheurs et chercheuse en éducation *See* Association of Educational Researchers of Ontario

Association ontarienne des ex-parlementaires *See* Ontario Association of Former Parliamentarians

Association ontarienne des professeurs de langues vivantes *See* Ontario Modern Language Teachers Association

Association ontarienne des services de réhabilitation pour enfants *See* Ontario Association of Children's Rehabilitation Services

Association ontarienne des sociétés de l'aide à l'enfance *See* Ontario Association of Children's Aid Societies

Association ontarienne des Sourd(e)s francophones (AOSF)
3349, ch Navan, Orléans ON K4B 1H9
www.aosf-ontario.ca
www.facebook.com/aosfontario
vimeo.com/aosfontario
Aperçu: *Dimension:* petite; *Envergure:* provinciale; fondée en 1995
Mission: L'AOSF est un organisme sans but lucratif qui favorise le regroupement des personnes franco-ontariennes vivant avec une surdité afin de répondre à leurs besoins et à leurs aspirations. Son but est de permettre à la communauté sourde de s'épanouir et de se développer.
Membre(s) du bureau directeur:
Michael McGuire, Président
mmcguire.aosf@hotmail.com

Association Ontarienne des Techniques *See* Ontario Association of Child & Youth Care

Association Ontario Danse *See* Dance Ontario Association

Association Ontario eleves a risque *See* Ontario Association For Students At Risk

Association paritaire pour la santé et la sécurité du travail - Administration provinciale
#10, 1220, boul Lebourgneuf, Québec QC G2K 2G4
Tél: 418-624-4801; *Téléc:* 418-624-4858
apssap@apssap.qc.ca
apssap.qc.ca
Aperçu: *Dimension:* moyenne; *Envergure:* provinciale
Mission: Supporter la prise en charge paritaire de la prévention en matière de santé, de sécurité et d'intégrité physique des personnes du secteur de l'Administration provinciale
Membre(s) du bureau directeur:
Colette Trudel, Directrice générale
ctrudel@apssap.qc.ca
Sylvie Bédard, Technicienne, Administration
sbedard@apssap.qc.ca

Association paritaire pour la santé et la sécurité du travail - Imprimerie et activités connexes
#450, 7450, boul Galeries d'Anjou, Anjou QC H1M 3M3
Tél: 514-355-8282; *Téléc:* 514-355-6818
info@aspimprimerie.qc.ca
www.aspimprimerie.qc.ca
Également appelé: ASP Inprimerie
Aperçu: *Dimension:* moyenne; *Envergure:* provinciale; Organisme sans but lucratif; fondée en 1983
Mission: Fournir aux employeurs et aux travailleurs du secteur imprimerie et activités connexes des services d'information, de

Canadian Associations / Association pour l'intégration sociale (Région de Québec) (AISQ)

Membre: Critères d'admissibilité: Personnes ayant une déficience intellectuelle et/ou un trouble envahissant du développement
Activités: Événements de sensibilisation: La semaine québécoise de la déficience intellectuelle; *Stagiaires:* Oui
Membre(s) du bureau directeur:
Valérie Poulin, Directrice générale
direction@aisrbs.com

Association pour l'intégration sociale (Région de Québec) (AISQ)
5225, 3e av ouest, Charlesbourg QC G1H 6G6
Tél: 418-622-4290; *Téléc:* 418-622-1683
aisq@aisq.org
www.aisq.org
www.facebook.com/aisqc
Aperçu: Dimension: petite; *Envergure:* locale; fondée en 1961
Mission: Soutenir et informer les familles de personnes vivant avec une déficience intellectuelle ainsi que les personnes elles-mêmes, et ce, tout en faisant la promotion et la défense de leurs droits.
Membre de: Association canadienne pour l'intégration communautaire; Association du Québec pour l'intégration sociale
Finances: Budget de fonctionnement annuel: $100,000-$250,000; *Fonds:* Principales sources : Centraide et Agence de la Santé et des Services sociaux de la Capitale-Nationale
Membre(s) du personnel: 5; 115 bénévole(s)
Membre: 321; *Montant de la cotisation:* 15 $ / année; *Critères d'admissibilite:* Parents d'un enfant présentant une déficience intellectuelle; professionnels; organismes; amis, frères, soeurs, grands parents; *Comités:* Prents-Soutien; Scolaire; Transition école-vieactive; Travail; Ressources résidentielles; Planifier l'avenir; Fratrie
Activités: Intervention communautaire; Soutien et accompagnement; Ateliers de langage (orthophonie); Ateliers frères-soeurs; Guides et outils de référence; Projet résidentiel APPART'enance; Promotion et campagnes de sensibilisation du grand public; *Événements de sensibilisation:* Semaine québécoise de la déficiance intellectuelle, mars; *Stagiaires:* Oui; *Bibliothèque:* Centre de documentation; rendez-vous
Membre(s) du bureau directeur:
Marie Boulanger-Lemieux, Directrice générale
mblemieux@aisq.org

Association pour l'intégration sociale (Région des Bois-Francs)
#105, 59, rue Monfette, Victoriaville QC G6P 1J8
Tél: 819-758-0574; *Téléc:* 819-758-8270
ais-bf@cdcbf.qc.ca
Également appelé: AIS Bois-Francs
Aperçu: Dimension: petite; *Envergure:* locale; fondée en 1981
Mission: Aider et soutenir les personnes ayant une déficience intellectuelle afin de leur permettre de vivre comme des citoyens et des citoyennes à part entière et de permettre à leur famille de s'épanouir de façon harmonieuse
Affiliation(s): Association du Québec pour l'intégration sociale
Activités: Accompagnement; café-rencontre; camp du jour; club jeunesse; soutien aux familles
Membre(s) du bureau directeur:
Valérie Jutras, Coordonnatrice

Association pour l'intégration sociale (Rouyn-Noranda) inc. (AIS)
1249, av Granada, Rouyn-Noranda QC J9Y 1G8
Tél: 819-797-9587; *Téléc:* 819-797-9553
administration@aisrn.com
www.aisrn.com
Aperçu: Dimension: petite; *Envergure:* locale; Organisme sans but lucratif; fondée en 1981
Mission: Promotion des intérêts et défense de droits des personnes vivant avec un handicap; promotion de l'integration sociale, culturelle, scolaire et professionelle; aide, entraide; service aux familles vivant avec une personne handicapée
Membre(s) du personnel: 3
Membre: Critères d'admissibilite: Parent d'enfant vivant avec une déficience intellectuelle et/ou physique
Activités: Camp de jour estival pour enfants (5-18 ans) vivant avec une déficience physique et/ou intellectuelle
Membre(s) du bureau directeur:
Mélanie Vachon, Directrice générale
melanievachon@aisrn.com

Association pour l'intégration sociale d'Ottawa (AISO)
235, rue Donald, Ottawa ON K1K 1N1
Tél: 613-744-2241; *Téléc:* 613-744-4898
info@aiso.org
www.aiso.org
Nom précédent: Association pour l'Intégration sociale d'Ottawa-Carleton
Aperçu: Dimension: grande; *Envergure:* locale; Organisme sans but lucratif; fondée en 1991
Mission: Favoriser l'autonomie et promouvoir l'intégration de la personne francophone intellectuellement handicapée au sein de la communauté franco-ontarienne d'Ottawa
Membre de: Association pour l'intégration communautaire de l'Ontario; Association canadienne pour l'intégration communautaire
Finances: Budget de fonctionnement annuel: $3 Million-$5 Million; *Fonds:* Centraide; Fondation Trillium
Membre(s) du personnel: 95; 10 bénévole(s)
Membre: 130; *Montant de la cotisation:* $10; *Critères d'admissibilite:* Familles, partenaires, intervenants; *Comités:* Exécutif; Finance
Activités: Tournoi de golf; expositions d'oeuvres d'art; *Service de conférenciers:* Oui
Membre(s) du bureau directeur:
Patricia Dostie, Directrice générale
pdostie@aiso.org
Madeleine Dubois, Présidente
Suzanne Rydzik, Vice-présidente

Association pour l'Intégration sociale d'Ottawa-Carleton
Voir Association pour l'intégration sociale d'Ottawa

Association pour la coordination des fréquences *See* Frequency Co-ordination System Association

Association pour la littérature, l'environnement et la culture au Canada *See* Association for Literature, Environment, & Culture in Canada

Association pour la microbiologie médicale et l'infectiologie Canada *See* Association of Medical Microbiology & Infectious Disease Canada

Association pour la prévention de la contamination de l'air et du sol (APCAS) / Air Waste Management Association - Québec Section
CP 49527, 5122, rue Côte des Neiges, Montréal QC H3T 2A5
Tél: 514-355-2675; *Téléc:* 514-355-4159
apcas@apcas.qc.ca
www.apcas.qc.ca
www.linkedin.com/groups/APCAS-Association-prévention-contamination-lair-4134138
Aperçu: Dimension: petite; *Envergure:* provinciale
Mission: Pour informer et d'éduquer dans les domaines de la gestion des déchets et l'assainissement de l'air, ainsi que de créer des occasions de réseautage pour ses membres
Finances: Budget de fonctionnement annuel: Moins de $50,000
10 bénévole(s)
Membre: 100; *Montant de la cotisation:* 50$
Membre(s) du bureau directeur:
Pierre Carabin, Président

Association pour la promotion des droits des personnes handicapées
CP 814, 2435, rue Saint-Jean-Bâptiste, Jonquière QC G7X 7W6
Tél: 418-548-5832; *Téléc:* 418-548-5291
apdph@videotron.ca
Aperçu: Dimension: petite; *Envergure:* locale; Organisme sans but lucratif; fondée en 1972
Mission: Trouver des solutions et des moyens aux problèmes rencontrés relatifs à la santé, à l'éducation, aux loisirs et à l'intégration sociale des personnes handicapées; sensibiliser la population; informer et assister les parents et les personnes handicapées et offrir des activités de loisirs adaptés aux besoins des personnes handicapées
Affiliation(s): Association du Québec pour l'intégration sociale
Finances: Budget de fonctionnement annuel: $100,000-$250,000
Membre: 100-499; *Montant de la cotisation:* 75$; *Critères d'admissibilite:* Personne handicapée
Activités: Diverses activités récréatives et sociocommunautaires; arts plastiques; terrain de jeux; chorale; danse; discothèque; ligue de quilles
Membre(s) du bureau directeur:
Geneviève Siméon, Directrice générale

Association pour la promotion des services documentaires scolaires (APSDS)
#5, 7870, rue Madeleine-Huguenin, Montréal QC H1L 6M7
Tél: 514-588-9400
apsds@apsds.org
apsds.org
www.facebook.com/APSDS.QC
twitter.com/apsds_
Aperçu: Dimension: moyenne; *Envergure:* provinciale; fondée en 1989
Mission: APSDS est une association professionnelle qui contribue au développement des services documentaires dans les commissions scolaires du Québec, dans les écoles primaires et secondaires, publiques et privées, et qui en assure la promotion.
Membre: Comités: Activités; Communications; Mise en candidature; Organisation du CMD; Recherche et développement; Recrutement
Membre(s) du bureau directeur:
Anne-Marie Roy, Présidente

Association pour la protection automobile *See* Automobile Protection Association

Association pour la protection des intérêts des consommateurs de la Côte-Nord
872, rue de Puyjalon, 2e étage, Baie-Comeau QC G5C 1N1
Tél: 418-589-7324; *Téléc:* 418-589-7088
apic@groupespopulaires.org
Également appelé: APIC Côte-Nord
Aperçu: Dimension: petite; *Envergure:* locale; Organisme sans but lucratif; fondée en 1978 surveillée en 1978 par Coalition des associations de consommateurs du Québec
Mission: Promouvoir les intérêts des consommateurs dans tous les aspects de la consommation; grouper les consommateurs de la région Côte-Nord
Membre de: Coalition des associations de consommateurs du Québec (CACQ)
Finances: Budget de fonctionnement annuel: $50,000-$100,000
Membre: 1199; *Montant de la cotisation:* 5$ individu
Activités: Aide de planification budgétaire; ateliers; centre de documentation; traitement des plaintes; informations; *Bibliothèque*

Association pour la recherche au collégial (ARC)
a/s Cégep du Vieux Montréal, #A7.76, 255, rue Ontario est, Montréal QC H2X 1X6
Tél: 514-843-8491; *Téléc:* 514-982-3448
arc@cvm.qc.ca
vega.cvm.qc.ca/arc
Aperçu: Dimension: petite; *Envergure:* provinciale; fondée en 1988
Mission: Promouvoir le développement de la recherche au collegial
Membre(s) du personnel: 7
Activités: Belle Rencontres; colloques; remise de prix
Membre(s) du bureau directeur:
Lynn Lapostolle, Directice générale

Association pour la santé environnementale du Québec (ASEQ) / Environmental Health Association of Québec (EHA Québec)
CP 364, Saint-Sauveur QC J0R 1R0
Tél: 450-240-5700; *Téléc:* 450-227-9648
office@aseq-ehaq.ca
www.aeha-quebec.ca
www.facebook.com/184591904921401
twitter.com/aseq_ehaq
Aperçu: Dimension: petite; *Envergure:* locale
Mission: La mission de l'ASEQ est la protection de l'environnement et la santé humaine au plan individuel et collectif en sensibilisant, soutenant et éduquant la population en regard les produits toxiques et les pesticides. Numéro d'enregistrement d'organisme de bienfaisance: BN 810116624RR0001.
Affiliation(s): EHA Nova Scotia; EHA Ontario; EHA Alberta; EHA BC
Membre: Montant de la cotisation: $5
Membre(s) du bureau directeur:
Rohini Peris, Président

Association pour la santé publique de l'Ontario *See* Ontario Public Health Association

Association pour la santé publique du Québec (ASPQ) / Québec Public Health Association
#102, 4529, rue Clark, Montréal QC H2T 2T3
Tél: 514-528-5811; *Téléc:* 514-528-5590
info@aspq.org
www.aspq.org

formation, de conseil et de recherche pour favoriser la prise en charge de la prévention dans les entreprises
Finances: *Budget de fonctionnement annuel:* $500,000-$1.5 Million
Membre(s) du personnel: 8
Membre: 1-99
Activités: Formations de groupe: Action sur les machines: Évacuation en cas d'incendie; Introduction à la prévention; Superviser avec diligence; Enquête accident; Formateur chariot; Formation de formateurs SIMDUT; *Stagiaires:* Oui; *Bibliothèque:* rendez-vous
Membre(s) du bureau directeur:
Marie Ménard, Directrice générale
mmenard@aspimprimerie.qc.ca

Association paritaire pour la santé et la sécurité du travail - Secteur Affaires municipales (APSAM)
#710, 715, rue du Square-Victoria, Montréal QC H2Y 2H7
Tél: 514-849-8373; *Téléc:* 514-849-8833
Ligne sans frais: 800-465-1754
Autres numéros: www.apsam.com/blogue
info@apsam.com
www.apsam.com
www.facebook.com/apsamsst
twitter.com/APSAM
plus.google.com/+apsam
Aperçu: *Dimension:* moyenne; *Envergure:* provinciale; fondée en 1986
Finances: *Budget de fonctionnement annuel:* $500,000-$1.5 Million
Membre: 100; *Montant de la cotisation:* .13$/100$ de masse salariale
Membre(s) du bureau directeur:
Denise Soucy, Directrice générale
dsoucy@apsam.com
Guylaine Chevalier, Agente de bureau, Comptabilité
gchevalier@apsam.com
Steve Langlois, Technicien, Informatique
slanglois@apsam.com
Publications:
• L'APSAM
Type: Revue; *Frequency:* Trimestriel

Association paritaire pour la santé et la sécurité du travail - Textiles primaires *Voir* Préventex - Association paritaire du textile

Association paritaire pour la santé et la sécurité du travail du secteur affaires sociales
#950, 5100, rue Sherbrooke est, Montréal QC H1V 3R9
Tél: 514-253-6871; *Téléc:* 514-253-1443
Ligne sans frais: 800-361-4528
www.asstsas.qc.ca
ca.linkedin.com/in/asstsas
www.facebook.com/305696879444973
twitter.com/InfosASSTSAS
Aperçu: *Dimension:* moyenne; *Envergure:* provinciale
Mission: Pour promouvoir la santé et la sécurité et à assurer la formation et l'information du public
Membre(s) du personnel: 30
Membre: 14 associations
Membre(s) du bureau directeur:
Diane Parent, Directrice générale, 514-253-6871 Ext. 230
Meetings/Conferences:
• Association paritaire pour la santé et la sécurité du travail du secteur affaires sociales (ASSTSAS) colloque régionale 2018, 2018, QC
Scope: Local
Publications:
• Objectif prévention [publication Association paritaire pour la santé et la sécurité du travail du secteur affaires sociales]
Type: Magazine; *Frequency:* 4 pa.
• Sans pépins [publication Association paritaire pour la santé et la sécurité du travail du secteur affaires sociales]
Type: Magazine; *Frequency:* 3 pa.; *ISSN:* 1481-3882

Association patronale des entreprises en construction du Québec (APECQ)
#6550, ch de la Côte-de-Liesse, 2e étage, Montréal QC H4T 1E3
Tél: 514-739-2381; *Téléc:* 514-341-1216
Ligne sans frais: 800-371-2381
info@apecq.org
www.apecq.org
www.linkedin.com/groups/APECQ-Association-patronale-entreprises-construction-4799833
www.facebook.com/516728745061135
twitter.com/APECQ
www.youtube.com/user/APECQ2002
Aperçu: *Dimension:* moyenne; *Envergure:* provinciale; fondée en 1897
Mission: Défendre et promouvoir les intérêts de ses entreprises membres et de leur offrir des services de qualité pour soutenir le développement de leurs affaires
Membre de: Association des gens d'affaires et professionnels du Québec; Conseil du Patronat; Chambre de Commerce
Finances: *Fonds:* Cotisations; commandites
Membre(s) du personnel: 22
Membre: *Montant de la cotisation:* Barème; *Comités:* Activités; Finances; Formation; Interventions politiques; Mutuelle; Rémunération et Ressources humaines; Salle de plans
Activités: Colloques; séminaires; congrès; tournoi de golf; partie d'huîtres
Membre(s) du bureau directeur:
Linda Marchand, Directrice générale
linda.marchand@apecq.org
Christian Thériault, President

Association pétrolière et gazière du Québec (APGQ) / Quebec Oil and Gas Association (QOGA)
#200, 140, Grande Allée est, Québec QC G1R 5P7
Tél: 418-261-2941
info@apgq-qoga.com
www.apgq-qoga.com
Aperçu: *Dimension:* grande; *Envergure:* provinciale
Mission: L'APGQ a été créée afin d'encourager le dialogue sur le potentiel d'une nouvelle industrie au Québec.
Membre: 20
Meetings/Conferences:
• 10th Annual Quebec Oil and Gas Association Conference 2018, 2018, QC
Scope: Provincial

Association Portugaise De L'Ile De L'Ouest *Voir* Associaça Portuguesa do West Island

Association Portugaise De Sainte-Thérèse *Voir* Associaça Portuguesa de Ste-Thérèse

Association Portugaise du Saint-Esprit *Voir* Associaça Portuguesa Espirito Santo

Association pour aînés résidant à Laval (APARL)
#110, 4901, rue St-Joseph, Laval QC H7C 1H6
Tél: 450-661-5252; *Téléc:* 450-661-2497
www.aparl.org
Nom précédent: Aide aux personnes âgées en résidence à Laval inc
Aperçu: *Dimension:* petite; *Envergure:* locale; Organisme sans but lucratif; fondée en 1974
Mission: Offrir aux aînés l'intégration sociale, les services et les ressources nécessaires qui brisent leur isolement afin de conserver leur autonomie et leur maintien à domicile; favoriser la participation; encourager
Membre de: Table de concertation; Centre local de services communautaires; Corporation de Développement Communautaire
Membre(s) du personnel: 8
Membre: *Montant de la cotisation:* 15$; *Critères d'admissibilite:* Ainés actifs et en perte d'autonomie
Activités: Cours; ateliers; café-causerie; Pignon sur rue; *Stagiaires:* Oui; *Service de conférenciers:* Oui
Membre(s) du bureau directeur:
Sylvie Brunet, Directrice générale

Association pour l'amélioration des sols et des récoltes de l'Ontario *See* Ontario Soil & Crop Improvement Association

Association pour l'amélioration du sol et des cultures du Nouveau-Brunswick *See* New Brunswick Soil & Crop Improvement Association

Association pour l'asthme et l'allergie alimentaire du Québec *Voir* Asthme et allergies Québec

L'association pour l'avancement des études scandinaves au Canada *See* Association for the Advancement of Scandinavian Studies in Canada

Association pour l'avancement des sciences et des techniques de la documentation (ASTED)
#387, 2065, rue Parthenais, Montréal QC H2K 3T1
Tél: 514-281-5012; *Téléc:* 514-281-8219
info@asted.org
asted.org
www.facebook.com/asted.org
Aperçu: *Dimension:* moyenne; *Envergure:* provinciale surveillé par Canadian Health Libraries Association
Mission: Pour promouvoir les intérêts de ses membres
Membre: *Montant de la cotisation:* Barème, en fonction de revenu annuel
Membre(s) du bureau directeur:
Cossette, Président par intérim
Gagnon, Secrétaire-trésorière
Meetings/Conferences:
• Association pour l'avancement des sciences et des techniques de la documentation (ASTED) Congrès des professionnels de l'information 2018, 2018, QC
Scope: Provincial
Contact Information: Courriel: info@congrescpi.com; site Internet: congrescpi.com

Association pour l'éducation permanente dans les universités du Canada *See* Canadian Association for University Continuing Education

Association pour l'enseignement de la géographie et de l'environnement en Ontario *See* Ontario Association for Geographic & Environmental Education

Association pour l'enseignement de la science et de la technologie au Québec (AESTQ)
9601, rue Colbert, Anjou QC H1J 1Z9
Tél: 514-948-6422; *Téléc:* 514-948-6423
info@aestq.org
www.aestq.org
Nom précédent: Association des professeurs de sciences de Québec
Aperçu: *Dimension:* moyenne; *Envergure:* provinciale; fondée en 1964
Mission: Avancement de l'enseignement des sciences et des technologies
Finances: *Budget de fonctionnement annuel:* $250,000-$500,000
Membre(s) du personnel: 2; 50 bénévole(s)
Membre: 600+; *Montant de la cotisation:* Barème
Membre(s) du bureau directeur:
Camille Turcotte, Directrice générale
camille.turcotte@aestq.org

Association pour l'histoire de la science et de la technologie au Canada *See* Canadian Science & Technology Historical Association

Association pour l'intégration communautaire de l'Outaouais (APICO)
405, boul Maloney est, Gatineau QC J8P 6Z8
Tél: 819-669-6219; *Téléc:* 819-669-7967
apico@bellnet.ca
www.apico.ca
www.facebook.com/403660446331598
twitter.com/APICO1957
Aperçu: *Dimension:* petite; *Envergure:* locale; Organisme sans but lucratif; fondée en 1957
Mission: Faciliter l'intégration sociale et communautaire des personnes ayant une déficience intellectuelle
Affiliation(s): Association du Québec pour l'intégration sociale
Membre: 350; *Montant de la cotisation:* 10$ individuel; 15$ famille
Activités: Service de répit (Programmes défis); conférences; boules de Noël; soirées; sorties
Membre(s) du bureau directeur:
Stéphane Viau, Directeur général, 819-669-6219 Ext. 212
stephane.viau.apico@bellnet.ca

Association pour l'intégration sociale - Région Beauce-Sartigan
12625, 1e av, Saint-Georges QC G5Y 2E4
Tél: 418-228-5021
ais.rbs@aisrbs.com
www.aisrbs.com
Également appelé: L'A.I.S. Beauce-Sartigan
Aperçu: *Dimension:* petite; *Envergure:* locale; Organisme sans but lucratif; fondée en 1988
Mission: Promouvoir l'intégration sociale; travailler à la défense des droits des personnes ayant une déficience intellectuelle; soutenir les familles en offrant du répit; informer la population en général et la sensibiliser
Membre de: Regroupement des Associations de personnes handicapées région Chaudière-Appalaches
Affiliation(s): Association du Québec pour l'intégration sociale
Membre(s) du personnel: 3

www.facebook.com/AssociationPourLaSantePubliqueDuQuebec
aspq
twitter.com/ASPQuebec
Aperçu: Dimension: moyenne; *Envergure:* provinciale; Organisme sans but lucratif; fondée en 1943 surveillé par Canadian Public Health Association
Mission: Favoriser un regard critique sur les enjeux de santé publique au Québec en constituant un regroupement volontaire, autonome, multidisciplinaire et multisectoriel de personnes et d'organisations provenant des milieux tant institutionnels et professionnels que communautaires; offre un espace à ses membres pour développer des prises de position communes ou concertées, appuyer des politiques favorables à la santé et au bien-être et développer des coalitions et des projets en collaboration avec d'autres partenaires de santé publique ou du milieu
Membre(s) du personnel: 17
Membre: 36 membres institutionnels; 172 membres individuels; *Montant de la cotisation:* 46$ pour un an; *Comités:* Finances, comptabilité et vérification; Gouvernance et mise en candidature; Vie associative; Ressources humaines; Appréciation de la contribution de la DG
Membre(s) du bureau directeur:
Lilianne Bertrand, Présidente
Lucie Granger, Directrice générale, 514-528-5811 Ext. 225
lgranger@aspq.org
Prix, Bourses:
• Prix Jean-Pierre Bélanger

Association pour la sécurité des bébés et des tout petits
See Infant & Toddler Safety Association

Association pour la voix études au Québec / Association for the Voice of Education in Quebec
1455, boul de Maisonneuve ouest, #H-711, Montréal QC H3G 1M8
Ligne sans frais: 888-994-9177
info@aveq-nous.ca
www.aveq-nous.ca
Aperçu: Dimension: moyenne; *Envergure:* provinciale
Mission: Vise à regrouper la communauté étudiante universitaire du Québec dans le but de défendre leurs intérêts politiques, sociaux et économiques
Membre: *Critères d'admissibilite:* Les étudiantes universitaire du Québec
Membre(s) du bureau directeur:
Jean-René Leblanc Gadoury, Coordinateur
coord.gen@aveq-nous.ca

Association pour le commerce des produits biologiques
See Canada Organic Trade Association

Association pour le développement de la personne handicapée intellectuelle du Saguenay (ADHIS)
766, rue du Cénacle, Chicoutimi QC G7H 2J2
Tél: 418-543-0093; *Téléc:* 866-896-0820
adhis@bellnet.ca
www.adhis.ca
Aperçu: Dimension: petite; *Envergure:* locale; fondée en 1976
Mission: Travailler à la défense des droits des personnes vivant avec une déficience intellectuelle, apporter du support aux parents et voir à l'amélioration de la qualité de vie des personnes
Affiliation(s): Association du Québec pour l'intégration sociale
Membre(s) du personnel: 20
Membre: *Montant de la cotisation:* 5$ régulier; 10$ soutien/famille; *Critères d'admissibilite:* Parent, personne handicapée; ami
Activités: Brunch annuel, semaine québécoise de la déficience intellectuelle; loisirs samedi; intégration en terrain de jeux; sensibilisation dans les écoles; camps; discothèque
Membre(s) du bureau directeur:
Sylvie Jean, Directrice générale

Association pour les applications pédagogiques de l'ordinateur au postsecondaire (APOP)
850, av de Vimy, Québec QC G1S 0B7
Tél: 581-981-7002
info@apop.qc.ca
apop.qc.ca
Aperçu: Dimension: moyenne; *Envergure:* provinciale
Mission: Regroupe des professeurs, des professionnels et des cadres des collèges du Québec qui s'intéressent à l'utilisation pédagogique des nouvelles technologies et de l'ordinateur
Finances: Budget de fonctionnement annuel: Moins de $50,000
Membre(s) du personnel: 1; 100 bénévole(s)
Membre: 500; *Montant de la cotisation:* 20$

Activités: *Service de conférenciers:* Oui
Membre(s) du bureau directeur:
Lucia Lepage, Présidente

Association pour les droits des non-fumeurs *See* Non-Smokers' Rights Association

Association pour les neurinomes acoustiques du Canada *See* Acoustic Neuroma Association of Canada

L'Association professionnelle des agents du service extérieur *See* Professional Association of Foreign Service Officers

L'Association professionnelle des cadres de la fonction publique du Canada *See* Association of Professional Executives of the Public Service of Canada

Association professionnelle des designers d'intérieur du Québec (APDIQ)
Maison de l'Architecture, du Design et de l'Urbanisme (MADU), #406, 420, rue McGill, Montréal QC H2Y 2G1
Tél: 514-284-6263
info@apdiq.com
www.apdiq.com
Nom précédent: Société des designers d'intérieurs du Québec
Aperçu: Dimension: moyenne; *Envergure:* provinciale; Organisme sans but lucratif; fondée en 1935 surveillé par Interior Designers of Canada
Mission: Promouvoir la reconnaissance des designers d'intérieur comme ordre professionnel; assurer la qualité de leurs services; les regrouper pour faire évoluer leur profession; veiller aux intérêts du public; édicter et assurer le respect des règles d'éthique professionnelle
Finances: Budget de fonctionnement annuel: $100,000-$250,000
Membre(s) du personnel: 3
Membre: 700; *Montant de la cotisation:* Barème; *Critères d'admissibilite:* Designer d'interieur
Activités: *Listes de destinataires:* Oui
Membre(s) du bureau directeur:
Marie-Claude Parenteau-Lebeuf, Directrice générale, 514-284-6263 Ext. 272
mcp.lebeuf@apdiq.com

Association professionnelle des écrivains de la Sagamie-Côte-Nord (APES)
#304, 240, rue Bossé, Chicoutimi QC G7J 1L9
Tél: 418-698-1176
apescn@hotmail.com
www.apescn.org
Aperçu: Dimension: petite; *Envergure:* provinciale; Organisme sans but lucratif; fondée en 1994
Mission: L'association se consacre: à la création individuelle et collective (publication de textes dans des recueils et organes de communications régionaux); au développement d'échanges créateurs avec les membres des autres communautés artistiques au Saguenay-Lac Saint-Jean et dans d'autres régions du Québec; au développement de l'intérêt du public pour l'écriture et pour la lecture; à la promotion et à la diffusion des ouvrages de ses membres; à la défense des intérêts socio-économiques et moraux de ses membres; à la représentation de ses membres auprès des pouvoirs publics
Membre: 29
Activités:: *Bibliothèque:* Centre de documentation
Membre(s) du bureau directeur:
Yvon Paré, Président

Association professionnelle des enseignantes et enseignants en commerce (APEC)
a/s Stéphanie Dubois, 1455, boul Casavant est, Saint-Hyacinthe QC J2S 8S8
www.profapec.com
www.facebook.com/apec.commerce
Nom précédent: Association provinciale de l'enseignement commercial
Aperçu: Dimension: petite; *Envergure:* provinciale; Organisme sans but lucratif; fondée en 1970
Mission: Informer le milieu enseignant en Administration Commerce et informatique de tout ce qui se fait, se dit sur les programmes de notre secteur, surtout les aspects pédagogiques de notre métier; être agent de liaison entre les enseignants de la Province
Membre de: Conseil pédagogique interdisciplinaire du Québec (CPIQ)
Membre(s) du bureau directeur:
Stéphanie Dubois, Présidente
stephanie.dubois@epsh.qc.ca

Association professionnelle des entreprises en logiciels libres (APELL)
#100, 7373, rue Lajeunesse, Montréal QC H2R 2H7
Courriel: info@apell.ca
www.apell-quebec.ca
twitter.com/apellqc
Aperçu: Dimension: moyenne; *Envergure:* provinciale; fondée en 2008
Mission: Assurer la représentation de membres; la promotion des avantages que représente le logiciel libre
Membre: *Critères d'admissibilite:* Entreprises spécialisées dans le logiciel libre
Membre(s) du bureau directeur:
Bégin Eric, Président

Association professionnelle des ingénieurs du gouvernement du Québec (ind.) (APIGQ) / Association of Professional Engineers of the Government of Québec (Ind.)
Complex Iberville Trois, #218, 2960, boul Laurier, Québec QC G1V 4S1
Tél: 418-683-3633; *Téléc:* 418-683-6878
info@apigq.qc.ca
www.apigq.qc.ca
Aperçu: Dimension: moyenne; *Envergure:* provinciale; fondée en 1986
Mission: Pour représenter les intérêts de leurs membres
Membre: 10 sections; *Critères d'admissibilite:* Ingénieur; *Comités:* Exécutif; Surveillance; Classification; Ministériel des relations professionnelles; Négociation; Organisateur du Colloque des ingénierus de l'État; Équité salariale; Assurances; Déontologie et du champ de pratique exclusif; Griefs; Révision des griefs; Statuts et réglements; Stratégie, d'action et d'information; Suffrage universel
Membre(s) du bureau directeur:
Michel Gagnon, Président

Association professionnelle des internes et résidents de Terre-Neuve *See* Professional Association of Internes & Residents of Newfoundland

Association professionnelle des pharmaciens salariés du Québec (APPSQ)
3560, rue la Verendrye, Sherbrooke QC J1L 1Z6
Tél: 819-563-6464; *Téléc:* 819-563-6464
Ligne sans frais: 877-565-6464
appsq@hotmail.com
Aperçu: Dimension: moyenne; *Envergure:* provinciale
Mission: De defendre des intérêts des pharmaciens salariés du Québec

Association professionnelle des résidents de l'Alberta *See* Professional Association of Residents of Alberta

Association professionnelle des résidents des provinces maritimes *See* Professional Association of Residents in the Maritime Provinces

Association professionnelle des résidents et internes du Manitoba *See* Professional Association of Residents & Interns of Manitoba

Association professionnelle des techniciennes et techniciens en documentation du Québec (APTDQ)
594, rue des Érables, Neuville QC G0A 2R0
Tél: 418-909-0608; *Téléc:* 418-909-0608
info@aptdq.org
www.aptdq.org
www.facebook.com/aptdq
twitter.com/aptdq
Nom précédent: Association professionnelle des techniciens en documentation du Québec
Aperçu: Dimension: moyenne; *Envergure:* provinciale; Organisme sans but lucratif; fondée en 1988
Mission: Regrouper les techniciens en documentation; promouvoir auprès des employeurs le caractère professionnel de ce travail; défendre les intérêts de ses membres auprès des employeurs et de l'État; fournir des services de toute nature en relation avec les buts de l'association; favoriser le développement de la profession; développer les échanges entre professionnels
Membre: *Montant de la cotisation:* Barème; *Critères d'admissibilite:* Technicien/technicienne en documentation du Québec; *Comités:* Congrès/colloques; formation continue; bulletin; recrutement; prix Manon-Bourget; reconnaissance du bénévolat; site Web et réseaux sociaux
Activités: Formation; service d'aide à l'emploi
Membre(s) du bureau directeur:

Christian Fortin, Président
Prix, Bourses:
• Prix Manon-Bourget
Avoir contribué de façon exceptionnelle au prestige de la profession
Meetings/Conferences:
• Association professionnelle des techniciennes et techniciens en documentation du Québec 16e congrès 2018, 2018
Scope: Provincial
Publications:
• L'Info-documentation [publication Association professionnelle des techniciennes et techniciens en documentation du Québec]
Accepts Advertising
Profile: Les derniers développements sur la bibliothéconomie, la gestion documentaire et les archives

Association professionnelle des techniciens en documentation du Québec *Voir* Association professionnelle des techniciennes et techniciens en documentation du Québec

Association provinciale de l'enseignement commercial *Voir* Association professionnelle des enseignantes et enseignants en commerce

Association provinciale des constructeurs d'habitations du Québec inc. (APCHQ) / Provincial Association of Home Builders of Québec
5930, boul Louis-H.-Lafontaine, Anjou QC H1M 1S7
Tél: 514-353-9960; *Téléc:* 514-353-4825
Ligne sans frais: 800-468-8160
www.apchq.com
www.linkedin.com/company/apchq/
www.facebook.com/apchq
twitter.com/APCHQ
www.youtube.com/APCHQinc/
Aperçu: Dimension: moyenne; *Envergure:* provinciale; fondée en 1961
Mission: Depuis 1997, l'APCHQ est la plus importante gestionnaire de mutuelles de prévention du domaine de la construction. Étant le seul agent négociateur patronal des relations de travail dans le secteur résidentiel, elle défend les intérêts de quelque 12 000 employeurs et 25 000 travailleurs
Membre: 3 600
Membre(s) du bureau directeur:
Mario Dargis, Président
Luc Bélanger, Directeur général

Abitibi-Témiscamingue
5930, boul Louis-H.-Lafontaine, Montréal QC H1M 1S7
Tél: 514-353-9960; *Téléc:* 514-353-4825
Ligne sans frais: 800-468-8160
www.apchq.com
Membre(s) du bureau directeur:
Benoit Mottard, Directeur général

Beauce-Appalaches
505, 90e rue, Saint-Georges QC G5Y 3L1
Tél: 418-228-8393; *Téléc:* 418-227-8000
www.apchq.com/beauceappalaches
Membre(s) du bureau directeur:
David Boudreau, Président
Maxime Tanguay, Directeur général
mtanguay@apchq-ba.com

Bois-Francs
CP 737, #200, 1097, rue Notre-Dame ouest, Victoriaville QC G6P 7W7
Tél: 819-758-5741; *Téléc:* 819-758-6007
apchq@apchqboisfrancs.com
www.apchq.com/boisfrancs
www.facebook.com/apchq.boisfrancs
Membre(s) du bureau directeur:
Carl Lafontaine, Directeur général

Centre du Quebec
1051, boul St-Joseph, Drummondville QC J2C 2C4
Tél: 819-477-3638; *Téléc:* 819-477-1711
Ligne sans frais: 888-771-1155
apchq.cdq@cgocable.ca
www.apchq.com/centreduquebec
Membre(s) du bureau directeur:
Bobby Rainville, Président
Denis Sauvageau, Directeur général

Est-du-Quebec
243, rue Saint-Germain est, Rimouski QC G5L 1B6
Tél: 418-722-6622; *Téléc:* 418-725-4362
Ligne sans frais: 800-463-9004
apchq@apchqestduquebec.com
www.apchq.com/estduquebec
Membre(s) du bureau directeur:
Justin Dionne, Président
Alain Bernier, Directeur général

Estrie
#300, 100, rue Belvédère sud, Sherbrooke QC J1H 4B5
Tél: 819-563-9643; *Téléc:* 819-563-0000
Ligne sans frais: 888-563-9335
apchq@apchq-estrie.com
www.apchq.com/estrie
www.facebook.com/ApchqEstrie
Membre(s) du bureau directeur:
Sylvain Mathieu, Directeur général
smathieu@apchq-estrie.com

Haute-Yamaska
1380, rue Denison ouest, Saint-Alphonse de Granby QC J0E 2A0
Tél: 450-777-3177; *Téléc:* 450-777-8399
Ligne sans frais: 800-989-3177
info@apchqhauteyamaska.com
www.apchq.com/hauteyamaska
Membre(s) du bureau directeur:
Hinda Sifoued, Directrice générale

Mauricie-Lanaudière
Centre de services Mauricie, 4800, rue Raymond-Bellemare, Trois-Rivières QC G9B 0G3
Tél: 819-376-5634; *Téléc:* 819-376-5445
Ligne sans frais: 877-376-5634
apchq@apchqmauricielanaudiere.com
www.apchq.com/mauricie
Membre(s) du bureau directeur:
Maxime Rodrigue, Directeur général
mrodrigue@apchq-ml.com

Montérégie-Suroît
#200, 21, boul de la Cité-des-Jeunes est, Vaudreuil-Dorion QC J7V 0N3
Tél: 450-371-1363; *Téléc:* 450-510-3003
info@apchqmonteregie-suroit.com
Membre(s) du bureau directeur:
Nathalie Mercier, Directrice générale

Montréal métropolitain
5800, boul Louis-H.-Lafontaine, Anjou QC H1M 1S7
Tél: 514-354-8722
Membre(s) du bureau directeur:
Linda Marchand, Directeur général

Outaouais
149, ch de la Savane, Gatineau QC J8T 5C1
Tél: 819-561-7000; *Téléc:* 819-561-0186
Ligne sans frais: 800-561-7001
www.apchq.com/outaouais
www.facebook.com/apchqoutaouais
twitter.com/APCHQOutaouais
Membre(s) du bureau directeur:
Benoît Mottard, Directeur général régional
bmottard@apchqoutaouais.com

Québec
1720, boul Père-Lelièvre, Québec QC G1M 3J6
Tél: 418-682-3353; *Téléc:* 418-682-3851
Ligne sans frais: 877-775-3353
apchqquebec@apchqquebec.ca
www.apchq.com/quebec
Membre(s) du bureau directeur:
Martine Savard, Directrice générale

Saguenay
1479, boul Saint-Paul, Chicoutimi QC G7J 3Y3
Tél: 418-549-8046; *Téléc:* 418-549-3409
Membre(s) du bureau directeur:
Marie-Josée Bouchard, Directrice générale

Association provinciale des enseignantes et enseignants du Québec (APEQ) / Québec Provincial Association of Teachers (QPAT)
#1, 17035, boul Brunswick, Kirkland QC H9H 5G6
Tél: 514-694-9777; *Téléc:* 514-694-0189
Ligne sans frais: 800-361-9870
www.qpat-apeq.qc.ca
www.facebook.com/qpatapeq
Aperçu: Dimension: moyenne; *Envergure:* provinciale surveillé par Canadian Teachers' Federation
Membre: *Comités:* Adult Education; Finance & Budget; Human Rights & Social Justice; Membership Plans; New Teachers; Nominations; Vocational Education
Membre(s) du bureau directeur:
Alan Lombard, Executive Director
Meetings/Conferences:
• Association provinciale des enseignantes et enseignants du Québec/Québec Provincial Association of Teachers Convention 2018, November, 2018
Scope: Provincial

Association provinciale des parents fransaskois *Voir* Association des parents fransaskois

Association Provinciale des Professeurs d'Immersion et du Programme Francophone (APPIPF) / Provincial French Immersion & Francophone Programme Teachers' Association
a/s Conseil scolaire de Coquitlam, 1100, av Winslow, Coquitlam BC V3J 2G3
Tél: 604-937-6392; *Téléc:* 604-936-6129
Nom précédent: Association provinciale des professeurs de l'immersion et du program-cadre BC
Aperçu: Dimension: petite; *Envergure:* provinciale
Mission: Promouvoir et améliorer tous les aspects de l'enseignement au programme d'immersion et au programme francophone.
Membre de: BC Teachers' Federation
Membre(s) du bureau directeur:
Sophie Bergeron, Présidente
sbergeron@sd43.bc.ca

Association provinciale des professeurs de l'immersion et du program-cadre BC *Voir* Association Provinciale des Professeurs d'Immersion et du Programme Francophone

Association pulmonaire du Canada *See* Canadian Lung Association

Association pulmonaire du Nouveau-Brunswick *See* New Brunswick Lung Association

Association pulmonaire du Québec *See* Québec Lung Association

Association Québec Snowboard (AQS) / Québec Snowboard Association
4545, av Pierre-de Coubertin, Montréal QC H1V 0B2
Tél: 514-621-4600
evenementsquebecsnowboard.ca
quebecsnowboard.ca
www.facebook.com/AssociationQuebecSnowboard
twitter.com/aqsnowboard
Aperçu: Dimension: petite; *Envergure:* provinciale surveillé par Canadian Snowboard Federation
Membre de: Canadian Snowboard Federation
Membre(s) du bureau directeur:
Patrick Lussier, Président

Association québécoise d'aviron *Voir* Aviron Québec

Association québécoise d'information scolaire et professionnelle (AQISEP)
801, rue des Agates, Québec QC G2L 2N4
Tél: 418-847-1781; *Téléc:* 418-634-0566
aqisep@bellnet.ca
www.aqisep.qc.ca
Aperçu: Dimension: petite; *Envergure:* provinciale; fondée en 1963
Mission: Offrir aux membres un service d'information, de soutien et d'accompagnement dans leurs interventions professionnelles; assurer le développement continu de leurs compétences; développer et promouvoir l'information scolaire et professionnelle
Membre: *Montant de la cotisation:* Barème; *Critères d'admissibilite:* Professionnels des réseaux de l'éducation et de la main-d'oeuvre
Membre(s) du bureau directeur:
Gaston Leclerc, Président

Association québécoise d'urbanisme (AQU)
CP 27, Montréal QC H3C 1C5
Tél: 514-277-0228; *Téléc:* 514-277-0093
info@aqu.qc.ca
www.aqu.qc.ca
Aperçu: Dimension: petite; *Envergure:* provinciale; Organisme sans but lucratif; fondée en 1978
Mission: La promotion de l'urbanisme et de l'aménagement du territoire
Finances: *Budget de fonctionnement annuel:* Moins de $50,000
Membre(s) du personnel: 1; 1 bénévole(s)
Membre: 700; *Montant de la cotisation:* 35$ étudiant; 100$ individuel; 370$ collectif
Membre(s) du bureau directeur:
Pierre Dauphinais, Président

Association québécoise de canoë-kayak de vitesse (AQCKV)
4545, av Pierre-de Coubertin, Montréal QC H1V 0B2
Tél: 514-252-3086
canoekayakquebec.com
www.facebook.com/100275890167157
Également appelé: Canoë Kayak Québec
Aperçu: *Dimension:* moyenne; *Envergure:* provinciale; Organisme sans but lucratif; fondée en 1979 surveillé par CanoeKayak Canada
Mission: Promouvoir les activités de canoë-kayak de vitesse au Québec
Membre de: CanoeKayak Canada
Finances: *Budget de fonctionnement annuel:* $50,000-$100,000
Membre: 2 000
Activités: *Stagiaires:* Oui; *Bibliothèque:* rendez-vous
Membre(s) du bureau directeur:
Christine Granger, Directrice générale
cgranger@canoekayakquebec.com
Franck Gomez, Directeur technique
fgomez@canoekayakquebec.com

Association Québécoise de chirurgie
CP 216, Succ. Desjardins, #3000, 2, Complexe Desjardins, Montréal QC H5B 1G8
Tél: 514-350-5107; Téléc: 514-350-5157
info@chirurgiequebec.ca
www.chirurgiequebec.ca
www.facebook.com/DPCAQC
twitter.com/AQCChirurgieQub
Nom précédent: Association des chirurgiens généraux du Québec
Aperçu: *Dimension:* moyenne; *Envergure:* provinciale surveillé par Fédération des médecins spécialistes du Québec
Mission: Objectifs sont la protection et défense des intérêts professionnels collectifs des chirurgiens et l'enseignement chirurgical continu
Membre(s) du personnel: 2
Membre(s) du bureau directeur:
Mario Viens, Président
Chantale Jubinville, Directrice

Association québécoise de commercialisation de poissons et de fruits de mer (AQCMER) / Quebec Fish and Seafood Marketing Association
CP 43050, 1859, boul René-Laennec, Laval QC H7M 6A1
Tél: 450-973-3388; Téléc: 450-973-3381
info@aqcmer.org
www.aqcmer.com
Aperçu: *Dimension:* petite; *Envergure:* provinciale; Organisme sans but lucratif; fondée en 1989
Mission: Promouvoir et accroître la commercialisation des poissons et fruits de mer tout en maintenant des liens étroits avec les différentes associations de l'industrie des pêches, de l'aquaculture en eau douce et de la mariculture
Membre de: Réseau Pêches du Québec
Membre: 34; *Critères d'admissibilité:* Distributeur; chaînes alimentaires; transformateurs

Association québécoise de défense des droits des personnes retraitées et préretraitées (AQDR)
#304, 7105, rue Saint-Hubert, Montréal QC H2S 2N1
Tél: 514-935-1551
Ligne sans frais: 877-935-1551
info@aqdr.org
www.aqdr.org
www.facebook.com/aqdrnationale
twitter.com/aqdrnationale
www.youtube.com/user/aqdrnational
Aperçu: *Dimension:* moyenne; *Envergure:* provinciale; fondée en 1979
Mission: Défense des droits culturels, économiques et sociaux des personnes retraitées et pré-retraitées
Finances: *Budget de fonctionnement annuel:* $250,000-$500,000
Membre(s) du personnel: 3; 9 bénévole(s)
Membre: 36 000 individuels; 20 000 associés; *Montant de la cotisation:* 20$; *Critères d'admissibilité:* 50 ans et plus
Activités: AGA; Assemblée des présidents; Colloques; *Service de conférenciers:* Oui; *Listes de destinataires:* Oui; *Bibliothèque:* Centre de documentation; Bibliothèque publique rendez-vous
Prix, Bourses:
• Prix Yvette Brunet
Décerné à la section reconnue annuellement comme la plus active dans son milieu pour la défense des droits de ses concitoyens

Association québécoise de doit comparé (AQDC) / Quebec Society of Comparitive Law
a/s Université d'Ottawa, Faculté de droit, #308, 57, rue Louis Pasteur, Ottawa ON K1N 6N5
Tél: 613-562-5800; Téléc: 613-562-5121
www.aqdc.qc.ca
Aperçu: *Dimension:* petite; *Envergure:* provinciale; fondée en 1960
Mission: Pour sensibiliser le public aux problèmes et des défauts dans le droit comparé
Membre: *Montant de la cotisation:* 35$ Adultes; 15$ Étdiants aux cycles supérierus à temps plein
Activités: Colloques; Concours; Ateliers
Membre(s) du bureau directeur:
Nathalie Vézina, Présidente, Conseil d'administraion

Association québécoise de doit constitutionel (AQDC)
Faculté de droit, Université Laval, 1030, av des Sciences-Humaines, Québec QC G1V 0A6
Tél: 418-656-2131; Téléc: 418-656-7230
info@aqdc.org
www.aqdc.org
Aperçu: *Dimension:* moyenne; *Envergure:* provinciale; fondée en 2005
Mission: Pour diffuser les connaissances sur le droit constitutionnel au Québec
Membre: *Montant de la cotisation:* 50$ Adultes; 20$ Étudiants
Activités: Congès
Membre(s) du bureau directeur:
Daniel Turp, Président, Conseil d'administraion
d@nielturpqc.org

Association québécoise de gérontologie (AQG)
6510, rue de Saint-Vallier, Montréal QC H2S 2P7
Tél: 514-387-3612; Téléc: 514-387-0352
Ligne sans frais: 888-387-3612
info@aqg-quebec.org
www.aqg-quebec.org
www.facebook.com/AQG.Quebec
Aperçu: *Dimension:* moyenne; *Envergure:* provinciale; Organisme sans but lucratif; fondée en 1978
Mission: Promouvoir la qualité des services offerts aux personnes âgées, ainsi que la formation du personnel oeuvrant dans le domaine de la gérontologie; favoriser la recherche; analyser, inspirer et critiquer les politiques et les législations gouvernementales; favoriser la circulation de l'information et provoquer des échanges entre personnes et groupes s'intéressant au vieillissement; sensibiliser la collectivité et les individus à leur vieillissement personnel ainsi qu'au phénomène du vieillissement
Membre de: Association canadienne de gérontologie
Affiliation(s): Association canadienne-française pour l'avancement des sciences
Membre(s) du personnel: 2
Membre: *Montant de la cotisation:* 150$ corporatif; 65$ régulier; 55$ retraité; 30$ étudiant; *Comités:* Formation; Régional; Exécutif
Activités: Congrès annuel; *Bibliothèque:* rendez-vous
Membre(s) du bureau directeur:
Chantal Meessen, Directrice générale

Association québécoise de joueurs d'échechs handicapeés visuels (AQJEHV)
2495, rue de Lorimier, Longueuil QC J4K 3P5
Tél: 514-447-2792
Ligne sans frais: 855-283-8453
info@aqjehy.org
aqjehv.org
Aperçu: *Dimension:* petite; *Envergure:* locale; fondée en 2009
Mission: Encourager les personnes ayant une déficience visuelle de pratiquer les échecs et développer des compétences qui peuvent être utilisés à l'intérieur et en dehors du jeu
Membre: *Critères d'admissibilite:* Toute personne vivant au Québec qui est aveugle et qui veut jouer d'échecs; des gens et des organisme qui croient aux buts et objectifs de l'association
Activités: *Evénements de sensibilisation:* Tournoi d'échechs invitation Jean-Marie Lebel (novembre)
Membre(s) du bureau directeur:
Emile Ouellet, Président, Conseil d'administration

Association québécoise de l'épilepsie
#204, 1650, boul de Maisonneuve ouest, Montréal QC H3H 2P3
Tél: 514-875-5595; Téléc: 514-875-6734
aqe@cooptel.qc.ca
www.associationquebecoiseepilepsie.com
Aperçu: *Dimension:* moyenne; *Envergure:* provinciale; Organisme sans but lucratif; fondée en 1960
Mission: Veiller au mieux-être des personnes épileptiques et à leurs familles; promouvoir les droits des personnes épileptiques; sensibiliser le public à l'épilepsie; promouvoir l'intégration scolaire et au travail
Membre: 6 association régionale

Épilepsie - Section de Québec
1411, boulevard Père-Lelièvre, Québec QC G1M 1N7
Tél: 418-524-8752; Téléc: 418-524-5882
epilepsiequebec@megaquebec.net
www.epilepsiequebec.com
Mission: Un organisme à but non lucratif qui a sa charte depuis 1960 et qui a porté jusqu'en 1990 le nom de La Ligue de l'Épilepsie du Québec. Sa mission est de veiller au mieux-être des personnes épileptiques à travers la province.
Membre(s) du bureau directeur:
Nicole Bélanger, Directrice générale

Épilepsie Abitibi-Témiscamingue
115, rue du Terminus ouest, Rouyn-Noranda QC J9X 2P7
Tél: 819-279-7992
epilepsieat@yahoo.fr
www.ae-at.qc.ca
Mission: Un organisme à but non lucratif qui a sa charte depuis 1960 et qui a porté jusqu'en 1990 le nom de La Ligue de l'Épilepsie du Québec. Sa mission est de veiller au mieux-être des personnes épileptiques à travers la province.
Membre(s) du bureau directeur:
Jacques Bouffard, Président

Épilepsie Côte-Nord
652, av Dequen, Sept-Iles QC G4R 2R5
Tél: 418-968-2507
Ligne sans frais: 866-968-2507
epilepsiecn@globetrotter.net
Mission: Un organisme à but non lucratif qui a sa charte depuis 1960 et qui a porté jusqu'en 1990 le nom de La Ligue de l'Épilepsie du Québec. Sa mission est de veiller au mieux-être des personnes épileptiques à travers la province.
Membre de: Epilepsy Canada

Épilepsie Gaspésie-sud
176, boul Gérard D. Lévesque ouest, Paspébiac QC G0C 2K0
Tél: 418-752-6819; Téléc: 418-752-5959
info@epilepsiegaspesiesud.com
www.epilepsiegaspesiesud.com
Membre de: Epilepsy Canada
Membre(s) du bureau directeur:
Gilles Aspirot, Président

Épilepsie Granby et régions
17, boul Mountain nord, 2e étage, Granby QC J2G 9M5
Tél: 450-378-8876
Ligne sans frais: 866-374-5377
info@epilepsiegranby.com
www.epilepsiegranby.com
Mission: Un organisme à but non lucratif qui a sa charte depuis 1960 et qui a porté jusqu'en 1990 le nom de La Ligue de l'Épilepsie du Québec. Sa mission est de veiller au mieux-être des personnes épileptiques à travers la province.
Membre de: Epilepsy Canada
Membre(s) du bureau directeur:
Anne Roy, Coordonnatrice, Membres
anie@epilepsiegranby.com

Épilepsie Outaouais
#111, 115, boul Sacré-Coeur, Gatineau QC J8X 1C5
Tél: 819-595-3331; Téléc: 819-771-3286
EpilepsieOutaouais@videotron.ca
www.epilepsieoutaouais.org
Mission: De soutenir les personnes atteintes d'épilepsie et leurs familles et d'interpréter auprès du public leurs besoins dans tous les domaines.
Membre de: Epilepsy Canada
Membre(s) du bureau directeur:
Roger Hébert, Directeur général

Épilepsie régionale pour personnes épileptiques de la région 02
CP 1633, 371, rue Racine est, Chicoutimi QC G7H 6Z5
Tél: 418-549-9888; Téléc: 418-549-3547
arpe@bellnet.ca
Mission: Un organisme à but non lucratif qui a sa charte depuis 1960 et qui a porté jusqu'en 1990 le nom de La Ligue de l'Épilepsie du Québec. Sa mission est de veiller au mieux-être des personnes épileptiques à travers la province.
Membre de: Epislepsy Canada
Membre(s) du bureau directeur:

Nicole Bouchard, Coordonnatrice

Association québécoise de l'industrie de la pêche (AQIP) / Québec Fish Processors Association
Place de la Cité, Tour Cominar, #0150, 2640, boul Laurier, Québec QC G1V 5C2
Tél: 418-654-1831; Téléc: 418-654-1376
info@aqip.com
www.aqip.com
Aperçu: *Dimension:* moyenne; *Envergure:* provinciale; fondée en 1978
Mission: Défendre les intérêts professionnels des industries québécoises de la transformation des produits marins; travailler au développement des services; aider à l'amélioration de la productivité en usines
Membre de: CRCD Gaspésie des Îles
Finances: *Budget de fonctionnement annuel:* $250,000-$500,000
Membre: 46 (35 membres industriels et 11 membres associés)
Activités: Négociations des plans conjoints

Association québécoise de l'industrie de la peinture (AQIP)
#103, 9900, boul Cavendish, Montréal QC H4M 2V2
Tél: 514-745-2611; Téléc: 514-745-2031
Aperçu: *Dimension:* petite; *Envergure:* provinciale

Association québécoise de l'industrie du disque, du spectacle et de la vidéo (ADISQ)
6420, rue Saint-Denis, Montréal QC H2S 2R7
Tél: 514-842-5147; Téléc: 514-842-7762
info@adisq.com
www.adisq.com
www.facebook.com/galaadisq
twitter.com/ADISQ_
Aperçu: *Dimension:* moyenne; *Envergure:* provinciale; fondée en 1978
Mission: Promouvoir les intérêts des producteurs de disques, spectacles et vidéos
Membre(s) du personnel: 17
Membre: 250; *Montant de la cotisation:* Barème; *Critères d'admissibilité:* Entreprises oeuvrant dans le milieu de la production d'enregistrements sonores, de spectacles ou de vidéos
Activités: *Service de conférenciers:* Oui; *Listes de destinataires:* Oui; *Bibliothèque*
Membre(s) du bureau directeur:
Julie Gariépy, Directrice générale, 514-842-5147 Ext. 227
Prix, Bourses:
• ADISQ Awards
The event honours the best musical achievement produced in Québec during the past year

Association québécoise de la distribution de fruits et légumes (AQDFL) / Québec Produce Marketing Association (QPMA)
#740, 6020, rue Jean-Talon est, Saint-Léonard QC H1S 3B1
Tél: 514-355-4330; Téléc: 514-355-9876
info@aqdfl.ca
www.aqdfl.ca
twitter.com/aqdfl
Aperçu: *Dimension:* moyenne; *Envergure:* provinciale; Organisme sans but lucratif; fondée en 1948
Mission: Créer un environnement propice à la commercialisation des fruits et légumes au Québec
Finances: *Budget de fonctionnement annuel:* $500,000-$1.5 Million
Membre(s) du personnel: 5
Membre: 500+; *Montant de la cotisation:* Barème; *Critères d'admissibilité:* Individus ou entreprises reliés de près ou de loin à l'industrie des fruits et légumes
Activités: Activités de reseautage; Campagne de promotion de la consommation de fruits et légumes ("J'aime 5 à 10 portions par jour."); *Événements de sensibilisation:* Congrès; Tournoi Golf; Partie d'huîtres; Tournoi de Poker
Membre(s) du bureau directeur:
Sophie Perreault, President & CEO

Association québécoise de la dysphasie
3958, rue Dandurand, Montréal QC H1X 1P7
Tél: 514-495-4118; Téléc: 514-495-8637
Ligne sans frais: 800-495-4118
direction@dysphasie.qc.ca
www.aqea.qc.ca
Nom précédent: Association québécoise pour les enfants atteints d'audimutité

Aperçu: *Dimension:* moyenne; *Envergure:* provinciale; fondée en 1986
Mission: Regrouper les parents d'enfants dysphasiques ou atteints d'audimutité; sensibiliser la communauté à la réalité que vivent ces enfants; informer les parents de leurs droits et des divers services dont ils peuvent bénéficier; identifier leurs besoins; susciter la création de nouveaux services; colliger et encourager les recherches faites sur les dysphasies et l'audimutité
Membre: *Montant de la cotisation:* 25$ membre régulier; 50$ membre corporatif; *Critères d'admissibilité:* Parents d'enfants dysphasiques; professionnels
Activités: Ateliers; conférences; congrès; symposium; formation pour parents ou professionnels
Membre(s) du bureau directeur:
Caroline Ricard, Présidente

Association québécoise de la fibromyalgie (AQF)
#225, 2465, rue Honoré-Mercier, Laval QC H7L 2S9
Tél: 450-933-6530
fqf@fibromyalgie-fqf.org
www.aqf.ca
Nom précédent: Association de la fibromyalgie du Québec
Aperçu: *Dimension:* moyenne; *Envergure:* provinciale; fondée en 1989
Mission: Sensibiliser la population face à la maladie par la défense des droits des personnes atteintes dans les différentes régions du Québec

Association québécoise de la fibrose kystique (AQFK) *Voir* Fibrose kystique Québec

Association québécoise de la gestion parasitaire (AQGP)
#403, 2030, boul Pie-IX, Montréal QC H1V 2C8
Tél: 514-355-3757; Téléc: 514-355-4159
Ligne sans frais: 800-663-2730
aqgp@spg.qc.ca
www.aqgp.ca
Nom précédent: Association des spécialistes en extermination du Québec
Aperçu: *Dimension:* petite; *Envergure:* provinciale; fondée en 1968
Mission: Promouvoir le professionnalisme de ses membres - en les représentant auprès des instances régissant l'industrie de l'extermination et du public en général; en s'assurant de la conformité de ses membres par l'élaboration de normes et de règlements spécifiques; en contribuant à l'accroissement de leurs connaissances techniques et scientifiques par l'accès à l'information et l'élaboration de programmes de formation adaptés
Membre de: Canadian Pest Management Association
Membre: 125
Membre(s) du bureau directeur:
Jean-Pierre Lamy, Président
André Maheu, Vice-président

Association québécoise de la pastorale de la santé *Voir* Association des intervenantes et des intervenants en soins spirituels du Québec

Association québécoise de la production d'énergie renouvelable (AQPER)
#807, 276, rue Saint-Jacques, Montréal QC H2Y 1N3
Tél: 514-281-3131
www.aqper.com
www.facebook.com/AQPER-199415180195136
twitter.com/AssociationERQc
Aperçu: *Dimension:* moyenne; *Envergure:* provinciale
Mission: D'accroître la production d'énergie renouvelable de source indépendante et d'en maximiser la valorisation dans Québec
Membre: *Critères d'admissibilité:* Des personnes ou des organismes qui participe ou s'intéresse au développement de la production indépendante d'électricité de source renouvelable au Québec; *Comités:* Biogaz; Biomasse; Communications et affaires sociales; Éolien; Hydraulique
Membre(s) du bureau directeur:
Jean-François Samray, Directeur général

Association québécoise de la production médiatique (AQPM)
#950, 1470, rue Peel, Montréal QC H3A 1T1
Tél: 514-397-8600; Téléc: 514-392-0232
www.aqpm.ca
Nom précédent: Association des producteurs de films et de télévision du Québec

Aperçu: *Dimension:* moyenne; *Envergure:* provinciale; fondée en 1966
Mission: Représente les entreprises de production indépendante en cinéma, en télévision et en web au Quebec
Membre(s) du personnel: 16
Membre: 150+ corporations; *Critères d'admissibilité:* Entreprises dont les actionnaires et administrateurs possèdent une expérience en production
Activités: Représentation, relations de travail, communications
Membre(s) du bureau directeur:
Hélène Messier, Présidente
hmessier@aqpm.ca

Association québécoise de la quincaillerie et des matériaux de construction (AQMAT) / The Building Materials Retailers Association of Québec
#200, 476, rue Jean-Neveu, Longueuil QC J4G 1N8
Tél: 450-646-5842; Téléc: 450-646-6171
information@aqmat.org
www.aqmat.org
Nom précédent: Association des détaillants de matériaux de construction du Québec
Aperçu: *Dimension:* moyenne; *Envergure:* provinciale; Organisme sans but lucratif; fondée en 1940
Mission: Promouvoir l'intérêt général de ses membres-clients engagés dans la vente au détail de matériaux de construction et de quincaillerie, en leur offrant une panoplie de produits et services visant à faciliter la gestion de leurs commerces, des Québécois et la rénovation
Affiliation(s): Conseil québécois du commerce de détail
Membre: 720; *Montant de la cotisation:* 375$ fournisseurs et associés; 325$ détaillants
Activités: Assurances collectives; cours; quatres réunions du Conseil d'Administration; mémoires aux instances gouvernementales; Opération Ratios (tous les deux ans); participation aux Congrès des Associations-Soeurs; programme de recrutement et de formation; rencontres régionales; deux tournois de golf annuels; taux préférentiel MasterCard et Visa; programme de réduction sur carburant; mutuelle de prévention; lois et règlements abrégés; guide de référence et de bonnes pratiques sur l'étiquetage et l'exactitude des prix
Membre(s) du bureau directeur:
Richard Darveau, Président-chef de la direction
rdarveau@aqmat.org

Association québécoise de la schizophrénie *Voir* Société québécoise de la schizophrénie

Association québécoise de lutte contre la pollution atmosphérique (AQLPA)
473, rue Principale, Saint-Léon-de-Standon QC G0R 4L0
Tél: 418-642-1322
Ligne sans frais: 855-702-7572
info@aqlpa.com
www.aqlpa.com
www.facebook.com/aqlpa
twitter.com/AQLPA
Aperçu: *Dimension:* petite; *Envergure:* provinciale; fondée en 1982
Mission: L'Association québécoise de lutte contre la pollution atmosphérique (AQLPA) est un organisme qui s'est donnée pour mandat de contribuer à la protection de l'air et de l'atmosphère entourant notre planète, à la fois pour la santé des humains et des écosystèmes qu'elle abrite
Membre: 415
Membre(s) du bureau directeur:
André Bélisle, Président, 418-642-1322 Ext. 221
andre.belisle@aqlpa.com
Jocelyne Lachapelle, Directrice générale par intérim
jocelyne.lachapelle@aqlpa.com
Meetings/Conferences:
• Association québécoise de lutte contre la pollution atmosphérique Coquetel bénéfice 2018, 2018
Scope: Provincial

Association québécoise de pédagogie collégiale (AQPC)
Cégep marie-victorin, 7000, rue Marie-Victorin, Montréal QC H2G 1J6
Tél: 514-328-3805; Téléc: 514-328-3824
info@aqpc.qc.ca
www.aqpc.qc.ca
Aperçu: *Dimension:* moyenne; *Envergure:* provinciale; Organisme sans but lucratif; fondée en 1981
Mission: Alimenter la réflexion sur la pédagogie collégiale et promouvoir le développement pédagogique dans le réseau collégial québécois

Finances: *Budget de fonctionnement annuel:*
$250,000-$500,000
Membre(s) du personnel: 3
Membre: 1000; *Montant de la cotisation:* 50$; *Critères d'admissibilite:* Enseignants; professionnels & cadres de l'éducation collégiale
Activités: Colloque annuel; publication d'ouvrages pédagogiques; stages
Membre(s) du bureau directeur:
Fanny Kingsbury, Directeur général
dg@aqpc.qc.ca
Meetings/Conferences:
• Association québécoise de pédagogie collégiale 38e colloque annuel, June, 2018, Saint-Hyacinthe, QC
Scope: National

Association québécoise de prévention du suicide (AQPS)
#230, 1135, Grande Allée ouest, Québec QC G1S 1E7
Tél: 418-614-5909; *Téléc:* 418-614-5906; *Crisis Hot-Line:* 866-277-3553
reception@aqps.info
www.aqps.info
www.facebook.com/preventiondusuicide
twitter.com/AQPS_Quebec
www.youtube.com/user/AQPSQuebec#p/a
Aperçu: *Dimension:* petite; *Envergure:* provinciale; fondée en 1986
Mission: L'Association québécoise de prévention du suicide réunit les organisations et les citoyens qui souhaitent voir diminuer significativement le nombre de décès par suicide au Québec.
Membre: 150
Membre(s) du bureau directeur:
Jérôme Gaudreault, Directeur général, 418-614-5909 Ext. 36
Catherine Rioux, Coordonnatrice des communications, 418-614-5909 Ext. 33

Association québécoise de promotion du tourisme socioculturel (AQPTSC)
CP 1000, Succ. M, 4545, av Pierre-de Coubertin, Montréal QC H1V 3R2
Tél: 514-252-3139; *Téléc:* 514-254-9464
aqptsc@sympatico.ca
Aperçu: *Dimension:* moyenne; *Envergure:* provinciale
Mission: Association appuyant les groupes associatifs et favorisant le tourisme thématique et les échanges culturels

Association québécoise de racquetball (AQR) / Quebec Racquetball Association
4545, av Pierre-de Coubertin, Montréal QC H1V 0B2
Tél: 514-252-3062
info@sports-4murs.qc.ca
www.racquetball.qc.ca
www.facebook.com/427582940621028
Aperçu: *Dimension:* petite; *Envergure:* provinciale surveillé par Racquetball Canada
Mission: Promouvoir le développement du racquetball au Québec en offrant différentes opportunités aux adeptes, tout en encourageant la participation sportive à travers un ensemble de services et de programmes
Membre de: Racquetball Canada; Sports-Québec; Regroupement Loisir Québec
Finances: *Budget de fonctionnement annuel:*
$50,000-$100,000; *Fonds:* Éducation, Loisir et Sport Québec
Membre(s) du personnel: 4
Membre: 10 000; *Montant de la cotisation:* Barème
Activités: Tournois; championnats; formation d'arbitres et d'entraîneurs; *Stagiaires:* Oui
Membre(s) du bureau directeur:
Rino Langelier, Président
rinolang@hotmail.com

Association québecoise de soins palliatifs
CP 321, Succ. Chef, Granby QC J2G 8E5
Tél: 514-826-9400; *Téléc:* 438-238-1336
info@aqsp.org
www.aqsp.org
twitter.com/PalliatifQc
Aperçu: *Dimension:* moyenne; *Envergure:* provinciale; fondée en 1990
Mission: Offrir aux intervenants de différentes disciplines de soins et de services, un organisme de référence et d'échange en soins palliatifs; favoriser le perfectionnement par la formation, le raffinement des soins et la recherche, pour assurer une meilleure qualité de vie aux malades atteints de maladie à issue fatale

Finances: *Budget de fonctionnement annuel:* Moins de $50,000
Membre: 1 200; *Montant de la cotisation:* 65$; *Critères d'admissibilite:* Intervenants en soins palliatifs; bénévoles
Activités: Conférences
Membre(s) du bureau directeur:
Alberte Déry, Présidente, Conseil d'administration
Marlène Côté, Vice-présidente, Conseil d'administration
Francine Lamarche, Coordonnatrice
Meetings/Conferences:
• 28e congrès annuel d'Association québécoise de soins palliatifs, 2018
Description: La réunion accueille des médecins, des professionnels et des bénévoles qui sont intéressés par les soins palliatifs. Le but de la conférence est de partager les expériences et de connaissances entre ceux dans le milieu des soins palliatifs.

Association québécoise de sports pour paralytiques cérébraux (AQSPC)
4545, av Pierre-de Coubertin, Montréal QC H1V 0B2
Tél: 514-252-3143; *Téléc:* 514-254-1069
www.sportpc.qc.ca
www.facebook.com/189413534433667
Aperçu: *Dimension:* petite; *Envergure:* provinciale surveillé par Canadian Cerebral Palsy Sports Association
Membre de: Canadian Cerebral Palsy Sports Association
Membre(s) du bureau directeur:
José Malo, Directrice générale, 514-252-3143 Ext. 3742
jmalo@sportpc.qc.ca

Association québécoise de Vol Libre (AQVL)
CP 321, Succ. St-Paul D'abbotsford, Québec QC J0E 1A0
Courriel: info@aqvl.qc.ca
aqvl.qc.ca
Aperçu: *Dimension:* petite; *Envergure:* locale; fondée en 1978
Mission: Promouvoir l'activité du Vol Libre au Québec; intermédiaire entre l'association canadienne et les membres québécois; publier le Survol Québec
Affiliation(s): Association Canadienne de Vol Libre
Finances: *Budget de fonctionnement annuel:* Moins de $50,000
10 bénévole(s)
Membre: 240; *Montant de la cotisation:* 150$; *Critères d'admissibilite:* Pilote de parapente ou de delta-plane
Activités: *Listes de destinataires:* Oui
Membre(s) du bureau directeur:
Christian Grenier, Président
president@aqvl.qc.ca
Patrick Dupuis, Secrétaire

Association québécoise des allergies alimentaires (AQAA)
6020, rue Jean Talon est, Saint-Léonard QC H1S 3B1
Tél: 514-990-2575
Ligne sans frais: 800-990-2575
allergies-alimentaires.org
Aperçu: *Dimension:* petite; *Envergure:* provinciale; fondée en 1990
Mission: A pour mission d'offrir du support et de l'information, de promouvoir l'éducation et la prévention, ainsi que d'encourager la recherche sur les allergies alimentaires et l'anaphylaxie
Membre de: Food Allergy & Anaphylaxis Alliance
Membre(s) du personnel: 7
Membre: *Comités:* Scientifique
Activités: Journée annuelle; ateliers de formation; consultations par professionnels; support téléphonique; *Stagiaires:* Oui; *Service de conférenciers:* Oui
Membre(s) du bureau directeur:
Daniel Lapointe, Directeur général
dlapointe@aqaa.qc.ca

Association québécoise des archivistes médicales; Association des archivistes médicales de la province de Québec *Voir* Association des Gestionnaires de l'information de la santé du Québec

Association québécoise des arénas et des installations récréatives et sportives (AQAIRS)
4545, av Pierre-de Coubertin, Montréal QC H1V 0B2
Tél: 514-252-5244; *Téléc:* 514-252-5220
info@aqairs.ca
www.aqairs.ca
Nom précédent: Association des Arénas du Québec
Aperçu: *Dimension:* moyenne; *Envergure:* provinciale; fondée en 1979

Mission: Contribuer au respect et à l'amélioration des normes visant les arénas et des installations récréatives et sportives au profit des participants aux activités qui s'y déroulent
Membre: 400 membres réguliers; 100 membres affaires; *Montant de la cotisation:* Barème
Activités: Sessions de formation; publication
Membre(s) du bureau directeur:
Luc Toupin, Directeur général, 514-252-5244 Ext. 3
ltoupin@loisirpublic.qc.ca

Association québécoise des auteurs dramatiques (AQAD)
187, rue Sainte-Catherine est, 3e étage, Montréal QC H2X 1K8
Tél: 514-596-3705; *Téléc:* 514-596-2953
info@aqad.qc.ca
www.aqad.qc.ca
Aperçu: *Dimension:* petite; *Envergure:* nationale; fondée en 1990
Mission: Défendre les droits et les intérêts moraux, sociaux, économiques et professionnels des auteurs dramatiques, des librettistes, des adaptateurs et des traducteurs francophones, québécois et canadiens
Finances: *Fonds:* Conseil des arts et des lettres du Québec
Membre(s) du personnel: 4
Membre: *Montant de la cotisation:* 80$
Activités: Librairie virtuelle ADEL; ateliers de formation; laboratoires; bureau de consultation
Membre(s) du bureau directeur:
Marie-Eve Gagnon, Directrice par intérim
megagnon@aqad.qc.ca

Association québécoise des avocats et avocates de la défense (AQAAD)
445, boul Saint-Laurent, Montréal QC H2Y 3T8
Tél: 514-954-3426; *Téléc:* 514-954-3451
Ligne sans frais: 800-361-8495
info@aqaad.com
www.aqaad.com
Aperçu: *Dimension:* petite; *Envergure:* provinciale; fondée en 1995
Mission: Défendre les droits et intérêts des avocats qui pratiquent le droit pénal
Membre: 800; *Montant de la cotisation:* 57,49$; *Comités:* Relations avec le Barreau du Québec; Relations avec la magistrature; Relations et intervention auprès du gouvernement du Québec; Relations et intervention auprès du gouvernement fédéral; Relations avec la Commission des services juridiques; Relations avec les médias; Relations avec l'A.A.D.M. et l'A.A.D.Q.; Finances et trésorerie; Règlements de l'AQAAD; Agenda annuel; C-10; Colloque annuel; Prix de l'AQAAD; Relations avec les associations canadiennes de défense; C-2; Jurisprudence; Pratique privée; Service de recherches et relations avec les universités; Demandes d'intervention
Membre(s) du bureau directeur:
Joëlle Roy, Présidente, Conseil d'administration, 450-530-3202, Fax: 450-530-2511
gagne_roy@videotron.ca

Association québécoise des avocats et avocates en droit de l'immigration (AQAADI)
#500, 445, boul Saint-Laurent, Montréal QC H2Y 3T8
Tél: 514-954-3471; *Téléc:* 514-954-3451
Ligne sans frais: 800-361-8495
www.aqaadi.com
Aperçu: *Dimension:* petite; *Envergure:* provinciale; fondée en 1991
Mission: Pour informer les avocats de l'immigration des modifications apportées aux lois sur l'immigration, et de créer une communauté d'avocats en immigration qui peuvent partager leurs expériences et s'entraider
Membre: 190; *Comités:* Qualité des services; Comité de formation; AQAADI pour les femmes et les enfants
Membre(s) du bureau directeur:
Jean-Sébastien Boudreault, Président, Conseil d'administration
jsboudreault@gmail.com

Association québécoise des banques alimentaires et des Moissons; Fédération des Moissons du Québec inc. *Voir* Les banques alimentaires du Québec

Association québécoise des cadres scolaires (AQCS)
#170, 1195, av Lavigerie, Québec QC G1V 4N3
Tél: 418-654-0014; *Téléc:* 418-654-1719
info@aqcs.ca
www.aqcs.ca
www.linkedin.com/company-beta/3495357

www.facebook.com/230806163669399
twitter.com/ACSQ_LT
www.youtube.com/user/ACSQ72
Nom précédent: Association des cadres scolaires du Québec
Aperçu: *Dimension:* moyenne; *Envergure:* provinciale; Organisme sans but lucratif; fondée en 1972
Mission: Valoriser le statut professionnel de ses membres et promouvoir leurs intérêts professionnels et économiques; Collaborer avec les autorités gouvernementales et les organismes intéressés, au développement ordonné du système scolaire, par une participation constante et adéquate à l'élaboration et à la mise en oeuvre des politiques relatives à l'éducation
Affiliation(s): Table nationale de lutte contre l'homophobie du réseau scolaire; Success for Youth Foundation; Olympiades Réussite Jeunesse; Grand défi Pierre Lavoie; Quebec Entrepreneurship Contest; Provincial Issue Table on Violence, Youth & the School Environment; Allô prof; Le Point en administration de l'éducation
Membre(s) du personnel: 13
Membre: Over 50,000; *Critères d'admissibilite:* Personnel d'encadrement de l'éducation
Activités:; *Bibliothèque:* rendez-vous
Membre(s) du bureau directeur:
Mario Champagne, Président
presidence@aqcs.ca
Jean-François Parent, Directeur général, 418-654-0014 Ext. 222
jfparent@aqcs.ca
Prix, Bourses:
• Prix Reconnaissance

L'Association québécoise des centres de la petite enfance (AQCPE)
#401, 7245, rue Clark, Montréal QC H2R 2Y4
Tél: 514-326-8008; *Téléc:* 514-326-3322
Ligne sans frais: 888-326-8008
info@aqcpe.com
www.aqcpe.com
www.facebook.com/aqcpe
twitter.com/aqcpe
www.youtube.com/user/aqcpe1
Aperçu: *Dimension:* moyenne; *Envergure:* provinciale; fondée en 2003
Mission: A pour mandat la concertation des acteurs du réseau, la représentation politique de ses membres et la promotion des centres de la petite enfance, et services de soutien; représente les employeurs du secteur des CPE à l'occasion de négociations, en matière de relations du travail et de main-d'oeuvre; l'AQCPE est reconnue par le Min. de la Famille et des Aînés pour les négociations provinciales
Affiliation(s): Association des services de garde en milieu scolaire du Québec; Carrefour action municipal et famille; Centrale des syndicats du Québec; Fédération canadienne des services de garde à l'enfance; Fédération des femmes du Québec; Fédération des travailleurs et travailleuses du Québec; Fédération québécoise des organismes communautaires famille; Réseau de la santé et des services sociaux
Membre(s) du personnel: 24
Membre: 13 associations
Membre(s) du bureau directeur:
Claude Deraîche, Directeur, Communications, 514-326-8008 Ext. 207
claude.deraiche@aqcpe.com

Association québécoise des critiques de cinéma (AQCC)
a/s Cinémathèque québécoise des critiques de cinéma, 335, boul de Maisonneuve est, Montréal QC H2X 1K1
aqcc.ca
Aperçu: *Dimension:* petite; *Envergure:* provinciale; Organisme sans but lucratif; fondée en 1973
Mission: Regrouper l'ensemble des personnes reconnues par l'Association comme oeuvrant au Québec dans le domaine de la critique cinématographique
Membre: *Montant de la cotisation:* 40$; *Critères d'admissibilite:* Oeuvrer dans le domaine de la critique cinématographique au Québec
Activités: Remise de prix cinématographiques; composition de jurys

Association québécoise des cyclothymiques *Voir* Revivre - Association Québécoise de soutien aux personnes souffrant de troubles anxieux, dépressifs ou bipolaires

Association Québécoise des dépanneurs en alimentation (AQDA)
#501, 1, av Holiday, Montréal QC H9R 5N3
Tél: 514-240-3934; *Téléc:* 514-630-6989
info@acda-aqda.ca
www.acda-aqda.ca
Aperçu: *Dimension:* moyenne; *Envergure:* provinciale surveillé par Canadian Convenience Stores Association
Affiliation(s): Canadian Convenience Stores Association; Western Convenience Stores Association; Ontario Convenience Stores Association; Atlantic Convenience Stores Association
Membre(s) du bureau directeur:
Michel Gadbois, Président
mgadbois@depanneurscanada.ca

Association québécoise des directeurs et directrices d'établissement d'enseignement retraités
#100, 7855, boul Louis-H.-Lafontaine, Anjou QC H1K 4E4
Tél: 514-353-3254
info@aqder.ca
www.aqder.ca
twitter.com/AQDER_National
Également appelé: AQDER
Aperçu: *Dimension:* moyenne; *Envergure:* provinciale; fondée en 1976
Mission: Développer les services nécessaires pour que les membres puissent vivre une retraite de qualité.
Membre(s) du bureau directeur:
Guy Lessard, Président

Association québécoise des directeurs et directrices du loisir municipal *Voir* Association québécoise du loisir municipal

Association québécoise des écoles de français langue étrangère (AQEFLE)
a/s Collège de Jonquière, 2505, rue St-Hubert, Jonquière QC G7X 7W2
Tél: 418-542-0352; *Téléc:* 418-542-3536
Ligne sans frais: 800-622-0352
www.aqefle.com
Aperçu: *Dimension:* moyenne; *Envergure:* provinciale
Mission: Fournir à des jeunes adultes et des adultes professionnels une compétence en français langue seconde
Finances: *Budget de fonctionnement annuel:* Moins de $50,000
Membre(s) du personnel: 4; 3 bénévole(s)
Membre: 7 écoles; *Critères d'admissibilite:* Etre une institution collégiale ou universitaire reconnue par le ministère de l'Éducation du Québec; offrir des cours de français langue seconde; être agréée par les membres de l'association
Membre(s) du bureau directeur:
Pierre Lincourt, Président
pierre_lincourt@uqac.ca

Association québécoise des éditeurs de magazines (AQEM)
a/s Félix Maltais, 4475, rue Frontenac, Montréal QC H2H 2S2
Tél: 514-844-2111
info@magazinesquebec.com
www.magazinesquebec.com
Aperçu: *Dimension:* petite; *Envergure:* provinciale; Organisme sans but lucratif; fondée en 1991
Mission: De promouvoir le développement de l'industrie du magazine dans son ensemble et défendre les intérêts de ses membres.
Membre: 44; *Montant de la cotisation:* Barème dépendent des ventes; *Critères d'admissibilite:* Éditeurs de magazines
Membre(s) du bureau directeur:
Robert Goyette, Président

Association québécoise des Éducateurs du primaire *Voir* Association québécoise des enseignantes et des enseignants du primaire

Association québécoise des éducatrices et éducateurs spécialisés en arts plastiques (AQÉSAP)
c/o Laurence Borys, Secrétaire Exécutive de l'AQÉSAP, 2761, rte 125 nord, Saint-Donat-de-Montcalm QC J0T 2C0
Tél: 819-323-6537
info@aqesap.org
www.aqesap.org
www.facebook.com/AQESAP.org
twitter.com/AQESAP
Aperçu: *Dimension:* petite; *Envergure:* provinciale; fondée en 1967
Mission: De promouvoir et de défendre la qualité de l'enseignement des arts, de stimuler la recherche et de favoriser le partage d'expériences pédagogiques par le biais de formations, de colloques, de congrès et de sa revue Vision.
Membre: *Montant de la cotisation:* 75$ individu; 37.50$ étudiant/retraité; 175$ entreprise; *Comités:* Gouvernance; Finances; Site web; Base de données et inscription en ligne
Membre(s) du bureau directeur:
Michel Lemieux, Président
presidence@aqesap.org

Association québécoise des enseignantes et des enseignants du primaire (AQEP)
Université de Montréal, CP 6128, Succ. Centre-Ville, Montréal QC H3C 3J7
Téléc: 866-941-2737
Ligne sans frais: 866-940-2737
info@aqep.org
www.aqep.org
www.facebook.com/AQEP.ORG
twitter.com/AQEP_
Nom précédent: Association québécoise des Éducateurs du primaire
Aperçu: *Dimension:* moyenne; *Envergure:* provinciale
Mission: Promouvoir et valoriser la profession d'enseignantes et d'enseignants; créer, organiser, administrer et développer un fond pour promouvoir l'avancement de la pédagogie; acquérir et développer des compétences au regard de la profession; favoriser l'excellence de l'acte d'enseigner; collaborer avec tout organisme poursuivant des buts similaires; être la source de référence et de ralliement pour la communauté enseignante primaire dans le but de favoriser l'avancement et l'excellence afin de promouvoir et valoriser l'acte d'enseigner. Notre contribution fera en sorte que la communauté enseignante du primaire puisse permettre à chaque personne la composant de se réaliser professionnellement, dans le plaisir, en faisant preuve d'innovation et de créativité
Membre: 1,000; *Montant de la cotisation:* 50$
Activités: Enseignement primaire; formation continue; organisation d'un congrès annuel; publication de Vivre le primaire; *Service de conférenciers:* Oui
Membre(s) du bureau directeur:
Audrey Cantin, Présidente
presidence@aqep.org

Association québécoise des enseignants de français langue seconde (AQEFLS) / Québec Association of Teachers of French as a Second Language
#228, 7400, boul Saint-Laurent, Montréal QC H2R 2Y1
Tél: 514-276-6470; *Téléc:* 514-276-3350
info@aqefls.org
www.aqefls.org
twitter.com/AQEFLS
Aperçu: *Dimension:* moyenne; *Envergure:* provinciale; fondée en 1979
Mission: Promouvoir l'enseignement du français langue seconde et les aspects qui s'y rattachent; coordonner et encourager les recherches d'ordre pratique dans le domaine de la pédagogie et dans tout autre domaine touchant l'enseignement du français langue seconde; permettre la diffusion des derniers développements de la recherche et les techniques dans le domaine de l'enseignement du français langue seconde
Affiliation(s): Fédération internationale des professeurs de français
Membre(s) du personnel: 1; 10 bénévole(s)
Membre: 500+; *Critères d'admissibilite:* L'Association réunit des enseignants qui oeuvrent dans les secteurs public et privé, de la maternelle à l'université, qu'il s'agisse d'organismes à vocation éducative ou d'entreprises industrielles ou commerciales; les secteurs du régulier, de l'immersion, et de l'accueil y sont représentés
Membre(s) du bureau directeur:
Carlos Carmona, Président

L'association québécoise des fournisseurs de services pétroliers et gaziers du Québec (AFSPC) / Oil & Gas Services Association of Québec (OGSAQ)
QC
Tél: 418-391-1155
info@afspg.com
www.afspg.com
Aperçu: *Dimension:* petite; *Envergure:* provinciale; fondée en 2011
Mission: L'AFSPG a été créé dans le but de pouvoir développer le gaz de schiste au Québec et surtout, de pouvoir améliorer le présent mais, avant tout, l'avenir de chaque Québécois. Dans les prochaines années, l'AFSPG souhaite être en mesure de créer plus de deux cents puits par année au Québec, où l'on

retrouve des sources de gaz schiste. Pour ce faire, ils utiliseront les plus grandes mesures de sécurité lors de l'extraction des gaz, limitant les chances de contaminations des sols environnants.
Membre: 60

Association québécoise des groupes d'ornithologues *Voir* Regroupement QuébecOiseaux

Association québécoise des industries de nutrition animale et céréalière (AQINAC)
#200, 4790, rue Martineau, Saint-Hyacinthe QC J2R 1V1
Tél: 450-799-2440; *Téléc:* 450-799-2445
info@aqinac.com
www.aqinac.com
twitter.com/AQINAC
Aperçu: *Dimension:* grande; *Envergure:* provinciale; fondée en 1963
Mission: Ôtre le leader dans la défense et la promotion du secteur de la nutrition et de la production animale tout en contribuant au développement d'une industrie agroalimentaire moderne et durable
Membre(s) du personnel: 8
Membre: 225+ sociétés; *Montant de la cotisation:* 900$ minimum; *Critères d'admissibilite:* Produits et/ou services en agro-alimentaire
Membre(s) du bureau directeur:
Yvan Lacroix, Président-directeur général
yvan.lacroix@aqinac.com
Cynthia Vallée, Agente, Communication/Événements
cynthia.vallee@aqinac.com

Association québécoise des infirmières et intervenants en recherche clinique (AQIIRC)
4200, rue Molson, Montréal QC H1Y 4V4
Tél: 514-935-2501; *Téléc:* 514-935-1799
info@aqiirc.qc.ca
aqiirc.qc.ca
www.facebook.com/aqiirc.asso?sk=wall
Aperçu: *Dimension:* petite; *Envergure:* provinciale; Organisme sans but lucratif; fondée en 1991
Mission: Regrouper les infirmières et infirmiers qui travaillent dans tous les domaines de la recherche clinique et promouvoir leurs rôles; soutenir la participation active des membres dans l'élaboration et la réalisation d'études cliniques; créer un réseau de sources d'information et d'entraide pour les membres et favoriser leur perfectionnement
Finances: *Budget de fonctionnement annuel:* Moins de $50,000
Membre: 300; *Montant de la cotisation:* 90$; *Critères d'admissibilite:* Infirmiers et infimières licenciés; *Comités:* Adhésion; Journal; Site web; Congrès; Réseau de ressources en recherche
Activités: Séances de formation; congrès; conférences
Membre(s) du bureau directeur:
Lucie Tremblay, Présidente
Meetings/Conferences:
• Association québécoise des infirmières et intervenants en recherche clinique Congrès 2018, May, 2018
Scope: Provincial
Publications:
• Portail infOIIQ
Type: Portail internet; *Editor:* Lauréanne Marceau
Profile: Portail d'actualités officiel de l'Ordre des infirmières et infirmiers du Québec

Association québécoise des informaticiennes et informaticiens indépendants (AQIII) / Québec Association for ICT Freelancers
974, rue Michelin, Laval QC H7L 5B6
Tél: 514-388-6147
Ligne sans frais: 888-858-7777
aqiii@aqiii.org
www.aqiii.org
www.linkedin.com/company/aqiii
www.facebook.com/AQIII.org
twitter.com/aqiii
Aperçu: *Dimension:* moyenne; *Envergure:* provinciale; fondée en 1993
Mission: Offrir une communauté de partage aux consultants indépendants en TIC afin qu'ils bénéficient des forces d'un réseau pour favoriser leur réussite et préserver leur liberté d'entrepreneuriat indépendant
Finances: *Fonds:* Commanditaires, subventions, tarifs
Membre(s) du personnel: 7
Membre: 1,800; *Montant de la cotisation:* 215$; *Comités:* Entente fournisseurs; Fiscalité; Gouvernance/Éthique; Marketing/Membership; Technologie; Relations avec les donneurs d'ouvrage
Activités: Activités de réseautage; Formation et ateliers; Soutenir les consultants indépendants et micro-entrepreneurs en TIC; *Service de conférenciers:* Oui
Membre(s) du bureau directeur:
Jean-Marc Longpré, Président
Caroline De Guire, Directrice générale
carolinedeguire@aqiii.org

Association québécoise des interprètes du patrimoine (AQIP)
CP 11003, Succ. Succ. Le Plateau, Gatineau QC J9A 0B6
Tél: 819-595-2190
aqip@aqip.ca
www.aqip.ca
www.facebook.com/AssoQuebecoiseInterpretePatrimoine
Aperçu: *Dimension:* moyenne; *Envergure:* provinciale; Organisme sans but lucratif; fondée en 1977
Mission: Stimuler la communication entre les individus et les organismes intéressés à l'interprétation du patrimoine naturel, culturel, historique et industriel; promouvoir l'interprétation du patrimoine québécois auprès des gouvernements, des organismes, des médias et du public en général; stimuler l'acquisition de connaissances et la recherche liée à l'interprétation du patrimoine
Finances: *Budget de fonctionnement annuel:* Moins de $50,000
Membre: 150; *Montant de la cotisation:* 10$ étudiant; 35$ individuel; 100$ affilié
Activités: Séminaire de formation et de perfectionnement; congrès thématique
Membre(s) du bureau directeur:
Gabrielle Normand, Présidente
Christian Arcand, Vice Présidente
Éliane Bélec, Secrétaire
Prix, Bourses:
• Prix du mérite en interprétation du patrimoine

Association québécoise des joueurs de dames (AQJD)
4545, av Pierre-de Coubertin, Montréal QC H1V 3R2
Tél: 514-252-3032
dames@fqjr.qc.ca
dames.quebecjeux.org
Aperçu: *Dimension:* petite; *Envergure:* provinciale; fondée en 1973
Mission: Favoriser le développement et la promotion du jeu de dames
Membre de: Fédération Canadienne des Jeux de Dames
Membre: *Montant de la cotisation:* 5$
Activités: Championnat provincial annuel; compétitions; jeux électroniques; logiciels; système de cote-classement
Membre(s) du bureau directeur:
Mario Bélanger, Président

Association Québécoise des Loisirs Folkloriques (AQLF)
471, ch de l'Église, Sainte-Barbe QC J0S 1P0
Tél: 450-373-5577; *Téléc:* 450-373-5577
info@quebecfolklore.qc.ca
www.quebecfolklore.qc.ca
Aperçu: *Dimension:* moyenne; *Envergure:* provinciale; fondée en 1975
Mission: Préserver et promouvoir le folklore québécois
Membre(s) du personnel: 3
Membre: *Montant de la cotisation:* 20$ individuel; 30$ familial; 50$ groupe; 100$ associatif; *Critères d'admissibilite:* Musiciens; chanteurs; danseurs; adepts
Activités: Gala Folklorique; compétition; soirée folklorique; *Service de conférenciers:* Oui
Membre(s) du bureau directeur:
Gérald Cyr, Président
Michel Mallette, Sec.-trés.

Association québécoise des marionnettistes (AQM)
Centre UNIMA-CANADA (section Québec), #300, 7755, boul Saint-Laurent, Montréal QC H2R 1X1
Tél: 514-522-1919
info@aqm.ca
www.aqm.ca
www.facebook.com/175003799226012
twitter.com/AQMarionnette
Également appelé: Union internationale de la marionnette - Canada
Aperçu: *Dimension:* petite; *Envergure:* provinciale; fondée en 1981
Mission: Représenter ses membres et créer un terrain propice aux échanges, aux actions communes et à la réflexion sur la pratique de l'art de la marionnette
Membre de: Conseil québécois du théatre; Académie québécoise du théatre
Membre: 150+; *Montant de la cotisation:* 42$ ami; 60$ organise culturel; 66$ artiste professionnel; 120$ compagnie artistique professionnelle; *Critères d'admissibilite:* Professionnel de la marionnette; *Comités:* Animation du milieu; AQM-UNIMA; Communications Web; Revue Marionnettes; Formation
Activités: Renseigne ses membres sur tout ce qui touche la marionnette au Québec et à l'étranger; organise des rencontres, des débats, des expositions, des colloques qui suscitent des échanges entre les diverses pratiques artistiques; *Stagiaires:* Oui; *Listes de destinataires:* Oui; *Bibliothèque:* Centre de documentation
Membre(s) du bureau directeur:
Hélène Ducharme, Directrice artistique & générale

Association québécoise des organismes de coopération internationale (AQOCI) / Québec Association of International Cooperation
#540, 1001, rue Sherbrooke est, Montréal QC H2L 1L3
Tél: 514-871-1086; *Téléc:* 514-871-9866
aqoci@aqoci.qc.ca
www.aqoci.qc.ca
www.facebook.com/aqoci
twitter.com/aqoci
www.youtube.com/aqoci
Aperçu: *Dimension:* moyenne; *Envergure:* internationale; fondée en 1976
Mission: Soutenir le travail des membres afin de permettre leur développement en s'inspirant des principes de solidarité et de coopération; favoriser l'échange pour mieux coordonner les actions communautaires; regrouper les organismes de coopération et d'éducation à la solidarité oeuvrant au Québec
Membre de: Canadian Council for International Cooperation/Conseil canadien pour la coopération internationale
Affiliation(s): Réseau québécois sur l'intégration continentale; Conseil canadien pour la coopération internationale
Finances: *Budget de fonctionnement annuel:* $500,000-$1.5 Million
Membre(s) du personnel: 9
Membre: 69; *Critères d'admissibilite:* Regroupements d'organismes de coopération internationale
Activités: *Stagiaires:* Oui; *Service de conférenciers:* Oui
Membre(s) du bureau directeur:
Michèle Asselin, Directeur général, 514-871-1086 Ext. 202
masselin@aqoci.qc.ca
Publications:
• AQOCI [Association québécoise des organismes de coopération internationale] rapport annuel
Frequency: Annuellement

Association québécoise des orthophonistes et des audiologistes (AQOA)
#102, 7229, rue Saint-Denis, Montréal QC H2R Ee3
Tél: 514-369-8929
admin@aqoa.qc.ca
www.aqoa.qc.ca
Aperçu: *Dimension:* petite; *Envergure:* provinciale; Organisme sans but lucratif; fondée en 1996
Mission: Défendre les droits et les intérêts des orthophonistes et audiologistes du Québec auprès de diverses instances, gouvernementales, syndicales, etc.
Affiliation(s): Ordre des orthophonistes et audiologistes du Québec, Mouvement pour l'adhésion aux traitements, Orthophonie et audiologie Canada, Association des jeunes bègues du Québec
Finances: *Budget de fonctionnement annuel:* Moins de $50,000
Membre: *Critères d'admissibilite:* Orthophonistes et audiologistes québécois; *Comités:* Pratique privée
Membre(s) du bureau directeur:
Philippe Fournier, Président
Prix, Bourses:
• Prix Phénix
Eligibility: C'est un prix pour un membre de l'AQOA qui est un exemple d'excellence dans sa profession.

Association québécoise des parents d'enfants handicapés visuels (AQPEHV) / Quebec Association for Parents of Visually Impaired Children (QAPVIC)
#203, 10, boul Churchill, Greenfield Park QC J4V 2L7
Tél: 450-465-7225; *Téléc:* 450-465-5129
Ligne sans frais: 888-849-8729
www.aqpehv.qc.ca

Canadian Associations / Association québécoise des personnes de petite taille (AQPPT) / Association of Little People of Quebec

Aperçu: *Dimension:* petite; *Envergure:* provinciale; fondée en 2004
Finances: *Fonds:* Ministère de la Santé et des Services sociaux du Québec
Membre: *Critères d'admissibilité:* Les parents d'enfants (0 à 21 ans) ayant une déficience visuelle.
Membre(s) du bureau directeur:
Roland Savard, Directeur général
direction.generale@aqpehv.qc.ca

Association québécoise des personnes de petite taille (AQPPT) / Association of Little People of Quebec
#308, 6300, av du Parc, Montréal QC H2V 4H8
Tél: 514-521-9671; *Téléc:* 514-521-3369
info@aqppt.org
www.aqppt.org
www.facebook.com/AQPPT
Aperçu: *Dimension:* petite; *Envergure:* provinciale; Organisme sans but lucratif; fondée en 1976
Mission: Promouvoir des intérêts et défendre les droits des personnes de petite taille et faciliter leur intégration scolaire, sociale et professionnelle.
Finances: *Budget de fonctionnement annuel:* $100,000-$250,000
Membre(s) du personnel: 3; 47 bénévole(s)
Membre: 397; *Montant de la cotisation:* 25-50 famille; 25$ soutien; 50$ organisme; *Critères d'admissibilité:* Etre une personne de petite taille, ou un parent, ou membre soutien
Activités: Information médicale; soutien aux membres; sensibilisation auprès de la population et dans les écoles; concertation et actions sur les dossiers comme l'accessibilité, le transport adapté, l'intégration au travail; promotion et défense des droits des personnes de petite taille; *Service de conférenciers:* Oui; *Bibliothèque:* Centre de documentation; Not open to public
Membre(s) du bureau directeur:
Normande Gagnon, Co-fondatrice

Association québécoise des pharmaciens propriétaires (AQPP) / Québec Association of Pharmacy Owners
4378, av Pierre-de Coubertin, Montréal QC H1V 1A6
Tél: 514-254-0676; *Téléc:* 514-254-1288
Ligne sans frais: 800-361-7765
info@aqpp.qc.ca
www.aqpp.qc.ca
twitter.com/VotrePharmacien
www.youtube.com/user/VotrePharmacien
Aperçu: *Dimension:* moyenne; *Envergure:* provinciale; fondée en 1970
Mission: Assurer l'étude, la défense et le développement des intérêts économiques, sociaux et professionnels de ses membres.
Membre(s) du personnel: 12
Membre: 1 930
Activités: *Service de conférenciers:* Oui; *Listes de destinataires:* Oui
Membre(s) du bureau directeur:
Normand Cadieux, Vice-président exécutif et directeur général

Association québécoise des phytothérapeutes (AQP)
3805, rue Bélair, Montréal QC H2A 2C1
Tél: 514-722-8888; *Téléc:* 514-722-5164
Ligne sans frais: 800-268-5878
associatio1@bellnet.ca
www.aqp-annspq.ca
Également appelé: Association des naturopathes et naturothérapeutes spécialisés en phytothérapie
Aperçu: *Dimension:* moyenne; *Envergure:* provinciale; fondée en 1969
Mission: Regrouper les phytothérapeutes; favoriser l'atteinte d'un niveau de compétence supérieure; assurer la protection du public; contribuer à l'avancement de la phytothérapie.
Membre: 500+; *Critères d'admissibilité:* Phytothérapeutes; naturopathes; naturothérapeutes; étudiants

Association Québécoise des Pompiers Volontaires et Permanents *Voir* Fédération Québécoise des Intervenants en Sécurité Incendie

Association québécoise des professeures et professeurs de français *Voir* Association québécoise des professeurs de français

Association québécoise des professeurs de français (AQPF)
1151, André-Charpentier, LeMoyne QC J4R 1S9
Tél: 450-923-9422
info@aqpf.qc.ca
www.aqpf.qc.ca
www.facebook.com/aqpfqc
Nom précédent: Association québécoise des professeures et professeurs de français
Aperçu: *Dimension:* moyenne; *Envergure:* nationale; Organisme sans but lucratif; fondée en 1967
Mission: Les principaux champs d'intervention sont - la didactique et l'enseignement du français langue maternelle du préscolaire à l'université; l'enseignement du français aux adultes; l'alphabétisation; l'enseignement du français langue seconde; promotion de la langue française, de la culture québécoise et de la francophonie
Affiliation(s): Fédération internationale des professeurs de français
Finances: *Budget de fonctionnement annuel:* $50,000-$100,000
30 bénévole(s)
Membre: 600; *Montant de la cotisation:* 10-50; *Critères d'admissibilité:* Enseignants, professeurs, chercheurs, conseillers pédagogiques, cadres, éditeurs
Activités: Rencontres pédagogiques, sociales, culturelles; commission pédagogique; commission linguistique; *Service de conférenciers:* Oui
Membre(s) du bureau directeur:
Marie-Hélène Marcoux, Présidente
marie-helene.marcoux@csnavigateurs.qc.ca
Isabelle Péladeau, Vice-présidente (intérim), Administration
isapeladeau@sympatico.ca
Prix, Bourses:
- Prix littéraires des enseignants AQPF-ANEL
- Prix d'innovation en enseignement de la poésie
- Prix de reconnaissance du meilleur étudiant
Meetings/Conferences:
- Association québécoise des professeurs de français Congrès 2018, 2018, QC
Scope: National

Association québécoise des professionnels d'insolvabilité
See Quebec Association of Insolvency & Restructuring Professionals

Association québécoise des professionnels de la réorganisation et de l'insolvabilité *See* Quebec Association of Insolvency & Restructuring Professionals

Association québécoise des réalisateurs et réalisatrices de cinéma et de télévision *Voir* Association des réalisateurs et réalisatrices du Québec

Association québécoise des salons du livre (AQSL)
#100, 60, rue St-Antoine, Trois-Rivières QC G9A 0C4
Téléc: 819-376-4222
Ligne sans frais: 888-542-2075
info@aqsl.org
www.aqsl.org
Aperçu: *Dimension:* moyenne; *Envergure:* provinciale; fondée en 1978
Mission: De promouvoir du livre, du périodique et de la lecture; De défendre les intérêts des Salons membres et favoriser la recherche, la documentation, les contacts professionnels, la création et la diffusion du livre
Membre de: Société de développment des entreprises culturelles.
Membre: 9; *Critères d'admissibilité:* Salon du livre au Québec
Membre(s) du bureau directeur:
Julie Brosseau, Présidente
direction@sltr.qc.ca

Abitibi-Témiscamingue
150, av du Lac, Rouyn-Noranda QC J9X 4N5
Tél: 819-797-4610; *Téléc:* 819-764-6375
info@slat.qc.ca
www.slat.qc.ca
Membre(s) du bureau directeur:
Ginette Vézina, Presidente
ginettevc@hotmail.com

Côte-Nord
#12, 652, av de Quen, Sept-Iles QC G4R 2R5
Tél: 418-968-4634; *Téléc:* 418-962-3684
slcn@cgocable.ca
www.salondulivrecotenord.com
Membre(s) du bureau directeur:
Mélanie Devost, Directrice générale

Estrie
#104, 138, rue Wellington nord, Sherbrooke QC J1H 5C5
Tél: 819-563-0744; *Téléc:* 819-563-3630
salondulivredelestrie@bellnet.ca
www.salondulivredelestrie.com
Membre(s) du bureau directeur:
Ghislaine Thibault, Directrice générale
Lucie Nicol, Présidente
lunic2@videotron.ca

Montréal
#430, 300, rue Saint-Sacrement, Montréal QC H2Y 1X4
Tél: 514-845-2365; *Téléc:* 514-845-7119
slm.info@videotron.ca
www.salondulivredemontreal.com
Membre(s) du bureau directeur:
Francine Bois, Directrice générale

Outaouais
CP 7, #301, 115, rue Principale, Gatineau QC J9H 3M2
Tél: 819-775-4873; *Téléc:* 819-775-3812
info@slo.qc.ca
www.slo.qc.ca
Membre(s) du bureau directeur:
Anne-Marie Trudel, Directrice générale
amtrudel@slo.qc.ca

Québec
26, rue St-Pierre, Québec QC G1K 8A3
Tél: 418-692-0010; *Téléc:* 418-692-0029
info@silq.ca
www.silq.ca
Membre(s) du bureau directeur:
Philippe Sauvageau, Président/Directeur général
psauvageau@silq.ca

Rimouski
CP 353, #105, 110, rue de l'Évêche est, Rimouski QC G5L 7C3
Tél: 418-723-7456; *Téléc:* 418-725-4543
slrinfo@globetrotter.net
www.salondulivrederimouski.ca
Membre(s) du bureau directeur:
Robin Doucet, Directeur général

Saguenay-Lac-St-Jean
2675, boul du Royaume, Jonquière QC G7X 7W4
Tél: 418-542-7294; *Téléc:* 418-542-3525
info@salondulivre.ca
www.salondulivre.ca
Membre(s) du bureau directeur:
Sylvie Marcoux, Directrice générale
marcoux.syl@videotron.ca

Trois-Rivières
#100, 60, rue St-Antoine, Trois-Rivières QC G9A 0C4
Tél: 819-376-5308; *Téléc:* 819-376-4222
info@sltr.qc.ca
www.sltr.qc.ca
Membre(s) du bureau directeur:
Julie Brosseau, Directrice générale
direction@sltr.qc.ca

Association québécoise des sports en fauteuil roulants *Voir* Parasports Québec

Association québécoise des techniques de l'environnement *Voir* Réseau environnement

Association québécoise des technologies (AQT) / Quebec Technology Association (QTA)
32, rue des Soeurs-Grises, Montréal QC H3C 2P8
Tél: 514-874-2667; *Téléc:* 514-874-1568
info@aqt.ca
www.aqt.ca
www.linkedin.com/groups/AQT-Association-qu%C3%A9b%C3%A9coise-technologies-Quebec-51115
twitter.com/aqtech
www.youtube.com/user/AQTechno/videos?view=0
Nom précédent: Centre de promotion du logiciel québécois; Réseau inter logiQ
Aperçu: *Dimension:* moyenne; *Envergure:* provinciale; fondée en 1990
Mission: Aider et soutenir les entrepreneurs en logiciel et multi média du Québec dans le développement de leur entreprise sur les scènes locales et internationale
Membre de: Canadian Advanced Technology Association; Information Technology Association of Canada; Fédération de l'Informatique du Québec
Finances: *Budget de fonctionnement annuel:* $500,000-$1.5 Million

Membre(s) du personnel: 14
Membre: 500; *Montant de la cotisation:* 325$ à 1250$ selon le nombre d'employés et le statut de l'entreprise; *Critères d'admissibilite:* Développeurs de logiciels du Québec
Activités: *Service de conférenciers:* Oui; *Listes de destinataires:* Oui
Membre(s) du bureau directeur:
Nicole Martel, Présidente directrice générale, 514-874-2667 Ext. 105
nmartel@aqt.ca

Association québécoise des transports (AQTr)
Bureau de Montréal, #200, 1255, boul Robert-Bourassa, Montréal QC H3B 3B2
Tél: 514-523-6444; *Téléc:* 514-523-2666
aqtr.com
www.facebook.com/AQTransports
twitter.com/AQTransports
Aperçu: *Dimension:* grande; *Envergure:* provinciale; fondée en 1965
Mission: Assumer un leadership technique; définir des règles en matière de sécurité et d'environnement; Favoriser l'échange international des expertises; promouvoir la recherche et le développement des expertises et des produits en transport; promouvoir la formation dans le domaine des transports; Assumer la représentativité de l'AQTR par la participation aux principaux forums sur les transports; Contribuer à servir la société par l'éducation et l'information du grand public
Finances: *Budget de fonctionnement annuel:* $500,000-$1.5 Million
Membre(s) du personnel: 7; 100 bénévole(s)
Membre: 950; *Montant de la cotisation:* Barème; *Critères d'admissibilite:* Secteur privé - Ingénieur conseils; Entrepreneurs; Fournisseurs et manufacturiers; Laboratoires; Transporteurs; Architectes et urbanistes; Étudiants; Spécialistes en environnement; Secteur public et parapublic - Ministères; Municipalités; Maisons d'enseignement; Sociétés de transport; Autres sociétés, départements et services publics; *Comités:* Directions techniques - Infrastructures de transport; Transport des personnes; Circulation; Sécurité dans les transports; Transport aérien; Recherche et développement; Comités - Transport des marchandises; Environnement; Revue; Congrès; Activités municipales
Activités: Regrouper les personnes impliquées dans les techniques du transport; Encourager les échanges multidisciplinaires et favoriser la collaboration entre différents secteurs; Recommander toute mesure permettant de développer des techniques du transport; *Listes de destinataires:* Oui
Membre(s) du bureau directeur:
Marc Des Rivières, Président
Dominique Lacoste, Présidente-directrice générale
Prix, Bourses:
• Grands prix d'excellence en transport
• Prix Josef-Hode-Keyser
• Prix Guy-Paré, Reconnaissance aux bénévoles
• Prix du Président, Reconnaissance aux bénévoles
• Prix Meilleure conférence, Reconnaissance aux bénévoles
• Programme de bourses d'études de l'AQTr
• Concours de mémoire AIPCR-Québec
Meetings/Conferences:
• 53e Congrès et Salon des transports: l'innovation, ça nous transporte!, April, 2018, Centre des congrès de Québec, Québec, QC
Scope: National
Publications:
• Routes et Transports [a publication of Association québécoise du transport et des routes inc.]
Type: Revue; *Frequency:* q.

Association québécoise des traumatisés craniens (AQTC)
#106, 911, rue Jean-Talon est, Montréal QC H2R 1V5
Tél: 514-274-7447; *Téléc:* 514-274-1717
www.aqtc.ca
www.facebook.com/AQTC.montreal.laval
Aperçu: *Dimension:* moyenne; *Envergure:* provinciale; Organisme sans but lucratif; fondée en 1986
Mission: De défendre et promouvoir les droits et les intérêts des personnes traumatisés cranio-cérébrales et de leurs familles et de favoriser le maintien ou l'amélioration de la qualité de vie; AQTC Laval: 220, av du Parc, (514) 274-7447
Finances: *Fonds:* Gouvernement provincial - SAAQ
Membre(s) du personnel: 11; 68 bénévole(s)
Membre: 427; *Critères d'admissibilite:* Personnes ayant subi un traumatisme cranio cérébral; les proches et les professionnels

Activités: Camp de vacances; activités; ateliers; services pour les proches; bénévolat interne et externe
Membre(s) du bureau directeur:
Pierre Mitchell, Directeur général
Pascal Brodeur, Adjoint à la direction, 514-274-7447 Ext. 233

Association québécoise des traumatisés crâniens (AQTC)
#106, 911, rue Jean-Talon est, Montréal QC H2R 1V5
Tél: 514-274-7447; *Téléc:* 514-274-1717
www.aqtc.ca
www.facebook.com/AQTC.montreal.laval
Aperçu: *Dimension:* petite; *Envergure:* provinciale; fondée en 1989
Mission: Accompagner les victimes de lésions cérébrales traumatiques en fournissant des loisirs activites, ateliers de groupe, et des informations
Membre de: Regroupement des associations de personnes traumatisées craniocérébrals du Québec / Coalition of Associations of Craniocerebral Trauma in Quebec
Membre(s) du personnel: 11
Membre: *Critères d'admissibilite:* Personnes du Québec qui ont survécu à une blessure traumatique du cerveau, de leurs familles, et amis; Toute personne intéressée à en apprendre davantage sur les lésions cérébrales traumatiques
Activités: Des activités de loisirs pour les professionnels formés à la psychologie et la récréologie, afin d'aider ceux qui ont souffert d'une lésion cérébrale traumatique; Organiser des ateliers de groupe qui mettent l'accent sur ??l'intégration pour les victimes de lésions cérébrales; Sensibiliser le public aux lésions cérébrales; Se référant à des personnes ressources appropriées; Fournir de l'information sur les blessures traumatiques au cerveau; Collaborer avec d'autres organismes communautaires; *Service de conférenciers:* Oui
Membre(s) du bureau directeur:
Pierre Mitchell, Executive Director, 514-274-7447 Ext. 224
Manon Beaudoin, Présidente
Céline Martel, Vice-présidente
Denyse Rousselet, Secrétaire
Nathalie Boucher, Intervenante psychosociale, 514-274-7447 Ext. 222
Publications:
• Association québécoise des traumatisés crâniens rapport annuel
Type: Yearbook; *Frequency:* Annually
• Phoenix
Type: Newspaper; *Frequency:* Quarterly
Profile: Reports & photographs of association happenings

Association québécoise des troubles d'apprentissage (AQETA) / Learning Disabilities Association of Québec (LDAQ)
#502, 740, rue Saint-Maurice, Montréal QC H3C 1L5
Tél: 514-847-1324; *Téléc:* 514-281-5187
Ligne sans frais: 877-847-1324
adj.adm@aqeta.qc.ca
www.aqeta.qc.ca
www.facebook.com/aqeta.provinciale
twitter.com/AQDRnationale
Aperçu: *Dimension:* moyenne; *Envergure:* provinciale; Organisme sans but lucratif; fondée en 1966 surveillé par Learning Disabilities Association of Canada
Mission: Faire connaître les troubles d'apprentissage; faire la promotion des besoins et des droits collectifs des enfants et des adultes qui vivent avec des troubles d'apprentissage
Membre de: Learning Disabilities Association of Canada
Finances: *Fonds:* Provinciaux; fédéraux
Membre(s) du personnel: 9
Membre: *Montant de la cotisation:* 20$ étudiant; 40$ régulier; 100$ Institutionnel
Activités: Informer les parents; travailler avec les intervenants; recruter et former des bénévoles; développer un partenariat avec le monde des affaires et les centres d'emploi pour favoriser l'intégration des jeunes; représentation; informer les intervenants en éducation et santé; *Service de conférenciers:* Oui; *Bibliothèque:* Centre de ressources; rendez-vous Not open to public
Membre(s) du bureau directeur:
Lise Bibaud, Directrice générale, 514-847-1324

Association québécoise des troubles d'apprentissage - section Outaouais
#203, 109, rue Wright, Gatineau QC J8X 2G7
Tél: 819-777-3126; *Téléc:* 819-777-5423
info@aqetaoutaouais.qc.ca
www.aqetaoutaouais.qc.ca

Aperçu: *Dimension:* petite; *Envergure:* locale; Organisme sans but lucratif; fondée en 1978
Mission: Répond aux besoins des personnes ayant des troubles d'apprentissage pour ainsi promouvoir l'intégration au niveau de l'éducation et de la vie communautaire en Outaouais
Membre de: Troubles d'apprentissage - association Canadienne
Finances: *Fonds:* Centraide; Agence de dévelop. de réseaux locaux de services de santé et de services sociaux
Membre(s) du personnel: 4
Membre: *Montant de la cotisation:* 20$ étudiant; 40$ régulier 100$ institution; *Critères d'admissibilite:* Adultes et enfants de 6 à 12 ans ayant des troubles d'apprentissage
Activités: Camp du samedi; camp d'été; écoute active; références; *Stagiaires:* Oui; *Service de conférenciers:* Oui; *Bibliothèque:* La découverte; rendez-vous
Membre(s) du bureau directeur:
Josée Lavigne, Présidente
Paul Morin, Directeur général
aqetaoutaouais@videotron.ca

Association québécoise des utilisateurs de l'ordinateur au primaire-secondaire (AQUOPS)
#1, 6818, rue Saint-Denis, Montréal QC H2S 2S2
Tél: 514-948-1234; *Téléc:* 514-948-1231
accueil@aquops.qc.ca
www.aquops.qc.ca
twitter.com/AQUOPS
Aperçu: *Dimension:* moyenne; *Envergure:* provinciale
Mission: Grouper en association les utilisateurs de l'ordinateur ainsi que les personnes intéressées au développement et à l'utilisation des technologies de l'information et des communications dans l'enseignement primaire et secondaire
Membre(s) du personnel: 11; 11 bénévole(s)
Activités: Ateliers; colloques; journées thématiques
Membre(s) du bureau directeur:
Patrick Beaupré, Président
patrick.beaupre@aquops.qc.ca
Prix, Bourses:
• Prix CHAPO
Décerné à des personnes ou groupes du monde scolaire, culturel ou commercial afin de souligner la qualité de leur engagement et de leur travail dans le domaine de l'intégration des technologies de l'information et de la communication (TIC)
Meetings/Conferences:
• Association québécoise des utilisateurs de l'ordinateur au primaire-secondaire (AQUOPS) Colloque 2018, March, 2018, Québec, QC
Scope: Provincial

Association québécoise du chauffage au mazout (AQCM) / Quebec Oil Heating Association
#202, 2, Place du Commerce, Ile-des-Soeurs QC H3E 1A1
Tél: 514-285-1150
info@petcommunication.ca
www.lemazout.org
Aperçu: *Dimension:* moyenne; *Envergure:* provinciale; fondée en 1957
Mission: Pour protéger les intérêts des utilisateurs, ainsi que le public; de promouvoir les avantages de l'huile de chauffage auprès des consommateurs; pour représenter et défendre les intérêts de ses membres au sein de l'industrie.
Membre: 18; *Critères d'admissibilite:* Entreprises qui commercialisent et fabriquent pétrole

Association québécoise du loisir municipal (AQLM)
4545, av Pierre-de Coubertin, Montréal QC H1V 0B2
Tél: 514-252-5244; *Téléc:* 514-252-5220
infoaqlm@loisirmunicipal.qc.ca
www.loisirmunicipal.qc.ca
Nom précédent: Association québécoise des directeurs et directrices du loisir municipal
Aperçu: *Dimension:* moyenne; *Envergure:* provinciale; Organisme sans but lucratif; fondée en 1999
Mission: Intégrer le domaine de vie communautaire au mandat de loisir; Affirmer la maîtrise d'oeuvre de la municipalité en loisir; faire valoir le service municipal de loisir comme partenaire du réseau des organisations locales (institutionnelles et associatives); Promouvoir l'expertise des professionnels du loisir; démontrer l'utilité et les bénéfices du loisir; Développer des pratiques professionnelles en loisir
Membre de: Regroupement loisir Québec
Finances: *Fonds:* Ponctuelles pour projets de recherches 15 bénévole(s)
Membre: 700 actif + 90 associés + 12 étudiants; *Montant de la cotisation:* 172-700; *Critères d'admissibilite:* Professionnel en loisir; *Comités:* Arts et culture; Formation; Formation scolaire;

Plan stratégique; Programme de reconnaissance et prix Excellence
Activités: *Service de conférenciers:* Oui
Membre(s) du bureau directeur:
Luc Toupin, Directeur général
ltoupin@loisirmunicipal.qc.ca
Pierre Waters, Directeur, Services aux membres affaires
pwatters@loisirmunicipal.qc.ca
Joëlle Derulle, Conseillère, Formations et développement
jderulle@loisirmunicipal.qc.ca

Association Québécoise du Lymphoedème (AQL) / Lymphedema Association of Québec (LAQ)
6565, rue St-Hubert, Montréal QC H2S 2M5
Tél: 514-979-2463
aql@infolympho.ca
www.infolympho.ca
www.facebook.com/AQL.LAQ
Aperçu: *Dimension:* moyenne; *Envergure:* provinciale; Organisme sans but lucratif
Meetings/Conferences:
• 14e Congrès annuel de l'Association québécoise du lymphoedème, 2018, QC
Scope: Provincial

Association québécoise du personnel de direction des écoles (AQPDE)
#235, 3291, ch Ste-Foy, Québec QC G1X 3V2
Tél: 418-781-0700; Téléc: 418-781-0276
info@aqpde.ca
www.aqpde.ca
Aperçu: *Dimension:* moyenne; *Envergure:* provinciale; fondée en 1967
Mission: Défendre et promouvoir les intérêts professionnels, sociaux et économiques des membres, favoriser leur participation et établir une concertation avec les autres organismes du réseau de l'éducation pour assurer les meilleures conditions de ses membres
Membre de: AFIDES International
Finances: *Budget de fonctionnement annuel:* $250,000-$500,000
Membre(s) du personnel: 3
Membre: 500; *Montant de la cotisation:* 1.2% du salaire; *Critères d'admissibilite:* Cadre des établissements scolaires
Activités: Congrès au 2 ans
Membre(s) du bureau directeur:
Danielle Boucher, Présidente

Association québécoise du théâtre amateur inc. *Voir* Fédération québécoise du théâtre amateur

Association québécoise du transport aérien (AQTA)
Aéroport international Jean-Lesage, #600, 6e av de l'Aéroport, Québec QC G2G 2T5
Tél: 418-871-4635; Téléc: 418-871-8189
aqta@aqta.ca
www.aqta.ca
Aperçu: *Dimension:* moyenne; *Envergure:* provinciale; Organisme sans but lucratif; fondée en 1975
Mission: Voué à la défense et la promotion des intérêts de tous les secteurs du transport aérien
Membre(s) du personnel: 2
Membre: 135; *Montant de la cotisation:* Barème; *Critères d'admissibilite:* Transporteurs aériens et fournisseurs de produits et services liés à l'aviation
Membre(s) du bureau directeur:
Jean-Marc Dufour, Président-directeur général
Publications:
• AIR: Le magazine de l'AQTA

Association québécoise Plaidoyer-Victimes (AQPV)
#201, 4305, rue d'Iberville, Montréal QC H2H 2L5
Tél: 514-526-9037; Téléc: 514-526-9951
aqpv@aqpv.ca
www.aqpv.ca
Également appelé: Plaidoyer-Victimes
Aperçu: *Dimension:* petite; *Envergure:* provinciale; Organisme sans but lucratif; fondée en 1984
Mission: Défense des droits et des intérêts des victimes d'actes criminels par la discussion, la sensibilisation, la formation, la concertation et la recherche
Membre(s) du personnel: 3
Membre: 242; *Montant de la cotisation:* 55$ individu; 65$ associatif; 130$ partenaire; *Critères d'admissibilite:* Toutes personnes ou organismes s'intéressant à la problématique des victimes d'actes criminels

Activités: *Stagiaires:* Oui; *Service de conférenciers:* Oui; *Listes de destinataires:* Oui
Membre(s) du bureau directeur:
Marie-Hélène Blanc, Directrice générale

Association québécoise pour l'évaluation d'impacts (AQEI)
CP 59042, Succ. Bourg-Royal, Québec QC G2L 2W6
Tél: 514-397-0316
aqei@aqei.qc.ca
www.aqei.qc.ca
www.linkedin.com/company/aqei
www.facebook.com/aqei1
twitter.com/AQEImpacts
Aperçu: *Dimension:* moyenne; *Envergure:* provinciale
Mission: Regrouper toute personne, professionnelle ou non, intéressée par l'évaluation d'impacts et à son utilisation dans le processus de planification et de prise de décision
Affiliation(s): International Association for Impact Assessment
Membre: *Montant de la cotisation:* Barème; *Comités:* Communications; Membership; Mémoire et avis; Programmation
Membre(s) du bureau directeur:
Marie-Hélène Léger, Coordonnatrice

Association québécoise pour l'hygiène, la santé et la sécurité du travail (AQHSST)
CP 52, 89, boul de Bromont, Bromont QC J2L 1A9
Tél: 450-776-2169
Ligne sans frais: 888-355-3830
info@aqhsst.qc.ca
www.aqhsst.qc.ca
www.linkedin.com/pub/aqhsst-ca/37/9b0/30b
www.facebook.com/pages/AQHSST/118417061527266
twitter.com/AQHSST
Aperçu: *Dimension:* moyenne; *Envergure:* provinciale; Organisme sans but lucratif; fondée en 1978
Mission: Promouvoir les connaissances relatives à l'hygiène industrielle par l'échange et la vulgarisation de l'information; Faire la promotion des connaissances dans des domaines connexes pouvant avoir un impact sur la santé et la sécurité du travail tels la sécurité, l'ergonomie et l'environnement; étudier les législations pertinentes et toute action gouvernementale relatives à ses champs d'activités et faire les représentations qu'elle juge à propos; Encourager la reconnaissance de la compétence de ses membres
Finances: *Budget de fonctionnement annuel:* $100,000-$250,000
Membre(s) du personnel: 2; 20 bénévole(s)
Membre: 475; *Montant de la cotisation:* 30$ membre étudiant; 125$ membre individuel; 325$ membre corporatif; *Comités:* Comité de formation; Comité des communications et du service à la clientèle
Activités: Congrès annuel; Formations; Activités associatives; regroupement de professionnels; *Bibliothèque:* UNF Library; Bibliothèque publique
Membre(s) du bureau directeur:
Nicolas Perron, Président, 450-774-9131, Fax: 450-261-2107
Amélie Trudel, Vice-présidente, 514-849-8373, Fax: 514-849-8873
France de Repentigny, Secrétaire, 514-982-2553, Fax: 514-283-6737
Christine Venditto, Trésorière
Prix, Bourses:
• Prix Antoine-Aumont de l'AQHSST
• Prix Méritas
• Bourse 3M
• Bourse Levitt sécurité Ltée
Meetings/Conferences:
• Congrès annuel de l'Association québécoise pour l'hygiène, la santé et la sécurité du travail 2018, 2018, QC
Scope: Provincial

Association québécoise pour la maîtrise de l'énergie (AQME) / Québec Association of Energy Managers (QAEM)
#750, 255, boul Crémazie est, Montréal QC H2M 1L5
Tél: 514-866-5584; Téléc: 514-874-1272
info@aqme.org
www.aqme.org
twitter.com/MaitriseEnergie
www.youtube.com/user/2729AQME
Aperçu: *Dimension:* moyenne; *Envergure:* provinciale; Organisme sans but lucratif; fondée en 1985
Mission: Contribuer à la promotion de la maîtrise de l'énergie au Québec pour une utilisation et une exploitation optimales des ressources et pour le respect de l'environnement

Membre(s) du personnel: 14
Membre: 800; *Montant de la cotisation:* Barème; *Critères d'admissibilite:* Utilisateur ou fournisseur d'énergie; *Comités:* Bâtiment; Industriel; Organisateur de la Soirée de crustacés et moules annuelle; Organisateur du congrès annuel; Organisateurs des Classiques de golf annuelles; Relève; Technique et jury du Concours Énergia; Transport; Exécutif
Activités: Congrès annuel, concours Énergia, party homards, tournois de golf; *Stagiaires:* Oui
Membre(s) du bureau directeur:
Jean Lacroix, Président/directeur général, 514-866-5584 Ext. 225
jlacroix@aqme.org

Association Québécoise pour la Santé Mentale des Nourrisson (AQSMN)
CP 10009, Saint-Jean-sur-Richelieu QC J2W 0G6
Tél: 514-598-8413
info@aqsmn.org
www.aqsmn.org
Aperçu: *Dimension:* petite; *Envergure:* provinciale
Mission: De promouvoir la recherche dans les domaines de la santé et le développement mental du nourrisson; pour étudier la santé mentale des parents.
Membre: *Montant de la cotisation:* 20$ étudiant; 60$ individu; 100$ organisme; *Critères d'admissibilite:* Cliniciens et de chercheurs
Membre(s) du bureau directeur:
Alain Lebel, Président

Association québécoise pour la thérapie conjugale et familiale *See* Québec Association of Marriage & Family Therapy

Association québécoise pour le loisir des personnes handicapées (AQLPH)
858, rue Laviolette, Trois-Rivières QC G9A 5J1
Tél: 819-693-3339
info@aqlph.qc.ca
www.aqlph.qc.ca
Aperçu: *Dimension:* moyenne; *Envergure:* provinciale; fondée en 1978
Mission: Promouvoir le droit à un loisir de qualité (éducatif, sécuritaire, valorisant et de détente); promouvoir la participation et la libre expression de la personne face à son loisir; promouvoir l'accès à tous les champs d'application du loisir (tourisme, plein air, sport et activité physique, loisir scientifique, socio-éducatif et socioculturel) pour toutes les personnes handicapées du Québec sans restriction d'âge, de sexe, ni de type d'handicap
Membre de: Alliance de vie active pour les canadiens; Canadiennes ayant un handicap
Membre: 14; *Critères d'admissibilite:* Associations régionales
Activités: "Destination Loisirs": une rencontre sportive, récréative et culturelle d'envergure provinciale de type participative où on y retrouve des activités sportives, de loisirs, touristiques et sociales pratiquées dans la plupart des régions tels le hockey-balle, le mini-golf, les quilles, etc.; *Bibliothèque:* Centre de documentation AQLPH; rendez-vous
Membre(s) du bureau directeur:
Marc St-Onge, Directeur

AlterGo
#340, 525, rue Dominion, Montréal QC H3J 2B4
Tél: 514-933-2739; Téléc: 514-933-9384
info@altergo.ca
www.altergo.ca
Membre(s) du bureau directeur:
Élise Blais, Présidente

ARLPH Abitibi-Témiscamingue
330, rue Perreault est, Rouyn-Noranda QC J9X 3C6
Tél: 819-762-8121
www.ulsat.qc.ca/arlphat/
Membre(s) du bureau directeur:
Laurent Juteau, Coordonateur Programme
ljuteau@ulsat.qc.ca

ARLPH Centre du Québec
La Place Rita St-Pierre, #236, 59, rue Monfette, Victoriaville QC G6P 1J8
Tél: 819-758-5464; Téléc: 819-758-4375
arlphcq@cdcbf.qc.ca
www.arlphcq.com

ARLPH Chaudière-Appalaches
5501, rue St-Georges, Lévis QC G6V 4M7
Tél: 418-833-4495; Téléc: 418-833-7214
arlphca@videotron.ca
www.arlphca.com

Membre(s) du bureau directeur:
Amélie Richard, Directrice régionale
ARLPH Côte-Nord
#218, 859, rue Bossé, Baie-Comeau QC G5C 3P8
Tél: 418-589-5774; *Téléc:* 418-589-4612
Ligne sans frais: 888-330-8757
info@urlscn.qc.ca
www.urlscn.qc.ca
Membre(s) du bureau directeur:
Pierre LeBreux, Directeur général
lebreux.pierre@urlscn.qc.ca
ARLPH de la Capitale-Nationale
CP 1000, Succ. M, 4545, av Pierre-De Coubertin, Montréal QC H1V 3R2
Tél: 514-252-3144
info@aqlph.qc.ca
www.aqlph.qc.ca
Membre(s) du bureau directeur:
Guylaine Laforest, Directrice
ARLPH Estrie
5182, boul Bourque, Sherbrooke QC J1N 1H4
Tél: 819-864-0864; *Téléc:* 819-864-1864
csle@abacom.com
www.csle.qc.ca/fr/arlpphe
Membre(s) du bureau directeur:
Claire Gaudreault, Directrice régionale
ARLPH Lanaudière
200, rue de Salaberry, Joliette QC J6E 4G1
Tél: 450-752-2586; *Téléc:* 450-759-8749
Ligne sans frais: 800-752-2586
arlphl@cepap.ca
Membre(s) du bureau directeur:
Paulette Goulet, Présidente
ARLPH Laurentides
#100, 300, rue Longpré, Saint-Jérôme QC J7Y 3B9
Tél: 450-431-3388; *Téléc:* 450-436-2277
arlphl@videotron.ca
www.arlphl.org
Membre(s) du bureau directeur:
Kevin Hoskins, Président
Bernard Oligny, Directeur général
ARLPH Laval
#215A, 387, bouls des Prairies, Laval QC H7N 2W4
Tél: 450-668-2354; *Téléc:* 450-668-2226
info@arlphl.ca
www.arlphl.qc.ca
Membre(s) du bureau directeur:
Rachid Ababou, Président
Louise Langevin, Directrice régionale
ARLPH Saguenay/Lac St-Jean
138, rue Price ouest, Chicoutimi QC G7H 1J8
Tél: 418-545-4132; *Téléc:* 418-545-7271
arlph@cybernaute.com
www.lavilla.ca/arlph
Membre(s) du bureau directeur:
Francine Vigneault, Présidente
URLS Bas St-Laurent
#304, 38, rue St-Germain est, Rimouski QC G5L 1A2
Tél: 418-723-5036; *Téléc:* 418-722-8906
info@urls-bsl.qc.ca
www.urls-bsl.qc.ca
www.facebook.com/urlsbsl
twitter.com/urlsbsl
Membre(s) du bureau directeur:
Lucille Porlier, Directrice générale
lucilleporlier@urls-bsl.qc.ca
URLS Gaspésie/Iles de la Madeleine
CP 99, 8, boul Perron est, Caplan QC G0C 1H0
Tél: 418-388-2121; *Téléc:* 418-388-2133
informations@urlsgim.com
www.urlsgim.com
www.facebook.com/urlsgim
Membre(s) du bureau directeur:
Nicolas Méthot, Directeur général
nicolas.methot@urlsgim.com
URLS Mauricie
260, rue Dessureault, Trois-Rivières QC G8T 9T9
Tél: 819-691-3075; *Téléc:* 819-373-6046
urls@urlsmauricie.com
www.urlsmauricie.com
Membre(s) du bureau directeur:
Jean-Marc Gauthier, Directeur général
URLS Outaouais
#209, 390, av de Buckingham, Gatineau QC J8L 2G7

Tél: 819-663-2575; *Téléc:* 819-281-6369
info@loisirsportoutaouais.com
www.urlso.qc.ca
Membre(s) du bureau directeur:
Frédérique Delisle, Directrice générale
direction@loisirsportoutaouais.com
Zone loisir Montérégie
3800, boul Casavant ouest, Saint-Hyacinthe QC J2S 8E3
Tél: 450-771-0707
infozlm@zlm.qc.ca
www.zlm.qc.ca
Membre(s) du bureau directeur:
Jean Lemonde, Directeur général
jlemonde@zlm.qc.ca

Association québécoise pour le tourisme équestre et l'équitation de loisir du Québec
1025, ch du Plan-Bouchard, Blainville QC J7C 4K7
Tél: 450-434-1433; *Téléc:* 450-434-8826
quebec@cheval.qc.ca
www.cheval.qc.ca
Également appelé: Québec à cheval
Aperçu: *Dimension:* moyenne; *Envergure:* provinciale; fondée en 1980
Mission: Assurer le développement de la randonnée équestre dans ses dimensions de plein air et de tourisme; inventorier et soutenir le développement de sentiers équestres; promouvoir par tous les moyens la randonnée et le tourisme équestres; sensibiliser les adeptes de l'équitation à une pratique sécuritaire de l'activité
Membre(s) du personnel: 6
Membre: 50 institutionnel; 7,000 individu
Activités: Stages et cliniques de formation; Équi-Livres; *Stagiaires:* Oui; *Service de conférenciers:* Oui
Membre(s) du bureau directeur:
Julie Villeneuve, Directeur général

Association québécoise pour les enfants atteints d'audimutité *Voir* Association québécoise de la dysphasie

L'Association récréative *See* The Recreation Association

Association régionale de football Laurentides Lanaudière (ARFLL)
3585, montée Gagnon, Terrebonne QC J6Y 1K8
Tél: 514-318-5376
arfll-lfl@hotmail.com
www.arfll.com
www.facebook.com/ARFLL
Aperçu: *Dimension:* petite; *Envergure:* locale; fondée en 2000
Mission: Promouvoir le football auprès de tous les jeunes
Membre: 700
Membre(s) du bureau directeur:
Charles Guitard, Président intérimaire

Association régionale de la communauté francophone de Saint-Jean inc. (ARCf)
67, ch Ragged Point, Saint John NB E2K 5C3
Tél: 506-658-4600; *Téléc:* 506-658-3984
arcf@arcf.ca
www.arcf-sj.org
www.facebook.com/arcfsaintjean
twitter.com/ARCfdeSaintJean
www.instagram.com/arcfdesaintjean
Nom précédent: Conseil communautaire Samuel-de-Champlain
Aperçu: *Dimension:* moyenne; *Envergure:* locale; Organisme sans but lucratif; fondée en 1985
Mission: Donner aux francophones du Saint-Jean métropolitain le meilleur milieu de vie au Nouveau-Brunswick
Membre de: Conseil provincial des sociétés culturelles; Chambre de commerce de Saint John; Société canadienne des directeurs d'association
Affiliation(s): Chevaliers de colomb; Scouts et guides; Association sportive
Finances: *Budget de fonctionnement annuel:* $1.5 Million-$3 Million; *Fonds:* Subventions gouvernementales; commandites; activités-bénéfices et commerciales
Membre(s) du personnel: 60; 350 bénévole(s)
Membre: 100-499; *Critères d'admissibilite:* Appuie le développement de la communauté francophone
Activités: Leur proposant des rencontres avec des artistes de la scène dans le cadre de la Série Rido et d'une programmation socio-culturelle diversifiée; *Bibliothèque:* Bibliothèque Le Cormoran
Membre(s) du bureau directeur:
Michel Côté, Directeur général
michel.cote@arcf.ca

Publications:
• Le Ceki's'passe [a publication of Association régionale de la communauté francophone de Saint-Jean inc.]
Type: Bulletin électronique; *Price:* Gratuit
Profile: Des informations sur ce qui se passe chaque semaine dans la communauté francophone de Saint-Jean
• Franco [a publication of Association régionale de la communauté francophone de Saint-Jean inc.]
Type: Magazine
Profile: Le magazine qui contient des souvenirs célébrant les 30 ans du Centre scolaire-communautaire Samuel-de-Champlain
• Le Saint-Jeannois [a publication of Association régionale de la communauté francophone de Saint-Jean inc.]
Type: Newsletter; *Frequency:* 10 fois par an; *Price:* Gratuit
Profile: Offre aux francophones une tribune de choix pour souligner leurs succès et pour publiciser leurs activités
• Les Z'affaires culturelles [a publication of Association régionale de la communauté francophone de Saint-Jean inc.]
Type: Bulletin électronique; *Price:* Gratuit
Profile: Des informations sur les nombreuses activités rassembleuses pour la communauté francophonede Saint-Jean

Association régionale de la police de York *See* York Regional Police Association

Association régionale de ringuette Laval
3235, boul St-Martin est, Laval QC H7E 5G8
Tél: 450-664-1917
ringuettelaval.org
Aperçu: *Dimension:* petite; *Envergure:* provinciale surveillé par Ringuette-Québec
Membre de: Ringuette-Québec
Membre(s) du bureau directeur:
Eric Allard, Président

Association Régionale de Ringuette Richelieu Yamaska
QC
www.ringuette-quebec.qc.ca/regionale_richelieu-yamaska.php
Aperçu: *Dimension:* petite; *Envergure:* provinciale surveillé par Ringuette-Québec
Membre de: Ringuette-Québec

Association régionale des maisons de transition *See* Regional Halfway House Association

Association régionale du sport étudiant de l'Abitibi-Témiscamingue *Voir* Réseau du sport étudiant du Québec Abitibi-Témiscamingue

Association régionale du sport étudiant de l'Est du Québec *Voir* Réseau du sport étudiant du Québec Est-du-Québec

Association régionale du sport étudiant de la Côte-Nord *Voir* Réseau du sport étudiant du Québec Côte-Nord

Association régionale du sport étudiant de la Mauricie *Voir* Réseau du sport étudiant du Québec, secteur Mauricie

Association régionale du sport étudiant de Montréal *Voir* Réseau du sport étudiant du Québec Montréal

Association régionale du sport étudiant de Québec et Chaudière-Appalaches *Voir* Réseau du sport étudiant du Québec Chaudière-Appalaches

Association régionale du sport étudiant du Saguenay-Lac St-Jean *Voir* Réseau du sport étudiant du Québec Saguenay-Lac St-Jean

Association régionale du sport étudiant Lac Saint-Louis *Voir* Réseau du sport étudiant du Québec Lac Saint-Louis

Association régionale du sport étudiant Laurentides-Lanaudière *Voir* Réseau du sport étudiant du Québec Laurentides-Lanaudière

Association régionale du sport scolaire *See* Greater Montreal Athletic Association

Association Renaissance de la région de l'Amiante
76, rue Saint-Joseph nord, Thetford Mines QC G6G 3N8
Tél: 418-335-5636
as.ren@bellnet.ca
www.facebook.com/363464490479376
Aperçu: *Dimension:* petite; *Envergure:* locale
Mission: Défendre les droits des personnes ayant une déficience intellectuelle et de leur famille; faciliter l'intégration sociale de ces personnes
Affiliation(s): Association du Québec pour l'intégration sociale

Membre: *Critères d'admissibilité:* Personne vivant avec une déficience intellectuelle ou un trouble envahissant du développement et sa famille
Activités: Information; orientation; activités éducatives; parrainage; activités sociales; samedi-répit; camp de vacances pour enfants; groupes d'entraide pour parents et pour personnes intégrées au marché du travail
Membre(s) du bureau directeur:
Johanne Lessard, Coordonnatrice

Association renaissance des personnes traumatisées crâniennes du Saguenay-Lac-Saint-Jean (ARPTC)
2223, boul du Saguenay, Jonquière QC G7S 4H5
Tél: 418-548-9366; *Téléc:* 418-548-9369
Ligne sans frais: 855-548-9366
arptc@arptc.org
www.arptc.org
Aperçu: *Dimension:* petite; *Envergure:* locale; fondée en 1995
Mission: Pour aider les personnes dans la région du Saguenay-Lac-Saint-Jean du Québec qui ont été touchés par les conséquences de lésions cérébrales; Pour aider les membres de la famille des personnes qui ont subi une lésion cérébrale
Membre de: Regroupement des associations de personnes traumatisées craniocérébrales du Québec / Coalition of Associations of Craniocerebral Trauma in Quebec
Membre(s) du personnel: 9
Activités: Protéger les droits des personnes souffrant de lésions cérébrales; Accroître la sensibilisation et fournir des informations sur les lésions cérébrales; Offrir un soutien psychosocial
Membre(s) du bureau directeur:
Jonathan Jean-Vézina, Directeur général
direction@arptc.org

Association royale de golf du Canada *See* Golf Canada

Association salers du Canada *See* Salers Association of Canada

Association scientifique canadienne de la viande *See* Canadian Meat Science Association

Association Sclérose en Plaques Rive-Sud (ASPRS)
3825, rue Windsor, Saint-Hubert QC J4T 2Z6
Tél: 450-926-5210; *Téléc:* 450-926-5215
info@asprs.qc.ca
www.asprs.qc.ca
www.linkedin.com/company/association-sclérose-en-plaques-rive-sud
twitter.com/asprs2
Aperçu: *Dimension:* petite; *Envergure:* locale; fondée en 1976
Mission: Aider des gens qui a sclérose en plaques de surmonter avec leur maladie s'engageant dans des activités sociales
Membre(s) du personnel: 10
Membre: *Critères d'admissibilité:* Toute personne avec de sclérose en plaques et leurs parents
Membre(s) du bureau directeur:
Nancy Caron, Directrice générale
nancy.caron@asprs.qc.ca

Association SeCan *See* SeCan Association

Association sectorielle services automobiles
#150, 8, rue de la Place-du-Commerce, Brossard QC J4W 3H2
Tél: 450-672-9330; *Téléc:* 450-672-4835
Ligne sans frais: 800-363-2344
info@autoprevention.org
www.autoprevention.org
twitter.com/AutoPrevention
www.youtube.com/autoprevention
Également appelé: Auto Prévention
Aperçu: *Dimension:* moyenne; *Envergure:* provinciale
Mission: Aider les travailleurs et les employeurs du secteur des services automobiles à prendre en charge la santé et la sécurité au travail, afin d'éliminer les risques d'accidents et de maladies professionnelles
Membre(s) du bureau directeur:
Sylvie Mallette, Directrice Générale
Publications:
• Auto Prévention [publication Association sectorielle services automobiles]
Type: Journal; *Frequency:* 4 pa.

Association sectorielle: Fabrication d'équipement de transport et de machines (ASFETM) / Sectorial Association: Transportation Equipment & Machinery Manufacturing (SATEMM)
#202, 3565, rue Jarry est, Montréal QC H1Z 4K6
Tél: 514-729-6961; *Téléc:* 514-729-8628
Ligne sans frais: 888-527-3386
info@asfetm.com
www.asfetm.com
Aperçu: *Dimension:* grande; *Envergure:* provinciale; Organisme sans but lucratif; fondée en 1983
Mission: Aider les employeurs et les travailleurs à prévenir les accidents du travail et les maladies professionnelles, en faisant pour eux de la recherche, en leur dispensant de l'information, de la formation et de l'assistance technique qui visent essentiellement à rendre impossibles les accidents et les maladies au travail, et en privilégiant, à cette fin, l'élimination de cette possibilité à sa source même selon un processus de participation paritaire
Membre de: National Safety Council (USA); Association du camionnage du Québec
Finances: *Budget de fonctionnement annuel:* $500,000-$1.5 Million
Membre(s) du personnel: 20
Membre: 8 groupes corporatifs - 3 patronaux + 5 syndicaux; *Critères d'admissibilité:* Etre une association patronale ou syndicale du secteur
Activités: Programme d'action annuel (30 projets); journées de sessions et de formation; colloques; *Service de conférenciers:* Oui
Membre(s) du bureau directeur:
Claude Boisvert, Directeur général
cboisvert@asfetm.com
Chantal Lauzon, Adjoint au directeur
clauzon@asfetm.com
Publications:
• Fiches techniques [a publication of Association sectorielle - Fabrication d'équipement de transport et de machines]
• Santé + Sécurité [a publication of Association sectorielle - Fabrication d'équipement de transport et de machines]
Type: Magazine

Association Sépharade Francophone *Voir* Communauté sépharade unifiée du Québec

Association Simmental du Québec *See* Québec Simmental Association

Association Sportive de Ringuette Brossard
CP 210, 8000, boul Leduc, Brossard QC J4Y 0E9
Courriel: communications@ringuetteroussillon.ca
www.ringuettebrossard.com
www.facebook.com/AssociationSportiveDeRinguetteDeBrossard
twitter.com/ARRoussillon
Également appelé: Ringuette Brossard
Aperçu: *Dimension:* petite; *Envergure:* provinciale surveillé par Ringuette-Québec
Membre de: Ringuette-Québec
Membre(s) du bureau directeur:
Sylvain Lebel, President
slebel1@sympatico.ca

Association sportive des aveugles du Québec inc. (ASAQ)
4545, av Pierre-de Coubertin, Montréal QC H1V 3R2
Tél: 514-252-3178
infoasaq@sportsaveugles.qc.ca
www.sportsaveugles.qc.ca
Aperçu: *Dimension:* petite; *Envergure:* provinciale; fondée en 1979 surveillé par Canadian Blind Sports Association Inc.
Mission: Promouvoir la pratique du sport amateur auprès des personnes handicapées de la vue et de favoriser ainsi leur intégration
Membre(s) du personnel: 5
Membre: 135; *Montant de la cotisation:* 15$
Activités: *Service de conférenciers:* Oui
Membre(s) du bureau directeur:
Nathalie Chartrand, Directrice générale

Association sportive des sourds du Québec inc. (ASSQ)
4545, av Pierre-de Coubertin, Montréal QC H1V 0B2
Tél: 514-252-3049
www.assq.org
www.facebook.com/ASSQ1
twitter.com/@ASSQ_Nouvelles
www.youtube.com/user/1ASSQ
Nom précédent: Association amateur des sports des sourds du Québec; Fédération sportive des sourds du Québec inc.
Aperçu: *Dimension:* moyenne; *Envergure:* provinciale; fondée en 1968 surveillé par Canadian Deaf Sports Association
Mission: Promouvoir le sport, les loisirs et l'activité physique chez les personnes sourdes et malentendantes du Québec
Membre de: Canadian Deaf Sports Association
Membre(s) du bureau directeur:
Suzanne Laforest, Directrice générale
slaforest@assq.org
Audrey Beauchamp, Coordinatrice, Projets et des communications
abeauchamp@assq.org
Caroline Hould, Chargée des programmes
chould@assq.org

Association sportive et communautaire du Centre-Sud (ASCCS)
2093, rue de la Visitation, Montréal QC H2X 3C9
Tél: 514-522-2246; *Téléc:* 514-522-6702
centre@asccs.qc.ca
asccs.qc.ca
www.linkedin.com/groups/Association-sportive-communautaire-CentreSud-3621278
www.facebook.com/103895026361019
twitter.com/ASCCSMontreal
Aperçu: *Dimension:* petite; *Envergure:* locale; fondée en 1974
Mission: Pour améliorer la qualité de vie des résidents de la région en offrant des activités de loisirs abordables
Membre: *Montant de la cotisation:* 15$ Adultes; 7$ Jeunes; 10$ Aînés
Activités: Sports; Activités d'arts et culture; Activités aquatiques
Membre(s) du bureau directeur:
Stéphane Proulx, Directeur adjoint, 514-522-2246 Ext. 223
sproulx@asccs.qc.ca

L'Association St.Vincent et Grenadines de Montrèal Inc. *See* St. Vincent & the Grenadines Association of Montreal Inc.

Association syndicale des employées de production et de service (ASEPS)
CP 1063, Saint-Lazare QC J7T 2Z7
Tél: 450-455-8346; *Téléc:* 450-455-9731
Ligne sans frais: 877-455-8346
aseps@aseps.qc.ca
aseps.qc.ca
Aperçu: *Dimension:* petite; *Envergure:* locale; fondée en 1996
Mission: Hausser le statut économique et social de ses membres; appuyer les personnes qui la recherche; promouvoir le plein-emploi, les activités éducatives, législatives et politiques
Finances: *Budget de fonctionnement annuel:* Moins de $50,000
Membre(s) du personnel: 2
Membre: 850; *Montant de la cotisation:* 5-8/semaine; *Critères d'admissibilité:* Salariés
Membre(s) du bureau directeur:
Donald A. Caron, Président
dcaron@aseps.qc.ca
Guillaume Caron, Vice-Président
guicaron@aseps.qc.ca
Paul-André Gagnon, Vice-Président, 819-269-3359
Daniel Guénette, Secrétaire
Jean-Claude Gobeil, Vice-Président

Association technique canadienne du bitume *See* Canadian Technical Asphalt Association

Association technique des pâtes et papiers du Canada *See* Pulp & Paper Technical Association of Canada

Association to Reunite Grandparents & Families *See* CANGRANDS Kinship Support

Association touristique Chaudière-Appalaches *Voir* Tourisme Chaudière-Appalaches

Association touristique des Iles-de-la-Madeleine *Voir* Tourisme Îles-de-la-Madeleine

Association touristique des Laurentides *Voir* Tourisme Laurentides

Association touristique du Saguenay-Lac-Saint-Jean *Voir* Association touristique régionale du Saguenay-Lac-Saint-Jean

Association touristique régionale de Charlevoix
495, boul de Comporté, La Malbaie QC G5A 3G3
Tél: 418-665-4454; *Téléc:* 418-665-3811
Ligne sans frais: 800-667-2276
info@tourisme-charlevoix.com
www.tourisme-charlevoix.com
www.facebook.com/tourismecharlevoix

twitter.com/gocharlevoix
www.youtube.com/user/TourismeCharlevoix
Également appelé: Tourisme Charlevoix
Aperçu: *Dimension:* moyenne; *Envergure:* locale; Organisme sans but lucratif surveillé par Associations touristiques régionales associées du Québec
Mission: Accueil, promotion, développement de Charlevoix en tourisme
Finances: *Budget de fonctionnement annuel:* $1.5 Million-$3 Million

Association touristique régionale du Saguenay-Lac-Saint-Jean
#100, 412, boul Saguenay est, Chicoutimi QC G7H 7Y8
Tél: 418-543-3536; *Téléc:* 418-543-1805
Ligne sans frais: 855-253-8387
admin@tourismesaglac.net
www.saguenaylacsaintjean.ca
www.linkedin.com/tourisme-saguenay-lac-saint-jean
www.facebook.com/TourismeSaguenayLacSaintJean
twitter.com/Saguenay_Lac
www.youtube.com/SaguenayLacStJean
Également appelé: Tourisme Saguenay-Lac-Saint-Jean; ATR Saguenay-Lac-Saint-Jean
Nom précédent: Association touristique du Saguenay-Lac-Saint-Jean
Aperçu: *Dimension:* moyenne; *Envergure:* locale; Organisme sans but lucratif; fondée en 1977 surveillée par Associations touristiques régionales associées du Québec
Mission: Au service et à l'écoute de ses membres et de l'industrie touristique régionale dans son ensemble, elle est une organisation de concertation dont les principales activités visent à promouvoir à développer la qualité de l'expérience touristique, à assurer l'accueil et l'information et la mise en marché
Membre de: l'Association des ATR Associées du Québec
Finances: *Budget de fonctionnement annuel:* $1.5 Million-$3 Million
Membre(s) du personnel: 16
Membre: 612; *Critères d'admissibilite:* Tourisme
Activités: *Événements de sensibilisation:* Lancement de saison; Grands Prix du tourisme québécois
Membre(s) du bureau directeur:
Julie Dubord, Directrice générale
jdubord@tourismesaglac.net
Sylvianne Dufour, Adjointe à la direction générale
directiongenerale@tourismesaglac.net

Association Trot & Amble du Québec (ATAQ) / Québec Trotting & Pacing Society
#216, 5375, rue Paré, Montréal QC H4P 1P7
Tél: 514-731-9484
Ligne sans frais: 800-731-9484
courses@qc.aira.com
www.trotetamble.ca
Aperçu: *Dimension:* moyenne; *Envergure:* provinciale
Mission: Coopérer avec les promoteurs afin de s'assurer de la bonne conduite des programmes de courses aux différents hippodromes du Québec; améliorer les lois et règlements en vue de favoriser le sport des courses sous harnais; représenter et aider tous les members; encourager et promouvoir les courses d'élevage québécois et les courses régulières; collaborer avec les différents organismes afin d'établir un juste équilibre pour le bien-être de l'industrie
Membre: *Montant de la cotisation:* Barème
Activités: Service d'assurances; activités sociales; promotion
Membre(s) du bureau directeur:
Marc Camirand, Président
Gilles Fortier, Secrétaire général, 514-731-9484

L'Association ukrainienne-canadienne des droits civils *See* Ukrainian Canadian Civil Liberties Association

Association universitaire canadienne d'études nordiques *See* Association of Canadian Universities for Northern Studies

L'Association Zoroastrianne du Québec (AZQ) / Zoroastrian Associaton of Québec (ZAQ)
PO Box 35, Stn. Beaconsfield, Beaconsfield QC H9W 5T6
Tel: 514-426-9929
quebeczoroastrians@gmail.com
zaq.org
www.facebook.com/www.zaq.org
twitter.com/ZAQGROUP
Overview: A small provincial charitable organization founded in 1984
Mission: Pour préserver et promouvoir le patrimoine religieux, culturel, social et historique de zoroastriens vivant au Québec

Affiliation(s): Federation of North American Zoroastrian Associations
Chief Officer(s):
Dolly Dastoor, President
dollydastoor@sympatico.ca

Association/Troubles Anxieux du Québec *Voir* Association/Troubles de l'Humeur et d'Anxiété au Québec

Association/Troubles de l'Humeur et d'Anxiété au Québec (ATHAQ)
QC
Courriel: info@athaq.com
www.athaq.com
Nom précédent: Association/Troubles Anxieux du Québec
Aperçu: *Dimension:* petite; *Envergure:* provinciale; Organisme sans but lucratif, fondée en 1991 surveillé par Anxiety Disorders Association of Canada
Mission: Formée par un groupe de professionnels oeuvrant dans le domaine des troubles anxieux et de ses comorbidités avec pour but de collaborer au niveau des soins, de l'enseignement, de la recherche, de la formation médicale et de l'information du public
Membre: 12 membres actifs; 8 membres consultants; *Critères d'admissibilite:* Psychiatres; psychologues; omnipraticiens; professionnels de la sant, mentale
Activités: Information; recherche; conférences; émissions pour télévision
Membre(s) du bureau directeur:
Cédric Aubé, Consultant

Associations de retraités des universités et collèges du Canada *See* College & University Retiree Associations of Canada

Associations touristiques régionales associées du Québec (ATRAQ) / Québec Regional Tourist Associations Inc.
#330, 1575, boul de l'Avenir, Laval QC H7S 2N5
Tél: 450-686-8358; *Téléc:* 450-686-9630
Ligne sans frais: 877-686-8358
information@atrassociees.com
www.atrassociees.com
www.facebook.com/ATRassociees
twitter.com/atrassociees
www.youtube.com/user/ATRassociees
Aperçu: *Dimension:* moyenne; *Envergure:* provinciale; Organisme sans but lucratif; fondée en 1981
Mission: Regrouper l'ensemble des associations touristiques régionales oeuvrant au Québec en vue de les représenter et défendre leurs intérêts collectifs; les promouvoir et leur offrir des services; contribuer ainsi au développement de l'industrie touristique québécoise
Membre(s) du personnel: 10
Membre: 21 ATR; *Critères d'admissibilite:* Etre une association touristique régionale reconnue par le ministère du tourisme du Québec
Activités: Grands Prix du Tourisme Québébécois; Bourse des Médias
Membre(s) du bureau directeur:
François-G. Chevrier, Président-Directeur général
francoisgchevrier@atrassociees.com

Associaton des éleveurs Ayrshire du Canada *See* Ayrshire Breeders Association of Canada

Associés bénévoles qualifiés au service des jeunes (ABQSJ)
#8146, rue Drolet, Montréal QC H2P 2H5
Tél: 514-948-6180
info@abqsj.org
www.abqsj.org
www.facebook.com/pages/ABQSJ/132550216834026
Aperçu: *Dimension:* petite; *Envergure:* provinciale; Organisme sans but lucratif
Mission: Former des bénévoles qui viennent en aide aux jeunes en difficulté
Membre(s) du personnel: 2
Membre: *Comités:* Coordination des stages; Bulletin; Publicité et levées de fonds; Chaîne téléphonique
Activités: *Service de conférenciers:* Oui
Membre(s) du bureau directeur:
Sandra Murphy, Présidente
Ginette Charron-Matte, Vice-présidente

Assyrian Association *See* Welfare Committee for the Assyrian Community in Canada

Asthma Society of Canada (ASC) / Société canadienne de l'asthme
#401, 124 Merton St., Toronto ON M4S 2Z2
Tel: 416-787-4050; *Fax:* 416-787-5807
Toll-Free: 866-787-4050
info@asthma.ca
www.asthma.ca
www.facebook.com/AsthmaSocietyofCanada
twitter.com/AsthmaSociety
Overview: A medium-sized national charitable organization founded in 1974
Mission: To optimize the health of people with asthma through education & asthma awareness
Member of: Canadian Network for Asthma Care
Affiliation(s): Family Physicians Asthma Group of Canada; Health Canada Laboratory Centre for Disease Control's National Asthma Control Task Force
Finances: *Annual Operating Budget:* $500,000-$1.5 Million; *Funding Sources:* Donations; special events; partnerships & sponsorships
Staff Member(s): 5
Membership: *Fees:* Schedule available; *Committees:* Executive; Nominations; Medical & Scientific Advisory; Finance; Program Development; Communications; Financial Development; Education
Activities: Research funding; national education website; toll-free Asthma Infoline; educational brochures & print materials; newsletter & magazine; annual fundraising; public awareness events; *Awareness Events:* National Asthma Awareness Month, May; *Speaker Service:* Yes; *Library:* Open to public
Chief Officer(s):
Vanessa Foran, President & CEO, 416-787-4050 Ext. 102
Jenna Reynolds, Director, Programs & Services, 416-787-4050 Ext. 101
Zhen Liu, Office Manager, 416-787-4050 Ext. 105

Asthme et allergies Québec
#880, #2600, boul Laurier, Québec QC G1V 4W2
Tél: 418-627-3141
Ligne sans frais: 877-627-3141
info@asthmeallergies.com
asthmeallergies.com
www.facebook.com/asthmeetallergiesquebec
Également appelé: Asthmédia
Nom précédent: Association pour l'asthme et l'allergie alimentaire du Québec
Aperçu: *Dimension:* petite; *Envergure:* provinciale; Organisme sans but lucratif; fondée en 1986
Mission: Informer les personnes souffrant d'asthme et d'allergie alimentaire sur leur problème de santé et sur les difficultés vécues par ces dernières dans leur vie quotidienne
Membre: *Montant de la cotisation:* $20
Activités: Ligne d'écoute; Conférences; Centre de documentation; Info-lettres
Membre(s) du bureau directeur:
Gervais Bélanger, Directeur général

Ataxia of Charlevoix-Saguenay Foundation *Voir* Fondation de l'Ataxie Charlevoix-Saguenay

ATD Fourth World Movement Canada *Voir* Mouvement ATD Quart Monde Canada

Atelier d'histoire Hochelaga-Maisonneuve
2929, av Jeanne-d'Arc, Montréal QC H1W 3W2
Tél: 514-899-9979; *Téléc:* 514-259-6466
videosepmedia@videotron.ca
Aperçu: *Dimension:* petite; *Envergure:* locale; Organisme sans but lucratif; fondée en 1978
Mission: Promouvoir l'intérêt pour l'histoire; utiliser tout processus d'animation pour oeuvrer au sein de la collectivité, des milieux populaires et scolaires; mettre en valeur les églises historiques d'Hochelaga-Maisonneuve
Finances: *Budget de fonctionnement annuel:* $50,000-$100,000
Membre(s) du personnel: 5; 5 bénévole(s)
Membre: 20; *Montant de la cotisation:* 10$
Activités: Expositions de photos anciennes; visites dans les écoles; visites guidées d'églises et bâtiments patrimoniaux de Montréal; *Bibliothèque:* Centre de documentation; Bibliothèque publique
Membre(s) du bureau directeur:
Paul Labonne, Directeur

Atelier de Formation Socioprofessionnelle de la Petite-Nation
358, rue Rossy, Saint-André-Avellin QC J0V 1W0

Canadian Associations / L'Atelier des lettres

Tél: 819-983-6373; *Téléc:* 819-983-6368
atelier@afspn.qc.ca
www.atelierfspn.org
www.facebook.com/LAtelierFspn
Également appelé: Atelier FSPN
Aperçu: *Dimension:* petite; *Envergure:* locale; fondée en 1987
Mission: Pour aider les personnes handicapées physiques et mentales à trouver un emploi
Membre(s) du personnel: 15
Membre(s) du bureau directeur:
Katherine Provost, Directrice générale

L'Atelier des lettres
1710, rue Beaudry, Montréal QC H2L 3E7
Tél: 514-524-0507; *Téléc:* 514-524-0222
latelier@qc.aira.com
www.atelierdeslettres.org
Aperçu: *Dimension:* petite; *Envergure:* locale
Mission: Pour réduire le degré d'analphabétisme entre les adultes vivant dans la région Centre-Sud, ainsi que pour améliorer la vie des gens qui sont analphabètes et à sensibiliser la population à l'analphabétisme
Membre(s) du personnel: 3
Membre: *Montant de la cotisation:* Gratuit
Membre(s) du bureau directeur:
Francine Lefebvre, Coordinatrice
coordination@qc.aira.com

Atelier habitation Montréal
#206, 55, av Mont-Royal ouest, Montréal QC H2T 2S6
Tél: 514-270-8488; *Téléc:* 514-270-6728
info@atelierhabitationmontreal.org
atelierhabitationmontreal.org
Aperçu: *Dimension:* petite; *Envergure:* locale; fondée en 1978
Mission: Pour offrir un soutien et des connaissances à ceux qui souhaitent créer des logements communautaires
Membre(s) du personnel: 9
Membre(s) du bureau directeur:
Robert Manningham, Directeur général
r.manningham@atelierhabitationmontreal.org

Atelier RADO Inc. (RADO)
CP 432, 325, rue St-François, Edmundston NB E3V 3L1
Tél: 506-735-6313; *Téléc:* 506-735-5803
rado@nb.aibn.com
www.nb-shopping.com/rado.htm
Aperçu: *Dimension:* petite; *Envergure:* locale; Organisme sans but lucratif; fondée en 1983
Mission: Alléger le fardeau de la pauvreté au sein des personnes à faibles revenus dans le comté du Madawaska
Membre de: Association of Food Banks & C.V.A.'s for New Brunswick; Canadian Association of Food Banks
Finances: *Budget de fonctionnement annuel:* $250,000-$500,000
Membre(s) du personnel: 6; 10 bénévole(s)
Membre: 1-99
Activités: Banque alimentaire; cuisine communautaire; comptoir vestimentaire; services d'urgence
Membre(s) du bureau directeur:
David Couturier, Personne ressource

Athabasca & District Chamber of Commerce (ADCofC)
PO Box 3074, Athabasca AB T9S 2B9
www.athabascachamber.org
www.facebook.com/AthabascaDistrictChamberOfCommerce
Overview: A small local organization founded in 1976
Member of: Alberta Chamber of Commerce
Affiliation(s): Canadian Chambers of Commerce
Finances: *Funding Sources:* Membership fees
Activities: Canada Day; Customer Appreciation Day, 3rd Friday in July
Awards:
• High School Graduation Math Award

Athabasca Native Friendship Centre Society
4919 - 53 St., Athabasca AB T9S 1L1
Tel: 780-675-3086; *Fax:* 780-675-3063
anfcs@telusplanet.net
anfca.com/friendship-centres/athabasca
Overview: A small local organization founded in 1988 overseen by Alberta Native Friendship Centres Association
Mission: The Society is a non-profit, social services agency administering programs & services to meet the needs of all Aboriginal people of the region, both transient & resident.
Member of: Alberta Native Friendship Centres Association (ANFCA)

Activities: Offering a comprehensive range of services, such as diabetes initiative, summer & after-school programs for children, court liaison, job training, housing consultation, language/literacy classes, recreational activities, health-related programs, low-cost clothing distriubtion
Chief Officer(s):
Laureen Houle, Executive Director

Athabasca University Faculty Association (AUFA) / Association des professeurs de l'Université d'Athabasca
PO Box 2250, Athabasca AB T9S 2B7
Tel: 780-675-6282; *Fax:* 780-675-6182
Toll-Free: 800-788-9041
aufahq@athabascau.ca
www.aufa.ab.ca
twitter.com/aufacultyassoc
Overview: A small local organization founded in 1973
Mission: To protect, enhance & improve salaries, benefits & working conditions of the AUFA membership
Member of: Canadian Association of University Teachers; Confederation of Alberta Faculty Associations
Affiliation(s): Alberta Federation of Labour; Canadian Labour Congress
Finances: *Annual Operating Budget:* Less than $50,000
Staff Member(s): 2; 14 volunteer(s)
Membership: 400; *Member Profile:* All Athabasca University academic and professional staff; *Committees:* Social Development; Equity; Communications; Grievance
Activities: Engaging in collective bargaining
Chief Officer(s):
Nick Driedger, Executive Director, 780-675-6967
nickdriedger@athabascau.ca

Athabasca University Students' Association *See* Athabasca University Students' Union

Athabasca University Students' Union (AUSU)
Energy Sqaure, #500, 10109 - 106th St. NW, Edmonton AB T5J 3L7
Tel: 780-497-7000
Toll-Free: 855-497-7003
ausu@ausu.ca
www.ausu.org
www.linkedin.com/company/athabasca-university-students%27?-union
www.facebook.com/AthaUSU
twitter.com/AthabascaUSU
Previous Name: Athabasca University Students' Association
Overview: A small local organization founded in 1992
Mission: To advocate on behalf of its student members, as well as for universal accessibility to quality post-secondary education; To promote the development of open & distance education; To provide educational opportunities & services for members; To enhance the recognition of members
Member of: Canadian Alliance of Students' Associations; Athabascha University Board of Governors; Athabasca University Faculty Council
Finances: *Annual Operating Budget:* $500,000-$1.5 Million; *Funding Sources:* Student fees
Staff Member(s): 4; 9 volunteer(s)
Membership: 35,000; *Fees:* $3 per undergraduate credit course at Athabasca University; *Member Profile:* All undergraduate Athasbasca University Students; *Committees:* Awards; Finance; Member Engagement & Communications
Activities: Advocating for Athabasca University students at the university, provincial & federal levels; Liaisoning with university to negotiate issues & fees; Providing services to Athabasca University undergraduate students
Chief Officer(s):
Sarah Cornett, Executive Director
executivedirector@ausu.org
Donette Kingyens, Coordinator, Communications & Member Services
services@ausu.org
Awards:
• Academic Achievement Scholarships
; *Amount:* $1,000
• AUSU Bursaries
; *Amount:* $1,000
• Balanced Student Awards
; *Amount:* $1,000
• Computer Bursaries
• Emergency Bursaries
; *Amount:* $700

• Health Care Bursary
; *Amount:* $1,000
• Returning Student Awards
; *Amount:* $1,000
• Single Parent Bursary
; *Amount:* $1,000
• Student Service Awards
; *Amount:* $1,000
• Travel Bursaries
; *Amount:* $1,000
Publications:
• AUSU [Athabasca University Students' Union] Newsletter
Type: Newsletter
• The Voice [a publication of the Athabasca University Students' Union]
Type: Magazine; *Frequency:* Weekly; *Editor:* Karl Low
Profile: Consists of articles created by Athabasca University students; offers news, ideas, & opinion pieces

The Athletes Association of Canada *See* AthletesCAN

Athletes International
#2702, 3550, rue Jeanne Mauce, Montréal QC H2X 3P7
Tel: 514-982-9989; *Fax:* 514-982-0111
Toll-Free: 800-344-1810
info@athletes-int.com
www.athletes-int.com
twitter.com/athletesint
Overview: A small national organization
Mission: To promote a sense of community & sharing in Canadian sport; To offer discounted products & services, to members of the Canadian sport community, through partners
Membership: *Member Profile:* Canadian sport community
Activities: Offering benefits in areas such as airfare, travel insurance, & hotel reservations
Chief Officer(s):
Peter Schleicher, President
pschleicher@athletes-int.com

AthletesCAN
PO Box 60039, Stn. Findlay Creek, Ottawa ON K1T 0K9
Tel: 613-526-4025; *Fax:* 613-526-9735
Toll-Free: 888-832-4222
info@athletescan.com
www.athletescan.com
www.facebook.com/AthletesCAN
twitter.com/AthletesCAN
instagram.com/athletescan
Also Known As: The Association of Canada's National Team Athletes
Previous Name: The Athletes Association of Canada
Overview: A medium-sized national organization founded in 1992
Mission: To work with others in leadership, advocacy & education to ensure a fair, responsive & supportive sport system for athletes
Staff Member(s): 3
Membership: 3,000+
Chief Officer(s):
Ashley LaBrie, Interim Executive Director, 613-526-4025 Ext. 224
alabrie@athletescan.com
Renee Ridout, Chief Content Curator
rridout@athletescan.com
Rob Little, Development Officer
rlittle@athletescan.com
Awards:
• AthletesCAN Leadership Award
Contact: Rachal Fleury, rfleury@athletescan.com

Athletic Therapists' Association of British Columbia *See* Athletic Therapy Association of British Columbia

Athletic Therapy Association of British Columbia (ATABC)
#200, 4170 Still Creek Dr., Burnaby BC V5C 6C6
Tel: 604-918-5077
info@athletictherapybc.ca
www.athletictherapybc.ca
www.facebook.com/264629906893091
twitter.com/ATABC
Previous Name: Athletic Therapists' Association of British Columbia
Overview: A small provincial organization founded in 1994
Mission: ATABC is a non-profit organization that represents athletic therapists in the province. It ensures that all of its members are in good standing with the Canadian Athletic

Therapists Association. It promotes injury prevention, immediate care & rehabilitation of musculoskeletal injuries.
Member of: Canadian Athletic Therapists Association
5 volunteer(s)
Membership: 1-99; *Member Profile:* Certified athletic therapists & certification candidates
Activities: Sports medical coverage throughout BC; *Speaker Service:* Yes
Chief Officer(s):
Sandy Zinkowski, President
Meetings/Conferences:
• Athletic Therapists Association of BC 13th Annual Member's Meeting, 2018
Scope: Provincial

Athletics Alberta
Percy Page Centre, 11759 Groat Rd., Edmonton AB T5M 3K6
Tel: 780-427-8792; *Fax:* 780-427-8899
Other Communication: www.flickr.com/photos/athleticsalberta
info@athleticsalberta.com
www.athleticsalberta.com
www.linkedin.com/groups/Athletics-Alberta-1997317
www.facebook.com/AthleticsAlberta
twitter.com/athleticsAB
www.youtube.com/user/AthleticsAB
Previous Name: Alberta Track & Field Association
Overview: A medium-sized provincial organization founded in 1969 overseen by Athletics Canada
Mission: To encourage participation & development of excellence in athletics (track & field, cross-country, & road-running)
Member of: Athletics Canada
Finances: *Funding Sources:* Lottery dollars; fundraising; membership fees
Staff Member(s): 3
Membership: *Committees:* Administration; Programs; Personnel; Executive; Marketing
Chief Officer(s):
Linda Blade, President
Peter Ogilvie, Executive Director
peterogilvie@athleticsalberta.com
Sheryl Mack, Office Manager
sherylmack@athleticsalberta.com

Athletics Canada / Athlétisme Canada
#105, 2141 Thurston Dr., Ottawa ON K1G 6C9
Tel: 613-260-5580; *Fax:* 613-260-0341
Other Communication: www.flickr.com/photos/athleticscanada
www.athletics.ca
www.facebook.com/AthleticsCanada
twitter.com/AthleticsCanada
Previous Name: Canadian Track & Field Association
Overview: A large national organization
Mission: To promote & encourage participation via competitions from the grass roots level through to the very highest level of proficiency; To assist coaches, officials & executives in fulfilling their goals through courses, conferences & clinics; To provide regular communication lines with members; To continually review & update technical programs; To assist in the research & investigation of potential new facilities; To engender more public awareness, interest & acceptance of the sport of track & field
Member of: International Association of Athletics Federations
Affiliation(s): International Amateur Athletic Federation
Staff Member(s): 20
Membership: *Committees:* Athlete's Council; Awards; Competition; Finance; Governance & Nominating; Human Resources; National Team; Officials; Rules
Activities: Offering national team events
Chief Officer(s):
Rob Guy, CEO
rguy@athletics.ca
Sylvie King, CFO
sylvie.king@athletics.ca
Mathieu Gentès, COO
mgentes@athletics.ca
Awards:
• Athletics Canada Annual Awards

Athletics Manitoba
#416, 145 Pacific Ave., Winnipeg MB R3B 2Z6
Tel: 204-925-5745
www.athleticsmanitoba.com
Overview: A medium-sized provincial organization founded in 1978 overseen by Athletics Canada
Mission: The governing and sanctioning organization for Track and field, Road Running and Cross Country in the province of Manitoba.
Member of: Athletics Canada; Sport Manitoba
Chief Officer(s):
Grant Mitchell, President
Chris Belof, Manager, Competition & Program
chris.belof@athleticsmanitoba.com
Awards:
• Athletics Manitoba Awards

Athletics New Brunswick (ANB) / Athlétisme du Nouveau-Brunswick
66 Belle Foret St., Dieppe NB E1A 8X9
Tel: 506-855-5003; *Fax:* 506-855-5011
anb@anb.ca
www.anb.ca
www.facebook.com/AthNB
twitter.com/AthNB
Overview: A medium-sized provincial organization founded in 1968 overseen by Athletics Canada
Mission: To act as the provincial sports organization for the sports of track & field & cross-country running
Member of: Athletics Canada
Membership: *Fees:* Schedule available
Activities: *Speaker Service:* Yes; *Rents Mailing List:* Yes
Chief Officer(s):
Bill MacMackin, President
Bill.MacMackin@anb.ca
Germain Landry, Vice-President
Germain.Landry@anb.ca
Gabriel (Gabe) LeBlanc, Director, Technical
anb@anb.ca
Camilla MacDougall, Registrar
Camilla.MacDougall@anb.ca

Athletics Nova Scotia
5516 Spring Garden Rd, 4th Fl., Halifax NS B3J 1G6
Tel: 902-425-5450; *Fax:* 902-425-5606
www.athleticsnovascotia.ca
Overview: A small provincial organization overseen by Athletics Canada
Mission: The Association is a non-profit, amateur sport governing body that develops, coordinates & promotes track & field, road running & cross-country running in Nova Scotia.
Member of: Athletics Canada
Staff Member(s): 2
Membership: *Fees:* $60 club athlete; $75 independent athelete; $30 independent coach; $20 Run Jump Throw athlete; *Member Profile:* Track & field clubs
Chief Officer(s):
Anitra Stevens, Executive Director
Joanthan Doucette, Manager, Coaching & Officiating
Awards:
• Athletics Nova Scotia Awards

Athletics Ontario
#211, 3 Concorde Gate, Toronto ON M3C 3N7
Tel: 416-426-7215; *Fax:* 416-426-7358
www.athleticsontario.ca
www.facebook.com/135196239850966
twitter.com/athleticsont
Previous Name: Ontario Track & Field Association
Overview: A medium-sized provincial organization founded in 1974 overseen by Athletics Canada
Mission: To promote & encourage participation via competitions from the grass roots level through to the very highest level of proficiency; To assist coaches, officials & executives in fulfilling their goals through courses, conferences & clinics; to provide regular communication lines with members; To continually review & update technical programs; To assist in the research & investigation of potential new facilities; To engender more public awareness, interest, & acceptance of the sport of track & field
Member of: Athletics Canada
Staff Member(s): 8
Chief Officer(s):
John Craig, Managing Director
Roman Olszewski, Director, Technical Services
roman.otfa@cogeco.ca
Anthony Biggar, Manager, Communications & Public Relations
anthonybiggar@athleticsontario.ca
Publications:
• Athletics Magazine
Type: Magazine; *Accepts Advertising*; *Editor:* Cecil Smith; Hazel North
Profile: Articles, event highlights, conference information, & athlete profiles

Athletics PEI
PO Box 302, 40 Enman Cres., Charlottetown PE C1A 7K7
www.athleticspei.ca
Overview: A small provincial organization
Member of: Athletics Canada

Athletics Yukon
4061 - 4th Ave., Whitehorse YT Y1A 1H1
athleticsyukon@gmail.com
www.athleticsyukon.ca
www.facebook.com/pages/Athletics-Yukon/149557131815078
Overview: A small provincial organization overseen by Athletics Canada
Mission: To promote & encourage athletics as a life-long pursuit
Member of: Athletics Canada; Sport Yukon
Affiliation(s): Boreal Adventure Running Association; Mount Lorne Mis-Adventure Race; Run Dawson
Membership: *Fees:* $15 youth & senior; $30 regular; $60 family
Activities: Administering the sports of: Road Racing; Cross Country Running; Track & Field; Snowshoeing; & Race Walking
Chief Officer(s):
Ben Yu Schott, President

Athlétisme Canada *See* Athletics Canada

Athlétisme du Nouveau-Brunswick *See* Athletics New Brunswick

Athmajothi Tamils Association
#101, 7125 rue Waverly, Montréal QC H2S 3J1
Tel: 514-271-9731
Overview: A small local organization

Atikokan & District Association for the Developmental Services *See* Community Living Atikokan

Atikokan Chamber of Commerce
PO Box 997, 214 Main St. West, Atikokan ON P0T 1C0
Tel: 807-597-1599; *Fax:* 807-597-2726
Toll-Free: 888-334-2332
info@atikokanchamber.com
www.atikokanchamber.com
Overview: A small local charitable organization founded in 1952
Mission: To fairly represent the business & community concerns of Atikokan; To provide educational services to the business community & interested public
Member of: Sunset Country Travel Association; Northwestern Ontario Associated Chambers of Commerce
Affiliation(s): Canadian Chamber of Commerce
Finances: *Annual Operating Budget:* Less than $50,000; *Funding Sources:* Membership dues
Staff Member(s): 1; 20 volunteer(s)
Membership: 47; *Fees:* $30 individual; $80-$390 business; $80 non-profit; *Committees:* Social; Retail; Tourism; Membership; Special Events
Activities: Organizing events, such as annual general meeting, business awards, contests with Atikokan Auto, & Home & Leisure Show; *Awareness Events:* Small Business Week; *Speaker Service:* Yes; *Rents Mailing List:* Yes
Chief Officer(s):
Ange Sponchia, General Manager

Atikokan Native Friendship Centre (ANFC)
PO Box 1510, #307, 309 Main St., Atikokan ON P0T 1C0
Tel: 807-597-1213; *Fax:* 807-597-1473
atikokaninfo.com/business/atikokan-native-friendship-centre
Overview: A small local charitable organization founded in 1983
Mission: To serve as a meeting place for urban, Aboriginal people and also community members regardless of nationality; To provide an Aboriginal Family Support program for families with children up to 6 years old (includes parent relief/ mom/dads & tots, prenatal and postnatal support); To provide health outreach services, healing & wellness services, family violence initiatives, crisis intervention services, seniors care support services, cultural events, educational assistance, food bank, resource library, community support &d assistance for newcomers & community referral services.
Member of: Ontario Federation of Indian Friendship Centres
Finances: *Funding Sources:* Heritage Canada
Membership: 1-99
Activities: Drop in Centre; clothing depot; Ashandiwin Food Bank; arts & crafts; recreation programs; referrals; family intervention; support services; job search skills; dabber bingo; *Library:* Open to public
Chief Officer(s):
Sarah Laurich, Executive Director
sarahlaurich@gmail.com

Atkinson Charitable Foundation
#702, 1 Yonge St., Toronto ON M5E 1E5
Tel: 416-368-5152; *Fax:* 416-865-3619
info@atkinsonfoundation.ca
www.atkinsonfoundation.ca
www.facebook.com/AtkinsonFoundation
twitter.com/AtkinsonCF
Overview: A small provincial charitable organization founded in 1942
Mission: To advance social & economic justice in Ontario; To mobilize people across various disciplines & interests; To collaborate with other shareholders to achieve an equitable society
Activities: Advocating for policies & practices that address social issues
Chief Officer(s):
Colette Murphy, Executive Director
Ausma Malik, Director, Social Engagement
Jenn Miller, Director, Social Investment
Patricia Thompson, Director, Social Impact
Farah Malik, Manager, Finance
Phillip Roh, Administrative Coordinator

Atlantic Alliance of Family Resource Centres *See* Valley Family Resource Centre Inc.

The Atlantic Alliance of Family Resource Centres
#1, 110 Richmond St, Woodstock NB E7M 2N9
Tel: 506-325-2299; *Fax:* 506-328-8896
anna.hayes@frc-crf.com
Overview: A medium-sized local organization
Member of: Canadian Association of Family Resource Programs (FRP Canada)
Chief Officer(s):
Anna-Marie Hayes, Contact

Atlantic Association of Applied Economists (AAAE)
1701 Hollis St., 13th Fl., Halifax NS B3J 3M8
Tel: 902-420-4601
www.cabe.ca/aaae
Overview: A medium-sized provincial organization overseen by Canadian Association for Business Economics
Mission: To provide opportunities for professional development & networking with other economists & analysts
Member of: Canadian Association for Business Economics
Chief Officer(s):
Sarah Miller, President, 902-420-4639
Tara Ainsworth, Treasurer, 902-420-4601

Atlantic Association of CBDCs
PO Box 40, 54 Loggie St., Mulgrave NS B0E 2G0
Tel: 902-747-2232; *Fax:* 902-747-2019
info@cbdc.ca
www.cbdc.nf.ca
www.youtube.com/user/AtlanticCBDCs
www.facebook.com/AACBDC
twitter.com/CBDCatlantic
Previous Name: Provincial Association of CBDCs
Overview: A small provincial organization
Mission: To oversee Community Business Development Corporations in Atlantic Canada
Affiliation(s): Pan Canadian Community Futures Network
Finances: *Funding Sources:* Atlantic Canada Opportunities Agency
Chief Officer(s):
Roseanne Leonard, Managing Director
roseanne.leonard@cbdc.ca

Atlantic Association of Community Business Development Corporations
PO Box 40, 54 Loggie St., Mulgrave NS B0E 2G0
Tel: 902-747-2232; *Fax:* 902-747-2019
Toll-Free: 888-303-2232
info@cbdc.ca
www.cbdc.ca
www.facebook.com/AACBDC
twitter.com/CBDCatlantic
www.youtube.com/user/AtlanticCBDCs
Also Known As: Atlantic Association of CBDCs
Overview: A medium-sized local organization
Mission: To promote the development of small business & job creation
Affiliation(s): Pan Canadian Community Futures Network
Membership: 41
Chief Officer(s):
Basil Ryan, Chief Operating Officer

Atlantic Association of Prosthetists & Orthotists
c/o Orthotics Prosthetics Canada, #202, 300 March Rd., Ottawa ON K2K 2E2
Overview: A small provincial organization overseen by Orthotics Prosthetics Canada
Mission: To promote quality patient care & a high standard of professionalism in the prosthetic & orthotic profession in the Atlantic region
Membership: *Member Profile:* Certified prosthetic & orthotic practitioners & registered technicians in the Atlantic provinces; Allied health professionals & suppliers; Students in the prosthetic & orthotic field; Retired individuals
Activities: Encouraging continuing education
Chief Officer(s):
Elizabeth Harris, President

Atlantic Building Supply Dealers Association (ABSDA)
70 Englehart St., Dieppe NB E1A 8H3
Tel: 506-858-0700; *Fax:* 506-859-0064
www.absda.ca
twitter.com/absdadealers
Previous Name: Maritime Lumber Dealers Association
Overview: A medium-sized local organization founded in 1955
Mission: To keep membership informed of new trends & developments in the industry; to provide a forum to discuss mutual problems & ideas; to provide continuing education programs for members
Staff Member(s): 3
Membership: 625; *Member Profile:* Properly established lumber & building materials retailers
Activities: *Library:*
Chief Officer(s):
Don Sherwood, President
sherwood@absda.ca
Brian Warr, Chair

Atlantic Canada Centre for Environmental Science (ACCES)
Saint Mary's University, 923 Robie St., Halifax NS B3H 3C3
Tel: 902-496-8234; *Fax:* 902-420-5261
www.smu.ca
Overview: A medium-sized local organization founded in 1991
Mission: To foster interdisciplinary research related to the environment
Membership: *Member Profile:* Saint Mary's University faculty members; Professionals interested in environmental science

Atlantic Canada Cruise Association (ACCA)
PO Box 1, Chester Basin NS B0J 1K0
Tel: 902-273-3330; *Fax:* 902-273-3331
info@atlanticcanadacruise.com
www.atlanticcanadacruise.com
Overview: A medium-sized provincial organization
Mission: To have Atlantic Canada as a preferred cruise destination in North America and lead the growth and development of the cruise industry in Atlantic Canada.
Membership: 10 ports + 14 organizations
Chief Officer(s):
Corryn Morrissey, Chair
cmorrissey@chaipei.com

Atlantic Canada Fish Farmers Association (ACFFA)
226 Limekiln Rd., Letang NB E5C 2A8
Tel: 506-755-3526; *Fax:* 506-755-6237
info@atlanticfishfarmers.com
atlanticfishfarmers.com
www.facebook.com/150506105026651
twitter.com/AtlFishFarmers
www.youtube.com/user/acffavideos
Previous Name: New Brunswick Salmon Growers Association
Overview: A small provincial organization founded in 1987
Mission: To act as the voice of Atlantic Canada's salmon farming industry; To implement fish health initiatives to produce high-quality finfish
Affiliation(s): Atlantic Canada Aquaculture Industry Research & Development Network (ACAIRDN)
Staff Member(s): 7
Membership: 25; *Fees:* Schedule available; *Member Profile:* Salmon farming producers in New Brunswick; Companies & organizations that support the industry
Activities: Liaising with governments; Promoting fish health & welfare & social responsibility; Developing training programs; Fostering a positive image for finfish aquaculture in Atlantic Canada; Participating in management & research initiatives with related organizations, such as the Aquaculture Association of Canada, the National Fish Health Working Group, the Bay of Fundy Marine Resource Planning, & the Musquash Marine Protected Area Steering Committee
Chief Officer(s):
Pamela Parker, Executive Director
Tobi Taylor, Manager, Operations
Betty House, Coordinator, Research & Development
Jim Hanley, Manager, Wharf

Atlantic Canada Pipe Band Association (ACPBA)
c/o Tara Wilcox, Cox & Palmer, Purdy's Wharf, Tower 1, #1100, 1959 Upperwater St., Halifax NS B3J 3N2
www.acpba.ca
www.facebook.com/208959232515981
twitter.com/acpba
Overview: A small local charitable organization founded in 1965
Finances: *Annual Operating Budget:* Less than $50,000
Membership: 250; *Committees:* Music & Grading
Chief Officer(s):
Tara Wilcox, Secretary

Atlantic Canada Trail Riding Association (ACTRA)
c/o Pat Rideout, 3540 Rte. 890, Hillgrove NB E4Z 5W6
www.ac-tra.ca
Overview: A small local organization founded in 1980 overseen by Canadian Long Distance Riding Association
Mission: To promote safe horsemanship & friendly competition in the long distance trail competition
Member of: Canadian Long Distance Riding Association
Membership: *Fees:* $17.50
Awards:
• ACTRA Award
• Mileage Awards
Publications:
• ACTRA [Atlantic Canada Trail Riding Association] Newsletter
Type: Newsletter; *Frequency:* 5 pa.

Atlantic Canada Water & Wastewater Association (ACWWA)
131 Shrewsbury Rd., Dartmouth NS B2V 2R6
Tel: 902-434-6002; *Fax:* 902-435-7796
contact@acwwa.ca
www.acwwa.ca
twitter.com/ACWWA
Overview: A medium-sized local organization
Mission: To improve drinking water in Atlantic Canada
Member of: American Water Works Association (AWWA); Water Environment Federation (WEF)
Membership: 430+; *Fees:* Schedule available; *Member Profile:* Water professionals in Atlantic Canada, from the industries of provision, contracting, utility management, operations, system design, consulting & academia; *Committees:* Scholarship; Conference; Operator Involvement; Education; Government Affairs; Magazine; Young Professionals; Membership; Volunteer; Media; Website; Technical Papers; Water For People; Cross Connection Control; Government Relations
Activities: Providing training & information about the water & wastewater industry to members; Enhancing government relations; Offering networking opportunities
Chief Officer(s):
Clara Shea, Executive Director
Kendall Mason, Director, Communication
Awards:
• Silent Hero Award
Awarded to recognize outstanding contributions of water & wastewater operations in each Atlantic Canadian provinces
• Young Professional of the Year Award
Presented to honour a young professional member of the ACWWA for outstanding contributions to the water & wastewater industry
• Volunteer Recognition Award
Awarded to honour outstanding contributions from a volunteer or group of volunteers
• Project of the Year - Engineering Award/Environmental Award
Awarded to a municipality or utility to recognize outstanding projects in Atlantic Canada that show innovation & high standards of technology in water or wastewater projects
• Fuller Award
Awarded to honour a member of ACWWA for outstanding service in the water supply field
• Ira P. MacNab Award
Awarded to honour notable service to the water industry
• Bedell Award
Awarded to acknowledge exceptional service to a Water Environmnent Federation (WEF) member association
Meetings/Conferences:
• Atlantic Canada Water & Wastewater Association 2018 71st

Annual Conference, September, 2018, Sydney, NS
Scope: Provincial
Description: A trade show, plus educational sessions & networking opportunities for Atlantic Canada's water professionals
Publications:
• AWWA Wastewater Operator Field Guide
Type: Booklet; *Price:* $65
Profile: Information used daily by wastewater system operators
• AWWA Water Operator Field Guide
Type: Booklet; *Price:* $65
Profile: Information for water treatment plant operators & water distribution operators
• Go with the Flow [a publication of the Atlantic Canada Water & Wastewater Association]
Type: Magazine; *Accepts Advertising*
• Operator Certification Study Guide [a publication of the Atlantic Canada Water & Wastewater Association]
Type: Booklet; *Price:* $85
Profile: Information for water treatment & water distribution operators
• Wastewater Operator Certification Study Guide
Type: Booklet; *Price:* $85
Profile: Sample questions & answer for wastewater operator certification exams

Atlantic Canadian Anti-Sealing Coalition
contact@antisealingcoalition.ca
www.antisealingcoalition.ca
www.facebook.com/260618610812
twitter.com/GreySealHugger
Overview: A medium-sized provincial organization
Mission: The Atlantic Canadian Anti-Sealing Coalition is a collection of individuals and groups from across the Atlantic Region working to end the commercial seal hunt by peaceful and legal means.
Membership: 285 individual; 10 organizations

Atlantic Canadian Organic Regional Network (ACORN) / Réseau régional du l'industrie biologique du Canada atlantique
PO Box 6343, 131 B Main St., Sackville NB E4L 1G6
Toll-Free: 866-322-2676
admin@acornorganic.org
www.acornorganic.org
www.facebook.com/acornorganic
twitter.com/acornorganic
www.instagram.com/acornorganic
Overview: A medium-sized provincial organization founded in 2000
Mission: To act as the voice of organics in Atlantic Canada
Member of: Volunteer Canada; Organic Materials Review Institute
Affiliation(s): Canadian Organic Growers
Staff Member(s): 1; 100 volunteer(s)
Membership: 300; *Fees:* $50 individual; $100 business; $250 sustaining
Chief Officer(s):
Janice Melanson, Executive Director

Atlantic Chamber of Commerce (ACC) / Chambre de commerce de l'Atlantique
PO Box 2291, Windsor NS B0N 2T0
Tel: 902-698-0265; *Fax:* 902-678-7420
www.apcc.ca
www.facebook.com/122204667965417
Previous Name: Atlantic Provinces Chambers of Commerce
Overview: A large provincial organization founded in 1896
Mission: To create an environment in which Chambers & Boards of Trade in Atlantic Canada can achieve their full potential & represent the business community in a unified & effective manner
Staff Member(s): 4
Membership: 300; *Member Profile:* New Brunswick Chamber of Commerce; Nova Scotia Chamber of Commerce; Newfoundland & Labrador Chamber of Commerce; PEI Chamber of Commerce; *Committees:* Provincial Division Advisory
Chief Officer(s):
Sheri Somerville, Chief Executive Officer, 506-654-6863
sheri@atlanticchamber.ca
Tracy Beaver, Manager
tracy@atlanticchamber.ca
   Fredericton
   270 Rookwood Ave., Fredericton NB E3B 2M2
   Tel: 902-698-0265

   Moncton
   910 Main St., Moncton NB E1C 1G6
   Tel: 506-857-3980

Atlantic Collegiate Athletic Association (ACAA) / Association Atlantique du Sport Collegial (AASC)
PO Box 95, Hubbards NS B0J 1T0
Tel: 902-857-0592
acaa@eastlink.ca
acaa.ca
Previous Name: Nova Scotia College Conference
Overview: A small provincial organization founded in 1967
Mission: To govern intercollegiate sports in the Atlantic provinces
Member of: Canadian Collegiate Athletic Association
Affiliation(s): Pacific Western Athletic Association; Alberta Colleges Athletic Conference; Réseau du sport étudiant du Québec; Ontario Colleges Athletic Association
Activities: Soccer; volleyball; badminton; basketball; golf; cross country
Chief Officer(s):
Ron O'Flaherty, Chair

Atlantic Community Newspapers Association *See* Newspapers Atlantic

Atlantic Concrete Association (ACA) / Association béton Atlantique (ABA)
#301, 3845 Joseph Howe Dr., Halifax NS B3L 4H9
Tel: 902-443-4456; *Fax:* 902-404-8074
info@atlanticconcrete.ca
www.atlanticconcrete.ca
www.facebook.com/atlanticconcrete
twitter.com/atlanticconc
Previous Name: Atlantic Provinces Ready-Mixed Concrete Association
Overview: A medium-sized provincial organization founded in 1966 overseen by Canadian Ready Mixed Concrete Association
Mission: To promote the use of ready-mixed concrete while providing leadership to the industry through the exchange of ideas & information
Member of: Canadian Ready Mixed Concrete Association; Road Builders Association of New Brunswick; Canadian Poured Concrete Wall Association; Construction Associations in NB, NS, & PEI
Affiliation(s): Canadian Portland Cement Association
Finances: *Funding Sources:* Membership fees
Staff Member(s): 1
Membership: *Fees:* Schedule available; *Member Profile:* Producers & Associates; *Committees:* Marketing; Technical & Plant Certification; Membership; Executive; Quality & Professional Affairs; Environment; Safety; Annual Golf Tournament
Chief Officer(s):
Mary Macaulay, Executive Director
Awards:
• Atlantic Concrete Association Memorial Scholarship
Meetings/Conferences:
• Atlantic Concrete Association 2018 General Meeting, February, 2018, Play Del Carmen

Atlantic Conference of Independent Schools (ACIS)
708 Main St., Wolfville NS B4P 1G4
Tel: 902-542-2237
gmitchell@landmarkeast.org
Overview: A small local organization overseen by Canadian Accredited Independent Schools
Mission: To promote the role of independent school education in the Maritime provinces; To coordinate educational, sporting & other activities of mutual interest to member schools
Affiliation(s): Canadian Association of Independent Schools

Atlantic Convenience Store Association (ACSA)
#B, 100 Ilsley Ave., Dartmouth NB B3B 1L3
Tel: 902-880-9733
theacsa.ca
Overview: A medium-sized provincial organization founded in 2008 overseen by Canadian Convenience Store Association
Mission: To represent convenience store retailers in the Atlantic provinces
Affiliation(s): Canadian Convenience Stores Association; Western Convenience Stores Association; Association Québécoise des dépanneurs en alimentation; Ontario Convenience Stores Association
Finances: *Funding Sources:* Membership fees
Membership: *Member Profile:* Major convenience store companies; independent owners; food retailers; suppliers & wholesalers; oil companies; gasoline & automotive product vendors
Chief Officer(s):
Mike Hammoud, President
hammoud@conveniencestores.ca

Atlantic Council of Canada (ACC) / Conseil atlantique du Canada (CAC)
#102, 165 University Ave., Toronto ON M5H 3B8
Tel: 416-979-1875; *Fax:* 416-979-0825
info@atlantic-council.ca
www.atlantic-council.ca
www.linkedin.com/company/atlantic-council-of-canada
www.facebook.com/TheAtlanticCouncilOfCanada
twitter.com/NATOCanada
www.youtube.com/user/TheAtlanticCouncil
Previous Name: Canadian Atlantic Coordinating Committee
Overview: A medium-sized international charitable organization founded in 1966
Mission: To inform Canadians of the purpose & benefits of Canada's membership in the Atlantic Alliance & NATO.
Affiliation(s): NATO; Atlantic Treaty Association - Paris, France
Membership: *Fees:* $125 2 people; $75 regular; $50 young professionals/senior; $25 student
Activities: *Internships:* Yes; *Speaker Service:* Yes
Chief Officer(s):
Julie Lindhout, President
Hugh Segal, Chair

Atlantic Dairy Council (ADC)
PO Box 9410, Stn. A, #700, 6009 Quinpool Rd., Halifax NS B3K 5S3
Tel: 902-425-2445; *Fax:* 902-425-2441
info@adcrecycles.com
www.adcrecycles.com
Overview: A medium-sized local organization
Mission: To maintain good relations among those engaged in dairy processing & distribution industries; to provide opportunities for industry training courses; & to enable united action on any matter concerning the welfare of the dairy trade 15 volunteer(s)
Membership: 80
Chief Officer(s):
John K. Sutherland, Executive Secretary

The Atlantic District of The Wesleyan Church
1830 Mountain Rd., Moncton NB E1G 1A9
Tel: 506-383-8326; *Fax:* 506-383-8333
office@atlanticdistrict.com
www.atlanticdistrict.com
Previous Name: The Wesleyan Church of Canada - Atlantic District
Overview: A medium-sized local organization founded in 1966
Chief Officer(s):
HC Wilson, District Superintendent
wilsonhc@twccanada.ca

Atlantic Division, CanoeKayak Canada (ADCKC)
PO Box 295, 34 Boathouse Lane, Dartmouth NS B2Y 3Y3
Tel: 902-425-5450; *Fax:* 902-425-5606
www.adckc.ca
www.facebook.com/196999566862
twitter.com/ADCKC
instagram.com/adckc/
Previous Name: CanoeKayak Canada - Atlantic Division
Overview: A small local organization overseen by CanoeKayak Canada
Member of: CanoeKayak Canada; Sport Nova Scotia
Chief Officer(s):
Robin Thomson, General Manager
robin@adckc.ca
Jeff Houser, Regional Coach
regionalcoach@adckc.ca

Atlantic Episcopal Assembly (AEA) / Assemblée des évêques de l'Atlantique
3 Oakley Ave., Halifax NS B3M 3G6
Tel: 902-443-9325
Overview: A small local organization founded in 1967 overseen by Canadian Conference of Catholic Bishops
Finances: *Annual Operating Budget:* Less than $50,000
Membership: 12; *Member Profile:* Bishops from Prince Edwards Island, Nova Scotia, New Brunswick & Newfoundland & Labrador; *Committees:* Executive; Social Affairs
Chief Officer(s):
Gérald LeBlanc, Secretary-Treasurer
geraldleblanc2@gmail.com

Canadian Associations / Atlantic Federation of Musicians, Local 571 (AFM, Local 571)

Anthony Mancini, President

Atlantic Federation of Musicians, Local 571 (AFM, Local 571)
16 Balcomes Dr., Halifax NS B3N 1H9
Tel: 902-479-3200; *Fax:* 902-479-1312
Toll-Free: 866-240-4809
admin@cfm571.ca
www.atlanticmusicians.org
Overview: A small provincial organization founded in 1953
Affiliation(s): American Federation of Musicians of the United States & Canada
Finances: *Funding Sources:* Membership fees
Staff Member(s): 2
Membership: 500; *Fees:* $155 initiation; $175 annually; *Member Profile:* Professional musicians united through the American Federation of Musicians
Chief Officer(s):
Tom Roach, President
troach@ns.sympatico.ca
Varun Vyas, Secretary-Treasurer
varun@cfm571.ca

The Atlantic Film Festival Association (AFFA)
PO Box 36139, Halifax NS B3J 3S9
Tel: 902-422-3456; *Fax:* 902-422-4006
festival@atlanticfilm.com
www.atlanticfilm.com
Previous Name: ScreenScene-Film & Television for Young People
Overview: A medium-sized international charitable organization founded in 1981
Mission: To promote & to build a strong film industry in Atlantic Canada
Member of: Atlantic Film Festival Association
Staff Member(s): 10
Activities: A 10-day celebration of film & video from around the world, Atlantic Film Festival, Sept.; Strategic Partners, an international co-production market focusing on film & TV and early stage projects, Sept.; The ViewFinders: International Film Festival for Youth, a 5-day event in the spring; AlFresco filmFesto, the AFFA's outdoor summer film series, held on the Halifax waterfront.
Chief Officer(s):
Wayne Carter, Executive Director

Atlantic Filmmakers Cooperative (AFCOOP)
PO Box 2043, Stn. M, Halifax NS B3J 2Z1
Tel: 902-405-4474; *Fax:* 902-405-4485
membership@afcoop.ca
afcoop.ca
www.facebook.com/117025119810
twitter.com/afcoop
www.youtube.com/afcoophalifax
Overview: A small local organization founded in 1973
Mission: To provide a space where media artists can meet & produce films; to give members access to production equipment & facilities
Member of: Cooperative Associations of Nova Scotia
Affiliation(s): Independent Film & Video Alliance; Academy of Canadian Cinema & TV; Linda Joy Busby Media Arts Foundation; Atlantic Independent Media; Atlantic Film Festival
Finances: *Funding Sources:* Canada Council; NS Dept. of Tourism, Culture & Heritage; NFB; NS Film Development Corp.
Staff Member(s): 3
Membership: *Fees:* $70 full; $40 associate; $180 production; *Member Profile:* Participation in making of film; taken film-related courses; demonstrate interest in co-op & function in community
Activities: Super 8, super 16 & 35mm film class; equipment workshop; animation classes; self-made films; five, three, one minute film program; *Library:* AFCOOP Video & Film Library; Open to public
Chief Officer(s):
Martha Cooley, Executive Director
director@afcoop.ca

Atlantic Fishing Industry Alliance
#10, 3045 Robie St., Halifax NS B3K 4P6
Tel: 902-446-4477
Overview: A medium-sized provincial organization founded in 1999
Mission: To represent organizations in the harvesting, processing and marketing sectors of the commercial fishing industry in the Maritime Provinces.

Atlantic Floor Covering Association (AFA)
#2, 1246 Rocky Lake Dr., Waverley NS B2R 1R5

Tel: 902-861-1889; *Fax:* 902-861-1910
afa@eastlink.ca
atlanticfloorcovering.ca
Overview: A small provincial organization founded in 1987
Member of: National Floorcovering Association
9 volunteer(s)
Membership: 65; *Fees:* $200-$400 dealer/retailer; $250 distributor/manufacturer; $75 installer
Chief Officer(s):
Cathy Cochrane, Executive Director
Darryl Johnson, President
Awards:
• Educational Grants "Floor Knowledge"

Atlantic Food & Beverage Processors Association / Association de l'industrie alimentaire de l'Atlantique
36 Albert St., Moncton NB E1C 1A9
Tel: 506-857-4255
info@atlanticfood.ca
www.atlanticfood.ca
Previous Name: New Brunswick Food & Beverage Processors Association
Overview: A medium-sized national organization founded in 1999
Mission: To actively support the food processors in Atlantic Canada in their efforts to operate efficiently & profitably
Membership: 400; *Fees:* Free
Activities: Regulator training programs; Industry conferences; Leading export trade missions
Chief Officer(s):
Greg Fash, Executive Director
Lee Turner, Board President

Atlantic Halfway House Association (AHHA) / Association de maison de transition atlantique (AMTA)
c/o Stacey Dort, 3170 Romans Ave., Halifax NS B3L 3W9
halfwayhouses.ca/en/region/ahha
Overview: A small provincial organization overseen by Regional Halfway House Association
Mission: To help offenders reintegrate themselves into society
Member of: Regional Halfway House Association

Atlantic Health Promotion Research Centre (AHPRC)
Dalhousie University, PO Box 15000, 1318 Robie St., Halifax NS B3H 4R2
Tel: 902-494-2240; *Fax:* 902-494-3594
ahprc@dal.ca
www.ahprc.dal.ca
Overview: A medium-sized local organization founded in 1993
Affiliation(s): Canadian Consortium for Health Promotion Research
Finances: *Funding Sources:* Dalhousie University; Health Canada; Nova Scotia Department of Health & Wellness; Health foundations
Chief Officer(s):
Lois Jackson, Scientific Director
lois.jackson@dal.ca

Atlantic Institute for Market Studies (AIMS)
Park West Centre, #204, 287 Lacewood Dr., Halifax NS B3M 3Y7
Tel: 902-429-1143
aims@aims.ca
www.aims.ca
www.facebook.com/AtlanticInstituteforMarketStudies
twitter.com/AIMST
www.youtube.com/user/AtlanticInstMarkStud
Overview: A small local charitable organization founded in 1994
Mission: To conduct research regarding economic & social issues that are relevant to Canadians.
Staff Member(s): 4
Activities: Promotes practical research in areas of employment insurance, social welfare & the impact of free trade on the region; *Speaker Service:* Yes
Chief Officer(s):
Marco Navarro-Genie, President & CEO
marco.navarro-genie@aims.ca

The Atlantic Jewish Council
#508, 5670 Spring Garden Rd., Halifax NS B3J 1H6
Tel: 902-422-7491; *Fax:* 902-425-3722
atlanticjewishcouncil@theajc.ns.ca
theajc.ns.ca
www.facebook.com/AtlanticJewishCouncil
www.flickr.com/photos/atlanticjewishcouncil
Overview: A medium-sized local organization

Member of: The Centre for Israel & Jewish Affairs
Affiliation(s): Jewish Federations of Canada - UIA
Staff Member(s): 8
Chief Officer(s):
Jon M. Goldberg, Executive Director, 902-422-7491 Ext. 222

Atlantic Marksmen Association
PO Box 181, Stn. Dartmouth Main, Dartmouth NS B2Y 3Y3
www.atlanticmarksmen.ca
Overview: A small local organization founded in 1954
Member of: Shooting Federation of Canada
Membership: 200; *Fees:* $200 senior, plus induction fee of $100; $30 juniors (18 & under)
Activities: Owns & operates two range facilities
Chief Officer(s):
Sean Hansen, President

Atlantic Mission Society (AMS)
joan@thechos.ca
pccweb.ca/ams
Overview: A medium-sized national organization founded in 1976 overseen by Presbyterian Church in Canada
Mission: To support missions with prayer, study & service
Member of: Presbyterian Church in Canada
Chief Officer(s):
Jennifer Whitfield, President
ajwhitfield@nl.rogers.com
Publications:
• The Presbyterian Message [a publication of the Atlantic Mission Society]
Type: Magazine

Atlantic Motion Picture Exhibitors Association
c/o Empire Theatres Ltd., 190 Chain Lake Dr., Halifax NS B3S 1C5
Tel: 902-876-4848
Overview: A small local organization
Member of: The Motion Picture Theatre Associations of Canada

Atlantic Pest Management Association (APMO)
51 Duke St., Bedford NS B4A 2Z2
Tel: 902-835-2304; *Fax:* 902-835-0953
pestworldapma.net/apma/
Overview: A small local organization
Member of: Canadian Pest Management Association
Chief Officer(s):
Don McCarthy, President
microkil@ns.sympatico.ca

Atlantic Planners Institute (API) / Institut des Urbanistes de l'atlantique (IVA)
35 Ascot Ct., Fredericton NB E3B 6C4
Tel: 506-455-7203; *Fax:* 506-455-1113
apiexecutivedirector@gmail.com
www.atlanticplanners.org
Overview: A medium-sized provincial organization overseen by Canadian Institute of Planners
Mission: To represent professional planners in New Brunswick, Prince Edward Island, Nova Scotia, Newfoundland & Labrador.
Affiliation(s): Canadian Institute of Planners
Finances: *Funding Sources:* Membership fees
Membership: *Fees:* $170; *Member Profile:* Professional planner in the four Atlantic Provinces of Canada; New Brunswick, Newfoundland and Labrador, Nova Scotia, and Prince Edward Island.; *Committees:* Membership; Professional Practice Review; Continuous Professional Learning
Chief Officer(s):
Jennifer Griffiths, Executive Director
Meetings/Conferences:
• Atlantic Planners Institute Conference 2018, October, 2018, Moncton, NB
Scope: Provincial
Description: Theme: "Planning in a New Environment"

Atlantic Provinces Art Gallery Association (APAGA) / Association des galeries d'art des provinces de l'Atlantique (AGAPA)
c/o Kevin Rice, Confederation Centre of the Arts, 145 Richmond St., Charlottetown NS C1A 1J1
apagaagapa.wordpress.com
Overview: A small provincial organization founded in 1975
Mission: To pursue & promote high standards of excellence in care & presentation of works of art in public art galleries in the Atlantic region; To encourage the closest possible cooperation between art galleries, museums & artists; To serve as an advisory body in matters of professional interest

Membership: 46 institutional; *Member Profile:* Open to art galleries in Atlantic region supported at least in part by public funds; registered as charitable organization (gallery or its umbrella organization); at least one full-time paid professionally qualified staff member
Chief Officer(s):
Kevin Rice, President
krice@confederationcentre.com
Awards:
• Lifetime Achievement Award

Atlantic Provinces Association of Landscape Architects (APALA)
PO Box 38051, Stn. Burnside, Dartmouth NS B3B 1X2
info@apala.ca
www.apala.ca
Overview: A medium-sized provincial organization overseen by Canadian Society of Landscape Architects
Mission: To promote, improve & advance the profession; to maintain standards of professional practice & conduct consistent with the need to serve & to protect the public interest; to support improvement &/or conservation of the natural, cultural, social & built environment
Member of: Canadian Society of Landscape Architects
Membership: 83; *Member Profile:* Individuals in the process of completing or having completed a program in landscape architecture & organizations involved in the landscape business
Chief Officer(s):
Angela Morin, Secretary-Treasurer
angela@sagehousedesign.ca
Daniel Glenn, President
dkg@glenngroup.ca

Atlantic Provinces Athletic Therapists Association (APATA) / Association des Therapeuets de Sport des Provinces Altantique (ATSPA)
c/o Memorial University, PO Box 4200, 2300 Elizabeth Ave., St. John's NL A1C 5S7
Tel: 709-737-3442
info@apata.ca
www.apata.ca
Overview: A small provincial organization
Member of: Canadian Athletic Therapists Association
Membership: *Committees:* Ethics; Insurance Billing
Chief Officer(s):
Colin King, President
colin.king@acadiau.ca
Awards:
• Diane Webster Memorial Award

Atlantic Provinces Chambers of Commerce *See* Atlantic Chamber of Commerce

Atlantic Provinces Council on the Sciences; Atlantic Provinces Inter-University Committee on the Sciences *See* Science Atlantic

Atlantic Provinces Economic Council (APEC) / Conseil économique des provinces de l'Atlantique
#500, 5121 Sackville St., Halifax NS B3J 1K1
Tel: 902-422-6516; *Fax:* 902-429-6803
info@apec-econ.ca
www.apec-econ.ca
twitter.com/APECatlantic
Overview: A medium-sized provincial organization founded in 1954
Mission: To be the leading advocate for the economic development of the Atlantic region and accomplishes this by: monitoring and analysing current and emerging economic trends and policies; communicating the results of this analysis to its mbmers on a regular basis; consulting with a wide audience; dissminating its research and policy analysis to business, gov't, and the community at large; advocating the appropriate public and private sector policy responses.
Staff Member(s): 9
Membership: *Fees:* Schedule available
Activities: *Speaker Service:* Yes; *Library:* by appointment
Chief Officer(s):
Elizabeth Beale, President & CEO
elizabeth.beale@apec-econ.ca

Atlantic Provinces Education Foundation *See* Council of Atlantic Ministers of Education & Training

Atlantic Provinces Library Association (APLA)
c/o Kenneth C. Rowe Management Bldg., Dalhousie University, Stn. 15000, #4010, 6100 University Ave., Halifax NS B3H 4R2
contact@apla.ca
www.apla.ca
www.linkedin.com/groups/4224326/profile
twitter.com/APLAcontact
Previous Name: Maritime Library Association
Overview: A medium-sized provincial organization founded in 1918
Mission: To promote library & information service & workers throughout the Atlantic region; To represent & support the interests of persons who work in libraries in the Atlantic provinces; To cooperate with other library associations & similar organizations; To develop & offer effective continuing education programs
Membership: *Fees:* Schedule available; *Member Profile:* Students, individuals, & institutions engaged in library study or services in the provinces of New Brunswick, Nova Scotia, Prince Edward Island, & Newfoundland & Labrador; *Committees:* Advocacy; Communications & Public Relations; Grow a Library Fund
Activities: Establishing interest groups; Disseminating information to members; Holding an annual conference
Chief Officer(s):
Suzanne van den Hoogen, President, 902-867-4535
svandenh@stfx.ca
Awards:
• Carin Alma E. Somers Scholarship
Annual scholarship to assist a Canadian citizen who is an Atlantic Provinces resident needing financial assistance to undertake or complete a Library & Information Science degree; *Amount:* $2,000 *Contact:* Vice-President: Kathryn Rose, E-mail: kathrynr@mun.ca
• Memorial Trust
Financial assistance is available for study & research *Contact:* Heather Sanderson, Phone: 902-420-5541; E-mail: heather.sanderson@smu.ca
• First Timer's Conference Grant
Grants are allocated to members of APLA, residing in Atlantic Canada, to attend his or her first APLA annual conference *Contact:* Vice-President: Kathryn Rose, E-mail: kathrynr@mun.ca
• Merit Award
To honour an individual who has made an outstanding contribution to library services in the Atlantic Provinces
• General Activities Fund Grant
Provision of funds for projects that will further the aims of the APLA *Contact:* President: Suzanne van den Hoogen, Phone: 902-867-4535; E-mail: svandenh@stfx.ca
• Advocacy Award
Awarded to honour exemplary library promotion, advocacy & outreach; *Amount:* $500 *Contact:* Jocelyne Thompson, Phone: 506-458-7053; E-mail: jlt@unb.ca
Meetings/Conferences:
• Atlantic Provinces Library Association 2018 Annual Conference, 2018
Scope: Provincial
Description: An educational program to support the interests & concerns of the library community in the Atlantic provinces
Publications:
• APLA [Atlantic Provinces Library Association] Bulletin
Type: Journal; *Frequency:* Quarterly; *Accepts Advertising*; *Editor:* Alison Ambi & Patricia Langille; *ISSN:* 0001-2203
Profile: Happenings in all sectors of librarianship in the Atlantic provinces

Atlantic Provinces Linguistic Association (APLA) / Association de linguistique des provinces atlantiques (ALPA)
c/o Saint Mary's University, Dept. of Modern Languages & Classics, Halifax NS B3H 3C3
www.unb.ca/apla-alpa
Overview: A small provincial organization founded in 1977
Mission: To promote the study of languages & linguistics in Atlantic Canada
Finances: *Annual Operating Budget:* Less than $50,000; *Funding Sources:* Membership dues; national government
Membership: 7 institutional; *Fees:* $30 individual; $15 student; $50 institution
Chief Officer(s):
Raymond Mopoho, President
Egor Tsedryk, Treasurer
egor.tsedryk@smu.ca
Publications:
• Linguistica Atlantica
Editor: Prof. Catherine Borin
Profile: Annual academic journal

Atlantic Provinces Numismatic Association (APNA)
c/o Dartmouth Seniors' Service Centre, 45 Ochterloney St., Dartmouth NS B2Y 4M7
Overview: A medium-sized provincial organization founded in 1958
Member of: Royal Canadian Numismatic Association

Atlantic Provinces Ready-Mixed Concrete Association *See* Atlantic Concrete Association

Atlantic Provinces Special Education Authority / Commission d'enseignement spécial des provinces de l'Atlantique
5940 South St., Halifax NS B3H 1S6
Tel: 902-424-8500; *Fax:* 902-423-8700; *TTY:* 902-424-8500
apsea@apsea.ca
www.apsea.ca
Overview: A small provincial organization founded in 1975
Mission: To provide educational services to children & youth who are visually impaired & hard of hearing
Activities: *Library:* APSEA Library
Chief Officer(s):
Bertram Tulk, Superintendent
tulkb@apsea.ca
Publications:
• Seen and Heard [a publication of the Atlantic Provinces Special Education Authority]
Type: Newsletter
Profile: News & updates for members

Atlantic Provinces Trial Lawyers Association (APTLA)
PO Box 2618, Central RPO, Halifax NS B3J 3N5
Tel: 902-446-4446; *Fax:* 902-425-9552
Toll-Free: 866-314-4446
www.aptla.ca
Overview: A medium-sized provincial organization
Mission: The Atlantic Provinces Trial Lawyers Association is a plaintiff-oriented organization dedicated to obtaining legal redress for those who have suffered injury or injustice, and to preserving the rights of the injured to full and fair compensation.
Staff Member(s): 6
Membership: *Member Profile:* Trial lawyers
Chief Officer(s):
David Gauthier, President
dgg@gauthierlaw.ca
Elizabeth Ann (Libby) Kinghorne, Executive Director
libbykinghorne@aptla.ca
Meetings/Conferences:
• Atlantic Provinces Trial Lawyers Association Annual Plaintiff Practice Conference, November, 2018, Delta Halifax, Halifax, NS
Scope: Provincial

Atlantic Provinces Trucking Association (APTA)
#800, 105 Englehart St., Dieppe NB E1A 8K2
Tel: 506-855-2782; *Fax:* 506-853-7424
Toll-Free: 866-866-1679
www.apta.ca
www.linkedin.com/groups/Atlantic-Provinces-Trucking-Association-4811425
www.facebook.com/aptaTrucking
twitter.com/APTA_Trucking
Overview: A medium-sized provincial organization founded in 1950 overseen by Canadian Trucking Alliance
Mission: To promote an efficient, safe & environmentally sound trucking industry in Atlantic Canada
Staff Member(s): 4
Membership: 325+; *Fees:* Schedule available; *Member Profile:* Open to anyone having an interest in the trucking industry in Atlantic Canada, including common carriers, owner-operators & private fleets; *Committees:* Associated Trades Council; Safety Council; Charity; Human Resource & Education; Marine; Legislative; Future Leaders
Activities: Improving infrastructure; Establishing training programs; Holding an annual meeting; *Rents Mailing List:* Yes
Chief Officer(s):
Vicki McKibbon, Chair
Dave Miller, Vice Chair
Ruby Murphy-Collins, Treasurer
Awards:
• Safety to Motor Transporation Award
Sponsored by Laurentian General Insurance Company; presented to an individual actively involved in promoting road & safety in the trucking industry
• Service to Industry Award
Sponsored by Trailmobile Canada; awarded to the person who

Canadian Associations / Atlantic Publishers Marketing Association (APMA)

has made the greatest contribution to the industry in the past year
• Driver of the Year Award
Sponsored by Volvo GM Canada Heavy Truck Corporation; recognizes all-round distinction in driving, courtesy, safety & community activity
• Dispatcher of the Year Award
Sponsored by Volvo GM Canada Heavy Truck Corporation; recognizes all-round distinction in driving, courtesy, safety & community activity
• Professional Driver Coach Award
Sponsored by Volvo GM Canada Heavy Truck Corporation; recognizes all-round distinction in driving, courtesy, safety & community activity
Publications:
• Atlantic Provinces Trucking Association Annual Report
Type: Report

Atlantic Publisher Association *See* Atlantic Publishers Marketing Association

Atlantic Publishers Marketing Association (APMA)
1484 Carlton St., Halifax NS B3H 3B7
Tel: 902-420-0711; *Fax:* 902-423-4302
www.atlanticpublishers.ca
www.facebook.com/AtlanticBooksToday
twitter.com/abtmagazine
Previous Name: Atlantic Publisher Association
Overview: A medium-sized provincial organization founded in 1990 overseen by Association of Canadian Publishers
Mission: To promote the growth & development of Canadian-owned publishing houses based in Atlantic Canada; To provide a common platform for publishers & individuals involved in Atlantic Canada's publishing industry to share ideas & information; To represent members to all levels of government; To liaison with associations & organizations to further the interests of the Canadian publishing industry; To promote the sale of publications by publishers
Member of: Access Copyright
Affiliation(s): Association of Canadian Publishers
Finances: *Annual Operating Budget:* $250,000-$500,000; *Funding Sources:* Government grants; Sales
Staff Member(s): 5
Membership: 35; *Fees:* Schedule available; *Member Profile:* Publishers from Atlantic Canada; *Committees:* Reading Guides; Atlantic Books Today; Chapters; Professional Development; Education; Digital
Activities: Publishing catalogues three times a year; Publishing Atlantic Books Today; Publishing seasonal gift guides two times a year; Advocating for Atlantic publishers in all four Atlantic provinces; Organizing professional development sessions; *Internships:* Yes
Chief Officer(s):
Carolyn Guy, Executive Director
cguy@atlanticpublishers.ca
Chris Benjamin, Managing Editor
editorial@atlanticpublishers.ca
Meetings/Conferences:
• Atlantic Publishers Marketing Association 2018 Annual General Meeting, 2018
Scope: Provincial
Publications:
• Atlantic Books Today
Type: Magazine; *Frequency:* 3 pa; *Accepts Advertising; Editor:* Chris Benjamin; *Price:* Free
Profile: An information source about books written & published in Atlantic Canada

Atlantic Region Aboriginal Lands Association
c/o Joe Sabattis, 77 French Village Rd., Kingsclear NB E3E 1K3
Tel: 506-363-3028
Overview: A small provincial organization founded in 2000 overseen by National Aboriginal Lands Managers Association
Staff Member(s): 1
Chief Officer(s):
Joe Sabattis, Chair
joesabattis@kingsclear.ca

Atlantic Salmon Federation (ASF) / Fédération du saumon atlantique
15 Rankin Mill Rd., Chamcook NB E5B 3A6
Tel: 506-529-4581
Toll-Free: 800-565-5666
membership@asf.ca
www.asf.ca
www.facebook.com/AtlanticSalmonFederation
twitter.com/SalmonNews
www.youtube.com/user/ASFatlanticsalmon
Overview: A large international charitable organization founded in 1948
Mission: To protect, conserve & restore wild Atlantic salmon & their ecosystems
Finances: *Annual Operating Budget:* Greater than $5 Million; *Funding Sources:* Membership
Staff Member(s): 35
Membership: 8,000; *Fees:* $50
Activities: Sharing knowledge with adults & children about wild Atlantic salmon; Conducting scientific research; *Internships:* Yes
Library: Atlantic Salmon Federation Library
Chief Officer(s):
Bill Taylor, President & Chief Executive Officer, 506-529-1034
btaylor@asf.ca
Geoff Giffin, Executive Director, Regional Programs, 506-650-8371
ggiffin@asf.ca
Jonathan Carr, Executive Director, Research & Environment, 506-529-1385
jcarr@asf.ca
Bill Mallory, Executive Vice-President & CFO, 506-529-1386
wmallory@asf.ca
Kirsten Rouse, Executive Director, Development, 506-529-1037
krouse@asf.ca
Martin Silverstone, Editor, Atlantic Salmon Journal, 514-457-8737
silverstonem@videotron.ca
Awards:
• Olin Fellowships
Presented annually to individuals who seek to improve their knowledge & skills while searching for solutions to challenges in Atlantic salmon biology, conservation, & management *Deadline:* March 15; *Amount:* $1,000-$3,000 *Contact:* Olin Fellowships, Atlantic Salmon Federation, PO Box 5200, St. Andrews, NB, E5B 3S8
• T.B. (Happy) Fraser Award
Presented annually to an individual who has made outstanding contributions to wild Atlantic salmon conservation at a regional or national level
• Lee Wulff Conservation Award
Presented annually to an individual who has made outstanding contributions to wild Atlantic salmon conservation
• Atlantic Salmon Federation Roll Of Honor
Presented annually to individuals who demonstrate outstanding commitment to wild Atlantic salmon conservation at the grass-roots level
• Affiliate of the Year Award
To recognize outstanding leadership in wild Atlantic salmon conservation within the Atlantic Salmon Federation's affiliate structure
Publications:
• Atlantic Salmon Federation Annual Report
Type: Yearbook; *Frequency:* Annually
Profile: Information about the federation's current projects that impact Atlantic salmon restoration plus future strategies
• Atlantic Salmon Federation Newsletter
Type: Newsletter
Profile: Updates on activities of the Federation
• Atlantic Salmon Journal
Type: Journal; *Accepts Advertising; Editor:* Martin Silverstone
Profile: Issues surrounding wild Atlantic salmon, including protection of the species
• Incidence & Impacts of Escaped Farmed Atlantic Salmon "Salmo Salar" in Nature
Type: Report; *Number of Pages:* 114; *Author:* Eva B. Thorstad et al.
Profile: The impacts of escaped farmed salmon
• Prince Edward Island Nitrate Report
Type: Report
Profile: The problem of nitrates entering streams & lakes
• State of the Population - Atlantic Salmon
Type: Report
Profile: A backgrounder on the Atlantic salmon population, featuring statistics, tables, & graphs

Atlantic Standardbred Breeders Association (ASBA)
PO Box 65, Port Hood NS B0E 2W0
Tel: 902-787-2869; *Fax:* 902-787-2214
the.maclennans@ns.sympatico.ca
www.atlanticsiresstakes.ca/contact.html
Overview: A small local organization
Mission: To promote the breeding of standardbred horses in the Atlantic provinces
Staff Member(s): 1; 10 volunteer(s)
Membership: 700 individual
Activities: Sponsoring the Atlantic Sires Stakes program
Chief Officer(s):
Lynne MacLennan, Executive Director/Manager

Atlantic Standardbred Breeders Association
c/o Lynne MacLennan, PO Box 65, Port Hood NS B0E 2W0
Tel: 902-787-2869; *Fax:* 902-787-2214
Overview: A small local organization
Mission: To promote the breeding of standardbred horses in the Atlantic provinces
Member of: Prince Edward Island Harness Racing Industry Association
Activities: Sponsoring the Atlantic Sires Stakes program
Chief Officer(s):
Lynne MacLennan, Contact
the.maclennans@ns.sympatico.ca

Atlantic Therapeutic Touch Network (ATTN) / Le réseau Toucher Thérapeutique de l'Atlantique
PO Box 24073, 21 MicMac Blvd., Dartmouth NS B3A 4T4
info@atlanticttn.com
www.atlanticttn.com
www.facebook.com/725635027565929
Overview: A small local organization founded in 1996
Chief Officer(s):
Judy Donovan-Whitty, Coordinator & Secretary

Atlantic Tire Dealers Association (ATDA)
93 Henderson St., Riverview NB E1B 4B6
Tel: 506-386-4306; *Fax:* 506-387-3987
www.atda.ca
Overview: A medium-sized local organization founded in 1960
Membership: 126
Chief Officer(s):
Frank Connor, Executive Director
fconnor@nbnet.nb.ca

Atlantic Turfgrass Research Foundation (ATRC)
Nova Scotia Agricultural College, 20 Rock Garden Rd., Truro NS B2N 5E3
Tel: 902-456-8571
Overview: A small provincial organization founded in 1992
Mission: To advance the turfgrass industry in Atlantic Canada
Activities: Researching turfgrass systems, in areas such as irrigation efficiency & water conservation & management
Chief Officer(s):
David Davey, President
Kevin Wentzell, Secretary

Atlantic Universities Athletic Association *See* Atlantic University Sport Association

Atlantic University Sport Association (AUS)
#403, 5657 Spring Garden Rd., Halifax NS B3J 3R4
Tel: 902-425-4235; *Fax:* 902-425-7825
www.atlanticuniversitysport.com
www.facebook.com/AtlanticUniversitySport
twitter.com/AUS_SUA
www.youtube.com/ATLuniversitysport
Also Known As: Atlantic University Sport
Previous Name: Atlantic Universities Athletic Association
Overview: A medium-sized local organization founded in 1974
Mission: To advance student athletes & university sport
Member of: Canadian Interuniversity Sport Association
Finances: *Funding Sources:* Memberships; Partners
Staff Member(s): 4
Membership: 11 institutional, 2,000 individuals; *Fees:* Schedule available; *Member Profile:* Institutions of higher learning
Chief Officer(s):
Philip M. Currie, Executive Director
pcurrie@atlanticuniversitysport.com

Atlantic Wildlife Institute
220 Cookville Rd., Cookville NB E4L 1Z8
Tel: 506-364-1902
www.atlanticwildlife.ca
www.facebook.com/AtlanticWildlife
twitter.com/atlanticwild
Overview: A small local organization
Chief Officer(s):
Barry Rothfuss, Co-Founder/Executive Director
Pam Novak, Co-Founder

Atlaz Sheltered Workshop *See* JVS of Greater Toronto

Atlin Board of Trade
PO Box 106, Atlin BC V0W 1A0
Tel: 250-651-7717
Overview: A small local organization founded in 1904
Mission: To promote & improve trade, commerce & the economic, civic & social welfare of the district
Affiliation(s): Yukon Chamber of Commerce; BC Chamber of Commerce
Finances: *Annual Operating Budget:* Less than $50,000; *Funding Sources:* Membership fees; donations
12 volunteer(s)
Membership: 40; *Fees:* $40
Chief Officer(s):
George Holman, President

ATM Industry Association Canada Region (ATMIA)
c/o Curt Binns, Executive Director, #218, 10520 Yonge St., Unit 35B, Richmond Hill ON L4C 3C7
Tel: 416-970-7954; *Fax:* 905-770-6230
www.atmia.com/regions/canada
www.linkedin.com/company/atm-industry-association
twitter.com/ATM_Industry
www.youtube.com/user/TheATMIA
Overview: A large international organization
Mission: To promote ATM convenience, growth, & usage worldwide; to protect the ATM industry's assets, interests, & reputation; to provide education, networking opportunities, & best practices
Membership: 5,000 worldwide; *Fees:* Schedule available
Activities: Consulting; training; networking; newsletters; conferences
Chief Officer(s):
Curt Binns, Executive Director, Canada
curt.binns@atmia.com
Publications:
• ATMIA [ATM Industry Association Canada] Canada E-Newsletter
Type: Newsletter

Attractions Ontario
#504, 344 Bloor St. West, Toronto ON M5S 3A7
Tel: 416-868-4386; *Fax:* 416-868-0386
Toll-Free: 877-557-3386
www.attractionsontario.ca
www.facebook.com/attractionsontario
twitter.com/AttractionsOnt
Overview: A small provincial organization founded in 1983
Mission: To develop effective marketing programs that increase attendance for members' attractions.
Staff Member(s): 5
Membership: *Fees:* Schedule available dependant on annual admissions or attendance; *Member Profile:* Public & privately owned attractions in such categories as amusement parks, historical sites, cultural activities, arts & entertainment & adventure
Chief Officer(s):
Tamara Russell, President
Troy Young, Executive Director
tyoung@attractionsontario.ca

Au bas de l'échelle (ABE)
#305, 6839A, rue Drolet, Montréal QC H2S 2T1
Tél: 514-270-7878; *Téléc:* 514-270-7726
abe@aubasdelechelle.ca
www.aubasdelechelle.ca
Aperçu: *Dimension:* petite; *Envergure:* provinciale; Organisme sans but lucratif; fondée en 1975
Mission: Défense des droits des non syndiqué(e)s; service d'information sur les lois du travail; information sur les droits des personnes non-syndiquées
Finances: *Budget de fonctionnement annuel:* $100,000-$250,000; *Fonds:* Gouvernement régional, provincial, fédéral, membres, dons etc.
Membre(s) du personnel: 6; 40 bénévole(s)
Membre: 200 individu; *Montant de la cotisation:* 5$ sans emploi; 12$ individu; *Critères d'admissibilite:* Travailleuses et travailleurs non-syndiqués
Activités: *Stagiaires:* Oui; *Service de conférenciers:* Oui

Au Coup de pouce Centre-Sud inc.
2338, rue Ontario est, Montréal QC H2K 1W1
Tél: 514-521-2439; *Téléc:* 514-521-5763
admin@aucoupdepouce.qc.ca
www.aucoupdepouce.qc.ca
Aperçu: *Dimension:* petite; *Envergure:* locale; fondée en 1973
Mission: Pour habiliter l'individu ainsi que l'intégration économique et sociale des personnes démunies; identifier les besoins prioritaires en éducation populaire aux gens du quartier Sainte-Marie; alphabétisation, accès à l'internet, initiation à l'informatique, ateliers, clubs, babillard d'emploi
Affiliation(s): Centraide du Grand Montréal
Membre(s) du personnel: 2
Membre: *Comités:* Journal; Événements
Membre(s) du bureau directeur:
Gisèle Caron, Coordinatrice
gisele@aucoupdepouce.qc.ca

Auctioneers Association of Alberta
RR#1, Red Deer AB T4N 5E1
Tel: 403-340-2070; *Fax:* 403-340-2019
www.albertaauctioneers.com
Overview: A small provincial organization founded in 1934
Mission: To develop standards of ethics for the profession; to help member become bonded; to lobby governments on laws & issues which affect the industry & keeps its members abreast of any news.
Membership: *Committees:* AMVIC & Automotive; Archives; Education; Membership & Nominating; Legislative; Surety; Convention; All Around Canadian Championships; Finance & Investment; Communications
Activities: Annual conference; trade fairs
Chief Officer(s):
Don Montgomery, President, 403-350-0523
Publications:
• The Alberta Auctioneer
Type: newsletter; *Frequency:* 3 pa

Auctioneers Association of Ontario
30959 Wyatt Rd., RR#6, Strathroy ON N7G 3H7
Tel: 519-232-4138; *Fax:* 519-232-9166
execdir@auctioneersassociation.com
www.auctioneersassociation.com
www.facebook.com/AuctioneersAssociationOntario
Overview: A small provincial organization
Chief Officer(s):
Rick Rittenhouse, President
salesrit@mergetel.com

Audio Engineering Society (AES)
AES Toronto Section, PO Box 292, #32E, 223 Pioneer Dr., Kitchener ON N2P 1L9
Tel: 519-894-5308
torontoaes@torontoaes.org
www.torontoaes.org
www.linkedin.com/groups?mostPopular=&gid=2023730
Overview: A small national organization
Mission: Dedicated to audio technology.
Chief Officer(s):
Blair Francey, Chair
Karl Machat, Secretary
Frank Lockwood, Vice Chair

Audit Bureau of Circulations *See* Alliance for Audited Media

Auditing Association of Canada (AAC) / L'Association canadienne de vérification
9 Forest Rd., Whitby ON L1N 3N7
Tel: 905-404-9511
admin@auditingcanada.com
www.auditingcanada.com
Previous Name: Canadian Environmental Auditing Association
Overview: A medium-sized international organization
Mission: To represent & promote the auditing profession; To advance public interest by enabling members to provide quality services
Membership: *Fees:* $30 plus GST student members; $230 plus GST general members; *Member Profile:* Auditors in environmental, health & safety, & related areas from across Canada, such as ISO 14001 & OHSAS 18001 registration auditors; Students who are interested in environmental & health & safety auditing; Corporations that support association activities
Activities: Certifying auditors; Upholding a code of ethics; Offering educational programs; Providing opportunities to network with colleagues; Offering information about government legislation & activities; Partnering with similar organizations
Chief Officer(s):
Don Fraser, Executive Director
Sue Keane, President
Meetings/Conferences:
• 2018 Auditing Association of Canada Annual Conference, 2018
Scope: National
Publications:
• Auditing Association of Canada Membership Directory
Type: Directory

Audition Québec
#001, 1951, boul de Maisonneuve est, Montréal QC H2K 2C9
Tél: 514-278-9633; *Téléc:* 514-278-9075
www.auditionquebec.org
www.facebook.com/auditionquebec
twitter.com/auditionquebec
Nom précédent: Association des devenus sourds et des malentendants du Québec
Aperçu: *Dimension:* petite; *Envergure:* provinciale; fondée en 1982
Mission: Défense des droits; intégration des personnes avec problèmes auditifs; assistance à la recherche sur la surdité; assistance pour l'obtention des aides techniques aux personnes ayant un handicap auditif
Finances: *Budget de fonctionnement annuel:* $50,000-$100,000; *Fonds:* Ministère de la santé et des services sociaux du Québec
Membre(s) du personnel: 1; 50 bénévole(s)
Membre: 350; *Montant de la cotisation:* 25$; *Critères d'admissibilite:* Devenus sourds; malentendants
Activités: Support moral pour personnes malentendantes; Cours d'ordinateur
Membre(s) du bureau directeur:
Daniel Morel, Président
Ronald Choquette, Secrétaire

Augustines de la Miséricorde de Jésus
2655, rue Guillaume - Le Pelletier, Québec QC G1C 3X7
Tél: 418-628-8860
secretaire@augustines.org
www.augustines.org
Aperçu: *Dimension:* petite; *Envergure:* locale; fondée en 1957
Mission: Les trois dimensions de la vie spirituelle des Augustines d'hier et de demain sont: communion fraternelle; louange et intercession; et miséricorde

Aurora & District Historical Society, Inc. *See* Aurora Historical Society, Inc.

Aurora Chamber of Commerce
#321, 6 - 14845 Yonge St., Aurora ON L4G 6H8
Tel: 905-727-7262; *Fax:* 905-841-6217
info@aurorachamber.on.ca
www.aurorachamber.on.ca
www.facebook.com/AuroraChamberON
twitter.com/ChamberinAurora
Overview: A small local organization
Member of: Ontario Chamber of Commerce; Canadian Chamber of Commerce
Staff Member(s): 6
Membership: *Fees:* Schedule available; *Committees:* Advocacy & Government Relations; Finance; Governance; Member Services & Marketing; BAA; Golf; Home Show
Chief Officer(s):
Sandra Watson, Interim Manager
s.watson@aurorachamber.on.ca

Aurora Historical Society, Inc.
Hillary House, National Historic Site, 15372 Yonge St., Aurora ON L4G 1N8
Tel: 905-727-8991
ahs@aurorahs.com
aurorahistoricalsociety.ca
www.facebook.com/HillaryHouseNHS
www.youtube.com/user/HillaryHouseNHS
Previous Name: Aurora & District Historical Society, Inc.
Overview: A small local charitable organization founded in 1963
Mission: To promote local awareness of & committment to heritage matters
Member of: Ontario Historical Society; Canadian Museums Association; Ontario Museum Association
Staff Member(s): 2
Membership: *Fees:* $10 student; $20 individual; $35 family; $75 corporate; $200 life; *Committees:* Restoration; Fundraising; Finance
Activities: Operates Aurora Museum & Hillary House; *Library:* Open to public
Chief Officer(s):
John McIntyre, President

Aurora House
PO Box 3779, The Pas MB R9A 1S4
Tel: 204-623-7427; *Fax:* 204-623-3901
Toll-Free: 877-977-0007; *Crisis Hot-Line:* 204-623-5497
auroratp@mts.net
www.aurorahouse-sharethecare.com
www.facebook.com/pages/Aurora-House/187177044629222

Canadian Associations / Aurora King Baseball Association (AKBA)

Also Known As: The Pas Committee for Women in Crisis Inc.; My Sister's House
Overview: A small local charitable organization founded in 1982
Mission: To address the issue of domestic violence; whether a woman & her children require a safe haven from an immediate abusive situation, or the woman is seeking to create change in her life, Aurora House & My Sister's House exist to empower the woman, providing programs & resources that promote & facilitate growth, self-esteem & understanding of the personal power to independently make choices; offers safe haven, education, information & resources that women & children require
Member of: Manitoba Association of Women's Shelters
Activities: Crisis line operation; residential services for women fleeing abusive relationships; walk-in follow up service; child support; Victims First Cell Phone; Second Stage Housing; presentations to schools, worksites; information booths at public events; tollfree number to nearest shelter 1-877-977-0007 (collect calls accepted); *Internships:* Yes; *Speaker Service:* Yes; *Library:* Open to public by appointment
Chief Officer(s):
Dawna Pritchard, Executive Director

Aurora King Baseball Association (AKBA)
PO Box 34040, Stn. Hollandview, 446 Hollandview Trail, Aurora ON L4G 0G3
info@akba.ca
www.akba.ca
www.linkedin.com/company/aurora-king-baseball-association
www.facebook.com/AuroraKingBaseball
twitter.com/aurorakingbball
Merged from: Aurora Minor Baseball Association; King Township Baseball Association
Overview: A medium-sized local organization
Chief Officer(s):
Matt Giesen, President
president@akba.ca

Ausable Bayfield Conservation Foundation
71108 Morrison Line, RR#3, Exeter ON N0M 1S5
Tel: 519-235-2610; *Fax:* 519-235-1963
Toll-Free: 888-286-2610
info@abca.on.ca
www.abca.on.ca
Overview: A small local organization founded in 1974
Mission: Raising funds for conservation, preservation & protection of the natural landscapes of the Ausable River, Bayfield River & Packhill Creek watersheds
Finances: *Annual Operating Budget:* Less than $50,000
Staff Member(s): 2; 9 volunteer(s)
Membership: 1-99
Activities: Conservation Dinner Auction
Chief Officer(s):
Tom Prout, General Manager/Sec.-Treas., 519-235-261 Ext. 234

Australian Cattle Dog Rescue of Ontario (ACDRO)
PO Box 249, 762 Upper James St., Hamilton ON L9C 3A2
Tel: 905-973-6687
Overview: A small provincial organization
Mission: To provides for the rescue, care, and adoption of needy Australian Cattle Dogs
Activities: Trio Kennel Club Show, Cowtown; booths at various pet shows
Chief Officer(s):
Sarah Mombourquette, Director
sarahm@acdro.com

Australian Football League Ontario (AFLO)
The Exchange Tower, PO Box 99, #3680, 130 King St. West, Toronto ON M5X 1B1
Tel: 416-304-0032
exec@aflontario.com
www.aflontario.com
www.facebook.com/AFLOntario
twitter.com/AFLOntario
Also Known As: AFL Ontario
Overview: A medium-sized provincial organization founded in 1989
Mission: To organize amateur Australian football competitions in Ontario & Québec.
Member of: AFL Canada
Membership: 11 clubs
Chief Officer(s):
Martin Walter, President

Australian Wine Society of Toronto (AWS)
c/o 39 Sierra Ct., Maple ON L6A 2E5
info@aws.ca
www.aws.ca
Overview: A small local organization founded in 1985
Mission: To encourage a greater awareness of the varietals, diversity & styles of Australian wines.
Membership: *Fees:* $35 single; $60 couple
Activities: Australian wine fair; monthly tastings & dinners
Chief Officer(s):
Malcolm Cocks, Chair

Australia-New Zealand Association (ANZA)
3 West 8 Ave., Vancouver BC V5Y 1M8
Tel: 604-876-7128
info@anzaclub.org
www.anzaclub.org
www.facebook.com/anzaclubvancouver
twitter.com/anzaclub
Also Known As: The ANZA Club
Overview: A medium-sized international organization founded in 1935
Mission: To foster friendly relations between British Columbia, Canada, Australia & New Zealand
Finances: *Funding Sources:* Membership dues; hall rentals; pub
Membership: *Fees:* $10
Activities: *Library:* Not open to public
Awards:
- Member of the Year
- Board Member of the Year

Austrian Canadian Edelweiss Club of Regina Inc
320 Maxwell Cres., Regina SK S4N 5Y1
Tel: 306-721-6388; *Fax:* 306-721-9980
austrianclubregina@gmail.com
www.austrianclubregina.ca
Also Known As: Austrian Club
Overview: A small local organization founded in 1974
Mission: To promote Austrian culture within the community of Regina; to provide social, educational, recreational & athletic programs, projects & gatherings; to assist newcomers of Austrian origin to establish themselves in Canada; to learn & advance within Canadian culture & citizenship
Affiliation(s): Canadian German Congress; Saskatchewan German Council; Austrian Canadian Council
Chief Officer(s):
John Josst, President

Autism Calgary Association
#174, 3359 - 27th St. NE, Calgary AB T1Y 5E4
Tel: 403-250-5033; *Fax:* 403-250-2625
info@autismcalgary.com
www.autismcalgary.com
www.facebook.com/autismcalgary
twitter.com/autismcalgary
Overview: A small local organization
Mission: Provides support, information and education to families
Staff Member(s): 5
Membership: *Fees:* Free
Chief Officer(s):
Lyndon Parakin, Executive Director, 403-250-5033 Ext. 223
lyndon@autismcalgary.com
Publications:
- The Autism Echo
Type: Newsletter; *Frequency:* Quarterly

Autism Canada / Société canadienne d'autisme
PO Box 366, Bothwell ON N0P 1C0
Tel: 519-695-5858; *Fax:* 519-695-5757
Toll-Free: 866-476-8440
www.autismcanada.org
www.linkedin.com/company/autism-canada
www.facebook.com/autismcanada
twitter.com/autismcanada
Also Known As: Autism Society Canada
Overview: A medium-sized national charitable organization founded in 1976
Mission: To provide support on a national basis to people affected by autism & related conditions through the collective efforts of Canadian provincial & territorial autism societies; To provide information & general referrals to the public regarding autism & related conditions; To promote public awareness of autism & related conditions; To encourage research in fields related or relevant to autism & related conditions; To communicate with government, agencies, & other organizations on behalf of persons affected by autism & related conditions; To promote actions to ensure people with autism & related conditions live in an environment that supports their well-being & enables them to reach their full potential; To promote & encourage the convening of conferences focused on autism & related conditions
Member of: Autism Society Ontario; World Autism Organization
Finances: *Annual Operating Budget:* $100,000-$250,000
Staff Member(s): 2
Membership: 3,000; *Committees:* ASD Advisory; Finance & Audit; Governance & Nominating; Marketing & Communications; Professional Advisors
Activities: *Awareness Events:* ICare4Autism Conference, July
Chief Officer(s):
Don Blane, Chair
Laurie Mawlam, Executive Director
laurie@autismcanada.org

Autism Nova Scotia (ANS)
5945 Spring Garden Rd., Halifax NS B3H 1Y4
Tel: 902-446-4995; *Fax:* 902-446-4997
Toll-Free: 877-544-4495
info@autismns.ca
www.autismnovascotia.ca
www.facebook.com/AutismNovaScotia
twitter.com/autismns
Previous Name: The Provincial Autism Centre
Overview: A small provincial charitable organization founded in 2002 overseen by Autism Society Canada
Mission: To advocate for, educate the public about, & provide support to, persons with autism/pervasive developmental disorders & their families
Affiliation(s): Society for Treatment of Autism
Finances: *Funding Sources:* Fundraising
Membership: *Fees:* $10 individual
Activities: *Speaker Service:* Yes; *Rents Mailing List:* Yes; *Library:* Open to public
Publications:
- Autistics Aloud
Type: Newsletter; *Frequency:* Quarterly
Profile: Displays the many talents amongst the autistic community, explores relevant issues and provides vital insight into autistic life.

Autism Ontario
#004, 1179 King St. West, Toronto ON M6K 3C5
Tel: 416-246-9592; *Fax:* 416-246-9417
Toll-Free: 800-472-7789
www.autismontario.com
www.facebook.com/autismontarioprovincial
twitter.com/AutismONT
Also Known As: Autism Society Ontario
Previous Name: Ontario Society for Autistic Citizens
Overview: A medium-sized provincial charitable organization founded in 1973 overseen by Autism Society Canada
Mission: To ensure that individuals with autism spectrum disorders are provided the means to achieve quality of life as respected members of society
Finances: *Funding Sources:* Membership dues; fundraising
Membership: *Fees:* $50 individual/family; $90 professional/researcher; $250 group; $500 lifetime individual/family; *Member Profile:* Anyone with an interest in autism: parents, friends, family, professionals
Activities: *Speaker Service:* Yes
Chief Officer(s):
Marg Spoelstra, Executive Director
marg@autismontario.com

Autism Society Alberta (ASA)
3639 26 St. NE, Calgary AB T1Y 5E1
Toll-Free: 877-777-7192
info@autismalberta.ca
www.autismalberta.ca
www.facebook.com/autismalberta
twitter.com/AutismSocietyAB
Overview: A medium-sized provincial charitable organization founded in 1972 overseen by Autism Society Canada
Mission: To improve the understanding of autism throughout Alberta by the dissemination of information to parents, health care workers, educators, government, private agencies & the public
Affiliation(s): Edmonton Autism Society; Autism Calgary Association; Autism Society Central Alberta
Finances: *Funding Sources:* Donations; Membership fees
Membership: *Member Profile:* Parents of autistic individuals; Groups
Activities: Summer recreational program; Christmas Party; support groups; hosting guest lecturers; *Speaker Service:* Yes
Chief Officer(s):
Deborah Barrett, President

Carole Anne Patenaude, Secretary

Autism Society Manitoba
825 Sherbrook St., Winnipeg MB R3A 1M5
Tel: 204-783-9563; Fax: 204-975-3027
info@autismmanitoba.com
www.autismmanitoba.com
www.facebook.com/AutismSocietyOfManitoba
twitter.com/manitobaautism
Overview: A small provincial charitable organization founded in 1977 overseen by Autism Society Canada
Mission: To enhance the quality of life of people with Autism Spectrum Disorder & their families; To promote full inclusion, dignity & development of personal skills & abilities for our members
Membership: Fees: $25
Activities: Educational resources; advocacy; structured social opportunities; Speaker Service: Yes; Library: Open to public

Autism Society Newfoundland & Labrador (ASNL)
PO Box 14078, St. John's NL A1B 4G8
Tel: 709-722-2803; Fax: 709-722-4926
info@autism.nf.net
www.autism.nf.net
twitter.com/AutismSocietyNL
Overview: A medium-sized provincial charitable organization founded in 1987 overseen by Autism Society Canada
Mission: To promote the diagnosis, treatment, education & integration into the community of all autistic persons; To provide information about autism; To promote research; To promote integrated care for autistic persons; To encourage the formation of parent support groups around the province
Finances: Funding Sources: Donations; government employment grants
Staff Member(s): 25
Membership: 600
Activities: Parent Support Meetings; Summer Leisure Time & Recreation; Speaker Service: Yes
Chief Officer(s):
Scott Crocker, Executive Director
scrocker@autism.nf.net

Autism Society Northwest Territories
5204 - 54th St., Yellowknife NT X1A 1W8
Tel: 867-446-0985; Fax: 867-873-4124
info@nwtautismsociety.org
www.nwtautismsociety.org
www.facebook.com/nwtautismsociety
Overview: A small provincial organization overseen by Autism Society Canada
Mission: To ensure that autistic individuals & their families have access to resources
Activities: Support & information groups
Chief Officer(s):
Denise McKee, President

Autism Society of British Columbia
#303, 3701 East Hastings St., Burnaby BC V5C 2H6
Tel: 604-434-0880; Fax: 604-434-0801
Toll-Free: 888-437-0880
info@autismbc.ca
www.autismbc.ca
www.facebook.com/autismbc
twitter.com/autismbc
Overview: A small provincial charitable organization founded in 1975 overseen by Autism Society Canada
Mission: To promote awareness of autism & the needs of families with a child or adult with autism; To provide advocacy, resources, & referrals to families of people with autism in BC
Staff Member(s): 8
Membership: 300 families; Fees: Adult client, student $5; family, professional $25; $100 institution/school/business; Lifetime $500; Member Profile: Parents of children with autism & professionals working in the autism field
Activities: Library: Not open to public
Chief Officer(s):
Laurie Guerra, President
Anya Walsh, Executive Director

Nanaimo Branch
PO Box 180, Stn. A, Nanaimo BC V9R 5K9
Tel: 250-714-0801; Fax: 250-714-0802
www.autismbc.ca/nanaimo.php
twitter.com/autismbcvanisle
Chief Officer(s):
Alexandria Stuart, Coordinator
astuart@autismbc.ca

Prince George Branch
13950 Athabasca Rd., Prince George BC V2N 5X9
Tel: 250-963-0803; Fax: 250-963-0804
www.autismbc.ca/prince_george.php
Chief Officer(s):
Heather Borland, Coordinator
hborland@autismbc.ca

Autism Society of PEI
PO Box 3243, Charlottetown PE C1A 8W5
Tel: 902-566-4844
Toll-Free: 888-360-8681
www.autismsociety.pe.ca
www.facebook.com/autismsocietypei
twitter.com/AutismSocietyPE
Overview: A small provincial organization overseen by Autism Society Canada
Mission: To provide austim resources to families in PEI
Membership: Fees: $10 family; $50 professional
Chief Officer(s):
Nathalie Walsh, Executive Director
nathalie@autismsociety.pe.ca

Autism Speaks Canada
#120, 2450 Victoria Park Ave., Toronto ON M2J 4A2
Tel: 416-362-6227; Fax: 416-362-6228
Toll-Free: 888-362-6227
Other Communication:
canadianfamilyservices@autismspeaks.org
www.autismspeaks.ca
www.facebook.com/AutismSpeaksCanada
twitter.com/autismspeaksCAN
Previous Name: National Alliance for Autism Research
Overview: A medium-sized national organization
Mission: To fund & accelerate biomedical research focusing on autism spectrum disorders
Activities: Awareness Events: World Autism Awareness Day, April 2
Chief Officer(s):
Jill Farber, Executive Director

Autism Treatment Services of Saskatchewan See Autism Treatment Services of Canada

Autism Yukon
108 Copper Rd., Whitehorse YT Y1A 2Z6
Tel: 867-667-6406
info@autismyukon.org
www.autismyukon.org
www.facebook.com/162869033819118
Overview: A small provincial organization overseen by Autism Society Canada
Mission: To provide support for individuals & families affected by autism
Membership: Fees: $10
Chief Officer(s):
Shirley Chua-Tan, Vice-President

Auto Sport Québec (ASQ)
CP 1000, Succ. M, 4545, av Pierre-de Coubertin, Montréal QC H1V 3R2
Tél: 514-252-3052; Téléc: 514-254-5369
info@lasq.ca
lasq.ca
Nom précédent: Fédération Auto-Québec
Aperçu: Dimension: moyenne; Envergure: provinciale; fondée en 1973
Mission: Pour représenter les responsables du sport automobile
Membre(s) du personnel: 8
Activités: Stagiaires: Oui; Listes de destinataires: Oui
Membre(s) du bureau directeur:
Gilles Villeneuve, Président et Directeur Général

AUTO21 - The Automobile of the 21st Century See AUTO21 Network of Centres of Excellence

AUTO21 Network of Centres of Excellence
401 Sunset Ave., Windsor ON N9B 3P4
Tel: 519-253-3000; Fax: 519-971-3626
info@auto21.ca
www.auto21.ca
www.linkedin.com/groups?about=&gid=2804256
www.facebook.com/AUTO21
twitter.com/auto21nce
www.youtube.com/user/AUTO21NCE
Also Known As: AUTO21
Previous Name: AUTO21 - The Automobile of the 21st Century

Overview: A medium-sized national organization founded in 2001
Mission: To partner the public & private secotrs in applied automotive R&D
Member of: Networks of Centres of Excellence
Finances: Annual Operating Budget: Greater than $5 Million; Funding Sources: Federal government; Private sector
Staff Member(s): 11
Membership: 200 researchers + 120 industry & government partners
Activities: Automotive research; Internships: Yes
Chief Officer(s):
Peter Frise, CEO & Scientific Director
Michelle Watters, COO & Executive Director
Stephanie Campeau, Director, Public Affairs & Communications

Automobile et touring club du Québec Voir CAA Québec

Automobile Journalists Association of Canada (AJAC) / Association des journalistes automobile du Canada
PO Box 398, Stn. Main, Cobourg ON K9A 4L1
Tel: 519-563-8417
www.ajac.ca
Overview: A small national organization founded in 1981
Mission: To report on new vehicles & new industry trends in various print and broadcast media.
Membership: Fees: Schedule available; Member Profile: Working automobile journalists & automotive industry public relations representatives
Activities: Art of the Automobile Competition; Rents Mailing List: Yes
Chief Officer(s):
Siobhan Duffield, Event Coordinator
siobhan@ajac.ca
Awards:
• Car of the Year Awards

Automobile Protection Association (APA) / Association pour la protection automobile
292, boul St-Joseph ouest, Montréal QC H2V 2N7
Tel: 514-272-5555; Fax: 514-273-0797
apamontreal@apa.ca
www.apa.ca
www.facebook.com/AutomobileProtectionAssociation
twitter.com/APA_LEMONAID
Overview: A medium-sized national organization founded in 1969
Mission: To inform & represent the public on major automobile-related issues
Finances: Annual Operating Budget: $500,000-$1.5 Million
Staff Member(s): 15
Membership: 10,000; Fees: $77+ tax
Activities: Internships: Yes; Speaker Service: Yes; Library: by appointment

Toronto Office
#1319, 2 Carlton St., Toronto ON M5B 1J3
Tel: 416-204-1444; Fax: 416-204-1985
apatoronto@apa.ca
www.apa.ca

Automotive Aftermarket Retailers of Ontario
#10, 5100 South Service Rd., Burlington ON L7L 6A5
Tel: 905-634-4040; Fax: 905-634-6274
Toll-Free: 800-268-5400
aaro@aaro.ca
www.aaro.ca
Overview: A medium-sized provincial organization
Mission: To advance the Interests of the Independent Sector of the Automotive Service Industry.
Chief Officer(s):
Rudy Graf, President
grafauto@on.aibn.com
Diane Freeman, Executive Director
execdirector@aaro.ca

Automotive Industries Association of Canada (AIAC) / Association des industries de l'automobile du Canada
#1400, 180 Elgin St., Ottawa ON K2P 2K3
Tel: 613-728-5821; Fax: 613-728-6021
Toll-Free: 800-808-2920
info@aiacanada.com
www.aiacanada.com
www.linkedin.com/company/aia-canada
www.facebook.com/AIAofCanada
twitter.com/AIAOFCANADA

Canadian Associations / Automotive Parts Manufacturers' Association (APMA)

Overview: A large national organization founded in 1964
Mission: To represent the automotive aftermarket industry in Canada; To promote, educate, & represent members
Finances: *Funding Sources:* Membership dues
300 volunteer(s)
Membership: 4,000 organizations; *Fees:* Dues based on the confirmed sales volumes of the individual members; *Member Profile:* Open to wholesalers, warehouse distributors, mass merchandisers, specialty groups & oil company headquarters, manufacturers, rebuilders, national distributors, manufacturers' agents, international exporters, allied organizations that supply goods &/or services to members of the association not for resale to warehouse distributors or wholesalers; *Committees:* Audit & Finance; Canada Night; Collision Council; Division Chairs; Young Executive Society
Activities: Offering correspondence courses (parts specialist training; sales training; jobber management; dangerous goods, WHMIS & hazardous waste); Providing insurance services (benefits & pensions); government relations; *Awareness Events:* Car Care Month, May; Car Safety Month, October; *Speaker Service:* Yes
Chief Officer(s):
Jean-François Champagne, President
jf.champagne@aiacanada.com
France Daviault, Vice-President
Luciana Nechita, Director, Public Affairs
Ibtihal Ridha, Senior Manager, Finance
Patty Kettles, Senior Manager, Member Relations
Rosa Azizi, Coordinator, Operations
Courtney DeLaura, Coordinator, Communications
Awards:
• AIA & the Global Automotive Aftermarket Symposium (GAAS) Scholarship Program
For students in secondary education; *Amount:* $1,000
• Hans McCorriston Motive Power Machinist Grant Program
For students in a motive power machinist course; *Amount:* $500
• The Arthur Paulin Automotive Aftermarket Scholarship Award
For students in an automotive program; *Amount:* $700
Atlantic Division
Chief Officer(s):
Lynn Cormier, Chair

Automotive Parts Manufacturers' Association (APMA)
#801, 10 Four Seasons Pl., Toronto ON M9B 6H7
Tel: 416-620-4220; *Fax:* 416-620-9730
www.apma.ca
www.linkedin.com/groups/2654454
twitter.com/APMACanada
Overview: A large national organization founded in 1952
Mission: To promote the manufacture in Canada of automotive parts, systems, components, materials, tools, equipment & supplies, & also the provision of services used in the automotive industry & in particular for the original equipment market; To engage in activities in support of the welfare of the members of the Association
Staff Member(s): 4
Membership: 400+ corporate; *Fees:* Schedule available; *Member Profile:* Canadian producers of parts, components, systems, tools, equipment & services for the automotive & truck manufacturing industries worldwide; 3 categories: Regular - manufacturers in Canada independent of vehicle companies; Canadian manufacturers which are divisions or affiliates of vehicle companies; International associates - manufacturers outside Canada interested or involved in the Canadian market & industry; Other associates - not manufacturers but interested in keeping in touch with industry trends & developments; *Committees:* Annual Conference; Connected Vehicle Working Group; Environment, Energy, Health & Safety; Innovation & Technology; Marketing & Strategic Initiatives; Strategic Purchasing
Activities: Conducting an emissions survey
Chief Officer(s):
Barry Jones, Chair
Flavio Volpe, President
Meetings/Conferences:
• Automotive Parts Manufacturers' Association 22nd Annual Automotive Outlook Conference 2018, 2018
Scope: National
Publications:
• APMA [Automotive Parts Manufacturers' Association] Newsletter
Type: Newsletter
Profile: APMA activities, issues & news delivered electronically

• Lead, Reach & Connect [a publication of the Automotive Parts Manufacturers' Association]
Type: Magazine; *Editor:* Alexandra Walld

Automotive Recyclers Association of Atlantic Canada (ARAAC)
Tel: 519-858-8761
araac@execulink.com
araac.ca
Previous Name: Maritime Auto Wreckers Association
Overview: A medium-sized provincial organization founded in 1972
Mission: ARAAC is the forum for channeling information, establishing the highest ethical and environmental standards of its membership, and is the official representative in the Atlantic Provinces for the Automotive Recyclers of Canada
Member of: Automotive Recyclers of Canada
Membership: *Member Profile:* Automotive recyclers (wholesale and retail recycled auto parts dealers); Suppliers of end-of-life vehicles to provincial shredding facilities; *Committees:* Government Affairs; Meetings; Membership; Nominations
Chief Officer(s):
Dalbert Livingstone, President, 902-892-0138
20dally1818@hotmail.com
Meetings/Conferences:
• Automotive Recyclers Association of Atlantic Canada 2018 Annual Meeting & Trade Show, May, 2018, Atlantica Hotel Halifax, Halifax, NS
Scope: Provincial

Automotive Recyclers Association of Manitoba (ARM)
PO Box 43049, Stn. Kildonan Place, Winnipeg MB R2C 5G5
Tel: 204-654-2726
www.arm.mb.ca
Overview: A medium-sized provincial organization
Mission: To provide quality recycled auto parts; To serve its customers & communities; To help the environment
Member of: Automotive Recyclers of Canada
Membership: *Member Profile:* Automotive recyclers (wholesale and retail recycled auto parts dealers); Suppliers of end-of-life vehicles to provincial shredding facilities
Chief Officer(s):
Alec Gilman, President, 204-633-2540, Fax: 204-633-0723

Automotive Recyclers of Canada (ARC)
134 Langarth St. East, London ON N6C 1Z5
Tel: 519-858-8761
info@autorecyclers.ca
autorecyclers.ca
twitter.com/autorecyclersCA
Overview: A large national organization founded in 1997
Mission: To act as the national voice for provincial member automotive recycling associations
Membership: 7 associations; *Member Profile:* Automotive recycling associations
Chief Officer(s):
Steve Fletcher, Managing Director
Publications:
• Canadian Auto Recyclers [a publication of Automotive Recyclers of Canada]
Type: Magazine; *Frequency:* Annually; *Editor:* Mike Davey

Automotive Retailers Association of British Columbia
#1, 8980 Fraserwood Ct., Burnaby BC V5J 5H7
Tel: 604-432-7987; *Fax:* 604-432-1756
reception@ara.bc.ca
www.ara.bc.ca
www.facebook.com/autoretailers
twitter.com/autoretailers
Overview: A medium-sized provincial organization founded in 1951
Mission: To enhance the image & competitive status of association members throughout BC & ensure high quality service to protect the road safety of the motoring public
Member of: Automotive Recyclers of Canada
Finances: *Funding Sources:* Membership dues
Membership: 1,000+; *Fees:* $525 associate; $656.25 full member; $262.50 branch/cross-divisional; *Member Profile:* Automotive aftermarket industry
Chief Officer(s):
Ken McCormack, President
kenmccormack@ara.bc.ca

Autonomous Federation of Collegial Staff (Ind.) *Voir* Fédération autonome du collégial (ind.)

Autorité des marchés financiers (AMF)
Place de la Cité, tour Cominar, #400, 2640, boul Laurier, Québec QC G1V 5C1
Tél: 418-525-0337; *Téléc:* 418-525-9512
Ligne sans frais: 877-525-0337
www.lautorite.qc.ca
www.linkedin.com/company/1128549
www.facebook.com/Bonnesquestions
twitter.com/lautorite
Aperçu: *Dimension:* moyenne; *Envergure:* provinciale; fondée en 2004 surveillé par Canadian Securities Administrators
Membre de: Canadian Securities Administrators
Membre(s) du bureau directeur:
Andrée Mayrand, Présidente
Michel Lespérance, Secrétaire
Louis Morisset, Président-directeur général
Publications:
• Bulletin de l'Autorité des marchés financiers
Type: Newsletter; *Frequency:* hebdomadaire
• L'Info-Autorité [publication Autorité des marchés financiers]
Type: Newsletter; *Frequency:* au 2 mois
• Rapport annuel de gestion de l'Autorité des marchés financiers [publication de Autorité des marchés financiers]
Type: Report; *Frequency:* annuel
Montréal
Tour de la Bourse, CP 246, 800, rue du Square-Victoria, 22e étage, Montréal QC H4Z 1G3
Tél: 514-395-0337; *Téléc:* 514-873-3090

Autorités canadiennes en valeurs mobilières *See* Canadian Securities Administrators

Aux Prismes Plein air et culture
CP 476, Succ. C, Montréal QC H2L 4K4
Tél: 514-990-7674
info@auxprismes.qc.ca
www.auxprismes.qc.ca
Aperçu: *Dimension:* petite; *Envergure:* locale
Mission: Association sans but lucratif pour gais, lesbiennes et amis/amies - tous les âges, sexes et orientations sexuelles; activités sociales, culturelles, sportives
Membre: *Montant de la cotisation:* 15$

Auxiliaires bénévoles de l'Hôpital de Chibougamau
51, 3e rue, Chibougamau QC G8P 1N1
Tél: 418-748-2676
Aperçu: *Dimension:* petite; *Envergure:* locale
Membre(s) du bureau directeur:
Priscilla Ratthé, Présidente, 418-748-6453

Avataq Cultural Institute
#360, 4150, rue Sainte-Catherine ouest, Montréal QC H3Z 2Y5
Tel: 514-989-9031; *Fax:* 514-989-8789
Toll-Free: 800-361-5029
avataq@avataq.qc.ca
www.avataq.qc.ca
Overview: A small provincial organization founded in 1980
Mission: To promote & protect the Inuit language & culture in Nunavik
Activities: *Library:* Open to public by appointment
Chief Officer(s):
Charlie Arngaq, President

The Avian Preservation Foundation (APF)
77 Long Island Cres., Unionville ON L3P 7M1
www.aacc.ca/apf.htm
Overview: A medium-sized national charitable organization
Mission: To support recognized expert aviculturists who are endeavouring to breed rare & endangered avian species; to establish a Canadian breeding centre for rare & endangered avian species; to establish a monitoring body for captive avian stocks in Canada through surveys & computer software; to create & maintain a breeding program throughout Canada for avian species currently listed as endangered; to create a captive preservation program for rare & endangered species within zoos, bird parks & sanctuaries where re-introduction into the natural habitat is not possible or practical
Member of: Avicultural Advancement Council of Canada
Finances: *Annual Operating Budget:* Less than $50,000
12 volunteer(s)
Membership: 250; *Fees:* $35
Chief Officer(s):
Jeremy Faria, President

Aviation Alberta (AVA)
Edmonton International Airport, 3715 - 56th Ave. East, Edmonton AB T9E 0V4

Tel: 780-890-0006
aviationalberta@gmail.com
www.aviationalberta.com
Previous Name: Alberta Aerospace Association
Overview: A small provincial organization founded in 2004
Mission: To be a catalyst for industry growth & the recognized voisce of aerospace, airport & aviation interests in Alberta; To serve its membership & promote the growth & prosperity of aerospace, airports & aviation in Alberta through collaboration, communication, training, education, research & advocacy
Affiliation(s): Aeropsace Industries Association of Canada; Aerospace Industry Association of British Columbia; Air Transport Association of Canada; Association for Unmanned Vehicles International; Association for Unmanned Vehicles International-Canada; Canada Aviation Museum; Canada's Aviation Hall of Fame; Canadian Airports Council; Canadian Association of Defence & Security Industries; Canadian Aviation Maintenance Council; Canadian Business Aircraft Association; Canadian Owners & Pilots Association; Civil Air Search & Rescue Association of Canada; Manitoba Aerospace Association; UVSI-Canada
Membership: 226; *Fees:* $40-$1,650; *Member Profile:* Aircraft/airline operators; aerospace; airport operators & uvs (unmanned vehicle systems)
Chief Officer(s):
Bram Tilroe, Acting Chair
Awards:
- President's Award
- Airport Operator Award
- Private Pilot Advanced Training
- Commercial Pilot Advanced Training
- AME or Avionics Technology
- UVS Robotics Technology
- Reilly Memorial Award

Avicultural Advancement Council of Canada (AACC)
77 Long Island Cres., Unionville ON L3P 7M1
www.aacc.ca
Overview: A medium-sized national licensing organization founded in 1972
Mission: To establish & maintain a national association of interested societies & individuals to promote the advancement of aviculture in Canada; To represent the Canadian avicultural community internationally; To disseminate information; to support recognized expert aviculturalists; To assist all levels of government in preparing informed legislation & policy relating to aviculture; To establish standards for the exhibition of birds in Canada; To provide a national identification leg band registry; To establish an avian species preservation program in Canada
Affiliation(s): American Singer Canary Club of Canada; Assoc. des amateurs d'oiseaux de la Mauricie; Assoc. des éléveurs d'oiseaux de Montréal; BC Avicultural Society; BC Exotic Bird Society; Budgerigar & Foreign Bird Society; Cage Bird Society of Hamilton; Calgary Canary Club; Canadian Dove Assoc.; Canadian Gloster Club; Cowichan Valley & Upper Island Cage Bird Club; Durham Avicultural Society; Edmonton Avicultural Association; Essex-Kent Cage Bird Society; Feather Fanciers Club; Golden Triangle Parrot Club; Kamloops Aviculturalist Society; London & District Cage Bird Society; Manitoba Canary & Finch Club
Finances: *Annual Operating Budget:* Less than $50,000; *Funding Sources:* Membership dues; Donations
12 volunteer(s)
Membership: 300 individual + 40 institutional; *Fees:* $35; *Member Profile:* Breeders, exhibitors & fanciers of birds; Clubs that subscribe to the principles of association
Activities: *Library:* Not open to public
Chief Officer(s):
Jeremy Faria, President
Gary D'Ornellas, Ring Registrar
bandsaacc@gmail.com
Awards:
- Canadian First Breeding Awards
Meetings/Conferences:
- Avicultural Advancement Council of Canada 80th Canadian National Cage Bird Show & Expo, 2018
Scope: National
Contact Information: URL: www.national-birdshow.com
Publications:
- The Avicultural Journal [a publication of the Avicultural Advancement Council of Canada]
Type: Journal; *Frequency:* q.

Aviron Québec (AQA)
4545, av Pierre-de Coubertin, Montréal QC H1V 0B2
Tél: 514-252-3191
info@avironquebec.ca
www.avironquebec.ca
Nom précédent: Association québécoise d'aviron
Aperçu: *Dimension:* moyenne; *Envergure:* provinciale; fondée en 1981 surveillé par Rowing Canada Aviron
Membre de: Rowing Canada Aviron
Membre(s) du bureau directeur:
Karol Sauvé, Contact, 514-252-3191
karolsauve@avironquebec.ca

Avocats Hors Québec (AHQ) / Quebec Lawyers Abroad
445, boul St-Laurent, Montréal QC H2Y 3T8
www.avocatshorsquebec.org
Aperçu: *Dimension:* moyenne; *Envergure:* provinciale
Mission: Pour défendre les intérêts des membres du Barreau du Québec qui travaillent à l'étranger
Membre: *Critères d'admissibilite:* Membres du Barreau du Québec
Membre(s) du bureau directeur:
Lucie Laplante, Présidente, Conseil d'administration

Avocats sans frontières Canada (ASFC) / Lawyers Without Borders Canada (LWBC)
#230, 825, rue St-Joseph est, Québec QC G1K 3C8
Tél: 418-907-2607; *Téléc:* 418-948-2241
info@asfcanada.ca
www.asfcanada.ca
www.facebook.com/asfcanada.ca
Également appelé: Abogados sin fronteras
Aperçu: *Dimension:* grande; *Envergure:* nationale
Mission: Pour aider à défendre les droits humains dans les endroits où ils sont le plus négligés
Membre: *Montant de la cotisation:* 15$
Activités: *Conférences;* *Séminaires;* *Stagiaires:* Oui
Membre(s) du bureau directeur:
Migues Baz, Président, Conseil d'administration

Avon Chamber of Commerce
PO Box 2188, Windsor NS B0N 2T0
Tel: 902-799-1185
info@avonchamberofcommerce.ca
www.avonchamberofcommerce.ca
www.facebook.com/theAvonChamber
twitter.com/avonchamber
Previous Name: West Hants Chamber of Commerce; Windsor Board of Trade
Overview: A small local organization founded in 1972
Mission: To improve the business climate for members by increasing awareness, being proactive in public policy & providing workshops, seminars & information sessions
Membership: 82; *Fees:* $86.25
Activities: Offering networking opportunities, programs, training, & educational events
Chief Officer(s):
Jeffrey Barrett, President
Joanna Gould-Thorpe, Vice-President

The Avon Trail
PO Box 21148, Stratford ON N5A 7V4
info@avontrail.ca
www.avontrail.ca
Overview: A small local charitable organization founded in 1975
Mission: To promote an interest in hiking & maintain hiking trails
Member of: Hike Ontario
Membership: *Fees:* $30 family; $20 individual/organization/youth; $15 student; *Committees:* Conservancy
Activities: Trail winds through river valleys, farm lands & festival country of Southern Ontario, from the Grand Valley to the Thames Valley Trail (100 km); guided hikes year round
Chief Officer(s):
Karen Hill, President

AWIC Community & Social Services (AWIC)
1761 Sheppard Ave., Toronto ON M2J 0A5
Tel: 416-499-4144; *Fax:* 416-499-4077
awic@bellnet.ca
www.awic.info
www.facebook.com/185101574859967
Previous Name: Association of Women of India in Canada
Overview: A small local organization
Mission: To assist newcomers to achieve full integration & participation in Canadian life while maintaining their culture & heritage
Membership: *Fees:* One year: $5; Five year: $20

Chief Officer(s):
Chitra Sunder, President
Vanita Pais, Director
Publications:
- AWIC Newsletter

Awo Taan Healing Lodge Society
PO Box 6084, Stn. A, Calgary AB T2H 2L3
Tel: 403-531-1970; *Fax:* 403-531-1977; *Crisis Hot-Line:* 403-531-1972
www.awotaan.org
www.facebook.com/awotaan
twitter.com/AwoTaan1
www.youtube.com/user/awotaan
Previous Name: Calgary Native Women's Shelter Society
Overview: A small local organization founded in 1992
Mission: To offer safe accommmodation, a full-service emergency shelter, counselling, support, & referrals to women & their children who consider themselves to be physically, emotionally, or sexually abused.
Member of: Calgary Regional Shelter Directors Network; Associaton of Directors & Volunteer Resources: Volunteer Calgary; Volunteer Collective
Affiliation(s): Alberta Council of Women's Shelters
Finances: *Funding Sources:* Provincial, municipal government; United Way
Membership: *Fees:* $5
Activities: Gala Dinner; Golf Tournament
Chief Officer(s):
Josie Nepinak, Executive Director

Aylmer Heritage Association *Voir* Association du Patrimoine d'Aylmer

Aylsham & District Board of Trade
PO Box 187, Aylsham SK S0E 0C0
Tel: 306-862-4849; *Fax:* 306-862-4506
Overview: A small local organization
Staff Member(s): 9; 200 volunteer(s)
Chief Officer(s):
Gwen Anderson, Secretary

Ayrshire Breeders Association of Canada (ABAC) / Associaton des éleveurs Ayrshire du Canada
4865, boul Laurier ouest, Saint-Hyacinthe QC J2S 3V4
Tel: 450-778-3535; *Fax:* 450-778-3531
info@ayrshire-canada.com
www.ayrshire-canada.com
www.facebook.com/ayrshire.canada
twitter.com/AyrshireCanada
Also Known As: Ayrshire Canada
Overview: A large national organization
Mission: To bring Ayrshire breeders together for the purpose of cooperating in their efforts to further the interests of the breed; To promote breeding of purebred Ayrshire cattle in Canada; To establish breeding standards; To cooperate with industry partners to enhance programs
Finances: *Annual Operating Budget:* $500,000-$1.5 Million
Staff Member(s): 5
Membership: 1,200
Activities: *Speaker Service:* Yes; *Rents Mailing List:* Yes
Chief Officer(s):
Michel Bourdeault, Executive Director
michel@ayrshire-canada.com
Awards:
- Award of Merit Award
- Master Breeder Award
- Honorary Member Award

The Azorean House of Ontario *See* Casa dos Acores do Ontário

Azrieli Foundation
#202, 22 St. Clair Ave., Toronto ON M4T 2S3
Tel: 416-322-5928; *Fax:* 416-322-5930
info@azrielifoundation.org
www.azrielifoundation.org
www.facebook.com/AzrieliMemoirs
twitter.com/AzrieliMemoirs
Overview: A medium-sized international charitable organization founded in 1989
Mission: To meet & extend the philanthropic goals of the late David J. Azrieli; To promote & preserve Jewish heritage & memory; To work towards a strong Jewish future in Israel & the diaspora
Activities: Funding institutions; Developing programs in the areas of science & medicine, education, architecture, arts, &

Canadian Associations / B'nai Brith Canada (BBC)

community development; Operating the Azrieli Institute for Educational Empowerment; Publishing memoirs & diaries written by survivors of the Holocaust; Supporting research on neurodevelopment
Chief Officer(s):
Naomi Azrieli, Chair & CEO

B'nai Brith Canada (BBC)
15 Hove St., Toronto ON M3H 4Y8
Tel: 416-633-6224; *Fax:* 416-630-2159
toronto@bnaibrith.ca
www.bnaibrith.ca
www.facebook.com/bnaibrithcanada
twitter.com/bnaibrithcanada
Also Known As: Children of the Covenant
Overview: A large national charitable organization founded in 1875
Mission: To bring men & women of the Jewish faith together in fellowship to serve the Jewish community through combating anti-Semitism, bigotry & racism in Canada & abroad; To carry out activities which ensure the security & survival of the State of Israel & Jewish communities worldwide
Affiliation(s): B'nai Brith International
Finances: *Annual Operating Budget:* $1.5 Million-$3 Million; *Funding Sources:* Private donations; Membership dues
Staff Member(s): 35
Membership: 20,000 families; *Fees:* Schedule available; *Member Profile:* Open to individuals 18 years of age & of Jewish faith; *Committees:* Affordable Housing Program; Centre for Community Action; Department of Government Relations; The League for Human Rights; Institute for International Affairs
Activities: Operating educational & community volunteer projects; *Awareness Events:* Annual Golf Tournament; Award of Merit Dinner; *Internships:* Yes; *Speaker Service:* Yes; *Rents Mailing List:* Yes; *Library:* Open to public by appointment
Chief Officer(s):
Michael Mostyn, Chief Executive Officer

Midwest Region
#C403, 123 Doncaster St., Winnipeg MB R3N 2B2
Tel: 204-487-9623; *Fax:* 204-487-9648
winnipeg@bnaibrith.ca

Québec Region
#202, 7155, rue Côte Saint-Luc, Montréal QC H4V 1J2
Tel: 514-733-5377; *Fax:* 514-342-9632
montreal@bnaibrith.ca

B'nai Brith Canada Institute for International Affairs
15 Hove St., Toronto ON M3H 4Y8
Tel: 416-633-6224; *Fax:* 416-630-2159
Toll-Free: 844-218-2624
bnb@bnaibrith.ca
www.bnaibrith.ca
www.facebook.com/bnaibrithcanada
twitter.com/bnaibrithcanada
www.instagram.com/bnaibrithcanada
Overview: A small international organization
Mission: To identify & fight human rights abuses throughout the world, with special emphasis on Jewish communities worldwide
Staff Member(s): 2; 3 volunteer(s)
Membership: 100
Activities: Advocacy & community mobilization; Public education; Media liaison; Fact finding missions; Briefs & consultations with government & non-government; Organizations; Publications
Chief Officer(s):
Eric Bissell, President
Frank Dimant, Executive Vice-President

B'nai Brith Women of Eastern Canada; Jewish Women International of Canada *See* Act To End Violence Against Women

B'nai Brith Youth Organization (BBYO)
Lake Ontario Region, #1-22, 4700 Bathurst St., Toronto ON M2R 1W8
Tel: 416-398-2004; *Fax:* 416-398-5780
info@bbyo.ca
www.bbyo.ca
www.facebook.com/lorbbyo
twitter.com/lorbbyo
Overview: A medium-sized provincial organization
Mission: To educate young people about the richness of Jewish culture & heritage
Finances: *Annual Operating Budget:* $500,000-$1.5 Million
Membership: *Fees:* $75; *Member Profile:* Jewish youth in grades seven through twelve

Chief Officer(s):
Kevin Goodman, Executive Director, 416-398-2004 Ext. 1
kgoodman@bbyo.ca

Northwest Canada Region (BBYO)
#1607, 90 Ave. SW, Calgary AB T2V 4V7
Tel: 403-444-3161
nwcbbyo.org
twitter.com/nwcbbyo
Chief Officer(s):
Kira Blumer, Regional Director
kblumer@bbyo.org

Red River Region (BBYO)
123 Doncaster St., Winnipeg MB R3M 0S3
Tel: 204-477-7547
members.shaw.ca/nlerner
twitter.com/BBYORedRiverReg

B2ten
QC
b2ten.ca
twitter.com/B2ten
Overview: A small national charitable organization founded in 2005
Mission: To help Canadian athletes achieve success in the sporting world, particularly in an international context.
Finances: *Funding Sources:* Donations

Baby's Breath
PO Box 21053, St Catharines ON L2M 7X2
Tel: 905-688-8884; *Fax:* 905-688-3300
Toll-Free: 800-363-7437
www.babysbreathcanada.ca
www.facebook.com/babysbreathca
twitter.com/babysbreathca
Previous Name: Canadian Foundation for the Study of Infant Deaths
Overview: A small national charitable organization founded in 1973
Mission: To support & represent families in Canada who are coping with the loss of an infant; To promote research on the health or medical conditions associated with infant deaths & stillbirths
Affiliation(s): SIDS International
Finances: *Funding Sources:* Individual; corporate donations
Membership: *Fees:* $25 individual; *Committees:* Medical & Research Advisory
Activities: *Speaker Service:* Yes; *Library:* Open to public by appointment
Chief Officer(s):
Wendy Potter, Chair
Awards:
• Dr. Sydney Segal Research Grant
Publications:
• The Baby's Breath
Type: Newsletter; *ISSN:* 1192-9294
Profile: Foundation information & events, medical updates
• Sam's Story [a publication of Baby's Breath]
Author: Fiona Chin-Yee
Profile: Resource for youngs SIDS siblings accompanied by a parents' guide

Bach Elgar Choir
86 Homewood Ave., Hamilton ON L8P 2M4
Tel: 905-527-5995; *Fax:* 905-527-0555
bachelgar@gmail.com
www.bachelgar.com
www.facebook.com/bachelgar
Overview: A medium-sized local charitable organization founded in 1905
Mission: To provide choral music of excellent quality & broad-based appeal to the community; To act as a cultural & educational resource
Affiliation(s): Ontario Choral Federation; Hamilton & Region Arts Council; Council for Business & the Arts in Canada; Canadian Conference of the Arts
Finances: *Funding Sources:* Municipal & provincial governments; foundation; fundraising; ticket sales
Staff Member(s): 2
Membership: *Member Profile:* Admittance to choir by audition
Activities: *Rents Mailing List:* Yes; *Library*
Chief Officer(s):
Alexander Cann, Artistic Director

Back Country Horsemen of British Columbia (BCHBC)
c/o Carol Creasy, Comp. 6, Site 10, RR#1, Sorrento BC V0E 2W0
Tel: 250-835-8587
ccreasy07@gmail.com
www.bchorsemen.org
Overview: A small provincial organization
Mission: To preserve & enhance public lands for use by equestrians; To offer a safe learning atmosphere for persons interested in trail riding & the wilderness experience; To act as a voice for members in dealing with provincial & municipal governing agencies on matters of concern to trail riders
Finances: *Funding Sources:* Membership fees
Membership: 584; *Fees:* $35; *Member Profile:* Equestrians of any age interested in trail riding & the back country of British Columbia; *Committees:* Trails; Chapter Communications; Education
Activities: Providing information about trails; Offering educational clinics about trail riding; Organizing monthly meetings; Collaborating with other groups, such as Scouts Canada, to work on projects such as bridge building; Increasing public awareness of the association
Chief Officer(s):
Ybo Plante, President, 250-743-3356
president@bchorsemen.org
Brian Wallace, Vice-President, 250-569-2324
hbwally@gmail.com
Sharon Pickthorne, Treasurer, 250-337-1818
oneoonone@telus.net
Publications:
• Back Country Horsemen of British Columbia Provincial Newsletter
Type: Newsletter
Profile: Association information, such as upcoming events & meetings

Alberni Valley Chapter
Alberni Valley BC
Tel: 250-720-1298
Mission: To inform & educate members about trail riding & British Columbia's back country
Chief Officer(s):
Melody Francoeur, Contact
melodyfrancoeur@shaw.ca

Aldergrove Chapter
Aldergrove BC
Tel: 604-856-4433
Mission: To provide education to equestrians about trail riding in British Columbia's back country
Chief Officer(s):
Brian Harder, Contact, 604-941-9888
bharder@usw.ca
Carleigh Paterson, Vice-Chair, 604-308-1962

Kamloops Chapter
Kamloops BC
Tel: 778-469-0041
Mission: To inform & educate equestrians in the Kamloops area
Chief Officer(s):
Wendy Harris, Contact
alwendyharris@shaw.ca
• Back Country Horsemen of British Columbia Kamloops Chapter Newsletter
Type: Newsletter; *Accepts Advertising*; *Editor:* Rick Weik
Profile: Information & announcements about the Kamloops chapter

Kootenay Chapter
Kootenay BC
Tel: 250-367-9834
Mission: To offer a safe learning environment for persons interested in trail riding & the wilderness experience
Chief Officer(s):
Rick Fillmore, Contact
ricof@direct.ca

Northwest Chapter
BC
Tel: 250-846-9251
Mission: To preserve, protect, & ride the trails of northwestern British Columbia; To educate equestrians through clinics
Chief Officer(s):
Floyd Kennedy, Contact

Canadian Associations / Badminton Ontario (BON)

- Back Country Horsemen of British Columbia Northwest Chapter Newsletter
Type: Newsletter; Author: Eileen Shorter

Okanagan Chapter
Okanagan BC
Tel: 250-763-3962
Mission: To offer educational clinics to equestrians in the Okanagan area
Chief Officer(s):
Joanne Poole, Contact

- Back Country Horsemen of British Columbia Okanagan Chapter Newsletter
Type: Newsletter; Editor: Anne Smith
Profile: Updates & announcements from the Okanagan Chapter

Powell River Chapter
Powell River BC
Tel: 604-487-1337
Mission: To provide a learning environment for persons interested in trail riding & the wilderness experience
Chief Officer(s):
Lynn Whittle, Contact
lynn.w@shaw.ca

Robson Valley Chapter
BC
Tel: 250-569-2324
Chief Officer(s):
Brian Wallace, Contact
hbwally@gmail.com

Shuswap Chapter
Shuswap BC
Tel: 778-257-7700
Affiliation(s): Horse Council of British Columbia
Chief Officer(s):
Linda Buchanan, Contact
lindaturtlevalley@gmail.com

- Back Country Horsemen of British Columbia Shuswap Chapter Newsletter
Type: Newsletter; Editor: Susan Noltner
Profile: Shuswp chapter updates & announcements

South Cariboo Chapter
Cariboo BC
Tel: 250-395-6492
Mission: To enhance & preserve public lands for use by equestrians
Chief Officer(s):
Peter Reid, Contact
peterreid99@hotmail.com

Vancouver Island - North Chapter
BC
Tel: 250-337-1818
Mission: To enhance & improve public lands for use by equestrians; To provide educational clinics for members
Chief Officer(s):
Sharon Pickthorne, Contact
oneonone@telus.net

Vancouver Island Chapter
BC
Tel: 250-245-4204
Mission: To provide educational clinics in trail riding, including safety, courtesy & environmental awareness, for persons on Vancouver Island; To preserve & enhance public lands for use by equestrians; To ensure Canadians maintain access to use horses & mules on public lands
Chief Officer(s):
Lynn deVries, Contact

Yarrow Chapter
Yarrow BC
Tel: 604-854-1245
Mission: To provide educational clinics in trail riding for person in the Yarrow area; To preserve & enhance public lands for use by equestrians; To offer a voice for members on issues related to the back country
Chief Officer(s):
Rose Schroeder, Contact
milkmaid@shaw.ca
John Gardener, Vice-Chair, Membership, 604-794-7272
Karin Smith, Secretary, 604-792-3902
Linda Kuhr, Treasurer, 604-823-7456
Peter Kuhr, Coordinator, Education, 604-823-7456
Gene Peters, Coordinator, Work Bee, 604-823-4672
Rose Schroeder, Coordinator, Trails, 604-854-1245

- Back Country Horsemen of British Columbia Yarrow Chapter Newsletter

Type: Newsletter; Editor: Kelly Hawes
Profile: Information & announcements from the Yarrow chapter

Back to the Bible Canada
PO Box 246, Stn. A, Abbotsford BC V2T 6Z6
Toll-Free: 800-663-2425
info@backtothebible.ca
www.backtothebible.ca
www.facebook.com/BTTBCanada
twitter.com/BTTBC
Also Known As: The Good News Broadcasting Association of Canada
Overview: A small national charitable organization
Mission: To provide teachings through Christian radio & multimedia to engage & encourage people in God's Word across Canada & around the world
Member of: Canadian Council of Christian Charities; Evangelican Fellowship of Canada
Staff Member(s): 6
Chief Officer(s):
Byron Reaume, CFO & Director of Stewardship
Bob Beasley, CEO

Badlands Historical Centre
335 - 1st St. East, Drumheller AB T0J 0Y0
Tel: 403-823-2593
landsbad@telus.net
Previous Name: Drumheller Museum Society
Overview: A small local organization
Mission: The Centre displays exhibits on the history of Drumheller Valley from the age of dinosaurs, up through the ice ages & into modern times.

Badminton Alberta
c/o Alberta Badminton Centre, 60 Patterson Blvd. SW, Calgary AB T3H 2E1
Tel: 403-297-2722; Fax: 403-297-2706
Toll-Free: 888-397-2722
members@badmintonalberta.ca
www.badmintonalberta.ca
www.facebook.com/170234779702176
Previous Name: Alberta Badminton Association
Overview: A medium-sized provincial organization founded in 1928 overseen by Badminton Canada
Mission: To promote the sport of badminton in Alberta
Member of: Badminton Canada; International Badminton Federation
Finances: Funding Sources: Alberta Sport Recreation Parks & Wildlife Foundation
Staff Member(s): 4
Membership: 7000 members; 350 affliated clubs; Fees: Schedule available; Member Profile: Athletes, clubs, coaches, & officials; Committees: Executive
Chief Officer(s):
Jeff Bell, Executive Director, 403-297-2108
jbell@badmintonalberta.ca

Badminton BC
#110, 12761 - 16 Ave., Surrey BC V4A 1N2
Tel: 604-385-3595
info@badmintonbc.com
www.badmintonbc.com
www.facebook.com/badmintonBC
twitter.com/b2dmintonbc
instagram.com/badminton_bc
Overview: A medium-sized provincial organization founded in 1925 overseen by Badminton Canada
Mission: To provide leadership to develop & promote badminton in BC by increasing the membership base, facilitating a higher standard of participation through competitive & development opportunities for players, coaches, officials & volunteers
Member of: Sport BC; International Badminton Federation
Finances: Funding Sources: Government grants; Fundraising; Sponsorships
Staff Member(s): 5
Membership: Fees: $15; Member Profile: Recreational & competitive players, coaches, & officials; Committees: Executive; Nominations; Governance Review; Risk Management; Finance & Audit; Regional/Sport Development; Membership; Performance; Competitions; Officials; Coaches; Judicial
Activities: Organizing tournaments, athlete training, & coaching; Speaker Service: Yes; Library: Badminton Resource Library; Open to public
Chief Officer(s):
Penny Gardner, Executive Director, 604-333-3599
executivedirector@badmintonbc.com

Meetings/Conferences:
- Badminton BC Annual General Meeting & Congress 2018, 2018, BC
Scope: Provincial

Badminton Canada
#401, 700 Industrial Ave., Ottawa ON K1G 0Y9
Tel: 613-569-2424; Fax: 613-748-5724
badminton@badminton.ca
www.badminton.ca
www.facebook.com/BadmintonCanada
twitter.com/BdmintonCanada
Previous Name: Canadian Badminton Association
Overview: A medium-sized national organization
Mission: To provide centralized support, &/or leadership in furthering member association objectives, act as custodian of the laws of badminton & to foster outstanding player development; to act for its members in helping to assure national & international class competition for Canada's outstanding badminton players, & to establish Canada as a leading participant in international badminton
Affiliation(s): International Badminton Federation
Staff Member(s): 3
Chief Officer(s):
Joe Morissette, Executive Director
morissette@badminton.ca

Badminton New Brunswick See Badminton New Nouveau Brunswick

Badminton New Nouveau Brunswick (BNNB)
NB
www.bnnb.ca
www.facebook.com/bnnb.ca
Previous Name: Badminton New Brunswick
Overview: A small provincial organization overseen by Badminton Canada
Mission: To organize junior & senior badminton tournaments
Member of: Badminton Canada
Membership: Member Profile: Players, coaches, & officials residing in New Brunswick who are members of organized badminton clubs or teams within the province & who may participate in any National or Provincial event
Chief Officer(s):
Eric Fortin, President

Badminton Newfoundland & Labrador Inc. (BNL)
PO Box 8082, St. John's NL A1B 3M9
Tel: 902-830-8529
badmintonnl@badmintonnl.ca
www.badmintonnl.ca
www.facebook.com/285446971492858
www.youtube.com/user/NLBadminton
Overview: A small provincial organization founded in 1969 overseen by Badminton Canada
Mission: To act as the governing body for badminton in Newfoundland & Labrador
Member of: Sport Newfoundland & Labrador
Finances: Annual Operating Budget: $50,000-$100,000
Staff Member(s): 1
Membership: 1-99; Member Profile: School & community badminton clubs for recreational & competitive players at junior or senior levels
Activities: Organizing sanctioned tournaments & events
Chief Officer(s):
John Gillam, President/Provincial Coach

Badminton Ontario (BON)
#209, 3 Concorde Gate, Toronto ON M3C 3N7
Tel: 416-426-7195; Fax: 416-426-7346
info@badmintonontario.ca
www.badmintonontario.ca
www.facebook.com/badmintonontario
twitter.com/badmntonontario
www.youtube.com/user/cweculture
Previous Name: Ontario Badminton Association
Overview: A medium-sized provincial organization founded in 1925 overseen by Badminton Canada
Mission: To provide an organized, structured environment for the activity of badminton; To promote & develop badminton in Ontario
Affiliation(s): Badminton World Federation
Finances: Annual Operating Budget: $50,000-$100,000; Funding Sources: Ministry of Citizenship, Culture & Recreation
Staff Member(s): 1; 60 volunteer(s)
Membership: 1,000; Fees: Schedule available; Member Profile: Badminton players; clubs; coaches; officials

Activities: *Awareness Events:* Provincial Championships
Chief Officer(s):
Ian Moss, President
ian.moss@badmintonontario.ca

Badminton Québec
4940, rue Hochelaga est, Montréal QC H1V 1E7
Tél: 514-252-3066; *Téléc:* 514-252-3175
info@badmintonquebec.com
www.badmintonquebec.com
www.facebook.com/BadmintonQuebec
twitter.com/@BadmintonQc
Également appelé: Fédération québécoise de badminton inc.
Aperçu: *Dimension:* grande; *Envergure:* provinciale; fondée en 1929 surveillé par Badminton Canada
Mission: Promouvoir et développer le sport sur tout le territoire québécois en regroupant tous ses membres, les personnes et associations intéressées au rayonnement de notre discipline
Membre de: Fédération internationale de badminton
Membre(s) du personnel: 6
Activités: *Stagiaires:* Oui
Membre(s) du bureau directeur:
Chantal Brouillard, Directrice générale
chantal.brouillard@badmintonquebec.com
Christian Guibourt, Directeur technique
christian.guibourt@badmintonquebec.com

Baffin Regional Chamber of Commerce (BRCC)
Building 987-C, PO Box 59, Iqaluit NU X0A 0H0
Tel: 867-979-4654; *Fax:* 867-979-2929
www.baffinchamber.ca
Overview: A small local organization founded in 1987
Mission: To foster, promote & improve business development throughout the Baffin Region & Canada
Finances: *Funding Sources:* Membership fees; project management & administration fees; profits from the annual Nunavut Trade Show & Conference
Membership: *Fees:* $25-$150; *Member Profile:* Baffin businesses & professionals; *Committees:* Communications; Chamber Relations; Trade Show
Activities: *Awareness Events:* Community Economic Development Weeks
Chief Officer(s):
Chris West, Executive Director
execdir@baffinchamber.ca

The Bahá'í Community of Canada / La communauté bahá'íe du Canada
Bahá'í National Centre, 7200 Leslie St., Thornhill ON L3T 6L8
Tel: 905-889-8168; *Fax:* 905-889-8184
Other Communication: Alt. URL: www.bahainews.ca
secretariat@cdnbnc.org
www.ca.bahai.org
www.facebook.com/Bahai.Community.of.Canada
www.flickr.com/photos/103796735@N05
Overview: A large national charitable organization founded in 1844
Mission: To teach the oneness of humanity, the common divine source of all the great religions, equality of the sexes & harmony of science & religion; headquarters in Haifa, Israel; 5-6 million adherents in 214 countries & territories; Canada's 30,000 Bahá'ís are located in some 1,200 localities, some of which elect local governing councils called Spiritual Assemblies; National Spiritual Assembly of Baha'is of Canada incorporated by Act of Parliament in 1949
Member of: Bahá'í International Community
Affiliation(s): Bahá'í International Community
Finances: *Annual Operating Budget:* Greater than $5 Million; *Funding Sources:* Contributions from members
Staff Member(s): 30
Membership: 30,000+
Activities: Study circles; Devotional gatherings; Junior youth spiritual empowerment program; Children's classes; *Awareness Events:* Unity in Diversity Week, Nov.; *Speaker Service:* Yes; *Library:* by appointment Not open to public
Chief Officer(s):
Karen McKye, Secretary-General
Gerald Filson, Director, Public Affairs
externalaffairs@cdnbnc.org
Corinne Box, Director, Government Relations, 613-233-3712
ogr@bcc-cbc.org

Bahá'í Community of Ottawa
211 McArthur Ave., Ottawa ON K1L 6P6
Tel: 613-742-8250
www.bahai-ottawa.org
twitter.com/OttawaBahais
Overview: A small local organization
Mission: To support the development of the Bahá'í Faith Community in Ottawa, Ontario.
Membership: 9 sectors
Chief Officer(s):
Corinne Box, Director, Government Relations, 613-233-3712
ogr@bcc-cbc.org

Baie Verte & Area Chamber of Commerce
PO Box 578, Baie Verte NL A0K 1B0
Tel: 709-532-4204; *Fax:* 709-532-4252
bvachamber@nf.aibn.com
www.bvachamber.com
Overview: A small local organization
Membership: 47; *Fees:* Schedule available based on number of employees.; *Committees:* Mining Conference
Chief Officer(s):
Lloyd Hayden, President
Kira Rideout, Business Administrator

Bakery Council of Canada *See* Baking Association of Canada

Baking Association of Canada (BAC) / Association canadienne de la boulangerie
#202, 7895 Tranmere Dr., Mississauga ON L5S 1V9
Tel: 905-405-0288; *Fax:* 905-405-0993
Toll-Free: 888-674-2253
info@baking.ca
www.baking.ca
Previous Name: Bakery Council of Canada
Overview: A medium-sized national organization founded in 1947
Mission: To further the interests of Canadian retail, in-store, & wholesale bakers, through advocacy & effective programs at the regional & national level
Member of: Retailer's Bakery Association; Conseil de la Boulangerie du Québec
Membership: 2,500; *Fees:* Schedule available; *Member Profile:* Retail bakers; in-store bakers; commercial bakers; suppliers; *Committees:* Education; Technical; Food Safety
Activities: *Library:* Not open to public
Chief Officer(s):
Paul Hetherington, President & CEO
Ahmed Mutaher, Director, Business Development - Events & Exhibitions
amutaher@baking.ca
Johanne Trudeau, Director, Food & Nutrition Policy
Meetings/Conferences:
• Bakery Congress 2018 Trade Show & Conference, 2018, Montréal, QC
Scope: National
Contact Information: Ahmed Mutaher, E-mail: amutaher@baking.ca
• Bakery Showcase 2018, April, 2018, The International Centre, Mississauga, ON
Scope: National
Contact Information: Ahmed Mutaher, E-mail: amutaher@baking.ca
Publications:
• BAC [Baking Association of Canada] E-Newsletter
Type: Newsletter; *Frequency:* twice a month; *Accepts Advertising*
Profile: Industry information & forthcoming events
• The Bulletin [a publication of the Baking Association of Canada]
Type: Newsletter; *Frequency:* 10 pa
Profile: Industry information & forthcoming events

BALANCE for Blind Adults
#302, 4920 Dundas St. West, Toronto ON M9A 1B7
Tel: 416-236-1796; *Fax:* 416-236-4280
info@balancefba.org
www.balancefba.org
www.facebook.com/balanceforblindadults
twitter.com/balancefba
Overview: A medium-sized local charitable organization founded in 1986
Mission: To provide instruction & support to individuals with visual impairment to enable them to live independently & confidently in their community; To promote independence, decision making, & self-fulfillment
Staff Member(s): 9
Membership: *Member Profile:* Application assessment process & must be responsible adult 18 years of age & older, self motivated to enhance his/her independence, able to live alone without supervision, & have sufficient resources to cover living expenses
Activities: Teaching daily living skills, orientation & mobility, community access & awareness, & life skills
Chief Officer(s):
Susan Archibald, Executive Director

Balle au mur Québec (BAMQ) / Québec Handball Association
CP 1000, Succ. M, 4545, av Pierre-de-Coubertin, Montréal QC H1V 3R2
Tél: 514-252-3062; *Téléc:* 514-252-3103
info@sports-4murs.qc.ca
www.balleaumur.qc.ca
www.facebook.com/BalleAuMurQuebecBamq
Aperçu: *Dimension:* moyenne; *Envergure:* provinciale; fondée en 1971
Affiliation(s): Association canadienned de Balle au mur
Finances: *Budget de fonctionnement annuel:* $50,000-$100,000; *Fonds:* Gouvernement provincial
Membre(s) du personnel: 2; 10 bénévole(s)
Membre: 10 institutionnel; 1 000 individu
Membre(s) du bureau directeur:
Michel Séguin, Directeur général

Ballet British Columbia
601 Smithe St., Vancouver BC V6G 5G1
Tel: 604-732-5003; *Fax:* 604-732-4417
info@balletbc.com
www.balletbc.com
www.facebook.com/BalletBC
twitter.com/BalletBC
www.youtube.com/user/BalletBC1
Overview: A medium-sized provincial charitable organization founded in 1986
Mission: To commission & perform a balanced repertoire rooted in classical technique, which encompasses the best new ballets & late 20th century classics
Member of: Vancouver Cultural Alliance
Finances: *Funding Sources:* Government; corporate & private donations
Staff Member(s): 17
Activities: *Internships:* Yes; *Speaker Service:* Yes
Chief Officer(s):
Branislav Henselmann, Executive Director
bhenselmann@balletbc.com
Emily Molnar, Artistic Director

Ballet Creole
101 Portland St., Toronto ON M8Y 1B1
Tel: 416-960-0350; *Fax:* 416-960-2067
info@balletcreole.org
www.balletcreole.org
www.facebook.com/ballet.creole
Overview: A small local charitable organization founded in 1990
Mission: To preserve & promote traditional & contemporary African & Caribbean dance styles; To build a dance legacy in Canada; To bring cultures together through entertainment, as well as education, accessibility & archival projects
Finances: *Funding Sources:* Ontario Ministry of Culture; Toronto Arts Council; Ontario Arts Council; private donations
Chief Officer(s):
Patrick Parson, Artistic Director
patrick@balletcreole.org

Ballet Jörgen
c/o George Brown College, Casa Loma Campus, Building C, #126, 160 Kendal Ave., Toronto ON M5R 1M3
Tel: 416-961-4725; *Fax:* 416-415-2865
info@balletjorgen.ca
www.balletjorgen.ca
www.facebook.com/balletjorgencanada
twitter.com/balletjorgenca
Overview: A small local charitable organization founded in 1987
Mission: To operate exclusively as a charitable organization to administer & employ its property, assets & rights for the purpose of raising the public's awareness of ballet as an art form by establishing, maintaining & operating a ballet company; To advance knowledge & increase public recognition of ballet by developing a repertoire of original dance productions for performance, film & video for the benefit of the community at large; To advance artistic appreciation & education of the general public of choreography as a distinctive art form by commissioning & making available to the public presentations by a variety of choreographers
Affiliation(s): George Brown Dance
Finances: *Funding Sources:* Individuals; government; corporate
Membership: *Committees:* Finance & Audit

Tel: 902-422-1301; *Fax:* 902-422-7251
info@thebethisrael.com
www.jewishhalifax.com
www.facebook.com/thebethisrael
Overview: A small local organization founded in 1894
Membership: 180 families
Activities: Beth Israel Synagogue; Hebrew school; kosher supervision; gift shop
Chief Officer(s):
Steven Zatzman, President
Publications:
• The Beth
Frequency: Quarterly

Barreau de Montréal / Bar of Montréal
Palais de Justice, #980, 1, rue Notre-Dame est, Montréal QC H2Y 1B6
Tél: 514-866-9392; *Téléc:* 514-866-1488
info@barreaudemontreal.qc.ca
www.barreaudemontreal.qc.ca
Aperçu: *Dimension:* moyenne; *Envergure:* locale; Organisme sans but lucratif; fondée en 1849
Mission: Administrer une corporation professionnelle
Finances: *Budget de fonctionnement annuel:* 500,000$-1.5 Million
Membre(s) du personnel: 8; 300 bénévole(s)
Membre: 11 500; *Montant de la cotisation:* 50-200; *Critères d'admissibilite:* Avocat
Activités: Dîners; Conféderences; Colloques; Tournoi de golf; Tournoi de tennis; Tournoi de badminton; *Evénements de sensibilisation:* Salon Visez Droit; *Service de conférenciers:* Oui
Membre(s) du bureau directeur:
Doris Larrivée, Directrice générale
dlarrivee@barreaudemontreal.qc.ca
Gislaine Dufault, Directrice des communications
gdufault@barreaudemontreal.qc.ca

Le Barreau des Territoires du Nord-Ouest *See* Law Society of the Northwest Territories

Barreau du Haut-Canada *See* Law Society of Upper Canada

Barreau du Nouveau-Brunswick *See* Law Society of New Brunswick

Barrhead & District Chamber of Commerce
PO Box 4524, Barrhead AB T7N 1A4
admin@barrheadchamberofcommerce.com
barrheadchamberofcommerce.com
Overview: A small local organization
Mission: To enhance the development of business by providing a liaison between local business & the rest of the community
Member of: Alberta Chamber of Commerce
Finances: *Annual Operating Budget:* Less than $50,000; *Funding Sources:* Membership fee
Membership: 69
Activities: Promoting local shopping & tourism; Providing educational speakers & seminars; Participating in town & country beautification; Supporting farming communities; *Library:* Open to public
Chief Officer(s):
Dave Sawatzky, President
president@barrheadchamberofcommerce.com

Barrhead Animal Rescue Society (BARS)
c/o Terry Colborne, PO Box 4702, Barrhead AB T7N 1A5
Tel: 780-307-6590
www.barrheadanimalrescue.org
www.facebook.com/BarrheadAnimalRescueSociety
Overview: A medium-sized local charitable organization founded in 2010
Mission: Dedicated to ensuring the humane treatment of all animals in the Town of Barrhead, the County of Barrhead and surrounding areas.
Finances: *Funding Sources:* Private donations
Chief Officer(s):
Terry Colbourne, President

Barrhead Association for Community Living (BACL)
4815 - 51 Ave., Barrhead AB T7N 1M1
Tel: 780-674-5051; *Fax:* 780-674-5023
bacl@xplornet.com
Overview: A small local charitable organization founded in 1973
Mission: To promote the welfare of people with handicaps & their families; To promote a community that embraces all people
Member of: Alberta Association for Community Living
Activities: *Internships:* Yes; *Speaker Service:* Yes

Barrhead Gem Seekers
c/o Laura Tywoniuk, 5508 - 58 Ave., Barrhead AB T7N 1C7
Tel: 780-674-4341
Overview: A small local organization founded in 1978
Mission: To promote & encourage interest in gem & mineral hobby
Member of: Alberta Federation of Rock Clubs
Chief Officer(s):
Laura Tywoniuk, Contact

Barrie & District Association of REALTORS Inc.
30 Mary St., Barrie ON L4N 1S8
Tel: 705-739-4650
www.barrie.realtors.ca
www.linkedin.com/company/barrie-&-district-association-of-realtors-inc-
www.facebook.com/BDARInc
twitter.com/barrierealtors
Previous Name: Barrie & District Real Estate Board Inc.
Overview: A small local organization overseen by Ontario Real Estate Association
Mission: To provide continuing education, Multiple Listing Service (MLS), statistical information & many other services to its members; To promote a high standard of business practices
Membership: 800; *Member Profile:* Real estate sales agents

Barrie & District Real Estate Board Inc. *See* Barrie & District Association of REALTORS Inc.

Barrie Agricultural Society *See* Essa & District Agricultural Society

Barrie Gem & Mineral Society Inc.
PO Box 143, Barrie ON L4M 4S9
Overview: A small local organization
Mission: To foster an interest in the earth sciences & related lapidary arts
Member of: Central Canadian Federation of Mineralogical Societies

Barrie Literacy Council
#244, 80 Bradford St., Barrie ON L4N 6S7
Tel: 705-728-7323; *Fax:* 705-728-7155
barrie_literacy@on.aibn.com
www.barrieliteracy.ca
www.facebook.com/BarrieLiteracyCouncil
Overview: A small local charitable organization founded in 1979
Mission: To help adults improve their basic reading, writing & math skills to reach their goals & improve their self-esteem
Member of: Laubach Literacy of Canada, Ontario
Affiliation(s): Community Literacy of Ontario; Learning Disabilities Association of Ontario; Simcoe/Muskoka Literacy Network
Finances: *Funding Sources:* Donations; Ministry of Training, Colleges & Universities
Staff Member(s): 6; 89 volunteer(s)
Membership: 150; *Committees:* Public Relations; Tutor Training; Finance; Planning & Evaluation; Social; Internal Communications; Fundraising; Volunteer Management; Student Liasion; Members-at-Large
Activities: Training adults in basic reading, writing, math; training tutors; *Speaker Service:* Yes; *Library:* Not open to public
Chief Officer(s):
Judy DesRoches, Executive Director

Barrie Native Friendship Centre (BNFC)
175 Bayfield St., Barrie ON L4M 3B4
Tel: 705-721-7689; *Fax:* 705-721-7418
Overview: A small local charitable organization founded in 1987
Mission: To promote social activities, community awareness, culture-language, information/resources, employment/education/staffing, children's programs; to assist urban Natives; to work in cooperation with non-Native community
Member of: Ontario Federation of Indian Friendship Centres
Membership: *Fees:* Free seniors; $10 adult; $20 family; *Member Profile:* Native & non-native membership
Activities: Culture-based Native programming; youth, family support, employment & training; healing & wellness; monthly meetings
Chief Officer(s):
Samantha Kinoshameg, Executive Director
executivedirector@bnfc.ca

Barrie Parents of Twins and More *See* Simcoe County Parents of Multiples

Barrie Post Polio Association
57 Henry St., Barrie ON L4N 1C6
Overview: A small local charitable organization
Mission: A self help group working with Ontario March of Dimes for those suffering from the late effects of poliomyelitis & for any other interested persons
Membership: *Fees:* $10
Chief Officer(s):
Pauline Berry, Contact
pberry@marchofdimes.ca

Barriere & District Chamber of Commerce
PO Box 1190, Barriere BC V0E 1E0
Tel: 250-672-9221
Overview: A small local organization
Affiliation(s): Canadian Chamber of Commerce
Finances: *Annual Operating Budget:* Less than $50,000; *Funding Sources:* Membership dues; fundraising
Membership: 25; *Fees:* Schedule available

Barriere & District Food Bank Society
4748 Gilbert Rd., Barriere BC V0E 1E0
Tel: 250-672-0029
Overview: A small local organization overseen by Food Banks British Columbia
Member of: Food Banks British Columbia
Membership: *Fees:* $2

Barrington & Area Chamber of Commerce
Box 1, Comp 7, Barrington NS B0W 1E0
Tel: 902-723-0091
barringtonchamberofcommerce@gmail.com
www.barringtonareachamber.com
www.facebook.com/barringtonareachamber
Overview: A small local organization founded in 1990
Membership: 50; *Fees:* Businesses with 9 or less employees: $50; businesses with 10-49 employees: $100; businesses with 50+ employees: $175; *Member Profile:* Individuals, corporations, businesses or firms in the Municipality of Barrington or the Town of Clark's Harbour
Chief Officer(s):
Kathy Johnson, Coordinator

Barrow Bay & District Sports Fishing Association (BB&DSFA)
PO Box 987, Lions Head ON N0H 1W0
Fax: 519-793-3363
barrowbayfishing@hotmail.com
www.bltg.com/bbdsfa
Overview: A small local organization founded in 1993
Member of: Ontario Federation of Anglers & Hunters
Affiliation(s): Ontario Federation of Anglers & Hunters
Finances: *Annual Operating Budget:* $50,000-$100,000; *Funding Sources:* Membership dues; fundraising; government grants
Membership: 92; *Member Profile:* Anglers, residents & associates who reside or who have seasonal residences in the vicinity of Barrow Bay & Lion's Head, Ontario, Canada
Publications:
• Barrow Bay & District Sports Fishing Association Newsletter
Type: Newsletter; *Author:* Jim Halliday

Barth Syndrome Foundation of Canada
#115, 162 Guelph St., Georgetown ON L7G 5X7
Tel: 905-873-2391
Toll-Free: 888-732-9458
www.barthsyndrome.ca
www.facebook.com/barthsyndromecanada
Overview: A medium-sized national charitable organization
Mission: To find research grants into the cause, treatments & cure for Barth Syndrome; To assist Canadian families & physicians dealing with the disease
Affiliation(s): Barth Syndrome Foundation Inc.
Finances: *Funding Sources:* Donations
Chief Officer(s):
Susan Hone, President

Base Borden Soaring (BBSG)
PO Box 286, Borden ON L0M 1C0
Tel: 705-424-1200
ourplace@csolve.net
users.csolve.net/~ourplace/contents.htm
Overview: A small local organization founded in 1974
Member of: Soaring Association of Canada
Membership: *Fees:* $50
Chief Officer(s):
Ray Leiska

Canadian Associations / Baseball Alberta (BA)

Baseball Alberta (BA)
11759 Groat Rd. NW, 2nd Fl., Edmonton AB T5M 3K6
Tel: 780-427-8943; *Fax:* 780-427-9032
registrar@baseballalberta.com
www.baseballalberta.com
www.facebook.com/baseballalberta
twitter.com/BaseballAlberta
Also Known As: Alberta Baseball Association
Overview: A large provincial organization founded in 1967 overseen by Baseball Canada
Mission: To promote & develop baseball in Alberta; To provide life & leadership skills for all genders through baseball; To encourage fun & fair play
Member of: Western Canada Baseball Association; Edmonton International Baseball Foundation
Affiliation(s): Alberta Amateur Baseball Council
Finances: *Funding Sources:* Membership dues; government; corporate
Staff Member(s): 3
Membership: *Fees:* Schedule available
Activities: Programs include: Rally Cap; Winterball; Reaching Baseball Ideals; Long Term Athlete Development; Canadian Sport for Life; National Coaching Certification Program; programs for girls & women
Chief Officer(s):
Darren Dekinder, Executive Director & Registrar, 780-427-9014
registrar@baseballalberta.com
Awards:
• Baseball Alberta Life Members
• Ted Rudd Minor Coach Award
• President's Award
• Wally A. Footz Builders Award
• Aurora Baseball Association Coach of the Year Award
• Murray Service Umpire of the Year Award
• Baseball Alberta Umpire Hall of Fame Award
• Junior Umpire of the Year Award
• Baseball Alberta Players of the Year
• Baseball Alberta Associations of the Year
• EIBF Bill Chmiliar Award of Merit

Baseball BC
#310, 15225 - 104th Ave., Surrey BC V3R 6Y8
Tel: 604-586-3310; *Fax:* 604-586-3311
info@baseball.bc.ca
www.baseball.bc.ca
www.facebook.com/233202485008
twitter.com/Baseball_BC
Previous Name: BC Amateur Baseball Association
Overview: A medium-sized provincial organization overseen by Baseball Canada
Mission: To support the development of baseball & the aspirations of its members; To offer oppourtunities & setting procedures, standards, & policies
Finances: *Funding Sources:* Government of B.C., Legacies Now, Rawlings Sporting Goods, Prostock Athletic Supply, Toronto Blue Jays, All Sport Insurance, Gatorade, Sport B.C.
Membership: 4,500
Chief Officer(s):
David Laing, Executive Director, 604-586-3312
davidlaing@baseball.bc.ca

Baseball Canada / Fédération canadienne de baseball amateur
#A7, 2212 Gladwin Cres., Ottawa ON K1B 5N1
Tel: 613-748-5606; *Fax:* 613-748-5767
info@baseball.ca
www.baseball.ca
www.facebook.com/baseballcanada
twitter.com/baseballcanada
instagram.com/baseballcanada;
youtube.com/baseballcanadamedia
Also Known As: Canadian Federation of Amateur Baseball
Overview: A large national charitable organization founded in 1964
Mission: To promote the development of baseball across Canada through support of provincial organizations & design of programs, including athletes, coaches, events, umpires & partner groups
Member of: International Baseball Association; Confederation of PanAmerican Baseball
Affiliation(s): Canadian Olympic Association
Finances: *Funding Sources:* Federal government; membership fees; sponsors; sales; program revenues
Staff Member(s): 9
Activities: Hosts seven national championships; selects three national teams for international competition; National Skill Competition; Coach & Umpire Certification; Baseball Canada Cup; Honda Hit-Run-Throw; *Internships:* Yes; *Library:* by appointment
Chief Officer(s):
Jason Dickson, President
Don Paulencu, Vice-President
Jody Frowley, Treasurer
Jim Baba, Director General
jbaba@baseball.ca

Baseball New Brunswick (BNB) / Baseball Nouveau-Brunswick
#13, 900 Hanwell Rd., Fredericton NB E3B 6A2
Tel: 506-451-1329; *Fax:* 506-451-1325
director@baseballnb.ca
www.baseballnb.ca
www.facebook.com/BaseballNB
twitter.com/NB_Selects
Overview: A medium-sized provincial organization founded in 1989 overseen by Baseball Canada
Mission: To promote & govern baseball in New Brunswick.
Affiliation(s): Sport New Brunswick; Baseball Atlantic
Finances: *Funding Sources:* Provincial government
Staff Member(s): 1
Membership: 5841; *Member Profile:* Baseball players, coaches, officials, volunteers & administrators.; *Committees:* Financial; High Performance; Hall of Fame; Personnel; Linguistics
Chief Officer(s):
David Watling, President
bnbwatling@rogers.com
David Dion, Executive Director

Baseball Nouveau-Brunswick See Baseball New Brunswick

Baseball Nova Scotia (BNS)
5516 Spring Garden Rd., 4th Fl., Halifax NS B3J 1G6
Tel: 902-425-5454; *Fax:* 902-425-5606
baseball@sportnovascotia.ca
www.baseballnovascotia.com
www.facebook.com/baseballnovascotia
twitter.com/baseball_ns
instagram.com/baseballnovascotia
Overview: A medium-sized provincial organization overseen by Baseball Canada
Mission: To represent baseball teams & leagues under the jurisdiction of BaseballCanada.
Member of: Canadian Federation of Amateur Baseball
Membership: *Fees:* Schedule available
Chief Officer(s):
Brandon Guenette, Executive Director
Trevor Wamback, Technical Director
twamback@sportnovascotia.ca
Brennan Curry, Coordinator, Programs
bcurry@sportnovascotia.ca

Baseball Ontario
#3, 131 Sheldon Dr., Cambridge ON N1R 6S2
Tel: 519-740-3900; *Fax:* 519-740-6311
baseball@baseballontario.com
www.baseballontario.com
www.facebook.com/BaseballOntario
twitter.com/BaseballOntario
instagram.com/baseball_ontario
Overview: A medium-sized provincial organization founded in 1918 overseen by Baseball Canada
Member of: CSAE
Affiliation(s): Little League Ontario
Finances: *Annual Operating Budget:* $500,000-$1.5 Million
Staff Member(s): 2
Membership: 18 organizations
Activities: Coaching; Umpiring; Elite Player Development; Insurance; Tournaments; Communications; *Awareness Events:* Spring Break Camp; AGM
Chief Officer(s):
Mary-Ann Smith, Administrative Director
maryann@baseballontario.com

Baseball PEI
40 Enman Cres., Charlottetown PE C1E 1E6
Tel: 902-368-4203; *Fax:* 902-368-4548
www.baseballpei.ca
www.facebook.com/BaseballPEI
twitter.com/BaseballPEI1
Previous Name: Prince Edward Island Amateur Baseball Association
Overview: A medium-sized provincial organization founded in 1967 overseen by Baseball Canada
Mission: To promote & develop minor & amateur baseball in PEI
Finances: *Annual Operating Budget:* Less than $50,000
Membership: *Fees:* Schedule available
Activities: Tournaments including Bantam, Pee Wee, and Midget levels.
Chief Officer(s):
Don LeClair, President
Randy Byrne, Executive Director

Bashaw & District Chamber of Commerce
PO Box 645, Bashaw AB T0B 0H0
Tel: 780-372-3087
bashawcc@gmail.com
www.enjoybashaw.com
Overview: A small local organization
Mission: To serve as the voice of Bashaw & District business
Chief Officer(s):
Dustin Hemingson, Chair

Basketball Alberta
Percy Page Centre, 11759 Groat Rd., 2nd Fl., Edmonton AB T5M 3K6
Tel: 780-427-9044; *Fax:* 780-427-9124
www.basketballalberta.ca
www.facebook.com/BasketballAlberta
twitter.com/BasketballAB
Overview: A medium-sized provincial organization founded in 1975 overseen by Canada Basketball
Mission: To be premier facilitators of participation, development, and excellence in basketball. To champion the sport of basketball as a game for life by inspiring unity facilitating development and delivering superior value.
Finances: *Funding Sources:* Provincial government; self-generated
Staff Member(s): 6
Membership: *Fees:* $11 per athlete
Chief Officer(s):
Bob Mitchell, President
bmitchell@basketballalberta.ab.ca
Paul Sir, Executive Director
psir@basketballalberta.ab.ca

Basketball BC
#210, 7888 - 200th St., Langley BC V2Y 3J4
Tel: 604-888-8088; *Fax:* 604-888-8323
info@basketball.bc.ca
www.basketball.bc.ca
www.facebook.com/basketballbc
twitter.com/BasketballBC
Overview: A medium-sized provincial organization overseen by Canada Basketball
Mission: To be British Columbia's leading resource for basketball; To build the game of basketball
Member of: Sport BC
Finances: *Funding Sources:* Government grant; fundraising; membership dues
Staff Member(s): 7
Membership: *Fees:* $15
Chief Officer(s):
Lawrie Johns, Executive Director, 604-455-2812
ljohns@basketball.bc.ca

Basketball Manitoba
145 Pacific Ave., Winnipeg MB R3B 2Z6
Tel: 204-925-5775; *Fax:* 204-925-5929
info@basketball.mb.ca
www.basketball.mb.ca
www.linkedin.com/company/basketball-manitoba
www.facebook.com/basketballmanitoba
twitter.com/basketballmb
www.youtube.com/user/baskmanbaskman
Overview: A medium-sized provincial organization founded in 1976 overseen by Canada Basketball
Mission: To operate as the provincial sport governing body for basketball in Manitoba; To ensure all Manitobians have access to the programs run by the association & that the game of basketball is enjoyed by as many people as possible
Staff Member(s): 4
Membership: *Committees:* Technical
Chief Officer(s):
Adam Wedlake, Executive Director
awedlake@basketball.mb.ca

Basketball New Brunswick (BNB) / Basketball Nouveau-Brunswick
#13, 900 Hanwell Rd., Fredericton NB E3B 6A2

Tel: 506-472-4667; *Fax:* 506-451-1325
info@basketball.nb.ca
www.basketball.nb.ca
www.facebook.com/BasketballNB
twitter.com/BasketballNB
Overview: A large provincial organization founded in 1979 overseen by Canada Basketball
Mission: To promote, develop & encourage sport & recreation aspects of basketball in New Brunswick; To assist in establishment of basketball clubs throughout New Brunswick; To liaise with government & private agencies interested in promoting & supporting basketball
Affiliation(s): New Brunswick Association of Approved Basketball Officials; New Brunswick Interscholastic Athletic Association
Finances: *Annual Operating Budget:* $500,000-$1.5 Million; *Funding Sources:* Membership dues; Provincial government; Programs
Staff Member(s): 3
Membership: *Member Profile:* All players competing in provincial championships; minor association members
Activities: Offering National Coaching Certification, an Elite Development Program, & junior officials development
Chief Officer(s):
Lori Wall, President
Carolyn Peppin, Executive Director
carolyn.peppin@basketball.nb.ca
Kim Flemming, Office Administrator
kim.flemming@basketball.nb.ca
Awards:
• Service Awards
• Play Fair Awards

Basketball Newfoundland *See* Newfoundland & Labrador Basketball Association

Basketball Nouveau-Brunswick *See* Basketball New Brunswick

Basketball Nova Scotia
5516 Spring Garden Rd., 3rd Fl., Halifax NS B3J 1G6
Tel: 902-425-5450; *Fax:* 902-425-5606
bnsadmin@basketball.ns.ca
basketballnovascotia.com
www.facebook.com/BasketballNovaScotia
twitter.com/BasketballNS
www.instagram.com/basketballnovascotia
Overview: A small provincial organization overseen by Canada Basketball
Mission: To promote & encourage the game of basketball throughout the province
Member of: Sport Canada
Affiliation(s): Sport Nova Scotia
Finances: *Annual Operating Budget:* $250,000-$500,000; *Funding Sources:* Government grants; Membership fees; Special events
Staff Member(s): 3; 12 volunteer(s)
Membership: 4,000; *Fees:* Schedule available
Activities: Offering the National Coaching Certificate Program; Facilitating player development programs & camps; Organizing tournaments
Chief Officer(s):
David Wagg, Executive Director
bnsexecutivedirector@sportnovascotia.ca

Basketball NWT
PO Box 44, Yellowknife NT X1A 2N1
www.bnwt.ca
www.facebook.com/bnwt.ca
Overview: A medium-sized provincial organization overseen by Canada Basketball
Mission: The Association encourages participation in basketball, develops athletes, & provides opportunities for cultural & social interchange among all involved in the sport
Affiliation(s): Steve Nash Youth Basketball; Sport North; Arctic Winter Games
Chief Officer(s):
Damien Healy, President & Executive Director

Basketball PEI
#101, 40 Enman Cres., Charlottetown PE C1E 1E6
Tel: 902-368-4986; *Fax:* 902-368-4548
Toll-Free: 800-247-6712
Other Communication: Toll-Free Fax: 1-800-235-5687
www.basketballpei.ca
twitter.com/basketballpei

Overview: A medium-sized provincial organization overseen by Canada Basketball
Mission: To develop basketball in the province of Prince Edward Island in a fun environment
Activities: Developing the skills needed to play basketball successfully
Chief Officer(s):
Katie Hamilton, Executive Director
katie@basketballpei.ca

Basketball Saskatchewan (BSI)
2205 Victoria Ave., Regina SK S4P 0S4
Fax: 306-525-4009
basketball@basketballsask.com
www.basketballsask.com
www.facebook.com/basketballsask
twitter.com/basketballsask
Previous Name: Saskatchewan Basketball
Overview: A medium-sized provincial licensing charitable organization founded in 1988 overseen by Canada Basketball
Mission: To support & improve basketball opportunities in Saskatchewan
Affiliation(s): Sask Sport
Finances: *Funding Sources:* Sask Sport; Fundraising
Staff Member(s): 2
Membership: 12,000; *Fees:* $35 active; $12 associate; $3.50 affiliate; *Member Profile:* Ages 9 to 60
Activities: *Speaker Service:* Yes; *Library:* Open to public
Chief Officer(s):
Greg Lucas, Executive Director, 306-780-9264
glucas@basketballsask.com
Dave Werry, Coordinator, High Performance, 306-780-9249
dwerry@basketballsask.com

Basketball Yukon
YT
www.basketballyukon.ca
Overview: A medium-sized provincial organization overseen by Canada Basketball
Mission: To assist in player & coaching development in the North; to lead the territory's basketball community through programs & services benefitting all levels of play
Affiliation(s): Sport Yukon, Canada Basketball
Chief Officer(s):
Tim Brady, President

Bateau-Dragon Canada *See* Dragon Boat Canada

Bathurst & District Labour Council
PO Box 114, Bathurst NB E2A 3Z1
Overview: A small local organization
Member of: New Brunswick Federation of Labour
Chief Officer(s):
John Gagnon, Contact, 506-545-0651
gagnonjohn@yahoo.com

Bathurst Jewish Community Centre *See* Prosserman Jewish Community Centre

Bathurst Volunteer Centre de Bénévolat Inc. (BVC)
464 King Ave., Bathurst NB E2A 1P6
Tel: 506-549-5955; *Fax:* 506-549-5866
info@bvc-cbb.ca
www.bvc-cbb.ca
Overview: A small local charitable organization founded in 1981
Mission: To provide basic needs to families in Chaleur who are unable to provide for themselves
Member of: Canadian Association of Food Banks; New Brunswick Association of Food Banks
Staff Member(s): 3
Activities: clothing exchange; food action programs; meals-on-wheels
Chief Officer(s):
Michel Godin, Manager
manager@bvc-cbb.ca

Bâtiments Durables Canada *See* Sustainable Buildings Canada

Baton New Brunswick (BNB)
20 Adams St., Tide Head NB E3N 4T3
Tel: 506-759-7113
www.batonnb.ca
Overview: A small provincial organization overseen by Canadian Baton Twirling Federation
Mission: To govern baton twirling in New Brunswick
Member of: Canadian Baton Twirling Federation
Membership: *Committees:* Technical; Membership

Chief Officer(s):
Nadine LeBelle-Déjario, President

Baton Twirling Association of British Columbia (BTABC)
22411 Westminster Hwy., Richmond BC V6V 1B6
Tel: 604-722-1595
batonbc@gmail.com
www.bcbaton.com
www.facebook.com/batontwirlingbc
twitter.com/BatonTwirlingBC
www.instagram.com/batontwirlingbc
Also Known As: Baton Twirling BC
Overview: A small provincial organization overseen by Canadian Baton Twirling Federation
Mission: To be the provincial governing body for the sport of baton twirling in British Columbia
Member of: Canadian Baton Twirling Federation
Finances: *Funding Sources:* Province of British Columbia
Activities: Competitions; Training
Chief Officer(s):
Shannon Webster, Chair
Nancey Forsman, Membership Officer

Batshaw Youth & Family Centres
5, parc Weredale, Westmount QC H3Z 1Y5
Tel: 514-989-1885
www.batshaw.ca
Overview: A small local organization founded in 1992
Mission: To intervene with children and families in situations of abuse, neglect, abandonment & when youth have serious behaviour problems, providing psychosocial, rehabilitation & social integration services.
Staff Member(s): 719
Membership: *Committees:* Executive; Governance & Ethics; Verifitication; Service Quality & Vigilance; Human Resources
Activities: *Library:* Centre de documentation
Chief Officer(s):
Judy Martin, President
Lesley Hill, Executive Director

Batten Disease Support & Research Association - Canadian Chapter (BDSRA)
www.bdsra.org
www.facebook.com/bdsra
twitter.com/bdsra
Overview: A small national charitable organization founded in 1994
Finances: *Annual Operating Budget:* Less than $50,000
Membership: 1-99; *Fees:* $20 family
Activities: Family support; public awareness; research
Chief Officer(s):
Margie Frazier, Executive Director, BDSRA
mfrazier@bdsra.org
Bev Maxim, Canada President
bevmaxim@yahoo.ca

Battle River Historical Society
PO Box 2936, 1001 - 1st Ave., Wainwright AB T9W 1S9
Tel: 780-842-3115
battleriverhs@gmail.com
Overview: A small local charitable organization founded in 1983
Mission: To preserve past & present history of Wainwright & district; to promote interest in history; to collect historical materials
Member of: Alberta Museums Association; Canadian Council for Railway Heritage
Finances: *Funding Sources:* Donations; grants
Activities: The Wainwright & District Museum

Battle River Research Group (BRRG)
PO Box 339, 4804 - 43 Ave., Forestburg AB T0B 1N0
Tel: 780-582-7308; *Fax:* 780-582-7312
Toll-Free: 866-828-6774
www.battleriverresearch.com
www.facebook.com/BattleRiverResearchGroup
twitter.com/BRRG_Ag
www.instagram.com/brrg_ag
Overview: A small local organization overseen by Agricultural Research & Extension Council of Alberta
Mission: To support agricultural research, in order to make agriculture more sustainable
Member of: Agricultural Research & Extension Council of Alberta
Membership: *Fees:* $20 individual (annual); $50 individual (3 years); $100 corporate
Chief Officer(s):

Canadian Associations / Battle River Soccer Association

Martina Alder, Coordinator, Extension & Environmental Program
env@battleriverresearch.com
Sarah Hall, Coordinator, Crop Program
crops@battleriverresearch.com
Publications:
• Over the Fenceline [a publication of the Battle River Research Group]
Type: Newsletter

Battle River Soccer Association
PO Box 5558, Leduc AB T9E 2A1
Tel: 780-717-1962
admin@battleriversoccer.com
www.battleriversoccer.com
Overview: A small local organization founded in 1983 overseen by Alberta Soccer Association
Mission: Physical office address: Quality Inn, #116, 501 - 11th Ave., Nisku, AB T9E 7N5
Member of: Alberta Soccer Association; Federation Internationale de Football Association; Canada Soccer Association
Affiliation(s): Breton Soccer Association; Calmar Soccer Association; Devon Soccer Association; Leduc Soccer Association; Millet Soccer Association; New Sarepta Soccer Association; Pigeon Lake Soccer Association; Thorsby Soccer Association; Warburg Soccer Association; Wetaskiwin Soccer Association
Membership: 3,000 players in 10 associations; *Committees:* Human Resources; Bylaw Review/ Financial Policy; IT
Chief Officer(s):
Craig Cooper, President
ck_cooper@yahoo.ca
Sara Letourneau, Office Administrator

Battlefords Agricultural Society (BAS)
PO Box 668, North Battleford SK S9A 2Y9
Tel: 306-445-2024; *Fax:* 306-445-3352
b.exhibition@sasktel.net
agsociety.com
www.facebook.com/113736988690080
twitter.com/BfordsAg
Previous Name: Battlefords Exhibition Association
Overview: A small local charitable organization founded in 1884
Mission: To promote improvements in agriculture & community development; to provide facilities for educational & leisure programs
Member of: Saskatchewan Association of Agricultural Societies & Exhibitions
Staff Member(s): 4
Membership: *Fees:* $40; *Member Profile:* Families, ages 16-85
Activities: Trade shows, quarter horse shows, raffles, chuckwagon races, 4H Regional Show, children's festival
Chief Officer(s):
Dana Alexander, President
Jocelyn Ritchie, General Manager

Battlefords Chamber of Commerce
PO Box 1000, Hwy. 16 & 40 East, North Battleford SK S9A 3E6
Tel: 306-445-6226; *Fax:* 306-446-0188
b.chamber@sasktel.net
www.battlefordschamber.com
www.facebook.com/battlefordschamber
Previous Name: North Battleford Chamber of Commerce
Overview: A small local organization founded in 1905
Member of: Canadian Chamber of Commerce; Saskatchewan Chamber of Commerce
Affiliation(s): Institution of Association Executives; Tourism Industry Association of Saskatchewan
Finances: *Funding Sources:* Membership dues
Staff Member(s): 3
Membership: *Fees:* Schedule available
Chief Officer(s):
Brendon Bootman, President
Linda Machniak, Executive Director
lindamachniak@sasktel.net

Battlefords Dance Festival Association *See* Svoboda Dance Festival Association

Battlefords Exhibition Association *See* Battlefords Agricultural Society

Battlefords Indian & Métis Friendship Centre
960 - 103 St., North Battleford SK S9A 1K2
Tel: 306-445-8216
nbimfc@sasktel.net
www.afcs.ca/battleford-friendship-centre.html
www.facebook.com/366725376804735
Also Known As: Battlefords Friendship Centre
Overview: A small local charitable organization founded in 1969
Member of: Aboriginal Friendship Centres of Saskatchewan
Membership: *Member Profile:* Aboriginal people

Battlefords Interval House Society
2092 - 102 St., North Battleford SK S9A 1H7
Tel: 306-445-2742; *Fax:* 306-446-2520; *Crisis Hot-Line:* 306-445-2742
Overview: A small local charitable organization founded in 1980
Mission: Provides 16-bed shelter; transportation; education/health promotion on anti-violence; life skills training advocate; court work advocate; partnership with agencies of justice, education, social services, health
Member of: Partnership Promoting Violence-Free Communities
Affiliation(s): Provincial Association of Transition Houses (PATHS)
Finances: *Funding Sources:* Provincial government
Staff Member(s): 14; 3 volunteer(s)
Membership: 30 individual; *Fees:* $5

The Battlefords Music Festival
PO Box 1301, North Battleford SK S9A 3L8
Tel: 306-445-0182
Overview: A small local charitable organization
Affiliation(s): Saskatchewan Music Festival Association
25 volunteer(s)
Membership: 30 individual
Chief Officer(s):
Kelly Waters, Contact

Battlefords United Way Inc.
#203, 891 - 99th St., North Battleford SK S9A 0N8
Tel: 306-445-1717
buw@sasktel.net
www.battlefordsunitedway.ca
Overview: A small local charitable organization founded in 1967 overseen by United Way of Canada - Centraide Canada
Mission: To improve lives & build community by engaging individuals & mobilizing collective action
Finances: *Funding Sources:* Donations
Activities: *Library:* by appointment
Chief Officer(s):
Brendon Boothman, Chair
Jana Blais, Treasurer

Bay of Islands SPCA; Bay of Islands Society for the Prevention of Cruelty to Animals *See* NL West SPCA

Bay of Quinte Dental Society (BQDS)
c/o John Marinovich, 257 Dundas St. East, Trenton ON K8V 1M1
Tel: 613-392-3939; *Crisis Hot-Line:* 613-961-0033
quintedentists.com
Overview: A small local organization overseen by Canadian Dental Association
Mission: To provide direction & education for dentistry within the Bay of Quinte region; To provide dental treatment & education for people in the community
Member of: Ontario Dental Association (ODA)
Membership: 62; *Member Profile:* Dentists & Dental Specialists
Chief Officer(s):
John Marinovich, President
john@marinovichgroup.com

Bay St. George Chamber of Commerce
35 Carolina Ave., Stephenville NL A2N 3P8
Tel: 709-643-5854; *Fax:* 709-643-6398
www.bsgcc.org
www.facebook.com/119729931434739
twitter.com/BSGCOC
Previous Name: Stephenville Chamber of Commerce
Overview: A small local organization founded in 1955
Mission: To promote & enhance economic growth towards a viable community
Membership: *Fees:* $10 student; $25 retired; $55 individual; $85-$500 business
Chief Officer(s):
Tom Rose, President

Bay St. George Folk Arts Council
c/o Aldonna O'Keefe, 45 Birch Dr., Kippens NL A2N 3P2
Tel: 709-643-9395
www.bsgfolkart.ca
www.facebook.com/profile.php?id=100008655662316&fref=ts
Overview: A small local organization founded in 2007
Membership: 25
Chief Officer(s):
Aldonna O'Keefe, Chair
amrokeefe@gmail.com
Debbie Hawco, Treasurer
debbiehawco@eastlink.ca

Baycrest Foundation
3560 Bathurst St., 2nd Fl., Toronto ON M6A 2E1
Tel: 416-785-2875; *Fax:* 416-785-4296
donations@baycrest.org
www.baycrest.org/give
Overview: A small local charitable organization founded in 1979
Mission: To raise money on behalf of the Baycrest Centre, which helps funds research for age related diseases
Finances: *Annual Operating Budget:* Less than $50,000
Chief Officer(s):
Josh Cooper, President & CEO, 416-785-2500 Ext. 2415
jcooper@baycrest.org

Bayfield & Area Chamber of Commerce
PO Box 2065, Bayfield ON N0M 1G0
Tel: 519-565-2499
Toll-Free: 800-565-2499
info@villageofbayfield.com
www.villageofbayfield.com
Overview: A small local organization
Mission: To promote the businesses & community of Bayfield
Membership: 1-99; *Fees:* $200
Activities: *Awareness Events:* Sail & Canvas, 3rd weekend in June

BBM Bureau of Measurement; Bureau of Broadcast Measurement; BBM Canada *See* Numeris

BC & Yukon Heart Foundation *See* Heart & Stroke Foundation of British Columbia & Yukon

BC Adaptive Snowsports (BCAS)
780 Marine Dr. SW, Vancouver BC V6P 5Y7
Tel: 604-333-3630
info@bcadaptive.com
www.bcadaptive.com
linkedin.com/company/the-disabled-skiers-association-of-bc
www.facebook.com/bcadaptive
twitter.com/BC_adaptive
Previous Name: Disabled Skiers Association of BC
Overview: A medium-sized provincial charitable organization founded in 1973 overseen by Canadian Association for Disabled Skiing
Mission: To promote adaptive skiing, snowboarding, & mountain accessbility as a form of rehabiliation for participants with physical disabilities; To contribute to an inclusive & healthy lifestyle for residents of British Columbia
Member of: BC Disability Sports; Canadian Association for Disabled Skiing
Finances: *Annual Operating Budget:* $100,000-$250,000; *Funding Sources:* Donations, Corporate sponsors; Government
Staff Member(s): 7; 700 volunteer(s)
Membership: 1,326; *Fees:* $46 participant; $41 volunteer/instructor
Activities: Offering adaptive snow sports throughout BC; *Awareness Events:* Scotiabank Charity Challenge; Black Diamond Gala; Sun Peaks Grand Golf Tournament; *Speaker Service:* Yes
Chief Officer(s):
Jason Campbell, Interim CEO & Director, Fund Development, 604-333-3630 Ext. 205
jason@bcadaptive.com

BC Alliance for Arts & Culture
#100, 938 Howe St., Vancouver BC V6Z 1N9
Tel: 604-681-3535; *Fax:* 604-681-7848
info@allianceforarts.com
www.allianceforarts.com
www.facebook.com/AllianceforArtsandCulture
twitter.com/AllianceArts
www.youtube.com/user/AllianceArtsCulture
Previous Name: Vancouver Cultural Alliance
Overview: A medium-sized provincial organization founded in 1986
Mission: To project a strong voice for the local arts community; To promote the activities of the arts through a variety of programs, services & marketing strategies; To increase public awareness of & accessibility to the arts & culture
Member of: Canadian Conference of the Arts; Tourism Vancouver

Finances: *Funding Sources:* British Columbia Arts Council; City of Vancouver; metro Vancouver
Membership: 350+; *Fees:* $25 student; $80 individual; $160-$650 organization/business; *Member Profile:* Inviduals & organizations interested in arts & culture in British Columbia
Activities: Offering training & employment programs; Providing professional development activities & public education; *Library:* Arts Resource Centre; Open to public
Chief Officer(s):
Brenda Leadley, Executive Director, 604-681-3535 Ext. 209
brenda@allianceforarts.com
Nancy Lanthier, Director, Communications, 604-681-3535 Ext. 212
nancy@allianceforarts.com
Beverly Edgecomb, Manager, Member Relations, 604-681-3535 Ext. 207
bev@allianceforarts.com

BC Amateur Baseball Association *See* Baseball BC

BC Artificial Insemination Centre *See* Westgen

BC Assocation for Crane Safety (BCACS)
PO Box 48883, Stn. Bentall, 595 Burrard St., Vancouver BC V7X 1A8
Tel: 604-336-4699; *Fax:* 604-339-4510
info@bcacs.ca
bcacs.ca
Overview: A small provincial organization founded in 2005
Mission: To create a safer workplace for those in the crane hoisting industry as well as to promote the industry
Chief Officer(s):
Ron Karras, Chair, Board of Directors

BC Association for Individualized Technology and Supports (BCITS)
#103, 366 East Kent Ave. South, Vancouver BC V5X 4N6
Tel: 604-326-0175; *Fax:* 604-326-0176
Toll-Free: 866-326-1245
info@bcits.org
www.bcits.org
Overview: A medium-sized provincial charitable organization
Mission: To help meet the needs of people with severe disabilities who require assistive technologies & supports
Activities: Provincial Respiratory Outreach Program; Technology for Independent Living; Discharge Planning
Chief Officer(s):
Christine Gordon, Chair
Ruth Marzetti, Executive Director
Richard Bing, Office Administrator

BC Association of Legal Assistants *See* British Columbia Paralegal Association

BC Association of Performing Arts Festivals *See* Performing Arts BC

BC Biotech *See* LifeSciences British Columbia

BC Cheerleading Association (BCCA)
BC
www.bccheerleading.ca
Overview: A small provincial organization overseen by Cheer Canada
Mission: To maintain athleticism & safety in cheerleading in British Columbia.
Member of: Cheer Canada
Chief Officer(s):
Krista Gerlich-Fitzgerald, Chair

BC Chinese Music Association (BCCMA)
#303, 8495 Ontario St., Vancouver BC V5X 3E8
Tel: 604-327-8807; *Fax:* 604-327-8606
mail@bccma.net
www.bccma.net
www.facebook.com/bccma
www.youtube.com/user/bccma
Overview: A small provincial charitable organization founded in 1995
Mission: To share & promote Chinese music; To use music to strengthen Canada's understanding of Chinese culture
Activities: Organizing concerts, classes, & instrument exhibitions
Chief Officer(s):
S.K. Lee, Honorary President

BC Chinese Soccer Federation (BCCSF)
#114, 4940 No. 3 Rd., Richmond BC V6X 3A5
Tel: 604-207-8711
www.bccsf.info
Overview: A small provincial organization
Mission: To promote the sport of soccer; To oversee the Multi-Nation Recreation League
Activities: Holding soccer tournaments; Offering a youth training program

BC Construction Safety Alliance (BCCSA)
#400, 625 Agnes St., New Westminster BC V3M 5Y4
Tel: 604-636-3675; *Fax:* 604-636-3676
Toll-Free: 877-860-3675
www.bccsa.ca
www.facebook.com/SafetyInConstruction
twitter.com/BCCSABeSafe
Previous Name: Construction Safety Network
Overview: A small provincial organization founded in 2001
Mission: To partner with WorkSafeBC to promote a positive occupational health & safety culture for the construction industry
Staff Member(s): 9
Chief Officer(s):
Mike McKenna, Executive Director
mmckenna@bccsa.ca

BC Disc Sports Society *See* British Columbia Disc Sports

BC Egg Producers *See* British Columbia Egg Marketing Board

BC English Teachers' Association *See* British Columbia Teachers of English Language Arts

BC Federation of School Athletic Associations *See* BC School Sports

BC First Party
#106, 2130 York Ave., Vancouver BC V6K 1C3
Tel: 604-710-2100
www.bcfirst.ca
www.facebook.com/bcfirst
twitter.com/bcfirst
www.youtube.com/user/TheBCFirstParty
Also Known As: BC First
Overview: A small provincial organization
Membership: *Fees:* $10 individual; $20 family
Chief Officer(s):
John Twigg, Party Leader

BC Freestyle Ski Association
#636, 280 Nelson St., Vancouver BC V6B 2E2
Tel: 604-398-8830
info@bcfreestyle.com
bcfreestyle.com
www.facebook.com/BCFreestyleSkiAssociation
twitter.com/bcfreestyle
Overview: A small provincial organization overseen by Canadian Freestyle Ski Association
Mission: To develop, promote & coordinate the sport of freestyle skiing in British Columbia.
Member of: Canadian Freestyle Ski Association
Chief Officer(s):
Adrian Taggart, President

BC Friends of Schizophrenics *See* British Columbia Schizophrenia Society

BC Games Society
#200, 990 Fort St., Victoria BC V8V 3K2
Tel: 250-387-1375; *Fax:* 250-387-4489
www.bcgames.org
www.facebook.com/BCGamesSociety
twitter.com/BCGames1
www.instagram.com/bcgames1
Previous Name: British Columbia Games Society
Overview: A small provincial organization
Mission: To provide event management leadership in the creation of development opportunities for individuals, sport organizations & host communities
Staff Member(s): 8
Chief Officer(s):
Kelly Mann, President & CEO
kellym@bcgames.org

BC Hands & Voices
1965 Rodger Ave., Port Coquitlam BC V3C 1B8
info@bchandsandvoices.com
www.bchandsandvoices.com
Overview: A small provincial charitable organization
Mission: BC Hands & Voices supports families with children who are deaf or hard of hearing.

Membership: *Fees:* $15 individual; $25 agency

BC Helicopter & Snowcat Skiing Operators Association *See* HeliCat Canada

B.C. Horseshoe Association
c/o Sam Tomasevic, 7987 Graham Ave., Burnaby BC V3N 1V8
Tel: 604-525-2186
administrator@bchorseshoe.com
www.bchorseshoe.com
Overview: A small provincial organization overseen by Horseshoe Canada
Mission: To promote the sport of horseshoe pitching in British Columbia.
Member of: Horseshoe Canada
Membership: 346
Chief Officer(s):
Sam Tomasevic, President
samtom@telus.net

BC Kosher; Orthodox Rabbinical Council of British Columbia *See* Kosher Check

BC Lacrosse Association (BCLA)
#101, 7382 Winston St., Burnaby BC V5A 2G9
Tel: 604-421-9755; *Fax:* 604-421-9775
info@bclacrosse.com
www.bclacrosse.com
www.facebook.com/481524661862119
twitter.com/BCLacrosse
www.youtube.com/user/BCLacrosseA
Overview: A medium-sized provincial organization overseen by Canadian Lacrosse Association
Mission: Promotes and regulates the sport of lacrosse in British Columbia
Member of: Canadian Lacrosse Association
Staff Member(s): 5
Chief Officer(s):
Rochelle Winterton, Executive Director
rochelle@bclacrosse.com
Dave Showers, Technical Director
dave@bclacrosse.com
Awards:
• The "Gary" Award
• Hugh Gifford Merit Award
• Tom Gordon Plaque
• Norm Wright Merit Award
• Ted Fridge Family SPIRIT Award
• Ruth Seward Merit Award
• Jimmy Gunn Merit Award
• John Cavallin Merit Award
• Bill McBain Merit Award
• Art Daoust Merit Award
• Dal Martin Merit Award
• Leon Hall Merit Award
• Irvine-Calder-Nevard Merit Award
• President's Awards
Meetings/Conferences:
• BC Lacrosse Association Annual General Meeting 2018, 2018, BC
Scope: Provincial

BC Lymphedema Association (BCLA)
PO Box 42603, Stn. Columbia Square, New Westminster BC V3M 6L7
Toll-Free: 866-991-2252
info@bclymph.org
www.bclymph.org
Overview: A medium-sized provincial charitable organization founded in 2006
Mission: To raise awareness about lymphedema; To represent & support lymphedema patients
Membership: *Fees:* $35 individual; $100 professional; $200 corporate; *Member Profile:* Lymphedema patients & professionals; *Committees:* Healthcare Advisory; Executive; Fundraising & Development; Marketing & Communications; Program
Chief Officer(s):
Lucette Wesley, President

BC Motels, Campgrounds, Resorts Association *See* British Columbia Lodging & Campgrounds Association

BC Motor Transport Association *See* British Columbia Trucking Association

BC Northern Real Estate Association
2609 Queensway, Prince George BC V2L 1N3

Tel: 250-563-1236; Fax: 250-563-3637
inquiries@bcnreb.bc.ca
Overview: A medium-sized local organization founded in 1966 overseen by British Columbia Real Estate Association
Member of: The Canadian Real Estate Association
Chief Officer(s):
Alexandra Goseltine, Executive Director
agoseltine@bcnreb.bc.ca

BC Parents in Crisis Society *See* Parent Support Services Society of BC

BC People First Society
BC
www.selfadvocatenet.com
www.facebook.com/bcpeoplefirst/timeline?ref=page_internal
Overview: A small provincial organization founded in 2000 overseen by People First of Canada
Mission: To change attitudes towards individuals with disabilities; To encourage self-advocacy among individuals with disabilities; To provide information & mentoring services; To raise public awareness about disabilities in the community
Affiliation(s): Community Living British Columbia (CLBC)
Activities: Disseminating information through self-advocacy website; Posting a job board; Hosting a Speakers Bureau
Chief Officer(s):
Bryce Schaufelberger, Contact

BC Rainbow Alliance of the Deaf
BC
info@bcrad.com
www.bcrad.com
www.facebook.com/BCRAD.YVR
Overview: A medium-sized provincial organization founded in 2004
Mission: The British Columbia Rainbow Alliance of the Deaf (BCRAD) is an educational and social recreation organization for all people on the Deaf and queer spectrums.
Affiliation(s): North West Rainbow Alliance of the Deaf
Chief Officer(s):
Zoée Montpetit, President

BC Rural & Multigrade Teachers' Association (BCRMTA)
www.bcruralteachers.org
Previous Name: British Columbia Rural Teachers' Association
Overview: A small provincial organization founded in 1982
Mission: To support teachers of multi-grade classrooms who live & teach in small communities
Affiliation(s): British Columbia Teachers Federation
Finances: *Annual Operating Budget:* Less than $50,000
Membership: 1-99; *Fees:* $20; *Member Profile:* BC teachers working/living in rural areas
Chief Officer(s):
Christina MacDonald, Treasurer
cgmac11@telus.net
Awards:
• Lottie Bowron Memorial Bursary
• Professional Development Travel Grants
Publications:
• The Rural Root [a publication of the BC Rural & Multigrade Teachers' Association]
Type: Newsletter; *Frequency:* 2-3 pa; *Editor:* Erika Momeyer

BC Sailing Association
#195, 3820 Cessna Dr., Richmond BC V7B 0A2
Tel: 604-333-3628; Fax: 604-333-3626
crew@bcsailing.bc.ca
www.bcsailing.bc.ca
www.facebook.com/bcsailing
Also Known As: BC Sailing
Overview: A medium-sized provincial organization overseen by Sail Canada
Mission: The provincial sport authority for sailing
Member of: Sail Canada; Sport BC
Affiliation(s): International Sailing Federation
Finances: *Funding Sources:* Provincial government; membership fees; programs
Staff Member(s): 3
Membership: 5,000; *Fees:* Schedule available
Chief Officer(s):
Tine Moberg-Parker, Executive Director
tmpsailing@shaw.ca

BC School Sports (BCSS)
Sydney Landing, #2003A, 3713 Kensington Ave., Burnaby BC V5B 0A7
Tel: 604-477-1488; Fax: 604-477-1484
info@bcschoolsports.ca
www.bcschoolsports.ca
www.facebook.com/224539464369947
twitter.com/bcschoolsports
Previous Name: BC Federation of School Athletic Associations
Overview: A medium-sized provincial charitable organization founded in 1968 overseen by School Sport Canada
Mission: To encourage student participation in extra-curricular athletics, assist schools in the development & delivery of their programs & provide governance for interschool competition
Member of: School Sport Canada; Sport BC
Affiliation(s): USA National Federation of State High Schools
Finances: *Annual Operating Budget:* $500,000-$1.5 Million; *Funding Sources:* Membership fees; government; sponsors; advertising
Staff Member(s): 3; 6 volunteer(s)
Membership: 400; *Fees:* Schedule available; *Member Profile:* Accredited secondary school in British Columbia; *Committees:* Administrators; Coaching Development; Competitive Standards; Disciplinary; Eligibility; Scholarship & Awards
Activities: Provincial championships; advocacy; regulatory services; fundraising services; coaching conference; leadership camp; *Awareness Events:* Milk Run; Spirit Week; National School Sports Week, Oct.
Chief Officer(s):
Sydney Landing, Executive Director
Shannon Key, Manager, Sport
skey@bcschoolsports.ca
Awards:
• Merit Award
• Coach of the Year Award
• Oustanding School Award
• Honour Award
• Bert & Greta Quartermaine Scholarship
Eligibility: Student athletes who show excellence in both badminton & academic endeavors
• Dave Gifford Memorial Scholarship
• Zone Scholarships

BC Smallbore Rifle Association *See* British Columbia Target Sports Association

BC Soccer Referees Association
8130 Selkirk St., Vancouver BC V6P 4H7
bcreferees@gmail.com
www.bcsra.com
www.facebook.com/BcSoccerRefereesAssociation
Overview: A small provincial organization
Mission: To support referees in the province of British Columbia.
Membership: *Fees:* $10 (18 & under); $25 (19 & over)
Chief Officer(s):
Chris Wattam, President
chris.wattam@shaw.ca
Meetings/Conferences:
• BC Soccer Referees Association AGM 2018, 2018
Scope: Provincial

BC Society of Transition Houses (BCSTH)
#325, 119 West Pender St., Vancouver BC V6B 1S5
Tel: 604-669-6943; Fax: 604-682-6962
Toll-Free: 800-661-1040
info@bcsth.ca
bcsth.ca
www.facebook.com/BCSTH
twitter.com/BCSTH
www.youtube.com/BCYSTH
Overview: A small provincial organization
Mission: To educate, promote & advocate on issues of violence against women; to support an organization that provides or seeks to provide shelter &/or services to women & their children who experience violence
Finances: *Funding Sources:* Government; members; fundraising
Membership: *Fees:* $75 individual; $150 agency; $300 full member; *Member Profile:* Shelters for abused women & their children
Activities: *Library:* BCSTH Library; Not open to public
Chief Officer(s):
Shabna Ali, Executive Director

BC Taekwondo Association
#101, 32885 Ventura Ave., Abbotsford BC V2S 6A3
www.bctaekwondo.org
Overview: A small provincial organization founded in 1994
Mission: To govern the sport of Tae Kwon Do in British Columbia.
Chief Officer(s):
Michael Smith, President
Darryl Mitchell, Treasurer/Secretary
dmitchell@axisls.com

BC Track & Field Association *See* British Columbia Athletics

BC Trappers' Association (BCTA)
c/o Alana Leclerc, PO Box 1063, Prince George BC V2L 4V2
Tel: 250-962-5452; Fax: 250-962-5462
info@bctrappers.bc.ca
bctrappers.bc.ca
Overview: A small provincial organization
Membership: *Member Profile:* Licensed trappers in British Columbia
Chief Officer(s):
Brian Dack, President
Meetings/Conferences:
• 73rd BC Trappers Association AGM & Convention, April, 2018, Coast Kamloops Hotel & Conference Centre, Kamloops, BC
Scope: Provincial

BC Water Ski Association *See* Water Ski & Wakeboard British Columbia

BCADA - The New Car Dealers of BC
#70, 10551 Shellbridge Way, Richmond BC V6X 2W9
Tel: 604-214-9964; Fax: 604-214-9965
info@newcardealers.ca
www.newcardealers.ca
Previous Name: Motor Dealers' Association of BC; BC Automobile Dealers' Association
Overview: A medium-sized provincial organization founded in 1942
Mission: To promote benefits & heighten awareness of issues of interest to members
Member of: Canadian Automobile Dealers' Association
Staff Member(s): 7
Membership: 345 dealerships; *Fees:* Schedule available; *Member Profile:* New vehicle franchise - car & truck
Chief Officer(s):
Blair Qualey, President & CEO
bqualey@newcardealers.ca

Beach Hebrew Institute
109 Kenilworth Ave., Toronto ON M4L 3S4
Tel: 416-694-7942
info@beachhebrewinstitute.ca
www.beachhebrewinstitute.ca
Overview: A small local organization
Membership: *Fees:* $450 single adult; $700 dual adult
Publications:
• The Weekly Huddle [a publication of Beach Hebrew Institute]
Type: Newsletter; *Frequency:* Weekly

Beachville District Historical Society
584367 Beachville Rd., Beachville ON N0J 1A0
Tel: 519-423-6497; Fax: 519-423-6935
www.beachvilledistrictmuseum.ca
Overview: A small local organization founded in 1973
Mission: To preserve & promote the history & culture of Beachville, Southwest Oxford, & Zorra Township
Member of: Ontario Historical Society
Membership: 56; *Fees:* $5 individual; $10 family
Activities: Beachville District Museum
Chief Officer(s):
Eleanor Reeves, Chair

Bear River Board of Trade
Bear River NS
bearriver.ns@gmail.com
bearriver.ca/bear-river-board-of-trade2
Overview: A small local organization founded in 1905
Membership: *Committees:* Community Greenhouse & Waterfront Gardens; Municipal Property, First Impressions; Pedestrian & Vehicle Safety; Bylaws
Chief Officer(s):
Larry Knox, President

Bear River Historical Society
PO Box 182, Bear River NS B0S 1B0
BearRiverHistory@gmail.com
bearrivermuseum.wordpress.com
www.facebook.com/133976233381746
Overview: A small local charitable organization founded in 1987
Activities: Operates community museum & archives

Chief Officer(s):
Rosamond McCue, President
Bonnie MacLeod, Secretary & Communications Contact
Publications:
• Bear River Tributary
Type: newsletter

Beaton Institute
Cape Breton University, PO Box 5300, 1250 Grand Lake Rd., Sydney NS B1P 6L2
Tel: 902-563-1329; *Fax:* 902-562-8899
beaton@cbu.ca
www.cbu.ca/beaton
www.facebook.com/thebeatoninstitute
twitter.com/beatoninstitute
www.youtube.com/user/thebeatoninstitute
Previous Name: Beaton Institute of Cape Breton Studies
Overview: A small local charitable organization founded in 1957
Mission: To collect & conserve the social, economic, political & cultural history of Cape Breton Island
Affiliation(s): Council of Nova Scotia Archives; Iona Connection Co-operative Limited; Cape Breton Genealogical Association; Association of Canadian Archivists; Society of American Archivists
Finances: *Annual Operating Budget:* $100,000-$250,000
Staff Member(s): 5
Activities: *Library:* Open to public
Chief Officer(s):
Catherine Arseneau, BA, MA, Manager, 902-563-1326
catherine_arseneau@cbu.ca

Beaton Institute of Cape Breton Studies *See* Beaton Institute

Beaumont Coin Discovery Group
c/o Ron Darbyshire, 4907 - 114 St., Edmonton AB T6H 3L5
Tel: 780-436-4335
coinguy@telus.net
Overview: A small local organization
Chief Officer(s):
Ron Darbyshire, Director

Beausejour & District Chamber of Commerce
PO Box 224, Beausejour MB R0E 0C0
Tel: 204-268-3502
beausejourchamber@gmail.com
ourhomeyourhome.ca
www.facebook.com/BeausejourDistrictChamber
twitter.com/BjourChamber
Overview: A small local organization founded in 1939
Mission: To serve commerce & community; To promote the economic, civic, educational & cultural interests of the town of Beausejour & area
Finances: *Annual Operating Budget:* Less than $50,000; *Funding Sources:* Membership dues
Staff Member(s): 1; 10 volunteer(s)
Membership: 87
Chief Officer(s):
Liz Pasieczka, Executive Director

BeautyCouncil (BC)
899 West 8th Ave., Vancouver BC V5Z 1E3
Tel: 604-871-0222; *Fax:* 604-871-0299
Toll-Free: 800-663-9283
info@beautycouncil.ca
beautycouncil.ca
www.facebook.com/beautycouncilwesterncanada
twitter.com/beautycouncil
www.pinterest.com/beautycouncil
Previous Name: Cosmetologists' Association of British Columbia; Cosmetology Industry Association of British Columbia
Overview: A small provincial licensing organization founded in 1929
Mission: To strive for the highest standards of excellence in professional cosmetology services through its member enhancement programs & to service the public through education & knowledge.
Finances: *Funding Sources:* Licence fees
Staff Member(s): 5
Membership: *Fees:* $30 honoree/trainee; $65 individual; $100 company; $150 company & individual; *Member Profile:* Licenced in hair, esthetics, nail technology or barbering
Activities: Regional shows; *Library:* Not open to public
Chief Officer(s):
Bill Moreland, Chair
Debbie Nickel, Executive Director
debbie.nickel@beautycouncil.ca

Awards:
• Hazel Kinnon Award
• Achievement Award

Beaver Party of Canada (BPOC) / Parti Castor du Canada (PCDC)
392 Cariboo Dr., Nanaimo BC V9R 7E1
Tel: 250-755-1183
Other Communication: Leader: 33344 King Rd., PO Box 3100, Abbotsford BC V2S 4P4
info@beaverparty.ca
www.beaverparty.ca
Also Known As: Beaver Party
Overview: A medium-sized national organization founded in 2015
Mission: To become a majority government in the Canadian parliament by: 17% flat taxes and increased GDP funding (1% Canadian Space Agency, 3% defence, 7% education including free post-secondary, and 12% health care); restorative justice and prison reform, starting with automatic parole, education, decriminalization and legalization of cannabis, and implementing 24/7 court services; and environmental protection policies (Clean Water Act and Environment and Climate Change Plan & Policy).
Finances: *Annual Operating Budget:* Greater than $5 Million; *Funding Sources:* Public donations
Staff Member(s): 24; 338 volunteer(s)
Membership: 100-499; *Fees:* $25
Activities: *Awareness Events:* International Prisoner Justice Day; *Internships:* Yes; *Speaker Service:* Yes; *Library:* Records; Open to public
Chief Officer(s):
Kelvin Purdy, Leader
leader@beaverparty.ca
Wayne Whiting, Chief Agent
Leona Whiting, Records Officer
records@beaverparty.ca
Publications:
• Did You Know? [a publication of the Beaver Party of Canada]
Type: Newsletter; *Frequency:* Quarterly; *Accepts Advertising*; *Price:* Free to members
Profile: Provides monthly updates to members

Beaverhill Bird Observatory (BBO)
PO Box 1418, Edmonton AB T5J 2N5
beaverhillbirds@gmail.com
www.beaverhillbirds.com
www.facebook.com/BeaverhillBirdObservatory
twitter.com/beaverhillbirds
Overview: A small local charitable organization
Mission: To promote study of resident & migratory birds & other aspects of natural history at Beaverhill Lake & elsewhere
Membership: *Fees:* $10; *Member Profile:* Biologists; Nature lovers
Activities: Documenting & monitoring changes in the avian species that utilize the Beaverhill area; Promoting an interest in the conservation of birds; Encouraging nature activities
Publications:
• The Willet [a publication of the Beaverhill Bird Observatory]
Type: Newsletter

Beaverlodge Chamber of Commerce
PO Box 303, Beaverlodge AB T0H 0C0
Tel: 780-354-8785
beavercc@telus.net
www.beaverlodgechamber.ca
Overview: A small local organization
Mission: To promote businesses; To influence government policy in areas of interest; To strengthen relationships between business & community
Member of: Alberta Chamber of Commerce
Membership: 50; *Fees:* $25 individuals; $100 businesses
Chief Officer(s):
Callie Balderston, President

Beaverlodge Food Bank
400 - 10th St., Beaverlodge AB T0H 0C0
Tel: 780-354-8069
Overview: A small local charitable organization founded in 1989 overseen by Food Banks Alberta Association
Member of: Food Banks Alberta Association
Activities: Christmas Hamper program

Beaverton District Chamber of Commerce
PO Box 29, Beaverton ON L0K 1A0
Tel: 705-426-2051
chamber@beavertononlakesimcoe.com
www.beavertononlakesimcoe.com

Overview: A small local organization founded in 1989
Affiliation(s): Ontario Chamber of Commerce
Finances: *Funding Sources:* Membership fee
Membership: *Fees:* $95
Chief Officer(s):
Rossie Baillie, President, 705-426-7616
rossiebaillie48@gmail.com

Beaverton Thorah Eldon Historical Society
PO Box 314, 284 Simcoe St., Beaverton ON L0K 1A0
Tel: 705-426-9641
bte.hist.soc@bellnet.ca
www.btehs.com
Overview: A small local charitable organization founded in 1976
Mission: To depict the history of the communities of Beaverton, Thorah, & Eldon; To provide genealogical & history resources, such as local newspapers, census information, church registers, & assessment rolls
Finances: *Funding Sources:* Donations; Fundraising; Grants
Membership: *Fees:* $20 / year; *Committees:* Antique Show; Education; Genealogy; History; Membership; Museum Gift Shop; Program; Property
Activities: Operating the Beaver River Museum, which consists of a log house, a brick house (c. 1900), & a mid-19th century stone jail; Hosting history meetings
Chief Officer(s):
George Hewitt, President
Heather Salzman, Curator
Ken Alsop, Archivist
Publications:
• The Beaverton Story: Harvest of Dreams
Type: Book; *Price:* $30
• Continuing Dreams: The Second Beaverton Story
Type: Book; *Price:* $30

Bechtel Foundation of Canada
#350, 1981, av McGill College, Montréal QC H3A 3A8
Tel: 514-871-1711; *Fax:* 514-871-1392
www.bechtel.com
Overview: A small provincial organization founded in 1949
Mission: To finance educational activities in engineering & the support of community & national health, welfare & cultural organizations
Staff Member(s): 165
Chief Officer(s):
John McVey, General Manager
jmcvey@bechtel.com

Bed & Breakfast Association of the Yukon (BBAY)
PO Box 31518, Whitehorse YT Y1A 6K8
info@yukonbandb.org
www.yukonbandb.org
Overview: A small provincial organization
Mission: To support and promote both the individual members and the B&B industry, to broaden public awareness, understanding and appreciation of the B&B industry in the Yukon, & to represent the B&B industry where a unified voice is needed and appropriate.
Chief Officer(s):
Mo Hartigan, President

Bedeque Bay Environmental Management Association (BBEMA)
PO Box 8310, 1929 Nodd Rd., Emerald PE C0B 1M0
Tel: 902-886-3211
www.bbema.ca
www.facebook.com/140016226032255
Overview: A small local organization founded in 1992
Mission: To provide a framework for citizen-based education and action that reduced soil erosion, maintained water quality and improved the ecosystem.
Membership: *Fees:* $20 single; $25 family; $10 student; $50-$250 corporate

Beef Cattle Research Council (BCRC)
#180, 6815 - 8th St. NE, Calgary AB T2E 7H7
Tel: 403-275-8558; *Fax:* 403-274-5686
info@beefresearch.ca
www.beefresearch.ca
www.facebook.com/BeefResearch
twitter.com/BeefResearch
www.youtube.com/beefresearch
Overview: A medium-sized national organization founded in 1997
Mission: Canada's national industry-led funding agency for beef research.
Affiliation(s): Canadian Cattlemen's Association (CCA)

Canadian Associations / Beef Farmers of Ontario (BFO)

Finances: Funding Sources: Producer-paid national levy; government funding
Chief Officer(s):
Andrea Brocklebank, Research Manager
brocklebanka@beefresearch.ca
Reynold Bergen, Science Director

Beef Farmers of Ontario (BFO)
130 Malcolm Rd., Guelph ON N1K 1B1
Tel: 519-824-0334; *Fax:* 519-824-9101
info@ontariobeef.com
www.ontariobeef.com
www.facebook.com/BeefFarmersofOntario
twitter.com/OntarioBeef
Previous Name: Ontario Beef Improvement Association; Ontario Cattlemen's Association
Overview: A medium-sized provincial organization founded in 1963
Mission: To foster a sustainable & profitable beef industry in Ontario; To provide programs & serivces to support local cattlemen's associations & provincial cattlemen in general; To lobby on issues at the provincial & national level
Member of: Canadian Cattlemen's Association
Staff Member(s): 13
Membership: *Member Profile:* Cattle producers in Ontario;
Committees: Cow / Calf; Feedlot; Research
Activities: Providing education & information to Ontario cattlemen; Engaging in advocacy activities on behalf of the Ontario beef industry; Liaising with government; Initiating studies, programs, & reviews; Encouraging economically sustainable production methods; Promoting Quality Starts Here programs to beef producers across Ontario; Developing domestic & export markets Promoting beef
Chief Officer(s):
Dave Stewart, Executive Director
Paul Stiles, Assistant Manager
Lianne Appleby, Manager, Communications
Jamie Thomas, Coordinator, Market Information
Lisa Turney, Coordinator, Research & Projects
Jen Snively, Policy Advisor
Awards:
• The Environmental Stewardship Award
Meetings/Conferences:
• Beef Farmers of Ontario 2018 Annual General Meeting, 2018, ON
Scope: Provincial
Description: An opportunity for Ontario's beef farmers to help set policy direction on cattle industry issues
Publications:
• OCA [Ontario Cattlemen's Association] Weekly Update
Type: Newsletter; *Frequency:* Weekly; *Editor:* Lianne Appleby
• Ontario Beef
Type: Magazine; *Frequency:* 5 pa; *Accepts Advertising; Editor:* Lianne Appleby; *Price:* Free for members of the OntarioCattlemen's Association
Profile: Information for producers, featuring articles of interest in the beef industry, research, market information, producer profiles, & current policy issues
• Ontario Cattlemen's Association Production Guides
Type: Guide
Profile: Production information of a wide variety of topics
• The Ontario Steakholder
Type: Newsletter; *Frequency:* Irregular; *Editor:* Lianne Appleby
Profile: A timely publication for Ontario's MPs & MPPs to connect them with Ontario's beef farmers

Beef Improvement Ontario (BIO)
#205, 660 Speedvale Ave. West, Guelph ON N1K 1E5
Tel: 519-767-2665; *Fax:* 519-767-2502
Toll-Free: 855-246-2333
info@biobeef.com
www.biobeef.com
Overview: A small provincial organization
Mission: To provide genetic & management products & services to breeders & feeders of beef cattle & enhance the competitive position of the Ontario beef industry
Affiliation(s): Agricultural Adaptation Council; Canadian Dairy Network; Centre of Genetic Improvement of Livestock; Igenity; Ontario Cattlemen's Association
Staff Member(s): 11
Chief Officer(s):
Mike Buis, President
Mike McMorris, General Manager
mmcmorris@bridgingintelligence.com

Beehive Adult Service Centre, Inc.
1119 Station St., Aylesford NS B0P 1C0
Tel: 902-847-9696; *Fax:* 902-847-9189
beehiveasc@eastlink.ca
www.beehiveasc.ca
www.facebook.com/533202606766142
Overview: A small local organization
Member of: DIRECTIONS Council for Vocational Services Society

Beehive Support Services Association
PO Box 6007, 5225 - 55A St., Drayton Valley AB T7A 1R6
Tel: 780-542-3113; *Fax:* 780-542-3115
www.beehivesupportservicesassocation.com
www.facebook.com/206749966033185
Previous Name: Drayton Valley Association for Community Living
Overview: A small local charitable organization founded in 1975
Mission: To support and promote the welfare of people with disabilities.
Member of: Alberta Association for Community Living; Alberta Association of Rehabilitation Centres
Membership: *Fees:* $10
Activities: Supporting the community through recycling initiatives like the Drayton Valley Bottle Depot.
Chief Officer(s):
Jacqueline Crawford, Executive Director, 780-542-3113 Ext. 222

Beekeepers' Association of Niagara Region
St Catharines ON
Tel: 905-934-4913
Overview: A small local organization
Mission: To offer education on beekeeping skills to person in the Niagara area
Member of: Ontario Beekeepers' Association
Membership: *Member Profile:* Beekeepers of the Niagara region
Activities: Organizing monthly meetings at the Niagara Regional Police Station Community Room in Welland to share information about beekeeping & association business; Providing networking opportunities for local beekeepers; Assisting beekeepers in handling issues in the beekeeping industry
Chief Officer(s):
George Dubanow, President, 905-934-4913
panosmarg@gmail.com

Beiseker & District Chamber of Commerce
PO Box 277, Beiseker AB T0M 0G0
Tel: 403-947-3875
Overview: A small local organization
Chief Officer(s):
Iris Balson, Contact, 403-947-3920

Belgian Canadian Business Association *See* Belgian Canadian Business Chamber

Belgian Canadian Business Chamber (BCBC)
PO Box 508, 161 Bay St., 27th Fl., Toronto ON M5J 2S1
Tel: 416-816-9154
www.belgiumconnect.com
www.linkedin.com/company/belgian-canadian-business-chamber
www.facebook.com/BelgiumConnect
twitter.com/Belgiumconnect
Previous Name: Belgian Canadian Business Association
Overview: A small international organization founded in 1988
Mission: The Belgian Canadian Business Chamber (BCBC) is based in Toronto & works to foster contacts & relationships for members who share an interest in developing business & trade opportunities between Canada & Belgium.
Member of: European Union Chamber of Commerce in Canada
Membership: *Fees:* Individuals: $60, Corporate: $300-$3,000;
Member Profile: Membership is open to anyone interested in developing or expanding their business relationship with Belgium.
Activities: Business seminars; Business with Belgium; Belgians in Canada; networking events; Frites Night; joint events with other European chambers
Chief Officer(s):
Vacant, President & Chief Executive Officer
Christian Frayssignes, Vice-President & EUCCAN Representative
André van der Heyden, Vice-President & Chief Operating Officer
Grégory Oleffe, Treasurer & Chief Financial Officer
William Van Loo, Board Secretary
Idalia Obregón, Executive Director
Anne Popoff, Events Director

The Belinda Stronach Foundation (TBSF)
Toronto ON
www.tbsf.ca
www.youtube.com/user/TheTBSFChannel
Overview: A small national charitable organization founded in 2008
Mission: Assists girls and women and Aboriginal youth in Canada and youth in developing nations to achieve a better life through the provision of programs that enhance basic health and education, improve economic and political independence and that promote civic involvement.
Activities: Spread the Net campaign
Chief Officer(s):
Belinda Stronach, President & CEO

Bell Aliant Pioneers
PO Box 1430, Saint John NB E2L 4K2
Toll-Free: 800-565-1436
www.bellaliantpioneers.com
Overview: A large provincial organization overseen by TelecomPioneers of Canada
Mission: To act as the largest corporate-based volunteer organization in Atlantic Canada
Membership: 9000; *Member Profile:* Current & former Bell Aliant employees
Chief Officer(s):
Chantal MacDonald, President, 506-452-4775
chantal.macdonald@bellaliant.ca

Newfoundland and Labrador
PO Box 25, Mount Pearl NL A1N 2C1
Tel: 709-758-6323
Chief Officer(s):
Bernie Molloy, President, Metro Club
bernie.molloy@bellaliant.ca

Nova Scotia
PO Box 880, Halifax NS S4P 3Y2

Prince Edward Island
PO Box 820, Charlottetown PE C1A 7M1
Tel: 902-629-5250
Chief Officer(s):
Joseph Rowledge, Contact
joseph.rowledge@bellaliant.ca

Belleville & District Chamber of Commerce (BCC)
5 Moira St., Belleville ON K8P 2S3
Tel: 613-962-4597; *Fax:* 613-962-3911
Toll-Free: 888-852-9992
info@bellevillechamber.ca
www.bellevillechamber.ca
www.facebook.com/126461154084001
twitter.com/BCC1864
Overview: A small local organization founded in 1864
Mission: To be recognized as the voice of business in promoting & nurturing a prosperous Belleville & district community: To act as a strong advocate of business in ensuring sound government policies which will create sustainable economic growth; To promote tourism & by developing partnership in education, training & the environment; To provide a means of networking amongst members to enable both business & personal development opportunities
Member of: Ontario Chamber of Commerce; Canadian Chamber of Commerce
Finances: *Funding Sources:* Fundraising; tourism promotion revenue; membership fees
Membership: *Fees:* Schedule available
Chief Officer(s):
Richard Davis, President
Bill Saunders, CEO
bill@bellevillechamber.ca

Belleville Police Association / Association de la police de Belleville
93 Dundas St. East, Belleville ON K8N 1C2
Tel: 613-966-0882; *Fax:* 613-966-1834
Overview: A small local organization
Chief Officer(s):
Peter Goulah, President

Benevolent & Protective Order of Elks of Canada
#100, 2629 - 29 Ave., Regina SK S4S 2N9
Tel: 306-359-9010; *Fax:* 306-565-2860
Toll-Free: 888-843-3557
grandlodge@elks-canada.org
www.elks-canada.org
Also Known As: Elks of Canada

Overview: A medium-sized national licensing charitable organization founded in 1913
Mission: To promote & support community needs, through volunteer efforts of local lodges
Finances: *Annual Operating Budget:* $1.5 Million-$3 Million; *Funding Sources:* Membership dues
Staff Member(s): 8
Membership: 20,000; *Fees:* $42
Chief Officer(s):
Bill Blake, National Executive Director
bblake@elks-canada.org
Sebastian Merk, Manager, Finance & Administration
smerk@elks-canada.org

Benevolent Irish Society of Prince Edward Island (BIS)
Benevolent Irish Society Hall, PO Box 34, 582 North River Rd., Charlottetown PE C1A 7K4
Tel: 902-892-2367
www.benevolentirishsocietyofpei.com
www.facebook.com/bishallpei
Overview: A small provincial organization founded in 1825
Mission: To enhance & preserve Irish heritage & culture; To assist the poor & indigent of all denominations; To promote friendship & unity among Irish people & their descendants for mutual benefit
Member of: Canadian Association of Irish Studies; Festivals & Events PEI
Finances: *Annual Operating Budget:* Less than $50,000; *Funding Sources:* Membership; special events
50 volunteer(s)
Membership: 160; *Fees:* $20; *Member Profile:* Men & women of Irish descent; *Committees:* Charitable; Culture; Finance; Heritage; Newsletter; Property; Social
Activities: Ceilidh at the Irish Hall; lecture series; St. Patrick's Parade; pub nights; Irish dance lessons
Chief Officer(s):
Shane O'Neill, Secretary

Bénévoles Canada *See* Volunteer Canada

Benfica House of Toronto *See* Casa do Benfica

Bengough Agricultural Society
PO Box 411, Bengough SK S0C 0K0
Tel: 306-268-2855
Overview: A small local charitable organization founded in 1915
Mission: To improve agriculture & the quality of life in the community by educating members & the community; to provide a community forum for discussing agricultural issues; to foster community development & community spirit; to help provide markets for Saskatchewan products; to encourage conservation of natural resources, including soil conservation, reforestation, rural & urban beautification
Member of: Saskatchewan Association of Agricultural Societies & Exhibitions
Membership: *Member Profile:* Area residents striving to promote our community through education & entertainment
Activities: Horse show & fair; trade show; farmers market
Chief Officer(s):
Rocky Kaufman, President, 306-268-4248
Awards:
• Bengough Agricultural Society Agricultural Scholarship
To any Bengough high school student for post-secondary education studying agriculture; *Amount:* $200

Bennington Heights Community Orchestra; East York Symphony Orchestra *See* Orchestra Toronto

The Benoit Labre House *Voir* La Maison Benoit Labre

Le Berceau de Kamouraska inc.
4, rue Lauzier, rte 132 est, Kamouraska QC G0L 1M0
Tél: 418-492-5099
Aperçu: *Dimension:* petite; *Envergure:* locale; fondée en 1993
Mission: Préservation et conservation d'un lieu historique et parc commémoratif racontant l'histoire du Berceau de Kamouraska.

Bereaved Families of Ontario (BFO)
PO Box 10015, Stn. Watline, Mississauga ON L4Z 4G5
info@bereavedfamilies.net
www.bereavedfamilies.net
Overview: A medium-sized provincial charitable organization founded in 1978
Mission: To create programs, services & resources to support bereaved families; To be committed to self-help & mutual aid, with a focus on families who have experienced the death of a child
Member of: Ontario Self-Help Network
Finances: *Funding Sources:* Individual & corporate solicitations; Foundations
1000 volunteer(s)
Membership: 12 affiliates; *Member Profile:* Bereaved parents, bereaved young people & others who wish to support
Activities: Telephone support; One-to-One support; Group sessions; Family nights; Volunteer training; Workshops for health professionals & others; *Speaker Service:* Yes; *Library:* Resource Centre; Not open to public
Chief Officer(s):
Carolyn Baltaz, Chair
Lloyd Lindsay, Vice-Chair

Cornwall
216 Montreal Rd., Cornwall ON K6H 1B4
Tel: 613-936-1455; *Fax:* 613-936-9689
bfcornwall@on.aibn.com
bfocornwall.ca
www.facebook.com/bfo.cornwall
Chief Officer(s):
Francis Reading, President

Durham Region
1050 Simcoe St. North, Oshawa ON L1G 4W5
Tel: 905-579-4293; *Fax:* 905-579-7403
Toll-Free: 800-387-4870
admin@bfodurham.net
www.bfodurham.net
Chief Officer(s):
Jane Carter, Executive Director

Halton/Peel
Centre for Grief & Healing, #610, 33 City Centre Dr., Mississauga ON L5B 2N5
Tel: 905-848-4337; *Fax:* 905-848-4338
Toll-Free: 877-826-3566
info@bereavedfamilies.ca
www.bereavedfamilies.ca
Chief Officer(s):
Barbara Bathurst, Executive Director

South Central Region
#2B, 300 Fennell St. East, Hamilton ON L9A 1T2
Tel: 905-318-0070; *Fax:* 905-318-9181
bfoscr.ca
www.facebook.com/147021168642545
twitter.com/bfohb
Chief Officer(s):
Mark Carr, Executive Director

Kingston
Unit 14 Business Centre, #1422, 993 Princess St., Kingston ON K7L 1H3
Tel: 613-634-1230
bfo@kingston.net
www.bfo-kingston.ca
www.facebook.com/bfokingston
twitter.com/BFOKingston
Chief Officer(s):
Jennifer Fowler, Executive Director

Midwestern Region
The Family Centre, 65 Hanson Ave., Kitchener ON N2C 2H6
Tel: 519-603-0196; *Fax:* 519-603-0198; *Crisis Hot-Line:* 844-437-3247
support@bfomidwest.org
www.bfomidwest.org
www.facebook.com/BFOMR
twitter.com/BFOMR
www.pinterest.com/BFOMR
Chief Officer(s):
Jaime Bickerton, Executive Director
jaime@bfomidwest.org
Carly Kowalik, Program Coordinator
carly@bfomidwest.org

London - Southwest Region
#4, 571 Wharncliffe Rd. South, London ON N6J 2N6
Tel: 416-686-1573; *Fax:* 416-686-1573
bflondon@rogers.com
bfolondon.ca
www.facebook.com/bfosw
Chief Officer(s):
Cathy Howe, Executive Director

Ottawa Region
#303, 211 Bronson Ave., Ottawa ON K1R 6H5
Tel: 613-567-4278
office@bfo-ottawa.org
www.bfo-ottawa.org
Chief Officer(s):
Laurie Rail, Executive Chair

Peterborough
403 McDonnel St., Peterborough ON K9H 2X5
Tel: 705-743-7233
Toll-Free: 866-887-2912
Chief Officer(s):
Gary Beamish, Chair

Toronto
#202, 250 Merton St., Toronto ON M41 1B1
Tel: 416-440-0290
info@bfotoronto.ca
www.bfotoronto.ca
www.facebook.com/bfotoronto
twitter.com/bfotoronto
www.youtube.com/user/BFOToronto
Chief Officer(s):
Aruna Ogale, Executive Director
aogale@bfotoronto.ca

York Region
#203, 17070 Yonge St., Newmarket ON L3Y 8Z4
Tel: 905-898-6265; *Fax:* 905-898-5870
Toll-Free: 800-969-6904
bfoyr@bellnet.ca
www.bfoyr.com
www.facebook.com/bfoyr
twitter.com/bfoyr
Chief Officer(s):
Christine Gougen, Bereavement Services Coordinator

Bereavement Authority of Ontario (BAO)
#505, 100 Sheppard Ave. East, Toronto ON M2N 6N5
Tel: 647-483-2645; *Fax:* 647-748-2645
Toll-Free: 844-493-6356
info@thebao.ca
www.thebao.ca
Overview: A medium-sized provincial licensing organization founded in 2016
Mission: To regulate licensed funeral establishments & related operators, directors, & representatives
Membership: *Committees:* Cemetery, Crematorium & Municipal; Faith-Based; Funeral & Transfer Services
Chief Officer(s):
Carey Smith, Registrar & CEO, 647-483-2645 Ext. 202
carey.smith@thebao.ca
Lisa Padgett, Manager, Office of the Registrar, 647-483-2645 Ext. 202
lisa.padgett@thebao.ca

Bereavement Ontario Network (BON)
174 Oxford St., Woodstock ON N4S 6B1
Tel: 519-290-0219
info@bereavementontarionetwork.ca
www.bereavementontarionetwork.ca
Overview: A medium-sized provincial charitable organization
Mission: To connect organizations & individuals throughout the province that work in the field of grief, bereavement, & mourning as professionals & volunteers
Chief Officer(s):
Susan McCoy, Chair
smccoy2140@rogers.com
Meetings/Conferences:
• Bereavement Ontario Network 28th Annual Fall Conference 2018, 2018, ON
Scope: Provincial

Bernard Betel Centre for Creative Living
1003 Steeles Ave. West, Toronto ON M2R 3T6
Tel: 416-225-2112; *Fax:* 416-225-2097
reception@betelcentre.org
www.betelcentre.org
Also Known As: Betel Centre
Overview: A small local charitable organization founded in 1965
Mission: To maximize the quality of life for seniors in the community & reflecting Jewish values
Member of: Ontario Community Support Association; Older Adult Centres of Ontario; Association of Ontario Health Centres
400 volunteer(s)
Membership: 2,000; *Fees:* $18 community; $40 complete; *Member Profile:* Seniors living in the community
Activities: Over 50 recreational, educational & health promotion programs; wellness screening clinics; community support services; kosher meals; *Internships:* Yes; *Library*
Chief Officer(s):
Adam Silver, Executive Director
adams@betelcentre.org

Canadian Associations / Bertie Historical Society (BHS)

Bertie Historical Society (BHS)
c/o Fort Erie Historical Museum, PO Box 339, Ridgeway ON L0S 1N0
Tel: 905-894-5322; *Fax:* 905-894-6851
museum@forterie.on.ca
Overview: A small local organization founded in 1969
Mission: To operate the Fort Erie Historical Museum
Activities: Monthly speakers; annual trip; supports local museum; *Speaker Service:* Yes
Chief Officer(s):
Earl Plato, Past President, 905-894-5322
earlplato@enoreo.on.ca

Berwick & District Ringette Association
NS
ringette.wordpress.com
Overview: A small local organization overseen by Ringette Nova Scotia
Member of: Ringette Nova Scotia
Chief Officer(s):
Marlene Connell, President
ron.connell@ns.sympatico.ca

Berwick Food Bank
100 South St., Berwick NS B0P 1E0
Tel: 902-538-1996
Overview: A small local organization
Member of: Nova Scotia Food Bank Association; Atlantic Alliance of Food Banks & C.V.A.'s

Berwyn & District Chamber of Commerce
PO Box 144, Berwyn AB T0H 0E0
Tel: 780-618-9675
Overview: A small local organization
Member of: Alberta Chamber of Commerce

Best Buddies Canada (BBC) / Vrais Copains
#907, 1243 Islington Ave., Toronto ON M8X 1Y9
Tel: 416-531-0003; *Fax:* 416-531-0325
Toll-Free: 888-779-0061
info@bestbuddies.ca
www.bestbuddies.ca
www.facebook.com/BestBuddiesCanada
twitter.com/BestBuddiesCND
www.youtube.com/user/bestbuddiescanada
Overview: A medium-sized national charitable organization founded in 1995
Mission: To enhance communities by offering one-to-one friendships & leadership development opportunities for people with intellectual & developmental disabilities
Member of: Best Buddies International
Finances: *Funding Sources:* Corporate & individual donations; foundation grants
Staff Member(s): 9
Membership: 80 chapters; 2,000 participants; *Committees:* Fundraising; Program; Gala; Strategic Planning
Activities: Annual gala; *Speaker Service:* Yes
Chief Officer(s):
Stephen Pinnock, Executive Director
sp@bestbuddies.ca
Ethel Maamo, Manager, Programs
ethelm@bestbuddies.ca

Better Business Bureau of Central & Northern Alberta
16102 - 100 Ave. NW, Edmonton AB T5P 0P3
Tel: 780-482-2341; *Fax:* 780-482-1150
Toll-Free: 800-232-7298
info@edmonton.bbb.org
edmonton.bbb.org
www.facebook.com/BBBCentralandNorthernAlberta
twitter.com/EdmontonBBB
Overview: A medium-sized local organization founded in 1957 overseen by Council of Better Business Bureaus
Mission: To handle inquiries & complaints; To provide an ad review program; To educate the public
Finances: *Funding Sources:* Membership fees
Staff Member(s): 14
Membership: 3,200; *Fees:* Based on number of employees
Activities: *Speaker Service:* Yes
Chief Officer(s):
Chris Lawrence, President & CEO
chris@edmonton.bbb.org

Better Business Bureau of Eastern & Northern Ontario & the Outaouais / Bureau d'éthique commerciale de l'Est et Nord de l'Ontario et l'Outaouais
#505, 700 Industrial Ave., Ottawa ON K1G 0Y9
Tel: 613-237-4856; *Fax:* 613-237-4878
Toll-Free: 877-859-8566
info@ottawa.bbb.org
www.bbb.org/ottawa
www.facebook.com/BBBottawa
twitter.com/BBBottawa
Overview: A medium-sized local organization founded in 1937 overseen by Council of Better Business Bureaus
Mission: To promote & foster the highest ethical relationship between business & the public through voluntary self-regulation, consumer & business education, & service excellence
Finances: *Funding Sources:* Membership fees
Membership: 2,100; *Fees:* $230-$850; *Committees:* Governance; Marketing; Human Resources; Finance; Membership
Chief Officer(s):
Christina Hlusko, Chair
Awards:
• Annual Torch Awards for Marketplace Trust

Better Business Bureau of Mainland BC
#404, 788 Beatty St., Vancouver BC V6B 2M1
Tel: 604-682-2711; *Fax:* 604-681-1544
Toll-Free: 888-803-1222
contactus@mbc.bbb.org
mbc.bbb.org
www.linkedin.com/groups?gid=1323147
www.facebook.com/BBBmainlandBC
twitter.com/BBB_BC
Overview: A medium-sized local organization founded in 1939 overseen by Council of Better Business Bureaus
Mission: To promote, develop & encourage an ethical marketplace
Finances: *Annual Operating Budget:* $500,000-$1.5 Million; *Funding Sources:* Membership dues
Staff Member(s): 20; 24 volunteer(s)
Membership: 4,000; *Fees:* $310+
Activities: *Awareness Events:* Annual "Scam Jam"; *Speaker Service:* Yes

Better Business Bureau of Manitoba & Northwest Ontario
1030B Empress St., Winnipeg MB R3G 3H4
Tel: 204-989-9010; *Fax:* 204-989-9016
Toll-Free: 800-385-3074
Other Communication: Complaints, E-mail: complaints@bbbmb.ca
ceo@bbbmb.ca
manitoba.bbb.org
www.facebook.com/197313847036123
Previous Name: Better Business Bureau of Winnipeg & Manitoba
Overview: A medium-sized provincial organization founded in 1930 overseen by Council of Better Business Bureaus
Mission: To encourage ethical business practices through self-regulation in Manitoba.
Finances: *Annual Operating Budget:* $250,000-$500,000; *Funding Sources:* Business memberships
Staff Member(s): 6
Membership: 1,000 corporate; *Fees:* $220-$2,000; *Member Profile:* Satisfactory performance as per Better Business Bureau; *Committees:* Executive; Finance; Human Resources; Membership; Public Service
Activities: Business performing reporting; complaint handling; business & consumer information; *Speaker Service:* Yes

Better Business Bureau of Mid-Western & Central Ontario
354 Charles St., Kitchener ON N2G 4L5
Tel: 519-579-3080; *Fax:* 519-570-0072
Toll-Free: 800-459-8875
mwco.bbb.org
www.facebook.com/234049259942145
Previous Name: Better Business Bureau of Mid-Western Ontario
Overview: A medium-sized local organization founded in 1976 overseen by Council of Better Business Bureaus
Mission: To encourage ethical business practices through self-regulation in Mid-Western Ontario.
Finances: *Funding Sources:* Membership fees
Staff Member(s): 10
Membership: 2,600; *Fees:* $300 - $800; *Member Profile:* Businesses
Chief Officer(s):
Ric Borski, President

Better Business Bureau of Mid-Western Ontario *See* Better Business Bureau of Mid-Western & Central Ontario

Better Business Bureau of Saskatchewan (BBB of SK)
980 Albert St., Regina SK S4R 2P7
Tel: 306-352-9259; *Fax:* 306-565-6236
Toll-Free: 877-352-9259
info@sask.bbb.org
www.bbb.org/saskatchewan
www.linkedin.com/company/better-business-bureau-of-saskatchewan-inc-
www.facebook.com/BBBSask
twitter.com/BBBSask
Also Known As: BBB Serving Saskatchewan
Overview: A medium-sized provincial organization founded in 1981 overseen by Council of Better Business Bureaus
Mission: To promote & foster high ethical relationships between business & the public through voluntary self-regulation, consumer & business education, & service excellence; To serve as a marketplace where buyers & sellers trust one another
Member of: Council of Better Business Bureaus
Finances: *Annual Operating Budget:* $500,000-$1.5 Million; *Funding Sources:* Accreditation fees; Event fees; Sponsorships
Staff Member(s): 5; 12 volunteer(s)
Membership: 1,100; *Committees:* Governance; Executive; Audit; Accreditation
Activities: Offering alternative dispute resolution services, advertising review, investigation of marketplace practices, & public education about scams & frauds; Raising consumer awareness; Providing business & ethics training, networking, & speakers bureau; *Speaker Service:* Yes; *Library:* BBB Internal
Chief Officer(s):
Karen Smith, Chief Executive Officer
ksmith@sask.bbb.org
Awards:
• Torch Awards for Ethics
Given to businesses that show ethical leadership through ongoing social responsibility *Eligibility:* Registered businesses operating in Saskatchewan for 1 year or more *Deadline:* January
Publications:
• The Echo [a publication of the Better Business Bureau of Saskatchewan]
Type: Newsletter
Profile: Information for businesses

Better Business Bureau of Southern Alberta *See* Better Business Bureau Serving Southern Alberta & East Kootenay

Better Business Bureau of the Maritime Provinces; Better Business Bureau of Nova Scotia *See* Better Business Bureau Serving the Atlantic Provinces

Better Business Bureau of Vancouver Island
#220, 1175 Cook St., Victoria BC V8V 4A1
Tel: 250-386-6348; *Fax:* 250-386-2367
Toll-Free: 877-826-4222
Other Communication: Complaints, E-mail: complaints@vi.bbb.org
info@vi.bbb.org
vi.bbb.org
www.linkedin.com/company/better-business-bureau-of-vancouver-island
www.facebook.com/BBBVancouverIsland
twitter.com/VIBBB
www.youtube.com/user/BBBVancouverIsland
Overview: A small local organization founded in 1962 overseen by Council of Better Business Bureaus
Mission: Committed to the principle that fair dealing is good business for both buyer & seller & the majority of buyers & sellers are honest & responsible
Member of: Council of Better Business Bureaus Virginia
Finances: *Annual Operating Budget:* $250,000-$500,000; *Funding Sources:* Membership dues
Staff Member(s): 10; 2 volunteer(s)
Membership: 2,000; *Fees:* $395-895
Activities: Reliability reports; fraud warnings; reliability reports on charitable organizations; arbitration between members & customer(s) involved; *Speaker Service:* Yes
Chief Officer(s):
Vern Fischer, President
Rosalind Scott, Executive Director

Better Business Bureau of Western Ontario
PO Box 2153, #308, 200 Queens Ave., London ON N6A 4E3
Tel: 519-673-3222
Toll-Free: 877-283-9222
Other Communication: Complaints, E-mail: complaints@westernontario.bbb.org
info@westernontario.bbb.org
westernontario.bbb.org
www.facebook.com/BBBWesternOnt
twitter.com/BBB_Western_Ont
Overview: A medium-sized local licensing organization founded in 1983 overseen by Council of Better Business Bureaus
Mission: To promote the vitality of the free enterprise system & ethical business practices; To serve the concerns of business & the consuming public
Finances: Annual Operating Budget: $250,000-$500,000; *Funding Sources:* Membership dues
Staff Member(s): 6; 18 volunteer(s)
Membership: 1,284; *Fees:* Based on company size; *Member Profile:* For profit business; *Committees:* Membership; Marketing; Executive; Finance; Charitable Review
Activities: Speaker Service: Yes
Chief Officer(s):
Jan Delaney, President
jdelaney@westernontario.bbb.org
Chris Lavoie, Manager, Operations
chris@westernontario.bbb.org
Marlene Aquilina-Bock, Coordinator, Business Development
marlene@london.bbb.org
Awards:
• Business Integrity Award
Includes $2,500 scholarship for post-secondary education to be awarded by the winning company

Better Business Bureau of Windsor & Southwestern Ontario
See IntegrityLink

Better Business Bureau of Winnipeg & Manitoba
See Better Business Bureau of Manitoba & Northwest Ontario

Better Business Bureau Serving Southern Alberta & East Kootenay
#350, 7330 Fisher St. SE, Calgary AB T2H 2H8
Tel: 403-531-8784; *Fax:* 403-640-2514
Other Communication: Complaints, E-mail: complaints@calgary.bbb.org
info@calgary.bbb.org
calgary.bbb.org
www.facebook.com/CalgaryBBB
twitter.com/calgarybbb
www.youtube.com/user/BBBServingSouthernAB
Previous Name: Better Business Bureau of Southern Alberta
Overview: A medium-sized local organization founded in 1955 overseen by Council of Better Business Bureaus
Mission: To promote & encourage ethical practices in retail market for goods & services through provision of a wide range of consultative, informative & conciliatory arbitration services for businesses & consumers.
Finances: Annual Operating Budget: $500,000-$1.5 Million; *Funding Sources:* Membership fees
Staff Member(s): 20; 10 volunteer(s)
Membership: 3,000; *Fees:* $395 base fee; *Member Profile:* Company free of legal or ethical transgressions; *Committees:* Executive; Board of Directors
Activities: Ethics Award; *Speaker Service:* Yes
Awards:
• Ethics Awards

Better Business Bureau Serving the Atlantic Provinces
#303, 1888 Brunswick St., Halifax NS B3J 3J8
Tel: 902-422-6581; *Fax:* 902-429-6457
Toll-Free: 877-663-2363
info@ap.bbb.org
atlanticprovinces.bbb.org
www.facebook.com/300802543311820
twitter.com/BBBAtlantic
Previous Name: Better Business Bureau of the Maritime Provinces; Better Business Bureau of Nova Scotia
Overview: A medium-sized provincial organization founded in 1949 overseen by Council of Better Business Bureaus
Mission: To provide mutually beneficial relationships between buyer & seller based on responsible business practices
Finances: Annual Operating Budget: $250,000-$500,000; *Funding Sources:* Membership dues
Staff Member(s): 13; 75 volunteer(s)
Membership: 1,400

Chief Officer(s):
Don MacKinnon, President

Bi Unité Montréal (BUM)
CP 476, Succ. C, Montréal QC H2L 4K4
Courriel: info@biunitemontreal.org
www.algi.qc.ca/asso/bum/
Aperçu: Dimension: petite; Envergure: locale
Mission: Association à but non lucratif; a pour mission de fair connaître la bisexualité et de rassembler les bisexuel(le)s dans un lieu commun pour qu'ils/qu'elles puissent s'informer, se divertir, et se supporter.

Biathlon Alberta
Bob Niven Training Centre, #102, 88 Canada Olympic Rd. SW, Calgary AB T3B 5R5
Tel: 403-202-6548
info@biathlon.ca
www.biathlon.ca
www.facebook.com/588814881135031
twitter.com/biathlonab
Overview: A small provincial organization founded in 1980 overseen by Biathlon Canada
Mission: To promote, develop & maintain biathlon in Alberta
Member of: Biathlon Canada; Alberta Ski & Snowboard Association
Finances: Annual Operating Budget: $100,000-$250,000
Staff Member(s): 2; 300 volunteer(s)
Membership: 12 clubs + 357 individual; *Fees:* Schedule available
Chief Officer(s):
Darcy Gullacher, General Manager
Karin Kaarsoo, President

Biathlon BC
BC
Tel: 604-230-0481
biathlonbc.ca
www.facebook.com/Biathlon-BC-181268575258202
twitter.com/BiathlonBC
instagram.com/biathlonbc
Overview: A small provincial organization overseen by Biathlon Canada
Mission: To promote Biathlon throughout British Columbia as a recreational & competitive sport.
Member of: Biathlon Canada
Membership: *Fees:* Schedule available
Chief Officer(s):
Tony Tsang, President
president@biathlonbc.ca

Biathlon Canada
#100, 1995 Olympic Way, Canmore AB T1W 2T6
Tel: 403-678-4002; *Fax:* 403-678-3644
info@biathloncanada.ca
www.biathloncanada.ca
www.linkedin.com/company/biathlon-canada
www.facebook.com/BiathlonCanada
twitter.com/biathloncanada
Overview: A medium-sized national charitable organization founded in 1976
Mission: To act as the governing body for the sport of biathlon in Canada
Affiliation(s): International Biathlon Union; Canadian Olympic Committee
Finances: Funding Sources: Sport Canada; Canadian Olympic Committee (COC); International Biathlon Union (IBU); Coaching Association of Canada (CAC)
Staff Member(s): 8
Membership: *Fees:* Schedule available; *Committees:* Human Resources & Compensation; Finance & Audit; Revenue Generation & Marketing; Officials; Canadian International Biathlon Union
Chief Officer(s):
Andy Holmwood, General Manager
aholmwood@biathloncanada.ca

Biathlon Manitoba
Sport for Life Centre, 145 Pacific Ave., Winnipeg MB R3B 2Z6
Tel: 204-925-5687
biathlon@sportmanitoba.ca
biathlonmanitoba.ca
www.facebook.com/biathlonmanitoba
twitter.com/BiathlonMB
Overview: A small provincial organization overseen by Biathlon Canada

Mission: To be the provincial governing body for the sport of biathlon in Manitoba
Member of: Biathlon Canada
Chief Officer(s):
Lin-P'ing Choo-Smith, President
choosmith@gmail.com
Lorraine Mitchell, Vice President
lorraine@clutterdenied.com

Biathlon Newfoundland & Labrador
Mount Pearl NL
info@biathlonnl.ca
www.facebook.com/biathlonnl
twitter.com/biathlonnl
Overview: A small provincial organization overseen by Biathlon Canada
Mission: To be the provincial governing body for the sport of biathlon in Newfoundland & Labrador
Member of: Biathlon Canada
Membership: 3 clubs; *Fees:* Schedule available
Chief Officer(s):
Gary Dawson, Contact

Biathlon Nouveau-New Brunswick
11051 Hwy. 430, Trout Brook NB E9E 1R5
Tel: 506-627-0217; *Fax:* 506-622-6162
biathlon@biathlonnb.ca
www.biathlonnb.ca
Also Known As: Biathlon NB
Overview: A small provincial organization overseen by Biathlon Canada
Mission: To be the provincial governing body for the sport of biathlon in New Brunswick
Member of: Biathlon Canada
Membership: *Fees:* $20 non-competitor; $25-$90 competitor; $150 club; *Committees:* Marketing & Fundraising; Coaching Development; Membership; Officials
Chief Officer(s):
Ray Kokkonen, President, 506-627-6437
kokkonen@nbnet.nb.ca
Cindy Bovenizer, Vice President, 506-684-3907
bovenizeraustin@yahoo.ca
Mike Lushinton, Secretary, 506-684-5688
carlalushinton@gmail.com
Paula Septon, Treasurer, 506-622-8047
paula.septon@bellaliant.ca

Biathlon Nova Scotia
c/o Sport Nova Scotia, 5516 Spring Garden Rd., Halifax NS B3J 1G6
Tel: 902-425-5454; *Fax:* 902-425-5606
admin@biathlonns.ca
www.biathlonns.ca
www.facebook.com/biathlonns
Overview: A small provincial organization overseen by Biathlon Canada
Mission: To be the provincial governing body for the sport of biathlon in Nova Scotia
Member of: Biathlon Canada
Membership: *Fees:* Schedule available; *Committees:* Marketing; Fundraising; Technical; Officials
Chief Officer(s):
Karen Purcell, President
Colleen Thompson, Secretary
Jylene Ryan, Treasurer

Biathlon Ontario
61 Kayla Cres., Collingwood ON L9Y 5K8
www.biathlonontario.ca
www.facebook.com/BiathlonOntario
Also Known As: BiON
Overview: A small provincial organization overseen by Biathlon Canada
Mission: To be the provincial governing body for the sport of biathlon in Ontario
Member of: Biathlon Canada
Membership: 7 clubs
Chief Officer(s):
Alex Dumond, President
alexandre.dumond@gmail.com
Christine Piche, Vice President, Administration
pichec10@gmail.com

Biathlon Prince Edward Island
2759 Glasgow Rd., Hunter River PE C0A 1N0
Tel: 902-964-3294
Other Communication: Alt. Phone: 902-314-2587

biathlonpei@gmail.com
www.facebook.com/biathlonpei
Also Known As: Biathlon PEI
Overview: A small provincial organization founded in 2005 overseen by Biathlon Canada
Mission: To be the provincial governing body for the sport of biathlon in Prince Edward Island
Member of: Biathlon Canada; Sport PEI Inc.
Activities: Programs for athletes of all levels
Chief Officer(s):
Bob Bentley, President
Steve Woodman, Secretary, 902-566-8003
steven.woodman@vac-acc.gc.ca

Biathlon Saskatchewan
1860 Lorne St., Regina SK S4P 2L7
Tel: 306-780-9236; *Fax:* 306-780-9462
sask.ski@sasktel.net
www.biathlonsask.ca
Overview: A small provincial organization founded in 2005 overseen by Biathlon Canada
Mission: To be the provincial governing body for the sport of biathlon in Saskatchewan
Member of: Biathlon Canada
Membership: 6 clubs
Chief Officer(s):
Doug Sylvester, Provincial Head Coach
doug.sylvester@sasktel.net
Alana Ottenbreit, Executive Director
sask.ski@sakstel.net

Biathlon Yukon
PO Box 31673, Whitehorse YT Y1A 6L3
Tel: 867-633-5717
biathlonyukon@gmail.com
www.biathlonyukon.org
Overview: A small provincial organization overseen by Biathlon Canada
Mission: To enhance opportunities for all Yukon persons in their pursuit of excellence & in their enjoyment of participation in biathlon
Member of: Biathlon Canada; Sport Yukon
Chief Officer(s):
Bill Curtis, President

The Bible Holiness Mission *See* The Bible Holiness Movement

The Bible Holiness Movement / Mouvement de sainteté biblique
PO Box 223, Stn. A, Vancouver BC V6C 2M3
Tel: 250-492-3376
www.bible-holiness-movement.com
Previous Name: The Bible Holiness Mission
Overview: A medium-sized international charitable organization founded in 1949
Mission: To emphasize the original Methodist faith of salvation & scriptural holiness, with principles of discipline, non-conformity & non-resistance; To administer overseas indigenous missionary centres in West Africa, the Philippines, East Africa, South Korea, India & the West Indies
Member of: Christian Holiness Partnership; National Black Evangelical Association; Anti-Slavery International
Affiliation(s): Religious Freedom of Council of Christian Minorities; Christians Concerned for Racial Equality
Finances: *Annual Operating Budget:* $100,000-$250,000; *Funding Sources:* Unsolicited gifts from Christian believers
Staff Member(s): 16; 6 volunteer(s)
Membership: 93,658 worldwide in 89 countries; 954 Canadian; *Fees:* None
Activities: *Internships:* Yes; *Speaker Service:* Yes; *Library:* Bible Holiness Movement Library; by appointment
Chief Officer(s):
Wesley H. Wakefield, Bishop-General
Publications:
• Hallelujah Magazine
Type: Magazine; *Frequency:* Bimonthly; *Editor:* Wesley H. Wakefield

The Bible Holiness Movement
PO Box 223, Stn. A, Vancouver BC V6C 2M3
www.bible-holiness-movement.com
Previous Name: Religious Freedom Council of Christian Minorities
Overview: A small local organization founded in 1979
Mission: To act as a sponsored organization of the Bible Holiness Movement. The Bible Holiness Movement is an aggressive Christian evangelistic and missionary movement.
Finances: *Annual Operating Budget:* Less than $50,000
4 volunteer(s)
Activities: *Speaker Service:* Yes; *Library:* by appointment
Awards:
• Religious Freedom Essay Contest Award

The Bible League of Canada / Société canadienne pour la distribution de la Bible
PO Box 368, Stn. Main, 399 Main St. West, Grimsby ON L3M 4H8
Tel: 905-319-9500; *Fax:* 905-319-0484
Toll-Free: 800-363-9673
ministry@bibleleague.ca
www.bibleleague.ca
www.facebook.com/BibleLeagueCanada
twitter.com/BibleLeagueCan
www.youtube.com/user/BibleLeagueCanada
Previous Name: World Home Bible League
Overview: A large national charitable organization founded in 1949
Mission: To spread the living word of God worldwide
Member of: Canadian Council of Christian Charities; International Association of Bible Leagues
Affiliation(s): The Bible League
Finances: *Annual Operating Budget:* $3 Million-$5 Million; *Funding Sources:* Donations
Staff Member(s): 15
Activities: Adult Ministry; Children's Ministry; Persecuted Church; Starting new churches; *Speaker Service:* Yes; *Library:* The Bible League of Canada Library
Chief Officer(s):
Paul Richardson, President
Awards:
• Bible League Canada Grants
Bible League Canada Grants for Canadians are awarded primarily based on a needs criteria and the completion of a grant application form. *Eligibility:* Needs-based criteria & completion of a grant application form.
Publications:
• Joy Report
Type: Newsletter; *Frequency:* Quarterly

Bibles & Literature in French Canada (BLF)
Quebec Field Office, 256, rue Marc Aurele Fortin, Lachute QC J8H 3W7
Tél: 450-562-7859; *Téléc:* 450-562-7859
info@blfcanada.org
www.blfcanada.org
Également appelé: BLF Canada
Aperçu: *Dimension:* petite; *Envergure:* provinciale
Mission: BLF Canada distribue une littérature de qualité afin de permettre de présenter, à ces millions de Canadiens, celui qui seul peut leur apporter la vraie vie.
Membre(s) du bureau directeur:
Toe-Blake Roy, Director
toeblake@blfcanada.org

Bibles for Missions Foundation (BFM)
Head Office, 45515 Knight Rd., Chilliwack BC V2R 5L2
Tel: 604-858-4980
admin@missionthriftstore.com
www.missionthriftstore.com
www.facebook.com/279261462189925
Overview: A large international charitable organization founded in 1989
Mission: To operate thrift stores across Canada to generate funds for Bible League Canada
Member of: The Bible League of Canada (TBLC)
Finances: *Funding Sources:* Donations
Chief Officer(s):
Casey Langbroek, CEO

Bibliographical Society of Canada (BSC) / Société bibliographique du Canada (SBC)
PO Box 19035, Stn. Walmer, 360 Bloor St. West, Toronto ON M5S 3C9
secretary@bsc-sbc.ca
www.bsc-sbc.ca
www.facebook.com/207539352655326
Overview: A small national organization founded in 1946
Mission: To encourage the learning & practice of bibliography; To further the study, research & publication of book history & print culture; To promote preservation & conservation of archival & published materials
Membership: *Fees:* $80 regular; $35 student; $50 retired; $100 institutional; *Member Profile:* Individuals & organizations interested in supporting & participating in bibliographical research & publication; *Committees:* Communications; Awards; Fellowships; Publications
Chief Officer(s):
Nancy Earle, President
president@bsc-sbc.ca
David Fernandez, Secretary
secretary@bsc-sbc.ca
Meetings/Conferences:
• Bibliographical Society of Canada 2018 Annual Meeting, 2018
Scope: National
Publications:
• Bulletin [a publication of the Bibliographical Society of Canada]
Type: Newsletter; *Frequency:* Semi-annually; *ISSN:* 0709-3756
Profile: Society news
• Papers of the Bibliographical Society of Canada
Type: Journal; *Frequency:* Semi-annually; *ISSN:* 0067-6896
Profile: Papers submitted by any scholar studying bibliography

Les bibliothèques publiques des régions de la Capitale-Nationale et Chaudière-Appalaches
a/s Réseau BIBLIO de la Capitale-Nationale, 3189, rue Albert-Demers, Charny QC G6X 3A1
Tél: 418-832-6166; *Téléc:* 418-832-6168
www.abpq.ca/fr/capitale-nationale-et-chaudieres-appalaches
Aperçu: *Dimension:* moyenne; *Envergure:* locale; Organisme sans but lucratif; fondée en 1984
Mission: Regrouper les responsables des bibliothèques publiques de ces régions; promouvoir et défendre les intérêts de ces bibliothèques; représenter le secteur des bibliothèques publiques des ces régions au sein des organismes à caractères culturel et social.
Membre de: Association des bibliothèques publiques du Québec
Membre: 9; *Critères d'admissibilite:* Bibliothèques publiques du Québec
Membre(s) du bureau directeur:
Marjorie Gagnon, Administratrice

Les bibliothèques publiques du Québec; Association des directeurs de bibliothèques publiques du Québec *Voir* Association des bibliothèques publiques du Québec

Bicycle Newfoundland & Labrador
PO Box 13241, Stn. A, St. John's NL A1B 4A5
admin@bnl.nf.ca
www.bnl.nf.ca
www.facebook.com/BicycleNL
twitter.com/BicycleNL
Overview: A small provincial organization overseen by Cycling Canada Cyclisme
Membership: *Fees:* Schedule available

Bicycle Nova Scotia (BNS)
5516 Spring Garden Rd., 4th Fl., Halifax NS B3J 1G6
Tel: 902-425-5454; *Fax:* 902-425-5606
staff@bicycle.ns.ca
www.bicycle.ns.ca
www.facebook.com/bicyclenovascotia
twitter.com/bicyclens
Overview: A small provincial organization overseen by Cycling Canada Cyclisme
Mission: To act as the governmnent body for cycling in Nova Scotia & to advocate for on & off road cycling
Member of: Canadian Cycling Association
Membership: *Fees:* $15 supporting; $25 general; $125 club
Activities: All aspects of cycling in Nova Scotia
Chief Officer(s):
Susanna Fuller, Co-President, Recreation & Transportation
susanna.fuller@bicycle.ns.ca
Lola Doucet, Co-President, Competition
lola.doucet@bicycle.ns.ca

Bicycle Trade Association of Canada *See* Canadian Independent Bicycle Retailers Association

Bicyclette sans frontiers *See* Bikes Without Borders

Bicycling Association of BC *See* Cycling British Columbia

Bide Awhile Animal Shelter Society
PO Box 50029, Stn. Southdale, 67 Neptune Cres., Dartmouth NS B2Y 4S2
Tel: 902-469-9578; *Fax:* 902-463-6173
bideawhile@bideawhile.org
www.bideawhile.org
www.facebook.com/bideawhile
twitter.com/bideawhile
Overview: A small local charitable organization founded in 1969

Mission: To rescue & care for abandoned animals with the hope of rehoming them; to promote spaying & neutering; to cultivate respect for animals through outreach.
Member of: Canadian Federation of Humane Societies
Finances: *Funding Sources:* Donations; small businesses; calendar sales
Membership: 500-999; *Fees:* $10 student/senior; $25 individual; $45 family; $135 patron; $200 bronze; $400 silver; $600 gold
Activities: Spook's Memorial Kitty Fund; Pet of the Day Contest
Chief Officer(s):
Nancy Mansfield, President
nancy.mansfield@bellaliant.net
Darrold Gould, Executive Director
darroldgould@bideawhile.org

La Biennale de Montréal
#304, 460, rue Sainte-Catherine ouest, Montréal QC H3B 1A7
Tél: 514-521-7340
info@biennalemontreal.org
www.biennalemontreal.org
Aperçu: *Dimension:* petite; *Envergure:* locale
Mission: D'analyser la relation que existe entre les pratiques en art contemporain et les disccours historiques sur le futur, d'une part, et nos modes de projection actuels dans l'avenir.
Membre(s) du bureau directeur:
Lydie Bochatay, Adjointe à la direction
lydie.bochatay@biennalemontreal.org

Big Brothers & Big Sisters of Québec *Voir* Association des Grands Frères et Grandes Soeurs du Québec

Big Brothers & Sisters of Kings & Annapolis Counties *See* Big Brothers Sisters of Nova Scotia

Big Brothers Big Sisters of Alberta
AB
Toll-Free: 800-404-4483
Overview: A medium-sized provincial charitable organization overseen by Big Brothers Big Sisters of Canada
Affiliation(s): Big Brothers Big Sisters of Canada

Big Brothers Big Sisters of Calgary & Area
5945 Centre St. SW, Calgary AB T2H 0C2
Tel: 403-777-3535; *Fax:* 403-777-3525
bbbs.calgary@bigbrothersbigsisters.ca
www.bbbscalgary.com
www.facebook.com/BBBSCalgary
twitter.com/BBBSCalgary
Affiliation(s): Big Brothers Big Sisters of Canada
Chief Officer(s):
Laurel Wood, Chair
Karen Orser, President & Chief Executive Officer
calgary.ea@bigbrothersbigsisters.ca

Big Brothers Big Sisters of Edmonton & Area
10135 - 89 St., Edmonton AB T5H 1P6
Tel: 780-424-8181; *Fax:* 780-426-6689
Toll-Free: 855-424-8181
bgcbigs.ca
www.facebook.com/BGCBigs
twitter.com/BGCBigs
Affiliation(s): Boys & Girls Clubs of Edmonton & Area
Chief Officer(s):
DeAnn Hunter, President
Liz O'Neill, Executive Director, 780-822-2525
liz.oneill@bgcbigs.ca
Kerry Woodland, Director, Service Delivery, 780-822-2518
kerry.woodland@bgcbigs.ca

Big Brothers Big Sisters of Red Deer & District
c/o Youth & Volunteer Centre, 4633 - 49th St., Red Deer AB T4N 1T4
Tel: 403-342-6500; *Fax:* 403-342-7734
www.bbbsreddeer.ca
www.facebook.com/BBBSRedDeer
twitter.com/BBBSRedDeer
Affiliation(s): Big Brothers Big Sisters of Canada; United Way of Central Alberta; Boys & Girls Clubs of Red Deer
Chief Officer(s):
Kris Fleckenstein, Chair
Jacquie Boyd, Executive Director, 403-342-6500 Ext. 105
jacquieb@youthhq.ca

Big Brothers Big Sisters of British Columbia
BC
Toll-Free: 800-404-4483
Overview: A medium-sized provincial charitable organization overseen by Big Brothers Big Sisters of Canada
Affiliation(s): Big Brothers Big Sisters of Canada

Big Brothers Big Sisters of Prince George
777 Kinsmen Pl., Prince George BC V2M 6Y7
Tel: 250-563-7410; *Fax:* 250-564-5217
reception@bbbspg.ca
www.bbbspg.ca
www.facebook.com/bbbspg
twitter.com/bbbspg
instagram.com/bbbspg
Affiliation(s): Big Brothers Big Sisters of Canada
Chief Officer(s):
Wende Bracklow, President
Tim Bennett, Executive Director
tim.bennett@bigbrothersbigsisters.ca

Big Brothers Big Sisters of the Okanagan
#102, 151 Commercial Dr., Kelowna BC V1X 7W2
Tel: 250-765-2661
Toll-Free: 800-404-4483
www.bigs.bc.ca
www.facebook.com/BigBrothersBigSistersOkanagan
twitter.com/BBBSOkanagan
Affiliation(s): Big Brothers Big Sisters of Canada
Chief Officer(s):
Ted Gross, President
Helen Brownrigg, Executive Director, 250-765-2661 Ext. 103
helen.brownrigg@bigbrothersbigsisters.ca

Big Brothers Big Sisters of Victoria & Area
230 Bay St., Victoria BC V9A 3K5
Tel: 250-475-1117; *Fax:* 250-475-1197
Toll-Free: 877-475-1114
reception.victoria@bigbrothersbigsisters.ca
www.bbbsvictoria.com
www.facebook.com/bbbsvictoria
twitter.com/bbbs_victoria
pinterest.com/bbbsvictoria
Affiliation(s): Big Brothers Big Sisters of Canada; United Way
Chief Officer(s):
Steve Chubby, President
Rhonda Brown, Executive Director, 250-475-1117 Ext. 47
rhonda.brown@bigbrothersbigsisters.ca

Big Brothers of Greater Vancouver
#102, 1193 Kingsway, Vancouver BC V5V 3C9
Tel: 604-876-2447; *Fax:* 604-876-2446
www.bigbrothersvancouver.com
www.facebook.com/bigbrothersvancouver
twitter.com/bigbrosonline
Mission: Serving the communities of: Sunshine Coast, Darcy, Squamish, Whistler, Pemberton, Surrey, Coquitlam, Vancouver & the Sea-to-Sky Corridor
Chief Officer(s):
Stephanie Hollingshead, Chair
Valerie Lambert, Executive Director, 604-876-2447 Ext. 223
valerie.lambert@bigbrothersbigsisters.ca

Big Brothers Big Sisters of Canada (BBBSC) / Les Grands Frères Grandes Soeurs du Canada
Toronto Eaton Centre, Galleria L1, #110A, 220 Yonge St., Toronto ON M5B 2H1
Tel: 905-639-0461
Toll-Free: 800-263-9133
www.bigbrothersbigsisters.ca
www.facebook.com/bigbrothersbigsistersofcanada
twitter.com/bbbsc
www.youtube.com/bbbscanada
Overview: A medium-sized national charitable organization founded in 1981
Mission: To provide leadership to member agencies as they develop programs to meet the changing needs of young people
Finances: *Funding Sources:* Private corporations; Public donations
Membership: 116 agencies
Activities: *Library:* Resource Centre; by appointment Not open to public
Chief Officer(s):
Peter Coleridge, President & Chief Executive Officer, 905-639-0461 Ext. 47
peter.coleridge@bigbrothersbigsisters.ca
Matthew Chater, Vice-President, Service & Organizational Development, 905-639-0461 Ext. 42

Big Brothers Big Sisters of Eastern Newfoundland
The Village Shopping Centre, PO Box 10, 430 Topsail Rd., St. John's NL A1E 4N1
Tel: 709-368-5437; *Fax:* 709-368-5477
Toll-Free: 877-513-5437
info@helpingkids.ca
www.helpingkids.ca
www.facebook.com/BBBSEasternNL
twitter.com/BBBSEasternNL
Previous Name: Big Brothers/Big Sisters of St. John's Mount Pearl
Overview: A small local charitable organization founded in 1975 overseen by Big Brothers Big Sisters of Canada
Affiliation(s): Big Brothers Big Sisters of Canada
Chief Officer(s):
Doug Skinner, Chair
Kelly Leach, Executive Director
kelly.leach.bigbrothersbigsisters.ca

Big Brothers Big Sisters of Manitoba
MB
Toll-Free: 800-404-4483
Overview: A medium-sized provincial charitable organization overseen by Big Brothers Big Sisters of Canada
Affiliation(s): Big Brothers Big Sisters of Canada

Big Brothers Big Sisters of Morden-Winkler
ALG Professional Centre, PO Box 450, 309 Main St., Winkler MB R6W 4A6
Tel: 204-325-9707
www.bigbrothersbigsisters.ca/mordenwinkler
www.facebook.com/BigBrothersBigSistersOfMordenWinkler
twitter.com/bbbsmw
Affiliation(s): Big Brothers Big Sisters of Canada
Chief Officer(s):
Vince Sheppard, President
Michael Penner, Executive Director, 204-325-9707
michael.penner@bigbrothersbigsisters.ca

Big Brothers Big Sisters of Portage la Prairie
15 Tupper St. South, Portage la Prairie MB R1N 1W7
Tel: 204-857-4397; *Fax:* 204-857-4397
www.bigbrothersbigsisters.ca/portage
Affiliation(s): Big Brothers Big Sisters of Canada
Chief Officer(s):
Auna-Marie Brown, Co-President
Cathy Pedden, Co-President
Dawn Froese, Executive Director
dawn.froese@bigbrothersbigsisters.ca

Big Brothers Big Sisters of Winnipeg
532 Ellice Ave., Winnipeg MB R3B 1Z2
Tel: 204-988-9200; *Fax:* 204-813-4704
bbbswpg@bigbrothersbigsisters.ca
www.bigwinnipeg.com
www.facebook.com/bbbswinnipeg
twitter.com/BBBSWpg
Affiliation(s): Big Brothers Big Sisters of Canada; United Way of Winnipeg
Chief Officer(s):
Ian Coupland, President
Greg Unger, Executive Director, 204-988-9206 Ext. 101
greg.unger@bigbrothersbigsisters.ca

Big Brothers Big Sisters of New Brunswick
NB
Toll-Free: 800-404-4483
Overview: A medium-sized provincial charitable organization overseen by Big Brothers Big Sisters of Canada
Affiliation(s): Big Brothers Big Sisters of Canada

Big Brothers Big Sisters of Miramichi
115 Maher St., Miramichi NB E1N 4B4
Tel: 506-778-2444; *Fax:* 506-778-1855
contact@bbbsmiramichi.com
www.bbbsmiramichi.com
www.facebook.com/miramichibbbs
twitter.com/bbbs_bgc
Affiliation(s): Big Brothers Big Sisters Canada; Boys & Girls Club Miramichi
Chief Officer(s):
Charlene Maguire MacKnight, Chair
Sheree A. Allison, Executive Director

Big Brothers Big Sisters of Moncton
22 Church St., #T240, Moncton NB E1C 7E6
Tel: 506-857-3047; *Fax:* 506-857-0929
reception.moncton@bigbrothersbigsisters.ca
www.bigbrothersbigsisters.ca/moncton
www.facebook.com/BigBrothersBigSistersMoncton
www.pinterest.com/MonctonBBBS
Affiliation(s): Big Brothers Big Sisters of Canada
Chief Officer(s):
Brett Murphy, President

Canadian Associations / Big Brothers Big Sisters of Nova Scotia

Peter MacDonald, Executive Director
peter.macdonald@bigbrothersbigsisters.ca

Big Brothers Big Sisters of Nova Scotia
NS
Toll-Free: 800-404-4483
Overview: A medium-sized provincial charitable organization overseen by Big Brothers Big Sisters of Canada
Affiliation(s): Big Brothers Big Sisters of Canada

Big Brothers Big Sisters of Greater Halifax
PO Box 307, 86 Ochterloney St., Dartmouth NS B2Y 3Y5
Tel: 902-466-5437; *Fax:* 902-465-4281
halifax@bigbrothersbigsisters.ca
www.bigbrothersbigsistershalifax.ca
www.facebook.com/BBBSHalifax
twitter.com/bbbshalifax
www.youtube.com/user/BBBSHalifax
Affiliation(s): Big Brothers Big Sisters of Canada
Chief Officer(s):
Peter Crowther, Chair
Carol Goddard, Executive Director, 902-700-8347
carol.goddard@bigbrothersbigsisters.ca

Big Brothers Big Sisters of Pictou County
PO Box 781, 74 Stellarton Rd., New Glasgow NS B2H 5G2
Tel: 902-752-6260; *Fax:* 902-752-6262
bigbrothers@eastlink.ca
www.bbbsofpc.com
Affiliation(s): Big Brothers Big Sisters Canada
Margie Grant-Walsh, Executive Director
margie.grantwalsh@bigbrothersbigsisters.ca

Big Brothers Sisters of the Annapolis Valley
136 Exhibition St., Kentville NS B4N 4E5
Tel: 902-678-8641; *Fax:* 902-678-8641
Toll-Free: 877-328-8671
annapolis.valley@bigbrothersbigsisters.ca
www.bbbsannapolisvalley.ca
www.facebook.com/bbbsav
Affiliation(s): Big Brothers Big Sisters of Canada
Chief Officer(s):
Jonathan Leard, Agency Manager, 902-678-8641 Ext. 101
jonathan.leard@bigbrothersbigsisters.ca

Big Brothers Big Sisters of Ontario
ON
Toll-Free: 800-404-4483
Overview: A medium-sized provincial charitable organization overseen by Big Brothers Big Sisters of Canada
Affiliation(s): Big Brothers Big Sisters of Canada

Big Brothers & Big Sisters of Toronto
#501, 2345 Yonge St., Toronto ON M4P 2E5
Tel: 416-925-8981; *Fax:* 416-925-4671
infotoronto@bigbrothersbigsisters.ca
www.bbbst.com
www.linkedin.com/company/big-brothers-big-sisters-of-toronto
www.facebook.com/BigBrothersBigSistersToronto
twitter.com/BBBSToronto
www.youtube.com/user/bike4tykes
Affiliation(s): Big Brothers Big Sisters of Canada
Chief Officer(s):
Calvin Younger, Chair
Leanne Nicolle, President & Chief Executive Officer, 416-925-8981 Ext. 4105
leanne.nicolle@bigbrothersbigsisters.ca

Big Brothers Big Sisters of Barrie & District
PO Box 261, 168 Bayfield St., Barrie ON L4M 4T2
Tel: 705-728-0515; *Fax:* 705-728-2965
mentor@bbbsbarrie.com
www.bigbrothersbigsisters.ca/barrie
www.facebook.com/216393495057704
twitter.com/BBBSBarrie
Affiliation(s): Big Brothers Big Sisters of Canada
Chief Officer(s):
Janice Leroux, President
Marianne Arbour, Executive Director
marianne.arbour@bigbrothersbigsisters.ca

Big Brothers Big Sisters of Chatham-Kent
137 Queen St., Chatham ON N7M 2G7
Tel: 519-351-1582; *Fax:* 519-351-1621
www.bigbrothersbigsistersofchatham-kent.com
www.facebook.com/bbbsck
twitter.com/bbbsck
Affiliation(s): Big Brothers Big Sisters of Canada; United Way; Goodlife Kids Foundation
Chief Officer(s):
Carmen Titus, President

Nan Stuckey, Executive Director
nan.stuckey@bigbrothersbigsisters.ca

Big Brothers Big Sisters of Ottawa (BBBSO)
#12, 1645 Woofroffe Ave., Ottawa ON K2G 1W2
Tel: 613-247-4776; *Fax:* 613-247-2240
info@bbbso.ca
www.bbbso.ca
www.linkedin.com/company/318325
www.facebook.com/BBBSO
twitter.com/BBBSO
Affiliation(s): Big Brothers Big Sisters of Canada
Chief Officer(s):
Tina Hill, President
Susan Ingram, Executive Director, 613-247-4776 Ext. 316
susani@bbbso.ca

Big Brothers Big Sisters of South Niagara
800 Niagara St., #JJ4, Welland ON L3C 5Z4
Tel: 905-735-0570; *Fax:* 905-735-2122
admin.southniagara@bigbrothersbigsisters.ca
www.bbbsinniagara.ca
www.facebook.com/bigbrothersbigsisterssn
twitter.com/BBBS_SNiagara
Affiliation(s): Big Brothers Big Sisters of Canada; United Way
Chief Officer(s):
Peter Papp, President
Barb Van Der Heyden, Executive Director, 905-735-0570 Ext. 223
barb.vanderheyden@bigbrothersbigsisters.ca

Big Brothers Big Sisters of Thunder Bay
704 McKenzie St., Thunder Bay ON P7C 3L4
Tel: 807-623-0292
gladys@ourkidscount.ca
www.ourkidscount.ca
www.facebook.com/bigbrothersbigsistersofthunderbay
twitter.com/BBBSThunderBay
Affiliation(s): Big Brothers Big Sisters of Canada
Chief Officer(s):
Cyndi Sereda, Chair
Gladys Berringer, Executive Director
gladys@ourkidscount.ca

Big Brothers Big Sisters of Prince Edward Island
2 St. Peters Rd., Charlottetown PE C1A 5N2
Tel: 902-569-5437; *Fax:* 902-892-5593
Toll-Free: 877-411-3729
Other Communication: Summerside Office: 902-436-8122
pei.bigbrothersbigsisters.ca
www.facebook.com/bbbspei
twitter.com/BBBSPEI
www.pinterest.com/bbbspei
Overview: A medium-sized provincial organization founded in 1975 overseen by Big Brothers Big Sisters of Canada
Affiliation(s): Big Brothers Big Sisters of Canada
Chief Officer(s):
Stephanie Rainnie, Chair
Myron Yates, Executive Director, 902-368-7760
myron.yates@bigbrothersbigsisters.ca

Big Brothers Big Sisters of Saskatchewan
SK
Toll-Free: 800-404-4483
Overview: A medium-sized provincial charitable organization overseen by Big Brothers Big Sisters of Canada
Affiliation(s): Big Brothers Big Sisters of Canada

Big Brothers Big Sisters of Regina & Area
2333 Albert St., Regina SK S4P 2V8
Tel: 306-757-3900; *Fax:* 306-206-1255
www.bigbrothersofregina.com
www.facebook.com/BigBrothersRegina
twitter.com/BigBroRegina
Affiliation(s): Big Brothers Big Sisters of Canada
Chief Officer(s):
Ash Noureldin, Executive Director, 306-757-3900 Ext. 1
ash.noureldin@bigbrothersbigsisters.ca

Big Brothers Big Sisters of Saskatoon
182 Wall St., Saskatoon SK S7K 1N4
Tel: 306-244-8197; *Fax:* 306-244-4171
office@bbbssaskatoon.org
www.bbbssaskatoon.org
www.facebook.com/BBBSSaskatoon
twitter.com/BBBSSaskatoon
Affiliation(s): Big Brothers Big Sisters of Canada
Chief Officer(s):
Melanie Weiss, President

Kim Megyesi, Executive Director, 306-244-8197 Ext. 2-233
kim.megyesi@bigbrothersbigsisters.ca

Big Brothers Big Sisters of Yukon
305 Wood St., Whitehorse YT Y1A 2E7
Tel: 867-668-7911
bbbsyukon@gmail.com
www.bigbrothersbigsisters.ca/yukon
www.facebook.com/BigBrothersBigSistersOfYukon
Overview: A small local organization
Affiliation(s): Big Brothers Big Sisters of Canada
Chief Officer(s):
Angela Krueger, Executive Director

Big Brothers/Big Sisters of St. John's Mount Pearl *See* Big Brothers Big Sisters of Eastern Newfoundland

Big Game Society of Nova Scotia
PO Box 305, Windsor NS B0N 2T0
Tel: 902-798-4036
www.biggamesocietyofns.com
www.facebook.com/1526752454233939
Overview: A small provincial organization founded in 1988
Mission: To preserve big game in Nova Scotia; To promote research & advocate for policies on big game
Membership: *Fees:* $15 active member; $12 scorer/associate member
Chief Officer(s):
Doug Titus, President

Big Rideau Lake Association (BRLA)
PO Box 93, Portland ON K0G 1V0
Tel: 613-272-3629
brla@brla.on.ca
www.brla.on.ca
Overview: A medium-sized local organization founded in 1911
Mission: To protect & conserve Big Rideau Lake and share its resources.
Membership: *Fees:* $60 individual; $180 corporate
Chief Officer(s):
Doug Good, President
president@brla.on.ca

Big River Chamber of Commerce
PO Box 159, Big River SK S0J 0E0
Tel: 306-469-2124; *Fax:* 306-469-4409
Overview: A small local organization
Activities: *Rents Mailing List:* Yes

Big Salmon River Anglers Association
Saint John NB
Tel: 506-634-1679; *Fax:* 506-653-7072
Overview: A small local organization
Member of: Atlantic Salmon Federation; New Brunswick Wildlife Federation
Affiliation(s): Moncton Fish and Game Association; Northumberland Salmon Protection Association; Atlantic Salmon For Northern Maine
Chief Officer(s):
Paul P. Elson, Contact
pelson@nbnet.nb.ca

Big Sisters Association of Barrie & District *See* Big Brothers Big Sisters of Ontario

Biggar & District Agricultural Society
Biggar SK
Overview: A small local charitable organization
Mission: To promote improvement of agriculture & improve the quality of life in the community; To provide a community forum for discussion of agricultural issues; To encourage conservation of natural resources
Member of: Saskatchewan Association of Agricultural Societies & Exhibitions
Affiliation(s): Saskatchewan Provincial Association of Fairs
100 volunteer(s)
Membership: 20; *Fees:* $5; *Member Profile:* Residents of Biggar; *Committees:* Advertising
Activities: Biggar Rodeo Days

Biggar & District Arts Council
Majestic Theatre, 322 Main St., Biggar SK S0K 0M0
biggardistrictartscouncil@yahoo.ca
www.facebook.com/16279732308
www.myspace.com/biggardistrictartscouncil
Overview: A small local organization
Mission: To provide the opportunity for local residents to experience quality professional performances & visual art

exhibits within their own community
Member of: Organization of Saskatchewan Arts Councils
Chief Officer(s):
Jan Phillip, President

Biggar & District Chamber of Commerce
PO Box 489, 202 - 3rd Ave. West, Biggar SK S0K 0M0
Tel: 306-948-3317; *Fax:* 306-948-5134
townofbiggar.com
Overview: A small local charitable organization
Mission: To support & promote economic growth for the business, community & its residents
Member of: Saskatchewan Chamber of Commerce
Finances: *Annual Operating Budget:* Less than $50,000; *Funding Sources:* Membership dues
Membership: 1-99; *Fees:* Schedule available

Bike Ottawa
PO Box 248, Stn. B, Ottawa ON K1P 6C4
info@bikeottawa.ca
www.bikeottawa.ca
www.facebook.com/BikeOttawa
twitter.com/BikeOttawa
Previous Name: Citizens for Safe Cycling
Overview: A medium-sized local organization founded in 1984
Mission: To promote cycling as fun, healthy, safe, economical, & environmentally-friendly transportation & recreation
Chief Officer(s):
Heather Shearer, President
president@bikeottawa.ca

Bike to Work BC Society (BTWBC)
PO Box 74591, Stn. Kitsilano, Vancouver BC V6K 4P4
www.biketowork.ca
www.facebook.com/biketowork.bc
twitter.com/BiketoworkBC
www.instagram.com/biketoworkbc
Overview: A small provincial organization founded in 2008
Mission: To help communities in BC deliver successful Bike to Work & Bike to School events; To encourage as many people as possible to experience the benefits of commuting by bicycle
Finances: *Funding Sources:* Donations; Government
Staff Member(s): 2
Activities: Organizing events by securing & sharing resources; *Awareness Events:* Bike to Work Week, May; Bike to School Week, May
Chief Officer(s):
Penny Noble, Executive Director, 604-805-5637
pnoble@biketowork.ca
Terri-Lynn Gifford, Program Coordinator
terri-lynn@biketowork.ca

Bikes Without Borders (BWB) / Bicyclette sans frontiers
25 Havelock St., Toronto ON M6H 3B3
Tel: 416-432-4801
info@bikeswithoutborders.org
www.bikeswithoutborders.org
www.facebook.com/bikeswithoutborders
twitter.com/BWB_Canada
www.youtube.com/user/bikeswithoutborders/videos
Overview: A small international charitable organization founded in 2004
Mission: To use bikes & bike-related solutions as a tool for development in marginalized communities; To promote the bicycle as a means of improving accessibility to health services, economic & educational opportunity, & independence
Finances: *Annual Operating Budget:* Less than $50,000; *Funding Sources:* Donations; Sponsorships; Grants
Staff Member(s): 3; 6 volunteer(s)
Activities: Organizing & promoting events & initiatives, including the Great Bike Recycle, Pedal Powered Hope Project, & Pedal-Powered Development; *Internships:* Yes; *Speaker Service:* Yes
Chief Officer(s):
Tanya Smith, Executive Director
tanya@bikeswithoutborders.org
Kelsey Abbott, Director, Operations
kelsey@bikeswithoutborders.org

Billy Graham Evangelistic Association of Canada (BGEAC)
20 Hopewell Ave. NE, Calgary AB T3J 5H5
Tel: 403-219-2300; *Fax:* 403-250-6567
Toll-Free: 800-293-3717
info@bgea.ca
www.billygraham.ca
www.facebook.com/BillyGrahamEvangelisticAssociationOfCanada
twitter.com/BGEAnews
www.youtube.com/user/BillyGrahamCanada
Also Known As: BGEA of Canada
Overview: A medium-sized national charitable organization founded in 1968
Mission: To expose those who are searching to the message of Christ; To help edify the Christian body in Canada
Affiliation(s): Bill Graham Evangelistic Association USA
Finances: *Annual Operating Budget:* Greater than $5 Million; *Funding Sources:* Donations
Staff Member(s): 30
Activities: Television & radio broadcasts; schools of evangelism; evangelistic crusades; teaching seminars
Chief Officer(s):
Fred Weiss, Executive Director
fweiss@samaritan.ca

The Bimetallic Question
Stock Exchange Tower, PO Box 883, Montréal QC H4Z 1K2
info@bimetallicquestion.org
www.bimetallicquestion.org
Also Known As: The Sherlock Holmes Society of Montréal
Overview: A small local organization founded in 1979
Mission: To bring together those people who enjoy Sherlock Holmes & the Victorian world in which he flourished
Membership: 35; *Fees:* $20

Bimose Tribal Council
598 Lakeview Dr., Kenora ON P9N 3P7
Tel: 807-468-5551; *Fax:* 807-468-3908
reception@bimose.ca
www.bimose.ca
Overview: A small local organization
Mission: Council services include: assisting communities to establish & maintain effective & efficient financial systems; helping communities & individuals access economic development opportunities, & develop sustainable businesses; educational counseling, assistance with tuition, advice to educational authorities & Boards; technical advisory services.
Staff Member(s): 28
Membership: *Member Profile:* Membership services are provided for the following First Nations:Asubpeescheewagong Netum Anishinabek; Eagle Lake; Iskatewizaagegan # 39; Lac Des Mille Lacs; Naotkamegwanning; Obashkaandagaang; Ochiichagwe'Babigo'Ining; Shoal Lake # 40; Wabaseemoong Independent Nations; Wabauskang; Wabigoon Lake Ojibway
Chief Officer(s):
Don Morrison, Executive Director, 807-468-5551 Ext. 236
dmorrison@bimose.ca

Binbrook Agricultural Society (BAS)
PO Box 244, 2600, RR #56, Binbrook ON L0R 1C0
Tel: 905-692-4003; *Fax:* 905-692-1434
Other Communication: President, e-mail: president@binbrookagriculturalsociety.org
info@binbrookagriculturalsociety.org
www.binbrookagriculturalsociety.org
twitter.com/BinbrookFair
Overview: A small local organization founded in 1854
Affiliation(s): Ontario Association of Agricultural Societies; Canadian Association of Exhibitions
Finances: *Annual Operating Budget:* Less than $50,000; *Funding Sources:* Regional government
Staff Member(s): 1; 140 volunteer(s)
Membership: 175 individual; 18 associate; *Fees:* $5 individual; $5 associate
Activities: Annual Fall Fair; agricultural education & awareness programs

Bio-dynamic Agricultural Society of British Columbia
2478 East 23rd Ave., Vancouver BC V5R 1A2
Tel: 778-869-4060
bdcertification@yahoo.com
Overview: A small provincial licensing organization
Affiliation(s): Certified Organic Associations of BC
Chief Officer(s):
Doug Helmer, Treasurer
Grant Watson, Administrator

BioNova
#124, 1344 Summer St., Halifax NS B3H 0A8
Tel: 902-421-5705; *Fax:* 902-421-2733
info@bionova.ca
www.bionova.ca
www.facebook.com/109904885741796
twitter.com/NSLifeSciences
www.youtube.com/user/NSLifeSciences
Also Known As: Nova Scotia Biotechnology & Life Sciences
Overview: A small provincial organization
Mission: To advocate for Nova Scotia's life sciences industry; to educate by telling positive news stories related to the life sciences industries; to build the life sciences community within the province; to provide member companies with support & resources to allow them to grow & be more prosperous
Membership: 53 organizations; *Fees:* Schedule available; *Member Profile:* Companies working in pharmaceuticals/vaccines, medical technologies, natural health products/nutraceuticals, bio IT & bioproducts; research organizations; service providers
Activities: *Awareness Events:* National Biotechnology Week, Sept.; Biotech & Beer, Nov.
Chief Officer(s):
Brian Lowe, Chair
Scott Moffitt, Managing Director
smoffitt@bionova.ca

Biophysical Society of Canada (BSC) / La société de biophysique du Canada
c/o Department of Physics, Simon Fraser University, 8888 University Dr., Burnaby BC V5A 1S6
www.biophysicalsociety.ca
Overview: A medium-sized national organization founded in 1985 overseen by Canadian Federation of Biological Societies
Mission: To promote biophysical research & education; to encourage cross-feeding of ideas between the physical & biological sciences; to foster & support scientific meetings, workshops & discussions in biophysics; to represent Canadian biophysics & biophysicists
Finances: *Funding Sources:* Membership dues
Membership: *Fees:* $100 lab; $60 regular; $25 student/post doc/emeritus
Activities: *Speaker Service:* Yes
Chief Officer(s):
John E. Baenziger, President
Awards:
• Student Poster Award

BIOQuébec / Québec Bio-Industries Business Network
#205, 1460, boul de l'Innovation, Bromont QC J2L 0J8
Tél: 514-360-4565; *Téléc:* 450-919-0827
direction@bioquebec.com
www.bioquebec.com
Nom précédent: Conseil des bio-industries du Québec; Association québécoise des bio-industries
Aperçu: *Dimension:* moyenne; *Envergure:* provinciale; Organisme sans but lucratif; fondée en 1997
Mission: Ôtre le porte-parole des entreprises biotechnologiques du Québec; favoriser le développement et la mise en valeur des biotechnologies et des bioindustries québécoises, et ce au bénéfice de ses membres; To promote the development & the upgrading of biotechnologies; to supply strategic information of technical & economical content as well as carry out projects, events & activities; to stimulate collaboration between private industry, governments & universities; to stimulate the growth of structuring economical activities in this field; to act as a spokesman for the bio-industry in Québec
Finances: *Fonds:* Federal Office of Regional Development - Québec; membership fees; Laval Technopole
Membre: 172 entreprises; *Montant de la cotisation:* Barème basé sur le nombre d'employés
Activités: Colloques, conférences, expositions
Membre(s) du bureau directeur:
Anie Perrault, Directrice générale
aperrault@bioquebec.com
Prix, Bourses:
• Genesis Awards

BioTalent Canada
#300, 130 Slater St., Ottawa ON K1P 6E2
Tel: 613-235-1402; *Fax:* 613-233-5741
Toll-Free: 866-243-2472
corporate@biotalent.ca
www.biotalent.ca
www.linkedin.com/in/biotalentcanada
www.facebook.com/biotalentcanada
twitter.com/BioTalentCanada
www.youtube.com/biotalentcanada
Previous Name: Biotechnology Human Resource Council
Overview: A small national organization founded in 1997

Canadian Associations / BIOTECanada

Mission: Help Canadian companies & academia develop the highly skilled staff necessary for commercial success; facilitate industry involvement in skills training & knowledge upgrading for employees; help the Canadian biotechnology sector strategically manage its workforce with human resource tools & HR intelligence services; facilitate the entry of new workers to the biotech sector through the communication of job opportunities to a broad audience
Member of: Global Bioscience Partnership; The Alliance of Sector Councils; Bio (Biotechnology Industry Organization)
Staff Member(s): 5
Chief Officer(s):
Rob Henderson, President & CEO
François Schubert, Chair
Norma K. Biln, Vice-Chair
Reg Joseph, Treasurer

BIOTECanada
#600, 1 Nicholas St., Ottawa ON K1N 7B7
Tel: 613-230-5585
info@biotech.ca
www.biotech.ca
www.linkedin.com/company/biotecanada
twitter.com/biotecanada
Previous Name: Canadian Institute of Biotechnology; Industrial Biotechnology Association of Canada
Overview: A medium-sized national organization founded in 1987
Mission: To provide a unified voice fostering an environment that responds to the needs of the biotechnology industry & research community, both nationally & internationally
Affiliation(s): AAFC Grains Innovation Roundtable Steering Committee; ACOA Atlantic Innovation Fund; Algonquin College Biotechnology Program Advisory Board; BIO Business Solutions Advisory Board; BIO International Convention Program Committee; BIO International Convention International Committee; Biorefinery Knowledge Network; Canadian Agri-Food Policy Institute Advisory Committee; DFAIT Life Sciences Advisory Board; DFAIT International Readiness Committee; EDC Stakeholder Roundtable; Environment Canada Scientific Expert Group for NSN(o); Health Canada Food Regulatory Advisory Committee
Finances: *Funding Sources:* Membership dues; government; sponsorship
Staff Member(s): 9
Membership: *Member Profile:* Biotechnology industry & regional groups; *Committees:* Industrial & Environmental; Vaccine Industry
Activities: Policy & regulatory advocacy; communications; human resources; *Rents Mailing List:* Yes
Chief Officer(s):
David Main, Chair
Andrew Casey, President & CEO
andrew.casey@biotech.ca

Biotechnology Human Resource Council *See* BioTalent Canada

Birchmount Bluffs Neighbourhood Centre (BBNC)
93 Birchmount Rd., Toronto ON M1N 3J7
Tel: 416-396-4310; *Fax:* 416-396-4314
contact@bbnc.ca
www.bbnc.ca
www.facebook.com/birchmountbluffs
twitter.com/bbncentre
Overview: A medium-sized local charitable organization
Mission: To provide programs and supports and foster social inclusion within the community, with a focus on individuals that face a barrier to service.
Finances: *Annual Operating Budget:* $1.5 Million-$3 Million; *Funding Sources:* Government, United Way, Donations
750 volunteer(s)
Membership: *Fees:* Youth free; $15 individual; $40 family; *Committees:* Executive; Personnel; Finance; Fundraising; Access & Equity; Nominations
Chief Officer(s):
Enrique Robert, Executive Director
enrique@bbnc.ca

Bird Studies Canada (BSC)
PO Box 160, 115 Front St., Port Rowan ON N0E 1M0
Fax: 519-586-3532
Toll-Free: 888-448-2473
generalinfo@birdscanada.org
www.bsc-eoc.org
www.facebook.com/birdscanada
twitter.com/BirdStudiesCan

Previous Name: Long Point Bird Observatory
Overview: A small provincial charitable organization founded in 1960
Mission: To advance the understanding, appreciation & conservation of wild birds & their habitats, in Canada & elsewhere, through studies that engage the skills, enthusiasm, & support of its members volunteers, staff & the interested public
Member of: Federation of Ontario Naturalists
Affiliation(s): Bird Life International; Partners in Flight; Ontario Bird Banding Association; James L. Baillie Memorial Fund; Newfoundland and Labrador Murre Conservation Fund
Finances: *Annual Operating Budget:* $1.5 Million-$3 Million; *Funding Sources:* Corporate sponsors; general donations; membership fees
Staff Member(s): 45
Membership: 5,000-14,999; *Fees:* $25 student; $35 individual; $50 household; $100 contributing; $175 sustaining; $1000 lifetime; $2,500 patron; *Committees:* Long Point Bird Observatory (LPBO) Committee; National Science Advisory Council
Activities: Monitoring several species as part of the requirement of the Species at Risk Act (SARA); Implementing international training in order to foster good conservation and research in Latin America; *Internships:* Yes; *Rents Mailing List:* Yes; *Library:* by appointment
Chief Officer(s):
David Love, Chair
Awards:
• Baillie Fund Regular Grant, Baillie Fund Grant Program
Eligibility: Non-profit organizations *Deadline:* December; *Amount:* $1,000-5,000 *Contact:* Andrew Coughlan, Phone: 866-518-0212; E-mail: acoughlan@birdscanada.org
• Baillie Fund Small Grant, Baillie Fund Grant Program
Eligibility: Individuals or organizations *Deadline:* January; *Amount:* $250-1,000 *Contact:* Andrew Coughlan, Phone: 866-518-0212; E-mail: acoughlan@birdscanada.org
• Baillie Fund Student Research Award, Baillie Fund Grant Program
Eligibility: Graduate students *Deadline:* February; *Amount:* $1,000 *Contact:* Andrew Coughlan, Phone: 866-518-0212; E-mail: acoughlan@birdscanada.org
• Murre Conservation Fund Grant
Eligibility: Eligible recipients are Canadian & include: non-profit organizations; aboriginal organizations; associations & wildlife management boards; research, academic & educational institutions; for profit organizations such as small businesses, companies, corporations, & industry associations; local organizations such as community associations & groups, seniors' & youth groups, & service clubs; & provincial, territorial, municipal & local governments *Deadline:* November *Contact:* Becky Stewart, E-mail: bstewart@birdscanada.org
• Doug Tarry Bird Study Award
To foster the development of ornithological interests in Canadian teenagers *Eligibility:* Canadian teenagers ranging in age from 13-17 years old *Deadline:* April

Birks Family Foundation / Fondation de la famille Birks
#1200, 615, boul René-Lévesque ouest, Montréal QC H3B 1P5
secretarytreasurer@birksfamilyfoundation.ca
www.birksfamilyfoundation.ca
Overview: A small local charitable organization founded in 1961
Awards:
• Birks Family Foundation Grant
Eligibility: Registered charity; in support of Canadian universities, hospitals, health care, social services or the development of Canadian culture.

Birth Control & Venereal Disease Information Centre
#403, 960 Lawrence Ave. West, Toronto ON M6A 3B5
Tel: 416-789-4541; *Fax:* 416-789-0762
info@BirthControlVD.org
www.birthcontrolvd.org
Overview: A small provincial organization founded in 1972
Mission: To help maintain sexual health with an emphasis on education & prevention. To provide patient-centred service in a caring, non-judgmental manner.

Birthright International / Accueil Grossesse
777 Coxwell Ave., Toronto ON M4C 3C6
Tel: 416-469-4789; *Fax:* 416-469-1772; *Crisis Hot-Line:* 800-550-4900
info@birthright.org
www.birthright.org
Overview: A medium-sized international charitable organization founded in 1968

Mission: To provide non-judgmental support to women facing an unplanned pregnancy, helping them carry their baby to term
Finances: *Funding Sources:* Donations
Membership: 300 chapters
Activities: Counselling; *Speaker Service:* Yes
Chief Officer(s):
Louise R. Summerhill, Co-President
Mary Berney, Co-President
Stephenie Fox, Co-President

Drummondville Chapter
1190, rue Goupil, Drummondville QC J2B 4Z7
Tel: 819-478-7474

Halifax Chapter
#201-2, 1521 Grafton St., Halifax NS B3J 2B9
Tel: 902-422-3400
Toll-Free: 800-550-4900

Lethbridge Chapter
#503, 740 - 7 Ave. South, Lethbridge AB T1J 0N9
Tel: 403-320-1003
Toll-Free: 800-550-4900

Moncton Chapter
#107, 236 St. George St., Moncton NB E1C 1W1
Tel: 506-382-2227
Toll-Free: 800-550-4900

Ottawa Chapter
#302, 200 Isabella St., Ottawa ON K1S 1V7
Tel: 613-231-5683
Toll-Free: 800-550-4900

Regina Chapter
#202, 1771 Rose St., Regina SK S4P 1Z4
Tel: 306-359-1862

Vancouver Chapter
#1107, 207 West Hastings St., Vancouver BC V6B 1H7
Tel: 604-687-7223
Toll-Free: 800-550-4900

Birtle & District Chamber of Commerce
PO Box 278, Birtle MB R0M 0C0
Tel: 204-842-3234
Overview: A small local organization
Finances: *Funding Sources:* Membership fees
Membership: *Member Profile:* Business owners & private individuals

Bison Producers of Alberta
501 - 11 Ave., Nisku AB T9E 7N5
Tel: 780-955-1995; *Fax:* 780-955-1990
info@bisoncentre.com
bisoncentre.com
Merged from: Alberta Bison Commission; Alberta Bison Association; Peace Country Bison Association
Overview: A small local organization
Member of: Canadian Bison Association
Membership: *Fees:* $236.25

Black Academic Scholarship Fund (BASF) / Fonds d'études académiques pour les Noirs
3270, rue Prince-Charles, Saint-Hubert QC J3Y 4X4
Other Communication: Scholarship Information, E-mail: scholarship@basfund.ca
info@basfund.ca
www.basfund.ca
Overview: A small local charitable organization founded in 1991
Mission: To enhance the economic status of visible minorities by providing educational opportunities
Finances: *Funding Sources:* Donations; Sponsorships; Fundraising
Activities: Promoting entrepreneurship & professional excellence; Offering career counselling services; Providing financial support to young people who are studying at accredited institutions; Sponsoring youth programs; *Awareness Events:* Jackie Robinson International Golf Tournament (golf@basfund.ca)

Black Artists Network of Nova Scotia (BANNS)
NS
Tel: 902-430-3560
admin@banns.ca
www.banns.ca
Overview: A small provincial organization founded in 1991
Mission: BANNS is a non-profit, multi-disciplinary arts association that seeks to develop the African Nova Scotian arts community.
Activities: B Space Gallery & Arts Centre; Preston Cultural Festival; Voices Black Theatre Ensemble; African Nova Scotian Quiltmakers Initiative

Black Business & Professional Association (BBPA)
#210, 675 King St. West, Toronto ON M5V 1M9
Tel: 416-504-4097; Fax: 416-504-7343
information@bbpa.org
www.bbpa.org
www.facebook.com/thebbpa
twitter.com/thebbpa
www.youtube.com/user/TheOfficialBBPA
Overview: A medium-sized national organization founded in 1983
Mission: To address discrimination in business, employment, education, housing, policing, political representation & immigration; to encourage entrepreneurship; to identify & reward excellence & achievement; to cooperate with other organizations with similar purposes to influence public opinion & public policy on matters of social & economic justice
Membership: Fees: $25 student/senior; $50 under 30; $100 regular; $175 family; $300 business
Chief Officer(s):
Pauline Christian, President
Awards:
• Harry Jerome Scholarships
Aimed at helping young people who may lack resources for further education; Amount: Five $2,000 annual awards

Black Business Initiative (BBI)
Centennial Bldg., #910, 1660 Hollis St., Halifax NS B3J 1V7
Tel: 902-426-8683; Fax: 902-426-8699
Toll-Free: 888-664-9333
bbi@bbi.ns.ca
www.bbi.ca
www.linkedin.com/company/black-business-initiative
www.facebook.com/blackbusinessns
twitter.com/blackbusinessns
www.youtube.com/user/BBIvideo
Overview: A small provincial organization
Mission: To grow the Black presence in business sectors including high-tech, manufacturing, tourism & culture
Membership: Committees: Executive; Finance; Governance; Lending; BBI Site; Services
Activities: Operating the Black Business Centre; strategic planning; regional business development; loan fund
Chief Officer(s):
Emmanuel Itiveh, Director, Entrepreneurship
Ayo D. Makanjuola, Director, Corporate Services
Laurissa Manning, Director, Stakeholder & Community Relations
Njabulo Nkala, Director, Innovation & Growth
Awards:
• The Black Business Initiative Society's Entrepreneur of the Year
• The Hector Jacques Award of Business Excellence
Publications:
• Annual Business Directory [a publication of the Black Business Initiative]
Type: Directory; Frequency: Annual
Profile: Black business listings & community resource information
• Black to Business [a publication of the Black Business Initiative]
Type: Magazine; Frequency: q.

Black Coalition for AIDS Prevention
20 Victoria St., 4th Fl., Toronto ON M5C 2N8
Tel: 416-977-9955; Fax: 416-977-7664
info@black-cap.com
www.black-cap.com
www.facebook.com/blackcapto
Also Known As: Black CAP
Overview: A medium-sized national organization founded in 1987 overseen by Canadian AIDS Society
Mission: To reduce the spread of HIV infection in Black communities; To enhance the quality of life for Black people living with or affected by HIV/AIDS
Member of: Ontario AIDS Network
Finances: Annual Operating Budget: $250,000-$500,000; Funding Sources: Ontario Ministry of Health & Long-Term Care; Health Canada; Toronto Public Health; Private donations
Staff Member(s): 6; 60 volunteer(s)
Membership: 40; Fees: $10+
Activities: Community workshops & forums; Training of community professionals & volunteers; Development of culturally specific education materials; Support & counselling; Speaker Service: Yes
Chief Officer(s):
Shannon Thomas Ryan, Executive Director
s.ryan@black-cap.com

Black Coalition of Québec / La Ligue des Noirs du Québec
5201, boul Decarie, Montréal QC H3W 3C2
Tel: 514-489-3830
info@liguedesnoirs.org
www.liguedesnoirs.org
Overview: A small local organization
Mission: The Coalition speaks for the Black community in the defence of individual human rights and against all forms of discrimination
Chief Officer(s):
Peterson Frederick, President

Black Community Resource Centre (BCRC)
#497, 6767, ch de la Côte-des-Neiges, Montréal QC H3S 2T6
Tel: 514-342-2247; Fax: 514-342-2283
info@bcrcmontreal.com
bcrcmontreal.com
Overview: A medium-sized local organization
Mission: To help English-speaking visible minority youth achieve their full potential
Activities: Information & referral; Support to schools; Conference, meeting & workshop support; Documentation Centre; Document translation; Web design; Workshops for adults & youth; Mini-Poste project; Expressing Life project
Publications:
• Semaji
Type: Newsletter; Frequency: Q

Black Creek Conservation Project
PO Box 98552, 873 Jane St., Toronto ON M6N 5A6
Tel: 416-661-6600; Fax: 416-661-6898
bccp@rogers.com
www.bccp.ca
Previous Name: Black Creek Project of Toronto Inc.
Overview: A small local organization founded in 1982
Mission: To preserve & rehabilitate the Black Creek watershed; To support a healthy, diverse, & sustainable ecosystem
Member of: Federation of Ontario Naturalists
Finances: Annual Operating Budget: $50,000-$100,000; Funding Sources: Government; private
Staff Member(s): 5; 2500 volunteer(s)
Membership: 45; Fees: $20/year general membership; $35/year group membership; $10/year youth membership
Activities: Tree planting; garbage clean-up; environmental lectures; erosion control; wetland creation; Awareness Events: Clean Toronto Together Event, April; Black Creek Earth Day Event, April; Rents Mailing List: Yes
Chief Officer(s):
Gaspar Horvath, President and Director
ghorvath@trca.on.ca
Publications:
• Kingfisher Newsletter
Type: Newsletter; Frequency: irregular

Black Creek Project of Toronto Inc. See Black Creek Conservation Project

Black Cultural Society for Nova Scotia
10 Cherry Brook Rd., Cherry Brook NS B2Z 1A8
Tel: 902-434-6223; Fax: 902-434-2306
Toll-Free: 800-465-0767
contact@bccns.com
www.bccns.com
www.facebook.com/188265867860941
Overview: A medium-sized provincial charitable organization founded in 1977
Mission: To create among members of the Black community an awareness of their past, their heritage & identity; to provide programs & activities to explore, learn about, understand & appreciate Black history, achievements & experiences in Canadian life.
Member of: Multicultural Association of Nova Scotia
Membership: Fees: $15 student/senior; $25 individual; $50 family/group; $100 corporate
Activities: Operates the Black Cultural centre for Nova Scotia; Speaker Service: Yes; Library: Open to public
Chief Officer(s):
Leslie Oliver, President

Black Educators Association of Nova Scotia (BEA)
2136 Gottingen St., Halifax NS B3K 3B3
Tel: 902-424-7036; Fax: 902-424-0636
Toll-Free: 800-565-3398
info@theblackeducators.ca
www.theblackeducators.ca
Overview: A medium-sized provincial charitable organization founded in 1969
Mission: To monitor & ensure the development of an equitable education system, so that African Nova Scotians are able to achieve their maximum potential
Affiliation(s): National Council of Black Educators of Canada
Finances: Funding Sources: Department of Canadian Heritage
Membership: Fees: $30 regular; $20 associate; $15 member at large; $10 student; $100 organization; Committees: Operations; Community Involvement; Curriculum; Professional Development; Membership; Personnel
Activities: Community workshops; provincial conferences
Chief Officer(s):
Ken Fells, President
Robert Upshaw, Executive Director
Awards:
• BEA Bursary Fund
; Amount: $400

Black Law Students' Association of Canada (BLSA) / L'Association des etudiants noirs en droit du Canada
Admin@blsacanada.com
www.blsacanada.com
www.facebook.com/blsacanada
twitter.com/BLSAC
Overview: A small national organization founded in 1991
Mission: A national organization committed to supporting and enhancing academic and professional opportunities for black law students in both official languages.
Chief Officer(s):
Moses Gashirabake, President
President@blsacanada.com
Meetings/Conferences:
• Black Law Students Association of Canada 27th Annual National Conference, February, 2018, Hotel Omni Mont-Royal, Montréal, QC
Scope: National
Description: Theme: "Advancing the Vision: Continuing in the Spirit of Excellence"
Contact Information: E-mail: conference@blsacanada.com

Black Loyalist Heritage Society (BLHS)
PO Box 1194, 98 Birchtown Rd., Shelburne NS B0T 1W0
Tel: 902-875-1310; Fax: 902-875-1352
Toll-Free: 888-354-0772
blackloyalist@blackloyalist.com
www.blackloyalist.com
www.facebook.com/111527972216141
Overview: A small local organization
Mission: To promote the history of Black Loyalists
Staff Member(s): 3
Membership: Fees: $20 individual; $25 family; $40 organization/business
Chief Officer(s):
Beverly Cox, Site Manager, 902-875-1606
beverly@blackloyalist.com

Black River-Matheson Chamber of Commerce
PO Box 518, Matheson ON P0K 1N0
chamber@brmchamberofcommerce.org
www.brmchamberofcommerce.org
Also Known As: BRM Chamber of Commerce
Overview: A small local organization
Mission: To promote commerce in the community
Member of: Canadian Chamber of Commerce
Membership: 53; Fees: $40 private; $95 non-profit; $95 1-11 employees; $175 12-50 employees; $275 51+ employees

Black Studies Centre (BSC)
1968, boul de Maisonneuve ouest, Montréal QC H3H 1K5
Tel: 514-933-0798
Overview: A medium-sized local organization founded in 1970
Mission: To provide a wide range of services to the Montreal community & to its various institutions; To be committed to the continued educational development of Montreal's Black community & to the recognition of the contributions they have made in helping Montreal to grow as a city
Chief Officer(s):
Clarence S. Bayne, President

Black Theatre Workshop (BTW)
#432, 3680, rue Jeanne-Mance, Montréal QC H2X 2K5
Tel: 514-932-1104
info@blacktheatreworkshop.ca
www.blacktheatreworkshop.ca

www.facebook.com/BlackTheatreWorkshop
twitter.com/BTW_Tweets
Overview: A medium-sized national charitable organization founded in 1972
Mission: To encourage & promote the development of a Black & Canadian theatre, rooted in a literature that reflects the creative will of Black Canadian writers & artists, & the creative collaborations between Black & other artists; To strive to create a greater cross-cultural understanding by its presence & the intrinsic value of its work
Finances: *Funding Sources:* Individual donations; Ticket revenue; Government funding
Activities: Performing season series; Touring schools and community centres in the greater Montreal area for Black History Month
Chief Officer(s):
Quincy Armorer, Artistic Director, 514-932-1104 Ext. 222
ad@blacktheatreworkshop.ca
Adele Benoit, General Manager, 514-932-1104 Ext. 221
gm@blacktheatreworkshop.ca
Awards:
• Gloria Mitchell-Aleong Award
Eligibility: Artists between the ages of 20 and 35 who demonstrate notable ability in the performing arts *Deadline:* November 27; *Amount:* $500
• The Victor Phillips Youth Award
Eligibility: Artists under the age of 20 who excel in both academics and the performing arts *Deadline:* November 27; *Amount:* $1,000

Blackfalds & District Chamber of Commerce
PO Box 249, Blackfalds AB T0M 0J0
Tel: 403-885-2386; *Fax:* 403-885-2386
info@blackfaldslive.ca
www.blackfaldslive.ca
Overview: A small local organization

Bladder Cancer Canada (BCC) / Cancer de la vessie Canada
#1000, 4936 Yonge St., Toronto ON M2N 6S3
Toll-Free: 866-674-8889
info@bladdercancercanada.org
www.bladdercancercanada.org
www.linkedin.com/company/2599127
www.facebook.com/BladderCancerCanada
twitter.com/BladderCancerCA
www.youtube.com/user/BladderCancerCA
Overview: A medium-sized national charitable organization founded in 2009
Mission: To improve patient support by having a patient to patient support system in place; To offer information about available treatment options; To create greater awareness of bladder cancer
Finances: *Annual Operating Budget:* $50,000-$100,000; *Funding Sources:* Private donations; fundraisers
Chief Officer(s):
Ken Bagshaw, Chair
Tammy Northam, Executive Director

Blaine Lake & District Chamber of Commerce
c/o Blaine Lake Town Office, PO Box 10, Blaine Lake SK S0J 0J0
Tel: 306-497-2531; *Fax:* 306-497-2511
blainelakecofc@sasktel.net
www.blainelake.ca/business/chamber.html
Overview: A small local organization
Mission: To unite the efforts of business & community to ensure economic health & social well being of Blaine Lake & District
Member of: Saskatchewan Chamber of Commerce, SaskTourism
Finances: *Annual Operating Budget:* Less than $50,000; *Funding Sources:* Annual silent auction; Membership fees
Membership: 58; *Fees:* Schedule available; *Member Profile:* Business
Activities: Annual Banquet; Community Candle Service; Cabin Drop; community events; community bulletin board; Community Contribution Awards

Blairmore Board of Trade *See* Crowsnest Pass Chamber of Commerce

Blankets for Canada Society Inc.
#217, 210A - 12A St. North, Lethbridge AB T1H 2J1
Tel: 403-329-6586; *Fax:* 403-381-8668
www.blankets4canada.ca
Also Known As: B4C
Overview: A small national charitable organization founded in 1998
Mission: To create blankets for those Canadians who are without shelter or in need of warmth; To support organizations who care for these people
Finances: *Annual Operating Budget:* Less than $50,000
250 volunteer(s)
Membership: 23; *Fees:* $20
Activities: Knit, crochet, quilt blankets for distribution
Chief Officer(s):
Nancy Panting, Founder
Publications:
• The Joiner [a publication of Blankets for Canada Society]
Type: Newsletter

Blenheim & District Chamber of Commerce
PO Box 1353, Blenheim ON N0P 1A0
Tel: 519-676-6555
blenheimontario.com/chamber-of-commerce
Overview: A small local organization founded in 1977
Finances: *Annual Operating Budget:* Less than $50,000
2 volunteer(s)
Membership: 51
Chief Officer(s):
Frank Vercouteren, President
Betty Russell, Secretary, 519-676-8090

Blind Bowls Association of Canada (BBAC)
SK
bbacanada.org
Overview: A small national organization
Mission: To govern the sport of bowls in Canada; to promote the interests of visually impaired lawn bowlers in Canada & around the world.
Chief Officer(s):
Vivian Berkeley, President
vberkeley@sympatico.ca
Shirley Ahern, Secretary
shirice@sympatico.ca

Blind River Chamber of Commerce (BRCC)
PO Box 998, Blind River ON P0R 1B0
Tel: 705-356-5715; *Fax:* 705-356-5720
chamber@blindriver.com
www.brchamber.ca
www.facebook.com/BRChamberofCommerce
twitter.com/BRChamber
Overview: A small local organization founded in 1951
Mission: To be the recognized voice of business committed to the enhancement of economic prosperity in our area
Member of: Ontario Chamber of Commerce; Northeastern Chamber of Commerce
Affiliation(s): Algoma Kinniwabi Travel Association
Membership: 160; *Fees:* Schedule available based on number of employees; *Committees:* Moonlight Madness; Small Business Week; Golf
Activities: Moonlight madness & summer sidewalk sale; retail events; Chamber Golf Classic
Chief Officer(s):
Alex Solomon, President, 705-356-7212
Garnet Young, Treasurer, 705-849-2245

Blind Sailing Association of Canada (BSAC)
17 Boustead Ave., Toronto ON M6R 1Y7
Tel: 416-489-2433
info@blindsailing.ca
www.blindsailing.ca
www.facebook.com/385889524843037
twitter.com/blindcansail
Overview: A small national organization founded in 2002
Mission: To provide opportunities for the blind to learn to sail, thus boosting skills, confidence & self-esteem
Member of: Ontario Sailing Association; Sail Canada
Membership: *Fees:* $40

Blind Sports Nova Scotia
NS
info@blindsportsnovascotia.ca
www.blindsportsnovascotia.ca
twitter.com/blindsportsns
Overview: A small provincial organization overseen by Canadian Blind Sports Association Inc.
Mission: Blind Sports Nova Scotia is an organization that presents sport & recreational activities for visually impaired athletes in Nova Scotia.
Member of: Canadian Blind Sport Association; Sport Nova Scotia
Membership: *Member Profile:* Adults, age 19+ (but 14+ are welcome, too)
Chief Officer(s):
Peter Parsons, Chair
Charlie MacDonald, Secretary

Blissymbolics Communication International (BCI)
#425, 1210 Don Mills Rd., Toronto ON M3B 3N9
www.blissymbolics.ca
Overview: A small international charitable organization founded in 1975
Mission: BCI is a non-profit, charitable organization that has the license for the use and publication of Blissymbols designed for persons with communication, language, & learning difficulties, severe speech & physical impairments.
Affiliation(s): Ontario Federation for Cerebral Palsy
Finances: *Funding Sources:* Federal & provincial governments, Ontario Crippled Children's Centre, Easter Seal society, charitable foundations, donations
Activities: BCI trains professionals, assists users, offers consultation, continues technology & software development.; *Internships:* Yes; *Speaker Service:* Yes; *Library:* Open to public
Chief Officer(s):
Shirley McNaughton, Co-Chair

Bloc québécois (BQ)
#502, 3750, boul Crémazie est, Montréal QC H2A 1B4
Tél: 514-526-3000; *Téléc:* 514-526-2868
Ligne sans frais: 888-448-1880
www.blocquebecois.org
www.facebook.com/blocquebecois
twitter.com/blocquebecois
www.youtube.com/user/blocquebecois
Aperçu: *Dimension:* moyenne; *Envergure:* provinciale; fondée en 1990
Finances: *Budget de fonctionnement annuel:* $500,000-$1.5 Million
Membre(s) du personnel: 8; 1500 bénévole(s)
Membre: 110 000; *Montant de la cotisation:* 5$
Membre(s) du bureau directeur:
Martine Ouellet, Chef
Mario Beaulieu, Président

Block Parent Program of Canada (BPPCI) / Programme Parents-Secours du Canada
PO Box 7, 50 Dunlop St. East, Lower Level, Barrie ON L4N 6S7
Tel: 705-792-4245; *Fax:* 705-792-4245
Toll-Free: 800-663-1134
info@blockparent.ca
www.blockparent.ca
www.facebook.com/blockparent
Overview: A large national charitable organization founded in 1968
Mission: To provide immediate assistance through a safety network; To offer supporting community education programs
Finances: *Annual Operating Budget:* $100,000-$250,000; *Funding Sources:* Federal grants; Corporate sponsor; Donations
Staff Member(s): 2
Membership: 12 provincial & territorial programs; 900+ community members; *Fees:* $1,500 to set up a program in a neighbourhood with 25,000 students & three elementary schools
Activities: Educational materials on safety; *Awareness Events:* National Block Parent Week, Oct. *Library:* Safety Video Library; Not open to public
Chief Officer(s):
Linda Patterson, President
Awards:
• National Block Parent Award
Publications:
• Block Parent Program of Canada Inc. Communiqué
Type: Newsletter

Alberta Block Parent Association (ABPA)
220 Doveview Cres. SE, Calgary AB T2B 1Y6
Tel: 403-262-2864
albertabpa@hotmail.com
www.albertablockparent.com
Member of: Block Parent Program of Canada Inc.
Chief Officer(s):
Donna Fox, President

Block Parent Program of Winnipeg
466 Gertrude Ave., Winnipeg MB R3L 0M8
Tel: 204-284-7562
teresamel@xplornet.ca
www.winnipegblockparents.mb.ca
Member of: Block Parent Program of Canada Inc.
Chief Officer(s):

George Jarvis, President
New Brunswick Block Parent Association (NBBPAI)
NB
Tel: 506-446-5992
lindapatterson100@gmail.com
Member of: Block Parent Program of Canada Inc.
Nova Scotia Block Parent Advisory Board
NS
Tel: 902-849-3525
byrnemg@hotmail.com
Member of: Block Parent Program of Canada Inc.
Ontario Block Parent Program (OBPPI)
ON
Member of: Block Parent Program of Canada Inc.
Chief Officer(s):
Marg Rooke, Acting Chair
mrooke@blockparent.on.ca

Block Rosary Group of Ontario
22 Norman Ross Dr., Markham ON L3S 3E8
Tel: 905-472-3194
Also Known As: The Block Rosary Crusaders
Overview: A small provincial charitable organization founded in 1982
Mission: To encourage families & friends to pray the Holy Rosary together; To pray for the ill, the deceased, & those in need of help spiritually & otherwise; To pray for peace & unity in families, communities, & the world
Affiliation(s): Archdiocese of Toronto
Finances: *Funding Sources:* Donations
Membership: 10 groups, with 500+ families & 80 coordinators; *Member Profile:* Catholic families in Durham Region, York Region & Metro Toronto, Ontario; *Committees:* Picnic; Carey Ohio; Anniversary; Living Rosary; Christmas Party
Activities: Organizing pilgrimages to Carey, Ohio, the Shrine of Our Lady of Fatima in Youngstown, New York & Midland, Ontario; Providing faith instruction; Offering prayer groups; Hosting social events such as summer picnics, anniversary dances & family Christmas parties
Chief Officer(s):
Jaime Marasigan, Contact
jmarasigan@sympatico.ca

Block Watch Society of British Columbia (BCBPS)
#120, 12414 - 82nd Ave., Surrey BC V3W 3E9
Tel: 604-418-3827; *Fax:* 604-501-2509
Toll-Free: 877-602-3358
blockwatch@blockwatch.com
blockwatch.com
Overview: A small provincial charitable organization founded in 1986
Mission: To build safe neighbourhoods across British Columbia; To encourage bonds among local residents & businesses to create a crime free area through community participation; To assist in the reduction of crime; To improve relations between police & communities
Membership: 88 societies; *Member Profile:* Members who watch for suspicious activity in their neighbourhoods
Activities: Partnering with police; Supporting Block Watch programs throughout British Columbia; Increasing crime awareness; Sharing knowledge of security measures, through the provision of resource materials; Training captains & co-captains
Chief Officer(s):
Colleen Staresina, President, 604-502-6287, Fax: 604-502-6539
colleen.staresina@rcmp-grc.gc.ca
Gary O'Brien, Vice-President, 250-754-2345
Gary.OBrien@rcmp-grc.gc.ca
Jenniffer Sanford, Secretary, 604-529-2494, Fax: 604-529-2422
Blockwatch@nwpolice.org
Michelle Wulff, Treasurer, 604-393-3000, Fax: 604-819-0865
michelle.wulff@rcmp-grc.gc.ca
Awards:
• Safe Communities Grant
• Crime Prevention Award
Publications:
• Block Watch Society of British Columbia Newsletter
Type: Newsletter
Profile: Information about crime trends, security, & society events

Blomidon Naturalists Society (BNS)
PO Box 2350, Wolfville NS B4P 2N5
bns@valleynature.ca
www.blomidonnaturalists.ca
twitter.com/bns1974
Overview: A small local charitable organization founded in 1974
Mission: To encourage & develop an understanding & appreciation of nature
Member of: Nature Nova Scotia, Nature Canada
Finances: *Annual Operating Budget:* $50,000-$100,000; *Funding Sources:* Membership dues
15 volunteer(s)
Membership: 250; *Fees:* $30 adult/family; $1 junior
Activities: Monthly meetings; field trips; bird counts; astronomy sessions
Chief Officer(s):
Soren Bondrup-Neilsen, President
Pat Kelly, Secretary
Awards:
• Robie Tufts Young Naturalist Award
Publications:
• Blomidon Naturalists Society Newsletter
Type: Newsletter; *Frequency:* Quarterly; *Number of Pages:* 48
Profile: Published once every season of the year around the equinoxes & solstices.

Blonde d'Aquitaine du Québec
1395, rte 122, Notre-Dame-du-Bon-Conseil QC J0C 1A0
Tél: 819-336-3966; *Téléc:* 819-336-2883
www.blondaquitaineqc.com
Aperçu: *Dimension:* petite; *Envergure:* provinciale
Membre de: Canadian Blonde d'Aquitaine Association
Membre(s) du bureau directeur:
Clemency Landry, President
Maureen Landry, Secretary

Blood Ties Four Directions Centre
307 Strickland St., Whitehorse YT Y1A 2J9
Tel: 867-633-2437; *Fax:* 867-633-2447
Toll-Free: 877-333-2437
bloodties@klondiker.com
www.bloodties.ca
Previous Name: AIDS Yukon Alliance
Overview: A small provincial charitable organization founded in 1988 overseen by Canadian AIDS Society
Mission: To acts as an information & support centre; to promote public awareness of AIDS/AIDS & hepatitis C and aid in their prevention; to assist people living with HIV/AIDS & hep C.
Member of: Pacific AIDS Network
Finances: *Funding Sources:* Government grants
Staff Member(s): 6
Membership: *Member Profile:* PHA's, families, friends, interested parties
Activities: Support group; treatment information; outreach; *Speaker Service:* Yes; *Library:* Resource Library; Open to public
Chief Officer(s):
Patricia Bacon, Executive Director
executivedirector@bloodties.ca

BloodWatch
PO Box 51523, 2140A Queen St. East, Toronto ON M4E 3V7
Tel: 647-272-7381
info@bloodwatch.org
www.bloodwatch.org
www.facebook.com/bloodwatch.org
twitter.com/BloodWatchOrg
Overview: A small national organization
Mission: To preserve the safety of the public blood system in Canada
Activities: Advocating for blood safety & the non-commodification of blood; Offering information about The Krever Inquiry & the consequences of tainted blood
Chief Officer(s):
Kat Lanteigne, Executive Director

The Bloom Group
391 Powell St., Vancouver BC V6A 1G5
Tel: 604-606-0300; *Fax:* 604-606-0309
info@thebloomgroup.org
www.thebloomgroup.org
Previous Name: St. James Community Service Society
Overview: A small local organization founded in 1961
Mission: To offer aid & assistance to those who are in need; To eliminate poverty & homelessness
Finances: *Annual Operating Budget:* Greater than $5 Million; *Funding Sources:* Regional & federal government
Membership: 1-99; *Fees:* $5 individual
Chief Officer(s):
Jonathan Oldman, Executive Director, 604-606-0307
joldman@thebloomgroup.org

Blue Line Racing Association
Edmonton AB
bluelineracing@live.ca
bluelineracing.ca
www.facebook.com/214136468679819
Overview: A small local charitable organization founded in 1996
Mission: To promote safe & legal alternatives to street racing in Edmonton
Finances: *Funding Sources:* Donations
5 volunteer(s)
Chief Officer(s):
Mike Wynnyk, Constable, Contact

Blue Mountain Foundation for the Arts (BMFA)
PO Box 581, 163 Hurontario St., Collingwood ON L9Y 4E8
Tel: 705-445-3430; *Fax:* 705-445-0840
admin@bmfa.on.ca
www.bmfa.on.ca
www.facebook.com/212400128776550
twitter.com/BMFA_ArtsCentre
Overview: A medium-sized local organization founded in 1975
Mission: To make the arts an integral part of life in southern Georgian Bay community; To develop talent & broaden appreciation of the arts; To nurture excellence in the arts; To work with other community groups; To foster wide variety of opportunities for creative expression; To broaden range of quality programs which are offered to increase public participation & fundraising
Staff Member(s): 1; 100 volunteer(s)
Membership: 375; *Fees:* Schedule available; *Committees:* Performing Arts; Performing Arts for Youth; Publications; Visual Arts; Policy; Planning; Finance
Chief Officer(s):
Deborah Mobbs, Executive Director
Susan Cook, Adminstrator, 705-445-3430
admin@bmfa.on.ca

Blue Mountains Chamber of Commerce
PO Box 477, Thornbury ON N0H 2P0
Tel: 519-599-1200; *Fax:* 519-599-2567
info@bluemountainschamber.ca
www.bluemountainschamber.ca
Previous Name: Thornbury & District Chamber of Commerce
Overview: A small local organization
Membership: 131; *Fees:* $55 non-profit; $155 business; $120 banner ad; *Committees:* Executive; Membership; Events; Finance; Nominating; Economic Development; Chamber Building; Community Watch; Sparc Competition
Chief Officer(s):
Dolf Jansen, President

Blue Water Chamber of Commerce
PO Box 204, St Georges MB R0E 1V0
Tel: 204-367-9970
bluewaterchamber@hotmail.com
Overview: A small local organization
Member of: Manitoba Chamber of Commerce
Chief Officer(s):
Diane Dube, President
cdc@granite.mb.ca

Bluegrass Music Association of Canada (BMAC)
399 Fichault Rd., Rutherglen ON P0H 2E0
Tel: 705-776-7754
www.bluegrasscanada.org
www.facebook.com/bluegrasscanada.org
Overview: A small national organization
Mission: To preserve & promote bluegrass & old-time music in Canada; To support individuals, groups & organizations involved in bluegrass & old-time music; To lead & promote education among fans, clubs, bands & artists
Affiliation(s): International Bluegrass Music Association; Canadian Country Music Association; The Ontario Council of Folk Festivals; Northern Ontario Country Music Association
Membership: *Fees:* $20 individual
Chief Officer(s):
David Porter, Vice-President

Bluewater Recycling Association (BRA)
415 Canada Ave., Huron Park ON N0M 1Y0
Tel: 519-228-6678; *Fax:* 519-228-6656
info@bra.org
www.bra.org
Overview: A small local organization founded in 1989
Mission: To provide ethical, innovative, effective resource-management services; To carry out the mission efficiently, safely & in an environmentally responsible manner,

ultimately enabling our members to meet their environmental commitments
Finances: *Annual Operating Budget:* Greater than $5 Million
Staff Member(s): 55
Membership: 21; *Fees:* Schedule available; *Member Profile:* Municipalities
Activities: *Speaker Service:* Yes
Chief Officer(s):
Francis Veilleux, President
Publications:
• Bluewater Recycling Newsletter
Type: Newsletter

Bluffton & District Chamber of Commerce
PO Box 38, Bluffton AB T0C 0M0
Tel: 403-843-6805; *Fax:* 403-843-3392
blufftonabchamber@gmail.com
www.facebook.com/176503109373804
Overview: A small local organization
Mission: To promote local businesses & community groups
Activities: Organizing & sponsoring trade fairs

BMW Club of Canada *See* BMW Clubs Canada

BMW Club of Regina *See* BMW Clubs Canada

BMW Clubs Canada (BMWCC) / Le Club BMW du Canada
c/o National Secretary, 4635, av Doherty, Montréal QC H4B 2B2
info@bmwclub.ca
www.bmwclub.ca
www.facebook.com/BMW.Canada
Previous Name: BMW Club of Canada
Overview: A medium-sized national organization founded in 1973
Mission: The umbrella organization is comprised of regional chapter clubs that actively provide a variety of events to promote the enjoyment & sharing of good will & fellowship derived from owning a BMW automobile or motorcycle.
Member of: International Council of BMW Clubs
Finances: *Annual Operating Budget:* $100,000-$250,000; *Funding Sources:* Membership dues
Membership: 800; *Fees:* $40-$60 (depending on local chapter)
Activities: Driving schools; motorsport; social activities; technical information; *Speaker Service:* Yes
Chief Officer(s):
Phil Abrami, President
Awards:
• Participation Trophy
• Competition Trophy

Atlantic Canada Chapter
#607, 105 Dunbrack St., Halifax NS B3M 3G7
Tel: 902-443-6369
info@bmwclubatlantic.ca
bmwclubatlantic.ca
twitter.com/BMWClubAtlantic
www.flickr.com/photos/55144543@N08

BMW Car Club of BC
PO Box 3452, 349 West Georgia St., Vancouver BC V6B 3Y4
info@bmwccbc.org
www.bmwccbc.org
Chief Officer(s):
David Gray, President
david@bmwccbc.org

BMW Car Club of Ottawa
PO Box 23179, Ottawa ON K2A 4E2
info@bmwccottawa.org
bmwccottawa.org
Chief Officer(s):
Chris Pawlowicz, President, Webmaster
chris@pawlowicz.ca

BMW Club of Manitoba
2071 Portage Ave., Winnipeg MB R3J 0K9
info@bmwpower.ca
bmwclubmanitoba.com
twitter.com/BMWclubMB
Chief Officer(s):
Jeremy Choy, Contact

BMW Club of Québec
4535, av du Parc, Montréal QC H2V 4E4
info@bmwquebec.ca
bmwquebec.ca

BMW Club of Saskatchewan
3655 Wetmore Cres., Regina SK S4V 2C2
hello@bmwsask.com
bmwsask.com
www.facebook.com/bmwsask
twitter.com/bmwsask

Northern Alberta BMW Club
PO Box 52024, Edmonton AB T6G 2T5
info@nabmwclub.ca
www.nabmwclub.ca
www.facebook.com/NorthernAlbertaBmwClub
twitter.com/NABMWyeg
Chief Officer(s):
Vince Paniak, President
vpaniak@nabmwclub.ca

Southern Alberta BMW Club
3 Canova Rd. SW, Calgary AB T2W 2K5
Fax: 403-281-4463
email@bmwcsa.ca
www.bmwcsa.ca
Chief Officer(s):
Brian Deboeck, President
president@bmwcsa.ca

Trillium Chapter
#530, 4936 Yonge St., Toronto ON M2N 6S3
Fax: 866-801-9185
trillium@bmwclub.ca
www.trillium-bmwclub.ca
Chief Officer(s):
Jennifer Venditti, President
jennifer.venditti@trillium-bmwclub.ca

Vancouver Island BMW Club
PO Box 30181, Stn. Saanich Centre, Victoria BC V8X 5E1
island@bmwclub.ca
www.bmwccvi.ca

Board of Canadian Registered Safety Professionals (BCRSP) / Conseil canadien des professionnels en sécurité agréés
#100, 6700 Century Ave., Mississauga ON L5N 6A4
Tel: 905-567-7198; *Fax:* 905-567-7191
Toll-Free: 888-279-2777
info@bcrsp.ca
www.bcrsp.ca
www.linkedin.com/company/board-of-canadian-registered-safety-professionals?trk=nav_account_sub_nav_company_admin
www.twitter.com/bcrsp
Previous Name: Association for Canadian Registered Safety Professionals
Overview: A medium-sized national licensing organization founded in 1976
Mission: To protect & promote occupational health & safety, environmental safety, & public safety, through the registration of qualified health & safety professionals committed to a code of ethics
Affiliation(s): Canadian Network of National Associations of Regulators; Institute for Credentialing Excellence (ICE); International Network of Safety & Health Practitioner Organisations (INSHPO)
Finances: *Annual Operating Budget:* $250,000-$500,000; *Funding Sources:* Membership dues
Staff Member(s): 5; 130 volunteer(s)
Membership: 2,000; *Fees:* $125; *Member Profile:* Successfully completed high school or equivalency; three years of continuous safety experience & current employment of at least 50% in a safety practitioners role
Activities: CRSP designation (the Board evaluates qualifications of candidates & members against established standards)
Chief Officer(s):
Daniel T. Lyons, Chair
Nicola Wright, Executive Director

Board of Directors of Drugless Therapy, Naturopathy (Ontario) *See* The College of Naturopaths of Ontario

Board of Examiners in Optometry in B.C. *See* College of Optometrists of BC

Board of Registration for Social Workers in B.C. *See* British Columbia College of Social Workers

Boating BC Association
#130, 10691 Shellbridge Way, Richmond BC V6X 2W8
Tel: 604-248-8906; *Fax:* 604-270-3644
info@boatingbc.ca
www.boatingbc.ca
www.linkedin.com/company/boating-bc-association
www.facebook.com/BoatingBC
twitter.com/boatingbc
www.youtube.com/channel/UCyvMWT5_eNm_0LBJFbXiZSw
Previous Name: British Columbia Marine Trades Association
Overview: A medium-sized provincial organization founded in 1957
Mission: To act as the voice of the BC recreational marine industry
Affiliation(s): BC Yacht Brokers Association; BC Bareboat Charters Association
Finances: *Annual Operating Budget:* $50,000-$100,000
Membership: 293 corporate; *Fees:* $100-395
Chief Officer(s):
Don Prittie, President, 250-656-5566
gm@canoecovemarina.com
Lisa Geddes, Executive Director, 604-248-8906
lisa@boatingbc.ca
Mike Short, First Vice-President & Treasurer, 604-278-9787
mike@vancouvermarina.com

Boating Ontario
15 Laurier Rd., Penetanguishene ON L9M 1G8
Tel: 705-549-1667; *Fax:* 705-549-1670
Toll-Free: 888-547-6662
info@boatingontario.ca
www.boatingontario.ca
Previous Name: Ontario Marine Operators Association
Overview: A medium-sized provincial organization founded in 1967
Mission: To promote recreational boating throughout Ontario
Membership: 460+ individual marinas + 160 trade members; *Member Profile:* Ontario marinas; Yacht clubs; Marine dealers; Associated companies
Activities: Lobbying on behalf of the industry; Providing information; Encouraging safe boating; Participating in boat shows; Offering workshops
Chief Officer(s):
Dick Peever, President, 519-524-4409, Fax: 519-524-2301
Graham Lacey, Vice-President, 705-383-2295, Fax: 705-383-2243
Al Donaldson, Executive Director, 705-549-1667, Fax: 705-549-1670
Ed Leeman, Secretary, 613-583-7973
Bob Eaton, Director, Environmental Services, 705-326-9359, Fax: 705-326-3827
Publications:
• Boating Ontario: Marinas & Destination Guide
Type: Directory; *Frequency:* Annually
Profile: A guide to more than 450 marina members of the Ontario Marine Operators Association, with information about their facilities & services
• Enviro Boater
Type: Manual
Profile: Suggestions for environment-friendly boating, produced by the Ontario Marine Operators Association, the Canadian Power & Sail Squadrons, & other interested organizations
• Marina News
Type: Newsletter; *Frequency:* 8 pa; *Price:* Free with membership in the Ontario Marine Operators Association
Profile: Business suggestions & industry news, for members of the Ontario Marine Operators Association

The Bob Rumball Centre for the Deaf (BRCD)
2395 Bayview Ave., Toronto ON M2L 1A2
Tel: 416-449-9651; *Fax:* 416-449-8881; *TTY:* 416-449-2728
info@bobrumball.org
www.bobrumball.org
www.facebook.com/86097284911
Overview: A large local organization founded in 1979
Mission: To provide opportunities for a higher quality of life for deaf people while preserving & promoting their language & culture; To foster & develop good relations with the community at large & actively promote the Centre; To work closely with the various ministries of the provincial government & related agencies
Member of: Ontario Mission of the Deaf
Finances: *Annual Operating Budget:* $3 Million-$5 Million; *Funding Sources:* Government; user fees; private & public donations
Staff Member(s): 75; 200 volunteer(s)
Activities: Adult education and residential program; Day and early years programs; Preschool program; Progressive independent living; Senior Supportive Housing; Sign language services; Volunteer services; *Internships:* Yes; *Speaker Service:* Yes; *Library*
Chief Officer(s):
Jane Hooey, Chair

Bob Rumball Foundation for the Deaf
2395 Bayview Ave., Toronto ON M2L 1A2
Tel: 416-449-9651; *TTY:* 416-449-2728
Other Communication: 416-640-0723
fundraising@bobrumball.org
www.bobrumball.org
www.facebook.com/86097284911
twitter.com/BobRumball
www.instagram.com/bobrumball
Previous Name: Ontario Mission of the Deaf
Overview: A small local organization founded in 1872
Mission: To meet the social, recreational, educational & spiritual needs of the deaf community & raise funds for The Bob Rumball Centre for the Deaf in Toronto, The Bob Rumball Associations for the Deaf in Milton, The Bob Rumball Long Term Care Home for the Deaf in Barrie & The Bob Rumball Camp for the Deaf in Parry Sound.
Chief Officer(s):
Derek Rumball, Executive Director

Bobcaygeon & Area Chamber of Commerce
PO Box 388, 21 Canal St. East, Bobcaygeon ON K0M 1A0
Tel: 705-738-2202; *Fax:* 705-738-1534
Toll-Free: 800-318-6173
www.bobcaygeon.org
www.facebook.com/Bobcaygeon-Chamber-of-Commerce-147571458647966
twitter.com/BobcaygeonCofC
Overview: A small local organization
Mission: To promote Bobcaygeon as a tourist area; To promote business in the area
Member of: Ontario Chamber of Commerce
Affiliation(s): Kawartha Lakes Associated Chambers of Commerce
Finances: *Funding Sources:* Membership dues; Ministry of Transportation
Membership: 200; *Fees:* $175; $65 associate or non-profit
Chief Officer(s):
Kent Leckie, President

Bobsleigh Canada Skeleton
c/o Canada Olympic Park, #329, 151 Canada Olympic Rd. SW, Calgary AB T3B 6B7
Tel: 403-247-5950; *Fax:* 403-202-6561
info@bobsleigh.ca
www.bobsleigh.ca
www.facebook.com/BobsleighCanadaSkeleton
twitter.com/BobsleighCAN
Overview: A medium-sized national charitable organization founded in 1990
Mission: To strive to create Olympic & world champions
Member of: Canadian Olympic Association
Affiliation(s): Fédération internationale de bobsleigh et de tobogganing
Finances: *Funding Sources:* Government & corporate sponsorship
Staff Member(s): 8
Activities: Operating national teams in men's & women's bobsleigh & skeleton; Hosting national & international events
Chief Officer(s):
Don Wilson, CEO

Boissevain & District Chamber of Commerce
PO Box 734, Boissevain MB R0K 0E0
Tel: 204-534-6488
admin@boissevain.ca
www.boissevain.ca
Overview: A small local organization
Mission: To promote the business of Boissevain & area
60 volunteer(s)
Membership: 60+; *Fees:* $20-$95; *Committees:* Tourism; Agriculture; Beautification
Activities: Organizing events such as Farm Focus Day; Providing information to members
Chief Officer(s):
Ken Hole, President

Boîte à science - Conseil du loisir scientifique du Québec
1150, boul René-Lévesque ouest, porte 16, Québec QC G1S 1V7
Tél: 418-658-1426; *Téléc:* 418-658-1012
info@boiteascience.com
www.boiteascience.com
www.facebook.com/BoiteAScience
twitter.com/Boiteascience
www.instagram.com/boiteascience

Nom précédent: Conseil du loisir scientifique de Québec
Aperçu: *Dimension:* moyenne; *Envergure:* locale; Organisme sans but lucratif; fondée en 1981
Mission: Éveiller, prioritairement chez les jeunes, leur intérêt pour les science et la technologie
Finances: *Budget de fonctionnement annuel:* $500,000-$1.5 Million; *Fonds:* Gouvernement; autofinancement; levées de fonds
Membre(s) du personnel: 8; 250 bénévole(s)
Membre: 8
Activités: Club des Débrouillards; Expo-sciences régionale; Aventure scientifique; Innovateur à l'école; Salle de découvertes; Défi apprenti-génie; Voilà Science!; Centres de table scientifiques; la Science dans ma classe; Pop science; *Stagiaires:* Oui; *Service de conférenciers:* Oui
Membre(s) du bureau directeur:
Dominique Tremblay, Directrice générale
dominiquetremblay@boiteascience.com

Les Bolides
3350, rue Ontario est, Montréal QC H1W 1P7
Tél: 514-522-7773
info@lesbolides.org
www.lesbolides.org
Aperçu: *Dimension:* petite; *Envergure:* locale
Mission: Ligue de quilles

BOMA Québec
#900, 500, rue Sherbrooke ouest, Montréal QC H3A 3C6
Tél: 514-282-3826; *Téléc:* 514-844-7556
Ligne sans frais: 855-682-3826
boma@boma-quebec.org
www.boma-quebec.org
www.linkedin.com/groups/BOMA-Québec-Association-propriétaires-gestionnaires-5155168
twitter.com/BOMAQc
Nom précédent: Association des propriétaires et administrateurs d'immeubles du Québec
Aperçu: *Dimension:* moyenne; *Envergure:* provinciale; fondée en 1927
Mission: Représenter les intérêts des propriétaires et des gérants d'édifices commerciaux et à bureaux au Québec
Membre de: Building Owners & Managers Association of Canada
Membre: 228; *Montant de la cotisation:* Barème; *Comités:* Affairs gouvernementales; conseil Québec métropolitan; communications; énergie et gestion technique; envrionnement; fête de Noël et activités sociales; formation; gestion des immeubles; golf; golf Québec métropolitan; membres affaires; normes et réglementations; recrutement; recrutement Québec métropolitan; relève; sécurité et mesures d'urgence
Activités: Déjeuner-causerie; cours de formation
Membre(s) du bureau directeur:
Anne Marie Guèvremont, Président
Linda Carbone, Directrice générale

Bon Accord/Gibbon Food Bank *See* Bon Accord/Gibbons Food Bank

Bon Accord/Gibbons Food Bank
5016 50th St., Gibbons AB T0A 1N0
Tel: 780-923-2344
bonaccordgibbonsfoodbank@gmail.com
www.facebook.com/395041237294596
Previous Name: Bon Accord/Gibbon Food Bank
Overview: A small local organization overseen by Food Banks Alberta Association
Mission: A registered charity, BN: 118813328RR0001
Member of: Food Banks Alberta Association

Le Bon Pilote inc.
#511, 445, rue Jean-Talon ouest, Montréal QC H3N 1R1
Tél: 514-593-5454; *Téléc:* 514-419-6954
lebonpilote@videotron.ca
www.lebonpilote.com
www.linkedin.com/company/2609230
twitter.com/lebonpilote
Aperçu: *Dimension:* petite; *Envergure:* locale
Mission: Pour aider les personnes ayant une déficience visuelle en leur fournissant des services et en développant de nouveaux services pour faire avancer leur cause
Affiliation(s): Institut Nazareth & Louis-Braille; MAB-Mackay; Agence de la santé et des services sociaux de Montréal; Agence de la santé et des services sociaux de la Montérégie; Les BusBoys.com, site pour les employés / retraités de la STM

Membre: *Montant de la cotisation:* Barème; *Critères d'admissibilite:* Les personnes ayant une déficience visuelle ou amblyope
Membre(s) du bureau directeur:
John D. Gill, Directeur général, 514-531-5330
johngill@videotron.ca

Bonavista Area Chamber of Commerce (BACC)
PO Box 280, Bonavista NL A0C 1B0
Tel: 709-468-7747; *Fax:* 709-468-2495
www.bacc.ca
Overview: A small local organization founded in 2002
Mission: To create a business climate of competitiveness, profitability & job creation for all businesses on the northern section of the Bonavista Peninsula; To improve the general civic & social welfare of the region
Finances: *Annual Operating Budget:* Less than $50,000
10 volunteer(s)
Membership: 1-99
Chief Officer(s):
Neal Tucker, President
Awards:
• Order of the Bonavista Area Chamber of Commerce
• Long Service Awards

Bonavista Historic Townscape Foundation (BHTF)
PO Box 10, Bonavista NL A0C 1B0
Tel: 709-468-2880; *Fax:* 709-468-7253
Other Communication: Alternate Phone: 709-468-7547; e-mail: info@garricktheatre.ca
garrickboxoffice@nf.aibn.com
www.garricktheatre.ca
www.facebook.com/garricktheatre
twitter.com/Garrick_Theatre
Overview: A small local organization founded in 1998
Finances: *Annual Operating Budget:* Less than $50,000
Staff Member(s): 5; 20 volunteer(s)
Membership: 1-99
Activities: Operating the Garrick Theatre
Chief Officer(s):
Ray Troke, Manager
David Bradley, Contact, 709-737-8232

Bonnechere Soaring Club
ON
Tel: 613-584-4636
Overview: A small local organization
Member of: Soaring Association of Canada

Bonnyville & District Chamber of Commerce
PO Box 6054, Hwy. 28 West, Bonnyville AB T9N 2G7
Tel: 780-826-3252; *Fax:* 780-826-4525
admin@bonnyvillechamber.com
www.bonnyvillechamber.com
Overview: A small local organization
Mission: To act as the voice of local business
Member of: Alberta Chamber of Commerce; Canadian Chamber of Commerce
Finances: *Funding Sources:* Membership dues
Membership: *Fees:* Schedule available
Activities: Organizing & promoting events such as rodeos, business seminars, & Golf Scramble
Chief Officer(s):
Tom Allan, President

Bonnyville & District Fine Arts Society
PO Box 5086, 4900 - 49 St., Bonnyville AB T9N 2G3
Tel: 780-826-3986; *Fax:* 780-826-2959
Overview: A small local organization
Mission: To encourage & facilitate appreciation & involvement in the arts in Bonnyville & district
Member of: Alberta Municipal Association for Culture
Finances: *Funding Sources:* Fees; donations; Alberta Community Development Grants; fundraising bingos & performances
Activities: "Touch of Class" Performance Series
Chief Officer(s):
Patricia Perry, President

Bonnyville Canadian Native Friendship Centre
PO Box 5399, 4711 - 50 Ave., Bonnyville AB T9N 2G5
Tel: 780-826-3374; *Fax:* 780-826-2540
bcnfced@incentre.net
www.facebook.com/bonnyvillefriendshipcentre
Overview: A small local organization founded in 1971 overseen by Alberta Native Friendship Centres Association

Canadian Associations / Book & Periodical Council (BPC)

Mission: To create a healthy, productive community through innovative & cultural services
Member of: Alberta Native Friendship Centres Association
Finances: *Funding Sources:* Membership dues
Membership: *Fees:* $5-10

Book & Periodical Council (BPC)
#107, 192 Spadina Ave., Toronto ON M5T 2C2
Tel: 416-975-9366; *Fax:* 416-975-1839
info@thebpc.ca
www.thebpc.ca
Overview: A medium-sized national organization founded in 1975
Mission: To increase the level of awareness & the use of Canadian materials by the general public & in educational systems at all levels; To ensure the public has an adequate & representative range of Canadian books & periodicals in sales outlets, library systems & educational institutions; To strengthen book & periodical distribution systems; To support the development of new & existing Canadian-owned companies & encourage their growth & expansion; To improve market conditions & contractual arrangements as well as promotion & publicity given to Canadian writers & their work; To encourage the development of writing & publishing projects of social & cultural importance; To improve the cultural & economic climate in which the Canadian book & periodical industries exist; To discourage expansion of foreign ownership in all sectors of the book & periodical publishing industries
Member of: Canadian Conference of the Arts
Finances: *Funding Sources:* Membership fees
100 volunteer(s)
Membership: 12 full + 15 associate associations + 5 affiliates; *Fees:* Schedule available; *Committees:* Freedom of Expression; Freight; Appointed Task Forces
Activities: *Awareness Events:* Freedom to Read Week, February
Chief Officer(s):
Anita Purcell, Chair
Meetings/Conferences:
• Book Summit 18, June, 2018, Harbourfront Centre, Toronto, ON
Scope: National
Contact Information: www.booksummit.ca

Book Publishers Association of Alberta (BPAA)
10523 - 100 Ave., Edmonton AB T5J 0A8
Tel: 780-424-5060; *Fax:* 780-424-7943
www.bookpublishers.ab.ca
www.facebook.com/ABbookpub
Previous Name: Alberta Publishers Association
Overview: A medium-sized provincial organization founded in 1975 overseen by Association of Canadian Publishers
Mission: To work for maintenance & growth of strong book publishing houses owned & controlled in Alberta; To speak for common interests of constituent members; To liaise & cooperate with other associations for the good of the Canadian publishing industry
Member of: Canadian Booksellers Association; Alberta Library Association; Edmonton Arts Council; Access Copyright; Book & Periodical Council; Edmonton Small Press Association; Alberta Cultural Industries Association
Affiliation(s): Publishers Association of the West
Finances: *Annual Operating Budget:* $100,000-$250,000; *Funding Sources:* Membership fees; grants; projects
Staff Member(s): 2
Membership: 29 companies; *Fees:* $300 supporting; $750 full
Activities: Offering professional development sessions & publishing resources; Read Alberta eBooks collection, offered through participating regional library systems; *Awareness Events:* Alberta Book Fair; *Library:* Not open to public
Chief Officer(s):
Kieran Leblanc, Executive Director
Awards:
• Alberta Book Publishing Awards
To recognize outstanding achievements in Alberta publishing; nine awards are given - Alberta Publisher of the Year, Alberta Trade Book of the Year, Alberta Book Design Award, Alberta Book Cover Design Award, Alberta Educational Book of the Year, Alberta Childrens' Book of the Year, Alberta Book Illustration Award, Alberta Scholarly Book, Alberta Emerging Publisher of the Year *Eligibility:* Alberta-based publishers who primarily publish original Canadian books

Boost Child & Youth Advocacy Centre (CYAC)
890 Yonge St., 11th Fl., Toronto ON M4W 3P4
Tel: 416-515-1100; *Fax:* 416-515-1227
Toll-Free: 855-424-1100
info@boostforkids.org
www.boostforkids.org
www.facebook.com/BoostforKids
twitter.com/boostforkids
Overview: A medium-sized local charitable organization founded in 1981
Mission: To prevent child abuse & violence; To ensure that children & youth grow up in safe environments; To offer services to children & their families
Activities: Raising awareness; Offering training & education programs; Providing resources
Chief Officer(s):
Karyn Kennedy, President & CEO
kennedy@boostforkids.org

Boot'n Bonnet British Car Club
c/o Brian & Linda Thomas, 92 Wyona Lane, Wolfe Island ON K0H 2Y0
Tel: 613-385-1947
www.bootnbonnet.ca
Overview: A small national organization founded in 1990
Member of: British Car Council of Canada
Finances: *Annual Operating Budget:* Less than $50,000; *Funding Sources:* Membership dues; events
10 volunteer(s)
Membership: 250+; *Fees:* $30
Activities: Car tours; meetings; barbeques; *Awareness Events:* British Car Day, Aug.; Autojumble
Chief Officer(s):
Brian Thomas, Contact, Membership
ThomasB@QueensU.Ca
Linda Thomas, Contact, Membership
ThomasL@QueensU.Ca
Publications:
• The Spanner [a pubication of the Boot'n Bonnet British Car Club]
Type: Newsletter; *Frequency:* Quarterly

Border Boosters Square & Round Dance Association (BBSRDA)
Toll-Free: 866-206-6696
www.squaredance.qc.ca
Previous Name: Québec Square & Round Dance Clubs
Overview: A medium-sized local organization founded in 1952 overseen by Canadian Square & Round Dance Society
Mission: To promote square & round dancing in the Québec, eastern Ontario & northern New York area
Membership: 14 clubs
Activities: Supporting member clubs; Holding two dances a year
Chief Officer(s):
Stephanie Charters, President

Border Cities Real Estate Board *See* Windsor-Essex County Real Estate Board

Boreal Institute for Northern Studies (1960-1990) *See* Canadian Circumpolar Institute

Bosnian Canadian Relief Association (BCRA)
122 North Queen St., Toronto ON M8Z 2E4
Tel: 416-236-9411; *Fax:* 416-237-0656
bosnianrelief.org
www.facebook.com/BosnianCanadianReliefAssociation
Also Known As: Bosnian Islamic Association Gazi Husrev-Beg
Overview: A small international organization founded in 1992
Mission: To provide humanitarian aid for the victims in Bosnia & Herzegovina
Affiliation(s): Bosnian Canadian Community Association
Finances: *Funding Sources:* Provincial grant; private donations
Activities: *Speaker Service:* Yes; *Library:* Documentation Centre; Open to public by appointment

Bosnian Islamic Association (BIAGH)
122 North Queen St., Toronto ON M8Z 2E4
Tel: 416-233-5967
www.biaghb.com
www.facebook.com/BosnianIslamicAssociationGaziHusrevBeg
Also Known As: Gazi Husrev-Beg
Previous Name: Association of Islamic Community Gazi Husrev-Beg
Overview: A small local organization founded in 1977
Mission: To respond to the religious needs of the Bosnian Islamic community
Membership: *Member Profile:* Bosnian Canadians
Activities: Providing classes, lectures, & workshops in Islamic education & national folklore for children, youth, & adults; Offering recreational activities, such as soccer & karate; Hosting special programs to observe religious holidays; Performing marriage ceremonies by the Imam; Providing counselling for individuals & families; Offering assistance with wills & Janazah; Cooperating with other Bosnian organizations

Boston Terrier Rescue Canada
PO Box 21001, 22 Baskin Dr. East, Arnprior ON K7S 3X6
Fax: 855-287-7817
Toll-Free: 855-287-3778
www.bostonterrierrescuecanada.com
www.facebook.com/BostonTerrierRescueCanada
twitter.com/btrescuecanada
www.youtube.com/user/BTRescueCanada
Overview: A medium-sized national charitable organization
Mission: To rescue & rehabilitate Boston Terriers & Boston Terrier mixes by providing temporary foster homes & permanent homes
Activities: Education; Advocacy
Chief Officer(s):
Margot Arsenault, President

Bothwell-Zone & District Historical Society
PO Box 271, Bothwell ON N0P 1C0
Tel: 519-695-3619
historicbothwell@hotmail.com
www.historicbothwell.ca
Also Known As: Bothwell-Zone Oil Museum
Overview: A small local charitable organization founded in 1990
Mission: To establish & maintain the Bothwell-Zone Oil Museum to depict & preserve the history, production methods, & equipment of primitive oil technology used in the 19th & 20th century as the world was striving to find a product to light their homes
Affiliation(s): Ontario Historical Society
Finances: *Annual Operating Budget:* Less than $50,000
Activities: Black Gold Days; Bothwell-Zone Oil Museum; *Speaker Service:* Yes; *Library:* by appointment

Bouctouche Chamber of Commerce / Chambre de commerce de Bouctouche
PO Box 2104, Bouctouche NB E4S 2J2
Tel: 506-743-2411; *Fax:* 506-743-8991
chambouc@nb.aibn.com
www.bouctouche.ca/en/business/chamber-of-commerce
www.facebook.com/LaChambreDeCommerceDeBouctouche
Overview: A small local organization founded in 1947
Mission: To be the spokesperson for the businesses of the region; To help develop economic growth & a better quality of life in Bouctouche
Member of: Atlantic Chamber of Commerce; New Brunswick Chamber of Commerce; Chambre de Commerce du Canada
Finances: *Funding Sources:* Bingo; golf tournament
Activities: *Rents Mailing List:* Yes

Bouffe pour tous/Moisson Longueuil
911, boul Roalnd-Therrien, Longueuil QC J4J 4L3
Tél: 450-670-5449
Aperçu: *Dimension:* petite; *Envergure:* locale
Mission: Faciliter l'approvisionnement en d'enrées alimentaires aux familles démunies et personnes seules depuis plus de 12 ans; familles monoparentales, gens sans emploi, gens aux prises avec des problèmes de drogues ou de violence
Membre: 1 200; *Critères d'admissibilite:* Les familles et les personnes dans le besoin

Boundary Country Regional Chamber of Commerce
PO Box 379, Midway BC V0H 1M0
Tel: 250-442-7263
info@boundarychamber.com
www.boundarychamber.com
Previous Name: Chamber of Commerce of the City of Grand Forks, Grand Forks Board of Trade
Overview: A small local organization founded in 1899
Mission: To improve the economic growth & well-being of the community; To promote businesses; To provide opportunities for members
Member of: Canadian Chamber of Commerce; BC Chamber of Commerce
Finances: *Annual Operating Budget:* $50,000-$100,000; *Funding Sources:* Membership fees; municipal & provincial fees for service
Staff Member(s): 2; 12 volunteer(s)
Membership: 142; *Fees:* Schedule available

Activities: Providing information & resources; Organizing networking opportunities; Supporting community events; Advocating for businesses; *Library:* Business Resource Library
Chief Officer(s):
Kathy Wright, Executive Director

Boundary District Arts Council (BDAC)
PO Box 2636, Grand Forks BC V0H 1E0
boundaryarts@yahoo.ca
boundaryarts.org
www.facebook.com/108200982601187
Overview: A small local organization founded in 1976
Mission: To promote art in the Boundary area by investing in various artistic productions
Member of: Assembly of BC Arts Councils
Membership: 19; *Fees:* $20; *Member Profile:* Arts groups
Chief Officer(s):
Michele Garrison, President
michele.shellygarrison@gmail.com

Boundary Organic Producers Association (BOPA)
PO Box 675, Grand Forks BC V0H 1H0
Tel: 250-442-5840
Overview: A small local licensing organization
Affiliation(s): Certified Organic Associations of BC
Finances: *Annual Operating Budget:* Less than $50,000
Staff Member(s): 1
Membership: 10-15 certified organic operators & associate members; *Fees:* $25; *Member Profile:* Organic producers & processors; *Committees:* Certification
Activities: Organic certification of producers & processors
Chief Officer(s):
Karl Lilgert, President
Christine Carlson, Administrator
christine@slowkettle.org

Boundless Adventures Association
7513 River Rd., RR#1, Palmer Rapids ON K0J 2E0
Tel: 416-658-7059; *Fax:* 613-758-2196
office@theboundlessschool.com
www.theboundlessschool.com
www.facebook.com/theboundlessschool
www.flickr.com/photos/boundlesshighschool
Also Known As: The Boundless School
Overview: A small local charitable organization founded in 1984
Mission: To improve the lives of marginalized youth, adults & children at risk through counselling, social rehabilitation, alternative education and outdoor adventure.
Chief Officer(s):
Steven Gottlieb, Executive Director

Bow Island / Burdett District Chamber of Commerce
PO Box 1001, Bow Island AB T0K 0G0
Tel: 403-545-6222; *Fax:* 403-545-6042
chamber@bowislandchamber.com
www.bowislandchamber.com
Overview: A small local organization founded in 1951
Mission: To present various events & promotions
Member of: Alberta Chamber of Commerce; Red Coat Trail Association
Finances: *Funding Sources:* Trade fair; Las Vegas Days; Rentals; Membership dues
Membership: 80+; *Fees:* $60; *Member Profile:* Businesses; Farmers
Activities: Organizing an annual trade fair, Las Vegas Days, & a rodeo barbecue
Chief Officer(s):
Bernice Deleenheer, President
Chandra Lane, Vice-President

Bow Valley Food Bank
PO Box 8071, 20 Sandstone Terrace, Canmore AB T1W 2T8
Tel: 403-678-9488
admin@bowvalleyfoodbank.ca
www.bowvalleyfoodbank.ca
Overview: A small local charitable organization founded in 1994 overseen by Food Banks Alberta Association
Mission: To provide a supply of emergency food in crisis situations; To build partnerships with other community organizations dedicated to fighting hunger; To raise awareness of hunger everywhere
Member of: Food Banks Alberta Association; Food Banks Canada

Bowden Historical Society
PO Box 576, Bowden AB T0M 0K0
Tel: 403-224-2122
2201@shawbiz.ca
www.bowdenpioneermuseum.com
Overview: A small local charitable organization founded in 1976
Mission: To create appreciation of our community & identity through the collection & preservation of historical artifacts & stories from Bowden.
Affiliation(s): Alberta Museums Associations
Finances: *Funding Sources:* Grants; membership dues; donations; fundraising
Membership: *Fees:* $10
Activities: Operates Bowden Pioneer Museum
Chief Officer(s):
Syd Cannings, President

Bowen Island Arts Council (BIAC)
PO Box 211, Bowen Island BC V0N 1G0
Tel: 604-947-2454; *Fax:* 604-947-2460
admin@biac.ca
www.biac.ca
Overview: A small local charitable organization founded in 1988
Mission: To support & promote art & culture on Bowen Island through direct support to artists & performing groups; to operate a gallery & performance space on Bowen Island
Affiliation(s): Assembly of BC Arts Councils
Finances: *Funding Sources:* Local grant; provincial grant; membership fees; donations
Staff Member(s): 2
Membership: *Fees:* $25 individual; $35 family; $45 organization; *Committees:* Gallery; Cultural Development; Communications; Community Hall & Arts Centre
Activities: Operates the multi-purpose gallery at Artesan Square for Bowen's Arts Council; sponsors performances & exhibits; links more specialized arts groups on Bowen Island; organizes the Bowen Art Walk, Studio Tours, & BC Cultural Crawl; produces the Classical Concert Series; *Speaker Service:* Yes
Chief Officer(s):
Carol Cram, President
Jacqueline M. Massey, Executive Director
Karen Watson, Gallery Coordinator/Curator

Bowen Island Chamber of Commerce
PO Box 199, 432 Cardena Rd., Bowen Island BC V0N 1G0
Tel: 604-947-9024
Overview: A small local organization

Bowen Nature Club
RR#1, CL-27, Bowen Island BC V0N 1G0
Tel: 604-947-9562
bowennatureclub@gmail.com
bowennatureclub.blogspot.ca
Overview: A small local organization founded in 1985
Mission: To promote the enjoyment of nature through environmental appreciation & conservation; To encourage wise use & conservation of natural resources & environmental protection
Member of: Federation of BC Naturalists
Membership: 21; *Fees:* $18 individual; $22 family
Chief Officer(s):
Jlonka Bally-Brown, President
jbally1@hotmail.com

Bowhunters Association of Nova Scotia
PO Box 705, Lower Sackville NS B4N 3J1
bansinformation@gmail.com
www.bowhuntersns.com
www.facebook.com/groups/BowhuntersAssociationofNovaScotia
Overview: A small provincial organization
Mission: To promote wildlife conservation & ethical bowhunting in Nova Scotia
Membership: *Fees:* $20 single; $20 (+ $5 for each additional member) family
Activities: Organizing events; Offering educational courses on ethical bowhunting
Chief Officer(s):
John Landry, President

Bowling Federation of Alberta
Percy Page Centre, 11759 Groat Rd., 2nd Floor, Edmonton AB T5M 3K6
Tel: 780-422-8251; *Fax:* 780-644-4632
bpaa@bowlab.ca
www.bowlfedab.ca
Overview: A small provincial organization
Mission: To promote competitive & noncompetitive bowling in Alberta
Membership: 5 associations
Chief Officer(s):
Annette Bruneau, President
Grady Long, Executie Director
gradyed@bowlfedab.ca

Bowling Federation of Canada / Fédération des quilles du Canada
250 Shields Ct., #10A, Markham ON L3R 9W7
Tel: 905-479-1560
info@canadabowls.ca
www.canadabowls.ca
Overview: A medium-sized national organization
Mission: To promote & foster the sport of bowling in Canada; To promote among the recognized national organizations in Canada, sportmanship, good fellowship, & the continued interest in the future development of bowling throughout Canada
Affiliation(s): Bowling Proprietors Association of Canada; Canadian 5-pin Bowlers Association; Canadian Tenpin Federation.
Chief Officer(s):
Bob Randall, President, 604-533-2695
brandall@shaw.ca
Sheila Carr, Administrator, 613-744-5090
c5pba@c5pba.ca

Bowling Federation of Saskatchewan
#101, 1805 - 8th Ave., Regina SK S4R 1E8
Tel: 306-780-9412; *Fax:* 306-780-9455
bowling@sasktel.net
saskbowl.com
twitter.com/SaskBowl
Overview: A medium-sized provincial organization founded in 1984
Mission: Working together through cooperation & harmonization to access & allocate funding for our members programs & services in order to enhance the sport of bowling
Member of: Sask Sport; Bowling Federation of Canada
Finances: *Funding Sources:* Sask Lotteries; sponsorship; fundraising
Chief Officer(s):
Rhonda Sereda, Executive Director

Bowling Proprietors' Association of BC
#209, 332 Columbia St., New Westminster BC V3L 1A6
Tel: 604-522-2990; *Fax:* 604-522-2055
bowl4fun@bowlbc.com
www.bowlbc.com
www.facebook.com/BowlBc
Also Known As: Bowl BC
Overview: A small provincial organization founded in 1954
Mission: To provide opportunities for people to bowl at their individual level
Activities: Adult, youth & seniors tournaments
Chief Officer(s):
Gord Wiffen, President

Bowling Proprietors' Association of Canada (BPAC)
#10A, 250 Shields Ct., Markham ON L3R 9W7
Tel: 905-479-1560; *Fax:* 905-479-8613
info@bowlcanada.ca
www.bowlcanada.ca
www.facebook.com/Bowl-Canada-703790949700789
twitter.com/bowlcanada
www.youtube.com/c/bowlcanada
Also Known As: Bowl Canada
Overview: A small national organization
Mission: The aim of this association is to improve general conditions in the bowling industry, to promote to the general public the benefits of bowling, to create a better relationship between the many bowling establishments across Canada and to encourage any and all practices which are in the best interests of the game.
Membership: 500 bowling centres
Activities: Youth Bowling Canada (YBC); Sunshine Bowlers; Club 55+.
Chief Officer(s):
Paul Oliveira, Executive Director
paul@bowlcanada.ca

Bowling Proprietors' Association of Ontario (BPAO)
#202, 500 Alden Rd., Markham ON L3R 5H5
Tel: 905-940-8200; *Fax:* 905-940-8201
info@bowlontario.ca
www.bowlontario.ca
Also Known As: Bowl Ontario

Canadian Associations / Bowls British Columbia

Overview: A medium-sized provincial organization founded in 1953
Mission: To improve conditions in bowling industry; To protect members from unreasonable legislation; To bring attention to the pleasures of bowling
Affiliation(s): Bowling Proprietors' Association of Canada
Membership: 124 bowling centres; *Member Profile:* Bowling centre ownership
Awards:
- Annual Director's Service Award
- Player Award for Perfect Game
- Volunteer 5, 10, 20, 25 Year Service Awards
- Member of the Year Award

Bowls British Columbia
c/o Jackie West, 2168 Stirling Cres., Courtenay BC V9N 9X1
info@bowlsbc.com
bowlsbc.com
twitter.com/bowlsbc
Also Known As: Bowls BC
Overview: A medium-sized provincial organization founded in 1925 overseen by Bowls Canada Boulingrin
Mission: To foster & promote the game of Lawn Bowls; To make the game available to all in accordance within the Canadian Human Rights Code within the Province of British Columbia
Affiliation(s): World Bowls Board; World Indoor Bowls Board
Activities: *Library:* BBC Library at Pacific Indoor Bowls Club; Not open to public
Chief Officer(s):
Jim Aitken, President, 604-904-8834
bowlsbc.prez@yahoo.ca
Harry Carruthers, Vice-President, 604-985-2241
hcarruthers@telus.net
Diane Fulton, Secretary
pacu@shaw.ca
Carolle Allen, Treasurer
cjallen@live.ca
Awards:
- Bowls BC Volunteer Awards
Publications:
- Bowls British Columbia Newsletter
Type: Newsletter; *Editor:* Marueen Johston
Profile: Timely information for members

Bowls Canada Boulingrin (BCB)
#206, 33 Roydon Pl., Nepean ON K2E 1A3
Tel: 613-244-0021; *Fax:* 613-244-0041
Toll-Free: 800-567-2695
office@bowlscanada.com
www.bowlscanada.com
www.facebook.com/BCBOfficial
twitter.com/BCBBowls
Previous Name: Lawn Bowls Canada Boulingrin
Overview: A medium-sized national charitable organization founded in 1902
Mission: To promote, foster & safeguard the sport of indoor & outdoor lawn bowling in all its forms in Canada, through events & programs
Member of: World Bowls Board; International Women's Bowls Board; World Indoor Bowls Council
Affiliation(s): Commonwealth Games Association of Canada
Finances: *Annual Operating Budget:* $250,000-$500,000; *Funding Sources:* Membership dues; marketing; advertising; merchandising; donations
Staff Member(s): 4; 100 volunteer(s)
Membership: 15,000; 252 clubs; *Fees:* $11; *Committees:* Team Canada; National Officials
Activities: Canadian championships; Canadian Senior Triples; Canadian Junior Championships; Under 25 World Junior Cup Qualifier; Canadian Mixed Pairs Championships; Canadian Indoor Singles.
Chief Officer(s):
Anna Mees, Executive Director, 613-244-0021 Ext. 101
amees@bowlscanada.com

Bowls Manitoba
145 Pacific Ave., Winnipeg MB R3B 2Z6
Tel: 204-925-5694; *Fax:* 204-925-5792
bowls@shawbiz.ca
www.bowls.mb.ca
www.facebook.com/BowlsMBInc
twitter.com/BowlsManitoba
Previous Name: Manitoba Lawn Bowling Association
Overview: A medium-sized provincial organization overseen by Bowls Canada Boulingrin
Mission: To promote lawnbowling in the province of Manitoba; To host various lawnbowling events
Member of: Sport Manitoba
Affiliation(s): Bowls Canada Boulingrin; World Bowls Ltd
Chief Officer(s):
Cathy Derewianchuk, Executive Director, 204-925-5694

Bowls Saskatchewan Inc.
#102, 1860 Lorne St., Regina SK S4P 2L7
Tel: 306-780-9426
bowlsask@sasktel.net
www.bowls.sk.ca
www.facebook.com/Bowls-Saskatchewan-732190793489071
Also Known As: Saskatchewan Lawn Bowling Association
Overview: A medium-sized provincial organization founded in 1991 overseen by Bowls Canada Boulingrin
Mission: To promote & expand the sport of bowls, which contains programs that accommodate/challenge all those interested, with the result that bowls becomes a high profile sport
Finances: *Annual Operating Budget:* $50,000-$100,000; *Funding Sources:* Saskatchewan lotteries
Staff Member(s): 1
Membership: 503 in 9 clubs; *Fees:* Schedule available; *Committees:* Executive; Officiating; Coaching; Sport for All
Activities: Learn to Bowl; Junior; Clinics; summer & fall tournaments; Regina Mixed Pairs Open Tournament
Chief Officer(s):
Denise Eberle, Executive Director
Duncan Holness, President
daholness@hotmail.com

Boxing Alberta
Percy Page Centre, 11759 Groat Rd., Edmonton AB T5M 3K6
Tel: 780-427-6515; *Fax:* 780-427-1205
www.boxingalberta.com
Previous Name: Alberta Amateur Boxing Association
Overview: A small provincial organization overseen by Canadian Amateur Boxing Association
Member of: Canadian Amateur Boxing Association
Staff Member(s): 2
Membership: 46 clubs
Chief Officer(s):
Roland Labbe, President
cvcwest@telus.net
Dennis Belair, Executive Director
dbelair@telus.net

Boxing BC Association
PO Box 23065, Stn. RPO 11, Prince George BC V2N 6Z2
Tel: 250-964-7750; *Fax:* 250-964-7787
information@boxing.bc.ca
www.boxing.bc.ca
www.facebook.com/489238011141309
Previous Name: British Columbia Amateur Boxing Association
Overview: A small provincial organization founded in 1985 overseen by Canadian Amateur Boxing Association
Mission: To provide all citizens of British Columbia access to & participation in the opportunities, programs & activities
Member of: Canadian Amateur Boxing Association
Finances: *Annual Operating Budget:* $100,000-$250,000
Staff Member(s): 1; 150 volunteer(s)
Membership: 1,100 in 42 clubs; *Fees:* Schedule available; *Member Profile:* Competitors, coaches, officials, associated volunteers
Activities: Club shows, tournament highlights & provincial championships & Golden Gloves tournaments; *Awareness Events:* Golden Gloves, March; *Internships:* Yes

Boxing Manitoba
#421, 145 Pacific Ave., Winnipeg MB R3B 2Z6
Tel: 204-925-5658; *Fax:* 204-925-5792
info@boxingmanitoba.com
www.boxingmanitoba.com
www.facebook.com/BoxingManitoba
twitter.com/boxingmanitoba
Previous Name: Manitoba Amateur Boxing Association
Overview: A small provincial organization overseen by Canadian Amateur Boxing Association
Mission: To govern the sport of boxing in Manitoba.
Member of: Canadian Amateur Boxing Association
Chief Officer(s):
Alan Hogg, President
president@boxingmanitoba.com
Roland Vandal, Vice-President & Technical Director
technical@boxingmanitoba.com

Boxing New Brunswick Boxe
413 Millidge Ave., Saint John NB E2K 2N3
Tel: 506-652-8251
nbref@yahoo.ca
boxingnb.com
Also Known As: Boxing NB Boxe
Overview: A small provincial organization overseen by Canadian Amateur Boxing Association
Mission: To govern the sport of boxing in New Brunswick.
Member of: Canadian Amateur Boxing Association
Chief Officer(s):
Ed Blanchard, President

Boxing Newfoundland & Labrador
NL
www.boxingnewfoundlandandlabrador.ca
Overview: A small provincial organization overseen by Canadian Amateur Boxing Association
Mission: To govern the sport of boxing in Newfoundland & Labrador.
Member of: Canadian Amateur Boxing Association; Sport NL
Chief Officer(s):
Mike Summers, President
mgsone@hotmail.com

Boxing Nova Scotia
NS
www.boxingnovascotia.com
www.facebook.com/BoxingNovaScotia
twitter.com/boxnovascotia
Overview: A small provincial organization overseen by Canadian Amateur Boxing Association
Mission: To govern the sport of boxing in Nova Scotia.
Member of: Canadian Amateur Boxing Association
Affiliation(s): Sport Nova Scotia; Nova Scotia Health Promotion & Protection
Membership: *Fees:* Schedule available

Boxing Ontario
#202, 3 Concorde Gate, Toronto ON M3C 3N7
Tel: 416-426-7250; *Fax:* 416-426-7367
info@boxingontario.com
www.boxingontario.com
www.facebook.com/boxingontario
twitter.com/BoxingOntario
Overview: A small provincial licensing organization founded in 1972 overseen by Canadian Amateur Boxing Association
Mission: This is the only governing body for amateur boxing in Ontario. It aims to organize, promote, develop interest & participation in the sport in the province.
Member of: Canadian Amateur Boxing Association
Affiliation(s): Association International de Boxe Amateur (AIBA); Ontario Ministry of Health Promotion
Finances: *Annual Operating Budget:* $250,000-$500,000; *Funding Sources:* Membership, Fundraising, Ministry of Tourism and Recreation
Staff Member(s): 3
Membership: 80 clubs; *Fees:* Schedule available
Activities: Governing amateur boxing; sanctioning amateur events
Chief Officer(s):
Matt Kennedy, Executive Director
mkennedy@boxingontario.com

Boxing Saskatchewan
1860 Lorne St., Regina SK S4P 2L7
Tel: 306-780-9305
boxingsask@sasktel.net
www.boxingsask.com
Also Known As: Saskatchewan Amateur Boxing Association
Overview: A small provincial organization overseen by Canadian Amateur Boxing Association
Mission: This is a non-profit society that enforces rules & regulations governing amateur boxing in the province. It also promotes the formation of new clubs.
Member of: Canadian Amateur Boxing Association
Affiliation(s): Canadian Amateur Boxing Association
Finances: *Funding Sources:* Sask Sport
Membership: 23 clubs
Chief Officer(s):
Graham Craig, Executive Director

The Boy Scouts Association - Canadian General Council
See Scouts Canada

Boyle & District Chamber of Commerce
PO Box 496, Boyle AB T0A 0M0

Tel: 780-689-2465; Fax: 780-689-2082
boylechamber.blogspot.ca
Overview: A small local organization
Mission: To promote & support businesses in the Boyle area
Membership: 25

Boyle Food Bank Association
PO Box 728, Boyle AB T0A 0M0
Overview: A small local charitable organization overseen by Food Banks Alberta Association

Boyle Street Community Services
10116 - 105 Ave. NW, Edmonton AB T5H 0K2
Tel: 780-424-4106; Fax: 780-425-2205
info@boylestreet.org
boylestreet.org
www.facebook.com/BoyleStreetCommunityServices
twitter.com/BoyleStreet
Overview: A small local organization founded in 1971
Mission: Boyle Street Community Services is a non-profit Edmonton agency which assists individuals and families challenged by homelessness and poverty.
Chief Officer(s):
Julian Daly, Executive Director, 780-424-4106 Ext. 204
jdaly@boylestreet.org

Boys & Girls Clubs of Alberta
11759 Groat Rd. NW, Edmonton AB T5M 3K6
Tel: 780-415-1734
Overview: A medium-sized provincial organization overseen by Boys & Girls Clubs of Canada
Member of: Boys & Girls Clubs of Canada
Staff Member(s): 2
Membership: 47,000

Boys & Girls Club of Airdrie
1003 Allen St., Airdrie AB T4B 1B3
Tel: 403-948-3331; Fax: 403-948-5132
info@bgcairdrie.com
airdrie.bgccan.com
www.facebook.com/BGCAirdrie
twitter.com/BGCAirdrie
Chief Officer(s):
Sean Hunter, President

Boys & Girls Club of Bashaw & Area
4903 - 50 Ave., Bashaw AB T0B 0H0
Tel: 780-372-4048; Fax: 780-372-3586
bashawyouthfoundation@hotmail.com
Chief Officer(s):
Angela Richardson, Executive Director

Boys & Girls Club of Bonnyville
PO Box 7733, 4714 - 48th St., Bonnyville AB T9N 2J1
Tel: 780-826-3037; Fax: 780-826-6488
byc@town.bonnyville.ab.ca
www.facebook.com/bgc.bonnyville
Chief Officer(s):
McKenzie Davies, Executive Director

Boys & Girls Club of Calgary (BGCC)
731 - 13 Ave. NE, Calgary AB T2E 1C8
Tel: 403-276-9981; Fax: 403-276-9988
info@bgcc.ab.ca
www.calgaryboysandgirlsclub.ca
www.linkedin.com/company/boys-and-girls-clubs-of-calgary
www.facebook.com/BGCCalgary
twitter.com/bgcc1939
Chief Officer(s):
Jeff Dyer, Chief Executive Officer

Boys & Girls Club of Cochrane and Area
PO Box 1554, 111 - 5th Ave. West, Cochrane AB T4C 1B5
Tel: 403-981-2020; Fax: 403-981-9555
info@bgccochrane.ca
www.bgccochrane.ca
www.facebook.com/bgccochrane

Boys & Girls Club of Crowsnest Pass
PO Box 1176, Stn. Coleman, 2114 - 127 St., Blairmore AB T0K 0M0
Tel: 403-562-8664; Fax: 403-562-8664
admin@bgccnp.com
bgccnp.blogspot.ca
www.facebook.com/BoysandGirlsClubCNP
twitter.com/BGCCNP
Chief Officer(s):
Steph Olsen, Administrator, 403-562-8664
admin@bgccnp.com

Boys & Girls Club of Edson & District
Griffiths Park Centre, PO Box 6032, 5414 - 6th Ave., Edson AB T7E 1S9
Tel: 780-723-7240; Fax: 780-723-7240
info@bgcedson.com
www.bgcedson.com
www.facebook.com/boysandgirlsclubofedson
Chief Officer(s):
Clare Hemsley, Board Director

Boys & Girls Club of the Foothills
PO Box 904, 611 - 3rd St. SW, Black Diamond AB T0L 0H0
Tel: 403-933-4066; Fax: 403-933-4068
exdirect@telus.net
www.bgcfoothills.com
www.facebook.com/bgcfcanada
Chief Officer(s):
Shirley Puttock, Executive Director

Boys & Girls Club of Fort Saskatchewan
10090 - 93 Ave., Fort Saskatchewan AB T8L 1N4
Tel: 780-992-0103; Fax: 780-998-0405
fortsaskboysandgirlsclub@hotmail.com
fortsask.bgccan.com
twitter.com/@FortSaskBGC
www.youtube.com/user/bgccan
Chief Officer(s):
Wendy Serink, Executive Director, 780-992-0103 Ext. 23
wserink@telusplanet.net

Boys & Girls Club of Leduc
#102, 4330 Black Gold Dr., Leduc AB T9E 3C3
Tel: 780-986-3121; Fax: 780-986-3137
www.bgcleduc.com
www.facebook.com/BGCleduc
twitter.com/bgcleduc
www.youtube.com/user/edbgleduc/videos
Chief Officer(s):
Shawna Bissell, Executive Director
executivedirector@bgcleduc.ca

Boys & Girls Club of Lethbridge & District
1405 - 8th Ave. North, Lethbridge AB T1H 6N9
Tel: 403-327-6423; Fax: 403-327-1711
info@bgclethbridge.com
www.bgclethbridge.com
www.facebook.com/bgclethbridge
twitter.com/bgclethbridge
Chief Officer(s):
Lyndsay Montina, Board President
board@bcglethbridge.com

Boys & Girls Club of Olds & Area
PO Box 4186, 5021 - 51st St., Olds AB T4H 1P6
Tel: 403-556-2466; Fax: 780-796-3639
boysgirlsolds@live.com
olds.bgccan.com
www.facebook.com/OldsBandGclub
twitter.com/OldsBandGClub
Chief Officer(s):
Raelynn Notley, Board Chair

Boys & Girls Club of St. Paul & District
PO Box 1009, 4821 - 50 Ave., St Paul AB T0A 3A0
Tel: 780-645-6769; Fax: 780-645-3650
Chief Officer(s):
Janelle Peters, President

Boys & Girls Club of Slave Lake
PO Box 232, 409 - 6th Ave., Slave Lake AB T0G 2A2
Tel: 780-805-1778
bgclub.slavelake@gmail.com
www.facebook.com/351464944949523
Chief Officer(s):
Melissa Mood, Executive Director

Boys & Girls Club of Strathcona County
3 Spruce Ave., Sherwood Park AB T8A 2B6
Tel: 780-416-1500; Fax: 780-416-2901
info@scbgc.com
www.scbgc.com
twitter.com/bgcstrathcona
Chief Officer(s):
Tyler Roed, Program Coordinator
tyler@scbgc.com

Boys & Girls Club of Wetaskiwin
5109 - 51 St., Wetaskiwin AB T9A 2A5
Tel: 780-352-4643; Fax: 780-352-7780
info@wetaskiwinyouth.ca
www.wetaskiwinyouth.ca
Chief Officer(s):
Sherri Senger, President

Boys & Girls Club of Whitecourt
PO Box 2053, 76 Sunset Blvd., Whitecourt AB T7S 1P7
Tel: 780-778-6696; Fax: 780-778-3464
recepwhitecourtbgc@gmail.com
whitecourt.bgccan.com
twitter.com/BGClubWct
Chief Officer(s):
Cathy Branton, Executive Director

Boys & Girls Club of Wolf Creek
PO Box 4115, #4, 5004 - 54 St., Ponoka AB T4J 1R5
Tel: 403-783-3112; Fax: 403-783-3108
www.ponokayouthcentre.com
Chief Officer(s):
Beth Reitz, Executive Director
beth@ponokayouthcentre.com

Boys & Girls Clubs of Edmonton & Area
10135 - 89 St., Edmonton AB T5H 1P6
Tel: 780-424-8181; Fax: 780-426-6689
Toll-Free: 855-424-8181
general.edmonton@bgcbigs.ca
bgcbigs.ca
facebook.com/BGCBigs
twitter.com/BGCBigs
Affiliation(s): Big Brothers Big Sisters of Edmonton & Area
Chief Officer(s):
Liz O'Neill, Executive Director, 780-822-2525
liz.oneill@bcbigs.ca

Boys & Girls Clubs of Red Deer & District
4633 - 49th St., Red Deer AB T4N 1T4
Tel: 403-342-6500; Fax: 403-342-7734
info@youthhq.ca
youthhq.ca
www.facebook.com/bgcreddeer
twitter.com/BBBSRedDeer
Chief Officer(s):
Jacquie Boyd, Executive Director, 403-342-6500 Ext. 105
jacquieb@youthhq.ca

Camrose Boys & Girls Club
4516 - 54th St., Camrose AB T4V 4W7
Tel: 780-672-8004; Fax: 780-672-8002
www.camroseboysandgirlsclub.com

Clearwater Boys & Girls Club
4928 - 49th St., Rocky Mountain House AB T4T 1B1
Tel: 403-845-5609
clearwaterbgc@live.com
clearwater.bgccan.com
www.facebook.com/clearwater.bgc.39
twitter.com/ClearwaterBGC
Chief Officer(s):
Hayley Hellum, Executive Director

Fort McMurray Boys & Girls Club
20 Riedel St., Fort McMurray AB T9H 3E1
Tel: 780-791-7775; Fax: 780-743-9359
ed@fmbgc.ca
fmbgc.ca
Chantal Beaver, President

Saddle Lake Boys & Girls Club
404D - 50 St., Saddle Lake AB T0A 3T0
Tel: 780-726-4170; Fax: 780-726-3754
slbgclub@gmail.com
Chief Officer(s):
Natalie Cardinal, Executive Director

Stettler & District Boys & Girls Club
Heartland Youth Centre, PO Box 876, 5002 - 47 St., Stettler AB T0C 2L0
Tel: 403-742-5437; Fax: 403-742-4700
hycstett@telus.net
stettler.bgccan.com
www.facebook.com/heartlandyouthcenter
Chief Officer(s):
Winnie Bissett, Executive Director

Boys & Girls Clubs of British Columbia
BC
Overview: A medium-sized provincial organization overseen by Boys & Girls Clubs of Canada
Member of: Boys and Girls Clubs of Canada

Boys & Girls Club of Kamloops
John Tod Centre, 150 Wood St., Kamloops BC V2B 0G6
Tel: 250-554-5437; Fax: 250-554-2756
admin@bgckamloops.com
www.bgckamloops.com
www.facebook.com/bgckamloops
twitter.com/BGCKamloops

Canadian Associations / Boys & Girls Clubs of Canada (BGCC) / Clubs garçons & filles du Canada

Chief Officer(s):
Traci Anderson, Executive Director, 250-554-5437 Ext. 205
exdir@bgckamloops.com

Boys & Girls Club of Williams Lake & District
17 - 4th Ave. South, Williams Lake BC V2G 1J6
Tel: 250-392-5730; *Fax:* 250-392-5743
oeprations@bgcwilliamslake.com
www.bgcwilliamslake.com
www.facebook.com/BoysAndGirlsClubOfWilliamsLake
Chief Officer(s):
Jay Goddard, Chair

Boys & Girls Club Services of Greater Victoria
#301, 1195 Esquimalt Rd., Victoria BC V8A 3N6
Tel: 250-384-9133; *Fax:* 250-384-9136
info@bgcvic.org
www.bgcvic.org
www.facebook.com/bgcvic
Chief Officer(s):
Dalyce Dixon, Executive Director, 250-384-9133 Ext. 216
DDixon@bgcvic.org

Boys & Girls Clubs of Central Vancouver Island
20 - 5th St., Nanaimo BC V9R 1M7
Tel: 250-754-3215; *Fax:* 250-754-4771
reception@bgccvi.com
www.bgccvi.com
www.facebook.com/bandgclubofcvi
twitter.com/bgccvi
Chief Officer(s):
Ian Kalina, Executive Director, 250-754-3215
ikalina@bgccvi.com

Boys & Girls Clubs of South Coast B.C.
2875 St. George St., Vancouver BC V5T 3R8
Tel: 604-879-6554; *Fax:* 604-879-6525
info@bgcbc.ca
www.bgcbc.ca
twitter.com/BGCyvr

Cranbrook Boys & Girls Club
1404 - 2nd St. North, Cranbrook BC V1C 3L2
Tel: 250-426-3830; *Fax:* 250-426-3036
bgccranbrook.ca
Chief Officer(s):
Mike Paugh, Chair

Okanagan Boys & Girls Clubs
1434 Graham St., Kelowna BC V1Y 3A8
Tel: 250-762-3914; *Fax:* 250-762-6562
www.boysandgirlsclubs.ca
www.facebook.com/OKboysandgirls
twitter.com/OKboysandgirls
www.youtube.com/user/OKBoysandGirlsClub
Chief Officer(s):
Diane Entwistle, Chief Executive Officer
dentwistle@boysandgirlsclubs.ca

Boys & Girls Clubs of Canada (BGCC) / Clubs garçons & filles du Canada
National Office, #400, 2005 Sheppard Ave. East, Toronto ON M2J 5B4
Tel: 905-477-7272; *Fax:* 416-640-5331
info@bgccan.com
www.bgccan.com
www.facebook.com/BGCCAN
twitter.com/BGCCAN
www.youtube.com/user/bgccan
Overview: A large national charitable organization founded in 1947
Mission: To provide a safe, supportive place where children & youth can experience new opportunities, overcome barriers, build positive relationships, & develop confidence & skills for life
Member of: Coalition of National Voluntary Organizations; Coalition for the Rights of Children
Finances: *Funding Sources:* Private sector donations
40 volunteer(s)
Membership: 200,000 individuals; 99 Clubs nationally; *Member Profile:* Children & youth, ages 0-21
Activities: Offering national programs, such as Active Living & Stay in School; Providing residential & day camping experiences; Offering street youth outreach; *Library:* Not open to public
Chief Officer(s):
Phil McDowell, Chair
Owen Charters, President & Chief Executive Officer
Marlene Deboisbriand, Vice-President, Programming & Member Services
Mathieu Chantelois, Vice-President, Marketing & Development
Carleen Dehaney, Vice-President, Finance & Operations

Denise Silverstone, Director, National Programs
Mary O'Connell, Manager, Communications Services
Karen McCullagh, Western Region Director, 403-936-0899
kmccullagh@bgccan.com
Sandra Morris, Central Region Director, 416-535-9675
smorris@bgccan.com
Jennifer Bessell, Newfoundland & Labrador Region Director
jbessell@bgccan.com
Debbie Cooper, Maritime Region Director
dcooper@bgccan.com
Line St-Amour, Québec Region Director
Carrie Wagner-Miller, Pacific Regional Director, 250-762-3989 Ext. 124
cwmiller@bgccan.com
Meetings/Conferences:
• Boys and Girls Clubs of Canada 2018 National Conference, May, 2018, Delta Prince Edward, Charlottetown, PE
Scope: National
Publications:
• Boys & Girls Clubs of Canada Newsletter
Type: Newsletter

Boys & Girls Clubs of Canada Foundation / Fondation des Clubs Garçons et Filles du Canada
Boys and Girls Clubs of Canada, #400, 2005 Sheppard Ave. East, Toronto ON M2J 5B4
Tel: 905-477-7272; *Fax:* 416-640-5331
www.bgccan.com
www.facebook.com/BGCCAN
twitter.com/BGCCAN
www.instagram.com/bgccan
Overview: A large national organization founded in 1995
Mission: To support the Boys & Girls Clubs of Canada
Finances: *Annual Operating Budget:* $1.5 Million-$3 Million; *Funding Sources:* Donations
Chief Officer(s):
David Mather, Chair

Boys & Girls Clubs of Manitoba
MB
Overview: A medium-sized provincial organization overseen by Boys & Girls Clubs of Canada
Member of: Boys & Girls Clubs of Canada

Boys & Girls Clubs of Winnipeg
#300, 61 Juno St., Winnipeg MB R3A 0B9
Tel: 204-982-4940; *Fax:* 204-982-4950
reception@wbgc.mb.ca
www.bgcwinnipeg.ca
www.facebook.com/bgcwinnipeg
twitter.com/BGCWinnipeg
Chief Officer(s):
Ron Brown, President & Chief Executive Officer
brown@wbgc.mb.ca

Thompson Boys & Girls Club
365 Thompson Dr., Thompson MB R8N 1N2
Tel: 204-778-7575
www.bgcthompson.ca
www.facebook.com/BoysGirlsClubOfThompson
twitter.com/@BGCThompson
Chief Officer(s):
Regina DaSilva-Gibbons, Executive Director
director@bgcthompson.ca

Boys & Girls Clubs of New Brunswick
NB
Overview: A P S organization overseen by Boys & Girls Clubs of Canada
Member of: Boys & Girls Clubs of Canada

Boys & Girls Club Miramichi
115 Maher St., Miramichi NB E1N 4B4
Tel: 506-778-2444; *Fax:* 506-778-1855
contact@bgcmiramichi.com
www.bbbsmiramichi.com
www.facebook.com/miramichibbbs
Mission: Their mission is to enrich the lives of children through mentoring.
Chief Officer(s):
Sheree A. Allison, Executive Director

Boys & Girls Club of Dieppe
76 Emmanuel St., Dieppe NB E1A 2J5
Tel: 506-857-3807; *Fax:* 506-869-8181
office@dbgc.org
www.dbgc.org
www.facebook.com/105281836175045
Chief Officer(s):

Bob Hebert, Executive Director, 506-857-3807 Ext. 111

Boys & Girls Club of Charlotte County
54 Disher Lane, Dufferin NB E3L 3H6
Tel: 506-466-4300; *Fax:* 506-466-4303
goldrush@bgccc.ca
bgccc.ca
Jessica Hall, Executive Director
ed@bgccc.ca

Boys & Girls Club of Fredricton
499 Canterbury Dr., Fredericton NB E3B 4M4
Tel: 506-472-5112; *Fax:* 506-472-8947
www.fbgc.ca
www.facebook.com/frederictonboysandgirlsclub
twitter.com/boysandgirlsf
Chief Officer(s):
Karen MacAlpine, Executive Director

Boys & Girls Club of Moncton
15 Everett St., Moncton NB E1C 3Z6
Tel: 506-858-0949; *Fax:* 506-855-7848
www.bgcmoncton.com
www.facebook.com/BoysandGirlsClubofMoncton
twitter.com/BGC_Moncton
Chief Officer(s):
Daniel M. LeBlanc, Executive Director, 506-858-0949 Ext. 101
daniel.leblanc@bgcmoncton.com

Boys & Girls Club of Riverview
PO Box 7416, 50 Runnymeade Rd., Riverview NB E1B 4T9
Tel: 506-387-7070; *Fax:* 506-387-6997
info@bgcriverview.com
www.bgcriverview.com
www.facebook.com/bgcriverview
twitter.com/bgcriverview

Boys & Girls Club of Saint John Inc.
PO Box 2441, 1 Paul Harris St., Saint John NB E2L 3V9
Tel: 506-634-2011; *Fax:* 506-648-0804
www.sjbgclub.com
www.facebook.com/saintjohnclub
Chief Officer(s):
Amy Shanks, Executive Director

Boys & Girls Club of Salisbury
2699 Fredericton Rd., Salisbury NB E4J 2E1
Tel: 506-372-5873; *Fax:* 866-854-5696
salbg@rogers.com
www.bgcsalisbury.com
Chief Officer(s):
Evelyn Tingley-Holt, Executive Director

Grand Manan Boys & Girls Club
#1, 1021 Rte. 776, Grand Manan NB E5G 4E5
Tel: 506-662-3653; *Fax:* 506-662-8479
www.facebook.com/gmbgclub

Petitcodiac Boys & Girls Club
45 Corey Ave., Petitcodiac NB E4Z 4G3
Tel: 506-756-2841; *Fax:* 506-756-1912
littletykes@nb.aibn.com
www.pettyboysgirlsclub.ca
Chief Officer(s):
Derrick Beardsworth, Executive Director

Boys & Girls Clubs of Newfoundland & Labrador
NL
Overview: A medium-sized provincial organization overseen by Boys & Girls Clubs of Canada
Member of: Boys & Girls Clubs of Canada

Boys & Girls Club of Botwood
PO Box 1049, 3 Military Rd., Botwood NL A0H 1E0
Tel: 709-257-3191; *Fax:* 709-257-4293
bbgclub@nf.aibn.com
www.facebook.com/boysgirlsclub.botwood
Chief Officer(s):
Darlene Rice, Executive Director

Boys & Girls Club of St. John's
PO Box 5012, St. John's NL A1C 5V3
Tel: 709-579-0181; *Fax:* 709-579-0182
www.bgclub.ca
www.facebook.com/bgcstjohns
twitter.com/BGC_of_StJohns
Chief Officer(s):
Jane Henderson, Executive Director, 709-579-0181 Ext. 204
jhenderson@bgcstjohns.ca

Gander Boys & Girls Club
Gander Arts & Culture Centre, 155 Airport Blvd., Gander NL A1V 1W5
Tel: 709-256-7803; *Fax:* 709-256-7040

Canadian Associations / Boys & Girls Clubs of Ontario

Chief Officer(s):
Brenda Paul, Executive Director
brenda.paul@nfld.net

James Hornell Boys & Girls Club - Buchans
1 Williams Turnpike, Buchans NL A0H 1G0
Tel: 709-672-3342; *Fax:* 709-672-3345
www.facebook.com/jameshornellboysandgirlsclub
Chief Officer(s):
Gary Noftle, Executive Director

Norris Arm Boys & Girls Club
95 Citizen's Dr., Norris Arm NL A0G 3M0
Tel: 709-653-2225; *Fax:* 709-653-2227
Chief Officer(s):
Betty Saunders, Executive Director

St. Anthony & Area Boys & Girls Club
272 West St., St Anthony NL A0K 4S0
Tel: 709-454-2582; *Fax:* 709-454-2052
www.facebook.com/StAnthonyAreaBoysGirlsClub
Chief Officer(s):
Colleen Loder, Executive Director
colleen@stanthonybgclub.com

Upper Island Cove Boys & Girls Club
PO Box 190, Stn. Conception Bay, Upper Island Cove NL A0A 4E0
Tel: 709-589-2943; *Fax:* 709-589-2943
Chief Officer(s):
Mose Drover, President

Wabana Boys & Girls Club
PO Box 539, 266 Quigley's Line, Bell Island NL A0A 4H0
Tel: 709-488-2288; *Fax:* 709-488-2226

Boys & Girls Clubs of Nova Scotia
NS
Overview: A medium-sized provincial organization overseen by Boys & Girls Clubs of Canada
Member of: Boys & Girls Clubs of Canada
Chief Officer(s):
Debbie Cooper, Regional Director
dcooper@bgccan.com

Boys & Girls Club of Preston
180 Lower Partridge River Rd., East Preston NS B2Z 1G8
Tel: 902-829-2665

Boys & Girls Club of Truro & Colchester
40 Douglas St., Truro NS B2N 2E7
Tel: 902-895-5008; *Fax:* 902-893-1171
www.bgctruro.ca
www.facebook.com/BoysAndGirlsClubOfTruroAndColchester
twitter.com/BGCTC2013
Chief Officer(s):
Amanda McNea, Acting Director of Operations

Boys & Girls Club of Yarmouth
11 Bond St., Yarmouth NS B5A 1P6
Tel: 902-742-9103; *Fax:* 902-742-5915
www.facebook.com/bgcysummercamp

Boys & Girls Clubs of Greater Halifax
50 Caledonia Rd., Dartmouth NS B2X 1K8
Tel: 902-435-3204
info@bgcgh.ca
www.bgcgh.ca
www.facebook.com/bgcghfx
twitter.com/BGCGreaterHfx
Chief Officer(s):
Henk van Leeuwen, Chief Executive Officer, 902-435-9916

Boys & Girls Clubs of Cape Breton
111 West St., Sydney NS B1N 1S2
Tel: 902-567-0240
wpyc@ns.sympatico.ca
www.bgccb.ca
www.facebook.com/theWPYC
twitter.com/bgc_whitneypier
Chief Officer(s):
Chester Borden, Executive Director

Boys & Girls Clubs of Ontario
ON
Overview: A medium-sized provincial organization overseen by Boys & Girls Clubs of Canada
Member of: Boys & Girls Clubs of Canada
Chief Officer(s):
Sandra Morris, Regional Director
smorris@bgccan.com
Serena Surujbali, Program Coordinator
ssurujbali@bgccan.com

Albion Boys & Girls Club
#14, 21 Panorama Crt., Toronto ON M9V 3S6
Tel: 416-740-3704; *Fax:* 416-740-7124
www.albionneighbourhoodservices.com
Chief Officer(s):
Susan Hall, President

Boys & Girls Club of Cornwall/SDG
506 First St. East, Cornwall ON K6H 1L7
Tel: 613-935-9015; *Fax:* 613-935-5615
staff@bgccornwallsdg.com
www.bgccornwallsdg.com
www.facebook.com/BGCCornwallSDG
twitter.com/BGCCornwallSDG
Chief Officer(s):
Kim Baird, Chair

Boys & Girls Club of Durham
433 Eulalia Ave., Oshawa ON L1H 2C6
Tel: 905-728-5121; *Fax:* 905-728-5126
www.bgcdurham.com
www.facebook.com/BGCDurham
twitter.com/BGClubDurham
Chief Officer(s):
Lisa McNee-Baker, Executive Director, 905-728-5121 Ext. 222
lmcneebaker@bgcdurham.com

Boys & Girls Club of East Scarborough
100 Galloway Rd., Toronto ON M1E 1W7
Tel: 416-281-0262; *Fax:* 416-281-0458
info@esbgc.org
www.esbgc.org
www.facebook.com/boysandgirlsclubofeastscarborough
twitter.com/esbgc
www.youtube.com/eastscarboroughbgc
Chief Officer(s):
Utcha Sawyers, Executive Director

Boys & Girls Club of Kingston & Area
Robert Meek Downtown Youth Centre, 559 Bagot St., Kingston ON K7K 3E1
Tel: 613-542-3306; *Fax:* 613-542-7964
www.bgckingston.ca
www.facebook.com/bgclubkingston
twitter.com/BGCKingstonON
Chief Officer(s):
Harold Parsons, Executive Director, 613-542-3306 Ext. 222
harold@bgckingston.ca

Boys & Girls Club of London
184 Horton St., London ON N6B 1K8
Tel: 519-434-9114; *Fax:* 519-432-9306
info@bgclondon.ca
www.bgclondon.ca
www.facebook.com/BGCLpage
twitter.com/BGCLondon
Chief Officer(s):
Chris Harvey, Chief Executive Officer, 519-434-9115 Ext. 259
charvey@bgclondon.ca

Boys & Girls Club of Niagara
8800 McLeod Rd., Niagara Falls ON L2H 0Y8
Tel: 905-357-2444; *Fax:* 905-357-7401
boysandgirlsclub@bgcn.cagara.org
www.boysandgirlsclubniagara.org
www.facebook.com/BGCofNiagara
twitter.com/BGCofNiagara
Chief Officer(s):
JoAnne Turner, Executive Director

Boys & Girls Club of North Simcoe
North Simcoe Sports & Recreation Centre, 527 Len Self Blvd., Midland ON L4R 5N6
Tel: 705-526-6159; *Fax:* 705-526-3844
club@bgcnorthsimcoe.com
www.bgcnorthsimcoe.com
www.facebook.com/BGCMidlandON
twitter.com/BGCMidlandON
Chief Officer(s):
Amanda Giles, Executive Director
amanda@bgcnorthsimcoe.com

Boys & Girls Club of Ottawa
2825 DuMaurier Ave., Ottawa ON K2B 7W3
Tel: 613-232-0925; *Fax:* 613-230-0891
www.bgcottawa.org
www.facebook.com/BGCOttawa
twitter.com/bgcottawa
Chief Officer(s):
Colleen Mooney, Executive Director, 613-232-0925 Ext. 241
cmooney@bgcottawa.org

Boys & Girls Club of Peel
247 McMurchy Ave. South, Brampton ON L6Y 1Z4
Tel: 905-712-1789; *Fax:* 905-451-9014
info@bgcpeel.org
www.bgcpeel.org
www.facebook.com/BoysandGirlsClubPeel
twitter.com/peelbgc
Chief Officer(s):
Jim Turner, Executive Director, 905-712-1789 Ext. 101
jturner@bgcpeel.org

Boys & Girls Club of Sarnia-Lambton
180 North College Ave., Sarnia ON N7T 7X2
Tel: 519-337-3651; *Fax:* 519-337-7281
boysandgirls@primus.ca
www.bgcsarnia.com
Chief Officer(s):
Diane MacLeod, Executive Director
dmacleod@bgcsarnia.com

Boys & Girls Clubs of Brantford
2 Edge St., Brantford ON N3T 6H1
Tel: 519-752-2964; *Fax:* 519-752-6530
bgcrecep@teksavvy.com
www.bgcbrant.ca
www.facebook.com/bgcbrant
www.twitter.com/BGCBRANT
Chief Officer(s):
Deanna Searle, Executive Director, 519-752-2964 Ext. 114
bgced@teksavvy.com

Boys & Girls Clubs of Hamilton
45 Ellis Ave., Hamilton ON L8H 4L8
Tel: 905-549-2814; *Fax:* 905-549-2313
info@kboysandgirlsclub.com
www.kboysandgirlsclub.com
www.facebook.com/BGCHamilton
twitter.com/BGCHamilton
Chief Officer(s):
Glenn Harkness, Executive Director, 905-549-2814 Ext. 226
glenn@kboysandgirlsclub.com

Boys & Girls Clubs of Kawartha Lakes
107 Lindsay St. South, Lindsay ON K9V 2M5
Tel: 705-324-4493; *Fax:* 705-878-8605
info@bgckl.com
www.bgckl.com
www.facebook.com/bgckl
twitter.com/BGCKL
www.youtube.com/user/BGCKL
Chief Officer(s):
Scott Robertson, Executive Director

Boys & Girls Clubs of Pembroke
PO Box 1354, 1144 Lea St., Pembroke ON K8A 6Y6
Tel: 613-735-1933; *Fax:* 613-735-1730
www.boysandgirlsclubofpembroke.com
www.facebook.com/bgcpembroke
twitter.com/bgcpembroke
Chief Officer(s):
Rhodina Turner, Executive Director
executivedirector@boysandgirlsclubofpembroke.org

Boys & Girls Clubs of Thunder Bay
270 Windsor St., Thunder Bay ON P7B 1V6
Tel: 807-623-0354; *Fax:* 807-622-5000
tbbgc@tbaytel.net
www.tbayboysandgirlsclub.org
www.facebook.com/BGtbayclubfb
twitter.com/boysandgirlstb
Chief Officer(s):
Albert Aiello, Executive Director, 807-623-0354 Ext. 112
tbbgc@tbaytel.net

Boys & Girls Clubs of West Scarborough
313 Pharmacy Ave., Toronto ON M1L 3E7
Tel: 416-755-9215; *Fax:* 416-755-7521
wsncc@wsncc.on.ca
www.wsncc.org
www.facebook.com/WestScarborough
Chief Officer(s):
Cynthia du Mont, Executive Director, 416-755-9215 Ext. 232
cdumont@wsncc.org

Boys & Girls Clubs of York Region
#11, 17705 Leslie St., Newmarket ON L3Y 6A1
Tel: 289-470-5306; *Fax:* 905-953-8241
bgcyr@socialenterprise.ca
www.bgcyr.ca
www.facebook.com/152201321457331
twitter.com/BGCYorkRegion

Braeburn Boys & Girls Club
#108, 75 Tandridge Cres., Toronto ON M9W 2N9
Tel: 416-745-3113; *Fax:* 416-745-9108
braeburn.bgccan.com

Dovercourt Boys & Girls Club
180 Westmoreland Ave., Toronto ON M6H 3A2
Tel: 416-536-4102; *Fax:* 416-536-2015
www.dovercourtkids.com
www.facebook.com/dovercourtkids
twitter.com/dovercourtkids
Chief Officer(s):
Sheldon Taylor, Executive Director, 416-536-4102 Ext. 205
sheldon@dovercourtkids.com

Eastview (Toronto) Boys & Girls Club
c/o Eastview Neighbourhood Community Centre, 86 Blake St., Toronto ON M4J 3C9
Tel: 416-392-1750; *Fax:* 416-392-1175
contact@eastviewcentre.com
www.eastviewcentre.com
facebook.com/EastviewNeighbourhoodCommunityCentre
twitter.com/eastviewcentre
Chief Officer(s):
Kerry Bowser, Executive Director

St. Alban's Boys & Girls Club
843 Palmerston Ave., Toronto ON M6G 2R8
Tel: 416-534-8461; *Fax:* 416-534-8860
info@stalbansclub.ca
www.stalbansclub.ca
www.facebook.com/stalbansbgclub
twitter.com/stalbansbgc
www.youtube.com/user/bgcYouthTube
Chief Officer(s):
Chris Foster, Executive Director, 416-534-8461 Ext. 222
chris@stalbansclub.ca

Toronto Kiwanis Boys & Girls Clubs
101 Spruce St., Toronto ON M5A 2J3
Tel: 416-925-2243; *Fax:* 416-925-9885
www.believeinkids.ca
www.facebook.com/BelieveInKids
twitter.com/tkbgc
Chief Officer(s):
Ian Edward, Executive Director, 416-925-2243 Ext. 22
iedward@believeinkids.ca

Boys & Girls Clubs of Prince Edward Island
PE
Also Known As: Boys & Girls Clubs of P.E.I.
Overview: A small provincial organization overseen by Boys & Girls Clubs Of Canada
Member of: Boys & Girls Clubs of Canada

Boys & Girls Club of Charlottetown
35 St. Peters Rd., Charlottetown PE C1A 5N1
Tel: 902-892-1817
programs@bgcharlottetown.com
www.charlottetownbg.com
www.facebook.com/BoysandGirlsChtown
twitter.com/ChtownBoysGirls
Chief Officer(s):
Amanda Beazley, Executive Director

Boys & Girls Club of Summerside
364 Notre Dame St., Summerside PE C1N 1S6
Tel: 902-436-9403; *Fax:* 902-436-9610
ssidebgclub@eastlink.ca
ssidebgclub.com
www.facebook.com/274826235970026
twitter.com/bgcsummerside
Chief Officer(s):
Adam Binkley, Executive Director

Wellington & Area Boys & Girls Club
PO Box 78, 24 Mill Rd., Wellington ON C0B 2E0
Tel: 902-854-3174; *Fax:* 902-854-2586
Chief Officer(s):
Michele MacDonald, Executive Director

Boys & Girls Clubs of Québec
QC
Aperçu: Dimension: moyenne; *Envergure:* provinciale surveillé par Boys & Girls Clubs of Canada
Membre de: Boys & Girls Clubs of Canada
Membre(s) du bureau directeur:
Marlene Deboisbriand, Vice-President, Member Services
mdeboisbriand@bgccan.com

Boys & Girls Club of LaSalle
8600, rue Hardy, LaSalle QC H8N 2P5
Tel: 514-364-4661; *Fax:* 514-364-3907
info@bgclasalle.com
www.bgclasalle.com
www.facebook.com/TheBoysandGirlsClubofLaSalle
Membre(s) du bureau directeur:
Mark Branch, Executive Director

Club Garçons et Filles - Local des jeunes des Jardins Fleuris
#1, 800, rue des Pompons, Sherbrooke QC J1E 2Z5

Dawson Boys & Girls Club
666, av Woodland, Montréal QC H4H 1V8
Tel: 514-767-9967; *Fax:* 514-767-7336
info-registration@centredawson.ca
dawson.bgccan.com
www.facebook.com/RepaireJeunesseDawson
twitter.com/dccverdun
Pietro Bozzo, Executive Director
direction@centredawson.ca

Maison Coup De Pouce Trois-Rivières
5591, rue Jean-Paul-Lavergne, Trois-Rivières QC G8Y 3Y5
Tel: 819-693-7036

Régional des maisons de jeunes de Québec
164, av Proulx, Québec QC G1M 1W7
Membre(s) du bureau directeur:
Richard Desjardins, Executive Director

Repaire jeunesse de Sherbrooke - Ascot
1520, rue Dunant, Sherbrooke QC J1H 4A2

Boys & Girls Clubs of Saskatchewan
SK
Overview: A medium-sized provincial organization overseen by Boys & Girls Clubs of Canada
Member of: Boys & Girls Clubs of Canada

Battlefords Boys & Girls Club
1301 - 104th St., North Battleford SK S9A 1N9
Tel: 306-445-0002; *Fax:* 306-446-1313
info@battlefordsboysandgirlsclub.ca
www.battlefordsboysandgirlsclub.com
www.facebook.com/614828391880265
Chief Officer(s):
Nicole Combres, Executive Director
executivedirector@battlefordsboysandgirlsclub.ca

Boys & Girls Club of Yorkton
54C Smith St. West, Yorkton SK S3N 1J4
Tel: 306-783-2582; *Fax:* 306-783-2502
admin@boysandgirlsclubofyorkton.ca
www.boysandgirlsclubofyorkton.ca
www.facebook.com/BGCYorkton
twitter.com/BGCYorkton
Chief Officer(s):
Lorraine Moeller, Executive Director
lorraine@boysandgirlsclubofyorkton.ca
Lorraine Moeller, Executive Director
edbgcyorkton@sasktel.net

Boys & Girls Clubs of Saskatoon
#105, 135 Robin Cres., Saskatoon SK S7L 6M3
Tel: 306-244-7820; *Fax:* 306-244-0089
office@bgcsaskatoon.com
www.bgcsaskatoon.com
www.facebook.com/bgcsaskatoon
Chief Officer(s):
Wanda Desjardin, Chief Executive Officer, 306-244-7820
wanda@bgcsaskatoon.com

Boys & Girls Clubs of Yukon
306 Alexander St., Whitehorse YT Y1A 2L6
Tel: 867-393-2824; *Fax:* 867-667-2108
info@bgcyukon.com
www.bgcyukon.com
www.facebook.com/bgcyukon
Overview: A small provincial organization overseen by Boys & Girls Clubs of Canada
Chief Officer(s):
Lindsay Cornell, Executive Director, 867-393-2824 Ext. 201
ed@bgcyukon.com

Bracebridge Chamber of Commerce
1 Manitoba St., 2nd Fl., Bracebridge ON P1L 1S4
Tel: 705-645-5231
Toll-Free: 866-645-8121
chamber@bracebridgechamber.com
www.bracebridgechamber.com
www.facebook.com/BracebridgeChamberofCommerce
twitter.com/BracebridgeCofC
Overview: A small local organization founded in 1952
Mission: To promote the commercial, industrial, agricultural & civic welfare of Bracebridge & the surrounding district; To help members enhance their quality of business
Member of: Canadian Chamber of Commerce
Finances: *Annual Operating Budget:* $100,000-$250,000;
Funding Sources: Membership dues; fee for service to operate Visitor Centre; federal & provincial governments; advertising; events
Staff Member(s): 2; 17 volunteer(s)
Membership: 315; *Fees:* $105-$1,000; *Committees:* Advocacy & Communications; Business Community Growth & Events; Chamber Revenue; Finance; Governance
Activities: Providing networking opportunities & education;
Internships: Yes
Chief Officer(s):
Brenda Rhodes, Executive Director
brenda@bracebridgechamber.com
Marny Mowat, Administrative Assistant
marny@bracebridgechamber.com
Awards:
• Business Achievement Awards
Publications:
• Bracebridge/Muskoka Map [a publication of the Bracebridge Chamber of Commerce]

Bracebridge Historical Society
PO Box 376, Bracebridge ON P1L 1T7
Tel: 705-645-5501; *Fax:* 705-645-0385
info@octagonalhouse.com
www.octagonalhouse.com
Also Known As: Woodchester Villa
Overview: A small local charitable organization founded in 1978
Mission: To operate & maintain historical sites & museums in Bracebridge
Finances: *Funding Sources:* Town of Bracebridge; provincial government

Bradford Board of Trade
PO Box 1713, 61 Holland St. East, Bradford ON L3Z 2B9
Tel: 905-778-8727
info@bradfordboardoftrade.com
www.bradfordboardoftrade.com
www.facebook.com/BBTVoice
twitter.com/BBTVoice
Overview: A small local organization
Mission: To sustain & promote local businesses
Chief Officer(s):
Cliff Ngai, President, 905-775-2323
president@bradfordboardoftrade.com
Rebecca Davis, Office Administrator
administration@bradfordboardoftrade.com

Bragg Creek Chamber of Commerce
PO Box 216, Bragg Creek AB T0L 0K0
Tel: 403-949-0004
info@visitbraggcreek.com
visitbraggcreek.com
Overview: A small local organization
Mission: To work together to increase development; To foster improvements that benefit the whole community; To strengthen trade & commerce; To improve the economic, civic, & social welfare of the area
Membership: 220+; *Fees:* $130; *Member Profile:* Business owners & professionals
Chief Officer(s):
Suzanne Jackett, President
suzanne@braggcreekchamber.com
Marcella Campbell, Treasurer
marcella@braggcreekchamber.com

Braille Literacy Canada (BLC)
c/o CNIB Library, 1929 Bayview Ave., Toronto ON M4G 3E8
Tel: 416-480-7522; *Fax:* 416-480-7700
info@blc-lbc.ca
www.canadianbrailleauthority.ca
www.linkedin.com/company/3502741
www.facebook.com/brailleliteracycanada
twitter.com/@brllitcan
Previous Name: Canadian Braille Authority
Overview: A small national organization founded in 1990
Mission: To promote braille as a primary medium for persons who are blind; To enables all Canadians who require braille to access information to have braille literacy; To sets up systems that allow blind persons to access print information in braille
Membership: *Fees:* $20; $200 life; $250 corporate;
Committees: UEB Implementation; Web Site; Transactional

Documents; Teaching and Learning; French Braille; Braille Promotion; Grants
Chief Officer(s):
Jen Goulden, President

Brain Care Centre (BCC)
#305, 11010 - 101 St. NW, Edmonton AB T5H 4B9
Tel: 780-477-7575; *Fax:* 780-474-4415
Toll-Free: 800-425-5552
www.braincarecentre.com
www.facebook.com/BrainCareC
twitter.com/BrainCareCentre
www.youtube.com/user/braincarecentreyeg
Previous Name: Northern Alberta Brain Injury Society
Overview: A small local charitable organization founded in 1983
Mission: To support people affected by acquired brain injury in northern Alberta
Finances: *Funding Sources:* Membership fees; Donations; Fundraising
Staff Member(s): 18
Membership: *Fees:* Donations; *Member Profile:* Persons in northern Alberta who are affected by brain injury; Families of individuals affected by brain injury
Activities: Coordinating services for people affected by acquired brain injury in northern Alberta; Providing information & referrals, through programs such as the information line 780-479-1757, ext. 34; Advocating on behalf of persons affected by acquired brain injury; Offering leisure & recreational activities; Providing one to one supportive counselling & support groups; Organizing educational workshops, such as Understanding Brain Injury; Liaising with the community to increase awareness about brain injury services; *Awareness Events:* Kick-off to Brain Injury Awareness Month Breakfast, early June *Library:* Northern Alberta Brain Injury Society Library Resource Centre
Chief Officer(s):
Garnet Cummings, Executive Director
Stephanie Boldt, President
Awards:
• Ginny Awards
• Patrick Hirschi Lifetime Achievement Award
Meetings/Conferences:
• Brain Care Centre 2018 Defying Limitations Gala, 2018
Scope: Provincial
Publications:
• NABIS News
Type: Newsletter; *Frequency:* Quarterly; *Price:* Free with membership in the Northern Alberta Brain Injury Society

Brain Injury Association of Alberta (BIAA)
4916 - 50th St., Red Deer AB T4N 1X7
Tel: 403-309-0866; *Fax:* 403-342-3880
Toll-Free: 888-533-5355
biac-aclc.ca/alberta
Overview: A small provincial organization founded in 1986 overseen by Brain Injury Association of Canada
Mission: To support acquired brain injury survivors, their families, caregivers, & professionals in Alberta; To provide information for individuals & organizations working with brain injury communities
Finances: *Funding Sources:* Fundraising
Membership: *Fees:* Free, courtesy membership for brain injury survivors; $10 individuals; $15 families; $20 professionals & organizations
Activities: Promoting prevention of acquired brain injury; Raising awareness of acquired brain injury; Engaging in advocacy activities; Developing partnerships; Providing education
Chief Officer(s):
Meloni Lyon, President
Shelly Wieser, Secretary

Brain Injury Association of Canada (BIAC) / Association canadienne des lésés cérébraux
#200, 440 Laurier Ave. West, Ottawa ON K1R 7X6
Tel: 613-762-1012; *Fax:* 613-782-2228
Toll-Free: 866-977-2492
info@braininjurycanada.ca
www.braininjurycanada.ca
www.facebook.com/braininjurycanada
twitter.com/BIACACLC
www.youtube.com/user/BrainInjuryCanada
Overview: A medium-sized national organization founded in 2003
Mission: To improve the quality of life for persons affected by acquired brain injury; To promote the prevention of brain injuries, through legislation & education in Canada

Finances: *Funding Sources:* Donations; Fundraising
Activities: Raising awareness of acquired brain injury; Providing education; Facilitating research; Engaging in advocacy activities; *Awareness Events:* Brain Injury Awareness Month, June
Chief Officer(s):
Barb Butler, Co-President
RJ Riopelle, Co-President
Harry Zarins, Executive Director
Meetings/Conferences:
• Brain Injury Canada Semi-Annual Conference 2018, 2018
Scope: National
• Brain Injury Canada Annual Conference 2018, October, 2018, Ottawa, ON
Scope: National
Publications:
• Brain Injury Association of Canada Annual Report
Type: Yearbook
• Impact: Pathways Ahead [a publication of Brain Injury Canada]
Type: Newsletter; *Editor:* Barb Butler
Profile: Happenings at the Brain Injury Association of Canada, plus news from across Canada

Brain Injury Association of Nova Scotia (BIANS)
PO Box 8804, Halifax NS B3K 5M4
Tel: 902-473-7301; *Fax:* 902-473-7302
info@braininjuryns.com
braininjuryns.com
www.facebook.com/357100817645932
Previous Name: Nova Scotia Head Injury Association
Overview: A small provincial organization founded in 1988 overseen by Brain Injury Association of Canada
Mission: To promote an environment throughout Nova Scotia that is responsive to the lifelong needs of persons affected by acquired brain injury
Finances: *Funding Sources:* Donations; Fundraising
Activities: Promoting the prevention of acquired brain injury in Nova Scotia; Increasing public awareness of acquired brain injury; Providing a framework for self-help for people with acquired brain injuries in the province; Lobbying on behalf of people with acquired brain injury; Liaising with both regional & provincial governments; Promoting research, quality care, & rehabilitation; Offering education, such as information; Providing support, such as peer support; Offering referrals; *Speaker Service:* Yes
Chief Officer(s):
Leona Burkey, Executive Director
Ryan Blood, President
Shelley Pick, Vice-President
Patrick MacConnell, Secretary
Publications:
• BIANS News
Type: Newsletter; *Accepts Advertising; Editor:* Mary Bourgeois
Profile: Association happenings, such as upcoming events & chapter news, plus articles & profiles

Brain Injury Coalition of Prince Edward Island (BICPEI)
#5, 81 Prince St., Charlottetown PE C1A 4R3
Tel: 902-314-4228
info@biapei.com
www.bicpei.com
www.facebook.com/243812565693892
Overview: A small provincial organization overseen by Brain Injury Association of Canada
Mission: To contribute to an environment that is responsive to the needs of peoples affected with a brain injury in Prince Edward Island; To promote brain injury prevention
Finances: *Funding Sources:* Fundraising
Membership: *Member Profile:* Persons with brian injury & their families in Prince Edward Island
Activities: Promoting public awareness of the causes & consequences of brain injuries in Prince Edward Island; Education persons about brain injuries & their prevention; Providing information to individuals & organizations which serve the brain injury community; Offering advocacy services for persons with brain injury & their families; Promoting enhanced rehabilitation programs & facilities in Prince Edward Island; Liaising with other brain injury organizations & related groups; *Library:* Brain Injury Coalition of Prince Edward Island Resource Centre

Brain Tumour Foundation of Canada (BTFC) / La Fondation canadienne sur les tumeurs cérébrales
#301, 620 Colborne St., London ON N6B 3R9
Tel: 519-642-7755; *Fax:* 519-642-7192
Toll-Free: 800-265-5106
www.braintumour.ca
www.facebook.com/BrainTumourFoundationofCanada
twitter.com/BrainTumourFdn
www.youtube.com/BrainTumourFdn
Overview: A small national charitable organization founded in 1982
Mission: To find a cure for brain tumors & to improve the quality of life for those affected; To fund brain tumor research; to provide patient & family support services; To educate the public
Member of: North American Brain Tumor Coalition; Canadian Alliance of Brain Tumor Organizations
Finances: *Funding Sources:* Group, individual, corporations & organization donations; fundraising events
Staff Member(s): 20
Activities: Support the Brain Tumor Tissue Bank; resource handbooks; pamphlets; books & videos dealing with brain tumors; support groups; national telephone support system; education & awareness; information displays in healthcare facilities; children's storybooks; *Awareness Events:* Brain Tumour Foundation of Canada Information Days; Brain Tumour Awareness Month, Oct.
Chief Officer(s):
Carl Cadogan, CEO
Publications:
• BrainStorm
Type: Newsletter

Bramalea Stamp Club
Brampton ON
webmaster@bramaleastampclub.org
www.bramaleastampclub.org
Overview: A small local organization founded in 1975
Member of: Royal Philatelic Society of Canada; Grand River Valley Philatelic Association; Greater Toronto Area Philatelic Association
Finances: *Funding Sources:* Membership dues; fundraising; show
Membership: 40; *Fees:* $15 individual; $20 family; *Member Profile:* Stamp collectors & philatelists
Chief Officer(s):
Bob Thorne, President

Brampton Arts Council (BAC)
24A Alexander St., Brampton ON L6V 1H6
Tel: 905-874-2919; *Fax:* 905-874-2921
info@artsbrampton.ca
www.artsbrampton.ca
www.youtube.com/bactalkbac
Overview: A small local charitable organization founded in 1978
Mission: To foster & promote arts within the City of Brampton; To educate public in the arts by providing various artistic presentations designed to raise level of aesthetic appreciation
Affiliation(s): Community Arts Ontario; Canadian Conference of the Arts; Brampton Board of Trade; Ontario Arts Council; Arts West
Staff Member(s): 2; 50 volunteer(s)
Membership: 43 corporate + 4 student + 90 individual; *Fees:* Schedule available; *Committees:* Finance & Administration; Planning; Publicity; Bi-Consultative; Bingo; Policy
Activities: Artists' Alley; Studio Tour; *Library:* Open to public
Chief Officer(s):
Marnie Richards, Executive Director
mrichards@artsbrampton.ca
Awards:
• Arts Person of the Year
• BAC/Royal Bank School Artistic Achievement Awards

The Brampton Board of Trade (BBOT)
#101, 36 Queen St. East, Brampton ON L6V 1A2
Tel: 905-451-1122
admin@bramptonbot.com
www.bramptonbot.com
www.linkedin.com/company/2087561
www.facebook.com/BramptonBOT
twitter.com/BramptonBOT
www.youtube.com/user/BramptonBoT
Overview: A small local organization founded in 1887
Mission: To represent & actively promote the interests of Brampton business, members & the private enterprise system
Member of: Ontario Chamber of Commerce; Canadian Chamber of Commerce
Membership: 883; *Fees:* Schedule available
Chief Officer(s):
Steve Sheils, Chief Executive Officer
ssheils@bramptonbot.com

Canadian Associations / Brampton Caledon Community Living (BCCL)

Carrie Andrews, Operations Manager
candrews@bramptonbot.com
Glenn Williams, Chair

Brampton Caledon Community Living (BCCL)
34 Church St. West, Brampton ON L6X 1H3
Tel: 905-453-8841; *Fax:* 905-453-8853
info@bramptoncaledoncl.ca
www.bramptoncaledoncl.ca
www.facebook.com/BramptonCaledonCommunityLiving
Overview: A small local organization founded in 1958
Mission: To support people with intellectual disabilities & their families; To ensure that people with intellectual disabilities have the resources & opportunities to actively participate in all aspects of community life
Member of: Community Living Ontario; Ontario Agencies Supporting Individuals with Special Needs; Advocacy Resource Centre for the Handicapped
Finances: *Funding Sources:* Ministry of Community of Social Services; Region of Peel; United Way; the Trillium Foundation; fundraising
Chief Officer(s):
Arlette Brobyn, President
Jim Triantafilou, Executive Director
jimt@bramptoncaledoncl.ca

Brampton Horticultural Society
PO Box 92546, 160 Main St. South, Brampton ON L6W 4R1
bramhort@hotmail.com
bramptonhort.org
Overview: A small local charitable organization founded in 1895
Member of: Ontario Horticultural Association
Membership: *Fees:* $19 single; $26 family; $14 senior single; $20 senior family; $2.50 junior
Chief Officer(s):
Fran Caldwell, President
Wendy Lovegrove, Secretary

Brampton Office *See* Heart & Stroke Foundation of Ontario

Brampton Real Estate Board (BREB)
#401, 60 Gillingham Dr., Brampton ON L6X 0Z9
Tel: 905-791-9913; *Fax:* 905-791-9430
Other Communication: bramptonrealestateboard.wordpress.com
info@breb.org
www.breb.org
www.facebook.com/theBREB
www.youtube.com/user/TheBREBTV
Overview: A small local organization founded in 1955 overseen by Ontario Real Estate Association
Mission: To help members achieve their real estate related goals
Member of: The Canadian Real Estate Association; Brampton Board of Trade
Staff Member(s): 7
Chief Officer(s):
Gerry Verdone, Executive Officer, 905-791-9913 Ext. 227
eo@breb.org

Brampton-Mississauga & District Labour Council *See* Peel Regional Labour Council

Brandon Chamber of Commerce
1043 Rosser Ave., Brandon MB R7A 0L5
Tel: 204-571-5340; *Fax:* 204-571-5347
info@brandonchamber.ca
brandonchamber.ca
www.facebook.com/156031967812208
twitter.com/BdnChamber
Overview: A medium-sized local organization
Mission: To encourage growth in the Brandon community by fostering a progressive business environment, favourable to enhancing existing & attracting new business
Member of: Manitoba Chambers of Commerce; Canadian Chamber of Commerce
Finances: *Annual Operating Budget:* $250,000-$500,000
Staff Member(s): 4
Membership: 593; *Committees:* Government Relations; Events; Membership; Business Development
Chief Officer(s):
Carolynn Cancade, General Manager, 204-571-5342

Brandon Economic Development Board *See* Economic Development Brandon

Brandon Friendship Centre
836 Lorne Ave., Brandon MB R7A 0T8
Tel: 204-727-1407; *Fax:* 204-726-0902
bfcinc@mts.net
Overview: A small local charitable organization
Mission: To provide services to the community with an emphasis on Aboriginal culture.
Activities: Services include: Brandon Aboriginal Youth Activity Centre; Parent Child Centre Program; Portage Aboriginal HeadStart Program; Brandon Friendship Centre Housing Authority; Kokum's Little Friends Daycare

Brandon Humane Society
2200 - 17 St. East, Brandon MB R7A 7M6
www.brandonhumanesociety.ca
www.facebook.com/307039086058890
Also Known As: Brandon Society for the Prevention of Cruelty to Animals
Overview: A small local organization founded in 1946 overseen by Canadian Federation of Humane Societies
Mission: To provide care for & homes for abused companion animals; To educate the public about the value of humane treatment of animals
Member of: Canadian Federation of Humane Societies
75 volunteer(s)
Membership: *Fees:* $10 individual; $20 family
Chief Officer(s):
Tracy Munn, Shelter Manager

Brandon Police Association (BPA) / Association de la police de la ville de Brandon
c/o Brandon Police Service, 1020 Victoria Ave., Brandon MB R7A 1A9
Tel: 204-729-2345; *Fax:* 204-726-1323
police.brandon.ca
Overview: A small local licensing organization founded in 1956
Mission: The Association represents the city police employees, negotiating a collective agreement with the city on their behalf.
Affiliation(s): Manitoba Police Association; Canadian Police Association
Membership: 125; *Member Profile:* Member/employee of Brandon Police
Activities: *Internships:* Yes; *Library:* Not open to public
Chief Officer(s):
Kevin Loewen, President

Brandon Real Estate Board (BREB)
857 - 18 St., Unit B, Brandon MB R7A 5B8
Tel: 204-727-4672; *Fax:* 204-727-8331
info@breb.mb.ca
www.breb.mb.ca
Overview: A small local organization overseen by Manitoba Real Estate Association
Mission: To provide real estate support for Realtors in Brandon.
Member of: The Canadian Real Estate Association
Staff Member(s): 3
Chief Officer(s):
Cam Toews, President
Annette Wiebe, Executive Officer
eo@breb.mb.ca

Brandon University Faculty Association (BUFA) / Association des professeurs de l'Université de Brandon
Clark Hall, Brandon University, #333, 270 - 18th St., Brandon MB R7A 6A9
Tel: 204-727-7347
www.bufa.org
Overview: A small local organization founded in 1978
Mission: To represent the faculty members in negotiating collective agreements
Member of: Canadian Association of University Teachers; Manitoba Organization of Faculty Associations
Staff Member(s): 1
Chief Officer(s):
Todd Fugleberg, President, 204-571-8577
Maureen Barrett, Administrator
barrett@brandonu.ca

Brandon University School of Music
Queen Elizabeth II Music Building, 270 - 18th St., Brandon MB R7A 6A9
Tel: 204-727-7388; *Fax:* 204-728-6839
music@brandonu.ca
www.brandonu.ca/music
Overview: A small local organization
Membership: *Member Profile:* Brandon University students
Chief Officer(s):
Greg Gatien, Acting Dean, 204-727-7363
gatieng@brandonu.ca

Branscombe Family Foundation
4785 Drummond Rd., Niagara Falls ON L2E 6C8
Tel: 905-358-0484; *Fax:* 905-358-1841
administration@branscombefamilyfoundation.com
www.branscombefamilyfoundation.com
Overview: A small local charitable organization founded in 1977
Mission: To improve health care & social programs for the people of The Regional Municipality of Niagara; To encourage higher education for students graduating from secondary schools
Finances: *Funding Sources:* Donations; Frank & Mildred Branscombe & River Realty Development (1976) Inc.
Activities: Supporting charitable & educational organizations in the Niagara Region & Ontario; Offering grants & scholarships

Brant *See* Habitat for Humanity Canada

Brant Community Social Planning Council
Brantford ON
Tel: 519-754-1081
Overview: A small local organization founded in 1989
Mission: To enhance the quality of life for all citizens in Brant County by facilitating effective planning in conjunction with an informed & involved community

Brant Family & Children's Services
PO Box 774, 70 Chatham St., Brantford ON N3T 5R7
Tel: 519-753-8681; *Fax:* 519-753-6090
Toll-Free: 888-753-8681; *TTY:* 519-753-8323
www.brantfacs.ca
Previous Name: Children's Aid Society of Brant
Overview: A small local organization founded in 1894
Mission: To provide child welfare & family services in Brantford, Brant, Six Nations, & New Credit; To foster & build healthy families & family relationships through guidance & education
Member of: Ontario Association of Children's Aid Societies
Affiliation(s): Contact Brant; Lansdowne Children's Centre; St. Leonard's Community Services; Brant County Health Unit; Nova Vita Domestic Violence Prevention Services
Finances: *Annual Operating Budget:* Greater than $5 Million
Activities: Providing child & family services; Working with other local associations to achieve goals
Chief Officer(s):
Andrew Koster, Executive Director

Brant Historical Society (BHS)
57 Charlotte St., Brantford ON N3T 2W6
Tel: 519-752-2483
www.brantmuseums.ca
www.facebook.com/BrantMuseums
twitter.com/Branthistorical
www.youtube.com/user/branthistorical
Overview: A small local charitable organization founded in 1908
Mission: To collect, preserve & share the history & heritage of Brantford/Brant County & Six Nations/New Credit
Member of: Ontario Historical Society; Ontario Museums Association
Membership: *Fees:* $20 student; $25 individual; $40 family
Activities: Operates Brant Museum & Archives; Publication of local history for Brantford/Brant County; Lecture series; *Speaker Service:* Yes; *Library:* Open to public
Chief Officer(s):
Lana Jobe, Executive Director

Brant Skills Centre
#1, 225 Fairview Dr., Brantford ON N3R 7E3
Tel: 519-758-1664; *Fax:* 519-758-9394
twitter.com/brantskills
Previous Name: Literacy Council of Brantford & District
Overview: A small local charitable organization founded in 1984
Mission: To help adults improve their literacy & essential skills & increase their independence; To teach adults employability skills
Member of: Laubach Literacy of Canada, Ontario
Finances: *Annual Operating Budget:* $50,000-$100,000; *Funding Sources:* Ministry of Training, Colleges and Universities - Employment Ontario
Staff Member(s): 5; 88 volunteer(s)
Activities: Offering one-to-one & small group tutoring; Facilitating workshops
Chief Officer(s):
Lori Bruner, Executive Director

Brant United Way (BUW)
125 Morrell St., Brantford ON N3T 4J9
Tel: 519-752-7848; *Fax:* 519-752-7913
info@brantunitedway.org

www.brantunitedway.org
www.facebook.com/BrantUnitedWay
twitter.com/brantunitedway
Overview: A small local charitable organization founded in 1953 overseen by United Way of Canada - Centraide Canada
Mission: To help people in their time of need
Finances: *Funding Sources:* Campaigns; donations
Staff Member(s): 9
Activities: *Speaker Service:* Yes
Chief Officer(s):
Sherry Haines, Executive Director

Brantford & District Association for Community Living See Community Living Brantford

Brantford & District Labour Council
PO Box 8, #201, 1100 Clarence St. South, Brantford ON N3S 7N8
Tel: 519-753-9142; *Fax:* 519-753-9747
www.brantfordlabourcouncil.ca
Overview: A small local organization overseen by Ontario Federation of Labour
Chief Officer(s):
Garry Mac Donald, President
Roxanne Bond, Recording Secretary

Brantford CADORA See CADORA Ontario Association Inc.

Brantford Lapidary & Mineral Society Inc. (BLMS)
1 Sherwood Dr., Brantford ON N3T 1N3
brantfordlapclub@live.ca
www.brantfordlapidarymineral.ca
Overview: A small local organization founded in 1964
Mission: To increase interest in the earth sciences & related lapidary arts
Membership: *Fees:* $15 single membership; $18 family
Activities: Offering lapidary training; Providing equipment access; Organizing monthly meetings; Arranging field trips; *Library:* Brantford Lapidary & Mineral Society Library
Chief Officer(s):
Ernie Edmonds, President, 519-583-9457
Awards:
• Brantford Lapidary and Mineral Society Inc. Awards
Eligibility: Presented annually to students enrolled in an Earth Sciences program in the Faculty of Science at the University of Waterloo who have achieved a minimum overall average of 75%; *Amount:* $1,000 each
Publications:
• The Telephone City Crystal [a publication of the Brantford Lapidary & Mineral Society, Inc.]
Type: Newsletter; *Editor:* Marcel LeBlanc
Profile: Information about lapidary & minerals, equipment advice, & forthcoming events

Brantford Musicians' Association (BMA)
101 Chatham St., Brantford ON N3T 2P3
Tel: 519-752-7973; *Fax:* 519-752-7973
Toll-Free: 800-463-6333
musicians@bellnet.ca
www.brantfordmusicians.org
Also Known As: AFM Local 467
Overview: A small local organization founded in 1907
Mission: To unite professional musicians; to secure improved wages, hours & working conditions for professional musicians; To promote live music in the community
Member of: American Federation of Musicians
Finances: *Annual Operating Budget:* Less than $50,000; *Funding Sources:* Membership fees
Staff Member(s): 1; 8 volunteer(s)
Membership: 202; *Fees:* $125; *Member Profile:* Professional musicians
Activities: Annual showcase of talent; annual "Bring Your Axe Night"
Chief Officer(s):
Rusty James, President
Marg Conway, Secretary

Brantford Numismatic Society
PO Box 28015, Stn. North Park Plaza, Brantford ON N3R 7K5
Tel: 519-759-5137
Overview: A small local organization
Member of: Ontario Numismatic Association
Chief Officer(s):
Len Trakalo, Contact
ltrakalo@rogers.com

Brantford Police Association (BPA)
344 Elgin St., Brantford ON N3S 7P6
Tel: 519-756-6621
Overview: A small local organization founded in 1946
Mission: To represent its members during collective bargaining negotiations.
Member of: Police Association of Ontario
Membership: *Member Profile:* Brantford Police officers and staff

Brantford Regional Chamber of Commerce See Chamber of Commerce of Brantford & Brant

Brantford Regional Real Estate Association Inc. (BRREA)
106 George St., Brantford ON N3T 2Y4
Tel: 519-753-0308; *Fax:* 519-753-8638
brantfordreb@rogers.com
www.brrea.com
www.linkedin.com/company/brantford-regional-real-estate-association
www.facebook.com/BrantfordRegionalRealEstateAssociation
twitter.com/_BRREA
www.youtube.com/BRREAssociation
Overview: A small local organization overseen by Ontario Real Estate Association
Mission: To provide real estate support for realtors working in Brantford
Member of: The Canadian Real Estate Association
Staff Member(s): 4
Membership: 300 relators in 24 organizations; *Committees:* Political Affairs; Community Awareness; Education; MLS/Technology
Chief Officer(s):
Viktoria Tumilowicz, Executive Officer
viktoria@brrea.com

Brantford Stamp Club
c/o Paul James, 64 Lorne Cres., Brantford ON N3T 4L7
www.brantfordstamp.org
Overview: A small local organization founded in 1937
Member of: Royal Philatelic Society of Canada; Grand River Valley Philatelic Association
Finances: *Funding Sources:* Membership dues; annual stamp show
Membership: 50; *Fees:* $15 single; $20 family; $3 children; $7 associate; *Member Profile:* Those interested in postage stamps & postal history; *Committees:* Executive; Annual Stamp Show
Activities: *Awareness Events:* Brantford Stamp Club Annual Show
Chief Officer(s):
Paul James, President, 519-751-3513
pjames@execulink.com

Brantford Symphony Orchestra Association Inc.
PO Box 24012, 185 King George Rd., Brantford ON N3R 7X3
Tel: 519-759-8781; *Fax:* 519-759-0842
administrator@brantfordsymphony.ca
www.brantfordsymphony.ca
www.facebook.com/Brantford.Symphony
twitter.com/bsobrant
Overview: A small local charitable organization overseen by Orchestras Canada
Mission: To provide enduring access to the best symphonic entertainment, giving people of all ages opportunities for musical growth & education
Finances: *Funding Sources:* Performance revenue; Corporate & individual donations
Staff Member(s): 3; 40 volunteer(s)
Membership: 100-499
Activities: *Awareness Events:* Annual Book Fair, April; *Speaker Service:* Yes
Chief Officer(s):
Maureen Wills, Co-President
m_wills@rogers.com
Joann Alho, Co-President
joannalho@gmail.com
Philip Sarabura, Conductor/Music Director
philip@philipsarabura.com

Brantwood Foundation
25 Bell Lane, Brantford ON N3T 1E1
Tel: 519-753-2658
www.brantwood.ca/brantwood-foundation
Overview: A small local charitable organization founded in 1982
Mission: To raise funds for the Brantwood Centre, a facility that provides services to challenged individuals in Brantford and Brant County.
Finances: *Funding Sources:* Provincial government; Brant United Way; private sector
Activities: Golf tournament; fundraising for Brantwood Centre
Chief Officer(s):
Emilie Brown, Coordinator, Public Relations & Fundraising
publicrelations@brantwood.ca

Break Open Ticket Program Management Alliance (BOTPMA)
ON
Overview: A small provincial organization founded in 1992
Mission: Entrepreneurs whose members provide fundraising products, services & leadership for the charitable gaming industry in Ontario
Membership: *Fees:* $500; *Member Profile:* Registered suppliers of Break Open Tickets & services to Ontario's charitable sector

Breakfast Cereals Canada (BCC)
#600, 100 Sheppard Ave. East, Toronto ON M2N 6N5
Tel: 416-510-8024; *Fax:* 416-510-8043
breakfastcereals.ca
Overview: A medium-sized national organization founded in 1983
Mission: To provide a forum for members to review issues of significance to the breakfast industry; to represent industry with government
Affiliation(s): Food & Consumer Products Manufacturers of Canada
Membership: 4; *Member Profile:* Cereal manufacturers only: General Mills Canada Corporation, Kellogg Canada Inc., Post Foods Canada Corporation & Quaker
Chief Officer(s):
Kathryn Fitzwilliam, Contact
kathrynf@fcpc.ca

Breakfast for Learning (BFL)
#206, 2084 Danforth Ave., Toronto ON M4C 1J9
Toll-Free: 800-627-7922
www.breakfastforlearning.ca
www.facebook.com/BreakfastforLearning
twitter.com/breakfastlearn
Overview: A medium-sized national charitable organization founded in 1992
Mission: To support breakfast, lunch, & snack nutrition programs in schools across Canada; To ensure that children are properly nourished so that they may reach their full potential
Activities: Funding school-based nutrition programs
Publications:
• Breakfast for Learning Annual Report
Type: Yearbook; *Frequency:* Annually

Breast Cancer Action (BCA) / Sensibilisation au cancer du sein
#301, 1390 Prince of Wales Dr., Ottawa ON K2C 3N6
Tel: 613-736-5921; *Fax:* 613-736-8422
info@bcaott.ca
www.bcaott.ca
www.facebook.com/BCAOttawa
twitter.com/BCAOttawa
Overview: A medium-sized local charitable organization founded in 1993
Mission: To develop programs focused on raising awareness & providing education on breast cancer; To offer support, information & resources for individuals & families affected by breast cancer; To promote the exchange of information among organizations
Finances: *Funding Sources:* Private donations; fundraisers
Staff Member(s): 2
Membership: *Fees:* $95
Activities: *Awareness Events:* Annual Walk/Fun Run, June; *Library:* Open to public
Chief Officer(s):
Karen Graszat, Executive Director
executivedirector@bcaott.ca

Breast Cancer Action Nova Scotia (BCANS)
Mill Cove Plaza, #205, 967 Bedford Hwy., Bedford NS B4A 1A9
Tel: 902-465-2685; *Fax:* 902-484-6436
bcans@bcans.ca
www.bcans.ca
www.facebook.com/BreastCancerActionNovaScotia
twitter.com/BCANSBedford
Overview: A medium-sized provincial charitable organization founded in 1994
Mission: To address the obstacles faced by those living with breast cancer; To provide information; To create a support network for those with breast cancer
Affiliation(s): Keller Williams Realty (Harold Shea)

Canadian Associations / Breast Cancer Society of Canada (BCSC) / Société du cancer du sein du Canada

Finances: *Annual Operating Budget:* $100,000-$250,000; *Funding Sources:* Donations
Membership: *Fees:* $10; *Committees:* Advocacy; Network; Pink Spring
Activities: Monthly educational talks; *Awareness Events:* Pink Spring Celebration Dinner, Dance, Fashion Show & Auction, Spring *Library:* Rosanna Bechtel Memorial Library
Meetings/Conferences:
• Breast Cancer Action Nova Scotia 2018 Annual General Meeting, 2018, NS
Scope: Provincial
Description: A business meeting for members, featuring reports from committee chairs
Publications:
• Atlantic Breast Cancer Net E-Newsletter
Type: Newsletter; *Price:* Free with membership in Breast Cancer Action Nova Scotia

Breast Cancer Society of Canada (BCSC) / Société du cancer du sein du Canada
420 East St. North, Sarnia ON N7T 6Y5
Tel: 519-336-0746; *Fax:* 519-336-5725
Toll-Free: 800-567-8767
bcsc@bcsc.ca
www.bcsc.ca
www.linkedin.com/company/breast-cancer-society-of-canada
www.facebook.com/breastcancersocietyofcanada
twitter.com/bcsc
www.youtube.com/user/BreastCancerSociety
Also Known As: Breast Cancer Society
Overview: A large national charitable organization founded in 1991
Mission: To support research into the prevention, detection, & treatment of breast cancer
Member of: Canadian Cancer Research Alliance
Finances: *Annual Operating Budget:* $250,000-$500,000; *Funding Sources:* Donations; Fundraising
Staff Member(s): 5; 100 volunteer(s)
Activities: Facilitating fundraising events; Funding breast cancer research; *Awareness Events:* Dress for the Cause, October; Pam Greenaway-Kohlmeier Memorial Golf Tournament; Mother's Day Walk
Chief Officer(s):
Kimberly Carson, CEO
kcarson@bcsc.ca
Virginia Hutton, Director, Development
vhutton@bcsc.ca
Dawn Hamilton, National Manager, Partnerships & Events
dhamilton@bcsc.ca
Neil Wiernik, National Manager, Digital Marketing & Social Media
Diane Renaud, Office Administrator
drenaud@bcsc.ca
Publications:
• Breast Cancer Society of Canada Newsletter
Type: Newsletter
Profile: Recent information about the society & research endeavours

Breeders of Belgian Horses Association of Québec *Voir*
Association des éleveurs de chevaux Belge du Québec

Brereton Field Naturalists' Club Inc. (BFN)
PO Box 1084, Barrie ON L4M 5E1
bfnclub.org
www.facebook.com/123840057676677
Overview: A small local charitable organization founded in 1951
Mission: To acquire & disseminate knowledge of natural history; to protect & preserve wildlife; to stimulate public interest in nature & its preservation
Affiliation(s): Federation of Ontario Naturalists
Finances: *Annual Operating Budget:* Less than $50,000; *Funding Sources:* Membership fees
95 volunteer(s)
Membership: 125; *Fees:* $10 student; $15 corresponding; $25 individual; $30 family; *Committees:* Conservation; Education; Field Trips; Newsletter; Program
Activities: Bird-watching outings; nature strolls; lunches; *Speaker Service:* Yes; *Library:* BFN Library; by appointment Not open to public
Chief Officer(s):
Brian Gibbon, Contact, 705-726-8969
bwg@backland.net
Publications:
• The Blue Heron
Type: Newsletter; *Frequency:* Annually

Brethren in Christ (BIC)
2700 Bristol Circle, Oakville ON L6H 6EH
Tel: 905-339-2335; *Fax:* 905-337-2120
office@canadianbic.ca
www.canadianbic.ca
www.facebook.com/BICCanada
twitter.com/BICCanada
vimeo.com/user10271482
Overview: A medium-sized international charitable organization founded in 1788
Member of: Evangelical Fellowship of Canada
Affiliation(s): Mennonite Central Committee; Canadian Holiness Federation
Finances: *Annual Operating Budget:* $500,000-$1.5 Million; *Funding Sources:* Congregational giving
Staff Member(s): 8
Membership: 3,450 + 43 congregations in Canada; *Member Profile:* North American membership is about 20,000 with significant churches in other countries including India, Japan, Zambia, Zimbabwe, Nicaragua, Cuba, Venezuela, Columbia, South Africa
Activities: *Speaker Service:* Yes; *Rents Mailing List:* Yes
Chief Officer(s):
Doug Sider, Executive Director
doug.sider@canadianbic.ca

Breton & District Chamber of Commerce
PO Box 850, Breton AB T0C 0P0
Tel: 780-696-4888
Overview: A small local organization

Breton & District Historical Society
PO Box 696, 4711 - 51 St., Breton AB T0C 0P0
Tel: 780-696-2551
bretonmuse@yahoo.com
Overview: A small local charitable organization founded in 1978
Mission: To present information & exhibits about Black history, community development, agriculture, & lumbering in Breton, Alberta
Finances: *Funding Sources:* Donations; Fundraising; Sponsorships
Activities: Operating the Breton & District Historical Museum; Restoring the Keystone Cemetery & honouring Black families who settled in the area
Chief Officer(s):
Allan Goddard, Contact

Brewers Association of Canada / L'association des brasseurs du Canada
#650, 45 O'Connor St., Ottawa ON K1P 1A4
cheers@beercanada.com
www.beercanada.com
www.linkedin.com/company/beer-canada
www.facebook.com/BeerCanadaCheers
twitter.com/beercanada
Also Known As: Beer Canada
Overview: A large national organization founded in 1943
Mission: To represent brewing companies operating in Canada; To collect information & statistics about the brewing industry; To provide information about the industry to the public
Membership: 50 brewers
Activities: Promoting the responsible use of alchohol; *Library*
Chief Officer(s):
Luke Harford, President
Luke Chapman, Director, Economics & Technical Affairs
Ed Gregory, Director, Policy & Research
Tanya Bernier, Manager, Office & Finance
Brittany Moorcroft, Manager, Member Services & Communications

Brewery, Winery & Distillery Workers Union - Local 300
7128 Gilley Ave., Burnaby BC V5J 4X2
Tel: 604-434-5155; *Fax:* 604-434-7333
brew300@telus.net
www.brew300.ca
Overview: A small provincial organization founded in 1925
Member of: National Union of Public and General Employees
Affiliation(s): BC Government & Service Employees' Union
Finances: *Annual Operating Budget:* $500,000-$1.5 Million
Staff Member(s): 3
Membership: 880; *Fees:* 1.5% of gross
Chief Officer(s):
Roy Graham, President

Brewing & Malting Barley Research Institute (BMBRI) / Institut de recherche - brassage et orge de maltage
PO Box 1497, Stn. Main, Winnipeg MB R3C 2Z4
Tel: 204-927-1407
info@bmbri.ca
www.bmbri.ca
Overview: A medium-sized national organization founded in 1948
Mission: To support the development & evaluation of new malting barley varieties in Canada
Staff Member(s): 2
Membership: 8 corporate; *Fees:* Schedule available; *Member Profile:* Commercial brewing or malting companies
Chief Officer(s):
Michael Brophy, President & CEO, 204-927-1401
mbrophy@bmbri.ca

Brian Bronfman Family Foundation (BBFF) / Fondation de la famille Brian Bronfman
#900, 1000, de la Gauchetière ouest, Montréal QC H3B 5H4
www.bronfman.ca
Overview: A large national charitable organization founded in 2006
Mission: To advance Brian Bronfman's philanthropic ideals; To achieve a peaceful & just society
Chief Officer(s):
Brian Bronfman, President

Brian Webb Dance Co.
PO Box 53092, Edmonton AB T5N 4B8
Tel: 780-452-3282
webbcdf@shaw.ca
www.bwdc.ca
www.facebook.com/BrianWebbDanceCompany
twitter.com/BrianWebbDance
instagram.com/brianwebbdanceco
Overview: A small local charitable organization founded in 1979
Mission: To produce & present contemporary dance; To build new works through collaboration
Staff Member(s): 5
Activities: *Awareness Events:* Art Auction
Chief Officer(s):
Brian Webb, Artistic Director

Bricklayers, Masons Independent Union of Canada (CLC) / Syndicat indépendant des briqueteurs et des maçons du Canada (CTC)
PO Box 105, #307, 1263 Wilson Ave., Toronto ON M3M 3G3
Tel: 416-247-9841; *Fax:* 416-241-9636
localone.ca
Overview: A medium-sized national organization
Membership: 1,500 + 1 local
Chief Officer(s):
Fernando Da Cunha, Vice President
John Meiorin, Secretary-Treasurer

Bridge Adult Service Society
16 Station St., Amherst NS B4H 0C2
Tel: 902-667-8433; *Fax:* 902-667-8433
b.workshop@ns.sympatico.ca
Overview: A small local organization
Member of: DIRECTIONS Council for Vocational Services Society
Chief Officer(s):
Susan Thibodeau, Executive Director/Manager

Bridges
#2, 670 Prince St., Truro NS B2N 1G6
Tel: 902-897-6665; *Fax:* 902-897-0569
bridges@bridgesinstitute.org
bridgesinstitute.org
Overview: A small local organization founded in 1991
Mission: To help to end men's violence against women
Chief Officer(s):
Tod Augusta-Scott
tod@bridgesinstitute.org

Bridges Family Programs Association
477 - 3rd St. SE, Medicine Hat AB T1A 0G8
Tel: 403-526-7473; *Fax:* 403-504-2459
bridgesfamilyprograms.org
Also Known As: BRIDGES
Previous Name: Parents of the Handicapped of Southeastern Alberta
Overview: A small local charitable organization founded in 1977

Mission: To work with families by building on their strengths, providing support, information & advocacy to make a positive difference in the lives of each person, family & community; families are able to access information & support which will assist them to meet their needs & enjoy safe, loving, healthy relationships & environments
Finances: *Funding Sources:* Provincial Government
Activities: Summer Program - Camp Wannacombac; Bridges Program; Healthy Start; Building Blocks; Best Babies; *Library:* Resource Centre; by appointment Not open to public

Bridgetown & Area Chamber of Commerce (BACC)
PO Box 467, Bridgetown NS B0S 1C0
www.bridgetownareachamber.com
www.facebook.com/baccsociety
twitter.com/baccsociety
Overview: A small local organization
Membership: *Fees:* $100 large business; $50 medium business; $30 small business; $20 individual
Chief Officer(s):
Jennifer D'Aubin, President
Gerry Bezanson, Secretary

Bridgetown & Area Historical Society
PO Box 645, 12 Queen St., Bridgetown NS B0S 1C0
Tel: 902-665-4530
www.jameshousemuseum.com/home/bahs
www.facebook.com/162556040569444?fref=ts
Also Known As: James House Museum
Overview: A small local charitable organization founded in 1979
Mission: To promote interest in local history of Bridgetown & area
Member of: Federation of Nova Scotia Heritage
Affiliation(s): Nova Scotia Museum - Halifax
10 volunteer(s)
Membership: 65 lifetime + 50 individual; *Fees:* $10 individual yearly; $20 family yearly; $100 lifetime; *Member Profile:* Interest in museum & history & archives; *Committees:* Maintenance; Special Events; Tea Room; Victoria Garden
Activities: Operates seasonal museum; *Library:* by appointment
Chief Officer(s):
Kathy Howland, Administrator/Curator

Bridgewater & Area Chamber of Commerce (BACC)
373 King St., Bridgewater NS B4V 1B1
Tel: 902-543-4263
www.bridgewaterchamber.com
www.facebook.com/100619843315571
Overview: A small local organization founded in 1899
Mission: To act as the voice of the business community in Bridgewater, Nova Scotia & the surrounding area
Membership: *Fees:* Schedule available based on number of employees; *Member Profile:* Any individual, business, or organization in Bridgewater, Nova Scotia & the surrounding region
Activities: Advocating on behalf of businesses to all levels of government; Partnering with other business associations & community organizations; Hosting community events; Providing training; Offering networking opportunities
Chief Officer(s):
Dan Hennessey, Executive Director
Awards:
• Entrepreneurship Scholarship
• Business Excellence Awards: Entrepreneur, Small Business, Large Business, President's Award
Publications:
• BACC [Bridgewater & Area Chamber of Commerce] Buzz
Type: Newsletter; *Price:* Free

Brier Island Chamber of Commerce
PO Box 74, Westport NS B0V 1H0
Overview: A small local organization
Chief Officer(s):
Harold Graham, President

Brighton-Cramahe Chamber of Commerce
Brighton Community Resource Centre, 1 Young St., Brighton ON K0K 1H0
Tel: 613-475-2775
info@brightonchamber.ca
www.brightonchamber.ca
Previous Name: AppleRoute Country Chamber of Commerce
Overview: A small local organization founded in 1994
Mission: To serve businesses in Brighton & surrounding area
Member of: Ontario Chamber of Commerce
Finances: *Annual Operating Budget:* $50,000-$100,000; *Funding Sources:* Membership fees; Fund raising

Staff Member(s): 1; 10 volunteer(s)
Membership: 150; *Fees:* $150-$875; *Member Profile:* Local business owners; *Committees:* Economic; Membership; Tourism
Activities: Organizing business breakfasts; Providing tourism information, economic strategy, & business referrals
Chief Officer(s):
Burke Friedrichkeit, President

British Canadian Chamber of Trade & Commerce
#1411, 215 Fort York Blvd., Toronto ON M5V 4A2
Tel: 416-816-9154
www.bcctc.ca
Overview: A medium-sized international organization
Mission: To foster reciprocal trading between Canada & the U.K.
Membership: *Fees:* Schedule available
Chief Officer(s):
Thomas O'Carroll, Vice-President, Central
tocarroll@bcctc.ca
Idalia Obregón, Executive Director
idalia@bcctc.ca

British Columbia & Yukon Chamber of Mines *See* Association for Mineral Exploration British Columbia

British Columbia & Yukon Community Newspapers Association (BCYCNA)
9 West Broadway, Vancouver BC V5Y 1P1
Tel: 604-669-9222; *Fax:* 604-684-4713
Toll-Free: 866-669-9222
info@bccommunitynews.com
www.bccommunitynews.com
www.linkedin.com/company/220705
Overview: A medium-sized local organization founded in 1920 overseen by Canadian Community Newspapers Association
Mission: To encourage excellence in the publishing of community newspapers; To promote the welfare & interests of the community newspaper industry; To improve standards in journalism & newspaper publishing; To facilitate the exchange of information among members; To develop & promote programs & services that benefit members
Member of: Canadian Community Newspapers Association
Finances: *Annual Operating Budget:* $250,000-$500,000
Staff Member(s): 3
Membership: 106; *Fees:* Schedule available; *Committees:* Finance; Marketing/Community classifieds; Membership; CCNA; Awards Gala/Professional Development; Scholarships; Government Relations; Press Council; Independents; Stewardship
Activities: Organizing Ma Murray Awards Gala; Offering scholarships; Providing industry advancement opportunities; *Rents Mailing List:* Yes
Chief Officer(s):
George Affleck, General Manager
gm@bccommunitynews.com
Kerry Slater, Manager, Special Projects
kerry@bccommunitynews.com
Cora Schupp, Manager, Accounting & Community Classifieds, 604-248-4206
accounting@bccommunitynews.com
Awards:
• Ma Murray Gala Awards
Celebrates member newspapers in journalism, photography, & more
Meetings/Conferences:
• British Columbia & Yukon Community Newspapers Association 2018 Annual General Meeting, 2018
Scope: Provincial

British Columbia Aboriginal Child Care Society (ACCS)
#102, 100 Park Royal South, West Vancouver BC V7T 1A2
Tel: 604-913-9128; *Fax:* 604-913-9129
reception@acc-society.bc.ca
www.acc-society.bc.ca
www.facebook.com/aboriginal.childcare
Overview: A small provincial organization
Mission: To develop & provide quality Aboriginal child care services in British Columbia; To support community-based child care services to ensure children develop as First Nations with a distinct language & culture
Affiliation(s): Canadian Child Care Federation
Finances: *Funding Sources:* British Columbia Ministry of Children & Family Development; Membership fees; Donations
Staff Member(s): 7
Membership: *Fees:* $15 student; $25 individuals; $100 organizations & centres; $200 associate members; *Member Profile:* Organizations & centres, such as early childhood, preschool, & out-of-school care programs that serve Aboriginal families throughout British Columbia; Individuals, such as administrators in Aboriginal child care, early childhood educators who are Aboriginal or who work with Aboriginal children, elders, parents of Aboriginal children, & Aboriginal students enrolled in ECE or ECD; Associate members who are interested in the objectives of the society
Activities: Initiating research on Aboriginal child care issues; Providing research reports; Presenting training workshops in various communities; Offering networking activities; *Library:* British Columbia Aboriginal Child Care Society Resource Library
Chief Officer(s):
Mary Teegee, President
Karen Isaac, Executive Director
karen@acc-society.bc.ca
Mary Burgaretta, Advisor, Aboriginal Child Care
mary@acc-society.bc.ca
Kirsten Bevelander, Advisor, Child Care
kirsten@acc-society.bc.ca
Pepper Brewster, Resource Librarian
library@acc-society.bc.ca
Dawn Westlands, Program Coordinator, Singing Frog Aboriginal Head Start Preschool
coordinator@sf.acc-society.bc.ca
Dawn Westlands, Program Coordinator, Eagle's Nest Aboriginal Head Start Preschool
coordinator@en.acc-society.bc.ca
Awards:
• British Columbia Aboriginal Child Care Society Aboriginal Child Care Recognition Award
Presented to an early childhood educator or caregiver for their contribution to the well-being of Aboriginal children in British Columbia *Contact:* Awards Committee, *Fax:* 604-913-9129
Publications:
• Caring For Our Children
Type: Newsletter; *Frequency:* Quarterly; *Editor:* David Wu; *Price:* Free with British Columbia Aboriginal Child Care Societymembership
Profile: Articles & information about the British Columbia Aboriginal Child Care Society's policies, library, training, events, & funding

British Columbia Aboriginal Lands Managers (BCALM)
c/o Shuswap First Nation, PO Box 2847, #3A-492, Arrow Rd., Invermere BC V0A 1K0
Tel: 250-349-5281; *Fax:* 250-342-6301
Overview: A small provincial organization founded in 2012 overseen by National Aboriginal Lands Managers Association
Staff Member(s): 1
Chief Officer(s):
Latrica (Terry) Nicholas, Chair
latricanic@gmail.com

British Columbia Aboriginal Network on Disability Society (BCANDS)
1179 Kosapsum Cres., Victoria BC V9A 7K7
Tel: 250-381-7303; *Fax:* 250-381-7312
Toll-Free: 888-815-5511; *TTY:* 888-815-5511
bcands@bcands.bc.ca
www.bcands.bc.ca
www.linkedin.com/company/3252163
www.facebook.com/386847191382585
twitter.com/bcands1
Overview: A small provincial charitable organization founded in 1991
Mission: To promote the betterment of Aboriginal people with disabilities
Staff Member(s): 9
Membership: *Member Profile:* Aboriginal people with disabilities
Activities: Advocacy; *Speaker Service:* Yes; *Library:* BCANDS Aboriginal Health Resource Centre
Chief Officer(s):
Stephen Lytton, President
Ruby Reid, Secretary-Treasurer
Neil Belanger, Executive Director

British Columbia Alpine Ski Association
#403, 1788 West Broadway, Vancouver BC V6J 1Y1
Tel: 604-678-3070; *Fax:* 604-678-8073
office@bcalpine.com
www.bcalpine.com
Overview: A small local organization
Mission: To promote the sport of alpine skiing in British Columbia

Staff Member(s): 8
Membership: 35 ski clubs; Fees: Schedule available
Chief Officer(s):
Bruce Goldsmid, CEO
bruceg@bcalpine.com
Awards:
• Dave Murray Ski Foundation Bursary
Eligibility: Financial need; athletic ability; sportsmanship; leadership; Amount: $750
• Bob Parsons' Memorial Fund Bursary
Eligibility: Leadership, dedication to sport, financial need, recommendation; Amount: $1000
• Ski Canada Magazine Bursary
Eligibility: K2 level athlete, financial need, potential; Amount: $1000
• RTA Nancy Greene Ski League Bursary
Eligibility: Member of the RTA NGSL program, financial need, sportsmanship Deadline: January 31; Amount: Four $100 bursaries

British Columbia Alternate Education Association (BCAEA)
c/o British columbia Teachers' Federation, #100, 550 West 6th Ave., Vancouver BC V5Z 4P2
Tel: 604-871-2283; Fax: 604-871-2286
Toll-Free: 800-663-9163
www.bctf.ca/bcaea
Overview: A small provincial organization
Mission: To help at-risk youth who are unsuccessful in the main stream educational system; to promote alternative education throughout the province and makes recommendations to the BC Teachers' Federation; to distribute $6500 in bursaries each year.
Affiliation(s): BC Teacher's Federation
Membership: Fees: $15 student/retired; $30 BCTF member; $50 non-BCTF member
Activities: Annual conference, Jan.
Chief Officer(s):
Mike Shaw, President, 250-768-3253, Fax: 778-476-5939
mike.shaw@telus.net
Awards:
• Student Bursary
Eligibility: Graduate student continuing at post-secondary institution Deadline: March 15; Amount: Five $500 awards
• Student Achievement Award
Eligibility: Student who shows responsibility, motivation, mastery skills Deadline: March 15; Amount: Fifteen $100 awards
• Kathi Hughes Innovative Programming Award
Eligibility: Teacher who shares unique program at Annual Conference Deadline: March 15; Amount: $500

British Columbia Amateur Bodybuilding Association (BCABBA)
#325, 1865 Dilworth Dr., Kelowna BC V1Y 9T1
support@bcabba.org
www.bcabba.org
www.facebook.com/BCAmateurBodybuildingAssoc
www.youtube.com/channel/UCVspmcLC0klJ9ng8bnA-YnA
Overview: A small provincial organization overseen by Canadian Bodybuilding Federation
Mission: To be the provincial governing body for the sport of amateur bodybuilding in British Columbia
Member of: Canadian Bodybuilding Federation; International Federation of Bodybuilding
Membership: Fees: $75 competitive
Chief Officer(s):
Sandra Wickham, President
Tamara Knight, Coordinator, Membership
tzonefitness@telus.net

British Columbia Amateur Boxing Association See Boxing BC Association

British Columbia Amateur Hockey Association (BCAHA) / Association de hockey amateur de la Colombie-Britannique
6671 Oldfield Rd., Saanichton BC V8M 2A1
Tel: 250-652-2978; Fax: 250-652-4536
info@bchockey.net
www.bchockey.net
www.facebook.com/BCHockeySource
twitter.com/BCHockey_Source
www.instagram.com/bchockeysource;
www.youtube.com/user/BCHockeySource
Also Known As: BC Hockey
Overview: A medium-sized provincial organization founded in 1919 overseen by Hockey Canada
Mission: To foster, improve & perpetuate amateur hockey in BC
Member of: Hockey Canada
Finances: Annual Operating Budget: $500,000-$1.5 Million
Staff Member(s): 7; 2000 volunteer(s)
Membership: 60,000 individual + 4,500 referees; Fees: Schedule available; Member Profile: Amateur hockey teams/leagues/associations; referees' organizations
Chief Officer(s):
Bill Ennos, Director, Programs
bennos@bchockey.net

British Columbia Amateur Softball Association (BCASA)
#201, 8889 Walnut Grove Dr., Langley BC V1M 2N7
Tel: 604-371-0302; Fax: 604-371-0344
Other Communication: Alt. E-mail: admin@softball.bc.ca
info@softball.bc.ca
www.softball.bc.ca
www.facebook.com/softball.bc
Also Known As: Softball BC
Overview: A medium-sized provincial organization overseen by Canadian Amateur Softball Association
Mission: To promote, govern & build the sport of Softball in British Columbia
Member of: Canadian Amateur Softball Association
Membership: Fees: Schedule available; Member Profile: Softball players, coaches, umpires
Chief Officer(s):
Rick Benson, Chief Operating Officer
rbenson@softball.bc.ca
Jeana Boyd, Coordinator, Programs
programcoordinator@softball.bc.ca

British Columbia Amateur Wrestling Association See British Columbia Wrestling Association

British Columbia Angus Association
#15, 3805 Patten Dr., Armstrong BC V0E 1B2
Tel: 250-249-5469; Fax: 250-249-5469
www.bcangus.ca
Overview: A small provincial organization
Member of: Canadian Angus Association
Affiliation(s): B.C. Junior Angus Association
Membership: 253; Fees: $50 regular; $7.50 junior
Chief Officer(s):
Tom de Waal, President
tom@harvestholsteins.com
Lorraine Sanford, National Director
alsanford@hotmail.com

British Columbia Apartment Owners & Managers Association (BCAOMA)
#203, 1847 West Broadway, Vancouver BC V6J 1Y6
Tel: 604-733-9440; Fax: 604-733-9420
Toll-Free: 877-700-9440
questions@bcaoma.com
www.bcapartmentowners.com
www.facebook.com/BCAOMA
twitter.com/BCAOMA
pinterest.com/bcaoma
Previous Name: Greater Vancouver Apartment Owners Association
Overview: A medium-sized provincial organization founded in 1964
Mission: To promote & sustain with a unified voice, residential rental housing in the province of British Columbia
Finances: Funding Sources: Membership fees
Staff Member(s): 6
Membership: 1,200; Fees: Schedule available; Member Profile: Must own or manage residential rental property in BC
Activities: Education; practical advice & assistance; employee benefits program; recommended trades & suppliers; tenancy agreements/applications & other forms & stationery; garbage disposal; advertising vacancies; credit checks
Chief Officer(s):
Valerie MacLean, CEO
Awards:
• Building Manager Graduate Scholarship
Awarded each year to the top Building Manager graduate from the Building Manager Certificate Program offered by the Vancouver Community College of Continuing Education

British Columbia Archery Association (BCAA)
PO Box 64727, Sunwood Square, Port Coquitlam BC V3B 0H1
Tel: 250-992-5586
www.archeryassociation.bc.ca
www.facebook.com/BCAA.Archery
Overview: A small provincial organization overseen by Archery Canada Tir à l'Arc
Mission: To promote & support the sport of archery in British Columbia
Member of: Archery Canada Tir à l'Arc; Sport BC
Affiliation(s): World Archery Federation
Finances: Funding Sources: Ministry of Community, Sport & Cultural Development; Sport BC
Membership: Fees: $70 adult; $60 youth; $150 family; $150 club
Activities: Tournaments; Newsletters; Information on certification
Chief Officer(s):
Ron Ostermeier, President, 778-990-2724
president@archeryassociation.bc.ca
Sonia Schina, Executive Director Ext. 7782412724
execdirector@archeryassociation.bc.ca
Publications:
• To The Point [a publication of the British Columbia Archery Association]
Type: Newsletter; Frequency: monthly; Price: Free download
Profile: Competetion results; Information on program offerings, meetings and internal advertisments

British Columbia Art Teachers' Association (BCATA)
c/o B.C. Teachers' Federation, #100, 550 West 6th Ave., Vancouver BC V5Z 4P2
Tel: 250-248-4662; Fax: 250-248-4628
Toll-Free: 800-663-9163
psac41@bctf.ca
bcata.ca
twitter.com/BCArtTeachers
Also Known As: BC Art Teachers' Association
Overview: A small provincial organization
Mission: To support & promote quality art education for all British Columbia students; to provide a network for art educators at the Primary, Intermediate & Graduation levels, & provides opportunities for professional development & collaboration.
Affiliation(s): B.C. Teachers' Federation; Canadian Society for Education through Art (CSEA); National Art Education Association (NAEA)
Membership: Fees: $57.75 non-BCTF members; $35 BCTF member; $20 BCTF retired member/student
Chief Officer(s):
Regan Rasmussen, Co-President, 250-478-5548, Fax: 250-472-2349
rrasmussen@shaw.ca
Eileen Ryan, Co-President, 604-576-4138
ryan_e@surreyschools.ca
Publications:
• BCATA Journal for Art Teachers
Type: journal; Price: $10 members; $15 non-members
Profile: Members share their experiences in art education.
• Visually Speaking
Type: newsletter

British Columbia Art Therapy Association (BCATA)
#101, 1001 West Broadway, Dept. 123, Vancouver BC V6H 4E4
Tel: 604-878-6393
Other Communication: admin@bcarttherapy.com
info@bcarttherapy.com
www.bcarttherapy.com
Overview: A small provincial organization founded in 1978
Mission: To foster the professional development of art therapy in British Columbia; To govern the standards & practice of the profession of art therapy & its practitioners; To uphold the British Columbia Art Therapy Association Code of Ethics
Membership: Fees: $20 students; $40 retired members; $60 associate members; $115 professional & registered members; Member Profile: Any person who is interested in the therapeutic use of art; Committees: Membership; Registration
Activities: Offering professional registration for art therapists in British Columbia; Hosting professional development programs; Promoting research
Chief Officer(s):
Michelle Oucharek-Deo, President
president@bcarttherapy.com
Debora Broadhurst, Vice-President
vp@bcarttherapy.com
Carolyn Simpson, Corresponding Secretary
corresponding@bcarttherapy.com
Charlotte Spafford, Treasurer
treasurer@bcarttherapy.com
Morgan Reinsbakken, Chair, Membership
membership@bcarttherapy.com

Publications:
- BCATA [British Columbia Art Therapy Association] Newsletter

Type: Newsletter; *Frequency:* Quarterly; *Editor:* Geri Nolan Hilfiker
Profile: Information about professional development workshops, book reviews, updates about the association, & regional news for art therapists in British Columbia & western Canada

British Columbia Association for Behaviour Analysis (BC-ABA)
PO Box 64743, Stn. Sunwood Square, Coquitlam BC V3B 6S0
info@bc-aba.org
bc-aba.org
Overview: A small provincial organization
Membership: Fees: $25 student; $30 full

British Columbia Association for Charitable Gaming
#401, 151 - 10090 152nd St., Surrey BC V2R 8X8
Tel: 604-568-8649
Toll-Free: 888-672-2224
www.bcacg.com
www.facebook.com/167363223281218
twitter.com/bcacg
Overview: A large provincial organization founded in 1997
Mission: To represent charities' interests in British Columbia by addressing the concerns of charities with licensing & access to gaming revenue
Chief Officer(s):
David Sheach, Executive Director
executivedirector@bcacg.com
Meetings/Conferences:
- BC Association for Charitable Gaming 2018 Symposium, 2018, BC

Scope: Provincial

British Columbia Association for Community Living; British Columbians for Mentally Handicapped People *See* Inclusion BC

British Columbia Association for Marriage & Family Therapy (BCAMFT)
PO Box 3958, Stn. Main, 349 West Georgia St., Vancouver BC V6B 3Z4
Tel: 604-687-6131
info@bcamft.bc.ca
www.bcamft.bc.ca
www.facebook.com/BCAMFT
Overview: A small provincial organization
Mission: To support family well-being through preventative programs & social actions, promotes education & training for therapists & provides a province-wide, professional network.
Member of: American Association for Marriage & Family Therapy
Finances: *Funding Sources:* Membership dues
Membership: Fees: $291 clinical/independent; $175 associate/pre-clinical; $206 affiliate; $67 student
Chief Officer(s):
Janey Komm, President
janey.cunningham@gmail.com

British Columbia Association for Regenerative Agriculture (BCARA)
PO Box 95004, Stn. Kingsgate, Vancouver BC V5T 2T8
Tel: 604-441-8215
bcara.admin@gmail.com
www.certifiedorganic.bc.ca/cb/bcara.php
www.facebook.com/BCARA.Cert
Overview: A small provincial organization
Mission: To operate a program certifying organic farms & products
Affiliation(s): Certified Organic Associations of BC
Membership: 43; *Committees:* Certification
Chief Officer(s):
Gwen Huber, Administrator

British Columbia Association of Aboriginal Friendship Centres (BCAAFC)
551 Chatham St., Victoria BC V8T 1E1
Tel: 250-388-5522; Fax: 250-388-5502
Toll-Free: 800-990-2432
frontdesk@bcaafc.com
www.bcaafc.com
www.facebook.com/BCAAFC
twitter.com/bcaafc
Overview: A medium-sized provincial organization overseen by National Association of Friendship Centres
Mission: To promote the betterment of Aboriginal Friendship Centres in British Columbia by acting as a unifying body for the Centres; To establish & maintain communications between Aboriginal Friendship Centres, other associations, & government
Staff Member(s): 20
Membership: 25 friendship centres; *Member Profile:* Friendship Centres in British Columbia
Activities: Advising government on programs & services to assist Aboriginal Friendship Centres
Chief Officer(s):
Paul Lacerte, Executive Director
Awards:
- First Citizens Fund Student Bursary

Eligibility: Sponsored & non-sponsored students registered full-time in a minimum two-year academic program at a recognized post-secondary institution in BC; eligible applicants must be of Aboriginal ancestry and maintain a minumum 2.5 GPA; *Amount:* $700 per semester for non-sponsored students; $350 per semester for sponsored students
- Post-Secondary Student Support Program

Eligibility: NWT or Nunavut Inuit students who have been living in BC for 12 consecutive months; BC registered members who do not have a Band membership/affiliation; status Indian students who are affiliated with a BC First Nation but do not have a Band membership
Meetings/Conferences:
- Aboriginal Youth 2018 16th Annual Gathering Our Voices Conference, March, 2018, Richmond, BC

Scope: Provincial
Description: Hosted by the British Columbia Association of Aboriginal Friendship Centres & their Provincial Aboriginal Youth Council
Contact Information: Manager, Events: Nadine Collison, E-mail: ncollison@bcaafc.com, Phone: 250-388-5522, ext. 210
Publications:
- BC Association of Aboriginal Friendship Centres Annual Report

Type: Report; *Frequency:* Annually

British Columbia Association of Agricultural Fairs & Exhibitions (BCAAFE)
#20, 16655 - 64th Ave., Surrey BC V3S 3V1
Tel: 778-574-4082
www.bcfairs.ca
www.facebook.com/BCFairs
twitter.com/BCFairs
Also Known As: BC Fairs
Previous Name: The Provincial Agricultural Fairs Association
Overview: A small provincial organization founded in 1910
Mission: To celebrate the importance of agriculture in British Columbia; To represent agricultural fairs, exhibitions, & related events throughout British Columbia; To work with other organizations to raise awareness of British Columbia agriculture
Member of: Canadian Association of Fairs & Exhibitions; International Association of Fairs & Expositions; Volunteer Canada
Finances: *Annual Operating Budget:* $250,000-$500,000; *Funding Sources:* Membership fees; Fundraising; Government grants; Advertising revenues
Staff Member(s): 2; 20 volunteer(s)
Membership: 86; *Fees:* $100-$1,100; *Committees:* By-Laws & Policies; Communications; Conference Planning; Government Relations; Membership Development; Provincial Awards
Activities: Educating the public about the importance of agriculture; Offering resources & services to agricultural exhibitions & fairs; Providing networking & educational opportunities; Raising awareness of agricultural fairs, exhibitions & festivals; *Speaker Service:* Yes; *Library:* Resource Library; Open to public
Chief Officer(s):
Tom Harter, President
Janine Saw, Executive Director
jbsaw@bcfairs.ca
Amanda Schaffner, Office Assistant
bcfairsassistant@gmail.com
Awards:
- BC Fairs Scholarship

Eligibility: Youth entering post-secondary education *Deadline:* May; *Amount:* $2,000
Meetings/Conferences:
- 108th BC Fairs Conference, October, 2018, Hotel Grand Pacific, Victoria, BC

Scope: Provincial
Publications:
- BC Fairs LiveWire

Type: Newsletter; *Frequency:* Quarterly; *Accepts Advertising*
Profile: Developments on the agricultural fair circuit across British Columbia
- Guide to BC's Fairs & Exhibitions

Type: Brochure; *Editor:* Janine Saw
Profile: Lists & promotes the annual fairs, exhibitions & festivals in British Columbia

British Columbia Association of Broadcasters (BCAB)
BC
www.bcab.ca
www.facebook.com/126523200745913
twitter.com/bcabinfo
Overview: A medium-sized provincial organization
Mission: To unify the broadcasting community in British Columbia
Membership: *Member Profile:* Private broadcasters in radio & television; associate members in the advertising & business communities
Activities: Community programs; annual conference
Chief Officer(s):
James Stewart, President
james.stuart@bellmedia.ca
Awards:
- Humanitarian Award

Meetings/Conferences:
- BC Association of Broadcasters 71st Annual Conference, May, 2018, Manteo Resort, Kelowna, BC

Scope: Provincial

British Columbia Association of Clinical Counsellors (BCACC)
#14, 2544 Dunlevy St., Victoria BC V8R 5Z2
Tel: 250-595-4448; Fax: 250-595-2926
Toll-Free: 800-909-6303
hoffice@bc-counsellors.org
www.bc-counsellors.org
linkedin.com/company/bc-association-of-clinical-counsellors
www.facebook.com/196801843685705
twitter.com/bccounsellors
Overview: A small provincial organization founded in 1988
Mission: To promote and regulate the practice of Registered Clincial Counsellors in BC and beyond
Membership: Fees: $436 active; $218 student; *Member Profile:* Registered Clinical Counsellors
Activities: *Rents Mailing List:* Yes; *Library:* Not open to public
Publications:
- Insights

Editor: Diane Payette
Profile: Magazine, three issues published annually

British Columbia Association of Family Resource Programs
#332, 505-8840 - 210th St., Langley BC V1M 2Y2
Tel: 778-590-0045
info@frpbc.ca
www.frpbc.ca
www.facebook.com/frpbc
twitter.com/frpbc
www.instagram.com/frpbc
Also Known As: FRP-BC
Overview: A small provincial organization founded in 1989
Mission: To raise awareness of the importance of community-based Family Resources Programs
Member of: Canadian Association of Family Resource Programs (FRP Canada)
Finances: *Annual Operating Budget:* $100,000-$250,000
Staff Member(s): 3
Membership: 150
Chief Officer(s):
Sherry Sinclair, Executive Director
executivedirector@frpbc.ca
Nicky Logins, Vice-President
nlogins@sfrs.ca
Ramsay Malange, Research Director
researcher@frpbc.ca

British Columbia Association of Healthcare Auxiliaries
#200, 1333 West Broadway, Vancouver BC V6H 4C6
Tel: 236-999-4752
info@bchealthcareaux.org
www.bchealthcareaux.org
Overview: A medium-sized provincial organization founded in 1945
Mission: To promote education & high standards of performance in order to ensure success for member auxiliaries

Membership: 80
Chief Officer(s):
Judith McBride, Executive Director

British Columbia Association of Insolvency & Restructuring Professionals (BCAIRP)
c/o Grant Thornton Alger Inc., #1600, 333 Seymour St., Vancouver BC V6B 0A4
Tel: 604-687-2711; Fax: 604-685-6569
www.bcairp.ca
Previous Name: British Columbia Insolvency Practitioners Association
Overview: A small provincial organization founded in 1979 overseen by Canadian Association of Insolvency & Restructuring Professionals
Member of: Canadian Association of Insolvency & Restructuring Professionals
Affiliation(s): Canadian Institute of Chartered Accountants
Membership: Member Profile: Licensed trustees in bankruptcy
Activities: Internships: Yes; Speaker Service: Yes
Chief Officer(s):
Michelle Madrigga, President
michelle.madrigga@ca.gt.com

British Columbia Association of Kinesiologists (BCAK)
#102, 211 Columbia St., Vancouver BC V6A 2R5
Tel: 604-601-5100; Fax: 604-305-0424
office@bcak.bc.ca
www.bcak.bc.ca
www.linkedin.com/groups/3812454
www.facebook.com/BC.Association.of.Kinesiologists
twitter.com/BCKinesiology
Overview: A small provincial organization founded in 1991
Mission: To uphold the standards of the profession of kinesiology; To promote the applications of kinesiology to other professionals & to the community; To assist in professional development; To encourage the exchange of ideas
Finances: Funding Sources: Membership dues & services
Membership: Fees: $50 student & academic; $175 associate; $175 non-practicing member; $300 practicing member; Member Profile: Registered kinesiologists; Students in kinesiology programs; Committees: Membership
Chief Officer(s):
Edward Reynolds, Executive Director

British Columbia Association of Laboratory Physicians (BCALP)
BC
www.bcalp.ca
Overview: A small provincial organization
Chief Officer(s):
Christopher Sherlock, President, 604-806-8422
csherloc@mail.ubc.ca

British Columbia Association of Mathematics Teachers (BCAMT)
c/o British Columbia Teachers' Federation, #100, 550 West 6th Ave., Vancouver BC V5Z 4P2
Tel: 604-871-2283
Toll-Free: 800-663-9163
www.bcamt.ca
Overview: A small provincial organization
Member of: BC Teachers' Federation
Membership: Fees: $40 BCTF members; $20 students & retired teachers; $58.50 non-BCTF members
Chief Officer(s):
Ron Coleborn, President
ron.coleborn@sd41.bc.ca
Michael Pruner, Vice-President
mpruner@nvsd44.bc.ca
Debbie Loo, Treasurer
debbie.loo@sd41.bc.ca
Meetings/Conferences:
• British Columbia Association of Mathematics Teachers 2018 New Teachers' Conference, January, 2018, Surrey, BC
Scope: Provincial

British Columbia Association of Medical Radiation Technologists (BCAMRT)
Central Office, #102, 211 Columbia St., Vancouver BC V6A 2R5
Tel: 604-682-8171; Fax: 604-305-0424
Toll-Free: 800-990-7090
office@bcamrt.bc.ca
www.bcamrt.bc.ca
Overview: A medium-sized provincial organization founded in 1951 overseen by Canadian Association of Medical Radiation Technologists
Mission: To manage the professional affairs of medical radiation technologists in British Columbia; To advocate for the profession of medical radiation technology across the province
Membership: 2,000; Member Profile: Medical radiation technologists throughout British Columbia; Committees: Advocacy; Annual General Conference; Awards; Commencement; Education Advisory; Finance; Professional Development; Student Secretary; Website & Technology
Activities: Upholding the Canadian Association of Medical Radiation Technologists code of ethics; Communicating with stakeholders; Offering information about radiography, nuclear medicine, magnetic resonance imaging, & radiation therapy; Providing continuing education programs
Chief Officer(s):
Jacqueline Wallace, President
Awards:
• Young Professional Award
• Member Recognition Awards
• Research Award
• Innovative Leadership Award
• President's Award
• Excellence in Teaching Award
• Paragon Award
Presented annually by Bracco Diagnostics Inc. to the BC student who achieves the highest marks in the province in the CAMRT Certification Examination
Meetings/Conferences:
• BC Association of Medical Radiation Technologists 2018 Annual General Conference, 2018
Scope: Provincial
Description: Speakers present on a variety of educational topics as well as tips for the workplace and health and wellness.

British Columbia Association of People Who Stutter (BCAPS)
8582 Flowering Pl., Burnaby BC V5A 4B4
Fax: 888-301-2227
Toll-Free: 888-301-2227
info@bcaps.ca
www.bcaps.ca
www.facebook.com/bcaps123
twitter.com/BCAPS1
Overview: A small provincial organization
Mission: To encourage & assist local support groups for people who stutter
Membership: Fees: $10 individual; $15 family
Chief Officer(s):
Kim Block, President
Publications:
• B.C. Blockbuster
Type: Newsletter; Frequency: Quarterly

British Columbia Association of Professionals with Disabilities
714 Warder Place, Victoria BC V9A 7H6
Tel: 250-361-9697
info@bcprofessionals.org
www.bcprofessionals.org
Overview: A small provincial organization founded in 2003
Mission: Provincially incorporated non-profit association dedicated to maximizing the inclusion, job retention, and advancement of current and future professionals with disabilities
Affiliation(s): Canadian Association of Professionals with Disabilities

British Columbia Association of School Business Officials (BCASBO)
#208, 1118 Homer St., Vancouver BC V6B 6L5
Tel: 604-687-0595; Fax: 604-687-8118
executivedirector@bcasbo.ca
www.bcasbo.ca
Previous Name: British Columbia School District Secretary-Treasurers' Association
Overview: A small provincial organization
Mission: To uphold professional standards of ethics, competence, & leadership in British Columbia's school district corporate & business administration
Membership: Fees: $1000 first member from a school district; $700 second & subsequent members from a school district; Member Profile: British Columbia business officials who work in school districts, such as secretary-treasurers, assistant secretary-treasurers, accountants, payroll supervisors, comptrollers, benefits supervisors, human resources managers, & information systems managers; Committees: Executive; Annual General Meeting; Strategic Planning; Accounting Advisory; BCeSIS Steering; Audit Program Advisory; Carbon Neutral; Capital Advisory; Education Advisory; Education Resource Acquisition; Leadership Development; Membership; Payroll & Benefits Advisory; PLNet Steering; School District Telecommunications Advisory; Shared Practice Working; Technical Review; Transportation; Web Site Content Management; Work Force Planning Steering
Activities: Providing professional development opportunities; Facilitating the exchange of ideas & concerns; Liaising with the province's Ministry of Education
Chief Officer(s):
Greg Frank, President, 604-296-6900 Ext. 661004, Fax: 604-296-6910
president@bcasbo.ca
Lyle Boyce, Executive Director, 778-420-4210, Fax: 604-687-8118
executivedirector@bcasbo.ca
Allan Reed, Secretary-Treasurer, 250-561-6800, Fax: 250-561-6889
SecretaryTreasurer@bcasbo.ca
Meetings/Conferences:
• 2018 BC Association of School Business Officials Annual General Meeting, May, 2018, Penticton, BC
Scope: Provincial
Publications:
• School Business: Newsletter of the British Columbia Association of School Business Officials
Type: Newsletter; Editor: Alba Urban
Profile: BCASBO meeting minutes, upcoming events, reports, member news, & articles

British Columbia Association of School Psychologists (BCASP)
c/o Barbara Nichols, 7715 Loedel Cres., Prince George BC V2N 0A5
executives@bcasp.ca
www.bcasp.ca
Overview: A small provincial organization
Mission: To represent the interests of school psychologists and to further the standards of school psychology practice in order to promote effective service to all students and their families.
Chief Officer(s):
Douglas Agar, President
president@bcasp.ca
Meetings/Conferences:
• BC Association of School Psychologists Conference 2018, 2018, BC
Scope: Provincial

British Columbia Association of Social Workers (BCASW) / Association des travailleurs sociaux de la Colombie-Britannique
#402, 1755 West Broadway, Vancouver BC V6J 4S5
Tel: 604-730-9111; Fax: 604-730-9112
Toll-Free: 800-665-4747
bcasw@bcasw.org
www.bcasw.org
Overview: A medium-sized provincial organization founded in 1956
Mission: Represents member concerns regarding the practice of social work in BC, professional education & regulation.
Member of: Canadian Association of Social Workers
Affiliation(s): End Legislated Poverty; End the Arms Race Coalition; BC Human Rights Coalition
Finances: Annual Operating Budget: $100,000-$250,000; Funding Sources: Membership fees
Membership: 800; Fees: Schedule available; Committees: Executive; Health Practice Enhancement; Health Social Work Advocacy; Multiculturalism & Antiracism; Perspectives
Activities: Speaker Service: Yes
Chief Officer(s):
Dianne Heath, Executive Director
dheath@bcasw.org
Meetings/Conferences:
• BC Association of Social Workers Annual General Meeting 2018, 2018, BC
Scope: Provincial
Publications:
• Perspectives [a publication of the British Columbia Association of Social Workers]
Type: Magazine

British Columbia Association of Specialized Victim Assistance & Counselling Programs See Ending Violence Association of British Columbia

British Columbia Association of Speech-Language Pathologists & Audiologists (BCASLPA)
#402, 1755 Broadway West, Vancouver BC V6J 4S5
Tel: 604-420-2222; *Fax:* 604-736-5606
Toll-Free: 877-222-7572
contact@bcaslpa.ca
www.bcaslpa.ca
www.linkedin.com/groups/4281068/profile
www.facebook.com/bcaslpa
twitter.com/bcaslpa
Overview: A small provincial charitable organization founded in 1957
Mission: To connect people with language, swallowing & hearing disorders with professionals in BC; To represent speech & hearing professionals; To provide information about disorders & treatments
Member of: Pan-Canadian Alliance of Speech-Language Pathology and Audiology Associations
Affiliation(s): Canadian Association of Speech Language Pathologists & Audiologists
Finances: *Annual Operating Budget:* $100,000-$250,000
Staff Member(s): 2; 25 volunteer(s)
Membership: 800; *Fees:* Schedule available; *Committees:* Government Affairs; School Affairs; Audiology; Speech Language Pathology; Private Practice; Continuing Education
Activities: Continuing education; research; standards of practice; *Awareness Events:* Speech & Hearing Month, May; *Internships:* Yes; *Speaker Service:* Yes; *Library:* by appointment
Chief Officer(s):
Kate Chase, President
kate.chase@yahoo.ca
Meetings/Conferences:
• BC Association of Speech/Language Pathologists & Audiologists 2018 Conference, 2018, BC
Scope: Provincial
Publications:
• Vibrations [a publication of the British Columbia Association of Speech-Language Pathologists & Audiologists]
Editor: Marianne Bullied

British Columbia Association of Teachers of Modern Languages (BCATML)
c/o BC Teachers' Federation, #100, 550 West 6th Ave., Vancouver BC V5Z 4P2
Tel: 604-871-2283; *Fax:* 604-871-2286
psac51@bctf.ca
www.bcatml.org
www.facebook.com/bcatml
twitter.com/bcatml
Overview: A small provincial organization
Mission: To promote & advance the teaching of modern languages throughout BC.
Member of: BC Teachers' Federation
Affiliation(s): Canadian Assoc. of Second Language Teachers
Membership: *Fees:* $40 BCTF member; $63 non BCTF member/institution; $15 retired teacher/student
Activities: annual conference
Chief Officer(s):
Rome Lavrencic, President
rlavrenc@sd40.bc.ca
Meetings/Conferences:
• BC Association of Teachers of Modern Languages 2018 Conference, 2018, BC
Scope: Provincial

British Columbia Association of the Appraisal Institute of Canada See The Appraisal Institute of Canada - British Columbia

British Columbia Athletics
#2001, 3713 Kensington Ave., B. Oslo Landing, Burnaby BC V5B 0A7
Tel: 604-333-3550; *Fax:* 604-333-3551
bcathletics@bcathletics.org
www.bcathletics.org
www.facebook.com/BCAthletics1
twitter.com/bc_athletics
Also Known As: BC Amateur Athletics Association
Previous Name: BC Track & Field Association
Overview: A medium-sized provincial licensing organization overseen by Athletics Canada
Mission: To promote, encourage & develop excellence by creating opportunities in athletics (track & field, road-running & cross-country running)
Member of: Athletics Canada; Sport BC
Staff Member(s): 9
Membership: *Fees:* Schedule available; *Committees:* Track & Field; Road Running; Cross Country; Masters; Junior Development; Masters
Activities: *Internships:* Yes; *Speaker Service:* Yes; *Rents Mailing List:* Yes; *Library:* Open to public
Chief Officer(s):
Brian McCalder, President & CEO
brian.mccalder@bcathletics.org

British Columbia Aviation Council (BCAC)
PO Box 31040, RPO Thunderbird, Langley BC V1M 0A9
Tel: 604-278-9330; *Fax:* 888-833-1507
info@bcaviationcouncil.org
www.bcaviationcouncil.org
twitter.com/bcac1938
www.flickr.com/photos/63124160@N08
Also Known As: BC Aviation Council
Overview: A small provincial organization founded in 1938
Mission: A member-driven organization that represents and promotes the shared interests of the aviation community; Aims to promote, stimulate & encourage the development, growth & advancement of aviation and aerospace in British Columbia
Affiliation(s): Air Cadet League of Canada, BC Provincial Committee; ATAC; BCGA; CCAA; COPA; CPPC; Hope Air; Manitoba Aviation Council; NATA; PNAA; Quarter Century in Aviation Club; Saskatchewan Aviation Council; Unmanned Systems Canada; Vancouver Board of Trade
Finances: *Funding Sources:* Membership fees
Membership: *Committees:* Airport; Air Operators; Awards/Scholarships; Communications; Endowment; Governance; Membership; Silve Wings Awards/Events; Youth Engagement
Chief Officer(s):
Candace McKibbon, Executive Director
cmckibbon@bcaviationcouncil.org
Donna Farquar, Executive Administrator
Awards:
• Aviation Entrepreneur of the Year, BCAC Industy Awards
Awarded annually to a leading air industry individual or organization that advances aviation in BC through innovative product development, new business ventures or cost saving initiatives*Location:* British Columbia *Deadline:* May 31
• William Templeton Award, BCAC Industy Awards
Awarded annually for outstanding initiative and achievment in the successful development of a community airport, regional airport, heliport or floatplane landing*Location:* British Columbia *Deadline:* May 31
• BCAC Environmental Award, BCAC Industy Awards
Awarded annually within the aviation community for an outstanding environmental initiative, program or accomplishment in one of more areas of: protection, rejuvenation, & awareness*Location:* British Columbia *Deadline:* May 31
• Robert S. Day Trophy, BCAC Industy Awards
Awarded annually in recognition of outstanding excellence, contribution & leadership for the promotion and development of aviation in BC *Eligibility:* An individual or organization based in BC with a recognizable contribution to the province*Location:* British Columbia *Deadline:* May 31
• Back & Bevington Air Safety Award, BCAC Industy Awards
Awarded annually for the mose significant contribution to Air Safety in BC*Location:* British Columbia *Deadline:* May 31
• Lifetime Achievement Award, BCAC Industy Awards
Awarded annually in recognition of outstanding leadership, promotion& consistent contribution to the continuous development of aviation in BC*Location:* British Columbia *Deadline:* May 31
• Pilot Training Scholarships
Anderson Family Flight Training ($5000); Commercial Pilot Scholarships: Al Michaud Memorial Scholarship ($5000), Conair Group Commerical Aviation Training Scholarship ($3000), Michelle Ward Memorial Scholarship ($2000); Commercial Float Plane Scholarship: Harbour Air Advanced Float Plane Endorsement Scholarship; Private Pilot: Anne & Rudi Bauer Memorial Scholarship ($1000); Commericial/Private Pilot/AME/Airport Ops - Female Scholarship: Mary Swain Memorial Aviation Training Scholarship ($1000); BC Aviation Council Flight Instructor Training Scholarship ($1000)*Location:* British Columbia *Deadline:* May 31
• Aviation Maintenance Engineering (AME) Scholarship
Barry & Jim Aviation Maintenance Graduate Scholarship ($3000) *Eligibility:* Recent graduate from an AME program in BC*Location:* British Columbia *Deadline:* May 31; *Amount:* $3000
• Airport Operations & Management Scholarships
BCAC Airports Committee Airport Operations/Management Training Scholarships ($2000); William Templeton Airport Operations Management Training Scholarship ($1000)*Location:* British Columbia *Deadline:* May 31
• General Scholarships
Alexander Holburn Beaudin + Lang, Ernie Alexander Memorial Scholarship ($2000); BC Aviation Council "Career" Training Scholarship ($1000)*Location:* British Columbia *Deadline:* May 31
Publications:
• The Frequent Flyer
Type: E-Newsletter; *Frequency:* monthly; *Number of Pages:* 10
Profile: Information relevant to members of the British Columbia aviation community

British Columbia Bailiffs Association (BCBA)
c/o Accurate Effective Bailiffs, 6139 Trapp Ave., Burnaby BC V3N 2V3
Tel: 604-526-3737
Overview: A small provincial organization
Mission: To assist members to develop their professional expertise
Membership: 1-99; *Member Profile:* British Columbia recovery & liquidation experts

British Columbia Ball Hockey Association (BCBHA)
9107 Norum Rd., Delta BC V4C 3H9
Tel: 604-998-1410
info@bcbha.com
www.bcbha.com
www.facebook.com/BCBallHockey
twitter.com/_BCBallHockey
Overview: A small provincial organization founded in 1980
Mission: To govern the sport of ball hockey in British Columbia; To establish bylaws & regulations, in order to ensure a safe & fun activity; To uphold the rules& regulations of ball hockey
Affiliation(s): Canadian Ball Hockey Association
Finances: *Funding Sources:* Sponsorships
Membership: *Fees:* Schedule available; *Member Profile:* Ball hockey leagues in British Columbia which follow the rules & regulations of the British Columbia Ball Hockey Association & the Canadian Ball Hockey Association
Activities: Promoting ball hockey in British Columbia; Assisting in the establishment of ball hockey leagues in the province; Disseminating rulebooks; Organizing provincial championships; Providing certification programs for officials; Resolving disputes
Chief Officer(s):
Mike Schweighardt, President, 604-998-1400 Ext. 201
president@bcbha.com
Darsh Grewall, Technical Director, 604-998-1400 Ext. 206
technical@bcbha.com

British Columbia Bed & Breakfast Innkeepers Guild
#305, 1845 Bellevue Ave., North Vancouver BC V7V 1B2
info@bcinnkeepers.com
www.bcsbestbnbs.com
www.facebook.com/BCBandBInnkeepersGuild
pinterest.com/bcinnkeepers
Previous Name: Western Canada B&B Innkeepers Association
Overview: A medium-sized provincial licensing organization founded in 1993
Mission: To increase the awareness of an optional accommodation for visitors & business travellers
Membership: *Fees:* Schedule available; *Member Profile:* Bed & Breakfast Innkeepers in British Columbia; *Committees:* Membership; Website; Brochure; Moyra Turner Award; Policy & Procedures; Communications; Standards & Ethics
Chief Officer(s):
Dennis Cyr, Secretary/Treasurer

British Columbia Bee Breeders' Association (BCBBA)
c/o Brenda Jager, 948 Harrison Way, Gabriola BC V0R 1X2
Tel: 250-755-5834
dencor.ca/BCBBA
Overview: A small provincial organization founded in 1987
Mission: Promoting and encouraging bee breeding in British Columbia.
Chief Officer(s):
Barry Denluck, President, 250-900-5159
President@BCBeeBreeders.ca
Axel Krause, Secretary, 250-608-7397
secretary@BCBeeBreeders.ca

British Columbia Bison Association
c/o Bill Bouffioux, President, RR#1, Site 1, Comp 1, Fort St. John BC V1J 4M6

Canadian Associations / British Columbia Blind Sports & Recreation Association (BCBSRA)

Tel: 250-785-4183
xybison@pris.ca
www.bcbuffalo.ca
Previous Name: British Columbia Interior Bison Association
Overview: A small provincial organization
Mission: To promote the bison industry as a economically & environmentally sustainable business
Member of: Canadian Bison Association
Membership: 60; *Fees:* $150
Chief Officer(s):
Bill Bouffioux, President
Isobel Vere, Secretary
ttonka@ttonka.ca

British Columbia Blind Sports & Recreation Association (BCBSRA)
#170, 5055 Joyce St., Vancouver BC V5R 6B2
Tel: 604-325-8638; *Fax:* 604-325-1638
Toll-Free: 877-604-8638
info@bcblindsports.bc.ca
www.bcblindsports.bc.ca
www.facebook.com/BCBlindSports
twitter.com/bc_blind
Also Known As: BC Blind Sports
Overview: A medium-sized provincial charitable organization founded in 1975 overseen by Canadian Blind Sports Association Inc.
Mission: To provide sports, physical recreation & fitness activities & programs for persons of all ages who are blind/visually impaired; to alleviate isolating & inhibiting effects of blindness/visual impairment; to improve physical capabilities & self-image of blind/visually impaired individuals by providing opportunities for them to learn; to encourage, promote & maintain interest in & cooperation with all such amateur sports & recreation organizations.
Finances: *Funding Sources:* Private donations; provincial government
Membership: *Fees:* $15 athlete; $5 supporting; *Member Profile:* Legally blind athletes; sighted guides; coaches; parents whose children are blind
Activities: Operates in nine regions: Kootenays, Thompson/Okanagan, Fraser Valley, Cariboo/North East, Vancouver/Squamish; Vancouver Island/South, Vancouver Island/North, North West, Fraser River/Delta; fundraisers; trade shows; workshops; *Speaker Service:* Yes
Chief Officer(s):
Brian Cowie, President
Tami Grenon, Vice-President
Meetings/Conferences:
• British Columbia Blind Sports & Recreation Association Annual General Meeting 2018, 2018
Scope: Provincial

British Columbia Blueberry Council
#275, 32160 South Fraser Way, Abbotsford BC V2T 1W5
Tel: 604-864-2117; *Fax:* 604-864-2197
info@bcblueberry.com
www.bcblueberry.com
Also Known As: BC Blueberries
Overview: A small provincial organization
Mission: To use promotion, research, industry education & relationship building to enhance the development of the blueberry industry
Membership: 800+; *Committees:* Finance; Promotions; Industry Relations; Research; ED Support; Bird Management
Chief Officer(s):
Jack Bates, Chair

British Columbia Bottle & Recycling Depot Association (BCBRDA)
#33030, 11198 - 84th Ave., Delta BC V4C 8E6
Tel: 604-930-0003; *Fax:* 604-930-0060
Other Communication: www.mydepot.ca
www.bcbda.com
Overview: A small provincial organization founded in 1997
Mission: To further the interests of association members through representation; To support a healthy environment by promoting recycling programs
Finances: *Funding Sources:* Membership fees
Membership: *Member Profile:* Bottle depots in British Columbia
Activities: Liaising with government & industry partners; Assisting the public by maintaining a website with information about depot locations, sales, & what each depot accepts for recycling
Chief Officer(s):
Corinne Atwood, Executive Director

British Columbia Brain Injury Association (BCBIA)
c/o Sea to Sky Meeting Management Inc., #206, 201 Bewicke Ave., North Vancouver BC V7M 3M7
Tel: 604-984-1212; *Fax:* 604-984-6434
Toll-Free: 877-858-1788
info@brainstreams.ca
www.brainstreams.ca
www.facebook.com/brainstreams
twitter.com/brainstreams
www.youtube.com/user/brainstreams
Overview: A small provincial organization founded in 1982 overseen by Brain Injury Association of Canada
Mission: To promote a better quality of life for those living with acquired brain injury in British Columbia
Finances: *Funding Sources:* Membership fees; Ministry of Children & Families; Donations; Sponsorships
Membership: *Fees:* $10 individuals; $25 families; $50 professional; $100 non-profit associations; $150 corporate; 200 diamond executive memberships
Activities: Promoting prevention of acquired brain injury throughout British Columbia; Providing education, resources, & referrals; Lobbying on behalf of persons affected by acquired brain injury; Supporting survivors of acquired brain injury, their families, & caregivers
Chief Officer(s):
Patti Flaherty, President
Publications:
• The Synaptic Post
Type: Newsletter; *Frequency:* Quarterly

British Columbia Broadband Association (BCBA)
248 Reid St., Quesnel BC V2J 2M2
Tel: 250-992-1230
info@bcba.ca
www.bcba.ca
Overview: A medium-sized provincial organization
Mission: To be the principal voice of the telecommunications & service provider industry in British Columbia
Membership: 58; *Fees:* $285
Chief Officer(s):
Bob Allen, President
Meetings/Conferences:
• 14th Annual BC Broadband Conference, May, 2018, Radisson Hotel, Richmond, BC
Scope: Provincial
Publications:
• British Columbia Broadband Association Newsletter
Type: Newsletter

British Columbia Broiler Hatching Egg Producers' Association (BCBHEC)
PO Box 191, Abbotsford BC V4X 3R2
Tel: 604-864-7556
association@bcbhec.com
www.bcbhec.com
Also Known As: BC Hatching Eggs
Overview: A small provincial licensing organization founded in 1963
Mission: To establish a better understanding & appreciation with the public & other interested parties regarding the industry; to stimulate & encourage improvements related to sales & scientific development in the field; to promote the exchange of ideas in an effort to find solutions to problems in the broiler hatching egg industry; to encourage economical plans to assists producers; & to provide better contact with hatcheries, feed suppliers, processors, & broiler growers.
Affiliation(s): BC Broiler Hatching Egg Commission; Sustainable Poultry Farming Group; British Columbia Agriculture Council; British Columbia Poultry Association; Environmental Farm Planning
Membership: *Committees:* Biosecurity Committee; Emergency Response Committee
Chief Officer(s):
Bryan Brandsma, President

British Columbia Broomball Society (BCBS)
BC
Overview: A small provincial organization overseen by Ballon sur glace Broomball Canada
Member of: Ballon sur glace Broomball Canada

British Columbia Business Educators Association (BCBEA)
c/o BC Teachers Federation, #100, 550 West 6th Ave., Vancouver BC B5Z 4P2
Tel: 604-871-2283; *Fax:* 604-871-2286
Toll-Free: 800-663-9163
bcbea.ca@gmail.com
bcbea.ca
www.facebook.com/bcbea.ca
twitter.com/bcbea
Overview: A small provincial organization
Mission: To support business education teachers at elementary, middle, & secondary schools who teach courses in business education & related fields.
Member of: BC Teachers' Federation
Membership: *Fees:* $23 student/retired; $35 BCTF member; $59.92 Non-BCTF member
Activities: Representation at regional, provincial & international conferences
Chief Officer(s):
Harmale Sangha, President
sangha_h@sd36.bc.ca

British Columbia Call Centre Association *See* British Columbia Contact Centre Association

British Columbia Camping Association
BC
info@bccamping.org
bccamping.org
www.facebook.com/BCcampingassociation
Overview: A medium-sized provincial organization overseen by Canadian Camping Association
Mission: To facilitate the development of organized camping in order to provide educational, character-building & constructive recreational experiences for all people; to develop awareness & appreciation of the natural environment
Member of: Canadian Camping Association
Membership: 55; *Fees:* $30 individual; $230 camp
Activities: *Rents Mailing List:* Yes
Chief Officer(s):
Margo Dunnet, President
president@bccamping.org
Stephanie Mikalishen, Secretary
Conor Lorimer, Treasurer
treasurer@bccamping.org
Meetings/Conferences:
• BC Camps Conference & Trade Show 2018, January, 2018, Stillwood Camp and Conference Centre, Lindell Beach, BC
Scope: Provincial

British Columbia Cancer Foundation (BCCF)
#150, 686 West Broadway, Vancouver BC V5Z 1G1
Tel: 604-877-6040; *Fax:* 604-877-6161
Toll-Free: 888-906-2873
bccfinfo@bccancer.bc.ca
www.bccancerfoundation.com
www.facebook.com/BCCancerFoundation
twitter.com/bccancer
Overview: A medium-sized provincial charitable organization founded in 1935
Mission: To reduce the incidence of cancer, reduce the mortality rate from cancer, & improve the quality of life for those living with cancer, through the acquisition, development, & stewardship of resources
Affiliation(s): British Columbia Cancer Research Centre; British Columbia Cancer Agency
Finances: *Annual Operating Budget:* Greater than $5 Million
Chief Officer(s):
Douglas Nelson, President & Chief Executive Officer
Luigi (Lou) Del Gobbo, Chief Financial Officer & Vice-President
Patsy Worrall, Vice-President, Marketing & Communications
Cindy Dopson, MBA, CHRP, Director, Human Resources

British Columbia Captive Insurance Association *See* Canadian Captive Insurance Association

British Columbia Care Providers Association (BCCPA)
Metrotower I, #738, 4710 Kingsway, Burnaby BC V5H 4M2
Tel: 604-736-4233; *Fax:* 604-736-4266
info@bccare.ca
www.bccare.ca
www.linkedin.com/groups/BC-Care-Providers-Association-5003096
www.facebook.com/bccareproviders
twitter.com/BCCareProviders
www.youtube.com/bccareproviders
Also Known As: Care Online
Overview: A small provincial organization founded in 1977 overseen by Canadian Alliance for Long Term Care
Mission: To provide the best possible care for seniors by supporting change, & promoting the growth & success of the

Mission: To advance the public school education & well-being of children in British Columbia
Finances: *Annual Operating Budget:* $500,000-$1.5 Million; *Funding Sources:* Ministry of Education; membership dues
Staff Member(s): 6; 40 volunteer(s)
Membership: 1,036; *Fees:* $65; *Member Profile:* Parent advisory council of BC public school/school district
Activities: *Speaker Service:* Yes
Chief Officer(s):
Terry Berting, President
terryberting@bccpac.bc.ca
Carla Giles, COO
Awards:
- George Matthews Award
- Bev Hosker Motivational Award
- BCCPAC Educational Award
; *Amount:* $500

British Columbia Conference of MB Churches (BCMB)
#101, 32310 South Fraser Way, Abbotsford BC V2T 1X1
Tel: 604-853-6959; *Fax:* 604-853-6990
Toll-Free: 888-653-9933
office@bcmb.org
www.bcmb.org
www.facebook.com/BCMBConference
Overview: A small provincial organization overseen by Canadian Conference of Mennonite Brethren Churches
Mission: To foster & encourage a movement of churches led by healthy leaders who spread God's values to friends, neighbours, and the world
Chief Officer(s):
Rob Thiessen, Conference Minister, 604-853-6959 Ext. 106
rob@bcmb.org
Meetings/Conferences:
- British Columbia Conference of MB Churches Annual Convention 2018, 2018, BC
Scope: Provincial
Contact Information: Assistant, Administration & Communications: Tamara Okoti, E-mail: tamara@bcmb.org

British Columbia Conservation Foundation (BCCF)
#206, 17564 - 56A Ave., Surrey BC V3S 1G3
Tel: 604-576-1433; *Fax:* 604-576-1482
hoffice@bccf.com
www.bccf.com
Overview: A medium-sized provincial organization founded in 1969
Mission: To contribute significantly to the perpetuation and expansion of fish and wildlife populations through the efficient implementation of projects in the field.
Staff Member(s): 3
Activities: Four regional offices
Chief Officer(s):
Deborah Gibson, Executive Director

British Columbia Conservative Party
#327, 1434 Ironwood St., Campbell River BC V9W 5T5
Tel: 250-434-2550
Toll-Free: 866-800-9025
info@bcconservative.ca
www.bcconservative.ca
www.facebook.com/BCConservativeParty
twitter.com/TheChoice4BC
www.youtube.com/bcconservativeparty
Also Known As: BC Conservative Party
Overview: A small provincial organization
Membership: *Fees:* $10
Chief Officer(s):
Scott Anderson, Interim Leader

British Columbia Construction Association (BCCA)
#401, 655 Tyee Rd., Victoria BC V9A 6X5
Tel: 250-475-1077; *Fax:* 250-475-1078
info@bccassn.com
www.bccassn.com
www.facebook.com/ThisisBCCA
twitter.com/WeBuildBC
www.youtube.com/user/BCCASSN
Overview: A large provincial organization founded in 1969 overseen by Canadian Construction Association
Mission: To provide excellence in the representation of & service to British Columbia's construction industry
Finances: *Funding Sources:* Membership dues; Group benefit plan; Industry forms; Publications
Staff Member(s): 27
Membership: 2,000 companies + 4 regional associations
Chief Officer(s):
Chris Atchison, President
Abigail Fulton, Vice-President
Warren Perks, Vice-President & Director, Industry Practices
Publications:
- British Columbia Construction Association Member Bulletin
Type: Bulletin
- Construction File [a publication of the British Columbia Construction Association]
Type: Newsletter
- Green Building Market Update [a publication of the British Columbia Construction Association]
Type: Newsletter
- Issue Update [a publication of the British Columbia Construction Association]
Type: Newsletter

Northern Regional Construction Association (NRCA)
3851 - 18th Ave., Prince George BC V2N 1B1
Tel: 250-563-1744; *Fax:* 250-563-1107
www.nrca.ca
Chief Officer(s):
Mike Fawcett, Chair
Scott Bone, Chief Executive Officer
sbone@nrca.ca

Southern Interior Construction Association (SICA)
#104, 151 Commercial Dr., Kelowna BC V1X 7W2
Tel: 250-491-7330; *Fax:* 250-491-3929
www.sica.bc.ca
www.facebook.com/SICABC
twitter.com/sicabc
www.youtube.com/user/SICA1969
Chief Officer(s):
Jason Henderson, Chief Executive Officer

Vancouver Island Construction Association (VICA)
1075 Alston St., Victoria BC V9A 3S6
Tel: 250-388-6471; *Fax:* 250-388-5183
Toll-Free: 877-847-6471
info@vicabc.ca
www.vicabc.ca
www.facebook.com/VIConstructionAssoc
twitter.com/VICA_BC
David Flint, Chair
Rory Kulmala, Chief Executive Officer
rorykulmala@vicabc.ca

Vancouver Regional Construction Association (VRCA)
3636 - 4th Ave. East, Vancouver BC V5M 1M3
Tel: 604-294-3766; *Fax:* 604-298-9472
info@vrca.ca
www.vrca.bc.ca
www.linkedin.com/company/1540219
www.facebook.com/VanConstruction
twitter.com/VanConstruction
Chief Officer(s):
Fiona Famulak, President, 604-293-6585
president@vrca.ca

British Columbia Contact Centre Association (BC CCA)
#102, 211 Columbia St., Vancouver BC V6A 2R5
Tel: 604-682-0296; *Fax:* 604-681-4545
info@bccontactcentre.com
www.bccallcentre.com
Previous Name: British Columbia Call Centre Association
Overview: A small provincial organization
Mission: To connect call centre employees & users with suppliers & government representatives
Finances: *Funding Sources:* Sponsorships
Membership: 100+; *Member Profile:* Call centre educators, managers, supervisors, consultants, & vendor suppliers;
Committees: Finance; Programs; Marketing & Communications; Sponsorship; Membership
Activities: Promoting growth of the contact centre industry; Conducting "boot camps" for those wishing to gain employment in customer service & sales; Exchanging best practices; Offering networking opportunities; Providing information sessions
Chief Officer(s):
Jean Mitchell, President, 604-622-7839
jean_mitchell@bcit.ca
Awards:
- Vendor of the Year
- Community Spirit Award
- Employee of the Year
- Contact Centre of the Year

Publications:
- British Columbia Contact Centre Association Newsletter
Type: Newsletter

British Columbia Contract Cleaner's Association (BCCCA)
1522 10th Ave., New Westminster BC V3M 3J2
info@bccca.ca
www.bccca.ca
Overview: A small provincial organization
Mission: To advance the interests of contract cleaners in the province of British Columbia
Membership: *Fees:* $170 primary; $195 associate; *Member Profile:* Organizations engaged in the contract cleaning industry
Chief Officer(s):
Barbara Hall, President

British Columbia Co-operative Association (BCCA)
#212, 1737 - 3rd Ave. West, Vancouver BC V6J 1K7
Tel: 604-662-3906; *Fax:* 604-662-3968
general@bcca.coop
www.bcca.coop
www.facebook.com/bc.cooperativeassociation
twitter.com/bc_coop
Overview: A medium-sized provincial organization
Mission: To promote & develop the co-operative economy in British Columbia
Finances: *Annual Operating Budget:* $500,000-$1.5 Million
Membership: 47; *Fees:* Sliding scale; *Member Profile:* Co-operatives; credit unions; non profit organizations
Activities: Promotion & development of co-operatives in BC; *Internships:* Yes
Chief Officer(s):
Carol Murray, Executive Director
murray@bcca.coop

British Columbia Cooperative Learning Provincial Specialist Association
c/o British Columbia Teachers' Federation, #100, 550 West 6th Ave., Vancouver BC V5Z 4P2
Tel: 604-871-2283
bccla.weebly.com
Overview: A small provincial organization
Mission: To foster and promote cooperative learning and cooperative schools in British Columbia.
Membership: *Fees:* $25 BCTF member; $10 student
Chief Officer(s):
Mike Galliford, President
mgalliford@sd43.bc.ca

British Columbia Council for Exceptional Children (BCCEC)
#17, 7511 No. 4 Rd., Richmond BC V6Y 4K4
info@bccec.org
www.bccec.org
Overview: A medium-sized provincial organization overseen by Council for Exceptional Children
Chief Officer(s):
Karen Jew, President

British Columbia Council for Families (BCCF)
#208, 1600 West 6th Ave., Vancouver BC V6J 1R3
Tel: 604-678-8884; *Fax:* 604-678-8886
bccf@bccf.ca
www.bccf.ca
www.linkedin.com/company/bc-council-for-families
www.facebook.com/BCFamilies
twitter.com/BC_Families
Also Known As: The Council
Overview: A medium-sized provincial charitable organization founded in 1977
Mission: To strengthen, encourage & support families through information, education, research & advocacy
Finances: *Annual Operating Budget:* $500,000-$1.5 Million; *Funding Sources:* Membership fees; sale of publications; government; foundations
Staff Member(s): 5; 12-2 volunteer(s)
Membership: 515; *Fees:* $25 student; $35 individual & family; $55 group; $150 corporate; *Member Profile:* Organizations & individuals interested in family well-being
Activities: *Awareness Events:* National Family Week; Intergenerational Week; Intl. Family Day - Connect with Kindness; *Internships:* Yes; *Speaker Service:* Yes
Chief Officer(s):
Sylvia Tremblay, President

Canadian Associations / British Columbia Courthouse Library Society

Joel B. Kaplan, Executive Director, 604-678-8884 Ext. 102, Fax: 604-678-8886
joelk@bccf.ca
Tina Albrecht, Manager, Communications
tinaa@bccf.ca
Awards:
• Distinguished Service to Families Award

British Columbia Courthouse Library Society
800 Smithe St., Vancouver BC V6Z 2E1
Tel: 604-660-2841; *Fax:* 604-660-2821
Toll-Free: 800-665-2570
librarian@courthouselibrary.ca
www.courthouselibrary.ca
twitter.com/theclbc
Also Known As: Courthouse Libraries BC
Overview: A medium-sized provincial organization
Mission: To offer legal information services to librarians, legal professionals, & the public
Activities: *Library:* Vancouver Courthouse Library
Chief Officer(s):
Alan Ross, Chair

British Columbia Cranberry Marketing Commission (BCCMC)
PO Box 162, Stn. A, Abbotsford BC V2T 6Z5
Tel: 604-897-9252
cranberries@telus.net
www.bccranberries.com
www.facebook.com/bccranberries
twitter.com/BCcranberries
instagram.com/bccranberries
Overview: A small provincial organization founded in 1968
Mission: To regulate cranberry farming in BC

British Columbia Cricket Association *See* British Columbia Mainland Cricket League

British Columbia Crime Prevention Association (BCCPA)
#120, 12414 - 82nd Ave., Surrey BC V3W 3E9
Tel: 604-501-9222; *Fax:* 604-501-2261
Toll-Free: 888-405-2288
info@bccpa.org
www.bccpa.org
www.facebook.com/255950554446178
twitter.com/crimeprevention
Overview: A medium-sized provincial charitable organization founded in 1978
Mission: To promote active community participation in crime prevention initiatives through awareness & education
Member of: Better Business Bureau; Canadian Security Association
12 volunteer(s)
Membership: 377; *Fees:* $65 individual; $35 student; $85 non-government; $140 government; $265 business; *Member Profile:* All who are concerned about crime; *Committees:* Education - Awareness; Development - Innovation; Administration - Management; Financial - Funding Management
Activities: *Awareness Events:* Golf Tournament & Silent Auction, June; *Speaker Service:* Yes; *Library:* Open to public
Chief Officer(s):
Marcie Flamand, President
Meetings/Conferences:
• 2018 BC Crime Prevention Association Training Symposium, 2018, BC
Scope: Provincial

British Columbia Criminal Justice Association (BCCJA)
3894 Commercial St., Vancouver BC V5N 4G2
info@bccja.com
www.bccja.com
Overview: A small provincial organization
Mission: To promote cooperation concerning the problems of crime & its consequences
Member of: Canadian Criminal Justice Association
Activities: Providing education & information on criminal justice issues; Encouraging professional networking opportunities; Promoting debate on issues within the criminal justice system; Fostering study of problems in the field; Providing advocacy
Chief Officer(s):
Tim Veresh, President
Publications:
• Sources & Resources
Type: Newsletter

Profile: Information for criminal justice & related professionals in British Columbia

British Columbia Culinary Arts Specialist Association
c/o British Columbia Teachers' Federation, #100, 550 West 6th Ave., Vancouver BC V5Z 4P2
bccasa.ca
twitter.com/BCCASAchef
Overview: A small provincial organization founded in 2000
Mission: To run culinary classes for students in British Columbia
Member of: BC Teachers' Federation
Chief Officer(s):
Eric MacNeill, President, 250-751-3409
emacneil@sd68.bc.ca

British Columbia Dairy Association
3236 Beta Ave., Burnaby BC V5G 4K4
Tel: 604-294-3775; *Fax:* 604-294-8199
Toll-Free: 800-242-6455
contactus@bcdairy.ca
www.bcdairyfoundation.ca
www.linkedin.com/company/bcdairy
www.facebook.com/bcdairy
twitter.com/bcmilk
www.youtube.com/MustDrinkMoreMilkTV
Merged from: BC Dairy Foundation; BC Milk Producers Association
Overview: A small provincial organization founded in 2011
Mission: To coordinate, plan, produce & administer dairy products promotion, education & public relations programs best suited to meet the needs of the dairy industry in British Columbia.
Activities: The Cold Crew; Dairy Farm Tours.
Chief Officer(s):
Dave Eto, Executive Director

British Columbia Dance Educators' Association (BCDEA)
c/o BC Teachers' Federation, #100, 550 West 6th Ave., Vancouver BC V5Z 4P2
Tel: 604-871-2283
Toll-Free: 800-663-9163
psac73@bctf.ca
www.bcdea.ca
twitter.com/BCDanceEd
Overview: A small provincial organization
Mission: Organization for teachers of dance in BC public schools.
Member of: BC Teachers' Federation
Chief Officer(s):
Kim Wolski, President
Meetings/Conferences:
• BC Dance Educators' Association Conference 2018, 2018, BC
Scope: Provincial

British Columbia Deaf Sports Federation (BCDSF)
#4, 320 Columbia St., New Westminster BC V3L 1A6
Fax: 604-526-5010; *TTY:* 604-526-5010
info@bcdeafsports.bc.ca
www.bcdeafsports.bc.ca
www.facebook.com/139556792849947
twitter.com/bcdeafsports
Overview: A medium-sized provincial charitable organization founded in 1975 overseen by Canadian Deaf Sports Association
Mission: To provide & support the development of competitive sporting events in BC among deaf & hard of hearing athletes; to encourage training for deaf coaches; to provide financial assistance to deaf athletes to participate in local, provincial & national competitions
Member of: Canadian Deaf Sports Association
Affiliation(s): BC Sport & Fitness Council for the Disabled
Finances: *Annual Operating Budget:* $100,000-$250,000; *Funding Sources:* Grants; gaming; membership fees; donations
Staff Member(s): 1
Membership: 300
Chief Officer(s):
Marilyn Loehr, Director, Membership
mloehr@bcdeafsports.bc.ca

British Columbia Dental Association
#400, 1765 - 8th Ave. West, Vancouver BC V6J 5C6
Tel: 604-736-7202; *Fax:* 604-736-7588
Toll-Free: 888-396-9888
info@yourdentalhealth.ca
www.bcdental.org
www.facebook.com/yourdentalhealth

Overview: A medium-sized provincial organization founded in 1998 overseen by Canadian Dental Association
Mission: To act as the voice of dentistry in British Columbia; To prevent oral disease
Membership: 2,900+; *Member Profile:* All dentists licensed to practise in British Columbia; Retired dentists & dentists unable to practise because of disability; Dentists who reside outside British Columbia; Students
Activities: Advocating for access to dental care for everyone in British Columbia; Raising public awareness of oral health; *Awareness Events:* Oral Health Month, April
Chief Officer(s):
Ann Heald, Director, Operations
aheald@bcdental.org
Meetings/Conferences:
• Pacific Dental Conference 2018, March, 2018, Vancouver, BC
Scope: Provincial
Contact Information: Address: Pacific Dental Conference, #305, 1505 West 2nd Ave., Vancouver, BC V6H 3Y4; Phone: 604-736-3781; E-mail: info@pdconf.com; URL: www.pdconf.com
• Pacific Dental Conference 2019, 2019, BC
Scope: Provincial
Contact Information: Address: Pacific Dental Conference, #305, 1505 West 2nd Ave., Vancouver, BC V6H 3Y4; Phone: 604-736-3781; E-mail: info@pdconf.com; URL: www.pdconf.com
Publications:
• the bridge [a publication of the British Columbia Dental Association]
Type: Magazine; *Frequency:* Bimonthly; *Accepts Advertising*
Profile: Issues that affect dentists in British Columbia
• British Columbia Dental Association Annual Fee Guide
Type: Guide; *Frequency:* Annually; *Accepts Advertising*
Profile: A reference published for dentists each January

British Columbia Dental Hygienists' Association (BCDHA)
#307, 9600 Cameron St., Burnaby BC V3J 7N3
Tel: 604-415-4559; *Fax:* 604-415-4579
Toll-Free: 888-305-3338
info@bcdha.bc.ca
www.bcdha.bc.ca
www.facebook.com/101954289892034
twitter.com/BCDHA
Overview: A small provincial organization founded in 1964
Mission: To promote the profession in British Columbia; To advocate on behalf of dental hygienists
Member of: Canadian Dental Hygienists' Association (CDHA)
Staff Member(s): 5
Membership: 3,000; *Member Profile:* Dental hygienists in British Columbia
Activities: Offering continuing education; Providing information about career opportunities for dental hygienists
Chief Officer(s):
Brenda Morris, Chair
upperislanddirector@bcdha.bc.ca
Jodi Noble, Vice-Chair
victoriadirector@bcdha.bc.ca
Cindy Fletcher, Executive Director
cfletcher@bcdha.bc.ca
Publications:
• Outlook
Type: Newsletter; *Frequency:* 3 pa; *Accepts Advertising*
Profile: Educational articles & association updates

British Columbia Disc Sports (BCDSS)
PO Box 21723, 1424 Commercial Dr., vancouver BC V5L 5G3
discbc@bcdss.ca
discbc.com
Also Known As: The Disc Sports Provincial Sport Organization (PSO)
Previous Name: BC Disc Sports Society
Overview: A small provincial organization
Mission: To be the provincial governing body of disc sports in British Columbian
Affiliation(s): BC Ultimate
Membership: 187; *Fees:* $5 through a recognized club; $10 individual
Activities: Disc golf; double disc court; freestyle; goaltimate; guts; ultimate
Chief Officer(s):
Craig Sheather, President

British Columbia Diving
#114, 15272 Croydon Dr., Surrey BC V3S 0Z5
Tel: 604-531-5576; *Fax:* 604-542-0387
www.bcdiving.ca

workers of British Columbia; To act as the single voice for workers' rights in British Columbia
Affiliation(s): 50+ unions
Staff Member(s): 7
Membership: 500,000+; *Member Profile:* British Columbia workers from affiliated unions in over 800 locals
Activities: Promoting the rights of working people; Providing educational opportunities; Publishing reports; Engaging in political, social, & community action; Promoting occupational health & safety; Organizing campaigns around issues such as minimum wage, working alone, & childcare; Supporting affiliated unions during labour disputes
Chief Officer(s):
Jim Chorostecki, Executive Director
Jaime Matten, Director, Communications
Meetings/Conferences:
• BC Pension Leadership Forum 2018, February, 2018
Scope: Provincial
Description: Hosted by the British Columbia Federation of Labour & SHARE
Contact Information: E-mail: bcfed@bcfed.ca
• British Columbia Federation of Labour 2018 Convention, November, 2018
Scope: Provincial
Description: A meeting held every two years to set the direction of the labour movement in British Columbia, attended by rank & file trade union members
Contact Information: E-mail: bcfed@bcfed.ca

British Columbia Federation of Police Officers See British Columbia Police Association

British Columbia Fencing Association (BCFA)
#15, 12900 Jack Bell Dr., Richmond BC V6V 2V8
www.fencing.bc.ca
twitter.com/FENCINGBC
Also Known As: Fencing BC
Overview: A small provincial organization overseen by Canadian Fencing Federation
Mission: To promote fencing in BC; To set policies & procedures which govern programs & events
Membership: 15; *Fees:* $40 individual; $65 club
Chief Officer(s):
John French, President
president.bcfa@gmail.com
Meetings/Conferences:
• British Columbia Fencing Association Annual General Meeting 2018, 2018, BC
Scope: Provincial

British Columbia Ferry & Marine Workers' Union (CLC) (BCFMWU) / Syndicat des travailleurs marins et de bacs de la Colombie-Britannique (CTC)
1511 Stewart Ave., Nanaimo BC V9S 4E3
Tel: 250-716-3454; *Fax:* 250-716-3455
Toll-Free: 800-663-7009
mailroom@bcfmwu.com
www.bcfmwu.com
www.facebook.com/BCFerryandMarineWorkersUnion
twitter.com/BCFMWU
vimeo.com/user53145424
Also Known As: Ferry Workers' Union
Overview: A medium-sized provincial organization founded in 1977
Mission: To seek the best possible wage standards & improvements in the conditions of employment for ferry & marine workers in BC & to represent members in protecting & maintaining their rights; to act as the representative of the membershipto safeguard & promote economic & social benefits & justice for all workers, unionized & non-unionized
Member of: National Union of Public and General Employees
Affiliation(s): BC Government & Employees Union; BC Federation of Labour; Canadian Labour Congress; International Transport Workers Federation (ITF); National Union of Public & General Employees (NUPGE); International Labour Organization
Finances: *Annual Operating Budget:* $1.5 Million-$3 Million; *Funding Sources:* Union dues
Staff Member(s): 9
Membership: 4,400; *Fees:* $60 initiation fee; 1.5% of gross monthly income; *Committees:* Asbestos; Communications; Convention; Education; Finance; First nations Vision; Hours of Work; Human Rights; Occupational Health and Safety; Solidarity; Young Workers
Activities: Child daycare for members; engagement in educational, legislative, political, civic, social, welfare, community & other activities

Chief Officer(s):
Graeme Johnston, Provincial President
graemejohnston@bcfmwu.com
Kevin Lee, Provincial 1st Vice President
kevinlee@bcfmwu.com
Shawna Walsh, Provincial 2nd Vice President
shawnawalsh@bcfmwu.com
Brian Lalli, Provincial Secretary Treasurer
brianlalli@bcfmwu.com
Awards:
• BC Ferry & Marine Workers' Union Awards
Eligibility: BCGMWU members, or an immediate relative of; enrolment in a university, college or technical program *Deadline:* June 1; *Amount:* $1,000, $500 & $250
Publications:
• Assembly Station [a publication of the BC Ferry & Marine Workers' Union]
Type: Newsletter; *Frequency:* irregular; *Accepts Advertising*; *Number of Pages:* 12; *Price:* Free download
Profile: Contains news, imformation and highlights relevant to members of the BC Ferry & Mairine Workers' Union

British Columbia Festival Association See British Columbia Drama Association

British Columbia Fishing Resorts & Outfitters Association (BCFROA)
PO Box 3301, #106, 1383 McGill Rd., Kamloops BC V2C 6B9
Tel: 250-374-6836; *Fax:* 250-374-6640
Toll-Free: 866-374-6836
bcfroa@bcfroa.ca
www.bcfroa.ca
www.facebook.com/wheretofishinbc
twitter.com/Fish_BC
www.youtube.com/user/BCFROA; pinterest.com/bcfroa
Overview: A small provincial organization founded in 1974
Mission: Works with the public & private sector to protect areas currently in use; to preserve the wildlife experience in BC for the enjoyment of future generations; a lobby group whose members are dedicated to providing a quality outdoor experience
Member of: Outdoor Recreation Council of British Columbia
Finances: *Annual Operating Budget:* $100,000-$250,000; *Funding Sources:* Membership dues; funding programs; promotions; sponsorships
Membership: 130+; *Fees:* $105-$519.75; *Member Profile:* Resort owner or angling & hunting guide
Activities: Marketing; lobbying; advocacy
Chief Officer(s):
Matt Jennings, Executive Director

British Columbia Floor Covering Association (BCFCA)
#2-19299 - 94 Ave., Surrey BC V4N 4E6
Tel: 604-881-4944; *Fax:* 604-881-4744
Toll-Free: 866-575-9928
info@bcfca.com
www.bcfca.com
Overview: A small provincial organization overseen by National Floor Covering Association
Mission: To communicate standards & codes to its members & to encourage industry development by offering training seminars & disseminating current information related to the industry; to act as the public voice of the provincial floor covering industry, & lobbies on its behalf.
Membership: 140; *Fees:* $550 dealers; $650 distributors; *Member Profile:* Manufacturers, distributors, retail stores, installers of flooring products; *Committees:* Grievance; Social; Membership; Education
Chief Officer(s):
Scott Rust, President

British Columbia Floorball Federation (BCFF)
3183 Edgemont Blvd., North Vancouver BC V7R 2N8
Tel: 778-385-7825
info@bcfloorball.com
www.bcfloorball.com
www.facebook.com/BCFloorball
twitter.com/bcfloorball
Overview: A small provincial organization overseen by Floorball Canada
Mission: To be the provincial governing body for the sport of floorball in British Columbia
Member of: Floorball Canada
Affiliation(s): WheelchairFloorball.com; JuniorFloorball.com
Membership: $10-$50
Chief Officer(s):
Blair Zimmerman, President

British Columbia Folklore Society (BCFS)
7345 Seabrook Rd., Central Saanich BC V8M 1M9
Tel: 250-652-7614
info@folklore.bc.ca
www.folklore.bc.ca
Overview: A small provincial charitable organization founded in 1994
Mission: To collect and preserve the traditional and contemporary folklife and folklore of the people of British Columbia.
Member of: BC Heritage Society
Activities: *Library:* British Columbia Folklore Society Reference Library; by appointment

British Columbia Food Technolgists (BCTF)
c/o Nilmini Wijewickreme, SGS Canada, 50-655 West Kent Ave. North, Vancouver BC V6P 6T7
Other Communication: membership@bcft.ca;
employment@bcft.ca
info@bcft.ca
www.bcft.ca
twitter.com/bcfoodtech
Overview: A small provincial organization overseen by Canadian Institute of Food Science & Technology
Mission: To advance food science & technology in British Columbia
Member of: Canadian Institute of Food Science & Technology; Institute of Food Technologists
Affiliation(s): Packaging Association of British Columbia; British Columbia Food Protection Association; British Columbia Nutraceutical Network
Membership: *Member Profile:* Scientists & technologists from government, academia, & industry; *Committees:* Advertising; Banquet; Membership; Program
Activities: Engaging in advocacy activities; Offering networking opportunities
Chief Officer(s):
Reena Mistry, Chair
chair@bcft.ca
Jenny Li, Secretary
jli@shafer-haggart.com
Thu Pham, Treasurer
Erin Friesen, Chair, Membership
membership@bcft.ca
Peter Taylor, Chair, Program, Banquet, & Suppliers' Night Committee
taylor58@telus.net
Nilmini Wijewickreme, Chair, Advertising
nilmini_wijewickreme@sgs.com
Meetings/Conferences:
• British Columbia Food Technologists Suppliers' Night 2018, 2018, BC
Scope: Provincial
Description: A learning event featuring over 100 supplier exhibits of interest to food scientists, research & development technologists, & senior managers & purchasers from food & beverage companies
Publications:
• Tech Talk: The British Columbia Food Technolgists Newsletter
Type: Newsletter; *Frequency:* Monthly; *Accepts Advertising*; *Editor:* Brian Jang; *Price:* Free with membership in British Columbia Food Technolgists
Profile: Association information, meetings, & food-related activities on the local & international scene, for persons involved in areas suchas food processing, research, product development, quality control, sales, & management

British Columbia Freedom of Information & Privacy Association (FIPA-BC)
#103, 1093 West Broadway, Vancouver BC V6H 1E2
Tel: 604-739-9788; *Fax:* 604-739-9148
fipa@fipa.bc.ca
www.fipa.bc.ca
twitter.com/bcfipa
Overview: A small provincial organization founded in 1990
Mission: To defend & improve public access to information in a world where quality of information & speed of access equals power; To defend personal privacy in a world where our personal information travels at the speed of light & its use is increasingly beyond our control
Staff Member(s): 2; 10 volunteer(s)
Membership: 150; *Fees:* $10 student/senior; $25 individual; $250 organization
Activities: Law reform; public legal education; public assistance; legal & policy research; legal & administrative interventions;

Canadian Associations / British Columbia Fruit Growers' Association

legislation; freedom of information & privacy awards/seminars; *Speaker Service:* Yes; *Library:* by appointment
Chief Officer(s):
Vincent Gogolek, Executive Director
Joyce Yan, Program Director
Awards:
• Freedom of Information & Privacy Awards
Publications:
• The Privacy Handbook: A Practical Guide to Your Privacy Rights in British Columbia and How to Protect Them
Number of Pages: 183; *Price:* $15

British Columbia Fruit Growers' Association
880 Vaughan Ave., Kelowna BC V1Y 7E4
Tel: 250-762-5226; *Fax:* 250-861-9089
info@bcfga.com
www.bcfga.com
www.facebook.com/208331935875260
Overview: A medium-sized provincial organization
Mission: To represent fruit growers' interests in British Columbia
Membership: *Member Profile:* Fruit growers in British Columbia
Activities: Lobbying the government for positive change to risk management programs, such as crop insurance & the Net Income Stablization Program; Providing services & products to growers
Chief Officer(s):
Joe Sardinha, President
Meetings/Conferences:
• BC Fruit Growers' Association 129th Annual General Meeting 2018, 2018, BC
Scope: Provincial
Contact Information: Email: info@bcfga.com

British Columbia Fuchsia & Begonia Society
c/o #17, 910 Fort Fraser Rise, Port Coquitlam BC V3C 6K3
info@bcfuchsiasociety.com
www.bcfuchsiasociety.com
Overview: A small provincial organization founded in 1961
Mission: To encourage the cultivation & promotion of fuchsias, begonias, ferns, gesnerieads & all other shade-loving plants
Member of: BC Council of Garden Clubs
Finances: *Annual Operating Budget:* Less than $50,000; *Funding Sources:* Membership dues; plant sales; raffles
185 volunteer(s)
Membership: 185; *Fees:* $20 single; $30 multiple
Activities: Meetings; workshops; plant sales; speaking to the community & other garden clubs; *Awareness Events:* Annual Show & Competition; *Speaker Service:* Yes; *Library:* Not open to public
Chief Officer(s):
Fran Carter, President
fccarter@hotmail.ca
Lorna Herchenson, Int'l Corresponding Secretary
lherchenson@telus.net

British Columbia Funeral Association (BCFA)
#211, 2187 Oak Bay Ave., Victoria BC V8R 1G1
Tel: 250-592-3213; *Fax:* 250-592-4362
Toll-Free: 800-665-3899
info@bcfunerals.com
www.bcfunerals.com
www.facebook.com/bcfunerals
twitter.com/bcfunerals
Also Known As: BC Funeral Association
Overview: A medium-sized provincial organization founded in 1912
Mission: To promote, through education, communication, & leadership, the highest standards of ethics & service in the funeral profession
Finances: *Funding Sources:* Membership dues; Sponsorships
Membership: *Member Profile:* Licensed funeral providers
Activities: Liaising with government representatives about legislation, regulations, & policies; Providing a province-wide toll-free line for information & referral; Offering continuing education programs; Organizing conferences & seminars; Providing Funeral Service Apprenticeship Training for British Columbia; Increasing public awareness
Chief Officer(s):
Sharla MacKay, President
Lori Cascaden, Executive Director
lori@bcfunerals.com
Meetings/Conferences:
• 2018 BC Funeral Association Annual Conference & General Meeting, May, 2018, River Rock Resort, Richmond, BC
Scope: Provincial

British Columbia Games Society *See* BC Games Society

British Columbia Genealogical Society (BCGS)
PO Box 88054, Stn. Lansdowne Mall, Richmond BC V6X 3T6
Tel: 604-502-9119; *Fax:* 604-502-9119
bcgs@bcgs.ca
www.bcgs.ca
Overview: A medium-sized provincial charitable organization founded in 1971
Mission: To perpetuate the heritage of BC; To collect, preserve & publish material relevant to promotion of ethical principles, scientific methods & effective techniques in genealogical & historical research
Member of: Canadian Federation of Genealogical & Family History Societies
Affiliation(s): Richmond Heritage; City of Richmond Archives
Finances: *Annual Operating Budget:* Less than $50,000; *Funding Sources:* Membership dues; Donations; Fundraising
60 volunteer(s)
Membership: 650+; *Fees:* $45 indivdual; $10 family associate; $22.50 student; $45 Affiliate society; *Member Profile:* Individuals interested in genealogy & related fields of local history, biography, heraldry & other aspects of historical research; *Committees:* British Columbia Research; Publications; Education; Cemetery; Library
Activities: Records of BC cemeteries; Publishes & sells transcripts; Exchange of journals with other societies all over the world; Research of various countries; *Library:* BCGS Walter Draycott Library & Resource Centre; Open to public
Chief Officer(s):
Eunice Robinson, President

British Columbia Golf Association (BCGA)
#116, 7198 Vantage Way, Delta BC V4G 1K7
Tel: 604-279-2580; *Fax:* 604-952-0060
Toll-Free: 888-833-2242
info@britishcolumbiagolf.org
www.britishcolumbiagolf.org
www.facebook.com/BritishColumbiaGolf
twitter.com/bc_golfer
Also Known As: British Columbia Golf
Overview: A large provincial licensing organization founded in 1922 overseen by Golf Canada
Mission: To promote interest in golf in BC; To protect the mutual interests of member clubs & their members; To establish & enforce uniformity in the rules of the game; To establish, control, & conduct amateur championships, matches & competitions; To interest & develop junior golfers; To select all teams to represent BC in national & international matches
Affiliation(s): Canadian Golf Foundation; Professional Golf Association of BC; Canadian Ladies Golf Association of BC; Golf Course Superintendents Association of BC; International Association of Golf Administrators; National Golf Foundation; Pacific Coast Golf Association; Pacific Northwest Golf Association
Finances: *Funding Sources:* Government; Sponsorship; Membership
Staff Member(s): 10
Activities: *Rents Mailing List:* Yes; *Library:* Open to public
Chief Officer(s):
Kris Jonasson, CEO
kris@britishcolumbiagolf.org
Deborah Pyne, Managing Director, Player Development
debbie@britishcolumbiagolf.org
Andy Fung, Director, Finance & Administration
andy@britishcolumbiagolf.org
Susan White, Senior Manager, Field Operations
susan@britishcolumbiagolf.org
Corrie Wong, Manager, Membership
corrie@britishcolumbiagolf.org

British Columbia Golf Superintendents Association (BCGSA)
PO Box 807, Lake Cowichan BC V0R 2G0
Tel: 250-749-6703; *Fax:* 250-749-6702
admin@bcgsa.com
www.bcgsa.com
Overview: A small provincial organization founded in 1995
Mission: To promote the professional recognition of golf course superintendents; To uphold the association's code of ethics
Membership: 300+; *Member Profile:* Turfgrass professionals involved in golf course maintenance & the science of turf management
Activities: Participating in turfgrass research; Exchanging knowledge related to golf course care; Sponsoring educational opportunities to benefit members
Chief Officer(s):
Ginny Tromp, Executive Administrator

Dean Piller, President, 250-658-4445
dpiller@telus.net
Mike Ferdinandi, Secretary/Treasurer
mike.ferdinandi@vancouver.ca
Publications:
• BCGSA Newsletter
Type: Newsletter

British Columbia Government & Service Employees' Union (BCGEU) / Syndicat des fonctionnaires provinciaux et de service de la Colombie-Britannique
4911 Canada Way, Burnaby BC V5G 3W3
Tel: 604-291-9611; *Fax:* 604-291-6030
Toll-Free: 800-663-1674
www.bcgeu.ca
Previous Name: British Columbia Government Employees' Union
Overview: A medium-sized provincial organization
Member of: National Union of Public and General Employees
Affiliation(s): BC Federation of Labour; Canadian Labour Congress
Finances: *Annual Operating Budget:* Greater than $5 Million; *Funding Sources:* Membership dues
Staff Member(s): 170
Membership: 67,000; *Member Profile:* Persons who work in direct government services, including the protection of children, the provision of financial assistance to the poor, the protection of the environment, the management of natural resources, the care of the mentally ill in institutions, the staffing of provincial correctional facilities, the fighting of forest fires, & the provision of the government's technical & clerical services
Chief Officer(s):
Judi Filion, Treasurer
Darryl Walker, President

British Columbia Government Employees' Union *See* British Columbia Government & Service Employees' Union

British Columbia Grapegrowers' Association (BCGA)
451 Atwood Rd., Grand Forks BC V0H 1H9
Tel: 877-762-4652; *Fax:* 250-442-4076
Toll-Free: 877-762-4652
www.grapegrowers.bc.ca
Previous Name: Association of British Columbia Grape Growers
Overview: A medium-sized provincial organization founded in 1960
Mission: The Association represents all commercial Columbia on agricultural issues and concerns. It works with other industry organizations, with procincial and federal agricultural organizations and all levels of government to represent, promote and advance the interests of all grapegrowers in British Columbia.
Finances: *Annual Operating Budget:* Less than $50,000; *Funding Sources:* Membership dues
Staff Member(s): 1; 10 volunteer(s)
Membership: 250; *Fees:* $150 minimum; *Committees:* Viticulture; Crop Insurance
Chief Officer(s):
Manfred Freese, President

British Columbia Ground Water Association (BCGWA)
1708 - 197A St., Langley BC V2Z 1K2
Tel: 604-530-8934; *Fax:* 604-530-8934
secretary@bcgwa.org
www.bcgwa.org
Overview: A small provincial organization
Staff Member(s): 2
Membership: *Member Profile:* Corporations that employ persons who work in water well contracting, manufacturing, or supplying materials & equipment; Individuals employed by a company or who belong to an association affiliated with the ground water industry
Activities: Offering workshops & seminars; Promoting research & standards in water well construction; Liaising with government agencies
Chief Officer(s):
Joan Perry, Secretary
Publications:
• British Columbia Ground Water Association Newsletter
Type: Newsletter; *Frequency:* Quarterly

British Columbia Hang Gliding & Paragliding Association (BCHPA)
BC
www.bchpa.ca
Previous Name: Hang Gliding Association of British Columbia
Overview: A small provincial organization
Mission: To protect, maintain & improve flying sites throughout the province.
Chief Officer(s):
Margit Nance, President
margitnance@show.ca

British Columbia Herb Growers Association (BCHGA)
998 Skeena Dr., Kelowna BC V1V 2K7
Tel: 604-824-2833
Overview: A small provincial organization founded in 1997
Mission: To promote & enhance herb growing in British Columbia; To represent herb growers
Finances: *Funding Sources:* Sponsorships
Membership: 50; *Fees:* $50 individuals; $75 foreign memberships; $125 corporations; *Member Profile:* Individuals & corporations involved in the herb business, such as researchers, educators, growers, manufacturers, processors, buyers, distributors, retailers, & service providers
Activities: Facilitating research; Providing networking opportunities; Offering market information; Organizing workshops; Supporting herb marketing
Publications:
• BCHGA [British Columbia Herb Growers Association] Newsletter
Type: Newsletter; *Frequency:* Quarterly; *Accepts Advertising*
Profile: Upcoming meetings, trade shows, & educational opportunities, association reports, & articles
• British Columbia Herb Growers Association Annual Report
Type: Yearbook; *Frequency:* Annually
• British Columbia Herb Growers Association Directory
Type: Directory
Profile: Listing of association members with contact information

British Columbia Hereford Association (BCHA)
c/o Vic Redekop, 25440 - 16th Ave., Aldergrove BC V4W 2R7
Tel: 250-557-4348; *Fax:* 250-557-4468
www.bchereford.ca
Overview: A small provincial organization founded in 1921
Mission: To produce Hereford seedstock to meet the demands of British Columbia's commercial cattle industry
Membership: 170; *Member Profile:* Purebred Hereford breeders in British Columbia
Activities: Organizing field days, shows, & sales; *Awareness Events:* Hereford Week In Canada, August
Chief Officer(s):
Daryl Kirton, Director
3-d-l@telus.net
Publications:
• BC Bulletin
Type: Newsletter

British Columbia Heritage Party *See* Christian Heritage Party of British Columbia

British Columbia Historical Federation (BCHF)
PO Box 5254, Stn. B, Victoria BC V8R 6N4
info@bchistory.ca
www.bchistory.ca
www.facebook.com/bchistoricalfederation
Overview: A medium-sized provincial charitable organization founded in 1922
Mission: To encourage interest in the history of British Columbia through financial support, research, & presentation
Member of: Heritage Council of British Columbia
Finances: *Annual Operating Budget:* Less than $50,000; *Funding Sources:* Heritage Trust of BC; Donations
100+ volunteer(s)
Membership: 350 +; *Fees:* Schedule available; *Member Profile:* Historic societies, museums, archives, historic sites;
Committees: Advocacy; Historic Trails & Sites
Activities: Disseminating publications; Offering awards & scholarships; Holding an annual conference
Chief Officer(s):
Gary Mitchell, President, 250-381-6607
Sandra Martins, Secretary
Awards:
• Lieutenant-Governor's Medal for Historical Writing
Established 1983; Lieutenant-Governor's Medal for Historical Writing, three Certificates of Merit, & cash awards given annually to authors of best books on any facet of BC history *Eligibility:* Book about B.C. history, published within the competition year *Deadline:* December 31; *Amount:* $2,500 *Contact:* Maurice Guibord, Vice-President, E-mail: vp2@bchistory.ca
• W. Kaye Lamb Essay Scholarships
Essay must be between 1500 and 5000 words, on a topic related to B.C. history *Eligibility:* Essay written by a student registered in university/college in B.C.; *Amount:* $750-1000 *Contact:* Marie Elliot
• BCHF Recognition Awards
Eligibility: Article that has appeared in the journal "British Columbia History" *Deadline:* March 1; *Amount:* $250 *Contact:* Shannon Bettles, BCHF Recognition Committee, E-mail: director3@bchf.ca
• Historic Website Competition
Awarded to recognize an individual or group initiative in creating a website about BC history *Deadline:* December 31; *Amount:* $250
• Anne & Philip Yandle Best Article Award
Eligibility: Author of an article published in British Columbia History magazine; *Amount:* $250
Meetings/Conferences:
• British Columbia Historical Federation 2018 Conference & Annual General Meeting, May, 2018, Nakusp, BC
Scope: Provincial
Contact Information: E-mail: info@bchistory.ca
Publications:
• BCHF [British Columbia Historical Federation] News
Type: Newsletter; *ISSN:* 1710-1433
Profile: News & updates for members
• British Columbia History [a publication of the British Columbia Historical Federation]
Type: Magazine; *Frequency:* 4 pa.; *Editor:* Andrea Lister; *ISSN:* 1710-7881; *Price:* $20
Profile: Contains information about the history of British Columbia using articles, maps, photos, & insight into localarchives

British Columbia Hog Marketing Commission
PO Box 8000-280, Abbotsford BC V2S 6H1
Tel: 604-287-4647; *Fax:* 604-820-6647
info@bcpork.ca
bcpork.ca
Also Known As: BC Pork
Overview: A small provincial organization founded in 1980
Chief Officer(s):
Geraldine Auston, Contact

British Columbia Honey Producers Association (BCHPA)
PO Box 1650, Comox BC V9M 8A2
www.bcbeekeepers.com
Overview: A small provincial organization founded in 1920
Mission: To promote the keeping of bees in British Columbia, using the most suitable methods; To represent the interest of beekeepers in British Columbia
Member of: Canadian Honey Council
Finances: *Funding Sources:* Membership fees; Donations
Membership: *Fees:* $40, 0-25 hives; $50, 26-50 hives; $60, 51-150 hives; $70, 151-300 hives; $120, 301-500 hives; $130, 501-1,000 hives; $200, more than 1,000 hives; *Member Profile:* Honey producers in British Columbia
Activities: Engaging in advocacy activities; Liaising with both the provincial & federal government & the media; Providing education & information, through symposiums & the association website; Offering group liability insurance; Educating the public, through instructional programs & exhibitions; Facilitating networking opportunities for infomation exchange
Meetings/Conferences:
• BC Honey Producers Association 2018 Semi-Annual AGM, March, 2018, Kamloops, BC
Scope: Provincial
• BC Honey Producers Association 2018 Annual General Meeting, Convention & Trade Show, 2018
Scope: Provincial
Publications:
• BeesCene
Type: Newsletter; *Frequency:* Quarterly; *Price:* Free with membership in the British Columbia Honey Producers Association

British Columbia Hospice Palliative Care Association (BCHPCA)
#1100, 1200 West 73rd Ave., Vancouver BC V6P 6G5
Tel: 604-267-7024; *Fax:* 604-267-7026
Toll-Free: 877-410-6297
office@bchpca.org
www.bchpca.org
Overview: A medium-sized provincial charitable organization
Mission: To ensure the quality of life for all British Columbians affected by life-limiting illness, death, & bereavement; To act as a collective voice in British Columbia, advocating for hospice palliative care at all levels
Member of: Canadian Hospice Palliative Care Association
Finances: *Annual Operating Budget:* $250,000-$500,000; *Funding Sources:* Grants; Donations
Staff Member(s): 2
Membership: 100-499; *Fees:* Schedule available, based upon annual budget; *Member Profile:* Organizations & individuals from British Columbia & the Yukon that provide palliative care
Activities: Encouraging the study of hospice & palliative care & providing educational resources; Increasing public awareness & support of programs; Promoting recognized standards of care; Providing communication networks; *Library:* Not open to public
Chief Officer(s):
Lorraine Gerard, Executive Director
ed@bchpca.org
Awards:
• British Columbia Hospice Palliative Care Association Award of Excellence
To honour achievement in the field of hospice palliative care in British Columbia, in either a paid or volunteer position *Deadline:* April *Contact:* Bonnie Atwood, Assistant, Administration, E-mail: office@bchpca.org
• British Columbia Hospice Palliative Care Association Research Award in Honour of Michael Downing
Deadline: April; *Amount:* $500 *Contact:* Bonnie Atwood, Assistant, Administration, E-mail: office@bchpca.org
• Awards Recognizing Enhanced End-of-Life Care for British Columbians
Funded by the Sovereign Order of St. John of Jerusalem, Knights Hospitaller, & administered by the British Columbia Hospice Palliative Care Association *Deadline:* April; *Amount:* $5,000 *Contact:* Bonnie Atwood, Assistant, Administration, E-mail: office@bchpca.org
• British Columbia Hospice Palliative Care Association Volunteer Award
To recognize personal achievements of volunteers working in the field of hospice palliative care in British Columbia *Deadline:* April *Contact:* Bonnie Atwood, Assistant, Administration, E-mail: office@bchpca.org
Meetings/Conferences:
• British Columbia Hospice Palliative Care Association 2018 Conference, May, 2018, BC
Scope: Provincial
Description: An annual meeting of members, with guest speakers, exhibits, regional meetings, the presentation of awards, & networking sessions
Contact Information: Assistant, Administration: Bonnie Atwood, E-mail: office@bchpca.org

British Columbia Hotel Association (BCHA)
#200, 948 Howe St., Vancouver BC V6Z 1N9
Tel: 604-681-7164; *Fax:* 604-681-7649
Toll-Free: 800-663-3153
www.bchotelassociation.com
twitter.com/bchotelassoc
Overview: A small provincial organization founded in 1917
Mission: To promote excellence & professionalism in the accommodation & hospitality industry of British Columbia; To advocate for the interests of British Columbia's hotel industry; To improve & increase the tourism & hospitality industry in British Columbia; To enhance the financial viability of members
Membership: 650 hotel members + 200 associate members
Activities: Providing educational & training opportunities; Offering marketing services; Liaising with government organizations & regulatory authorities; Recommending improvements in law
Chief Officer(s):
David Wetsch, President
Al McCreary, Treasurer
James Chase, Chief Executive Officer
james@bchotelassociation.com
Cailey Murphy, Coordinator, Communications, 604-443-4751
cailey@bchotelassociation.com
Louise Thompson, Coordinator, Member Services
Publications:
• InnFocus
Type: Magazine; *Frequency:* Quarterly; *Accepts Advertising*; *Editor:* Cailey Murphy

Canadian Associations / British Columbia Industrial Designer Association (BCID)

Profile: Feature articles about British Columbia's hotel industry, plus association reports
• InnTouch
Type: Newsletter; *Frequency:* Bi-weekly; *Editor:* Cailey Murphy
Profile: Current information about British Columbia's hospitality industry

British Columbia Human Rights Coalition *See* Community Legal Assistance Society

British Columbia Industrial Designer Association (BCID)
PO Box 33943, Vancouver BC V6J 4L7
Tel: 604-608-3204; *Fax:* 604-608-3204
email@bcid.com
www.bcid.com
Overview: A small provincial organization overseen by Association Of Canadian Industrial Designers
Mission: To act as the public voice for its members; to represent their interests nationally; to maintain a set of standards to preserve the integrity of the profession; to keep a register of professional industrial designers in the province.
Membership: *Member Profile:* Available to any permanent, legal resident of B.C., Alberta, or Sask. who has obtained at least an undergraduate degree, with a major in industrial design, and whose primary professional responsibility as a practioner or educator is with industrial design.

British Columbia Insolvency Practitioners Association *See* British Columbia Association of Insolvency & Restructuring Professionals

British Columbia Institute of Agrologists (BCIA)
2777 Claude Rd., Victoria BC V9B 3T7
Tel: 250-380-9292; *Fax:* 250-380-9233
Toll-Free: 877-855-9291
admin@bcia.com
www.bcia.com
Overview: A medium-sized provincial licensing organization founded in 1947 overseen by Agricultural Institute of Canada
Finances: *Annual Operating Budget:* $250,000-$500,000; *Funding Sources:* Membership dues
Staff Member(s): 3; 20 volunteer(s)
Membership: 950; *Fees:* $150; *Member Profile:* Professional agrologists
Activities: *Internships:* Yes
Chief Officer(s):
Robert Moody, Executive Director
p.ag@bcia.com
Meetings/Conferences:
• British Columbia Institute of Agrologists 71st Annual General Meeting & Conference 2018, 2018, BC
Scope: Provincial

British Columbia Institute of Technology Faculty & Staff Association (BCIT FSA)
3700 Willingdon Ave., #SE16-116, Burnaby BC V5G 3H2
Tel: 604-432-8695; *Fax:* 604-432-8348
fsa@bcit.ca
www.bcitfsa.ca
www.linkedin.com/groups/2420205
www.facebook.com/BCITFSA
twitter.com/BCITFSA
Overview: A medium-sized provincial organization founded in 1964
Mission: To defend & advance the employment interests of members, through representation; To improve employment conditions for members; To celebrate & protect members; To improve standards in education
Member of: Canadian Association of University Teachers; BC Federation of Labour
Finances: *Annual Operating Budget:* $500,000-$1.5 Million; *Funding Sources:* Membership dues
Staff Member(s): 9; 100 volunteer(s)
Membership: 1,600; *Committees:* Bargaining; Collective Agreement; Department Rights & Responsibilities; FSA-CUPE Bargaining; Instructional Development; Internal Audit; Investment; ITS Reclassification; Joint Benefits; Joint Labour Management; Rehabilitation
Activities: Engaging in collective bargaining, advocacy, & labour relations activities; Liaising with government & the community; Promoting the association & its members
Chief Officer(s):
Teresa Place, President
Paul Reniers, Executive Director, 604-432-8696
preniers@bcit.ca

Publications:
• FSA Voice [a publication of the British Columbia Institute of Technology Faculty & Staff Association]
Type: Newsletter
Profile: Association reports & activities, plus articles about employment issues

British Columbia Institute of the Purchasing Management Association of Canada *See* Supply Chain Management Association - British Columbia

British Columbia Interior Bison Association *See* British Columbia Bison Association

British Columbia International Commercial Arbitration Centre (BCICAC)
#348, 1275 West 6th Ave., Vancouver BC V6H 1A6
Tel: 604-684-2821; *Fax:* 604-736-9233
Toll-Free: 877-684-2821
admin@bcicac.com
www.bcicac.com
Overview: A medium-sized international organization founded in 1986
Mission: To provide effective alternative dispute resolution services to our clients
Membership: *Member Profile:* Arbitrators & mediators
Chief Officer(s):
Patrick Williams, President & Director

British Columbia Investment Agriculture Foundation (IAF)
PO Box 8248, 808 Douglas Victoria, 3rd Fl., Victoria BC V8W 2Z7
Tel: 250-356-1662; *Fax:* 250-953-5162
Other Communication: Funding Inquiries e-mail:
funding@iafbc.ca
info@iafbc.ca
www.iafbc.ca
www.linkedin.com/company/3638464
www.facebook.com/InvestAgBC
twitter.com/IAFBC
Also Known As: Investment Agriculture Foundation of BC
Overview: A medium-sized provincial organization founded in 1996
Mission: To encourage growth & innovation in the agriculture & agri-food industry across British Columbia
Finances: *Funding Sources:* Federal & provincial government
Chief Officer(s):
Ken Bates, Chair
Peter Donkers, Executive Director, 250-356-6654
pdonkers@iafbc.ca
Awards:
• Award of Excellence for Innovation in Agriculture & Agri-Food
• BC Buy Local Award of Excellence
Publications:
• Growing Tomorrow [a publication of British Columbia Investment Agriculture Foundation]
Type: Newsletter; *Frequency:* 3 pa

British Columbia Katahdin Sheep Association
c/o Christopher & Christine Page, Venner Brook Farm, 9166 Chemainus Rd., Chemainus BC V0R 1K0
Tel: 250-246-4140
vennerbrookfarm@hotmail.com
www.katahdinsheep.com
Overview: A small provincial organization overseen by Canadian Katahdin Sheep Association Inc.
Mission: To develop British Columbia's Katahdin sheep industry
Membership: 1-99; *Member Profile:* Katahdin sheep breeders in British Columbia
Chief Officer(s):
Hans Bissig, Contact, 250-428-3365
bissigl@hotmail.com

British Columbia Landscape & Nursery Association (BCLNA)
#102, 19289 Langley Bypass, Surrey BC V3S 6K1
Tel: 604-575-3500; *Fax:* 604-574-7773
Toll-Free: 800-421-7963
www.bclna.com
www.linkedin.com/groups/2387526
www.facebook.com/bclna
twitter.com/bclna
Previous Name: British Columbia Nursery Trades Association
Overview: A medium-sized provincial organization founded in 1953 overseen by Canadian Nursery Landscape Association

Mission: To work together to improve quality & standards of the landscape horticulture industry
Member of: BC Agriculture Council; Canadian Nursery Landscape Association
Finances: *Annual Operating Budget:* $1.5 Million-$3 Million; *Funding Sources:* Membership dues; CanWest Horticultural Show
Staff Member(s): 6
Membership: 500+; *Fees:* $370-$980, based on gross sales; *Member Profile:* Nurserymen, garden centre operators, landscape & maintenance contractors, sod growers, arborists & suppliers from across British Columbia
Activities: Offering educational seminars & certification programs
Chief Officer(s):
Hedy Dyck, Chief Operating Officer

British Columbia Law Institute (BCLI)
University of British Columbia, 1822 East Mall, Vancouver BC V6T 1Z1
Tel: 604-822-0142; *Fax:* 604-822-0144
Toll-Free: 800-565-5297
bcli@bcli.org
www.bcli.org
www.linkedin.com/company/2281377
www.facebook.com/BCLawInstitute
twitter.com/BCLawInstitute
Overview: A small provincial charitable organization founded in 1997
Mission: To perform research & studies to change & modernize law in British Columbia
Staff Member(s): 4
Activities: *Awareness Events:* GREATdebate
Chief Officer(s):
Kathleen Cunningham, Executive Director
kcunningham@bcli.org
Krista James, National Director
kjames@bcli.org

British Columbia Liberal Party
PO Box 28131, Vancouver BC V6C 3T7
Tel: 604-606-6000; *Fax:* 604-632-0253
Toll-Free: 800-567-2257
contact@bcliberals.com
www.bcliberals.com
www.facebook.com/BCLiberals
twitter.com/bcliberals
www.youtube.com/user/BCLiberals
Also Known As: BC Liberal Party
Overview: A small provincial organization overseen by The Liberal Party of Canada
Chief Officer(s):
Sharon White, Party President

British Columbia Libertarian Party (BCLP)
#703, 1180 Falcon Dr., Coquitlam BC V3E 2K7
Tel: 604-944-2845
info@libertarian.bc.ca
www.libertarian.bc.ca
Overview: A small provincial organization founded in 1986 overseen by The Libertarian Party of Canada
Mission: To advocate civil liberties & private property rights, including drug legalization & ending coercive taxation
Affiliation(s): Foundation for Research on Economics & the Environment
Activities: *Speaker Service:* Yes
Chief Officer(s):
Clayton Welwood, Leader

British Columbia Library Association (BCLA)
#150, 900 Howe St., Vancouver BC V6Z 2M4
Tel: 604-683-5354; *Fax:* 604-609-0707
Toll-Free: 888-683-5354
bclaoffice@bcla.bc.ca
www.bclaconnect.ca
twitter.com/bclaconnect
Overview: A large provincial licensing charitable organization founded in 1911
Mission: To encourage library development throughout British Columbia; To coordinate library services to various parts of the province; To promote cooperation between libraries; To advance the mutual interests of libraries & library personnel
Finances: *Funding Sources:* Membership dues; Donations; Sponsorships
Membership: 700+; *Fees:* Schedule available; *Member Profile:* Individuals in the library profession in British Columbia; Supporters of libraries in British Columbia; Libraries; Companies

& organizations providing products or services to libraries; *Committees:* Continuing Education; Copyright; Diversity & Multicultural Services; Information Policy; Intellectual Freedom; Resolutions; Mentorship
Activities: Coordinating projects to improve library services & information access; Providing workshops & seminars; Preparing briefs to government; Sponsoring scholarships & awards; Providing an online job posting service; Liaising with similar organizations across Canada; Co-hosting the British Columbia Library Conference, featuring educational sessions, speakers, meetings, social events, & a trade show
Chief Officer(s):
Annette DeFaveri, Executive Director
execdir@bcla.bc.ca
Cassie McFadden, Office Manager
Awards:
- Helen Gordon Stewart Award
; *Amount:* Plaque; life membership in the association
- Honourary Life Membership
; *Amount:* Plaque; life membership in the association
- Achievement in Library Service
; *Amount:* Plaque
- Keith Sacré Library Champion Award
; *Amount:* Plaque; Invitation to awards banquet
- BCLA President's Award
- Merit Awards
- Ken Haycock Student Conference Award
; *Amount:* $300; conference registration
- Alice Bacon Continuing Education Scholarship
; *Amount:* No less than $100
- Harry Newsom Memorial Award
; *Amount:* Varies
- Virginia Chisholm Memorial Award
; *Amount:* $185; basic conference registration
- Academic Librarians Section Outstanding Contribution Award
- Young Adult & Children's Services Section Award
Meetings/Conferences:
- British Columbia Library Association (BCLA) Library Conference 2018, 2018, BC
Scope: Provincial

British Columbia Library Association Library Technicians' & Assistants' Section
#150, 900 Howe St., Vancouver BC V6Z 2M4
bclaconnect.ca/ltas
twitter.com/bclaltas
Overview: A small provincial organization overseen by British Columbia Library Association (BCLA)
Mission: To establish an inclusive, province-wide organization which supports & promotes the role of library technicians & assistants, regardless of formal training or certification, through education, communication, & advocacy.
Chief Officer(s):
Krissy Bublitz, Chair
ltaschair@gmail.com

British Columbia Library Trustees' Association (BCLTA)
#108, 9865 - 140th St., Surrey BC V3T 4M4
Tel: 604-913-1424
Toll-Free: 888-206-1245
office@bclta.ca
www.bclta.ca
www.facebook.com/392761817401045
twitter.com/BCLTA
Overview: A small provincial charitable organization founded in 1977
Mission: To develop & support library trustees who govern local public libraries in British Columbia; To advance public library service in the province
Affiliation(s): British Columbia Library Association
Finances: *Funding Sources:* Grants; Sponsorships; Membership dues
Staff Member(s): 2
Membership: 71 library boards, with 700+ library trustees; *Fees:* Schedule available for library boards, $100 associate; *Member Profile:* Institutional membership for library boards, featuring general membership privileges for each individual trustee; Associate membership for library systems or persons interested in libraries
Activities: Promoting literacy & library services; Engaging in advocacy activities; Liaising with the provincial government's Public Library Services Branch; Providing educational opportunities for members; Offering networking opportunities
Chief Officer(s):

Barbara Kelly, Executive Director
execdir@bctla.ca
Awards:
- Nancy Bennett Merit Award
- Super Trustee Award
- Library Advocate Award
Meetings/Conferences:
- British Columbia Library Trustees' Association 2018 Annual General Meeting, 2018
Scope: Provincial
Publications:
- BCLTA Bulletin [a publication of the British Columbia Library Trustees' Association]
Type: Newsletter; *Frequency:* Monthly; *Accepts Advertising*;
Price: Free with British Columbia Library Trustees' Association membership
Profile: News articles, events & stories of interest to BCLTA members
- British Columbia Library Trustees' Association Annual Report
Type: Yearbook; *Frequency:* Annually
- The Effective Board Member [a publication of the British Columbia Library Trustees' Association]
Type: Handbook; *Price:* Free with BCTLA membership; $8 for non-members
Profile: A British Columbia public library trustee educational resource
- Taking the Lead [a publication of the British Columbia Library Trustees' Association]
Type: Handbook; *Price:* Free with British Columbia Library Trustees' Associationmembership
Profile: Educational resource for British Columbia public library board chairs

British Columbia Lions Society for Children with Disabilities (BCLS)
3981 Oak St., Vancouver BC V6H 4H5
Tel: 604-873-1865; *Fax:* 604-873-0166
Toll-Free: 800-818-4483
info@easterealsbcy.ca
www.easterseals.bcy.ca
www.facebook.com/EasterSealsBCY
twitter.com/EasterSealsBCY
Also Known As: Lions Society of BC; Easter Seals; BC Lions Foundation for Children with Disabilities
Overview: A large provincial charitable organization founded in 1952
Mission: To provide as many services as possible to children with disabilities; To enhance the lives of children with special needs; To give children with disabilities self-esteem, self-confidence, & a sense of independence
Member of: Easter Seals Canada
Affiliation(s): Easter Seal House Society; 24 HR Relay Society
Finances: *Funding Sources:* Appeals & lotteries; events; donations from Lions Clubs; estates & gifts to societies; foundations
Activities: Camping Programs - three camps, to any child between the age of 6 & 18 with a disability, free of charge; Patient Care Grants - offers financial assistance for some medical treatments not covered by BC Med; Easter Seal Houses - three houses for families to stay while their sick child is in for medical treatment; *Awareness Events:* Paper Eggs, March; 24-Hour Relay for the Kids, June; Drop-Zone, September; Scotiabank Easter Seals Regatta, July; Timmy's Christmas Telethon, December; *Rents Mailing List:* Yes; *Library*
Victoria Office
2095 Granite St., Victoria BC V8S 3G5
Tel: 250-370-0518; *Fax:* 250-370-5098
Toll-Free: 888-868-2822
info@forthekidsbc.org

British Columbia Literacy Council (BCLCIRA)
c/o Sir Wilfred Grenfell Elementary School, 3323 Wellington Ave., Vancouver BC V5R 4Y3
Tel: 604-713-4844; *Fax:* 604-713-4846
www.readingbc.ca
Also Known As: Council No: CF300
Overview: A small provincial organization overseen by International Reading Association
Chief Officer(s):
Dianna Mezzarobba, Coordinator

British Columbia Lodging & Campgrounds Association (BCLCA)
#209, 3003 St. John's St., Port Moody BC V3H 2C4
Tel: 778-383-1037; *Fax:* 604-945-7606
www.bclca.com

www.facebook.com/TravellinginBritishColumbia
twitter.com/TravellinginBC
www.instagram.com/travelinbc
Previous Name: BC Motels, Campgrounds, Resorts Association
Overview: A medium-sized provincial organization founded in 1944
Mission: To promote the public's utilization of member lodging & campground businesses; To monitor & make representation to governments on legislation affecting the interests of British Columbia's lodging & campground businesses; To speak for the membership on matters of general or specific interest; To encourage members to strive for excellence in accommodation & service
Finances: *Annual Operating Budget:* $250,000-$500,000
Staff Member(s): 3
Membership: 625; *Fees:* $280; *Member Profile:* Accommodation businesses such as: motel, hotel, campground, RV Park, resort or B&B in the province of British Columbia
Activities: Marketing & promotion; group purchasing discounts; lobbying; education & industry standards
Chief Officer(s):
Joss Penny, Executive Director
jpenny@bclca.com

British Columbia Lung Association (BCLA)
2675 Oak St., Vancouver BC V6H 2K2
Tel: 604-731-5864; *Fax:* 604-731-5810
Toll-Free: 800-665-5864
info@bc.lung.ca
www.bc.lung.ca
www.facebook.com/BCLungAssociation
twitter.com/BCLungAssoc
Previous Name: Anti-Tuberculosis Society
Overview: A medium-sized provincial charitable organization founded in 1906 overseen by Canadian Lung Association
Mission: To support lung health research, education, prevention, & advocacy; To help people manage respiratory diseases, including asthma, COPD (chronic bronchitis & emphysema), lung cancer, sleep apnea, & tuberculosis
Finances: *Funding Sources:* Donations; Sponsorships; Fundraising
Membership: *Committees:* Executive; Medical Advisory
Activities: Providing money to physicians & scientists doing research in British Columbia on lung diseases; Offering breathing test events; *Awareness Events:* The Staircimb for Clean Air, February; The Bicycle Trek for Life & Breath, September
Chief Officer(s):
Scott McDonald, President & CEO
Kelly Ablog-Morrant, Director, Health Education & Program Services
Chris Lam, Manager, Development
Katrina van Bylandt, Manager, Communications
Debora Wong, Manager, Finance & Administration
Marissa McFadyen, Coordinator, Special Events
Meetings/Conferences:
- British Columbia Lung Association 15th Annual Air Quality & Health Workshop 2018, February, 2018, Vancouver, BC
Scope: Provincial
Publications:
- British Columbia Lung Association Annual Report
Type: Yearbook; *Frequency:* Annually
- Your Health [a publication of the British Columbia Lung Association]
Type: Magazine; *Frequency:* Semiannually; *Editor:* Katrina van Bylandt
Profile: Health information for medical & health promoters, educators, donors to the Lung Association, & persons interested in respiratoryhealth

British Columbia Lupus Society (BCLS)
#210, 888 West 8th Ave., Vancouver BC V5Z 3Y1
Tel: 604-714-5564
Toll-Free: 866-585-8787
info@bclupus.org
www.bclupus.org
Also Known As: BC Lupus Society
Overview: A medium-sized provincial charitable organization founded in 1977 overseen by Lupus Canada
Mission: To provide education & support to Lupus patients & their friends & families; to increase public awareness of lupus
Membership: *Fees:* $20 individual; $25 family
Activities: *Awareness Events:* Lupus Awareness Month, Oct.; World Lupus Day, May 10
Chief Officer(s):

Josie Bradley, President

British Columbia Mainland Cricket League (BCMCL)
PO Box 100, 12886 - 96th Ave., Surrey BC V3V 6A8
Fax: 604-909-2669
info@bcmcl.ca
www.bcmcl.org
www.facebook.com/bcmcl.ca
twitter.com/bcmcl
www.youtube.com/thebcmcl
Previous Name: British Columbia Cricket Association
Overview: A small provincial organization overseen by Cricket Canada
Member of: Cricket Canada
Chief Officer(s):
Nazir Desai, President, 778-318-6630
ndesai7@hotmail.com
Mohammed Talha Patel, Secretary, 604-445-9752
surreystars@hotmail.com

British Columbia Marijuana Party
307 Hastings St. West, Vancouver BC V6B 1H6
Tel: 604-683-1750
www.cannabisculture.com
www.facebook.com/CCMagazineOnline
twitter.com/cannabisculture
www.instagram.com/cannabisculture
Also Known As: BC Marijuana Party
Overview: A small provincial organization
Chief Officer(s):
Marc Emery, Party Leader

British Columbia Marine Trades Association See Boating BC Association

British Columbia Maritime Employers Association (BCMEA)
#500, 349 Railway St., Vancouver BC V6A 1A4
Tel: 604-688-1155; *Fax:* 604-684-2397
www.bcmea.com
www.linkedin.com/company/1556948
www.facebook.com/BCMEA
twitter.com/editorbcmea
Overview: A medium-sized provincial organization founded in 1963
Mission: To respond to the needs of members; To represent the interests of members; To provide labour relations services to British Columbia's waterfront employers
Membership: 59 organizations; *Member Profile:* Ship owners; Stevedores; Bulk terminal operators; *Committees:* Executive; Finance
Activities: Offering labour relations, training & information services
Chief Officer(s):
Terry Duggan, President & Chief Executive Officer
Mike Leonard, Senior Vice President, Employee Relations & Dispatch
John Beckett, Vice President, Training, Safety, & Recruitment
Eleanor Marynuik, Vice President, Human Resources

British Columbia Marketing Board (BCMB) See British Columbia Farm Industry Review Board

British Columbia Medical Association See Doctors of BC

British Columbia Milk Marketing Board
#200, 32160 South Fraser Way, Abbotsford BC V2T 1W5
Tel: 604-556-3444; *Fax:* 604-556-7717
info@milk-bc.com
www.milk-bc.com
Overview: A small provincial organization
Mission: To promote, control & regulate the production, transportation, packing, storing & marketing of milk, fluid milk & manufactured milk products within British Columbia
Staff Member(s): 13
Chief Officer(s):
Ben Janzen, Chair
bjanzen@milk-bc.com
Robert Delage, General Manager
rdelage@milk-bc.com

British Columbia Miniature Horse Club (BCMHC)
1620 Baldy Mountain Rd., Shawnigan Lake BC V0R 2W2
Tel: 250-743-1183
pipb@shaw.ca
www.bcminiaturehorseclubs.com
Overview: A small provincial organization founded in 1978
Mission: To share information about the miniature horse breed

Membership: *Fees:* $5 youth members; $25 individuals; $35 families; *Member Profile:* Adults & youth, in British Columbia, who are interested in the miniature horse breed; Members do not have to be horse owners
Activities: Organizing educational clinics to help members with their show skills; Hosting shows for miniature horses; Presenting demonstrations at equine functions; Participating in parades to increase awareness of the miniature horse breed; Providing networking opportunities for the exchange of information
Chief Officer(s):
Jason Walmsley, President, 604-856-1419
Jazbo@telus.net
Marie O'Neill, Vice-President, 604-514-1467
omarie@telus.net
Jo Anne Barnhill, Secretary, 604-856-7812
barnhill@uniserve.ca
Heather Ward, Treasurer, 604-858-9650
sunnyvalehjward@telus.net
Rebecca Bermudez, Editor, Newsletter, 604-316-5060
bec@pipsqueakpaddocks.com
Lavon Read, Show Secretary, 360-659-1711
Publications:
• British Columbia Miniature Horse Club Newsletter
Type: Newsletter; *Editor:* Rebecca Bermudez
Profile: Club news & announcements

British Columbia Mountaineering Club
PO Box 20042, Vancouver BC V5Z 0C1
Tel: 604-268-9502
info@bcmc.ca
www.bcmc.ca
Overview: A small provincial organization founded in 1907
Mission: BCMC is a group of active individuals who organize mountaineering & skiing trips throughout the year. The primary mode of locomotion is pedestrian to allow appreciation of the mountains with least environmental impact. The Club is also active in conservation, trail & hut construction, trail maintenance, mountain safety & education.
Affiliation(s): Federation of Mountain Clubs of BC
16 volunteer(s)
Membership: 500 individual; *Fees:* $45 individual; $68 couple; $23 youth/senior; $800 lifetime; *Committees:* Conservation
Activities: Hiking; climbing; mountaineering; backcountry skiing; snowshoeing; hiking, backpacking; *Library:* by appointment
Chief Officer(s):
David Scanlon, President

British Columbia Municipal Safety Association (BCMSA)
20430 Fraser Hwy., Langley BC V3A 4G2
Fax: 778-278-0029
www.bcmsa.ca
www.facebook.com/167587416635419?sk=wall
Overview: A small provincial organization
Mission: The central purpose of the BC Municipal Safety Association is to improve worker health and safety through the sharing of knowledge and resources within local government.
Chief Officer(s):
Cathy Cook, Executive Director, 778-278-3486
ccook@bcmsa.ca
Meetings/Conferences:
• 2018 BC Municipal OH&S Conference, 2018, BC
Scope: Provincial

British Columbia Museums Association (BCMA)
675 Belleville St., Victoria BC V8W 9W2
Tel: 250-356-5700
bcma@museumsassn.bc.ca
www.museumsassn.bc.ca
www.facebook.com/BCMuseumsAssn
twitter.com/bcmuseumsassn
Also Known As: BC Museums Association
Overview: A medium-sized provincial charitable organization founded in 1957
Mission: To promote the protection & preservation of the objects, specimens, records & sites significant to the natural, creative & human history of British Columbia; To aid in the improvement of museums & galleries as educational institutions; To assist in the development of the museum profession; To support & advocate for the museum community of British Columbia
Member of: Canadian Museums Association
Finances: *Funding Sources:* Government; Membership fees; Services fees; Sponsorships; Donations
Staff Member(s): 2; 20 volunteer(s)

Membership: 500; *Fees:* Schedule available; *Member Profile:* Individual/institution subscribing to the aims of the BCMA; *Committees:* Advocacy; Awards; Membership; Professional Development
Activities: Providing professional development opportunities for members & non-members; Holding an annual conference; Providing information networking for members & non-members; Advocating on behalf of institutions, trustees, professional staff & volunteers; *Internships:* Yes; *Speaker Service:* Yes
Chief Officer(s):
Erica Mattson, Executive Director
executivedirector@museumsassn.bc.ca
Heather Jeliazkov, Manager, Marketing & Membership Services
hjeliazkov@museumsassn.bc.ca
Awards:
• Corporate Service Award
Eligibility: A business or corporation that has been innovative in its support to the museum, art gallery or archives
• Award of Merit
Eligibility: An individual, institution or agency that has made a recent outstanding, innovative, or creative achievement in the museum or art gallery fields in BC
• Distinguished Service Award
Eligibility: An individual who has made a substantial & noteworthy contribution, on a provincial basis, to the museum, art gallery, archives, or heritage field
• Barrie Hardcastle Bursary
This award is used toward training in financial administration & management; funds may cover tuition or registration fees, travel, & textbooks *Eligibility:* Staff & volunteers of current Institutional BCMA Members
• Joe Nagel Technology Bursary
This bursary will assist the recipient in implementing an innovative use of technology in the museum, art gallery, or heritage fields *Eligibility:* BCMA members in good standing
Meetings/Conferences:
• British Columbia Museums Association 2018 Annual Conference, 2018
Scope: Provincial
Publications:
• Roundup [a publication of the British Columbia Museum Association]
Type: Magazine; *Frequency:* q.; *Accepts Advertising*; *Editor:* Jane Lemke; *Price:* Free with membership in the BCMA
Profile: A resource containing informative articles on current issues & events, profiles on feature members of the museumcommunity, & professional development opportunities

British Columbia Music Educators' Association (BCMEA)
c/o British Columbia Teachers' Federation, #100, 550 West 6th Ave., Vancouver BC V5Z 4P2
bcmusiced@gmail.com
www.bcmusiced.ca
Overview: A small provincial organization founded in 1957
Mission: To promote excellence in music education in British Columbia schools; To advocate for music education in British Columbia; To foster music appreciation
Member of: British Columbia Teachers' Federation
Membership: *Fees:* $36 retired persons & students; $60 British Columbia Teachers' Federation members; $87.92 non-BCTF members; *Member Profile:* Music educators in British Columbia; Persons interested in music education; Retired educators; Students
Activities: Promoting music education in British Columbia schools; Providing professional development activities; Liaising with partner organizations; Offering networking opportunities
Chief Officer(s):
Mandart Chan, President, 250-478-5501, Fax: 250-478-2879
bcmea.vp1@gmail.com
Meetings/Conferences:
• BC Music Educators' Association 2018 Annual Conference, October, 2018, River Rock Casino Resort, Richmond, BC
Scope: Provincial
Description: Professional development activities & exhibits for British Columbia teachers
Contact Information: www.bcmeaconference.com
Publications:
• The BC Music Educator
Type: Journal; *Frequency:* Quarterly; *Accepts Advertising*
Profile: Articles, plus music course, festival, & conference offerings

British Columbia Muslim Association (BCMA)
12300 Blundell Rd., Richmond BC V6W 1B3

Tel: 604-270-2522; Fax: 604-244-9750
bcma@shawcable.com
www.thebcma.com
www.facebook.com/bcmuslimassociation
twitter.com/thebcma1
Overview: A large provincial organization founded in 1966
Mission: To represent Sunni Muslims in British Columbia; To promote the interests of the Muslim community
Finances: *Funding Sources:* Donations; Fundraising
Membership: 40,000; *Member Profile:* Sunni Muslims throughout British Columbia
Activities: Developing & maintaining religious, cultural, & educational facilities; Owning & operating Mosques; Providing funeral & burial facilities; Providing locations for prayers; Operating the British Columbia Muslim School Richmond & the Surrey Muslim School; Offering educational opportunities; Providing social services to youth, adults, & seniors; Organizing social & recreational activities; Cooperating with other Muslim organizations; Promoting community awareness about Islam; Disseminating information about Islam
Chief Officer(s):
Saiyad Ali, Administrator
administrator@thebcma.com

Abbotsford Branch
1980 Salton Rd., Abbotsford BC V2S 3W7
Tel: 778-552-1354
abbotsford@thebcma.com
abbotsford.thebcma.com
Chief Officer(s):
Amir Zeb, Chair, 778-240-0133
Yaqoob Shah, Secretary
Nabeek Akhtar, Treasurer, 604-308-4972

Burnaby Branch
5060 Canada Way, Burnaby BC V5E 3N2
Tel: 604-294-2824; *Fax:* 604-244-9750
www.bcmaburnaby.org
Chief Officer(s):
Hazra Ismail, Chair
hazra7866@yahoo.ca
Khatoon Nisha Zuber, Secretary
nishazuber@hotmail.com
Tazul Ali, Treasurer

Kelowna Branch
1120 Hwy. 33N, Kelowna BC V1X 1Z2
Tel: 250-979-1370
kelowna@thebcma.com
kelowna.thebcma.com
Chief Officer(s):
Mostafa Shoranick, Chair

Nanaimo Branch
Islamic Centre of Nanaimo, 905 Hecate St., Nanaimo BC V9R 4K7
Tel: 250-754-3471
nanaimo@thebcma.com
nanaimo.thebcma.com

North Shore Branch
2300 Kirkstone Rd., North Vancouver BC V7J 3M3
Tel: 604-980-4613
northshore@thebcma.com
northshore.thebcma.com
Chief Officer(s):
Mohammad Rahamatulla, Chair
raham9@yahoo.com

Prince George Branch
PO Box 23025, Stn. College Heights, Prince George BC V2N 6Z2
Tel: 250-277-1791; *Fax:* 604-244-9750
bcma.pgchapter@gmail.com
pg.thebcma.com
Chief Officer(s):
Mostafa Mohammed, Chair, 250-564-5412
dr.mm_201210@yahoo.ca
Hassan Tahir, Secretary
Khalid Bashir, Treasurer, 250-612-7384
kbashir10@gmail.com

Richmond Branch
12300 Blundell Rd., Richmond BC V6W 1B3
Tel: 604-244-9750
richmond@thebcma.com
Richmond.thebcma.com
Chief Officer(s):
Syed Tariq Kamal, Chair, 604-716-3510
Asif R. Butt, Secretary
Abdul Fayun Khan, Treasurer

Mohammed Gul, Director, Social Services
Mohsin Chaudhry, Director, Youth
Mahmood Awan, Director, Membership
Shahzad Mansoory, Director, Sports
Ismail Patel, Director, Education

Surrey Delta Branch
12407 - 72nd Ave., Surrey BC V3W 2M5
Tel: 604-596-7834
surreydelta@thebcma.com
surrey.thebcma.com

Surrey East Branch
13585 - 62nd Ave., Surrey BC V6X 2J3
Tel: 604-597-7863
surreyeast@thebcma.com
surreyeast.thebcma.com
Chief Officer(s):
Iltaf Sahib, Chair
iltafsahib@gmail.com

Vancouver Branch
4162 Welwyn St., Vancouver BC V5N 3Z2
Tel: 604-873-1787
vancouver@thebcma.com
vancouver.thebcma.com
Chief Officer(s):
Hakim Mohammed, Chair

Victoria Branch
2218 Quadra St., Victoria BC V8T 4C6
Tel: 250-995-1422
bcmavictoria@gmail.com
www.masjidal-iman.com
Chief Officer(s):
Belkacem Chergui, Chair

British Columbia Native Women's Association
144 Briar Ave., Kamloops BC V2B 1C1
Tel: 250-554-4556; *Fax:* 250-554-4573
www.facebook.com/bc.nativewomensassociation
Overview: A medium-sized provincial organization overseen by Native Women's Association of Canada

British Columbia Nature (Federation of British Columbia Naturalists) (FBCN)
c/o Parks Heritage Centre, 1620 Mount Seymour Rd., North Vancouver BC V7G 2R9
www.bcnature.ca
Previous Name: Nature Council of British Columbia
Overview: A medium-sized provincial organization founded in 1969
Mission: To protect biodiversity, species at risk, & natural areas throughout British Columbia; To present a unified voice on conservation & environmental issues
Finances: *Funding Sources:* Membership fees; Donations; Fundraising
Membership: 50+ local nature clubs; *Fees:* $20; *Member Profile:* Naturalists, biologists, academics, environmentalists, nature experts, local natural history groups, & nature clubs throughout British Columbia; *Committees:* Awards; Communications; Conservation; Education
Activities: Providing educational opportunities; Coordinating stewardship projects
Chief Officer(s):
Betty Davison, Office Manager, 604-985-3057
manager@bcnature.ca
Meetings/Conferences:
• BC Nature 2018 Annual General Meeting, 2018
Scope: Provincial
Description: An annual meeting of naturalists, environmentalists, biologists, & academics who are members of British Columbia Nature
Publications:
• BC Nature Magazine
Type: Magazine; *Frequency:* Quarterly; *Accepts Advertising*; *Price:* Free with membership in the British Columbia Nature (Federation of BC Naturalists)
Profile: Club news, conservation information, & book reviews

British Columbia Naturopathic Association (BCNA)
2238 Pine St., Vancouver BC V6J 5G4
Tel: 604-736-6646; *Fax:* 604-736-6048
Toll-Free: 800-277-1128
bcna@bcna.ca
www.bcna.ca
www.facebook.com/BCNaturopathicAssociation
twitter.com/BCnaturopath
www.youtube.com/user/BCNaturopathicAssoc

Overview: A small provincial organization founded in 1993 overseen by The Canadian Association of Naturopathic Doctors
Mission: To act on behalf of the naturopathic profession in British Columbia; To advance the welfare of members of the profession
Affiliation(s): Canadian Association of Naturopathic Doctors
Membership: *Member Profile:* Licensed NDs (naturopathic physicians) in British Columbia, specializing in disease prevention & clinical nutrition; Public members
Activities: Promoting services provided by the naturopathic profession; Offering referrals; Engaging in collective bargaining & advocacy activities; Providing educational opportunities; *Awareness Events:* Naturopathic Medicine Week, first week of May
Publications:
• Your Health
Type: Newsletter; *Frequency:* Quarterly
Profile: Research & articles

British Columbia Netball Association
BC
Tel: 604-293-1820
mwebb1@shaw.ca
bcnetball.ca
www.facebook.com/BCNetballAssoc
twitter.com/BCNetball
Also Known As: BC Netball
Overview: A small provincial organization overseen by Netball Canada
Mission: To oversee the sport of netball in British Columbia.
Member of: Netball Canada
Affiliation(s): International Federation of Netball Associations
Chief Officer(s):
Ann Willcocks, President

British Columbia Neurofibromatosis Foundation (BCNF)
PO Box 5339, Victoria BC V8R 6S4
Toll-Free: 800-385-2263
info@bcnf.bc.ca
www.bcnf.bc.ca
www.facebook.com/10150157765325565
twitter.com/BC_NF
Overview: A small provincial charitable organization founded in 1984
Mission: To empower individuals with NF & their families to reach their full potential by providing support, education & research funding to find a cure
Member of: INFA - International NF Association
Affiliation(s): National NF Foundation
Finances: *Funding Sources:* Grants; fundraising events; membership dues; donations
Staff Member(s): 2
Membership: *Member Profile:* Individuals with neurofibro materials
Activities: Physician awareness campaign & various community awareness events; *Library:* Open to public
Chief Officer(s):
Desirée Sher, Executive Director

British Columbia Non-Profit Housing Association (BCNPHA)
#220, 1651 Commercial Dr., Vancouver BC V5L 3Y3
Tel: 604-291-2600; *Fax:* 604-291-2636
Toll-Free: 800-494-8859
admin@bcnpha.ca
www.bcnpha.ca
www.linkedin.com/company/bc-non-profit-housing-association
www.facebook.com/bcnpha
twitter.com/BCNPHA
Also Known As: BC Non-Profit Housing Association
Overview: A small provincial organization founded in 1993
Mission: To support non-profit housing providers in British Columbia, by offering services; To strive towards safe & affordable housing for tenants in the province; To encourage excellence, through best practices
Affiliation(s): BC Housing; Canada Mortgage & Housing Corporation
Finances: *Funding Sources:* CMHC; Sponsorships
Membership: *Fees:* $70-$500; *Member Profile:* Individuals; Non-profit housing societies; Non-profit organizational associations; For-profit service organizations
Activities: Offering core courses, workshops, & seminars led by BCNPHA-certified instructors; Engaging in advocacy activities at both the provincial & national levels; Liaising with public, private, & non profit sectors; Participating in policy development

Chief Officer(s):
Kishone Tony Roy, CEO
kishone@bcnpha.ca
Jill Atkey, Managing Director
jill@bcnpha.ca
Dean Pogas, Director, Operations & Communications
dean@bcnpha.ca
Ian Cullis, Director, Asset Management
ian@bcnpha.ca
Publications:
• BCNPHA eNews [a publication of British Columbia Non-Profit Housing Association]
Type: Newsletter; Price: Free
• British Columbia Non-Profit Housing Association Membership Directory
Type: Directory; Frequency: Annually
• British Columbia Non-Profit Housing Association Annual Report
Type: Yearbook; Frequency: Annually
• InfoLink [a publication of British Columbia Non-Profit Housing Association]
Type: Newsletter; Frequency: Bimonthly; Accepts Advertising; Editor: Dean Pogas; Price: Free with British Columbia Non-ProfitHousing Association membership; $20 non-members
Profile: News updates, resources, & articles related to British Columbia's non-profit housing sector
• Supplier Directory [a publication of British Columbia Non-Profit Housing Association]
Type: Directory
Profile: Listings of British Columbia Non-Profit Housing Association associate members, who offer professional services or products, &suppliers, recommended by non-profit housing providers

British Columbia Northern Real Estate Board
2609 Queensway, Prince George BC V2L 1N3
Tel: 250-563-1236; Fax: 250-563-3637
inquiries@bcnreb.bc.ca
boards.mls.ca/bcnreb
Overview: A small local organization overseen by British Columbia Real Estate Association
Chief Officer(s):
Dorothy Friesen, President

British Columbia Nurse Practitioner Association (BCNPA)
27656 - 110th Ave., Maple Ridge BC V2W 1P6
info@bcnpa.org
www.bcnpa.org
www.facebook.com/BCNPA
twitter.com/BCNPA
Overview: A small provincial organization
Mission: To represent nurse practitioners on a variety of issues with stakeholders, such as British Columbia's health authorities & the British Columbia Ministry of Health; To develop a professional environment in which nurse practitioners can provide accessible, efficient, & effective healthcare; To foster the role of nurse practitioners as autonomous healthcare providers
Membership: Fees: $90/year, associate members & students; $240/year, active members; Member Profile: Nurse practitioners from across British Columbia; Nurses interested in the nurse practitioner practice; Nurse practitioner students
Activities: Advancing the professional interests of nurse practitioners in British Columbia; Providing educational resources; Sponsoring clinical education by healthcare experts; Liaising with government & other health disciplines; Offering networking opportunities; Promoting awareness of the role of nurse practitioners
Chief Officer(s):
Kathleen Fyvie, President
Meetings/Conferences:
• 13th Annual BC Nurse Practitioner Association Conference 2018, June, 2018, Vancouver Island Conference Centre, Nanaimo, BC
Scope: Provincial

British Columbia Nursery Trades Association See British Columbia Landscape & Nursery Association

British Columbia Nurses' Union (BCNU) / Syndicat des infirmières de la Colombie-Britannique
4060 Regent St., Burnaby BC V5C 6P5
Tel: 604-433-2268; Fax: 604-433-7945
Toll-Free: 800-663-9991
Other Communication: Toll Free Fax: 1-888-284-2222
www.bcnu.org
www.linkedin.com/company/british-columbia-nurses'-union
www.facebook.com/OurNursesMatter
twitter.com/BCNursesUnion
www.youtube.com/user/TheBCNursesUnion
Overview: A large provincial organization founded in 1981
Mission: To defend nurses' individual rights & the rights of the nursing profession as a whole; To protect & advance the well-being of members & the community at large
Member of: Canadian Federation of Nurses' Union
Finances: Funding Sources: Membership dues
Activities: Providing support & services for members; Advocating & representing on behalf of members; Engaging in collective bargaining; Providing bursaries & other grants; Rents Mailing List: Yes
Chief Officer(s):
Gayle Duteil, President, 604-908-2268
gayleduteil@bcnu.org
Awards:
• BCNU Member Education Bursary
• LPN (Licensed Practical Nurse) Education Bursary
• Student Nurse Education Bursary
Meetings/Conferences:
• British Columbia Nurses' Union Convention 2018, May, 2018, Hyatt Regency Vancouver, Vancouver, BC
Scope: Provincial

British Columbia Occupational Health Nurses Professional Practice Group See Occupational Nurses' Specialty Association of British Columbia

British Columbia Oyster Growers' Association See British Columbia Shellfish Growers Association

British Columbia Paint Manufacturers' Association (BCPMA)
c/o Cloverdale Paint Inc., #400, 2630 Croydon Dr., Surrey BC V3Z 6T3
Tel: 604-596-6261
helpdesk@cloverdalepaint.com
www.cloverdalepaint.com
Overview: A small provincial organization founded in 1933
Mission: To act as the voice of paint manufacturers in British Columbia; To promote the welfare of association members
Membership: 1-99; Member Profile: Paint manufacturing companies in British Columbia
Activities: Engaging in advocacy activities related to the paint manufacturing industry in British Columbia; Liaising with various levels of government

British Columbia Paleontological Alliance (BCPA)
c/o THe Exploration Place, PO Box 1779, Prince George BC V2L 4V7
www.bcfossils.ca
Overview: A small provincial organization
Mission: To advance the science of paleontology in the province by fostering public awareness, scientific collecting and education & by promoting communication among all those interested in fossils
Membership: 5 regional societies; Member Profile: Paleontology organizations
Chief Officer(s):
Tom Cockburn, Chair

British Columbia Paralegal Association (BCPA)
PO Box 75561, RPO Edgemont Village, North Vancouver BC V7R 4X1
info@bcparalegalassociation.com
www.bcparalegalassociation.com
www.facebook.com/BCParalegalAssn
Previous Name: BC Association of Legal Assistants
Overview: A small provincial organization founded in 1979
Mission: To promote the use of academically trained legal assistants within the legal community
Finances: Funding Sources: Membership fees
10 volunteer(s)
Membership: 700; Fees: $25 student; $75 voting/associate; $125 corporate; Member Profile: An educational background sufficient to satisfy Directors of Proficiency as LA; Committees: Education; Membership; Program; Newsletter
Activities: Educational seminars; meetings
Chief Officer(s):
Yves Moisan, President
yves@bcparalegalassociation.com
Carmen Marolla, Vice-President
carmen@bcparalegalassociation.com
Maryann Reinhardt, Secretary
maryann@bcparalegalassociation.com
Rose Singh, Vice-President, Education & Certification
rose@bcparalegalassociation.com

British Columbia Paraplegic Association; Canadian Paraplegic Association See Spinal Cord Injury British Columbia

British Columbia Parent-Teacher (Home & School) Federation See British Columbia Confederation of Parent Advisory Councils

British Columbia Party
7665 Sapperton Ave., Burnaby BC V3N 4C9
Tel: 604-220-3742
Also Known As: BC Party
Overview: A small provincial organization founded in 1998
Chief Officer(s):
Graham Gifford, Contact
graham.giff@gmail.com

British Columbia Persons with AIDS Society See Positive Living BC

British Columbia Pharmacy Association (BCPhA)
#1530, 1200 West 73rd Ave., Vancouver BC V6P 6G5
Tel: 604-261-2092; Fax: 604-261-2097
Toll-Free: 800-663-2840
info@bcpharmacy.ca
www.bcpharmacy.ca
twitter.com/bc_pharmacy
Overview: A medium-sized provincial organization founded in 1968
Mission: To support & advance the economic & professional well-being of members, with the goal that they will provide improved health care in British Columbia
Finances: Funding Sources: Membership fees
Membership: 2,200 pharmacists + 700 pharmacies; Member Profile: Pharmacists registered with the College of Pharmacists of British Columbia; Pharmacies licensed by the College of Pharmacists of British Columbia; Persons with an interest in pharmacy who are not registered with the College of Pharmacists of British Columbia; Pharmacy students; Persons retired from active pharmacy
Activities: Communicating with other groups, agencies, & governments; Developing & maintaining education for members; Promoting ethical & competent professional activities of members
Chief Officer(s):
Geraldine Vance, Chief Executive Officer
geraldine.vance@bcpharmacy.ca
Cyril Lopez, Chief Operating Officer, Member & Corporate Services
cyril.lopez@bcpharmacy.ca
Angie Gaddy, Director, Communications
angie.gaddy@bcpharmacy.ca
Meetings/Conferences:
• BC Pharmacy Association Annual Conference 2018, May, 2018, Fairmont Empress, Victoria, BC
Scope: National
Attendance: 300+
Publications:
• The Tablet [a publication of the British Columbia Pharmacy Association]
Type: Magazine; Frequency: Bimonthly; Accepts Advertising; Editor: Angie Gaddy; Price: Free with membership in the British Columbia PharmacyAssociation
Profile: News, comment, & analysis of topics important to pharmacists in British Columbia

British Columbia Philatelic Society
19659 Poplar Dr., Pitt Meadows BC V3Y 1Z3
Tel: 604-984-0989
verdraco@uniserve.com
www.bcphilatelic.org
Overview: A medium-sized provincial organization founded in 1919
Mission: To publicize the hobby of philately
Affiliation(s): Royal Philatelic Society of Canada; American Philatelic Society; Northwest Federation of Stamp Clubs
Finances: Funding Sources: Membership dues; Gerald E. Wellburn Philatelic Foundation
Membership: 80; Fees: $7.50 students under age 18; $20 individuals; $30 families; Member Profile: Stamp & postal-history collectors in British Columbia
Activities: Conducting weekly meetings at West Burnaby United Church; Hosting montly auctions, "Swap & Shop Socials" & exhibitions; Liaising with clubs across North America & abroad; Library: British Columbia Philatelic Society Philatelic Library
Chief Officer(s):
Tom Balabanov, President

Leslie Upton, Secretary
Derren J. Carman, Treasurer
Publications:
• British Columbia Philatelic Society Newsletter
Type: Newsletter; *Frequency:* 3 pa
Profile: Information distributed to society members
• Greater Victoria & Vancouver Area Stamp Show & Bourse Listing of Events & Stamp Directory
Type: Directory
Profile: Listings of dealers, stores, clubs, & local shows

British Columbia Physical Education Provincial Specialist Association *See* Physical Education in British Columbia

British Columbia Play Therapy Association (BCPTA)
#335, 2818 Main St., Vancouver BC V5T 0C1
Tel: 778-710-7529
bcplaytherapy.ca
www.facebook.com/196439843813637
Overview: A small provincial organization founded in 1993
Mission: To promote the status of play therapy in British Columbia, encourage sound play therapy principles; promote high standards of professional and ethical conduct; and nurture the professional development of play therapists within a supportive association.
Membership: 120; *Fees:* $50 annual; $30 student; *Member Profile:* Professionals who work with children, youth, adults and family members; *Committees:* Education; E-newsletter; Membership; Website
Meetings/Conferences:
• BC Play Therapy Association 2018 Conference, 2018, BC
Scope: Provincial

British Columbia Podiatric Medical Association (BCPMA)
#220, 445 Mountain Hwy., North Vancouver BC V7J 2L1
Tel: 604-985-3338; *Fax:* 604-682-2766
info@bcpodiatrists.ca
www.bcpodiatrists.ca
Overview: A small provincial organization
Membership: *Fees:* $510
Activities: Providing a list of podiatrists who are licensed & registered with the College of Podiatric Surgeons of British Columbia; Offering information about foot care to British Columbians; Hosting & participating in health events for the public; *Speaker Service:* Yes
Chief Officer(s):
Howard Green, President

British Columbia Police Association
#202, 190 Alexander St., Vancouver BC V6A 1B5
Tel: 604-685-6486; *Fax:* 604-685-5228
contact@bc-pa.ca
www.bc-pa.ca
Previous Name: British Columbia Federation of Police Officers
Overview: A medium-sized provincial organization
Mission: To represent the interests of its members
Member of: Canadian Police Association
Membership: 2,500
Chief Officer(s):
Tom Stamatakis, President

British Columbia Powerlifting Association (BCPA)
#222, 12085 - 228 St., Maple Ridge BC V2X 6M2
bc-powerlifting.com
www.facebook.com/291376977556248
Overview: A small provincial organization founded in 2011 overseen by Canadian Powerlifting Union
Mission: To promote powerlifting throughout British Columbia
Member of: Canadian Powerlifting Union; International Powerlifting Federation
Membership: *Fees:* $60 first time; $85 general; $60 special olympics; $25 associaite
Chief Officer(s):
Joe Oliveira, President, 604-734-2932
olivejoe1969@gmail.com

British Columbia Prader-Willi Syndrome Association (BCPWSA)
2133 Chilcotin Cres., Kelowna BC V1V 2N9
www.bcpwsa.com
www.facebook.com/bcpwsa
Overview: A small provincial charitable organization founded in 1982
Mission: To provide an understanding & awareness of PWS by supporting those who have the syndrome, their families & all who come in contact with PWS

3 volunteer(s)
Membership: *Fees:* $25 individual
Chief Officer(s):
Heather Beach, President
president@bcpwsa.com
Cheryl Gagne, Treasurer
treasurer@bcpwsa.com
Frances Robinson, Secretary
secretary@bcpwsa.com

British Columbia Primary Teachers Association (BCPTA)
c/o BC Teachers' Federation, #100, 550 West 6th Ave., Vancouver BC V5Z 4P2
Tel: 604-871-2283; *Fax:* 604-871-2286
Toll-Free: 800-663-9163
www.bcpta.ca
www.facebook.com/340793353262
twitter.com/BCprimaryteach
Overview: A small provincial organization founded in 1958
Mission: To foster & promote the cause of early childhood education in British Columbia; To provide leadership in professional development; To provide BCTF with a source of consultation on matters affecting early childhood education & primary teachers in British Columbia
Member of: BC Teachers' Federation
Finances: *Annual Operating Budget:* $100,000-$250,000
15 volunteer(s)
Membership: 1,000-4,999; *Fees:* Schedule available
Activities: *Speaker Service:* Yes
Chief Officer(s):
Janine Fraser, President
psa55@bctf.ca
Meetings/Conferences:
• BC Primary Teachers' Association Spring Event 2018, 2018, BC
Scope: Provincial

British Columbia Principals & Vice-Principals Association (BCPVPA)
#200, 525 - 10 Ave. West, Vancouver BC V5Z 1K9
Tel: 604-689-3399; *Fax:* 604-877-5380
Toll-Free: 800-663-0432
www.bcpvpa.bc.ca
twitter.com/bcpvpa
www.youtube.com/user/BCPVPAVideos
Overview: A medium-sized provincial organization founded in 1988
Mission: To provide legal and contractual services advice, organize student leadership activities, and provide professional development programs
Member of: Canadian Society of Association Executives
Chief Officer(s):
Shelley Green, President
sgreen@bcpvpa.bc.ca
Kit Krieger, Executive Director
kkrieger@bcpvpa.bc.ca

British Columbia Printing & Imaging Association (BCPIA)
PO Box 75218, Stn. White Rock, Surrey BC V4A 0B1
Tel: 604-542-0902
www.bcpia.org
Previous Name: British Columbia Printing Industries Association
Overview: A medium-sized provincial organization
Mission: To be the voice of the BC printing industry & its employees; to provide services & benefits which encourage fellowship, education, community involvement & high standards in business conduct.
Member of: Canadian Printing Industries Association
Affiliation(s): Printing Industries of America
Membership: 60 companies; *Fees:* Schedule available
Activities: *Library:* Industry Reference Library; Not open to public
Chief Officer(s):
Marilynn Knoch, Executive Director
mknoch@bcpia.org

British Columbia Printing Industries Association *See* British Columbia Printing & Imaging Association

British Columbia Professional Fire Fighters' Burn Fund
#463, 4800 Kingsway, Burnaby BC V5H 4J2

Tel: 604-436-5617; *Fax:* 604-436-3057
info@burnfund.org
www.burnfund.org
Overview: A small provincial charitable organization founded in 1978
Mission: The charitable arm of the BC Professional Fire Fighters Association; Helps with burn prevention programs; help burn survivors
Affiliation(s): BC Professional Fire Fighters Association
Finances: *Funding Sources:* Donations; BC Professional Fire Fighters Assocation
Chief Officer(s):
Tony Burke, Executive Director
tj@burnfund.org

British Columbia Professional Golfers Association *See* Professional Golfers' Assocation of British Columbia

British Columbia Provincial Renal Agency (BCPRA)
#700, 1380 Burrard St., Vancouver BC V6Z 2H3
Tel: 604-875-7340
bcpra@bcpra.ca
www.bcrenalagency.ca
www.facebook.com/BCRenalAgency
twitter.com/BCRenalAgency
www.youtube.com/user/BCRenalAgency
Overview: A large provincial organization founded in 1997
Mission: To make BC a leader in kidney care delivery in Canada, through enhancing the network of kidney care, providing a coordinated patient-focused information system & monitoring & maintaining quality & standards of care
Finances: *Annual Operating Budget:* Greater than $5 Million; *Funding Sources:* Provincial government
Membership: *Committees:* Emergency Management Planning; Executive; Facilities & Equipment Planning; Glomerulonephritis; Hemodialysis; Hemodialysis Technical Group; Home Hemodialysis; Information Management Council; Kidney Care; Medical Advisory; Palliative Care; Peritoneal Dialysis; Pharmacy & Formulary; Renal Administrators; Renal Educators Group
Activities: Planning & monitoring province-wide kidney care services; Developing province-wide clinical standards & guidelines; Developing funding models; Measuring & reporting on patient & system results; Supporting research & development; *Awareness Events:* Western Canada PD Days
Meetings/Conferences:
• BC Kidney Days 2018, November, 2018, JW Marriott Parq Vancouver, Vancouver, BC
Scope: Provincial
Description: Unites clinicians & administrators from BC, Canada, & the United States to discuss current research, trends, clinical treatment & surgical breakthroughs in renal patient care.
Contact Information: URL:
www.bcrenalagency.ca/bc-kidney-days
Publications:
• PROMIS UpDate
Type: Newsletter
Profile: Up-to-date information about projects & system features, distributed every eight to ten weeks
• Renal News [a publication of the British Columbia Provincial Renal Agency]
Type: Newsletter; *Frequency:* Quarterly
Profile: Information about projects & practices across British Columbia's renal network

British Columbia Psychogeriatric Association (BCPGA)
PO Box 47028, 1030 Denman St., Vancouver BC V6G 3E1
Fax: 888-835-2451
www.bcpga.com
twitter.com/BCPGA1
Overview: A small provincial organization founded in 1997
Mission: A professional association of clinicians working in the field of mental health and older adults.
Chief Officer(s):
Nancy Jokinen, Co-President, 250-960-5111
jokinenn@unbc.ca
Dawn Hemingway, Co-President, 250-960-5694
Dawn.Hemingway@unbc.ca
Meetings/Conferences:
• 2018 BC Psychogeriatric Association Conference, 2018, BC
Scope: Provincial

British Columbia Psychological Association (BCPA)
#402, 1177 West Broadway, Vancouver BC V6H 1G3
Tel: 604-730-0501; *Fax:* 604-730-0502
Toll-Free: 800-730-0522
www.psychologists.bc.ca

Canadian Associations / British Columbia Public Interest Advocacy Centre (BCPIAC)

www.linkedin.com/groups/3997897
www.facebook.com/bcpsychologists
twitter.com/bcpsychologists
www.youtube.com/user/bcpsychologists
Overview: A medium-sized provincial organization
Mission: To promote & advance the profession of psychology in British Columbia
Staff Member(s): 1
Membership: *Committees:* Advocacy; BCPA Awards; Community Engagement; Continuing Education; Disaster Response Network; Membership; Psychologically Healthy Workplace Awards
Chief Officer(s):
Rick Gambrel, Executive Director
rick.gambrel@psychologists.bc.ca
Inky Kang, Coordinator, Marketing & Advertising
inkyung.kang@psychologists.bc.ca
Priya Bangar, Coordinator, Education
priya.bangar@psychologists.bc.ca

British Columbia Public Interest Advocacy Centre (BCPIAC)
#208, 1090 West Pender St., Vancouver BC V6E 2N7
Tel: 604-687-3063; *Fax:* 604-682-7896
support@bcpiac.com
www.bcpiac.com
www.facebook.com/443550842340768
twitter.com/BCPIAC
Overview: A small provincial organization founded in 1981
Mission: To advance the interests of groups that are generally unrepresented or underrepresented in issues of major public concern, such as welfare, disability, human, farmworkers & consumers rights
Finances: *Funding Sources:* Law Foundation of BC
Staff Member(s): 6
Activities: Advocating for a legal system that provides fair representation access to all individuals, regardless of income & social status; Communicating with the BC Ombudsperson to push for equal welfare service access; Providing legal representation to marginalized people of colour who excperience racial discrimination
Chief Officer(s):
Tannis Braithwaite, Executive Director
tbraithwaite@bcpiac.com
Grace Matsutani, Administrator
grace@bcpiac.com

British Columbia Purebred Sheep Breeders' Association (BCPSBA)
c/o Jan Carter, 3606 Ferguson Rd., Port Alberni BC V9Y 8L4
Tel: 250-723-8214
cottonwoodfarm@telus.net
www.bcsheep.com
Overview: A small provincial organization
Mission: To encourage a general & constant improvement in sheep breeding & a better organization of the interests of purebred sheep breeders of the province; to advance the interests of its members through cooperation with other industry organizations, & the governments, provincial & federal.
Member of: British Columbia Sheep Federation; Canadian Sheep Breeders Association
Finances: *Funding Sources:* Membership dues; fundraising
Membership: 83; *Fees:* $20; $10 junior
Activities: Sheep shows; fair displays & events
Chief Officer(s):
Anna Green, President, 250-546-6545
anna@otterlakefarm.ca

British Columbia Racquetball Association (BCRA)
BC
info@racquetballbc.ca
www.racquetballbc.ca
twitter.com/bcracquetball
Overview: A medium-sized provincial charitable organization founded in 1970 overseen by Racquetball Canada
Member of: Racquetball Canada
Finances: *Funding Sources:* Fundraising; SportsFunder Lottery; Sponsorships
Membership: *Fees:* $15
Activities: Supporting tournaments; Providing rules, skills, & junior development clinics; Hosting school programs

British Columbia Railway Historical Association (BCRHA)
1148 Balmoral Rd., Victoria BC V8T 1B1
bcrha@shaw.ca
www.trainweb.org/bcrha
Overview: A small provincial charitable organization founded in 1961
Mission: To preserve railway exhibits, manuscripts & film related to the BC railways
Member of: Heritage Society of BC
Finances: *Funding Sources:* Donations; book sales; membership dues
Membership: *Fees:* Annual $15; *Member Profile:* Interest in BC railway history
Activities: Research & publication of books on BC railway history; *Library:* British Columbia Railway Historical Association Library; Not open to public

British Columbia Raspberry Industry Council *See* Raspberry Industry Development Council

British Columbia Ready Mixed Concrete Association *See* Concrete B.C.

British Columbia Real Estate Association (BCREA)
PO Box 10123, #1420, 701 Georgia St. West, Vancouver BC V7Y 1C6
Tel: 604-683-7702; *Fax:* 604-683-8601
bcrea@bcrea.bc.ca
www.bcrea.bc.ca
twitter.com/bcrea
Overview: A large provincial organization founded in 1976
Mission: To promote the interests of & advocate for the real estate profession; To secure public support & trust in the profession; To promote property rights & real estate related issues; To ensure high standards of ethics & professionalism through ongoing education of realtors
Member of: The Canadian Real Estate Association
Affiliation(s): National Association of Realtors - USA
Finances: *Funding Sources:* Membership fees; Education programs
13 volunteer(s)
Membership: 12 real estate boards; *Member Profile:* Board or association of realtors in British Columbia; *Committees:* Audit; Legislative; Education; Standard Forms; Government Relations
Activities: Offering the Applied Real Estate Course & continuing professional education seminars; *Library:* by appointment Not open to public
Chief Officer(s):
Robert Laing, Chief Executive Officer, 604-742-2787
rlaing@bcrea.bc.ca
Melinda Entwistle, Chief Operating Officer, 604-742-2798
mentwistle@bcrea.bc.ca
Damian Stathonikos, Director, Communications & Public Affairs, 604-742-2793
dstathonikos@bcrea.bc.ca
Publications:
• The Bulletin [a publication of the British Columbia Real Estate Association]
Type: Newsletter; *Frequency:* Quarterly
• Commercial Leading Indicator [a publication of the British Columbia Real Estate Association]
Type: Report; *Frequency:* Quarterly
• The Condominium Manual [a publication of the British Columbia Real Estate Association]
Type: Guide; *Author:* Mike Mangan; *ISBN:* 0-9865416-0-5; *Price:* $49.95
• Connections: Advocacy News from the British Columbia Real Estate Association
Type: Newsletter; *Frequency:* Quarterly
• Housing Forecasts & Forecast Updates [a publication of the British Columbia Real Estate Association]
Type: Report; *Frequency:* Quarterly
• Legally Speaking [a publication of the British Columbia Real Estate Association]
Type: Newsletter; *Frequency:* 8 pa; *Author:* J. Clee et al.
• Mortgage Rate Forecasts [a publication of the British Columbia Real Estate Association]
Type: Report; *Frequency:* Quarterly

British Columbia Recreation & Parks Association (BCRPA)
#301, 470 Granville St., Vancouver BC V6C 1V5
Tel: 604-629-0965; *Fax:* 604-629-2651
Toll-Free: 866-929-0965
Other Communication: registration@bcrpa.bc.ca
bcrpa@bcrpa.bc.ca
www.bcrpa.bc.ca
twitter.com/bcrpa
Overview: A medium-sized provincial charitable organization founded in 1958 overseen by Canadian Parks & Recreation Association
Mission: To establish & sustain healthy lifestyles & communities in British Columbia
Finances: *Funding Sources:* Membership fees; Donations
Staff Member(s): 15
Membership: *Fees:* Free, 1st year students; $60 individual goverment members; $245 individual independent members; Schedule based on population for local governments; *Member Profile:* Local governments, such as municipalities & regional districts; Corporations or commercial organizations; Not-for-profit organizations & educational institutions, connected to park, recreation, & cultural sectors; Individuals who work for or who are connected to a local government member; Students
Activities: Advocating accessibility & inclusiveness to recreation & physical activity; Providing training & resources; Distributing manuals on topics such as fitness theory, aquatic fitness group fitness, weight training, & yoga fitness
Chief Officer(s):
Darryl Condon, President
Holly-Ann Burrows, Manager, Communication, 604-629-0965 Ext. 233
hburrows@bcrpa.bc.ca
Sandra Couto, Manager, Finance, 604-629-0965 Ext. 222
scouto@bcrpa.bc.ca
Sara Ferguson, Clerk, 604-629-0965 Ext. 221
Awards:
• BCRPA Friend of the Sector Award
Awarded to honour excellence, innovation, & creativity by those outside the field of parks & recreation
• BCRPA Provincial Awards
Awarded to recognize outstanding programs & dedicated professionals who make a difference in the parks & recreation sector; includes categories for oustanding achievement, merit, facility excellence, program excellence, parks & open spaces, and management innovation
Meetings/Conferences:
• British Columbia Recreation & Parks Association 2018 41st Annual ProvincialParks & Grounds Spring Training, February, 2018, Coast Hotel & Convention Centre, Langley, BC
Scope: Provincial
Description: Continuing education sessions that cover a wide range of interests for parks & grounds professionals
• British Columbia Recreation & Parks Association Symposium 2018, April, 2018, The Westin Bayshore, Vancouver, BC
Scope: Provincial
Description: An annual meeting of interest to parks & recreation professionals & volunteers, as well as elected officials from across British Columbia
• British Columbia Recreation & Parks Association Provincial Ripple Effects: Aquatics Workshop 2018, 2018
Scope: Provincial
Description: A two-day conference which occurs every two years, presenting operations, programming, & best practices for aquatics professionals
Publications:
• British Columbia Recreation & Parks Association Annual Report
Type: Yearbook
• Recreation & Parks BC
Type: Magazine; *Frequency:* Quarterly; *Accepts Advertising Profile:* Happenings in the parks & recreation sector

British Columbia Refederation Party
#573, 7360 - 137 St., Surrey BC V3W 1A3
Tel: 604-593-4833
info.bcr@bcrefed.com
www.bcrefed.com
www.facebook.com/bcrefed
Also Known As: BC Refed
Previous Name: Western Refederation Party of BC; Western Independence Party of BC
Overview: A small provincial organization founded in 2000
Mission: To advocate direct democracy & reform to Canadian federalism
Chief Officer(s):
Dale Marcell, President

British Columbia Registered Music Teachers' Association (BCRMTA)
c/o Registrar, PO Box 45537, Stn. Sunnyside, Surrey BC V4A 9N3
registrar@bcrmta.bc.ca
www.bcrmta.bc.ca
Overview: A medium-sized provincial organization founded in 1947

Mission: To raise the standard of the profession of music teaching in British Columbia; to promote the interests of music teachers in British Columbia
Membership: 1,000+ individual; *Committees:* Canada Music Week; Standing Rules & By-Laws; Archives; Website; Professional Development; Young Artists Tour & BC Piano Competition
Activities: 22 branches in BC
Chief Officer(s):
Cynthia Taylor, President
president@bcrmta.bc.ca
Susan Olsen, Registrar

Abbotsford Branch
Abbotsford BC
Tel: 604-850-9224
www.abbotsfordmusicbcrmta.com
Chief Officer(s):
Jean Ritter, President
jeanacademy@gmail.com

Chilliwack Branch
Chilliwack BC
Tel: 604-847-9915
bcrmta.bc.ca/chilliwack-branch
Chief Officer(s):
Sherrie Van Akker, Contact
vanakker@telus.net

Coquitlam/Maple Ridge Branch
BC
Tel: 604-941-0109
bcrmta.bc.ca/coquitlammaple-ridge-2
Chief Officer(s):
Sandra Lee, President
sandrabraathenlee@hotmail.com

East Kootenay Branch
BC
Tel: 250-426-0165
cmw@caraspiano.ca
bcrmta.bc.ca/east-kootenay
Chief Officer(s):
Cara Webb, Contact

Kelowna Branch
Kelowna BC
Tel: 250-763-5873
www.kelownabcrmta.com
Chief Officer(s):
Deborah Batycki, Contact
batycki@telus.net

Mid-Island Branch
BC
Tel: 250-248-2249
makingmelodies@hotmail.com
www.musicnanaimo.com
Chief Officer(s):
Dianne Bohn, President
bdbohn@shaw.ca

Mission Branch
Mission BC
Tel: 604-826-3312
www.bcrmta.bc.ca/mission
Chief Officer(s):
Florence Graham, Contact

Nelson Branch
Nelson BC
Tel: 250-352-7625
acmacd@shaw.ca
www.bcrmta.bc.ca/nelson
Chief Officer(s):
Anne McDonald, President

North Island Branch
BC
Tel: 250-923-3731
bcrmta.bc.ca/north-island
Chief Officer(s):
Cynthia Taylor, Contact
cindytaylormusic@gmail.com

North Shore Branch
BC
Tel: 604-921-7204
bcrmta.bc.ca/north-shore
Chief Officer(s):
Valerie Cook, President
valeriecook@shaw.ca

Prince George Branch
Prince George BC
Tel: 250-963-7001
bcrmta.bc.ca/prince-george
Chief Officer(s):
Louise Phillips, Contact
louisephillips@hotmail.com

Richmond Branch
PO Box 39502, Stn. Broadmoor, Richmond BC V7A 5G9
Tel: 604-268-9559
info@bcrmta.com
www.bcrmta.com
Chief Officer(s):
Mimi Ho, President

Shuswap Branch
BC
bcrmta.bc.ca/shuswap
Chief Officer(s):
Jane Hein, President
janehein@telus.net

South Fraser (Surrey, North Delta, White Rock, Langley) Branch
BC
www.southfrasermusic.com

South Okanagan Branch
BC
bcrmta.bc.ca/south-okanagan

Sunshine Coast Branch
Gibsons BC
Tel: 604-885-6756
bcrmta.bc.ca/sunshine-coast
Chief Officer(s):
Val Anderson, Contact
valand@uniserve.com

Trail/Castlegar Branch
BC
Tel: 250-362-9526
bcrmta.bc.ca/trailcastlegar
Chief Officer(s):
Dawna Kavanagh, President
kavanagh@telus.net

Vancouver Branch
Vancouver BC
bcrmta@bcrmta.org
www.bcrmta.org

Vernon Branch
Vernon BC
Tel: 250-542-5873
bcrmta.bc.ca/vernon
Chief Officer(s):
Carol Stromberg, Contact
kcstromberg@yahoo.com

Victoria Branch
Victoria BC
Tel: 250-370-2551
bcrmtavictoria.webs.com
Chief Officer(s):
Patricia Williamson, President
pwilliamson@shaw.ca

British Columbia Restaurant & Foodservices Association (BCRFA)
#2, 2246 Spruce St., Vancouver BC V6H 2P3
Tel: 604-669-2239; *Fax:* 604-669-6175
Toll-Free: 877-669-2239
info@bcrfa.com
www.bcrfa.com
www.linkedin.com/company/bc-restaurant-&-foodservices-association-bcrfa-
www.facebook.com/BCRFA
twitter.com/BCRFA
Overview: A medium-sized provincial organization founded in 1977
Mission: To be the voice of the hospitality industry in British Columbia; the advocat of the restaurant industry.
Staff Member(s): 5
Membership: 3,000; *Fees:* $185 education; $325 restaurant-licenced; $275 restaurant-non licensed; $350 supplier; *Member Profile:* Restaurateurs, foodservice retailers, suppliers & educators.
Activities: *Speaker Service:* Yes
Chief Officer(s):
Ian Tostenson, President & CEO
itostenson@bcrfa.com

British Columbia Rhythmic Sportive Gymnastics Federation (BCRSGF)
#268, 828 West 8th Ave., Vancouver BC V5Z 1E2
Tel: 604-333-3485; *Fax:* 604-909-1749
bcrsgf@rhythmicsbc.com
www.rhythmicsbc.com
www.facebook.com/Rhythmicsbc
www.youtube.com/user/bcrsgf
Also Known As: BC Rhythmic Gymnastics Federation
Overview: A small provincial organization
Mission: To be the governing body of the sport of rhythmic gymnastics in British Columbia, including special olympics, Aethetic Group Gymnastics & men's rhythmic gymnastics.
Chief Officer(s):
Sashka Gitcheva, Program Coordinator

British Columbia Rifle Association (BCRA)
PO Box 2418, Stn. Sardis Main, Chilliwack BC V2R 1A7
contact@bcrifle.org
www.bcrifle.org
Overview: A medium-sized provincial organization founded in 1874
Mission: To create a public sentiment for the encouragement of marksmanship in all its trades among citizens of British Columbia, both as a sport & as a definite contribution to the defence of Canada
Member of: Dominion of Canada Rifle Association
Membership: *Fees:* Schedule available
Activities: BC Marksmanship Championships in 7 different shooting sports

British Columbia Ringette Association (BCRA) / Association de ringuette de Colombie-Britannique
#420, 789 West Pender St., Vancouver BC V6C 1H2
Tel: 604-629-4583
info@bcringette.org
www.bcringette.org
www.facebook.com/RingetteBC
twitter.com/bcringette
www.youtube.com/user/ringettebc
Overview: A small provincial organization founded in 1976 overseen by Ringette Canada
Mission: To promote ringette & allow for opportunities for people in British Columbia to play ringette.
Staff Member(s): 2
Membership: *Committees:* High Performance; Canada Winter Games; Officiating Development; Audit & Finance; Sport & Athlete Development; Coaching Development; House Provincials & Tournaments; Strategic Planning; Nomination & Sucession; Risk Management; Human Resources
Chief Officer(s):
Colin Ensworth, Manager, Sports Operations
manager@bcringette.org
Rob Tait, Chair
chair@bcringette.org
Awards:
• BCRA Scholarship

British Columbia Road Builders & Heavy Construction Association (BCRB&HCA)
#307, 8678 Greenall Ave., Burnaby BC V5J 3M6
Tel: 604-436-0220; *Fax:* 604-436-2627
info@roadbuilders.bc.ca
www.roadbuilders.bc.ca
twitter.com/BCRoadBuilders
Overview: A medium-sized provincial organization founded in 1965 overseen by Canadian Construction Association
Mission: To represent the interests of member companies to government, media, other organizations & the public
Member of: British Columbia Business Council; British Columbia Chamber of Commerce
Affiliation(s): Western Canada Roadbuilders Association; Canadian Construction Association
Finances: *Funding Sources:* Membership fees; Events
Membership: 100-499; *Fees:* Schedule available; *Member Profile:* Firms involved in asphalt & concrete manufacturing, grading, paving, blasting, road & bridge building & maintenance, utility construction & the supply of related goods & services; *Committees:* Construction; Maintenance; Service & Supply
Activities: Advocating for balanced, safe transportation systems & infrastructure development that promotes provincial economic growth; Conducting research; Providing networking opportunities; *Speaker Service:* Yes
Chief Officer(s):
Kelly Scott, President
Tanjeet Kalsi, Manager, Operations

Canadian Associations / British Columbia Rugby Union

Parveen Parhar, Manager, Communications & Membership
Meetings/Conferences:
• BC Road Builders Fall Conference, September, 2018, BC
Scope: Provincial
• BC Road Builders AGM, December, 2018, BC
Scope: Provincial
Publications:
• Blue Book Equipment Rental Rate Guide
Frequency: Annually; *Accepts Advertising*
Profile: Published by the BC Road Builders & Heavy Construction Association, in partnership with the provincial Ministry of Transportation
• The Voice
Type: Newsletter; *Frequency:* Bimonthly
Profile: Association activities, member profiles, industry news, & forthcoming events for British Columbia Road Builders & Heavy Construction Association members & industry partners

British Columbia Rugby Union
#203, 210 West Broadway, Vancouver BC V5Y 3W2
Tel: 604-737-3065; *Fax:* 604-737-3916
www.bcrugby.com
www.facebook.com/bcrugbyunion
twitter.com/bcrugbyunion
www.youtube.com/bcrugbyunion
Also Known As: BC Rugby
Overview: A medium-sized provincial organization founded in 1889 overseen by Rugby Canada
Mission: To promote, sustain & manage the game of rugby in BC in a manner that will ensure wide participation & the continuous development in a safe & responsible manner
Member of: Rugby Canada
Staff Member(s): 4
Membership: 14,000; *Fees:* Schedule available; *Committees:* Competition; Discipline; Youth; Medical Science; Appeal
Activities: *Library:* Open to public
Chief Officer(s):
Annabel Kehoe, Chief Executive Officer, 604-499-7494
Louise Wheeler, Manager, Member Services

British Columbia Rural Teachers' Association *See* BC Rural & Multigrade Teachers' Association

British Columbia Safety Authority
#200, 505 - 6th St., New Westminster BC V3L 0E1
Toll-Free: 866-566-7233
contact@technicalsafetybc.ca
www.technicalsafetybc.ca
www.linkedin.com/company/technical-safety-bc
www.facebook.com/technicalsafetyBC
twitter.com/TechSafetyBC
Also Known As: Technical Safety BC
Overview: A medium-sized provincial organization
Mission: To protect the residents of BC by ensuring the safety of mechanical systems, products, equipment & work practices
Chief Officer(s):
Catherine Roome, President & CEO

British Columbia Salmon Farmers Association (BCSFA)
#201, 911 Island Hwy., Campbell River BC V9W 2C2
Tel: 250-286-1636; *Fax:* 800-849-9430
Toll-Free: 800-661-7256
info@bcsalmonfarmers.ca
www.bcsalmonfarmers.ca
www.facebook.com/BCSalmonFarmers
twitter.com/BCSalmonFarmers
Overview: A small provincial organization founded in 1984
Mission: To act as the voice of British Columbia's farmed salmon industry; To advance the competitiveness & sustainable growth of the salmon farming industry; To increase fish farming opportunities in British Columbia
Finances: *Funding Sources:* Membership dues; Industry funding
Staff Member(s): 5
Membership: 41; *Fees:* $400 sustaining; Schedule, based upon revenue, for associate; *Member Profile:* Salmon farmers from British Columbia; Supply & service companies that support the salmon farming industry
Activities: Liaising with government; Educating the public; *Speaker Service:* Yes
Chief Officer(s):
Jeremy Dunn, Executive Director
jeremy@bcsalmonfarmers.ca
Sabrina Santoro, Manager, Communications
sabrina@bcsalmonfarmers.ca
Meetings/Conferences:
• British Columbia Salmon Farmers Association Annual General Meeting 2018, 2018
Scope: Provincial
Publications:
• British Columbia Salmon Farmers Association Annual Report
Type: Yearbook
• British Columbia Salmon Farmers Association Sustainability Progress Report
Type: Report

British Columbia Saw Filers Association (BCSFA)
6521 Orchard Hill Rd., Vernon BC V1H 1B6
Tel: 250-546-2234; *Fax:* 604-585-4014
info@bcsawfilers.com
www.bcsawfilers.com
Overview: A small provincial organization
Chief Officer(s):
Bruce Doroshuk, President
bruce.doroshuk@tolko.com
Meetings/Conferences:
• 2018 BC Saw Filers Association Annual General Meeting & Trade Show, 2018, BC
Scope: Provincial

British Columbia Schizophrenia Society
#1100, 1200 West 73rd Ave., Vancouver BC V6P 6G5
Tel: 604-270-7841; *Fax:* 604-270-9861
Toll-Free: 888-888-0029
prov@bcss.org
www.bcss.org
www.facebook.com/BCSchizophreniaSociety
twitter.com/BCSchizophrenia
www.youtube.com/user/bcssprov
Previous Name: BC Friends of Schizophrenics
Overview: A small provincial charitable organization founded in 1982 overseen by Schizophrenia Society of Canada
Mission: To alleviate the suffering caused by schizophrenia; To provide support & education; To increase public awareness & understanding of schizophrenia & other persistent mental illnesses; To promote research into the causes, treatment & cure of schizophrenia
Member of: Schizophrenia Society of Canada
Staff Member(s): 24
Activities: 30 branches in British Columbia; *Library:* Open to public
Chief Officer(s):
Deborah Conner, Executive Director

British Columbia School Counsellors' Association
PO Box 858, Terrace BC V8G 4R1
www.bcschoolcounsellor.com
Overview: A small provincial organization
Member of: BC Teachers' Federation
Chief Officer(s):
Jim Hooper, President
jhooper.bcsca@gmail.com

British Columbia School District Secretary-Treasurers' Association *See* British Columbia Association of School Business Officials

British Columbia School Superintendents Association (BCSSA)
#208, 1118 Homer St., Vancouver BC V6B 6L5
Tel: 604-687-0590; *Fax:* 604-687-8118
information@bcssa.org
www.bcssa.org
www.linkedin.com/company/bc-school-superintendents-association
twitter.com/BCSups
Overview: A small provincial organization
Mission: To provide equity & excellence in student learning; To develop competent, ethical, & visionary leaders
Membership: 250+; *Member Profile:* Superintendents, assistant superintendents, directors of instruction, & other senior executives from British Columbia's sixty school districts
Activities: Supporting professional development activities; Advocating for high quality public education; Providing networking opportunities
Chief Officer(s):
Tom Longridge, President
tom.longridge@sd72.bc.ca
Claire Guy, Executive Director
jmcelgunn@bcssa.org
Meetings/Conferences:
• BC School Superintendents Association Spring Forum 2018, April, 2018, Westin Bayshore, Vancouver, BC
Scope: Provincial
Description: Topics related to the British Columbia School Superintendents Association's Dimensions of Practice, featuring innovative & successful models of leadership
• BC School Superintendents Association Summer Leadership Academy 2018, August, 2018, BC
Scope: Provincial
• BC School Superintendents Association Fall Conference & AGM 2018, November, 2018, Westin Bayshore, Vancouver, BC
Scope: Provincial
Description: Themes include leadership, school effectiveness, & improvement
• BC School Superintendents Association Winter Conference 2018, 2018, BC
Scope: Provincial
Publications:
• Leadergram
Type: Newsletter
Profile: Information for BCSSA members

British Columbia School Trustees Association (BCSTA) / Association des commissaires d'écoles de Colombie-Britannique
1580 West Broadway, 4th Fl., Vancouver BC V6J 5K9
Tel: 604-734-2721; *Fax:* 604-732-4559
bcsta@bcsta.org
www.bcsta.org
www.linkedin.com/company/bc-school-trustees-association
twitter.com/bc_sta
Overview: A medium-sized provincial organization founded in 1905 overseen by Canadian School Boards Association
Mission: To promote effective boards of public school trustees working together for BC students; To improve student achievement through community engagement
Member of: School Boards Association (CSBA)
Staff Member(s): 12
Membership: 60 boards + 420 trustees; *Fees:* Schedule available; *Committees:* Education; Finance; Aboriginal Education
Chief Officer(s):
Mike Roberts, Chief Executive Officer, 604-235-2297
mroberts@bcsta.org
Jodi Olstead, Director, Finance & Human Resources, 604-235-2296
jolstead@bcsta.org
Mike P. Gagel, Director, Information & Education Technology, 604-235-2292
mgagel@bcsta.org
Awards:
• BCSTA Scholarships for Student Citizenship
Eligibility: Graduating BC public school students
Meetings/Conferences:
• British Columbia School Trustees Association 114th Annual General Meeting 2018, April, 2018, BC
Scope: Provincial

British Columbia Science Teachers' Association (BCScTA)
c/o Ashcroft Secondary School, PO Box 669, Ashcroft BC V0K 1A0
Tel: 250-453-9144; *Fax:* 250-453-2368
bcscta@gmail.com
www.bcscta.ca
Overview: A medium-sized provincial organization
Member of: BC Teachers' Federation
Membership: *Fees:* $35 BCTF member; $10 Student/Retiree/TOC
Chief Officer(s):
Grahame Rainey, President
Tim McCracken, 1st Vice-President
Meetings/Conferences:
• BC Science Teachers' Association Catalyst Conference 2018, October, 2018, Kelowna, BC
Scope: Provincial

British Columbia Scientific Cryptozoology Club (BCSCC)
BC
bcscc@bcscc.ca
bcscc.ca
Overview: A small provincial organization founded in 1989
Mission: To research & preserve the databases of cryptozoological animals internationally
Membership: *Fees:* $30 Canadian residents; $30 USD international residents; *Member Profile:* People involved with cryptozoological
Chief Officer(s):
Paul H. Leblond, Chairman & Founder

John Kirk, President & Founder

British Columbia Seafood Alliance (BCSA)
#1100, 1200 West 73rd Ave., Vancouver BC V6P 6G5
Tel: 604-377-9213; Fax: 604-683-4510
www.bcseafoodalliance.com
Overview: A medium-sized provincial organization
Mission: To represent the interests & values of a majority of BC's seafood industries to the federal & provincial governments & to the general public; to promote the conservation & environmentally sustainable use & production of seafood resources in BC; to foster an economically viable & internationally competitive seafood industry
Membership: 18
Chief Officer(s):
Christina Burridge, Executive Director
cburridge@telus.net

British Columbia Securities Commission (BCSC)
PO Box 10142, Stn. Pacific Centre, 701 West Georgia St., 12th Fl., Vancouver BC V7Y 1L2
Tel: 604-899-6500; Fax: 604-899-6506
Toll-Free: 800-373-6393
inquiries@bcsc.bc.ca
www.bcsc.bc.ca
www.linkedin.com/company/british-columbia-securities-commission
twitter.com/BCSC_Info
www.youtube.com/user/BCSC4Industry
Overview: A medium-sized provincial organization overseen by Canadian Securities Administrators
Mission: To regulate securities trading in British Columbia, through the administration of the Securities Act; To report to the Legislature, through the minister responsible for the administration of the Securities Act; To foster a fair & competitive securities market; To protect investors & market integrity
Member of: Canadian Securities Administrators
Finances: Annual Operating Budget: Greater than $5 Million; Funding Sources: Fees collected from market participants under the legislation
Staff Member(s): 190
Activities: Education investors & market participants; Monitoring compliance & demanding corrective action
Chief Officer(s):
Brenda Leong, Chair & Chief Executive Officer
Nigel P. Cave, Vice-Chair & Executive Commissioner
Publications:
• British Columbia Securities Commission Ethics & Conduct Policy
• British Columbia Securities Commission Governance Policy
• British Columbia Securities Commission Annual Report
Type: Report; Frequency: Annually

British Columbia Seniors Living Association (BCSLA)
#300, 3665 Kingsway, Vancouver BC V5R 5W2
Tel: 604-689-5949; Fax: 604-689-5946
Toll-Free: 888-402-2722
Other Communication: membership@bcsla.ca
info@bcsla.ca
www.bcsla.ca
Overview: A small provincial organization
Chief Officer(s):
Marlene Williams, Director, Membership Services
Meetings/Conferences:
• BC Seniors Living Association 2018 Conference, 2018, BC
Scope: Provincial

British Columbia Shake & Shingle Association
33017 - 14th Ave., Mission BC V2V 2P3
Tel: 604-826-7185
enquiries@bcshakeshingle.com
www.bcshakeshingle.com
Overview: A small provincial charitable organization founded in 1979
Mission: To coordinate the efforts of the member mills & associates with the objective of protecting & increasing the viability of the BC wood shake & shingle manufacturing industry
Affiliation(s): Cedar Shake & Shingle Bureau
Finances: Funding Sources: Membership fees; government
Membership: 18; Member Profile: Direct involvement in the shake & shingle industry
Activities: Internships: Yes; Rents Mailing List: Yes

British Columbia Sheet Metal Association (SMACNA-BC)
#315, 15225 - 104 Ave., Surrey BC V3R 6Y8
Tel: 604-585-4641; Fax: 604-584-9304
smacnabc@smacna-bc.org
www.smacna-bc.org
twitter.com/smacnabc
Also Known As: Sheet Metal & Air Conditioning Contractors National Association - BC Division
Overview: A medium-sized provincial organization founded in 1969
Mission: To promote financial stability in the sheet metal industry as well as to improve working conditions for their members
Membership: 69; Member Profile: Unionized sheet metal contractors throughout British Columbia (exluding Vancouver Island); Suppliers to the industry
Chief Officer(s):
Bruce E. Sychuk, Executive Director

British Columbia Shellfish Growers Association (BCSGA)
2002 Comox Ave., #F, Comox BC V9M 3M6
Tel: 250-890-7561
admin@bcsga.ca
www.bcsga.ca
Previous Name: British Columbia Oyster Growers' Association
Overview: A small provincial organization founded in 1948
Mission: To advance the sustainable growth & prosperity of the BC shellfish industry in a global economy by providing leadership & advocacy to members & stakeholders while maintaining the integrity of the marine environment
Member of: Canadian Aquaculture Industry Alliance; Aquaculture Association of Canada
Finances: Annual Operating Budget: $100,000-$250,000; Funding Sources: Membership fees
Staff Member(s): 1
Membership: 181; Fees: $500
Activities: Advocating for members & the industry; To engage in communications, research & development; Lobbying; Marketing; Offering member services
Chief Officer(s):
Steve Pocock, President, 250-285-2724
Darlene Winterburn, Executive Director, 250-890-7561
darlene@bcsga.ca

British Columbia Shorthand Reporters Association (BCSRA)
PO Box 130, 1027 Davie St., Vancouver BC V6E 4L2
Tel: 604-734-5311; Fax: 604-642-5177
Toll-Free: 866-207-2222
bcsra@bcsra.net
www.bcsra.net
Overview: A small provincial organization founded in 1975
Mission: To support the court reporting community & related fields in British Columbia; To uphold the professional standards & ethics of court reporters, broadcast captioners, & CART providers in the province
Finances: Funding Sources: Membership dues
Membership: Fees: $15 students; $35 associates/affiliates; $85 new graduates; $170 full members; Member Profile: Court / realtime reporters, broadcast captioners, & CART (communication acess realtime translation) providers in British Columbia
Activities: Engaging in advocacy activities on behalf of the profession; Providing public relations services
Chief Officer(s):
Debra Collos, President

British Columbia Shorthorn Association
16951 - 12 Ave., Surrey BC V3S 9M3
Tel: 604-536-2800; Fax: 604-538-6760
semiahmooshorthorns@shaw.ca
www.facebook.com/222735927770671
Overview: A small provincial organization
Mission: To raise shorthorn cattle
Member of: Canadian Shorthorn Association
Membership: 49
Chief Officer(s):
Gary Wood, President

British Columbia Simmental Association See Simmental Association of British Columbia

British Columbia Snowboard Association (BCSB)
PO Box 2040, Kelowna BC V1X 4K5
Tel: 250-442-6928
admin@bcsnowboard.com
bcsnowboard.com
www.facebook.com/BCSnowboardAssociation
twitter.com/bcsnowboard
www.instagram.com/bcsnowboard
Also Known As: BC Snowboard
Overview: A small provincial organization overseen by Canadian Snowboard Federation
Mission: To support snowboard athletes, coaches & officials in the province of British Columbia
Member of: Canadian Snowboard Federation
Membership: Fees: $30-$250
Activities: Riglet; Riders; Women's Snowboard; Aboriginal Snowboard; Para-Snowboard; Officials; Coaches; Judges
Chief Officer(s):
Cathy Astofooroff, Executive Director, 250-442-6928
cathy@bcsnowboard.com

British Columbia Snowmobile Federation (BCSF)
PO Box 277, 18 - 1st St., Keremeos BC V0X 1N0
Tel: 250-499-5117; Fax: 250-499-2103
Toll-Free: 877-537-8716
office@bcsf.org
www.bcsf.org
www.facebook.com/BCSnowmobileFederation
twitter.com/BCSnowmobile
instagram.com/bcsnowmobilefederation
Overview: A medium-sized provincial organization founded in 1965
Mission: To encourage & promote the sport of operating snowmobiles in BC by enhancing cooperation & communication between & among snowmobile clubs, recreation industry & racing divisions, the provincial government, other motorized recreational organizations & groups supportive of snowmobiling
Member of: Outdoor Recreation Council of British Columbia; Wilderness Tourism Association; BC Avalanche Association
Affiliation(s): International Snowmobile Council; Canadian Council of Snowmobile Organizations
Finances: Annual Operating Budget: $50,000-$100,000; Funding Sources: Membership fees
Staff Member(s): 1; 70 volunteer(s)
Membership: 6,000 individual + 70 clubs; Fees: Schedule available; Committees: Trails; Charities; Safety; Environment; Government Relations; Snow Show
Activities: Tread Lightly Program; Safety Training Program; SnoVision 2000 Program; Exemplary Service Recognition Program; Awareness Events: Snowarama (charity ride); Speaker Service: Yes; Rents Mailing List: Yes
Chief Officer(s):
Richard Cronier, President
president@bcsf.org
Donegal Wilson, Executive Director
Awards:
• BCSF Excellence Awards Program
Publications:
• BCSF [British Columbia Snowmobile Federation] Member Newsletter
Type: Newsletter
• SnoScene [a publication of the British Columbia Snowmobile Federation]
Type: Newsletter

British Columbia Soccer Association
#250, 3410 Lougheed Hwy., Vancouver BC V5M 2A4
Tel: 604-299-6401; Fax: 604-299-9610
info@bcsoccer.net
www.bcsoccer.net
twitter.com/1bcsoccer
Overview: A medium-sized provincial organization founded in 1907 overseen by Canadian Soccer Association
Mission: To promote & develop the sport of soccer in British Columbia
Member of: Canadian Soccer Association
Staff Member(s): 18
Chief Officer(s):
Jason Elligott, Executive Director
jasonelligott@bcsoccer.net

British Columbia Social Studies Teachers Association (BCSSTA)
c/o BC Teachers' Federation, #100, 550 West 6th Ave., Vancouver BC V5Z 4P2
Tel: 604-871-2283; Fax: 604-871-2286
Toll-Free: 800-663-9163
bcssta@gmail.com
bcssta.wordpress.com
twitter.com/bcssta
Overview: A small provincial organization

Mission: To support & improve the teaching of social studies
Member of: BC Teachers' Federation
Membership: Fees: Schedule available
Chief Officer(s):
Dale Martelli, President
Meetings/Conferences:
• BC Social Studies Teachers' Association Conference 2018, 2018, BC
Scope: Provincial

British Columbia Society for Male Survivors of Sexual Abuse (BCSMSSA)
3126 West Broadway, Vancouver BC V6K 2H3
Tel: 604-682-6482; Fax: 604-684-8883
www.bc-malesurvivors.com
Merged from: Vancouver Society for Male Survivors of Sexual Abuse; Victoria Male Survivors of Sexual Assault Soc.
Overview: A small provincial charitable organization founded in 1990
Mission: To provide treatment & support services to male survivors of sexual abuse & support for their families & partners; To acquire & develop education material & gather statistics; To establish new programs for male survivors within British Columbia or assist other agencies in setting up programs through training & consultation; To advocate for male survivors with government & the general population
Member of: British Columbia Association of Specialized Victim Assistance & Counselling Programs
Finances: Annual Operating Budget: $250,000-$500,000; Funding Sources: Provincial government, donations & foundation grants; Client-paid fees; Client compensation program
Staff Member(s): 13; 5 volunteer(s)
Activities: Individual & group therapy; Guidance & support through legal processes; Education through training programs; Video & manual production & sale; Awareness Events: Male Survivors of Sexual Abuse Awareness Month, Apr.; Internships: Yes; Speaker Service: Yes; Library
Chief Officer(s):
Daniel Kline, Executive Director

British Columbia Society for the Prevention of Cruelty to Animals
1245 East 7th Ave., Vancouver BC V5T 1R1
Tel: 604-681-7271
Toll-Free: 800-665-1868
info@spca.bc.ca
www.spca.bc.ca
www.facebook.com/bcspca
twitter.com/BC_SPCA
www.youtube.com/user/bcspcabc
Also Known As: BC SPCA
Overview: A medium-sized provincial charitable organization founded in 1895 overseen by Canadian Federation of Humane Societies
Mission: To protect & enhance the quality of life for domestic, farm, & wild animals in British Columbia
Member of: Canadian Federation of Humane Societies
4000 volunteer(s)
Membership: Fees: $25 regular; $15 senior; $100 associate/corporate; $250 lifetime
Chief Officer(s):
Marylee Davies, President

British Columbia Society of Electroneurophysiology Technologists (BCSET)
c/o EEG Department, Penticton Regional Hospital, 550 Carmi Ave., Penticton BC V2A 3G6
Tel: 250-492-1000; Fax: 250-492-9037
webmaster@bcset.org
www.bcset.org
Overview: A small provincial organization
Mission: A professional non-profit association dedicated to fostering excellence in diagnostic electroneurophysiology, furthering education and providing a forum for discussion and interaction.
Affiliation(s): Canadian Association of Electroneurophysiology Technologists
3 volunteer(s)
Membership: 1-99; Member Profile: Electroneurophysiology technologists in British Columbia
Chief Officer(s):
Tara Cassidy, President

British Columbia Society of Laboratory Science (BCSLS)
#720, 999 West Broadway, Vancouver BC V5Z 1K5
Tel: 604-714-1760; Fax: 604-738-4080
Toll-Free: 800-304-0033
bcsls@bcsls.net
www.bcsls.net
Previous Name: British Columbia Society of Medical Technologists
Overview: A medium-sized provincial organization founded in 1969 overseen by Canadian Society for Medical Laboratory Science
Mission: To provide members with representation, education, fellowship & leadership
Finances: Funding Sources: Membership dues; education programs
Staff Member(s): 2
Membership: Member Profile: Medical laboratory technologists & assistants in British Columbia; Committees: Congress; MLA Education Day
Activities: Fall Congress; Awareness Events: National Medical Laboratory Week, April; Internships: Yes; Speaker Service: Yes
Chief Officer(s):
Larry Wright, President
president@bcsls.net
Malcolm Ashford, Executive Director
malcolm@bcsls.net
Donna O'Neill, Director, Professional Development
education@bcsls.net
Dawn Hutchinson, Director, Marketing & Communications
marketing@bcsls.net

British Columbia Society of Landscape Architects (BCSLA)
#450, 355 Burrard St., Vancouver BC V6C 2G8
Tel: 604-682-5610; Fax: 604-681-3394
admin@bcsla.org
www.bcsla.org
www.linkedin.com/groups/BC-Society-Landscape-Architects-5074296
www.facebook.com/BCSocietyofLandscapeArchitects
twitter.com/BCSLA
Overview: A medium-sized provincial licensing organization founded in 1964 overseen by Canadian Society of Landscape Architects
Mission: To promote, improve & advance the profession; to maintain standards of professional practice & conduct consistent with the need to serve & protect the public interest; to support the improvement &/or conservation of the natural, cultural, social & built environment.
Member of: Canadian Society of Landscape Architects
Finances: Funding Sources: Membership dues; special events; sponsors
Membership: Fees: $623 landscape architect; $180 associate/intern; $42 student; $263 affiliate; $106 inactive; Member Profile: Must have university degree in landscape architecture followed by two years experience working for registered landscape architect; must complete series of exams.; Committees: Bylaws & Standards; Public & Professional Relations; Nominations; Finance; Credentials
Activities: Internships: Yes
Chief Officer(s):
Robert Evans, President

British Columbia Society of Medical Technologists See British Columbia Society of Laboratory Science

British Columbia Society of Prosthodontists (BCSP)
#220, 2425 Oak St., Vancouver BC V6H 3S7
Tel: 604-734-1232; Fax: 604-732-1719
www.bcprosthodontists.org
Overview: A small provincial organization
Mission: A non-profit organization made up of certified specialists in Prosthodontics.
Membership: 30; Member Profile: Certified specialists in Prosthodontics in the province of British Columbia.
Chief Officer(s):
Alec Cheng, President

British Columbia Society of Respiratory Therapists (BCSRT)
PO Box 4760, Vancouver BC V6B 4A4
Tel: 604-623-2227
www.bcsrt.ca
Overview: A medium-sized provincial organization founded in 1977
Mission: To represent the interests of the respiratory therapy profession in British Columbia; To promote best practices within the occupation; To uphold the British Columbia Society of Respiratory Therapists Standards for Professional Conduct, Code of Ethics, & Standards of Practice
Membership: Fees: Free, for first & second year students; $15 third year students; $20 affiliate; $75 corporate; $85 active/associate; Member Profile: Registered respiratory therapists of British Columbia; Non-practicing individuals; Students; Corporations
Activities: Promoting the role of registered respiratory therapists (RTs); Providing continuing educational oppotunities in respiratory care; Awarding grants; Liaisinig with regulators & national professional associations; Reviewing & revising standards of practice
Chief Officer(s):
Mike Giesbrecht, President
preselect.bcsrt@gmail.com
Meetings/Conferences:
• 2018 Annual Meeting of the BC Society of Respiratory Therapists, 2018, BC
Scope: Provincial

British Columbia Spaces for Nature
PO Box 673, Gibsons BC V0N 1V0
info@spacesfornature.org
www.spacesfornature.org
Overview: A medium-sized provincial charitable organization founded in 1989
Mission: To protect British Columbia's wilderness resource
Activities: Leading campaigns to protect wilderness areas throughout British Columbia; Library: British Columbia Spaces for Nature Library
Chief Officer(s):
Robert Ballantyne, Executive Member
Chloe O'Loughlin, Executive Member
Loretta Woodcock, Executive Member
Publications:
• Jobs & Environment: Moving British Columbia into the 21st Century
Type: Report; Number of Pages: 74
Profile: Policy options & recommendations for British Columbia's future
• Keeping the Special in Special Management Zones: A Citizens Guide [a publication of British Columbia Spaces for Nature]
Type: Report; Number of Pages: 143
Profile: Information about special management zones, or government designated land use planning areas, whereconservation is emphasized in management decisions
• Klinaklini Resource Analysis [a publication of British Columbia Spaces for Nature]
Type: Report; Number of Pages: 87
Profile: Suggestions for safeguarding the biodiversity of this interior-to-coastal watershed
• West Chilcotin Demonstration Project [a publication of British Columbia Spaces for Nature]
Type: Report; Number of Pages: 73
Profile: Collaboration between First Nations, the local community, the tourism industry, & the forest industry to create a sustainablefuture for the West Chilcotin

British Columbia Special Olympics See Special Olympics BC

British Columbia Speed Skating Association
PO Box 2023, Stn. A, Abbotsford BC V2T 3T8
Tel: 604-746-4349; Fax: 604-746-4549
www.speed-skating.bc.ca
www.facebook.com/BCSpeedSkating
twitter.com/BCSpeedSkating
www.instagram.com/BCSpeedSkating
Overview: A small provincial organization overseen by Speed Skating Canada
Mission: To foster the growth & development of Speed Skating in B.C.
Member of: Speed Skating Canada
Membership: Committees: Athlete Development; Coaching Development; Officials Development; Club & Membership Development; Competitions; Awards; Records; Risk Management
Chief Officer(s):
Ted Houghton, Executive Director, 604-309-8178
ted.houghton@shaw.ca
Awards:
• Athlete of the Year Awards
• Honour Roll Award
• Gagne Family Award

- Officials Award of Excellence
- Peter Williamson Memorial Trust Fund Bursary

Meetings/Conferences:
- British Columbia Speed Skating Association Annual General Meeting 2018, 2018, BC

Scope: Provincial

British Columbia Sporthorse - Sport Pony Breeders Group
c/o Shelley Fraser, 2547 - 208th St., Langley BC V2Z 2B1
Tel: 604-533-1228
www.bcsporthorses.com
Overview: A small provincial organization
Mission: To promote the breeding of sporthorses & sportponies in British Columbia; To organize shows for owners & breeders of sporthorses & sportponies to show their stock; To improve the breeding program
Membership: *Fees:* $25 senior (19 years & older); $15 junior (18 years & under); $35 family (parents & children 18 years & under); *Member Profile:* Owners & breeders of sporthorses & sportponies in British Columbia
Activities: Providing educational seminars & clinics about sporthorses & sportponies; Marketing British Columbia bred sporthorses & sportponies; Offering networking opportunities
Chief Officer(s):
Ulli Dargel, Entry Secretary, 604-421-6681
actionfilm@telus.net
Shelley Fraser, Entry Secretary, 604-534-8782
tiwi@telus.net

British Columbia Sports Hall of Fame & Museum
Gate A, BC Place Stadium, 777 Pacific Blvd. South, Vancouver BC V6B 4Y8
Tel: 604-687-5520; *Fax:* 604-687-5510
sportsinfo@bcsportshalloffame.com
www.bcsportshalloffame.com
www.facebook.com/bcsportshall
twitter.com/BCSportsHall
Overview: A medium-sized provincial charitable organization founded in 1966
Mission: To collect, preserve & display sports artifacts from BC's sporting history; to provide an exciting & educational environment for sports history
Member of: Canadian Museums Association; BC Museums Association
Affiliation(s): International Association of Sports Museums & Halls of Fame
Finances: *Funding Sources:* Corporate & private
Staff Member(s): 5; 50 volunteer(s)
Membership: 1-99
Activities: Champions Banquet & Tournament of Champions; *Awareness Events:* Banquet of Champions, Induction Ceremonies; *Internships:* Yes; *Library:* by appointment
Chief Officer(s):
Allison Mailer, Executive Director
allison.mailer@bcsportshalloffame.com
Jason Beck, Curator
jason.beck@bcsportshalloffame.com

British Columbia Square & Round Dance Federation
c/o President, 1459 Claudia Pl., Port Coquitlam BC V3C 2V5
Tel: 604-941-6392
Toll-Free: 800-335-9433
www.squaredance.bc.ca
www.facebook.com/BCSquareAndRoundDanceFederation
twitter.com/bcfedlive
Overview: A medium-sized provincial charitable organization overseen by Canadian Square & Round Dance Society
Mission: To provide healthy recreation at the community level for an affordable cost
Membership: *Member Profile:* Leaders; Dancers; Volunteers
Activities: Square dancing; Round dancing; Country dancing; Clogging; Wheelchair dancing; *Library:* BC Federation Library; Not open to public
Chief Officer(s):
Ken Crisp, President
kcrisp@telus.net

British Columbia Stone, Sand & Gravel Association (BCSSGA)
BC
Tel: 778-571-2670; *Fax:* 778-571-2680
gravelbc@telus.net
www.gravelbc.ca
Previous Name: Aggregate Producers Association of BC
Overview: A medium-sized provincial organization founded in 1988
Mission: To represent the aggregate industry in British Columbia, at all levels of government & in the community
Membership: *Fees:* Schedule available; *Member Profile:* Companies & organizations working in or involved with the aggregate industry in British Columbia
Activities: Networking for members; lessons for elementary children on the use of aggregate
Chief Officer(s):
Paul Allard, Executive Director
Awards:
- BCSSGA Annual Awards

British Columbia Summer Swimming Association (BCSSA)
#205, 2323 Boundary Rd., Vancouver BC V5M 4V8
Tel: 604-473-9447; *Fax:* 604-473-9660
office@bcsummerswimming.com
www.bcsummerswimming.com
www.facebook.com/bcsummerswimming
twitter.com/BCSSAstaff
Overview: A medium-sized provincial organization founded in 1958
Mission: To promote & encourage the development of athletes and volunteers through participation in water sport opportunities across British Colubia through member clubs
Membership: 60 clubs + 5,000 athletes
Activities: Speed swimming; diving; water polo; synchronized swimming
Chief Officer(s):
Danny Schilds, President
president@bcsummerswimming.com
Francis Cheung, Vice President
vp@bcsummerswimming.com

British Columbia Supercargoes' Association
#206, 3711 Delbrook Ave., North Vancouver BC V7N 3Z4
Tel: 604-813-8577
president@supercargoes.bc.ca
www.supercargoes.bc.ca
Overview: A small provincial organization founded in 1952
Mission: To provide expert marine cargo planning & onsite management & supervision of shiploading & discharge of all types of cargoes & vessels on the west coast of North America
Finances: *Funding Sources:* Membership dues
Membership: 9; *Member Profile:* Marine professionals in the shipping industry
Chief Officer(s):
Terry Stuart, President

British Columbia Surgical Society (BCSS)
#115, 1665 West Broadway, Vancouver BC V6J 5A4
Tel: 604-638-2843; *Fax:* 604-638-2938
www.bcss.ca
Overview: A small provincial organization founded in 1947
Mission: To further the teaching, practice, & science of the branches of surgery; to advance patient care
Finances: *Funding Sources:* Sponsorships
Activities: Promoting continuous learning; Facilitating the exchange of information among surgeons
Chief Officer(s):
Nam Nguyen, President
Meetings/Conferences:
- 2018 BC Surgical Society Annual Spring Meeting, May, 2018, Fairmont Chateau Whistler, Whistler, BC

Scope: Provincial

British Columbia Sustainable Energy Association (BCSEA)
PO Box 44104, Stn. Gorge Plaza, 2947 Tillicum Rd., Victoria BC V9A 7K1
Tel: 604-332-0025
info@bcsea.org
www.bcsea.org
ca.linkedin.com/company/bc-sustainable-energy-association
www.facebook.com/BCSEA
twitter.com/bcsea
www.youtube.com/BCSEA
Overview: A medium-sized provincial organization founded in 2004
Mission: To support the sustainable production, distribution & consumption of energy in British Columbia & beyond
Affiliation(s): Canadian Renewable Energy Association; Canadian Solar Industries Association; Canadian Wind Energy Association; Climate Action Network Canada; KyotoPLUS; Livable Region Coalition; NorthWest Energy Coalition; Oil Free Coast Alliance; Organizing for Change: Priorities for Environmental Leadership
Finances: *Funding Sources:* Donations
Membership: *Fees:* $30 student; $75 supporter; $120 leader; *Member Profile:* Individuals & organizations
Activities: Develops & undertakes educational programs, policy advocacy, public outreach & energy planning; Provide: Sustainable energy news & information, BC utilities commission interventions, energy directories, webinars, leadership training & other special events
Chief Officer(s):
Jessica McIlroy, Executive Director
Renee Lormé-Gulbrandsen, Administrative Director

British Columbia Table Tennis Association (BCTTA)
#208, 5760 Minoru Blvd., Richmond BC V6X 2A9
Tel: 604-270-3393
bctta@lightspeed.ca
www.bctta.ca
Overview: A small provincial organization overseen by Table Tennis Canada
Member of: Table Tennis Canada; Sport BC
Affiliation(s): International Table Tennis Federation
Membership: 200+; *Fees:* $30 voting members; $20 non-voting members
Chief Officer(s):
Amelia Ho, President

British Columbia Target Sports Association
PO Box 496, Kamloops BC V2C 5L2
targetsports@bctsa.bc.ca
www.bctsa.bc.ca
Previous Name: BC Smallbore Rifle Association
Overview: A small provincial organization
Mission: To promote target rifle sports in British Columbia
Member of: Shooting Federation of Canada
Finances: *Funding Sources:* Membership dues; donations; sports grants; entry fees
Membership: *Fees:* $25 family/senior; $10 junior; $10 associate; $25 club
Activities: Provincial/national championships

British Columbia Teacher Regulation Branch (BCCT)
#400, 2025 West Broadway, Vancouver BC V6J 1Z6
Tel: 604-660-6060; *Fax:* 604-775-4859
Toll-Free: 800-555-3684
www.bcteacherregulation.ca
Previous Name: British Columbia College of Teachers
Overview: A medium-sized provincial organization founded in 1987
Mission: To establish standards for the education, professional responsibility & competence of its members; To certify educators
Finances: *Funding Sources:* Application & membership fees
Staff Member(s): 22
Membership: 68,000+; *Fees:* $80; *Member Profile:* Certified educators in British Columbia; *Committees:* Finance; Discipline; Qualifications; Teacher Education Programs
Chief Officer(s):
Alison Hougham, Media Relations Contact
alison.hougham@gov.bc.ca

British Columbia Teacher-Librarians' Association (BCTLA)
c/o Grahame Rainey, Treasurer, #1607 - 511 Rochester Ave., Coquitlam BC V3K 0A2
www.bctf.ca/bctla
www.facebook.com/bctlaofficial
twitter.com/bctla
Overview: A medium-sized provincial organization founded in 1939
Mission: To promote the role of teacher-librarians within British Columbia's education community; To improve the learning & working condition in school library resource centres
Member of: British Columbia Teachers' Federation (BCTLA is a provincial specialist association of the BCTF)
Membership: *Fees:* Schedule available; *Member Profile:* Teacher-librarians throughout British Columbia
Activities: Supporting resource-based learning, cooperative planning, & teaching; Encouraging professional development; Advocating for strong school libraries
Chief Officer(s):
Jessica Bonin, President
bctla.jessica.bonin@gmail.com
Grahame Rainey, Treasurer
bctla@rainey.ca
Patricia Baisi, Secretary, 604-946-0095
dpbaisi@hotmail.com

Canadian Associations / British Columbia Teachers for Peace & Global Education (PAGE)

Awards:
- BC Teacher-Librarian of the Year Award
- BC New Teacher-Librarian of the Year Award
- Val Hamilton Lifetime Achievement Award
- BCTLA Distinguished Service Award
- BCTLA Honorary Life Membership Award
- BCTLA President's Award
- Ken Haycock Professional Development Grant; *Amount:* up to $350
- BCTLA Representative Speaker Grant; *Amount:* up to $350
- William H. Scott Memorial BCTLA Conference Grant; *Amount:* up to $350
- BCTLA Chapter Grants
- Regional BCTLA Conference Grant; *Amount:* $3,000
- BCTLA New Teacher/TTOC Conference Grant; *Amount:* $500
- New BCTLA Chapter Start-Up Grant

Contact: Marilyn Lunde, Coordinator, Chapters/Sections, E-mail: marilynlunde@gmail.com; Phone: 250-368-5591
Meetings/Conferences:
- British Columbia Teacher-Librarians' Association 2018 Provincial Conference, October, 2018, BC
Scope: Provincial
Description: A gathering of British Columbia's teacher-librarians for workshops, keynote presentations, & social events
Contact Information: bctlaconference.ca
Publications:
- The Bookmark [a publication of the British Columbia Teacher-Librarians' Association]
Type: Journal; *Frequency:* Quarterly; *ISSN:* 0381-6028
Profile: Developments in the field of teacher-librarianship, information about learning resources in British Columbia, & the promotion of literature appreciation

British Columbia Teachers for Peace & Global Education (PAGE)
c/o BC Teachers' Federation, #100, 550 West 6th Ave., Vancouver BC V5Z 4P2
Tel: 604-871-2283; *Fax:* 604-871-2286
Toll-Free: 800-663-9163
www.pagebc.ca
www.facebook.com/PAGEBC.CA
twitter.com/PAGE_BC
Overview: A small provincial organization founded in 1985
Mission: To maintain a network of teachers who support both local & international initiatives to make the world a more equitable & sustainable one; to foster awareness raising, professional development & activism, & encourage students to demonstrate humanitarian concern.
Affiliation(s): British Columbia Teachers' Federation
Finances: *Funding Sources:* Grant; membership fees
Membership: *Fees:* $10 student/retired; $25 BCTF member; $45 non-BCTF member
Chief Officer(s):
Greg van Vugt, President
gvanvugt@hotmail.com
Publications:
- The Global Educator
Type: journal

British Columbia Teachers of English Language Arts
c/o B.C. Teachers' Federation, #100, 550 West 6th Ave., Vancouver BC V5Z 4P2
Tel: 604-871-1848
Toll-Free: 800-663-9163
www.bctela.ca
Previous Name: BC English Teachers' Association
Overview: A medium-sized provincial organization
Member of: BC Teachers' Federation
Membership: *Fees:* $50; *Member Profile:* English Language Arts teachers from British Columbia & Yukon

British Columbia Teachers' Federation (BCTF) / Fédération des enseignants de la Colombie-Britannique
#100, 550 Wsst 6th Ave., Vancouver BC V5Z 4P2
Tel: 604-871-2283
Toll-Free: 800-663-9163
webinfo@bctf.ca
www.bctf.ca
www.facebook.com/BCTeachersFederation
twitter.com/bctf
www.youtube.com/bctfvids
Overview: A large provincial organization founded in 1917 overseen by Canadian Teachers' Federation
Mission: To represent 41,000 public school teachers in the province of British Columbia; To support 33 provincial specialist associations, such as the British Columbia Teacher-Librarians' Association & the British Columbia Music Educators' Association; To advocate for the professional, economic, & social goals of teachers
Member of: Canadian Labour Congress; British Columbia Federation of Labour
Membership: 41,000; *Member Profile:* Public school teachers in the province of British Columbia; *Committees:* Aboriginal Education Advisory; Adult Education Advisory; French Programs & Services; Action on Social Justice; Finance; Health & Safety Advisory; Income Security; Pensions; Professional Issues Advisory; PSA Council; Teachers Teaching on Call Advisory
Activities: Offering workshops & programs for members; Publishing research reports; Promoting a quality pluralistic public school system; Engaging in collective bargaining
Chief Officer(s):
Glen Hansman, President
ghansman@bctf.ca
Teri Mooring, Second Vice-President
tmooring@bctf.ca
Awards:
- Regional Social Justice Conference Fund
Designed to provide funding for social justice conferences to be held throughout the province; funding occurs on a biennial basis
- Local Social Justice Grants
Provide seed money for activities/projects that will bring about systemic change to social justice in schools, districts or communities in BC *Deadline:* April
- Ed May Social Responsibility Fund
The fund provides money to assist teachers in developing & implementing violence-prevention, antiracist, inclusive, gender-equity & multicultural resources *Deadline:* November
- Bob Rosen Social Justice Award
Awarded an individual who has made a sustained & significant contribution to social justice within the federation *Deadline:* Janury
Meetings/Conferences:
- British Columbia Teachers' Federation 103rd Annual General Meeting 2018, March, 2018, Hyatt Regency Hotel, Vancouver, BC
Scope: Provincial
- British Columbia Teachers' Federation Summer Leadership Conference 2018, 2018
Scope: Provincial
Publications:
- BC Legislature Watch [a publication of the British Columbia Teachers' Federation]
Type: Newsletter
Profile: Updates on education issues fron the BC legislature
- BCTF [British Columbia Teachers' Federation] News
Type: Newsletter; *Frequency:* Monthly
Profile: Significant issues for staff & PD representatives throughout British Columbia
- BCTF Pro-D News [a publication of the British Columbia Teachers' Federation]
Type: Newsletter; *Frequency:* Monthly
Profile: Updates on professional development issues
- Social Justice Newsletter [a publication of the British Columbia Teachers' Federation]
Type: Newsletter; *Frequency:* Semiannually
- Teacher Newsmagazine [a publication of the British Columbia Teachers' Federation]
Type: Magazine; *Frequency:* 6 pa; *Accepts Advertising*
Profile: Circulating to over 40,000 public school teachers, student teachers, retired teachers, teacher affiliates, parentadvisory councils, & university personnel in British Columbia
- TTOC Dispatch [a publication of the British Columbia Teachers' Federation]
Type: Newsletter
Profile: Newsletter for teachers teaching on call

British Columbia Team Handball Federation (BCTHF)
Vancouver BC
bchandball@gmail.com
bchandball.wix.com/bchandball
www.facebook.com/BCHandball
twitter.com/van_handball
Overview: A small provincial organization founded in 2003
Mission: To act as the governing body for handball in BC
Member of: Canadian Team Handball Federation
Membership: *Fees:* Schedule available
Chief Officer(s):
David Lee, Executive Director

British Columbia Technology Education Association
c/o L.V. Rogers Secondary School, 1004 Cottonwood St., Nelson BC V1L 3W2
Tel: 250-352-5538; *Fax:* 250-352-3119
info@bctea.org
www.bctea.org
Overview: A medium-sized provincial organization
Mission: To promote technology education in British Columbia schools
Member of: BC Teachers' Federation; Provincial Specialist Association
Membership: *Fees:* Schedule available
Chief Officer(s):
Mike Howard, President
mhoward@telus.net

British Columbia Technology Industries Association (BCTIA)
#900, 1188 West Georgia St., Vancouver BC V6E 4A2
Tel: 604-683-6159
info@bctia.org
www.bctia.org
www.linkedin.com/groupInvitation?gid=112219
www.facebook.com/bctia.org
twitter.com/bctia
www.youtube.com/user/bctiaTV
Also Known As: BC Technology Industries Association
Merged from: Electronic Manufacturers' Association of BC & the Information Technology Assn of Canada, BC Chapter
Overview: A medium-sized provincial organization founded in 1993
Mission: To support the growth of a strong knowledge economy in British Columbia; To act as the voice of the technology industry
Staff Member(s): 11
Membership: *Fees:* Schedule available; *Member Profile:* Companies of all sizes, from all sectors
Activities: Offering professional development activities; Delivering programs, such as Xcelerate, an executive education program & PODIUM, an industry promotion program; Advocating on behalf of the industry; Facilitating partnerships; Increasing public awareness
Chief Officer(s):
Bill Tam, President & Chief Executive Officer, 604-602-5230
btam@bctia.org
Cindy Pearson, Vice-President & Chief Operating Officer, 604-602-5234
cpearson@bctia.org
Peter Payne, Executive in Residence

British Columbia Tennis Association *See* Tennis BC

British Columbia Tenpin Bowling Association
North Vancouver BC
www.bctenpin.com
www.facebook.com/groups/199885590219513
twitter.com/bctenpin
www.instagram.com/bctenpin
Overview: A small provincial organization overseen by Canadian Tenpin Federation, Inc.
Mission: To oversee the sport of tenpin bowling in British Columbia.
Member of: Canadian Tenpin Federation, Inc.
Membership: *Committees:* Legislative, Policy & Procedures; Public Relations; Finance & Budget; Fundraising; Youth; Hall of Fame; Awards; Seniors; Coaching; Website; Scholarship
Chief Officer(s):
Mark Westerberg, President
Bruce Taylor, Vice-President
MaryAnne Madsen, Secretary
Miriam Reid, Treasurer

British Columbia Therapeutic Recreation Association (BCTRA)
PO Box 93597, Stn. Nelson Park, Vancouver BC V6E 4L7
Other Communication: membership@bctra.org
info@bctra.org
www.bctra.org
Overview: A small provincial organization founded in 1991
Mission: To represent Therapeutic Recreation Professionals & their practice within BC

Membership: *Fees:* $210; $110 supporting; $50 student
Chief Officer(s):
Brenda Kinch, President
president@bctra.org

British Columbia Therapeutic Riding Association (BCTRA)
3885B - 96th St., Delta BC V4K 3N3
Tel: 604-590-0897
ponypalstra@yahoo.ca
www.vcn.bc.ca/bctra
Overview: A small provincial charitable organization founded in 1986
Mission: To adhance the quality of life of people with disabilities
Member of: Canadian Therapeutic Riding Association; Horse Council of British Columbia
Affiliation(s): Horse Council BC; Sports & Fitness Council for the Disabled
Finances: *Funding Sources:* Membership dues; donations
Membership: *Fees:* $30 group/centre; $10 individual; *Member Profile:* Therapeutic riding centres/individuals
Activities: *Speaker Service:* Yes
Chief Officer(s):
Candice Miller, President

British Columbia Transplant Society (BCTS)
West Tower, #350, 555 West 12th Ave., Vancouver BC V5Z 3X7
Tel: 604-877-2240; *Fax:* 604-877-2111
Toll-Free: 800-663-6189
info@bct.phsa.ca
www.transplant.bc.ca
www.facebook.com/BCTransplant
twitter.com/BCTransplant
Overview: A medium-sized provincial organization founded in 1986
Mission: To lead & coordinate all activities related to organ transplantation & donation, ensuring high standards of quality & efficient management
Affiliation(s): University of British Columbia
Finances: *Funding Sources:* Provincial government; donations; private funding
Activities: Organ transplant services & research; *Speaker Service:* Yes
Chief Officer(s):
Ed Ferre, Director, Program Development & External Relations
Peggy John, Manager, Communications
Linda Irwin, Manager, Health Information

British Columbia Trucking Association (BCTA)
#100, 20111 - 93A Ave., Langley BC V1M 4A9
Tel: 604-888-5319; *Fax:* 604-888-2941
bcta@bctrucking.com
www.bctrucking.com
www.facebook.com/TruckingBC
twitter.com/BCTruckingAssoc
Previous Name: BC Motor Transport Association
Overview: A medium-sized provincial organization founded in 1913 overseen by Canadian Trucking Alliance
Mission: To act as the recognised voice of the commercial road transportation industry in British Columbia, by consulting & communicating with the industry, government & the public; To promote a prosperous, safe, efficient & responsible road transportation industry; To provide programs & services to members
Affiliation(s): Canadian Trucking Alliance, Motor Coach Canada
Finances: *Funding Sources:* Membership dues
Membership: 1,400+; *Fees:* Schedule available; *Member Profile:* Trucking companies operating in BC; Suppliers to trucking industry; *Committees:* Convention; Insurance; International; Labour; Freight Claims & Hazardous Goods; Safety; Truxpo; Vehicle Standards
Activities: Conferences; Training programs; *Speaker Service:* Yes; *Rents Mailing List:* Yes
Chief Officer(s):
Louise Yako, President & Chief Executive Officer
Awards:
• BCTA Motor Carrier Member Scholarship, BCTA Scholarships Program
Eligibility: Children of employees/owners of BCTA Motor Carrier Members who have either graduated from secondary school or have completed one or more previous years of post-secondary education at an accredited Canadian institution *Deadline:* July 1; *Amount:* $1,500; $1,000
• BCTA Associate Member Scholarship, BCTA Scholarships Program
Eligibility: Children of employees/owners of BCTA Associate Members who have either graduated from secondary school or have completed one or more previous years of post-secondary education at an accredited Canadian institution *Deadline:* July 1; *Amount:* $1,500; $1,000
Meetings/Conferences:
• British Columbia Trucking Association 2018 105th Annual General Meeting & Management Conference, 2018, BC
Scope: Provincial
Description: A meeting of members of the British Columbia motor carrier association

British Columbia Turkey Farms
#106, 19329 Enterprise Way, Surrey BC V3S 6J8
Tel: 604-534-5644; *Fax:* 604-534-3651
Other Communication: BC Turkey Association:
association@bcturkey.com
info@bcturkey.com
www.bcturkey.com
Also Known As: BC Turkey Marketing Board & BC Turkey Association
Overview: A small provincial organization founded in 1966
Mission: To represent BC's registered turkey farms; To work closely with all industry partners to promote safe, quality & nutritious turkey products
Member of: British Columbia Turkey Association
Finances: *Funding Sources:* Grower levy
Staff Member(s): 5
Membership: 65; *Member Profile:* Registered turkey farmers
Chief Officer(s):
Michel Benoit, General Manager & Marketing
info@bcturkey.com
Nancy Samson, Executive Assistant & Administration

British Columbia Ultrasonographers' Society (BCUS)
127 - 62nd Ave. East, Vancouver BC V5X 2E7
www.bcus.org
Overview: A small provincial organization founded in 1981
Mission: To promote & encourage the science & art of diagnostic medical sonography; provide a forum to promote the discussion of matters affecting the field; provide a place for professional growth
Membership: 1-99; *Fees:* $15 active/associate; $0 student
Chief Officer(s):
Vickie Lessoway, Executive Director

British Columbia Vegetable Marketing Commission (BCVMC)
#207, 15252- 32nd Ave., Surrey BC V3S 0R7
Tel: 604-542-9734; *Fax:* 604-542-9735
tom@bcveg.com
www.bcveg.com
Overview: A small provincial licensing organization
Staff Member(s): 5
Chief Officer(s):
Tom Demma, General Manager
tom@bcveg.com
David Taylor, Chair

British Columbia Veterinary Medical Association See College of Veterinarians of British Columbia

British Columbia Veterinary Technologists Association (BCVTA)
101 Todd Rd., Kamloops BC V5C 5A9
Tel: 250-319-0027; *Fax:* 866-319-1929
bcvta.com
Previous Name: Animal Health Technologists Association of BC
Overview: A small provincial organization founded in 1980
Mission: To promote, encourage & maintain the knowledge, ability & competence of members of the Association in the area of animal care; to establish minimum standards of training for members of the Association; to participate in the development of a standard level of provincial recognition as a profession
Member of: Canadian Association of Animal Health Technologists & Technicians
Finances: *Annual Operating Budget:* Less than $50,000; *Funding Sources:* Membership fees
Staff Member(s): 6
Membership: 310; *Fees:* $110 regular; $40 student; $15 non-resident; $100 renewal; *Member Profile:* Graduates of CVMA-accredited 2-year AHT program
Activities: *Awareness Events:* Animal Health Technologists Week, Oct.
Chief Officer(s):
Christine Watson, Executive Director
ed@bcvta.com
Lindsay Ramage, President
lindsaybcvta@yahoo.ca
Meetings/Conferences:
• BC Veterinary Technologists Association 2018 Conference, 2018, BC
Scope: Provincial

British Columbia Video Relay Services Committee
c/o WIDHH, 2125 West 7th Ave., Vancouver BC V6K 1X9
bcvrsc@gmail.com
bcvrs.ca
www.facebook.com/bcvrs
twitter.com/BCVRS
Also Known As: BCVRS Committee
Overview: A small provincial organization founded in 2008
Mission: To represent the deaf community's view on Video Relay Services
Chief Officer(s):
Lisa Anderson-Kellett, Communications Officer
lisa@bcvrs.ca

British Columbia Wall & Ceiling Association
#112, 18663 - 52nd Ave., Surrey BC V3S 8E5
Tel: 604-575-0511; *Fax:* 604-575-0544
info@bcwca.org
www.bcwca.org
Overview: A small provincial organization overseen by Northwest Wall & Ceiling Bureau
Mission: To represent British Columbia chapters of the Northwest Wall & Ceiling Bureau on issues related to the wall & ceiling industry; To improve & promote industry apprenticeship & training; To uphold a Code of Ethics
Finances: *Funding Sources:* Membership fees; Sponsorships
Membership: *Fees:* $800 contractors/associate members; $1,800 per chapter for suppliers/dealers' $2,000-$7,500 manufacturers; *Member Profile:* Professional from British Columbia's wall & ceiling industry, such as manufacturers, suppliers, & drywall & stucco contractors
Activities: Providing technical resources & educational seminars for members; Offering networking opportunities; *Library:* British Columbia Wall & Ceiling Association Resource Library
Chief Officer(s):
Cathy LaPointe, President
Leesa Matwick, Executive Director
Publications:
• The Trowel
Type: Magazine; *Frequency:* Bimonthly; *Accepts Advertising*; *Editor:* Jessica Krippendorf; *Price:* Free with membership in the British Columbia Wall & Ceiling Association
Profile: Information for BC Wall & Ceiling Association members & other construction professionals throughout western Canada

British Columbia Wall & Ceiling Association (BCWCA)
#112, 18663 - 52nd Ave., Surrey BC V3S 8E5
Tel: 604-575-0511; *Fax:* 604-575-0544
info@bcwca.org
www.bcwca.org
twitter.com/BCWCA
Overview: A small provincial organization
Chief Officer(s):
Murray Corey, Executive Director
Eric Brown, President

British Columbia Water & Waste Association (BCWWA)
#620, 1090 West Pender St., Vancouver BC V6E 2N7
Tel: 604-433-4389; *Fax:* 604-433-9859
Toll-Free: 877-433-4389
contact@bcwwa.org
www.bcwwa.org
www.linkedin.com/company/2646273
www.facebook.com/BCWWA
twitter.com/bcwwa
Overview: A medium-sized provincial organization founded in 1964
Mission: To safeguard public health & the environment through the sharing of skills, knowledge, experience & education; To provide a voice for the water & wastewater community in British Columbia & the Yukon
Member of: American Water Works Association (AWWA); Water Environment Federation (WEF); Canadian Water & Wastewater Association (CWWA)
Finances: *Funding Sources:* Membership fees; Courses; Seminars; Annual conference

Canadian Associations / British Columbia Water Polo Association

Membership: *Fees:* $25 students; $99 operators & individuals; *Member Profile:* British Columbia & Yukon professionals & students in the water & waste fields; *Committees:* Annual Conference; Cross Connection Control; Education Advisory Council; Young Professionals; Yukon; Drinking Water; Infrastructure Management; Risk & Resilience; SCADA & IT; Wastewater & Residuals Management; Water Sustainability; Wastewater Collection; Watershed Management
Activities: Promoting dialogue & information dissemination on environmental matters; Offering operator education & training opportunities (online training now available); Providing networking opportunities such as our Annual Conference; Certifying backflow assembly testers in British Columbia & Yukon through our Cross Connection Control program; Creating awareness of the value of water through Drinking Water Week, which occurs annually in May.; *Awareness Events:* Drinking Water Week, May *Library:* British Columbia Water & Waste Association Library
Chief Officer(s):
Carlie Hucul, Chief Executive Officer, 604-630-0011
chucul@bcwwa.org
Ashifa Dhanani, Project Manager, Small Water Systems (SWS)
adhanani@bcwwa.org
Marian Hands, Senior Manager, Education, 604-630-0093
mhands@bcwwa.org
Ally Trott, Coordinator, Member Services, 604-433-4389
atrott@bcwwa.org
Awards:
- Stanley S. Copp Award
- Personal Recognition Award
- Corporate Recognition Award
- Bridge Building Award
- Small Water Systems Award
- Victor M. Terry Award
- Water for People Kenneth J. Miller Award
- Okanagan College Bursary
- UBC Bursary

Meetings/Conferences:
- British Columbia Water & Waste Association 2018 46th Annual Conference & Trade Show, 2018, BC
Scope: Provincial
Description: A four day conference, including technical sessions & the chance to view current products at the trade show
Publications:
- Watermark
Type: Magazine; *Frequency:* Quarterly; *Accepts Advertising*; *Editor:* Carol Campbell
Profile: Calendar of events, product listings, new member listings, employment opportunities, informative articles, & reports on the annual conference, technical seminars & symposia

British Columbia Water Polo Association
#227, 3820 Cessna Dr., Richmond BC V7B 0A2
Tel: 604-333-3480; *Fax:* 604-333-3450
office@bcwaterpolo.ca
www.bcwaterpolo.ca
www.facebook.com/BCWPA
twitter.com/bcwaterpolo
www.instagram.com/bcwaterpolo
Also Known As: BC Water Polo
Overview: A medium-sized provincial organization founded in 1975 overseen by Water Polo Canada
Mission: To develop water polo in BC; to train provincal team & national team athletes
Member of: Water Polo Canada
Finances: *Funding Sources:* Direct access funding; sponsorshp; government grant; membership fees
Staff Member(s): 1; 300 volunteer(s)
Membership: 1,000; *Fees:* Schedule available; *Committees:* Technical Advisory
Activities: *Library:* Open to public

British Columbia Waterfowl Society
5191 Robertson Rd., RR#1, Delta BC V4K 3N2
Tel: 604-946-6980
www.reifelbirdsanctuary.com/bcws2.html
Also Known As: Reifel Bird Sanctuary
Overview: A medium-sized provincial charitable organization founded in 1963
Mission: To encourage conservation of wetlands; to spur public awareness on importance of conservation of estuaries; to operate George C. Reifel Migratory Bird Sanctuary.
Finances: *Annual Operating Budget:* $100,000-$250,000
Staff Member(s): 6; 40 volunteer(s)
Membership: 2,000; *Fees:* $20 single; $40 family; $500 life; *Committees:* Conservation; Publicity & Promotion; Operations; Membership Services
Activities: *Awareness Events:* Snow Goose Festival, Nov.; *Speaker Service:* Yes; *Library:* Not open to public
Chief Officer(s):
Kathleen Fry, Manager
Jack Bates, President

British Columbia Weightlifting Association (BCWA)
5249 Laurel Dr., Delta BC V4K 4S4
info@bcweightlifting.ca
www.bcweightlifting.ca
www.facebook.com/bcweightlifting
twitter.com/bcweightlifting
Also Known As: BC Weightlifting Association
Overview: A small provincial organization founded in 1969
Mission: To promote the sport of Olympic weightlifting in British Columbia
Affiliation(s): Canadian Weightlifting Federation
Finances: *Funding Sources:* Membership fees; Donations; Sponsorships
Membership: *Fees:* $25 youth athlete (12 & under); $40 student/junior (13-18); $55 standard; $110 family; $8 associate/volunteer; $50 club; *Member Profile:* Coaches; Officials: Youth (age 12 & under), student, senior, & master (age 35 & over) athletes; Volunteers
Activities: Providing information about championships
Meetings/Conferences:
- British Columbia Weightlifting Association Annual General Meeting 2018, 2018
Scope: Provincial

British Columbia Welsh Pony & Cob Association
c/o Debbie Miyashita, PO Box 192, Canoe BC V0E 1K0
Overview: A small provincial organization overseen by Welsh Pony & Cob Society of Canada
Mission: To promote the Welsh pony breed in British Columbia
Membership: 1-99; *Member Profile:* Persons in British Columbia who are involved with the Welsh pony breed; *Committees:* Northern; Interior; Fraser Valley
Activities: Offering networking opportunities for club members; Providing information about the Welsh breed to the public; Organizing the annual All Pony Show each July at Maple Ridge
Chief Officer(s):
Debbie Miyashita, Secretary, 250-804-2928
debbiem8@shaw.ca
Awards:
- Presidents Award
To recognize an outstanding contribution in the promotion of the Welsh pony breed
Meetings/Conferences:
- BC Welsh Pony & Cob Association 2018 Annual General Meeting, 2018, BC
Scope: Provincial
Publications:
- BC on the Move
Type: Newsletter; *Frequency:* Bimonthly; *Accepts Advertising*; *Editor:* Moya Petznick
Profile: Association activities, articles, & forthcoming events

Vancouver Island Region
c/o Philip Towell, 6033 Kellow Rd., Port Alberni BC V9Y 7L5
Tel: 250-724-1176
Mission: To promote the Welsh pony breed on Vancouver Island
Chief Officer(s):
Philip Towell, Contact, 250-724-1176

British Columbia Wheelchair Sports Association (BCWSA)
780 Southwest Marine Dr., Vancouver BC V6P 5Y7
Tel: 604-333-3520; *Fax:* 604-333-3450
Toll-Free: 877-737-3090
info@bcwheelchairsports.com
www.bcwheelchairsports.com
www.facebook.com/BCWSA
twitter.com/BCWSA
www.youtube.com/user/BCWheelchairSports
Overview: A medium-sized provincial charitable organization
Mission: To promote & develop wheelchair sport opportunities for British Columbians who identify with physical disabilities
Member of: Canadian Wheelchair Sports Association
Staff Member(s): 10
Membership: *Member Profile:* Individuals who identify with a disability & able bodied individuals
Activities: *Awareness Events:* Rick Hansen Wheels in Motion Event, June; *Speaker Service:* Yes
Chief Officer(s):
Gail Hamamoto, Executive Director, 604-333-3520 Ext. 201
gail@bcwheelchairsports.com
Awards:
- Junior Athlete of the Year
- Female Athlete of the Year Award
- Male Athlete of the Year Award
- Official of the Year Award
- Outstanding Community Service
- Volunteer of the Year Award

British Columbia Wine Institute (BCWI)
#107, 1726 Dolphin Ave., Kelowna BC V1Y 9R9
Tel: 250-762-9744; *Fax:* 250-762-9788
Toll-Free: 800-661-2294
info@winebc.com
www.winebc.org
twitter.com/winebcdotcom
Overview: A medium-sized provincial organization founded in 1990
Staff Member(s): 6
Membership: 119
Chief Officer(s):
Miles Prodan, President & CEO, 250-762-9744 Ext. 101
mprodan@winebc.com

British Columbia Women's Institutes (BCWI)
PO Box 36, 4395 Mountain Rd., Barriere BC V0E 1E1
Tel: 250-672-0259; *Fax:* 250-672-0259
info@bcwi.org
www.bcwi.ca
www.facebook.com/185390304847227
twitter.com/bcwi
www.youtube.com/user/BCWomensInstitute
Overview: A medium-sized provincial charitable organization founded in 1909 overseen by Federated Women's Institutes of Canada
Mission: To help discover, stimulate & develop leadership among women; to assist, encourage & support women to become knowledgeable & responsible citizens; to ensure basic human rights for women & to work towards their equality; to be a strong voice through which matters of utmost concern can reach the decision makers; to network with organizations sharing similar objectives; to promote the improvement of agricultural & other rural communities & to safeguard the environment
Member of: Associated Country Women of the World
Affiliation(s): BC Federation of Agriculture
Finances: *Annual Operating Budget:* $50,000-$100,000; *Funding Sources:* Membership dues; grants
Staff Member(s): 1
Membership: 1,800; *Fees:* $15
Activities: *Awareness Events:* Women's Institutes Week, Feb.; *Speaker Service:* Yes; *Library:* Open to public by appointment

British Columbia Wood Specialities Group Association
#200, 9292 - 200th St., Langley BC V1M 3A6
Tel: 604-882-7100; *Fax:* 604-882-7300
Toll-Free: 877-422-9663
info@bcwood.com
www.bcwood.com
www.facebook.com/bcwoodspecialtiesgroup
twitter.com/BC_Wood
Also Known As: BC Wood
Overview: A medium-sized provincial charitable organization founded in 1989
Mission: To assist BC manufacturers of value-added products achieve global competitiveness by providing essential marketing services to capitalize on new market opportunities
Finances: *Annual Operating Budget:* $1.5 Million-$3 Million; *Funding Sources:* Membership dues; provincial government; federal government
Staff Member(s): 11
Membership: 260; *Fees:* $500-$2,000; *Member Profile:* Manufacturers of value-added wood products in BC; *Committees:* Marketing
Activities: *Speaker Service:* Yes; *Library:* BC Wood Resource Library; by appointment
Chief Officer(s):
Brian Hawrysh, CEO, 604-882-7100 Ext. 244

British Columbia Wrestling Association (BCWA)
3333 Ardingley Ave., Burnaby BC V5B 4A5
Tel: 604-737-3092; *Fax:* 604-737-6043
info@bcwrestling.com

www.bcwrestling.com
www.facebook.com/bcwrestling
twitter.com/wrestlingBC
Also Known As: Wrestling BC
Previous Name: British Columbia Amateur Wrestling Association
Overview: A small provincial organization founded in 1979 overseen by Canadian Amateur Wrestling Association
Mission: To promote & enhance the well-being of young people through their participation in wrestling
Member of: Sport BC
Affiliation(s): BC School Sports
Staff Member(s): 2; 300 volunteer(s)
Membership: 2,200; *Member Profile:* Wrestlers, coaches, and officials
Activities: Camps; clinics; tournaments
Chief Officer(s):
Phil Cizmic, President, 250-923-0735
philip.cizmic@sd72.bc.ca

British Columbia's Children's Hospital Foundation (BCCHF)
938 West 28th Ave., Vancouver BC V5Z 4H4
Tel: 604-875-2444; *Fax:* 604-875-2596
Toll-Free: 888-663-3033
info@bcchf.ca
www.bcchf.ca
www.facebook.com/BCChildrens
twitter.com/BCCHF
www.youtube.com/user/bcchf
Overview: A small provincial charitable organization
Mission: To make positive differences in the lives of children by raising funds to support British Columbia's Children's Hospital & its related health partners
Member of: Children's & Women's Health Centre of British Columbia
Finances: *Annual Operating Budget:* $500,000-$1.5 Million
Staff Member(s): 35
Activities: *Awareness Events:* CMN Telethon, June 2-3
Chief Officer(s):
Don Lindsay, Chair
Teri Nicholas, President & CEO
Hitesh Kothary, Chief Financial Officer
Debora Sweeney, Chief Strategy Officer
Maria Faccio, Chief Philanthropy Offier
Lillian Hum, Chief Philanthropy Offier

British Columbian Francophone Youth Council *Voir* Conseil jeunesse francophone de la Colombie-Britannique

British Columbia-Yukon Halfway House Association (BCYHHA)
763 Kingsway, Vancouver BC V5V 3C2
contact@bcyhha.org
www.bcyhha.org
Overview: A small provincial organization overseen by Regional Halfway House Association
Mission: To help offenders with their reintegration into society
Member of: Regional Halfway House Association

British Council - Canada
#2800, 777 Bay St., Toronto ON M5G 2G2
CA-Accounts.Enquiries@britishcouncil.org
www.britishcouncil.ca
www.linkedin.com/company/british-council
www.facebook.com/BritishCouncilCanada
twitter.com/britishcouncil
www.instagram.com/britishcouncilcanada
Overview: A small international charitable organization
Mission: To encourage cultural, scientific, technological & educational cooperation between Britain & Canada
Staff Member(s): 5
Activities: Education, arts, science & information
Chief Officer(s):
Mariya Afzal, Country Director
Awards:
• Arts Grants
• UK/Canada Collaborative Programme
• British Chevening Scholarships
One year's postgraduate study at a British university in disciplines including: environmental studies, science, international relations, engineering
   Montréal Office
   #1940, 2000, av McGill College, Montréal QC H3A 3H3

British Exservicemen's Association
1143 Kingsway Ave., Vancouver BC V5V 3C9
Tel: 604-874-6510
britexassoc@shawbiz.ca
britishex.ca
Overview: A small local organization founded in 1958
Membership: *Member Profile:* Exservices & associates
Chief Officer(s):
Carolyn Crompton, President

British Isles Family History Society of Greater Ottawa (BIFHSGO)
PO Box 38026, Ottawa ON K2C 3Y7
Tel: 613-234-2520
queries@bifhsgo.ca
www.bifhsgo.ca
www.facebook.com/BIFHSGO
twitter.com/BIFHSGO
www.pinterest.ca/bisles3129
Overview: A small local charitable organization founded in 1994
Mission: To promote & encourage research & publishing of Canadian family histories by descendants of British Isles emigrants
Member of: Federation of Geneological Societies; Federation of Family History Societies
Finances: *Annual Operating Budget:* Less than $50,000; *Funding Sources:* Membership dues; conference fees
50 volunteer(s)
Membership: 515; *Fees:* $45 individual; $55 family; $45 institution; *Member Profile:* Interest in family history of descendants of ancestors who migrated from British Isles; *Committees:* Scottish Genealogy; Genetic Genealogy (DNA); Writing
Activities: Annual conference held in September; Monthly meetings & special interest group meetings; Quarterly journal: Anglo-Celtic Roots; *Library:* Brian O'Regan Memorial Library; Open to public
Chief Officer(s):
Barbara Tose, President
bifhsgopres@gmail.com
Publications:
• Anglo-Celtic Roots
Type: Journal; *Frequency:* Quarterly
Profile: Presents articles on Canadian and British Isles family and social history, as well as genealogical research techniques and practices

British Israel World Federation (Canada) Inc. (BIWF)
313 Sherbourne St., Toronto ON M5A 2S3
Tel: 416-921-5996; *Fax:* 416-921-9511
british-israel@bellnet.ca
www.britishisrael.ca
Overview: A small national charitable organization founded in 1929
Mission: To be a Federation of orthodox Christians of many denominations who believe the Bible to be the inspired word of God
Affiliation(s): The British-Israel-World Federation; BIWF (Queensland) Inc.; BIWF (NZ) Auckland Inc.; Canadian British-Israel Association Windsor, Ontario; The Association of the Covenant People (Vancouver, BC)
Staff Member(s): 2
Membership: 1,200; *Fees:* $10 non-voting; $15 voting
Activities: Monthly meetings; Conventions; *Speaker Service:* Yes
Publications:
• The Kingdom Herald
Profile: Magazine, 10 issues published annually

The British Methodist Episcopal Church of Canada (BME)
c/o BME Christ Church St. James, 460 Shaw St., Toronto ON M6G 3L3
Tel: 416-534-3831; *Fax:* 416-534-3367
info@bmechristchurch.org
www.bmechristchurch.org
Overview: A medium-sized national organization
Affiliation(s): African Methodist Episcopal Church
Membership: 130 churches

British North America Philatelic Society Ltd. (BNAPS)
c/o Andy Ellwood, 10 Doris Ave., Gloucester ON K1T 3W8
www.bnaps.org
Overview: A small international charitable organization founded in 1943
Mission: To collect stamps from pre-confederation Canada
Membership: *Fees:* $35; *Member Profile:* Individuals & families in Canada, the United States, & the United Kingdom who are interested in the hobby of collecting BNA philately; *Committees:* Convention; Elections; Ethics; Finance; Judging; Publications
Activities: Offering 21 study groups & 14 regional groups; Providing financial grants for activities to encourage young people to pursue a hobby in philately; *Speaker Service:* Yes; *Library:* The Horace W. Harrison Library
Chief Officer(s):
Eldon C. Godfrey, President
Andy Ellwood, Secretary
Publications:
• BNA Topics
Type: Journal; *Frequency:* Quarterly; *Number of Pages:* 80; *Editor:* Robert Lemire & Mike Street
Profile: Articles about BNA philately, as well as philatelic news, bood reviews, & postal history
• BNAPortraitS: The People's Publication of BNAPS
Type: Newsletter; *Frequency:* Quarterly; *Accepts Advertising*; *Editor:* Victor Willson
Profile: Society activities, study group & regional group news, awards, & membership information
• Canadian Philately - an Outline
Author: J. Burnett; F. Scrimgeour; V Wilson

Broadcast Educators Association of Canada (BEAC) / Association Canadienne de educateurs en radiodiffusion
beac.ca
www.facebook.com/BEACanada
twitter.com/BEACanada
Overview: A large national organization
Mission: To provide a forum to reflect on & respond collectively to issues & directions relevant to individual, institutonal & industry needs
Membership: *Fees:* $390 institutional; $37.45 individual; $50 associate; *Member Profile:* Administrators in radio, television, broadcast journalism & news media
Chief Officer(s):
Ashif Jivraj, President
ashif_jivraj@bcit.ca
Alana Gieck, Vice President
agieck@mtroyal.ca
Awards:
• BEAC National Awards

Broadcast Executives Society (BES)
PO Box 75150, 20 Bloor St. East, Toronto ON M4W 3T3
Tel: 416-899-0370
www.bes.ca
Overview: A medium-sized national organization founded in 1961
Mission: To serve as forum for the broadcast industry.
Membership: 300+; *Fees:* $169.50 GTA resident; $113 non-resident; *Member Profile:* Broadcasters, broadcast representatives, advertising agency personnel, advertisers, film producers, distributors & other parties interested in the business of broadcasting
Chief Officer(s):
John Tucker, Administrator

Broadcast Research Council of Canada (BRC)
#1005, 160 Bloor St. East, Toronto ON M4W 1B9
Tel: 416-413-3864; *Fax:* 416-413-3879
brc@tvb.ca
www.brc.ca
ca.linkedin.com/pub/brc-broadcast-research-council-of-canada/2 4/462/118
www.facebook.com/117260268358077
twitter.com/BroadcastBRC
Overview: A medium-sized national organization
Mission: To provide a forum for presentations relating to the broadcast advertising business; to provide awards to the most promising students at colleges that train people to enter the advertising business.
Membership: *Member Profile:* Membership in the BRC is open to advertisers, advertising agencies, media, media representatives, research companies, and organizations, and to students active in the field of research.
Chief Officer(s):
Robert DaSilva, President

Brock Information Centre *See* Information Brock

Brock University Faculty Association (BUFA) / Association des professeurs de l'Université Brock
Mackenzie-Chown Complex, Brock University, 500 Glenridge Ave., #D402, St Catharines ON L2S 3A1

Canadian Associations / Brockville & District Association for Community Involvement (BDACI)

Tel: 905-688-5550; Fax: 905-688-8256
bufa@brocku.ca
www.bufa.ca
www.facebook.com/212515592101908
twitter.com/BUFABrock
Overview: A small local organization founded in 1996
Mission: To influence conditions of employment, including promotion, tenure, pensions, sabbaticals & research grants.
Affiliation(s): Canadian Association of University Teachers; Ontario Confederation of University Faculty Associations
Finances: Funding Sources: Membership dues
Staff Member(s): 3
Membership: Member Profile: Brock University faculty & professional librarians; Committees: Negotiating; Academic & Professional Awards; Collective Agreement; Grievance Panel; Hiring Advice; Occupational Health & Safety; Pension; Communications; Social Justice; Status of Women
Chief Officer(s):
Linda Rose-Krasnor, President
linda.rose-krasnor@brocku.ca
Shannon Lever, Administrative Assistant
slever@brocku.ca

Brockville & District Association for Community Involvement (BDACI)
#4, 2495 Parkedale Ave., Brockville ON K6V 3H2
Tel: 613-345-4092; Fax: 613-345-7469
bdaci@ripnet.com
bdaci.com
Previous Name: Brockville & District Association for Community Living; Brockville & District Association for the Mentally Retarded
Overview: A medium-sized local charitable organization founded in 1956
Mission: To support people with intellectual disabilities & their families; To promote their full participation, as equal citizens, in community life
Member of: Community Living Ontario
Activities: Speaker Service: Yes
Chief Officer(s):
Beth French, Executive Director

Brockville & District Association for Community Living; Brockville & District Association for the Mentally Retarded See Brockville & District Association for Community Involvement

Brockville & District Chamber of Commerce
#1, 3 Market St. West, Brockville ON K6V 7L2
Tel: 613-342-6553; Fax: 613-342-6849
info@brockvillechamber.com
www.brockvillechamber.com
www.linkedin.com/groups/Brockville-District-Chamber-Commerce-4074940
www.facebook.com/brockvillechamber
twitter.com/brockvillechamb
Overview: A small local organization founded in 1906
Mission: To foster a competitive business environment in the Brockville region that benefits members of the community through the growth of jobs, wealth & quality of life
Member of: Ontario Chamber of Commerce; Canadian Chamber of Commerce
Finances: Annual Operating Budget: $50,000-$100,000; Funding Sources: Membership dues
Staff Member(s): 5; 15 volunteer(s)
Membership: 560+; Fees: Schedule available; Committees: Advocacy & Economic Development; Chamber Ambassadors; Executive; Finance; Human Resources; Membership; Nominating; Programming; Tourism; Young Professionals
Chief Officer(s):
Laura Good, President
Pam Robertson, Executive Director
Awards:
• Awards of Excellence

Brockville & District Multicultural Council Inc.
PO Box 1757, Brockville ON K6V 6K8
Tel: 613-342-1469
brkMulticulturalCommittee@yahoo.ca
www.brockvillemulticulturalfestival.com
Overview: A small local charitable organization founded in 1981
Mission: To preserve, maintain, & stimulate the creative expression of all cultures & folk art heritages through community interaction; to promote multiculturalism in Leeds & Grenville Counties; to offer assistance to newcomers & other Canadians in maintaining & nurturing their cultural heritage.
Affiliation(s): Ministry of Citizenship & Culture
Membership: Member Profile: Any cultural individual or group

Activities: Annual community festival; annual wine & cheese party; monthly meetings, 3rd Tuesday of each month; provides entertainment &/or cultural displays at various community functions
Chief Officer(s):
Bea Singh, Contact

Brome County Historical Society (BCHS) / La Société historique du Comté de Brome
130, ch Lakeside, Knowlton QC J0E 1V0
Tel: 450-243-6782
bchs@endirect.qc.ca
www.bromemuseum.com
Overview: A small local charitable organization founded in 1897
Mission: To preserve, research, & exhibit historical material about Brome County & its sites
Member of: Federation of Québec Historical Societies
Finances: Annual Operating Budget: $50,000-$100,000; Funding Sources: Admissions; book sales; donations; memberships; fundraising
Staff Member(s): 2; 5 volunteer(s)
Membership: 600; Fees: $25 single; $45 couple; $50 family; $350 life; Committees: Building; Finance; Fundraising; Heritage
Activities: Operating Brome County Historical Museum: Old Fire Hall, Marion L. Phelps Building, Centennial Building, County Court House & Tibbits Hill Pioneer School; Offering historical lectures; Library
Chief Officer(s):
Arlene Royea, Managing Director

The Bronte Historical Society
7 West Rivers St., Oakville ON L6L 6N9
Tel: 905-825-5552
brontehistoricalsociety@bellnet.ca
www.brontehistoricalsociety.ca
Overview: A small international charitable organization founded in 1893
Mission: To bring closer together all who honour the Brontë sisters; to act as the guardian of such letters, writings & personal belongings as could be acquired for the Museum; to dispel legend & false sentiments regarding the Brontë story
Finances: Funding Sources: Membership fees; donations; museum fees
Activities: General meetings, member gathering and fundraising events; Speaker Service: Yes
Chief Officer(s):
Judith Watkins, Canadian Representative

Brooks & District Chamber of Commerce
PO Box 400, 403 - 2 Ave. West, Brooks AB T1R 1B4
Tel: 403-362-7641; Fax: 403-362-6893
manager@brookschamber.ab.ca
www.brookschamber.ab.ca
www.facebook.com/BrooksandDistrictChamberofCommerce
twitter.com/BrooksChamber
Overview: A small local organization founded in 1947
Member of: Alberta Chamber of Commerce; Canadian Chamber of Commerce
Finances: Funding Sources: Sponsorship; trade show; membership fees; educational events
Staff Member(s): 2
Membership: 300; Fees: Schedule available based on number of employees; Member Profile: Businesses
Activities: Luncheons monthly; Internships: Yes; Speaker Service: Yes
Chief Officer(s):
Karen Vogelaar, Executive Director
Michelle Gietz, President
Awards:
• Business of the Year
• New Business of the Year
• Customer Service Excellence Award

Broomball Canada Federation See Ballon sur glace Broomball Canada

Broomball Federation of Ontario See Federation of Broomball Associations of Ontario

Broomball Newfoundland & Labrador
NL
Overview: A small provincial organization overseen by Ballon sur glace Broomball Canada
Member of: Ballon sur glace Broomball Canada

Brotherhood of Locomotive Engineers See Teamsters Canada Rail Conference

Brothers of Our Lady of Mercy Voir Frères de Notre-Dame de la Miséricorde

The Brothers of the Good Shepherd / Les Frères du Bon-Pasteur
Development Office, PO Box 1003, 10 Delaware Ave., Hamilton ON L8N 3R1
Tel: 905-528-9109; Fax: 905-528-6967
info@goodshepherdcentres.ca
www.goodshepherdcentres.ca
www.facebook.com/goodshepherdhamilton
twitter.com/goodshepherdham
www.youtube.com/channel/UCDb1lcEb-uKK3n_9kuBVbPg
Also Known As: Good Shepherd
Previous Name: Little Brothers of the Good Shepherd
Overview: A small local charitable organization founded in 1951
Finances: Annual Operating Budget: $500,000-$1.5 Million
Activities: Housing for battered women & children; residence for homeless youth; men's hostel; food bank & food line; speakers on topics dealing with violence & abuse; Speaker Service: Yes
Chief Officer(s):
Richard MacPhee, Executive Director

Bruce Children's Aid Society See Bruce Grey Child & Family Services

Bruce County Historical Society
PO Box 742, Southampton ON N0H 2L0
www.brucecountyhistory.on.ca
www.facebook.com/BruceCountyHS
Overview: A small local charitable organization founded in 1957
Mission: To bring together people concerned with the preservation of Bruce County's heritage; To collect & preserve historical items, accounts, manuscripts, books, etc.
Affiliation(s): Ontario Historical Society
30 volunteer(s)
Membership: 420; Fees: $20 annual; $500 lifetime
Chief Officer(s):
Joyce Osborne, Membership Secretary

Bruce Grey Child & Family Services (BGCFS)
1290 - 3rd Ave. East, Owen Sound ON N4K 2L5
Tel: 519-371-4453; Fax: 519-376-8934
Toll-Free: 855-322-4453
www.bgcfs.ca
Previous Name: Bruce Children's Aid Society
Merged from: The Children's Aid Societies of Bruce & Grey Counties
Overview: A small local organization founded in 2012
Mission: To protect children by providing supportive services to children & families through partnerships
Staff Member(s): 150
Chief Officer(s):
David F. Wyles, President
Phyllis Lovell, Executive Director

Bruce House
#402, 251 Bank St., Ottawa ON K2P 1X3
Tel: 613-729-0911; Fax: 613-729-0959
admin@brucehouse.org
www.brucehouse.org
www.facebook.com/MoreThanAHouse
twitter.com/MoreThanAHouse
Overview: A small local charitable organization founded in 1988 overseen by Canadian AIDS Society
Mission: To provide housing, compassionate care & support in Ottawa-Carleton for people living with HIV/AIDS, believing that everyone has the right to live & die with dignity; to operate a 7-bed residence staffed 24-hours a day for people who require extensive support & 34 rent-to-income apartment units for those able to live independently.
Member of: Ontario AIDS Network; Ontario Non-Profit Housing Association
Affiliation(s): City of Ottawa, Province of Ontario, government of Canada, a network of community centers & agencies, local hospitals, physicians, social service agencies, other local charitable agencies & organizations
Finances: Funding Sources: Ministry of Health; donations; RMOC; United Way

Bruce Peninsula Association for Community Living
PO Box 95, 314 George St., Wiarton ON N0H 2T0
Tel: 519-534-0553; Fax: 519-534-2739
bpacl@bmts.com
www.bpacl.com
Previous Name: Community Living Wiarton & District
Overview: A medium-sized local organization

Mission: To help people with disabilities fully participate in all aspects of society
Member of: Community Living Ontario
Chief Officer(s):
Michele Bell, Executive Director

Bruce Peninsula Environment Group (BPEG)
PO Box 1072, Lions Head ON N0H 1W0
info@bpeg.ca
www.bpeg.ca
Overview: A small local organization founded in 1989
Mission: BPEG is a group of people concerned about the environment & committed to preserving the unique ecology of the Bruce Peninsula. It promotes awareness of the region's diverse flora, fauna, geology & cultural history, & monitors human impact on them. It has planted trees, helped with water quality issues on farmland, encouraged wildlife with habitat improvement, & has been active in legislating for better forestry practices.
Member of: Great Lakes United; Ontario Environment Network; Durham Nuclear Awareness; Canadian Environmental Network; Grey-Bruce Power Council
Finances: *Annual Operating Budget:* Less than $50,000; *Funding Sources:* Membership fees; donations
8 volunteer(s)
Membership: 125; *Fees:* $25 family, $15 single; *Member Profile:* Residents of the Bruce Peninsula; *Committees:* Alternate Energy; Dark Sky; Media; Recycling; Sustainable Forestry
Activities: Earth Day; energy tour; monthly meetings; tree planting; road clean-ups; recycling; environmental awards; *Awareness Events:* Energy Tour, June 4; *Library:* by appointment
Chief Officer(s):
Jim Kuellmer, Chair
Awards:
• Bruce Peninsula Environment Group Award for Excellence

The Bruce Trail Association *See* The Bruce Trail Conservancy

The Bruce Trail Conservancy
PO Box 857, Hamilton ON L8N 3N9
Tel: 905-529-6821; *Fax:* 905-529-6823
Toll-Free: 800-665-4453
info@brucetrail.org
www.brucetrail.org
www.facebook.com/TheBruceTrailConservancy
Previous Name: The Bruce Trail Association
Overview: A medium-sized provincial charitable organization founded in 1963
Mission: To secure, develop & manage the Bruce Trail as a public footpath along the Niagara Escarpment from Queenston to Tobermory, thereby promoting preservation of the escarpment's ecological & cultural integrity & fostering an appreciation of its natural beauty. The Bruce Trail, designated as a UNESCO World Biosphere Reserve, is Canada's oldest and longest footpath.
Member of: Hike Ontario
Affiliation(s): Ontario Trails Council; Coalition on the Niagara Escarpment; Federation of Ontario Naturalists; Hike Ontario
Finances: *Funding Sources:* Memberships; donations; sales
Staff Member(s): 15; 1250 volunteer(s)
Membership: 8,500; *Fees:* $50; $125 organization
Activities: Land conservation; trail management & development; environmental hikes; *Speaker Service:* Yes; *Library:* by appointment
Chief Officer(s):
Beth Gilhespy, Executive Director
bgilhespy@brucetrail.org

Beaver Valley
PO Box 3251, Meaford ON N4L 1A5
www.beavervalleybrucetrail.org
www.facebook.com/BeaverValleyBruceTrailClub
Chief Officer(s):
Ros Rossetti, President, 519-538-1866
rosamundr@aol.com

Blue Mountains
PO Box 91, Collingwood ON L9Y 3Z4
hart@bmbtc.org
www.bmbtc.org

Caledon Hills
PO Box 65, Stn. Caledon Village, Caledon ON L7K 3L3
info@caledonbrucetrail.org
www.caledonbrucetrail.org
www.facebook.com/CaledonHillsBruceTrailClub

Dufferin Hi-Land
PO Box 698, Alliston ON L9R 2V9
www.dufferinbrucetrailclub.org
Chief Officer(s):
Carl Alexander, President
carlwalexander@gmail.com

Iroquoia
ON
info@iroquoia.on.ca
www.iroquoia.on.ca
www.facebook.com/IroquoiaBruceTrailClub
twitter.com/IroquoiaBruceTr
Chief Officer(s):
Cathie Mills, President

Niagara
5085 Alyssa Dr., Beamsville ON L0R 1B2
niagarabrucetrailclub@gmail.com
www.niagarabrucetrail.org
www.facebook.com/156401064406469
twitter.com/BTCNiagara1
www.instagram.com/niagarabrucetrailclub
Chief Officer(s):
Debbie Demizio, President

Peninsula
PO Box 2, Tobermory ON N0H 2R0
peninsulabrucetrailclub@gmail.com
www.pbtc.ca
www.facebook.com/pages/Peninsula-Bruce-Trail-Club/154060254652464
Chief Officer(s):
John Whitworth, President
ajwhitworth@rogers.com

Sydenham
PO Box 431, Owen Sound ON N4K 5P7
info@sydenhambrucetrail.ca
www.sydenhambrucetrail.ca
www.facebook.com/sydenhambrucetrailclub
Chief Officer(s):
Bob Knapp, President, 519-371-1255
rmknapp@yahoo.com

Toronto
PO Box 857, Hamilton ON L8N 3N9
Tel: 905-529-6821; *Fax:* 905-529-6823
Toll-Free: 800-665-4453
info@brucetrail.org
www.torontobrucetrailclub.org
Affiliation(s): Halton Hills Chapter
Chief Officer(s):
Todd Bardes, President

Buckskinners Muzzleloading Association, Limited
PO Box 4127, Stn. Champlain Place, 2493 Route 490, Dieppe NB E1A 6E8
Tel: 506-576-1959; *Fax:* 506-859-1249
buckskinnersweb@yahoo.com
buckskinnersweb.weebly.com
Overview: A small local organization founded in 1978
Mission: To promote good & safe blackpowder shooting, marksmanship & sportsmanship; to encourage & promote buckskinning knowledge & skills
Affiliation(s): New Brunswick Wildlife Federation
Finances: *Annual Operating Budget:* Less than $50,000
36 volunteer(s)
Membership: 36; *Fees:* $20 single; $35 family; *Member Profile:* Buckskinners, Civil War & pre-1840 re-enactors
Activities: Winter Rendezvous, Feb.; Summer Rendezvous, June
Chief Officer(s):
Shirley Stuart, Contact

Buddhist Association of Canada - Cham Shan Temple
7254 Bayview Ave., Toronto ON L3T 2R6
Tel: 905-886-1522
chamshantemple.askus@gmail.com
www.chamshantemple.org
www.facebook.com/temple.chamshan
twitter.com/temple_chamshan
Overview: A small national organization founded in 1973
Mission: In addition to the main worship hall & 2 congregation halls, the Buddhist temple also includes a Dharma seminary for the Chinese community to learn Buddhism.
Activities: Seminars, sutra reading groups, meditation retreats; Library
Chief Officer(s):
Dayi Shi, President & Abbot

Buddhist Churches of Canada *See* Jodo Shinshu Buddhist Temples of Canada

Buddies in Bad Times Theatre
12 Alexander St., Toronto ON M4Y 1B4
Tel: 416-975-9130; *Fax:* 416-975-9293
buddiesinbadtimes.com
www.facebook.com/buddiesinbadtimes
twitter.com/yyzbuddies
www.youtube.com/BIBTTV
Overview: A medium-sized local organization founded in 1979
Mission: To promote gay, lesbian, & queer theatrical expression
Finances: *Funding Sources:* Government; foundations
Staff Member(s): 18
Chief Officer(s):
Evalyn Parry, Artistic Director
evalyn@buddiesinbadtimes.com

Buffalo Lake Naturalists Club
PO Box 1802, Stettler AB T0C 2L0
BuffaloLakeNC@gmail.com
www.buffalolakenature.com
www.facebook.com/BuffaloLakeNaturalists
Overview: A small local organization founded in 1973
Mission: To promote the enjoyment of nature through environmental appreciation & conservation; To encourage wise use & conservation of natural resources & environmental protection
Member of: Federation of Alberta Naturalists
Finances: *Funding Sources:* Membership fees
Membership: *Fees:* $10 single; $20 family
Activities: Bird, plant & butterfly identification field trips; community projects; park planning & cleanup; Library

Buffalo Narrows Chamber of Commerce
PO Box 430, Buffalo Narrows SK S0M 0J0
Tel: 306-235-7442; *Fax:* 306-235-4416
Overview: A small local organization

Buffalo Narrows Friendship Centre
PO Box 189, 351 Buffalo St., Buffalo Narrows SK S0M 0J0
Tel: 306-235-4633; *Fax:* 306-235-4544
bnfc@sasktel.net
www.afcs.ca/buffalo-narrows.html
Overview: A small local organization
Chief Officer(s):
Brenda Chartier, Executive Director

BuildForce Canada
#1150, 220 Laurier Ave. West, Ottawa ON K1P 5Z9
Tel: 613-569-5552
Other Communication: eLearning Support: 1-866-793-6225;
support@buildforce.ca
info@buildforce.ca
www.buildforce.ca
Previous Name: Construction Sector Council
Overview: A medium-sized national organization founded in 2001
Mission: To identify critical human resources challenges in the construction industry; To find common solutions & approaches
Finances: *Funding Sources:* Government funding
Chief Officer(s):
Rosemary Sparks, Executive Director
Meetings/Conferences:
• 3rd National Construction & Maintenance Industry Strategy Summit 2019, 2019
Scope: National
Description: Biennial conference
Publications:
• BuildForce Magazine
Type: Magazine; *Accepts Advertising; Editor:* Shannon Savory

Building Energy Management Manitoba (BEMM)
#309, 23 - 845 Dakota St., Winnipeg MB R2M 5M3
Tel: 204-452-2098
info@bemm.ca
www.bemm.ca
Overview: A small provincial organization
Mission: To promote energy efficiency & management in the commercial, industrial, institutional & mult-residential building sectors
Membership: *Fees:* $150; *Member Profile:* Engineers, architects, property managers, contractors & energy management professionals; Representatives from government, school boards, hospitals & utility
Chief Officer(s):

Canadian Associations / Building Envelope Council of Ottawa Region (BECOR)

Robert Bisson, Treasurer, 204-945-8452
robert.bisson@gov.mb.ca
Rob Walger Glenday, Contact, Membership Inquiries & Website
info@bemm.ca
Meetings/Conferences:
• Building Energy Management Manitoba 2018 Better Buildings Conference, 2018
Scope: Provincial

Building Envelope Council of Ottawa Region (BECOR)
PO Box 7328, Stn. Vanier, Ottawa ON K1L 8E4
Tel: 819-956-3401; *Fax:* 819-956-3400
info@becor.org
www.becor.org
Overview: A small local charitable organization founded in 1988
Mission: To promote the pursuit of excellence in the design, construction & performance of the building envelope
Member of: National Building Envelope Council
Finances: *Annual Operating Budget:* Less than $50,000
Membership: 100-499; *Fees:* $75; $25 student; $300 corporate
Activities: Seminars, conferences; *Speaker Service:* Yes
Chief Officer(s):
Hélène Roche, President
helene.roche@nrc-cnrc.gc.ca
Peter Fridgen, Treasurer
fridgen@fridgen.ca

Building Futures Employment Society (BFES)
61 Glendale Ave., Lower Sackville NS B4C 3J4
Tel: 902-865-1797; *Fax:* 902-865-1797
www.buildfutures.ca
Www.facebook.com/BuildingFuturesBFES
Also Known As: FUTURES
Previous Name: Anchor Industries Society
Overview: A small local organization founded in 1973
Mission: To offer vocational & recreational programs & services to adults with intellectual challenges
Member of: DIRECTIONS Council for Vocational Services Society
Activities: Operates four businesses: The PrintShop, The OffShoot Shop, The Ladle Restaurant & All Wrapped Up; literary classes; employment programs
Chief Officer(s):
Marilyn Forest, Executive Director
Publications:
• Anchor Industries Society Newsletter
Type: Newsletter

Building Industry & Land Development Alberta
#328, 9707 - 110 St., Edmonton AB T5K 2L9
Tel: 780-424-5890
Toll-Free: 800-661-3348
info@bildalberta.ca
www.bildalberta.ca
twitter.com/BILDalberta
Also Known As: BILD Alberta
Merged from: Canadian Home Builders' Association - Alberta; Urban Development Institute - Alberta Division
Overview: A medium-sized provincial organization overseen by Canadian Home Builders' Association
Mission: To act as the voice of the residential construction industry in Alberta
Affiliation(s): Canadian Home Builders' Association
Staff Member(s): 10
Membership: 1,000-4,999; *Member Profile:* New home builders, renovators, developers, trade & supply companies, & professional services
Activities: *Speaker Service:* Yes
Chief Officer(s):
Carmen Wyton, Chief Executive Officer
carmen.wyton@bildalberta.ca
T.J. Keil, Executive Director
tj.keil@bildalberta.ca
Awards:
• Awards in Excellence in Housing
Yearly award for homebuilders
• Industry Leader Awards
Yearly award for homebuilders
• Safety Leadership Awards
Yearly award for homebuilders
Meetings/Conferences:
• BILD Alberta 2018 Spring Conference, April, 2018, Fairmont Banff Springs Hotel, Banff, AB
Scope: Provincial
Contact Information: Email: conference@bildalberta.ca

Publications:
• BILD Alberta Newsletter
Type: Newsletter
Profile: An information resource containing provincial activity & policy changes, discussions, & government relations work done by BILD Alberta

Central Alberta
#200, 6700 - 76 St., Red Deer AB T4P 4G6
Tel: 403-346-5321; *Fax:* 403-342-1301
info@chbacentralalberta.ca
www.chbaca.ca
Chief Officer(s):
Denie Olmstead, Chief Executive Officer

Edmonton Region
150 Summerside Gate SW, Edmonton AB T6X 0P5
Tel: 780-425-1020; *Fax:* 780-425-1031
info@chbaedmonton.ca
www.chbaedmonton.ca
www.facebook.com/515536701870378
twitter.com/chba_edmonton
Chief Officer(s):
Sharon Copithorne, Chief Executive Officer, 780-702-0323
scopithorne@chbaedmonton.ca

Grande Prairie Region
#104, 10127 - 121 Ave., Grande Prairie AB T8V 7V3
Tel: 780-538-4494; *Fax:* 780-513-4459
info@chbagp.com
www.chbagp.com
Chief Officer(s):
Kathy Nilsson, Executive Officer

Lethbridge Region (CHBA-LR)
#14, 495 WT Hill Blvd., Lethbridge AB T1J 1Y6
Tel: 403-328-2288
info@chbalethbridge.com
www.chbalethbridge.com
www.facebook.com/canadianhomebuildersassociationLR
twitter.com/chbaleth
Chief Officer(s):
Angela Zuba, Chief Executive Officer, 403-328-2288 Ext. 203

Medicine Hat & District
#5, 1311 Trans Canada Way SE, Medicine Hat AB T1B 1J1
Tel: 403-977-6722
chbamedicinehat.com
www.facebook.com/206974552667135
twitter.com/MedHatBuilders
Chief Officer(s):
Jackie Velcoff, Executive Officer
eo@chbamedicinehat.com

Building Industry & Land Development Association (BILD)
#100, 20 Upjohn Rd., Toronto ON M3B 2V9
Tel: 416-391-3445; *Fax:* 416-391-2118
Other Communication: Alternate Phone: 416-391-4663
info@bildgta.ca
www.bildgta.ca
www.linkedin.com/company/building-industry-and-land-development-association-bild-
www.facebook.com/bildgta
twitter.com/bildgta
www.youtube.com/user/BILDgta
Merged from: Greater Toronto Home Builders' Association; Urban Development Institute/Ontario
Overview: A medium-sized local organization overseen by Canadian Home Builders' Association
Mission: To represent the land development & renovation industry in the Greater Toronto Area
Staff Member(s): 16
Membership: 1,500 corporate; *Member Profile:* Home builders, land developers, renovators, land use & environmental planners, sub-contractors, manufacturers, lawyers, surveyors, architects, suppliers, professional & financial institutions; *Committees:* Administration; Communication & Events; Government Relations; Membership; Finance
Activities: Communicating with all levels of government to facilitate communication with the construction industry; Promoting the welfare of membership; Protecting the interests of customers through advocacy & representation
Chief Officer(s):
Bryan Tuckey, President & Chief Executive Officer
btuckey@bildgta.ca
Awards:
• BILD Awards
• Hall of Fame Award
• Chair's Award of Merit

• Member of the Year Award
• Associate Awards
• Lifetime Achievement Award
• Renovation & Custom Home Awards
Meetings/Conferences:
• Building Industry & Land Development Association Annual General Meeting 2018, 2018
Scope: Local

Building Industry & Land Development Calgary Region
#100, 7326 - 10th St. NE, Calgary AB T2E 8W1
Tel: 403-235-1911; *Fax:* 403-248-1272
info@bildcr.com
www.bildcr.com
www.linkedin.com/company/17918873
www.facebook.com/BILDCR
twitter.com/BILDCR
Also Known As: BILD Calgary Region
Merged from: Canadian Home Builders' Association - Calgary Region; Urban Development Institute (UDI) - Calgary
Overview: A small local organization founded in 1946
Mission: To represent & advocate for the building industry
220 volunteer(s)
Membership: 661; *Fees:* Schedule available
Chief Officer(s):
Guy Huntingford, CEO
guy.huntingford@bildcr.com
David Bears, Director, Programs
david.bears@bildcr.com
Beverly Jarvis, Director, Policy, Projects & Government Relations
beverly.jarvis@bildcr.com
Grace Lui, Director, Strategic Initiatives & Government Relations
grace.lui@bildcr.com
Val Veldhuyzen, Director, Finance & Administration
val.veldhuyzen@bildcr.com

The Building Materials Retailers Association of Québec *Voir* Association québécoise de la quincaillerie et des matériaux de construction

Building Officials' Association of British Columbia (BOABC)
#145, 10451 Shellbridge Way, Richmond BC V6X 2W8
Tel: 604-270-9516
info@boabc.org
www.boabc.org
Overview: A small provincial organization founded in 1954
Mission: To serve the public interest in building safety, health & welfare by advancing high, consistent standards of building official practice through the professional competence of its members
Staff Member(s): 2
Membership: 675; *Fees:* $441.26 regular/associate; $38.61 student/retired; *Member Profile:* Local government building officials & those involved in building design, construction, testing & research
Activities: Education seminars
Chief Officer(s):
Manjit S. Sohi, President
president@boabc.org

Building Owners & Managers Association - Atlantic *See* Building Owners & Managers Association - Nova Scotia

Building Owners & Managers Association - Canada
PO Box 61, #1801, 1 Dundas St. West, Toronto ON M5G 1Z3
Tel: 416-214-1912; *Fax:* 416-214-1284
info@bomacanada.ca
www.bomacanada.ca
www.facebook.com/pages/BOMA-Canada/107613392698316
twitter.com/BOMA_CAN
Also Known As: BOMA Canada
Overview: A medium-sized national organization
Mission: To represent the Canadian commerical real estate industry on matters of national concern; To develop a strong communications network between local associations; To promote professionalism of members through education programs & effective public relations activity
Affiliation(s): BOMA International
Membership: 2,000
Chief Officer(s):
Benjamin L, Shinewald, President/CEO
Meetings/Conferences:
• Building Owners & Managers Association 2018 Conference,

2018
Scope: National

Building Owners & Managers Association - Nova Scotia
PO Box 1597, Halifax NS B3J 2Y3
Tel: 902-425-3717; *Fax:* 902-431-7220
info@bomanovascotia.com
www.bomanovascotia.com
Also Known As: BOMA Nova Scotia
Previous Name: Building Owners & Managers Association - Atlantic
Overview: A medium-sized local organization
Mission: To actively represent our members, through education, networking & lobbying in matters affecting the ownership, management & operation of commercial properties
Member of: Building Owners & Managers Association of Canada
Membership: *Member Profile:* Owners, managers and suppliers of the commercial real estate industry
Chief Officer(s):
Rod Winters, President

Building Owners & Managers Association of British Columbia
#556, 409 Granville St., Vancouver BC V6C 1T2
Tel: 604-684-3916; *Fax:* 604-684-4876
bomabc@boma.bc.ca
www.boma.bc.ca
www.linkedin.com/company/boma-bc
Also Known As: BOMA BC
Overview: A medium-sized provincial organization founded in 1911
Mission: To represent the interests & concerns of building owners & managers in the commercial & office space industry in British Columbia
Member of: Building Owners & Managers Association of Canada; BOMA International
Affiliation(s): Heritage Canada; Vancouver Board of Trade; CSAE
Membership: 300; *Fees:* $266-$4,200 Corporate real estate; $266-$1,890 Corporate business; *Member Profile:* Individuals & firms that work in corporate real estate; Suppliers & service companies serving the building industry; Students enrolled in post-secondary programs related to real estate; *Committees:* Contact; Education; Emergency Response; Energy & Environment; Golf; Health & Safety; Luncheon Program; Quality Building; Sponsorship; Taxation
Chief Officer(s):
Paul LaBranche, President
pdl@boma.bc.ca
Muneesh Sharma, Director, Government Affairs
muneesh@boma.bc.ca
Daniel Klemky, Manager, Energy & Environment
daniel@boma.bc.ca
Kiomi Lutz, Manager, Member Services
kiomi@boma.bc.ca
Awards:
- EARTH Award
Eligibility: BOMA BC members with an environmentally conscious building that is located in British Columbia, at least three years old from date of occupancy, & at least 50% used as office space
- TOBY Award
Eligibility: BOMA members that own or manage a building that is at least three years old from date of occupancy & at least 50% used as office space
- Leasing Deal of the Year
Eligibility: Self-nominated landlord & broker teams
- Tenant Improvement of the Year
Eligibility: Self-nominated architectural & design companies or landlords
- PINNACLE Award
Eligibility: BOMA BC members

Building Owners & Managers Association of Edmonton
Standard Life Centre, #390, 10405 Jasper Ave., Edmonton AB T5J 3N4
Tel: 780-428-0419; *Fax:* 780-426-6882
www.bomaedmonton.org
Also Known As: BOMA Edmonton
Overview: A medium-sized local organization founded in 1958 overseen by Building Owners & Managers Association International
Mission: To represent the interests & concerns of building owners & managers in the commercial & office space industry in Edmonton
Member of: euilding Owners & Managers Association of Canada
Finances: *Funding Sources:* Membership dues; education programs; advertising
Staff Member(s): 2
Membership: *Fees:* Schedule available; *Member Profile:* Building owner/manager or service company to property management industry
Activities: *Library:* by appointment
Chief Officer(s):
Percy J. Woods, President & Chief Staff Officer
pwoods@bomaedm.ca

Building Owners & Managers Association of Manitoba
PO Box 3107, Winnipeg MB R3C 4E6
Tel: 204-777-2662; *Fax:* 204-777-0326
bomamanitoba.ca
www.linkedin.com/company/boma-manitoba
www.facebook.com/308490885833086
twitter.com/bomamanitoba
Also Known As: BOMA Manitoba
Overview: A medium-sized provincial organization founded in 1982
Mission: To represent the interests & concerns of building owners & managers in the commercial real estate industry in Manitoba
Member of: Building Owners & Managers Association of Canada; Building Owners & Managers Association International
Staff Member(s): 2
Membership: 250+; *Fees:* $895; *Member Profile:* Companies involved in commercial real estate ownership, development & management; *Committees:* Awards of Excellence; Education; Marketing & Development; Membership; Golf Tournament; Government Affairs/Advocacy; Building Operators & Engineers Group; Codes & Standards; Energy & Environment
Chief Officer(s):
Tom Thiessen, Executive Director
tom@bomamanitoba.ca
Awards:
- Awards of Excellence

Building Owners & Managers Association of Ottawa
#1005, 141 Laurier Ave. West, Ottawa ON K1P 5J3
Tel: 613-232-1875; *Fax:* 613-563-3908
administration@bomaottawa.org
www.bomaottawa.org
twitter.com/boma_ottawa
Also Known As: BOMA Ottawa
Overview: A small local organization founded in 1971
Member of: BOMA International
Finances: *Annual Operating Budget:* $500,000-$1.5 Million; *Funding Sources:* Membership dues
Membership: 450; *Fees:* Schedule available; *Committees:* Marketing; Membership; Planning & Policy; Awards; Education; Government Affairs; Security & Life Safety; Curling; Spring Golf; Fall Golf; Lunch; Ski
Chief Officer(s):
Dean Karakasis, Executive Director
executivedirector@bomaottawa.org

Building Owners & Managers Association Toronto
#1800, 1 Dundas St. West, Toronto ON M5G 1Z3
Tel: 416-596-8065; *Fax:* 416-596-1085
info@bomatoronto.org
www.bomatoronto.org
www.linkedin.com/company/boma-toronto
www.facebook.com/bomatoronto
www.youtube.com/user/BOMAtoronto
Also Known As: BOMA Toronto
Overview: A large local organization
Mission: To represent the interests & concerns of building owners & managers in the commercial & office space industry in the Greater Toronto Area
Member of: BOMA International
Membership: 600+; *Committees:* Awards; Education Advisory; Energy; Events; Executive; Regulatory Affairs & Environment; Security Risk Management Advisory Council; Young Professional
Chief Officer(s):
Susan Allen, President & CEO
sallen@bomatoronto.org
Bala Gnanam, Director, Sustainable Building Operations & Strategic Partnerships, 416-596-8065 Ext. 230
bgnanam@bomatoronto.org
Aaron Therrien, Senior Manager, Member Services, 416-596-8065 Ext. 220
atherrien@bomatoronto.org
Thomas Catania, Manager, Sponsorship, 416-596-8065 Ext. 226
tcatania@bomatoronto.org
Teresa Champagnie-Bent, Manager, Awards, 416-596-8065 Ext. 227
tcbent@bomatoronto.org
Fawzia Karim, Manager, Accounting, 416-596-8065 Ext. 225
fkarim@bomatoronto.org
Kseniia Khudorozhkova, Office Administrator, 416-596-8065 Ext. 228
kseniia@bomatoronto.org
Awards:
- Certificate of Excellence
- The Outstanding Building of the Year (TOBY) Award
- Earth Award
- Pinnacle Award
- Earth Hour Challenge Award

Building Owners & Managers Institute of Canada
#1201, 55 York St., Toronto ON M5J 1R7
Tel: 416-977-8700; *Fax:* 416-977-8800
Toll-Free: 888-821-9319
admin@bomicanada.com
www.bomicanada.com
Also Known As: BOMI Canada
Overview: A small national organization founded in 1974
Mission: Provides education for members of the commercial property industry, including certification for property managers, facilities professionals, systems personnel and systems supervisors
Chief Officer(s):
Jim Preece, President
jpreece@bomicanada.com

Building Supply Industry Association of British Columbia (BSIA of BC)
#2, 19299 - 94th Ave., Surrey BC V4N 4E6
Tel: 604-513-2205; *Fax:* 604-513-2206
Toll-Free: 888-711-5656
www.bsiabc.ca
Overview: A medium-sized provincial organization founded in 1938
Mission: To act as the official voice of the building supply industry in British Columbia; To provide services to members
Membership: *Fees:* $169 wholesale branches; $199 retail stores & manufacturer's agents; $399 associates & retail & wholesale head offices; *Member Profile:* Manufacturers; Wholesalers; Suppliers; Retailers who operate lumber yards, hardware stores, & home centres
Activities: Promoting the building supply industry in British Columbia; Liaising with government; Addressing concerns within the industry; Providing information to members; Hosting product knowledge evenings at the BSIA office
Chief Officer(s):
Thomas Foreman, President
thomas@bsiabc.ca
Marijoel Chamberlain, Coordinator, Member Services, & Manager, Trade Show
marijoel@bsiabc.ca
Jackie Trafton, Administrator
jackie@bsiabc.ca
Meetings/Conferences:
- Westcoast Building & Hardware Show 2018, 2018, BC
Scope: Provincial
Description: A trade show for members of the building supply industry, presenting educational opportunities & new & innovative products & services
Contact Information: Phone: 604-513-2205, E-mail: info@bsiabc.ca
Publications:
- BSIA e-news
Type: Newsletter; *Frequency:* Monthly; *Accepts Advertising*; *Price:* Free with membership in the Building Supply Industry Association of British Columbia
Profile: Industry & association news
- BSIA News Magazine
Type: Magazine; *Frequency:* 5 pa; *Accepts Advertising*; *Price:* Free with membership in the Building Supply Industry Association of British Columbia
Profile: A 40 to 60 page magazine, featuring association activities & in-depth articles for building supply dealers &

Canadian Associations / Bukas Loob sa Diyos Covenant Community / "Open in Spirit to God"

suppliers throughout British Columbia, who retail a wide range of home improvement supplies & materials
- Building Supply Industry Association of British Columbia Directory
Type: Directory; *Frequency:* Annually; *Accepts Advertising*; *Price:* Free with membership in the Building SupplyIndustry Association of British Columbia
Profile: An alphabetical & city listing of British Columbia's building material & hardware retailers & suppliers
- Building Supply Industry Association of British Columbia Retail Product Buying Guide
Type: Guide; *Frequency:* Annually; *Accepts Advertising*; *Price:* Free with membership in the Building Supply Industry Association of BritishColumbia
Profile: Information about industry related vendors & suppliers
- Occupational Health & Safety Policy & Procedures Manual
Type: Manual; *Price:* Free with membership in the BSIA of British Columbia; $19.95 non-members
Profile: A generic guide to the development of a specific manual for each business
- Retail Job Descriptions Handbook
Type: Handbook

Bukas Loob sa Diyos Covenant Community / "Open in Spirit to God"
2565 Bathurst Street, Toronto ON M6B 2Z3
Tel: 416-787-7003; *Fax:* 416-787-6677
BLD_Toronto_Secretariat@googlegroups.com
www.bldtoronto.org
Also Known As: BLD Toronto
Overview: A small local charitable organization
Mission: To be witnesses to the Word that others may hear & understand; To be counsellors with the Spirit, that others may have healing & wholeness; to be defenders in Christ of those who suffer injustice & oppression; To be charismatic in activities; to be faithful to the Magisterium of the Church; To ensure that all activities & teachings of a BLD district are in accordance with official doctrines & dogmas of the Church, through ecclesial authority of the local Archdiocese over each BLD district; To ensure that the activities of each BLD member are the pastoral responsibilities of the Spiritual Director, who is under the ecclesial authority of the Archdiocese of Manila; To ensure the structure of each BLD consists of one couple to act as Community Shepherd of the local district, & five district counsellor couples who, through prayer & discernment, listen to God's will on the BLD's direction
Affiliation(s): Archdiocese of Toronto
Finances: *Funding Sources:* Donations
Activities: Providing faith instruction; Offering programs for couples, singles, & youth, such as renewal programs & encounters; Organizing prayer groups, Living Word groups, & First Friday devotions; Conducting services for apostolic & pastoral groups, families, communities, married couples, missions, the separated, widowed & divorced, solo parents, & youth & children; Conducting teachings, praise, worship, & seminars, such as Life in the Spirit seminars
Chief Officer(s):
Pat Canlas, Contact
prcanlas316@rogers.com

Bulimia Anorexia Nervosa Association (BANA) / Association de la boulimie et d'anorexie mentale
#100, 1500 Ouellette Ave., Windsor ON N8X 1K7
Tel: 519-969-2112; *Fax:* 519-969-0227
info@bana.ca
www.bana.ca
www.linkedin.com/groups/Bulimia-Anorexia-Nervosa-Association-2223288
www.facebook.com/277063735753721
twitter.com/BANAWindsor
banawindsor.tumblr.com
Overview: A medium-sized local charitable organization founded in 1982
Mission: To reduce the incidence of bulimia & anorexia nervosa with preventative programs; To offer services in the form of group, family & individual counselling; To provide a hotline for the community; To maintain a library for community use; To provide an educational, preventative curriculum
Finances: *Annual Operating Budget:* $500,000-$1.5 Million; *Funding Sources:* Provincial government
Staff Member(s): 8; 30 volunteer(s)
Membership: 300
Activities: *Awareness Events:* Eating Disorder Awareness Week, early Feb.; *Internships:* Yes; *Speaker Service:* Yes; *Library:* Open to public
Chief Officer(s):
Luciana Rosu-Sieza, Executive Director
luciana@bana.ca

Bulkley Valley Community Arts Council
PO Box 3971, Smithers BC V0J 2N0
Tel: 250-847-8022
info@bvartscouncil.com
www.bvartscouncil.com
www.facebook.com/bvartscouncil
Overview: A small local organization founded in 1980
Mission: The Bulkley Valley Community Arts Council (BVCAC) is a long standing democratic organization constituted to increase awareness of and access to the arts for residents of the Bulkley Valley.
Member of: Assembly of BC Arts Councils
Staff Member(s): 6
Chief Officer(s):
Miriam Colvin, President
Melissa Sawatsky, Secretary

Bulkley Valley Naturalists (BVN)
15087 H. Kerr Rd., Telkwa BC V0J 2X2
www.bvnaturalists.ca
Overview: A small local organization founded in 1979
Mission: To promote the enjoyment of nature through environmental appreciation & conservation; To encourage wise use & conservation of natural resources & environmental protection.
Member of: Federation of BC Naturalists
Affiliation(s): Federation of BC Naturalists.
Membership: *Fees:* $20 individual; $25 family
Activities: Participating in Christmas bird count and midwinter Bald Eagle count; participating on advisory committees on land use; developing nature education programs, field trips for schools

Bully B'Ware
6 Beddingfield St., Port Moody BC V3H 3N1
Tel: 604-936-8000; *Fax:* 604-936-8000
Toll-Free: 888-552-8559
bully@direct.ca
www.bullybeware.com
Overview: A small international organization
Finances: *Annual Operating Budget:* Less than $50,000
Membership: 1-99
Activities: *Speaker Service:* Yes
Chief Officer(s):
Cindi Seddon, Contact
Alyson McLellan, Contact
Gesele Lajoie, Contact

BullyingCanada Inc.
PO Box 27009, Stn. Atl Superstore, 471 Smythe St., Fredericton NB E3B 9M1
Fax: 866-780-3592
Toll-Free: 877-352-4497
Other Communication: Toll-Free Fax: 1-866-780-3592; Donations: 1-877-459-7413
headoffice@bullyingcanada.ca
www.bullyingcanada.ca
www.facebook.com/bullyingcanada
twitter.com/bullyingcanada
Overview: A small national charitable organization founded in 2006
Mission: To offer information, help & support to everyone involved in bullying; To undertake anti-bullying initiatives, including school workshops & a 24/7 support line
Finances: *Annual Operating Budget:* Less than $50,000; *Funding Sources:* Donations
Staff Member(s): 3; 20 volunteer(s)
Activities: Offering scholarships; Providing school programs & book reviews; *Internships:* Yes; *Speaker Service:* Yes
Chief Officer(s):
Rob Benn-Frenette, O.N.B., Co-Executive Director
rob.benn-frenette@bullyingcanada.ca
Katie Thompson, Co-Executive Director
katie.thompson@bullyingcanada.ca
   Alberta Office
   #125, 8015 Roper Rd. NW, Edmonton AB T6E 6S4
   British Columbia Office
   #600, 1285 West Broadway, Vancouver BC V6H 3X8
   Ontario Office
   PO Box 120, #503, 7700 Hurontario St., Brampton ON L6Y 4M6

Bund Deutscher Karnevalsgesellschaften Kanada *See* German-Canadian Mardi Gras Association Inc.

Bureau canadien d'agrément en foresterie *See* Canadian Forestry Accreditation Board

Bureau canadien de l'éducation internationale *See* Canadian Bureau for International Education

Bureau canadien de reconnaissance professionnelle des spécialistes de l'environnement *See* Canadian Environmental Certification Approvals Board

Bureau canadien de soudage *See* Canadian Welding Bureau

Bureau canadien des ressources humaines en technologie *See* Canadian Technology Human Resources Board

Bureau d'assurance du Canada *See* Insurance Bureau of Canada

Bureau d'éthique commerciale de l'Est et Nord de l'Ontario et l'Outaouais *See* Better Business Bureau of Eastern & Northern Ontario & the Outaouais

Bureau de bois de sciage des Maritimes *See* Maritime Lumber Bureau

Bureau de la télévision du Canada *See* Television Bureau of Canada, Inc.

Bureau de promotion du commerce Canada *See* Trade Facilitation Office Canada

Bureau de tourisme et de congrés de Saint John *See* Tourism Saint John

Le Bureau des examinateurs en pharmacie du Canada *See* The Pharmacy Examining Board of Canada

Bureau des regroupements des artistes visuels de l'Ontario (BRAVO)
CP 53004, Succ. Rideau, Ottawa ON K1N 1C5
Tél: 819-457-1892
Ligne sans frais: 800-611-4789
info@bravoart.org
bravoart.org
www.facebook.com/artBRAVOvisuel
twitter.com/BRAVOmembres
www.youtube.com/user/dgbravo1
Aperçu: *Dimension:* petite; *Envergure:* provinciale; fondée en 1991
Mission: BRAVO est voué à la défense des intérêts individuels et collectifs de ses membres et ses activités répondent à ses besoins de communication, de représentation, de formation, de promotion et d'appui à la diffusion des arts visuels. Bref, BRAVO vise la dynamisation des arts visuels et médiatiques non seulement chez ses artistes, mais aussi dans toutes les communautés de l'Ontario.
Membre(s) du personnel: 2
Membre: 135; *Montant de la cotisation:* 15$ étudiant; 40$ associé; 50$ statutaire; 75$ institutionnel; *Critères d'admissibilite:* Artistes professionnels
Membre(s) du bureau directeur:
Yves Larocque, Directeur général et artistique

Bureau local d'intervention traitant du SIDA (BLITS)
#116, 59, rue Monfette, Victoriaville QC G6P 1J8
Tél: 819-758-2662; *Téléc:* 819-758-8270
Ligne sans frais: 866-758-2662
blits@cdcbf.qc.ca
www.blits.ca
www.facebook.com/BLITSvictoriaville
Aperçu: *Dimension:* petite; *Envergure:* locale; Organisme sans but lucratif; fondée en 1989
Membre: *Montant de la cotisation:* 5$ annuellement
Activités:: *Bibliothèque:* Bibliothèque publique
Membre(s) du bureau directeur:
Gabrielle Bergeron, Présidente
Maryse Laroche, Directrice
blitscoordo@cdcbf.qc.ca
Sylvie Bondon, Agente de bureau
Véronique Vanier, Agente d'éducation
blitsprojet@cdcbf.qc.ca

Bureau national d'examen d'assistance dentaire *See* National Dental Assisting Examining Board

Le bureau national d'examen dentaire du Canada *See* National Dental Examining Board of Canada

Bureau régional d'action sida (Outaouais) (BRAS)
#003, 109, rue Wright, Gatineau QC J8X 2G7

Tél: 819-776-2727; *Téléc:* 819-776-2001
Ligne sans frais: 877-376-2727
info@lebras.qc.ca
www.lebras.qc.ca
www.facebook.com/bureauregionaldactionsida
Aperçu: *Dimension:* petite; *Envergure:* locale; fondée en 1990
Mission: Développer et promouvoir des actions communautaires vizant l'amelioration de la qualité de vie de la population de l'Outaonais face au VIH/sida
Membre de: Réseau juridique canadien du VIH/Sida; Coalition des organismes communautaires québécois de lutte contre le sida; CATIE, TROCAO, CRIO
Membre(s) du personnel: 27
Membre: *Montant de la cotisation:* 5$
Activités: Soutien; éducation à la prévention; promotion et concertation; *Evénements de sensibilisation:* Journée mondiale de lutte contre le sida, ateliers VIH;Dèmystification de l'homosexualité; Realités de larue Journie de lutte à l'homophobie
Membre(s) du bureau directeur:
Sylvain Laflamme, Directeur général
dg@lebras.qc.ca
Prix, Bourses:
• Prix Lemieux-Tremblay

Burford Township Historical Society
141 Harley Rd., Harley ON N0E 1E0
Tel: 519-449-4658
info@BurfordTownshipMuseum.ca
burfordtownshipmuseum.ca
twitter.com/BurfordTHS
Overview: A small local charitable organization founded in 1986
Mission: To promote interest in the history of Burford Township; to preserve artifacts for the use of the public; Operation of the Burford Township Museum
Affiliation(s): Ontario Historical Society
Activities: Heritage Week events for school children; Strawberry Social & Garden Party; Old Fashioned Christmas Concert
Chief Officer(s):
Gary Jermy, Archivist
Linda Robbins, President

Burgess Shale Geoscience Foundation
PO Box 148, Field BC V0A 1G0
Tel: 250-343-6006; *Fax:* 250-343-6426
Toll-Free: 800-343-3006
info@burgess-shale.bc.ca
www.burgess-shale.bc.ca
www.facebook.com/BurgessShale
Overview: A small local organization founded in 1993
Mission: To increase the exposure of the genereal public to the earth sciences & in particular, to promote interest in geology & paleantology
Activities: Earth Science Guided Hikes Program; High School Research Project; Burgess Shale Learning Centre; Burgess Shale Discovery Centre
Chief Officer(s):
Randle Robertson, Executive Director
Jim Abbott, Chair

Burin Peninsula Chamber of Commerce
PO Box 728, Marystown NL A0E 2M0
Tel: 709-567-3340; *Fax:* 855-749-6880
burinpeninsulachamber@outlook.com
burinpeninsulachamber.com
www.facebook.com/BurinPeninsulaChamberOfCommerce
Overview: A small local organization founded in 1991
Mission: To promote local businesses & help them grow
Member of: Canadian Chamber of Commerce; Atlantic Provinces Chamber of Commerce
Staff Member(s): 6
Membership: *Fees:* Schedule available
Activities: *Speaker Service:* Yes; *Library:* Open to public
Chief Officer(s):
Loretta Lewis, President
Lisa MacLeod, Business Manager

Burke Mountain Naturalists
PO Box 52540, RPO Coquitlam Centre, Coquitlam BC V3B 7J4
burkemtnnats@gmail.com
www.burkemountainnaturalists.ca
www.facebook.com/BurkeMountainNaturalists
twitter.com/BurkeMtnNats
Overview: A small local charitable organization founded in 1989
Mission: The group is a non-profit society that promotes the enjoyment of nature through environmental appreciation & conservation. It advocates accessibility & maintenance of natural areas, particularly local ones. It is a registered charity, BN: 873847966RR0001.
Member of: BC Nature
Membership: 450; *Fees:* $33 single; $40 family/group
Activities: Monthly meetings; field trips & hikes; recording bird/flora sightings; preparing natural history brochures

Burlington Association for Nuclear Disarmament (BAND)
Burlington ON
Tel: 905-632-4774
band@cogeco.ca
Overview: A small international organization founded in 1983
Mission: To educate Canadians about the consequences of the nuclear arms race; To support the broader peace movement
Member of: Canadian Peace Alliance
Affiliation(s): November 16 Coalition; Abolition 2000; Halton Peace Network
Finances: *Annual Operating Budget:* Less than $50,000; *Funding Sources:* Membership fees; donations
Membership: 60 individual; *Fees:* $10; *Committees:* Letter Writing
Activities: Forum on Missile Defence; public forums on peace issues; *Speaker Service:* Yes
Chief Officer(s):
Doug W. Brown, Chair

Burlington Chamber of Commerce
#201, 414 Locust St., Burlington ON L7S 1T7
Tel: 905-639-0174; *Fax:* 905-333-3956
info@burlingtonchamber.com
www.burlingtonchamber.com
www.facebook.com/burlington.chamber
twitter.com/burlingtoncofc
www.youtube.com/user/BurlingtonChamber
Overview: A medium-sized local organization founded in 1947
Mission: To be the focus for business in Burlington; to encourage & promote a strong Burlington business community through sound practices that support social & economic development
Member of: Ontario Chamber of Commerce; Canadian Chamber of Commerce; Ontario Association of Marketing Directors; Ontario Chamber of Commerce Executives; Chamber of Commerce Executives of Canada
Finances: *Funding Sources:* Membership dues; programming
Staff Member(s): 6
Membership: *Fees:* Schedule available; *Committees:* Membership, Marketing & Communication; Programs; Political Action; Environment; Young Professional Network Organizing; Health Advocacy; SHiFT
Activities: *Speaker Service:* Yes; *Rents Mailing List:* Yes
Chief Officer(s):
Bruce Nicholson, Chair
Keith Hoey, President

Burlington Historical Society (BHS)
PO Box 93164, 1450 Headon Rd., Burlington ON L7M 4A3
info@burlingtonhistorical.ca
www.burlingtonhistorical.ca
Overview: A small local charitable organization founded in 1961
Mission: To bring together those people interested in the history of Burlington and district, and to stimulate public awareness in its local heritage.
Member of: Ontario Historical Society
Membership: *Fees:* $30 individual; $25 seniors; $40 family; *Member Profile:* Interest in local history
Activities: Sales tables at heritage events; monthly meetings; Heritage Week activities; Joseph Brant Day; *Library:* Galloway Room, Burlington Central Library; by appointment
Chief Officer(s):
Alan Harrington, President

BurlingtonGreen Environmental Association
3281 Myers Lane, Burlington ON L7N 1K6
Tel: 905-466-2171
www.burlingtongreen.org
www.facebook.com/burlington.green.environment
twitter.com/burlingtongreen
Overview: A medium-sized local organization
Mission: To advocate for local environmental issues
Finances: *Funding Sources:* Membership fees; Donations
Membership: *Fees:* $5 students; $20 individuals; $25 families; *Member Profile:* Citizens for a greener community
Activities: Establishing the BurlingtonGreen Youth Network which meets monthly; *Awareness Events:* BurlingtonGreen Eco-Film Festival
Chief Officer(s):
Amy Schnurr, Executive Director
Publications:
• BurlingtonGreen Environmental Association Newsletter
Type: Newsletter; *Frequency:* Annually
Profile: Information, eco-event listings, stories, & special bulletins
• BurlingtonGreen Youth Network Bulletin
Type: Newsletter
Profile: Information about volunteering, events, competitions, & scholarships
• Greening Tips
Type: Newsletter; *Frequency:* Monthly

Burn Survivors Association
c/o Camp BUCKO, #15549, 265 Port Union Rd., Toronto ON M1C 4Z7
Tel: 647-343-2267
Toll-Free: 877-272-8256
www.campbucko.ca
twitter.com/camp_bucko
Also Known As: Camp BUCKO
Overview: A small local charitable organization founded in 1979
Mission: To provide support & information for burn survivors & their families; To offer a safe & caring camp program for children, from ages 7 to 17, with burn injuries
Finances: *Funding Sources:* Donations; Fundraising
Membership: *Member Profile:* Burn survivors; Families & friends of burn survivors; Interested individuals
Activities: Operating Camp BUCKO summer camp for young burn survivors, featuring recreational & therapeutic activities; Offering volunteer camp positions to adult burn survivors
Publications:
• Survivor [a publication of the Burn Survivors Association]
Type: Newsletter
Profile: Information & reviews of Camp BUCKO experiences

Burnaby Arts Council (BAC)
6584 Deer Lake Ave., Burnaby BC V5G 3T7
Tel: 604-298-7322; *Fax:* 604-298-9465
info@burnabyartscouncil.org
www.burnabyartscouncil.org
Overview: A small local charitable organization founded in 1967
Mission: To promote artists in the community; To encourage access to the arts; to increase & broaden the opportunities for public enjoyment of & participation in cultural activities
Member of: Assembly of BC Arts Councils
Finances: *Annual Operating Budget:* $50,000-$100,000
Staff Member(s): 7; 13 volunteer(s)
Membership: 14 corporate + 125 individual; *Member Profile:* Engaged in arts or related activity; *Committees:* Administration; Communication; Executive; Gallery; Program
Activities: Christmas Craft Fair; Cavalcade of Stars; Artwalk; Summer Theatre; Members Showcase; *Library:* Open to public
Chief Officer(s):
Bill Thomson, President
Brian Daniel, Vice-President

Burnaby Association for Community Inclusion (BACI)
2702 Norland Ave., Burnaby BC V5B 3A6
Tel: 604-299-7851; *Fax:* 604-299-5921; *TTY:* 604-563-2579
reception@gobaci.com
www.gobaci.com
www.facebook.com/gobaci
twitter.com/gobaci/
Overview: A small local organization founded in 1956
Mission: Support services for people with developmental disabilities
Membership: *Committees:* Accreditation; Advocacy; Board Governance Review; Burnaby Association of Self Advocates; Committee on Seniors' Issues; Events & Hospitality; Audit; Employee Wellness; Labour Management; Occupational Health & Safety; Quality Assurance
Chief Officer(s):
Tanya Sather, Co-Executive Director, 604-292-1292
tanya.sather@gobaci.com
Richard Faucher, Co-Executive Director
richard.faucher@gobaci.com

Burnaby Board of Trade (BBOT)
#201, 4555 Kingsway, Burnaby BC V5H 4T8
Tel: 604-412-0100; *Fax:* 604-412-0102
admin@bbot.ca
www.bbot.ca
www.linkedin.com/company/burnaby-board-of-trade
www.facebook.com/burnabyboardoftrade

twitter.com/burnabybot
www.youtube.com/user/burnabyboardoftrade
Also Known As: Burnaby Chamber of Commerce
Overview: A medium-sized local organization founded in 1910
Mission: To make Burnaby a better place to live & do business
Member of: Canadian Chamber of Commerce
Finances: *Funding Sources:* Membership dues; fundraising
Staff Member(s): 8
Membership: *Fees:* Schedule available based on number of employees; *Member Profile:* Burnaby businesses from a large variety of industries
Activities: International Trade Mission; Education; Tourism Management; Lobbyist; *Rents Mailing List:* Yes
Chief Officer(s):
Paul Holden, CEO
Awards:
• Business Innovation
For ingenuity & innovation in business activities
• Entrepreneurial Spirit
For having demonstrated a highly entrepreneurial approach to launching a successful new business or new initiative
• Newsmaker of the Year
For having been widely recognized in the press for achievements as a Burnaby based business; helping to promote the city as a dynamic business location
• Business of the Year: Small Business
For a Burnaby business with less than 50 employees with annual revenues of up to 5 million, which has made an outstanding contribution in the combined area of business success, innovation & community service
• Burnaby Hall of Fame
For a Burnaby business which has demonstrated outstanding success over many years & had a positive & significant impact on the community
• Community Spirit Award
For an exceptional contribution promoting Burnaby through its community festivals, events or programs & business activities
• Community Service
For the strong support of local service agencies, businesses, civic projects, positive business/community relations & promotion of the arts
• Business Person of the Year
For a local business person who is an outstanding role model for business development & excellence
• Business of the Year
For a Burnaby business that has made an outstanding contribution in the areas of business success, innovation & community service

Burnaby Laphounds Club
3051 Aires Place, Burnaby BC V3J 7G1
Tel: 604-444-4464
Overview: A small local organization founded in 1957
Member of: Lapidary, Rock & Mineral Society of British Columbia
Chief Officer(s):
Nancy Dickson, Contact
nancyandallan@telus.net

Burnaby Multicultural Society (BMS)
6255 Nelson Ave., Burnaby BC V5H 4T5
Tel: 604-431-4131
info@thebms.ca
www.thebms.ca
Overview: A small local charitable organization founded in 1984
Mission: To raise awareness & appreciation of gender, racial, ethnic & cultural diversity in Canada
Member of: Affiliation of Multicultural Societies & Service Agencies of BC
Activities: Immigrant settlement & integration; Public education; Seniors programs; English classes; *Library:* Open to public by appointment
Chief Officer(s):
Ruminder Sadhra, President
bms.chair@shaw.ca
Rana Dhatt, Executive Director
rana.dhatt@thebms.ca

Burnaby Volunteer Centre Society
#203, 2101 Holdom Ave., Burnaby BC V5B 0A4
Tel: 604-294-5533
www.volunteerburnaby.ca
www.facebook.com/volunteerburnaby
twitter.com/volunteerbby
Also Known As: Volunteer Burnaby
Overview: A small local organization founded in 1979
Mission: To encourage volunteerism in local communities which in turn helps support non-profit organizations & neighbourhood events
Member of: Volunteer BC; Volunteer Canada
Finances: *Funding Sources:* All levels of government; donations; United Way
Staff Member(s): 4
Membership: 53; *Fees:* Schedule available based on budget for organizations; *Member Profile:* Agencies in need of volunteers; volunteers
Chief Officer(s):
Dave Baspaly, Executive Director
dave@volunteerburnaby.ca

Burnaby Writers' Society
Burnaby BC
Tel: 604-421-4931
info@bws.bc.ca
www.burnabywritersnews.blogspot.ca
Overview: A small local charitable organization founded in 1967
Mission: A community-oriented writers' group, dedicated to mutual support & encouragement of local talent; with a strong emphasis on skill development, marketing, & a professional approach to writing
Member of: Burnaby Arts Council
Finances: *Funding Sources:* Municipal Government
Membership: *Member Profile:* Membership ranges from novice writers to full-time professionals; from poets, short story writers & journalists to authors of science fiction, fantasy, mystery & romance novels

Burns Lake & District Chamber of Commerce
Heritage Centre, PO Box 339, 540 Hwy. 16, Burns Lake BC V0J 1E0
Tel: 250-692-3773; *Fax:* 250-692-3701
info@burnslakechamber.com
burnslakechamber.com
www.linkedin.com/company/burns-lake-&-district-chamber-of-commerce-&-visitor-centre
www.facebook.com/327936400553227
twitter.com/BurnsLakeBiz
instagram.com/visitburnslake
Overview: A small local organization founded in 1927
Mission: To have a vibrant business community; To serve & connect our members by providing the tools & information to grow, enhance & develop existing & new business
Member of: BC Chamber of Commerce; Canadian Chamber of Commerce; Northern BC Tourism Association
Finances: *Funding Sources:* Membership dues
Staff Member(s): 2
Membership: *Committees:* Governance & Conduct; Member Relations; Finance & Audit; Nominations
Activities: *Library:* Business Information Centre; Not open to public
Chief Officer(s):
Greg Brown, President

Burns Lake Christian Supportive Society
PO Box 1142, Burns Lake BC V0J 1E0
Tel: 250-692-7809; *Fax:* 250-692-7809
Overview: A small local organization
Mission: To provide services to special-needs citizens, their family, &/or advocates
Member of: British Columbia Association for Community Living
Staff Member(s): 1
Membership: 150; *Fees:* Schedule available
Activities: *Internships:* Yes

Burrows Trail Arts Council (BTAC)
PO Box 29, McCreary MB R0J 1B0
Tel: 204-835-2192
btac@mts.net
www.mts.net/~btac
Overview: A small local charitable organization founded in 1986
Member of: Manitoba Association of Community Arts Councils Inc.
Membership: *Fees:* $5 annually
Activities: *Library:* Open to public
Chief Officer(s):
Joyce Wiebe, President

Bus Carriers Federation *Voir* Fédération des transporteurs par autobus

Bus History Association, Inc. (BHA)
c/o Bernie Drouillard, 965 McEwan Ave., Windsor ON N9B 2G1
www.bus-history.org
Overview: A medium-sized national organization founded in 1963
Mission: To preserve & record data, information & other related materials of the bus industry, both within North America & worldwide
Member of: Canadian Transit Heritage Foundation
6 volunteer(s)
Membership: *Fees:* $45 Canadian resident; US$35 US resident; US$50 international; *Member Profile:* Persons interested in bus industry
Chief Officer(s):
Paul A. Leger, Chair
Bernard Drouillard, Secretary-Treasurer
bdrouillard3@cogeco.ca
Meetings/Conferences:
• Bus History Association 2018 Convention, 2018
Scope: National
Publications:
• Bus Industry [a publication of the Bus History Association, Inc.]
Type: Magazine; *Editor:* Loring Lawrence
Profile: Presents features on both historical & modern aspects of transit, with an emphasis on North America, but also includes overseas material aswell.

Business Council of British Columbia
#810, 1050 Pender St. West, Vancouver BC V6E 3S7
Tel: 604-684-3384; *Fax:* 888-488-5376
Other Communication: Media Contact Phone: 604-696-6582
info@bcbc.com
www.bcbc.com
www.linkedin.com/company/business-council-of-british-columbia
twitter.com/BizCouncilBC
Previous Name: Employers' Council of BC
Overview: A large provincial organization founded in 1966
Mission: To build a competitive & growing economy that provides opportunities for all who invest, work, & live in British Columbia
Finances: *Funding Sources:* Membership fees
Membership: 250 organizations; *Committees:* Communications; Environmental; Energy & Climate; Employee Relations; Human Capital; Indigenous Affairs & Reconciliation; Innovation & Productivity; NEXT Leaders Council
Chief Officer(s):
Greg D'Avignon, President & CEO
greg.davignon@bcbc.com
Jock Finlayson, Executive VP & Chief Policy Officer
jock.finlayson@bcbc.com
Cheryl Maitland Muir, Vice-President, Communications
cheryl.muir@bcbc.com
Ken Peacock, Chief Economist & Vice-President
ken.peacock@bcbc.com
Publications:
• BC Economic Review & Outlook [a publication of Business Council of British Columbia]
• Collective Bargaining Bulletin [a publication of Business Council of British Columbia]
Type: Bulletin
• Environment & Energy Bulletin [a publication of Business Council of British Columbia]
Type: Bulletin
• Human Capital Law & Policy [a publication of Business Council of British Columbia]
• Policy Perspectives [a publication of Business Council of British Columbia]
Type: Newsletter

Business Council of Canada / Conseil canadien des affaires
#1001, 99 Bank St., Ottawa ON K1P 6B9
Tel: 613-238-3727; *Fax:* 613-238-3247
info@thebusinesscouncil.ca
www.thebusinesscouncil.ca
www.linkedin.com/company/2403612
twitter.com/BizCouncilofCan
www.youtube.com/user/CdnCEOCouncil
Previous Name: Canadian Council of Chief Executives; Business Council on National Issues
Overview: A large national organization founded in 1976
Mission: To engage in policy work in Canada, North America, & the world
Membership: 100-499; *Member Profile:* Business leaders from 150 Canadian corporations
Activities: Working on national issues, such as taxation, fiscal & monetary policy, corporate governance, & competitiveness; Preparing presentations & reports
Chief Officer(s):

John Manley, P.C., O.C., President & CEO
Susan Scotti, Executive Vice-President, 613-288-3860
susan.scotti@thebusinesscouncil.ca
John R. Dillon, Corporate Counsel & Senior Vice-President, Policy, 613-288-3863
john.dillon@thebusinesscouncil.ca
Ross H. Laver, Senior Vice-President, Policy & Communications, 613-288-3862
ross.laver@thebusinesscouncil.ca
Nancy Wallace, Vice-President, Corporate Services, 613-288-3858
nancy.wallace@thebusinesscouncil.ca
Brian Kingston, Vice-President, Policy, International & Fiscal Issues, 613-288-3855
brian.kingston@thebusinesscouncil.ca
Valerie Walker, Vice-President, Talent & Skills, 613-288-3859
valerie.walker@thebusinesscouncil.ca
Cam Vidler, Vice-President, Economic Policy & Innovation, 613-288-3854
cam.vidler@thebusinesscouncil.ca
McKensi Patterson, Communications Officer, 613-288-3861
mckensi.patterson@thebusinesscouncil.ca
Publications:
• Business Council of Canada Annual Report
Type: Yearbook

Business Development Centre (Toronto)
#900, 1 Yonge St., Toronto ON M5E 1E5
Tel: 416-345-9437; *Fax:* 416-345-9044
torbiz@tbdc.com
www.tbdc.com
www.linkedin.com/groups?homeNewMember=&gid=2847142
www.facebook.com/TorontoBusinessDevelopmentCentre
twitter.com/theTBDC
Overview: A medium-sized international organization founded in 1990
Mission: To assist people in business (non-profit); to provide regular seminars on import/export; entrepreneurial training; community programs
Affiliation(s): Canadian Industrial Innovation Centre
Membership: *Member Profile:* Small business people; entrepreneurs
Activities: *Speaker Service:* Yes; *Library:* Open to public

Business Development Centre of Greater Fort Erie See Fort Erie Business Success & Loan Centre

Business for the Arts / Affairs pour les arts
174 Avenue Rd., Toronto ON M5R 2J1
Tel: 416-869-3016; *Fax:* 416-869-0435
www.businessforthearts.org
www.linkedin.com/company/businessforthearts
www.facebook.com/businessforthearts
twitter.com/businessftarts
www.flickr.com/photos/businessforthearts
Overview: A medium-sized national organization founded in 1974
Mission: To make the partnership between business & the arts more effective in supporting the nation's creative minds.
Finances: *Funding Sources:* Membership fees; special project sponsorships
Staff Member(s): 8
Membership: 36 corporate; *Fees:* $6500
Activities: artsVest; boardLink; artsScene; BFTA Annual Awards
Chief Officer(s):
James D. Fleck, Chair
Nichole Anderson, President & CEO
n_anderson@businessforthearts.org
Awards:
• John P. Fisher Award for Media Support of the Arts
Created by CBAC & Southam Inc. in honour of the late John P. Fisher, who was CBAC's Chairman from 1991-1996 and was also CEO of Southam Inc.; to recognize newspapers that combine a mixture of quality arts journalism with significant contributions of advertising, in-kind & volunteer support
• Edmund C. Bovey Award
To recognize individual members of the business community who contribute leadership, time, money & expertise to the arts; *Amount:* A sculpture to the winner & $20,000 distributed to the arts in a way specified by the winner
• National Post Awards for Business in the Arts
Created in 1979 to encourage the corporate sector's involvement with the visual & performing arts in Canada & to recognize this involvement

Business Practices & Consumer Protection Authority of British Columbia *See* Consumer Protection BC

Business Professional Association of Canada (BPA Canada)
www.bpacanada.com
twitter.com/bpacanada
Overview: A large national organization
Mission: To give members quality referrals while helping them build their client relationships
Membership: *Member Profile:* Business professionals
Activities: Holding weekly meetings; Hosting social networking events, seminars, & workshops
Chief Officer(s):
Mike Hurley, Director
   Ajax Chapter
   Ajax ON
   ajax@bpacanada.com
   Chief Officer(s):
   Jamie Abbott, President
   james@summitcma.ca
   Markham Corporate Chapter
   Markham ON
   markham@bpacanada.com
   Chief Officer(s):
   Sheri Kurtz, President, 905-201-8005
   Oshawa Chapter
   Oshawa ON
   oshawa@bpacanada.com
   Chief Officer(s):
   Chris Maeder, President, 905-443-1115
   chris.maeder@investorsgroup.com

Business Women's Network *Voir* Réseau des femmes d'affaires du Québec inc.

Business Women's Networking Association (BWNA)
Aurora ON
Tel: 289-466-6100
www.bwna.ca
Overview: A small local organization
Mission: To offer support & exchange information on issues unique to women in business.
Membership: *Fees:* $120; *Member Profile:* Entrepreneurial women in professional & service occupations who are self-employed and/or small business owners
Activities: Monthly meetings & lunches with speakers
Chief Officer(s):
Elina Bagshaw, President, Aurora Chapter
   King Chapter
   King City ON
   Tel: 905-939-8025
   Chief Officer(s):
   Jane Cameron, President

Butler Family Foundation
12420 - 102 Ave., Edmonton AB T5N 0M1
Tel: 780-488-1823
www.butlerfamilyfoundation.ca
Overview: A small local charitable organization founded in 2007
Mission: To foster the growth of healthy families & communities in Edmonton; To support children & families; To promote education & the pursuit of knowledge
Activities: Supporting Edmonton-based charities in the areas of early childhood education & care, community development, & sports & recreation
Chief Officer(s):
Shannon Butler, Executive Coordinator

Buy-Side Investment Management Association (BIMA)
c/o Zzeem, Inc., PO Box 38179, Toronto ON M5N 1B6
info@bima.ca
www.bima.ca
Overview: A small national organization founded in 2005
Mission: To help members reach & maintain a high level of success
Membership: 1-99
Activities: Networking opportunities; educational opportunities; representing member interests; semi-annual conferences
Chief Officer(s):
Justin Lord, President

Bytown Railway Society (BRS)
PO Box 47076, Ottawa ON K1B 5P9
Tel: 613-745-1201; *Fax:* 613-745-1201
info@bytownrailwaysociety.ca
www.bytownrailwaysociety.ca
www.facebook.com/bytownrailwaysociety
Overview: A small national charitable organization founded in 1969
Mission: To promote an interest in railways & railway history, with particular emphasis on Canadian railways.
Finances: *Funding Sources:* Publications sale; memberships
Activities: Restoration/preservation of owned railway equipment; *Library:* Bytown Railway Society Library; Open to public by appointment
Chief Officer(s):
David Stremes, President
Douglas Wilson, Vice President
Awards:
• Lifetime Achievement Award
To a person who has made a significant contribution to the society over a period of years
• Preservation Award
To a person or group of people for an outstanding preservation or restoration activity
Publications:
• Canadian Trackside Guide© 2017
Type: Guide; *Frequency:* a.; *Number of Pages:* 744; *Editor:* Earl Roberts & David Stremes; *Price:* $39.95
Profile: Comprehensive guide to Canadian Railways

CAA British Columbia (BCAA)
4567 Canada Way, Burnaby BC V5G 4T1
Tel: 604-268-5500; *Fax:* 604-268-5585
Toll-Free: 877-325-8888
info@bcaa.com
www.bcaa.com
Overview: A large provincial organization founded in 1906 overseen by Canadian Automobile Association
Mission: To provide motoring, travel, & insurance services to members in British Columbia & the Yukon
Member of: Canadian Automobile Association (CAA); American Automobile Association (AAA)
Finances: *Annual Operating Budget:* Greater than $5 Million; *Funding Sources:* Membership fees
Staff Member(s): 1000
Membership: 800,000
Activities: *Internships:* Yes
Chief Officer(s):
Shom Sen, President & CEO
Clayton Buckingham, Chief Financial Officer
Brent Cuthbertson, Chief Marketing Officer
Eric Hopkins, Chief Strategic Ventures Officer
Brenda Lowden, Chief Member Experience Officer
Salman Manki, Chief Legal Officer
Ken Ontko, Chief Information Officer
Grant Stockwell, Chief Automotive Officer
Publications:
• BCAA [British Columbia Automobile Association] Newsletter
Type: Newsletter
   Abbotsford Branch
   33338 South Fraser Way, Abbotsford BC V2S 2B4
   Tel: 604-870-3850; *Fax:* 604-870-3899
   Chilliwack Branch
   #1, 45609 Luckakuck Way, Chilliwack BC V2R 1A3
   Tel: 604-824-2720; *Fax:* 604-824-2749
   Coquitlam Branch
   #50, 2773 Barnet Hwy., Coquitlam BC V3B 1C2
   Tel: 604-268-5750; *Fax:* 604-268-5799
   Courtenay
   #17, 1599 Cliffe Ave., Courtenay BC V9N 2K6
   Tel: 250-703-2328; *Fax:* 250-703-2329
   Delta Branch
   7343 - 120 St., Delta BC V4C 6P5
   Tel: 604-268-5900; *Fax:* 604-268-5949
   Kamloops Branch
   #400, 500 Notre Dame Dr., Kamloops BC V2C 6T6
   Tel: 250-852-4600; *Fax:* 250-852-4637
   Kelowna Branch
   Burtch Plaza, #18, 1470 Harvey Ave., Kelowna BC V1Y 9K8
   Tel: 250-870-4900; *Fax:* 250-870-4937
   Langley Branch
   #10, 20190 Langley ByPass, Langley BC V3A 9J9
   Tel: 604-268-5950; *Fax:* 604-268-5999
   Maple Ridge
   #500, 20395 Lougheed Hwy., Maple Ridge BC V2X 2P9
   Tel: 604-205-1200; *Fax:* 604-205-1249
   Nanaimo Branch
   Metral Place, #400, 6581 Aulds Rd., Nanaimo BC V9T 6J6

Tel: 250-390-7700; *Fax:* 250-390-7739
Nelson Branch
596 Baker St., Nelson BC V1L 4H9
Tel: 250-505-1720; *Fax:* 250-505-1749
New Westminster Branch
501 - 6th St., New Westminster BC V3L 3B9
Tel: 604-268-5700; *Fax:* 604-268-5749
North Vancouver
1527 Lonsdale Ave., North Vancouver BC V7M 2J2
Tel: 604-205-1050; *Fax:* 604-990-1547
Penticton Branch
#100, 2100 Main St., Penticton BC V2A 5H7
Tel: 250-487-2450; *Fax:* 250-487-2479
Prince George Branch
River Point Shopping Centre, #100, 2324 Ferry Ave., Prince George BC V2N 0B1
Tel: 250-649-2399; *Fax:* 250-649-2397
Richmond Branch
Lansdowne Centre, #618, 5300 No. 3 Rd., Richmond BC V6X 2X9
Tel: 604-268-5850; *Fax:* 604-268-5899
Surrey
#D1, 15251 - 101 Ave., Surrey BC V3R 9V8
Tel: 604-205-1000; *Fax:* 604-205-1049
Vancouver - Broadway Branch
999 West Broadway, Vancouver BC V5Z 1K5
Tel: 604-268-5600; *Fax:* 604-268-5647
Vancouver - Kerrisdale Branch
2347 West 41st Ave., Vancouver BC V6M 2A3
Tel: 604-268-5800; *Fax:* 604-268-5848
Vernon Branch
Vernon Square, #103, 5710 - 24th St., Vernon BC V1T 9T3
Tel: 250-550-2400; *Fax:* 250-550-2429
Victoria - Broadmead Branch
#120, 777 Royal Oak Dr., Victoria BC V8X 4V1
Tel: 250-704-1750; *Fax:* 250-704-1789
Victoria - Downtown Branch
1262 Quadra St., Victoria BC V8W 2K7
Tel: 250-414-8320; *Fax:* 250-414-8369
West Vancouver Branch
#710, 2002 Park Royal South, West Vancouver BC V7T 2W4
Tel: 604-268-5650; *Fax:* 604-268-5699

CAA Manitoba
PO Box 1400, 870 Empress St., Winnipeg MB R3G 3H3
Tel: 204-262-6161
Toll-Free: 800-222-4357
contact@caamanitoba.com
www.caamanitoba.com
www.facebook.com/caamanitoba
twitter.com/caamanitoba
www.instagram.com/caamanitoba
Overview: A medium-sized provincial organization overseen by Canadian Automobile Association
Mission: To provide safety products & services to Manitobans
Membership: 200,000 individuals
Chief Officer(s):
Michael R. Mager, President & Chief Executive Officer

CAA Québec
444, rue Bouvier, Québec QC G2J 1E3
Tél: 418-624-2424
Ligne sans frais: 800-686-9243
www.caaquebec.com
www.linkedin.com/company/caa-quebec
www.facebook.com/caaQc
twitter.com/CAA_Quebec
www.pinterest.com/caaquebec
Nom précédent: Automobile et touring club du Québec
Aperçu: *Dimension:* grande; *Envergure:* provinciale; fondée en 1904 surveillé par Canadian Automobile Association
Mission: Veut assurer la sécurité et paix d'esprit à chacun de ses membres ainsi qu'à ses clients en leur offrant des services et des produits de très haute qualité dans les domaines de l'automobile, du voyage, de l'habitation et des services financiers
Affiliation(s): Alliance internationale du Tourisme; Fédération internationale de l'automobile
Membre: 1 100 000; *Montant de la cotisation:* 89$ CAA Classique; 150$ CAA Plus; 198$ CAA Premier
Activités: Services routiers; Services aux voyageurs - Agences de voyages et Auto-Touring; Assurances et services financiers; Services techniques; Services habitation

Publications:
• Magazine CAA-Québec
Type: Magazine
Boisbriand
2715, rue d'Annemasse, Boisbriand QC J7H 0A5
Tél: 450-435-3636
Brossard
#20, 8940, boul Leduc, Brossard QC J4Y 0G4
Tél: 450-465-0620
Gatineau
960, boul Maloney ouest, Gatineau QC J8T 3R6
Tél: 819-778-2225
Laval
#100, 3131, boul St-Martin ouest, Laval QC H7T 2Z5
Tél: 450-682-8100
Montréal
#100, 1180, rue Drummond, Montréal QC H3G 2R7
Tél: 514-861-5111
Pointe-Claire
1000, boul St-Jean, Pointe-Claire QC H9R 5P1
Tél: 514-426-2760
Québec
#202, 500, rue Bouvier, Québec QC G2J 1E3
Tél: 418-624-8222
Québec (Place de la Cité)
#133, 2600, boul Laurier, Québec QC G1V 4T3
Tél: 418-653-9200
Saguenay
#1100, 1700, boul Talbot, Saguenay QC G7H 7Y1
Tél: 418-545-8686
Saint-Léonard
7178, boul Langelier, Saint-Léonard QC H1S 2X6
Tél: 514-255-3560
Sherbrooke
2990, rue King ouest, Sherbrooke QC J1L 1Y7
Tél: 819-566-5132
Terrebonne
302, montée des Pionniers, Terrebonne QC J6V 1S6
Tél: 450-585-9797
Trois-Rivières
4085, boul des Récollets, Trois-Rivières QC G9A 6M1
Tél: 819-376-9393

Cabbagetown Community Arts Centre (CCAC)
422 Parliament St., Toronto ON M5A 2A2
Tel: 416-925-7222; *Fax:* 416-928-1741
theccac@yahoo.com
www.cabbagetownarts.org
Overview: A small local charitable organization founded in 1979
Mission: To provide underpriviledged children with the opportunity to learn music & art
Staff Member(s): 9
Chief Officer(s):
Sarah Patrick, Executive Director

Cabbagetown Preservation Association (CPA)
PO Box 82808, Stn. Cabbagetown, 467 Parliament St., Toronto ON M5A 3Y2
Tel: 416-964-8004
cpa@cabbagetownpa.ca
www.cabbagetownpa.ca
www.facebook.com/CabbagetownPreservationAssociation
Overview: A small local charitable organization founded in 1989
Mission: To preserve the architectural integrity of the Cabbagetown neighbourhood
Member of: Metro Area Heritage Group; Toronto Historical Association
Affiliation(s): Ontario Historical Association
Finances: *Annual Operating Budget:* Less than $50,000; *Funding Sources:* Membership dues; sale of t-shirts, book & postcards; provincial & corporate grants
100 volunteer(s)
Membership: 442; *Member Profile:* Members live in or are interested in this area of Toronto; *Committees:* Heritage Issues; Riverdale Farm & Riverdale Park Issues; Walking Tours; Tour of Homes; Cabbagetown People Program; Hidden Gardens & Private Spaces Tour
Activities: Walking tours; tea; public meetings, Nov. & Feb.; Historic Plaque Program; *Awareness Events:* Forsythia Festival, 1st Sunday in May; Cabbagetown Festival, 2nd weekend in Sept.; *Speaker Service:* Yes; *Library:* by appointment
Chief Officer(s):
David Pretlove, Co-Chair
Gilles Huot, Co-Chair
Mary Martin, Treasurer
Awards:
• Streetscapes in Bloom Award
• The Peggy Kurtin Award for Excellence in Restoration
Publications:
• The CPA [Cabbagetown Preservation Association] Newsletter
Type: Newsletter; *Frequency:* Quarterly

Cache Creek Chamber of Commerce
PO Box 460, Cache Creek BC V0K 1H0
Tel: 250-457-9312
cachecreekhusky@gmail.com
www.cachecreekvillage.com
Overview: A small local organization

CADORA British Columbia
PO Box 31120, RPO University Heights, Victoria BC V8N 6J3
Tel: 250-722-4791
www.cadorabc.com
Also Known As: Canadian Dressage Owners & Riders Association, Pacific Chapter
Overview: A small provincial organization overseen by Canadian Dressage Owners & Riders Association
Mission: To act as a unified voice on dressage issues in British Columbia; To develop & promote dressage in British Columbia
Membership: *Fees:* $10 senior members; $5 non-riding family members; $2.50 junior members; *Member Profile:* Junior & senior dressage riders & their non-riding family members from across British Columbia
Activities: Liaising with regulatory bodies on dressage issues; Encouraging participation in competitions & demonstrations; Offering awards, scholarships, & travel assistance programs; Increasing knowledge of good horsemanship; Presenting the CADORA BC Provincial Dressage Program, with educational clinics, seminars, & symposia throughout British Columbia
Chief Officer(s):
Courtenay Fraser, President, 778-232-1664
courtenay@courtenayfraser.com
Megan Andersen, Vice-President, 604-533-3130
admin@jctraining.ca
Stephanie Sutton, Secretary, 604-535-7477
Pamela Williams, Treasurer, 250-722-4791
pamw@shaw.ca
Country CADORA Chapter
c/o Linda Dieno, PO Box 10091, Aldergrove BC V4W 3Z5
Tel: 604-882-0120
cassabyrne@shaw.ca
Mission: To develop & promote dressage in the Surrey region of British Columbia
Chief Officer(s):
Linda Dieno, Contact
cassabyrne@shaw.ca
Courtenay CADORA Chapter
c/o Christal Quinn, 4722 Condensory Rd., Courtenay BC V9J 1R6
Tel: 250-334-2306
Mission: To develop dressage in the Courtenay area of British Columbia
Isobell Springett, Contact, 250-338-9834
isobell@mars.ark.com
Mid-Island CADORA Chapter
c/o Pam Williams, 2711 Ritten Rd., Nanaimo BC V9X 1W4
Tel: 250-722-4791
pamw@shaw.ca
Chief Officer(s):
Pam Williams, Contact, 250-722-4791
pamw@shaw.ca
North Central - Skeena CADORA Chapter
c/o Cindy Thiele, 1420 PG Pulpmill Rd., Prince George BC V2K 5P4
Tel: 250-563-2933
Mission: To promote dressage in British Columbia's North Central - Skeena area
Chief Officer(s):
Jodie Kennedy-Baker, Contact, 250-963-6866
jobaker@sd57.bc.ca
Cindy Thiele, Contact, 250-563-2933
thiele@mailscar.ca
Okanagan CADORA Chapter
c/o Suzanne Wallace, 7069 Nakiska Dr., Vernon BC V1B 3M5
Tel: 250-545-5573
suwallace@shaw.ca
Mission: To promote interest in dressage riding as in the Okanagan

Chief Officer(s):
Suzanne Wallace, Contact, 250-545-5573
suwallace@shaw.ca

Salt Spring CADORA Chapter
c/o Barb Murphy, 166 Lakefair Dr., Salt Spring Island BC V8K 1C7
Tel: 250-537-8470
bj55murphy@telus.net
Mission: To develop dressage on Saltspring Island
Chief Officer(s):
Barb Murphy, Contact, 250-537-8470
bj55murphy@telus.net

Vancouver - Richmond CADORA Chapter
c/o Sarah T. Simpson, 7273 Balaclava St., Vancouver BC V6N 1M7
Tel: 604-266-9202
stsimpson@shaw.ca
Mission: To develop & promote dressage in British Columbia's Vancouver - Richmond region
Anki Sjoholm, Contact, 604-274-8735
ankisjoholm@shaw.ca

CADORA Ontario Association Inc.
c/o Don Barnes, #13, 1475 Upper Gage Ave., Hamilton ON L8W 1E6
Tel: 905-387-2031
www.cadora.ca/cadora-ontario
www.facebook.com/CadoraOntario?fref=ts
Also Known As: Canadian Dressage Owners & Riders Association, Eastern Chapter
Overview: A small provincial organization overseen by Canadian Dressage Owners & Riders Association
Mission: To develop the talent, the art, & the sport of dressage in Ontario
Membership: *Member Profile:* Ontario dressage enthusiasts
Activities: Disseminating information to members about dressage; Presenting championships
Chief Officer(s):
Don Barnes, President, 905-387-2031
Dressagegames@aol.com
Awards:
• CADORA Ontario Riding Scholarship
To recognize the highest scoring champion at each level as determined at the Silver Dressage Championships
• Year-End Bronze Competitor Awards
To recognize the highest-placing competitor at all levels (training through fourth level)
• Ontario Provincial Sport Horse Dressage Award
To recognize the highest-placing competitor at all levels (training through fourth level) Contact: Susan Johnson, Phone: 905-549-4491; E-mail: suej99@hotmail.com
Publications:
• CADORA [Canadian Dressage Owners & Riders Association] Ontario Association Newsletter
Type: Newsletter; *Frequency:* Semiannually; *Editor:* Don Barnes
Profile: Association contact information, lists of members, application forms, championship results, meeting notices, & articles

Caledon CADORA Chapter
c/o Lynne Poole, PO Box 415, Schomberg ON L0G 1T0
www.caledondressage.com
Mission: To foster interest in the sport of dressage in Ontario's Caledon region
Affiliation(s): Dressage Canada; Equine-Hippeque Canada; Ontario Equestrian Federation; Toronto CADORA
Chief Officer(s):
Kristy Nahirniak, President & Show Secretary, 519-925-6256
knahirniak@sympatico.ca
Nina Barker, Vice-President & Treasurer, 705-534-2717
nbarker@csolve.net
Sean Antonello, Secretary & Sponsorship, 519-404-3852

Conestoga CADORA Chapter
c/o Philip Parkes, RR#2, Listowel ON N4W 3G8
www.conestogacadora.ca
Mission: To promote ownership of dressage horses; To foster participation in dressage riding
Member of: Equine Canada
Affiliation(s): Dressage Canada; Ontario Equestrian Federation
Chief Officer(s):
Philip Parkes, President, 519-588-8768
Philip@philipparkesequestrian.com
Chris Henderson, Secretary, 519-744-6319
chenders@uwaterloo.ca

Jane MacIntosh, Treasurer, 519-653-8290
jmacintosh@bellnet.ca
Karen Carter, Show Coordinator, 519-570-2375
randkcarter@sympatico.ca
Trish Faucette, Show Coordinator, 519-634-8147
jweber@golden.net
• Conestoga CADORA Newsletter
Type: Newsletter; *Editor:* Philip Parkes; *Price:* Free with membership in Conestoga CADORA
Profile: Chapter activities & announcements

Dressage Niagara Chapter
PO Box 231, Fonthill ON L0S 1E0
www.dressageniagara.com
www.facebook.com/166396176766652
Mission: To promote the sport of dressage in the Niagara Region of Ontario; To encourage participation in competitions
Member of: Equine Canada
Chief Officer(s):
Louise Kennedy, President
Cheryl Semotok, Vice-President
Kristy Barber, Treasurer
Deb Hildebrand, Secretary
• Annual Dressage Niagara Competition Handbook
Type: Yearbook; *Frequency:* Annually; *Accepts Advertising*
• Dressage Niagara Membership Directory
Type: Directory
• Dressage Niagara Newsletter
Type: Newsletter; *Frequency:* Quarterly; *Price:* Free with membership in Dressage Niagara
Profile: Club information

Glanbrook CADORA Chapter
c/o 12 Suncrest Ct., Cambridge ON N1S 4Z9
Tel: 519-620-8858
glanbrookcadora@gmail.com
www.glanbrookcadora.ca
Mission: To encourage ownership of dressage horses in the Glanbrook area of Ontario; To foster interest in the sport of dressage riding; To increase knowlege of good horsemanship
Member of: Equine Canada
Affiliation(s): Dressage Canada; Ontario Equestrian Federation
Chief Officer(s):
Judy Wanner, Area Representative, 905-333-5481
judithwanner@sympatico.ca
• Glanbrook CADORA Newsletter
Type: Newsletter; *Price:* Free with Glanbrook CADORA membership
Profile: Chapter activities & announcments

Greater Sudbury Chapter (GSDA)
c/o Ashley Czerkas, 4028 Regional Rd. 15, Chelmsford ON P0M 1L0
Tel: 705-855-2254
gsda@persona.ca
www.gsda.info
www.facebook.com/402568493165315
Mission: To promote the sport of dressage in the Greater Sudbury region; To increase understanding of good horsemanship
Affiliation(s): Equine-Hippique Canada; Dressage Canada
Chief Officer(s):
Connie Czerkas, President
connie_czerkas@personainternet.com
Vanessa Catto, Vice-President
vancatt@hotmail.com
Donna Keller, 1st Secretary
Ashley Czerkas, 2nd Secretary
ashley.czerkas@personainternet.com

Kawartha Lakes Dressage Chapter (KLDA)
c/o Lisa Hossack-Scott, 2833 Hwy. 28, RR#1, Duro ON K0L 1S0
Tel: 705-749-9726
klda@klda.ca
www.klda.ca
Mission: To foster the sport of dressage in the Kawartha Lakes area of Ontario
Affiliation(s): Dressage Canada
Chief Officer(s):
Miranda Trudeau, President
Lynne Milford, Secretary, Membership
Lisa Hossack-Scott, Treasurer
Jennifer Plumbtree, Communications
• The Centre Line
Type: Newsletter; *Accepts Advertising*; *Editor:* Jennifer Plumbtree

Profile: Chapter activities, such as meeting reports & show information

London Chapter (LDA)
c/o Devon Jamieson, 3783 Petrolia Line, Petrolia ON N0N 1R0
londondressage.com
Mission: To encourage the ownership of dressage horses; To foster interest & participation in dressage riding
Affiliation(s): Dressage Canada; Equine-Hippique Canada
Chief Officer(s):
Lynn Young, Chair, 519-542-1326
ryoung1@cogeco.ca
Devon Jamieson, Secretary, 519-312-4378
Stephanie Myslik, Treasurer, 519-649-8248
stephanie-murdoch@hotmail.com
• London Dressage Association Newsletter
Type: Newsletter; *Price:* Free with membership in the London Dressage Association
Profile: Club activities

Ottawa Area CADORA Chapter (OADG)
c/o Cathy Gordon, 819 Drummond Rd., R.R. 1, Carleton Place ON K7C 3P1
Tel: 613-257-5145
www.ottawadressage.ca
www.facebook.com/187355987992852
Mission: To develop the sport of dressage in the Ottawa area
Affiliation(s): Dressage Canada
Chief Officer(s):
Pierre Paquette, President, 613-821-6206
president@ottawadressage.ca
Laura-Lee Brenneman, Secretary/Treasurer, 613-421-1741
treasurer@ottawadressage.ca
Cathy Gordon, Director, Membership, 613-257-5145
membership@ottawadressage.ca
Peggy McQuaid, Coordinator, Education, 613-831-2692
education@ottawadressage.ca
Catherine Maguire, Director, Awards, 613-256-2725
awards@ottawadressage.ca
• Ottawa Area Dressage Group Newsletter
Type: Newsletter; *Frequency:* 8 pa; *Accepts Advertising*; *Editor:* Diana Bayer; *Price:* Free with Ottawa Area DressageGroup membership
Profile: Chapter activities, including show schedules, results, awards, forthcoming clinics & meetings, & updates on rules & regulations

Quinte St. Lawrence CADORA Chapter (QSLB)
c/o Sharrie Lynch, 4027 Shannonville Rd., Roslin ON K0K 2Y0
qslbinfo@gmail.com
www.qslb.ca
www.facebook.com/QSLBCadora
Mission: To encourage interest in the sport of dressage riding in the Quinte St. Lawrence region of Ontario; To increase understanding of good horsemanship
Affiliation(s): Dressage Canada
Chief Officer(s):
Micky Colton, President
mccolton@sympatico.ca
Shari Clark, Vice-President
sclark@kos.net
Jane Casson, Secretary/Treasurer
tjcasson@sympatico.ca
• Quinte St. Lawrence Branch Newsletter
Type: Newsletter; *Editor:* Alicia Finan
Profile: QSLB activities & announcements

Toronto CADORA Chapter
#1206, 15 Michael Power Pl., Toronto ON M9A 5G4
Tel: 905-640-1720
tcinfo@torontocadora.com
www.torontocadora.com
twitter.com/torontocadora
Mission: To promote the sport & art of dressage in the Toronto area; To nurture good horsemanship; To offer an education-focused & horse-friendly atmosphere
Chief Officer(s):
Sue Saunders, President
Mary Chamberlain, Secretary, Membership
mchamberlain@sympatico.ca
Sue Pallotta, Treasurer
• Track Right
Type: Newsletter; *Editor:* Andrea Wetzel; *Price:* Free with membership in the Toronto CADORA Chapter
Profile: Club activities

Canadian Associations / CAEO Québec

Windsor - Essex CADORA Chapter
c/o Sarah Reaume, 184 Texas Rd., Amherstburg ON N9V 2R7
windsoressexcadora.weebly.com
Mission: To foster participation in the sport of dressage riding in Ontario's Windsor - Essex region; To increase awareness of the sport of dressage riding
Member of: Equine Canada
Affiliation(s): Dressage Canada
Chief Officer(s):
Jenn Bauermann, President
Andrea Bingham, Treasurer
Jen Ingratta, Secretary
• Windsor - Essex Canadian Dressage Owners & Riders Association Members' Farm Directory
Type: Directory
• Windsor - Essex Canadian Dressage Owners & Riders Association Omnibus
Type: Handbook
Profile: Rules, regulations, & requirements for Windsor - Essex club awards

CAE Basses-Laurentides inc. *Voir* Réseau des SADC et CAE

CAE de la Rive-Sud inc. *Voir* Réseau des SADC et CAE

CAEO Québec
PO Box 55505, Stn. Maisonneuve, Montréal QC H1W 0A1
info@caeoquebec.org
www.caeoquebec.org
www.facebook.com/CAEOquebec
twitter.com/CAEOquebec
Previous Name: Gay Line
Overview: A small local charitable organization founded in 1976
Mission: To provide a listening & information telephone service for English-speaking gays, lesbians, bisexuals & transgendered people in Québec.
Affiliation(s): Gai Écoute
Membership: *Member Profile:* Lesbian; gay; bisexual; transgendered
Activities: *Speaker Service:* Yes; *Library:* Gay Line Resource Library; Not open to public
Chief Officer(s):
Nick Frate, Founder

Caisse de bienfaisance de la marine Royale Canadienne *See* Royal Canadian Naval Benevolent Fund

La Caisse des acteurs du Canada inc. *See* The Actors' Fund of Canada

Caisse Financial Group *Voir* Caisse Groupe Financier

Caisse Groupe Financier / Caisse Financial Group
#400, 205 Provencher Blvd., Winnipeg MB R2H 0G4
Tél: 204-237-8988; *Téléc:* 204-233-6405
Ligne sans frais: 866-926-0706
info@caisse.biz
www.caisse.biz
www.linkedin.com/company-beta/870979
Merged from: Fédération des Caisses populaires du Manitoba
Aperçu: Dimension: grande; *Envergure:* provinciale; fondée en 1937
Mission: Contribuer à l'essor économique et socio-culturel des manitobains en poursuivant le développement des services et du réseau financiers dont les avoirs sont gérés, administrés et contrôlés par des francophones
Affiliation(s): Mouvement Desjardins
Membre: 32,500+; *Critères d'admissibilite:* Résidant ou entreprise du Manitoba
Membre(s) du bureau directeur:
Réal Déquier, President
Joël Rondeau, Chief Executive Officer

Caledon Chamber of Commerce
12598 Hwy. 50 South, Bolton ON L7E 1T6
Tel: 905-857-7393; *Fax:* 905-857-7405
www.caledonchamber.com
www.facebook.com/caledon.chamber
twitter.com/ChamberCaledon
Overview: A small local organization founded in 1985
Mission: To promote, encourage & represent local business; To be the "voice of business" committed to the economic, social & environmental health of Caledon
Affiliation(s): Canadian Chamber of Commerce; Ontario Chamber of Commerce
Finances: *Funding Sources:* Membership dues; programs; trade show
Membership: *Fees:* Schedule available based on number of employees; *Committees:* Programs; Events; Advocacy/Policy; Marketing & Communication; Membership Development
Activities: Caledon Home Show; Headwaters Golf Classic; Caledon Women's Christmas Dinner; meetings; networking;
Library: Open to public
Chief Officer(s):
Warren Darnley, Chair
Awards:
• Business of the Year
• Property Improvement Awards
• Caledon Woman of the Year Recognition

Caledon Community Services (CCS)
Royal Cortyards, Upper Level, 18 King St. East, Bolton ON L7E 1E8
Tel: 905-584-2300; *Fax:* 905-951-2303
info@ccs4u.org
www.ccs4u.org
www.facebook.com/caledoncommunityservices
twitter.com/CaledonCS
www.youtube.com/user/CaledonCServices
Overview: A small local charitable organization founded in 1971 overseen by InformOntario
Mission: CCS is a health & social service organization with volunteer-delivered programs to provide the Caledon community with support in times of difficulty & change.
Member of: Ontario Community Support Association; Association of Community Information Centres in Ontario
Affiliation(s): Social Planning Council of Peel; Volunteer Centre of Peel
Finances: *Funding Sources:* United Way; Donations
Membership: *Member Profile:* Caledon residents
Activities: Community information; family & individual counselling; crisis support; support for seniors; housing; respite caregivers; Ontario Works Jobs Development; employment services; training; ESL classes
Chief Officer(s):
Monty Laskin, Chief Executive Officer

Caledon East & District Historical Society (CEDHS)
PO Box 37, Caledon East ON L7C 3L8
Tel: 905-584-0352
www.cedhs.ca
Overview: A small local organization founded in 1834
Mission: To promote & maintain the history of the Caledon East area
Member of: Ontario Historical Society
Finances: *Annual Operating Budget:* Less than $50,000;
Funding Sources: Membership fees; publications sales
10 volunteer(s)
Membership: 70; *Fees:* $15; *Committees:* Volunteer Executive
Activities: Maintaining archives; Offering tours; Organizing 5 meetings per year with speakers on historical subjects
Chief Officer(s):
Donna Davies, President
donnadavies@rogers.com
Publications:
• Settling the Hills
Type: Book; *Number of Pages:* 224; *Editor:* Donna Davies;
Price: $25
Profile: An early history of the area of Caledon East, with 160 b/w photos

Caledon Institute of Social Policy
1356 Wellington St. West, 2nd Fl., Ottawa ON K1Y 3C3
Tel: 613-729-3340
caledon@caledoninst.org
www.caledoninst.org
twitter.com/CaledonINST
Overview: A small national charitable organization founded in 1992
Mission: To research & analyze public policy; To inform & influence public opinion & foster discussion on poverty & social policy
Finances: *Funding Sources:* Maytree Foundation; Donations
Staff Member(s): 8
Chief Officer(s):
Sherri Torjman, Vice-President
torjman@caledoninst.org

Caledonia Regional Chamber of Commerce
PO Box 2035, 1 Grand Trunk Lane, Caledonia ON N3W 2G6
Tel: 905-765-0377
info@caledonia-chamber.com
www.caledonia-chamber.com
Overview: A small local organization
Chief Officer(s):
Krista Damant, President, 905-765-3223
Barb Martindale, Executive Director, 905-765-0377

Calgary & Area Medical Staff Society (CAPA)
c/o Alberta Medical Association, 350, 708 - 11 Ave. SW, Calgary AB T2R 0E4
Tel: 403-205-2093
audrey.harlow@albertadoctors.org
www.camss.ca
Previous Name: Calgary & Area Physician's Association
Overview: A small local organization
Mission: Represents physicians working in the Calgary Health Region in hospitals or in the community
Finances: *Funding Sources:* Membership dues
Membership: *Fees:* $275; *Member Profile:* All physicians working for the Calgary Health Region
Chief Officer(s):
Dave Lowery, Communications Director
Steve Patterson, President
steve.patterson@albertahealthservices.ca
Publications:
• Vital Signs
Type: Magazine; *Frequency:* Monthly; *Editor:* Dave Lowery

Calgary & Area Physician's Association *See* Calgary & Area Medical Staff Society

Calgary & District Labour Council (CDLC)
#321, 3132 - 26 St. NE, Calgary AB T1Y 6Z1
Tel: 403-262-2390; *Fax:* 403-262-2408
info@thecdlc.ca
www.thecdlc.ca
www.facebook.com/TheCDLC
twitter.com/calgarylabour
Overview: A large local organization founded in 1905 overseen by Alberta Federation of Labour
Mission: To maintain, strengthen, & protect Calgary's public & social institutions & programs
Member of: Alberta Federation of Labour
Affiliation(s): Canadian Labour Congress; Alberta Federation of Labour
Staff Member(s): 1
Membership: 60 unions representing 30,000 workers; *Member Profile:* Affiliated union locals; *Committees:* Finance; Labour Day BBQ; Political Action; S'ean Gillen Memorial Scholarship; United Way Partnership
Activities: *Awareness Events:* Labour Day BBQ, Sept.; May Day Arts Festival
Chief Officer(s):
Alex Shevalier, President
Awards:
• S'ean Gillen Memorial Scholarship

Calgary & District Target Shooters Association (CDTSA)
#142, 612 - 500 Country Hills Blvd., Calgary AB T3K 5K3
Tel: 403-275-3257
www.cdtsa.ca
Overview: A small local organization founded in 1981
Affiliation(s): Alberta Federation of Shooting Sports; Alberta Fish & Game Association; Alberta Black Powder Association; Alberta Metallic Silhouette Association
Finances: *Annual Operating Budget:* Less than $50,000
12 volunteer(s)
Membership: *Fees:* Schedule available

Calgary Aboriginal Arts Awareness Society (CAAAS)
#202B, 351 - 11 Ave. SW, Calgary AB T2R 0C7
Tel: 403-296-2227
Previous Name: Calgary Aboriginal Awareness Society
Overview: A small local charitable organization founded in 1988
Mission: To celebrate positive reinforcement, communication & outreach of the cultural continuum of traditional & contemporary practice of Aboriginal Professional Artists
Finances: *Annual Operating Budget:* $50,000-$100,000
Staff Member(s): 2; 40 volunteer(s)
Membership: 40; *Member Profile:* Calgary & area aboriginals & non-aboriginals
Activities: Art exhibition; theatre productions; literary & media arts; *Awareness Events:* Aboriginal Awareness Week, 3rd week June; *Speaker Service:* Yes

Calgary Aboriginal Awareness Society *See* Calgary Aboriginal Arts Awareness Society

Calgary Alpha House Society
203 - 15 Ave. SE, Calgary AB T2G 1G4
Tel: 403-234-7388; *Fax:* 403-705-0123
info@alphahousecalgary.com
www.alphahousecalgary.com
www.facebook.com/AlphaHouseSociety
twitter.com/alphahouseyyc
Also Known As: Alpha House
Overview: A small local organization founded in 1981
Mission: To provide drop-in/overnight shelter & short-term detoxification for males & females with alcohol &/or drug abuse issues
Staff Member(s): 22
Chief Officer(s):
Kathy Christiansen, Executive Director
kathy@alphahousecalgary.com

Calgary Association of Self Help
1019 - 7th Ave. SW, Calgary AB T2P 1A8
Tel: 403-266-8711; *Fax:* 403-266-2478
info@calgaryselfhelp.com
calgaryselfhelp.com
www.facebook.com/CalgaryAssociationofSelfHelp
twitter.com/yycselfhelp
Overview: A medium-sized local charitable organization founded in 1973
Mission: To provide client-centred, flexible services promoting the abilities of adults with mental illness through rehabilitation, counselling & social/leisure programs
Finances: *Funding Sources:* Provincial government; fundraising
Staff Member(s): 24
Chief Officer(s):
Anneisa Lauchlan, Chief Executive Officer, 403-266-8711 Ext. 222

Calgary Association of the Deaf (CgyAD)
63 Cornell Rd. NW, Calgary AB T2L 0L4
info@cad1935.ca
www.facebook.com/CgyAD
Overview: A small local organization
Affiliation(s): Alberta Association of the Deaf
Chief Officer(s):
Robyn Mackie, President

Calgary Birth Control Association *See* Calgary Sexual Health Centre

Calgary Boxing & Wrestling Commission *See* Calgary Combative Sports Commission

Calgary Canada-China Friendship Association (CCCFA)
Calgary AB
federation.tripod.com/calgary.html
www.facebook.com/cccfa1
Overview: A small international organization founded in 1974 overseen by Federation of Canada-China Friendship Associations
Mission: To develop friendship & understanding between Canadians in Alberta & the People's Republic of China
Member of: Federation of Canada-China Friendship Associations
Activities: Dinner meetings; tours to China; cultural education
Chief Officer(s):
Sheila Foster, President, 403-251-6369
fosterst@shaw.ca

Calgary Caribbean Cultural Association *See* Caribbean Community Council of Calgary

Calgary Catholic Immigration Society (CCIS)
1111 - 11 Ave. SW, 5th Fl., Calgary AB T2R 0G5
Tel: 403-262-2006; *Fax:* 403-262-2033
contact@ccis-calgary.ab.ca
www.ccisab.ca
www.facebook.com/298577383506539
twitter.com/ccis2
www.youtube.com/user/CCISTV
Overview: A small international organization
Mission: CCIS is a non-profit organization which provides settlement & integration services to immigrants & refugees in Southern Alberta.
Staff Member(s): 110; 2000 volunteer(s)

Activities: Pre-employment training & counseling; community outreach for families & seniors; temporary accommodation facility; Integrated Resettlement Program
Chief Officer(s):
Fariborz Birjandian, Executive Director

Brooks & County Immigration Services
PO Box 844, 500 Cassils Rd., Bay 2, Brooks AB T1R 1B5
Tel: 403-362-0404; *Fax:* 403-362-0435
info@bcis-brooks.ca
Mission: Provides settlement and integration services to all immigrants, refugees and temporary foreign workers.

Foothills Community Immigrant Services
PO Box 45043, 609 Centre St., 2nd Fl., High River AB T1V 1R7
Tel: 403-652-5325; *Fax:* 403-652-5350
highriver@ccis-calgary.ab.ca
Mission: Provides comprehensive settlement and integration services throughout the Municipal District of Foothills and Southern Alberta.

Margaret Chisholm Resettlement Centre
23 McDougall Ct. NE, Calgary AB T2E 8R3
Tel: 403-262-8132
mcrc@ccis-calgary.ab.ca
Mission: To provide temporary accommodation to newcomers as they begin the resettlement process in Calgary

Calgary Chamber of Commerce
#600, 237 - 8th Ave. SE, Calgary AB T2G 5C3
Tel: 403-750-0400
info@calgarychamber.com
www.calgarychamber.com
www.linkedin.com/company/calgary-chamber-of-commerce
www.facebook.com/CalgaryChamber
twitter.com/calgarychamber
Overview: A medium-sized local organization founded in 1891
Mission: To lead & serve the Calgary business community valuing its diversity
Staff Member(s): 18
Chief Officer(s):
Rob Hawley, Chair
Adam Legge, President & CEO
Rebecca Wood, Director, Member Services
rwood@calgarychamber.com

Calgary Chamber of Voluntary Organizations (CCVO)
#1175, 105 - 12 Ave. SE, Calgary AB T2G 1A1
Tel: 403-261-6655; *Fax:* 403-261-6602
info@calgarycvo.org
www.calgarycvo.org
www.facebook.com/nonprofitvoice
twitter.com/nonprofitvoice
Overview: A small local organization
Mission: To strengthen Calgary's voluntary sector & provide leadership on policy matters impacting the sector as a whole
Membership: *Fees:* Schedule available
Chief Officer(s):
David Mitchell, President & CEO, 403-910-5881
dmitchell@calgarycvo.org
Meetings/Conferences:
• 2018 Calgary Chamber of Voluntary Organizations Connections Conference, 2018, Calgary, AB
Scope: Local

Calgary Children's Foundation
c/o CHQR FM, #170, 200 Barclay Parade SW, Calgary AB T2P 4R5
Tel: 403-444-4337
Overview: A small local organization
Mission: To promote the mental & physical health & welfare of children & certain adults who are disadvantaged & reside within Alberta
Finances: *Funding Sources:* Donations
Activities: Pledge day; luncheon; golf tournament; *Awareness Events:* Pledge Day Radiothon
Chief Officer(s):
Betty Jo Kaiser, Administrator
bettyjo.kaiser@corusent.com

Calgary Chinese Cultural Society (CCCS)
#201, 116 - Ave. SW, Calgary AB T2P 0B9
Tel: 403-263-8830
Overview: A small provincial organization founded in 1975
Mission: To contribute to multiculturalism by promoting mutual understanding & cultural interaction between the Chinese community & fellow Canadians; to promote the construction of a multi-purpose cultural & educational centre in Chinatown; to contribute to charitable & community service; to promote cultural exchange & friendship between Canada & China
Member of: Alberta Chinese Community Congress; National Congress of Chinese Canadians
Activities: Operates Chinese language school

Calgary Civil Liberties Association *See* Alberta Civil Liberties Research Centre

Calgary Combative Sports Commission
c/o Compliance Services, Animal & Bylaw Services, City of Calgary, PO Box 2100, Stn. M #128, Calgary AB T2P 2M5
Tel: 403-648-6323; *Fax:* 403-221-3528
combativesportscommission@calgary.ca
www.calgary.ca
Previous Name: Calgary Boxing & Wrestling Commission
Overview: A small local licensing organization founded in 2007 overseen by Canadian Professional Boxing Council
Mission: The commission acts as a regulation body for professional combative sports within the City of Calgary.
Member of: Canadian Professional Boxing Federation
Membership: 1-99
Chief Officer(s):
Shirley Stunzi, Chair, 403-710-6148
Shirley.Stunzi@calgary.ca
Kent Pallister, Administrator

Calgary Community Living Society (CCLS)
#211, 4014 Macleod Trail South, Calgary AB T2G 2R7
Tel: 403-245-4665; *Fax:* 403-228-2132
ccls@telus.net
www.cclscalgary.com
Overview: A small local charitable organization founded in 1984
Mission: To empower families, through advocacy & education & support to create meaningful & inclusive community lives for their family members & friends with devleopmental disabiblities
Member of: Alberta Association for Community Living
Finances: *Funding Sources:* Grants; private donations; fundraising
Membership: *Fees:* $20; *Member Profile:* Persons with development disabilities, their families & friends
Activities: Calgary Family Network; Family Connection meetings; Coffee Talk meetings; referrals & resources; summer picnic; Christmas party; *Library:* CCLS Resource Library; Open to public

Calgary Co-operative Memorial Society (CCMS)
#204A, 223 - 12th Ave. SW, Calgary AB T2R 0G9
Tel: 403-248-2044
Toll-Free: 800-566-9959
admin@calgarymemorial.com
www.calgarymemorial.com
www.facebook.com/calgarycooperativememorialsociety
Also Known As: Calgary Memorial Society
Previous Name: Memorial Society of Calgary
Overview: A small local organization founded in 1966
Mission: To negotiate on behalf of members for funeral plans with contracted funeral providers to ensure dignified funerals as economically as possible.
Membership: *Fees:* $22.15; *Committees:* Governance; Service Provider; Presentations; Advertising; Legislative Watch; Nominating & AGM; Giving
Activities: *Speaker Service:* Yes
Chief Officer(s):
Tony Kasper, Chair
tonykasper@shaw.ca

Calgary Danish Businessmen's Association
c/o Danish Canadian Club, 727 - 11 Ave. SW, Calgary AB T2R 0E3
Tel: 403-261-9774; *Fax:* 403-261-6631
Overview: A small local organization founded in 1980
Mission: To encorage networking, friendship & the promotion of business knowledge in a social setting.
Member of: Federation of Danish Associations in Canada
Activities: Meetings with guest speaker, discussions on current business issues, & dinners
Chief Officer(s):
Vaughn Schuler, Contact, 403-207-3126
vschuler@devry.edu

Calgary Exhibition & Stampede
PO Box 1060, Stn. M, 1410 Olympic Way SE, Calgary AB T2P 2K8
Tel: 403-261-0101
Toll-Free: 800-661-1767

Other Communication: www.flickr.com/photos/calgarystampede
info@calgarystampede.com
www.calgarystampede.com
www.facebook.com/calgarystampede
twitter.com/calgarystampede
www.youtube.com/calgarystampede
Also Known As: Calgary Stampede
Overview: A large local organization founded in 1912
Mission: To preserve & promote Western heritage & values
Member of: Canadian Association of Fairs & Exhibitions
Finances: *Annual Operating Budget:* Greater than $5 Million
Staff Member(s): 1200; 2300 volunteer(s)
Activities: Presenting year-round events; *Internships:* Yes; *Speaker Service:* Yes
Chief Officer(s):
Warren Connell, CEO
Paul Rosenberg, Chief Operating Officer
Shelly Flint, Chief Financial Officer

Calgary Faceter's Guild
c/o Dave Biro, PO Box 395, Blackfalds AB T0M 0J0
www.afrc.ca/calgaryfacetersguild.htm
Overview: A small local organization
Mission: To promote and support the development of faceting and related activities, and to aid in the education of its members.
Member of: Alberta Federation of Rock Clubs; Gem & Mineral Federation of Canada.
Finances: *Funding Sources:* Membership
Chief Officer(s):
Dave Biro, Contact
dbiroret@telus.net

Calgary Field Naturalists' Society (CFNS)
PO Box 981, Stn. M, Calgary AB T2P 2K4
Tel: 403-239-6444
www.naturecalgary.com
www.facebook.com/naturecalgary
twitter.com/NatureYYC
Also Known As: Nature Calgary
Overview: A small local charitable organization founded in 1955 overseen by Federation of Alberta Naturalists
Mission: To promote enjoyment of nature through environmental appreciation & conservation; To encourage wise use & conservation of natural resources & environmental protection
Member of: Calgary Area Outdoor Council; Alberta Environmental Network
Finances: *Annual Operating Budget:* Less than $50,000; *Funding Sources:* Membership dues; donations; publications sale
185 volunteer(s)
Membership: 100-499; *Fees:* $20 regular; $25 family; *Committees:* Bird Study; Botany & Fungi Study; Nature Photography; Endangered Species; Natural Areas
Activities: 35 slide shows/presentations & over 100 field trips a year; Speaker Series; Bird Study Group; Botany Group; Field Trips; Banquet; *Speaker Service:* Yes
Chief Officer(s):
Andrew Hart, President
president@naturecalgary.com
Ed Kissinger, Treasurer
treasurer@naturecalgary.com
Awards:
• President's Award, Honorary Life Memberships

Calgary Firefighters Burn Treatment Society (CFFBTS)
2234 - 30 Ave. NE, Calgary AB T2E 7K9
Tel: 403-701-2876; *Fax:* 403-271-0744
info@cfbts.org
cfbts.org
www.facebook.com/hotstuffcalgary
twitter.com/hotstuffcalgary
Overview: A medium-sized local charitable organization founded in 1978
Mission: To raise funds for burn victims in burn units throughout Calgary & Southern Alberta
Finances: *Funding Sources:* Calendar sales; fundraisers; public donations; special events
Membership: 1,000
Chief Officer(s):
Jim Fisher, President
president@cfbts.org
Publications:
• Calgary Firefighters Burn Treatment Society Newsletter
Type: Newsletter

Calgary Folk Club
#85, 305 - 4625 Varsity Dr. NW, Calgary AB T3A 0Z9
Tel: 403-286-5651; *Fax:* 403-286-6534
manager@calgaryfolkclub.com
www.calgaryfolkclub.com
www.facebook.com/CalgaryFolkClub
twitter.com/calgfolkclub
Overview: A small local organization founded in 1972
Mission: To present 13 concerts from September to April featuring internationally touring folk artists
Finances: *Funding Sources:* Provincial government; local Arts Council
30 volunteer(s)
Membership: 200 individual; 350 associate; *Fees:* $195 individual
Chief Officer(s):
Donna McTaggart, Manager
donnamc@kaos-consulting.com
Suze Casey, Artistic Director
suze@beliefrepatterning.com

Calgary Food Bank
5000 - 11 St. SE, Calgary AB T2H 2Y5
Tel: 403-253-2059; *Fax:* 403-259-4240
info@calgaryfoodbank.com
www.calgaryfoodbank.com
www.linkedin.com/company/calgary-food-bank
www.facebook.com/calgaryfoodbank
twitter.com/CalgaryFoodBank
www.youtube.com/yycfoodbank
Overview: A small local charitable organization overseen by Food Banks Alberta Association
Mission: To gather & distribute quality emergency food to those in need
Member of: Food Banks Alberta Association

The Calgary Foundation
#700, 999 - 8 St. SW, Calgary AB T2R 1J5
Tel: 403-802-7700; *Fax:* 403-802-7701
info@thecalgaryfoundation.org
thecalgaryfoundation.org
www.facebook.com/TheCalgaryFoundation
twitter.com/CalgFoundation
Overview: A small local charitable organization founded in 1955
Mission: To act as a catalyst & a convener; To provide a meeting place, fostering partnerships, engaging citizens, & addressing needs; To promotes & facilitate philanthropy for the long term benefit of Calgary & area; To operate as a community builder, applying its resources, expertise, & leadership, in partnership with others, to identify needs, address community issues, & build a stronger community for the benefit of Calgary & area citizens; To strengthen the charitable sector to be better able to serve the existing & emerging needs of the Calgary & area community
Member of: Community Foundations of Canada; Council on Foundations
Finances: *Annual Operating Budget:* $3 Million-$5 Million; *Funding Sources:* Private donations
Staff Member(s): 18; 110 volunteer(s)
Activities: Friends of the Foundation Annual Celeration
Chief Officer(s):
Eva Friesen, President & CEO
efriesen@thecalgaryfoundation.org
Gerald M. Deyell, Chair

Calgary Health Trust
#800, 11012 Macleod Trail SE, Calgary AB T2J 6A5
Tel: 403-943-0615; *Fax:* 403-943-0628
fundraising@calgaryhealthtrust.ca
www.calgaryhealthtrust.ca
www.linkedin.com/company/calgary-health-trust
www.facebook.com/YYCHealthTrust
twitter.com/YYCHealthTrust
www.youtube.com/user/YYCHealthTrust
Overview: A small local charitable organization
Mission: To receive & distribute philanthropic health care gifts & funds across Calgary; To work closely with Alberta Health Services to identify key priorities for allocation of philanthropic support; To enhance the development of health care, patient care, technology, & services at medical centres across Calgary
Affiliation(s): Alberta Health Services
Finances: *Funding Sources:* Individual & corporate donations; Sponsorship; Lotteries; Fundraising
Staff Member(s): 45
Activities: Organizing lotteries & other fundraising events; Collecting donations & philanthropic gifts
Chief Officer(s):
Jill Olynyk, Chief Executive Officer
jill.olynyk@calgaryhealthtrust.ca
Susan Cuerrier, Chief Financial Officer
susan.cuerrier@calgaryhealthtrust.ca
Publications:
• Calgary Health Trust Annual Report
Type: Report; *Frequency:* Annually

Calgary Horticultural Society (CHS)
208 - 50 Ave. SW, Calgary AB T2S 2S1
Tel: 403-287-3469; *Fax:* 403-287-6986
office@calhort.org
www.calhort.org
www.facebook.com/calhort
twitter.com/yycgardening
Overview: A medium-sized provincial organization founded in 1907
Mission: To educate, promote & encourage gardening in the Calgary area
Affiliation(s): Royal Horticultural Society
Finances: *Funding Sources:* Membership fees; committee activities
Staff Member(s): 6
Membership: 5,000+; *Fees:* $25 students/seniors; $35 senior family; $45 individual/affiliate; $55 family; $245 corporate
Activities: Gardeners Fair; garden competition; plant exchanges; *Speaker Service:* Yes; *Library:* Not open to public
Chief Officer(s):
Kenna Burima, President
Elizabeth Jolicoeur, Executive Director

Calgary Humane Society
4455 - 110 Ave. SE, Calgary AB T2C 2T7
Tel: 403-205-4455; *Fax:* 403-723-6050
www.calgaryhumane.ca
www.facebook.com/CalgaryHumaneSociety
twitter.com/CalgaryHumane
www.youtube.com/user/CalgaryHumaneSociety
Overview: A medium-sized provincial charitable organization founded in 1922 overseen by Canadian Federation of Humane Societies
Mission: To foster humane treatment of animals & to promote values which demonstrate respect for animals
Member of: Alberta SPCA
Finances: *Funding Sources:* Donations; Memberships; Bequests; Services; Planned giving
Staff Member(s): 19
Membership: *Fees:* $10 senior; $15 youth; $40 individual; $250 lifetime
Activities: *Library:* Resource Centre; by appointment
Chief Officer(s):
Carrie Fritz, Executive Director

Calgary Immigrant Aid Society See Immigrant Services Calgary

Calgary Immigrant Women's Association (CIWA)
#200, 138 - 4th Ave. SE, Calgary AB T2G 4Z6
Tel: 403-263-4414; *Fax:* 403-264-3914
reception@ciwa-online.com
www.ciwa-online.com
www.linkedin.com/company/calgary-immigrant-women%27s-association
www.facebook.com/CIWAyyc
twitter.com/CIWA_yyc
www.youtube.com/user/CIWAvideos
Overview: A medium-sized local charitable organization founded in 1982
Mission: To promote & support the integration of immigrant women into the community & the larger Canadian society
Affiliation(s): Alberta/NWT Network of Immigrant Women; Alberta Association of Immigrant Serving Agencies
Finances: *Annual Operating Budget:* $1.5 Million-$3 Million; *Funding Sources:* All levels of government; corporate; individuals
Staff Member(s): 137; 696 volunteer(s)
Membership: 175; *Fees:* $10 individual; $25 organization; *Committees:* Fund Development; Public Relations; Finance; Personnel
Activities: CIWA Conference; youth program; new friends & neighbourhood groups; cross-cultural parenting program; family conflict program; skills training & employment program; volunteer program; language instruction for newcomers to Canada; Pebbles in the Sand; intake, settlement & referral services; integration project; women & youth safety program; childcare; baby club; accent reduction; Lifting the Bar; *Library:* Open to public

Chief Officer(s):
Beba Svigir, CEO, 403-444-1755
director@ciwa-online.com

Calgary Insurance Women See Insurance Professionals of Calgary

Calgary Japanese Community Association (CJCA)
2236 - 29th St. SW, Calgary AB T3E 2K2
Tel: 403-242-4143
cjcamain@shaw.ca
www.calgaryjca.com
Overview: A small local organization
Member of: National Association of Japanese Canadians
Membership: *Fees:* $15 individual/senior; $30 family; *Committees:* Advertising; Communications; Community & Seniors Foundation; Cultural; Fundraising; Membership; Social Events; Special Projects
Chief Officer(s):
Mari Sasaki, Office Administrator
cjcamain@shaw.ca
Publications:
• CJCA [Calgary Japanese Community Association] Q-Newsletter
Type: Newsletter; *Frequency:* Quarterly

Calgary Jewish Community Council See The Centre for Israel & Jewish Affairs

Calgary Law Library Group (CLLG)
c/o Osler, Hoskin & Harcourt LLP, #2500, 450 - 1st St. SW, Calgary AB T2P 5H1
calgarylawlibrarygroup@gmail.com
www.cllg.wildapricot.org
Overview: A small local organization
Mission: To promote the services of law librarians & legal information professionals; To represent the interests of law librarians & legal information professionals in Calgary & the surrounding area; To offer continuing education to members
Membership: *Fees:* Free, students; $40 individuals/affiliate; *Member Profile:* Persons in Alberta who provide services to libraries disseminating legal information; Individuals interested in legal information libraries; MLIS & Library Technician students; *Committees:* CLLG Guidelines; Education Grant; Program; Shelagh Mikulak Library Leadership Award; Student; Website
Activities: Facilitating networking opportunities with other professionals in many areas of librarianship; Providing professional development activities; Cooperating with other organizations
Chief Officer(s):
Annamarie Bergen, Co-Chair
chair.cllg@gmail.com
Elda Figueira, Co-Chair
Helen Mok, Secretary
secretary.cllg@gmail.com
Shelley Buckler, Treasurer
treasurer.cllg@gmail.com
Awards:
• Shelagh Mikulak Library Leadership Award
Awarded to an individual who displays innovation, respect, integrity, & leadership in the profession, as well as advocates for librarians/the librarian community as a whole; *Amount:* $500
• Education Grant
; *Amount:* $1,000
Meetings/Conferences:
• Calgary Law Library Group 2018 Annual General Meeting, 2018, Calgary, AB
Scope: Local
Description: An annual meeting of legal information professionals & law librarians from Calgary & the surrounding area
Publications:
• Calgary Law Library Group Directory of Members
Type: Directory

Calgary Marching Showband Association
Calgary Stampede, PO Box 1060, Stn. M, Calgary AB T2P 2K8
Tel: 403-261-9318; *Fax:* 403-233-7245
info@stampedeshowband.com
www.stampedeshowband.com
www.facebook.com/calgarystampede
twitter.com/calgarystampede
Also Known As: Calgary Stampede Showband
Overview: A small local organization
Chief Officer(s):
Michelle Fior, Chair
mfior@calgarystampede.com

Mike Jewitt, Director, Bands
mjewitt@calgarystampede.com
Scott A. Grant, General Contact
sgrant@calgarystampede.com

Calgary Meals on Wheels
5759 - 80 Ave. SE, Calgary AB T2C 4S6
Tel: 403-243-2834; *Fax:* 403-243-8438
info@mealsonwheels.com
www.mealsonwheels.com
www.linkedin.com/company/calgary-meals-on-wheels
www.facebook.com/calgarymealsonwheels
twitter.com/MealsOnWheelsca
Overview: A small local charitable organization founded in 1965
Mission: To build a stronger, caring community; To promote health & independence through the provision of nutritious & affordable meals to seniors & people in need
Finances: *Funding Sources:* Fees 46%; fundraising 27%; FCSS 18%; United Way 9%
Staff Member(s): 50; 730 volunteer(s)
Membership: 195; *Fees:* $10 group; $5 individual; *Member Profile:* Anyone who supports the Meals on Wheels mission; *Committees:* Capital Project; Operations; Finance & Audit; Governance; Marketing; Capital Campaign
Activities: *Awareness Events:* Meals on Wheels Awareness Week; *Internships:* Yes; *Speaker Service:* Yes
Chief Officer(s):
Janice Curtis, Executive Director
jcurtis@mealsonwheels.com
Chris Mattock, Coordinator, Marketing & Communications
marketing@mealsonwheels.com
Awards:
• Patricia Bourne Award
• Bill Girling Heart Award

Calgary Mennonite Centre for Newcomers Society See Centre for Newcomers Society of Calgary

Calgary Minor Soccer Association (CSMA)
#7, 6991 - 48 St. SE, Calgary AB T2C 5A4
Tel: 403-279-8686; *Fax:* 403-236-3669
info@calgaryminorsoccer.com
calgaryminorsoccer.com
www.facebook.com/calgaryminorsoccer
twitter.com/cmsasoccer
instagram.com/calgaryminorsoccer
Overview: A small local organization overseen by Alberta Soccer Association
Member of: Alberta Soccer Association
Staff Member(s): 12
Chief Officer(s):
Daryl Leinweber, Executive Director, 403-279-8686 Ext. 1007
execdirector@calgaryminorsoccer.com
Cory Letendre, Manager, 403-279-8686 Ext. 1002
operations@calgaryminorsoccer.com
Melissa Collinson, League Director, 403-279-8686 Ext. 1003
leagues@calgaryminorsoccer.com

Calgary Motor Dealers Association (CMDA)
#101, 7309 Flint Rd. SE, Calgary AB T2H 1G3
Tel: 403-974-0707; *Fax:* 403-974-0711
Toll-Free: 866-318-2632
www.calgarymotordealers.com
Overview: A small local organization founded in 1951
Affiliation(s): Motor Dealers Association of Alberta
Staff Member(s): 2; 25 volunteer(s)
Membership: 70; *Member Profile:* Franchised new vehicle dealers in Calgary
Chief Officer(s):
Jack Thompson, Executive Director

Calgary Musicians Association
#5, 606 Meredith Rd. NE, Calgary AB T2E 5A8
Tel: 403-264-6610; *Fax:* 403-264-6610
Toll-Free: 888-796-8742
info@calgarymusicians.org
calgarymusicians.org
www.facebook.com/CalgaryMusiciansAssociation
twitter.com/YYCmusicians
Overview: A medium-sized local organization founded in 1938
Mission: To establish & maintain working standards in the music industry, as well as to provide support to & to promote their members
Member of: American Federation of Musicians of the United States & Canada
Finances: *Annual Operating Budget:* $100,000-$250,000; *Funding Sources:* Membership dues

Staff Member(s): 1
Membership: 700; *Fees:* $185; $115 initiation fee
Activities: Improving wages & working conditions of musicians; collective bargaining; promotion of musicians; referral service; *Speaker Service:* Yes
Chief Officer(s):
Allistair Elliott, President

Calgary Native Women's Shelter Society See Awo Taan Healing Lodge Society

Calgary Numismatic Society (CNS)
PO Box 633, Calgary AB T2P 2J3
info@calgarynumismaticsociety.org
www.calgarynumismaticsociety.org
www.facebook.com/calgarynumismaticsociety
Overview: A small local organization founded in 1950
Mission: To promote the collection of coins, medals, & paper money
Member of: Canadian Numismatic Association
Finances: *Annual Operating Budget:* Less than $50,000; *Funding Sources:* Membership dues; special events
Membership: 75; *Fees:* $12 senior; $18 family; $3 youth
Activities: *Awareness Events:* Annual Spring Coin Show; Canada's Money Collector Show, July
Chief Officer(s):
Gordon Schiele, President
Publications:
• CNS [Calgary Numismatic Society] Bulletin
Type: Newsletter; *Editor:* Neil Probert

Calgary Olympic Development Association See WinSport Canada

Calgary Opera Association
Mamdani Opera Centre, 1315 - 7 St. SW, Calgary AB T2R 1A5
Tel: 403-262-7286; *Fax:* 403-263-5428
info@calgaryopera.com
www.calgaryopera.com
www.facebook.com/calgaryopera
twitter.com/CalgaryOpera
Overview: A small local organization founded in 1972
Mission: To enrich the cultural life of the community by celebrating musical art through the performance of professional opera
Member of: Opera America
Affiliation(s): Actors Equity Association
Finances: *Funding Sources:* Government; corporate; individual
Staff Member(s): 21
Chief Officer(s):
W.R. (Bob) McPhee, General Director & CEO

Calgary Parents of Multiple Births Association See Twins, Triplets & More Association of Calgary

Calgary Philatelic Society (CPS)
PO Box 1478, Calgary AB T2P 2L6
calphilso@calgaryphilatelicsociety.com
www.calgaryphilatelicsociety.com
Overview: A small local organization founded in 1922
Mission: To provide a meeting place for local stamp collectors to get together and share their interest in stamps and postal history.
Member of: Royal Philatelic Society of Canada; American Philatelic Society; American Topical Association
Affiliation(s): British North America Philatelic Society
Finances: *Funding Sources:* Membership fees
Membership: *Member Profile:* Stamp collectors; exhibitors; accumulators; *Committees:* Archives; Caltapex Show; Circuit Books; Dealer Bourse; Exhibits; Library; Life Members; Membership; Private Treaty Books; Programmes; Regular Auction; Sergeant-at-Arms; Silent Auction; Spring Show
Activities: Stamp collecting, auctions, shows & presentations; *Library:* Not open to public
Chief Officer(s):
Peter Fleck, President
president@calgaryphilatelicsociety.com
Awards:
• Founder's Award
• Life Membership Award
• Bob Monilaws Award
Publications:
• The Calgary Philatelist
Price: Free for members

Calgary Philharmonic Society (CPO)
#205, 8 Ave. SE, Calgary AB T2G 0K9

Canadian Associations / Calgary Police Association (CPA)

Tel: 403-571-0270; *Fax:* 403-294-7424
info@calgaryphil.com
www.calgaryphil.com
www.facebook.com/calgaryphil
twitter.com/calgaryphil
www.youtube.com/CalgaryPhilharmonic
Also Known As: Calgary Philharmonic Orchestra
Merged from: Alberta Philharmonic; Calgary Symphony
Overview: A large local charitable organization founded in 1955 overseen by Orchestras Canada
Mission: To provide audience with a rich, diverse & unequalled symphonic musical experience which earns broad community support
Member of: Orchestras Canada; Calgary Chamber of Commerce
Affiliation(s): American Symphony Orchestra League
Finances: *Annual Operating Budget:* Greater than $5 Million; *Funding Sources:* Federal, provincial & city grants; Corporate & individual donations; Sponsorships; Performance revenue
Staff Member(s): 90; 80 volunteer(s)
Membership: 1-99; *Fees:* $25; *Committees:* Artistic Administration; Development; Finance & Administration; Marketing & Sales
Activities: *Internships:* Yes *Library:* Music Library; Not open to public
Chief Officer(s):
Paul Dornian, President & CEO
pdornian@calgaryphil.com
Awards:
• Marley Rynd Scholarship
Eligibility: An advanced orchestral music student from the Mount Royal Conservatory or the University of Calgary Faculty of Music

Calgary Police Association (CPA)
Calgary AB
www.backtheblue.ca
Overview: A small local organization
Mission: To lobby government to influence the criminal justice system & promote the interests of the citizens of Calgary & the members; to bargain for improved wages, working conditions & benefits; to help members being investigated or charged with offences
Staff Member(s): 2
Membership: 1,800+; *Member Profile:* Members of Calgary police
Chief Officer(s):
Howard Burns, President
Mike Baker, Vice-President, Finance

Calgary Power Employees Association; TransAlta Employees' Association *See* United Utility Workers' Association

Calgary Real Estate Board Cooperative Limited (CREB)
300 Manning Rd. NE, Calgary AB T2E 8K4
Tel: 403-263-0530; *Fax:* 403-218-3688
info@creb.com
www.creb.com
Overview: A medium-sized local organization overseen by Alberta Real Estate Association
Member of: Alberta Real Estate Association; The Canadian Real Estate Association
Staff Member(s): 70
Membership: 5,200
Chief Officer(s):
Alan Tennant, Chief Executive Officer, 403-781-1359
alan.tennant@creb.ca

Calgary Residential Rental Association (CRRA)
4653 Macleod Trail SW, Calgary AB T2G 0A6
Tel: 403-265-6055; *Fax:* 403-265-9696
info@crra.ca
www.crra.ca
www.facebook.com/www.crra.ca
twitter.com/crra_ca
Overview: A small local organization founded in 1959
Mission: To provide representation & networking for the residential rental industry.
Finances: *Funding Sources:* Membership dues
Staff Member(s): 4
Membership: 1,000+; *Fees:* Schedule available dependant on number of units owned; *Member Profile:* Owners, managers and companies that service residential rental units in Calgary
Activities: Courses & seminars on educating landlords; annual trade show
Chief Officer(s):
Gerry Baxter, Executive Director
gerry@crra.ca

Calgary Rock & Lapidary Club
#13, 3650 - 19th St. NE, Calgary AB T2E 6V2
www.crlc.ca
www.facebook.com/CalgaryRockandLapidaryClub
twitter.com/CRLCrockhounds
Overview: A small local organization founded in 1959
Mission: To encourage interest in the study of rocks, minerals, gems, fossils & artifacts in Alberta & elsewhere
Member of: Alberta Federation of Rock Clubs
Affiliation(s): Gem & Mineral Federation of Canada
Membership: 250; *Fees:* $30 adult; $25 senior; $50 family; *Member Profile:* Persons with a common interest in the lapidary arts & earth sciences; *Committees:* Metaphysical; Pebble Pups; Resource; Show; Workshop
Activities: Collecting, working & exhibiting finished gemstones & geological specimens for public display; Organizing field trips for collecting lapidary materials; Offering study groups with hands-on sessions for children; *Library:* Calgary Rock and Lapidary Club Library; Not open to public
Chief Officer(s):
Stefan Gibbins, President
Publications:
• The Calgary Lapidary Journal
Type: Newsletter; *Frequency:* 8 pa

Calgary Round-Up Band Association (CRUB)
#3, 2451 Dieppe Ave. SW, Calgary AB T3E 7K1
Tel: 403-259-3120
info@roundupband.org
www.roundupband.org
www.facebook.com/CalgaryRoundUpBand
Overview: A small international charitable organization founded in 1956
Mission: To provide instruction, discipline & social activities for junior high school-aged musicians
Affiliation(s): Calgary Stampede Show Band; Calgary Stetson Show Band
Staff Member(s): 4; 290 volunteer(s)
Membership: 300 associates; 100 students; *Fees:* $750; *Member Profile:* Enrolled in music program; *Committees:* Recruiting; Publicity; Uniforming
Activities: Marching & Show Band Performances
Chief Officer(s):
Barry Hensch, President
president@roundupband.org
Earl Paddock, Executive Director
execdirector@roundupband.org

Calgary Seniors' Resource Society
3639 - 26 St. NE, Calgary AB T1Y 5E1
Tel: 403-266-6200; *Fax:* 403-269-5183
www.calgaryseniors.org
www.facebook.com/CalgarySeniors
twitter.com/Calgary_Seniors
Previous Name: Senior Citizens' Central Council of Calgary
Overview: A medium-sized local charitable organization founded in 1995
Mission: To enhance the quality of life & human dignity of seniors by supporting their independence through home services & community based programs
Member of: Alberta Council on Aging; Alberta Association on Gerontology
Affiliation(s): Calgary Homeless Foundation
Finances: *Funding Sources:* Family & Community Support Services; donations
Membership: *Fees:* $20; *Member Profile:* Individuals 55 years of age or over
Activities: Information, referral & advice; outreach services; escorted transportation; friendly visiting; ABCs' Fraud Awareness program; SeniorConnect program
Chief Officer(s):
Mark Kolesar, President

Calgary Sexual Health Centre
#304, 301 - 14 St. NW, Calgary AB T2N 2A1
Tel: 403-283-5580; *Fax:* 403-270-3209
generalmail@calgarysexualhealth.ca
www.calgarysexualhealth.ca
www.facebook.com/CalgarySexualHealthCentre
twitter.com/yycsexualhealth
Previous Name: Calgary Birth Control Association
Overview: A small local organization founded in 1972
Mission: To offer counselling & education services to help people consider their sexual & reproductive choices in informed & responsible ways.
Member of: Planned Parenthood Alberta; Planned Parenthood Federation of Canada
Activities: Pregnancy options; birth control; referrals; support groups; pregnancy tests; wontgetweird.com program; Resource Centre with books, pamphlets, tools, kits, & DVDs for sale; Training Centre with professional development programs; *Speaker Service:* Yes; *Library:* Open to public
Chief Officer(s):
Pam Krause, Executive Director
pkrause@calgarysexualhealth.ca

Calgary Sledge Hockey Association
Calgary AB
info@calgarysledgehockey.ca
calgarysledgehockey.ca
www.facebook.com/CalgarySledgeHockey
Overview: A small local charitable organization
Affiliation(s): Hockey Alberta; Hockey Canada
Membership: 3 teams
Chief Officer(s):
Dave TAylor, Director of Marketing, 403-891-9295

Calgary Soccer Federation
Calgary Soccer Centre, 7000 - 48 St. SE, Calgary AB T2C 4E1
Tel: 403-279-8453; *Fax:* 403-279-8796
www.calgarysoccerfederation.com
www.facebook.com/calgarysoccerfederation
twitter.com/calgarysoccer1
Overview: A small local organization overseen by Alberta Soccer Association
Member of: Alberta Soccer Association

Calgary Society of Independent Filmmakers (CSIF)
CommunityWise Resource Centre, #103, 223 - 12 Ave. SW, Calgary AB T2R 0G9
Tel: 403-205-4747
communications@csif.org
www.csif.org
twitter.com/CSIF
Overview: A small local organization founded in 1975
Mission: To promote film making as art, reflecting & challenging the changing cultural landscape through production & exhibition of films.
Finances: *Funding Sources:* Canada Council; Alberta Foundation for the Arts; Calgary Arts Development; Nat'l Film Board; AMAA; IMAA
Staff Member(s): 5
Membership: *Fees:* $40 associate; $60 production B; $15 library; *Committees:* Membership; Finance; Production; HR; Facilities; Programming; Communications; Strategic Planning; Policy
Activities: *Speaker Service:* Yes
Chief Officer(s):
Leah Nicholson, President
Bobbie Todd, Operations Coordinator

Calgary Society of Organists
6311 Crowchild Trail SW, Calgary AB T3E 5R6
Tel: 403-249-0764
cso@shaw.ca
members.shaw.ca/cso
Overview: A small local charitable organization
Mission: To promote and appreciate organ music in and around the Calgary area.
Membership: 150; *Fees:* $15
Chief Officer(s):
Howard Janzen, Treasurer
janzenh@shaw.ca

Calgary Stetson Show Band (CSSB)
#3, 2451 Dieppe Ave. SW, Calgary AB T3E 7K1
Tel: 403-258-0889
office@stetsonband.org
www.stetsonband.org
www.facebook.com/StetsonShowBand
twitter.com/StetsonShowBand
www.instagram.com/stetsonshowband
Overview: A small local organization
Mission: To provide Calgary & area students in grades 10-12 opportunities for personal development through advanced musicianship & performance
Membership: *Fees:* $750
Chief Officer(s):
Andrea Ciona, Band Director
banddirector@stetsonband.org

Calgary Tourist & Convention Bureau *See* Tourism Calgary

Calgary United Soccer Association
#183, 2880 Glenmore Trail SE, Calgary AB T2C 2E7
Tel: 403-270-0363; *Fax:* 403-270-0573
info@cusa.ab.ca
www.cusa.ab.ca
www.facebook.com/CalgaryUnitedSoccerAssociation
twitter.com/cusa_events
Overview: A small local organization overseen by Alberta Soccer Association
Member of: Alberta Soccer Association
Staff Member(s): 5
Chief Officer(s):
Pearl Doupe, Executive Director, 403-648-0861
pearl@cusa.ab.ca
Awards:
• A&J Buckler Trophy
• President's Award
• Lifetime Achievement Award
• Award of Merit
• Kieran McGarrigle Award

Calgary Urban Project Society (CUPS)
1001 - 10 Ave. SW, Calgary AB T2R 0B7
Tel: 403-221-8780; *Fax:* 403-221-8791
info@cupscalgary.com
cupscalgary.com
www.facebook.com/CUPSCalgary
twitter.com/CUPSCalgaryAB
www.youtube.com/user/CUPSCalgary1989
Also Known As: CUPS Community Health Centre
Overview: A small local charitable organization founded in 1988
Mission: To advance the quality of life & affirm the worth of all persons through a compassionate, Christ-centred, & holistic healing ministry directed especially to persons who have rejected or have been rejected or neglected by society
Finances: *Annual Operating Budget:* Greater than $5 Million; *Funding Sources:* Corporations; individual donors; foundations; government
Staff Member(s): 180; 564 volunteer(s)
Activities: *Awareness Events:* Christmas Wreath Campaign, Dec.
Chief Officer(s):
Carlene Donnelly, Executive Director
carlened@cupscalgary.com

Calgary Vietnamese Canadian Association
#203, 1829 - 54 St. SE, Calgary AB T2B 1N5
Tel: 403-272-4668; *Fax:* 403-272-4668
hnv-calgary@hotmail.com
www.hoinguoivietcalgary.net
Overview: A small local organization

Calgary Wildlife Rehabilitation Society (CWRS)
11555 - 85th St. NW, Calgary AB T3R 1J3
Tel: 403-266-2282; *Fax:* 403-266-2449
Other Communication: Wildlife Rescue e-mail:
wildlife@calgarywildlife.org
admin@calgarywildlife.org
calgarywildlife.org
www.facebook.com/calgarywildlife
twitter.com/calgarywildlife
Overview: A small local organization founded in 1993
Mission: To rescue, rehabilitate & release injured wild animals
Chief Officer(s):
Andrea Hunt, Executive Director
Jenna McFarland, Manager, Animal Care Operations

Calgary Women's Emergency Shelter Association (CWES)
#501, 1509 Centre St. NW, Calgary AB T2G 2E6
Tel: 403-290-1552; *Fax:* 403-237-7728
Toll-Free: 866-806-7233; *Crisis Hot-Line:* 403-234-7233
info@cwes.ca
www.calgarywomensshelter.com
www.facebook.com/calgarywomenemergencyshelter
twitter.com/end_abuse
www.youtube.com/user/CalgaryWomensShelter
Overview: A small local charitable organization founded in 1974
Mission: To provide support for women, children, men, & youth affected by family violence & abuse
Member of: Alberta Association of Services for Children & Families; Calgary Coalition Against Family Violence
Affiliation(s): Alberta Council of Women's Shelters; Calgary Domestic Violence Collective

Finances: *Funding Sources:* Provincial government; municipal government; federal government; charitable donations; United Way
Activities: Yearly Turning Points Fundraising Gala; *Speaker Service:* Yes
Chief Officer(s):
Shelly Norris, Board President
Kim Ruse, Executive Director

Calgary Women's Soccer Association (CWSA)
#110, 4441 - 76 Ave. SE, Calgary AB T2C 2G8
Tel: 403-720-6692; *Fax:* 403-720-6693
office@mycwsa.ca
www.womensoccer.ab.ca
www.facebook.com/124525960988252
Overview: A small local organization overseen by Alberta Soccer Association
Member of: Alberta Soccer Association
Staff Member(s): 5
Chief Officer(s):
Jacquie Herltein, Executive Director
execdir@mycwsa.ca
Awards:
• CWSA Scholarship
Eligibility: Individuals playing for a team within CWSA who are registered in a program/studies leading to a diploma/certificate; eligible individuals must have high academic standing & demonstrate excellence in leadership, community spirit & community involvement *Deadline:* September 30; *Amount:* 3 at $1,000

Calgary Youth Orchestra
c/o Mount Royal University Conservatory, 4825 Mount Royal Gate SW, Calgary AB T3E 6K6
Tel: 403-440-5978; *Fax:* 403-440-6594
cyo@mtroyal.ca
www.cyo.ab.ca
Overview: A small local organization overseen by Orchestras Canada
Mission: To provide the best possible musical experience for the talented young musicians of the Calgary region, in an art form that is considered one of the highest forms of expression
Member of: Orchestras Canada
Activities: Facilitating rehersals, workshops, concerts & tours
Chief Officer(s):
George Fenwick, Orchestra Manager

Calgary Zoological Society
1300 Zoo Rd. NE, Calgary AB T2E 7V6
Tel: 403-232-9300; *Fax:* 403-237-7582
Toll-Free: 800-588-9993
www.calgaryzoo.org
www.facebook.com/thecalgaryzoo
twitter.com/calgaryzoo
www.youtube.com/thecalgaryzoo
Overview: A large provincial charitable organization founded in 1929
Mission: To operate the Calgary Zoo, Botanical Garden & Prehistoric Park; to advocate on behalf of animals
Member of: Canadian Association of Zoos & Aquariums (CAZA); Association of Zoos & Aquariums (AZA)
Affiliation(s): Amphibian Ark; Tourism Calgary
Finances: *Annual Operating Budget:* $100,000-$250,000; *Funding Sources:* Donations; Sponsorships; Admission
Activities: Offering educational programs; Providing the Calgary Zoo's Endangered Species Reintroduction Research program
Chief Officer(s):
Clément Lanthier, President & CEO
Darryl Dziadyk, Director, Facilities, Grounds & Environment
Meetings/Conferences:
• Calgary Zoological Society 2018 AGM, 2018, AB
Scope: Provincial
Description: Members of the society receive voting rights at the annual meeting
Publications:
• Calgary Zoological Society WILD LIFE Member Blog
Frequency: Quarterly
Profile: Formerly WILD LIFE Magazine; provides weekly updates on conservation, travel & the Calgary Zoo

Call2Recycle Canada, Inc.
#606, 4576 Yonge St., Toronto ON M2N 6N4
Toll-Free: 888-224-9746
www.call2recycle.ca
www.linkedin.com/company/call2recycle
www.facebook.com/Call2Recycle

twitter.com/Call2Recycle
plus.google.com/109631060180236144576
Previous Name: Canadian Household Battery Association; Rechargeable Battery Recycling Corporation Canada
Overview: A small international organization
Mission: To recycle rechargeable battery & cell phones; to conduct public education campaigns & recycling programs
Finances: *Funding Sources:* Manufacturers & marketers of portable rechargeable batteries & products
Activities: *Awareness Events:* Waste Reduction Week, Oct.

Calypso Association of Manitoba
474 Gilmore Ave., Winnipeg MB R2G 2G6
Tel: 204-669-3439
Overview: A small provincial organization founded in 1982
Mission: To demonstrate the versatility & adaptability of Calypso

Cambrian Youth Orchestra *See* Sudbury Youth Orchestra Inc.

Cambridge Association for the Mentally Handicapped *See* Community Living Cambridge

Cambridge Association of Realtors Inc.
2040 Eagle St. North, Cambridge ON N3H 0A1
Tel: 519-623-3660; *Fax:* 519-623-8253
cambridge-admin@rogers.com
cambridgeassociationofrealtors.com
www.facebook.com/CambridgeAssociationOfRealtors
twitter.com/CamRealtors
Previous Name: Galt and District Real Estate Board; Real Estate Board of Cambridge
Overview: A small local organization founded in 1953 overseen by Ontario Real Estate Association
Member of: The Canadian Real Estate Association
Membership: 382

Cambridge Chamber of Commerce
750 Hespler Rd., Cambridge ON N3H 5L8
Tel: 519-622-2221; *Fax:* 519-622-0177
Toll-Free: 800-749-7560
cchamber@cambridgechamber.com
www.cambridgechamber.com
ca.linkedin.com/in/cambridgechamber
twitter.com/My_Chamber
www.youtube.com/thecambridgechamber
Overview: A medium-sized local organization founded in 1973
Member of: Canadian Chamber of Commerce; Ontario Chamber of Commerce
Finances: *Funding Sources:* Membership fees
Staff Member(s): 9
Membership: *Fees:* Schedule available
Activities: Operates Cambridge Visitor & Convention Bureau; Business Outlook dinner; Business After Hours; *Speaker Service:* Yes; *Rents Mailing List:* Yes
Chief Officer(s):
Greg Durocher, President & CEO
greg@cambridgechamber.com

Cambridge Literacy Council; Literacy Council of Kitchener-Waterloo *See* The Literacy Group of Waterloo Region

Cambridge Multicultural Centre *See* YMCA Immigrant & Community Services

Cambridge Self-Help Food Bank
54 Ainslie St. South, Cambridge ON N1R 3K3
Tel: 519-622-6550; *Fax:* 519-622-9076
www.cambridgefoodbank.on.ca
www.facebook.com/CambridgeFoodBank
twitter.com/CambFoodBank
Overview: A small local charitable organization
Mission: To distribute food to underpriviledged people; to provide programs that help people in need become self-sufficient
Staff Member(s): 20
Chief Officer(s):
Pat Singleton, Executive Director

Cambridge Tourism
750 Hespeler Rd., Cambridge ON N3H 5L8
Tel: 519-622-2336; *Fax:* 519-622-0177
Toll-Free: 800-749-7560
visit@cambridgechamber.com
www.cambridgetourism.com
www.facebook.com/pages/Visit-Cambridge-Ontario/249977815059176
www.pinterest.com/cambridgeon

Also Known As: Cambridge Visitor & Convention Bureau
Overview: A small local charitable organization founded in 1981
Mission: To develop tourism initiatives & build partnerships that pool ideas & resources to promote Cambridge as a viable travel destination, generating greater economic impact for the city & other tourism stakeholders.
Member of: Cambridge Chamber of Commerce; City of Cambridge
Affiliation(s): Ontario Motor Coach Association; Grand River County; Tourism Toronto; Southern Ontario Travel Organization; Canadian Society of Associations Executives
Finances: *Funding Sources:* 50% municipal government + 50% private sector
Membership: *Member Profile:* Private sector tourism organizations
Activities: Marketing; visitor services; tourism awareness; Annual Tourism Awards; *Library:* Tourist Information Resource Centre; Open to public

Cameco Capitol Arts Centre
20 Queen St., Port Hope ON L1A 3Z4
Tel: 905-885-1071; *Fax:* 905-885-9714
Toll-Free: 800-434-5092
info@capitoltheatre.com
www.capitoltheatre.com
www.facebook.com/CapitolTheatrePortHope
Overview: A medium-sized local organization founded in 1993
Mission: To provide the Northumberland County Area with the best in professional & community theatre music & dance & provide educational community & theatre arts program
180 volunteer(s)
Membership: 500; *Fees:* Schedule available, based upon donation
Chief Officer(s):
Antonio Sarmiento, General Manager & Artistic Director, 905-885-9060 Ext. 204
antonio@capitoltheatre.com
Shannon Oliver, Manager, Business, 905-885-9060 Ext. 206
shannon@capitoltheatre.com

CAMH Foundation
Bell Gateway Building, 100 Stokes St., 5th Fl., Toronto ON M6J 1H4
Tel: 416-979-6909; *Fax:* 416-979-6910
Toll-Free: 800-414-0471
foundation@camh.ca
www.supportcamh.ca
ca.linkedin.com/company/camh-foundation
www.facebook.com/end.stigma
twitter.com/endstigma
www.instagram.com/camhfoundation
Also Known As: Centre for Addiction & Mental Health Foundation
Overview: A small local charitable organization
Mission: To raise money on behalf of CAMH in order to improve the services provided to patients & to fund research
Staff Member(s): 52
Chief Officer(s):
Darrell Gregersen, President & CEO
Darrell.Gregersen@camh.ca

Camosun College Faculty Association (CCFA) / Association des professeurs du Collège Camosun
Camosun College, Young Bldg., #221, 3100 Foul Bay Rd., Victoria BC V8P 5J2
Tel: 250-370-3655
www.camosunfaculty.ca
Overview: A small local organization
Membership: 350 continuing, 150 term; *Committees:* Contract Management; Contract Negotiating; Disability; Human Rights & International Solidarity; Joint Occupational Safety & Health; Professional Development
Chief Officer(s):
Al Morrison, President, 250-370-3594
morrisona@camosun.bc.ca

Campaign for Nuclear Phaseout (CNP)
#412, 1 Nicholas St., Ottawa ON K1N 7B7
www.cnp.ca
Overview: A small national organization
Mission: The Campaign for Nuclear Phaseout (CNP) represents a coalition of Canadian public interest organizations concerned with the environmental consequences of nuclear power generation.
Affiliation(s): Canadian Coalition for Nuclear Responsibility; Concerned Citizens of Renfrew County and Area; Energy Probe; Greenpeace Canada; Sierra Club of Canada

Campaign Life Coalition (CLC)
#300, 104 Bond St., Toronto ON M5B 1X9
Tel: 416-204-9749; *Fax:* 416-204-1027
Toll-Free: 800-730-5358
clc@campaignlifecoalition.com
www.campaignlifecoalition.com
www.facebook.com/CampaignLifeCoalition
twitter.com/CampaignLife
Previous Name: Coalition for the Protection of Human Life
Overview: A medium-sized national organization
Mission: To protect human life from conception to natural death; to maintain representatives on Parliament Hill; to foster respect for life through adequate legal protection from abortion, infanticide, euthanasia & other life-threatening social & moral trends
Member of: Campaign Life Coalition of Canada
Chief Officer(s):
Jim Hughes, National President

Campbell River & Area Multicultural & Immigrant Services Association *See* Immigrant Welcome Centre

Campbell River & Courtenay District Labour Council
#2, 830 - 14th Ave., Campbell River BC V9W 4H4
Tel: 250-287-3884
crcdlc@gmail.com
www.crclabourcouncil.com
Overview: A small local organization overseen by British Columbia Federation of Labour
Mission: To promote the interests of affiliates in the Campbell River British Columbia area; To advance the economic & social welfare of workers
Affiliation(s): Canadian Labour Congress (CLC)
Membership: *Committees:* Membership; Miners' Memorial Day; Political Action; Labour History Conference; Labour Day Event
Activities: Offering educational opportunities; Lobbying local elected officials for the rights of workers; Conducting campaigns around labour issues, such as pensions; Taking part in a ceremony on the annual Day of Mourning to remember workers who have died or been injured while at work; Participating in the Annual Miners' Memorial Day; Supporting community organizations; Hosting monthly meetings to discuss council business & to hear union reports

Campbell River & District Association for Community Living
1153 Greenwood St., Campbell River BC V9W 3C5
Tel: 250-286-0391; *Fax:* 250-286-3732
www.cradacl.bc.ca
Overview: A small local organization
Mission: Provides advocates for local services to support people of all ages with special needs, their families and caregivers.
Membership: *Fees:* $5
Chief Officer(s):
Greg Hill, Executive Director
Winna Mitchell, President

Campbell River & District Chamber of Commerce
900 Alder St., Campbell River BC V9W 2P6
Tel: 250-287-4636; *Fax:* 250-286-6490
admin@campbellriverchamber.ca
www.campbellriverchamber.ca
www.facebook.com/CampbellRiverChamber
twitter.com/ChamberCR
www.youtube.com/user/CampbellRiverChamber
Overview: A medium-sized local organization founded in 1931
Member of: BC Chamber of Commerce
Finances: *Funding Sources:* Membership dues
Staff Member(s): 2
Membership: 500; *Fees:* $1000 growth; $500 connected; $275 builder; *Committees:* Executive; Finance & Budget; Nomination; Advocacy
Chief Officer(s):
Colleen Evans, President & CEO, 250-287-4513
colleen.evans@campbellriverchamber.ca

Campbell River & District Food Bank
1393 Marwalk Cres., Campbell River BC V9W 5V9
Tel: 250-286-3226; *Fax:* 250-286-3296
campbellriverfoodbank@gmail.com
Overview: A small local charitable organization overseen by Food Banks British Columbia
Mission: The agency provides food to those in need in the Campbell River area.
Member of: Food Banks British Columbia
Chief Officer(s):
Debbie Willis, Contact

Campbell River & District United Way
PO Box 135, Campbell River BC V9W 5A7
Tel: 250-702-2911
bvbayly@uwcnvi.ca
Overview: A small local organization overseen by United Way of Canada - Centraide Canada
Mission: To raise & distribute funds to member agencies that are providing support and services to residents in the Campbell River area
Member of: United Way of Canada

Campbell River Museum & Archives Society
PO Box 70, Stn. A, Campbell River BC V9W 4Z9
Tel: 250-287-3103; *Fax:* 250-286-0109
general.inquiries@crmuseum.ca
www.crmuseum.ca
www.facebook.com/100483307218
Also Known As: Museum at Campbell River
Overview: A small local charitable organization founded in 1958
Mission: To operate the museum, a 21,000-sq. ft. facility sitting on a 7-acre wooded lot; To exhibit a First Nations Gallery showing a coastal lifestyle with such themes as logging, floathouse, & the salmon industry.
Member of: Canadian Museums Association; BC Museums Association; Association of Cultural Executives
Finances: *Funding Sources:* All levels of government
Staff Member(s): 9
Membership: *Fees:* $30 individual; $40 family; $25 senior; $20 student; $45 business
Activities: Public & school programs; special exhibits; family events; field trips; guided tours; museum shop; *Library:* Archives Research Centre; Open to public
Chief Officer(s):
Dennis Fitzgerald, President
Sandra Parrish, Executive Director
sandra.parrish@crmuseum.ca

Campbellford & District Association for Community Living
See Community Living Campbellford/Brighton

Campbellford/Seymour Heritage Society
PO Box 1294, 113 Front St. North, Campbellford ON K0L 1L0
Tel: 705-653-2634
csheritage@persona.ca
www.csheritage.org
Overview: A small local charitable organization founded in 1983
Member of: Ontario Historical Society
Affiliation(s): Ontario Historical Society
Finances: *Annual Operating Budget:* Less than $50,000; *Funding Sources:* Fundraising; government grants
25 volunteer(s)
Membership: 50; *Fees:* $10 single; $5 under 18; $25 corporate; $15 family; $25 sponsor/patron; $20 model railroad club; *Committees:* Collections; Publicity; Computer; Building; Membership; Publications; Garden Displays
Activities: *Library:* Archives
Publications:
• Campbellford Memorial Hospital: 50 Years of Care Beyond Compare
Number of Pages: 103; *Editor:* Ann Rowe; *Price:* $20
• Gleanings: A History of Campbellford-Seymour
Number of Pages: 559; *Editor:* Margaret Crothers, Ann Rowe et al.; *Price:* $40
• A Walk Down Memory Lane: 150 Years of the Campbellford-Seymour Agricultural Society, 1854-2004
Number of Pages: 142; *Editor:* Ann Rowe; *Price:* $20

Campbellford-Seymour Chamber of Commerce *See* Trent Hills & District Chamber of Commerce

Campbellton Regional Chamber of Commerce / Chambre de commerce régional de Campbellton
41A Water St., Campbellton NB E3N 1A6
Tel: 506-759-7856
crcc@nbnet.nb.ca
www.facebook.com/517867708342924
Overview: A small local organization founded in 1985
Member of: Industrial Commission of Restigouche; NB Chamber of Commerce; Atlantic Provinces Chamber of Commerce; NB Economic Council
Affiliation(s): NB Chamber of Commerce; Atlantic Chamber of Commerce

Campground Owners Association of Nova Scotia (COANS)
c/o Tourism Industry Association of Nova Scotia, 2089 Maitland St., Halifax NS B3K 2Z8
Tel: 902-496-7474
www.campingnovascotia.com
Also Known As: Camping Nova Scotia
Overview: A medium-sized provincial organization founded in 1941 overseen by Canadian Camping Association
Mission: To provide the best camping experience possible throughout our diverse province; To improve standards at all the province's campgrounds; to provide leadership to this important segment of the provincial economy
Finances: *Funding Sources:* Membership dues; Conferences; Government grants
Chief Officer(s):
Jennifer Falkenham, General Manager
jennifer@tourism.ca

Camping Association of Nova Scotia *See* Camping Association of Nova Scotia & PEI

Camping Association of Nova Scotia & PEI (CANSPEI)
c/o Sports Nova Scotia, 5516 Spring Garden Rd., 4th Fl., Halifax NS B3J 1G6
Tel: 902-220-3280
info@canspei.ca
canspei.ca
www.facebook.com/CANSPEI
twitter.com/CANSPEI
Also Known As: Camping Association of NS & PEI
Previous Name: Camping Association of Nova Scotia
Overview: A medium-sized provincial organization founded in 1941 overseen by Canadian Camping Association
Mission: To support & serve the development of summer residential & organized camping in Nova Scotia & Prince Edward Island
Member of: Canadian Camping Association
Membership: *Fees:* $85; *Committees:* Awards & Recognition; Training & Education; Membership; Accreditation; Marketing & Advertising; New Program Development Grant
Activities: Camp accreditation; information about camping; training & education programs for professionals
Chief Officer(s):
Derek Mitchell, Executive Director
derekmitchell@venturepartner.ca

Camping in Ontario
#6, 1915 Clements Rd., Pickering ON L1W 3V1
Tel: 289-660-2192; *Fax:* 289-660-2146
Toll-Free: 877-672-2226
Other Communication: Tollfree Fax: 877-905-2714
info@campinginontario.ca
www.campinginontario.ca
www.facebook.com/CampingInOntario
twitter.com/CampInOntario
plus.google.com/+CampinginontarioCanada
Also Known As: Ontario Private Campground Association (OPCA)
Overview: A medium-sized provincial organization founded in 1969
Mission: To support & improve the operation of private campgrounds in Ontario by establishing standards, disseminating information & by representation in the tourist industry & at all levels of government
Member of: Tourism Industry Association of Canada; Tourism Federation of Ontario
Affiliation(s): Campgrounds Campings Canada; Go RVing Canada
Finances: *Funding Sources:* Member dues; sponsorship; educational activities
Staff Member(s): 4
Membership: 400+; *Fees:* Schedule available dependant on number of sites; *Member Profile:* Active - private campground operators who have legal authority to operate, have paid current annual dues & all other outstanding accounts owed to the association; Associate - person, firms, companies or organizations which provide products or services to the association or membership, & have paid current annual dues & all other outstanding accounts owed to the association; Affiliate - non-private parks, persons, firms, companies or organizations which do not provide products or services to the association or membership
Activities: Member education; marketing; advocacy; *Library*
Chief Officer(s):
Alexandra Anderson, Executive Director
opca@campinginontario.ca

Camping Québec
#700, 2001, rue de la Métropole, Longueuil QC J4G 1S9
Tél: 450-651-7396; *Téléc:* 450-651-7397
Ligne sans frais: 800-363-0457
www.campingquebec.com
Également appelé: Association des terrains de camping du Québec
Aperçu: *Dimension:* moyenne; *Envergure:* provinciale; fondée en 1962
Mission: Défendre les intérêts de nos membres; offrir des services de publications et promotion, des activitées, des escomptes sur achats et programmes divers.
Membre: *Critères d'admissibilité:* Exploitants de terrains de camping
Membre(s) du bureau directeur:
Natasha Bouchard, Présidente
Prix, Bourses:
- Prix de l'Excellence

Campus Gay Club (University of Manitoba) *See* Rainbow Resource Centre

CAMPUT (CAMPUT)
#646, 200 North Service Rd. West, Oakville ON L6M 2Y1
Tel: 905-827-5139; *Fax:* 905-827-3260
info@camput.org
www.camput.org
Also Known As: Canada's Energy & Utility Regulators
Previous Name: Canadian Association of Members of Public Utility Tribunals / Association canadienne des membres des tribunaux d'utilité publique
Overview: A medium-sized national organization founded in 1976
Mission: To improve public utility regulation in Canada
Affiliation(s): National Association of Regulatory Utility Commissioners (NARUC)
Membership: 14 member boards & commissions, & 7 associate member boards & commissions; *Member Profile:* Any Canadian tribunal, board, commission, or agency that is responsible for the economic regulation of utilities; Any Canadian energy tribunal, board, commission, or agency that makes binding decisions through adjudicative or quasi-judicial processes; *Committees:* Regulatory Affairs; Education
Activities: Educating & training commissioners & staff of public utility tribunals; Communicating with members; Liaising with parallel regulatory organizations
Chief Officer(s):
Terry Rochefort, Executive Director, 905-827-5139
rochefort@camput.org
Meetings/Conferences:
- 2018 CAMPUT Annual Conference, May, 2018, Royal York Hotel, Toronto, ON
Scope: National
Description: An annual event to address current regulatory issues & energy related subjects

Camrose & District Food Bank
PO Box 1936, 4524 - 54 St., Camrose AB T4V 1X8
Tel: 780-679-3220; *Fax:* 780-679-3221
nbaid@cable-lynx.net
Also Known As: Neighbourlink
Overview: A small local charitable organization founded in 1979 overseen by Food Banks Alberta Association
Mission: To provide food to those in need
Member of: Food Banks Alberta Association; World Vision
Finances: *Funding Sources:* Donations
Staff Member(s): 2; 500 volunteer(s)

Camrose Arts Society
Chuck MacLean Arts Centre, 5204 - 50 Ave., Camrose AB T4V 0S8
Tel: 780-672-4426; *Fax:* 780-672-2469
www.camrose.com
Overview: A small local charitable organization founded in 1979
Mission: To help people understand & value culture & the arts as integral to life
Member of: Alberta Municipal Association for Culture
Membership: *Fees:* Schedule available
Activities: Holding an art auction & Crafts Fest; Offering arts & recreation programs; *Library:* Open to public
Chief Officer(s):
Jane Cherry-Lemire, Arts Director
jcherry@camrose.ca

Camrose Association for Community Living (CAFCL)
Burgess Building, 4604 - 57 St., Camrose AB T4V 2E7
Tel: 780-672-0257; *Fax:* 780-672-7484
info@cafcl.org
www.cafcl.org
www.facebook.com/137368986301614
Overview: A medium-sized local charitable organization founded in 1962
Mission: To assist people to live in the community; a community that values & embraces all people
Member of: Alberta Association for Community Living; Alberta Association of Rehabilitation Centres
Finances: *Annual Operating Budget:* Greater than $5 Million
Staff Member(s): 101
Activities: Adult Residences; Adult Outreach; Respite Care; Skill Development; Rose Club - Drop In Centre; Fundraising; Sexuality Relationship; Parenting Support; Day Options Program; *Awareness Events:* Community Living Awareness Month; *Library:* Not open to public
Chief Officer(s):
Esther McDonald, CEO
Awards:
- Donor of the Year
- Volunteer of the Year

Camrose Chamber of Commerce
5402 - 48 Ave., Camrose AB T4V 0J7
Tel: 780-672-4217; *Fax:* 780-672-1059
www.camrosechamber.ca
www.facebook.com/CamroseChamberOfCommerce
Overview: A small local organization founded in 1908
Mission: To promote & maintain a proud & prosperous business community
Member of: Alberta Chamber of Commerce; Canadian Chamber of Commerce
Finances: *Funding Sources:* Membership dues; designated projects
Staff Member(s): 2
Membership: 390; *Fees:* Schedule available
Chief Officer(s):
Sharon Anderson, Executive Director
Tanya Fox, President
Awards:
- Jessie Burgess Memorial Award

Canada - Albania Business Council (CABC) / Conseil Commercial Canada - Albanie
#701, 165 University Ave., Toronto ON M5H 3B8
Tel: 416-979-1875; *Fax:* 416-979-0825
canadaalbaniabusinesscouncil.ca
Overview: A small local organization founded in 2010
Mission: To help encourage businesses to invest in & trade with Albania
Membership: *Fees:* $113 - $16,950; *Member Profile:* Corporations who support bilateral trade between Canada & Albania
Activities: Forums
Chief Officer(s):
Robert Baines, Executive Director
robert.baines@CanadaAlbaniaBusinessCouncil.ca
Abby Badwi, Chairman, Board of Directors

Canada - Newfoundland & Labrador Offshore Petroleum Board (C-NLOPB)
TD Place, #101, 140 Water St., St. John's NL A1C 6H6
Tel: 709-778-1400; *Fax:* 709-778-1473
information@cnlopb.ca
www.cnlopb.ca
twitter.com/CNLOPB
www.youtube.com/channel/UCooTeZWw7Bdgxeu7TzQQW4w
Mission: To apply the provisions of the *Atlantic Accord* & the *Atlantic Accord Implementation Acts* to all activities of operators in the Canada-Newfoundland & Labrador Offshore Area; To regulate the oil & gas industry for the Newfoundland & Labrador Offshore Area
Activities: Facilitating the exploration for & development of hydrocarbon resources; *Library:* Information Resources Centre
Chief Officer(s):
Scott Tessier, Chair & CEO
Ed Williams, Vice-Chair
Mike Baker, Director, Administration & Industrial Benefits
Dave Burley, Director, Environmental Affairs
Craig Rowe, Director, Exploration & Information Resources
Paul Alexander, Director & Chief Safety Officer, Safety

Jeff O'Keefe, Director & Chief Conservation Officer, Resource Management
John Kennedy, Director, Operations
Sean Kelly, Manager, Public Relations, 709-778-1418, Fax: 709-689-0713
skelly@cnlopb.ca
Publications:
• Canada - Newfoundland & Labrador Offshore Petroleum Board Annual Report
Type: Yearbook; *Frequency:* Annually
Profile: Contents include the board's role, objectives, & financial statements

Canada - Nova Scotia Offshore Petroleum Board (CNSOPB)
TD Centre, 1791 Barrington St., 8th Fl., Halifax NS B3J 3K9
Tel: 902-422-5588; *Fax:* 902-422-1799
info@cnsopb.ns.ca
www.cnsopb.ns.ca
twitter.com/CNSOPB
Mission: To regulate petroleum activities in the Nova Scotia Offshore Area
Activities: Issuing licences for offshore exploration & development; Collecting & distributing data
Chief Officer(s):
Stuart Pinks, P.Eng., Chief Executive Officer, 902-496-3206
spinks@cnsopb.ns.ca
Carl Makrides, Director, Resources, 902-496-0747
cmakrides@cnsopb.ns.ca
Christine Bonnell-Eisnor, Director, Regulatory Affairs & Finance, 902-496-0734
cbonnell@cnsopb.ns.ca
Shanti Dogra, General Counsel, 902-496-0736
sdogra@cnsopb.ns.ca
Troy MacDonald, Director, Information Services, 902-496-0734
tmacdonald@cnsopb.ns.ca
Stacy O'Rourke, Director, Communications, 902-410-6402
sorourke@cnsopb.ns.ca
Publications:
• Canada - Nova Scotia Offshore Petroleum Board Annual Report
Type: Yearbook; *Frequency:* Annually
Profile: A summary of offshore activities, healthy & safety initiatives, environmental protection, information services, & financial statements

Canada Bandy
Winnipeg MB
Overview: A small national organization
Mission: To govern the sport of bandy in Canada

Canada Basketball
#11, 1 Westside Dr., Toronto ON M9C 1B2
Tel: 416-614-8037; *Fax:* 416-614-9570
info@basketball.ca
www.basketball.ca
www.facebook.com/CanadaBasketball
twitter.com/CanBball
www.youtube.com/user/CanadaBasketball08
Also Known As: Canadian Basketball Association
Overview: A large national charitable organization founded in 1972
Mission: To develop the sport of basketball domestically & to contribute to the development of basketball internationally
Member of: International Basketball Federation
Affiliation(s): 10 provincial + 2 territorial associations; Canadian Interuniversity Athletic Union; Canadian Colleges Athletic Association; Canadian School Sports Federation; Toronto Raptors; Canadian Wheelchair Basketball Association; Canadian Association of Basketball Officials; National Association of Basketball Coaches of Canada; Women's Basketball Coaches Association
Staff Member(s): 32
Activities: National Teams; coaching programs; championships; direct mail; licensing; youth basketball programs; *Internships:* Yes
Chief Officer(s):
Michele O'Keefe, Executive Director
mokeefe@basketball.ca
Bryan Crawford, Senior Director, Operations
Maria-Leena Clarke, Director, Marketing & Partnerships
Andrea Driedger, Director, Finance

Canada BIM Council Inc.
PO Box 17017, Stn. Yonge-King, Toronto ON M5E 1Y2
Toll-Free: 877-778-5194
www.canbim.com
www.facebook.com/125791377505468
twitter.com/CanBIM
Also Known As: CanBIM
Overview: A small national organization
Mission: To serve & benefit members who work with Building Information Modeling (BIM) technologies in the fields of architecture, engineering, construction, building ownership & facility management, construction law & education
Membership: 53; *Fees:* $50-$25,000; *Committees:* Education; Technology; Trades; GC; Designers; Owners & FM; International; Marketing
Chief Officer(s):
Allan Partridge, President
Gerry Lattmann, Executive Director
glattmann@canbim.com

Canada Bulgaria Business Network
#1, 6 Hillholm Rd., Toronto ON M5P 1M2
info@canadabulgaria.com
www.canadabulgaria.com
Overview: A medium-sized national organization
Mission: To build & strengthen commercial & investment relations between Canada & Bulgaria; To unite Bulgaria-related companies & professionals; To assist members with business development
Membership: *Fees:* $100-$1,000 business; $50 individual; $25 student; *Committees:* Events; Membership
Activities: Offering networking & advertising opportunities; Organizing & providing educational & business seminars
Chief Officer(s):
Matey Nedkov, President

Canada China Business Council (CCBC) / Conseil commercial Canada Chine
#1501, 330 Bay St., Toronto ON M5H 2S8
Tel: 416-954-3800; *Fax:* 416-954-3806
ccbc@ccbc.com
www.ccbc.com
Previous Name: Canada-China Trade Council
Overview: A medium-sized international organization founded in 1978
Mission: To build business success in China & Canada by offering service & support, from direct operational support in China, to trade & investment advocacy on its members' behalf
Finances: *Funding Sources:* Corporations; Member dues
Membership: 200 Cdn. companies & organizations; *Fees:* Based on annual gross revenue; *Member Profile:* Companies, universities, non-profit corporations, government agencies; sectors ranging from agri-food, energy & manufacturing to business, legal & financial services, education & health care
Activities: Advice on export marketing; business consulting; joint venture negotiation; trade promotion; research; translation & interpretation; *Internships:* Yes; *Library:* Not open to public
Chief Officer(s):
Peter Kruyt, Chair
Sarah Kutulakos, Executive Director

Montréal Office
759, rue du Square-Victoria, #RC4, Montréal QC H2Y 2K3
Tel: 514-842-7837; *Fax:* 514-800-2189
Chief Officer(s):
Laurier Dubeau, Director
laurier@ccbc.com

Vancouver Office
#300, 1055 West Hastings St., Vancouver BC V6E 2E9
Tel: 604-681-8838
Chief Officer(s):
Lotta Ygartua, Director
lotta@ccbc.com

Canada Chinese Computer Association (CCCA)
PO Box 56551, Stn. Town Square, Markham ON L3R 0M6
Tel: 905-294-8891
ccca@theccca.com
www.theccca.com
Overview: A small national organization founded in 1993
Mission: To promote & protect the interests of Canada's Chinese computer business community
Affiliation(s): CCCA Charitable Foundation
Finances: *Funding Sources:* Membership fees; Income from events & services
Membership: *Fees:* $300 sponsors & directors; $50 voting members & media; *Member Profile:* Chinese computer business community in Canada
Activities: Communicating with members; Providing networking opportunities
Chief Officer(s):
Gordon Chan, President
John Tse, Vice-President
Eric Siu, Treasurer

Canada Cricket Umpires Association Inc. (CCUA)
ON
www.ccua.ca
Overview: A small national organization
Mission: To promote & advance cricket umpires throughout Canada.
Member of: West Indies Cricket Umpires Association

Canada Dance Festival Society
PO Box 1376, Stn. B, Ottawa ON K1P 5R4
Tel: 613-947-7000
info@canadadance.ca
www.canadadance.ca
www.facebook.com/Canadadancefest
twitter.com/canadadancefest
www.youtube.com/user/canadadancefestival
Overview: A small local charitable organization
Mission: To present diverse dance performances; To provide community networking & audience development
Staff Member(s): 6
Chief Officer(s):
Jeanne Holmes, Artistic Director
jholmes@canadadance.ca

Canada DanceSport (CDS)
www.dancesport.ca
www.facebook.com/262039667324976
Previous Name: Canadian Amateur DanceSport Association
Overview: A medium-sized national organization founded in 1978
Member of: World DanceSport Federation
Affiliation(s): World DanceSport Association
Chief Officer(s):
Sandy Brittain, President

Canada East Equipment Dealers' Association (CEEDA)
580 Bryne Dr, #C1, Barrie ON L4N 9P6
Tel: 705-726-2100; *Fax:* 705-726-2187
www.ceeda.ca
www.linkedin.com/groups/3210864/profile
www.facebook.com/189673951062605
twitter.com/ceedaCanadaEast
Previous Name: Ontario Retail Farm Equipment Dealers' Association
Overview: A medium-sized provincial organization founded in 1945
Mission: To promote the welfare of equipment trade retailers in the Maritimes & Ontario; To represent dealer interests in government legislation & regulation; To foster cooperation among manufacturers & distributors; To promote high standards for the retail equipment industry
Affiliation(s): North American Equipment Dealers' Association (NAEDA)
Membership: *Member Profile:* Farmstead, agricultural, powersport, & outdoor power equipment dealers from Ontario & the Maritimes
Activities: Liaising with educational institutions, equipment manufacturers, & provincial & federal governments; Providing training seminars; Collecting industry statistics; Disseminating timely information; Offering insurance counselling; Promoting safety
Chief Officer(s):
Craig Smith, Chair, 905-572-6714
oneils@mountaincable.net
Keith Stoltz, 1st Vice-Chair, 519-291-2151
keith@stoltzsales.com
Beverly J. Leavitt, President & CEO, 905-841-6888
bev@ceeda.ca
Carol Schoen, Secretary-Treasurer, 519-638-3317
cschoen2003@yahoo.com
Meetings/Conferences:
• Canada East Equipment Dealers' Association 2018 Annual Meeting & Convention, 2018
Scope: Provincial

Canada Employment & Immigration Union (CEIU) / Syndicat de l'emploi et de l'immigration du Canada (SEIC)
#1204, 275 Slater St., Ottawa ON K1P 5H9
Tel: 613-236-9634; *Fax:* 613-236-7871
Toll-Free: 855-271-3848

courchs@ceiu-seic.ca
ceiu-seic.ca
Overview: A large national organization founded in 1977 overseen by Public Service Alliance of Canada
Mission: To unite all the union members in the Canada Employment & Immigration Commission, the Department of Employment & Immigration & the Immigration Appeal Board, & anyone who wishes to join in a single union acting on their behalf by processing appeals & grievances; To unite all members by fostering an understanding of the fundamental differences between the interests of the members & those of the employer; To assure a union presence at the workplace through collective strength of membership
Membership: 21,702 + 279 locals; *Member Profile:* Co-workers in Canada Employment & Immigration Commission; Immigration Refugee Board; *Committees:* Call Centres'; Human Rights/Race Relations; Immigration & Refugee Board; Citizenship & Immigration Advisory
Chief Officer(s):
Marco Angeli, National President, 613-236-9634 Ext. 222
angelim@ceiu-seic.ca
Michelle Henderson, National Executive Vice-President, 613-236-9634 Ext. 223
hendersonm@ceiu-seic.ca
Awards:
- CEIU National Scholarships

British Columbia & Yukon Regional Office
#530, 789 West Pender St., Vancouver BC V6C 1H2
Tel: 604-436-3120; *Fax:* 833-240-7871
Toll-Free: 800-663-3151
bcytruo@ceiu-seic.ca
Chief Officer(s):
Steve Claxton, National Union Representative
claxtons@ceiu-seic.ca
Kathy Sand, National Union Representative
sandk@ceiu-seic.ca

Bureaux régionaux du Québec
#405, 1255, rue Carré Philips, Montréal QC H3B 3G1
Tél: 514-861-7342; *Téléc:* 514-861-7343
Ligne sans frais: 800-361-2871
Chief Officer(s):
Guy Boulanger, Représentant syndical sénior
boulang@ceiu-seic.ca
Sylvain Archambault, Représentant syndical national
archams@ceiu-seic.ca
Genadi Voinerchuk, Représentant syndical national
voinerchukg@ceiu-seic.ca

Manitoba, Saskatchewan, Alberta, Northwest Territories & Nunavut Regional Office
#402, 275 Broadway Ave., Winnipeg MB R3C 4M6
Tel: 204-957-1455; *Fax:* 204-943-0826
Toll-Free: 888-875-9576
Chief Officer(s):
Pamela Meier-Duthie, National Union Representative, Manitoba & Saskatchewan
meierduthiep@ceiu-seic.ca
Wes Todd, National Union Representative, Alberta, NWT & Nunavut
toddw@ceiu-seic.ca

New Brunswick & Prince Edward Island Regional Office
#206, 272 St. George St., Moncton NB E1C 1W5
Tel: 506-857-2220; *Fax:* 506-857-0848
Toll-Free: 888-441-5022
Chief Officer(s):
Mona Daigle, National Union Representative
daiglem@ceiu-seic.ca
Jérémie Leblanc, Administrative Assistant, NB, NS, PEI & NL
leblanj@ceiu-seic.ca

Newfoundland & Labrador Regional Office
PO Box 3123, Paradise NL A1L 3W3
Tel: 709-782-2622; *Fax:* 709-782-2644
Toll-Free: 866-782-2622
Chief Officer(s):
Denise Richey, National Union Representative
richeyd@ceiu-seic.ca

Nova Scotia Regional Office
Halifax NS
Tel: 902-455-7085; *Fax:* 902-455-2128
Toll-Free: 877-498-0277
Chief Officer(s):
Sharon Barbour, National Union Representative
barbous@ceiu-seic.ca

Ontario Regional Office
#1720, 2 Carlton St., Toronto ON M5B 1J3
Tel: 416-488-3000; *Fax:* 416-488-8319
Toll-Free: 800-268-8809
Chief Officer(s):
Todd Ferguson, National Union Representative
fergust@ceiu-seic.ca
Ram Sivapalan, National Union Representative
sivapar@ceiu-seic.ca
Chris Sloan, National Union Representative
sloanc@ceiu-seic.ca

Canada Eurasia Russia Business Association (CERBA)
1 First Canadian Place, #1600, 100 King St. West, Toronto ON M5X 1G5
Tel: 416-862-4403; *Fax:* 416-862-7661
www.cerbanet.org
ww.linkedin.com/company/canada-eurasia-russia-business-association
Overview: A medium-sized international organization founded in 1997
Mission: To enhance & support trade, investment, & good relations between Canada, Russia, & Eurasia; To act as the voice of Canadian business in Russia & Eurasia; to expand Canadian business activity in Eurasia
Finances: *Funding Sources:* Sponsors
Membership: 200+; *Member Profile:* Corporations; Individuals
Activities: Promoting bilateral business growth; Advocating & lobbying on government policy; Offering trade missions to & from Canada, Russia, & Eurasia; Providing networking opportunities; Offering seminars, conferences, & roundtables; Providing market intelligence & marketing; Partnering with organizations; *Awareness Events:* Annual Charity Auction
Chief Officer(s):
Lou Naumovski, National Chair
Katherine Balabanova, Regional Director, Toronto
Publications:
- CERBA [Canada Eurasia Russia Business Association] Newsletter
Type: Newsletter; *Frequency:* Quarterly; *Editor:* Elena Settles
Profile: CERBA events & news

Canada Fitness Survey (1985) *See* Canadian Fitness & Lifestyle Research Institute

Canada Foundation for Innovation (CFI) / Fondation canadienne pour l'innovation (FCI)
#450, 230 Queen St. East, Ottawa ON K1P 5E4
Tel: 613-947-6496; *Fax:* 613-943-2581
feedback@innovation.ca
www.innovation.ca
www.linkedin.com/company/canada-foundation-for-innovation
www.facebook.com/innovationincanada
twitter.com/innovationca
www.youtube.com/user/InnovationCanada
Overview: A small local organization founded in 1997
Mission: To fund research infrastructure; To strengthen the capacity of Canadian universities, colleges, research hospitals, & non-profit research institutions to carry out world-class research & technology development to benefit Canadians; To support economic growth; To increase job opportunities; To promote collaboration among research institutions in Canada
Finances: *Funding Sources:* Government
Staff Member(s): 75
Chief Officer(s):
Gilles G. Patry, President & CEO, 613-947-7260
Pierre Normand, Vice-President, External Relations & Communications, 613-943-0211
Manon Harvey, Vice-President, Finance & Corporate Services
manon.harvey@innovation.ca
Guy Levesque, Vice-President, Programs & Performance
Publications:
- Canada Foundation for Innovation / Fondation canadienne pour l'innovation Annual Report
Type: Yearbook; *Frequency:* Annually; *ISSN:* 1712-0608; *ISBN:* 978-0-9784394-1-5

Canada Fox Breeders' Association
c/o Melanie Williams, 30 Tanya Cres., Moncton NB E1E 4W5
Tel: 506-388-2087
cfba@nb.sympatico.ca
www.clrc.ca/foxes.shtml
Overview: A small national organization founded in 1920
Mission: To improve, advance, & protect the Canadian ranched fox industry; To assist breeders & producers of foxes in Canada
Affiliation(s): Canadian Livestock Records Corporation
Membership: *Fees:* $15 / year; *Member Profile:* Applicants for membership must own at least one ranch fox; *Committees:* Executive; Registration; Finance; Marketing & Promotion; Research & Development
Activities: Keeping a record of the breeding & origin of all purebred foxes bred in captivity; Promoting fox pelts; Assisting members with marketing
Chief Officer(s):
Melanie Williams, Secretary-Treasurer
Lorna Woolsey, Registrar, Canadian Livestock Records Corporation, 613-731-7110 Ext. 306
lorna.woolsey@clrc.ca

Canada Games Council (CGC) / Conseil des jeux du Canada
#701, 2197 Riverside Dr., Ottawa ON K1H 7X3
Tel: 613-526-2320; *Fax:* 613-526-4068
canada.games@canadagames.ca
www.canadagames.ca
www.facebook.com/CanadaGames
twitter.com/CanadaGames
www.youtube.com/cgc1967;
instagram.com/canadagamescouncil
Overview: A medium-sized national organization founded in 1967
Mission: The Canada Games Council is a well-established, national organization that fosters on-going partnerships with organizations at the municipal, provincial and national levels. It allocates resources in support of the following mission and strategic directions.
Finances: *Annual Operating Budget:* $250,000-$500,000; *Funding Sources:* Federal Government (operation costs); Federal Government, Provincial Government & host city (capital).
Staff Member(s): 9. 5000 volunteer(s)
Membership: *Committees:* Sport; Marketing; Communications; Operations
Activities: *Internships:* Yes
Chief Officer(s):
Sue Hylland, Chief Executive Officer
shylland@canadagames.ca
Patrick Kenny, Director, Marketing & Communications
pkenny@canadagames.ca

Canada Grains Council (CGC)
#476, 167 Lombard Ave., Winnipeg MB R3B 0T6
Tel: 204-925-2130; *Fax:* 204-956-9506
office@canadagrainscouncil.ca
www.canadagrainscouncil.ca
Overview: A large national organization founded in 1969
Mission: To be the primary networking group for those involved in the grain industry
Membership: 30 organizations; *Committees:* Management; Planning
Chief Officer(s):
Patti Miller, Chair
Mark Brock, Vice-Chair
Tyler Bjornson, President
president@canadagrainscouncil.ca
Meetings/Conferences:
- Canada Grains Council Canadian Global Crops Symposium 2018, March, 2018, Westin Harbour Castle, Toronto, ON
Scope: National

Canada Green Building Council (CaGBC) / Conseil du bâtiment durable du Canada (CBDCa)
#202, 47 Clarence St., Ottawa ON K1N 9K1
Tel: 613-241-1184; *Fax:* 613-241-4782
Toll-Free: 866-941-1184
info@cagbc.org
www.cagbc.org
www.linkedin.com/groups?mostPopular=&gid=1333997
www.facebook.com/CanadaGreenBuilding
twitter.com/CaGBC
www.youtube.com/user/CaGBC
Overview: A small national organization founded in 2002
Mission: To create buildings, homes, & communities across Canada that are environmentally responsible & high-performing; To advocate for green buildings
Finances: *Funding Sources:* Sponsorships
Activities: Developing best design practices; Providing educational materials for members
Chief Officer(s):
Andrew McAllan, Chair
Thomas Mueller, President & CEO
Sarah Burns, Vice-President, Communications & Marketing
sburns@cagbc.org

Canada Health Infoway / Inforoute Santé du Canada

Meetings/Conferences:
• Canada Green Building Council 2018 National Conference, 2018
Scope: National

Canada Health Infoway / Inforoute Santé du Canada
#1200, 1000, rue Sherbrooke ouest, Montréal QC H3A 3G4
Tel: 514-868-0550; *Fax:* 514-868-1120
Toll-Free: 866-868-0550
www.infoway-inforoute.ca
www.linkedin.com/company/canada-health-infoway
www.facebook.com/CanadaHealthInfoway
twitter.com/infoway
www.youtube.com/user/InfowayInforoute
Overview: A medium-sized national organization founded in 2001
Mission: To accelerate the development of compatible electronic health information systems, which provide healthcare professionals with rapid access to complete & accurate patient information, enabling better decisions about diagnosis & treatment
Finances: *Funding Sources:* Federal funding
Membership: *Member Profile:* Federal, provincial & territorial deputy ministers of health
Activities: Working to accelerate the implementation of electonic health record (EHR)
Chief Officer(s):
Michael Green, President & CEO

Halifax
#125, 200 Waterfront Dr., Bedford NS B4A 4J4
Tel: 902-832-0876; *Fax:* 902-835-4719
Toll-Free: 877-832-0876
Mission: To foster and accelerate the development and adoption of electronic health information systems with compatible standards and communications technologies on a pan-Canadian basis, with tangible benefits to Canadians; and to build on existing initiatives.

Toronto
#1300, 150 King St. West, Toronto ON M5H 1J9
Tel: 416-979-4606; *Fax:* 416-593-5911
Toll-Free: 888-733-6462
Mission: To foster and accelerate the development and adoption of electronic health information systems with compatible standards and communications technologies on a pan-Canadian basis, with tangible benefits to Canadians; and to build on existing initiatives.

Vancouver
Commerce Place, #1120, 400 Burrard St., Vancouver BC V6C 3A6
Tel: 604-682-0420; *Fax:* 604-682-8034
Toll-Free: 877-682-0420
Mission: To foster and accelerate the development and adoption of electronic health information systems with compatible standards and communications technologies on a pan-Canadian basis, with tangible benefits to Canadians; and to build on existing initiatives.

Canada India Village Aid Association (CIVA)
1822 West 2nd Ave., Vancouver BC V6J 1H9
projects@civaid.ca
www.civaid.ca
Overview: A small international charitable organization founded in 1981
Mission: To raise funds to support anti-poverty projects benefiting the peoples of rural India; to foster self-help & self-reliance, particularly through sustainable development & women's empowerment, collaborating with Indian non-profit agencies & organizations in various fields of development, education, health care, & environmental concern.
50 volunteer(s)
Activities: Health training programs; irrigation projects
Chief Officer(s):
Ashok Kotwal, Contact

Canada Israel Experience Centre (CIEC)
#220, 4600 Bathurst St., Toronto ON M2R 3V3
Tel: 416-398-6931; *Fax:* 416-631-6373
Toll-Free: 800-567-4772
ciec@ujafed.org
www.canadaisraelexperience.com
Overview: A small national organization
Mission: To maximize the number of young Canadian Jews participating in formal & informal educational experiences in Israel; to provide information on summer tours, kibbutz programs, Israel-related community activities, accredited programs & long-term stays in Israel
Affiliation(s): United Israel Appeal of Canada; CRB Foundation
Activities: Israel summer programs for youth; referrals to other programs with other organizations

Canada Korea Business Association (CKBA)
#2900, 550 Burrard St., Vancouver BC V6C 0A3
Tel: 604-631-3217; *Fax:* 604-631-3232
info@ckba.org
ckba.org
www.facebook.com/ckba.org
twitter.com/CkbaOrg
Overview: A small international organization founded in 1972
Mission: To increase understanding between business communities in Canada & Korea; To promote trade & capital investment between Canada & Korea
Finances: *Funding Sources:* Membership fees; Sponsorships; Donations
Staff Member(s): 13
Membership: *Fees:* $30 student; $110 individual; $350 corporate; *Member Profile:* Canadian companies that sell goods & services to Korea; Korean companies with branch offices in Canada; Service organizations, such as financial & legal organizations; Cultural organizations
Activities: Promoting technical cooperation & cultural educational relationships between Canada & Korea; Organizing a delegation visit to Korea each autumn; Hosting delegations from Korea in the areas of investment & trade; Arranging guest speakers, such as ambassadors, politicians, & business leaders; Donating to Korea related charities
Chief Officer(s):
John C.H. Kim, President & Secretary
Richard Hall, Vice-President
Jay Oh, Chief Financial Officer
Awards:
• Canada Korea Business Association Scholarship
To assist university students in British Columbia, who are studying Korean language & culture

Canada Media Fund (CMF)
#4, 50 Wellington St. East, Toronto ON M5E 1C8
Tel: 416-214-4400; *Fax:* 416-214-4420
Toll-Free: 877-975-0766
info@cmf-fmc.ca
www.cmf-fmc.ca
www.facebook.com/cmf.fmc
twitter.com/cmf_fmc
Overview: A medium-sized national organization
Mission: To provide funding to Canada's television & digital media industries through the following two streams: Experimental & Convergent.
Chief Officer(s):
Louis L. Roquet, Chair
Valerie Creighton, President & CEO
Stéphane Cardin, Vice-President, Industry & Public Affairs
Sandra Collins, Vice-President & CFO, Operations

Canada Nature *See* Nature Canada

Canada Organic Trade Association (COTA) / Association pour le commerce des produits biologiques (ACPB)
#7519, 1145 Carling Ave., Ottawa ON K1Z 7K4
Tel: 613-482-1717; *Fax:* 613-236-0743
www.ota.com/canada-ota
www.linkedin.com/company/organic-trade-association
www.facebook.com/OrganicTrade
twitter.com/OrganicTrade
Overview: A large national organization founded in 1985
Mission: To promote & protect the growth of organic trade in Canada; to benefit organic farmers, consumers, the environment & the economy; to provide information on ingredients, sourcing, certification, marketing, imports & exports, & a range of other concerns
Membership: *Fees:* Schedule available; *Member Profile:* Businesses engaged in the production, distribution, certification & promotion of organic products, including growers, shippers, importers & exporters, consultants, retailers & others supportive of organic agriculture & trade; *Committees:* COTA Advisory
Activities: *Awareness Events:* Parliament Day
Chief Officer(s):
Tia Loftsgard, Executive Director
tloftsgard@ota.com

Canada Porc International *See* Canada Pork International

Canada Pork International (CPI) / Canada Porc International
#900, 220 Laurier Ave. West, Ottawa ON K1P 5Z9
Tel: 613-236-9886; *Fax:* 613-236-6656
cpi@canadapork.com
www.canadapork.com
Overview: A medium-sized international organization founded in 1991
Mission: To carry out its responsibilities as the export development agency of the Canadian pork industry; To develop & implement international promotional efforts
Affiliation(s): Canadian Meat Council; Canadian Pork Council
Activities: Providing information to foreign customers about Canadian pork products; Liaising with the federal government & trading partners in matters of foreign market access issues; Informing the Canadian industry about changes in export markets
Chief Officer(s):
Martin Lavoie, President & CEO
Michael Young, Vice-President, Technical Programs & Marketing Services
young@canadapork.com
Joan Champagne, Finance Officer
César Urias, Director, Market Access & Government Programs Management
Kevin Mosser, Director, National Marketing
mosser@canadapork.com

Canada Safety Council (CSC) / Conseil canadien de la sécurité (CCS)
1020 Thomas Spratt Pl., Ottawa ON K1G 5L5
Tel: 613-739-1535; *Fax:* 613-739-1566
csc@safety-council.org
www.canadasafetycouncil.org
www.facebook.com/canada.safety
twitter.com/CanadaSafetyCSC
Overview: A large national charitable organization founded in 1968
Membership: *Fees:* $50 Individual; $250+ Corporate; $1,000+ Sustaining
Chief Officer(s):
Jack Smith, President
Raynard Marchand, General Manager, Programs
Publications:
• Safety Canada Online [a publication of Canada Safety Council]
Type: Newsletter; *Frequency:* q.
Profile: Electronic newsletter available to members & on the CSC website.

Canada Sans Pauvreté *See* Canada Without Poverty

Canada Saut à Ski *See* Ski Jumping Canada

Canada Sheep Council *See* Canadian Sheep Federation

Canada Taiwan Trade Association (CTTA)
#450, 1090 West Georgia St., Vancouver BC V6E 3V7
Tel: 604-682-2848; *Fax:* 604-285-3601
ctta@intergate.ca
Overview: A small international organization founded in 1988
Mission: To establish an active network of business contacts to develop trade and investment opportunities between Tawainese investors & local business communities; to promote a mutual understanding & an exchanging of business and cultural information between the various business broups of Canada & Taiwan.
Activities: Meetings; trade mission; trade show; golf tournament

Canada Tibet Committee (CTC)
1425, boul René-Lévesque ouest, 3e étage, Montréal QC H3G 1T7
Tel: 514-487-0665
ctcoffice@tibet.ca
www.tibet.ca
www.facebook.com/CanadaTibet
twitter.com/canadatibet
www.youtube.com/tibetchannel
Overview: A large national organization founded in 1987
Mission: To defend & promote human rights & democratic freedoms of Tibetan people; To encourage support for Tibet from the government of Canada
Finances: *Funding Sources:* Membership dues, Donations; Fundraising
Activities: *Library:* Dharma Resource Centre
Chief Officer(s):
Carole Samdup, Executive Director

Canada West Equipment Dealers Association (CWEDA)
2435 Pegasus Rd. NE, Calgary AB T2E 8C3
Tel: 403-250-7581; *Fax:* 403-291-5138
info@cweda.ca
www.cweda.ca
www.linkedin.com/groups/Canada-West-Equipment-Dealers-Association
twitter.com/cweda
www.youtube.com/user/CWEDA1
Also Known As: Canada West
Overview: A small provincial organization founded in 1941
Mission: To represent equipment dealers in Manitoba, Saskatchewan, Alberta & British Columbia; to provide its members with industry intelligence, business support, & acts as their voice in industry & manufacturer relations.
Member of: North American Equipment Dealers Association
Finances: *Funding Sources:* Membership fees; association services
Staff Member(s): 5
Membership: *Fees:* $500 dealer; $600 associate; *Member Profile:* Farm, industrial & outdoor power equipment dealers
Chief Officer(s):
Cameron Bode, President
bodecameron@southcountry.ca
John Schmeiser, Executive Vice-President & CEO
Awards:
• Merit Award (Dealer of the Year)
• Safety & Loss Control Award
• Outstanding Dealership Award

Canada West Foundation (CWF)
#110, 134 - 11th Ave. SE, Calgary AB T2G 0X5
Tel: 403-264-9535
Toll-Free: 888-825-5293
cwf@cwf.ca
www.cwf.ca
www.linkedin.com/company/2262878
twitter.com/CanadaWestFdn
Overview: A medium-sized local charitable organization founded in 1971
Mission: A leading source of strategic insight, conducting and communicating non-partisan economic and public policy research of importance to the four western provinces and all Canadians.
Finances: *Annual Operating Budget:* $1.5 Million-$3 Million; *Funding Sources:* Individuals; Corporations; Foundations; Governments
Staff Member(s): 18
Membership: 26 Board Members; *Fees:* $200 annual; $50 friends
Activities: Conducting research projects; *Internships:* Yes; *Speaker Service:* Yes; *Library:* Not open to public
Chief Officer(s):
Martha Hall Findlay, President & Chief Executive Officer
Colleen Collins, Vice-President, Research
collins@cwf.ca
Hector Humphrey, Director, Finance & Administration
humphrey@cwf.ca
Jamie Gradon, Manager, Communications
gradon@cwf.ca
Publications:
• Currents
Type: Bulletin; *Frequency:* Monthly; *Editor:* Doug Firby
Profile: Currents is a quarterly update on the state of the economy in Canada's four western provinces. It is sponsored by Canadian Western Bank.
• Window on the West
Type: Magazine; *Frequency:* Quarterly
Profile: Western economic issues & policies

Canada West Universities Athletic Association
PO Box 78090, Stn. Northside, Port Coquitlam BC V3B 7H5
Tel: 604-475-1213; *Fax:* 604-475-1997
sportsinfo@canadawest.org
www.canadawest.org
Overview: A small local organization
Mission: To organize inter-collegiate sporting events between members
Staff Member(s): 4
Membership: 17 universities; *Member Profile:* Western Canadian universities
Chief Officer(s):
Diane St. Denis, Executive Director
dstdenis@canadawest.org

Canada Without Poverty / Canada Sans Pauvreté
251 Bank St., 2nd Fl., Ottawa ON K2P 1X3
Tel: 613-789-0096; *Fax:* 613-566-3449
Toll-Free: 800-810-1076
info@cwp-csp.ca
www.cwp-csp.ca
www.facebook.com/106633876058589
twitter.com/CWP_CSP
Previous Name: National Anti-Poverty Organization
Overview: A medium-sized national charitable organization founded in 1971
Mission: To eradicate poverty in Canada by promoting income and social security for all Canadians, and by promoting poverty eradication as a human rights obligation.
Affiliation(s): Citizens for Public Justice; Public Interest Law Centre; Amnesty International Canada; Assembly of First Nations; Canadian Association of Social Workers; Canadian Co-operative Assocation; Canadian Council on Social Development; Canadian Labour Congress & a number of labour unions/organizations
Staff Member(s): 2
Activities: Dignity for All: The Campaign for a Poverty-free Canada; *Speaker Service:* Yes; *Library:* Resource Centre; Open to public by appointment
Chief Officer(s):
Leilani Farha, Executive Director
Megan Yarema, Director, Education & Outreach

Canada World Youth (CWY) / Jeunesse Canada Monde (JCM)
#300, 2330, rue Notre-Dame ouest, Montréal QC H3J 1N4
Tel: 514-931-3526; *Fax:* 514-939-2621
Toll-Free: 800-605-3526
info@cwy-jcm.org
www.canadaworldyouth.org
fr-fr.facebook.com/CanadaWorldYouth.JeunesseCanadaMonde
twitter.com/cwyjcm
Overview: A large international charitable organization founded in 1971
Mission: To increase people's ability to participate actively in the development of just, harmonious & sustainable societies; To create exceptional learning opportunities for communities, groups & individuals wishing to acquire skills & explore new ideas.
Member of: Canadian Council for International Cooperation; Youth Net International
Affiliation(s): World Assembly of Youth
Finances: *Annual Operating Budget:* Greater than $5 Million; *Funding Sources:* CIDA, fundraising activities; diversification programs.
Staff Member(s): 160; 3950 volunteer(s)
Activities: Youth Exchange Program (ages 17-20); Work Partner Program (ages 18-29); Customized Program; Joint Ventures Program; Other services include human resource development; north-south cooperation; educational exchanges; leadership & intercultural training; development education; group travel.; *Internships:* Yes
Chief Officer(s):
Louis Moubarak, President & CEO
Awards:
• Outstanding Canadian CWY Alumni Award
; *Amount:* $3,000
• Youth Innovation Award
; *Amount:* $3,000
• Outstanding Overseas CWY Alumni Award
; *Amount:* $3,000

Toronto Office
#602, 130 Spadina Ave., Toronto ON M5V 2L4
Toll-Free: 800-605-3526

Canada's Accredited Zoos & Aquariums (CAZA) / Aquariums et zoos accrédités du Canada (AZAC)
#400, 280 Metcalfe St., Ottawa ON K2P 1R7
Tel: 613-567-0099; *Fax:* 613-233-5438
Toll-Free: 888-822-2907
info@caza.ca
www.caza.ca
www.linkedin.com/company/canada's-accredited-zoos-and-aquariums---aquariums-et-zoos-accr-dit-s-du-canada
www.facebook.com/CAZA.AZAC
Previous Name: Canadian Association of Zoos & Aquariums
Overview: A medium-sized national charitable organization founded in 1975
Mission: To promote the welfare of animals; To provide input into legislative matters & government policy affecting the zoo & aquarium industry
Member of: IUCN, International Union for Conservation of Nature; The World Association of Zoos & Aquariums; Canadian Museums Association
Finances: *Funding Sources:* Donations
Membership: *Fees:* $55 associate; $65 professional; $25 student & retired professional; $250 supporting institutional; $400 commercial; schedule for educational; *Member Profile:* Zoo & aquarium professionals; *Committees:* Executive; Nominating; Ethics; Awards; Conservation & Education; National Awareness; Policy; Accreditation; Business Development; Government Relations; Membership Services; Finance; Arctic Biodiversity; Conference
Activities: Administering the CAZA Accreditation Program; Upholding the CAZA Code of Professional Ethics; Promoting education; Offering a mentoring program for institutions
Chief Officer(s):
Massimo Bergamini, Executive Director
Awards:
• Thomas Baines Award
Awarded to recognize outstanding achievement by a member in exhibit design, animal husbandry, or education
• Eleanor Oakes Award
Awarded to recognize outstanding achievement by a member in exhibit design, animal husbandry, or education on a smaller scale & budget
• Peter Karsten Conservation Award
Awarded to honour achievement in the field of conservation by a member or member institution
• Col. G.D. Dailley Award
Awarded to recognize achievement in propagation & management programs that contribute to the survival of at-risk animal populations
• Animal Enrichment Award
Awarded to recognize the creativity of design & implementation of an initiative that fosters animal enrichment through the creation of a positive environment that respects the species' needs
• Zoo & Aquarium Professional Award
Awarded to honour contributions to the zoo & aquarium field by a permanent staff member employed at a member institution
• Volunteer of the Year
Awarded to recognize the valuable contribution a volunteer has made to a member institution of CAZA/AZAC
• Certificate of Merit
Awarded to recognize & thank individuals for their outstanding contributions to CAZA/AZAC institutions
Meetings/Conferences:
• Canada's Accredited Zoos & Aquariums Annual Conference 2018, 2018
Scope: National
Description: A meeting of members to vote on the business of the association
Publications:
• Canadian Association of Zoos & Aquariums Membership Directory
Type: Directory
Profile: A listing of institutional, commercial, & affiliate members of the Canadian Association of Zoos & Aquariums
• CAZA [Canadian Association of Zoos & Aquariums] News
Type: Newsletter; *Frequency:* Bimonthly; *Editor:* G. Tarry; *Price:* Free with Canadian Association of Zoos & Aquariums membership
• CAZA [Canadian Association of Zoos & Aquariums] Annual Report
Type: Yearbook; *Frequency:* Annually
• Connecting Canadians to Nature: Strategic Plan [a publication of the Canadian Association of Zoos & Aquariums
Type: Report; *Number of Pages:* 16

Canada's Advanced Internet Development Organization (CANARIE)
#500, 45 O'Connor St., Ottawa ON K1P 1A4
Tel: 613-943-5454; *Fax:* 613-943-5443
info@canarie.ca
www.canarie.ca
www.linkedin.com/groups?mostPopular=&gid=3712846
www.facebook.com/CanarieInc
twitter.com/CANARIE_Inc
Overview: A medium-sized national organization founded in 1993
Mission: Canada's advanced internet development organization; to facilitate & promote the development of Canada's communications infrastructure; to stimulate next-generation products, applications & services; to communicate the benefits of an information-based society.

Canadian Associations / Canada's Aviation Hall of Fame (CAHF)

CANARIE also intends to act as a catalyst and partner with governments, industry and the research community to increase overall IT awareness, ensure continuing promotion of Canadian technological excellence and ultimately, foster long-term productivity and improvement of living standards.
Finances: *Funding Sources:* Government
Staff Member(s): 22
Membership: 100
Activities: Core programs: Advanced Networks; E-Business; E-Content; E-Health; E-Learning; *Speaker Service:* Yes
Chief Officer(s):
Jim Ghadbane, President & CEO, 613-944-5603
jim.ghadbane@canarie.ca
Nancy E. Carter, Chief Financial Officer, 613-943-5437
nancy.carter@canarie.ca
Awards:
• CANARIE IWAY Awards

Canada's Aviation Hall of Fame (CAHF)
PO Box 6090, Wetaskiwin AB T9A 2G1
Tel: 780-361-1351; *Fax:* 780-361-1239
Toll-Free: 800-661-4726
cahf2@telus.net
www.cahf.ca
www.facebook.com/CanadasAviationHallofFame1
www.youtube.com/user/cahf1973
Overview: A small national charitable organization founded in 1973
Mission: To preserve & publicize the names & deeds of those who have made a significant contribution to Canadian aviation; to house an extensive collection of personal items & memorabilia, as well as a library of about 2,500 books & over 12,000 periodicals.
Member of: Canadian Museums Association; Alberta Museums Association; Canadian Aeronautical Preservation Association
Membership: *Committees:* Operations
Activities: Annual induction ceremonies, May/June; *Library:* Documentation Centre; Open to public by appointment
Chief Officer(s):
Tom Appleton, Chair
Awards:
• Belt of Orion
Eligibility: An organization, group, society or association who has made an outstanding contribution to the advancement of aviation in Canada

Canada's History / Histoire Canada
PO Box 118, Stn. Main, Markham ON L3P 3J5
Tel: 905-946-8790; *Fax:* 905-946-1679
Toll-Free: 888-816-0997
memberservices@canadashistory.ca
www.canadashistory.ca
www.facebook.com/CanadasHistory
twitter.com/canadashistory
www.youtube.com/canadashistory;
www.flickr.com/photos/canadas_history
Previous Name: Canada's National History Society
Overview: A large national charitable organization founded in 1995
Mission: To promote greater popular interest in Canadian history
Finances: *Annual Operating Budget:* $1.5 Million-$3 Million; *Funding Sources:* Subscriptions; grants; corporate & individual support
Staff Member(s): 12
Membership: 47,004
Activities: *Rents Mailing List:* Yes; *Library:* by appointment
Chief Officer(s):
Janet Walker, President & CEO
jwalker@canadashistory.ca
Danielle Chartier, Manager, Marketing & Circulation
dchartier@canadashistory.ca
Joel Ralph, Director, Programs
jralph@canadashistory.ca
Awards:
• Governor General's History Award for Community Programming
Awarded to volunteer-led community organizations for creating innovating programming to commemorate Canadian heritage
Deadline: August 14; *Amount:* 2 awards of $2,500 (English & French)
• Governor General's History Award for Museums
• Governor General's History Award for Popular Media
Awarded to individuals who introduced historical Canadian characters & events to the national & international public; *Amount:* $5,000 & a medal
• Governor General's History Award for Scholarly Research
Awarded for a non-fiction work of Canadian history published in the last year that made the most significant contribution to an understanding of the Canadian past; *Amount:* $5,000
• Governor General's History Awards for Excellence in Teaching
Deadline: April 1; *Amount:* 6 prizes of $2,500 & the recipient's school will also receive $1,000
• Kayak Kids' Illustrated History Challenge, Student Awards
Eligibility: Children 7-14 years of age who have drawn comics or written illustrated stories about a topic in Canadian history
• Canadian Aboriginal Writing & Arts Challenge, Student Awards
Eligibility: Ages 14-29
Publications:
• Canada's History
Type: Magazine; *Frequency:* 6 pa; *Accepts Advertising*; *ISSN:* 1920-9894; *Price:* $32.95
• Kayak [a publication of Canada's History]
Type: Magazine; *Frequency:* 6 pa; *Price:* $16.95
Profile: For children from ages 7 to 11

Canada's Medical Technology Companies / Les Sociétés Canadiennes de Technologies Médicales
#900, 405 The West Mall, Toronto ON M9C 5J1
Tel: 416-620-1915
Toll-Free: 866-586-3332
www.medec.org
Also Known As: MEDEC
Previous Name: Association de l'industrie des technologies de la santé
Overview: A large national organization founded in 1987
Mission: To advocate for the adoption & use of medical technology by healthcare systems in Canada
Membership: *Committees:* Cardiovascular; Credentialing; Environment Protection; Federal Affairs; Health Technology; Human Resources; LabCANDx Steering; Laboratory/Medicine; Medical Imaging; Ontario; Procurement; Regulatory Affairs; Québec; Valeur de l'innovation; Vision Care; Western Canada; Wound Care
Activities: Promoting the medical technology industry; Acting as a liaison with federal & provincial governments, industry partners, stakeholders, & the public; Offering education activities, networking, support, & information; Providing advice on medical device regulations in Canada
Chief Officer(s):
Brian Lewis, President & CEO
ceo@medec.org
Iris Crawford, Vice-President, Finance & Operations
Nicole DeKort, Vice-President, Government Affairs
Klaus Stitz, Vice-President, Regulatory Affairs
Gerry Frenette, Executive Director, Public & Member Relations
Debbie Gates, Manager, Events & Education
Natasha Alves, Administrative Coordinator
Publications:
• ePULSE [a publication of Canada's Medical Technology Companies]
Type: Newsletter; *Frequency:* Weekly
• PULSE [a publication of Canada's Medical Technology Companies]
Type: Newsletter; *Frequency:* Weekly
Québec Office
#1515-A, 740, rue Notre-Dame ouest, Montréal QC H3C 3X6
Tél: 514-217-1167
Chief Officer(s):
Benoit Larose, Vice-présidente, 514-871-8096 Ext. 36
Western Office
Vancouver BC
Tel: 604-353-5233
Chief Officer(s):
Robert Rauscher, Vice-President

Canada's National Bible Hour (CNBH)
c/o Global Outreach Mission, PO Box 1210, St Catharines ON L2R 7A7
Tel: 905-684-1401; *Fax:* 905-684-3069
www.missiongo.org/cnbh
www.facebook.com/168935979827368
www.youtube.com/user/missiongo
Overview: A small national organization founded in 1925
Mission: The Hour is a bible-teaching ministry, & Canada's oldest religious broadcast, heard from coast to coast. It is sponsored by Global Outreach Mission (GOM), an organization dedicated to evangelism & missions.
Member of: Global Outreach Mission
Chief Officer(s):
Brian Albrecht, President, GOM

Canada's National Firearms Association (NFA)
PO Box 49090, Edmonton AB T6E 6H4
Tel: 780-439-1394; *Fax:* 780-439-4091
Toll-Free: 877-818-0393
Other Communication: Membership e-mail: membership@nfa.ca; Legal e-mail: legal@nfa.ca
info@nfa.ca
nfa.ca
www.facebook.com/NFACANADA
twitter.com/CanadasNFA
www.youtube.com/user/NFAfreedom
Previous Name: National Firearms Association
Overview: A large national organization founded in 1984
Mission: To support hunting & sport shooting rights in Canada
Finances: *Annual Operating Budget:* $500,000-$1.5 Million; *Funding Sources:* Membership fees; Donations
Staff Member(s): 1
Membership: 100,000+; *Fees:* $30 senior; $35 individual; $45 family; $60 business
Activities: Speeches & presentations; Political action; *Speaker Service:* Yes; *Library:* NFA Resources; Not open to public
Chief Officer(s):
Sheldon Clare, National President
sheldon@nfa.ca
Bill Rants, Trasurer
bill@nfa.ca
Meetings/Conferences:
• 2018 Annual General Meeting of Canada's National Firearms Association, 2018
Scope: National
Publications:
• Bulletin Français [a publication of Canada's National Firearms Association]
Type: Newsletter
Profile: The association's French-language newsletter
• Canadian Firearms Journal [a publication of Canada's National Firearms Association]
Type: Journal

Canada's National History Society *See* Canada's History

Canada's Oil Sands Innovation Alliance (COSIA)
#1700, 520 5th Ave. SW, Calgary AB T2P 3R7
Tel: 403-444-5282
info@cosia.ca
www.cosia.ca
twitter.com/COSIA_ca
Overview: A large international organization founded in 2012
Mission: To drive the growth of Canada's oil sands & improve environmental performance
Membership: 13 organizations; *Member Profile:* Regular members consist of universities, government agencies and companies involved in oilsands industry.
Chief Officer(s):
Dan Wicklum, Chief Executive
John Brogly, Director, Water & Tailings EPAs
Jenna Dunlop, Director, Land EPA
Publications:
• Collaborator [a publication of Canada's Oil Sands Innovation Alliance]
Type: Newsletter; *Frequency:* Quarterly

Canada's Public Policy Forum / Forum des politiques publiques du Canada
#1405, 130 Albert St., Ottawa ON K1P 5G4
Tel: 613-238-7160; *Fax:* 613-238-7990
mail@ppforum.ca
www.ppforum.com
www.facebook.com/publicpolicyforum
twitter.com/ppforumca
www.youtube.com/user/PublicPolicyForum;
flickr.com/photos/ppforumdotca
Overview: A medium-sized national organization founded in 1988
Mission: To promote better public policy & better public management through dialogue among leaders from the public, private, labour & voluntary sectors
Finances: *Annual Operating Budget:* $3 Million-$5 Million; *Funding Sources:* Private sector, government, academia
Staff Member(s): 25
Membership: 180; *Fees:* $1,130-$19,210
Chief Officer(s):
Larry Murray, Chair
David J. Mitchell, President & CEO
Julie Cafley, Vice-President
julie.cafley@ppforum.ca

Natasha Gauthier, Director, Communications
natasha.gauthier@ppforum.ca

Canada's Research-Based Pharmaceutical Companies; Pharmaceutical Manufacturers Association of Canada *See* Innovative Medicines Canada

Canada's Sports Hall of Fame / Temple de la renommée des sports du Canada
169 Canada Olympic Rd. SW, Calgary AB T3B 6B7
Tel: 403-776-1040
info@cshof.ca
www.sportshall.ca
www.facebook.com/CANsportshall
twitter.com/CANsportshall
www.instagram.com/cansportshall
Overview: A medium-sized national organization founded in 1955
Mission: To inspire Canadian identity & national pride by telling the compelling stories of those outstanding achievements that make up Canada's sports history.
Membership: 100-499
Chief Officer(s):
Marnie Krell, Director, Communications & Marketing
mkrell@cshof.ca
Janice Smith, Director, Exhibits & Programming
jsmith@cshof.ca
Ruth Cowan, Coordinator, Facility Rentals & Fund Development
rcowan@cshof.ca

Canada's Venture Capital & Private Equity Association (CVCA) / Association canadienne du capital de risque et d'investissement (ACCR)
#1201, 372 Bay St., Toronto ON M5H 2W9
Tel: 416-487-0519
cvca@cvca.ca
www.cvca.ca
www.linkedin.com/company/cvca
twitter.com/cvcacanada
Previous Name: Canadian Venture Capital Association
Overview: A small national organization
Mission: To provide advocacy, networking, information & professional development for venture capital & private equity professionals.
Finances: *Funding Sources:* Membership dues, Sponsorship
Membership: 200+ corporate members; 1,000+ individual members; *Fees:* Schedule available; *Member Profile:* Members include Canadian venture capital & private equity companies.; *Committees:* Executive; Nominating; Tax Policy; Government Relations; Membership; Regulatory, Reporting & Valuation; Finance; Conference; Awards; Young Private Capitalists; Communications & Research; Canadian Women in Private Equity; Model Documents; Internal
Activities: Researching; Encouraging investment from the Canadian institutional sector; Fostering international investment in Canadian venture capital & private equity funds
Chief Officer(s):
Dave Mullen, Chair
Mike Woollatt, Chief Executive Officer
Awards:
• Entrepreneur of the Year Award
• Deal of the Year Award
Meetings/Conferences:
• Invest Canada 2018: Canada's Private Equity & Venture Capital Conference, June, 2018, Calgary, AB
Description: Hosted by the Canadian Venture Capital & Private Equity Association and Réseau Capital
Publications:
• Canada's Venture Capital & Private Equity Association Members' Weekly Update
Type: Newsletter; *Frequency:* Weekly
Profile: CVCA events, investment statistics, press releases, special discounts to industry events, & industry happenings

Canada-Arab Business Council (CABC) / Conseil de commerce canado-arabe (CCCA)
#700, 1 Rideau St., Toronto ON K1N 8S7
Tel: 613-670-5853
info@c-abc.org
www.c-abc.org
www.linkedin.com/company/canada-arab-business-council
www.facebook.com/451940824838113
twitter.com/cdaarabbusiness
Previous Name: Canadian-Arab Business Council
Overview: A medium-sized international organization founded in 1983
Mission: To promote trade investment with Arab countries
Affiliation(s): Canadian Chamber of Commerce
Membership: *Fees:* Schedule available based on number of employees.
Chief Officer(s):
Peter Sutherland, President & CEO

Canada-China Bilateral Cooperation Association (CCBCA)
Oceanic Business Centre, #2300, 1066 West Hastings St., Vancouver BC V6E 3X2
Tel: 604-998-2369; *Fax:* 604-726-7669
tour2010@gmail.com
www.ccbca.org
Overview: A medium-sized international organization
Mission: To promote trade between Canada & China

Canada-China Trade Council *See* Canada China Business Council

Canada-Cuba Sports & Cultural Festivals (CCS&CF)
#3, 221 Trowers Rd., 2nd Fl., Woodbridge ON L4L 6A2
Tel: 905-850-0999; *Fax:* 905-850-0997
admin@canadacuba.com
canadacuba.com
www.youtube.com/user/CanadaCubaEvents
Overview: A medium-sized international organization founded in 1988
Mission: To represent Cuban organizations operating in sport, recreation, education & culture
Affiliation(s): Cuban Sports Federation; Institute of Music; Ministry of Culture; Havana Convention Centre; Casa del Caribe; Casa de las Americas
Chief Officer(s):
Jonathan Watts, President

Canada-Finland Chamber of Commerce
c/o Finnish Credit Union, 191 Eglinton Ave. East, Toronto ON M4P 1K1
Tel: 416-486-1533; *Fax:* 416-486-1592
info@canadafinlandcc.com
www.canadafinlandcc.com
www.linkedin.com/e/eabb6b-gbb4qf6x-6u/vgh/3194405/
www.facebook.com/?sk=2361831622
Overview: A medium-sized international organization founded in 1971
11 volunteer(s)
Membership: 55; *Fees:* $25-$75
Chief Officer(s):
Lauri Asikainen, President
lauri.asikainen@connecttheteam.com

CanadaGAP
#312, 245 Menten Pl., Ottawa ON K2H 9E8
Tel: 613-829-4711; *Fax:* 613-829-9379
info@canadagap.ca
www.canadagap.ca
Overview: A large national organization
Mission: To operate a food safety program for companies that produce & handle fruits & vegetables; To develop & disseminate manuals for Greenhouse & fruit & vegetable operations; To encourage Good Agricultural Practices (GAPs); To encourage best practices for food supply management
Affiliation(s): CanAgPlus
Finances: *Funding Sources:* Program fees
Staff Member(s): 7
Membership: 1,500+; *Fees:* Schedule available; *Member Profile:* Companies that produce & handle fruits & vegetables & are interested in participating in the food safety program
Activities: Auditing & certifying food operations based on the standards of the CanadaGAP program & the Hazard Analysis & Critical Control Point (HACCP) approach
Chief Officer(s):
Heather Gale, Executive Director
Meetings/Conferences:
• CanadaGAP Annual General Meeting 2018, 2018
Scope: National
Description: Includes a presentation of the year's financial statements & an annual report
Publications:
• CanadaGAP Annual Report
Type: Report
• CanadaGAP Audit Checklist
Type: Booklet
• CanadaGAP Food Safety Manual for Fresh Fruits & Vegetables
Type: Booklet; *Number of Pages:* 203
• CanadaGAP Food Safety Manual for Greenhouse Product
Type: Booklet; *Number of Pages:* 189

Canada-India Business Council (C-IBC) / Conseil de commerce Canada-Inde
#604, 80 Richmond St. West, Toronto ON M5H 2A4
Tel: 416-214-5947; *Fax:* 416-214-9081
info@canada-indiabusiness.com
www.canada-indiabusiness.com
www.linkedin.com/company/canada-india-business-council
www.facebook.com/197738980259340
twitter.com/c_ibc
Overview: A small international organization founded in 1982
Mission: To promote trade & investment between Canada & India by fostering direct contacts between Canadian & Indian business people; To advise the Canadian government with respect to policies & programs affecting Canada's relations with India; To serve as a forum for exchange of information & views between business executives of Canada & India on issues of importance to both countries; To provide information & advice to companies of both countries with respect to trade & investment matters in either country
Finances: *Funding Sources:* Membership & consulting fees
Staff Member(s): 2
Membership: 103; *Fees:* Schedule available; *Member Profile:* Entrepreneurs & corporations; *Committees:* Cleantech; Energy-Resources; Infrastructure; Education; Trade Policy
Activities: Developing trade, investment & services; Organizing trade missions, seminars & networking events; *Speaker Service:* Yes; *Library:* Not open to public
Chief Officer(s):
Pat Koval, Chair
Gary Comerford, President & CEO

Canada-Israel Cultural Foundation (CICF) / Fondation culturelle Canada-Israël
4700 Bathurst St., 2nd Fl., Toronto ON M2R 1W8
Tel: 416-932-2260
cicf@bellnet.ca
www.cicfweb.ca
Overview: A small international charitable organization founded in 1963
Mission: To act as a cultural bridge between Canada and Israel, promoting and supporting intercultural exchange with a special focus on young artists, and developing artistic life by awarding scholarships and grants
Staff Member(s): 2
Membership: *Fees:* $50 regular; $100 spondor; $500 patron
Activities: Bringing Israeli performers & artists to Canada
Chief Officer(s):
Cheryl Wetstein, Executive Director
  Ottawa Chapter
  73 Loch Isle Rd., Nepean ON K2H 8G7
  Tel: 613-726-0713; *Fax:* 613-728-3497

The Canada-Japan Society of British Columbia
PO Box 47071, #15, 555 West 12th Ave., Vancouver BC V5Z 3X0
canadajapansociety.bc.ca
Overview: A small provincial organization
Mission: To encourage & to increase the opportunities in British Columbia for the extension of friendship & understanding between the people of Canada & the people of Japan
Membership: *Fees:* $325 corporate; $100 individual; $35 retired/student

Canada-Japan Society of Montréal *Voir* Société Canada-Japon de Montréal

Canada-Japan Society of Toronto
Toronto ON
www.canadajapansociety.blogspot.com
www.linkedin.com/company/canada-japan-society
twitter.com/canadajapansoc
Overview: A small local organization
Mission: To provide opportunities to enhance understanding of Japan, Canada & Canada-Japan relations
Member of: Japanese and Canadian Community Network
Activities: *Awareness Events:* Bonenkai, December
Chief Officer(s):
Lisa Houston, Communications Director

Canada-Pakistan Association of the National Capital Region (CPA-NCR)
#34, 174 Colonnade Rd., Ottawa ON K2E 7J6
Tel: 613-875-1786
info@pcpa-ncr.org

www.cpa-ncr.org
www.facebook.com/cpa.ncr.ottawa
twitter.com/CPANCR
Overview: A small local organization
Mission: To help and establish the Pakistani community in Canada.
Member of: National Federation of Pakistani Canadians Inc.
Affiliation(s): National Association of Pakistani Canadians
Membership: *Fees:* $10 individual; $25 family
Chief Officer(s):
Anis Rehman, President

Canada-Poland Chamber of Commerce of Toronto
#102, 2680 Matheson Blvd. East, Toronto ON L4W 0A5
info@canada-poland.com
www.canada-poland.com
www.facebook.com/canadapolandchamber
twitter.com/canadapolandcct
www.youtube.com/channel/UCrDyCb2VQWf05irpRh6GK5g
Overview: A small international organization
Mission: To promote, develop & expand business, trade & investment opportunities between Canada & Poland
Membership: *Fees:* $50 student; $100 individual; $250 business; *Committees:* Communications; Engineering & Technology; Higher Education
Activities: Organizing events, such as the Polish-Cup Golf Tournament; *Library*
Chief Officer(s):
Wojciech Sniegowski, President

Canada-Singapore Business Association
c/o Edwards, Kenny & Bray, #1900, 1040 West Georgia St., Vancouver BC V6E 4H3
Tel: 604-464-0019; *Fax:* 604-464-0872
info@csba.ca
www.csba.ca
Overview: A small international organization founded in 1995
Mission: To promote the development of commerce between Singapore & Canada; to liaise with government & keeps it members abreast of related government programs; to serve as a forum in Canada for individuals & companies with mutual interest to exchange ideas & information.
Affiliation(s): CSBA Singapore; Vancouver Singapore Club
Finances: *Funding Sources:* Membership dues
Membership: *Fees:* $75 individual; $150 corporate
Activities: Meetings; seminars; workshops; networking; *Library:* Open to public
Chief Officer(s):
Brian M. Cole, Chair
colebm@telus.net

Canada-Sri Lanka Business Council (CSLBC)
58 Sundial Cres., Toronto ON M4A 2J8
Tel: 416-445-5390; *Fax:* 416-363-4601
cslbcbiz@rogers.com
www.cslbc.ca
Overview: A medium-sized international organization founded in 1990
Mission: To promote trade, investment, technological exchange, tourism & industrial cooperation between Canada & Sri Lanka
Activities: Networking; Providing business information; Annual President's Awards Gala
Chief Officer(s):
Upali Obeyesekere, President
Ganesan Sugumar, Vice President
Mohan Perera, General Secretary
Awards:
• President's Award
Publications:
• CSLBC [Canada-Sri Lanka Business Council] Newsletter
Type: Newsletter

Canada-Yukon Business Service Centre / Centre de services aux entreprises Canada-Yukon (CYBSC)
#101, 307 Jarvis St., Whitehorse YT Y1A 2H3
Tel: 867-633-6257; *Fax:* 867-667-2001
Toll-Free: 800-661-0543; *TTY:* 800-457-8466
yukon@cbsc.ic.gc.ca
Overview: A small provincial organization founded in 1997
Mission: To provide access to information & resources on federal & territorial government business services, programs, & regulations
Member of: Canada Business Network
Activities: Offering workshops; *Library:* Canada-Yukon Business Service Centre Reference Library; Open to public

Canadian & American Reformed Churches
comments@canrc.org
www.canrc.org
Also Known As: Canadian Reformed Churches
Overview: A large national organization
Mission: To exalt the Triune God by faithfully proclaiming the gospel of Jesus Christ
Membership: 50+ organizations

Canadian 4-H Council / Conseil des 4-H du Canada
Central Experimental Farm, 960 Carling Avenue, Building 106, Ottawa ON K1A 0C6
Tel: 613-759-1013; *Fax:* 613-759-1016
info@4-h-canada.ca
www.4-H-canada.ca
www.facebook.com/4HCanada
twitter.com/4HCanada
www.youtube.com/4hcanada
Previous Name: Canadian Council on 4-H Clubs
Overview: A large national charitable organization founded in 1933
Mission: To inspire youth across Canada to become contributing leaders in their communities; To support the development of Canada's rural youth
Finances: *Funding Sources:* Memberhip fees; Sponsorships; Donations; Wills & Bequests
Staff Member(s): 14; 7,70 volunteer(s)
Membership: 24,500+; *Fees:* $125 individual/alumni; *Committees:* Youth Advisory
Activities: Offering exchanges & scholarships which focus on citizenship; Providing leadership development opportunities
Chief Officer(s):
Shannon Benner, Chief Executive Officer
Sue Wood, Manager, Admissions
Awards:
• 4-H AgriVenture Scholarship Opportunity
Awarded to one student nationally, to be used toward an AgriVenture travel and work program.; *Amount:* $3,000
• CIBC 4-H Post-Secondary Education Scholarship
Funding may be used for tuition, books and/or lodging. *Eligibility:* 4-H members in their last year of high school or CEGEP; *Amount:* $2,500 (3)
• TD 4-H Agriculture Scholarship
Eligibility: 4-H members in their last year of high school who are planning to enroll in post-secondary education in an agriculture or agri-business related discipline.; *Amount:* $2,500 (10)
• Co-operators/4-H National Volunteer Leader of the Year Award
A volunteer leader is selected from each province, and a grand prize winner is selected from that group.; *Amount:* $1,100
• Sears in Your Community 4-H Club Grants Program
Provides funding support to 4-H groups that provide after-school programs so youth can have fun while developing leadership skills, citizenship, and life skills in a positive and safe environment. *Eligibility:* Available for any 4-H club in Canada; *Amount:* $1,000
• Agrium 4-H Youth Leadership Initiative
Challenges 4-H members to enhance their local communities by actively participating and practicing their leadership skills.
Eligibility: Available for any 4-H club in Canada; *Amount:* $50,000
Publications:
• L'avantage 4-H Advantage
Type: Magazine; *Frequency:* Semiannually; *Price:* Free
Profile: Coverage of national programs & 4-H activities across Canada
• Canadian 4-H Council Annual Report
Type: Yearbook; *Frequency:* Annually
Profile: Annual Report of the Canadian 4-H Council & Canadian 4-H Foundation

Alberta - Airdrie Office
Airdrie Office, 97 East Lake Ramp NE, Airdrie AB T4A 0C3
Tel: 403-948-8510; *Fax:* 403-948-2069
www.4h.ab.ca
Mission: To provide a place for youth to learn & grow; To organize outings, achievement days, & fundraiers; To participate in various activities in the community which meet the interests of youth, increase their knowledge, & develop life skills
Member of: Canadian 4-H Council
Chief Officer(s):
Margarite Stark, Director
margarite.stark@gov.ab.ca

British Columbia
2741 - 30 St., Vernon BC V1T 5C6
Tel: 250-545-0336; *Fax:* 250-545-0399
Toll-Free: 866-776-0373
mail@bc4h.bc.ca
www.bc4h.bc.ca
www.facebook.com/472654772849933
Mission: To provide young people with an oppourtunity to learn how to become productive, self-assured adults who can make their community and country a good place in which to live.
Chief Officer(s):
Claudette Martin, Manager
manager@bc4h.bc.ca

Manitoba
1129 Queens Ave, Brandon MB R7A 1L9
Tel: 204-726-6136
4hdirector@mymts.net
www.4h.mb.ca
Chief Officer(s):
Clayton Robins, Executive Director
crobins@4h.mb.ca

New Brunswick
#5, 267 Connell St., Woodstock NB E7M 1L2
Tel: 506-324-6244; *Fax:* 506-325-9266
nb4h@aernet.ca
www.nb4h.com
www.facebook.com/4HNEWBRUNSWICK
twitter.com/4HNB
Mission: To learn to do by doing

Newfoundland
PO Box 50, Calvert NL A0A 1N0
Tel: 709-727-3397
NL4-H@outlook.com
www.4hnl.ca
Chief Officer(s):
Shirley Barnable, President
shirleybarnable@gmail.com

Nova Scotia
Nova Scotia Department of Agriculture, 60 Research Dr., Bible Hill NS B6L 2R2
Tel: 902-843-3990; *Fax:* 902-843-3989
4hnovascotia@eastlink.ca
novascotia4h.ca
www.facebook.com/4HNovaScotia
twitter.com/@Official4HNS
Mission: Part of the 4-H Club which operates for youth between the ages of 7-21 and which offers various projects from livestock to scrapebooking.
Chief Officer(s):
Heather Williams, President
helw2002@hotmail.com

Ontario
PO Box 212, 111 Main St. North, Rockwood ON N0B 2K0
Tel: 519-856-0992; *Fax:* 519-856-0515
Toll-Free: 877-410-6748
inquiries@4-hontario.ca
www.4-hontario.ca
www.facebook.com/4hontario
twitter.com/4hontario
Mission: To work with members to develop leadership & life skills that equip them with tools to reach their full potential; To help youth focus on how their actions affect personal relationships, their community, the environment & society as a whole; To promote learning through experience
Member of: Canadian 4-H Council
Chief Officer(s):
Tammy Oswick-Kearney, President
Debra Brown, Executive Director
ed@4-hontario.ca

Prince Edward Island
PO Box 2000, #235, 40 Enman Cres., Charlottetown PE C1A 7N8
Tel: 902-368-4833; *Fax:* 902-368-6289
Toll-Free: 866-308-4833
pei4h@gov.pe.ca
www.pei4h.ca
www.facebook.com/pei4h
twitter.com/PEI4H
www.youtube.com/user/4HPEI
Mission: To provide leadership & skills development opportunities for youth; To raise agricultural awareness
Chief Officer(s):
Kelly Mullaly, Administrative Director
kjmullaly@gov.pe.ca

Canadian Associations / Canadian Academy of Child & Adolescent Psychiatry (CACAP) / Académie canadienne de psychiatrie de l'enfant et de l'adolescent

- The Link [a publication of Prince Edward Island 4-H Council]
Type: Newsletter; *Frequency:* Quarterly
Profile: Local, regional, provincial, & national 4-H news
Saskatchewan
3830 Thatcher Ave., Saskatoon SK S7R 1A5
Tel: 306-933-7727; *Fax:* 306-933-7730
info@4-h.sk.ca
www.4-h.sk.ca
Chief Officer(s):
Cera Youngson, Executive Director, 306-933-7729
manager@4-h.sk.ca

Canadian 5 Pin Bowlers' Association (C5PBA) / Association canadienne des cinq quilles (AC5Q)
#206, 720 Belfast Rd., Ottawa ON K1G 0Z5
Tel: 613-744-5090; *Fax:* 613-744-2217
www.c5pba.ca
www.facebook.com/117638274967514
Previous Name: Canadian Bowling Congress
Overview: A medium-sized national licensing charitable organization founded in 1978
Mission: The sports organization of male & female 5 pin bowlers provides programs & services to its members for their participation in organized 5-pin bowling. It also regulates bowling systems to standardize the sport.
Affiliation(s): Bowling Federation of Canada
Finances: *Funding Sources:* Membership fees; government; sponsors
Membership: 150,000; *Fees:* $7; *Member Profile:* Male & female 5 pin bowlers
Activities: Awards Program; *Library:* Not open to public
Chief Officer(s):
Dave Post, President
Sheila Carr, Executive Director
sheila.c5pba@gmail.com

Canadian Abilities Foundation
#803, 255 Duncan Mill Rd., Toronto ON M3B 3H9
Tel: 416-421-7944; *Fax:* 416-421-8418
abilities@bcsgroup.com
www.abilities.ca
twitter.com/abilitiescanada
Overview: A small national charitable organization founded in 1988
Mission: To provide information, inspiration & opportunity to Canadians with disabilities
Activities: *Internships:* Yes; *Speaker Service:* Yes; *Rents Mailing List:* Yes
Chief Officer(s):
Caroline Tapp-McDougall, Executive Director & Managing Editor
Publications:
- Abilities
Type: Magazine; *Frequency:* Quarterly; *Accepts Advertising*
Profile: For people with disabilities, their families, friends, & professionals

Canadian Aboriginal & Minority Supplier Council (CAMSC)
95 Berkeley St., Toronto ON M5A 2W8
Tel: 416-941-0004; *Fax:* 416-941-9282
info@camsc.ca
www.camsc.ca
Overview: A small national organization
Mission: Dedicated to the economic empowerment of Aboriginal & visible minority communities through business development & employment; to identify & certify Aboriginal & minority-owned businesses, & to integrate them into the supply chain of major corporations in Canada.
Activities: CAMCS Business Achievement Awards; Aboriginal & Minority Supplier Procurement Fair.
Chief Officer(s):
Cassandra Dorrington, President

Canadian Aboriginal AIDS Network (CAAN)
6520 Salish Dr., Vancouver BC V6N 2C7
Tel: 604-266-7616; *Fax:* 604-266-7612
www.caan.ca
www.facebook.com/CAAN.ca
twitter.com/caan_says
Overview: A medium-sized national organization
Mission: To provide support & advocacy for Aboriginal people living with or affected by HIV/AIDS, TB, aging, mental illness, or other co-morbidity issues
Staff Member(s): 10
Membership: 26 organizations; *Fees:* $50 full organization; $25 associate organizations; *Member Profile:* Aboriginal groups & associations; Aboriginals with AIDS; Associate organizations & individuals
Activities: *Awareness Events:* Aboriginal AIDS Awareness Week, December
Chief Officer(s):
Emma Palmantier, Chair
Ken Clement, Chief Executive Officer, 604-266-7616 Ext. 227
Merv Thomas, Manager, National Programs Communications, 604-266-7616 Ext. 226
Publications:
- Canadian Journal of Aboriginal Community-Based HIV/AIDS Research (CJACBR)
Type: Journal; *Frequency:* Annually; *Editor:* Renee Masching et al.
Profile: A peer-reviewed journal directed toward Aboriginal HIV/AIDS service organizations, Aboriginal people living with HIV/AIDS, community leaders, policy & decision-makers, & anyone with an interest in HIV/AIDS

Canadian Aboriginal Minerals Association (CAMA)
395 Loonway Rd., Capreol ON P0M 1H0
Tel: 705-858-4444; *Fax:* 705-858-4440
Toll-Free: 844-443-6452
info@aboriginalminerals.com
www.aboriginalminerals.com
www.facebook.com/CanadianAboriginalMineralsAssociation
twitter.com/aboriginalmine
Overview: A small national organization founded in 1992
Mission: To increase the understanding of the minerals industry & the Aboriginal communities' interests in lands & resources; To advance economic development, environmental protection, & mineral resource management in the Aboriginal community
Finances: *Funding Sources:* Sponsors
Activities: Providing networking opportunities between First Nations communities & industry; Advocating in Aboriginal community, land, & resource development; Presenting workshops across Canada
Chief Officer(s):
Hans Matthews, President

Canadian Aboriginal Veterans & Serving Members Association (CAV)
34 Kingham Pl., Victoria BC V9B 1L8
Tel: 250-900-5768
national-president@nationalalliance.ca
canadianaboriginalveterans.ca
Overview: A small national organization

Canadian Academic Accounting Association (CAAA) / Association canadienne des professeurs de comptabilité (ACPC)
245 Fairview Mall Dr., Toronto ON M2J 4T1
Tel: 416-486-5361; *Fax:* 416-486-6158
admin@caaa.ca
www.caaa.ca
twitter.com/caaa_acpc
Overview: A medium-sized national organization founded in 1976
Mission: To promote excellence in accounting education & research in Canada with particular reference to Canadian post-secondary accounting programs & Canadian issues
Membership: 100-499; *Fees:* $74-$185; *Committees:* Annual Conference; Education; George Baxter; Haim Falk; L.S. Rosen; Membership; Nominating; Research
Activities: *Rents Mailing List:* Yes
Chief Officer(s):
Alan J. Richardson, President
pres@caaa.ca
Jamison Aldcorn, Vice-President, Colleges
vpcolleges@caaa.ca
Sarah Gumpinger, Vice-President
vpatlarge@caaa.ca
Chi Ho Ng, Treasurer
treasurer@caaa.ca
Gina Létourneau, Secretary
secretary@caaa.ca
Meetings/Conferences:
- 2018 Canadian Academic Accounting Association Annual Conference, June, 2018, Calgary, AB
Scope: National
Description: Theme: "Accounting & Public Trust"
Publications:
- Accounting Perspectives
Type: Journal; *Frequency:* Quarterly; *Editor:* J. Efrim Boritz
Profile: Applied research on the discipline & practice of accounting
- Canadian Accounting Education & Research News (CAERN)
Type: Newsletter; *Frequency:* 3 pa
Profile: CAAA events, relations with granting agencies, research opportunities, professional activities, & announcements involving members & their associates
- Contemporary Accounting Research (CAR)
Type: Journal; *Frequency:* Quarterly
Profile: Academic research of interest to the Canadian accounting community

Canadian Academic Institute in Athens *See* Canadian Institute in Greece

Canadian Academies of Science *See* Council of Canadian Academies

Canadian Academy of Audiology (CAA) / Académie canadienne d'audiologie (ACA)
PO Box 22531, 300 Coxwell Ave., Toronto ON M4L 3B6
Tel: 647-794-7305
Toll-Free: 800-264-5106
contact@canadianaudiology.ca
www.canadianaudiology.ca
www.linkedin.com/groups/4068951
www.facebook.com/CanadianAcademyofAudiology
twitter.com/caaudiology
Overview: A medium-sized national organization founded in 1996
Mission: To represent the audiological community in Canada; To provide quality hearing health care & education to persons with, or at risk for, hearing or vestibular disorders; To maintain & advance ethical standards of practice
Membership: *Fees:* $35 student; $95 retired/international; $140 affiliate; $195 full; *Member Profile:* Audiologists from across Canada
Activities: Encouraging & facilitating research; Promoting & enhancing the profession of audiology; *Awareness Events:* Speech & Hearing Awarenss Month, May; National Audiology Week, Nov.
Chief Officer(s):
Marlene Bagatto, President
Salima Jiwani, President-Elect
Meetings/Conferences:
- Canadian Academy of Audiology 21st Annual Conference & Exhibition 2018, October, 2018, Sheraton on the Falls, Niagara Falls, ON
Scope: National
Description: Annual general meeting, educational sessions, speaker presentations, exhibits, & networking opportunities

Canadian Academy of Child & Adolescent Psychiatry (CACAP) / Académie canadienne de psychiatrie de l'enfant et de l'adolescent
#701, 141 Laurier Ave. West, Ottawa ON KIP 5J3
Tel: 613-288-0408; *Fax:* 613-234-9857
info@cacap-acpea.org
www.cacap-acpea.org
Previous Name: Canadian Academy of Child Psychiatry
Overview: A small national charitable organization founded in 1980
Mission: To advance the mental health of children, youth, & families; To promote the highest standards of patient care & service to children, youth, & families, incorporating a psychological, social, & biological approach
Membership: *Fees:* $325 full; $195 associate; $195 affliate; $260 international; *Member Profile:* Psychiatrists, specializing in the treatment of children & adolescents, & other professionals in Canada; *Committees:* Advocacy; Education; Fees & Tariffs; Industry Relations; Professional Standards; Research & Scientific; Website; Awards; Budget; Constitution; Credentials; Elections
Activities: Engaging in advocacy activities related to the mental health of children, youth, & families; Collaborating with other professional disciplines; Promoting research; Furthering the continuing education of practicing child & adolescent psychiatrists
Chief Officer(s):
Wade Junek, President
Elizabeth Waite, Executive Director
Alexa Bagnell, Secretary-Treasurer
Awards:
- Paul D. Steinhauer Advocacy Award
To recognize a member of the Canadian Academy of Child & Adolescent Psychiatry who has advocated for children, adolescents, & their families
- Naomi Rae-Grant Award
To recognize a member of the Canadian Academy of Child &

Adolescent Psychiatry who has done innovative work on an aspect of consultation, community intervention, or prevention
• Excellence in Education Award
To recognize a psychiatric educator who has made a significant contribution in undergraduate, postgraduate, continuing professional education, public education in child & adolescent mental health
Meetings/Conferences:
• Canadian Academy of Child and Adolescent Psychiatry 38th Annual Conference, September, 2018, Halifax, NS
Scope: National
Publications:
• Journal of the Canadian Academy of Child & Adolescent Psychiatry
Type: Journal; *Frequency:* Quarterly; *Accepts Advertising*;
Editor: Normand Carrey; *ISSN:* 1719-8429
Profile: Featuring original articles, clinical perspectives, & book reviews

Canadian Academy of Child Psychiatry See Canadian Academy of Child & Adolescent Psychiatry

Canadian Academy of Endodontics / L'Académie canadienne d'endodontie
#301, 400 St. Mary Ave., Winnipeg MB R3C 4K5
Tel: 204-942-2511; *Fax:* 204-956-4147
info@caendo.ca
www.caendo.ca
Overview: A small national organization founded in 1964
Mission: To advance endodontics by providing lectures, information, forums for interaction, & resources; To enhance the health of the public
Affiliation(s): Canadian Dental Association
Finances: *Funding Sources:* Membership dues; fees; convention; newsletter ads
Membership: *Fees:* $300 active; $250 associate; $200 academic; $15 retired/student; *Committees:* Standards of Practice; Scientific Advisory; Membership; Public Relations; Nominating; Communications
Chief Officer(s):
Simona Pesun, President
Ian Watson, Executive Director

The Canadian Academy of Engineering (CAE) / L'Académie canadienne du génie (ACG)
#1402, 180 Elgin St., Ottawa ON K2P 2K3
Tel: 613-235-9056; *Fax:* 613-235-6861
info@acad-eng-gen.ca
www.acad-eng-gen.ca
Overview: A medium-sized national charitable organization founded in 1987
Mission: To ensure that Canadian engineering expertise is applied to the benefit of all Canadians
Member of: International Council of Academies of Engineering & Technological Sciences (CAETS)
Finances: *Funding Sources:* Sponsorships
Staff Member(s): 2
Membership: 584; *Member Profile:* Accomplished engineers, nominated & elected by their peers; *Committees:* Fellowship; Honours & Awards; Finance; Investment
Activities: Increasing awareness of engineering in society; Promoting industrial competitiveness & environmental preservation; Advising on engineering education, research, & innovation; Developing relations with other professional engineering organizations
Chief Officer(s):
Kevin Goheen, Executive Director
Publications:
• Canadian Academy of Engineering Newsletter / Communiqué
Type: Newsletter; *Frequency:* Quarterly
Profile: Reports, updates, upcoming events, & activities of the Academy & its Fellows

Canadian Academy of Facial Plastic & Reconstructive Surgery (CAFPRS)
c/o Dr. Andres Gantous, #230, 30 The Queensway, Toronto ON M6R 1B5
Tel: 905-569-6965
Toll-Free: 800-545-8864
www.cafprs.com
Overview: A small national organization
Mission: To represent cosmetic & plastic surgeons in Canada
Membership: 60
Chief Officer(s):
Mark Taylor, President
Andres Gantous, Secretary-Treasurer

Canadian Academy of Geriatric Psychiatry (CAGP) / L'Académie canadienne de psychiatrie gériatrique (ACPG)
#6, 20 Crown Steel Dr., Markham ON L3R 9X9
Tel: 905-415-3917; *Fax:* 905-415-0071
Toll-Free: 855-415-3917
cagp@secretariatcentral.com
www.cagp.ca
www.facebook.com/CanadianAcademyofGeriatricPsychiatry
Overview: A small national organization
Mission: To promote mental health for elderly people in Canada
Member of: Council of Academies of the Canadian Psychiatric Association
Membership: *Fees:* $276.25 full/affiliate; Free for members in training; *Member Profile:* Geriatric psychiatrists; Physicians with fellowship from the RCPSC or CFPC; people with interests in geriatric psychiatry; *Committees:* Membership; Communications; Annual Scientific Meeting; Nominations; CAGP Awards; Education; Update in Geriatric Psychiatry; Geriatric Psychiatry Online Course; Finance
Activities: Encouraging education & research of members; Advocating for seniors' mental health; Developing guidelines for training in geriatric psychiatry; Providing networking opportunities; Promoting exchange of knowledge; Initiating the Canadian Coalition for Seniors Mental Health to implement research, education, & partnership development
Chief Officer(s):
Mark Rapoport, President
Maria Kardaris, Manager
Nancy Vasil, Co-Chair, Communications
Awards:
• Fellowship Award
• Resident Award
• Outstanding Contributions to Geriatric Psychiatry in Canada
• Lifetime Achievement in Geriatric Psychiatry
Publications:
• CAGP [Canadian Academy of Geriatric Psychiatry] E-newsletter
Type: Newsletter; *Frequency:* Quarterly
Profile: CAGP reports, meetings, awards, & statistics
• Canadian Journal of Geriatric Medicine & Psychiatry
Type: Journal
Profile: Peer-reviewed original research on the health & care of older adults, co-sponsored by the Canadian Academy of Geriatric Psychiatry & the Canadian Geriatrics Society

Canadian Academy of Periodontology (CAP) / Académie canadienne de parodontologie (ACP)
#201, 1815 Alta Vista Dr., Ottawa ON K1G 3Y6
Tel: 613-523-9800; *Fax:* 613-523-1968
info@cap-acp.ca
www.cap-acp.ca
Overview: A small national organization founded in 1958 overseen by Canadian Dental Association
Mission: To act as the national voice of periodontists; To promote excellence in the practice of periodontics; To establish standards of care & guidelines for therapy; To advance public knowledge & awareness of periodontal health
Affiliation(s): American Academy of Periodontology
Finances: *Funding Sources:* Sponsors
Membership: *Fees:* $250; *Member Profile:* Periodontists; *Committees:* CDSA; Mentorship program; Periodontal Education; RCDC; Web Site
Chief Officer(s):
Jean-Pierre Picard, President
jean-pierre.picard@forces.gc.ca
Claire D'Amour, Executive Secretary

Canadian Academy of Psychiatry & the Law (CAPL) / L'Académie canadienne de psychiatrie et droit (ACPD)
c/o Katie Hardy, Canadian Psychiatric Association, #701, 141 Laurier Ave. West, Ottawa ON K1P 5J3
Tel: 613-234-2815; *Fax:* 613-234-9857
capl@cpa-apc.org
www.capl-acpd.org
Overview: A small national organization founded in 1995 overseen by Canadian Psychiatric Association
Mission: To advance the science & practice of forensic psychiatry; To promote high standards of patient care & professional practice; To address issues related to forensic psychiatry
Finances: *Funding Sources:* Sponsors
Membership: *Fees:* $200 full, affiliate, & associate members; $75 members in training; *Member Profile:* Members of the Royal College of Physicians & Surgeons of Canada, or an equivalent organization; Psychiatrists with an interest in psychiatry & the law
Activities: Furthering the continuing education of practising forensic psychiatrists; Encouraging research in forensic psychiatry; Providing information to the public related to psychiatry & law
Chief Officer(s):
Johann Brink, MB ChB, FCPsych, President
Brad Booth, MD, FRCPC, DABP, Secretary
Awards:
• Bruno Cormier Award
• The CAPL Fellowship Award
Meetings/Conferences:
• Canadian Academy of Psychiatry & the Law Annual Conference, March, 2018, Fairmont Empress, Victoria, BC
Scope: National
Description: Information for psychiatrists working in law & psychiatry, & for any physicians interested in furthering their knowledge of this field
Publications:
• CAPL [Canadian Academy of Psychiatry & the Law] Newsletter
Type: Newsletter
Profile: Review of meeting presentations for CAPL members

Canadian Academy of Recording Arts & Sciences (CARAS) / Académie canadienne des arts et des sciences de l'enregistrement (ACASE)
345 Adelaide St. West, 2nd fl., Toronto ON M5V 1R5
Tel: 416-485-3135; *Fax:* 416-485-4978
Toll-Free: 888-440-5866
info@carasonline.ca
carasonline.ca
Overview: A medium-sized national charitable organization founded in 1975
Mission: To promote Canadian artists and music; To identify & reward the achievements of Canadian artists
Membership: *Fees:* $75 regular; $25 student; *Member Profile:* Individuals & artists who work in the Canadian music industry; Persons must hold a Canadian birth certificate or passport, or they must be a Canadian Landed Immigrant, with residency in Canada
Activities: Voting for the JUNO Awards; *Awareness Events:* JUNO Awards
Chief Officer(s):
Mark Cohon, Chair
Allan Reid, President & CEO, CARAS, The JUNO Awards & MusiCounts
allan@junoawards.ca
Meghan McCabe, Senior Manager, Communications
meghan@junoawards.ca
Awards:
• JUNO Fan Choice Award
• JUNO Award: Single of the Year
• JUNO Award: International Album of the Year
• JUNO Award: Album of the Year
• JUNO Award: Artist of the Year
• JUNO Award: Group of the Year
• JUNO Award: New Artist of the Year
• JUNO Award: New Group of the Year
• JUNO Award: Songwriter of the Year
• JUNO Award: Country Album of the Year
• JUNO Award: Adult Alternative Album of the Year
• JUNO Award: Alternative Album of the Year
• JUNO Award: Pop Album of the Year
• JUNO Award: Rock Album of the Year
• JUNO Award: Vocal Jazz Album of the Year
• JUNO Award: Contemporary Jazz Album of the Year
• JUNO Award: Traditional Jazz Album of the Year
• JUNO Award: Instrumental Album of the Year
• JUNO Award: Francophone Album of the Year
• JUNO Award: Children's Album of the Year
• JUNO Award: Classical Album of the Year - Solo or Chamber Ensemble
• JUNO Award: Classical Album of the Year - Large Ensemble or Soloist(s) With Large Ensemble Accompaniment
• JUNO Award: Classical Album of the Year - Vocal or Choral Performance
• JUNO Award: Classical Composition of the Year
• JUNO Award: Rap Recording of the Year
• JUNO Award: Dance Recording of the Year
• JUNO Award: R&B / Soul Recording of the Year
• JUNO Award: Reggae Recording of the Year
• JUNO Award: Aboriginal Album of the Year
• JUNO Award: Roots & Traditional Album of the Year - Solo
• JUNO Award: Roots & Traditional Album of the Year - Group

- JUNO Award: Blues Album of the Year
- JUNO Award: Contemporary Christian / Gospel Album of the Year
- JUNO Award: World Music Album of the Year
- JUNO Award: Jack Richardson Producer of the Year
- JUNO Award: Recording Engineer of the Year
- JUNO Award: Recording Package of the Year
- JUNO Award: Video of the Year
- JUNO Award: Music DVD of the Year

Publications:
- CARAS [Canadian Academy of Recording Arts & Sciences] News

Type: Newsletter; *Frequency:* 3 pa; *Price:* Free with Canadian Academy of Recording Arts & Sciences membership
Profile: Music industry happenings, MusiCounts updates, & JUNO Award news
- MusiCounts News

Type: Newsletter; *Frequency:* 3 pa; *Price:* Free with Canadian Academy of Recording Arts & Sciences membership
Profile: JUNO Award news, music industry happenings, & MusiCounts updates

Canadian Academy of Sport Medicine (CASM) / Académie canadienne de médecine du sport (ACMS)
#1400, 180 Elgin St., Ottawa ON K2P 2K3
Tel: 613-748-5851; *Fax:* 613-912-0128
Toll-Free: 877-585-2394
admin@casem-acmse.org
www.casm-acms.org
www.facebook.com/119018054888639
twitter.com/CASEMACMSE
Overview: A medium-sized national charitable organization founded in 1970
Mission: To promote excellence in the practice of medicine, as it applies to physical activity; To advance the art & science of sport medicine
Affiliation(s): World Federation of Sport Medicine
Finances: *Funding Sources:* Membership fees; Donations
Membership: *Member Profile:* All medical doctors; Residents & fellows; Medical students with an interest in sport medicine; *Committees:* Athletes with a Disability; Annual Symposium; Clinical Journal of Sport Medicine; Credentials (Diploma); Communications, Marketing & Membership; Fellowship; Official Languages; Paediatric Sport & Exercise Medicine; Timely Topics; Publications; Research; Selection; Sport Safety; Team Physician; Team Physician Development; Women's Issues in Sport Medicine; Interest Groups
Activities: Conducting research; Offering continuing medical education; Providing current information; Creating networking opportunities
Chief Officer(s):
Dawn Haworth, Executive Director
Publications:
- Canadian Academy of Sport Medicine Newsletter

Type: Newsletter; *Frequency:* Quarterly; *Price:* Free with membership in the Canadian Academy of Sport Medicine
- Clinical Journal of Sport Medicine

Type: Journal; *Price:* Free with regular membership in the Canadian Academy of Sport Medicine

Canadian Academy of the History of Pharmacy (CAHP) / Académie canadienne d'histoire de la pharmacie
4714 - 147 St., Edmonton AB T6H 5E7
www.cahp.ca
Overview: A small national organization founded in 1945
Mission: To provide research & historical information about pharmacy in Canada
Membership: 54 members + 10 schools of pharmacy; *Fees:* $10 individuals; $20 institutions
Activities: Collecting, publishing, & distributing historical information about pharmacy in Canada
Chief Officer(s):
Gary Cavanagh, President
John Bachynsky, Secretary & Treasurer
jbachynsky@pharmacy.ualberta.ca

Canadian Accredited Independent Schools (CAIS)
264 Welland Ave, #P, 2nd Fl., St Catharines ON L2R 2P8
Tel: 905-683-5658; *Fax:* 905-684-5057
www.cais.ca
www.linkedin.com/company/canadian-accredited-independent-schools-cais-
twitter.com/CAIS_Schools
Previous Name: Canadian Association of Independent Schools
Overview: A small national organization founded in 1979
Membership: 90 schools; *Fees:* $1000 + $17.35 per student; *Member Profile:* Independent schools which meet certain requirements, such as teaching a curriculum on a K-12 continuum & operating for at least five years
Activities: Fostering leadership in education
Chief Officer(s):
Anne-Marie Kee, Executive Director
akee@cais.ca
Tracey Nolan, Executive Assistant
tnolan@cais.ca
Publications:
- CAIS [Canadian Association of Independent Schools] Newsletter

Type: Newsletter; *Frequency:* Quarterly
Profile: Conference, course, & workshop information, upcoming events, & reports

Canadian Accredited Independent Schools Advancement Professionals (ISAPC)
isapcanada@gmail.com
www.isapc.ca
www.linkedin.com/groups/2071818/profile
www.facebook.com/ISAPCanada
twitter.com/isap_canada
Overview: A medium-sized national organization founded in 1981 overseen by Canadian Accredited Independent Schools
Mission: The Canadian Accredited Independent Schools Advancement Professionals is an association of development and advancement directors and officers.
Affiliation(s): Canadian Accredited Independent Schools
Membership: 340; *Member Profile:* Canadian independent school advancement professionals employed in development, alumni/ae relations, major gift fundraising, planned giving, event management, advancement support services, prospect researching, database management and communications
Chief Officer(s):
Laura Edwards, President
ledwards@yorkhouse.ca
Awards:
- Rising Star Award
- Mary Birt Award for Mentorship
- Sam Heaman Award
- Distinguished Award for Advancement Support Staff

Meetings/Conferences:
- Canadian Accredited Independent Schools Advancement Professionals Biennial National Conference 2019, 2019

Scope: National

Canadian Acoustical Association (CAA) / Association canadienne d'acoustique (ACA)
c/o C. Laroche, Faculty of Health Sciences, University of Ottawa, #3062, 451 Smyth Rd., Ottawa ON K1H 8M5
Tel: 613-562-5800; *Fax:* 613-562-5248
www.caa-aca.ca
Overview: A large national charitable organization
Mission: To foster communication among people working in all areas of acoustics in Canada; To promote the growth & practical application of knowledge in acoustics; To encourage education, research & employment in acoustics
Finances: *Funding Sources:* Membership; Subscriptions; Conference fees
20 volunteer(s)
Membership: 300 individuals + 80 organizations; *Fees:* $100 individual; $50 student; *Member Profile:* Individuals with an interest in acoustics, including students, professors, consultants & government
Activities: *Awareness Events:* Acoustics Week in Canada, October
Chief Officer(s):
Frank Russo, President, 416-979-5000 Ext. 2647
president@caa-aca.ca
Dalila Giusti, Treasurer, 905-660-2444 Ext. 228
treasurer@caa-aca.ca
Roberto Racca, Executive Secretary
secretary@caa-aca.ca
Awards:
- Student Presentation Awards

Awarded annually to undergraduate or graduate students making the best presentations during the technical sessions of Canadian Acoustics Week *Eligibility:* Application must be made at the time of submission of the abstract; *Amount:* Three awards of $500 each
- Bell Student Prize in Speech Communication & Hearing

Eligibility: For a graduate student enrolled in a Canadian academic institution & conducting research in the field of speech communication or behavioural acoustics; applicants must submit an application form & supporting documentation before the end of February of the year the award is to be made; *Amount:* $500
- Fessenden Student Prize in Underwater Acoustics

Awarded every two years *Eligibility:* For a graduate student enrolled at a Canadian university & conducting research in underwater acoustics or in a branch of science closely connected to underwater acoustics; applicants must submit an application & supporting documentation before the end of February of the year the award is to be made; *Amount:* $500
- Eckel Student Prize in Noise Control

Awarded annually for a graduate student pursuing studies in any discipline of acoustics & conducting research related to the advancement of the practice of noise control; *Amount:* $500
- Directors' Awards

Eligibility: The first author must study or work in Canada; all papers reporting new results, as well as review & tutorial papers are eligible; technical notes are not eligible; *Amount:* $250 for best student paper; $250 for best member paper published in Canadian Acoustics *Contact:* Chantal Laroche
- Shaw Postdoctoral Prize in Acoustics

Eligibility: For full-time research for 12 months for a highly qualified candidate holding a Ph.D. degree or the equivalent, who has completed all formal academic research training & who wishes to acquire up to two years supervised research training in an established setting; the proposed research must be related to some area of acoustics, psychoacoustics, speech communication or noise; applicants must submit an application form & supporting documentation; *Amount:* $3,000
- Student Prize in Psychological Acoustics

; *Amount:* $500
- Student Prize in Architectural & Room Acoustics

; *Amount:* $500
- Hétu Prize in Acoustics

; *Amount:* A book about acoustics & one-year subscription to Canadian Acoustics
- Canada-Wide Science Fair Award in Acoustics

; *Amount:* $1,000
- Student Travel Subsidies

; *Amount:* Travel to the CAA Conference
- Underwater Acoustics & Signal Processing Student Travel Award

; *Amount:* One $500 or two $250

Meetings/Conferences:
- Canadian Acoustical Association "Acoustics Week in Canada" Conference, November, 2018, Victoria, BC

Scope: National
Publications:
- Canadian Acoustics Journal [a publication of the Canadian Acoustical Journal]

Type: Journal; *Frequency:* Quarterly; *Editor:* Frank Russo; *Price:* Free to CAAmembers
Profile: Refereed articles, research, reviews, activities, new products, & news about acoustics & vibration

Canadian Acquirer's Association (CAA)
#1400, 2000, rue Mansfield, Montréal QC M3A 3A2
Tel: 514-842-0886
contact@acquirers.ca
www.acquirers.ca
Overview: A small national organization founded in 2008
Mission: To bring together payment professionals in Canada
Membership: *Member Profile:* Entrepreneurs in the field of electronic payments (credit, debit, gift card, EFT & other)
Chief Officer(s):
Adam Atlas, Founding President
atlas@adamatlas.com

Canadian Actors' Equity Association (CLC) (CAEA)
44 Victoria St., 12th Fl., Toronto ON M5C 3C4
Tel: 416-867-9165; *Fax:* 416-867-9246
Other Communication: membership@caea.com
info@caea.com
www.caea.com
Also Known As: Actors' Equity
Overview: A medium-sized national organization founded in 1976
Mission: To negotiate & administer collective agreements, provides benefit plans, information & support; to act as an advocate for its membership.
Membership: 6,000; *Fees:* $180; *Member Profile:* Performers, directors, choreographers, fight directors, & stage managers involved in live performance in theatre, opera, & dance in English Canada; *Committees:* Honours; Directors, Choreographers, & Fight Directors; Atlantic; Council Renewal; Diversity; Equity Independent & Small-Scale Theatre Resource;

Canadian Associations / Canadian Addiction Counsellors Certification Federation (CACCF) / Fédération canadienne d'agrément des conseillers en toxicomanie

Member Communications & Education; Opera; Stage Management
Chief Officer(s):
Allan Teichman, President
president@caea.com
Arden R. Ryshpan, Executive Director
execdir@caea.com
Lynn McQueen, Director, Communications
editor@caea.com
Publications:
• EQ
Type: Newsletter; *Frequency:* Quarterly; *Editor:* Barb Farwell
Profile: Information for equity members

Western Office (CAEA)
#510, 736 Granville St., Vancouver BC V6Z 1G3
Tel: 604-682-6173; *Fax:* 604-682-6174
woffice@caea.com
Chief Officer(s):
Jennifer Riedle, Business Representative
jennifer@caea.com

Canadian Addiction Counsellors Certification Board *See* Canadian Addiction Counsellors Certification Federation

Canadian Addiction Counsellors Certification Federation (CACCF) / Fédération canadienne d'agrément des conseillers en toxicomanie
81 Bruce St., #C, Kitchener ON N2B 1Y7
Tel: 519-772-0533; *Fax:* 519-772-0535
Toll-Free: 866-624-1911
info@caccf.ca
canadianaddictioncounsellors.org
www.linkedin.com/company/canadian-addiction-counsellors-certification-federation
www.facebook.com/CACCF
twitter.com/CACCF_Canada
Previous Name: Canadian Addiction Counsellors Certification Board
Overview: A medium-sized national organization
Mission: To offer credible certifications to all addiction specific counsellors in Canada; To promote & monitor the competency of addiction specific counsellors in Canada
Member of: International Certification & Reciprocity Consortium / Alcohol & Other Drug Abuse (IC&RC/AODA)
Staff Member(s): 3
Membership: 900+; *Fees:* $240 regular; $60 student; $50 retired; *Committees:* Certification
Chief Officer(s):
Jeff Wilbee, Executive Director
jeff@caccf.ca
Tom Gabriel, President
Publications:
• The Beacon
Type: Newsletter; *Frequency:* Semiannually

The Canadian Addison Society / La Société canadienne d'Addison
1 Palace Arch Dr., Toronto ON M9A 2S1
Toll-Free: 888-550-5582
Other Communication: newsletter@addisonsociety.ca
info@addisonsociety.ca
www.addisonsociety.ca
Overview: A small national charitable organization founded in 1990
Mission: To offer information about Addison's Disease; To assist in the education of the medical society & the public about Addison's Disease
Finances: *Funding Sources:* Donations
Membership: 111; *Fees:* $25
Activities: Providing support, through various groups
Chief Officer(s):
Harold Smith, President
president@addisonsociety.ca
Roger Steinmann, Vice-President
vicepresident@addisonsociety.ca
Rick Burpee, Secretary-Treasurer
secretary-treasurer@addisonsociety.ca
Meetings/Conferences:
• The Canadian Addison Society Annual General Meeting 2018, 2018
Scope: National
Publications:
• The Canadian Addison Society Newsletter
Type: Newsletter; *Frequency:* Quarterly
Profile: Society updates & current information regarding Addison's Disease

Canadian ADHD Resource Alliance (CADDRA)
#604, 3950 - 14th Ave., Markham ON L3R 0A9
Tel: 416-637-8583; *Fax:* 416-385-3232
info@caddra.ca
www.caddra.ca
Also Known As: Canadian Attention Deficit Hyperactivity Disorder Resource Alliance
Overview: A small national organization
Mission: To take a leadership role in ADHD research in Canada; to develop the Canadian ADHD Practice Guidelines (CAP-G); to facilitate development & implementation of training standards & guidelines; to share information amongst all stakeholder groups; to advocate to governments, teaching environments & employment organizations on ADHD
Membership: *Fees:* $200 full; $170 international/associate; $60 resident; *Member Profile:* Doctors who support patients & their families, who suffer from ADHD
Chief Officer(s):
Niamh McGarry, Executive Director
niamh.mcgarry@caddra.ca
Meetings/Conferences:
• Canadian ADHD Resource Alliance 14th Annual Conference, November, 2018, Hyatt Regency Calgary, Calgary, AB
Scope: National

Canadian Administrative Housekeepers Association *See* Canadian Association of Environmental Management

Canadian Adult Congenital Heart Network (CACH)
c/o BB&C, #100, 2233 Argentia Rd., Mississauga ON L5N 2K7
Tel: 905-826-6665; *Fax:* 905-826-4873
www.cachnet.ca
Overview: A small national organization founded in 1991
Mission: To promote the interests of Canadians born with heart defects
Affiliation(s): Toronto Congenital Cardiac Centre for Adults; Adult Congenital Heart Council
Finances: *Funding Sources:* Donations
Membership: *Fees:* $100 physicians & surgeons; $50 nurses, assistants & other professionals
Chief Officer(s):
Erwin Oechslin, President
Publications:
• The Beat
Type: Newsletter; *Editor:* Laura-Lee Walter
Profile: Stories, overviews, & clinic updates

Canadian Adult Recreational Hockey Association (CARHA)
#610, 1420 Blair Pl., Ottawa ON K1J 9L8
Tel: 613-244-1989; *Fax:* 613-244-0451
Toll-Free: 800-267-1854
hockey@carhahockey.ca
www.carhahockey.ca
www.facebook.com/carhahockey
twitter.com/CARHAHockey
Also Known As: CARHA Hockey
Previous Name: Canadian Oldtimers' Hockey Association
Overview: A medium-sized national charitable organization founded in 1975
Mission: To develop & provide a wide range of innovative hockey benefits & solutions to customers; To build & retain relationships among the adult recreational hockey community across Canada
Finances: *Funding Sources:* Membership; Sponsorship
Membership: *Fees:* $23; *Member Profile:* Men & women, 19 years of age or older
Activities: *Internships:* Yes
Chief Officer(s):
Michael S. Peski, President
mpeski@carhahockey.ca
Lori Lopez, Director, Business Operations
llopez@carhahockey.ca
Karen Hodgson, Manager, Member Services
kHodgson@carhahockey.ca
Laurie Snider, Coordinator, Member Services & Special Projects
lsnider@carhahockey.ca
Publications:
• Ice Chips
Type: Newsletter; *Frequency:* Quarterly

Canadian Advanced Technology Alliance (CATA Alliance) / Association canadienne de technologie de pointe
National Headquarters, #416, 207 Bank St., Ottawa ON K2P 2N2
Tel: 613-236-6550
info@cata.ca
www.cata.ca
twitter.com/CATAAlliance
Overview: A large national organization founded in 1978
Mission: To provide members with a network to establish partnerships, to match up with global business opportunities; To offer communication & advocacy services, notably in dealing with the government; To work to ensure that policies are favourable to Canadian technology companies; To maintain a research repository where members can access information to advance their agendas
Affiliation(s): Canadian Association of Internet Providers (CAIP)
Membership: *Member Profile:* Corporations with Canadian offices, engaged in research & development activities; International corporations in a collaboration with CATA; User industries; Service companies
Activities: Engaging in advocacy activities; Providing original & timely information for members & stakeholders; Supporting research projects
Chief Officer(s):
John Reid, President & CEO
Charles Duffet, Chief Digital Officer
Russ Roberts, Senior Vice-President, Tax & Finance
Kevin Wennekes, Chief Business Officer
Awards:
• Innovation & Leadership Awards
To recognize expertise, innovation, & leadership in the Canadian high-technology sector
• Sara Kirke Award
To recognize woman entrepreneurship, including outstanding technological innovation & corporate leadership

Canadian Adventist Teachers Network
c/o Seventh-day Adventist Church in Canada, 1148 King St. East, Oshawa ON L1H 1H8
Tel: 905-433-0011; *Fax:* 905-433-0982
education@adventist.ca
catnet.sdacc.org
Also Known As: CAT-net
Overview: A small national organization
Mission: Dedicated to promoting excellence in Christian education by helping facilitate communication and the exchange of ideas among Adventist educators.
Affiliation(s): Seventh-day Adventist Church in Canada
Chief Officer(s):
Dennis Marshall, General Vice-President & Director, Education
marshall.dennis@adventist.ca

Canadian Aerial Applicators Association (CAAA)
#202, 4505 - 99 St., Edmonton AB T6E 3N8
Tel: 780-413-0078; *Fax:* 780-413-0076
caaa@telusplanet.net
www.canadianaerialapplicators.com
Overview: A small national organization founded in 1986
Mission: To promote safety & continuing education within the industry, & to support professionalism amongst its members; to lobby federal & provincial government agencies to design policies; to advise regulatory agencies on the safe & efficient aerial application of pesticides & other crop inputs.
Affiliation(s): Bayer CropScience Canada Co.; BASF Canada, Inc.; Syngenta Crop Protection Canada, Inc.
Staff Member(s): 5
Membership: 172; *Fees:* Schedule available dependant on number of aircrafts & staff
Activities: Mentorship Program; training from ground crews to pilots; conference & tradeshow; *Internships:* Yes
Chief Officer(s):
Paul O'Carroll, President
Jill Lane, Executive Director
director@canadianaerialapplicators.com

Canadian Aeronautical Institute (CAI) *See* Canadian Aeronautics & Space Institute

Canadian Aeronautics & Space Institute (CASI) / Institut aéronautique et spatial du Canada
#104, 350 Terry Fox Dr., Ottawa ON K2K 2W5
Tel: 613-591-8787; *Fax:* 613-591-7291
Other Communication: membership@casi.ca
casi@casi.ca
www.casi.ca
Previous Name: Canadian Aeronautical Institute (CAI)
Merged from: Institute of Aircraft Technicians; Ottawa Aeronautical Society; US Institute of Aeronautical Science
Overview: A medium-sized national licensing organization founded in 1954

Mission: To advance the art, science, engineering, & applications of aeronautics & associated technologies in Canada; To provide a focus for communications and networking for aeronautics and & communities in Canada; To assist members in developming skills, exchanging information & sharing talents in their areas of interest
Affiliation(s): Canadian Air Cushion Technology Society; Canadian Navigation Society; Canadian Remote Sensing Society
Finances: *Funding Sources:* Member dues
Membership: 1,600; *Fees:* $39.55 juniors, $67.80 seriors, $101.70 regular; *Committees:* Executive; Admissions; Nominating; Senior Awards; Strategic Oversight; Student Activities
Activities: Facilitating communications among the Canadian aeronautics & space community; Developing members' skills; Publish journals, newsletters & a podcast
Chief Officer(s):
Ian Fejtek, President
Jacques Giroux, Vice President
Geoff Languedoc, Executive Director
Awards:
• F.W. (Casey) Baldwin Award
Presented for the best article published in the Canadian Aeronautics and Space Journal during the preceding calendar year
• Elvie L. Smith Scholarship
Awarded annually to a student who is following a post-secondary degree or diploma course recognized by the institute *Eligibility:* Nominee must be a Canadian citizen and student in good standing of CASI; must be entering their last year of undergraduate studies in the year they receive the scholarship; *Amount:* $5000
• Charles Luttman Scholarship
Awarded annually to a student who is following a post-secondary degree or diploma course recognized by the institute *Eligibility:* Nominee must be a Canadian citizen and student in good standing of CASI; must be entering their next-to-last year of undergraduate studies in the year they receive the scholarship; *Amount:* $3000
Meetings/Conferences:
• Canadian Aeronautics & Space Institute ASTRO 2018 Conference, May, 2018, Delta Québec, Québec, QC
Scope: International
Contact Information: Phone: 613-591-8787; E-mail: astro@casi.ca
Publications:
• Canadian Aeronautics & Space Journal (CASJ)
Type: Journal; *Frequency:* 3 pa; *Accepts Advertising; Editor:* Brendan Quine; *Price:* Free to members & corporate
Profile: Fundamental & applied research, new technologies & other developments in the aerospace sciences & related fields
• Canadian Journal of Remote Sensing (CJRS)/Journal canadien de télédétection
Type: Journal; *Frequency:* 6 pa; *Accepts Advertising; Editor:* Nicholas Coops; *Price:* Free to members & corporate partners
Profile: Technical research articles, notes & review papers on topics such as sensor & algorithm development, image processing techniques& other advances
• CASI [Canadian Aeronautics & Space Institute] Clipper
Type: E-newsletter; *Frequency:* Bimonthly
Profile: Information about the aeronautics, space & related communities, provides information on conferences, events and meetings; produced & distributed tomembers & corporate partners

Canadian Aerophilatelic Society (CAS) / La société canadienne d'aérophilatélie (SCA)
203A Woodfield Dr., Nepean ON K2G 4P2
www.aerophilately.ca
Overview: A small national organization founded in 1984
Mission: To represent Canadian aerophilatelists nationally & internationally
Membership: *Fees:* $20 members in Canada; $22 US residents; $25 members outside Canada; *Member Profile:* Canadians who are interested in world-wide aerophilately; Collectors throughout the world who are interested in Canadian aerophilately
Activities: Facilitating the exchange of information; Providing information about air mail stamps & covers; Selling covers; *Library:* Canadian Aerophilatelic Society Library
Chief Officer(s):
Steve Johnson, President
steverman@rogers.com

Brian Wolfenden, Secretary-Treasurer
bjnepean@trytel.com
Publications:
• The Canadian Aerophilatelist
Type: Newsletter; *Frequency:* Quarterly; *Editor:* Chris Hargreaves

Canadian Agencies Practicing Marketing Activation (CAPMA)
#107, 1 Eva Rd., Toronto ON M9C 4Z5
info@capma.org
www.capma.org
Overview: A medium-sized national organization founded in 2001
Mission: To raise the profile of the marketing industry; To provide members with the resources to grow as businesses
Member of: Institute of Communication Agencies
Membership: *Fees:* Based on number of employees; *Member Profile:* Marketing agencies in Canada
Activities: Developing networking opportunities
Chief Officer(s):
Troy Yung, President
Awards:
• PROMO! Award

Canadian Agency for Drugs & Technologies in Health (CADTH) / Agence canadienne des médicaments et des technologies de la santé (ACMTS)
#600, 865 Carling Ave., Ottawa ON K1S 5S8
Tel: 613-226-2553; *Fax:* 613-226-5392
Toll-Free: 866-988-1444
requests@cadth.ca
www.cadth.ca
www.linkedin.com/company/cadth
twitter.com/CADTH_ACMTS
www.youtube.com/user/CADTHACMTS
Previous Name: Canadian Coordinating Office for Health Technology Assessment
Overview: A medium-sized national organization founded in 1989
Mission: To offer evidence-based information & impartial advice to health care decision makers about the effectiveness of drugs & other health technologies
Finances: *Funding Sources:* Canadian federal, provincial, & territorial governments
Membership: *Member Profile:* Canadian health care decision makers
Activities: Assessing drugs & health technologies; Conducting drug reviews; Identifying optimal drug therapy
Chief Officer(s):
Brian O'Rourke, President & CEO
Awards:
• Canadian Agency for Drugs & Technologies in Health Award of Excellence
To recognize individuals whose achievements have advanced the fields of health technology assessment, evidence-based drug reviews, or optimal technology utilization in Canada
Meetings/Conferences:
• 2018 Canadian Agency for Drugs & Technologies in Health Symposium, April, 2018, Halifax, NS
Scope: National
Description: Theme: "Managing Health Technologies: Supporting Appropriate, Affordable, & Accessible Care"
Publications:
• Canadian Agency for Drugs & Technologies in Health Annual Report
Type: Yearbook; *Frequency:* Annually
• Canadian Agency for Drugs & Technologies in Health Technology Reports
Profile: Peer reviewed assessments of health care technologies & services
• CDR [Common Drug Review] Update
Type: Bulletin; *Price:* Free
Profile: Common Drug Review program initiatives & activities
• COMPUS [Canadian Optimal Medication Prescribing & Utilization Service] Communiqué
Type: Newsletter; *Price:* Free
Profile: Activities of the Canadian Optimal Medication Prescribing & Utilization Service
• Connection [a publication of the Canadian Agency for Drugs & Technologies in Health]
Type: Newsletter
Profile: Corporate newsletter of the Canadian Agency for Drugs & Technologies in Health

• Health Technology Update
Type: Newsletter; *Frequency:* 3 pa; *ISSN:* 1715-5568
Profile: Articles about new medical devices, procedures, & health systems
• Issues in Emerging Health Technologies
Type: Bulletin
Profile: Drug & non-drug technologies that are not yet used, or widely diffused, in Canada

Canadian Agricultural Economics & Farm Management Society *See* Canadian Agricultural Economics Society

Canadian Agricultural Economics Society (CAES) / Société canadienne d'agroéconomie (SCAE)
University Of Victoria, PO Box 1700, Stn. CSC, #360, Business & Economics Bldg., Victoria BC V8W 2Y2
Fax: 866-543-7613
caes.usask.ca
twitter.com/CAES_AgEcon
Previous Name: Canadian Agricultural Economics & Farm Management Society
Overview: A medium-sized national organization
Mission: To address problems related to the economics of food production & marketing & the quality of rural life through extension, research, teaching, & policy making in government & private industry
Affiliation(s): Agricultural Institute of Canada
Membership: 488; *Fees:* $125 regular; $30 student; $65 senior; $75 early career; *Member Profile:* Individuals with interest in agricultural economics
Chief Officer(s):
Valerie Johnson, Executive Director
valcaes@telus.net
Awards:
• Excellence in Farm Business Management
• Outstanding Ph.D. Thesis Award
• Outstanding Master's Thesis Award
• Outstanding Agribusiness Master's Project Award
• Outstanding Journal Article Award
• Publication of Enduring Quality Award
• Undergraduate Book Prize Award
Publications:
• Canadian Agricultural Economics Society Newsletter
Type: Newsletter
Profile: CAES news & activities
• Canadian Journal of Agricultural Economics [a publication of the Canadian Agricultural Economics Society]
Type: Journal; *Frequency:* 4 pa; *Price:* Free to members
Profile: International peer-reviewed journal about agricultural & resource economics

Canadian Agricultural Human Resource Council (CAHRC)
#404, 1410 Blair Pl., Ottawa ON K1J 9B9
Tel: 613-745-7457
info@cahrc-ccrha.ca
www.cahrc-ccrha.ca
www.linkedin.com/company/canadian-agricultural-human-resource-council
Overview: A medium-sized national organization
Mission: To raise awareness of, & provide solutions to, the human resource issues affecting Canada's agricultural industry
Membership: 19
Activities: Providing training & skills development services; Building Canada's agriculture workforce
Chief Officer(s):
Portia MacDonald-Dewhirst, Executive Director
macdonald-dewhirst@cahrc-ccrha.ca

Canadian Agricultural Safety Association (CASA) / Association canadienne de sécurité agricole (ACSA)
3325-C Pembina Hwy., Winnipeg MB R3V 0A2
Tel: 204-452-2272; *Fax:* 204-261-5004
Toll-Free: 877-452-2272
info@casa-acsa.ca
www.casa-acsa.ca
www.linkedin.com/company/canadian-agricultural-safety-association
www.facebook.com/planfarmsafety
twitter.com/planfarmsafety
www.youtube.com/planfarmsafety
Overview: A medium-sized national organization founded in 1993
Mission: To address problems of illness, injuries & accidental death in farmers, their families & agricultural workers; To improve health & safety conditions of those that live or work on Canadian farms

Canadian Associations / Canadian Agri-Marketing Association (CAMA)

Finances: *Annual Operating Budget:* $1.5 Million-$3 Million
Staff Member(s): 4
Membership: *Fees:* $100 personal, not-profit; $300 academia, producer, government, service/supply industry
Activities: *Library:* Open to public
Chief Officer(s):
Marcel L. Hacault, Executive Director
Denis Bilodeau, Chair
denisbilodeau@upa.qc.ca
Dean Anderson, Vice-Chair
dean.anderson@wsps.ca
Lauranne Sanderson, Treasurer
Meetings/Conferences:
• Canadian Agricultural Safety Association Conference 2018, 2018
Scope: National
Description: A forum for members, supporters, researchers and innovators to network, share, and learn about important trends and developments in agricultural safety.
Publications:
• CASA [Canadian Agricultural Safety Association] / ACSA [Association canadienne de sécurité agricole] Liaison
Type: Newsletter; *Frequency:* Monthly
Profile: News for members & interested individuals
• CASA [Canadian Agricultural Safety Association] Annual Report
Type: Yearbook; *Frequency:* Annually
Profile: Long term objectives of the association & financial statements

Canadian Agri-Marketing Association (CAMA)
22 Guyers Dr., RR#3, Port Elgin ON N0H 2C7
Tel: 519-389-6552
info@cama.org
www.cama.org
Overview: A medium-sized national organization founded in 1966
Mission: To promote the exchange & application of agricultural marketing ideas; To encourage high professional standards of agricultural marketing in Ontario
Affiliation(s): National Agri-Marketing Association (Canadian Agri-Marketing Association's USA counterpart)
Membership: *Member Profile:* Agribusiness marketing professionals from across Ontario, such as manufacturers, agencies, retailers & associations
Activities: Encouraging professional development; Creating networking opportunities with others in the industry in Ontario; Promoting interest in agri-marketing as a career
Chief Officer(s):
Mary Thornley, Executive Director, 519-389-6552
Publications:
• Agri-Marketing
Type: Newsletter; *Price:* Free with membership in the Canadian Agri-Marketing Association
• Canadian Agri-Marketing Association Membership Directory
Type: Directory; *Price:* Free with membership in the Canadian Agri-Marketing Association
Profile: A national directory of CAMA members

Canadian Agri-Marketing Association (Alberta) (CAMA)
22 Guyers Dr., RR#3, Port Elgin ON N0H 2C7
Alberta@cama.org
www.cama.org/chapters/alberta
Also Known As: CAMA Alberta
Overview: A medium-sized provincial organization founded in 1978 overseen by Canadian Agri-Marketing Association
Mission: To increase knowledge of ideas related to agri-marketing; To promote high professional standards of agricultural marketing
Affiliation(s): National Agri-Marketing Association (NAMA); CAMA Saskatchewan; CAMA Manitoba; CAMA Ontario; CAMA Québec
Membership: *Fees:* $140
Activities: Offering professional development seminars; Providing networking opportunities
Chief Officer(s):
Teresa Faulk, President, CAMA Alberta
Publications:
• CAMA [Canadian Agri-Marketing Association] Membership Directory
Type: Directory
Profile: Contact information for CAMA members throughout Canada
• MarketNews [a publication of the Canadian Agri-Marketing Association]

Type: Newsletter; *Frequency:* 5 pa
Profile: Association events & industry information for members

Canadian Agri-Marketing Association (Manitoba)
210 - 1600 Kenaston Blvd., Winnipeg MB R3P 0Y4
Tel: 204-799-2019; *Fax:* 204-257-5651
camamb@mts.net
www.cama.org/manitoba/ManitobaHome.aspx
Also Known As: CAMA Manitoba
Overview: A small provincial organization founded in 1985 overseen by Canadian Agri-Marketing Association
Mission: To promote excellence in agrimarketing
Affiliation(s): CAMA Ontario; CAMA Alberta; CAMA Saskatchewan
Finances: *Annual Operating Budget:* Less than $50,000
Staff Member(s): 1; 12 volunteer(s)
Membership: 125 individual; *Fees:* $100 individual; $25 student
Chief Officer(s):
Barbara Chabih, President

Canadian Agri-Marketing Association (Saskatchewan)
PO Box 4005, Regina SK S4P 3R9
Tel: 306-262-0733
camask@sasktel.net
www.cama.org/saskatchewan/saskatchewanHome.aspx
Also Known As: CAMA Saskatchewan
Overview: A medium-sized provincial organization overseen by Canadian Agri-Marketing Association
Mission: To operate as a networking organization for all sectors of Saskatchewan's agricultural industry
Membership: *Committees:* Events & Programs; Membership; Membership Communications; Promotions / Public Relations; Website
Chief Officer(s):
Lesley Kelly, President

Canadian AIDS Society (CAS) / Société canadienne du sida (SCS)
#100, 190 O'Connor St., Ottawa ON K2P 2R3
Tel: 613-230-3580; *Fax:* 613-563-4998
Toll-Free: 800-499-1986
casinfo@cdnaids.ca
www.cdnaids.ca
www.facebook.com/aidsida
twitter.com/CDNAIDS
www.instagram.com/cdnaids
Overview: A medium-sized national charitable organization founded in 1988
Mission: To strengthen the response to HIV/AIDS across Canada; To enrich the lives of people living with HIV/AIDS
Finances: *Funding Sources:* Membership fees; Sponsorships; Fundraising
Membership: 120+ organizations; *Fees:* Schedule available; *Member Profile:* Community-based AIDS organizations across Canada
Activities: Promoting awareness & education; Offering information; Advocating on federal public policy; Establishing networking groups; *Awareness Events:* AIDS Walk for Life; Annual World AIDS Day, December 1; *Speaker Service:* Yes
Chief Officer(s):
Greg Riehl, Chair
gregr@cdnaids.ca
Michael Sangster, Vice-Chair
mikes@cdnaids.ca
Gary Lacasse, Executive Director
gary.lacasse@cdnaids.ca
Gerry Croteau, Secretary
gerryc@cdnaids.ca
Janet MacPhee, Treasurer
janetm@cdnaids.ca
Janne Charbonneau, Officer, Communications
janne.charbonneau@cdnaids.ca
Lynne Belle-Isle, Manager, National Programs
lynne.belle-isle@cdnaids.ca
Tobias Keogh, Manager, Fundraising
tobias.keogh@cdnaids.ca
Awards:
• Canadian AIDS Society Leadership Award
National contributions made in the fight again HIV/AIDS
Publications:
• Canadian AIDS Society Annual Report
Type: Yearbook; *Frequency:* Annually
Profile: Society's achievements, finances, supporters, & volunteers

• InfoCAS
Type: Newsletter; *Frequency:* Quarterly; *Price:* Free
Profile: HIV/AIDS national policy, governmental news, & activities of member groups
• InFocus
Type: Newletter; *Frequency:* Semiannually
Profile: Examination of HIV/AIDS issues, ideas, & information

Canadian AIDS Treatment Information Exchange (CATIE) / Réseau canadien d'info-traitements sida
PO Box 1104, #505, 555 Richmond St. West, Toronto ON M5V 3B1
Tel: 416-203-7122; *Fax:* 416-203-8284
Toll-Free: 800-263-1638
info@catie.ca
www.catie.ca
www.linkedin.com/company/canadian-aids-treatment-information-exchange
www.facebook.com/CATIEInfo
twitter.com/CATIEInfo
www.youtube.com/user/catieinfo
Previous Name: Community AIDS Treatment Information Exchange
Overview: A small national charitable organization founded in 1990
Mission: To improve the health & quality of life of all people living with HIV/AIDS (PHAs) in Canada; To provide HIV/AIDS treatment information to PHAs, caregivers & AIDS service organizations who are encouraged to be active partners in achieving informed decision-making & optimal health care; To promote collaboration among affected populations
Member of: Canadian AIDS Society; Ontario AIDS Network; Ontario Hospital Association
Finances: *Annual Operating Budget:* $3 Million-$5 Million; *Funding Sources:* Government grants; Corporate sponsorship
Staff Member(s): 40
Membership: 3,000; *Member Profile:* HIV+ individuals; Allied health care professionals; Community health organizations; *Committees:* Aboriginal Advisory; Executive; Strategic Planning & Policy Development
Activities: Providing current & confidential treatment information; Supporting & connecting people with HIV; Developing current knowledge on HIV prevention & treatment; Working to ensure that frontline providers address HIV & hepatitis C issues; *Awareness Events:* World AIDS Day, Dec. 1; *Internships:* Yes; *Speaker Service:* Yes; *Library:* CATIE Ordering Centre; by appointment
Chief Officer(s):
John McCullagh, Chair
jmccullagh@catie.ca
Laurie Edmiston, Executive Director
ledmiston@catie.ca
Meetings/Conferences:
• Canadian AIDS Treatment Information Exchange 2018 Forum, 2018
Scope: National
Publications:
• The CATIE [Canadian AIDS Treatment Information Exchange] Exchange
Type: Newsletter; *Editor:* Jim Pollock
Profile: Forum on CATIE & frontline programs
• The Positive Side [a publication of the Canadian AIDS Treatment Information Exchange]
Type: Magazine; *Frequency:* s-a.; *Editor:* Debbie Koenig
Profile: A health & wellness magazine written for people living with HIV

Canadian Air Cushion Technology Society (CACTS)
c/o Canadian Aeronautics & Space Institute, #104, 350 Terry Fox Dr., Kanata ON K2K 2W5
Tel: 613-591-8787; *Fax:* 613-591-7291
www.casi.ca/canadian-air-cushion-tech-soc
Overview: A small national organization overseen by Canadian Aeronautics & Space Institute
Mission: To serve the air cushion technology (hovercraft) community throughout Canada; To advance the science, technologies, & applications of air cushion technology
Activities: Providing air cushion technology information; Liaising with other organizations interested in hovercraft
Chief Officer(s):
Jacques Laframboise, Society Chair
malina1@vif.com

Canadian Air Line Pilots Association *See* Air Line Pilots Association, International - Canada

Canadian Air Traffic Control Association (CATCA) / Association canadienne du contrôle du trafic aérien (ACCTA)
#304, 265 Carling Ave., Ottawa ON K1S 2E1
Tel: 613-225-3553; *Fax:* 613-225-8448
catca@catca.ca
www.catca.ca
www.facebook.com/CATCA5454
twitter.com/CATCA5454
Overview: A medium-sized national organization founded in 1959
Mission: To represent the air traffic controllers of Canada
Membership: *Committees:* Convention; Contract; Election; Occupational Health & Safety
Chief Officer(s):
Peter Duffey, President
Doug Best, Executive Vice-President
Meetings/Conferences:
• Canadian Air Traffic Control Association 2019 Convention, 2019, Calgary Tower, Springbank Tower & Edmonton ACC, Calgary, AB
Scope: National
Description: A biennial convention attended by delegates from regions across Canada

Canadian Airports Council (CAC) / Le conseil des aéroports du Canada
#600, 116 Lisgar St., Ottawa ON K2P 0C2
Tel: 613-560-9302; *Fax:* 613-560-6599
www.cacairports.ca
Overview: A large national organization founded in 1992
Mission: To lead the industry through effective lobbying, timely communications & the establishment of strategic alliances with other industry stakeholders, while promoting Canada's airports; To encourage consensus building in order to effectively represent unified airport positions to government, the aviation industry & the public
Member of: Airports Council International - North America (ACI-NA)
Affiliation(s): Air Transport Association of Canada (ATAC); Canadian International Freight Forwarders Association (CIFFA); Canadian Chamber of Commerce; Canadian Tourism Commission; Tourism Industry Association of Canada (TIAC)
Finances: *Funding Sources:* Sponsorships
Membership: 51; *Fees:* $1,500; *Member Profile:* Canadian airports (CAC members are also members of Airports Council International - North America)
Activities: Preparing submissions to governmental bodies & agencies
Chief Officer(s):
Daniel-Robert Gooch, President, 613-560-9302 Ext. 16
daniel.gooch@cacairports.ca
Holly Christian, Executive Assistant, 613-560-9302 Ext. 14
holly.christian@cacairports.ca
Awards:
• The CAC Air Cadet League of Canada Scholarship
• The CAC Gerry Bruno Scholarship
Recognizes students with high academic acheivement who are working toward a career in aviation managment, planning, marketing or policy; awarded every two years *Eligibility:* Any student registered in any associated Canadian university college or program *Deadline:* August 1; *Amount:* $5,000
Meetings/Conferences:
• Airports Canada Conference & Exhibition, 2018
Description: A targeted opportunity for key decision-makers to share ideas & gain the latest information on the best strategic & operational tools & practices concerning airports across Canada & internationally
Publications:
• The Airport Voice: News & Views
Type: Newsletter; *Price:* Free download
Profile: National & international news affecting Canadian airports
• The Canadian Airports Council Annual Report
Type: Yearbook; *Frequency:* Annually
Profile: Significant developments at the CAC & in the industry during the year

Canadian Alarm & Security Association *See* Canadian Security Association

Canadian Albacore Association (CAA)
PO Box 98093, 970 Queen St. East, Toronto ON M4M 1J8
www.albacore.ca
www.facebook.com/AlbacoreSailCan
twitter.com/AlbacoreSailCan
Overview: A small national organization founded in 1961
Mission: To promote & support the development of the Albacore fleet
Membership: *Fees:* $60 full member; $27 associate member; $21 youth member; *Member Profile:* Canadian owners & sailors of Albacore dinghies
Activities: Sharing news & information about Canadian Albacore sailing; Sponsoring events & regattas
Chief Officer(s):
Mary Neumann, Commodore
John Cawthorne, Treasurer
Publications:
• Shackles & Cringles
Type: Newsletter; *Frequency:* Quarterly; *Editor:* Jelena Balic; *Price:* Free to members

Canadian Alliance for Long Term Care (CALTC)
info@caltc.ca
www.caltc.ca
Overview: A medium-sized national organization
Mission: To ensure the delivery fo quality care to vulnerable citizens of Canada
Membership: *Member Profile:* Provincial associations & publicly funded long term care providers

Canadian Alliance of British Pensioners (CABP)
#202, 4800 Dundas St. West, Toronto ON M9A 1B1
Tel: 416-253-6402
Toll-Free: 888-591-3964
info@britishpensions.com
www.britishpensions.com
www.facebook.com/131267116913840
twitter.com/CABP_News
www.youtube.com/user/ICBPandCABP
Overview: A medium-sized national organization
Mission: To campaign politically to cease the freezing of British state pensions paid in certain countries
Member of: International Consortium of British Pensioners
Finances: *Funding Sources:* Membership fees; Campaigning
Membership: *Fees:* $25; $40 international; *Member Profile:* Current & soon to be expatriate British pensioners in Canada
Activities: Providing information & advice to members about British state pensions; Organizing public information meetings about the legal challenge against the United Kingdom government's pension-freezing policy
Chief Officer(s):
Sheila Telford, Chair
Publications:
• Justice
Type: Magazine; *Frequency:* Quarterly; *Price:* Free with membership in the Canadian Alliance of British Pensioners
Profile: Current information about pension issues & the Alliance's campaign to end pension discrimination

British Pensioners Association of Western Canada (BPAWC)
211 Fonda Way SE, Calgary AB T2A 4Z7
Tel: 403-730-0525
expats@britishpensioners.com
www.britishpensioners.com
Chief Officer(s):
Jonathan Macfarland, President

Canadian Alliance of Dance Artists (CADA ON) / Alliance canadiennes des artistes de danse
476 Parliament St., 2nd Fl., Toronto ON M4X 1P2
Tel: 416-657-2276
office@cada-on.ca
cadaontario.camp8.org
www.facebook.com/cadaontariochapter
twitter.com/cadaon
Overview: A small provincial organization founded in 1986
Mission: To advance the socioeconomic status & working conditions of professional dance artists in Ontario; To support the professional & artistic development of Ontario's dance artists
Affiliation(s): Canadian Alliance of Dance Artists, British Columbia Chapter
Finances: *Funding Sources:* Membership fees; Canadian Council of the Arts; The Ontario Trillium Foundation; Ontario Arts Council; Toronto Arts Council
Membership: 200; *Fees:* $80 professional artists; $60 emerging artists; $50 associates; *Member Profile:* Emerging & professional dance artists; Associate professionals; Dance students
Activities: Developing services & programs for the dance community in Ontario; Increasing public awareness of dance; Partnering with other arts service organizations; Advocating for the elevation of the status of the arts
Chief Officer(s):
Larissa Taurins-Crawford, Administrative Director

West Chapter (CADA BC)
c/o Scotiabank Dance Centre, 677 Davie St., 7th Fl., Vancouver BC V6B 2G6
Tel: 604-606-6414
office@cadawest.org
cadawest.org
facebook.com/CADAWest
twitter.com/CADAWest
Mission: To act as a unified voice for professional dance artists in British Columbia; To advance the socioeconomic status & working conditions of professional dance artists; To enable dance artists to attain their potential; To foster excellence in dance
Chief Officer(s):
Starr Muranko, Chair
Lexi Vajda, Secretary
Ben Shockey, Treasurer
Jessica Wadsworth, Program Manager

Canadian Alliance of Physiotherapy Regulators (CARP) / Alliance canadienne des organismes de réglementation de la physiothérapie (ACORP)
#501, 1243 Islington Ave., Toronto ON M8X 1Y9
Tel: 416-234-8800; *Fax:* 416-234-8820
email@alliancept.org
www.alliancept.org
Overview: A large national organization founded in 1987
Mission: To facilitate the sharing of information & build consensus on national regulatory issues in order to assist member regulators in fulfilling their mandate of protecting the public interest
Finances: *Annual Operating Budget:* $500,000-$1.5 Million
Staff Member(s): 8
Membership: 11 provincial physiotherapy regulators; *Fees:* Schedule available; *Member Profile:* Member boards must have provincial regulation respecting physiotherapists; *Committees:* CEO Review Committee; Governance and Nominations Committee; Evaluation Services Committee; Registrars' Committee
Activities: Credentialling; examinations
Chief Officer(s):
Katya Masnyk, Chief Executive Officer
Publications:
• Canadian Alliance of Physiotherapy Regulators Annual Report
Type: Report; *Frequency:* Annually; *Price:* Free

Canadian Alliance of Student Associations (CASA) / Alliance canadienne des associations étudiantes (ACAE)
#410, Slater St., Ottawa ON K1P 6E2
Tel: 613-236-3457; *Fax:* 613-236-2386
www.casa-acae.com
www.facebook.com/casa.acae
twitter.com/casadaily
www.youtube.com/user/CASAACAE;
www.flickr.com/photos/casa-acae
Overview: A medium-sized national organization founded in 1995
Mission: To be a national voice for Canada's post-secondary students
Finances: *Funding Sources:* Membership dues
Membership: 27; *Member Profile:* Student associations & student unions from across Canada
Chief Officer(s):
Shifrah Gadansetti, Chair
chair@casa.ca
Michael McDonald, Executive Director, 613-236-3457 Ext. 222
ed@casa.ca
MacAndrew Clarke, Officer, Government & Stakeholder Relations, 613-236-3457 Ext. 221
government@casa.ca
Lindsay Boyd, Officer, 613-236-3457 Ext. 224
communications@casa.ca
Rosanne Waters, Policy & Research Analyst, 613-236-3457 Ext. 227
policy@casa.ca

Canadian Alliance on Mental Illness & Mental Health (CAMIMH)
#702, 141 Laurier Ave. West, Ottawa ON K1P 5J3
Tel: 613-237-2144; *Fax:* 613-237-1674
www.facebook.com/FaceMentalIllness
twitter.com/miawcanada
www.flickr.com/photos/45033589@N02

Canadian Associations / Canadian Alopecia Areata Foundation (CANAAF)

Overview: A medium-sized national organization founded in 1998
Mission: An alliance of mental health organizations comprised of health care providers and organizations representing persons with mental illness and their families and caregivers.
Activities: *Awareness Events:* Mental Illness Awareness Week

Canadian Alopecia Areata Foundation (CANAAF)
227 Burton Grove, King City ON L7B 1C7
info@canaaf.org
canaaf.org
Overview: A medium-sized national charitable organization founded in 2009
Mission: To give support to people suffering from Alopecia Areata
Chief Officer(s):
Colleen Butler, President
colleen@canaaf.org

Canadian Amateur Bobsleigh & Luge Association *See* Canadian Luge Association

Canadian Amateur Boxing Association (CABA) / Association canadienne de boxe amateur (ACBA)
c/o Canadian Olympic Committee, 500, boul René-Lévesque ouest, Montréal QC H2Z 2A5
Tel: 514-861-3713; *Fax:* 514-819-9228
Toll-Free: 800-861-1319
info@boxingcanada.org
www.boxingcanada.org
www.facebook.com/BoxingCa
twitter.com/boxing_canada
Also Known As: Boxing Canada
Overview: A medium-sized national organization founded in 1969
Mission: To develop & maintain uniform rules & regulations to govern amateur boxing competitions in Canada; To develop coaches & officials; To organize national team programs, including development, training, & competition
Affiliation(s): International Amateur Boxing Association
Activities: Providing news & results about the sport
Chief Officer(s):
Roy Halpin, Executive Director
rhalpin@boxingcanada.org
Daniel Trépanier, Director, High Performance
dtrepanier@boxingcanada.org
Dionne Andree-Anne, Coordinator, Programs/Projects
adionne@boxingcanada.org
Awards:
• Male Rookie of the Year
• Female Rookie of the Year
• Male Boxer of the Year
• Female Boxer of the Year
• Most Courageous Boxer

Canadian Amateur DanceSport Association *See* Canada DanceSport

Canadian Amateur Musicians (CAMMAC) / Musiciens amateurs du Canada
85, rue Cammac, Harrington QC J8G 2T2
Tel: 819-687-3938; *Fax:* 819-687-3323
Toll-Free: 888-622-8755
national@cammac.ca
www.cammac.ca
www.linkedin.com/company/3007438
www.facebook.com/cammacmusic
twitter.com/cammac_music
www.youtube.com/user/CAMMACMusicCentre
Overview: A medium-sized national charitable organization founded in 1953
Mission: To create opportunities for musicians of all levels & ages to play music in a non-competitive environment
Finances: *Funding Sources:* Membership fees; Donations
Staff Member(s): 10; 50 volunteer(s)
Membership: 2,200; *Fees:* $30 students & seniors; $35 individuals; $55 families; $200 groups; *Member Profile:* Amateur musicians from across Canada & other countries
Activities: Offering a music library with over 10,000 scores; Maintaining the Lake MacDonald Music Centre site; Organizing summer musical programs; Developing school & community programs; *Awareness Events:* Festival CAMMAC; *Internships:* Yes *Library:* CAMMAC Music Library
Chief Officer(s):
Mathieu Lussier, Chair
Rosalind Bell, Secretary
Geneviève Morin, Treasurer
Guylaine Lemaire, Artistic Director
Publications:
• Canadian Amateur Musicians Annual Report
Type: Report; *Frequency:* Annually
  Montréal Region
  Montréal QC
  www.cammac.ca
  Mission: To offer music making activities in the Montréal area
  Chief Officer(s):
  Daniel Roussety, Co-President, 450-585-1146
  Micheline Tanguay, Co-President, 450-681-6950
  François Marcotte, Secretary, 514-658-0828
  frs.marcotte@videotron.ca
  Sally Campbell, Co-Treasurer, 514-842-3011
  Sean McCutcheon, Co-Treasurer, 514-842-3011
• Express
Type: Newsletter; *Frequency:* 5 pa; *Editor:* Peter Lowensteyn; *ISSN:* 1493-0129
Profile: Musical activities & happening in the Montréal area for members of Canadian Amateur Musicians, Montréal Region
  Ottawa-Gatineau Region
  309 Olmstead St., Ottawa ON K1L 7K2
  Tel: 613-860-1751
  ottawagatineau@cammac.ca
  www.cammac.ca
  Mission: To offer musical activities for amateur musicians in the Ottawa-Gatineau region
  Chief Officer(s):
  Janet Stevens, President
  Diana Winninger, Secretary
  Daniela Planka, Treasurer
• Canadian Amateur Musicians, Ottawa-Gatineau Region Newsletter
Type: Newsletter; *Frequency:* Quarterly; *Accepts Advertising*; *Editor:* Susan Isaac
Profile: News items, announcements, & event reports for members of the Canadian Amateur Musicians Ottawa-Gatineau region
  Québec Region
  Québec QC
  Tel: 418-659-7344
  cammac.quebec@gmail.com
  Mission: To provide music making opportunities for amateur musicians in the Québec City area
  Chief Officer(s):
  Mireille Barry, President
  Marie Garon, Secretary
  Toronto Region
  83 Bellefair Ave., Toronto ON M4L 3T7
  Tel: 416-421-0779
  toronto@cammac.ca
  Chief Officer(s):
  Tim Moody, President
  tim@timmoody.com
• CAMMAC [Canadian Amateur Musicians] Toronto Region Newsletter
Type: Newsletter; *Frequency:* 5 pa; *Accepts Advertising*; *Editor:* Riccarda Balogh; *Price:* Free with Canadian Amateur Musicians Toronto Regionmembership
Profile: Local CAMMAC Toronto news, articles, & information about forthcoming events

Canadian Amateur Radio Federation *See* Radio Amateurs of Canada Inc.

Canadian Amateur Softball Association
#212, 223 Colonnade Rd., Ottawa ON K2E 7K3
Tel: 613-523-3386; *Fax:* 613-523-5761
info@softball.ca
www.softball.ca
www.facebook.com/SoftballCanadaNSO
twitter.com/softballcanada
plus.google.com/108685588748854542444
Also Known As: Softball Canada
Overview: A medium-sized national organization founded in 1965
Mission: To develop & promote softball in Canada
Staff Member(s): 8
Membership: 13 provincial/territorial associations
Chief Officer(s):
Kevin Quinn, President, 902-368-3024
kevin.quinn1@pei.sympatico.ca
Hugh Mitchener, CEO, 613-523-3386 Ext. 3106
hmitchener@softball.ca

Canadian Amateur Synchronized Swimming Association *See* Synchro Canada

Canadian Amateur Synchronized Swimming Association (Manitoba Section) *See* Synchro Manitoba

Canadian Amateur Wrestling Association (CAWA) / Association canadienne de lutte amateur
#7, 5370 Canotek Rd., Gloucester ON K1J 9E6
Tel: 613-748-5686; *Fax:* 613-748-5756
info@wrestling.ca
www.wrestling.ca
www.linkedin.com/company/wrestling-canada-lutte
www.facebook.com/WrestlingCanada
twitter.com/wrestlingcanada
Also Known As: Wrestling Canada Lutte
Overview: A medium-sized national organization founded in 1970
Mission: To operate as the national sport governing body for Olympic style wrestling in Canada; To implement a long term athlete development model; To develop coaches, officials, & administrators; To achieve podium finishes for Canadian wrestlers at World Championships & Olympic Games
Finances: *Funding Sources:* Sponsorships
Membership: *Committees:* Executive; High Performance; Coaching Education & Certification; Science & Medical; International Team; Development; Marketing; Hall of Fame
Activities: Encouraging participation in Olympic wrestling in Canada; Liaising with provincial sport governing bodies; Selecting & preparing Canada's teams which compete at the world championships & multi-sport events, such as the Olympic Games; Overseeing three national championships & one international cup on an annual basis
Chief Officer(s):
Don Ryan, President
Tamara Medwidsky, Executive Director
tamara@wrestling.ca
Alex Davidson, Manager, High Performance
adavidson@wrestling.ca
Kyle Hunter, Manager, Domestic Development
kylehunter@wrestling.ca
Eric Smith, Coordinator, Finance & Administration
ericsmith@wrestling.ca
Meetings/Conferences:
• Canadian Amateur Wrestling Association / Association canadienne de lutte amateur 2018 Annual General Meeting, 2018
Scope: National

Canadian Amputee Golf Association (CAGA)
PO Box 6091, Stn. A, Calgary AB T2H 2L4
canamps@caga.ca
www.caga.ca
Overview: A small national organization founded in 2000
Mission: To provide support for amputees both before & after amputation; To raise awareness to the general population on the effects of amputation; To offer rehabilitation, through teaching amputees golf; To run amputee golf tournaments
Membership: *Fees:* $25; $150 lifetime
Chief Officer(s):
Gwen Davies, President

Canadian Amputee Sports Association (CASA) / Association canadienne des sports pour amputés
Toronto ON
www.canadianamputeesports.ca
Overview: A medium-sized national charitable organization founded in 1977
Mission: To promote & organize amateur sport competitions in Canada for persons who are without a limb or part of a limb; To promote research in prosthetic devices for sport activities; To select a Canadian national team for participation in international sports events for amputees
Affiliation(s): Canadian Paralympic Committee; Hockey Canada
Finances: *Funding Sources:* Membership dues
10 volunteer(s)
Membership: *Member Profile:* Amputees & other athletes

Canadian Andropause Society *See* Canadian Society for the Study of the Aging Male

Canadian Anesthesiologists' Society (CAS) / Société canadienne des anesthésiologistes (SCA)
#208, 1 Eglinton Ave. East, Toronto ON M4P 3A1
Tel: 416-480-0602; *Fax:* 416-480-0320
anesthesia@cas.ca

www.cas.ca
twitter.com/CASUpdate
Overview: A large national organization founded in 1943
Mission: To advance the medical practice of anesthesia throughout Canada
Affiliation(s): Canadian Anesthesia Research Foundation (CARF); CAS International Education Foundation (CAS IEF)
Staff Member(s): 8
Membership: *Fees:* $634 active; $562 associate; $509 associate, not residing in Canada; $85 active disabled/active fellow/anesthesia assistant/student/retired; *Member Profile:* Canadian anesthesiologists; *Committees:* Annual Meeting; Archives & Artifacts; By-Law & Constitution; Continuing Education & Professional Development; Ethics; Finance; Local Arrangements; Medical Economics/Physician Resources; Nominations; Patient Safety; Research Advisory; Scientific Affairs; Standards
Activities: Presenting professional development opportunities; Promoting excellent patient care; Supporting research
Chief Officer(s):
Debra M. Thomson, Executive Director
dthomson@cas.ca
Amanda Cormier, Director, Communications, Marketing & Events
acormier@cas.ca
Iris Li, Director, Finance, HR & IT
ili@cas.ca
Justine Gill, Manager, Education, Accreditation & Member Programs
jgill@cas.ca
Victor Gonzalez, Administrator, Member & Office
vgonzalez@cas.ca
Pascal Lalonde, Coordinator, Membership
plalonde@cas.ca
Awards:
• The Gold Medal
The highest award of the Canadian Anesthesiologists' Society for an individual who has made a significant contribution to anesthesia in Canada
• Clinical Teacher Award
To recognize excellence in the teaching of clinical anesthesia
• Clinical Practitioner Award
To recognize excellence in clinical anesthesia practice
• John Bradley Young Educator Award
To recognize excellence & effectiveness in education in anesthesia
• Research Recognition Award
To recognize a senior investigator who has sustained major contributions in anesthesia research in Canada
• Medical Student Prize
Eligibility: Full-time medical students in any Canadian medical school
• CAS Career Scientist Award in Anesthesia
• New Investigator Operating Grants
• Subspecialty Operating Grants
• Open Operating Grants
Meetings/Conferences:
• Canadian Anesthesiologists' Society 2018 74th Annual Meeting, June, 2018, Palais de Congrès, Montréal, QC
Scope: National
Description: A convention, with an exhibition pharmaceutical companies & equipment manufacturers
• Canadian Anesthesiologists' Society 2019 75th Annual Meeting, June, 2019, Telus Convention Centre, Calgary, AB
Scope: National
Description: A convention, with an exhibition pharmaceutical companies & equipment manufacturers
Publications:
• Anesthesia News [a publication of Canadian Anesthesiologists' Society]
Type: Newsletter; *Frequency:* Quarterly; *Editor:* Dr. David McKnight
Profile: Society updates, including events, prizes, & research
• Canadian Anesthesiologists' Society Annual Report
Type: Yearbook; *Frequency:* Annually
• Canadian Journal of Anesthesia / Journal canadien d'anesthésie
Type: Journal; *Frequency:* Monthly; *Editor:* Hilary P. Grocott, MD; *ISSN:* 0832-610X
Profile: Peer-reviewed clinical research, basic research, & expert reviews & opinions to assist anesthesiologists
• Guidelines to the Practice of Anesthesia
Price: $25

Canadian Angelman Syndrome Society (CASS) / Société canadienne du syndrome d'Angelman (SCSA)
PO Box 37, Priddis AB T0L 1W0
Tel: 403-931-2415
www.angelmancanada.org
Overview: A small national organization
Mission: To educate concerned families, medical & educational communities & the general public about Angelman Syndrome; To establish & maintain support systems; To promote research activities on the diagnosis, treatment, management & prevention of Angelman Syndrome; To fundraise
13 volunteer(s)
Membership: 1-99
Chief Officer(s):
John Carscallen, Secretary-Treasurer
cass@davincibb.net

Canadian Angus Association (CAA) / L'Association canadienne Angus
292140 Wagon Wheel Blvd., Rocky View County AB T4A 0E2
Tel: 403-571-3580; *Fax:* 403-571-3599
Toll-Free: 888-571-3580
cdnangus@cdnangus.ca
www.cdnangus.ca
www.facebook.com/CanadianAngusAssociation
twitter.com/cdnangus
youtube.com/user/CanadianAngusAssoc;
instagram.com/cdnangus
Also Known As: Canadian Aberdeen Angus Association
Overview: A small national organization founded in 1906
Mission: To offer services to enhance the growth & position of the Angus breed; To maintain breed purity
Member of: Canadian Beef Breeds Council
Affiliation(s): Canadian Red Angus Promotion Society; American Angus Association; American Red Angus Association; Mexican Angus Association; Australian Angus Association
Membership: *Fees:* Schedule available; *Member Profile:* Individuals, Partnerships; Incorporated companies
Activities: Maintaining breed registry
Chief Officer(s):
Brett Wildman, President, 780-785-3709
wildmanlivestock@hotmail.com
Rob Smith, Chief Executive Officer
ceo@cdnangus.ca
Awards:
• Auction Market of the Year Award
• Feedlot of the Year Award
Publications:
• Aberdeen Angus World [a publication of the Canadian Angus Association]
Type: Magazine; *Accepts Advertising; Editor:* Dave Callaway
• CAA [Canadian Angus Association] Breeder Handbook
Type: Newsletter
• CAA [Canadian Angus Association] Newsletter
Type: Newsletter
Profile: Angus news & events

Canadian Animal Health Institute (CAHI) / Institut canadien de la santé animale (ICSA)
#102, 160 Research Lane, Guelph ON N1G 5B2
Tel: 519-763-7777; *Fax:* 519-763-7407
cahi@cahi-icsa.ca
www.cahi-icsa.ca
Overview: A medium-sized national organization founded in 1968
Mission: To work closely with allied industry groups for the betterment of Canadian agriculture; To foster & maintain a regulatory & legislative climate which will encourage member companies to develop & market useful animal health products & services; To promote the proper use of animal health & nutrition products by livestock & poultry farmers through user education information programs; To develop a public information program which enhances appreciation of the contributions the animal health & nutrition industry makes to the economy & society
Finances: *Funding Sources:* Membership dues
Staff Member(s): 3
Membership: 60 organizations
Chief Officer(s):
Jean Szkotnicki, President
Tracey Firth, Director, Programs
Awards:
• Industry Leadership Award
Meetings/Conferences:
• Canadian Animal Health Institute Annual Meeting 2018, June, 2018, Pillar & Post, Niagara-on-the-Lake, ON
Scope: National
Publications:
• CAHI [Canadian Animal Health Institute] Resource Directory
Type: Directory; *Frequency:* Biennially
Profile: Listings of CAHI members, veterinary associations, government agencies related to animal health, commodity organizations, & CAHI's foreign sisterorganizations
• Inforum [a publication of the Canadian Animal Health Institute]
Type: Newsletter; *Frequency:* 4 pa
Profile: Distributed to Canadian veterinarians in the Canadian Veterinary Journal

Canadian Anthropology Society (CASCA) / Société canadienne d'Anthropologie
c/o Karli Whitmore, #301, 125, rue Dean de la Londe, Baie d'Urfe QC H9X 3TB
Other Communication: membership@anthropologica.ca
www.cas-sca.ca
www.facebook.com/132028862261
twitter.com/CASCATweet
Overview: A small national organization
Mission: To promote anthropology in Canada
Member of: World Council of Anthropological Associations
Membership: *Fees:* Schedule available
Activities: Supporting anthropological research; Sharing anthropological knowledge with the academic community & the public; *Awareness Events:* Third Annual Anthropology Film Festival
Chief Officer(s):
Martha Radice, President
Udo Krautwurst, Treasurer
Charles Menzies, Secretary
Publications:
• Anthropologica
Type: Journal; *Frequency:* Semiannually; *Editor:* Andrew Lyons; *Price:* Free to CASCA members
Profile: Peer-reviewed articles about social & cultural issues
• Culture: The Newsletter for the Canadian Anthropology Society
Type: Newsletter; *Editor:* Daphne Winlan & Karine Vanthuyne
Profile: News, book notes

Canadian Anti-Counterfeiting Network (CACN)
#300, 180 Attwell Dr., Toronto ON M9W 6A9
Tel: 647-260-3090; *Fax:* 416-679-9234
cacn@electrofed.com
www.cacn.ca
twitter.com/BuyTheRealThing
Overview: A small national organization
Mission: The Canadian Anti-Counterfeiting Network (CACN) is a coalition of individuals, companies firms and associations that have united in the fight against product counterfeiting and copyright piracy in Canada and Internationally.
Membership: *Fees:* $1,500
Chief Officer(s):
Wayne Edwards, Chair
wedwards@electrofed.com

Canadian Anti-Money Laundering Institute (CAMLI)
PO Box 427, Merrickville ON K0G 1N0
Tel: 613-283-9659; *Fax:* 613-526-9384
contactus@camli.org
www.camli.org
www.linkedin.com/company/canadian-anti-money-laundering-institute-camli-
twitter.com/CAMLIorg
Overview: A small national organization
Mission: CAMLI is an education and resource forum for anti-money laundering compliance professionals.
Membership: *Fees:* Two-year general membership: $400 + HST; *Member Profile:* Canadian-based and international compliance professionals
Activities: Training Programs
Meetings/Conferences:
• Canadian Anti-Money Laundering Institute 2018 Conference, 2018
Scope: National

Canadian Antique Phonograph Society (CAPS)
122 Major St., Toronto ON M5S 2L2
info@capsnews.org
www.capsnews.org
Overview: A small national organization founded in 1970
Mission: To share information about phonographs, gramophones, all types of sound recordings of historical importance, ephemera & related memorabilia with emphasis on the history of the phonograph & recorded sound in Canada.

Canadian Associations / Canadian Apheresis Group (CAG) / Groupe canadien d'aphérèse

Membership: 225+; *Fees:* $35
Activities: 8 meetings with presentations annually
Chief Officer(s):
Mike Bryan, President
Bill Pratt, Treasurer

Canadian Apheresis Group (CAG) / Groupe canadien d'aphérèse
#199, 435 St. Laurent Blvd., Ottawa ON K1K 2Z8
Tel: 613-748-9613; *Fax:* 613-748-6392
cag@cagcanada.ca
www.cagcanada.ca
Overview: A small national organization founded in 1980
Mission: To provide a forum for information exchange among apheresis practioners in Canada; To promote clinical research in apheresis
Membership: Representatives from 40 apheresis units in 19 medical centers in Canada; *Member Profile:* Physicians; Nurses
Activities: Collecting & reviewing information on apheresis procedures
Chief Officer(s):
Gail Rock, Chair

Canadian Apparel Federation (CAF) / Fédération canadienne du vêtement
#708, 151 Slater St., Ottawa ON K1P 5H3
Tel: 613-231-3220; *Fax:* 613-231-2305
info@apparel.ca
www.apparel.ca
www.linkedin.com/company/canadian-apparel-federation
www.facebook.com/102242196491712
twitter.com/caf_apparel
Previous Name: Canadian Apparel Manufacturers Institute
Overview: A large national organization
Mission: To provide a forum for provincial apparel associations representing the vast majority of the country's manufacturers; To exercise leadership in relations with government, suppliers & the general public
Finances: *Funding Sources:* Membership fees; sponsorship
Membership: *Fees:* Schedule available; *Member Profile:* Canadian firms engaged in apparel manufacture or marketing, & suppliers to the apparel industry
Activities: Industry information & resources
Chief Officer(s):
Bob Kirke, Executive Director
bkirke@apparel.ca
Publications:
• Apparel Directory
Type: Directory
Profile: Listings of manufacturers, importers, & designers in all apparel categories
• CAF/FCV [Canadian Apparel Federation/Fédération canadienne du vêtement] Bulletin
Type: Newsletter
• Directory of Suppliers to the Apparel Industry
Type: Directory
Profile: Listings of suppliers of textiles, trimmings, technology, & services

Canadian Apparel Manufacturers Institute *See* Canadian Apparel Federation

Canadian Applied & Industrial Mathematics Society (CAIMS) / Société canadienne de mathématiques appliquées et industrielles (SCMAI)
c/o Prof. Sharene Bungay, Dept. of Comp. Science, Memorial University, St. John's NL A1B 3X5
www.caims.ca
Overview: A small national organization
Chief Officer(s):
Jianhong Wu, President
wujh@mathstat.yorku.ca
Publications:
• Canadian Applied & Industrial Mathematics Society Newsletter
Type: Newsletter; *Frequency:* Quarterly
• Canadian Applied Mathematics Quarterly
Type: Journal; *Frequency:* Quarterly; *Editor:* Jack W. Macki; T. Bryant Moodie

Canadian Apprenticeship Forum (CAF) / Forum canadien sur l'apprentissage
#404, 2197 Riverside Dr., Ottawa ON K1H 7X3
Tel: 613-235-4004
www.caf-fca.org
www.linkedin.com/company/2231800
www.facebook.com/cafapprenticeship
twitter.com/CAF_FCA
www.youtube.com/user/cafapprenticeship
Overview: A small national organization
Mission: To bring together the key participants who make up the Canadian apprenticeship community
Staff Member(s): 6
Membership: *Fees:* $100 contributor; $1,000 supporter; $3,000 patron; $5,000 champion
Activities: Promotion of apprenticeship; inventory/information project; accessibility & barriers to apprenticeship; common core
Chief Officer(s):
Sarah Watts-Rynard, Executive Director

Canadian Aquaculture Industry Alliance (CAIA) / Alliance de l'industrie canadienne de l'aquiculture
PO Box 81100, Stn. World Exchange Plaza, #705, 116 Albert St., Ottawa ON K1P 1B1
Tel: 613-239-0612; *Fax:* 613-239-0619
info@aquaculture.ca
www.aquaculture.ca
www.facebook.com/155794491097836
twitter.com/CDNaquaculture
www.youtube.com/channel/UCgg1cyvyiLcDP8lF81oHAWg
Overview: A medium-sized national organization founded in 1987
Mission: To represent the interests of aquaculture operators, feed companies, suppliers, & provincial finfish & shellfish aquaculture associations on both the national & international scenes; To ensure the international competitiveness of the Canadian aquaculture industry
Membership: *Member Profile:* Aquaculture operators; Feed companies; Suppliers; Provincial shellfish & finfish aquaculture associations
Activities: Advocating for Canadian aquaculture issues; Fostering cooperation among various aquaculture interests; Promoting a positive image of the Canadian aquaculture industry; Encouraging the consumption of aquaculture products from Canada
Chief Officer(s):
Ruth Salmon, Executive Director, 613-239-0612, Fax: 613-239-0619
ruth.salmon@aquaculture.ca
Clare Backman, President

Canadian Arab Federation (CAF) / La Fédération Canado-Arabe
1057 McNicoll Ave., Toronto ON M1W 3W6
Tel: 416-493-8635; *Fax:* 416-493-9239
Toll-Free: 866-886-4675
info@caf.ca
www.caf.ca
Overview: A medium-sized national organization founded in 1967
Mission: To represent Canadian Arabs on issues related to public policy; To protect civil liberties & the equality of human rights
Member of: African Canadian Social Development Council
Finances: *Funding Sources:* Donations
Membership: 40+ organizations; *Member Profile:* Arab-Canadian associations throughout Canada
Activities: Providing educational opportunities; Increasing public awareness; Liaising with all levels of government on issues important to Canadian Arabs; Handling media relations; Encouraging community empowerment, through civic participation; Promoting Arab & Muslim culture; Combatting racism; Fundraising; Offering networking opportunities; Providing job search workshops; Offering meeting rooms; Providing Arabic classes; *Speaker Service:* Yes; *Library:* Canadian Arab Federation Community Resource Library; Open to public
Chief Officer(s):
Farid Ayad, President
Abdallah Alkrunz, Vice-President, East
Mohamed El Rashidy, Vice-President, West
Publications:
• CAF [Canadian Arab Federation] Weekly Bulletin
Type: Newsletter; *Frequency:* Weekly
Profile: Current events, articles, & event announcements

Canadian Arabian Horse Association *See* Canadian Arabian Horse Registry

Canadian Arabian Horse Registry (CAHR)
c/o Arabian Horse Association, 10805 E. Bethany Dr., Aurora CO 80014 USA
Tel: 303-696-4500; *Fax:* 303-696-4599
info.cahr@arabianhorses.org
www.cahr.ca
Previous Name: Canadian Arabian Horse Association
Overview: A small national organization founded in 1958
Mission: To register purebred Arabian horses in Canada; to establish standards of breeding practices; to serve the needs of Arabian horse owners
Affiliation(s): Canadian Equestrian Federation
Membership: *Fees:* $65 annual; $75 non-resident; $170 3-year; $750 life; *Member Profile:* Owners of Arabian horses
Activities: Encouraging the development of Arabian horses in Canada; maintaining efficient inspection; developing Arabian horse show rules in Canada; maintaining the Canadian Partbred Arabian Register for registering Half-Arabians & Anglo-Arabians
Chief Officer(s):
Christine Tribe, Registrar
Marcia Friesen, President
Robert Sproule, Secretary-Treasurer
Publications:
• Canadian Arabian Horse News [a publication of the Canadian Arabian Horse Registry]
Type: Magazine; *Accepts Advertising*; *Editor:* Nicole Toren
Profile: Features include Canadian show results

Canadian Archaeological Association (CAA) / Association canadienne d'archéologie
www.canadianarchaeology.com
Overview: A small national charitable organization founded in 1968
Mission: To publish & disseminate archaeological knowledge in Canada; To encourage archaeological research & conservation efforts; To promote cooperation among archaeological societies & agencies
Membership: *Fees:* $30-$40 students; $70-$100 regular; $125 institutional; *Member Profile:* Professional, avocational & student archaeologists; General public; *Committees:* Aboriginal Heritage; Puclic Advocacy; Student's; Membership; Cultural Resource Management; Heritage & Legislation Policy; Public Communication Awards; James & Margaret Pendergast Award; Weetaluktuk Award; Smith-Wintemberg Award
Activities: Fostering cooperation with aboriginal groups; Promoting activities advantageous to archaeology; Advocating nationally
Chief Officer(s):
Gary Warrick, President
president@canadianarchaeology.com
Jennifer Campbell, Vice President
vice-president@canadianarchaeology.com
Joanne Braaten, Secretary-Treasurer
secretary-treasurer@canadianarchaeology.com
Awards:
• Public Communication Awards
Contact: Meaghan Peuramaki-Brown, Committee Chair, E-mail: mmpeuram@ucalgary.ca
• Weetaluktuk Award
Contact: Gary Coupland, Committee Chair, E-mail: coupland@chass.utoronto.ca
• James & Margaret Pendergast Award
Contact: Bjorn O. Simonsen, Committee Chair, E-mail: bjorno@shaw.ca
• Smith-Wintemberg Award
Contact: Eldon Yellowhorn, Committee Chair, E-mail: ecy@sfu.ca
Meetings/Conferences:
• Canadian Archaeological Association Annual Meeting 2018, 2018, Winnipeg, MB
Scope: National
• Canadian Archaeological Association Annual Meeting 2019, 2019, Québec, QC
Scope: National
• Canadian Archaeological Association Annual Meeting 2020, 2020, Edmonton, AB
Scope: National
Publications:
• CAA [Canadian Archaeological Association] Newsletter / Bulletin de l'ACA [Association d'archéologie canadienne
Type: Newsletter; *Frequency:* Semiannually; *Editor:* Karen Ryan; *Price:* Free with membership in the CanadianArchaeological Association
Profile: A spring & fall publication
• Canadian Journal of Archaeology / Journal canadien d'archéologie
Type: Journal; *Frequency:* Semiannually; *Editor:* Dr. Gerry Oetelaar; *Price:* Free with membership in the Canadian ArchaeologicalAssociation
Profile: Documents the processes & results of Canadian archaeology

Canadian Architectural Certification Board (CACB) / Conseil canadien de certification en architecture (CCCA)
#710, 1 Nicholas St., Ottawa ON K1N 7B7
Tel: 613-241-8399; Fax: 613-241-7991
info@cacb.ca
www.cacb.ca
Overview: A medium-sized national licensing organization founded in 1976
Mission: The Canadian Architectural Certification Board fulfills two seperate but related mandates: 1- Administer a program of accreditation of the Canadaian schools of architecture in accordance with "Conditions and Procedures for Accreditation" approved by the CCAC and the CCUSA and 2- Administer a program of certification of the educational qualifications of indivdual applicants in accordance withe criteria contained within the "Education Standard" approved by the CCAC.
Finances: Annual Operating Budget: $100,000-$250,000; Funding Sources: Collateral organizations
Staff Member(s): 3; 100 volunteer(s)
Membership: Member Profile: Professional associations; university schools of architecture
Activities: Certification of educational qualifications for architects; accreditation of Canadian University Schools of Architecture
Chief Officer(s):
Branko Kolarevic, President
Myriam Blais, Vice-President

Canadian Arctic Resources Committee
488 Gladstone Ave., Ottawa ON K1N 8V4
Tel: 613-759-4284; Fax: 613-237-3845
Toll-Free: 866-949-9006
davidg@carc.org
www.carc.org
www.facebook.com/168782596508551
Overview: A medium-sized national organization
Mission: The Canadian Arctic Resources Committee (CARC) is a citizens' organization dedicated to the long-term environmental and social well being of northern Canada and its peoples.
Chief Officer(s):
Ben McDonald, Acting Chair

Canadian Arm Wrestling Federation (CAWF)
c/o Tracey Arnold, Secretary-Treasurer, 1635 - 8th Ave., Saskatoon SK S7K 2X8
www.cawf.ca
Overview: A medium-sized national organization overseen by World Armwrestling Federation
Mission: To oversee & promote the sport of arm wrestling in Canada.
Member of: World Armwrestling Federation
Membership: 3,500; Fees: $20
Chief Officer(s):
Rick Pinkney, President
Joey Costello, Vice-President
Tracey Arnold, Secretary-Treasurer
tarnold001@hotmail.com
Anthony Dall'Antonia, Director, Communications
vancouverarm@hotmail.com
Awards:
• The John Miazdzyk Award
For dedication to the sport of arm wrestling.

Canadian Armenian Business Council Inc. (CABC) / Conseil commercial canadien-arménien inc.
#102, 2425 de Salaberry, Montréal QC H3M 1L2
Tel: 514-333-7655; Fax: 514-333-7280
info@cabc.ca
www.cabc.ca
Overview: A small national organization founded in 1985
Mission: To promote & serve the Armenian business community; To act as a marketing tool for North American Armenian businesses
Membership: Fees: $60 individuals; $100 corporations; $25 students; Committees: Membership; Events; Publications; Recognition of Excellence; Youth; Inter-trade; Sponsorships & Grants; Public Relations
Activities: Increasing communication & cooperation between Armenians in business; Providing business courses; Conducting market research; Promoting trade & investments; Participating in international trade missions
Chief Officer(s):
Paul Nahabedian, President, 514-878-5111, Fax: 514-878-5070
paul.nahabedian@rbc.com
Publications:
• CABC [Canadian Armenian Business Council Inc.] Business Directory
Type: Directory

The Canadian Art Foundation
#330, 215 Spadina Ave., Toronto ON M5T 2C7
Tel: 416-368-8854; Fax: 416-368-6135
Toll-Free: 800-222-4762
info@canadianart.ca
www.canadianart.ca
www.facebook.com/canadianart
twitter.com/canartca
vimeo.com/channels/canadianart; canadianart.tumblr.com
Overview: A medium-sized national charitable organization founded in 1991
Mission: To foster & support the visual arts in Canada & to celebrate artists & their creativity with a program of events, lectures, competitions, publications & educational initiatives.
Member of: Canadian Magazine Publishers Association
Finances: Annual Operating Budget: $500,000-$1.5 Million; Funding Sources: Government grants; ad sales; circulation; private
Staff Member(s): 5; 1 volunteer(s)
Activities: Programs include: Gallery Events; Film Festival; International Speaker Series; Tours; Writing Prize; Anne Lind International Program; RBC Canadian Painting Competition; Editorial Residency; & School Hop.; Internships: Yes; Rents Mailing List: Yes
Chief Officer(s):
Debra Campbell, Co-Chair
Gabe Gonda, Co-Chair
Publications:
• Canadian Art
Type: Magazine; Frequency: Quarterly; Accepts Advertising; Editor: Richard Rhodes; ISSN: 0825-3854; Price: $24 Canada; $34 USA; $42 International - plus applicable taxes

Canadian Art Therapy Association (CATA) / L'association canadienne d'art thérapie
PO Box 658, Stn. Main, Parksville BC V9P 2G7
cata15.wildapricot.org
www.linkedin.com/company/3574360
www.facebook.com/142451825860747
instagram.com/cata_photos_acat
Overview: A small national organization founded in 1977
Mission: To promote the development & maintenance of professional standards of art therapy training, registration, research, & practice in Canada; To heighten awareness of art therapy as an important mental health discipline
Membership: Fees: $25 students; $50 associate members; $70 professional members; $95 registered members; Member Profile: Art therapists, who have a R.C.A.T.,or equivalent; Art therapists, who have finished professional post-graduate training & are active in the field; Individuals interested in the promotion of art therapy may be associate members; Students, who are enrolled in a Canadian graduate art therapy program
Activities: Facilitating the exchange & collaboration of art therapists, students, & professionals in related fields; Fostering research; Organizing educational opportunities, such as lectures, seminars, & workshops
Chief Officer(s):
Haley Toll, President
cata.president@gmail.com
Michelle Winkel, Vice-President
catavicepresident@gmail.com
Sharona Bookbinder, Treasurer
cata.treasurer@gmail.com
Rajni Sharma, Chair, Communications
catacommunications@gmail.com
Awards:
• Art Therapy Student Bursary
; Amount: $1,000
• Research Award for an Art Therapy Student
; Amount: $1,000
• Research Award for a Registered Art Therapist
; Amount: $1,000
Publications:
• Canadian Art Therapy Association Directory
Type: Directory
Profile: Listings of professional & registered art therapists, who are members of the Canadian Art Therapy Association & who chose to be listed in the directory
• Canadian Art Therapy Association Journal
Type: Journal; Frequency: Semiannually; Editor: Marilyn Magnuson; ISSN: 0832-2473; Price: Free with membership CATA; $30 non-members in Canada; $35 in the U.S.A; $40 intl.
• Canadian Art Therapy Association Newsletter
Type: Newsletter; Frequency: 3 pa

Canadian Arthritis & Rheumatism Society See Arthritis Society

Canadian Arthritis Network (CAN) / Le Réseau canadien de l'arthrite
#8-400-6-1, 700 University Ave., Toronto ON M5G 1Z5
Tel: 416-586-4770; Fax: 416-586-8395
can@arthritisnetwork.ca
www.arthritisnetwork.ca
www.facebook.com/102841629761794
twitter.com/commcan
Overview: A medium-sized national organization founded in 1998
Mission: To improve the quality of life for people with arthritis; To support integrated, trans-disciplinary research & development, with a focus upon inflammatory joint diseases, osteoarthritis, & bioengineering for restoration of joint function
Member of: Networks of Centres of Excellence
Affiliation(s): The Arthritis Society; Canadian Institute of Health Research Institute of Musculoskeletal Health & Arthritis
Finances: Funding Sources: Grants; Federal government
Membership: 200 researchers; Member Profile: Canadian arthritis researchers & clinicians; Canadian academic institutions; Committees: Legacy Steering
Activities: Partnering with clinicians, academics, government, industry, voluntary agencies, & consumers; Facilitating the commercialization of new discoveries
Chief Officer(s):
Robin Armstrong, Chair
Kate Lee, Managing Director, 416-586-3167
klee2@mtsinai.on.ca
Claire Bombardier, Co-Scientific Director
Monique Gignac, Co-Scientific Director
Publications:
• Annual Report of the Canadian Arthritis Network
Type: Yearbook; Frequency: Annually
• Arthritis in Canada
Type: Report
Profile: Impacts of arthritis on Canadians, plus information about ambulatory care, prescription medications, & hospital services
• Research Excellence at the Canadian Arthritis Network
Type: Report; Number of Pages: 20

Canadian Artists Representation (CARFAC) / Le Front des artistes canadiens
#250, 2 Daly Ave., Ottawa ON K1N 6E2
Tel: 613-233-6161; Fax: 613-233-6162
Toll-Free: 866-344-6161
membership@carfac.ca
www.carfac.ca
www.facebook.com/CARFACNational
twitter.com/carfacnational
Overview: A large national organization founded in 1968
Mission: To act as a national voice for Canada's professional visual artists; To promote a socio-economic climate that is conducive to the production of visual arts
Member of: Canadian Conference of the Arts (CCA); International Association of Artists; Coalition for Cultural Diversity
Affiliation(s): Creators Rights Alliance (CRA); Access Copyright
Finances: Funding Sources: Donations
Membership: Member Profile: Professional Canadian visual artists
Activities: Defending artists' economic & legal rights; Conducting research; Educating the public about dealing fairly with artists
Chief Officer(s):
Ingrid Mary Percy, National President & Spokesperson
Paddy Lamb, Vice President
Yael Brotman, Secretary
David Yazbeck, Treasurer
Publications:
• Calendar [a publication of Canadian Artists' Representation]
Type: Newsletter; Frequency: s-a.; Editor: Melissa Gruber; April Britski; ISSN: 1495-558X
Profile: Information for professional artists & association news

Canadian Artists Representation Copyright Collective Inc.
See Copyright Visual Arts

Canadian Artists' Representation British Columbia
#100, 938 Howe St., Vancouver BC V6Z 1N9

Canadian Associations / Canadian Artists' Representation Manitoba / Le Front des artistes canadiens de Manitoba

Tel: 604-519-4669
bc@carfac.ca
www.carfacbc.org
www.linkedin.com/company/carfac-bc
www.facebook.com/carfacbc
twitter.com/Carfacbc
www.youtube.com/user/carfacbc
Overview: A medium-sized provincial organization overseen by Canadian Artists' Representation
Mission: To assist BC visual artists to advance their professional status & economic potential; to provide informational services to assist in the development of the visual artist & the visual arts as a profession; to research, publish & otherwise provide educational information for the development of the visual arts professional & for the benefit of all Canadians interested in the visual arts; to advocate the role & value of the visual arts in BC & beyond; to assist & encourage members of the visual arts profession to make individual & group contributions to the growth & development of the visual arts in Canada
Membership: 181
Chief Officer(s):
Julie McIntyre, President

Canadian Artists' Representation Manitoba / Le Front des artistes canadiens de Manitoba
#407, 100 Arthur St., Winnipeg MB R3B 1H3
Tel: 204-943-7211; *Fax:* 204-942-1555
carfac-mbcontact@mts.net
Also Known As: CARFAC Manitoba
Overview: A small provincial organization founded in 1981 overseen by Canadian Artists' Representation
Mission: To protect & promote the social economic interests of practising visual artists in Manitoba; to lobby the government on issues related to the field, including copyright issues; to provide artists & the public with current information on such events as exhibitions, workshops & art classes.
Member of: Canadian Artists' Representation
Activities: Workshops; *Internships:* Yes; *Library:* Open to public

Canadian Artists' Representation Maritimes
2575 Elm St., Halifax NS B3L 2Y5
Tel: 516-454-3285
Other Communication: membership.carfac@gmail.com
elmstreetstudio@ns.sympatico.ca
www.carfacmaritimes.org
Overview: A medium-sized local organization founded in 2003 overseen by Canadian Artists' Representation
Mission: To defend artists' economic & legal rights in the Maritime provinces; To educate the public on fair dealing with artists
Membership: *Fees:* $20 student; $40 professional artist & individual associate; $60 professional artist couple; $80 institutional associate; $250 sustaining member; *Member Profile:* Professional visual artists living & working in Nova Scotia, New Brunswick, & Prince Edward Island
Activities: Engaging in advocacy activities; Facilitating communications among artists; Providing information to members
Chief Officer(s):
Susan Tooke, President
Publications:
• The / Le Studio
Type: Newsletter; *Frequency:* Monthly
Profile: Updates about the organization for members

Canadian Artists' Representation Ontario / Le Front des artistes canadiens de l'Ontario
#372, 401 Richmond St. West, Toronto ON M5V 3A8
Tel: 416-340-8850; *Fax:* 416-340-7653
Toll-Free: 877-890-8850
carfacontario@carfacontario.ca
www.carfacontario.ca
www.facebook.com/CARFAC-Ontario-6450654849
twitter.com/carfacontario
Also Known As: CARFAC Ontario
Overview: A medium-sized provincial organization founded in 1968 overseen by Canadian Artists' Representation
Mission: To protect the rights of visual artists; To develop policies & services to help artists, curators, art patrons, galleries, & other stakeholders
Member of: Canadian Artists' Representation/Front des artistes canadiens
Finances: *Funding Sources:* Donations
Staff Member(s): 4
Membership: 734 individuals + 31 organizations; *Fees:* Schedule available; *Member Profile:* Professional visual & media artists based in Ontario
Activities: Offering professional development courses & services; Advocating for the rights of visual artists; Hosting workshops; Providing resources
Chief Officer(s):
Sally Lee, Executive Director
sl@carfacontario.ca
Victoria Glizer, Manager, Operations
Publications:
• Dispatch: CARFAC [Canadian Artists' Representation] Ontario Newsletter
Type: Newsletter; *Frequency:* Quarterly; *Accepts Advertising*
Profile: Business & artistic resource for CARFAC members

Canadian Artists' Representation Saskatchewan
1734A Dewdney Ave., Regina SK S4R 1G6
Tel: 306-522-9788; *Fax:* 306-522-9783
programs@carfac.sk.ca
www.carfac.sk.ca
www.facebook.com/CARFACSASK
twitter.com/CARFACSASK
www.instagram.com/carfacsask
Also Known As: CARFAC SASK
Overview: A medium-sized provincial organization overseen by Canadian Artists' Representation
Mission: To improve the status of Saskatchewan visual artists; To advocate on behalf of practising visual artists in Saskatchewan
Affiliation(s): CARFAC National; CARFAC Copyright Collective; International Association of Art
Finances: *Funding Sources:* Donations
Membership: *Fees:* Schedule available; *Member Profile:* Visual artists in Saskatchewan
Activities: Providing education & resources to visual artists; Conducting research; Consulting with arts & cultural organizations & other provincial agencies; *Library:* CARFAC SASK Resource Centre
Chief Officer(s):
Wendy Nelson, Executive Director
director@carfac.sk.ca
Publications:
• CARFAC SASK [Canadian Artists' Representation Saskatchewan] Newsletter
Type: Newsletter; *Frequency:* 10 pa; *Price:* Free for CARFAC SASK members
Profile: CARFAC SASK & CARFAC National news, events & exhibitions, educational opportunities, grant information, cultural developments, research, & articlesfor visual artists
• The Saskatchewan Gallery Survey
Frequency: Triennially; *Price:* Free to CARFAC SASK members
Profile: A guide to the galleries of Saskatchewan
• Visual Arts Handbook
Frequency: Triennially; *Price:* Free to Saskatchewan residents
Profile: A guide for artists, art gallery personnel, art dealers, collectors, librarians, & educators in the visual arts in Saskatchewan

Saskatoon Office
#203, 416 - 21st St. East, Saskatoon SK S7K 0C2
Tel: 306-933-3206; *Fax:* 306-933-2053
membership@carfac.sk.ca

Canadian Arts Presenting Association (CAPACOA) / Association canadienne des organismes artistiques
#200, 17 York St., Ottawa ON K1N 5S7
Tel: 613-562-3515; *Fax:* 613-562-4005
mail@capacoa.ca
www.capacoa.ca
www.linkedin.com/company/capacoa
www.facebook.com/CAPACOA
twitter.com/capacoa
Overview: A large national charitable organization founded in 1985
Mission: To promote the development of the presentation of the arts in Canada; To promote & encourage greater knowledge & appreciation of the presentation of the performing arts; To encourage touring of artists & attractions throughout all regions of Canada; To provide information on artists & attractions touring regionally & nationally; To assist presenters of the arts in Canada with coordination of bookings; To provide opportunities for professional development of presenters in Canada; To promote communication & understanding between presenters of the arts in Canada; To provide forum for exchange of views concerning presentation of the performing arts generally; To provide information on regional & federal policies which relate to presentation of the arts; To provide the opportunity to make contacts nationwide
Finances: *Annual Operating Budget:* $250,000-$500,000
Staff Member(s): 3
Membership: 140 organizations; *Fees:* Schedule available
Activities: Raising public awareness about the arts; Offering networking & professional development opportunities; Supporting research projects focused on the presentation of the performing arts; *Rents Mailing List:* Yes
Chief Officer(s):
Sue Urquhart, Executive Director
sue.urqhart@capacoa.ca
Mélanie Bureau, Manager, Operations
melanie.bureau@capacoa.ca
Meetings/Conferences:
• Canadian Arts Presenting Association / Association canadienne des organismes artistiques 2018 30th Annual Conference, 2018
Scope: National

Canadian Asian Studies Association (CASA) / Association canadienne des études asiatiques (ACEA)
c/o Dept. of Geography, Université du Québec à Montréal, PO Box 8888, Stn. Centre Ville, Pavillon Hubert Aquin Local A-4310, Montréal QC H3C 3P8
Tel: 514-848-2280; *Fax:* 514-848-4514
casa_acea@yahoo.ca
www.casa-acea.ca
Overview: A medium-sized national organization founded in 1968
Mission: To expand & disseminate knowledge about Asia in Canada
Finances: *Funding Sources:* Sponsorships
Membership: *Fees:* $35 students; $45 unwaged or retired members; $60 regular members; $75 families; $100 institutions; $250 corporate sustaining members
Activities: Publishing monographs, such as South Asia Between Turmoil & Hope
Chief Officer(s):
André Laliberté, Secretary
andre.laliberte@uottawa.ca
Prashant Keshavmurthy, Treasurer
prashant.keshavmurthy@mcgill.ca
Awards:
• Best Canadian Dissertation on East Asia Award Competition
• Chiang Ching-Kuo Foundation Fellowship Award
; *Amount:* $10,000 each, for up to 2 doctoral fellowships; $22,000, for 1 post-doctoral fellowship

Canadian Assembly of Narcotics Anonymous (CANA)
PO Box 812, Stn. Edmonton Main, Edmonton AB T5J 2L4
www.canaacna.org
Previous Name: Narcotics Anonymous
Overview: A small national organization founded in 1989
Mission: To help addicts who suffer from the disease of addiction
Membership: *Member Profile:* Anyone regardless of age, race, religion, sexual identity or preference
Activities: *Speaker Service:* Yes; *Library:* Open to public by appointment

British Columbia Region
PO Box 1695, Stn. A, Vancouver BC V6C 2P7
Tel: 604-873-1018
www.bcrna.ca

Canada Atlantic Region
PO Box 26025, 407 Westmorland Rd., Saint John NB E2J 4M3
Toll-Free: 800-564-0228
contact.us@carna.ca
www.carna.ca

Golden Triangle Area
#311, 23-500 Fairway Rd. South, Kitchener ON N2C 1X3
Tel: 519-651-1121
Toll-Free: 866-311-1611
www.gtascna.org

Hamilton Area
PO Box 57067, Stn. Jackson, 2 King St. West, Hamilton ON L8P 4W9
Tel: 905-522-0332; *Crisis Hot-Line:* 888-811-3887
www.nahamilton.org

Narcotiques Anonymes
5496, rue Notre-Dame est, Montréal QC H1N 2C4

Ligne sans frais: 855-544-6362
info@naquebec.org
www.naquebec.org
Ontario Region
PO Box 5939, Stn. A, Toronto ON M5W 1P3
www.orscna.org

Canadian Assessment, Vocational Evaluation & Work Adjustment Society (CAVEWAS) / Association canadienne des évaluateurs de capacités de travail société (ACECTS)
#310, 4 Cataraqui St., Kingston ON K7K 1Z7
Tel: 613-531-9210
Toll-Free: 866-560-3838
www.cavewas.com
Previous Name: Canadian Association for Vocational Evaluation & Work Adjustment
Overview: A small national organization
Mission: To identify & resolve issues relevant to vocational rehabilitation & career transition services
Activities: Certified Vocational Evaluator (CVE) Designation
Chief Officer(s):
Phillip W. Boswell, President
pwboswell@telus.net

Canadian Associated Air Balance Council (CAABC)
Tel: 905-886-6513; *Fax:* 905-886-6513
mail@designtest.ca
www.caabc.org
Overview: A small national organization founded in 1970
Mission: To promote independent testing & balancing of mechanical systems; to produce standards to advance the industry
Affiliation(s): Associated Air Balance Council
Finances: *Funding Sources:* Membership fees
Staff Member(s): 1; 18 volunteer(s)
Membership: 20; *Fees:* $3,000; *Committees:* Membership; Technical; Standards
Chief Officer(s):
Surrinder S. Sahota, President

Canadian Associates of Ben-Gurion University of the Negev
National & Toronto Office, #506, 1000 Finch Ave. West, Toronto ON M3J 2V5
Tel: 416-665-8054; *Fax:* 416-665-8055
bgutoronto@bengurion.ca
www.bengurion.ca
www.facebook.com/119559301437197
twitter.com/BenGurionCanada
www.youtube.com/user/BenGurionUniversity
Overview: A small international charitable organization founded in 1975
Mission: To raise funds for needy & worthy students, for scholarships, to attend Ben-Gurion University
Activities: *Speaker Service:* Yes
Chief Officer(s):
Mark Mendelson, Chief Executive Officer
markmendelson@bengurion.ca

Montréal Office
#400, 4950, rue Queen Mary, Montréal QC H3W 1X3
Tel: 514-937-8927; *Fax:* 514-937-8920
bgumontreal@sympatico.ca
Chief Officer(s):
Agar Grinberg, Executive Director
agargrinberg@bengurion.ca

Winnipeg Office
#C309, 123 Doncaster St., Winnipeg MB R3N 2B2
Tel: 204-942-7347; *Fax:* 204-944-8041
bguwinnipeg@bengurion.ca
Chief Officer(s):
Ariel Karabelnicoff, Executive Director
arielkarabelnicoff@bengurion.ca

Canadian Association Against Sexual Harassment in Higher Education *See* Canadian Association for the Prevention of Discrimination & Harassment in Higher Education

Canadian Association for American Studies (CAAS) / Association d'études américaines au Canada (AEAC)
c/o Bryce Traister, Prof. & Chair, Dept. of English, Western Univ., 2G02, 1151 Richmond St., London ON N6A 3K7
webmaster@american-studies.ca
www.american-studies.ca
www.facebook.com/groups/75085833950
twitter.com/CAASCanada
Overview: A small national organization founded in 1964
Mission: To encourage study & research concerning the United States; To examine the implications of American studies for Canada & the world
Chief Officer(s):
Bryce Traister, President
traister@uwo.ca
Adam Beardsworth, Vice-President
Luke Bresky, Secretary
Priscilla L. Walton, Treasurer
Meetings/Conferences:
• Canadian Association for American Studies 2018 Conference, 2018
Scope: National
Publications:
• Canadian Review of American Studies
Type: Journal; *Frequency:* 3 pa; *Accepts Advertising*; *Price:* Free with membership in the Canadian Association forAmerican Studies
Profile: The journal features essays & reviews related to the culture of the United States & relations between the United States & Canada

Canadian Association for Anatomy, Neurobiology, & Cell Biology (CAANCB) / Association canadienne d'anatomie, de neurobiologie et de biologie cellulaire (ACANBC)
University of Manitoba, #128, 745 Bannatyne Ave., Winnipeg MB R3E 0J9
Tel: 204-789-3483; *Fax:* 204-789-3920
www.caancb.blogspot.com
Previous Name: Canadian Association of Anatomists / Association Canadienne d'Anatomie
Overview: A small national organization founded in 1956 overseen by Canadian Federation of Biological Societies
Mission: To advance knowledge of anatomy; To represent anatomical sciences throughout Canada
Finances: *Funding Sources:* Membership fees
Membership: *Member Profile:* Elected members are individuals who have contributed to the development of the science; Associate members are persons who are interested in the discipline; Graduate students; Retired persons (emeritus members)
Chief Officer(s):
William H. Baldridge, Secretary
william.baldridge@dal.ca
Sari S. Hannila, Treasurer
hannila@cc.umanitoba.ca
Awards:
• Murray L. Barr Junior Scientist Award
• J.C.B. Grant Award
• C.P. Leblond Research Presentation Award (2)
; *Amount:* $400
• Research Publication Award of the CAANCB / ACANBC Chairs
; *Amount:* $250
• Arthur W. Ham Graduate Student Award
• Travel / Meeting Awards (2)
Publications:
• CAANCB [Canadian Association for Anatomy, Neurobiology, & Cell Biology] Anchor
Type: Newsletter

Canadian Association for Astrological Education (CAAE)
226 Cromwell Ave., Oshawa ON L1J 4T8
Tel: 905-725-9179
thecaae@gmail.com
www.thecaae.com
www.facebook.com/theCAAE
Overview: A medium-sized national organization founded in 1993
Mission: To advance astrological education in Canada through the provision of a standardized curriculum
Membership: *Member Profile:* Associate members consist of individuals with a working knowledge of astrology or an astrological resume; Student members consist of students who are taking at least one astrology class with a CAAE teacher
Activities: Offering astrological courses & examinations
Chief Officer(s):
Joan Ann Evelyn, President

Canadian Association for Business Economics (CABE) / Association canadienne de science économique des affaires
PO Box 898, Stn. B, Ottawa ON K1P 5P9
Toll-Free: 855-222-3321
info@cabe.ca
www.cabe.ca
www.facebook.com/CABEconomics
twitter.com/CABE_Economics
Overview: A medium-sized national organization founded in 1975
Mission: To represent the interests of business economists in Canada; To enhance the professionalism of business economists
Affiliation(s): International Federation of Associations of Business Economists; National Association of Business Economists (Canadian Association for Business Economics's sister organization in the United States)
Membership: 900+; *Fees:* Schedule available; *Member Profile:* Canadian professionals in the field of business economics, including economists in businesses, governments, associations & other organizations
Activities: Creating a network with other other applied economists to discuss business economics & related subjects; Promoting the study of business economics in Canada; Liaising with other national & international organizations of business economists; Offering professional development activities, such as workshops
Chief Officer(s):
Paul Jacobson, President
pmj@jciconsult.com
Publications:
• CABE [Canadian Association for Business Economics, Inc.] Membership Directory
Type: Directory; *Price:* Free with membership in Canadian Association for Business Economics
• CABE [Canadian Association for Business Economics, Inc.] News
Type: Newsletter; *Price:* Free with membership in Canadian Association for Business Economics
• Canadian Business Economics
Type: Journal; *Price:* Free with membership in Canadian Association for Business Economics

Canadian Association for Child & Play Therapy
PO Box 24010, Guelph ON N1E 6V8
Tel: 519-827-1506; *Fax:* 519-827-1825
membership@cacpt.com
www.cacpt.com
Overview: A small national organization
Mission: To advance & promote play therapy; To set high professional & ethical play therapy practice standards; To support research & professional training in the play therapy field
Membership: *Fees:* $40 student; $60 general; $75 professional; $140 certified; $200 agency; *Member Profile:* Professional association for the field of child psychotherapy & play therapy in Canada
Chief Officer(s):
Elizabeth A. Sharpe, Executive Director
elizabeth@cacpt.com
Publications:
• Playground Magazine [a publication of the Canadian Association for Child & Play Therapy]
Type: Magazine; *Frequency:* Quarterly; *Accepts Advertising*;
Editor: Lorie Walton
Profile: Information on Play Therapy; Association information & upcoming events

Canadian Association for Clinical Microbiology & Infectious Diseases (CACMID) / Association canadienne de microbiologie clinique et des maladies contagieuses
c/o National Microbiology Laboratory, 1015 Arlington St., Winnipeg MB R3E 3R2
Fax: 204-789-2097
www.cacmid.ca
www.facebook.com/CACMID
twitter.com/cacmid
Overview: A small national charitable organization founded in 1932
Mission: To enhance the cooperation of professionals specializing in clinical microbiology & infectious disease; To act as the voice for clinical microbiology & infectious disease professionals; To develop standards in the field of clinical microbiology
Membership: *Fees:* $50 regular member; $20 student & retired members; $800 sustaining member; *Member Profile:* Medical & clinical microbiologists; Infectious disease physicians; Medical technologists; Laboratory scientists & managers; Research technologists

Activities: Promoting education & research
Chief Officer(s):
Jeff Fuller, President
jeff.fuller@albertahealthservices.ca
Matthew W. Gilmour, Secretary-Treasurer
Matthew.Gilmour@cacmid.ca
Meetings/Conferences:
• Canadian Association for Clinical Microbiology and Infectious Diseases Annual Conference 2018, May, 2018, Vancouver, BC
Scope: National
Publications:
• CACMID [Canadian Association for Clinical Microbiology & Infectious Diseases] Membership Directory
Type: Directory

Canadian Association for Commonwealth Literature & Language Studies (CACLALS) / Association canadienne pour l'étude des langues et de la littérature du Commonwealth

c/o Kristina Fagan, Department of English, University of Saskatchewan, 9 Campus Dr., Saskatoon SK S7N 5A5
www.caclals.ca
Overview: A small international organization founded in 1973
Mission: To promote the study of Commonwealth literature in Canada; To encourage the reading of Canadian literature abroad
Affiliation(s): Association for Commonwealth Literature & Language Studies (ACLALS)
Membership: *Fees:* $20 students & unwaged persons; $50 regular members; *Member Profile:* Teachers, scholars, writers, & students who are interested in Commonwealth & postcolonial literature
Chief Officer(s):
Susan Gingell, President
Kristina Fagan, Secretary-Treasurer
Neil ten Kortenaar, Editor, Chimo
kortenaar@utsc.utoronto.ca
Meetings/Conferences:
• Canadian Association for Commonwealth Literature & Language Studies Conference 2018, May, 2018, University of Regina, Regina, SK
Scope: National
Description: Keynote speakers, roundtables, sessions, & readings
Publications:
• Chimo: The Newsjournal of the Canadian Association for Commonwealth Literature & Language Studies
Type: Newsletter; *Frequency:* Semiannually; *Editor:* Neil ten Kortenaar
Profile: Association activities, conference information, & member news

Canadian Association for Commonwealth Literature & Language Studies (CACLALS)

c/o Dept. of English & Film Studies, Wilfrid Laurier University, 75 University Ave., Waterloo ON N2L 3C5
www.caclals.ca
Overview: A small international organization founded in 1964
Mission: To promote Commonwealth Literature Studies, organize seminars & workshops, arrange lectures by writers & scholars; To disseminate knowledge
Member of: The Commonwealth
Affiliation(s): Commonwealth Consortium of Education; International Federation for Modern Languages & Literatures
Finances: *Annual Operating Budget:* Less than $50,000
30 volunteer(s)
Membership: 1,600; *Member Profile:* Professors; researchers; practitioners; students; public; *Committees:* Conference; Afrikan Participation; First Nations; Indigenous & Dalit; South Asian
Activities: Chapters in Canada, Europe, India, Malaysia, South Africa, Sri Lanka, South Pacific, West Indies & USA
Chief Officer(s):
Mariam Pirbhai, President

Canadian Association for Community Living (CACL) / Association canadienne pour l'intégration communautaire

20-850 King St. West, Oshawa ON L1J 8N5
Tel: 416-661-9611; *Fax:* 905-436-3587
Toll-Free: 855-661-9611
inform@cacl.ca
www.cacl.ca
www.facebook.com/canadianacl
twitter.com/cacl_acic
www.youtube.com/canadianacl
Previous Name: Canadian Association for the Mentally Retarded
Overview: A large national charitable organization founded in 1958
Mission: To ensure the following for people with intellectual disabilities: the same rights, & access to choice, services, & supports as others; the same opportunities to live in freedom & dignity with the necessary supports to do so; & the ability to articulate & realize their rights & aspirations
Member of: Inclusion International
Affiliation(s): People First of Canada; Council of Canadians with Disabilities (CCD); National Alliance for Children & Youth; Active Living Alliance; Canadian Council on Social Development (CCSD); Canadian Coalition for the Rights of Children (CCRC); Canadian Institute of Child Health (CICH); Canadian Caregiver Coalition; Canadian Down Syndrome Society (CDSS); Family Service Canada; DisAbled Women's Network Canada (DAWN)
Finances: *Funding Sources:* Government of Canada; Assessments from provincial & territorial associations; Fundraising; Donations; Sponsorships
Membership: 10 provincial associations + 3 territorial associations (consisting of 400 local associations & 40,000+ members); *Member Profile:* Family members & others who work for the benefit of people with an intellectual disability
Activities: Defending the rights & advocating for the interests of individuals with intellectual disabilities; Promoting research; Engaging with governments; Raising awareness of inclusion; *Speaker Service:* Yes; *Library:* Canadian Association for Community Living Resource Centre; Open to public by appointment
Chief Officer(s):
Joy Bacon, President
Michael Bach, Executive Vice-President
mbach@cacl.ca
Sue Talmey, Director, Finance & Administration
stalmey@cacl.ca
Tara Brinston Levandier, Director, Policy & Program Operations
tbrinston@cacl.ca
Gordon Porter, Director, Inclusive Education Initiatives
inclusiveeducation@cacl.ca
Agata Zieba, Senior Officer, Communications
azieba@cacl.ca
Publications:
• Coming Together [a publication of the Canadian Association for Community Living]
Type: Newsletter
Profile: The Canadian Association for Community Living's family newsletter, featuring stories of families
• Education Watch [a publication of the Canadian Association for Community Living]
Type: Newsletter; *Frequency:* Quarterly
Profile: Inclusive education across Canada
• INFO@ [a publication of the Canadian Association for Community Living]
Type: Newsletter; *Frequency:* Bimonthly
Profile: Up-to-date topics & issues within the Canadian Association for Community Living & its members & affiliates
• Institution Watch [a publication of the Canadian Association for Community Living]
Type: Newsletter
Profile: Produced by the People First of Canada - CACL Joint Task Force on Deinstitutionalization
• Invisible No More [a publication of the Canadian Association for Community Living]
Type: Book; *Number of Pages:* 160; *Author:* Vincenzo Pietropaolo
Profile: A photography book chronicling the lives of individuals with intellectual disabilities
• National Report Card on Inclusion [a publication of the Canadian Association for Community Living]
Type: Report; *Frequency:* Annual
Profile: The purpose is to track the progress of inclusion in Canadian society
• Povery Watch [a publication of the Canadian Association for Community Living]
Type: Newsletter; *Frequency:* Quarterly
Profile: A publication from the Canadian Association for Community Living's National Action Committee on Disability Supports, Income, & Employment

Canadian Association for Community Living - Antigonish

83 Kirk St., Antigonish NS B2G 1Y7
Tel: 902-863-5024; *Fax:* 902-863-0090
info@caclantigonish.ca
caclantigonish.ca
www.facebook.com/CACLworkshop
Also Known As: CACL - Antigonish
Overview: A small local organization overseen by Nova Scotia Association for Community Living
Member of: DIRECTIONS Council for Vocational Services Society; Nova Scotia Association for Community Living
Finances: *Funding Sources:* Government; revenue; donations; fundraising

Canadian Association for Community Living - Clare Branch

1711 Hwy. 1, Church Point NS B0W 1M0
Tel: 902-769-3253; *Fax:* 902-769-0002
www.caclclare.ca
www.facebook.com/317155121790228
Also Known As: L'Atelier De Clare
Overview: A small local organization founded in 1979
Mission: To help members become productive members of society through work placements & the development of life skills
Member of: DIRECTIONS Council for Vocational Services Society; Canadian Association for Community Living - Clare Branch
Staff Member(s): 17; 5 volunteer(s)
Chief Officer(s):
Brigette Robicheau, Acting Executive Director
brobicheau@caclclare.ca

Canadian Association for Composite Structures & Materials (CACSMA) / Association canadienne pour les structures et matériaux composites (ACSMAC)

c/o J. Denault, Industrial Materials Institute, Ntl. Research Council, 75 boul Mortange, Boucherville QC J4B 6Y4
Tel: 450-641-5149; *Fax:* 450-641-5105
www.cacsma.ca
Overview: A medium-sized national organization founded in 1988
Mission: To support composites companies in Canada; To promote Canadian composites capabilities; To encourage the application of composites in all sectors
Membership: *Fees:* $20 students; $60 individuals; $250 corporate members; *Member Profile:* Canadian individuals & corporate members, such as government employees, teachers, researchers, research centers, consultants, technologists, materials specialists, fabricators, equipment manufacturers, suppliers, & distributors
Activities: Informing members of scientific & technological developments in the composites industry; Liaising with government; Fostering research & development alliances; Creating networking opportunities with other national & international materials organizations
Chief Officer(s):
Suong V. Hoa, President, 514-848-2424 Ext. 3139, Fax: 514-848-3178
hoasuon@alcor.concordia.ca
Mehdi Hojjati, Secretary, 514-283-9209, Fax: 514-283-9445
Mehdi.Hojjati@nrc-cnrc.gc.ca
Johanne Denault, Treasurer, 450-641-5149, Fax: 450-641-5105
Johanne.Denault@imi.cnrc-nrc.gc.ca

Canadian Association for Conservation of Cultural Property (CAC) / Association canadienne pour la conservation et la restauration des biens culturels (ACCR)

c/o Danielle Allard, #419, 207 Bank St., Ottawa ON K2P 2N2
Tel: 613-231-3977; *Fax:* 613-231-1406
coordinator@cac-accr.com
www.cac-accr.ca
www.facebook.com/289264431135291
Previous Name: Canadian Association for Conservation; International Institute for Conservation of Historic & Artistic Works - Canadian Group
Overview: A small national organization founded in 1974
Mission: To promote conservation of Canadian cultural property
Finances: *Funding Sources:* Membership fees; Sponsorships
Membership: *Member Profile:* Persons interested in the field of conservation, such as professional conservation practitioners & individual & institutional collectors; *Committees:* Communication; Translations; CAC Grants & Awards; Membership; Job Descriptions; Bulletin; Journal; Conference Planning; Central Conference; Training; Workplace Issues; Fundraising; Marketing, Sales & Promotions; Emerging Conservators
Activities: Disseminating information to conservators about technical advances; Offering professional development activities; Providing networking opportunities
Chief Officer(s):
Cindy Colford, President
president@cac-accr.ca

Jessica Lafrance, Vice-President
jessca.lafrance@live.ca
Susannah Kendall, Secretary
sookendall@yahoo.com
Michael Harrington, Treasurer
mharrington@jhgconsulting.com
Awards:
• Charles Mervyn Ruggles Award
• Training Activity Grant
• Professional Development Grant to Attend a Conservation Conference, Workshop or Seminar
• Professional Development Grant to Attend the Annual CAC Conference &/or Workshop
Meetings/Conferences:
• Canadian Association for Conservation 2018 44th Annual Conference, May, 2018, Kingston, ON
Scope: National
Description: Educational sessions & a tradeshow
Publications:
• Canadian Association for Conservation Bulletin
Type: Newsletter; *Frequency:* Quarterly
Profile: Association activities
• Canadian Association for Conservation Conference Program & Abstracts
Type: Abstracts; *Frequency:* Annually
Profile: Abstracts from the association's annual conference
• Canadian Association for Conservation Directory of Members
Type: Directory; *Frequency:* Annually; *Accepts Advertising;*
Editor: Anne Sinclair
Profile: Contact information for association members
• Code of Ethics & Guidance for Practice
Price: $10
• The Journal of the Canadian Association for Conservation
Type: Journal; *Frequency:* Annually; *Editor:* Irene Karsten; Carole Dignard
Profile: Peer reviewed articles about the conservation of cultural property, including treatments & research
• Selecting & Employing a Conservator in Canada
Profile: Assistance to select a conservator to preserve, repair, & restore objects

Canadian Association for Conservation; International Institute for Conservation of Historic & Artistic Works - Canadian Group *See* Canadian Association for Conservation of Cultural Property

Canadian Association for Co-operative Education *See* Co-operative Education & Work-Integrated Learning Canada

Canadian Association for Corporate Growth *See* Association for Corporate Growth, Toronto Chapter

Canadian Association for Curriculum Studies (CACS)
c/o Canadian Society for the Study of Education, #204, 260 Dalhousie St., Ottawa ON K1N 7E4
Tel: 613-241-0018; *Fax:* 613-241-0019
csse-scee@csse.ca
csse-scee.ca/associations/cacs-acec
twitter.com/cacs_acec
Overview: A small national organization overseen by Canadian Society for the Study of Education
Mission: To support inquiries into & discussions of curricula that are of interest to Canadian educators
Member of: Canadian Society for the Study of Education
Chief Officer(s):
Avril Aitken, President
aaitken@bishopsu.ca

Canadian Association for Dental Research (CADR) / Association canadienne de recherches dentaires (ACRD)
c/o Western University, 1151 Richmond St., London ON N6A 5B8
Tel: 519-661-2111
www.cadr-acrd.ca
Overview: A medium-sized national organization
Mission: To advance research & increase knowledge in order to improve oral health in Canada; To support & represent Canadian oral health researchers
Member of: International Association for Dental Research
Membership: *Member Profile:* Oral health researchers in Canada, who are interested in the furtherance of research in fields related to dental science; Persons interested in the latest reserach (affiliate members); Students interested in dental research; Retired persons who have been members of the association
Activities: Communicating & applying research findings; Presenting awards & scholarships
Chief Officer(s):
Joy M. Richman, President, 604-822-3568
richman@dentistry.ubc.ca
Patrick Flood, Vice-President
pflood@ualberta.ca
Fernanda Almeida, Secretary-Treasurer
falmeida@dentistry.ubc.ca
Meetings/Conferences:
• Canadian Association for Dental Research 42nd Annual Meeting, March, 2018, Fort Lauderdale, FL
Scope: International
Description: In conjunction with the 47th Annual Meeting of the American Association of Dental Research & the 96th General Session & Exhibition of the International Association for Dental Research
• Canadian Association for Dental Research 43rd Annual Meeting, June, 2019, Vancouver, BC
Scope: International
Description: In conjunction with the 48th Annual Meeting of the American Association of Dental Research & the 97th General Session & Exhibition of the International Association for Dental Research
• Canadian Association for Dental Research 44th Annual Meeting, March, 2020, Washington, DC
Scope: International
Description: In conjunction with the 49th Annual Meeting of the American Association of Dental Research & the 98th General Session & Exhibition of the International Association for Dental Research
Publications:
• CADR [Canadian Association for Dental Research]/ACRD [Association canadienne de recherches dentaires] Division Annual Report
Type: Yearbook; *Frequency:* Annually

Canadian Association for Disabled Skiing (CADS) / Association canadienne pour les skieurs handicapés (ACSH)
791 Strathcona Dr. SW, Calgary AB T3H 1N8
Tel: 587-315-5870; *Fax:* 866-531-9644
disabledskiing.ca
Overview: A medium-sized national charitable organization founded in 1976
Mission: To assist individuals with a disability to participate in recreational & competitive snow skiing & snowboarding
Finances: *Funding Sources:* Sponsorships; Donations
1900 volunteer(s)
Membership: 1,130 disabled members; *Fees:* $25
Activities: Ensuring that programs are delivered at an appropriate level of expertise, through the work of a technical committee; Providing information about adaptive equipment;
Awareness Events: CADS Ski Improvement & Race Development Festival, March
Chief Officer(s):
Maureen O'Hara-Leman, Executive Director
executive.director@disabledskiing.ca
Publications:
• The Perspective: CADS National Newsletter
Type: Newsletter; *Editor:* Karen Elliott
Profile: Reports from the Canadian Association for Disabled Skiing, plus programming & forthcoming events

Canadian Association for Disabled Skiing - Alberta (CADS Alberta)
11759 Groat Rd., Edmonton AB T5M 3K6
Tel: 780-427-8104; *Fax:* 780-422-2663
info@cadsalberta.ca
www.cadsalberta.ca
www.facebook.com/CADSAB
twitter.com/CADSAlberta
Overview: A small provincial charitable organization founded in 1961 overseen by Canadian Association for Disabled Skiing
Mission: CADS Alberta is a volunteer-based organization assisting individuals with a disability to lead fuller lives through active participation in recreational & competitive snow skiing & snowboarding. It is a registered charity, BN: 133967406RR0001.
Member of: Canadian Association for Disabled Skiing
Affiliation(s): Canadian Ski Instructors' Alliance (CSIA), Canadian Association of Snowboard Instructors (CASI)
Finances: *Annual Operating Budget:* $50,000-$100,000
500 volunteer(s)
Membership: 800+; *Fees:* $40
Chief Officer(s):
Edward Shaw, President
president@cadsalberta.ca
Sharon Veeneman, Executive Coordinator
Awards:
• Eileen Lloyd Award
• John Hanson Award
• Volunteer of the Year Award
• Coach of the Year Award
• Instructor of the Year Award
Calgary Zone
CADS Calgary, Canada Olympic Park, 88 Canada Olympic Rd. SW, Calgary AB T3B 5R5
Tel: 403-286-8050
info@cadscalgary.ca
www.cadscalgary.ca
twitter.com/CADSCalgary
Chief Officer(s):
John Bowman, Chair
chair@cadscalgary.ca
Edmonton Zone
CADS Edmonton, PO Box 35073, 10818 Jasper Ave., Edmonton AB T5J 0B7
Tel: 780-669-3856
info@cadsedmonton.ca
www.cadsedmonton.ca
www.facebook.com/150695641627414
twitter.com/CADSEdmonton
Chief Officer(s):
Dale Loyer, President
Rocky Mountain Zone
Rocky Mountain Adaptive Sports Centre, #2, 201 Carey, Canmore AB T1W 2R7
Tel: 403-431-1354
info@rockymountainadaptive.com
www.rockymountainadaptive.com
Chief Officer(s):
Jamie McCulloch, Executive Director, 403-431-1154
jamie@rockymountainadaptive.com

Canadian Association for Disabled Skiing - National Capital Division (CADS-NCD)
1216 Bordeau Grove, Ottawa ON K1C 2M7
Tel: 819-827-4378
www.cads-ncd.ca
Overview: A medium-sized provincial charitable organization overseen by Canadian Association for Disabled Skiing
Mission: To provide disabled individuals with skiing opportunities
Member of: Canadian Association for Disabled Skiing
Membership: *Committees:* Technical
Chief Officer(s):
Bernie Simpson, President
berniesimpson@outlook.com

Canadian Association for Disabled Skiing - New Brunswick
c/o Lloyd Gagnon, 59 rue Carrier, Edmundston NB E3V EY2
Tel: 506-739-9662
Overview: A medium-sized provincial charitable organization overseen by Canadian Association for Disabled Skiing
Mission: To provide skiing opportunities for individuals with disabilities
Member of: Canadian Association for Disabled Skiing
Chief Officer(s):
Lloyd Gagnon, President
lloyd@disabledskiing.ca
Jim Bowland, Technical Coordinator
jimbowland.cadsnb@nb.sympatico.ca

Canadian Association for Disabled Skiing - Newfoundland & Labrador Division
6 Albany Pl., St. John's NL A1E 1Y2
Tel: 709-753-3625; *Fax:* 709-777-4884
disabledskiing.ca/?page_id=123
Also Known As: CADS Newfoundland/Labrador
Overview: A small provincial organization overseen by Canadian Association for Disabled Skiing
Member of: Canadian Association for Disabled Skiing
Chief Officer(s):
Marg Tibbo, Representative
margaret.tibbo@easternhealth.ca

Canadian Association for Disabled Skiing - Nova Scotia
c/o Alpine Ski Nova Scotia, 5516 Spring Garden Rd., 4th Fl., Halifax NS B3J 1G6

Canadian Associations / Canadian Association for Disabled Skiing - Ontario

Tel: 902-425-5450; Fax: 902-425-5606
alpinens@sportnovascotia.ca
disabledskiing.ca/provincial-programs/nova-scotia
Also Known As: CADS Nova Scotia
Overview: A medium-sized provincial organization overseen by Canadian Association for Disabled Skiing
Member of: Alpine Canada Alpin; Canadian Association for Disabled Skiing
Finances: Annual Operating Budget: $250,000-$500,000
Staff Member(s): 1; 5 volunteer(s)
Membership: 1-99
Chief Officer(s):
Lorraine Burch, Executive Director

Canadian Association for Disabled Skiing - Ontario
145 Dew St., King City ON L7B 1L1
Tel: 647-280-1307
www.disabledskiingontario.com
www.facebook.com/cads.ontario
twitter.com/cads_ontario
www.flickr.com/photos/cadsontario
Also Known As: CADS Ontario
Overview: A medium-sized provincial organization overseen by Canadian Association for Disabled Skiing
Mission: To provide a skiing program for people with disabilities
Member of: Canadian Association for Disabled Skiing
Chief Officer(s):
Gwen Binsfeld, President

Canadian Association for Distance Education (CADE); Association for Media & Technology in Education in Canada (AMTEC) See Canadian Network for Innovation in Education

Canadian Association for Educational Psychology (CAEP) / L'association Canadienne en psychopedagogie (ACP)
c/o Canadian Society for the Study of Education, #204, 260 Dalhousie St., Ottawa ON K1N 7E4
Tel: 613-241-0018; Fax: 613-241-0019
caepacp.wordpress.com
www.facebook.com/CAEP.ACP
Overview: A small national organization founded in 1997 overseen by Canadian Society for the Study of Education
Mission: To research, discuss, & encourage the study of educational psychology
Member of: Canadian Society for the Study of Education
Membership: Fees: $10 regular & international; $5 student/retired/low income
Activities: CAEPtalks Canada
Chief Officer(s):
Jess Whitley, President
jwhitley@uottawa.ca
Awards:
• Robbie Case Memorial Award
• G.M. Dunlop Distinguished Contribution Awards (Graduate Student Award)
• Carol Crealock Award
• Exceptionality Education International Book of the Year Award
Publications:
• CAEP [Canadian Association for Educational Psychology] Newsletter
Type: Newsletter; Frequency: Semiannually
• CAEP/ACP [Canadian Association for Educational Psychology] Dialogic
Profile: Collections of articles on a specific topic

Canadian Association for Enterostomal Therapy (CAET) / Association canadienne des stomathérapeutes
66 Leopolds Dr., Ottawa ON K1V 7E3
Fax: 613-834-6351
Toll-Free: 888-739-5072
office@caet.ca
www.caet.ca
Overview: A small national charitable organization founded in 1981
Mission: To promote high standards for nursing practice in the area of enterostomal therapy
Membership: 350+; Member Profile: Nurses specializing in the care of patients with challenges in wound, ostomy, & continence;
Committees: National Conference Planning; Political Action; Professional Development and Practice; Informatics and Research; Marketing
Activities: Promoting education & research; Providing networking opportunities
Chief Officer(s):
Paulo DaRosa, President
paulo_darosa@rogers.com
Elise Rodd-Nielsen, Treasurer
eliserodd@hotmail.com
Catherine Harley, Executive Director
catherine.harley@sympatico.ca
Awards:
• President's Award
Eligibility: Awarded for excellence in ET Nursing.
Meetings/Conferences:
• Canadian Association for Enterostomal Therapy National Conference 2018, May, 2018, Victoria, BC
Scope: National
Description: Theme: "Turn Knowledge into Action: Education in Specialized Wound, Ostomy & Continence Care"
Publications:
• CAET [Canadian Association for Enterostomal Therapy] Membership Directory
Type: Directory
• The Link: The Official Publication of the CAET [Canadian Association for Enterostomal Therapy]
Type: Newsletter; Frequency: 3 pa; Accepts Advertising; Price: Free to CAET members
Profile: Reports, research projects, clinical papers, review articles, & industry news

Canadian Association for Familial Ataxias Voir Association canadienne des ataxies familiales

Canadian Association for Food Studies (CAFS) / L'Association canadienne des études sur l'alimentation
c/o Centre for Studies in Food Security, Ryerson University, 350 Victoria St., Toronto ON M5B 2K3
Tel: 416-979-5000; Fax: 416-979-5362
cafsadmin@foodstudies.ca
cafs.landfood.ubc.ca
www.linkedin.com/groups/Canadian-Association-Food-Studies-3916447?home=&gid=3916447&trk=anet_ug_hm
www.facebook.com/CAFSpage
twitter.com/CAFSfoodstudies
Overview: A small national organization founded in 2005
Mission: Aims to allow researchers from diverse disciplines working at universities as well as public and community based organizations to meet regularly to identify research priorities and to share research findings on diverse issues dealing with food security concerns.
Membership: Fees: $75 regualr; $30 student
Meetings/Conferences:
• Canadian Association for Food Studies 13th Annual Assembly, 2018
Scope: National

Canadian Association for Free Expression (CAFE)
PO Box 332, Stn. B, Toronto ON M9W 5L3
Tel: 905-897-7221; Fax: 905-277-3914
cafe@canadafirst.net
www.canadianfreespeech.com
Overview: A small national organization founded in 1981
Mission: To protect Canadian civil liberties; To promote free speech & discussion as essential parts to a functioning democracy
Activities: Researching threats to freedom of speech; Informing media of concerns about threats to freedom of speech & freedom of belief; Engaging in lobbying activities & court interventions
Publications:
• The Free Speech Monitor
Frequency: 10 pa; Price: $15
Profile: CAFE research on threats to freedom of speech

Canadian Association for Graduate Studies (CAGS) / Association canadienne pour les études supérieures (ACES)
#301, 260 St. Patrick St., Ottawa ON K1N 5K5
Tel: 613-562-0949; Fax: 613-562-9009
info@cags.ca
www.cags.ca
Overview: A medium-sized national charitable organization founded in 1962
Mission: To promote excellence in graduate education; To foster research, scholarship, & creative activity; To provide a nationwide link for the exchange of information between graduate schools & granting councils, research, business, & industrial sectors, & all levels of government; To hold meetings & conferences; To publish materials to advance graduate education; To develop & maintain national standards for graduate degree programs; To support the regular external evaluation of these standards; To deal with other matters of concern to Deans & Associate Deans of graduate studies
Member of: Canadian Consortium for Research; Association of Universities & Colleges of Canada
Finances: Annual Operating Budget: $250,000-$500,000;
Funding Sources: Subscriptions
Staff Member(s): 2
Membership: 58 Canadian universities with graduate programs + 2 national graduate student associations + 3 federal research-granting agencies & organizations; Fees: Schedule available; Member Profile: Institutional members are Canadian universities with graduate programs & which are members of the Association of Universities & Colleges of Canada. Graduate student association members are national associations with objectives consistent with CAGS. Corresponding members are related national & international organizations & Canadian institutions with plans for graduate programs. Sustaining members are nonprofit and for-profit organizations which provide services to graduate studies & research. Federal research-granting agency membership is open to federal research-granting agencies.
Chief Officer(s):
Sally Rutherford, Executive Director
sally.rutherford@cags.ca
John Doering, President, 204-474-9887
jay_doering@umanitoba.ca
Gary Slater, Vice-President, 613-562-5800 Ext. 1234
deangrad@uottawa.ca
Sue Horton, Sec.-Treas., 519-888-4567 Ext. 33439
sehorton@uwaterloo.ca
Awards:
• CAGS [Canadian Association for Graduate Studies] / UMI [University Microfilms International] Distinguished Dissertation Awards
To honour doctoral students whose dissertations make an unique contribution to the areas of engineering, medical sciences, & natural sciences or fine arts, humanities, & social sciences
• CAGS [Canadian Association for Graduate Studies] / ETS Educational Testing Service] Award for Excellence & Innovation
Presented to a member institution or one its graduate programs for excellence & innovation in enhancing the graduate student experience
Meetings/Conferences:
• Canadian Association for Graduate Studies 56th Annual Conference, November, 2018, Fort Garry Hotel, Winnipeg, MB
Scope: National
Description: A yearly conference held at the end of October or the beginning of November, including plenary & breakout sessions, workshops, the presentation of awards, & the Killam Lecture related to graduate studies
Publications:
• Canadian Association for Graduate Studies Statistical Report
Type: Yearbook; Frequency: Annually
Profile: A report on registration in graduate studies at Canadian universities for association members only

Canadian Association for Health Services & Policy Research (CAHSPR) / Association canadienne pour la recherche sur les services et les politiques de la santé (ACRSPS)
292 Somerset St. West, Ottawa ON K2P 0J6
Tel: 613-288-9239; Fax: 613-599-7805
info@cahspr.ca
www.cahspr.ca
www.facebook.com/CAHSPR
twitter.com/CAHSPR
www.youtube.com/CAHSPR
Previous Name: Canadian Health Economics Research Association
Overview: A small national organization founded in 1983
Mission: To provide a multidisciplinary association fostering and supporting linkages between researchers and decision makers; knowledge translation and exchange; education and training; and advocacy for research and its more effective use in planning, practice and policy-making.
Finances: Funding Sources: Membership dues
Membership: 450; Fees: $175 individual; $75 student; Member Profile: Health services & policy researchers; Decision makers; Practitioners; Students; Users of research from organizations & industry; Representatives from sponsor organizations;
Committees: Collaborative Healthcare Improvement Partnerships; Cancer; Health and Human Resources; Maternal

and Child Health; Mental Health; Primary Health Care; Student Working Group
Chief Officer(s):
Steve Morgan, President
Adalsteinn (Steini) Brown, President-Elect
Meetings/Conferences:
• Canadian Association for Health Services and Policy Research 2018 Conference, May, 2018, Hotel Bonaventure, Montréal, QC
Scope: National
Description: Theme: "Shaping the Future of Canada's Health Systems"
Publications:
• CAHSPR [Canadian Association for Health Services & Policy Research] Newsletter
Type: Newsletter; *Frequency:* Weekly
Profile: CAHSPR activities & upcoming events, career opportunities, links to course materials for student members, research & policy items of interest to members
• Healthcare Policy
Type: Journal; *Frequency:* Quarterly

The Canadian Association for HIV Research (CAHR) / L'Association Canadienne de recherche sur le HIV (ACRV)
#744, 1 Rideau St., Ottawa ON K1N 8S7
Tel: 613-241-5785; *Fax:* 613-670-5701
info@cahr-acrv.ca
www.cahr-acrv.ca
www.facebook.com/CanadianAssociationforHIVResearch
twitter.com/CAHR_ACRV
Overview: A medium-sized national charitable organization founded in 1991
Mission: Focuses on HIV/AIDS research & education
Staff Member(s): 3
Membership: 1,000+; *Fees:* $50 HIV community member/other; $75 community-based researcher; $150 academic researcher
Chief Officer(s):
Robert Hogg, President
Carol Strike, Secretary
Curtis Cooper, Treasurer
Andrew Matejcic, Executive Director
Shelley Mineault, Project Coordinator
Erin Love, Project Coordinator
Meetings/Conferences:
• 27th Annual Canadian Conference on HIV/AIDS Research, April, 2018, Vancouver, BC
Scope: National

Canadian Association for Humane Trapping (CAHT)
PO Box 36534, Stn. Eastgate, 75 Centennial Pkwy North, Hamilton ON L8E 2P0
info@caht.ca
www.caht.ca
Overview: A medium-sized national charitable organization founded in 1954
Mission: To reduce & eliminate suffering of animals trapped for whatever reason; To work with governments, trappers, the commercial fur industry, animal welfare organizations & the public-at-large to bring about actual trapping improvements
Member of: World Conservation Union; Fur Institute of Canada; World Wildlife Fund; Canadian Nature Federation; Canadian Federation of Humane Societies
Finances: *Funding Sources:* Membership fees; Bequests; Donations
Staff Member(s): 3
Membership: 750; *Fees:* $10; *Committees:* Trap research & development
Activities: *Speaker Service:* Yes
Chief Officer(s):
Carl Bandow, Executive Director
Donald Mitton, Project Director
Donna Bandow, Coordinator, Grants & Fundraising
Publications:
• The CAHT [Canadian Association for Humane Trapping] Bulletin
Type: Newsletter; *Number of Pages:* 16

Canadian Association for Immunization Research & Evaluation
950 West 28th Ave., Vancouver BC V5Z 4H4
Tel: 604-875-2422; *Fax:* 604-875-2635
caire@cfri.ca
www.caire.ca
Overview: A small national organization
Mission: To promote vaccinology research in Canada; To represent the interests of individuals in the vaccinology research field; To stimulate public interest in vaccine studies & vaccine-preventable diseases; To disseminate information from research studies to health professionals & the public
Membership: *Committees:* Management; Research Sponsor Activity
Chief Officer(s):
Brian Ward, Interim Chair

Canadian Association for Information Science (CAIS) / Association canadienne des sciences de l'information (ACSI)
www.cais-acsi.ca
Overview: A small national organization founded in 1970
Mission: To advance information science in Canada by encouraging & facilitating the exchange of information on the use, access, retrieval, organization, management, & dissemination of information
Membership: *Member Profile:* Information scientists, librarians, archivists, computer scientists, educators, journalists, documentalists, economists & others who support the objectives of the Canadian Association for Information Science
Activities: Publishing a journal; Organizing annual conference
Chief Officer(s):
Vivian Howard, President
vivian.howard@dal.ca
Dinesh Rathi, Vice-President
drathi@ualberta.ca
Philippe Mongeon, Secretary & Treasurer
philippe.mongeon@umontreal.ca
Publications:
• Canadian Journal of Information & Library Science
Type: Journal; *Frequency:* Quarterly; *Accepts Advertising*; *Editor:* Valerie Nesset; *ISSN:* 1920-7239; *Price:* Free for personal or institutional members of CAIS;$95 Canada; $110 other countries
Profile: Research, reviews of books, software & technology, & letters to the editor

Canadian Association for Integrative & Energy Therapies (CAIET)
Tel: 416-221-5639; *Fax:* 416-221-7126
www.caiet.org
www.facebook.com/epccanada
twitter.com/CEPConference
Overview: A small national organization
Mission: A Canadian nonprofit organization of licensed mental health professionals and related energy and integrative health practitioners promoting knowledge and understanding of Energy Psychology and related fields.
Membership: *Fees:* $95 regular; $550 corporate
Chief Officer(s):
Sharon Cass-Toole, President & Executive Director
Meetings/Conferences:
• Canadian Energy Psychology Conference 2018, October, 2018, Toronto, ON
Scope: National
Contact Information: www.epccanada.ca

Canadian Association for Interpretation See Interpretation Canada - A Professional Association for Heritage Interpretation

Canadian Association for Irish Studies (CAIS) / L'Association canadienne pour les études irlandaises
c/o School of Canadian-Irish Studies, Concordia University, 1455, boul de Maisonneuve ouest, #H1001, Montréal QC H3G 1M8
info@irishstudies.ca
www.irishstudies.ca
Overview: A small international charitable organization founded in 1974
Mission: To encourage the study of Irish culture in Canada
Membership: *Fees:* $35 students; $75 regular & senior members; $110 family; *Member Profile:* Individuals in Canada & throughout the world who are interested in the promotion of Irish culture in Canada
Activities: Supporting discussions of current issues in Irish studies
Chief Officer(s):
Jane McGaughey, President
jane.mcgaughey@concordia.ca
Jean Talman, Communications Officer
jean.talman@utoronto.ca
Publications:
• CAIS [Canadian Association for Irish Studies] Newsletter
Type: Newsletter; *Frequency:* Semiannually; *Editor:* Michael Quigley; *Price:* Free for CAIS members
Profile: Announcements & information from the association
• The Canadian Journal of Irish Studies (CJIS) / Revue canadienne d'études irlandaises (RCÉI)
Type: Journal; *Frequency:* Semiannually; *Editor:* Rhona Richman Kenneally; *Price:* Free for CAIS members
Profile: Research, book reviews, & general interest writing about aspects of the life of Ireland, especially workwith a Canadian dimension

Canadian Association for Israel Philately (CAFIP)
11 Evening Side Rd., Thornhill ON L3T 4K1
Tel: 416-879-4298
Overview: A small international organization founded in 1952
Mission: To promote the study of postage stamps & the postal history of Israel
Affiliation(s): Society of Israel Philately; World Philatelic Congress; Royal Philatelic Society of Canada; American Philately Society
Membership: *Member Profile:* Interest in Israel, Judaica & Holy Land philatelics
Activities: Meets second Wed. of each month at Bet Joseph Lubavitch, 44 Edinburgh St. E. Toronto; *Library*
Chief Officer(s):
Morty Wagman, Contact

Canadian Association for Japanese Language Education (CAJLE)
PO Box 75133, 20 Bloor St. East, Toronto ON M4W 3T3
cajle.pr@gmail.com
www.cajle.info
Overview: A small national organization founded in 1988
Mission: Promotes Japanese language education in Canada.
Membership: 200; *Fees:* $45 regular; $30 student; $120 institutional
Activities: Annual conference, lectures, workshops, publication of academic journals and newsletters
Chief Officer(s):
Ikuko Komuro-Lee, President
Meetings/Conferences:
• Canadian Association for Japanese Language Education Annual Conference 2018, August, 2018, Huron University College, London, ON
Scope: National
Description: Theme: "Diversity & Assessment: Exploring the Significance of Assessment in a Diversifying Society"

Canadian Association for Laboratory Accreditation Inc. (CALA)
#102, 2934 Baseline Rd., Ottawa ON K2H 1B2
Tel: 613-233-5300; *Fax:* 613-233-5501
Other Communication: Feed: www.cala.ca/rss_news.rss
webmaster@cala.ca
www.cala.ca
www.linkedin.com/company/canadian-association-for-laboratory-accreditation-cala-
www.facebook.com/161209647296775
Overview: A medium-sized national organization founded in 1989
Mission: To provide internationally-recognized accreditation services; To assist laboratories in the achievement of high levels of scientific & management excellence; To improve environmental quality & public health & safety
Member of: Asia Pacific Laboratory Accreditation Cooperation; International Laboratory Accreditation Cooperation
Finances: *Annual Operating Budget:* $3 Million-$5 Million; *Funding Sources:* Membership fees; service fees
Staff Member(s): 15; 150 volunteer(s)
Membership: 500; *Fees:* $50 individual; $450 institution; *Member Profile:* Individuals, consultants, institutions, industrial organizations, regulatory agencies, laboratory equipment suppliers, & user groups interested in the work of environmental analytical laboratories; *Committees:* Board of Directors; Finance & Audit; Nominating; Regulatory Affairs; Strategy & Risk
Activities: Advocating for change in protecting public health & safety; Educating the public & raising awareness of laboratory accreditation; Offering training opportunities, such as workshops & web-based education; Conducting site audits & proficiency testing to evaluate the performance of laboratories; Granting accreditation to laboratories, based on decisions of the CALA Accreditation Council; *Speaker Service:* Yes
Chief Officer(s):
C. Charlie Brimley, President & CEO
cbrimley@cala.ca
Brenda Dashney, Chief Financial Officer
bdashney@cala.ca

Canadian Associations / Canadian Association for Laboratory Animal Science (CALAS) / Association canadienne pour la science des animaux de laboratoire (ACSAL)

Ken Middlebrook, Manager, Proficiency Testing
kmiddlebrook@cala.ca
Andrew Morris, Manager, Data & Information
amorris@cala.ca
Awards:
• John Lawrence Student Scholarship
Eligibility: Post-secondary students who have completed a 2-month work term in a CALA member laboratory, with submission of a scientific paper *Deadline:* August; *Amount:* $1,000
Meetings/Conferences:
• Canadian Association for Laboratory Accreditation 2018 Annual General Meeting, 2018
Scope: National
Publications:
• Canadian Association for Laboratory Accreditation Inc. Annual Report
Type: Yearbook; *Frequency:* Annually
• Canadian Association for Laboratory Accreditation Inc. Newsletter
Type: Newsletter; *Frequency:* Quarterly; *Editor:* Andrew Morris
Profile: Information & news about CALA programs & services
• Canadian Association for Laboratory Accreditation Inc. Brochure
Type: Brochure

Canadian Association for Laboratory Animal Science (CALAS) / Association canadienne pour la science des animaux de laboratoire (ACSAL)
#640, 144 Front St., Toronto ON M5J 2L7
Tel: 416-593-0268; *Fax:* 416-979-1819
Other Communication: membership@calas-acsal.org
office@calas-acsal.org
calas-acsal.org
Overview: A small national organization founded in 1961
Mission: To elevate standards of laboratory animal science; To promote excellence in research; To eliminate inhumane & unnecessary use of animals in research; To enhance animal welfare
Finances: *Funding Sources:* Membership fees; Sponsorships
Membership: 1,000; *Member Profile:* Veterinarians; Physicians; Researchers; Technicians; Administrators; Students; Institutions; *Committees:* Awards; Marketing; Membership; Educational; Regional Chapter; Symposium; Continuing Education
Activities: Providing information about the animal science industry; Offering networking opportunities; Providing continuing education to advance the knowledge & skills of persons who work with laboratory animals
Chief Officer(s):
Jacqui Sullivan, Board Liaison
jacqui@calas-acsal.org
Khadijah Hewitt, Contact, Membership & Registry Relations
khadijah@calas-acsal.org
Wendy Ansell, Registrar, Symposium
wendy@calas-acsal.org
Alysone Will, Contact, Finance
alysone@calas-acsal.org
Khadijah Hewitt, Coordinator, Membership & Registry
Publications:
• Canadian Association for Laboratory Animal Science Members' Magazine
Type: Magazine; *Frequency:* Bimonthly; *Price:* Free with membership in the Canadian Association for Laboratory Animal Science

Canadian Association for Latin American & Caribbean Studies (CALACS) / Association canadienne des études latino-américaines et caraïbes (ACELAC)
c/o Juan Pablo Crespo Vasquez, York Research Tower, York University, #8-17, 4700 Keele St., Toronto ON M3J 1P3
Tel: 416-736-2100; *Fax:* 519-971-3610
calacs@yorku.ca
www.can-latam.org
Overview: A medium-sized national organization founded in 1969
Mission: To facilitate networking & the exchange of information among those engaged in teaching & research on Latin America & the Caribbean in Canada & abroad; To foster throughout Canada, especially within the universities, colleges, & other centres of higher education, the expansion of information on & interest in Latin America & the Caribbean; To represent the academic & professional interest of Canadian Latin Americanists
Member of: Canadian Council of Area Studies Learned Societies

Finances: *Funding Sources:* International Development Research Council
Membership: 350; *Fees:* $80 regular; $23 student; $90 institution; *Member Profile:* Academics; Students; NGO officers; Government officials; *Committees:* Advisory; Organizing
Chief Officer(s):
Pablo Crespo Vasquez Juan, Contact, Administration
Steven Palmer, Secretary-Treasurer, 519-253-3000 Ext. 2329
spalmer@uwindsor.ca
Meetings/Conferences:
• Canadian Association for Latin American & Caribbean Studies 2018 Congress, May, 2018, Université du Québec à Montréal, Montréal, QC
Scope: National
Publications:
• CALACS [Canadian Association for Latin American & Caribbean Studies] Bulletin
Type: Newsletter
Profile: Information & announcements for members about the activities of the association
• Canadian Journal of Latin American and Caribbean Studies (CJLACS)
Type: Journal; *Frequency:* Semiannually; *Accepts Advertising*; *Editor:* Catherine Krull
Profile: Articles, research, debates, & reviews of recent publications on Latin America & the Caribbean

Canadian Association for Leisure Studies (CALS) / Association canadienne d'études en loisir
c/o Recreation & Leisure Studies, Faculty of Applied Health Sciences, University of Waterloo, Waterloo ON N2L 3G1
www.cals.uwaterloo.ca
Overview: A small national organization founded in 1981
Membership: *Member Profile:* Canadian & international practitioners & scholars with an interest in recreation & leisure services & research
Activities: Establishing the Research Group on Leisure & Aging
Chief Officer(s):
Heather Mair, President
hmair@uwaterloo.ca
Dawn Trussell, Vice-President & Treasurer
Karen Gallant, Secretary
Meetings/Conferences:
• Canadian Association for Leisure Studies Canadian Congress on Leisure 2020, 2020
Scope: National
Description: A triennial meeting at the Canadian Congress on Leisure Research.
Publications:
• Leisure / Loisir
Type: Journal; *Frequency:* Quarterly; *ISSN:* 1492-7713
Profile: Scholarly papers in the field of leisure, recreation, sport, parks, tourism, & the arts

Canadian Association for Medical Education (CAME) / Association canadienne pour l'éducation médicale (ACÉM)
#100, 2733 Lancaster Rd., Ottawa ON K1B 0A9
Tel: 613-730-0687; *Fax:* 613-730-1196
came@afmc.ca
www.came-acem.ca
Overview: A medium-sized national organization founded in 1987
Mission: To improve medical education in Canada; To promote excellence & scholarship in medical education; To support educational development; To encourage research in medical education
Finances: *Annual Operating Budget:* $100,000-$250,000
Staff Member(s): 1; 40 volunteer(s)
Membership: 680; *Fees:* $10 students; $25 residents; $150 regular membership; *Member Profile:* Medical educators in Canada; Faculty members; Residents; Students; *Committees:* Executive; Finance; Awards; Nominating
Activities: Advocating for medical education & medical educators; Offering networking opportunities; Providing professional development activities, such as workshops
Chief Officer(s):
Allyn Walsh, President
Shelley Ross, Secretary
Anurag Saxena, Treasurer
Ming-Ka Chan, Coordinator, Membership
Susan Lieff, Liaison Officer
Awards:
• CAME Ian Hart Award for Distinguished Contribution to Medical Education

To recognize senior faculty who have made an exceptional contribution to medical education
• CAME Meridith Marks New Educator's Award
To recognize persons in the first phase of their professional career *Contact:* Mary Digout, E-mail: came@afmc.ca
Meetings/Conferences:
• Canadian Conference on Medical Education 2018, April, 2018, Halifax Convention Centre, Halifax, NS
Scope: National
Contact Information: www.mededconference.ca
Publications:
• CAME [Canadian Association for Medical Education] Newsletter
Type: Newsletter
Profile: Articles & commentaries of interest to Canadian medical educators
• CAME [Canadian Association for Medical Education] E-Bulletin
Type: Newsletter; *Frequency:* Monthly
Profile: Current association information, such as announcements, upcoming meetings, grant opportunities, & career postings

Canadian Association for Mine & Explosive Ordnance Security (CAMEO)
1009 Oak Cres., Cornwall ON K6J 2N2
Tel: 613-937-0686; *Fax:* 613-937-4643
www.cameo.org
Also Known As: CAMEO Landmine Clearance
Overview: A small international charitable organization
Mission: To engage in humanitarian mine clearance; to engage in humanitarian explosive ordnance disposal; to engage in live-firing area clearance & environmental clean-up; to engage in land mine & explosive ordnance awareness training; to engage in land mine & battle area surveys; to provide training & assistance to others in the carrying out of all of the above activities
Affiliation(s): Gurkha Security Guards' EOD Trust; Defence Remediation Incorporated; Canadian Landmine Research Network; Operation Save Innocent Lives - Sudan; Wolf's Flat Ordnance Disposal Corporation; Sécuriplus; AGRA Inc.; Somali-Canadian Aid; Christian Council of Mozambique; New Sudan Council of Churches; Igreja Evangélica Unida - Comunhao Anglicana em Angola
Activities: Landmine clearance in Southern Sudan; *Speaker Service:* Yes
Chief Officer(s):
James D. McGill, Executive Director, President & CEO
megill@cameo.org

Canadian Association for Neuroscience (CAN)
c/o DeArmond Management, 2661 Queenswood Dr., Victoria BC V8N 1X6
Tel: 250-472-7644
info@can-acn.org
can-acn.org
www.facebook.com/can.acn
twitter.com/CAN_ACN
Overview: A large national organization
Mission: To promote communication among Canadian neuroscientists & encourage research related to the nervous system; To educate about current neuroscience research
Chief Officer(s):
Julie Poupart, Director, Communications
Meetings/Conferences:
• 2018 12th Annual Canadian Neuroscience Meeting, May, 2018, Vancouver, BC
Scope: National
Description: Neuroscientists meet to discuss neuroscience research in Canada.

Canadian Association for Nursing Research (CANR) / Association canadienne pour la recherche infirmière
c/o Caroline Porr, Memorial University of Newfoundland, St. John's NL A1C 5S7
Tel: 709-777-7103
www.canresearch.ca
Overview: A medium-sized national organization
Mission: To foster practice-based nursing research & research-based nursing practice across Canada
Member of: Canadian Nursing Association
Membership: *Fees:* $20 students/retired persons/affiliates; $35 regular members; *Member Profile:* Nurses; Students; Persons committed to the association's purposes
Activities: Providing information about research & funding; Educating professionals & the public about nursing research &

its link to practice; Advocating for members' interests; Liaising with governments & other nursing organizations
Chief Officer(s):
Caroline Porr, President
cporr@mun.ca
Patrice Drake, Treasurer
mpdrake@upei.ca
Awards:
• Outstanding New Investigator Award
• Promotion of Research Based Practice Award
• Practitioner-Researcher Award
• Nurse Researcher Award

Canadian Association for Pastoral Practice & Education See Canadian Association for Spiritual Care

Canadian Association for People Who Stutter (CAPS) See Canadian Stuttering Association

Canadian Association for Pharmacy Distribution Management (CAPDM) / Association canadienne de la gestion de l'approvisionnement pharmaceutique (ACGAP)
#301A, 3800 Steeles Ave. West, Woodbridge ON L4L 4G9
Tel: 905-265-1706; *Fax:* 905-265-9372
www.capdm.ca
www.linkedin.com/company/canadian-association-for-pharmacy-distribution-management-capdm-
www.facebook.com/182173808506667
Previous Name: Canadian Wholesale Drug Association
Overview: A large national organization founded in 1964
Mission: To act as a resource & an advocacy voice for its members to advance the pharmacy distribution system as an effective, efficient, & safe delivery system for patient health care in Canada
Finances: *Funding Sources:* Membership dues; Conference fees
Staff Member(s): 4
Membership: 1-99; *Fees:* Schedule available; *Member Profile:* Pharmacy supply chain industry trading partners, including full consolidated distributors, allied distributors, self-distributing pharmacy chains, manufacturers, & service providers;
Committees: Customer Service; Electronic Signature; Government Relations; Pandemic Preparedness; Member Services; Safe & Secure Supply Chain
Activities: *Library:*
Chief Officer(s):
John Targett, Chair
David W. Johnston, President & CEO
david@capdm.ca
Terri Hay, Vice-President, Industry & Member Relations
terri@capdm.ca
Allison Chan, Manager, Member Services & Events
allison@capdm.ca
Meetings/Conferences:
• Canadian Association for Pharmacy Distribution Management 2018 Executive Conference, January, 2018
Scope: National
• Canadian Association for Pharmacy Distribution Management 2018 Annual Conference, May, 2018, The Diplomat Beach Resort, Hollywood, FL
Scope: National
• Canadian Association for Pharmacy Distribution Management 2018 September Member Forum, September, 2018, Angus Glen Golf Club, Markham, ON
Scope: National
Contact Information: Allison Chan, Phone: 905-265-1706, ext. 223, Email: allison@capdm.ca
Publications:
• Guidebook on Government Prescription Drug Reimbursement Plans & Related Programs
Price: $75 for members; $125 for non-members
Profile: Details on each provincial drug benefit program
• Industry Trends Reports
Price: Free for members; $49.95 for non-members
Profile: Statistics & highlights information related to the distribution & consumption of health care goods & services in Canada
• Pharmacy Who's Who
Type: Directory; *Price:* $180
Profile: Lists retail chains, banners & franchises, manufacturers, distributors, goods & service suppliers, pharmacy associations, top retailers, & post-graduate educational programs

Canadian Association for Photographic Art (CAPA) / L'Association canadienne d'art photographique
PO Box 357, Logan Lake BC V0K 1W0
Tel: 604-523-2378; *Fax:* 604-523-2333
capa@capacanada.ca
capacanada.ca
www.facebook.com/TheCanadianAssociationForPhotographicArt
Merged from: National Association for Photographic Art; Colour Photographic Association of Canada
Overview: A medium-sized national organization founded in 1998
Mission: To promote the advancement of photography as an art form in Canada
Affiliation(s): Fédération Internationale de l'Art Photographique
Finances: *Funding Sources:* Membership dues
Membership: *Fees:* Schedule available
Activities: Exhibitions, seminars, workshops, & field trips; sponsors Camera Canada College, an annual summer weekend of field trips, seminars, & camaraderie held in a different city each year
Chief Officer(s):
Jacques S. Mailloux, President
president@capacanada.ca
Publications:
• Canadian Camera
Type: Magazine; *Frequency:* Quarterly; *Number of Pages:* 40+; *Price:* Subscription with membership
Profile: Articles about photography, photography tips, photographs from competitions, CAPA news, & profiles of member clubs

Canadian Association for Population Therapeutics (CAPT)
c/o Peggy Kee, Sunnybrook Health Sciences Centre, 2075 Bayview Ave., #E240, Toronto ON M4N 3M5
Tel: 416-480-6100; *Fax:* 416-480-6025
www.capt-actp.com
Overview: A small national organization founded in 1996
Mission: To advance the sound development of population-based studies of therapeutic interventions; To provide a forum for the reporting, scientific discussion & dissemination of the data derived from population-based therapeutic research, as an information resource for medical decision-making in the best interests of the individual patient & the public well-being
Membership: 100-499; *Fees:* $50 individual; $25 students
Chief Officer(s):
Peggy Kee, Administrative Officer
peggy.kee@sunnybrook.ca
Meetings/Conferences:
• Canadian Association for Population Therapeutics Conference 2018, 2018
Scope: National

Canadian Association for Prior Learning Assesment (CAPLA) / L'Association canadienne pour la reconnaissance des acquis
PO Box 56001, RPO Minto Place, Ottawa ON K1R 7Z1
Tel: 613-860-1747
info@capla.ca
www.capla.ca
Overview: A small national organization founded in 1994
Mission: Provides the expertise, advocacy and support for the development of prior learning assessment in Canada through its workshops, quarterly newsletter and education and training activities.
Chief Officer(s):
Bonnie Kennedy, Executive Director
b.kennedy@quicklinks.on.ca

Canadian Association for Production & Inventory Control; American Production & Inventory Control Society See Association for Operations Management

Canadian Association for Renewable Energies (CARE) / Association canadienne pour les énergies renouvelables
7885 Jock Trail, Ottawa ON K0A 2Z0
Tel: 613-663-5400; *Fax:* 613-822-4987
www.renewables.ca
twitter.com/renewablesca
Also Known As: we c.a.r.e
Overview: A small national organization founded in 1998
Mission: To promote feasible applications of renewable energies
Finances: *Annual Operating Budget:* Less than $50,000; *Funding Sources:* Membership fees
Staff Member(s): 1
Membership: *Member Profile:* Supporters of renewable energies
Activities: Undertaking research to optimize renewable energy technologies; *Speaker Service:* Yes
Chief Officer(s):
Bill Eggertson, Executive Director
eggertson@renewables.ca
Publications:
• Refocus Weekly [a publication of the Canadian Association for Renewable Energies]
Type: Newsletter; *Frequency:* Weekly; *Accepts Advertising*
Profile: News, reports, & events from around the world
• Renewable Energy Focus
Type: Magazine; *Accepts Advertising*
Profile: Debate & dialogue between industry, research, government agencies, & financial organizations throughout the world on topics such as biomass, biogass, hydroelectricity, wind, waves, solararchitecture, & fuel cells

Canadian Association for Sandplay Therapy (CAST)
c/o Dave Rogers, Treasurer, #232, 220 Century Rd., Spruce Grove AB T7X 3X7
www.sandplay.ca
Overview: A small national organization founded in 1993
Mission: To promote the development of sandplay in Canada by providing training, offering opportunities for professional exchange, and maintaining guidelines for professional practice.
Member of: International Society for Sandplay Therapy (ISST)
Activities: Training program; workshops & information meetings
Chief Officer(s):
Barbara Dalziel, President

Canadian Association for School Health (CASH)
16629 - 62A Ave., Surrey BC V3S 9L5
Tel: 604-575-3199
info@cash-aces.ca
www.cash-aces.ca
Overview: A small national organization
Mission: Provincial/area coalitions who promote the health of youth through a school-related health program called Comprehensive School Health (CSH); to develop & implements projects, activities & services that follow the CSH approach. This approach helps community agencies, parents, educators, & health professionals work together.
Member of: International School Health Network
Activities: *Library:* Canadian Centre on Community & School Health

Canadian Association for Scottish Studies (CASS)
Dept. of History, Centre for Scottish Studies, University of Guelph, 50 Stone Rd. East, Guelph ON N1G 2W1
Tel: 519-824-4120
scottish@uoguelph.ca
www.uoguelph.ca/arts/scottish
www.facebook.com/scottishstudies
twitter.com/ScottishStudies
Overview: A small national organization founded in 1971
Mission: To promote interest in Scottish history, literature, & culture
Affiliation(s): Scottish Studies Foundation
Chief Officer(s):
James E. Fraser, Chair & Director, Guelph Centre for Scottish Studies
Publications:
• International Review of Scottish Studies
Type: Journal; *Frequency:* Annually; *Editor:* James E. Fraser; *ISSN:* 0703-1580; *Price:* Free online
Profile: Articles & reviews related to Scottish history & culture

Canadian Association for Security & Intelligence Studies (CASIS) / Association canadienne pour les études de renseignement et de sécurité (ACERS)
PO Box 71007, RPO L'Esplanade, Ottawa ON K2P 2L9
ecretariat@casis.ca
www.casis.ca
Overview: A small national organization founded in 1985
Mission: To provide informed debate in Canada on security & intelligence issues; To facilitate awareness & understandingof the intelligence & security community
Membership: *Fees:* $75 general member; $40 student; *Member Profile:* Academics; Government officials; Lawyers; Journalists; Concerned citizens
Activities: Encouraging research & fostering accumulation of knowledge
Chief Officer(s):
Greg Fyffe, President
Sarah Jane Corke, Vice-President
Robert Crawhall, Treasurer

Canadian Associations / Canadian Association for Size Acceptance (CASA)

Canadian Association for Size Acceptance (CASA)
#511, 99 Dalhousie St., Toronto ON M5B 2N2
Tel: 416-861-0217; *Fax:* 416-861-1668
Overview: A small local organization founded in 1997
Mission: To lobby against & raises awareness of discrimination towards people of size.
Member of: International Size Acceptance Association; National Association to Advance Fat Acceptance
Activities: Conducts media interviews; educates children, teachers, medical professionals & public about the dangers & health effects of dieting; maintains database of plus size services

Canadian Association for Social Work Education (CASWE) / Association canadienne pour la formation en travail social (ACFTS)
#410, 383 Parkdale Ave., Ottawa ON K1Y 4R4
Tel: 613-792-1953
Toll-Free: 888-342-6522
admin@caswe-acfts.ca
caswe-acfts.ca
Previous Name: National Committee of Schools of Social Work; Canadian Association of Schools of Social Work (CASSW)
Overview: A small national charitable organization founded in 1967
Mission: To advance university education for the profession of social work; To accredit professional social work educational programs, based on high educational standards; To increase understanding of the nature & role of social work practice & social welfare
Membership: 38 university departments or schools of social work; *Fees:* $30 unwaged persons; $35 retired faculty; $40 students; $60 field & sessional instructors & alumni; $80 faculty; $100 - $5000 Insitutions; *Member Profile:* University faculties, schools, & departments offering professional education in social work at the undergraduate, graduate, & post-graduate levels, & accredited by the CASWE / ACFTS Board of Accreditation; University departments or schools planning to operatie programs in social work; Individuals, such as university social work current or retired teachers, field instructors, administrators, alumni or students; *Committees:* Nominating; Educational Policy; International Affairs; Student; Field Education; Social Policy & Advocacy; Francophone Social Work in Linguistic Minority Contexts; Diversity
Activities: Formulating educational policies; Promoting research related to social work practice; Exchanging information & ideas with other national & international social work associations
Chief Officer(s):
Carolyn Campbell, President, -, 902-494-1188
Carolyn.Campbell@dal.ca
Sylvie Renaud, Coordinator, Accreditation
accred@caswe-acfts.ca
Sheri McConnell, Vice-President
smcconne@mun.ca
John Flynn, Treasurer
jflynn033@uottawa.ca
Sharon Leslie, Office Administrator, 613-792-1953 Ext. 221
admin@caswe-acfts.ca
Alexandra Wright, PhD, Executive Director
awright@caswe-acfts.ca
Meetings/Conferences:
• Canadian Association for Social Work Education Conference 2018, May, 2018, University of Regina, Regina, SK
Scope: National
Description: Theme: "Honouring Reconciliation & Respecting our Differences"
Publications:
• Canadian Association for Social Work Education Directory of Schools
Type: Directory; *Price:* Free with membership in the Canadian Association for Social Work Education
• Canadian Social Work Review / Revue canadienne de service social
Type: Journal; *Frequency:* Semiannually; *Editor:* David Este; *Price:* Free with membership in the Canadian Association for Social Work Education
Profile: A peer-reviewed journal, featuring original research, critical analyses, & debates that affect social work educators,practitioners, & students

Canadian Association for Spiritual Care (CASC) / Association canadienne de soins spirituels (ACSS)
#27, 1267 Dorval Dr., Oakville ON L6M 3Z4
Tel: 289-837-2272; *Fax:* 289-837-4800
Toll-Free: 866-442-2773
www.spiritualcare.ca
Previous Name: Canadian Association for Pastoral Practice & Education
Overview: A medium-sized national organization founded in 1965
Mission: To be a national multifaith organization committed to the professional education, certification & support of people involved in spiritual care, counselling & education
Finances: *Funding Sources:* Membership dues
Membership: *Fees:* $185 associate members, with any amount of CPE or PCE training, & corporate members; $395 certified specialists or teaching supervisors; *Member Profile:* Persons involved in a variety of ministries, in settings such as parishes, prisons & correctional facilities, pastoral counselling centres, health care facilities & industrial facilities
Activities: Offering educational programs for both clergy & lay persons; Providing certification for supervisors & specialists; Creating networking opportunities
Chief Officer(s):
Tony Sedfawi, Executive Director
office@spiritualcare.ca
Kathy Greig, Manager
kathy@spiritualcare.ca
Meetings/Conferences:
• Annual Canadian Association for Spiritual Care Conference: Exploring Spiritual Landscapres through the Arts, April, 2018, Deerhurst, ON
Scope: National
Publications:
• Canadian Association for Pastoral Practice & Education Handbook
Type: Handbook
Profile: Information about accreditation, certification, & practice
• CAPPE [Canadian Association for Pastoral Practice & Education] / ACEPEP National E-Newsletter
Type: Newsletter; *Price:* Free with membership in the Canadian Association for Pastoral Practice & Education
• CAPPE [Canadian Association for Pastoral Practice & Education] / ACEPEP Annual Report
Type: Yearbook; *Frequency:* Annually; *Price:* Free with membership in the Canadian Association for Pastoral Practice & Education

Canadian Association for Student Robotics See FIRST Robotics Canada

Canadian Association for Studies in Co-operation (CASC) / Association canadienne pour les études sur la coopération (ACEC)
c/o Centre for the Study of Co-operatives, University of Saskatchewan, 101 Diefenbaker Pl., Saskatoon SK S7N 5B8
casc.acec@usask.ca
www.coopresearch.coop
www.linkedin.com/groups/4411516
www.facebook.com/CCRNRCRC
twitter.com/CCRNRCRC
www.youtube.com/user/CCRNRCRC
Overview: A small national organization founded in 2000
Mission: To promote research on co-operatives in Canada
Membership: *Member Profile:* Researchers, scholars, & practitioners working in the area of co-operatives
Chief Officer(s):
Fiona Duguid, President
Awards:
• Lemaire Co-operative Studies Award
Postgraduate & undergraduate awards to encourage students to undertake studies which will help them to contribute to the development of co-operatives in Canada or elsewhere; disciplines include: housing, planning, environmental studies, engineering, geography, science, architecture; *Amount:* $1,000-$3,000
• Alexander Fraser Laidlaw Fellowship
Postgraduate award for students in: housing, environmental studies, planning, geography, science, architecture, civil engineering, engineering; the fellowship is awarded on the basis of the applicant's academic record & the importance of the proposed research activities to the development of the co-operative movement in Canada or elsewhere; *Amount:* $1,000
• Amy & Tim Dauphinee Scholarships for Studies in Co-operation
For graduate students in the following disciplines: cooperatives, housing, planning, environmental studies, geography, science, architecture, civil engineering, engineering; awards based on the applicant's academic records & on the importance of the proposed research activities to the development of the co-operative movement in Canada or abroad; *Amount:* $3,000

Meetings/Conferences:
• 2018 Canadian Association for Studies in Co-operation Conference, 2018
Scope: National
Publications:
• CASC [Canadian Association for Studies in Co-operation] Newsletter
Type: Newsletter

Canadian Association for Studies in the Bahá'í Faith See Association for Bahá'í Studies

Canadian Association for Suicide Prevention (CASP) / L'Association canadienne pour la prévention du suicide (ACPS)
285 Benjamin Rd., Waterloo ON N2J 3Z4
Tel: 519-884-1470
casp@suicideprevention.ca
www.suicideprevention.ca
www.facebook.com/CanadianAssociationforSuicidePrevention
twitter.com/casp_ca
Overview: A small national charitable organization founded in 1985
Mission: To reduce the suicide rate; To minimize the harmful consequences of suicide
Finances: *Funding Sources:* Donations; Memoriams; Fundraising
Membership: *Fees:* $30 students; $50 individuals; $150 agencies
Activities: Advocating for policy development; Liaising with provincial, territorial, & federal governments; Providing educational services; Offering information & resources to communities; Facilitating research; Developing the Sharing the Healing Fund & the Network Fund to increase the availability of grief groups; *Awareness Events:* World Suicide Prevention Day, September
Chief Officer(s):
Karen Letofsky, President
Tana Nash, Executive Director
Meetings/Conferences:
• Canadian Association for Suicide Prevention 2018 Annual Conference, 2018
Scope: National

Canadian Association for Supported Employment (CASE)
c/o AiMHi, 950 Kerry St., Prince George BC V2M 5A3
Tel: 250-564-6408; *Fax:* 250-564-6801
www.supportedemployment.ca
www.facebook.com/CanadianAssocSupportedEmployment
twitter.com/casecanada
Overview: A medium-sized national organization
Mission: To promote workplace inclusion for Canadians with disabilities through supported employment
Membership: *Fees:* $25 individual; $100 organization; *Member Profile:* Individuals & organizations that are interested in working towards full employment for all members of our community
Chief Officer(s):
Tracy Williams, President
Meetings/Conferences:
• Canadian Association for Supported Employment 2018 Conference, June, 2018, Halifax Convention Centre, Halifax, NS
Scope: National

Canadian Association for Teacher Education (CATE) / Association canadienne pour la formation des enseignants (ACFE)
c/o Canadian Society for the Study of Education, #204, 260 Dalhousie St., Ottawa ON K1N 7E4
Tel: 613-241-0018; *Fax:* 613-241-0019
cate-acfe.ca
Overview: A medium-sized national charitable organization founded in 1978 overseen by Canadian Society for the Study of Education
Mission: To encourage scholarly study & research in education, with special emphasis on teacher education; to provide for the membership a national forum for the presentation & discussion of significant studies in education, with special emphasis on teacher education
Member of: Canadian Society for the Study of Education
Finances: *Annual Operating Budget:* Less than $50,000; *Funding Sources:* Membership dues; grants
Membership: 300; *Member Profile:* Open to faculty in education departments & students researching & developing teacher education; *Committees:* Awards
Chief Officer(s):

Jodi Nickel, President
jnickel@mtroyal.ca
Awards:
• CATE Award for Contributions to Research in Teacher Education
• CATE Thesis & Dissertation Awards of Recognition
Meetings/Conferences:
• Canadian Association for Teacher Education 2018 Annual Conference, May, 2018, University of Regina, Regina, SK
Scope: National
Publications:
• CATE [Canadian Association for Teacher Education] Newsletter
Type: E-Newsletter; *Frequency:* Quarterly
• Polygraph Book Series [publications of the Canadian Association for Teacher Education]
Type: Series
Profile: Titles in the series include: Canadian Perspectives on Initial Teacher Environmental Education Praxis; Handbook of Canadian Research inInitial Teacher Education; The Complexity of Hiring, Supporting, and Retaining New Teachers Across Canada; Foundations in Teacher Education: A Canadian Perspective
• Working Conference Publications [publications of the Canadian Association for Teacher Education]
Profile: Titles include: What Should Canada's Teachers Know? Teacher Capacities: Knowledge, Beliefs and Skills; Change and progress inCanadian teacher education: Research on recent innovations in teacher preparation in Canada; Becoming Teacher: Sites for Teacher Development in Canadian Teacher Education

Canadian Association for the Advancement of Music & the Arts (CAAMA)
1525 Trotwood Ave., Mississauga ON L5G 3Z8
info@caama.org
www.caama.org
Overview: A large national organization founded in 1991
Mission: To further the independent music industry, in Canada & abroad; To ensure that laws regarding the music industry are favourable to members
Membership: *Fees:* $50 company; $10 individual; *Member Profile:* Individuals & groups affiliated with the Canadian sound recording industry
Activities: Organizing Canadian Music Week; Conducting musician seminars
Chief Officer(s):
Patti Jannetta, President

Canadian Association for the Advancement of Netherlandic Studies (CAANS) / Association canadienne pour l'avancement des études néerlandaises (ACAEN)
c/o Secretary, 613 Huycks Point Rd., Wellington ON K0K 3L0
www.caans-acaen.ca
www.facebook.com/29784957106215
Overview: A small national organization founded in 1971
Mission: To stimulate awareness & interest in & to promote the study of Netherlandic languages (Dutch, Flemish, Afrikaans), as well as Netherlandic literature, history & culture; to provide a forum for discussion in these areas, hold an annual conference, publish research & sponsor relevant cultural & scholarly activities such as meetings, presentations, lectures & discussions
Affiliation(s): Congress of the Social Sciences and Humanities
Finances: *Funding Sources:* Membership fees; University of Windsor subsidies; Netherlandic Language Union
Membership: *Fees:* $30 individuals & institutions; $25 seniors; $20 students
Chief Officer(s):
Michiel Horn, President
schuhhorn@sympatico.ca
Paul de Laat, Secretary-Treasurer
pgdelaat@gmail.com
Publications:
• CAAN [Canadian Association for the Advancement of Netherlandic Studies] Newsletter / Bulletin de l'ACAEN
Type: Newsletter; *Frequency:* 3 pa; *Editor:* Mary Eggermont-Molenaar
• Canadian Journal of Netherlandic Studies / Revue canadienne d'études néerlandaises
Type: Journal; *Frequency:* Semiannually; *Editor:* Basil D. Kingstone; *ISSN:* 0225-0500

Canadian Association for the Advancement of Women & Sport & Physical Activity (CAAWS) / Association canadienne pour l'avancement des femmes du sport et de l'activité physique (ACAFS)
801 King Edward Ave., #N202, Ottawa ON K1N 6N5
Tel: 613-562-5667; *Fax:* 613-562-5668
caaws@caaws.ca
www.caaws.ca
www.facebook.com/CAAWS
twitter.com/caaws
Overview: A medium-sized national organization founded in 1981
Mission: To promote an equitable sport & physical activity system, in which girls & women are participants & leaders; To foster equitable support & diverse opportunities, in sport & physical activity for females across Canada
Finances: *Funding Sources:* Donations
Activities: Fostering positive experiences for women in sport & physical activitythroughout Canada; Providing education on issues related to female participation in sport & physical activity; Creating community awareness about the value of an equitable sport & physical activity system; Collaborating with related organizations to foster an equitable system; Presenting awards, grants, & scholarships
Chief Officer(s):
Karin Lofstrom, Executive Director
klofstrom@caaws.ca
Sydney Millar, Manager, National Program
snmillar@caaws.ca
Haley Wolfenden, Manager, Communications, Marketing & Events
hwolfenden@caaws.ca
Awards:
• Breakthrough Awards
Presented annually to outstanding nominees who have used innovative ideas & alternative approaches to encourage & enable more girls & women to participate/lead/coach in sport & physical activity *Contact:* Karin Lofstrom
• Girls@Play Nike Youth Award
• CAAWS/Nike Girls@Play MVP Grant
Monthly grant awarded to a female athlete, coach, official or sport/recreation organization to help make their sporting goals & dreams *Contact:* www.caaws.ca/girlsatplay/grants/index.html
• Stacey Levitt Scholarships
Eligibility: Awarded each year on behalf of the Levitt family & in memory of Stacey Levitt, who was killed while jogging in 1995 after being hit by a car; *Amount:* $500 & a copy of "I am a Rose"
Publications:
• Health Benefits of Physical Activity for Girls & Women
Profile: A research project on the topic of health benefits & risks of physical activity for girls & women
• In Her Voice: An Exploration of Young Women's Sport & Physical Activity Experiences
Profile: A report, based on group conversations with women, from the ages of 13 to 17, from diverse communities across Canada
• Including Transitioned & Transitioning Athletes in Sport - Issues, Facts, & Perspectives
Profile: Information about gender transition & sport participation
• Making the Most of Your Opportunities: A Media Guide for Athletes & Their Coaches
Price: $15
Profile: Information about effective self-promotion
• On the Move
Type: Handbook
Profile: A practical guide for programmers, coaches teachers, volunteers, & parents to create a female-only program
• Seeing the Invisible, Speaking about the Unspoken: A Position Paper on Homophobia in Sport
Number of Pages: 11
• Sex Discrimination in Sport - An Update
Type: Report; *Number of Pages:* 20; *Author:* Hilary Findlay
• Success Stories: Increasing Opportunities for Girls & Women in National & Multi-Sport Organizations
Number of Pages: 25
• Women on Boards: A Guide to Getting Involved
Number of Pages: 72
Profile: Information for women on governing boards & in senior roles of organizations

Canadian Association for the History of Nursing (CAHN) / Association canadienne pour l'histoire du nursing
College of Nursing, University of Saskatchewan, 4440 - 4th Ave., Regina SK S4T 0H8
www.cahn-achn.ca
Overview: A small national charitable organization founded in 1987
Mission: To promote interest in the history of nursing; To develop scholarship in the field
Member of: Canadian Nurses Association
Affiliation(s): Canadian Nurses Association
Finances: *Funding Sources:* Memberships; Donations
Membership: *Fees:* $60 registered nurses; $30 retired nurses, students & associate members
Activities: Promoting the preservation of historical nursing materials; Hosting forums; Supporting innovations in teaching nursing history; Advancing historical research
Chief Officer(s):
Helen Vandenberg, President
president@cahn-achn.ca
Awards:
• The Dr. Margaret Allemang Scholarship for the History of Nursing
• Vera Roberts Endowment Fund for Nursing Research
Meetings/Conferences:
• Canadian Association for the History of Nursing 2018 Annual Conference, June, 2018
Description: Theme: "Tracing Nurses' Footsteps: Nursing & the Tides of Change"
Publications:
• CAHN [Canadian Association for the History of Nursing] / ACHN [Association canadienne pour l'histoire du nursing] Newsletter
Type: Newsletter; *Frequency:* Semiannually
Profile: Reports, articles, book reviews, research items, announcements, & letters to the editor

Canadian Association for the Mentally Retarded *See* Canadian Association for Community Living

Canadian Association for the Practical Study of Law in Education (CAPSLE) / Association canadienne pour une étude pratique de la loi dans le système éducatif
c/o Lori Pollock, 37 Moultrey Cres., Georgetown ON L7G 4N4
Tel: 905-702-1710; *Fax:* 905-873-0662
info@capsle.ca
capsle.ca
Overview: A small national organization founded in 1989
Mission: To provide an open forum for the practical study of legal issues affecting education
Membership: *Fees:* $35 student; $95 regular; $275 corporate; *Member Profile:* Teachers, administrators, board members, trustees, unions, school board associations, educators, academics, students, government & lawyers
Chief Officer(s):
Robert Weir, President
president@capsle.ca

The Canadian Association for the Prevention of Consumption & Other Forms of Tuberculosis; The Canadian Tuberculosis & Respiratory Disease Associa *See* Canadian Lung Association

Canadian Association for the Prevention of Discrimination & Harassment in Higher Education (CAPDHHE) / L'association canadienne pour la prévention de la discrimination et du harcèlement en milieu d'enseignement supérieur (ACPDHMES)
c/o University of British Columbia, Vancouver BC V6T 1Z2
Tel: 604-822-4859; *Fax:* 604-822-3260
amlong@ubc.ca
www.capdhhe.org
Previous Name: Canadian Association Against Sexual Harassment in Higher Education
Overview: A medium-sized national organization founded in 1985
Mission: To provide professional development for individuals employed at colleges & universities in the area of discrimination & harassment
Membership: 150; *Fees:* $100 regular; $25 student; $300 institutional
Chief Officer(s):
Milé Komlen, President
komlenm@mcmaster.ca
Sonya Nigam, Vice President
snigam@uottawa.ca
Meetings/Conferences:
• Canadian Association for the Prevention of Discrimination and Harassment in Higher Education 2018 Conference, 2018
Scope: National

Canadian Associations / Canadian Association for the Study of Adult Education (CASAE) / Association canadienne pour l'étude de l'éducation des adultes (ACÉÉA)

Canadian Association for the Study of Adult Education (CASAE) / Association canadienne pour l'étude de l'éducation des adultes (ACÉÉA)
#204, 260 Dalhousie St., Ottawa ON K1N 7E4
Tel: 613-241-0018; *Fax:* 613-241-0019
casae.aceea@csse.ca
www.casae-aceea.ca
Overview: A small national charitable organization founded in 1981
Mission: To promote the study of adult education; To facilitate research; to share knowledge in adult education
Membership: *Fees:* $100 regular; $40 student, retired, & unwaged members; *Member Profile:* Individuals, institutions & agencies interested in the study of adult education; *Committees:* Constitutional; Archives; Peer Review Committee for Canadian and International Papers
Chief Officer(s):
Shauna Butterwick, Co-President
shauna.butterwick@ubc.ca
Carole Roy, Co-President
croy@stfx.ca
Meetings/Conferences:
• Canadian Association for the Study of Adult Education 2018 Conference, May, 2018, University of Regina, Regina, SK
Scope: National
Publications:
• Canadian Journal for the Study of Adult Education (CJSAE) / Revue canadienne pour l'étude de l'éducation des adultes (RCÉÉA)
Type: Journal; *Editor:* Tom Nesbit
Profile: Reports of research, reviews of literature, & essays about issues in adult & continuingeducation
• CASAE [Canadian Association for the Study of Adult Education] / ACÉÉA Directory
Type: Directory
Profile: Listings of all CASAE / ACÉÉA members & faculty engaged in adult education
• The Learning Edge / La Fine pointe [a publication of the Canadian Association for the Study of Adult Education]
Type: Newsletter
Profile: Newsletter / Bulletin of the Canadian Association for the Study of Adult Education / Association Canadiennepour l' Étude de l' Éducation des Adults on research projects, regional developments, publications, new programs, & institutional reports

Canadian Association for the Study of Discourse & Writing (CASDW) / Association canadienne de rédactologie (ACR)
c/o W. Brock MacDonald, Woodsworth College, University of Toronto, 119 St. George St., Toronto ON M5S 1A9
casdwacr.wordpress.com
Previous Name: Canadian Association of Teachers of Technical Writing (CATTW)/L'Association canadienne de professeurs de rédaction technique et scientifique (ACPRTS)
Overview: A small national organization
Mission: To advance the study & teaching of discourse, writing, & communication in both academic & nonacademic settings
Member of: Canadian Federation for the Humanities & Social Sciences (CFHSS)
Finances: *Funding Sources:* Membership dues
Membership: *Fees:* $25 retirees & students; $40 regular members; *Member Profile:* Researchers, teachers, & practitioners who study & teach written & oral communication
Activities: Supporting writing in digital environments; Providing networking opportunities
Chief Officer(s):
W. Brock MacDonald, Treasurer, Membership, 416-978-0246, Fax: 416-978-6111
wb.macdonald@utoronto.ca
Awards:
• The Joan Pavelich Award for the Best Dissertation in Writing Studies
• Best Article Award
Meetings/Conferences:
• Canadian Association for the Study of Discourse & Writing Annual Conference 2018, May, 2018, University of Regina, Regina, SK
Scope: National
Description: Held during the Congress of the Social Sciences & Humanities; involves opportunities for speakers to hold lengthy discussions & forge networking relationships
Publications:
• Canadian Journal for Studies in Discourse & Writing
Type: Journal; *Price:* Free with membership in the Canadian Association for the Study of Discourse &Writing
Profile: Peer-reviewed journal with articles & reviews for teachers, practitioners, & researchers

Canadian Association for the Study of Educational Administration (CASEA) / Association canadienne pour l'étude de l'administration scolaire (ACÉAS)
c/o Canadian Society for the Study of Education, #204, 260 Dalhousie St., Ottawa ON K1N 7E4
Tel: 613-241-0018; *Fax:* 613-241-0019
csse-scee.ca/associations/casea-aceas
Overview: A small national organization overseen by Canadian Society for the Study of Education
Mission: To promote the study of educational administration among scholars & practitioners
Member of: Canadian Society for the Study of Education
Chief Officer(s):
Jacqueline Kirk, President
kirkj@brandonu.ca

Canadian Association for the Study of Indigenous Education (CASIE) / Association canadienne pour l'étude de l'education des autochtones (ACÉFÉ)
c/o Canadian Society for the Study of Education, #204, 260 Dalhousie St., Ottawa ON K1N 7E4
Tel: 613-241-0018; *Fax:* 613-241-0019
www.casieaceea.org
Overview: A medium-sized national organization founded in 2008 overseen by Canadian Society for the Study of Education
Member of: Canadian Society for the Study of Education
Chief Officer(s):
Mark Aquash, President
oshogeeshik@yahoo.com

Canadian Association for the Study of International Development (CASID) / L'Association canadienne d'études du développement international (ACEDI)
c/o The Canadian Federation for the Humanities & Social Sciences, #300, 275 Bank St., Ottawa ON K2P 2L6
Tel: 613-238-6112; *Fax:* 613-238-6114
www.casid-acedi.ca
Overview: A medium-sized national organization
Mission: To be a national, bilingual, interdisciplinary & pluralistic association devoted to the study of international development
Member of: Social Science Federation of Canada
Finances: *Annual Operating Budget:* $100,000-$250,000; *Funding Sources:* International Development Research Centre
Membership: 182; *Fees:* $14-$135
Activities: Annual conferences; Cross-Canada tours of development specialists; Facilitates networking among students, academics, researchers & policymakers involved in international development; Provides a limited amount of travel grants to assist graduate students & others to participate in the annual conference
Chief Officer(s):
Ann Miller, Contact
amiller@fedcan.ca
Publications:
• Canadian Journal of Development Studies / Revue canadienne d'études du développement
Type: Journal; *Frequency:* Quarterly; *Editor:* Henry Rempel & Scott Simon; *ISSN:* 0225-5189; *Price:* $110 institutions; $65 individuals; $35 students
Profile: International & interdisciplinary journal about development issues, with contributions from allcountries of the developing world
• CASID [Canadian Association for the Study of International Development] / ACÉDI Bulletin
Type: Newletter
Profile: News, publications, announcements, & events

Canadian Association for the Study of the Liver (CASL) / Association canadienne pour l'étude du foie
c/o BUKSA Strategic Conference Services, #307, 10328 - 81st Ave., Edmonton AB T6C 3T5
Tel: 780-436-0983
casl@hepatology.ca
www.hepatology.ca
Overview: A small national organization
Mission: To eliminate liver disease
Affiliation(s): International Association for the Study of the Liver (IASL)
Membership: *Fees:* Free for students & trainees; $200 associate; $300 regular & international; *Member Profile:* Scientists & healthcare professionals with a interest in liver diseases, such as gastroenterologists, hepatologists, transplant surgeons, radiologists, & pediatricians; Undergraduates & post-graduate students, residents, fellows, & trainees; *Committees:* Education; Membership; Research
Activities: Engaging in advocacy activities; Promoting education & research
Chief Officer(s):
Rick Schreiber, President
Kelly Burak, Secretary-Treasurer
Marc Bilodeau, President-Elect
Meetings/Conferences:
• Canadian Liver Meeting 2018, February, 2018, Intercontinental Toronto Hotel Center, Toronto, ON
Scope: National
Description: Meeting of the Canadian Association for the Study of the Liver (CASL), the Canadian Network on Hepatitis C (CANHEPC), & the Canadian Association of Hepatology Nurses (CAHN)
Publications:
• Canadian Journal of Gastroenterology & Hepatology [a publication of the Canadian Association for the Study of the Liver]
Type: Journal; *Price:* Free with membership in the Canadian Association for the Study of the Liver

Canadian Association for the Study of Women & Education (CASWE) / Association canadienne pour l'étude sur les femmes et l'éducation (ACÉFÉ)
c/o Canadian Society for the Study of Education, #204, 260 Dalhousie St., Ottawa ON K1N 7E4
Tel: 613-241-0018; *Fax:* 613-241-0019
canadianwomenineducation.net
twitter.com/CASWE1
Overview: A small national organization overseen by Canadian Society for the Study of Education
Member of: Canadian Society for the Study of Education
Membership: *Fees:* $10-39
Activities: Research projects; resources for graduate students
Chief Officer(s):
Kathy Sanford, President
ksanford@uvic.ca
Awards:
• Achievement Award
• Graduate Student Awards
• Carol Crealock Memorial Award

Canadian Association for the Teachers of French as a First Language *Voir* Alliance canadienne des responsables et enseignants en français (langue maternelle)

Canadian Association for Theatre Research (CATR) / Association canadienne de la recherche théâtrale (ACRT)
catr.membership@gmail.com
www.catracrt.ca
twitter.com/catr_acrt
Previous Name: Association for Canadian Theatre History
Overview: A small national organization founded in 1976
Mission: To focus on theatre, drama, & performance in a Canadian context, including acting, directing, practical matters of theatre, historiography, & the teaching, reception, theory, & literary criticism of drama
Member of: Humanities & Social Sciences Federation of Canada; Canadian Conference of the Arts; International Federation for Theatre Research
Finances: *Funding Sources:* Membership dues
Membership: *Fees:* $40-$150; *Member Profile:* Academics; Students; Libraries; *Committees:* McCallum Scholarship; Saddlemyer; Godin; Plant; O'Neill; CATR
Activities: *Library:* Graduate Centre for Study of Drama; by appointment
Chief Officer(s):
Sasha Kovacs, Secretary
sashakovacs@gmail.com
Barry Freeman, Coordinator, Membership
Awards:
• McCallum Scholarship
Meetings/Conferences:
• Canadian Association for Theatre Research 2018 Conference, May, 2018, Kingston, ON
Scope: National

Canadian Association for Translation Studies *See* Association canadienne de traductologie

Canadian Association for University Continuing Education (CAUCE) / Association pour l'éducation

permanente dans les universités du Canada (AEPUC)
c/o Centre for Continuing & Distance Education, U. of Saskatchewan, #464, 221 Cumberland Ave. North, Saskatoon SK S7N 1M3
Tel: 306-966-5604; Fax: 306-966-5590
cauce.secratariat@usask.ca
www.cauce-aepuc.ca
Overview: A medium-sized national charitable organization founded in 1974
Mission: To enlarge the quality & scope of educational opportunities for adults at the university level
Membership: Fees: Schedule available; Member Profile: Deans, practitioners, & senior administrative personnel with careers in university continuing education in Canada; Committees: Executive; Professional Development; Communications & Publications; Conference Development; Marketing Awards; Membership; Nominations; Program Awards; Research & Information
Activities: Offering professional development activities, such as a teleconference series
Chief Officer(s):
Cathy Kelly, President, 519-888-4873, Fax: 519-746-4607
cathy.kelly@uwaterloo.ca
Awards:
• Marketing Awards
To recognize marketing work in continuing education Deadline: March Contact: Marilou Cruz, m1cruz@ryerson.ca
• Program Awards
To recognize excellence in continuing education programs Deadline: March Contact: Heather Stamp-Nunes, hstampnunes@mun.ca
Meetings/Conferences:
• CAUCE 2018: The 65th Annual Conference & General Meeting of the Canadian Association for University Continuing Education, May, 2018, Dalhousie University, Halifax, NS
Scope: National
Description: Theme: "Over the Horizon: The Future of Work & Learning Opportunities for Continuing Education"
Publications:
• The Bulletin
Type: Newsletter
Profile: Current information for Canadian Association for University Continuing Education members

Canadian Association for Vocational Evaluation & Work Adjustment See Canadian Assessment, Vocational Evaluation & Work Adjustment Society

Canadian Association for Williams Syndrome (CAWS)
19 Pereverzoff Pl., Prince Albert SK S6X 1A8
Tel: 306-922-3230; Fax: 306-922-3457
caws.sasktelwebhosting.com
Overview: A small national charitable organization founded in 1984
Mission: To support William syndrome individuals & their families; To advance education, research, & knowledge of the genetic disorder known as Williams Syndrome
Finances: Funding Sources: Donations; Fundraising
Activities: Supporting research; Increasing awareness of Williams Syndrome; Sharing information; Library: Canadian Association for Williams Syndrome Resource Centre
Chief Officer(s):
Gloria Manhussier, Editor/Secretary
mahussier.m@sasktel.net
Publications:
• Canadian Association for Williams Syndrome Newsletter
Type: Newsletter; Frequency: Quarterly
Profile: News, resources, & medical & educational information from across Canada

CAWS - Alberta
c/o Mary Kueller, 10733 St. Gabriel Rd., Edmonton AB T6A 3S7
Chief Officer(s):
Misty Kuefler, Chairperson
MKuefler@vsm.ab.ca

CAWS - British Columbia
c/o Cindy Sanford, PO Box 26206, Richmond BC V6Y 3V3
Chief Officer(s):
Cindy Sanford, Provincial Contact, 604-564-7779
cawsbc@yahoo.com

CAWS - Manitoba
c/o Coralee Crowe, 27 Regis Dr., Winnipeg MB R2N 1J9
Chief Officer(s):
Coralee Crowe, Vice Chair, 204-479-7734
dcrowe@mymts.net

CAWS - New Brunswick
c/o Michelle Dobbin, 28 West Ave., Sackville NB E4L 4P1
Chief Officer(s):
Michelle Dobbin, Provincial Contact, 506-536-0821
dobbinwm@gmail.com

CAWS - Newfoundland
c/o April Williams, 1680 A. Torbay Rd., Torbay NL A1K 1H2
Chief Officer(s):
April Williams, Provincial Contact
aprildswilliams@hotmail.com

CAWS - Nova Scotia
c/o Christena Cote, NS
Tel: 902-422-8670

CAWS - Ontario
c/o Monique & John Plessas, 163 Wolverleigh Blvd., Toronto ON M4C 1S1
Tel: 416-269-7030
Chief Officer(s):
Monique Plessas, Toronto Contact
John Plessas, Toronto Contact
momslilangel@rogers.com

CAWS - Québec
c/o Jocelyne Z'Graggen, 108, 59e av, Saint-Hippolyte QC J8A 1N9
Chief Officer(s):
Jocelyne Z'Graggen, Provincial Contact, 450-563-3574
coeurachanter@bellnet.ca

CAWS - Saskatchewan
c/o Gloria Mahussier, 19 Pereverzoff Pl., Prince Albert SK S6X 1A8
Chief Officer(s):
Kelly Fraser, Provincial Contact
schmister@hotmail.com

Canadian Association for Young Children (CAYC) / Association canadienne pour les jeunes enfants (ACJE)
31 Pinedale Dr., Prospect Bay NS B3T 1Z6
www.cayc.ca
Overview: A medium-sized national charitable organization founded in 1974
Mission: To influence policies & programs affecting critical issues related to the education & welfare of Canadian young children from birth through age nine
Finances: Funding Sources: Membership fees
Membership: Fees: $30 students & seniors; $100 regular; $120 associations & institutions; $135 international; Member Profile: Parents; Teachers; Caregivers; Administrators; Students
Activities: Promoting & providing professional development opportunities
Chief Officer(s):
Rebecca Kelley, President
becky.kelley@cayc.ca
Iris Berger, Chair, Publications
iris.berger@cayc.ca
Vicki Brown, Contact, Membership Service
membership@cayc.ca
Awards:
• Friends of Children Award
Publications:
• Journal of Childhood Studies [a publication of the Canadian Association for Young Children]
Type: Journal; Frequency: Triannually; Accepts Advertising; Editor: Laurie Kocher; Veronica Pacini
Profile: For CAYC members & professionals concerned with early childhood development & primary education

Alberta/North West Territories
c/o Linda O'Donoghue, Bow Valley College, 345 - 6th Ave. SE, Calgary AB T2G 4V1
Chief Officer(s):
Becky Kelley, Co-Director
becky.kelley@cayc.ca
Linda O'Donoghue, Co-Director
linda.odonoghue@cayc.ca
• CAYC [Canadian Association for Young Children]: Alberta / NWT Newsletter
Type: Newsletter; Editor: Jayne Clarke & Elizabeth Ashton
Profile: Upcoming events, new regulations, book reviews, website resources, & information

British Columbia/Yukon
c/o Kathleen Kummen, Capilano University, #374, 2055 Purcell Way, North Vancouver BC V8B 0B1
Tel: 604-986-1911
Chief Officer(s):
Kathleen Kummen, Provincial Director
kathleen.kummen@cayc.ca

Manitoba/Nunavut
Chief Officer(s):
Joanna Malkiewicz, Provincial Director
joanna.malkiewicz@cayc.ca

New Brunswick, Prince Edward Island & Nova Scotia
Chief Officer(s):
Sherry Riggs, Provincial Director
sherry.riggs@cayc.ca

Newfoundland & Labrador
Chief Officer(s):
Margaret Fair, CAYC President & Provincial Contact
margaret.fair@cayc.ca

Ontario
c/o Anne Marie Coughlin, London Bridge Child Care Services, 550 Fanshawe Park Rd., London ON N5X 1L1
Chief Officer(s):
Anne Marie Coughlin, Provincial Director
annemarie.coughlin@cayc.ca

Québec
c/o Fiona Rowlands, Dept. of Education, Concordia University, 1455, boul de Maisonneuve ouest, #LB-579, Montréal QC H3G 1M8
Tel: 514-848-2424
Chief Officer(s):
Fiona Rowlands, Provincial Director
fiona.rowlands@cayc.ca

Saskatchewan
Chief Officer(s):
Kari Nagel, Provincial Director
kari.nagel@cayc.ca
• CAYC [Canadian Association for Young Children] Saskatchewan Newsletter
Type: Newsletter; Frequency: Semiannually
Profile: Information & forthcoming events

Canadian Association of Accredited Mortgage Professionals; Canadian Institute of Mortgage Brokers & Lenders See Mortgage Professionals Canada

Canadian Association of Acupuncture & Traditional Chinese Medicine (CAACTM)
c/o Chinese Medicine & Acupuncture Clinic of Toronto, 3195 Sheppard Ave. East, 2nd Fl., Toronto ON M1T 3K1
Tel: 416-493-8447; Fax: 416-493-9450
Toll-Free: 888-299-9799
info@caatcm.com
www.caatcm.com
Overview: A small national organization founded in 1994
Mission: To promote & improve the practice of traditional Chinese medicine & acupuncture in the prevention & treatment of diseases, & the restoration & maintenance of health; To implement acceptable standards of practice within the profession
Membership: 2,366; Fees: $185 first year; $100 renewal; Member Profile: Graduates of a traditional Chinese medicine university & acupuncturists with knowledge of traditional Chinese medicine with at least 5 years of experience; students of traditional Chinese medicine & acupuncture

Canadian Association of Administrators of Labour Legislation (CAALL) / Association canadienne des administrateurs de la législation ouvrière (ACALO)
CAALL Secretariat, Phase II, Place du Portage, 165, rue Hôtel-de-Ville, 8e étage, Gatineau QC K1A 0J2
Tel: 819-654-4123; Fax: 819-654-4125
Other Communication: Alt. Phone: 819-654-4125
CAALL-secretariat@hrsdc-rhdsc.gc.ca
www.caall-acalo.org
Overview: A small national organization founded in 1938
Mission: To provide a forum for federal, provincial, & territorial senior officials; to develop agenda, background papers, & logistics for meetings of Ministers responsible for Labour; To follow-up on issues as directed by Ministers
Affiliation(s): Canadian Centre on Occupational Health & Safety; National Association of Government Labor Officials; Association of Workers Compensation Board of Canada
Membership: Member Profile: Federal, provincial, & territorial departments of labour; Heads of occupational safety & health agencies; Committees: International Labour Affairs; Conciliation & Mediation; Labour Standards; Occupational Health & Safety; Strategic Labour Policy
Activities: Library: CAALL Resource Library

Canadian Associations / Canadian Association of Aesthetic Medicine (CAAM) / L'association canadienne de médecine esthétique

Publications:
- CAALL [Canadian Association of Administrators of Labour Legislation] Monthly Bulletin
Type: Newsletter; *Frequency:* Monthly
Profile: National & international articles

Canadian Association of Advanced Practice Nurses *See* Nurse Practitioner Association of Canada

Canadian Association of Aerial Surveyors *See* Geomatics Industry Association of Canada

Canadian Association of Aesthetic Medicine (CAAM) / L'association canadienne de médecine esthétique
#220, 445 Mountain Hwy., North Vancouver BC V7J 2L1
Tel: 604-988-0450; *Fax:* 604-929-0871
info@caam.ca
www.caam.ca
Overview: A small national organization founded in 2003
Mission: CAAM is the face of aesthetic medicine in Canada, comprising of a multidisciplinary group of aesthetic physicians from various backgrounds and interests.
Activities: *Library:* CAAM Library
Chief Officer(s):
Susan Roberts, Executive Director
s.roberts@caam.ca
Meetings/Conferences:
- Canadian Association of Aesthetic Medicine 15th Annual Conference, October, 2018, Hilton Toronto/Markham Suites Conference Centre, Toronto, ON
Scope: National

Canadian Association of Agri-Retailers (CAAR)
#628, 70 Arthur St., Winnipeg MB R3B 1G7
Tel: 204-989-9300; *Fax:* 204-989-9306
Toll-Free: 800-463-9323
info@caar.org
www.caar.org
www.linkedin.com/company/caar—canadian-association-of-agri-retailers
twitter.com/CdnAgRetail
Previous Name: Western Fertilizer & Chemical Dealers Association
Overview: A medium-sized national organization founded in 1978
Mission: To represent & protect the interests of Canadian agricultural retailers
Staff Member(s): 6
Membership: *Fees:* $485 primary retailer; $285 branch retailer; $1295 primary supplier; $485 agricultural media publishers; free for schools & branch suppliers; *Member Profile:* Canadian agricultural retailer members, who provide farmers with the products & services required for agricultural production; Canadian suppliers, who manufacture the products sold by retailers; *Committees:* Executive Council; Finance; Membership Development & Services; Facility & Transport Logistics; Convention; Communication & Public Relations; Stewardship & Agronomy; Government Affairs & Industry Relations
Activities: Liaising with provincial & national governments; Engaging in advocacy actitivities; Offering networking opportunities for agricultural suppliers & retailers; Providing information & training events
Chief Officer(s):
Lynda Nicol, Director, Member Services, 204-989-9305
lynda@caar.org
Lisa Defoort, Manager, Event & Creative, 204-989-9313
lisa@caar.org
Awards:
- Agronomist of the Year
To honour agronomic knowledge, customer satisfaction, commitment to continuing education, & community & industry leadership *Deadline:* December
- Retailer of the Year
To recognize a retailer who provides exceptional customer service, plus environmental stewardship & community & industry leadership *Deadline:* December; *Amount:* $2,000
- Retailer Hall of Fame
A lifetime achievement award in the agri-retail industry *Deadline:* December; *Amount:* $2,000
- 4R Agri-Retailer Award
Honours a CAAR member location that has shown leadership in the adoption of 4R Nutrient Stewardship (Right Source @ Right Rate, Right Time, Right Place) into business practices*Deadline:* December; *Amount:* $1,000
- Chairman's Award
Awarded to an individual who is a strong supporter of the Association and the agri-retail industry in general *Deadline:* December
Meetings/Conferences:
- Canadian Association of Agri-Retailers Conference 2018, February, 2018, Saskatoon, SK
Scope: National
Description: A conference & exhibition featuring the annual general meeting, educational workshops, guest speaker sessions, the presentation of awards, & networking events
Publications:
- CAAR [Canadian Association of Agri-Retailers] Roster
Type: Directory
Profile: A networking tool with hundreds of listings of businesses & organizations, as well as the Supplier's Guide & the CAARPerk$ Guide (formerly the Member BenefitsGuide)
- The CAAR Network [[a publication of the Canadian Association of Agri-Retailers]
Type: Newsletter; *Accepts Advertising*
Profile: Includes member-focused information, including agricultural news & knowledge
- CCA [Certified Crop Advisors] Examiner
Type: Newsletter; *Frequency:* Quarterly
Profile: Offers 4 Continuing Education Units (CEUs) towards the Certified Crop Advisor program through a self-study exam
- The Communicator [a publication of the Canadian Association of Agri-Retailers]
Type: Magazine; *Accepts Advertising*
Profile: Focuses on the issues & successes of Canadian agri-retail; features companies, equipment, & innovations that are leading theagricultural industry

The Canadian Association of Amateur Oarsmen *See* Rowing Canada Aviron

Canadian Association of Ambulatory Care (CAAC)
#200, 100 Consilium Pl., Toronto ON M1H 3E3
canadianambulatorycare@gmail.com
www.canadianambulatorycare.com
twitter.com/ambulatorycare
Overview: A small national organization founded in 2012
Mission: To enhance the ambulatory care field in Canada
Membership: *Fees:* $45
Chief Officer(s):
Denyse Henry, Chief Executive Officer
caacceo1@gmail.com
Jatinder Bains, President
caacpresident@gmail.com
Julia Young, Vice-President, Finance & Sponsorship
caactreasurer1@gmail.com
Edna Pasaoa, Vice-President, Membership & Promotions
caacmembership@gmail.com
Sherrol Palmer, Vice-President, Education
caaceducation@gmail.com
Adam Saporta, Vice-President, Special Projects
caacspecialprojects1@gmail.com
Vinder Nat, Vice-President, Communications & Stakeholders Relations
caaccommunications@gmail.com
Ellie Lee, Vice-President, Web Design & Publications
caacrelations@gmail.com
Jing Zhou, Secretary
Meetings/Conferences:
- 2018 Canadian Association of Ambulatory Care Conference, June, 2018, Ottawa, ON
Scope: National
Description: Theme: "Strategies for Improving the Patient Experience in Ambulatory Care"

Canadian Association of Anatomists / Association Canadienne d'Anatomie *See* Canadian Association for Anatomy, Neurobiology, & Cell Biology

Canadian Association of Animal Health Technologists & Technicians *See* Registered Veterinary Technologists & Technicians of Canada

Canadian Association of Apheresis Nurses (CAAN) / Association Canadienne des Infirmiers et Infirmieres d'Apheresis
Canadian Apheresis Group, #199, 435 St. Laurent Blvd., Ottawa ON K1K 2Z8
Tel: 613-748-9613; *Fax:* 613-748-6392
apheresisnurses@live.ca
www.apheresisnurses.org
Overview: A small national organization founded in 1992
Mission: To establish apheresis standards; To promote & collect information on all apheresis procedures including plasma exchange, cytapheresis, photopheresis & stem cell collection
Member of: World Apheresis Association
Affiliation(s): Canadian Apheresis Group; Canadian Nurses Association
Membership: *Member Profile:* Professional nurses
Activities: Offering regional education days
Publications:
- Canadian Association of Apheresis Nurses Newsletter
Type: Newsletter

Canadian Association of Apiculturists *See* Canadian Association of Professional Apiculturists

Canadian Association of Aquarium Clubs (CAOAC)
#223, 1717 60th St. SE, Calgary AB T2A 7Y7
amtowell@shaw.ca
www.caoac.ca
Overview: A medium-sized national organization founded in 1959
Mission: A non-profit corporation and are composed of member aquarium, reptile & amphibian, pond & water garden, and similar clubs or societies from across Canada and the Northeast United States.
Chief Officer(s):
Ron Bishop, President
ron.bishop2@sympatico.ca
Meetings/Conferences:
- 2018 Canadian Association of Aquarium Clubs Convention, 2018
Scope: National

Canadian Association of Bariatric Physicians & Surgeons (CABPS) / L'Association canadienne des medecins et chirurgiens bariatrique (ACMCB)
#210, 2800 - 14th Ave., Markham ON L3R 0E4
Tel: 416-491-2886; *Fax:* 416-491-1670
cabps@associationconcepts.ca
cabps.ca
cabps.linkedin.com/company/cabps
www.facebook.com/pages/CABPS/215143185313177
twitter.com/Cabps_Obesity
Overview: A small national organization
Mission: Represents Canadian specialists interested in the treatment of obesity and severe obesity for the purposes of professional development and coordination and promotion of common goals.
Affiliation(s): International Federation for the Surgery of Obesity and Metabolic Disorders
Membership: *Fees:* $195 active member; $95 associate/affiliate; *Member Profile:* Physicians, surgeons and allied health care professionals who express an interest in the clinical management of obesity or who have a research interest in any aspect of obesity or its related co-morbid diseases.
Chief Officer(s):
Mehran Anvari, President, 905-522-2951
anvari@mcmaster.ca

Canadian Association of Black Journalists
42 Charles St. East, Toronto ON M4Y 1T4
cabj.wordpress.com
www.linkedin.com/groups/Canadian-Association-Black-Journalists-Communicators-2024462
www.facebook.com/186302344752083
Overview: A small national organization founded in 1996
Mission: Dedicated to both diversifying Canada's newsrooms, and promoting journalism as a viable career for African-Canadian youth.
Member of: National Black Alliance
Membership: *Fees:* $65 full; $50 associate; $40 supporting; $20 student; *Member Profile:* Committed to building relationships among Black journalists & other media communicators; welcomes everyone who supports goals & values; encourages people of colour to enter the industry; students welcome
Activities: Professional development
Awards:
- Scholarships
Two scholarships awarded yearly to second year journalism or radio/television arts students; *Amount:* $1,000

Canadian Association of Black Lawyers (CABL) / L'Association des Avocats Noirs du Canada
#300, 20 Toronto St., Toronto ON M5C 2B8
info@cabl.ca
www.cabl.ca
www.linkedin.com/groups/3951435/profile
www.facebook.com/150574661678680
twitter.com/cablnational

Canadian Associations / Canadian Association of Career Educators & Employers (CACEE) / Association canadienne des spécialistes en emploi et des employeurs (ACSEE)

Overview: A medium-sized national organization founded in 1996
Mission: To bring together law professionals & other interested Canadians to cultive & maintain The Association of Black Professionals in Canada
Chief Officer(s):
Shawn Richard, President
Rosemarie Mercury, Vice President
Esi Codjoe, Secretary
Charlene Theodore, Treasurer

British Columbia Chatper (CABL BC)
BC
www.cabl.ca/chapters/bc-chapter

Canadian Association of Blue Cross Plans (CABCP) / Association Canadienne des Croix Bleue (ACCB)
PO Box 2005, #610, 185 The West Mall, Toronto ON M9C 5P1
Toll-Free: 866-732-2583
www.bluecross.ca
Also Known As: Blue Cross Canada
Overview: A small national licensing organization founded in 1955
Mission: To maintain & monitor standards of performance by association members; to ensure members manage effectively supplementary health, dental, life insurance, & disability income products on an individual and group basis
Affiliation(s): Blue Cross (USA); Blue Shield (USA); International Federation of Health Funds
Membership: *Member Profile:* Independent Blue Cross Member Plans in Canada

Alberta Blue Cross
Blue Cross Place, 10009 - 108th St. NW, Edmonton AB T5J 3C5
Tel: 780-498-8100
Toll-Free: 800-661-6995
www.ab.bluecross.ca
www.linkedin.com/company/16959
www.facebook.com/AlbertaBlueCross
twitter.com/ABBluecross
vimeo.com/albertabluecross
Mission: To provide supplementary health care & related benefit programs & services
Chief Officer(s):
Ray R. Pisani, President/CEO
• Alberta Blue Cross Annual Report
Type: Yearbook; *Frequency:* Annually

Manitoba Blue Cross
PO Box 1046, Stn. Main, Winnipeg MB R3C 2X7
Tel: 204-775-0151; *Fax:* 204-786-5965
Toll-Free: 800-873-2583
www.mb.bluecross.ca
Mission: To offer services within the supplementary health care & travel benefit fields to all Manitobans
Chief Officer(s):
Andrew Yorke, President & CEO

Medavie Blue Cross/Atlantic Blue Cross Care/Service Croix Bleue de l'Atlantique
PO Box 220, 644 Main St., Moncton NB E1C 8L3
Toll-Free: 800-667-4511
www.medavie.bluecross.ca
www.facebook.com/MedavieBlueCross
twitter.com/MedavieBC
www.youtube.com/MedavieBlueCross
Chief Officer(s):
Pierre-Yves Julien, CEO

Ontario Blue Cross
#610, 185 The West Mall, Toronto ON M9C 5P1
Tel: 416-646-2585; *Fax:* 800-893-0997
Toll-Free: 866-732-2583
bco.indhealth@ont.bluecross.ca
www.useblue.com
Mission: To provide health & travel insurance in Ontario
• Ontario Blue Cross Annual Report
Type: Yearbook; *Frequency:* Annually

Pacific Blue Cross
c/o British Columbia Life & Casualty Company (BC Life), PO Box 7000, Vancouver BC V6B 4E1
Tel: 604-419-2000; *Fax:* 604-419-2990
Toll-Free: 888-275-4672
www.pac.bluecross.ca
www.linkedin.com/company/pacific-blue-cross
www.facebook.com/pacificbluecross
twitter.com/pacbluecross
Mission: To provide extended health & dental benefits
Chief Officer(s):
Jan K. Grude, President/CEO
Gerry Smith, Chair
• Pacific Blue Cross Annual Report
Type: Yearboook; *Frequency:* Annually

Québec Blue Cross/Croix Bleue du Québec
#9B, 550, rue Sherbrooke ouest, Montréal QC H3A 3S3
Tel: 514-286-7686; *Fax:* 866-286-8358
Toll-Free: 877-909-7686
info@qc.croixbleue.ca
www.qc.croixbleue.ca
Mission: To offer health & travel insurance in Québec
• Québec Blue Cross Annual Report
Type: Yearbook; *Frequency:* Annually

Saskatchewan Blue Cross
PO Box 4030, 516 - 2nd Ave. North, Saskatoon SK S7K 3T2
Tel: 306-244-1192; *Fax:* 306-652-5751
Toll-Free: 800-667-6853
www.sk.bluecross.ca
www.linkedin.com/company/saskatchewan-blue-cross
www.facebook.com/sk.push2play
twitter.com/SKBlueCross
Chief Officer(s):
G.N. (Arnie) Arnott, President/CEO

Canadian Association of Broadcast Consultants (CABC) / Association Canadienne des Consultants en Radito-télédiffusion (ACCR)
c/o D.E.M. Allen & Associates Ltd., 130 Cree Cres., Winnipeg MB R3J 3W1
Tel: 204-889-9202; *Fax:* 204-831-6650
www.cabc-accr.ca
Overview: A medium-sized national organization
Membership: 14
Chief Officer(s):
Joseph Sadoun, President, 514-934-3024
jsadoun@yrh.com
Kerry Pelser, Secretary-Treasurer, 204-889-9202
kpelser@dema.mb.ca

Canadian Association of Broadcasters (CAB) / Association canadienne des radiodiffuseurs (ACR)
#770, 45 O'Connor St., Ottawa ON K1P 1A4
Tel: 613-233-4035; *Fax:* 613-233-6961
Overview: A medium-sized national organization founded in 1926
Mission: To act as the national voice of Canada's private broadcasters
Member of: Radio Starmaker Fund
Finances: *Funding Sources:* Membership fees
Membership: 80+; *Member Profile:* Private broadcasters from the radio, television, & specialty sectors
Activities: Engaging in copyright advocacy
Chief Officer(s):
Sylvie Bissonnette, CFO & Vice-President, Finance, 613-233-4035 Ext. 221
sbissonnette@cab-acr.ca
Awards:
• Jim Allard Broadcast Journalism Scholarship
Established 1983; awarded annually to an aspiring broadcaster enrolled in a broadcast journalism program at a Canadian college or university, who best combines academic achievement with natural talent; *Amount:* $2,500
• Ruth Hancock Memorial Scholarships
Award established jointly in 1975 by the association, the Broadcast Executives Society & Canadian Association of Broadcast Representatives; presented annually to three Canadian students enrolled in recognized communications courses; *Amount:* 3 at $1,500
Publications:
• CAB [Canadian Association of Broadcasters] Update
Type: Newsletter; *Frequency:* Irregular
Profile: CAB activities & priorities

Canadian Association of Business Incubation (CABI)
#2002A, 1 Yonge St., Toronto ON M5E 1E5
Tel: 416-345-9937; *Fax:* 416-345-9044
info@cabi.ca
www.cabi.ca
twitter.com/cabimember
Previous Name: Canadian Association of Business Incubators
Overview: A small national organization
Mission: The Canadian Association of Business Incubation, (CABI) is a national organization of member organizations whose members are dedicated to creating employment and economic activity through the development of enterprises supported by the business incubation industry.
Membership: *Fees:* $425
Chief Officer(s):
Gail Gillian-Bain, President & COO
ggillian@cabi.ca
Meetings/Conferences:
• Canadian Acceleration and Business Incubation Leadership Summit 2018, 2018
Scope: National

Canadian Association of Business Incubators *See* Canadian Association of Business Incubation

Canadian Association of Business Valuators (CABV) *See* Canadian Institute of Chartered Business Valuators

Canadian Association of Cardio-Pulmonary Technologists (CACPT)
PO Box 848, Stn. A, Toronto ON M5W 1G3
contactus@cacpt.ca
www.cacpt.ca
Overview: A small national organization founded in 1970
Mission: To establish maintain high standards for Registered Cardio-Pulmonary Technologists
Affiliation(s): Canadian Cardiovascular Society; Canadian Cardiovascular Congress
Membership: *Member Profile:* Technologists employed in the Heart Catheterization Laboratories &/or Pulmonary Function Laboratories; *Committees:* Education; Pulmonary; Cardiac
Chief Officer(s):
Glenda Ryan, President
president@cacpt.ca

Canadian Association of Cardiovascular Prevention & Rehabilitation (CACPR)
1390 Taylor Ave., Winnipeg MB R3M 3V8
Tel: 204-928-7870
admin@cacpr.ca
www.cacpr.ca
www.facebook.com/1CACPR
twitter.com/CACPR_1
Overview: A small national organization founded in 1991
Mission: To provide research & advocacy in cardiovascular disease prevention & rehabilitation
Staff Member(s): 5
Membership: *Fees:* $150 associate/regular; $180 international; $60 retired; $75 student; *Member Profile:* Health professionals in cardiac rehabilitation; *Committees:* Membership; Knowledge Transfer; CV Edge Publication; Research; Marketing; CACPR Registry Project
Activities: *Awareness Events:* Walk of Life for Cardiac Rehabilitation
Chief Officer(s):
Linda Smith, Executive Director
lsmith@cacpr.ca
Katelin Gresty, Special Projects
kgresty@cacpr.ca
Awards:
• Canadian Cardiac Rehabilitation Foundation Graduate Scholarship Awards
To recognize the research of graduate students in the area of cardiac rehabilitation & to reflect CACR's support of their educational endeavours in this area; *Amount:* Four awards of $3,000 each
Publications:
• Current Issues in Cardiac Rehabilitation & Prevention (CICRP)
Type: Newsletter; *Frequency:* Semiannually; *Editor:* Scott Lear; *Price:* Free to members
Profile: Articles, research, reviews, national news, & events
• Journal of Cardiopulmonary Rehabilitation & Prevention (JCRP)
Type: Journal; *Price:* Free for members; $263 non-members

Canadian Association of Career Educators & Employers (CACEE) / Association canadienne des spécialistes en emploi et des employeurs (ACSEE)
#200, 411 Richmond St. East, Toronto ON M5A 3S5
Fax: 416-929-5256
Toll-Free: 866-922-3303
www.cacee.com
www.linkedin.com/company/cacee
twitter.com/followCACEE
Previous Name: ACCIS - The Graduate Workforce Professionals
Overview: A medium-sized national organization founded in 1946

Mission: To facilitate the process of matching graduates with employment; a partnership of employer recruiters & career educators providing information, advice & services to students, employers & career centre personnel in the areas of career planning & student recruitment
Member of: International Network of Graduate Recruitment & Development Associations
Staff Member(s): 6
Membership: *Fees:* Schedule available; *Member Profile:* Career services professionals and employers; *Committees:* Executive; Awards & Recognition; Communications; Diversity; Education; Elections; Ethics; Performance; Business School Working Group; Membership
Chief Officer(s):
Dan Relihan, President
relihan.dan@gmail.com
Meetings/Conferences:
• 2018 Canadian Association of Career Educators & Employers National Conference, May, 2018, Waterloo, ON
Scope: National
Attendance: 250-350

Canadian Association of Certified Planning Technicians (CACPT)
PO Box 69006, 1900 King St. East, Hamilton ON L8K 6R4
Tel: 905-578-4681; *Fax:* 905-578-9581
director@cacpt.org
www.cacpt.org
twitter.com/CACPTech
Overview: A small national licensing organization founded in 1979
Mission: To maintain high standards for Planning Technicians & other related planning professionals
Membership: *Fees:* $205 full; $145 associate; $30 student; *Committees:* Budget; Outreach/Promotional; Web; Conference; Merit; Newsletter; Registration; Seneca Accreditation
Chief Officer(s):
George Zajac, Executive Director
director@cacpt.org
Cathy Burke, Administrative Assistant
admin@cacpt.org
Awards:
• CACPT Student Merit Awards
Presented annually to a student in each recognized college training program
• CACPT Merit Awards
Publications:
• Techtalk
Type: Newsletter; *Editor:* Rebecca Dahl

Canadian Association of Chemical Distributors (CACD) / Association canadienne des distributeurs de produits chimiques (ACDPC)
#1, 1160 Blair Rd., Burlington ON L7M 1K9
Tel: 905-332-8777; *Fax:* 905-332-0777
www.cacd.ca
www.linkedin.com/company/canadian-association-of-chemical-distributors
www.facebook.com/youbethechemistcanada
twitter.com/cacd_cathy
www.youtube.com/user/CatherineCACD
Overview: A medium-sized national organization founded in 1986
Staff Member(s): 5; 180 volunteer(s)
Membership: 46 companies; *Fees:* Schedule available based on sales; *Member Profile:* Chemical distributing companies; *Committees:* Financial Reporting; Health & Safety; Montréal Chapter; Operation & Logistics; Regulatory Affairs; Responsible Distribution; Western Chapter; You be The Chemist
Activities: Collaborating with government to establish policies
Chief Officer(s):
Cathy Campbell, President, 905-844-9140 Ext. 21
ccampbell@cacd.ca
Meetings/Conferences:
• Canadian Association of Chemical Distributors 32nd Annual General Meeting, 2018
Scope: National
Description: An event featuring keynote speakers
Publications:
• The Chemunicator
Type: Magazine; *Frequency:* 3 pa; *Accepts Advertising*; *Editor:* Catherine Wieckowska
Profile: Canadian Association of Chemical Distributors reports, plus news & information for the chemical distribution industry

Canadian Association of Chiefs of Police (CACP) / Association canadienne des chefs de police (ACCP)
#100, 300 Terry Fox Dr., Kanata ON K2K 0E3
Tel: 613-595-1101; *Fax:* 613-383-0372
cacp@cacp.ca
www.cacp.ca
Overview: A medium-sized national organization founded in 1905
Mission: To encourage & develop cooperation among all Canadian police organizations & members in pursuit & attainment of common objects to create & develop the highest standards of efficiency in law enforcement through the fostering & encouragement of police training, education & research; To promote & maintain a high standard of ethics, integrity, honour & conduct in profession of law enforcement; To encourage & advance the study of modern & progressive practices in prevention & detection of crime; To foster uniformity of police practices & cooperation for the protection & security of the people of Canada
Member of: Canadian Society of Association Executives; International Association of Chiefs of Police
Finances: *Annual Operating Budget:* $500,000-$1.5 Million; *Funding Sources:* Federal & provincial government sustaining grants; Membership fees; Publications
Staff Member(s): 7
Membership: 766 active & associate; *Fees:* $375; *Member Profile:* Police executives; corporate executives; *Committees:* Crime Prevention/Community Policing; Drug Abuse; Electronic Crime; Human Resources; Informatics; Law Amendments; National Police Service; Organized Crime; POLIS; Policing with Aboriginal Peoples; Private Sector Liaison; National Security
Activities: Library;
Chief Officer(s):
Dale McFee, O.O.M., President
Meetings/Conferences:
• Canadian Association of Chiefs of Police 2018 113th Annual Conference, August, 2018, Halifax Convention Centre, Halifax, NS
Scope: National
Description: Conference sessions & exhibits

Canadian Association of Child Neurology (CACN) / L'Association canadienne de neurologie pédiatrique (ACNP)
#709, 7015 Macleod Trail SW, Calgary AB T2H 2K6
Tel: 403-229-9544; *Fax:* 403-229-1661
www.cnsfederation.org
Overview: A small national organization founded in 1991 overseen by Canadian Neurological Sciences Federation
Mission: To advance knowledge about the development of the nervous system from conception, as well as the diseases of the nervous system in children; To improve treatment of young people with neurological handicaps
Membership: 100; *Fees:* $80 junior members; $250 associate members; $440 active members; *Member Profile:* Pediatric neurologists in Canada
Activities: Engaging in advocacy activities
Awards:
• President's Prize
Awarded for the best paper in pediatric neuroscience by a resident or fellow *Contact:* Marika Fitzgerald, *E-mail:* marika-fitzgerald@cnsfederation.org
Publications:
• Canadian Association of Child Neurology Membership Directory
Type: Directory

Canadian Association of College & University Student Services (CACUSS) / Association des services aux étudiants des universités et collèges du Canada (ASEUCC)
#202, 720 Spadina Ave., Toronto ON M5S 2T9
Tel: 647-345-1116
contact@cacuss.ca
www.cacuss.ca
www.facebook.com/cacuss
twitter.com/cacusstweets
Overview: A medium-sized national organization founded in 1977 overseen by Universities Canada
Mission: To represent & serve persons who work in Canadian post-secondary institutions in student affairs & services; To offer advocacy & assistance on issues that affect the quality of student life on Canadian university & college campuses
Member of: Universities Canada; Council for the Advancement of Standards in Higher Education
Membership: *Fees:* Schedule available; *Member Profile:* Individuals who work in Canadian post-secondary institutions in student affairs & services; Institutions; Students
Activities: Providing professional development services & programs for members
Chief Officer(s):
Janet Mee, President
David Newman, President-Elect
Jennifer Hamilton, Executive Director, 416-889-7650
cacuss-ed@cacuss.ca
Awards:
• CACUSS Award of Honour
To honour a distinguished contribution to the development & promotion of student services *Contact:* Corinna Fitzgerald, *E-mail:* cfitzger@stfx.ca
• CACUSS Life Membership Award
Eligibility: A retired member recommended by a divisional president *Deadline:* February *Contact:* Corinna Fitzgerald, *E-mail:* cfitzger@stfx.ca
• Special Projects Fund
To support projects that will have value to Canadian Association of College & University Student Services members *Eligibility:* Any current member of the Canadain Association of College & University Student Services *Contact:* Corinna Fitzgerald, *E-mail:* cfitzger@stfx.ca
Meetings/Conferences:
• Canadian Association of College & University Student Services 2018 Conference, June, 2018, PEI Convention Centre, Charlottetown, PE
Scope: National
Publications:
• CACUSS [Canadian Association of College & University Student Services] Member Directory
Type: Directory
Profile: For members only
• Campus Crime: University Liability for Failure to Protect Its Students
Type: Monograph; *Author:* D.R.R. DuPlessis
• Canadian Association of College & University Student Services Communiqué
Type: Newsletter; *Frequency:* 3 pa; *Accepts Advertising*; *Price:* Free with membership; $64.20 individual non-members
Profile: News, articles, updates, opinion pieces, letters to the editor, artwork, & photographs related to college & university student services in Canada
• Growing Together in Service
Type: Monograph; *Author:* W.A. Stewart
• Making the Connection: Civic Leadership Development on Post Secondary Campuses through Community Service Learning
Type: Monograph; *Author:* Cheryl Rose
• Procedural Fairness for University & College Students
Type: Monograph; *Author:* Lynn M. Smith
• Suicide Risk Management on the Post-Seconday Campus
Type: Monograph; *Author:* Judy Murphy

Canadian Association of Communicators in Education (CACE) / Association canadienne des agents de communication en éducation (ACACE)
#310, 1390 Prince of Wales Dr., Ottawa ON K2C 3N6
www.cace-acace.org
www.linkedin.com/company/canadian-association-for-communicators-in-education
www.facebook.com/cace.acace
twitter.com/caceacace
Overview: A medium-sized national organization founded in 1984
Mission: To support teaching & learning through effective communication strategies; To help with the development of professional communication services in the education industry; To foster student success through communication
Finances: *Annual Operating Budget:* $50,000-$100,000; *Funding Sources:* Membership fees; Conference fees; Professional development fees
Staff Member(s): 1; 15 volunteer(s)
Membership: 125; *Fees:* $150 associate; $195 full; *Member Profile:* Educational marketing & communications professionals in Canada
Activities: Offering regional workshops & networking opportunities; Increasing awareness of the role of communicators in education; Establishing standards; Promoting a code of ethics
Chief Officer(s):
Catherine Shedden, President, 705-324-6776
catherine.shedden@tldsb.on.ca

Canadian Associations / Canadian Association of Critical Care Nurses (CACCN) / Association canadienne des infirmières et infirmiers en soins intensifs (ACIISI)

Bruce Buruma, 1st Vice-President, 403-342-3708
bruce.buruma@rdpsd.ab.ca
Meetings/Conferences:
• Canadian Association of Communicators in Education 2018 Annual General Meeting, 2018
Scope: National
Publications:
• CACE [Canadian Association of Communicators in Education] Membership Directory
Type: Directory
• CACE [Canadian Association of Communicators in Education] Annual Report
Type: Yearbook; *Frequency:* Annually

Canadian Association of Community Financial Service Providers *See* Canadian Payday Loan Association

Canadian Association of Community Health Centres (CACHC) / Association canadienne des centres de santé communautiare
#500, 340 College St., Toronto ON M5T 3A9
Tel: 416-922-5694; *Fax:* 866-404-6040
www.cachc.ca
www.linkedin.com/groups/Canadian-Assoc-Community-Health-Centres-4322814
www.facebook.com/CACHC.ACCSC
twitter.com/CACHC_ACCSC
www.youtube.com/user/CACHCandACCSC
Overview: A medium-sized national organization founded in 1995
Mission: To support provincially-based community health centre organizations in Canada; to represent community health centre organizations nationally; to improve health services in Canadian communities; to promote community health centre organizations for the delivery of primary health care
Finances: *Annual Operating Budget:* $100,000-$250,000; *Funding Sources:* Membership dues; special contributions; conference revenue; donations
Staff Member(s): 3
Membership: 75; *Fees:* Schedule available based on annual budget; *Member Profile:* Community health care centres
Chief Officer(s):
Scott Wolfe, Executive Director
swolfe@cachc.ca
Jane Moloney, Chair
Michelle Hurtubise, Treasurer

Canadian Association of Community Television Users & Stations (CACTUS)
177, rte Principale est, Sainte-Cécile-de-Masham QC J0X 2W0
Tel: 819-456-2237
cactus.independentmedia.ca
twitter.com/CACTUS62
Overview: A small national organization
Mission: To improve access to local media & media production training & equipment in Canada
Membership: 25+ organizations; *Member Profile:* Community television channels & producing groups; Individuals in th broadcasting industry
Chief Officer(s):
Cathy Edwards, Executive Director
cedwards@timescape.ca

Canadian Association of Conference Interpreters *Voir* Association camadienne des interprètes de conférence

Canadian Association of Credit Counselling Services (CACCS)
PO Box 189, Grimsby ON L3M 4G3
Toll-Free: 800-263-0260
info@caccs.ca
www.caccs.ca
www.facebook.com/195249373845789
twitter.com/finfitscore
Overview: A medium-sized national charitable organization
Mission: The Canadian Association of Credit Counselling Services (CACCS) represents a Canada-wide network of accredited, not-for-profit agencies & affiliates offering preventative education & confidential services to clients experiencing financial difficulties. With a focus on financial counselling education, accreditation of agencies & certification of Financial Counsellors, CACCS is also committed to national research & policy initiatives concerning personal finance & industry advocacy.
Chief Officer(s):
Henrietta Ross, CEO

Canadian Association of Critical Care Nurses (CACCN) / Association canadienne des infirmières et infirmiers en soins intensifs (ACIISI)
PO Box 25322, London ON N6B 6B1
Tel: 519-649-5284; *Fax:* 519-649-1458
Toll-Free: 866-477-9077
caccn@caccn.ca
www.caccn.ca
www.facebook.com/121001477977759
blog.caccn.ca/wordpress
Previous Name: National Society of Critical Care Nurses
Overview: A medium-sized national organization founded in 1983
Mission: To maintain & enhance the quality of patient- & family-centred care throughout Canada; To develop standards of critical care nursing practice
Member of: CNA Network; WFCCN; WFPICCS
Finances: *Funding Sources:* Membership; advertising revenue; conference registration
Staff Member(s): 1
Membership: 1,200; *Fees:* $50 students; $75/year or $140/2 years, regular & associate members; *Member Profile:* Canadian critical care nurses who work in, or have an interest in, the care of neonatal, paediatric or adult patients; International members; Students
Activities: Advocating for critical care nurses across Canada; Responding to the educational needs of critical care nurses; Presenting educational funds & awards; Offering networking opportunities; Publishing position statements on topics of significance to the critical care nursing profession
Chief Officer(s):
Christine Halfkenny-Zellas, Chief Operating Officer
Meetings/Conferences:
• Dynamics 2018: The Annual National Convention & Product Exhibition of the Canadian Association of Critical Care Nurses, September, 2018, Calgary, AB
Scope: National
Description: Featuring programming to enhance education, clinical practice, research, & leadership.
Contact Information: Toll-Free Phone: 1-866-477-9077; E-mail: caccn@caccn.ca
Publications:
• CACCN [Canadian Association of Critical Care Nurses] Standards for Critical Care Nursing Practice
Price: Free with membership in the Canadian Association ofCritical Care Nurses
Profile: A resource for nurses, administrators, & other health care professionals
• CACCN [Canadian Association of Critical Care Nurses] Annual Report
Type: Yearbook; *Frequency:* Annually; *Price:* Free with membership in the Canadian Association of Critical Care Nurses
• Canadian Journal of Critical Care Nursing
Type: Journal; *Frequency:* Quarterly; *Accepts Advertising*; *Editor:* Paula Price, RN PhD; *Price:* Free with membership in the Canadian Association of Critical Care Nurses
Profile: A peer reviewed critical care nursing journal
British Columbia Chapter
Vancouver BC
bclm@caccn.ca
www.caccn.ca
Mission: To support critical care nurses in British Columbia to provide the best possible care to critically ill patients
Chief Officer(s):
Vena Camenzuli, Contact
Greater Edmonton Chapter
PO Box 52191, Edmonton AB T6G 2C5
greateredmonton@caccn.ca
www.caccn.ca
Mission: To foster the best possible nursing care in the greater Edmonton district
Liane Manz, President
• Canadian Association of Critical Care Nurses, Greater Edmonton Chapter, Newsletter
Type: Newsletter; *Editor:* Sara Pretzlaff
Profile: Chapter activities, conference reviews, & future plans
London Regional Chapter
ON
londonregional@caccn.ca
www.caccn.ca
Mission: To represent critical care nurses in the London & southwestern Ontario area
Chief Officer(s):
Alison Rowlands, President
alison.rowlands@lhsc.on.ca
Jane Moore, Secretary
jpm@golden.net
Dianne Morley, Treasurer
diane.morley@lhsc.on.ca
Denise Geroux, Contact, Education
denise.geroux@lhsc.on.ca
Janet Taylor, Contact, Newsletter
janet.taylor@lhsc.on.ca
• Canadian Association of Critical Care Nurses, London Regional Chapter, Newsletter
Type: Newsletter; *Editor:* Janet Taylor; *Price:* Free with membership in the CACCN London regional chapter
• Canadian Association of Critical Care Nurses, London Regional Chapter, Annual Report
Type: Yearbook; *Frequency:* Annually; *Price:* Free with membership in the CACCN London regional chapter
Manitoba Chapter
MB
manitoba@caccn.ca
www.caccn.ca
Mission: To promote & advance critical care nursing in Manitoba
Chief Officer(s):
Tannis Sidloski, President, 204-235-3493
tsidloski@sbgh.mb.ca
Sara Unrau, Chair, Publicity & Newsletter
sunrau@sbgh.mb.ca
• Canadian Association of Critical Care Nurses, Manitoba Chapter, Newsletter
Type: Newsletter; *Frequency:* Semiannually; *Editor:* Sara Unrau
Profile: Chapter initiatives, executive reports, awards, current events, professional development information, & upcoming educationalopportunities
Montréal Chapter
Montréal QC
montreal@caccn.ca
www.caccn.ca
Mission: To support critical care nurses in the Montréal area to attain excellence in their nursing practice; To implement standards of critical care nursing practice; To address political & professional issues
Chief Officer(s):
Christine Echegaray-Benites, Co-President
Mélanie Gauthier, Co-President
New Brunswick Chapter
NB
newbrunswick@caccn.ca
www.caccn.ca
www.facebook.com/482650845176504
Mission: To promote critical care nursing across New Brunswick
Chief Officer(s):
Joe Carr, President, New Brunswick
Nova Scotia Chapter
NS
novascotia@caccn.ca
www.caccn.ca
Mission: To act as the voice of critical care nursing in Nova Scotia
Chief Officer(s):
Ashley Mowatt, President
Barb Fagan, BOD Liaison
Ottawa Regional Chapter
Ottawa ON
ottawaregional@caccn.ca
www.caccn.ca
Mission: To work as the voice of critical care nurses in Ottawa & the surrounding region
Chief Officer(s):
Marilyn White, President
• Canadian Association of Critical Care Nurses, Ottawa Regional Chapter, Newsletter
Type: Newsletter
Profile: Chapter information for members
Saskatchewan Chapter
SK
saskatchewan@caccn.ca
www.caccn.ca
Mission: To support critical care nurses in Saskatchewans
Chief Officer(s):
Jennifer Graf, President, 306-535-1960
jengarf@gmail.com
Jennifer Graf, Vice-President

- Canadian Association of Critical Care Nurses, Saskatchewan Chapter, Newsletter
Type: Newsletter; Editor: Shelley Anderson
Profile: Chapter activities, executive reports, conference reviews, & forthcoming events

Southern Alberta
Calgary AB
calgary@caccn.ca
www.caccn.ca
www.facebook.com/caccn.southernalberta
Chief Officer(s):
Tricia Bray, President
Ashley Altenbeck, Secretary
Susan Gerritsen, Treasurer

- Canadian Association of Critical Care Nurses, Calgary Chapter, Annual Report
Type: Yearbook; Frequency: Annually

Toronto Chapter
PO Box 79660, 1995 Weston Rd., Toronto ON M9N 3W9
caccn.executive@gmail.com
www.torontocaccn.ca
Chief Officer(s):
Ingrid Daley, President
Jo-Ann Fernando, Secretary
Natalia Lavrencic, Treasurer
Alicia Jones-Harmer, Coordinator, Education
Primrose Mharapara, Contact, Membership
- Critical Connections
Type: Newsletter; Accepts Advertising; Editor: Teresa Robitaille
Profile: Executive reports, articles, & forthcoming events

Canadian Association of Crown Counsel (CACC) / Association canadienne des juristes de l'État (ACJE)
PO Box 30, #1015, 180 Dundas St. West, Toronto ON M5G 1Z8
Tel: 416-260-4888; Fax: 416-977-1460
info@cacc-acje.ca
www.cacc-acje.ca
Overview: A small national organization
Mission: To represent the collective interests of its members on a national level
Membership: Member Profile: Crown prosecutors & Crown lawyers
Chief Officer(s):
Rick Woodburn, President, 902-424-7670

Canadian Association of Customs Brokers See Canadian Society of Customs Brokers

Canadian Association of Defence & Security Industries (CADSI) / Association des industries canadiennes de défense et de sécurité (AICDS)
#300, 251 Laurier Ave. West, Ottawa ON K1P 5J6
Tel: 613-235-5337; Fax: 613-235-0784
cadsi@defenceandsecurity.ca
www.defenceandsecurity.ca
twitter.com/cadsicanada
Previous Name: Canadian Defence Industries Association
Overview: A medium-sized national organization founded in 1985
Mission: To represent Canadian defence & security industries domestically & internationally
Staff Member(s): 4
Membership: Fees: Schedule available, based on number of defence & security employees; Member Profile: Registered, legal, private-sector companies with Canadian operations & whose business interests include defence & / or security; Canadian non-commercial organizations or companies which have an interest in defence & security; Committees: Small Medium Enterprise; Events; Government Relations; International; Contracts & Business
Activities: Engaging in advocacy activities; Offering business development information & activities to members; Organizing educational events; Providing networking opportunities
Chief Officer(s):
Janet Thorsteinson, Vice-President, Policy & Government Relations, 613-235-5337 Ext. 25
Jennifer Giguere, Director, Domestic & International Events, 613-235-5337 Ext. 33
Steven Hillier, Director, Development, Marketing, & Membership, 613-235-5337 Ext. 22
Nicolas Todd, Director, Policy & Government Relations, 613-235-5337 Ext. 37
Publications:
- Canadian Defence & Security Directory
Type: Directory; Frequency: Annually; Price: Free
Profile: An inventory of member firms' capabilities, plus information on Canadian government departments & agencies that work with defence & security industries, prepared for members, government departments, foreign embassies, Canadian trade commissioners, & military attaches abroad
- ENews Bulletin
Type: Newsletter; Frequency: Weekly
Profile: Recent developments in the defence & security sectors, & Canadian Association of Defence & Security Industries events & activities

Canadian Association of Direct Response Insurers (CADRI)
#301, 250 Consumers Rd., Toronto ON M2J 4V6
Tel: 416-773-0101; Fax: 416-495-8723
cadri@cadri.com
www.cadri.com
Overview: A medium-sized national organization
Mission: To support & represent direct response insurers to benefit consumers
Membership: Member Profile: Insurers who are involved in the sales & servicing of property & casualty insurance products in Canada, through direct response marketing & distribution
Activities: Researching to support advocacy; Providing information on direct response insurance
Chief Officer(s):
Alain Thibault, President
Ruth Abrahamson, Association Manager
manager@cadri.com

Canadian Association of Drilling Engineers (CADE)
PO Box 957, Stn. M, Calgary AB T2P 2K4
Tel: 403-971-0311
Toll-Free: 877-801-1820
info@cadecanada.com
www.cadecanada.com
www.linkedin.com/groups?home=&gid=3309291
twitter.com/cade_can
Overview: A medium-sized national organization founded in 1974
Mission: To provide a forum for the exchange of technical drilling knowledge & expertise
Affiliation(s): Canadian Association of Oilwell Drilling Contractors
Finances: Funding Sources: Membership dues
Membership: 500+; Fees: $10 student; $47.50 retiree; $95 full member; Member Profile: Individuals who work in the petroleum industry
Chief Officer(s):
Ken Holmes, President
ken.holmes@rpsgroup.com
John Garden, Vice President
john@deadeye.ab.ca
Publications:
- Canadian Well Construction Journal [a publication of the Canadian Association of Drilling Engineers]
Type: Journal

Canadian Association of Electroneurophysiology Technologists Inc. (CAET) / Association canadienne des technologues en électroneurophysiologie inc. (ACTE)
c/o St. Boniface Hospital, 409 Taché Ave., Winnipeg MB R2H 2A6
Tel: 204-233-8563
www.caet.org
Overview: A small national organization founded in 1951
Mission: To advance the knowledge, science, & technology of electroneurophysiology in Canada
Affiliation(s): Canadian Board of Registration of Electroencephalograph Technologists Inc. (CBRET)
Finances: Funding Sources: Membership fees; Sponsorships
Membership: Fees: $60 regular; $50 associate; $65 new regular; $55 new associate; Committees: Nomination/Accreditation/Training Standards; Education/Scientific Committee/Technical Standards; By-Laws
Activities: Promoting technical standards of electroneurophysiology
Chief Officer(s):
Joanne Nikkel, President
joanne.nikkel@caet.org
Bruce Goddard, Vice-President
bruce.goddard@caet.org
Jodi Kent, Secretary & Registrar
jodi.kent@caet.org
Meetings/Conferences:
- Canadian Association of Electroneurophysiology Technologists 2018 Annual General Meeting, 2018
Scope: National
Publications:
- Canadian Association of Electroneurophysiology Technologists Inc. Membership Directory
Type: Directory

Canadian Association of Elizabeth Fry Societies (CAEFS) / Association canadienne des sociétés Elizabeth Fry (ACSEF)
#701, 151 Slater St., Ottawa ON K1P 5H3
Tel: 613-238-2422; Fax: 613-232-7130
Toll-Free: 800-637-4606
admin@caefs.ca
www.caefs.ca
www.facebook.com/138252919680859
twitter.com/CAEFS
www.youtube.com/user/CAEFSElizabethFry
Overview: A medium-sized national charitable organization founded in 1978
Mission: To work with & on behalf of women & girls involved with the justice system, in particular criminalized women; To offer services & programs to women in need, advocating for reforms & offering fora within which the public may be informed about & participate in all aspects of the justice system as it affects women
Affiliation(s): Canadian Association of Sexual Assault Centres; Congress of Black Women; National Anti-Poverty Organization; Equality for Gays & Lesbians Everywhere; National Associations Active in Criminal Justice; National Action Committee on the Status of Women; National Association of Women & the Law; National Organization of Immigrant & Visible Minority Women of Canada; National Voluntary Organizations; Native Women's Association of Canada; Pauktuutit, the Inuit Women's Association; Women's Legal Education & Action Fund; National Council of Women of Canada; United Way National Agencies Committee
Finances: Funding Sources: Dept. of Solicitor General; Corporate & individual donations
Membership: 24 societies
Activities: Monitoring, participating in, & advocating for fairness & equality within the justice system; Cooperating with other organizations which share its commitment to equality & fairness for girls & women; Encouraging & providing opporties; Raising community awareness of social & economic disadvantages & of systemic inequalities; Internships: Yes; Speaker Service: Yes; Library: Open to public by appointment
Chief Officer(s):
Kathi Heim, Interim Executive Director

Central Okanagan Elizabeth Fry Society
#104, 347 Leon Ave., Kelowna BC V1Y 8C7
Tel: 250-763-4613; Fax: 250-763-4272
www.empowerific.com
www.facebook.com/empowerific
twitter.com/empowerific
Chief Officer(s):
Michelle Novakowski, Executive Director

Council of Elizabeth Fry Societies of Ontario
c/o Canadian Association of Elizabeth Fry Societies, #701, 151 Slater St., Ottawa ON K1P 5H3
Toll-Free: 800-637-4606
info@cefso.ca
www.cefso.ca
Chief Officer(s):
Bryonie Baxter, President
president@cefso.ca

Elizabeth Fry Society for the Regional Municipality of Waterloo
58 Queen St. South, Kitchener ON N2G 1V6
Tel: 519-579-6732; Fax: 519-579-6367
e.f.society@gmail.com
www.cefso.ca/waterloo.html
Chief Officer(s):
Patrice Butts, Manager

Elizabeth Fry Society of Calgary
1730 - 10 Ave. SW, Calgary AB T3C 0K1
Tel: 403-294-0737; Fax: 403-262-0285
Toll-Free: 877-398-3656
reception@elizabethfry.ab.ca
www.elizabethfrycalgary.ca
www.facebook.com/232422026837022
Chief Officer(s):
Barbara Hagen, Executive Director

Elizabeth Fry Society of Cape Breton
16C Levatte Cres., Sydney NS B1N 3K3
Tel: 902-539-6165; *Fax:* 902-539-1683
efrycb@eastlink.ca
Chief Officer(s):
Darlene McEachern, Executive Director

Elizabeth Fry Society of Edmonton (EFSE)
10523 - 100th Ave. NW, Edmonton AB T5J 0A8
Tel: 780-421-1175; *Fax:* 780-425-8989
Toll-Free: 866-421-1175; *Crisis Hot-Line:* 780-482-4357
officemanager@efryedmonton.ab.ca
www.efryedmonton.ab.ca
www.facebook.com/EFryEdmonton
twitter.com/EFryEdmonton
Chief Officer(s):
Toni Sinclair, Executive Director, 780-784-2201
director@efryedmonton.ab.ca
• Awakening the Spirit: A Process for Change [a publication of the Elizabeth Fry Society of Edmonton]
Type: Book
• Building Paths: Employment Needs of Provincially Sentenced Women [a publication of the Elizabeth Fry Society of Edmonton]
Type: Book; *Number of Pages:* 101
• Building Pathways: The Employment Needs of Federally Sentenced Women [a publication of the Elizabeth Fry Society of Edmonton]
Type: Book; *Number of Pages:* 103
• Changing Paths [a publication of the Elizabeth Fry Society of Edmonton]
Type: Manual; *Number of Pages:* 74; *Author:* Bev Sochatsky & Sarah Stewart; *ISBN:* 0-9731470-5-9
Profile: The curriculum guide for the Changing Paths Literacy & Life Skills program
• Nobody There: Making Peace with Motherhood [a publication of the Elizabeth Fry Society of Edmonton]
Type: Book; *Number of Pages:* 192
• Solitude & Cold Storage: Women's Journeys of Endurance in Segregation [publication of the Elizabeth Fry Society of Edmonton]
Type: Book; *Number of Pages:* 144; *Author:* Joane Martel; *ISBN:* 0-9686247-0-7

Elizabeth Fry Society of Greater Vancouver
237 East Columbia St., New Westminster BC V3L 3W4
Tel: 604-520-1166; *Fax:* 604-520-1169
Toll-Free: 888-879-9593
info@elizabethfry.com
www.elizabethfry.com
www.facebook.com/EFryVancouver
twitter.com/EFryVancouver
Chief Officer(s):
Shawn Bayes, Executive Director

Elizabeth Fry Society of Hamilton
85 Holton Ave. South, Hamilton ON L8M 2L4
Tel: 905-527-3097; *Fax:* 905-527-4278
Toll-Free: 866-216-3379
www.efryhamilton.org
Chief Officer(s):
Leanne Kilby, Executive Director
lkilby@efryhamilton.org

Elizabeth Fry Society of Kingston
127 Charles St., Kingston ON K7K 1V8
Tel: 613-544-1744
Toll-Free: 888-560-3379
info@efrykingston.ca
efrykingston.ca
Chief Officer(s):
Trish Crawford, Executive Director

Elizabeth Fry Society of Mainland Nova Scotia
1 Tulip St., Dartmouth NS B3A 2S3
Tel: 902-454-5041; *Fax:* 902-455-5913
Toll-Free: 877-619-1354
efrymns.ca
Chief Officer(s):
Tammy Gloade, Executive Director
ed@efrymns.ca

Elizabeth Fry Society of Manitoba
544 Selkirk Ave., Winnipeg MB R2W 2M9
Tel: 204-589-7335; *Fax:* 204-589-7338
Toll-Free: 800-582-5655
administration@efsmanitoba.org
www.efsmanitoba.org
Chief Officer(s):
Tracy Booth, Executive Director
executivedirector@efsmanitoba.org

Elizabeth Fry Society of Northwestern Ontario
217 South Algoma St., Thunder Bay ON P7B 3C3
Tel: 807-623-1319
www.cefso.ca
Chief Officer(s):
Erin Bellavance, Coordinator

Elizabeth Fry Society of Ottawa
#309, 211 Bronson Ave., Ottawa ON K1R 6H5
Tel: 613-237-7427; *Fax:* 613-237-8312
Toll-Free: 800-611-4755
info@efryottawa.com
www.efryottawa.com
Chief Officer(s):
Bryonie Baxter, Executive Director
bryonie.baxter@efryottawa.com

Elizabeth Fry Society of Peel Halton
#LL-01, 24 Queen St. East, Brampton ON L6V 1A3
Tel: 905-459-1315; *Fax:* 905-459-1322
efry@efrypeelhalton.ca
www.efrypeelhalton.ca
Chief Officer(s):
Deborah Riddle, Executive Director

Elizabeth Fry Society of Peterborough
223C Aylmer St. North, Peterborough ON K9J 3K3
Tel: 705-749-6809; *Fax:* 705-749-6818
Toll-Free: 800-820-7384
info@efryptbo.org
www.efryptbo.org
www.facebook.com/ElizabethFrySocietyOfPeterborough
twitter.com/Efry_society
Chief Officer(s):
Lesley Hamilton, President

Elizabeth Fry Society of Saint John
PO Box 23012, Saint John NB E2J 4M1
Tel: 506-635-8851; *Fax:* 506-635-8851
Toll-Free: 866-301-8800
efry@nb.aibn.com
www.facebook.com/173421546050588
Chief Officer(s):
Marianna Stack, President

Elizabeth Fry Society of Saskatchewan (EFSS)
#600, 245 - 3 Ave. South, Saskatoon SK S7M 1M4
Tel: 306-934-4606; *Fax:* 306-652-2933
Toll-Free: 888-934-4606
info@elizabethfrysask.org
www.elizabethfrysask.org
Chief Officer(s):
Sue Delanoy, Executive Director
executivedirector@elizabethfrysask.org

Elizabeth Fry Society of Simcoe County
102 Maple Ave., Barrie ON L4N 1S4
Tel: 705-725-0613
www.elizabethfrysociety.com
Chief Officer(s):
Tracy Wood, Executive Director
tracyw@elizabethfrysociety.com

Elizabeth Fry Society of Sudbury
204 Elm St. West, Sudbury ON P3C 1V3
Tel: 705-673-1364; *Fax:* 705-673-2159
Toll-Free: 855-381-1364
info@efrysudbury.com
efrysudbury.com

Kamloops & District Elizabeth Fry Society
827 Seymour St., Kamloops BC V2C 2H6
Tel: 250-374-2119
admin@kamloopsefry.com
www.kamloopsefry.com
www.facebook.com/KamloopsEFry
Chief Officer(s):
Jennifer Murphy, President

Prince George & District Elizabeth Fry Society
1575 - 5th Ave., Prince George BC V2L 3L9
Tel: 250-563-1113; *Fax:* 250-563-8765
www.pgefry.bc.ca
Chief Officer(s):
Kathi Heim, Executive Director
kathi@pgefry.bc.ca

Société Elizabeth Fry du Québec
5105, ch de la Côte St-Antoine, Montréal QC H4A 1N8
Tél: 514-489-2116; *Téléc:* 514-489-2598
info@elizabethfry.qc.ca
www.elizabethfry.qc.ca
www.linkedin.com/company/société-elizabeth-fry-du-québec
www.facebook.com/1570742069815865

Chief Officer(s):
Ruth Gagnon, Directrice générale, 514-489-2116 Ext. 222
direction@elizabethfry.qc.ca

South Cariboo Elizabeth Fry Society
PO Box 603, 601 Bancroft St., Ashcroft BC V0K 1A0
Tel: 250-453-9656; *Fax:* 250-453-2034

Toronto Elizabeth Fry Society
215 Wellesley St. East, Toronto ON M4X 1G1
Tel: 416-924-3708
Toll-Free: 855-924-3708
info@efrytoronto.org
www.efrytoronto.org
www.linkedin.com/groups?gid=3384615
www.facebook.com/elizabethfrytoronto
twitter.com/efry_toronto
Chief Officer(s):
Gemma Napoli, Executive Director, 416-924-3708 Ext. 253
gnapoli@efrytoronto.org

Canadian Association of Environmental Law Societies (CAELS)
Overview: A medium-sized national organization
Mission: The Canadian Association of Environmental Law Societies (CAELS) is a networking project connecting environmental law students across the country. CAELS will allow law students to interact with their peers and professors, practitioners and environmental professionals.
1 volunteer(s)
Meetings/Conferences:
• Canadian Association of Environmental Law Societies 2018 Conference, 2018
Scope: National

Canadian Association of Environmental Management
c/o Homewood Health Centre, 150 Delhi St., Guelph ON N1E 6K9
Tel: 519-824-1010; *Fax:* 519-824-1827
www.caenvironmentalmanagement.com
Previous Name: Canadian Administrative Housekeepers Association
Overview: A small national organization founded in 1972
Mission: To promote the professional growth & development of its members & help them improve the environmental & housekeeping services they offer.
Finances: *Funding Sources:* Advertising; membership dues
Membership: *Fees:* $80 individual; $140 organization; $40 additional member; *Member Profile:* Managers, supervisors, self-employed people, corporate & associate members involved in the environmental services field
Activities: Conference & trade shows; *Speaker Service:* Yes
Chief Officer(s):
Keith Sopha, President
sophkeit@homewood.org

Canadian Association of Exposition Management (CAEM) / Association canadienne des directeurs d'expositions
PO Box 218, #2219, 160 Tycos Dr., Toronto ON M6B 1W8
Tel: 416-787-9377; *Fax:* 416-596-1808
Toll-Free: 866-441-9377
info@caem.ca
www.caem.ca
Previous Name: Association of Trade & Consumer Exhibitions
Overview: A medium-sized national organization founded in 1983
Mission: To represent & improve the exposition & trade show industry in Canada
Finances: *Funding Sources:* Membership fees; Sponsorships
Membership: *Member Profile:* Professional trade & consumer show producers & managers, & industry suppliers
Activities: Promoting Canada's exposition & trade show industry; Offering networking opportunities; Providing professional development sessions
Chief Officer(s):
Serge Micheli, Executive Director, 416-787-9377 Ext. 224
smicheli@caem.ca
Lisa McDonald, President
Sherry Kirkpatrick, 1st Vice-President
Catherine MacNutt, 2nd Vice-President
Jennifer Allaby, Secretary
Mike Russell, Treasurer
Michael Dargavel, Office Manager, 416-787-9377 Ext. 225

Canadian Association of Fairs & Exhibitions (CAFE) / Association canadienne des foires et expositions
PO Box 21053, Stn. WEPO, Brandon MB R7B 3W8
Toll-Free: 800-663-1714
info@canadian-fairs.ca
www.canadian-fairs.ca
www.facebook.com/canadianfairs
twitter.com/CdnAssocofFairs
Overview: A large national charitable organization founded in 1924
Mission: To provide leadership in the development of the Canadian fair industry; To represent the Canadian fairs & exhibitions sector at the national level
Member of: Imagine Canada
Affiliation(s): International Association of Fairs & Exhibitions; Provincial Associations of Agricultural Societies; Outdoor Amusement Business Association; Showmens League of Canada; Canadian 4H Council
Finances: *Annual Operating Budget:* $250,000-$500,000; *Funding Sources:* Membership fees
Membership: *Fees:* Schedule available; *Member Profile:* Recognized fair or exhibition established under Provincial Act; firms & organizations which derive significant percentage of annual income from providing products & services to fair organizations
Activities: Workshops; CAFE Learning Forums; insurance program
Chief Officer(s):
Gregg Korek, President
Christina Franc, Executive Director
christina@canadian-fairs.ca
Awards:
- Canadian Fair Champion
- Roll of Honour
- Innovation Award
- Future Leader Award
- Jack Libbert Memorial Service Member of the Year

Meetings/Conferences:
- Canadian Association of Fairs & Exhibitions Annual Convention 2018, November, 2018, Banff, AB
Scope: National

Publications:
- Canadian Fair & Exhibition National Industry Directory [a publication of the Canadian Association of Fairs & Exhibitions]
Frequency: Annually
Profile: Listings of CAFE members & fair dates
- Canadian Fair News [a publication of the Canadian Association of Fairs & Exhibitions]
Frequency: Quarterly
Profile: Industry information including agricultural issues, government programs & regulations, trends, & association programs

Canadian Association of Family Enterprise *See* Family Enterprise Xchange

Canadian Association of Family Resource Programs / Association canadienne des programmes de ressources pour la famille
#149, 150 Isabella St., Ottawa ON K1S 1V7
Tel: 613-237-7667; *Fax:* 613-237-8515
Toll-Free: 866-637-7226
Other Communication: www.parentsmatter.ca
info@frp.ca
www.frp.ca
www.facebook.com/frpcanada
twitter.com/frpcanada
www.youtube.com/user/FRPCanada
Also Known As: FRP Canada
Previous Name: Canadian Association of Toy Libraries
Overview: A medium-sized national charitable organization founded in 1976
Mission: To promote the well-being of families, through provision of leadership, consultation, & resources to organizations which care for children & support families; To act as the national voice for family resource programs; To advance social policy, research, resource development, & training for those who support the capacity of families to raise their children
Member of: National Alliance for Children & Youth
Finances: *Funding Sources:* Donations; Membership fees; Grants
Staff Member(s): 3
Membership: 500+ organizations; *Fees:* Schedule available; *Member Profile:* Canadian community-based family resource programs
Activities: Offering training in areas such as child development, literacy, & early learning; Researching topics, such as family development, to assist family resource programs; Providing a network for family resource programs; Promoting family support programs to communities; Publishing numerous resources, such as newcomer resources; *Awareness Events:* National Family Week
Chief Officer(s):
Kelly Stone, Executive Director
kellystone@frp.ca

Meetings/Conferences:
- Family Resource Program Conference 2019, 2019
Scope: National
Description: A biennial conference, presenting a keynote speaker, a panel discussion, workshops, & exhibits

Publications:
- Canadian Association of Family Resource Programs Annual Report
Type: Yearbook; *Frequency:* Annually
- Discovering Our Capacities
Type: Study; *Editor:* Deborah Sullivan; *Price:* $12 members; $15 non-members
Profile: The philosophies & perspectives of informal community support systems & more formal service delivery systems
- The Evaluation of Family Resource Programs: Challenges & Promising Approaches
Editor: Peter Gabor; *Price:* $15 members; $18 non-members
Profile: Ideas to improve evaluation of family resource programs
- e-Valuation: Building Evaluation Capacity in the Family Resource Sector
Type: Report; *Editor:* Peter Gabor; *Price:* $15 members; $18 non-members
Profile: A detailed guide to employing the evaluation system & tools developed for family resource programs
- Finding Our Way: A Participatory Evaluation Method for Family Resource Programs
Type: Manual; *Number of Pages:* 200; *Editor:* Diana Ellis; *Price:* $28 members; $32non-members
Profile: A guide for family resource programs, featuring a glossary, samply tools, & an annotated bibliography
- FRP Canada Member Directory [a publication of the Canadian Association of Family Resource Programs]
Type: Directory
Profile: A listing of more than 500 family resource programs throughout Canada, such as Ontario Early Years Centres & CertifiedCanadian Family Educators
- Improving Facilities: Innovative Approaches for Community Programs
Type: Guide; *Editor:* Patrick Chen; Janice MacAulay; *Price:* $24 members; $28 non-members
Profile: Tips to improve facilities, including checklists, forms, & a bibliography
- Making Choices: Parenting Program Inventory
Price: $20 members; $25 non-members
Profile: Information for practitioners & parents
- Responsibility & Accountability: What Community-Based Programs Need to Know
Type: Book; *Number of Pages:* 64; *Price:* $15 members; $18 non-members
Profile: Liability for community organizations
- Supporting Fathers
Type: Handbook; *Editor:* B. Beauregard; F. Brown; K. Kidder; *Price:* $22 members; $27 non-members
Profile: A guide for program staff to improve their programs for fathers
- Synergy: Integrated Approaches in Family Support
Type: Report; *Price:* $27 members; $32 non-members
Profile: Experiences surrounding the provision of comprehensive services for families in Canada
- Tensions & Possibilities: Forging Better Links Between Family Resource Programs & Child Welfare
Type: Report; *Number of Pages:* 104; *Editor:* Janice MacAulay; *Price:* $20 members; $25 non-members
Profile: Practices for family resource programs in relation to child welfare issues, featuring charts & checklists
- Weaving Literacy into Family & Community Life
Editor: Suzanne Smythe; Lee Weinstein; *Price:* $25 members; $30 non-members
Profile: A resource featuring the following booklets: Book 1-Literacy in our Lives; Book 2-Creating Learning Environments for Children; Book 3-Community-BasedFamily Literacy Partnerships - 3 Case Studies; Book 4-Literacy Initiatives in Family Resource Programs; & Book 5: A Literacy Workers' Guide to FRPs
- Working With Parent Groups: A Handbook for Facilitators
Type: Handbook; *Editor:* Betsy Mann; *Price:* $25 members; $29 non-members
Profile: Ideas & a list of resources for strengthening parents' ability to fill their role

Canadian Association of Farm Advisors (CAFA)
PO Box 270, Seven Sisters Falls MB R0E 1Y0
Tel: 204-348-3578
Toll-Free: 877-474-2871
Other Communication: Cell Phone Contact: 204-340-2500
info@cafanet.com
www.cafanet.com
www.linkedin.com/groups/3443736
www.facebook.com/FarmAdvisors
twitter.com/CAFANET
Overview: A medium-sized national organization founded in 2001
Mission: To assist farm producers & agribusinesses by improving the advice provided to them; to improve the education & professionalism of farm advisors; to represent farm advisors on issues of concern
Finances: *Funding Sources:* Sponsorships
Staff Member(s): 1
Membership: *Fees:* $385 regular; $130 associate; $100 student; *Member Profile:* Agribusinesses; Agricultural economists; Agrologists; Agronomists; Farm producers; Educators; Appraisers; Bankers, accountants, commodity traders, financial planners, trust officers, & insurance agents; Lawyers; Consultants; Marketing representatives; Media members; & Veterinarians
Activities: Increasing the skills & knowledge of farm advisors; Providing better access to farm advice; Offering networking opportunities; *Awareness Events:* Regional Conferences; *Speaker Service:* Yes; *Library:* CAFA Library
Chief Officer(s):
Chris Corbett, Chair
Liz Robertson, Executive Director

Meetings/Conferences:
- Canadian Association of Farm Advisors 2018 Conference, 2018
Scope: National

Publications:
- Cultivating Business [a publication of the Canadian Association of Farm Advisors]
Type: Magazine; *Frequency:* Annually; *Accepts Advertising*
Profile: CAFA news & events from across Canada for farmers & their advisors

Canadian Association of Film Distributors & Exporters (CAFDE) / Association canadienne des distributeurs et exportateurs de films (ACDEF)
#1605, 85 Albert St., Ottawa ON K1P 6A4
Tel: 613-238-3557
info@CAFDE.ca
cafde.ca
Previous Name: National Association of Canadian Film & Video Distributors
Overview: A medium-sized national organization founded in 1991
Mission: To foster & promote the health of the Canadian motion picture industry by strengthening the Canadian owned & controlled distribution/export sector
Affiliation(s): Association des producteurs de films et de television du Québec
Finances: *Funding Sources:* Membership dues
Membership: 9; *Member Profile:* Canadian owned & controlled film & television distributors; *Committees:* Copyright; Inter-Provincial Restrictions; Classification & Censorship; Theatrical; Home Video; Television & Airlines; Cable Fund; Export Issues; Festivals
Chief Officer(s):
Hussain Amarshi, President

Canadian Association of Financial Institutions in Insurance (CAFII) / Association canadienne des institutions financières en assurance (ACIFA)
#255, 55 St. Clair Ave. West, Toronto ON M4V 2Y7
Tel: 416-494-9224; *Fax:* 416-967-6320
info@cafii.com
www.cafii.com
Overview: A small national organization founded in 1997
Mission: To develop an efficient & effective, open & flexible insurance marketplace; to provide a voice for financial institutions that sell insurance through a range of distribution methods

Finances: *Funding Sources:* Annual fees of members
Membership: *Member Profile:* Organizations that sell insurance through a variety of methods, such as agents & brokers, travel agents, call centres, direct mail, DTIs, & the Internet; Organizations that sell insurance in all major lines of business
Activities: Working with governments & regulators to develop a legislative & regulatory framework for the insurance sector; Monitoring, analyzing, & offering information & advice to members; Communicating with consumers & the media; Supporting training & professional development; Researching to support association objectives
Chief Officer(s):
Brendan Wycks, Executive Director
Publications:
• CAFII [Canadian Association of Financial Institutions in Insurance] Monthly Newsletter
Type: Newsletter; *Frequency:* Monthly; *Editor:* Lawrie Savage & Associates
Profile: Updates for CAFII members
• Regulatory Updates [a publication of the Canadian Association of Financial Institutions in Insurance]
Type: Newsletter; *Frequency:* Monthly
Profile: Information for CAFII members

Canadian Association of Fire Chiefs (CAFC) / Association canadienne des chefs de pompiers (ACCP)
#702, 280 Albert St., Ottawa ON K1P 5G8
Tel: 613-270-9138
Toll-Free: 800-775-5189
www.cafc.ca
www.linkedin.com/in/canadian-association-of-fire-chiefs-82ba052a
twitter.com/cafc2
Overview: A medium-sized national organization
Mission: To lead & represent the Canadian Fire Service on public safety issues with the vision of being nationally recognized as the fire service voice of authority
Affiliation(s): International Association of Fire Chiefs
Membership: 1,000; *Fees:* $190 + GST
Activities: *Rents Mailing List:* Yes; *Library:* Fire Services Resource Centre; Open to public
Chief Officer(s):
Robert Simonds, President
Pierre Voisine, Secretary
Lee Grant, Treasurer
Meetings/Conferences:
• Canadian Association of Fire Chiefs Fire-Rescue Canada 2018, September, 2018, Ottawa, ON
Scope: National
Description: Speaker presentations, seminars, & workshops for the fire & emergency services community from across Canada & the United States
Contact Information: Director, Events & Operations: Vicky Constantineau, E-mail: vconstantineau@cafc.ca
Publications:
• Canadian Association of Fire Chiefs Directory of Members
Type: Directory; *Frequency:* Annually
Profile: Includes CAFC leadership listings & updated bylaws
• Fire Chief Magazine
Type: Magazine; *Frequency:* Quarterly
Profile: Important issues about fire services

The Canadian Association of Fitness Professionals / Association canadienne des professionnels en conditionnement physique
#110, 225 Select Ave., Toronto ON M1X 0B5
Tel: 416-493-3515; *Fax:* 416-493-1756
Toll-Free: 800-667-5622
info@canfitpro.com
www.canfitpro.com
www.linkedin.com/groups?gid=1773770&trk=hb_side_g
www.facebook.com/canfitpro
twitter.com/canfitpro
www.youtube.com/user/canfitpro/featured
Also Known As: Can-Fit-Pro
Overview: A medium-sized national licensing organization founded in 1993
Mission: Can-Fit-Pro takes today's fitness professionals' challenges & creates tomorrow's solutions through ongoing relative knowledge & personal enrichment
Member of: National Fitness Leadership Advisory Committee
Finances: *Annual Operating Budget:* $1.5 Million-$3 Million; *Funding Sources:* Sponsorship; private; membership dues; courses
Staff Member(s): 10; 400 volunteer(s)
Membership: 30,000; *Member Profile:* Interest in fitness industry
Activities: Certification & standards for fitness instructors & personal trainers, who work at private & public fitness facilities; continuing education; events & six conferences a year
Chief Officer(s):
Maureen Hagan, Executive Director
Kathy Ash, Contact, Administration

Canadian Association of Food Banks *See* Food Banks Canada

Canadian Association of Foodservice Professionals (CAFP) / Association canadienne des professionnels des services alimentaires
CAFP National Office, #130, 10691 Shellbridge Way, Richmond BC V6X 2W8
Tel: 604-248-0215; *Fax:* 604-270-3644
Toll-Free: 877-599-2237
national@cafp.ca
www.cafp.ca
twitter.com/wearecafp
Previous Name: Canadian Food Service Executives Association
Overview: A large national organization founded in 1901
Mission: To enhance the prestige of the food service profession through improving standards of service; To promote education in the industry & to provide increased opportunity for youth to train for the food service profession; To promote research in food service & nutrition; To work for food service regulation & legislation in the public interest; To promote through good fellowship & personal association new opportunities for increased management efficiency & exchange of professional information
Staff Member(s): 1; 22 volunteer(s)
Membership: 1,050
Chief Officer(s):
Marc Haine, President
president@cafp.ca
Dwayne Botchar, Vice-President, Membership
membership@cafp.ca
Lorne Deutsch, Vice-President, National Communications
communications@cafp.ca
Meetings/Conferences:
• 2018 Canadian Association of Foodservice Professionals National Conference, May, 2018, Pacific Gateway Hotel, Vancouver, BC
Scope: National
Publications:
• Food Bites [a publication of the Canadian Association of Foodservice Professionals]
Type: Newsletter
• Quick Bites [a publication of the Canadian Association of Foodservice Professionals]
Type: Newsletter

Calgary Branch
Chief Officer(s):
Kim Flamand, President
Helen Scott, National Director
Maggie da Silva Porter, Secretary
Division de Montréal
Chief Officer(s):
Béatrice Martin, Présidente
beatrice.martin@berthelet.com
Edmonton Branch
CAFPedmonton@gmail.com
Chief Officer(s):
Marc Haine, President
Darrell Lindstrom, CFE, National Director
Halifax/Dartmouth Branch
Chief Officer(s):
Lisa Slauenwhite, President
Delores Smith, CFE, National Director/Vice-President, Public Relations & Recruitment
dasmith@accesswave.ca
London Branch
Chief Officer(s):
Lin Yuan-Su, President
0610@hotmail.com
Tammy Latta, Vice-President, Membership
tlatta@nms.on.ca
New Brunswick Branch
Chief Officer(s):
Jeff Williams, President
Esther Archibald, CFE, National Director
Northumberland Branch
Chief Officer(s):
David Breen, President
breen.dave@hfx.sysco.ca
Ottawa Branch
Chief Officer(s):
Frances Furmankiewicz, President
Leesa Franklin, CFE, National Director/Past President
Chantal Cheff, Vice-President, Membership
chantal.cheff@leisureworld.ca
Toronto Branch
toronto@cafp.com
Chief Officer(s):
Nancy Hewittlo, President
Rosie Maclean, National Director/Sargeant-at-Arms
Vancouver Branch
Chief Officer(s):
Simon Tse, President
tosimontse@gmail.com
Susan Cox, National Director/Past President
Lezlie Smith, Vice-President, Membership
lezlie.smith@telus.net

Canadian Association of Foot Care Nurses (CAFCN)
c/o Pat MacDonald, President, 110 Linden Park Bay, Winnipeg MB R2R 1Y3
secretary@cafcn.ca
www.cafcn.ca
Previous Name: Foot Care Canada
Overview: A large national organization founded in 2005
Mission: To advance the practice of foot care through a collaborative and networking process for all individuals providing foot care.
Membership: *Fees:* $50 per year; *Member Profile:* Nurses registered in Canada, who specialize in foot care; *Committees:* Education; Policy; Conference; Website; Newsletter; Nominations; Public Relations; Bylaw
Chief Officer(s):
Pat MacDonald, President
president@cafcn.ca
Meetings/Conferences:
• The 9th Canadian Association of Foot Care Nurses AGM & Conference 2018, May, 2018, DoubleTree by Hilton Hotel & Conference Centre, Regina, SK

Canadian Association of Former Parliamentarians (CAFP) / L'Association canadienne des ex-parlementaires (ACEP)
House of Commons, PO Box 1, 131 Queen St., Ottawa ON K1A 0A6
Tel: 613-947-1690; *Fax:* 613-947-1764
Toll-Free: 888-567-4764
exparl@parl.gc.ca
www.exparl.ca
Overview: A small national organization founded in 1987
Mission: To provide support to the government, fostering good relations between Senate, House of Commons & former parliamentarians; to raise funds to promote the knowledge, education & experience of the principles & operation of democratic & parliamentary procedure.
Finances: *Funding Sources:* Membership dues; grant
Staff Member(s): 3
Membership: *Fees:* $125; *Member Profile:* Former Senators & Members of the House of Commons
Chief Officer(s):
Andy Mitchell, President
Publications:
• Beyond the Hill
Type: Magazine; *Frequency:* Quarterly; *Editor:* Dorothy Dobbie

Canadian Association of Foundations of Education (CAFE) / Association canadienne des fondements de l'éducation (ACFE)
c/o Canadian Society for the Study of Education, #204, 260 Dalhousie St., Ottawa ON K1N 7E4
Tel: 613-241-0018; *Fax:* 613-241-0019
cafe.acefe@gmail.com
www.cafe-acefe.com
Overview: A medium-sized national organization founded in 1971 overseen by Canadian Society for the Study of Education
Mission: To provide a forum for discussing the contribution of the social sciences & humanities (eg. history of education, philosophy of education, sociology of education) to educational theory, research & practice
Member of: Canadian Society for the Study of Education

Canadian Associations / Canadian Association of Freediving & Apnea (CAFA)

Finances: *Annual Operating Budget:* Less than $50,000; *Funding Sources:* Membership fees
Membership: 100-499; *Fees:* $10 regular & international; $5 student/retired/low income; *Member Profile:* Professors & graduate students in education foundations; *Committees:* Executive; Emerging Scholars; Special Interest Group
Chief Officer(s):
Kurt Clausen, President
Awards:
• CAFE Publication Award
• Outstanding Dissertation/Thesis Recognition Award
• Outstanding Advising & Mentoring Award
• Distinguished Service Award
Publications:
• CAFE [Canadian Association of Foundations of Education] Newsletter
Type: Newsletter; *Frequency:* Quarterly

Canadian Association of Freediving & Apnea (CAFA)
19640 - 34A Ave., Lengley BC V3A 7W6
Other Communication: Board, E-mail:
board@freedivecanada.com
www.freedivecanada.com
Overview: A small national organization
Mission: To further the sport of freediving in Canada & abroad.
Membership: *Fees:* $25 full; $50 associate
Chief Officer(s):
Andrew Hogan, President
president@freedivecanada.com

Canadian Association of Gastroenterology / Association canadienne de gastroentérologie
#224, 1540 Cornwall Rd., Oakville ON L6J 7W5
Tel: 905-829-2504; *Fax:* 905-829-0242
Toll-Free: 888-780-0007
general@cag-acg.org
www.cag-acg.org
www.linkedin.com/company/canadian-association-of-gastroenterology
www.facebook.com/canadianassociationofgastroenterology
twitter.com/CanGastroAssn
Overview: A small national organization founded in 1962
Mission: To support & engage in the study of gastroenterology; To promote patient care, research, teaching & professional development in the field; To promote & maintain the highest ethical standards of practice
Affiliation(s): Canadian Medical Association; World Organization of Gastroenterology
Staff Member(s): 6
Membership: 1,100; *Fees:* schedule; *Member Profile:* Doctors; scientists; health care providers; *Committees:* Administrative Affairs; Education Affairs; Clinical Affiars; Research Affairs; Nominations; Operations
Chief Officer(s):
Paul Sinclair, Executive Director
Sandra Daniels, Senior Manager
Cathy Mancini, Office Administrator
Meetings/Conferences:
• Canadian Digestive Diseases Week: Canadian Association of Gastroenterology Annual Scientific Conference 2018, February, 2018, Toronto, ON
Scope: National
• Canadian Digestive Diseases Week: Canadian Association of Gastroenterology Annual Scientific Conference 2019, February, 2019, Banff, AB
Scope: National
• Canadian Digestive Diseases Week: Canadian Association of Gastroenterology Annual Scientific Conference 2020, February, 2020, Montréal, QC
Scope: National
• Canadian Digestive Diseases Week: Canadian Association of Gastroenterology Annual Scientific Conference 2021, February, 2021, Banff, AB
Scope: National

Canadian Association of General Surgeons (CAGS) / Association canadienne des chirurgiens généraux (ACCG)
PO Box 1428, Stn. B, Ottawa ON K1P 5R4
Tel: 613-882-6510
cags@cags-accg.ca
www.cags-accg.ca
www.facebook.com/220880261312881
twitter.com/CAGS_ACCG

Overview: A medium-sized national charitable organization founded in 1977
Mission: To assist all general surgeons with continuing education; facilitate & promote surgical research; develop policies & new ideas in the areas of clinical care, education & research
Affiliation(s): Canadian Medical Association; Royal College of Physicians & Surgeons of Canada
Finances: *Funding Sources:* Membership fees; Corporate funding
Staff Member(s): 1
Membership: *Fees:* $350 full; $35 associate; $10 medical student; $0 senior/retired; *Member Profile:* General surgeons; *Committees:* Clinical Practice; Continuing Professional Development; Acute Care; Endoscopic & Larascopic Surgery; Endocrine, Head & Neck; International Surgery; Membership; Professionalism; Oncology; Post-Graduate Education; Program; Research; Hepatobiliary; Executive
Chief Officer(s):
Debrah Wirtzfeld, President
Jasmin Lidington, Executive Director
jlidington@cags-accg.ca
Meetings/Conferences:
• 2018 Canadian Surgery Forum, September, 2018, Delta Hotel St. John's & The St. John's Convention Centre, St. John's, NL
Scope: National
Contact Information: URL: www.canadiansurgeryforum.com
Publications:
• CAGS [Canadian Association of General Surgeons] Newsletter
Type: Newsletter
Profile: Association news, conference highlights, & research

Canadian Association of Genetic Counsellors (CAGC) / Association Canadienne des conseillers en génétique (ACCG)
PO Box 52083, Oakville ON L6J 7N5
Tel: 905-847-1363; *Fax:* 905-847-3855
Other Communication: president@cagc-accg.ca
CAGCOffice@cagc-accg.ca
www.cagc-accg.ca
Overview: A small national organization
Mission: To promote high standards of practice; To encourage professional growth; To increase public awareness of the profession; To offer certification in genetic counselling
Membership: 1-99; *Fees:* $100 full, associate; $50 student; *Member Profile:* Genetic counsellors
Meetings/Conferences:
• Canadian Association of Genetic Counsellors 2018 Annual Education Conference, 2018
Scope: National

Canadian Association of Geographers (CAG) / Association canadienne des géographes
Department of Geography, McGill University, #425, 805, rue Sherbrooke ouest, Montréal QC H3A 2K6
Tel: 514-398-4946; *Fax:* 514-398-7437
valerie.shoffey@cag-acg.ca
www.cag-acg.ca
Overview: A medium-sized national organization founded in 1951
Mission: To promote the discipline of geography in Canada & internationally
Member of: Humanities & Social Science Federation of Canada; Canadian Federation of Earth Sciences; International Geographical Union
Affiliation(s): L'l'association professionelle des géographes du Québec; Association of American Geographers; Institute of British Geographers
Membership: *Member Profile:* Practicing geographers from the public & private sectors & universities across Canada & internationally; Students
Activities: Promoting geographic education; Disseminating geographic research; Collaborating with other national & international geographic organizations
Chief Officer(s):
Anne Godlewska, President
anne.godlewska@queensu.ca
Mary-Louise Byrne, Secretary-Treasurer
mlbyrne@wlu.ca
Ian MacLachlan, Editor, The Canadian Geographer
TCG.editor@cag-acg.ca
Valerie Shoffey, Editor, The CAG Newsletter
valerie.shoffey@cag-acg.ca
Meetings/Conferences:
• Canadian Association of Geographers 2018 Annual Meeting, August, 2018, Québec City Convention Centre, Québec, QC
Scope: National
Publications:
• The CAG [Canadian Association of Geographers] Newsletter
Type: Newsletter; *Frequency:* Quarterly; *Editor:* Valerie Shoffey; *Price:* Free with membership in the Canadian Association of Geographers
Profile: News about members, employment opportunities & announcements, technical features, Statistics Canada news, research highlights, & studentinformation
• The CAG [Canadian Association of Geographers] Annual Directory
Type: Directory; *Frequency:* Annually; *Editor:* Kim Falcigno (kimfalcigno@shaw.ca); *Price:* Free with membership in the Canadian Association of Geographers
Profile: Listings of CAG members, academic staff, research activities, & current publications of Canadian university geographydepartments & government agencies
• The Canadian Geographer (TCG) / Le Géographe canadien (LGC)
Type: Journal; *Frequency:* Quarterly; *Editor:* Ian MacLachlan; *Price:* Free with membership in theCanadian Association of Geographers
Profile: Philosophical, theoretical, & methodological subjects of interest to scholars & geographers in Canada & worldwide

Atlantic Division (ACAG)
c/o James Boxall, GIS Centre, Killam Library, Dalhousie University, 6225 University Ave., Halifax NS B3H 4H8
community.smu.ca/acag
Mission: To promote the study, research, & application of geography throughout the Atlantic provinces; To serve geographers who reside in Newfoundland & Labrador, Prince Edward Island, Nova Scotia, & New Brunswick
Chief Officer(s):
Colin Laroque, President
claroque@mta.ca
James Boxall, Secretary-Treasurer
James.Boxall@Dal.ca
• Canadian Association of Geographers, Atlantic Division Annual Report
Type: Yearbook; *Frequency:* Annually

Ontario Division (CAGONT)
c/o Wayne Forsythe, Dept. of Geography, Ryerson University, Toronto ON M5B 2K3
www.geography.ryerson.ca/cagont
Mission: To promote the study, teaching, research, & application of geography, especially in Ontario
Chief Officer(s):
Wayne Forsythe, President, 416-979-5000 Ext. 7141
forsythe@geography.ryerson.ca
Peter Kedron, Vice-President, 416-979-5000 Ext. 7147
pkedron@ryerson.ca

Prairie Division (PCAG)
c/o D. Eberts, J.R. Brodie Science Ctr., Dept of Geography, Brandon U., #4-09, 270 - 18th St., Brandon MB R7A 6A9
pcag.uwinnipeg.ca
Mission: To encourage geographic study, research, & applications in Saskatchewan, Manitoba, & North Dakota
Chief Officer(s):
Dirk de Boer, President
dirk.deboer@usask.ca
Derrek Eberts, Secretary-Treasurer
ebertsd@BrandonU.ca
• Prairie Perspectives: Geographical Essays
Type: Yearbook; *Frequency:* Annually
Profile: Proceedings of the prairie division's annual meeting

Western Division (WDCAG)
c/o H. Jiskoot, Water & Environmental Science Bldg., U. of Lethbridge, 4401 University Dr., Lethbridge AB T1K 3M4
www.geog.uvic.ca/dept/wcag
Mission: To promote geographic education & research in Alberta, British Columbia, Yukon, & the Northwest Territories
Theresa Garvin, President
Theresa.Garvin@ualberta.ca
Craig Coburn, Secretary-Treasurer
hester.jiskoot@uleth.ca
• Canadian Association of Geographers Western Division Newsletter
Type: Newsletter; *Frequency:* Semiannually; *Editor:* C. Beaney (claire.beaney@ufv.ca)
Profile: Updates distributed to members
• Occasional Papers in Geography of the Canadian Assn of Geographers, Western Division: Proceedings of the Annual Conference
Type: Yearbook; *Frequency:* Annually

• Western Geography
Type: Journal; *Editor:* Neil Hanlon (hanlon@unbc.ca)
Profile: Original scholarly work on geographical themes, focussing on western Canada & its surrounding regions

Canadian Association of Geophysical Contractors (CAGC)
#1045, 1015 - 4 St. SW, Calgary AB T2R 1J4
Tel: 403-265-0045; *Fax:* 403-265-0025
info@cagc.ca
www.cagc.ca
www.linkedin.com/groups?gid=3696242
www.facebook.com/166335486730528
Overview: A small national organization founded in 1977
Mission: To act as the voice of business in the Canadian seismic industry; To promote the Canadian geophysical industry
Membership: 600; *Committees:* Source Magazine; Chainsaw Certification; Buried Facilities; Blasters Harmonization; Seismic Blasters; Seismic Permit Agent
Activities: Working with governments, stakeholders, & communities; Promoting hight ethical standards throughout the geophysical industry; Providing health & safety training
Chief Officer(s):
Cam Moore, Chair
cam@cossackland.ca
Mike Doyle, President
mjd@cagc.ca
Publications:
• The Source: The Voice of Business in the Canadian Seismic Industry
Type: Magazine; *Frequency:* Quarterly
Profile: Canadian Association of Geophysical Contractors membership news, awards, & upcoming events

Canadian Association of Gift Planners (CAGP) / Association canadienne des professionnels en dons planifiés (ACPDP)
#201, 1188 Wellington St. West, Ottawa ON K1Y 2Z5
Tel: 613-232-7991; *Fax:* 613-232-7286
Toll-Free: 888-430-9494
communications@cagp-acpdp.org
www.cagp-acpdp.org
twitter.com/CAGP_ACPDP
Overview: A medium-sized national organization founded in 1992
Mission: To advance the work of professionals in gift planning; To ensure professionals adhere to the CAGP-ACPDP code of ethics; To advocate for a favourable legislative regime for philanthropy
Finances: *Funding Sources:* Membership fees; Sponsorships
Membership: 1,350; *Fees:* $290 individual; $85 student; *Member Profile:* Individuals involved in the gift planning process of registered charitable organizations or foundations, as well as fundraising consultants, lawyers, accountants, financial planners, life insurance representatives, trust officers, & other professionals
Activities: Fostering the development & growth of gift planning; Developing strategic partnerships; Creating awareness of charitable giving; Providing education opportunities; Offering networking opportunities; *Library*
Chief Officer(s):
Ruth MacKenzie, Executive Director, 613-232-7991 Ext. 223
rmackenzie@cagp-acpdp.org
Nancy Shore, Coordinator, Membership, 613-232-7991 Ext. 227
nshore@cagp-acpdp.org
Jean-Marie Niangoran, Coordinator, Accounting & Finance, 613-232-7991 Ext. 221
jmniangoran@cagp-acpdp.org
Awards:
• Friend of CAGP / Ami de l'ACPDP
Individuals & organizations which exemplify the spirit & vision of CAGP *Contact:* Coordinator, Programs: Sharyon Smith, E-mail: education@cagp-acpdp.org
Meetings/Conferences:
• 25th Annual Canadian Association of Gift Planners 2018 National Conference, April, 2018, Winnipeg, MB
Scope: National
Description: An annual spring meeting, featuring educational workshops, experienced speakers, & exhibits
Contact Information: www.cagpconference.org
Publications:
• The Planner
Type: Newsletter
Profile: CAGP-ACPDP news, statistics, education updates, & career information

Canadian Association of Hepatology Nurses (CAHN) / Association canadienne des infirmières et infirmiers en hépatologie
c/o Lori Lee Walston, 506 Fader St., New Westminster BC V3L 3T5
www.cahn.ca
Overview: A small national organization
Mission: To represent & support hepatology nurses throughout Canada; To encourage liver health & to prevent illness; To improve the standards of practice in hepatology nursing; To promote the excellent care of persons with liver related health problems & disorders
Affiliation(s): Canadian Nurses Association (CNA); Canadian Association for the Study of Liver Disease (CASL); Canadian Liver Foundation (CLF)
Membership: *Member Profile:* Nurses in Canada who practice hepatology; *Committees:* Executive; Awards; Communications; Conference Planning; Education; Standards & Competencies
Activities: Establishing Hepatology Nursing Standards of Practice; Promoting research in hepatology nursing; Sharing information about hepatology; Providing continuing education for professionals in hepatology & clients; Engaging in advocacy activities; Offering networking opportunities
Chief Officer(s):
Donna Zukowski, President
president@cahn.ca
Maria Schmidt, Secretary
Lori Lee Walston, Treasurer
treasurer@cahn.ca
Meetings/Conferences:
• Canadian Association of Hepatology Nurses 2018 Annual General Meeting, February, 2018, InterContinental Hotel, Toronto, ON
Scope: National
Publications:
• Canadian Association of Hepatology Nurses Newsletter
Type: Newsletter; *Frequency:* Quarterly
Profile: Updates on issues affecting hepatology nurses, forthcoming educational opportunities, award information, & association membership news

Canadian Association of Heritage Professionals (CAPHC) / Association canadienne d'experts-conseils en patrimoine (ACECP)
190 Bronson Ave., Ottawa ON K1R 6H4
Tel: 613-569-7455
admin@cahp-acecp.ca
www.caphc.ca
www.facebook.com/121466461265655
Previous Name: Association of Heritage Consultants
Overview: A medium-sized national organization founded in 1987
Mission: To represent & further the professional interests of heritage consultants active in both the private & public sectors; To establish & maintain principles & standards of practice for heritage consultants; To enhance awareness & appreciation of heritage resources, & the contribution of heritage consultants; To foster communication among private practitioners, public agencies, & the public at large in matters related to heritage conservation
Affiliation(s): ICOMOS International (International Council on Monuments & Sites); ICOMOS Canada - English-Speaking Committee
Membership: *Fees:* $25 student; $50 subscriber/retired; $180 intern; $290 professional; *Member Profile:* Practitioners active in either private or public sector in fields allied to heritage conservation; *Committees:* Advocacy; Annual General Meeting & Nominations; Business Development; Communications; Conference & Awards; Corporate Planning; Education; Ethics & Conduct; Governance; Government Liaison; Membership
Activities: Offering the following range of services by members: archaeology, anthropology, conservation, curation, design & planning, education, heritage administration, landscape design, photography, illustration & recording, & restoration
Chief Officer(s):
Jill Taylor, President
Julie Harris, Secretary
Publications:
• Canadian Association of Professional Heritage Consultants Forum
Type: Newsletter; *Accepts Advertising*
Profile: Articles on conservation, CAPHC / ACECP news & events

• CAPHC [Canadian Association of Professional Heritage Consultants] Membership Directory
Type: Directory; *Accepts Advertising*

Canadian Association of Home & Property Inspectors (CAHPI) / Association canadienne des inspecteurs de biens immobiliers
PO Box 76065, Stn. Morgan's Grant, 832 March Rd., Ottawa ON K2W 0E1
Tel: 613-832-3536
Toll-Free: 888-748-2244
info@cahpi.ca
www.cahpi.ca
www.facebook.com/cahpi.ca
Previous Name: Canadian Association of Home Inspectors
Overview: A small national organization founded in 1982
Mission: To promote & enhance the professionalism & competency of professional home & property inspectors
Affiliation(s): American Association of Home Inspectors (ASHI)
Finances: *Annual Operating Budget:* $100,000-$250,000
Staff Member(s): 1; 15 volunteer(s)
Membership: 1,000; *Fees:* $175; *Committees:* By-law & Policy; Executive; Public Relations; Research & Development
Activities: Establishing & maintaining a national standard for the education, certification, & professional practice of Canadian home & property inspectors; Enabling transferability of certification within all Canadian home & property inspector provincial organizations; Offering evaluation & public awareness campaigns for consumer protection; Developing programs for home & property inspectors & associations; Organizing National Conference; *Speaker Service:* Yes
Chief Officer(s):
Graham Clarke, President
president@cahpi.ca
Brian Hutchinson, Vice-President, 902-452-8858
vicepresident@cahpi.ca
Sharry Featherston, Executive Director
sharry@cahpi.ca
Awards:
• Stephen Greenford Award
Presented to an individual who has furthered the development of the Home Inspection profession nationally
• President's Award
Presented to an individual who has furthered the development of the Home Inspection profession in his/her Provincial/Regional Association
• Michael Ludolph Memorial Award
• Tropea / Hipperson Memorial Award
Meetings/Conferences:
• Canadian Association of Home & Property Inspectors 2018 National Conference, 2018
Scope: National
Publications:
• The Canadian Home Inspector Magazine
Type: Magazine; *Frequency:* Biannually; *Accepts Advertising*; *Editor:* Sharry Featherston; *Price:* Free with CAHPI membership
Profile: Information on the home inspection profession for CAHPI provincial & regional members

Association des inspecteurs en bâtiments du Québec (AIBQ)
#204, 7811, boul Louis H. Lafontaine, Montréal QC H1K 4E4
Tél: 514-352-2427; *Téléc:* 514-355-8248
Ligne sans frais: 877-644-2427
www.aibq.qc.ca
www.facebook.com/AIBQ.QC.CA
Mission: To ensure a proper control of the building inspection practice in Québec
Chief Officer(s):
Pascal Parent, Président

Atlantic Chapter
info@cahpi-atl.com
www.cahpi-atl.com
Mission: To define the qualifications & performance requirements of Registered Home Inspectors; To regulate members; To grant the designation, Registered Home Inspector, to qualified practitioners in Nova Scotia, New Brunswick, Newfoundland, & Price Edward Island
Chief Officer(s):
Julie Peck, Registrar

Manitoba Chapter
PO Box 66024, Winnipeg MB R3K 2E7
info@cahpi.mb.ca
www.cahpi.mb.ca

Mission: To promote the professional pre-purchase home inspection industry in Manitoba; To provide continuing educational opportunities to member inspectors in Manitoba

Ontario Association of Home Inspectors (OAHI)
#205, 1515 Matheson Blvd., Mississauga ON L4W 2P5
Tel: 416-256-0960; *Fax:* 905-624-4360
Toll-Free: 888-744-6244
www.oahi.com
www.linkedin.com/groups/2398169
Mission: To enhance the technical skills & professional practice of home inspectors in Ontario; To educate & discipline in order to maintain high professional standards
Chief Officer(s):
Murray Parish, President

Saskatchewan Chapter
PO Box 20045, Stn. Cornwall Centre, Regina SK S4P 4J7
Toll-Free: 888-748-2244
www.cahpi-sk.ca
Mission: To maintain & regulate national standards in home inspections in Saskatchewan
Chief Officer(s):
Jim Nichols, Contact, Membership

Canadian Association of Home Inspectors *See* Canadian Association of Home & Property Inspectors

Canadian Association of Immersion Teachers *Voir* Association canadienne des professeurs d'immersion

Canadian Association of Immunohematologists *See* Canadian Society for Transfusion Medicine

Canadian Association of Importers & Exporters / Association canadienne des importateurs & exportateurs
PO Box 149, 777 Bay St., Toronto ON M5G 2C8
Tel: 416-595-5333
info@iecanada.com
www.iecanada.com
www.linkedin.com/groups/1853004
www.facebook.com/1638214366455924
twitter.com/iecanada
Also Known As: IE Canada
Previous Name: Canadian Importers Association Inc.
Overview: A large national organization founded in 1932
Mission: To be the voice of Canadian importers & exporters; To support Canadian importers & exporters so that they remain profitable & competitive in a global market
Finances: *Funding Sources:* Membership fees; Sponsorships
Membership: 4,000 trade professionals; *Fees:* $1395-$2795; *Member Profile:* Importers; Exporters; Distributors; Agents; *Committees:* Manufacturing, Retail & Distribution; Oil, Mining & Gas; Food
Activities: Providing information about Canadian customs & trade policy; Liaising with government
Chief Officer(s):
Joy Nott, CCS, P.Log, President
jnott@iecanada.com
Keith Mussar, VP, Regulatory Affairs & Co-Chair, Food Committee
kmussar@iecanada.com
Paulette Niedermier, Vice-President, Operations & Administration
James Sutton, Director, Advocacy
Andrea MacDonald, Director, Communications
amacdonald@iecanada.com
Awards:
• Trade Compliance Leadership Award
To recognize a Canadian customs compliance and trade professional who has been providing leadership, innovation and advocacy on behalf of their own company and other importers and exporters in Canada.
• Best Practices in Trade Compliance Processes Award
To recognize the corporate accomplishment of implementing new processes intended to improve trade efficiencies or trade compliance.
• Greening the Supply Chain Award
To recognize a Canadian company that has initiated, implemented and proven corporate commitment to the greening of the supply chain and reducing their carbon footprint.
• Beth Travis Memorial I.E. Canada Member of the Year Award
To recognize an outstanding I.E.Canada member who represents the spirit of the Association: to be the leading voice of the Canadian trade community and to represent and advocate on behalf of importers and exporters to influence change.

Meetings/Conferences:
• Canadian Association of Importers & Exporters 2018 Annual Conference, 2018
Scope: National
Publications:
• Canadian Association of Importers & Exporters Membership Directory
Type: Directory; *Price:* Free with membership in the Canadian Association of Importers & Exporters
Profile: A source for establishing contacts in international trade
• I.E. Now
Type: Newsletter; *Frequency:* Monthly; *Editor:* Andrea Macdonald; *Price:* Free with membership in the Canadian Association of Importers & Exporters
Profile: Articles about international trade & customs
• I.E. Today
Type: Newsletter; *Frequency:* Daily; *Accepts Advertising*; *Editor:* M. Weaver (mweaver@iecanada.com); *Price:* Free with membership in the Canadian Association of Importers & Exporters
Profile: News about trade & customs issues, plus activities of the Canadian Association of Importers & Exporters, including the presentation of awards, educational opportunities, &previews & reviews of conferences
• Importing into Canada
Type: Guide; *Price:* $49.95
Profile: Information about how to establish an importing business, including current rules & regulations for bringing goods into the country
• Mon I.E.
Type: Newsletter; *Frequency:* Monthly; *Editor:* C. Sivière (csiviere@iecanada.com); *Price:* Free with membership in the Canadian Association of Importers & Exporters
Profile: Customs & international trade articles

Canadian Association of Income Trusts Investors (CAITI) / Association canadienne d'investissement dans des fiducies de revenu
#1062, 1930 Yonge St., Toronto ON M4S 1Z4
contact@caiti.info
www.caiti.info
Overview: A small national organization
Mission: Mission is to preserve the viability and sustainability of the Canadian income trust market, for the benefit of Canadians saving for retirement now and in the future
Chief Officer(s):
Brent D. Fullard, President & CEO

Canadian Association of Independent Credit Counselling Agencies (CAICCA)
#306, 15225 - 104th Ave., Surrey BC V3R 6Y8
Tel: 604-588-9491; *Fax:* 604-588-9007
Toll-Free: 877-588-9491
info@caicca.org
www.caicca.ca
Overview: A small national organization
Mission: To maintain a Code of Ethics for the independent credit counselling industry; to liaise with appropriate provincial regulatory bodies; to promote & educate consumers & the credit granting industry on services provided by the association
Finances: *Annual Operating Budget:* $100,000-$250,000
Membership: 7; *Fees:* $100
Chief Officer(s):
Margaret Johnson, President

Canadian Association of Independent Life Brokerage Agencies (CAILBA)
#1300, 60 Adelaide St. East, Toronto ON M5C 3E4
Tel: 416-548-4223
info@caliba.com
www.cailba.com
www.linkedin.com/company-beta/10963663
Overview: A large national organization
Mission: To lobby provincial & federal governments on legislative issues affecting the life & health insurance brokerage industry; to provide a forum for networking & relationship building among members, insurance companies & industry vendors
Affiliation(s): The National Association of Independent Life Brokerage Agencies (NAILBA); IFB Independent Financial Brokers; Canadian Life and Health Insurance Association (CLHIA); Advocis, The Financial Advisors Association of Canada
Membership: 70+ member companies; *Fees:* $2,500 MGAs & Industry Affiliates; $3,125 Industry Suppliers & Solution Providors; *Member Profile:* Life & health insurance brokerage agencies; *Committees:* Technology; Compliance - Legislative Affairs; Compliance - Regulatory Affairs

Activities: Monthly Board Meetings; CAILBA Information Series (teleconferences)
Chief Officer(s):
Michael Williams, President
mwilliams@bfgon.com
Clementine Peacock, Executive Director
Andrew Harris, Administrator
Meetings/Conferences:
• CAILBA 2018 National Conference & AGM, May, 2018, Fairmont le Château Frontenac, Québec, QC
Scope: National

Canadian Association of Independent Living Centres *See* Independent Living Canada

Canadian Association of Independent Schools *See* Canadian Accredited Independent Schools

Canadian Association of Insolvency & Restructuring Professionals (CAIRP) / Association canadienne des professionnels de l'insolvabilité et de la réorganisation (ACPIR)
277 Wellington St. West, Toronto ON M5V 3H2
Tel: 416-204-3242; *Fax:* 416-204-3410
info@cairp.ca
www.cairp.ca
www.linkedin.com/company/3239103
www.facebook.com/CAIRP.ca
twitter.com/CAIRP_ACPIR
Previous Name: Canadian Insolvency Practitioners Association
Overview: A medium-sized national organization founded in 1979
Mission: To develop, educate, support & give value to members; To foster the provision of insolvency, business recovery service with integrity, objectivity & competence, in a manner that instils the highest degree of public trust; To advocate for a fair, transparent, & effective system of insolvency/business recovery administration throughout Canada
Member of: Insol International
Affiliation(s): The Canadian Institute of Chartered Accountants
Finances: *Funding Sources:* Membership dues
Staff Member(s): 9
Membership: 1,480; *Member Profile:* Completion of National Insolvency Qualification Program (NIQP) offered jointly by CAIRP & the Superintendent of Bankruptcy
Activities: Working with the federal government on joint committees concerning policy, legislation, education programs & Oral Boards for trustee licence candidates; Providing education programs; *Speaker Service:* Yes
Chief Officer(s):
Mark Yakabuski, President & COO
mark.yakabusk@cairp.ca
Bea Casey, Director, CAIRP Education Programs
bea.casey@cairp.ca
Ali R. Hemani, Director, Finance & Administration
ali.hemani@cairp.ca
Meetings/Conferences:
• 2018 Canadian Association of Insolvency & Restructuring Professionals Annual Conference, August, 2018, Charlottetown, PE
Scope: National
Description: Technical sessions plus networking opportunities & social events
Publications:
• Chair's Newsletter [a publication of the Canadian Association of Insolvency & Restructuring Professionals]
Type: Newsletter
Profile: CAIRP news
• Rebuilding Success [a publication of the Canadian Association of Insolvency & Restructuring Professionals]
Type: Magazine; *Frequency:* Semiannually; *Accepts Advertising*; *Editor:* Jon Waldman
Profile: CAIRP information, articles, & buyer's guide

Canadian Association of Insurance Women (CAIW) / Association canadienne des femmes d'assurance (ACFA)
c/o Sovereign General Insurance Co., 1718 Argyle St., 4th Fl., Halifax NS B3J 3N6
Tel: 902-492-4970; *Fax:* 902-492-0440
www.caiw-acfa.com
www.linkedin.com/groups/CAIW-ACFA-Canadian-Association-Insurance-4254216
Overview: A medium-sized national organization founded in 1966
Mission: To enhance the value of member associations
Finances: *Funding Sources:* Sponsorships

Activities: Providing education & networking opportunities
Chief Officer(s):
Laura Greening, President
laura.greening@sovgen.com
Cheryl Morton, Treasurer
cmortoncaiw@gmail.com

Canadian Association of Internes & Residents See Resident Doctors of Canada

Canadian Association of Internet Providers See Canadian Association of Wireless Internet Service Providers

Canadian Association of Interventional Cardiology (CAIC) / Association canadienne de cardiologie d'intervention
3, boul Lakeview, Beaconsfield QC H9W 4P8
Toll-Free: 877-990-9044
info@caic-acci.org
www.caic-acci.org
Overview: A small national organization
Mission: To advance the discipline, development, & implementation of interventional cardiology
Member of: Canadian Cardiology Society
Membership: 100+; *Member Profile:* Members Canadian Cardiovascular Society; Cardiologists who specialize in hemodynamic interventions; Trainees in Cardiology (or Fellows in interventional cardiology) may apply for Affiliate-in-Training membership
Chief Officer(s):
Eric Cohen, President
Kevin McKenzie, Executive Director
Warren J. Cantor, Treasurer

Canadian Association of Journalists (CAJ) / L'Association canadienne des journalistes
PO Box 117, Stn. F, Toronto ON MRY 2L4
Tel: 647-968-2393
www.caj.ca
www.linkedin.com/company/canadian-association-of-journalists
www.facebook.com/CdnAssocJournalists
twitter.com/CAJ
Previous Name: Centre for Investigative Journalism
Overview: A medium-sized national organization founded in 1978
Mission: To promote excellence in journalism; to encourage & promote investigative journalism
Finances: *Funding Sources:* Membership fees; media corporations; advertising
Membership: *Fees:* $20 student; $45 first time; $75 regular; $120 couple; $100 associate; $65 retired
Activities: *Internships:* Yes; *Speaker Service:* Yes; *Rents Mailing List:* Yes
Chief Officer(s):
Nick Taylor-Vaisey, President
nick@caj.ca
Awards:
• Award for Journalistic Excellence in Conflict Analysis
• CAJ/Canada NewsWire Student Award of Excellence in Journalism
• The CAJ Awards
Awards presented for the top investigative report published or broadcast in the following media: Newspaper/Newswire (open category), Newspaper (circulation under 25,000), Magazine, TV, Radio, Faith & Spirituality, Photojournalism, Computer assisting reporting & the Don McGillivray award for Best Investigative Report *Deadline:* January; *Amount:* $1,000 *Contact:* John Dickins
Meetings/Conferences:
• Canadian Association of Journalists 2018 Annual Conference, May, 2018, Hyatt Regency Toronto, Toronto, ON
Scope: National
Publications:
• Media
Type: Magazine; *Frequency:* 3 pa; *Accepts Advertising*; *Number of Pages:* 32; *Editor:* David McKie; *Price:* Free with CAJ membership; $14.98/yr
Profile: Investigative stories as well as analytical pieces about the practice of journalism in Canada
• The Wire
Type: Newsletter; *Frequency:* Quarterly
Profile: CAJ news & activities, articles, & profiles

Canadian Association of Labour Media (CALM) / Association canadienne de la presse syndicale (ACPS)
PO Box 10624, Stn. Bloorcourt, Toronto ON M6H 4H9
Tel: 581-983-4397; *Fax:* 581-983-4397
editor@calm.ca
www.calm.ca
www.facebook.com/canadian.association.of.labour.media
twitter.com/CanLabourMedia
Overview: A medium-sized national organization founded in 1976
Mission: To provide training, labour-friendly news, & graphics for labour communicators
Affiliation(s): Canadian Labour Congress
Staff Member(s): 4
Membership: 300+; *Fees:* Schedule available; *Member Profile:* Union publication editors
Activities: Producing stories & graphics for members to use in their newsletters; Organizing training sessions
Chief Officer(s):
Chris Lawson, President
Martin Lukacs, Executive Editor
Nora Loreto, Executive Editor
Awards:
• Best Overall Publication
• Excellence in Layout & Design
• Excellence in Writing
• Best Photograph
• Best Cartoon
• Best Illustration
• Ed Finn Award
• Morden Lazarus Prize
• Cliff Scotton Prize
• Breaking Barriers Award
• Muckraking Award
• Best Audio-Visual Production
• Best Public Advocacy Audio-Visual Production
• Best Commercial Television Ad
• Best Commercial Radio Ad
• Best Poster
• Best Print Ad
• Best Moving Billboard
• Best Flyer or Brochure
• Dennis McGann Stroke-of-Genius Award
• Best Overall Website
• Best Website Content
• Best Website Design
• Best Cyberunion
Meetings/Conferences:
• Canadian Association of Labour Media Conference 2018, May, 2018, Lord Nelson Hotel, Halifax, NS
Publications:
• CALMideas [a publication of the Canadian Association of Labour Media]
Type: Newsletter
Profile: Information for editors about how to compile a newsletter
• Union Editor's Handbook / Rédacteurs en chef syndicaux [a publication of the Canadian Association of Labour Media]
Type: Handbook; *Number of Pages:* 28; *Price:* $7
Profile: A guide for union editors
• What is Copyright?
Type: Booklet; *Number of Pages:* 8; *Price:* $5
• What's Libel?: Say What You Want Without Getting Sued
Type: Booklet; *Number of Pages:* 16; *Price:* $5

Canadian Association of Law Libraries (CALL) / Association canadienne des bibliothèques de droit (ACBD)
#200, 411 Richmond St. East, Toronto ON M5A 3S5
Tel: 647-346-8723
office@callacbd.ca
www.callacbd.ca
www.linkedin.com/groups/2006070/profile
www.facebook.com/callacbd
twitter.com/callacbd
Overview: A medium-sized national organization founded in 1963
Mission: To promote law librarianship; To develop Canadian law libraries; To promote access to legal information
Membership: 400; *Fees:* $15 student; $57 retired; $85 unwaged; $170 active; *Member Profile:* Individuals who represent a variety of law library interests; *Committees:* Cataloguing; Committee to Promote Research; Communications; Conference Planning; Copyright; KF Modified Classification; Membership Development; Professional Development; Scholarships & Awards; Vendor Liaison
Activities: Fostering cooperation among Canadian law libraries; Encouraging professional development; Creating networking opportunities for persons engaged in or interested in law library work; Cooperating with related organizations; Conducting surveys; Organizing special interest groups, such as academic law libraries, access services & resource sharing, courthouse & law society libraries, Department of Justice / Attorney General libraries, knowledge management, prison library, & private law libraries
Chief Officer(s):
Connie Crosby, President
Awards:
• Hugh Lawford Award for Excellence in Legal Publishing
An annual award to recognize excellence in legal publishing.
• Denis Marshall Memorial Award for Excellence in Law Librarianship
This award is an honour bestowed upon a current member of CALL/ACBD who has provided outstanding service to the Association and/or enhanced the profession of law librarianship in the recent past.; *Amount:* $3,000
• Canadian Law Library Review Featured Article Award
Given annually to the author of a feature length article published in Canadian Law Library Review / Revue canadienne des bibliothèques de droit.; *Amount:* $500
• Diana M. Priestly Memorial Scholarship
To support professional development in the field.; *Amount:* $2,500
• James D. Lang Memorial Scholarship
The scholarship is designed to support attendance at a continuing education program, be it a workshop, certificate program or other similar activity deemed appropriate by the CALL/ACBD Scholarships and Awards Committee.
• CALL Research Grant
Established to provide members with financial assistance to carry out research in areas of interest to members/to the association; *Amount:* up to $3,000
• CALL Education Reserve Fund Grant
Awards money to members to further their education
• Eunice Beeson Memorial Travel Fund
Assists members of the Association by covering travel costs to attend the annual meeting
• Northern Exposure to Leadership Grant
To support individuals to attend the Northern Exposure to Leadership Institute
• Janine Miller Fellowship
Provides funding for one member to attend the Law via the Internet Conference; *Amount:* $2,500
Meetings/Conferences:
• Canadian Association of Law Libraries 2018 Conference, 2018
Scope: National
Contact Information: www.callacbd.ca/Conference
• Canadian Association of Law Libraries Annual General Meeting 2018, 2018
Scope: National
Publications:
• Canadian Law Library Review [a publication of the Canadian Association of Law Libraries]
Type: Journal; *Frequency:* Quarterly; *Price:* $90
• CALL [Canadian Association of Law Libraries] Annual Directory
Type: Directory; *Frequency:* Annually; *Price:* Free with membership in the Canadian Association of Law Libraries
Profile: Listings of CALL members, officers, & committee & special interest group chairs
• In Session [a publication of the Canadian Association of Law Libraries]
Type: Newsletter; *Frequency:* Monthly; *Accepts Advertising*; *Price:* Free with membership in the Canadian Association of Law Libraries
Profile: News & updates for members

Canadian Association of Learned Journals (CALJ) / Association canadienne des revues savantes (ACRS)
PO Box 20304, Ottawa ON K1N 1A3
info@calj-acrs.ca
www.calj-acrs.ca
www.facebook.com/1164120333598476
twitter.com/caljacrs
Overview: A small national organization founded in 1990
Mission: To ensure the well-being of learned journals in Canada, through promotion, education, & lobbying
Membership: 100+; *Fees:* Schedule available; *Member Profile:* Canadian journals of scholarly work in the humanities & social sciences
Chief Officer(s):
Ken Clavette, Executive Director
Publications:
• Best Practices Guide to Scholarly Journal Publishing

Canadian Associations / Canadian Association of MAiD Assessors & Providers (CAMAP)

Type: Handbook; *Price:* $40 non-member journals & Canadian & international research libraries

Canadian Association of Legal Translators *Voir* Association canadienne des juristes-traducteurs

Canadian Association of MAiD Assessors & Providers (CAMAP)
326 - 1964 Fort St., Victoria BC V8R 6R3
camap.web@gmail.com
www.camapcanada.ca
Overview: A medium-sized national organization
Mission: To provide support for Medical Assistance in Dying (MAiD) assessors & providers; To serve as a leader in determining MAiD standards; To provide information about MAiD to the healthcare community & the public
Membership: *Fees:* $90; *Member Profile:* Physicians, nurse practitioners, & other industry professionals involved in the assessment & provision of Medical Assistance in Dying services; Individuals interested in supporting CAMAP's work
Activities: Offering MAiD resources, including guidelines, books, & journals; Providing information about MAiD tools; *Library:* Open to public
Chief Officer(s):
Stefanie Green, Administrator, 250-592-4710, Fax: 250-592-4712
camap.office@gmail.com
Meetings/Conferences:
• Canadian Association of MAiD Assessors & Providers 2018 Medical Assistance in Dying Conference, May, 2018, Shaw Centre, Ottawa, ON
Scope: National
Contact Information: www.maidconference.ca

Canadian Association of Management Consultants (CMC-Canada) / Association canadienne des conseillers en management
#701, 372 Bay St., Toronto ON M5H 2W9
Tel: 416-860-1515; *Fax:* 416-860-1535
Toll-Free: 800-268-1148
consulting@cmc-canada.ca
www.cmc-canada.ca
www.linkedin.com/company/canadian-association-of-management-consultants
www.facebook.com/153670124764294
twitter.com/CMCCanada1
cmc-yonemitsu.blogspot.ca;
www.youtube.com/user/CMCCanada1
Previous Name: Institute of Certified Management Consultants of Canada
Overview: A medium-sized national licensing organization founded in 1963
Mission: To foster excellence & integrity in the management consulting profession; To administer the Certified Management Consultant (CMC) designation in Canada; To advance the practice & profile of the profession of management consulting in Canada; To promote ethical standards
Member of: International Council of Management Consulting Institutes (ICMCI)
Finances: *Annual Operating Budget:* $1.5 Million-$3 Million
Staff Member(s): 8; 100 volunteer(s)
Membership: 2,850+; *Fees:* $499; *Member Profile:* Persons in the business of management consulting across Canada; *Committees:* National Certification; National Advocacy; Professional Development Operations; Marketing & Communications; Operations Review; Insight Editorial Board
Activities: Advocating for the profession in both government & public settings; Providing education, professional development, training, certifications, & job postings; Offering networking opportunities; Organizing events; *Speaker Service:* Yes; *Library:* CMCCentral
Chief Officer(s):
Jac van Beek, Chief Executive Officer
Mary Blair, Managing Director
mblair@cmc-canada.ca
Sylvia Biggs, Director, Business Development & Partnerships
sbiggs@cmc-canada.ca
Sarah McIntosh, Manager, Certification
smcintosh@cmc-canada.ca
Jordan Sandler, Manager, Marketing & Communications
jsandler@cmc-canada.ca
Emma Girduckis, Coordinator, Events & Communications
Eva Melakuova, Coordinator, Membership
Publications:
• CMC [Canadian Association of Management Consultants] Annual Report
Type: Yearbook; *Frequency:* Annually
• cNotes [a publication of the Canadian Association of Management Consultants]
Type: Newsletter; *Frequency:* s-a; *Editor:* Jordan Sandler
• Consult [a publication of the Canadian Association of Management Consultants]
Type: Magazine; *Frequency:* s-a
Profile: Magazine dedicated to management consulting, including industry insights & profiles on industry professionals.
• Management Consulting Industry Study
Type: Report; *Price:* $50 members & non-members
• Management Consulting: An Introduction to the Methodologies, Tools & Techniques of the Profession
Price: $100 members; $200 non-members

Canadian Association of Medical Biochemists (CAMB) / Association des médecins biochimistes du Canada (AMBC)
2083 Black Friars Rd., Ottawa ON K2A 3K6
Tel: 613-680-8526; *Fax:* 613-249-3557
camb.ambc@gmail.com
www.camb-ambc.ca
Overview: A small national organization founded in 1975
Chief Officer(s):
Andrew don Wauchope, President

Canadian Association of Medical Cannabis Dispensaries (CAMCD) / Association canadienne de dispensares de cannabis médical (ACDCM)
200 - 225 West 8th Ave., Vancouver BC V5Y 1N3
www.camcd-acdcm.ca
www.facebook.com/CAMCD.ca
Overview: A large national organization
Mission: To promote safe & affordable medical cannabis access; To lobby for the rights of medical cannabis patients
Membership: 25; *Member Profile:* Medical marijuana dispensaries that are certified under the CAMCD Dispensary Certification Program
Chief Officer(s):
Jeremy Jacob, President

Canadian Association of Medical Device Reprocessing (CAMDR)
147 Parkside Dr., Oak Bluff MB R4G 0A6
info@camdr.ca
www.camdr.ca
Overview: A small national organization
Mission: CAMDR seeks to address numerous issues including patient safety, infection prevention & control, technology assessments, vendor relations, organizational management, and education.
Membership: *Fees:* $50
Chief Officer(s):
Abdool Karim, President
Meetings/Conferences:
• Canadian Association of Medical Device Reprocessing 2018 Conference, October, 2018, Halifax, NS
Scope: National

Canadian Association of Medical Oncologists (CAMO) / Association canadienne des oncologues médicaux (ACOM)
PO Box 35164, Stn. Westgate, Ottawa ON K1Z 1A2
Tel: 613-415-6033; *Fax:* 866-839-7501
camo@royalcollege.ca
www.cos.ca/camo
Overview: A small national organization
Membership: *Fees:* no charge for residents, associate members, & emeritus; $50 corresponding & senior members; $250 active members; *Committees:* Annual Scientific Meeting; Continuing Medical Education; Fellowship; Nominating; Human Resources
Activities: Providing continuing professional development opportunities; Facilitating communication among medical oncologists
Chief Officer(s):
Christopher Lee, President
Alexi Campbell, Executive Director
Bruce Colwell, Secretary-Treasurer
Publications:
• Canadian Association of Medical Oncologists Membership Directory
Type: Directory
Profile: Offers access to medical oncologists throughout Canada

Canadian Association of Medical Radiation Technologists (CAMRT) / Association canadienne des technologues en radiation médicale (ACTRM)
#1300, 180 Elgin St., Ottawa ON K2P 2K3
Tel: 613-234-0012; *Fax:* 613-234-1097
Toll-Free: 800-463-9729
info@camrt.ca
www.camrt.ca
www.linkedin.com/company/1432897
www.facebook.com/CAMRTactrm
twitter.com/CAMRT_ACTRM
Overview: A medium-sized national licensing organization founded in 1942
Mission: To act as the certifying body for medical radiation technologists & therapists throughout Canada
Member of: International Society of Radiographers & Radiological Technologists
Membership: 10 provincial associations, sharing a membership of approximately 12,000; *Member Profile:* Persons from the disciplines of radiological technology, magnetic resonance, nuclear medicine, & radiation therapy
Activities: Administering national certification exams for the disciplines of radiological technology, magnetic resonance, nuclear medicine, & radiation therapy; Offering continuing education; *Awareness Events:* MRT Week, November
Chief Officer(s):
François Couillard, Chief Executive Officer
fcouillard@camrt.ca
Carrie Bru, Director, Education
cbru@camrt.ca
Mark Given, Director, Professional Practice
mgiven@camrt.ca
Karen Morrison, Director, Membership & Events
kmorrison@camrt.ca
Fahad Sami, Director, Finance & Administration
fsami@camrt.ca
Christopher Topham, Director, Advocacy & Communications
ctopham@camrt.ca
Awards:
• Dr. Petrie Memorial Award
An essay competition award
• L.J. Cartwright Student Award
An essay competition award
• E.I. Hood Award
An essay competition award
• Sister Mary Arthur "Sharing the Light" Award
An essay competition award
• CR/PACS Technology Award
An essay competition award
• Bayer MR Award
An essay competition award
• George Reason Memorial Award
An exhibit competition award
• Philips Award
An exhibit competition award
• Dr. Marshall Mallett Student Award
An exhibit competition award
• Bracco Diagnostics Canada MR Poster Award
An exhibit competition award
• Dr. Marshall Mallett "Lamp of Knowledge" Award
A CAMRT honorary award
• Welch Memorial Lecture
A CAMRT honorary award
• Life Membership Award
A CAMRT honorary award
• Honorary Life Membership Award
A CAMRT honorary award
• Award for Early Professional Achievement
A CAMRT honorary award
Meetings/Conferences:
• Canadian Association of Medical Radiation Technologists 76th Annual General Conference, 2018, Vancouver, BC
Scope: National
Description: Joint conference with The Canadian Association of Nuclear Medicine (CANM)
Publications:
• CAMRT [Canadian Association of Medical Radiation Technologists] Newsletter
Type: Newsletter; *Frequency:* Quarterly; *Accepts Advertising*
Profile: Canadian Association of Medical Radiation Technologists articles, education activities, & events
• Canadian Association of Medical Radiation Technologists Annual Report
Type: Yearbook; *Frequency:* Annually

- Journal of Medical Imaging & Radiation Sciences
Type: Journal; *Frequency:* Quarterly; *Accepts Advertising;*
Editor: Lisa Di Prospero
Profile: A peer-reviewed journal of articles on recent research, professional practices, new technology, & book reviews

Canadian Association of Medical Teams Abroad (CAMTA)
103 Laurier Dr., Edmonton AB T5R 5P6
Tel: 780-486-7161; *Fax:* 403-223-9020
info@camta.com
camta.com
www.facebook.com/237638586268756
twitter.com/camta
Overview: A small national charitable organization founded in 2001
Mission: CAMTA provides orthopedic surgeries to pediatric and adult patients in Ecuador.
Finances: Annual Operating Budget: $250,000-$500,000
Membership: Member Profile: Edmonton-based health care practitioners and lay people.
Chief Officer(s):
Marc Moreau, President
Francisco Gallardo, Secretary
Veronica Kong, Executive Director

Canadian Association of Members of Public Utility Tribunals / Association canadienne des membres des tribunaux d'utilité publique *See* CAMPUT

Canadian Association of Message Exchanges, Inc. *See* Canadian Call Management Association

Canadian Association of Midwives (CAM) / L'Association canadienne des sages-femmes (ACSF)
59, av Riverview, Montréal QC H3R 3R9
Tel: 514-807-3668; *Fax:* 514-738-0370
admin@canadianmidwives.org
www.canadianmidwives.org
www.facebook.com/CanadianMidwives
Overview: A medium-sized national organization
Mission: Promotion, support and uniting of the proffession of midwifery in Canada
Membership: 882; *Fees:* $100; *Committees:* CAM International; National Working Group for the Emergency Skills Workshop for Midwives (ESW); Ghislaine Francoeur Fund; Canadian Journal of Midwifery Research and Practic; CAM Conference Program; Scientific Abstract Review; Insurance/Risk Management
Chief Officer(s):
Tonia Occhionero, Executive Director
Meetings/Conferences:
• Canadian Association of Midwives Annual Conference & Exhibit 2018, October, 2018, Hilton Lac-Leamy, Gatineau, QC
Scope: National

Canadian Association of Mining Equipment & Services for Export *See* Mining Suppliers Trade Association Canada

Canadian Association of Mobile Entertainers & Operators (CAMEO) *See* Canadian Professional DJ Association Inc.

Canadian Association of Moldmakers (CAMM)
c/o St. Clair College (FCEM), PO Box 16, 2000 Talbot Rd. West, Windsor ON N9A 6S4
Tel: 519-255-7863; *Fax:* 519-255-9446
info@camm.ca
www.camm.ca
Previous Name: Windsor Association of Moldmakers
Overview: A small national licensing organization founded in 1981
Mission: To address the concerns of Canadian mold making companies & to present a united voice on legislative issues to provincial & federal governments
Finances: Funding Sources: Corporate sponsorships
Staff Member(s): 1
Membership: Fees: $850; *Member Profile:* Mold makers & their mold making network
Activities: Supporting training & education of mold makers; Conducting an annual wage & fringe benefit survey; Offering networking opportunities
Chief Officer(s):
Jonathon Azzopardi, Chair
Publications:
• CAMM [Canadian Association of Mould Makers] Newsletter
Type: Newsletter
Profile: Industry news & technical information

• Canadian Association of Mould Makers Membership Directory
Type: Directory
Profile: Listing of member companies

Canadian Association of Montessori Teachers (CAMT)
312 Oakwood Crt., Newmarket ON L3Y 3C8
Tel: 416-755-7184; *Fax:* 866-328-7974
info@camt100.ca
www.camt100.ca
www.facebook.com/montessoriCAMT
Overview: A small national organization
Mission: To advance the standards of Montessori teaching & to improve the quality of Montessori education throughout Canada
Activities: Organizing workshops & conferences
Chief Officer(s):
Claudia Langlois, President
Meetings/Conferences:
• Canadian Association of Montessori Teachers 2018 Mini-Conference, April, 2018, Woodland Cultural Centre, Brantford, ON
Scope: National
Description: Theme: "Walking the Path to Reconciliation"

Canadian Association of Movers (CAM) / Association canadienne des déménageurs (ACD)
PO Box 26004, Stn. Churchill, Mississauga ON L5L 5W7
Tel: 905-848-6579; *Fax:* 866-601-8499
Toll-Free: 866-860-0065
admin@mover.net
www.mover.net
www.linkedin.com/company-beta/293837
www.facebook.com/canadianmover
Overview: A medium-sized national organization
Mission: To protect & further the interests of owner-managed moving & storage companies through the provision of leadership, motivation, research, education, programs of mutual benefit, consultation & technical advice for members
Member of: International Association of Movers; American Moving & Storage Association; British Association of Movers; Pan American International Movers Association
Affiliation(s): American Moving & Storage Association; British Association of Removers; International Association of Movers
Finances: Annual Operating Budget: $250,000-$500,000; *Funding Sources:* Membership; Advertising
Membership: 404; *Fees:* $500 movers in Canada/affiliates; $600 suppliers/international movers; $165 branches; *Committees:* Board of Directors; Conference; International; Marketing & Internet; Membership; Supplier
Activities: Government & political affairs; membership development; volunteer participation & recognition; van lines; public affairs & publications; research & development; education & training; professional ethics & standards; organizational competency
Chief Officer(s):
Patrick Greaney, President, 905-848-6579
pgreaney@mover.net
Perry Thorne, Chairman, 416-289-3047
perry@gregandsonsmoving.com
Cam Carswell, Vice Chairman, 306-934-3335
ccarswell@sasktel.net
David Ogilvy, Secretary/Treasurer, 146-777-2722
godilvy@ogilvy.ca
Awards:
• Distinguished Service Award
• Innovators Award
• Industry/Public Service Award
• Industry Achievement Award
• Agent of the Year Award
• Independent Mover of the Year Award
Meetings/Conferences:
• Canadian Association of Movers 2018 Annual Conference & Trade Show, November, 2018, Crowne Plaza, Niagara Falls, ON
Scope: National
Publications:
• The Canadian Mover [a publication of the Canadian Association of Movers]
Type: Magazine
• The Mover's Edge [a publication of the Canadian Association of Movers]
Type: Newsletter

Canadian Association of Municipal Administrators (CAMA)
PO Box 128, Stn. A, Fredericton NB E3B 4Y2

Toll-Free: 866-771-2262
www.camacam.ca
Overview: A small national organization
Mission: To advance excellence in municipal management throughout Canada
Affiliation(s): Local Government Managers Australia (LGMA); New Zealand Society of Local Government Managers (SOLGM); Society of Local Authority Chief Executives (SOLACE); International City / County Management Association (ICMA)
Finances: Funding Sources: Memberships fees; Sponsorships
Membership: 462; *Fees:* Schedule available, based on population of municipality; *Member Profile:* Senior managers from Canadian municipalities, such as city managers, chief administrative officers, & commissioners; Affiliate members are those who work closely with municipal administrators
Activities: Providing professional development in municipal management; Offering networking opportunities
Chief Officer(s):
Marie-Hélène Lajoie, President
Jennifer Goodine, Executive Director
Meetings/Conferences:
• Canadian Association of Municipal Administrators 2018 47th Annual Conference & Annual General Meeting, May, 2018, Fredericton Convention Centre, Fredericton, NB
Scope: National
Description: Information & a trade show for senior managers from Canadian municipalities throughout Canada
Publications:
• Canadian Association of Municipal Administrators e-Brief
Type: Newsletter; *Frequency:* Semimonthly
Profile: Association happenings, including conference information, workshops, & membership news

Canadian Association of Music Libraries, Archives & Documentation Centres (CAML) / Association canadienne des bibliothèques, archives et centres de documentation musicaux inc. (ACBM)
Edward Johnson Bldg., University of Toronto, 80 Queen's Park Cres., Toronto ON M5S 2C5
caml-acbm.org
Previous Name: Canadian Music Library Association
Overview: A small national organization founded in 1971
Mission: To represent librarians, researchers, & archivists in the field of music
Affiliation(s): Canadian University Music Society (CUMS); International Association of Music Libaries (IAML); Library & Archives Canada
Membership: Fees: $86 individual; $115 institutional; $76 paraprofessional/student/retired; *Member Profile:* Librarians, archivists, researchers, & institutions in the field of music; Any person interested in the collection, preservation, organization, & study of music
Activities: Providing information to members; Arranging networking opportunities
Chief Officer(s):
Kyla Jemison, Membership Secretary
kyla.jemison@utoronto.ca
Meetings/Conferences:
• Canadian Association of Music Libraries, Archives & Documentation Centres 2018 Conference, May, 2018, University of Regina, Regina, SK
Scope: National
Description: A national meeting covering issues & information of interest to music librarians, archivists, & researchers
Publications:
• CAML [Canadian Association of Music Libraries, Archives & Documentation Centres] Review / Revue de l'ACBM
Type: Journal; *Frequency:* 3 pa; *Editor:* Cathy Martin; *ISSN:* 1496-9963; *Price:* Free with membership in the Canadian Association of Music Libraries
Profile: Information of interest to members of the Canadian Association of Music Libraries, Archives &Documentation Centres, including conference reports, articles, & book & CD reviews
• Directory of Music Collections in Canada
Type: Directory; *Editor:* Carol Ohlers
Profile: An up-to-date listing of major music collections in Canadian institutions

Canadian Association of Music Therapists (CAMT) / Association canadienne des musicothérapeutes (AMC)
#5, 1124 Gainsborough Rd., London ON N6H 5N1
Fax: 519-641-0431
Toll-Free: 800-996-2268

info@musictherapy.ca
www.musictherapy.ca
Overview: A medium-sized national licensing organization founded in 1974
Mission: To promote excellence in music therapy practice & education in Canadian clinical, educational, & community settings
Affiliation(s): World Federation of Music Therapy
Finances: *Funding Sources:* Membership; Book sales; Conference fees
Membership: *Fees:* $60 students, interns, & retired & inactive therapists; $75 graduate students; $225 associate menbers; $195 accredited therapists; $330 corporate; *Member Profile:* Accredited music therapists; Unaccredited graduates of a CAMT recognized music therapy training program; Students; Individuals who support the music therapy profession & its aims; Corporate members
Activities: Accrediting music therapists; Setting standards for music therapy training; Increasing awareness of music therapy; Providing guidance & information to members; Representing members in matters related to practice & government legislation; *Internships:* Yes *Library:* Canadian Association for Music Therapy Library; by appointment
Awards:
• Norma Sharpe Award
Awarded to an MTA who has made an outstanding contribution to the field of music therapy in Canada
• Peer Recognition Award
Meetings/Conferences:
• Canadian Association of Music Therapists 2018 Conference, May, 2018, Sheraton Hotel Newfoundland, St. John's, NL
Scope: National
Description: Theme: "Keeping Us Anchored: Music Therapy, Connection & Culture"
Publications:
• CAMT [Canadian Association for Music Therapy] Newsletter
Type: Newsletter; *Frequency:* Quarterly
• Canadian Association for Music Therapy Conference Proceedings
Frequency: Annually
Profile: Proceedings from each CAMT national conference
• The Canadian Association for Music Therapy Member Sourcebook
Type: Directory
• The Canadian Journal of Music Therapy
Type: Journal; *Frequency:* Annually; *Accepts Advertising*; *Editor:* Kevin Kirkland
Profile: Peer-reviewed papers about music therapy knowledge & practice

Music Therapy Association of British Columbia
c/o Capilano College, 2055 Purcell Way, North Vancouver BC V7N 3H5
Tel: 604-924-0046; *Fax:* 604-983-7559
Toll-Free: 800-424-0556
info@mtabc.com
www.mtabc.com
www.facebook.com/141974696573
twitter.com/musictherapybc
www.youtube.com/channel/UCiLiJ0Aj_3TLcmCatxASwBg
Mission: To advocate for music therapists in matters related to standards of professional practice, salary scales, ethics, and promotion of the field with other organizations, government agencies, unions and employer groups.
Chief Officer(s):
Gemma Isaac, President
president@mtabc.com

Canadian Association of Mutual Insurance Companies (CAMIC) / Association canadienne des compagnies d'assurance mutuelles (ACCAM)
#205, 311 McArthur Ave., Ottawa ON K1L 6P1
Tel: 613-789-6851; *Fax:* 613-789-7665
www.camic.ca
Overview: A small national organization founded in 1980
Mission: To provide information, research, advocacy to its members in areas of general concerns & to negotiate supply agreements for goods & services of common needs. Objectives: to promote a strong, health and competitive insurance market; to support regulatory efficiency and legislative change; to inform member companies on matters affecting the industry and to build consensus on action plans; to promote self-regulation for the property and casualty insurance industry
Member of: International Cooperative & Mutual Insurance Federation; National Association of Mutual Insurance Companies
Finances: *Funding Sources:* Membership fees; conventions; commissions
Staff Member(s): 2
Membership: 106 corporate; *Fees:* Schedule available; *Member Profile:* Mutual insurance company; mutual reinsurance company or subsidiary of mutual insurance company
Chief Officer(s):
Normand Lafrenière, President
nlafreniere@camic.ca

The Canadian Association of Naturopathic Doctors (CAND) / Association canadienne des docteurs en naturopathie
#200, 20 Holly St., Toronto ON M2S 3B1
Tel: 416-496-8633; *Fax:* 416-496-8634
Toll-Free: 800-551-4381
www.cand.ca
www.facebook.com/NaturopathicDrs
twitter.com/naturopathicdrs
Previous Name: Canadian Naturopathic Association
Overview: A medium-sized national organization founded in 1955
Mission: CAND is a not-for-profit professional organization that promotes naturopathic medicine to the public, insurance companies & corporations. CAND encourages professional, educational & networking activities among its members, & standardization of educational requirements for practitioners
Membership: *Member Profile:* Naturopathic doctors; students of naturopathic medicine; suppliers
Activities: Advocacy, education; *Awareness Events:* Naturopathic Medicine Week, May
Chief Officer(s):
Shawn O'Reilly, Executive Director
Alex McKenna, Marketing Director

Canadian Association of Nephrology Nurses & Technologists (CANNT) / Association canadienne des infirmières et infirmiers et technologues de néphrologie (ACITN)
PO Box 10, 59 Millmanor Place, Delaware ON N0L 1E0
Tel: 519-652-6767; *Fax:* 519-652-5015
Toll-Free: 877-720-2819
cannt@cannt.ca
www.cannt.ca
www.facebook.com/160999717295820
twitter.com/CANNT1
Overview: A small national organization founded in 1968
Mission: To improve the care of renal patients through support of educational opportunities for association members; To evaluate the performance & competence of nephrology nurses & technologists against the CANNT Standards of Practice
Affiliation(s): Kidney Foundation of Canada; Canadian Nurses Association
Finances: *Annual Operating Budget:* $250,000-$500,000; *Funding Sources:* Sponsorships; Fundraising
Membership: 537; *Fees:* $75; $35 student; *Member Profile:* Individuals involved in the care of patients with renal disease; *Committees:* Bursary
Activities: Disseminating knowledge; Promoting excellence in practice & quality care; Participating in exam development activities with the CNA
Chief Officer(s):
Anne Moulton, RN, CNeph(C), President, 905-522-1155 Ext. 33916
CANNT.president@gmail.com
Melanie Wiggins, Treasurer & Coordinator, Website
CANNT.webtreasurer@gmail.com
Publications:
• CANNT [Canadian Association of Nephrology Nurses & Technologists] Journal / Journal ACITN
Type: Journal; *Frequency:* Quarterly; *Editor:* Gillian Brunier; *Price:* Free with CANNT membership

Canadian Association of Neuropathologists (CANP) / Association canadienne de neuropathologistes
c/o Service d'Anatomo-pathologie, CHA Hopital de l'Enfant-Jesus, 1401, 18e rue, Québec QC G1J 1Z4
Tel: 418-649-5725; *Fax:* 418-649-5856
www.canp.ca
Overview: A small national charitable organization founded in 1960
Mission: To promote the professional & educational objectives of neuropathologists; To ensure high standards in the neuropathology field
Affiliation(s): International Society of Neuropathology
Finances: *Funding Sources:* Membership dues
Membership: *Member Profile:* Devote majority of time to neuropathology
Chief Officer(s):
Marc Del Bigio, President
Peter Gould, Secretary-Treasurer
peter.gould@fmed.ulaval.ca

Canadian Association of Neuroscience Nurses (CANN) / Association canadienne des infirmiers et infirmières en sciences neurologiques (ACIISN)
c/o Janet White, #212, 324 Larry Uteck Blvd., Halifax NS B3M 0E7
www.cann.ca
twitter.com/CANNinfo
Overview: A small national organization founded in 1969
Mission: To prevent illness & to improve health outcomes for people with, or at risk for, neurological disorders; To establish standards of practice for neuroscience nurses
Member of: World Federation of Neuroscience Nurses
Affiliation(s): Canadian Nurses Association; Canadian Congress of Neurological Sciences; Canadian Brain & Nerve Health Coalition (CBANHC); Canadian Council on Donation and Transplantation (CCDT); National Stroke Leadership Group; Canadian Association of Brain Tumor Coalition (CABTO); Think First
Membership: *Fees:* $85 general; $65 associate; *Member Profile:* Registered nurses who are licensed to practise in Canada & are working in neurological or neurosurgical nursing; Registered nurses who live outside Canada & are associate members; Individuals practising in a related discipline in the neurosciences; Registered nurses with an interest in neuroscience nursing; Students; *Committees:* Canadian Journal of Neuroscience Nursing; Communications & Marketing; Program; Scientific
Activities: Offering continuing education opportunities; Providing networking possibilities; Promoting research; Facilitating access to recent research; Collaborating with individuals & other groups to prevent illness & to improve health outcomes
Chief Officer(s):
Jill Kamensek, President
Jodi Dusik-Sharpe, Vice-President & Secretary
Mark Bonin, Treasurer
mabonin62@gmail.com
Janet White, Chair, Membership
Meetings/Conferences:
• Canadian Association of Neuroscience Nurses 2018 49th Annual General Meeting, June, 2018, Atlantica Hotel Halifax, Halifax, NS
Scope: National
Description: Scientific sessions offering professional development for neuroscience nurses
Publications:
• Canadian Journal of Neuroscience Nursing (CJNN) / Le journal canadien des infirmiers et infirmières en sciences neurologiques
Type: Journal; *Frequency:* Quarterly; *Accepts Advertising*; *Price:* Free withmembership in the Canadian Association of Neuroscience Nurses
Profile: A peer reviewed journal, distributed to neuroscience nurses & medical libraries

Canadian Association of Nordic Ski Instructors (CANSI) / Association canadienne des moniteurs de ski nordique
c/o Secrétariat, 164, rue Adrien-Robert, Gatineau QC J8Y 3S2
Tel: 819-360-6700; *Fax:* 819-778-0017
Other Communication: Membership Inquiries, E-mail: membership@cansi.ca
office@cansi.ca
www.cansi.ca
www.facebook.com/162657427089855
Overview: A small national organization founded in 1976
Mission: To promote & advance cross-country & Telemark skiing in Canada, establishing standards, & offering levels of certification in technique & training
Membership: *Fees:* Schedule available; *Member Profile:* Completed Level I Cross Country or Telemark course
Activities: Providing resources to instuctors; liaising nationally & internationally with the Nordic disciplines; coordinating national level courses
Chief Officer(s):
Gaétan Lord, President
Françoise Chatenoud, Office Coordinator
   Atlantic Region
   c/o 3 Westview Ave., Corner Brook NL A2H 3B7

Tel: 709-634-9962
info@atlantic.cansi.ca
Chief Officer(s):
Keith Payne, Regional Representative
Central Region - MB, NU, & SK
info@central.cansi.ca
Chief Officer(s):
Katrina Froese, Regional Representative
Mountain Region - AB & NT
c/o John Gallagher, 2003 Olympic Way, Canmore AB T1W 2T6
info@mountain.cansi.ca
Ontario Region
Toll-Free: 888-226-7446
info@ontario.cansi.ca
Joseph Ferri, Director, Finance
finance-dir@ontario.cansi.ca
Pacific Region - BC & YT
c/o Canada West Mountain School, 47 West Broadway, Vancouver BC V5Y 1P1
pacific@cansi.ca
Chief Officer(s):
Jamie Sterling, Coordinator, Communications
Québec Region
QC
Courriel: info@quebec.cansi.ca
www.cansi-quebec.ca
Chief Officer(s):
Gaetan Lord, Président
Charles Blair, Secretary-Treasurer

Canadian Association of Nuclear Medicine (CANM) / Association canadienne de médecine nucléaire (ACMN)
PO Box 4383, Stn. E, Ottawa ON K1S 5B4
Tel: 613-882-5097
canm@canm-acmn.ca
www.canm-acmn.ca
Overview: A small national organization founded in 1971
Mission: To strive for excellence in the practice of diagnostic & therapeutic nuclear medicine; to promote the continued professional competence of nuclear medicine specialists; to establish guidelines of clinical practice; to encourage biomedical research
Affiliation(s): Canadian Medical Association; Society of Nuclear Medicine - USA; Canadian Association of Radiation Protection
Finances: *Funding Sources:* Membership dues
Membership: *Fees:* $300 Full; Free for Residents; *Member Profile:* Physicians who have received certification in nuclear medicine; Scientists associated with nuclear medicine; Medical radiation technologists; Medically qualified practitioners working in the discipline of nuclear medicine; Trainees
Chief Officer(s):
Andrew Ross, President
Francois Lamoureux, Vice-President
Glenn Ollenberger, Secretary-Treasurer
Awards:
• Emeritus Award
• Eric Lepp Clinical Vignettes
Meetings/Conferences:
• CANM [Canadian Association of Nuclear Medicine] 2018 Annual Scientific Meeting, March, 2018, Marriott Vancouver Pinnacle Downtown, Vancouver, BC
Scope: National

Canadian Association of Numismatic Dealers (CAND) / Association canadienne des marchands numismatiques
c/o Jo-Anne Simpson, Executive Secretary, PO Box 10272, Stn. Winona, Stoney Creek ON L8E 5R1
Tel: 905-643-4988; *Fax:* 905-643-6329
email@cand.org
www.cand.org
Overview: A small national organization founded in 1975
Mission: To ensure professionalism by members of the association
Membership: *Member Profile:* Persons engaged in the retail numismatic trade, such as coin dealers, foreign exchange dealers, bullion dealers, & paper money dealers
Activities: Upholding the Code of Ethics
Chief Officer(s):
Michael Findlay, President
ccdn@bconnex.net
Paul Koolhaas, Vice-President
paul.koolhaas@sympatico.ca

Wendy Hoare, Secretary-Treasurer
jhoare@jeffreyhoare.on.ca
Meetings/Conferences:
• Canadian Association of Numismatic Dealers 2018 Annual Convention, January, 2018, Sheraton Hamilton Hotel, Hamilton, ON
Scope: National
Contact Information: Tom Kennedy, E-mail: cand@cogeco.ca, Phone: 519-271-8825

Canadian Association of Nurses in HIV/AIDS Care (CANAC) / Association canadienne des infirmières et infirmiers en sidologie
St. Paul's Hospital, #B552, 1081 Burrard St., Vancouver BC V6Z 1Y6
admin@canac.org
www.canac.org
Overview: A small national charitable organization founded in 1991
Mission: The Canadian Association of Nurses in AIDS Care (CANAC) is a national professional nursing organization committed to fostering excellence in HIV/AIDS nursing, promoting the health, rights and dignity of persons affected by HIV/AIDS and to preventing the spread of HIV infection.
Affiliation(s): Canadian Nurses Association
Finances: *Funding Sources:* Membership dues; fundraising; special projects
Membership: *Fees:* $40 associate/student; $50 regular; *Member Profile:* Nurses; support mission of CANAC; corporate & associate
Chief Officer(s):
Janna Campbell, Executive Assistant
Meetings/Conferences:
• Canadian Association of Nurses in HIV/AIDS Care 26th Annual Conference 2018, April, 2018, Coast Coal Harbour Hotel, Vancouver, BC
Scope: National
Description: Theme: "Acting Up, Reducing Harm: Clinical Practice & Advocacy in the Context of Crisis"
Publications:
• Connection: The Newsletter of the Canadian Association of Nurses in AIDS Care
Type: Newsletter; *Frequency:* 3 pa; *Editor:* Jennifer Shaw
Profile: CANAD / ACIIS news & reports, conference information, events, resources, & employment opportunities

Canadian Association of Nurses in Oncology (CANO) / Association canadienne des infirmières en oncologie (ACIO)
#301, 750 West Pender St., Vancouver BC V6C 2T7
Tel: 604-874-4322; *Fax:* 604-874-4378
cano@malachite-mgmt.com
www.cano-acio.ca
www.facebook.com/336467099484
twitter.com/CANO_ACIO
www.youtube.com/user/CANOACIO
Overview: A medium-sized national organization founded in 1984
Mission: To advocate for improved cancer care for all Canadians
Affiliation(s): Canadian Nurses Association; International Society of Cancer Nurses; Canadian Oncology Societies
Finances: *Funding Sources:* Membership dues; sponsorships
Staff Member(s): 4
Membership: *Fees:* $100 regular/associate/affiliate; $50 student/non-working; *Member Profile:* Registered Nurses involved in or interested in cancer nursing; *Committees:* Connections; Education; Marketing; Recognition of Excellence; Research
Chief Officer(s):
Tracy Truant, President
Jyoti Bhardwaj, Executive Director
Meetings/Conferences:
• Canadian Association of Nurses in Oncology Annual Conference 2018, October, 2018, Charlottetown, PE
Scope: National
Description: Theme: "Excellence in Oncology: Our Patients, Our Passion"
Publications:
• Canadian Oncology Nursing Journal
Type: Journal; *Frequency:* Quarterly; *Editor:* Margaret I. Fitch
• CANO [Canadian Association of Nurses in Oncology] Connections
Type: Newsletter

Canadian Association of Occupational Therapists (CAOT) / Association canadienne des ergothérapeutes (ACE)
#100, 34 Colonnade Rd., Ottawa ON K2E 7J6
Tel: 613-523-2268; *Fax:* 613-523-2552
Toll-Free: 800-434-2268
membership@caot.ca
www.caot.ca
www.facebook.com/CAOT.ca
twitter.com/CAOT_ACE
Overview: A large national organization founded in 1926
Mission: To develop & promote the profession of occupational therapy in Canada & abroad; To assist occupational therapists achieve excellence in their professional practice by offering services, products, events, & networking opportunities
Affiliation(s): World Federation of Occupational Therapists
Staff Member(s): 29
Membership: 12,000+; *Fees:* Schedule available; *Member Profile:* Occupational therapists who have graduated from an occupational therapy program accredited by the Canadian Association of Occupational Therapistsor recognized by the World Federation of Occupational Therapists; Individuals interested or involved in occupational therapy; Graduate students; Retired occupational therapists
Activities: Providing access to the latest developments in occupational therapy practice & research; Offering a mentoring program; Organizing continuing education opportunities; Advocating on behalf of occupational therapists; *Rents Mailing List:* Yes; *Library*
Chief Officer(s):
Janet Craik, Executive Director, 613-523-2268 Ext. 244
jcraik@caot.ca
Havelin Anand, Director, Government Affairs & Policy, 613-523-2268 Ext. 230
hanand@caot.ca
Suzanne Maurice, Director, Administration, 613-523-2268 Ext. 228
smaurice@caot.ca
Pat Underwood, Director, Communications, 613-523-2268 Ext. 229
punderwood@caot.ca
Vicky Wang, Director, Finance, 613-523-2268 Ext. 227
finance@caot.ca
Awards:
• Fellowship Award
• Award for Leadership in Occupational Therapy
• Honorary Membership
• Award for Innovative Practice
• Muriel Driver Memorial Lectureship
• Dr. Helen P. LeVesconte Award for Volunteerism in the Canadian Association of Occupational Therapists
• Award of Merit
• Life Membership
• Citation Award
• Certificate of Appreciation
• Student Award
• Golden Quill Award
• Outstanding Occupational Therapist of the Year Award
Meetings/Conferences:
• Canadian Association of Occupational Therapists Conference 2018, June, 2018, Sheraton Vancouver Wall Centre, Vancouver, BC
Scope: National
Publications:
• Canadian Association of Occupational Therapists Annual Report
Type: Yearbook; *Frequency:* Annually
Profile: A review of association activities during the past year, plus financial information
• Canadian Journal of Occupational Therapy [a publication of the Canadian Association of Occupational Therapists]
Type: Journal; *Frequency:* 5 pa; *Accepts Advertising*; *Editor:* Helene Polatajko; *ISSN:* 0008-4174
Profile: Professional peer-reviewed scientific journal promotingadvancement in research & education
• Enabling Occupation II: Advancing an Occupational Therapy Vision for Health, Well-being & Justice through Occupation
Author: Elizabeth Townsend, Helen Polatajko; *ISBN:* 978-1-895437-76-8
Profile: A study & practice guide, focussing on occupation-basedenablement
• Occupational Therapy Now [a publication of the Canadian Association of Occupational Therapists]
Type: Magazine; *Frequency:* bi-m.; *Accepts Advertising*

Canadian Associations / Canadian Association of Occupational Therapists - British Columbia (CAOT-BC)

Profile: Practice magazine, with clinical applications of recent research & theory, evidence-based practice, & product reviews

Canadian Association of Occupational Therapists - British Columbia (CAOT-BC)
c/o National Office, #100, 34 Colonnade Rd., Ottawa ON K2E 7J6
Tel: 613-523-2268; *Fax:* 613-523-2552
Toll-Free: 800-434-2268
www.caot.ca/default.asp?pageid=4125
twitter.com/Caot_bc
Overview: A medium-sized provincial organization
Mission: To promote the profession of occupational therapy throughout the province & represent its members to regional health boards & government, health professional groups & the public; to foster the growth & development of the profession in BC; to provide a variety of services to its members including continuing education, reentry & participation in professional issues
Member of: Canadian Association of Occupational Therapists
Membership: *Member Profile:* Occupational therapists; affiliate organizations; students
Activities: *Rents Mailing List:* Yes
Chief Officer(s):
Giovanna Boniface, Managing Director
gboniface@caot.ca
Awards:
• British Columbia Citation Award
To acknowledge the contribution to the health & well-being of Canadians of an occupational therapist living in British Columbia
• Outstanding OT of the Year
To recognize an occupational therapist living in British Columbia who has made an outstanding contribution to the profession throughout his or her career.

Canadian Association of Oilwell Drilling Contractors (CAODC)
#2050, 717 - 7th Ave. SW, Calgary AB T2P 0Z3
Tel: 403-264-4311; *Fax:* 403-263-3796
Other Communication: Membership e-mail: membership@caodc.ca
info@caodc.ca
www.caodc.ca
www.linkedin.com/company/5607531
www.facebook.com/thecaodc
twitter.com/thecaodc
www.youtube.com/user/TheCAODC
Overview: A large national organization founded in 1949
Mission: To represent drilling rig contractors; To provide ongoing means of communication between drilling & well servicing contractors, governments, other industry sector participants, & the general public; To improve standards for safety & training, equipment & technical procedures; To coordinate programs between government bodies & contractors; To oversee the Rig Technician Trade & Apprenticeship Program in Alberta, British Columbia, & Saskatchewan
Membership: 32 Drilling Division; 77 Service Rig Division; 180 Associate Division; 2 Offshore Division; *Fees:* Schedule available; *Member Profile:* Upstream Canadian petroleum drilling contractors (land-based & offshore) service rig contractors & associate companies; *Committees:* Accounting & Taxation (Drilling); Communications; Engineering & Technical; Executive Human Resources; Forecasting; Health, Safety & Training (Drilling); Information Technology; Legal & Contracts (Drilling); Rig Technician Apprenticeship; Saskatchewan Health, Safety & Training
Activities: *Library:* Open to public by appointment
Chief Officer(s):
Mark A. Scholz, President
John Bayko, Vice-President, Communications
Steven Berg, Vice-President, Operations
Shirley Challand, Manager, Administration
Awards:
• CAODC Scholarship Program
• CAODC Occupational Health & Safety (OHS) Scholarship Program
Publications:
• CAODC [Canadian Association of Oilwell Drilling Contractors] The Hitch
Type: Magazine; *Frequency:* 3 pa; *Accepts Advertising*
Profile: Reports on issues about Canada's oil industry. drilling forecasts, & CAODC committee updates
• CAODC [Canadian Association of Oilwell Drilling Contractors] Members Directory
Type: Directory; *Frequency:* Annual
Profile: Available online

Canadian Association of Optometrists (CAO) / Association canadienne des optométristes (ACO)
234 Argyle Ave., Ottawa ON K2P 1B9
Tel: 613-235-7924; *Fax:* 613-235-2098
Toll-Free: 888-263-4676
info@opto.ca
www.opto.ca
www.facebook.com/CanadianOpto
twitter.com/CanadianOpto
Overview: A large national organization founded in 1941
Mission: To represent & assist the profession of optometry in Canada; To improve the quality, availability, & accessibility of vision & eye care
Affiliation(s): Eye Health Council of Canada
Finances: *Funding Sources:* Membership fees; Sponsorships
Membership: 4,600+; *Fees:* Schedule available; *Member Profile:* Doctors of optometry in Canada; *Committees:* Diabetes; Government Relations; Children Vision Initiative; National Public Education; Executive
Activities: Liaising with government; Engaging in advocacy activities; Providing professional development & educational opportunities; Conducting research; Offering information; Promoting ethical decision-making; *Awareness Events:* Children's Vision Month, September
Chief Officer(s):
Laurie Clement, CEO
lclement@opto.ca
Rhona Lahey, Director, Communications & Marketing, 613-235-7924 Ext. 213
Maria Georgescu, Manager, Finance & Operations, 613-235-7924 Ext. 217
Marie-Therese Robinson, Office Administrator, 613-235-7924 Ext. 216
Awards:
• Canadian Optometric Education Fund (COETF) Annual Awards Program
• Vision Champion Award
Awarded to recognize individuals & organizations outside of the eye care professional industry who have worked to improve eye health & vision care in Canada
Meetings/Conferences:
• Canadian Association of Optometrists 2019 36th Biennial Congress, July, 2019, Victoria, BC
Scope: National
Attendance: 600
Publications:
• Canadian Journal of Optometry [a publication of the Canadian Association of Optometrists]
Type: Journal; *Frequency:* q.; *Accepts Advertising;* *Editor:* Dr. B. Ralph Chou, OD, MSc; *ISSN:* 0045-5075; *Price:* Free with CAO membership, $70 (Canada) or $80 (USA/overseas) without CAO membership
Profile: Features articles on clinical practice, research, case studies, & practicemanagement tips

Canadian Association of Oral & Maxillofacial Surgeons (CAOMS) / Association canadienne de spécialistes en chirurgie buccale et maxillo-faciale (ACSCBMF)
#100, 32 Colonnade Rd., Ottawa ON K2E 7J6
Tel: 613-721-1816; *Fax:* 613-721-3581
Toll-Free: 888-369-5641
caoms@caoms.com
www.caoms.com
Overview: A medium-sized national organization founded in 1953
Mission: To support & meet the needs of oral & maxillofacial surgeons in Canada
Finances: *Funding Sources:* Membership fees; Sponsorships
Membership: *Fees:* Free, for honorary, retired, & student members; $250 affiliate, supporting, & life members; $500 active members; *Member Profile:* Any individual who is certified & licensed to practice the specialty of oral & maxillofacial surgery in a Canadian province or territory; Affiliate members are persons in a foreign country who hold membership in that country's national organization for oral & maxillofacial surgeons; Students enrolled full-time in an accredited program for the training of oral & maxillofacial surgeons
Activities: Providing professional development opportunities; Offering networking events
Chief Officer(s):
Ian Ross, President
Pierre-Éric Landry, Executive Director
pierre.eric.landry@me.com
Awards:
• Distinguished Service Award
To recognize Canadian Association of Oral & Maxillofacial Surgeons members who have made a contribution to benefit the specialty of oral & maxillofacial surgery or the association

Canadian Association of Orthodontists (CAO) / Association canadienne des orthodontists (aco)
#210, 2800 - 14th Ave., Toronto ON L3R 0E4
Tel: 416-491-3186; *Fax:* 416-491-1670
Toll-Free: 877-226-8800
cao@associationconcepts.ca
www.cao-aco.org
www.facebook.com/CAOSmiles
twitter.com/CAOSmile
Overview: A medium-sized national organization founded in 1949
Mission: To advance the science & art of orthodontics; To promote the highest quality of orthodontic care in Canada; To act as the official voice of Canadian orthodontic specialists
Finances: *Funding Sources:* Membership fees; Sponsorships
Membership: 500+; *Member Profile:* Educationally qualified orthodontic specialists, registered with a Dental Regulatory Authority; Graduate & postgraduate students enrolled in a Commission on Dental Accreditation program; Academic members who have completed a university level program in orthodontics & are employed full-time in an orthodontic program; *Committees:* Nominations; Bulletin; Communications; President - CFAO; Insurance; Membership; Policy & Procedures & By-laws; WFO - Country; National Scientific Session; New & Younger Members; Database / Directory; History, Archives, & Media; CAO / AAO; Planning & Priorities; Standards of Practice; Sponsorship; WFO; CAO / CDA; CAO Web; Eucators
Activities: Promoting standards of excellence in orthodontic education; Striving for higher standards of excellence in the practice of orthodontics; Promoting public awareness of the benefits of orthodontic health care; Protecting the rights of members
Chief Officer(s):
Robert Kinniburgh, President
Sheila Smith, First Vice-President
Michael Wagner, Second Vice-President
Michael W. Patrician, Secretary-Treasurer
Dan Pollit, Chair, Communications
dpollit@rogers.com
Meetings/Conferences:
• 2018 Canadian Association of Orthodontists Annual Conference, 2018
Scope: National
Description: A scientific session with exhibits
• Canadian Association of Orthodontists 2018 70th Annual Scientific Session, September, 2018, Westin Bayshore Hotel, Vancouver, BC
Scope: National
Description: A scientific session with exhibits
• Canadian Association of Orthodontists 2019 71st Annual Scientific Session, September, 2019, Delta Fredericton Hotel & Fredericton Convention Centre, Fredericton, NB
Scope: National
Description: A scientific session with exhibits
Publications:
• Canadian Association of Orthodontists Bulletin
Type: Newsletter; *Frequency:* Semiannually; *Editor:* Dr. Jim Poslun; *Price:* Free with membership in the Canadian Association of Orthodontists
Profile: Updates on the association & the profession
• Canadian Association of Orthodontists Directory
Type: Directory; *Frequency:* Biennially; *Editor:* Dr. Stephen Roth; *Price:* Free with membership in the Canadian Association of Orthodontists
Profile: A listing of all Canadian Association of Orthodontists members
• Canadian Association of Orthodontists Membership Manual
Type: Manual; *Price:* Free with membership in the Canadian Association of Orthodontists
Profile: Information about orthodontic practice, such as GST & insurance guidelines
• Presidential News
Type: Newsletter; *Price:* Free with membership in the Canadian Association of Orthodontists
Profile: Information from the Canadian Association of Orthodontists' president
• Recommendations on Infection Control for Orthodontic Practice
Price: Free with membership in the Canadian Association of Orthodontists

Canadian Association of Paediatric Health Centres (CAPHC) / Association canadienne des centres de santé pédiatriques
c/o Canadian Association of Paediatric Health Centres, #104, 2141 Thurston Dr., Ottawa ON K1G 6C9
Tel: 613-738-4164; Fax: 613-738-3247
info@caphc.org
www.caphc.org
www.facebook.com/ACCSP.CAPHC
twitter.com/CAPHCTweets
Previous Name: Canadian Association of Paediatric Hospitals
Overview: A medium-sized national organization founded in 1968
Mission: To improve the health of children within Canada through research activities & through advocacy with governments & health care organizations; To provide information exchange amongst members
Staff Member(s): 7
Chief Officer(s):
Elaine Orrbine, President & Chief Executive Officer
eorrdine@caphc.org
Doug Maynard, Associate Director
dmaynard@caphc.org
Meetings/Conferences:
- Canadian Association of Paediatric Health Centres Annual Conference 2018, October, 2018, Saskatoon, SK
Scope: National

Canadian Association of Paediatric Hospitals *See* Canadian Association of Paediatric Health Centres

Canadian Association of Paediatric Surgeons (CAPS) / Association de la chirurgie infantile canadienne
c/o Children's Hospital Of Winnipeg, 840 Sherbrook St., #AE401, Winnipeg MB R3A 1S1
Tel: 204-787-1246; Fax: 204-787-4618
admin@caps.ca
www.caps.ca
www.facebook.com/CAPSsurgeons
twitter.com/CAPSsurgeons
Overview: A medium-sized national organization
Mission: To improve the surgical care of infants & children in Canada
Finances: *Funding Sources:* Membership dues, donations.
Membership: *Fees:* $500; *Member Profile:* Paediatric surgeons who are active, candidates, or honorary
Chief Officer(s):
B.J. Hancock, Secretary-Treasurer

Canadian Association of Palynologists (CAP) / Association canadienne des palynologues
c/o Dr. Mary A. Vetter, Luther College, University of Regina, Regina SK S4S 0A2
www.scirpus.ca/cap/cap.shtml
Overview: A small national organization founded in 1978
Mission: To advance all aspects of palynology in Canada
Affiliation(s): International Federation of Palynological Societies (IFPS)
Finances: *Funding Sources:* Membership dues
Membership: 57; *Fees:* $10; *Member Profile:* Palynologists from universities, government agencies, & industries; Persons with an interest in Canadian palynology
Activities: Promoting cooperation between palynologists & persons in related fields of study; *Library:* CAP Library
Chief Officer(s):
Francine McCarthy, President
fmccarthy@brocku.ca
Mary A. Vetter, Secretary-Treasurer
mary.vetter@uregina.ca
Florin Pendea, Editor, CAP Newsletter
ifpendea@Lakeheadu.ca
Awards:
- Canadian Association of Palynologists Annual Student Research Award
To recognize students' contributions to palynological research
Contact: Matthew Peros, E-mail: mperos@uottawa.ca
Publications:
- CAP [Canadian Association of Palynologists] Newsletter
Type: Newsletter; *Frequency:* Semiannually; *Editor:* Dr. Terri Lacourse; *Price:* Free with membership in theCanadian Association of Palynologists
Profile: Reports about fieldwork, analytical methods, & research in Canadian palynology, plus essays & conference information

Canadian Association of Paralegals (CAO) / Association canadienne des parajuristes
a/s Mrs. Cara Subirana, 2606, av Adhémar-Raynault, L'Assomption QC J5W 0E1
info@caplegal.ca
www.caplegal.ca
Overview: A small national organization
Mission: To promote the paralegal profession; to provide support and an exchange of ideas between colleagues and members, in order to better the skills of the paralegals; to offer continuing education, such as conferences, seminars and discussion groups; and to supply valuable information to paralegals useful in their field of practice, law firms, private businesses, Canadian public corporations and others.
Chief Officer(s):
Dominique Myner, Chair
Publications:
- Liaison [a publication of the Canadian Association of Paralegals]
Type: Newsletter; *Editor:* Tina Paliotta

Canadian Association of Pathologists (CAP) / Association canadienne des pathologistes (ACP)
#310, 4 Cataraqui St., Kingston ON K7K 1Z7
Tel: 613-507-8528
Toll-Free: 866-531-0626
info@cap-acp.org
cap-acp.org
www.linkedin.com/in/capacp
www.facebook.com/canadian.association.pathologists
twitter.com/CAPACP
Overview: A medium-sized national charitable organization founded in 1949
Mission: To maintain high standards for patient practices and care for pathologists and laboratory medicine.
Membership: *Fees:* Schedule available; *Committees:* Awards; Special Archives; Continuing Professional Development; Professional Affairs; Annual Meeting; Membership; Nominating; Executive; Membership; National Standards for High Complexity Laboratory Testing; Resource Development; Workload & Workforce
Activities: Providing professional development opportunities; Offering networking opportunities; Providing information about developments in laboratory medicine
Chief Officer(s):
Martin Trotter, President
Heather Dow, Manager
Publications:
- The CAP [Canadian Association of Pathologists] Newsletter
Type: Newsletter; *Frequency:* Quarterly; *Accepts Advertising*
Profile: Available to members only
- CAP [Canadian Association of Pathologists] Membership Directory
Type: Directory; *Frequency:* Annually

Canadian Association of Pension Supervisory Authorities (CAPSA) / Association canadienne des organismes de contrôle des régimes de retraite (ACOR)
c/o CAPSA Secretariat, PO Box 85, 5160 Yonge St., 18th Fl., Toronto ON M2N 6L9
Tel: 416-590-7081; Fax: 416-226-7878
Toll-Free: 800-668-0128
capsa-acor@fsco.gov.on.ca
www.capsa-acor.org
Overview: A small national organization founded in 1974
Mission: To facilitate an efficient & effective pension regulatory system in Canada
Member of: Joint Forum of Financial Market Regulators
Affiliation(s): National Pension Compliance Officers Association; Canadian Council of Insurance Regulators; Canadian Securities Administrators; Canadian Insurance Services Regulatory Organizations
Membership: 12; *Member Profile:* Canadian pension supervisory authorities
Activities: Developing policies to harmonize pension law across Canada
Chief Officer(s):
Neil Mohindra, Manager, Policy
Publications:
- CAPSA [Canadian Association of Pension Supervisory Authorities] / ACOR Communiqué
Type: Newsletter
Profile: Information for stakeholders about CAPSA's priorities & initiatives

Canadian Association of Perinatal & Women's Health Nurses (CAPWHN) / Association canadienne des infirmières et infirmiers en périnatalité et en santé des femmes
2781 Lancaster Rd., Ottawa ON K1B 1A7
Tel: 613-730-4192; Fax: 613-730-4314
Toll-Free: 800-561-2416
admin@capwhn.ca
www.capwhn.ca
www.facebook.com/CAPWHN
twitter.com/CAPWHN
Previous Name: Association of Women's Health, Obstetric & Neonatal Nurses Canada
Overview: A medium-sized national organization founded in 2010
Mission: To improve the health of women & newborns; To strengthen the nursing profession in Canada
Staff Member(s): 1
Membership: 500+; *Member Profile:* Women's health, obstetric & newborn nurses from across Canada; *Committees:* Advocacy & Health Policy; Membership; Research; Nominations
Activities: Promoting the health of women & newborns; Engaging in advocacy activiities; Conducting research; Disseminating information about health policy, clinical practice & management; Providing education at the local, provincial & national level; Developing a professional network to share ideas
Chief Officer(s):
Sharon Dore, RN, PhD, President
Fabienne Morton, RN, Treasurer
Rita Assabgui, Executive Director
Meetings/Conferences:
- 2018 Canadian Association of Perinatal & Women's Health Nurses National Conference, October, 2018, Ottawa, ON
Scope: National
Publications:
- CAPWHN [Canadian Association of Perinatal & Women's Health Issues] Newsletter
Type: Newsletter; *Frequency:* 3 pa; *Accepts Advertising*
Profile: Activities of CAPWHN & its chapters in the Atlantic provinces, Québec, Ontario, Manitoba & Saskatchewan, & Alberta & British Columbia

Canadian Association of Personal Property Appraisers (CAPPA)
463 King St. East, Toronto ON M5G 1L6
Tel: 416-364-3730
www.cpa-cappa.com
Also Known As: Canadian Professional Appraisers (CPA)
Overview: A small national organization founded in 1989
Mission: To accredit appraisers with proper experience, training, & qualifications & who subscribe to a code of ethics
Membership: *Member Profile:* Qualified individuals who have at least 5 years experience in their field.
Chief Officer(s):
John A. Libby, President
libbygallery@rogers.com
Daniel D. Zakaib, Vice-President, 416-987-8750
dzack@rogers.com

Canadian Association of Petroleum Land Administration (CAPLA)
First St. Plaza, #620, 138 - 4th Ave. SE, Calgary AB T2G 4Z6
Tel: 403-452-6497; Fax: 403-452-6627
office@caplacanada.org
www.caplacanada.org
www.linkedin.com/groups/3877780/profile
www.facebook.com/caplacanada
twitter.com/caplacanada
Overview: A medium-sized national organization founded in 1994
Mission: To establish recognized standards of excellence & influence the energy industry
Staff Member(s): 7; 300 volunteer(s)
Membership: 1,800+; *Fees:* $75 student; $175 active; $75 retired; *Member Profile:* Individuals working in land asset management; *Committees:* Awards; Certification; Conference; Education Delivery & Facilitation; Education Development; Events; Executive; Knowledge Bank; Leadership Forum; Member Services; Mentorship; NEXUS Editorial; Social Media; Surface Stakeholder Engagement
Activities: Leadership & education programs; Professional Development; Voluntary certificate program; Networking opportunities
Chief Officer(s):
Matt Worthy, General Manager, 403-452-6591
matt@caplacanada.org

Awards:
- President's Award
- Outstanding Volunteer Award
- Rising Star Award
- T. Cathy Miller Champion Award
- CAPLA Committee of the Year Award
- Myra Drumm Memorial Student Achievement Award

Publications:
- NEXUS [a publication of the Canadian Association of Petroleum Land Administration]
Type: Magazine; *Frequency:* Quarterly; *Accepts Advertising;* *Editor:* Katherine Matiko
Profile: Industry information & association news

Canadian Association of Petroleum Landmen (CAPL)
#1600, 520 - 5 Ave. SW, Calgary AB T2P 3R7
Tel: 403-237-6635; *Fax:* 403-263-1620
reception@landman.ca
www.landman.ca
www.linkedin.com/groups/3919817/profile
www.facebook.com/936358049739811
twitter.com/CAPLCanadian
Merged from: Alberta Landmen's Association
Overview: A medium-sized national organization founded in 1948
Mission: To enhance all facets of the landman profession in Canada
Finances: *Annual Operating Budget:* $1.5 Million-$3 Million
Membership: 1,500+
Activities: Liaising with government departments & other resource based associations; Communicating with members; Providing professional development opportunities; Offering networking events
Chief Officer(s):
Larry Buzan, President
Noel Millions, Vice President
Meetings/Conferences:
- 39th Annual Canadian Association of Petroleum Landmen Conference 2018, September, 2018, Regina, SK
Scope: National
Publications:
- Canadian Association of Petroleum Landmen Membership Directory
Type: Directory; *Price:* Free access with membership in the Canadian Association of Petroleum Landmen
- CAPL [Canadian Association of Petroleum Landmen] Annual Report
Type: Yearbook; *Frequency:* Annually
- The Negotiator: The Magazine of the Canadian Association of Petroleum Landmen
Type: Magazine; *Frequency:* 10 pa; *Accepts Advertising;* *Editor:* K. Rennie, M. Innes, & J. Frese; *Price:* Free with membership in the CanadianAssociation of Petroleum Landmen
Profile: Feature articles, CAPL conference information, & CAPL news & events

Canadian Association of Petroleum Producers (CAPP) / Association canadienne des producteurs pétroliers
#2100, 350 - 7 Ave. SW, Calgary AB T2P 3N9
Tel: 403-267-1100; *Fax:* 403-261-4622
Other Communication: membership@capp.ca
communication@capp.ca
www.capp.ca
www.linkedin.com/groupRegistration?gid=2632445
www.facebook.com/OilGasCanada
twitter.com/oilgascanada
www.youtube.com/cappvideos
Merged from: Canadian Petroleum Association; Independent Petroleum Association of Canada
Overview: A large national organization founded in 1992
Mission: To represent companies that produce Canada's natural gas & crude oil; To enhance the economic sustainability of the Canadian upstream petroleum industry; To ensure work is conducted in a safe & environmentally & socially responsible manner; To work with government to develop regulatory requirements
Membership: 100+ producer members + 150 associate members; *Member Profile:* Individuals or companies that provide services, such as drilling, banking & computing, for Canada's oil & gas industry; *Committees:* Industry Equalization Steering Committee
Activities: Reviewing, analyzing, & recommending industry policy positions; Participating in regulatory change dialogues; Representing the industry on multi-sector international, federal & provincial consultation bodies; Communicating with governments, regulators, stakeholders & the public; Offering seminars & workshops; Providing industry trends, statistics & research information; Informing members of industry standards & guidelines; Monitoring pipeline expansions; Improving coordinated land use planning processes
Chief Officer(s):
Tim McMillan, President
tim.mcmillan@capp.ca
Terry Abel, Executive Vice President
terry.abel@capp.ca
Jeff Gaulin, Vice President, Communications
jeff.gaulin@capp.ca
Nick Schultz, Vice President, Pipeline Regulation & General Counsel
schultz@capp.ca
Ben Brunnen, Vice President, Oil Sands
ben.brunnen@capp.ca
Awards:
- President's Award
Meetings/Conferences:
- Canadian Association of Petroleum Producers (CAPP) Scotiabank Energy Symposium 2018, April, 2018
Scope: National
Description: High-profile speakers on energy and industry discussion panels.
Contact Information: Email: communication@capp.ca, Phone: 403-267-1100

Canadian Association of Pharmacy in Oncology (CAPhO) / L'Association canadienne de pharmacie en oncologie (ACPhO)
c/o Sea to Sky Meeting Management Inc., #206, 201 Bewicke Ave., Winnipeg MB V7M 3M7
Tel: 778-338-4142; *Fax:* 704-984-6434
info@capho.org
www.capho.ca
www.facebook.com/109491585819684
twitter.com/CAPhO_ACPhO
Overview: A small national organization
Mission: CAPhO, the national forum for oncology pharmacy practitioners & other health care professionals, promotes the practice of oncology pharmacy in Canada, by providing educational opportunites, upholding professional practice standards, & developing the profession as a specialty area of pharmacy practice.
Membership: *Fees:* $50 pharmacy technician & pharamacy assistant; $75 pharmacist; $67.50 joint CAPhO/ISOPP; $50 supporting; $25 student; $2500 corporate; *Member Profile:* Members include oncology pharmacy practitioners & other health care professionals interested in oncology pharmacy.; *Committees:* Awards; Communications; Education; Membership; Conference Planning; Undergraduate Pharmacy Education Task Force
Activities: Facilitating communication; Fostering the development of pharmacy-based research; Promoting occupational health & safety issues
Chief Officer(s):
Joan Fabbro, President
president@capho.org
Mark Pasetka, President-Elect
presidentelect@capho.org
Lori Emond, Treasurer
treasurer@capho.org
Awards:
- Long Time Service Award
- CAPhO Distinguished Service Award
Meetings/Conferences:
- Canadian Association of Pharmacy in Oncology Conference 2018, May, 2018, Hilton Lac-Leamy, Gatineau, QC
Scope: National
Publications:
- CAPhO [Canadian Association of Pharmacy in Oncology] Newsletter
Type: Newsletter; *Frequency:* 3 pa

Canadian Association of Pharmacy Students & Interns (CAPSI) / Association canadienne des étudiants et internes en pharmacie (ACEIP)
144 College St., Toronto ON M5S 3M2
www.capsi.ca
www.facebook.com/439833150533
twitter.com/capsinational
Overview: A medium-sized national organization founded in 1968
Mission: To prepare members for moral, social, ethical obligations to be upheld in the profession of pharmacy; To promote high standards of pharmacy education throughout Canada; To promote means by which members may enhance their professional knowledge & skills; To promote mutual interests & liaison with international pharmacy students, interns & society at large
Affiliation(s): International Pharmacy Student Foundation; Canadian Pharmaceutical Association; Academy of Students; Canadian Society of Hospital Pharmacists
Finances: *Annual Operating Budget:* Less than $50,000
Membership: 3,500+; *Member Profile:* Pharmacy student or intern; *Committees:* Finance; Objectives
Activities: *Internships:* Yes
Chief Officer(s):
Caitlin McGrath, President
pres@capsi.ca
Natasha Szabolcs, Vice-President, Communications
vpcom@capsi.ca
Robyn St. Croix, Executive Secretary
secretary@capsi.ca
Awards:
- Pharmaceutical Care Poster Competition
Teams of up to 3 students compete locally by preparing a pharmaceutical care case work-up in poster form; *Amount:* $250 travel subsidy to PDW; membership to Canadian Society of Hospital Pharmacists
- Compounding Competition
Students compete locally by analysing & preparing pharmacy compound; *Amount:* $250 travel subsidy to PDW
- Patient Interview Competition
Individual students compete locally by conducting a 15 minute patient interview; *Amount:* $250 travel subsidy to PDW; USPDI V.1-2
- Literary Challenge
Individual students compete locally by composing articles relevant to Pharmacy; *Amount:* $500 travel subsidy to PDW; recognition in the Canadian Pharmaceutical Journal
Publications:
- CAPSIL [Canadian Association of Pharmacy Students & Interns] / JACEIP
Type: Newsletter; *Frequency:* 3pa; *Editor:* Darren Reithmeier
Profile: CAPSI national updates & information about current issues in pharmacy & letters & submissions from Canadian pharmacy students

Canadian Association of Pharmacy Technicians (CAPT)
#164, 9-6975 Meadowvale Town Centre Circle, Mississauga ON L5N 2V7
Tel: 416-410-1142; *Fax:* 416-410-1142
www.capt.ca
www.linkedin.com/company/canadian-association-of-pharmacy-technicians-—-capt
www.facebook.com/capt.ca
twitter.com/capt4u
Overview: A medium-sized national organization founded in 1983
Mission: To act as the voice of pharmacy technicians
Member of: Canadian Council on Continuing Education in Pharmacy.
Membership: *Fees:* $75; $45 student; *Member Profile:* Pharmacy technicians, assistants, & aides throughout Canada
Activities: Increasing awareness of the value & role of pharmacy technicians; Providing information to members
Chief Officer(s):
Colleen Norris, President
cnorris@capt.ca
Robert Solek, Vice-President
rsolek@capt.ca
Sheena Deane, Director, Finance
sdeane@capt.ca
Lois Battcock, Director, Administration
lbattcock@capt.ca
Samantha Jenkins, Director, Internal Affairs
sjenkins@capt.ca
Mona Sousa, Director, Membership
msousa@capt.ca
Hayley Roberts, Director, Promotions & Public Relations
hroberts@capt.ca
Meetings/Conferences:
- Canadian Association of Pharmacy Technicians 2018 Professional Development Conference, May, 2018, Whistler, BC
Scope: National

Publications:
• The Mortar [a publication of the Canadian Association of Pharmacy Technicians]
Type: Journal; *Price:* Free with membership in the Canadian Association of Pharmacy Technicians
Profile: A continuing education resource
• Tech Talk [a publication of the Canadian Association of Pharmacy Technicians]
Type: Newsletter

Canadian Association of Photographers & Illustrators in Communications *See* Canadian Association of Professional Image Creators

Canadian Association of Physical Medicine & Rehabilitation (CAPM&R) / Association canadienne de médecine physique et de réadaptation
#310, 4 Cataraqui St., Kingston ON K7K 1Z7
Tel: 613-507-0480; *Fax:* 866-531-0626
info@capmr.ca
www.capmr.ca
www.facebook.com/capmr.ca
twitter.com/CAPM_R
Overview: A medium-sized national organization
Mission: The CAPM&R represents and promotes the interests of the speciality of physiatry in Canada by providing and maintaining a national forum and network. It advances and increases awareness of the specialty through strategic alliances and partnerships, public policy, and professional and practice development.
Membership: *Fees:* $350 active; $150 associate; $100 corresponding; $20 resident; $0 medical student/retired; *Member Profile:* Active members: Certified specialists in physical medicine and rehab; Associate Members: physicians from other speciality fields such as rheumatology, orthopedic surgery, and neurosciences, medical scientists with a PhD, Residents; medical student members; Corresponding members: physiatrists, other physicians, and medical scientists residing outside Canada.; *Committees:* Executive; Continuing Professional Development; Education; Nominating; Research; Scientific Program; Royal College Specialty Committee in Physical Medicine and Rehabilitation
Chief Officer(s):
Rodney Li Pi Shan, President
Heather Dow, Executive Director
Meetings/Conferences:
• Canadian Association of Physical Medicine & Rehabilitation 66th Annual Scientific Meeting, May, 2018, Whitehorse, YT
Scope: National

Canadian Association of Physician Assistants (CAPA)
#704, 265 Carling Ave., Ottawa ON K1S 2E1
Tel: 613-248-2272; *Fax:* 613-521-2226
Toll-Free: 877-744-2272
admin@capa-acam.ca
capa-acam.ca
www.facebook.com/CAPA.ACAM
twitter.com/CAPAACAM
Overview: A small national organization
Mission: To develop Canadian health care; To advocate for members; To promote the delivery of patient-centered quality health care
Membership: 500; *Member Profile:* Canadian physician assistants
Chief Officer(s):
Patrick Nelson, Executive Director
Meetings/Conferences:
• 2018 Canadian Association of Physician Assistants Annual Conference, October, 2018, Fairmont Empress, Victoria, BC
Scope: National

Canadian Association of Physicians for the Environment (CAPE)
#405, 215 Spadina Ave., Toronto ON M5T 2C7
Tel: 416-306-2273; *Fax:* 416-960-9392
info@cape.ca
www.cape.ca
twitter.com/CAPE_Doctors
Overview: A small national organization founded in 1994
Mission: To act as a national voice of physicians on issues surrounding health & the environment; To address issues of environmental degradation to protect & promote human health
Affiliation(s): International Society of Doctors for the Environment (ISDE)
Finances: *Funding Sources:* Membership fees; Donations
Membership: *Member Profile:* Physicians; Health care workers; Citizens across Canada
Activities: Providing educational opportunities; Liaising with other national & international organizations; Designing the online resource, Children's Environmental Health Project; Advocating for laws, standards, & policies to promote health & protect the environment
Chief Officer(s):
Kim Perrotta, Executive Director
Publications:
• CAPE [Canadian Association of Physicians for the Environment] News
Type: Newsletter
Profile: Association news & information on the health implications of environmental issues

Canadian Association of Physicians of Indian Heritage (CAPIH)
115 Charingcross St., Brantford ON N3R 2H8
Tel: 519-304-1718; *Fax:* 519-304-4635
Toll-Free: 888-982-2744
info@capih.ca
www.capih.ca
Overview: A medium-sized national organization founded in 2005
Mission: To arrange continuing medical educations meetings & seminars; to provide resources, services & expertise within Canada & in the Third World as needed
Affiliation(s): American Association of Physicians of Indian Origin (AAPI)
Finances: *Annual Operating Budget:* Less than $50,000; *Funding Sources:* Membership dues
1 volunteer(s)
Membership: 600; *Fees:* $100 Affiliate, General; $50 Resident, associate; $25 student; $500 corporate; *Member Profile:* Physicians; residents; medical students; *Committees:* Education; Entertainment; Community Liaison
Activities: Continuing education seminars; networking; travel seminars
Chief Officer(s):
Kempe S. Gowda, President
Joseph Kurian, CEO

Canadian Association of Physicians with Disabilities
70 Hillsdale Ave. West, Toronto ON M5P 1G1
Tel: 416-485-9461; *Fax:* 416-485-9461
feedback@capd.ca
www.capd.ca
Overview: A small national organization
Mission: CAPD provides a national forum for physicians with disabilities, opening avenues for exchange of ideas & information, particularly as these apply to clinical practice. It aims to improve the quality of care & of life for people with disabilities by influencing clinical education & research in matters pertaining to both patients & physicians with disabilities. It also acts as a vehicle to inform & educate the public at large regarding the many facets of disabilities & to be proactive in influencing policies & laws.
Affiliation(s): Canadian Medical Association
Finances: *Annual Operating Budget:* Less than $50,000
Membership: 1-99; *Member Profile:* Physicians with disabilities & those interested in disabilities
Chief Officer(s):
Ophelia Lynn MacDonald, Contact

Canadian Association of Physicists (CAP) / Association canadienne des physiciens et physiciennes (ACP)
555 King Edward Ave., 3rd Fl., Ottawa ON K1N 7N5
Tel: 613-562-5614; *Fax:* 613-562-5615
cap@uottawa.ca
www.cap.ca
www.facebook.com/CanadianAssociationOfPhysicists
twitter.com/CAPhys
Overview: A medium-sized national organization founded in 1945
Mission: To serve as a platform for physicists to meet & exchange information, ideas & knowledge; To increase awareness & visibility of physics & Canadian physicists; To encourage Canadians to study physics; To address science policy & funding issues in the physics field
Member of: Canadian Consortium for Research & the Partnership Group for Science & Engineering
Affiliation(s): Chemical Institute of Canada; Canadian Organization of Medical Physicists; American Physical Society; Institute of Physics; Mexican Physical Society; Brazilian Physical Society
Finances: *Funding Sources:* Membership dues; Annual congress
Staff Member(s): 3
Membership: 1,600+; *Fees:* Schedule available; *Member Profile:* Individuals who have a Bachelor's degree in physics or four years of experience in the physics field; Corporations or firms that provide products or services to physicists; Canadian university & college physics departments; Research institutes or laboratories that employ physicists; *Committees:* Certification; Encourage Women in Physics; Liaison; Science Policy
Activities: Engaging in political lobbying & advocacy for the advancement of science policy in Canada; *Awareness Events:* Art of Physics Competition
Chief Officer(s):
Francine Ford, Executive Director
Awards:
• CAP-INO Medal for Outstanding Achievement in Applied Photonics
• CAP/DCMMP Brockhouse Medal
• CAP Herzberg Medal
• CAP Medal for Outstanding Achievement in Industrial & Applied Physics
• CAP Medal for Lifetime Achievement in Physics
• CAP-CRM Prize in Theoretical & Mathematical Physics
• CAP-TRIUMF Vogt Medal in Subatomic Physics
• CAP Award for Excellence in Teaching High School/CEGEP Physics
• CAP Medal for Excellence in Teaching Undergraduate Physics
• CAP-COMP Peter Kirkby Memorial Medal for Outstanding Service to Canadian Physics
Meetings/Conferences:
• Canadian Association of Physicists Congress 2018, June, 2018, Dalhousie University, Halifax, NS
Scope: National
Publications:
• Physics in Canada [a publication of the Canadian Association of Physicists]
Type: Journal; *Editor:* Béla Joós
Profile: Articles on physics topics; news about the field of physics; book reviews

Canadian Association of Police Educators (CAPE) / Association canadienne des intervenants en formation policière (ACIFP)
c/o Wayne Jacobsen, 1430 Victoria Ave. East, Brandon MB R7A 2A9
Tel: 204-725-8700
cape.educators@gmail.com
cape-educators.ca
www.facebook.com/593948850654424
Overview: A small national organization
Mission: To promote law enforcement training & education through the guidance of research, program development, knowledge transfer, network facilitation & collaborative training initiatives; to providve advice & input on national & regional law enforcement training & educations trends/needs; to promote a commitment to training
Membership: *Member Profile:* Police educators
Chief Officer(s):
Catherine Wareham, Secretary
Catherine.Wareham@GeorgianCollege.ca
Wayne Jacobsen, President
jacobsew@assiniboine.net
Meetings/Conferences:
• Canadian Association of Police Educators 2018 Conference, June, 2018, Pacific Region Training Centre, Chilliwack, BC
Scope: National
Publications:
• E-Journal [a publication of Canadian Association of Police Educators]
Type: Electronic journal

Canadian Association of Police Governance (CAPG) / Association canadienne des commissions de police
#204, 78 George St., Ottawa ON K1N 5W1
Tel: 613-344-2384; *Fax:* 613-344-2385
communications@capg.ca
capg.ca
Overview: A medium-sized national organization founded in 1989
Mission: To improve the effectiveness of civilian bodies that govern local police services
Finances: *Funding Sources:* Membership dues; Conference

Canadian Associations / Canadian Association of Prawn Producers (CAPP)

Membership: *Fees:* $290-$5,800 police boards/municipal advisory committees; $585 non-police board organizations; *Member Profile:* Canadian police governing bodies; *Committees:* Governance; Member Engagement & Advocacy; Research & Policy; Conference; First Nations Police Governance; Executive
Activities: Determining adequare personnel levels; Budgeting for the needs of the police service; Monitoring the budget; Reviewing the performance of the service; Hiring the Chief of Police; Evaluating the Chief of Police; Labour relations; Discipline; Policy development; *Library:* Canadian Association of Police Boards Library; by appointment
Chief Officer(s):
Mary Anne Silverthorn, Preisdent
Sandy Smallwood, Vice Preisdent
Micki Ruth, Treasurer
Brian Boudreau, Secretary
Awards:
• Emil Kolb Award for Excellence in Police Governance
Meetings/Conferences:
• Canadian Association of Police Governance Conference 2018, August, 2018, Fort Gary Hotel, Winnipeg, MB
Scope: National
Contact Information: capgconference.ca

Canadian Association of Prawn Producers (CAPP)
1362 Revell Dr., Manotick ON K4M 1K8
Tel: 613-692-8249; *Fax:* 613-692-8250
office@shrimp-canada.com
www.shrimp-canada.com
Overview: A large national organization
Mission: To represent the interests of Canadian at-sea producers of coldwater shrimp; To advocate for sustainable & responsible resource management; To provide a platform through which Canadian prawn producers can communicate their issues to government & the general public
Chief Officer(s):
Bruce Chapman, Executive Director

Canadian Association of Pregnancy Support Services
#304 - 4820 Gaetz Ave., Red Deer AB T4N 4A4
Tel: 403-347-2827; *Fax:* 403-343-2847
Toll-Free: 866-845-2151
www.capss.com
www.facebook.com/CanadianAssociationOfPregnancySupportServices?ref=str
twitter.com/CAPSS_RD
Overview: A small national organization
Mission: A Christian national ministry dedicated to providing support for life and sexual health by partnering with Pregnancy Centres across Canada.
Affiliation(s): Evangelical Fellowship of Canada; Canadian Council of Christian Charities
Chief Officer(s):
Lola French, Executive Director, 403-347-2827
lola@capss.com
Meetings/Conferences:
• 2018 Canadian Association of Pregnancy Support Services Conference, April, 2018, Niagara Falls, ON
Scope: National

Canadian Association of Principals (CAP) / Association canadienne des directeurs d'école
#220, 300 Earl Grey Dr., Kanata ON K2T 1C1
Tel: 613-839-0768; *Fax:* 613-622-0258
info@cdnprincipals.org
www.cdnprincipals.org
www.facebook.com/599842980034960
twitter.com/CdnPrincipals
Overview: A medium-sized national charitable organization founded in 1977
Mission: To represent the professional perspectives of principals & vice-principals at the national level & to provide the leadership necessary to ensure quality educational opportunities for Canadian students.
Finances: *Funding Sources:* Membership fees; projects; professional development.
Membership: *Fees:* $10; *Member Profile:* Principals & vice principals
Chief Officer(s):
Jill Sooley-Perley, Executive Assistant
Jameel Aziz, President
jaziz@sd73.bc.ca
Awards:
• CAP Student Leadership Award
• Distinguished School Principal Award
• Elementary Grade School Award

Canadian Association of Private Language Schools (CAPLS)
12880 - 54A Ave., Surrey BC V3X 3C9
Tel: 604-507-2577; *Fax:* 604-502-0373
info@capls.com
Overview: A medium-sized national organization

Canadian Association of Professional Academic Librarians (CAPAL)
PO Box 19543, Toronto ON M4W 3T9
capalibrarians@gmail.com
capalibrarians.org
twitter.com/CAPALacbap
Overview: A medium-sized national charitable organization founded in 2013
Mission: To represent the interests of professional academic librarians in relation to the areas of education, standards, professional practice, ethics, & core principles.
Membership: *Fees:* $50.82 employed; $49.18 associate; $20.88 student; $22.52 retired/unemployed; *Committees:* Advocacy; Communications; Diversity & Equity; Education & Professional Development; Membership; Nominations; Publications; Research & Scholarship; Student
Chief Officer(s):
Colleen Burgess, Chair, Communications
Meetings/Conferences:
• Canadian Association of Professional Academic Librarians 2018 Annual Conference, 2018
Scope: National
Publications:
• Canadian Journal of Academic Librarianship [a publication of the Canadian Association of Professional Academic Librarians]
Type: Journal; *Frequency:* Semiannually; *Editor:* Monica S. Fazekas et al.; *Price:* Free of charge
Profile: Peer-reviewed journal publishing articles ontopics related to academic librarians & the profession of academic librarianship
• CAPAL [Canadian Association of Professional Academic Librarians] Connections
Type: Newsletter; *Editor:* Juliya Borie et al.
Profile: News & updates for members

Canadian Association of Professional Apiculturists (CAPA) / Association Canadienne des Professionels de l'Apiculture (ACPA)
PO Box 373, Aylesford NS B0P 1C0
www.capabees.com
Also Known As: CAPABEES
Previous Name: Canadian Association of Apiculturists
Overview: A medium-sized local organization founded in 1959
Mission: To disseminate information on the management of bees
Membership: *Member Profile:* Persons who study, educate, & administrate in the fields of apiculture & pollination, such as federal & provincial apiculturists, extension apiculturists, teaching or research apiculturalists, apicultural technicians, & apiary inspectors; Associate members include graduate students involved in apicultural projects, technicians associated with apicultural personnel or apicultural projects, representatives of appropriate agriculture & agri-food branches & the Canadian Honey Council, plus members of the Apiary Inspectors of America & the American Association of Professional Apiculturists
Activities: Conducting research; Liaising with the Canadian Honey Council & other professional apiculturists; Co-administering the Canadian Bee Research Fund with the Canadian Honey Council
Chief Officer(s):
Rheal Lafreniere, President, Executive Commitee
Rheal.Lafreniere@gov.mb.ca
Awards:
• Student Merit Award
Eligibility: Canadian students or international students attending Canadian universities who have contributed to the development of apiculture; *Amount:* $600
Publications:
• A Guide to Managing Bees for Crop Pollination
• Honey Bee Disease & Pests

Canadian Association of Professional Art Conservators See Canadian Association of Professional Conservators

Canadian Association of Professional Conservators (CAPC) / Association canadienne des restaurateurs professionnels (ACRP)
c/o Canadian Museums Association, #400, 280 Metcalfe St., Ottawa ON K2P 1R7
Fax: 613-233-5438
www.capc-acrp.ca
Previous Name: Canadian Association of Professional Art Conservators
Overview: A small national organization founded in 1971
Mission: To foster high standards within the conservation profession through accreditation; To facilitate public access to professional conservators
Affiliation(s): Canadian Museums Association; Canadian Association for the Conservation of Cultural Property (CAC)
Membership: *Member Profile:* Conservators; Conservation scientists
Activities: Maintaining standards of members established in the Code of Ethics & Guidance for Practice of the Canadian Association for the Conservation of Cultural Property & of the Canadian Association of Professional Conservators
Chief Officer(s):
Marianne Webb, President, 604-741-0521
mw@mariannewebb.com
Heidi Sobol, Vice-President, 416-586-5583
heidis@rom.on.ca
Greg Kelley, Treasurer, 416-947-1498
gkelley@gregkelley.com
Publications:
• CAPC [Canadian Association of Professional Conservators] Information for Collectors & Custodians
Type: Brochure
Profile: Available to CAPC members
• CAPC [Canadian Association of Professional Conservators] Membership Directory
Type: Directory
Profile: Membership list of accredited CAPC members
• Code of Ethics & Guidance for Practice of the Canadian Association for Conservation of Cultural Property & the CAPC
Profile: Published jointly by the Canadian Association for Conservation of Cultural Property & the Canadian Associationof Professional Conservators
• Selecting & Employing a Conservator in Canada
Profile: Published jointly by the Canadian Association for Conservation of Cultural Property & the Canadian Association of Professional Conservators
• What is Conservation?
Profile: Published jointly by the Canadian Association for Conservation of Cultural Property & the Canadian Association of Professional Conservators

Canadian Association of Professional Employees (CAPE) / Association canadienne des employés professionnels (ACEP)
World Exchange Plaza, 100 Queen St., 4th Fl., Ottawa ON K1P 1J9
Tel: 613-236-9181; *Fax:* 613-236-6017
Toll-Free: 800-265-9181
general@acep-cape.ca
www.acep-cape.ca
Previous Name: Economists', Sociologists' & Statisticians' Association
Merged from: Canadian Union of Professional & Technical Employees; Social Science Employees Association
Overview: A medium-sized national organization founded in 1915
Mission: To negotiate & monitor collective agreement for all federal government economists, sociologists & statisticians.
Affiliation(s): International Labour Organization
Finances: *Annual Operating Budget:* $500,000-$1.5 Million; *Funding Sources:* Membership dues
Staff Member(s): 19
Membership: 5,000 institutional + 50 associate; *Fees:* $35/month; *Member Profile:* Federal government employees in the ES category & research officers at the Library of Parliament.; *Committees:* Collective Bargaining; Finance; Human Rights; Pensions
Chief Officer(s):
Claude Poirier, President, 613-236-9181
cpoirier@acep-cape.ca

Canadian Association of Professional Image Creators (CAPIC) / Association canadienne de photographes et illustrateurs de publicité
#202, 720 Spadina Ave., Toronto ON M5S 2T9

Tel: 416-462-3677; Fax: 416-929-5256
Toll-Free: 888-252-2742
info@capic.org
www.capic.org
www.facebook.com/CAPICnational
twitter.com/followCAPIC
Previous Name: Canadian Association of Photographers & Illustrators in Communications
Overview: A small national organization founded in 1978
Mission: To safeguard & promote the rights of photographers, illustrators, & digital artists who work in the Canadian communications industry
Affiliation(s): American Society of Media Photographers (ASMP)
Membership: 1030+
Activities: Advocating for professional photographers, illustrators, & digital artists; Working for copyright protection; Maintaining industry standards; Offering educational programs
Chief Officer(s):
Hai Au Bui, President
nationalpresident@capic.org

  Montréal Chapter
  Montréal QC
  Courriel: communications@capicmontreal.ca
  capicmontreal.ca
  www.linkedin.com/company/capic-montreal
  www.facebook.com/capicmontreal
  twitter.com/capicmontreal
  Chief Officer(s):
  Hai Au Bui, Président
  evenements@capicmontreal.ca

  Prairie Chapter
  Calgary AB
  capicprairie.tumblr.com
  www.facebook.com/CAPICPrairie
  twitter.com/capicprairie
  Chief Officer(s):
  Michele Ramberg, VP Communications & Events, 403-242-4328
  prairiecommunications@capic.org

  Vancouver Chapter
  Vancouver BC
  capicvancouver@capic.org
  www.facebook.com/capicvancouver
  twitter.com/capicvancouver
  Chief Officer(s):
  Rick Etkin, Interim President, 604-875-0535
  vancouverpresident@capic.org

Canadian Association of Professional Immigration Consultants (CAPIC) / Association Canadienne des Conseillers Professionnels en Immigration (ACCPI)
#602, 245 Fairview Mall Dr., Toronto ON M2J 4T1
Tel: 416-483-7044; Fax: 416-309-1985
info@capic.ca
www.capic.ca
www.facebook.com/684073984953919
twitter.com/capicaccpi
Merged from: Association of Immigration Counsel of Canada; Organization of Professional Immigration Consultants
Overview: A small national organization founded in 2005
Mission: To represent Certified Canadian Immigration Consultants (CCIC), or full members of the Canadian Society of Immigration Consultants (CSIC)
Finances: *Funding Sources:* Membership fees; Sponsorships
Membership: *Member Profile:* Professional immigration consultants in Canada; Students; *Committees:* Executive; Governance; Finance; Membership; Communication; Education & Training; Policy; Lobbying
Activities: Lobbying; Providing information & education; Communicating by social media; Offering opportunities to network with peers
Chief Officer(s):
Katarina Onuschak, Executive Director, 416-483-7044 Ext. 25, Fax: 416-483-0884
executive@capic.ca
Monica Poon, National Coordinator
admin@capic.ca
Christopher Daw, Director, Lobbying, 519-342-5342
lobbying@capic.ca
Lynn Gaudet, Director, Communications, 403-229-9256, Fax: 403-262-9169
communication@capic.ca

Deepak Kohli, Director, Membership, 416-877-5264
membership@capic.ca
Tanveer Sharief, Director, Education & Training, 403-975-7530
education@capic.ca

Canadian Association of Professional Pet Dog Trainers (CAPPDT)
3226 Cambourne Cres., Mississauga ON L5N 5G2
Toll-Free: 877-748-7829
generalinfo@cappdt.ca
www.cappdt.ca
Overview: A medium-sized national organization founded in 1994
Mission: To further the concept of dog-friendly & humane training techniques; To provide a single source of access to educational opportunities, peer networking & event advertising
Membership: 500; *Fees:* $60 professional; $40 associate; *Member Profile:* Dog obedience trainers & instructors
Chief Officer(s):
Pat Renshaw, Chair, 519-925-9542
chair@cappdt.ca
Publications:
• CAPPDT [Canadian Association of Professional Pet Dog Trainers] Forum
Type: Newsletter; *Frequency:* Quarterly; *Accepts Advertising*
Profile: Information about training, business, legislation, & rescue

Canadian Association of Professional Regulatory Affairs (CAPRA) / Association canadienne des professionnels en réglementation (ACPR)
#795, 2425 Matheson Blvd. East, Mississauga ON L4W 5K4
Tel: 905-615-6885
administrator@capra.ca
www.capra.ca
Overview: A small national organization founded in 1982
Mission: To provide a formal professional identity & recognition for regulatory affairs professionals in the pharmaceutical/healthcare field
Membership: 900; *Fees:* $49; *Member Profile:* Pharmaceutical regulatory affairs professionals; *Committees:* Executive; Finance; Executive Advisory; SOP and Policy; Election; Symposium; Education Day; Dinner Meeting; AGM; Annual Face-to-Face; Marketing; Publications; Student Relations; Website; Programming; Webinar; Volunteer Recognition
Chief Officer(s):
Mary Speagle, Chair, 905-690-5775

Canadian Association of Professional Speakers (CAPS)
#300, 1370 Don Mills Rd., Toronto ON M3B 3N7
Tel: 416-847-3355; Fax: 416-441-0591
Toll-Free: 877-847-3350
info@canadianspeakers.org
www.canadianspeakers.org
www.linkedin.com/groups?gid=105645
Overview: A small national organization
Mission: To help speakers succeed through partnerships, market development & accreditation.
Affiliation(s): International Federation for Professional Speakers
Finances: *Funding Sources:* Membership dues
Membership: *Fees:* $495 regular; $250 GSF dual/retired; *Member Profile:* Humourists; sports celebrities; business strategists; health experts; personal growth coaches; economists; doctors; lawyers, etc.
Activities: 10 Chapters across Canada; *Rents Mailing List:* Yes

Canadian Association of Professionals with Disabilities
714 Warder Place, Victoria BC V9A 7H6
Tel: 250-361-9697
info@canadianprofessionals.org
www.canadianprofessionals.org
Overview: A medium-sized national organization founded in 2003
Mission: To address issues affecting professionals with disabilities
Finances: *Funding Sources:* Donations
Activities: Supporting self-advocacy; Sharing knowledge; Providing mentorship opportunities

Canadian Association of Programs in Public Administration (CAPPA)
c/o Johnson-Shoyama Graduate School of Public Policy, Univ. of Regina, 3737 Wascana Pkwy., Regina SK S4S 0A2

Tel: 306-585-5463; Fax: 306-585-5461
www.cappa.ca
Overview: A small national organization founded in 1975
Mission: To improve methods of teaching public administration
Affiliation(s): Institute of Public Administration of Canada
Membership: *Fees:* $400 programs with graduate school; $250 institutional
Chief Officer(s):
Kathy Brock, President

Canadian Association of Prosthetists & Orthotists *See* Orthotics Prosthetics Canada

Canadian Association of Provincial Cancer Agencies (CAPCA)
#300, 1 University Ave., Toronto ON M5J 2P1
Tel: 416-619-5744; Fax: 416-915-9224
info@capca.ca
www.capca.ca
Overview: A small national charitable organization founded in 1998
Mission: To support the reduction of the burden of cancer, through effective leadership & collaboration between the provincial cancer agencies
Staff Member(s): 3
Membership: 10; *Member Profile:* Provincial Cancer agencies; *Committees:* Systemic Therapy Safety Committee; Primary Care Policy Advisory Committee
Chief Officer(s):
Eshwar Kumar, Chair
Brent Schacter, Chief Executive Officer, 204-787-2128, Fax: 204-786-0196
brent.schacter@cancercare.mb.ca

Canadian Association of Provincial Court Judges (CAPCJ) / L'Association canadienne des juges de cours provinciales
150 Bond St. East, Oshawa ON L1G 0A2
Tel: 905-743-2820
www.judges-juges.ca
Overview: A medium-sized national organization founded in 1973
Mission: To ensure the soundness of provincial & territorial courts across Canada; To promote judicial independence & the rule of law
Finances: *Funding Sources:* Membership dues; Federal & provincial grants
Membership: 1,000; *Member Profile:* Provincial & territorial judges throughout Canada; *Committees:* Communications; Equality & Diversity; Conference; Journal; Webmaster; National Education; Atlantic Education; Prairies & Territories Education; National Judicial Institute Representative; New Judges Education Program; Compensation; Professional Responsibility & Judicial Independence; Law; History Project; Liaison with Judicial & Legal Organizations; Judicial Counselling; Electronic Newsletter; Access to Justice; Strategic Plan Review / C.A.P.C.J. Handbook; Judicial Education; Judicial Ethics
Activities: Monitoring the status of provincially-appointed judges; Engaging in advocacy activities; Participating in law reform; Providing education; Disseminating information
Chief Officer(s):
David Walker, President
Mayland McKimm, 1st Vice-President
Robert David Gorin, 2nd Vice-President
Yvan Poulin, 3rd Vice-President
Joseph De Filippis, Treasurer
Jacques Nadeau, Secretary
Awards:
• Justice Award
Meetings/Conferences:
• Canadian Association of Provincial Court Judges 2018 Annual Conference, 2018
Scope: National
Publications:
• Canadian Association of Provincial Court Judges Newsletter
Type: Newsletter
Profile: Association news, events, membership information, & legal anecdotes
• CAPCJ [Canadian Association of Provincial Court Judges] Handbook
Type: Handbook; *Editor:* Judge Sheila Whelan
• Provincial Judges' Journal / Journal des juges provinciaux
Type: Journal; *Frequency:* Semiannually; *Editor:* Judge Brigitte Volpe
Profile: Association reports plus articles

Canadian Associations / Canadian Association of Psychosocial Oncology (CAPO) / Association Canadienne d'oncologie psychosociale (ACOP)

Canadian Association of Psychosocial Oncology (CAPO) / Association Canadienne d'oncologie psychosociale (ACOP)
#1, 189 Queen St. East, Toronto ON M5A 1S2
Tel: 416-968-0207; *Fax:* 416-968-6818
capo@funnel.ca
www.capo.ca
Overview: A small national charitable organization founded in 1986
Mission: To promote excellence in psychosocial oncology services
Finances: *Funding Sources:* Membership fees; Donations; Sponsorships
Membership: *Fees:* $60 affiliate, student, & retired members; $150 full members; *Member Profile:* Clinicians, researchers, educators, & others committed to treating & studying th psychological, social, spiritual, & emotions aspects of cancer
Activities: Encouraging interdisciplinary excellence in psychosocial research, education, & clinical practice; Developing standards & practice guidelines; Offering educational programs; Advocating for access to psychosocial care & services; Providing a national network for the exchange of ideas
Chief Officer(s):
Shane Sinclair, President, 403-220-2925, Fax: 403-284-4803
sinclair@ucalgary.ca
Carole Mayer, Vice-President, 705-522-6237 Ext. 2700
cmayer@hsnsudbury.ca
Doris Howell, Secretary, 416-946-4501 Ext. 3419
doris.howell@uhn.on.ca
Nelson Byrne, Treasurer, 289-848-2039, Fax: 844-457-7683
drbyrne@connectcancersupport.ca
Anthony Laycock, Association Manager
Meetings/Conferences:
• Canadian Association of Psychosocial Oncology 2018 Conference, May, 2018, Toronto, ON
Scope: National
Description: Theme: "Tailored & Targeted Interventions: The New Psychosocial Frontier"
Publications:
• The Emotional Facts of Life with Cancer: A Guide to Counselling & Support for Patients, Families, & Friends
Type: Booklet; *Number of Pages:* 32; *Editor:* Beth Kapusta
Profile: Information about professional support to help people cope with cancer
• Oncology Exchange
Type: Journal; *Price:* Free with membership in the Canadian Association of Psychosocial Oncology
Profile: A Canadian interdisciplinary journal

Canadian Association of Public Health Dentistry (CAPHD) / Association canadienne de santé dentaire publique (ACSDP)
c/o Andrea Richard, PO Box 602, Manitouwadge ON P0T 2C0
info@caphd.ca
www.caphd.ca
Previous Name: Canadian Society of Public Health Dentists
Overview: A small national organization
Mission: To advocate for dental public health in order to improve the oral health of Canadians; To promote oral health
Affiliation(s): Canadian Dental Association
Finances: *Funding Sources:* Membership dues
Membership: *Fees:* $250 suport; $125 full; $35 retired/student; *Member Profile:* Dentists; University professors; Dental hygienists; Dental therapists; Dental assistants; Denturists; Public health administrators; *Committees:* Membership; Scientific Conference; Policy Advocacy; Communications
Chief Officer(s):
Carlos Quiñonez, President
Andrea Richard, Executive Director

Canadian Association of Radiation Oncologists *See* Canadian Association of Radiation Oncology

Canadian Association of Radiation Oncology (CARO) / Association canadienne de radio-oncologie (ACRO)
#6, 20 Crown Steel Dr., Markham ON L3R 9X9
Tel: 905-415-3917; *Fax:* 905-415-0071
Toll-Free: 855-415-3917
caro-acro@secretariatcentral.com
www.caro-acro.ca
Previous Name: Canadian Association of Radiation Oncologists
Overview: A small national organization founded in 1986
Mission: To act as the voice of radiation oncology in Canada; To promote high standards of patient care, radiation oncology research, & education
Affiliation(s): Royal College of Physicians & Surgeons of Canada; Canadian Medical Association; Canadian Association of Medical Radiation Technologists; Canadian Organization of Medical Physicists; Canadian Association of Nurses in Oncology
Membership: 755; *Fees:* Free for fellows, residents, & retired persons; $50 associates; $363 regular members; $1,000 corporate members; *Member Profile:* Radiation oncologists in Canada; Radiation oncology fellows & residents; *Committees:* Annual Scientific Meeting; Education; Finance; History & Archives; Manpower & Standards of Care in Radiation Oncology; Membership; Nominating; Residents & Fellows; Website; Liaison
Chief Officer(s):
Eric Vigneault, President
Jacqueline Spayne, Secretary-Treasurer
Meetings/Conferences:
• Canadian Association of Radiation Oncology 2018 Annual Scientific Meeting, September, 2018, Le Centre Sheraton Montréal Hôtel, Montréal, QC
Scope: National
Description: Joint meeting held in partnership with the Canadian Organization of Medical Physicists (COMP) & the Canadian Association of Medical Radiation Technologists (CAMRT)
Publications:
• CARO [Canadian Association of Radiation Oncology] Code of Ethics
• Physician / Industry Relationships Guidelines
Profile: Guidelines established by the Canadian Association of Radiation Oncology to assist physicians
• Radiosurgery Scope of Practice in Canada

Canadian Association of Radiologists (CAR) / L'Association canadienne des radiologistes
#600, 294 Albert St., Ottawa ON K1P 6E6
Tel: 613-860-3111; *Fax:* 613-860-3112
info@car.ca
www.car.ca
Overview: A medium-sized national organization founded in 1937
Mission: Voluntary organization representing the goals & the interests of imaging specialists; to promote the clinical, educational, research & political goals of Canadian radiology to members, organized radiology, medical associations, government & the public
Affiliation(s): Canadian Medical Association
Finances: *Funding Sources:* Membership dues; corporate
Staff Member(s): 13
Membership: *Fees:* Schedule available; *Member Profile:* Radiologists & residents-in-training
Activities: *Rents Mailing List:* Yes
Chief Officer(s):
Adele Fifield, CEO, 613-860-3111 Ext. 200
afifield@car.ca
Awards:
• Gold Medal & Young Radiologist Award
Meetings/Conferences:
• Canadian Association of Radiologists 81st Annual Scientific Meeting, April, 2018, Le Centre Sheraton, Montréal, QC
Scope: National
Description: Theme: "Artificial Intelligence in Radiology: Present & Future"
Publications:
• Canadian Association of Radiologists Journal / Journal de l'Association canadienne de radiologiste
Type: Journal; *Frequency:* 5 pa; *Accepts Advertising*; *Editor:* Craig Coblentz, MD, FRCPC; *ISSN:* 0846-5371
Profile: Scientific review of radiology in Canada

Canadian Association of Railway Suppliers (CARS) / Association canadienne des fournisseurs de chemins de fer
#901, 99 Bank St., Ottawa ON K1P 6B9
Tel: 613-237-3888; *Fax:* 613-237-4888
info@railwaysuppliers.ca
www.railwaysuppliers.ca
Previous Name: Canadian Railway & Transit Manufacturers Association
Overview: A medium-sized national organization founded in 1991
Mission: To help members maximize their business opportunities; To influence decisions made on the federal and provincial levels that affect the rail industry
Staff Member(s): 2
Membership: 130+ companies; *Fees:* Schedule available; *Member Profile:* Companies that supply products & services to Canadian railways; *Committees:* Government Relations & International Trade; CARS Scholarship; Membership & Marketing; CARS Western
Activities: Staff meet regularly with members of parliment, senior policy advisors and civil servants to inform and deliver a clear message to its members; hold committees, conferences, trade shows, workshops & industry meetings
Chief Officer(s):
Sylvia Newell, President
sylvie_newell@railwaysuppliers.ca
Awards:
• CARS Scholarship Fund
Provides financial assistance to one or more current memebers and immediate family to continue education in the rail industry; or one or more students in a given year enrolled in a program whose pursuit will result in an application to the railway industry *Eligibility:* Students undertaking a university or college degree in a discipline that will benefit the railway industry; must be a memeber of the CARS or be related to a member who has been in good standing for two or more years *Deadline:* April 30; *Amount:* $5,000 *Contact:* Sylvia Newell,
sylvia_newell@railwaysuppliers.com
Meetings/Conferences:
• National Railway Day Conference 2018, November, 2018, Westin Hotel, Ottawa, ON
Description: The event will bring suppliers, railways and government bodies together to celebrate the railway industry

Canadian Association of Recycling Industries (CARI) / Association canadienne des industries du recyclage (ACIR)
#1906, 130 Albert St., Ottawa ON K1P 5G4
Tel: 613-728-6946; *Fax:* 705-835-6196
info@cari-acir.org
www.cari-acir.org
www.linkedin.com/company/canadian-association-of-recycling-industries-cari-
twitter.com/CARI_Recycling
Overview: A medium-sized national organization founded in 1941
Mission: To address issues facing the recycling industry in Canada & internationally; To promote commercial recycling activities
Membership: 260+; *Member Profile:* Canadian companies in the recycling sector, from small scrap yards to large processing plants
Activities: Providing information on government legislation, environment & safety regulations, & new technology; Organizing networking events; Working to solve scrap metal theft; Developing cost cutting services for members; *Speaker Service:* Yes
Chief Officer(s):
Tracy Shaw, President & CEO
tracy@cari-acir.org
Donna Turner, Director, Events
donna@cari-acir.org
Marie Binette, Manager, Communications
marie@cari-acir.org
Meetings/Conferences:
• Canadian Association of Recycling Industries (CARI) 2018 Annual Convention, June, 2018, Hilton Hotels & Suites, Niagara Falls, ON
Scope: National
Publications:
• Canadian Association of Recycling Industries Membership Directory
Type: Directory; *Frequency:* Annually
Profile: Listings of contact information for the recycling industry

Canadian Association of Refugee Lawyers
281 Eglinton Ave. East, Toronto ON M4P 1L3
info@carl-acaadr.ca
www.carl-acadr.ca
www.facebook.com/CARLadvocates
twitter.com/CARLadvocates
Overview: A medium-sized national organization founded in 2011
Mission: To advocate for the rights of refugees & forced migrants; To research issues related to refugees; To promote equitable practices in the treatment of refugees in Canada
Finances: *Funding Sources:* Donations
Membership: 300; *Fees:* $90 standard; $50 associate/NGO/articling students; free for students; *Member Profile:* Refugee lawyers; Academics in refugee studies; Law students; *Committees:* Advocacy; Legal Research; Litigation; Membership & Education; Research; Sustainability
Activities: Litigation; Research; Advocacy; Education

Chief Officer(s):
Mitchell Goldberg, President

Canadian Association of Regulated Importers (CARI) / Association canadienne des importateurs règlementés
#206, 1545 Carling Ave., Ottawa ON K1Z 8P9
Tel: 613-738-1729; *Fax:* 613-733-9501
www.cariimport.org
Overview: A medium-sized national organization founded in 1986
Mission: To ensure the right & ability for importers to do business like other businesses & to create one voice for commodities on the import control list or otherwise controlled by regulations.
Finances: *Funding Sources:* Membership dues
Membership: 60+; *Member Profile:* Import permit holder - poultry, cheese, beef
Activities: *Speaker Service:* Yes

Canadian Association of Rehabilitation Professionals Inc.
See Vocational Rehabilitation Association of Canada

Canadian Association of Rent to Own Professionals (CAROP)
info@carop.ca
www.carop.ca
plus.google.com/?partnerid=ogpy0
Overview: A small national organization founded in 2014
Mission: The Canadian Association of Rent to Own Professionals is the collective voice of rent-to-own professionals across Canada.
Membership: 1-99
Chief Officer(s):
Ron Geddert, President

Canadian Association of Research Administrators (CARA) / Association canadienne des administratrices et des administrateurs de recherche (ACAAR)
#1710, 350 Albert St., Ottawa ON K1R 1B1
Tel: 289-244-3744
webinars@cara-acaar.ca
cara-acaar.ca
www.linkedin.com/groups/4978586/profile
twitter.com/@cara_acaar
Previous Name: Canadian Association of University Research Administrators
Overview: A small national organization founded in 1971 overseen by Universities Canada
Mission: To advance the research administrator profession; To improve the efficiency & effectiveness of research administration at post-secondary institutions; To advocate for its membership through representation & unity; To foster & encourage collaboration with organizations in related disciplines
Member of: Universities Canada; Canadian Consortium for Research
Affiliation(s): National Council of University Research Administrators; Society of Research Administrators; Association of University Technology Managers; Canadian Association of University Business Officers; Canadian Association of Research Ethics Boards; Research Administrators' Group Network
Finances: *Funding Sources:* Membership dues
Staff Member(s): 2
Membership: 900+; *Fees:* $150; *Member Profile:* Individuals with direct or indirect involvement in research administration
Activities: Offering professional development opportunities; Holding an annual national conference; Partnering with international sister organizations to advance communication, networking, & development; Organizing a mentor program; *Library:* O3 Resource Library; Not open to public
Chief Officer(s):
Sarah Lampson, Executive Director, 289-442-2992
executive_director@cara-acaar.ca
Awards:
• Walter Hitschfeld Award
 Deadline: December *Contact:* Sarah Lampson, Executive Director, E-mail: executive_director@cara-acaar.ca
• Research Management Excellence Award
 Deadline: December *Contact:* Sarah Lampson, Executive Director, E-mail: executive_director@cara-acaar.ca
• Dan Chase Distinguished Service Awards
 Deadline: December *Contact:* Sarah Lampson, Executive Director, E-mail: executive_director@cara-acaar.ca
• The Directors' Award for Inter-Institutional Collaboration
 Deadline: December *Contact:* Sarah Lampson, Executive Director, E-mail: executive_director@cara-acaar.ca
• The Innovation Award
 Deadline: December *Contact:* Sarah Lampson, Executive Director, E-mail: executive_director@cara-acaar.ca
• The Community Builder Award
 Deadline: December *Contact:* Sarah Lampson, Executive Director, E-mail: executive_director@cara-acaar.ca
• The Unsung Hero Awards
 Deadline: December *Contact:* Sarah Lampson, Executive Director, E-mail: executive_director@cara-acaar.ca
Meetings/Conferences:
• Canadian Association of Research Administrators 2018 Annual Conference, May, 2018, Westin Ottawa, Ottawa, ON
 Scope: National
 Description: Theme: "Research Administration: Resilience in a Time of Change"
 Contact Information: Manager, Professional Development & Membership Services: Nina Darkeff, E-mail: conference@cara-acaar.ca, Phone: 289-244-3744

Canadian Association of Research Libraries (CARL) / Association des bibliothèques de recherche du Canada (ABRC)
#203, 309 Cooper St., Ottawa ON K2P 0G5
Tel: 613-482-9344
info@carl-abrc.ca
www.carl-abrc.ca
twitter.com/carlabrc
Overview: A medium-sized national charitable organization founded in 1976
Mission: To provide leadership to the Canadian research library community; To address issues affecting research libraries, such as federal research policy, copyright, open access publication, & preservation; To encourage broad access to scholarly information; To seek public policy encouraging of research
Membership: 31 libraries; *Member Profile:* Academic research libraries throughout Canada, as well as Library & Archives Canada & National Science Library; *Committees:* Advancing Research; Building Capacity; Assessment; Policy
Activities: Facilitating effective scholarly communication; Engaging in advocacy activities; Encouraging research partnerships
Chief Officer(s):
Susan Haigh, Executive Director, 613-482-9344 Ext. 101
susan.haigh@carl-abrc.ca
Katherine McColgan, Manager, Administration & Programs, 613-482-9344 Ext. 102
katherine.mccolgan@carl-abrc.ca
Awards:
• CARL Award for Distinguished Service to Research Librarianship
 Awarded annually to an individual who has made a substantial local, national, or international contribution to research librarianship; *Amount:* $1,000
• CARL Award of Merit
 To honour a Canadian who has made an outstanding contribution to research librarianship
• CARL Research in Librarianship Grant
 Deadline: August 15
Meetings/Conferences:
• Canadian Association of Research Libraries Spring General Meeting 2018, April, 2018, Regina, SK
 Scope: National
Publications:
• CARL [Canadian Association of Research Libraries] / ABRC E-Lert / Cyberavis Weekly News Bulletin
 Type: Newsletter; *Frequency:* Weekly
 Profile: Coverage of scholarly communication & journals, access to published government information, innovation, copyright, &research
• CARL [Canadian Association of Research Libraries] / ABRC [Association des bibliothèques de recherche du Canada] Statistics
 Frequency: Annually; *Price:* $50
• CARL [Canadian Association of Research Libraries] Annual Report
 Type: Yearbook; *Frequency:* Annually
• CARL [Canadian Association of Research Libraries] Members' Handbook / Manuel des Membres
 Type: Handbook; *Number of Pages:* 49
 Profile: By-laws, structures, procedures, awards, policies, & plans

Canadian Association of Retired Persons *See* CARP

Canadian Association of Retired Teachers (CART) / Association Canadienne des Enseignantes et des Enseignants Retraités (ACER)
c/o Canadian Teachers' Federation, 2490 Don Reid Dr., Ottawa ON K1H 1E1
Tel: 613-232-1505; *Fax:* 613-232-1886
info@acer-cart.org
www.acer-cart.org
Overview: A small national organization
Mission: To facilitate & promote liaison & mutual assistance among its member organizations; To promote the interests of its member organizations; To develop strategies for joint action on matters of common concern to member organizations; To cooperate with other organizations on matters of common concern
Activities: Promoting & supporting public education
Chief Officer(s):
Roger Régimbal, Executive Director
Publications:
• Canadian Association of Retired Teachers Newsletter
 Type: Newsletter

Canadian Association of Rhodes Scholars (CARS)
c/o Arthur R.A. Scace, PO Box 142, #3910, Toronto-Dominion Bank Tower, Toronto ON M5K 1H1
www.canadian-rhodes-scholars.ca
Overview: A medium-sized international organization
Mission: To further higher education; To assist in the administration of the Rhodes Scholarships in Canada; To represent members' views to the Warden & the Rhodes Trust
Membership: *Fees:* $30; *Member Profile:* Rhodes Scholars who reside in Canada; *Committees:* Mentoring; Sailing Dinner
Activities: Promoting social interaction among Rhodes Scholars
Chief Officer(s):
John Rayner, Treasurer
Publications:
• Canadian Association of Rhodes Scholar Newsletter
 Type: Newsletter; *Frequency:* 3 pa; *Editor:* John Fraser

Canadian Association of Road Safety Professionals (CARSP) / Association canadienne des professionnels de la sécurité routière (ACPSER)
St Catharines ON
info@casp.ca
www.carsp.ca
twitter.com/CARSPInfo
Overview: A small national organization
Mission: The association preserves & shares professional experience regarding road safety. It promotes research & professional development & facilitates communication & cooperation among road safety groups & agencies.
Membership: *Fees:* $65 regular, $10 student; Schedule for groups; *Member Profile:* Professionals involved in the research, management & delivery of road safety in Canada; *Committees:* Membership; Marketing
Activities: Disseminating traffic safety information; Acting as an influential voice for road safety professionals to communicate information to policy-makers
Chief Officer(s):
Brenda Suggett, Executive Administrator
Brian Jonah, President
Jennifer Kroeker-Hall, Vice-President
Publications:
• Canadian Traffic Safety Digest
 Type: Newsletter; *Frequency:* Monthly
 Profile: Compilation of traffic safety information from throughout Canada
• Proceedings of Canadian Multidisciplinary Road Safety Conferences
 Profile: Proceedings of past conferences hosted by the Canadian Association of Road Safety Professionals
• The Safety Network / Réseau-sécurité
 Type: Newsletter; *Frequency:* Quarterly
 Profile: Articles, news, & research concerning road & motor vehicle safety for CARSP members

Canadian Association of SAS Users (CASU) / Association canadienne des utilisateurs SAS (ACUS)
280 King St. East, 5th Fl., Toronto ON M5A 1K7
Tel: 416-363-4424; *Fax:* 416-363-5399
twitter.com/SASCanada
Overview: A medium-sized national organization founded in 1991
Mission: To provide support to all Canadian SAS user groups; to assist them in the most efficient & effective use of the SAS

system for information delivery; to provide updates on research & development of institute software & services.
Chief Officer(s):
Carl Farrell, Executive Vice President, SAS Americas

Canadian Association of School Administrators See Canadian Association of School System Administrators

Canadian Association of School Social Workers & Attendance Counsellors (CASSWAC)
c/o Garden Valley School Div., PO Box 1330, 750 Triple East Blvd., Winkler MB R6W 4B3
Tel: 204-325-8335
www.casswac.ca
Overview: A medium-sized national organization founded in 1982
Mission: To provide professional development & networking opportunities for school social workers & attendance counsellors in Canada; To enhance the quality of school social work & attendance counselling
Finances: *Annual Operating Budget:* Less than $50,000; *Funding Sources:* Membership dues
8 volunteer(s)
Membership: 230; *Fees:* $35; *Member Profile:* Working in school system in non-teaching counselling role
Chief Officer(s):
Jessica Askin, Vice-President
jessica.askin@gvsd.ca
Publications:
• CASSWAC [Canadian Association of School Social Workers & Attendance Counsellors] Newsletter
Type: Newsletter
Profile: News of current trends & issues

Canadian Association of School System Administrators (CASSA) / Association canadienne des administrateurs et des administratrices scolaires (ACGCS)
1123 Glenashton Dr., Oakville ON L6H 5M1
Tel: 905-845-2345; *Fax:* 905-845-2044
www.cassa-acgcs.ca
twitter.com/CASSAACGCS
Previous Name: Canadian Association of School Administrators
Overview: A medium-sized national organization founded in 1975
Mission: To promote & enhance effective administration & leadership in provision of quality education in Canada; to provide a national voice on educational matters; to promote & provide opportunity for professional development to the membership; to promote communication & liaison with national & international organizations having an interest in education; to provide a variety of services to the membership; to recognize outstanding contributions to education in Canada
Affiliation(s): College of Alberta School Superintendents; Manitoba Association of School Superintendents; Ontario Catholic Supervisory Officers' Association; Ontario Public Supervisory Officials' Association; Association of Administrators of English Schools of Québec; Association of Nova Scotia Educational Administrators; School Administrators of Prince Edward Island; Newfoundland & Labrador Association of Superintendents of Education; Association of Directors General of English School Boards of Québec; New Brunswick School Superintendents Association
Finances: *Annual Operating Budget:* $50,000-$100,000; *Funding Sources:* Affiliate sponsorship
Staff Member(s): 1; 1 volunteer(s)
Membership: 1,000; *Fees:* Schedule available; *Member Profile:* Provincial & territorial associations or a designated segment whose members hold adminstrative & leadership responsibility for a school system, region, district, division, province or territory; Associate - educational administrators for whom there is no provincial or territorial association; Professors of educational administration; Retired administrators who are not members of provincial organizations; Graduate students of educational administration
Activities: Facilitating annual workshops; Providing representation and services for members
Chief Officer(s):
Ken Bain, Executive Director, 905-520-1112
ken_bain@cassa-acgcs.ca
Awards:
• Distinguished Service Award
Eligibility: Any present or recent CASSA member who has demonstrated outstanding ability and leadership *Deadline:* May
• XEROX - EXL Award
Eligibility: CASSA members who exhibit exemplary leadership and have enhanced the nature of school administration through service *Deadline:* May
Meetings/Conferences:
• Canadian Association of School System Administrators Annual Conference 2018, July, 2018, Ottawa Westin Hotel, Ottawa, ON
Scope: National
Publications:
• Leaders & Learners
Type: Newsletter; *Accepts Advertising*; *Editor:* Tara Lee Wittchen
Profile: CASA news & events, & articles
• Leaders & Learners
Type: Magazine; *Frequency:* 2 pa; *Accepts Advertising*; *Editor:* Shannon Savory
Profile: CASA news & events, & articles

Canadian Association of Schools of Nursing (CASN) / Association canadienne des écoles de sciences infirmières (ACESI)
#450, 1145 Hunt Club Rd., Ottawa ON K1V 0Y3
Tel: 613-235-3150; *Fax:* 613-235-4476
inquire@casn.ca
www.casn.ca
www.linkedin.com/company/canadian-association-of-schools-of-nursing-association-canadienne-des-ecole-de-sciences-infirmieres
www.facebook.com/574645555928679
twitter.com/CASN43
Previous Name: Canadian Association of University Schools of Nursing
Overview: A medium-sized national charitable organization founded in 1942 overseen by Universities Canada
Mission: To represent Canadian nursing programs; To act as the national voice for nursing education & nursing research
Member of: Universities Canada; Association of Accrediting Agencies of Canada (AAAC); Canadian Consortium for Research; Network for the Advancement of Health Services Research
Affiliation(s): Association of Universities and Colleges of Canada (AUCC)
Finances: *Annual Operating Budget:* $500,000-$1.5 Million; *Funding Sources:* Membership fees; services
Membership: *Member Profile:* Universities & colleges that offer all or part of an undergraduate or graduate degree in nursing; *Committees:* Accreditation Bureau; Advocacy; Awards & Nominations; Clinical Education; Education; Graduate Studies; Public Health Task Force; Research & Scholarship; Strategic Planning; Task Force on Nurse Practitioner Education; Task Force on Nursing Master's Education; Task Force on Governance
Chief Officer(s):
Cynthia Baker, Executive Director, 613-235-3150 Ext. 26
cbaker@casn.ca
Awards:
• Award for Academic Administrative Excellence
Eligibility: Any member of a CASN member school (dean, director, head, chair, vice-dean, assistant dean, etc.) who is, or has been, responsible for the administration of the school, or faculty, the undergraduate program, the graduate program, or the research program during the last three academic years.
• Ethel Johns Award
Eligibility: Any present or former faculty member of CASN member school.
• Award for Excellence in Nursing Education
Eligibility: Any professor of a CASN member school may be nominated.
• Award for Excellence in Nursing Research
Eligibility: Any faculty member of a CASN member school may be nominated.
• Wendy McBride Award for Accreditation Reviewer Excellence
Eligibility: Any current CASN reviewer who has participated in an accreditation review in the last two years. The nominee can be any participating member of the on-site review team.
Meetings/Conferences:
• Canadian Nursing Education Conference 2018, May, 2018, Montréal, QC
Scope: National
Description: Theme: "Canadian Nursing Education: Responding to a Changing World"
Publications:
• Canadian Association of Schools of Nursing NewsUpdate
Type: Newsletter

Canadian Association of Science Centres (CASC) / L'Association canadienne des centres de sciences (ACCS)
100 Ramsey Lake Rd., Sudbury ON P3E 5S9
Tel: 705-522-6825
info@casc-accs.com
www.canadiansciencecentres.ca
Overview: A medium-sized national organization founded in 1985
Mission: Creates synergy among Canada's science centres and science-related museums, assists in finding solutions to the challenges faced by these public institutions, and provides a single voice before government.
Membership: *Fees:* Based on operating budget
Chief Officer(s):
Catherine Paisley, President
David Desjardins, Treasurer
Meetings/Conferences:
• Canadian Association of Science Centres 2018 Annual Conference, 2018
Scope: National

Canadian Association of Second Language Teachers (CASLT) / Association canadienne des professeurs de langues secondes (ACPLS)
2490 Don Reid Dr., Ottawa ON K1H 1E1
Tel: 613-727-0994
Toll-Free: 877-727-0994
admin@caslt.org
www.caslt.org
www.facebook.com/groups/607794879275425
twitter.com/CASLT_ACPLS
Overview: A medium-sized national organization founded in 1970
Mission: To promote & advance nationally learning of second languages; To encourage activities & research in field of second language; To create opportunities for professional development; To promote research & information exchange among second language educators
Member of: Canadian Association for Japanese Language Education; Canadian Association of Applied Linguistics; Canadian Teachers' Federation; Society for Educational Visits and Exchanges in Canada; Canadian Parents for French; Canadian Association of Immersion Teachers; French for the Future
Finances: *Annual Operating Budget:* $250,000-$500,000; *Funding Sources:* Government; Membership dues
Staff Member(s): 4; 10 volunteer(s)
Membership: 4,500 individual; *Fees:* $0 Students; $15 Affiliates; $45 Regular; $250 Institutions; *Member Profile:* Interest in second language education; *Committees:* Nominating Committee; Awards; Performance Appraisal; Special Initiatives Fund; Membership & Provincial Association Partnerships; Communications & Marketing; Organization Capacity Building; Policy Review & Development; Board Advisory; Ad hoc (Technology); Anglais Langue Seconde; Common Framework & Portfolio for Student Teachers of Languages)
Activities: Providing professional development, educational publications, networking activities, & research & resource development; *Speaker Service:* Yes
Chief Officer(s):
Francis Potié, Executive Director
francispotie@caslt.org
Saousan Maadarani, Administrative Assistant
Awards:
• H.H. Stern Award
; *Amount:* $500
• Prix Robert Roy Award
Eligibility: Must have been an active member of the CASLT for at least 2 years; must have distinguished his or herself in teaching, research, or writing to the improvement of second language teaching & learning in Canada
• Lifetime Membership Award
Meetings/Conferences:
• Language Without Borders 2019 Conference, May, 2019, Fredericton, NB
Publications:
• CASLT [Canadian Association of Second Language Teachers] FSL Newsletter
Type: Newsletter; *Frequency:* Monthly; *Price:* Free
Profile: CASLT activities & events, teacher tips, suggested resources & web links, & new teaching & learning materials for teachers with an interest inFrench
• CASLT [Canadian Association of Second Language Teachers] ESL & Modern Languages Newsletter

Type: Newsletter; *Frequency:* Monthly; *Price:* Free
Profile: News about teaching & learning resources & Web links, in addition to CASLT events & activities for teachers of English, Spanish, German, French, Chinese, Japanese & other languages
• Réflexions [a publication of the Canadian Association of Second Language Teachers]
Type: Magazine; *Frequency:* 3 pa; *Number of Pages:* 24
Profile: Articles by researchers, resource reviews, conference information, Web links, & CASLT news & projects for CASLT members

Canadian Association of Sexual Assault Centres (CASAC) / Association canadienne des centres contre les agressions à caractère sexuel (ACCCACS)
77 East 20th Ave., Vancouver BC V5V 1L7
Tel: 604-876-2622; *Fax:* 604-876-8450
casac01@shaw.ca
www.casac.ca
Overview: A medium-sized national charitable organization founded in 1977
Mission: To work for an end to violence against women & toward women's equality; to provide a national voice for anti-rape workers.
Membership: *Member Profile:* Centres that work to prevent sexual assault & provide assistance to those who have been victims of sexual assault
Activities: *Speaker Service:* Yes; *Library*

Canadian Association of Slavists (CAS) / Association canadienne des slavistes
Alumni Hall, Dept. of History & Classics, University of Alberta, #2, 28 Tory Bldg., Edmonton AB T6G 2H4
Tel: 780-492-2566; *Fax:* 780-492-9125
csp@ulberta.ca
www.ualberta.ca/~csp/cas/contact.html
Overview: A medium-sized national organization founded in 1954
Mission: To operate a learned society comprising scholars & professionals with interests in the social, economic, & political life of Slavic people, in addition to their languages, cultures, & histories; To promote understanding of Slavic societies & dialogue; To disseminate information about the past & present of the Slavic world
Member of: Canadian Federation for the Humanities & Social Sciences (CFHSS)
Affiliation(s): The Canadian Association for Ukrainian Studies (CAUS)
Finances: *Funding Sources:* Membership fees; Grants; Gifts
Membership: 500-999; *Fees:* $70 Cdn; $45 Cdn emeritus; $90 Cdn joint; $35 student & underemployed; $600 life; foreign $70, $45 foreign emeritus; $95 foreign joint; *Member Profile:* Members include scholars engaged in teaching & research in the area of Central & East European Studies, including university, college, & secondary school teachers & librarians. Individuals interested in the aims of CAS may join as associate members.; *Committees:* Programme; Nominating; International Relations
Activities: *Rents Mailing List:* Yes
Chief Officer(s):
Megan Swift, President, 250-721-7504, Fax: 250-721-7319
maswift@uvic.ca
R. Carter Elwood, Honorary President
relwood@ccs.carleton.ca
Bohdan Nebesio, Sec.-Treas., 905-688-5550 Ext. 5211
bnebesio@brocku.ca
Elena Baraban, Vice-President
elena_baraban@umanitoba.ca
Reid Allan, Vice-President
russky@unb.ca
Bohdan Nebesio, Sec.-Treas., 905-688-5550 Ext. 5211
bnebesio@brocku.ca
Awards:
• Canadian Association of Slavists Undergraduate & Graduate Student Essay Awards
Best undergraduate & graduate level essays *Deadline:* September
Meetings/Conferences:
• Canadian Association of Slavists 2018 Annual Conference, May, 2018, University of Regina, Regina, SK
Scope: National
Description: Annual conference held in conjunction with yearly congress of the Canadian Federation for the Humanities and Social Sciences.
Publications:
• Canadian Slavonic Papers / Revue Canadienne des Slavistes: An Interdisciplinary Journal Devoted to Central and Eastern Europe
Type: Journal; *Frequency:* Quarterly; *Editor:* Heather J. Coleman; Svitlana Krys; *Price:* Free with membership in the Canadian Association of Slavists
Profile: A forum for scholars from disciplines such as language & linguistics, literature, history, political science, sociology, economics, anthropology, geography, & the arts
• The CAS [Canadian Association of Slavists] Newsletter
Type: Newsletter; *ISSN:* 0381-6133; *Price:* Free for members of the Canadian Association of Slavists
Profile: Information about the association's activities

Canadian Association of Smallmouth Anglers (CASA)
2858 Agricola, Halifax NS B3K 4E6
www.casa-website.com
www.facebook.com/canadianassociationofsmallmouthanglers
Overview: A small provincial organization founded in 1989
Mission: To promote Smallmouth bass fishing in Nova Scotia; To raise awareness on conservation & management issues surrounding Smallmouth bass
Membership: *Fees:* $20 adult; $10 junior; $30 family
Activities: Hosting four family tournaments each year
Chief Officer(s):
Mike LaPierre, President
president@casa-website.com

Canadian Association of Snowboard Instructors (CASI) / Association canadienne des moniteurs de surf des neiges (ACMS)
60 Canning Cres., Cambridge ON N1T 1X2
Tel: 519-624-6593; *Fax:* 519-624-6594
Toll-Free: 877-976-2274
Other Communication: Toll free fax: 866-471-6594
headoffice@casi-acms.com
www.casi-acms.com
www.facebook.com/CASIACMS
twitter.com/casiacms
www.youtube.com/casiacms
Overview: A medium-sized national licensing organization founded in 1994
Mission: To promote the sport of snowboarding, snowboard instruction & coaching & the professions of snowboard teaching & coaching in Canada by training & certifying snowboard instructors & coaches; to ensure that a standard of safe & efficient snowboard instruction is maintained.
Member of: Canadian Ski Council
Affiliation(s): Canadian Ski Instructors Alliance; Canadian Snowboard Federation
Membership: *Fees:* $91.33 regular; $48.36 associate; $26.34 student; $142.85 affiliate; *Committees:* Technical & Educational
Activities: Instructor & coaching certification courses; *Internships:* Yes; *Speaker Service:* Yes
Chief Officer(s):
Dan Genge, Executive Director
dgenge@casi-acms.com

Canadian Association of Social Workers (CASW) / Association canadienne des travailleurs sociaux (ACTS)
#402, 383 Parkdale Ave., Ottawa ON K1Y 4R4
Tel: 613-729-6668; *Fax:* 613-729-9608
casw@casw-acts.ca
www.casw-acts.ca
www.facebook.com/Canadian.Association.of.Social.Workers
Overview: A medium-sized national organization founded in 1926
Mission: To represent Canadian professional social workers; To strengthen & advances the social work profession in Canada; To preserve excellence within the profession
Affiliation(s): International Federation of Social Workers
Staff Member(s): 4
Membership: *Fees:* $50 individual affiliate; $0 individual student; *Member Profile:* British Columbia Association of Social Workers; Alberta College of Social Workers; Saskatchewan Association of Social Workers; Manitoba Association of Social Workers; Ontario Association of Social Workers; New Brunswick Association of Social Workers; Nova Scotia Association of Social Workers; Newfoundland & Labrador Association of Social Workers; Prince Edward Island Association of Social Workers; The Association of Social Workers of Northern Canada
Activities: Promoting social justice for Canadians; Producing position papers on topics such as poverty & women's income; *Library:* Canadian Association of Social Workers Library; by appointment
Chief Officer(s):
Fred Phelps, Executive Director
Publications:
• Canadian Association of Social Workers Code of Ethics & Guidelines for Ethical Practice
• Canadian Social Work
Type: Journal; *Frequency:* Annually
Profile: Current issues of interest to the Canadian social work community
• CASW [Canadian Association of Social Workers] Bulletin
Type: Newsletter; *Frequency:* Semiannually
Profile: Canadian Association of Social Workers initiatives & activities, plus activities within the International Federation of Social Workers
• CASW [Canadian Association of Social Workers] Reporter
Type: Newsletter; *Frequency:* Monthly
Profile: Events, opportunities, & initiatives of interest to social workers

Canadian Association of Specialized Kinesiology
PO Box 214, Tamworth ON K0K 3G0
Toll-Free: 888-490-1340
office@canask.org
www.canask.org
www.facebook.com/219459068073143
twitter.com/CanASK1
Also Known As: CanASK
Overview: A small national organization
Mission: To link association members to international affiliates; To promote & support the specialized kinesiology community of Canada
Affiliation(s): International Kinesiology College; Touch for Health Kinesiology Association (USA); The Energy Kinesiology Association (USA)
Membership: *Fees:* $65 general members; $125 practitioners & instructors; $35 students
Activities: Providing resources
Chief Officer(s):
Heather Phillips, President
Publications:
• Canadian Association of Specialized Kinesiology Membership Directory
Type: Directory; *Frequency:* Annually
Profile: Listing of instructors, practitioners, general members, & student members
• Reaching Out [a publication of the Canadian Association of Specialized Kinesiology]
Type: Newsletter; *Frequency:* Quarterly
Profile: News & information about kinesiology subjects, proposed bylaws, book reviews, reports from kinesiologists, & articles from NorthAmerican conferences

Canadian Association of Speech-Language Pathologists & Audiologists *See* Speech-Language & Audiology Canada

Canadian Association of Sport Sciences *See* Canadian Society for Exercise Physiology

Canadian Association of Staff Physician Recruiters (CASPR)
info@caspr.ca
caspr.ca
linkd.in/sFXJUG
on.fb.me/tgfzQp
twitter.com/CanadianASPR
Overview: A medium-sized national organization
Mission: The Canadian Association of Staff Physician Recruiters (CASPR) is a professional organization from across Canada whose members primary role is to recruit physicians for their communities, local hospitals and other healthcare organizations.
Membership: *Committees:* Education; Sponsorship; Communication; Membership; Barriers to Physician Recruitment; Conference
Chief Officer(s):
Amanda English, Development & Operations Coordinator
Meetings/Conferences:
• Canadian Association of Staff Physician Recruiters 2018 Conference, April, 2018, Fredericton, NB
Scope: National

Canadian Association of Statutory Human Rights Agencies (CASHRA) / Association canadienne des commissions et conseil des droits de la personne (ACCCDP)
#170, 99 - 5th Ave., Ottawa ON K1P 5P5
www.cashra.ca

Overview: A medium-sized national charitable organization founded in 1972
Mission: An umbrella organization for the federal, provincial and territorial human rights commissions.
Membership: 12 organizations
Meetings/Conferences:
• 2018 Canadian Association of Statutory Human Rights Agencies Annual Conference, 2018
Scope: National

Canadian Association of Student Financial Aid Administrators (CASFAA)
c/o Treasurer, University of Manitoba, 422 University Centre, Winnipeg MB R3T 2N2
Tel: 204-474-9532
info@casfaa.ca
www.casfaa.ca
Overview: A medium-sized national organization founded in 1979
Mission: Represents financial aid administrators & awards officers in universities & colleges across Canada
Membership: 100-499; *Fees:* $200 full/associate/affiliate; $25 student; $1,000 corporate
Chief Officer(s):
John Boylan, President
john.boylan@ubc.ca
Jane Lastra, Treasurer
jane.lastra@umanitoba.ca
Meetings/Conferences:
• Canadian Association of Student Financial Aid Administrators 2018 Annual Conference, May, 2018
Scope: National

Canadian Association of Swine Veterinarians (CASV) / Association Canadienne des Vétérinaires Porcins (ACVP)
Tel: 519-273-7170
www.casv-acvp.ca
Overview: A small national organization founded in 2003
Mission: To support members; To discuss issues affecting members; To offer a nation voice on issues that affect pork production; To enhance knowledge of animal welfare, herd health management, & food safety
Membership: *Member Profile:* Canadian veterinarians who have a special interest in swine; Persons in industry, academia, & government
Activities: Facilitating networking opportunities; Encouraging professional development; Promoting communications among organizations with similar interests
Chief Officer(s):
John Harding, Chair, 306-966-7070
john.harding@usask.ca
George Charbonneau, President, 519-273-7170
gcharbon@swineservices.ca

Canadian Association of Teachers of Technical Writing (CATTW)/L'Association canadienne de professeurs de rédaction technique et scientifique (ACP *See* Canadian Association for the Study of Discourse & Writing

Canadian Association of the Deaf (CAD) / Association des sourds du Canada (ASC)
#606, 251 Bank St., Ottawa ON K2P 1X3
Tel: 613-565-2882; *Fax:* 613-565-1207; *TTY:* 613-565-8882
info@cad.ca
www.cad.ca
www.facebook.com/1940CADASC
twitter.com/CADASC
Overview: A medium-sized national charitable organization founded in 1940
Mission: To protect & promote the rights, needs, & concerns of deaf Canadians
Affiliation(s): World Federation of the Deaf; Council of Canadians with Disabilities
Finances: *Funding Sources:* Government funding; Fundraising; Membership fees; Grants
Staff Member(s): 5
Membership: 300,000; *Fees:* Schedule available; *Member Profile:* Affiliated organizations at the non-national level;
Committees: Community Action; Finance & Audit; Governance
Activities: *Speaker Service:* Yes; *Rents Mailing List:* Yes; *Library*
Chief Officer(s):
Frank Folino, President
ffolino@cad.ca
James Roots, Executive Director
Pavel Chernousov, Project Coordinator

Canadian Association of Thoracic Surgeons (CATS) / Association canadienne des chirurgiens thoraciques
#300, 421 Gilmour St., Ottawa ON K2P 0R5
cats@canadianthoracicsurgeons.ca
www.canadianthoracicsurgeons.ca
Overview: A medium-sized national organization
Mission: To represent thoracic surgeons across Canada
Membership: *Fees:* No charge for residents; $250 full members; *Member Profile:* A medical graduate of a Canadian medical school (or equivalent), who has received full-time training in a thoracic surgery training program, accredited by the Royal College of Physicians & Surgeons of Canada; Physicians with postgraduate training in thoracic surgery engaged in a practice related to thoracic surgery; Residents in a field related to thoracic surgery; Persons who have retired from the active practice of thoracic surgery or other related professional activity; Organizations with interests compatible with the interests of the association; Physicians or scientists outside Canada;
Committees: Executive; Research; Continuing Professional Development; Bylaws; Standards of Practice; Communication / Web
Activities: Conducting clinical & laboratory research; Participating in health care planning, such as standards of practice
Chief Officer(s):
Drew Bethune, President
Andrew Seely, Secretary-Treasurer & Chair, Programs
Meetings/Conferences:
• 2018 Canadian Association of Thoracic Surgeons Annual Meeting, September, 2018, St. John's, NL
Scope: National

Canadian Association of Token Collectors (CATC)
PO Box 21018, Stn. Meadowvale, Mississauga ON L5N 6A2
www.nunet.ca/catc.htm
Overview: A small national organization founded in 1972
Mission: To provide information on token collecting, from early colonial to modern trade dollars
Affiliation(s): Ontario Numismatic Association (ONA); Canadian Numismatic Association (CNA)
Membership: *Fees:* $20
Chief Officer(s):
Harry N. James, President
harrynj@sympatico.ca
Publications:
• Numismatica Canada
Type: Newsletter; *Frequency:* Quarterly
Profile: Detailed information about token collecting throughout history for CATC members

Canadian Association of Tour Operators (CATO)
#1011, 7B Pleasant Blvd., Toronto ON M4T 1K2
Tel: 416-485-8232; *Fax:* 416-485-0112
info@cato.ca
www.cato.ca
Overview: A medium-sized national organization founded in 1983
Mission: To act as a voice on behalf of tour operators in dealing with government at all levels in Canada & abroad; To maintain a high standard of ethical practice in the business of tour operators; To promote public confidence & awareness of the business of tour operators
Affiliation(s): Association des Tours Opérateurs du Québec (ATOQ)
Membership: *Fees:* Schedule available; *Member Profile:* Professional outbound tour companies operating in Canada
Activities: Providing market research & industry surveys; Offering crisis management & public relations; Providing networking opportunities; Increasing knowledge & skills of members; Promoting cooperation between tour operators & suppliers
Chief Officer(s):
Pierre LePage, Executive Director

Canadian Association of Toy Libraries *See* Canadian Association of Family Resource Programs

Canadian Association of Transplantation
114 Cheyenne Way, Ottawa ON K2J 0E9
Toll-Free: 877-968-9449
admin@cst-transplant.ca
www.cst-transplant.ca
Overview: A medium-sized national organization
Mission: Health professionals committed to facilitating & enhancing the transplant process

Membership: 600; *Fees:* $50 associate/trainee; $200 full;
Committees: Communications; Education; Ethics; Grants & Awards; Leading Clinical Practice; Governance & Nominations; Public Policy; Research; Scientific Meetings; Standards
Activities: *Awareness Events:* National Organ & Tissue Donation Awareness Week, April
Chief Officer(s):
Steven Paraskevas, President

Canadian Association of University & College Teachers of French *Voir* Association des professeurs de français des universités et collèges canadiens

Canadian Association of University Business Officers (CAUBO) / Association canadienne du personnel administratif universitaire (ACPAU)
#315, 350 Albert St., Ottawa ON K1R 1B1
Tel: 613-230-6760; *Fax:* 613-563-7739
info@caubo.ca
www.caubo.ca
Overview: A medium-sized national charitable organization founded in 1937 overseen by Universities Canada
Mission: To promote the professional & effective management of the administrative, financial & business affairs of higher education; To have the professional standards of its members & to strengthen the contribution of higher education to the well being of Canada
Member of: Universities Canada
Finances: *Annual Operating Budget:* $3 Million-$5 Million; *Funding Sources:* Membership fees; training & development fees; non-due revenue
Staff Member(s): 12; 112 volunteer)
Membership: 143 Post secondary institutions; 60 corporate; 15 associate; *Fees:* Schedule available; *Member Profile:* Member of AUCC or federated or affiliated with member of AUCC;
Committees: Board of Directors; Executive
Activities: Organizing workshops, online courses, outreach programs, webinars, seminars & conferences; Offering faculty bargaining services; *Library:* Knowledge Centre
Chief Officer(s):
Nathalie Laporte, Executive Director, 613-230-6760 Ext. 268
nlaporte@caubo.ca
Tamara Nemchin, Associate Director
tnemchin@caubo.ca
Awards:
• Ken Clements Award
Recognizes a university administrator who has made outstanding contributions to the activities of the organization
• CAUBO Quality & Productivity Awards
Designed to recognize, reward & share university achievements in improving the quality & reducing the cost of higher education programs & services; National & Regional categories *Eligibility:* Awards evaluated on portability, originality, quality impact, productivity impact, & involvement; *Amount:* National: first prize $10,000; second prize $5,000; third prize $3,000
Meetings/Conferences:
• Canadian Association of University Business Officers 2018 Annual Conference, June, 2018, Simon Fraser University, Vancouver, BC
Scope: National
Publications:
• CAUBO [Canadian Association of University Business Officers] Connection
Type: Newsletter
• Debt Management Guide
Profile: A guide for CAUBO members
• Financial Information of Universities & Colleges
Frequency: Annually
Profile: Prepared by Statistics Canada for the Canadian Association of University Business Officers
• Financial Reporting Guide
Profile: Accounting principles & standards of disclosure used in Canadian univeristy published financial statements
• A Guide for Faculty Collective Bargaining: Issues, Strategies, Communication
Profile: Assistance to university administrators in managing critical events on campus
• Investment Survey
Profile: A compilation of the Canadian Universities' Investment Survey results published by the CAUBO Treasury & Investment Committee
• A Point of No Return: The Urgent Need for Infrastructure Renewal at Canadian Universities
Profile: Survey to measure the accumulated deferred maintenance on Canadian university campuses

- University Manager
Type: Magazine; *Frequency:* Quarterly; *Accepts Advertising*; *Editor:* Christine Hanlon
Profile: Promotes the effective management of administrative, financial & business affairs at universities & colleges

Canadian Association of University Research Administrators *See* Canadian Association of Research Administrators

Canadian Association of University Schools of Music *See* Canadian University Music Society

Canadian Association of University Schools of Nursing *See* Canadian Association of Schools of Nursing

Canadian Association of University Teachers (CAUT) / Association canadienne des professeures et professeurs d'université (ACPPU)
2705 Queensview Dr., Ottawa ON K2B 8K2
Tel: 613-820-2270; *Fax:* 613-820-7244
acppu@caut.ca
www.caut.ca
www.linkedin.com/company/canadian-association-of-university-teachers
www.facebook.com/CAUT.ACPPU
twitter.com/CAUT_ACPPU
Overview: A large national organization founded in 1951
Mission: To act as the national voice for academic staff; To promote academic freedom; To improve the quality & accessibility of post-secondary education in Canada
Affiliation(s): Association of Canadian Community Colleges; Canadian Association for Graduate Studies; Canadian Association of University Business Officers; Canadian Education Association; Canadian Federation for the Humanities and Social Sciences & other discipline-based associations; Canadian Federation of Students; Education International; Network for Education & Academic Rights; Coalition of Contingent Academic Labour
Finances: *Funding Sources:* Membership fees
Staff Member(s): 35
Membership: 68,000+; *Member Profile:* Canadian university teachers, librarians, researchers, & other academic professionals; General & contract academic staff; Retired academic staff; Graduate students; *Committees:* Academic Freedom & Tenure; Collective Bargaining & Economic Benefits; Contract Academic Staff; Equity; Librarians & Archivists; Clinical Faculty; Francophones
Activities: Offering courses & workshops; Conducting research about post-secondary education in Canada; Engaging in advocacy activities; Advising member associations in dealing with health & safety issues; *Awareness Events:* Fair Employment Week, October
Chief Officer(s):
David Robinson, Executive Director, 613-820-2270 Ext. 199
Pam Foster, Director, Research & Political Action, 613-820-2270 Ext. 195
Valérie Dufour, Director, Communications, 613-820-2270 Ext. 198
Awards:
• Milner Memorial Award
To recognize a distinguished contribution to the cause of academic freedom
• Sarah Shorten Award
To recognize outstanding achievements in the promotion of the advancement of women in Canadian universities
• Academic Librarians' & Archivists' Distinguished Service Award
To recognize outstanding service by academic librarians or faculty who have contributed to the advancement of the status &/or working conditions of academic librarians at Canadian universities
• Donald C. Savage Award
To honour & to recognize outstanding achievements in the promotion of collective bargaining in Canadian universities
• J.H. Stewart Reid Memorial Fellowship Trust
Awarded annually to a student registered in a doctoral program at a Canadian university. *Eligibility:* PhD students *Deadline:* April 30; *Amount:* $5000
• Excellence in Education Journalism Award
To recognize and promote in-depth and thoughtful coverage of issues related to post-secondary education in Canada.
• Equity Award
To recognize post-secondary academic staff who have demonstrated an outstanding commitment to challenging exclusionary behaviours and practices such as racism and homophobia and by so doing have made post-secondary education in Canada more inclusive.

• Academic Freedom Award
Honours individuals for significant efforts to promote & defend academic freedom in their colleges or universities
• Dedicated Service Award
Honours individuals for desmonstrating exceptional service to their faculty associations
• Distinguished Academic Award
Recognizes academics who excel in teaching, research, service to the institution & service to the community
• Bernice Schrank Award
Recognizes oustanding contributions to the enforcement of academic staff workplace rights through grievance & arbitration
Meetings/Conferences:
• Canadian Association of University Teachers Forum for Presidents 2018, January, 2018, Ottawa, ON
Scope: National
Description: Information for academic staff association presidents
Publications:
• CAUT [Canadian Association of University Teachers] / ACPPU Bulletin
Frequency: 10pa; *Accepts Advertising*; *Editor:* Liza Duhaime; *Price:* $25 Canada; $35 USA; $65 International
Profile: For CAUT members, politicians, reporters, & those interested in post-secondary education
• CAUT [Canadian Association of University Teachers] Almanac of Post-Secondary Education
Frequency: Annually
Profile: Statistical information about universities & colleges for students, academic staff, journalists, & the public
• CAUT [Canadian Association of University Teachers] Education Review
Profile: Policy concerns related to post-secondary education
• CAUT [Canadian Association of University Teachers] Newswire
Type: Newsletter; *Frequency:* Monthly
Profile: Information for member association communications officers & newsletter editors
• Equity Review [a publication of Canadian Association of University Teachers]

Canadian Association of University Teachers of German (CAUTG) / L'Association des professeurs d'allemand des universités canadiennes (APAUC)
c/o Michel Mallet, Université de Moncton, 18, av Antonine-Maillet, Moncton NB E1A 3E9
www.cautg.org
Overview: A small national organization founded in 1961
Mission: To promote studies & research in Germanic Studies at the post-secondary level
Member of: Canadian Association of Teachers of German (CATG); Canadian Federation of the Humanities & Social Sciences
Affiliation(s): Deutscher Akademischer Austauschdienst (DAAD); Goethe Institute
Activities: Sponsoring & organizing programs for scholars; Coordinating a summer job program for Canadian students in Germany; Sponsoring a language program abroad; Participating in an exchange of teaching assistants
Chief Officer(s):
Michel Mallet, Secretary
secretary@cautg.org
James M. Skidmore, Treasurer
treasurer@cautg.org
Publications:
• CAUTG [Canadian Association of University Teachers of German] / APAUC Bulletin
Type: Newsletter; *Frequency:* Annually; *ISSN:* 1193-817X
• CAUTG [Canadian Association of University Teachers of German] / APAU Directory
Type: Directory; *Frequency:* Annually
Profile: A directory of departments of German at Canadian universities & colleges
• Seminar: A Journal of Germanic Studies
Type: Journal; *Frequency:* Quarterly; *ISSN:* 0037-1939
Profile: A scholarly publication about Germanic literature, media, & culture

Canadian Association of Veterans in United Nations Peacekeeping (CAVUNP) / Association Canadienne des Vétérans des Forces de la Paix pour les Nations Unies
PO Box PO Box 46026, RPO Beacon Hill, 2339 Ogilvie Rd., Gloucester ON K1J 9M7
Tel: 613-746-3302
cavunp@rogers.com
www.cavunp.org

Overview: A small national organization founded in 1986
Mission: To perpetuate the memories of fallen comrades; to provide assistance to serving & retired Canadian peacekeepers & their families; to provide education about peacekeeping & peacekeepers
Member of: Veterans Affairs Canada Advisory Committee on the New Veterans Charter; Veterans Affairs Canada Veterans Week Advisory Committee; Veterans Affairs Canada Pacific Region Advisory Council; The Joint Veterans Affairs & National Defence Centre for the Care of Injured and Retired Members of the CF
Membership: *Member Profile:* Retired & serving Canadian military (Regular & Reserve), Royal Canadian Mounted Police, & civilian personnel who have served on United Nations Peacekeeping Missions
Activities: Cooperating with other veterans' organizations; Donating literature on Canada's participation in the United Nations Peacekeeping Forces to schools & public libraries; *Awareness Events:* Canadian Peacekeeping Day, Aug. 9; International Day of United Nations Peacekeepers, May 29
Chief Officer(s):
Ronald R. Griffis, National President, 902-538-3399
J. Robert O'Brien, Chair
gunkeob@yahoo.com
Paul Greensides, National Secretary-Treasurer
cavunp@rogers.com
Publications:
• The Thin Blue Line / Sur la corde raide en bleu
Type: Newsletter; *Editor:* John Stuart
Profile: Association news & activities from chapters across the country

Buffalo 461 Chapter (Hamilton)
c/o Chapter President, 28 Goldwin St., Hamilton ON L9G 6V9
Tel: 905-385-8045
Chief Officer(s):
Douglas Furchner, President
retiredppcli@yahoo.ca
Paul A. Hale, Contact, Chapter Membership, 905-794-2109
cavunpbuffalo461@hotmail.com

Calgary Chapter
c/o Chapter President, 39 Cedardale Hill SW, Calgary AB T2W 5A6
Tel: 403-251-0056
www.cavunp.ab.ca
Chief Officer(s):
Robert F.M. Titus, President
rfmtitus@shaw.ca
Barry T. Wood, Contact, Chapter Membership, 403-254-2882
bwood.un@shaw.ca

Camp Maple Leaf Chapter
c/o Chapter President, 412 Court St. North, Thunder Bay ON P7A 4X1
Tel: 807-475-0803
Chief Officer(s):
Robert L. Manns, President, 807-475-0803
Sydney Bouchard, Contact, Chapter Membership, 807-475-4475

Central Ontario Chapter
c/o Chapter President, 69 Brown Wood Drive, Barrie ON L4M 6M6
Tel: 705-727-1746
Chief Officer(s):
Fernand O. Taillefer, President
taillefer1746@rogers.com
Laurette G. Bedard, Contact, Chapter Membership, 705-429-1547
mlbedard@sympatico.ca

Colonel John Gardam Chapter
c/o Chapter President, 1815 Chopin Place, Orléans ON K1C 5G1
Tel: 613-834-9274
Chief Officer(s):
Wayne R. MacCullough, President
wrmac50@rogers.com
Trevor E. Luten, Contact, Chapter Membership, 613-830-7437
trevor.luten@sympatico.ca

Dartmouth - Halifax Chapter
NS
cavunp-dartmouth.tripod.com
Chief Officer(s):
Shawn E. Kennedy, President
shawn.kennedy450@gmail.com

Canadian Associations / Canadian Association of Wholesale Sales Representatives (CAWS) / Association canadienne des représentants de ventes en gros

Al J. Simpson, Contact, Chapter Membership, 902-465-6761
jackdusty51@gmail.com

Edmonton Chapter
c/o Chapter President, #4PH, 8340 Jasper Ave., Edmonton AB T5H 4C6
Tel: 780-429-7232
Chief Officer(s):
Arthur Adamson, President
artadamson@shaw.ca

Kingston Limestone Chapter
c/o Chapter President, 69 Chesterfield Dr., Amherstview ON K7N 1M5
Tel: 613-384-8527
Chief Officer(s):
Jim (Harold) James, President
hethjim@cogeco.ca

LCpl David W. Young Chapter
c/o Chapter President, 11 Goshen St., Tillsonburg ON N4G 2T7
Tel: 519-688-9212
Chief Officer(s):
Edward J. Weil, President
e-mweil@kwic.com

LGen. R.R. Crabbe Chapter
c/o Past President, 1408 - 233 Booth Dr., Winnipeg MB R3J 3M4
Tel: 204-832-3030
www.cavunp-winnipeg.com
Chief Officer(s):
Bob Barry, Past President

MCpl Mark Isfeld Memorial Chapter
c/o Chapter President, 909 Foreshaw Road, Victoria BC V9A 6M1
Tel: 250-383-8227
Chief Officer(s):
James P. MacMillan-Murphy, President, 250-889-0944
macmurph2@shaw.ca
Scott Laird, Contact, Chapter Membership, 250-383-2808
slaird2@telus.net

MGen. Lewis W. Mackenzie Chapter
c/o Chapter President, 37 Highland Drive, George's River NS B1Y 3G3
Tel: 902-794-8908
cavunplewis.tripod.com
Chief Officer(s):
Ronald V. Clarke, President, 902-794-8908
babetootie@eastlink.ca
John R. Horvath, Contact, Chapter Membership, 902-539-9953
jhorvath@syd.eastlink.ca

Niagara Chapter
c/o Chapter President, 4525 Garden Gate Terrace, Beamsville ON L0R 1B9
Tel: 905-563-9911
Chief Officer(s):
Kevin Wadden, President
kwadden@cogeco.ca
Earle Topley, Contact, Chapter Membership, 905-574-4164

North Saskatchewan Chapter
c/o Chapter President, 307 Cowley Rd., Saskatoon SK S7N 3Z3
Tel: 306-933-9847
members.shaw.ca/nschapter
Chief Officer(s):
Michael W. Titus, President
mjtitus@shaw.ca
Kenneth W. Lowther, Contact, Chapter Membership, 306-384-8208
kwl1@shaw.ca

Peterborough Chapter
c/o Bill Steedman, #205, 811 Sherbrooke St., Peterborough ON K9J 2R2
Tel: 705-743-0115
Chief Officer(s):
Bob Ware, President

Prince Edward Island Chapter
c/o Chapter President, #11, 319 Shakespeare Dr., Stratford PE C1B 2Y4
Tel: 902-892-4403
Chief Officer(s):
Peter R. Van Iderstine, President, 902-892-4403
vanider@pei.sympatico.ca

Prince George & Northern British Columbia Chapter
c/o Royal Canadian Legion Branch 43, 1335 7th Ave., Prince George BC V2L 3N9
Chief Officer(s):
Peter M. Engensperger, Contact, Chapter Membership, 250-981-0140
pdt@canada.com

South Saskatchewan Chapter
c/o Chapter President, 37 Lake St., Regina SK S4S 4A7
Tel: 306-584-7308
Chief Officer(s):
Kenneth C. Garbutt, President
kgarbutt@accesscomm.ca
Wesley D. Kopp, Contact, Chapter Membership, 306-584-0678

Spr Christopher Holopina Chapter
c/o Chapter President, 533 - 16th Street, Brandon MB R7A 4Y2
Tel: 204-728-7951
Chief Officer(s):
Yves Lacerte, President, 204-728-7951
good2sea_u@yahoo.com
Martin Haller, Contact, Chapter Membership, 204-727-5009
bdfc@mts.net

Stony Plain Chapter
c/o Chapter President, Box 17, Site 12, RR#2, Carvel AB T0E 0H0
Tel: 780-963-7768
Chief Officer(s):
Norman A. Westwell, President
njwest@telus.net
Herbert Ross Reid, Contact, Chapter Membership, 780-963-8636
hrreid@telus.net

Succursale MGén Alain R. Forand
23, rue Létourneau, Saint-Jean-sur-Richelieu QC J3W 1B3
Tél: 450-359-4776
onuforand.org
Chief Officer(s):
Robert Chouinard, Président, 450-359-4776
choufam@videotron.ca
France Gagné, Secrétaire de Succursale, 514-772-8519
gafrance@hotmail.com

Wainwright Chapter
c/o Chapter President, 1833 - 1A Street Crescent, Wainwright AB T9W 1N4
Tel: 780-842-6495
Chief Officer(s):
Ronald F. McBride, President, 780-842-6495
mcbride3@telus.net

Western Newfoundland Chapter
c/o Chapter President, 18 Hillside Road, Corner Brook NL A2H 1A6
Tel: 709-639-1163
Chief Officer(s):
Michael S. Martin, President
michaelmartin@nf.sympatico.ca
Winston Childs, Chapter Secretary, 709-634-6428
wdchilds@nl.rogers.com

William C. Hall VC, Greenwood Chapter
c/o Chapter President, PO Box 1152, 883 Carol St., Greenwood NS B0P 1N0
Tel: 902-765-6755
Chief Officer(s):
Nelson G. Mullen, President
nelbel@eastlink.ca

Canadian Association of Volunteer Bureaux Centres *See* Volunteer Canada

Canadian Association of Wholesale Sales Representatives (CAWS) / Association canadienne des représentants de ventes en gros
PO Box 70003, 1725 Avenue Rd., Toronto ON M5M 0A3
Tel: 416-782-8961; *Fax:* 416-782-5876
info@caws.ca
www.caws.ca
Overview: A medium-sized national organization founded in 1983
Mission: To represent comission sales agents on a national level; To serve as an umbrella organization for affiliate markets across Canada
Membership: *Fees:* $300 full; $150 associate; *Member Profile:* Commissioned sales agents selling apparel
Chief Officer(s):
Kim Crawford, President
kim-crawford@hotmail.com

Canadian Association of Wireless Internet Service Providers / Association des fournisseurs de service internet sans fil
#300, 162 Metcalfe St., Ottawa ON K2P 1P2
Toll-Free: 844-370-0404
info@canwisp.ca
www.canwisp.ca
Also Known As: Canwisp
Previous Name: Canadian Association of Internet Providers
Overview: A small national organization founded in 1996
Mission: To foster the growth of a healthy & competitive Internet service industry in Canada through collective & cooperative action on issues of mutual interest
Member of: Canadian Advanced Technology Alliance (CATAAlliance)
Finances: *Annual Operating Budget:* $250,000-$500,000
Staff Member(s): 4
Membership: 100; *Fees:* Schedule available; *Member Profile:* Internet service providers; suppliers to the internet industry
Chief Officer(s):
Eric Lay, Executive Director
Cathi Malette, Manager, Member Services
cmalette@cata.ca
Meetings/Conferences:
• 2018 SP Conference & Annual General Meeting, March, 2018, Ottawa, ON

Canadian Association of Women Executives & Entrepreneurs (CAWEE) / Association canadienne des femmes cadres et entrepreneurs
#1600, 401 Bay St., Toronto ON M5H 2Y4
Tel: 416-756-0000; *Fax:* 416-756-0000
contact@cawee.net
www.cawee.net
www.linkedin.com/groups/2294616/profile
Overview: A medium-sized national organization founded in 1976
Mission: To provide an environment for successful businesswomen to grow & develop, both professionally & personally, through business & community involvement
Member of: International Alliance of Women
Finances: *Funding Sources:* Membership dues; Sponsors
10 volunteer(s)
Membership: 200 corporate/individual; *Fees:* $260; *Member Profile:* At least two years of middle-management experience; *Committees:* Program; Business Owners; Member Communications; Public Relations; Finance & Administration; Legislative; Resources; Membership
Activities: *Speaker Service:* Yes; *Rents Mailing List:* Yes
Chief Officer(s):
Lois Volk, President, 416-460-5221
loisvolk@invis.ca
Amya Greenleaf Brassert, Director, Policy & Administration, 416-454-5112
amygbrassert@rogers.com
Heather Freed, Director, Sponsorship, 416-806-5478
sponsorship@cawee.net
Marie May, Director, Membership, 416-622-7823
marie@mayandcompany.ca
Awards:
• ExtraOrdinary Woman
Presented to one woman each year in recognition of her dedication to herself & other women in their pursuit of personal, professional & financial achievement
• Canadian Association of Women Executives and Entrepreneurs Scholarship (CAWEE)
Eligibility: Female student of the York University's MBA program at the Schulich School of Business who shows a strong interest in advancing the status of women in business.
Publications:
• Acclaim
Type: Newsletter; *Frequency:* Quarterly
Profile: CAWEE news, activities, & member information & articles

Canadian Association of Wooden Money Collectors (CAWMC)
PO Box 2643, Stn. M, Calgary AB T2P 3C1
www.nunet.ca/cawmc
Overview: A small international organization founded in 1975
Finances: *Funding Sources:* Membership dues

Membership: *Fees:* $5 youth; $10 Canadian & USA members; $20 international members; *Member Profile:* Collectors of Canadian wooden money, tokens, & souvenirs
Activities: Facilitating networking opportunities; Distributing information of interest to wooden money collectors; Conducting C.A.W.M.C. mail auctions
Chief Officer(s):
Norm Belsten, Contact
nbelsten@sympatico.ca
Publications:
• Timber Talk
Type: Newsletter; *Accepts Advertising*; *Price:* Free with membership in the Canadian Association of Wooden Money Collectors
Profile: Current information & articles of interest to woooden money collectors

Canadian Association of Wound Care (CAWC) / Association canadienne du soin des plaies
#608, 920 Yonge St., Toronto ON M4W 3C7
Tel: 416-485-2292; *Fax:* 416-485-2291
Toll-Free: 866-474-0125
info@cawc.net
www.cawc.net
www.facebook.com/woundcarecanada
twitter.com/WoundCareCanada
Also Known As: Wounds Canada
Overview: A medium-sized national organization founded in 1995
Mission: To advance wound care in Canada by focussing on public policy, clinical practice, education, research, & international communications
Staff Member(s): 8
Membership: *Fees:* $100 + HST clinician & industry personnel; $75 + HST student, retiree, patient, & lay caregiver; *Member Profile:* Health care professionals, industry participants, patients & caregivers
Chief Officer(s):
Peggy Ahearn, Executive Director
Patricia Coutts, President
Christine Pearson, Treasurer
Meetings/Conferences:
• Canadian Association of Wound Care 2018 Spring Conference, May, 2018, RBC Convention Centre, Winnipeg, MB
Scope: National
• Canadian Association of Wound Care 2018 Fall Conference, 2018
Scope: National
Description: Educational components of the conference include basic clinical, advanced clinical, research, & public policy & education
Publications:
• Wound Care Canada: The Official Publication of the Canadian Association of Wound Care
Type: Newsletter; *Accepts Advertising*; *Editor:* Fiona Hendry; *ISSN:* 1708-6884
Profile: Clinical practice articles, education, & research of interest toclinicians, patients, cargivers, & industry

Canadian Association of Zoos & Aquariums *See* Canada's Accredited Zoos & Aquariums

Canadian Association on Gerontology (CAG) / Association canadienne de gérontologie (ACG)
c/o University of Toronto, #160, 500 University Ave., Toronto ON M5G 1V7
Toll-Free: 855-224-2240
www.cagacg.ca
www.linkedin.com/company/canadian-association-on-gerontology
www.facebook.com/CdnAssocGero
twitter.com/cagacg
Overview: A medium-sized national charitable organization founded in 1971
Mission: To develop the theoretical & practical understanding of individual & population aging through multidisciplinary research, practice, education & policy analysis in gerontology; To seek the improvement of the conditions of life of elderly people in Canada
Member of: International Association of Gerontology & Geriatrics
Finances: *Funding Sources:* Membership dues; Annual conference; Donations; Corporate sponsorships
20 volunteer(s)
Membership: 500 individuals & organizations; *Fees:* $175 individual; $250 organization; $90 senior/student; *Member Profile:* Academics; health care professionals

Activities: *Rents Mailing List:* Yes
Chief Officer(s):
Verena Menec, Vice-President
Anthony Lombardo, PhD, Executive Director
Alison Phinney, Secretary-Treasurer
Awards:
• CAG Honorary Membership
Candidate has made a significant contribution to gerontology; *Amount:* Life membership
• CAG Distinguished Member Award
Recognizes a CAG member who has contributed significantly to furthering objectives & activities of the CAG
• The CAG Donald Menzies Bursary
To support post-baccalaureate students registered in a program of study focused on aging or the aged; *Amount:* $1,500
• The CAG Margery Boyce Bursary
To support post-baccalaureate students who have made a significant contribution to their community through volunteer activities with or on behalf of seniors & who are registered in a program of study focused on aging or the aged; *Amount:* $500
• CAG Award for Contribution to Gerontology
To recognize an individual who has recently made an outstanding contribution to the field of aging; *Amount:* Certificate
Meetings/Conferences:
• Canadian Association on Gerontology 2018 47th Annual Scientific & Educational Meeting, October, 2018, Vancouver, BC
Scope: National
Description: A multi-discplinary conference for persons interested in individual & population aging
Publications:
• Abuse & Neglect of Older Canadians: Strategies for Change
• CAG [Canadian Association on Gerontology] Newsletter / Bulletin d'information de l'ACG
Type: Newsletter; *Frequency:* Quarterly
Profile: Information about conferences, events, students, publications, & CAG news
• Canadian Association on Gerontology Conference Program Books
Frequency: Biennially
• Canadian Association on Gerontology Policy Statements & Issues Papers
• Canadian Journal on Aging [a publication of the Canadian Association on Gerontology]
Frequency: Quarterly; *Accepts Advertising*; *Editor:* Dr. Paul Stolee; *ISSN:* 0714-9808; *Price:* $30student; $71 individual; $115 institution
Profile: A refereed publication with articles about aging concerned with biology, practice, social sciences, & psychology
• National Forum on Closing the Care Gap

Canadian Association on Water Pollution Research & Control *See* Canadian Association on Water Quality

Canadian Association on Water Quality (CAWQ) / Association canadienne sur la qualité de l'eau (ACQE)
PO Box 5050, Burlington ON L7R 4A6
Tel: 289-780-0378
www.cawq.ca
Also Known As: Canadian National Committee of the International Association on Water Quality
Previous Name: Canadian Association on Water Pollution Research & Control
Overview: A medium-sized national charitable organization founded in 1967
Mission: To promote research of scientific, technological, legal & administrative aspects of water pollution research & control; To further the exchange of information & the practical application of such research for public benefit
Member of: International Association on Water Quality
Finances: *Funding Sources:* Membership fees; Subscriptions; Grants
Membership: 10 corporate + 210 individual; *Fees:* Schedule available; *Member Profile:* Individuals, organizations & students engaged in water quality & pollution research & control
Chief Officer(s):
Chris Marvin, President, 905-319-6919, Fax: 905-336-6430
chris.marvin@ec.gc.ca
Yves Comeau, Secretary, 514-340-4711 Ext. 3728, Fax: 514-340-5918
yves.comeau@polymtl.ca
Hubert Cabana, Treasurer, 819-821-8000 Ext. 65457, Fax: 819-821-7974
hubert.cabana@usherbrooke.ca
Meetings/Conferences:
• Canadian Association on Water Quality 53rd CENTRAL Canadian Symposium on Water Quality Research 2018, 2018
Scope: National
Description: A gathering of people in diverse fields of water quality research to present innovations in engineering, science, & policy.
Publications:
• Canadian Association on Water Quality Annual Report
Frequency: Annually
• IWA's Water 21
Type: Newsletter; *Frequency:* Bimonthly
• Water Quality Research Journal of Canada
Type: Journal; *Frequency:* Quarterly; *Editor:* Ronnie Gehr; *Price:* Free for individual CAWQ members; $250 Canada & USA; $295 International
Profile: Peer-reviewed scholarly & review articles & original research on topics such as the impact of pollutants & contaminants on aquatic ecosystems,aquatic species at risk, water treatment & quality, conservation, & water pollution policies

Canadian Astronomical Society (CASCA) / Société canadienne d'astronomie
c/o R. Hanes, Dept. of Physics, Engineering, Physics & Astronomy, 64 Bader Lane, Stirling Hall, Queen's University, Kingston ON K7L 3N6
Tel: 613-533-6000; *Fax:* 613-533-6463
casca@astro.queensu.ca
www.casca.ca
Overview: A medium-sized national organization founded in 1971
Finances: *Funding Sources:* Membership dues
Membership: 420; *Fees:* $60
Chief Officer(s):
Gilles Joncas, President
CASCA-President@astro.queensu.ca
Nadine Manset, Secretary
CASCA-Secretary@astro.queensu.ca
Leslie Sage, Press Officer
CASCApressofficer@gmail.com
Meetings/Conferences:
• Canadian Astronomical Society 2018 Annual Meeting, 2018
Scope: National
Description: Annual meetings are open to all interested persons, but the presentation of scientific papers is restricted to members or applicants for membership & speakers invited by the Local Organizing Committee
Publications:
• Cassiopeia
Type: Newsletter; *Frequency:* Quarterly; *Editor:* Brian Martin
Profile: Observatory news, meeting & departmental reports, events, & instrumentation ideas

Canadian Atherosclerosis Society *See* Canadian Society of Atherosclerosis, Thrombosis & Vascular Biology

Canadian Athletes Now Fund / Fonds des Athlétes Canadiens (FDAC)
106 Berkeley St., Toronto ON M5A 2W7
Tel: 416-487-4442
Toll-Free: 866-937-2012
Other Communication: Alt. E-mail: athleterelations@CanadianAthletesNow.ca
info@canadianathletesnow.ca
www.canadianathletesnow.ca
www.facebook.com/CANFund
www.youtube.com/user/CanadianAthletesNow
Also Known As: See You In CAN Fund; CAN Fund
Overview: A medium-sized national charitable organization
Mission: To provide financial assistance to amateur athletes in Canada. It is a registered charity: 856858642RR0003.
Finances: *Funding Sources:* Fundraising
Chief Officer(s):
Jane Roos, Founder & Executive Director

Canadian Athletic Therapists Association (CATA) / Association canadienne des thérapeutes du sport
#300, 400 - 5th Ave. SW, Calgary AB T2P 0L6
Tel: 403-509-2282; *Fax:* 403-509-2280
Toll-Free: 888-509-2282
info@athletictherapy.org
www.athletictherapy.org
www.facebook.com/catacanada
twitter.com/CATA_Canada
Overview: A medium-sized national licensing organization founded in 1968
Mission: To deliver care through injury prevention, emergency services & rehabilitative techniques

Canadian Associations / Canadian Authors Association (CAA)

Staff Member(s): 2; 65 volunteer(s)
Membership: 1,000-4,999; *Fees:* $204.95; *Member Profile:* Certified Athletic Therapists; Certification candidates; *Committees:* Canadian Board of Certification for Athletic Therapy; Education; Marketing, Sponsorship & Insurance Billing; Program Accreditation; Member Services; High-Performance Providers; International Relations; Financial Advisory; Ethics; Ombudsperson; President's Committee
Activities: Monitoring of professional standards; Hosting conferences
Chief Officer(s):
Darryl Thorvaldson, President
Sandy Jespersen, Executive Director, 416-549-1682
executivedirector@athletictherapy.org
Awards:
• Hall of Fame Award
• Special Recognition Award
• Merit Award
• Distinguished Athletic Therapy Educator Award
• Writing Award
• Outstanding SAT Award
• Evert Van Beek Award
• Volunteer Appreciation Award
• Student Leadership Award
• Research Grant
• Larry Ashley Memorial Scholarship Award
• Annual Scholarship Award
Meetings/Conferences:
• Canadian Athletic Therapists Association 52nd National Conference, May, 2018, Québec, QC
Scope: National
Publications:
• Athletic Therapy Today [a publication of the Canadian Athletic Therapists Association]
Frequency: Semiannually
• CATA [Canadian Athletic Therapists Association] Newsletter
Type: Newsletter; *Number of Pages:* 4

Canadian Atlantic Coordinating Committee *See* Atlantic Council of Canada

---

Canadian Authors Association (CAA)
#203, 6 West St. North, Orillia ON L3V 5B8
Tel: 705-325-3926
admin@canadianauthors.org
canadianauthors.org
Overview: A medium-sized national charitable organization founded in 1921
Mission: To promote & protect Canadian authors & their works; To act as a voice for writers
Affiliation(s): La Société des écrivains canadiens
Finances: *Funding Sources:* Membership fees; Donations
Membership: *Fees:* $50 students; $150 professional or associate members; *Member Profile:* Professional members who have had work published or performed; Associate members who do not qualify for professional membership; Full-time students
Activities: Encouraging work of artistic & literary merit; Providing networking & marketing opportunities
Chief Officer(s):
Anita Purcell, Executive Director
Jessica Wiles, Executive Director
Awards:
• Canadian Authors Association MOSAID Technologies Inc. Award for Fiction
For a full-length novel
• Canadian Authors Association Lela Common Award for Canadian History
For historical non-fiction on a Canadian subject
• Canadian Authors Association Poetry Award
For a book of poetry by one poet
• Canadian Authors Association Carol Bolt Award for Drama
For the best English-language play for adults by an author who is a Canadian or landed immigrant
• Canadian Authors Association - BookLand Press Emerging Writer Award
For a Canadian or landed immigrant writer, under age 30, showing promise in the area of literary creation
• Allan Sangster Award
Awarded to a CAA member for extraordinary service to the association
Meetings/Conferences:
• Canadian Authors Association 2018 Conference, 2018
Scope: National
Description: Educational seminars, awards, readings, & networking opportunities
Publications:
• The Canadian Writer's Guide
Type: Book; *ISBN:* 1-55041-740-1; *Price:* $36
Profile: A comprehensive resource for Canadian writers, featuring articles on topics such as book contracts, copyright, editing, as well as listings of workshops, retreats, & writing schools
• National Newsline [a publication of the Canadian Authors Association]
Type: Newsletter; *Frequency:* Quarterly; *Accepts Advertising*; *ISSN:* 0833-8558; *Price:* Free with Canadian Authors Association membership

Edmonton (Alberta Branch)
PO Box 52007, Edmonton AB T6G 2T5
branchline@canauthorsalberta.ca
www.canauthorsalberta.ca
www.facebook.com/175817798054
twitter.com/CAAAlberta
Mission: To provide guidance & recognition to writers throughout Alberta
Chief Officer(s):
Leanne Myggland-Carter, Operations Manager & Communications Manager
• The Branch Line
Type: Newsletter; *Frequency:* 8 pa; *Number of Pages:* 8
Profile: National & branch news, as well as book reviews & forthcoming Alberta literary events

Kelowna (Okanagan Branch)
c/o 31355 Shannon Pl., Westbank BC V4T 1L3
Mission: To assist writers in the Okanagan area of British Columbia
Chief Officer(s):
Sterling Haynes, Contact
jshaynes@shaw.ca
• Branch Echo
Type: Newsletter; *Accepts Advertising*
Profile: Okanagan branch activities

Kitchener (Waterloo-Wellington Branch)
Kitchener ON
canadianauthors.org/waterloo-wellington
Mission: To encourage & protect writers in the Waterloo-Wellington region of Ontario
Chief Officer(s):
Vanessa Ricci-Thode, President
waterlooauthors@gmail.com
• The Water Well
Type: Newsletter; *Frequency:* Quarterly
Profile: Articles, plus news from the Waterloo-Wellington branch
• Words From Here
Type: Book
Profile: An anthology of works from the Waterloo-Wellington branch

Niagara Branch (CAA Niagara)
PO Box 1512, 4 Queen St., St Catharines ON L2R 3B0
www.canauthorsniagara.org
Mission: To support local writers in the Niagara region; To help writers create & publish works
Chief Officer(s):
Charlotte King, President, 905-937-1901
gctoasties@gmail.com
• Literary Gifts
Type: Booklet; *Frequency:* Annually
Profile: A yearly Christmas booklet
• Stroke Of The Pen
Type: Newsletter; *Frequency:* Quarterly; *Editor:* Anne Osborne
Profile: Niagara branch activities & forthcoming events

National Capital Region Branch (CAA / NCR)
Ottawa ON
www.canadianauthors.org/nationalcapitalregion
twitter.com/caa_ncr
Mission: To assist writers in Ottawa & the surrounding region; To act as a collective voice for writers in the area
Chief Officer(s):
Arlene Smith, President
NCRadmin@canadianauthors.org
• Byline
Type: Magazine; *Frequency:* Quarterly; *Editor:* Sharyn Heagle; *Price:* Free to members of the Canadian Authors Association, National Capital Region Branch
Profile: Local current events, articles, & stories of interest to writers

Peterborough (Peterborough & Area Branch)
PO Box 2412, Peterborough ON K9J 7Y8
ptbocaa@gmail.com
www.canauthors-peterborough.ca
Mission: To help writers in Peterborough, Ontario, & the surrounding region
Chief Officer(s):
J.R. Maclean, President
president@canauthors-peterborough.ca
Amanda Fife, Vice-President
Stephen Thompson, Secretary
Val Crowley, Treasurer
• E-Line Newsletter
Type: Newsletter
Profile: Peterborough & Area Branch activities & forthcoming events
• Shoreline Reflections: A Collection of Short Stories & Poetry
Type: Book; *ISBN:* 978-0-9738308-2-8; *Price:* $14.95
Profile: Short stories & poetry, presented by members of the Canadian Authors Association Peterborough & Area Branch

Toronto Branch
Toronto ON
caatoronto@gmail.com
www.canauthorstoronto.org
Mission: To provide assistance to writers in Toronto & the surrounding area
Chief Officer(s):
Christopher Canniff, President
president@canauthorstoronto.org
Farah Mawani, Secretary
• The Authors' Quarterly
Type: Newsletter; *Frequency:* Quarterly; *Accepts Advertising*
Profile: Toronto branch activities, member news, & announcements
• Gathered Streams: A Collection of Works by Members of the CAA Toronto Branch
Type: Book; *Editor:* Sharon Crawford & Jake Hogeterp
Profile: An anthology of literary works by writers of the Canadian Authors Association, Toronto Branch

Vancouver Branch
PO Box 45019, RPO Ocean Park, South Surrey BC V4A 9L1
Tel: 604-788-9501
vaninfo@canadianauthors.org
canadianauthors.org/vancouver
www.facebook.com/CanadianAuthorsVancouver
Mission: To assist writers in Vancouver, British Columbia
Chief Officer(s):
Margo Bates, President
Grant Brandson, Secretary
Jean Kay, Treasurer
• West Coast Writers
Type: Newsletter; *Frequency:* Quarterly; *Editor:* Carol Tulpar & Barbara Mumford
Profile: Articles, member news from Vancouver, plus forthcoming branch events

---

Canadian Automated Buildings Association *See* Continental Automated Buildings Association

---

Canadian Automatic Merchandising Association (CAMA) / L'Association canadienne d'auto-distribution
Member Services, #100, 2233 Argentia Rd., Mississauga ON L5N 2X7
Fax: 905-826-4873
Toll-Free: 888-849-2262
info@vending-cama.com
www.vending-cama.com
www.facebook.com/10047975738697
twitter.com/CAMA_Vending
Overview: A medium-sized national organization founded in 1953
Mission: To represt the intersts of Vending Operators, Machine Manufacturers, and Product and Service Suppliers in Canada.
Staff Member(s): 2
Membership: 156; *Fees:* Schedule available; *Member Profile:* Equipment & product suppliers & vending operators
Chief Officer(s):
Ed Kozma, President
edward.kozma@meigroup.com
Amanda Curtis, Executive Director
acurtis@vending-cama.com

Canadian Automatic Sprinkler Association (CASA)
#302, 335 Renfrew Dr., Markham ON L3R 9S9
Tel: 905-477-2270; *Fax:* 905-477-3611
info@casa-firesprinkler.org
www.casa-firesprinkler.org

www.linkedin.com/groups/3904166/profile
twitter.com/CASAFS
Overview: A medium-sized national organization founded in 1961
Mission: To advance the fire sprinkler art as applied to the conservation of life & property from fire
Member of: National Trade Contractors Coalition of Canada
Staff Member(s): 10
Chief Officer(s):
John Galt, President
jgalt@casa-firesprinkler.org

Canadian Automobile Association (CAA) / Association canadienne des automobilistes
National Office, 60 Commerce Valley Dr. East, Thornhill ON L3T 7P9
Tel: 905-771-3000; *Fax:* 905-771-3101
Toll-Free: 800-222-4357
generalenquiry@national.caa.ca
www.caa.ca
www.facebook.com/CAANational
twitter.com/CAA
www.youtube.com/TheCAAChannel
Overview: A large national organization founded in 1913
Mission: To promote, develop & implement programs & information related to the rights, responsibilities, & needs of the motorist as a consumer
Affiliation(s): Alliance internationale de tourisme; Fédération internationale de l'automobile; Federacion interamericana de touring y automovil-clubes; Commonwealth Motoring Conference; American Automobile Association
Finances: *Funding Sources:* Membership dues
Membership: 9 clubs serving 6,000,000
Activities: Roadside assistance; driver training; insurance; travel packages; Savings & Rewards program; *Speaker Service:* Yes; *Library:* Canadian Automobile Association Library

Canadian Automobile Association Atlantic
Corporate Office & Saint John Member Service Centre, 378 Westmorland Rd., Saint John NB E2J 2G4
Tel: 506-634-1400; *Fax:* 506-653-9500
Toll-Free: 800-561-8807
www.atlantic.caa.ca
www.facebook.com/CAA.Atlantic
twitter.com/CAA_Atlantic
Also Known As: CAA Atlantic
Overview: A medium-sized provincial organization overseen by Canadian Automobile Association
Mission: To serve New Brunswick, Newfoundland & Labrador, Nova Scotia, & Prince Edward Island
Membership: 200,000 individuals

Canadian Automobile Association Niagara
3271 Schmon Pkwy., Thorold ON L2V 4Y6
Tel: 905-984-8585; *Fax:* 905-688-0289
Toll-Free: 800-263-3616
caaniagara.ca
www.facebook.com/CAANiagara
twitter.com/CAANiagara
www.youtube.com/user/CAANiagara1
Also Known As: CAA Niagara
Overview: A medium-sized local organization overseen by Canadian Automobile Association

Canadian Automobile Association North & East Ontario
2151 Thurston Dr., Ottawa ON K1G 6C9
Tel: 613-820-1890; *Fax:* 613-820-4646
Toll-Free: 800-267-8713
Other Communication: Membership e-mail:
membership@caaneo.on.ca
contactcaa@caaneo.on.ca
www.caaneo.ca
www.facebook.com/CAANEO
twitter.com/CAANEO
www.youtube.com/user/TheCAANEOChannel
Also Known As: CAA North & East Ontario
Overview: A medium-sized local organization founded in 1964 overseen by Canadian Automobile Association
Mission: To deliver automotive, travel, insurance & related services to members & advocate on their behalf
Membership: *Fees:* Schedule available
Activities: Providing automotive, travel, & insurance services; *Speaker Service:* Yes
Chief Officer(s):
Jack Campbell, Chair

Canadian Automobile Association Saskatchewan
200 Albert St. North, Regina SK S4R 5E2
Tel: 306-791-4314; *Fax:* 306-949-4461
Toll-Free: 800-564-6222
caa.admin@caasask.sk.ca
caasask.ca
www.linkedin.com/company/521051
twitter.com/caasaskatchewan
www.youtube.com/caasask
Also Known As: CAA Saskatchewan
Overview: A medium-sized provincial organization overseen by Canadian Automobile Association
Mission: To guarantee excellent emergency road assistance, travel, & insurance services; To provide services, products, programs, & representations to government in order to meet the needs of members, clients, & employees
Member of: Canadian Automobile Association of Canada
Membership: 185,000; *Fees:* $33 a la carte; $77 basic; $115 plus; $144 premier; $146 plus RV; $175 premier RV
Chief Officer(s):
Fred Titanich, President

Canadian Automobile Association South Central Ontario
60 Commerce Valley Dr. East, Thornhill ON L3T 7P9
Tel: 416-221-4300; *Fax:* 905-771-3101
Toll-Free: 800-268-3750
Other Communication: blog.caasco.com
membership@caasco.ca
www.caasco.ca
www.facebook.com/106112779480473
twitter.com/caasco
www.youtube.com/caasouthcentralON
Also Known As: CAA South Central Ontario
Previous Name: Canadian Automobile Association Toronto
Overview: A medium-sized local organization founded in 1903 overseen by Canadian Automobile Association
Mission: To enrich the driving experience of members by providing travel, insurance & automotive services & information
Finances: *Funding Sources:* Membership fees
Membership: 1,900,000
Activities: Offering roadside services, CAA driver training, CAA-approved vehicle repair facilities, insurance services, & travel services
Chief Officer(s):
Bill Carter, Chair
Jay Woo, President & CEO
Jeff LeMoine, Consultant, Communications, 905-771-4709
jlem@caasco.ca
Publications:
• CAA [Canadian Automobile Association] eLetter
Type: Newsletter; *Frequency:* Monthly
Profile: CAA programs, advice, consumer information, & membership savings
• CAA [Canadian Automobile Association] Waves
Type: Newsletter; *Frequency:* Monthly
Profile: Tavel newsletter with information such as destinations, deals, & tips
• CAA [Canadian Automobile Association South Central Ontario] Magazine
Type: Magazine; *Frequency:* Quarterly; *Editor:* Tracy Howard
Profile: Publication for members includes CAA, automotive, insurance, travel, & lifestyle information
• Extraordinary Explorations [a publication of the Canadian Automobile Association]
Frequency: Quarterly
Profile: Travel ideas & vacation experiences

Canadian Automobile Association Toronto *See* Canadian Automobile Association South Central Ontario

Canadian Automobile Chamber of Commerce *See* Canadian Vehicle Manufacturers' Association

Canadian Automobile Dealers' Association (CADA) / Corporation des associations de détaillants d'automobiles (CADA)
#303, 123 Commerce Valley Dr. East, Thornhill ON L3T 7W8
Tel: 905-940-4959
Toll-Free: 800-463-5289
www.cada.ca
twitter.com/cdnautocada
Previous Name: Federation of Automobile Dealer Associations of Canada
Overview: A large national organization founded in 1941
Mission: To deal with issues of a national nature which affect the well-being of franchised automobile & truck dealers in Canada
Membership: 3,200 dealers representing 140,000 people; *Member Profile:* Franchised new automobile dealers in Canada
Chief Officer(s):
John White, President & CEO
jwhite@cada.ca
Awards:
• Canadian Automobile Dealers' Association Business in Automotive Management Scholarship
; *Amount:* $2,000
Publications:
• Canadian Auto Dealer
Type: Magazine; *Frequency:* 8 pa; *ISSN:* 1715-8737; *Price:* $16.95 Canada; $29.95 USA
Profile: For dealer principals & senior managers at Canadian automobile dealerships
• Driving Canada's Future: Background Information & Statistics
• Energuide
• Turning the Lights on Leasing: Consumer Guide to Vehicle Leasing
Profile: A publication for consumers from the Canadian Automobile Dealers Association, Canadian Vehicle Manufacturers Association, Association of International AutomobileManufacturers of Canada & the Canadian Finance and Leasing Association

Ottawa Office
#1403, 222 Queen St., Ottawa ON K1P 5V9
Tel: 613-230-2079
Toll-Free: 800-465-3054

Canadian Automobile Insurance Rate Regulators Association (CARR)
PE
www.carrorg.ca
Overview: A small national organization founded in 2008
Mission: To provide a forum for members to share best practices, identify issues & participate in educational opportunities
Membership: 1-99
Activities: Educational opportunities; conferences
Chief Officer(s):
Allison MacEwen, Chair
Heather Walker, Contact, 902-892-3501, Fax: 902-566-4076
HWalker@irac.pe.ca
Kate Paisley, Administrative Coordinator, 506-643-7806
kate.paisley@nbib-canb.org
Publications:
• CARR [Canadian Automobile Insurance Rate Regulators Association] Emissions
Type: Newsletter

Canadian Automobile Sport Clubs - Ontario Region Inc. (CASC-OR)
1100 Barmac Dr., Toronto ON M9L 2X3
Tel: 416-667-9500; *Fax:* 416-667-9555
Toll-Free: 877-667-9505
office@casc.on.ca
www.casc.on.ca
Overview: A medium-sized provincial organization founded in 1964
Mission: To provide leadership, management, advocacy & the administrative services, facilities & equipment necessary to enable members to maximize their enjoyment & participation in motorsport; to maintain controls & standards necessary for safe competition
Affiliation(s): British Automobile Racing Club; British Empire Motor Club; BMW Club of Canada; Canadian Race Communications Association; Canadian Timing Association; Canadian Volvo Club; Deutscher Automobil Club; HADA Motorsport Club; Kitchener Waterloo Rally Club; London Auto Sport Club; Motorsport Club of Ottawa; Maple Leaf Rally Club; Motorsport Marshalling Services; Mazda Sportscar Owners Club; Oshawa Motor Sport Club; Ontario Z Car Owners Association; Peterborough Motor Sports Club; Race Drivers Guild of Canada; Saab Club of Canada; St. Catharines Motor Club; St. Lawrence Automobile Club
Finances: *Funding Sources:* Licences; permits; event services
Membership: 30 clubs; *Member Profile:* Motorsport professionals & enthusiasts; *Committees:* Race
Activities: International Auto Show Exhibitor; Ontario Regional Driving Championships; *Speaker Service:* Yes; *Library:* by appointment
Chief Officer(s):

Canadian Associations / Canadian Automotive Repair & Service Council

Peter Jackson, Secretary
secretary@casc.on.ca
Perry Iannuzzi, President
president@casc.on.ca

Canadian Automotive Repair & Service Council
c/o Cars Training Network, 81 Osborne Rd., Courtice ON L1E 2R3
Fax: 855-813-2111
Toll-Free: 855-813-2101
info@carstraining.net
www.carsondemand.com
Also Known As: CARS Council
Overview: A small national organization founded in 1991
Mission: To serve as a virtual gathering place to access training & education programs, to research industry issues, & to learn of new skills, technologies & trends.
Member of: Alliance of Sector Councils; Society for Applied Learning Technology; Canadian Collision Industry Forum; Automotive Industries Association of Canada; Association of Accrediting Agencies of Canada; Canadian Apprenticeship Forum
Affiliation(s): CARS Institute
Membership: *Member Profile:* Employers & employees in automotive repair & service; technicians; business owners; educators
Activities: National accreditation program; workshops; *Library:* Not open to public

Canadian Avalanche Association (CAA)
PO Box 2759, 110 MacKenzie Ave., Revelstoke BC V0E 2S0
Tel: 250-837-2435; *Fax:* 866-366-2094
www.avalancheassociation.ca
Overview: A medium-sized national organization founded in 1982
Mission: To foster & support a professional environment for avalanche safety operations in Canada; To represent the avalanche community to stakeholders
Finances: *Funding Sources:* Donations
Activities: Establishing technical standards; Providing technical training courses for professional avalanche workers, wilderness guiding operations, government programs (Parks Canada & provincial parks), & highway, railway, mining, forestry, & construction operations
Chief Officer(s):
Joe Obad, Executive Director
jobad@avalancheassociation.ca
Kristin Anthony-Malone, Manager, Operations
kmalone@avalancheassociation.ca
Emily Grady, Manager, Industry Training Program
egrady@avalancheassociation.ca
Meetings/Conferences:
• Canadian Avalanche Association 2018 Annual General Meeting & Spring Conference, 2018
Scope: National
Description: An introduction for technicians & supervisors from transportation & utility & resource sectors, such as forestry, mining, & railways, who manage winter operations & avalanche hazard programs
Publications:
• Avalanche Accidents in Canada
Profile: Volume 1 - 1955 to 1976; Volume 2 - 1943 to 1978; Volume 3 - 1978 to 1984; Volume 4 - 1984 to 1996; Volume 5 - 1996 to 2007
• The Avalanche Journal [a publication of the Canadian Avalanche Association]
Type: Journal; *Frequency:* Quarterly; *Accepts Advertising*; *Price:* $30 Canada; $40 USA;$45 international
Profile: Research, reports from alpine countries, publication & product reviews, plus techniques, tools, & tips for avalanche safety
• Guidelines for Snow Avalanche Risk Determination & Mapping in Canada
Type: Guide; *Price:* $20
Profile: A technical reference for avalanche consultants & others, featuring concepts for the determination of avalanche risks, plus guidelines for avalanchemapping & acceptable risks
• Land Managers Guide for Snow Avalanche Hazards in Canada
Type: Guide; *Price:* $20
Profile: A guide to help land managers & consultants recognize & mitigate potential snow avalanche hazards
• Observation Guidelines & Recording Standards for Weather, Snowpack, & Avalanches (OGRS)
Type: Guide
Profile: A technical guide for professional avalanche safety operations & research in Canada

Canadian Aviation Artists Assocation (CAAA)
3800 Jennifer Rd., Victoria BC V8P 3X2
Tel: 250-380-3876
canadianaviationartistsassoc@gmail.com
www.aviationartists.ca
www.facebook.com/167043893392787
Overview: A small local organization founded in 1997
Mission: To advance aviation art in Canada
Finances: *Annual Operating Budget:* Less than $50,000
3 volunteer(s)
Membership: 30; *Fees:* $60 Canadian artists; $65 American artists; $70 artists outside North America; *Member Profile:* All artists interested in creating aviation art
Activities: Art shows; annual conference
Chief Officer(s):
Eric Mitchell, President, Board of Directors, 250-380-0876
ericmitchell@telus.net
Publications:
• AerialViews
Type: Newsletter
Profile: CAAA news; members' gallery; artist profiles; articles on technique

Canadian Aviation Historical Society (CAHS)
PO Box 2700, Stn. D, Ottawa ON K1P 5W7
www.cahs.ca
Overview: A small national charitable organization founded in 1962
Mission: To support & encourage research into Canadian aeronautoical history; To foster the collection and dissemination of knowledge; To stimulate interest in and to further the appreciation and understanding of the influence of aviation on Canada's development and in the world
Finances: *Funding Sources:* Donations
Membership: *Fees:* $50 Canadian members; $60 USA; $70 international; *Member Profile:* Individuals with an interest in the history of aviation
Activities: Supporting research in Canadian aeronautical history
Chief Officer(s):
Gary Williams, National President, 306-543-8123
Gord McNulty, National Vice President
Rachel Heide, Treasurer, 613-443-9975
Jim Bell, Secretary, 204-293-5402
Awards:
• Doug MacRitchie Memorial Scholarship
Location: Centennial College
Meetings/Conferences:
• Canadian Aviation Historical Society (CAHS) National Convention and Annual General Meeting, May, 2018, Sheraton Cavalier Hotel, Calgary, AB
Description: Featuring speaker sessions, meet & greets, and a field trip to participate in CHAA's Fly Day
Publications:
• Canadian Aviation Historical Society Journal
Type: Journal; *Frequency:* Quarterly; *Editor:* Bill March; *Price:* Free with CAHS membership
Profile: Articles & news about Canadian aviation history
• The Canadian Aviation Historical Society Newsletter
Type: Newsletter
Profile: Information for CAHS members

Calgary Chapter
#1021, 3235 - 56 St. NE, Calgary AB T1Y 2X7
Tel: 403-274-3711
www.cahs.ca/chapters/calgary
Chief Officer(s):
Richard Boer, Chapter President

Manitoba Chapter
c/o 819 Ashburn St., Winnipeg MB R3G 3C8
Tel: 204-293-5402
cahswyg@cahs.ca
www.cahs.ca/welcome-to-the-manitoba-chapter
Chief Officer(s):
James A. Bell, Chapter President

Montréal Chapter
101, rue Oakland, Beaconsfield QC H9W 5C8
Tel: 514-481-8786
www.cahs.ca/chapters/montreal
Chief Officer(s):
Don Baird, Secretary
Graham Batty, Treasurer, 514-217-5369
graham@bagpiping.com
• L'Avion
Type: Newsletter; *Frequency:* Bimonthly; *Editor:* Pat Barrett
Profile: Historical articles, chapter activities, reviews, & upcoming events

New Brunswick Chapter
c/o 346 Summit Dr., Saint John NB E2J 3M2
turnbullchapter@gmail.com
www.facebook.com/TurnbullNBChapter
Chief Officer(s):
Jim Sulis, Chapter President
• Contact
Type: Newsletter; *Price:* Free for Canadian Aviation Historical Society, Turnbull Chapter members

Ottawa Chapter
c/o 728 Thicket Way, Orléans ON K4A 3B6
Tel: 613-841-6349
www.cahs.ca/chapters/ottawa
Chief Officer(s):
Timothy Dubé, Chapter President
cahsyow@cahs.ca
Rachel Lea Heide, Secretary-Treasurer
• The Observair
Type: Newsletter; *Frequency:* 8 pa; *Price:* Free for Canadian Aviation Historical Society, Ottawa Chapter members
Profile: Meeting reports, historical articles, upcoming events, & reviews of aviation books

Prince Edward Island "Carl F. Burke, MBE" Chapter
#110, 1 St. John Ave., Stratford PE C1B 2B4
www.cahs.ca/chapters/prince-edward-island
Chief Officer(s):
Andy Anderson, Chapter President
• Prince Edward Island "Carl F. Burke, MBE" Chapter Newsletter
Type: Newsletter
Profile: Historical articles

Regina "Roland Groome" Chapter
526 Black Dr., Regina SK S4X 2V9
Tel: 306-543-8123
www.cahs.ca/chapters/regina
Chief Officer(s):
Gary Williams, Chapter President
president@cahs.ca

Toronto Chapter
65 Sussex Ave., Toronto ON M5S 1J8
www.cahs.ca/chapters/toronto
Chief Officer(s):
George Topple, Chapter President
george.topple@gmail.com
• Flypast
Type: Newsletter; *Frequency:* 8 pa; *Price:* Free for Canadian Aviation Historical Society, Toronto Chapter members
Profile: Chapter activities, report, & upcoming events

Vancouver Chapter
3489 Lakedale Ave., Burnaby BC V5A 3E2
Tel: 604-420-6065
www.cahs.ca/chapters/vancouver
Chief Officer(s):
J.E. (Jerry) Vernon, Chapter President

Canadian Aviation Maintenance Council *See* Canadian Council for Aviation & Aerospace

Canadian Badminton Association *See* Badminton Canada

Canadian Ball Hockey Association (CBHA) / Association canadienne de hockey-balle
9107 Norum Rd., Delta BC V4C 3H9
Tel: 604-638-1480; *Fax:* 604-998-1410
info@cbha.com
www.cbha.com
www.facebook.com/BallHockeyCanada
twitter.com/CanBallHockey
Overview: A medium-sized national organization founded in 1977
Mission: To promote the sport of ball hockey; To arrange championships
Membership: *Member Profile:* Leagues, teams, players, associations
Chief Officer(s):
George Gortsos, Executive Director

Canadian Band Association (CBA) / Association canadienne des harmonies
131 Rouge Rd., Winnipeg MB R3K 1J5
Tel: 204-663-1226
mbband@shaw.ca
www.canadianband.org
Overview: A medium-sized national charitable organization founded in 1934
Mission: To promote & develop the musical educational & cultural values of band & band music in Canada

Finances: *Annual Operating Budget:* Less than $50,000; *Funding Sources:* Membership dues
Membership: 2,600; *Fees:* $30
Activities: Organizing events, concert programs, competitions, & National Youth Band
Chief Officer(s):
John Balsille, Executive Director
Publications:
• Canadian Winds [a publication of the Canadian Band Association]
Type: Journal; *Frequency:* Biannually; *Accepts Advertising*; *Editor:* Tim Maloney; *Price:* $210
Profile: A professional journal for members of the Canadian Band Association that seeks to be a scholarly and pedagogical text accessible to all music educators

Canadian Band Directors Association (Ontario) Inc. *See* Ontario Band Association

Canadian Bankers Association (CBA) / Association des banquiers canadiens
PO Box 348, Stn. Commerce Court West, 199 Bay St., 30th Fl., Toronto ON M5L 1G2
Tel: 416-362-6092; *Fax:* 416-362-7705
Toll-Free: 800-263-0231
inform@cba.ca
www.cba.ca
www.linkedin.com/company/canadian-bankers-association
www.facebook.com/YourMoneySeniors
twitter.com/CdnBankers
www.youtube.com/user/cdnbankers
Overview: A large national organization founded in 1893
Mission: To advocate for policies that contribute to a beneficial banking system
Membership: 61 banks; *Member Profile:* Domestic banks; Foreign bank subsidiaries; Foreign bank branches operating in Canada; Lending branches
Activities: Promoting financial literacy among Canadians
Chief Officer(s):
Cameron Fowler, Chair, Executive Council
Terry Campbell, President
Andrew Perez, Manager, Media Relations, 416-362-6093 Ext. 219
aperez@cba.ca
  Montréal Office
  #2480, 1800, av McGill College, Montréal QC H3A 3J6
  Tel: 514-840-8747; *Fax:* 514-282-7551
  Ottawa Office
  #1421, 50 O'Connor St., Ottawa ON K1P 6L2
  Tel: 613-234-4431

Canadian Banking Ombudsman *See* Ombudsman for Banking Services & Investments

Canadian Baptist Ministries (CBM)
7185 Millcreek Dr., Mississauga ON L5N 5R4
Tel: 905-821-3533; *Fax:* 905-826-3441
communications@cbmin.org
www.cbmin.org
www.facebook.com/cbmin.org
Merged from: Canadian Baptist International Ministries; Canadian Baptist Federation
Overview: A large national organization founded in 1995
Mission: To partner with local churches around the world to bring hope, healing & reconciliation through word & deed
Member of: Canadian Council of Christian Charities
Affiliation(s): Canadian Baptists of Western Canada; Canadian Baptists of Ontario & Quebec; Baptist World Alliance; Convention of Atlantic Baptist Churches; Union d'Églises Baptists Francophones au Canada; Atlantic Baptist Women; Canadian Baptist Women of Ontario & Quebec
Finances: *Annual Operating Budget:* Greater than $5 Million; *Funding Sources:* Member churches; individuals; CIDA
Staff Member(s): 112; 540 volunteer(s)
Membership: 250,000 + 1,000 churches; *Member Profile:* Members of churches affiliated with the four conventions/unions; *Committees:* Public Affairs
Activities: Partners in Mission - 75 missionaries serving in Asia, Africa, Latin America, Europe & Canada; The Sharing Way - relief & development ministries in 13 countries, working in areas of agricultural & community development, community health, etc.; Canadian Baptist Volunteers - short-term ministry opportunities; Canada Caucus - consensus building among the churches in Canada; *Library:* Daniel Global Mission Resource Room
Chief Officer(s):

Malcolm Card, President
Norm Hubley, Treasurer

Canadian Baptists of Ontario & Quebec (CBOQ)
5 International Blvd., Toronto ON M9W 6H3
Tel: 416-622-8600; *Fax:* 416-622-2308
info@baptist.ca
baptist.ca
www.facebook.com/cboqcommunity
twitter.com/cboq
vimeo.com/cboq
Previous Name: Baptist Convention of Ontario & Québec
Overview: A large provincial organization founded in 1889 overseen by Canadian Baptist Ministries
Mission: A family of churches building Christ's kingdom; Supports & enables member churches to be healthy, mission congregations as they serve God together
Member of: Canadian Baptist Ministries
Affiliation(s): Baptist Women of Ontario & Quebec; McMaster Divinity College; Canadian Council of Churches; Evangelical Fellowship of Canada; Canadian Council of Christian Charities; Convention of Atlantic Baptist Churches; Canadian Baptists of Western Canada; French Union of Baptist Churches
Finances: *Annual Operating Budget:* $3 Million-$5 Million; *Funding Sources:* Member churches
Staff Member(s): 15
Membership: 375
Activities: *Internships:* Yes *Library:* Canadian Baptist Ministries Library; Open to public
Chief Officer(s):
Tim McCoy, Executive Minister
tmccoy@baptist.ca

Canadian Baptists of Western Canada (CBWC)
#201, 221 10th Ave. SE, Calgary AB T2G 0V9
Tel: 403-228-9559; *Fax:* 403-228-9048
Toll-Free: 800-820-2479
office@cbwc.ca
www.cbwc.ca
www.facebook.com/115787141838284
twitter.com/@TheCBWC
www.youtube.com/user/CanadianBaptists
Previous Name: The Baptist Union of Western Canada
Overview: A medium-sized local charitable organization founded in 1908 overseen by Canadian Baptist Ministries
Mission: The Canadian Baptists of Western Canada is a Christ-centred community of churches.
Affiliation(s): Baptist World Alliance; Canadian Baptist Ministries; North American Baptist Fellowship; Evangelical Fellowship of Canada; Canadian Council Of Churches
Finances: *Funding Sources:* Church congregations
Staff Member(s): 30
Membership: 183 congregations representing 100,000 worshippers; *Committees:* Western Canada Missions; Evangelism; Finance; Youth
Activities: *Internships:* Yes
Chief Officer(s):
Bob Webber, Director, Ministry, 403-228-9559 Ext. 311
bwebber@cbwc.ca
  Alberta & NWT Regional Office
  #201, 221 10th Ave SE, Calgary AB T2G 0V9
  Tel: 403-228-9559; *Fax:* 403-228-9048
  Toll-Free: 800-820-2479
  office@cbwc.ca
  cbwc.ca
  www.facebook.com/115787141838284
  twitter.com/@TheCBWC
  www.youtube.com/user/CanadianBaptists
  Chief Officer(s):
  Dennis Stone, Regional Minister, 780-462-2176
  dstone@cbwc.ca
  British Columbia & Yukon Regional Office
  7175 Royal Oak Avenue, Burnaby BC V5J 4J3
  Tel: 604-420-7646; *Fax:* 604-422-8696
  Toll-Free: 800-596-7772
  bcyarea@cbwc.ca
  cbwc.ca/regions/british-columbiayukon
  Chief Officer(s):
  Rob Ogilvie, Regional Minister, 604-420-7646
  rogilvie@cbwc.ca
  Heartland Regional Office
  PO Box 37239, #3, 4621 Rae St., Regina SK S4S 7K4
  Tel: 306-789-2900; *Fax:* 306-789-2902
  Toll-Free: 866-789-2940
  heartland@cbwc.ca

Chief Officer(s):
Mark Doerksen, Manager
mdoerksen@cbwc.ca

Canadian Bar Association *Voir* Association du barreau canadien

Canadian Bar Association (CBA) / Association du barreau canadien (ABC)
#500, 865 Carling Ave., Ottawa ON K1S 5S8
Tel: 613-237-2925; *Fax:* 613-237-0185
Toll-Free: 800-267-8860
Other Communication: Alternative Phone: 613-237-1988
info@cba.ca
www.cba.org
www.linkedin.com/company/canadian-bar-association
www.facebook.com/CanadianBarAssociation
twitter.com/CBA_News
www.youtube.com/user/cbaspin
Overview: A large national organization founded in 1921
Mission: To promote improvements in the law; to promote improvements in the administration of justice; to promote individual lawyer training; to advocate in the public interest; to represent the profession on a national & international level; to promote the interests of the CBA; to promote equality in the profession
Affiliation(s): Canadian Association of Law Teachers; Canadian Law Information Council; Commonwealth Bar Association; Inter-American Bar Association; International Bar Association; Union internationale des avocats
Finances: *Annual Operating Budget:* Greater than $5 Million
Staff Member(s): 70
Membership: 36,000+; *Fees:* Schedule available by province; *Member Profile:* Open to lawyers, notaries, judges, law students, persons with a recognized law degree but not licensed to practise or retired from active practice of law, law administrators; membership is voluntary in all but British Columbia & New Brunswick; *Committees:* Awards; Communications; Continuing Legal Education; Equality; Ethics & Professional Issues; International Development; Judicial Compensation & Benefits Commitee; Law Day; Legal Aid; Legislation & Law Reform; Membership; Resolutions, Constitution & ByLaws; Supreme Court of Canada
Activities: Law for the Future Fund; legal aid; law reform initiatives; insurance & financial services for members; advocacy; Canadian Bar Foundation; *Awareness Events:* National Law Day, April
Chief Officer(s):
John Hoyles, CAE, Chief Executive Officer
Janet M. Fuhrer, President
Awards:
• Pro Bono Award
• Justica Award
• CBA President's Award
• The Douglas Miller Award
• The Louis St-Laurent Award of Excellence
• PAJLO Student Essay Contest
• Ramon John Hnatyshyn Award for Law
• Viscount Bennett Fellowship
Meetings/Conferences:
• Canadian Bar Association Annual General Meeting 2018, February, 2018, Delta Hotels Ottawa City Centre, Ottawa, ON
Scope: National
  Alberta Branch
  #1725, 311 - 6 Ave. SW, Calgary AB T2P 3H2
  Tel: 403-263-3707; *Fax:* 403-265-8581
  communications@cba-alberta.org
  www.cba.org/alberta
  www.facebook.com/cba.alberta
  twitter.com/cbaalberta
  Chief Officer(s):
  Marian De Souza, President
  mdesouza@lawyersassist.ca
  Steven Mandziuk, QC, Vice-President
  smandziuk@finning.ca
  British Columbia Branch
  845 Cambie St., 10th Fl., Vancouver BC V6B 5T3
  Tel: 604-687-3404; *Fax:* 604-669-9601
  Toll-Free: 888-687-3404
  cba@bccba.org
  www.bccba.org
  Chief Officer(s):
  Caroline Nevin, Executive Director
  cnevin@bccba.org

Canadian Associations / Canadian Bar Insurance Association (CBIA)

Division du Québec
#1935, 500, Place d'Armes, Montréal QC H2Y 2W2
Tél: 514-393-9600; Téléc: 514-393-3350
Ligne sans frais: 877-393-9601
info@abcqc.qc.ca
www.abcqc.qc.ca
Chief Officer(s):
Martin Thibault, Directeur, Développement des affaires et du service aux membres
mthibault@abcqc.qc.ca
Manitoba Branch
#1020, 444 St. Mary Ave., Winnipeg MB R3C 3T1
Tel: 204-927-1210; Fax: 204-927-1212
admin@cba-mb.ca
www.cba.org/Manitoba
Chief Officer(s):
Scott Abel, President
sabel@patersons.ca
New Brunswick Branch
422 York St., Fredericton NB E3B 3P7
Tel: 506-452-7818; Fax: 506-459-7959
cbanb@cbanb.com
www.nb-cba.org
Chief Officer(s):
Denise Cameron Scott, Executive Director
Newfoundland Branch
Elizabeth Business Centre, PO Box 16, #107, 49-55 Elizabeth Ave., St. John's NL A1A 1W9
Tel: 709-579-5783; Fax: 709-726-4166
cba-nl@cba.org
www.cba.org/newfoundland/
Chief Officer(s):
Ashley Woodford, Executive Director
Northwest Territories
PO Box 1985, Stn. Main, Yellowknife NT X1A 2N9
Tel: 867-669-7739; Fax: 867-873-6344
info@cba-nt.org
www.cba.org/northwest
Pamela Naylor, Executive Director
pamela@cba-nt.org
Nova Scotia Branch
#1050, 5991 Spring Garden Rd., Halifax NS B3H 1Y6
Tel: 902-422-1905; Fax: 902-423-0475
cbainfo@cbans.ca
www.cba.org/ns
Chief Officer(s):
Tina Tucker, Executive Director
Ontario Bar Association (OBA)
#300, 20 Toronto St., Toronto ON M5C 2B8
Tel: 416-869-1047; Fax: 416-869-1390
Toll-Free: 800-668-8900
info@oba.org
www.oba.org
www.facebook.com/OntarioBarAssociation
twitter.com/obatoday
Chief Officer(s):
Steve Pengelly, Executive Director, 416-869-1047 Ext. 323
spengelly@oba.org
Prince Edward Island Branch
49 Water St., Charlottetown PE C1A 1A3
Tel: 902-566-1590; Fax: 902-566-3352
cbapei@eastlink.ca
www.cba.org/pei/
Chief Officer(s):
Jane Smith, Executive Director
Saskatchewan Branch
Canada Building, #306, 105 - 21st St. East, Saskatoon SK S7K 0B3
Tel: 306-244-3898; Fax: 306-652-3977
Toll-Free: 800-242-8288
cba.sk@sasktel.net
www.cba.org/saskatchewan
Chief Officer(s):
Brenda Hesje, Executive Director
Yukon Branch
PO Box 31712, Stn. Main Street, Whitehorse YT Y1A 6L3
Tel: 867-393-4769; Fax: 867-393-4769
cbayukon@northwestel.net
www.cba.org/yukon/
Chief Officer(s):
Laura Davidson, Executive Director

Canadian Bar Insurance Association (CBIA)
#500, 5 Park Home Ave., Toronto ON M2N 6L4
Tel: 416-221-4119; Fax: 416-221-6064
Toll-Free: 800-267-2242
customerservice@barinsurance.com
www.barinsurance.com
www.linkedin.com/company/canadian-bar-insurance-association-cbia-
www.facebook.com/barinsurance
twitter.com/cbia_aabc
Overview: A small national organization founded in 1982
Mission: To arrange for the provision of insurance & financial services to members of the legal community, their families, & their employees
Staff Member(s): 20
Activities: Employing insurance experts to design, price, & manage products; Offering services & information to members of the legal profession; Speaker Service: Yes
Chief Officer(s):
Henry Kugler, President & Chief Executive Officer
h.kugler@barinsurance.com
Dawn Marchand, Vice-President, Marketing & Direct Distribution
d.marchand@barinsurance.com
Publications:
• Canadian Bar Insurance Association Annual Report
Type: Report; Frequency: a.

Canadian Baton Twirling Federation (CBTF) / Fédération baton canadienne
c/o Jeff Johnson, 35 Ridge Dr., Toronto ON M4T 1B6
Fax: 416-484-1672
www.cbtf.ca
www.facebook.com/CBTFCA
twitter.com/cbtfca
Overview: A medium-sized national charitable organization founded in 1979
Member of: World Baton Twirling Federation
Membership: Committees: Technical
Chief Officer(s):
Jeff Johnson, President
Lisa Wilde, Secretary
Michelle Bretherick, Treasurer

Canadian Battle of Normandy Foundation See Canadian Battlefields Foundation

Canadian Battlefields Foundation
c/o Canadian War Museum, 1 Vimy Pl., Ottawa ON K1R 1C2
Tel: 613-731-7767
cbf.fccb@gmail.com
www.canadianbattlefieldsfoundation.ca
www.facebook.com/220483754647284?ref=ts&fref=ts
twitter.com/CBFFCCB
Previous Name: Canadian Battle of Normandy Foundation
Overview: A medium-sized national charitable organization founded in 1992
Mission: To act with Le Mémorial to educate the international public with respect to Canada's role in the Second World War & to educate Canadians through providing scholarships, bursaries & prizes to carry on research into military history; to raise & disburse funds to support these activities.
Finances: Annual Operating Budget: Less than $50,000; Funding Sources: Grants; donations; membership fees
4 volunteer(s)
Membership: 300; Fees: $25 individuals; $100 associations; $200 corporations; Committees: Communications; Education; Executive; Finance; Trust Fund
Activities: Canadian Normandy Bursary Programme; university-accepted credit course on WW II; maintenance of Canadian Memorial Garden, Caen, France; Speaker Service: Yes
Chief Officer(s):
H.G. Needham, Treasurer
Charles Belzile, President
Antonio Lamer, Honorary Patron

Canadian Beef
Eastern Office, #210, 2550 Argentia Rd., Mississauga ON L5N 5R1
Tel: 905-821-4900; Fax: 905-821-4915
Toll-Free: 888-248-2333
info@canadabeef.ca
www.canadabeef.ca
www.facebook.com/LoveCDNBeef
twitter.com/canadianbeef
www.youtube.com/user/LoveCDNBeef
Overview: A medium-sized national organization
Mission: To build consumer demand for beef
Member of: Market development division of the Canadian Cattlemen's Association
Activities: Speaker Service: Yes
Chief Officer(s):
Francis Andres, Executive Vice President
Ron Glaser, Vice President
Joyce Parslow, Marketing & Consumer Relations
Western Office
#146, 6715 - 8th St. NE, Calgary AB T2E 7H7
Tel: 403-275-5890; Fax: 403-275-9288

Canadian Beef Breeds Council (CBBC)
#165, 6715 - 8th St. NE, Calgary AB T2E 7H7
Tel: 403-730-0350
info@canadianbeefbreeds.com
www.canadianbeefbreeds.com
www.facebook.com/BeefGenetics
twitter.com/CanBeefBreeds
Overview: A medium-sized national organization founded in 1994
Mission: To represent & promote the purebred cattle sector both domestically & internationally
Finances: Funding Sources: Government; corporate sponsors
Staff Member(s): 3
Membership: 16 associations; Committees: Governance; Animal Health; Scientific Advancement; Market Development Niche Breeds
Activities: Presentations; trade missions; hosts international speakers
Chief Officer(s):
Michael Latimer, Executive Director
mlatimer@beefbreeds.ca

Canadian Belgian Blue Association (CBBA)
c/o Marie Goubau, 1489 Concession 1, Lefaivre ON K0B 1J0
Tel: 613-731-7110; Fax: 613-731-0704
info@lagantoise.com
www.belgianblue.ca
Overview: A small national organization founded in 1986
Mission: To provide for registration of Belgian Blue in Canada; To promote the Belgian Blue
Affiliation(s): Canadian Livestock Records Corporation
Membership: 1-99; Fees: $100 initial membership; $50 annual renewal of membership; $10 junior membership (under 18 years of age); Member Profile: Breeders of Belgian Blue cattle in Canada; Committees: Executive; Finance; Registration; Breed Improvement; Information; Nominating
Activities: Maintaining a record of ancestry & origin of Belgian Blue in Canada; Supervising breeders of Belgian Blue
Chief Officer(s):
Sam Dunlop, President
ulsterbelgianblues@hotmail.com
Ken Miller, Secretary-Treasurer
kejab@sasktel.net

Canadian Belgian Horse Association
17150 Concession 10, Schomberg ON L0G 1T0
Tel: 905-939-1186; Fax: 905-939-7547
cbha@csolve.net
www.canadianbelgianhorse.com
Overview: A small national organization founded in 1907
Mission: To promote the Belgian breed of horse
Membership: 793; Fees: $50
Chief Officer(s):
Terry Morrow, President
morrowsbelgians@sympatico.ca
Publications:
• Canadian Belgian Banner
Type: Magazine; Accepts Advertising; Price: Free with membership

Canadian Beverage Association / Association canadienne des boissons
WaterPark Place, 20 Bay St., 11th Fl., Toronto ON M5J 2N8
Tel: 416-362-2424; Fax: 416-362-3229
info@canadianbeverage.ca
www.canadianbeverage.ca
www.linkedin.com/company/canadian-beverage-association
www.facebook.com/CanadianBeverageAssociation
twitter.com/CanadaBev
Previous Name: Refreshments Canada; Canadian Bottlers of Carbonated Beverages; Canadian Soft Drink Association
Overview: A medium-sized national organization founded in 1942

Mission: To represent beverage bottlers, distributors, franchise houses & industry suppliers on a variety of issues
Finances: *Annual Operating Budget:* $500,000-$1.5 Million
Staff Member(s): 8
Membership: 45 organizations; *Member Profile:* Manufacturers & distributors of beverages & their suppliers
Activities: *Library:* by appointment Not open to public
Chief Officer(s):
Jim Goetz, President
jim@canadianbeverage.ca
Carolyn Fell, Senior Director, Communications
carolyn@canadianbeverage.ca
Megan Boyle, Senior Director, Government Affairs
megan@canadianbeverage.ca

Canadian Bible Society (CBS) / Société biblique canadienne
National Support Office, 10 Carnforth Rd., Toronto ON M4A 2S4
Tel: 416-757-4171; *Fax:* 416-757-3376
Toll-Free: 800-465-2425
Other Communication: Online Store E-mail:
custserv@biblesociety.ca
info@biblesociety.ca
www.biblesociety.ca
www.facebook.com/CanadianBibleSociety
twitter.com/CanadianBible
pinterest.com/canadianbible
Overview: A large national charitable organization founded in 1904
Mission: To translate, publish, & distribute Bibles, New Testaments & other Scriptures throughout Canada & Bermuda
Member of: United Bible Societies
Finances: *Funding Sources:* Donations; Sale of gifts; Fundraising
Activities: Offering various programs to share God's Word, such as Operation Bible for the Canadian military, & welcoming newcomers to Canada with God's message
Chief Officer(s):
Jonathan Dent, National Director
Mark Hirowatari, Interim Chief Financial Officer
mhirowatari@biblesociety.ca
Layla Velasquez, Director, Development, Marketing & Communication
lvelasquez@biblesociety.ca
Publications:
• Canadian Bible Society Annual Report
Type: Yearbook; *Frequency:* Annually
• Canadian Bible Society e-Updates
Type: Newsletter
• Daily Bible Reading [a publication of the Canadian Bible Society]
Type: Guide
• Taste & See [a publication of the Canadian Bible Society]
Type: E-Book; *Price:* Free from website
Profile: An overview of the Bible

British Columbia District Office
700 Kingsway St., Vancouver BC V5V 3C1
Tel: 604-872-6691; *Fax:* 604-872-0562
Toll-Free: 800-661-7437
vancouver@biblesociety.ca
www.biblesociety.ca/districts/britishcolumbia
Chief Officer(s):
Amie Wiebe, District Director, Southern BC
awiebe@biblesociety.ca

Central Ontario District Office
10 Carnforth Rd., Toronto ON M4A 2S4
Tel: 416-689-3437; *Fax:* 416-757-3376
centralontario@biblesociety.ca
www.biblesociety.ca/districts/ontariocentral
Chief Officer(s):
Don Miller, Director
dmiller@biblesociety.ca

Central Ontario District Office
10 Carnforth Rd., Toronto ON M4A 2S4
Tel: 416-689-3437; *Fax:* 416-757-3376
centralontario@biblesociety.ca
www.biblesociety.ca/districts/ontariocentral
Chief Officer(s):
Don Miller, District Director
dmiller@biblesociety.ca

Eastern Ontario District Office
315 Lisgar St., Ottawa ON K2P 0E1
Tel: 613-236-3910; *Fax:* 613-236-2431
ottawa@biblesociety.ca
www.biblesociety.ca/districts/ontarioeastern

Chief Officer(s):
Don Miller, Director of Ministry Advancement

Manitoba District Office
952 St. Mary's Rd., Winnipeg MB R2M 3R8
Tel: 204-257-8835; *Fax:* 204-254-2411
winnipeg@biblesociety.ca
www.biblesociety.ca/districts/manitoba
Chief Officer(s):
Len Bachiu, District Director
lbachiu@biblesociety.ca

New Brunswick District Office
c/o Crandall University (Murray Bldg), PO Box 6004, 333 Gorge Rd., Moncton NB E1C 9L7
Tel: 506-858-1067; *Fax:* 506-858-1068
Toll-Free: 888-242-5397
www.biblesociety.ca/districts/newbrunswick
Chief Officer(s):
Lorne K. Freake, District Director
lfreake@biblesociety.ca

Newfoundland & Labrador District Office
PO Box 8113, 7 Stamp's Lane, St. John's NL A1E 3C9
Tel: 709-722-7929; *Fax:* 709-722-9105
Toll-Free: 888-242-5397
www.biblesociety.ca/districts/newfoundlandandlabrador
Chief Officer(s):
Lorne Freake, District Director
lfreake@biblesociety.ca

North Alberta District Office
8749 - 53 Ave. NW, Edmonton AB T6E 5E9
Tel: 780-439-7729; *Fax:* 780-439-1676
Toll-Free: 877-439-7729
alberta@biblesociety.ca
www.biblesociety.ca/districts/albertanorth
Chief Officer(s):
Marvin Busenius, District Director
mbusenius@biblesociety.ca

Northern Ontario District Office
315 Lisgar St., Ottawa ON K2P 0E1
Tel: 613-236-3910; *Fax:* 613-236-2431
ottawa@biblesociety.ca
www.biblesociety.ca/districts/ontarionorthern
Chief Officer(s):
Don Miller, District Director
dmiller@biblesociety.ca

Nova Scotia District Office
c/o Crandall University (Murray Bldg), PO Box 6004, 333 Gorge Rd., Moncton NB E1C 9L7
Tel: 506-858-1067; *Fax:* 506-858-1068
Toll-Free: 888-242-5397
www.biblesociety.ca/districts/nova-scotia
Chief Officer(s):
Lorne K. Freake, Director of Ministry Advancement
lfreake@biblesociety.ca

Prince Edward Island District Office
c/o Crandall University (Murray Bldg), PO Box 6004, 333 Gorge Rd., Moncton NB E1C 9L7
Tel: 506-858-1067; *Fax:* 506-858-1068
Toll-Free: 888-242-5397
www.biblesociety.ca/districts/princeedwardisland
Chief Officer(s):
Bill Dean, District Director

Québec District Office
1025, rue Saint-Jean, Québec QC G1R 1R9
Tél: 418-692-2698; *Téléc:* 418-692-4616
Ligne sans frais: 855-692-2698
quebec@biblesociety.ca
www.biblesociety.ca/districts/quebec
Chief Officer(s):
Francis Lemieux, French Ministry Promotions Officer
flemieux@societebiblique.ca

Saskatchewan District Office
PO Box 1931, Stn. Main, #201, 401 - 43rd. St. East, Saskatoon SK S7K 3S5
Tel: 306-664-2480; *Fax:* 306-664-2480
Toll-Free: 800-667-4691
saskatoon@biblesociety.ca
www.biblesociety.ca/districts/saskatchewan
Chief Officer(s):
Leonard Bachiu, District Director

South Alberta District Office
8749 - 53 Ave., NW, Edmonton AB T6E 5E9
Tel: 403-261-4827; *Fax:* 403-439-1676
Toll-Free: 877-439-7729

alberta@biblesociety.ca
www.biblesociety.ca/districts/albertasouth
Chief Officer(s):
Marvin Busenius, Director, Ministry Advancement
mbusenius@biblesociety.ca

Southwestern Ontario District Office
#206, 385 Frederick St., Kitchener ON N2H 2P2
Tel: 416-522-3485
london@biblesociety.ca
www.biblesociety.ca/districts/ontario_southwestern
Chief Officer(s):
Alana Reeve, Regional Representative
areeve@biblesociety.ca

Canadian Billiards & Snooker Association (CBSA)
www.cbsa.ca
www.facebook.com/CanadianBilliardsSnookerAssociation
Overview: A medium-sized national organization founded in 1974
Member of: Canadian Olympic Committee
Affiliation(s): Cue Sports for Canada; World Pool-Billiard Association; Bill Congress of America; International Billiards & Snooker Federation
Activities: Providing championship information
Chief Officer(s):
Randall Morrison, President
randall.morrison@cbsa.ca
John White, Vice-President
john.white@cbsa.ca
Candace Campbell, Secretary
candace.campbell@cbsa.ca
Frank Kakouros, Treasurer
frank.kakouros@cbsa.ca

Canadian Biochemical Society *See* Canadian Society for Molecular Biosciences

Canadian Bioethics Society (CBS) / Société canadienne de bioéthique
c/o Amy Middleton, Administrator, PO Box 33, Hubbards NS B0J 1T0
info@bioethics.ca
www.bioethics.ca
Merged from: Canadian Society of Bioethic; Société canadienne de la bioéthique médicale
Overview: A small national charitable organization founded in 1988
Mission: To facilitate knowledge sharing related to bioethics; To discover solutions to bioethical problems by promotion of research & dissemination of information
Finances: *Funding Sources:* Donations
Membership: 600+; *Fees:* $39 student; $139 individual; $546 supporting organization; *Member Profile:* Professional individuals & institutions interested in ethics & health research & practice
Activities: Promoting teaching of bioethics
Chief Officer(s):
Ghislaine Cleret de Langavant, President, 514-873-9791
president@bioethics.ca
Priya Somascanthan, Treasurer
Awards:
• CBS Distinguished Service Award
• CBS Lifetime Achievement Award
Meetings/Conferences:
• 2018 Canadian Bioethics Society Conference, May, 2018, Dalhousie University, Halifax, NS
Scope: National
Publications:
• Canadian Bioethics Society Newsletter
Type: Newsletter; *Accepts Advertising*; *Editor:* Stacey Page
Profile: Articles. book reviews, CBS activities, & upcoming events of interest to CBS members

Canadian Biogas Association
#900, 275 Slater St., Ottawa ON K1P 5H9
Tel: 613-822-1004
jgreen@biogasassociation.ca
www.biogasassociation.ca
www.linkedin.com/groups/3854330/profile
www.facebook.com/168782246502009
twitter.com/BiogasOntario
Previous Name: Agrienergy Producers' Association of Ontario
Overview: A medium-sized provincial organization founded in 2008
Mission: To promote biogas opportunitites, shape policies that impact biogas, provide resources & offer technical expertise to address challenges in development

Canadian Associations / Canadian Biomaterials Society (CSB) / Société canadienne des biomatériaux (SCB)

Membership: 100+; *Fees:* $675 small business; $2,000 large business; *Member Profile:* Members of the biogas industry, including farmers, munipicalitites, technology developers, consultants, finance & insurance firms & other affiliate representatives
Activities: Supporting research; Outreach events

Canadian Biomaterials Society (CSB) / Société canadienne des biomatériaux (SCB)
www.biomaterials.ca
www.linkedin.com/groups/Canadian-Biomaterials-Society-Societe-Canadienne-4267244
Overview: A small national organization overseen by International Union of Societies for Biomaterials Science & Engineering
Mission: To develop biomaterials science, technology, & education in Canadian industries, universities, & governments
Member of: International Union of Societies for Biomaterials Science & Engineering
Membership: *Fees:* $100 corporate members; $50 regular members; $25 students
Chief Officer(s):
Diego Mantovani, Representative, International Union of Societies - Biomaterials Science/Engineeri
Ze Zhang, Representative, International Union of Societies - Biomaterials Science/Engineeri
Rosalind Labow, Treasurer
rlabow@ottawaheart.ca
Lauren Flynn, Secretary
lauren.flynn@chee.queensu.ca
Meetings/Conferences:
• 34th Annual Meeting of the Canadian Biomaterials Society 2018, May, 2018, Victoria, BC

Canadian Bison Association (CBA) / Association canadienne du bison
PO Box 3116, #200, 1660 Pasqua St., Regina SK S4P 3G7
Tel: 306-522-4766; *Fax:* 306-522-4768
cba1@sasktel.net
www.canadianbison.ca
www.facebook.com/CanadianBisonAssociation
twitter.com/CanadianBisonAs
Overview: A medium-sized national licensing charitable organization founded in 1984
Mission: To develop the bison industry; to maintain the production of bison in a natural state (no growth hormones, chemicals, feed lots, free-range management); to be the voice for commercial breeders; to assist in the formation of regulations & guidelines in commercial production & management of Canadian Plains Bison & to promote the product & awareness of the bison industry
Member of: Canadian Livestock Records Corporation
Affiliation(s): BC Bison Associaion; Bison Producers of Alberta; Saskatchewan Bison Association; Manitoba Bison Associaion; Ontario Bison Associaion; Union Québecoise du Bison
Finances: *Funding Sources:* Membership fees; convention; show & sale
Staff Member(s): 3; 10 volunteer(s)
Membership: 560; *Fees:* Schedule available; *Member Profile:* Active - own bison; associate - interest in bison industry
Activities: Bison Show & Sale; Annual Convention
Chief Officer(s):
Terry Kremeniuk, Executive Director, 306-522-4762
cba2@sasktel.net

Canadian Blind Sports Association Inc. (CBSA) / Association canadienne des sports pour aveugles inc.
#325, 5055 Joyce St., Vancouver BC V5R 6B2
Tel: 604-419-0480; *Fax:* 604-419-0481
Toll-Free: 866-604-0480
info@canadianblindsports.ca
www.canadianblindsports.ca
www.facebook.com/canadianblindsports
Overview: A medium-sized national charitable organization founded in 1976
Mission: To facilitate opportunities for Canadians who are legally blind to participate in amateur sport at the national/international level, & to thereby enhance a healthy lifestyle & individual well-being.
Affiliation(s): International Blind Sports Association; Canadian Paralympic Committee; Active Living Alliance
Finances: *Annual Operating Budget:* $250,000-$500,000; *Funding Sources:* Donations; government; membership dues
Staff Member(s): 2
Activities: *Rents Mailing List:* Yes

Chief Officer(s):
Jane D. Blaine, Chief Executive Officer
jane@canadianblindsports.ca

Canadian Blonde d'Aquitaine Association
c/o Canadian Livestock Records Corp., 2417 Holly Ln., Ottawa ON K1V 0M7
Tel: 613-731-7110; *Fax:* 613-731-0704
cbda@clrc.ca
www.canadianblondeassociation.ca
Overview: A medium-sized national organization founded in 1972
Mission: To improve the practice of breeding Blonde d'Aquitaine cows
Member of: Canadian Beef Breeds Council
Finances: *Funding Sources:* Registration of animals
Membership: 178
Chief Officer(s):
Dave Kamelchuk, President
Publications:
• Canadian Blonde d'Aquitaine Association's Newsletter
Type: Newsletter; *Frequency:* Quarterly; *Accepts Advertising*
Profile: Articles, events, & programs for association members

Canadian Blood & Marrow Transplant Group (CBMTG) / Société Canadienne de greffe de cellules souches hematopoietiques
#400, 570 West 7th Ave., Vancouver BC V5Z 1B3
Tel: 604-874-4944; *Fax:* 604-874-4378
cbmtg@malachite-mgmt.com
www.cbmtg.org
Overview: A small national organization
Mission: To provide leadership in the field of blood & marrow transplantation (BMT); to recognize & promote advances in clinical care; to promote basic, translational & clinical research & education; to represent BMT issues to government agencies, health care organizations & the public; to collaborate with fellow organizations
Finances: *Funding Sources:* Membership dues
Membership: *Fees:* $130 physician/PhD; $110 allied health membership;$1,500 - $7,500 corporate; $400 - $1,600 organizations, based on no. of members; *Member Profile:* Those with sustained interest in blood & marrow transplantation; professionals, students & interested companies; *Committees:* Executive; Education; Laboratory
Chief Officer(s):
Ana Torres, Executive Director
ana.torres@malachite-mgmt.com
Meetings/Conferences:
• Canadian Blood & Marrow Transplant Group 2018 Annual Conference, June, 2018, Delta Hotel, Ottawa, ON
Scope: National
Publications:
• CBMTG [Canadian Blood & Marrow Transplant Group] Newsletter
Type: Newsletter; *Frequency:* Quarterly; *Editor:* Nancy Henderson
Profile: Professional news; case studies; clinical papers; questions; letters to the editor; industry news

Canadian Blood Services (CBS) / Société canadienne du sang
1800 Alta Vista Dr., Ottawa ON K1G 4J5
Tel: 613-739-2300; *Fax:* 613-731-1411
Toll-Free: 888-236-6283
feedback@blood.ca
www.blood.ca
www.linkedin.com/company/canadian-blood-services
www.facebook.com/itsinyoutogive
twitter.com/itsinyoutogive
www.youtube.com/18882DONATE
Previous Name: Canadian Red Cross - Blood Services
Overview: A medium-sized national organization founded in 1998
Mission: To manage the blood supply for Canadians; To ensure blood safety
Finances: *Funding Sources:* Fundraising
Activities: Screening donors; Collecting & processing blood; Managing the OneMatch Stem Cell & Marrow Network; Producing publications about blood, plasma, & platelet donation
Chief Officer(s):
Leah Hollins, Chair
Graham D. Sher, Chief Executive Officer
Publications:
• BloodNotes [a publication of Canadian Blood Services]

Type: Newsletter
Profile: Information & educational articles for hospital customers
• Canadian Blood Services Annual Report
Type: Yearbook; *Frequency:* Annually

Ancaster
35 Stone Church Rd., Ancaster ON L9K 1S5
Toll-Free: 888-236-6283
Chief Officer(s):
Dunbar Russel, Regional Representative, Ontario
Barrie
#100, 231 Bayview Dr., Barrie ON L4N 4Y5
Toll-Free: 888-823-6283
Brandon
c/o Westman Collection Site, Town Centre, 800 Rosser Ave., Brandon MB R7A 6N5
Toll-Free: 888-236-6283
Burlington
1250 Brant St., Burlington ON L7P 1X8
Toll-Free: 888-236-6283
Calgary
737 - 13th Ave., Calgary AB T2R 1J1
Toll-Free: 888-236-6283
Chief Officer(s):
Mike Shaw, Regional Representative, Alberta, Saskatchewan, Manitoba, Northwest Territories, & Nunavut
Charlottetown
85 Fitzroy St., Charlottetown PE C1A 1R6
Toll-Free: 888-236-6283
Chief Officer(s):
Jeff Scott, Regional Representative, Atlantic
Corner Brook
3 Herald Ave., Corner Brook NL A2H 4B8
Toll-Free: 888-236-6283
Edmonton
8249 - 114th St., Edmonton AB T6G 2R8
Toll-Free: 888-236-6283
Guelph
130 Silvercreek Pkwy. North, Guelph ON N1H 7Y5
Toll-Free: 888-236-6283
Halifax
#252, 7071 Bayers Rd., Halifax NS B3L 2C2
Toll-Free: 888-236-6283
Chief Officer(s):
Jeff Scott, Regional Representative, Atlantic
Kelowna
#103, 1865 Dilworth Dr., Kelowna BC V1Y 9T1
Toll-Free: 888-236-6283
Kingston
850 Gardiners Rd., Kingston ON K7M 3X9
Toll-Free: 888-236-6283
Kitchener-Waterloo
94 Bridgeport Rd. East, Waterloo ON N2J 2J9
Toll-Free: 888-263-3283
Lethbridge
Lethbridge Centre Mall, #220, 200 - 4 Ave. South, Lethbridge AB T1J 4C9
Toll-Free: 888-236-6283
London
820 Wharncliffe Rd. South, London ON N6J 2N4
Toll-Free: 888-236-6283
Chief Officer(s):
Dunbar Russel, Regional Representative, Ontario
Mississauga
#15, 785 Britannia Rd. West, Mississauga ON L5V 2Y1
Toll-Free: 888-236-6283
Moncton
500 Mapleton Rd., Moncton NB E1G 0N3
Toll-Free: 888-236-6283
Oshawa
1300 Harmony Rd. North, Oshawa ON L1K 2B1
Toll-Free: 888-236-6283
Ottawa
1575 Carling Ave., Ottawa ON K1Z 7M3
Tel: 613-560-7440
Toll-Free: 888-236-6283
Chief Officer(s):
Dunbar Russel, Regional Representative, Ontario
Ottawa - Alta Vista Dr. - National Fundraising Office
1800 Alta Vista Dr., Ottawa ON K1G 4J5
Tel: 613-739-2300; *Fax:* 613-739-2141
Toll-Free: 888-236-6283
campaignforcanadians.ca
Chief Officer(s):

Penny Holmes-Tuor, Manager
penny.holmes-tuor@blood.ca
Peterborough
55 George St. North, Peterborough ON K9J 3G2
Toll-Free: 888-236-6283
Prince George
2277 Westwood Dr., Prince George BC V2N 4V6
Toll-Free: 888-236-6283
Red Deer
#5, 5020 - 68th St., Red Deer AB T4N 7B4
Toll-Free: 888-236-6283
Regina
2571 Broad St., Regina SK S4P 4H6
Toll-Free: 888-236-6283
Chief Officer(s):
Mike Shaw, Regional Representative, Alberta, Saskatchewan, Manitoba, Northwest Territories, & Nunavut
Saint John
405 University Ave., Saint John NB E2L 4G7
Toll-Free: 888-236-6283
Chief Officer(s):
Jeff Scott, Regional Representative, Atlantic
St Catharines
#395, 397 Ontario St., St Catharines ON L2N 4M8
Toll-Free: 888-236-6283
St. John's
7 Wicklow St., St. John's NL A1B 3Z9
Toll-Free: 888-236-6283
Chief Officer(s):
Jeff Scott, Regional Representative, Atlantic
Sarnia
Bayside Mall, 150 Christina St. North, Sarnia ON N7T 7W5
Toll-Free: 888-236-6283
Saskatoon
325 - 20th St. East, Saskatoon SK S7K 0A9
Toll-Free: 888-236-6283
Chief Officer(s):
Mike Shaw, Regional Representative, Alberta, Saskatchewan, Manitoba, Northwest Territories, & Nunavut
Sudbury
235 Cedar St., Sudbury ON P3B 1M8
Tel: 705-674-4003
Toll-Free: 888-236-6283
Chief Officer(s):
Dunbar Russel, Regional Representative, Ontario
Sudbury - National Contact Centre
235 Cedar St., Sudbury ON P3B 1M8
Tel: 705-674-4003; *Fax:* 705-674-7165
Toll-Free: 888-236-6283
Surrey
15285 - 101 Ave., Surrey BC V3R 8X8
Toll-Free: 888-236-6283
Sydney
850 Grand Lake Rd., Sydney NS B1P 5T9
Toll-Free: 888-236-6283
Toronto - Bay & Bloor
Manulife Centre, 55 Bloor St. West, 2nd Fl., Toronto ON M4W 1A5
Toll-Free: 888-236-6283
Toronto - College St.
67 College St., Toronto ON M5G 2M1
Toll-Free: 888-236-6283
Chief Officer(s):
Dunbar Russel, Regional Representative, Ontario
Toronto - King Street
163 King St. West, Main Fl., Toronto ON M5H 4H2
Toll-Free: 888-236-6283
Vancouver - Oak Street
4750 Oak St., Vancouver BC V6H 2N9
Tel: 604-707-3400
Toll-Free: 888-236-6283
Vancouver - Standard Life
888 Dunsmur St., 2nd Fl., Vancouver BC V6C 3K4
Toll-Free: 888-236-6283
Victoria
3449 Saanich Rd., Victoria BC V8X 1W9
Toll-Free: 888-236-6283
Windsor
3909 Grand Marais Rd. East, Windsor ON N8W 1W9
Toll-Free: 888-236-6283
Winnipeg
777 William Ave., Winnipeg MB R3E 3R4

Toll-Free: 888-236-6283
Chief Officer(s):
Mike Shaw, Regional Representative, Alberta, Saskatchewan, Manitoba, Northwest Territories, & Nunavut

Canadian Board Diversity Council (CBDC) / Conseil canadien pour la diversité administrative (CCDA)
#502, 180 Bloor St. West, Toronto ON M5S 2V6
Tel: 416-361-1475
inquiries@boarddiversity.ca
www.boarddiversity.ca
www.linkedin.com/company/882730
twitter.com/diverseboards
Overview: A medium-sized national organization founded in 2009
Mission: To conduct research on diversity on Canadian corporate boards; To provide governance education programming; to educate members & the governance community onboard diversity best practices & principles; To build a network of business leaders who are committed to diversity
Affiliation(s): Women's Executive Network
Staff Member(s): 5
Activities: Governance education; Research; Rankings; Report Cards on board diversity; Diversity 50 list (diversity50@boarddiversity.ca); Summits & roundtables
Chief Officer(s):
Sherri Stevens, Owner & CEO

Canadian Board for Respiratory Care Inc. (CBRC) / Le Conseil canadien des soins respiratoires inc. (CCSR)
#103, 1083 Queen St., Halifax NS B3H 0B2
Tel: 902-492-4387; *Fax:* 902-492-0045
cbrc@cbrc.ca
www.cbrc.ca
Overview: A small national organization founded in 1989
Mission: To produce examinations used to test respiratory therapists prior to entering active practice
Chief Officer(s):
Julie Brown, Secretary/Treasurer

Canadian Board of Examiners for Professional Surveyors (CBEPS) / Le Conseil canadien des Examinateurs pour les Arpenteurs-géomètres (CCEAG)
#100E, 900 Dynes Rd., Ottawa ON K2C 3L6
Tel: 613-274-7115; *Fax:* 613-723-5558
registrar@cbeps-cceag.ca
www.cbeps-cceag.ca
Overview: A medium-sized national organization
Mission: Establishes, assesses and certifies the academic qualifications of individuals who apply to become land surveyors and/or geomatics professionals in Canada, except for Quebec.
Staff Member(s): 2
Chief Officer(s):
Jean-Claude Tétreault, Registrar

Canadian Board of Marine Underwriters (CBMU)
#100, 2233 Argentia Rd., Mississauga ON L5N 2X7
Tel: 905-826-4768; *Fax:* 905-826-4873
cbmu@cbmu.com
www.cbmu.com
www.linkedin.com/groups/4581774/profile
twitter.com/TheCBMU
Overview: A medium-sized national organization founded in 1917
Mission: To procure & disseminate information of interest to marine underwriters & others; To facilitate the exchange of views & ideas which work to improve the marine underwriting industry & marine insurance; To promote & protect the interest of the underwriting community
Member of: International Union of Marine Insurers
Finances: *Funding Sources:* Membership dues
Membership: *Member Profile:* Marine underwriters; associate - brokers, surveyors, maritime lawyers, government representatives, members of international underwriting boards & others involved in related activities; *Committees:* Underwriting; Claims & Loss Prevention; Legislative; Program & Education; Communications; Finance & Assessments
Chief Officer(s):
Roger Fernandes, President, 416-368-8200 Ext. 1
rffernandes@gaic.com
Jennifer Yung, Administrator
cbmu@cbmu.com
Halyna Troian, Secretary-Treasurer
htroian@cbmu.com

Meetings/Conferences:
• 2018 Canadian Board of Marine Underwriters Spring Conference, May, 2018, Queen's Landing Hotel, Niagara-on-the-Lake, ON
Scope: National

Canadian Board of Registration of Electroencephalograph Technologists Inc. (CBRET)
c/o Hospital for Sick Children, 555 University Ave., 6th Fl, Atrium 6C, Toronto ON M5G 1X8
Tel: 416-813-6545; *Fax:* 416-813-6709
cbret.org
Overview: A small national licensing organization founded in 1972 overseen by Canadian Association of Electroneurophysiology Technologists, Inc.
Mission: To offer registration & certification procedures for the electroneurodiagnostic profession of electroencephalography (EEG), as regulated by the College of Physicians & Surgeons in each province & territory; To conduct written & oral-practical examinations to determine the knowledge & skills of EEG technologists
Affiliation(s): Canadian Association of Electroneurophysiology Technologists (CAET)
Activities: Reviewing qualifications of foreign-trained electroencephalograph technologists before they come to Canada, & advising them if they meet the prerequisites for the registration examination; Maintaining liaison with the Canadian Association of Electroneurophysiology Technologists (CAET)
Chief Officer(s):
Rohit Sharma, Registrar

Canadian Boating Federation / Fédération nautique du Canada
#330, 24, ch St-Louis, Salaberry-de-Valleyfield QC J6T 1M4
Tel: 450-377-4122; *Fax:* 450-377-5282
cbfnc@cbfnc.ca
www.cbfnc.ca
Overview: A small national organization
Membership: *Member Profile:* Organizations that promote boating; Racing members; Officiating members; Crew members, who maintain racing equipment; Individuals who are neither owners nor drivers in any racing class, but who are interested in racing activities, may be associate members
Activities: Coordinating races; Maintaining rules; Establishing a code of ethics; Sharing race results
Chief Officer(s):
Derek Anderson, President

Canadian Bodybuilding Federation (CBBF) / Fédération canadienne de culturisme
www.cbbf.ca
www.facebook.com/CanadianBodybuildingFederationCBBF
Overview: A small national organization
Mission: To act as the governing body for amateur bodybuilding, fitness, & body fitness (figure) competition
Affiliation(s): British Columbia Amateur Bodybuilding Association; Alberta Bodybuilding Association; Saskatchewan Amateur Bodybuilders Association (SABBA); Manitoba Amateur Bodybuilding Association; Ontario Physique Association (OPA); Association des Physiques Québécois; New Brunswick Physique & Figure Association; Nova Scotia Amateur Bodybuilders Association; Newfoundland & Labrador Amateur Bodybuilding Association
Activities: Qualifying competitors for the three IFBB World Championships; Posting championship results
Chief Officer(s):
Georgina Dunnington, Chair
Publications:
• Rules/Regulations Documents [a publication of the Canadian Bodybuilding Federation]
Type: Guides
Profile: A series of documents outlining rules for various competition categories

Canadian Boer Goat Association *See* Canadian Meat Goat Association

Canadian Bond Investors' Association (CBIA) / Association canadienne des investisseurs obligataires (ACIO)
#123, 20 Carlton St., Toronto ON M5B 2H5
Tel: 416-585-3000
info@bondinvestors.ca
bondinvestors.ca
Overview: A small national organization founded in 2011
Mission: To be the independent voice of Canada bond investors

Canadian Associations / Canadian Book Professionals Association (CanBPA)

Membership: 30+; *Fees:* $2,000 institutional; $1,000 affiliate; *Member Profile:* Canadian fixed income institutional investor organizations
Activities: Advocating on behalf of members; providing market information & expertise; providing educational opportunities
Chief Officer(s):
Peter Waite, Executive Director

Canadian Book Professionals Association (CanBPA)
info@canbpa.ca
canbpa.ca
www.facebook.com/136875019696314
twitter.com/canbpa
Merged from: Book Publishing Professionals Association (BPPA); Young Publishers of Canada (YPC)
Overview: A medium-sized national organization
Mission: To foster networking, provide educational opportunities & idea sharing, & job & career information & postings for book professionals of all kinds, including publishers, librarians, booksellers & agents
Activities: Seminars; networking, social events & other programming; career information

Canadian Book Publishers' Council; Canadian Textbook Publishers Institute *See* Canadian Publishers' Council

Canadian Bookbinders & Book Artists Guild (CBBAG) / Guilde canadienne des relieurs et des artisans du livre
#207, 80 Ward. St., Toronto ON M6H 4A6
Tel: 416-581-1071
cbbag@cbbag.ca
www.cbbag.ca
www.facebook.com/groups/77394956232
Overview: A medium-sized national charitable organization founded in 1983
Mission: To create a spirit of community among hand workers in the book arts & those who love books; to promote greater awareness of the book arts; to increase educational opportunities, & foster excellence through exhibitions, workshops, lectures, & publications.
Affiliation(s): Ontario Crafts Council
Finances: *Funding Sources:* Membership fees; donations; grants
Membership: *Fees:* $25 student; $60 Canadian; $70 American/overseas; $70 family/institution; $80 American families/insitutions; $35 American students; *Member Profile:* Hand workers or interest in book arts; *Committees:* Communications; Events; National Education; Membership; Publications; Volunteers
Activities: Workshops; exhibitions; program meetings; suppliers list; book art fairs; *Library:* Open to public by appointment
Chief Officer(s):
Mary McIntyre, President

Canadian Bookkeepers Alliance *See* Canadian Bookkeepers Association

Canadian Bookkeepers Association
#482, 283 Danforth Ave., Toronto ON M4K 1N2
Fax: 866-804-4617
Toll-Free: 866-451-2204
www.c-b-a.ca
Previous Name: Canadian Bookkeepers Alliance
Overview: A small national organization
Mission: To promote, support, provide for & encourage Canadian bookkeepers; to promote & increase the awareness of Bookkeeping in Canada as a professional discipline; to support national, regional & local networking among Canadian Bookkeepers; to provide information on leading-edge procedures, education & technologies that enhance the industry, as well as, the Canadian bookkeeping professional; to support & encourage responsible & accurate bookkeeping practices throughout Canada
Membership: *Fees:* Schedule available
Activities: *Awareness Events:* Annual Conference
Chief Officer(s):
Guy Desmarais, President
president@canadianbookkeepersassociation.com

Canadian Booksellers Association (CBA)
c/o Retail Council of Canada, #800, 1881 Yonge St., Toronto ON M4S 3C4
Toll-Free: 888-373-8245
Overview: A medium-sized national organization founded in 1952
Mission: To promote a high standard of business methods & ethics among members; To define & expand the role of booksellers within the Canadian publishing process; To provide professional advice to prospective & practising booksellers
Affiliation(s): Retail Council of Canada
Finances: *Annual Operating Budget:* $250,000-$500,000
Staff Member(s): 4
Membership: 800; *Fees:* Schedule available; *Member Profile:* Booksellers; publishers; wholesalers; distributors; *Committees:* Membership; Research Advisory; Advocacy Policy; Communications; Campus; Supplier Relations; Technology
Activities: *Rents Mailing List:* Yes
Chief Officer(s):
Darryl Julott, Contact
djulott@retailcouncil.org
Awards:
• Book Design of the Year
• Specialty Bookseller of the Year
• Distributor of the Year
• Editor of the Year
• Fiction Book of the Year
• Author of the Year
• Bookseller of the Year
• Campus Bookseller of the Year
• Non-Fiction Book of the Year
• Marketing Achievement of the Year
• Publisher of the Year
• Sales Rep of the Year
Publications:
• Canadian Bookseller
Type: Magazine; *Frequency:* Quarterly; *Accepts Advertising;*
Price: $24
Profile: Trade magazine with news & analysis of the book industry
• Canadian Bookselling Primer
Profile: Information for new hires in Canadian book retailing
• CBA [Canadian Booksellers Association] Membership Directory
Type: Directory
• CBA [Canadian Booksellers Association] Sourcebook
Profile: Listing of publishers, distributors, wholesalers, & suppliers
• Introduction to Bookselling
Type: Manual
Profile: Tips & tools of the bookselling trade

Canadian Botanical Association (CBA) / Association botanique du Canada (ABC)
PO Box 160, Aberdeen SK S0K 0A0
Tel: 306-253-4654; *Fax:* 306-253-4744
Toll-Free: 888-993-9990
www.cba-abc.ca
Overview: A small national organization founded in 1965
Mission: To represent Canadian Botany & botanists nationally & internationally; to respond quickly & professionally on matters that are of concern to Canadian botanists.
Affiliation(s): Botanical Society of America
Finances: *Funding Sources:* Membership
Membership: *Fees:* $55 regular; $25 student/retired; $1000 lifetime; $500 senior lifetime; *Member Profile:* Professional botanists; academics; research scientists; *Committees:* Conservation; Development & Membership
Activities: Ecology; Mycology; Structure & development; Systematics & phytogeography; Teaching; *Library:* Not open to public
Chief Officer(s):
Fédeerique Guinel, President, 519-884-0710 Ext. 2230
fguinel@wlu.ca
Anne Bruneau, Vice-President, 514-343-2121
anne.bruneau@umontreal.ca
Santokh Singh, Secretary
santokh.singh@botany.ubc.ca
Jane Young, Treasurer, 250-960-5861
youngj@unbc.ca
Awards:
• Iain & Sylvia Taylor Award
• Mary E. Elliott Service Award
• Lionel Cinq-Mars Award
• John Macoun Travel Bursary
• Undergraduate Student Regional Awards
• Lawson Medal
Publications:
• Botany
Type: Journal; *Frequency:* Monthly; *Editor:* Cecily Pearson; *ISSN:* 1480-3305
• CBA [Canadian Botanical Association] / ABC [Association botanique du Canada] Bulletin
Type: Bulletin; *Frequency:* 3 pa; *Editor:* Christine D. Maxwell

Canadian Botanical Conservation Network (CBCN) / Le Réseau canadien pour la conservation de la flore
c/o Science Department, Royal Botanical Gardens, PO Box 399, 680 Plains Rd., Hamilton ON L8N 3H8
Tel: 905-527-1158; *Fax:* 905-577-0375
www.rbg.ca/cbcn
www.facebook.com/RoyalBotanicalGardens
twitter.com/RBGCanada
www.youtube.com/user/royalbotanicalgarden
Overview: A small national organization founded in 1994
Mission: To preserve the biological diversity of Canada's rare & endangered native plant species, wild habitats & ecosystems
Membership: *Member Profile:* Individuals & organizations with an interest in conservation of plant diversity
Activities: Promoting preservation of native plant species, wild habitats, & ecosystems through education & conservation programs; *Library:* CBCN Library
Publications:
• CBCN [Canadian Botanical Conservation Network] Newsletter
Type: Newsletter; *Frequency:* Quarterly; *Editor:* Dr. David A. Galbraith; *ISSN:* 1480-8218
Profile: Plant conservation & biodiversity news, CNCN member news, & upcoming events

Canadian Bottled Water Association (CBWA) / Association canadienne des embouteilleurs d'eau
#617, 7357 Woodbine Ave., Markham ON L3R 6R3
Tel: 416-618-1763; *Fax:* 877-354-2788
www.cbwa.ca
Overview: A medium-sized national licensing organization founded in 1992
Mission: To represent the Canadian bottled water industry; To ensure a high standard of quality for bottled water
Member of: International Council of Bottled Water Associations
Membership: *Member Profile:* Canadian bottled water companies; Equipment manufacturers; Suppliers; Distributors
Activities: Providing educational opportunities
Chief Officer(s):
Elizabeth Griswold, Executive Director
griswold@cbwa.ca
Meetings/Conferences:
• 30th Annual Canadian Bottled Water Association Convention & Trade Show, 2018
Scope: National
Publications:
• Canadian Bottled Water Association Suppliers Guide
Type: Guide
• Canadian Bottled Water Association Products & Services Index
Type: Guide

Canadian Bowling Congress *See* Canadian 5 Pin Bowlers' Association

Canadian Braille Authority *See* Braille Literacy Canada

Canadian Brain Tumour Consortium (CBTC)
c/o Sunnybrook Health Sciences Centre, #402A, 2075 Bayview Ave., Toronto ON M4N 3M5
Tel: 416-480-4766; *Fax:* 416-480-5054
headquarters@cbtc.ca
www.cbtc.ca
Overview: A small national organization founded in 1998
Mission: To act as a national investigator network in the treatment of pediatric & adult patients with brain tumour
Affiliation(s): Canadian Congress of Neurological Sciences
Finances: *Funding Sources:* Client sponsorship agreements
Membership: 129; *Fees:* $250; *Member Profile:* Brain tumour specialists & researchers; *Committees:* Credentials; Scientific
Activities: Developing multi-centre brain tumour research projects in Canada; Liaising with industry to execute clinical trials; Influencing government policy; Disseminating knowledge

Canadian Brain Tumour Tissue Bank
London Health Sciences Centre, University of Western Ontario, 339 Windermere Rd., #C7108, London ON N6A 5A5
Tel: 519-663-3427; *Fax:* 519-663-2930
www.braintumor.ca
Also Known As: Brain Tumor Tissue Bank
Overview: A small national organization
Mission: To supply optimally collected brain tumour tissue to researchers all over the country, internationally & locally in the hopes that some day the cause of & the cure for brain tumours

will be found
Affiliation(s): The Brain Tumour Foundation of Canada
Finances: *Funding Sources:* Brain Tumor Foundation of Canada
Chief Officer(s):
Marcela White, Coordinator
marcela.white@lhsc.on.ca

Canadian Breast Cancer Network (CBCN) / Réseau canadien du cancer du sein (RCCS)
#602, 331 Cooper St., Ottawa ON K2P 0G5
Tel: 613-230-3044; *Fax:* 613-230-4424
Toll-Free: 800-685-8820
cbcn@cbcn.ca
www.cbcn.ca
www.facebook.com/168424759878914
twitter.com/CBCN
www.youtube.com/user/CBCNvideos
Overview: A medium-sized national organization founded in 1994
Mission: To act as the national voice of breast cancer survivors
Finances: *Funding Sources:* Donations
Staff Member(s): 4
Membership: *Member Profile:* Individuals & groups, such as health care professionals, persons affected by breast cancer, & breast cancer care groups
Activities: Promoting education & awarness; Influencing research & health care policy; Supporting individuals affected by breast cancer
Chief Officer(s):
Cathy Ammendolea, President
Craig Faucette, Operations Manager
Sharon Young, Vice President
Publications:
• Network News [a publication of the Canadian Breast Cancer Network]
Type: Newsletter; *Accepts Advertising*
• Outreach [a publication of the Canadian Breast Cancer Network]
Type: Newsletter

Canadian Bridge Federation (CFB) / La Fédération canadienne incorporée de bridge
2719 East Jolly Pl., Regina SK S4V 0X8
Tel: 306-761-1677; *Fax:* 306-789-4919
www.cbf.ca
www.facebook.com/Canadian.Bridge.Federation
Overview: A small national organization founded in 1960
Mission: To conduct grassroot bridge events in Canada; to select & subsidize teams to World Championships.
Affiliation(s): American Contract Bridge League
Finances: *Funding Sources:* Membership fees; game fees
Staff Member(s): 2
Membership: *Fees:* $12 regular; $8 students/first time members
Chief Officer(s):
Janice Anderson, Executive Director
jan@cbf.ca
Nader Hanna, President
zone3@cbf.ca

Canadian Broadcast Standards Council (CBSC) / Conseil canadien des normes de la radiotélévision (CCNR)
PO Box 3265, Stn. D, Ottawa ON K1P 6H8
Tel: 613-233-4607; *Fax:* 613-233-4826
Toll-Free: 866-696-4718
info@cbsc.ca
www.cbsc.ca
Overview: A medium-sized national organization founded in 1990
Mission: To administer standards established by Canada's private broadcasters; To address concerns raised by viewers or listeners about broadcast programs
Finances: *Annual Operating Budget:* $500,000-$1.5 Million
Staff Member(s): 3; 80 volunteer(s)
Membership: 700
Chief Officer(s):
Andrée Noël, National Chair
anoel@cbsc.ca

Canadian Broiler Hatching Egg Marketing Agency *See* Canadian Hatching Egg Producers

Canadian Brown Swiss & Braunvieh Association / L'association canadienne de la Suisse Brune et de la Braunvieh
RR#5 5653 Hwy. 6 North, Guelph ON N1H 6J2
Tel: 519-821-2811; *Fax:* 519-763-6582
brownswiss@gencor.ca
www.browncow.ca
www.facebook.com/117089315003708
Overview: A small national organization founded in 1914
Mission: To encourage, develop & regulate breeding of Brown Swiss & Braunvieh dairy cattle.
Member of: Canadian Beef Breeds Council
Finances: *Funding Sources:* Membership fees
Staff Member(s): 1
Membership: *Member Profile:* Owner/operator
Chief Officer(s):
Renald Dumas, President, 418-453-2896
renciedumas@hotmail.ca
Jessie Weir, Secretary Manager
  Alberta Braunveih Association
  RR#1, Leduc AB T9E 2X1
  Tel: 780-986-1726; *Fax:* 780-986-3069
  swisstraditionbv@yahoo.ca
  Member of: Canadian Brown Swiss Association
  Chief Officer(s):
  Verena Peden, Contact

Canadian Bureau for International Education (CBIE) / Bureau canadien de l'éducation internationale (BCEI)
#1550, 220 Laurier Ave. West, Ottawa ON K1P 5Z9
Tel: 613-237-4820; *Fax:* 613-237-1073
communications@cbie.ca
www.cbie-bcei.ca
www.linkedin.com/company-beta/1560528
www.facebook.com/cbie.ca
twitter.com/cbie_bcei
www.youtube.com/user/cbiebcei
Previous Name: Canadian Service for Overseas Students & Trainees
Overview: A large international charitable organization founded in 1966
Mission: To be the national voice advancing Canadian international education by creating & mobilizing expertise, knowledge, opportunity & leadership
Member of: Canadian Consortium for International Education
Affiliation(s): UNESCO Canada; National Consortium of Scientific & Educational Societies
Finances: *Funding Sources:* Membership dues; Government; Contracts
Staff Member(s): 80
Membership: *Fees:* Schedule available; *Member Profile:* Canadian institutions involved in international education; *Committees:* Education Abroad Advisory; Immigration Advisory; Annual Conference Advisory
Activities: Promoting lifelong learning; Administering formal courses & training programs; Organizing non-formal study visits, exchanges, work attachments & other international development experiences; Managing scholarships; Promoting research; Engaging in advocacy activities; *Awareness Events:* International Education Week, mid November; *Internships:* Yes; *Speaker Service:* Yes; *Rents Mailing List:* Yes
Chief Officer(s):
Karen McBride, President & CEO, 613-237-4820 Ext. 222
kmcbride@cbie.ca
Basel Alashi, Vice President, International Partnerships, 613-237-4820 Ext. 253
balashi@cbie.ca
Awards:
• Celanese Canada Internationalist Fellowships
• CIDA Awards for Canadians
Up to 50 awards of up to $15,000 awarded annually
• United Nations Fellowships
• Lucent Global Science Scholars
Meetings/Conferences:
• Canadian Bureau for International Education 2018 Annual Conference, 2018
Scope: National
Description: The Conference features professional development workshops, concurrent sessions and networking opportunities.

Canadian Bureau for the Advancement of Music (CBAM)
#208, 40 Wynford Dr., Toronto ON M3C 1J5
Tel: 647-352-4015
admin@cbam.ca
www.cbam.ca
Overview: A medium-sized national charitable organization founded in 1919
Mission: To promote music (piano) education program for elementary school students
Staff Member(s): 2
Chief Officer(s):
Howard Hutt, President

Canadian Burn Survivors Community (CBSC)
110 Bambrick Rd., Middle Sackville NS B4E 0J4
www.canadianburnsurvivors.ca
www.facebook.com/298455086834875
Overview: A small national organization founded in 2006
Mission: To provide support to burn survivors
Membership: *Member Profile:* Burn victims; Fire-fighters; Burn unit staff; advisors
Chief Officer(s):
Barbara Anne Hodge, Chair

Canadian Business Aircraft Association Inc. *See* Canadian Business Aviation Association

Canadian Business Aviation Association (CBAA) / Association canadienne de l'aviation d'affaires (ACAA)
#700, 1 Rideau St., Ottawa ON K1N 8S7
Tel: 613-236-5611; *Fax:* 613-236-2361
www.cbaa-acaa.ca
www.linkedin.com/company-beta/9473794
twitter.com/CBAAconvention
Previous Name: Canadian Business Aircraft Association Inc.
Overview: A medium-sized national organization founded in 1961
Mission: To represent & promote the Canadian business aviation community globally, advocating safety, security & efficiency
Affiliation(s): National Business Aviation Association; International Business Aviation Council; European Business Aircraft Association
Finances: *Funding Sources:* Membership dues; convention/tradeshow
Staff Member(s): 7
Membership: Approx. 400 comapnies & organizations; *Fees:* Schedule available; *Member Profile:* owns or operates a Canadian privately or state registered aircraft as an aid to conduct its business; Commercial: owns or operates Canadian commercially registered aircraft; Associate: businesses primarily concerned with aviation activities, including the manufacture of aircraft; Affiliate: owns or operates aircraft exclusively registered in a nation other than Canada
Activities: Leadership; excellence; collaboration; ethics
Chief Officer(s):
Rudy Toering, President & CEO, 613-236-5611 Ext. 238
rtoering@cbaa.ca
Aime O-Connor, Executive Assistant & Director, Administration, 613-236-5611 Ext. 228
aoconnor@cbaa.ca
Lindsay Berndt, Manager, Membership & Community Services, 613-236-5611 Ext. 221
lberndt@cbaa.ca
Awards:
• Honorary Lifetime Membership Award
Recognizes an individual who has made a significant contribution to the CBAA *Eligibility:* Candidates must have made a significatn contribution to the CBAA; must be retired from the CBAA member company for which the worked during the time of significant contribution
• Award of Merit
Granted to a person, company or group in recognition of an outstanding contribution to aviation *Eligibility:* Not necessary for recipient to be a memeber of CBAA; based on nominations
• Pilot Safety Award, Safety Award
Eligibility: Awards granted to pilots of CBAA member companies who have completed 1,500 or more consecutive accident-free hours flown while in a business aircraft
• Company Safety Award, Safety Award
Eligibility: Awards granted to member companies which have completed 1,500 or more accident-free consecutive hours flown in the operation of business aircraft
• Annual Scholarship to Canadian Schedulers & Dispatchers
Eligibility: Students or air cadets registered for aviation courses, or Canadian citizens or permanent residents who work for a CBAA-member company *Deadline:* June 1; *Amount:* $10,000
Contact: Aime O'Connor, aoconnor@cbaa.ca
• CBAA Regional Top Amateur Pilot Award
Granted in conjunction with the John C. Webster Memorial Trohpy Competition and honours one top finalist in the region where the convention is held. *Eligibility:* Winner will be identified

Canadian Associations / Canadian Business for Social Responsibility (CBSR)

through the Webster Memorial Trohpy Competetion; *Amount:* $1,500
• Hope Air Philanthropist of the Year Award
Recognizes philanthropic leadership by a CBAA member who has shown dedication to Hope Air's mission of removing the barriers that separate Canadians from the specialized healthcare they require *Eligibility:* A CBAA member who has provided leadership, service and/or outstanding support to Hope Air (through financial or in-kind support;, encouragement and motivation; or leadership in a philanthropic or community-involved role); *Amount:* $1,500
Meetings/Conferences:
• Canadian Business Aviation Association's 2018 Convention and Exhibition, June, 2018, Waterloo, ON
Description: Exhibitions & static displays; educational & information sessions
Publications:
• The Canadian Business Aviation Association 2016 Buyer's Guide
Type: Magazine; *Frequency:* a.; *Accepts Advertising*; *Number of Pages:* 16
Profile: Provides information on industry suppliers, CBAA activities and acts as a year-round reference to CBAA 2016 exhibitors, sponsers & speakers
• The Canadian Business Aviation Association Annual Report
Type: Report; *Frequency:* a.; *Number of Pages:* 4
Profile: Provides highlights on the yearly activity of the CBAA
• The Canadian Business Aviation Association News Brief
Type: Newsletter; *Number of Pages:* 6
Profile: Provides news highlights, information and annoucements concerning the CBAA

Atlantic Provinces Chapter
c/o AG Aviation Ltd., PO Box 2564, Balmoral NB E8E 2W7
Tel: 506-759-4629
Chief Officer(s):
Peter Bing, Chapter Chair
peter.bing@sobeys.com

Edmonton Chapter
Edmonton AB
Chief Officer(s):
Marty Hope, Chapter Co-Chair
mhope@millarwestern.com
Keith Tilley, Chapter Co-Chair
kjtilley@gmail.com

Ontario Chapter
c/o Wilson Aircraft, #353, 14845 - 6 Yonge St., Aurora ON L4G 6H8
Tel: 905-713-1059
Chief Officer(s):
Carla Libralato, Chapter Co-Chair
carla@skycharter.com
Mike Casey, chapter Co-Chair
mcasey@fssalliance.com

Québec Chapter
c/o Skyservice Business Aviation, 9785, av Ryan, Dorval QC H9P 1A2
Tel: 514-636-5250

Saskatchewan Chapter
c/o Executive Air Service, 2710 Airport Rd., Regina SK S4W 1A3
Tel: 306-787-2431; *Fax:* 306-787-1424
cbaa.sk@gmail.com
Chief Officer(s):
Jim Thompson, Chapter Chair
jim.thompson@gov.sk.ca

Vancouver Chapter
Vancouver BC
Chief Officer(s):
Jody Maclean, Co-Chair
jody@andersonair.ca
Suli Umar, Co-Chair
suli.bizjet@gmail.com

Canadian Business for Social Responsibility (CBSR)
#300, 215 Spadina Ave., Toronto ON M5T 2C7
Tel: 416-703-7435; *Fax:* 416-703-7475
www.cbsr.ca
www.linkedin.com/company/canadian-business-for-social-responsibility-cbsr-
www.facebook.com/CBSRNews
twitter.com/cbsrnews
www.flickr.com/photos/cbsr
Overview: A small national organization founded in 1995
Mission: To help Canadian companies create a positive social, environmental, & economic effect on society
Membership: *Member Profile:* Leading Canadian corporations interested in advancing CSR policies & practices
Activities: Offering climate consultancy services; *Speaker Service:* Yes
Chief Officer(s):
Leor Rotchild, Executive Director
Publications:
• The Climate Change Guide
Type: Manual; *Price:* $35
Profile: Steps outlining responsibilities, opportunities, & risks regarding climate change

Canadian Business Press (CBP) / La Presse spécialisée du Canada
4195 Dundas St. West, Toronto ON M8X 1Y4
Tel: 416-239-1022
Overview: A small national organization founded in 1920
Mission: To represent the interests of Canadian business, professional & farm press. It fosters communication among members of the industry, & encourages cooperation between the private sector & the government; to serve as a prime source of information for & about the industry.
Finances: *Funding Sources:* Membership dues
Membership: *Member Profile:* Publishers of business publications in Canada
Chief Officer(s):
John Kerr, Chair
Awards:
• Kenneth R. Wilson Awards
Recognize excellence in writing & graphic design (17 categories) in specialized business/professional publications; open to all business publications, regardless of CBP membership, that are published in English &/or French; all awards, except the Harvey Southam Editorial Career Award, require an entry fee *Contact:* krwawards@cbp.ca

Canadian Cable Systems Alliance (CCSA)
447 Gondola Point Rd., Quispamsis NB E2E 1E1
Tel: 506-849-1334; *Fax:* 506-849-1338
info@ccsa.cable.ca
www.ccsa.cable.ca
Overview: A medium-sized national organization
Mission: To act as the voice of Canadian independent cable companies
Finances: *Funding Sources:* Sponsorships
Membership: 115+ companies; *Fees:* $750 minimum; *Member Profile:* Canadian independent cable companies
Activities: Making representations to regulatory bodies on issues which affect members; Partnering with vendors; Offering contract administration; Providing cooperative marketing initiatives; Facilitating networking opportunities
Chief Officer(s):
Donna Robertson, Chair
Dale Cook, Contact, Membership
dcook@ccsa.cable.ca
Awards:
• Canadian Cable Systems Alliance Member of the Year Award
Meetings/Conferences:
• Connect 2018, 2018
Scope: National

Canadian Call Management Association (CAM-X)
#10, 24 Olive St., Grimsby ON L3M 2B6
Tel: 905-309-0224; *Fax:* 905-309-0225
Toll-Free: 800-896-1054
info@camx.ca
www.camx.ca
www.facebook.com/pages/CAM-X/118064931573806
twitter.com/CAM-XAssociation
Previous Name: Canadian Association of Message Exchanges, Inc.
Overview: A medium-sized national organization founded in 1964
Mission: To promote the welfare of the message-handling industry & related services through the encouragement & maintenance of high standards of ethics & services; the exchange of information & the rendering of mutual aid & assistance between member organizations.
Finances: *Annual Operating Budget:* $50,000-$100,000; *Funding Sources:* Membership dues; seminars
Staff Member(s): 1
Membership: 100; *Fees:* $150-$1,680; *Member Profile:* Call centres; TAS; teleservices; *Committees:* Development; Member Services; Public Relations; Telephone Co. Liaison
Activities: Service Level Award Program; education seminars; annual convention; mentoring program
Chief Officer(s):
Linda Osip, Executive Director
linda@camx.ca
Awards:
• Award of Excellence
Meetings/Conferences:
• 54th CAM-X Annual Convention & Trade Show, October, 2018
Scope: National

Canadian Camping Association (CCA) / Association des camps du Canada (ACC)
c/o Jill Dundas, Girl Guides Ontario, 100-180 Duncan Mill Rd., Toronto ON M3B 1Z6
www.ccamping.org
www.facebook.com/CanadianCampingAssociation
twitter.com/ccampingorg
Overview: A large national charitable organization founded in 1936
Mission: To develop & promote organized camping for all populations across Canada; To further the interests & welfare of children, youth, & adults through camping; To encourage high standards in camping
Member of: Canadian Camping Association
Affiliation(s): International Camping Fellowship; American Camp Association; Outdoor Council of Canada; Canadian Canoe Museum; SmartBoater.ca
Finances: *Funding Sources:* Provincial Camping Associations, corporate sponsors and private contributions.
Membership: 9 provincial camping associations, representing more than 700 camps throughout Canada; *Member Profile:* Provincial camping associations
Activities: Providing information about camping developments & regulations; Engaging in advocacy activities; Guiding camping leaders
Chief Officer(s):
Jill Dundas, President, 416-526-4102
jill.dundas@sympatico.ca
Awards:
• Ron Johnstone Lifetime Achievement Award
• Jack Pearse Award of Honour
• CCA / ACC Awards of Excellence
• Research Awards of Excellence
• Special Recognition Awards

Canadian Cancer Society (CCS) / Société canadienne du cancer
National Office, #300, 55 St Clair Ave. West, Toronto ON M4V 2Y7
Tel: 416-961-7223; *Fax:* 416-961-4189
Toll-Free: 800-268-8874
ccs@cancer.ca
www.cancer.ca
www.facebook.com/canadiancancersociety
twitter.com/cancersociety
www.youtube.com/user/CDNCancerSociety
Overview: A large national charitable organization founded in 1938
Mission: To collect donations to fund cancer research in Canada; to disseminate information on cancer prevention & treatments, advocating for healthy environment & lifestyle to reduce the incidence of cancer; to offer individual & group support programs for caregivers, family & friends of cancer patients
Affiliation(s): Canadian Breast Cancer Research Alliance; Canadian Prostate Cancer Research Initiative; Canadian Tobacco Control Research Initiative; Canadian Strategy for Cancer Control; Chronic Disease Prevention Alliance of Canada
Finances: *Funding Sources:* Donations
Staff Member(s): 1200; 1700 volunteer(s)
Membership: 10 provincial & territorial divisions
Activities: Advocating for social & political change to control & reduce cancer; promoting methods of prevention; providing the Cancer Information Service; *Awareness Events:* Daffodil Month, April; Childhood, Men's, & Ovarian Cancer Awareness Month, September; Breast Cancer Awareness Month, October
Chief Officer(s):
Robert Lawrie, Chair
Lynne Hudson, President & CEO
Paula Roberts, Vice President, Marketing & Communications
Arlene Teti, Chief Human Resources Officer
Awards:
• O. Harold Warwick Prize, Canadian Cancer Society Awards for Excellence in Cancer Research
; *Amount:* $20,000 toward the recipient's research program

- Robert L. Noble Prize, Canadian Cancer Society Awards for Excellence in Cancer Research
; *Amount:* $20,000 toward the recipient's research program
- The William E. Rawls Prize, Canadian Cancer Society Awards for Excellence in Cancer Research
; *Amount:* $20,000 toward the recipient's research program
- Bernard and Francine Dorval Prize, Canadian Cancer Society Awards for Excellence in Cancer Research
; *Amount:* $20,000 toward the recipient's research program
Publications:
- Canadian Cancer Statistics [a publication of Canadian Cancer Society]
Frequency: Annually
Profile: Report of cancer incidence & mortality in Canada

Alberta & Northwest Territories Division
#200, 325 Manning Rd. NE, Calgary AB T2E 2P5
Tel: 403-205-3966; *Fax:* 403-205-3979
Toll-Free: 800-661-2262
info@cancer.ab.ca
www.cancer.ca
www.facebook.com/CanadianCancerSocietyABNWT
twitter.com/ccs_AlbertaNWT
Mission: To eradicate cancer & enhance the quality of life of people living with cancer. To achieve this mission by funding research on all types of cancer, providing the public with comprehensive information about cancer & risk reduction, advocating for healthy public policy, as well as offering supportive care services to cancer patients, family members & friends.
Chief Officer(s):
Michael Permack, Chair
Dan Holinda, Executive Director
- Believe
Type: Magazine; *Frequency:* Semiannually; *Editor:* Deanna Kraus; *Price:* Free for people living with cancer, & Canadian Cancer Society volunteers & donors
Profile: Support services, cancer information, research, supporters, advocacy, & prevention

British Columbia & Yukon Division
565 West 10th Ave., Vancouver BC V5Z 4J4
Tel: 604-872-4400; *Fax:* 604-872-4113
Toll-Free: 800-663-2524
frontdesk@bc.cancer.ca
www.facebook.com/CanadianCancerSocietyBCY
twitter.com/cancersocietybc
Chief Officer(s):
Faye Wightman, Executive Director
Cheryl Swallow, Vice-President, Finance & Administration

Division du Québec
5151, boul de l'Assomption, Montréal QC H1T 4A9
Tél: 514-255-5151; *Téléc:* 514-255-2808
webmestre@quebec.cancer.ca
www.facebook.com/sccquebec
twitter.com/SCC_Quebec
Chief Officer(s):
Suzanne Dubois, Directrice générale
André Léger, Directeur, Finances
- Canadian Cancer Society's Annual Report - Québec Division
Type: Yearbook; *Frequency:* Annually
Profile: Financial report & description of society activities submitted to the delegates of the general assembly

Manitoba Division
193 Sherbrook St., Winnipeg MB R3C 2B7
Tel: 204-774-7483; *Fax:* 204-774-7500
Toll-Free: 888-532-6982
info@mb.cancer.ca
www.facebook.com/CCSManitoba
twitter.com/CancerSocietyMB
Chief Officer(s):
Elmer Gomes, Chair
Reta Faryon, Contact
rfaryon@mb.cancer
- Community Services Directory
Type: Directory
Profile: Listings of support programs, hair donation programs, home care, transportation, stop smoking programs, & places to find a prosthesis or wig
- Society News
Type: Newsletter
Profile: Volunteer information, upcoming events, & methods of prevention

New Brunswick Division
PO Box 2089, 133 Prince William St., Saint John NB E2L 3T5
Tel: 506-634-6272; *Fax:* 506-634-3808
ccsnb@nb.cancer.ca
www.facebook.com/CanadianCancerSocietyNB
twitter.com/CancerSocietyNB
Chief Officer(s):
Michael Costello, Chair
Anne McTiernan-Gamble, Chief Executive Officer

Newfoundland & Labrador Division
Daffodil Place, PO Box 8921, 70 Ropewalk Ln., St. John's NL A1B 3R9
Tel: 709-753-6520; *Fax:* 709-753-9314
Toll-Free: 888-753-6520
ccs@nl.cancer.ca
Chief Officer(s):
Matthew Piercey, Chief Executive Officer
mpiercey@nl.cancer.ca
Natasha Denty, Manager, Finance & Operations
- Canadian Cancer Society - Newfoundland & Labrador Division Community Report
Type: Yearbook; *Frequency:* Annually

Nova Scotia Division
5826 South St., Halifax NS B3H 1S6
Tel: 902-423-6183; *Fax:* 902-429-6563
Toll-Free: 800-639-0222
ccs.ns@ns.cancer.ca
www.facebook.com/CancerSocietyNS
twitter.com/cancersocietyNS
Mission: To overcome cancer; To create healthy lives for Nova Scotians
Chief Officer(s):
David Landrigan, Chair
Kendra Morton, Director, Development
- Canadian Cancer Society - Nova Scotia Division Annual Report
Type: Yearbook; *Frequency:* Annually

Ontario Division
#500, 55 St. Clair Ave. West, Toronto ON M4V 2Y7
Tel: 416-488-5400; *Fax:* 416-488-2872
Toll-Free: 800-268-8874
webmaster@ontario.cancer.ca
Chief Officer(s):
Mark Hierlihy, Executive Director
Rowena Pinto, Vice-President, Public Affairs & Strategic Initiatives
Lesley Ring, Vice-President, Development & Marketing
- Hope Blooms
Type: Newsletter; *Frequency:* Monthly
Profile: Cancer research updates, tips to reduce risk of cancer, upcoming events, volunteer profiles

Prince Edward Island Division
#1, 1 Rochford St., Charlottetown PE C1A 9L2
Tel: 902-566-4007; *Fax:* 902-628-8281
info@pei.cancer.ca
www.cancer.ca/pei
www.facebook.com/CancerSocietyPE
twitter.com/CancerSocietyPE
Chief Officer(s):
Marlene Mulligan, Executive Director
mmulligan@pei.cancer.ca
- Cancer Quarterly
Type: Newsletter; *Frequency:* Quarterly

Saskatchewan Division
1910 McIntyre St., Regina SK S4P 2R3
Tel: 306-790-5822; *Fax:* 306-569-2133
Toll-Free: 877-977-4673
ccssk@sk.cancer.ca
www.facebook.com/jointhefight.sk
twitter.com/jointhefight_sk
Chief Officer(s):
Susan Holmes, Chair
Keith Karasin, Executive Director

Canadian Cancer Society Research Institute
#300, 55 St. Clair Ave. West, Toronto ON M4V 2Y7
Tel: 416-961-7223; *Fax:* 416-961-4189
research@cancer.ca
www.cancer.ca/research
Previous Name: National Cancer Institute of Canada
Overview: A medium-sized national organization founded in 2009
Mission: To act as a strong voice in the cancer research community; To support a broad range of projects that involve Canadian investigators across the spectrum of cancer research
Staff Member(s): 10
Activities: Funding promising cancer research; Sponsoring clinical trials to test new drugs; Offering programs to train, develop, & support cancer researchers; Establishing peer review panels to review applications to conduct studies; Presenting awards; Collaborating with other research organizations, such as the Canadian Breast Cancer Research Alliance & the Canadian Tobacco Control Research Initiative
Chief Officer(s):
Sian Bevan, Vice-President, Research, 416-934-5308
sian.bevan@cancer.ca
Lori Moser, Manager, Programs, 416-934-5310
lori.moser@cancer.ca
Publications:
- Research Connection [a publication of the Canadian Cancer Society Research Institute]
Type: Newsletter
Profile: News for cancer researchers, including information about research grants

Canadian Cancer Survivor Network (CCSN)
#210, 1750 Courtwood Cres., Ottawa ON K2C 2B5
Tel: 613-898-1871
info@survivornet.ca
survivornet.ca
www.facebook.com/CanadianSurvivorNet
twitter.com/survivornetca
Overview: A large national organization
Mission: To help cancer patients & their families cope with their situation; To educate the public about the costs of cancer
Staff Member(s): 4
Membership: *Committees:* Asbestos & Mesothelioma Advisory Council; Breast Cancer Advisory Council; IT & Web Advisory; Prostate Cancer Advisory Council
Chief Officer(s):
Jackie Manthorne, President & CEO
jmanthorne@survivornet.ca

Canadian Canoe Association *See* CanoeKayak Canada

Canadian Canola Growers Association (CCGA)
#400, 1661 Portage Ave., Winnipeg MB R3J 3T7
Tel: 204-788-0090; *Fax:* 204-788-0039
Toll-Free: 866-745-2256
ccga@ccga.ca
www.ccga.ca
Overview: A small national organization founded in 1984
Mission: To supprt canola producers by voicing their concerns about national & international issues
Affiliation(s): Alberta Canola Prorducers Commission; Saskatchewan Canola Development Commission; Manitoba Canola Growers; BC Grain Producers Association; Ontario Canola Growers
Staff Member(s): 12
Membership: 5; *Member Profile:* Canola growers & producer associations
Chief Officer(s):
Rick White, General Manager, 204-789-8810
rickw@ccga.ca
Kelly Green, Director, Communications, 204-789-8821
kellyg@ccga.ca

Canadian Capital Markets Association (CCMA) / Association canadienne des marchés des capitaux (ACMC)
85 Richmond St. West, Toronto ON M5H 2C9
Tel: 416-410-1050
info@ccma-acmc.ca
www.ccma-acmc.ca
Overview: A medium-sized national organization founded in 2000
Mission: To make recommendations to meet the challenges & opportunities facing Canadian & international capital markets; To enhance the competitiveness of capital markets in Canada
Membership: *Committees:* Board of Directors; Sell-Side; Buy-Side; Custodian; Communications & Education Working Group; Legal / Regulatory Working Group
Chief Officer(s):
Jamie Anderson, Secretary
Publications:
- CCMA [Canadian Capital Markets Association] News
Type: Newsletter
Profile: Information about the association's current initiatives

Canadian Captive Insurance Association (CCIA)
BC
info@canadiancaptive.com
www.canadiancaptive.com
www.linkedin.com/company/2232242

Canadian Associations / Canadian Carbonization Research Association (CCRA)

www.facebook.com/canadiancaptive
twitter.com/canadiancaptive
Previous Name: British Columbia Captive Insurance Association
Overview: A small provincial organization founded in 1992
Mission: To represent association members; to promote the captive insurance industry in British Columbia
Membership: Fees: $100 new company; $25 existing company; *Member Profile:* Individuals interested in British Columbia captives
Activities: Providing professional development opportunities; Reviewing proposed legislative changes; Making recommendations to regulators regarding changes to legislation
Chief Officer(s):
Baddeley Michael, Contact, 604-608-6182 Ext. 112
michael.baddeley@integrogroup.com
Day Kevin, Contact, 888-388-1112
kevin@riskebiz.com
Neil MacLean, Contact, 604-844-5507
nmaclean@guildyule.com
Barb Murray, Contact, 604-443-2476
barb.murray@aon.ca

Canadian Carbonization Research Association (CCRA)
c/o Ted Todoschuk, PO Box 2460, 1330 Burlington St. East, Hamilton ON L8N 3J5
Tel: 905-548-4796; *Fax:* 905-548-4653
www.cancarb.ca
Overview: A small national organization founded in 1965
Mission: To fund coke & coal research in Canada for benefit of member companies
Finances: Funding Sources: Membership fees
Membership: 7 corporate; *Member Profile:* Coal producer, coke producer or related to coal/coke products; *Committees:* Technical
Chief Officer(s):
Ted Todoschuk, Contact
ted.todoschuk@arcelormittal.com

Canadian Cardiac Rehabilitation Foundation See Cardiac Health Foundation of Canada

Canadian Cardiovascular Society (CCS) / Société canadienne de cardiologie
#1403, 222 Queen St., Ottawa ON K1P 5V9
Tel: 613-569-3407; *Fax:* 613-569-6574
Toll-Free: 877-569-3407
info@ccs.ca
www.ccs.ca
www.facebook.com/141084722576966
twitter.com/SCC_CCS
Previous Name: Canadian Heart Association
Overview: A medium-sized national organization founded in 1947
Mission: To promote cardiovascular health & care through knowledge translation, dissemination of research & encouragement of best practices, professional development & leadership in health policy
Member of: World Heart Federation; Inter-American Society of Cardiology; Canadian Coalition for High Blood Pressure Prevention & Control; American Society of Cardiology
Affiliation(s): Canadian Society of Clinical Perfusionists; Canadian Society of Cardiology Technologists; Canadian Association of Cardiopulmonary Technologists; Canadian Medical Association; Royal College of Physicians & Surgeons of Canada; Canadian Council of Cardiovascular Nursing
Finances: Funding Sources: Membership dues; programs & activities
Membership: 2,000+; *Fees:* $485; *Member Profile:* Physicians, surgeons or scientists, whose primary interest is in practice of cardiology & cardiovascular surgery or research in related fields
Activities: Consensus conference development; continuing professional development; advocacy; *Rents Mailing List:* Yes; *Library:* Not open to public
Chief Officer(s):
Heather Ross, President
Anne Ferguson, Chief Executive Officer
Awards:
• Annual Achievement Award
• Harold N. Segall Award of Merit
• Research Achievement Award
• Distinguished Teacher Award
• Young Investigator Award
Meetings/Conferences:
• 2018 Canadian Cardiovascular Congress, October, 2018, Toronto, ON
Scope: National
Publications:
• The Canadian Journal of Cardiology
Type: Journal; *Editor:* Dr. E.R. Smith; *Price:* Free with CCS membership
Profile: Research reports, health outcomes, ethics, review articles, policy, political issues, & case reports concerning cardiovascular medicine

Canadian Career Development Foundation (CCDF) / Fondation canadienne pour le développement de carrière (FCDC)
#202, 119 Ross Ave., Ottawa ON K1Y 0N6
Tel: 613-729-6164; *Fax:* 613-729-3515
Toll-Free: 877-729-6164
information@ccdf.ca
www.ccdf.ca
twitter.com/CCDFFCDC
Overview: A medium-sized national charitable organization founded in 1979
Mission: To advance the understanding & practice of career development.
Affiliation(s): International Association for Educational & Vocational Guidance
Finances: Funding Sources: Government grants; contracts; donations
Staff Member(s): 8
Activities: Expert consultation on career development issues; professional development courses; workshops on quality & accountability; clearinghouse of resources; *Speaker Service:* Yes; *Library:* by appointment Not open to public
Chief Officer(s):
Lynne Bezanson, Executive Director
l.bezanson@ccdf.ca
Sareena Hopkins, Co-Executive Director
s.hopkins@ccdf.ca

Canadian Caregiver Coalition (CCC-CCAN) / Coalition canadienne des aidants et aidantes naturels
110 Argyle Ave., Ottawa ON K2P 1B4
Tel: 613-233-5694; *Fax:* 613-230-4376
Toll-Free: 888-866-2273
info@ccc-ccan.ca
www.ccc-ccan.ca
Overview: A medium-sized national organization
Mission: To join with caregivers, service providers, policy makers & other stakeholders to identify & respond to the needs of caregivers in Canada

Canadian Caribbean Amateur Golfers Association (CCAGA)
#718, 7305 Woodbine Ave, Markham ON L3R 3V7
Fax: 905-420-8421
info@ccaga.ca
www.ccaga.ca
Overview: A small local organization founded in 1980
Mission: A Not-For-Profit Association offering beginners and amateur golfers the opportunity to play and compete among each other
Membership: Fees: $125 single; $200 family; $100 associate (non-playing)

Canadian Carpet Institute / Institut canadien du tapis
#200, 435 St. Laurent Blvd., Ottawa ON K1K 2Z8
Tel: 613-749-3265; *Fax:* 613-745-8753
info@canadiancarpet.org
www.canadiancarpet.org
Overview: A medium-sized national organization founded in 1963
Mission: To serve as a forum in developing industry consensus for action on common problems & opportunities; To enhance the well-being of the Canadian carpet industry by any & all means consistent with the members & the public interest
Member of: Healthy Indoors Partnership; National Floor Covering Association; World Carpet & Rug Council
Finances: Funding Sources: Membership dues
9 volunteer(s)
Membership: 5 mills + 6 suppliers + 1 carpet cushion; *Fees:* Based on sales; *Member Profile:* Canadian carpet manufacturers & suppliers; *Committees:* Technical Affairs
Activities: Providing information to the carpet industry & consumers
Chief Officer(s):
Carl Hulme, President
Alexandre Lacroix, Vice-President
Raymonde Lemire, Manager, Administration

Canadian Cartographic Association (CCA) / Association canadienne de cartographie
c/o Paul Heersink, 39 Wales Ave., Markham ON L3P 2C4
Fax: 416-446-1639
treasurer@cca-acc.org
www.cca-acc.org
Overview: A small national organization founded in 1975
Mission: To promote interest in cartographic materials; To encourage research in the field of cartography; To advance education in cartography
Affiliation(s): International Cartographic Association
Membership: 16; *Fees:* $45 student/retired/institution; $90 regular members; $110 family membership; $200 corporate; *Member Profile:* Individuals with an interest in mapping
Activities: Facilitating the exchange of information; Organizing a biannual exhibit of Canadian cartography; Collaborating with sister organizations
Chief Officer(s):
Elise Pietroniro, Secretary
secretary@cca-acc.org
Paul Heersink, Treasurer
Meetings/Conferences:
• 43rd Canadian Cartographic Association Conference 2018, May, 2018, Nova Scotia Community College, Lawrencetown, NS
Scope: National
Description: Theme: "Community Mapping: Place-Making Through Maps"
Publications:
• Cartographica
Type: Journal; *Frequency:* Quarterly; *ISSN:* 0317-7173; *Price:* Free with CCA membership
Profile: Cartographica also appears as a monograph on a single topic
• Cartouche
Type: Newsletter; *Frequency:* Quarterly; *Editor:* Patricia Connor Reid; *Price:* Free with CCA membership
Profile: Association activities, forthcoming events, articles, products, & news

Canadian Carwash Association (CCA)
#340, 4195 Dundas St. West, Toronto ON M8X 1Y4
Tel: 416-239-0339; *Fax:* 416-239-1076
office@canadiancarwash.ca
www.canadiancarwash.ca
twitter.com/canadiancarwash
Overview: A small national organization founded in 1961
Mission: To promote the benefits of professional carwashing
Affiliation(s): International Carwash Association
Finances: Annual Operating Budget: Less than $50,000
Staff Member(s): 7; 20 volunteer(s)
Membership: 200; *Fees:* $210 carwash operator, manufacturer/supplier, detail shop; *Member Profile:* Carwash operators; manufacturers; suppliers to the carwash industry
Activities: Legislation & regulatory activity; auto industry communications; professionalism & increasing profitability; environmental awareness
Chief Officer(s):
Scott Murray, President, 905-662-6595
Awards:
• Ted Snyders Memorial Award
Meetings/Conferences:
• Canadian Carwash Association Annual General Meeting 2018, March, 2018, Toronto Congress Centre, Toronto, ON
Scope: National
Publications:
• Octane
Type: Magazine; *Frequency:* Quarterly; *Price:* $48 Canada
Profile: Publication about the car wash & petroleum industry, including a yearly buyer's guide & a guide to the CARWACS tradeshow
• Wash Volume Report: National Report
Frequency: Quarterly; *Price:* Free with CCA membership
Profile: Comparison of carwash performance across Canada
• Wash Volume Report: Regional Market
Frequency: Quarterly; *Price:* Free with CCA membership
Profile: Comparison of carwash performance within regions
• WASH-word
Type: Newsletter

Canadian Casting Federation
c/o Toronto Sportsmen's Association, #66, 2700 Dufferin St., Toronto ON M6B 4J3

Tel: 416-487-4477; *Fax:* 416-487-4478
info@torontosportsmens.ca
www.torontosportsmens.ca/Casting.html
Overview: A small national organization founded in 1978
Mission: To teach casting skills, covering fly, bait & spinning
Affiliation(s): Toronto Sportsmen's Association; Ontario Fly & Bait Casting Association
Activities: *Awareness Events:* Canadian Casting Championships

Canadian Cat Association (CCA) / Association féline Canadienne (AFC)
Bldg. 12, #102, 5045 Orbitor Dr., Mississauga ON L4W 4Y4
Tel: 905-232-3481; *Fax:* 289-232-9481
office@cca-afc.com
www.cca-afc.com
www.facebook.com/100474523335824
Overview: A small national organization founded in 1961
Mission: To improve all breeds of cats in Canada, & maintains a registry of purebred lineages; to serve as a source for cat-related news, including information on shows, & an online breeders' showcase.
Staff Member(s): 2
Membership: *Fees:* $50 individual; $60 family; $15 junior; *Committees:* Benefit Shows; Legislative; Ethics; Publications; Public Relations; Standards; CCA Awards & Scoring; Technology; Website; Clerking; Board of Examiners; Membership; Fundraising
Chief Officer(s):
Bob Gleason, President, 519-433-2947
robertgleason@rogers.com
Sandra Dawes, Administrator & Registrar
sandra@cca-afc.com
Publications:
• Chat Canada Cats
Type: Magazine; *Frequency:* Annually; *Editor:* Sylvie Lamoureux St. Mathias

Canadian Catholic Biblical Association *See* Catholic Biblical Association of Canada

Canadian Catholic Campus Ministry (CCCM)
#307, 47 Queen's Park Cres. East, Toronto ON M5S 2C3
Tel: 416-506-0183; *Fax:* 416-978-7827
www.cccm.ca
www.facebook.com/252224265072
Also Known As: Canadian Catholic Students Association
Overview: A small national charitable organization
Mission: To unite Catholic students on Canadian post-secondary campuses; To nurture Christian student leadership
Affiliation(s): International Movement of Catholic Students - Canada
Finances: *Funding Sources:* Donations
Membership: *Member Profile:* Persons who support the purpose of the association
Activities: Supporting prayerful, pastoral action; *Awareness Events:* Catholic Students' Week, March
Chief Officer(s):
Kidd Sue, Chair & Atlantic Representative
sukidd@upei.ca
Martha Fauteux, Vice-Chair & Central Representative
mfauteux@uwaterloo.ca
Nancy Quan, Western Representative
Nancy.quan@stmu.ab.ca
Chrisandra Skipper, Central Representative
cskipper@assumptionu.ca
Robert Corbeil, National Coordinator, 879-743-7197, Fax: 855-488-0807
nc@cccm.ca

Canadian Catholic Conference *See* Canadian Conference of Catholic Bishops

Canadian Catholic Historical Association - English Section (CCHA) / Société canadienne d'histoire de l'église catholique - Section anglaise
c/o St. Michael's College, 81 St. Mary St., Toronto ON M5S 1J4
Tel: 905-893-9754; *Fax:* 416-934-3444
www.cchahistory.ca
twitter.com/cchahistory
Overview: A medium-sized national organization founded in 1933
Mission: The Association promotes interest & research in the history of the Canadian Catholic Church, its dioceses, religious communities, institutions, parishes, buildings, sites, & personalities. It is divided into English & French sections.

Finances: *Annual Operating Budget:* Less than $50,000; *Funding Sources:* Membership fees; donations
11 volunteer(s)
Membership: 100-499; *Fees:* $50 Canadian; US$50 American; $30 student; $60 French-English
Activities: Annual scholarly conference at the Canadian Congress
Chief Officer(s):
G. Edward MacDonald, President-General
gemacdonald@upei.ca
Edward Jackman, Secretary-General
revedjackman@rogers.com
Awards:
• James F. Kenney Prize
Eligibility: Awarded for the best essay on any aspect of the history of Catholicism in Canada written in a course by an undergraduate student in any university.; *Amount:* $500 *Contact:* Dr. Edward MacDonald, gemacdonald@upei.ca
• G.E. Clerk Award
Eligibility: Scholars who have distinguished themselves in Catholic studies, publishing, teaching, archival work, or administration. *Contact:* Dr. Edward MacDonald, gemacdonald@upei.ca
• Paul Bator Award
This award recognizes the best article published in Historical Studies in the previous two years. *Contact:* Dr. Edward MacDonald, gemacdonald@upei.ca
History Office
#508, 10 St. Mary St., Toronto ON M4Y 1P9
Tel: 416-968-3683; *Fax:* 416-975-1588
terence.fay@utoronto.ca

Canadian Catholic Historical Association - French Section
Voir Société canadienne d'histoire de l'Église Catholique - Section française

Canadian Catholic School Trustees' Association (CCSTA) / Association canadienne des commissaires d'écoles catholique
Catholic Education Centre, 570 West Hunt Club Rd., Nepean ON K2G 3R4
Tel: 613-224-4455; *Fax:* 613-224-3187
ccsta@ocsb.ca
www.ccsta.ca
Overview: A medium-sized national organization founded in 1960
Mission: To protect the right to Catholic education in Canada; To promote excellence in Catholic education across Canada
Member of: National Catholic Education Association (US)
Finances: *Funding Sources:* Sponsorships
Membership: 8 associations representing 80 Catholic school boards; *Member Profile:* Provincial & territorial Catholic school trustees' associations in Canada
Activities: Promoting Catholic education; Providing professional development opportunities for trustees; Collaborating with the Canadian Conference of Catholic Bishops; Liaising with Canadian government agencies & other Catholic education organizations; *Awareness Events:* Catholic Education Week
Chief Officer(s):
Mike St. Amand, President
mike@ashlycw.com
Marino Gazzola, Vice-President
marino.gazzola@sympatico.ca
Julian Hanlon, Executive Director
julian.hanlon@ocsb.ca
Meetings/Conferences:
• Canadian Catholic School Trustees' Association 2018 AGM, June, 2018, Delta Hotels Grand Okanagan Resort, Kelowna, BC
Contact Information: ccsta@ocsb.ca
• Canadian Catholic School Trustees' Association 2019 AGM, May, 2019, Canmore, AB
Contact Information: ccsta@ocsb.ca
Publications:
• Build Bethlehem Everywhere - A Statement on Catholic Education
Type: Book
• CCSTA [Canadian Catholic School Trustees' Association] Newsletter
Type: Newsletter
Profile: Includes CCSTA activities, conferences, & provincial reports

Canadian Cattle Breeders' Association (CCBA) / Société des éleveurs de bovins canadiens (SEBC)
4865, boul Laurier ouest, Saint-Hyacinthe QC J2S 3V4

Tel: 450-774-2775; *Fax:* 450-774-9775
www.clrc.ca/canadiancattle.shtml
Overview: A medium-sized national organization founded in 1895
Member of: Canadian Livestock Records Corporation
Finances: *Annual Operating Budget:* $50,000-$100,000; *Funding Sources:* Membership dues
Staff Member(s): 1
Membership: 93; *Fees:* Schedule available
Chief Officer(s):
Jim Washer, Secretary-Treasurer
ahebert@csrlinc.com

Canadian Cattlemen's Association (CCA)
#180, 6815 - 8 St. NE, Calgary AB T2E 7H7
Tel: 403-275-8558; *Fax:* 403-274-5686
feedback@cattle.ca
www.cattle.ca
www.facebook.com/Canadian-Cattlemens-Association-333965336775693/
twitter.com/CdnCattlemen
www.instagram.com/Canadiancattlemens
Overview: A large national organization founded in 1932
Mission: To act as the national voice of beef producers across Canada; To produce high-quality beef products; To maintain a profitable Canadian beef industry; To use management practices that protect the health of the animal & protect the environment
Finances: *Funding Sources:* Fee assessments to provincial cattle organization members; National Check-off Agency
Staff Member(s): 24
Membership: *Committees:* Environment; Animal Care; Animal Health & Meat Inspection; Value Creation & Competitiveness; Foreign Trade; Domestic Ag-Policy & Regulations; Convention; Executive & Finance
Activities: Collaborating with other agricultural sectors & food industries on matters of mutual concern; Providing a mentorship program
Chief Officer(s):
Dan Darling, President
Dennis Laycraft, Executive Vice President
Rob McNabb, General Manager, Operations
Fawn Jackson, Manager, Environment and Sustainability
Meetings/Conferences:
• Canadian Cattlemen's Association 2018 Annual General Meeting, March, 2018, Ottawa Marriott Hotel, Ottawa, ON
Scope: National
Description: An opportunity for members to address industry issues & to elect officers
Publications:
• Canadian Cattlemen's Association By-laws
Number of Pages: 20
• Canadian Cattlemen's Association Policy Manual
Type: Manual; *Number of Pages:* 26
Profile: Topics include animal care, animal health, meat inspection, environment, finance, foreign trade, value creation, & competitiveness
• CCA [Canadian Cattlemen's Association] Monthly Report
Type: Report; *Frequency:* Monthly
Profile: CCA news & information about the beef producing industry
• CCA [Canadian Cattlemen's Association] Annual Report
Frequency: Annually
Profile: Executive, division, committee, provincial association, & financial reports
• CCA [Canadian Cattlemen's Association] News
Type: Newsletter; *Frequency:* Semimonthly; *Price:* Free
Profile: Recent association & industry information
Ottawa Office
#1207, 350 Sparks St., Ottawa ON K1R 7S8
Tel: 613-233-9375; *Fax:* 613-233-2860
Chief Officer(s):
John Masswohl, Director, Government & International Relations

Canadian CED Network / Réseau canadien de DÉC
PO Box 199E, 59, rue Monfette, Victoriaville QC G6P 1J8
Tel: 819-795-3056; *Fax:* 819-795-3056
Toll-Free: 877-202-2268
info@ccednet-rcdec.ca
ccednet-rcdec.ca
www.linkedin.com/company/canadian-community-economic-development-network
www.facebook.com/CCEDNet
twitter.com/CCEDNet_RCDEC
www.youtube.com/user/ccednet
Overview: A large national organization

Canadian Associations / Canadian Celiac Association (CCA) / L'Association canadienne de la maladie coeliaque

Mission: To strengthen communities in Canada by creating economic opportunities that improve local social & environmental conditions.
Member of: National Congress for Community Economic Development
Staff Member(s): 3
Membership: *Fees:* Schedule available
Chief Officer(s):
Mike Toye, Executive Director
mtoye@ccednet-rcdec.ca

Canadian Celiac Association (CCA) / L'Association canadienne de la maladie coeliaque
Bldg. 1, #400, 5025 Orbitor Dr., Mississauga ON L4W 4Y5
Tel: 905-507-6208; *Fax:* 905-507-4673
Toll-Free: 800-363-7296
info@celiac.ca
www.celiac.ca
www.facebook.com/CCAceliac
twitter.com/ccaceliac
www.pinterest.ca/canadianceliac
Also Known As: Celiac Canada
Previous Name: Canadian Celiac Sprue Association
Overview: A large national charitable organization founded in 1972
Mission: To increase awareness of celiac & dermatitis herpetiformis among government institutions, health care professionals & the public; To provide information about the disease & a gluten-free diet; To encourage research through the establishment of the J.A. Campbell Research Fund
Finances: *Funding Sources:* Donations
Membership: *Fees:* $65 new; $50 renewal
Activities: Providing awareness & education programs; engaging in advocacy activities; *Awareness Events:* Celiac Awareness Month, Oct.
Chief Officer(s):
Anne Wraggett, President
Awards:
- J.A.Campbell Research Grant
; *Amount:* $25,000 maximum
- J.A.Campbell Young Investigator Award
; *Amount:* $5,000
Meetings/Conferences:
- 2018 Canadian Celiac Association National Conference, 2018
Scope: National
Publications:
- Acceptability of Food & Food Ingredients for the Gluten Free Diet
Type: Dictionary; *Price:* Free for new members of the Canadian Celiac Association; $10 non-members
- Celiac News
Type: Newsletter; *Frequency:* 3 pa; *Price:* Free with CCA membership
Profile: Up-to-date information about the diesease & a gluten-free diet

Belleville & Quinte Chapter
c/o Karen Y. Brooks, PO Box 293, Bloomfield ON K0K 1G0
chapter.on.bellville.quinte@celiac.ca
Chief Officer(s):
Karen Brooks, President
karenybrooks@sympatico.ca

Calgary Chapter
#1A, 2215 - 27 Ave. NE, Calgary AB T2E 8J2
Tel: 403-237-0304; *Fax:* 403-269-9626
info@calgaryceliac.ca
calgaryceliac.com
www.facebook.com/155433831171925
Chief Officer(s):
Cindy Casper, Coordinator, Events
- Calgary Chapter Newsletter
Type: Newsletter; *Frequency:* Quarterly

Edmonton Chapter
#220, 5615 - 101 Ave. NW, Edmonton AB T6A 3Z7
Tel: 780-485-2949; *Fax:* 780-485-2940
info@celiacedmonton.ca
www.celiacedmonton.ca
www.facebook.com/296692389521
twitter.com/edmontonceliac
Chief Officer(s):
Don Briggs, President
- Celiac Circular
Type: Newsletter; *Frequency:* Bimonthly; *Price:* Free for members of the Canadian Celiac Association Edmonton Chapter; $20 non-members

Fredericton Chapter
#226, 527 Beaverbrook Ct., Fredericton NB E3B 1X6
fred.celiac@gmail.com
Chief Officer(s):
Angela Welch, President, 506-454-3222

Hamilton/Burlington Chapter
PO Box 65580, Stn. Dundas, Dundas ON L9H 6Y6
Tel: 905-572-6775
hamiltonceliacchapter@gmail.com
www.glutenfreehamilton.ca
Chief Officer(s):
Laura Harrison, President
Wendy Stewart, Treasurer
- Hamilton Celiac News
Type: Newsletter; *Frequency:* Quarterly; *Accepts Advertising*; *Editor:* Laura Harrison
Profile: Upcoming events, meeting reports, celiac friendly restaurants, & recipes

Kamloops Chapter
2672 Qu'Appelle Blvd., Kamloops BC V2E 2H7
Tel: 250-319-9978
www.kamloopsceliac.org
www.facebook.com/275537332507738
Chief Officer(s):
Eileen Gordon, Secretary, 250-374-6185
- Canadian Celiac Association Kamloops Chapter Newsletter
Type: Newsletter

Kelowna Chapter
PO Box 21031, Stn. Orchard Park, Kelowna BC V1Y 9N8
Tel: 250-763-7159
kelownaceliac.org
www.facebook.com/KelownaCeliac
twitter.com/KelownaCeliac
Chief Officer(s):
Irene Thompson, President
rithomp@telus.net
Marie Ablett, Help-line Contact
dougmarieablett1@shaw.ca

Kingston Chapter
Kingston ON
info@kingstonceliac.ca
www.kingstonceliac.ca
Chief Officer(s):
Sue Jennett, President

Kitchener/Waterloo Chapter
1412 - 16 Barrel Yards Blvd., Waterloo ON N2L 0C4
kwceliac@sympatico.ca
Chief Officer(s):
Elizabeth Popham, President, 519-580-5982

London Chapter
PO Box 27051, London ON N5X 3X5
info@londonceliac.org
www.londonceliac.org
Chief Officer(s):
Helen Olmstead, President

Manitoba - West Chapter
#11, 83 Silverbirch Dr., Brandon MB R7B 1A8
Tel: 204-727-8445
chapter.mb.westernmanitoba.ca@celiac.ca
Chief Officer(s):
Debbie Barrett, Contact
deborahb22012@yahoo.ca

Manitoba Chapter
#204, 825 Sherbrook St., Winnipeg MB R3A 1M5
Tel: 204-772-6979
office@manitobaceliac.com
www.manitobaceliac.com
www.facebook.com/176000709214214
twitter.com/manitobaceliac
Chief Officer(s):
Dorothy Macintyre, President
- Celi-Yak
Type: Newsletter; *Frequency:* Quarterly; *Price:* Free for Manitoba Chapter members
Profile: Food & product information, recipes & restaurants, health news, & upcoming events

Moncton Chapter
PO Box 1576, Moncton NB E1C 9X4
monctonceliacchapter.org
www.facebook.com/249496635102956
Chief Officer(s):
Jo-Anne Wilson, President
Aline Farrell, Vice-President
Dave Saunders, Treasurer
- Canadian Celiac Association Moncton Chapter Newsletter
Type: Newsletter; *Editor:* Mike Murphy

Newfoundland & Labrador Chapter
38 East Meadows Ave., St. John's NL A1A 3M5
celiacnl.ca
www.facebook.com/199683166751767
Chief Officer(s):
Lisa Dooley, President, 709-693-4213
glutenfreenuggets@outlook.com

Nova Scotia Chapter
Tacoma Plaza, #14, 50 Tacoma Dr., Dartmouth NS B2W 3E6
Tel: 902-464-9222; *Fax:* 902-435-6747
info@celiacns.ca
www.celiacns.ca
www.facebook.com/celiacns
twitter.com/ccaceliac
Chief Officer(s):
Marg Gorveatt, Coordinator, Office Operations
- Canadian Celiac Association Halifax Chapter
Type: Newsletter; *Frequency:* Quarterly
Profile: Recent issues dealing with Celiac Disease & Dermatitis Herpetiformis, chapter updates, & recipes

Ottawa Chapter
PO Box 39035, Stn. Billings Bridge, Ottawa ON K1H 1A1
Tel: 613-786-1335
www.ottawaceliac.ca
Chief Officer(s):
Samantha Maloney, President
- Ottawa Chapter Newsletter
Type: Newsletter; *Editor:* Quintin Wight; *Price:* Free for Ottawa Chapter members
Profile: Upcoming events, issues, gluten-free product information, & recipes

Peterborough & Area Chapter
Peterborough ON
Tel: 905-372-2361
www.celiacpeterborough.ca
Mission: To help celiacs & their families adjust to gluten-free living
Chief Officer(s):
Shirley Stewart, Contact
shirleystewart26@gmail.com
- Peterborough & Area Chapter Newsletter
Type: Newsletter; *Frequency:* 3 pa; *Accepts Advertising*; *Editor:* Leslee Horton; *Price:* Free with Peterborough & Area Chapter membership

Prince Edward Island Chapter
PO Box 1921, Charlottetown PE C1A 7N5
Tel: 902-724-2189
info@celiacpei.ca
www.celiacpei.ca
Chief Officer(s):
JoAnn Doughart, President
- Canadian Celiac Association Charlottetown Chapter
Type: Newsletter; *Editor:* Jim Hancock; Gay Hancock

Québec Chapter
Montréal QC
Tél: 514-893-9856
info@celiacquebec.ca
celiacquebec.ca

Regina Chapter
PO Box 1773, Regina SK S4P 3C6
chapter.sk.regina@celiac.ca
Chief Officer(s):
Audrey Webb, President

Saint John Chapter
NB
chapter.nb.saintjohn@celiac.ca

St Catharines Chapter
PO Box 29003, 125 Carlton St., St Catharines ON L2R 7P9
Tel: 905-988-9475
chapter.on.st.catharines@celiac.ca
Chief Officer(s):
Lynne Turcotte, President
lturcotte@cogeco.ca

Saskatoon Chapter
PO Box 8935, Saskatoon SK S7K 6S7
chapter.sk.saskatoon@celiac.ca
www.facebook.com/164568043600499
Chief Officer(s):
Penny Fairbrother, President
- Celiac Digest
Type: Newsletter; *Accepts Advertising*; *Editor:* Jennifer Holmes

Thunder Bay Chapter
739 Harold Cr., Thunder Bay ON P7C 5H8
Tel: 807-623-5572
www.celiactbay.ca
Chief Officer(s):
Deb Paris, President
• Celiac News
Type: Newsletter; *Frequency:* Y; *Editor:* A. Peat, K. Smith, & B. Knott
Profile: Information with a local emphasis to support & educate people with celiac disease

Toronto Chapter
PO Box 23056, 550 Eglinton Ave. West, Toronto ON M5N 3A8
Tel: 416-781-9140
www.torontoceliac.org
Chief Officer(s):
Joni Brinder, President
• Toronto Chapter Newsletter
Type: Newsletter; *Accepts Advertising*; *Editor:* Danny Weill & Alanna Weill

Vancouver Chapter
#306, 1385 West 8th St., Vancouver BC V6H 3V9
Tel: 604-736-2229
Toll-Free: 877-736-2240
info@vancouverceliac.ca
www.vancouverceliac.ca
twitter.com/VancouverCCA
Chief Officer(s):
Jason Klatt, Director
• Celiac News
Type: Newsletter; *Frequency:* 3 pa; *Accepts Advertising*; *Editor:* Jane Kamimura & Joy Swaddling
Profile: Vancouver area news, recipes, restaurant reviews, & upcoming events

Victoria Chapter
PO Box 5457, Stn. B, Victoria BC V8R 6S8
Tel: 250-472-0141
victoriaceliacs@hotmail.ca
www.victoriaceliac.org
Chief Officer(s):
Nancy Adrian, President
• Victoria Celiac News
Type: Newsletter; *Frequency:* Bimonthly; *Accepts Advertising*; *Editor:* Christine Rushforth
Profile: Gluten free diet information

Canadian Celiac Sprue Association *See* Canadian Celiac Association

Canadian Celtic Arts Association
c/o Jean Talman, 81 St. Mary St., Toronto ON M5S 1J4
info@canadiancelticarts.ca
www.canadiancelticarts.ca
Overview: A small national organization founded in 1979
Mission: To promote Celtic culture; To serve as a link between the diverse Celtic communities in Canada
Finances: *Funding Sources:* Membership dues; Donations
Membership: *Fees:* $15 students & seniors; $20 families
Activities: Encouraging Celtic artistic creation, research, study, literature, music, art, & thought; Providing artistic & literary events, programs, & festivals
Chief Officer(s):
Janice Chan, President
president@canadiancelticarts.ca
Donald Gillies, Treasurer
treasurer@canadiancelticarts.ca
Jean Talman, Membership Secretary & Coordinator, Programmes
membership@canadiancelticarts.ca
Publications:
• Canadian Celtic Arts Association Newsletter
Type: Newsletter; *Editor:* Leah Morrigan
Profile: Literary & artistic reviews, viewpoints, & Celtic-related events

Canadian Centre for Advanced Film Studies *See* Canadian Film Centre

Canadian Centre for Architecture (CCA) / Centre Canadien d'Architecture
1920, rue Baile, Montréal QC H3H 2S6
Tel: 514-939-7026
Other Communication: Bookstore e-mail: books@cca.qc.ca
info@cca.qc.ca
www.cca.qc.ca
www.facebook.com/cca.conversation
twitter.com/ccawire
www.youtube.com/CCAChannel
Overview: A large national licensing charitable organization founded in 1979
Mission: To advance knowledge, promote public understanding, widen thought & debate on the art of architecture, its history, theory, practice & role in society
Affiliation(s): International Council of Museums (ICOM); International Confederation of Architectural Museums (ICAM); American Association of Museums (AAM); Canadian Museums Association (CMA); Société des musées québécois (SMQ); Société des directeurs des musées Montréal (SDMM); Research Library Group (RLG); Independent Research Libraries Association (IRLA); Association of Research Institutes in Art History (ARIAH); Institut de recherche en histoire de l'architecture
Finances: *Annual Operating Budget:* Greater than $5 Million; *Funding Sources:* Donors; sponsors; government
Staff Member(s): 77; 50 volunteer(s)
Membership: 1,800; *Fees:* Schedule available; *Member Profile:* Professors, students & practitioners of architecture; families; general public
Activities: International exhibitions; lectures & colloqia; film & video screenings; concerts; guided tours; school programs; research activities; CCA Bookstore; *Internships:* Yes; *Library:* Open to public by appointment
Chief Officer(s):
Phyllis Lambert, Founding Director Emeritus
Bruce Kuwabara, Chair, Board of Trustees
Mirko Zardini, Director
Publications:
• CCA [Canadian Centre for Architecture] E-Newsletter
Type: Newsletter
• CCA [Canadian Centre for Architecture] Bookstore Newsletter
Type: Newsletter

Canadian Centre for Creative Technology *See* Shad Valley International

Canadian Centre for Ethics & Corporate Policy (CCECP)
#1801, 1 Yonge St., Toronto ON M5E 1W7
Tel: 416-368-7525; *Fax:* 416-369-0515
info@ethicscentre.ca
www.ethicscentre.ca
www.linkedin.com/company/2455638
twitter.com/ethicscentre
Also Known As: EthicsCentre CA
Overview: A small national charitable organization founded in 1988
Mission: To ensure the use of ethical values in the decision making processes of businesses & other organizations; To promote ethical decision making; To act as a forum for discussion & debate
Finances: *Annual Operating Budget:* $50,000-$100,000; *Funding Sources:* Membership; Donations; Sponsorships
Staff Member(s): 2; 20 volunteer(s)
Membership: 42 corporate; 45 individual; *Fees:* $20 student; $50 individual; $250-$10,000 organization; *Committees:* Communications; Events; Executive; Membership; Nominating & Governance
Activities: Organizing luncheon & breakfast speaker's series, roundtables & senior management workshops; Publishing newsletter; Engaging in student outreach; *Speaker Service:* Yes
Chief Officer(s):
Neil St. John, Executive Director
neil@ethicscentre.ca
Lois Marsh, Administrator
lmarsh@ethicscentre.ca
Publications:
• Management Ethics [a publication of the Canadian Centre for Ethics & Corporate Policy]
Type: Newsletter
Profile: Articles on ethics, corporate governance & corporate responsibility

Canadian Centre for Ethics in Sport (CCES) / Centre canadien pour l'éthique dans le sport
#350, 955 Green Valley Cres., Ottawa ON K2C 3V4
Tel: 613-521-3340; *Fax:* 613-521-3134
Toll-Free: 800-672-7775
info@cces.ca
www.cces.ca
www.facebook.com/CanadianCentreforEthicsInSport
twitter.com/EthicsInSport
www.youtube.com/ccesonline
Overview: A medium-sized national organization founded in 1991
Mission: Foster ethical sport for all Canadians
Affiliation(s): True Sport Foundation
Staff Member(s): 50
Chief Officer(s):
David Zussman, Chair
Paul Melia, President & CEO
pmelia@cces.ca

Canadian Centre for Fisheries Innovation (CCFI) / Centre canadien d'innovations des pêches
PO Box 4920, St. John's NL A1C 5R3
Tel: 709-778-0517; *Fax:* 709-778-0516
ccfi@mi.mun.ca
www.ccfi.ca
Previous Name: Centre for Fisheries Innovation
Overview: A medium-sized national organization founded in 1989
Mission: To work with the fishing industry to improve productivity & profitability of fishery through science & technology
Member of: Newfoundland Ocean Industries Association; Aquaculture Association of Canada; Fisheries Council of Canada; St. John's Board of Trade
Affiliation(s): Memorial University of Newfoundland; Marine Institute
Staff Member(s): 5
Activities: Engaging in aquaculture, harvesting, processing & equipment development; Undertaking research & development projects; Disseminating information
Chief Officer(s):
Robert Verge, Managing Director, 709-778-0542
Robert.Verge@mi.mun.ca

Canadian Centre for International Studies & Cooperation
Voir Centre canadien d'étude et de coopération internationale

Canadian Centre for Investigation & Prevention of Torture
See Canadian Centre for Victims of Torture

Canadian Centre for Occupational Health & Safety (CCOHS) / Centre canadien d'hygiène et de sécurité au travail (CCHST)
135 Hunter St. East, Hamilton ON L8N 1M5
Tel: 905-572-2981; *Fax:* 905-572-2206
Toll-Free: 800-668-4284
clientservices@ccohs.ca
www.ccohs.ca
www.facebook.com/CCOHS
twitter.com/ccohs
Overview: A large national charitable organization founded in 1978
Mission: To promote the total well-being—physical, psychological & mental health—of working Canadians by providing information, training, education, management systems & solutions that support health, safety, & wellness programs
Finances: *Annual Operating Budget:* Greater than $5 Million; *Funding Sources:* Government & revenue from product sales
Staff Member(s): 85
Membership: *Fees:* Optional membership packages from $25 - $500/ yr.
Activities: Provides a variety of public service initiatives at no charge to users, such as OSH Answers, Inquiry Service, Newsletters, Webinars & Podcasts; services for specialty resources provided on a cost recovery basis include databases, publications, & training & education; *Speaker Service:* Yes; *Library:* Documentation Resources; by appointment
Chief Officer(s):
Gareth Jones, Acting President & CEO
Ivy Lumia, Corporate Secretary
Meetings/Conferences:
• Canadian Centre for Occupational Health & Safety Forum, 2018
Scope: National
Publications:
• The Health & Safety Report [a publication of the Canadian Centre for Occupational Health & Safety]
Type: Newsletter; *Frequency:* Monthly; *Price:* Free
Profile: Workplace health & safety news, plus information & tips
• Liaison [a publication of the Canadian Centre for Occupational Health & Safety]
Type: Newsletter; *Frequency:* Bimonthly
Profile: CCOHS developments, resources, & initiatives

Canadian Centre for Policy Alternatives (CCPA) / Centre canadien de politique alternative
#500, 251 Bank St., Ottawa ON K2P 1X3
Tel: 613-563-1341; Fax: 613-233-1458
ccpa@policyalternatives.ca
www.policyalternatives.ca
www.facebook.com/policyalternatives
twitter.com/ccpa
www.youtube.com/user/policyalternatives
Overview: A medium-sized national organization founded in 1980
Mission: To promote research on economic & social issues facing Canada; To monitor current developments in economy & study important trends that affect Canadians; To demonstrate thoughtful alternatives to the limited perspectives of business, research institutes & government agencies; To put forward research that reflects concerns of women & men, labour & business, churches, cooperatives & voluntary agencies, governments, minorities, disadvantaged & fortunate individuals
Membership: 12,000+
Activities: Publishing research reports; Organizing public symposiums & conferences
Chief Officer(s):
Bruce Campbell, Executive Director
Publications:
• The CCPA Monitor [a publication of the Canadian Centre for Policy Alternatives]
Type: Magazine; Frequency: 6 pa; Editor: Stuart Trew; Price: Free to CCPA members
Profile: Includes articles on social, climiate, & economic justice, with a focus on CCPA's research
• Our Schools/Our Selves [a publication of the Canadian Centre for Policy Alternatives]
Type: Journal; Frequency: q.; Price: $70
Profile: A forum for debate & discussion on topics like Aboriginal education, anti-racism classroom programs, commercialism, child care, & sexeducation

British Columbia Office
#1400, 207 West Hastings St., Vancouver BC V6B 1H7
Tel: 604-801-5121; Fax: 604-801-5122
ccpabc@policyalternatives.ca
www.policyalternatives.ca/offices/bc
Chief Officer(s):
Seth Klein, Director

Manitoba Office
#205, 765 Main St., Winnipeg MB R2W 3N5
Tel: 204-927-3200; Fax: 204-927-3201
ccpamb@policyalternatives.ca
www.policyalternatives.ca/offices/manitoba
www.facebook.com/CCPAMB
twitter.com/CCPAMB
www.youtube.com/policyalternatives
Chief Officer(s):
Molly McCracken, Director

Nova Scotia Office
PO Box 8355, Halifax NS B3K 5M1
Tel: 902-240-0926
ccpans@policyalternatives.ca
www.policyalternatives.ca/offices/nova-scotia
www.facebook.com/CCPANS
twitter.com/CCPANS
www.youtube.com/policyalternatives
Chief Officer(s):
Christine Saulnier, Director

Saskatchewan Office
2835 - 13th Ave., #G, Regina SK S4T 1N6
Tel: 306-924-3372; Fax: 306-586-5177
ccpasask@sasktel.net
www.policyalternatives.ca/offices/saskatchewan
Chief Officer(s):
Simon Enoch, Director

Canadian Centre for Stress & Well-Being See Canadian Centre for Wellbeing

Canadian Centre for Studies in Publishing (CCSP)
Simon Fraser University at Harbour Centre, 515 West Hastings St., Vancouver BC V6B 5K3
Tel: 778-782-5242; Fax: 778-782-5239
ccsp-info@sfu.ca
publishing.sfu.ca
Overview: A small international charitable organization founded in 1987
Mission: Dedicated to the development of publishing in Canada & internationally
Membership: Member Profile: Educators; publishers; students
Activities: Teaching, research, innovation & information centre; Internships: Yes; Speaker Service: Yes; Library: CCSP Resource Library; by appointment

Canadian Centre for Victims of Torture (CCVT)
194 Jarvis St., 2nd Fl., Toronto ON M5B 2B7
Tel: 416-363-1066; Fax: 416-363-2122
www.ccvt.org
www.facebook.com/115015798517911
twitter.com/ccvt_toronto
Previous Name: Canadian Centre for Investigation & Prevention of Torture
Overview: A medium-sized national charitable organization founded in 1983
Mission: To offer support & arrange medical, legal & social care for torture victims & their families; to increase public awareness in Canada & abroad of torture & its effects upon survivors & their families
Member of: Canadian Council for Refugees; Toronto Refugee Affairs Council; Ontario Council of Agencies Serving Immigrants; Multicultural Health Association; Canadian Network for the Health of Survivors of Torture & Organized Violence
Finances: Annual Operating Budget: $1.5 Million-$3 Million
Staff Member(s): 30
Membership: Committees: Health; Legal; Volunteer Advisory; Public Education
Activities: Internships: Yes; Speaker Service: Yes; Rents Mailing List: Yes; Library: Resource Centre; Open to public
Chief Officer(s):
Mulugeta Abai, Executive Director
mabai@ccvt.org

Canadian Centre for Wellbeing
PO Box 83030, Stn. Victoria Park, Toronto ON M4B 3N2
Tel: 647-560-4824
info@ccfw.ca
www.ccfw.ca
Previous Name: Canadian Centre for Stress & Well-Being
Overview: A small national organization founded in 1982
Mission: To provide education about stress management; To increase health & wellness
Activities: Counselling; Offering resources about stress management skills

Canadian Centre on Disability Studies (CCDS)
56 The Promenade, Winnipeg MB R3B 3H9
Tel: 204-287-8411; Fax: 204-284-5343; TTY: 204-475-6223
ccds@disabilitystudies.ca
www.disabilitystudies.ca
Overview: A small national charitable organization founded in 1995
Mission: To research, educate, & disseminate information on disability issues
Staff Member(s): 9
Membership: Fees: $100 business/organization; $20 individual; $10 student/senior
Chief Officer(s):
Susan Hardie, Executive Director, 204-287-8411 Ext. 25
shardie@disabilitystudies.ca
Publications:
• CCDS [Canadian Centre on Disability Studies] Bulletin
Type: Newsletter; Frequency: Quarterly

Canadian Centre on Substance Abuse See Canadian Centre on Substance Use & Addiction

Canadian Centre on Substance Use & Addiction (CCSA) / Centre canadien sur les dépendances et l'usage de substances (CCLAT)
#500, 75 Albert St., Ottawa ON K1P 5E7
Tel: 613-235-4048; Fax: 613-235-8101
media@ccsa.ca
www.ccsa.ca
www.linkedin.com/company/canadian-centre-on-substance-abuse-ccsa-
twitter.com/CCSAcanada
www.youtube.com/user/CCSACCLAT
Previous Name: Canadian Centre on Substance Abuse
Overview: A medium-sized national charitable organization founded in 1988
Mission: To minimize the harm associated with addictions, including substance abuse & problem gambling
Finances: Annual Operating Budget: Greater than $5 Million; Funding Sources: Canada's Drug Strategy
Staff Member(s): 55
Activities: Providing information on substance use issues; Offering reference information; Providing evidence based policy guidance to governments; Sharing treatment knowledge & best practices on substance use & addiction; Awareness Events: National Drug Awareness Week, Nov. Library: CCSA Library Collection; by appointment
Chief Officer(s):
Rita Notarandrea, CEO
Rhowena Martin, Deputy Chief Executive Officer
Amy Porath, Director, Research & Policy
Anne Richer, Director, Finance
Andrea Brasset, Interim Director, Public Affairs & Communications
Darlene Pinto, Director, Human Resources
Rebecca Jesseman, Director, Information Systems & Web Services
Kim Dudley, Associate Director, Strategic Partnerships & Knowledge Mobilization
Publications:
• Action News [a publication of the Canadian Centre on Substance Use & Addiction]
Type: Newsletter; Frequency: Quarterly; ISSN: 1701-4522
Profile: Current events related to substance abuse
• Canadian Centre on Substance Abuse Annual Report
Type: Yearbook; Frequency: Annually
• Directory of Fetal Alcohol Spectrum Disorder (FASD) Information & Support Services in Canada
Type: Directory; ISSN: 1715-4197
Profile: Listings of organizations & individuals that provide an FASD related service in Canada

The Canadian Centre/International P.E.N. (PEN)
#301, 24 Ryerson Ave., Toronto ON M5T 2P3
Tel: 416-703-8448; Fax: 416-703-3870
queries@pencanada.ca
www.pencanada.ca
www.facebook.com/PENCanadaCentre
twitter.com/PENCanada
www.youtube.com/canadapen
Also Known As: PEN Canada
Overview: A medium-sized international charitable organization founded in 1926
Mission: To foster understanding among writers of all nations; to fight for freedom of expression wherever it is endangered; to work for preservation of world's literature
Member of: Network on International Human Rights
Finances: Funding Sources: Donations; events
Staff Member(s): 4
Membership: 1,000; Fees: $25 student; $75 regular; Member Profile: Poets, playwrights, essayists (including nonfiction writers), editors, novelists & journalists who have produced at least one book of substantial literary value; editors who have worked at their profession for at least five years & edited at least five books eligible under the above criteria; translators who have translated at least five eligible books; playwrights who have had at least one play produced by an Equity company; associate - those who share PEN's goals but who do not quality for membership; reduced rate of membership available to students who wish to form or join established PEN chapter at a university or community college
Activities: Library: Not open to public
Chief Officer(s):
Philip Slayton, President
Tasleem Thawar, Executive Director
tthawar@pencanada.ca

Canadian Cerebral Palsy Sports Association (CCPSA) / Association canadienne de sport pour paralytiques cérébraux (ACPSA)
#104, 720 Belfast Rd., Ottawa ON K1G 0Z5
Tel: 613-748-1430
info@ccpsa.ca
www.ccpsa.ca
www.facebook.com/112866075626
Overview: A medium-sized national charitable organization founded in 1985
Mission: To act as umbrella group for all provincial cerebral palsy sport organizations; To design programs that are designed for athletes with cerebral palsy & non-progressive head injuries
Affiliation(s): Cerebral Palsy International Sports & Recreation Association; International Paralympic Committee
Finances: Annual Operating Budget: $500,000-$1.5 Million; Funding Sources: Government of Canada, Dept. of Heritage; Sport Canada; donations; fundraising
Staff Member(s): 3; 11 volunteer(s)

Membership: 2,500; *Fees:* $25-200; *Committees:* Coaching; Boccia; Classification; Athletics
Activities: Programs include cycling, soccer, athletics & boccia, swimming, bowls, powerlifting
Chief Officer(s):
Jennifer Larson, Interim Executive Director, 613-748-1430 Ext. 2
jlarson@ccpsa.ca

The Canadian Chamber of Commerce / La Chambre de commerce du Canada
#420, 360 Albert St., Ottawa ON K1R 7X7
Tel: 613-238-4000; *Fax:* 613-238-7643
info@chamber.ca
www.chamber.ca
www.linkedin.com/company/the-canadian-chamber-of-commerce-canada-
www.facebook.com/CanadianChamberofCommerce
twitter.com/CdnChamberofCom
www.youtube.com/user/CdnChamberofCommerce
Overview: A large national organization founded in 1925
Mission: To create a climate for competitiveness, profitability & job creation for enterprises of all sizes in all sectors across Canada. Offices in Ottawa, Toronto, Montreal & Calgary
Member of: International Chamber of Commerce
Affiliation(s): Canadian Services Coalition; Canadian Society of Association Executives; C.D. Howe Institute; Chamber of Commerce Executives of Canada; Forum for International Trade Training; International Chamber of Commerce; World Chambers Federation
Finances: *Annual Operating Budget:* Greater than $5 Million
Staff Member(s): 33
Membership: 450+ chambers of commerce + 200,000 businesses across Canada; *Fees:* Schedule available; *Committees:* Business Law; Competition Law & Policy; Economic Policy; Human Resources Policy; Innovations; Intellectual Property; International Affairs; Natural Resources & Environment; Ottawa Liaison; SME; Taxation; Territorial Policy; Transportation & Infrastructure
Chief Officer(s):
David Paterson, Chair
Perrin Beatty, President & CEO
pbeatty@chamber.ca
Guillaum (Will) Dubreuil, Director, Public Affairs & Media Relations
gdubreuil@chamber.ca
Meetings/Conferences:
• Canadian Chamber of Commerce 2018 AGM and Convention, September, 2018, Thunder Bay, ON
Scope: National

Calgary Office
PO Box 38057, Calgary AB T3K 5G9
Tel: 403-271-0595; *Fax:* 403-226-6930

Montréal Office
#560, 999, boul de Maisonneuve ouest, Montréal QC H3A 3L4
Tel: 514-866-4334; *Fax:* 514-866-7296

Toronto Office
#901, 55 University Ave., Toronto ON M5J 2H7
Tel: 416-868-6415; *Fax:* 416-868-0189

Canadian Chapter of the International Council of Community Churches *See* Christian Catholic Church Canada

Canadian Charolais Association (CCA)
2320 - 41 Ave. NE, Calgary AB T2E 6W8
Tel: 403-250-9242; *Fax:* 403-291-9324
cca@charolais.com
www.charolais.com
www.facebook.com/cdncharolais
twitter.com/canCharolais
Overview: A medium-sized national organization founded in 1958
Mission: To be leaders in predictable beef genetics; to register, record, transfer & promote Canadian Charolais; to provide services for membership
Member of: Canadian Beef Breeds Council
Finances: *Annual Operating Budget:* $500,000-$1.5 Million; *Funding Sources:* Registration & transfer of Charolais cattle
Membership: 1,100; *Fees:* $25 junior; $65 associate; *Member Profile:* Owner of registered Charolais cattle
Chief Officer(s):
Mel Reekie, General Manager
mreekie@charolais.com
Awards:
• CCA Scholarship
; *Amount:* $1,000

• Dale Norheim Memorial Scholarship
; *Amount:* $1,500

Canadian Chemical Producers' Association *See* Chemistry Industry Association of Canada

Canadian Chianina Association
c/o Barb Jack, PO Box 45, Meskanaw SK S0K 2W0
Tel: 306-864-3644; *Fax:* 306-864-2936
www.clrc.ca/chianina.shtml
Overview: A small national organization founded in 1972
Mission: To provide for registration of Chianina cattle in Canada
Member of: Canadian Livestock Records Corporation
Membership: *Fees:* $50 initiation fee; $25 annual membership; *Member Profile:* Breeders of Canadian Chianina cattle
Chief Officer(s):
Barb Jack, Secretary Manager, 306-864-3644, Fax: 306-864-2936

Canadian Chicken Marketing Agency *See* Chicken Farmers of Canada

Canadian Chihuahua Rescue & Transport (CCRT)
PO Box 83023, 5899 Leslie St., Toronto ON M2H 3R9
Toll-Free: 877-783-7333
info@ccrt.net
www.ccrt.net
Overview: A small national charitable organization founded in 1999
Mission: To rescue & provide necessary veterinary care for homeless & abused Chihuahua & Chihuahua mix breed dogs throughout Canada
Finances: *Funding Sources:* Adoption fees; Sponsorships; Donations; Purchases from store
Activities: Assisting in finding homes for pets; Microchipping, spaying, neutering, & vaccinating Chihuahuas placed through the organization; Educating Chihuahua owners & the public about the breed

Canadian Child Abuse Association
PO Box 42066, Stn. Acadia, Calgary AB T2J 7A6
Tel: 403-289-8385
www.ccaa.org
www.facebook.com/takingaction
Previous Name: Canadian Society for the Investigation of Child Abuse
Overview: A small national charitable organization founded in 1985
Mission: To support professionals, witnesses, & victims involved in the investigation of child abuse
Activities: Providing educational resources & services; Engaging in advocacy activities; Conducting research
Chief Officer(s):
Alice Gifford, Coordinator, Communications
aliceg@ccaa.org

Canadian Child Care Federation (CCCF) / Fédération canadienne des services de garde à l'enfance (FCSGE)
#600, 700 Industrial Ave., Ottawa ON K1G 0Y9
Tel: 613-729-5289; *Fax:* 613-729-3159
Toll-Free: 800-858-1412
info@cccf-fcsge.ca
www.cccf-fcsge.ca
www.facebook.com/groups/5657406573
www.youtube.com/user/Qualitychildcare
Previous Name: Canadian Child Day Care Federation
Overview: A large national charitable organization founded in 1987
Mission: To promote excellence in child care & early learning
Affiliation(s): Assn of Early Childhood Educators of AB; AB Family Child Care Assn; Assn of Early Childhood Educators of NL; Assn of Early Childhood Educators of ON; Assn of Early Childhood Educators of QC; BC Aboriginal Child Care Society; BC Family Child Care Assn; Certification Council of Early Childhood Educators of NS; Early Childhood Care & Education NB; Early Childhood Development Assn of PEI; Early Childhood Educators of BC; Home Child Card Assn of ON; MB Child Care Assn; NS Child Care Assn; SK Early Childhood Assn; YT Child Cars Assn
Finances: *Funding Sources:* Donations; Sponsorships
Membership: 11,000+; *Fees:* $35 student; $65 individual; $90 organization; *Member Profile:* Individuals who support the goals of the Canadian Child Care Federation, such as educators & policy makers; organizations, such as educational institutions & child care organizations

Activities: Conducting research; providing resources to enrich curriculum & to increase understanding of child development, including numerous books, guides and kits; offering professional development opportunities; promoting child health & safety; establishing partnerships; *Awareness Events:* National Child Day
Chief Officer(s):
Don Giesbrecht, Chief Executive Officer, 613-729-5289 Ext. 220
dgiesbrecht@cccf-fcsge.ca
Claire McLaughlin, Manager, Publications & Marketing, 613-729-5289 Ext. 221
cmclaughlin@cccf-fcsge.ca
Awards:
• Award for Excellence in Child Care
To honour persons who have made an outstanding contribution to the field of child care
Meetings/Conferences:
• Canadian Child Care Federation 2018 Annual General Meeting, 2018
Scope: National
Publications:
• Interaction [a publication of Canadian Child Care Federation]
Type: Magazine; *Frequency:* Quarterly; *Accepts Advertising*; *Editor:* Claire McLaughlin; *Price:* Free with membership in the Canadian Child Care Federation; $50/year for non-members
Profile: News, opinions, current research, & practice information from across Canada on topics such as family based care, health,& best practices

Canadian Child Day Care Federation *See* Canadian Child Care Federation

Canadian Children's Book Centre (CCBC)
#217, 40 Orchard View Blvd., Toronto ON M4R 1B9
Tel: 416-975-0010; *Fax:* 416-975-8970
info@bookcentre.ca
www.bookcentre.ca
www.facebook.com/kidsbookcentre
twitter.com/kidsbookcentre
Overview: A medium-sized national charitable organization founded in 1976
Mission: To promote the reading, writing, & illustrating of Canadian books for young readers, providing programs, publications & resources for teachers, librarians, authors, illustrators, publishers, booksellers & parents.
Affiliation(s): Book & Periodical Council; Book Promoters Association of Canada; Canadian Booksellers Association; Canadian Coalition of School Libraries
Finances: *Funding Sources:* Canada Council for the Arts; Canadian Heritage; TD Bank Financial Group; Imperial Oil Foundation
Staff Member(s): 6
Membership: *Fees:* $45 senior/student; $75 individual; $150 associate; $500 corporate; $1,000 patron; *Member Profile:* Teachers, librarians, authors, illustrators, publishers, booksellers, wholesalers & parents
Activities: TD Canadian Children's Book Week; TD Grade One Book Giveaway Program; resource libraries of Canadian Children's books in Toronto, Halifax, Edmonton, Vancouver & Winnipeg; Regional Officers in Alberta, British Columbia, Manitoba & Nova Scotia; *Library:* Open to public by appointment
Chief Officer(s):
Charlotte Teeple, Executive Director
charlotte@bookcentre.ca
Shannon Howe Barnes, Coordinator, Programs
shannon@bookcentre.ca
Meghan Howe, Coordinator, Library
meghan@bookcentre.ca
Awards:
• The Norma Fleck Award for Canadian Children's Non-Fiction
Rewards excellence in outstanding work of non-fiction for young people by a Canadian author, published in previous calendar year; jury members include a teacher, a librarian, a reviewer & a bookseller; *Amount:* $10,000
• The Geoffrey Bilson Award for Historical Fiction for Young People
Rewards excellence in outstanding work of historical fiction for young people by a Canadian author, published in previous calendar year; judges are: a writer, bookseller, children's books specialist, historian, librarian; *Amount:* $5,000
• TD Canadian Children's Literature Award
; *Amount:* $30,000
Publications:
• Canadian Children's Book News
Type: Magazine; *Frequency:* Quarterly; *Accepts Advertising*
Profile: New Canadian children's books, industry issues, profiles of publishers & bookstores, & author & illustrator interviews

Canadian Associations / Canadian Children's Opera Company (CCOC)

• CCBC [Canadian Children's Book Centre] Newsletter
Type: Newsletter; *Frequency:* Monthly
• Theme Guide
Frequency: Annually
Profile: Theme guides, with over 200 book selections for reading & interest levels ranging from junior kindergarten to young adult, on a different topic each year, including adventure, mystery, sports, multiculturalism, families & friends, the environment, book illustrations, Canada & the sea
Edmonton
Herbert T. Coutts Education Library, University of Alberta, Edmonton AB T6G 2G5
Tel: 780-492-1460
Chief Officer(s):
Katherine Koch, Contact
Vancouver
Education Library, University of British Columbia, 2125 Main Mall, Vancouver BC V6T 1Z4
Tel: 604-822-0940
Chief Officer(s):
Jo-Anne Naslund, Contact
Winnipeg
Elizabeth Dafoe Library, University of Manitoba, 25 Chancellors Circle, Winnipeg MB R3T 2N2
Tel: 204-480-1053
Chief Officer(s):
Kyle Feenstra, Contact
Halifax
Mount Saint Vincent University Library, 166 Bedford Hwy., Halifax NS B3M 2J6
Tel: 902-457-6403
Chief Officer(s):
Meg Raven, Contact

Canadian Children's Opera Company (CCOC)
227 Front St. East, Toronto ON M5A 1E8
Tel: 416-366-0467; *Fax:* 416-366-9204
info@canadianchildrensopera.com
www.canadianchildrensopera.com
www.facebook.com/110622059017962
twitter.com/OperaKidsCanada
Overview: A small national charitable organization founded in 1968
Mission: To be the foremost children's operatic chorus in Canada; To achieve international recognition
Member of: Ontario Choral Federation; Opera for Youth Inc.; Canadian Conference for the Arts
Finances: *Annual Operating Budget:* $500,000-$1.5 Million
Staff Member(s): 13
Membership: 200; *Fees:* Schedule available
Chief Officer(s):
Ken Hall, Managing Director
Dean Burry, Artistic Director

Canadian Children's Optimist Foundation (CCOF) / Fondation Optimiste des enfants canadiens (FOEC)
#200, 5205, boul Metropolitain est, Montréal QC H1R 1Z7
Tel: 514-593-4401; *Fax:* 514-721-1104
Toll-Free: 800-363-7151
info@ccof-foec.org
ccof-foec.org
www.facebook.com/ccof.foec
Overview: A small national charitable organization founded in 1988
Mission: To support Optimist International & its member clubs in Canada
Affiliation(s): Optimist International
Membership: *Committees:* Outsourcing; Club Grant; Gift Planning; Governance; Spread Relief
Chief Officer(s):
Vince Parker, President
Jacques Pelland, Secretary-Treasurer
jacques.pelland@optimist.org
Nadège Fortier, Administrative Director
nadege.fortier@optimist.org

Canadian Chiropractic Association (CCA) / Association chiropratique canadienne (ACC)
#6, 186 Spadina Ave., Toronto ON M5T 3B2
Tel: 416-585-7902; *Fax:* 416-585-2970
Toll-Free: 877-222-9303
info@chiropractic.ca
www.chiropractic.ca
www.linkedin.com/company/canadian-chiropractic-association
www.facebook.com/canadianchiropracticassociation
twitter.com/CanChiroAssoc
www.youtube.com/CanChiroAssoc
Overview: A large national organization founded in 1953
Mission: To see every Canadian have full & equitable access to chiropractic care; To promote the integration of chiropractic into the Canadian health care system
Affiliation(s): Canadian Chiropractic Examining Board; Canadian Chiropractic Historical Association; Canadian Chiropractic Protective Association; Canadian Chiropractic Research Foundation; Canadian Federation of Chiropractic Regulatory & Educational Accrediting Boards; Canadian Memorial Chiropractic College; Université Du Québec • Trois-Rivières Programme De Doctorat En Chiropratique; World Federation of Chiropractic
Finances: *Funding Sources:* Membership fees; Corporate partnerships
Staff Member(s): 13
Membership: 7,000+; *Fees:* $245 1st year of licensure; $291 2nd year of licensure/Other; $485 3rd/subsequent years of licensure; *Member Profile:* Graduates of accredited chiropractic colleges, who are licensed by their provincial licensing offices, & who are members of their provincial associations
Activities: Raising public awareness of the benefits of chiropractic care; Facilitating research; Advocating for the needs of the chiropractic profession; Communicating timely information with registered members
Chief Officer(s):
Alison Dantas, CEO, 416-585-7902 Ext. 226
adantas@chiropractic.ca
Meetings/Conferences:
• Canadian Chiropractic Association National Convention & Tradeshow 2018, 2018
Scope: National
Publications:
• Canadian Chiropractic Association Membership Directory [a publication of the Canadian Chiropractic Association]
Type: Directory; *Price:* Free with CCA membership
Profile: A listing of all associate members
• Canadian Chiropractic Association Update
Type: Newsletter
• The CCA [Canadian Chiropractic Association] Report
Type: Newsletter; *Price:* Free with CCA membership
• Journal of the Canadian Chiropractic Association (JCCA)
Frequency: Quarterly; *Accepts Advertising*; *Editor:* Kent Stuber; *ISSN:* 1715-6181; *Price:* Free with CCA membership; $30 Canadian non-members; $74 foreign
Profile: Peer-reviewed research & communication between the CCA & its members

Canadian Chiropractic Examining Board (CCEB) / Conseil canadien des examens chiropratiques
#230, 1209 - 59th Ave. SE, Calgary AB T2H 2P6
Fax: 403-230-3321
exams@cceb.ca
www.cceb.ca
Overview: A small national organization founded in 1962
Mission: To provide high quality exams for licensure
Member of: National Certification Commission
Membership: *Member Profile:* Provincial chiropractic licensing boards
Activities: Clinical competency evaluation & cognitive skill examinations; annual general meeting

Canadian Chiropractic Research Foundation (CCRF) / La Fondation canadienne pour la recherche en chiropratique
#6, 186 Spadina Ave., Toronto ON M5T 3B2
Tel: 416-585-7902; *Fax:* 416-585-2970
Toll-Free: 877-222-9303
www.canadianchiropracticresearchfoundation.com
Previous Name: Chiropractic Foundation for Spinal Research
Overview: A small national charitable organization founded in 1976
Mission: To fund & facilitate health services & research related to the practice of chiropractic
Affiliation(s): Canadian Chiropractic Association; Canadian Institute for Health Research
Finances: *Funding Sources:* Donations; Foundation memberships; Fundraising
Membership: *Fees:* $125 bronze; $500 silver; $1000 gold; $5000 platinum; $10000 benefactor; $25000 heritage
Activities: Assisting doctors of chiropractic to obtain Masters & PhD degrees; Liaising with other organizations; Creating a university-based chiropractic research chair in each province
Chief Officer(s):
Drew Potter, President
dpotter@chiropractic.ca

Canadian Chito-Ryu Karate-Do Association
89 Curlew Ave., Toronto ON M3A 2P8
Tel: 416-444-5310
info@canadianchitoryu.ca
www.canadianchitoryu.ca
www.youtube.com/channel/UCBzr2eWZs8oJHXOBKgY0fYg
Overview: A small national organization founded in 1991
Mission: Committed to understanding and propagating the karate-do of its founder O'Sensei Dr. Tsuyoshi Chitose.
Chief Officer(s):
David Smith, President
Derek J. Ryan, Vice-President

Canadian Christian Business Federation (CCBF)
26 Blueridge Ct., Guelph ON N1H 6S6
Tel: 519-837-9172
ccbfed@gmail.com
www.ccbf.org
www.facebook.com/ccbfed
twitter.com/ccbfed
Overview: A medium-sized national organization
Mission: To help members enhance their faith & success through professional development, support, & Christian fellowship
Membership: 450; *Member Profile:* Christian business leaders & professionals
Activities: Offering biblically-based professional development programs & resources
Chief Officer(s):
Keith Knight, Executive Director

Canadian Christian Relief & Development Association (CCRDA)
374 North Scugog Crt., Bowmanville ON L1C 3K2
Tel: 289-385-7307; *Fax:* 519-885-5225
ccrdacoordinator@gmail.com
www.ccrda.ca
Previous Name: CCCC Relief & Development Group (R&D Group).
Overview: A small national charitable organization founded in 1984
Mission: Building partnerships to effectively provide emergency relief, facilitate sustainable development, promote justice, and speak with one voice on behalf of the world's poor and disadvantaged peoples.
Membership: 41; *Fees:* $120-$1,800; *Member Profile:* Canadian Christian organizations involved in relief, development, and/or justice who are committed to integrated, transformational development.

Canadian Church Press (CCP)
8 MacDonald Ave., Hamilton ON L8P 4N5
Tel: 905-521-2240
cdnchurchpress@hotmail.com
www.canadianchurchpress.com
www.facebook.com/CanadianChurchPress
twitter.com/CdnChurchPress
Overview: A small national organization founded in 1957
Mission: To foster helpfulness among editors & publishers of its member publications; To deal cooperatively with editorial & publishing problems that do, or may, affect more than one member publication; To encourage higher standards of religious journalism in order to enable its member publications to render more useful service
Finances: *Funding Sources:* Sponsorships
Membership: 56; *Fees:* $50-$215 periodical; $30 associate; *Member Profile:* Christian publications in Canada
Activities: Offering fellowship for members; Supporting members; Conducting professional development workshops in annual convention
Chief Officer(s):
Ian Adnams, President
Saskia Rowley, Vice-President
Jim O'Leary, Treasurer
Awards:
• General Canadian Church Press Awards
• A.C. Forrest Award
Meetings/Conferences:
• Canadian Church Press/Association of Roman Catholic Communicators of Canada Convention 2018, May, 2018, Sheraton Hamilton, Hamilton, ON
Publications:
• Canadian Church Press Membership Directory
Type: Directory

Profile: Listings of publication members, associate members, & honorary life members

Canadian Circulation Management Association *See* Circulation Management Association of Canada

Canadian Circulations Audit Board Inc. (CCAB) / Office canadien de vérification de la diffusion
Div. of BPA International, #800, 1 Concorde Gate, Toronto ON M3C 3N6
Tel: 416-487-2418; *Fax:* 416-487-6405
www.bpaww.com
Overview: A medium-sized national organization founded in 1937
Mission: To issue standardized statements of data reported by a member; to verify the figures shown in these statements by auditors' examination of any & all records considered by the corporation to be necessary; to disseminate such data for the benefit of any individual or company requiring such information
Finances: *Funding Sources:* Membership fees
Membership: *Fees:* Schedule available
Chief Officer(s):
Tim Peel, Contact
mpeel@bpaww.com

Canadian Circumpolar Institute (CCI) / Institut circumpolaire canadien
University of Alberta, #1-42, Pembina Hall, Edmonton AB T6G 2H8
Tel: 780-492-4512; *Fax:* 780-492-1153
www.cci.ualberta.ca
Previous Name: Boreal Institute for Northern Studies (1960-1990)
Overview: A small international organization founded in 1990
Mission: To promote & support research, education, & training related to the boreal & circumpolar regions of the Arctic & Antactica; To enhance awareness of polar environments
Member of: University of Alberta
Finances: *Funding Sources:* Grants; Donations
Membership: 500-999
Activities: Developing & facilitating interdisciplinary circumpolar research & education; Facilitating communication among northern researchers; Awarding grants & scholarships; Providing outreach programs; Publishing three to five titles each year in subject areas related to the north; Disseminating information about circumpolar areas; *Library:* The Canadian Circumpolar Collection (CCC), U of Alberta Library; Open to public
Chief Officer(s):
Marianne S. Douglas, Director, 780-492-0055, Fax: 780-492-1153
marianne.douglas@ualberta.ca
Anita Dey Nuttall, Associate Director, Research Advancement, 780-492-9089, Fax: 780-492-1153
anitad@ualberta.ca
Lindsay Johnston, Circumpolar Librarian & Public Service Mgr, Cameron Library, 780-492-5946
lindsay.johnston@ualberta.ca
Elaine L. Maloney, Managing Editor, CCI Press, 780-492-4999, Fax: 780-492-1153
elaine.maloney@ualberta.ca
Publications:
• Canadian Circumpolar Institute Occasional Publications Series
Type: Monographs; *Editor:* Elaine L. Maloney, CCI Press; *ISSN:* 0068-0303
Profile: Conference proceedings & collections of papers
• Circumpolar Research Series
Type: Monographs; *Editor:* Elaine L. Maloney, CCI Press; *ISSN:* 0838-133X
Profile: Scholarly research on circumpolar situations & concerns
• Northern Hunter-Gatherers Research Series
Editor: Elaine L. Maloney, CCI Press; *ISSN:* 1707-522X
Profile: Interdisciplinary research about the hunting & gathering peoples of arctic, boreal, & sub-arctic regions
• Northern Reference Series [publications of the Canadian Circumpolar Institute]
Editor: Elaine L. Maloney, CCI Press; *ISSN:* 1192-5620
Profile: Bibliographies, literature reviews, annotated bibliographies, & review papers
• Solstice Series [publications of the Canadian Circumpolar Institute]
Editor: Elaine L. Maloney, CCI Press; *ISSN:* 1709-5824
Profile: Case studies & community-based models

Canadian Civil Liberties Association (CCLA) / Association canadienne des libertés civiles
#900, 90 Eglinton Ave. East, Toronto ON M4P 2Y3
Tel: 416-363-0321; *Fax:* 416-861-1291
mail@ccla.org
www.ccla.org
www.facebook.com/cancivlib
twitter.com/cancivlib
www.youtube.com/cancivlib
Overview: A medium-sized national organization founded in 1964
Mission: To protect the civil liberties, human rights, & democratic freedoms of all Canadians
Staff Member(s): 12
Membership: *Fees:* $150 sustaining; $75 regular; $10 student
Activities: Operating as a law reform organization; *Awareness Events:* Rights Watch; Celebrating Canada Gala; *Internships:* Yes *Library:* Canadian Civil Liberties Association Library
Chief Officer(s):
Michael Bryant, Executive Director & General Counsel
Publications:
• CCLA [Canadian Civil Liberties Association] Newsnotes
Frequency: 3 pa
Profile: News & events regarding Canadian civil liberties

Canadian Clean Power Coalition (CCPC)
c/o David Butler, 64 Chapala Heath, Calgary AB T2X 3P9
Tel: 403-606-0973; *Fax:* 403-256-0424
www.canadiancleanpowercoalition.com
Overview: A medium-sized national organization founded in 2000
Mission: To secure a future for coal-fired electricity generation, along with a mix of fuels such as solar, wind hydro, & nuclear; To research & develop clean coal technology
Membership: *Member Profile:* Canadian & American energy producers in the coal, hydro, natural gas, wind, solar & nuclear power sectors
Activities: Addressing environmental issues with governments & stakeholders
Chief Officer(s):
David Butler, Executive Director
dave.butler@cleanerpower.ca

The Canadian Club of Toronto
Royal York Hotel, 100 Front St. West, Fl. MM, Toronto ON M5J 1E3
Tel: 416-364-5590; *Fax:* 416-364-5676
info@canadianclub.org
www.canadianclub.org
www.facebook.com/193517383995
twitter.com/cdnclubto
Overview: A medium-sized local organization
Mission: To host speakers & leaders from politics, business, science, art & the media; programming is accessible to everyone through cable broadcasts & online webcasts
Finances: *Funding Sources:* Membership fees; ticket sales
Membership: *Fees:* $80 individual; $160 corporate
Chief Officer(s):
Alison Loat, President
Lynn Chou, Executive Director
lchou@canadianclub.org

Canadian Coalition Against the Death Penalty (CCADP) / Coalition canadien contre la peine de mort
80 Lillington Ave., Toronto ON M1N 3K7
Tel: 416-693-9112; *Fax:* 416-693-9112
info@ccadp.org
www.ccadp.org
www.facebook.com/70610338689
www.youtube.com/ccadpmedia
Overview: A small national organization founded in 1998
Mission: To provide information about abuses of the death penalty internationally; To ensure Canada does not return to the death penalty
Finances: *Funding Sources:* Donations
Activities: Raising funds for the wrongly convicted; *Speaker Service:* Yes
Chief Officer(s):
Tracy Lamourie, Director & Founder
Dave Parkinson, Director & Founder

Canadian Coalition for Fair Digital Access (CCFDA) / Coalition canadienne pour un accès équitable à la technologie digitale (CCAETD)
c/o #1300, 100 Queen St., Ottawa ON K1P 1J9
Tel: 613-238-2090; *Fax:* 613-238-9380
information@ccfda.ca
www.ccfda.ca
Overview: A medium-sized national organization founded in 2002
Mission: The Canadian Coalition for Fair Digital Access (CCFDA) was established to advocate the concerns of Canadian businesses, consumers and individuals affected by the copyright levy regime Canada. CCFDA members include major Canadian retailers, consumer product manufacturers and technology companies.
Membership: 14; *Member Profile:* Major Canadian retailers; consumer product manufacturers; technology companies
Chief Officer(s):
Fraser Smith

Canadian Coalition for Farm Animals (CCFA) / Coalition Canadienne pour la Protection des Animaux de Ferme
#200/140, 131 Bloor St. West, Toronto ON M5S 1R8
info@humanefood.ca
www.humanefood.ca
www.facebook.com/canadiancoalitionforfarmanimals
Overview: A medium-sized national organization founded in 2002
Mission: To promote the welfare of animals raised for food in Canada through public education, legislative change & consumer choice
Finances: *Funding Sources:* Donations
Membership: 27 organizations; *Fees:* None
Chief Officer(s):
Stephanie Brown, Director

Canadian Coalition for Genetic Fairness (CCGF) / Coalition Canadienne pour L'Equité Génétique (CCEG)
#400, 151 Frederick St., Kitchener ON N2H 2M2
Tel: 519-749-7063; *Fax:* 519-749-8965
Toll-Free: 800-998-7398
info@ccgf-cceg.ca
www.ccgf-cceg.ca
www.facebook.com/FightingGeneticDiscrimination
twitter.com/GeneticFairness
Overview: A medium-sized national organization
Mission: The CCGF/CCEG is a coalition of organizations dedicated to preventing genetic discrimination for all Canadians.
Finances: *Funding Sources:* Donations; Fundraising
Membership: 17 member organizations

Canadian Coalition for Good Governance (CCGG)
PO Box 22, #3304, 20 Queen St. West, Toronto ON M5H 3R3
Tel: 416-868-3576
www.ccgg.ca
Overview: A medium-sized national organization
Mission: To improve the performance of publicly traded corporations through the promotion of good governance practices across Canada
Membership: 47; *Member Profile:* Pension funds, mutual funds & third party money managers.; *Committees:* Finance & Audit; Governance & Nominating
Chief Officer(s):
Stephen Erlichman, Executive Director
serlichman@ccgg.ca
Awards:
• Governance Gavel Awards
Publications:
• Report on Clawback Provisions [a publication of the Canadian Coalition for Good Governance]
Type: Report
• Report on Voting Results [a publication of the Canadian Coalition for Good Governance]
Type: Report
• Shareholder Democracy Study [a publication of the Canadian Coalition for Good Governance]
Type: Report; *Frequency:* irregular

Canadian Coalition for Immunization Awareness & Promotion *See* Immunize Canada

Canadian Coalition for Nuclear Responsibility (CCNR) / Regroupement pour la surveillance du nucléaire (RSN)
53, rue Dufferin, Hampstead QC H3X 3T4
Tel: 514-489-5118
ccnr@web.ca
www.ccnr.org
Overview: A small national organization founded in 1975
Mission: To research all issues related to nuclear energy, whether civilian or military — including non-nuclear alternatives — especially those pertaining to Canada.

Canadian Associations / Canadian Coalition for Seniors Mental Health (CCSMH)

Affiliation(s): Environment Liaison Centre - International; Friends of the Earth - Canada; Canadian Peace Alliance; Abolition 2000
Chief Officer(s):
Gordon Edwards, President

Canadian Coalition for Seniors Mental Health (CCSMH)
c/o Baycrest, West Wing, Old Hospital, #311, 3560 Bathurst St., Toronto ON M6A 2E1
Tel: 613-233-1619; *Fax:* 613-614-9450
www.ccsmh.ca
twitter.com/CCSMH
Overview: A small national organization founded in 2002
Mission: To promote the mental health of seniors by connecting people, ideas and resources.
Finances: *Funding Sources:* Public Health Agency of Canada: Population Health Fund; Canadian Institutes of Health Research: Institute of Aging
Chief Officer(s):
Bonnie Schroeder, Executive Director
director@ccsmh.ca

Canadian Coalition for the Rights of Children (CCRC)
c/o Justice for Children, #1203, 415 Yonge St., Toronto ON M5B 2E7
Tel: 416-920-1633; *Fax:* 416-920-5855
info@rightsofchildren.ca
rightsofchildren.ca
Overview: A small national organization founded in 1989
Mission: To promote respect for the rights of children; To implement the UN Convention on the Rights of the Child.
Membership: *Fees:* $300 large organizations; $200 medium organizations; $100 small organizations; $50 individual; $5 students; $0 youth under 18
Chief Officer(s):
Cheryl Milne, Chair

Canadian College & University Food Service Association (CCUFSA)
c/o Drew Hall, University of Guelph, Gordon St., Guelph ON N1G 2W1
Tel: 519-824-4120; *Fax:* 519-837-9302
mcollins@hrs.uoguelph.ca
www.ccufsa.on.ca
Overview: A medium-sized national organization
Mission: To enhance the quality of campus life through the growth & development of food service operations in colleges & universities
Membership: 160; *Fees:* $25-$295
Chief Officer(s):
Lee Elkas, President, 519-885-1211 Ext. 32704
laelkas@connect.uwaterloo.ca
David Boeckner, Executive Director, 519-824-4120 Ext. 52222
boeckner@uoguelph.ca
Gerard Hayes, Secretary-Treasurer, 250-371-5660
ghayes@tru.ca
Meetings/Conferences:
• Canadian College & University Food Service Association Conference 2018, June, 2018, Blue Mountain Resort, Collingwood, ON
Scope: National
Publications:
• CCUFSA [Canadian College & University Food Service Association] Magazine
Profile: Association information & articles

Canadian College of Emergency Medical Services (CCEMS)
c/o Edmonton General Hospital, 4712 - 91 Ave., Edmonton AB T6B 2L1
Tel: 780-451-4437
Toll-Free: 800-797-4437
info@ccofems.org
www.ccofems.org
twitter.com/ccofems
Overview: A medium-sized national organization founded in 1988
Mission: To provide training & education for emergency medical services professionals
Chief Officer(s):
Greg Clarkes, President
greg@ccofems.org

Canadian College of Health Leaders (CCHL) / Collège canadien des leaders en santé (CCLS)
292 Somerset St. West, Ottawa ON K2P 0J6
Tel: 613-235-7218; *Fax:* 613-235-5451
Toll-Free: 800-363-9056
Other Communication: communications@cchse.org
info@cchl-ccls.ca
www.cchl-ccls.ca
www.linkedin.com/company/canadian-college-of-health-leaders
www.facebook.com/CCHL.National
twitter.com/CCHL_CCLS
www.youtube.com/HealthLeadersCanada
Previous Name: Canadian College of Service Executives
Overview: A large national organization founded in 1970
Mission: To advance excellence in health leadership; To act as a collective voice for the profession
Member of: Health Action Lobby; Coalition for Public Health in the 21st Century
Finances: *Funding Sources:* Membership dues; Advertising; Sponsorships
Staff Member(s): 25
Membership: 3,000 individuals; 80+ companies; *Fees:* $2,000 corporate; $475 active; $225 active-reduce; $50 student; $245 associate; $145 retired; free for lifelong members (25 years+); *Member Profile:* Individuals & corporations from all health sectors throughout Canada; Students; Retired members
Activities: Offering a competency-based certification program; Advocating for the profession; Providing professional development resources & opportunities; Preparing position papers on topics such as pandemic planning & patient safety; Offering a forum for the exchange of best practices
Chief Officer(s):
Ray J. Racette, President & Chief Executive Office, 613-235-7218 Ext. 227
rracette@cchl-ccls.ca
Jaime Cleroux, Vice-President, Corporate Partnership Excellence, 613-235-7218 Ext. 235
jcleroux@cchl-ccls.ca
Sylvie M. Deliencourt, Director, Certification, Leadership Development & Chapter Support, 613-235-7218 Ext. 233
sdeliencourt@cchl-ccls.ca
Carolyn Farrington, Chief Financial Officer, 613-235-7218 Ext. 228
cfarrington@cchl-ccls.ca
Kathy Ivey, Manager, Marketing & Communications, 613-235-7218 Ext. 229
kivey@cchl-ccls.ca
Awards:
• 3M Health Care Quality Team Awards
To recognize innovation, quality, & teamwork *Contact:* Cindy MacBride, Manager Awards & Sponsorships, Phone: 613-235-7218, ext. 213, E-mail: cmacbride@cchl-ccls.ca
• College Honorary Life Member Award
To honour longstanding College members who have contributed significantly to Canada's health system *Contact:* Cindy MacBride, Manager Awards & Sponsorships, Phone: 613-235-7218, ext. 13, E-mail: cmacbride@cchl-ccls.ca
• College Award for Distinguished Service
To recognize individual or corporate members for significant contribution to the College *Contact:* Cindy MacBride, Manager Awards & Sponsorships, Phone: 613-235-7218, ext. 13, E-mail: cmacbride@cchl-ccls.ca
• Chapter Awards for Distinguished Service
To honour an individual or corporate member who has made a significant contribution to their chapter *Contact:* Cindy MacBride, Manager Awards & Sponsorships, Phone: 613-235-7218, ext. 13, E-mail: cmacbride@cchl-ccls.ca
• Award of Excellence in Mental Health & Quality Improvement
An award for high quality papers submitted as a component of the Certified Health Executive (CHE) program *Contact:* Cindy MacBride, Manager Awards & Sponsorships, Phone: 613-235-7218, ext. 13, E-mail: cmacbride@cchl-ccls.ca
• Energy & Environmental Stewardship Award
Awarded to a health care organization that has implemented programs that demonstrate environmental responsibility, such as the preservation of natural resources, the reducion of energy usage, & effective waste diversion solutions *Contact:* Cindy MacBride, Manager Awards & Sponsorships, Phone: 613-235-7218, ext. 13, E-mail: cmacbride@cchl-ccls.ca
• Excellence in Patient Safety Award
To recognize individuals or teams that improve workplace & patient safety *Contact:* Cindy MacBride, Manager Awards & Sponsorships, Phone: 613-235-7218, ext. 13, E-mail: cmacbride@cchl-ccls.ca
• Innovation Award for Health Care Leadership
Awarded to a senior executive for innovation in their organization *Contact:* Cindy MacBride, Manager Awards & Sponsorships, Phone: 613-235-7218, ext. 13, E-mail: cmacbride@cchl-ccls.ca
• Mentorship Award
Presented to a leader who is committed to mentoring & inspiring health care leadership *Contact:* Cindy MacBride, Manager Awards & Sponsorships, Phone: 613-235-7218, ext. 13, E-mail: cmacbride@cchl-ccls.ca
• Nursing Leadership Award
To honour persons committed to excellence in patient centered care & leadership *Contact:* Cindy MacBride, Manager Awards & Sponsorships, Phone: 613-235-7218, ext. 13, E-mail: cmacbride@cchl-ccls.ca
• President's Award for Outstanding Corporate Membership in the College
Presented to a corporate member who has helped the College achieve its mission *Contact:* Cindy MacBride, Manager Awards & Sponsorships, Phone: 613-235-7218, ext. 13, E-mail: cmacbride@cchl-ccls.ca
• Robert Wood Johnson Awards
Awarded to one student from each of the six Canadian universities offering graduate programs in health services administration *Contact:* Cindy MacBride, Manager Awards & Sponsorships, Phone: 613-235-7218, ext. 13, E-mail: cmacbride@cchl-ccls.ca
• Robert Zed Young Health Leader Award
To recognize a Canadian health care leader who has demonstrated leadership in improving the effectiveness & sustainability of the nation's health system *Contact:* Cindy MacBride, Manager Awards & Sponsorships, Phone: 613-235-7218, ext. 13, E-mail: cmacbride@cchl-ccls.ca
Meetings/Conferences:
• National Health Leadership Conference 2018, June, 2018, St. John's, NL
Scope: National
Description: Theme: "Creating the Winning Conditions for Change"
Publications:
• Canadian College of Health Service Annual Report
Type: Report; *Frequency:* a.
• Code of Ethics for Members of the Canadian College of Health Service Executives
Price: Free
Profile: A guide for professional & personal behaviour
• Communiqué [a publication of the Canadian College of Health Leaders]
Type: Newsletter; *Frequency:* Monthly; *Accepts Advertising*; *Price:* Free with membership
Profile: College & member news, initiatives in health care, & career opportunities for members
• Healthcare Management FORUM
Type: Journal; *Frequency:* q.; *Accepts Advertising*; *Editor:* Ron Lindstrom; *ISSN:* 0840-4704; *Price:* Free for active members of the College; $90 individuals in Canada; $212 institutions
Profile: Peer-reviewed articles about Canadian health services management issues, theory, & practice

Assiniboia (Saskatchewan) Regional Chapter
SK
www.cchl-ccls.ca
Chief Officer(s):
John Knoch, Chair
john.knoch@schr.sk.ca

Bluenose (Nova Scotia & Prince Edward Island) Regional Chapter
NS
www.cchl-ccls.ca
Mission: To advance & recognize excellence in health leadership in Nova Scotia & Prince Edward Island
Chief Officer(s):
Heather Wolfe, Chair
heather.wolfe@cehha.nshealth.ca
• Canadian College of Health Service Executives, Bluenose Chapter, News Update
Type: Newsletter; *Frequency:* Quarterly
Profile: Chapter activities & upcoming events for Bluenose members
• Canadian College of Health Service Executives, Bluenose Chapter, Annual Report
Frequency: Annually
Profile: Review of chapter programs & services

British Columbia Interior Regional Chapter
BC
www.cchl-ccls.ca
Chief Officer(s):

Paul Gallant, Chair
paul@gallanthealthworks.com
British Columbia Lower Mainland Regional Chapter
BC
www.cchl-ccls.ca
Chief Officer(s):
Paul Gallant, Chair
paul@gallanthealthworks.com
Moe Baloo, Vice-Chair
mbaloo@providencehealth.bc.ca
Zahida Esmail, Treasurer
zahidaesmail@gmail.com
David Thompsom, National Board Rep
dthompson@providencehealth.bc.ca
• Canadian College of Health Leaders British Columbia Lower Mainland Regional Chapter Executive Mentoring Program Handbook
Type: Handbook
Profile: Information for mentors & mentees
Eastern Ontario Regional Chapter
ON
www.cchl-ccls.ca
Chief Officer(s):
Jennifer Proulx, Chair
jen@proulx.info
Joanne Bezzubetz, Vice-Chair
jbezzubetz@gmail.com
Paul Caines, Secretary
• Canadian College of Health Service Executives Eastern Ontario Chapter Newsletter
Type: Newsletter
Profile: Chapter activities & upcoming professional development events
Greater Toronto Area Regional Chapter
Toronto ON
www.cchl-ccls.ca
Mission: To foster mentorship among health care leaders in the Greater Toronto Region; To engage early careerists in order to develop leadership skills; To provide information & facilitate knowledge exchange in the Greater Toronto Region
Chief Officer(s):
Sean J. Molloy, Chair
seanmolloyis@gmail.com
Hamilton & Area Regional Chapter
ON
www.cchl-ccls.ca
Chief Officer(s):
Bryan Herechuk, Chair
bherechu@stjosham.on.ca
Ajay Bhardwaj, Vice-Chair
ajaybhardwaj@hotmail.com
• Canadian College of Health Leaders Hamilton & Area Regional Chapter News
Type: Newsletter
Profile: Chpater happenings & upcoming events
LEADS Collaborative
Toll-Free: 800-363-9056
leads@cchl-ccls.ca
www.leadscollaborative.ca
www.linkedin.com/company/leads-collaborative
www.facebook.com/LEADSleaders
twitter.com/LEADSleaders
Mission: To provide health care professionals with leadership development services using the LEADS in a Caring Environment (LEADS) framework
Chief Officer(s):
Brenda Lammi, Director
blammi@leadscanada.net
Lynne Marleau, Coordinator, Administrative & Communications
lmarleau@leadscanada.net
Anne Marie Lecompte, Program Leader
amlecompte@leadscanada.net
Manitoba Regional Chapter
c/o Donald Solar, Parkview Place Care Centre, 440 Edmonton St., Winnipeg MB R3B 2M4
Tel: 204-942-5291
www.cchl-ccls.ca
Mission: To support & assist health care leaders in Manitoba
Chief Officer(s):
Israel Mendez, Chair
imendez.mba2007@ivey.ca
Donald Solar, Treasurer
donald.solar@reveraliving.com

Randy Lock, Secretary
randy.lock@shaw.ca
Midnight Sun (Yukon, Northwest Territories, & Nunavut) Regional Chapter
NT
www.cchl-ccls.ca
Chief Officer(s):
Wayne Overbo, Chair
wayne_overbo@gov.nt.ca
Donna L. Allen, Treasurer
donna_allen@gov.nt.ca
NEON Lights (Northeastern Ontario) Regional Chapter
c/o Patty MacDonald, Canadian Mental Health Association, #100, 111 Elm St., Sudbury ON P3C 1T3
Tel: 705-675-7252
www.cchl-ccls.ca
Mission: To promote & recognize excellence in health care leadership in northeastern Ontario
Chief Officer(s):
Patty MacDonald, Chair
pmacdonald@cmha-sm.on.ca
Cathy Bailey, Secretary-Treasurer
cathy.bailey@ne.ccac-ont.ca
• NEON Lights Regional Chapter Chair Update
Type: Newsletter; *Frequency:* Irregular
Profile: News from the national Canadian College of Health Leaders, as well as local activities & professional development events
New Brunswick Regional Chapter
NB
www.cchl-ccls.ca
Chief Officer(s):
Connor Atchison, Secretary
atchison.connorm@gmail.com
Thomas Maston, Treasurer
tom.maston@gnb.ca
Nancy Roberts, Chair
Nancy.Roberts@gnb.ca
Newfoundland & Labrador Regional Chapter
NL
www.cchl-ccls.ca
Chief Officer(s):
Cathy Hoyles, Chair
cathy.hoyles@easternhealth.ca
Mollie Butler, Vice-Chair
mollie.butler@easternhealth.ca
Sharon Paulette Lehr, Treasurer
sharon.lehr@easternhealth.ca
Northern & Central Saskatchewan Regional Chapter
Saskatoon SK
www.cchl-ccls.ca
Chief Officer(s):
Sandra Blevins, Chair
sandra.blevins@saskatoonhealthregion.ca
Northern Alberta Regional Chapter
AB
www.cchl-ccls.ca
Mission: To support & promote management excellence in health services throughout northern Alberta
Chief Officer(s):
Brenda Rebman, Contact
brebman@futuresrpi.com
Jewel Buksa, Contact
jewel@buksa.com
• Leader to Leader
Type: Newsletter
Profile: Chapter information, reports, membership information, & upcoming events
Northern British Columbia Regional Chapter
BC
chapters@cchl-ccls.ca
www.cchl-ccls.ca
Northwestern Ontario Regional Chapter
ON
www.cchl-ccls.ca
Québec Regional Chapter
QC
www.cchl-ccls.ca
Chief Officer(s):
Martin Beaumont, President
martin.beaumont.csssnl@ssss.gouv.qc.ca
Diane Boivin, Vice-President
dianeboivin1@videotron.ca

Linda August, Secretary
linda.august@ssss.gouv.qc.ca
William-Jean Côté, Treasurer
willcote@bell.net
Southern Alberta Regional Chapter
AB
www.cchl-ccls.ca
Chief Officer(s):
Brenda Rebman, Director
brebman@futuresrpi.com
Southwestern Ontario Regional Chapter
c/o Paul Heinrich, North Bay Regional Health Centre, PO Box 2500, 50 College Dr., North Bay ON P1B 5A4
Tel: 705-474-8600
www.cchl-ccls.ca
Mission: To support & advocate for the health services profession in southwestern Ontario
Chief Officer(s):
Julie Campbell, Chair
juliemaycampbell@gmail.com
Paul Heinrich, Director
paul.heinrich@nbrhc.on.ca
• Canadian College of Health Service Executives, Southwestern Ontario Regional Chapter, Newsletter
Type: Newsletter
Profile: Chapter reports & upcoming events, plus news from the national Canadian College of Health Service Executives
Starlight (Canadian Forces Health Services Group) Regional Chapter
www.cchl-ccls.ca
Mission: To advance health leadership within the Canadian Forces Health Services Group
Chief Officer(s):
Stephan Plourde, Chair
Steve_plourde@hotmail.com
William-Jean Côté, Secretary
willcote@bell.net
Vancouver Island Regional Chapter
BC
www.cchl-ccls.ca
Chief Officer(s):
Tim Orr, Chair
timothy.orr@viha.ca
Bart Johnson, Treasurer
bart.johnson@viha.ca

Canadian College of Medical Geneticists (CCMG) / Collège canadien de généticiens médicaux
#310, 4 Cataraqui St., Kingston ON K7K 1Z7
Tel: 613-507-8345; *Fax:* 866-303-0626
info@ccmg-ccgm.org
www.ccmg-ccgm.org
Overview: A small national licensing charitable organization founded in 1975
Mission: To establish & maintain professional & ethical standards for medical genetics services in Canada; To certify individuals who provide medical genetics services; to encourage research activities
Affiliation(s): Canadian Association of Genetic Counsellors (CAGC)
Membership: *Fees:* $475 regular; $250 associate affiliate; $100 fellow-in-training member affiliate; *Committees:* Accreditation of Centres; Awards & Nominations; CAGC / CCMG; Clinical Practice; Constitution & Bylaws; Credentials; Education; Ethics & Public Policy; Examinations; Examinations; Laboratory Practice; Metabolics; Training; Scientific Program
Activities: Ensuring a high quality of service is delivered to the public; Informing government & the public about the importance of medical genetics & advances in medical genetics; Offering continuing education; Lobbying for continued universal access to medical genetics services
Chief Officer(s):
Gail Graham, President
Sean Young, Treasurer
Awards:
• Linda Stevens Fund Trainee Award
Meetings/Conferences:
• Canadian College of Medical Geneticists 2018 Annual Meeting, June, 2018
Scope: National
Description: Theme: "The Future is Now"
Publications:
• CCMG [Canadian College of Medical Geneticists] Newsletter
Type: Newsletter

- CCMG [Canadian College of Medical Geneticists] Membership Directory
Type: Directory

The Canadian College of Naturopathic Medicine (CCNM)
1255 Sheppard Ave. East, Toronto ON M2K 1E2
Tel: 416-498-1255
Toll-Free: 866-241-2266
www.ccnm.edu
www.linkedin.com/in/ccnmalumni
www.facebook.com/myccnm
twitter.com/myccnm
www.youtube.com/myccnm
Overview: A medium-sized national licensing organization
Mission: To promote naturopathic medicine; To educate its students & expand members' knowledge about naturopathic medicine
Chief Officer(s):
Colleen McQuarrie, Chair

Canadian College of Neuropsychopharmacology (CCNP)
c/o Rachelle Anderson, Dept. of Psychiatry, University of Alberta, #IE7.19, 8440 - 112 St., Walter MacKenzie Centre, Edmonton AB T6G 2B7
Tel: 780-407-6543; *Fax:* 780-407-6672
Rachelle@ccnp.ca
www.ccnp.ca
Overview: A small national organization
Mission: To promote the development of neuropsychopharmacology in Canada & internationally; To encourage the quality of research & treatment in the field of neuropsychopharmacology
Membership: *Fees:* $100/yr. fellow members; $25/yr. junior & retired members; *Member Profile:* Clinical & basic science researchers; *Committees:* Awards; Nominating; Finance; Public Relations & Liaison; Membership; Clinical Affairs
Activities: Providing a forum for researchers to exchange ideas & experience in neuropsychopharmacology; Liaising with government organizations, educational institutions, industry, the public, & related scientific bodies
Chief Officer(s):
Paul Albert, President
Marco Leyton, Vice-President
Darrell Mousseau, Secretary
Lalit Srivastava, Treasurer
Meetings/Conferences:
- Canadian College of Neuropsychopharmacology 41st Annual Meeting 2018, June, 2018, UBC Robson Square, Vancouver, BC
Scope: National
Publications:
- CCNP [Canadian College of Neuropsychopharmacology] Newsletter
Type: Newsletter; *Editor:* Rachelle Anderson
Profile: College information, including meeting & membership news
- Journal of Psychiatry & Neuroscience
Type: Journal; *Frequency:* Bimonthly; *Editor:* Russell T. Joffe; Simon N. Young; *ISSN:* 1180-4882
Profile: Original research & reviews in basic & clinical science, as well as emerging issues in biological & clinical psychiatry

Canadian College of Physicists in Medicine (CCPM) / Collège canadien des physiciens en médecine
PO Box 72124, RPO Kanata North, Kanata ON K2K 2P4
Tel: 613-599-3491; *Fax:* 613-435-7257
admin@medphys.ca
www.ccpm.ca
Overview: A small national organization founded in 1979
Mission: To identify, through certification, individuals who have acquired & maintained a standard of knowledge & skill essential to the practice of medical physics, in order to serve the public
Affiliation(s): Canadian Organization of Medical Physicists (COMP)
Membership: *Member Profile:* Individuals with a graduate degree in medical physics, physics, science with physics as a major, or another field accepted by the College board; Members must have patient-related experience in physics as applied to medicine; Candidates must also pass examinations; Fellowship applicants must have made significant contributions in clinical service, education, or research related to medical physics
Chief Officer(s):
Nancy Barrett, Executive Director
nancy@medphys.ca
Horacio Patrocinio, CCPM Registrar
registrar@ccpm.ca
Matthew G. Schmid, President
mschmid@bccancer.bc.ca
Awards:
- Harold E Johns Travel Award
To assist the individual to extend his or her knowledge by travelling to another centre or institution with the intent of gaining further experience in his or her chosen field, or, alternately, to embark on a new field of endeavour in medical physics.
Eligibility: College member under 35 who became a member within the previous three years.; *Amount:* $2000
Publications:
- InterACTIONS!
Type: Newsletter; *Frequency:* Quarterly; *Accepts Advertising*; *Editor:* Dr. Parminder Basran
Profile: News from the Canadian Organization of Medical Physicists & the Canadian College of Physicists in Medicine for members

Canadian College of Professional Counsellors & Psychotherapists (CCPCP)
PO Box 23045, Vernon BC V1T 9L8
Tel: 250-558-7700
Toll-Free: 866-704-4828
inquiry@ccpcp.ca
www.ccpcp.ca
Overview: A small national organization founded in 2006
Mission: To represent College members & persons who seek counselling & psychotherapy services; To establish & enforce standards of practice
Membership: *Fees:* Schedule available
Chief Officer(s):
Kristi Novakowski, Registrar

Canadian College of Service Executives *See* Canadian College of Health Leaders

Canadian Collegiate Athletic Association (CCAA) / Association canadienne du sport collégial (ACSC)
2 St. Lawrence Dr., Cornwall ON K6H 4Z1
Tel: 613-937-1508; *Fax:* 613-937-1530
sandra@ccaa.ca
www.ccaa.ca
www.facebook.com/CCAAsportsACSC
twitter.com/CCAAsportsACSC
www.youtube.com/ccaasportsacsc;
instagram.com/ccaasportsacsc
Overview: A medium-sized national organization founded in 1974
Mission: To operate as the national governing body for men's & women's college sport in Canada
Affiliation(s): Atlantic Colleges Athletic Association; Fédération québécoise du sport étudiant; Ontario Colleges Athletic Association; Alberta Colleges Athletic Conference; British Columbia Colleges Athletic Association
Staff Member(s): 1; 100 volunteer(s)
Membership: 108 institutional
Chief Officer(s):
Sandra Murray-MacDonell, Executive Director
sandra@ccaa.ca

Canadian Colombian Professional Association (CCPA)
2408 Gladacres Lane, Oakville ON L6M 0G4
treasurer@ccpassociation.com
www.ccpassociation.com
Also Known As: Canadian Coalition of Professionals from the Americas
Overview: A small local organization founded in 1952
Mission: To promote the interaction of Canadians of Hispanic descent & to strengthen the Canadian Hispanic community
8 volunteer(s)
Membership: *Fees:* $30 Members; $15 Spouses; *Member Profile:* People who are born in Columbia or who are of Columbian origin & their spouses
Activities: Conferences; Networking; Mentoring
Chief Officer(s):
Paula Calderon, President, Board of Directors

Canadian Columbian Professional Association (CCPA)
c/o Andrew Carvajal, Desloges Law Group, #700, 69 Yonge St., Toronto ON M5E 1K3
www.ccpassociation.com
www.linkedin.com/groups/4167715/profile
www.facebook.com/CadColPA
twitter.com/cadcolpa
Overview: A small national organization founded in 2001
Mission: To support the integration of Hispanic professionals into the Canadian workforce; to facilitate the exchange of information among Canadian Hispanic groups & professionals
Member of: Professional Immigrant Networks
Affiliation(s): Toronto Region Immigrant Employment Council
Activities: Professional development activites
Chief Officer(s):
Andrew Carvajal, President
Nestor Paez, Treasurer

Canadian Commercial Arbitration Centre *Voir* Centre canadien d'arbitrage commercial

Canadian Commission for UNESCO (CCUNESCO) / Commission canadienne pour l'UNESCO
PO Box 1047, 150 Elgin St., Ottawa ON K1P 5V8
Tel: 613-566-4414; *Fax:* 613-566-4405
Toll-Free: 800-263-5588
ccunesco@unesco.ca
www.unesco.ca
Overview: A medium-sized international organization founded in 1957
Mission: To promote Canadian participation in the programmes & activities of UNESCO; To advise the government of Canada on its policies toward UNESCO; To act as a forum for Canadian civil society & government to discuss matters relating to UNESCO
Affiliation(s): Canada Council for the Arts; Network of 180 national commissions for UNESCO
Finances: *Funding Sources:* Division of the Canada Council for the Arts
Staff Member(s): 11
Membership: 200; *Member Profile:* Associations; institutions; government departments & agencies; *Committees:* Sectoral-commissions on education, natural & social sciences, culture & communication
Activities: *Rents Mailing List:* Yes
Chief Officer(s):
Sébastien Goupil, Secretary-General, 613-566-4414 Ext. 5557
sebastien.goupil@unesco.ca
Meetings/Conferences:
- Canadian Commission for UNESCO 58th Annual General Meeting, 2018, 2018
Publications:
- Contact: Bulletin of the Canadian Commission for UNESCO
Type: Newsletter; *Frequency:* Semiannually; *ISSN:* 1705 7981
Profile: Commission news, events, & articles
- Share the Road
Type: Magazine; *Author:* Sheila Duggan; *ISSN:* 978-0-9780369-3-5
Profile: Publication launched for International Adult Learners' Week 2008

Canadian Commission of Military History *Voir* Commission canadienne d'histoire militaire

Canadian Committee for the Theory of Machines & Mechanisms *Voir* Commission canadienne pour la théorie des machines et des mécanismes

Canadian Committee for World Press Freedom
1400 - 100 Queen St., Ottawa ON K1P 1J9
info@ccwpf-cclpm.ca
www.ccwpf-cclpm.ca
www.facebook.com/CanadianCommitteeforWorldPressFreedom
twitter.com/CDN_WPF
Overview: A small national organization founded in 2008
Mission: To defend & advocate for freedom of press in Canada; To address press freedom issues & free expression violations
Chief Officer(s):
Shawn McCarthy, President
Awards:
- CCWPF Press Freedom Award
Deadline: February; *Amount:* $1,000
- Spencer Moore Award

Canadian Committee of Byzantinists
Talbot College, Univ. of Western Ontario, London ON N6A 3K7
Tel: 519-661-3045; *Fax:* 519-850-2388
Overview: A small national organization founded in 1965
Mission: To network among Canadian Byzantinists; to promote communications & exchange of information; to promote

Byzantine Studies in Canada
Member of: Association internationale des études byzantines
Finances: *Annual Operating Budget:* Less than $50,000
Membership: 30; *Fees:* $15; *Member Profile:* Academic: professors & university students
Chief Officer(s):
Geoffrey Greatrex, President
Publications:
• Canadio-Byzantina
Type: Newsletter; *Frequency:* Annually
Profile: Scholarly work on Byzantium for CCB members & institutions worldwide

Canadian Committee of Graduate Students in Education (CCGSE) / Comité canadien des étudiants et étudiantes aux cycles supérieurs en éducation (CCÉÉCSÉ)
c/o Canadian Society for the Study of Education, #204, 260 Dalhousie St., Ottawa ON K1N 7E4
Tel: 613-241-0018; *Fax:* 613-241-0019
csse-scee.ca/associations/ccgse-ccee
Overview: A small national organization overseen by Canadian Society for the Study of Education
Mission: To be the graduate student caucus within the Canadian Society for the Study of Education
Member of: Canadian Society for the Study of Education
Membership: *Fees:* $10-39
Chief Officer(s):
Josianne Robert, President
josianne.robert2@usherbrooke.ca

Canadian Committee of Lawyers & Jurists for World Jewry
c/o Raphael Barristers, #202, 1137 Centre St., Thornhill ON L4J 3M6
Tel: 416-594-1812; *Fax:* 416-594-0868
Toll-Free: 855-594-1812
braphael@raphaelbar.com
Also Known As: Jewish Civil Rights Educational Foundation of Canada
Overview: A small international organization founded in 1973
Mission: To promote the welfare of Jewish people in foreign countries whether they wish to emigrate or remain where they are; to undertake advocacy work on behalf of individuals or groups that have suffered discrimination at the hands of their government
Activities: *Speaker Service:* Yes; *Rents Mailing List:* Yes
Chief Officer(s):
Bert Raphael, President
Awards:
• Human Rights Award
• Arthur Maloney Prize for Advocacy

Canadian Committee on Cataloguing / Comité canadien de catalogage
Library & Archives Canada, 550, boul de la Cité, Gatineau QC K1A 0N4
Tel: 613-996-5115
Toll-Free: 866-578-7777
BAC.Normesdecatalogage-Cataloguingstandards.LAC@canada.ca
www.bac-lac.gc.ca
Overview: A medium-sized national organization founded in 1974
Mission: To formulate policy on questions concerning cataloguing & bibliographic control, including subject analysis, referred to it by any of the organizations represented on the Committee; to provide representative Canadian opinion for presentation at international meetings, committees & working groups; actively involved with the revision of the Anglo-American Cataloguing Rules.
Chief Officer(s):
Christine Oliver, Chair
christine.oliver@uottawa.ca

Canadian Committee on Labour History (CCLH) / Comité canadien sur l'histoire du travail
c/o Canadian Committee on Labour History, Athabasca University, #1200, 10011 - 109 St. NW, Edmonton AB T5J 3S8
Tel: 780-497-3412; *Fax:* 780-421-3298
cclh@athabascau.ca
www.cclh.ca
twitter.com/CCLHTweets
Previous Name: Committee on Canadian Labour History
Overview: A medium-sized national organization founded in 1971
Mission: To promote & publish scholarly research in the area of Canadian labour history & related topics
Member of: Canadian Magazine Publishers Association; Canadian Association of Learned Journals
Affiliation(s): International Association of Labour History Institutions; Canadian Historical Association; Conference of Historical Journals; Council of Editors of Learned Journals
Finances: *Annual Operating Budget:* $50,000-$100,000
Staff Member(s): 2
Membership: 800; *Fees:* $25
Chief Officer(s):
G.S. Kealey, Treasurer
gkealey@unb.ca
Awards:
• Forsey Prize
Publications:
• Labour / Le Travail: Journal of Canadian Labour Studies / Revue d'Études Ouvrières Canadiennes
Type: Journal; *Frequency:* Semiannually; *Number of Pages:* 350; *Editor:* Bryan D. Palmer; *ISSN:* 0700-3862
Profile: Articles, reviews, documents, & reports about the historical perspective on Canadian workers, aswell as international work of interest to Canadian labour studies

Canadian Committee on MARC / Comité canadien du MARC
Description Division, Service Branch, Library & Archives Canada, 395 Wellington St., Ottawa ON K1A 0N4
Fax: 819-934-4388
BAC.MARC21.LAC@bac-lac.gc.ca
www.marc21.ca/040010-203-e.html
Overview: A medium-sized national organization founded in 1976
Mission: To act as a Canadian MARC Advisory Committee to the National Library by examining the MARC 21 communication formats & making recommendations on the formats; To examine MARC 21 communication formats as a medium for the exchange of machine-readable bibliographic information in Canada; To establish procedures for receiving, evaluating & making recommendations on proposed national & international standards for the representation in machine-readable form of bibliographic information & other related standards; To maintain liaison with its constituent organizations & relevant outside agencies
Affiliation(s): Library & Archives Canada
Chief Officer(s):
Bill Leonard, Contact, 613-716-3379

The Canadian Committee to Protect Journalists *See* Canadian Journalists for Free Expression

Canadian Common Ground Alliance
c/o Alberta One-Call Corporation, #104, 4242 7th St. SE, Calgary AB T2G 2Y8
info@canadiancga.com
www.canadiancga.com
www.facebook.com/206712292676354
twitter.com/CanadianCGA
Overview: A medium-sized national organization
Mission: To ensure public safety; To protect the environment & underground infrastructure of Canada
Membership: *Fees:* $2,000 corporate/association; $100 individual; *Committees:* Best Practices; Damage Information Reporting Tool & Statistics
Chief Officer(s):
Mike Sullivan, Executive Director
msullivan@canadiancga.com

Canadian Communication Association (CCA) / Association canadienne de communication (ACC)
c/o Department of Communication Studies, Wilfred Laurier University, 75 University Ave. West, Waterloo ON N2L 3C5
www.acc-cca.ca
Overview: A small national organization founded in 1980
Mission: To advance communication research and studies in the belief that a better understanding of communication is crucial to building a vibrant society.
Member of: Social Science Federation of Canada
Membership: *Fees:* $85 regular; $75 part time/sessional/retired; $30 student; $250 institutional
Chief Officer(s):
Penelope Ironstone, President
pironstone@wlu.ca

Canadian Communications Foundation (CCF)
Toronto ON
www.broadcasting-history.ca
Overview: A medium-sized national organization
Mission: To document the history of Canadian broadcasting on the foundation's online electronic database.
Chief Officer(s):
Pip Wedge, President
Fil Fraser, Vice-President

Canadian Community Newspapers Association (CCNA)
#200, 890 Yonge St., Toronto ON M4W 3P4
Tel: 416-923-3567; *Fax:* 416-923-7206
Toll-Free: 877-305-2262
info@newspaperscanada.ca
www.newspaperscanada.ca
Overview: A medium-sized national organization founded in 1919
Mission: To be the national voice of the community press in Canada
Membership: 700+ newspapers; *Member Profile:* Each regional association has its own criteria for full active membership.
Chief Officer(s):
John Hinds, President & CEO
Awards:
• Premier Awards
Awards are presented in the following categories: Outstanding Columnist, Local Cartoon, Editorial Writing, Community Service, Agricultural Edition, House Ad, Reporter Initiative, News Story, Environmental Writing, Best Ad Design
• Special Competition Awards
Awards are given in following areas: Best Spot News Photo, Best Feature Photo, Best Sports Photo, Best Christmas Edition, Best Sports Page, Best Special Section, Best Historical Story, Best Newspaper Promotion, Best Feature Story, Best Photo Essay, Best Feature Series, Best Agricultural Story
• General Excellence Awards
Awards are presented to newspapers for general excellence by circulation category, & include presentations to the Best All-Round Newspaper, Best Front Page, & Best Editorial Page

Canadian Community Reinvestment Coalition (CCRC)
PO Box 821, Stn. B, Ottawa ON K1P 241
Tel: 613-789-5753; *Fax:* 613-241-4758
info@cancrc.org
www.cancrc.org
Overview: A medium-sized national organization
Mission: To increase the accountability of Canada's financial institutions, increase their reinvestment in the Canadian ecomony, strengthen Canada's economy, strengthen community economic development efforts across Canada, & develop leadership in the Canadian financial sevices consumer movement.
Membership: 100; *Fees:* $25-$250

Canadian Comparative Literature Association (CCLA) / Association canadienne de littérature comparée (ACLC)
c/o Markus Reisenleitner, Department of Humanities, York University, 217 Vanier College, Toronto ON M3H 1P3
complit.ca
Overview: A small national organization founded in 1969
Affiliation(s): International Comparative Literature Association; Congress of the Humanities & Social Sciences
Membership: *Fees:* $30 students, retired, unemployed, & under employed persons; $60 regular members; $75 joint membership; $375 life membership; *Member Profile:* Scholars interested in comparative literature from across Canada
Activities: Organizing educational meetings & networking opportunities for members
Chief Officer(s):
Karin Beeler, President
beeler@unbc.ca
Susan Ingram, Vice-President
singram@yorku.ca
Pascal Gin, Secretary
pascal_gin@carleton.ca
Markus Reisenleitner, Treasurer
mrln@yorku.ca
Meetings/Conferences:
• Canadian Comparative Literature Association 2018 Congress, May, 2018, Regina, SK
Scope: National
Description: Theme: "Gathering Diversities"
Publications:
• Canadian Review of Comparative Literature / Revue canadienne de littérature comparée

Type: Journal; *Price:* Free with joint membership in the Canadian Comparative Literature Association

Canadian Concrete Masonry Producers Association (CCMPA)
PO Box 1345, 1500 Avenue Rd., Toronto ON M5M 3X0
Tel: 416-495-7497; *Fax:* 416-495-8939
Toll-Free: 888-495-7497
information@ccmpa.ca
www.ccmpa.ca
www.linkedin.com/company-beta/16200827
www.facebook.com/CanadianConcreteMasonryProducers
twitter.com/CCMasonryPA
Previous Name: Ontario Concrete Block Association
Overview: A medium-sized national organization founded in 1962
Mission: To work on behalf of concrete masonry producers
Member of: Masonry Canada
Finances: *Annual Operating Budget:* $100,000-$250,000; *Funding Sources:* Membership dues
Staff Member(s): 2
Membership: 25 manufacturers
Activities: Marketing; Professional development; Research
Chief Officer(s):
Marina de Souza, Executive Director
Paul Hargest, President
phargest@boehmerblock.com
Marcus Poirier, Vice President
mporier@permacon.ca

Canadian Concrete Pipe Association (CCPA) / Association canadienne des fabricants de tuyaux de béton (ACTB)
205 Miller Dr., Halton Hills ON L7G 6G4
Tel: 905-877-5369; *Fax:* 905-877-5369
info@ccpa.com
www.ccpa.com
www.linkedin.com/groups?trk=groups_management_submission_queue-h-dsc&gid=1920373
www.youtube.com/user/CanadianConcretePipe
Overview: A medium-sized national organization founded in 1992
Mission: To coordinate research & development, promotion, education & federal government relations programs pertaining to the marketing of high quality precast concrete waste water & storm drainage products in Canada.
Member of: Federation of Canadian Municipalities
Affiliation(s): Ontario Concrete Pipe Association; Tubecon; American Concrete Pipe Association
Finances: *Annual Operating Budget:* Less than $50,000; *Funding Sources:* Membership dues; research grants
Staff Member(s): 2; 30 volunteer(s)
Membership: 35; *Member Profile:* Manufacturers of concrete pipes & related products; suppliers to manufacturers
Activities: Software development; product development; market research; *Speaker Service:* Yes; *Library:* Data Centre; Open to public
Chief Officer(s):
John Greer, Chair

Canadian Condominium Institute (CCI) / Institut canadien des concominiums
#210, 2800 - 14th Ave., Markham ON L3R 0E4
Tel: 416-491-6216; *Fax:* 416-491-1670
Toll-Free: 866-491-6216
info@cci.ca
www.cci.ca
twitter.com/cci_national
Overview: A medium-sized national organization founded in 1982
Mission: To provide education, information, awareness & access to expertise by, but also for, its members; To serve as a central clearinghouse & research centre on condominium issues & activities across the country; To provide objective research for practitioners & government agencies regarding all aspects of condominium operations; To offer professional assistance; To improve legislation & represent condominiums
Affiliation(s): Association of the Canadian Condominium Institute
24 volunteer(s)
Membership: 1,200; *Member Profile:* Condominium Corporations; Professionals; Individuals; Business Partners; *Committees:* Executive; Finance; Nominations; Chapter Relations; Membership; Communications; Education; Government Relations; Constitution
Activities: Providing an information hotline for answers to questions related to the condominium industry & condominium living; Holds an Annual General Meeting
Chief Officer(s):
Alison Nash, Executive Director, 416-491-6216 Ext. 109
alison@associationconcepts.ca
Laura Fairley, Operations Manager, 416-491-6216 Ext. 108
laura@associationconcepts.ca
Publications:
• CCI [Canadian Condominium Institute] Newsletter
Type: Newsletter

CCI-Golden Horseshoe Chapter
PO Box 37, Burlington ON L7R 3x8
Tel: 905-631-0124; *Fax:* 416-491-1670
Toll-Free: 844-631-0124
admin@cci-ghc.ca
www.cci-ghc.ca
www.facebook.com/CCIGHC
twitter.com/CCIGHC
Chief Officer(s):
Nathan Helder, President

CCI-Huronia Chapter
PO Box 95, Barrie ON L4M 4S9
Tel: 705-431-5213; *Fax:* 705-431-5213
info@ccihuronia.com
www.ccihuronia.com

CCI-London & Area Chapter
PO Box 51022, 1593 Adelaide St. North, London ON N5X 4P9
Tel: 519-453-0672; *Fax:* 519-642-4726
ccisw@cci-sw.on.ca
www.cci-sw.on.ca
www.facebook.com/TheCanadianCondominiumInstituteLondonAreaChapter
twitter.com/CCILondonArea
Chief Officer(s):
Chris DiPietro, President

CCI-Manitoba Chapter
PO Box 48067, Stn. Lakewood, Winnipeg MB R2J 4A3
Tel: 204-794-1134
ccimanitoba@cci.ca
cci-manitoba.ca
www.facebook.com/ccimanitoba
twitter.com/ccimanitoba
Chief Officer(s):
Maureen Hancharyk, President, 204-781-7098

CCI-New Brunswick Chapter
PO Box 363, Stn. A, Fredericton NB E3B 4Z9
Tel: 506-447-1511
ccinewbrunswick@cci.ca
cci-newbrunswick.ca
www.facebook.com/ccinewbrunswick
twitter.com/ccinewbrunswick
Chief Officer(s):
Léo-Guy LeBlank, President

CCI-Newfoundland & Labrador Chapter
Churchill Square, PO Box 23060, St. John's NL A1B 4J9
ccinewfoundland@cci.ca
cci-newfoundland.ca
www.facebook.com/cci.newfoundland
twitter.com/CCINewfoundland
Chief Officer(s):
Carol Burke, President

CCI-North Alberta Chapter
Kingsway Business Center, #37, 11810 Kingsway Ave. NW, Edmonton AB T5G 0X5
Tel: 780-453-9004; *Fax:* 780-452-9003
info@ccinorthalberta.com
www.ccinorthalberta.com
Chief Officer(s):
Anand Sharma, President
anand@csmgmtinc.ca

CCI-North Saskatchewan Chapter
PO Box 7074, Saskatoon SK S7K 4J1
Tel: 306-652-0311; *Fax:* 306-652-0373
northsaskatchewan@cci.ca
cci-northsaskatchewan.ca
www.facebook.com/ccinorthsaskatchewan
twitter.com/CCINorthSask
Chief Officer(s):
Donna Singbeil, President

CCI-Northwestern Ontario Chapter
PO Box 10692, Thunder Bay ON P7B 6V1
Tel: 807-346-5690; *Fax:* 807-344-1507
nwontario@cci.ca
www.cci-nwontario.ca
twitter.com/cci_nwo
Chief Officer(s):
Dan Kelly, President

CCI-Nova Scotia Chapter
#135, #3-644 Portland St., Dartmouth NS B2W 2M3
Tel: 902-222-4002
info@ccinovascotia.ca
www.ccinovascotia.ca
www.facebook.com/CCINovaScotia
twitter.com/nova_cci

CCI-Eastern Ontario Chapter
PO Box 32001, 1386 Richmond Rd., Ottawa ON K2B 1A1
Tel: 613-755-5145; *Fax:* 613-755-4086
info@cci-easternontario.ca
cci-easternontario.ca
twitter.com/CCIEastOntario
Chief Officer(s):
Nancy Houle, President

CCI-South Alberta Chapter
PO Box 38107, Calgary AB T3K 4Y0
Tel: 403-253-9082; *Fax:* 403-220-1215
administrator@ccisouthalberta.com
www.ccisouthalberta.com
www.facebook.com/ccisouthalberta
twitter.com/CCI_South_AB
Chief Officer(s):
Andrew Fulcher, President

CCI-South Saskatchewan Chapter
PO Box 3784, Regina SK S4P 3N8
Toll-Free: 866-491-6216
cci-ssk@cci.ca
cci-southsaskatchewan.ca
Chief Officer(s):
Dawna Matthews, President

CCI-Toronto & Area Chapter
#210, 2800 - 14th Ave., Markham ON L3R 0E4
Tel: 416-491-6216; *Fax:* 416-491-1670
info@ccitoronto.org
www.ccitoronto.org
www.facebook.com/CCIToronto
twitter.com/CCIToronto
instagram.com/ccitoronto
Chief Officer(s):
Sally Thompson, President

CCI-Vancouver Chapter
PO Box 17577, Stn. The Ritz, Vancouver BC V6E 0B2
Tel: 866-491-6216; *Fax:* 866-502-1670
contact@ccivancouver.ca
www.ccivancouver.ca
www.facebook.com/CCIVancouver
twitter.com/CCIVancouver
Chief Officer(s):
Paul Murcutt, President

CCI-Windsor - Essex County Chapter
PO Box 22015, 11500 Tecumseh Rd. East, Windsor ON N8N 5G6
Tel: 519-978-3237; *Fax:* 519-978-9042
cci-windsor.ca
www.facebook.com/cciwindsor
twitter.com/cciwindsor
Chief Officer(s):
Troy Humber, President, 519-300-6288

Canadian Conference of Catholic Bishops (CCCB) / Conférence des évêques catholiques du Canada (CECC)
2500 Don Reid Dr., Ottawa ON K1H 2J2
Tel: 613-241-9461; *Fax:* 613-241-8117
cecc@cccb.ca
www.cccb.ca
www.facebook.com/123711474340639
twitter.com/CCCB_CECC
www.youtube.com/user/cccbadmin
Previous Name: Canadian Catholic Conference
Overview: A small national charitable organization founded in 1943
Mission: To exercise pastoral functions for Catholics in Canada
Staff Member(s): 40
Membership: *Member Profile:* Diocesan bishops in Canada; Coadjutor Bishops; Auxiliary Bishops; Titular Bishops of any rite within the Catholic Church

Activities: Providing aid to developing countries & Christian education; Offering a forum for bishops to share experiences & insights; Promoting the teaching of the Catholic Church in circumstances from conception to natural death; Preparing & providing educational resources; Strengthening the role of the family
Chief Officer(s):
Paul Bowman, Director, 613-241-9461 Ext. 229
Frank Leo, Jr., C.S.S., General Secretary, 613-241-9461 Ext. 206
gensec@cccb.ca
Publications:
• At Home with the Word
Type: Yearbook; *Frequency:* Annually; *Price:* $9
• Children's Daily Prayer
Type: Yearbook; *Frequency:* Annually; *ISBN:* 978-1-56854-662-9; *Price:* $18
• Daily Prayer
Type: Yearbook; *Frequency:* Annually; *Price:* $15
• A Simple Guide to the Daily Mass Readings
Type: Yearbook; *Frequency:* Annually; *Price:* $3
• Sourcebook for Sundays & Seasons
Type: Yearbook; *Frequency:* Annually; *ISBN:* 978-1-56854-674-2; *Price:* $18
• Workbook for Lectors & Gospel Readers
Type: Yearbook; *Frequency:* Annually; *ISBN:* 978-0-88997-572-9; *Price:* $15

Canadian Conference of Mennonite Brethren Churches (CCMBC)
1310 Taylor Ave., Winnipeg MB R3M 3Z6
Tel: 204-669-6575; *Fax:* 204-654-1865
Toll-Free: 888-669-6575
karen.hume@mbchurches.ca
www.mennonitebrethren.ca
www.linkedin.com/company/canadian-conference-of-mennonite-brethren-churches
www.facebook.com/mbconf
twitter.com/CdnMBConf
Overview: A medium-sized national organization founded in 1945
Mission: To glorify God, to nurture & equip members to live the Christian life & to mobilize them for ministry
Finances: *Funding Sources:* Donations
Staff Member(s): 19
Membership: 31,264; 256 Mennonite Brethren congregations; *Committees:* Mennonite Central Committee; Mennonite Disaster Service; Manitoba Missions/Service
Activities: *Library:* Centre for MB Studies; Open to public
Chief Officer(s):
Willy Reimer, Executive Director, 855-256-3211
willy.reimer@mbchurches.ca
Publications:
• Le Lien
Frequency: Bimonthly; *Editor:* Jean Biéri; *ISSN:* 1716-5016; *Price:* $16/year: Canada, $20/year: international
Profile: Written in French, the publication serves the conference's francophone churches in Québec
• MB Chinese Herald
Frequency: Bimonthly; *Editor:* Joseph Kwan; *ISSN:* 1911-8783
Profile: Written in Chinese, the Herald serves the conference's Chinese community
• Mennonite Brethren Herald
Frequency: Monthly; *Accepts Advertising*; *Editor:* Laura Kalmar; *ISSN:* 0025-9349; *Price:* Free for Canadian MB Church members; from $25.20 to $27.60 for non-members
Profile: Feature articles, columns, letters, news, people, & events for the Mennonite Brethren community
• Mennonite Historian
Type: Newsletter; *Frequency:* Quarterly; *Editor:* Jon Isaak; *Price:* $15/yr., $28/2 yrs., $40/3 yrs.

Canadian Conference of Pharmaceutical Faculties *See* Association of Faculties of Pharmacy of Canada

Canadian Conference of the Arts (CCA) / Conférence canadienne des arts
#406, 130 Slater St., Ottawa ON K1P 6E2
Tel: 613-238-3561; *Fax:* 613-238-4849
info@ccarts.ca
www.ccarts.ca
www.linkedin.com/company/canadian-conference-of-the-arts-la-conf-rence-canadienne-des-arts
www.facebook.com/CanArts
twitter.com/CanadianArts
Overview: A medium-sized national charitable organization founded in 1945
Mission: To ensure the lively existence & continued growth of the arts & the cultural industries in Canada; To increase the Canadian materials (works created, produced, & performed by Canadians) available to Canadians; To improve the quality of life for all artists & arts groups; To unite members to work for interests of all artists & whole cultural community; To work closely with other arts service organizations to formulate policies & advocate their adoption by governments
Finances: *Annual Operating Budget:* $500,000-$1.5 Million; *Funding Sources:* Membership fees; Publication sales; Conference fees; Government subsidies (federal, provincial)
Staff Member(s): 7
Membership: 800; *Fees:* Schedule available; *Member Profile:* Persons from all arts disciplines, & all cultural industries; major arts institutions & festivals; regional & community arts councils; provincial & national associations in every discipline; individuals who support goals & aspirations of artists in Canada
Activities: Advocating on behalf of Canada's artists & art organizations; Encouraging & procuring public funding & support for the arts; Communicating & collaborating to change policy affecting artists & art organizations; *Library:* by appointment
Chief Officer(s):
Alain Pineau, National Director
Anne-Marie Des Roches, Associate Director, Senior Policy Advisor
Awards:
• Keith Kelly Award for Cultural Leadership
• Diplôme d'honneur
Established in 1954; presented annually to Canadians who have contributed outstanding service to the arts; recipients have included Vincent Massey, Wilfrid Pelletier, Maureen Forrester, Floyd Chalmers, Gabrielle Roy, Glenn Gould, Alfred Pellan, Bill Reid, Antonine Maillet

Canadian Congress of Neurological Sciences *See* Canadian Neurological Sciences Federation

Canadian Connemara Pony Society (CCPS)
PO Box 291, RR 9, Saskatoon SK S7K 1P3
Tel: 306-374-1703
www.canadianconnemara.org
Previous Name: American Connemara Association - Western Canada
Overview: A small local organization founded in 1956
Mission: To assist & promote the breeding, registration, training, exhibition & general use of the Connemara Pony for pleasure, sport, equestrian competition, & therapeutic horsemanship in North America; To preserve the unique qualities of the Connemara through encouraging selective breeding for type & conformation as described in the Society's Standards for the Breed; To assist & promote local, national & international equestrian competition; To keep the members of the Society informed in all matters concerning the Connemara
Affiliation(s): American Connemara Pony Society
Membership: *Fees:* $15 junior; $20 associate & non-resident; $40 senior; *Committees:* Arbitration; Awards; Historical Archives; Inspections; Membership; Newsletter; Nominating; Promotions; Registration; Webpage
Chief Officer(s):
Susan MacDougall, President
Elsie Priddy, Secretary-Treasurer

Canadian Conservation Institute (CCI) / Institut canadien de conservation (l'ICC)
1030 Innes Rd., Ottawa ON K1B 4S7
Tel: 613-998-3721; *Fax:* 613-998-4721
Toll-Free: 866-998-3721; *TTY:* 819-997-3123
cci-icc.services@pch.gc.ca
www.cci-icc.gc.ca
www.facebook.com/cci.conservation
Overview: A medium-sized national organization founded in 1972
Mission: To promote the proper preservation & care of moveable cultural heritage in Canada; To advance the science, technology, & practice of conservation; To support the heritage community in Canada
Affiliation(s): CCI is a Special Operating Agency within the Department of Canadian Heritage
Activities: Working with Canadian heritage institutions, such as historic sites, art galleries, libraries, & museums; Conducting conservation research; Offering learning opportunities; Disseminating conservation information; *Library:* Canadian Conservation Institute Library
Chief Officer(s):
Jeanne Inch, Director General & Chief Operating Officer
Publications:
• CCI [Canadian Conservation Institute] News
Type: Newsletter; *Editor:* Barbara Patterson; Linda Leclerc
Profile: Canadian Conservation Institute services, learning opportunities, library acquisitions, & new publications

Canadian Construction Association (CCA) / Association canadienne de la construction (ACC)
#1900, 275 Slater St., Ottawa ON K1P 5H9
Tel: 613-236-9455; *Fax:* 613-236-9526
cca@cca-acc.com
www.cca-acc.com
twitter.com/ConstructionCAN
www.youtube.com/user/ConstructionCAN
Overview: A large national organization founded in 1918
Mission: To act as the national voice of the construction industry; To serve, promote, & enhance the construction industry by acting on behalf of its members in matters of national concern
Membership: 20,000 members + 65 partner associations; *Committees:* Standard Practices; Innovation & Technology; Business & Market Development; Industry Advocacy & Regulatory Affairs; Gold Seal
Chief Officer(s):
Chris McNally, Chair
Mary Van Buren, President, 613-236-9455 Ext. 414
Mark Belton, Director, Finance, 613-236-9455 Ext. 418
mbelton@cca-acc.com
Awards:
• CCA Awards of Excellence
• CCA Awards of Recognition
• CCA Person of the Year
• CCA Excellence in Innovation Award
• CCA Environmental Achievement Award
• CCA International Business Award
• CCA National Safety Award
• CCA Partner Association Award of Excellence
• CCA Community Leader Award
• CCA Gold Seal Association Award
• CCA General Contractor Award of Recognition
• CCA Trade Contractor Award of Recognition
• CCA Civil Infrastructure Award of Recognition
• CCA Manufacturers, Suppliers & Services Award of Recognition
Meetings/Conferences:
• Canadian Construction Association 100th Annual Conference 2018, March, 2018, Banff, AB
Scope: National
Description: Theme: "Building to New Heights"
Contact Information: Director, Meetings & Conferences: Chantal Montpetit, Phone: 613-236-9455 ext. 406; E-mail: infoconference@cca-acc.com; conference.cca-acc.com
Publications:
• CCA [Canadian Construction Association] Weekly
Type: Newsletter; *Frequency:* Weekly

Canadian Construction Women (CCW)
#700, 555 Burrard St., Vancouver BC V7X 1M8
info@constructionwomen.org
www.constructionwomen.org
www.linkedin.com/company/canadian-construction-women-ccw-
www.facebook.com/cdnconstructionwomen
twitter.com/constructionw
www.instagram.com/constructionw
Overview: A small national organization
Mission: To attract & retain women in the construction industry
Finances: *Funding Sources:* Sponsorships
Membership: *Fees:* $300 corporate; $100 individuals
Activities: Supporting & mentoring members; Providing networking opportunities; Offering chances to learn
Chief Officer(s):
Marie-France Venneri, President
president@constructionwomen.org
Publications:
• Canadian Construction Women Member Directory
Type: Directory
Profile: Listing of contacts representing a cross section of the industry
• Under the Hard Hat
Type: Newsletter; *Frequency:* Monthly
Profile: Publication informs members of approaching events

Canadian Consumer Specialty Products Association (CCSPA) / Association canadienne de produits de consommation spécialisés (ACPCS)
#800, 130 Albert St., Ottawa ON K1P 5G4

Canadian Associations / Canadian Contemporary Dance Theatre (CCDT)

Tel: 613-232-6616; *Fax:* 613-233-6350
assoc@ccspa.org
www.ccspa.org
twitter.com/CCSPA_ACPCS
Previous Name: Canadian Manufacturers of Chemical Specialties Association
Overview: A medium-sized national organization founded in 1958
Mission: Represents the specialty chemical & formulated products industry; promotes the interests of member companies by providing a national voice, encouraging ethical practices, negotiating with government, & fostering industry cooperation
Finances: *Funding Sources:* Membership fees
Staff Member(s): 3
Membership: 35; *Fees:* Schedule available; *Committees:* Registered Products; Soap & Detergent/Environment; Public Affairs
Activities: *Rents Mailing List:* Yes
Chief Officer(s):
Shannon Coombs, President, 613-232-6616 Ext. 11
coombss@ccspa.org
Nancy Hitchins, Director, Administration & Member Services, 613-232-6616 Ext. 12
hitchinsn@ccspa.org
Awards:
• Chevalier Award Scholarship
; *Amount:* $2,500
Meetings/Conferences:
• 2018 CCSPA Annual Government Interface, April, 2018, Marriott Hotel, Ottawa, ON
Scope: National

Canadian Contemporary Dance Theatre (CCDT)
509 Parliament St., Toronto ON M4X 1P3
Tel: 416-924-5657; *Fax:* 416-924-4141
info@ccdt.org
www.ccdt.org
www.facebook.com/CanadianContemporaryDanceTheatre
twitter.com/CCDTdance
Overview: A small national organization founded in 1980
Mission: To promote dance theatre to young people
Membership: *Member Profile:* Dancers under age 20
Chief Officer(s):
Deborah Lundmark, Artistic Director & Resident Choreographer
Michael de Coninck Smith, Managing Director & Tour Manager

The Canadian Continence Foundation / Fondation d'aide aux personnes incontinentes (Canada)
PO Box 417, Peterborough ON K9J 6Z3
Tel: 705-750-4600; *Fax:* 705-750-1770
Toll-Free: 800-265-9575
www.canadiancontinence.ca
www.linkedin.com/groups/3694602
www.facebook.com/canadian.continence
twitter.com/cdncontinence
www.youtube.com/user/canadiancontinence
Previous Name: The Simon Foundation for Continence Canada
Overview: A large national charitable organization founded in 1986
Mission: To act as a source of information, education & support for incontinent individuals; To increase public awareness & influence government policy
Affiliation(s): Simon Foundation-USA
Activities: Montréal Helpline; *Awareness Events:* Incontinence Awareness Month, Nov.; *Speaker Service:* Yes
Chief Officer(s):
Adrian Wagg, President
Jacqueline Cahill, Executive Director
Publications:
• The Source: Your Guide to Better Bladder Control
Type: Guide

Canadian Contractors Association (CCA)
#4, 5660 - 10 St. NE, Calgary AB T2E 8W7
Tel: 403-509-3922; *Fax:* 403-270-8518
Toll-Free: 877-509-3925
chad@canadiancontractors.info
www.canadiancontractors.info
Overview: A medium-sized national organization
Mission: To provide information & services to the independant consultant & contractor market
Activities: Providing insurance benefits to self-employed or independent contractors
Chief Officer(s):
Chad Pimm, Chief Operations Officer
chad.p@rpibi.com

Michelle Hennessy, Director, Marketing
mh@michellehennessy.com

Canadian Convenience Stores Association (CCSA) / Association Canadienne des dépanneurs en alimentation (ACDA)
#205, 2140 Winston Park Dr., Oakville ON L6H 5V5
Tel: 905-845-9339; *Fax:* 905-845-9340
Toll-Free: 877-934-3968
info@theccsa.ca
www.theccsa.ca
Overview: A large national organization founded in 2006
Mission: To be the industry voice for all convenience store matters; To provide a forum for concerns & issues
Affiliation(s): Western Convenience Stores Association; Ontario Convenience Stores Association; Association Québécoise des dépanneurs en alimentation; Atlantic Convenience Stores Association; National Convenience Stores Distributors Association
Finances: *Funding Sources:* Membership fees
Membership: 31,000; *Member Profile:* Major convenience store companies; Independent owners; Food retailers; Suppliers & wholesalers; Gasoline & automotive product vendors
Activities: Online Responsible Retail Training program; Combating contraband tobacco
Chief Officer(s):
Satinder Chera, President

Canadian Convention of Southern Baptists *See* CNBC

Canadian Co-operative Association (CCA) / Association des coopératives du Canada (ACC)
#400, 275 Bank St., Ottawa ON K2P 2L6
Tel: 613-238-6711; *Fax:* 613-567-0658
www.coopscanada.coop
www.facebook.com/CoopsInCanada
twitter.com/cca_intl
www.youtube.com/user/CCAottawa
Overview: A large national organization founded in 1987
Mission: To develop co-operatives in other countries; To promote the co-operative model; To unite co-operatives from various industry sectors & regions of Canada
Affiliation(s): Conseil canadien de la coopération et de la mutualité; Co-operative Development Initiative (co-managed by CCA and CCCM); Co-operative Development Foundation of Canada (CDF)
Finances: *Funding Sources:* Donations
Membership: 2,000+ organizations; *Member Profile:* Co-operatives in Canada, which represent over nine million co-operative & credit union members
Activities: Supporting members through the provision of financial or technical resources; *Awareness Events:* Co-op Week, Oct.
Chief Officer(s):
Patrice Pratt, Chair
Michael Casey, Executive Director, 613-238-6711 Ext. 244
Brian Coburn, Director, Operations, 613-238-6711 Ext. 223
Ingrid Fischer, Director, Business Development, 613-238-6711 Ext. 238
Donna Miller, Director, Human Resources, 613-238-6711 Ext. 213
Awards:
• Canadian Co-operative Achievement Award
To recognize individual contributions to the co-operative movement in Canada
• Global Co-operator Award
To honour an individual who demonstrates commitment to the international development work of the Canadian Co-operative Association & the Co-operative Development Foundation of Canada
• Alexander Fraser Laidlaw Fellowship, CASC Scholarships
• Amy & Tim Dauphinee Scholarship, CASC Scholarships
• Lemaire Co-operative Studies Award, CASC Scholarships
Publications:
• Canadian Co-operative Association Annual Report
Type: Yearbook; *Frequency:* Annually
Profile: A summary of the association's activities
• Co-operative News Briefs [a publication of the Canadian Co-operative Association]
Type: Newsletter; *Frequency:* Semimonthly; *Price:* Free
Profile: Information for those with an interest in co-operative sector developments in Canada & throughout the world
• Co-operatives Helping Fuel a Green Economy [a publication of the Canadian Co-operative Association]
Type: Booklet; *Author:* Patti Giovanninni; *Editor:* John Anderson

• Ethno-cultural & Immigrant Co-operatives in Canada [a publication of the Canadian Co-operative Association]
Type: Booklet; *Author:* Patti Giovannini; *Editor:* John Anderson; Donna Balkan
• Governance Matters [a publication of the Canadian Co-operative Association]
Type: Newsletter; *Frequency:* 8 pa
Profile: Governance issues for the co-operative leader
• International Development Digest [a publication of the Canadian Co-operative Association]
Type: Digest; *Frequency:* 3 pa
Profile: Information about international co-operative development efforts undertaken on behalf of CCA's Canadian credit union & co-operativemembers
• International Development Review [a publication of the Canadian Co-operative Association]
Type: Yearbook; *Frequency:* Annually
Profile: Annual highlights from the Canadian Co-operative Association's international development program
• International Dispatch [a publication of the Canadian Co-operative Association]
Type: Newsletter; *Frequency:* 6 pa
Profile: News & views about co-operatives & credit unions around the world & the war on poverty
• The Lay of the Land: Local Food Initiatives in Canada [a publication of the Canadian Co-operative Association]
Type: Booklet; *Number of Pages:* 53; *Author:* Adrian Egbers; *Editor:* Lynne Markell
Profile: Information about the area of local food, within & outside the co-operativesector
• New futures: Innovative Uses of the Co-op Model [a publication of the Canadian Co-operative Association]
Type: Booklet; *Number of Pages:* 30; *Author:* Brenda Heald; *Editor:* Donna Balkan; *ISBN:* 978-0-88817-102-3
Profile: Profiles of Canadian co-ops that use the co-op model
• Working Together for Local Food [a publication of the Canadian Co-operative Association]
Type: Booklet; *Number of Pages:* 63; *Author:* Adrian Egbers; Stefan Epp; *Editor:* Lynne Markell; *ISBN:* 978-0-88817-103-0
Profile: Profiles of successful local food co-ops

Canadian Co-operative Wool Growers Ltd. (CCWG)
PO Box 130, 142 Franktown Rd., Carleton Place ON K7C 3P3
Tel: 613-257-2714; *Fax:* 613-257-8896
ccwghq@wool.ca
www.wool.ca
Overview: A medium-sized national organization founded in 1918
Mission: To operate as a producer-owned wool marketing cooperative; To collect, grade, & market, the majority of the Canadian wool clip to the global market; To retail farm supplies & animal health & identification products
Staff Member(s): 35
Membership: 1,200
Chief Officer(s):
Eric Bjergso, General Manager
ericb@wool.ca

Canadian Coordinating Office for Health Technology Assessment *See* Canadian Agency for Drugs & Technologies in Health

Canadian Copper & Brass Development Association (CCBDA)
#210, 65 Overlea Blvd., Toronto ON M4H 1P1
Tel: 416-391-5599; *Fax:* 416-391-3823
Toll-Free: 877-640-0946
library@copperalliance.ca
www.coppercanada.ca
www.facebook.com/coppercanada
twitter.com/coppercanada
Overview: A medium-sized national organization founded in 1958
Mission: To promote, foster & stimulate use of products of Canadian copper & brass industry; To represent & support the primary producers fabricators, manufacturers, & consumers of copper & copper alloys in Canada, by increasing industry & public awareness of copper's capabilites & advantages compared to other metals & materials, & by providing technical services related to copper's use
Member of: Copper Alliance
Affiliation(s): International Copper Association
Finances: *Annual Operating Budget:* $250,000-$500,000
Staff Member(s): 2
Membership: 13 corporate; *Fees:* $1,500+; *Member Profile:* Primary copper producers, fabricators, & manufacturers

Activities: *Library:* Open to public by appointment
Chief Officer(s):
Stephen Knapp, Executive Director
Publications:
• Canadian Copper [a publication of the Canadian Copper & Brass Development Association]
Type: Magazine
Profile: Articles on mining, electrical equipment, wire, natural gas systems, architecture, & other copper topics

Canadian Copyright Institute (CCI)
#107, 192 Spadina Ave., Toronto ON M5T 2C2
Tel: 416-975-1756; *Fax:* 416-975-1839
info@thecci.ca
www.thecci.ca
Overview: A medium-sized national organization founded in 1965
Mission: To encourage a better understanding of the law of copyright on the part of members, public & users of copyright material; To engage in & foster research in copyright law
Affiliation(s): Book & Periodical Council
Finances: *Funding Sources:* Membership fees
25 volunteer(s)
Membership: 45 individual + 19 corporate + 47 affiliate; *Fees:* $75 individual; *Member Profile:* Interest in copyright & concern to encourage its use in public interest
Activities: *Library:* by appointment
Chief Officer(s):
Anne McClelland, Administrator

Canadian Corporate Counsel Association (CCCA) / Association canadienne des conseillers juridiques d'entreprises
#1210, 20 Toronto St., Toronto ON M5C 2B8
Tel: 416-869-0522; *Fax:* 416-869-0946
ccca@ccca-cba.org
www.ccca-accje.org
twitter.com/CCCA_News
Overview: A medium-sized national organization founded in 1987
Mission: To provide quality education, information & other services & resources of specific interest to corporate counsel in Canada, & to facilitate communication & networking among such counsel
Member of: Canadian Bar Association
Affiliation(s): Malaysian Corporate Counsel Association; Corporate Lawyers Association of South Africa; Australian Corporate Lawyers Association; Hong Kong Corporate Counsel Association; Singapore Corporate Counsel Association; Corporate Lawyers Association of New Zealand
Finances: *Annual Operating Budget:* $250,000-$500,000
Staff Member(s): 5
Membership: 10,000; *Fees:* Schedule available; *Member Profile:* Members of the Canadian Bar Association; employed by & providing legal services to any business enterprise, association, institution, non-profit organization, crown corporation, regulatory body or government agency or department providing funding or assistance programs to any of the foregoing
Activities: *Speaker Service:* Yes; *Rents Mailing List:* Yes
Chief Officer(s):
Christine Staley, Executive Director, 416-869-0522 Ext. 203
cstaley@ccca-cba.org
Awards:
• Robert V.A. Jones Award
Contact: CCCA Awards Nominations Committee, E-mail: kunsworth@ccca-cba.org
• Community Builder Award
Contact: CCCA Awards Nominations Committee, E-mail: kunsworth@ccca-cba.org
• Professional Contribution Award
Contact: CCCA Awards Nominations Committee, E-mail: kunsworth@ccca-cba.org
• Special Contribution Award
Contact: CCCA Awards Nominations Committee, E-mail: kunsworth@ccca-cba.org
• Up & Comer Award
Contact: CCCA Awards Nominations Committee, E-mail: kunsworth@ccca-cba.org
• Innovation Award
Contact: CCCA Awards Nominations Committee, E-mail: kunsworth@ccca-cba.org
Meetings/Conferences:
• Canadian Corporate Counsel Association 2018 National Conference, April, 2018, Fairmont Royal York Hotel, Toronto, ON
Scope: National
Description: Theme: "Beyond Borders: Business & Law in the Global Village"
Publications:
• CCCA Magazine [a publication of the Canadian Corporate Counsel Association]
Type: Magazine; *Frequency:* Quarterly; *Accepts Advertising*;
Editor: Lynne Kryku; *ISSN:* 1913-0562
Profile: Publishes articles about issues regarding corporate law, as well as articles pertaining to theinterests of coorporate lawyers

Canadian Corps Association
201 Niagara St., Toronto ON M5V 1C9
Tel: 416-504-6694
Overview: A small national organization founded in 1934

The Canadian Corps of Commissionaires / Le Corps Canadien des Commissionnaires
National Office, #201, 100 Gloucester St., Ottawa ON K2P 0A4
Tel: 613-688-0710; *Fax:* 613-688-0719
Toll-Free: 877-322-6777
info@commissionaires.ca
www.commissionaires.ca
www.linkedin.com/company/commissionaires-canada
www.facebook.com/CommissionairesCanada
Also Known As: Commissionaires
Overview: A large national organization founded in 1925
Mission: To create meaningful employment opportunities for former members of the Canadian Forces, the Royal Canadian Mounted Police & others who wish to contribute to the security & well-being of Canadians
Member of: Canadian Society for Industrial Security; American Society for Industrial Security
Finances: *Annual Operating Budget:* Greater than $5 Million; *Funding Sources:* Self-funded
Staff Member(s): 8; 20 volunteer(s)
Membership: 20,000; *Member Profile:* Armed Forces, RCMP & others (varies by Division)
Activities: Strong national federation of Divisions, working in harmony to be the preferred provider of security services
Chief Officer(s):
Harry Harsch, RCN, Chief of Staff
Awards:
• Commissionaires Long Service Medal
• Commissionaires Distinguished Service Medal
• Commissionaires Meritorious Service Medal

British Columbia Division
#801, 595 Howe St., Vancouver BC V6C 2T5
Tel: 604-646-3330; *Fax:* 604-681-9864
Toll-Free: 877-322-6777
info@commissionaires.bc.ca
www.commissionaires.bc.ca
Chief Officer(s):
Chris Mitchell, MHS, CEO

Division de Montréal
#700, 1001, rue Sherbrooke est, Montréal QC H2L 1L3
Tél: 514-273-8578; *Téléc:* 514-277-1922
Ligne sans frais: 877-322-6777
info@cccmtl.ca
www.commissionnairesquebec.ca
Chief Officer(s):
Marc Parent, Chef de la direction

Division du Québec
#700, 1001 rue Sherbrooke est, Montréal QC H2L 1L3
Tél: 514-273-8578; *Téléc:* 514-277-1922
Ligne sans frais: 877-322-6777
info@cccmtl.ca
commissionnairesquebec.ca
www.linkedin.com/company/2843379
www.facebook.com/211839285575785
Chief Officer(s):
Marc Parent, Chef de la direction
Francis Giguère, Coordonnateur, Communication/marketing

Great Lakes-Toronto Division
2947 Portland Dr., Oakville ON L6H 5S4
Tel: 416-364-4496; *Fax:* 416-364-5395
Toll-Free: 866-364-4496
toronto@commissionaires-cgl.ca
www.commissionaires-cgl.ca
Chief Officer(s):
Tom Prins, President & CEO

Hamilton Division
#208, 151 York Blvd., Hamilton ON L8R 3M2
Tel: 905-527-2775; *Fax:* 905-527-9948
Toll-Free: 800-241-9988
cccham@on.aibn.com
www.commissionaireshamilton.com
Chief Officer(s):
J.L. (John) Livingstone, CD, CEO

Kingston Division
737 Arlington Park Pl., Kingston ON K7M 8M8
Tel: 613-634-4432; *Fax:* 613-389-0743
Toll-Free: 877-346-0363
kingstoncorps@thecommissionaires.com
Chief Officer(s):
Michael Robert Voith, MSC, CD, PEng, CEO

Manitoba Division
290 Burnell St., Winnipeg MB R3G 2A7
Tel: 204-942-5993; *Fax:* 204-942-6702
Toll-Free: 877-322-6777
admin@commissionaires.mb.ca
www.commissionaires.mb.ca
www.linkedin.com/company/commissionaires-manitoba
Chief Officer(s):
Tom Reimer, MMM CD, Chief Executive Officer

New Brunswick & Prince Edward Island Division
160 Mark Dr., Saint John NB E2J 4H5
Tel: 506-634-8000; *Fax:* 506-646-2400
Toll-Free: 877-322-6777
cccnbpei@nb.sympatico.ca
www.commissionaires.ca
Chief Officer(s):
Peter Kramers, Chief Executive Officer

Newfoundland & Labrador Division
83 Thorburn Rd., #C, St. John's NL A1B 3M2
Tel: 709-754-0757; *Fax:* 709-754-0116
Toll-Free: 877-322-6777
info@commissionaires.nl.ca
www.commissionaires.nl.ca
Chief Officer(s):
James G. Lynch, CEO
jlynch@commissionaires.nl.ca

North Saskatchewan Division (CNSD)
1219 Idylwyld Dr. North, Saskatoon SK S7L 1A1
Tel: 306-244-6588; *Fax:* 306-244-6191
Toll-Free: 877-244-6588
ccc@commissionairesnsask.ca
Chief Officer(s):
Mike Cooper, CEO

Northern Alberta, Northwest Territories & Nunavut Division
10633 - 124 St., Edmonton AB T5N 1S5
Tel: 780-451-1974; *Fax:* 780-452-9389
Toll-Free: 877-322-6777
nalberta@commissionaires.ab.ca
www.commissionaires.ab.ca
Chief Officer(s):
John D. Slater, MBA, CD, Chief Executive Officer

Nova Scotia Division
1472 Hollis St., Halifax NS B3J 1V2
Tel: 902-429-8101; *Fax:* 902-444-8590
Anne James, Director, Human Resources
ajames@commissionaires.ns.ca

Ottawa Division
24 Colonnade Rd., Ottawa ON K2E 7J6
Tel: 613-231-6462; *Fax:* 613-567-1517
Toll-Free: 877-322-6777
staff@commissionaires-ottawa.on.ca
www.commissionaires-ottawa.on.ca
Chief Officer(s):
Paul A. Guindon, CEO

South Saskatchewan Division
Alpine Village Mall, 122 Albert St., Regina SK S4R 2N2
Tel: 306-757-0998; *Fax:* 306-352-5494
Toll-Free: 866-757-0998
southsask@commissionaires.sk.ca
Chief Officer(s):
Colin King, CD, CEO

Southern Alberta Division
1107 - 53 Ave. NE, Calgary AB T2E 6X9
Tel: 403-244-4664; *Fax:* 403-228-0623
Toll-Free: 877-322-6777
www.commissionaires-salta.ca
Chief Officer(s):
Steve Gagnon, MEng, CEO

Victoria, the Islands & Yukon Division
928 Cloverdale Ave., Victoria BC V8X 2T3

Canadian Associations / Canadian Correspondence Chess Association (CCCA) / L'Association canadienne des échecs par correspondance (ACEC)

Tel: 250-727-7755; Fax: 250-727-7355
Toll-Free: 877-532-5009
www.commissionairesviy.ca
www.linkedin.com/company/10090662
www.facebook.com/cmrevictoria
twitter.com/CVIYSecurity
Chief Officer(s):
Gary Paulson, CEO

Canadian Correspondence Chess Association (CCCA) / L'Association canadienne des échecs par correspondance (ACEC)
c/o Manny Migicovsky, 1669, Country Rte 4, RR#1, L'Orignal QC K0B 1K0
Tel: 613-632-3166
ccca@cogeco.ca
correspondencechess.com/ccca
Overview: A small national charitable organization
Mission: To promote chess playing via mail & e-mail both nationally & internationally
Member of: Chess Federation of Canada
Membership: Fees: $30 regular; $27 senior/youth; $35 USA; $40 international
Chief Officer(s):
Manny Migicovsky, President
Publications:
• Check!
Type: Newsletter; Editor: Michael Egan, Games Editor

Canadian Corrugated Containerboard Association / Association canadienne du cartonnage ondulé et du carton-caisse
#3, 1995 Clark Blvd., Brampton ON L6T 4W1
Tel: 905-458-1247; Fax: 905-458-2052
info@cccabox.org
www.cccabox.org
Previous Name: Paper Packaging Canada
Overview: A medium-sized national organization overseen by Paper & Paperboard Packaging Environmental Council
Mission: To represent containerboard mill sites, corrugator plants, sheet plants & related industries; to work together with other players in the paper industry to develop an agenda of common concerns & issues
Membership: 1-99
Activities: Networking & information sharing; seminars; conference & trade fair; annual golf tournament; Awareness Events: Golf Tournament, June
Chief Officer(s):
Peter Moore, Chair
David Andrews, Executive Director, 905-458-1247
davidandrews@cccabox.org

Canadian Cosmetic, Toiletry & Fragrance Association (CCTFA) / Association canadienne des cosmétiques, produit de toilette et parfums
#102, 420 Britannia Rd. East, Mississauga ON L4Z 3L5
Tel: 905-890-5161; Fax: 905-890-2607
cctfa@cctfa.ca
www.cctfa.ca
Overview: A medium-sized national organization founded in 1928
Mission: To encourage trust & confidence in the Canadian cosmetic, toiletry & fragrance industry & in the safety, efficacy & quality of its products; To be the principapal voice of the personal care industry, including cosmetic-like drug products & cosmetic-like natural health products (NHP), interfacing on a timely basis with governemtn & elected representatives, to ensure development & effective representationof industry positions on a ll regulatory issues; to have the personal care industyr perceived by consumers at large as being socially concerned, responsible & involved with Canadian society; this will be primarily achieved through the CCTFA Foundation & the Look Good Feel Better program.
Finances: Annual Operating Budget: $500,000-$1.5 Million
Membership: 64 active companies + 79 associate companies + 10 retail private brand companies + 14 custom manufacturer members
Chief Officer(s):
Myles Robinson, Chair

Canadian Cosmetics Careers Association Inc. (CCCA)
48 Fenton Lane, Port Hope ON L1A 0A3
Tel: 416-410-9175
www.cccacosmetics.com
Overview: A small national organization
Mission: To advance professional development in the cosmetics industry; to provide opportunities for development in the Canadian cosmetics industry through accreditation
Activities: Offering the cosmetics correspondence course
Publications:
• Canadian Cosmetics Careers Association Inc. Membership Roster
Type: Directory; Frequency: Annually
Profile: Listing of current members for all members
• The CCCA [Canadian Cosmetics Careers Association Inc.] Newsletter
Type: Newsletter; Frequency: 3 pa
Profile: Information about events, new products, reviews, awards, trends in the retail environment, association news, & member profiles

Canadian Council for Aboriginal Business (CCAB) / Conseil canadien pour le commerce autochtone
#310, Berkeley St., Toronto ON M5A 4J5
Tel: 416-961-8663; Fax: 416-961-3995
info@caab.com
www.ccab.com
www.facebook.com/CanadianCouncilforAboriginalBusiness
twitter.com/ccab_national
Previous Name: Canadian Council for Native Business
Overview: A medium-sized national charitable organization founded in 1984
Mission: To promote full participation of Aboriginal communities in the Canadian economy
Finances: Funding Sources: Private sector
Staff Member(s): 9
Membership: 550+; Fees: $1,000 small business; $2,500-$5,000 business; $7,500-$10,000 partner business
Activities: Providing tools, training, network building, major business awards & national events; Internships: Yes; Speaker Service: Yes
Chief Officer(s):
J.P. Gladu, President & CEO, 416-961-8663 Ext. 235
jpgladu@ccab.com
David Abbott, Vice President, Operations, 416-961-8663 Ext. 223
dabbott@ccab.com
Ken Montour, Manager, Membership Relations, 416-961-8663 Ext. 229
kmontour@ccab.com

The Canadian Council for Accreditation of Pharmacy Programs (CCAPP) / Le Conseil canadien de l'agrément des programmes de pharmacie
Leslie Dan Faculty of Pharmacy, University of Toronto, #1207, 144 College St., Toronto ON M5S 3M2
Tel: 416-946-5055; Fax: 416-978-8511
ccappinfo@phm.utoronto.ca
www.ccapp-accredit.ca
Overview: A medium-sized national organization founded in 1992
Mission: To accredit pharmacy academic programs offered at Canadian universities
Staff Member(s): 2
Chief Officer(s):
Wayne Hindmarsh, Executive Director, 416-946-5055, Fax: 416-978-8511
Catherine Schuster, Coordinator, Pharmacy Technician Programs Accreditation
Publications:
• Annual Report & Directory of Accredited Programs [publication of The Canadian Council for Accreditation of Pharmacy Programs]
Frequency: Annually
Profile: Annual report features a list of approved Faculties of Pharmacy

Canadian Council for Aviation & Aerospace (CCAA) / Conseil canadien de l'aviation et de l'aérospatiale
#105, 1785 Alta Vista Dr., Ottawa ON K1G 3Y6
Tel: 613-727-8272; Fax: 613-727-7018
Toll-Free: 800-448-9715
www.avaerocouncil.ca
Previous Name: Canadian Aviation Maintenance Council
Overview: A medium-sized national licensing organization founded in 1992
Mission: To develop occupational training standards & facilitate the implementation of a human resources strategy for the Canadian Aviation Maintenance Industry
Finances: Annual Operating Budget: $250,000-$500,000; Funding Sources: Aviation maintenance industry; Human Resources Development Canada; Federal government
Membership: 1,000-4,999; Committees: CCAA Board of Directors; CCAA Audit; CCAA Nominating; CCAA Accreditation Board; CCAA Certification Board; CCAA National Standing Trade Advisory; CCAA Youth Internship Advisory (YIAC)
Activities: Certification; accreditation; training; youth programs; Internships: Yes
Chief Officer(s):
Robert Donald, Executive Director, 613-727-8272 Ext. 222
rdonald@avaerocouncil.ca

Canadian Council for Human Resources in the Environment Industry See Environmental Careers Organization of Canada

Canadian Council for International Co-operation (CCIC) / Conseil canadien pour la coopération internationale
39 McArthur Ave., Ottawa ON K1L 8L7
Tel: 613-241-7007; Fax: 613-241-5302
Other Communication: www.flickr.com/photos/ccciccic
info@ccic.ca
www.ccic.ca
www.facebook.com/ccciccic
twitter.com/CCCICCIC
www.youtube.com/user/CCICable
Overview: A large national organization founded in 1968
Mission: To work globally to achieve sustainable human development; To seek to end global poverty; To promote social justice & human dignity for all
Finances: Funding Sources: Federal government
4 volunteer(s)
Membership: 80 organizations; Fees: Schedule available; Member Profile: Non-profit organizations working in Canada & overseas, including religious & secular development groups, professional associations, & labour unions; These work with NGOs, cooperatives, & citizens' groups in Africa, Asia, & Latin America to meet basic needs for food, shelter, education, health, & sanitation; Many groups conduct policy research & campaign with their southern partners for fair trade, global security, children's rights, biodiversity, or the forgiveness of multilateral debt; Some members work exclusively in Canada, designing education materials for use in classrooms & resource centres; All members must adhere to a Code of Ethics which governs their financial management, communications with the public, & administration
Activities: Monitoring & analyzing federal policies on foreign affairs, aid, trade, debt & defence & communicating findings to members & the public; Engaging Canadians in a collective search for development alternatives; Internships: Yes; Speaker Service: Yes
Chief Officer(s):
Julia Sánchez, President & CEO
jsanchez@ccic.ca
Anna Campos, Officer, Finance & Administration
acampos@ccic.ca
Jessica Ruano, Officer, Communications
jruano@ccic.ca
Fraser Reilly-King, Senior Policy Analyst
freillyking@ccic.ca
Publications:
• Au Courant [a publication of the Canadian Council for International Co-operation]
Type: Newsletter; Frequency: Semiannually; ISSN: 118-604X
Profile: News, analysis, & opinion about domestic & international economic policy, development aid, & foreign policy
• Who's Who in International Development [a publication of the Canadian Council for International Co-operation]
Type: Directory
Profile: Listing of CCIC members working to end global poverty

Canadian Council for Native Business See Canadian Council for Aboriginal Business

The Canadian Council for Public-Private Partnerships (CCPPP) / Le Conseil canadien pour les partenariats public-privé
#608, 55 University Ave., Toronto ON M5J 2H7
Tel: 416-861-0500
partners@pppcouncil.ca
www.pppcouncil.ca
ca.linkedin.com/company/the-canadian-council-for-public-private-partnerships
twitter.com/pppcouncil
www.youtube.com/user/CCPPPVideo

Overview: A medium-sized national organization founded in 1993
Mission: To act as a proponent for improvements in the quality & cost of public services provided to Canadians through innovative partnerships between the public & private sectors
Affiliation(s): Federation of Canadian Municipalities; Canadian Water & Wastewater Association
Finances: *Annual Operating Budget:* $250,000-$500,000; *Funding Sources:* Membership fees
Staff Member(s): 7
Membership: 400 organizations; *Fees:* $380 individual; $350 public/non-profit; $1,000 corporate; $3,650 sponsor; *Committees:* Executive; Communications & Government Relations; Awards; Research; Nominating
Activities: *Library:* by appointment
Chief Officer(s):
Mark Romoff, President & CEO, 416-861-9917
mromoff@pppcouncil.ca
Dave Trafford, Director, Communications & Media Relations, 416-861-0605 Ext. 210
dtrafford@pppcouncil.ca
Awards:
• CCPPP National Awards
To honour governments &/or public institutions & their private sector partners who have demonstrated excellence & innovation in the establishment of public-private partnerships
Meetings/Conferences:
• The Canadian Council for Public-Private Partnerships 2018 26th Annual Conference, November, 2018
Scope: National

Canadian Council for Reform Judaism (CCRJ)
#301, 3845 Bathurst St., Toronto ON M3H 3N2
Tel: 416-630-0375; *Fax:* 416-630-5089
ccrj@ccrj.ca
www.ccrj.ca
www.linkedin.com/groups?gid=1300517
www.facebook.com/reformjudaism
twitter.com/urj
www.youtube.com/urjweb
Previous Name: Canadian Council of Reform Rabbis
Overview: A medium-sized national organization
Mission: The CCRJ is the Canadian region of the Union for Reform Judasim Congregations, & serves as the umbrella organization for Reform Judaism in Canada, representing about 30,000 affiliated members in 27 Reform Congregations.
Member of: Union for Reform Judaism
Chief Officer(s):
Paul Leszner, President
CCRJPresident@ccrj.ca
Morris Cooper, Vice-President
CCRJVicePresident@ccrj.ca
Ron Lubarsky, Secretary/Treasurer
ron.lubarsky@rogers.com

Canadian Council for Small Business & Entrepreneurship (CCSBE) / Conseil canadien des PME et de l'entrepreneuriat (CCPME)
c/o Pat Sargeant, Women's Enterprise Centre of Manitoba, #100, 207 Donald St., Winnipeg MB R3C 1M5
Tel: 204-988-1873; *Fax:* 902-988-1871
ccsbesecretariat@wecm.ca
www.ccsbe.org
www.linkedin.com/groups/CCSBE-CCPME-2431087
twitter.com/CCSBE2013
Overview: A medium-sized national organization founded in 1979
Mission: The Canadian Council for Small Business and Entrepreneurship (CCSBE-CCPME) is a national membership-based organization promoting and advancing the developmet of small business and entreprenurship through research, education and training, networking, and dissemination of scholarly and policy-oriented information.
Affiliation(s): International Council for Small Business
Chief Officer(s):
Sandra Altner, President
saltner@wecm.ca
Francine Schlosser, Secretary
fschloss@uwindsor.ca
Meetings/Conferences:
• Canadian Council for Small Business & Entrepreneurship 2018 Conference, May, 2018, Dalhousie University, Halifax, NS
Scope: National

Canadian Council for the Advancement of Education (CCAE) / Le Conseil canadien pour l'avancement de l'éducation
#310, 4 Cataraqui St., Kingston ON K7K 1Z7
Tel: 613-531-9213; *Fax:* 613-531-0626
admin@ccaecanada.org
www.ccaecanada.org
twitter.com/CCAECanada
Overview: A medium-sized national organization founded in 1993
Mission: To promote excellence in educational advancement through networking opportunities, professional development, & mutual support
Finances: *Annual Operating Budget:* $500,000-$1.5 Million; *Funding Sources:* Membership fees
Membership: 1,000-4,999; *Fees:* Schedule available; *Member Profile:* Representatives of Canadian universities, colleges, institutes, & independent schools who may be employed in alumni administration, communications, fundraising, external relations, advancement services, public affairs, enrolment management, or related disciplines
Chief Officer(s):
Mark Hazlett, Executive Director
haz@ccaecanada.org
Melana Soroka, President
Kathy Arney, Vice-President
kathy_arney@banff.centre.ca
Kathy Butler, Vice-President
kbutler@okanagan.bc.ca
Ivan Muzychka, Vice-President
ivanm@mun.ca
Awards:
• Canadian Council for the Advancement of Education Prix D'Excellence
Deadline: March
• Canadian Council for the Advancement of Education Paul Webb Scholarship
To fund professional development for a person working in the area of alumni relations *Deadline:* April; *Amount:* $500
• TD Insurance Meloche Monnex Fellowships in Advancement
For persons judged to be best suited to work in the field of educational advancement, based upon qualities of intellect, character, aptitude, & relevant experience *Deadline:* January *Contact:* Terry Cockerline & Randy Paquette, Co-Chairs, E-mail: fellowships@ccaecanada.org
• Canadian Council for the Advancement of Education Ontario Regional Chapter Scholarship
To promote professional development within the advancement profession *Eligibility:* Candidate must be employed by a CCAE member institution in Ontario *Location:* Ontario *Deadline:* April; *Amount:* $500
• Canadian Council for the Advancement of Education Richard Lim Professional Development Scholarship
To promote integration between the different areas of advancement *Eligibility:* A person employed by a Canadian Council for the Advancement of Education member institution in Ontario, who wishes to attend a professional seminar, workshop, or conference within a different stream of the advancement profession from the position presently held *Location:* Ontario *Deadline:* April; *Amount:* $500
Meetings/Conferences:
• Canadian Council for the Advancement of Education National Conference 2018, June, 2018, Westin Nova Scotian Hotel, Halifax, NS
Scope: National
Description: An annual national gathering, with keynote speakers, plenary sessions, roundtables, & the presentation of awards

Canadian Council for the Americas (CCA) / Conseil Canadien pour les Amériques
TD Centre, PO Box 1175, 77 King St. West, Toronto ON M5K 1P2
Tel: 416-367-4313
info@ccacanada.com
www.ccacanada.com
www.linkedin.com/company/canadian-council-for-the-americas
www.facebook.com/CCACanada
twitter.com/CCACanada
www.youtube.com/user/CCATorontoOffice
Overview: A medium-sized international organization founded in 1987
Mission: To address Canadian political & economic issues, particularly trade & investment; To foster stronger economic ties between Canada & the regions of Latin America & the Caribbean
Finances: *Funding Sources:* Membership dues; events
Staff Member(s): 2
Membership: 40; *Fees:* $100 individual; $250 corporate; *Member Profile:* Canadian companies & financial institutions interested in trade outside of Canada
Chief Officer(s):
Jonathan Hausman, Chair

Canadian Council for the Americas - British Columbia (CCA-BC)
1295 Johnston St., Vancouver BC V6H 3R9
Tel: 604-868-8678
info@cca-bc.com
www.cca-bc.com
Overview: A medium-sized international organization founded in 1987
Mission: To increase business & trade between British Columbia & Latin America
Staff Member(s): 4; 10 volunteer(s)
Membership: 550; *Fees:* $150-$5,000
Activities: Hosting events
Chief Officer(s):
André Nudelman, Chair
anudelman@cca-bc.com

Canadian Council for Tobacco Control (CCTC) / Conseil canadien pour le contrôle du tabac
#508, 75 Albert St., Ottawa ON K1P 5E7
Tel: 613-567-3050; *Fax:* 613-567-2730
Toll-Free: 800-267-5234
www.facebook.com/158829997464616
twitter.com/CdnCouncilTC
Previous Name: Canadian Council on Smoking & Health
Overview: A medium-sized national charitable organization founded in 1974
Mission: To envision a strong & effective tobacco control movement; To diminish the adverse impact to the health of Canadians caused by tobacco industry products; To increase the effectiveness & capacity of individuals & organizations involved in tobacco control, to achieve a smoke free society in Canada; To prevent tobaccco use; To persuade & help smokers to stop using tobacco products; To educate Canadians about the marketing strategies & tactics of the tobacco industry & the adverse effects tobacco products have on the health of Canadians
Finances: *Funding Sources:* Federal & provincial governments
Activities: *Awareness Events:* National Non-Smoking Week/Weedless Wednesday, Jan.; World No Tobacco Day, May; *Speaker Service:* Yes; *Library:* National Clearing House for Tobacco & Health; Not open to public
Awards:
• Award of Excellence

Canadian Council of Archives (CCA) / Conseil canadien des archives
#1912, 130 Albert St., Ottawa ON K1P 5G4
Tel: 613-565-1222; *Fax:* 613-565-5445
Toll-Free: 866-254-1403
info@archivescanada.ca
archivescanada.ca/AboutCCA
Overview: A medium-sized national charitable organization founded in 1985
Mission: To facilitate development of Canadian archival system & its coordination; To make recommendations to system's operation & financing; To develop & facilitate implementation & management of programs to assist archival community; To communicate archival needs & concerns to decision-makers, researchers, & the general public.
Finances: *Funding Sources:* Federal government
Membership: *Member Profile:* National archivist & delegates from 2 national associations & provincial/territorial Council of Archives; *Committees:* Copyright; Canadian Committee on Archival Description; Preservation; Standards
Activities: Control of Holdings program; Professional Development & Training program; Special Projects program; Preservation Management program; Preservation Training & Information program.
Chief Officer(s):
Lara Wilson, Chair
ljwilson@uvic.ca
Christina Nichols, Executive Director
cnichols@archivescanada.ca

Canadian Council of Cardiovascular Nurses (CCCN) / Conseil canadien des infirmières et infirmiers en nursing cardiovasculaire (CCINC)
#202, 300 March Rd., Ottawa ON K2K 2E2

Canadian Associations / Canadian Council of Christian Charities (CCCC)

Tel: 613-599-9210; Fax: 613-595-1155
info@cccn.ca
www.cccn.ca
www.facebook.com/124535634406687
Overview: A medium-sized national organization founded in 1973
Mission: To promote & maintain high standards of cardiovascular nursing through education, research, health promotion, strategic alliances, & advocacy
Member of: Canadian Nursing Association; Canadian Society of Association Executives
Affiliation(s): Heart & Stroke Foundation of Canada; Canadian Coalition for High Blood Pressure Prevention & Control; Canadian Cardiovascular Society
Finances: Funding Sources: Membership fees; Sponsorships; Conference registration
Staff Member(s): 2; 20 volunteer(s)
Membership: 1,300; Fees: $85 regular; $42 RN students; Member Profile: Canadian nurses interested in heart health; Practicing nurses in the cardiovascular field; Committees: Professional Education; Research; Health Promotion; Board of Directors
Activities: Developing ongoing professional nursing education in the cardiovascular field; Promoting cardiovascular nursing research; Participating in health promotion activities; Collaborating with other organizations on issues involving cardiovascular nursing
Chief Officer(s):
David Miriguay, Executive Director, 613-599-9210 Ext. 1
david@cccn.ca
Awards:
• Lynne Child Cardiovascular Nursing Certification Award
• Mae Gallant Cardiovascular Nursing Student Award
• Cardiovascular Nursing Clinical Excellence Award
• Cardiovascular Nursing Research Excellence Award
• Cardiovascular Nursing Leadership Excellence Award
• Cardiovascular Nursing Health Promotion & Advocacy Excellence Award
• Honorary Lifetime Member Award
Meetings/Conferences:
• Canadian Council of Cardiovascular Nurses 2018 Spring Nursing Conference & Annual General Meeting, May, 2018, DoubleTree Fallsview Resort & Spa, Niagara Falls, ON
Scope: National
• Canadian Council of Cardiovascular Nurses 2018 Fall Conference, 2018
Scope: National
Description: Held during the Canadian Cardiovascular Congress; includes sessions showcasing the wide range of clinical & research work in the cardiovascular research field
Publications:
• Canadian Council of Cardiovascular Nurses Annual Report
Type: Yearbook; Frequency: Annually
Profile: A review of the council's year
• Canadian Council of Cardiovascular Nurses Newsletter
Type: Newsletter; Frequency: Monthly
Profile: Current events of the council, including conferences, award presentations, & members in the news
• Canadian Journal of Cardiovascular Nursing (CJCN)
Type: Journal; Frequency: Quarterly; Accepts Advertising; Editor: Suzanne Fredericks; Price: Free for members of the Canadian Council of Cardiovascular Nurses; $75 non-members
Profile: The peer reviewed official publication of the Canadian Journal of Cardiovascular Nursing, featuring original articles about healthcare issues related to cardiovascular health & illness & research information

Canadian Council of Chief Executives; Business Council on National Issues See Business Council of Canada

Canadian Council of Christian Charities (CCCC)
#1, 43 Howard Ave., Elmira ON N3B 2C9
Tel: 519-669-5137; Fax: 519-669-3291
www.cccc.org
www.linkedin.com/company/canadian-council-of-christian-charities
www.facebook.com/CCCCCharities
twitter.com/ccccharities
Overview: A medium-sized national licensing charitable organization founded in 1972
Mission: To encourage the Canadian Christian community to a biblical stewardship of all He has entrusted to us by integrating practical concepts of administration, development & accountability with the spiritual concerns of ministry
Finances: Annual Operating Budget: $500,000-$1.5 Million
Staff Member(s): 17; 56 volunteer(s)
Membership: 3,300; Fees: $30-$765+
Activities: Education; training on legal, financial & leadership issues
Chief Officer(s):
John Pellowe, Chief Executive Officer
Publications:
• CCCC [Canadian Council of Christian Charities] Bulletin
Type: Newsletter; Frequency: 5-7 pa; Accepts Advertising; Editor: Heather Hanson; ISSN: 0838-6803; Price: Free with CCCC membership; $45 non-members
Profile: CCCC news & information & legislative developments for executives, administrators, & stewardship representatives of Christian charitiesoperating under Canadian law
• Charities Handbook
Price: Free with CCCC membership; $95 non-members

The Canadian Council of Churches (CCC) / Le conseil Canadien des églises
47 Queen's Park Cres. E, 3rd Fl., Toronto ON M5S 2C3
Tel: 416-972-9494; Fax: 416-927-0405
Toll-Free: 866-822-7645
info@councilofchurches.ca
www.councilofchurches.ca
www.facebook.com/CCC.CCE
twitter.com/ccc_cce
Overview: A large national charitable organization founded in 1944
Mission: To represent the belief in the Lord Jesus Christ as God & Saviour; To fulfill together the common calling to the glory of one God, Father, Son & Holy Spirit
Affiliation(s): Citizens for Public Justice; Friendship Ministries Canada; Oikocredit; The Yonge Street Mission
Finances: Funding Sources: Member churches
Staff Member(s): 6; 2 volunteer(s)
Membership: 25 denominations of Anglican, Evangelical, Free Church, Eastern & Oriental Orthodox, Protestant & Catholic traditions
Activities: Sponsoring of Project Ploughshares; Maintaining dialogue with all faith groups
Chief Officer(s):
Alyson Barnett-Cowan, President

Canadian Council of Conservative Synagogues (CCCS)
37 Southbourne Ave., Toronto ON M3H 1A4
Tel: 416-635-5340
canadianccs.weebly.com
Overview: A small national organization
Mission: To support & promote cooperative programming among members
Membership: 5
Activities: Developing youth programs
Chief Officer(s):
Robyn Esar, Coordinator, Youth
youth@canadianccs.org

Canadian Council of Engineering Technicians and Technologists (CCETT) See Canadian Council of Technicians & Technologists

Canadian Council of Forest Ministers (CCFM) / Conseil canadien des ministres des forêts
c/o Policy, Economics & Industry Branch, Natural Resources Canada, 580 Booth St., Ottawa ON K1A 0E4
ccfm@nrcan-rncan.gc.ca
www.ccfm.org
Mission: The Canadian Council of Ministers (CCFM) was established in 1985 to give sufficient attention to forest issues. CCFM stimulates the development of policies & initiatives for strengthening the forest sector, including the forest resource & its use. It provides leadership, addresses national & international issues & sets the direction for stewardship & sustainable management of Canada's forests. The CCFM is composed of the 14 federal, provincial & territorial ministers responsible for forests. The CCFM undertakes activities primarily through ad hoc fora, committees & working groups. CCFM initiatives include: Climate Change; Wildland Fires; Forest Pests; Forest in Mind Program; & A Vision for Canada's Forests: 2008 & Beyond. National Forestry Database Program: nfdp.ccfm.org; National Forest Information System: nfis.org
Chief Officer(s):
Amanda Dacyk, Policy Analyst, CCFM Secretariat

Canadian Council of Human Resources Associations See Chartered Professionals in Human Resources

Canadian Council of Independent Laboratories (CCIL) / Conseil canadien des laboratoires indépendants
PO Box 41027, Ottawa ON K1G 5K9
Tel: 613-746-3919; Fax: 613-746-4324
ccil@magma.ca
www.ccil.com
Overview: A medium-sized national licensing organization founded in 1993
Mission: Represents the independent testing industry in Canada.
Staff Member(s): 9
Membership: 330
Activities: Speaker Service: Yes
Chief Officer(s):
Derwyn L. Reuber, Executive Director
dreuber@ccil.com
Jeffrey Pike, President
jeffrey.pike@alsglobal.com

Canadian Council of Insurance Regulators See Financial Services Commission of Ontario

Canadian Council of Insurance Regulators (CCIR) / Conseil canadien des responsables de la réglementation d'assurance (CCRRA)
CCIR Secretariat, PO Box 85, 5160 Yonge St., Toronto ON M2N 6L9
Tel: 416-590-7290; Fax: 416-226-7878
ccir-ccrra@fsco.gov.on.ca
www.ccir-ccrra.org
Overview: A small national organization
Mission: To facilitate an effective regulatory system in Canada to serve the public interest; To enhance consumer protection
Membership: Member Profile: Regulators of insurance across Canada
Activities: Working cooperatively with other financial services regulators; Developing insurance policies; Harmonizing insurance policy & regulation across jurisdictions
Chief Officer(s):
Carolyn Rogers, Chair
Patrick Déry, Vice-Chair
Philip Howell, Vice-Chair
Doug Murphy, Vice-Chair
Carol Shelvin, Policy Manager
Publications:
• Canadian Council of Insurance Regulators Meeting Highlights
Frequency: Semiannually
Profile: Summaries of the annual Canadian Council of Insurance Regulators Spring & Fall Meetings

Canadian Council of Ministers of the Environment (CCME) / Conseil canadien des ministres de l'environnement
#360, 123 Main St., Winnipeg MB R3C 1A3
Tel: 204-948-2090
info@ccme.ca
www.ccme.ca
Mission: CCME is comprised of the environment ministers from the federal, provincial & territorial governments. These 14 ministers normally meet at least once a year to discuss national environmental priorities & determine work to be carried out under the auspices of CCME. The Council seeks to achieve positive environmental results, focusing on issues that are national in scope & that require collective attention by a number of governments. CCME aims to assist its members to meet their mandate of protecting Canada's environment. CCME serves as a principal forum for members to develop national strategies, norms, & guidelines that each environment ministry across the country can use. CCME is not another level of government regulator, but a council of government ministers holding similar responsibilities.
Finances: Annual Operating Budget: $1.5 Million-$3 Million; Funding Sources: Federal, provincial & territorial governments
Staff Member(s): 9
Membership: 1-99; Committees: Air Management; Climate Change; Water Management; Soil Quality Guildelines Task Group; Waste Management Task Group
Chief Officer(s):
Catherine McKenna, Minister, Environment & Climate Change Canada, 819-938-3813
ec.ministre-minister.ec@canada.ca
Michael Goeres, Executive Director, 204-948-2172
mgoeres@ccme.ca

Canadian Council of Montessori Administrators (CCMA)
#102, 4953 Dundas St. West, Toronto ON M9A 1B6
Tel: 416-239-1166; *Fax:* 416-239-9544
Toll-Free: 800-954-6300
ccma@bellnet.ca
www.ccma.ca
twitter.com/ccmamontessori
Overview: A medium-sized national organization
Mission: To support Montessori administrators in Canada; to offer expertise in Montessori school administration & the Montessori method of education
Membership: *Fees:* $300 + $6 per full-day student + $4 per half-day student; *Member Profile:* Montessori School Administrators
Chief Officer(s):
Terry Gouie

Canadian Council of Motor Transport Administrators (CCMTA) / Conseil canadien des administrateurs en transport motorisé (CCATM)
#404, 1111 Prince of Wales, Ottawa ON K2C 3T2
Tel: 613-736-1003; *Fax:* 613-736-1395
info@ccmta.ca
www.ccmta.ca
www.linkedin.com/company-beta/3011130
www.youtube.com/channel/UC1VcXHx1vc5z0njwotrwOZw
Overview: A medium-sized national charitable organization founded in 1940
Mission: To provide collaborative leadership in addressing Canadian road safety priorities
Finances: *Funding Sources:* Member assessments; Special projects; Membership fees
Membership: 100-499; *Fees:* $475 associate; *Member Profile:* Members elected from provincial, territorial & federal governments; associate members are elected from transportation-related organizations; *Committees:* Drivers & Vehicles; Compliance & Regulatory Affairs; Road Safety Research & Policies
Activities: Developing strategies & programs; Managing a communications network, called the Interprovincial Record Exchange system; *Rents Mailing List:* Yes
Chief Officer(s):
Allison Fradette, Executive Director, 613-736-1003 Ext. 263
afradette@ccmta.ca
Martin Rochon, Director, Administration & Services, 613-736-1003 Ext. 252
mrochon@ccmta.ca
Awards:
• Road Safety Award
Recognizes strategies aimed at reducing injury and death on Canada's roads *Eligibility:* CCMTA Members and Associates who demonstrate a commitment to reduce fatalities and serious road injuries; a unique or creative attempt to advance road safety; supports one or more of the Road Safety 2025 objectives *Deadline:* March 16 *Contact:* Martin Rochon, mrochon@ccmta.ca
• Jennie Howe Government Member Award
Honours a CCMTA member whose primary function is directly associated with the coordination, administration, regulation and control of motor vehicle transportation and highway safety; and who has made a significant contribution to CCMTA *Eligibility:* Candidate must be a CCMTA member-government representative for a minimum of three years; Program committee Chairs and Board Members are not eligible *Deadline:* March 16
• Sean McAlister Service Recognition Award
Honours an individual who has been an active member of the Board of Directors, a program committee of project group for more than five years, upon their retirement from a CCMTA volunteer poistion *Eligibility:* Retiring individuals *Contact:* Martin Rochon, mrochon@ccmta.ca
• CCMTA-Police Partnership Award
Honours the achievements and service of active police officers or units in developing key relationships involved in highway transportation safety at the local, regional, provincial/territorioal or national level *Contact:* Eileen Melnick-McCarthy, emelnick@ccmta.ca
Meetings/Conferences:
• Canadian Council of Motor Transport Administrators 2018 Annual Meeting, June, 2018, Quebec City, QC
Scope: National
Description: Educational events, an exhibition, a working forum where important decisions are made, & an excellent networking opportunity for government decision-makers & members of the private sector
Contact Information: Phone: 613-736-1003 Fax: 613-736-1395, E-mail: ccmta-secretariat@ccmta.ca
• Canadian Council of Motor Transport Administrators 2019 Annual Meeting, June, 2019, Ottawa, ON
Scope: National
Description: Educational events, an exhibition, a working forum where important decisions are made, & an excellent networking opportunity for government decision-makers & members of the private sector
Contact Information: Phone: 613-736-1003 Fax: 613-736-1395, E-mail: ccmta-secretariat@ccmta.ca
• Canadian Council of Motor Transport Administrators 2020 Annual Meeting, May, 2020, Charlottetown, PE
Scope: National
Description: Educational events, an exhibition, a working forum where important decisions are made, & an excellent networking opportunity for government decision-makers & members of the private sector
Contact Information: Phone: 613-736-1003 Fax: 613-736-1395, E-mail: ccmta-secretariat@ccmta.ca
Publications:
• CCMTA [Canadian Council of Motor Transport Administrators] Newsletter
Type: Newsletter; *Frequency:* q.; *Number of Pages:* 13; *Price:* Free download
Profile: Current projects & initiatives of CCMTA
• CCMTA [Canadian Council of Motor Transport Administrators] Year in Review
Type: Report; *Frequency:* a.; *Number of Pages:* 45; *ISBN:* 978-1-927993-21-7; *Price:* Free download
Profile: Highlights annual news, activities and achievements of the CCMTA
• Maintenance & Periodic Inspections Standards (PMVI)
Type: Guide; *Frequency:* a.; *Number of Pages:* 207; *Price:* Free download; $20 hard copy
Profile: Provides a guide to maintenance & inspection standards for Canadian motorists

Canadian Council of Muslim Theologians (CCMT)
#211, 1825 Markham Rd., Toronto ON M1B 4Z9
Tel: 416-900-0962; *Fax:* 416-981-3247
Toll-Free: 866-243-2268
info@jucanada.org
www.jucanada.org
www.facebook.com/Canadiancouncil
twitter.com/JU_Canada
Overview: A medium-sized national organization
Mission: To promote the doctrines of Islam; To preserve the Shari'ah; To obtain religious freedom; To offer religious guidance; To provide help for the poor & distressed; To sanction halal foods
Member of: Jami'yyatul Ulama Canada
Membership: *Member Profile:* Muslim scholars in the field of Shari'ah who have graduated from Islamic universities
Chief Officer(s):
Abdullah Kapodrawee, Ameer

Canadian Council of Muslim Women (CCMW) / Conseil canadien des femmes musulmanes
PO Box 154, Gananoque ON K7G 2T7
Tel: 613-382-2847
info@ccmw.com
www.ccmw.com
www.linkedin.com/company/ccmw
www.facebook.com/CCMWNational
twitter.com/ccmwcanada
Overview: A medium-sized national organization founded in 1982
Mission: To assist Muslim women in participating effectively in Canadian society; To promote mutual understanding with women of other faiths; To strengthen the bonds of sisterhood among Muslim communities & individuals; To achieve equity & empowerment for Muslim women in Canada
Finances: *Annual Operating Budget:* Less than $50,000; *Funding Sources:* Fundraising; Public funds; Government
Staff Member(s): 2; 30 volunteer(s)
Membership: 100+; *Member Profile:* Practising Muslim women
Activities: Implementing projects & toolkits; *Awareness Events:* Women Who Inspire Awards Brunch; *Speaker Service:* Yes
Chief Officer(s):
Nuzhat Jafri, President
nuzhatjafri@gmail.com
Alia Hogben, Executive Director, 613-382-2847
aliahogben@gmail.com
Awards:
• Lila Fahlman Scholarships
Eligibility: Muslim women students who are enrolled in a full-time graduate or undergraduate diploma at a Canadian college or university & involved in civic engagement or volunteer work *Deadline:* May; *Amount:* $1,000
Publications:
• CCMW [Canadian Council of Muslim Women] National Newsletter
Type: Newsletter

Canadian Council of Practical Nurse Regulators (CCPNR)
c/o College of Licensed Practical Nurses of British Columbia, #260, 3480 Gilmore Way, Burnaby BC V5G 4Y1
Tel: 778-373-3101
ccpnr@clpnbc.org
www.ccpnr.ca
Overview: A medium-sized national organization
Mission: To ensure the safety of the public through the regulation of Licensed/Registered Practical Nurses
Membership: *Committees:* Executive
Chief Officer(s):
Carina Herman, Chair
chair@ccpnr.ca

Canadian Council of Professional Certification (CCPC)
1 Edenmills Dr., Toronto ON M1E 4L1
Tel: 416-724-5339; *Fax:* 905-727-1061
www.ccpcglobal.com
www.linkedin.com/company/ccpc-global
www.facebook.com/267324543281480
twitter.com/CCPCGlobal
Also Known As: CCPC Global
Overview: A large national licensing organization
Mission: To grant certification & professional designation to qualified applicants
Membership: *Fees:* Schedule available
Activities: Offering courses & certifications in business, coaching, customer service & leadership training, counselling, nutrition management, spirituality, & community service
Awards:
• NET Institute Scholarship Program
Publications:
• Canadian Council of Professional Certification Manuals
Type: Book
Profile: A series of manuals & standards for each certification offered by the Council
Calgary - Western Canada Regional Office
#3404, 3000 Somervale Ct. SW, Calgary AB T2Y 4J2
Tel: 403-201-2123; *Fax:* 403-254-8385

Canadian Council of Professional Engineers *See* Engineers Canada

Canadian Council of Professional Fish Harvesters (CCPFH) / Conseil canadien des pêcheurs professionnels (CCPP)
#712, 1 Nicholas St., Ottawa ON K1N 7B7
Tel: 613-235-3474; *Fax:* 613-231-4313
www.ccpfh-ccpp.org
www.facebook.com/CCPFHCCPP
twitter.com/CCPFH_CCPP
Overview: A medium-sized national organization founded in 1995
Mission: To represent the interests of professional fish harvesters across Canada in their dealings with the federal, provincial & territorial governments on national issues of common concern; To act as a national industry sector council to plan & implement training & adjustment & human resources programs for the fish harvesting industry in Canada
Membership: *Member Profile:* Fish harvesters; Captains & crew members
Chief Officer(s):
Pierre Verreault, Executive Director, 613-235-3474 Ext. 223
Jean Lanteigne, President
Ronnie Heighton, Vice President
Kim Olsen, Vice President, West Coast
Bill Broderick, Vice President, East Coast
O'Neil Cloutier, Treasurer
Keith Paugh, Secretary
Publications:
• Canadian Council of Professional Fish Harvesters Newsletter
Type: Newsletter; *Frequency:* Quarterly
Profile: News & information from the council & industry

Canadian Associations / Canadian Council of Professional Geoscientists (CCPG) / Conseil Canadien des Géoscientifiques Professionnels (CCGP)

Canadian Council of Professional Geoscientists (CCPG) / Conseil Canadien des Géoscientifiques Professionnels (CCGP)
#200, 4010 Regent St., Burnaby BC V5C 6N2
Tel: 604-412-4888; *Fax:* 604-433-2494
info@ccpg.ca
www.ccpg.ca
Overview: A small national organization
Mission: To develop consistent high standards for licensure and practice of geoscience, facilitate national and international mobility, and promote the recognition of Canadian professional geoscientists.
Chief Officer(s):
Oliver Bonham, Chief Executive Officer
obonham@ccpg.ca

Canadian Council of Reform Rabbis *See* Canadian Council for Reform Judaism

Canadian Council of Snowmobile Organizations (CCSO) / Conseil canadien des organismes de motoneige (CCOM)
PO Box 21059, Thunder Bay ON P7A 8A7
Tel: 807-345-5299
ccso.ccom@tbaytel.net
www.ccso-ccom.ca
www.facebook.com/126035004176384
twitter.com/ccsosnow
Overview: A large national organization founded in 1974
Mission: To provide leadership & support to organized snowmobiling in Canada
Activities: Promoting the welfare & betterment of snowmobile recreational activities; Cooperating with provincial & federal officials, other organizations, & the public on issues affecting snowbiles; Coordinating legislative activities; Promoting a code of ethics for snowmobiling; Completing the Trans-Canadian Snowmobile Trail; *Awareness Events:* National Safety Week, January; Take a Friend Snowmobiling Week, February
Chief Officer(s):
Dennis Burns, Executive Director
Awards:
• Outstanding Snowmobile Dealership, CCSO Excellence Awards
• Outstanding Organized Snowmobile-Related Company, CCSO Excellence Awards
• Outstanding Snowmobile Tourism Promotion & Development, CCSO Excellence Awards
• Outstanding Snowmobile Club, CCSO Excellence Awards
• Outstanding Snowmobile Family, CCSO Excellence Awards
• Outstanding Snowmobiler, CCSO Excellence Awards
• Outstanding Youth - The Pete Greenlaw Award, CCSO Excellence Awards
• Outstanding Groomer Operator, CCSO Excellence Awards
• CCSO President's Award, CCSO Excellence Awards
• CCSO Environment Award - The Pat Whiteway Award, CCSO Excellence Awards
Meetings/Conferences:
• 50th Annual International Snowmobile Congress 2018, June, 2018, Halifax, NS
Scope: International
Publications:
• CCSO [Canadian Council of Snowmobile Organizations] / CCOM [Conseil canadien des organismes de motoneige] News Bulletin
Type: Newsletter

Canadian Council of Teachers of English Language Arts (CCTELA)
#10, 730 River Rd., Winnipeg MB R2M 5A4
Tel: 204-255-1676; *Fax:* 204-253-2562
cctela.52@gmail.com
www.cctela.ca
Overview: A medium-sized national organization founded in 1967
Mission: To provide a national voice in education relating to English Language Arts; to serve as a forum for communication among provincial councils concerning English Language Arts; to provide a system of communication & cooperation for teachers of English Language Arts at all levels in Canada; to encourage research, experimentation & investigation in English Language Arts teaching; to sponsor, promote & lobby for programs of benefit to Canadian students.
Affiliation(s): International Federation of Teachers of English
Finances: *Annual Operating Budget:* Less than $50,000; *Funding Sources:* Membership fees; Journal subscriptions
Staff Member(s): 1; 15 volunteer(s)

Membership: 400; *Fees:* Regular: $60; Institution: $90; Undergraduate Student or Retiree: $35; *Member Profile:* Open to teachers of English & Language Arts
Activities: *Speaker Service:* Yes
Chief Officer(s):
Linda Ferguson, Executive Director

Canadian Council of Technicians & Technologists (CCTT) / Conseil canadien des techniciens et technologues
#405, 2197 Riverside Dr., Ottawa ON K1H 7X3
Tel: 613-238-8123; *Fax:* 613-238-8822
cctt@cctt.ca
www.cctt.ca
www.linkedin.com/company/canadian-council-of-technicians-&-technologists
twitter.com/CCTTCanada
Previous Name: Canadian Council of Engineering Technicians and Technologists (CCETT)
Overview: A large national organization founded in 1973
Mission: To advocate on behalf of Canada's certified technicians & technologists; To establish & maintain national competency standards
Activities: Providing accreditation & insurance services; *Awareness Events:* National Technology Week, Nov.
Chief Officer(s):
Rick Tachuk, President & CEO, 613-238-8123 Ext. 224
rtachuk@cctt.ca
Darlene Pilon, Manager, Finance, 613-238-8123 Ext. 221
dpilon@cctt.ca
Valery Vidershpan, Manager, Projects, 613-238-8123 Ext. 225
vvidershpan@cctt.ca
Gordon Griffith, Coordinator, Programs, 613-238-8123 Ext. 223
ggriffith@cctt.ca
Meetings/Conferences:
• Canadian Council of Technicians & Technologists (CTTT) 2018 National Technology Conference, 2018
Scope: National
Publications:
• Innovation Weekly [a publication of the Canadian Council of Technicians & Technologists]
Type: Newsletter; *Frequency:* Weekly
Profile: News for technology professionals across Canada, including credential information, awards, & awareness activities

The Canadian Council of the Blind (CCB) / Le Conseil canadien des aveugles
#100, 20 James St., Ottawa ON K2P 0T6
Tel: 613-567-0311; *Fax:* 613-567-2728
Toll-Free: 877-304-0968
www.ccbnational.net
www.facebook.com/ccbnational
twitter.com/ccbnational
Overview: A medium-sized national charitable organization founded in 1944
Mission: To promote the well-being of individuals who are blind or vision-impaired through higher education, profitable employment, & social association; To create a closer relationship between blind & sighted friends; To organize a nation-wide organization of people who are blind & vision-impaired & groups of blind persons throughout Canada; To promote measures for the conservation of sight & the prevention of blindness
Affiliation(s): World Blind Union
Finances: *Funding Sources:* Telemarketing; Product sales
Membership: *Member Profile:* Registered legally blind; Persons with a condition that will lead to blindness; Deafblind persons
Activities: Providing peer support; *Awareness Events:* White Cane Week, February; *Internships:* Yes; *Speaker Service:* Yes
Chief Officer(s):
Louise Gillis, National President
Lori Fry, First Vice-President
Jim Tokos, Second Vice-President
Awards:
• Book of Fame Citation
The Book of Fame was donated to the Council in 1958 by the disbanded Comrades Club of Toronto; it contains the names & citations of outstanding blind Canadians selected yearly by the eight divisions & the National Board of Directors of the Council; each recipient of a citation is presented with a framed photograph of the appropriate page in the book
• Award of Merit
Established 1952; presented to a Canadian, blind or sighted, who has rendered outstanding work for the blind; *Amount:* A gold medal & clasp, a specially printed & bound citation & honorary life membership in the CCB

Publications:
• Canadian Council of the Blind / Le Conseil Canadien des Aveugles Newsletter
Type: Newsletter; *Frequency:* Monthly
Profile: Available electronically or in large print format, the newsletter features articles on issues affecting the blind & visually impaired, products for the blind, competition results, & CCB updates & events
• White Cane Week Magazine
Type: Magazine; *Frequency:* Annually; *Accepts Advertising*; *Editor:* Mike Potvin
Profile: CCB news & information, White Cane Week review & events, & a resource guide for the blind & vision impaired

Canadian Council of University Physical Education & Kinesiology Administrators (CCUPEKA) / Conseil canadien des administrateurs universitaires en éducation physique et kinésiologie (CCAUEPK)
c/o Dr. J. Starkes, Department of Kinesiology, McMaster University, Hamilton ON L8S 4K1
www.ccupeka.ca
Overview: A small national organization founded in 1971 overseen by Universities Canada
Mission: To serve as an accrediting body for physical education & kinesiology programs at universities in Canada; To offer a voice for academics, through lobbying initiatives
Member of: Universities Canada
Membership: *Member Profile:* Administrators of physical education & kinesiology programs at Canadian universities
Activities: Offering a forum for discussion among members
Chief Officer(s):
Angela Belcastro, President

Canadian Council on 4-H Clubs *See* Canadian 4-H Council

Canadian Council on Africa
#700, 1 Rideau St., Ottawa ON K1N 8S7
Tel: 613-565-3011
www.ccafrica.ca
www.linkedin.com/groups/4471230
www.facebook.com/CCAFRICA.CCAFRIQUE
twitter.com/ccafrica2012
www.youtube.com/ccafrica1
Also Known As: CCAfrica
Overview: A medium-sized international organization founded in 2002
Mission: To promote trade & investment between Canada & Africa
Chief Officer(s):
Nola Kianza, President & CEO
nola.kianza@ccafrica.ca
Chris Kianza, Vice-President, Business Development & Member Relations
chris.kianza@ccafrica.ca
Publications:
• The Rising Africa [a publication of the Canadian Council on Africa]
Type: Magazine
Québec Office
#123, 1320 boul Graham, Ville Mont-Royal QC H3P 3C8
Tel: 514-758-3011
Chief Officer(s):
Leonie Perron, Director, International Development & Events
leonie.perron@ccafrica.ca
Toronto - Central Office
161 Bay St., 27th Fl., Toronto ON M5J 2S1
Tel: 416-572-2129
Western Office
#102, 10208 - 120 St., Edmonton AB T5K 2W2
Tel: 780-915-1110
Chief Officer(s):
Frank Kense, Vice-President
frank.kense@ccafrica.ca

Canadian Council on Animal Care (CCAC) / Conseil canadien de protection des animaux (CCPA)
#800, 190 O'Connor St., Ottawa ON K2P 2R3
Tel: 613-238-4031; *Fax:* 613-238-2837
ccac@ccac.ca
www.ccac.ca
Overview: A medium-sized national organization founded in 1968
Mission: To act on behalf of the people of Canada to ensure, through programs of education, assessment & persuasion, that the use of animals in Canada, where necessary for research, teaching & testing, employs physical & psychological care

according to acceptable scientific standards; To promote an increased level of knowledge, awareness, & sensitivity to the relevant ethical principles
Membership: 22 organizations; *Committees:* Planning & Priorities; Finance; Guidelines; Education & Training; Assessments
Activities: *Library:* Open to public by appointment
Chief Officer(s):
Louise Desjardins, Executive Director, 613-238-4031 Ext. 224
ldesjardins@ccac.ca
Michael Baar, Director, Assessment & Certification, 613-238-4031 Ext. 226
mbaar@ccac.ca
Gilly Griffin, Director, Standards, 613-238-4031 Ext. 225
ggriffin@ccac.ca
Sandra MacInnis, Director, Public Affairs & Communications, 613-238-4031 Ext. 237
smacinnis@ccac.ca
Felicetta Celenza, Coordinator, Events, 613-238-4031 Ext. 252
fcelenza@ccac.ca
Publications:
• Canadian Council on Animal Care Workshop Proceedings
• CCAC [Canadian Council on Animal Care] Annual Report
Frequency: Annually
• CCAC [Canadian Council on Animal Care] Guidelines
Frequency: Irregular
Profile: Topics include procurement of animals used in science, laboratory animal facilities, the care and use of wildlife, antibody production, institutional animal user training,transgenic animals, & animal use protocol review
• CCAC [Canadian Council on Animal Care] Guide to the Care & Use of Experimental Animals
• Resource: The Newsletter of the Canadian Council on Animal Care (CCAC)
Type: Newsletter; *Frequency:* Semiannually; *Editor:* Clément Gauthier, PhD; *ISSN:* 0700-5237
Profile: Articles about laboratory animal science; news about current issues & events related to the CCAC

The Canadian Council on Continuing Education in Pharmacy (CCCEP) / Le conseil canadien de l'éducation permanente en pharmacie
#210, 2002 Quebec Ave., Saskatoon SK S7K 1W4
Tel: 306-652-7790; *Fax:* 306-652-7795
Other Communication: Executive Director e-mail:
exec.dir@cccep.ca
cccep@cccep.ca
www.cccep.ca
Overview: A small national licensing organization founded in 1973
Mission: To act as the national coordinating & accrediting body for continuing education in pharmacy in Canada; To enhance the quality of continuing pharmacy education; To advance pharmacy practice
Finances: *Annual Operating Budget:* $250,000-$500,000
Membership: 15; *Member Profile:* Organizations interested in promoting the quality of continuing professional development for pharmacy professionals
Activities: Establishing policy & criteria for accreditation; Accrediting continuing education programs provided to pharmacists; Promoting the standardization of continuing pharmacy education
Chief Officer(s):
Barbara Thomas, President
Publications:
• The Canadian Council on Continuing Education in Pharmacy Annual Report
Type: Yearbook; *Frequency:* Annually

Canadian Council on Ecological Areas (CCEA)
c/o Environmental Stewardship, Environment & Climate Change Canada, #3, 351, boul St-Joseph, Gatineau QC K1A 0H3
Tel: 819-934-6064; *Fax:* 819-994-4445
mark.richardson@ec.gc.ca
www.ccea.org
Overview: A small national organization founded in 1982
Mission: To facilitate the establishment of a comprehensive network of protected areas which are linked together in a system that will protect Canada's terrestrial & aquatic diversity in perpetuity
Chief Officer(s):
Mark Richardson, Sec.-Manager
mark.richardson@ec.gc.ca

Canadian Council on Health Services Accreditation; Canadian Council on Health Facilities Accreditation *See* Accreditation Canada

Canadian Council on International Law (CCIL) / Conseil canadien de droit international (CCDI)
275 Bay St., Ottawa ON K1R 5Z5
Tel: 613-235-0442; *Fax:* 613-232-8228
manager@ccil-ccdi.ca
www.ccil-ccdi.ca
www.linkedin.com/groups/Canadian-Council-on-International-Law-4787358?gid=4787358&mostPopular=&trk=tyah
www.facebook.com/240331419338849
www.twitter.com/ccil_ccdi
Overview: A small international charitable organization founded in 1972
Mission: To bring together scholars of international law & organizations engaged in teaching & research at Canadian universities; To encourage & conduct studies in international law with a view to its progressive development & codification; To foster the study of legal aspects of Canada's international problems & to advocate their solution in accordance with existing or developing principles of international law.
Affiliation(s): Société québécoise de droit international; American Society of International Law; Japanese Association of International Law
Finances: *Annual Operating Budget:* $50,000-$100,000; *Funding Sources:* Membership fees, donations, government project funding
Staff Member(s): 1; 24 volunteer(s)
Membership: 400; *Fees:* $85 individual; $45 student; *Member Profile:* Leading scholars; students of international law; government & practising lawyers from both public & private sectors
Activities: Speakers series; *Speaker Service:* Yes; Library
Chief Officer(s):
Adrienne Jarabek, President
Elizabeth Macaulay, Manager
manager@ccil-ccdi.ca
Awards:
• John E. Read Medal
• Ronald St. John Macdonald Young Scholars Award
Meetings/Conferences:
• Canadian Council on International Law 47th Annual Conference, 2018
Scope: International

Canadian Council on Rehabilitation & Work (CCRW) / Le Conseil canadien de la réadaptation et du travail (CCRT)
#105, 477 Mount Pleasant Rd., Toronto ON M4S 2L9
Tel: 416-260-3060; *Fax:* 416-260-3093
Toll-Free: 800-664-0925; *TTY:* 416-260-9223
info@ccrw.org
www.ccrw.org
www.linkedin.com/company/2458107
www.facebook.com/CCRW.org
twitter.com/ccrw
Overview: A medium-sized national charitable organization founded in 1976
Mission: To improve employment opportunities for persons with disabilities in Canada; To promote the equitable & meaningful employment of persons with disabilities
Activities: Connecting employers with job seekers who have disabilities; Offering an ethno-cultural portal for youth with disabilities; Assisting workplaces, with the Job Accommodation Service; Conducting research in the area of employment for people with disabilities; Providing an employment program for employers & job seekers, known as the Workplace Essential Skills Partnership; Creating awareness of skilled trade careers for youth, by developing skilled trades information & workshops
Chief Officer(s):
Maureen Haan, President & Chief Executive Officer, 416-260-3060 Ext. 222
mhaan@ccrw.org
Monica Winkler, Senior Administrator, 416-260-3060 Ext. 227
mwinkler@ccrw.org
Publications:
• Ability & Enterprise (A&E) [a publication of the Canadian Council on Rehabilitation & Work]
Type: Newsletter
Profile: CCRW news & information
• CCRW [Canadian Council on Rehabilitation & Work] Annual Report
Type: Yearbook; *Frequency:* Annually

Canadian Council on Smoking & Health *See* Canadian Council for Tobacco Control

Canadian Council on Social Development (CCSD) / Conseil canadien de développement social (CCDS)
PO Box 13713, Kanata ON K2K 1X6
Tel: 613-236-8977
info@ccsd.ca
www.ccsd.ca
Previous Name: Canadian Welfare Council
Overview: A large national charitable organization founded in 1920
Mission: To develop & promote progressive social policies, on issues such as child well-being, poverty, housing, employment, cultural diversity, & social inclusion
Finances: *Funding Sources:* Membership fee; Donations; Sponsorships; United Way; Research contracts; Sale of publications
Activities: Conducting research; Providing information; Consulting with others involved in the field; Engaging in advocacy activities; Educating the public
Chief Officer(s):
Peggy Taillon, President & CEO, 613-236-8977 Ext. 22
taillon@ccsd.ca
Katherine Scott, Vice-President, Research & Policy, 613-236-8977 Ext. 21
scott@ccsd.ca
Nancy Shipman, Vice-President, Strategic Communications & Social Media, 613-236-8977 Ext. 29
shipman@ccsd.ca
Michel Frojmovic, Manager, Community Data Program, 613-236-8977 Ext. 23
Publications:
• Canadian Fact Book on Poverty [a publication of the Canadian Council on Social Development]
Frequency: Irregular
• CCSD [Canadian Council on Social Development] Annual Report
Type: Yearbook; *Frequency:* Annually
• Personal Security Index [a publication of the Canadian Council on Social Development]
Frequency: Irregular
• Progress of Canada's Children & Youth [a publication of Canadian Council on Social Development]
Frequency: Irregular

Canadian Counselling & Psychotherapy Association (CCPA) / L'Association canadienne de counseling et de psychothérapie (ACCP)
#6, 203 Colonnade Rd. South, Ottawa ON K2E 7K3
Tel: 613-237-1099; *Fax:* 613-237-9786
Toll-Free: 877-765-5565
www.ccpa-accp.ca
www.facebook.com/CCPA.ACCP
twitter.com/ccpa_accp
Previous Name: Canadian Counselling Association
Overview: A medium-sized national organization founded in 1965
Mission: To enhance the counselling profession in Canada; To promote policies & practices which support the provision of accessible, competent, & accountable counselling services throughout the human lifespan, & in a manner sensitive to the pluralistic nature of society
Finances: *Funding Sources:* Membership dues
Staff Member(s): 11
Membership: 4,600; *Fees:* Schedule available; *Member Profile:* Professionally trained counsellors in fields of education, employment & career development, social work, business, industry, mental health, public service agencies, government & private practice; *Committees:* Executive; Governance; Risk Management; Quality Assurance & Sustainability; Regulation & Policy; Appeals; Ethics; Certification; Awards
Activities: Organizing annual conference
Chief Officer(s):
Natasha Caverley, President
president@ccpa-accp.ca
Barbara MacCallum, Chief Executive Officer
bmaccallum@ccpa-accp.ca
Meetings/Conferences:
• Canadian Counselling and Psychotherapy Association 2018 Conference, May, 2018, Delta Hotel, Winnipeg, MB
Scope: National
Attendance: 5000+
Contact Information:
www.ccpa-accp.ca/continuing-education/annual-conference

Canadian Associations / Canadian Country Music Association (CCMA) / Association de la musique country canadienne

Alberta & Northwest Territories Chapter
AB
Chief Officer(s):
Kathy Offet Gartner, President
president@abnwtchapter.ca

British Columbia Chapter
BC
www.ccpa-accp.ca/en/chapters/britishcolumbia
Chief Officer(s):
Paul Yeung, President

Career Development Chapter
www.ccpa-accp.ca/en/chapters/careercounsellors
Chief Officer(s):
Jessica Isenor, President
jisen010@uottawa.ca

Counsellor Educators Chapter
www.ccpa-accp.ca/en/chapters/counsellereducator
Chief Officer(s):
Patrice Keats, President

Creative Arts in Counselling Chapter
www.ccpa-accp.ca/en/chapters/creativeartsincounselling
Chief Officer(s):
Amy Mackenzie, President
amy.mackenzie@gmail.com

Indigenous Circle Chapter
www.ccpa-accp.ca/chapters/indigenous-circle
Chief Officer(s):
Jamie Warren, President
jwarrencounselling@gmail.com

National Capital Region Chapter
Ottawa ON
Chief Officer(s):
Nicholas Renaud, President
nicholas.renaud@gmail.com

Pastoral & Spiritual Care in Counselling Chapter
www.ccpa-accp.ca/en/chapters/pastoralspiritualcare
Chief Officer(s):
Gerard Vardy, President

Private Practitioners Chapter
www.ccpa-accp.ca/en/chapters/privatepractitioners
Chief Officer(s):
Corrine Hendricken-Eldershaw, President
corrinealz@eastlink.ca

School Counsellors Chapter
www.ccpa-accp.ca/en/chapters/schoolcounsellors
Chief Officer(s):
Belinda Josephson, President
gjosephson@eastlink.ca

Social Justice Chapter
www.ccpa-accp.ca/en/chapters/socialjustice
Chief Officer(s):
Linda Wheeldon, Chair
linda.wheeldon@acadiau.ca
Andria Hill-Lehr, Chair
andrialehr@yahoo.ca

Canadian Counselling Association *See* Canadian Counselling & Psychotherapy Association

Canadian Country Music Association (CCMA) / Association de la musique country canadienne
#200, 120 Adelaide St. East, Toronto ON M5C 1K9
Tel: 416-947-1331; *Fax:* 416-947-5924
country@ccma.org
www.ccma.org
www.facebook.com/CCMAOfficial
twitter.com/ccmaofficial
Overview: A medium-sized national organization founded in 1976
Mission: To protect the heritage & advocate the development of Canadian country music both in Canada & worldwide
Finances: Funding Sources: Membership dues; sponsorship
Staff Member(s): 6
Membership: Fees: $75; *Member Profile:* Industry & corporate members have direct & substantial involvement required in country music, applicable to advertising, artists, broadcast personnel, producers, & record/video companies
Activities: Offering events & programs to increase awareness & appreciation for Canadian country music, such as Country Music Week & Discovery Program; *Awareness Events:* Country Music Week, Sept.
Chief Officer(s):
Don Green, President
dgreen@ccma.org
Ted Ellis, Chair

Mike Denney, Secretary-Treasurer
Awards:
• CCMA Music Awards
Awards in 10 categories are presented annually to outstanding performers; 35 citations honour individuals & organizations that have made a significant contribution to country music
Publications:
• The Book: CCMA Source Guide
Type: Directory
Profile: Lists country music contacts
• The Source
Type: Newsletter; *Frequency:* Monthly
Profile: Timely information about the country music industry

Canadian Courier & Logistics Association (CCLA)
PO Box 333, #119, 660 Eglinton Ave. East, Toronto ON M4G 2K2
Tel: 416-696-9995; *Fax:* 416-696-9993
Toll-Free: 877-766-6604
info@canadiancourier.org
www.canadiancourier.org
twitter.com/CCLA4
Previous Name: Canadian Courier Association
Overview: A medium-sized national organization founded in 1986
Mission: To serve the needs, promote the interests & concerns, & enhance the reputation of the courier industry in Canada regardless of size or type of operation
Staff Member(s): 2
Membership: Fees: $927 supplier; $1,850 resource partner; *Member Profile:* Couriers & time sensitive logistics service providers in Canada; *Committees:* Cargo Security; Customs; Courier Process; Environment & Energy; Regulatory; Urban Mobility; Weights & Measures
Activities: Luncheon seminars; golf tournament
Chief Officer(s):
David Turnbull, President & CEO
dturnbull@canadiancourier.org
Awards:
• Courier Executive of the Year Award

Canadian Courier Association *See* Canadian Courier & Logistics Association

Canadian Cowboys' Association (CCA)
PO Box 1027, Regina SK S4P 3B2
Tel: 306-931-2700; *Fax:* 306-721-2701
canadiancowboys@sasktel.net
www.canadiancowboys.ca
www.facebook.com/CCARodeo
twitter.com/CCA_Rodeo
www.youtube.com/user/CanadianCowboysAssn
Overview: A small national organization founded in 1963
Mission: To sanction over 50 rodeos in Western Canada; to serve as a source of competition information, maintaining schedules & records of standings & results.
Chief Officer(s):
Shylo Claypool, President

Canadian Crafts Federation (CCF) / Fédération canadienne des métiers d'art (FCMA)
PO Box 1231, Fredericton NB E3B 5C8
Tel: 506-462-9560
info@canadiancraftsfederation.ca
www.canadiancraftsfederation.ca
Overview: A medium-sized national charitable organization founded in 1998
Mission: To represent provincial & territorial crafts councils & the Canadian crafts sector; To advance & promote the vitality & excellence of Canadian crafts nationally & internationally to the benefit of Canadian craftspeople & the community at large
Affiliation(s): World Crafts Council
Finances: Annual Operating Budget: Less than $50,000; *Funding Sources:* Membership fees; grants
Staff Member(s): 1; 10 volunteer(s)
Membership: 19 organizations; 8 individuals; *Fees:* Schedule available; *Member Profile:* Craft Council members consist of provincial or territorial craft organizations in Canada; Affiliate members consist of organizations, institutions, or associations involved with contemporary fine craft; Honourary members consist of individuals recognized for their contributions to the Canadian craft industry
Activities: Campaigning for funding & programs on behalf of crafts professionals
Chief Officer(s):
Maegen Black, Director
maegen@canadiancraftsfederation.ca

Awards:
• Robert Jekyll Award for Leadership in Craft
Meetings/Conferences:
• Canadian Crafts Federation 2018 13th Annual National Craft Conference, October, 2018
Scope: National

Canadian Credit Institute Educational Foundation (CCIEF)
#216C, 219 Dufferin St., Toronto ON M6L 3J1
Tel: 416-572-2615; *Fax:* 416-572-2619
Toll-Free: 888-447-3324
geninfo@creditedu.org
www.creditedu.org
Overview: A small national organization founded in 1967
Mission: To provide funding in support of credit initiatives to enhance performance of professionals dedicated to excellence.
Staff Member(s): 7
Chief Officer(s):
Nawshad Khadaroo, General Manager
nkhadaroo@creditedu.org
Awards:
• The CCIEF Scholarship
To promote education through the Credit Institute of Canada by providing financial support to students in pursuit of the CCP (Certified Credit Professional) designation. *Eligibility:* Financial need; at least two years experience in the credit/financial field with a long term goal in the credit or financial management field(s); Canadian resident; participates in local community or volunteer program and will provide a letter of reference; *Amount:* up to $2000

Canadian Credit Union Association (CCUA) / Association canadienne des coopératives financières (ACCF)
Corporate Office, #1000, 151 Yonge St., Toronto ON M5C 2W7
Tel: 416-232-1262
Toll-Free: 800-649-0222
Other Communication: Alt. E-mails: conferences@ccua.com; webinars@ccua.com
inquiries@ccua.com
www.ccua.com
www.linkedin.com/company/canadian-credit-union-association
www.facebook.com/CCUA.ACCF
twitter.com/CCUA_ACCF
www.youtube.com/channel/UCFUZjJjJ6jCnYLYfBgDU7EA
Previous Name: Credit Union Central of Canada; Canadian Cooperative Credit Society
Overview: A large national organization founded in 1953
Mission: To act as the national voice for the Canadian credit union system; To facilitate the national cooperative movement; To provide services to ensure best practices are met at all credit unions; To develop opportunities for cooperative growth
Affiliation(s): Concentra Financial
Staff Member(s): 46
Membership: 5 provincial credit union centrals + 1 federation of caisses populaires; *Member Profile:* Provincial credit union centrals; Federation of caisses populaires; *Committees:* Legislative & Regulatory Affairs Advisory; Credit Union Growth & Innovation; National Marketing Advisory; Professional Development & Education Advisory; Credit Union Social Responsibility; National Young Leaders; National Lenders; Research Advisory; CEO Payments Strategy; Central Compliance Managers Working Group; Government Relations Working Group; Basel III Capital Working Group
Activities: Providing liquidity for the Canadian system; Establishing the National Mentorship Program, to match employees in senior positions with high potential employees
Chief Officer(s):
Martha Durdin, President & CEO
Korinne Collins, Vice-President, Professional Development & Education
Stephen Fitzpatrick, Vice-President & CFO, Corporate Services
Jennifer McGill, Vice-President, Communications & Marketing
Brenda O'Connor, Vice-President, General Counsel & Corporate Secretary
Chris White, Vice-President, Government Relations
Awards:
• Community Economic Development Award
• Hall of Fame Award
• Innovation Award
• Young Leaders Award
• Social Responsibility Award
Meetings/Conferences:
• Canadian Credit Union Association 2018 National Conference for Canada's Credit Unions, April, 2018, Toronto, ON

Scope: National
Contact Information: Conference Registrar, E-mail: conferences@ccua.com
Publications:
• Canadian Central Annual Report [a publication of the Canadian Credit Union Association]
Type: Yearbook; *Frequency:* Annually
• CONNECTIONS [a publication of the Canadian Credit Union Association]
Type: Newsletter
Profile: Takes the place of former newsletters Intelegram & the Policy & Advocacy Report.
• Credit Union/Caisse Populaire Information Survey [a publication of the Canadian Credit Union Association]
Type: Survey
• Enterprise: The Voice of Canadian Credit Unions [a publication of the Canadian Credit Union Association]
Type: Magazine; *Accepts Advertising*
Profile: Coverage of issues that impact Canada's credit union sector, such as restructuring, technology, & marketing
• Largest 100 Credit Unions [a publication of the Canadian Credit Union Association]
Type: Report; *Frequency:* Semi-Annually
• National System Results [a publication of the Canadian Credit Union Association]
Type: Report; *Frequency:* Quarterly
Profile: Financial information from the Canadian credit union system
  Ottawa Office
  #320, 100 Queen St., Ottawa ON K1P 1J9
  Tel: 613-238-6747

Canadian Criminal Justice Association (CCJA) / Association canadienne de justice pénale (ACJP)
#101, 320 Parkdale Ave., Ottawa ON K1Y 4X9
Tel: 613-725-3715; *Fax:* 613-725-3720
ccja-acjp@ccja-acjp.ca
www.ccja-acjp.ca
www.facebook.com/1134943779881932
twitter.com/AcjpCcja
www.youtube.com/channel/UCK7h-KJz2RCamFaSSxzKFcg
Overview: A medium-sized national charitable organization founded in 1919
Mission: To promote a humane, equitable & effective criminal justice system in Canada
Affiliation(s): Academy of Criminal Justice Sciences; Alberta Criminal Justice Association; American Correctional Association; British Columbia Criminal Justice Association; Criminal Justice Association of Ontario; Manitoba Criminal Justice Association; New Brunswick Prince Edward Island Criminal Justice Association; Nova Scotia Criminal Justice Association; Société de criminologie du Québec
Finances: *Annual Operating Budget:* $250,000-$500,000; *Funding Sources:* Government grants; publication sales; fundraising
Staff Member(s): 3; 50 volunteer(s)
Membership: 700; *Fees:* $25-$500; *Member Profile:* Legal corporations, partnerships & entities; Students; Individuals who wish to support the association; *Committees:* Awards; Membership Strategies; Policy Review; Public Awareness & Visibility; Public Education Resources
Activities: *Library:* Not open to public
Chief Officer(s):
Roland LaHaye, President
Irving Kulik, Executive Director
Publications:
• Canadian Journal of Criminology & Criminal Justice
Type: Journal; *Frequency:* Quarterly; *Price:* $55 student; $100 individual; $210 institutional
Profile: Peer-reviewed scientific journal with articles based on research & experimentation for researchers, practitioners, justice administrators, academics, & those interestedin recent criminological findings
• CCJA [Canadian Criminal Justice Association] Newsletter
Type: Newsletter; *Frequency:* Biweekly
Profile: News from across Canada with CCJA member input
• The Directory of Services for Victims of Crime
Type: Directory
Profile: Listing of agencies & services for victims throughout Canada
• The Justice Directory of Services
Type: Directory
Profile: Listing of Canadian federal, provincial, & voluntary services in the field of criminal justice & corrections

• The Justice Report
Type: Magazine; *Frequency:* Quarterly; *Editor:* Nancy Wright
Profile: Opinion pieces by professional journalists, articles by partners in the criminal justice system, recent court decision reports, inmate opinions, & upcoming events

Canadian Critical Care Society (CCCS) / Société canadienne de soins intensifs
#6, 20 Crown Steel Dr., Toronto ON L3R 9X9
Tel: 905-415-3917; *Fax:* 905-415-0071
Toll-Free: 855-415-3917
cccs@secretariatcentral.com
www.canadiancriticalcare.org
www.facebook.com/269898849687697
Overview: A medium-sized national organization
Mission: To promote & develop critical care medicine in Canada
Affiliation(s): Canadian Medical Association; World Federation of Societies of Intensive & Critical Care Medicine
Membership: *Committees:* Clinical; Communications; Education; Ethics; Knowledge Translation; Liaisons; Meetings; Membership & Finance; Scientific
Chief Officer(s):
Alison Fox-Robichaud, President
Meetings/Conferences:
• Canadian Critical Care Conference 2018, February, 2018, Four Seasons Resort, Whistler, BC
Scope: National
Contact Information: www.canadiancriticalcare.ca

Canadian Croatian Congress (CWC) / Kanadsko Hrvatski Kongres
3550 Commercial St., Vancouver BC V5A 4E9
Tel: 604-871-7190; *Fax:* 604-879-2256
crowc@shaw.ca
www.crocc.org
Overview: A large international charitable organization founded in 1993
Mission: To unite & network Croatian associations & institutions throughout the world, & to assist in their successful functioning
Member of: United Nations
Affiliation(s): Croatian World Congress
Finances: *Annual Operating Budget:* $250,000-$500,000; *Funding Sources:* Membership dues; donations
Staff Member(s): 20; 125 volunteer(s)
Membership: *Member Profile:* Croatian community; *Committees:* Lobby; Humanitarian; Sports; Schools; Cultural; Investment; Emigration; Youth; Internet
Activities: *Library:* by appointment
Chief Officer(s):
Ivan Curman, President, 604-871-9170, Fax: 604-879-2256
crocc@shaw.ca

Canadian Crop Hail Association (CCHA)
c/o Co-operative Hail Insurance Company Ltd., 2709 - 13th Ave., Regina SK S4P 3A8
Overview: A small national organization
Mission: To represent insurers who write crop hail insurance in Alberta, Saskatchewan, & Manitoba
Membership: 11; *Member Profile:* Companies that sell crop hail insurance to producers in western Canada, such as Additional Municipal Hail Ltd., Agriculture Financial Services Corporation, Butler Byers Hail Insurance Ltd., Canadian Hail Agencies Inc., Co-operative Hail Insurance Company, Manitoba Agricultural Services Corporation, McQueen Agencies Ltd., Farmers Hail Insurance Agencies, Ltd., Rain & Hail Insurance Service, Ltd., Henderson Hail Agencies Ltd., & Wray Agencies Ltd.
Chief Officer(s):
Murray Bantle, Chair, 306-522-8891
Brian Tainsh, Media Contact, Alberta, 403-782-8232
David Van Deynze, Media Contact, Manitoba, 204-239-3252

Canadian Crossroads International (CCI) / Carrefour canadien international
#201, 49 Bathurst St., Toronto ON M5V 2P2
Tel: 416-967-1611; *Fax:* 416-967-9078
Toll-Free: 877-967-1611
info@cintl.org
www.cintl.org
www.linkedin.com/company/crossroads-international
www.facebook.com/CanadianCrossroads
twitter.com/CrossroadsIntl
www.youtube.com/user/CanadianCrossroads
Overview: A medium-sized international charitable organization founded in 1958
Mission: To reduce poverty & increase women's rights around the world; To work with local organizations in West Africa, Southern Africa & South America; To uphold ethical relationships with stakeholders; To help develop programs & meet development goals of developing countries; To support the exchange of skilled volunteers
Member of: Canadian Council for International Cooperation
Finances: *Annual Operating Budget:* $100,000-$250,000; *Funding Sources:* CIDA; Private donations
Staff Member(s): 23; 200 volunteer(s)
Membership: 12; *Committees:* National Program; National Alumni Association; National Fundraising; National Finance; Personnel; Nominating; Executive
Activities: *Internships:* Yes
Chief Officer(s):
Susan Watts, Chair
Julie Mills, Treasurer
Beatriz Gonzalez, Officer, Communications & Public Outreach, 416-967-1611 Ext. 224
beatriz@cintl.org
  Montréal Office
  #100, 3000, rue Omer-Lavallée, Montréal QC H1Y 3R8
  Tél: 514-528-5363; *Téléc:* 514-528-5367
  quebec@cintl.org
  www.facebook.com/Carrefourcanadien
  Mission: Carrefour canadien international (CCI) est un organisme sans but lucratif qui reçoit l'appui de l'Agence canadienne de développement international (ACDI), de bailleurs de fonds gouvernementaux et non gouvernementaux ainsi que de donateurs individuels provenant des quatre coins du globe.
  Chief Officer(s):
  Nicolas Gersdorff, Agent de communication, nouveaux média Ext. 222

Canadian Crude Quality Technical Association (CCQTA)
www.ccqta.com
Overview: A medium-sized national organization
Mission: The CCQTA facilitates the resolution of common crude oil quality issues by establishing direct lines of communications among crude oil stakeholders. Note: CCQTA does not have a permanent office location
Membership: 75; *Fees:* $1,000-$2,000; *Member Profile:* Any subscriber that is engaged in any commercial activity of the petroleum industry and who pays the initial and subsequent annual fees.

Canadian Cue Sport Association (CCS)
87 Brightstone Gardens SE, Calgary AB T2Z 0C6
Tel: 403-271-9221
pplted@hotmail.com
www.cdnqsport.com
Overview: A small national organization founded in 2003
Mission: To manage a Canadian billiards Championship Program & to provide sanctioning of billiard leagues
Membership: *Fees:* $50 individual; $20 per player in leagues, depending on league size; *Member Profile:* Leagues; Individual Players
Chief Officer(s):
Ted Harms, President

Canadian Culinary Federation (CCFCC) / Fédération Culinaire Canadienne
30 Hamilton Ct., Riverview NB E1B 3C3
Tel: 506-387-4882; *Fax:* 506-387-4884
Other Communication: membership@ccfcc.ca
admin@ccfcc.ca
www.ccfcc.ca
www.facebook.com/CCFCC
twitter.com/CdnChefs
Previous Name: Canadian Federation of Chefs & Cooks; Canadian Federation of Chefs de Cuisine
Overview: A large national organization founded in 1963
Mission: To promote a Canadian food culture both nationally & internationally; To encourage professional excellence among chefs & cooks throughout Canada
Member of: World Association of Chefs' Societies
Membership: *Fees:* $115 / year + $30 initiation fee, national members & members at large; $55 / year, Canadian Forces members; $30 / year, junior members; *Member Profile:* Cook apprentices; Journeyman cooks; Professional chefs; Culinary professionals; *Committees:* Honour Society; Finance; Ethics; Culinary Team; Junior Membership; National Convention; National Elections; National Marketing; National Membership
Activities: Creating learning opportunities
Chief Officer(s):
Donald A. Gyurkovits, Chair
chairman@ccfcc.ca

Canadian Associations / Canadian Cultural Society of The Deaf, Inc. (CCSD)

Roy Butterworth, Executive Director
admin@ccfcc.ca
Awards:
• Chef of the Year
Eligibility: A chef that best exemplifies the elements of professionalism, dedication to the craft of cooking and has applied themselves to the success of Branch work.
Meetings/Conferences:
• 55th Annual Canadian Culinary Federation 2018 National Convention, June, 2018, Charlottetown, PE
Scope: National
Publications:
• Mise en Place
Type: Newsletter; *Frequency:* Quarterly; *Accepts Advertising*
Profile: Informative articles for members of the Canadian Culinary Federation

Brandon Branch
Brandon MB
Tel: 204-667-4647
Chief Officer(s):
Paul Lemire, President
pilot11@shaw.ca

Calgary Branch
#496, 130 - 5403 Crowchild Trail NW, Calgary AB T3B 4Z1
president@calgarychefs.com
www.calgarychefs.com
www.facebook.com/259373817454055
Chief Officer(s):
Fred Malley, President

Chapitre Outaouais
Outaouais QC
Tél: 613-673-9295
Chief Officer(s):
Stephane Paquet, Président

Edmonton Branch
9797 Jasper Ave., Edmonton AB T5J 1N9
Tel: 780-475-2433; *Fax:* 780-426-1874
admin@edmontonchefs.ca
www.edmontonchefs.ca
Chief Officer(s):
Stanley Townsend, President
president@edmontonchefs.ca

Halifax Branch
PO Box 31457, Halifax NS B3K 5Z1
Tel: 902-433-0261; *Fax:* 902-433-0261
www.nsacc.ca
Chief Officer(s):
John St. John, President
john.stjohn@nscc.ca

Hamilton Branch
25 Roselle Pl., Stoney Creek ON L8G 1R2
admin@ccfhamilton.ca
www.ccfhamilton.ca
twitter.com/HamiltonChefs

Kingston Branch
925 Hudson Dr., Kingston ON K7M 5V4
Tel: 613-384-1746
Chief Officer(s):
Ian Sarfin, President
isarfin@cogeco.ca

Lethbridge Branch
PO Box 1021, Lethbridge AB T1J 4A2
www.southernalbertachefs.com
www.facebook.com/175006825913901
twitter.com/SAACmedia
Chief Officer(s):
Debbie Clause, President

London Branch
London ON
Tel: 519-615-9487
Chief Officer(s):
Mike A. Pitre, President
chefmikepitre@gmail.com

Moncton Branch
Moncton NB
Tel: 506-384-7026
Chief Officer(s):
Lana Manuge, President
chefroy@nbnet.nb.ca

Montréal Branch
Montréal QC
Tél: 450-467-5972
Chief Officer(s):
Denis Parent, Président
parent-denis@videotron.ca

Muskoka Branch
PO Box 773, Barrie ON L4M 4Y5
Tel: 705-791-2434
www.ccfmuskoka.com
www.facebook.com/302353886554323
Chief Officer(s):
Daniel Clements, President
danielclements@rogers.com

North Vancouver Island
PO Box 3156, Courtenay BC V9N 5N4
Tel: 250-897-3134
info@northvancouverislandchefs.com
www.northvancouverislandchefs.com
Chief Officer(s):
Lesley Stav, President
lesley.stav@northvancouverislandchefs.com

Okanagan Branch
PO Box 2612, Stn. Banks Center, Kelowna BC V1X 6A7
secretary@okanaganchefs.com
www.okanaganchefs.com
www.facebook.com/okanaganchefs
twitter.com/okanaganchefs
Chief Officer(s):
Bernard Casavent, President
president@okanaganchefs.com

Ottawa Branch
Ottawa ON
Tel: 613-836-0268
www.ccfccottawa.ca
www.facebook.com/CCFCC.Ottawa.ca
twitter.com/CCFCC_Ottawa
Chief Officer(s):
Russell Weir, President, 613-238-1500
weirr@algonquincollege.com

Prince Edward Island Branch
PO Box 581, Charlottetown PE C1A 7L1
Chief Officer(s):
Jeff McCourt, President, 902-629-9445
mccourtjeff1@gmail.com

Québec
Québec QC
Tel: 418-871-8737
Chief Officer(s):
Martens Didier, Président
martdidier@hotmail.com

Regina Branch
PO Box 3162, Regina SK S4P 3G7
ccfccregina@live.ca
www.ccfccregina.ca
www.facebook.com/ccfccregina
Chief Officer(s):
Trent Brears, President
president@ccfccregina.ca

St. John's Branch
St. John's NL
Tel: 709-437-6519
ccfccstjohnsbranch@nf.sympatico.ca
Chief Officer(s):
Andrew Hodge, President
andrew_hodge@hotmail.com

Saskatoon Branch
Saskatoon SK
Tel: 306-652-1780
askus@ccfccsaskatoonbranch.org
www.ccfccsaskatoonbranch.org
Chief Officer(s):
Anthony J. McCarthy, President
anthonym@saskatoonclub.com

Toronto Branch
PO Box 1093, Stn. A, Toronto ON M5V 1G6
administrator@escoffiertoronto.com
www.escoffiertoronto.com
www.facebook.com/308371625923106
Chief Officer(s):
Cornelia Volino, President
president@escoffiertoronto.com

Vancouver Branch
PO Box 2007, Stn. Main, Vancouver BC V6B 3P8
www.bcchefs.com
www.facebook.com/BritishColumbiaChefsAssociation
twitter.com/BCChefs
Chief Officer(s):
Edgar Rahal, President
president@bcchefs.com

Victoria Branch
1735 Kingsberry Cres., Victoria BC V8P 2A8
Tel: 778-430-7977
info@ccfccvictoria.ca
www.ccfccvictoria.ca
www.facebook.com/174851829250060
twitter.com/CCFCCVictoria
Chief Officer(s):
Jamie Martinuea, President
president@ccfccvictoria.ca

Windsor Branch
788 South Pacific Ave., Windsor ON N8X 2X2
info@culinaryguildofwindsor.ca
www.culinaryguildofwindsor.ca
Chief Officer(s):
Helmut Market, President
president@culinaryguildofwindsor.ca

Winnipeg Branch
PO Box 1072, Winnipeg MB R3C 2X4
www.winnipegchefs.org
Chief Officer(s):
Brent Prockert, President
chefbrent@shawbiz.ca

Canadian Cultural Society of The Deaf, Inc. (CCSD)
The Distillery Historic District, 34 Distillery Lane, Toronto ON M5A 3C4
info@deafculturecentre.ca
www.deafculturecentre.ca
www.facebook.com/deafculturecentre
twitter.com/DeafCulture
Also Known As: Deaf Culture Centre
Overview: A medium-sized national charitable organization founded in 1973
Mission: To ensure that the cultural needs of deaf & hard-of-hearing people are being met; To concentrate efforts in the areas of the performing arts, sign language, deaf literature, the visual arts, & heritage resources
Membership: *Fees:* $100; *Member Profile:* 8 provincial cultural societies across Canada
Activities: Provides programs on culture, history, visual & performing artists (Deaf), with ongoing workshops, exhibits, school tours & virtual displays; gift shop showcasing Deaf artists' work; *Internships:* Yes
Chief Officer(s):
Joanne Cripps, Executive Director
jcripps@deafculturecentre.ca

Canadian Curling Association (CCA) / Association canadienne de curling
1660 Vimont Ct., Orléans ON K4A 4J4
Tel: 613-834-2076; *Fax:* 613-834-0716
Toll-Free: 800-550-2875
Other Communication:
www.flickr.com/photos/seasonofchampions
boc@curling.ca
www.curling.ca
www.facebook.com/curlingcanada
twitter.com/curlingcanada
www.youtube.com/ccacurling
Also Known As: Curling Canada
Overview: A large national organization founded in 1990
Mission: To attract, retain & advance participants to grow the sport of curling
Affiliation(s): World Curling Federation
Staff Member(s): 16
Membership: *Committees:* Finance & Audit; Governance; CEO Performance & Compensation; Appointment Suggestions; Hall of Fame & Awards; Constitutional Review
Activities: Organizing championships; Facilitating tournaments, camps, & development programs
Chief Officer(s):
Patricia Ray, Chief Operating Officer, 613-834-2076 Ext. 154
pray@curling.ca
Al Cameron, Director, Communications & Media Relations, 403-463-5500
acameron@curling.ca
Awards:
• Volunteer of the Year Award
Based on contributions from the previous curling season; national volunteer of the year receives an all-expense paid weekend trip to Nokia Brier or Scott Tournament of Hearts, where they will be recognized during a playoff game

- Award of Achievement
Commemorative plaque presented in recognition of individuals who have contributed significantly to any aspect of Canadian curling operations *Deadline:* March
- Ray Kingsmith Award
Awarded to an individual who parallels the level of involvement & commitment exemplified by Ray Kingsmith *Deadline:* March
- Board of Governors Special Recognition Award
Awarded to an individual or organization who has significantly impacted Canadian curling through their contributions or achievements *Deadline:* December 31
- Eight Ender Awards
Awarded to teams who score Eight Enders; *Amount:* Pins & Certificates

Canadian Curly Horse Association
PO Box 35, Sunnybrook AB T0C 2M0
Tel: 780-789-2125
curlys@sunnybrookstables.com
www.curlyhorse.ca
Overview: A small national organization founded in 1993
Mission: To promote hypo-allergenic curly horses & to gather together owners of curly horses to share knowledge & activities
Membership: *Fees:* $35 Canadians; $45 Americans
Chief Officer(s):
Maureen Ivan, President, 403-450-7213
maureen.i@rockinhorsecurlies.ca

Canadian Cutting Horse Association (CCHA)
RR#3, Innisfail AB T4G 1T8
Tel: 403-227-4444; *Fax:* 403-227-3030
www.ccha.ca
Overview: A small national organization founded in 1953
Mission: To promote the cutting horse, a specially trained horse to isolate or cut an individual animal from large cattle herds
Finances: *Funding Sources:* Membership fees; Sponsorships
Activities: Hosting cutting horse competitions
Chief Officer(s):
Les Timmons, President, 250-573-5350
Jamie Couilliard, Vice-President, 403-247-3563
Connie Delorme, National Administrator
Geoff Thomas, Secretary-Treasurer, 403-347-6900
Awards:
- CCHA Sportsmanship Award
Eligibility: Person must be an active youth, amateur, non-pro, or open competitor, who displays a positive attitude, kindness, & helpfulness in & around shows
Publications:
- The Canadian Cutter
Type: Newsletter
   British Columbia
   c/o Lynn Graham, 640 Lister Rd., Kamloops BC V2H 0B8
   Tel: 250-578-8244; *Fax:* 250-578-8244
   Chief Officer(s):
   Campbell Garrard, President
   Lynn Graham, Secretary
   Saskatchewan
   c/o Elaine Good, PO Box 1064, Fillmore SK S0G 1N0
   Tel: 306-722-3643; *Fax:* 306-722-3643
   Chief Officer(s):
   Les Jack, President
   Elaine Good, Secretary/Treasurer

Canadian Cycling Association *See* Cycling Canada Cyclisme

Canadian Cystic Fibrosis Foundation *See* Cystic Fibrosis Canada

Canadian Cytology Council *See* Canadian Society of Cytology

Canadian Daily Newspaper Association *See* Newspapers Canada

Canadian Dairy Commission (CDC) / Commission canadienne du lait (CCL)
NCC Driveway, Bldg. 55, 960 Carling Ave., Ottawa ON K1A 0Z2
Tel: 613-792-2000; *Fax:* 613-792-2009; *TTY:* 613-792-2082
carole.cyr@cdc-ccl.gc.ca
www.cdc-ccl.gc.ca
Overview: A medium-sized national organization founded in 1966
Mission: To provide efficient producers of milk & cream with the opportunity of obtaining a fair return for their labour & investment; to provide consumers of dairy products with a continuous & adequate supply of high quality dairy products
Staff Member(s): 65
Activities: Sets support prices for butter & skim milk powder which provincial authorities use to set milk prices for the domestic markets; develops policies & programs which meet the needs of the industry
Chief Officer(s):
Carole Cyr, Communications Officer
Meetings/Conferences:
- Canadian Dairy Commission Annual Public Meeting 2018, January, 2018, Delta City Centre Hotel, Ottawa, ON
Scope: National

Canadian Dam Association (CDA) / Association canadienne des barrages (ACB)
PO Box 2281, Moose Jaw SK S6TH 7W6
www.cda.ca
Merged from: Canadian National Committee on Large Dams
Overview: A small national organization founded in 1989
Mission: To monitor the technical, environmental, social, economic, legal, & administrative aspects of dams in Canada; To ensure the safe operation of dams across Canada
Member of: Society of the Engineering Institute of Canada; International Commission on Large Dams
Finances: *Funding Sources:* Membership fees; Conferences; Advertising
Membership: *Fees:* $5 students; $40 individuals; $350 corporate members; $700 corporate sponsors; *Member Profile:* Individuals, students, & corporations with an interest in dam safety, such as dam owners, engineers, technologists, researchers, government agencies, hydro companies, & equipment manufacturers & suppliers
Activities: Promoting the adoption of regulatory policies & safety guidelines for dams & reservoirs in Canada; Fostering inter-provincial cooperation; Offering education & outreach about dams
Chief Officer(s):
Wayne Phillips, Executive Director
Awards:
- Inge Anderson Award of Merit
Contact: Tony Bennett, Awards Committee Chair, Phone: 905-262-2667
- Gary Salmon Memorial Scholarship
Contact: Tony Bennett, Awards Committee Chair, Phone: 905-262-2667
- Peter Halliday Award for Service
Contact: Tony Bennett, Awards Committee Chair, Phone: 905-262-2667
- Published Paper Award of Excellence
Contact: Tony Bennett, Awards Committee Chair, Phone: 905-262-2667
- Research Award
Contact: Tony Bennett, Awards Committee Chair, Phone: 905-262-2667
- Student Achievement Award
Contact: Tony Bennett, Awards Committee Chair, Phone: 905-262-2667
- Meritorious Achievement Award
Contact: Tony Bennett, Awards Committee Chair, Phone: 905-262-2667
Meetings/Conferences:
- Canadian Dam Association 2018 Annual Conference, October, 2018, Québec City Convention Centre, Québec, QC
Scope: National
Description: Featuring technical paper presentations, workshops, tours, exhibitor presentations, & a social program
Publications:
- Canadian Dam Association Bulletin
Type: Magazine; *Frequency:* Quarterly; *Accepts Advertising*; *Editor:* A. Kirkham (allan.kirkham@opg.com); *Price:* Free with membership in the Canadian Dam Association
Profile: Information from the Canadian Dam Association to help members remain informed about the association, the board, awards, conferences, & suppliers &buyers
- Dam Safety Guidelines
Type: Guidelines; *Number of Pages:* 82; *Price:* $60 each, plus GST, for CDA members; $100 each, plus GST, for non-members
Profile: A Canadian Dam Association publication, with a companion series of English language technical bulletins (235 pages)
- Dams in Canada
Type: CD; *Price:* $60 each, plus GST, for CDA members; $100 each, plus GST, for non-members
Profile: Featuring chapters, with photographs, drawings, & text, on water resources, water supply, irrigation, hydroelectric dams, & flood control dams, plus the Dams in Canada Register, with information about over 900dams

Canadian Dance Teachers' Association (CDTA) / Association canadienne des professeurs de danse
#38, 6033 Shawson Dr., Mississauga ON L5T 1H8
Tel: 905-564-2139; *Fax:* 905-564-2211
canadiandanceteachers@bellnet.ca
www.cdtanational.ca
www.facebook.com/236169423103547
Overview: A medium-sized national licensing organization founded in 1949
Mission: To advance education in the field of dance & maintain throughout Canada an organization of qualified dance teachers; to promote friendship & the exchange of ideas & information among the dance teachers of Canada, to provide an organization to represent Canadian dance teachers internationally
Member of: World Dance & Dancesport Council
Finances: *Annual Operating Budget:* Less than $50,000
Staff Member(s): 1
Membership: 1,000-4,999; *Member Profile:* Professional dancers, owners of dance schools, professional dance teachers; *Committees:* Executive; Division for each: Ballet, Ballroom, International Folk Dance, Scottish Dance Arts, Stage including Tap, Jazz, Baton & Acrobatics
Activities: Offering lessons in ballroom, ballet, tap, jazz, acrobatics, baton, Scottish dance arts, modern & national dancing
Chief Officer(s):
Georgina Church, President
   Alberta Branch
   c/o President, 14 Dumas Cres., Red Deer AB T4R 2S1
   Tel: 403-346-6333
   albertacdta@shaw.ca
   www.albertacdta.ca
   Chief Officer(s):
   Julie Dionne, President
   British Columbia Branch
   PO Box 31547, Pitt Meadows BC V3Y 2G7
   bcdta2009@gmail.com
   www.cdtabc.ca
   Chief Officer(s):
   Steve Nikleva, President
   snikleva@shaw.ca
   Ontario Branch
   #38, 6603 Shawson Dr., Mississauga ON L5T 1H8
   Tel: 905-564-2139; *Fax:* 905-564-2211
   canadiandanceteachers@bellnet.ca
   cdtaont.com
   www.facebook.com/236169423103547
   Chief Officer(s):
   Sue Romeril, President
   Québec Branch
   QC
   Saskatchewan Branch
   c/o President, PO Box 1402, Humboldt SK S0K 2A0
   Tel: 306-682-2635; *Fax:* 306-585-1634
   cdtaskbranch@hotmail.com
   www.cdtaskbranch.com
   Mission: To promote interaction between dance teachers & through this exchange improve the standard for dancing & teaching
   Chief Officer(s):
   Paula Puetz, President

Canadian Day Care Advocacy Association *See* Child Care Advocacy Association of Canada

Canadian Deaf Curling Association (CDCA) / Association de Curling des Sourdes du Canada
Vancouver BC
Tel: 604-734-2250; *Fax:* 604-734-2254; *TTY:* 250-539-3264
www.deafcurlcanada.org
Also Known As: Deaf Curl Canada
Overview: A small national organization overseen by Canadian Deaf Sports Association
Mission: To provide deaf & hard of hearing curlers with opportunities across Canada
Member of: Canadian Deaf Sports Association; Canadian Curling Association
Affiliation(s): British Columbia Deaf Sports Federation; Alberta Deaf Curling Association; Saskatchewan Deaf Sports Association; Manitoba Deaf Curling Association; Ontario Deaf Curling Association; Association de Curling des Sourds du Quebec; Nova Scotia Deaf Curling Association

Canadian Associations / Canadian Deaf Golf Association (CDGA) / Association Canadienne de Golf des Sourds

Chief Officer(s):
Bradford Bentley, President
president@deafcurlcanada.org
Allard Thomas, Vice-President
Susanne Beriault, Secretary
cdca-secretary@gmail.com
David Pickard, Treasurer
dpickard@telus.net
Dean Sutton, Chief Technical Director
curlingtd@shaw.ca

Canadian Deaf Golf Association (CDGA) / Association Canadienne de Golf des Sourds
#20, 51 Sholto Drive, London ON N6G 2E9
cdga1993.wixsite.com/cdga
Overview: A small national organization overseen by Canadian Deaf Sports Association
Mission: To aid in the development of leadership & golfing skills among deaf golfers across Canada
Member of: Canadian Deaf Sports Association
Membership: Fees: $10
Chief Officer(s):
Dana McCarthy, President
cdgapresident@gmail.com
Peter Mitchell, Vice-President
pmitchell25@rogers.ca
Paul Landry, Secretary
pauljlandry@shaw.ca
Adam Redmond, Treasurer
cdgatreasurer@gmail.com
Aurele Bourgeois, Director
abourgeois10@cogeco.ca

Canadian Deaf Ice Hockey Federation (CDIHF)
ON
www.cdihf.deafhockey.com
www.facebook.com/canada.deafhockey?fref=ts&ref=br_tf
twitter.com/CDNdeafhockey
Previous Name: Canadian Hearing Impaired Hockey Association
Overview: A small national charitable organization founded in 1983 overseen by Canadian Deaf Sports Association
Mission: To offer ice hockey programs for deaf & hard of hearing participants; To administer a hockey team to represent Canada internationally
Member of: Canadian Deaf Sports Association
Affiliation(s): Canadian Hockey Association; Ontario Deaf Sports Association, Inc.
Finances: Funding Sources: Donations; Sponsorships
Activities: Hosting training camps & hockey schools; Organizing the CDIHC Hockey Championships; Participating in the World Deaf Ice Hockey Championship
Chief Officer(s):
Mark Dunn, President
mark.dunn@deafhockey.com

Canadian Deaf Sports Association (CDSA) / Association des sports des sourds du Canada (ASSC)
#202, 10217, boul Pie IX, Montréal QC H1H 3Z5
Tel: 514-321-8686; Fax: 514-321-8349; TTY: 514-321-2937
info@assc-cdsa.com
www.assc-cdsa.com
www.facebook.com/assc.cdsa
twitter.com/ASSC_CDSA
Overview: A medium-sized national licensing charitable organization founded in 1964
Mission: To promote & facilitate the practice of fitness, amateur sports & recreation among deaf people of all ages in Canada from the local recreational level to Olympics calibre
Member of: Canadian Deaf & Hard of Hearing Forum; Canadian Paralympic Committee; Canadian Sports Coalition.
Affiliation(s): International Committee of Sports for the Deaf
Staff Member(s): 3
Membership: Committees: Finance; Communications; Governance; Human Resources
Chief Officer(s):
Alain Turpin, Chief Executive Officer
alain.turpin@assc-cdsa.com
Gigi Fiset, Manager, Operational Services & Events
gigi.fiset@assc-cdsa.com

Canadian Deafblind & Rubella Association (Ontario Chapter) Inc. See Canadian Deafblind Association (National)

Canadian Deafblind Association (National) (CDBA) / Association canadienne de la surdicécité (Bureau National)
PO Box 421, #14, 1860 Appleby Line, Burlington ON L7L 7H7
Fax: 905-319-2027
Toll-Free: 866-229-5832
info@cdbanational.com
www.cdbanational.com
www.facebook.com/cdbanational
twitter.com/CDBANational
Overview: A medium-sized national charitable organization
Mission: To promote awareness, education & support for people who are deafblind, in order to enhance their well-being
Chief Officer(s):
Carolyn Monaco, President
carolyn.monaco@sympatico.ca
Tom McFadden, National Executive Director

Alberta Chapter
AB
Tel: 780-554-6083
www.deafblindalberta.ca
Chief Officer(s):
Nicole Sander, Vice-President
nicsander@me.com

British Columbia Chapter
227 - 6th St., New Westminster BC V3L 3A5
Tel: 604-528-6170; Fax: 604-528-6174
www.cdbabc.ca
Mission: To promote public awareness of deafblindness as a unique disability; To work with government & other agencies to initiate the development of assistance programs for the deafblind; To act as a resource in addressing the needs of individuals who are deafblind
Member of: CDBA National; Inclusion BC; Council of Service Providers; Shared Vision Team; Canadian National Society of the Deafblind (CNSDB); Special Education Partners Group
Chief Officer(s):
Theresa Tancock, Coordinator, Family Services
theresa@cdbabc.ca

Canadian Deafblind Association - New Brunswick Inc.
#495 B Prospect St., #H, Fredericton NB E3B 9M4
Tel: 506-452-1544; Fax: 506-451-8309; TTY: 506-452-1544
www.cdba-nb.ca
www.facebook.com/CDBANB
Chief Officer(s):
Kevin Symes, Executive Director
k.symes@cdba-nb.ca

Ontario Chapter
50 Main St., Paris ON N3L 2E2
Tel: 519-442-0463; Fax: 519-442-1871
Toll-Free: 877-760-7439; TTY: 519-442-6641
info@cdbaontario.com
www.cdbaontario.com
www.facebook.com/cdbaontario
twitter.com/CDBAOntario
Mission: To provide support & services to individuals who are deafblind & their families throughout the province
Chief Officer(s):
Cathy Proll, Executive Director

Saskatchewan Chapter
83 Tucker Cres., Saskatoon SK S7H 3H7
Tel: 306-374-0022; Fax: 306-374-0004
cdba.sk@shaw.ca
Chief Officer(s):
Dana Heinrichs, Executive Director

Canadian Deals & Coupons Association (CDCA)
Toronto ON
info@canadiandealsassociation.com
www.canadiandealsassociation.com
www.linkedin.com/company/canadian-deals-association
www.facebook.com/CanadianDealsandCouponAssociation
twitter.com/DealsCouponsCAN
Overview: A large national organization founded in 2010
Mission: To provide services to companies in the retail industry, in order to promote specials & coupons
Membership: Member Profile: Coupon providers; Distributors; Retailers; Manufacturers; Technology & Service providers; Industry Individuals
Chief Officer(s):
Albert S. Bitton, President

Canadian Decorators' Association (CDECA)
#202, 10 Morrow Ave., Toronto ON M6R 2J1
Tel: 416-231-6202; Fax: 416-489-1713
Toll-Free: 866-878-2155
info@cdeca.com
www.cdeca.com
www.linkedin.com/groups?mostRecent=&gid=3909610
www.facebook.com/CanDecorators
twitter.com/CDECAnational
Overview: A small national organization
Mission: The Canadian Decorators' Association (CDECA) is a professional not-for-profit Association representing interior decorators and interior designers, and Affiliate businesses across Canada.
Membership: 500+; Fees: $300 accredited; $120 student
Chief Officer(s):
Seamus Gearin, Executive Director
office@cdeca.com

Canadian Defence Industries Association See Canadian Association of Defence & Security Industries

Canadian Dental Assistants Association (CDAA) / Association canadienne des assistants(es) dentaires (ACAD)
#1150, 45 O'Connor St., Ottawa ON K1P 1A4
Tel: 613-521-5495
Toll-Free: 800-345-5137
info@cdaa.ca
www.cdaa.ca
twitter.com/CDAA_ACAD
Overview: A medium-sized national organization founded in 1945
Mission: To foster opportunities for growth; To be the voice for Canadian dental assistants; To represent the interests of provincial & military dental associations
Finances: Funding Sources: Transfer fees from provincial associations
Staff Member(s): 2
Membership: 15,000-49,999; Committees: Audit & Financial; Awards; Bylaws & Governance; Knowledge Transference
Activities: Government relations; Advocacy; Knowledge & Research; Awareness Events: Dental Assistants Week, March; Library
Chief Officer(s):
Michelle Fowler, President
Tammy Thomson, Vice-President
Publications:
• The CDAA [Canadian Dental Assistants Association] Journal
Type: Journal; Frequency: Semiannually; Number of Pages: 32; Price: $45 Canada; $50 USA; $60 international
Profile: Articles, information, & services for individuals involved in the dental assisting profession

Canadian Dental Association (CDA) / L'Association dentaire canadienne (ADC)
1815 Alta Vista Dr., Ottawa ON K1G 3Y6
Tel: 613-523-1770
reception@cda-adc.ca
www.cda-adc.ca
www.facebook.com/CanadianDentalAssociation
twitter.com/CdnDentalAssoc
Overview: A large national organization founded in 1902
Mission: To represent & advance dentistry nationally & internationally; To promote oral health
Affiliation(s): FDI World Dental Federation
Staff Member(s): 35
Membership: 15,000+; Fees: $512.53
Activities: Awareness Events: National Oral Health Month, April
Library: Sydney Wood Bradley Memorial Library; by appointment
Chief Officer(s):
Randall Croutze, President
Awards:
• Medal of Honour
• Honourary Membership Award
• Distinguished Service Award
• Award of Merit
• Oral Health Promotion Award
• Special Friend of Canadian Dentistry Award
Publications:
• Canadian Dental Association Member News
Type: Newsletter
• CD Alert [a publication of the Canadian Dental Association]
Type: Newsletter
Profile: Industry trends, best practices, & timely information
• Dentistry News
Type: Newsletter

- Directory of Dental Regulatory Authorities & Provincial / Territorial Associations
Type: Directory
Profile: Listing of contact information
- Highlights Reports [a publication of the Canadian Dental Association]
- Journal of the Canadian Dental Association (JCDA)
Type: Journal; *Frequency:* 11 pa; *Editor:* John O'Keefe
Profile: National, peer-reviewed, science-based, clinical practice information available in both paper & electronic format

Canadian Dental Hygienists Association (CDHA) / Association canadienne des hygiènistes dentaires
1122 Wellington St. West, Ottawa ON K1Y 2Y7
Tel: 613-224-5515; *Fax:* 613-224-7283
Toll-Free: 800-267-5235
info@cdha.ca
www.cdha.ca
www.facebook.com/theCDHA
twitter.com/theCDHA
www.youtube.com/thecdha
Overview: A medium-sized national licensing organization founded in 1964
Mission: To act as the collective voice of dental hygiene in Canada; To advance the profession in support of members; To contribute to the health & well-being of the public
Finances: *Funding Sources:* Membership fees
Staff Member(s): 18
Membership: 17,000; *Fees:* Schedule available; *Member Profile:* Dental hygienists - academics & clinicians
Activities: National standards; education reform; code of ethics; *Library:* Open to public
Chief Officer(s):
Ondina Love, Chief Executive Officer
olove@cdha.ca
Laura Sandvold, Director, Finance & Operations
lsandvold@cdha.ca
Angie D'Aoust, Director, Marketing & Communications
adaoust@cdha.ca
Ann Wright, Director, Dental Hygiene Practice
awright@cdha.ca
Brigitte Gauthier, Manager, Membership Services
bgauthier@cdha.ca

Canadian Dental Protective Association (CDOA)
#300, 1100 Burloak Dr., Burlington ON L7L 6B2
Tel: 416-491-5932; *Fax:* 416-239-3443
Toll-Free: 800-876-2372
info@cdpa.com
www.cdpa.com
www.linkedin.com/company/canadian-dental-protective-association
www.facebook.com/canadiandentalprotectiveassociation
twitter.com/CDPA_Assistance
Overview: A medium-sized national organization founded in 1994
Mission: To enhance the practice of dentistry by providing risk management education, information, assistance, & support for members
Finances: *Funding Sources:* Membership fees
Staff Member(s): 1; 6 volunteer(s)
Membership: 1,200; *Fees:* $1,152.60
Chief Officer(s):
Robert Katz, President
Jimmy Ho, Treasurer
Lionel Lenkinski, Executive Director

Canadian Dental Therapists Association (CDTA)
87 Brookland St., Antigonish NS B2G 1W1
admin@dental-therapists.com
wwww.dental-therapists.com
www.facebook.com/410493672365099
Overview: A medium-sized national organization founded in 1972
Mission: To cultivate, promote, & sustain the art & science of dental therapy; To maintain the honour & interests of the dental therapy profession; To contribute toward the improvement of the health of the public
Chief Officer(s):
Sajiev Thomas, Contact
sajiev@dental-therapists.com

Canadian Depression Glass Association (CDGA)
PO Box 41564, Brampton ON L6Z 4R1
Overview: A medium-sized international organization founded in 1976
Mission: To serve as the voice for Canadian collectors & dealers of Depression Glass; members across Canada & the U.S.
Membership: *Fees:* $20; $50 for three years
Chief Officer(s):
Walter Lemiski, Contact
Publications:
- Canadian Depression Glass Review
Type: Journal
Profile: Articles, dealer & shop directory, show notices, ads for buyers & sellers, glass book reviews, & member letters

Canadian Depression Research & Intervention Network (CDRIN)
c/o CDRIN Secretariat, Mood Disorders Society of Canada, #736, 304 Stone Rd. West, Guelph ON N1G 4W4
info@cdrin.org
www.cdrin.org
www.linkedin.com/company/canadian-depression-research-and-intervention-network
www.facebook.com/CDRIN.org
twitter.com/CDRINorg
Overview: A medium-sized national organization founded in 2013
Mission: To create & share knowledge that leads to more effective prevention, early diagnosis, & treatment of depression, Post-Traumatic Stress Disorder, & related illnesses
Affiliation(s): Mood Disorders Society of Canada; Mental Health Commission of Canada
Finances: *Funding Sources:* Federal funding
Membership: *Committees:* Depression Hubs National Advisory; Finance, Audit & Risk; Governance & Nominating; Resource Development
Chief Officer(s):
David Pilon, Chair
Zul Merali, Scientific Director
Phil Upshall, Officer
Meetings/Conferences:
- Canadian Depression Research & Intervention Network Conference 2018, 2018
Scope: National

Canadian Dermatology Association (CDA) / Association canadienne de dermatologie (ACD)
#425, 1385 Bank St., Ottawa ON K1H 8N4
Tel: 613-738-1748; *Fax:* 613-738-4695
Toll-Free: 800-267-3376
info@dermatology.ca
www.dermatology.ca
www.facebook.com/CdnDermatology
twitter.com/cdndermatology
Overview: A medium-sized national organization founded in 1925
Mission: To advance the science of medicine & surgery related to the health of the skin; To support & advance patient care; To represent dermatologists in Canada
Affiliation(s): Canadian Medical Association; American Academy of Dermatology
Finances: *Funding Sources:* Membership fees; Sponsorships
Staff Member(s): 10
Membership: *Fees:* Free for residents, fellows, life members, & honorary members; $200 international members; $225 associate members; $325 dematologist members; *Member Profile:* Dermatologists who have received certification from the Royal College of Physicians & Surgeons of Canada, or a diploma from the American Board of Dermatology; International members who are practicing dermatologist in any country other than Canada & the United States; Residents & fellows; Associate members who are interested in dermatology
Activities: Providing continuing medical education for members; Offering public education on diseases of the skin, hair, & nails; Increasing awareness about sun safety & other aspects of skin care (e-mail: educational.material@dermatology.ca); Presenting awards for educational & professional accomplishments (e-mail: info@dermatology.ca); *Awareness Events:* National Sun Awareness Week *Library:* The Robert Jackson Library & Archives
Chief Officer(s):
Vince Bertucci, President
Chantal Courchesne, Chief Executive Officer
ccourchesne@dermatology.ca
Robyn Hopkins, Director, Finance
rhopkins@dermatology.ca
Nimmi Sidhu, Coordinator, Communications
nsidhu@dermatology.ca
Awards:
- Public Education Award
Entries accepted in the categories of not-for-profit organizations, industry, & media (print, radio, & television)
- Edwin Brown - Canadian Dermatology Association Endowment Fund
Awarded to a researcher
- Award of Honour
Open to persons, who are not members of the medical profession
- Young Dermatologists' Volunteer Award
To recognize a young Canadian Dermatology Association member, in private practice, who offers volunteer medical & dermatological services to the community
- Barney Usher Research Award in Dermatology
To honour a Canadian Dermatology Association member who submits the best manuscript for original work relevant to dermatology
- Award of Merit
To recognize a Canadian Dermatology Association member for excellence in leadership & excellence in contributions made to the Canadian Dermatology Association
- President's Cup
Presented to a recipient, selected by the Canadian Dermatology Association president, in recognition of assistance to the president &/or the association
Meetings/Conferences:
- Canadian Dermatology Association 2018 93rd Annual Conference, June, 2018, Montréal, QC
Scope: National
Description: Oral & poster presentations on subjects relevant to practicing dermatologists
- Canadian Dermatology Association 2019 94th Annual Conference, June, 2019, Calgary, AB
Scope: National
Description: Oral & poster presentations on subjects relevant to practicing dermatologists
Publications:
- Canadian Dermatology Association eBulletin
Type: Newsletter; *Frequency:* Monthly; *Price:* Free with membership in the Canadian DermatologyAssociation
Profile: CDA activities, articles of personal & professional interest, political reports, & news from regional dermatologic associations
- Journal of Cutaneous Medicine & Surgery [a publication of the Canadian Dermatology Association]
Type: Journal; *Accepts Advertising*; *Editor:* Dr. Jason Rivers; *Price:* Free withmembership in the Canadian Dermatology Association
Profile: Reviews, basic & clinical science articles, editorials, case reports, & letters to the editor

Canadian Dexter Cattle Association (CDCA) / Société canadienne des bovins Dexter
2417 Holly Lane, Ottawa ON K1V 0M7
Tel: 613-731-7110; *Fax:* 613-731-0704
ron.black@clrc.ca
www.dextercattle.ca
Overview: A medium-sized national organization founded in 1986
Mission: To preserve & promote the breeding of good quality Dexter cattle in Canada
Member of: Canadian Livestock Records Corporation; Canadian Beef Breeds Council
Finances: *Annual Operating Budget:* Less than $50,000; *Funding Sources:* Membership dues; Registration fees
7 volunteer(s)
Membership: 100; *Fees:* $50; *Committees:* Marketing & Promotion; Newsletter; Classification; Constitution
Chief Officer(s):
Adrian Hykaway, President
hykaway@mcsnet.ca
Publications:
- Dexter Cattle in Canada
Frequency: Annually
Profile: A herd book of the Dexter breed

Canadian Diabetes Association See Diabetes Canada

Canadian Diamond Drilling Association (CDDA)
City Centre Building, #337, 101 Worthington St. East, North Bay ON P1B 1G5
Tel: 705-476-6992; *Fax:* 705-476-9494
office@cdda.ca
www.canadiandrilling.com
Previous Name: Canadian Drilling Association

Overview: A medium-sized national organization founded in 1938
Mission: To foster the commercial interests of members; to promote the simplifications, standardization & interchangeability of diamond drilling equipment; to recognize the safety & health of employees; to foster the protection of the natural environment; to secure the elimination of unfair or uneconomic practices within the industry & freedom from unjust or unlawful exactions; to establish & maintain uniformity & equity in the customs & commercial usages of the diamond drilling business; to acquire & disseminate valuable business information; to promote communication among those engaged in the industry
Member of: National Drilling Association; Canadian Association of Mining Equipment & Services for Export; Prospectors & Developers Association of Canada
Finances: *Annual Operating Budget:* $50,000-$100,000; *Funding Sources:* Membership dues
Staff Member(s): 1
Membership: 100; *Fees:* $100 individual; $500 associate; $1,000-$5,100 active member
Activities: *Rents Mailing List:* Yes
Chief Officer(s):
Louise Lowe, Manager, 705-476-6992

Canadian Die Casters Association (CDCA) / Association canadienne des mouleurs sous pression
#3, 247 Barr St., Renfrew ON K7V 1J6
Fax: 613-432-6840
Toll-Free: 866-809-7032
info@diecasters.ca
www.diecasters.ca
Overview: A small national organization founded in 1980
Mission: To assist die casters in dealing with governments & other organizations on industry issues; To provide a united voice for members
Staff Member(s): 1
Membership: *Fees:* Schedule available, based upon gross sales volume; *Member Profile:* Canadian die casters
Activities: Conducting annual meetings, trade shows, & workshops
Chief Officer(s):
Bonnie James, Executive Director
Awards:
• Canadian Die Casters Association Bursary Program

Canadian Dietetic Association *See* Dietitians of Canada

Canadian Digestive Health Foundation (CDHF) / Fondation canadienne for la promotion de la santé digestive
#455, 2525 Old Bronte Rd., Oakville ON L6M 4J2
Tel: 905-847-2002
www.cdhf.ca
www.linkedin.com/company/649009
www.facebook.com/CDHFdn
twitter.com/TheCDHF
www.youtube.com/user/CDHFtube
Overview: A medium-sized national charitable organization founded in 1994 overseen by Canadian Association of Gastroenterology
Mission: To raise funds for the protection, promotion, & improvement of digestive health
Finances: *Funding Sources:* Donations; Government funding; Corporate sponsors
Staff Member(s): 3
Chief Officer(s):
Richard Fedorak, President
Catherine Mulvale, Executive Director
Publications:
• Canadian Digestive Health Foundation Newsletter
Type: Newsletter
Profile: Current information from digestive health experts across Canada

Canadian Direct Marketing Association *See* Canadian Marketing Association

Canadian Disaster Child Care Society (CDCC)
329 - 30th Ave. South, Cranbrook BC V1C 3K8
Tel: 250-489-0036; *Fax:* 250-489-0038
disasterchildcare@shaw.ca
www.members.shaw.ca/disasterchildcare
Overview: A small national organization
Mission: Trains volunteers to provide specialized childcare that focuses on using play to help children work through their feelings and regain control over their environment following a disaster
Activities: Has worked following the Montreal Ice Storm; with Kosovar children who came to Canada under Operation Parasol

Canadian Disaster Restoration Group (CDRG)
#5, 1084 Kenaston Rd., Ottawa ON K1B 3P5
Tel: 613-736-9222; *Fax:* 613-736-1002
Toll-Free: 866-736-9222
storm@cdrg.ca
www.cdrg.ca
www.facebook.com/117026655044784
twitter.com/CDRG_RedTeam
Also Known As: cdrg+RedTeam
Overview: A medium-sized national organization founded in 2004
Mission: To provide disaster restoration services through their network of member companies across Canada
Membership: 60+
Chief Officer(s):
Simon Frigon, Founder & CEO
Michel Lapensee, Chief Financial Officer
Stephanie Delaney, Remediation Consultant

The Canadian Don't Do Drugs Society
PO Box 1053, 7B Pleasant Blvd., Toronto ON M4T 1K2
Tel: 416-923-3779; *Fax:* 416-923-0083
Toll-Free: 800-883-7761
www.skddd.org
www.linkedin.com/company/2802976
www.facebook.com/smartkidsdontdodrugs
twitter.com/SKDDD_SmartKidz
www.youtube.com/user/TheSmartkidz
Also Known As: Smart Kids Don't Do Drugs
Overview: A small national charitable organization founded in 1994
Mission: To aide children & parents in the fight against the ravages of drugs in our society
Chief Officer(s):
Robert O'Reilly, Executive Director

Canadian Donkey & Mule Association (CDMA)
PO Box 12716, Lloydminster AB T7V 0Y4
Tel: 780-875-6362
donkeyandmule@live.ca
www.donkeyandmule.com
Overview: A small national organization founded with 1976
Mission: To operate registry for donkeys & recordation for mules; to promote use, well-being & protection of donkeys & mules; to assist in training & placing donkeys for disabled riding.
Affiliation(s): American Donkey & Mule Society; British Donkey Breed Society; Breed Societies of Britain, Australia, Sweden, Holland, Germany, New Zealand
Finances: *Funding Sources:* Membership dues & charity auction
Membership: *Fees:* $20 junior; $40 single; $50 family; $50 foreign; *Member Profile:* Owner, breeder, manager, or supporter of donkeys & mules
Chief Officer(s):
Chris Schlosser, Secretary
kindatinyfarms@telus.net
Kim Baerg, President
kimbaerg@hotmail.com

Canadian Door Institute of Dealers, Manufacturers & Distributors (CDI) / Institut canadien de concessionnaires, manufacturiers et distributeurs de portes
#210, 2800 - 14th Ave., Markham ON L3R 0E4
Tel: 905-814-9260; *Fax:* 416-491-1670
info@cdi-door.com
www.cdi-door.com
www.facebook.com/CDI.National
Overview: A medium-sized national organization
Mission: To improve the standards of Canada's door industry
Membership: *Fees:* $135-$450; *Member Profile:* Manufacturers; Distributors; Dealers; Suppliers
Activities: Providing education, training, services & certification programs
Chief Officer(s):
Mike Plecash, President

The Canadian Doukhobor Society (CDS)
215 - 33 Ave. South, Creston BC V0G 1G1
Tel: 250-204-2931
spirit-wrestlers.com/CDS
Overview: A small national charitable organization founded in 1930
Mission: To promote brotherhood, universal peace & the spiritual growth of our members
Member of: Council of Doukhobors in Canada
Finances: *Funding Sources:* Membership donations
Membership: *Member Profile:* Groups & organizations who respect Doukhobor ideals & principles as stated in statute
Chief Officer(s):
Beth Terriff, Secretary-Treasurer
Alex Wishlow, President
awishlow@kootenay.com

Canadian Dove Association (CDA)
c/o John House, PO Box 135, Plattsville ON N0J 1S0
canadiandoveassociation.weebly.com
Overview: A small national organization founded in 1977
Mission: To better inform fanciers about dove & foreign pigeons of the world
Member of: Avicultural Advancement Council of Canada
Finances: *Funding Sources:* Membership dues; donations
Membership: *Fees:* $7 junior; $25 family/senior; $40 international
Activities: Propagation to prevent extinction
Chief Officer(s):
John House, Secretary-Treasurer
David House, President

Canadian Down Syndrome Society (CDSS) / Société canadienne du syndrome de Down
#103, 2003 - 14 St. NW, Calgary AB T2M 3N4
Tel: 403-270-8500; *Fax:* 403-270-8291
Toll-Free: 800-883-5608
www.cdss.ca
www.facebook.com/cdndownsyndrome
twitter.com/CdnDownSyndrome
www.youtube.com/user/CdnDownSyndrome
Overview: A medium-sized national charitable organization founded in 1987
Mission: To ensure equitable opportunities for all Canadians with Down Syndrome
Finances: *Funding Sources:* Health Canada; Grants; Donations; Membership
43 volunteer(s)
Membership: 1,400; *Fees:* $20 individual/family; $40 group; *Member Profile:* Families & individuals with Down syndrome; Educators; Medical professionals; *Committees:* Resource Council (Medical & Educational); National Funding; Public Awareness; Fund Raising; Membership; Adult Issues; Nominating
Activities: Providing information & education; Researching; Engaging in advocacy activities; Increasing public awareness; Offering family support & networking; Working in collaboration with other local groups & national organizations toward the realization of common objectives; *Awareness Events:* National Down Syndrome Awareness Week, November *Library:* Resource Centre & Library; by appointment
Chief Officer(s):
Laura LaChance, Chair
Kirk Crowther, Executive Director
Lynette Gowie, Office Manager
Kaitlyn Pecson, Manager, Communications
Jenny Morrow, Manager, Development
Corrine Grieve, Manager, Resource
Shannon Thomas, Coordinator, Communications & Membership
Meetings/Conferences:
• 31st Canadian Down Syndrome Conference, May, 2018, Hamilton, ON
Scope: National
Publications:
• Canadian Down Syndrome Society Newsletter
Type: Newsletter; *Frequency:* Quarterly
• CDSS [Canadian Down Syndrome Society] Calendar
Frequency: Annually
• CDSS [Canadian Down Syndrome Society] Information Series
Profile: Topics include Teaching Children with Down Syndrome, Toilet Training Your Child with Down Syndrome, Stubborn Behaviour, Registered Educational Savings Plan, Taxation,Wills & Trusts, Obstructive Sleep Apnea Syndrome, & Stop Running by Building Skills: Behavioural Approach

Canadian Dressage Owners & Riders Association
c/o Donald J. Barnes, #13, 1475 Upper Gage Ave., Hamilton ON L8T 1E6
Tel: 905-387-2031
dressagegames@aol.com
www.cadora.ca
www.facebook.com/CadoraInc

twitter.com/CadoraInc
instagram.com/CadoraInc
Also Known As: CADORA Inc.
Overview: A medium-sized national organization founded in 1969
Mission: To promote interest in dressage riding as a sport throughout Canada; To develop the sport consistent with the principles of the international governing body of the equestrian Olympic disciplines; To ensure progressions leading to competitive International levels
Member of: Equine Canada; Ontario Equestrian Federation
Affiliation(s): Dressage Canada
Finances: *Funding Sources:* Fundraising; Donations; Membership fees
Membership: *Member Profile:* Dressage riders from across Canada
Activities: Providing educational workshops & clinics; Coordinating competitions & matches; Presenting awards; Arranging demonstrations of dressage riding in all areas of Canada
Chief Officer(s):
Donald J. Barnes, President & Editor, Omnibus
David Rosensweig, Coordinator, National Clinic
dhr@live.ca
Publications:
• Cadora INK [a publication of the Canadian Dressage Owners & Riders Association]
Type: Newsletter; *Frequency:* Quarterly; *Accepts Advertising*;
Editor: Lisa Macklem
Profile: Competitions & results, workshops, clinics, events, meetings, feature articles, reviews, & regional reports
• Omnibus [a publication of the Canadian Dressage Owners & Riders Association]
Editor: Donald J. Barnes; *Price:* Free with membership in the Canadian Dressage Owners & Riders Association
Profile: Information about the CADORA National Awards Program, the Cadora L-Inc Program, the Cadora Education Sponsorship Plan, as well as EC/DC, FEI, & Cadora Inc dressage tests

Canadian Drilling Association *See* Canadian Diamond Drilling Association

Canadian Drug Manufacturers Association *See* Canadian Generic Pharmaceutical Association

Canadian Drug Policy Coalition (CDPC) / Coalition canadienne des politiques sur les drogues
c/o Centre for Applied Research in Mental Health & Addiction, SFU, #2400, 515 West Hastings St., Vancouver BC V6B 5K3
mail@drugpolicy.ca
www.drugpolicy.ca
www.linkedin.com/company/candrugpolicy
www.facebook.com/CANdrugpolicy
twitter.com/CANdrugpolicy
Overview: A medium-sized national organization founded in 2009
Mission: To promote a safe & healthy Canada in which drug policy & legislation are based on human rights, justice, & social inclusion; To engage Canadians to support innovative responses to drug related problems; To work to alter & improve Canada's drug policies
Finances: *Funding Sources:* Corporate sponsorship
Chief Officer(s):
Donald MacPherson, Executive Director
donaldmacpherson@drugpolicy.ca
Publications:
• Getting to Tomorrow: A Report on Canadian Drug Policy [a publication of the Canadian Drug Policy Coalition]
Type: Report; *Author:* Connie Carter & Donald MacPherson; *Editor:* Caroline Mousseau
Profile: A report examining the role of current federal drug policies in the maintenance of safety & health; Cites the need for an improved support system for drug users

Canadian Dupuytren Society / Société canadienne de Dupuytren
107, av de Marlin Crescent, Pointe-Claire QC H9S 5B2
Overview: A small national charitable organization
Mission: To raise awareness of Dupuytren's contracture
Chief Officer(s):
Paule Gauthier

Canadian Dyslexia Association (CDA) / Association canadienne de la dyslexie
57, rue du Couvent, Gatineau QC J9H 3C8
Tel: 613-853-6539; *Fax:* 819-684-0672
info@dyslexiaassociation.ca
www.dyslexiaassociation.ca
Overview: A medium-sized national charitable organization founded in 1991
Affiliation(s): Canadian Dyslexia Centre, Heritage Academy
Finances: *Funding Sources:* National Literacy Secretariat
Activities: *Internships:* Yes; *Speaker Service:* Yes; *Library:* by appointment

Canadian Economics Association (CEA) / Association canadienne d'économique
Department of Economics, Brock Univ., 500 Glenridge Ave., St Catharines ON L2S 3A1
Tel: 905-688-5550
www.economics.ca
Overview: A small national organization founded in 1967
Mission: To represent academic economists; To advance economic knowledge
Member of: Social Science Federation of Canada
Finances: *Funding Sources:* Membership fees
Membership: 1,800; *Fees:* $20 students & retirees; $50 regular; *Member Profile:* Academic economists in Canada & abroad; Undergraduate & graduate students at degree-granting universities; Retired members, age 65 or older
Activities: Encouraging study & research; Furthering discussion of economic questions; Listing employment opportunities
Chief Officer(s):
Vivian Tran, Executive Director
office@economics.ca
Charles Beach, President
beachc@econ.queensu.ca
Frances Woolley, Vice-President
Robert Diamond, Secretary-Treasurer
robert.dimand@brocku.ca
Awards:
• John Rae Prize
Presented every two years, in recognition of research excellence; *Amount:* $10,000
• Doug Purvis Memorial Prize
To honour a work of excellence relating to Canadian economic policy; *Amount:* $10,000
• Harry G. Johnson Prize
For the author or authors of the paper judged to be the best paper published in the Canadian Journal of Economics; *Amount:* $5,000
• Robert Mundell Prize
For the young author or authors of the paper judged to be the best paper published in the Canadian Journal of Economics; *Amount:* $3,000
• John Vanderkamp Prize
For the best paper published in Canadian Public Policy; *Amount:* $2,000
• The Mike McCracken Award for Economic Statistics
To recognize contributions to the development or use of official economic statistics
Meetings/Conferences:
• Canadian Economics Association 52nd Annual Conference 2018, June, 2018, McGill University, Montreal, QC
Scope: National
Description: An annual conference held during the last week of May or the first week of June
• Canadian Economics Association 52nd Annual Conference 2019, 2019, Banff Centre for Arts & Creativity, Banff, AB
Scope: National
Description: An annual conference held during the last week of May or the first week of June
• Canadian Economics Association 52nd Annual Conference 2020, 2020, University of Toronto, Toronto, ON
Scope: National
Description: An annual conference held during the last week of May or the first week of June
Publications:
• Canadian Economics Department Directory [a publication of the Canadian Economics Association]
Type: Directory
Profile: Contact information for economic departments across Canada
• Canadian Journal of Economics / Revue canadienne d'économique [a publication of the Canadian Economics Association]
Type: Journal; *Editor:* D. Green (journals@economics.ca); *Price:* Free with membership in the Canadian Economics Association
Profile: Theoretical & empirical papers in all areas of economics
• Canadian Public Policy [a publication of the Canadian Economics Association]
Type: Journal; *Frequency:* Quarterly; *Accepts Advertising*;
Editor: Herb Emery (cpp.adp@gmail.com); *ISSN:* 0317-0861
Profile: An examination of public policy problems in Canada, written for advisers & decision makers in business organizations & governments, & policy researchers in universities & private institutions
• Directory of Canadian Academic Economists [a publication of the Canadian Economics Association]
Type: Directory
Profile: Rank & contact information for academic economists throughout Canada

Canadian Ecumenical Action *See* Multifaith Action Society

Canadian Eczema Society for Education & Research *See* Eczema Society of Canada

Canadian Education & Research Institute for Counselling
Foundation House, #300, 2 St. Clair Ave. East, Toronto ON M4T 2T5
Tel: 416-929-2510; *Fax:* 416-923-2536
admin@ceric.ca
www.ceric.ca
www.linkedin.com/company/canadian-education-and-research-institute-for-counselling-ceric-
www.facebook.com/cericca
twitter.com/ceric_ca
Overview: A medium-sized national charitable organization
Mission: To promote & provide education & research programs for individuals working or interested in the career counselling & development field; To enhance the quality & accessibility of counselling services in Canada
Membership: *Committees:* Content & Learning; Marketing, Communications & Web Services; Practical & Academic Research
Activities: Developing career advancement initiatives
Chief Officer(s):
Riz Ibrahim, Executive Director
riz@ceric.ca
Awards:
• Etta St John Wileman Award
• Graduate Student Award
Eligibility: Full-time graduate students who have submitted a one-page career development article on the ContactPoint or OrientAction websites
• Elizabeth McTavish Bursary
Eligibility: Non-profit, community-based organizations
Publications:
• CERIC [Canadian Education & Research Institute for Counselling] Annual Report
Type: Yearbook; *Frequency:* Annually

Canadian Education & Training Accreditation Commission (CETAC)
#310, 590 Queen St., Fredericton NB E3B 7H9
Tel: 613-800-0340
www.cetac.ca
Overview: A medium-sized national organization founded in 1984
Mission: To assure students & the general public of the quality of Canada's post-secondary institutions & the programs they offer; To assist the institutions in continuously improving themselves & the education provided to students

Canadian Education Association (CEA) / Association canadienne d'éducation (ACE)
#703, 60 St. Clair Ave. East, Toronto ON M4T 1N5
Tel: 416-591-6300; *Fax:* 416-591-5345
Toll-Free: 866-803-9549
info@edcan.ca
www.edcan.ca
www.linkedin.com/company/canadian-education-association-cea-association-canadienne-d-ducation-ace-
www.facebook.com/cea.ace
twitter.com/EdCanNet
www.youtube.com/user/CdnEducAssn
Also Known As: EdCan Network
Overview: A medium-sized national charitable organization founded in 1891
Mission: To promote educational change in Canada
Member of: Magazines Canada; Imaging Canada
Finances: *Funding Sources:* Provincial departments of education; Publication sales; Membership fees; Fees for service; Forums

Staff Member(s): 6
Membership: 350; *Fees:* $50 student; $120 individual; $360 non-profit organization; $540 corporate; $750 (plus fee based on enrolment) school district; $1,000 faculty; *Committees:* Executive; Council; Editorial Board
Activities: Providing information for school boards & organizations; Producing publications; Offering leadership courses; Providing a conversations series
Chief Officer(s):
Ron Canuel, President & Chief Executive Officer
rcanuel@cea-ace.ca
Gilles Latour, Chief Operating Officer
glatour@cea-ace.ca
Max Cooke, Director, Communications
mcooke@cea-ace.ca
Mia San Jose, Manager, Circulations & Membership
Awards:
• Whitworth Award for Education Research

Canadian Education Exchange Foundation (CEEF) / Fondation canadienne des echanges educatifs
#4, 250 Bayview Dr., Barrie ON L4N 4Y8
Tel: 705-739-7596; *Fax:* 705-739-7764
www.ceef.ca
www.facebook.com/CEEFexchanges
Overview: A medium-sized national organization

Canadian Educational Researchers' Association (CERA)
c/o Canadian Society for the Study of Education, #204, 260 Dalhousie St., Ottawa ON K1N 7E4
Tel: 613-241-0018; *Fax:* 613-241-0019
www.ceraacce.ca
Overview: A small national organization overseen by Canadian Society for the Study of Education
Mission: To improve the quality & quantity of educational research; To act as the voice for the educational research community throughout Canada
Member of: Canadian Society for the Study of Education
Affiliation(s): Canadian Society for the Study of Education (CSSE)
Membership: *Fees:* $10 regular & international; $5 student/retired/low income; *Member Profile:* Educational researchers who are members of the Canadian Society for the Study of Education; Associate members who have an interest in educational research & who believe in the goals of the association; Graduate students
Activities: Promoting & supporting research in education; Mentoring students; Organizing networking events
Chief Officer(s):
Christopher DeLuca, President
cdeluca@queensu.ca
Laurie Hellsten-Bzovey, Executive Officer
laurie.hellsten@usask.ca
Awards:
• Audet-Allard Award
• R.W.B. Jackson Award
• Todd Rogers Research Award
• David Bateson New Scholar Award

Canadian Educational Resources Council (CERC)
#203, 250 Merton St., Toronto ON M4S 1B1
Tel: 416-322-7011; *Fax:* 416-322-6999
www.cerc-ca.org
Overview: A medium-sized national organization
Mission: Seeks to enhance elementary and secondary education in Canada by developing mutually beneficial relationships with the educational community that result in the development and acquisition of high quality learning resources and improved student achievement.
Member of: Canadian Education Association; Canadian Copyright Institute; Access Copyright
Chief Officer(s):
Gerry McIntyre, Executive Director

Canadian Egg Marketing Agency *See* Egg Farmers of Canada

Canadian Electric Wheelchair Hockey Association (CEWHA)
#920, 200 Yorkland Blvd., Toronto ON M2J 5C1
Tel: 416-757-8544; *Fax:* 416-490-9334
info@cewha.ca
www.cewha.ca
www.facebook.com/cewha
twitter.com/canadianewha
www.youtube.com/cewhanational
Overview: A small national charitable organization founded in 1980
Mission: To provide a hockey program for persons with disabilities who have limited upper body strength & mobility
Finances: *Funding Sources:* Donations; Sponsorships; Fundraising
Membership: 200 players + 80 volunteers; *Member Profile:* All persons with disabilities who would benefit from an electric wheelchair in competitive sport & daily living
Activities: Offering recreation & social programs; Organizing national tournaments
Chief Officer(s):
John Blackburn, Executive Director

Canadian Electrical Contractors Association (CECA) / Association canadienne des entrepreneurs électriciens (ACEE)
41 Maple St., Uxbridge ON L9P 1C8
Tel: 416-491-2414; *Fax:* 416-765-0006
ceca@ceca.org
www.ceca.org
www.facebook.com/595431040611335
Overview: A medium-sized national organization founded in 1955
Mission: To represent electrical contractors at the national level
Member of: National Trade Contractors Coalition of Canada
Affiliation(s): National Electrical Contractors Association (International Chapter); Canadian Construction Association; Canadian Standards Association
Membership: 8,000 contractors employing 70,000 persons; *Member Profile:* Provincial & territorial electrical contractor groups
Activities: Numerous publications on topics such as management, codes & standards, safety, marketing & more; access to employee group benefits
Chief Officer(s):
David Mason, President
Kevin Ashley, Vice-President

Canadian Electrical Manufacturers Representatives Association (CEMRA)
#300, 180 Attwell Dr., Toronto ON M9W 6A9
Tel: 905-602-8877; *Fax:* 416-679-9234
Toll-Free: 866-602-8877
info@electrofed.com
www.electrofed.com
Overview: A medium-sized national organization founded in 1980
Mission: To represent over 300 member companies that manufacture, distribute & service electrical, electronics & telecommunications products
Member of: Electro-Federation Canada; Electrical Council
5 volunteer(s)
Membership: 300+ member companies; *Member Profile:* Independent sales representatives in the electrical industry
Chief Officer(s):
Jim Taggart, President & CEO
jtaggart@electrofed.com

Canadian Electricity Association (CEA) / Association canadienne de l'électricité (ACE)
#1500, 275 Slater St., Ottawa ON K1P 5H9
Tel: 613-230-9263; *Fax:* 613-230-9326
info@electricity.ca
www.electricity.ca
www.linkedin.com/company/canadian-electricity-association
www.facebook.com/canadianelectricityassociation
twitter.com/CDNElectricity
powerforthefuture.ca/blog
Overview: A large national organization founded in 1891
Mission: To be the national voice for safe, secure & sustainable electricity for Canadians; To provide its members with value-added products & services to advance the strategic interests of Canada's electricity community
Staff Member(s): 30
Membership: 38 Corporate Utility Members; 66 Corporate Partner Members; 14 Associate Members; *Member Profile:* Corporate Utility Members consist of companies that generate, transmit, & distribute electrical energy to customers throughout Canada; Corporate Partner Members consist of manufacturers & suppliers serving the electricity sector; *Committees:* Human Resources; Occupational Health and Safety; Technology
Activities: Analyzing national & international business issues; Providing a national forum for the electricity business; Advocating industry views; Helping companies in evolving markets; Communicating findings about concerns such as mercury emissions & electric & magnetic fields; *Library:* Canadian Electricty Association Library
Chief Officer(s):
Sergio Marchi, President & CEO
Francis Bradley, Chief Operating Officer
bradley@electricity.ca
Richard Lussier, CPA, CMA, Vice-President, Operations
lussier@electricity.ca
Devin McCarthy, Vice-President, Public Affairs & US Policy
mccarthy@electricity.ca
David Martinek, Director, Communications
martinek@electricity.ca
Publications:
• Annual Service Continuity Report on Distribution System Performance in Electrical Utilities
Type: Yearbook; *Frequency:* Annually; *Price:* $250 members; $800 non-members
Profile: Produced by the Performance Excellence & Benchmarking program of the Canadian Electricity Association, the report containsinformation about industry standard metrics for electricity distribution, including system average interruption frequency index & the system average interruption duration index
• The CEA [Canadian Electricity Association] Member Directory & Resource Guide
Type: Directory; *Frequency:* Annually; *Price:* $15 members; $65 non-members
Profile: Contact information for the Canadian electricity industry's major players, in addition to information about the operations of the CanadianElectricity Association's member companies
• Electricity Annual
Type: Yearbook; *Frequency:* Annually
Profile: The Canadian Electricity Association's yearly industry review
• Forced Outage Performance of Transmission Equipment [a publication of the Canadian Electricity Association]
Type: Yearbook; *Frequency:* Annually; *Price:* $550 members; $1,400 non-members
Profile: Produced by the Performance Excellence & Benchmarking program of the Canadian Electricity Association, thereport addresses the performance of transmission equipment in Canada
• Generation Equipment Status [a publication of the Canadian Electricity Association]
Type: Yearbook; *Frequency:* Annually; *Price:* $550 members; $1,400 non-members
Profile: Produced by the Performance Excellence & Benchmarking program of the Canadian Electricity Association, the report features informationon the performance of electrical generating units in Canada

Canadian Employee Assistance Program Association (CEAPA) / Association canadienne des programmes d'aide aux employés (ACPAE)
1031 Portage Ave., Winnipeg MB R3G 0R8
Tel: 204-944-7063
www.ceapaonline.com
Overview: A medium-sized national organization founded in 1995
Mission: To promote the concept of Employee Assistance Programs in Canada & to provide networking opportunities for EAP practitioners & programs
Finances: *Funding Sources:* Membership dues
19 volunteer(s)
Membership: 200; *Fees:* $35 individual; $100 corporate
Activities: *Speaker Service:* Yes
Chief Officer(s):
Tony Showchuk, President
tony.showchuk@sasktel.com
Maria Besenski, Treasurer
Maria.besenski@saskatoon.ca
Awards:
• Workplace Excellence
Recognizing organiations that are committed to improving well being of employees
• EAP Union Excellence
Recognizing the contributions that Union members have brought to the field of EAP
• Individual Excellence
Recognizing individuals that contribute to the overall well being of fellow employees & families in dealing with challenges/changes

Canadian Employee Relocation Council (CERC)
#1010, 180 Dundas St. W., Toronto ON M5G 1Z8

Tel: 416-593-9812; *Fax:* 416-593-1139
Toll-Free: 866-357-2372
info@cerc.ca
www.cerc.ca
www.facebook.com/151161928253133
twitter.com/CERC_CA
Overview: A small national organization founded in 1982
Mission: To provide leadership, services & assistance to members enabling them to effectively serve relocated families by addressing issues that impact the relocation industry, domestically & internationally
Finances: *Annual Operating Budget:* $100,000-$250,000
Staff Member(s): 2; 70 volunteer(s)
Membership: 550; *Fees:* $50 student; $155 individual; $275 associate; $475 corporate
Activities: *Library:* Not open to public
Chief Officer(s):
Stephen Cryne, President/CEO
Meetings/Conferences:
• Canadian Employee Relocation Council 2018 Conference, 2018
Scope: National
Publications:
• Bi-Annual Survey [a publication of the Canadian Employee Relocation Council]
Frequency: Semiannually; *Price:* Free for CERC members
Profile: Survey on employee relocation policies
• CERC [Canadian Employee Relocation Council] News
Type: Newsletter; *Frequency:* Monthly; *Price:* Free with CERC membership
Profile: Current industry news & information
• CERC [Canadian Employee Relocation Council] Perspectives Magazine
Type: Magazine; *Frequency:* Quarterly; *Price:* Free with CERC membership
Profile: Analysis of issues & trends in relocation
• CERC [Canadian Employee Relocation Council] Membership Roster
Type: Directory; *Price:* Free for Canadian Employee Relocation Council members
• Relocation Policies
Price: Free for CERC corporate members

Canadian Energy Efficiency Alliance (CEEA) / L'Association de l'efficacité énergétique du Canada
1485 Laperriere Ave., Ottawa ON K1Z 7S8
Tel: 613-722-2269; *Fax:* 613-729-6206
info@energyefficiency.org
www.energyefficiency.org
www.linkedin.com/groups?gid=4036109
www.facebook.com/111344902257508
twitter.com/CdnEnergyEffic
Overview: A medium-sized national organization founded in 1995
Mission: To promote the economic & environmental benefits of energy efficiency; To work with the federal & provincial governments, & stakeholders, to ensure energy efficiency is a priority for all sectors of the economy
Affiliation(s): Canadian Energy Efficiency Centre
Finances: *Annual Operating Budget:* $250,000-$500,000; *Funding Sources:* Membership dues & projects
Membership: 25,000; *Fees:* $80-$15,000; *Member Profile:* Businesses providing energy efficiency products or services in Canada
Activities: Establishing a National Energy Efficiency Centre to be North America's energy technology showcase; Provide research on energy efficiency & its advancement; Create networking opportunities for members & stakeholders; Support effective energy efficiency polices, programs, codes & standards; Help members develop, promote & deliver energy efficient products & services; Annual meetings
Chief Officer(s):
Elizabeth McDonald, President & CEO
elizabethmcdonald@energyefficiency.org
Natalia Kaliberda, Client Manager
natalia.kaliberda@thewillowgroup.com

Canadian Energy Law Foundation (CELF)
1959 Upper Water St., Halifax NS B3J 3N2
Tel: 902-420-3328; *Fax:* 902-420-1417
info@energylawfoundation.ca
www.energylawfoundation.ca
Previous Name: Canadian Petroleum Law Foundation
Overview: A small national organization founded in 1963
Mission: To foster the development & improvement of law relating to or affecting the phases of the petroleum & natural gas industries; To raise the standards of the administration & practice of the law; To encourage a better knowledge & understanding of the law
Membership: *Fees:* $525 Class A (firms of 5+ lawyers); $105 Class B (firms of 1-4 laywers); *Member Profile:* Legal practitioners from law firms, companies, governmental entities, administrative bodies, professional societies & institutions of learning
Chief Officer(s):
Ryan Konotopsky, President
president@energylawfoundation.ca
Awards:
• Graduate Scholarship in Law
; *Amount:* Up to $20,000
• Undergraduate Scholarships/Prizes in Law
; *Amount:* $2,500 per prize

Canadian Energy Pipeline Association (CEPA) / Association canadienne de pipelines d'énergie
#1110, 505 - 3rd St. SW, Calgary AB T2P 3E6
Tel: 403-221-8777; *Fax:* 403-221-8760
aboutpipelines@cepa.com
www.cepa.com
www.facebook.com/aboutpipelines
twitter.com/aboutpipelines
www.youtube.com/aboutpipelines;
www.slideshare.net/aboutpipelines
Overview: A medium-sized national organization founded in 1993
Mission: To represent Canada's transmission pipeline companies; To ensure a strong transmission pipeline industry
Staff Member(s): 14; 200 volunteer(s)
Membership: *Member Profile:* Canada's pipeline companies that transport natural gas & crude oil throughout North America; *Committees:* Damage Prevention Regulations; Emergency Security Management; Environment; Health & Safety; Land Issues Task Force; Pipeline Integrity; Aboriginal Affairs; Climate Change; Corporate Tax; Commodity Tax; Pipeline Abandonment Obligations; Pipeline Economics; Property Tax; Regulatory Accounting; Regulatory Policy
Activities: Liaising with government regarding industry practices
Chief Officer(s):
Chris Bloomer, President & Chief Executive Officer
Jim Donihee, Chief Operating Officer
Patrick Smyth, Director, Safety & Engineering
Awards:
• Environmental Management Award
• Environmental Achievement Award
• Spill Prevention Award

Canadian Energy Research Institute (CERI)
#150, 3512 - 33 St. NW, Calgary AB T2L 2A6
Tel: 403-282-1231; *Fax:* 403-284-4181
info@ceri.ca
www.ceri.ca
twitter.com/ceri_canada
Overview: A medium-sized national organization founded in 1975
Mission: To provide public, industry & government individuals with information concerning all aspects of energy
Membership: 150; *Committees:* Research Advisory
Activities: *Speaker Service:* Yes; *Library:* I.N. McKinnon Memorial Library
Chief Officer(s):
Allan Fogwill, President & CEO
David McWhinney, Vice President, Finance & Operations
Dinara Millington, Vice President, Research
Lisa Rollins, Vice President, Marketing & Communications
Meetings/Conferences:
• Canadian Energy Research Institute 2018 Petrochemical Conference, June, 2018, Kananaskis, AB
Scope: National

Canadian Energy Workers' Association (CEWA)
9908 - 106 St., Edmonton AB T5K 1C4
Tel: 780-420-7887; *Fax:* 780-420-7881
cewa@cewa.ca
www.cewa.ca
Previous Name: Canadian Utilities & Northland Utilities Employees' Association; Alberta Power Employees' Association
Overview: A small national organization founded in 1969
Mission: To represent the interests of members, by serving as a bargaining agent for matters related to working relations with employers
Activities: Engaging in problem solving between members & management; Creating programs for members in the areas of safety, security & skills development; Seeking opportunities to organize & represent workers; Offering an annual bursary program
Chief Officer(s):
Christine Robinson, Interim Manager, Business, 780-977-3418
crobinson@cewa.ca

Canadian Engineering Education Association (CEEA) / Association canadienne de l'éducation en génie (ACEG)
c/o Design Engineering, University of Manitoba, E2-262 EITC, 75 Chancellors Circle, Winnipeg MB R3T 5V6
Tel: 204-474-7113; *Fax:* 204-474-7676
ceea@umanitoba.ca
ceea.ca
Overview: A medium-sized national organization
Mission: Aims to enhance the competence and relevance of graduates from Canadian Engineering schools through continuous improvement in engineering education.
Membership: *Fees:* $25 individual; $100 professional; $500 institutional/affiliate
Chief Officer(s):
Susan McCahan, President
Meetings/Conferences:
• Canadian Engineering Education Association 2018 Conference, June, 2018, University of British Columbia, Vancouver, BC
Scope: National

Canadian Entertainment Conference *See* Canadian Organization of Campus Activities

Canadian Environment Industry Association (CEIA)
#410, 215 Spadina Ave., Toronto ON M5T 2C7
Tel: 416-531-7884
info@oneia.ca
www.oneia.ca
www.linkedin.com/groups/3999411/profile
twitter.com/ONEIAnetwork
www.youtube.com/user/ONEIAmedia
Overview: A large national organization
Mission: To promote the interests and development of Canadian companies supplying environmental technologies, products & services
Membership: 1,500
Chief Officer(s):
Derek Webb, President & Chief Executive Officer
Alex Gill, Executive Director
Marjan Lahuis, Manager, Operations

Canadian Environment Industry Association - British Columbia Chapter *See* British Columbia Environment Industry Association

Canadian Environment Industry Association - Ontario Chapter *See* Ontario Environment Industry Association

Canadian Environmental Auditing Association *See* Auditing Association of Canada

Canadian Environmental Certification Approvals Board (CECAB) / Bureau canadien de reconnaissance professionnelle des spécialistes de l'environnement
#200, 308 - 11th Ave. SE, Calgary AB T2G 0Y2
Tel: 403-233-7484; *Fax:* 403-264-6240
certification@eco.ca
www.cecab.org
Overview: A small national licensing organization founded in 1998
Mission: CECAB is a professional autonomous body providing national certification for Canadian environmental practitioners.
Finances: *Annual Operating Budget:* $250,000-$500,000; *Funding Sources:* Industry; HRDC; CCHREI
Staff Member(s): 3
Membership: 700+; *Fees:* CEDIT $50; CCEP $150-300; *Member Profile:* Environmental practitioners from all provinces & territories, representing all disciplines.; *Committees:* Certification; Discipline; Ethics; Professional Development
Chief Officer(s):
Victor Nowicki, Chair

Canadian Environmental Defence Fund *See* Environmental Defence

Canadian Associations / Canadian Environmental Grantmakers' Network (CEGN) / Réseau canadien des subventionneurs en environnement (RCSE)

Canadian Environmental Grantmakers' Network (CEGN) / Réseau canadien des subventionneurs en environnement (RCSE)
c/o Foundation House, 2 St. Clair Ave. East, Toronto ON M4T 2T5
Tel: 647-288-8891
info@cegn.org
www.cegn.org
twitter.com/cegn
Overview: A medium-sized national organization founded in 1995
Mission: To develop an effective network of environmental grantmakers in Canada by facilitating information-sharing, collaboration, training & professional development, research, & communications
Membership: *Member Profile:* Private, community, public & corporate foundations; government & corporate funding programs that give grants in support of Canadian environment
Chief Officer(s):
Pegi Dover, Executive Director
pegi_dover@cegn.org
Meetings/Conferences:
• Canadian Environmental Grantmakers' Network 2018 Conference, May, 2018, The Banff Centre, Banff, AB
Scope: National
Contact Information: Executive Director: Pegi Dover; Email: pegi_dover@cegn.org; Phone: 647-288-8891

Canadian Environmental Law Association (CELA) / Association canadienne du droit de l'environnement
#301, 130 Spadina Ave., Toronto ON M5V 2L4
Tel: 416-960-2284; *Fax:* 416-960-9392
articling@cela.ca
www.cela.ca
www.facebook.com/CanadianEnvironmentalLawAssociation
twitter.com/CanEnvLawAssn
Overview: A medium-sized national organization founded in 1970
Mission: To advocate for environmental law reform; To act in court or during hearings on behalf of citizens' groups & individuals who would otherwise be unable to afford legal assistance
Finances: *Funding Sources:* Legal Aid Ontario
Staff Member(s): 15; 1 volunteer(s)
Activities: *Library:* Resource Library for the Environment & the Law; by appointment
Chief Officer(s):
Tracy Tucker, Office Manager/Executive Assistant, 416-960-2284 Ext. 210
tracy@cela.ca

Canadian Environmental Network (RCEN) / Réseau canadien de l'environnement
14 Manchester Ave., Ottawa ON K1Y 1Y9
Tel: 613-728-9810; *Fax:* 613-728-2963
secretary@rcen.ca
rcen.ca
www.facebook.com/CanadianEnvironmentalNetwork
twitter.com/RCEN
www.youtube.com/user/RCEN1
Overview: A large national organization founded in 1977
Mission: To promote ecologically sound ways of life; To enhance members' work to restore, protect, & promote a clean & sustainable environment
Membership: *Member Profile:* Canadian non-profit, non-governmental organizations with a focus on environmental concerns
Activities: Providing communication & networking services for members
Chief Officer(s):
Josh Brandon, Chair
chair@rcen.ca
Publications:
• Getting Answers: A Guide to the Environmental Petitions Process
Type: Guide; *Number of Pages:* 27
• Ideas for a More Effective Environmental Movement in Canada
Number of Pages: 17; *Author:* Jerry DeMarco
• Mercury . . . A Global Toxin: Perspectives on Initiatives & Programs on Coal-Fired Power Plants & Mercury Emissions
Number of Pages: 114; *Author:* Anna Tilman
Profile: Coal-fired Power Plants - Mercury Emissions; Canada-wide Standards for Mercury Electric PowerGenerating Sector; Strategies & Control Technologies for Reducing Mercury Emissions; Mercury Emission Trading; U.S. Regulatory Action on Mercury & Coal-Fired Plants; Global Initiatives on Mercury
• Mercury . . . A Public Concern, including Analysis of Mercury Emissions from Coal-Fired Power Plants & Canada-Wide Standards
Number of Pages: 198; *Author:* Anna Tilman
Profile: Government Programs-Mercury; Canada-wide Standards for Mercury Electric Power GeneratingSector; Mercury Data from Coal-Fired Plants; Cumulative Emissions-The True Loading Picture; U.S. Regulatory Action on Mercury & Coal-Fired Plants; Recommendations for Canada-wide Standards for Mercury
• Participating in Federal Public Policy: A Guide for the Voluntary Sector
Type: Guide
Profile: A resource to assist voluntary organizations participate in the federal public policy development process
• RCEN [Canadian Environmental Network] e-Bulletin
Type: Newsletter; *Frequency:* Weekly
Profile: Up-to-date information about RCEN activities & news of interest for RCEN members
• RCEN [Canadian Environmental Network] Annual Report
Type: Yearbook; *Frequency:* Annually
Profile: A review of the network's activities & audited financial statements
• RCEN [Canadian Environmental Network] Youth Friendly Guide: Youth Guide to Policy Change for Intergenerational Partnerships
Type: Guide
Profile: A guidebook of interest to organizations wanting to make their operations youth-friendly
• RCEN [Canadian Environmental Network] Biodiversity Best Practices Handbook
Type: Handbook

Canadian Environmental Technology Advancement Corporation - West (CETAC)
3608 - 33rd St. NW, Calgary AB T2L 2A6
Tel: 403-777-9595; *Fax:* 403-777-9599
cetac@cetacwest.com
cetacwest.com
www.linkedin.com/company-beta/2128202
www.facebook.com/431936763529236
Also Known As: CETAC-West
Overview: A medium-sized national organization founded in 1994
Mission: To be committed to helping small & medium-sized enterprises that are engaged in the development & commercialization of new environmental technologies
Finances: *Funding Sources:* Provincial & federal government
Staff Member(s): 8
Activities: Technical research assistance, regulatory counsel & a range of consulting & referral services
Publications:
• CETAC [Canadian Environmental Technology Advancement Corporation] Focus
Type: Newsletter; *Frequency:* Quarterly

Canadian Epilepsy Alliance (CAE) / L'Alliance canadienne de l'épilepsie (ACE)
c/o President, 351 Kenmount Rd., St. John's NL A1B 3P9
Tel: 709-722-0502; *Fax:* 709-722-0999
www.epilepsymatters.com
Overview: A medium-sized national charitable organization founded in 1998
Mission: To promote independence & quality of life for people with epilepsy & their families, through support services, information, advocacy, & public awareness
Finances: *Funding Sources:* Membership fees; donations; grants; shared costs
Membership: *Member Profile:* Epilepsy organizations across Canada
Activities: *Speaker Service:* Yes
Chief Officer(s):
Gail Dempsey, President
executivedirector@epilepsynl.com
Publications:
• Epilepsy Matters: The Newsletter of the Canadian Epilepsy Alliance
Type: Newsletter; *Frequency:* 3 pa
Profile: National thematic journal about epilepsy issues for persons with epilepsy & their caregivers

Canadian ETF Association (CETFA)
c/o Horizons Exchange Traded Funds, #700, 26 Wellington St. East, Toronto ON M5E 1S2
www.cetfa.ca
twitter.com/cetfassn
www.youtube.com/cetfassn
Overview: A small national organization founded in 2011
Mission: To promote awareness of the Canadian exchange trade fund (ETF) industry
Membership: 6 member firms + 17 affiliate firms + 13 portfolio managers; *Fees:* $7,500; *Member Profile:* Any Canadian Exchange Traded Fund provider
Activities: Increasing ETF education for both retail & institutional investors; Providing industry statistics; Ensuring the adoption of best practice standards by the ETF industry
Chief Officer(s):
Howard Atkinson, Founding Managing Director & Chair, 416-777-5167
hatkinson@horizonsetfs.com

Canadian Ethnic Journalists' & Writers' Club *See* Canadian Ethnic Media Association

Canadian Ethnic Media Association (CEMA)
24 Tarlton Rd., Toronto ON M5P 2M4
Tel: 416-488-0048
canadianethnicmedia.com
Previous Name: Canadian Ethnic Journalists' & Writers' Club
Overview: A small national organization founded in 1978
Mission: To promote & preserve the value of the ethnic media in Canada; To advance understanding of Canada's cultural diversity
Membership: *Fees:* Schedule available; *Member Profile:* Print, broadcast, & web journalists & writers; journalism students
Activities: Promoting multiculturalism; Providing opportunities for members to exchange ideas; Cooperating with similar organizations
Chief Officer(s):
Madeline Ziniak, Contact
madeline.ziniak@gmail.com
Awards:
• CEMA Awards
Up to nine plaques are offered annually to jounalists in print, radio, television & innovation; awards are given to journalists for excellence in their field; competition is open to all journalists, in any language, whether or not they are members of the Club; a single award is also given to writers of a published work of fact, fiction or poetry in book form.

Canadian Ethnic Studies Association (CESA) / Société canadienne d'études ethniques (SCEE)
c/o University of Calgary, Social Science, #909, 2500 University Dr. NW, Calgary AB T2N 1N4
Tel: 403-220-7372
Other Communication: Alt. E-mail: ces@cc.umanitoba.ca
cesa@ucalgary.ca
cesa.uwinnipeg.ca
Previous Name: Inter University Committee on Canadian Slavs (IUCCS)
Overview: A medium-sized national organization founded in 1971
Mission: To encourage scholarly debate about theoretical & practical issues in Canadian ethnic studies
Membership: *Fees:* Schedule available
Activities: Promoting & supporting education in Canadian ethnic studies; Liaising with related organizations; Encouraging understanding of diverse cultural heritages; Providing networking opportunities among scholars
Chief Officer(s):
Shibao Guo, President
guos@ucalgary.ca
Evangelia Tastsoglou, Vice-President
evie.tastsoglou@smu.ca
Henry P.H. Chow, Secretary-Treasurer
Henry.Chow@uregina.ca
Awards:
• Howard Palmer Memorial Scholarship Award
Publications:
• Canadian Ethnic Studies / Études ethniques au Canada
Type: Journal; *Frequency:* 3 pa; *Editor:* Lloyd L. Wong
Profile: Scholarly articles, book reviews & research notes about immigration, ethnicity, inter-group relations, & the history & cultural life ofethnic groups in Canada

Canadian Ethnocultural Council (CEC) / Conseil ethnoculturel du Canada
#400, 176 Gloucester St., Ottawa ON K2P 0A6
Tel: 613-230-3867; *Fax:* 613-230-8051
cec@web.net

www.ethnocultural.ca
www.youtube.com/user/EthnoCanada
Overview: A medium-sized national organization founded in 1980
Mission: To represent a cross-section of ethnocultural groups across Canada.
Membership: 33 national organizations
Activities: *Speaker Service:* Yes; *Library:* by appointment
Chief Officer(s):
Dominic Campione, President

Canadian Evaluation Society (CES) / Société canadienne d'évaluation
#3, 247 Barr St., Renfrew ON K7V 1J6
Fax: 613-432-6840
Toll-Free: 855-251-5721
secretariat@evaluationcanada.ca
www.evaluationcanada.ca
www.linkedin.com/groups/8172963
facebook.com/ces.sce
twitter.com/CES_SCE
Overview: A medium-sized national organization founded in 1981
Mission: To advance evaluation for its members & the public; To establish & maintain CES as the recognized national organization which represents the evaluation community; To provide a forum for the advancement of theory & practice of evaluation; To develop competencies, ethics, & standards to improve the practice of evaluation; To advocate for high-quality evaluation with practitioners, local chapters, nationally & internationally; To promote the use of evaluation in society
Member of: International Organization for Cooperation in Education; Réseau francophone d'évaluation; Consortium of Universities for Evaluation Education
Affiliation(s): American Evaluation Society; Australasian Evaluation Society
Finances: *Annual Operating Budget:* $100,000-$250,000
Staff Member(s): 4; 200 volunteer(s)
Membership: 1,800 individual; *Fees:* $195 individual & international; $100 senior; $95 full-time student; *Member Profile:* Members come from a variety of work settings & backgrounds including the federal, provincial & municipal governments; social, health & service organizations; academic institutions & private firms; members represent disciplines ranging from psychology, sociology, social work, education, economics, health sciences, administration, political science & policy sciences to accounting, engineering, urban & regional planning; *Committees:* Executive; Communication & Marketing; Governance & Process; Professional Learning
Activities: Providing professional development training, webinars, workshops, & online courses; Organizing annual conference; Developing promotion & outreach initiatives; *Internships:* Yes; *Speaker Service:* Yes; *Rents Mailing List:* Yes; *Library:* Evaluation Grey Literature Database; by appointment Not open to public
Chief Officer(s):
Harry Cummings, President
president@evaluationcanada.ca
Rebecca Mellett, Executive Director
ed@evaluationcanada.ca
Awards:
• Award for Contribution to Evaluation in Canada
• CES Award for Service to the Society
To honour those members who have made an exemplary contribution in the service of the Society
• Student Essay Award
Given to the best student essay dealing with some aspect of evaluation; *Amount:* $500 as well as travel & registration costs to attend the CES Annual Conference
Meetings/Conferences:
• Canadian Evaluation Society 2018 National Conference, May, 2018, Hyatt Regency Calgary, Calgary, AB
Scope: National
Description: Theme: "Co-creation"
Contact Information: Conference website:
c2018.evaluationcanada.ca
Publications:
• Canadian Evaluation Society Newsletter
Type: Newsletter; *Frequency:* Weekly
• Canadian Journal of Program Evaluation
Type: Journal; *Frequency:* Semiannually; *Editor:* Robert Schwartz; *ISSN:* 0834-1516
Profile: Articles, book reviews, & research & practice notes about the theory & practice of program evaluation in Canada

Canadian Examiners in Optometry (CEO) / Examinateurs canadiens en optométrie (ECO)
#403, 37 Sandiford Dr., Stouffville ON L4A 7X5
Tel: 905-642-1373; *Fax:* 905-642-3786
administration@ceo-eco.org
www.ceo-eco.org
Overview: A medium-sized national organization
Mission: To assess the competence of individual optometrists in the practice of optometry; To provide assessment results to the individuals & to relevant regulators; To provide mechanisms to evaluate the quality of practice of optometrists in Canada
Membership: 10; *Member Profile:* Provincial optometry regulators

Canadian Executive Service Organization (CESO) / Service d'assistance canadienne aux organismes (SACO)
#800, 700 Bay St., Toronto ON M5G 1Z6
Tel: 416-961-2376; *Fax:* 416-961-1096
Toll-Free: 800-268-9052
info@ceso-saco.com
www.ceso-saco.com
www.linkedin.com/company/ceso-canadian-executive-service-organization-
www.facebook.com/cesosaco
twitter.com/cesosaco
www.youtube.com/CESOSACO
Overview: A large international charitable organization founded in 1967
Mission: To enhance the socio-economic well-being of the peoples & the communities of Canada, developing nations & emerging market economies
Member of: Canadian Council for International Cooperation
Finances: *Funding Sources:* Government
4000 volunteer(s)
Membership: 800; *Committees:* Executive; National Development; Audit; Nominations & Governance; Finance & Administration; Compensation; Volunteer Liaison
Chief Officer(s):
Wendy Harris, President & Chief Executive Officer
wharris@ceso-saco.com
Gale Lee, Director, International Services (Asia, Americas & the Caribbean)
glee@ceso-saco.com
Apollinaire Ihaza, Director, International Services (Africa & Haiti)
apollinaire@ceso-saco.com
Michelle Ng, Director, Finance
mng@ceso-saco.com
Olivia Goudou, Director, Communications & Engagement
ogoudou@ceso-saco.com
Publications:
• Canadian Executive Service Organization Annual Report
Type: Yearbook; *Frequency:* Annually
  Montréal
  #500, 1001 rue Sherbrooke est, Montréal QC H2L 1L3
  Tel: 514-875-7226; *Fax:* 514-875-6928
  Toll-Free: 800-268-9052
  info@saco-ceso.com

Canadian Explosive Technicians' Association (CETA) / Association canadienne des techniciens en explosif
Explosive Disposal Unit, Halton Regional Police Service, 1151 Bronte Rd., Oakville ON L6M 3L1
www.cetatechs.com
Overview: A small national organization founded in 1992
Mission: To enhance public safety by supporting & advocating for explosive technicians
Membership: 500; *Fees:* $200; *Member Profile:* Police & military bomb technicians throughout Canada
Activities: Offering professional development opportunities

Canadian Explosives Industry Association (CEAEC)
164, Ruskin, Beaconsfield QC H9W 2Y2
www.ceaec.ca
Overview: A medium-sized national organization
Mission: To promote & represent the general interests of distributors, manufacturers, & users of explosives; To promote & maintain high standards concerning the use, handling, & transport of explosives; To co-operate with government authorities in the promotion of safety standards; To encourage the adoption & adherence to uniform legislation concerning the Canadian explosives industry
Finances: *Funding Sources:* Membership dues
Staff Member(s): 1
Membership: 27; *Fees:* Schedule available; *Member Profile:* Corporations, firms, or individuals carrying on business as a distributor, manufacturer, or transporter of blasting explosives in Canada; Corporations, firms, or individuals involved with providing goods & services to the Canadian explosives industry
Activities: Communicating with government authorities in the interest of explosives safety legislation; Facilitating working relations between explosives manufacturers & distributors
Chief Officer(s):
Nicholas Ebsworth, Executive Director
n.ebsworth@ceaec.ca

Canadian Fabry Association / L'association canadienne de fabry
52 Glen Forest Dr., Hamilton ON L8K 5V8
www.fabrycanada.com
Overview: A medium-sized national organization
Mission: To educate the public & offer information on treatments; To encourage & support research; To increase facilities for those suffering from the disease
Activities: *Awareness Events:* National Patient Conference, June
Chief Officer(s):
Gina Costantino, President

Canadian Faculties of Agriculture & Veterinary Medicine (CFAVM) / Facultés d'agriculture et de médecine vétérinaire du Canada
#204, 532 Montreal Rd., Ottawa ON K1K1 4R4
Tel: 613-822-4442
info@acfavm.ca
www.cfavm.ca
Previous Name: Association of Faculties of Veterinary Medicine in Canada
Overview: A medium-sized national organization founded in 1991 overseen by Universities Canada
Member of: Universities Canada
Membership: 13 universities (8 faculties + 5 schools)
Activities: Coordination of teaching, research & extension programs
Chief Officer(s):
Roger Larson, P.Ag., Executive Director

Canadian Fallen Firefighters Foundation / Fondation canadienne des pompiers morts en service
#200, 440 Laurier Ave. West, Ottawa ON K1R 7X6
Tel: 613-786-3024; *Fax:* 613-782-2228
info@cfff.ca
www.cfff.ca
www.facebook.com/CFFF.FCPMS
Overview: A small national charitable organization founded in 2003
Mission: To serve all firefighters & their families in time of need. This registered, non-profit, charitable organization is made up of members of the Canadian Fire Service and other interested citizens dedicated to honouring Canada's fallen firefighters.
Affiliation(s): Canadian Fire Service
Finances: *Annual Operating Budget:* $100,000-$250,000
Staff Member(s): 3; 1000 volunteer(s)
Membership: 180,000; *Member Profile:* Firefighters & their families; *Committees:* Design of Monument; Funding; Executive
Activities: *Awareness Events:* National Memorial Ceremony, 2nd Sun. in Sept.; *Speaker Service:* Yes
Chief Officer(s):
Robert Kirkpatrick, President
Douglas Wylie, 1st Vice-President
Mike McKenna, 2nd Vice-President
John Clare, Treasurer
Publications:
• Firefighter Life Safety
Type: Newsletter; *Frequency:* Monthly
Profile: Published in conjunction with the Everyone Goes Home program, for members of fire service, the newsletter contains steps to eliminate line-of-duty deaths & injuries, best practices collectedfrom fire departments, upcoming firefighter life safety events, & implementation of safety & survival plans

Canadian Families & Corrections Network (CFCN)
PO Box 35040, Kingston ON K7L 5S5
Tel: 613-541-0743
Toll-Free: 888-371-2326
national@cfcn-rcafd.org
www.cfcn-rcafd.org
Overview: A small national charitable organization
Mission: To assist families affected by criminal behaviour, incarceration, & community reintegration
Finances: *Funding Sources:* Donations

Membership: *Fees:* $10 students, seniors, & underwaged persons; $30 individuals; $65 non-profit agencies; $175 corporate memberships
Activities: Offering family support; Providing orientation on restorative justice; Referring families to community resources; Providing visitor resource centres at institutions; Offering information, such as "Telling the children about incarceration" & "Maintaining a relationship with children during incarceration"
Chief Officer(s):
Louise Leonardi, Executive Director
Publications:
• Child-Friendly Practices within the Prison Setting
Number of Pages: 26; *Author:* Margaret Holland
Profile: Written with Lori Ann Bevins-Yeomans & Joyce Waddell-Townsend of Children Visiting Prisons-Kingston Inc.
• Families & Corrections Journal
Type: Journal; *Price:* Free
Profile: Articles with news & information about Canadian families & corrections
• One Day at a Time: Writings on Facing the Incarceration of a Friend or Family Member
Number of Pages: 39
• Staying Involved: A Guide for Incarcerated Fathers
Type: Guide
Profile: A joint initiative of Pro Bono Queen's University & Canadian Families & Corrections Network
• Time Together & The Directory of Canadian Services to the Families of Adult Offenders
Number of Pages: 95; *Author:* Lloyd Withers
Profile: A survival guide for families & friends visiting in Canadian federal prisons
• Time's Up: A Reintegration Toolkit for families
Number of Pages: 36; *ISBN:* 0-9688923-5-3
• Waiting at the Gate: Families, Corrections, & Restorative Justice
Number of Pages: 242; *Price:* $25

Canadian Fanconi Anemia Research Fund / La Fondation canadienne de recherche de l'anémie de Fanconi
PO Box 38157, Toronto ON M5N 3A9
Tel: 416-489-6393; *Fax:* 416-489-6393
admin@fanconicanada.org
www.fanconicanada.org
Also Known As: Fanconi Canada
Overview: A small national organization
Mission: To raise money for research into finding a cure &/or treatments for Fanconi anemia; to raise awareness about the disease; to provide support to affected Canadian families

Canadian Farm & Industrial Equipment Institute *See* Association of Equipment Manufacturers - Canada

Canadian Farm Animal Care Trust
#306, 92 Caplan Ave., Barrie ON L4N 0Z7
Tel: 705-436-5776; *Fax:* 705-436-3551
www.canfact.ca
Also Known As: CANFACT
Overview: A small national charitable organization founded in 1989
Mission: To encourage the development & use of systems that subject farm animals to the minimum amount of stress, distress or injury in the rearing, transportation & slaughter of these animals
Finances: *Annual Operating Budget:* $50,000-$100,000
15 volunteer(s)
Activities: *Speaker Service:* Yes
Chief Officer(s):
Tom Hughes, President

Canadian Farm Builders Association (CFBA)
PO Box 24029, Stn. Bullfrog, Guelph ON N1E 6V8
Tel: 519-824-0809; *Fax:* 519-824-2477
cfba@cfba.ca
www.cfba.ca
Overview: A small national organization founded in 1980
Mission: To promote & advance the construction of structurally efficient, environmentally sound, efficient farm buildings in Canada; To promote & advance the standards of farm structures through research, education & practical application
Finances: *Annual Operating Budget:* Less than $50,000
Staff Member(s): 1
Membership: 240; *Fees:* Schedule available
Chief Officer(s):
Sally Akroyd Bombino, General Manager

Canadian Farm Business Management Council *See* Farm Management Canada

Canadian Farm Writers' Federation (CFWF)
PO Box 250, Ormstown QC J0S 1K0
Fax: 450-829-2226
Toll-Free: 877-782-6456
secretariat@cfwf.ca
cfwf.wildapricot.org
Overview: A small national organization founded in 1955
Mission: To serve the interests of agricultural journalists
Affiliation(s): British Columbia Farm Writers' Association (BCFWA); Alberta Farm Writers' Association (AFWA); Saskatchewan Farm Writers' Association (SFWA); Manitoba Farm Writers' & Broadcasters' Association; Eastern Canada Farm Writers' Association (ECFWA)
Membership: 380+; *Member Profile:* Agricultural journalists, such as editors, reporters, & broadcasters; Journalists in business & government who are responsible for agricultural communications
Activities: Providing networking opportunities; Offering professional development
Chief Officer(s):
Lisa Guenther, President
Tamara Leigh, Vice-President
tamara.leigh@agr.gc.ca
Hugh Maynard, Secretary-Treasurer, 877-782-6456 Ext. 704
hugh@quanglo.ca
Christina Franc, Administrator, 877-782-6456 Ext. 706
christina@quanglo.ca
Meetings/Conferences:
• 2018 Canadian Farm Writers Federation Conference, 2018
Scope: National
Publications:
• The Farm Journalist: Newsletter of the Canadian Farm Writers' Federation
Type: Newsletter; *Frequency:* Bimonthly; *Editor:* Christina Franc
Profile: News for farm jouralists, information sources, events, launches, awards, & professional development information

Canadian Federal Pilots Association (CFPA) / Association des pilotes fédéraux du Canada (APFC)
#107, 18 Deakin St., Ottawa ON K2E 8B7
Tel: 613-230-5476; *Fax:* 613-230-2668
cfpa@cfpa-apfc.ca
www.cfpa-apfc.ca
Previous Name: Aircraft Operations Group Association (Ind.)
Overview: A medium-sized provincial charitable organization
Finances: *Annual Operating Budget:* Greater than $5 Million
Staff Member(s): 2
Membership: 15,000-49,999; *Member Profile:* Professional pilots employed by Transport Canada Aviation Group, Transportation Safety Board & NAV Canada; *Committees:* Professional Standards; Pay & Benefits
Activities: *Internships:* Yes; *Library*
Chief Officer(s):
Greg McConnell, Chair
Denis Brunelle, Vice-Chair
Ron Graham, Secretary-Treasurer
Greg Holbrook, Director, Operations

Canadian Federation for the Humanities & Social Sciences (CFHSS) / Fédération Canadienne des Sciences Humaines
#300, 275 Bank St., Ottawa ON K2P 2L6
Tel: 613-238-6112; *Fax:* 613-238-6114
info@ideas-idees.ca
www.ideas-idees.ca
www.linkedin.com/company/canadian-federation-for-the-humanities-and-social-sciences
www.facebook.com/ideas.idees
twitter.com/ideas_idees
www.youtube.com/user/IdeasIdees
Overview: A medium-sized national organization
Mission: To support and advance Canada's research in the humanities & social science fields
Finances: *Funding Sources:* Public and Private sponsorship, educational institutions
Staff Member(s): 16
Membership: 80 scholarly associations, 79 universities & colleges, 6 affiliates
Chief Officer(s):
Camille Ferrier, Communications Officer
cferrier@ideas-idees.ca

Canadian Federation of Agriculture (CFA) / Fédération canadienne de l'agriculture (FCA)
21 Florence St., Ottawa ON K2P 0W6
Tel: 613-236-3633; *Fax:* 613-236-5749
info@canadian-farmers.ca
www.cfa-fca.ca
www.facebook.com/189161978085033
twitter.com/CFAFCA
Overview: A large national organization founded in 1935
Mission: To coordinate the efforts of agricultural producer organizations throughout Canada for the purpose of promoting their common interests through collective action; to promote & advance the social & economic conditions of those engaged in agricultural pursuits; to assist in formulating & promoting national agricultural policies to meet changing national & international conditions
Member of: International Federation of Agriculture Producers; World Farmers Organisation
Affiliation(s): BC Agriculture Council; Keystone Agricultural Producers (Manitoba); Ontario Federation of Agriculture; L'Union des producteurs agricoles (Québec); Coopérative fédérée de Québec; NS Federation of Agriculture; PEI Federation of Agriculture; Agriculture Producers Assoc. of New Brunswick; Newfoundland & Labrador Federation of Agriculture; Dairy Farmers of Canada; Canadian Egg Marketing Agency; Chicken Farmers of Canada; Canadian Turkey Marketing Agency; Canadian Broiler Hatching Egg Marketing Agency; Canadian Sugar Beet Producers' Assoc.; Canadian Pork Council; Wild Rose Agricultural Producers
Finances: *Annual Operating Budget:* $500,000-$1.5 Million; *Funding Sources:* Membership fees
Staff Member(s): 8
Membership: 22 provincial farm organizations, national/regional commodity organizations; *Member Profile:* Farm organization or farmer co-op
Activities: *Awareness Events:* Food Freedom Day, Feb. 12; *Internships:* Yes; *Library:* by appointment
Chief Officer(s):
Ron Bonnett, President
Errol Halkai, Acting Executive Director, 613-236-3633 Ext. 2323
errol@canadian-farmers.ca
Jessica Goodfellow, Director, Communications
communications@cfafca.ca
Meetings/Conferences:
• Canadian Federation of Agriculture 2018 Annual Meeting, 2018
Scope: National

Canadian Federation of Aircraft Maintenance Engineers Associations (CFAMEA) / Fédération Canadienne des associations de techniciens d'entrien d'aéronefs (FCATEA)
c/o AME Association of Ontario, PO Box 160, Stn. Toronto AMF, Mississauga ON L5P 1B1
Tel: 905-673-5681; *Fax:* 905-673-6328
www.cfamea.com
Also Known As: Aircraft Maintenance Engineers Association
Overview: A medium-sized national organization
Mission: To constitute a body that will be recognized, & will be available for consultations regarding the regulation of any matter in the aviation industry, which affects or may affect Aircraft Maintenance Engineers or any other person in the Aviation Maintenance Professions
Finances: *Funding Sources:* Membership dues
Membership: 5 regional associations; *Member Profile:* Canadian AME Associations
Activities: Liaison with government concerning aircraft maintenance & AME licensing; *Awareness Events:* Canadian Aviation Regulatio nAdvisory Council (CARAC) Annual Meeting
Chief Officer(s):
Uli Huber, President, 902-499-2315
uli@cfamea.com
Meetings/Conferences:
• Canadian Aviation Regulation Advisory Council (CARAC) 17th Plenary Meeting, February, 2018
Scope: National

AME Association (Atlantic) Inc.
126 Gulliver Dr., Fredericton NB E3A 3C5
Tel: 506-472-0462; *Fax:* 626-452-1153
www.atlanticame.ca
www.facebook.com/atlanticame
Chief Officer(s):
Ben L. McCarty, President
ben@cfamea.com

Central AME Association
PO Box 42055, Stn. Ferry Rd., Winnipeg MB R3J 3X7

Canadian Associations / The Canadian Federation of Business & Professional Women's Clubs (CFBPWC) / Fédération canadienne des clubs des femmes de carrières commerciales et professionnelles (FCCFCCP)

Tel: 204-945-1974
camea@mymts.net
camea.ca
Chief Officer(s):
Kerry Bews, General Manager
Ontario AME Association
c/o Skyservice F.B.O. Inc., PO Box 160, Stn. Toronto AMF, Mississauga ON L5P 1B1
Tel: 905-673-5681; *Fax:* 905-673-6328
www.ame-ont.com
Chief Officer(s):
Warren Couch, President
Pacific AME Association
#314, 5400 Airport Rd. South, Richmond BC V7B 1B4
Tel: 604-279-9579
pamea@telus.net
www.pamea.ca
Western AME Association
PO Box 21101, Edmonton AB T6R 2V4
Tel: 780-462-1173; *Fax:* 780-413-0076
info@wamea.com
www.wamea.com
www.linkedin.com/company/wamea
www.facebook.com/WAMEAWAMEA
twitter.com/WAMEAWAMEA
Chief Officer(s):
Rod Fihser, President

Canadian Federation of Amateur Roller Skaters *See* Roller Sports Canada

Canadian Federation of Apartment Associations (CFAA) / Fédération canadienne des Associations de propriétaires immobiliers
#640, 1600 Carling Ave., Ottawa ON K1Z 1G3
Tel: 613-235-0101; *Fax:* 613-238-0101
admin@cfaa-fcapi.org
www.cfaa-fcapi.org
twitter.com/CFAAConference
Overview: A small national organization founded in 1995
Mission: To represent members on political & economic issues at the national level & to facilitate the exchange of information & materials amongst members while maintaining the highest professional & ethical standards in all activities
Finances: *Annual Operating Budget:* Less than $50,000; *Funding Sources:* Membership fees; donations
Staff Member(s): 1
Membership: 17 landlord organizations; *Fees:* Schedule available; *Committees:* Conference & AGM; Government Relations; Membership
Chief Officer(s):
John Dickie, President
David Benes, Administrator
Meetings/Conferences:
• Canadian Federation of Apartment Associations Rental Housing Conference 2018, May, 2018, Coast Coal Harbour Hotel, Vancouver, BC
Scope: National
Publications:
• CFAA [Canadian Federation of Apartment Associations] - FCAPI Annual Report
Type: Yearbook; *Frequency:* Annually
• National Outlook [a publication of the Canadian Federation of Apartment Associations]
Type: Newsletter; *Frequency:* Quarterly
Profile: CFAA-FCAPI information & events, best practices, successful programs & legislation news from across Canada

Canadian Federation of Aromatherapists / La fédération canadienne d'aromathérapistes
124 Sweet Water Cres., Richmond Hill ON L4S 2B4
Tel: 519-746-1594; *Fax:* 519-746-9493
cfamanager@cfacanada.com
www.cfacanada.com
www.facebook.com/CanadianAromatherapy
twitter.com/cfaaromatherapy
Overview: A medium-sized national organization founded in 1993
Mission: To maintain a register of aromatherapy practitioners, schools, & instructors who meet established minimum standards; To act as a unified voice of the profession; To maintain the highest ethical standards of the profession
Membership: *Fees:* $150 international; $140 professional/Aromatologist/Aromacologist/non-practicing/professional instructor; $85 affiliate; $45 student
Chief Officer(s):
Danielle Sade, Past President
daniellesade@hotmail.ca

The Canadian Federation of Business & Professional Women's Clubs (CFBPWC) / Fédération canadienne des clubs des femmes de carrières commerciales et professionnelles (FCCFCCP)
2913 Centre St. North, Calgary ON T2E 2V9
www.bpwcanada.com
www.ca.linkedin.com/in/bpwcanada
facebook.com/bpw.canada
twitter.com/bpwcan
Also Known As: BPW Canada
Overview: A large national organization founded in 1930
Mission: To develop & encourage women to pursue business, the professions & industry; To work toward the improvement of economic, employment & social conditions for women; To work for high standards of service in business, the professions, industry & public life; To stimulate interest in federal, provincial & municipal affairs; To encourage women to participate in the business of government at all levels; To encourage & assist women & girls to acquire further education & training
Member of: International Federation of Business & Professional Women
Finances: *Funding Sources:* Membership fees
Membership: 2,500; *Fees:* $30; *Member Profile:* Active - one who is actively engaged in renumerative occupation in business, profession or industry at the time of acceptance into membership; Associate - one who is not engaged in renumerative occupation & who has not been an active member of a club; Student; *Committees:* Federation Promotion; Health; International; Personal Development & Mentoring; Programs/Projects; Public Affairs; Resolutions & Briefs; Ways & Means; Young BPW
Activities: *Awareness Events:* Convention; *Internships:* Yes
Chief Officer(s):
Jenny Gukamani-Abdulla, President
president@bpwcanada.com
Linda Davis, First Vice President
firstvp@bpwcanada.com
Karen Gorgerat, Vice President, Resolutions
resolutions@bpwcanada.com
Amanda McLaren, Secretary
secretary@bpwcanada.com
Lila Smith, Treasurer
treasurer@bpwcanada.com
Meetings/Conferences:
• Business & Professional Women of Canada National Convention 2018, August, 2018
Scope: National
Description: An opportunity to educate & empower Canadian women to improve economic, political, employment, & social conditions
Publications:
• BPW Connections - Coast to Coast / Connexions BPW - d'un océan à l'autre
Type: Newsletter; *Frequency:* Quarterly; *Editor:* Sue Calhoun & Judy Hagerman
Profile: BPW Canada news from across the country
• Handbook for Club Members
Abbotsford
34136 Alma St., Abbotsford BC V2T 5P3
bpwabbotsford@gmail.com
www.bpwabbotsford.ca
www.linkedin.com/groups?gid=4150531&trk=myg_ugrp_ovr
www.facebook.com/bpwabbotsford
twitter.com/BPWAbbotsford
Chief Officer(s):
Maggie Reimer, President
Barrie
Barrie ON
www.bpwbarrie.com
www.facebook.com/195875163776382?sk=wall&filter=12
twitter.com/BPWBarrie
Brampton
#154, 10 George St. North, Brampton ON L6X 1R2
contact@bpw-brampton.com
bpwbrampton.com
Chief Officer(s):
Pat Dowling, President
Calgary
#244, 1811 - 4 St. SW, Calgary AB T2S 1W2
Tel: 403-230-6042
info@bpwcalgary.com
www.bpwcalgary.com
www.linkedin.com/groups?gid=2303046&trk=hb_side_g
www.facebook.com/BPWCalgary
twitter.com/BPWCalgary
Chief Officer(s):
Barb Francis, President
Cambridge
Cambridge ON
amy.phillips@live.com
www.bpwcambridge.org
Durham
PO Box 66126, Stn. Town Centre, 1355 Kingston Rd., Pickering ON L1V 6P7
bpwdurham.com
www.facebook.com/BPWDurham
Chief Officer(s):
Joanne Cox, President
Greater Moncton
PO Box 29162, Stn. North End, Moncton NB E1G 4R3
Tel: 506-874-0887
info@monctonbpw.com
www.monctonbpw.com
www.facebook.com/209150065818445
twitter.com/BPWmoncton
Chief Officer(s):
Jolene Barrieau, President
Greater Sudbury
PO Box 2593, Stn. A, Sudbury ON P3A 4S9
Tel: 705-671-2022
bpwgreatersudbury.com
Kitchener-Waterloo
Kitchener ON
www.bpwkw.com
Chief Officer(s):
Elaine Mortensen, President, 519-585-0186
elaine.mortensen@sunlife.com
London
5 Hart Cres., London ON N6E 3A3
membership@bpwlondon.com
www.bpwlondon.com
ca.linkedin.com/in/bpwlondoncanada
facebook.com/bpwlondoncanada
twitter.com/bpwlondoncanada
Mission
PO Box 3232, Mission BC V2V 4J4
www.bpwmission.ca
www.facebook.com/BPWMission
twitter.com/BPWMission
Chief Officer(s):
Connie Friesen, President
Mississauga
PO Box 31, 145 Queen St. South, Streetsville ON L5M 2B7
info@bpwmississauga.com
bpwmississauga.com
www.linkedin.com/in/bpwmississauga
www.facebook.com/BpwMississauga
twitter.com/BPWMiss
Chief Officer(s):
Asha Singh, President, 416-564-2742
Niagara Falls
Niagara Falls ON
www.bpwniagara.com
www.facebook.com/bpw.niagara
Chief Officer(s):
Nancy Broerse, President
nancy@infodiva.ca
North Toronto
#201, 29 Gervais Dr., Toronto ON M3C 1Y9
Tel: 416-510-8387
info@bpwnorthtoronto.com
www.bpwnorthtoronto.com
Chief Officer(s):
Linda Rice, President
Ontario
#201, Bramalea Rd., Brampton ON L6T 2W4
www.bpwontario.org
ca.linkedin.com/in/bpwontario
www.facebook.com/bpw.ontario.3
twitter.com/bpwontario
Chief Officer(s):
Linda Davis, President
Québec
www.bpwprovincialquebec.ca
Chief Officer(s):

Canadian Associations / Canadian Federation of Business School Deans (CFBSD) / Fédération canadienne des doyens des écoles d'administration (FCDEA)

Julie Leclerc, President
Regina
PO Box 1911, Regina SK S4P 3E1
Tel: 306-585-9177
contact@reginabpw.org
reginabpw.org
twitter.com/BPWRegina
Chief Officer(s):
Karen Meban, President
Saskatoon
PO Box 22, Saskatoon SK S7K 3K1
www.bpwsaskatoon.com
www.linkedin.com/groups/BPW-Saskatoon-Inc-4426447/about
www.facebook.com/BPWSaskatoon
twitter.com/@BPWSaskatoonInc
Chief Officer(s):
Tammy Richmond, President
president@bpwsaskatoon.com
Toronto
Toronto ON
www.bpwtoronto.com
Victoria
Victoria BC
info@bpwvictoria.com
www.bpwvictoria.com
Chief Officer(s):
Margo Almond, President
Winnipeg Central
34 Park Grove Dr., Winnipeg MB R2J 3L6
Tel: 204-257-0589
winnipegcentral.bpw.ca
Chief Officer(s):
Sharla Wasylyshen, President

Canadian Federation of Business School Deans (CFBSD) / Fédération canadienne des doyens des écoles d'administration (FCDEA)
3000, ch de la Côte-Sainte-Catherine, Montréal QC H3T 2A7
Tel: 514-340-7116; *Fax:* 514-340-7275
info@cfbsd.ca
www.cfbsd.ca
Previous Name: Canadian Federation of Deans of Management & Administrative Studies
Overview: A small national organization founded in 1976
Mission: To encourage the professional development of business school administrators; To promote excellence in management education; To represent management education to the government, the business community, & the media
Membership: 60 university level business schools, representing 3,000 faculty members & 150,000 students; *Member Profile:* Deans & directors from Canadian faculties of management & business in Canada; Associate industry & international members; *Committees:* Management Education Research; Communications
Activities: Monitoring public policy; Engaging in advocacy activities; Providing research & information services; Raising the profile of management education; Assisting member institutions in the improvement of their programs
Chief Officer(s):
Timothy Daus, Executive Director
daus@cfbsd.ca
Bahram Dadgostar, Chair
Jerry Tomberlin, Vice-Chair
Robert Mantha, Secretary-Treasurer

Canadian Federation of Chefs & Cooks; Canadian Federation of Chefs de Cuisine *See* Canadian Culinary Federation

Canadian Federation of Chiropractic Regulatory & Educational Accrediting Boards (CFCREAB)
#2301, 30 Gloucester St., Toronto ON M4Y 1L6
Tel: 416-697-7458
www.chirofed.ca
Previous Name: Canadian Federation of Chiropractic Regulatory Boards
Overview: A medium-sized national organization founded in 1978
Mission: To promote unified standards for the operations of all licensing & regulatory boards; To aid in problems confronting individual boards; To promote & aid cooperation between chiropractic learning boards & regulatory boards
Finances: *Annual Operating Budget:* $100,000-$250,000

Membership: 11; *Member Profile:* Provincial & territorial organizations having jurisdiction over licences, registration, testing or discipline of doctors of chiropractic
Chief Officer(s):
H. James Duncan, Chief Executive Officer

Canadian Federation of Chiropractic Regulatory Boards *See* Canadian Federation of Chiropractic Regulatory & Educational Accrediting Boards

Canadian Federation of Deans of Management & Administrative Studies *See* Canadian Federation of Business School Deans

Canadian Federation of Earth Sciences (CFES) / Fédération canadienne des sciences de la Terre
c/o Scott Swinden, 3 Crest Rd., Halifax NS B3M 2W1
Tel: 902-444-3525; *Fax:* 902-444-7802
info@swindengeoscience.ca
earthsciencescanada.org
Previous Name: Canadian Geoscience Council
Overview: A medium-sized national organization founded in 1972
Mission: To promote coordination & cooperation in activities in Canadian geoscientific education; to advise on science policy involving the earth sciences; to provide an informed opinion to the public of Canada on matters of public concern.
Finances: *Annual Operating Budget:* $100,000-$250,000; *Funding Sources:* Geological Survey of Canada; member societies
Membership: 15 organizations
Chief Officer(s):
Scott Swinden, President

Canadian Federation of Engineering Students (CFES) / Fédération canadienne des étudiants et étudiantes en génie
#300, 55 Metcalfe St., Ottawa ON K1P 6L5
info@cfes.ca
www.cfes.ca
www.facebook.com/cfes.fceg
www.instagram.com/cfes.fceg
Overview: A medium-sized national organization founded in 1969
Mission: To act as a unified voice for engineering students both nationally & internationally; To assist engineering students in both personal & professional growth; To be aware of & communicate changes in society which affect the engineering profession & engineering students
Affiliation(s): BEST (Board of European Students of Technology)
Finances: *Funding Sources:* Sponsorships
Membership: 75,000; *Member Profile:* Engineering students across Canada; *Committees:* Education; Official Languages; Information Technology; Outreach
Activities: Facilitating the exchange of information between members; Recognizing student achievements; Supporting an all-encompassing education for engineering students; Offering complementary education courses
Chief Officer(s):
Zenon Kripki, President
president@cfes.ca
Publications:
• CFES [Canadian Federation of Engineering Students] eBulletin
Type: Newsletter
Profile: Federation activities, commissioner reports, & upcoming events
• Project [a publication of the Canadian Federation of Engineering Students]
Type: Magazine; *Frequency:* Semiannually; *Accepts Advertising*; *Price:* Distributed to schools for engineering students
Profile: Relevant articles for engineering students across Canada

Canadian Federation of Friends of Museums (CFFM) / Fédération canadienne des amis de musées (FCAM)
#400, 280 Metcalfe St., Ottawa ON K2P 1R7
Tel: 613-567-0099; *Fax:* 613-233-5438
info@cffm-fcam.ca
www.cffm-fcam.ca
www.facebook.com/146503988697066
Overview: A medium-sized national charitable organization founded in 1977
Mission: To serve as source of information & expertise for friends of museums; To serve as communications network & national voice for those who are dedicated to the support &

promotion of museums for the benefit of all Canadians
Affiliation(s): Canadian Museums Association; International Council of Museums Canada; World Federation of Friends of Museums
Finances: *Funding Sources:* Membership dues; Donations 10 volunteer(s)
Membership: 242 individual + 140 institutions; *Fees:* $40 for individuals; $50-$200 for institutions; *Member Profile:* Individuals & organizations that support museums & heritage sites in Canada; *Committees:* Advisory; By-Laws; Growth & Development; Finance; Fundraising & Special Projects; Nominations; Strategic Alliance
Chief Officer(s):
Bruce Bolton, President
Publications:
• CFFM [Canadian Federation of Friends of Museums] Newsletter
Type: Newsletter
• Significant Treasures / Trésors parlants
Number of Pages: 320; *Price:* $7.50 + $5 postage & handling
Profile: Organized by province, the resource presents information about Canadian museums, their significant objects, & their location on city maps

Canadian Federation of Humane Societies (CFHS) / Fédération des sociétés canadiennes d'assistance aux animaux
#102, 30 Concourse Gate, Ottawa ON K2E 7V7
Tel: 613-224-8072; *Fax:* 613-723-0252
Toll-Free: 888-678-2347
info@cfhs.ca
www.cfhs.ca
www.linkedin.com/company/canadian-federation-of-humane-societies
www.facebook.com/HumaneCanada
twitter.com/cfhs
www.youtube.com/user/CanadianHumane
Overview: A large national charitable organization founded in 1957
Mission: To support its member animal welfare organizations across Canada in promoting respect & humane treatment toward all animals
Finances: *Annual Operating Budget:* $500,000-$1.5 Million; *Funding Sources:* Donations
Staff Member(s): 6
Membership: *Member Profile:* Any society devoted to the prevention of cruelty to or suffering of animals; *Committees:* Executive; Fundraising; Finance & Audit; Membership; Governance, Compensation & Nomination; McGrand Trust Management
Activities: *Speaker Service:* Yes; *Library:* Open to public by appointment
Chief Officer(s):
Barbara Cartwright, CEO
barbara@cfhs.ca
Luna Allison, Manager, Communications & Marketing
lunaa@cfhs.ca
Meetings/Conferences:
• 2018 Canadian Federation of Humane Societies National Animal Welfare Conference, April, 2018, Hyatt Regency Calgary, Calgary, AB
Scope: National
Publications:
• Animal Welfare in Focus
Type: Newsletter; *Frequency:* Semiannually; *Price:* Free for CFHS member societies, donors, & the public upon request
Profile: Up-to-date information about the CFHS & member societies, & animal welfare news from Canada & abroad
• Canadian Federation of Humane Societies Factsheets
Price: Free
Profile: Information about companion animals, wildlife, & farm animal welfare issues
• CFHS [Canadian Federation of Humane Societies] Annual Report
Type: Yearbook; *Frequency:* Annually

Canadian Federation of Independent Business (CFIB) / Fédération canadienne de l'entreprise indépendante
#401, 4141 Yonge St., Toronto ON M2P 2A6
Tel: 416-222-8022; *Fax:* 416-222-4337
Toll-Free: 888-234-2232
cfib@cfib.ca
www.cfib-fcei.ca
www.linkedin.com/company/62788
www.facebook.com/CFIB

Tel: 613-234-8252; *Fax:* 613-234-8221
Toll-Free: 888-220-9606
cfuwgen@rogers.com
www.cfuw.org
www.facebook.com/cfuw.fcfdu
twitter.com/cfuwcfdu
Overview: A large national organization founded in 1919
Mission: To pursue knowledge, promote education & improve the status of women & human rights; To participate actively in public affairs in a spirit of cooperation & friendship
Finances: *Annual Operating Budget:* $250,000-$500,000; *Funding Sources:* Membership dues
Staff Member(s): 5; 30 volunteer(s)
Membership: 9,000 individuals in 107 clubs; *Member Profile:* Women university graduates; *Committees:* Education; Fellowships; Finance; International Relations; Libraries & Creative Arts; Communication; Resolutions; Status of Women & Human Rights; Membership
Activities: Annual General Meetings; Advocacy; Funding for Education; Community Service; Lifelong Learning; Women's Leadership
Chief Officer(s):
Robin Jackson, Executive Director, 613-234-8252 Ext. 102
cfuwed@rogers.com
Betty Dunlop, Manager, Fellowship Program, 613-234-8252 Ext. 104
fellowships@cfuw.org
Sarah Schattmann, Coordinator, Advocacy, 613-234-8252 Ext. 106
cfuwadvocacy@rogers.com
Ryszard Kowalski, Developer, Bookkeeper & Software, 613-234-8252 Ext. 107
cfuwfin@rogers.com
Meetings/Conferences:
• Canadian Federation of University Women 2018 AGM & Conference, 2018
Scope: National
Publications:
• CFUW [Canadian Federation of University Women] History & Heroines
Profile: An eight volume series tracing Canadian Federation of University Women's historical highlights decade by decade
• CFUW [Canadian Federation of University Women] Women In Action
Profile: Published several times each year on select intiatives surrounding women's issues, such as employment insurance, education for all, HIV & AIDS, childcare, & security& prosperity
• CFUW [Canadian Federation of University Women]: A Year in Action
Frequency: Annually
• Communicator / La Communicatrice [a publication of the Canadian Federation of University Women]
Type: Newsletter; *Frequency:* 5 pa
Profile: CFUW's current events from across Canada

Canadian Federation of Vietnamese Associations of Canada *See* Vietnamese Canadian Federation

Canadian Feed Industry Association *See* Animal Nutrition Association of Canada

Canadian Feed The Children (CFTC)
#123, 6 Lansing Sq., Toronto ON M2J 1T5
Tel: 416-757-1220; *Fax:* 416-757-3318
Toll-Free: 800-387-1221
contact@canadianfeedthechildren.ca
www.canadianfeedthechildren.ca
www.linkedin.com/company/canadian-feed-the-children
www.facebook.com/CanadianFeedTheChildren
twitter.com/cdnfeedchildren
www.youtube.com/user/canadianfeed
Overview: A medium-sized international charitable organization founded in 1986
Mission: To alleviate the impact of poverty on children; To work with local partners overseas & in Canada to enhance the well-being of children & the self-sufficiency of their families & communities
Member of: Canadian Council for International Cooperation
Finances: *Annual Operating Budget:* Greater than $5 Million; *Funding Sources:* Foundations; private contributions
Staff Member(s): 13
Membership: *Committees:* Finance & Audit; Nomination & Governance
Activities: *Speaker Service:* Yes
Chief Officer(s):
Debra Kerby, President & CEO

Anne Marshall, Chief Financial Officer
Peter Timmerman, Vice-President, Programs
Gail Black, Vice-President, Development
Jennifer Watson, Vice-President, Communications

Canadian Fence Industry Association (CFIA) / Association canadienne de l'industrie de la clôture
PO Box 516, 22 John St., Drayton ON N0G 1P0
Tel: 519-638-0101; *Fax:* 519-489-2805
info@cfia.ca
www.cfia.ca
Overview: A medium-sized national licensing organization founded in 1968
Mission: To ensure the industry maintains high standards of quality of work as well as ethics
Member of: American Fencing Association
Finances: *Funding Sources:* Membership dues
Membership: 170; *Fees:* $350; *Member Profile:* Residential & commercial manufacturers; retailers; installers
Chief Officer(s):
Martin McCooey, President
president@cfia.ca
Bob Bignell, Executive Secretary
execsecretary@cfia.ca
  Ontario
  c/o Medallion Fence, 10651 Keele St., Maple ON L6A 3Y9
  Tel: 905-832-2922; *Fax:* 905-832-1564
  Chief Officer(s):
  Sid Isenberg, President
  sid@medallionfence.com
  Québec
  a/s Clôture Solival Inc., 5274, boul Cléroux, Laval QC H7T 2E8
  Tel: 450-682-1318; *Fax:* 450-682-0061
  quebecpres@cfia.ca
  Chief Officer(s):
  Kim Raymond, President
  kraymond@cloturesolival.com
  Western
  c/o Align Fence Inc., 11403 - 199 St., Edmonton AB T5S 2C6
  Tel: 780-438-7300
  westernpres@cfia.ca
  Chief Officer(s):
  Justin Reyolds, President

Canadian Fencing Federation (CFF) / Fédération canadienne d'escrime
44 - 1554 Carling Ave., Ottawa ON K1Z 7M4
Tel: 613-323-5605; *Fax:* 647-476-2402
cff@fencing.ca
www.fencing.ca
www.facebook.com/168914029806258
twitter.com/fencingcanada
Also Known As: Fencing Canada
Overview: A medium-sized national charitable organization founded in 1971
Mission: To promote & develop the sport of fencing in Canada; To foster an environment of collaboration & excellence; To encourage the growth of fencing
Member of: International Fencing Federation; Sport Matters
Affiliation(s): Fédération internationale d'escrime
Finances: *Annual Operating Budget:* $500,000-$1.5 Million; *Funding Sources:* Membership fees; Government; Olympic Association
Staff Member(s): 4; 25 volunteer(s)
Membership: 6,000; *Fees:* $22.50; *Committees:* Competitions; Domestic Development; High Performance; Historical; Officials; Veterans; Wheelchair Fencing
Activities: Planning competitions; *Internships:* Yes
Chief Officer(s):
Caroline Sharp, Executive Director
ed@fencing.ca
Tim Stang, Technical Director, 905-324-1222
td@fencing.ca
Meetings/Conferences:
• Canadian Fencing Federation 2018 Annual General Meeting, 2018
Scope: National

Canadian Ferry Association (CFA) / Association canadienne des traversiers (ACT)
c/o Mr. Serge Buy, 70 George St., 3rd Fl., Ottawa ON K1N 5V9
Tel: 613-686-3838; *Fax:* 866-851-5689
info@canadianferry.ca
www.canadianferry.ca

www.linkedin.com/groups/4733824/profile
twitter.com/cdnferry
Overview: A small national organization founded in 1987
Mission: To establish & maintain a standard of professional & technical excellence in the operation of Canadian ferries; To promote & protect the interests of members of the association
Finances: *Funding Sources:* Sponsorships
Membership: 90; *Fees:* $250-$12,000 owner/operator, in relation to fleet size & tonnage; $1,000 industry participant; $200 associate member; *Member Profile:* Major ferry owners, operators & industry stakeholders in Canada
Activities: Providing opportunities for discussion of matters of interest to members; Promoting the safety, reliability, & efficiency of Canadian ferry operators; Providing representation at regulatory forums such as CMAC; Provide reports, newsletter, press releases & videos
Chief Officer(s):
Serge Buy, Executive Director
sbuy@canadianferry.ca
Christine Helm, Events Manager
chelm@canadianferry.ca
Alyson Queen, Communications
aqueen@canadianferry.ca
Chris Frantz, Project Manager
cfrantz@canadianferry.ca
Meetings/Conferences:
• Canadian Ferry Association's Conference, September, 2018, Whistler, BC
Description: Provides industry-specific workshops, networking, exhibitors & a speaker series
Publications:
• [Canadian Ferry Association] Keeping Canada Moving: A Survey of the Ferry Sector in Canada
Type: Report; *Frequency:* a.; *Number of Pages:* 35; *Price:* Free download
Profile: Data on the ferry sector in Canada
• CFA [Canadian Ferry Association] Annual Report
Type: Report; *Frequency:* a.; *Number of Pages:* 15; *Price:* Free download
Profile: Offered in English & French, provides information about members of the CFOA & the organization in general
• Ferry Horizons [Canadian Ferry Association]
Type: Magazine; *Frequency:* s-a.; *Accepts Advertising*; *Number of Pages:* 15; *Price:* Free download
Profile: Offered in English & French, provides information about members of the CFA & the organization in general

Canadian Fertility & Andrology Society (CFAS) / Société canadienne de fertilité et d'andrologie
#301, 1719, rue Grand Trunk, Montréal QC H3K 1M1
Tel: 514-524-9009; *Fax:* 514-524-2163
info@cfas.ca
www.cfas.ca
Previous Name: Canadian Society for the Study of Fertility
Merged from: Canadian Andrology Society
Overview: A medium-sized national charitable organization founded in 1954
Mission: To speak on behalf of interested parties in the field of assisted reproductive technologies & research in reproductive sciences
Finances: *Funding Sources:* Membership fees; Sponsorships
Staff Member(s): 2
Membership: 625+; *Fees:* $25 trainees; $100 non-MDs; $150 medical doctors; *Member Profile:* Reproductive healthcare specialists & scientists, such as gynecologists, obstetricians, reproductive endocrinologists, psychologists, social workers, nurses, laboratory technicians, research scientists, ethicists, & lawyers; Medical students, interns, residents, graduate students, & fellows; *Committees:* Awards; Communications; Finance; Governance; Government Relations; Professional Development; Scientific Program
Activities: Establishing practice guidelines & standards; Providing continuing professional development credits, as recognized by the Royal College of Physicians & Surgeons of Canada; Offering public education
Chief Officer(s):
Jeff Roberts, President
Jason Min, Vice-President
Jason Hitkari, Director, Continuing Professional Development
Jay Baltz, Treasurer
Meetings/Conferences:
• Canadian Fertility & Andrology Society 2018 64th Annual Meeting, September, 2018, Le Westin Montreal, Montréal, QC
Scope: National
Description: Educational presentations, a trade show, &

networking opportunities for persons involved in the field of reproductive medicine
• Canadian Fertility & Andrology Society 2019 65th Annual Meeting, September, 2019, The Westin Ottawa, Ottawa, ON
Scope: National
Description: Educational presentations, a trade show, & networking opportunities for persons involved in the field of reproductive medicine
Publications:
• CFAS [Canadian Fertility & Andrology Society] Communiqué
Type: Newsletter
Profile: CFAS information & events, plus articles
• Presidents' Annual Report [a publication of the Canadian Fertility & Andrology Society]
Type: Yearbook; *Frequency:* Annually

Canadian Fertilizer Institute *See* Fertilizer Canada

Canadian Field Hockey Association *See* Field Hockey Canada

Canadian Film & Television Production Association *See* Canadian Media Production Association

Canadian Film Centre (CFC) / Centre canadien du film
2489 Bayview Ave., Toronto ON M2L 1A8
Tel: 416-445-1446; *Fax:* 416-445-9481
info@cfccreates.com
www.cfccreates.com
www.facebook.com/cfccreates
twitter.com/cfccreates
instagram.com/cfccreates; vimeo.com/user3482071
Previous Name: Canadian Centre for Advanced Film Studies
Overview: A medium-sized national charitable organization founded in 1988
Mission: To operate as Canada's foremost film, televion, & new media institution; To advance Canadian creative talent, content, & values worldwide, through training, production, promotion & investment
Finances: *Funding Sources:* Government grants; private sector
Staff Member(s): 53
Chief Officer(s):
Slawko Klymkiw, Chief Executive Officer, 416-445-1446 Ext. 203
sklymkiw@cfccreates.com

Canadian Film Institute (CFI) / Institut canadien du film (ICF)
#120, 2 Daly Ave., Ottawa ON K1N 6E2
Tel: 613-232-6727; *Fax:* 613-232-6315
info@cfi-icf.ca
www.cfi-icf.ca
www.facebook.com/CanadianFilmInstitute
twitter.com/Canadian_Film
www.youtube.com/user/CanadianFilmInstitut
Overview: A medium-sized national charitable organization founded in 1935
Mission: To promote Canadian cinema; To assist in locating sources for rental or purchase of individual films & videos; To give subject & content information on theatrical & non-theatrical films & videos from both private & public sources; To give general information on Canadian & international film, video, & television production, distribution, exhibition, & related subjects
Finances: *Funding Sources:* All levels of government; Sponsorships; Fundraising
200 volunteer(s)
Membership: 450; *Fees:* $15
Activities: Operating a cinema & information centre; Organizing festivals & conferences; *Awareness Events:* Cafe Ex: *Rents Mailing List:* Yes; *Library:* by appointment
Chief Officer(s):
Susan Scotti, Chair
Tom McSorley, Executive Director & Secretary
Michael Leong, Treasurer

Canadian Filmmakers Distribution Centre (CFMDC)
#245, 401 Richmond St. West, Toronto ON M5V 3A8
Tel: 416-588-0725
cfmdc@cfmdc.org
www.cfmdc.org
www.facebook.com/cfmdcmembers
Overview: A medium-sized national organization founded in 1967
Mission: To promote & distribute the work of independent Canadian filmmakers.
Staff Member(s): 8

Membership: 550 individual; *Fees:* $75 filmmaker; $35 student; $50 research; *Member Profile:* Individuals interested in independent Canadian film or production company; generally film-makers distributed by centre
Activities: *Library:* Open to public by appointment
Chief Officer(s):
Lauren Howes, Executive Director
director@cfmdc.org

Canadian Finance & Leasing Association (CFLA) / Association canadienne de financement et de location (ACFL)
#301, 15 Toronto St., Toronto ON M5C 2E3
Tel: 416-860-1133; *Fax:* 416-860-1140
Toll-Free: 877-213-7373
info@cfla-acfl.ca
www.cfla-acfl.ca
www.linkedin.com/company/1360377
Merged from: Canadian Automotive Leasing Association; Equipment Lessors Association of Canada
Overview: A medium-sized national organization founded in 1973
Mission: To ensure an environment in Canada where asset-based financing, equipment & vehicle-leasing industry can be profitable
Finances: *Annual Operating Budget:* $500,000-$1.5 Million; *Funding Sources:* Membership fees; events fees
Staff Member(s): 5; 120 volunteer(s)
Membership: 200+ companies; *Member Profile:* Represents the asset-based financing, equipment & vehicle-leasing industry in Canada, ranging from large multinationals to regional financing companies; *Committees:* Accounting; Auto Finance Working Group; Board of Directors; Education & Program; Fleet; Government Relations; Legal; Membership; Small Ticket Funders; Tax; Technology
Activities: *Speaker Service:* Yes; *Library:* Resource Centre; Not open to public
Chief Officer(s):
David Powell, President & CEO, 416-860-1133 Ext. 24
david.powell@cfla-acfl.ca
Matthew Poirier, Director, Policy, 416-860-1133 Ext. 26
matthew@cfla-acfl.ca
Lalita Sirnaik, Manager, Finance & Administration, 416-860-1133 Ext. 22
lalita@cfla-acfl.ca
Meetings/Conferences:
• Canadian Finance & Leasing Association 2018 Conference, 2018
Scope: National

Canadian Finnsheep Breeders' Association
Box 10, Site 10, RR#4, Stony Plain AB T7Z 1X4
Tel: 888-963-0416
info@finnsheep.ca
www.finnsheep.ca
Overview: A small national organization founded in 1969
Mission: To encourage, develop, & regulate the breeding of Finnsheep; To protect & assist Finnsheep breeders
Affiliation(s): Canadian Livestock Records Corporation
Membership: 1-99; *Fees:* $10 / year; *Member Profile:* Individuals, partnerships, shareholders, companies, or firms engaged in the breeding & propagation of Finnsheep across Canada; *Committees:* Executive; Registration; Special Committees
Activities: Establishing breeding standards; Maintaining records of the breeding & origin of Finnsheep; Compiling statistics of the industry; Supervising breeders of Finnsheep to prevent fraud
Chief Officer(s):
Kathy Playdon, President, 888-963-0416
Lorna Woolsey, Registrar, 613-731-7110 Ext. 306, *Fax:* 613-731-0704
Laura Lee Mills, Registrar (French), 613-731-7110 Ext. 314, *Fax:* 613-731-0704

Canadian Fire Alarm Association (CFAA)
#3-4, 85 Citizen Ct., Markham ON L6G 1A8
Tel: 905-944-0030; *Fax:* 905-479-3639
Toll-Free: 800-529-0552
admin@cfaa.ca
www.cfaa.ca
Overview: A small national organization founded in 1973
Mission: To maximize the effectiveness and use of fire alarm systems in the protection of life and property in Canada.
Finances: *Annual Operating Budget:* $500,000-$1.5 Million; *Funding Sources:* Membership, registration and training fees
Staff Member(s): 4; 100 volunteer(s)

Membership: 400; *Fees:* $20 student; $50 associate; $225 participating; $500 sustaining; *Committees:* Education; Marketing & Communications; Industry Affairs; Revitalization & Membership; Technicians; Finance; Governance
Activities: Technician Training; Technician Registration; Authority Having Jurisdiction (AHJ) Fire Alarm Training; Building Owner/Manager Fire Alarm Training; Fire Alarm Standards and Legislation; *Internships:* Yes; *Speaker Service:* Yes
Chief Officer(s):
Steve Clemens, Executive Director, 905-944-0030
sclemens@cfaa.ca
Ruth Kavanagh, Office Supervisor, 905-944-0030
Awards:
• Fire Alarm Technology Program High Achievement
Eligibility: Graduate of a Canadian Fire Alarm Technology Program *Deadline:* June 1, annually; *Amount:* $500
Publications:
• Canadian Fire Alarm Association Journal
Type: Journal
Profile: Canadian Fire Alarm Industry News and Updates for AHJ's, Building Owners/Managers and those in the fire alarm manufacturing or service industry.

Canadian Fire Safety Association (CFSA)
#210, 2800 - 14th Ave., Markham ON L3R 0E4
Tel: 416-492-9417; *Fax:* 416-491-1670
cfsa@taylorenterprises.com
www.canadianfiresafety.com
Overview: A medium-sized national organization founded in 1971
Mission: To promote fire safety through seminars, safety training courses, scholarships & regular meetings.
Finances: *Funding Sources:* Membership fees
Membership: *Fees:* Schedule available; *Member Profile:* Membership represents a broad cross-section of government, business & education including architects, engineers, fire officials, building officials, fire protection consultants, manufacturers, the insurance industry, teachers & students.
Chief Officer(s):
David Moors, President
davidmorris@firetronics.ca
Carolyne Vigon, Administrator
carolyne@taylorenterprises.com

Canadian Fisheries Association *See* Fisheries Council of Canada

Canadian Fitness & Lifestyle Research Institute (CFLRI) / Institut canadien de la recherche sur la condition physique et le mode de vie
#201, 185 Somerset St. West, Ottawa ON K2P 0J2
Tel: 613-233-5528; *Fax:* 613-233-5536
www.cflri.ca
Previous Name: Canada Fitness Survey (1985)
Overview: A medium-sized national charitable organization founded in 1980
Mission: To conduct research, monitor trends, & make recommendations to increase physical activity & improve health in Canada
Finances: *Funding Sources:* Fitness / Active Living Program Unit of Health Canada; Contracts; Grants; Publication sales; Donations
Activities: Providing education about leading active & healthy lives; Developing a provider-based intervention known as PACE Canada; Conducting surveys, such as The Canadian Physical Activity Levels Among Youth (CAN PLAY)
Chief Officer(s):
Nancy Dubois, Chair
Christine Cameron, President
Makda Araia, Research Analyst
Publications:
• Capacity Study [a publication of the Canadian Fitness & Lifestyle Research Institute]
Frequency: Annually
Profile: Information to increase physical activity in the Canadian workplace
• Kids CANPLAY [a publication of the Canadian Fitness & Lifestyle Research Institute]
Profile: Information to encourage children to be active at home, at school, & in the community
• The Lifestyle Tips [a publication of the Canadian Fitness & Lifestyle Research Institute]
Profile: Practical suggestions for integrating physical activity into daily life
• Physical Activity Monitor [a publication of the Canadian Fitness & Lifestyle Research Institute]

Frequency: Irregular; *ISBN:* 1-895724-49-X
Profile: Report presents trends in physical activity among Canadian workers
• The Research File [a publication of the Canadian Fitness & Lifestyle Research Institute]
; *ISSN:* 1188-6641
Profile: Ongoing series of research summaries about physical activity, for professionals

Canadian Fjord Horse Association
c/o Canadian Livestock Records Corp., 2417 Holly Ln., Ottawa ON K1V 0M7
Tel: 613-731-7110; *Fax:* 613-731-0704
directors@cfha.org
www.cfha.org
www.facebook.com/canadianfjord
twitter.com/canadianfjord
www.youtube.com/canadianfjord
Overview: A small national organization founded in 1977
Mission: To operate under the Animal Pedigree Act; To assure the success of the purebred registered Norwegian Fjord Horse in Canada
Member of: Fjord Horse International Association (FHI); Canadian Livestock Records Corporation
Membership: *Fees:* $40 regular; $25 junior/additional members; *Member Profile:* Owners & admirers of the Fjord Horse in Canada; *Committees:* Promotions; Membership; Education & Evaluation
Activities: Registering animals & keeping pedigrees; Providing education about the Norwegian Fjord Horse; Raising awareness & understanding of the breed; Encouraging members to show the Norwegian Fjord Horse
Chief Officer(s):
Carol Boehm, President, 250-838-7782
Lauralee Mills, CLRC Contact
lauralee.mills@clrc.ca
Publications:
• Canadian Fjord Horse Association Newsletter
Type: Newsletter; *Editor:* Darlene Shewfelt

Canadian Flag Association (CFA) / Association canadienne de vexillologie (ACV)
409 - 60 C Line, Orangeville ON L9W 0A9
cfa.acv@gmail.com
cfa-acv.tripod.com
www.facebook.com/317266027131
Overview: A small national organization founded in 1985
Mission: To gather, organize & disseminate flag information with particular emphasis on flags having some association with Canada; to promote vexillology; to encourage & facilitate exchange of ideas between flag scholars, flag makers, flag collectors, flag designers & flag historians
Member of: Fédération Internationale des Associations Vexillologiques
Finances: *Funding Sources:* Membership fees
Membership: *Member Profile:* Flag historians (vexillologists); flag collectors; flag makers; flag retailers; flag archivists
Activities: *Speaker Service:* Yes; *Rents Mailing List:* Yes; *Library:* by appointment
Chief Officer(s):
Kevin Harrington, President
Publications:
• Flagscan
Frequency: Quarterly; *Editor:* Kevin Harrington; *ISSN:* 0833-1510

Canadian Flooring, Cleaning & Restoration Association / Association canadienne du couvre-plancher, nettoyage et restauration
PO Box 30015, 333 Mountainview Rd. South, Georgetown ON L7G 6J8
Tel: 905-822-2280
info@cfcra.ca
www.cfcra.ca
www.linkedin.com/company/9368939
www.facebook.com/CFCRA
twitter.com/TheCFCRA
Overview: A small national organization
Mission: To improve the floor covering & cleaning industries in Canada; To promote proper moisture measurement & mitigation
Affiliation(s): Institute of Inspection Cleaning & Restoration Certification; International Inspection, Cleaning & Restoration Council of Associations
Membership: *Fees:* $150-$500
Activities: Offering services & events to members
Chief Officer(s):

Sharon Fenton, Executive Director

Canadian Fluid Power Association (CFPA) / Association canadienne d'énergie fluide
#25, 1250 Marlborough Ct., Oakville ON L6H 2W7
Tel: 905-844-6822
info@cfpa.ca
www.cfpa.ca
www.linkedin.com/groups?gid=4704028
twitter.com/CANADIANFPA
Overview: A medium-sized national organization founded in 1974
Mission: To build public awareness of fluid power technology; To provide a forum for the exchange of information & opinions; To represent the Canadian fluid power industry to government, educational institutions & other organizations; To ensure that members' concerns are known to those in government; To ensure that students are able to be properly prepared for careers in the fluid power industry; To ensure that members are kept abreast of the latest developments in the fluid power industry; To grow & develop fluid power technology in Canada
Member of: National Fluid Power Association
Finances: *Annual Operating Budget:* Less than $50,000; *Funding Sources:* Membership fees; Sponsorships; Golf tournament
Staff Member(s): 1; 10 volunteer(s)
Membership: 45; *Fees:* Schedule available; *Member Profile:* Manufacturers, distributors, assemblers, educators, consultants & designers of fluid power components, systems & services; *Committees:* Communications; Education & Careers; Industrial Relations; Market Insight
Activities: Representing the fluid power industry on the Canadian advisory committee with regard to the drafting of international standards; Representing the fluid power industry in the formulation of applicable national standards; *Speaker Service:* Yes
Chief Officer(s):
Trish Torrance, Association Manager
Awards:
• Canadian Fluid Power Scholarship
; *Amount:* $500
Meetings/Conferences:
• Canadian Fluid Power Association Annual General Meeting 2018, 2018
Scope: National
Publications:
• CFPA [Canadian Fluid Power Association] Newsletter
Type: Newsletter

Canadian Food Exporters Association (CFEA) / Association canadienne des exportateurs à l'alimentation (ACEA)
Two Morneau Shepell Centre, #900, 895 Don Mills Rd., Toronto ON M3C 1W3
Tel: 416-445-3747; *Fax:* 416-639-2110
info@cfea.com
www.cfea.com
www.facebook.com/canadianfoodexportersassociation
twitter.com/cfea
www.instagram.com/cfeacdn
Overview: A medium-sized national organization founded in 1996
Mission: To enhance export efforts in the food & beverage industry; To raise the international profile of Canadian food & beverage products; To increase the export sales of food & beverage products
Affiliation(s): Food Beverage Canada (FBC)
Membership: *Member Profile:* Food & beverage manufacturers which export or wish to expand into new markets
Activities: Increasing exporting by small to medium-sized food & beverage processors & manufacturers; Providing a Central Information Clearinghouse & information network; Offering workshops; Coordinating trade shows & developing trade missions; Providing assistance in meeting technical regulations; Offering an in-house label service
Publications:
• Canadian Food Exporters Association Member Directory
Type: Directory
Profile: Contact information distributed to Canadian Food Exporters Association members & potential buyers
• CFEA [Canadian Food Exporters Association] E-News
Type: Newsletter; *Frequency:* Weekly
Profile: Canadian Food Exporters Association activities, industry trends, & market news & intelligence

Canadian Food for Children (CFFC)
1258 Lakeshore Rd. East, Mississauga ON L5E 1E9
Tel: 905-274-9239
cffc.aasimone@yahoo.ca
www.canadianfoodforchildren.net
Overview: A small national charitable organization founded in 1985
Mission: To raise funds, gather goods, & purchase food for the hungry in developing countries
Affiliation(s): Universal Aide Society
Finances: *Funding Sources:* Donations; Corporate sponsorships
Membership: *Member Profile:* Individuals who care about the poor of the world, & who volunteer for the non-denominational, registered charity, which operates under the Society's Act & the guidelines of Revenue Canada
Activities: Collecting supplies that are donated by a variety of groups; Conducting tours of the Langley, British Columbia depot for school students; Issuing tax receipts for cash & "gifts in kind" tax receipts for donated materials; Operating a thrift shop; Fundraising
Chief Officer(s):
Andrew Simone, Co-Founder
Joan Simone, Co-Founder

Canadian Food for the Hungry International
#1, 31741 Peardonville Rd., Abbotsford BC V2T 1L2
Tel: 604-853-4262; *Fax:* 604-853-4332
Toll-Free: 800-667-0605
info@fhcanada.org
www.fhcanada.org
www.facebook.com/Poverty.Revolution
twitter.com/fhcanada/
Overview: A medium-sized international charitable organization
Mission: To help developing countries overcome poverty through Christianity
Chief Officer(s):
Ben Hoogendoorn, President & CEO

Canadian Food Service Executives Association *See* Canadian Association of Foodservice Professionals

Canadian Food Service Supervisors Association *See* Canadian Society of Nutrition Management

Canadian Foodgrains Bank (CFGB)
PO Box 767, #400, 393 Portage Ave., Winnipeg MB R3C 2L4
Tel: 204-944-1993; *Fax:* 204-943-2597
Toll-Free: 800-665-0377
Other Communication: www.flickr.com/photos/foodgrainsbank
cfgb@foodgrainsbank.ca
foodgrainsbank.ca
www.facebook.com/CanadianFoodgrainsBank
twitter.com/FoodgrainsJames
www.youtube.com/user/foodgrainsbank
Also Known As: Foodgrains Bank
Overview: A large international charitable organization founded in 1983
Mission: To provide a Christian response to hunger; To share resources with & support hungry populations outside Canada to achieve food security; To reduce hunger in developing countries
Finances: *Funding Sources:* Donations (cash & grain); Fundraising
Membership: 15; *Member Profile:* Canadian churches & church-related agencies
Activities: Improving community development; Protecting & building sustainable economic livelihoods; Encouraging peace-building; Strengthening Canadian & international policy & action towards hunger issues; Increasing public awareness & engagement
Chief Officer(s):
Jim Cornelius, Executive Director, 204-944-1993 Ext. 225
jcornelius@foodgrainsbank.ca
Publications:
• Canadian Foodgrains Bank Annual Report
Type: Yearbook; *Frequency:* Annually
• Table Talk [a publication of Canadian Foodgrains Bank Association Inc.]
Type: Newsletter; *Frequency:* s-a.; *Number of Pages:* 6

Canadian Football Hall of Fame & Museum
58 Jackson St. West, Hamilton ON L8P 1L4
Tel: 905-528-7566; *Fax:* 905-528-9781
info@cfhof.ca
www.cfhof.ca
www.facebook.com/CFHOFandM

Canadian Associations / Canadian Football League (CFL) / Ligue canadienne de football (LCF)

twitter.com/cfhof
www.youtube.com/user/CFHOFandM
Overview: A small national charitable organization founded in 1963
Mission: The Hall & Museum commemorate & promote the names & careers of those who have contributed to the development of Canadian football. Artifacts & other memorabilia that relate to the history of the sport are collected, preserved, documented, & exhibited. Education programs offered to students, grades K-8. The Hall & Museum are a non-profit, registered charity, BN: 106845993RR0001.
Finances: *Annual Operating Budget:* $100,000-$250,000
Staff Member(s): 2; 70 volunteer(s)
Activities: Induction weekend; Grey Cup week; school outreach program; gift shop; collections; *Library:* by appointment
Chief Officer(s):
Dave Marler, Chair
Mark DeNobile, Executive Director
mark@cfhof.ca
Christopher Alfred, Curator
chris@cfhof.ca

Canadian Football League (CFL) / Ligue canadienne de football (LCF)
50 Wellington St. East, 3rd Fl., Toronto ON M5E 1C8
Tel: 416-322-9650; *Fax:* 416-322-9651
www.cfl.ca
www.facebook.com/CFL
twitter.com/CFL
www.youtube.com/CFL
Overview: A large national licensing organization founded in 1958
Affiliation(s): Canadian Football League Players' Association (CFLPA); Canadian Football League Alumni Association (CFLAA); Football Canada; Canadian Interuniversity Sport (CIS); Canadian Football Hall of Fame; Canadian Football Officials Association
Membership: 9 CFL teams
Activities: *Awareness Events:* Grey Cup Championship Game; *Rents Mailing List:* Yes
Chief Officer(s):
Randy Ambrosie, Commissioner
Greg Dick, Senior Vice-President, Operations & Finance
Glen Johnson, Senior Vice-President, Football
Christina Litz, Senior Vice-President, Marketing & Content
Matt Maychak, Vice-President, Communications & Public Affairs

Canadian Football League Alumni Association (CFLAA)
17 Kinnell St., Hamilton ON L8R 2J8
Tel: 905-639-6359
Toll-Free: 877-890-7272
www.cflaa.ca
www.facebook.com/cflaa
twitter.com/CFL_Alumni
www.youtube.com/user/CFLAlumniAssociation
Overview: A large national organization
Mission: To foster a lifelong connection between the Canadian Football League & its alumni; To provide support to the alumni community
Finances: *Funding Sources:* Donations
Chief Officer(s):
Leo Ezerins, Executive Director

Canadian Football League Players' Association (CFLPA) / Association des joueurs de la ligue de football canadienne
175 Barton St. East, Stoney Creek ON L8E 2K3
Tel: 905-664-0852; *Fax:* 905-664-9653
Toll-Free: 800-616-6865
admin@cflpa.com
www.cflpa.com
www.facebook.com/CFLPA
twitter.com/cflpa
www.youtube.com/user/cflpa
Overview: A small national organization founded in 1965
Mission: The Canadian Football League Players' Association was established in 1965 & has since that time represented the professional football players in the Canadian Football League with the objective of establishing fair & reasonable working conditions for the players.
Membership: approx. 400 + 8 locals
Chief Officer(s):
Jeff Keeping, President
Marwan Hage, 1st Vice-President
Brian Ramsay, Executive Director

Awards:
• Tom Pate Award
Publications:
• Canadian Football League Players' Association Negotiation Booklet
• Canadian Football League Players' Association Salary Survey
• CFLPA [Canadian Football League Players' Association] Newsletter
Type: Newsletter

Canadian Football Officials Association (CFOA) / Association Canadienne des Officiels de Football (ACOF)
www.cfoa-acof.ca
Overview: A medium-sized national organization founded in 1969
Chief Officer(s):
Ron Paluzzi, Secretary-Treasurer
rpaluzzi@3macs.com

Canadian Forage & Grassland Association (CFGA) / Association Canadienne pour les Plantes Fourragères (ACPF)
125 Patterson Cres., Brandon MB R7A 6T7
Tel: 204-726-9393; *Fax:* 204-726-9703
www.canadianfga.ca
Overview: A small national organization
Mission: The CFGA/ACPF is the national voice for all sectors of the forage and grassland industry. Its main role is to uphold our robust forage industry and realize the potential of the domestic and export forage market.
Membership: *Fees:* $1500 overseas exporters; $250 US exporters, patrons; *Committees:* Producer/User; Forage Export & Domestic Development; Research & Extension
Chief Officer(s):
Wayne Digby, Executive Director
w_digby@canadianfga.ca

Canadian Forces Logistics Association - Montréal
c/o Léo Gravelle, 2093, rue Montarville, Saint-Bruno-de-Montarville QC J3V 3V8
Overview: A small national organization
Mission: To promote the interests of the Canadian Forces Logistics Branch & serves to exchange information between serving & retired logisticians & other interested parties.
Membership: *Fees:* $15
Chief Officer(s):
Léo Gravelle, Treasurer

Canadian Forestry Accreditation Board (CFAB) / Bureau canadien d'agrément en foresterie
18 Pommel Cres., Kanata ON K2M 1A2
Tel: 613-599-7259; *Fax:* 613-599-8107
cfab@cfab.ca
www.cfab.ca
Overview: A medium-sized national organization founded in 1989
Mission: Responsible for the accreditation of Canadian university forestry baccalaureate programs for the purpose of meeting academic requirements for professional registration.
Affiliation(s): Association of BC Forest Professionals; Association of Newfoundland-Labrador Registered Professional Foresters; Association of Registered Professional Foresters of New Brunswick; Association of Saskatchewan Forestry Professionals; College of Alberta Professional Foresters Association; Ordre des ingénieurs forestiers du Québec; Registered Professional Foresters Association of Nova Scotia; Canadian Institute of Forestry
Chief Officer(s):
Lorne F. Riley, Executive Director

Canadian Forestry Association (CFA) / Association forestière canadienne
c/o The Canadian Institute of Forestry, PO Box 99, 6905 Hwy. 17 West, Mattawa ON P0H 1V0
Tel: 705-744-1715; *Fax:* 705-744-1716
www.canadianforestry.com
Overview: A large national charitable organization founded in 1900
Mission: To advocate for the wise use & protection of Canada's forest, water, & wildlife resources; To nurture economic & environmental health, through the management & conservation of forest resources; To provide a national voice for provincial forestry agencies
Affiliation(s): Canadian Institute of Forestry
Finances: *Funding Sources:* Donations

Activities: Advising the federal government of forest policy; Increasing public awareness about the protection of forests; *Awareness Events:* National Forest Week, Sept.
Chief Officer(s):
Dave Lemkay, General Manager
Publications:
• Canadian Forestry Association Teaching Kit, Volume 1: Canada's Forests - Learning from the Past, Building for the Future
Type: Kit; *Number of Pages:* 32
Profile: A tool for educators to help young people in junior to senior grades understand the importance ofprotecting & conserving forests
• Canadian Forestry Association Teaching Kit, Volume 2: Canada's Forests - A Breath of Fresh Air
Type: Booklet; *Number of Pages:* 40
Profile: An exploration of climate change & its effects on Canadian forests
• Canadian Forestry Association Teaching Kit, Volume 3: Canada's Forests - All Things Big & Small
Type: Booklet; *Number of Pages:* 40
Profile: An examination of biodiversity in Canada's forests for the junior to intermediate grade levels
• Canadian Forestry Association Teaching Kit, Volume 4: Canada's Forests - Source of Life
Type: Booklet; *Number of Pages:* 48
Profile: Information about forest sustainability for students from grade 4 to 7
• Canadian Forestry Association Teaching Kit, Volume 5: Canada's Forest - A Fine Balance
Type: Booklet; *Number of Pages:* 44
Profile: Information & activities about the decline of wildlife habitat & species at risk, for students from grade 4 to grade 12
• Canadian Forestry Association Teaching Kit, Volume 6: Canada's Forests & Wetlands - Our Natural Water Filters
Type: Booklet; *Number of Pages:* 40
Profile: Forest, wetland, & water issues presented for children in grades 5 to 8
• Canadian Forestry Association Teaching Kit, Volume 7: The Boreal Forest - A Global Legacy
Type: Booklet; *Number of Pages:* 48
Profile: A teaching kit about the boreal forest intended for students from age 5 to 18
• Canadian Forestry Association Teaching Kit, Volume 8: Canada's Boreal Forest - Tradition & Transition
Type: Booklet; *Number of Pages:* 44
Profile: An exploration of the boreal forest & the interdependence that exists between the forest & Canadians
• Canadian Forestry Association Teaching Kit User Guide
Type: Guide
Profile: Activities for the entire class, group activities, activities for partners, games, outdoor activities, research, student presentations, & activities with Aboriginalcontent

Canadian Forestry Association of New Brunswick (CFANB) / Association forestière canadienne du Nouveau-Brunswick (AFCNB)
#248, 1350 Regent St., Fredericton NB E3C 2G6
Tel: 506-452-1339; *Fax:* 506-452-7950
Toll-Free: 866-405-7000
info@cfanb.ca
www.cfanb.ca
www.facebook.com/EnvirothonNB
www.youtube.com/cfanb
Also Known As: The Tree House
Overview: A medium-sized provincial charitable organization founded in 1939 overseen by Canadian Forestry Association
Mission: To champions trees & forests of New Brunswick; To promote environmental, commercial, recreational, & inspirational benefits; To encourages conservation & wise use of natural resources
Finances: *Funding Sources:* Membership fees; Government grants; Foundation support
20 volunteer(s)
Membership: 75; *Fees:* Schedule available; Individual membership $25; *Member Profile:* Open
Activities: *Awareness Events:* National Forest Week, September; Arbor Day, May
Chief Officer(s):
Bernard Daigle, President
Doug Hiltz, Treasurer/Secretary

Canadian Foundation for AIDS Research (CANFAR) / Fondation canadienne de recherche sur le SIDA
#602, 200 Wellington St. West, Toronto ON M5V 3C7

Tel: 416-361-6281; Fax: 416-361-5736
Toll-Free: 800-563-2873
www.canfar.com
www.facebook.com/canfar
twitter.com/canfar
www.youtube.com/user/CANFAR; www.flickr.com/photos/canfar
Overview: A medium-sized national charitable organization founded in 1987
Mission: To raise awareness in order to fund research into all aspects of HIV infection & AIDS
Finances: *Annual Operating Budget:* $500,000-$1.5 Million
Staff Member(s): 5; 70 volunteer(s)
Membership: 60; *Member Profile:* Anyone who actively participates in betterment of the Foundation; *Committees:* Scientific Advisory
Activities: Raising funds for AIDS research; *Speaker Service:* Yes
Chief Officer(s):
Christopher Bunting, President & CEO, 416-361-6281 Ext. 229
cbunting@canfar.com
Publications:
• CANFAR [Canadian Foundation for AIDS Research] Annual Report
Frequency: Annually
• Catalyst [a publication of the Canadian Foundation for AIDS Research]
Type: Newsletter
Profile: CANFAR's programs & fundraising events, reports on advances in HIV / AIDS, & updates on research
• Funding Leading-Edge Research: Canada's HIV/AIDS epidemic, the global HIV / AIDS crisis & CANFAR
Author: S.E. Read, R.S. Remis, J.K. Stewart

Canadian Foundation for Climate & Atmospheric Sciences (CFCAS) / Fondation canadienne pour les sciences du climat et de l'atmosphère (FCSCA)
#901, 350 Sparks St., Ottawa ON K1R 7S8
Tel: 613-238-2223; *Fax:* 613-238-2227
info@cfcas.org
www.cfcas.org
Overview: A medium-sized national charitable organization founded in 2000
Mission: To fund university-based research on climate, & atmospheric & related oceanic work in Canada
Finances: *Annual Operating Budget:* Greater than $5 Million
Activities: Responding to national needs or scientific imperatives; Providing grants
Chief Officer(s):
Dawn Conway, Executive Director
conway@cfcas.org
Denny Alexander, Officer, Communications
alexander@cfcas.org
Tim Aston, Officer, Science
aston@cfcas.org
Publications:
• CFCAS [Canadian Foundation for Climate & Atmospheric Sciences] News
Type: Newsletter
Profile: Foundation happenings, research news, & grant information

Canadian Foundation for Dietetic Research (CFDF)
#604, 480 University Ave., Toronto ON M5G 1V2
Tel: 416-642-9309; *Fax:* 416-596-0603
info@cfdr.ca
www.cfdr.ca
Overview: A medium-sized national charitable organization
Mission: To provide grants for research in dietetics & nutrition
Finances: *Funding Sources:* Donations
Chief Officer(s):
Sarah Hewko, Chair

Canadian Foundation for Drug Policy
70 MacDonald St., Ottawa ON K2P 1H6
Tel: 613-236-1027; *Fax:* 613-238-2891
eoscapel@ca.inter.net
www.cfdp.ca
Overview: A small national organization founded in 1993
Mission: To examine drug policies & their effects; to act as a forum for the exchange of views in regards to drug policy reform
Finances: *Funding Sources:* Donations
Chief Officer(s):
Eugene Oscapella, Contact
eoscapel@ca.inter.net

Canadian Foundation for Economic Education (CFEE) / Fondation d'éducation économique
#201, 110 Eglinton Ave. West, Toronto ON M4R 1A3
Tel: 416-968-2236; *Fax:* 416-968-0488
Toll-Free: 888-570-7610
mail@cfee.org
www.cfee.org
twitter.com/cfee1
vimeo.com/cfee/videos
Overview: A medium-sized national charitable organization founded in 1974
Mission: To enhance the economic capabilities of Canadians
Affiliation(s): Organisation for Economic Co-operation & Development (OECD); Child & Youth Finance International; Association of Asia Pacific Countries (APEC)
Finances: *Funding Sources:* Sponsorships; Project activity
Staff Member(s): 9
Activities: Engaging in research activities; Producing resources, such as teaching kits & student materials; Distributing resources to educators across Canada; Developing curriculum, workshops, seminars, & conferences; Providing advisory services; Collaborating with provincial ministries & departments of education; Partnering with various organizations & associations on various projects; *Awareness Events:* Talk With Our Kids About Money Day, April
Chief Officer(s):
Gary Rabbior, President
grabbior@cfee.org
Publications:
• Building Futures in Canada [a publication of the Canadian Foundation for Economic Education]
Type: Online Resource
Profile: Stories of immigrants to Canada (www.buildingfuturesincanada.ca)
• Building Futures in Manitoba [a publication of the Canadian Foundation for Economic Education]
Type: Teaching Resource
Profile: Seeks to integrate basic economic & financial education into the Manitoba curriculum in grades 4-10(buildingfuturesinmanitoba.com)
• The Canadian Economy: The Big Picture [a publication of the Canadian Foundation for Economic Education]
Type: Booklet
Profile: A model of the economy that reveals how the system works
• Catching the Wave [a publication of the Canadian Foundation for Economic Education]
Type: Report
Profile: Research on factors that foster entrepreneurial initiative & success
• Classroom Edition [a publication of the Canadian Foundation for Economic Education]
Type: Teaching Resource
Profile: Education news & resources for teachers (news from the Globe & Mail); custom lesson plans (classroomedition.ca)
• Dayplanner for Newcomers to Canada [a publication of the Canadian Foundation for Economic Education]
Type: Online Resource
Profile: Interactive dayplanner to help newcomers to Canada settle (cfeedayplanner.com)
• Entrepreneurship: The Spirit of Adventure [a publication of the Canadian Foundation for Economic Education]
Type: Teaching Resource
Profile: For those interested in learning more about entrepreneurship (cfeespiritofadventure.com)
• Managing Your Money in Canada [a publication of the Canadian Foundation for Economic Education]
Type: Online Resource
Profile: Artcilees on how to financially plan for various life events
• Money & Youth [a publication of the Canadian Foundation for Economic Education]
Type: Book; *Number of Pages:* 125
Profile: A resource & teacher's guide to help young people learn how to take control of their financial future

Canadian Foundation for Healthcare Improvement (CFHI) / Fondation canadienne pour l'amélioration des services de santé (FCASS)
#200, 150 Kent St., Ottawa ON K1P 0E4
Tel: 613-728-2238; *Fax:* 613-728-3527
Other Communication: registration@cfhi-fcass.ca
info@cfhi-fcass.ca
www.cfhi-fcass.ca
www.linkedin.com/company/canadian-foundation-for-healthcare-improvement
www.facebook.com/107329739320566
twitter.com/cfhi_fcass
www.youtube.com/user/CHSRF
Previous Name: Canadian Health Services Research Foundation
Overview: A large national organization founded in 1996
Mission: To fund management & policy research in health services; To support applied health services & nursing researchers; To support the synthesis & dissemination of research results; To support the use of research results by decision makers in the health system
Finances: *Annual Operating Budget:* Greater than $5 Million; *Funding Sources:* Government grants & endowments
Activities: Collaborating with regions, provinces, territories to improve healthcare systems; *Awareness Events:* CEO Forum; *Internships:* Yes; *Speaker Service:* Yes
Chief Officer(s):
R. Lynn Stevenson, Chair
Maureen O'Neil, O.C., President
Maria Judd, Vice-President, Programs
Maria.Judd@cfhi-fcass.ca
Publications:
• Canadian Foundation for Healthcare Improvement Annual Report
Type: Yearbook; *Frequency:* Annually
Profile: Organizational highlights from the past year
• It's Happening Now [a publication of the Canadian Foundation for Healthcare Improvement]
Type: Newsletter; *Frequency:* Monthly
Profile: Current reports & activities from the Canadian Foundation for Healthcare Improvement
• Pass it on! [a series of publications from the Canadian Foundation for Healthcare Improvement]
Profile: Innovative approaches to successful changes in healthcare

Canadian Foundation for Masorti Judaism (CFMJ)
#508, 1000 Finch Ave. West, Toronto ON M3J 2V5
Tel: 416-667-1717
Toll-Free: 866-357-3384
info@masorti.ca
www.masorti.ca
Overview: A medium-sized international charitable organization founded in 1979
Mission: To support the Masorti (Conservative) Movement in Israel, which promotes scholarship, Zionism & religious tolerance & pluralism, within the context of modern Israeli society
Chief Officer(s):
Jennifer Gorman, Executive Director
Publications:
• Traditions
Type: Newsletter
Profile: Masorti news & programs

Canadian Foundation for Pharmacy (CFP) / Fondation canadienne pour la pharmacie
5809 Fieldon Rd., Mississauga ON L5M 5K1
Tel: 905-997-3238; *Fax:* 905-997-4264
www.cfpnet.ca
www.linkedin.com/groups/Canadian-Foundation-Pharmacy-7473036
Previous Name: Canadian Foundation for the Advancement of Pharmacy
Overview: A medium-sized national charitable organization founded in 1945
Mission: To provide programs for the advancement of the pharmacy profession in Canada
Affiliation(s): Canadian Pharmacists Association
Finances: *Funding Sources:* Individual & corporate donations
Activities: *Library:* Not open to public
Chief Officer(s):
Marshall Moleschi, President
Dayle Acorn, Executive Director
dacorn@cfpnet.ca
Awards:
• Pharmacy Research Awards
These awards are designed to give special recognition to deserving students pursuing postgraduate work in Canadian faculties of pharmacy; *Amount:* Two awards of $1,000 each available for the best poster & podium presentations
• Clinical Practice
• Pharmacy Administration
• Professional Practice Awards
Established 1973; the purpose of these awards is to support student initiatives designed to foster public health awareness;

two awards of $1,000 & $500 are given; open to pharmacy graduates on a national competition basis
• Industrial Pharmacy Awards
Established 1977; these awards are intended to honour distinguished performance of undergraduate pharmacy students participating in the PMAC Industrial Pharmacy Studentship Program; two awards of $1,000 & $500 are given; open to students registered in Canadian schools of pharmacy who have completed Industrial Pharmacy Summer Studentship Program
• Hospital Pharmacy Awards
Established 1956; the purpose of these awards is to recognize excellence of performance by students participating in an accredited hospital pharmacy residency program in Canada; two awards of $1,000 & $500 are given; open to Canadian pharmacy graduates

Canadian Foundation for Physically Disabled Persons (CFPDP)
#265, 6 Garamond Ct., Toronto ON M3C 1Z5
Tel: 416-760-7351; Fax: 416-760-9405
info@cfpdp.com
www.cfpdp.com
www.facebook.com/cffpdp
twitter.com/cffpdp
Overview: A small national charitable organization founded in 1984
Mission: To provide financial assistance to organizations sharing concern for physically disabled adults; To help create awareness in the public & business communities, & in government of the needs of physically disabled adults in the areas of housing, employment, education, accessibility, sports & recreation, & research
Finances: Funding Sources: Private fundraising
Staff Member(s): 2
Activities: Great Valentine Gala; Terry Fox Hall of Fame luncheon; Rolling Rampage 10K wheelchair race; Speaker Service: Yes
Chief Officer(s):
Vim Kochhar, Chair
vimkochhar@sympatico.ca
Dorothy Price, Executive Director
dorothyprice@sympatico.ca
Awards:
• Canadian Helen Keller Centre Awards

Canadian Foundation for the Advancement of Pharmacy
See Canadian Foundation for Pharmacy

Canadian Foundation for the Love of Children
See Kids Kottage Foundation

Canadian Foundation for the Study of Infant Deaths
See Baby's Breath

Canadian Foundation for Ukrainian Studies (CFUS) / Fondation canadienne des études ukrainiennes
620 Spadina Ave., Toronto ON M5S 2H4
Tel: 416-766-9630; Fax: 416-766-0599
Toll-Free: 877-766-9630
admin@cfus.ca
www.cfus.ca
Overview: A small national charitable organization founded in 1975
Mission: To encourage & advance university-level Ukrainian studies for the development of the Ukrainian community in Canada; To promote knowledge of Ukraine's history & culture in order to develop sound relations with Ukraine
Finances: Funding Sources: Fundraising; Donations; Bequests; Endowments; Government funding
Activities: Supporting Ukrainian studies, research, & publishing; Providing scholarships & awards to students; Administering endowment funds

Canadian Foundation on Compulsive Gambling (Ontario)
See Responsible Gambling Council (Ontario)

Canadian Foundation on Fetal Alcohol Research (CFFAR) / Fondation canadienne de la recherche dur l'alcoolisation foetale (FCRAF)
#62, 2192 Queen St. East, Toronto ON M4E 1E6
info@fasdfoundation.ca
www.fasdfoundation.ca
Overview: A medium-sized national organization founded in 2007
Mission: The Canadian Foundation on Fetal Alcohol Research (CFFAR), is an independent, non-profit foundation created to promote interest and fund research related to the short and long-term bio-medical, psychological and social effects of alcohol consumption during pregnancy, and the prevention of fetal alcohol spectrum disorders (FASD).
Chief Officer(s):
Louise Nadeau, Chair

Canadian Foundry Association (CFA) / Association des fonderies canadiennes (AFC)
#1500, 1 Nicholas St., Ottawa ON K1N 7B7
Tel: 613-789-4894; Fax: 613-789-5957
info@foundryassociation.ca
www.foundryassociation.ca
Overview: A medium-sized national organization founded in 1975
Mission: To assist & represent the membership in dealing with government on industry specific issues; To communicate information to the industry, which will assist its members in strengthening their own competitive position & ensuring a strong Canadian foundry industry
Member of: Canadian Society of Association Executives
Membership: 50 organizations; Fees: Fees based on sales volume; Member Profile: Pour metal castings or supplier to the industry; Committees: Education; Environment; Membership; Occupational Health & Safety
Activities: Rents Mailing List: Yes
Chief Officer(s):
Judith Arbour, Executive Director
judy@foundryassociation.ca
William Monaghan, Secretary-Treasurer
Meetings/Conferences:
• Canadian Foundry Association 2018 Issues Meeting, March, 2018, Waterfront Banquet & Conference Centre, Hamilton, ON
Scope: National
Description: Technical committees work on issues to represent members' interests
• Canadian Foundry Association Annual Meeting 2018, 2018
Scope: National
Description: A gathering of members to address issues facing the Canadian foundry industry

Canadian Frailty Network
Kidd House, 100 Stuart St., Kingston ON K7L 3N6
Tel: 613-549-6666
www.cfn-nce.ca
Overview: A medium-sized national organization
Mission: To improve care of older Canadians living with frailty through research & knowledge sharing; To ensure that the needs of older adults are recognized by promoting change in health & social care systems
Finances: Funding Sources: Government
Membership: 400 researchers; 44 hospitals; 20 industry & business partners; 100 community agencies; 20 government agencies; Committees: Citizen Engagement; Education & Training; International Scientific Advisory; Knowledge Translation; Research Management; Scientific Review
Activities: Funding research projects; Recruiting & training Highly Qualified Personnel through the CFN Interdisciplinary Training Program
Chief Officer(s):
Carol Barrie, Executive Director & COO
Peter Aitken, Manager, Partnerships, Development & Government Relations
Kate Cooke, Manager, Communications & Corporate Initiatives
Perry Kim, Manager, Research & Intellectual Property

Canadian Franchise Association (CFA) / Association canadienne de la franchise
#116, 5399 Eglinton Ave. West, Toronto ON M9C 5K6
Tel: 416-695-2896; Fax: 416-695-1950
Toll-Free: 800-665-4232
info@cfa.ca
www.cfa.ca
Previous Name: Association of Canadian Franchisors
Overview: A medium-sized national organization founded in 1967
Mission: To promote & represent franchise excellence through a national association of businesses united by a common interest in ethical franchising
Finances: Annual Operating Budget: $1.5 Million-$3 Million
Staff Member(s): 23
Membership: 400 franchisors + 100 franchise support service; Member Profile: Regular - franchising for at least two years in Canada as franchisor; franchise support service - provides products or services to franchisors.; Committees: FSS; Awards; Board of Directors; Convention; Editorial & Program; Franchise Advisory; Legal & Legislature; Membership.
Activities: Speaker Service: Yes
Chief Officer(s):
Lorraine McLachlan, President & CEO
Gary Martini-Wong, Manager, Finance & Accounting
Awards:
• Award of Excellence in Franchise Relations
Meetings/Conferences:
• Canadian Franchise Association 2018 National Convention, April, 2018, Ottawa, ON
Scope: National

Canadian Fraternal Association (CFA) / Association canadienne des sociétés fraternelles
c/o FaithLife Financial, 470 Weber St. North, Waterloo ON N2J 4G4
Tel: 519-886-4610; Fax: 519-886-0350
www.cfa-afc.org
Overview: A small national organization founded in 1891
Mission: To promote the general benefit welfare system by uniting fraternal benefit societies in all matters of mutual concern & public interest
Membership: Member Profile: Fraternal societies
Chief Officer(s):
Gordon Kennedy, Secretary-Treasurer
gkennedy@faithlifefinancial.ca
Karen Bjerland, President

Canadian Freestyle Ski Association / Association canadienne de ski acrobatique
808 Pacific St., Vancouver BC V6Z 1C2
Tel: 604-714-2233; Fax: 604-714-2232
Toll-Free: 877-714-2232
info@freestyleski.com
www.freestyleski.ca
www.linkedin.com/company/8580796
www.facebook.com/CanFreestyleSki
twitter.com/canfreestyleski
instagram.com/canfreestyleski
Overview: A medium-sized national organization
Mission: The national governing body of the sport of freestyle skiing with a mandate to develop the sport within Canada; to represent our country internationally; to promote the safe development of the sport; to promote excellence in national & international competitions
Affiliation(s): Canadian Ski & Snowboard Association
Finances: Annual Operating Budget: $500,000-$1.5 Million
Membership: 2,000; Fees: $10
Activities: Rents Mailing List: Yes
Chief Officer(s):
Bruce Robinson, Chief Executive Officer
brucerobinson@freestyleski.com

Canadian Friends of Bar-Ilan University (CFBIU)
#214, 1750 Steeles Ave. West, Concord ON L4K 2L7
Tel: 905-660-3563; Fax: 905-660-1612
Toll-Free: 888-248-2720
admin@cfbiu.org
www.cfbiu.org
www.facebook.com/barilancanada
www.youtube.com/barilanuniversity
Overview: A small international organization
Mission: To raise money for Bar-Ilan University
Finances: Funding Sources: Donations
Activities: Public lectures; Speaker Service: Yes
Chief Officer(s):
Gabi Weisfeld, President

Eastern Region
#612, 5858, rue Côte-des-Neiges, Montréal QC H3S 2S1
Tel: 514-731-7893

Western Region
#124, 3495 Cambie St., Vancouver BC V5Z 4R3
Toll-Free: 888-248-2720

Canadian Friends of Beth Hatefutsoth
1170, rue Peel, Montréal QC H3B 4P2
Tel: 514-878-5290
Overview: A small national organization
Mission: To raise funds for Beit Hatefutsoth through membership, & to bring travelling exhibits from Israel

Canadian Friends of Bikur Cholim Hospital
329 Joicey Blvd., Toronto ON M5N 2V8
Tel: 416-781-6960
Overview: A small international organization
Mission: To support & raise funds for Bakir Cholim Hospital in Jerusalem
Chief Officer(s):

David Kleiner, Secretary-Treasurer
dkleiner@danatrading.com

Canadian Friends of Boys Town Jerusalem
#200, 2788 Bathurst St., Toronto ON M6B 3A3
Tel: 416-789-7241; *Fax:* 416-789-1090
Toll-Free: 866-989-7241
www.btjcanada.com
Overview: A small local organization founded in 1973
Mission: To take boys of high potential from all parts of Israel from junior high school, high school & colleges of mechanical & electrical engineering & expose them to a high level of technological, academic, & religious training; To raise funds for Boys Town Jerusalem in order to provide education for boys from disadvantaged backgrounds
Finances: *Annual Operating Budget:* $100,000-$250,000; *Funding Sources:* Foundation grants; Events; Direct mail; Major gifts
Staff Member(s): 2; 10 volunteer(s)
Membership: *Committees:* Board of Directors
Chief Officer(s):
Jules Kronis, President
Sharon E. Anisman, Executive Director
sharon@btjcanada.com
Debbie Basch, Administrative Assistant
debbie@btjcanada.com

Canadian Friends of Burma (CFOB) / Les amis canadiens de la Birmanie
#206, 145 Spruce St., Ottawa ON K1R 6P1
Tel: 613-237-8056; *Fax:* 613-563-0017
cfob@cfob.org
www.cfob.org
Overview: A medium-sized international organization founded in 1991
Mission: To promote democracy & human rights in Burma by working within the global movement, & educating & activating Canadian involvement in the struggle for peace in Burma
Member of: Burma Advisory Group; Network on International Human Rights; Canadian Council for Refugees
Affiliation(s): World University Service of Canada; Canadian Asia Pacific Working Group; Peacefund Canada; Canadian Peacebuilding Coordinating Committee
Finances: *Funding Sources:* International Centre for Human Rights & Democratic Development; Private foundations; Donors 3 volunteer(s)
Membership: 1,200 donor contacts; *Fees:* Suggested donation: $25 regular; $15 low income; $100 institution
Activities: *Speaker Service:* Yes; *Library:* CFOB Library; Open to public by appointment
Chief Officer(s):
Tin Maung Htoo, Executive Director
Awards:
• Thakore Foundation Award

Canadian Friends of Peace Now (Shalom Achshav) (CFPN)
#517, 119-660 Eglinton Ave. East, Toronto ON M4G 2K2
Tel: 416-322-5559; *Fax:* 416-322-5587
Toll-Free: 866-405-5387
info@peacenowcanada.org
www.peacenowcanada.org
www.facebook.com/CanadianFriendsofPeaceNow
Overview: A small national charitable organization founded in 1982
Mission: CFPN supports Peace Now, a peace movement in Israel that sponsors dialogue between Israelis & Palestinians, & advocates a 2-state solution for co-existence. CFPN organizes lectures in Canada & sponsors visits by Israeli & Palestinian peace activists. It is a registered charity, BN: 119147320RR0001.
Member of: Canadian Jewish Congress
Finances: *Annual Operating Budget:* $50,000-$100,000; *Funding Sources:* Private donations
Staff Member(s): 1
Activities: Public lectures; *Speaker Service:* Yes
Chief Officer(s):
David Brooks, Co-Chair, Ottawa
Gabriella Goliger, Co-Chair, Ottawa
Sheldon Gordon, Chair, Toronto
Stephen Scheinberg, Chair, Montréal

Canadian Friends of Schizophrenics See Schizophrenia Society of Canada

Canadian Friends of the Hebrew University (CFHU) / Association des amis canadiens de l'Université Hébraïque
PO Box 65, #3020, 3080 Yonge St., Toronto ON M4N 3N1
Tel: 416-485-8000; *Fax:* 416-485-8565
Toll-Free: 888-432-7398
info@cfhu.org
www.cfhu.org
www.facebook.com/CFHUFriendsandAlumni
twitter.com/CdnFriendsHU
www.youtube.com/user/CdnFriendsHU
Overview: A small international organization
Mission: To develop & promote awareness of, leadership in, & financial support for the Hebrew University of Jerusalem.
Staff Member(s): 10
Activities: Sponsors educational programs
Chief Officer(s):
Rami Kleinmann, President & CEO
rkleinmann@cfhu.org
Miriam Pilc-Levine, National Director, Communications & Marketing
mpilc-levine@cfhu.org
Publications:
• CFHU eNewsletter [a publication of the Canadian Friends of the Hebrew University]
Type: Newsletter; *Frequency:* Monthly

Calgary Chapter
120 - 7 Ave. SW, Calgary AB T2P 0W4
Tel: 403-297-0605; *Fax:* 403-253-1944
calgary@cfhu.org
Chief Officer(s):
Cheryl Baron, President

Edmonton Chapter
#7200, JCC - 156 St., Edmonton AB T5R 1X3
Tel: 780-444-0809; *Fax:* 780-444-4019
edmonton@cfhu.org

Montréal Chapter
#720, 1310, av Greene, Montréal QC H3Z 2B2
Tel: 514-932-2133; *Fax:* 514-932-3749
mtl@cfhu.org
Chief Officer(s):
Simon Bensimon, Director
sbensimon@cfhu.org

Ottawa Chapter
2430 Georgina Dr., Ottawa ON K2B 7M7
Tel: 613-829-3150; *Fax:* 613-726-0096
ott@cfhu.org
Chief Officer(s):
Jon Reider, Executive Director
jreider@cfhu.org

Toronto Chapter
PO Box 65, #3020, 3080 Yonge St., Toronto ON M4N 3N1
Tel: 416-485-8000; *Fax:* 416-485-8565
tor@cfhu.org
Chief Officer(s):
Elan Divon, Director
edivon@cfhu.org

Vancouver Chapter
#204, 950 West 41st Ave., Vancouver BC V5Z 2N7
Tel: 604-257-5133; *Fax:* 604-257-5144
vanc@cfhu.org
Chief Officer(s):
Dina Wachtel, Western Region Director
dwachtel@cfhu.org

Winnipeg Chapter
#206, 1700 Corydon Ave., Winnipeg MB R3N 0K1
Tel: 204-942-3085; *Fax:* 204-943-6211
wpg@cfhu.org
Chief Officer(s):
Sharon Zalik, Director
szalik@cfhu.org

Canadian Friends of Ukraine (CFU)
South Building, 620 Spadina Ave., 2nd Fl., Toronto ON M5S 2H4
Tel: 416-964-6644; *Fax:* 416-964-6085
canfun@interlog.com
www.canadianfriendsofukraine.com
www.facebook.com/Canadian-Friends-of-Ukraine-264273896939710/
Overview: A small international organization founded in 1089
Mission: To strengthen Canadian-Ukrainian relations; To promote democracy & reform in Ukraine
Finances: *Funding Sources:* Donations
Activities: Providing technical assistance & support for government institutions, hospitals, libraries, & educational institutions; Promoting international awarenss to strengthen democracy; Supporting projects that encourage legislative reform, public access to information, & human rights; Opening Canadian library centres in eastern & southern Ukraine
Chief Officer(s):
Lisa Shymko, Executive Director
Awards:
• Teachers Awards
To recognize teachers in Ukrainian-language schools & teachers of Ukrainian-language courses

Canadian Friends of Yeshiva University (CFYU)
#300, 4580 Dufferin St., Toronto ON M3H 5Y2
Tel: 416-783-6960; *Fax:* 416-783-9854
canada@yu.edu
www.yu.edu/canadian-friends
www.facebook.com/166648253367786
Overview: A small international charitable organization
Mission: To support Yeshiva University's Canadian students & alumni; to raise the University's profile in Canada; to bring our spiritual, intellectual and creative resources to Canadian Jewish communities-and to raise the funds needed to make all of this possible.
Member of: Yeshiva University
Staff Member(s): 4
Chief Officer(s):
Stuart Haber, National Director
stuart.haber@yu.edu

Canadian Friends Service Committee (CFSC) / Secours Quaker Canadien
60 Lowther Ave., Toronto ON M5R 1C7
Tel: 416-920-5213
www.quakerservice.ca
www.facebook.com/CFSCQuakers
twitter.com/CFSCQuakers
Also Known As: Religious Society of Friends (Quakers)
Overview: A medium-sized national charitable organization founded in 1931
Mission: To unify & expand the concerns of Friends (Quakers)
Member of: The Canadian Council of Churches; Kairos: Canadian Ecumenical Justice Initiatives; Project Ploughshares; Canadian Council for Refugees; War Resistors Support Campaign
Finances: *Annual Operating Budget:* $500,000-$1.5 Million; *Funding Sources:* Individuals; meetings
Staff Member(s): 7; 40 volunteer(s)
Membership: *Committees:* Finance; Personnel; Quakers Fostering Justice; Quaker Indigenous Rights; Quaker Peace
Activities: Participating in peace & social justice work; *Internships:* Yes; *Speaker Service:* Yes; *Library:* Friends House Library; Not open to public
Chief Officer(s):
Jennifer Preston, Administrator, Finance
jennifer@quakerservice.ca
Matthew Legge, Coordinator, Administrative & Communications
matt@quakerservice.ca
Publications:
• Quaker Concern [a publication of Canadian Friends Service Committee]
Type: Newsletter; *Frequency:* 3 pa
Profile: CFSC information & feature articles on CFSC concerns

Canadian Fruit Wholesalers Association See Canadian Produce Marketing Association

Canadian Fuels Association / Association canadienne des carburants
#1000, 275 Slater St., Ottawa ON K1P 5H9
Tel: 613-232-3709; *Fax:* 613-236-4280
canadianfuels.ca
www.linkedin.com/company/canadianfuels----carburantsca
www.facebook.com/CanadianFuels
twitter.com/CanadianFuels
Previous Name: Canadian Petroleum Products Institute
Overview: A large national organization founded in 1989
Mission: To represent its membership to governments on issues related to business, the environment & health & safety in the petroleum products sector; To ensure its own adherence to the Competition Act, & provide a competition compliance program & training sessions to all staff & members
Membership: 10; *Member Profile:* Companies engaged in petroleum refining, marketing & distribution

Activities: Training & education; news releases, reports & technical documents; Driver Certification Program for petroleum transport drivers
Chief Officer(s):
Peter Boag, President
president@canadianfuels.ca
Awards:
• Distinguished Service to Humanism Award
Publications:
• Canadian Fuels Association Annual Review
Type: Report
Profile: Tough questions about the future of transportation fuels in Canada
• Fuels for Life [a publication of the Canadian Fuels Association]
Type: Report; *Number of Pages:* 60
Profile: Discussion paper on Canada's future transportation fuels choices

Eastern Canada Division
#1000, 275 Slater St., Toronto ON K1P 5H9
Tel: 514-284-7754; *Fax:* 514-284-3301
Chief Officer(s):
Carol Montreuil, Vice-President
Ontario Division
#1100, 151 Yonge St., Toronto ON M5C 2W7
Tel: 416-492-5677; *Fax:* 416-492-2514
Chief Officer(s):
Lisa Stilborn, Vice-President
Western Division
#2100, 350 - 7th Ave. SW, Calgary AB T2P 3N9
Tel: 403-266-7565
Chief Officer(s):
Brian Ahearn, Vice-President

Canadian Fujianese Friendship Association
#101, 1258 West Broadway, Vancouver BC V6H 0A9
Tel: 604-232-1255; *Fax:* 604-909-6865
fujiancanadaorg@gmail.com
www.fujiancanada.org
Overview: A small national organization
Mission: To help members adapt to Canadian society; To provide members with information & assistance; To promote the exchange of culture & information between Fujian & Canada

The Canadian Fur Trade Development Institute
#1270, 1435, rue Saint-Alexandre, Montréal QC H3A 2G4
Tel: 514-844-1945; *Fax:* 514-844-8593
Toll-Free: 800-376-9996
Overview: A medium-sized national organization

Canadian Galloway Association (CGA) / Société canadienne Galloway
c/o CLRC, 2417 Holly Lane, Ottawa ON K1V 0M7
Tel: 613-731-7110; *Fax:* 613-731-0704
galloway@clrc.ca
www.galloway.ca
Overview: A medium-sized national organization founded in 1882
Mission: To promote & regulate the breeding of Galloways, Belted Galloways & White Galloways in Canada
Member of: Canadian Beef Breeds Council; Canadian Livestock Records Corporation
Finances: *Annual Operating Budget:* Less than $50,000; *Funding Sources:* Registrations; memberships; donations
Membership: 100-499; *Member Profile:* Breeders of purebred Galloway cattle; *Committees:* Promotion; Breed Advancement; Belted Galloway; White Galloway; A.I. & E.T.; Policy Manual
Chief Officer(s):
Brian Robertson, President, 403-392-2535
trirway.livestock@gmail.com
Ron Black, Secretary-Treasurer

Canadian Gaming Association (CGA)
#503, 131 Bloor St. West, Toronto ON M5S 1P7
Tel: 416-304-7800; *Fax:* 416-304-7805
info@canadiangaming.ca
www.canadiangaming.ca
Overview: A large national organization
Mission: To act as the voice of companies & organizations involved in the gaming & entertainment industry throughout Canada; To foster a greater understanding of the gaming industry
Finances: *Funding Sources:* Membership fees; Sponsorships; Canadian Gaming Summit delegate fees
Membership: *Fees:* Schedule available, based upon annual gross corporate revenues; *Member Profile:* Representatives of the Canadian gaming industry, such as manufacturers, suppliers & operators
Activities: Liaising with governmental agencies & industry stakeholders; Advocating for the Canadian gaming & entertainment industry; Initiating accurate industry data; Providing information about the gaming industry to elected officials, decision makers, the media, & general public; Offering networking opportunities for members
Chief Officer(s):
William P. Rutsey, President & CEO
Paul Burns, Vice-President, 416-304-6870
pburns@canadiangaming.ca
Meetings/Conferences:
• Canadian Gaming Summit 2018, June, 2018, Niagara Falls, ON
Scope: International
Description: A conference & trade show for representatives from gaming & regulatory agencies, First Nations gaming, provincial lotteries, casinos, race tracks, & charitable gaming organizations
Contact Information: www.canadiangamingsummit.com
Publications:
• Canadian Gaming Business Magazine
Type: Magazine; *Accepts Advertising*; *Price:* Free with membership in the Canadian Gaming Association
• Canadian Gaming Update
Type: Newsletter
Profile: Information about current issues & events which affect Canada's gaming industry

Canadian Gas Association (CGA) / Association canadienne du gaz
#1220, 350 Albert St., Ottawa ON K1R 1A4
Tel: 613-748-0057; *Fax:* 613-748-9078
info@cga.ca
www.cga.ca
www.linkedin.com/company/canadian-gas-association
twitter.com/GoSmartEnergy
Overview: A large national organization founded in 1907
Mission: To act as the voice of the natural gas distribution industry in Canada
Membership: *Member Profile:* Natural gas distribution companies, transmission companies, equipment manufacturers and other service providers
Activities: Advancing policy positions with federal & provincial decision makers; Developing educational information
Chief Officer(s):
Timothy M. Egan, President & CEO, 613-748-0057 Ext. 300
Meetings/Conferences:
• Canadian Gas Association 2018 Regulatory Course, March, 2018, Ottawa, ON
Scope: National
Contact Information: E-mail: help@canaevents.com
• Canadian Gas Association 2018 Operations, Engineering & Integrity Conference, April, 2018, Winnipeg, MB
Scope: National
Contact Information: E-mail: help@canaevents.com
• Canadian Gas Association Gas Measurement & Regulation School 2018, June, 2018, Edmonton, AB
Scope: National
Contact Information: E-mail: help@canaevents.com
• Canadian Gas Association 2019 Regulatory Course, March, 2019, Calgary, AB
Scope: National
Contact Information: E-mail: help@canaevents.com
• Canadian Gas Association 2019 Engineering Conference, March, 2019, Calgary, AB
Scope: National
Contact Information: E-mail: help@canaevents.com
• Canadian Gas Association 2019 Operations Conference, April, 2019, London, ON
Scope: National
Contact Information: E-mail: help@canaevents.com
• Canadian Gas Association Gas Measurement & Regulation School 2019, June, 2019, Quebec City, QC
Scope: National
Contact Information: E-mail: help@canaevents.com
Publications:
• Canadian Gas Association Market Updates
Profile: Topics include natural gas markets pre-heating season, post-heating season, supply, & demographics
• Canadian Gas Association Membership Directory
Type: Directory
Profile: Available for current CGA members
• Energy [a publication of the Canadian Gas Association]
Type: Magazine; *Accepts Advertising*; *Editor:* Timothy Egan
Profile: A publication dedicated to the role of energy in Canada, with a focus on natural gas; features profiles on key players in Canada & abroad,reviews on current issues & debates in the industry, & information on the politics of energy

Canadian Gas Processors Association *See* Gas Processing Association Canada

Canadian Gay Archives *See* Canadian Lesbian & Gay Archives

Canadian Gelbvieh Association (CGA)
5160 Skyline Way NE, Calgary AB T2E 6V1
Tel: 403-250-8640; *Fax:* 403-291-5624
gelbvieh@gelbvieh.ca
www.gelbvieh.ca
Overview: A medium-sized national organization founded in 1972
Mission: To promote Gelbvieh cattle in Canada & their registration.
Member of: Canadian Beef Breeds Council
Finances: *Funding Sources:* Membership fees; Purebred cattle registrations & transfers
Staff Member(s): 1
Membership: 121; *Fees:* $125; *Member Profile:* Cattlemen & women
Chief Officer(s):
Darrell Hickman, President
darrell.hickman@lakelandc.ab.ca
Wendy Belcher, Secretary Manager

Canadian Gemmological Association (CGA)
#105, 55 Queen St. East, Toronto ON M5C 1R6
Tel: 647-466-2436; *Fax:* 416-366-6519
www.canadiangemmological.com
Overview: A small national licensing organization founded in 1958
Mission: To set a standard for excellence in the practice of gemmology
Affiliation(s): Gemmological Association & Gem Testing Laboratory of Great Britain
Membership: *Fees:* $150 annually
Activities: Providing training in gemmology; Liaising with governments to set guidelines for sales, marketing, & appraising; Offering a forum for gemmologists to share knowledge; *Library:* CGA Library
Chief Officer(s):
Donna Hawrelko, FGA, FCGmA, President
JoAnne Larmond, Office Administrator
Publications:
• The Canadian Gemmologist
Type: Journal; *Frequency:* Quarterly; *Price:* Free with CGA membership

Canadian General Standards Board (CGSB) / Office des normes générales du Canada (ONGC)
Place Du Portage III, #6B1, 11, rue Laurier, Gatineau QC K1A 1G6
Tel: 819-956-0425; *Fax:* 819-956-1634
Toll-Free: 800-665-2472
ncr.cgsb-ongc@tpsgc-pwgsc.gc.ca
www.tpsgc-pwgsc.gc.ca/ongc-cgsb
Previous Name: Canadian Government Specifications Board
Overview: A medium-sized national organization founded in 1934
Mission: To develop standards, through accreditation with the Standards Council of Canada; To offer conformity assessment services, including product certification & registration of quality & environmental management systems, conforming to ISO standards
Member of: American Society for Quality; Business Forms Management Association; Canadian Safe Boating Council; Standards Engineering Society
Affiliation(s): Standards Council of Canada; National Standards Authority of Ireland; Standards & Industrial Research Institute of Malaysia; Business & Institutional Furniture Manufacturers' Association; American Society for Testing & Materials; Canadian Centre for Occupational Health & Safety; Information Handling Services; Canadian International Development Agency; Canadian Society for Nondestructive Testing, Inc.; Techstreet; Provincial Territorial Committee on Building Standards; Canadian Council of Fire Marshals & Fire Commissioners
Finances: *Annual Operating Budget:* $3 Million-$5 Million
Staff Member(s): 53; 5000 volunteer(s)
Membership: 1,000-4,999
Activities: *Library:* Sales Centre; Open to public
Chief Officer(s):

Begonia Lojk, Acting Director, 819-956-0383
begonia.lojk@tpsgc-pwgsc.gc.ca

Canadian Generic Pharmaceutical Association (CGPA) / L'Association canadienne du médicament générique (ACMG)
#409, 4120 Yonge St., Toronto ON M2P 2B8
Tel: 416-223-2333; Fax: 416-223-2425
info@canadiangenerics.ca
www.canadiangenerics.ca
www.facebook.com/CanadianGenerics
twitter.com/CdnGenerics
Previous Name: Canadian Drug Manufacturers Association
Overview: A large national organization founded in 1984
Mission: To promote an environment which supports & enhances the provision of affordable generic & innovative medications to Canadians & patients around the world through research, development & manufacturing of pharmaceuticals & fine chemicals in Canada
Member of: International Generic Pharmaceutical Association
Finances: *Annual Operating Budget:* $1.5 Million-$3 Million; *Funding Sources:* Membership fees
Staff Member(s): 6
Membership: 17 corporate; *Fees:* % of sales; *Member Profile:* Generic pharmaceutical company; *Committees:* Government Relations; Intellectual Property; Market Growth; Scientific Affairs
Activities: *Speaker Service:* Yes; *Library:* by appointment
Chief Officer(s):
Jim Keon, President
jim@canadiangenerics.ca

Canadian Genetic Diseases Network (CGDN) / Réseau canadien sur les maladies génétiques (RCMG)
#201, 2150 Western Pkwy., Vancouver BC V6T 1Z4
Tel: 604-221-7300
Overview: A medium-sized national organization founded in 1990
Mission: A nation-wide consortium of Canada's top investigators & core-technology facilities in human genetics, partnered with colleagues from industry to conduct leading-edge research within an "Institute without Walls"; to achieve international competitiveness in scientific research with social & economic benefits
Finances: *Funding Sources:* Federal government; industry; foundations
Publications:
• CGDN [Canadian Genetic Diseases Network] Annual Report
Type: Yearbook; *Frequency:* Annually

Canadian GeoExchange Coalition (CGC) / Coalition canadienne de l'énergie géothermique
#109, 7240 rue Waverly, Montréal QC H2R 2Y8
Tel: 514-807-7559; Fax: 514-807-8221
info@geoexchange.ca
www.geo-exchange.ca
Overview: A medium-sized national organization
Mission: To develop industry standards; To expand the market for geoexchange technology in Canada
Member of: Energy Dialogue Group
Membership: 126; *Fees:* Schedule available; *Member Profile:* Organizations involved with residential & commercial heating & air conditioning; *Committees:* Training; Technology
Activities: Providing information, training & certification; Increasing public awareness; Working with stakeholders to foster the growth of the Canadian geoexchange industry; Liaising with provincial ministries of energy in Canada
Chief Officer(s):
Ted Kantrowitz, President & CEO, 514-807-7559 Ext. 24
ted@geoexchange.ca
Manon Narbonne, Comptroller, 514-807-7559
accounting@geoexchange.ca
Meetings/Conferences:
• 13th International Energy Agency Heat Pump Conference, 2020
Scope: International
Description: Promotes heat pumping technologies through discussions, networking, and information exchange.

Canadian Geophysical Union (CGU) / Union géophysique canadienne (UGC)
c/o Dept. of Geology & Geophysics, University of Calgary, ES #278, 2500 University Dr. NW, Calgary AB T2N 1N4
Tel: 403-220-5596; Fax: 403-284-0074
cgu@ucalgary.ca
www.cgu-ugc.ca
www.facebook.com/442350399250129
twitter.com/CGU_UGC
Overview: A medium-sized national organization founded in 1973
Mission: To bring together & promote the geophysical sciences; To provide a focus for geophysicists at Canadian universities, government agencies, & industry in fields of study encompassing the composition & processes of the whole earth, including hydrology, space studies, & geology
Finances: *Annual Operating Budget:* Less than $50,000
Staff Member(s): 1; 12 volunteer(s)
Membership: 500; *Fees:* $30 full; $15 associate
Chief Officer(s):
Brian Branfireun, President, 519-661-211 Ext. 89221
bbranfir@uwo.ca
Richard Petrone, Treasurer
Maria Strack, Secretary
Meetings/Conferences:
• Canadian Geophysical Union 2018 Joint Annual Meeting, June, 2018, Niagara Falls, ON
Scope: National
Publications:
• Elements: The Newsletter of the Canadian Geophysical Union / Le Bulletin de l'union géophysique canadienne
Type: Newsletter; *Frequency:* Semiannually; *Accepts Advertising; Editor:* Ed S. Krebes; *Price:* Free to CGUmembers
Profile: CGU information, announcements, events, awards, officers, & section & committee news

Canadian Geoscience Council *See* Canadian Federation of Earth Sciences

Canadian Geotechnical Society (CGS)
8828 Pigott Rd., Richmond BC V7A 2C4
Tel: 604-277-7527; Fax: 604-277-7529
Toll-Free: 800-710-9867
www.cgs.ca
Overview: A small national organization
Membership: *Committees:* Computing; Education; Heritage; Landslides; Professional Practice; Transportation Geotechnique; Mining Geotechnique
Chief Officer(s):
Wayne Gibson, P.Eng., Administrator
cgs@cgs.ca
Victor Sowa, P.Eng., P.Geo., Secretary General
vsowacgs@dccnet.com
Meetings/Conferences:
• 71st Canadian Geotechnical Conference, September, 2018, Edmonton, AB
Scope: National
Description: Theme: "Transportation Geotechnique - Moving Forward"
Contact Information: www.geoedmonton2018.ca

Canadian Geriatrics Society (CGS) / Société canadienne de gériatrie (SCG)
#6, 20 Crown Steel Dr., Markham ON L3R 9X9
Tel: 905-415-3917; Fax: 905-415-0071
Toll-Free: 855-415-3917
www.canadiangeriatrics.ca
twitter.com/CanGeriSoc
Previous Name: Canadian Society of Geriatric Medicine
Overview: A small national organization founded in 1981
Mission: To promote excellence in the medical care of the elderly; To support high standards of research on geriatrics; To disseminate information about the clinical care of the elderly
Member of: Royal College of Physicians & Surgeons of Canada
Affiliation(s): Canadian Association of Gerontology
Membership: *Fees:* $170; *Member Profile:* Physicians with an interest in geriatrics; *Committees:* Foundation; CPD; Communications; Specialty; Membership; Awards; Education; Continuing Professional Development
Activities: Annual general meeting; advocacy
Chief Officer(s):
Karen Fruetel, President
Meetings/Conferences:
• Canadian Geriatrics Society 38th Annual Scientific Meeting, April, 2018, Montréal, QC
Scope: National

Canadian German Chamber of Industry & Commerce Inc. (CGCIC) / Deutsch-Kanadische Industrie- und Handelskammer
#1500, 480 University Ave., Toronto ON M5G 1V2
Tel: 416-598-3355; Fax: 416-598-1840
info@germanchamber.ca
kanada.ahk.de
www.facebook.com/AHKCanada
twitter.com/ahkcanada
Also Known As: German Trade Commission
Overview: A large international organization founded in 1968
Mission: To promote trade & investment between Germany & Canada; offices in Toronto & Montreal
Member of: Association of German Chambers of Industry & Commerce, Berlin
Finances: *Annual Operating Budget:* $1.5 Million-$3 Million; *Funding Sources:* German government grants; own resources
Staff Member(s): 22
Membership: 500+ Canadian & German firms; *Fees:* $80-$5,000
Activities: Offering German Marketing Services: market background information, identification of partners, publication packages, letters of introduction to German companies; Representing several major Trade Fairs (Cologne, Frankfurt, Hamburg, Stuttgart, Dusseldorf, Nuremberg); Providing technical inspection services; refund of the German Value Added Tax (VAT); *Library:* Open to public
Chief Officer(s):
Thomas Beck, President & CEO
Publications:
• Canadian German Headlines: CGCIC Newsletter [a publication of the Canadian German Chamber of Industry & Commerce Inc.]
Type: Newsletter; *Frequency:* Monthly; *Accepts Advertising*
Profile: CGCIC member news, articles concerning the Canadian & German business community, news about theCanadian & German economy, updated economic data, & Chamber & other events
• Kanada - groses Land, grose Potentiale [a publication of the Canadian German Chamber of Industry & Commerce Inc.]
Type: Brochure
Profile: First-hand experiences of Canadian subsidiaries of German companies
• Membership Directory of the Canadian German Chamber of Industry & Commerce
Type: Directory
• Opportunities for German companies in the Canadian mining sector
Type: Study
Profile: Focuses on the potential of the Canadian market for raw materials
   Montréal
   #200, 410, rue St-Nicolas, Montréal QC H2Y 2P5
   Tel: 514-844-3051; Fax: 514-844-1473
   info.montreal@germanchamber.ca
   Chief Officer(s):
   Anna-Lena Gruenagel, Contact
   Anna-lena.gruenagel@germanchamber.ca

Canadian Gerontological Nursing Association (CGNA) / Association canadienne des infirmières et infirmiers en gérontologie
www.cgna.net
Overview: A medium-sized national charitable organization founded in 1984
Mission: To promote gerontological nursing practice standards & educational programs in gerontological nursing; To promote the health of elderly persons; To promote networking opportunities; To support & disseminate gerontological nursing research; To represent members to government, education, professional & other appropriate bodies
Affiliation(s): Canadian Nurses Association
Finances: *Annual Operating Budget:* $50,000-$100,000
5 volunteer(s)
Membership: 500-999; *Fees:* Schedule available
Activities: *Library:*
Chief Officer(s):
Veronique Boscart, RN, MScN, MEd, President
vboscart@conestogac.on.ca
Michelle Heyer, Treasurer
Awards:
• Ann C. Beckingham Scholarship
• Memorial Scholarship
Meetings/Conferences:
• Canadian Gerontological Nursing Association 2019 20th Biennial Conference, May, 2019, Calgary, AB
Scope: National
Contact Information: cgna2019.ca
Publications:
• The Canadian Gerontological Nurse [a publication of the Canadian Gerontological Nursing Association]
Type: Newsletter; *Frequency:* Quarterly

Canadian Associations / Canadian Gift Association / Association canadienne de cadeaux

- Gerontological Nursing Competencies & Standards of Practice
Type: Document; *Price:* $13 members; $16 non-members
- Perspectives [a publication of the Canadian Gerontological Nursing Association]
Type: Journal; *Frequency:* Quarterly; *ISSN:* 0831-7445

Canadian Gift Association / Association canadienne de cadeaux
42 Voyager Ct. South, Toronto ON M9W 5M7
Tel: 416-679-0170; *Fax:* 416-679-0175
Toll-Free: 800-611-6100
info@cangift.org
www.cangift.org
www.linkedin.com/company/canadian-gift-association
www.facebook.com/CanadianGift
twitter.com/cangift
www.youtube.com/user/cgtassoc
Also Known As: CanGift
Overview: A medium-sized national organization founded in 1976
Mission: To create & manage sales opportunities for the gift industry
Finances: *Funding Sources:* Membership fees; programs
Membership: 1,400; *Fees:* $850 silver; $1000 gold; *Member Profile:* Manufacturers; distributors; wholesalers
Activities: *Speaker Service:* Yes
Chief Officer(s):
Ellen Turk, Chair
Awards:
- Supplier & Sales Rep. of the Year
- Best Giftware of the Year
- Retailer of the Year
Meetings/Conferences:
- Toronto Gift Fair Spring, January, 2018, The International Centre & Congress Centre, Toronto, ON
Scope: Local
Attendance: 24,600
Description: The Toronto Gift Fair is Canada's largest temporary trade gift fair.
- Alberta Gift Fair Spring, February, 2018, Edmonton Expo Centre, Edmonton, AB
Scope: Local
Attendance: 16,000
Description: The Alberta Gift Fair contains Western Canada's most comprehensive collection of products and services, catering to the specialized needs of retailers, sales representatives and manufacturers.
Publications:
- Canadian Gift & Tableware Association Research Publications
Profile: Information on opening a giftware store & developing a business plan, for members, retailers, & industry insiders
- Market Monitor [a publication of the Canadian Gift & Tableware Association]
Frequency: Semiannually
Profile: Analysis on timely & relevant topics such as internet retailing, market size, & channels of distribution related to the Canadian giftware market &industry, for CGTA members only
- MarketPulse [a publication of the Canadian Gift & Tableware Association]
Frequency: Semiannually
Profile: Survey results, based on consumer retail purchase activity, to provide stakeholders information on bestselling categories & trends
- Retail News [a publication of the Canadian Gift & Tableware Association]
Profile: Business publication for gift retailers, with information on operating more profitable businesses, distributed to gift stores throughout Canada
- SalesPulse [a publication of the Canadian Gift & Tableware Association]
Frequency: Quarterly
Profile: Based on surveys of giftware retailers, information includes sales, margins, & inventories, to provide an outlook on the upcoming quarter

Canadian Girls Rodeo Association
PO Box 6152, Stn. D, Calgary AB T2P 2C8
Tel: 403-563-5212
cgraentries@gmail.com
www.cgra.ca
Overview: A small national charitable organization founded in 1957
Mission: To promote girls' rodeo sports in Canada; to organize, control, supervise & manage girls' rodeo events for the benefit, safety & protection of the cowgirls
Finances: *Funding Sources:* Bingo; raffles; rodeos
Membership: *Fees:* $100 senior; $70 junior; $25 non-active
Chief Officer(s):
Deb Hambling, President
d.hambling@hotmail.com

Canadian Global Campaign for Education
321 Chapel St., Ottawa ON K1N 7Z2
Tel: 613-232-3569; *Fax:* 613-232-7435
info@cgce.ca
www.cgce.ca
www.facebook.com/126466670779367
twitter.com/join1goal
Overview: A medium-sized international organization founded in 2004
Member of: Global Campaign for Education
Finances: *Funding Sources:* Government
Membership: 18
Activities: *Awareness Events:* Global Action Week
Chief Officer(s):
Karen Mundy, Contact

Canadian Goat Society (CGS) / La Société canadienne des éléveurs de chèvres
2417 Holly Ln., Ottawa ON K1V 0M7
Tel: 613-731-9894; *Fax:* 613-731-0704
cangoatsoc@rogers.com
goat.softcorp.ca
Overview: A medium-sized national organization founded in 1917
Mission: To maintain the integrity of herdbooks, providing accurate evaluation programs for performance and type and promoting the responsible and humane treatment of goats.
Member of: Ontario Farm Animal Council
Membership: *Fees:* $56
Activities: *Library:* Not open to public
Chief Officer(s):
Arnold Steeves, President
arnsfarm@nb.sympatico.ca

Canadian Golf Foundation *See* Golf Canada Foundation

Canadian Golf Hall of Fame & Museum (CGHF) / Musée et Temple canadien de la renommée du golf
Glen Abbey Golf Club, 1333 Dorval Dr., Oakville ON L6M 4X7
Tel: 905-849-9700
cghf@golfcanada.ca
www.rcga.org
Also Known As: Canadian Golf Museum
Overview: A small national charitable organization founded in 1971 overseen by Golf Canada
Mission: Celebrates the outstanding individuals of Canadian golf: amateur and professional players, and others who have played a key role in the evolution of the game of golf in Canada. Open year round, with a shortened schedule during the winter months.
Member of: Ontario Museum Association; Canadian Museum Association; Ontario Archives Association; Canadian Association for Sport Heritage; International Sports Heritage Association
Finances: *Funding Sources:* Golf Canada
Activities: *Library:* Canadian Golf Hall of Fame & Museum Library; Open to public
Chief Officer(s):
Karen Hewson, Managing Director, Heritage Services, 905-849-9700 Ext. 213
khewson@golfcanada.ca
Meggan Gardner, Curator, 905-849-9700 Ext. 412
mgardner@golfcanada.ca

Canadian Golf Superintendents Association (CGSA) / Association canadienne des surintendants de golf
#201, 5399 Eglinton Ave. West, Toronto ON M9C 5K6
Tel: 416-626-8873
Toll-Free: 800-387-1056
cgsa@golfsupers.com
www.golfsupers.com
www.facebook.com/151227228150
twitter.com/GolfSupers
Overview: A medium-sized national organization founded in 1966
Mission: To promote excellence in golf course management & environmental responsibility; To uphold the Canadian Golf Superintendents Association Principles Of Professional Practice & Code of Ethics & Conduct
Member of: Canadian Turfgrass Research Foundation
Finances: *Funding Sources:* Sponsorships
Membership: 1,500; *Fees:* Schedule available; *Member Profile:* Golf course superintendents & turfgrass specialists in Canada; *Committees:* Environment; Communications, Marketing, & Public Relations; Professional Development & Research; Conference & Events; Member Services; Equipment Technicians Advisory
Activities: Providing continuing professional development opportunities for members; Sponsoring research projects; Establishing the Master Superintendent Designation Program; Offering networking opportunities; *Awareness Events:* Canadian International Turfgrass Conference and Trade Show, annual *Library:* CGSA Office Library
Chief Officer(s):
Kathryn Wood, Director, Professional Development & Meetings, 905-602-8873 Ext. 222
kwood@golfsupers.com
Lori Micucci, Manager, Member Services, 905-602-8873 Ext. 226
lmicucci@golfsupers.com
Awards:
- Toro Future Superintendent of the Year Award
Deadline: June
- Bayer Superintendent of the Year Award
Deadline: June
- Environmental Award
Deadline: November
- Equipment Technician of the Year Award
Deadline: November
- Gordon Witteveen Award
Deadline: November
- John B. Steel Award
Deadline: November
- Student Scholarships
Eligibility: CGSA member students currently enrolled in at least the second year of a recognized turfgrass program of two years or longer; mechanic course students are also eligible *Deadline:* November; *Amount:* $2,500
Meetings/Conferences:
- Canadian Golf Course Management Conference & Trade Show 2018, 2018
Scope: International
Description: An international conference & trade show featuring over 100 exhibitors
Contact Information: Director, Professional Development & Meetings: Kathryn Wood, Phone: 519-589-9282, Email: kwood@golfsupers.com
Publications:
- CGSA [Canadian Golf Superintendents Association] Membership Directory
Type: Directory; *Frequency:* Annually; *Price:* Free with Canadian Golf Superintendents Association membership
Profile: Listings of CGSA members, members' clubs, & industry affiliates, for members only
- GreenMaster [a publication of the Canadian Golf Superintendents Association]
Type: Magazine; *Frequency:* 6 pa; *Price:* $36 (Canada); $46 (US & International)
Profile: Informative articles of interest to golf course superintendents
- Greenmatter E-News [a publication of the Canadian Golf Superintendents Association]
Type: Newsletter; *Frequency:* Monthly
Profile: Current issues, regional news, & product information

Canadian Good Roads Association; Roads & Transportation Association of Canada *See* Transportation Association of Canada

Canadian Government Specifications Board *See* Canadian General Standards Board

Canadian Grand Masters Fiddling Association (CGMFA)
101 Centrepointe Dr., Ottawa ON K2G 5K7
Tel: 613-727-6641
Other Communication: Membership E-mail: members@canadiangrandmasters.ca
cgmfa@canadiangrandmasters.ca
www.canadiangrandmasters.ca
www.facebook.com/CanadianGrandMasters
twitter.com/CGMFA
Previous Name: Canadian Grand Masters Fiddling Championship
Overview: A small national organization founded in 1986
Mission: To preserve the rich heritage of Canadian fiddling
Activities: *Awareness Events:* Annual Canadian Grand Masters Competition; Annual Canadian Grand Master Fiddle Camp
Chief Officer(s):
Ron Bourque, President

Randy Foster, Vice-President
Margaret Côté, Secretary
Todd Thompson, Treasurer & Chair, Finance, Corporations, & By-Laws
Publications:
• Canadian Fiddler
Type: Newsletter; *Frequency:* Quarterly; *Accepts Advertising;*
Price: Free for members
Profile: Articles about fiddlers, information about traditional fiddling, fiddling & stepdancing competitions, contest results, & upcoming events across Canada

Canadian Grand Masters Fiddling Championship *See* Canadian Grand Masters Fiddling Association

Canadian Grandparents' Rights Association (CGRA)
#207, 14980 - 104 Ave., Surrey BC V3R 1M9
Tel: 604-585-8242; *Fax:* 604-585-8241
Toll-Free: 866-585-8242
www.CanadianGrandparentsRightsAssociation.com
Overview: A medium-sized national organization founded in 1986
Mission: Promotes, supports, and assists Grandparents and their families in maintaining or re-establishing family ties and family stability where the family has been disrupted; especially those ties between grandparents and grandchildren.
Member of: Grand Parents Raising Grandchildren
Finances: *Funding Sources:* Donations; Membership fees; BC Gaming
Activities: *Speaker Service:* Yes; *Library:* by appointment
  Yukon (GRAY)
  Whitehorse YT
  Tel: 867-821-3821
  yukon-seniors-and-elders.org/gray/gray_home.htm
  Mission: To assist grandparents with questions about access to or custody of their grandchildren
Chief Officer(s):
Eleanor Millard, Contact

Canadian Group Psychotherapy Association (CGPA)
c/o First Stage Enterprises, #109, 1 Corcorde Gate, Toronto ON M3C 3N6
Tel: 416-426-7229; *Fax:* 416-726-7280
Toll-Free: 866-433-9695
admin@cgpa.ca
www.cgpa.ca
www.linkedin.com/company/5054194
twitter.com/National_CGPA
Overview: A small national organization founded in 1990
Mission: To promote excellence in standards of training, practice, & research; To encourage & provide for the education of mental health professionals in group psychotherapy
Member of: International Association for Group Psychotherapy & Group Processes (IAGP)
Finances: *Funding Sources:* Sponsorships
Membership: *Fees:* $150 full members; $75 student/retiree; *Member Profile:* Canadian group psychotherapists
Activities: Developing national standards for training & practice; Encouraging scientific research; Sponsoring workshops; Disseminating information about educational programs
Chief Officer(s):
Joan-Dianne Smith, President
Colleen Wilkie, Secretary
Jessica Kerr, Contact
Awards:
• Martin Fisher Training Award
• The Jackman Training Award
• CGPF Endowments Conference Scholarships
Meetings/Conferences:
• 2018 Canadian Group Psychotherapy Association Conference, 2018
Scope: National
Publications:
• The Chronicle: The Newsletter of the Canadian Group Psychotherapy Association
Type: Newsletter; *Editor:* Colleen Wilkie, PhD
Profile: Articles, committee reports, section news, & Canadian Group Psychotherapy Foundation news

Canadian Guernsey Association
5653 Hwy. 6 North, RR#5, Guelph ON N1H 6J2
Tel: 519-836-2141; *Fax:* 519-763-6582
info@guernseycanada.ca
www.guernseycanada.ca
Overview: A medium-sized national organization founded in 1905
Mission: To provide services to breeders of Guernsey dairy cattle including records, awards, promotion, sales & shows.
Affiliation(s): Canadian Livestock Records Corporation; Joint Classification Board; Agriculture & Agri-Food Canada; Canadian Dairy Network
Finances: *Funding Sources:* Membership dues; registration fees
Membership: *Fees:* $85; *Member Profile:* Breeders & owners of Guernsey cattle
Activities: Shows; sales
Chief Officer(s):
Jesse Weir, Administrator

Canadian Guide Dogs for the Blind (CGDB)
National Office & Training Centre, PO Box 280, 4120 Rideau Valley Dr. North, Manotick ON K4M 1A3
Tel: 613-692-7777; *Fax:* 613-692-0650
info@guidedogs.ca
www.guidedogs.ca
Overview: A medium-sized national charitable organization founded in 1984
Mission: To assist visually-impaired Canadians with their mobility by providing & training them in the use of professionally trained guide dogs
Member of: International Guide Dog Federation; Assistance Dogs International, Inc.
Finances: *Funding Sources:* Donations; Fundraising; Gift Shop
Chief Officer(s):
Jane Thornton, Co-Founder & Chief Operating Officer
Publications:
• Side by Side [a publication of the Canadian Guide Dogs for the Blind]
Type: Newsletter; *Frequency:* s-a.

Canadian Guild of Crafts / Guilde canadienne des métiers d'art
1460B, rue Sherbrooke ouest, Montréal QC H3G 1K4
Tel: 514-849-6091; *Fax:* 514-849-7351
Toll-Free: 866-477-6091
info@canadianguild.com
www.canadianguildofcrafts.com
www.facebook.com/187315447973358
Overview: A medium-sized national charitable organization founded in 1906
Mission: To preserve, encourage & promote Canadian crafts; to organize & sponsor exhibitions of the work of recognized & promising artists in the fields of arts & crafts; to educate interested groups about Canadian & native crafts through tours & lectures
Finances: *Annual Operating Budget:* $250,000-$500,000; *Funding Sources:* Membership fees; sales; donations
Staff Member(s): 7
Membership: 1-99; *Fees:* $50 individual; $50 affiliated group
Activities: Temporary exhibitions; gallery; permanent collection; *Internships:* Yes; *Speaker Service:* Yes; *Library:* Archives; Open to public
Chief Officer(s):
Diane Labelle, Director

Canadian Guild of Crafts (Ontario); Ontario Craft Foundation *See* Ontario Crafts Council

Canadian Gymnastics Federation *See* Gymnastics Canada Gymnastique

Canadian Hackney Society
PO Box 142, 2698 - 8 Line Rd., Metcalfe ON K0A 2P0
Tel: 613-821-2676
www.hackney.ca
Overview: A small national organization founded in 1892
Member of: Canadian Livestock Records Corporation
Affiliation(s): Canadian Equestrian Federation; Ontario Hackney Association; Atlantic Hackney Association; Western Canada Hackney Association; American Hackney Horse Association
Finances: *Funding Sources:* Membership fees; registration fees; fundraising
Membership: *Fees:* $15 junior; $25 regular; $500 lifetime
Activities: *Speaker Service:* Yes; *Rents Mailing List:* Yes; *Library:* by appointment
Chief Officer(s):
Christy Stewart, Executive Director
castewart@bell.net

Canadian Hadassah WIZO (CHW)
#208, 90 Eglinton Ave. East, Toronto ON M4P 2Z3
Tel: 416-477-5964; *Fax:* 416-977-5965
info@chw.ca
www.chw.ca
www.linkedin.com/company/chw
www.facebook.com/CanadianHadassahWIZO
twitter.com/CHWdotCA
www.youtube.com/user/CHWOrganization
Also Known As: Hadassah-WIZO Organization of Canada
Overview: A large national charitable organization founded in 1917
Mission: To extend material & moral support of Jewish women of Canada to needy individuals in Hadassah-WIZO welfare institutions in Israel; To encourage Jewish & Hebrew culture in Canada
Affiliation(s): Canadian Jewish Congress; Canadian Zionist Federation; National Council of Women of Canada; United Nations Association; Women's International Zionist Organization; Hadassah International
Finances: *Funding Sources:* Fundraising
Staff Member(s): 10
Membership: 10,000+; *Fees:* $36; *Committees:* Fundraising; Advocacy; Programming
Activities: Fundraising; Operating youth clubs & summer camps; *Awareness Events:* National Officers Meeting, Aug.; National Convention, Nov.
Chief Officer(s):
Claudia Goldman, National President
Alina Ianson, Executive Director
Publications:
• Canadian Hadassah WIZO Annual Donor Report
Type: Report; *Frequency:* Annually
• Orah Magazine [a publication of Canadian Hadassah WIZO]
Type: Magazine; *Editor:* Alina Ianson; *ISSN:* 1209-7039
Profile: Features CHW initiatives in Israel, news, & donor profiles
  Calgary
  1607 - 90th Ave. SW, Calgary AB T2V 4V7
  Tel: 403-253-4612; *Fax:* 403-640-1100
  info@calgary.chw.ca
  www.chw.ca/calgary
  Chief Officer(s):
  Aviva Cheuk, President
  Edmonton
  #200, 10220 - 156th St., Edmonton AB T5P 2R1
  Tel: 780-444-6985
  info@edmonton.chw.ca
  www.chw.ca/edmonton
  Chief Officer(s):
  Stephanie Hendin, Contact
  London
  London ON
  Tel: 519-439-3383
  info@london.chw.ca
  www.chw.ca/london
  Chief Officer(s):
  Michelle Bottner, President
  Montréal
  #3405, 6900, boul Decarie, Montréal QC H3X 2T8
  Tel: 514-933-8461; *Fax:* 514-933-6483
  info@montreal.chw.ca
  www.chw.ca/montreal
  www.facebook.com/CHWMontreal
  Chief Officer(s):
  Sheila Nemtin Levine, President
  Ottawa
  1301 Prince of Wales Drive, Ottawa ON K2C 1N2
  Tel: 613-699-0802; *Fax:* 613-274-7015
  info@ottawa.chw.ca
  www.chw.ca/ottawa
  Chief Officer(s):
  Sophie Frenkel, Co-President
  Linda Senzilet, Co-President
  Toronto
  #638A, 209 Sheppard Ave. West, Toronto ON M3H 2S1
  Tel: 416-630-8373; *Fax:* 416-630-2370
  info@toronto.chw/ca
  www.chw.ca/toronto
  Chief Officer(s):
  Fran Luborsky, President
  Vancouver
  #304B, 950 West 41st Ave., Vancouver BC V5Z 2N7
  Tel: 604-257-5160; *Fax:* 604-257-5164
  office@vancouver.chw.ca
  www.chw.ca/vancouver
  Chief Officer(s):
  Stephanie Rusen, President

Canadian Associations / Canadian Haflinger Association (CHA)

Victoria
Victoria BC
Tel: 250-479-4040
grillamine@gmail.com
www.chw.ca/victoria
Chief Officer(s):
Marilyn Weisbart, President

Canadian Haflinger Association (CHA)
RR#1, Burgessville ON N0J 1C0
Tel: 519-424-2521
mattway@execulink.com
www.haflinger.ca
Overview: A small national organization founded in 1981
Mission: To promote Haflinger horses in Canada
Finances: *Annual Operating Budget:* Less than $50,000
Staff Member(s): 5
Membership: 150; *Fees:* $35
Chief Officer(s):
Jim Hird, President
jim_hird@yahoo.com
Mike Ready, Vice-President
never_ready@hotmail.com
Mary Sexsmith, Sec.-Treas.
Publications:
• Chatter [a publication of the Canadian Haflinger Association]
Type: Newsletter; *Frequency:* Quarterly
Profile: Upcoming shows & events, articles & stories

Canadian Handball Association (CHA) / Fédération de balle au mur du Canada
Toronto ON
www.canadianhandball.com
Overview: A medium-sized national organization
Mission: To promote handball in Canada
Membership: 3,000
Chief Officer(s):
Chris Simmons, President

Canadian Hard of Hearing Association (CHHA) / Association des malentendants canadiens (AMEC)
#205, 2415 Holly Lane, Ottawa ON K1V 7P2
Tel: 613-526-1584; *Fax:* 613-526-4718
Toll-Free: 800-263-8068; *TTY:* 613-526-2692
chhanational@chha.ca
www.chha.ca
www.facebook.com/CHHANational
twitter.com/CHHA_AMEC
Overview: A medium-sized national charitable organization founded in 1982
Mission: To act as the voice of all hard of hearing Canadians; To promote the integration of hard of hearing people into society
Finances: *Annual Operating Budget:* $250,000-$500,000; *Funding Sources:* Membership fees; Conference registration fees; Advertising; Sponsorships; Donations
Staff Member(s): 3; 300 volunteer(s)
Membership: 2,000; *Fees:* $30 regular members; $50 family units; $30 Student; $300 Coporation; $120 not-for-profit organization; $350 lifetime; *Member Profile:* Any person or organization that supports the objectives of the Canadian Hard of Hearing Association, including hard of hearing individuals & family members
Activities: Raising public awareness about issues important to hard of hearing persons
Chief Officer(s):
Lorin MacDonald, President
Glenn Martin, Executive Director
gmartin@chha.ca
Awards:
• Bette Moulton Award
• Marilyn Dahl Award of Merit
• Charles Laszlo Award of Technical Excellence
• Winnifred C. Cory Award of Merit
• Lynn Wheadon Education Award
• Young Adult Award of Excellence
Meetings/Conferences:
• Canadian Hard of Hearing Association 2018 National Conference, 2018
Scope: National
Publications:
• Listen / Écoute [a publication of the Canadian Hard of Hearing Association]
Type: Magazine; *Frequency:* 3 pa; *Accepts Advertising; Price:* $5
Profile: Hearing health issues, technology, & the concerns of hard of hearing individuals

Alberta - Calgary Branch
c/o 63 Cornell Rd. NW, Calgary AB T2L 0L4
Tel: 403-284-6224; *Fax:* 403-824-6224
info@chha-calgary.ca
www.chha-calgary.ca
Chief Officer(s):
Terry Webb, President

Alberta - Edmonton Branch
#10, 9912 - 106 St., Edmonton AB T5K 1C5
Tel: 780-428-6622; *Fax:* 780-420-6661; *TTY:* 780-628-6622
chha-ed@shaw.ca
www.chha-ed.com
Chief Officer(s):
Marilyn Kingdon, President

Alberta - Lethbridge Branch
1010 - 18A St. North, Lethbridge AB T1H 3J3
Tel: 403-328-2929
Chief Officer(s):
Doreen Gyorkos, President
dgyorkos@telusplanet.net

British Columbia - BC Main Chapter
#101, 9300 Nowell St., Chilliwack BC V2P 4V7
Tel: 604-795-9238; *Fax:* 604-795-9628
Toll-Free: 866-888-2442
info@chha-bc.org
www.chha-bc.org
www.facebook.com/127952830548757
Chief Officer(s):
Marilyn Dahl, President

British Columbia - BC Parents' Branch
c/o 10150 Gillanders Rd., Chilliwack BC V2P 6H4
Tel: 604-819-5312; *Fax:* 604-794-3960
info@chhaparents.bc.ca
www.chhaparents.bc.ca
Chief Officer(s):
Willetta Les, Administrator

British Columbia - Chilliwack Branch
c/o BC Chapter, #101, 9300 Nowell St., Chilliwack BC V2P4V71
Tel: 604-795-9238
info@chha-bc.org
Chief Officer(s):
Scott Secord, President

British Columbia - Comox Valley
PO Box 433, Lazo BC V0R 2K0
Tel: 250-339-5770
Chief Officer(s):
Sarah Trotter, President
fstrotter@shaw.ca

British Columbia - HEAR Branch
#60, 5221 Oakmount Cres., Burnaby BC V5H 4R4
Tel: 604-438-2500
Chief Officer(s):
Betty MacGillivray, Acting President
bettymac@telus.net

British Columbia - North Shore Branch (CHHA-NSB)
600 West Queens Rd., North Vancouver BC V7N 2L3
Tel: 604-926-5222; *Fax:* 604-925-2286
chha_nsb@telus.net
www.chha-nsb.com
Chief Officer(s):
Mike Hocevar, President
mikehocevar@gmail.com

British Columbia - Vancouver Branch
c/o 2125 West 7th Ave., Vancouver BC V6K 1X9
Tel: 778-358-9955
chhavancouver@gmail.com
www.chhavancouver.ca
Chief Officer(s):
Ruth Warick, President

Manitoba Chapter
c/o SMD Self-Help Clearinghouse, 825 Sherbrook St., Winnipeg MB R3A 1M5
Tel: 204-975-3037; *Fax:* 204-975-3027
mbchha@mts.net
www.chha-mb.ca
Chief Officer(s):
Gladys Nielsen, Contact

New Brunswick - Moncton Branch
809 Bernard St., Dieppe NB E1A 5Y2
Tel: 506-855-3799
Chief Officer(s):
Rhéal Léger, President
legerrh@rogers.com

New Brunswick Chapter
74 Alvic Pl., Saint John NB E2M 5G1
Tel: 506-657-7643; *Fax:* 506-657-7643
winslow@nbnet.nb.ca
Chief Officer(s):
Ian Hamilton, President

Newfoundland - Exploits Valley Branch
576 Main St., Bishops Falls NL A0H 1C0
chha-evb@nl.rogers.com
Chief Officer(s):
Lillian Menchenton, President

Newfoundland - Gander Branch
77 Fraser Rd., Gander NL A1V 1L1
Tel: 709-256-7935
Chief Officer(s):
Cal Carter, President
c-carter@nl.rogers.com

Newfoundland - Happy Valley Goose Bay Branch
Happy Valley-Goose Bay NL A0P 1C0
Chief Officer(s):
Cyril Peach, President
cgpeach@hotmail.com

Newfoundland - Labrador West Branch
813 Carol Dr., Labrador City NL A2V 1S9
Tel: 709-944-5253
Chief Officer(s):
Jerome Gover, President
rgover@nf.sympatico.ca

Newfoundland - Western NL Branch
4 Ingrid Ave., Corner Brook NL A2H 6P2
Tel: 709-639-9547
Chief Officer(s):
Virginia Brake, President
vbrake@nf.sympatico.ca

Newfoundland & Labrador Chapter
1081 Topsail Rd., Mount Pearl NL A1N 5G1
Tel: 709-753-3224; *Fax:* 709-753-5640
info@chha-nl.ca
www.chha-nl.nl.ca
Chief Officer(s):
Robert Young, President

Northwest Territories - Yellowknife Branch
Aven Court, #5A, 5710 - 50th Ave., Yellowknife NT X1A 1E9
Tel: 867-873-4735
Chief Officer(s):
Esther Braden, President
ebraden@theedge.ca

Ontario - Hamilton Branch
c/o #122, 762 Upper James St., Hamilton ON L9C 3A2
Tel: 905-575-4964
info@chha-hamilton.ca
www.chha-hamilton.ca
Chief Officer(s):
Rob Diehl, President

Ontario - Kingston Hard of Hearing Club
#517, 829 Norwest Rd., Kingston ON K7P 2N3
Tel: 613-378-2457
Chief Officer(s):
Margaret Shenton, President
mshenton@sympatico.ca

Ontario - National Capital Region
c/o #205, 2415 Holly Lane, Ottawa ON K1V 7P2
Tel: 613-526-1584; *Fax:* 613-526-4718
alena@chhancr.com
chhancr.com
Chief Officer(s):
Louise Normand, President
alena@chhancr.com

Ontario - Sudbury Branch
#101, 435 Notre Dame Ave., Sudbury ON P3C 5K6
Tel: 705-523-5695; *Fax:* 705-523-8621
Toll-Free: 866-300-2442; *TTY:* 705-523-5695
chha@vianet.ca
www.chhasudbury.com
Chief Officer(s):
Lorraine O'Brien, President

Ontario - York Branch
147 Primeau Dr., Aurora ON L4G 6Z6
www.chha-york.com
Chief Officer(s):
Dan McDonnell, President
dmac773@gmail.com

Prince Edward Island Chapter
RR#1 Augustine Cove, Borden-Carleton PE C0B 1X0
Tel: 902-855-2382; *Fax:* 902-885-3282
Chief Officer(s):
Annie Lee MacDonald, President
annmerdon@pei.sympatico.ca

Québec - Outaouais Branch
25, rue des Rapides, Gatineau QC J8T 5K2
Chief Officer(s):
Carole Willans, Interim President
cwillans@chha.ca

Québec Chapter
25, rue des Rapides, Gatineau QC J8T 5K2
Chief Officer(s):
Carole Willans, President
cwillans@chha.ca

Saskatchewan - Regina Branch
c/o 2341 Broad St., Regina SK S4P 1Y9
Tel: 306-457-3259; *Fax:* 306-757-3252
Toll-Free: 800-565-3323
Chief Officer(s):
Gloria Knous, President
glochha@sasktel.net

Canadian Hardware & Housewares Manufacturers' Association (CHHMA) / Association canadienne des fabricants de produits de quincaillerie et d'articles ménagers
#101, 1335 Morningside Ave., Toronto ON M1B 5M4
Tel: 416-282-0022
www.chhma.ca
twitter.com/theCHHMA
Overview: A large national organization founded in 1966
Mission: To assist members to sell more & do it more profitably
Finances: *Funding Sources:* Membership dues
Membership: 200+ companies; *Fees:* Schedule available; *Member Profile:* Manufacture products; Agency representing manufacturer or service to manufacturer; *Committees:* Executive; Business Events & Spring Conference; Quebec
Chief Officer(s):
Sam Moncada, President, 416-282-0022 Ext. 125
smoncada@chhma.ca
Maureen Hizaka, Director, Operations, 416-282-0022 Ext. 123
mhizaka@chhma.ca
Michael Jorgenson, Manager, Marketing & Communications, 416-282-0022 Ext. 134
mjorgenson@chhma.ca
Pam Winter, Coordinator, Events, 416-282-0022 Ext. 121
pwinter@chhma.ca
Awards:
• The CHHMA Scholarship Awards
Eligibility: Children of member company employees *Deadline:* July 15; *Amount:* $1,000 per year (first two years of post-secondary studies)
Meetings/Conferences:
• CHHMA [Canadian Hardware & Housewares Manufacturers Association] Spring Conference & AGM 2018, April, 2018, Mississauga Convention Centre, Mississauga, ON
Scope: National

Canadian Hardwood Plywood & Veneer Association (CHPVA) / Association canadienne du Contreplaqué et de Placages de bois dur (ACCPBD)
89, av Godfrey, Saint-Sauveur QC J0R 1R5
Tel: 450-227-4048; *Fax:* 450-227-7827
www.chpva.com
Overview: A medium-sized national organization
Mission: To protect the interests & conserve the rights of those involved in the manufacture & distribution of hardwood veneer & plywood & their suppliers in Canada.
Membership: 54; *Fees:* Schedule available; *Member Profile:* Manufacturers of hardwood plywood & vaneer; Furniture & cabinetry manufacturers; Wholesalers; Industry suppliers; *Committees:* Technical; Marketing
Chief Officer(s):
Gaëtan Lauzon, Executive Vice President
glauzon@chpva.ca
Carole Aussant, Coordinator
caussant@chpva.ca

Canadian Harm Reduction Network
#1904, 666 Spadina Ave., Toronto ON M5S 2H8
Tel: 416-928-0279; *Fax:* 416-966-9512
Toll-Free: 800-728-1293
noharm@canadianharmreduction.com
www.canadianharmreduction.com
www.facebook.com/noharmcanada
twitter.com/noharmcanada
youtube.com/noharmcanada
Overview: A small national organization
Mission: To reduce the social, health & economic harms associated with drugs & drug policies
Affiliation(s): Drug Policy Alliance

Canadian Harvard Aircraft Association (CHAA)
PO Box 175, 244411 Airport Rd., Tillsonburg ON N4G 4H5
Tel: 519-842-9922
info@harvards.com
www.harvards.com
www.facebook.com/canadianharvards
twitter.com/CdnHarvards
Overview: A small local organization founded in 1985
Mission: To restore, preserve, maintain, display & demostrate the Harvard aircraft & others associated with the RCAF.
Membership: *Fees:* $50 general; $75 family; $500 lifetime; $15 18 & under; $1000 sponsor; *Committees:* Fundraising; Membership; Volunteer
Activities: Harvard & Tiger Moth ground schools; formation workshops; aircraft maintenance training
Chief Officer(s):
Pat Hanna, President & Chair
p_hanna@harvards.com
Terry Scott, Director, Public Relations
t_scott@harvards.com
Publications:
• The Roar
Type: Newsletter; *Frequency:* Quarterly

Canadian Hatching Egg Producers (CHEP) / Producteurs d'oufs d'incubation du Canada (POIC)
21 Florence St., Ottawa ON K20 0W6
Tel: 613-232-3023; *Fax:* 613-232-5241
info@chep-poic.ca
www.chep-poic.ca
Previous Name: Canadian Broiler Hatching Egg Marketing Agency
Overview: A medium-sized national organization founded in 1986
Mission: To ensure that our members produce enough hatching eggs to meet the needs of the broiler industry
Member of: Canadian Federation of Agriculture
Finances: *Funding Sources:* Farmer levies
Membership: 230 farmers; *Member Profile:* Farmers in British Columbia, Alberta, Saskatchewan, Manitoba, Ontario & Québec
Chief Officer(s):
Jack Greydanus, Chair
Giuseppe Caminiti, General Manager

Canadian Hays Converter Association
#201, 1600 - 15th Ave. SW, Calgary AB T3C 0Y2
Tel: 403-245-6923; *Fax:* 403-244-3128
haysconverter@shaw.ca
Overview: A small national organization
Mission: To develop & regulate the breeding of Hays Converter cattle; To establish & implement breeding & performance standards for Hays Converter cattle; To register Hays Converter cattle in cooperation with the Canadian Livestock Records Corporation; To maintain a record of the pedigrees of Hays Converter cattle
Member of: Canadian Beef Breeds Council
Affiliation(s): Canadian Livestock Records Corporation
Membership: *Fees:* $50 active & associate members; $20 junior members
Activities: Promoting the breeding & development of Hays Converter cattle in Canada; Publishing data & information on the industry; Supervising breeders of Hays Converter cattle
Chief Officer(s):
Terri Worms, Secretary-Manager
Lisa Hutt, Registrar, Canadian Livestock Records Corporation, 613-731-7110 Ext. 312
lisa.hutt@clrc.ca

Canadian Health Coalition (CHC) / Coalition canadienne de la santé
#212, 251 Bank St., Ottawa ON K2P 1X3
Tel: 613-688-4973
hello@healthcoalition.ca
www.healthcoalition.ca
www.facebook.com/CanadianHealthCoalition
twitter.com/healthcoalition
www.youtube.com/user/HealthCoalition
Overview: A large national organization founded in 1979
Mission: To create good health; To preserve & strengthen the Canada Health Act, the foundation of Medicare; To make the health care system democratic, accountable & representative; To provide a continuum of care from large institutions to the home; To protect our investment in the skills & abilities of our health care workers; To ensure fair wages for all health care providers; To eliminate profit-making from illness; To reduce over-prescribing & make drugs affordable; To stop fee-for-service payments; To expand methods of health care & the role of non-physician health providers
Finances: *Funding Sources:* Donations
Activities: *Speaker Service:* Yes
Chief Officer(s):
Adrienne Silnicki, National Director, Policy & Advocacy
asilnicki@healthcoalition.ca
Amélie Baillargeon, National Director, Operations & Projects
amelie@healthcoalition.ca

Canadian Health Economics Research Association *See* Canadian Association for Health Services & Policy Research

Canadian Health Food Association (CHFA) / Association canadienne des aliments de santé
#302, 235 Yorkland Blvd., Toronto ON M2J 4Y8
Tel: 416-497-6939; *Fax:* 416-497-3214
Toll-Free: 800-661-4510
info@chfa.ca
www.chfa.ca
www.facebook.com/CanadianHealthFoodAssociation
twitter.com/cdnhealthfood
instagram.com/canadianhealthfoodassociation
Previous Name: Health Food Dealers Association
Overview: A medium-sized national organization founded in 1964
Mission: To act as the voice of the natural products industry; To promote natural & organic products as an integral part of health & well-being; To ensure the growth of the natural & organic industry
Membership: 1,000+; *Member Profile:* Suppliers of natural products &/or organics; Retailers of natural health products &/or health foods; Associate members, such as farmers, organic certification providers, health practitioners, gyms, industry consultants, & media
Activities: Supporting & empowering members; Seeking scientific advice from the Expert Scientific Advisory Panel; Engaging in advocacy & outreach activities; Offering education; Providing networking opportunities; *Awareness Events:* National Health Food Month, November
Chief Officer(s):
Don Smith, Chair
Helen Long, President
Awards:
• Hall of Fame Award
Meetings/Conferences:
• Canadian Health Food Association (CHFA) West 2018, February, 2018, Vancouver Convention Centre, West Building, Vancouver, BC
Scope: Provincial
Description: A conference & trade show attended by owners, managers, employees, & nutrition & health care practitioners from pharmacies, health stores, grocery stores, specialty stores, & online retailers
Contact Information: Phone: 416-497-6939, Toll-Free Phone: 1-800-661-4510, E-mail: info@chfa.ca
• Canadian Health Food Association (CHFA) East 2018, September, 2018, Metro Toronto Convention Centre, South Building, Toronto, ON
Scope: Provincial
Attendance: 2,900
Description: A trade event, featuring exhibits from leading suppliers, manufacturers, distributors, & brokers of natural health products & organics
Contact Information: Phone: 416-497-6939, Toll-Free Phone: 1-800-661-4510, E-mail: info@chfa.ca
• Canadian Health Food Association (CHFA) Québec 2019, May, 2019, Palais des congrès de Montréal, Montréal, QC
Scope: Provincial
Description: A conference & trade show designed for owners & decision makers from both small & large establishments, such as natural & health food retail stores, specialty stores, food chains, & pharmacies
Contact Information: Phone: 416-497-6939, Toll-Free Phone: 1-800-661-4510, E-mail: info@chfa.ca
Publications:
• Canadian Health Food Association Annual Report

Canadian Associations / Canadian Health Information Management Association (CHIMA)

Type: Yearbook; *Frequency:* Annually
Profile: Activities of the association during the past year
• Canadian Health Food Association Asssociate Member Directory
Type: Directory; *Frequency:* Monthly
Profile: A membership directory exclusively for members
• Canadian Health Food Association e-News
Type: Newsletter; *Frequency:* Weekly; *Price:* Free with membership in the Canadian Health Food Association
Profile: Latest developments in the natural health & organic products industry
• Canadian Health Food Association Member Bulletins
Type: Newsletter; *Frequency:* Irregular; *Price:* Free with membership in the Canadian Health Food Association
Profile: Recent news in the natural health & organic products industry
• Canadian Health Food Association Retail Member Directory
Type: Directory; *Frequency:* Monthly
Profile: A listing with contact information
• Canadian Health Food Association Supplier Member Directory
Type: Directory; *Frequency:* Monthly
Profile: A membership directory exclusively for members
• Membership that Matters! [a publication of the Canadian Health Food Association]
Type: Newsletter; *Price:* Free with membership in the Canadian Health Food Association
Profile: Information for members to help their businesses prosper
• NATURALeHealthy [a publication of the Canadian Health Food Association]
Type: Newsletter; *Frequency:* Monthly; *Price:* Free with membership in the Canadian Health Food Association
• Research & Your Health
Type: Newsletter; *Frequency:* Quarterly; *Number of Pages:* 8; *Price:* Free with membership in the Canadian Health Food Association
Profile: Abstracts about the value of natural health products

Canadian Health Information Management Association (CHIMA)
99 Enterprise Dr. South, London ON N6N 1B9
Tel: 519-438-6700; *Fax:* 519-438-7001
Toll-Free: 877-332-4462
www.echima.ca
www.linkedin.com/groups/4445368/profile
www.facebook.com/OfficialCHIMA
twitter.com/E_CHIMA
Previous Name: Canadian Health Record Association
Overview: A medium-sized national organization founded in 1942
Mission: To contribute to the promotion of wellness & the provision of quality healthcare through excellence in health information management; To assure competency of practice through credentialling, standards, & continuing education; To promote value of health information management professionals
Affiliation(s): International Federation of Health Information Management Associations; American Health Information Management Association
Finances: *Funding Sources:* Membership & exam revenues; promotional products & services; continuing education; services & events
Staff Member(s): 13
Membership: 5,000 members; *Member Profile:* Graduate of recognized health information management program & successful challenge Canadian College of Health Information Management (CCHIM) certification examination
Activities: *Speaker Service:* Yes
Chief Officer(s):
Gail Crook, CEO & Registrar, 519-438-6700 Ext. 227
gail.crook@echima.ca
Tasha Clipperton, Coordinator, Member Services
tasha.clipperton@echima.ca
Awards:
• Tribute to Excellence Award
Awarded to a CHIMA member whose professional practice exemplifies excellence in health information management
• Volunteer Award
Awarded to a CHIMA member who has made significant & impactful contributions to the delivery of services to CHIMA through volunteerism
• Promising New Professional Award
Awarded to graduate student member who demonstrates outstanding academic achievement & displays excellent work ethic

Meetings/Conferences:
• Canadian Health Information Management Association National Conference 2018, 2018
Scope: National
Contact Information: Director, Professional Development: Paula Weisflock, Phone: 519-438-6700, ext. 222, E-mail: paula.weisflock@echima.ca
Publications:
• An Essential Guide to Clinical Documentation Improvement [publication of Canadian Health Information Management Association]
Type: Report; *Author:* C. Grant & A. Jamal
Profile: White Paper discussing optical clinical documentation practices
• CHIMA [Canadian Health Information Management Association] Connection
Type: Newsletter; *Frequency:* Bimonthly
Profile: Industry news & events
• Human Resources Outlook 2014-2019 [a publication of Canadian Health Information Management Association]
Type: Report
Profile: Discusses key industry changes & their impact on Health Informatics & Health Information Management professions

Manitoba Chapter
MB
mbnuchapter@echima.ca
mbnu.echima.ca
Chief Officer(s):
Ric Van Amelsvoort-Barran, Chair
rvanamelsvoortbarran@manitoba-ehealth.ca
Chantal Plaetinck, Secretary-Treasurer

New Brunswick Chapter
NB
nbchapter@echima.ca
nb.echima.ca
Chief Officer(s):
Jeannette Blanchard, Chair
jeannette.blanchard@horizonnb.ca
Susanne Surette, Secretary-Treasurer

Newfoundland & Labrador Chapter
NL
nlchapter@echima.ca
nl.echima.ca
Chief Officer(s):
Jennifer Gushue, Chair
jennifer.gushue@easternhealth.ca
Jennifer Butler, Secretary-Treasurer

Ontario Chapter
ON
onchapter@echima.ca
on.echima.ca
Chief Officer(s):
Stephanie Tambeau, Chair
stambeaudia@gmail.com

Canadian Health Libraries Association (CHLA) / Association des bibliothèques de la santé du Canada (ABSC)
468 Queen St. East, #LL02, Toronto ON M5A 1T7
Tel: 416-646-1600; *Fax:* 416-646-9460
info@chla-absc.ca
www.chla-absc.ca
www.facebook.com/CHLA.ABSC
twitter.com/chlaabsc
instagram.com/chla_absc
Overview: A large national organization founded in 1976
Mission: To lead health librarians towards excellence
Membership: *Fees:* $50 students, unemployed & retired persons; $125 regular members; $250 institutions; *Member Profile:* Health librarian; Institutions; Students
Activities: Facilitating the transfer of knowledge in health sciences; Offering professional development events; Providing grants for members to attend continuing education events; Engaging in advocacy activities; Providing networking opportunities; *Rents Mailing List:* Yes
Chief Officer(s):
Lindsay Alcock, President
president@chla-absc.ca
Sophie Regalado, Secretary
secretary@chla-absc.ca
Lindsey Sikora, Director, Public Relations
pr@chla-absc.ca
Awards:
• CHLA/ABSC Canadian Hospital Librarian of the Year Award
Awarded to recognize the contribution of an individual hospital librarian to the advancement of health care & health librarianship in Canada *Deadline:* February 1 *Contact:* Past President, CHLA: Jeanna Hough, E-mail: past-president@chla-absc.ca
• CHLA/ABSC Emerging Leader Award
Awarded to recognize the skills, energy & enthusiasm that new health science librarians contribute to the profession as a whole *Deadline:* February 1 *Contact:* Past President, CHLA: Jeanna Hough, E-mail: past-president@chla-absc.ca
• CHLA/ABSC Flower Award for Innovation
Recognizes librarians or teams of librarians who have created or demonstrated improvements in health sciences library services for the profession through innovation & creativity *Deadline:* February 1 *Contact:* Past President, CHLA: Jeanna Hough, E-mail: past-president@chla-absc.ca
• JCHLA/JABSC Student Paper Prize
Awarded to a library & information science or library technician student who submits the best unpublished aper on health sciences librarianship *Deadline:* April 30 *Contact:* Editor, JCHLA: Cari Merkley, E-mail: editor@chla-absc.ca
• Margaret Ridley Charlton Award of Outstanding Achievement
Honours a librarian who has made a significant contribution to the field of health sciences librarianship in Canada *Deadline:* February 1 *Contact:* Past President, CHLA: Jeanna Hough, E-mail: past-president@chla-absc.ca
• CHLA/ABSC Chapter and Interest Group Initiatives Fund
Supports & recognizes special initiatives, programs or activities undertaken by CHLA/ABSC chapters & interest groups that further the objectives of CHLA/ABSC
• CHLA/ABSC Professional Development Grant
Awarded to enhance access to professional development opportunities for individual members
• CHLA/ABSC Research Grant
Awarded to foster & support research in the field of health science librarianship by providing funding to CHLA/ABSC members who are conducting research in this particular field
• CHLA/ABSC Rural & Remote Opportunities Grant
Awarded to support continuing education activities to benefit CHLA/ABSC members in rural or remote communities
Meetings/Conferences:
• 2018 Canadian Health Libraries Association (CHLA) / Association des bibliothèques de la santé du Canada (ABSC) 42nd Annual Conference, 2018
Scope: National
Description: An annual May or June gathering of health science librarians to participate in continuing education courses & lectures, & to view products & services related to their work
Publications:
• Canadian Health Libraries Association Annual Report
Type: Report; *Frequency:* Annually
• CHLA [Canadian Health Libraries Association] / ABSC Directory & Membership List
Type: Directory
Profile: For members only
• Journal of the Canadian Health Libraries Association / Journal de l'association des bibliothèques de la santé du Canada
Type: Journal; *Frequency:* Quarterly; *Accepts Advertising*; *Editor:* Cari Merkley; *ISSN:* 1708-6892
Profile: Feature articles, book reviews, & news
• Standards for Library & Information Services in Canadian Healthcare Facilities
Type: Monograph; *ISBN:* 0-9692171-4-5; *Price:* $30 Canadian Health Libraries Association; $35 Non-members
• Workload Measurement Systems: A Guide for Libraries
Type: Monograph; *ISBN:* 0-9692171-3-7; *Price:* $30 Canadian Health Libraries Association; $40 Non-members

Canadian Health Record Association *See* Canadian Health Information Management Association

Canadian Health Services Research Foundation *See* Canadian Foundation for Healthcare Improvement

Canadian Healthcare Engineering Society (CHES) / Société canadienne d'ingénierie des services de santé (SCISS)
#310, 4 Cataraqui St., Kingston ON K7K 1Z7
Tel: 613-531-2661; *Fax:* 613-531-0626
ches@eventsmgt.com
www.ches.org
Previous Name: Canadian Hospital Engineering Society
Overview: A medium-sized national organization founded in 1980
Mission: To be a forum for exchange of information & ideas related to excellence in communication & professional development in healthcare facilities management

Membership: 700 individual; *Fees:* $130; *Committees:* Communications; Governance; Membership/Recognition; Partnerships & Advocacy; Professional Development
Activities: Awareness Events: National Healthcare Facilities Engineering Week, October
Chief Officer(s):
Mitch Weimer, President
Meetings/Conferences:
• 38th Annual Conference of the Canadian Healthcare Engineering Society, September, 2018, St. John's Convention Centre, St. John's, NL
Scope: National
Description: Theme: "Smarter Infrastructure for Enhanced Patient Outcomes"

Canadian Hearing Impaired Hockey Association See Canadian Deaf Ice Hockey Federation

Canadian Hearing Instrument Practitioners Society (CHIPS)
#259, 185-9040 Blundell Rd., Richmond BC V6Y 1K3
www.chipscanada.com
Overview: A small national organization founded in 1998
Mission: The national professional organization for Hearing Instrument Practitioners who provide hearing healthcare services for hard of hearing people in Canada.
Member of: International Hearing Society
Membership: Fees: $275 Board Certified Hearing Instrument Specialist, Graduate, Provisional, Corporate Members; $100 Industrial Members; $50 Associate Members
Chief Officer(s):
Allen Kirkham, Chair

Canadian Hearing Society (CHS) / Société canadienne de l'ouïe
271 Spadina Rd., Toronto ON M5R 2V3
Tel: 416-928-2500; *Fax:* 416-928-2506
Toll-Free: 877-347-3427; *TTY:* 877-216-7310
info@chs.ca
www.chs.ca
www.facebook.com/chssco
twitter.com/CHSCanada
www.youtube.com/user/CHSCanadaTV
Overview: A large national charitable organization founded in 1940
Mission: To provide services that enhance the independence of deaf, deafened, & hard of hearing people, & that encourage prevention of hearing loss
Finances: Annual Operating Budget: Greater than $5 Million; *Funding Sources:* Ontario government service contracts; Product sales; United Way
Staff Member(s): 450
Activities: Providing counselling services, employment services, a hearing aid program, Ontario Interpreter Service, general social services, & sign language classes; Engaging in advocacy activities; *Awareness Events:* Hearing Awareness Month, May; Deaf Awareness Week, third week of Sept.; *Internships:* Yes; *Speaker Service:* Yes
Chief Officer(s):
Julia Dumanian, President & CEO
Stephanus Greeff, Vice-President, Finance & Corporate Services
Gary Malkowski, Vice-President, Stakeholder & Employer Relations
Barrie Office
#1412, 64 Cedar Pointe Dr., Barrie ON L4N 5R7
Tel: 705-737-3190; *Fax:* 705-722-0381; *TTY:* 877-872-0585
Belleville Office
Bayview Mall, #51, 470 Dundas St. East, Belleville ON K8N 1G1
Tel: 613-966-8995; *Fax:* 613-966-8365; *TTY:* 877-872-0586
Chief Officer(s):
Jen Vander Heyden, Program Assistant
jvanderheyden@chs.ca
Brantford Office
#139, 225 Colborne St., Brantford ON N3T 2H2
Tel: 519-753-3162; *Fax:* 519-753-7447; *TTY:* 877-843-0370
Chief Officer(s):
Victoria Baby, Regional Director
Brockville Sub-Office
#205, 68 William St., Brockville ON K6V 4V5
Tel: 613-498-3933; *Fax:* 613-498-0363
Toll-Free: 877-817-8209; *TTY:* 877-817-8209
info@chs.ca
Chief Officer(s):
Brian McKenzie, Regional Director

Chatham-Kent Office
75 Thames St., 2nd Fl., Chatham ON N7L 1S4
Tel: 519-354-9347; *Fax:* 519-354-2083; *TTY:* 877-872-0589
Chief Officer(s):
Brian McKenzie, Regional Director
Cornwall Office
#203, 4 Montreal Rd., Cornwall ON K6H 1B1
Fax: 613-521-0838
Toll-Free: 877-866-4445; *TTY:* 888-697-3650
Chief Officer(s):
Michel David, Regional Director
Durham Regional Office
Braemor Center Plaza, #7, 575 Thornton Rd. North, Oshawa ON L1J 8L5
Tel: 905-404-8490; *Fax:* 905-404-2012
Toll-Free: 888-697-3617; *TTY:* 888-697-3617
webmaster@chs.ca
Chief Officer(s):
Maggie Doherty-Gillbert, Regional Director
Elliot Lake Office
c/o St. Joseph's General Hospital, 70 Spine Rd., Elliot Lake ON P5A 1X2
Tel: 705-848-5306; *Fax:* 705-848-3937
Toll-Free: 877-634-0179
Chief Officer(s):
Silvy Coutu, Regional Director
Guelph Office
#200, 2 Quebec St., Guelph ON N1H 2T3
Tel: 519-821-4242; *Fax:* 519-821-8846
Toll-Free: 888-697-3611
webmaster@chs.ca
Chief Officer(s):
Victoria Baby, Regional Director
Hamilton Office
21 Hunter St. East, 2nd Fl., Hamilton ON L8N 1M2
Tel: 905-522-0755; *Fax:* 905-522-1336
Toll-Free: 888-224-7247; *TTY:* 877-817-8208
Kingston Regional Office
Frontenac Mall, 1300 Bath Rd., #D4, Kingston ON K7M 4X4
Tel: 613-544-1927; *Fax:* 613-544-1975
Toll-Free: 877-544-1927; *TTY:* 877-817-8209
Chief Officer(s):
Deborah Martin, Manager, Administration & Support Services
dmartin@chs.ca
London Regional Office
181 Wellington St., London ON N6B 2K9
Tel: 519-667-3325; *Fax:* 519-667-9668; *TTY:* 888-697-3613
Mississauga
#300, 2227 South Millway, Mississauga ON L5L 3R6
Tel: 905-608-0271; *Fax:* 905-608-8241
Toll-Free: 866-603-7161; *TTY:* 877-634-0176
Chief Officer(s):
Victoria Baby, Regional Director
Muskoka Office
#103, 175 Manitoba Street, Bracebridge ON P1L 1S3
Tel: 705-645-8882; *Fax:* 705-645-0182
Toll-Free: 877-840-8882; *TTY:* 877-872-0585
webmaster@chs.ca
Chief Officer(s):
Maggie Doherty-Gillbert, Regional Director
North Bay Office
#7, 140 King St. West, North Bay ON P1B 5Z7
Tel: 705-474-8090; *Fax:* 705-474-6075; *TTY:* 877-634-0174
Chief Officer(s):
Silvy Coutu, Regional Director
Ottawa Regional Office
#600, 2197 Riverside Dr., Ottawa ON K1H 7X3
Tel: 613-521-0509; *Fax:* 613-521-0838; *TTY:* 888-697-3650
Chief Officer(s):
Michel David, Regional Director
mdavid@chs.ca
Peterborough Office
315 Reid St., Peterborough ON K9J 3R2
Tel: 705-743-1573; *Fax:* 705-741-0708
Toll-Free: 800-213-3848; *TTY:* 888-697-3623
Sarnia Office
420 East St. North, Sarnia ON N7T 6Y5
Tel: 519-337-8307; *Fax:* 519-337-6886
Toll-Free: 877-634-0178; *TTY:* 877-634-0178
Chief Officer(s):
Marilyn Reid, Regional Director
Sault Ste. Marie Regional Office
130 Queen St. East, Sault Ste Marie ON P6A 1Y5

Tel: 705-946-4320; *Fax:* 705-256-7231
Toll-Free: 855-819-9169; *TTY:* 877-634-0179
Chief Officer(s):
Wayne King, Regional Program Manager
Simcoe York Regional Office
#105, 713 Davis Dr., Newmarket ON L3Y 2R3
Tel: 905-715-7511; *Fax:* 905-715-7109
Toll-Free: 877-715-7511; *TTY:* 877-817-8213
webmaster@chs.ca
Chief Officer(s):
Maggie Doherty-Gilbert, Regional Director
Sudbury Regional Office
1233 Paris St., Sudbury ON P3E 3B6
Tel: 705-522-1020; *Fax:* 705-522-1060
Toll-Free: 800-479-4562; *TTY:* 877-817-8205
Chief Officer(s):
Maureen Beaudry, Counsellor
Thunder Bay Regional Office
Victoriaville Centre, #35, 125 Syndicate Ave. South, Thunder Bay ON P7E 6H8
Tel: 807-623-1646; *Fax:* 807-623-4815
Toll-Free: 866-646-0514; *TTY:* 877-634-0183
Timmins Office
20 Wilcox St., Timmins ON P4N 3K6
Tel: 705-268-0771; *Fax:* 705-268-4598
Toll-Free: 877-872-0580; *TTY:* 877-872-0580
webmaster@chs.ca
Chief Officer(s):
Silvy Coutu, Regional Director
Toronto (Central) Region
271 Spadina Rd., Toronto ON M5R 2V3
Tel: 416-928-2504; *Fax:* 416-928-2523
Toll-Free: 877-215-9530
tr.frontdesk@chs.ca
Chief Officer(s):
Stephanie Ozorio, Regional Director
Waterloo Regional Office
#200, 120 Ottawa St. North, Kitchener ON N2H 3K5
Tel: 519-744-6811; *Fax:* 519-744-2390
Toll-Free: 800-668-5815; *TTY:* 888-697-3611
Windsor Regional Office
300 Giles Blvd. East, #A3, Windsor ON N9A 4C4
Tel: 519-253-7241; *Fax:* 519-253-6630; *TTY:* 877-216-7302

Canadian Hearing Society Foundation See Hearing Foundation of Canada

Canadian Heart Association See Canadian Cardiovascular Society

Canadian Heartland Training Railway
Camrose Heritage Railway Station & Park, 4407 - 47 Ave., Camrose AB T4V 1X2
Tel: 403-601-8731; *Fax:* 403-601-8704
www.chtr.ca
Overview: A small national organization
Mission: To support the practical training needs of the railway industry in Canada & around the world
Member of: Railway Association of Canada; Railway Suppliers Association of Canada
Activities: Offers training & support for Shortline & Industrial Railways in Canada
Chief Officer(s):
Joe Bracken, President
joebracken@chtr.ca

Canadian Heavy Oil Association (CHOA)
#2310, 144 - 4th Ave. SW, Calgary AB T2P 3N4
Tel: 403-269-1755; *Fax:* 403-453-0179
e-suggestions@choa.ab.ca
www.choa.ab.ca
www.linkedin.com/company/canadian-heavy-oil-association
twitter.com/CDN_CHOA
Overview: A medium-sized national organization
Mission: To provide a technical, educational, & social forum for people employed in, or associated with, the oil sands & heavy oil industries
Finances: Funding Sources: Membership fees; Sponsorships
Membership: 2,000; *Fees:* $25 student; $125 regular; *Member Profile:* Individuals employed in heavy oil exploration & production, service & supply, consulting, & government; Students; *Committees:* Executive; Finance & Audit; Governance & Nominations; Sponsorship & Networking; Member Policy; Professional Programs; Regional & External Policy

Activities: Providing continuing education; Offering networking opportunities with industry peers; *Library:* Canadian Heavy Oil Association Library; by appointment Not open to public
Chief Officer(s):
Stephen Arseniuk, President, 403-718-8821
Kerri Markle, Executive Director
Awards:
• CHOA Scholarships
; *Amount:* $2,000
• CHOA Bursary Program
To support students with financial needs to pursue programs that mat lead to work in the heavy oil industry
Meetings/Conferences:
• Canadian Heavy Oil Association 2018 Slugging it Out Conference, April, 2018, BMO Centre Stampede Park, Calgary, AB
Scope: National
Publications:
• CHOA [Canadian Heavy Oil Association] Handbook
Type: Handbook; *Price:* $60
Profile: Topics include markets & logistics, environment & regulatory best management practices, geology & geophysics, geostatistics, geomechanics, reservoir & wellbore simulation, drilling & completions, field testing, bitumen / heavy oil upgrading, & heavy oil research
• Journal of the Canadian Heavy Oil Association
Type: Journal; *Frequency:* Quarterly; *Accepts Advertising*; *Editor:* Deborah Jaremko
Profile: Feature articles, technology information, news from the association, scholarship winners, volunteer recognition, & sponsor information

Canadian Hematology Society (CHS) / Société canadienne d'hématologie
#199, 435 St. Laurent Blvd., Ottawa ON K1K 2Z8
Tel: 613-748-9613; *Fax:* 613-748-6392
chs@uniserve.ca
www.canadianhematologysociety.org
Overview: A small national organization founded in 1971
Mission: To represent members of the Society & provide information about hematology
Membership: *Fees:* $75 active; *Member Profile:* Canadian physicians & scientists with an interest in the discipline
Chief Officer(s):
Aaron Schimmer, President
Publications:
• Canadian Hematology Society Membership Directory
Type: Directory
• Canadian Hematology Society Newsletter
Type: Newsletter; *Frequency:* 3 pa

Canadian Hemerocallis Society
16 Douville Ct., Toronto ON M5A 4E7
Tel: 416-362-1682
www.distinctly.on.ca/chs
Also Known As: National Daylily Society of Canada
Overview: A small national organization
Mission: To promote, encourage & foster the development & improvement of the genus Hemerocallis
Membership: *Fees:* $25
Chief Officer(s):
John P. Peat, President
jpeat@distinctly.on.ca

Canadian Hemochromatosis Society (CHS) / Société canadienne de l'hémochromatose
#285, 7000 Minoru Blvd., Richmond BC V6Y 3Z5
Tel: 604-279-7135; *Fax:* 604-279-7138
Toll-Free: 877-223-4766
office@toomuchiron.ca
www.toomuchiron.ca
www.linkedin.com/groups/Canadian-Hemochromatosis-Society-1096237
www.facebook.com/TooMuchIron
twitter.com/IronOutCanada
www.youtube.com/user/toomuchiron
Overview: A medium-sized national charitable organization founded in 1982
Mission: To increase awareness among the public & medical community with regards to the importance of family screening, early diagnosis & treatment of Hemochromatosis
Member of: International Association of Haemochromatosis Societies
Affiliation(s): Haemochromatosis Society of Great Britain; Haemochromatosis Society of Southern Africa; American Hemochromatosis Society Inc.; Association hémochromatose France; Haemochromatosis Society Australia; Iron Disorders Institute of America
Finances: *Funding Sources:* Donations; membership dues
Membership: *Fees:* Lifetime: $895 professional; $750 family; $500 individual; $295 senior
Activities: Maintains a central registry of members & donors & their families; also provides support & information, speakers, & a Medical Advisory Board; *Awareness Events:* National Hemochromatosis Awareness Week, last week of May
Chief Officer(s):
Patrick Haney, President & Chair
Bob Rogers, Executive Director & CEO
Publications:
• Iron Filings: Newsletter of The Canadian Hemochromatosis Society
Type: Newsletter; *Frequency:* Semiannually; *Price:* Free for members
Profile: Current research, news about hemochromatosis, dietary information, stories, & CHS member information

Canadian Hemophilia Society (CHS) / Société canadienne de l'hémophilie (SCHQ)
#301, 666, rue Sherbrooke ouest, Montréal QC H3A 1E7
Tel: 514-848-0503; *Fax:* 514-848-9661
Toll-Free: 800-668-2686
chs@hemophilia.ca
www.hemophilia.ca
www.facebook.com/CanadianHemophiliaSociety
twitter.com/CHShemophilia
www.youtube.com/user/CanadianHemophilia
Overview: A medium-sized national charitable organization founded in 1953
Mission: To find a cure & to provide services to people with hemophilia or other inherited bleeding disorders; To serve persons infected with HIV or hepatitis through blood & blood products; To enhance the health & quality of life of individuals affected by inherited bleeding disorders
Affiliation(s): World Federation of Hemophilia
Finances: *Annual Operating Budget:* $500,000-$1.5 Million; *Funding Sources:* Donations
Staff Member(s): 20; 200 volunteer(s)
Membership: 10; *Committees:* Blood Safety & Supply; Chapter Relations; Governance; HIV & Hepatitis National; International Projects; Program; Youth
Activities: Providing information, programs & services to people with inherited bleeding disorders, healthcare providers & communities; Conducting research; Developing standards of care; Offering education & support; Fundraising; *Awareness Events:* Hemophilia Day, Apr. 17; *Internships:* Yes; *Speaker Service:* Yes
Chief Officer(s):
David Page, National Executive Director
dpage@hemophilia.ca
Hélène Bourgaize, National Director, Chapter Relations & Human Resources
hbourgaize@hemophilia.ca
Deborah Franz Currie, National Director, Resource Development
dcurrie@hemophilia.ca
Publications:
• All About Carriers
Number of Pages: 133
Profile: Comprehensive guide, for carriers of hemophilia A or B
• All About von Willebrand Disease
Number of Pages: 86
Profile: A comprehensive guide, for persons with the disease
• Canadian Hemophilia Society Annual Report & Financial Statement
Frequency: Annually
• Factor Deficiencies
Profile: A series of publications, with topics such as Factor XI Deficiency, An Inherited Bleeding Disorder, for patients, families, & healthcare providers
• Hemophilia Today
Type: Magazine; *Frequency:* 3 pa; *Editor:* François Laroche
Profile: Current news & relevant issues to inform the hemophilia & bleeding disorders community

Alberta Chapter
PO Box 44171, Edmonton AB T5V 1N6
Toll-Free: 800-668-2686
albertachapter@hemophilia.ca
www.hemophilia.ca/en/provincial-chapters/alberta
Chief Officer(s):
Hillary Nemeth, Co-President
Sheri Spady, Co-President

British Columbia Chapter
PO Box 21161, Stn. Maple Ridge Sq., Maple Ridge BC V2X 1P7
Tel: 778-230-9661
chsbc@shaw.ca
www.hemophiliabc.ca
Mission: To help improve the lives of people with hemophilia
Chief Officer(s):
Curtis Brandell, President

Hemophilia Manitoba
944 Portage Ave., Winnipeg MB R3G 0R1
Tel: 204-775-8625; *Fax:* 204-774-9403
Toll-Free: 866-775-8625
info@hemophiliamb.ca
www.hemophiliamb.ca
www.facebook.com/186587534783298
twitter.com/HemophiliaMB
www.youtube.com/user/hemophiliamb
Chief Officer(s):
Christine Keilback, Executive Director

Hemophilia Ontario
#10100, 4711 Yonge St., Toronto ON M2N 6K8
Tel: 416-972-0641; *Fax:* 888-958-0307
Toll-Free: 888-838-8846
www.hemophilia.ca/en/provincial-chapters/ontario
Chief Officer(s):
Matthew Maynard, Interim Executive Director
mmaynard@hemophilia.on.ca

Hemophilia Saskatchewan
2366 Ave. C North, Saskatoon SK S7L 5X5
Tel: 306-653-4366
Toll-Free: 866-953-4366
hemosask@hemophilia.ca
www.hemophiliask.ca/hemophilia-saskatchewan.html
www.facebook.com/HemophiliaSaskatchewan
twitter.com/HemophiliaSask
Chief Officer(s):
Wendy Quinn, President

New Brunswick Chapter
#173, 337 Rothesay Ave., Saint John NB E2J 2C3
Tel: 506-608-0031
www.hemophilia.ca/en/provincial-chapters/new-brunswick
Chief Officer(s):
Victoria Watts, President
president@chsnb.com

Newfoundland & Labrador Chapter
25 Main Rd., Cavendish NL A0B 1J0
chsnlcc@nf.sympatico.ca
hemophilia.ca/en/provincial-chapters/newfoundland-and-labrador
Chief Officer(s):
Jenny Jacobs, President

Nova Scotia Chapter
17 Malcolm Lucas Dr., Enfield NS B2T 1A8
Tel: 902-883-7111
nshemophiliasociety@hotmail.com
www.hemophilia.ca/en/provincial-chapters/nova-scotia
Chief Officer(s):
Betty-Anne Hines, President

Prince Edward Island Chapter
PO Box 2951, Charlottetown PE C1A 8C5
www.hemophilia.ca/en/provincial-chapters/prince-edward-island
Chief Officer(s):
Shelley Mountain, President

Section Québec
#514, 2120, rue Sherbrooke est, Montréal QC H2K 1C3
Tél: 514-848-0666; *Téléc:* 514-904-2253
Ligne sans frais: 877-870-0666
info@schq.org
www.hemophilia.ca/fr/sections-provinciales/quebec
www.facebook.com/27424888399
Affiliation(s): Partenaire Santé Québec/COCQSida
Chief Officer(s):
François Laroche, Président

Canadian Hereford Association (CHA) / Association canadienne Hereford
5160 Skyline Way NE, Calgary AB T2E 6V1
Tel: 403-275-2662; *Fax:* 403-295-1333
Toll-Free: 888-836-7242
herefords@hereford.ca
www.hereford.ca
twitter.com/CAN_Hereford

Overview: A medium-sized national organization founded in 1890
Mission: To promote the consistent & economical production of beef; To strive to meet & exceed consumer expectations for tender, juicy, & flavourful beef products, through performance measurement, genetic selection, appropriate handling, feeding, & processing
Member of: Canadian Beef Breeds Council
Affiliation(s): Canadian Cattlemens Association
Finances: *Funding Sources:* Membership fees; breeding records
Staff Member(s): 10
Membership: *Fees:* $150 standard; $50 young guns; $15 junior; *Member Profile:* Purebred breeders; farmers & ranchers; *Committees:* Marketing; Show; Pedigree; Hereford Breed Improvement
Activities: Organizing the Annual Hereford Convention, the National Hereford Youth Conference, & the National Hereford Show
Chief Officer(s):
Gordon Stephenson, General Manager
gm@hereford.ca
Publications:
• Canadian Hereford Association Member Directory
Type: Directory
• Canadian Hereford Digest
Type: Magazine; *Accepts Advertising*
Profile: Information about the beef breed for purebred & commercial cattle producers

Canadian Heritage Information Network (CHIN) / Réseau canadien d'information sur le patrimoine (RCIP)
15, rue Eddy, 7e étage, Gatineau QC K1A 0M5
Tel: 819-994-1200; *Fax:* 819-994-9555
Toll-Free: 800-520-2446; *TTY:* 888-997-3123
service@chin.gc.ca
www.rcip-chin.gc.ca
Overview: A medium-sized national organization founded in 1972
Mission: To engage national & international audiences in Canadian heritage, through leadership & innovation in digital content, partnerships, & lifelong learning opportunities
Member of: Canadian Museums Association; International Committee for Documentation (CIDOC); Museum Computer Network.
Staff Member(s): 43
Membership: 1,500+; *Member Profile:* Canadian museums & heritage institutions
Activities: *Awareness Events:* Canadian Multiculturalism Day, June 27; *Internships:* Yes; *Speaker Service:* Yes
Chief Officer(s):
Claudette Lévesque, Acting Director General, 819-934-5016
Paul Lima, Senior Policy Advisor, 819-934-5019
Julie Marion, Director, Program Development, 819-934-5024

The Canadian Heritage of Québec *Voir* L'Héritage canadien du Québec

Canadian Highland Cattle Society (CHCS) / Société canadienne des éleveurs de bovins Highland
121 Rang 5 East, Saint-Donat-de-Rimouski QC G0K 1L0
Tel: 418-739-4477; *Fax:* 418-739-4477
highland@chcs.ca
www.chcs.ca
Overview: A small national organization founded in 1964
Mission: To regulate & promote breeding of Highland cattle in Canada.
Finances: *Funding Sources:* Membership fees
Membership: *Fees:* $60 resident; $12 youth; $72 non-resident; $1200 life
Chief Officer(s):
Marise Labrie, Secretary-Manager

Canadian Historical Association (CHA) / Société historique du Canada (SHC)
#1912, 130 Albert St., Ottawa ON K1P 5G4
Tel: 613-233-7885; *Fax:* 613-565-5445
cha-shc@cha-shc.ca
www.cha-shc.ca
www.facebook.com/215430858536628
twitter.com/CndHistAssoc
Overview: A large national charitable organization founded in 1922
Mission: To encourage historical research; To stimulate public interest in history; To promote the preservation of Canadian heritage
Member of: Canadian Federation for the Humanities and Social Sciences; International Committee of Historical Sciences
Finances: *Annual Operating Budget:* $100,000-$250,000; *Funding Sources:* Membership dues; Publication revenue
Staff Member(s): 1; 24 volunteer(s)
Membership: 1,100; *Fees:* Schedule available; *Member Profile:* Interest in history; *Committees:* Advocacy; Affiliated; Annual Meeting; CHA Bulletin Editors; Equity, Diversity & Accessibility; Graduate Student Liaison; History Department Chairs; IHAF Liaison; International Committee of Historical Sciences Liaison; Nominating; Outreach & Partnerships; Prizes; Publications; Teaching
Activities: Publishing historical works & documents; Lobbying archives, museums, governments, & granting agencies in the interest of historians, particularly on issues relating to the preservation of heritage materials & public access to historical documents
Chief Officer(s):
Michel Duquet, Executive Director
mduquet@cha-shc.ca
Awards:
• The Clio Prizes
• Albert B. Corey Prize
Established 1966 & jointly sponsored by the CHA & the American Historical Association; awarded every two years to the best book dealing with the history of Canadian-American relations or the history of both countries; *Amount:* $1,000
• The Wallace K. Ferguson Prize
Established 1979; awarded annually for outstanding work in a field of history other than Canadian; *Amount:* $1,000
• Jean-Marie Fecteau Prize
Awarded for the best article published in a peer-reviewed journal (including student journals) by a PhD or MA-level student, in French or in English.; *Amount:* $250
• John Bullen Prize
Awarded to the outstanding PhD thesis on a historical topic in a Canadian university by a Canadian citizen or landed immigrant
Deadline: December; *Amount:* $500
• François-Xavier Garneau Medal
The Senior CHA Prize; awarded every five years to a book which represents an outstanding Canadian contribution to history; *Amount:* $2,000
• Sir John A. Macdonald Prize
Established 1976; awarded annually for the nonfiction work of Canadian history "judged to have made the most significant contribution to an understanding of the Canadian past"; *Amount:* $5,000
Meetings/Conferences:
• Canadian Historical Association 2018 Annual Meeting, May, 2018, University of Regina, Regina, SK
Scope: National
Description: An event for historians to showcase their research & to discuss issues related to the discipline
• Canadian Historical Association 2019 Annual Meeting, 2019, University of British Columbia, Vancouver, BC
Scope: National
Description: An event for historians to showcase their research & to discuss issues related to the discipline
Publications:
• Becoming a Historian
Editor: Franca Iacovetta et al.
Profile: Handbook with guidance & advice for graduate history students & junior history professors
• CHA [Canadian Historical Association] Short Books
Number of Pages: 200; *Editor:* Pierre-Yves Saunier
Profile: Series on international themes & issues, for undergraduate students & the educated public
• CHA [Canadian Historical Association] Bulletin
Frequency: 3 pa; *Accepts Advertising*; *Editor:* Martin Laberge & Robert Talbot; *ISSN:* 0382-4764
Profile: News & comments of interest to professional historians in Canada
• Immigration & Ethnicity in Canada [a publication of the Canadian Historical Association]
Editor: Marlene Epp; *ISSN:* 2292-7441
Profile: Series presents concise histories of aspects of immigration & ethnicity in Canada
• Journal of the Canadian Historical Association / Revue de la Société historique du Canada
Type: Journal; *Frequency:* Annually; *Editor:* Jacqueline Holler et al.; *ISSN:* 1712-6274
Profile: Best papers presented at CHA's annual meeting

Canadian Historical Association, Archives Section *See* Association of Canadian Archivists

Canadian History of Education Association (CHEA) / L'Association canadienne d'histoire de l'éducation (ACHE)
University of Saskatchewan, College of Education, 28 Campus Dr., Saskatoon SK S7N 0X1
www.ache-chea.ca
www.facebook.com/achechea
twitter.com/CHEA_ACHE
Overview: A small national organization
Chief Officer(s):
Kristina Llewellyn, President
Meetings/Conferences:
• Canadian History of Education Association 20th Biennial Conference, 2018
Scope: National

Canadian HIV Trials Network (CTN) / Réseau canadien pour les essais VIH
#588, 1081 Burrard St., Vancouver BC V6Z 1Y6
Tel: 604-806-8327; *Fax:* 604-806-8005
Toll-Free: 800-661-4664
ctninfo@hivnet.ubc.ca
www.hivnet.ubc.ca
www.linkedin.com/company/2287403
www.facebook.com/CIHR.CTN
twitter.com/CIHR_CTN
www.youtube.com/user/CIHRCTN
Overview: A medium-sized national organization founded in 1990
Mission: To develop treatments, vaccines & a cure for HIV disease & AIDS through the conduct of scientifically sound & ethical clinical trials
Finances: *Annual Operating Budget:* $3 Million-$5 Million; *Funding Sources:* Health Canada
Staff Member(s): 30
Chief Officer(s):
Aslam Anis, National Director
Marina Klein, National Co-Director
Sharon Walmsley, National Co-Director
   Atlantic Region
   QEII Health Sciences Centre - Victoria General Hospital, 5790 University Ave., Halifax NS B3H 1V7
   Tel: 902-473-2700
   Ontario Region
   University of Ottawa at Ottawa General Hospital, 501 Smyth Rd., Ottawa ON K1H 8L6
   Pacific Region
   St. Paul's Hospital, John Ruedy Immunodeficiency Clinic, 1081 Burrard St., Vancouver BC V6Z 1Y6
   Prairie Region
   Southern Alberta HIV Clinic, #3223, 1213 - 4 St. SW, Calgary AB T2R 0X7
   Québec Region
   Institut thoracique de Montréal, 3650, rue St-Urbain, Montréal QC H2X 2P4
   Toronto & Area Office
   Sunnybrook Health Science Centre, 2075 Bayview Ave., Toronto ON M4N 3M5
   Tel: 416-480-5900

Canadian HIV/AIDS Legal Network / Réseau juridique canadien VIH/sida
#600, 1240 Bay St., Toronto ON M5R 2A7
Tel: 416-595-1666; *Fax:* 416-595-0094
info@aidslaw.ca
www.aidslaw.ca
www.facebook.com/CanadianHIVAIDSLegalNetwork
twitter.com/aidslaw
www.youtube.com/aidslaw
Overview: A medium-sized national charitable organization founded in 1992 overseen by Canadian AIDS Society
Mission: To promote the human rights of people living with & vulnerable to HIV/AIDS, in Canada & internationally; through research, legal & policy analysis, education, advocacy & community mobilization
Finances: *Annual Operating Budget:* $500,000-$1.5 Million; *Funding Sources:* Federal government; donations; corporations; various international organizations
Staff Member(s): 13
Membership: *Fees:* $50 individual; US$100 international individual; Organizations: schedule based on annual budget; *Member Profile:* Community AIDS organizations; harm reduction organizations

Canadian Associations / Canadian Hockey League

Activities: Projects on legal & ethical issues raised by HIV/AIDS; *Internships:* Yes *Library:* Resource Centre; by appointment
Chief Officer(s):
Richard Elliot, Executive Director, 416-595-1666 Ext. 229
Janet Butler-McPhee, Director of Communications, 416-595-1666 Ext. 228
Awards:
• Awards for Action on HIV/AIDS & Human Rights
To recognize individuals or organizations that have made an outstanding contribution to addressing HIV/AIDS & human rights issues
Publications:
• HIV / AIDS Policy & Law Review
Type: Journal; *Editor:* David Garmaise; *ISSN:* 1712-624X; *Price:* $75 Canada; $125 international
Profile: Analysis & summaries of current developments in HIV/AIDS-related policy and law from an international perspective
• Legal Network News
; *ISSN:* 1488-0997

Canadian Hockey League
#201, 305 Milner Ave., Toronto ON M1B 3V4
Tel: 416-332-9711; *Fax:* 416-299-8787
www.chl.ca
twitter.com/CHLHockey
www.instagram.com/chlhockey
Overview: A large national organization
Mission: To act as the umbrella organization for the three major junior hockey leagues in Canada: Ontario Hockey League, Western Hockey League & Quebec Major Junior Hockey League
Activities: Mastercard Memorial Cup; Home Hardware Top Prospects Game; Subway Super Series; CHL Import Draft; *Rents Mailing List:* Yes
Chief Officer(s):
David E. Branch, President
Gilles Courteau, Vice-President
Ron Robison, Vice-President
Ray Hollowell, Director, Finance
rhollowell@chl.ca
Cole Butterworth, Director, Business Operations
cbutterworth@chl.ca
Paul Krotz, Director, Communications
pkrotz@chl.ca
Christina Sloan, Director, Corporate Partnerships
csloan@chl.ca
Awards:
• Player of the Year
• Top Prospect Award
• Sportsman of the Year
• Rookie of the Year
• Top Scorer of the Year
• Humanitarian of the Year
• Scholastic Player of the Year
• Brian Kilrea CHL Coach of the Year
• Goaltender of the Year
• Defenceman of the Year

Canadian Hoisting & Rigging Safety Council / Conseil Canadien de la sécurité du levage et du gréage
PO Box 282, Stn. B, Ottawa ON K1P 6C4
Tel: 604-336-4699; *Fax:* 604-336-4510
input@chrsc.ca
chrsc.ca
Overview: A large national organization
Mission: To create standardized regulations throughout the nation with regards to cranes, hoisting & rigging
Chief Officer(s):
Fraser Cocks, Chair, Board of Directors

Canadian Holistic Nurses Association (CHNA) / Association canadienne des infirmières en soins holistiques
www.chna.ca
www.facebook.com/CHNA.ca
Overview: A small national organization founded in 1986
Mission: To further the development of holistic nursing practice; To promote CHNA standards of practice
Affiliation(s): Canadian Nurses Association
Membership: *Fees:* $60 full members/retired; $50 associate members; $30 students
Activities: Adhering to CNA Nursing Practice Standards & the CNA Code of Ethics for Nurses; Promoting holistic nursing practice, education, & research; Influencing the health care system; Supporting members; Providing networking opportunities
Chief Officer(s):
Linda Muzio, President
Connie McDonald, Secretary
Publications:
• Canadian Holistic Nurses Association Member Directory
Type: Directory
• Canadian Holistic Nurses Association Newsletter
Type: Newsletter; *Editor:* Wendy Snefjella

Canadian Home & School & Parent-Teacher Federation *See* Canadian Home & School Federation

Canadian Home & School Federation (CHSF) / Fédération canadienne des associations foyer-école (FCAFE)
618 Bronson Settlement Rd., Red Bank Queens County NB E4A 2K9
www.canadianhomeandschoolfederation.ca
Previous Name: Canadian Home & School & Parent-Teacher Federation
Overview: A large national charitable organization founded in 1927
Mission: To improve the quality of Canadian public education available to children & youth; To act as the national voice of parents with children in public schools
Affiliation(s): Canadian Education Association; Breakfast for Learning; Canadian Teachers Federation; Canadian Association of Principals; Centre for Science in Public Interest; Media Awareness; Council of Ministers of Education Canada
Membership: *Member Profile:* Parents with children in public schools who belong to provincial affiliates
Activities: Advocating for children & youth; Promoting the health & social well-being of children & youth
Chief Officer(s):
Diane Power, President
Arlene Morell, Vice-President
Deb Couzens, Secretary
Leola Langille, Treasurer
Publications:
• Effective Beginnings: A Guide to New Partnerships in Schools
Author: J. Mansfield; *Editor:* M. Durkin & H. Kingdon; *ISBN:* 0-921077-27-0

Canadian Home Builders' Association (CHBA) / Association canadienne des constructeurs d'habitations
#500, 150 Laurier Ave. West, Ottawa ON K1P 5J4
Tel: 613-230-3060; *Fax:* 613-232-8214
chba@chba.ca
www.chba.ca
www.facebook.com/chbanational
twitter.com/chbanational
Previous Name: Housing & Urban Development Association of Canada
Overview: A large national organization founded in 1943
Mission: To assist its members in serving the needs & meeting the aspirations of Canadians for housing; To be the voice of the residential construction industry in Canada; To achieve an environment in which members can operate profitably; To promote affordability & choice in housing for all Canadians; To support the professionalism of members
Membership: *Member Profile:* New home builders; Renovators; Trade contractors; Leading manufacturers; Suppliers; Warranty program providers; Government housing agents; Service people; Professionals; *Committees:* Canadian Renovators' Council; Executive; Executive Officers' Council; Manufacturers' Council; Modular Construction Council; National Marketing; Net Zero Energy Housing Council; Professional Development; Technical Research; Urban Council
Activities: Promoting the interests of housing consumers; Liaising with all levels of government; Working to influence decision-makers on issues such as taxation & regulatory reform; Developing courses & workshops; Distributing industry news; *Awareness Events:* Renovation Month, October; New Homes Month
Chief Officer(s):
Kevin Lee, Chief Executive Officer
Awards:
• New Home Award
• Home Renovation Award
• Net Zero Home Award
• Community Development Award
• Marketing Award
• Marketing Excellence Award
• Design Excellence Award
Meetings/Conferences:
• Canadian Home Builders' Association 2018 75th National Conference, March, 2018, Fairmont Empress, Victoria, BC
Scope: National
Description: Featuring the Canadian Home Builders' Association Annual Meeting of Members, provincial caucus meetings, guest speakers, the association's annual economic session, presentation of the National SAM Awards, social events, & networking opportunities
Contact Information: Director, Conferences & Special Events: Lynda Barrett, E-mail: conference@chba.ca
Publications:
• Canadian Home Builders' Association Builders' Manual
Type: Book; *Frequency:* 6 pa; *Accepts Advertising*; *ISBN:* 0-86506-062-2; *Price:* $65
Profile: Contains tips for building energy-efficient housing
• Home Builder Magazine [a publication of the Canadian Home Builders' Association]
Type: Magazine; *Frequency:* 6 pa; *Accepts Advertising*; *ISSN:* 0840-4348
Profile: An information resource containing installation tips, technology developments & building techniques, homeimprovement ideas, & home design inspiration
• Industry Highlights [a publication of the Canadian Home Builders' Association]
Type: Newsletter; *Frequency:* Daily
Profile: Features media on housing issues & developments, with CHBA commentary
• Marketing Today [a publication of the Canadian Home Builders' Association]
Type: Newsletter; *Frequency:* bi-m.
Profile: An information resource for marketing & sales professionals; covers market research, consumer trends, & sales advice
• National Update [a publication of the Canadian Home Builders' Association]
Type: Newsletter; *Frequency:* Monthly
Profile: Features Association news & updates
• Net Zero News [a publication of the Canadian Home Builders' Association]
Type: Newsletter
• Pule Survey [a publication of the Canadian Home Builders' Association]
Type: Report; *Frequency:* a.
Profile: Survey of home builders providing insight into housing trends, market conditions, & construction practices
• Week in Review [a publication of the Canadian Home Builders' Association]
Type: Newsletter; *Frequency:* Weekly
Profile: Features a wrap-up of mnajor housing stories, with CBHA commentary

Canadian Home Builders' Association - British Columbia (CHBA BC)
c/o Bldg. NW5, British Columbia Institute of Technology Campus, 3700 Willingdon Ave., Burnaby BC V5G 3H2
Tel: 604-432-7112; *Fax:* 604-432-9038
Toll-Free: 800-933-6777
info@chbabc.org
www.chbabc.org
www.facebook.com/CHBABC
twitter.com/CHBABC
www.flickr.com/photos/104243952@N02
Overview: A medium-sized provincial organization founded in 1967 overseen by Canadian Home Builders' Association
Mission: To act as the voice of British Columbia's residential construction industry; To foster an environment for effectiveness & professionalism in the industry; To maintain affordability & profitability in British Columbia's housing industry
Staff Member(s): 5
Membership: 1,500; *Member Profile:* New home builders & renovators; Land developers; Trade contractors; Product & material manufacturers; Building product suppliers; Lending institutions; Insurance providers; Service professionals; *Committees:* Marketing; Education and Training; Government Relations; Technical Research; Renovator's Council
Activities: Liaising with the provincial government on province-wide initiatives; offering courses for Master Builder credential; providing government information & reference materials; offering technical support services; *Library:* CHBA BC Technical & Video Library
Chief Officer(s):
Neil Moody, Chief Executive Officer, 604-432-7112 Ext. 304
neilmoody@chbabc.org

Awards:
• Georgie Awards
To celebrate excellence in home building
Meetings/Conferences:
• Canadian Home Builders' Association of British Columbia Annual General Meeting 2018, 2018, BC
Scope: Provincial

Central Interior
921C Laval Cres., Kamloops BC V2C 5P4
Tel: 250-828-1844; *Fax:* 250-828-6611
info@chbaci.ca
www.chbaci.ca
www.facebook.com/114764955227340
twitter.com/CHBACI
Chief Officer(s):
Rose Choy, Office Manager
rose@chbaci.ca

Central Okanagan
#216, 1884 Spall Rd., Kelowna BC V1Y 4R1
Tel: 250-681-3988
info@cbaokanagan.ca
cbaokanagan.ca
www.facebook.com/121441914604188
twitter.com/CHBACI
Chief Officer(s):
Sherri Paiement, Executive Officer

Fraser Valley
PO Box 365, Abbotsford BC V2T 6Z6
Tel: 604-755-9306; *Fax:* 604-755-0223
info@chbafv.com
www.chbafv.com
www.linkedin.com/in/chba-fraser-valley-8753a228
www.facebook.com/chba.fraservalley
twitter.com/chbafv
Chief Officer(s):
Christy MacLeod, Executive Director
christy@chbafv.com

Northern BC
#115, 1705 - 3rd Ave., Prince George BC V2L 3G7
Tel: 250-563-3306
admin@chbanorthernbc.ca
www.chbanorthernbc.ca
Chief Officer(s):
Donna Maskell, Executive Assistant

Rocky Mountain
PO Box 2602, Fernie BC V0B 1M0
Tel: 250-420-1102
Chief Officer(s):
Jolanda Redeker, Executive Officer

Sea to Sky
PO Box 337, Whistler BC V0N 1B0
Tel: 604-902-2110
info@chba.com
www.seatoskychba.com
Chief Officer(s):
Alex Tavuchis, President

South Okanagan
104 Dunant Cres., Penticton BC V2A 3E9
Tel: 250-493-0001
www.chbaso.org
www.facebook.com/CHBASO
twitter.com/CHBASO
Chief Officer(s):
Carol Sudchak, Executive Officer

Vancouver Island
170 Wallace St., Nanaimo BC V9R 5B1
Tel: 250-755-1366; *Fax:* 250-714-1155
www.chbacvi.com
Chief Officer(s):
Kelsey Botting, Interim Executive Officer
kelsey@chbacvi.com

Canadian Home Builders' Association - New Brunswick / Association canadienne des constructeurs d'habitations - Nouveau-Brunswick
#207, 403 Regent St., Fredericton NB E3B 3X6
Tel: 506-459-7219; *Fax:* 506-450-4924
nbhome@nbhome.nb.ca
www.nbhomebuilders.ca
www.facebook.com/CHBANB
Overview: A small provincial organization founded in 1986 overseen by Canadian Home Builders' Association
Mission: To represent residential construction industry for New Brunswick consumers, members & government; To improve the performance of the housing industry
Staff Member(s): 2
Membership: *Member Profile:* Builders, renovators, developers, electricians, roofers, plumbers, suppliers, energy consultants, municipalities, government
Activities: Advocating at all levels of government to represent membership; *Awareness Events:* Presidents' Cup Golf Tournament; *Speaker Service:* Yes; *Rents Mailing List:* Yes; *Library:* by appointment
Chief Officer(s):
Claudia Simmonds, Chief Executive Officer
Awards:
• Awards of Excellence

Greater Fredericton
#207, 403 Regent St., Fredericton NB E3B 3X6
Tel: 506-459-7219; *Fax:* 506-450-4924
chbanb@nb.aibn.com
www.frederictonhomebuilders.com
Chief Officer(s):
Mallory Carter, Executive Officer

Greater Moncton
#2, 297 Collishaw St., Moncton NB E1C 9R2
Tel: 506-852-3377; *Fax:* 506-852-3871
gmhba@monctonhomebuilders.com
www.monctonhomebuilders.com
Chief Officer(s):
Denise Charron, Executive Officer

Saint John Region
PO Box 2581, Saint John NB E2L 4S8
Tel: 506-672-7487; *Fax:* 506-738-8145
sjhba@nb.aibn.com
Chief Officer(s):
Linda Smith, Executive Officer

Sussex
PO Box 4733, Sussex NB E4E 5L9
Tel: 506-432-1534; *Fax:* 506-433-5906
Chief Officer(s):
Juanita Carhart, Executive Officer
juanita.carhart@gmail.com

Canadian Home Builders' Association - Newfoundland Labrador (CHBA-EN)
435 Blackmarsh Rd., St. John's NL A1E 1T7
Tel: 709-753-2000; *Fax:* 709-753-7469
Toll-Free: 800-265-2800
admin@chbanl.ca
chbanl.ca
www.facebook.com/CHBANL
twitter.com/chba_nl
www.youtube.com/user/CHBANL
Overview: A medium-sized provincial organization founded in 1956 overseen by Canadian Home Builders' Association
Mission: To act as the voice of the residential construction industry in Newfoundland & Labrador
Staff Member(s): 3
Membership: 29 local associations + 4,000 member companies; *Member Profile:* Builders, developers, renovators, trade contractors, manufacturers, suppliers, landscape & lawn care organizations, financial & mortgage companies, associations, boards, & housing corporations, business services, media
Activities: Facilitating networking opportunities; Delivering the R-2000 Initiative & EnerGuide for New Houses Program in Newfoundland and Labrador; Providing updates on standards, codes, & regulations; Offering consumer information & seminars; Presenting sales & marketing awards; Liaising with municipal planning departments & the provincial government; *Awareness Events:* New Homes Month; Renovation Month *Library:* Consumer Resource Centre
Chief Officer(s):
Victoria Belbin, Chief Executive Officer
ceo@chbanl.ca
Awards:
• Building Excellence & Residential Growth (BERG) Awards
Meetings/Conferences:
• Canadian Home Builders' Association - Newfoundland Labrador 35th Annual Home Show 2018, April, 2018, The Glacier, Mount Pearl, NL
Scope: Provincial
Description: An event showcasing residential construction products & services; allows visitors to network with suppliers & consumers alike
Contact Information: Manager, Office Administration: Kelly Rogers, E-mail: admin@chbanl.ca

Publications:
• Canadian Home Builders' Association - Newfoundland Labrador Member Directory
Type: Directory

Canadian Home Builders' Association - Northern British Columbia
#115, 1705 - 3rd Ave., Prince George BC V2L 3G7
Tel: 250-563-3306; *Fax:* 250-563-3815
admin@chbanorthernbc.ca
www.chbanorthernbc.ca
www.facebook.com/chbaofnorthernbc
twitter.com/CHBA_NBC
www.instagram.com/chbanorthernbc
Overview: A small local organization founded in 1974
Mission: To represent the interests of professionals & businesses in the home building sector of northern British Columbia
Member of: Canadian Home Builders' Association - British Columbia
Membership: 75; *Member Profile:* Developers, sub-contractors, builders, renovators, suppliers, financial organizations, & government agencies involved in the home building & renovating business in Prince George, British Columbia & the surrounding region
Activities: Engaging in advocacy activities for the home building industry; Hosting monthly Builder's Liason meetings with local building officials; Providing training; Offering networking opportunities; Promoting a Code of Ethics; *Awareness Events:* CHBA Northern BC Home Show
Chief Officer(s):
Terri McConnachie, Executive Officer
Publications:
• Canadian Home Builders' Association - Northern British Columbia Membership Directory
Type: Directory; *Frequency:* Annually; *Accepts Advertising*
Profile: Features contact information for companies involved in the home building sector

Canadian Home Builders' Association - Prince Edward Island (CHBA-PEI)
#212A, 420 University Ave., Charlottetown PE C1A 7Z5
Tel: 902-367-6125
chba-pei.ca
www.facebook.com/CHBAPEI
twitter.com/CHBA_PEI
plus.google.com/110164647965189349176
Overview: A small provincial organization founded in 2009 overseen by Canadian Home Builders' Association
Mission: To be the voice of the residential construction industry in PEI; To achieve an environment in which membership can operate profitably; To promote affordability & choice in housing in PEI
Membership: 20; *Member Profile:* New home builders, renovators, developers, trades, manufacturers, suppliers & professionals; Companies & individuals that do business in Prince Edward Island & beyond
Activities: Holding monthly dinner meetings; Facilitating seminars
Chief Officer(s):
Todd MacEwen, Executive Officer
todd@chba-pei.ca

Canadian Home Builders' Association - Saskatchewan
#2, 3012 Louise St., Saskatoon SK S7J 3L8
Tel: 306-955-5188; *Fax:* 306-373-3735
Toll-Free: 888-955-5188
Previous Name: Saskatchewan Home Builders' Association
Overview: A medium-sized provincial organization founded in 1974 overseen by Canadian Home Builders' Association
Mission: To act as the voice of the residential construction industry in Saskatchewan; To promote professionalism in the industry
Membership: *Member Profile:* Builders, education & training institutions, government & non-profit agencies, manufacturers, suppliers, renovators, contractors, & professional services
Activities: Cooperating with local, federal, & provincial governments to address industry issues; Providing training services
Chief Officer(s):
Errol Fisher, Chair

Regina & Region
#100, 1801 MacKay St., Regina SK S4N 6E7
Tel: 306-546-5223; *Fax:* 306-569-9144
www.reginahomebuilders.ca

Canadian Associations / Canadian Home Care Association (CHCA) / Association canadienne de soins et services à domicile

Chief Officer(s):
Stu Niebergall, President & Chief Executive Officer
s.niebergall@reginahomebuilders.com
Saskatoon & Region
#2, 3012 Louise St., Saskatoon SK S7J 3L8
Tel: 306-955-5188; *Fax:* 306-373-3735
www.saskatoonhomebuilders.com
www.facebook.com/SaskatoonHomeBuilders
twitter.com/saskatoonhba
Chief Officer(s):
Dave Hepburn, Chief Executive Officer

Canadian Home Care Association (CHCA) / Association canadienne de soins et services à domicile
#302, 2000 Argentia Rd., Mississauga ON L5N 1W1
Tel: 905-567-7373
chca@cdnhomecare.ca
www.cdnhomecare.ca
twitter.com/CdnHomeCare
www.youtube.com/user/cdnhomecare
Overview: A medium-sized national organization founded in 1990
Mission: To promote the development, integration, delivery, public awareness & evaluation of quality home care services in Canada; To provide national leadership to strengthen & unify the home care sector; To collect & disseminate information about home care; To encourage or commission research; To influence policy & legislation; To establish a code of ethics
Membership: 600; *Fees:* $200-$6,000; *Member Profile:* Organizations & individuals involved in coordination & delivery, research & policy making, funding & management of home care services
Activities: Current areas of focus: national standards; research; communication & liaison with other national organizations; education opportunities for members
Chief Officer(s):
Réal Cloutier, President
Nadine Henningsen, Executive Director
nhenningsen@cdnhomecare.ca
Meetings/Conferences:
• Canadian Home Care Association 2018 International Home Care Summit, 2018
Scope: National

Canadian Home Furnishings Alliance (CHFA)
Toronto International Centre, PO Box 85, 6900 Airport Rd., #C, Mississauga ON L4V 1E8
Tel: 905-678-4678; *Fax:* 905-677-5212
info@chfaweb.ca
www.chfaweb.ca
Overview: A medium-sized national organization
Mission: To represent manufacturers, importers, & distributors of furniture, furnishings, fixtures, & accessories
Finances: *Funding Sources:* Membership fees
Membership: 22; *Member Profile:* Active members consist of Ontario-based manufacturers, importers, or distributors of residential home furnishings; Affiliate members consist of suppliers serving Ontario's home furnishings industry
Activities: *Awareness Events:* Golf Classic Tournament & Dinner
Chief Officer(s):
Murray Vaughan, President
murray@chfaweb.ca

Canadian Honey Council / Conseil canadien du miel
#218, 51519 RR#220, Sherwood Park AB T8E 1H1
Toll-Free: 877-356-8935
chc-ccm@honeycouncil.ca
www.honeycouncil.ca
twitter.com/honeycouncil
Overview: A medium-sized national organization founded in 1940
Mission: To promote, develop & maintain cooperation among all persons, organizations & government personnel involved with Canadian beekeeping industry
Affiliation(s): Apimondia
Finances: *Annual Operating Budget:* $50,000-$100,000
Staff Member(s): 1
Membership: 375; *Fees:* Schedule available; *Member Profile:* Beekeeping organizations; *Committees:* Membership
Activities: Providing resources & information about the bee industry; Developing honey production & bee management practices; Promoting Canadian honey; *Speaker Service:* Yes; *Rents Mailing List:* Yes
Chief Officer(s):
Rod Scarlett, Executive Director
Awards:
• Fred Rathje Memorial Award

Canadian Horse Breeders' Association (CHBA) / Société des Éleveurs de Chevaux Canadiens
#108, 59, rue Monfette, Victoriaville QC G6P 1J8
Tel: 819-367-2195; *Fax:* 819-367-2195
www.lechevalcanadien.ca
www.facebook.com/SECC.CHBA
Overview: A medium-sized international organization founded in 1895
Mission: To preserve & improve the Canadian horse; To promote & maintain breed standards; To provide services to breeders of the Canadian horse
Affiliation(s): Canadian Livestock Records Corporation
Membership: 1,100; *Fees:* $450 lifetime members; $45 / year active & junior members & supporters; $30 physical supporters over age 18; $10 physical supporters under age 18; *Member Profile:* Owners or co-owners of registered Canadian horses, from Canada, the United States, & Europe, who are at least 18 years of age; Junior members under 18 years of age; *Committees:* By-laws; Promotion; Annual General Meeting; Judgement & Classification; Futurity
Activities: Monitoring the registration, identification, & the keeping of the stud book for Canadian horses; Grading
Chief Officer(s):
Marie Josee Proulx, President, 819-367-2195
Pierre Lalonde, Vice-President, 819-278-4414, *Fax:* 819-278-3054
pierre.lalonde@xplornet.ca
David Campbell, Secretary-Treasurer
Dale Myggland, Director, Western Canada & Maritimes, & USA Representative, 780-842-4975, *Fax:* 780-842-6248
dmygg@telusplanet.net
Raymond Robichaud, Director, Ontario, 613-931-2060
fermerayann@yahoo.ca
Sandra Rowe, Director, Québec, 418-272-1264
lacadienne32@hotmail.com
Laura Lee Mills, Registrar, 613-731-7110 Ext. 314, *Fax:* 613-731-0704
lauralee.mills@clrc.ca
Publications:
• Le cheval canadien
Type: Newsletter; *Frequency:* 3 pa; *Price:* Free with membership in the Canadian Horse Breeders' Association

Atlantic District
c/o Christie Riddell, 2626 South Rawdon Rd., RR#1, Mount Uniacke NS B0N 1Z0
www.canadianhorseatlantic.ca
Mission: To preserve, protect, & promote the Canadian horse breed
Chief Officer(s):
April Watson, President
watsonnhc@gmail.com
Nicole Sullivan, Secretary-Treasurer
hymagnum@gmail.com
• Canadian Horse Breeders' Association Atlantic District Club Newsletter
Type: Newsletter; *Editor:* Cathy Arsenault
Rocky Mountain District (CHARMD)
c/o Heather Poff, 27131 Twp. Rd. 524, Spruce Grove AB T7X 3M9
Tel: 780-499-8458
dpoff@telus.net
www.canadianhorsebreeders.com
Mission: To preserve & promote the Canadian horse
Chief Officer(s):
Dale Myggland, President
dmygg@telusplanet.net
Patti Juutiand, Vice-President
spjuuti@mac.com
• Canadian Horse Breeders' Association Rocky Mountain District Newsletter
Type: Newsletter; *Price:* $20

Canadian Horse Heritage & Preservation Society (CHHAPS)
c/o Judi Hayward, Five Winds Farm, 1745 Lockyer Rd., Roberts Creek BC V0N 2W1
chhaps.ca
Overview: A small international organization
Mission: To preserve the traditional type of Canadian horse; To ensure responsible care & stewardship of heritage animals; To recognize the heritage of the Canadian horse to the history of Canada
Membership: *Fees:* $35 / year all categories of membership; *Member Profile:* Owners & admirers of the Canadian horse breed, from any location, who are interested in the preservation of the Canadian horse; Junior members under 19 years of age
Activities: Promoting the Canadian horse breed; Educating members & the public about the Canadian horse breed, through clinics & educational events with guest speakers; Sponsoring shows & events for the Canadian horse; Encouraging the exchange of information with other horse organizations
Chief Officer(s):
Judi Hayward, Contact, Membership
judihayward@dccnet.com
Meetings/Conferences:
• Canadian Horse Heritage & Preservation Society 2018 Annual General Meeting, 2018
Scope: National
Publications:
• Canadian Horse Heritage & Preservation Society Newsletter
Type: Newsletter; *Frequency:* Quarterly; *Price:* Free with membership in the Canadian Horse Heritage & Preservation Society

Canadian Horticultural Council (CHC) / Conseil canadien de l'horticulture
#102, 2200 Prince of Wales Dr., Ottawa ON K2E 6Z9
Tel: 613-226-4880; *Fax:* 613-226-4497
admin@hortcouncil.ca
www.hortcouncil.ca
twitter.com/chc_cch
Overview: A large national organization founded in 1922
Mission: To improve horticultural & allied industries including production, grading, packing, transportation, storage & marketing
Member of: CanAgPlus
Affiliation(s): Canadian Potato Council; International Federation for Produce Standards; Potatoes Canada
Finances: *Annual Operating Budget:* $500,000-$1.5 Million
Staff Member(s): 10
Membership: 120+ organizations; *Fees:* Amount based on national farm cash receipts; *Member Profile:* Organizations promoting development of horticultural industry; horticultural commodity organizations; federal & provincial government agriculture departments; *Committees:* Apple & Fruit; Business Risk Management; Crop, Plant Protection & the Environment; Greenhouse; Industry Standards & Food Safety; Labour; Potato; Trade & Marketing; Vegetable
Activities: *Library:*
Chief Officer(s):
Alvin Keenan, President
Meetings/Conferences:
• Canadian Horticultural Council Annual General Meeting 2018, March, 2018
Scope: National
Description: Members come together to deal with the challenges and opportunities facing Canada's horticultural industry.
Publications:
• Fresh Thinking [a publication of the Canadian Horticultural Council]
Type: Magazine; *Frequency:* s-a.
• Hort Shorts [a publication of the Canadian Horticultural Council]
Type: Newsletter

Canadian Horticultural Therapy Association (CHTA)
PO Box 74628, 2768 West Broadway, Vancouver BC V6K 4P4
admin@chta.ca
www.chta.ca
www.facebook.com/119374542077
Overview: A small national organization
Mission: To promote the use & awareness of horticulture as a therapeutic modality; horticultural therapy is a process which uses plants, horticultural activities, & the natural world to promote awareness & well-being by improving the body, mind, & spirit
Membership: *Fees:* $35 student; $55 individual; $95 corporate; *Member Profile:* Professionals such as occupational therapists, physiotherapists, recreation therapists, social workers, nurses, psychologists, landscape architects & designers, horticulturists, & people who have a passion for gardening
Chief Officer(s):
Christina Klein, Chair
chair@chta.ca

Canadian Hospice Palliative Care Association (CHPCA) / Association canadienne de soins palliatifs (ACSP)
Annex D, Saint-Vincent Hospital, 60 Cambridge St. North, Ottawa ON K1R 7A5
Tel: 613-241-3663; *Fax:* 613-241-3986
Toll-Free: 800-668-2785
Other Communication: Info Line: 1-877-203-4636
info@chpca.net
www.chpca.net
www.facebook.com/CanadianHospicePalliativeCare
twitter.com/CanadianHPCAssn
Overview: A large national charitable organization founded in 1991
Mission: To provide leadership in the pursuit of excellence in the care of people approaching death in Canada, in order to lessen suffering, loneliness, & grief; To develop national standards of practice for hospice palliative care
Member of: Quality End of Life Care Coalition; HEAL; Carers Canada; Health Charities Council of Canada
Finances: *Funding Sources:* Federal government; membership dues; corporate sponsors; sale of resources; donations
Staff Member(s): 10
Membership: *Member Profile:* Members include Canadian & international health care organizations, providers, & volunteers.; *Committees:* Executive; Finance; Organizational Development; Awards; Hastened Death
Activities: Raising awareness of hospice palliative care; Increasing knowledge & skills of health care providers & volunteers; Supporting research; Advocating for improved hospice palliative care policy, resource allocation, & supports for caregivers; *Awareness Events:* National Hospice Palliative Care Week, May; Hike for Hospice Palliative Care, May
Chief Officer(s):
Sharon Baxter, Executive Director
Sandie Lessard, Finance Officer
Cheryl Spencer, Coordinator, Administration & Events
Awards:
• CHPCA Champion Award
• CHPCA Leadership Award
• Award of Excellence
• Award of Pediatric Excellence
• Media Award
• Balfour Mount Champion Award
Publications:
• AVISO [a publication of Canadian Hospice Palliative Care Association]
Type: Newsletter; *Frequency:* Biannually
• Canadian Hospice Palliative Care Association Monthly Update
Type: Newsletter; *Frequency:* Monthly
Profile: Events, research news, awards, policy news, & resources
• Directory of Hospice Palliative Care Services
Type: Directory
Profile: Information on the availability of hospice palliative care services across Canada, featuring listings of programs & services, contact information, population served, & area of care

Canadian Hospital Engineering Society *See* Canadian Healthcare Engineering Society

Canadian Hotel Marketing & Sales Executives (CHMSE)
26 Avonhurst Rd., Toronto ON M9A 2G8
Tel: 416-252-9800; *Fax:* 416-252-7071
info@chmse.com
www.chmse.com
www.linkedin.com/groups?home=&gid=3020813
twitter.com/CHMSE
Overview: A medium-sized provincial organization founded in 1980
Mission: To be the leading association in providing professional development opportunities to sales & marketing executives within the Canadian hospitality industry
Finances: *Annual Operating Budget:* $50,000-$100,000; *Funding Sources:* Membership dues; strategic partnerships; sponsorships
Staff Member(s): 1; 12 volunteer(s)
Membership: 100; *Fees:* $299; $99 long distance; $25 application fee; *Member Profile:* Hotel members - employed in sales capacity in the hotel industry; Affiliate members - representatives of organizations which provide goods & services to the hotel industry; *Committees:* Membership; Programs; Communications; Students; Fundraising; Educational Development; Affiliates
Activities: Training programs for hospitality & sales professionals
Chief Officer(s):
Shelley Macdonald, Executive Director
Christopher White, President
christopher.white@eatonhotels.com
Publications:
• Canadian Hotel Marketing & Sales Executives Directory
Type: Directory
Profile: Listing of members
• Key Access
Type: Newsletter; *Frequency:* 3 pa; *Accepts Advertising*

Canadian Household Battery Association; Rechargeable Battery Recycling Corporation Canada *See* Call2Recycle Canada, Inc.

Canadian Housing & Renewal Association (CHRA) / Association canadienne d'habitation et de rénovation urbaine (ACHRU)
#902, 75 Albert St., Ottawa ON K1P 5E7
Tel: 613-594-3007; *Fax:* 613-594-9596
info@chra-achru.ca
www.chra-achru.ca
www.facebook.com/CHRA.ACHRU.ca
twitter.com/CHRA_ACHRU
www.youtube.com/user/CanadianHousing/
Overview: A medium-sized national organization founded in 1968
Mission: To provide access to adequate & affordable housing
Finances: *Annual Operating Budget:* $250,000-$500,000; *Funding Sources:* Federal & provincial governments; private
Staff Member(s): 6
Membership: 250; *Fees:* Schedule available; *Member Profile:* Directors, managers, employees & tenants of territorial, provincial, municipal & private non-profit housing corporations, housing authorities & rehabilitation program agencies, elected representatives, academics, housing consultants, municipal planners, tenants associations & others interested in the field.; *Committees:* Executive; Finance; Nominations & Awards; Resolutions; Personnel; Membership Development; International; Policy Advisory
Activities: Increasing public awareness of housing issues & inequalities through advocacy, research, communications & promotes excellence in the management of social housing through education & training; *Rents Mailing List:* Yes
Chief Officer(s):
Jeff Morrison, Executive Director
jmorrison@chra-achru.ca

Canadian Human Rights Foundation *See* Equitas - International Centre for Human Rights Education

Canadian Hydrogen & Fuel Cell Association (CHFCA)
#900, 1188 West Georgia St., Vancouver BC V6E 4A2
Tel: 604-283-1040; *Fax:* 604-283-1043
info@chfca.ca
www.chfca.ca
www.linkedin.com/groups?mostPopular=&gid=3145006?mostPopular=&gid=3145006
www.facebook.com/poweringnow
twitter.com/poweringnow
www.youtube.com/chfca
Merged from: Canadian Hydrogen Association (CHA) & Hydrogen & Fuel Cells Canada (H2FCC)
Overview: A small national organization founded in 2009
Mission: To act as the collective voice of the hydrogen & fuel cell technologies & products sector; To support Canadian corporations, educational institutions, & governments which develop & deploy hydrogen & fuel cell products & services in Canada
Membership: 70 organizations; *Fees:* Schedule available, based upon number of employees; *Member Profile:* Hydrogen & fuel cell technology & component firms; Fuelling system organizations; Fuel storage services; Engineering firms; Financial services
Activities: Increasing awareness of the economic, environmental, & social benefits of hydrogen & fuel cells; Supporting the development of regulations, codes, & standards; Facilitating demonstration projects, such as Hydrogen Village & the Hydrogen Highway; Supporting the safe & widespread application & commercialization of hydrogen & fuel cell products; Engaging in advocacy activities; Liasing with government stakeholders; Providing information to governments, media & the pubblic; Offering networking opportunities for members
Chief Officer(s):
Eric Denhoff, President & Chief Executive Officer, 604-760-7176
edenhoff@chfca.ca
Meetings/Conferences:
• Hydrogen + Fuel Cells 2018 International Conference, 2018
Scope: International
Publications:
• Canadian Capabilities Guide: Canada's Hydrogen & Fuel Cell Industry
Type: Guide
Profile: Profiles & critical information about companies & organizations in Canada's hydrogen & fuel cell sector
• Canadian Fuel Cell Commercialization Roadmap Update: Progress of Canada's Hydrogen & Fuel Cell Industry
Type: Guide
Profile: ISSN: 978-1-100-10468-360537E
• Canadian Hydrogen & Fuel Cell Association Newsletter
Type: Newsletter; *Frequency:* Quarterly
Profile: Association member news & successes
• Canadian Hydrogen & Fuel Cell Sector Profile
Type: Guide
Profile: Statistics about Canada's hydrogen & fuel cell sector

Canadian Hydrographic Association (CHA) / Association canadienne d'hydrographie
#1205, 4900 Yonge St., Toronto ON M2N 6A6
Tel: 416-512-5815
www.hydrography.ca
Overview: A small national organization founded in 1966
Mission: To advance the development of hydrography & associated activities in Canada; to further the knowledge & professional development of members; to enhance & demonstrate the public need for hydrography; & to help the development of hydrographic sciences in developing countries; & to embrace the desciplines of marine cartography, hydrographic surveying, offshore exploration, marine geodesy, & tidal studies.
Member of: International Federation of Hydrographic Societies
Affiliation(s): Canadian Institute of Geomatics; The Hydrographic Society
Finances: *Funding Sources:* Membership dues; Conferences & seminars; Sponsorships
Membership: *Fees:* Schedule available; *Member Profile:* Hydrographers; Workers in associated disciplines; persons interested in hydrography & marine cartography; *Committees:* Lighthouse; Student Award; Hydrographic; Website
Activities: Operating a Student Award Program; *Library:* Gerry Wade Memorial Library; by appointment
Chief Officer(s):
Rob Hare, National President
wabbit@shaw.ca
Kirsten Greenfield, National Secretary
kirsten.greenfield@pwgsc-tpsgc.gc.ca
Christine Delbridge, National Treasurer, 905-336-4745
Christine.Delbridge@dfo-mpo.gc.ca
Awards:
• Canadian Hydrographic Association Award
Awarded to a student at any Canadian university or technological college who must be continuing into second year of a program in one of the following fields of study: hydrography, cartography, geomatics, survey sciences; award based on 70% or better GPA & financial need; *Amount:* $2,000 scholarship
Publications:
• Lighthouse: The Journal of the Canadian Hydrographic Association
Type: Journal; *Frequency:* Semiannually; *Number of Pages:* 60; *Price:* $20 Canada; $25 international
Profile: Timely scientific, technical, & non-technical articles about hydrography in Canada, news from the industry, & CHA activities & events
   Atlantic Branch
   PO Box 1006, Dartmouth NS B2Y 4A2
   Tel: 902-426-0574
   Chief Officer(s):
   Bruce Anderson, Vice-President
   Bruce.Anderson@dfo-mpo.gc.ca
   Central Branch
   867 Lakeshore Rd., Burlington ON L7R 4A6
   email@mcquestmarine.com
   Chief Officer(s):
   Ken McMillan, Vice-President
   Ottawa Branch
   615 Booth St., Ottawa ON K1A 0E6
   Tel: 613-995-5249
   Chief Officer(s):

Kian Fadaie, Vice-President
Kian.Fadaie@dfo-mpo.gc.ca
Pacific Branch
9860 West Saanich Rd., Sidney BC V8L 4B2
Tel: 250-363-6669; *Fax:* 250-363-6323
Chief Officer(s):
Craig Lessels, Vice-President
Craig.Lessels@dfo-mpo.gc.ca
Québec Branch
53, rue St-Germain ouest, Rimouski QC G5L 4B4
Tel: 418-775-0812; *Fax:* 418-775-0654
Chief Officer(s):
Bernard Labrecque, Vice-President
Bernard.labrecque@dfo-mpo.gc.ca

Canadian Hydropower Association (CHA) / Association canadienne de l'hydroélectricité
#1402 - 150 Metcalfe St., Ottawa ON K2P 1P1
Tel: 613-751-6655; *Fax:* 613-751-4465
info@canadahydro.ca
canadahydro.ca
www.linkedin.com/company-beta/1031125
twitter.com/CanadaHydro
www.youtube.com/c/CanadaHydroCaAssociation
Overview: A large national organization founded in 1998
Mission: To provide leadership for the responsible growth & prosperity of the Canadian hydropower industry
Membership: 50; *Fees:* $10 students; $126.63 individuals or universitites; $1,261.94 associations; $1,261.94-247,450 corporations or generators; *Member Profile:* Owners of hydroelectric facilities; Individuals directly or indirectly involved in a Canadian hydroelectric activity
Chief Officer(s):
Jacob Irving, President, 613-751-6655 Ext. 3
jacob@canadahydro.ca
Anne-Raphaëlle Audouin, Manager, 613-751-6655 Ext. 2
anne@canadahydro.ca
Meetings/Conferences:
• 18th Annual Hydropower Forum 2018, 2018
Scope: National

Canadian Hypnosis Association (CHA)
121 Wallis St., Parksville BC V9P 1K7
Tel: 250-248-0480
www.canadianhypnosisassociation.ca
Previous Name: Canadian Hypnotherapy Association
Overview: A small national organization founded in 1977
Mission: To determine standards for hypnotherapy in Canada & to promote the therapeutic value of hypnosis
Finances: *Funding Sources:* Fees
Membership: *Fees:* $100 full member; $35 student; $25 non-practising; *Member Profile:* Training or practising hypnotherapists
Chief Officer(s):
Joe Friede, President

Canadian Hypnotherapy Association *See* Canadian Hypnosis Association

Canadian Ice Carvers' Society / Société des sculpteurs de glace
ON
Tel: 613-836-1798
www.canadianicecarverssociety.com
Previous Name: Ottawa-Hull Ice Carvers' Society
Overview: A small international licensing organization founded in 1987
Mission: To promote mutual friendship & harmony amongst members & to pursue higher social recognition, artistic expression & technical perfection of ice carving through activities such as demonstrations, education & workshops
Finances: *Funding Sources:* Contracts
Membership: *Member Profile:* Knowledge or interest in ice carving
Activities: Winterlude; Crystal Garden - ice carving competition
Chief Officer(s):
Ikuo Kanbayashi, President
ikanbayashi@rogers.com

Canadian Icelandic Horse Federation (CIHF)
c/o Canadian Livestock Records Corporation, 2417 Holly Lane, Ottawa ON K1V 0M7
Tel: 613-731-7110; *Fax:* 613-731-0704
Toll-Free: 877-731-7110
www.cihf.ca
Overview: A small national organization founded in 1979
Mission: To promote & maintain the purity of the Icelandic horse; To keep record of breeding & registration of Icelandic horse under the Canadian National Livestock Record System; To promote the awareness & secure the integrity of purebred Icelandic horses
Member of: European Friends of the Icelandic Horse
Finances: *Funding Sources:* Equipment sales
Membership: 150; *Committees:* Breeding; Education; Membership & Breed Promotion; Multi Media; Sponsorship; Sport; World Championships; Youth
Activities: *Speaker Service:* Yes
Chief Officer(s):
Victoria Stoncius, Vice-President
vicky.stoncius@hotmail.com

Canadian Image Processing & Pattern Recognition Society (CIPPRS) / Association canadienne de traitement d'images et de reconnaissance des formes (ACTIRF)
Dept. of Computer Sciences, Univ. of Western Ontario, Middlesex College 383, London ON N6A 5B7
Tel: 519-661-2111; *Fax:* 519-661-3515
www.cipprs.org
Overview: A medium-sized national organization
Mission: To promote research & development activities in image & signal processing for solving pattern recognition problems.
Affiliation(s): Canadian Information Processing Society
Finances: *Funding Sources:* Conferences; membership fees
Membership: *Fees:* $30 regular; $20 student
Chief Officer(s):
John Barron, Treasurer
barron@csd.uwo.ca
Greg Dudek, President
dudek@cim.dot.mcgill.edu
Awards:
• Distinguished Service Award
• Young Investigator Award

Canadian Imaging Trade Association (CITA) / Association canadienne de l'industrie de l'imagerie
#300, 180 Attwell Dr., Toronto ON M9W 6A9
Tel: 905-602-8877
cita@electrofed.com
www.electrofed.com/cita/
Previous Name: Canadian Photo Video Trade Association
Overview: A medium-sized national organization founded in 1955
Mission: To promote traditional & emerging imaging technologies (manufacturers/importers & distributors of photographic & electronic imaging equipment & sensitized materials)
Finances: *Annual Operating Budget:* $50,000-$100,000; *Funding Sources:* Membership fees
Staff Member(s): 1
Membership: 40 corporate + 5 associate + 7 senior/lifetime; *Fees:* Schedule available; *Member Profile:* Actively involved in manufacturing/distribution of photo imaging equipment supplies; *Committees:* Legislation; Industry Statistics; Promotion; Convention
Activities: CITA is part of a special committee that works in conjunction with the Canadian Standards Association to rationalize & simplify specifications of photo & imaging equipment, so that new products may reach the Canadian market more quickly; *Library*
Chief Officer(s):
Dori Gospodaric, General Manager
Awards:
• Dealer of the Year Award
Publications:
• Image Line
Type: Newsletter
Profile: CITA activities

Canadian Importers Association Inc. *See* Canadian Association of Importers & Exporters

Canadian Independent Adjusters' Association (CIAA) / Association canadienne des experts indépendants (ACEI)
Centennial Centre, #100, 5401 Eglinton Ave. West, Toronto ON M9C 5K6
Tel: 416-621-6222; *Fax:* 416-621-7776
Toll-Free: 877-255-5589
info@ciaa-adjusters.ca
www.ciaa-adjusters.ca
Overview: A medium-sized national organization founded in 1953
Mission: To provide leadership for independent adjusters in Canada; To develop & maintain high standards of professionalism; To represent the interests of independent adjusters at the regional, provincial, & national levels
Membership: *Member Profile:* Canadian independent adjusters
Activities: Engaging in advocacy activities; Providing continuing education; Liaising with government, industry, & the public; Offering networking opportunities
Chief Officer(s):
Patricia M. Battle, Executive Director, 416-621-6222, Fax: 416-621-7776
pbattle@ciaa-adjusters.ca
Fred R. Plant, President, 506-853-8507, Fax: 506-853-8501
fred.plant@scm.ca
Heather Matthews, 1st Vice-President, 519-578-5540, Fax: 519-578-2868
Heather.Matthews@crawco.ca
Gary Ellis, 2nd Vice-President, 902-628-9090, Fax: 902-628-9093
gary.ellis@amgclaims.ca
Monica Kuzyk, Secretary, 866-952-2876, Fax: 519-888-9704
mkuzyk@curocanada.com
John Seyler, Treasurer, 905-238-4985, Fax: 905-238-2735
jseyler@integrated-ins.ca
Meetings/Conferences:
• CIAA's 34th Annual General Meeting & Conference, 2018
Scope: National
Publications:
• CIAA [Canadian Independent Adjusters' Association] National Claims Manual
Type: Directory; *Frequency:* Annually; *Accepts Advertising*; *Number of Pages:* 150; *Price:* $45
Profile: Comprehensive resource publication for insurance claims management professionals throughout Canada, featuring sections such as provinciallegal limitation periods, insurance institutes, councils, & superintendents, provincial educational & licensing requirements, & Canadian ICPB offices
• Claims Canada
Type: Journal; *Frequency:* Bimonthly; *Accepts Advertising*; *Editor:* Laura Kupcis
Profile: Incorporating the previously titled magazine, The Canadian Independent Adjuster, the national property & casualty insurance claims & loss magazine interests stakeholders in the insurance claimsmanagement & adjustment process

Canadian Independent Bicycle Retailers Association (CIBRA) / Association canadienne des détaillants de vélos isdépendants (ACDVI)
43 Hanna Ave., Toronto ON M6K 1X1
Tel: 416-427-2870
www.cibra.bike
www.facebook.com/CIBRA.Bike
twitter.com/cibrabike
Previous Name: Bicycle Trade Association of Canada
Overview: A small national organization founded in 2014
Mission: To serve the needs of Canada's independent bike retailers & contribute to the development of the bicycle retail industry as a whole
Finances: *Annual Operating Budget:* $500,000-$1.5 Million; *Funding Sources:* Membership fees; Trade show revenue; Publications revenue
Membership: *Fees:* $197.75 retailer; schedule for suppliers, based upon revenue; *Member Profile:* Independent bicycle retailers, suppliers, distributors, & manufacturers across Canada
Activities: *Rents Mailing List:* Yes
Chief Officer(s):
Kevin Senior, President
Publications:
• SPOKE'n [a publication of the Canadian Independent Bicycle Retailers Association]
Type: Newsletter; *Frequency:* q.
Profile: Features articles, information, news & industry updates

Canadian Independent Film Caucus *See* Documentary Organization of Canada

Canadian Independent Music Association (CIMA)
30 St. Patrick St., 2nd Fl., Toronto ON M5T 3A3
Tel: 416-485-3152
www.cimamusic.ca
www.linkedin.com/company/canadian-independent-music-association
twitter.com/_CIMAmusic

Previous Name: Canadian Independent Record Production Association (CIRPA)
Overview: A medium-sized national organization founded in 1975
Mission: To lobby governments for support & copyright reform; To raise the profile of Canadian music abroad by promoting the industry at international events
Affiliation(s): Canadian Music Industry Database
Finances: *Funding Sources:* Membership dues; Projects; Government subsidies; Corporate sponsors
Staff Member(s): 9
Membership: 375 organizations; *Fees:* Schedule available; *Member Profile:* Canadian-owned companies & representatives involved in music; membership includes record producers, labels, & studios; managers; agents; licensors; video producers & directors; artists; *Committees:* Executive; Finance & Audit; Government Affairs; Ontario Advisory; Music Export Liaison; Talent Selection
Activities: *Internships:* Yes
Chief Officer(s):
Stuart Johnston, President, 416-485-3152 Ext. 232
stuart@cimamusic.ca
Donna Murphy, Vice-President, Operations, 416-485-3152 Ext. 225
donna@cimamusic.ca
Lisa Fiorilli, Coordinator, Research & Communications, 416-485-3152 Ext. 223
lisa@cimamusic.ca

Canadian Independent Record Production Association (CIRPA) *See* Canadian Independent Music Association

Canadian Independent Telephone Association (CITA) / Association canadienne du téléphone indépendant
c/o Creative Events Management, #205, 1402 Queen St. West, Alton ON L7K 0C3
Tel: 519-940-0935; *Fax:* 519-940-1137
www.cita.ca
Overview: A medium-sized national organization founded in 1905
Mission: To promote the increase & improvement of telephone service in Canada; to promote & protect the common business interest of members; to produce & distribute literature; to represent the industry before regulatory bodies, either federal or provincial.
Finances: *Funding Sources:* Membership fees; showcase
Membership: 29 + 100 associate; *Fees:* Schedule available; *Member Profile:* Independant phone companies; Telephone equipment & service providers
Chief Officer(s):
Margi Taylor, General Manager, 519-940-0935
mhtaylor@allstream.net

Canadian Indigenous Nurses Association (CINA)
50 Driveway, Ottawa ON K2P 1E2
Tel: 613-724-4677
info@anac.on.ca
www.indigenousnurses.ca
twitter.com/aboriginalnurse
Previous Name: Aboriginal Nurses Association of Canada; Indian & Inuit Nurses of Canada
Overview: A large national charitable organization founded in 1974
Mission: To work with & on behalf of Aboriginal nurses to promote the development & practice of Aboriginal nursing in order to improve the health of Aboriginal people
Member of: Canadian Nurses Association
Affiliation(s): Health Canada; Canadian Nurses Association
Membership: 100-499; *Fees:* $60 regular; $20 student; $120 organization subscription; *Member Profile:* Regular - registered nurses with Aboriginal ancestry; Associate - health care workers, non-Aboriginal registered nurses & LPNs; Student - any full-time student of nursing
Activities: Recruiting; Supporting members; Consulting; Researching; Educating; *Awareness Events:* Aboriginal Nurses Day, May 13; *Library*
Chief Officer(s):
Lisa Bourque-Bearskin, President
Ada Roberts, Vice-President
Meetings/Conferences:
• Canadian Indigenous Nurses Association 2018 Annual General Meeting, 2018
Scope: National
Publications:
• The Aboriginal Nurse [a publication of the Canadian Indigenous Nurses Association]
Type: Newsletter; *Frequency:* 3 pa; *Accepts Advertising; Editor:* Connie Toulouse; *Price:* Free with membership in the Aboriginal Nurses Association of Canada

Canadian Industrial Relations Association *Voir* Association canadienne des relations industrielles

Canadian Industrial Transportation Association *See* Freight Management Association of Canada

Canadian Infectious Disease Society *See* Association of Medical Microbiology & Infectious Disease Canada

Canadian Information Centre for International Credentials (CICIC) / Centre d'information canadien sur les diplômes internationaux
#1106, 95 St. Clair Ave. West, Toronto ON M4V 1N6
Tel: 416-962-9725; *Fax:* 416-962-2800
www.cicic.ca
www.linkedin.com/company/cicic---cicdi
www.facebook.com/CICIC.CICDI
twitter.com/CICIC_CICDI
Also Known As: CICDI
Overview: A medium-sized national organization founded in 1990 overseen by Council Of Ministers Of Education, Canada
Mission: To collect, organize, & distribute information; To act as a national clearinghouse & referral service; To support the recognition & portability of Canadian & international educational & occupational qualifications
Member of: Enic-Naric Networks; Imagine Education in Canada

Canadian Information Processing Society (CIPS) / L'Association canadienne de l'informatique (ACI)
National Office, #801, 5090 Explorer Dr., Mississauga ON L4W 4T9
Tel: 905-602-1370; *Fax:* 905-602-7884
Toll-Free: 877-275-2477
info@cips.ca
www.cips.ca
www.linkedin.com/groups/71785/profile
www.facebook.com/187610094599781
twitter.com/cips
Overview: A large national charitable organization founded in 1958
Mission: To define & foster the IT profession; To encourage & support the IT practitioner; To advance the theory & practice of IT, while safeguarding the public interest
Member of: International Federation for Information Processing; Institute for Certification of Computer Professionals; South Asian Regional Computer Confederation
Affiliation(s): British Computer Society; Australian Computer Society; Association for Computing Machinery
Membership: 6,000; *Fees:* Schedule available; *Member Profile:* Open to business people, scientists, educators & others who make their careers in information technology (IT)
Activities: Awarding the Information Systems Professional of Canada (I.S.P.) designation
Chief Officer(s):
Jon Nightingale, Chair, Governance Committee
Awards:
• GALA Award
• C.C. Gotlieb CIPS Contribution Award
• Goodfellow Award
The highest award available to CIPS members, awarded to those who have made an outstanding contribution to CIPS & to information processing in Canada
• Marilyn Harris IT Professionalism Award
For members who are recognized by their peers for their integrity & expertise, for their outstanding achievements in fields related to information processing, & who have a high degree of competence in their field
• Gary Hadford Professional Achievement Award
Alberta Chapter
PO Box 21085, #202, 5405 - 99th St. NW, Edmonton AB T6E 3N8
Tel: 780-431-9311; *Fax:* 780-413-0076
Toll-Free: 844-431-9311
alberta@cips.ca
ab.cips.ca
Chief Officer(s):
Shauna Prokopchuk, Association Manager
British Columbia Chapter
#102, 211 Columbia St., Vancouver BC V6A 2R5
Tel: 604-681-2796; *Fax:* 604-681-4545
bc@cips.ca
bc.cips.ca
Chief Officer(s):
Jude Pillainayagam, President
Manitoba Chapter
PO Box 2610, Winnipeg MB R3C 4B3
manitoba@cips.ca
mb.cips.ca
Chief Officer(s):
Linda Hunter, President
Newfoundland & Labrador Chapter
PO Box 21053, St. John's NL A1A 5B2
nl@cips.ca
nl.cips.ca
Chief Officer(s):
Cheryl Lundrigan, President
Nova Scotia Chapter
PO Box 1612, Stn. Halifax Central, Halifax NS B3J 2Y3
cipsns@cips.ca
ns.cips.ca
Chief Officer(s):
Jim Nicoll, Secretary
Ontario Chapter
cipsontario.ca
Réseau Action TI
Tour ouest, #355, 550, rue Sherbrooke ouest, Montréal QC H3A 1B9
Tél: 514-840-1240
info@actionti.com
www.actionti.com
www.linkedin.com/groups/90428
www.facebook.com/ActionTI
twitter.com/ActionTI
Chief Officer(s):
Louis Dagenais, Président
Saskatchewan Chapter
PO Box 20073, Stn. Cornwall Center, Regina SK S4P 4J7
Tel: 306-352-1392
saskatchewan@cips.ca
sk.cips.ca
Chief Officer(s):
Shaun Herron, President
• Canadian Information Processing Society Saskatchewan Chapter Annual Report
Type: Report; *Frequency:* Annually

Canadian Injured Workers Alliance (CIWA) / L'Alliance canadienne des victimes d'accidents et de maladies du travail (ACVAMT)
1201 Jasper Dr., Thunder Bay ON P7B 6R2
Tel: 807-345-3429; *Fax:* 807-344-8683
Toll-Free: 877-787-7010
ciwa@tbaytel.net
www.ciwa.ca
Overview: A medium-sized national organization founded in 1990
Mission: To support & strengthen the work of local & provincial groups by providing a forum for exchanging information & experiences
Finances: *Annual Operating Budget:* $100,000-$250,000
Staff Member(s): 3; 20 volunteer(s)
Membership: 100-499; *Member Profile:* Provincial injured workers organizations
Activities: Offering conferences & workshops; Providing leadership training; Conducting a survey on the re-employment of injured workers; Engaging in research; *Speaker Service:* Yes; *Library:* Resource Centre; Not open to public
Chief Officer(s):
Bill Chedore, National Coordinator, 905-517-1718
basev@hotmail.com
Publications:
• Highlights [a publication of the Canadian Injured Workers Alliance]
Type: Newsletter; *Frequency:* Quarterly; *Price:* $5 injured worker & unemployed; $10 individual; $15 organization
Profile: Information about provincial & national developments, government policies, & CIWA projects for injured workers' groups

Canadian Innovation Centre (CIC)
c/o Waterloo Research & Technology Park, #15, 295 Hagey Blvd., Waterloo ON N2L 6R5
Tel: 519-885-5870; *Fax:* 519-513-2421
Toll-Free: 800-265-4559
info@innovationcentre.ca
www.innovationcentre.ca

Canadian Associations / The Canadian Institute (CI) / L'Institut canadien

www.linkedin.com/company/canadian-innovation-centre
twitter.com/innovationctre
Overview: A medium-sized national organization founded in 1981
Mission: To advance innovation by helping our clients make better business decisions through information, education & commercialization.
Staff Member(s): 10
Activities: *Library:* by appointment
Chief Officer(s):
Ted Cross, Chair
Josie Graham, CEO & Director, Projects and Studies
Awards:
• Market Research Services
Assists individuals & established companies in commercializing their technologies & business ventures; will conduct preliminary & detailed market research, evaluate commercial potential, manage development & testing, assist in venture planning, provide training & education programs, & promote international technologies available for license *Eligibility:* Individual entrepreneurs, inventors/innovators & small businesses
• The Inventor's Assistance Program
Provides an objective evaluation of a new idea which considers technical feasibility, available legal protection & market competition *Eligibility:* Individual entrepreneurs, inventors/innovators or small businesses

Canadian Insolvency Practitioners Association *See*
Canadian Association of Insolvency & Restructuring Professionals

The Canadian Institute (CI) / L'Institut canadien
1329 Bay St., Toronto ON M5R 2C4
Tel: 416-927-7936; *Fax:* 416-927-1563
Toll-Free: 877-927-7936
customerservice@canadianinstitute.com
www.canadianinstitute.com
Overview: A small national organization
Mission: To monitor trends in public policy, the law, & major industry sectors; To provide business intelligence for Canadian decision-makers
Affiliation(s): American Conference Institute (New York); C5 (London, UK)
Finances: *Funding Sources:* Sponsorships; Conference fees
Activities: Organizing conferences, executive briefings, & summits for senior delegates; Publishing materials for conferences

Canadian Institute for Advanced Research (CIFAR) / Institut canadien de recherches avancées (ICRA)
#1400, 180 Dundas St. West, Toronto ON M5G 1Z8
Tel: 416-971-4251; *Fax:* 416-971-6169
Toll-Free: 888-738-1113
info@cifar.ca
www.ciar.ca
www.linkedin.com/company/canadian-institute-for-advanced-research
www.facebook.com/CIFAR
twitter.com/cifar_news
Overview: A medium-sized national organization founded in 1982
Mission: To stimulate leading-edge research projects vital to Canada's future prosperity.
Staff Member(s): 14
Membership: 400
Activities: Programs in cosmology, superconductivity, evolutionary biology, population health, human development, earth system evolution, the science of soft surfaces & interfaces, economic growth, nanoelectronics
Chief Officer(s):
Alan Bernstein, President/CEO, 416-971-4255
abernstein@cifar.ca

Canadian Institute for Child & Adolescent Psychoanalytic Psychotherapy (CICAPP)
17 Saddletree Trail, Brampton ON L6X 4M5
Tel: 416-690-5464; *Fax:* 416-690-2746
info@cicapp.ca
www.cicapp.ca
Previous Name: Toronto Child Psychoanalytic Program
Overview: A small national organization founded in 1981
Mission: To provide training in psychodynamic child therapy; to foster the growth of the profession in Canada; to have input in shaping government policies; to promote ongoing research in child psychotherapy
Membership: 55; **Fees:** $215
Chief Officer(s):
Suzanne Pearen, Administrator
suzanne_pearen@rogers.com

Canadian Institute for Conflict Resolution (CICR) / Institut canadien pour la résolution des conflits
c/o St. Paul University, 223 Main St., Ottawa ON K1S 1C4
Tel: 613-235-5800; *Fax:* 613-235-5801
Toll-Free: 866-684-2427
info@cicr-icrc.ca
www.cicr-icrc.ca
Overview: A medium-sized national charitable organization founded in 1988
Mission: To foster, develop & communicate resolution processes for individuals, organizations & communities in Canada & internationally; to embody, within the conflict resolution process, the positive attributes of common sense, sensitivity, compassion & spirituality.
Activities: Works with a number of community organizations in areas such as community mediation training & conflict resolution processes, addressing such issues as multiculturalism, race relations & community relations; provides hands-on workshops
Chief Officer(s):
Brian Strom, Executive Director

Canadian Institute for Energy Training (CIET) / Institut canadien de formation de l'énergie
#5600, 100 King St. West, Toronto ON M5X 1C9
Tel: 647-255-3107
Toll-Free: 800-461-7618
info@cietcanada.com
www.cietcanada.com
Overview: A medium-sized national organization founded in 1994
Mission: To focus on the advancement of energy efficiency in industrial, commercial & public sector organizations; To provide effective training solutions for the incorporation of energy management into organizational management priorities
Finances: *Funding Sources:* Fees for service
Activities: Offers the following training courses: Certified Energy Manager (CEM); Certified Measurement & Verification Professional (CMVP); Certified Energy Auditor (CEA); Certified Building Commissioning Professional (CBCP); Certified Professional in Energy Performance Contracting (CIET); Building Operator Certification (BOC); Certified in the Use of RETScreen; International Energy Efficiency Financing Protocol (IEEFP); ISO 50001 Standard Implementation; and more
Chief Officer(s):
Douglas Tripp, President

Canadian Institute for Health Information (CIHI) / Institut canadien d'information sur la santé (ICIS)
#600, 495 Richmond Rd., Ottawa ON K2A 4H6
Tel: 613-241-7860; *Fax:* 613-241-8120
Other Communication: help@cihi.ca
communications@cihi.ca
www.cihi.ca
www.facebook.com/141785889231388
twitter.com/CIHI_ICIS
www.youtube.com/user/CIHICanada
Overview: A small national organization founded in 1994
Mission: To collect, analyze, & provide information about the health system in Canada & the health of Canadians; To support persons who use data for health & health-services research
Finances: *Funding Sources:* Federal, provincial, & territorial governments
Activities: Maintaining health databases, measurements, & standards; Developing reports; Raising awareness about services; *Speaker Service:* Yes
Chief Officer(s):
David O'Toole, President & Chief Executive Officer, 613-694-6500
dotoole@cihi.ca
Brent Diverty, Vice-President, Programs, 613-694-6501
BDiverty@cihi.ca
Anne McFarlane, Vice-President, Western Canada & Developmental Initiatives, 250-220-2211
AMcFarlane@cihi.ca
Louise Ogilvie, Vice-President, Corporate Services, 613-694-6503
LOgilvie@cihi.caca
Jeremy Veillard, Vice-President, Research & Analysis, 416-549-5361
JVeillard@cihi.ca
Publications:
• Canadian Institute for Health Information Annual Report
Type: Yearbook; *Frequency:* Annually
• CIHI [Canadian Institute for Health Information] Directions ICIS [Institut canadien d'information sur la santé]
Type: Newsletter; *ISSN:* 1201-0383
CIHI Montréal
#300, 1010, rue Sherbrooke ouest, Montréal QC H3A 2R7
Tel: 514-842-2226; *Fax:* 514-842-3996
Chief Officer(s):
Caroline Heick, Executive Director, Ontario and Quebec, 416-549-5517
CHeick@cihi.ca
CIHI St. John's
#701, 140 Water St., St. John's NL A1C 6H6
Tel: 709-576-7006; *Fax:* 709-576-0952
Chief Officer(s):
Stephen O'Reilly, Executive Director, Atlantic Canada, 709-733-7064
SOReilly@cihi.ca
CIHI Toronto
#300, 4110 Yonge St., Toronto ON M2P 2B7
Tel: 416-481-2002; *Fax:* 416-481-2950
Chief Officer(s):
Caroline Heick, Executive Director, Ontario and Quebec, 416-549-5517
CHeick@cihi.ca
CIHI Victoria
#600, 880 Douglas St., Victoria BC V8W 2B7
Tel: 250-220-4100; *Fax:* 250-220-7090

Canadian Institute for Historical Microreproductions *See* Canadiana

Canadian Institute for Jewish Research (CIJR) / Institut canadien de recherche sur le Judaïsme (ICRJ)
PO Box 175, Stn. H, Montréal QC H3G 2K7
Tel: 514-486-5544; *Fax:* 514-486-8284
cijr@isranet.org
www.isranet.org
www.facebook.com/162536567136089
twitter.com/cijr
Overview: A small national charitable organization founded in 1988
Mission: To increase public understanding of Jewish Israel & general Jewish world issues
Activities: Bringing up-to-date informtion about Jewish world-related issues to Jewish & non-Jewish communities, the media, & students; Maintaining the Middle East & Jewish World Databank, an archive of Jewish, Israel, & Middle East materials; Presenting regular Insider Briefing seminars & Community Colloquia
Chief Officer(s):
Jack Kincler, National Chair
Baruch Cohen, Research Chair
Frederick Krantz, Director
Ira Robinson, Associate Director
Publications:
• Canadian Institute for Jewish Research Daily Isranet Briefing
Type: Newsletter; *Frequency:* Daily; *Price:* Free with membership in the Canadian Institute for Jewish Research
Profile: Current issues affecting Jewish people, read by more than 60,00 people around the world
• Communiqué Isranet
Type: Newsletter; *Frequency:* Weekly; *Price:* Free with membership in the Canadian Institute for Jewish Research
Profile: Articles, documents, & opinion pieces about current issues impacting Jewish people
• Dateline: Middle East
Type: Magazine; *Price:* Free with membership in the Canadian Institute for Jewish Research
Profile: A magazine for students
• Israfax
Type: Magazine; *Frequency:* Quarterly; *Editor:* Frederick Krantz; *Price:* Free with membership in the Canadian Institute forJewish Research
Profile: Articles from international newspapers, journals, magazines, documents, & websites collected & distributed throughout Canada & around the globe

Canadian Institute for Mediterranean Studies (CIMS) / Institut canadien d'études méditerranéennes
c/o Carr Hall, Department of Italian Studies, University of Toronto, 100 St. Joseph St., Toronto ON M5S 1J4
sites.utoronto.ca/cims
Merged from: Society for Mediterranean Studies; Canadian Mediterranean Institute

Overview: A medium-sized national charitable organization founded in 1996
Mission: To study all aspects of Mediterranean culture & civilization, past & present
Finances: *Funding Sources:* Membership fees; Donations
Membership: *Fees:* Schedule available; *Member Profile:* Scholars interested in Mediterranean studies; Persons with an interest in the Mediterranean world
Activities: Facilitating research; Organizing public lectures; Sponsoring international interdisciplinary conferences
Chief Officer(s):
Mario Crespi, Executive Director
mario.crespi@utoronto.ca
Publications:
• Canadian Institute for Mediterranean Studies Bulletin
Type: Newsletter; *Frequency:* Semiannually; *Price:* Free with Canadian Institute for Mediterranean Studies membership
Profile: Canadian Institute for Mediterranean Studies activities
• Scripta Mediterranea
Type: Journal; *Frequency:* Annually; *Price:* Free with Canadian Institute for Mediterranean Studies membership
Profile: Refereed scholarly journal, with articles & reviews on all aspects of Mediterranean culture & civilization, past & present

Ottawa
Desmarais Building, University of Ottawa, #1160, 55 Laurier Ave. East, Ottawa ON K1N 6N5
Tel: 819-684-8768
cimsottawa@gmail.com
Chief Officer(s):
Louise Terrillon-Mackay, President

Canadian Institute for NDE
135 Fennell Ave. West, Hamilton ON L8N 3T2
Tel: 905-387-1655; *Fax:* 905-574-6080
Toll-Free: 800-964-9488
info@cinde.ca
www.cinde.ca
www.facebook.com/297023083473
Also Known As: CINDE
Merged from: Canadian Society for Nondestructive Testing; NDE Institute of Canada
Overview: A medium-sized national organization founded in 1964
Mission: To advance scientific, engineering, technical knowledge in the field of nondestructive testing; To gather & disseminate information relating to nondestructive testing useful to individuals & beneficial to the general public; To promote nondestructive testing through courses of instruction, lectures, meetings, publications, conferences, etc.
Member of: NDE Institute of Canada
Finances: *Annual Operating Budget:* $100,000-$250,000
Staff Member(s): 1
Membership: 50 corporate + 20 associate + 20 student + 20 senior/lifetime + 1,000 individual + 50 subscriptions; *Fees:* $60 individual; $160 sustaining; $475 corporate; *Committees:* Finance & Audit; Governance; Long Range Planning; Member Services; Nomination & Awards
Chief Officer(s):
Glenn Tubrett, Chief Executive Officer
g.tubrett@cinde.ca
Publications:
• CINDE [Canadian Institute for NDE] Journal
Type: Journal; *Frequency:* Bimonthly; *Accepts Advertising*; *Price:* Free with Canadian Institute for NDE membership; $80 Canada; $110 USA; $135 overseas
Profile: Canadian Institute for NDE chapter reports, conferences, members, & board of directors, industry & international news, business directory, & new products supplies & services

Canadian Institute for Neutron Scattering (CINS)
Bldg. 459, Station 18, Canadian Neutron Beam Centre, Chalk River Labs, Chalk River ON K0J 1J0
Tel: 613-584-8297; *Fax:* 613-584-4040
www.cins.ca
Overview: A small international organization
Mission: To advance neutron scattering research; To promote the neutron scattering in science & technology
Membership: 400; *Member Profile:* Persons interested in neutron scattering research from government, academia, & industry; Graduate students
Activities: Providing educational activities
Chief Officer(s):
Dominic Ryan, President
dhryan@physics.mcgill.ca
Niki Schrie, Secretary-Treasurer
Niki.Schrie@nrc-cnrc.gc.ca

Canadian Institute for Radiation Safety *See* Radiation Safety Institute of Canada

Canadian Institute for Research in Nondestructive Examination (CINDE)
135 Fennell Ave. West, Hamilton ON L8N 3T2
Tel: 905-387-1655; *Fax:* 905-574-6080
Toll-Free: 800-964-9488
www.cinde.ca
www.facebook.com/297023083473
Also Known As: Canadian Institute for NDE
Overview: A small national organization
Mission: To foster, coordinate & disseminate results of research, development & application of new or advanced NDE techniques in Canada; to promote technology transfer by encouraging collaboration between universities, research organizations & industrial or governmental users; to raise the profile of NDE research in Canada by publicizing the need for & economic benefits arising from advances in NDE
Membership: 100; *Member Profile:* Open to applied scientists & engineers who have a professional interest in conductor application of research in NDE
Activities: *Rents Mailing List:* Yes
Chief Officer(s):
Larry Cote, President and CEO, 905-387-1655 Ext. 225
l.cote@cinde.ca

Canadian Institute for the Administration of Justice (CIAJ) / Institut canadien d'administration de la justice (ICAJ)
Faculté de droit, Univ. de Montréal, PO Box 6128, Stn. Centre-Ville, #A3421, 3101, chemin de la Tour, Montréal QC H3C 3J7
Tel: 514-343-6157; *Fax:* 514-343-6296
ciaj@ciaj-icaj.ca
www.ciaj-icaj.ca
www.linkedin.com/groups?about=&gid=4113891
www.facebook.com/ciaj.icaj
twitter.com/ciaj_icaj
Overview: A medium-sized national charitable organization founded in 1974
Mission: To improve the quality of justice for all Canadians
Finances: *Annual Operating Budget:* $100,000-$250,000; *Funding Sources:* Membership fees
Staff Member(s): 5
Membership: 1,678; *Fees:* $10 student; $75 retired; $150 individual; *Member Profile:* Anyone interested in the administration of justice; *Committees:* Administrative Tribunals; Communications; Court Administration; Criminal Law Reform Task Force; Education; Executive; Finance & Fundraising; International Initiatives; Membership; Nominations; Research
Chief Officer(s):
Michèle Moreau, Executive Director
Donna Ventress, Coordinator, Publications & Communications
Meetings/Conferences:
• Canadian Institute for the Administration of Justice 2018 Annual Conference, October, 2018, Westin Ottawa, Ottawa, ON
Scope: National
Description: Theme: "Justice & Mental Health"
Publications:
• CIAJ [Canadian Institute for the Administration of Justice] Newsletter
Type: Newsletter; *Frequency:* Irregular
Profile: CIIAJ information, conferences, events & awards, legislative information

Canadian Institute for the Relief of Pain & Disability (CIRPD)
National Office, #204, 916 West Broadway, Vancouver BC V5Z 1K7
Tel: 604-684-4148; *Fax:* 604-684-6247
Toll-Free: 800-872-3105
admin@cirpd.org
www.cirpd.org
www.linkedin.com/groups/Canadian-Institute-Relief-Pain-Disability-2262962
www.facebook.com/CIRPD
twitter.com/cirpd
www.youtube.com/user/cirpdadmin
Previous Name: Physical Medicine Research Foundation
Overview: A small national charitable organization founded in 1985
Mission: To improve diagnosis & treatment for pain sufferers; To prevent & reduce pain & disability & improve the quality of life for people who suffer from muscle & joint pain
Affiliation(s): Canadian Cochrane Centre

Finances: *Annual Operating Budget:* $250,000-$500,000; *Funding Sources:* Donations
Staff Member(s): 5
Membership: *Fees:* $12 people with chronic pain; $75 individual/organization; *Committees:* Nominations
Activities: Offering educational & research programs; Disseminating evidence-informed best practices; Establishing regional & international health care committees to bring together academics & clinicians from all health care disciplines to prevent & reduce disability; *Library:* Canadian Institute for the Relief of Pain & Disability Library
Chief Officer(s):
Marc I. White, Executive Director
Adrienne Hook, President
William Dyer, Secretary
Janette Lyons, Treasurer
Awards:
• Woodbridge Grants & Awards Program
Categories include traffic & auto engineering related research; diagnosis & treatment related research; & disability prevention related research *Contact:* Dr. Jack Richman, Research Chair, Phone: 905-678-2924
Publications:
• Canadian Institute for the Relief of Pain & Disability Annual Report
Type: Yearbook; *Frequency:* Annually

Canadian Institute for Theatre Technology (CITT) / L'Institut Canadien des Technologies Scénographiques (ICTS)
#404, 4529, rue Clark, Montréal QC H2T 2T3
Tel: 514-504-9998; *Fax:* 514-504-9997
Toll-Free: 888-271-3383
info@citt.org
www.citt.org
www.facebook.com/CITTICTS
twitter.com/CITTICTS
Overview: A small national organization founded in 1990
Mission: To work for the betterment of the Canadian live performance community; To promote safe & ethical work practices
Affiliation(s): United States Institute for Theatre Technology (USITT); l'Organisation Internationale des Scénographes, Techniciens et Architectes de Théâtre / International Organization of Scenographers, Theatre Architects, & Technicians
Membership: *Member Profile:* Theatre consultants & architects; Managers; Designers; Manufacturers; Suppliers; Technicians; Educators; Students; *Committees:* Annual Conference Programming; Finance; Fundraising; Membership Recruitment & Retention; Nomination
Activities: Encouraging industry standards; Engaging in advocacy activities; Promoting research; Organizing professional development activities for members; Offering networking opportunities; Recognizing excellent work
Chief Officer(s):
Adam Mitchell, President
Monique Corbeil, National Coordinator
Awards:
• Dieter Penzhorn Memorial Award (for significant service to CITT / ICTS)
• CITT / ICTS Educational Achievement Award
• The Ron Epp Memorial Award for Professional Achievement
• CITT / ICTS Supplier (Corporate) Achievement Award
• CITT / ICTS Award of Technical Merit
• The Honorary Membership Award
Meetings/Conferences:
• Canadian Institute for Theatre Technology Rendez-vous 2018 Annual Conference & Trade Show, August, 2018, St Catharines, ON
Scope: National
Publications:
• Canadian Institute for Theatre Technology Annual Report & Annual General Meeting Minutes
Type: Yearbook; *Frequency:* Annually
• Canadian Institute for Theatre Technology / L'Institut Canadien des Technologies Scénographiques Member Directory
Type: Directory
Profile: List of members by name, province, & caucus
• Stageworks
Type: Newsletter; *Accepts Advertising*
Profile: News from the national office & the International Organization of Scenographers, Theatre Architects, & Technicians, plus awards information

Canadian Associations / Canadian Institute in Greece (CIG)

Alberta Section
AB
alberta@citt.org
www.citt-alberta.org
Chief Officer(s):
Kevin Humphrey, Chair
Josh Gennings, Secretary
Mark Belkie, Treasurer
• Behind the Scene [a publication of the Canadian Institute for Theatre Technology, Alberta Section]
Type: Newsletter
Profile: Information & upcoming events from the Alberta Section of the Canadian Institute for Theatre Technology

Atlantic Region Section
atlantic@citt.org
www.citt.org/atlantic.html
Jim Wilson, Section Committe Member, New Brunswick
Karl Simmons, Section Committe Member, Newfoundland & Labrador

British Columbia Section
BC
bc@citt.org
www.citt.org/british_columbia.html
Chief Officer(s):
Jim Dobbs, Chair
Matt Frankish, Vice-Chair
Ace Martens, Secretary
Colin MacDuff, Treasurer

Ontario Section
PO Box 72051, 1630 Danforth Ave., Toronto ON M4C 1H0
ontario@citt.org
www.citt.org/ontario.html
Chief Officer(s):
Sharon Secord, Chair
James McKernan, Secretary
Victor Svenningson, Treasurer

Québec Section (CQICTS)
PO Box 85041, 345, boul Laurier, Mont-Saint-Hilaire QC J3H 5W1
cqicts@citt.org
www.citt.org/quebec.html
www.facebook.com/CITTICTS
Mission: To contribute to the development of the theatre technology sector in Québec; To promote excellence in theatre technology
Member of: Quebec Council of Human Resources & Culture
Chief Officer(s):
Michel Desbiens, Chair
Martin Saintonge, Vice-Chair
Monique Corbeil, Secretary
Gilles Benoist, Treasurer

Canadian Institute in Greece (CIG)
Dionysiou Aiginitou 7, Athens GR-115 28 Greece
Tel: 30-210-722-3201; *Fax:* 30-210-725-7968
info@cig-icg.gr
www.cig-icg.gr
www.facebook.com/pages/The-Canadian-Institute-in-Greece/173666819462
twitter.com/CIGICG
www.youtube.com/channel/UCFJEoGzs3NPPdo-2qa1vNKA
Previous Name: Canadian Academic Institute in Athens
Overview: A small international organization founded in 1974
Mission: To promote academic & cultural exchanges between Canada & Greece; to serve the needs of Canadian scholars in Greece
Staff Member(s): 4
Membership: *Fees:* Schedule available; *Member Profile:* People interested in Greek history; *Committees:* Fellowship; Libray; Permits; Publications; Bulletin
Chief Officer(s):
David W. Rupp, Director
drupp@cig-icg.gr

Canadian Institute of Actuaries (CIA) / Institut canadien des actuaires (ICA)
Secretariat, #1740, 360 Albert St., Ottawa ON K1R 7X7
Tel: 613-236-8196; *Fax:* 613-233-4552
head.office@cia-ica.ca
www.cia-ica.ca
twitter.com/CIA_Actuaries
Overview: A large national organization founded in 1965
Mission: To set & ensure educational & professional standards for members; To operate a review & disciplinary system; To maintain liaison with government authorities & other professions & organizations; To promote research
Membership: *Fees:* $1,280 fellow; $1,087 associate (5 years or more); $375 associate (less than 5 years), affiliate & correspondent; *Member Profile:* Actuaries who meet policy on education & work experience requirements
Activities: Engaging in advocacy activities; Sponsoring programs for the education of members; Library
Chief Officer(s):
Michel C. Simard, Executive Director
executive.director@cia-ica.ca
Lynn Blackburn, Director, Professional Practice & Volunteer Services
lynn.blackburn@cia-ica.ca
Les Dandridge, Director, Communications & Public Affairs
les.dandridge@cia-ica.ca
Jacques Leduc, Director, Operations, Finance, & Administration
jacques.leduc@cia-ica.ca
Alicia Rollo, Director, Membership, Education & Professional Development
alicia.rollo@cia-ica.ca
Meetings/Conferences:
• Canadian Institute of Actuaries 2018 Annual Meeting, June, 2018, Toronto, ON
Scope: National
Publications:
• (e)Bulletin: The Monthly Newsletter of the CIA [Canadian Institute of Actuaries]
Type: E-Newsletter; *Frequency:* Monthly
Profile: Institute news & announcements

Canadian Institute of Biotechnology; Industrial Biotechnology Association of Canada *See* BIOTECanada

Canadian Institute of Bookkeeping (CIB)
PO Box 963, 31 Adelaide St. East, Toronto ON M5C 2K3
Tel: 416-925-9420; *Fax:* 416-929-8815
info@cibcb.com
www.cibcb.com
Overview: A small national organization
Mission: To promote the advancement of certified bookkeepers; To prepare persons for professional positions in a financial environment; To establish educational, ethical, & professional standards in the bookkeeping profession; To protect the public
Finances: *Funding Sources:* Membership fees
Membership: *Fees:* $50 enrolment fee; $240 certified bookkeeper; $192 associate; $156 student; *Member Profile:* Individuals working in the bookkeeping / accounting field, who have completed Level I & Level II of the academic program; Students, who are completing the academic & experience requirements to become certified
Activities: Enforcing the Code of Professional Conduct of CIB; Providing the CIB professional development program; Raising public awareness of certified bookkeepers
Publications:
• Canadian Institute of Bookkeeping Newsletter
Type: Newsletter; *Frequency:* Quarterly; *Price:* Free to members of the Canadian Institute of Bookkeeping
Profile: Information from the Institute

Canadian Institute of Chartered Business Planners (CICBP)
#210, 1117 First St. SW, Calgary AB T2R 0T9
Tel: 403-457-5144; *Fax:* 403-457-5133
Other Communication: Alternate E-mail: admin@cicbp.ca
info@cicbp.ca
www.cicbp.ca
Overview: A small national organization
Mission: To ensure high standards of practice & professionalism in business planning; To represent & protect the profession; To protect the public interest
Membership: *Member Profile:* Business planning professionals from across Canada; Members, who meet requirements, are entitled to use the designation, Chartered Business Planner (CBP); Students enrolled in the Institute's program or other programs accredited by the Institute
Activities: Training & certifying business planning professionals; Providing professional development opportunities; Promoting the specialized profession of business planning
Publications:
• Business Planning Review
Frequency: Semiannually
Profile: Articles & papers on business planning
• The Chartered Business Planner
Type: Newsletter; *Frequency:* Quarterly
Profile: Institute activities & members announcements

Canadian Institute of Chartered Business Valuators (CICBV) / L'Institut canadien des experts en évaluation d'entreprises
#710, 277 Wellington St. West, Toronto ON M5V 3H2
Tel: 416-977-1117; *Fax:* 416-977-7066
Toll-Free: 866-770-7315
admin@cicbv.ca
cicbv.ca
Previous Name: Canadian Association of Business Valuators (CABV)
Overview: A medium-sized national licensing organization founded in 1971
Mission: To develop high professional standards for Canadian Chartered Business Valuators; To manage the Chartered Business Valuator (CBV) designation; To govern members of the Institute with a strict Code of Ethics & Practice Standards
Staff Member(s): 8
Membership: 1,700+; *Fees:* $860; *Member Profile:* Chartered Business Valuators in Canada, who work in the areas of corporate finance, securities valuation, disputes, & compliance; *Committees:* Accreditation/Membership; Audit; Awards; Communications; Conduct & Discipline; Continuing Education; Education; Executive; FCBV/LIFE Membership Selection; International; Nominating; Professional Practice & Standards; Publications; Research Institute; Strategic Planning; Liaison; Workshops
Activities: Offering professional development opportunities; Developing programs to test members; Encouraging research; Facilitating the exchange of ideas; Promoting the profession of business valuations; *Library:* Canadian Institute of Chartered Business Valuators Library
Chief Officer(s):
Mary Jane Andrews, President & CEO
maryjane.andrews@cicbv.ca
Bob Boulton, Director, Education & Standards
robert.boulton@cicbv.ca
Isabel Natale, Coordinator, Program
isabel.natale@cicbv.ca
Megan Rousseau, Manager, Communications
megan.rousseau@cicbv.ca
Deborah Pelle Hanlon, Manager, Events
deborah.hanlon@cicbv.ca
Judith Roth, Manager, Information Technology & Member Services
judith.roth@cicbv.ca
Publications:
• The Business Valuator [a publication of the Canadian Institute of Chartered Business Valuators]
Type: Newsletter; *Frequency:* Quarterly
Profile: CICBV's activities, members, & students
• Canadian Institute of Chartered Business Valuators Handbook
Frequency: Annually
Profile: CICBV's by-laws, code of ethics, practice standards, policies, & member list
• Canadian Institute of Chartered Business Valuators Casebook
Profile: Summary of significant legal & tax cases related to valuation
• Canadian Institute of Chartered Business Valuators Bibliography
Profile: Listing of articles & conference papers published by the CICBV
• Canadian Institute of Chartered Business Valuators Annual Report
Type: Yearbook; *Frequency:* Annually
Profile: Summary of the Institute's yearly highlights
• The Journal of Business Valuation [a publication of the Canadian Institute of Chartered Business Valuators]
Type: Journal; *Frequency:* Semiannually
Profile: Articles & papers related to the field of business valutation, plus the proceedings of the Canadian Institute ofChartered Business Valuators' biennial conferences
• The Valuation Law Review [a publication of the Canadian Institute of Chartered Business Valuators]
Frequency: Annually
Profile: Publication consists of corporate securities law, family law, & taxation

Canadian Institute of Child Health (CICH) / Institut canadien de la santé infantile
#300, 384 Bank St., Ottawa ON K2P 1Y4
Tel: 613-230-8838; *Fax:* 613-230-6654
cich@cich.ca
profile.cich.ca
www.facebook.com/313427342097626
twitter.com/CICH_ICSI

Overview: A medium-sized national charitable organization founded in 1977
Mission: To promote the health & well-being of Canadian children through consultation, collaboration, research & advocacy by building alliances & coalitions & by creating resources on health promotion, disease & injury prevention relevant to child & family health in Canada; To identify issues of concern by monitoring the health & well-being of children in Canada; To promote & improve the health & well-being of mothers & infants in all settings; To promote the healthy physical development of children in a safe environment & reduce childhood injuries; To promote the healthy psycho-social development of children in supportive & nurturing environments; To facilitate empowerment of individuals & communities to achieve the above goals for Canadian children & their families; To facilitate collaborative work between consumers, professional, non-professional & government agencies that results in appropriate actions for identified needs
Member of: Canadian Coalition for the Prevention of Developmental Disabilities; Coalition of National Voluntary Organizations; Canadian Coalition on the Rights of the Child; Children's Alliance; Breastfeeding Committee for Canada; National Literacy & Health Program
Affiliation(s): Canadian Children's Environmental Health Network; Key Institution of Childwatch International; International Network for Child Health, Environment & Safety; WHO/European Environment Agency Working Group on the Environment & Children's Health
Finances: *Funding Sources:* Government; Membership fees; Donations; Sale of publications; Sponsors; Foundations
185 volunteer(s)
Membership: 565; *Fees:* $15 youth; $35 individual; $65 hospital; $75 educational institution; $85 corporate
Chief Officer(s):
Janice Sonmen, Executive Director
Publications:
• Child Health [a publication of the Canadian Institute of Child Health]
Type: Newsletter; *Frequency:* Quarterly; *ISSN:* 0838-9683; *Price:* Free with CICH membership
Profile: National news about child health & well-being issues

Canadian Institute of Credit & Financial Management *See* Credit Institute of Canada

Canadian Institute of Cultural Affairs / Institut canadien des affaires culturelles
#405, 401 Richmond St. West, Toronto ON M5V 3A8
Tel: 416-691-2316
ica@icacan.org
www.icacan.org
www.facebook.com/ICAInternational
Also Known As: ICA Canada
Overview: A small national charitable organization founded in 1976
Mission: To empower people to develop leadership capacity; To contribute to positive social change
Finances: *Funding Sources:* Membership fees; Donations; Sponsorships
Staff Member(s): 3
Membership: *Committees:* Program Advisory
Activities: Presenting programs such as the Courage to Lead Program, the Youth as Facilitative Leaders Program (a skills development & mentorship program), & the Listen to the Drumming Program (to help communities in Kenya & Tanzania develop their own way to alleviate the HIV/AIDS crisis)
Chief Officer(s):
Nan Hudson, Executive Director
Publications:
• L'art de la discussion structurée 100 applications concrèt [a publication of the Canadian Institute of Cultural Affairs]
Author: R. Brian Stanfield; *Price:* $38.00
• The Art of Focused Conversation [a publication of the Canadian Institute of Cultural Affairs]
Author: R. Brian Stanfield; *ISBN:* 0-86571-416-9; *Price:* $21.95
• The Art of Focused Conversation for Schools [a publication of the Canadian Institute of Cultural Affairs]
Author: Jo Nelson; *ISBN:* 0-86571-435-5; *Price:* $21.95
• The Courage to Lead: Transform Self, Transform Society [a publication of the Canadian Institute of Cultural Affairs]
Author: R. Brian Stanfield; *ISBN:* 1-4759-1001-0; *Price:* $29.95
• More Than 50 Ways to Build Team Consensus [a publication of the Canadian Institute of Cultural Affairs]
Author: R. Bruce Williams; *ISBN:* 0-932935-48-6; *Price:* $38.95

• The Social Progress Triangles [a publication of the Canadian Institute of Cultural Affairs]
Author: Jon C. Jenkins & Maureen R. Jenkins; *Price:* $31.95
• Transformational Strategy [a publication of the Canadian Institute of Cultural Affairs]
Author: Bill Staples; *ISBN:* 1-4759-6839-6; *Price:* $29.95
• The Workshop Book [a publication of the Canadian Institute of Cultural Affairs]
Author: R. Brian Stanfield; *ISBN:* 0-86571-470-3; *Price:* $22.95

Canadian Institute of Energy (British Columbia) (CIE)
#26, 181 Ravine Dr., Port Moody BC V3H 4T3
Tel: 604-949-1346; *Fax:* 604-469-3717
cienergybc@gmail.com
cienergybc.blogspot.ca
Overview: A small provincial organization founded in 1979
Mission: To provide a perspective on energy technology, business & policy, nationally & internationally, for those affected professionally or personally by energy issues; To encourage energy research, education & dissemination of topical information; To provide an unbiased forum for discussion & debate
Finances: *Funding Sources:* Membership fees
6 volunteer(s)
Membership: 500; *Fees:* $60 individual; $750 organization; *Member Profile:* Professionally involved in all aspects of energy, whether in exploring for sources, conducting energy research, converting or using energy, or in energy planning
Activities: *Speaker Service:* Yes; *Rents Mailing List:* Yes
Chief Officer(s):
Penny Cochrane, Chair
Charles Bois, Director
John Oliver, Treasurer
Awards:
• Energy Scholarship
• Energy Research & Development Award
• Applied Energy Innovation Award

Canadian Institute of Entrepreneurship (CIE)
coordinator@cienow.com
www.canadianinstituteofentrepreneurship.com
Overview: A small national organization
Mission: To promote education in entrepreneurship; To act as a registrar & facilitator
Membership: *Member Profile:* Students interested in obtaining the CIE designation, CE, Certified Entrepreneur; Persons with the designation, CE, Certified Entrepreneur
Activities: Granting the CIE Certification academic designation, in partnership with Canadian post-secondary institutions; Offering mentoring services
Publications:
• CIE Newsletter
Type: Newsletter
Profile: Information for student members & Certified Entrepreneurs

Canadian Institute of Financial Planners (CIFPs)
#600, 3660 Hurontario St., Mississauga ON L5B 3C4
Tel: 647-723-6450; *Fax:* 647-723-6457
Toll-Free: 866-933-0233
cifps@cifps.ca
www.cifps.ca
Overview: A medium-sized national organization founded in 1972
Mission: To train & qualify advisors to become Certified Financial Planners; To represent members on matters of common interest
Finances: *Funding Sources:* Sponsorships
Membership: 3,500+; *Member Profile:* Canadian financial planners; Financial planning students
Activities: Providing continuing education, mentorship, & support services; Advocating on issues that affect the financial planning profession in Canada; Promoting the financial planning profession to the public
Chief Officer(s):
Keith Costello, President & Chief Executive Officer
Anthony Williams, Vice-President, Academic Affairs
Andrew Cunningham, Director, Information Services
Robert Jeffrey, Director, Member Relations
Odele Burton, Corporate Secretary
Meetings/Conferences:
• Canadian Institute of Financial Planners 16th Annual National Conference 2018, June, 2018, Halifax Marriott Harbourfront, Halifax, NS
Scope: National

Publications:
• Canadian Institute of Financial Planners Magazine
Type: Magazine
Profile: Information about current trends & practices in the financial planning profession
• Canadian Institute of Financial Planners Newsletter
Type: Newsletter
Profile: Information about the Institute's activities & events for its members

Canadian Institute of Food Science & Technology (CIFST) / Institut canadien de science et technologie alimentaires (ICSTA)
#1311, 3-1750 The Queensway, Toronto ON M9C 5H5
Tel: 905-271-8338; *Fax:* 905-271-8344
cifst@cifst.ca
www.cifst.ca
www.linkedin.com/groups/7472160
twitter.com/cifst_icsta
Overview: A medium-sized national organization founded in 1951
Mission: To advance food science & technology; To act as a voice for scientific issues related to the Canadian food industry
Affiliation(s): British Columbia Food Technologists
Finances: *Funding Sources:* Sponsorships
Membership: 1,200+; *Fees:* $43 student; $87.50 retired; $195 professional/associate; $550 sustaining; *Member Profile:* Food industry professionals from across Canada, such as scientists & technologists in industry, academia, & government; *Committees:* Awards; Canadian Food Insights Magazine Editorial Advisory; Conference; Fellow Selection; Membership Renewal; Nominating; Scientific Expert Council & Scientific Expert Panels
Activities: Exchanging scientific, educational, & business information; Engaging in advocacy activities; Liaising with related national & international organizations, such as Agriculture & Agri-Food Canada (AAFC) & the International Union of Food Science & Technology (IUFoST); Promoting professional development; Establishing Subject Interest Divisions, such as food process engineering, functional foods, government & regulatory affairs, microbiology, nutrition, packaging, & sensory evaluation
Chief Officer(s):
Michael Nickerson, President
Carol Ann Burrell, Executive Director, 905-271-8338, Fax: 905-271-8344
caburrell@cifst.ca
Meetings/Conferences:
• 2018 Canadian Institute of Food Science & Technology National Conference, 2018
Scope: International
Publications:
• Canadian Food Insights [a publication of the Canadian Institute of Food Science & Technology]
Type: Magazine

Alberta Section
c/o Hisham Karami, Alberta Health Services, Queen Elizabeth II Hosp., Grande Prairie AB T8N 7E9
www.cifst.ca
Chief Officer(s):
Michael Gänzle, Chair, 780-492-0774, Fax: 780-492-4265
mgaenzle@ualberta.ca
Mirko Betti, Secretary-Treasurer, 780-248-1598
mirko.betti@ales.ualberta.ca
Hisham Karami, Director, Membership, 780-710-2071
hishamkarami@hotmail.com

Atlantic Section
c/o Joy Shinn, PEI Healthy Eating Alliance, #220, 40 Enman Cres., Charlottetown PE C1E 1E6
Tel: 902-940-9782
cifst.atlantic@gmail.com
www.cifst.ca
Chief Officer(s):
H.P. Vasantha Rupasinghe, Chair
vrupasinghe@dal.ca

Manitoba Section
c/o M. Samelo, Manitoba Harvest Hemp Foods, #1108, 40 Dalhousie Dr., Winnipeg MB R3T 2Y7
manitobasection@cifst.ca
www.cifst.ca
twitter.com/CIFSTMB
Chief Officer(s):
Kevin Segall, Chair, 204-475-6207 Ext. 16, Fax: 204-284-6407
ksegall@burcon.ca
Maria Evelyn Samelo, Secretary

Canadian Associations / Canadian Institute of Forestry (CIF) / Institut forestier du Canada (IFC)

Carol Nabanoba Musoke, Treasurer, 204-226-0292
• Canadian Institute of Food Science & Technology, Manitoba Section
Type: Yearbook; *Frequency:* Annually
Profile: Reports from executives & financial statements

Ontario Section
5 Fenwood Circle, Peterborough ON K9J 6M4
Tel: 866-437-6030; *Fax:* 866-719-5396
OntarioSection@cifst.ca
www.cifst.ca
Chief Officer(s):
Maureen Taylor, Chair, 905-567-2555 Ext. 29, Fax: 905-567-2556
maureen@theingredientcompany.com
• SciTech
Type: Newsletter; *Editor:* James Summers
Profile: Current activities of the Toronto section for members

Québec Section
c/o Manon Cloutier, 130, Place de Naples, Laval QC H7M 4A6
Tel: 450-663-6503; *Fax:* 450-663-6503
www.cifst.ca
Chief Officer(s):
Sam Choucha, Chair, 514-421-0303
sam.choucha@univarcanada.com
• Canadian Institute of Food Science & Technology, Québec Section Annual Report
Type: Yearbook; *Frequency:* Annually
Profile: A summary of the previous year's activities

Canadian Institute of Forestry (CIF) / Institut forestier du Canada (IFC)
PO Box 99, 6905 Hwy. 17 West, Mattawa ON P0H 1V0
Tel: 705-744-1715; *Fax:* 705-744-1716
Other Communication: questions@cif-ifc.org
admin@cif-ifc.org
www.cif-ifc.org
facebook.com/groups/5380633929
twitter.com/cif_ifc
youtube.com/user/CIFtube
Previous Name: Canadian Society of Forest Engineers
Overview: A large national organization founded in 1908
Mission: To act as the national voice of forest practitioners
Member of: International Union of Societies of Foresters
Affiliation(s): Forests without Borders; Canadian Forestry Association
Finances: *Funding Sources:* Membership dues; Sponsorships
Membership: 2,200; *Fees:* $39.55 students; $67.80 retired members; $50 sustaining individuals; $111.87 active members & spousal; $192.10 current active members; *Member Profile:* Foresters; Forest technicians & technologists; Educators; Scientists, such as biologists & ecologists; Students; Others with a professional interest in forestry; *Committees:* National board of Directors; Executive; Awards; Silver Ring Accreditation
Activities: Providing national leadership in forestry; Promoting competence & knowledge of forestry for professionals; Presenting a national electronic lecture series; Providing workshops & seminars; Fostering public awareness & understanding of forestry issues; Presenting rings to graduates of Canadian forest technical & forestry baccalaureate programs; Offering field tours; Establishing demonstration forests; Providing networking opportunities; Liaising with the Canadian Council of Forest Ministers; *Speaker Service:* Yes
Chief Officer(s):
Johnathan Lok, President
Megan Smith, Vice President
Alex Drummond, 2nd Vice President
Al Stinson, Past President
Awards:
• International Forestry Achievement Award
To recognize outstanding achievement in international forestry
• James M. Kitz Award
To honour contributions of forest practitioners who are new to the profession
• Canadian Forest Management Group Achievement Award
To honour outstanding achievement by teams & groups of natural resource managers, researchers, & NGO groups in the field of forest resource related activities in Canada
• Canadian Forestry Achievement Award
To recognize outstanding achievement in forestry in Canada
• Canadian Forestry Scientific Achievement Award
To honour unique achievement in forestry research in Canada
• Presidential Award
Presented to individuals who have made significant or consistent contributions to the practice & profession of forestry
• Section of the Year Award
Awarded to sections that exemplify the objects of the Canadian Institute of Forestry
• Tree of Life Award
To honour persons who have made superior contributions to forest renewal, sustainable forest resource management, or sustained yield integrated management of the forest & its intrinsic resources
• Gold Medal
For graduating students, selected by the head of each school, from each forestry baccalaureate school & each forestry diploma school in Canada
• Honourary Members
For a non-member who has made outstanding contributions to the advancement of forestry
• J. Michael Waldram Memorial Model Forest Fellowship
For a Canadian Aboriginal youth enrolled in at least their second year in either a degree or diploma program in natural resource management at a Canadian university or college
• Fellows of the Institute
To recognize a member or ex-member who has made outstanding contributions to the advancement of forestry or to the Candian Institute of Forestry
Meetings/Conferences:
• Canadian Institute of Forestry 110th AGM 2018, September, 2018, Grande Prairie, AB
Scope: National
Publications:
• Canadian Institute of Forestry Annual Report
Type: Yearbook; *Frequency:* Annually
• Canadian Institute of Forestry E-news
Type: Newsletter; *Frequency:* Bimonthly
Profile: Information about the Institute, such as conferences, section updates, & member resources
• The Forestry Chronicle: The Official Journal of the Canadian Institute of Forestry
Type: Journal; *Frequency:* Bimonthly; *Accepts Advertising*;
Editor: Brian Haddon; *Price:* $100 personal electronic & print; $300 multi-users electronic & print
Profile: Practical & applied science & information for forest management planning & operations

Canadian Institute of Forestry, Newfoundland & Labrador (CIF-NL)
PO Box 793, Stn. Main, Corner Brook NL A2H 6G7
newfoundland-labrador@cif-ifc.org
cif-ifc.org/site/newfoundland_labrador
Overview: A small provincial organization
Mission: To advance the stewardship of Canada's forest resources, provide national leadership in forestry, promote competence among forestry professionals, and foster public awareness of Canadian and international forestry issues.
Chief Officer(s):
Allan Masters, Director

Canadian Institute of Gemmology (CIG) / Institut canadien de gemmologie
c/o School of Jewellery Arts, PO Box 57010, Vancouver BC V5K 5G6
Tel: 604-530-8569
Toll-Free: 604-530-8569
Other Communication: gemlab@cigem.ca
info@cigem.ca
www.cigem.ca
www.facebook.com/CanadianInstituteOfGemmology
twitter.com/CIGemNews
Also Known As: Pacific Institute of Gemmology
Overview: A small national organization founded in 1990
Mission: To serve the jewellery industry & the general public
Member of: European Parliament of Art Schools for Jewellery and Crafts
Activities: Offering C.I.G courses & training; Providing GemForum - The Information Exchange
Chief Officer(s):
Wolf Kuehn, Executive Director
Publications:
• CIGem News: The Newsletter of the Canadian Institute of Gemmology
Type: Newsletter; *Frequency:* Monthly
• Gemmology Canada
Type: Magazine; *Editor:* J. Wolf Kuehn; *ISSN:* 0846-3611
Profile: Articles written by students of the Canadian Institute of Gemmology & other contributors

Canadian Institute of Geomatics (CIG) / Association canadienne des sciences géomatiques
#100D, 900 Dynes Rd., Ottawa ON K2C 3L6
Tel: 613-224-9851; *Fax:* 613-224-9577
admincig@magma.ca
www.cig-acsg.ca
www.linkedin.com/grps?gid=1095187&trk=myg_ugrp_ovr
Overview: A medium-sized national organization founded in 1882
Mission: Geomatics is commonly defined as a "discipline aimed at managing geographic data by means of the science & technology used to acquire, store, process, display & distribute them"; To advance the development of geomatics sciences in Canada; To enhance & demonstrate the public usefulness of geomatics; To further the professional development of its members; To foster cooperation between & promote unity of purpose among Canadian geomatics organizations; To represent & promote Canadian interests in geomatics internationally
Affiliation(s): International Federation of Surveyors; International Society for Photogrammetry & Remote Sensing; International Cartographic Association; Commonwealth Association of Canada Lands Surveyors; Canadian Council of Land Surveyors; Canadian Hydrographic Association
Finances: *Annual Operating Budget:* $100,000-$250,000; *Funding Sources:* Membership fees; Events; Contributions
Staff Member(s): 3; 30 volunteer(s)
Membership: 1,500; *Fees:* $140 member; $50 student; *Committees:* Cartography; Education; Engineering & Mining; Geodesy; Geospatial Data Infrastructures; Hydrography; GPS; Land Surveying; Land Information Management; Photogrammetry; Remote Sensing; Urban Regional Information; Annual Conferences
Activities: Geographical information systems (GIS); global positioning systems & remote sensing as tools & techniques in environmental monitoring & planning (ie. sustainable development); *Library:* by appointment
Chief Officer(s):
Alex Giannelia, President, 416-203-9858, Fax: 416-203-9843
ag@airsensing.com
Awards:
• Hans Klinkenberg Memorial Scholarship
• Jim Jones Award
Awarded to the Institute member who makes the most valuable contribution to the articles and departments section of Geomatica; *Amount:* $500
• John Carroll Geodesy Award
Eligibility: Undergraduate students in university programs leading to an accredited degree with surveying as a specialty; *Amount:* $500
• Student Award
• Lou Sebert Library Award
Awarded to the best published literary work on a subject in the field of Canadian geomatics
• Samuel Gamble Award
Publications:
• Geomatica [a publication of the Canadian Institute of Geomatics]
Type: Journal; *Frequency:* Quarterly; *Accepts Advertising*;
Editor: Izaak de Rijcke; *Price:* $290
Profile: Formerly the CISM Journal ACSGC, the surveying & mapping publication features both scientific & practical information, conferences, reviews, industry news, & new products

Canadian Institute of International Affairs / Institut canadien des affaires internationales *See* Canadian International Council

Canadian Institute of Iridology
PO Box 13576, Stn. Best Buy, Mississauga ON L5N 8G5
Tel: 416-231-6298; *Fax:* 905-824-0063
iridologyplus@hotmail.com
www.cdninstiridology.com
Overview: A small national organization founded in 1989
Mission: To provide a professional teaching forum in the field of iridology
Affiliation(s): The Iridologists' Association of Canada (Ir.A.C.)
Activities: Offering training in the practice of iris analysis, including the Practitioner Diploma Program in Clinical Iridology

Canadian Institute of Management (CIM) / Institut canadien de gestion
National Office, 15 Collier St., Lower Level, Barrie ON L4M 1G5
Tel: 705-725-8926; *Fax:* 705-725-8196
Toll-Free: 800-387-5774

office@cim.ca
www.cim.ca
Overview: A medium-sized national licensing organization founded in 1942
Mission: To promote the senior management profession by offering a series of educational programs from single courses to professional certification
Finances: *Funding Sources:* Corporate sponsorship
Membership: *Fees:* Schedule available; *Member Profile:* Canadian leaders in the management profession
Activities: Offering educational opportunities to enhance managerial skills; Certifying managers
Chief Officer(s):
Matthew Jelavic, President
president@cim.ca
Betty Smith, Secretary
pastpresident@cim.ca
Deb Daigle, Treasurer
treasurer@cim.ca
Publications:
• Canadian Manager Magazine
Type: Magazine; *Frequency:* Quarterly; *Accepts Advertising;*
Editor: Sheila Sproule; *Price:* Free to CIM members
Profile: Information about management developments
• Tips from the Top
Type: Newsletter; *Frequency:* Monthly; *Price:* Free for CIM members

Alberta - Northern & NWT Branch
PO Box 610, Stn. Main, Edmonton AB T5J 2K8
Tel: 780-455-7951
northernalberta@cim.ca
Affiliation(s): Faculty of Extension, University of Alberta
Chief Officer(s):
Garry Kalawarny, Regional President, Western & Central
central@cim.ca

Alberta - Southern Branch
PO Box 53222, Stn. Marlborough, Calgary AB T2A 7L9
Tel: 705-725-8926; *Fax:* 705-725-8196
Toll-Free: 800-387-5774
cimsouthalberta@gmail.com
Affiliation(s): University of Calgary; Southern Alberta Institute of Technology; Mount Royal College; Olds College; Red Deer College; DeVry Canada
Chief Officer(s):
Garry Kalawarny, Regional President, Western & Central
central@cim.ca

British Columbia & Yukon Branch
PO Box 346, 4974 Kingsway, Burnaby BC V5J 4M9
bc@cim.ca
Chief Officer(s):
Garry Kalawarny, Regional President, Western & Central
central@cim.ca

Manitoba - Winnipeg Branch
1150 Waverley St., #B2, Winnipeg MB R3T 0P4
Tel: 204-474-8653
cim.winnipeg@mts.net
www.cim-winnipeg.ca
Affiliation(s): University of Manitoba
Chief Officer(s):
Clayton McPherson, President
Garry Kalawarny, Regional President, Western/Central
central@cim.ca
• Manitoba Manager
Type: Newsletter; *Frequency:* Quarterly
Profile: Branch news, upcoming events, & articles

Maritime Branch
PO Box 463, Port Williams NS B0P 1T0
Tel: 902-670-0746
info@maritimecim.com
www.maritimecim.com
Chief Officer(s):
Katherine Hanks, President

Newfoundland & Labrador Branch
49 Anthony Ave., St. John's NL A1E 1X5
Tel: 709-437-7075; *Fax:* 709-437-7079
newfoundlandandlabrador@cim.ca
cimnl.ca
www.facebook.com/184069228310762
Affiliation(s): Memorial University; Keyin College; Eastern College
Chief Officer(s):
Ken Noseworthy, Regional President, Eastern
eastern@cim.ca

Ontario - Grand Valley Branch
#167, 55 Northfield Dr. East, Waterloo ON N2K 3T6
Toll-Free: 800-387-5774
grandvalley@cim.ca
www.facebook.com/cimgrv
twitter.com/cimgrandvalley
Affiliation(s): Conestoga College; Wilfrid Laurier University
Chief Officer(s):
Lorraine Gignac, Regional President, Ontario East
onteast@cim.ca

Ontario - Hamilton Branch
PO Box 57035, Stn. Jackson Square, Hamilton ON L8P 4W9
Tel: 905-561-9889; *Fax:* 866-774-2226
admin@cim-hamilton.com
cim-hamilton.com
Affiliation(s): Mohawk College; McMaster University
Chief Officer(s):
Don Spaetzel, President, 905-690-1164
dspaetzel@cogeco.ca
• The Hamilton Scene
Type: Newsletter

Ontario - Lake Simcoe Branch
PO Box 1060, Barrie ON L4M 5E1
Tel: 705-326-6577
infolakesimcoe@cim.ca
Affiliation(s): Georgian College of Applied Arts & Technology
Chief Officer(s):
Lorraine Gignac, Regional President, Ontario East
onteast@cim.ca
• Lake Simcoe Manager
Type: Newsletter

Ontario - London Branch
PO Box 611, Stn. B, London ON N6A 4Y4
Tel: 519-681-4168; *Fax:* 519-668-7866
cimlonbr@sympatico.ca
Affiliation(s): University of Western Ontario
Chief Officer(s):
Beth Lahey, Regional President, Ontario West
ontwest@cim.ca
• London Manager
Type: Newsletter

Ontario - Niagara Branch
#264, 17 - 7000 McLeod Rd., Niagara Falls ON L2G 7K3
Toll-Free: 800-387-5774
niagara@cim.ca
Affiliation(s): Niagara College of Applied Arts & Technology; Brock University
Chief Officer(s):
Beth Lahey, Regional President, Ontario West
ontwest@cim.ca

Ontario - Ottawa Valley Branch
#303, 320 Croyden Ave., Ottawa ON K2B 5P3
Tel: 613-831-0379
ottawa@cim.ca
Affiliation(s): Carleton University; Algonquin College; St. Lawrence College; University of Ottawa
Chief Officer(s):
Lorraine Gignac, Regional President, Ontario East
onteast@cim.ca

Ontario - Sarnia Branch
258 Ross Ave., Sarnia ON N7T 1J9
Tel: 519-336-3544
sarnia@cim.ca
Affiliation(s): Lambton College

Ontario - Toronto Branch
#210, 2800 - 14th St., Markham ON L3R 0E4
toronto@cim.ca
Affiliation(s): University of Toronto; Ryerson University; York University; Centennial College; Humber College; George Brown College; Seneca College

Québec - Montréal Branch (CIM)
#200, 2140, boul Marie-Victorin, Longueuil QC J4G 1A9
Tél: 450-674-6775; *Téléc:* 450-646-9333
montreal@cim.ca
Affiliation(s): Concordia University; McGill University; Université de Montréal; UNiversity du Québec; Sherbrooke Université
Chief Officer(s):
Pierre Jutras, Président
Caroline Coulombe, Secrétaire-Trésorière
Pierre Henri, Président régional, Québec
quebec@cim.ca

Saskatchewan - Saskatoon/Regina Branch
PO Box 8055, Saskatoon SK S7K 4R7
Fax: 866-812-0654
Toll-Free: 800-387-5774
saskatoon-regina@cim.ca
Affiliation(s): University of Saskatchewan; CIM Distance Education
Chief Officer(s):
Garry Kalawarny, Regional President, Western & Central
central@cim.ca

Canadian Institute of Marketing / Institut canadien du marketing
205 Miller Dr., Georgetown ON L7G 6G4
Tel: 905-877-5369
www.professionalmarketer.ca
www.linkedin.com/groups?mostPopular=&gid=105823
twitter.com/regprofmarketer
www.youtube.com/user/canadianmarketer
Overview: A medium-sized international charitable organization founded in 1982
Mission: To improve the practice of marketing in Canada by encouraging the adoption of professional standards & qualifications by practitioners & employers, & by sponsoring activities related to marketing education & training; To be a means by which those engaged in all aspects of marketing as a professional activity can represent their views & interests to governments & agencies
Member of: Asia Pacific Marketing Federation
Affiliation(s): Affiliated with 20 other Institutes of Marketing around the world
Membership: Over 50,000; *Fees:* Schedule available; *Member Profile:* No corporate memberships; each person has to apply for, & earn, the right of membership
Activities: Accredited marketing programs in the following colleges & universities: Algonquin College, Atkinson College, BC Institute of Technology, Seneca, Centennial, Concordia, Kingston College (Vancouver), Mount Allison, Ottawa, Ryerson, St. Lawrence College, University of Toronto, York University, Brock University; *Speaker Service:* Yes
Chief Officer(s):
A. Grant Lee, Executive Director
grant.lee@professionalmarketer.ca
Faythe Pal, Chair
faythe@handsoftimeinc.com
John Jackson, Secretary-Treasurer
humanist.officiant@me.com
Shiv Seechurn, Registrar
shivseechurn@rogers.com
Publications:
• Canadian Institute of Marketing Membership Directory
Type: Directory
Profile: Listing of members
• Canadian Institute of Marketing Services Directory
Type: Directory
Profile: Listing of accredited professionals who have the qualifications & experience to provide services in marketing
• Marketing Canada
Type: Journal; *Frequency:* Quarterly; *Accepts Advertising;*
Editor: A. Grant Lee
Profile: Articles related to marketing theory, case studies, standards & ethics, & applications of principles

Canadian Institute of Mining & Metallurgy *See* Canadian Institute of Mining, Metallurgy & Petroleum

Canadian Institute of Mining, Metallurgy & Petroleum (CIM) / Institut canadien des mines, de la métallurgie et du pétrole (ICM)
CIM National Office, #1250, 3500, boul de Maisonneuve ouest, Westmount QC H3Z 3C1
Tel: 514-939-2710; *Fax:* 514-939-2714
cim@cim.org
www.cim.org
Previous Name: Canadian Institute of Mining & Metallurgy
Overview: A large national organization founded in 1898
Mission: To act as a resource sector that is broadly recognized & respected as an angine for sustainable growth & prosperity
Membership: 12,000+; *Member Profile:* Professionals in the Canadian minerals, metals, materials, & energy sectors, from industry, government, & academia; *Committees:* Central Publications; Audit; Bulletin; By-Laws; CIM Valuation of Mineral Properties; Education; Estimation Guidelines; Human Resources; International Advisory Liaison; Membership; President Elect Nominating; Public Affairs; Special Volumes
Activities: Providing technical forums, conferences & professional networking opportunities; Offering continuing education programs & courses; Liasing with government

Canadian Associations / Canadian Institute of Planners (CIP) / Institut canadien des urbanistes (ICU)

departments; Commissioning special volumes & reports & publishing technical papers; *Speaker Service:* Yes; *Library:* Canadian Institute of Mining, Metallurgy & Petroleum Library
Chief Officer(s):
Angela Hamlyn, Executive Director, 514-393-2710 Ext. 1303
ahamlyn@cim.org
Marilou Reboulis, Administrative Assistant, 514-939-2710 Ext. 1337
mreboulis@cim.org
Awards:
• CIM Awards
The institute administers 27 awards recognizing achievement in mining, metallurgy & petroleum industries
• CIM Journalism Awards
Established 1985; presented to print, radio & television journalists in Canada for balanced & technically accurate news reporting, feature writing, radio & television broadcasting that best enhance public understanding of the minerals industry & its contribution to the economic & social well-being of Canada; *Amount:* $500 first prizes
• Medals for Bravery
Established 1933; medals are awarded in recognition of great valour displayed to save life in mines or plants of Canadian mining companies; an award is made only in a case where a person knowingly risks his/her life in attempting to rescue a fellow worker
• The Order of Santa Barbara
Established 1968; a silver medal is awarded to any woman who has made a significant contribution to the welfare of a mining community in Canada
Meetings/Conferences:
• 25th World Mining Congress & Expo, June, 2018, Astana
Scope: International
Attendance: 1,500
• Canadian Institute of Mining, Metallurgy & Petroleum 2018 Convention, 2018
Description: A mining event, featuring a technical program, workshops, field trips, a student program, & a social program
Contact Information: convention.cim.org
Publications:
• CIM [Canadian Institute of Mining, Metallurgy & Petroleum] Magazine
Type: Magazine; *Frequency:* 7 pa; *Accepts Advertising*; *ISSN:* 1718-4177; *Price:* Free for members; $160 non-members in Canada
Profile: Editorials, technical information, industry events, & industry information
• CIM [Canadian Institute of Mining, Metallurgy & Petroleum] Directory
Type: Directory; *Frequency:* Annually
Profile: Listing of individual & corporate CIM members
• CIM [Canadian Institute of Mining, Metallurgy & Petroleum] Reporter
Frequency: Annually
Profile: Official publication of the annual CIM Conference & Exhibition, for all registered delegates & visitors
• CIM [Canadian Institute of Mining, Metallurgy & Petroleum] Canadian Metallurgical Quarterly
Frequency: Quarterly; *ISSN:* 0008-4433
Profile: Publishes original contributions on all aspects of metallurgy and materials science, including mineral processing, hydrometallurgy, pyrometallurgy, materials processing, physical metallurgy and the service behaviour of materials.

Canadian Institute of Planners (CIP) / Institut canadien des urbanistes (ICU)
#1112, 141 Laurier Ave. West, Ottawa ON K1P 5J3
Tel: 613-237-7526; *Fax:* 613-237-7045
Toll-Free: 800-207-2138
general@cip-icu.ca
www.cip-icu.ca
Overview: A medium-sized national organization founded in 1919
Mission: To advance professional planning excellence, through the delivery of membership & public services in Canada & abroad
Affiliation(s): Alberta Professional Planners Institute; Saskatchewan Professional Planners Institute; Atlantic Planners Institute; Manitoba Professional Planners Institute; Ontario Professional Planners Institute; Ordre des urbanistes du Québec; Planning Institute of British Columbia
Finances: *Funding Sources:* Membership fees
Membership: 7,500; *Member Profile:* Professional community & regional planners employed in the private sector in the consulting & land development industries & in the public sector at all levels of government.
Activities: *Awareness Events:* World Town Planning Day, November; *Internships:* Yes; *Rents Mailing List:* Yes; *Library*
Chief Officer(s):
Steven Brasier, CAE, Executive Director
sbrasier@cip-icu.ca
Meetings/Conferences:
• Canadian Institute of Planners 2018 Conference, July, 2018, Winnipeg, MB
Scope: National
• Canadian Institute of Planners 2019 Conference, July, 2019, Ottawa, ON
Scope: National
• Canadian Institute of Planners 2020 Conference, July, 2020, Whistler, BC
Scope: National

Canadian Institute of Plumbing & Heating (CIPH) / Institut canadien de plomberie et de chauffage
#504, 295 The West Mall, Toronto ON M9C 4Z4
Tel: 416-695-0447
Toll-Free: 800-639-2474
info@ciph.com
www.ciph.com
www.linkedin.com/company/ciph
www.facebook.com/355926634482039
www.twitter.com/ciphnews
www.youtube.com/channel/UCx8_LwmTSuOmOr0lyp7sLGQ
Overview: A large national organization founded in 1933
Mission: To act as a unified voice for plumbing, heating, hydronic, PVF, & waterworks across Canada
Membership: 250; *Member Profile:* Companies throughout Canada that manufacture, sell, & distribute plumbing, heating, hydronic, PVF, & waterworks products & services; *Committees:* Executive / Finance; Nominating; Membership; Government Affairs; Region Hydronics; Charity Committee for Habitat for Humanity Canada; Manufacturers' Agents; Wholesalers' Division; Manufacturers' Division; Education & Training Council; Plumbing Industry Advisory Council; Canadian Hydronics Council; Industrial Pipe, Valve, & Fittings Council
Activities: Liaising with governments & organizations; Influencing the development of standards & codes; Raising awareness of safety; Providing education; Offering networking opportunities to share best practices
Chief Officer(s):
Ralph Suppa, CAE, President & General Manager
r.suppa@ciph.com
Elizabeth McCullough, CDE, General Manager, Trade Shows
e.mccullough@ciph.com
Kevin Wong, Technical Advisor
k.wong@ciph.com
Stephen Apps, Manager, Program
s.apps@ciph.com
Matt Wiesenfeld, Manager, Program
m.wiesenfeld@ciph.com
Meetings/Conferences:
• Canadian Institute of Plumbing & Heating 2018 Annual Business Conference, June, 2018, Fairmont Chateau Whistler, Whistler, BC
Scope: National
Publications:
• Advocacy Link [a publication of the Canadian Institute of Plumbing & Heating]
Type: Newsletter
Profile: A summary of information about the Canadian Institute of Plumbing & Heating. the Industrial Pipes, Valves, & Fittings Council, & theCanadian Hydronics Council, involving code & standards, public safety, & education
• Canadian Institute of Plumbing & Heating Member Directory
Type: Directory
Profile: Listing of members by head office, plus further information such as sales offices & contacts
• CIPH [Canadian Institute of Plumbing & Heating] EconoLink
Profile: Results from surveys
• CIPH [Canadian Institute of Plumbing & Heating] Wholesalers Sales Statistics
Frequency: Monthly; *Price:* $325
Profile: A summary of sales survey results in six regions by product groups
• Pipeline
Type: Newsletter; *Frequency:* 3-4 pa
Profile: Information about the hydronics, plumbing, & PVF industries, educational products, trade shows, & association activities for Canadian Institute of Plumbing & Heating members, industry stakeholders, &government
Atlantic Region
c/o Mike Lovegrove, Wolseley Canada, 1270 St. George Blvd., Moncton NB E1E 3S1
Tel: 506-853-8020; *Fax:* 506-858-7186
Chief Officer(s):
Mike Lovegrove, Region President
mike.lovegrove@wolseleyinc.ca
Kathy Saunders, Region Coordinator, 902-497-1084, Fax: 902-443-6888
kathysaunders@bellaliant.net
British Columbia Region
c/o Kathryn Kuboseek, 15316 Sequoia Dr., Surrey BC V3S 8N4
Tel: 778-867-5956; *Fax:* 604-594-5091
ciphbc@shaw.ca
www.ciph.com/en/British-Columbia
twitter.com/CIPHBC
Chief Officer(s):
Tim Main, President, 778-777-5083
tim.main@xyleminc.com
Kathryn Fallis, Region Coordinator
Calgary, Alberta Region
PO Box 4520, Stn. C, Calgary AB T2T 5N3
Tel: 403-244-4487; *Fax:* 403-244-2340
Chief Officer(s):
Mike Stringer, President, 403-256-4900, Fax: 403-256-1208
sales@stringersales.com
Connie Pruden, Region Coordinator, 403-244-4487, Fax: 403-244-2340
conniep@associationsplus.ca
• CIPH [Canadian Institute of Plumbing & Heating] Updater - Calgary Region
Type: Newsletter
Profile: Local upcoming events, training opportunities, & member news
Edmonton, Alberta, Region
c/o Linda Wood Edwards, PO Box 11021, Stn. Main, Edmonton AB T5J 3K3
Tel: 780-918-4200
Chief Officer(s):
Linda Wood Edwards, Region Coordinator
edmonton@ciph.com
• Backflow
Type: Newsletter
Profile: Upcoming events, course information, & regional activities
Manitoba Region
c/o Lisa Carbonneau, PO Box 2737, Winnipeg MB R3C 4B3
Tel: 204-832-1512; *Fax:* 204-897-8094
Chief Officer(s):
Ryan Bristow, Region President, 204-772-4341, Fax: 204-772-4402
rbristow@equipcoltd.com
Lise Carbonneau, Region Coordinator
whirlwind@shaw.ca
• Overflow
Type: Newsletter; *Editor:* Alan Thompson (alatho@ipexinc.com)
Profile: Upcoming events, company profiles, & region activities
Newfoundland Region
c/o Sheri Slaney, 16 Argus Pl., St. John's NL A1A 5N2
Tel: 709-753-4222; *Fax:* 709-753-6641
ciph.nl@gmail.com
Chief Officer(s):
John Ozon, Region President, 709-753-1670
jozon@kerrcontrols.ca
Sheri Slaney, Region Coordinator, 709-753-4222
Ontario Region
c/o Nancy Barden, 5827 - 6th Line, RR#1, Hillsburgh ON N0B 1Z0
Tel: 519-855-6474; *Fax:* 519-855-1747
Chief Officer(s):
Jon Leeson, Region President, 416-213-1585 Ext. 144
jleeson@desco.ca
Nancy Barden, Region Coordinator
barden@sympatico.ca
• The Flow
Type: Newsletter
Profile: Information about upcoming events & profiles
Québec Region
c/o Claude Robitaille, #106, 4460, ch des Cageux, Montréal QC H7W 2S7
Tél: 514-989-1002; *Téléc:* 514-681-1941

Chief Officer(s):
Claude Robitaille, Region Coordinator
claude.robitaille@mtaplus.com
Gilles Legault, Region President, 450-655-9588, Fax: 450-641-2737
glegault@ajpsylvain.com
• The Good Tip
Type: Newsletter
Profile: Information about forthcoming events & industry news
Saskatchewan Region
c/o Nicole Ursu, Uponor Ltd., PO Box 6030, Regina SK S4N 5T6
Chief Officer(s):
Nicole Ursu, Region President, 306-591-1883
nicole.ursu@uponor.com
Lovella Jones, Region Coordinator
lovella.jones@b-creative.ca
• Connection [a publication of Canadian Institute of Plumbing & Heating, Saskatchewan Region]
Type: Newsletter
Profile: Upcoming events, educational opportunities, & regional news

Canadian Institute of Public & Private Real Estate Companies *See* Real Property Association of Canada

Canadian Institute of Public Health Inspectors (CIPHI) / Institut Canadien des inspecteurs en santé publique (ICISP)
#720, 999 West Broadway Ave., Vancouver BC V5Z 1K5
Tel: 604-739-8180; *Fax:* 604-738-4080
Toll-Free: 888-245-8180
Other Communication: office@ciphi.ca
questions@ciphi.ca
www.ciphi.ca
www.facebook.com/CIPHI.ICISP
twitter.com/ciphi_national
Previous Name: Canadian Institute of Sanitary Inspectors
Overview: A medium-sized national licensing organization founded in 1934
Mission: To protect the health of all Canadians; To advance the environmental & health sciences; To enhance the field of public health inspection through certification, information, & advocacy
Affiliation(s): National Environmental Health Association (NEHA)
Membership: 1,000-4,999; *Fees:* Schedule available; *Member Profile:* Canadian public health inspectors; Environmental health officers; *Committees:* Retirees Advisory
Activities: Providing professional development opportunities; *Awareness Events:* Environmental Public Health Week (EPHW), January; *Speaker Service:* Yes
Chief Officer(s):
Ann Thomas, National President
president@ciphi.ca
Meetings/Conferences:
• Canadian Institute of Public Health Inspectors 84th National Educational Conference 2018, 2018
Scope: National
Description: Featuring the presentation of Institute awards
Publications:
• Canadian Institute of Public Health Inspectors National Newsletter
Type: Newsletter
• Environmental Health Review [a publication of the Canadian Institute of Public Health Inspectors]
Type: Journal; *Frequency:* Quarterly; *Editor:* Andrew Papadopoulos; *Price:* Free for Canadian Institute of Public Health Inspectors members

Canadian Institute of Quantity Surveyors (CIQS)
#19, 90 Nolan Ct., Markham ON L3R 4L9
Tel: 905-477-0008; *Fax:* 905-477-6774
admin@ciqs.org
www.ciqs.org
www.linkedin.com/groups/Canadian-Institute-Quantity-Surveyors-4837923
www.facebook.com/112909992224092
twitter.com/CIQS_Official
Overview: A medium-sized national organization
Mission: To represent the quantity surveying & construction estimating profession in Canada
Staff Member(s): 2
Membership: *Member Profile:* Professional Quantity Surveyors, Associate Quantity Surveyors, Construction Estimator Certified (CEC), Associate Construction Estimator, and fullnad part-time students.

Chief Officer(s):
Lois Metcalfe, Executive Director
execdir@ciqs.org
Mark Gardin, Chair
president@ciqs.org

Canadian Institute of Quantity Surveyors - British Columbia
c/o Canadian Institute of Quantity Surveyors, #19, 90 Nolan Ct., Markham ON L3R 4L9
Fax: 905-477-6774
Toll-Free: 866-345-1168
info@ciqs-bc.org
www.ciqs-bc.org
Overview: A small provincial organization overseen by Canadian Institute of Quantity Surveyors
Member of: Canadian Institute of Quantity Surveyors
Finances: *Annual Operating Budget:* Less than $50,000
Membership: 350 individual
Chief Officer(s):
Indu Elapatha, President

Canadian Institute of Quantity Surveyors - Maritimes
PO Box 38131, Dartmouth NS B3B 1T0
info@ciqs-maritimes.org
www.ciqs-maritimes.org
Overview: A small provincial organization founded in 1979 overseen by Canadian Institute of Quantity Surveyors
Mission: To promote & advance professional status of quantity surveyors; To collaborate with other professions & organizations in the construction industry
Member of: Canadian Institute of Quantity Surveyors
Finances: *Annual Operating Budget:* Less than $50,000; *Funding Sources:* Membership dues
Membership: 100+; *Member Profile:* Examination of technical subject & work experience
Chief Officer(s):
David Dooks, President
Merrill Varner, Secretary

Canadian Institute of Quantity Surveyors - Ontario
#19, 90 Nolan Ct., Markham ON L3R 4L9
Tel: 905-477-3222; *Fax:* 905-477-6774
info@ciqs-ontario.org
www.ciqs-ontario.org
Also Known As: CIQS - Ontario
Overview: A small provincial organization overseen by Canadian Institute of Quantity Surveyors
Mission: To maintain high standards for the industry & help its members gain employment
Member of: Canadian Institute of Quantity Surveyors
Chief Officer(s):
Lois Metcalfe, Administrator
lois.metcalfe@ciqs-ontario.org

Canadian Institute of Realtors *See* Real Estate Institute of Canada

Canadian Institute of Resources Law (CIRL) / Institut canadien du droit des ressources
Murray Fraser Hall, University of Calgary, #3353, 2500 University Dr. NW, Calgary AB T2N 1N4
Tel: 403-220-3200; *Fax:* 403-282-6182
cirl@ucalgary.ca
www.cirl.ca
twitter.com/ResourcesLaw
Overview: A small national charitable organization founded in 1979
Mission: To undertake and promote research, education and publication on the law relating to Canada's renewable and non-renewable natural resources.
Finances: *Funding Sources:* Public and Private Sectors; Non-Governmental Organizations
Staff Member(s): 17
Activities: Sponsoring conferences, workshops & courses on aspects of resources law; *Library:* Open to public by appointment
Chief Officer(s):
Allan Ingelson, LLM; JD; BSc; B, Executive Director, 403-220-3975
allan.ingelson@ucalgary.ca
Ian Holloway, PhD, Chair
Publications:
• Canada Energy Law Service
Profile: Looseleaf guide to the regulatory regimes administered by the National Energy Board & the Alberta Energy & Utilities Board

• CIRL [Canadian Institute of Resources Law] Annual Report
Type: Yearbook; *Frequency:* Annually
• Resources [a publication of the Canadian Institute of Resources Law]
Type: Newsletter; *Frequency:* Quarterly; *ISSN:* 0714-5918; *Price:* Free
Profile: Commentary on matters of concern in natural resources law & policy, developments in resources case & statute law, & CIRL new publications,courses, & conferences

Canadian Institute of Sanitary Inspectors *See* Canadian Institute of Public Health Inspectors

Canadian Institute of Steel Construction (CISC) / Institut canadien de la construction en acier (ICCA)
#200, 3760 - 14th Ave., Markham ON L3R 3T7
Tel: 905-946-0864; *Fax:* 905-946-8574
info@cisc-icca.ca
www.cisc-icca.ca
www.linkedin.com/company/986081
www.facebook.com/cisc.icca.ca
twitter.com/cisc_icca
Overview: A medium-sized national organization founded in 1942
Mission: To promote good design & safety, together with efficient & economical use of steel as a means of expanding the construction markets for structural steel, joists & platework
Member of: Standards Council of Canada; Canadian Standards Association; Canadian Welding Bureau; Welding Institute of Canada; Canadian Steel Trade & Employment Congress; Canadian Construction Association; Construction Specifications Canada; Transportation Association of Canada
Affiliation(s): Canadian Steel Construction Council; Steel Structures Education Foundation
Staff Member(s): 14
Membership: 885; *Fees:* Schedule available; *Member Profile:* Organizations & individuals involved in the steel construction industry
Activities: *Speaker Service:* Yes; *Library:* by appointment
Chief Officer(s):
Jim McLagan, Chair
Ed Whalen, President
ewhalen@cisc-icca.ca

Canadian Institute of Stress (CIS)
Toronto ON
Tel: 416-236-4218
info@stresscanada.org
www.stresscanada.org
www.facebook.com/TheCanadianInstituteOfStress
Overview: A small national organization founded in 1979
Mission: To provide programs & tools for individuals & workplaces to handle stress
Activities: Providing certification training; Offering web-based distance education for professionals; *Speaker Service:* Yes
Chief Officer(s):
Richard Earle, Managing Director
earle@stresscanada.org

Canadian Institute of Surveying *See* Association of Canada Lands Surveyors

Canadian Institute of the Arts for Young Audiences *See* Vancouver International Children's Festival

Canadian Institute of Traffic & Transportation (CITT) / Institut canadien du trafic et du transport
#400, 10 King St. East, Toronto ON M5C 1C3
Tel: 416-363-5696; *Fax:* 416-363-5698
info@citt.ca
www.citt.ca
www.linkedin.com/company/citt
twitter.com/CITTLogistics
Overview: A medium-sized national organization founded in 1958
Mission: To promote high standards of professionalism among transportation logisticians
Staff Member(s): 7
Membership: 2,000+
Activities: Provides a CLLP certification program; courses on logistics and business management; SCL webinar series
Chief Officer(s):
Pina Melchionna, B.A., LL.B, M.B, President & CEO, 306-227-1096
pmelchionna@citt.ca

Chrissy Aitchison, Senior Manager, Marketing & Strategic Initiatives, 416-363-5696 Ext. 28
caitchison@citt.ca
Jennifer Traer, Senior Manager, Member Support & Events, 416-363-5695 Ext. 32
jtraer@citt.ca
Marysa MacKinnon, Member & Events Administrator, 416-363-5696 Ext. 21
mmackinnon@citt.ca
Maria Murjani, Manager, Programs & Student Support, 416-363-5696 Ext. 24
mmurjani@citt.ca
Meetings/Conferences:
• Canada Logistics Conference 2018, October, 2018, Vancouver, BC
Description: Annual leadership conference for supply chain logistics professionals

Canadian Institute of Transportation Engineers (CITE) / Institut Canadien des ingénieurs en transports
PO Box 25118, 1221 Weber St. East, kitchener ON N2A 4A5
Tel: 202-785-0060; *Fax:* 202-785-0609
webmaster@cite7.org
www.cite7.org
www.linkedin.com/company-beta/1030321/
www.facebook.com/itecanada
twitter.com/itecanada
Overview: A large international organization overseen by Institute of Transportation Engineers
Mission: To facilitate the application of technology & scientific principles for modes of ground transportation in Canada
Affiliation(s): Canadian Urban Transit Association; Transport Association of Canada; Intelligent Transportation Systems Society of Canada; Canadian Parking Association
Membership: 2,000+; *Member Profile:* Transportation engineers, planners, technologists & students across Canada
Activities: Promoting professional development; Supporting education; Encouraging research; Increasing public awareness; Exchanging professional information; Maintaining a central point of reference & pro-active action
Chief Officer(s):
Jen Malzer, P.Eng., President, 403-880-9786
Edward Soldo, P.Eng., FITE, Vice President, 519-661-2500 Ext. 4936
Julia Salvini, P.Eng., Secretary-Treasurer, 519-591-0426
Meetings/Conferences:
• Canadian Institute of Transportation Engineers 2018 Conference, June, 2018, Shaw Conference Centre, Edmonton, AB
Scope: National

Canadian Institute of Ukrainian Studies (CIUS) / Institut canadien d'études ukrainiennes
#4-30, Pembina Hall, University of Alberta, Edmonton AB T6G 2H8
Tel: 780-492-2972; *Fax:* 780-492-4967
cius@ualberta.ca
www.cius.ca
www.facebook.com/canadian.institute.of.ukrainian.studies
Overview: A small national organization founded in 1976
Mission: To develop Ukrainian scholarship in Canada; To organize research in Ukrainian & Ukrainian-Canadian studies
Finances: *Funding Sources:* University of Alberta operating budget; Grants for projects; Income from endoment funds; Donations
Staff Member(s): 10
Activities: Directing the Kowalsky Program for the Study of Eastern Ukraine; Coordinating the Kule Ukrainian Canadian Studies Centre; Operating the Peter Jacyk Centre for Ukrainian Historical Research; Directing the Stasiuk Program for the Study of Contemporary Ukraine; Operating the Ukrainian Language Education Centre (E-mail: ulec@ualberta.ca); Managing the Ukrainian Knowledge Internet Portal Project Office (E-mail: ukip@ualberta.ca); Supporting Ukrainian studies internationally; Organizing lectures & a seminar series
Chief Officer(s):
Volodymyr Kravchenko, Director
cius.director@ualberta.ca
Publications:
• CIUS [Canadian Institute of Ukrainian Studies] Newsletter
Type: Newsletter; *Editor:* B. Klid, M. Soroka, & M. Yurkevich; *ISSN:* 1485-7979
Profile: Information about the institute's endowment funds, grants, awards, seminars & lectures, new publications, & researchprograms

• Journal of Ukrainian Studies
Type: Journal; *Frequency:* Semiannually
Profile: Scholarly journal about Ukrainian & Ukrainian-Canadian studies, featuring articles, reviews, literary translations, & guides to research
Toronto Office
University of Toronto, #308, 256 McCaul St., Toronto ON M5T 1W5
Tel: 416-978-6934; *Fax:* 416-978-2672
Chief Officer(s):
Frank E. Sysyn, Director
f.sysyn@utoronto.ca
Roman Senkus, Senior Editor, CIUS, 416-978-8669
r.senkus@utoronto.ca
• Internet Encyclopedia of Ukraine
Type: Encyclopedia; *Editor:* Roman Senkus (r.senkus@utoronto.ca)
Profile: A comprehensive work in English on Ukrainian history, geography, people, culture, & economy

Canadian Institute of Underwriters (CIU)
c/o Marian Kingsmill, DKCI Events (David Kingsmill Consultants Inc.), PO Box 91516, Stn. Roseland Plaza, 3023 New St., Burlington ON L7R 4L6
www.ciu.ca
Overview: A medium-sized national organization
Finances: *Funding Sources:* Sponsorships
Membership: *Fees:* $110; *Member Profile:* Members have attained their Fellow of the Academy of Life Underwriting & possess a minimum of five years experience in life & health underwriting; Associate members have attained their Associate of Academy of Life Underwriting & possess a minimum of two years experience of life & health underwriting
Activities: Facilitating the exchange of ideas on issues that affect the insurance industry; Providing educational opportunities
Chief Officer(s):
Merv Gillson, Chair
merv.gillson@logiq3.com
Linda Wisleski, Treasurer
linda_wislesky@swissre.com
Russell Shaw, Incoming Treasurer
russell.shaw@rbc.com
Meetings/Conferences:
• Canadian Institute of Underwriters Annual General Meeting 2018, June, 2018, Marriott Bloor-Yorkville, Toronto, ON
Scope: National

Canadian Institutional Research & Planning Association (CIRPA) / Association canadienne de planification et de recherche institutionnelles (ACPRI)
c/o Concordia University, 1455, boul de Maisonneuve ouest, Montréal QC H3G 1M8
Tel: 514-848-2424
www.cirpa-acpri.ca
www.linkedin.com/groups/CIRPA-ACPRI-Canadian-Institutional-Research-4083906
Previous Name: Canadian Institutional Researchers & Planners Association
Overview: A small national organization founded in 1994
Mission: To promote the professional interests of its members; to advance research on post-secondary education in general & to encourage studies of the operation of post-secondary institutions in particular; to promote good practice in institutional policy-making, management, planning & research; to encourage a closer cooperation between researchers on post-secondary education & institutional researchers, planners, managers & policy-makers; to encourage comparative studies of post-secondary systems
Affiliation(s): Association of Institutional Research; European Air
Membership: 230; *Fees:* $100; $50 student; *Committees:* Nominations
Chief Officer(s):
Sharon Schultz, President

Canadian Institutional Researchers & Planners Association
See Canadian Institutional Research & Planning Association

Canadian Insurance Accountants Association (CIAA) / Association canadienne des comptables en assurance
#301, 250 Consumers Rd., Toronto ON M2J 4V6
Tel: 416-494-1440
ciaa@ciaa.org
www.ciaa.org

Overview: A medium-sized national organization founded in 1934
Mission: To promote study, research, & development of management & insurance accounting
Membership: *Fees:* $160; *Member Profile:* Active members are employed by an insurance / reinsurance company, insurance / reinsurance broker, or an insurance agency; Associate members are involved in the supply of specialized knowledge or services to the insurance industry
Activities: Providing a professional development program, including courses, seminars, speakers, & conferences; Facilitating networking opportunities within the industry; *Speaker Service:* Yes
Chief Officer(s):
Lisa Isaacs, Account Executive
Meetings/Conferences:
• Canadian Insurance Accountants Association 2018 54th Annual Conference, September, 2018, Fairmont Montebello, Montebello, QC
Scope: National
Publications:
• Canadian Insurance Accountants Association Membership Directory
Type: Directory; *Frequency:* Annually
Profile: Listings of CIAA members with their contact information

Canadian Insurance Claims Managers Association (CICMA)
c/o Insurance Bureau of Canada, PO Box 121, #2400, 777 Bay St., Toronto ON M5G 2C8
Tel: 416-362-2031; *Fax:* 416-361-5952
www.cicma.ca
Overview: A small national organization founded in 1952
Mission: To maintain a high standard of ethics among those who handle general insurance claims; To promote the general insurance industry in matters related to the settlement of claims; To advance administration to result in just settlement of claims
Membership: *Member Profile:* Active members include officers of a general insurance company who are engaged in the administration of claims, & employees of general insurance companies whose responsibility involves the management of employees who administer claims; Life members have an established record of outstanding service in the association; Honorary members are senior officers of an association, government department, or administrative body; Associate members are persons who were previously active members in good standing; *Committees:* Arbitration; Communication; Constitution; Education; IBC Liaison; Membership/Association Enhancement; Treasurer; Website
Activities: Administering the Canadian Inter-Company Arbitration Agreement; Facilitating information exchange; Promoting mediation or arbitration to resolve claims
Chief Officer(s):
Patrick O'Hara, President
pohara@millenniuminsurance.ca

Canadian Integrative Network for Death Education & Alternatives (CINDEA)
contact@cindea.ca
www.cindea.ca
Overview: A small national organization
Mission: To provide support for the pan-death movement & end-of-life practitioners
Member of: National Home Funeral Alliance
Membership: *Fees:* $20/year; *Member Profile:* Individuals engaged or interested in pan-death care
Activities: Offering pan-death information & resources
Chief Officer(s):
Pashta MaryMoon, Director

Canadian Intergovernmental Conference Secretariat (CICS) / Secrétariat des conférences intergouvernementales canadiennes
PO Box 488, Stn. A, 222 Queen St., 10th Fl., Ottawa ON K1N 8V5
Tel: 613-995-2341; *Fax:* 613-996-6091
info@scics.gc.ca
www.scics.gc.ca
twitter.com/cics_info
Mission: CICS was established in 1973 by the First Ministers as an agency of the federal & provincial governments. Governments recognized a need for a mechanism to serve, on a continuing basis, conferences of First Ministers & a growing number of intergovernmental meetings. CICS serves federal-provincial First Ministers' meetings, the Annual Premiers' Conference, the Eastern Canadian Premiers' & New England

Governors' Conference & the Western Premiers' Conference. The core of the Secretariat's work is providing services to multilateral meetings of Ministers & Deputy Ministers in virtually every sector of government activity. The Secretariat's services are available to federal, provincial & territorial departments that are called upon to organize & chair such meetings. The agency's mandate & sole program are designed to relieve its clients of the numerous & various technical & administrative tasks associated with the planning & conduct of senior level intergovernmental conferences. The CICS maintains through its Information Services section, a document archives (including audio-visual & photographic material) for the use of governments & the general public. The information contained in the archives is made available, as appropriate, to government institutions at the federal, provincial & territorial levels while unclassified material is also available to the public on request.
Chief Officer(s):
André McArdle, Secretary, 613-995-2345

Canadian International Air Show (CIAS)
Press Bldg., Exhibition Place, 210 Princes' Blvd., 2nd Fl., Toronto ON M6K 3C3
Tel: 416-263-3650; *Fax:* 416-263-3654
info@cias.org
cias.org
www.facebook.com/torontoairshow
twitter.com/TorontoAirshow
Also Known As: Canadian Exhibition Airshows Inc.
Overview: A medium-sized local organization founded in 1949
Mission: To entertain the Toronto community with world-class air shows; to provide customized opportunities for our corporate partners; to support community groups through involvement in fund-raising & outreach programs
Member of: International Council of Air Shows; NorthEast Council of Airshows; Etobicoke Chamber of Commerce
Finances: *Funding Sources:* Metropolitan Toronto; independent sponsorship

Canadian International Council (CIC) / Conseil international du Canada
6 Hoskin Ave., Toronto ON M5S 1H8
Tel: 416-946-7209
Other Communication: www.opencanada.org
info@thecic.org
www.thecic.org
www.facebook.com/CanadianInternationalCouncil
twitter.com/TheCIC
www.youtube.com/user/onlinecicvideos
Previous Name: Canadian Institute of International Affairs / Institut canadien des affaires internationales
Overview: A medium-sized international charitable organization founded in 1928
Mission: To strengthen Canada's role in international affairs; To advance research & dialogue on international affairs
Finances: *Funding Sources:* Private supporters
Staff Member(s): 9
Membership: *Fees:* $75 regular; $45 young professional (under 35 years of age); $20 student; *Member Profile:* Individuals & organizations interested in international affairs
Activities: Conducting policy research; Offering a fellowship program; Presenting seminars, discussions, & study groups
Chief Officer(s):
Keith Martin, Acting President
Publications:
• The 9 Habits of Highly Effective Resource Economies [a publication of the Canadian International Council]
Type: Report; *Number of Pages:* 89; *Author:* Madeline Drohan
Profile: A research report on Canada's rich natural resource endowment & oppportunities that can contributeto Canada's future prosperity
• Behaviour of Chinese SOEs [a publication of the Canadian International Council]
Type: Report; *Number of Pages:* 25; *Author:* Margaret Keenan
• Canadian International Council Annual Report
Type: Report
• Intellectual Property Report [a publication of the Canadian International Council]
Type: Report; *Number of Pages:* 96
• International Journal [a publication of the Canadian International Council]
Type: Journal; *Editor:* Brian Bow; *Price:* $38 with regular CIC membership; $29 with student CIC membership
Profile: Scholarly articles on international relations
• Issues in Canada-China Relations [a publication of the Canadian International Council]
Type: Report; *Number of Pages:* 427; *Author:* Pitman Potter

• Open Canada: A Global Positioning Strategy for a Networked Age [a publication of the Canadian International Council]
Type: Report; *Number of Pages:* 93; *Author:* Edward Greenspon; *ISBN:* 0-9866175-1-2
• Strategic Studies Working Group Papers [a publication of the Canadian International Council]
Type: Report; *Author:* Thomas Keenan
Profile: A research report on technological security

Canadian International Dragon Boat Festival Society (CIDBFS)
Creekside Community Centre, 1 Athletes Way, Vancouver BC V5Y 0B1
Tel: 604-688-2382; *Fax:* 866-571-9004
info@dragonboatbc.ca
dragonboatbc.ca
www.facebook.com/thedragonboatbc
twitter.com/dragonboatbc
Also Known As: Rio Tinto Alcan Dragon Boat Festival
Previous Name: Dragon Boat Festival Society
Overview: A small national organization founded in 1989
Mission: To foster learning & exploration of Canada's diverse multicultural heritage through performing, visual & culinary arts, & dragon boat-racing
Member of: Vancouver Cultural Alliance
Finances: *Funding Sources:* Government; corporate; donations; fund-raising
Staff Member(s): 12; 1000 volunteer(s)
Activities: Annual 3 day multicultural festival; year long education program on multiculturalism; *Speaker Service:* Yes
Chief Officer(s):
Ann Phelps, Executive Director

Canadian International DX Club (CIDX)
PO Box 67063, Stn. Lemoyne, Saint-Lambert QC J4R 2T8
cidxclub@yahoo.com
www.anarc.org/cidx
Overview: A small international organization founded in 1962
Mission: To serve radio enthusiasts throughout the world
Member of: Association of North American Radio Clubs
Finances: *Funding Sources:* Membership fees
Membership: *Fees:* $10 members for outside Canada or the U.S.A.; $15 Canadian & U.S.A. members; *Member Profile:* Members of the radio monitoring community from around the world
Activities: Providing education about radio; Promoting the radio hobby
Publications:
• Messenger
Type: Newsletter; *Frequency:* Monthly; *Price:* Free with membership in the Canadian International DX Club
Profile: Information on all aspects of radio, such as AM, FM, shortwave, pirate broadcasting, & Internet & satellite radio

Canadian International Freight Forwarders Association (CIFFA) / Association des transitaires internationaux canadiens (ATIC)
#480, 170 Attwell Dr., Toronto ON M9W 5Z5
Tel: 416-234-5100; *Fax:* 416-234-5152
Toll-Free: 866-282-4332
secretariat@ciffa.com
www.ciffa.com
www.linkedin.com/company-beta/782966
www.facebook.com/CiffaInc
twitter.com/CIFFAInc
Overview: A large international organization founded in 1948
Mission: To represent & support members of the Canadian international freight forwarding industry in providing the highest level of quality & professional services to their clients
Member of: Federation internationale des associations de transitaires et assimiles
Affiliation(s): International Federation of Freight Forwarders Associations
Finances: *Annual Operating Budget:* $500,000-$1.5 Million; *Funding Sources:* Membership dues; education fees
Staff Member(s): 5; 20 volunteer(s)
Membership: 188 regular + 94 associate; *Fees:* $1,145-$2,545 regular; $770 associate; *Member Profile:* Canadian companies involved in freight forwarding; *Committees:* Airfreight; By Laws; Customs & Co-chair; Education; Ethics & Standards; FIATA; Finance; Judicial; Membership; Seafreight
Activities: CIFFA Professional Training Program; education courses; dangerous goods courses, topical workshops
Chief Officer(s):
Gary Vince, President, 289-562-6601, Fax: 905-564-1380

Bruce Rodgers, Vice-President, National Product Customs, 905-673-5254, Fax: 905-677-0587
Wendy Trudeau, Managing Director, Transportation, 905-677-7381
Angelo Loffredi, Vice President, International Trade & Special Accounts, 514-343-0044, Fax: 514-343-2635
Awards:
• CIFFA Scholarship Program
To promote higher learning in international trade, logistics & commerce; Increase awareness of freight forwarding as a career; Support the children of CIFFA Regular Members' employees in achieving highter learning *Eligibility:* Child of an employee of a CIFFA Regular Member company as of June 1 of the award year; Student entering any year of undergraduate/graduate studies at an accredited Canadian university or college; Enrolled in international trade, logistics or businesses course leading to a diploma or degree *Deadline:* August; *Amount:* 2 installments of $1500 during the first and second years of study
• Donna Letterio Leadership Award
The award recognizes a woman in the global freight logistics sector who has demonstrated professionalism, commitment, leadership and a passion for excellence *Eligibility:* Any woman in international freight forwarding, transportation or global logistics who demonstrates excellence in professionalism, commitment and leadership *Deadline:* March 10
Meetings/Conferences:
• CIFFA Annual General Meeting, 2018
Publications:
• The Forwarder [a publication of Canadian International Freight Forwarders Association, Inc.]
Type: Magazine; *Accepts Advertising*
  Central Division
  PO Box 159, Stn. Toronto AMF, Mississauga ON L5P 1B1
  Tel: 905-362-6000
  Chief Officer(s):
  Jodie Wilson, Chair
  jodie.wilson@lcnav.com
  Eastern Division
  c/o Milgram International Shipping, #400, 645, rue Wellington, Montréal QC H3C 0L1
  Tel: 514-288-2358
  Chief Officer(s):
  Angelo Loffredi, Chair
  aloffredi@milgram.com%20
  Western Division
  c/o Courtney Agencies Ltd., #802, 535 Thurlow St., Vancouver BC V6E 3L2
  Tel: 604-684-7505
  Chief Officer(s):
  Paul Courtney, Chair
  paul@courtney.ca

Canadian International Grains Institute
#1000, 303 Main St., Winnipeg MB R3C 3G7
Tel: 204-983-5344; *Fax:* 204-983-2642
cigi@cigi.ca
www.cigi.ca
www.facebook.com/278582516605
twitter.com/CigiWinnipeg
www.youtube.com/user/CIGIwinnipeg
Overview: A medium-sized international organization founded in 1972
Mission: To provide educational programs & technical activities in support of market development & promotion of world markets for Canada's grains, oilseeds & special crops
Finances: *Funding Sources:* Canadian Wheat Board; International Markets Bureau of Agriculture; Agri-Food Canada
Staff Member(s): 35
Activities: Provides an average of 35 programs annually
Chief Officer(s):
JoAnne Buth, Chief Executive Officer
jbuth@cigi.ca
Heather Johnson, Director, Communications, 204-983-7678
hjohnson@cigi.ca

Canadian International Institute of Applied Negotiation (CIIAN) / L'Institut international canadien de la négociation pratique
68B Raddarz Rd., RR#2, Eganville ON K0J 1T0
Tel: 613-237-9050
ciian@ciian.org
www.ciian.org
www.facebook.com/145938635447384
twitter.com/CIIAN

Overview: A small international organization founded in 1992
Mission: To build sustainable peace at local, national, & international levels
Activities: Offering conflict prevention, dispute resolution, & peacebuilding programming, such as the Domestic Program, the International Program, the Violence Prevention Early Response Unit, & Special Programs; Providing courses & workshops, including a Certificate Program in Peacebuilding & Conflict Resolution; Conferring the professional designation of Registered Practitioner in Dispute Resolution (RPDR); Developing resources such as research papers, manuals, & videos; *Speaker Service:* Yes
Chief Officer(s):
Benjamin Hoffman, President
Evan Hoffman, Executive Director
ehoffman@ciian.org
Publications:
• CIIAN [Canadian International Institute of Applied Negotiation] News
Type: Newsletter; *Accepts Advertising*
Profile: Information about Canadian International Institute of Applied Negotiation projects, such as clinics & courses, scholarships, & forthcomingpublications
• The Mediator's Handbook for Durable Peace
Type: Handbook; *Author:* Evan Hoffman
Profile: The presentation of an original model of durable peace, plus practical tactics
• New Math for Human Relations
Type: Handbook; *Author:* Dr. Benjamin Hoffman; *Price:* $10
• The Peace Guerilla Handbook
Type: Handbook; *Author:* Dr. Benjamin Hoffman; *Price:* $11
Profile: Information for persons who must prevent violence or build peace

Canadian Internet Registration Authority (CIRA)
#306, 350 Sparks St., Ottawa ON K1R 7S8
Tel: 613-237-5335; *Fax:* 800-285-0517
www.cira.ca
www.linkedin.com/groups?gid=2456714
www.facebook.com/cira.ca
twitter.com/ciranews
www.youtube.com/ciranews
Overview: A small national organization founded in 1987
Mission: To operate the dot-ca internet country code.
Staff Member(s): 6
Membership: *Member Profile:* Individuals who own a .ca domain name
Chief Officer(s):
Byron Holland, President & CEO

Canadian Interoperability Technology Interest Group (CITIG)
c/o Canadian Association of Chiefs of Police, #100, 300 Terry Fox Dr., Kanata ON K2K 0E3
Tel: 613-595-1101
www.citig.ca
Overview: A medium-sized national organization founded in 2007
Mission: To improve communications interoperability in the field of Canadian public safety
Affiliation(s): Canadian Association of Chiefs of Police (CACP); Canadian Association of Fire Chiefs (CAFC); Paramedic Chiefs of Canada (PCC)
Membership: 1,250; *Fees:* Free; *Member Profile:* First responders; members of government, non-governmental organizations, associations, academia & industry
Chief Officer(s):
Lance Valcour, O.O.M., Executive Director

Canadian Interuniversity Athletic Union *See* Canadian Interuniversity Sport

Canadian Interuniversity Sport (CIS) / Sport interuniversitaire canadien (SIC)
#N205, 801 King Edward, Ottawa ON K1N 6N5
Tel: 613-562-5670; *Fax:* 613-562-5669
feedback@universitysport.ca
www.cis-sic.ca
www.facebook.com/cissports
twitter.com/CIS_SIC
www.youtube.com/universitysport; www.instagram.com/CIS_SIC
Previous Name: Canadian Interuniversity Athletic Union
Overview: A medium-sized national organization overseen by Universities Canada
Mission: To act as the national governing body for men's & women's university sport in Canada
Member of: Universities Canada
Affiliation(s): Atlantic University Sport; Québec Student Sport Federation; Ontario University Athletics; Canada West Universities Athletic Association
Staff Member(s): 9
Membership: 55 institutional (these are also members of four regional associations)
Chief Officer(s):
Drew Love, Interim Chief Operating Officer, 613-568-5670 Ext. 26
dlove@universitysport.ca
Debbie Villeneuve, Director, Finance & Administration, 613-568-5670 Ext. 24
villeneuve@universitysport.ca

Canadian Intravenous Nurses Association *See* Canadian Vascular Access Association

Canadian Investor Protection Fund (CIPF) / Fonds canadien de protection des épargnants (FCPE)
First Canadian Place, PO Box 481, #2610, 100 King St. West, Toronto ON M5X 1E5
Tel: 416-866-8366; *Fax:* 416-360-8441
Toll-Free: 866-243-6981
info@cipf.ca
www.cipf.ca
Previous Name: National Contingency Fund
Overview: A medium-sized national organization founded in 1969
Mission: To foster a healthy & active capital market in Canada by contributing to the security & confidence of investors who have accounts with members of sponsoring self-regulatory organizations
Membership: 100-499; *Member Profile:* Investment dealers who are members of our sponsoring self-regulatory organizations; *Committees:* Audit, Finance & Investment; Governance, Nominating & Human Resources; Coverage; Industry Risk
Chief Officer(s):
Rozanne E. Reszel, President & Chief Executive Officer
Barbara Love, Senior Vice-President & Secretary
Linda Pendrill, Chief Financial Officer
Ilana Singer, Vice-President
Tammy Smith, Director, Risk Assessment
Donna Yiu, Director, Industry Policy & Risk

Canadian Investor Relations Institute (CIRI) / Institut canadien de relations avec les investisseurs
#601, 67 Yonge St., Toronto ON M5E 1J8
Tel: 416-364-8200; *Fax:* 416-364-2805
enquiries@ciri.org
www.ciri.org
Previous Name: National Investor Relations Institute Canada (NIRI Canada)
Overview: A medium-sized national organization founded in 1990
Mission: To advance the practice of investor relations; To raise the stature of the profession in Canada; To act as the voice of investor relations professionals throughout Canada
Finances: *Funding Sources:* Corporate donations
Membership: 600+; *Member Profile:* Executives who are responsible for communications between public corporations, the financial community, & investors, such as IR practitioners, IR consultants, & IR vendors; *Committees:* Audit; Certification Curriculum; Certification Governance; Corporate Donation Program; Editorial Board; Human Resources, Compensation & Corporate Governance; Issues; Membership; Resource & Education
Activities: Advancing the professional competency of members through professional development sessions; Engaging in advocacy activities; Encouraging research
Chief Officer(s):
Yvette Lokker, President & Chief Executive Officer, 416-364-8200 Ext. 224
ylokker@ciri.org
Salisha Hosein, Director, Professional Development & Communications, 416-364-8200 Ext. 228
shosein@ciri.org
Kaitlin Beca, Coordinator, Programming, 416-364-8200 Ext. 221
kbeca@ciri.org
Karen Clutsam, Coordinator, Membership, 416-364-8200 Ext. 229
kclutsam@ciri.org
Jane Maciel, Executive Assistant & Specialist, Publications, 416-364-8200 Ext. 222
jmaciel@ciri.org
Meetings/Conferences:
• Canadian Investor Relations Institute 31st Annual Conference, June, 2018, Toronto Marriott Downtown, Toronto, ON
Scope: National
Publications:
• CIRI [Canadian Investor Relations Institute] Newsline
Type: Newsletter; *Frequency:* Bimonthly; *Accepts Advertising*;
Price: Free for Canadian Investor Relations Institute members
Profile: In-depth information about regulatory & accounting issues, capital markets, & IR practices, for members
• CIRI [Canadian Investor Relations Institute] wIRed
Type: Newsletter; *Frequency:* Weekly
Profile: Institute activities, job listings, & professional development events, for persons involved in the investor relations field
• CIRI [Canadian Investor Relations Institute] Membership Directory
Type: Directory
Profile: Listings of the Institute's members & their contact information
• A Guide to Developing an IR Program [a publication of the Canadian Investor Relations Institute]
• Investor Relations Compensation & Responsibilities Survey [a publication of the Canadian Investor Relations Institute]
• IR Focus [a publication of the Canadian Investor Relations Institute]
Frequency: Bimonthly; *Price:* Free for Canadian Investor Relations Institute members
Profile: Distributed with Newsline, the publication addresses a single professional challenge
• Issues Bulletin [a publication of the Canadian Investor Relations Institute]
Price: Free for Canadian Investor RelationsInstitute members
Profile: A production of the CIRI Issues Committee to update members on current developments affecting investor relations
• Standards & Guidance for Disclosure [a publication of the Canadian Investor Relations Institute]
Price: Free for Canadian Investor Relations Institute members
Profile: Featuring a Model Disclosure Policy template

Canadian Iris Society (CIS)
c/o Ed Jowett, 1960 Sideroad 15, RR#2, Tottenham ON L0G 1W0
Tel: 905-936-9941
cdniris@gmail.com
www.cdn-iris.ca
Overview: A small national organization founded in 1946
Mission: To encourage, improve & extend the cultivation of the Iris & to collaborate with other societies for this purpose, as well as to regulate the nomenclature & colour classification of this flower.
Finances: *Funding Sources:* Membership dues; iris auctions
Membership: *Fees:* $20 1 year; $50 3 years; *Member Profile:* Amateur gardeners; gardening experts; horticulturists
Activities: June Iris Shows: Royal Botanical Gardens, Hamilton; Iris sales & auctions; *Awareness Events:* June Iris Shows
Chief Officer(s):
Ed Jowett, President
jowettfarm@copper.net
Nancy Kennedy, Secretary
xkennedy@sympatico.ca

Canadian ISBN Agency (ISBN) / Agence canadienne de l'ISBN
Library & Archives Canada, 395 Wellington St., Ottawa ON K1A 0N4
Tel: 819-994-6872; *Fax:* 819-977-7517
Toll-Free: 866-578-7777
isbn@lac-bac.gc.ca
www.collectionscanada.gc.ca/isn/041011-1000-e.html
Also Known As: Canadian International Standard Book Number Agency
Overview: A small national organization founded in 1974
Member of: Library & Archives Canada
Affiliation(s): International ISBN Agency
Activities: Assigns ISBNs for Canadian book publishers

Canadian IT Law Association / Association canadienne du droit des technologies de l'information
c/o Lisa Ptack, PO Box 918, 1 Promenade Circle, Thornhill ON L4J 8G7
www.it-can.ca
Also Known As: IT Can
Overview: A medium-sized national organization founded in 1997
Mission: To develop & encourage the use of technology law in Canada

Membership: *Fees:* Schedule available
Chief Officer(s):
Simon Hodgett, President, Executive Commitee
shodgett@osler.com
Lisa Ptack, Executive Director
lisa.ptack@rogers.com

Canadian Italian Business & Professional Association (CIBPA) / Association des gens d'affaires & professionnels italo-canadiens
#310, 8370, boul Lacordaire, Montréal QC H1R 3Y6
Tel: 514-254-4929; *Fax:* 514-254-4920
info@cibpamontreal.com
www.cibpamontreal.com
www.facebook.com/cibpa.montreal
twitter.com/CIBPAMONTREAL
Overview: A medium-sized international organization founded in 1949
Mission: To encourage high ethical standards & professional development; To voice concerns in order to protect the interests of members
Membership: 400+; *Member Profile:* Business people & professionals of Italian origin or descent
Activities: Fostering trade & business dealings between members; Providing a bursary program
Chief Officer(s):
Giovanni Chieffallo, President
Carole Gagliardi, Vice-President, Communications
Mike Goriani, Vice-President, Events
Roberto Rinaldi, Vice-President, Membership
Sam Spatari, Vice-President, Finance
Luisa Papa, Administrative Secretary

Canadian Italian Business & Professional Association of Ottawa (CIBPA)
1026 Baseline Rd., Ottawa ON K2C 0A6
info@cibpaottawa.com
www.cibpa-ottawa.com
Overview: A small local organization founded in 1961
Mission: CIBPA promotes the recreational, cultural, social, artistic, charitable, business and professional activities of Italian Canadians in the National Capital Region and also encourages the participation of Italian Canadians in the economic and public affairs of this region and Canada.
Membership: 1-99; *Fees:* $95 regular; $25 student
Chief Officer(s):
Gino Milito, President
Awards:
• CIBPA Ottawa Scholarship Awards

Canadian Italian Heritage Foundation (CIHF)
11 Director Ct., Woodbridge ON L4L 4S5
Tel: 905-850-4500; *Fax:* 905-850-4516
Overview: A medium-sized national charitable organization
Mission: To work with the Italian Canadian community to undertake projects in collaboration with other existing organizations that support & promote Italian heritage & culture through activities within Canada
Chief Officer(s):
Michael Tibollo, President
Awards:
• Canadian Italian Heritage Foundation Scholarship Award
Eligibility: Must be between 16 and 28; must have one parent that is of Canadian-Italian descent

Canadian Jesuits International (CJI)
70 Saint Mary St., Toronto ON M5S 1J3
Tel: 416-465-1824
Toll-Free: 800-448-2148
cji@jesuits.ca
www.canadianjesuitsinternational.ca
www.facebook.com/canadianjesuitsinternational
twitter.com/CJIyouth4others
Also Known As: Canadian Jesuit Missions
Overview: A medium-sized national charitable organization founded in 1955
Mission: Committed to the service of faith & the promotion of justice for the poor of the world; especially dedicated to the educational needs of women, children, elderly & indigenous people at home & abroad
Staff Member(s): 5
Activities: Support projects in Africa, India, Nepal, Jamaica, & Ukraine
Chief Officer(s):
Jenny Cafiso, Director
Publications:
• Mission News [a publication of Canadian Jesuits International]

Type: Newsletter; *Frequency:* 3 pa
Profile: News & stories about people in developing countries

Canadian Jewellers Association (CJA)
#600, 27 Queen St. East, Toronto ON M5C 2M6
Tel: 416-368-7616; *Fax:* 416-368-1986
Toll-Free: 800-580-0942
www.canadianjewellers.com
Overview: A medium-sized national organization founded in 1923
Mission: To provide its members with information, services & techonology that allow them to flourish in their profession
Member of: The World Jewellery Confederation
Finances: *Funding Sources:* Trade show; membership dues
Membership: 1,090; *Fees:* Schedule available; *Member Profile:* Retailers; manufacturers; wholesalers; supply sector; *Committees:* Accredited Appraiser Program; Charity; Diamonds/Colored Stones; Ethics; Investment/Audit; Government Relations; Marketing/Public Relations; Membership Benefits; Membership Review; Insurance; Watch/Supply; Executive; Young Professional Networking
Activities: Benefits; series of industry-related courses of study; *Rents Mailing List:* Yes; *Library:* Tiffany/Gerstein Library; Not open to public
Chief Officer(s):
David Ritter, President & CEO

Canadian Jewish Congress See The Centre for Israel & Jewish Affairs

Canadian Jiu-jitsu Council
PO Box 543, Madoc ON K0K 2K0
Tel: 613-473-4366
www.jiujitsucouncil.ca
Overview: A medium-sized national organization founded in 1968
Mission: A non-profit educational Martial Arts organization under the Canadian Province of Ontario Charter. The CJC is administered by a volunteer group of senior Black Belts whose objective is to guide and assist the growth of Jiujitsu in a friendly, healthy environment and to help more people get more benefits, knowledge and pleasure from the Martial Art and Science of Jiujitsu.
Membership: *Fees:* $40 club; $40 black belts; $25 senior students; $10 junior students
Chief Officer(s):
Robert Walthers, President
rwalther@kos.net

Canadian Journalism Foundation (CJF) / La Fondation pour le journalisme canadien
#500, 59 Adelaide St. East, Toronto ON M5C 1K6
Tel: 416-955-0394; *Fax:* 416-532-6879
www.cjf-fjc.ca
www.facebook.com/cjfprograms
twitter.com/cjffjc
Overview: A medium-sized national charitable organization founded in 1990
Mission: To honour outstanding achievements in the field of journalism in Canada through grants, awards & scholarships; to promote & support programs & seminars at or in conjunction with qualified educational institutions in journalism.
Finances: *Annual Operating Budget:* $250,000-$500,000; *Funding Sources:* Media and non-media corporations and foundations; membership dues.
Staff Member(s): 3
Activities: *Internships:* Yes
Chief Officer(s):
Natalie Turvey, Executive Director
nturvey@cjf-fjc.ca
Wendy Kan, Program Manager
wkan@cjf-fjc.ca

Canadian Journalists for Free Expression (CJFE) / Journalistes canadiens pour la liberté d'expression
PO Box 407, #1101, 555 Richmond St. West, Toronto ON M5V 3B1
Tel: 416-515-9622; *Fax:* 416-515-7879
cjfe@cjfe.org
www.cjfe.org
www.facebook.com/167459509971053
twitter.com/canadacjfe
Previous Name: The Canadian Committee to Protect Journalists
Overview: A medium-sized national charitable organization founded in 1982

Mission: To promote freedom of expression
Member of: International Freedom of Expression Exchange (IFEX)
Finances: *Funding Sources:* Membership fees; donations; foundation grants
Staff Member(s): 12; 2 volunteer(s)
Membership: 300+; *Fees:* $25; *Member Profile:* Journalists; writers; producers; editors; publishers & others interested; *Committees:* Journalists in Exile
Activities: IFEX Clearing House operates an Action Alert Network & disseminates information on freedom of the press to organizations & individuals around the world; operates a Journalists in Distress Fund; training programs for journalists living in the developing world; *Awareness Events:* Word On The Street; World Press Freedom Day, May 3
Chief Officer(s):
Tom Henheffer, Executive Director
Arnold Amber, President
Awards:
• Canadian International Press Freedom Awards

Canadian Junior Chamber See Junior Chamber International Canada

Canadian Junior Football League (CJFL)
www.cjfl.org
www.facebook.com/166507583399023
twitter.com/cjflnews
Overview: A large national organization founded in 1908
Mission: To foster community involvement & a positive environment; To teach discipline, perseverance & cooperation
Member of: Football Canada
Membership: 18 teams; *Member Profile:* Young men aged 17-22
Activities: Canadian Bowl (National championship)
Chief Officer(s):
Jim Pankovich, Commissioner
Todd Wilson, Deputy Commissioner
Paul Shortt, Executive Director
Ryan Watters, Director, Communications & Digital Media
Awards:
• Stewart MacDonald Executive of the Year
• Life Membership
• Ed Henick Meritorious Service
• Past Commissioners Community Service
• Gord Currie Coach of the Year
• Rookie of the Year
• Larry Wruck Defensive Player of the Year
• Peter Dalla Riva Offensive Player of the Year
• Intergold Cup Champions
• Jostens Cup Champions
• Leader Post Trophy Champions
• Armadale Cup Champions
• Paul Kirk Memorial Trophy
• John M Bannerman Memorial Trophy
• Canadian Bowl Champions

Canadian Junior Golf Association (CJGA)
#6, 170 West Beaver Creek Rd., Richmond Hill ON L4B 1L6
Tel: 905-731-6388; *Fax:* 905-731-6058
Toll-Free: 877-508-1069
info@cjga.com
www.cjga.com
www.facebook.com/cjga.ca
twitter.com/CJGA
Overview: A medium-sized national organization founded in 1993
Mission: To provide competition & instruction to junior golfers in Canada
Staff Member(s): 28
Activities: Golf tours & competitions; kids programs
Chief Officer(s):
Earl M. Fritz, Executive Director
earl.fritz@cjga.com

Canadian Katahdin Sheep Association Inc. (CKSA)
c/o Canadian Livestock Records Corporation, 2417 Holly Lane, Ottawa ON K1V 0M7
Tel: 613-731-7110; *Fax:* 613-731-0704
katahdin@clrc.ca
www.katahdinsheep.com
Overview: A small national organization founded in 1995
Mission: To provide a system for the development, identification, & registration of Katahdin sheep in Canada, through the Canadian Livestock Records Corporation Inc.; To address issues of concern to the Katahdin sheep industry; To

Canadian Associations / Canadian Kendo Federation (CKF) / Fédération canadienne de kendo

expand the industry
Affiliation(s): Canadian Livestock Records Corporation
Membership: 80; *Fees:* $10 junior members; $25 associate members; $50 renewed farm memberships, individual, or company; $60 new farm memberships; $1,000 life memberships; *Member Profile:* Persons, partnerships, or farms that own at least one Canadian-registered Katahdin sheep
Activities: Establishing & maintaining selective breeding standards; Promoting Katahdin sheep; Maintaining records of the transfer of ownership of Katahdin sheep; Compiling & publishing data relating to Katahdin sheep; Assisting in the implementation of research programs; Educating the public & members of the association
Chief Officer(s):
Louis L'Arrivee, President, 306-769-8981, Fax: 306-769-8916
landjlarrivee@sasktel.net
Bonnie Ramsey, Vice-President, 204-662-4588, Fax: 204-662-4588
wickedsheep@hotmail.com
Ron Black, Secretary-Treasurer, 613-731-7110 Ext. 303, Fax: 613-731-0704
ron.black@clrc.ca
Lorna Woolsey, Registrar, 613-731-7110 Ext. 306, Fax: 613-731-0704
lorna.woolsey@clrc.ca
Laura Lee Mills, Registrar (French), 613-731-7110 Ext. 314, Fax: 613-731-0704
lauralee.mills@clrc.ca
Meetings/Conferences:
• Canadian Katahdin Sheep Association 2018 Annual General Meeting, 2018
Scope: National
Publications:
• Canadian Katahdin Sheep Association Breed Guidebook
Type: Guidebook
Profile: Characteristics, standards, procedures, identification, & registration
• Canadian Katahdin Sheep Association Newsletter
Type: Newsletter; *Frequency:* Quarterly; *Accepts Advertising*; *Editor:* Duane Rose; *Price:* Free with membership in the Canadian Katahdin Sheep Association
Profile: Association updates, articles, & photographs of Katahdin sheep

Canadian Kendo Federation (CKF) / Fédération canadienne de kendo
c/o Christian D'Orangeville, 65, rue Saint-Paul ouest, Montréal QC H2Y 35S
www.kendo-canada.com
www.facebook.com/KendoCanada
twitter.com/KendoCanada
Also Known As: Kendo Federation
Overview: A small national organization
Mission: To support Kendo, Iaido, & Jodo in Canada
Finances: *Funding Sources:* Membership fees; Donations; Sale of CKF souvenirs
Membership: *Fees:* $15 junior (age 15 & under); $35 regular; $75 club; *Committees:* Kendo Grading; Iaido Grading; Jodo Grading; Finance; Internal Review; Budget & Event; Team Canada; Secretary's; CKF History
Chief Officer(s):
Christian D'Orangeville, President
cdorangeville@kendo-canada.com

Canadian Kennel Club (CKC) / Club canin canadien
#400, 200 Ronson Dr., Toronto ON M9W 5Z9
Tel: 416-675-5511; *Fax:* 416-675-6506
Toll-Free: 855-364-7252
Other Communication: orderdesk@ckc.ca
information@ckc.ca
www.ckc.ca
www.facebook.com/CKC4thedogs
twitter.com/CKC4thedogs
instagram.com/ckc4thedogs
Overview: A large national organization founded in 1888
Mission: To provide registry services for all breeds of purebred dogs; To provide governance for all CKC approved events; To encourage, guide, & advance the interests of purebred dogs & their owners & breeders in Canada
Finances: *Annual Operating Budget:* Greater than $5 Million; *Funding Sources:* Membership dues; Service fees
Staff Member(s): 45; 50 volunteer(s)
Membership: 18,000; *Fees:* $51 basic; $102 premier; *Committees:* Executive Performance and Compensation Review; Board Orientation & Education; Breed Standards; Club Recognition; Breeder Relations; Event Officiating; Genetics & Medical; Legislation; Strategic Planning; Responsible Dog Ownership; Communications; Appeal; Audit; Discipline; Registration
Activities: Promoting shows & events; Offering registry services; Providing information about dogs; *Speaker Service:* Yes; *Library:* CKC Library; Open to public
Chief Officer(s):
Lance Novak, Executive Director
ed@ckc.ca
Sherry Weiss, Manager, Events
sweiss@ckc.ca
Andrew Patton, Manager, Marketing & Communications
apatton@ckc.ca
Diane Draper, Manager, Regulatory
ddraper@ckc.ca
Publications:
• Breeders' Showcase [a publication of the Canadian Kennel Club]
Accepts Advertising
• The Bulletin [a publication of the Canadian Kennel Club]
Type: Newsletter; *Frequency:* Monthly; *Price:* Free with CKC membership
• Directory of Breeders [a publication of the Canadian Kennel Club]
Type: Directory; *Accepts Advertising*
• Directory of Suppliers [a publication of the Canadian Kennel Club]
Type: Directory
• Dogs Annual [a publication of the Canadian Kennel Club]
Type: Yearbook; *Frequency:* Annually; *Price:* Free with CKC membership
• Dogs in Canada [a publication of the Canadian Kennel Club]
Type: Magazine; *Frequency:* Monthly; *Accepts Advertising*; *Price:* Free with CKC membership
Profile: Expert advice on topics such as dog behaviour, training, health, & nutrition
• Judges Directory [a publication of the Canadian Kennel Club]
Type: Directory
• Official Section [a publication of the Canadian Kennel Club]
Price: Free with Canadian Kennel Club membership

Canadian Kennel Club Foundation (CKCF)
#402, 200 Ronson Dr., Toronto ON M9W 5Z9
Tel: 416-674-3698
Toll-Free: 877-887-2523
info@ckcf.ca
www.ckcf.ca
Overview: A medium-sized national charitable organization
Mission: To improve the lives of dogs in Canada; To strengthen the relationship between dogs & humans; To promote canine health research; To empower communities to raise awareness on responsible dog ownership
Activities: Supporting research & projects focused on improving canine health
Awards:
• Health Research Grants
Eligibility: Individual researchers or research teams led by a primary investigator *Deadline:* July
• Pawsitivity Grants
Eligibility: Eligible recipients for funds from a registered charity

Canadian Kitchen Cabinet Association (CKCA) / Association canadienne de fabricants d'armoires de cuisine (ACAC)
1485 Laperriere Ave., Ottawa ON K1Z 7S8
Tel: 613-567-9171; *Fax:* 613-729-6206
info@ckca.ca
www.ckca.ca
Overview: A medium-sized national organization founded in 1968
Mission: To promote the interests & conserve the rights of those engaged in the manufacture of kitchen cabinets, bathroom vanities & related millwork as well as their suppliers & dealers.
Membership: 112; *Fees:* Schedule available; *Member Profile:* Manufacturers; Suppliers; Dealers; Associates
Chief Officer(s):
Jake Wolter, President

Canadian Knifemaker's Guild
PO Box 35022, Stn. Nelson Park, London ON N5W 5Z6
info@canadianknifemakersguild.com
canadianknifemakersguild.com
Overview: A small national organization founded in 1994
Mission: To increase public awareness of knifemakers, not as makers of weapons, but as skilled & versatile craftspeople producing high quality knives
Membership: 40; *Fees:* $30-$150; *Member Profile:* Anyone involved in the craft of knifemaking
Chief Officer(s):
Wolfgang Loerchner, President
Wally Hayes, Vice-President

Canadian Laboratory Suppliers Association (CLSA) / Association canadienne de fournisseurs de laboratoire
#131, 525 Highland Rd. West, Kitchener ON N3M 5P4
Tel: 519-650-8028; *Fax:* 519-653-8749
www.clsassoc.com
Overview: A medium-sized national organization
Mission: The Canadian Labratory Suppliers Association is a group of scientific companies committed to promoting and serving the Canadian laboratory marketplace. It provides a non-competitive environment for executives of Canada's leading scientific suppliers to share ideas and concepts. The CLSA's objective is to provide market analysis on the scientific industry, and to understand and discuss issues that influence the Canadian laboratory scientific market.
Finances: *Funding Sources:* Membership dues
Membership: 52 companies; *Fees:* Schedule available; *Member Profile:* Labratory supply Companies in Canada; *Committees:* New Members; Survey; Exhibits & Promotions; Resources; Social
Activities: Lab exhibits; market data & salary surveys
Chief Officer(s):
Alan Koop, President & Chair

Canadian Labour Congress (CLC) / Congrès du travail du Canada (CTC)
National Headquarters, 2841 Riverside Dr., Ottawa ON K1V 8X7
Tel: 613-521-3400; *Fax:* 613-521-4655
www.canadianlabour.ca
www.facebook.com/clc.ctc
twitter.com/canadianlabour
www.youtube.com/canadianlabour
Overview: A large national licensing organization founded in 1956
Mission: To represent the interests of affiliated workers across Canada; To act as an umbrella organization for affiliated regional labour councils, provincial federations, Canadian unions, & international unions
Membership: 3,000,000+; *Member Profile:* Affiliated workers in various occupations throughout Canada
Activities: Lobbying politicians; Organizing campaigns & rallies; Representing the Canadian labour movement when dealing with the media & business
Chief Officer(s):
Hassan Yussuff, President
president@clc-ctc.ca
Kerry Pither, Director, Communications, 613-294-2203
Kpither@clc-ctc.ca
Meetings/Conferences:
• Canadian Labour Congress 2018 National Convention, 2018
Scope: National
Description: A convention for members of the labour movement to develop an Action Plan, based on committee reports, resolutions, & the discussion of policies

Atlantic Regional Office
2282 Mountain Rd., Moncton NB E1G 1B4
Tel: 506-858-9350; *Fax:* 506-858-9571
atlantic@clc-ctc.ca
www.canadianlabour.ca/atlantic-region
Mission: To serve labour councils & federations in New Brunswick, Nova Scotia, Prince Edward Island, & Newfoundland & Labrador
Chief Officer(s):
Alex Furlong, Director
afurlong@clc-ctc.ca
Serge Landry, Representative, New Brunswick & PEI
slandry@clc-ctc.ca
Kelly Roche, Representative, Newfoundland & Labrador
kroche@clc-ctc.ca
Tony Tracy, Representative, Nova Scotia
ttracy@clc-ctc.ca

Ontario Regional Office
#401, 15 Gervais Dr., Toronto ON M3C 1Y8
Tel: 416-441-3710; *Fax:* 416-441-4073
ontario@clc-ctc.ca
canadianlabour.ca/about-clc/contact-us#ontario
Chief Officer(s):
Erin Harrison, Director
eharrison@clc-ctc.ca

Eddie Ste-Marie, Representative
estemarie@clc-ctc.ca
Gogi Bhandal, Representative
gbhandal@clc-ctc.ca
Medhi Kouhestaninejad, Representative
mkouhestaninejad@clc-ctc.ca
Lisa Bastien, Representative
lbastien@clc-ctc.ca
Mojdeh Cox, Representative
mcox@clc-ctc.ca
Pacific Regional Office
#201, 5118 Joyce St., Vancouver BC V5R 4H1
Tél: 604-430-6766; *Téléc:* 604-430-6762
pacific@clc-ctc.ca
canadianlabour.ca/about-clc/contact-us#pacific
Mission: To work with labour councils & federations of labour in British Columbia & the Yukon
Chief Officer(s):
Orion Irvine, Director
oirvine@clc-ctc.ca
Ron Stipp, Representative
rstipp@clc-ctc.ca
Chantel O'Neill, Representative
coneill@clc-ctc.ca
Prairie Regional Office
1888 Angus St., Regina SK S4T 1Z4
Tel: 306-525-6137; *Fax:* 306-525-9514
prairie@clc-ctc.ca
canadianlabour.ca/about-clc/contact-us#prairie
Mission: To work with labour councils & federations of labour in Alberta, Manitoba, Saskatchewan, the Northwest Territories, & Nunavut
Chief Officer(s):
Darla Leard, Regional Director
dleard@clc-ctc.ca
Cori Longo, Representative, Alberta
clongo@clc-ctc.ca
Cindy Murdoch, Representative, Manitoba
cmurdoch@clc-ctc.ca
Wendy Daku, Representative, Saskatchewan
wdaku@clc-ctc.ca
Québec Regional Office
#12100, 565, boul Crémazie est, Montréal QC H2M 2W3
Tél: 514-383-8000; *Téléc:* 514-383-8004
Ligne sans frais: 877-897-0057
www.ftq.qc.ca
www.facebook.com/laFTQ
twitter.com/ftqnouvelles
Chief Officer(s):
Isabelle Coulombe, Directrice, 514-383-8027
icoulombe@ftq.qc.ca

Canadian Labour International Film Festival (CLiFF)
Toronto ON
Tel: 416-579-0481
info@labourfilms.ca
labourfilms.ca
Overview: A medium-sized national organization founded in 2009
Mission: To produce a labour-oriented film festival in Canada, featuring films about workers & their conditions from Canada & around the world; To provide a venue where working people can tell their own stories in their own words & images; To encourage the production of films about working people
Activities: Partnering with other labour organizations; Assisting organizations & communities across Canada to host a film festival
Chief Officer(s):
Frank Saptel, Festival Founder & Director

Canadian LabourWatch Association
#205, 125A - 1030 Denman St., Vancouver BC V6G 2M6
Fax: 888-864-7390
Toll-Free: 888-652-2687
www.labourwatch.com
Overview: A small national organization
Mission: To protect the rights of employees with respect to labour relations
Membership: 12; *Fees:* $1,000+; *Member Profile:* National & provincial industry associations; Law firms
Activities: Offering resources & research on unionization
Chief Officer(s):
John Mortimer, President
john@labourwatch.com

Canadian Lacrosse Association (CLA) / Association canadienne de crosse (ACC)
Gladstone Sports & Health Centre, #310, 18 Louisa St., Ottawa ON K1R 6Y6
Tel: 613-260-2028; *Fax:* 613-260-2029
info1@lacrosse.ca
www.lacrosse.ca
www.facebook.com/CanadianLacrosseAssociation
twitter.com/LacrosseCanada
Overview: A medium-sized national licensing charitable organization founded in 1867
Mission: To promote, develop & preserve the sport of Lacrosse & its heritage as Canada's national summer sport.
Affiliation(s): International Lacrosse Federation; International Federation of Women's Lacrosse Associations; Fédération internationale d'Inter-crosse; Canadian Lacrosse Foundation; Sport Canada; Coaching Association of Canada
Finances: *Annual Operating Budget:* $250,000-$500,000; *Funding Sources:* Sport Canada; membership fees; sponsors; donations; sales
Staff Member(s): 3
Membership: 11 provincial organizations; *Fees:* $350 - $1,050; *Member Profile:* Provincial associations/leagues; *Committees:* Equipment Review; Transfer Review; Appeals; Discipline; Aboriginal Development
Activities: *Awareness Events:* Lacrosse Week, 3rd week of May; *Internships:* Yes; *Speaker Service:* Yes; *Rents Mailing List:* Yes
Chief Officer(s):
Joanne Thomson, Executive Director
joanne@lacrosse.ca
Britany Gordon, Coordinator, Events & Communications
britany@lacrosse.ca

Canadian Lacrosse Hall of Fame
PO Box 308, 65 - 6th Ave., New Westminster BC V3L 4Y6
Tel: 604-527-4640; *Fax:* 604-527-4641
info@canadianlacrossehalloffame.com
www.canadianlacrossehalloffame.org
Overview: A small national organization founded in 1967
Mission: To present the history of lacrosse in Canada & to induct worthy receipients into the Hall of Fame
Activities: *Library:* Canadian Lacrosse Hall of Fame Archives; by appointment
Chief Officer(s):
Allan Blair, Curator

Canadian Lactation Consultant Association (CLCA) / Association canadienne des consultantes en lactation
4 Innovation Dr., Dundas ON L9H 793
Tel: 905-689-3980; *Fax:* 905-689-1465
clca-accl@gmail.com
www.clca-accl.ca
www.linkedin.com/groups/Canadian-Lactation-Consultant-Association-CLCAACCL-4367040
www.facebook.com/welcomeback/requests/#!/CLCA.ACCL
twitter.com/cdnlactation
Overview: A small national organization founded in 1986
Affiliation(s): International Lactation Consultant Association
Activities: *Library:* CLCA/ACCL Lending Library; by appointment
Chief Officer(s):
Lauretta Williams, Administrator

Canadian Land Reclamation Association (CLRA) / Association canadienne de réhabilitation des sites dégradés (ACRSD)
c/o ManageWise, Inc., PO Box 21085, Edmonton AB T6R 2V4
Tel: 780-437-0044
www.clra.ca
www.linkedin.com/company/canadian-land-reclamation-association
Overview: A small national organization founded in 1975
Mission: To encourage involvement in reclamation projects of disturbed land
Member of: International Affiliation of Land Reclamationists
Finances: *Funding Sources:* Membership dues; Sponsorships
Membership: *Fees:* $15 full-time students & retirees; $50 regular members; $200 corporate members; *Member Profile:* Individuals & corporations interested in or engaged in reclamation activities
Activities: Facilitating the exchange of information & experience; Encouraging education in the field of land reclamation
Chief Officer(s):
Andrea McEachern, President
Shauna Prokopchuk, Coordinator
Marisa Hemmes, Coordinator, Membership & Communications
Awards:
• Dr. Edward M. Watkin Award
To recognize contributions that advance the progress of reclamation or the association
• Noranda Land Reclamation Award
To recognize outstanding achievement in land reclamation in Canada
• Linda Jones Memorial Award
Awarded to two students annually who are in a reclamation related program at a Canadian post-secondary institution; *Amount:* $1,000
Meetings/Conferences:
• Canadian Land Reclamation Association / Association canadienne de réhabilitation des sites dégradés 2018 43rd Annual General Meeting, 2018
Scope: National
Description: Business affairs of the association
Publications:
• Canadian Land Reclamation Association Annual Meeting Proceedings
Type: Yearbook; *Frequency:* Annually
• Canadian Reclamation [a publication of the Canadian Land Reclamation Association]
Type: Magazine; *Frequency:* s-a.; *Accepts Advertising*; *Editor:* Tracy Patterson; *ISSN:* 1701-722X
Profile: Articles & illustrations
• Reclamation Newsletter [a publication of the Canadian Land Reclamation Association]
Type: Newsletter; *Frequency:* s-a.
Profile: Articles & updates on all aspects of reclamation

Alberta Chapter
AB
www.clra.ca
Chief Officer(s):
Andrea Granger, Past President
granger.andrea@cleanharbors.com

Canadian Laser Aesthetic Surgery Society *See* The Canadian Laser and Aesthetic Specialists Society

The Canadian Laser and Aesthetic Specialists Society (CLASS)
2334 Heska Rd., Pickering ON L1V 2P9
Fax: 905-837-1125
Toll-Free: 877-578-0336
www.class.ca
Previous Name: Canadian Laser Aesthetic Surgery Society
Overview: A small national organization founded in 1997
Mission: To disseminate information & promote quality in all forms of aesthetic laser surgery; To promote communication between medical specialties to further awareness, education, & professional development
Finances: *Funding Sources:* Membership dues; Corporate sponsors
Membership: *Fees:* $250; *Member Profile:* Physicians who have achieved a specialty certification in either Dermatology, Plastic Surgery, Otolaryngology, or Ophthalmology
Activities: Hosting annual symposium; Providing a member directory
Chief Officer(s):
Karen Edstrom, President

Canadian Law & Economics Association
Faculty of Law, University of Toronto, 84 Queen's Park Cres., Toronto ON M5S 2C5
Tel: 416-978-0210; *Fax:* 416-978-7899
www.canlecon.org
Overview: A small national organization
Chief Officer(s):
Nadia Gulezko, Contact
n.gulezko@utoronto.ca

Canadian Law & Society Association (CLSA) / Association canadienne droit et société (ACDS)
info@acds-clsa.org
www.acds-clsa.org
Overview: A small national organization founded in 1985
Mission: To encourage socio-legal inquiry both domestically & internationally
Member of: Canadian Federation for the Humanities & Social Sciences
Membership: *Fees:* Annually, $140 individual; $30 student/post doc sessional; $50 Emeritus; *Member Profile:* Scholars from

many disciplines, with an interest in the place of law in economic political, cultural and social life
Activities: Awaring prizes for scholarship
Chief Officer(s):
Lyndsay Campbell, President
Nicole O'Byrne, Vice President
Thomas McMorrow, Vice President
Meetings/Conferences:
• Canadian Law & Society Association Annual Mid-Winter Meeting 2018, January, 2018
Scope: National
• Canadian Law & Society Association Annual Meeting 2018, June, 2018
Scope: National
Publications:
• Canadian Journal of Law & Society / La Revue Canadienne Droit et Société (CJLS / RCDS)
Type: Journal; *Frequency:* Semiannually; *Accepts Advertising*; *Editor:* D. Moore; M. Valverde; M. Coutu; *ISSN:* 0829-3201; *Price:* Free with CLSA / ACDSmembership; $90 Canada; $110 International
Profile: Original academic research in the field of law & society scholarship
• The CLSA / ACDS Bulletin
Type: Newsletter; *Frequency:* Semiannually; *Editor:* Kimberley White; *Price:* Free with CLSA / ACDS membership
Profile: Forum for for CLSA members to share information on developments & issues affecting Canadian law & society research

Canadian Lawyers Association for International Human Rights (CLAIHR)
www.claihr.ca
www.facebook.com/claihr
twitter.com/CLAIHR
Overview: A small national organization
Mission: To promote human rights globally through legal education, advocacy & law reform; to promote awareness of human rights issues within the legal community in Canada.
Membership: *Fees:* $50 general; $25 student

Canadian Lawyers Insurance Association (CLIA) / Association d'assurances des juristes canadiens (AAJC)
Office of the General Manager, #510, 36 Toronto St., Toronto ON M5C 2C5
Tel: 416-408-5293; *Fax:* 416-408-3721
info@clia.ca
www.clia.ca
Overview: A small national organization founded in 1988
Mission: To provide a reliable source of insurance on a non-profit basis; To ensure availability of reasonably priced insurance, & that premium rates reflect the loss experience of Canadian lawyers; To stabilize premiums in both mandatory & excess layers
Staff Member(s): 2
Membership: *Member Profile:* Participating law societies, which agree on standard limits & policy terms, in Alberta, Saskatchewan, Manitoba, New Brunswick, Nova Scotia, Prince Edward Island, Newfoundland & Labrador, Yukon, Northwest Territories, & Nunavut
Activities: Providing professional liability insurance for Canadian lawyers; Managing a Voluntary Excess Program in the provinces of British Columbia & Ontario, through the Canadian Bar Excess Liability Association
Chief Officer(s):
Patrick Mahoney, General Manager
Norma Ibbetson, Assistant General Manager, 416-408-5294
Publications:
• Canadian Lawyers Insurance Association Annual Report
Type: Yearbook; *Frequency:* Annually
Profile: A summary of the association's yearly activities
• Loss Prevention Bulletin [a publication of the Canadian Lawyers Insurance Association]
Type: Newsletter; *Editor:* Karen L. Dyck
Profile: Claim prevention techniques to help lawyers minimize the likelihood of being sued for malpractice
• Loss Prevention eBytes [a publication of the Canadian Lawyers Insurance Association]
Price: Loss prevention information for CLIA insured lawyers
• Safe & Effective Practice [a publication of the Canadian Lawyers Insurance Association]
Number of Pages: 106; *Author:* Jean Côté; *Editor:* Barry Vogel, Q.C.; *Price:* Free to members of the legal profession

Canadian League Against Epilepsy (CLAE)
c/o Secretariat Central, #6, 20 Crown Steel Dr., Markham ON L3R 9X9
Tel: 905-415-3917
clae@secretariatcentral.com
www.claegroup.org
Overview: A small national organization
Mission: To help Canadians affected by epilepsy; To develop therapeutic & preventative strategies to prevent the effects of epilepsy
Affiliation(s): Canadian Epilepsy Alliance; American Epilepsy Society; North American Commission for Epilepsy
Finances: *Funding Sources:* Donations; Fundraising
Membership: *Fees:* $50 junior; $100 allied heatlh professionals; $150 active; *Member Profile:* Medical & basic sciences professionals, including physicians, neuropsychologists, & nurses; Students
Activities: Increasing awareness about epilepsy; Educating Canadians about epilepsy; Providing professional development opportunities; Supporting epilepsy research
Chief Officer(s):
Jorge Burneo, President
Mary Lou Smith, Secretary
David Steven, Treasurer

Canadian League of Composers / La Ligue canadienne de compositeurs
Chalmers House, 20 St. Joseph St., Toronto ON M4Y 1J9
Tel: 416-964-1364; *Fax:* 416-961-7189
Toll-Free: 877-964-1364
info@composition.org
composition.org
www.facebook.com/143305345702145
twitter.com/CLC_LCC
Overview: A small national organization
Mission: To represent the interests of composers & to monitor & influence the conditions that affect their livelihood & public image
Membership: 400; *Fees:* $60; *Committees:* Executive; Advocacy; Awards; Communications; Professional; Membership
Chief Officer(s):
Christopher Reiche, President
Elisha Denburg, General Manager

Canadian Lebanon Society of Halifax
c/o Community Centre, 255 Bedford Hwy., Halifax NS B3M 2K5
Tel: 902-444-4257
cls_halifax@hotmail.com
Overview: A small local organization founded in 1938
Mission: To act as the voice of Nova Scotia's Lebanese community; To service the Lebanese people of Nova Scotia; To promote the heritage & culture of the Lebanese community
Activities: Producing radio programs, a magazine, & festivals to promote the culture of the Lebanese community; Providing education about Lebanese culture & the Arabic language to youth; *Awareness Events:* Multicultural Festival, June; Annual Lebanese Summer Festival, July; Labanon's Independence Day, November

Canadian Lesbian & Gay Archives (CLGA)
PO Box 699, Stn. F, 34 Isabella St., Toronto ON M4Y 1N1
Tel: 416-777-2755
queeries@clga.ca
www.clga.ca
www.facebook.com/116735553447
twitter.com/clgarchives
Previous Name: Canadian Gay Archives
Overview: A medium-sized national charitable organization founded in 1973
Mission: To acquire, preserve & make available to the public information in any medium about lesbians & gays, with an emphasis on Canada.
Affiliation(s): Association of Canadian Archivists; Ontario Association of Archives
Finances: *Annual Operating Budget:* Less than $50,000
Staff Member(s): 1; 25 volunteer(s)
Membership: 1,200
Activities: *Library:* James Fraser Library; Open to public by appointment
Chief Officer(s):
Robert Windrum, President

Canadian Library Association *See* Canadian Federation of Library Associations

Canadian Life & Health Insurance Association Inc. (CLHIA) / Association canadienne des compagnies d'assurances de personnes inc. (ACCAP)
#2300, 79 Wellington St. West, Toronto ON M5K 1G8
Tel: 416-777-2221; *Fax:* 416-777-1895
Toll-Free: 888-295-8112
Other Communication: Ottawa: 613-230-0031; Montreal: 514-854-9004
info@clhia.ca
www.clhia.ca
twitter.com/clhia
Previous Name: Canadian Life Insurance Association
Overview: A large national organization founded in 1894
Mission: To represent the interests of member life & health insurance companies
Membership: 100-499; *Member Profile:* Life & health insurers licensed to do business in Canada; Insurance-related organizations
Activities: Facilitating the exchange of information about best practices & current developments; Compiling information & statistics
Chief Officer(s):
Dean Connor, Chair
Paul Mahon, President
Publications:
• Canadian Life & Health Insurance Facts
Type: Report; *Frequency:* a.
Profile: Statistics on life & health insurance ownership & purchases, life & health insurance companies' income & expenses, pension plan coverages, assets & obligations, & operations inCanada
• A Guide to Disability Insurance
Type: Booklet; *Number of Pages:* 20
Profile: A guide to understanding options for income replacement in the event of disability
• A Guide to Life Insurance
Type: Booklet; *Number of Pages:* 36
Profile: Consumer publication about types of policies, agent services, riders & dividends, & premiums
• A Guide to Long-Term Care Insurance
Type: Booklet; *Number of Pages:* 12
Profile: Resource to assist consumers
• A Guide to Supplementary Health Insurance
Type: Booklet; *Number of Pages:* 20
Profile: Resource to assist consumers
• A Guide to the Coordination of Benefits
Type: Booklet; *Number of Pages:* 12
Profile: Assistance in navigating the claims process
• A Guide to Travel Health Insurance
Type: Booklet; *Number of Pages:* 12
Profile: A review of the supplementary health insurance needed by Canadians when they travel ouside the province or country
• In The Loop
Type: Newsletter; *Frequency:* Monthly; *Price:* Free with Claim Section Industry Associate status
Profile: Industry updates
• Key Facts About Segregated Fund Contracts
Type: Booklet; *Number of Pages:* 12
Profile: A guide for investors
• Provincial Facts & Figures
Type: Report; *Frequency:* a.
Montréal Office
#630, 1001, boul de Maisonneuve ouest, Montréal QC H3A 3C8
Tel: 514-845-9004; *Fax:* 514-845-6182
Ottawa Office
#400, 46 Elgin St., Ottawa ON K1P 5K6
Tel: 613-230-0031; *Fax:* 613-230-0297

Canadian Life & Health Insurance OmbudService *See* OmbudService for Life & Health Insurance

Canadian Life Insurance Association *See* Canadian Life & Health Insurance Association Inc.

Canadian Life Insurance Medical Officers Association (CLIMOA) / Association Canadienne des Directeurs Médicaux en Assurance-Vie (ACDMAV)
#100, 32 Colonnade Rd., Ottawa ON K2E 7J6
Tel: 613-721-7061; *Fax:* 613-721-3581
climoa@unconventionalplanning.com
www.climoa.com
Overview: A small national organization
Mission: To help develop & coordinate doctors & others working in the health & life insurance industry

Membership: *Fees:* $200 active; $100 associate; $35 emeritus; *Committees:* Medical Education; Professional Relations
Activities: Meetings; presentations
Chief Officer(s):
Bruce Boyd, President

Canadian Lifeboat Institution
PO Box 30066, Stn. Moncton, 12051 #1 Rd., Richmond BC V7E 1T5
Tel: 604-760-5218
info@canadianlifeboatinstitution.org
www.canadianlifeboatinstitution.org
www.facebook.com/CanadianLifeboatInstitutionInc
twitter.com/CLI_Lifeboat
Overview: A medium-sized national charitable organization founded in 1981
Mission: To support & provide local, provincial & national marine search & rescue services; To promote safety & accident prevention at sea
Finances: *Funding Sources:* Donations
Activities: Offering safety education programs
Chief Officer(s):
Bob McIlwaine, President
Awards:
• Patron's Medal

Canadian Limousin Association (CLA)
#13, 4101 - 19th St. NE, Calgary AB T2E 7C4
Tel: 403-253-7309; *Fax:* 403-253-1704
Toll-Free: 866-886-1605
limousin@limousin.com
www.limousin.com
www.facebook.com/CanadianLimousin
twitter.com/cdnlimousin
Overview: A large international organization founded in 1970
Mission: To provide collective service for Limousin breeders in Canada; To record registration & produce Records of Performance on all registered aninals; To promote & inform producers about Limousin cattle; To develop & implement educational agricultural programs
Member of: Canadian 4H; Canadian Beef Breeds Council
Finances: *Annual Operating Budget:* $250,000-$500,000; *Funding Sources:* Registration of limousin cattle; Membership dues
Staff Member(s): 6; 11 volunteer(s)
Membership: 750; *Fees:* Schedule available; *Member Profile:* Limousin cattle breeders; *Committees:* Advertising & Promotion; Breed Improvement; Export; Junior
Activities: *Library:* by appointment
Chief Officer(s):
Tessa Verbeek, General Manager, 413-636-1066
tverbeek@limousin.com
Awards:
• Show Cattle of the Year Awards
Publications:
• Canadian Limousin Association Newsletter
Type: Newsletter; *Frequency:* Monthly
Profile: Information about breeders & breeding, sales, & beef industry trends
• Limousin Voice [a publication of the Canadian Limousin Association]
Frequency: Quarterly; *Accepts Advertising*; *Editor:* Bryan Kostiuk; *Price:* $35
Profile: Includes a bull issue, a herd reference issue & a harvest of value issue

Canadian Linguistic Association (CLA) / Association canadienne de linguistique (ACL)
c/o University of Toronto Press, Journals Division, 5201 Dufferin Ave., Toronto ON M3H 5T8
www.cla-acl.ca
Overview: A medium-sized national organization
Mission: To advance scientific study of linguistics & language in Canada
Member of: Humanities & Social Sciences Federation of Canada
Affiliation(s): International Permanent Committee of Linguists
Finances: *Funding Sources:* Membership dues
6 volunteer(s)
Membership: 400 institutional + 360 individual; *Fees:* $45 individual; $50 institution
Chief Officer(s):
France Martineau, President
fmartin@uOttawa.ca
Ileana Paul, Secretary
ileana@uwo.ca
Carrie Dyck, Treasurer
cdyck@mun.ca
Meetings/Conferences:
• Canadian Linguistic Association 2018 Conference, May, 2018, University of Regina, Regina, SK
Scope: National
Description: Information from all areas of linguistics
Publications:
• The Canadian Journal of Linguistics
Type: Journal; *Frequency:* Quarterly; *Accepts Advertising*;
Editor: Sarah Cummins; *ISSN:* 0008-4131; *Price:* Free with CLA membership; $65
Profile: Articles, as well as book reviews, about topics such as linguistic theory, phonology, phonetics, semantics, syntax, linguistic description ofnatural languages, historical linguistics, psycholinguistics, sociolinguistics, & first & second language acquisition

Canadian Literacy & Learning Network (CLLN) / Rassemblement canadien pour l'alphabétisation (RCA)
342A Elgin St., Ottawa ON K2P 1M6
Tel: 613-563-2464; *Fax:* 613-563-2504
clln@literacy.ca
www.literacy.ca
www.facebook.com/195237923820101
twitter.com/Cdn_Literacy
Overview: A medium-sized national charitable organization founded in 1978
Mission: To act as a national voice for literacy for Canadians
Member of: Prince Edward Island Literacy Alliance Inc.
Finances: *Funding Sources:* Membership fees; Donations; employement & social development canada
Membership: *Member Profile:* Provincial & territorial literacy coalitions & organizations; Individual who support the mission & goals of MCL
Activities: Providing networking opportunities; Researching; Preparing special reports, such a briefs to the House of Commons; Liaising with government; Informing the general public about issues related to adult literacy; Developing & strengthening learners through the Learners Advisory Network; Communicating & collaborating to ensure Canadians have access to quality literacy education; Supporting people & organizations involved with adult literacy education
Chief Officer(s):
Lindsay Kennedy, President & CEO, 613-563-2464 Ext. 222
lkennedy@literacy.ca

Canadian Literary & Artistic Association / Association littéraire et artistique canadienne inc.
PO Box 20035, Stn. De Vinci, Repentigny QC J5Y 0K6
Tel: 514-993-1556
alaican@aei.ca
www.alai.ca
Also Known As: ALAI Canada
Overview: A small national organization founded in 1978
Mission: To promote & protect copyright & study questions regarding the protection & the applicability of these rights
Member of: International ALAI
Finances: *Funding Sources:* Membership fees
Membership: 145 individuals; *Fees:* $125 individuals; $160 institutions; $60 students; *Member Profile:* Any person interested in copyright who endorses the goals of ALAICanada
Activities: Conferences, seminars & congresses; Publishes documents dealing with copyright; Holds educational & training sessions; *Speaker Service:* Yes
Chief Officer(s):
Geneviève Barsalou, Director

Canadian Liver Foundation (CLF) / Fondation canadienne du foie (FCF)
#801, 3100 Steeles Ave. East, Toronto ON L3R 8T3
Tel: 416-491-3353; *Fax:* 905-752-1540
Toll-Free: 800-563-5483
clf@liver.ca
www.liver.ca
www.facebook.com/CanadianLiverFoundation
twitter.com/CdnLiverFdtn
www.youtube.com/user/clfwebmaster
Overview: A large national charitable organization founded in 1969
Mission: To reduce the incidence & impact of all liver disease by funding liver research & education; promote liver health through programs & publications
Finances: *Funding Sources:* Donations; Fundraising; Government grants
Membership: *Fees:* $25
Activities: Programs for parents, youth; publications; *Awareness Events:* Help Fight Liver Disease Month, March; *Speaker Service:* Yes; *Rents Mailing List:* Yes; *Library:* Open to public
Chief Officer(s):
Gary A. Fagan, President & CEO
gfagan@liver.ca
Veronica Herfindahl, National Director, Marketing & Communications
vherfindahl@liver.ca
Karen Seto, National Director, Professional Partnerships & Programs
kseto@liver.ca
Billie Potkonjak, National Director, Health Promotion & Patient Services, Research Grants Administrati
bpotkonjak@liver.ca

Atlantic Canada Chapter
#103-406, 287 Lacewood Dr., Halifax NS B3M 3Y7
Tel: 902-423-8538
Toll-Free: 866-423-8538
atlantic@liver.ca

British Columbia/Yukon Chapter
#109, 828 West 8th Ave., Vancouver BC V5Z 1E2
Tel: 604-707-6430; *Fax:* 604-681-6067
Toll-Free: 800-856-7266
Chief Officer(s):
Monica Chui, Director, Regional Business Development, Western Canada
mchui@liver.ca

Chatham/Kent Chapter
PO Box 23, Chatham ON N7M 5K1
Tel: 519-682-9805; *Fax:* 519-682-2184
clfchatham@liver.ca
Chief Officer(s):
Sheila Hughes, Development Manager
shughes@liver.ca

Sarnia/Lambton/London Chapter
PO Box 1011, Sarnia ON N7T 7K2
Tel: 519-336-5223
Chief Officer(s):
Sheila Hughes, Development Manager
shughes@liver.ca

Manitoba Chapter
PO Box 1583, Lac du Bonnet MB R0E 1A0
Tel: 204-345-2434
Chief Officer(s):
Bianca Pengelly, Reginal Coordinator
bpengelly@liver.ca

Moncton Chapter
#110, 1127B Main St., Moncton NB E1C 1H1
atlantic@liver.ca

Montréal Chapter
#1430, 1000, rue de la Gauchetière ouest, Montréal QC H3B 4W5
Tél: 514-876-4170; *Téléc:* 514-876-4172
Chief Officer(s):
Anne Brisson, Regional Coordinator
abrisson@liver.ca

Windsor/Essex Chapter
PO Box 29023, 3395 Walker Rd., Windsor ON N8W 3R0
Tel: 519-974-8008
clfwindsor@liver.ca
Chief Officer(s):
Sheila Hughes, Development Manager
shughes@liver.ca
Todd Hebert, Regional Director
thebert@liver.ca

Southern Alberta/Calgary/Edmonton Chapter
#309, 1010 - 1st Ave. NE, Calgary AB T2E 7W7
Tel: 403-276-3390; *Fax:* 403-276-3423
Toll-Free: 888-557-5516
Debralee Fernets, Regional Manager
debralee@liver.ca

Toronto/GTA Chapter
#801, 3100 Steeles Ave. East, Markham ON L3R 8T3
Tel: 416-491-3353; *Fax:* 905-752-1540
Toll-Free: 800-563-5483
Chief Officer(s):
Jennifer Turack, Regional Coordinator
jturack@liver.ca

Canadian Associations / Canadian Livestock Records Corporation (CLRC) / Société canadienne d'enregistrement des animaux

Canadian Livestock Records Corporation (CLRC) / Société canadienne d'enregistrement des animaux
2417 Holly Lane, Ottawa ON K1V 0M7
Tel: 613-731-7110; *Fax:* 613-731-0704
Toll-Free: 877-833-7110
clrc@clrc.ca
www.clrc.ca
Previous Name: Canadian National Live Stock Records
Overview: A medium-sized national organization founded in 1905
Mission: To serve the Canadian seed stock industry; to be responsible to the member breed associations & Agriculture Canada for the maintenance of records, issuance of certificates, endorsement of changes of ownership, enrolment of members, registration of individuals, identification letters, collection of fees & the deposit of same into the appropriate breed association account
Finances: *Annual Operating Budget:* $500,000-$1.5 Million; *Funding Sources:* Fees for service
Staff Member(s): 8
Membership: 1-99; *Fees:* Schedule available; *Member Profile:* Livestock associations
Activities: *Library:* Open to public
Chief Officer(s):
Jim Washer, General Manager, 613-731-7110 Ext. 303
j.washer@clrc.ca

Canadian Llama & Alpaca Association (CLAA)
2320 - 41 Ave. NE, Calgary AB T2W 6W8
Tel: 403-250-2165; *Fax:* 403-291-9324
Toll-Free: 800-717-5262
info@claacanada.com
www.claacanada.com
Overview: A medium-sized national organization founded in 1987
Mission: To set up & maintain a reputable registry for Canadian llamas & alpacas
Staff Member(s): 1
Membership: 718; *Fees:* $195 alpaca; $140 llama
Chief Officer(s):
Susan Wipfli, President
skwipfli@sympatico.ca

Canadian Lowline Cattle Association (CLCA)
c/o Lee Monteith, PO Box 84, Edam SK S0M 0V0
Tel: 306-397-2584
www.canadianlowline.com
Overview: A small national organization founded in 1997
Mission: To support Lowline cattle breeders across Canada; To gain exposure & acceptance of the Lowline cattle breed in the agricultural world
Member of: Canadian Beef Breeds Council
Affiliation(s): Canadian Livestock Records Corporation
Membership: 1-99; *Member Profile:* Breeders of Lowline cattle in Canada
Activities: Providing information about Lowline cattle
Chief Officer(s):
Lee Monteith, General Manager
cmonteith@littleloon.ca
Publications:
• Sales Catalogue
Type: Catalogue

Canadian Luge Association / Association canadienne de luge
#323, 151 Canada Olympic Rd. SW, Calgary AB T3B 6B7
Tel: 403-202-6581
www.luge.ca
www.facebook.com/138340422883168
twitter.com/LugeCanada
Previous Name: Canadian Amateur Bobsleigh & Luge Association
Overview: A medium-sized national organization founded in 1990
Mission: To provide leadership & pursue success in promotion & development of all aspects of luge.
Finances: *Funding Sources:* donations; Fast Track Capital
Staff Member(s): 4
Membership: *Member Profile:* Provincial associations fully recognized by national association
Activities: *Internships:* Yes
Chief Officer(s):
Tim Farstad, Executive Director
tfarstad@luge.ca

Canadian Luing Cattle Association
c/o Blacketlees Farm, RR#4, Rimbey AB T0C 2J0
Tel: 403-843-0094; *Fax:* 403-843-0094
iaineaitken@gmail.com
www.luingcattle.com/luing.html
Overview: A small national organization founded in 1975
Mission: To develop & regulate the breeding of Luing cattle in Canada; To protect & assist breeders
Affiliation(s): Canadian Livestock Records Corporation
Membership: 1-99; *Fees:* $35 / year; $10 junior membership (until member's 18th birthday); *Member Profile:* Breeders of Luing cattle in Canada
Activities: Encouraging the breeding of Luing cattle in Canada; Maintaining the Luing cattle breed in Canada; Compiling statistics about the industry; Publishing data & documents related to to breeding of Luing cattle; Supervising breeders of Luing cattle
Chief Officer(s):
Jeff Longard, President, 780-682-3805
Paul Galbraith, Vice-President, 250-346-3100
Iain Aitken, Secretary-Treasurer, 403-843-0094, Fax: 403-843-0094
ieaitken@hotmail.com
Lisa Hutt, Registrar, 613-731-7110 Ext. 312, Fax: 613-731-0704
lisa.hutt@clrc.ca

Canadian Lumber Standards Accreditation Board (CLSAB)
#102, 28 Deakin St., Ottawa ON K2E 8B7
Tel: 613-482-2480; *Fax:* 613-482-6044
info@clsab.ca
www.clsab.ca
Overview: A medium-sized national organization founded in 1960
Mission: To monitor the identification & certification of lumber used in or exported from Canada, or manufactured in accordance with Canadian standards; To provide lumber grading agencies with the authority to supervise lumber manufacturers; To review & advise upon grading rules & standards
Finances: *Funding Sources:* Membership dues; Assessment fees
Membership: 11; *Member Profile:* Lumber regulatory inspection & grading agencies; *Committees:* Executive; Operations
Chief Officer(s):
Chuck Dentelbeck, President & CEO

Canadian Lung Association (CLA) / Association pulmonaire du Canada
National Office, #502, 885 Meadowlands Dr., Ottawa ON K2C 3N2
Tel: 613-569-6411
Toll-Free: 888-566-5864
info@lung.ca
www.lung.ca
www.facebook.com/canadianlungassociation
twitter.com/canlung
www.youtube.com/user/TheLungAssociation
Previous Name: The Canadian Association for the Prevention of Consumption & Other Forms of Tuberculosis; The Canadian Tuberculosis & Respiratory Disease Association
Overview: A large national charitable organization founded in 1900
Mission: To improve & promote lung health across Canada
Finances: *Funding Sources:* Donations; Fundraising; Sponsorships
Activities: Advocating for improvements to care for lung disease patients; Providing lung health information to governments & the public; Funding medical research; Coordinating the Christmas Seal campaign; *Awareness Events:* National Non-Smoking Week, January; Lung Cancer Month, November; COPD Awareness Week, November
Chief Officer(s):
Terry Dean, President & Chief Executive Officer
Debbie Smith, Chief Privacy Officer
dsmith@lung.ca
Janet Sutherland, Director, Canadian Thoracic Society/Canadian Respiratory Health Professiona
Marketa Stastna, Manager, Marketing & Communications
Meetings/Conferences:
• Canadian Respiratory Conference 2018, April, 2018, Vancouver, BC
Scope: National
Attendance: 650
Description: Jointly organized by the Canadian Lung Association, the Canadian Thoracic Society, & the Canadian Respiratory Health Professionals
Publications:
• Canadian Lung Association Annual Report
Type: Yearbook; *Frequency:* Annually

Canadian Lutheran World Relief (CLWR)
#600, 177 Lombard Ave., Winnipeg MB R3B 0W5
Tel: 204-694-5602; *Fax:* 204-694-5460
Toll-Free: 800-661-2597
clwr@clwr.mb.ca
www.clwr.org
www.linkedin.com/company/canadian-lutheran-world-relief
www.facebook.com/CanadianLutheranWorldRelief
twitter.com/CanLWR
www.youtube.com/user/CLWRvideo; instagram.com/canlwr
Overview: A large national charitable organization founded in 1946
Mission: To provide development programming in Africa, Asia, Latin America, & the Middle East; To provide emergency relief in case of disaster; To enable sponsorships for refugee resettlement in Canada; To focus on development, peace building, alternative approaches to trade, education, & community building
Member of: Canadian Foodgrains Bank; The Lutheran World Federation; ACT Alliance; Canadian Churches in Action; Canadian Council for International Cooperation; Manitoba Council for International Cooperation; Saskatchewan Council for International Cooperation
Finances: *Funding Sources:* Evangelical Lutheran Church of Canada; Lutheran Church-Canada; Canadian Lutherans; Government
Staff Member(s): 23
Activities: *Speaker Service:* Yes
Chief Officer(s):
Robert Granke, Executive Director, 204-631-0113
rgranke@clwr.mb.ca
Carla Blakley, Director, Community Relations, 204-631-0504
carla@clwr.org
Patricia Maruschak, Director, Programs, 204-631-0116
patricia@clwr.org
Diana Koldyk, Director, Finance, HR & Administration, 204-631-0507
diana@clwr.org
Publications:
• Canadian Lutheran World Relief Annual Report
Type: Yearbook; *Frequency:* Annually
Profile: Distributed to CLWR donors
• Canadian Lutheran World Relief Bulletin of Reports
Type: Yearbook; *Frequency:* Annually
Profile: CLWR activities & financial information
• CLWR [Canadian Lutheran World Relief] News Briefs
Type: Newsletter; *Frequency:* Weekly
Profile: Summary of significant CLWR-related news events in Canada or around the world
• CLWR [Canadian Lutheran World Relief] Monthly Briefs
Frequency: Monthly
Profile: Information for constituents about events in the developing world & the response of Canadians
• Four Corners [a publication of the Canadian Lutheran World Relief]
Type: Newsletter; *Frequency:* Semiannually
Profile: News about alternative trade to create opportunities for artists in the developing world
• Partnership Newsletter [a publication of the Canadian Lutheran World Relief]
Type: Newsletter; *Frequency:* Quarterly; *ISSN:* 1916-2308
Profile: Inspirational stories about people in the developing world

Eastern Regional Office
#101, 470 Weber St. North, Waterloo ON N2L 6J2
Tel: 519-725-8777; *Fax:* 519-725-8776
Toll-Free: 888-255-0150
Chief Officer(s):
Jennifer Ardon, Contact
jardon@clwr.mb.ca

Western Regional Office
80 East 10 Ave., New Westminster BC V3L 4R5
Tel: 604-540-9760; *Fax:* 604-540-9795
Toll-Free: 888-588-6686
clwr@clwrbc.ca
Chief Officer(s):
Fikre M. Tsehai, Development Manager

Canadian Lyme Disease Foundation / Fondation canadienne de la maladie de lyme
2495 Reece Rd., Westbank BC V4T 1N1
Tel: 250-768-0978; *Fax:* 250-768-0946
www.canlyme.org

www.facebook.com/143033619666
twitter.com/canlyme
Also Known As: CanLyme
Overview: A small national charitable organization
Mission: To advance research about Lyme Disease in Canada
Affiliation(s): International Lyme & Associated Diseases Society (ILADS)
Finances: *Funding Sources:* Donations; Fundraising
Activities: Providing Canadian Lyme Disease news & research; *Library:* Canadian Lyme Disease Foundation Library
Chief Officer(s):
Jim Wilson, President & Founder
jimwilson@telus.net

Canadian Lymphedema Framework (CLF)
#204, 4800 Dundas St. West, Toronto ON M9A 1B1
Tel: 647-693-1083
admin@canadalymph.ca
www.canadalymph.ca
Overview: A small national charitable organization founded in 2009
Mission: To advance the treatment of lymphedema & related disorders in Canada; To promote lymphedema research, practices, & clinical development
Affiliation(s): International Lymphedema Framework
Membership: *Committees:* Scientific
Chief Officer(s):
Anna Kennedy, Executive Director

Canadian Machinery Vibration Association (CMVA) / Association canadienne en vibrations de machines (ACVM)
#1260, 225 The East Mall, Toronto ON M9B 0A9
Tel: 416-622-1170; *Fax:* 416-622-5376
val@cmva.com
www.cmva.com
Overview: A small national organization founded in 1993
Mission: A not-for-profit association dedicated to the advancement of machinery condition monitoring technologies.
Finances: *Annual Operating Budget:* $100,000-$250,000
Membership: 550; *Fees:* $120 individual; $750 corporate
Chief Officer(s):
Andy Woodcock, Executive Director
awoodcock@cmva.com
Publications:
• Good Vibes
Type: Newsletter; *Frequency:* Quarterly; *Editor:* Val Zacharias

Canadian Magen David Adom for Israel (CMDA) / Magen David Adom canadien pour Israël
#3155, 6900, boul Decarie, Montréal QC H3X 2T8
Tel: 514-731-4400; *Fax:* 514-731-2490
Toll-Free: 800-731-2848
info@cmdai.org
www.cmdai.org
www.linkedin.com/company/10863533
www.facebook.com/CanadianMagenDavidAdom
twitter.com/CanadianMDA
www.youtube.com/user/CanadianMDA
Overview: A small international charitable organization founded in 1976
Mission: To raise funds to purchase medical supplies to be sent to Israel
Member of: International Red Cross
Affiliation(s): Magen David Adom, Israel
Finances: *Annual Operating Budget:* $250,000-$500,000
Staff Member(s): 1
Membership: 1,200; *Fees:* $18+; *Committees:* Executive; Finance; Marketing; Membership; Personnel
Activities: Fundraising events; concerts; guest speakers; games night; board meetings; *Awareness Events:* Israel Day, March; Israeli Street Festival, May or June; Mall Exhibitions
Chief Officer(s):
Sidney Benizri, National Executive Director
sbenizri@cmdai.org

Calgary Chapter
PO Box 73112, RPO Woodbine, Calgary AB T2W 6E4
Tel: 403-251-6802
www.cmdai.org/calgary/
Chief Officer(s):
James Cohen, Co-Chair
s_s_wainer@shaw.ca

London Chapter
116 Maxwell Crt., London ON N5X 1Z3
Tel: 519-455-5411
www.cmdai.org/london/

Chief Officer(s):
Naomi Sheinbaum, Co-Chair
naomi8@sympatico.ca

Ottawa Chapter
95 Beaver Ridge, Ottawa ON K2E 6E5
Tel: 613-224-2500
www.cmdai.org/ottawa/
Chief Officer(s):
Seymour Eisenberg, President
seyeis@rogers.com

Toronto Chapter
#508, 4580 Dufferin St., Toronto ON M3H 5Y2
Tel: 416-780-0034; *Fax:* 416-780-0343
Toll-Free: 888-858-2632
toronto@cmdai.org
www.cmdai.org/toronto/
Chief Officer(s):
Iris Ehrent, Administrative Coordinator

Vancouver Chapter
#318, 101-1001 West Broadway, Vancouver BC V6H 4E4
Tel: 604-873-5244; *Fax:* 604-873-5246
vancouver@cmdai.org
www.cmdai.org/vancouver/

Canadian Maine-Anjou Association (CMAA)
5160 Skyline Way NE, Calgary AB T2E 6V1
Tel: 403-291-7077; *Fax:* 403-291-0274
cmaa@maine-anjou.ca
www.maine-anjou.ca
www.facebook.com/848369091908255
Overview: A small national organization founded in 1970
Mission: To encourage, develop, & regulate the breeding of Main-Anjou cattle in Canada
Member of: Canadian Beef Breeds Council
Membership: *Member Profile:* Breeders engaged in propagation & breeding of Maine-Anjou cattle
Chief Officer(s):
Scott McCormack, President
Tracy Wood, Secretary
Brian Brown, Treasurer
Publications:
• The Maine Mail [a publication of the Canadian Maine-Anjou Association]
Type: Magazine; *Frequency:* Bi-annually; *Accepts Advertising*

Canadian Management Centre
#320, 33 Yonge St., Toronto ON M5E 1G4
Tel: 416-214-6047
Toll-Free: 877-262-2519
cmcinfo@cmcoutperform.com
www.cmcoutperform.com
www.linkedin.com/company/35861
twitter.com/canadianmgmt
www.youtube.com/user/CdnMgmtCtr
Overview: A large national organization
Mission: To play a key role in strengthening the ability of Canada's business leaders, managers, & organizations to compete & succeed in today's challenging & changing business environment; To provide a full range of professional development & management education services to companies, government agencies, & individuals
Affiliation(s): American Management Association International
Activities: *Speaker Service:* Yes; *Rents Mailing List:* Yes; Library
Chief Officer(s):
John Wright, President & Managing Director
Patrice Penaud, Vice-President, Business Development
Bernadette Smith, Vice-President, Talent Solutions
Mai Thao, Director, Marketing

Canadian Manufactured Housing Institute (CMHI)
#500, 150 Laurier Ave. West, Ottawa ON K1P 5J4
Tel: 613-563-3520; *Fax:* 613-232-8600
cmhi@cmhi.ca
www.cmhi.ca
www.linkedin.com/company/canadian-manufactured-housing-institute
twitter.com/CMHI_ICHU
plus.google.com/105246295798437075142
Overview: A medium-sized national organization founded in 1953
Mission: To be the voice of the manufactured housing industry in Canada; to seek, identify & solidify the development of new, profitable market opportunities for manufactured housing, both domestically & internationally; to promote housing affordability for all Canadians.

Membership: *Fees:* $1000 national; $400 regional; *Member Profile:* Manufacturers; retailers; suppliers
Activities: *Library:* Not open to public
Chief Officer(s):
Dale Ball, President

Canadian Manufacturers & Exporters (CME) / Manufacturiers et Exportateurs Canada
#620, 55 Standish Ct., Mississauga ON L5R 4B2
Tel: 905-672-3466; *Fax:* 905-672-1764
www.cme-mec.ca
twitter.com/cme_mec
www.youtube.com/manufacturingTV
Previous Name: Alliance of Manufacturers & Exporters Canada
Merged from: Canadian Manufacturers' Association (1871); Canadian Exporters' Association (1943)
Overview: A large national organization founded in 1996
Mission: To continuously improve the competitiveness of Canadian industry & to expand export business by: aggressive, effective advocacy to government at all levels; delivering timely, relevant information, programs & support of superior quality & value; providing opportunities for education, learning & professional growth; & promoting the development & implementation of advanced technology
Finances: *Funding Sources:* Membership fees; Publication sales; Services
Membership: 5,000-14,999; *Fees:* Schedule available; *Member Profile:* Manufacturers, exporters, exporting companies, businesses & institutions servicing the manufacturing & exporting sectors
Activities: *Awareness Events:* Canadian Manufacturing Week, 2nd week of Oct.; *Speaker Service:* Yes
Chief Officer(s):
Dennis Darby, President & CEO
president@cme-mec.ca
Mathew Wilson, Senior Vice-President, 647-808-8231
mathew.wilson@cme-mec.ca
Nancy Coulas, Director, Energy & Environment Policy
nancy.coulas@cme-mec.ca
Marie Morden, Director, Partnerships & Stakeholder Relations
marie.morden@cme-mec.ca
David Suess, Director, Manufacturing Skills Centre
david.suess@cme-mec.ca
Susan Kallsen, Executive Assistant & Corporate Secretary
susan.kallsen@cme-mec.ca
Meetings/Conferences:
• Canadian Manufacturers & Exporters 2018 LEAN Conference, June, 2018, RBC Convention Center, Winnipeg, MB
Scope: National
Contact Information: www.embracingexcellence.ca
Publications:
• 20/20: Canada's Industry Association Magazine [a publication of Canadian Manufacturers & Exporters]
Type: Magazine; *Frequency:* Bimonthly; *Accepts Advertising*; *Editor:* Marie Morden
Profile: Information for Canadian industry to compete in the global economy, on subjects such as globalcompetitiveness, workforce capability, energy, environment & efficiency, financial services, logistics, innovation, & CME strategy
• CME [Canadian Manufacturers & Exporters] Newsletter
Type: Newsletter
• Manufacturing Pulse [a publication of Canadian Manufacturers & Exporters]
Type: Newsletter; *Author:* Mike Holden

Alberta Division
#531, 10060 Jasper Ave., Edmonton AB T5J 3R8
Tel: 780-965-4691
ab.cme-mec.ca
Chief Officer(s):
David MacLean, Vice-President
david.maclean@cme-mec.ca

Association des manufacturiers et des exportateurs du Québec (MEQ)
#201, 360, rue Saint-Jacques, Montréal QC H2Y 1P5
Tél: 514-866-7774; *Téléc:* 514-866-9447
Ligne sans frais: 800-363-0226
info@meq.ca
qc.cme-mec.ca
Chief Officer(s):
Éric Tétrault, Président
eric.tetrault@meq.ca
Pierre Léger, Directeur général
pierre.leger@meq.ca

British Columbia Division
#2163, 13353 Commerce Pkwy, Richmond BC V6V 3A1

Canadian Associations / Canadian Marfan Association (CMA) / Association du syndrome de Marfan

Tel: 604-713-7800; Fax: 604-713-7801
bc.cme-mec.ca
twitter.com/cme_bc
www.youtube.com/cmebc1
Chief Officer(s):
Andrew Wynn-Williams, Vice-President, 604-713-7803 Ext. 5290
andrew.wynnwilliams@cme-mec.ca
Manitoba Division
67 Scurfield Blvd., #B, Winnipeg MB R3Y 1G4
Tel: 204-949-1454; Fax: 204-943-3476
mb.info@cme-mec.ca
mb.cme-mec.ca
Chief Officer(s):
Ron Koslowsky, Vice-President
ron.koslowsky@cme-mec.ca
New Brunswick & Prince Edward Island Division
PO Box 416, Stn. Frederiction A, Fredericton NB E3B 4Z9
Tel: 506-259-0358
nb.cme-mec.ca
Chief Officer(s):
Joel Richardson, Vice-President
joel.richardson@cme-mec.ca
Newfoundland & Labrador Division
#207, 90 O'Leary Ave., St. John's NL A1B 2C7
Tel: 709-685-5820
nfl.cme-mec.ca
Chief Officer(s):
David Haire, Vice-President
david.haire@cme-mec.ca
Nova Scotia Division
#106, 3667 Strawberry Hill St., Halifax NS B3K 5A8
Tel: 902-422-4477; Fax: 902-422-9563
Chief Officer(s):
Michel Raymond, Divisional Vice President, 902-802-2662
michel.raymond@cme-mec.ca
Jacqui Squires, Office Manager, 902-476-2706
jacqui.squires@cme-mec.ca
Ontario Division
#620, 55 Standish Ct., Mississauga ON L5R 4B2
Tel: 905-672-3466; Fax: 905-672-1764
Toll-Free: 800-268-9684
on.cme-mec.ca
Chief Officer(s):
Ian Howcroft, Vice-President
ian.howcroft@cme-mec.ca

Canadian Manufacturers of Chemical Specialties Association *See* Canadian Consumer Specialty Products Association

Canadian Marfan Association (CMA) / Association du syndrome de Marfan
PO Box 42257, Stn. Centre Plaza, 128 Queen St. South, Mississauga ON L5M 4Z0
Tel: 905-826-3223; Fax: 905-826-2125
Toll-Free: 866-722-1722
info@marfan.ca
www.marfan.ca
www.facebook.com/CanadianMarfanAssociation
twitter.com/CanadianMarfan
Overview: A medium-sized national charitable organization founded in 1986
Member of: International Federation of Marfan Syndrome Associations; Thoracic Aortic Disease (TAD) Coalition; Canadian Organization for Rare Disorders
Finances: *Funding Sources:* Donations; Fundraising
Staff Member(s): 2
Membership: *Fees:* Donation
Activities: Increasing awareness of Marfan Syndrome through publications & information packages; Producing videos; Organizing presentations, seminars & conferences across Canada; Organizing Marfan regional support groups; Fostering & supporting research; *Awareness Events:* National Marfan Awareness Week, 3rd week of November; *Internships:* Yes
Library: Canadian Marfan Association Resource Centre; by appointment Not open to public
Chief Officer(s):
Barry Edington, Executive Director

The Canadian Marine Industries and Shipbuilding Association (CMISA) / Association de la construction navale du Canada
#1502, 222 Queen St., Ottawa ON K1P 5V9
Tel: 613-232-7127; Fax: 613-238-5519
canadianshipbuilding.com

Previous Name: Shipbuilding Association of Canada; Canadian Maritime Industries Association
Overview: A medium-sized national organization founded in 1995
Mission: Represents the interests of the Canadian shipbuilding, ship repair & associated marine equipment & services industries
Finances: *Funding Sources:* Membership dues
Membership: 1-99; *Fees:* Schedule available; *Member Profile:* Canadian organizations engaged in provision of services, products &/or facilities related to ship design, shipbuilding & ship repair, must be 65% Canadian content/owned; *Committees:* Technical; Finance; Personnel; International Marketing; Procurement Outlook; SAC/Government Working Groups
Activities: *Rents Mailing List:* Yes
Chief Officer(s):
Peter Cairns, President

Canadian Marine Manufacturers Association *See* National Marine Manufacturers Association Canada

Canadian Marine Pilots' Association (CMPA) / Association des pilotes maritimes du Canada (APMC)
c/o Tristan Laflamme, #901, 50 O'Connor St., Ottawa ON K1P 6L2
Tel: 613-220-8954
apmc-cmpa@apmc-cmpa.ca
www.marinepilots.ca
Overview: A small national organization founded in 1966
Mission: To represent Canadian marine pilots; To raise awareness of marine pilots' role to protect public safety; To ensure a healthy Canadian marine sector
Member of: International Maritime Pilots' Association; Canadian Merchant Service Guild
Membership: 400; *Member Profile:* Marine pilots in Canada
Activities: Upholding a Code of Conduct for Canadian pilots; Contributing to matters of safety & regulatory issues; Collaborating with marine stakeholders to maintain a vibrant marine sector
Chief Officer(s):
Simon Pelletier, President
Bernard Boissonneault, Vice-President
Laurentian Region
Mike Burgess, Vice-President
Great Lakes Region
Kevin Vail, Vice-President
Pacific Region
Andrew Rae, Vice-President
Atlantic Region
Tristan Laflamme, Executive Director & General Counsel
Meetings/Conferences:
• Canadian Marine Pilots' Association 6th Congress, 2018
Scope: National
Publications:
• The Canadian Pilot: The CMPA Newsletter
Type: Newsletter
Profile: Information, articles, & forthcoming events for pilots & other stakeholders in the industry

The Canadian Maritime Law Association / L'Association canadienne de droit maritime
#900, 1000, rue de la Gauchetière ouest, Montréal QC H3B 5H4
Tel: 514-954-3184; Fax: 514-954-1905
cmla@cmla.org
www.cmla.org
Overview: A medium-sized national organization founded in 1951
Mission: To promote the study & advancement of maritime law in Canada; To promote the harmonization of maritime law internationally
Member of: Comité maritime international
Finances: *Funding Sources:* Membership fees
Membership: 300+; *Fees:* $150 individual; $500 organization; $30 student; *Member Profile:* Individual, association, or corporate body resident in Canada; *Committees:* Executive (Board of Directors); Arctic Issues; Arrest & Sales of Ships; Carriage of Goods; Carriage of Passengers; CMI Liaison; Communications; Continuing Legal Education; Customs/Immigration/Stowaways; Federal Courts Act & Rules; Finance & Investment; Fisheries; General Average; IMO Liaison; Legislative & Regulatory; Limitation of Liability; Marine Environment; Marine Insurance; Membership; Nominating; Piracy; Places of Refuge; Ports & Harbours; Ratification of Maritime Convention; Salvage & Wreck; Seafarers; Tetley Award; Transportation Safety Board; Young Members
Chief Officer(s):
Marc D. Isaacs, President
marc@isaacsco.ca
Robert C. Wilkins, Secretary-Treasurer
rwilkins@blg.com

Canadian Marketing Association (CMA) / Association canadienne du marketing (ACM)
#603, 55 University Ave., Toronto ON M5J 2H7
Tel: 416-391-2362; Fax: 416-441-4062
Toll-Free: 800-267-8805
info@thecma.ca
www.the-cma.org
www.linkedin.com/groups/47336
www.facebook.com/cdnmarketing
twitter.com/Cdnmarketing
www.youtube.com/user/canadianmarketing
Previous Name: Canadian Direct Marketing Association
Overview: A large national organization founded in 1967
Mission: To be the pre-eminent marketing association in Canada representing the integration & convergence of all marketing disciplines, channels & technologies
Affiliation(s): European Direct Marketing Association; Direct Marketing Association - USA
Finances: *Annual Operating Budget:* $1.5 Million-$3 Million; *Funding Sources:* Membership dues; events
Staff Member(s): 28; 400 volunteers
Membership: 800 corporate; 1,200 total; *Member Profile:* Membership includes corporations & organizations which encompass Canada's major business sectors & which represent the integration & convergence of all marketing disciplines, channels & technologies; supports 480,000 jobs & generates more than $51 billion in overall annual sales; *Committees:* Special Interest Councils - Branding & Strategic Planning; Customer Relationship Management; Database & Marketing Technology; Integrated Marketing Communications; Not-for-Profit; Contact Centre; Direct Mail; E-Marketing
Activities: Responds to public policy issues; participates in a variety of government-led task forces & working groups on issues such as privacy, electronic commerce, consumer protection, the prevention of telemarketing fraud, & unsolicited bulk e-mail; forms internal task forces to develop self-regulatory policies on standards of business practice, ethics, privacy, & marketing to children & teenagers; enforces Code of Ethics & Standards of Practice & Privacy Code; *Rents Mailing List:* Yes
Chief Officer(s):
John Wiltshire, President & CEO
Awards:
• CMA Awards
20 categories; direct response campaigns from all media are considered
• CMA Student Awards
Meetings/Conferences:
• Canadian Marketing Association CMAinsights, February, 2018
Scope: National
Description: CMAinsights will feature multiple content streams; focusing on both the marketer and the data practitioner.
• Canadian Marketing Association CMAideas, February, 2018
Scope: National
Description: Brings together a unique conference of creators, innovators and leaders with insights from unlikely places and undiscovered territories.
• Canadian Marketing Association CMAdigital, June, 2018
Scope: National
• Canadian Marketing Association CMAideas, September, 2018
Scope: National
Description: Brings together a unique conference of creators, innovators and leaders with insights from unlikely places and undiscovered territories.
• Canadian Marketing Association CMAmedia, October, 2018
Scope: National
• Canadian Marketing Association CMAfuture, November, 2018
Scope: National
Description: A look at the newest methods, strategies and technology on the horizon
Publications:
• Canadian Marketing Association Membership Directory & Buyers' Guide
Type: Directory; *Accepts Advertising*
Profile: Listing of companies & their services
• CMA [Canadian Marketing Association] Guide to E-mail Marketing
Type: Guide
Profile: Theory, best practices & practical advice, for marketers
• CMA [Canadian Marketing Association] Fundraiser's Handbook
Type: Handbook; *Number of Pages:* 35; *Price:* $15 members;

$25 non-members
Profile: A guide to measurement & evaluation

Association du marketing relationne
#109, 1744, rue William, Montréal QC H3J 1R4
Tél: 514-904-1927
info@relationnel.ca
relationnel.ca
www.linkedin.com/groups?gid=1743317
www.facebook.com/AMRQuebec
twitter.com/AMRQuebec
www.youtube.com/user/AMRQuebec
Chief Officer(s):
Alex Langlois, Président

Calgary Chapter
PO Box 5071, Stn. A, Calgary AB T2H 1X1
Tel: 403-860-8745; *Fax:* 403-974-2043
info@calgarycma.com
www.calgarycma.com
www.linkedin.com/companies/433702
twitter.com/calgarycma
www.flickr.com/calgarycma
Chief Officer(s):
Jim Carter, President
jim.carter@theclient.ca

Manitoba Chapter
PO Box 1973, Winnipeg MB R3C 3R3
Tel: 204-284-5642
www.cmamanitoba.com
www.facebook.com/marketingmanitoba
twitter.com/cma_manitoba
Chief Officer(s):
Kevin Gordon, Interim President
president@cmamanitoba.com

Ottawa Chapter
PO Box 8024, Stn. Alta Vista, Ottawa ON K1G 3H6
Fax: 613-248-4667
info@cmaottawa.com
www.cmaottawa.com
Chief Officer(s):
Sharon Daly, President
s.daly@calian.com

Canadian Masonry Contractors' Association (CMCA)
Canada Masonry Centre, 360 Superior Blvd., Mississauga ON L5T 2N7
Tel: 905-564-6622; *Fax:* 905-564-5744
www.canadamasonrycentre.com/cmca
Overview: A medium-sized national organization founded in 1967
Mission: To advance masonry technology, skills development & the use of masonry products in construction across Canada.
Member of: National Trade Contractors Coalition of Canada
Affiliation(s): Ontario Masonry Contractors' Association; Metro Mason Contractors Association; Canada Masonry Centre
Finances: *Funding Sources:* Membership dues
Activities: *Speaker Service:* Yes; *Library:* by appointment

Association des entrepreneurs en maçonnerie du Québec
#101, 4097, boul Saint-Jean Baptiste, Montréal QC H1B 5V3
Tél: 514-645-1113; *Téléc:* 514-645-1114
Ligne sans frais: 866-645-1113
aemq@aemq.com
www.aemq.com
www.linkedin.com/company/aemq---association-des-entrepreneurs-en-maçonnerie-du-québec
www.facebook.com/171902572902949
Chief Officer(s):
Marco Tommasel, Président

British Columbia & Yukon Chapter
3636 - 4th Ave. East, Vancouver BC V5M 1M3
Tel: 604-291-1458; *Fax:* 604-291-9482
info@masonrybc.org
www.masonrybc.org

Manitoba Masonry Contractors' Association
Manitoba Masonry Institute, 1447 Waverley St., Winnipeg MB R3T 0P7
Tel: 204-949-0688
mmi_mmca@mts.net
www.manitobamasonry.ca

Masonry Contractors' Association of Alberta, Northern Region
PO Box 44157, RPO Garside, Edmonton AB T5V 1N6
Tel: 780-851-7013; *Fax:* 780-851-7013
mcaanorth@mca-canada.com
www.mca-canada.com
Chief Officer(s):
Karen Schneider, Contact

Masonry Contractors' Association of Alberta, Southern Region
#169, 132-250 Shawville Blvd. SE, Calgary AB T2Y 2Z7
Tel: 587-998-4023
mcaasouth@mca-canada.com
www.mca-canada.com
Chief Officer(s):
Danine McDougall, Contact

Ontario Masonry Contractors' Association
360 Superior Blvd., Mississauga ON L5T 2N7
Tel: 905-564-6622
www.canadamasonrycentre.com/omca

Saskatchewan Masonry Institute
532 - 2nd Ave. North, Saskatoon SK S7K 2C5
Tel: 306-665-0622; *Fax:* 306-665-0621
info@saskmasonry.ca
www.saskmasonry.ca
Chief Officer(s):
Rob Walchuk, President

Canadian Massage Therapist Alliance (CMTA) / Alliance Canadienne de Massothérapeutes
#16, 1724 Quebec Ave., Saskatoon SK S7K 1V9
Tel: 306-384-7077
info@crmta.ca
www.crmta.ca
www.facebook.com/CRMTA
Overview: A medium-sized national organization founded in 1991
Mission: To foster & advance the art, science & philosophy of massage therapy through nationwide cooperation in a professional, ethical & practical manner for the betterment of health care in Canada
Finances: *Funding Sources:* Membership dues
Membership: 9; *Member Profile:* Provincial organizations
Activities: *Awareness Events:* National Massage Therapy Awareness Week, Sept.

Canadian Masters Athletic Association (CMAA)
Tel: 416-380-2503
canadianmasters.ca
Previous Name: Canadian Masters Track & Field Association
Overview: A medium-sized national organization founded in 1972
Finances: *Funding Sources:* Membership fees
Membership: 1,527; *Member Profile:* Men & women 30 and up
Chief Officer(s):
Paul Osland, President
paul.osland@hotmail.com
Sherry Watts, Contact, Membership
pacertraining@yahoo.ca
Publications:
• The MASTERpiece
Type: Newsletter; *Frequency:* Irregular; *Price:* Free with CMAA membership
Profile: News, results, & upcoming events for Masters

Canadian Masters Cross-Country Ski Association (CMCSA) / Association canadienne des maîtres en ski de fond
2 MacNeil Cres., Stephenville NL A2N 3E3
Tel: 709-643-3259
www.canadian-masters-xc-ski.ca
Overview: A medium-sized national organization founded in 1980
Mission: To promote Masters cross-country skiing across Canada, establish rules & regulations for activities, & representing members at meetings at the WMA.
Affiliation(s): World Masters Cross-Country Ski Association; Cross-Country Canada
Finances: *Funding Sources:* Membership fees
Membership: *Fees:* $20; $35 in Québec; *Member Profile:* 30 years of age & over
Activities: Cross country ski races in Canada & abroad; Masters World Cup; Canadian Masters National Championships
Chief Officer(s):
Bruce Legrow, National Director
bruce.legrow@nf.sympatico.ca
Publications:
• Canadian Masters Cross-Country Ski Association Newsletter
Type: Newsletter; *Frequency:* Irregular; *Price:* Free with CMCSA membership
Profile: Information & upcoming events for Masters skiers

Alberta
c/o Dave Rees, 12 Spray Village, Canmore AB T1W 2T5
Tel: 403-707-5565
Chief Officer(s):
Dave Rees, Director
rees.ski@gmail.com

British Columbia
c/o Mike Bell, 4193B Gordon Dr., Kelowna BC V1W 1S4
Tel: 250-540-1273
Chief Officer(s):
Mike Bell, Director
mikebell10@gmail.com

Manitoba
c/o Danielle Papin, 126 Sherbrun St., Winnipeg MB R3G 2K4
Tel: 204-772-2535
Chief Officer(s):
Danielle Papin, Director
dpapin@mts.net

New Brunswick
c/o Roger Lévesque, 94 Pioneer Ave., Balmoral NB E8E 1E1
Tel: 506-826-2534
Chief Officer(s):
Roger Levesque, Director

Newfoundland/Labrador
c/o Bruce Legrow, 2 MacNeil Cres., Stephenville NL A2N 3E3
Tel: 709-643-3259
Chief Officer(s):
Bruce LeGrow, Director
bruce.legrow@nf.sympatico.ca

Ontario
ON
Chief Officer(s):
Deborah De Pass, Director, Membership
deb.depass@gmail.com

Québec
c/o Rock Ouimet, 546, rue de la Tourelle, Québec QC G1R 1E3
Chief Officer(s):
Rock Ouimet, Director
rock.ouimet@gmail.com

Saskatchewan
c/o Robin Butler, 531 Emmeline Key, Saskatoon SK S7J 5G8
Tel: 306-373-6658
Chief Officer(s):
Robin Butler, Director
skirobin@sasktel.net

Yukon
c/o Mary Whitley, 1 Chalet Cres., Whitehorse YT Y1A 3H1
Tel: 867-668-2903
Chief Officer(s):
Mary Whitley, Director
whitley@polarcom.com

Canadian Masters Track & Field Association *See* Canadian Masters Athletic Association

Canadian Mathematical Society (CMS) / Société mathématique du Canada
#209, 1725 St Laurent Blvd., Ottawa ON K1G 3V4
Tel: 613-733-2662
office@cms.math.ca
www.cms.math.ca
www.facebook.com/canmathsoc
Overview: A medium-sized international charitable organization founded in 1945
Mission: To promote & advance the discovery, learning & application of mathematics
Member of: National Consortium for Scientific Societies
Finances: *Annual Operating Budget:* $500,000-$1.5 Million; *Funding Sources:* Membership; publications; donations
Staff Member(s): 9; 210 volunteer(s)
Membership: 1,068; *Fees:* $56-$280 individual; $110-$1,180 institution; *Member Profile:* University professors; students; teachers & mathematicians; *Committees:* Education; Electronic Services; Finance; Advancement of Mathematics; Human Rights; International Affairs; Mathematical Competitions; Nominating; Publications; Research; Women in Mathematics
Activities: Meetings; publishing; competitions; mathematics awareness; electronic services; represents the Canadian mathematical community to federal & provincial governments; *Speaker Service:* Yes; *Rents Mailing List:* Yes
Chief Officer(s):

Yvette Roberts, Manager, Finance & Operations, 613-733-2662 Ext. 788
finances@cms.math.ca
Denise Charron, Manager, Memberships & Publications, 613-733-2662 Ext. 777
mpagent@cms.math.ca
Sarah Watson, Manager, Meetings & Events, 613-733-2662 Ext. 733
meetings@cms.math.ca
Awards:
• Canadian Mathematical Olympiad
Annual mathematics competition established to provide an opportunity for students to perform well on the Canadian Open Mathematics Challenge & to complete on a national basis. Fifteen cash prizes
Meetings/Conferences:
• 2018 Canadian Mathematical Society Summer Meeting, June, 2018, Fredericton, NB
Scope: National
Publications:
• Canadian Journal of Mathematics (CJM)
Type: Journal
• Canadian Mathematical Bulletin (CMB)
Type: Journal
• Canadian Mathematical Society Notes
Type: Journal

Canadian Meat Council (CMC) / Conseil des viandes du Canada
#930, 220 Laurier Ave. West, Ottawa ON K1P 5Z9
Tel: 613-729-3911; *Fax:* 613-729-4997
info@cmc-cvc.com
www.cmc-cvc.com
www.facebook.com/cmccvc
twitter.com/CMCCVC
Previous Name: Meat Packers Council of Canada
Overview: A medium-sized national organization founded in 1919
Mission: To express the views of the membership with government, all elements of the food industry, consumer organizations, the research & academic community, & the media; To foster high standards of industry integrity, & a vast range of wholesome, nutritional meat products
Finances: *Funding Sources:* Membership dues
Staff Member(s): 7
Membership: 66; *Member Profile:* Federally inspected packers & processors of meat; *Committees:* Pork; Technical; Beef & Veal
Activities: Responding to members' needs; Contributing to the competitiveness of the industry at both domestic & international levels; Providing a forum for members to discuss & consider matters relating to government regulations & activities, competitiveness, & dealings with other national trade associations; Working towards a free & expanding market environment; *Speaker Service:* Yes; *Library:* Council Library
Chief Officer(s):
Chris White, President & CEO, 613-729-3911 Ext. 25
chris@cmc-cvc.com
Jorge Correa, Vice-President, Market Access & Technical Affairs, 613-729-3911 Ext. 23
jorge@cmc-cvc.com
Meetings/Conferences:
• 98th Annual Canadian Meat Council Conference 2018, 2018
Scope: National
Description: A meeting with a technical symposium & exhibits, a general session, as well as the announcement of scholarship recipients
Publications:
• Food Service Meat Manual / Manuel des vaindes pour les services alimenaires
Type: Manual; *Number of Pages:* 40+; *Price:* $30 for 1-9 copies; $25 for 10+copies
Profile: The third revised edition that outines the cutting & trimming technniqes for 86 cuts of meat

Canadian Meat Goat Association (CMGA) / Canadienne de la Chèvre de Boucherie
#12, 449 Laird Rd., Guelph ON N1G 4W1
Tel: 519-824-2942; *Fax:* 519-824-2534
info@canadianmeatgoat.com
www.canadianmeatgoat.com
Previous Name: Canadian Boer Goat Association
Overview: A small national organization founded in 1995
Mission: To support the development of a profitable meat goat breeding stock & meat industry in Canada; to provide animal registration; to establish breeding standards; to promote the industry & raise consumer demand for chevon
Member of: Canadian Livestock Records Corporation
Membership: *Fees:* $75 active members; $50 associate members; $20 junior members (persons under 18 years); *Member Profile:* Commercial meat goat & purebred seed stock producers across Canada
Activities: Creating educational tools for commercial meat goat & purebred seed stock producers; partnering in research; introducing a youth program; developing marketing tools in order to expand the market; representing members at agricultural events throughout Canada
Chief Officer(s):
Stuart Chutter, President, 306-599-9152
stuchutt@hotmail.com
Publications:
• Canadian Meat Goat Association Membership Directory
Type: Directory; *Frequency:* Annually
• Canadian Meat Goat Journal
Type: Journal; *Frequency:* Quarterly; *Accepts Advertising; Price:* Free with Canadian Meat Goat Association membership
Profile: Management of goats; business practices; goat health issues, & marketing

Canadian Meat Science Association (CMSA) / Association scientifique canadienne de la viande (ASCB)
Dept. of Agricultural, Food & Nutritional Science, Univ. of Alberta, #4-10, Agriculture / Forestry Centre, Edmonton AB T6G 2P5
admin@cmsa-ascv.ca
www.cmsa-ascv.ca
Overview: A medium-sized national organization
Mission: To promote the application of science & technology to the production, processing, packaging, distribution, preparation, evaluation, & utilization of all meat & meat products; To develop & promote useful, coordinated research, educational techniques, & service activities
Membership: 13 corporate members; *Fees:* $60 professional; $200 corporate; $0 students; *Member Profile:* Individuals & corporations with an interest in the science of meat & meat products; *Committees:* Promotion & Membership; Education; Newsletter; Nominations & Elections; Symposium; Website & Electronic Communications; Audit
Activities: Providing forums & networking opportunities for discussion & dissemination of information; Promoting recognition of people engaged in meat science
Chief Officer(s):
Eric Pouliot, President
eric.pouliot@cepoq.com
Bethany Uttaro, Sec.-Treas.
bethany.uttaro@agr.gc.ca
Awards:
• Percy Gitelman Memorial Scholarship
Sponsored jointly by the Canadian Meat Science Association and Newly Weds Foods, Inc.; *Amount:* $3,000
• CMC Associate Members Scholarship
To honour a promising graduate student who is studying Meat Science in Canada; *Amount:* 3,000
Publications:
• Canadian Meat Science Association Membership Directory
Type: Directory; *Frequency:* Annually
Profile: A listing of persons & organizations throughout Canada with an interest in meat science
• CMSA [Canadian Meat Science Association] News
Type: Newsletter; *Frequency:* Quarterly
Profile: Activities of the meat sector & the association for CMSA members

Canadian Media Directors' Council (CMDC)
#1097, 1930 Yonge St., Toronto ON M4S 1Z4
Tel: 416-967-7282
www.cmdc.ca
www.facebook.com/canadianmedialeadership
twitter.com/CMDCCanada
Overview: A small national organization founded in 1966
Mission: To advance media advertising in Canada; To create more efficient processes to execute and administer media transactions by adopting industry-wide standards
Membership: 38; *Member Profile:* Media professionals who represent advertising & media management companies in Canada
Activities: Liaising with government, media sellers, & advertising organizations; Providing continuing education program for media professionals
Chief Officer(s):
Janet Callaghan, President, 416-921-4049
jsc@janetcallaghan.com
Meetings/Conferences:
• Canadian Media Directors' Council 2018 Annual Conference, 2018
Scope: National
Publications:
• CMDC [Canadian Media Directors' Council] Media Digest
Type: Guide; *Frequency:* Annually

Canadian Media Guild (CMG) / La Guilde canadienne des médias
#810, 310 Front St. West, Toronto ON M5V 3B5
Tel: 416-591-5333
Toll-Free: 800-465-4149
info@cmg.ca
www.cmg.ca
twitter.com/CMGLaGuilde
Previous Name: Canadian Wire Service Guild
Overview: A medium-sized national organization founded in 1950
Mission: To advance the interests of Guild members through collective bargaining
Affiliation(s): CWA/SCA Canada
Membership: 6,000; *Member Profile:* Members work in the Canadian media & become part of a democratic trade union
Activities: Promoting good working environments; Providing training & education to assist members
Chief Officer(s):
Dominique Bondar, Office Coordinator
dominique@cmg.ca
Jeanne d'Arc Umurungi, Director, Communications
jeannedarc@cmg.ca
Publications:
• G-Force
Type: Newsletter; *Frequency:* Quarterly; *Editor:* Karen Wirsig
Profile: Media issues & information for CMG members

Halifax Regional Office
#133, 1657 Barrington St., Halifax NS B3J 2A1
Tel: 902-471-6070
Chief Officer(s):
Gerald Whelan, Staff Representative, Atlantic Office
gerry@cmg.ca

Ottawa Regional Office
Ottawa ON
Toll-Free: 819-230-6769
Chief Officer(s):
Olivier Desharnais-Roy, Staff Representative
olivier@cmg.ca

Vancouver Regional Office
Vancouver BC
Tel: 604-642-2554
Chief Officer(s):
Jean Broughton, Staff Representative, Western Office
jean@cmg.ca

Canadian Media Production Association (CMPA)
601 Bank St., 2nd Fl., Ottawa ON K1S 3T4
Tel: 613-233-1444; *Fax:* 613-233-0073
Toll-Free: 800-656-7440
ottawa@cmpa.ca
www.cmpa.ca
www.linkedin.com/company/canadian-media-production-association-cmpa-
www.facebook.com/theCMPA
twitter.com/CMPA_Updates
www.youtube.com/CMPAOnline
Previous Name: Canadian Film & Television Production Association
Overview: A medium-sized national organization founded in 1990
Mission: To represent the interests of media companies engaged in the production & distribution of English language television programs, feature films, & new media content throughout Canada
Membership: 300 companies; *Committees:* Audit; Canada Media Fund Working Group; Copyright; CRTC Regulatory; Digital Business Export; Feature Film; Industrial Relations; Internal Finance; International Business & Production Finance; Membership Strategy & Outreach; Mentorship; New Business Model; Public Affairs; Terms of Trade Working Group
Activities: *Library:*
Chief Officer(s):
Michael Hennessy, President & Chief Executive Officer, 613-688-0946 Ext. 328

Jane Cheesman, Chief Financial Officer, 613-688-0947 Ext. 330
jane.cheesman@cmpa.ca
Marc Séguin, Senior Vice-President, Policy, 613-688-0948 Ext. 323
marc.seguin@cmpa.ca
Jay Thomson, Vice-President, Broadcasting Policy & Regulatory Affairs, 613-688-0949 Ext. 322
jay.thomson@cmpa.ca
Susanne Vaas, Vice-President, Corporate & International Affairs, 613-688-0950 Ext. 337
susanne.vaas@cmpa.ca
Anne Trueman, Director, Communications & Media, 613-688-0951 Ext. 327
anne.trueman@cmpa.ca
Sarolta Csete, Manager, National Mentorship Program & e-Services, 613-688-0952 Ext. 338
sarolta.csete@cmpa.ca
Lisa Moreau, Manager, Member Services & Special Events, 613-688-0900 Ext. 329
lisa.moreau@cmpa.ca
Meetings/Conferences:
• Canadian Media Producers Association's Prime Time in Ottawa 2018, January, 2018, Ottawa, ON
Scope: National
Contact Information: www.primetimeinottawa.ca
Publications:
• Canadian Media Production Association's Note to Members
Type: Newsletter; *Price:* Free with membership in the Canadian Media Production Association
Profile: Containing pertinent industry information

Canadian Medical & Biological Engineering Society (CMBES) / Société canadienne de génie biomédical inc. (SCGB)
1485 Laperriere Ave., Ottawa ON K1Z 7S8
Tel: 613-728-1759
secretariat@cmbes.ca
www.cmbes.ca
twitter.com/cmbesociety
Overview: A medium-sized national organization founded in 1965
Mission: To advance the theory & practice of medical device technology; To advance individuals who are engaged in interdisciplinary work involving medicine, engineering, & the life sciences; To represent the interests of biomedical & clinical engineering to government agencies
Affiliation(s): International Federation for Medical and Biological Engineering (IFMBE)
Membership: 100-499; *Fees:* $130 full; $45 associate; $35 student/retired; $60 student instutional; Schedule for corporate membership based on number of members per group
Activities: Offering continuing education; Providing networking opportunities; *Awareness Events:* Biomedical / Clinical Engineering Appreciation Week
Chief Officer(s):
Martin Poulin, President
martin.poulin@viha.ca
Mike Capuano, Vice-President
capuamik@hhsc.ca
Awards:
• Outstanding Canadian Biomedical Engineer Award
Awarded to a Canadian biomedical engineer who has made notable contributions in the field of biomedical engineering
Eligibility: A professional engineer who is a CMBES member in good standing & engaged in biomedical engineering in Canada
• Outstanding Canadian BMET Award
Presented to a Canadian Biomedical Equipment Technician (BMET) who displays exellence in the field of biomedical engineering technology through ability, service, or contributions
Eligibility: A professional engineer who is a CMBES member in good standing & engaged in biomedical engineering in Canada
• Early Career Achievement Award
Awarded to recognize young professionals who have demonstrated outstanding performance & achievement in the early stages of their careers through client services, technical ability, or development achievements *Eligibility:* A CMBES member who graduated from a post-secondary program related to biomedical engineering & who has been working in the field for a maximum of five years
Meetings/Conferences:
• Canadian Medical & Biological Engineering Society 2018 41st Annual National Conference, May, 2018, Delta Prince Edward Island, Charlottetown, PE
Scope: National

Publications:
• Canadian Medical & Biological Engineering Society Conference Proceedings & Abstracts
• Canadian Medical & Biological Engineering Society Career Booklet
Type: Booklet
Profile: Information for guidance counselors & employment centers
• Clinical Engineering Standards of Practice [a publication of the Canadian Medical & Biological Engineering Society]
Type: Guide; *ISBN:* 978-0-919529-36-6; *Price:* Free with Cdn. Medical & Biological Engineering Society membership; $50 non-members
Profile: Criteria for health care institutions on the management of medical devices, the education& certification requirements for clinical engineers & biomedical engineering technologists & technicians & the promotion of professional development
• CMBES [Canadian Medical & Biological Engineering Society Inc.] Newsletter
Type: Newsletter; *Editor:* Dr. Gnahoua Zoabli; Pamela Wilson; *ISSN:* 1499-4089
Profile: Society activities, conferences, events, awards, chapters, & events

Canadian Medical Association (CMA) / Association médicale canadienne (AMC)
1209 Michael St., Ottawa ON K1J 7T2
Tel: 613-731-8610; *Fax:* 613-236-8864
Toll-Free: 888-855-2555
Other Communication: cmatechsupport@cma.ca (Technical Support)
cmamsc@cma.ca
www.cma.ca
www.linkedin.com/company/canadian-medical-association
www.facebook.com/CanadianMedicalAssociation
twitter.com/CMA_Docs
www.youtube.com/user/CanadianMedicalAssoc
Overview: A large national organization founded in 1867
Mission: To act as the national voice of physicians in Canada; To serve the Canadian medical community; To promote the highest standards of health & health care
Member of: World Medical Association
Affiliation(s): Assn. of Cdn. Medical Colleges; Cdn. Anesthesiologists' Soc.; Cdn. Assn. of Medical Biochemists; Cdn. Assn. of Physicians with Disabilities; Cdn. Assn. of Physicians for the Environment; Cdn. Assn. of Radiation Oncologists; Cdn. Fedn. of Medical Students; Cdn. Infectious Disease Soc.; Cdn. Neurological/Neurosurgical/Clinical Neurophysiologists Societies; Cdn. Ophthalmological Soc.; Cdn. Orthopaedic Assn.; Cdn. Paediatric Soc.; Cdn. Psychiatric Assn; Cdn. Rheumatology Assn.; Cdn. Soc. of Addiction Medicine; Cdn. Soc. of Internal Medicine; Cdn. Soc. of Nuclear Medicine; Cdn. Soc. of Otolaryngoly
Membership: 83,000+; *Member Profile:* Practising physicians; Residents; Retired physicians; Students; *Committees:* Ethics; Political Action; Health Care & Promotion; Health Policy & Economics; Education & Professional Development
Activities: Providing national & provincial advocacy; Offering practice management solutions; Providing courses through the CMA's Physician Management Institute, a leadership development program designed for physicians in the Canadian health care system
Chief Officer(s):
Cindy Forbes, President
Brian Brodie, Chair
Granger Avery, President-Elect
Awards:
• Medal of Honour
Contact: Chair, Committee on Archives & Awards, Phone: 1-800-663-7336, ext. 2243, E-mail: Julie.perron@cma.ca
• Medal of Service
Contact: Chair, Committee on Archives & Awards, Phone: 1-800-663-7336, ext. 2243, E-mail: Julie.perron@cma.ca
• May Cohen Award for Women Mentors
Contact: Chair, Committee on Archives & Awards, Phone: 1-800-663-7336, ext. 2243, E-mail: Julie.perron@cma.ca
• Sir Charles Tupper Award for Political Action
Contact: Chair, Committee on Archives & Awards, Phone: 1-800-663-7336, ext. 2243, E-mail: Julie.perron@cma.ca
• F.N.G. Starr Award
Contact: Chair, Committee on Archives & Awards, Phone: 1-800-663-7336, ext. 2243, E-mail: Julie.perron@cma.ca
• Award for Excellence in Health Promotion
Contact: Chair, Committee on Archives & Awards, Phone: 1-800-663-7336, ext. 2243, E-mail: Julie.perron@cma.ca

• Awards for Young Leaders
Contact: Chair, Committee on Archives & Awards, Phone: 1-800-663-7336, ext. 2243, E-mail: Julie.perron@cma.ca
• Dr. William Marsden Award in Medical Ethics
Contact: Chair, Committee on Archives & Awards, Phone: 1-800-663-7336, ext. 2243, E-mail: Julie.perron@cma.ca
• Physician Misericordia Award
Contact: Chair, Committee on Archives & Awards, Phone: 1-800-663-7336, ext. 2243, E-mail: Julie.perron@cma.ca
Meetings/Conferences:
• Canadian Medical Association 2018 151st Annual Meeting, August, 2018, Winnipeg, MB
Scope: National
Description: A meeting, featuring a business session to consider business & matters referred by the General Council
Publications:
• Canadian Health Magazine
Type: Magazine; *Frequency:* Quarterly; *Accepts Advertising*; *Editor:* Diana Swift; *Price:* $12 / year
Profile: A health & wellness resource for patients in a physician's waiting room
• Canadian Journal of Surgery (CJS)
Type: Journal; *Frequency:* Bimonthly; *Accepts Advertising*; *Editor:* E.J. Harvey, MD; G.L. Warnock, MD; *ISSN:* 0008-428X; *Price:* $35 Canadian students & residents; $175 Canadian individuals; $270 institutions
Profile: Continuing medical education for Canadian surgical specialists
• Canadian Medical Association Complete Home Medical Guide
Type: Book; *ISSN:* 1-55363-054-8; *Price:* $51.95 members
Profile: An 1104 page authoritative & user-friendly resource for physicians to recommend to patients
• Canadian Medical Association Conference Updates
Profile: The latest news from major clinical meetings
• Canadian Medical Association Journal (CMAJ)
Type: Journal; *Frequency:* Semimonthly; *Accepts Advertising*; *Editor:* Paul C. Hébert; *ISSN:* 0820-3946; *Price:* $35 / issue Canadian; $40 / issue USA
Profile: Peer-reviewed original research, review articles, practice updates, drug alerts, health news, & commentaries for clinicians, available online& in print
• CMA [Canadian Medical Association] Bulletin
Type: Newsletter; *Frequency:* Semimonthly; *Editor:* Patrick Sullivan; Steve Wharry
Profile: A communication from the Canadian Medical Association, with news stories of interest to Canadian physicians, inserted in the Canadian MedicalAssociation Journal
• CMA [Canadian Medical Association] Driver's Guide: Determining Medical Fitness to Operate Motor Vehicles
Type: Guide; *Price:* Free for Canadian Medical Association members
Profile: Examples of sections include the following: Functional assessment - emerging emphasis; Reporting - when & why; Drivingcessation; Aging; Vision; Respiratory diseases; Psychiatric illness; Cardiovascular diseases; Seat belts & air bags; Motorcycles & off-road vehicles; Aviation; Railway; & Appendices
• CMA [Canadian Medical Association] Leadership Series: MD Pulse
Type: Magazine; *Price:* $8.95 / copy members; $14.95 nonmembers
Profile: Results of the National Physician Survey, prepared by the Canadian Medical Association in collaboration with the College of Family Physicians of Canada & theRoyal College of Physicians & Surgeons of Canada
• CMA [Canadian Medical Association] Leadership Series: Primary Care Reform
Type: Magazine; *Editor:* Dr. Albert Schumacher
Profile: An outline of primary care reform initiatives throughout Canada
• CMA [Canadian Medical Association] Leadership Series: Elder Care - Issues & Options
Type: Magazine; *Price:* $8.95 / copy members; $14.95 nonmemebers
Profile: An examination of the medical, social, & ethical dimensions of care for older patients
• CMA [Canadian Medical Association] Leadership Series: Women's Health - Research & Practice Issues for Canadian Physicians
Type: Magazine; *Price:* $8.95 / copy members; $14.95 nonmemebers
Profile: Published by the Canadian Medical Association in partnership with the Centre for Research inWomen's Health
• CMA [Canadian Medical Association] Complete Book of Mother & Baby Care

Canadian Associations / Canadian Medical Foundation (CMF) / La Fondation médicale canadienne

Type: Book; *Number of Pages:* 264; *Editor:* Anne Biringer MD, CCFP,FCFP; *ISBN:* 978-1-55363-154-5; *Price:* $24 members
Profile: Care for a mother & her baby, from conception to age three
• Future Practice
Type: Magazine; *Frequency:* Irregular; *Editor:* Pat Rich
Profile: Information for physicians about health information technology in Canada
• History of the Canadian Medical Association, 1954-94
Type: Book; *Number of Pages:* 388; *Author:* John Sutton Bennett, MD; *ISBN:* 0-920169-83-X; *Price:* $19.95 members
Profile: A comprehensive account of important events that continue to affect medicine in Canada
• Honour Due: the Story of Dr. Leonora Howard King
Type: Book; *Number of Pages:* 236; *Author:* Margaret I. Negodaeff-Tomsik; *ISBN:* 0-920169-33-3; *Price:* $19.95 members
Profile: The story of the first Canadian to work as a physician in China
• Lessons Learned: Reflections of Canadian Physician Leaders
Type: Book; *Number of Pages:* 123; *Editor:* Chris Carruthers, MD; *ISBN:* 978-1-897490-09-9; *Price:* $16.95 members
• MD Lounge
Type: Magazine; *Editor:* Dr. Francine Lemire et al.
Profile: Information & advice to strengthen relations between general practitioners, family physicians, & other specialists, published by the Canadian Medical Association in partnership with The Royal College of Physicians & Surgeons of Canada & the College of Family Physicians of Canada
• PMI [Physician Management Institute] Newsletter: Leadership for Physicians
Type: Newsletter
Profile: Information about leadership theories & techniques

Canadian Medical Cannabis Industry Association See Cannabis Canada Association

Canadian Medical Foundation (CMF) / La Fondation médicale canadienne
#407, 1500 Bank St., Ottawa ON K1H 1B8
Tel: 613-518-6010
info@cmf.ca
www.medicalfoundation.ca
twitter.com/CdnMedicalFound
www.youtube.com/CdnMedicalFoundation
Overview: A large national charitable organization founded in 1987
Mission: To improve health outcomes in Canada by providing programs for vulnerables communities, offering assistance to physicians-in-training & other organizations, & engaging in philanthropic activity
Finances: *Annual Operating Budget:* $1.5 Million-$3 Million
Staff Member(s): 3
Activities: Medical Education Program; Medical Outreach Program; Physician Health & Well-being Program; annual golf tournament; *Library:* Not open to public
Chief Officer(s):
Lee Gould, President & CEO
lee.gould@cmf.ca
Publications:
• Best Practice [a publication of the Canadian Medical Foundation]
Type: Newsletter; *Frequency:* Quarterly

The Canadian Medical Protective Association / Association canadienne de protection médicale
PO Box 8225, Stn. T, Ottawa ON K1G 3H7
Tel: 613-725-2000; *Fax:* 613-725-1300
Toll-Free: 800-267-6522
inquiries@cmpa.org
www.cmpa-acpm.ca
www.linkedin.com/company/canadian-medical-protective-association
twitter.com/CMPAmembers
www.youtube.com/user/cmpamembers
Overview: A large national organization founded in 1901
Mission: To offer advice, assistance, & resources to members facing medical-legal issues; To provide compensation to patients proven to have been hurt by negligent care
Membership: *Fees:* Schedule available; *Committees:* Audit; Case Review; Executive; Extent of Assistance; Government; Human Resources & Compensation; Investment; Member & Stakeholder Relations; Nominating; Pension; Safe Medical Care
Activities: Providing professional development programs & resources
Chief Officer(s):
Hartley Stern, Executive Director & CEO
Meetings/Conferences:
• The Canadian Medical Protective Association 2018 Annual Meeting, August, 2018, Winnipeg, MB
Publications:
• CMPA [The Canadian Medical Protective Association] Perspective
Type: Magazine; *Frequency:* q.

Canadian MedicAlert Foundation / Fondation canadienne MedicAlert
Morneau Shepell Centre II, #600, 895 Don Mills Rd, Toronto ON M3C 1W3
Tel: 416-696-0267; *Fax:* 800-392-8422
Toll-Free: 800-668-1507
customerservice@medicalert.ca
www.medicalert.ca
www.facebook.com/medicalertcanada
twitter.com/medicalertCA
www.youtube.com/medicalertCA
Also Known As: MedicAlert
Overview: A large national charitable organization founded in 1961
Mission: To provide lifelong access to personal & medical information in order to protect & save the lives of its members; MedicAlert is a non-profit organization that provides all Canadians with medical protection in an emergency situation
Affiliation(s): MedicAlert Foundation International
Finances: *Funding Sources:* Membership fees; donations
Staff Member(s): 60
Membership: 1 million + individuals + 12 board; *Fees:* Schedule available
Activities: Membership includes a stainless steel bracelet or necklet engraved with medical information, member ID number & a 24-hour emergency hotline number available in 140 languages worldwide; members also receive a wallet card that lists medications & the names & phone numbers of physicians & emergency contacts; *Awareness Events:* MedicAlert Month, May; *Internships:* Yes; *Speaker Service:* Yes
Chief Officer(s):
Robert Ridge, MBA, President & CEO
Dorothy Griesbach, CPA, Director & CPO, Finance & Corporate Affairs

Canadian MedTech Manufacturers' Alliance (CMMA)
#900, 405 The West Mall, Toronto ON M9C 5J1
Tel: 416-620-1915; *Fax:* 416-620-1595
Toll-Free: 866-586-3332
www.medec.org
twitter.com/medec_canada
Merged from: Trillium Medical Technology Association & MEDEC
Overview: A medium-sized national organization founded in 2011
Mission: To encourage the development of medical technology & to help this technology grow in international markets
Membership: *Member Profile:* Medical technology companies
Chief Officer(s):
Brian Lewis, President & CEO
ceo@medec.org
Iris Crawford, Vice-President, Finance & Operations
Gerry Frenette, Executive Director, Public & Member Relations
Debbie Gates, Manager, Events & Education
Natasha Alves, Coordinator, Administration
Christina D'Costa, Coordinator, Business Development

Canadian Melanoma Foundation (CMF)
c/o Div. of Dermatology, Univ. of British Columbia, 835 - 10th Ave. West, Vancouver BC V5Z 4E8
Tel: 604-875-4747; *Fax:* 604-873-9919
www.derm.ubc.ca/division/cmf/cmf1.htm
Overview: A small national organization
Mission: A non-profit organization dedicated to improving cancer prevention and cure.

Canadian Memorial Chiropractic College (CMCC)
6100 Leslie St., Toronto ON M2H 3J1
Tel: 416-482-2340; *Fax:* 416-646-1114
Toll-Free: 800-463-2923
communications@cmcc.ca
www.cmcc.ca
Overview: A medium-sized national organization founded in 1945
Mission: To advance the art, science & philosophy of chiropractic; To educate chiropractors; To further the development of the chiropractic profession; To improve the health of society
Member of: Canadian Chiropractic Association
Finances: *Funding Sources:* Membership fees; Student tuition; Donations
Membership: 1,600; *Fees:* $715; *Member Profile:* Chiropractors across Canada & internationally
Activities: *Awareness Events:* Run/Walk for Chiropractic Education; *Speaker Service:* Yes; *Library:* CC Clemmer Health Sciences Library; by appointment
Chief Officer(s):
David Gryfe, Chair
Rahim Karim, Vice-Chair
Publications:
• CMCC [Canadian Memorial Chiropractic College] Annual Report
Type: Yearbook; *Frequency:* Annually
• CMCC [Canadian Memorial Chiropractic College] Academic Calendar
Frequency: Annually
Profile: Academic programs & course descriptions
• CMCC [Canadian Memorial Chiropractic College] Research Report
Frequency: Irregular
Profile: A summary of research activities undertaken at CMCC
• Primary Contact: A Magazine for Canadian Chiropractors
Type: Magazine; *Frequency:* 3 pa; *Editor:* Shannon Clark
Profile: Articles, continuing education, CMCC events, & members

Canadian Mental Health Association (CMHA) / Association canadienne pour la santé mentale (ACSM)
#1110, 151 Slater St., Ottawa ON K1P 5H3
Tel: 613-745-7750
info@cmha.ca
www.cmha.ca
www.facebook.com/CANMentalHealth
twitter.com/CMHA_NTL
www.youtube.com/user/cmhanational
Overview: A large national charitable organization founded in 1918
Mission: To promote mental health as well as support the resilience & recovery of people experiencing mental illness, through advocacy, education, research & service
Affiliation(s): Canadian Alliance on Mental Illness & Mental Health; Canadian Health Network
Finances: *Annual Operating Budget:* $3 Million-$5 Million; *Funding Sources:* Donations & bequests; corporate support; affiliated CMHA fees
Staff Member(s): 11; 10,0 volunteer(s)
Activities: *Awareness Events:* Mental Health Week, May; National Conference & AGM, TBC
Chief Officer(s):
Patrick Smith, National Chief Executive Officer
Cal Crocker, Chair
Sarika Gundu, National Director, Workplace Mental Health Program
Fardous Hosseiny, National Director, Policy
Awards:
• Strengthening CMHA Award
• C.M. Hincks Award
• Consumer Involvement Award
Meetings/Conferences:
• Canadian Mental Health Association 2018 National Conference, October, 2018, Montréal, QC
Scope: National
Publications:
• CMHA [Canadian Mental Health Association] Annual Report
Type: Report; *Frequency:* a.
Profile: Details of CMHA initiatives & achievements

   Alberta Division
   Capital Place, #320, 9707 - 110 St. NW, Edmonton AB T5K 2L9
   Tel: 780-482-6576; *Fax:* 780-482-6348
   alberta@cmha.ab.ca
   alberta.cmha.ca
   William (Bill) Bone, Chair

   British Columbia Division
   #1200, 1111 Melville St., Vancouver BC V6E 3V6
   Tel: 604-688-3234; *Fax:* 604-688-3236
   Toll-Free: 800-555-8222
   info@cmha.bc.ca
   www.cmha.bc.ca
   www.facebook.com/CMHABCDIVISION

twitter.com/cmhabc
www.youtube.com/cmhabc
Chief Officer(s):
Beverly Gutray, Chief Executive Officer
bev.gutray@cmha.bc.ca
Division du Québec
#326, 911, rue Jean-Talon est, Montréal QC H2R 1V5
Tél: 514-849-3291; *Téléc:* 514-849-8372
info@acsm.qc.ca
www.acsm.qc.ca
www.facebook.com/189002251132456
twitter.com/ACSMDivisionQc
www.youtube.com/user/ACSMQC
Chief Officer(s):
Renée Ouimet, Directrice
reneeouimet@acsm.qc.ca
Manitoba Division
930 Portage Ave., Winnipeg MB R3G 0P8
Tel: 204-982-6100; *Fax:* 204-982-6128
office@cmhawpg.mb.ca
winnipeg.cmha.ca
www.facebook.com/cmha.manitoba
twitter.com/MbDivisionCMHA
www.youtube.com/user/CMHAWpg
Chief Officer(s):
Stephanie Skakun, Acting Executive Director
New Brunswick Division
#202, 403 Regent St., Fredericton NB E3B 3X6
Tel: 506-455-5231; *Fax:* 506-459-3878
cmhanb.ca
www.facebook.com/CMHANB
Chief Officer(s):
Christa Baldwin, Executive Director
christa.baldwin@cmhanb.ca
Newfoundland & Labrador Division
70 The Boulevard, 1st Fl., St. John's NL A1A 1K2
Tel: 709-753-8550; *Fax:* 709-753-8537
Toll-Free: 877-753-8550
office@cmhanl.ca
www.cmhanl.ca
www.facebook.com/247087668665555
twitter.com/CMHANL
www.youtube.com/user/cmhanational
Chief Officer(s):
George Skinner, Executive Director
Nova Scotia Division
63 King St., Dartmouth NS B2Y 2R7
Tel: 902-466-6600; *Fax:* 902-466-3300
Toll-Free: 877-466-6606
cmhans@bellaliant.com
novascotia.cmha.ca
www.facebook.com/cmhansdivision
twitter.com/cmhansdivision
pinterest.com/cmhanovascotia
Chief Officer(s):
Gail Gardiner, Executive Director
Ontario Division
#2301, 180 Dundas St. West, Toronto ON M5G 1Z8
Tel: 416-977-5580; *Fax:* 416-977-2813
Toll-Free: 800-875-6213
info@ontario.cmha.ca
ontario.cmha.ca
www.facebook.com/cmha.ontario
twitter.com/CMHAOntario
www.youtube.com/cmhaontario
Chief Officer(s):
Camille Quenneville, CEO
cquenneville@ontario.cmha.ca
Prince Edward Island Division
PO Box 785, 178 Fitzroy St., Charlottetown PE C1A 7L9
Tel: 902-566-3034; *Fax:* 902-566-4643
division@cmha.pe.ca
pei.cmha.ca
www.facebook.com/CMHAPEIDivision
Chief Officer(s):
Reid Burke, Executive Director
Saskatchewan Division
2702 - 12th Ave., Regina SK S4T 1J2
Tel: 306-525-5601; *Fax:* 306-569-3788
Toll-Free: 800-461-5483
contactus@cmhask.com
www.cmhask.com
www.facebook.com/255440253328
Chief Officer(s):

Dave Nelson, Executive Director
daven@cmhask.com
Yukon Division
6 Bates Cres., Whitehorse YT Y1A 4T8
Tel: 867-668-7144
cmha.ca@gmail.com
twitter.com/CMHAYukon
Chief Officer(s):
Dudley Morgan, Executive Director

Canadian Merchant Navy Veterans Association Inc. (CMNVA) / L'Association des Anciens Combattants de la marine marchande canadienne Inc.
2108 Melrick Pl., Sooke BC V9Z 0M9
Tel: 250-642-2638; *Fax:* 250-642-3332
Overview: A medium-sized national organization founded in 1990
Mission: To renew old friendships & bring together ex-Canadian merchant seamen; to promote increased recognition of the role of the merchant navy during wartime; to liaise with government to obtain full benefits & pension as recognized veterans
Finances: *Funding Sources:* Membership dues; donations
Membership: *Member Profile:* Canadian citizen who sailed on Canadian or allied deep-sea ships during WWI or II or Korean conflict; former allied merchant seamen who sailed during WWII or Korean conflict; family members of veterans; associate - peacetime Canadian seafarers
Activities: Quarterly meetings within branches; *Speaker Service:* Yes
Chief Officer(s):
Bruce Ferguson, President

Canadian Merchant Service Guild (CMSG) / Guilde de la marine marchande du Canada (GMMC)
#234, 9 Antares Dr., Ottawa ON K2E 7V5
Tel: 613-727-6079; *Fax:* 613-727-6079
cmsgott@on.aibn.com
www.cmsg-gmmc.ca
Overview: A medium-sized national licensing organization founded in 1919
Mission: To promote the social, economic, cultural, educational & material interests of ships' masters, chief engineers, officers, pilots & of other persons whose employment is directly related to maritime operations
Affiliation(s): International Transport Workers' Federation (ITF)
Chief Officer(s):
Mark Boucher, National President
Publications:
• Canadian Merchant Service Guild Bulletin
Type: Newsletter; *Frequency:* Irregular
Profile: Information for CMSG members
• Canadian Merchant Service Guild News
Type: Magazine; *Frequency:* Irregular; *Editor:* Mark Boucher
Profile: CMSG activities & branch news
Eastern Branch
c/o Quebec Office, #108, 3107, av Hôtels, Québec QC G1W 4W5
Tel: 418-650-6471; *Fax:* 418-650-1484
cmsg-gmmc.qc@bellnet.ca
www.cmsg-gmmc.ca
Mission: To act as a voice for the interests of Canadian Ships' Officers and has been instrumental in successfully lobbying for improvement to a host of regulations directly related to the safety of life at sea and the well-being of all seafarers.
Chief Officer(s):
Edward Day, President
Western Branch
#310, 218 Blue Mountain St., Coquitlam BC V3K 4H2
Tel: 602-939-8990; *Fax:* 602-939-8950
cmsgwb@cmsg.org
www.cmsg-gmmc.ca
Mission: To act as a voice for the interests of Canadian Ships' Officers and has been instrumental in successfully lobbying for improvement to a host ofregulations directly related to the safety of life at sea and the well-being of ll seafarers.
Chief Officer(s):
Mike Armstrong, President

Canadian Meteorological & Oceanographic Society (CMOS) / Société canadienne de météorologie et d'océanographie (SCMO)
PO Box 3211, Stn. D, Ottawa ON K1P 6H7
Tel: 613-990-0300
cmos@cmos.ca

www.cmos.ca
www.linkedin.com/groups/Canadian-Meteocean-Group-6515104/about
twitter.com/cmos_scmo
Previous Name: Canadian Meteorological Society
Overview: A large national charitable organization founded in 1967
Mission: To advance meteorology & oceanography in Canada
Member of: Canadian Consortium for Research; Partnership Group for Science & Engineering
Finances: *Annual Operating Budget:* $500,000-$1.5 Million; *Funding Sources:* Membership fees; Donations; Congress resignation fees
Staff Member(s): 9; 3 volunteer(s)
Membership: 800; *Fees:* $80 regular; $53 retired; $53 associate; $20 student; $226 sustaining; $160 corporate; *Member Profile:* Meteorologists & oceanographers; Persons interested in meteorology & oceanography; Corporations & institutions; Government organizations; Students; *Committees:* Accreditation; Students; External Relations; Fellows; Awards: Scholarships; Scientific; Audit; Nominating
Activities: Participating in School Science Fairs; Accrediting consultants in meteorology & oceanography; Providing advice & suggestions to government & its departments on meteorological & oceanographic issues; Publications; Scholarships; Prizes & Awards; Public lectures; *Speaker Service:* Yes
Chief Officer(s):
Gordon Griffith, Executive Director, 613-990-0300, Fax: 613-993-3174
exec-dir@cmos.ca
Doug G. Steyn, Director, Publications, 604-827-5517, Fax: 613-993-3174
publications@cmos.ca
Bourque Sheila, Director, Education & Outreach
education@cmos.ca
Qing Liao, Office Manager, 613-991-4494, Fax: 613-993-3174
accounts@cmos.ca
Awards:
• Postgraduate Scholarship
• Undergraduate Scholarship
• Tertia M.C. Hughes Memorial Prize
• The J.P. Tully Medal in Oceanography
May be awarded each year to a person whose scientific contributions have had a significant impact on Canadian oceanography
• The President's Prize
May be awarded each year to a member or members of the Society for a recent paper or book of special merit in the fields of meteorology or oceanography. *Eligibility:* Paper must have been published in Atmosphere-Ocean, The CMOS bulletin, SCMO or another referred journal
• François J. Saucier Prize in Applied Oceanography
May be awarded each year to a member or members of the Society for an outstanding contribution to the application of oceanography in Canada
• The Rube Hornstein Medal in Operational Meteorology
May be awarded each year to an individual for outstanding operational meteorological service. The work for which the prize is granted may be cumulative over a period of years or may be a single notable achievement
• Dr. Andrew Thomson Prize in Applied Meteorology
May be awarded each year to a member or members of the Society for an outstanding contribution to the application of meteorology in Canada
• Neil J. Campbell Award for Exceptional Volunteer Service
The award may be made for an exceptional contribution in a single year or for contributions over an extended period.
Meetings/Conferences:
• 52nd Canadian Meteorological & Oceanographic Society Congress, June, 2018, Halifax Convention Centre, Halifax, NS
Scope: National
Description: Theme: "Marine & Environmental Risks & Impacts"
Publications:
• Atmosphere-Ocean
Type: Journal; *Frequency:* Quarterly; *ISSN:* 0705-5900; *Price:* $50 individual; $125 institution
Profile: Scientific journal with original research, survey articles, & comments on published papers in the fields of atmospheric, oceanographic, & hydrological sciences
• Canadian Meteorological & Oceanographic Society Annual Review
Frequency: Annually; *Price:* Free with Canadian Meteorological & OceanographicSociety membership
Profile: Summaries of the Canadian Meteorological &

Canadian Associations / Canadian Meter Study Group

Oceanographic Society yearly activities & the audited financial statement
• Canadian Meteorological & Oceanographic Society Annual Congress Program & Abstracts
Type: Yearbook; *Frequency:* Annually; *Price:* Free withCMOS membership; $50 non-members & institutions
Profile: Guide to the Canadian Meteorological & Oceanographic Society Annual Congress sessions & abstracts of papers to be presented
• CMOS [Canadian Meteorological & Oceanographic Society] Bulletin SCMO [Société canadienne de météorologie et d'océanographie]
Frequency: Bimonthly; *Accepts Advertising; Editor:* Paul-André Bolduc; *Price:* Free with CMOS / SCMO membership; $80 non-members & institutions
Profile: Technical articles, conferences, & events related to meteorology, oceanography, climatology, & meteorological & oceanographic history
• The Edmonton Tornado & Hailstorm: A Decade of Research
Author: R. Charlton, B. Kachman, L. Wojtiw; *Price:* $10
• Numerical Methods in Atmospheric & Oceanic Modelling: The André J. Robert Memorial Volume
Number of Pages: 634; *Editor:* C. Lin, R. Laprise, & H. Ritchie; *ISBN:* 0-9698414-4-2; *Price:* $39.95
Profile: Refereed papers by scientists on the art & science of numerical modelling, for students & researchers

Alberta Centre
Edmonton AB
Tel: 780-492-6706; *Fax:* 780-492-2030
Chief Officer(s):
Paul Myers, Vice Chair
pmyers@ualberta.ca
British Columbia Interior (Kelowna)
Prince George BC
Tel: 250-960-5785
Chief Officer(s):
Peter Jackson, Chair
peterj@unbc.ca
British Columbia Lower Mainland Centre
Vancouver BC
Tel: 604-822-2821
Chief Officer(s):
William Hsieh, Chair
whsieh@eos.ubc.ca
Centre de Québec
Québec QC
Tél: 418-654-3764; *Téléc:* 418-654-2600
yves_gratton@ete.inrs.ca
Chief Officer(s):
Yves Gratton, Chair
Centre de Rimouski
Rimouski QC
Chief Officer(s):
Yvonnick Le Clainche, Président
Halifax Centre
Dartmouth NS
Tel: 902-426-9963
Chief Officer(s):
Blair Greenan, Chair
Blair.Greenan@dfo-mpo.gc.ca
Montréal Centre
Montréal QC
Tel: 514-384-9990; *Fax:* 514-384-1598
Chief Officer(s):
Rabah Hammouche, Secretary-Treasurer
rabah@enviromet.qc.ca
New Brunswick Chapter
Fredericton NB
Tel: 506-477-3257; *Fax:* 506-453-4581
Chief Officer(s):
William Ward, President
Newfoundland Centre
St. John's NL
Tel: 709-772-8963; *Fax:* 709-772-4105
Chief Officer(s):
Fraser Davidson, Chair
Fraser.Davidson@dfo-mpo.gc.ca
Len Zedel, Secretary, 709-737-3106
zedel@mun.ca
Ottawa Centre
Ottawa ON
Tel: 613-831-5851
Chief Officer(s):

Ann McMillan, Chair
mcmillan@storm.ca
Saskatchewan Centre
Saskatoon SK
Tel: 306-933-8122
Chief Officer(s):
Virginia Wittrock, Chair
wittrock@src.sk.ca
Toronto Centre
Toronto ON
Tel: 416-736-2100; *Fax:* 416-739-5817
Chief Officer(s):
Tom McElroy, Chair
TMcElroy@yorku.ca
Oscar Koren, Secretary, 905-669-2365
okoren@sympatico.ca
Vancouver Island Centre
Victoria BC
Tel: 250-363-8233
Chief Officer(s):
Gregory Flato, Chair
greg.flato@ec.gc.ca
Winnipeg Centre
Winnipeg MB
Tel: 204-983-4513; *Fax:* 204-983-0109
Chief Officer(s):
Jim Slipec, Chair
jim.slipec@ec.gc.ca

Canadian Meteorological Society *See* Canadian Meteorological & Oceanographic Society

Canadian Meter Study Group
#903, 24 Marilyn Dr., Guelph ON N1H 8E9
www.postalhistorycanada.net/php/StudyGroups/Meter/
Overview: A small national organization
Mission: To study the history of Canadian metered mail in Canada
Affiliation(s): Postal History Society of Canada
Membership: *Member Profile:* Individuals interested in the history of Canadian postage meters
Chief Officer(s):
Ross W. Irwin, Contact
Publications:
• Canada Meter Study Group Newsletter
Type: Newsletter

Canadian Micrographic Society; Canadian Information & Image Management Society *See* Association for Image & Information Management International - 1st Canadian Chapter

Canadian Micro-Mineral Association
660 Heathcliffe Place, Waterloo ON N2T 2P3
canadianmicrominerals.ca
Overview: A small national organization founded in 1964
Mission: To promote education & interest in mineralogy & to encourage fellowship & goodwill among its members
Member of: Gem & Mineral Federation of Canada
Membership: 1-99; *Fees:* $15
Activities: Micro Symposium; Micro Workshop
Chief Officer(s):
Frank Ruehlicke, President, 519-880-2716
ruehlicke@rogers.com

Canadian Midwifery Regulators Consortium (CMRC) / Consortium canadien des ordres des sages-femmes (CCOSF)
c/o College Of Midwives of Manitoba, #235, 500 Portage Ave., Winnipeg MB R3C 3X1
Tel: 204-783-4520; *Fax:* 204-779-1490
www.cmrc-ccosf.ca
Overview: A small national organization founded in 2000
Mission: To facilitate inter-provincial mobility, to advocate for legislation, regulation, and standards of practice that support access to a high standard of midwifery care across the country, and to provide a forum for Canadian regulators to discuss and take action on issues of mutual concern.
Affiliation(s): College of Midwives of British Columbia; Alberta Midwifery Health Disciplines Committee; College of Midwives Manitoba; College of Midwives of Ontario; Ordres des sages-femmes du Québec; Northwest Territories Health Professional Licensing (Midwifery)
Chief Officer(s):
Kris Robinson, Chairperson

Canadian Militaria Preservation Society (CMPS)
c/o MilArm Co. Ltd., 10769 - 99 St., 2nd Fl., Edmonton AB T5H 4H6
Tel: 780-424-5281; *Fax:* 800-894-7598
milarm@telus.net
www.milarm.com
www.facebook.com/milarmguns
www.youtube.com/user/TheMILARMchannel
Overview: A small local organization founded in 2000
Mission: To collect military items with an emphasis on Canadian militari
Affiliation(s): Royal Alberta Museum; Heritage Community Foundation
Activities: Producing a website & virtual museum on Alberta's homefront during World War II; Operating a museum containing Canadian militaria from 1812 to the present
Chief Officer(s):
Allan Kerr, Curator
R. Gordon McGowan, President

Canadian Military Colleges Faculty Association (CMCFA) / Association des professeurs(es) des collèges militaires du Canada (APCMC)
PO Box 577, Stn. 120 Clarence St., Kingston ON K7L 4W5
Tel: 613-541-6000; *Fax:* 613-544-5966
Other Communication: Alt. Phone: 613-544-6879
cmcfa-apcmc.ca
Overview: A small national organization
Mission: To represent academic faculty at the Royal Military College of Canada, Royal Military College St. Jean, & the Canadian Forces College
Affiliation(s): Canadian Association of University Teachers (CAUT); Ontario Confederation of University Faculty Associations (OCUFA); National Joint Council (NJC)
Membership: *Committees:* Grievance; Compensation & Benefits
Chief Officer(s):
Jean-Marc Noel, President
president@cmcfa-apcmc.ca

Canadian Milking Shorthorn Society (CMSS)
203 Ferry Rd., Cornwall PE C0A 1H4
Tel: 902-439-9386; *Fax:* 902-436-0551
milking.shorthorn@gmail.com
www.cmss.on.ca
www.facebook.com/milkingshorthorn
Overview: A small national organization founded in 1920
Mission: To promote & encourage the development of milking shorthorn cattle.
Member of: Canadian Shorthorn Association
Membership: *Fees:* $25 junior; $85 individual; $40 new member; *Member Profile:* Breeders; *Committees:* Show; Genetic Improvement; Promotion/Youth
Activities: American Milking Shorthorn Society Convention; National Milking Shorthorn Show.
Chief Officer(s):
Ryan Barrett, Secretary-Manager
Dave Prinzen, President, 613-393-5087
daprinzen@sympatico.ca

Canadian Mineral Analysts (CMA) / Analystes des minéraux canadiens
c/o John Gregorchuk, 444 Harold Ave. West, Winnipeg MB R2C 2E2
Tel: 204-224-1443
www.canadianmineralanalysts.com
Overview: A small national organization founded in 1969
Mission: To promote communication among analysts in the mining industry & persons engaged in analytical procedures & the development of methods
Membership: *Fees:* $25 students & retired individuals; $40 new & renewing members; $1000 corporate members; *Member Profile:* Analysts employed in the mineral industry; Technical personnel connected with the provision of analyses
Activities: Providing educational opportunities; Assisting in the development of methods for element analysis; Compiling methods manuals for members; Liaising with laboratories of the Canadian mining industry; Supporting the Certified Assayers Foundation of British Columbia
Chief Officer(s):
John Gregorchuk, Managing Secretary, 204-224-1443
jgregorchuk@mts.net
Sean Murry, Treasurer, 604-270-2252
smurry@vwr.com
Awards:
• Canadian Mineral Analysts Scholarships

Awarded for courses in mineral sciences & chemical technology at Canadian colleges *Eligibility:* Students currently enrolled in a chemical engineering technician or analytical chemistry program at a recognized Canadian post-secondary institution; *Amount:* up to $1,000
Meetings/Conferences:
• Canadian Mineral Analysts Annual Conference & Exhibition 2018, September, 2018, Prestige Mountain Resort & Conference Centre, Rossland, BC
Scope: National
Contact Information: www.2018cma.com
Publications:
• Proceedings of the Canadian Mineral Analysts / Analystes des minéraux canadiens Annual Meeting
Type: Yearbook; *Frequency:* Annually; *Price:* Free with CMA / SMA membership
• QC / QA Manual [a publication of the Canadian Mineral Analysts]
Type: Manual; *Price:* $30

Canadian Mineral Processors Society (CMP)
555 Booth St., Ottawa ON K1A 0G1
www.cmpsoc.ca
twitter.com/cmpsoc1
Overview: A medium-sized national organization overseen by Canadian Institute of Mining, Metallurgy & Petroleum
Mission: To provide an open forum for Mineral Processing Operators across the world to network & communicate; To encourage participation throughout its membership
Chief Officer(s):
Janice Zinck, Secretary, 613-995-4221
janice.zinck@canada.ca
Awards:
• Mineral Processor of the Year
• A.R. MacPherson Comminution Award
• Bill Moore Special Achievement Award
• Lifetime Achievement Award
• Ray MacDonald Volunteer Award
• CMP Conference Best Presentation Award
Meetings/Conferences:
• Canadian Mineral Processors 50th Annual Conference 2018, January, 2018, Westin Hotel, Ottawa, ON
Scope: National
Description: Theme: "Past, Present & Future: Celebrating 50 Years of Innovation"

Canadian Mining Industry Research Organization (CAMIRO)
1545 Maley Dr., Sudbury ON P3A 4R7
Tel: 705-673-6595; *Fax:* 705-673-6588
info@camiro.org
www.camiro.org
Overview: A small national organization
Mission: To manage collaborative mining research in the divisions of exploration, mining, & metallurgical processing; To contribute to the safety, growth, & competitiveness of the Canadian mineral industry
Membership: *Member Profile:* Corporations & organizations who wish to further the objects of the association
Activities: Initiating applied research
Chief Officer(s):
Peter Golde, Managing Director

Canadian Modern Pentathlon Association *See* Pentathlon Canada

Canadian Morgan Horse Association (CMHA) / Association des chevaux Morgan canadien inc.
PO Box 286, Port Perry ON L9L 1A3
Tel: 905-982-0060; *Fax:* 905-982-0097
info@morganhorse.ca
www.morganhorse.ca
Overview: A medium-sized national licensing organization founded in 1968
Member of: Equine Canada
Affiliation(s): British Columbia Interior Morgan Horse Club; New Brunswick Morgan Horse Club; Nova Scotia Morgan Horse Club; Ontario Morgan Horse Club; Saskatchewan Morgan Horse Club
Membership: *Fees:* Schedule available; *Committees:* Awards; Equine Canada; Historical; Membership; Part Morgan; Promotion; Youth
Chief Officer(s):
Melissa MacKenzie, President, 506-832-5515
morgans@nb.sympatico.ca
Tina Collins, Eastern Vice-President, 905-715-4042
tina.collins@equiman.com

Charlene Dalen-Brown, Western Vice-President, 306-500-5998
cdalenbrown@gmail.com
Awards:
• Versatile Morgan Medallion Award
• Morgan Trail Awards
• Lifetime Mileage Awards
Meetings/Conferences:
• Canadian Morgan Horse Association 2018 AGM, March, 2018, Marriott Airport, Toronto, ON
Scope: National
Publications:
• The Canadian Morgan Magazine [a publication of the Canadian Morgan Horse Association]
Type: Magazine; *Accepts Advertising*; *Editor:* Sheri Wilson; *Price:* Free with CMHA membership; $25 Canada; $35 international
• Registry Books [publications of the Canadian Morgan Horse Association]
Profile: Volumes of Canadian registered Morgan Horses, for Morgan breeders & owners

Canadian Mortgage Brokers Association
#101, 1765 West 8th Ave., Vancouver BC V6J 5C6
Tel: 604-408-9989; *Fax:* 604-608-0977
Toll-Free: 877-371-2916
www.cmba-achc.ca
Overview: A medium-sized national organization
Mission: To enhance & support provincial mortgage broker associations; To ensure that standards of professionalism & ethics are met by members
Membership: 3
Activities: Representing members to government
Chief Officer(s):
Tannis Brissett, Executive Director

Canadian Motion Picture Distributors Association *See* Motion Picture Association - Canada

Canadian Motorcycle Association (CMA) / Association motocycliste canadienne
605 James St. North, 4th Fl., Hamilton ON L8L 1J9
Tel: 905-522-5705; *Fax:* 905-522-5716
registration@canmocycle.ca
www.canmocycle.ca
www.facebook.com/motorcyclingcanada
Overview: A medium-sized national licensing organization founded in 1946
Mission: To encourage & develop motorcycling for the benefit & enjoyment of its members
Affiliation(s): Fédération internationale motocycliste; Canadian Olympic Association; FIM North America Union
Finances: *Annual Operating Budget:* $500,000-$1.5 Million; *Funding Sources:* Membership fees; event fees
Staff Member(s): 4; 150 volunteer(s)
Membership: 100 club + 150 lifetime + 9,000 individual; *Fees:* $30; $15 family (per individual); *Member Profile:* Interest in motorcycling; *Committees:* Strategic Planning; Technical; Environmental; Awards; Nominations; Trials Advisory; Development of Alternative Energy Competition
Chief Officer(s):
Joseph Godsall, President
Marilyn Bastedo, Chief Executive Officer
mbastedo.cma@bellnet.ca

Canadian Mountain Arts Foundation (CMAF)
PO Box 8521, Canmore AB T1W 2V3
Tel: 403-609-2623
info@artsplacecanmore.com
artsplacecanmore.com
www.facebook.com/CMAFab
twitter.com/artscanmore
Overview: A small local charitable organization founded in 1996
Mission: CMAF is a volunteer-run charity with a mandate to increase and broaden the opportunities for the residents of the Bow Valley to enjoy and participate in the arts.
Staff Member(s): 4
Chief Officer(s):
Lynne MacLeod, President

Canadian Murray Grey Association (CMGA)
PO Box 157, Bragg Creek AB T0L OKO
Tel: 403-949-2199
cmgareg@telus.net
www.cdnmurraygrey.ca
Overview: A medium-sized national organization founded in 1970

Mission: To promote the genetics of Murray Grey Beef Cattle
Member of: Canadian Beef Breeds Council
Membership: *Fees:* $75 annual; $5 junior; $35 associate; $1000 lifetime; *Committees:* Financial; Promotion & Events; CBBC; Constitution; Herd Book; Nominating; Pedigree & Registration

Canadian Museums Association (CMA) / Association des musées canadiens
#400, 280 Metcalfe St., Ottawa ON K2P 1R7
Tel: 613-567-0099; *Fax:* 613-233-5438
Toll-Free: 888-822-2907
info@museums.ca
www.museums.ca
www.facebook.com/musecdn
twitter.com/musecdn
www.youtube.com/museumsdotca
Overview: A large national organization founded in 1947
Mission: To advance a strong, vital & valued Canadian museum sector
Affiliation(s): Alliance of Natural History Museums (ANHMC); Canadian Federation of Friends of Museum (CFFM); Council of Museums Canada; Canadian Association of Zoos & Aquariums; Canadian Association of Science Centres; Canadian Art Museums Directors' Association (CAMDO); ICOM Canada; Organization of Military Museums of Canada (OMMC); Department of Canadian Heritage
Finances: *Annual Operating Budget:* Greater than $5 Million; *Funding Sources:* Membership fees; Donations; Government grants
Membership: 2,000; *Fees:* $85 voting individual; $100 - $2,750 institution, based on operating budget; $50 senior & student; $100 affiliate & foreign; $250 corporate; *Member Profile:* Members include museum professionals in Canada & abroad, non-profit museums, art galleries, science centres, aquaria, archives, sport halls of fame, artist-run centres, zoos & historic sites throughout Canada
Activities: Providing professional development & networking opportunities for members; Collaborating with other national & international organizations; Creating & delivering projects & programs; *Awareness Events:* Canadian Museums Day, November 23; *Internships:* Yes
Chief Officer(s):
John G. McAvity, Executive Director & CEO, 613-567-0099 Ext. 226
jmcavity@museums.ca
Karen Bachmann, President
Jane Fullertown, VicePresident
Awards:
• The Awards of Outstanding Achievement
Deadline: November 15
• The Award of Distinguished Service
Deadline: November 15
• The Fellows of the CMA
Deadline: November 15
• The Barbara Tyler Award in Museum Leadership
Deadline: November 15
• ICOM Canada's International Achievement Award
Deadline: November 15
• The History Alive! Award of Excellence for History in Museums Presented by the Canadian Museums Association (CMA) in partnership with Canada's History Society *Deadline:* July
• The Museums & Schools Partnership Award
Presented by the Canadian Museums Association (CMA) & the Canadian Teachers' Federation *Deadline:* November 15
• The Museum Volunteer Award
Presented by the Canadian Museums Association (CMA) & the Canadian Federation of Friends of Museums (CFFM) *Deadline:* November 15
Meetings/Conferences:
• Canadian Museums Association 2018 Museum Enterprises Conference, January, 2018, Toronto, ON
Scope: National
Description: Keynote sessions, educational presentations, workshops, & networking opportunities for museum professionals involved in operations, admissions, retail, & food services
• Canadian Museums Association 71st National Conference 2018, April, 2018, Sheraton Vancouver Wall Centre, Vancouver, BC
Scope: National
Description: A conference & tradeshow for Canadian museum professionals, such as directors, administrators, & curators
Publications:
• Muse [a publication of the Canadian Museums Association]
Type: Magazine; *Frequency:* Bimonthly; *Accepts Advertising*;

Canadian Associations / Canadian Music Centre (CMC) / Centre de musique canadienne

Price: Free for members; $35 non-members in Canada; $46 U.S.A.; $55 international
Profile: Current issues, solutions to challenges, current projects, industry best practices, book reviews, Canadian & international news, & opinion pieces

Canadian Mushroom Growers' Association *See* Mushrooms Canada

Canadian Music Centre (CMC) / Centre de musique canadienne
20 St. Joseph St., Toronto ON M4Y 1J9
Tel: 416-961-6601
info@musiccentre.ca
www.musiccentre.ca
www.linkedin.com/company/the-canadian-music-centre
www.facebook.com/CanadianMusic
twitter.com/cmcnational
www.youtube.com/user/CanadianMusicCentre
Overview: A medium-sized national charitable organization founded in 1959
Mission: To stimulate the awareness, appreciation & performance of Canadian music
Member of: Canadian Conference of the Arts
Finances: *Annual Operating Budget:* $500,000-$1.5 Million; *Funding Sources:* 3 levels of government; Universities & arts bodies; Donations
Staff Member(s): 35; 5 volunteer(s)
Membership: 630 associate + 415 individual; *Fees:* Schedule available; *Member Profile:* Associate - composers selected by an adjudication committee; voting - individuals supporting or interested in work of the Centre
Activities: Offering a selection of music libraries; Providing repertoire consultation; Offering publishing, print & bind services; Renting out rehearsal & performance spaces; *Library:* Ettore Mazzolini Library; Open to public
Chief Officer(s):
Glenn Hodgins, Executive Director
ghodgins@musiccentre.ca
Ana-Maria Lipoczi, Manager, Music Services
alipoczi@musiccentre.ca
Awards:
• Harry Freedman Award
Awarded on alternating years beginning in 2010; Offers a composer the resources to refine a piece of work to generate a more definitive product *Eligibility:* An Associate Composer working in collaboration with one to six musicians, or a Canadian composer/performer; the piece submitted for nomination must have received no prior commercial recording *Deadline:* January; *Amount:* $1,500
• Toronto Emerging Composer Award
Awarded annually to support the creation of a new musical work or the completion of an existing music-based project *Eligibility:* Emerging composers living in the Greater Toronto Area; *Amount:* $6,000

British Columbia Region
837 Davie St., Vancouver BC V6Z 1B7
Tel: 604-734-4622; *Fax:* 604-734-4627
Toll-Free: 844-416-8742
bcregion@musiccentre.ca
Chief Officer(s):
Sean Bickerton, Regional Director
sean@musiccentre.ca

Ontario Region
20 St. Joseph St., Toronto ON M4Y 1J9
Tel: 416-961-6601; *Fax:* 416-961-7198
ontario@musiccentre.ca
Chief Officer(s):
Matthew Fava, Regional Director
mfava@musiccentre.ca

Prairie Region
University of Calgary, #320, 2500 University Dr. NW, 3rd Fl., Calgary AB T2N 1N4
Tel: 403-220-7403; *Fax:* 403-289-4877
prairie@musiccentre.ca
Mission: To provide an extensive collection of books, scores, music periodicals, & CDs; To make works of & information about Canadian composers easily accessible; To showcase Canadian music & composers
Member of: Canadian Music Centre
Chief Officer(s):
John Reid, Regional Director

Région du Québec (CMC)
#200, 1085, Côte du Beaver Hall, Montréal QC H2Z 1S5

Tél: 514-866-3477; *Téléc:* 514-866-0456
quebec@centremusique.ca
www.centremusique.ca
Chief Officer(s):
Claire Marchand, Regional Director
cmarchand@musiccentre.ca

Canadian Music Competitions Inc. *Voir* Concours de musique du Canada inc.

Canadian Music Educators' Association (CMEA) / Association canadienne des éducateurs de musique
info@cmea.ca
www.cmea.ca
www.facebook.com/CanadianMEA
twitter.com/CanadianMEA
Overview: A medium-sized national organization founded in 1959
Mission: To nurture a vital music learning community throughout Canada
Member of: International Society for Music Education
Affiliation(s): International Society for Music Education
Finances: *Annual Operating Budget:* $50,000-$100,000; *Funding Sources:* Membership fees
22 volunteer(s)
Membership: 2,200; *Fees:* $12-$50 non-affiliated; $50 affiliated; *Committees:* Research Council; Awards/Honorary Membership; Retired Teachers; Student Chapters; Strategic Planning; Teacher Education; Evaluation; Advocacy
Activities: *Internships:* Yes; *Speaker Service:* Yes; *Library*
Chief Officer(s):
Kirsten MacLaine, President
Publications:
• Canadian Music Educator [a publication of the Canadian Music Educators' Association]
Type: Newsletter

Canadian Music Festival Adjudicators' Association (CMFAA)
c/o Humbercrest United Church, 16 Baby Point Rd., Toronto ON M6S 2E9
Tel: 416-239-8530
www.cmfaa.ca
Overview: A small national organization founded in 1960
Finances: *Funding Sources:* Membership fees
Membership: 250; *Fees:* $40; *Member Profile:* Three successful festival adjudications
Activities: *Rents Mailing List:* Yes
Chief Officer(s):
Melvin Hurst, President
melvinhurst@gmail.com

Canadian Music Library Association *See* Canadian Association of Music Libraries, Archives & Documentation Centres

Canadian Music Week Inc. (CMW)
5355 Vail Ct., Mississauga ON L5M 6G9
Tel: 905-858-4747; *Fax:* 905-858-4848
cmw.net
www.facebook.com/canadianmusicweek
twitter.com/CMW_Week
Overview: A medium-sized national organization
Mission: To organize the annual Canadian Music Week festival, convention & trade show
Chief Officer(s):
Neill Dixon, President
neill@cmw.net
Verle Mobbs, General Manager
verle@cmw.net
Cameron Wright, Director, Festival
concerts@cmw.net

Canadian Musical Reproduction Rights Agency (CMRRA) / Agence canadienne des droits de production musicaux limitée
#320, 56 Wellesley St. West, Toronto ON M5S 2S3
Tel: 416-926-1966; *Fax:* 416-926-7521
inquiries@cmrra.ca
www.cmrra.ca
Overview: A small national organization founded in 1976
Mission: Represents the majority of music publishers & copyright owners doing business in Canada; on their behalf, issues licences & collects royalties for the reproduction of copyrighted musical works on CDs, cassettes & other sound carriers, & in films, TV programs & advertising; owned by the Canadian Music Publishers Association

Staff Member(s): 50
Membership: *Member Profile:* Music publishers
Activities: *Speaker Service:* Yes
Chief Officer(s):
David A. Basskin, President
Fred Merritt, Vice-President, Finance & Administration

Canadian Mutual Fund Association *See* Investment Funds Institute of Canada

Canadian National Accelerated Christian Education Association *See* Accelerated Christian Education Canada

Canadian National Association of Real Estate Appraisers (CNAREA)
PO Box 157, Qualicum Beach BC V9K 1S7
Fax: 866-836-6369
Toll-Free: 888-399-3366
hq@cnarea.ca
www.cnarea.ca
Overview: A small national organization founded in 1992
Mission: To certify & regulate real property appraisers in Canada; To raise the standards of the real property appraising profession; To protect consumers
Member of: The Canadian Employee Relocation Council (CERC); Canadian Association of Acredited Mortgage Proffessionals (CAAMP)
Affiliation(s): Appraisal Foundation (Washington DC, USA); Appraisal Foundation Advisory Council (TAFAC); National Association of Independent Fee Appraisers (NAIFA)
Membership: *Member Profile:* Canadian professional real property appraisers, such as those with the following designations: DAR (Designated Appraiser Residential), DAC (Designated Appraiser Commercial), DAC (Designated Appraiser Commercial with a Specialty in Agricultural), DRP (Designated Reserve Planner), Certified Appraisal Reviewer & CMAR (Certified Mortgage Appraisal Reviewer); Associate members are those who have an an interest in the appraisal profession or who work with professional appraisers; Candidates are persons who want to further their education & experience to earn a designation
Activities: Offering continuing education opportunities; Maintaining the professionalism of members; Ensuring that members abide by a Code of Ethics; Providing designated members with professional liability insurance for error & omissions
Chief Officer(s):
Steven G. Coull, Chief Executive Officer
ceo@cnarea.ca
James Carty, National President
jim@cartyappraisals.ca
Michel Beaudoin, National Vice-President
Robert B. Fraser, National Treasurer
rfraser16@cogeco.ca
Johnathan Carty, National Secretary
Publications:
• CNAREA [Canadian National Association of Real Estate Appraisers] Newsletter
Type: Newsletter
Profile: Association activities & changes in insurance coverage

Canadian National Association of Trained Nurses *See* Canadian Nurses Association

Canadian National Autism Foundation (CNAF)
PO Box 66512, 38 King St. East, Stoney Creek ON L8G 5E5
Tel: 905-930-8682; *Fax:* 905-930-9744
info@cnaf.net
www.cnaf.net
Overview: A small national charitable organization founded in 2000
Mission: To increase autism awareness; To assist families; To raise funds to support Canadian-based autism research
Chief Officer(s):
Tina Fougere, President & Founder

Canadian National Baton Twirling Association (CNBTA)
c/o Lisa Ross, Treasurer, 7208 Conc. 1, RR#2, Puslinch ON N0B 2J0
info@cnbta.org
www.cnbta.org
www.facebook.com/CNBTA
Overview: A small national organization
Mission: To promote the sport of baton twirling in Canada
Affiliation(s): National Baton Twirling Association - USA; Global Alliance of National Baton Twirling & Majorette Associations

Membership: *Fees:* $5-$40
Chief Officer(s):
Kevan Latrace, President
cnbta.prez@gmail.com
Darlene King, National Technical Director/Co-Founder
darleneking@shaw.ca

Canadian National Committee for Irrigation & Drainage (CANCID)
9 Corvus Crt., Ottawa ON K2E 7Z4
Tel: 613-237-9363; *Fax:* 613-594-5190
executivedirector@cwra.org
www.cwra.org
twitter.com/cwraed
Previous Name: International Commission on Irrigation & Drainage - Canadian National Committee
Overview: A small international organization
Mission: To promote research, development, & application of technology among those interested in irrigation, drainage, & flood control
Affiliation(s): Canadian Water Resources Association (CWRA); International Commission on Irrigation & Drainage (ICID); Canadian Committee on Irrigation and Drainage; Canadian Society for Hydrologic Sciences; Student and Young Professionals
Activities: Disseminating news about technical information & CANCID & ICID activities; Liaising with other ICID committees & related organizations
Chief Officer(s):
Brent Paterson, President, 403-381-5515, Fax: 403-381-5765
brent.paterson@gov.ab.ca
Laurie Tollefson, Secretary-Treasurer, 306-867-5404, Fax: 306-867-9656
tollefsonl@agr.gc.ca
Awards:
• Ken Thompson Scholarship
Eligibility: Graduate students whose programs of study focus on applied, natural, or social science aspects of water resources.; *Amount:* $2,000
• Dillon Scholarship
Eligibility: Graduate students whose programs of study focus on applied, natural, or social science aspects of water resources.; *Amount:* $5,000
• General Canadian Water Resources Association Scholarship
Eligibility: Graduate students whose programs of study focus on applied, natural, or social science aspects of water resources.; *Amount:* $1,500 (3)

Canadian National Energy Alliance (CNEA)
www.cnea.co
twitter.com/CNEA_for_AECL
Overview: A large national organization
Mission: To unite Canada's leading engineering & technology companies to manage Canada's radioactive waste & decommissioning responsibilities; To ensure that Canada's nuclear science capabilities continue to support the federal government's needs & responsibilities; To create & maintain an innovative agenda that supports Canada's existing science & technology needs as well as allows the association to pursue global nuclear initiatives
Affiliation(s): Atkins; CH2M; Fluor; SNC-Lavalin; Rolls-Royce Civil Nuclear Canada Ltd.
Activities: Overseeing the privatization, management, & operation of Canadian Nuclear Laboratories (CNL)
Chief Officer(s):
Lou Riccoboni, Contact, 613-723-8700 Ext. 73140
lou.riccoboni@CNEA.co

Canadian National Exhibition Association (CNEA) / Exposition nationale canadienne
Exhibition Place, Toronto ON M6K 3C3
Tel: 416-263-3800; *Fax:* 416-263-3838
info@theex.com
www.theex.com
Overview: A medium-sized national organization founded in 1879
Mission: The CNEA is responsible for the planning and presentation of the annual Canadian National Exhibition at Exhibition Place in Toronto, Ontario.
Membership: 125
Chief Officer(s):
Brian Ashton, President
Sarah Fink, Corporate Secretary, 416-263-5201
sfink@theex.com
Meetings/Conferences:
• Canadian National Exhibition 2018, August, 2018, Canadian National Exhibition Place, Toronto, ON
Scope: National

Canadian National Federation of Independent Unions (CNFIU) / Fédération canadienne nationale des syndicats indépendants (FCNSI)
PO Box 416, 36 Main St. North, Campbellville ON L0P 1B0
Tel: 905-854-6868; *Fax:* 905-854-6869
Toll-Free: 800-638-9438
info@cnfiu.com
www.cnfiu.com
Overview: A medium-sized national organization founded in 1980
Mission: To encourage & promote the formation of independent unions
Affiliation(s): Division of Laborers' International Union of North America
Finances: *Annual Operating Budget:* $100,000-$250,000
Staff Member(s): 16
Membership: 3,500
Chief Officer(s):
Ann Waller, National President
ann.waller@cnfiu.com
Paul Dickson, Secretary-Treasurer
treasurer@cnfiu.com

Canadian National Institute for the Blind (CNIB) / INCA (INCA)
1929 Bayview Ave., Toronto ON M4G 3E8
Toll-Free: 800-563-2642
info@cnib.ca
www.cnib.ca
www.facebook.com/myCNIB
twitter.com/CNIB
www.youtube.com/cnibnatcomm
Also Known As: The Canadian National Institute for the Blind/Institut national canadien pour les aveugles
Overview: A large national charitable organization founded in 1918
Mission: To ameliorate the condition of persons with vision loss in Canada; To prevent blindness; To promote sight enhancement services; To direct services to more than 100,000 Canadians with vision loss, provided through a network of more than 50 offices across the country; To provide library services, research, advocacy, public education, & accessible design consulting; To produce materials in alternative formats, including Braille & DAISY talking books; To supply assistive technologies for persons with vision loss
Affiliation(s): World Blind Union; International Agency for the Prevention of Blindness
Finances: *Funding Sources:* United Way; Government; Corporate funding; Private fundraising
Staff Member(s): 700
Activities: Counselling & referral; Rehabilitation teaching; Orientation & mobility training; Providing library services; Researching blindness prevention; *Library:* CNIB Library; Not open to public
Chief Officer(s):
John M. Rafferty, President & CEO
Craig Lillico, CFO & Corporate Secretary
Garry Nenson, Vice-President, Philanthropy & Social Enterprise
Maria Ash, Vice-President, Shared Services & Integration
Rob Hindley, Vice-President, Marketing & Social Enterprise
Diane Bergeron, Executive Director, Strategic Relations & Engagement
Diane.Bergeron@cnib.ca
Awards:
• Arthur Napier Magill Distinguished Service Award
To recognize outstanding service in work for the blind & prevention of blindness services *Deadline:* April 31 *Contact:* Jaclyn Lavigne, E-mail: jaclyn.lavigne@cnib.ca
• Guide Dog Assistance Fund
The fund is designed to cover extraordinary veterinary expenses for working guide dogs, & to provide financial support for Canadian conferences & training events which are for or about guide dogs & their users.
• Winston Gordon Award of Excellence in Accessible Technology
Presented to an individual or group who has made significant technological advances benefiting people with vision loss
• CNIB Post-Secondary Scholarships
This category of scholarships includes the following: The Bernice and Robert Gilbert Fund ($1,000); FJL Woodcock SAPA Scholarships ($1,000); CNIB General Scholarships ($3,000); The Dr. John and Olive Pyper Scholarship ($4,000); The Joyce Family Foundation Bursary ($4,000); The Barney Danson Scholarship ($5,000) *Eligibility:* Blind & visually impaired students who plan to study at the post-secondary level *Contact:* Shampa Bose, E-mail: shampa.bose@cnib.ca
• CNIB Master's Scholarships
This category of scholarships includes the following: CNIB Master's Scholarship ($12,500); Nalini Perera Little Lotus Bud Master's Scholarship ($5,000). *Eligibility:* Blind & visually impaired students who plan to study at the post-graduate level at a Canadian university *Contact:* Shampa Bose, E-mail: shampa.bose@cnib.ca
• Dr. Dayton M. Forman Memorial Award
To honour leadership in the advancement of library & information services for Canadians living with vision loss or print disabilities
• CNIB's Sense Scholarship
Eligibility: Students with vision loss enrolled in a post-secondary program or going into a post-secondary program; *Amount:* $500 *Contact:* Jeff deViller, E-mail: jeff.deViller@cnib.ca
Meetings/Conferences:
• 2018 CNIB National Braille Conference, 2018
Scope: National
Publications:
• The Canadian National Institute for the Blind Annual Report
Frequency: Annually
• Insight [a publication of the Canadian National Institute for the Blind]
Type: e-Newsletter; *Frequency:* Monthly; *Price:* Free
Profile: Vision health information, consumer products & assistive technologies, & upcoming events

Alberta-Northwest Territories Division
12010 Jasper Ave., Edmonton AB T5K 0P3
Tel: 780-488-4871; *Fax:* 780-482-0017
Toll-Free: 800-563-2642; *TTY:* 780-482-4089
alberta@cnib.ca
Chief Officer(s):
John Mulka, Regional Vice-President, Western Canada

British Columbia-Yukon Division
#200, 5055 Joyce St., Vancouver BC V5R 6B2
Tel: 604-431-2121; *Fax:* 604-431-2099
Toll-Free: 800-563-2642
bcyukon@cnib.ca
Chief Officer(s):
John Mulka, Regional Vice-President, Western Canada

Division du Québec (INCA)
3044, rue Delisle, Montréal QC H4C 1M9
Tél: 514-934-4622; *Téléc:* 514-934-2131
Ligne sans frais: 800-563-2642
Chief Officer(s):
Marie-Camille Blais, Directrice générale, Québec

Manitoba Division
1080 Portage Ave., Winnipeg MB R3G 3M3
Tel: 204-774-5421; *Fax:* 204-775-5090
manitoba@cnib.ca
Chief Officer(s):
Glenn Hildebrand, Chair

New Brunswick Division
22 Church St., #T120-22, Moncton NB E1C 0P7
Tel: 506-857-4240; *Fax:* 506-857-3019
Toll-Free: 800-536-2642
Chief Officer(s):
Pamela Gow-Boyd, Regional Vice-President, Atlantic Canada

Newfoundland & Labrador Division
70 The Boulevard, St. John's NL A1A 1K2
Tel: 709-754-1180; *Fax:* 709-754-2018
Toll-Free: 800-563-2642
Chief Officer(s):
Pamela Gow-Boyd, Regional Vice President, Atlantic Canada

Nova Scotia-PEI Division
6136 Almon St., Halifax NS B3K 1T8
Tel: 902-453-1480
Toll-Free: 800-563-2642
Chief Officer(s):
Pamela Gow-Boyd, Regional Vice-President, Atlantic Canada

Ontario Division
1929 Bayview Ave., Toronto ON M4G 3E8
Tel: 416-486-2500; *Fax:* 416-480-7700
Toll-Free: 800-563-2642; *TTY:* 416-480-8645
Chief Officer(s):
Len Baker, Regional Vice-President, Ontario & Quebec

Saskatchewan Division
2160 Broad St., Regina SK S4P 1Y5
Tel: 306-525-2571; *Fax:* 306-565-3300
Toll-Free: 800-563-2642
Chief Officer(s):
Christall Beaudry, Executive Director

Canadian Associations / Canadian National Millers Association (CNMA)

Canadian National Live Stock Records *See* Canadian Livestock Records Corporation

Canadian National Millers Association (CNMA)
#303, 236 Metcalfe St., Ottawa ON K2P 1R3
Tel: 613-238-2293; *Fax:* 613-271-1112
www.canadianmillers.ca
Overview: A medium-sized national organization
Mission: To serve as a vehicle for consultation between the milling industry, government departments & agencies; To promote regulatory & public policy environment that enhances international competitiveness; To provide international trade development to the industry; To disseminate information about the industry & Canadian wheat flour quality; To work directly & in cooperation with the trade offices abroad
Finances: *Annual Operating Budget:* $250,000-$500,000
Staff Member(s): 2
Membership: 10 companies; *Member Profile:* Wheat & oat processors; Producers of milled grain products
Chief Officer(s):
Gordon Harrison, President
gharrison@canadianmillers.ca
Donna Wiggins, Director, Administration
dwiggins@canadianmillers.ca

Canadian National Railways Police Association (Ind.) (CNRPA) / Association des policiers des chemins de fer nationaux du Canada (ind.)
c/o CN Headquarters, 935, rue de la Gauchetière ouest, Montréal QC H3B 2M9
Toll-Free: 800-465-9239
Also Known As: CNR Police Association
Overview: A small national organization founded in 1923
Chief Officer(s):
Gerry St. George, National President

Canadian Native Friendship Centre (CNFC)
11728 - 95 St., Edmonton AB T5G 1L9
Tel: 780-760-1900; *Fax:* 780-760-1900
www.cnfc.ca
www.facebook.com/CNFCEdmonton
Also Known As: CNFC Edmonton
Overview: A small local charitable organization founded in 1962 overseen by Alberta Native Friendship Centres Association
Mission: To improve the quality of life of Aboriginal Peoples in an urban environment by supporting self-determined activities encouraging equal access to & participation in Canadian society while respecting Aboriginal cultural distinctiveness
Member of: National Association of Friendship Centres; Alberta Native Friendship Centres Association
Finances: *Funding Sources:* Federal & provincial government; United Way; donations
Staff Member(s): 5
Activities: Food & clothing banks; Aboriginal cultural awareness programs; recreation; fine art; crafts; dance classes; *Speaker Service:* Yes; *Library:* Resource Centre; Open to public
Chief Officer(s):
Ron Walker, Executive Director

Canadian Natural Health Association (CNHA)
#105, 5 Wakunda Pl., Toronto ON M4A 1A2
Tel: 416-686-7056
Previous Name: Canadian Natural Hygiene Society
Overview: A medium-sized national charitable organization founded in 1960
Mission: To establish leadership in healthy, natural lifestyle education & support services; to assist by providing resources to help make people healthier
Finances: *Funding Sources:* Lectures; book sales; membership fees
Activities: Publication & sales of literature on health; lectures & courses on health; Counselling; publication of newsletter; *Internships:* Yes; *Speaker Service:* Yes; *Library:* Open to public by appointment

Canadian Natural Hygiene Society *See* Canadian Natural Health Association

Canadian Nature Federation *See* Nature Canada

Canadian Naturopathic Association *See* The Canadian Association of Naturopathic Doctors

Canadian Nautical Research Society (CNRS) / Société canadienne pour la recherche nautique
PO Box 34029, Ottawa ON K2J 4B0
Tel: 613-476-1177
www.cnrs-scrn.org
www.facebook.com/cnrs.scrn
twitter.com/CanNautResSoc
Overview: A medium-sized national charitable organization founded in 1982
Mission: To stimulate & promote nautical research in Canada; To enhance Canada's understanding of its maritime heritage; To foster communication in nautical affairs, to organize meetings, & to cooperate with other agencies promoting nautical research
Affiliation(s): International Commission for Maritime History
Finances: *Annual Operating Budget:* Less than $50,000; *Funding Sources:* Membership fees; donations
12 volunteer's
Membership: 45 institutional + 226 individual; *Fees:* $70 individual; $25 students; $95 institutional; +$10 for international; *Member Profile:* Individuals or groups that are interested or engaged in nautical research; *Committees:* Awards; Editorial; Executive
Chief Officer(s):
Christopher Madsen, President
cmv.madsen@yahoo.com
Awards:
• Keith Matthews Award
Awarded annually to recognize outstanding books & journal articles on nautical research
• Gerald Panting New Scholars Award
Eligibility: New scholars in the nautical research field
Meetings/Conferences:
• Canadian Nautical Research Society 2018 Conference & Annual General Meeting, June, 2018, Toronto, ON
Scope: National
Description: Theme: "Lower Lakes, Upper Lakes: Connecting Maritime Heritage"
Publications:
• Argonauta [a publication of the Canadian Nautical Research Society]
Type: Newsletter; *Frequency:* Quarterly; *Editor:* Isabel Campbell; Colleen McKee
Profile: Articles, research notes, & CNRS activities
• The Northern Mariner / Le Marin du nord [a publication of the Canadian Nautical Research Society]
Type: Journal; *Frequency:* Quarterly; *Editor:* Walter Lewis; *ISSN:* 1183-112X
Profile: Refereed essays, documents, & book reviews on naval & maritime history in the North Atlantic & NorthPacific, published in association with the North American Society for Oceanic History

Canadian Navigation Society (CNS)
c/o Canadian Aeronautics & Space Institute, #104, 350 Terry Fox Dr., Kanata ON K2K 2W5
Tel: 613-591-8787; *Fax:* 613-591-7291
www.casi.ca/canadian-navigation-society
Overview: A small national charitable organization overseen by Canadian Aeronautics & Space Institute
Mission: To advance the science, technologies, & applications of navigation
Activities: Promoting the publication of papers on topics related to navigation; Providing navigation & related technology information
Chief Officer(s):
Susan Skone, Society Chair
sskone@geomatics.ucalgary.ca

Canadian Netherlands Business & Professional Association Inc. (CNBPA)
c/o Tom Vandeloo, KPMG Canada, Bay Adelaide Centre, Toronto ON M5H 2S5
Tel: 416-981-3424; *Fax:* 416-981-3424
info@cnbpa.ca
www.cnbpa.ca
www.linkedin.com/groups/Canadian-Netherlands-Business-Professional-Association-144005
twitter.com/cnbpa
Previous Name: Netherlands Business & Professional Association
Overview: A small local organization founded in 1979
Mission: To promote the economic & social interests of association members
Membership: *Fees:* $60 individuals; $300 corporate memberships; *Member Profile:* Professionals & business people with Dutch interests
Activities: Facilitating interaction with other European business organizations in Canada; Offering networking opportunities
Chief Officer(s):
Tom Vandeloo, President
Publications:
• Canadian Netherlands Business & Professional Association Member Directory
Type: Directory; *Price:* Free with CNBPA membership

Canadian Network for Asthma Care *See* Canadian Network for Respiratory Care

Canadian Network for Environmental Education & Communication (EECOM) / Réseau canadien d'éducation et de communication relatives à l'environnement
c/o 336 Rosedale Ave., Winnipeg MB R3L 1L8
nswayze@eecom.org
www.eecom.org
www.facebook.com/112287385502920
Overview: A small national charitable organization founded in 1993
Mission: To advance environmental learning in Canada; To promote environmental literacy & environmental stewardship; To contribute to a sustainable future
Finances: *Funding Sources:* Donations
Membership: *Fees:* $10 associates; $20 students; $40 individuals; $115 not-for-profit organizations; $280 corporations & government; *Member Profile:* Environmental educators, practitioners, researchers, scientists, administrators, & business representatives
Activities: Offering networking opportunities; Providing professional development resources & activities; Liaising with other organizations
Chief Officer(s):
Natalie Swayzer, Executive Director, 204-221-2007
Grant Gardner, Chair, 709-737-8155
Rick Wishart, Treasurer, 204-467-3254
Awards:
• EECom Awards for Excellence in Environmental Education
Publications:
• EECOM News
Type: Newsletter; *Frequency:* Bimonthly; *Editor:* Sue Wallace; *Price:* Free with Canadian Network for Environmental Education & Communication membership
Profile: Conferences, members, regional reports, awards, & announcements

Canadian Network for Improved Outcomes in Systemic Lupus Erythematosus (CaNIOS)
Health Sciences Centre, #RR149, 800 Sherbrook St., Winnipeg MB R3A 1M4
Tel: 204-787-4734; *Fax:* 204-787-2475
www.canios.ca
www.facebook.com/CaniosRacple
twitter.com/Canios1
Overview: A medium-sized national organization founded in 1995
Mission: To allow Canadian researchers to address questions important to patients with lupus & their families
Finances: *Funding Sources:* Governmental agencies; Not-for-profit organizations & foundations
Membership: *Committees:* Scientific & Data Access; Advocacy & KTE; Fundraising; Membership; Authorship & Publication
Activities: Maintaining a database of lupus patients through the National Lupus Registry
Chief Officer(s):
Christine Peschken, Chair
Publications:
• CaNIOSIn Touch: CaNIOS Research Participants Newsletter
Type: Newsletter; *Frequency:* Semiannually

Canadian Network for Innovation in Education (CNIE) / Réseau canadien pour l'innovation en éducation (RCIÉ)
#204, 260 Dalhousie St., Ottawa ON K1N 7E4
Tel: 613-241-0018; *Fax:* 613-241-0019
cnie-rcie@cnie-rcie.ca
www.cnie-rcie.ca
www.facebook.com/CNIE.RCIE
twitter.com/CNIE_RCIE
Previous Name: Canadian Association for Distance Education (CADE); Association for Media & Technology in Education in Canada (AMTEC)
Merged from: Canadian Association for Distance Education; Association for Media & Technology in Education Canada
Overview: A medium-sized national charitable organization founded in 2007
Mission: To develop & promote the use of technologies, practices, & policies that foster access to learning for students
Membership: *Fees:* $100 individual; $50 student & retired membership; $350 organizational (first 4 members + $85 each additional member; *Committees:* Awards; Website; Professional

Development; International Relations; Sponsorship & External Relations
Chief Officer(s):
Lorraine Carter, Interim Co-President
lorrainec@nipissingu.ca
Diane Janes, Interim Co-President
diane_janes@cbu.ca
Sandy Hughes, Secretary-Treasurer
shughes@wlu.ca

Canadian Network for Respiratory Care (CNRC) / Réseau Canadien pour les soins respiratoires (RCSR)
16851 Mount Wolfe Rd., Caledon ON L7E 3P6
Tel: 905-880-1092; *Fax:* 905-880-9733
Toll-Free: 855-355-4672
info@cnrchome.net
www.cnrchome.net
Previous Name: Canadian Network for Asthma Care
Overview: A small national charitable organization founded in 1994
Mission: To certify healthcare professionals as asthma & rspiratory educators (CAEs & CREs)
Staff Member(s): 5
Membership: 21 organizations; *Member Profile:* Organizations & associations interested in respiratory health; Certified asthma & respiratory educators; *Committees:* Recertification; Certification Management; Exam; Item-writing; Medical Advisory; Strategic Planning; Finance/Fundraising; Conference Planning; Abstract
Chief Officer(s):
Cheryl Connors, Executive Director
Meetings/Conferences:
• Canadian Network for Respiratory Care National Respiratory Education Conference 2019, 2019

Canadian Network of National Associations of Regulators (CNNAR) / Réseau canadien des associations nationales d'organismes de réglementation (RCANOR)
528 River Rd., Ottawa ON K1V 1E9
Tel: 613-739-4376
www.cnnar.ca
Overview: A medium-sized national organization founded in 2003
Mission: To support the self-regulation of professionals and occupations; to increase the understanding of the Canadian public, governments and others, of the value of self-regulation; facilitate collaboration at the national level amongst our members, federal government agencies and other national and international groups; monitor and respond to federal legislation and policy; serve as an information clearing house on common issues; and develop and share resources.
Membership: *Fees:* $750
Meetings/Conferences:
• Canadian Network of Agencies for Regulation 2018 Conference, October, 2018, Fairmont Banff Springs, Banff, AB
Scope: National
Attendance: 400+

Canadian Network of Toxicology Centres (CNTC) / Réseau canadien des centres de toxicologie
University of Guelph, 50 Stone Rd E, Guelph ON N1G 2W1
Tel: 519-824-4120
Overview: A medium-sized national organization founded in 1983
Mission: To be recognized & respected for excellence in research, training, analysis & communication of information focused on critical toxicology issues for ecosystem & human health; to achieve this through innovative, multi-disciplinary teamwork & partnerships between the public & private sector
Affiliation(s): Metals in the Environment Research Network
Finances: *Annual Operating Budget:* $1.5 Million-$3 Million; *Funding Sources:* Environment Canada; grants from government & industrial companies & associations
Staff Member(s): 4
Activities: 4 themes - Human Health & Environmental Risk Assessment; Metal Speciation at the Biological Interface; Endocrine Disrupters & Reproductive/Endocrines Toxicology; Immunotoxicology; also conducts research on a contract basis for government or industry, develops educational materials on toxicology for secondary school programs across Canada; risk assessments of complex mixtures
Chief Officer(s):
Leonard Ritter, Executive Director
lritter@uoguelph.ca

Publications:
• CNTC [Canadian Network of Toxicology Centres] News
Type: Newsletter
Profile: Communication among CNTC member scientists & the public to increase education about toxicology
• CNTC [Canadian Network of Toxicology Centres] Science Briefs
Type: Newsletter
• CNTC [Canadian Network of Toxicology Centres] Annual Report
Type: Yearbook; *Frequency:* Annually
• CNTC [Canadian Network of Toxicology Centres] Annual Symposium Report
Type: Yearbook; *Frequency:* Annually

Canadian Network to Abolish Nuclear Weapons (CNANW)
30 Cleary Ave., Ottawa ON K2A 4A1
Tel: 613-233-1982; *Fax:* 613-233-9028
cnanw@web.ca
www.web.net/~cnanw/
Overview: A small national organization founded in 1996
Mission: CNANW and its members do work to educate the public, and conduct seminars, consultations and meetings with the public, officials and politicians in Canada and abroad. All this work is with the purpose of advancing the cause of nuclear disarmament and moving the world toward abolition of nuclear weapons
Affiliation(s): Les Artistes pour la paix; Canadian Coalition for Nuclear Responsiblity; Canadian Federation of University Women; Canadian Peace Alliance; Canadian Voice of Women for Peace; Canadian Pugwash Group; Centre de Ressources sur la Non-Violence; Lawyers for Social Responsibility; Physicians for Global Survival; Project Ploughshares; Science for Peace; United Nations Association in Canada; Veterans Against Nuclear Arms; World Conference on Religion & Peace; World Federalist Movement - Canada

Canadian Neurological Sciences Federation (CNSF) / Fédération des sciences neurologiques du Canada
143N - 8500 Macleod Trail SE, Calgary AB T2H 2N1
Tel: 403-229-9544; *Fax:* 403-229-1661
www.cnsfederation.org
Previous Name: Canadian Congress of Neurological Sciences
Overview: A medium-sized national organization
Mission: To support the neuroscience professions in Canada, particularly those members of the CNSF Societies, through education, advocacy, membership services & research promotion
Membership: 1,000-4,999; *Fees:* Schedule available; *Member Profile:* Neurology & neurosurgery residents & fellows; *Committees:* Professional Development; Scientific Program; Planning
Activities: Providing a national forum for communication; Offering continuing medical education to members & the neurological medical profession; Encouraging fundamental & applied research; Increasing public awareness about neurological disorders; Advocating on behalf of the profession
Chief Officer(s):
Dan Morin, Chief Executive Officer
dan-morin@cnsfederation.org
Marika Fitzgerald, Manager, Finance & Administration
marika-fitzgerald@cnsfederation.org
Donna Irvin, Administrator, Membership Services
donna-irvin@cnsfederation.org
Meetings/Conferences:
• Canadian Neurological Sciences Federation 2018 53rd Congress, June, 2018, Halifax, NS
Scope: National
Description: Courses, lectures, oral & digital poster presentations, plus exhibits & social events
Publications:
• Canadian Journal of Neurological Sciences
Type: Journal; *Frequency:* 6 pa; *Editor:* Dr. Robert Chen
Profile: Published through Cambridge Journals Online, a peer-reviewed clinical & basic neuroscience research articles, covering neurology, neurosurgery, clinicalneurophysiology, & pediatric neurology

Canadian Neurological Society (CNS) / Société canadienne de neurologie
#709, 7015 Macleod Trail SW, Calgary AB T2H 2K1
Tel: 403-229-9544; *Fax:* 403-229-1661
www.cnsfederation.org
Overview: A medium-sized national organization overseen by Canadian Neurological Sciences Federation

Mission: To promote & encourage all aspects of neurology, including research, education, assessment & accreditation; provide for annual scientific sessions to promote the knowledge & practice of neurology
Membership: 525; *Fees:* $355 full; $80 Junior; $250 associate; *Member Profile:* Neurologists, Neurology residents, those in other related medical fields
Chief Officer(s):
Dan Morin, CNSF CEO
dan-morin@cnsfederation.org
Marika Fitzgerald, CNSF Controller
marika-fitzgerald@cnsfederation.org
Awards:
• Francis McNaughton & André Barbeau Memorial Prizes
Best submitted papers based on work done during the neurology residency or in post-residency training; junior members or active members of the society within 2 years of obtaining certification are eligible; *Amount:* $1,000, inscribed scroll; up to $1,000 to cover expenses to attend the annual meeting of the Canadia
Publications:
• The Canadian Journal of Neurological Sciences
Type: Journal; *Frequency:* Bimonthly; *Accepts Advertising*; *Editor:* G. Bryan Young; *Price:* Free with CNS membership
Profile: Peer-reviewed original articles

Canadian New Music Network (CNMN) / Réseau canadien pour les musiques nouvelles (RCMN)
#200, 1085, Côte du Beaver Hall, Montréal QC H2Z 1S5
admin@reseaumusiquesnouvelles.ca
www.newmusicnetwork.ca
www.facebook.com/CNMN.RCMN
Overview: A medium-sized national organization founded in 2005
Mission: To improve communication, understanding & knowledge within the new music community; To represent the community in Canadian society, by working with the media, Canadian government & arts organizations
Affiliation(s): Canadian Music Centre; Upstream Music Association
Finances: *Funding Sources:* Government grants; Membership dues
Membership: 1,841; *Fees:* Schedule available; *Member Profile:* Artists, ensembles, orchestras, production companies, record labels, music educators, music media, musicologists, music lovers & fans who believe in the importance & value of creative music making in Canadian society
Activities: Offering website & online directory of members; Organizing biennial conference, regional meetings & tours
Chief Officer(s):
Jennifer Waring, President
Emily Hall, Administrator

Canadian Northern Society (CNS)
PO Box 1174, Camrose AB T4V 1X2
Tel: 780-672-3099
canadiannorthern@telus.net
www.canadiannorthern.ca
www.facebook.com/Canadian-Northern-Society/211046248914713
Overview: A small local charitable organization founded in 1986
Mission: To preserve three distinct railway depots and adjacent community parks (Big Valley, Camrose & Meeting Creek); a prairie grain elevator; & a number of artifacts related to both railway history and the collective history of rural Western Canada
Finances: *Funding Sources:* Donations; Fundraising; Grants; Workshops
Membership: *Fees:* $20 full members; $10 associate; *Committees:* Camrose Railway Station Park & Morgan Railway Garden; Meeting Creek Grain Elevator & Railway Station Heritage Site; Big Valley Railway Station & Roundhouse Interpretive Park; Canora Chronicle; Audit
Activities: Preserving railway station sites at Camrose, Big Valley & Meeting Creek, Alberta, as well as the grain elevator at Meeting Creek; Offer workshops and special activities
Chief Officer(s):
Lorrie Tiegs, President
Norm Prestage, Vice-President
Shawn I. Smith, Treasurer
Dean Tiegs, Secretary
secretary@canadiannorthern.ca
Publications:
• The Canora Chronicle
Type: Newsletter; *Frequency:* Quarterly; *Editor:* Dean Tiegs; Lorrie Tiegs; *Price:* Free with society membership
Profile: News about heritage tourism initiatives

Canadian Nuclear Association (CNA) / Association nucléaire canadienne
#1610, 130 Albert St., Ottawa ON K1P 5G4
Tel: 613-237-4262; Fax: 613-237-0989
info@cna.ca
www.cna.ca
www.linkedin.com/company/canadian-nuclear-association
www.facebook.com/TalkNuclear
twitter.com/talknuclear
www.youtube.com/talknuclear
Overview: A large national organization founded in 1960
Mission: To promote the orderly & sound development of nuclear energy for peaceful purposes in Canada & abroad; To promote & foster an environment favourable to the healthy growth of the uses of nuclear energy & radioisotopes; To encourage cooperation between various industries, utilities, educational institutions, government departments & agencies, which may have a common interest in the development of economic nuclear power & the uses of radioisotopes; To provide a forum for the discussion & resolution of problems which are of concern to the members, the industry, or the Canadian public; To stimulate cooperation with other associations with similar objectives & purposes
Finances: Funding Sources: Membership fees
Staff Member(s): 12
Membership: 100; Fees: Schedule available, based upon company size & activity; Member Profile: Industries & enterprises interested in the development & application of nuclear energy for peaceful purposes including uranium producers, reactor manufacturers, electrical utilities, engineering companies, banks, employee unions, departments of federal & provincial governments, educational establishments; Committees: Communications; Regulatory Affairs; Climate Change
Activities: Promoting cooperation among industries, utilities, institutions & agencies; Providing a forum for the exchange of information & discussion of issues; Developing a political environment & regulatory framework; Speaker Service: Yes
Chief Officer(s):
John Barrett, President & Chief Executive Officer
barrettj@cna.ca
Erin Polka, Communications Officer
polkae@cna.ca
George Christidis, Director, Government Affairs, 613-237-4262 Ext. 108
georgec@cna.ca
John Stewart, Director, Policy & Research, 613-237-4262 Ext. 103
stewartj@cna.ca
Marie-danielle Davis, Corporate Secretary/Director, Member Services, 613-237-4262 Ext. 102
davism@cna.ca
Meetings/Conferences:
• Canadian Nuclear Association Conference & Trade Show 2018, 2018
Scope: National
Contact Information: Email: conference@cna.ca
Publications:
• CNA [Canadian Nuclear Association] Newsletter
Type: Newsletter; Frequency: Bimonthly; Editor: Michelle Leslie
Profile: News & information on the nuclear industry
• Nuclear Canada Yearbook [a publication of the Canadian Nuclear Association]
Type: Yearbook; Frequency: Annually
Profile: Information about the Canadian nuclear industry & a buyers' guide of nuclear products & services
• Nuclear Energy Handbook [a publication of the Canadian Nuclear Association]
Profile: Basic & factual information about nuclear energy

Canadian Nuclear Society (CNS) / Société nucléaire canadienne (SNC)
655 Bay St., 17th Fl., Toronto ON M5G 2K4
Tel: 416-977-7620; Fax: 416-977-8131
cns-snc@on.aibn.com
www.cns-snc.ca
Previous Name: The technical society of the Canadian Nuclear Association (CNA)
Overview: A medium-sized national organization founded in 1979
Mission: To promote the exchange of information about nuclear science & technology & its applications; To foster the beneficial utilization of nuclear science
Member of: Engineering Institute of Canada (EIC)
Finances: Funding Sources: Sponsorships
Membership: Fees: $27.81 students; $48.41 retirees; $82.40 regular members; Member Profile: Individuals directly involved with nuclear technology; Students; Persons interested in nuclear topics; Committees: Program; CNA Interface; WIN Interface; COG Interface; OCI Interface; Branch Affairs; Education & Communication; Membership; Bulletin; Finance; Past Presidents'; Climate Change, The Nuclear Future, & Communication Advisory; Fusion; Honours & Awards; Universities / UNENE; Inter-society Relations; Young Generation; Representative to PAGSE
Activities: Providing education; Offering opportunities to network with colleagues in Canada & internationally
Chief Officer(s):
Adriaan Buijs, President
K.L. (Ken) Smith, Financial Administrator
Denise Rouben, Office Manager
cns-snc@on.aibn.com
Awards:
• W.B. Lewis Medal
Contact: The Chair, Honours & Awards Committee, 655 Bay St., 17th Fl. Toronto, ON M5G 2K4
• Ian McRae Award of Merit, Canadian Nuclear Society
Contact: The Chair, Honours & Awards Committee, 655 Bay St., 17th Fl. Toronto, ON M5G 2K4
• Outstanding Contribution Award, Canadian Nuclear Society
Contact: The Chair, Honours & Awards Committee, 655 Bay St., 17th Fl. Toronto, ON M5G 2K4
• Innovative Achievement Award, Canadian Nuclear Society
Contact: The Chair, Honours & Awards Committee, 655 Bay St., 17th Fl. Toronto, ON M5G 2K4
• Fellows of the Canadian Nuclear Society, Canadian Nuclear Society
Contact: The Chair, Honours & Awards Committee, 655 Bay St., 17th Fl. Toronto, ON M5G 2K4
• John S. Hewitt Team Achievement Award, Canadian Nuclear Society
Contact: The Chair, Honours & Awards Committee, 655 Bay St., 17th Fl. Toronto, ON M5G 2K4
• Education & Communication Award, Canadian Nuclear Society
Contact: The Chair, Honours & Awards Committee, 655 Bay St., 17th Fl. Toronto, ON M5G 2K4
• R.E. Jervis Award, Canadian Nuclear Society
Contact: The Chair, Honours & Awards Committee, 655 Bay St., 17th Fl. Toronto, ON M5G 2K4
• CNA International Award, Canadian Nuclear Society
Contact: The Chair, Honours & Awards Committee, 655 Bay St., 17th Fl. Toronto, ON M5G 2K4
• CNS President's Award, Canadian Nuclear Society
Contact: Chair, Honours & Awards Committee, 655 Bay St., 17th Fl. Toronto, ON M5G 2K4
Meetings/Conferences:
• Canadian Nuclear Society 38th Annual Conference, June, 2018, Sheraton Cavalier Saskatoon Hotel, Saskatoon, SK
Scope: National
Publications:
• Canadian Nuclear Society Bulletin
Type: Journal; Frequency: Quarterly; Editor: Ric Fluke; Price: Free with Canadian Nuclear Society membership
Profile: Society news, conference reports, technical papers, articles, & letters
• Canadian Nuclear Society Proceedings
Profile: Information from Canadian Nuclear Society conferences or symposia

Canadian Numismatic Association See Royal Canadian Numismatic Association

Canadian Numismatic Research Society (CNRS)
PO Box 1351, Victoria BC V8W 2W7
www.nunetcan.net/cnrs/cnrs.htm
Overview: A small national organization founded in 1963
Mission: To promote reseach & study of numismatics
Membership: Member Profile: Members are invited to join CNRS; Individuals must be engaged in numismatic research & have published the results of their research
Activities: Increasing public awareness & understanding of numismatics; Disseminating knowledge about numismatics related to Canada
Chief Officer(s):
Ronald Greene, Secretary/Treasurer
ragreene@telus.net
Publications:
• Numismatica Canada
Frequency: Quarterly; Price: $15 non-members
Profile: Information about Canadian tokens, medals, modern municipal trade dollars, & other numismatic topics, published in conjunction with the Canadian Association of Token Collectors

Canadian Nurse Continence Advisors Association (CNCA)
c/o Jennifer Skelly, St. Joseph's Healthcare, King Campus, 2757 King St. East, Hamilton ON L8G 5E4
Tel: 905-573-4823
www.cnca.ca
Overview: A small national organization
Mission: To protect the quality standard associated with being an NCA
Membership: Fees: $40 full; $30 affiliate; $20 student; Member Profile: Nurse Continence Advisors (NCA)
Chief Officer(s):
Jennifer Skelly, President
skelly@mcmaster.ca

Canadian Nursery Landscape Association (CNLA)
7856 Fifth Line South, Milton ON L9T 2X8
Tel: 905-875-1399; Fax: 905-875-1840
Toll-Free: 888-446-3499
info@cnla-acpp.ca
www.cnla-acpp.ca
www.linkedin.com/groups/985377
www.facebook.com/canadanursery
twitter.com/CNLA_ACPP
Previous Name: Canadian Nursery Trades Association; Landscape Canada
Overview: A medium-sized national organization founded in 1968
Mission: To coordinate provincial member groups in the Canadian horticultural industry; To set national standards; To work with government; To develop national priorities
Affiliation(s): Flowers Canada; Canadian Ornamental Plant Foundation; Associated Landscape Contractors of America; International Garden Centres Association; North American Plant Protection Organization; American Nursery & Landscape Association; International Ornamental Growers Association; Canadian Plant Protection Advisory Committee; Canadian Horticultural Council
Finances: Annual Operating Budget: $500,000-$1.5 Million; Funding Sources: Membership dues; publications; management fees
Staff Member(s): 8; 21 volunteer(s)
Membership: 3,210; Fees: Schedule available; Member Profile: Provincial landscape associations; Companies in the landscape industry; Suppliers to the landscape industry; Committees: Certification; Executive; Garden Centres; Growers; Human Resources; Insurance; Landscape; Standards
Activities: Advocating on behalf of members; Promoting horticultural research; Offering educational sessions & networking opportunities
Chief Officer(s):
Victor Santacruz, Executive Director
victor@cnla-acpp.ca
Awards:
• Award of Landscape Excellence
Publications:
• Canadian Standards for Nursery Stock
Price: Free with CNLA membership
Profile: A set of minimum professional standards for for the nursery industry
• CNLA [Canadian Nursery Landscape Association] Newsbrief
Type: Newsletter; Frequency: Bimonthly; Price: Free with CNLA membership
Profile: National news about the industry & the association
• CNLA [Canadian Nursery Landscape Association] Membership Directory
Type: Directory; Frequency: Annually; Price: Free with CNLA membership

Canadian Nursery Trades Association; Landscape Canada See Canadian Nursery Landscape Association

Canadian Nurses Association (CNA) / Association des infirmières et infirmiers du Canada
50 Driveway, Ottawa ON K2P 1E2
Tel: 613-237-2133; Fax: 613-237-3520
Toll-Free: 800-361-8404
cna@cna-aiic.ca
www.cna-aiic.ca
www.facebook.com/cnf.fiic
twitter.com/theCNF
www.youtube.com/user/CNAVideos
Previous Name: Canadian National Association of Trained Nurses

Overview: A large national organization founded in 1962
Mission: To advance the discipline of nursing; To advocate for public policy that incorporates the principles of primary health care & respects the principles, conditions & spirit of the Canada Health Act; To advance the regulation of Registered Nurses in the interest of the public; To advance international health policy & development in Canada
Member of: International Council of Nurses
Finances: *Annual Operating Budget:* $500,000-$1.5 Million; *Funding Sources:* Membership dues; Testing services; Sales & marketing
Staff Member(s): 5; 25 volunteer(s)
Membership: 11 provincial & territorial nursing associations, representing over 129,023 registered nurses; *Fees:* Schedule available; *Member Profile:* Provincial & territorial associations; Nursing students; National nursing groups, emerging groups & other groups
Activities: Collaborating with nurses, other health-care providers, health system stakeholders, & the public with the goal of sustaining quality practice & achieving positive client outcomes; Promoting awareness of the nursing profession; Setting standards for education, practice, research, & administration; *Awareness Events:* National Nursing Week, May; National Nursing Day, May 12 *Library:* Helen K. Mussallem Library
Chief Officer(s):
Mike Villeneuve, CEO
Donna Dewar, Director, Corporate Project Management & IT Services
ddewar@cna-aiic.ca
Joanne Lauzon, Director, Finance and Administration, 613-237-2159 Ext. 202
jlauzon@cna-aiic.ca
Carolyn Pullen, Director, Advocacy & Strategy, 613-237-2159 Ext. 521
cpullen@cna-aiic.ca
Awards:
• Jeanne Mance Award
To honour individuals who have made significant contributions to the health of Canadians & positively influenced nursing practice in Canada
• Employer Recognition Award
To recognize employers who demonstrate support for the certification process in nursing specialties
• CNA Order of Merit Awards
To honour excellence in five categories: clinical nursing practice, administration, education, research, and policy
Meetings/Conferences:
• Canadian Nurses Association 2018 Annual Meeting & Biennial Convention, June, 2018, Shaw Centre, Ottawa, ON
Scope: National
Attendance: 1,000+
Description: One of Canada's largest nursing conferences, featuring presentations, speakers, workshops, & the opportunity to view new products in the health-care marketplace
Contact Information: E-mail: conferences@cna-aiic.ca
Publications:
• Achieving Excellence in Professional Practice [a publication of the Canadian Nurses Association]
Type: Book; *ISBN:* 1-55119-024-9; *Price:* $24.95
Profile: A guide to enable groups to develop or revise professional standards
• Blueprint for the Canadian Nurse Practitioner Examination: Family/All Ages[a publication of the Canadian Nurses Association]
Type: Book; *ISBN:* 978-1-55119-958-0; *Price:* $69.95
Profile: An information source for candidates who plan to write the Canadian NursePractitioner Examination
• Canadian Nurse [a publication fo the Canadian Nurses Association]
Type: Magazine; *Frequency:* 6 pa
• CNA [Canadian Nurses Association] Annual Report
Type: Yearbook; *Frequency:* Annually
Profile: Highlights of the association's activities & achievements throughout the year
• CNA [Canadian Nurses Association] Now Newsletter
Type: Newsletter
• Code of Ethics for Registered Nurses [a publication of the Canadian Nurses Association]
Type: Book; *ISBN:* 1-55119-024-9; *Price:* $7
Profile: A statement of the ethical values of nurses
• Toward 2020: Visions for Nursing [a publication of the Canadian Nurses Association]
Type: Book; *Author:* Janet T. MacDonald et al.; *ISBN:* 978-1-55119-818-7; *Price:* $49.99

Profile: A toolkit that highlights the findings of CNA's study on the future of nursing

Canadian Nurses Foundation (CNF) / Fondation des infirmières et infirmiers du Canada
50 Driveway, Ottawa ON K2P 1E2
Tel: 613-680-0879; *Fax:* 613-237-3520
Toll-Free: 844-204-0124
info@cnf-fiic.ca
www.cnf-fiic.ca
www.facebook.com/CNF.FIIC
twitter.com/theCNF
Overview: A medium-sized national charitable organization founded in 1962
Mission: To promote the health of Canadians by enhancing nursing education & research
Finances: *Annual Operating Budget:* $500,000-$1.5 Million; *Funding Sources:* Special membership dues; corporate & individual donations
Staff Member(s): 5; 75 volunteer(s)
Membership: 10,000; *Fees:* Donation; *Committees:* CNF Nightingale Gala; Fundraising
Activities: Offering financial support to nurses & nursing students through grants & scholarships; Funding nurse-led research; *Internships:* Yes; *Speaker Service:* Yes
Chief Officer(s):
Christine Rieck Buckley, Chief Executive Officer
cbuckley@cnf-fiic.ca
Annette Martin, Director, Development
amartin@cnf-fiic.ca
Susan Fulford Hearn, Foundation Coordinator
shearn@cnf-fiic.ca
Awards:
• CNF Scholarships
Eligibility: Nurses & nursing students who are Canadian citizens or permanent residents studying at a Canadian college or university *Deadline:* March 31; *Amount:* $1,000-$10,000
Publications:
• Foundation Focus [a publication of the Canadian Nurses Foundation]
Type: Newsletter; *Editor:* Susan Hearn

Canadian Nurses Protective Society (CNPS) / Société de protection des infirmières et infirmiers du Canada (SPIIC)
#510, 1545 Carling Ave., Ottawa ON K1Z 8P9
Fax: 613-237-6300
Toll-Free: 800-267-3390
info@cnps.ca
www.cnps.ca
Overview: A small national organization founded in 1988
Mission: To offer legal liability protection related to nursing practice to eligible Registered Nurses
Affiliation(s): College & Association of Registered Nurses of Alberta; Saskatchewan Registered Nurses' Association; College of Registered Nurses of Manitoba; Registered Nurses' Association of Ontario; Nurses Association of New Brunswick; College of Registered Nurses of Nova Scotia; Association of Registered Nurses of Prince Edward Island; Association of Registered Nurses of Newfoundland & Labrador; Registered Nurses Association of the Northwest Territories & Nunavut; Yukon Registered Nurses Association
Activities: Providing legal & financial assistance for nurses in professional legal jeopardy; Offering information & educational opportunities about professional liability problems
Chief Officer(s):
Chantal Léonard, CEO
Publications:
• infoLAW
Profile: Topics include operating room nursing, malpractice lawsuits, medication errors, & the nurse as a witness

Canadian Nursing Informatics Association (CNIA)
937 Cromwell Dr., Ottawa ON K1V 6K3
www.cnia.ca
twitter.com/cnia_ca
Overview: A small national organization
Mission: To be the voice for Nursing Informatics in Canada; to catalyze the emergence of a new national association of nurse informaticians
Affiliation(s): Canadian Nurses Association
Finances: *Annual Operating Budget:* Less than $50,000
Membership: 300; *Fees:* $52.50 general/associate; $157.50 institutional; $26.25 student
Chief Officer(s):
June Kaminski, President

Canadian Nursing Students' Association (CNSA) / Association des étudiantes infirmières du Canada (AEIC)
#450, 1145 Hunt Club Rd., Ottawa ON K1V 0Y3
Tel: 613-235-3150
communications@cnsa.ca
www.cnsa.ca
www.facebook.com/CNSA.AEIC
twitter.com/cnsa1
www.youtube.com/user/CNSAAEIC
Previous Name: Canadian University Nursing Students' Association
Overview: A medium-sized national organization founded in 1971
Mission: To represent nursing students in Canada; To strive to enhance the legal, ethical, professional, & educational aspects of nursing
Affiliation(s): Canadian Nurses Association; Canadian Association of Schools of Nursing
Membership: *Member Profile:* Student bodies at a School of Nursing; Nursing students at a School of Nursing; Former individual members or distance members with a continuing interest in the association; Organizations or corporate bodies approved by the board of directors; *Committees:* Advocacy; Bilingualism & Translation; Community & Public Health; Diversity; Global Health; Indigenous Health Advocacy; Informatics; Research & Education
Activities: Promoting the nursing profession; Providing a communication link among Canadian nursing students; Encouraging education; Liaising with other organizations concerned with nursing; Increasing awareness of the existence of & the need for nursing research
Chief Officer(s):
Bryce Boynton, President
president@cnsa.ca
Sheren Anwar Siani, Vice-President
vp@cnsa.ca
Caitlyn Patrick, Director, Communications
communications@cnsa.ca
Kennedie Maidment, Director, Membership Services
services@cnsa.ca
Peter Stinnissen, Director, Bilingualism & Translation
translation@cnsa.ca
Karlee McKenzie, Director, National Conference
conference@cnsa.ca
Ashley Ahuja, Director, Career & Leadership
leadership@cnsa.ca
Meetings/Conferences:
• Canadian Nursing Students' Association 2018 National Conference, January, 2018, Nanaimo, BC
Scope: Provincial
Description: A conference to promote professional & personal development & discussion in the field of nursing
Publications:
• Canadian Nursing Students' Association Governing Bylaws
Profile: Some sections include rules, regulations, & policies of the association, the board of directors & officers, committees, membership, finances, amendments to bylaws, &meetings
• Canadian Nursing Students' Association Governing Rules & Regulations
Profile: Covering the power, duties, & meetings of the board of directors & officers, the duties & meetings of the regional executive, committees, & national & regionalconferences

Canadian Nutrition Society (CNS) / Société canadienne de nutrition (SCN)
1867 La Chapelle St., Ottawa ON K1C 6A8
Toll-Free: 888-414-7188
info@cns-scn.ca
www.cns-scn.ca
www.linkedin.com/groups?gid=4660487
www.facebook.com/canadiannutritionsociety
twitter.com/@CNS_SCN
Merged from: Canadian Society for Clinical Nutrition; Canadian Society for Nutritional Sciences
Overview: A medium-sized national organization founded in 2010
Mission: To promote nutrition science & education; To act as a voice for those engaged in furthering nutrition
Finances: *Funding Sources:* Membership fees; Sponsorships
Membership: *Fees:* Schedule available; *Member Profile:* Graduates of post-secondary institutions with degrees or diplomas in nutrition-related disciplines; Members of provincially regulated health care professions; Students; *Committees:* Advocacy; Annual Conference; Awards; Canadian Malnutrition

Canadian Associations / Canadian Obesity Network (CON) / Réseau Canadien en Obésité (RCO)

Task Force; Communications/Membership; Education; Ethics; Student Leadership
Activities: Advocating for the promotion of health & the prevention & treatment of disease; Lobbying for research funding; Providing input into policy formulation; Promoting the application of best practices; Offering professional development; Providing networking opportunities
Chief Officer(s):
Sarah Robbins, President
president@cns-scn.ca
David Ma, Vice-President, Research
Valerie Marchand, Vice-President, Health Professionals
Alison Duncan, Treasurer
Andrea Grantham, Executive Director
andrea@cns-scn.ca
Kathy Hare, Financial Administrator
kathy@cns-scn.ca
Awards:
• Khush Jeejeebhoy Award
To recognize the best application of clinical nutrition research findings to clinical practice
• Earle Willard McHenry Award
Awarded for distinguished service in the field of nutrition by a Canadian or Canadian-based individual
• Nestlé Nutrition Student & Trainee Award
The Nestlé Nutrition Student & Trainee Competition is part of the Canadian Nutrition Society Annual Meeting
• PhD Dissertation Award
Presented for outstanding research contributing to the degree of PhD
• Joanne Schweitzer Clinical Nutrition Research Abstract Award
• Centrum Foundation New Scientist Award for Outstanding Research
• IUNS Travel Subsidy Award
Meetings/Conferences:
• 2018 Canadian Nutrition Society Annual Conference, May, 2018, Halifax Convention Centre, Halifax, NS
Scope: National
Publications:
• CNS [Canadian Nutrition Society] Newsletter
Type: Newsletter

Canadian Obesity Network (CON) / Réseau Canadien en Obésité (RCO)
Li Ka Shing Centre for Health Research & Innovation, Univ. of Alberta, #1-116, 8602 - 112 St., Edmonton AB T6G 2E1
Tel: 780-492-8361; *Fax:* 780-492-9414
info@obesitynetwork.ca
www.obesitynetwork.ca
twitter.com/CanObesityNet
Overview: A small national organization founded in 2006
Mission: To foster knowledge translation, capacity building, & partnerships in the area of obesity in Canada; To find innovative & effective ways to treat & prevent obesity; To reduce the mental, physical, & economic burden of obesity
Staff Member(s): 8
Membership: 10,500; *Member Profile:* Obesity researchers; Health professionals; Stakeholders; Media members; *Committees:* Science
Activities: Facilitating networking among researchers, health professionals, policy makers, & stakeholders who are interested in obesity; Promoting research; Training researchers & practitioners; Building consensus on obesity policies; *Speaker Service:* Yes
Chief Officer(s):
Anton Hart, Chair
Arya M. Sharma, Scientific Director
Meetings/Conferences:
• Canadian Obesity Summit 2019, 2019
Scope: National
Publications:
• Best Weight: A Practical Guide to Office-Based Obesity Management
Number of Pages: 100; *Author:* Dr. Y. Freedhoff; Dr. A.M. Sharma
Profile: A practical guide to managing obesity in a clinical setting
• Conduit
Type: Magazine; *Frequency:* Quarterly; *Accepts Advertising;*
Editor: Brad Hussey
Profile: Articles about obesity research & networking activities throughout Canada
• Obesity + (Online Best Evidence Service In Tackling Obesity Plus)
Profile: Latest evidence for clinical practice on obesity

Canadian Occupational Health Nurses Association (COHNA) / Association canadienne des infirmières et infirmiers en santé du travail (ACIIST)
PO Box 25058, RPO Deer Park, Red Deer AB T4R 2M2
info@cohna-aciist.ca
www.cohna-aciist.ca
Previous Name: National Association of Occupational Health Nurses
Overview: A medium-sized national organization founded in 1984
Mission: To promote national standards for the occupational health nursing practice; To advance the profession by providing a national forum for the exchange of ideas & concerns; To enhance the profile of occupational health nurses; To improve the health & safety of workers; To contribute to the health of the community by providing quality health services to workers; To encourage continuing education
Affiliation(s): Canadian Nurses Association
Finances: *Annual Operating Budget:* Less than $50,000; *Funding Sources:* Membership dues
4 volunteer(s)
Membership: 2,400; *Fees:* $5; *Member Profile:* Member of provincial occupational health nurses group; *Committees:* Certification; Communication; Education; Finance
Activities: *Speaker Service:* Yes
Chief Officer(s):
Cathy Dormody, President
Anne Masters-Boyne, Secretary/Treasurer
Carmen Skelton, Vice President
ellencoe@telus.net

Canadian Occupational Therapy Foundation (COTF) / La Fondation canadienne d'ergothérapie (FCE)
CTTC Bldg., #3401, 1125 Colonel By Dr., Ottawa ON K1S 5R1
Tel: 613-523-2268; *Fax:* 613-523-2552
Toll-Free: 800-434-2268
www.cotfcanada.org
www.facebook.com/239464269434993
Overview: A medium-sized national charitable organization founded in 1983
Mission: To fund & promote research & scholarship in occupational therapy in Canada
Finances: *Annual Operating Budget:* $50,000-$100,000; *Funding Sources:* Donations; Canadian Assocation of Occupational Therapists
Staff Member(s): 2; 20 volunteer(s)
Membership: 1,500; *Committees:* Research; Scholarship
Activities: Competitions for research; scholarship
Chief Officer(s):
Sangita Kamblé, Executive Director, 613-523-2268 Ext. 241
skamble@cotfcanada.org
Anne McDonald, Executive Assistant, 613-523-2268 Ext. 226
amcdonald@cotfcanada.org
Awards:
• Masters & Docotral Scholarships
Awarded annually to members of CAOT enrolled full-time or part-time in a masters or doctoral program in a discipline related to occupational therapy research *Eligibility:* Occupational Therapy students enrolled in Masters or Doctoral Research based programs. Must be current members of CAOT *Deadline:* October 1; *Amount:* $1,500; $3,000
• COTF Research Grants
; *Amount:* $2,000; $5,000
• Janice Hines Memorial Award
Awarded annually to a member of CAOT for an activity which supports the transfer of knowledge of best practices in pediatric occupational therapy; *Amount:* $500
• Goldwin Howland Scholarship
Awarded to a member of CAOT who has demonstrated leadership & vision within the profession; *Amount:* $2,000
• Thelma Cardwell Scholarship
Awarded annually to a member of CAOT enrolled full-time in a masters or doctoral level program who is able to demonstrate an outstanding contribution to occupational therapy; *Amount:* $2,000

Canadian Office & Professional Employees Union (COPEU) / Le Syndicat canadien des employées et employés professionnels et de bureau (SEPB)
c/o Francine Doyon, #11100, 565 boul Crémazie est, Montréal QC H2M 2W2
copesepb.ca
Overview: A medium-sized national organization founded in 1933
Mission: A national labour union organization made up of 2 regional Councils and 39 Local unions comprising tens of thousands of members in several provinces across Canada.
Affiliation(s): Canadian Labour Congress (CLC)
Membership: 3,000,000; *Member Profile:* Office employees, technical and professional employees and sales representatives both in the private and public sectors.
Chief Officer(s):
Serge Cadieux, National President, 514-522-6511 Ext. 235, Fax: 514-522-9096
scadieux@copesepb.ca

Region 1 - Section locale 1012
#1.139, 8485, av Christophe-Colomb, Montréal QC H2M 0A7

Region 1 - Section locale 434
#250, 1200, av Papineau, Montréal QC H2K 4R5
Tél: 514-522-6511; *Téléc:* 514-528-7380
Ligne sans frais: 800-561-7372
sepb434@videotron.net
Chief Officer(s):
François Leduc, Président, 514-522-0434 Ext. 222

Region 1 - Section locale 463
1717, rue du Havre, Montréal QC H2K 2X3
Tél: 514-598-3259; *Téléc:* 514-598-3890
sepb463@gazmetro.com

Region 1 - Section locale 480
#250, 1200, av Papineau, Montréal QC H2K 4R5
Tél: 514-522-6511
Ligne sans frais: 800-561-7372
lucsabou@magma.ca

Region 1 - Section locale 526
CP 1980, 4010, rue St-Andre, Jonquière QC G7S 5K5
Tél: 418-622-5170
Ligne sans frais: 800-295-7372
langis_lapointe@abitibiconsolidated.com

Region 1 - Section locale 571
303, rue Notre-Dame est, 4e étage, Montréal QC H2Y 3Y8
Tél: 512-487-2419; *Téléc:* 514-872-3883
c_picotte@videotron.ca

Region 1 - Section locale 573
#250, 1200, av Papineau, Montréal QC H2K 4R5
Tél: 514-522-6511; *Téléc:* 514-522-9000
Ligne sans frais: 800-561-7372
573@sepb.qc.ca

Region 1 - Section locale 574
#250, 1200, av Papineau, Montréal QC H2K 4R5
Tél: 514-522-7574; *Téléc:* 514-522-0505
574@sepb.qc.ca
Chief Officer(s):
Loïc Breton, Président
lbreton@sepb.qc.ca

Region 1 - Section locale 575
#2200, 565, boul Crémazie est, Montréal QC H2M 2V7
Tél: 514-522-6511; *Téléc:* 514-522-5759
Ligne sans frais: 800-561-7372
sepb575.desjardins@videotron.net
www.sepb575.qc.ca

Region 1 - Section locale 576
444, rue Mountainview, Otterburn Park QC J3H 2K2
Tél: 450-672-4010; *Téléc:* 450-467-9347
rmace-burton@rsb.qc.ca

Region 1 - Section locale 577
3200, boul Souvenir ouest, #A105, Laval QC H7V 1W9
Tél: 450-621-5600
jfitch@swlauriersb.qc.ca

Region 1 - Section locale 578
13, boul St-Laurent est, Longueuil QC J4H 4B7
Tél: 450-647-5884; *Téléc:* 450-647-5099
sepbmarie-victorin@qc.aira.com

Region 1 - Section locale 579
500, boul Dollard, Outremont QC H2V 3G2
Tél: 514-271-1194; *Téléc:* 514-271-1981
579@sepb.qc.ca

Region 1 - Section locale 610
CP 96565, 895, de la Gauchetière ouest, Montréal QC H3B 5J8
Tél: 514-280-7139
info@spstm.ca

Region 1 - Section locale 611
#250, 1200, av Papineau, Montréal QC H2K 4R5
Tél: 514-522-6511; *Téléc:* 514-522-9000
Chief Officer(s):
Jacques Lamontagne, Président

Region 2 - Local 103
c/o Penny Wachter, President, 3145 Doran Rd., Pembroke ON K8A 6W8

Tel: 613-735-5496
cope103inthevalley@hotmail.com
Region 2 - Local 131
c/o Steve Reeves, President, 280 Willis Dr., Aurora ON L4G 7M3
Fax: 877-217-1437
Toll-Free: 800-746-5728
Region 2 - Local 151
c/o Assunta Young, President, PO Box 359, Marathon ON P0T 2E0
Tel: 807-229-2681; *Fax:* 807-229-3638
Region 2 - Local 225
c/o Daniel Mayville, President, PO Box 19, Stn. A, Ottawa ON K1N 8V1
Tel: 613-907-1626
correspondence@cope225sepb.ca
www.cope225sepb.ca
www.facebook.com/cope225sepb
Region 2 - Local 236
c/o Christine Bayko, President, 400 Westbury Cres., Thunder Bay ON P7C 4N4
Tel: 807-624-2255
chrisb@supercu.com
Region 2 - Local 24
c/o Frank Woit, President, 879 Callandar Bay Dr., Callander ON P0H 1H0
Tel: 705-752-1651
Frank.woit@sympatico.ca
Region 2 - Local 26
c/o Pauline Wallace, President, 433 Townline Rd., Sault Ste Marie ON P6A 6K4
Tel: 705-949-6444
Chief Officer(s):
Jacques Morin, Président
Region 2 - Local 290
c/o Teena O'Keefe, President, 151 North Service Rd., Burlington ON L7R 4C2
Tel: 800-263-9120; *Fax:* 905-632-4733
Region 2 - Local 343
c/o Liz Fong, President, #701, 555 Richmond St. West, Toronto ON M5V 3B1
Tel: 416-703-4448; *Fax:* 416-703-8520
Toll-Free: 888-224-5553
cope343@on.aibn.com
www.cope343.com
www.facebook.com/COPEOnt
twitter.com/PorterStrike
Region 2 - Local 429
c/o Judy McLeod, Kirkland Lake District Comp. School, PO Box 520, 60 Allen Ave., Kirkland Lake ON P2N 3J5
Tel: 705-567-4981; *Fax:* 705-568-8829
Region 2 - Local 454
c/o Maria Kullman, President, 1126 Roland St., Thunder Bay ON P7B 5M4
Tel: 807-345-6395; *Fax:* 807-344-8448
Region 2 - Local 468
c/o Valerie Francis-Roberts, President, PO Box 1202, #701, 555 Richmond St. West, Toronto ON M5V 3B1
Tel: 416-703-8515; *Fax:* 416-703-8520
jbest@copeontario.ca
Region 2 - Local 473
c/o Lynne Sims, President, 11 Golfview Cres., London ON N6C 5N1
Tel: 519-680-4013; *Fax:* 519-686-1392
Region 2 - Local 491
3731 Eastgate Dr. East, Regina SK S4Z 1A5
Tel: 306-525-5874; *Fax:* 306-781-8177
cope491.ca
Chief Officer(s):
Steve Smith, President
ssmith@cupe.ca
Region 2 - Local 521
c/o Bonnie Paterson, PO Box 7, Dryden ON P8N 2Y7
Tel: 807-223-8246; *Fax:* 807-223-8843
Region 2 - Local 523
c/o Shannon Lamontagne, President, 173 Lefebvre Peninsula Rd., Moonbeam ON P0L 2G0
Tel: 705-367-2799
shanron7@yahoo.ca
Chief Officer(s):
Ron Roberts, President
Susan Bellefeuille, Recording Secretary
Pauline Gauvin, Financial Secretary

Region 2 - Local 527
c/o Elaine Sinha, President, 580 Upper Wellington St., Hamilton ON L9A 3P9
Tel: 905-387-9843; *Fax:* 905-387-9919
Chief Officer(s):
Victor Lau, Secretary
Region 2 - Local 529
c/o Jody Etmanski, President, 372 Cartier St., North Bay ON P1B 8N5
Tel: 705-462-5030
raymondd@npsc.edu.on.ca
Region 2 - Local 550
PO Box 47108, Dundas SQ PO, 10 Dundas St. East, Toronto ON M5B 0A1
Tel: 416-671-3865
copelocal550@hotmail.com
www.copelocal550.ca
Region 2 - Local 81
C/o Dan Rogers, President, 1126 Roland St., Thunder Bay ON P7B 5H4
Tel: 807-473-3445
Region 2 - Local 96
c/o Cheryl Balacko, President, 319 River St., Thunder Bay ON P7A 3R3
Tel: 807-343-8335; *Fax:* 807-345-0428
cope96@tbaytel.net
Chief Officer(s):
Yves Ouellet, Président
Region 3 - Local 342
c/o Erin McGee, President, #403 D, 275 Broadway, Winnipeg MB R3C 4M6
Tel: 204-942-0899; *Fax:* 204-947-6513
Region 3 - Local 397
#109, 2709 - 12th Ave., Regina SK S4T 1J3
Tel: 306-352-4238; *Fax:* 306-347-2720
Toll-Free: 877-267-3397
cope397@sasktel.net
www.cope397.ca
www.facebook.com/COPE397
twitter.com/COPE397
Region 3 - Local 458
c/o Yvonne Bootsman, President, PO Box 11242, Edmonton AB T5J 3K5
Tel: 780-916-8997
cope458president@gmail.com
Region 4 - Local 378
4595 Canada Way, 2nd Fl., Burnaby BC V5G 1J9
Tel: 604-299-0378; *Fax:* 604-299-8211
Toll-Free: 800-665-6838
communications@cope378.ca
www.cope378.ca
www.facebook.com/COPE378
twitter.com/COPE378
www.youtube.com/378COPE
Mission: Part of the larger COPE National Union, Local 378, located in Burnaby, represents 12,000 employees of BC Hydro, Capilano University, TransLink, and other other workplaces throughout BC.
Affiliation(s): B.C. Federation of Labour, Canadian Labour Congress
Chief Officer(s):
Andy Ross, President
aross@cope378.ca
Lori Mayhew, Secretary-Treasurer
lmayhew@cope378.ca
David Black, Vice President
davidblack@cope378.ca

Canadian Office Products Association (COPA)
#101, 1335 Morningside Ave., Toronto ON M1B 5M4
Tel: 905-624-9462; *Fax:* 905-624-0830
info@copa.ca
www.copa.ca
www.linkedin.com/company/2675440
www.facebook.com/CanadianOfficeProductsAssociation
twitter.com/COPA_network
Previous Name: Stationery & Office Equipment Guild of Canada Inc.; Stationers' Guild of Canada Inc.
Overview: A small national organization founded in 1933
Mission: To help their memebers by providing them with business solutions that allow them to grow
Membership: *Fees:* Schedule available dependant on type of business & annual sales; *Committees:* Awards; Finance; Business Network; Logistics; Golf; Data Factory

Chief Officer(s):
Sam Moncada, President
smoncada@copa.ca

Canadian Oil Heat Association (COHA)
c/o COHA Ontario Chapter, #2, 22 Peel St., Lindsay ON K9V 3L8
Tel: 905-604-8884; *Fax:* 866-946-0316
Toll-Free: 855-336-8943
info@coha-ontario.ca
www.coha-ontario.ca
www.facebook.com/ilovecleanerheat
twitter.com/CanadianOilHeat
Also Known As: Cleaner Heat
Overview: A medium-sized national organization founded in 1983
Mission: To be the oil heat industry's voice in matters concerning provincial & federal regulators & government decision makers on matters of policy, safety & certification
Member of: Canadian Association Executives
Membership: 400+; *Fees:* $300 - $18,000; *Member Profile:* Oil dealers; Major oil companies; Equipment manufacturers; Wholesalers; Contractors & trainers
Activities: Promoting the benefits of residential fuel oil to the consumer public
Chief Officer(s):
Jim Wood, President, Ontario Chapter
jwood@mckeownandwood.com
Publications:
• COHA [Canadian Oil Heat Association] Directory
Type: Directory
Profile: Listing of equipment wholesalers & manufacturers, fuel oil suppliers, & service contractors
• Today's Oilheat Newsletter
Type: Newsletter

Canadian Oilseed Processors Association (COPA)
#2150, 360 Main St., Winnipeg MB R3C 3Z3
Tel: 204-956-9500; *Fax:* 204-956-9506
copa@mymts.net
www.copaonline.net
Previous Name: Canola Crushers of Western Canada
Overview: A small national organization founded in 1992
Mission: To represent Canadian oilseed producers
Staff Member(s): 3
Membership: 7; *Member Profile:* Major Oilseed Processors; *Committees:* Technical, Environmental & Safety; Oil Trading Rules; Meal Trading Rules; Food Feed Safety
Chief Officer(s):
Ken Stone, Chair

Canadian Oldtimers' Hockey Association *See* Canadian Adult Recreational Hockey Association

Canadian Olympic Committee (COC) / Comité olympique canadien
Corporate Office, #900, 21 St. Clair Ave. East, Toronto ON M4T 1L9
Tel: 416-962-0262; *Fax:* 416-967-4902
digital@olympic.ca
www.olympic.ca
www.facebook.com/teamcanada
twitter.com/teamcanada
www.youtube.com/teamcanada; instagram.com/teamcanada
Overview: A small national charitable organization founded in 1952
Mission: To be responsible for all aspects of Canada's involvement in the Olympic movement, including Canada's participation in the Olympic & Pan American Games & a wide variety of programs that promote the Olympic Movement in Canada through cultural & educational means.
Finances: *Annual Operating Budget:* Greater than $5 Million; *Funding Sources:* National & international sponsors
Staff Member(s): 26; 400 volunteer(s)
Membership: 400
Activities: *Speaker Service:* Yes
Chief Officer(s):
Christopher Overholt, CEO & Secretary General
Montréal
4141, av Pierre-de Coubertin, Montréal QC H1V 3N7
Tél: 514-861-3371
Ottawa
85 Albert St. 14th Fl., Ottawa ON K1P 6A4
Tel: 613-244-2020

Canadian Associations / Canadian Olympic Hall of Fame / Temple de la renommée olympique du Canada

Canadian Olympic Hall of Fame / Temple de la renommée olympique du Canada
c/o COC, #1400, 85 Albert St., Ottawa ON K1P 6A4
Tel: 613-244-2020; Fax: 613-244-0169
olympic.ca/canadian-olympic-hall-of-fame
Overview: A small national organization founded in 1948
Mission: To honor those who have served the cause of the Olympic Movement with distinction; those athletes, coaches, officials, administrators & volunteers whose dedication, sportsmanship & achievements have made an exemplary contribution to the Canadian Olympic Movement
Member of: Canadian Olympic Committee
Staff Member(s): 1; 6 volunteer(s)
Membership: 351

Canadian Oncology Societies (COS)
Fax: 613-247-3511
Toll-Free: 877-990-9044
info@cos.ca
www.cos.ca
Overview: A small national organization
Mission: To increase & exchange knowledge in the field of oncology; To promote the application of such knowledge in the prevention & diagnosis of cancer & the care of cancer patients & their families; To promote interdisciplinary approaches to patient care & research in cancer; To provide a forum for the presentation & discussion of scientific knowledge & advances in oncology; To further continuing education for groups & indivduals involved in the care of patients who require special attention; To support public cancer education programs; To support & assist the Canadian Cancer Society & the National Cancer Insitute; To advise government & other agencies on the provision of health services relevent to oncology
Affiliation(s): Canadian Association of Medical Oncologists; Canadian Hematology Society; Canadian Society of Surgical Oncology; Society of Gynecologic Oncologists of Canada; Canadian Association of Nursing in Oncology; Canadian Uro-Oncology Group.
Membership: 6 societies; *Committees:* Education
Chief Officer(s):
Charles Pitts, Administrator

Canadian Opera Company (COC) / Compagnie d'opéra canadienne
227 Front St. East, Toronto ON M5A 1E8
Tel: 416-363-6671; Fax: 416-363-5584
info@coc.ca
www.coc.ca
www.linkedin.com/company/canadian-opera-company
www.facebook.com/canadianoperacompany
twitter.com/canadianopera
www.youtube.com/canadianopera
Overview: A large national charitable organization founded in 1950
Mission: To produce opera of the highest international standard while attracting growing public support & participation in opera through increased accessibility & education; To attract, develop & promote young Canadian singers, musicians, stage directors, conductors, designers, technical personnel & administrators; To encourage Canadian librettists & composers to compose new works
Member of: Opera America
Affiliation(s): The Canadian Opera Foundation; Canadian Opera Volunteer Committee; Canadian Children's Opera Company
Finances: *Annual Operating Budget:* Greater than $5 Million; *Funding Sources:* Government; Corporate & individual donations; Box office revenue
Staff Member(s): 60; 1200 volunteer(s)
Membership: 350 President's Council + 3,750 friends + 400 aged 19-29; *Fees:* $75+; *Member Profile:* Interest in opera; *Committees:* Finance; Fundraising; Planning
Activities: Producing six mainstage operas; Performing numerous concerts; Participating in education & outreach programs for schools; Providing resources for educators; *Awareness Events:* Opera Chats; *Interactive Opera:* Opera at Harbourfront; *Internships:* Yes; *Speaker Service:* Yes; *Library:* Open to public
Chief Officer(s):
Alexander Neef, General Director
Johannes Debus, Music Director
Publications:
• eOpera [a publication of the Canadian Opera Company]
Type: Newsletter; *Price:* Free with online subscription
Profile: Company news involving information for early & discounted ticket access

Canadian Operational Research Society (CORS) / Société canadienne de recherche opérationelle (SCRO)
PO Box 2225, Stn. D, Ottawa ON K1P 5W4
www.cors.ca
Overview: A small national organization founded in 1958
Mission: To advance the theory & practice of O.R. in Canada; to stimulate & promote contacts between people interested in the subject
Finances: *Funding Sources:* Membership fees
Membership: *Fees:* $110 individual; $55 retired; $45 student; *Committees:* Education; Membership; Program; Public Relations; Publications; Awards; Past President's Advisory Board; SIG
Activities: Operational research; educational activities; *Speaker Service:* Yes
Chief Officer(s):
Corinne MacDonald, President
corinne.macdonald@dal.ca
Dionne Aleman, Secretary
aleman@mie.utoronto.ca
Awards:
• Harold Larnder Prize
• Omond Solandt Award
• Practice Prize Competition
• Student Prize Competition
• Award of Merit
• Service Awards
Publications:
• Canadian Operational Research Society Membership Directory
Type: Directory; *Price:* Free with CORS membership
Profile: Listing of CORS members
• CORS [Canadian Operational Research Society] Bulletin / Bulletin de la SCRO [Société canadienne de recherche opérationelle]
Type: Newsletter; *Frequency:* Quarterly; *Editor:* Lise Arseneau
Profile: CORS activities, section news, awards, competitions, meetings & conferences
• INFOR: Information Systems & Operational Research
Type: Journal; *Accepts Advertising; Editor:* Bernard Gendron; *ISSN:* 0315-5986; *Price:* $65 individual; $95 institution; $70-$100international
Profile: Scientific papers on theory, methodology, & practice of operational research & information systems

Canadian Ophthalmological Society (COS) / Société canadienne d'opthalmologie (SCO)
#110, 2733 Lancaster Rd., Ottawa ON K1B 0A9
Tel: 613-729-6779; Fax: 613-729-7209
cos@cos-sco.ca
www.cos-sco.ca
Overview: A medium-sized national organization founded in 1937
Mission: To assure the provision of optimal eye care to all Canadians by promoting excellence in ophthalmology & providing services to support its members in practice
Member of: Canadian Standards Association
Affiliation(s): Canadian Medical Association; Concilium Ophthalmological Universale
Finances: *Annual Operating Budget:* $500,000-$1.5 Million; *Funding Sources:* Membership dues; subscriptions; exhibits 2 volunteer(s)
Membership: 863 individual; *Fees:* Active: $500; Associate $200; Affiliate $200; Inter'l: $400; *Member Profile:* Physicians who have received certification of fellowship in opthamology from the Royal College of Family Physicians and Surgeons of Canada or has reveived a diploma of the American Board of Ophthalmology or their equivalent, or has received certification by the board of the province in which he or she practices, or holds other specialist qualifications in opthalmology as shall be acceptable to the Board
Activities: *Rents Mailing List:* Yes
Chief Officer(s):
Jennifer Brunet-Colvey, Chief Executive Officer
Rosalind O'Connell, Manager, Communications & Public Affairs
communications@cos-sco.ca
Meetings/Conferences:
• Canadian Ophthalmological Society 2018 Annual Meeting & Exhibition, May, 2018, Metro Toronto Convention Centre, Toronto, ON
Scope: National

Canadian Oral History Association (COHA) / Société canadienne d'histoire orale (SCHO)
c/o University of Winnipeg, 515 Portage Ave., Winnipeg MB R3B 2E9
www.canoha.ca
Previous Name: Oral History Committee, Canadian Historical Association
Overview: A small national organization founded in 1974
Mission: To encourage & support the creation & preservation of sound recordings which document the history & culture of Canada; to develop standards of excellence & increase competence in the field of oral history through study, education & research.
Finances: *Funding Sources:* Membership dues
Membership: *Fees:* $15 student; $20 individual; $30 institutional
Activities: *Rents Mailing List:* Yes; *Library:* by appointment
Chief Officer(s):
Nolan Reilly, President
Janis Thiessen, Secretary-Treasurer

Canadian Organic Growers Inc. (COG) / Cultivons Biologique Canada
#7519, 1145 Carling Ave., Ottawa ON K1Z 7K4
Tel: 613-216-0741; Fax: 613-236-0743
Toll-Free: 888-375-7383
office@cog.ca
www.cog.ca
www.facebook.com/CanadianOrganic
twitter.com/CanadianOrganic
Overview: A medium-sized national charitable organization founded in 1975
Mission: To conduct research into alternatives to traditional chemical & energy-intensive food growing practices; To provide a resource base & a forum open to all farmers & food growers interested in alternative agriculture; To foster the goals of a decentralized, bio-regionally-based food system; To endorse practices which promote & maintain long-term soil fertility, reduce fossil fuel uses, reduce pollution, recycle wastes & conserve non-renewable resources; To assist the farmer, grower, food processor & consumer, through education & demonstration, in understanding the value of organic foods
Member of: Canadian Environmental Network
Affiliation(s): Atlantic Canadian Organic Regional Network; Certified Organic Associations of British Columbia; Ecological Farmers Association of Ontario; Saskatchewan Organic Directorate
Finances: *Funding Sources:* Membership dues; Publications sale; Foundations; Governments
Membership: *Fees:* Donation based; *Member Profile:* Farmers; Gardeners; Consumers; Environmentalists; Writers; Wholesale marketers; *Committees:* Finance; Fundraising; Strategic Planning; Succession; By-laws & Policy & Procedures; *Chapters:* TCOG
Activities: *Awareness Events:* Organic Week, Sept. *Library:* Mail-Lending Library; Not open to public
Chief Officer(s):
Ashley St. Hilaire, Director, Operations
Awards:
• Mary Perlmutter Scholarship
Awarded annually to a graduate student whose work within a recognized research institution is deemed beneficial to organic growers
Publications:
• The Canadian Organic Grower
Price: $18 + HST
Profile: Canada's voice for organics-reaching over 2,500 farmers, gardeners and consumers across Canada.
• Organic Statistics
Profile: Statistical overview of the Canadian organic sector for Canada & by province
• Practical Skills Handbooks
Profile: Resources for organic, transitioning, & conventional farmers on topics such as organic field crops & organic livestock

Durham
ON
Tel: 905-263-9907
info@durhamorganicgardeners.com
durhamorganicgardeners.com
www.facebook.com/DurhamOrganicGardeners
twitter.com/cogdurham
Chief Officer(s):
Vincent Powers, Contact

Hamilton
Hamilton ON
greaterhamilton@cog.ca

Island Natural Growers (Gulf Islands)
106 Old Scott Rd., Salt Spring Island BC V8K 2L6
Tel: 250-537-5511
Chief Officer(s):

Rod Martens, Co-Chair, 250-931-1233
Anne Macey, Secretary

Organic Food Council of Manitoba
PO Box 68082, Stn. Osborne Village, Winnipeg MB R3L 2V9
Tel: 204-779-8546
organicfoodcouncil.org
www.facebook.com/OrganicFoodCouncilManitoba
Chief Officer(s):
Janine Gibson, Chapter Chair
Ottawa
Ottawa ON
Tel: 613-244-4000
cog.oso.chapter@cog.ca
cog.ca/ottawa
Chief Officer(s):
Adèle McKay, Project Manager
Perth/Waterloo/Wellington
ON
Toll-Free: 888-375-7383
office@cog.ca
www.cog.ca/pww
www.facebook.com/cogpww
twitter.com/cogpww
Toronto
Toronto ON
Tel: 647-367-7706
torontochapter@cog.ca
www.cogtoronto.org
www.facebook.com/COGTorontoChapter
Chief Officer(s):
Elizabeth Chrumka, Chapter Chair
Vancouver Island
BC
Tel: 250-642-3671
Chief Officer(s):
Mary Alice Johnson, Chapter Chair
mary@almfarms.org

Canadian Organization for Development through Education (CODE)
321 Chapel St., Ottawa ON K1N 7Z2
Tel: 613-232-3569; *Fax:* 613-232-7435
Toll-Free: 800-661-2633
codehq@code.ngo
www.code.ngo
www.facebook.com/codecan.org
www.youtube.com/user/TheCodecan
Previous Name: Overseas Book Centre
Overview: A large international charitable organization
Mission: To work with partners to bring tangible education results to the developing world for nearly 50 years; To enable people to learn by developing partnerships that provide resources for learning; To promote awareness & understanding; To encourage self-reliance
Member of: The Reading and Writing for Critical Thinking International Consortium; The Canadian Global Campaign for Education
Affiliation(s): CODE Foundation; CODE Incorporated; International Book Bank
Finances: *Annual Operating Budget:* Greater than $5 Million; *Funding Sources:* Private sponsorship; Donations
Staff Member(s): 17
Activities: Library
Chief Officer(s):
Scott Walter, Executive Director
swalter@code.ngo
Awards:
• The Burt Award for African Young Adult Literature
• The Burt Award for Caribbean Young Adult Literature
• The Burt Award for First Nations, Inuit and Métis Young Adult Literature
Publications:
• CODE Annual Report
Type: Yearbook; *Frequency:* Annually
Profile: A report published each autumn, with financial statements, program results, & articles from the field
• The CODE Reader
Type: Newsletter; *Frequency:* Semiannually

Canadian Organization for Rare Disorders (CORD)
#600, 151 Bloor St. West, Toronto ON M5S 1S4
Tel: 416-969-7464; *Fax:* 416-969-7420
Toll-Free: 877-302-7273
info@rarediscorders.ca
rarediscorders.ca
www.facebook.com/RareDisorders
twitter.com/Durhane
Overview: A small national charitable organization founded in 1995
Mission: To advocate for health policy that works for people with rare disorders; to promote research & services for all rare disorders in Canada; To increase access to genetic screening & genetic counselling for rare disorders
Member of: Canadian Coalition for Genetic Fairness
Finances: *Funding Sources:* Alberta Gaming and Liquor Commission; BIOTECanada; Canadian Genetic Diseases Network; Health Canada; Donations
Membership: *Fees:* $25 individual; $50 affiliate; corporate leader: schedule based on commitment level; *Member Profile:* Organizations that represent all those with rare disorders
Activities: Liaising with governments, industry, clinicians, & researchers; Providing information; Connecting affected families; Supporting the Expensive Drugs for Rare Disorders program; *Awareness Events:* Annual International Rare Disease Day, Feb.
Chief Officer(s):
Durhane Wong-Rieger, President & CEO
durhane@sympatico.ca
John Adams, Chair
Publications:
• THE LINK Newsletter
Type: Newsletter; *Frequency:* Annually
Profile: Articles, conferences, & CORD activities

Canadian Organization of Campus Activities (COCA)
#202, 509 Commissioners Rd. West, London ON N6J 1Y5
Tel: 519-690-0207; *Fax:* 519-681-4328
cocaoffice@coca.org
www.coca.org
Previous Name: Canadian Entertainment Conference
Overview: A medium-sized national organization founded in 1982
Mission: To strive to develop quality campus programming, through information sharing
Affiliation(s): National Association for Campus Activities (USA)
Finances: *Funding Sources:* Membership fees; Sponsorships
Staff Member(s): 1; 25 volunteer(s)
Membership: 65 colleges/universities; 100 companies/artists; *Fees:* $150 artists; $285 companies (associations, agencies, & suppliers); $300 institutions; *Member Profile:* Post-secondary institutions across Canada; Associate members, such as entertainers, booking agencies, artist management, & other suppliers to the campus entertainment & programming industry; *Committees:* Awards; National Conference; Education; Nominating; Communications; International Relations
Activities: Providing resources; Offering educational opportunities; Hosting national & regional conferences & meetings; Enabling blook booking with other schools; Providing networking opportunities with other members & campus buyers; Offering the COCA Job Network; Sponsoring regional events, such as Campus Idol & Campus Music Explosion; *Library:* Canadian Organization of Campus Activities Library; Not open to public
Chief Officer(s):
Earle Taylor, Executive Director, 519-690-0207, Fax: 519-681-3284
Kenney Fitzpatrick, Chair, 902-457-6123, Fax: 902-457-0444
kenney@mountstudents.ca
Shea Dahl, Chair, National Conference Committee, 604-822-5336, Fax: 604-822-9019
programs@ams.ubc.ca
Meetings/Conferences:
• Canadian Organization of Campus Activities 2018 National Conference, June, 2018, Fredericton, NB
Scope: National
Description: Educational sessions, plus showcases featuring music, films, & comedy, plus the Campus Activities Biz Hall trade show
Publications:
• Canadian Organization of Campus Activities Conference Manual
Type: Manual; *Frequency:* Annually
Profile: A manual from the Canadian Organization of Campus Activities National Conference
• COCA [Canadian Organization of Campus Activities] Membership Directory
Type: Directory
Profile: Available for Canadian Organization of Campus Activities members only
• COCA [Canadian Organization of Campus Activities] Notes
Type: Newsletter; *Frequency:* 3 - 4 pa; *Accepts Advertising*;
Editor: Bill Mahon; *Price:* Free with Canadian Organization of Campus Activities membership
Profile: Reports from regions throughout Canada plus information about upcoming events

Canadian Organization of Medical Physicists (COMP) / L'Organisation canadienne des physiciens médicaux (OCPM)
#202, 300 March Rd., Kanata ON K2K 2E2
Tel: 613-599-3491; *Fax:* 613-595-1155
www.comp-ocpm.ca
www.facebook.com/CanadianMedphys
twitter.com/MedphysCA
Overview: A small national organization founded in 1989
Mission: To encourage the application of physics in medicine; To develop & protect professional standards; To encourage certification by the Canadian College of Physicists in Medicine
Member of: International Organization of Medical Physics
Affiliation(s): Canadian College of Physicists in Medicine; American Association of Physicists in Medicine; Institute of Physics and Engineering in Medicine
Membership: *Member Profile:* Professional medical physicists who are practising in Canada; Scientists; Academics; Post-doctoral fellows; Graduate students in medical physics programs; National & international corporations; *Committees:* Awards & Nominations; Communications; Imaging; Professional Affairs; Quality Assurance & Radiation Safety Advisory; Science & Education
Activities: Promoting scientific knowledge & publication; Exchanging scientific or technical information; Promoting continuing education
Chief Officer(s):
Michelle Hilts, President
Nancy Barrett, Executive Director, 613-599-1948
nancy.barrett@comp-ocpm.ca
Gisele Kite, Administrator
gisele.kite@comp-ocpm.ca
Awards:
• Gold Medal
Deadline: April
• FCOMP Award
Deadline: April
• Sylvia Fedoruk Prize
Deadline: February
• CAP-COMP Peter Kirkby Memorial Medal
Publications:
• InterACTIONS
Type: Newsletter; *Frequency:* Quarterly; *Accepts Advertising*;
Editor: Dr. Christopher Thomas
Profile: Newsletter of the Canadian Organization of Medical Physicists (COMP) & the Canadian College of Physicists in Medicine (CCPM) for their members
• Medical Physics
Type: Journal; *Price:* Free with COMP membership
• Physics in Medicine & Biology
Type: Journal; *Price:* $385

Canadian Orienteering Federation (COF) / Fédération canadienne de course d'orientation
1239 Colgrove Ave. NE, Calgary AB T2E 5C3
Tel: 403-283-0807; *Fax:* 403-451-1681
info@orienteering.ca
www.orienteering.ca
www.facebook.com/orienteeringcanada
twitter.com/orienteeringcan
www.youtube.com/orienteeringcanada
Also Known As: Orienteering Canada
Overview: A large national organization founded in 1967
Mission: To provide leadership & resources to individuals involved in orienteering in Canada
Affiliation(s): International Orienteering Federation
Membership: *Member Profile:* Coaches, officials, volunteers, athletes, & youth leaders involved in orienteering; *Committees:* Celebration, Awards & Recognition; Coaching; Executive; Finance & Audit; Governance; High Performance; HR; Long Term Athlete Development; Major Events; Mountain Bike Orienteering; New Participant Recruitment; Nominations; Officials Program; Sass Peepre Junior Development; Ski Orienteering; Technical
Activities: *Rents Mailing List:* Yes
Chief Officer(s):
Tracy Bradley, Executive Director
Publications:
• Orienteering Canada Newsletter
Type: Newsletter

Canadian Ornamental Plant Foundation (COPF) / Fondation canadienne des plantes ornementales
PO Box 26029, Guelph ON N1E 6W1
Tel: 519-341-6761; Fax: 519-341-6748
Toll-Free: 800-265-1629
info@copf.org
www.copf.org
Overview: A small national organization founded in 1964
Mission: To encourage new plant development by strengthening relations between growers & breeders for the benefit of the horticulture industry
Member of: aanadian Horticultural Council; International Plant Propagators Society
Staff Member(s): 3
Membership: 660; Fees: Schedule available; Member Profile: Businesses involved in the horticulture industry
Activities: Rents Mailing List: Yes
Chief Officer(s):
Victoria Turner Shoemaker, Executive Director
victoria@copf.org

Canadian Orthopaedic Association (COA) / Association canadienne d'orthopédie
#620, 4060, rue Sainte-Catherine ouest, Westmount QC H3Z 2Z3
Tel: 514-874-9003; Fax: 514-874-0464
www.coa-aco.org
twitter.com/CdnOrthoAssoc
Overview: A medium-sized national organization founded in 1948
Mission: To provide continuing medical education & training for orthopaedic surgeons
Finances: Annual Operating Budget: $500,000-$1.5 Million
Staff Member(s): 4
Membership: 950 individual; 50 associate; Fees: $475 individual; $25 associate; Committees: Communications; Finance & Audit; Membership/Admission; Professional Practice; Standards
Chief Officer(s):
Douglas C. Thomson, Chief Executive Officer
Meetings/Conferences:
• Canadian Orthopaedic Association 2018 Annual Meeting, June, 2018, Victoria, BC
Scope: National
Publications:
• COA [Canadian Orthopaedic Association] Newsletter
Type: Newsletter; Frequency: Quarterly; Accepts Advertising; Editor: Dr. Alastair Younger; Price: Free with COA membership
Profile: Current events & ideas in orthopaedics

Canadian Orthopaedic Foundation (COF) / Fondation orthopédique du Canada (FOC)
PO Box 1036, Toronto ON M5K 1P2
Tel: 416-410-2341; Fax: 416-352-5078
Toll-Free: 800-461-3639
mailbox@canorth.org
whenithurtstomove.org
www.facebook.com/OrthopaedicFoundation
twitter.com/canorthofound
Overview: A medium-sized national charitable organization founded in 1965
Mission: To foster excellence in the provision of health care to patients with musculoskeletal disease or injury, in a cost effective manner, based on significant outcome studies, by supporting research, educating its members & securing funding from government & other health care funding agencies
Affiliation(s): World Orthopaedic Concern; Canadian Medical Association
Finances: Funding Sources: Membership dues
Staff Member(s): 4; 300 volunteer(s)
Membership: Committees: Medical & Scientific Review
Activities: Awareness Events: Hip Hip Hooray Orthopaedic Walk, May; Rents Mailing List: Yes
Chief Officer(s):
Geoffrey Johnston, Chair & President
James Hall, Vice Chair
Awards:
• I. Edouard Samson Award
Medal & $15,000 awarded for outstanding orthopaedic research by a young investigator; paper presented at the annual meeting of the Canadian Orthopaedic Research Society
Publications:
• OrthoLink
Type: Newsletter; Frequency: Quarterly
Profile: Information & practical tips for people interested in building & maintaining bone & joint health

Canadian Orthopaedic Nurses Association (CONA) / Association canadienne des infirmières et infirmiers en orthopédie
7714 - 80 Ave., Edmonton AB T6C 0S4
www.cona-nurse.org
Overview: A medium-sized national organization founded in 1978
Mission: To foster professional growth of the membership in the assessment, treatment & rehabilitation of individuals with neuromuscular & skeletal alterations; To promote nursing research related to orthopaedics
Affiliation(s): Canadian Nurses Association
Finances: Annual Operating Budget: Less than $50,000; Funding Sources: Membership dues; conference fees
Staff Member(s): 1; 8 volunteer(s)
Membership: 535 individual; 10 associate; Fees: $100 nurses; $75 other members of medical profession; $35 retired members; Member Profile: Active - registered nurse, associate - all other health professionals
Activities: Rents Mailing List: Yes
Chief Officer(s):
Candace Kenyon, President
Awards:
• CONA Certification Award
• CONA Conference Grant
• CONA Excellence in Orthopaedic Nursing Practice Award
• COA Literary Award
• CONA Speakers Fund Award
• Up & Coming Orthopaedic Nurse Award
• Lifetime Achievement Award
Meetings/Conferences:
• Canadian Orthopaedic Nurses Association 2018 Annual National Conference, May, 2018, Regina, SK
Scope: National
Publications:
• Orthroscope [a publication of the Canadian Orthopaedic Nurses Association]
Type: Newsletter; Frequency: Quarterly; Price: Free with CONA membership
Profile: National newsletter with current events in orthopaedic nursing

Canadian Orthopaedic Residents Association (CORA) / L'Association Canadienne des Residents en Orthopédie (ACRO)
#450, 4150, rue Sainte-Catherine ouest, Montréal QC H3Z 2Y5
Tel: 514-874-9003; Fax: 514-874-0464
coraweb@canorth.org
www.coraweb.org
Overview: A small national organization
Mission: To foster & promote research & education in the field of Orthopaedic Surgery
Chief Officer(s):
Nadia Murphy, President
nlmurphy@dal.ca
Meetings/Conferences:
• 2018 Canadian Orthopaedic Residents Association Annual Meeting, June, 2018, Victoria, BC
Scope: National

Canadian Orthopractic Manual Therapy Association
#207, 1150 - 100 Ave., Edmonton AB T5K 0J7
Tel: 780-482-7428; Fax: 780-488-2463
info@orthopractic.org
www.orthopractic.org
Overview: A medium-sized national organization
Mission: To provide the public, fellow healthcare professionals, government & funding agencies with guidelines on the provision of safe & effective manual therapy including mobilization & manipulation
Membership: 115; Fees: $100

Canadian Orthoptic Council / Conseil canadien d'orthoptique
CHUL, 2705, boul Laurier, Sainte-Foy QC G1V 4G2
Fax: 418-654-2188
info@orthopticscanada.org
www.orthopticscanada.org
Overview: A medium-sized national organization
Mission: To establish standards in the training of orthoptic students; To establish standards for orthoptic training centres; To provide examinations of orthoptic students in order to determine their proficiency in orthopotics & to award a certificate of competency to qualified students who pass the examinations; To require evidence of continuing education of certified orthoptists; To establish standards for the professional ethical conduct of certified orthoptists
Affiliation(s): Canadian Medical Association; Canadian Ophthalmological Society
Staff Member(s): 1
Chief Officer(s):
Louis-Etienne Marcoux, Secretary-Treasurer
Ann Haver, Administrative Coordinator

Canadian Outdoor Measurement Bureau See Canadian Out-of-Home Measurement Bureau

Canadian Out-of-Home Measurement Bureau (COMB)
#605, 111 Peter St., Toronto ON M5V 2H1
Tel: 416-968-3823; Fax: 416-968-9396
Toll-Free: 800-866-1189
www.comb.org
www.linkedin.com/company/canadian-out-of-home-measurement-bureau-comb-
Previous Name: Canadian Outdoor Measurement Bureau
Overview: A medium-sized national organization founded in 1965
Mission: To provide unbiased quantitative research; To aid members in the research & media measurement processes
Staff Member(s): 9
Membership: 19 companies + 2 advertisers + 43 advertising agencies; Member Profile: Out-of-home companies, advertising agencies & advertisers; Committees: Research
Chief Officer(s):
Rosanne Caron, President
rcaron@omac.comb.org

Canadian Overseas Telecommunications Union
2170, av Pierre Dupuy, Montréal QC H3C 3R4
Tel: 514-866-9015
cotu.ca
Overview: A large national charitable organization
Mission: To maintain the benefits of the members of the union through collective bargaining
Member of: Confederation of Canadian Unions
Chief Officer(s):
Daniel Séguin, President
president@cotu.ca

Canadian Owners & Pilots Association (COPA)
#903, 75 Albert St., Ottawa ON K1P 5E7
Tel: 613-236-4901; Fax: 613-236-8646
copa@copanational.org
www.copanational.org
www.facebook.com/COPAnational
twitter.com/copa_pres
Overview: A medium-sized national charitable organization founded in 1952
Mission: To serve as the voice of general aviation in Canada
Finances: Annual Operating Budget: $500,000-$1.5 Million; Funding Sources: Membership dues; advertising
Staff Member(s): 9; 20 volunteer(s)
Membership: 17,000; Fees: $60-$85 individual; $83-$108 family; $280-$305 corporate; $1,000-$1,350 lifetime; free for students enrolled in a CFTU; Member Profile: Pilots & aircraft owners; Corporate members; Committees: Awards; Awards Review; By-laws Review; Convention Review; Legal Advisory; Medical Advisory; Sea Plane; Strategic Planning
Activities: Offering insurance programs; Library: Canadian Owners & Pilots Association Library; Open to public
Chief Officer(s):
Bernard Gervais, President
bgervais@copanational.org
Awards:
• COPA Awards
Awards include: Award for Merit, Appreciation Award, President's Award and Literary Award Eligibility: Members of COPA; residents of Canada
Meetings/Conferences:
• Canadian Owners and Pilots Association Convention & Trade Show 2018, June, 2018, Saint John, NB
Publications:
• COPA [Canadian Owners & Pilots Association] Flight
Type: Magazine; Frequency: Monthly; Accepts Advertising; Editor: Michel Hell; Price: Free with COPA membership
Profile: Aviation news for members, flying students, aviation medical examiners, air cadets, & government officials
• COPA [Canadian Owners & Pilots Association] Aviation Guides
Price: Free for members
Profile: Booklets on topics such as cross border operations, buying an aircraft, aircraft operating costs, & private aerodromes

- COPA [Canadian Owners & Pilots Association] eFlight
Type: Newsletter; Frequency: Weekly
Profile: Worldwide news about the aviation industry

Canadian Paediatric Society (CPS) / Société canadienne de pédiatrie
#100, 2305 St. Laurent Blvd., Ottawa ON K1G 4J8
Tel: 613-526-9397; Fax: 613-526-3332
www.cps.ca
www.linkedin.com/company/canadian-paediatric-society
www.facebook.com/CanadianPaediatricSociety
twitter.com/canpaedsociety
www.youtube.com/canpaedsociety
Overview: A medium-sized national organization founded in 1922
Mission: To advocate for the health needs of children & youth; To provide continuing education to paediatricians; To establish national guidelines for paediatric care & practice
Member of: International Paediatric Association
Staff Member(s): 30
Membership: 3,000 individual; Member Profile: Certified paediatricians & associates; Committees: Action Committee for Children & Teens; Acute Care; Adolescent Health; Annual Conference; Awards; Bioethics; Community Paediatrics; Continuing Professional Development; Drug Therapy & Hazardous Substances; Fetus & Newborn; First Nations, Inuit & Métis Health; Healthy Active Living & Sports Medicine; Infectious Diseases & Immunization; Injury Prevention; Mental Health & Development Disabilities; Nutrition & Gastroenterology; Paediatric Human Resources Planning
Activities: Conducting Continuing Medical Education courses; Rents Mailing List: Yes; Library: Open to public
Chief Officer(s):
Jonathan Kronick, President
Marie Adèle Davis, Executive Director
madavis@cps.ca
Elizabeth Moreau, Director, Communications & Knowledge Translation
elizabethm@cps.ca
Awards:
- Ross Award
- CPS Awards for Excellence
- CPS Research Award
Meetings/Conferences:
- 95th Canadian Paediatric Society Annual Conference 2018, May, 2018, Québec City Convention Centre, Québec, QC
Scope: National
Contact Information: Phone: 613-526-9397 ext. 248, Email: meetings@cps.ca, www.annualconference.cps.ca
Publications:
- CPS [Canadian Paediatric Society] News
Type: Newsletter; Frequency: 5 pa; Accepts Advertising; Price: Free with CPS membership
Profile: Current society activities for CPS members
- Paediatrics & Child Health [a publication of the Canadian Paediatric Society]
Type: Journal; Accepts Advertising; Price: Free with CPS membership
Profile: Educational information & research reports for clinicians, parents, & caregivers

Canadian Pain Society / Société canadienne pour le traitement de la douleur
#301, 250 Consumers Rd., Toronto ON M2J 4V6
Tel: 416-642-6379; Fax: 416-495-8723
office@canadianpainsociety.ca
www.canadianpainsociety.ca
www.facebook.com/CanadianPain
twitter.com/canadianpain
Overview: A medium-sized national organization founded in 1982
Mission: To foster research on pain; To improve the management of patients with acute & chronic pain
Member of: International Association for the Study of Pain
Membership: 850; Fees: $45 trainees; $150 regular members; Member Profile: Health professionals & basic scientists with an interest in pain research & management; Students, residents, & interns at the pre-doctoral, doctoral, or pre-professional level; Committees: Awards; Nomination; Scientific Program
Chief Officer(s):
Brian Cairns, President
Marsha Campbell-Yeo, Secretary
Karim Mukhida, Treasurer
Emma Roberts, Manager
eroberts@canadianpainsociety.ca

Meetings/Conferences:
- Canadian Pain Society 2018 39th Annual Scientific Meeting, May, 2018, Hotel Bonaventure Montréal, Montréal, QC
Scope: National
Description: The exchange of current information about pain assessment, pain mechanisms, & pain management for healthcare professionals, scientists, & trainees from clinical, research, industry, & policy settings
Publications:
- The Canadian Journal of Pain [a publication of the Canadian Pain Society]
Type: Journal; Frequency: Quarterly
Profile: Featuring articles & information about the latest developments in the field of pain
- Canadian Pain Society Membership Directory
Type: Directory
Profile: Contact information for members
- CPS [Canadian Pain Society] Newsletter
Type: Newsletter; Frequency: Quarterly; Editor: Brittany Rosenbloom; Price: Free with membership in theCanadian Pain Society
Profile: Updates from the Canadian Pain Society, including book reviews, a trainee corner, training opportunities, & forthcoming events

Canadian Paint & Coatings Association (CPCA) / Association canadienne de l'industrie de la peinture et du revêtement
#608, 170 Laurier Ave. West, Ottawa ON K1P 5V5
Tel: 613-231-3604; Fax: 613-231-4908
cpca@canpaint.com
www.canpaint.com
www.linkedin.com/company/canadian-paint-and-coatings-association
www.facebook.com/CanadianPaint
twitter.com/Can_Paint
Overview: A medium-sized national organization founded in 1913
Mission: To represent the paint industry among the provincial, federal & municipal governments
Finances: Annual Operating Budget: $500,000-$1.5 Million
Staff Member(s): 4
Membership: 105 organizations; Member Profile: Manufacturers of paints & coatings for architectural, automotive, & industrial applications; Suppliers & distributors that provide materials & services to paint & coatings companies; Affiliate companies that manufacture equipment for the paint & coatings industry; Committees: Audit & Finance; Auto Refinishing Council; Chemical Management Plant - Paint & Coatings Working Group; Education & Training; Governance & Nominating; Health, Safety & Environment; Management Information; Product Stewardship
Activities: Offering seminars, educational materials, programs & services
Chief Officer(s):
Tim Vogel, Chair
Meetings/Conferences:
- 2018 Canadian Paint and Coatings Association Annual Conference & AGM, May, 2018, Toronto, ON
Scope: National
Description: Paint & coatings professionals gather to discuss the state of the Canadian paint & coatings industries.

Canadian Palomino Horse Association (CPHA)
c/o Lorraine Holdaway, 631 Hendershott Rd., RR#1, Hannon ON L0R 1P0
Tel: 905-692-4328
canadianpalomino@gmail.com
www.clrc.ca/palomino.shtml
Overview: A small national organization founded in 1952
Mission: To develop & promote the breeding of Palomino horses in Canada; To establish standards of breeding
Affiliation(s): Canadian Livestock Records Corporation
Membership: 15 regular; 9 lifetime; Fees: $20 regular annual membership; $75 life membership
Activities: Registering Palomino horses in Canada; Keeping a record of the breeding & origin of Palomino horses; Protecting & assisting breeders engaged in propagation & breeding; Compiling statistics on the industry
Chief Officer(s):
Lorraine Holdaway, Secretary
Laura Lee Mills, Registrar, 613-731-7110 Ext. 314
lauralee.mills@clrc.ca

Canadian Paper Money Society (CPMS)
Attn: Dick Dunn, PO Box 562, Pickering ON L1V 2R7

info@cpmsonline.ca
www.nunetcan.net/cpms.htm
Overview: A small national organization founded in 1964
Mission: To encourage & support historical studies of banks & other paper money issuing authorities in Canada, to preserve their history & statistical records, & through research & publishing the results thereof, ensure that information, documents & other evidence of Canada's financial development will be preserved.
Finances: Funding Sources: Membership dues
Membership: Fees: $30 printed; $20 digital
Chief Officer(s):
Dick Dunn, Secretary-Treasurer
Jared Stepleton, President
president@cpmsonline.ca

Canadian Paralympic Committee (CPC) / Comité paralympique canadien
#100, 85 Plymouth St., Ottawa ON K1S 3E2
Tel: 613-569-4333; Fax: 613-569-2777
www.paralympic.ca
www.facebook.com/CDNParalympics
twitter.com/CDNParalympics
www.youtube.com/user/CDNParalympics
Previous Name: Canadian Federation of Sport Organizations for the Disabled
Overview: A medium-sized national charitable organization founded in 1982
Mission: To support disabled athletes through the establishment of a sustainable Paralymic sport system; To inspire all disabled Canadians to participate in sports
Affiliation(s): International Paralympic Committee
Finances: Funding Sources: Government; private & public sector
Staff Member(s): 22
Membership: 28 national organizations; Member Profile: Any National Sport Organization for Athletes with a Disability or National Sport Organization representing a sport on the Paralympic program, provided that such organization is properly constituted in Canada & is the recognized Canadian member of the appropriate international federation; Committees: Athlete Council; Coach's Council; Development; External Representation; Finance & Audit; Governance; High Performance; Nominating; Operations & Human Resources; Revenue Generation & Government Relations
Activities: Internships: Yes; Speaker Service: Yes; Library: by appointment
Chief Officer(s):
Karen O'Neill, Chief Executive Officer, 613-569-4333 Ext. 223
koneill@paralympic.ca
Gaétan Tardif, President
Laurie Cairns, Executive Director, Corporate Services
lcairns@paralympic.ca
François Robert, Executive Director, Partnerships
frobert@paralympic.ca
Martin Richard, Executive Director, Communications & Marketing
mrichard@paralympic.ca
Catherine Gosselin-Després, Executive Director, Sport
cgosselin-despres@paralympic.ca

Canadian Paraplegic Association See Spinal Cord Injury Canada

Canadian Paraplegic Association - Newfoundland & Labrador See Spinal Cord Injury Newfoundland & Labrador

Canadian Paraplegic Association (Alberta) See Spinal Cord Injury Alberta

Canadian Paraplegic Association (Manitoba)
#211, 825 Sherbrook St., Winnipeg MB R3A 1M5
Tel: 204-786-4753; Fax: 204-786-1140
Toll-Free: 800-720-4933
winnipeg@canparaplegic.org
www.cpamanitoba.ca
Overview: A medium-sized provincial organization overseen by Spinal Cord Injury Canada
Mission: To represent persons with spinal cord injuries in Manitoba
Membership: Member Profile: Persons living with disabilities, their families, & supporters
Activities: Offering information services, rehabilitation counselling, peer support, community advocacy, & employment services
Chief Officer(s):

Ron Burky, Executive Director
rburky@canparaplegic.org
Darlene Cooper, Director, Rehabilitation Services
djcooper@canparaplegic.org

Canadian Paraplegic Association (New Brunswick) Inc. See Ability New Brunswick

Canadian Paraplegic Association (Nova Scotia)
Mumford Professional Centre, #255, 6960 Mumford Rd., Halifax NS B3L 4P1
Tel: 902-423-1277; *Fax:* 902-492-1213
Toll-Free: 800-889-1889
halifax@canparaplegic.org
www.thespine.ca
www.facebook.com/213554735333572
twitter.com/CPANS
www.youtube.com/user/CPANovaScotia
Overview: A medium-sized provincial organization overseen by Spinal Cord Injury Canada
Staff Member(s): 4
Activities: *Awareness Events:* Wheel & Win, Feb.; Sail Able, July
Chief Officer(s):
Gordon Pye, Chair
Angela Cook, Treasurer
Nancy Beaton, Executive Director
nbeaton@canparaplegic.org

Canadian Paraplegic Association (Prince Edward Island) See Spinal Cord Injury (Prince Edward Island)

Canadian Paraplegic Association (Saskatchewan) See Spinal Cord Injury Saskatchewan

Canadian Paraplegic Association Ontario See Spinal Cord Injury Ontario

Canadian Parents for French (CPF)
#1104, 170 Laurier Ave. West, Ottawa ON K1P 5V5
Tel: 613-235-1481; *Fax:* 613-230-5940
cpf@cpf.ca
www.cpf.ca
www.facebook.com/CanadianParentsForFrench
twitter.com/CPFNational
Overview: A large national charitable organization founded in 1977
Mission: To provide educational opportunities for young Canadians to learn & use the French language; To recognize & support English & French as Canada's two official languages; To create & promote opportunities for young Canadians to learn & use French as a second language
Finances: *Funding Sources:* Membership fees; Donations from individuals, foundations & corporations; Grants & contributions
Membership: *Fees:* $25 individual/family; $60 associate; *Member Profile:* Individuals, families & organizations interested in the promotion & creation of French second-language learning opportunities for young Canadians; *Committees:* Nominations; Bylaws; Strategic Planning; Membership Strategy; Advocacy
Activities: Organizing Concours d'Art Oratoire, a provincial/territorial public speaking competition for Core French, French immersion & French first language students; Training volunteers; *Speaker Service:* Yes; *Rents Mailing List:* Yes; *Library:* Not open to public
Chief Officer(s):
Nicole Thibault, National Executive Director, 613-235-1481 Ext. 224
nthibault@cpf.ca
Cathy Stone, Director, Operations, 613-235-1481 Ext. 221
cstone@cpf.ca
Publications:
• CPF [Canadian Parents for French] National News
Type: Newsletter; *Accepts Advertising; ISSN:* 1202-7384
Profile: CFP activities, plus news & opinions to support learning French as a second language
• Helping Your Child Become Bilingual: A Tool Kit for Parents
Type: Booklet; *Number of Pages:* 30; *Price:* Free with CPF membership
• The State of French-Second-Language Education in Canada
Type: Yearbook; *Frequency:* Annually; *Price:* Free with CPF membership
Profile: Assessments of French-second language programs across Canada & examinations of the quality of national & provincial & territorial support for French-second languageprograms

Canadian Parking Association (CPA)
#350, 2255 St. Laurent Blvd., Ottawa ON K1G 4K3
Tel: 613-727-0700; *Fax:* 613-727-3183
info@canadianparking.ca
www.canadianparking.ca
www.linkedin.com/company/2241893?trk=tyah
www.facebook.com/173429676044219?sk=wall
twitter.com/canadianparking
Also Known As: Association canadienne du stationnement
Overview: A medium-sized national organization founded in 1983
Mission: To represent the parking industry & provide a dynamic forum for learning & sharing to enhance member's ability to serve the public & improve the economic vitality of communities
Membership: 320; *Fees:* $520 full; *Member Profile:* Individuals associated with the public parking industry in Canada
Chief Officer(s):
Rick Duffy, President, 905-625-4370 Ext. 223
rduffy@wps-na.com
Daniel Germain, Vice President, 514-874-1208
daniele.germain@parkindigo.com
Awards:
• CPA Scholarship Fund
Eligibility: Registered CPA members, entering/enrolled in a full time studies bachelor or degree program *Deadline:* May 15; *Amount:* $2,000 x10
Meetings/Conferences:
• Canadian Parking Association 2018 Conference & Trade Show, September, 2018, Sheraton Centre Toronto, Toronto, ON
Scope: National
Publications:
• Parker [a publication of the Canadian Parking Association]
Type: Magazine; *Frequency:* q.; *Accepts Advertising; Number of Pages:* 40
Profile: Highlights, information and news relevant to members of the Canadian Parking Association

Canadian Parks & Recreation Association (CPRA) / Association canadienne des parcs et loisirs
PO Box 83069, 1180 Walkley Rd., Ottawa ON K1V 2M5
Tel: 613-523-5315
info@cpra.ca
www.cpra.ca
www.linkedin.com/in/cpra-acpl
www.facebook.com/168910893249240
twitter.com/CPRA_ACPL
Overview: A large national charitable organization founded in 1945
Mission: To advocate on the benefits of parks & recreation services
Membership: 13 provincial & territorial parks & recreation associations
Activities: Influencing policy direction; Promoting the benefits of parks & recreation; Providing information to members; Offering professional development opportunities; *Awareness Events:* Recreation & Parks Month, June
Chief Officer(s):
CJ Noble, Executive Director
cjnoble@cpra.ca
Visnja Zaborski Breton, Director, Communications
Awards:
• Award of Merit
• President's Award of Distinction
• Partnership Award
• Harry Boothman Bursary
Publications:
• The Benefits Catalogue
Type: Catalogue; *Number of Pages:* 200
Profile: Research outlining why parks, recreation, fitness, arts, & culture are important to the development of healthy individuals & communities
• Canadian Parks & Recreation Association Annual Report
Type: Yearbook; *Frequency:* Annually
• Canadian Parks & Recreation Association Research Reports
Profile: Topics include A Workbook on Child Health & Poverty: A Shared Vision for Health Children; Recreation & Children & Youth Living in Poverty: Barriers, Benefits & SuccessStories; & Bridging the Recreation Divide: Listening to Youth & Parents from Low-income Families across Canada
• CPRA [Canadian Parks & Recreation Association] E-News
Type: Newsletter; *Frequency:* Quarterly; *Price:* Free with CPRA membership
Profile: CPRA activities, conferences, awards, news, resources, initiatives, & research
• CPRA [Canadian Parks & Recreation Association] Tool Kits
Type: Kit
Profile: Topics of tool kits include Making All Recreation Safe, Relevant Recreation, & Everybody Gets to Play

Canadian Parks & Wilderness Society (CPAWS) / Société pour la nature et les parcs du Canada (SNAP)
#506, 250 City Centre Ave., Ottawa ON K1R 6K7
Tel: 613-569-7226; *Fax:* 613-569-7098
Toll-Free: 800-333-9453
www.cpaws.org
www.facebook.com/cpaws
twitter.com/cpaws
www.youtube.com/cpawsnational;
www.instagram.com/cpaws_national
Previous Name: National & Provincial Parks Association (NPPAC)
Overview: A medium-sized national charitable organization founded in 1963
Mission: To act as the Canadian voice for public wilderness protection
Finances: *Funding Sources:* Donations; Fundraising
Membership: 1,200; *Committees:* Conservation; Engagement; Governance
Activities: Increasing awareness & understanding of ecological principles; Providing educational programs; Liaising with government, First Nations, business, & other organizations
Chief Officer(s):
Éric Hébert-Daly, National Executive Director
Ellen Adelberg, Director, Communications & Marketing
eadelberg@cpaws.ca
Awards:
• Harkin Conservation Award
To honour individuals who have made a significant contribution to the conservation of Canada's parks & wilderness
Publications:
• Community Atlas Initiative [a publication of the Canadian Parks & Wilderness Society]
Profile: CPAWS works with communities near national parks to produce atlases about land use & the natural environment, such as the Gulf IslandsCommunity Atlas, the Riding Mountain Community Atlas, the St. Lawrence Islands Atlas, & the Bruce Penninsula Community Atlas
• CPAWS [Canadian Parks & Wilderness Society] Annual Report
Type: Yearbook; *Frequency:* Annually
Profile: CPAWS yearly highlights & financial information
• CPAWS [Canadian Parks & Wilderness Society] Research Reports
Frequency: Irregular
Profile: Conservation biology scientific report topics include Grizzly Challenge; Special Marine Areas in Newfoundland & Labrador; Ontario's Timber Harvesting Levels: Scienceor Wishful Thinking?; The State of the Alberta Parks & Protected Areas; & Uncertain Future: Woodland Caribou & Canada's Boreal Forest
• Gatineau Park: A Threatened Treasure
Type: Booklet; *Number of Pages:* 28
Profile: Information to ensure a sustainable future for Gatineau Park & its ecosystems
• More Than Trees: A Citizen's Guide to Making Conservation a Bigger Part of Forest Management
Type: Guide; *Number of Pages:* 91; *Editor:* Chris Henschel; Dave Pearce
Profile: A guide featuring advice fact sheets, compliance checklists, & the forest guardians reporting form
• Nahanni: Protected Forever
Type: Booklet; *Number of Pages:* 16
Profile: The expansion of the Nahanni National Park Reserve
Calgary - Southern Alberta Chapter
c/o Bob Niven Training Centre, Canada Olympic Park, 88 Canada Olympic Rd. SW, Calgary AB T3B 5R5
Tel: 403-232-6686; *Fax:* 403-232-6988
infosab@cpaws.org
www.cpaws-southernalberta.org
facebook.com/cpawssab
twitter.com/cpawssab
www.youtube.com/cpawsnational
Chief Officer(s):
Anne-Marie Syslak, Executive Director
amsyslak@cpaws.org
Katie Morrison, Director
kmorrison@cpaws.org
• Green Notes [a publication of the Canadian Parks & Wilderness Society Calgary - Southern Alberta Chapter]
Type: Newsletter; *Frequency:* Semiannually; *Editor:* Doug Firby
Profile: Articles & features about wilderness issues & campaigns

Edmonton - Northern Alberta Chapter
PO Box 52031, #800, 10025 - 106 St., Edmonton AB T6G 2T5
Tel: 780-424-5128
infonab@cpaws.org
www.cpawsnab.org
www.facebook.com/cpaws.northernalberta
twitter.com/cpawsnab
www.instagram.com/cpaws_nab
Mission: To maintain biodiversity & wilderness in northern Alberta
Chief Officer(s):
Alison Ronson, Executive Director
• Boreal Market News
Editor: Helene Walsh
Profile: Information for decision makers about developments in forest management
• News for the Wild
Type: Newsletter; *Frequency:* Semiannually; *Editor:* J. Gysbers; B. Ensslin; M. Avery; *Price:* Free for CPAWS members
Profile: Information about CPAWS campaigns in Alberta

Fredericton - New Brunswick Chapter (CPAWS NB)
180 St John St., Fredericton NB E3B 4A9
Tel: 506-452-9902
cpawsnb@nb.sympatico.ca
www.cpawsnb.org
www.facebook.com/CPAWSNewBrunswick
twitter.com/RCnature
Mission: To work towards the permanent protection of wilderness areas in New Brunswick
Chief Officer(s):
Roberta Clowater, Executive Director
• An Analysis of the Parks Act Review [a publication of the Canadian Parks & Wilderness Society Fredericton - NB Chapter]
Type: Report; *Author:* Kelsey Butler
• Climate Change Fact Sheets [a publication of the Canadian Parks & Wilderness Society Fredericton - NB Chapter]
Type: Report
Profile: A series of fact sheets highlighting the changes that New Brunswick will experience as a result of climate change
• Good Planning is Good Management [a publication of the Canadian Parks & Wilderness Society Fredericton - NB Chapter]
Type: Report; *Author:* Roberta Clowater & Steve Reid
Profile: Addresses the issues of land use planning & urban sprawl in NewBrunswick
• Resource Management Plan Framework for New Brunswick Provincial Parks: A Guide to Management Planning
Type: Report; *Author:* Kelsey Butler et al.

Halifax - Nova Scotia Chapter (CPAWS - NS)
PO Box 51086, Stn. Rockingham Ridge, Halifax NS B3M 4R8
Tel: 902-446-4155
cpawsns.org
www.facebook.com/cpawsns
twitter.com/cpawsnovascotia
www.youtube.com/cpawsns;
www.flickr.com/photos/64626833@N02
Mission: To conserve Nova Scotia's wild places in parks & other protected areas as well as areas of ocean
Chief Officer(s):
Martin Willison, President
Chris Miller, Biologist, National Conservation
Judith Cabrita, Administrator

Montréal - Québec Chapter (CPAWS Québec)
#303, 727, rue St-Urbain, Montréal QC H2R 2Y5
Tél: 514-278-7627
www.snapqc.org
www.facebook.com/SNAPQuebec
twitter.com/snapqc
www.youtube.com/channel/UCrE5HMtv8GnNtZCxplQVlsw
Mission: D'établir un réseau d'aires protégées au Québec
Chief Officer(s):
Alain Branchaud, Directeur général, 514-278-7627 Ext. 226

Ottawa - Ottawa Valley Chapter (CPAWS - OV)
190 Bronson Ave., Ottawa ON K1R 6H4
Tel: 613-232-7297; *Fax:* 613-569-7098
www.cpaws-ov-vo.org
www.facebook.com/cpawsov
twitter.com/cpaws_ottawa
www.youtube.com/user/cpawsov/
www.flickr.com/photos/50944355@N08/
Chief Officer(s):
John McDonnell, Executive Director

St. John's - Newfoundland & Labrador Chapter (CPAWS - NL)
The Environmental Gathering Place, PO Box 8732, 172 Military Rd., #301C, St. John's NL A1B 3T1
Tel: 709-726-5800
nlcoordinator@cpaws.org
www.cpawsnl.org
www.facebook.com/cpawsnl/
twitter.com/cpawsnl
www.youtube.com/user/cpawsnl;
www.flickr.com/photos/cpaws-nl
Mission: To foster management of protected areas in Newfoundland & Labrador; To promote the establishment of new marine & terrestrial protected areas in the province
Chief Officer(s):
Suzanne Dooley, Co-Executive Director
sdooley@cpaws.org
Tanya Edwards, Co-Executive Director
tedwards@cpaws.org
Emile Colpron, Coordinator, Marine
nlmarine@cpaws.org

Saskatoon - Saskatchewan Chapter
PO Box 25106, Stn. River Hts., Saskatoon SK S7K 2B1
Tel: 306-469-7876
www.cpaws-sask.org
www.facebook.com/cpaws.sask
twitter.com/cpawsSK
Mission: To establish protected areas on Crown lands in Saskatchewan; To promote responsible land use
Affiliation(s): Saskatchewan Environmental Society; Nature Saskatchewan; Silva Forest Foundation
Chief Officer(s):
Gord Vaadeland, Executive Director
gvaadeland@cpaws.org

Toronto - CPAWS Wildlands League Chapter
#380, 401 Richmond St. West, Toronto ON M5V 3A8
Tel: 416-971-9453; *Fax:* 416-979-3155
Toll-Free: 866-510-9453
info@wildlandsleague.org
www.wildlandsleague.org
www.facebook.com/259132727038
twitter.com/bewildon
www.instagram.com/wildlandsleague
Mission: To save, protect, & enhance wilderness areas throughout Ontario
Chief Officer(s):
Janet Sumner, Executive Director, 416-971-9453 Ext. 39
janet@wildlandsleague.org
• 2014 Caribou Report [a publication of the Canadian Parks & Wilderness Society]
Type: Report
• CPAWS [Canadian Parks & Wilderness Society] Wildlands League Chapter Annual Report
Type: Yearbook; *Frequency:* Annually
• Ontario's Timber Harvesting Levels [a publication of the Canadian Parks & Wilderness Society]
Type: Report
• Wild Notes [a publication of the Canadian Parks & Wilderness Society, Toronto Chapter]
Type: Newsletter; *Price:* Free with donations to the Wildlands League

Vancouver - British Columbia Chapter (CPAWS - BC)
#410, 698 Seymour St., Vancouver BC V6B 3K6
Tel: 604-685-7445; *Fax:* 604-685-6449
www.facebook.com/cpawsbc
twitter.com/CPAWSbc

Whitehorse - Yukon Chapter
PO Box 31095, 211 Main St., Whitehorse YT Y1A 5P7
Tel: 867-393-8080; *Fax:* 867-393-8081
info@cpawsyukon.org
cpawsyukon.org
www.facebook.com/CPAWS.Yukon
twitter.com/CPAWSYukon
www.youtube.com/cpawsyukon
Mission: To safeguard wilderness & wildlife in the Yukon
Chief Officer(s):
Gill Cracknell, Executive Director

Winnipeg - Manitoba Chapter (CPAWS Manitoba)
#3, 303 Portage Ave., Winnipeg MB R3B 2B4
Tel: 204-949-0782
info@cpawsmb.org
cpawsmb.org
www.facebook.com/cpawsmb.org
twitter.com/cpawsmb
www.instagram.com/cpawsmb
Chief Officer(s):
Ron Thiessen, Executive Director

Yellowknife - Northwest Territories Chapter
PO Box 1934, 5020 - 52nd St., Yellowknife NT X1A 2P5
Tel: 867-873-9893
cpawsnwt.org
www.facebook.com/cpawsnwt
Mission: To conserve the land, water, & wildlife of the Northwest Territories
Chief Officer(s):
Kris Brekke, Executive Director

Canadian Partnership for Children's Health & Environment (CPCHE) / Le Partenariat canadien pour la santé des enfants et l'environnement (PCSEE)
#301, 130 Spadina Ave., Toronto ON M5V 2L4
Tel: 416-960-2284
info@healthyenvironmentforkids.ca
www.healthyenvironmentforkids.ca
Overview: A medium-sized national organization
Mission: The Canadian Partnership for Children's Health and Environment (CPCHE) is an affiliation of groups with overlapping missions to improve children's environmental health in Canada. Working across traditional boundaries, CPCHE provides common ground for organizations working to protect children's health from environmental contaminants.
Chief Officer(s):
Erica Phipps, Director
erica@healthyenvironmentforkids.ca

Canadian Partnership for Consumer Food Safety Education
R.R. #22, Cambridge ON N3C 2V4
Tel: 519-651-2466; *Fax:* 519-651-3253
brenda.watson@canfightbac.org
www.canfightbac.org
www.facebook.com/347282142037165?fref=ts
twitter.com/CanFightBac
Overview: A medium-sized national charitable organization founded in 1997
Mission: To educate consumers about their role in food safety; to reduce the incidence of foodborne illness in Canada
Finances: *Annual Operating Budget:* $100,000-$250,000
Membership: 35+
Chief Officer(s):
Brenda Watson, Executive Director

Canadian Pasta Manufacturers Association (CPMA)
86 Armstrong St., Ottawa ON K1Y 2V7
Tel: 613-235-4010
www.pastacanada.com
Overview: A small national organization
Mission: To promote Canadian pasta as a healthy & affordable food choice
Finances: *Funding Sources:* Advancing Canadian Agriculture and Agri-Food (ACAAF) Program
Membership: *Member Profile:* Manufacturers of pasta made from durum wheat
Activities: Providing consumer education; Conducting surveys; Funding the health communications program called "Grains: They're Essential"; *Awareness Events:* World Pasta Day, Oct. 25

Canadian Pastry Chefs Guild Inc. (CPCG)
c/o Egon Keller, 36 Melrose Ave., Barrie ON L4M 2A7
Tel: 705-719-9654
www.canadianpastrychefsguild.ca
Overview: A small national organization founded in 2002
Mission: To promote trade education for pastry chefs throughout Canada; to improve trade standards
Membership: 200; *Fees:* $65; *Member Profile:* Members of the Guild, such as pastry chefs or executive pastry chefs in hotels, bakeries, restaurants, or wholesale & retail businesses, are approved by the Board of Directors & abide by a Code of Ethics; Members also include teachers & persons closely connected to the trade, such as equipment manufacturers & suppliers
Activities: Offering shows & competitions, recipes, & resources
Chief Officer(s):
Al Criminisi, President
al@lentia.com
Daniel Gonzalez, Vice-President
pastryman@sympatico.ca
Nyree Allen, Secretary
nyree.allen@gmail.com

Canadian Associations / Canadian Patient Safety Institute (CPSI) / Institut canadien pour la sécurité des patients

Egon Keller, CEO
freewind1@sympatico.ca
Publications:
• The Guild Journal
Type: Newsletter; *Editor:* Richard Crossman; *Price:* Free with Guild membership
Profile: Guild activities

Canadian Patient Safety Institute (CPSI) / Institut canadien pour la sécurité des patients
#1414, 10235 - 101 St., Edmonton AB T5J 3G1
Tel: 780-409-8090; *Fax:* 780-409-8098
Toll-Free: 866-421-6933
info@cpsi-icsp.ca
www.patientsafetyinstitute.ca
www.linkedin.com/companies/canadian-patient-safety-institute
www.facebook.com/PatientSafety
twitter.com/Patient_Safety
www.youtube.com/patientsafetycanada
Overview: A small national organization founded in 2003
Mission: To work with patients, healthcare providers, organizations, regulatory bodies, & governments to provide safer healthcare for Canadians; To promote leading practices for patient safety within Canada's health system
Finances: *Funding Sources:* Health Canada
Activities: Providing resources about patient safety; Identifying patient safety practices; Developing safety competencies; Promoting integration of patient safety practices into educational & training programs; *Awareness Events:* Canadian Patient Safety Week *Library:* Canadian Patient Safety Institute Library
Chief Officer(s):
Doug Cochrane, Chair
Hugh MacLeod, CEO
hmacleod@cpsi-icsp.ca
Cecilia Bloxom, Director, Communications
cbloxom@cpsi-icsp.ca
Publications:
• Patient Safety Matters: The CPSI Newsletter
Type: Newsletter
Profile: Institute updates, courses, appointments, profiles, funding, & upcoming events

Canadian Payday Loan Association (CPLA) / Association canadienne des prêteurs sur salaire (ACPS)
#1600, 25 Main St. West, Hamilton ON L8P 1H1
Tel: 905-522-2752; *Fax:* 905-522-2310
www.cpla-acps.ca
Previous Name: Canadian Association of Community Financial Service Providers
Overview: A small national organization founded in 2004
Mission: To represent the interests of the sector to governments & consumers, & to ensure that Association members adhere to national standards of best business practices for the industry
Staff Member(s): 2
Membership: 947 retail outlets; *Fees:* $1,000 per store; *Member Profile:* Small-sum unsecured short-term credit (payday loan) providers who operate retail outlets across Canada
Chief Officer(s):
Stan Keyes, President
stan.keyes@cpla-acps.ca
Marian Ross, Executive Assistant
marian.ross@cpla-acps.ca

Canadian Payments Association (CPA) / Association canadienne des paiements (ACP)
180 Elgin St., 12th Fl., Ottawa ON K2P 2K3
Tel: 613-238-4173; *Fax:* 613-233-3385
info@cdnpay.ca
www.cdnpay.ca
Overview: A medium-sized national organization founded in 1980
Mission: To establish & operate safe & efficient national clearing & settlements systems; To facilitate the interaction of its systems with others involved in the exchange, clearing & settlement of payments; To facilitate the development of new payment methods & technologies
Finances: *Funding Sources:* Membership dues
Staff Member(s): 80
Membership: 118; *Member Profile:* The Bank of Canada & all banks operating in Canada are required to be members. Other institutions eligible for membership are credit union centrals, federations of caisses populaires, trust companies, loan companies, other deposit-taking institutions, life insurance companies, securities dealers that are members of the Investment Dealers Association or the Bourse de Montréal, & money market mutual funds that meet certain requirements.; *Committees:* Executive; Finance; Stakeholder Advisory; Large-Value Transfer System (LVTS) Management; National Clearings; CPA Regulatory, Statutory and Policy Matters; Payments Risk; Cash Management Users
Activities: Monitoring payment system developments & related issues in Canada & abroad; *Library:* by appointment
Chief Officer(s):
Janet Cosier, Chair
Eric Wolfe, Deputy Chair
Publications:
• Canadian Payments Association Annual Review
Frequency: Annually
• Forum [a publication of the Canadian Payments Association]
Type: Newsletter; *Frequency:* Quarterly; *Editor:* Geoffroi Montpetit
Profile: Association activities & important payment developments

Canadian Payroll Association (CPA) / L'Association canadienne de la paie (ACP)
#1600, 250 Bloor St. East, Toronto ON M4W 1E6
Tel: 416-487-3380; *Fax:* 416-487-3384
Toll-Free: 800-387-4693
Other Communication: dialogue@payroll.ca
infoline@payroll.ca
www.payroll.ca
www.linkedin.com/company/the-canadian-payroll-association
twitter.com/cdnpayroll
Overview: A large national organization founded in 1978
Mission: To provide payroll leadership, through advocacy & education
Finances: *Funding Sources:* Membership fees; Education program; Training sessions
Membership: 20,000+ organizational & individual; *Fees:* Schedule available; *Member Profile:* Corporate, Professional & Associate memberships available
Activities: Providing the CPA Professional Development Series that covers all aspects of payroll training, including terminations, taxable benefits, year end reporting & new year requirements; *Awareness Events:* National Payroll Week, September; *Speaker Service:* Yes; *Library:* Infoline
Chief Officer(s):
Patrick Culhane, President & CEO
Meetings/Conferences:
• Canadian Payroll Association 36th Annual Conference & Trade Show, June, 2018, Ottawa, ON
Scope: National
Description: Theme: "Full Steam Ahead: 40 Years of Payroll Compliance"
Publications:
• CPA [The Canadian Payroll Association] E-Source
Type: Newsletter; *Frequency:* Bimonthly
Profile: Legislation & compliance updates, payroll & human resources tips, & professional development opportunities
• Dialogue [a publication of The Canadian Payroll Association]
Type: Magazine; *Frequency:* Bimonthly
Profile: Articles, products, legislative updates, trends, case-studies, & industry related news about payroll administration
• Your Payroll Privacy Questions Answered
Author: Murray Long; *ISBN:* 0-9736167-2-5; *Price:* $39.95
Profile: For people responsible for payroll & related functions

Canadian Peace Alliance (CPA) / Alliance canadienne pour la paix
PO Box 13, 427 Bloor St. West, Toronto ON M5S 1X7
Tel: 416-588-5555; *Fax:* 416-588-5556
cpa@web.ca
www.acp-cpa.ca
www.facebook.com/268544019838244
twitter.com/CanadianPeace
Overview: A medium-sized national organization founded in 1985
Mission: To involve Canadians in the worldwide movement to stop the arms race, ensure the non-violent settlement of disputes & guarantee the security & well-being of all peoples.
Affiliation(s): Canadian Network to Abolish Nuclear Weapons; International Peace Bureau
Finances: *Funding Sources:* Membership dues; donations
Staff Member(s): 1
Membership: 156 groups; *Fees:* Schedule available; *Member Profile:* Acceptance of statement of unity; *Committees:* Steering
Activities: Facilitates member group campaigns for peace & disarmament; quarterly clearinghouse mailings; *Internships:* Yes; *Speaker Service:* Yes; *Rents Mailing List:* Yes; *Library:* Resource Centre; by appointment
Chief Officer(s):
Sid Lacombe, Coordinator, 416-588-5555
cpa@web.ca

Canadian Peacebuilding Coordinating Committee *See* Peacebuild: The Canadian Peacebuilding Network

Canadian Peacekeeping Veterans Association (CPVA)
PO Box 905, Kingston ON K7L 4X8
Tel: 506-627-6437
info@cpva.ca
www.cpva.ca
Overview: A small national organization founded in 1991
Mission: To assist Canadians who have served on peacekeeping missions
Member of: National Council of Veterans
20 volunteer(s)
Membership: *Fees:* $20 regular; $25 associate; $100 group; *Member Profile:* Military, police & civilian veterans of peacekeeping missions; also open to those who served with Multinational Force & Observers, International Commission of Control & Supervision, International Commission for Supervision & Control
Activities: *Awareness Events:* Peacekeeping Memorial Day, Aug. 9; *Speaker Service:* Yes
Chief Officer(s):
Ray Kokkonen, President
kokkonen@nbnet.nb.ca

Canadian Pediatric Endocrine Group (CPEG) / Groupe canadien d'endocrinologie pédiatrique (GCEP)
c/o Robert Barnes, M.D., Montreal Children's Hospital, #316E, 2300, rue Tupper, Montréal QC H3H 1P3
Tel: 514-412-4315; *Fax:* 514-412-4264
www.cpeg-gcep.net
Overview: A small national organization
Mission: To promote the study of pediatric endocrinology
Membership: *Member Profile:* Paediatricians; Endocrinologists; Fellows in training; Nurses
Activities: Communicating information about pediatric endocrinology & diabetes
Chief Officer(s):
Robert Barnes, Secretary-Treasurer
Meetings/Conferences:
• 2018 Canadian Pediatric Endocrine Group Annual Scientific Meeting, February, 2018, Sheraton Vancouver Wall Centre, Vancouver, BC
Scope: National

Canadian Pediatric Foundation (CPF) / La fondation canadienne de pédiatrie
#100, 2305 St. Laurent Blvd., Ottawa ON K1G 4J8
Tel: 613-526-9397; *Fax:* 613-526-3332
www.cps.ca
www.linkedin.com/company/canadian-paediatric-society
www.facebook.com/CanadianPaediatricSociety
twitter.com/canpaedsociety
www.youtube.com/canpaedsociety
Overview: A medium-sized national organization founded in 1985
Mission: To promote improved health care & social well-being for the children of Canada, particularly for disadvantaged groups; To promote better standards of health care for children throughout the world, particularly where Canadian aid is active
Membership: 150; *Committees:* Action Committee for Children and Teens; Acute Care; Adolescent Health; Annual Conference; Awards; Bioethics; Community Paediatrics; Continuing Professional Development; Drug Therapy & Hazardous Substances; Fetus & Newborn; First Nations, Inuit & Métis Health; Healthy Active Living & Sports Medicine; Infectious Diseases & Immunization; Injury Prevention; Mental Health & Development Disabilities; Nutrition & Gastroenterology; Paediatric Human Resources Planning
Chief Officer(s):
Marie Adèle Davis, Executive Director, 613-526-9397 Ext. 226
madavis@cps.ca
Elizabeth Moreau, Director, Communications & Knowledge Translation
elizabethm@cps.ca
Jackie Millette, Director, Education, Committees & Sections
jackiem@cps.ca
Jane Cheesman, Director, Finance & Administration
janec@cps.ca

Meetings/Conferences:
• Canadian Pediatric Society 95th Annual Conference, May, 2018, Québec City Convention Centre, Québec, QC
Scope: National
Contact Information: www.annualconference.cps.ca

Canadian Pension & Benefits Institute (CPBI) / Institut canadien de la retraite et des avantages sociaux (ICRA)
CPBI National Office, 1175, av Union, Montréal QC H3B 3C3
Tel: 514-288-1222; *Fax:* 514-288-1225
Other Communication: members@cpbi-icra.ca
info@cpbi-icra.ca
www.cpbi-icra.ca
www.linkedin.com/company/canadian-pension-&-benefits-institute
twitter.com/cpbi_icra
Overview: A medium-sized national organization founded in 1960
Finances: *Annual Operating Budget:* $3 Million-$5 Million; *Funding Sources:* Membership fees; Sponsorships; Event registration fees
Membership: *Fees:* Free students; $35 associate; $250 regular; *Member Profile:* Persons involved in pension, benefits, & investment issues in Canada & the United States; *Committees:* Finance & Audit; Governance; Human Resources; Membership; Nominating; Program; Recognition
Activities: Analyzing best practices, related to to pensions, employee benefits, & investments; Offering continuing education; Facilitating the exchange of information; Providing member access to industry job postings
Chief Officer(s):
Peter G. Casquinha, Chief Executive Officer, 514-288-1222 Ext. 25
peter@cpbi-icra.ca
Meetings/Conferences:
• Canadian Pension & Benefits Institute Forum 2018, June, 2018, Fairmont Le Château Frontenac, Québec, QC
Scope: International
Publications:
• Canadian Pension & Benefits Institute Annual Report
Type: Yearbook; *Frequency:* Annually
• Canadian Pension & Benefits Institute Members' Directory
Type: Directory
Profile: Listing of Canadian Pension & Benefits Institute members & their contact information

Atlantic Region
1600 Bedford Hwy., Bedford NS B4A 1E8
Tel: 902-835-0391; *Fax:* 902-835-3628
atlantic@cpbi-icra.ca
www.cpbi-icra.ca
Mission: To provide members in Atlantic Canada with education & networking opportunities for the analysis of best practices & the exchange of information
Chief Officer(s):
Maria Hayes, Regional Administrator

Manitoba Region
80 Noble Ave., Winnipeg MB R2L 0J6
Tel: 204-667-5027; *Fax:* 204-477-5081
manitoba@cpbi-icra.ca
www.cpbi-icra.ca
Mission: To facilitate the exchange of best practices & information for pension, employee benefit, & investment professionals in Manitoba
Joan Turnbull, Regional Administrator
• Manitoba Momentum
Type: Newsletter
Profile: News from the CPBI Manitoba Regional Council, including upcoming local events, membership information, & credit updates

Northern Alberta Region
#3353, 11215 Jasper Ave., Edmonton AB T5K 0L5
Tel: 780-438-3398; *Fax:* 780-438-3399
albertanorth@cpbi-icra.ca
www.cpbi-icra.ca
Mission: To offer educational & networking opportunities to persons in northern Alberta involved in the pensions, employee benefits, & investments sectors
Shelly Petovar, Regional Administrator

Ontario Region
PO Box 64003, 200 Bay St., Toronto ON M5J 2T6
Fax: 905-643-2972
Toll-Free: 877-599-1414
ontario@cpbi-icra.ca
www.cpbi-icra.ca
Mission: To provide education & networking forums related to pensions, employee benefits, & investments in the Ontario region
Jackie Ablett, Regional Administrator

Pacific Region
PO Box 48542, Stn. Bentall, Vancouver BC V7X 1A3
Tel: 604-379-1946
pacific@cpbi-icra.ca
www.cpbi-icra.ca
Mission: To serve persons involved in the pensions, employee benefits, & investments sector in the Pacific region

Québec Region
1175, av Union, Montréal QC H3B 3C3
Tel: 514-288-7272; *Fax:* 514-288-1255
quebec@cpbi-icra.ca
www.cpbi-icra.ca
Mission: To facilitate the exchange of information & the analysis of best practices among persons employed in the fields of pensions, investments, & employee benefits in the Québec region
Chief Officer(s):
André Picard, Chair
Michèle Bernier, Treasurer
Myriam Beaudry, Regional Administrator

Saskatchewan Region
PO Box 353, White City SK S4L 5B1
Tel: 306-757-1013; *Fax:* 306-781-3316
saskatchewan@cpbi-icra.ca
www.cpbi-icra.ca
Mission: To support individuals involved in the pension, benefits, & investment sectors in Saskatchewan
Karen Lovelace, Regional Administrator
• CPBI [Canadian Pension & Benefits Institute] Saskatchewan News
Type: Newsletter; *Frequency:* 3 pa
Profile: Membership news, education updates, upcoming events, & sponsorship opportunities

Southern Alberta Region
PO Box 20065, 205 - 5th Ave. SW, Calgary AB T2P 4H3
Tel: 587-435-2724
albertasouth@cpbi-icra.ca
www.cpbi-icra.ca
Mission: To provide continuing education & networking opportunities for individuals involved in pensions, employee benefits, & investments in southern Alberta
Krista Esau, Regional Administrator

Canadian Peony Society / Société canadienne de la pivoine
PO Box 28027, RPO Parkdale, 468 Albert St., Waterloo ON N2L 6J8
Other Communication: membership@peony.ca
info@peony.ca
www.peony.ca
Overview: A small national organization founded in 1998
Mission: To promote the growing, improving and use of peonies in the garden and for home decoration; to encourage peony breeding to produce distinctly Canadian peony hybrids; to locate and record locally bred peonies, and produce a national registry of collections and their location; and, to sponsor an annual peony show and encourage regional shows.
Membership: *Fees:* $15 individual; $275 lifetime

Canadian Percheron Association / Association canadienne du cheval Percheron
Rolla BC
Tel: 250-759-4981; *Fax:* 888-423-0049
canadapercheron@uniserve.com
www.canadianpercherons.com
Overview: A small national organization
Mission: To develop & encourage the breeding of purebred Percheron horses in Canada; To establish standards of breeding; To regulate the breeding of purebred Percheron horses
Membership: *Fees:* $50
Activities: Keeping a record of the breeding & origin of Percheron horses; Protecting & assisting breeders of purebred Percheron horses in compliance with the Animal Pedigree Act; Compiling statistics on the Percheron industry
Chief Officer(s):
David Logies, President, 902-538-8505
Kathy Ackles, Contact
Publications:
• Canadian Percheron Broadcaster
Type: Magazine; *Accepts Advertising*

Canadian Peregrine Foundation (CPF)
#20, 25 Crouse Rd., Toronto ON M1R 5P8
Tel: 416-481-1233
Toll-Free: 888-709-3944
info@peregrine-foundation.ca
www.peregrine-foundation.ca
Overview: A small national organization founded in 1998
Mission: The Canadian Peregrine Foundation is a registered charity dedicated to assisting the recovery of the peregrine falcon and other raptors at risk.
Membership: *Fees:* $30 single; $40 family

Canadian Periodical Publishers' Association; Canadian Magazine Publishers Association (CMPA) *See* Magazines Canada

Canadian Personal Trainers Network *See* Certified Professional Trainers Network

Canadian Pest Control Association *See* Canadian Pest Management Association

Canadian Pest Management Association (CPMA) / Association canadienne de la gestion parasitaire (ACGP)
#360, 13 - 3120 Rutherford Rd., Vaughan ON L4K 0B2
Fax: 866-957-7378
Toll-Free: 866-630-2762
cpma@pestworld.org
pestworldcanada.net
Previous Name: Canadian Pest Control Association
Overview: A medium-sized national organization founded in 1943
Mission: To provide pest management information; To act as the voice of the pest management industry throughout Canada; Upholding the association's Code of Ethics
Affiliation(s): Pest Management Association of Alberta; Atlantic Pest Management Association; Structural Pest Management Association of Ontario; Association Québécoise de Gestion Parasitaire; Structural Pest Management Association of British Colombia; Manitoba Pest Management Association
Membership: *Member Profile:* Members of provincial & regional pest management associations; Suppliers
Activities: Offering training & networking opportunities; Conducting research; Offering assistance to consumers seeking a professional pest control company
Chief Officer(s):
Sandy Costa, President
sandy@greenleafpestcontrol.com
Meetings/Conferences:
• Pest Management Canada 2018, March, 2018
Scope: National
Description: Educational sessions, networking opportunities, & exhibits of products, services & techniques
Publications:
• Canada ePestWorld [a publication of the Canadian Pest Management Association]
Type: Newsletter; *Frequency:* Monthly; *Price:* Free with Canadian Pest Management Association membership
Profile: Timely national industry news & happenings, membership bulletins, & articles
• ePestWorld [a publication of the Canadian Pest Management Association]
Type: Newsletter; *Frequency:* Weekly
Profile: Industry information
• Pest Gazette [a publication of the Canadian Pest Management Association]
Type: Newsletter; *Frequency:* Quarterly; *Number of Pages:* 4
Profile: Educational information about seasonal pests for pest management consumers
• PestWorld [a publication of Canadian Pest Management Association]
Type: Newsletter; *Frequency:* Bimonthly; *Price:* Free with Canadian PestManagement Association membership
Profile: Business techniques & tips, analysis of the pest management industry, field stories, technical updates, & legislative news

Canadian Petroleum Law Foundation *See* Canadian Energy Law Foundation

Canadian Petroleum Products Institute *See* Canadian Fuels Association

Canadian Pharmacists Association (CPhA) / Association des pharmaciens du Canada
1785 Alta Vista Dr., Ottawa ON K1G 3Y6

Canadian Associations / Canadian Plowing Organization

Publications:
- CPIA [Canadian Plastics Industry Association] Annual Report

Type: Yearbook; *Frequency:* Annually

Western Region
#33020, 11198 - 84th Ave., Delta BC V4C 1L0
Tel: 604-581-1984; *Fax:* 604-581-1607

Canadian Plowing Council *See* Canadian Plowing Organization

Canadian Plowing Organization
38 Parkin St., Salisbury NB E4J 2N4
Tel: 506-372-9427
info@canadianplowing.ca
www.canadianplowing.ca
Previous Name: Canadian Plowing Council
Overview: A small national charitable organization founded in 1955
Mission: To preserve the art of match plowing in Canada; to promote the efficient operation & use of farm machinery; to promote improved farm productivity & yield efficiency through proper seed bed preparation & soil management
Affiliation(s): World Ploughing Organization
Finances: *Annual Operating Budget:* Less than $50,000; *Funding Sources:* Donations
1 volunteer(s)
Membership: 30 affiliated countries
Activities: Organizes an annual Canadian Championship Plowing Contest at which a Canadian Senior Champion Plowman, a Reserve Champion Plowman & a Canadian Junior Champion Plowman are declared
Chief Officer(s):
Gary Keith, Secretary

Canadian Plumbing & Mechanical Contractors Association, BC Branch *See* Mechanical Contractors Association of British Columbia

Canadian Plywood Association
#100, 375 Lynn Ave., North Vancouver BC V7J 2C4
Tel: 604-981-4190; *Fax:* 604-985-0342
info@canply.org
www.canply.org
Also Known As: CANPLY
Overview: A medium-sized national organization
Mission: Canadian plywood organization.
Finances: *Annual Operating Budget:* $1.5 Million-$3 Million
Staff Member(s): 14
Membership: 1-99
Chief Officer(s):
Judy White, Office Manager
Nick Nagy, President
nagy@certiwood.com

Canadian Podiatric Medical Association (CPMA) / Association médicale podiatrique canadienne
#2063, 61 Broadway Blvd., Sherwood Park AB T8H 2C1
Toll-Free: 888-220-3338
askus@podiatrycanada.org
www.podiatrycanada.org
Overview: A small national organization founded in 1924
Mission: To effectively serve & provide guidance to its members & the podiatry profession in Canada; to serve the public; to provide the authoritative national voice for podiatrists in Canada; to recognize a particular responsibility to contribute to the development of national positions & standards related to the podiatric medical profession through education, research, materials & personnel
Member of: Federation of International Podiatrists
Affiliation(s): Canadian Podiatric Education Foundation (CPEF)
Finances: *Annual Operating Budget:* $50,000-$100,000; *Funding Sources:* Membership dues; endorsement
Staff Member(s): 1
Membership: 250+; *Fees:* $300; *Member Profile:* Doctor of Podiatric Medicine; *Committees:* Insurance; Publications; Seal of Approval/Acceptance; By-Laws; Foot Health Awareness Month; Economic Development
Activities: Educational; political; *Awareness Events:* National Foot Health Awareness Month, May; *Internships:* Yes; *Rents Mailing List:* Yes
Chief Officer(s):
Jayne Jeneroux, Executive Director
Publications:
- CPMA [Canadian Podiatric Medical Association] Newsletter

Type: Newsletter; *Frequency:* Semiannually; *Price:* Free with CPMA membership

Canadian Poetry Association (CPA) / Association canadienne de la poésie
c/o Pooka Press, PO Box 2648, Stn. Main, Vancouver BC V5B 3W8
poemata@live.com
www.canadianpoetryassociation.webs.com
twitter.com/cpalit
Overview: A small national organization founded in 1985
Mission: To promote the reading, writing, publishing, purchasing & preservation of poetry in Canada through the individual efforts of its members
Finances: *Funding Sources:* Membership dues; Grants
Membership: *Fees:* $30 regular; $20 students/seniors; $40 international; $50 association; $150 library/bookstore; *Member Profile:* Poets & those interested in poetry
Activities: Operates a LISTSERV: cpa@sympatico.ca
Awards:
- Shaunt Basmajian Chapbook Award

Publications:
- Poemata

Type: Magazine; *Accepts Advertising;* *Editor:* Donna Allard; *ISSN:* 1203-6595
Profile: National forum for ideas, with markets, reviews, & CPA announcements, chapter reports & happenings

Atlantic Canada
#4-212, 331 Elmwood Dr., Moncton NB E1A 1X6

Canadian Police Association (CPA) / Association canadienne des policiers (ACP)
#100, 141 Catherine St., Ottawa ON K2P 1C3
Tel: 613-231-4168; *Fax:* 613-231-3254
cpa-acp@cpa-acp.ca
www.cpa-acp.ca
Overview: A large national organization founded in 1953
Mission: To promote the interests of police personnel & the public they serve; To provide a collective support network for Member Associations; To advocate for adequate & equitable resources for policing; To identify key national issues impacting Member Associations, and facilitate their resolution; To liaise with the international policing community on issues affecting Canadian police personnel
Staff Member(s): 4
Membership: 60,000 personnel + 160 police services; *Member Profile:* Rank & file police officers
Activities: *Library:* Canadian Police Association Library
Chief Officer(s):
Tom Stamatakis, President
Denis Côté, Vice-President
Meetings/Conferences:
- 2018 Biennial Canadian Police Association Conference, 2018

Scope: National

Canadian Polish Congress (CPC) / Congrès canadien polonais
3055 Lake Shore Blvd. West, Toronto ON M8V 1K6
Tel: 416-532-2876; *Fax:* 416-532-5730
kongres@kpk.org
www.kpk.org
Overview: A large national charitable organization founded in 1944
Mission: To represent Polish-Canadians & to defend their interests; To coordinate & support the work of Polish-Canadian organizations in Canada; To foster Polish culture & assist Polish immigrants; To inform Canadians about Poland's contribution to culture & to maintain liaisons with Poland
Member of: Canadian Ethnocultural Council
Affiliation(s): Polonia of the Free World; Canadian Polish Research Institute; Adam Mickiewicz Foundation; Polish Combattants Association; Polish National Union
Finances: *Funding Sources:* Membership fees
Membership: *Committees:* Checks & Balances; Dispute Resolution; Seniors
Activities: *Library:* Not open to public
Chief Officer(s):
Wladyslaw Lizon, President
president@kpk.org
Anna Mazurkiewicz, Secretary-General
cpcgeneralsecretary@kpk.org
Elizabeth Morgan, Treasurer
emorgan@kpk.org

Alberta Branch
PO Box 1912, Stn. Main, Edmonton AB T5J 2P3
Tel: 780-425-2172; *Fax:* 780-432-6295
www.kpkalberta.com
Chief Officer(s):
Jaroslaw Nowinka, President
j.nowinka@shaw.ca

British Columbia Branch
1134 Kingsway, Vancouver BC V5V 3C8
Tel: 604-725-8712
kpkbritishcolumbia@gmail.com
www.kpkbritishcolumbia.com
www.facebook.com/KPKBritishColumbia
Chief Officer(s):
Beata Grodkowska, President

Hamilton Branch
374 Aurora Cres., Burlington ON L7N 2A9
Tel: 905-637-9333
Chief Officer(s):
Stanislaw Warda, President
Stanley.warda097@sympatico.ca

Kitchener Branch
601 Wellington St. North, Kitchener ON N2H 5J6
Tel: 519-623-3460
www.kpk-kitchener.org
Chief Officer(s):
Urszula Walkowska, President
uw@appaut.com

Manitoba Branch
768 Mountain Ave., Winnipeg MB R2W 1L7
Tel: 204-338-2888; *Fax:* 204-589-7878
kongres@shaw.ca
www.kpkmanitoba.ca
Chief Officer(s):
Grazyna Galezowska, President

Mississauga Branch
Mississauga ON
mississauga.kpk@gmail.com
en.kpk-mississauga.org
www.youtube.com/user/kpkmississauga
Chief Officer(s):
Anna Mazurkiewicz, President, 905-206-0003
kpkmississauga@rogers.com

Niagara Branch
36 October Dr., St Catharines ON L2N 6J6
Tel: 905-934-3175
Chief Officer(s):
Jacek Kaminski, President

Oshawa Branch
418 Grange Ct., Oshawa ON L1G 7J1
Tel: 905-576-6726
kpkoshawa@gmail.com
Chief Officer(s):
Elizabeth Szczepanski, President

Ottawa Branch
Ottawa ON
www.kpk-ottawa.org
Chief Officer(s):
Piotr Nawrot, President
pnawrot@rogers.com

Québec Branch
63, rue Prince Arthur est, Montréal QC H2X 1B4
Tel: 514-285-4880; *Fax:* 514-624-0416
Chief Officer(s):
Edward Sliz, President
esliz@rogers.com

Sudbury Branch
291 Albinson St., Sudbury ON P3C 3W2
Tel: 705-673-1931
ahmrozewski@sympatico.ca
Chief Officer(s):
Andrzej H. Mrozewski, President
ahmrozewski@sympatico.ca

Thunder Bay Branch
90 Banning St., Thunder Bay ON P7B 3H7
Tel: 807-344-5530
Chief Officer(s):
Henryk Bystrzycki, President
bbystrzycki@tbaytel.net

Toronto Branch
206 Beverley St., Toronto ON M5T 1Z3
Tel: 416-971-9848; *Fax:* 416-971-9848
president@kpk-toronto.org
www.kpk-toronto.org
Chief Officer(s):
Juliusz Kirejczyk, President

Windsor Branch
2050 Willistead Cres., Windsor ON N8Y 1K5

Tel: 519-256-4172
Chief Officer(s):
Jerzy Barycki, President

Canadian Polish Foundation / Fondation canadienne-polonaise
2453 Lake Shore Blvd. West, Toronto ON M8V 1C5
Tel: 647-762-3876
cdnpolishfdn@yahoo.ca
www.facebook.com/270776979652952
Overview: A small local organization founded in 1998

Canadian Polish Society
43 Facer St., St Catharines ON L2M 5H4
Tel: 905-937-1413
office@canadianpolishsociety.com
www.canadianpolishsociety.com
www.facebook.com/102029093175788
Previous Name: Polish Society in Canada
Overview: A small local organization founded in 1928
Mission: To unite Canadians of Polish origin & Polish people in Canada; To represent Poles in all levels of government & political life; To create & to foster strong cultural, economic & social Polish community; To engage Polish business community in economic cooperation & exchange of information; To promote & preserve Polish cultural heritage & historical traditions; To organize cultural events & to assist & help Poles in need
Membership: 200+; *Member Profile:* Polish descent

Canadian Political Science Association (CPSA) / Association canadienne de science politique (ACSP)
#204, 260 Dalhousie St., Ottawa ON K1N 7E4
Tel: 613-562-1202; *Fax:* 613-241-0019
cpsa-acsp@cpsa-acsp.ca
www.cpsa-acsp.ca
Overview: A medium-sized national charitable organization founded in 1913
Mission: To encourage & develop political science & its relationship with other disciplines
Member of: Canadian Federation for the Humanities & Social Sciences; International Political Science Association; United Nations Educational, Scientific and Cultural Organization
Finances: *Annual Operating Budget:* $1.5 Million-$3 Million; *Funding Sources:* Membership fees; Institutional subscriptions to the Canadian Journal of Political Science; SSHRC grants; Provincial & federal funding
Staff Member(s): 2
Membership: 1,150 individuals; *Fees:* Schedule available; *Member Profile:* Individuals interested in CPSA objectives, including representatives of political science departments, students, politicians, public servants, & persons from the private sector
Activities: Offering grants, scholarships, & fellowships; Sponsoring the Parliamentary Internship Program; *Internships:* Yes; *Rents Mailing List:* Yes
Chief Officer(s):
Silvina Danesi, Executive Director
silvina_danesi@cpsa-acsp.ca
Awards:
• Conference Poster Prize
• Prize in Comparative Politics
• Prix francophone
• C.B. Macpherson Prize
• John McMenemy Prize
• Donald Smiley Prize
• Jill Vickers Prize
• Prize in International Relations
• Vincent Lemieux Prize
• Prize for Teaching Excellence
Meetings/Conferences:
• Canadian Political Science Association 2018 Annual Conference (within the Congress of the Humanities & Social Sciences), May, 2018, University of Regina, Regina, SK
Scope: National
Description: A conference including the association's business & committee meetings, special presentations, workshops, & exhibits
Contact Information: Administrator: Michelle Hopkins, E-mail: cpsa-acsp@cpsa-acsp.ca
• Canadian Political Science Association 2019 Annual Conference (within the Congress of the Humanities & Social Sciences), June, 2019, University of British Columbia, Vancouver, BC
Scope: National
Description: A conference including the association's business & committee meetings, special presentations, workshops, & exhibits
Contact Information: Administrator: Michelle Hopkins, E-mail: cpsa-acsp@cpsa-acsp.ca
Publications:
• Canadian Journal of Political Science [a publication of the Canadian Political Science Association]
Type: Journal; *Frequency:* q.; *Editor:* Graham White et al.; *ISSN:* 0008-4239; *Price:* Free formembers of the Canadian Political Science Association
Profile: A journal of articles & book reviews sent to 3,000 subscribers

Canadian Political Science Students' Association (CPSSA) / Association des Étudiants de Science Politique du Canada (AESPC)
University of Calgary, Dept. of Political Science, 2500 Universtiy Dr. NW, Calgary AB T2N 1N4
Tel: 613-562-1202; *Fax:* 613-241-0019
ca.linkedin.com/company/canadian-political-science-students%27-association
www.facebook.com/CPSSAAESPC
twitter.com/cpssa_aespc
instagram.com/cpssa_aespc
Overview: A medium-sized national organization founded in 1997
Mission: A national student organization representing students and student groups studying Political Science across the country.
Membership: *Committees:* Journal; Conference; Academic

Canadian Polo Association (CPA)
#100, 180 Renfrew Dr., Markham ON L3R 9Z2
Tel: 647-208-7656; *Fax:* 905-477-6897
info@polocanada.ca
www.polocanada.ca
www.facebook.com/polocanada
Also Known As: Polo Canada
Overview: A small national charitable organization founded in 1985
Mission: To develop & maintain standards of excellence for the sport of polo in Canada; To promote polo across the nation
Finances: *Funding Sources:* Membership fees; Donations
Membership: 12 clubs; *Fees:* $30 juniors; $60 adults; *Member Profile:* Individual junior & adult polo players, & clubs from across Canada
Activities: Supporting polo players & clubs across Canada; Providing resources; Raising awareness of polo & attracting new players to the game; Supporting training programs, educational workshops, & clinics for coaches, umpires, & players; Encouraging international competition; Offering junior polo programs; Facilitating communication between member clubs

Canadian Pony Club (CPC)
PO Box 127, Baldur MB R0K 0B0
Fax: 204-535-2289
Toll-Free: 888-286-7669
info@canadianponyclub.org
www.canadianponyclub.org
www.facebook.com/CanadianPonyClub
Overview: A medium-sized national organization founded in 1934
Mission: To encourage & instruct young people to ride & care for their horses, while promoting loyalty, character, & sportsmanship
Member of: Equine Canada
Affiliation(s): Ontario Equestrian Federation
Finances: *Funding Sources:* Fees
Membership: 3,500, in 150 branches; *Member Profile:* Young people between the ages of 6-21 who wish to learn all about horses; *Committees:* Awards & Recognition; Equine Canada; Finance; Governance; Horse Masters Program; Human Resources; Information Technology; Management; Marketing & Fundraising; National Communications; National Dressage; National Education; National Prince Philip Games; National Quiz; National Rally; National Show Jumping; National Testing; National Tetrathlon; Ombudsman; Risk Management; Strategic Planning
Activities: Instruction in dressage, show jumping, Tetrathlon
Chief Officer(s):
Danielle Valiquette, Executive Director
executivedirector@canadianponyclub.org
Val Crowe, Administrator
Awards:
• CPC Award of Excellence
Eligibility: CPC members attending or registered at a university or college; *Amount:* 2 at $1,000 + 1 at $500
• Examiners Emeritus
Eligibility: Retired National Examiners who have displayed exemplary service to the CPC
• National Chairs Award
Eligibility: Individuals who have displayed exemplary service to the CPC
Publications:
• Branch Rules & Regulations Documents [a publication of the Canadian Pony Club]
Type: Guide
• Educational Badge Program Manual [a publication of the Canadian Pony Club]
Type: Guide
• National Education Handbook [a publication of the Canadian Pony Club]
Type: Guide
• Study Guides Series [a publication of the Canadian Pony Club]
Type: Guide

Alberta Central
PO Box 71, Tees AB T0C 2N0
Tel: 403-747-3013
canadianponyclub.org/AlbertaCentral
Affiliation(s): Alberta Equestrian Federation
Chief Officer(s):
Liana Shaw, Regional Chair
lianabraun@hotmail.com

Alberta North
c/o 53315 Range Rd. 222, Ardrossan AB T8E 2M5
albertanorthregion@outlook.com
albertanorthregion.wix.com/abnorth
Chief Officer(s):
Carol Judd, Regional Chair

Alberta South
Lethbridge AB
canadianponyclub.org/AlbertaSouth
Chief Officer(s):
Danielle Williams, Regional Chair

British Columbia Interior North
bcin.webs.com
Chief Officer(s):
Sandy Agatiello, Regional Chair
sandyagatiello@yahoo.ca

British Columbia Islands
c/o 2040 Saddle Dr., Nanoose Bay BC V9L 5Z2
Tel: 250-468-7247
canadianponyclub.org/BCIS/
Chief Officer(s):
Tanya Richards, Regional Chair
tjrd@shaw.ca

British Columbia Lower Mainland
canadianponyclub.org/BCLM/wp
Chief Officer(s):
Melanie Rupp, Regional Chair
bclmchair@gmail.com

Central Ontario
Newmarket ON
centralontarioregion@ponyclub.ca
canadianponyclub.org/CentralOntario/
Chief Officer(s):
Laurie Blake, Regional Chair, 905-830-0552
ljblake@rogers.com

Manitoba
MB
canadianponyclub.org/Manitoba
Chief Officer(s):
Deborah Shepherd, Regional Chair
deb_shep1@yahoo.co.uk

New Brunswick/PEI
www.nb-peiponyclub.com
Chief Officer(s):
Lindsay Fleming, Regional Chair

Nova Scotia
Kentville NS
canadianponyclub.org/NS/
Chief Officer(s):
Valerie McDermott, Regional Chair
rustyanchorfarm@eastlink.ca

St. Lawrence/Ottawa Valley
canadianponyclub.org/SLOV/
Chief Officer(s):
Liz Tucker, Regional Chair
tuck9@can.rogers.com

Canadian Associations / Canadian Pony Society

Saskatchewan
c/o Pelmac Stables, PO Box 66, RR7, Site 707, Saskatoon SK S7K 1N2
Tel: 306-933-4615; *Fax:* 306-933-3189
www.saskponyclub.org
Chief Officer(s):
Nancy Hibbert, Regional Chair
Nanhib54@gmail.com
Western Ontario
ON
canadianponyclub.org/WesternOntario
Chief Officer(s):
Sherry Jackson, Regional Chair
wor@canadianponyclub.org

Canadian Pony Society
746629 Township Rd. 4, #RR2, Princeton ON N0J 1V0
Tel: 519-458-8231
www.clrc.ca/pony.shtml
Overview: A small national organization founded in 1901
Mission: To encourage, develop & regulate the breeding of ponies in Canada by establishing standards of breeding & by carrying out a system of registration under the Canadian Livestock Records Corporation
Affiliation(s): Canadian Livestock Records
Finances: *Annual Operating Budget:* Less than $50,000
3 volunteer(s)
Membership: 100-499; *Fees:* $25
Activities: Members show at local fairs, Royal Winter Fair etc.
Chief Officer(s):
Sandy Gunby, Secretary
Chris Bacher, Treasurer
Art Alderman, President

Canadian Poolplayers Association (CPA)
1000 Lake Saint Louis Blvd., Lake Saint Louis MO 63367 USA
Tel: 636-625-8611; *Fax:* 636-625-2975
playpool@wightman.ca
www.poolplayers.ca
www.facebook.com/34672444365
www.youtube.com/apaleagues
Also Known As: Canadian Pool League
Overview: A medium-sized national organization founded in 1989
Mission: Sanctions an international network of amateur pool leagues
Member of: Canadian Franchise Association
Affiliation(s): American Pool Players Association
Finances: *Funding Sources:* Membership dues
Staff Member(s): 4
Membership: 250,000; *Fees:* $25; *Member Profile:* Men & women over 19
Activities: Organized amateur pool league
Chief Officer(s):
Larry Hubbart, Contact
Lindsay Dobson, Contact

Canadian Population Society
520-17 Aberdeen St., Ottawa ON K1S 3J3
admin@canpopsoc.ca
www.canpopsoc.ca
Overview: A small national organization
Mission: To work toward the improvement of knowledge and understanding about the quantitative and qualitative characteristics of human population
Membership: *Fees:* $40 student; $75 regular; $350 lifetime; *Committees:* Awards; Canadian Federation of Humanities and Social Sciences; Federation of Canadian Demographers; International; Journal; National; Program; Student Paper Competition
Chief Officer(s):
Eric Fong, President
fong@chass.utoronto.ca
Feng Hou, Sec.-Treas.
feng.hou@statcan.ca
Awards:
• Canadian Population Society Award
This award honors a Canadian scholar every two years who has shown outstanding commitment to the profession of demography and whose cumulative work has contributed in important ways to the advancement of the discipline in Canada, through publications, teaching and/or service.
Meetings/Conferences:
• 2018 Canadian Population Society Annual Meeting, May, 2018, University of Regina, Regina, SK
Scope: National

Publications:
• Canadian Studies in Population
Type: Journal; *Editor:* Frank Trovato; *ISSN:* 03801 489; *Price:* Free with CPS membership
Profile: Joint demographic publication of the Canadian Population Society & the University of Alberta
• CPS [Canadian Population Society] Newsletter
Type: Newsletter; *Frequency:* Semiannually; *Editor:* Laurie Goldmann
Profile: For CPS members

Canadian Pork Council (CPC) / Conseil canadien du porc (CCP)
#900, 200 Laurier Ave. West, Ottawa ON K1P 5Z9
Tel: 613-236-9239; *Fax:* 613-236-6658
info@cpc-ccp.com
www.cpc-ccp.com
Previous Name: Canadian Swine Council
Overview: A medium-sized national organization founded in 1966
Mission: To provide a leadership role in a concerted effort involving all levels of industry & government toward a common understanding & action plan for achieving a dynamic & prosperous pork industry in Canada.
Member of: Canadian Federation of Agriculture
Membership: 9 provincial; *Member Profile:* Hog producer marketing organizations
Activities: International trade food safety; quality assurance; environmental programs; *Library:* Open to public by appointment
Chief Officer(s):
Jean-Guy Vincent, Chair

Canadian Porphyria Foundation Inc. (CPF) / La Fondation canadienne de la porphyrie
PO Box 1206, Neepawa MB R0J 1H0
Tel: 204-476-2800; *Fax:* 204-476-2800
Toll-Free: 866-476-2801
porphyria@cpf-inc.ca
www.cpf-inc.ca
Overview: A small national charitable organization founded in 1988
Mission: Dedicated to improving the quality of life for Canadians affected by the porphyrias through programs of awareness, education, service, advocacy & research; committed to promoting public & medical professional awareness; assembling, printing & distributing up-to-date educational information to physicians, health care personnel, diagnosed patients & others affected by porphyria; offering support programs to affected individuals & their families; promoting the family social welfare of affected individuals; educating & informing physicians & others in health care about the porphyrias so that early diagnosis & proper treatment will be realized; promoting & providing financial assistance for research; committed to encouraging, supporting & serving physicians & researchers in their efforts to find more effective treatments & to increasing physician, patient & community awareness & thereby cultivating support for research
Finances: *Annual Operating Budget:* $50,000-$100,000; *Funding Sources:* Fund-raising; Donations; Bequeaths; In memoriams; Philanthropic community
Staff Member(s): 3; 200 volunteer(s)
Membership: 2,500; *Member Profile:* People diagnosed with Porphyria & their families; medical personnel; interested persons, friends; *Committees:* Finance; Publicity; Newsletter; Member Services
Activities: Support groups, patient advocacy; confidential database, patient registry; educational information; list of safe/unsafe drugs; research fund development; fund-raising; *Awareness Events:* National Porphyria Day, June 1; *Speaker Service:* Yes
Chief Officer(s):
Lois J. Aitken, President/Executive Director
Publications:
• Canadian Porphyria Foundation National Newsletter
Type: Newsletter; *Frequency:* Semiannually
Profile: General information about porphyria

Canadian Port & Harbour Association *See* Association of Canadian Port Authorities

Canadian Portland Cement Association *See* Cement Association of Canada

Canadian Positive Psychology Association (CAPPA)
#703, 1 Eglinton Ave. East, Toronto ON M4P 3A1
Tel: 416-481-8930
info@positivepsychologycanada.com
www.positivepsychologycanada.com

Overview: A small national organization
Mission: A representative association for scholars and academics who are engaged in rigorous academic research in the field of positive psychology.
Membership: *Fees:* $90 regualr; $30 student; *Member Profile:* Researchers, clinicians, educators, students, business owners, coaches, consultants, medical experts.
Chief Officer(s):
Louisa Jewell, President
Meetings/Conferences:
• 4th Canadian Conference on Positive Psychology, May, 2018, University of Toronto, Toronto, ON
Scope: National

Canadian Postmasters & Assistants Association (CPAA) / Association canadienne des maîtres de poste et adjoints (ACMPA)
281 Queen Mary St., Ottawa ON K1K 1X1
Tel: 613-745-2095; *Fax:* 613-745-5559
mail@cpaa-acmpa.ca
cpaa-acmpa.ca
Overview: A medium-sized national organization founded in 1902
Affiliation(s): Canadian Labour Congress
Staff Member(s): 9
Membership: 6,364
Chief Officer(s):
Leslie A. Schous, National President
leslieschous@cpaa-acmpa.ca
Pierre Charbonneau, National Vice-President
pierrecharbonneau@cpaa-acmpa.ca
Shirley L. Dressler, National Vice President
shirleydressler@cpaa-acmpa.ca
Daniel L. Maheux, National Secretary-Treasurer
danielmaheux@cpaa-acmpa.ca
Publications:
• Communiqué
Type: Newsletter; *Frequency:* Semiannually; *Editor:* Karen E. MacDonald

Canadian Post-MD Education Registry (CAPER) / Système informatisé sur les stagiaires post-MD en formation clinique
#800, 265 Carling Ave., Ottawa ON K1S 2E1
Tel: 613-730-1204; *Fax:* 613-730-1196
caper@afmc.ca
www.caper.ca
twitter.com/CAPERCanada
Overview: A medium-sized national charitable organization founded in 1986
Mission: To provide accurate & timely data pertaining to Post-MD training & physician resources in Canada to assist medical schools, governments & other work longitudinal research pertaining to physicians training & supply
Affiliation(s): Association of Faculties of Medicine of Canada
Finances: *Funding Sources:* Medical organizations; federal, provincial & territorial governments
Chief Officer(s):
Lynda Buske, Interim Director
lbuske@caper.ca
Publications:
• CAPER [Canadian Post-MD Education Registry] Annual Census
Type: Report; *Frequency:* Annually; *ISSN:* 1712-9184
Profile: Annual census of post-M.D. trainees
• CAPER [Canadian Post-MD Education Registry] Provincial Reports
Type: Report; *Frequency:* Annually

Canadian Poultry & Egg Processors Council (CPEPC)
#400, 1545 Carling Ave., Ottawa ON K1Z 8P9
Tel: 613-724-6605; *Fax:* 613-724-4577
www.cpepc.ca
Overview: A medium-sized national organization
Mission: To foster a climate of continuous improvement within the Canadian feather industry recognizing the need for increasing competitiveness
Membership: *Member Profile:* Processors, packagers and distributors of chicken and turkey meat, graders and further processors of eggs and hatcheries in Canada
Chief Officer(s):
Robin Horel, President / CEO
robinhorel@cpepc.ca
Meetings/Conferences:
• Canadian Poultry and Egg Processors Council 2018

Convention, June, 2018, Montréal, QC
Scope: National

Canadian Power & Sail Squadrons (Canadian Headquarters) (CPS) / Escadrilles canadiennes de plaisance (ECP)
26 Golden Gate Ct., Toronto ON M1P 3A5
Tel: 416-293-2438; *Fax:* 416-293-2445
Toll-Free: 888-277-2628
hqg@cps-ecp.ca
www.cps-ecp.ca
www.facebook.com/CPSboat
twitter.com/cpsboat
www.youtube.com/CPSECP
Overview: A medium-sized national charitable organization founded in 1938
Mission: To increase awareness & knowledge of safe boating by educating & training members & the general public, by fostering fellowship among members, & establishing partnerships & alliances with organizations & agencies interested in boating
Member of: Canadian Safe Boating Council
Finances: *Annual Operating Budget:* $1.5 Million-$3 Million
Staff Member(s): 13; 5000 volunteer(s)
Membership: 34,000; *Fees:* $30; *Member Profile:* Must pass specified examination & pay dues on annual basis; *Committees:* Public Relations; Training Department
Activities: *Library:* Not open to public
Chief Officer(s):
Walter Kowalchuk, Executive Director, 416-293-2438 Ext. 0160
wkowalchuk@cps-ecp.ca
John Gullick, Manager, Government & Special Programs, 416-293-2438 Ext. 0155
jgullick@cps-ecp.ca
Meetings/Conferences:
• Canadian Power and Sail Squadrons National Conference 2018, October, 2018, Ottawa, ON
Scope: National

Canadian Powerlifting Federation *See* Canadian Powerlifting Union

Canadian Powerlifting Federation (CPF)
www.canadianpowerliftingfederation.com
www.facebook.com/Canadian-Powerlifting-Federation-CPF-117359724995464
Previous Name: Canadian Powerlifting Organization
Overview: A small national organization
Mission: Promoting powerlifting in Canada
Member of: World Powerlifting Congress; World Powerlifting Organization
Membership: *Member Profile:* Individuals & organizations, from across Canada, who are interested in powerlifting
Activities: Providing results from CPF meets & its affiliates

Canadian Powerlifting Organization *See* Canadian Powerlifting Federation

Canadian Powerlifting Union (CPU)
c/o Mike Armstrong, 4709 Fordham Cres. SE, Calgary AB T2A 2A5
Tel: 403-402-4142
www.powerlifting.ca
www.facebook.com/CDNpowerliftingunion
Previous Name: Canadian Powerlifting Federation
Overview: A medium-sized national organization founded in 1982
Mission: To oversee & regulate all IPF style powerlifting in Canada
Affiliation(s): International Powerlifting Federation
Membership: *Committees:* Anti-Doping; Coaching; Team Selection; Funding; ParaPowerlifting
Chief Officer(s):
Mark Giffin, President
mark@powerlifting.ca
Ryan Fowler, Chair, Coaching
rfowler@powerlifting.ca
Mike Armstrong, Secretary
mike@powerlifting.ca
Barry Antoniow, Treasurer
bantoniow@powerlifting.ca

Canadian Prader-Willi Syndrome Association *See* Foundation for Prader-Willi Research in Canada

Canadian Precast / Prestressed Concrete Institute (CPCI) / Institut canadien du béton préfabriqué et précontraint
PO Box 24058, Stn. Hazeldean, Ottawa ON K2M 2C3
Tel: 613-232-2619; *Fax:* 613-232-5139
Toll-Free: 877-937-2724
helpdesk@cpci.ca
www.cpci.ca
www.facebook.com/CPCIPrecast
Overview: A medium-sized national organization founded in 1961
Mission: To promote & advance the interests & general welfare of the structural precast/prestressed concrete industry, the architectural precast concrete industry & the post-tensioned concrete industry in Canada
Affiliation(s): Athena Institute; British Precast Concrete Federation; Cement Association of Canada; Construction Resource Initiatives Council; National Precast Concrete Association; Post-Tensioning Institute; Precast/Prestressed Concrete Institute; Royal Architectural Institute of Canada
Finances: *Annual Operating Budget:* $500,000-$1.5 Million
Staff Member(s): 4
Membership: 33 institutional; *Member Profile:* Manufacturers, suppliers, students, architects, engineers, or technicians in the precast/prestressed concrete industry
Activities: Developing marketing programs; Collecting & providing resources & information; Conducting research for the improvement of precast & prestressed concrete design & manufacturing; *Awareness Events:* National Precast Day, September; *Library:* Open to public
Chief Officer(s):
Rob Burak, President
robert.burak@cpci.ca
Brian Hall, Managing Director
brianhall@cpci.ca
Publications:
• CPCI [Canadian Precast / Prestressed Concrete Institute] Imagineering
Type: Magazine; *Accepts Advertising;* *Editor:* Brian J. Hall
Profile: Feature articles, industry updates, member directory, "tech talk", marketing information, president's messages

The Canadian Press (CP) / La presse canadienne
36 King St. East, Toronto ON M5C 2L9
Tel: 416-364-0321; *Fax:* 416-364-0207
Other Communication: archives@cpimages.com
editorial@thecanadianpress.com
www.thecanadianpress.com
www.linkedin.com/company/the-canadian-press
www.facebook.com/thecanadianpress
twitter.com/CdnPress
Overview: A large national organization founded in 1917
Mission: To operate as a national news cooperative, owned & financed by Canada's daily newspapers
Membership: 100 daily newspapers
Activities: Providing news & information services to more than 600 radio & television stations, cable TV systems, internet sites, & commercial clients, delivered by satellite & web server; Offering a Picture Service that delivers nearly 1,000 photos a week; *Library*
Chief Officer(s):
Stephen Meurice, Editor-in-Chief
Rose Kingdon, Director, Broadcast News, 416-364-0321
Graeme Roy, Director, News Photography, 416-507-2169
Andrea Baillie, Managing Editor, News Desks/Beats
Awards:
• The Canadian Press National Newspaper Awards
Honours excellence in the following categories: Breaking News, Best Sports Photo, & Best News Feature Photo
• George Gross Award
• Tom Hanson Photojournalism Award
• National Picture of the Year Awards
Calgary Bureau
#310, 131 - 9th Ave. SW, Calgary AB T2P 1K1
Tel: 403-233-7004; *Fax:* 403-262-7520
Edmonton Bureau
#504, 10109 - 106 St. NW, Edmonton AB T5J 3L7
Tel: 780-428-6107; *Fax:* 780-428-0663
www.thecanadianpress.com
Fredericton Bureau
Press Gallery, PO Box 6000, 96 St. John St., Fredericton NB E3B 5H1
Tel: 506-457-0746; *Fax:* 506-457-9708
Halifax Bureau
#701, 1888 Brunswick St., Halifax NS B3J 2L4
Tel: 902-422-8496; *Fax:* 902-425-2675
Chief Officer(s):
Rob Roberts, Chief, 902-422-1444
Atlantic Bureau
Montréal Bureau
#100, 215, rue St-Jacques, Montréal QC H2Y 1M6
Tél: 514-849-3212; *Téléc:* 514-282-6915
Ottawa Bureau
PO Box 595, Stn. B, Ottawa ON K1P 5P7
Tel: 613-236-4122; *Fax:* 613-238-4452
Chief Officer(s):
Heather Scoffield, Chief
Ottawa Bureau
Québec Bureau
#2.43, 1050, des Parlementaires, Québec QC G1R 5J1
Tel: 418-646-5377; *Fax:* 418-523-9686
Chief Officer(s):
Donald McKenzie, Chef de bureau
Regina Bureau
#335, Press Gallery, Legislative Bldg., 2405 Legislative Dr., Regina SK S4S 0B3
Tel: 306-585-1024; *Fax:* 306-585-1027
St. John's Bureau
The Fortis Bldg., PO Box 5951, #901, 139 Water St., St. John's NL A1C 5X4
Tel: 709-576-0687; *Fax:* 709-576-0049
Vancouver Bureau
#250, 840 Howe St., Vancouver BC V6Z 2L2
Tel: 604-687-1662; *Fax:* 604-687-5040
Victoria Bureau
#350, Press Gallery, Legislative Building, Victoria BC V8V 1X4
Tel: 250-384-4912; *Fax:* 250-356-9597
Washington Bureau
National Press Bldg., 1100 - 13th St. NW, Washington DC 20005 USA
Tel: 202-641-9734
Winnipeg Bureau
#101, 386 Broadway Ave., Winnipeg MB R3C 3R6
Tel: 204-988-1780; *Fax:* 204-942-4788

Canadian Printable Electronics Industry Association (CPEIA)
170 Cheyenne Way, Ottawa ON K2J 5S6
Tel: 613-795-8181
cpeia-acei.ca
www.linkedin.com/company/canadian-printable-electronics-industry-association-cpeia-
twitter.com/CPEIA_ACEI
Overview: A medium-sized national organization founded in 2014
Mission: The Canadian Printable Electronics Industry Association (CPEIA) connects key Canadian and international players in industry, academia and government to build a strong Canadian PE sector.
Membership: *Fees:* $50 students; $!00 indivuduals; $250 universities; $500 multinationals
Chief Officer(s):
Peter Kallai, Executive Director
pkallai@cpeia-acei.ca
Leo Valiquette, Director, Marketing and Communications

Canadian Printing Industries Association (CPIA) / Association canadienne de l'imprimerie (ACI)
#407, 2-2026 Lanthier Dr., Orléans ON K4A 0N6
Tel: 613-236-7208; *Fax:* 613-232-1334
Toll-Free: 800-267-7280
info@cpia-aci.ca
www.cpia-aci.ca
www.linkedin.com/company/canadian-printing-industries-association
Previous Name: Graphic Arts Industries Association; Canadian Printing & Imaging Association
Overview: A medium-sized national organization founded in 1939
Mission: To advance the quality of management in the printing & allied trades; to offer services through a network of local & related organizations including representations to various sectors; to enhance the image & profile of the industry
Affiliation(s): Printing Industries of America
Finances: *Annual Operating Budget:* $250,000-$500,000; *Funding Sources:* Membership dues
Staff Member(s): 2; 25 volunteer(s)

Canadian Associations / Canadian Printing Industries Scholarship Trust Fund

Membership: 300; *Member Profile:* Owners/senior executives of companies in pre-press, press, bindery & allied industries; *Committees:* Government Affairs; Membership
Activities: *Library:* Not open to public
Chief Officer(s):
Brian Ellis, Executive Director
brianellis@cpia-aci.ca
Sandy Stephens, Chair
sstephens@informco.com

Canadian Printing Industries Scholarship Trust Fund
11 Alderbrook Pl., Bolton ON L7E 1V3
Tel: 416-524-1954
www.printscholarships.ca
Overview: A medium-sized national organization founded in 1971
Mission: To provide financial aid to young individuals enrolled in programs related to the printing industry
Finances: *Funding Sources:* Donations
Chief Officer(s):
Bob Kirk, Administrator

Canadian Printing Ink Manufacturers' Association (CPIMA)
ON
Tel: 905-665-9310; *Fax:* 647-439-1572
www.cpima.org
Overview: A medium-sized national organization founded in 1932
Mission: To exchange information that will be of benefit to members, the ink industry, & the printing industry
Affiliation(s): Society of British Ink Manufacturers; National Association of Printing Ink Manufacturers; Oil & Colour Chemists Organization of Ontario; International Paint & Printing Ink Council; Radtech International North America
Finances: *Funding Sources:* Membership dues
Staff Member(s): 1
Membership: 6; *Member Profile:* Canadian ink manufacturers
Chief Officer(s):
Steve Marshall, President
Michelle Connolly, Executive Director
mconnolly@cpima.org
Awards:
• The Jim Glynn Award
Publications:
• Canadian Printing Ink Manufacturers Association Technical Bulletins
Type: Newsletter; *Frequency:* Irregular
Profile: Topics include environmental issues, printing inks & food packaging, scrap ink, & UV inks health & saftey

Canadian Private Copying Collective (CPCC)
#403, 150 Eglinton Ave. East, Toronto ON M4P 1E8
Tel: 416-486-6832; *Fax:* 416-486-3064
Toll-Free: 800-892-7235
inquiries@cpcc.ca
www.cpcc.ca
Overview: A medium-sized national organization founded in 1999
Mission: To collect & distribute private copying royalties through a levy system on blank CDs, cassettes and minidiscs
Membership: *Member Profile:* Songwriters; recording artists; music publishers; record companies
Chief Officer(s):
Anna Bucci, Executive Director
abucci@cpcc.ca

Canadian Process Control Association (CPCA)
146 Delarmbro Dr, Erin ON N0B 1T0
Tel: 519-833-7414
cpca@cpca-assoc.com
www.cpca-assoc.com
www.linkedin.com/groups/3153710
twitter.com/cpca_assoc
Previous Name: Industrial Instrument Manufacturers Association
Overview: A medium-sized national organization
Mission: To promote the industry & its members to customers, academia & public bodies; To provide a forum for the exchange of technical, industry & regulatory information; To develop industry statistics; To encourage professional & ethical behaviour & quality standards among members
Member of: Membership dues
Finances: *Annual Operating Budget:* $50,000-$100,000
Staff Member(s): 1

Membership: 40 corporate; *Fees:* Schedule available; *Committees:* Academic; Communications; Industrial Relations; Statistics
Chief Officer(s):
Trish Torrance, Manager
Awards:
• CPCA Scholarship
; *Amount:* $2,500
Meetings/Conferences:
• Canadian Process Control Association 2018 Annual General Meeting, 2018
Scope: National
Publications:
• CPCA [Canadian Process Control Association] Newsletter
Type: Newsletter

Canadian Produce Marketing Association (CPMA) / Association canadienne de la distribution de fruits et légumes
162 Cleopatra Dr., Ottawa ON K2G 5X2
Tel: 613-226-4187; *Fax:* 613-226-2984
question@cpma.ca
www.cpma.ca
Previous Name: Canadian Fruit Wholesalers Association
Overview: A medium-sized national organization founded in 1924
Mission: To increase the market for fresh fruits & vegetables in Canada, by encouraging cooperation & information exchange in all segments, at the domestic & international level
Affiliation(s): Canadian Horticultural Council
Finances: *Annual Operating Budget:* $1.5 Million-$3 Million; *Funding Sources:* Membership dues; Convention
Staff Member(s): 13; 40 volunteer(s)
Membership: 680; *Fees:* $1,139.25 active; $924 associate; $598.50 branch; *Member Profile:* Retailers, wholesalers, brokers, shippers, food service operators, carriers of fresh fruits & vegetables; *Committees:* Grower/Shipper; Marketing; Member services; NA Trade Task Force; Retail/Foodservice Marketing
Activities: *Library:*
Chief Officer(s):
Jim DiMenna, Chair
Ron Lemaire, President
Meetings/Conferences:
• Canadian Produce Marketing Association 93rd Annual Convention & Trade Show, April, 2018, Vancouver Convention Centre, Vancouver, BC
Scope: International
Description: Featuring business sessions, a trade show, a keynote speaker, & awards
Contact Information: www.convention.cpma.ca

Canadian Professional Association for Transgender Health (CPATH)
#201, 1770 Fort St., Ottawa ON V8R 1J5
Tel: 250-592-6183; *Fax:* 250-592-6123
info@cpath.ca
www.cpath.ca
Overview: A medium-sized national organization founded in 2008
Mission: CPATH is an interdisciplinary professional organization which works to support the health, wellbeing, and dignity of trans and gender diverse people.
Membership: *Fees:* $25-$175
Chief Officer(s):
Devon MacFarlane, President
Meetings/Conferences:
• Canadian Professional Association for Transgender Health Conference, 2019
Scope: National

Canadian Professional Boxing Council (CPBC)
www.canadianboxingcouncil.com
Overview: A large national organization founded in 1976
Mission: To act as the sanctioning body for professional boxing in Canada; To aid in the development of professional boxing & crown new deserving champions
Membership: *Committees:* Ratings
Activities: Crowning new champions; Working with promoters; Adhering to the uniform rules of boxing in all aspects of competition
Chief Officer(s):
Don Collette, President

Canadian Professional DJ Association Inc. (CPDJA)
PO Box 300, 3007 Kingston Rd., Toronto ON M1M 1P1

Tel: 416-234-2299; *Fax:* 866-964-2299
Toll-Free: 866-964-2299
www.cpdja.org
Previous Name: Canadian Association of Mobile Entertainers & Operators (CAMEO)
Overview: A small national organization
Mission: To provide benefits & programs to DJ Industry professionals at competitive rates & to provide a forum for these professionals to network & share information, mutual concerns & techniques
Membership: *Fees:* $64.95 general; $259 allied; $325 primary; $375 professional; *Member Profile:* DJs/KJs; Industry suppliers & retailers
Activities: Training; networking; promotion; service; information; dj directory
Chief Officer(s):
Dennis Hampson, Contact
dhampson@cpdja.ca

Canadian Professional Golfers' Association *See* Professional Golfers' Association of Canada

Canadian Professional Sales Association (CPSA) / Association canadienne des professionnels de la vente
#400, 655 Bay St., Toronto ON M5G 2K4
Tel: 416-408-2685; *Fax:* 416-408-2684
Toll-Free: 888-267-2772
Other Communication: salessuccess@cpsa.com
customerservice@cpsa.com
www.cpsa.com
www.linkedin.com/groups?gid=1589497
www.facebook.com/CanadianProfessionalSalesAssociation
twitter.com/cpsa
Overview: A large national organization founded in 1874
Mission: To develop & serve sales professionals
Finances: *Funding Sources:* Membership fees
Membership: 20,000+; *Fees:* $129 annual membership fee + $25 one-time administration fee; *Member Profile:* Sales & marketing professionals from throughout Canada; Students enrolled in a marketing program
Activities: Providing sales training programs; Offering networking opportunities
Chief Officer(s):
Kim Hansen, President & Managing Partner
Ann Mackenzie, Executive Director & CEO
Michael Jackson, Senior Vice President, Operations
Ian Macdonald, Treasurer
Awards:
• CPSA Travel Awards
• C.H. Barnes Award
• Sales Excellence Award
Publications:
• Contact
Type: Magazine
• Sales Connexion
Type: Newsletter; *Frequency:* Biweekly; *Accepts Advertising*
Profile: Sales news, articles, tips, & job postings

Canadian Progress Charitable Foundation (CPCF)
c/o Canadian Progress Club, #143, 75 Lavinia St., New Glasgow NS B2H 1N5
Fax: 888-337-9826
Toll-Free: 877-944-4726
info@progressclub.ca
www.progressclub.ca
Overview: A small national charitable organization founded in 1968
Mission: To assist the Canadian Special Olympics
Member of: Canadian Progress Club
Chief Officer(s):
Michele Russell, President

Canadian Progress Club / Club progrès du Canada
#143, 75 Lavinia St., New Glasgow NS B2H 1N5
Fax: 888-337-9826
Toll-Free: 877-944-4726
info@progressclub.ca
www.progressclub.ca
twitter.com/ProgressClub
Overview: A medium-sized national charitable organization founded in 1922
Mission: To assist those in need as well as creating & preserving a spirit of friendship that is sincere; to advance the best interests of the community in which that club is located.
Membership: 600 individuals in 30 clubs; *Member Profile:* Open to both men & women wishing to assist within their community

Chief Officer(s):
Juanita Soutar, National President
juanitasoutar@hotmail.com
Jana Cleary, National Business Administrator
jana.cleary@progressclub.ca

Alberta North Zone
PO Box 183, St Albert AB T8N 1N3
Tel: 780-491-3501; *Fax:* 780-460-6697
www.progressclubab.ca
Chief Officer(s):
Carol Fergusson, Zone Director

Halifax Cornwallis
PO Box 31170, Halifax NS B3K 5Y1
Tel: 902-454-2971
club@cpchalifaxcornwallis.ca
www.cpchalifaxcornwallis.ca
www.linkedin.com/company/canadian-progress-club-halifax-cornwallis
www.facebook.com/CanadianProgressClubHalifaxCornwallis

Stampede City
125 Inglewood Grove SE, Calgary AB T2G 5R4
Tel: 403-282-1400; *Fax:* 403-338-1197
bullshooters@telus.net
www.stampedecityprogressclub.com

Canadian Propane Association (CPA) / Association canadienne du propane (ACP)
#300, 100 Gloucester St., Ottawa ON K2P 0A2
Tel: 613-683-2270
info@propane.ca
www.propane.ca
www.linkedin.com/groups/4355062
twitter.com/CanadaPropane
Merged from: Propane Gas Association of Canada Inc.; Ontario Propane Association
Overview: A medium-sized national licensing organization founded in 2011
Mission: To act as the national voice of the Canadian propane industry; To supports its members in the development of a safe, environmentally responsible Canadian propane industry
Affiliation(s): Propane Training Institute (PTI), a division of the CPA; Liquefied Petroleum Gas Emergency Response Corporation, a wholly owned subsidiary of the CPA
Finances: *Annual Operating Budget:* $1.5 Million-$3 Million; *Funding Sources:* Membership dues
Staff Member(s): 13
Membership: 400+; *Fees:* Schedule available; *Member Profile:* Producers; Wholesalers; Retailers; Transporters; Manufacturers of appliances, cylinders & equipment; Associates; *Committees:* Codes & Standards; Training & Development; Transportation
Activities: Providing industry related training & emergency response; Promoting the interests of the industry; Engaging in regulatory relations; *Internships:* Yes
Chief Officer(s):
Nathalie St-Pierre, President & CEO, 613-683-2270
Mélanie Levac, Vice President, Regulatory Affairs & Safety, 613-799-0935
Allan Murphy, Vice President, Government Relations, 613-683-2278
Awards:
• Lifetime Industry Achievement Award
• PTI Trainer-of-the-Year Award
• CPA Student Scholarship Award
Meetings/Conferences:
• 2018 Canadian Propane Association Leadership Summit, 2018
Scope: National
Description: The summit provides the opportunity for leaders in the propane industy to share ideas & knowledge among each other
Publications:
• CPA [Canadian Propane Association] Newsletter
Type: Newsletter; *Frequency:* Monthly
Profile: For members
• CPA [Canadian Propane Association] Bulletin
Type: Newsletter; *Frequency:* Bimonthly
Profile: For members

Calgary Office
#1100, 744 - 4th Ave. SW, Calgary AB T2P 3T4
Tel: 403-543-6518; *Fax:* 403-543-6508
Toll-Free: 877-784-4636
training@propane.ca
www.propane.ca
Chief Officer(s):
Marlene Petit, Training Administrator, Propane Training Institute, 403-543-6507

Canadian Property Tax Association, Inc. (CPTA) / Association canadienne de taxe foncière, inc
#816, 5863 Leslie St., Toronto ON M2H 1J8
Tel: 416-493-3276; *Fax:* 416-493-3276
cpta@on.aibn.com
www.cpta.org
Overview: A medium-sized national organization founded in 1967
Mission: To facilitate the exchange of information about industrial & commercial property tax issues throughout Canada
Membership: *Fees:* $415 first member; $205 second member; $100 retired member; *Member Profile:* Canadian corporate property companies, associations, tax officers, tax consultants, lawyers, & government officials
Activities: Studying legislation & making representations to government; Providing networking opportunities; *Library:* Canadian Property Tax Association Resource Library
Chief Officer(s):
Monica Keller, 403-237-1189, Fax: 403-231-2809
mkeller@talisman-energy.com
Viviane Marcotte, Managing Director, National Office
cpta@on.aibn.com
Publications:
• Canadian Property Tax Association, Inc. Membership Directory
Type: Directory; *Frequency:* Annually; *Price:* Free with membership
Profile: Listing of Canadian Property Tax Association members, member companies, chapter executives, directors, & assessment offices
• Canadian Property Tax Association, Inc. Communications Update
Type: Directory; *Frequency:* 6 pa; *Price:* Free with membership
Profile: An information resource for members including articles on tax & assessment issues, chapter information, & upcoming meetings
• Tax Practices Across Canada & Appeals Procedures Manual [a publication of the Canadian Property Tax Association, Inc.]
Type: Book; *Frequency:* Annually; *Price:* Free with membership
Profile: A manual outlining procedures & tax practices that are unique to each province

Canadian Psychiatric Association (CPA) / Association des psychiatres du Canada
#701, 141 Laurier Ave. West, Ottawa ON K1P 5J3
Tel: 613-234-2815; *Fax:* 613-234-9857
Toll-Free: 800-267-1555
cpa@cpa-apc.org
www.cpa-apc.org
Overview: A medium-sized national organization founded in 1951
Mission: To forge a strong, collective voice for Canadian psychiatrists & to promote an environment that fosters excellence in the provision of clinical care, education & research
Affiliation(s): Canadian Medical Association; World Psychiatric Association
Finances: *Annual Operating Budget:* $1.5 Million-$3 Million; *Funding Sources:* Membership; government; industry; subscriptions
Staff Member(s): 22
Membership: 4,000; *Fees:* $562 active; $57 member-in-training; $195 associate/affiliate; $285 international; *Member Profile:* Members in following psychiatric practice interests: admin. psychiatry, adolescent/young adult psychiatry, affective disorders, alcohol & substance abuse disorder, psychoanalysis/psychodynamic therapy, anxiety disorder, attention deficit disorder, behaviorial & cognitive therapy, biological psychiatry, child abuse, conjoint therapy, community psychiatry, consultation-liaison, chronic care, chronic pain, development/learning disabilities, dissociative disorders, eating disorders, education, emergency & crisis intervention, epidemiology, family therapy, forensic psychiatry, gender disorders, general psychiatry, geriatric psychiatry, hospital psychiatry, infant/child psychiatry, inpatient/outpatient, marital & divorce therapy, mental retardation, mood disorders, occupational therapy, etc.; *Committees:* Education; Economics; Professional Standards & Practice; Provinces; Scientific & Research
Activities: Public Information Office responds to media & public information requests, & refers inquiries to member psychiatrists with interests &/or expertise in a specific area; Service Bureau provides a variety of administrative, financial, publishing & communication services to affiliated psychiatric organizations on a contract basis; CPA sponsors lectures & conference speakers; online access to electronic mail system, online conferencing, CPA bylaws, position & policy papers, calendar of events & publications; *Awareness Events:* Mental Illness Awareness Week, 2nd week of Oct.
Chief Officer(s):
Glenn Brimacombe, Chief Executive Officer
gbrimacombe@cpa-apc.org
Brenda Fudge, Director, Finance & Administration
bfudge@cpa-apc,org
Katie Hardy, Director, Professional & Membership Services
khardy@cpa-apc.org
Jadranka Bacic, Associate Director, Communications
jbacic@cpa-apc.org
Meetings/Conferences:
• Canadian Psychiatric Association 68th Annual Conference / 68e Conférence annuelle de l'Association des psychiatres du Canada, September, 2018, The Westin Harbour Castle, Toronto, ON
Scope: National
Attendance: 1,100
Contact Information: E-mail: conference@cpa-apc.org

Canadian Psychoanalytic Society (CPS) / Société canadienne de psychanalyse (SCP)
7000, ch Côte-des-Neiges, Montréal QC H3S 2C1
Tel: 514-738-6105
www.psychoanalysis.ca
Overview: A small national licensing organization founded in 1967
Mission: To promote psychoanalysis treatments & professionals
Affiliation(s): International Psychoanalytical Association
Activities: Conferences; workshops & meetings; *Library:* CPS Library; Not open to public
Chief Officer(s):
Andrew Brook, President
Awards:
• Douglas Levin Essay Prize
; *Amount:* Awarded biennially to candidates of the CPS branches
• Miguel Prados Essay Prize
; *Amount:* Awarded biennially to members of the CPS
• Citation of Merit
; *Amount:* Recognizes distinguished & enduring contributions by members to the profession of psychoanalysis

CPS Western Canadian Branch
c/o Nancy Briones, 7755 Yukon St., Vancouver BC V5X 2Y4
info1@wbcps.org
www.wbcps.org
Chief Officer(s):
David Heilbrunn, President

Ottawa Psychoanalytic Society
c/o Somerset Psychologists, #201, 125 Somerset St. West, Ottawa ON K2P 0H7
Tel: 613-236-5608
contact@ottawaps.ca
ottawaps.ca
www.facebook.com/OttawaPsychoanalyticSociety
Chief Officer(s):
Arthur Leonoff, Director

Québec English Branch
7000, ch Côte-des-Neiges, Montréal QC H3S 2C1
Tel: 514-342-7444; *Fax:* 514-342-1062
cpsqeb@qc.aira.com
www.psychoanalysismontreal.com
Chief Officer(s):
Erica Robertson, President

Société psychanalytique de Montréal
7000, ch de la Côte-des-Neiges, Montréal QC H3S 2C1
Tél: 514-342-5208; *Téléc:* 514-342-9990
spsymtl@qc.aira.com
www.psychanalysemontreal.org
Chief Officer(s):
Louis Brunet, Président

Société psychanalytique de Québec
1180, rue Charles-Albanel, Sainte-Foy QC G1X 4T9
Tél: 418-877-8445; *Téléc:* 418-877-7056
info@spq-scp.ca
www.spq-scp.ca

South Western Ontario Psychoanalytic Society
London ON

Toronto Psychoanalytic Society (TIP)
#203, 40 St. Clair Ave. East, Toronto ON M4T 1M9
Tel: 416-922-7770; *Fax:* 416-922-9988
torontopsychoanalysis.com
www.facebook.com/TorontoPsychoanalyticSociety
Chief Officer(s):
Rukhsana Bukhari, President

Canadian Associations / Canadian Psychological Association (CPA) / Société canadienne de psychologie (SCP)

Canadian Psychological Association (CPA) / Société canadienne de psychologie (SCP)
#702, 141 Laurier Ave. West, Ottawa ON K1P 5J3
Tel: 613-237-2144; *Fax:* 613-237-1674
Toll-Free: 888-472-0657
cpa@cpa.ca
www.cpa.ca
www.facebook.com/146082642130174
twitter.com/CPA_SCP
www.youtube.com/user/CPAVideoChannel
Overview: A medium-sized national organization founded in 1939
Mission: To improve the health & welfare of Canadians by promoting psychological research, education, & practice
Affiliation(s): Canadian Register of Health Service Providers in Psychology; Council of Provincial Associations of Psychologists; International Union of Psychological Science; Canadian Federation for the Humanities & Social Sciences
Finances: *Annual Operating Budget:* Less than $50,000; *Funding Sources:* Membership dues; Government grants
Staff Member(s): 17
Membership: 7,000+; *Member Profile:* Individuals with a masters or doctoral degree in psychology; Students enrolled in psychology or a related field; Foreign affiliates & special affiliates; retired members & fellows; *Committees:* Admin, Finance & Audit; Canadian National Committee for the International Union of Psychological Science; Convention; Education & Training; Ethicsl Fellows & Awards; Governance; International Affairs; Membership; Past Presidents; Professional Affairs; Public Policy; Publications; Scientific Affairs; Sections
Activities: Promoting the development & dissemination of psychological knowledge; Providing services to members; Advocating for psychology; Providing continuing education opportunities; *Awareness Events:* Mental Illness Awareness Week; *Rents Mailing List:* Yes
Chief Officer(s):
Karen R. Cohen, Chief Executive Officer, 613-237-2144 Ext. 323
executiveoffice@cpa.ca
Lisa Votta-Bleeker, Deputy CEO & Director, Science Directorate, 613-237-2144 Ext. 323
executiveoffice@cpa.ca
Phil Bolger, Chief Financial Officer, 613-237-2144 Ext. 329
pbolger@cpa.ca
Rozen Alex, Director, Practice Directorate, 613-237-2144 Ext. 334
practicedirectorate@cpa.ca
Seán Kelly, Director, Events, Membership & Association Development, 613-237-2144 Ext. 335
skelly@cpa.ca
Meetings/Conferences:
• Canadian Psychological Association 2018 29th International Congress on Applied Psychology, June, 2018, Montréal, QC
Scope: National
Attendance: 1,800
Contact Information: URL: www.icap2018.com, E-mail: icap2018@cpa.ca
• Canadian Psychological Association 2019 National Convention & Annual Meeting, May, 2019, Halifax Marriott Harbourfront, Halifax, NS
Scope: National
Attendance: 1,800
Description: Co-convention with NACCJPC
• Canadian Psychological Association 2020 National Convention & Annual Meeting, June, 2020, Hyatt Regency Calgary, Calgary, AB
Scope: National
Attendance: 1,800
• Canadian Psychological Association 2021 National Convention & Annual Meeting, June, 2021, Westin Ottawa Hotel, Ottawa, ON
Scope: National
Attendance: 1,800
Publications:
• Canadian Journal of Behavioural Science / La revue canadienne des sciences du comportement
Type: Journal; *Frequency:* Quarterly; *Accepts Advertising*;
Editor: Todd Morrison; *Price:* $119 + GST/HST individuals in Canada; $289.00 + GST/HSTinstitutions in Canada
Profile: Original, empirical articles in the following areas of psychology:abnormal, behavioural, community, counselling, educational, environmental, developmental, health, industrial-organizational, clinical neuropsychological, personality, psychometrics, & social
• The Canadian Journal of Experimental Psychology
Type: Journal; *Frequency:* Quarterly; *Accepts Advertising*;
Editor: Doug J. Mewhort; *ISSN:* 0008-4255; *Price:* $119 + GST/HST individuals in Canada; $289.00 + GST/HST institutions in Canada
Profile: A journal of original research papers from the field of experimental psychology, published in partnershipwith the American Psychological Association
• Canadian Psychology
Type: Journal; *Frequency:* Quarterly; *Accepts Advertising*;
Editor: Martin Drapeau, Ph.D.; *Price:* $119 + GST/HST individuals in Canada; $289.00 + GST/HST institutions inCanada
Profile: Generalist articles in areas of theory, research, & practice
• CPA [Canadian Psychological Association] News
Type: Newsletter; *Price:* Free with membership in the Canadian Psycological Association
Profile: Current information for members
• Psynopsis: Canada's Psychology Magazine
Type: Magazine; *Frequency:* Quarterly; *Accepts Advertising*;
Editor: Karen R. Cohen; *ISSN:* 1187-11809
Profile: Articles of interest to scientists, educators, & practitioners in psychology

Canadian Public Accountability Board (CPAB) / Conseil canadien sur la reddition de comptes (CCRC)
#900, 150 York St., Toronto ON M5H 3S5
Tel: 416-913-8260; *Fax:* 416-850-9235
Toll-Free: 877-520-8260
info@cpab-ccrc.ca
www.cpab-ccrc.ca
www.linkedin.com/company/1858673
twitter.com/CPAB_CCRC
Overview: A medium-sized national organization
Mission: To provide effective audit regulation of public companies in Canada
Staff Member(s): 50
Membership: *Committees:* Audit
Chief Officer(s):
Brian A. Hunt, Chief Executive Officer
John Mastrella, Chief Financial Officer & Senior Director, Interprovincial Relations
M. Jane Williamson, Vice-President, Inspections
Adrienne Jackson, Director, Communications
adrienne.jackson@cpab-ccrc.ca

Canadian Public Health Association (CPHA) / Association canadienne de santé publique (ACSP)
#404, 1525 Carling Ave., Ottawa ON K1Z 8R9
Tel: 613-725-3769; *Fax:* 613-725-9826
info@cpha.ca
www.cpha.ca
www.linkedin.com/company/113746
www.facebook.com/cpha.acsp
twitter.com/CPHA_ACSP
Overview: A large national charitable organization founded in 1910
Mission: To represent public health in Canada; To support universal & equitable access to the necessary conditions to achieve health for all Canadians; To provide links to the international public health community
Affiliation(s): World Health Organization; World Federation of Public Health Associations
Finances: *Funding Sources:* Membership fees; Donations
Membership: 2,000; *Fees:* $250 regular; $88 students; $100 retired persons; $265 international regular members; $107 international students; $120 international retired; *Member Profile:* Individuals who support Canadian Public Health Association objectives, & who are engaged or interested in community or public health activities, such as professionals in public health practice, researchers, professors, & government workers
Activities: Advising decision-makers about public health system reform; Liaising with provincial & territorial public health associations & national & international agencies & organizations; Publishing & disseminating research results; *Speaker Service:* Yes
Chief Officer(s):
Ardene Robinson Vollman, PhD, RN, CCHN(C, Chair
Susan Jackson, PhD, MSc, BSc, Chair-Elect
Annie Duchesne, MScPH, Director
Jacqueline Gahagan, PhD, Director
James Mintz, BA, Director
Manasi Parikh, Director
Awards:
• Aventis Pasteur International Award
• Ron Draper Health Promotion Award
• Certificate of Merit
• Student Award
• Honorary Life Membership
Awarded for exceptional excellence as an educator, researcher or practitioner in the field of public health, as demonstrated by achievements, valuable & outstanding research or distinguished service in the advancement of public health knowledge & practice
• R.D. Defries Award
The highest honour granted by the association; presented to the CPHA members who have made outstanding contributions in the broad field of public health; preference is given to Canadian contributions & individuals who have substantially supported the objectives of the association; the award carries with it an honorary life membership
• Janssen-Ortho Inc. Award
Presented to the candidate who has significantly advanced the cause, legitimized & stressed the responsibility & state of the art of public health
Meetings/Conferences:
• Canadian Public Health Association 2018 Conference, May, 2018, Montréal, QC
Scope: National
Description: A conference for policy-makers, researchers, environmental health professionals, academics, & students from across Canada
Contact Information: Conference Manager: Sarah Pettenuzzo, Phone: 613-725-3769, ext. 153
Publications:
• The Canadian Journal of Public Health
Type: Journal; *Frequency:* Bimonthly; *Accepts Advertising*;
Editor: Debra Lynkowski; *Price:* Free with membership in the Canadian Public Health Association
Profile: Articles on public health, including epidemiology, nutrition, family health, environmental health, sexually transmitted diseases, gerontology, behavioural medicine,rural health, health promotion, & public health policy
• Canadian Public Health Association Annual Report
Type: Yearbook; *Frequency:* Annually
• CPHA [Canadian Public Health Association] Health Digest
Frequency: Quarterly; *Editor:* Debra Lynkowski; *ISBN:* 0703-5624; *Price:* Free with membership inthe Canadian Public Health Association
Profile: Incorporates the international newsletter, Partners Around the World, plus articles from across Canada & around the world

Canadian Public Health Association - NB/PEI Branch
NB
nbpei.pha@gmail.com
Overview: A small provincial organization founded in 1952 overseen by Canadian Public Health Association
Mission: To maintain & improve the level of personal & community health
Chief Officer(s):
Tracey Rickards, President
Anne Lebans, Secretary-Treasurer

Canadian Public Health Association - NWT/Nunavut Branch (NTNUPHA)
PO Box 1709, Yellowknife NT X1A 2P3
Overview: A small provincial organization overseen by Canadian Public Health Association
Mission: To represent public health professionals
Chief Officer(s):
Cheryl Case, President

Canadian Public Personnel Management Association *See* International Personnel Management Association - Canada

Canadian Public Relations Society Inc. (CPRS) / La Société canadienne des relations publiques
#346, 4195 Dundas St. West, Toronto ON M8X 1Y4
Tel: 416-239-7034; *Fax:* 416-239-1076
admin@cprs.ca
www.cprs.ca
www.linkedin.com/groups/768077
www.facebook.com/CPRSNational
twitter.com/CPRSNational
Overview: A medium-sized national organization founded in 1948
Mission: To oversee the practice of public relations practitioners in Canada, to ensure the protection of the public interest; To advance the professional stature of public relations practitioners; To promote the ethical practice of public relations & communications management
Finances: *Funding Sources:* Membership fees; Sponsorships

Membership: 14 member societies; *Fees:* $270 member & associate ($50 initiation fee); $140 affiliate; *Member Profile:* Public relations practitioners in Canada; *Committees:* Audit & Investment; Awards; College of Fellows; Governance; Judicial & Ethics; Measurement; National Membership Task Force; Nominating; Professional Development; Public Relations & Communications
Activities: Offering professional development activities; *Speaker Service:* Yes; *Library:* Canadian Public Relations Society Resource Library
Chief Officer(s):
Karen Dalton, Executive Director
kdalton@cprs.ca
Kiki Cloutier, Director, Marketing, Communications & Events
kcloutier@cprs.ca
Lorianne Weston, Director, Accreditation & Education
accreditation@cprs.ca
Elizabeth Tang, Manager, Membership & Awards
etang@cprs.ca
Meetings/Conferences:
• Canadian Public Relations Society 2018 National Conference, May, 2018, Charlottetown, PE
Scope: National
Description: An education conference, with networking opportunities with public relations professionals from across Canada
Publications:
• Canadian Public Relations Society Annual Report
Type: Yearbook; *Frequency:* Annually
• Education Standard & Curriculum Guide
Type: Guide

CPRS Calgary
PO Box 2081, Stn. M, Calgary AB T2P 2M4
communications@cprscalgary.com
www.cprscalgary.org
www.facebook.com/CPRSCalgary
twitter.com/CPRSCalgary
Chief Officer(s):
Shawn Davis, President
president@cprscalgary.com
Melanie Simmons, Secretary
secretary@cprscalgary.com
Tammy Schwass, Director, Membership
membership@cprscalgary.com
• CPRS [Canadian Public Relations Society Inc.] Calgary Annual Report
Type: Yearbook; *Frequency:* Annually
Profile: The society's year in review
• Independent Consultant Directory [a publication of Canadian Public Relations Society Inc., Calgary]
Type: Directory
Profile: A directory to assist organizations in sourcing public relations & communications expertise in Calgary

CPRS Edmonton
PO Box 35068, Stn. Mid Town, Edmonton AB T5K 0L0
communications@cprsedmonton.ca
www.cprsedmonton.ca
www.linkedin.com/groups/5113537
www.facebook.com/CPRSEdmonton
twitter.com/cprsedmonton
Chief Officer(s):
Melissa Pennell, President
president@cprsedmonton.ca
Marjorie Henderson, Secretary
secretary@cprsedmonton.ca
Tim Conrad, Chair, Accreditation
accreditation@cprsedmonton.ca
Josie Hammond-Thrasher, Chair, Membership
membership@cprsedmonton.ca
• CPRS [Canadian Public Relations Society, Inc.] Edmonton Newsletter
Type: Newsletter; *Frequency:* Monthly
Profile: CPRS Edmonton board happenings, local news from the public relations field, resources, & case studies

CPRS Hamilton
PO Box 33517, Stn. Dundurn, Hamilton ON L8P 4X4
info@cprs-hamilton.ca
www.cprs-hamilton.ca
www.linkedin.com/groups?mostPopular&gid=768077
www.facebook.com/CPRSHamilton
twitter.com/CPRSHamilton
Mission: To serve public relations professionals from Hamilton, Halton, Niagara, & Southwestern Ontario
Chief Officer(s):
Mark Gregory, Co-President
mark@locomotionpr.ca
Lisa Stocco, Co-President
lstocco@grandriver.ca
Alex Anderson, Co-Chair, Communications
alexandria@alexandriaanderson.ca
Dustin Manley, Co-Chair, Communications
dustin@designedux.com

CPRS Manitoba
PO Box 441, Stn. Main, Winnipeg MB R3C 2H6
info@cprs.mb.ca
www.cprs.mb.ca
www.linkedin.com/company/3623660
www.facebook.com/CPRSManitoba
twitter.com/CPRSManitoba
Chief Officer(s):
Conor Lloyd, President
president@cprs.mb.ca
Tammy Sawatzky, Secretary
• CPRS [Canadian Public Relations Society Inc.] Manitoba Annual Report
Type: Yearbook; *Frequency:* Annually

CPRS New Brunswick
c/o Chris Williams, Department of Energy, #M100, 1 Germain St., Saint John NB E2L 4V1
Tel: 506-738-8064
www.cprs.ca/societies/nb.aspx
Chief Officer(s):
Wayne Knorr, Vice-President, 506-460-2181
wayne.knorr@fredericton.ca
Chris Williams, Chair, Membership
willcomm@nb.sympatico.ca

CPRS Newfoundland & Labrador
NL
cprsnlchapter@gmail.com
cprsnl.wordpress.com
www.facebook.com/CPRSNL
twitter.com/cprs_nl

CPRS Nova Scotia (CPRS-NS)
PO Box 1544, Halifax NS B3J 2Y3
www.cprsns.com
www.facebook.com/cprsns
twitter.com/cprsns
Chief Officer(s):
Alyson Murray, President

CPRS Ottawa-Gatineau
#102, 364 Cooper St., Ottawa ON K2P 2P3
info@cprsottawa.ca
www.cprsottawa.ca
www.linkedin.com/company/cprs-ottawa-gatineau
www.facebook.com/CPRSOttawaGatineau
twitter.com/CPRSOttawaGat
www.youtube.com/user/CPRSOttawaGatineau
Chief Officer(s):
Margaret Pearcy, President
president@cprsottawa.ca
Jason LaMontagne, Director, External Communications
externalcomms@cprsottawa.ca
• VOX [a publication of Canadian Public Relations Society Inc. Ottawa-Gatineau]
Type: Newsletter; *Frequency:* Bimonthly
Profile: Information about the society's activities in the National Capital Region

CPRS Prince Edward Island
c/o Anna MacDonald, Media Relations Officer, University of PEI, PO Box 16, Mount Stewart PE C0A 1T0
www.cprs.ca/societies/pei.aspx
Chief Officer(s):
Anna MacDonald, President
amacdonald@upei.ca
Kathy Maher, Vice-President
Doug Shackell, Secretary-Treasurer
Sheri Ostridge, Chair, Accreditation

CPRS Prince George
cprsnl@gmail.com
cprsnorthernlights.com
Chief Officer(s):
Jonathon Dyck, President
Shelly Burich, Co-Chair, Communications
Matt Wood, Co-Chair, Communications

CPRS Québec
#1700, 2001, boul Robert-Bourassa, Montréal QC H3A 2A6
Tél: 514-845-4441; *Téléc:* 514-228-7401
info@srq.qc.ca
www.sqprp.ca
www.linkedin.com/groups/1945719
www.facebook.com/SQPRP
twitter.com/sqprp
Chief Officer(s):
Annie Paré, Présidente

CPRS Regina
PO Box 472, Regina SK S4P 3A2
cprsreginamembership@gmail.com
www.cprsregina.sk.ca
www.linkedin.com/groups/4076984
www.facebook.com/CPRSregina
twitter.com/CPRS_Regina
Chief Officer(s):
Michelle James, President
cprsreginapresident@gmail.com
Ariane Whiting, Director, Membership
cprsreginamembership@gmail.com

CPRS Toronto
c/o Lois Marsh, CPRS Toronto Secretariat, #1801, 1 Yonge St., Toronto ON M5E 1W7
Tel: 416-360-1988; *Fax:* 416-369-0515
www.cprstoronto.com
Chief Officer(s):
Erica Silver, Co-President
president@cprstoronto.com
Danielle Kelly, Co-President
Lois Marsh, Secretary
marshl@marsh-executive.com
Heath Applebaum, Director, Education
heath@echocommunications.ca
Hilary Lawton, Director, Membership
hilarylawton@yahoo.ca
• CPRS [Canadian Public Relations Society Inc.] Toronto Member Directory
Type: Directory
Profile: For CPRS members only
• CPRS [Canadian Public Relations Society Inc.] Toronto Student Directory
Type: Directory
Profile: For CPRS members only
• New Perspective [a publication of the Canadian Public Relations Society Inc.]
Type: Newsletter; *Frequency:* Quarterly; *Accepts Advertising*
Profile: CPRS Toronto activities, meeting highlights, book reviews, profiles, & articles related to public relations

CPRS Vancouver
#102, 211 Columbia St., Vancouver BC V6A 2R5
Tel: 604-633-1433; *Fax:* 604-681-4545
admin@cprsvancouver.com
www.cprsvancouver.com
www.facebook.com/CPRSVancouver
twitter.com/CPRSVancouver
instagram.com/cprsvancouver
Chief Officer(s):
Emma Shea, President
Tanya Colledge, Director, Communications
Ange Frymire Fleming, Director, Accreditation
John Kageorge, Director, Membership

CPRS Vancouver Island (CPRS-VI)
c/o Marina Hawkeswood, Mainstay Communications, 1621 Dufferin Cres., Nanaimo BC V9S 5T4
info@cprs-vi.org
www.cprs-vi.org
www.linkedin.com/groups/2220945
www.facebook.com/CPRSVI
twitter.com/CPRS_VI
Chief Officer(s):
Peggy Kulmala, President
president@cprs-vi.org
Janina Stajic, Secretary
secretary@cprs-vi.org
Marina Hawkeswood, Chair, Communications
Marina Jaffey, Chair, Education
education@cprs-vi.org
Phil Saunders, Chair, Membership, 250-391-2526
membership@cprs-vi.org
• CPRS-VI [Canadian Public Relations Society Inc. - Vancouver Island] Newsletter
Type: Newsletter
Profile: Information for members, including local issues & coming events

Canadian Public Works Association (CPWA) / Association canadienne des travaux publics
#1150, 45 O'Connor St., Ottawa ON K1P 1A4
Tel: 202-218-6750
Toll-Free: 800-848-2792
www.cpwa.net
twitter.com/cpwatweets
Overview: A medium-sized national organization founded in 1986
Mission: To improve the quality of public works services for Canadian citizens; To share information about public works issues that are unique to Canada
Affiliation(s): American Public Works Association
Staff Member(s): 2
Membership: 2,250; *Member Profile:* Public works employees in Canada who are members of the American Public Works Association; Any person or organization in Canada with an interest in infrastructure & public works issues
Activities: Engaging in advocacy projects; Producing position statements; Facilitating the exchange of information for public works employees; Organizing outreach campaigns; Raising awareness of public works services; *Awareness Events:* National Public Works Week, May *Library:* Canadian Public Works Association Library
Chief Officer(s):
Scott Grayson, Executive Director, 800-848-2792 Ext. 6700
sgrayson@apwa.net
Anne Jackson, Director, Sustainability & CPWA Advocacy, 800-848-2792 Ext. 6750
ajackson@apwa.net
Alan Young, Consultant, Government Relations
young@tactix.ca
Laura Bynum, Contact, Media Relations, 800-848-2792 Ext. 6736
lbynum@apwa.net

Canadian Publishers' Council (CPC)
#203, 250 Merton St., Toronto ON M4S 1B1
Tel: 416-322-7011; *Fax:* 416-322-6999
www.pubcouncil.ca
Previous Name: Canadian Book Publishers' Council; Canadian Textbook Publishers Institute
Overview: A medium-sized national organization founded in 1910
Mission: To represent the interests of 18 companies who publish books & other media for elementary & secondary schools, colleges & universities, professional & reference, retail & library markets
Member of: Book & Periodical Council; CANARIE; Information Technology Association of Canada; Canadian Booksellers Association; Ontario Library Association
Affiliation(s): International Publishers Association
Finances: *Funding Sources:* Membership fees; project grants
Staff Member(s): 3
Membership: 18 firms; *Fees:* Schedule available; *Member Profile:* Incorporated in Canada with primary role as book publishing; 5 titles in print & publishing minimum 1 book per year; affiliate - engaged in related activities; honorary - service to Council; associate
Activities: Professional Development Seminar Program; *Library:* Not open to public
Chief Officer(s):
David Swail, Executive Director, External Relations, 416-322-7011 Ext. 222
dswail@pubcouncil.ca

Canadian Pulp & Paper Association See Forest Products Association of Canada

Canadian Pulp & Paper Association - Technical Section See Pulp & Paper Technical Association of Canada

Canadian Pulp & Paper Network for Innovation in Education & Research; Mechanical Wood-Pulps Network See Pulp & Paper Centre

Canadian Quarter Horse Association (CQHA)
c/o Sherry Clemens, Secretary, PO Box 2132, Moose Jaw SK S6H 7T2
Tel: 306-692-8393
admin@huntseathorses.com
www.cqha.ca
www.facebook.com/192652444096322
Overview: A small national organization
Mission: To address issues of concern to Canadian owners of American Quarter Horses; to be a communications vehicle for and with Canadian owners of American Quarter Horses; and to promote and market - both globally and within Canada - Canadian-bred and/or Canadian-owned American Quarter Horses.
Affiliation(s): American Quarter Horse Association
Chief Officer(s):
Haidee Landry, President
hmqh@hotmail.com
Meetings/Conferences:
• Canadian Quarter Horse Association 2018 Annual General Meeting, January, 2018, Sheraton Conference Centre, Red Deer, AB
Scope: National

Canadian Quaternary Association / Association canadienne pour l'étude du Quaternaire
c/o Kathryn Hargan, Department of Biology, Queen's University, 116 Barrie St., Kingston ON K7L 3N6
Tel: 613-533-6000
www.canqua.com
Also Known As: CANQUA
Overview: A small national organization founded in 1975
Mission: To study & advance knowledge of the quaternary period
Affiliation(s): Geological Association of Canada
Membership: 150; *Fees:* $0 students; $15 regular members; *Member Profile:* Persons interested in Canadian quaternary studies, such as geographers, geologists, biologists, botanists, archaeologists, & students
Activities: Disseminating information about the quaternary period; Cooperating with other quaternary associations
Chief Officer(s):
Sarah Finkelstein, President, 416-978-5613, Fax: 416-978-3938
finkelstein@es.utoronto.ca
Patrick Lajeunesse, Vice-President, 418-565-2131 Ext. 5879, Fax: 418-656-3960
patrick.lajeunesse@ggr.ulaval.ca
Kathryn Hargan, Secretary-Treasurer, 613-533-6000 Ext. 75143
kathrynhargan@gmail.com
Awards:
• W.A. Johnston Medal
To recognize professional excellence in quaternary science
• Aleksis Dreimanis Doctoral Scholarship
A student prize
• David Proudfoot Award
Awarded for the best student presentation at the Canadian Quaternary Association biennial meeting
• Guy Lortie Award
To recognize the best paper presented by a student at the Canadian Quaternary Association biennial meeting
Meetings/Conferences:
• Canadian Quaternary Association 2018 Conference, August, 2018
Scope: National
Description: Joint meeting with the American Quaternary Association (AMQUA)

Canadian Quilters' Association (CQA) / Association canadienne de la courtepointe (ACC)
6 Spruce St., Pasadena NL A0L 1K0
administration@canadianquilter.com
www.canadianquilter.com
www.facebook.com/canadianquilterassociation
Overview: A medium-sized national organization founded in 1981
Mission: The promotion of a greater understanding, appreciation & knowledge of the art, techniques & heritage of patchwork, appliqué & quilting; the promotion of the highest standards of workmanship & design in both traditional & innovative work the fostering of a climate of cooperation amongst quiltmakers across the country.
Finances: *Annual Operating Budget:* Less than $50,000; *Funding Sources:* Membership dues; fundraising
9 volunteer(s)
Membership: 1,800 individuals; 12 regional contacts; *Fees:* $56.50, 1 yr.; $101.70, 2 yr.
Activities: *Library:* Not open to public
Chief Officer(s):
Johanna Alford, President, 902-835-9780
Vivian Kapusta, Secretary/Publicist
Awards:
• Dorothy McMurdie Award
• Teacher of the Year
• Agnes Boal Bursary
Meetings/Conferences:
• Quilt Canada 2018, May, 2018, Vancouver Convention Centre, Vancouver, BC
Scope: National
Contact Information: E-mail: confcoordinator@canadianquilter.com

Canadian Race Communications Association (CRCA)
PO Box 307, Shannonville ON K0K 3A0
crcamarshal@live.com
www.crcamarshal.com
www.facebook.com/101660183249507
twitter.com/CRCA_Marshals
Overview: A medium-sized national licensing organization founded in 1959
Mission: To provide corner marshals for all forms of racing events
Membership: *Fees:* $15
Chief Officer(s):
Darrell Briggs, President
Michel Paquette, Director, Membership, 613-293-3741
membership@crca1.com
Publications:
• The Blue Flag [a publication of Canadian Race Communications Association]
Type: Newsletter; *Frequency:* Quarterly

Canadian Race Relations Foundation (CRRF)
#225, 6 Garamond Crt., Toronto ON M3C 1Z5
Tel: 416-703-4164; *Fax:* 416-441-2752
Toll-Free: 888-240-4936
info@crrf-fcrr.ca
www.crr.ca
www.linkedin.com/company/the-canadian-race-relations-foundation
www.facebook.com/699059076842903
twitter.com/CRRF
Overview: A medium-sized national organization
Mission: To eliminate racism and all forms of racial discrimination, and promote Canadian identity, belonging and the mutuality of citizenship rights and responsibilities for a more harmonious Canada.
Finances: *Annual Operating Budget:* $250,000-$500,000
Chief Officer(s):
Anita Bromberg, Executive Director, 416-441-2714
abromberg@crrf-fcrr.ca

Canadian Racing Pigeon Union Inc.
261 Tillson Ave., #C, Tillsonburg ON N4G 5X2
Tel: 519-842-9771; *Fax:* 519-842-8809
Toll-Free: 866-652-5704
crpu@crpu.ca
www.crpu.ca
www.facebook.com/226183050750688
Overview: A medium-sized national organization founded in 1929
Mission: To promote the sport of pigeon racing in Canada
Affiliation(s): Fédération colombophile internationale
Staff Member(s): 1
Membership: 1,500; *Fees:* $50 individual; $75 family
Chief Officer(s):
Chris Watson, President
president@crpu.ca
Denise Luscher, Administrator
denise@crpu.ca

Canadian Racquetball Association See Racquetball Canada

Canadian Radiation Protection Association (CRPA) / Association canadienne de radioprotection (ACRP)
PO Box 83, Carleton Place ON K7C 3P3
Tel: 613-253-3779; *Fax:* 888-551-0712
secretariat@crpa-acrp.ca
www.crpa-acrp.ca
www.linkedin.com/groups?gid=4296889
Overview: A small national organization founded in 1979
Mission: To develop scientific knowledge for protection from the harmful effects of radiation; To encourage research; To assist in the development of professional standards in the discipline
Affiliation(s): International Radiation Protection Association (IRPA)
Membership: *Fees:* $700 corporate members; $155 full or associate members; $30 students; *Member Profile:* Individuals with training who are engaged in the science & practice of radiation protection; *Committees:* Registered Radiation Safety Professionals; Conference; Students and Young Professionals; Professional Development; Communications; Bulletin Editorial Board; Translation; Membership; Archives; Nominations; Rules; Finance; International Liaison

Activities: Promoting educational opportunities
Chief Officer(s):
Jeff Dovyak, President
Ray Ilson, Treasurer
Publications:
• CRPA [Canadian Radiation Protection Association] Bulletin
Type: Newsletter; *Frequency:* Quarterly
Profile: For Canadian Radiation Protection Association members only

Canadian Radio Technical Planning Board *See* Radio Advisory Board of Canada

Canadian Railroad Historical Association (CRHA) / Association canadienne d'histoire ferroviaire
110, rue St-Pierre, Saint-Constant QC J5A 1G7
Tel: 450-632-2410; *Fax:* 450-638-1563
info@exporail.org
www.exporail.org/en
www.facebook.com/Exporail
twitter.com/Exporail
Also Known As: Exporail: The Canadian Railway Museum
Overview: A medium-sized national charitable organization founded in 1932
Mission: To collect, preserve & disseminate information/items relating to the history of railways in Canada
Finances: *Annual Operating Budget:* $1.5 Million-$3 Million
Membership: *Fees:* $50 regular; $110 friend of the museum; *Committees:* Executive; Collection; Membership; Audit
Activities: *Library:* Canadian Railroad Historical Association Library/Archives; by appointment Not open to public
Chief Officer(s):
C. Stephen Cheasley, President

Calgary & South-Western Division
4515 Dalhart Rd. NW, Calgary AB T3A 1B9
Tel: 403-652-7279
www.exporail.org/en/crha/divisions
Chief Officer(s):
D. Walter Edgar, Vice-President
walter@dweco.com

Charny Division
#103, 5314, av des Belles-Amours, Charny QC G6X 1P2
Tel: 418-832-1502
info@groupe-traq.com
www.groupe-traq.com
Chief Officer(s):
Louis-François Garceau, President

Esquimalt & Nanaimo Division
2414 Dryfe St., Victoria BC V8R 5T2
Tel: 250-514-6497
info@encrha.com
www.encrha.com

Kingston Division
PO Box 1714, Kingston ON K7L 5V5
intercolonialrailway.com/CRHA/
Chief Officer(s):
Douglas Smith, President
DRGsmith@sympatico.ca

New Brunswick Division
2847 Main St., Hillsborough NB E4H 2X7
Tel: 506-734-3195
www.crhanb.ca
Mission: The Canadian Railroad Historical Association (NB Division), known as the CRHA (NB), is New Brunswick's most active railway heritage group with its focus to provide all members of the general public with information regarding all aspects of railway transportation in the Province of New Brunswick and thereby to provide the education, enjoyment and entertainment of the general public

Niagara Division
PO Box 20311, Stn. Grantham, St Catharines ON L2M 7W7
Chief Officer(s):
Andy Panko, Division Representative
apanko@niagara.com

Pacific Coast Division
PO Box 1006, Stn. A, Vancouver BC V6C 2P1
railsmith@yahoo.ca

Prince George-Nechako-Fraser Division
PO Box 2408, Prince George BC V2N 2S6
Tel: 250-563-7351
trains@pgrfm.bc.ca

Rideau Valley Division
PO Box 962, 90 William St., Smiths Falls ON K7A 5A5
Tel: 613-283-5696

Selkirk Division
PO Box 2561, 719 Track St. W., Revelstoke BC V0E 2S0
Tel: 250-837-6060
railway@telus.net
www.railwaymuseum.com

Toronto & York Division
43 Marjory Ave., Toronto ON M4M 2Y2
Chief Officer(s):
Paul Bowles, Contact, 416-465-9910

Canadian Railway & Transit Manufacturers Association *See* Canadian Association of Railway Suppliers

Canadian Railway Club
PO Box 162, Stn. St-Charles, Kirkland QC H9H 0A3
Tel: 514-428-5903; *Fax:* 514-697-6238
info@canadianrailwayclub.ca
canadianrailwayclub.ca
Overview: A small national organization founded in 1902
Affiliation(s): Toronto Railway Club; Railway Associaiton of Canada; C.A.R.S.; WCRNA
Membership: *Fees:* $30; *Member Profile:* Current or retired employees of railway companies; Companies that produce railway accessories or services; Those associated with railway companies; *Committees:* Executive; Arrangements; Membership & Attendance; Audit; Advertising
Chief Officer(s):
Heather McGuire, Administrator
Tony Persechino, President

Canadian Ready Mixed Concrete Association (CRMCA)
#3, 365 Brunel Rd., Mississauga ON L4Z 1Z5
Tel: 905-507-1122; *Fax:* 905-890-8122
info@concretealberta.com
www.crmca.ca
Overview: A medium-sized national organization founded in 1981
Mission: To represent federally legislated issues impacting the members of the ready mixed concrete industry
Finances: *Annual Operating Budget:* $100,000-$250,000
Staff Member(s): 4; 40 volunteer(s)
Membership: 8 member associations; *Member Profile:* Each of Canada's provincial or regional ready mixed concrete associations; *Committees:* Technical; Marketing & Promotion; Environmental; Residential; Transportation; Pumping; Safety
Meetings/Conferences:
• CONEXPO-CON/AGG, March, 2020, Las Vegas, NV
Attendance: 130,000
Description: North American's largest construction trade show representing asphalt, aggregates, concrete, earthmoving, lifting, mining, and other utilities
Contact Information: Phone: 800-867-6060
• World of Conrete, January, 2018, Las Vegas, NV
Attendance: 55,000
Description: Annual event dedicated to conrete & masonry professionls
Publications:
• Concrete Energy Guide
Type: Handbook; *Number of Pages:* 52; *Author:* John Straube
• Environmental Product Declaration
Type: Handbook; *Number of Pages:* 24

The Canadian Real Estate Association (CREA) / Association canadienne de l'immeuble
200 Catherine St., 6th Fl., Ottawa ON K2P 2K9
Tel: 613-237-7111; *Fax:* 613-234-2567
Toll-Free: 800-842-2732
info@crea.ca
www.crea.ca
www.linkedin.com/company/1400987
www.facebook.com/CREA.ACI
twitter.com/CREA_ACI
www.youtube.com/user/CREACHANNEL
Overview: A large national organization founded in 1943
Mission: To enhance member professionalism, competency & profitability; To advocate government policies which improve the industry's market environment & enhance individual rights with respect to the ownership of real property
Affiliation(s): National Association of Realtors; International Real Estate Federation; International Consortium Real Estate Associations
Finances: *Funding Sources:* Membership dues; Publications
Staff Member(s): 5

Membership: 90,000 licensed or registered brokers/agents & salespeople in 103 real estate boards, 10 provincial associations & 1 territorial association
Chief Officer(s):
Gary Simonsen, Chief Executive Officer
Pauline Aunger, President
Publications:
• Canadian Real Estate Association Annual Report
• CREA [Canadian Real Estate Association] By-laws & Rules
Profile: An overview of the Association's policies & membership responsibilities
• Economic Impact of MLS Sales [a publication of the Canadian Real Estate Association]
Profile: A study exploring the spin-off economic activity created by homebuyers
• The Homebuyers' Road Map [a publication of the Canadian Real Estate Association]
Profile: An information toolkit designed to help homebuyers make informed decisions when choosing a home
• A Homeowner's Guide to Radon [a publication of the Canadian Real Estate Association]
Profile: A report outlining the health risks of colourless, odourless, & tasteless gas radon & its consequences for homeowners & homebuyers
• Integrated Accessbility Standards Regulation Policy [a publication of the the Canadian Real Estate Association]
Profile: A plan outlining the requirements of CREA's Integrated Accessibility Standards Regulation policy, as guided by theAccessibility for Ontarians Disability Act

Canadian Recording Industry Association *See* Music Canada

Canadian Recreation Facilities Council
PO Box 534, Cochrane AB T0C 1C0
Tel: 403-851-7626; *Fax:* 403-851-9181
info@crfc.ca
www.crfc.ca
Overview: A medium-sized national organization
Mission: To encourage full representation from all provinces & territories; to promote facility programs at the provincial/territorial & national levels; to facilitate the exchange of information; to identify & encourage the development of projects & programs of a national interest; to develop & deliver an unified position on issues of a national interest; to strive for financial self-sufficiency
Membership: 15; *Member Profile:* Provincial & Territorial Facility Associations
Chief Officer(s):
Larry Golby, Chair
944golby@telus.net
John Milton, Chief Executive Officer

Canadian Recreational Canoeing Association *See* Paddle Canada

Canadian Recreational Vehicle Association (CRVA) / Association canadienne du véhicule récréatif
110 Freelton Rd., Freelton ON L0R 1K0
www.crva.ca
Overview: A medium-sized national organization founded in 1975
Mission: To promote recreational vehicle lifestyle
Membership: *Fees:* $282.50-$339; *Member Profile:* Manufacturers of RVs & their suppliers

Canadian Recruiters Guild *See* Association of Professional Recruiters of Canada

Canadian Red Angus Promotion Society
RR#2, New Norway AB T0B 3L0
Tel: 780-678-9069; *Fax:* 780-855-2581
www.redangus.ca
www.facebook.com/CanadianRedAngus
twitter.com/CdnRedAngus
Overview: A small national organization founded in 1972
Mission: To promote & advertise Canadian Red Angus cattle
Member of: Canadian Angus Association
Finances: *Funding Sources:* Membership dues; fund-raising
Membership: 275; *Committees:* Promotion & Show; Advertising; CCA Liaison; Red Roundup
Activities: Annual Red Roundup Sale; Red Angus Shows; advertising & promotion
Chief Officer(s):
Brent Troyer, President, 519-321-1815
brenttroyer6@gmail.com

Canadian Red Cross (CRC) / La Société la Croix-Rouge canadienne
170 Metcalfe St., Ottawa ON K2P 2P2

Canadian Associations / Canadian Red Poll Cattle Association / Société Canadienne des Bovins Red Poll

Tel: 613-740-1900; Fax: 613-740-1911
Toll-Free: 800-418-1111
wecare@redcross.ca
www.redcross.ca
www.facebook.com/canadianredcross
twitter.com/redcrossCanada
www.youtube.com/user/canadianredcross
Overview: A large international charitable organization founded in 1896
Mission: To help people deal with situations that threaten: their survival & safety, their security & well-being, their human dignity, in Canada & around the world; To improve the lives of vulnerable people by mobilizing the power of humanity
Member of: International Red Cross & Red Crescent Societies
Affiliation(s): International Committee of the Red Cross; International Federation of Red Cross & Red Crescent Societies (Geneva)
Finances: Annual Operating Budget: Greater than $5 Million; Funding Sources: Public donations; United Way; Governments; Corporations
20,0 volunteer(s)
Activities: Providing international services & field operations, including emergency, water safety, & first aid services; Offering community services, such as veterans' services & home assistance; Violence, abuse & bullying prevention programs & services; International & Canadian disaster preparedness & response; Healthcare programs & services; Awareness Events: Red Cross Month, March; World Red Cross Day, May 8 Library: National Office Library; by appointment
Chief Officer(s):
Conrad Sauvé, President & CEO
Larry Mills, Chief Financial Officer
Ann Clancy, Chief of Staff
Amy Mapara, Corporate Secretary
Michel Léveillé, Chief Communications Officer
Publications:
• Be Ready, Be Safe
Type: Booklet; Number of Pages: 60; ISBN: 978-1-55104-506-1
Profile: An activity booklet for 12 & 13 year old children
• Bug Out Activity Booklet: Get the Facts on Germs
Type: Booklet
Profile: Booklets for ages 6 to 8, 9 to 11, & 12 to 13, plus a family guide for ages 4 to 13
• Bug Out Facilitator Guide: Get the Facts on Germs
Type: Guide
Profile: Booklets for educators & caregivers of children from ages 6 to 8, 9 to 11, & 12 to 13
• Canadian Red Cross Society Annual Report
Type: Yearbook; Frequency: Annually
Profile: A review of Canadian & international disaster management, health & homecare services, humanitarian issues, donations, & financial information
• Canadian Red Cross Society: Working to Serve Humanity 2010-2015
Type: Report; Number of Pages: 20
Profile: A strategic plan for the future
• Drowning Research: Water Safety Poll
Type: Survey; ISBN: 0
Profile: Canadian parents concerned about safety in backyard pools
• Expect the Unexpected Facilitator's Guide
Type: Guide
Profile: Guides for educators using the Emergency Preparedness Program with students aged 7 to 8, 9 to 11, & 12 to 13
• Facing Fear: Helping Young People Deal with Terrorism & Tragic Events
Type: Guide; ISBN: 1-55104-277-0
Profile: Booklets with activities & lesson plans for students aged 5 to 7, 8 to 10, 11 to 13, & 14 to 16
• Facing the Unexpected, Be Prepared
Type: Booklet; Number of Pages: 44; ISBN: 978-1-55104-504-7
Profile: An activity booklet for children ages 10 & 11
• Integrating Emergency Management & High-Risk Populations: Survey Report & Action Recommendations
Type: Report; Number of Pages: 58
Profile: Prepared for Public Safety Canada by Canadian Red Cross
• It Can Happen, Be Ready
Type: Booklet; Number of Pages: 36; ISBN: 978-1-55104-502-3
Profile: An activity booklet for 7 & 8 year old children
• Let's Plan for The Unexpected
Type: Booklet; Number of Pages: 52; ISBN: 978-1-55104-508-5
Profile: An activity booklet for families

• Social Media During Emergencies
Type: Survey
Profile: Exploring how to use social media during an emergency
• Survive the Peace: Landmine Education & Community Involvement Guide
Type: Guide; Number of Pages: 54
Profile: Background information about the landmine crisis, learning activities, & ways to take action
• Your Emergency Preparedness Guide
Type: Guide; Number of Pages: 36
Profile: A publication from Public Safety Canada, in collaboration with the Canadian Red Cross, the Canadian Association of Chiefs of Police, the Canadian Association of Fire Chiefs, St. JohnAmbulance, & The Salvation Army, available in print, audio, Braille, large print, diskette, & CD
Atlantic Zone Office
Burnside Industrial Park, 133 Troop Ave., Dartmouth NS B3B 2A7
Tel: 902-423-3680; Fax: 902-422-6247
Division du Québec
6, Place du Commerce, Verdun QC H3E 1P4
Tél: 514-362-2930; Téléc: 514-362-9991
Chief Officer(s):
Michel Léveillé, Directeur
Ontario Zone Office
5700 Cancross Ct., Mississauga ON L5R 3E9
Tel: 905-890-1000
Toll-Free: 877-356-3226
Western Zone Office
#100, 1305 - 11 Ave. SW, Calgary AB T3C 3P6
Tel: 403-541-6100; Fax: 403-541-6129

Canadian Red Cross - Blood Services See Canadian Blood Services

Canadian Red Poll Cattle Association / Société Canadienne des Bovins Red Poll
2417 Holly Lane, Ottawa ON K1V 0M7
Tel: 613-731-7110; Fax: 613-731-0704
Toll-Free: 877-731-7110
redpoll@clrc.ca
www.clrc.ca/redpoll.shtml
Overview: A medium-sized national organization founded in 1906
Mission: To encourage development & regulation of breeding of purebred Red Poll cattle in Canada for improvement of Canadian beef cattle industry
Member of: Canadian Livestock Records Corporation
Finances: Annual Operating Budget: Less than $50,000; Funding Sources: Membership dues; fees for service
Staff Member(s): 1; 13 volunteer(s)
Membership: 16; Fees: $60
Chief Officer(s):
Ron Black, Secretary-Treasurer

Canadian Regional Science Association Voir Association canadienne des sciences régionales

Canadian Register of Health Service Psychologists (CRHSP) / Répertoire canadien des psychologues offrant des services de santé (RCPOSS)
72 boul Saint-Raymond, Gatineau QC J8Y 1S2
Tel: 819-771-1441; Fax: 819-771-1444
info@crhspp.ca
www.crhspp.ca
Overview: A small national organization founded in 1985
Mission: To promote & protect public access to qualified health service providers in psychology
Membership: 1,000-4,999; Member Profile: Psychologists providing health services
Activities: Rents Mailing List: Yes
Chief Officer(s):
John MacDonald, Executive Director
Publications:
• Directory of Canadian Health Service Psychologists [a publication of the Canadian Register of Health Service Psychologists]
Type: Directory; Price: $26.25/AB, MB, NT, NU, PE, QC, SK, YT; $28/BC; $28.25/NB, NL, ON; $28.75 NS

Canadian Registry of Tennessee Walking Horse (CRTWH)
c/o Leslie Hunchuk, Box 12, Site 12, RR#1, Millard AB T0L 1K0
Tel: 403-931-2105
secretary@crtwh.ca

www.crtwh.ca
www.facebook.com/crtwh
Overview: A small international organization
Mission: To register & record purebred Tennessee Walking Horses, both in Canada & internationally; To preserve the historical attributes of the Tennessee Walking Horse breed; To encourage improvement in the quality of the breed
Member of: Equine Canada
Affiliation(s): Canadian Livestock Records Corporation
Membership: Fees: $10 youth members, under 18; $15 associate members; $25 full members; $35 non-Canadian residents; $200 individual life members; Member Profile: Canadian individuals, families, organizations, groups, corporations, & partnerships; International members
Activities: Promoting the Tennessee Walking Horse breed; Establishing standards of breeding; Cooperating with other breed associations & agricultural groups; Presenting awards
Chief Officer(s):
Fran Kerik, President
president@crtwh.ca
Bill Roy, Vice-President, 250-838-2066
vice-president@crtwh.ca
Leslie Hunchuk, Secretary, 403-931-2105
secretary@crtwh.ca
Dianne Little, Treasurer, 403-271-7391
treasurer@crtwh.ca
Publications:
• The Canadian Walker
Type: Newsletter
Profile: Association updates

Canadian Reiki Association (CRA)
#24, 2350 New St., Burlington ON L7R 4P8
Toll-Free: 800-835-7525
reiki@reiki.ca
www.reiki.ca
www.facebook.com/groups/6813158154
twitter.com/reikicanada
www.pinterest.com/canadianreikias
Overview: A small national organization founded in 1997
Mission: Provides members with a national voice; encourages high educational standards; promotes ethical practices & teaching; assists the public with referrals to practitioners & teachers; committed to enlightening & educating communites about Reiki
Member of: Volunteer Canada
Staff Member(s): 1
Chief Officer(s):
Bonnie Smith, President
bonnie@reiki.ca

Canadian Remote Sensing Society (CRSS) / Société canadienne de télédétection
c/o Canadian Aeronautics & Space Institute, #104, 350 Terry Fox Dr., Kanata ON K2K 2W5
Tel: 613-591-8787; Fax: 613-591-7291
casi@casi.ca
www.crss-sct.ca
Overview: A small national organization founded in 1978
Mission: To advance the art, science, engineering, & application of remote sensing in Canada; To uphold the Society's Code of Ethics
Member of: Canadian Aeronautics & Space Institute (CASI)
Activities: Disseminating technical remote sensing information; Developing a program for certification of remote sensing scientists & mapping scientists in GIS & photogrammetry
Chief Officer(s):
Monique Bernier, Chair
Anne Smith, Vice-Chair
Richard Fournier, Secretary-Treasurer
Meetings/Conferences:
• 39th Canadian Remote Sensing Society Conference 2018, 2018
Scope: National
Publications:
• Canadian Journal of Remote Sensing (CJRS) / Journal canadien de télédétection (JCT)
Type: Journal; Frequency: Bimonthly; Accepts Advertising; Editor: Nicholas Coops; Price: $211.68 Canada; $206.30 USA; $217.20 International
Profile: Research articles & notes, technical notes, & review papers on topics such asinformation processing methods, data acquisition, & applications

Canadian Renewable Fuels Association See Renewable Industries Canada

Canadian Rental Association (CRA) / Association de location du Canada
112B Scurfield Blvd., Winnipeg MB R3Y 1G4
Tel: 204-452-1836; *Fax:* 204-453-3569
Toll-Free: 800-486-9899
www.crarental.org
www.facebook.com/canadianrental
twitter.com/canadianrental
www.youtube.com/canadianrental
Previous Name: Rental Association of Canada
Overview: A small national organization founded in 1964
Finances: *Annual Operating Budget:* $100,000-$250,000
Staff Member(s): 2; 13 volunteer(s)
Membership: 500-999; *Committees:* Membership Benefit; Policy and Procedures; Social Media/Advertising; Trade Show; Website
Activities: *Library:* Not open to public
Chief Officer(s):
Mandy Maeren, Executive Director

Canadian Reprography Collective *See* Access Copyright

Canadian Research Institute for the Advancement of Women (CRIAW) / Institut canadien de recherches sur les femmes (ICREF)
#201, 240 Catherine St., Ottawa ON K2P 2G8
Tel: 613-422-2188
www.criaw-icref.ca
www.facebook.com/criaw.icref
twitter.com/criawicref
Overview: A medium-sized national organization founded in 1976
Mission: To advance the position of women in society through feminist & women-centred research; To encourage, coordinate & communicate research about the reality of women's lives & ensure an equal place for women & their experiences in the body of knowledge about Canada; To recognize & affirm the diversity of women's experiences; to demystify the research process & promote connections between research, social action & social change; To facilitate communication among feminist researchers & research organizations world-wide
Finances: *Annual Operating Budget:* $250,000-$500,000; *Funding Sources:* Government; donations; membership fees; sales of publications; administration of projects
Staff Member(s): 4
Membership: 1,000 individual + 25 institutional; *Fees:* $15 student/low income; $30 regular; $55 supporting; $150 sustaining; $100 institutional; *Member Profile:* Independent researchers; students; academics; policy makers; journalists; community activists & women's centres
Activities: *Speaker Service:* Yes; *Library:* Resource Centre; Open to public
Chief Officer(s):
Cindy Hanson, President
Jacqueline Neapole, Office Manager
Pat Hendrick, Finance Officer
Publications:
• CRIAW [Canadian Research Institute for the Advancement of Women] Papers
Profile: Topics in the series include the following: Canada's Early Women Writers: Texts in English to 1859; Canadian Women's Autobiography in English: AnIntroductory Guide for Researchers & Teachers; & Feminist Engagement with the Law: The Legal Recognition of the Battered Woman Syndrome
• Feminist Perspectives
Profile: Topics in the series include the following: Gender-sensitive Theory & the Housing Needs of Mother-led Families: Some Concepts & Some Buildings; Reclaiming Body Territory; Role Muddles: The Stereotyping ofFeminists; & Towards Family Policies in Canada With Women in Mind
• Feminist Voices
Profile: Topics in this series include the following: Diaries in English by women in Canada, 1753-1995: an Annotated Bibliography; Invoking Community: Rethinking the Health of Lesbian & Bisexual Women; & Making NewFeminisms: A Conversation Between a Feminist Mother & Daughter

Canadian Resident Matching Service (CARMS)
#300, 171 Nepean St., Ottawa ON K2P 0B4
Tel: 613-237-0075
Toll-Free: 877-227-6742
help@carms.ca
www.carms.ca
www.linkedin.com/company/carms
www.facebook.com/carms.ca
twitter.com/carms_ca
www.youtube.com/user/CaRMSvideo
Overview: A small national organization founded in 1982
Mission: National organization that serves both eligible applicants & post graduate programs by offering fair & equitable access to medical residency training in Canada
Staff Member(s): 44
Membership: *Committees:* Executive; Finance & Audit; Nominating; Research & Data Policy; Awards; Scope of Services
Chief Officer(s):
Sandra Banner, Executive Director/CEO

Canadian Resort & Recreational Development Association (1992) *See* Canadian Resort Development Association

Canadian Resort Development Association (CRDA)
13061 - 15 Ave., South Surrey BC V4A 1K6
Tel: 604-538-7001; *Fax:* 604-538-7101
info@crda.com
www.crda.com
Previous Name: Canadian Resort & Recreational Development Association (1992)
Overview: A small national organization founded in 1980
Mission: To raise a better understanding of the value of the vacation ownership product; to ensure fair & ethical treatment by all industry participants, through legislation or industry self-management; to educate & inform within the membership & outwardly to the public.
Affiliation(s): American Resort Development Association; All India Resort Development Association; Mexican Resort Development Association; Co-Operative Association of Resort Exchangers; Canadian Resort & Foodservices Association; Hotel Association of Canada; Resort Development Organisation
Membership: 47; *Fees:* $0 - $3,000; *Member Profile:* Resort developers; marketers; suppliers
Chief Officer(s):
Jon Zwickel, President & CEO

Canadian Respiratory Health Professionals (CRHP)
c/o Canadian Thoracic Society, #300, 1750 Courtwood Cres., Ottawa ON K2C 2B5
Tel: 613-569-6411; *Fax:* 613-569-8860
crhpinfo@lung.ca
crhp.lung.ca
www.facebook.com/334691136607567
Merged from: Cdn Nurses Respiratory, Cdn Physiotherapy Cardio-Respiratory, & Respiratory Therapy Societies
Overview: A small national organization founded in 2004 overseen by Canadian Lung Association
Mission: To promote lung health & the prevention of lung disease
Affiliation(s): Canadian Thoracic Society
Membership: *Fees:* $30 associate member; $45 full member; *Member Profile:* A multidisciplinary health professional section of The Canadian Lung Association, consisting of respiratory therapists, cardio-pulmonary physiotherapists, nurses, pharmacists, & other health professionals who work in the respiratory field
Activities: Advising the Canadian Lung Association on scientific matters, as well as professional & public education; Administering a research & fellowship program; Facilitating interprofessional collaboration
Chief Officer(s):
Janet Sutherland, Executive Director
Publications:
• Airwaves - The Newsletter of the Canadian Respiratory Health Professionals
Type: Newsletter; *Price:* Free with CRHP membership
Profile: Information for Canadian Respiratory Health Professionals members

Canadian Restaurant & Foodservices Association *See* Restaurants Canada

Canadian Retina Society / Société canadienne de la rétine
c/o Canadian Ophthalmological Society, 110 - 2733 Lancaster Rd., Ottawa ON K1B 0A9
Toll-Free: 800-267-5763
www.cos-sco.ca/cpd/canadian-retina-society-meeting
Overview: A medium-sized national organization
Mission: To promote & support retina specialists in Canada
Chief Officer(s):
Amin Kherani, President
Meetings/Conferences:
• Canadian Retina Society 2018 6th Annual Meeting, March, 2018, Fairmont Tremblant, Mont-Tremblant, QC
Scope: National

Canadian Retransmission Collective (CRC) / Société collective de retransmission du Canada (SCR)
74 The Esplanade, Toronto ON M5E 1A9
Tel: 416-304-0290; *Fax:* 416-304-0496
info@crc-scrc.ca
www.crc-scrc.ca
Overview: A small national organization
Mission: To retransmit of royalties paid for the use of programs in broadcast signals that are classed as 'distant', or not transitted by the originating signal
Staff Member(s): 5
Chief Officer(s):
Carol Cooper, President/CEO

Canadian Rheumatology Association (CRA) / Société canadienne de rhumatologie
#244, 12 - 16715 Yonge St., Newmarket ON L3X 1X4
Tel: 905-952-0698; *Fax:* 905-952-0708
info@rheum.ca
rheum.ca
Overview: A small national organization
Mission: To represent Canadian rheumatologists & promote their pursuit of excellence in arthritis care & research in Canada through leadership, education & communication
Affiliation(s): Canadian Medical Association, Royal College of Physicians & Surgeons of Canada
Membership: *Fees:* $400; *Member Profile:* Canadian & international rheumatologists; others with a focused area of interest in rheumatology; *Committees:* Access to Care; Human Resources; Education; Management; Scientific; Therapeutics; Canadian Initiative for Outcomes in Rheumatology Care
Chief Officer(s):
Cory Baillie, President
Jacob Karsh, Sec.-Treas.
Awards:
• Distinguished Rheumatologist Award
Eligibility: A CRA member; *Amount:* $5,000
• Distinguished Investigator Award
Eligibility: A CRA member; *Amount:* $2,500
• Teacher - Educator Award
Eligibility: A CRA member; *Amount:* $2,500
• Young Investigator Award
Eligibility: A CRA member; *Amount:* $2,500
• CRA/ARF Young Faculty Award for Excellence in Research
Eligibility: A CRA member; *Amount:* $1,250
• Dr. Philip S. Rosen Endowment Fund
; *Amount:* $1,000
• Ian Watson Memorial Award
; *Amount:* $1,000
• Best Abstract by an Undergraduate Student
; *Amount:* $1,000
Meetings/Conferences:
• 2018 Canadian Rheumatology Association Annual Scientific Meeting, February, 2018, Vancouver, BC
Scope: National
Publications:
• Journal of the Canadian Rheumatology Association
Type: Journal; *Frequency:* Quarterly

Canadian Rock Mechanics Association (CARMA) / Association canadienne de méchanique des roches
c/o Civil Engineering Department, University of Toronto, 35 St. George St., Toronto ON M5S 1A4
www.carma-rocks.com
Overview: A medium-sized national organization founded in 1980
Mission: To represent Canada to the international community of engineers working in the mining & civil engineering aspects of rock mechanics engineering
Member of: Canadian Geotechnical Society; Canadian Institute of Mining & Metallurgy
Affiliation(s): International Society for Rock Mechanics
6 volunteer(s)
Membership: 165
Chief Officer(s):
John Hadjigeorgiou, Chair
john.hadjigeorgiou@utoronto.ca
Luc Beauchamp, Secretary-Treasurer
lucbeauchamp@workplacesafetynorth.com
Awards:
• John Franklin Award
Recognizes an individual who has recently made an outstanding and published technical contribution in the fields of rock

Canadian Associations / Canadian Roofing Contractors' Association (CRCA) / Association canadienne des entrepreneurs en couverture (ACEC)

mechanics or rock engineering in Canada and/or internationally. Given biannually

Canadian Roofing Contractors' Association (CRCA) / Association canadienne des entrepreneurs en couverture (ACEC)
#100, 2430 Don Reid Dr., Ottawa ON K1H 1E1
Tel: 613-232-6724; *Fax:* 613-232-2893
Toll-Free: 800-461-2722
crca@roofingcanada.com
www.roofingcanada.com
Overview: A medium-sized national organization founded in 1960
Mission: To provide leadership & guidance to members of the Canadian roofing industry
Member of: Canadian Construction Association; National Trade Contractors Coalition of Canada; National Roofing Contractors Association
Affiliation(s): Construction Specifications Canada
Staff Member(s): 4
Membership: 380; *Member Profile:* Companies actively engaged in the roofing & related sheet metal contracting business in Canada; *Committees:* Board of Directors; Executive; National Technical; Associate Members
Chief Officer(s):
Bob Brunet, Executive Director
brunet@roofingcanada.com

Canadian Rope Skipping Federation (CRSF)
c/o Bonnie Popov, Registrar, 906 County Rd. 46, RR#3, Essex ON N8M 2X7
info@ropeskippingcanada.com
www.ropeskippingcanada.com
twitter.com/RopeSkippingCA
Also Known As: Rope Skipping Canada (RSC)
Previous Name: Canadian Skipping Association
Overview: A small national organization
Mission: To promote rope skipping as a fitness & recreational activity, as well as a competitive sport.
Membership: *Fees:* $20 full; $10 administrative; $7 recreational
Chief Officer(s):
Bonnie Popov, Registrar

Canadian Rose Society (CRS)
116 Belsize Dr., Toronto ON M4S 1L7
Tel: 416-266-6303
Canrosesociety@aol.com
canadianrosesociety.org
www.facebook.com/canadianrosesociety
Previous Name: Rose Society of Ontario
Overview: A medium-sized national charitable organization founded in 1955
Mission: To provide information about rose growing, speakers, judges, nurseries & suppliers, & rose shows; To correspond with people with similar interests throughout Canada & around the world
Member of: World Federation of Rose Societies
Affiliation(s): World Federation of Rose Societies
Finances: *Annual Operating Budget:* Less than $50,000; *Funding Sources:* Donations, membership fees, sales of goods & services
Membership: 500-999; *Fees:* $20 regular; $25 family; $30 affiliate society, nursery, institute;$35 U.S.A. members; $50 foreign; $15 all electronic subscriptions
Activities: *Speaker Service:* Yes; *Library:* Rose Book Library & Rose Slide Library
Chief Officer(s):
Barb Munton, Membership Sec.-Treas.
Publications:
• Canadian Rose Society Newsletter: Sharing your love of roses
Type: Newsletter
Profile: Business of the Canadian Rose Society & world rose news

Canadian Rugby Football Union *See* Football Canada

Canadian Rugby Union *See* Rugby Canada

Canadian Sablefish Association (CSA)
#24B, 12820 Trites Rd., Richmond BC V7E 3R8
Tel: 604-328-7835; *Fax:* 604-448-5382
info@canadiansablefish.com
www.canadiansablefish.com
Overview: A small national organization founded in 1987
Mission: To protect the interests & investments of sablefish fishermen & to explore & develop programs & policies for the protection & conservation of the Canadian sablefish resource & fishery

Canadian Safe Boating Council (CSBC) / Conseil canadien de la sécurité nautique
400 Consumers Rd., Toronto ON M2J 1P8
Tel: 905-820-4817
www.csbc.ca
Overview: A small national organization founded in 1991
Mission: To promote boating safety through the activities of our members & public awareness campaigns
Finances: *Annual Operating Budget:* $100,000-$250,000
100 volunteer(s)
Membership: 135; *Fees:* $500 patron; $150 - organization; $75 - individual; *Committees:* Symposium; PFD Task Force; CASBA Awards; Communications
Activities: Boating safety education; *Awareness Events:* Safe Boating Awareness Week; *Speaker Service:* Yes
Chief Officer(s):
Jean Murray, Chair
chair@csbc.ca

Canadian Safe Cannabis Society (CSCS)
405 Tranquille Rd., Kamloops BC V2B 3G9
Tel: 778-470-5858; *Fax:* 778-470-5859
ilikecannabis.ca
www.facebook.com/436016019940077
Overview: A large national organization
Mission: To assist eligible Canadian patients in safely acquiring medicinal cannabis
Chief Officer(s):
Carl Anderson, Director
carl@ilikecannabis.ca

Canadian Safe School Network (CSSN)
229 Niagara St., Toronto ON M6J 2L5
Tel: 416-977-1050
info@canadiansafeschools.com
www.canadiansafeschools.com
www.facebook.com/CanadianSafeSchoolNetwork
twitter.com/CndnSafeSchools
Overview: A small national organization founded in 1997
Mission: To reduce youth violence & to make our schools & communities safer
Staff Member(s): 5
Chief Officer(s):
Stuart Auty, President
Renee Goncalves, Coordinator, Communications & Event

Canadian Sanitation Supply Association; Canadian Sanitation Standards Association *See* International Sanitary Supply Association Canada

Canadian Schizophrenia Foundation *See* International Schizophrenia Foundation

Canadian Scholarship Trust Foundation (CST) / Fondation fiduciaire canadienne de bourses d'études
#1600, 2235 Sheppard Ave. East, Toronto ON M2J 5B8
Tel: 416-445-7377; *Fax:* 416-445-1708
Toll-Free: 877-333-7377
cstplan@cst.org
www.cst.org
www.linkedin.com/company/cst-consultants-inc.
www.facebook.com/CSTConsultants
twitter.com/CSTConsultants
www.youtube.com/CSTConsultants
Also Known As: CST Foundation
Overview: A small national charitable organization founded in 1960
Mission: To assist parents & others to save for post-secondary education of children, by way of the Canadian Scholarship Trust Plan
Chief Officer(s):
Sherry MacDonald, President/CEO
Peter Bethlenfalvy, CFO

Canadian School Boards Association (CSBA) / L'Association canadienne des commissions/conseils scolaires (ACCCS)
#400, 3 Place Ville Marie, Montréal QC H3B 2E3
Tel: 514-289-2988; *Fax:* 514-788-3334
info@cdnsba.org
www.cdnsba.org
www.facebook.com/cdnsba
twitter.com/cdnsba
Previous Name: Canadian School Trustees' Association
Overview: A large national organization founded in 1923
Mission: To support jurisdictional school board associations in their mandates; To advocate on national, collective interests of Canadian children; To promote the role democratically elected school boards play in ensuring quality & equitable education in Canada
Finances: *Annual Operating Budget:* $250,000-$500,000; *Funding Sources:* Membership fees from school & trustee board associations
Staff Member(s): 3; 23 volunteer(s)
Membership: 250 school boards; *Member Profile:* Provincial/territorial associations of school trustees, school boards & boards of school trustees or of school commissioners; *Committees:* Executive
Activities: *Rents Mailing List:* Yes; *Library*
Chief Officer(s):
Floyd Martens, President
Goronwy Price, Vice President
Meetings/Conferences:
• Canadian School Boards Association 2018 Annual Meeting, 2018
Scope: National
• Canadian School Boards Association / Association canadienne des commissions/conseils scolaires 2018 Congress, July, 2018, Halifax, NS
Scope: National
Publications:
• Anaphylaxis: A Handbook for School Boards
Type: Handbook; *Number of Pages:* 74; *ISBN:* 0-920632-80-7
• CSBA [Canadian School Boards Association] InfoBackgrounder
Type: Newsletter; *Frequency:* Irregular
Profile: Topics include the following: Child Care; High School Completion Rates; & Copyright

Canadian School Libraries (CSL)
299 Canterbury Dr., Waterloo ON N2K 3C1
www.canadianschoollibraries.ca
www.facebook.com/groups/1400617276832667
twitter.com/CdnSchoolLibrar
Overview: A medium-sized national organization
Mission: To contribute to professional research & development in the school library learning commons field in Canada; To help students across Canada improve their learning skills; To unite library practitioners & educators in Canada; To collaborate with other school library organizations, programs, & communities
Activities: Maintaining library learning commons standards; Providing education about library learning commons to school libraries; Offering professional opportunities; Supporting research on library learning commons; Developing & working with educational initiatives at the national & international levels
Chief Officer(s):
Anita Brooks Kirkland, Chair
Publications:
• Canadian School Libraries Journal
Type: Journal; *Frequency:* 3 pa; *Editor:* Derrick Grose; *ISSN:* 2560-7227
Profile: Information about school library research & practice

Canadian School Trustees' Association *See* Canadian School Boards Association

Canadian Science & Technology Historical Association (CSTHA) / Association pour l'histoire de la science et de la technologie au Canada (AHSTC)
PO Box 8502, Stn. T, Ottawa ON K1G 3H9
cstha-ahstc.ca
Overview: A medium-sized national charitable organization founded in 1980
Mission: To foster the study of Canada's scientific & technological heritage through research, publication, teaching & preservation of artifacts & records
Finances: *Annual Operating Budget:* Less than $50,000; *Funding Sources:* Membership fees
Membership: 150; *Fees:* $27
Activities: *Rents Mailing List:* Yes
Chief Officer(s):
Dorotea Gucciardo, President
Mahdi Khelfaoui, Secretary

Canadian Science Writers' Association *See* Science Writers & Communicators of Canada

Canadian Screen Institute *See* National Screen Institute - Canada

Canadian Search Dog Association (CSDA)
PO Box 37103, Stn. Lynnwood Postal Outlet, Edmonton AB T5R 5Y2
calgary.csda@outlook.com
canadiansearchdog.com
www.facebook.com/156258481071770
Previous Name: RCMP Civilian Search & Rescue Civilian Search Dog Program; RCMP Civilian Search Dog Association
Overview: A medium-sized provincial charitable organization founded in 1995
Mission: To generate a group of trained search workers & search dogs to aid the RCMP & other tasking agencies in the search for lost or missing persons
Finances: Funding Sources: Donations

Canadian Securities Administrators (CSA) / Autorités canadiennes en valeurs mobilières (ACVM)
CSA Secretariat, Tour de la Bourse, #2510, 800, rue du Victoria-Square, Montréal QC H4Z 1J2
Tel: 514-864-9510; Fax: 514-864-9512
csa-acvm-secretariat@acvm-csa.ca
www.securities-administrators.ca
twitter.com/CSA_News
Overview: A small national organization
Mission: To coordinate & harmonize regulation of the Canadian capital markets; To foster fair & efficient capital markets; To reduce the risk of failure of market intermediaries
Membership: 13; Member Profile: Securities regulators of Canada's provinces & territories
Activities: Developing the Canadian Securities Regulatory System (CSRS) to harmonize securities regulation, policy, & practice; Educating investors; Providing educational resources about securities & investing; Protecting investors from improper or fraudulent practices; Authorizing individuals who provide investment services to the public; Supervising market intermediaries; Maintaining the databases, SEDAR & SEDI
Chief Officer(s):
Louis Morisset, Chair
Publications:
• Investor Education Annual Activity Report [a publication of the Canadian Securities Administrators]
Type: Report; Frequency: Annually
Profile: A summary of education initiatives
• Report on Enforcement Activities [a publication of the Canadian Securities Administrators]
Type: Report
Profile: Highlights of how Canadian securities regulators protect investors & the marketplace

Canadian Securities Institute (CSI) / L'Institut canadien des valeurs mobilières
200 Wellington St. West, 15th Fl., Toronto ON M5V 3C7
Tel: 416-364-9130; Fax: 416-359-0486
Toll-Free: 866-866-2601
customer_support@csi.ca
www.csi.ca
www.linkedin.com/groups/3720042
www.facebook.com/csiglobal
twitter.com/CSIGlobalEd
www.youtube.com/user/CSIGlobalEd
Previous Name: Institute of Canadian Bankers
Overview: A large national organization founded in 1970
Mission: To enhance the knowledge of securities & financial industry professionals & promote knowledge & understanding of investing among the public
Affiliation(s): Investment Industry Regulatory Organization of Canada; Montreal Exchange; Toronto Stock Exchange; Canadian Venture Exchange
Activities: Granting CIM, PFP, MTI & CIWM professional designations as well as Fellow of the Canadian Securities Institute (FCSI) & Fellow, Institute of Canadian Bankers (FICB); Offering courses in areas such as Retail Banking, Financial Planning & Insurance, Investment Management & Trading, Wealth Management & private Banking, Business Banking, Leadership, Management & Compliance & Continuing Education.; Speaker Service: Yes
Chief Officer(s):
Marie Muldowney, Managing Director
Bureau de Montréal
#400, 625, boul René-Lévesque ouest, Montréal QC H3B 1R2

Canadian Securities Institute Research Foundation / Fondation de recherche de l'Institut canadien des valeurs mobilières
200 Wellington St. West, 15th Fl., Toronto ON M5V 3G2
Tel: 416-681-2262; Fax: 416-364-8952
hirwin@csi.ca
www.csifoundation.com
Previous Name: Investor Learning Centre of Canada
Overview: A small national organization founded in 1993
Mission: Encourages, considers & supports realistic & creative ideas for research in issues pertaining to the Canadian capital markets to benefit investors & other participants with a national &/or global perspective
Affiliation(s): Canadian Securities Institute (CSI)
Activities: Publications & seminars aimed at the novice investor; publications include: "How to Invest in Canadian Securities", "How to Read Financial Statements", "Investment Terms & Definitions", & "Career Oppoutunities in the Investment Industry"; Intelligent Investing seminar series provides a basic overview of investment principles, stocks, bonds, mutual funds & practical information on how to start investing & plan for retirement; Library: ILC Resource Centre

Canadian Security Association (CANASA) / L'Association canadienne de la sécurité
National Office, #201, 50 Acadia Ave., Markham ON L3R 0B3
Tel: 905-513-0622; Fax: 905-513-0624
Toll-Free: 800-538-9919
info@canasa.org
www.canasa.org
www.linkedin.com/company/canadian-security-association
www.facebook.com/canasanews
twitter.com/CANASA_News
Previous Name: Canadian Alarm & Security Association
Overview: A large national organization founded in 1977
Mission: To act as the national voice of the security industry; To promote & protect the interests of members; To increase public awareness of the security industry's effectiveness in reducing risk; To develop & promote programs consistent with the needs of members; To develop & promote programs which will lead to the reduction of false dispatches & improved response; To influence regulations affecting the members
Finances: Funding Sources: Membership fees; Trade show
Membership: 1,000 companies in 10 chapters; Fees: Schedule available; Member Profile: Includes installing & monitoring companies, manufacturers, distributors, consultants & public safety organizations; Members install &/or monitor over 85% of all alarm systems in Canada; Committees: CASC Council; Ethics; Fire & Burglar By-law; National Audit; National By-law & Policy; National Government Relations; National Leadership Forum; National Monitoring Station; National Nominating; Scholarship; Telecommunications Signal Problem Group
Activities: Organizing professional development courses; Hosting members' meetings; Library: by appointment
Chief Officer(s):
Patrick Shaw, Executive Director, 905-513-0622 Ext. 222
pstraw@canasa.org
Steve Basnett, Director, Trade Shows & Events, 905-513-0622 Ext. 224
sbasnett@canasa.org
Awards:
• CANASA National Scholarship Program
Ten scholarships are awarded annually; Amount: $1,000
Publications:
• Canadian Security Association Annual Report
Type: Yearbook
• Canadian Security Association Directory of Members
Type: Directory
Profile: Listing of agents, consulting companies, consultants, installer & installer - monitoring businesses, distributors, monitors, manufacturers, security dirctors, privateguard services, & single installers
• Inside Security [a publication of the Canadian Security Association]
Type: Newsletter
Atlantic Regional Council
Chief Officer(s):
Darron Parker, President
British Columbia Regional Council
BC
Chief Officer(s):
Stuart Armour, President
Luke Malcolm, Vice-President
Southern Alberta Regional Council
AB
Chief Officer(s):
Stephen Goodship, President
Barry Paisley, Vice-President
Northern Alberta Regional Council
AB
Chief Officer(s):
Patti Jones, President
Stephanie Prytuliak, Vice-President
Golden Horseshoe Regional Council
ON
Chief Officer(s):
Joseph Rossano, President
Prairie Regional Chapter
Chief Officer(s):
Lisa Boyer, President
Tara Webber, Vice-President
Central Ontario Regional Council
ON
Chief Officer(s):
Robert Moore, President
Trask Dittburner, Vice-President
Eastern Ontario Regional Council
ON
Chief Officer(s):
Chris Izatt, President
Québec Regional Council
QC
Chief Officer(s):
Denis Primeau, Président
Southwestern Ontario Regional Council
ON
Chief Officer(s):
Brian Gibbs, President
Angelo Bucciarelli, Vice-President

Canadian Security Traders Association, Inc. (CSTA)
PO Box 3, 31 Adelaide St. East, Toronto ON M5C 2J6
janice.cooper@canadiansta.org
www.canadiansta.org
Overview: A medium-sized national organization founded in 2000
Membership: Committees: Audit; Conference; CSTA/STA Relationship; Nominating; Sponsorship; Speakers; Website
Chief Officer(s):
Peggy Bowie, President, 416-926-5462
peggy_bowie@manulifeam.com
Meetings/Conferences:
• Canadian Security Traders Association 25th Annual Conference, August, 2018, Hilton Québec City, Québec, QC
Scope: National

Canadian Seed Growers' Association (CSGA) / Association canadienne des producteurs de semences
PO Box 8455, #202, 240 Catherine St., Ottawa ON K1G 3T1
Tel: 613-236-0497; Fax: 613-563-7855
seeds@seedgrowers.ca
www.seedgrowers.ca
Overview: A medium-sized national organization founded in 1904
Mission: To advance the Canadian seed industry; To advocate for the use of the seed certification as an integral part of quality & identity assurance programs; To develop & provide seed crop certification standards & regulations
Staff Member(s): 8
Membership: 4,300
Activities: Advancing the grower perspective on issues related to seed; Cooperating with researchers & growers to expand the use of pedigreed seed; Certifying pedigreed seed crops
Chief Officer(s):
Glyn Chancey, Executive Director, 613-236-0497 Ext. 224
gchancey@seedgrowers.ca
Meetings/Conferences:
• Canadian Seed Growers' Association Annual General Meeting 2018, July, 2018, Montréal, QC
Scope: National
Publications:
• Canadian Seed Growers' Acreage & Membership Report
Type: Report
• Canadian Seed Growers' Association Annual Report
Type: Report; Frequency: Annually
• Seed Scoop [a publication of the Canadian Seed Growers' Association]
Type: Newsletter; Frequency: Monthly

Canadian Associations / Canadian Seed Trade Association (CSTA) / Association canadienne du commerce des semences (ACCS)

Profile: Contains important updates on seed crop regulations & association programs & activities
• Seed to Succeed [a publication of the Canadian Seed Growers' Association]
Type: Magazine; *Frequency:* s-a.; *Price:* Free with CSGA membership
Profile: Provides insight into current issues in the seed sector

Canadian Seed Trade Association (CSTA) / Association canadienne du commerce des semences (ACCS)
#505, 2039 Robertson Rd., Ottawa ON K2H 8R2
Tel: 613-829-9527; *Fax:* 613-829-3530
www.cdnseed.org
www.facebook.com/cdnseed
twitter.com/SeedInnovation
Overview: A medium-sized national organization founded in 1923
Mission: To foster an environment conducive to researching, developing, distributing & trading seed and associated technologies
Finances: Funding Sources: Membership fees
Staff Member(s): 3
Membership: 128; *Fees:* Schedule available; *Member Profile:* Plant breeders & those involved with the seed manufacturing industry; *Committees:* Biotechnology; Forage & Turf Committee; International Committee; Researchers East; Researchers West; Oilseeds, Pulses & Western Cereals; Intellectual Property; Corn, Soybeans & Eastern Cereals
Chief Officer(s):
Patty Townsend, Chief Executive Officer, 613-829-9527 Ext. 223
Peter Entz, President

Canadian Self Storage Association (CSSA)
PO Box 188, Coldwater ON L0K 1E0
Fax: 519-941-0877
Toll-Free: 888-898-8538
info@cssa.ca
www.cssa.ca
ca.linkedin.com/groups/Canadian-Self-Storage-Association-4106636
www.facebook.com/CanadianSelfStorageAssociation
twitter.com/cdnselfstorage/
Overview: A medium-sized national organization
Mission: The Canadian Self Storage Association brings together industry members through leadership, information, products, networking, services and government representation.
Affiliation(s): American Self Storage Association
Membership: Fees: $499
Chief Officer(s):
Troy McLellan, President

Canadian Senior Pro Rodeo Association (CSPRA)
PO Box 393, Carseland AB T0J 0M0
Tel: 403-875-3242
info@canadaseniorrodeo.com
www.canadianseniorrodeo.com
Overview: A large national organization
Mission: To allow individuals over 40 to compete in rodeo events across Canada & North America
Finances: Funding Sources: Corporate & individual sponsors
Membership: Fees: $173.25; $26.25 associate
Activities: Hosting rodeos; events include saddle bronc riding, bareback riding, bull riding, tie down roping, team roping, ribbon roping, barrel racing, & steer wrestling
Chief Officer(s):
Michelle Atwood, Secretary

Canadian Service for Overseas Students & Trainees *See* Canadian Bureau for International Education

Canadian Sheep Breeders' Association (CSBA) / La société canadienne des éleveurs de moutons
PO Box 46, RR#2, Site 7, Bluffton AB T0C 0M0
Fax: 877-207-2541
Toll-Free: 866-956-1116
office@sheepbreeders.ca
www.sheepbreeders.ca
Overview: A medium-sized national organization
Mission: To represent & promote sheep breeders
Membership: 1,100; *Fees:* $50; *Committees:* Executive & Finance; Spot Parentage; Health/Scrapie Canada/Eradication Working Group; Constitution; Promotion/Education/Information; Breed Standards/International Association Recognition; Genetics/GenOvis/Research; Classic & Model/Template
Chief Officer(s):
Bruce Sinclair, President

Neil Versavel, Vice-President
Stacey White, General Manager

Canadian Sheep Federation / Fédération canadienne du mouton
130 Malcolm Rd., Guelph ON N1K 1B1
Tel: 613-652-1824; *Fax:* 866-909-5360
Toll-Free: 888-684-7739
info@cansheep.ca
www.cansheep.ca
Previous Name: Canada Sheep Council
Overview: A small national organization founded in 1990
Mission: To set national policy for the sheep industry; to endeavour to further the viability, expansion & prosperity of the Canadian sheep & wool industry.
Finances: Funding Sources: Provincial organizations; Federal funding
Staff Member(s): 2
Membership: 10 organizations; *Member Profile:* Canadian sheep producers
Chief Officer(s):
Philip Kolodychuk, Chair
philk@abnorth.com
Carlena Patterson, Executive Director
corlena@cansheep.ca

Canadian Sheet Steel Building Institute (CSSBI) / Institut canadien de la tôle d'acier pour le bâtiment (ICTAB)
#2A, 652 Bishop St. North, Cambridge ON N3H 4V6
Tel: 519-650-1285; *Fax:* 519-650-8081
info@cssbi.ca
www.cssbi.ca
www.linkedin.com/groups/Canadian-Sheet-Steel-Building-Institute-3886745
www.facebook.com/197469816960835
twitter.com/cssbi
Overview: A medium-sized national organization founded in 1961
Mission: To make steel the material of choice for building construction in Canada.
Membership: 29 corporate; *Member Profile:* Producers, fabricators & associates involved in the structural sheet steel industry
Chief Officer(s):
Meredith Perez, Manager, Marketing

Canadian Shiatsu Society of British Columbia (CSSBC)
123 Carrie Cates Ct., North Vancouver BC V7M 3K7
Tel: 604-349-8508
info@shiatsupractor.org
www.shiatsupractor.org
Overview: A small provincial organization
Mission: To set high educational & professional standards for Shiatsu Therapy in British Columbia; To provide the Shiatsupractor (SPR) certification
Membership: Fees: $100; *Member Profile:* Shiatsupractors in British Columbia

Canadian Shire Horse Association (CSHA)
c/o Maxine Campbell, PO Box 387, Dawson Creek BC V1G 4H3
www.canadianshirehorse.com
Overview: A small national organization
Mission: To encourage, develop and regulate purebred Shire horses in Canada.
Membership: Fees: $50 Canadian breeders; $30 associate members; $500 life memberships; *Member Profile:* Shire horse breeders & owners
Activities: Arranging procedures for registration of Shire horses; Setting standards for the breed; Providing information specific to Shire breeders & owners; Presenting show results for Shire horses
Publications:
• CSHA [Canadian Shire Horse Association] Newsletter
Type: Newsletter; *Price:* Free with membership in the Canadian Shire Horse Association

Canadian Shooting Sports Association (CSSA)
#204, 1143 Wentworth St. West, Oshawa ON L1J 8P7
Fax: 905-720-3497
Toll-Free: 888-873-4339
info@cdnshootingsports.org
cssa-cila.org
Merged from: Ontario Handgun Association; Ontario Smallbore Federation
Overview: A medium-sized national organization

Mission: To provide the knowledge, guidance & services to ensure the continuation promotion of the shooting sports & related activities & to represent their interests to the government, the regulatory bodies, the media & the public
Affiliation(s): Ontario Council of Shooters; Shooting Federation of Canada
Finances: Funding Sources: Membership fees
Membership: 15,000; *Fees:* $45 general; $80 family; $27 junior; $250 corporate; $950 life; *Member Profile:* Member of a recognized shooting club
Activities: To provide liability insurance & training courses

Canadian Shorthorn Association
Canada Centre Bldg., Exhibition Park, PO Box 3771, Regina SK S4P 3N8
Tel: 306-757-2212; *Fax:* 306-525-5852
info@canadianshorthorn.com
www.canadianshorthorn.com
Overview: A medium-sized national organization founded in 1886
Member of: Canadian Beef Breeds Council
Affiliation(s): Alberta Shorthorn Association; British Columbia Shorthorn Association; Maritime Shorthorn Association; New Brunswick Shorthorn Association; Nova Scotia Shorthorn Association; Ontario Shorthorn Association; Prince Edward Island Shorthorn Association; Quebec Shorthorn Association; Saskatchewan Shorthorn Association; Shorthorn Breeders of Manitoba Inc.
Finances: Annual Operating Budget: $100,000-$250,000
Staff Member(s): 2
Membership: 600; *Fees:* Schedule available
Chief Officer(s):
Bob Merkley, President
circlemshorthorns@telus.net
Belinda Wagner, Secretary-Treasurer

Canadian Simmental Association
#13, 4101 - 19 St. NE, Calgary AB T2E 7C4
Tel: 403-250-7979; *Fax:* 403-250-5121
Toll-Free: 866-860-6051
cansim@simmental.com
www.simmental.com
Overview: A small national organization founded in 1969
Mission: To encourage, develop, & regulate the breeding of Simmental cattle in Canada
Member of: Canadian Beef Breeds Council
Staff Member(s): 9
Membership: Fees: $25 youth; $50 annual membership initiation; $50 annual administration; $25 annual membership; $200 life membership
Activities: Registering Simmental cattle in Canada; Keeping a record of the breeding and origin of all Simmental cattle; Protecting & assisting breeders engaged in the propagation & breeding of Simmental cattle; Compiling statistics on the industry; *Library:* CSA Library
Chief Officer(s):
Fraser Redpath, President, 204-529-2560, Fax: 204-529-2560
redsim2@gmail.com
Kelly Ashworth, First Vice-President
jashworth@sasktel.net
Randy Mader, Second Vice-President
rrmader@xplornet.com
Bruce Holmquist, General Manager
bholmquist@simmental.com
Publications:
• Canadian Simmental Association Annual Report
Type: Yearbook; *Frequency:* Annually
• Commercial Country [a publication of the Canadian Simmental Association]
Type: Magazine; *Frequency:* Semiannually; *Accepts Advertising*
Profile: Information for the commercial industry
• CSA [Canadian Simmental Association] Member Enewsletter
Type: Newsletter; *Frequency:* Monthly
Profile: Beef information, CSA activities, registry information, & events
• Simmental Country
Type: Magazine; *Frequency:* Bimonthly; *Accepts Advertising*; *ISSN:* 1709-5212; *Price:* $42 Canada; $65 USA; $130 International
Profile: Advertising & marketing needs for breeders

Canadian Sinfonietta Youth Orchestra (CSYO)
c/o Canadian Sinfonietta, 107 Glengrove Ave. West, Toronto ON M4R 1P1
Tel: 416-716-6997
cs.youthorchestra@gmail.com

www.csyo.wordpress.com
twitter.com/csyouthorch
Previous Name: Toronto Cultural Youth Orchestra
Overview: A small local charitable organization founded in 1985 overseen by Orchestras Canada
Mission: To provide young musicians with quality orchestral experience to further their musical development
Membership: *Fees:* $180
Activities: Performing concerts, Participating in music competitions and festivals
Chief Officer(s):
Tak-Ng Lai, Music Director

Canadian Ski & Snowboard Association; Canadian Ski Association *See* Canadian Snowsports Association

Canadian Ski Council (CSC) / Conseil canadien du ski
#14, 76000 Hwy. 27, Woodbridge ON L4H 0P8
Tel: 905-856-4754
info@skicanada.org
www.skicanada.org
www.facebook.com/GoSkiingGoSnowboarding
twitter.com/cdnskicouncil
www.pinterest.com/gosnow
Overview: A medium-sized national organization founded in 1977
Mission: To encourage participation in recreational skiing & snowboarding.
Member of: Canadian Society of Association Executives; Tourism Industry Association of Canada.
Affiliation(s): Canadian Association for Disabled Skiing; Canadian Ski Instructors' Alliance; Canadian Ski Patrol; Canadian Association of Snowboard Instructors; Association des stations de ski du Québec; Atlantic Ski Area Association; Canadian Snowsports Association; Canada West Ski Areas Association; Ontario Snow Resorits Associations
Finances: *Funding Sources:* Sponsorship; associate membership; service fees; research
Membership: 11 organizations; *Committees:* Marketing & Research; Toronto Snow Show
Activities: Skier Development Programs; product development; research; *Speaker Service:* Yes; *Rents Mailing List:* Yes
Chief Officer(s):
Claude Péloquin, Chair
Patrick Arkeveld, President & CEO

Canadian Ski Instructors' Alliance (CSIA) / Alliance des moniteurs de ski du Canada
#401, 8615, boul Saint-Laurent, Montréal QC H2P 2M9
Tel: 514-748-2648; *Fax:* 514-748-2476
Toll-Free: 800-811-6428
national@snowpro.com
www.snowpro.com
www.facebook.com/CSIAAMSC
twitter.com/csiaamsc
www.youtube.com/user/CSIAAMSC
Overview: A large national organization founded in 1938
Mission: To promote professionalism & high standards for the profession of ski instruction; To certify ski instructors across Canada
Member of: Canadian Ski Council
Affiliation(s): International Ski Instructors' Association
Finances: *Funding Sources:* Membership dues
Staff Member(s): 15
Activities: Providing education & leadership that contributes to a vibrant mountain experience for the skiing public; *Internships:* Yes
Chief Officer(s):
Francois Morrison, Managing Director
fmorrison@snowpro.com
Lisa Cambise, Director, Shared Services
lisa@snowpro.com
Martin Jean, Director, Education & Membership Services
martinj@snowpro.com
Benoit Fournier, Coordinator, National Programs
benoit@snowpro.com
Publications:
• CSIA [Canadian Ski Instructors' Alliance] eBLAST
Type: Newsletter; *Frequency:* Monthly
Profile: CSIA activities
• Ski Pro
Type: Magazine; *Frequency:* Annually; *Accepts Advertising*;
Price: Free with CSIA membership
Profile: CSIA news, teaching tips, techniques, industry updates,

benefits, course schedules, job listings, & merchandise for ski instructors & coaches
Ontario
637 Hurontario St., Collingwood ON L9Y 2N6
Tel: 416-426-7261; *Fax:* 705-300-7135
info@csiaontario.com
www.csiaontario.com
www.facebook.com/csiaontario
twitter.com/csiaontario
Chief Officer(s):
Shelagh Mulveney, Office Administrator

Canadian Ski Marathon (CSM) / Marathon canadien de ski (MCS)
266, rue Viger, Papineauville QC J0V 1R0
Tel: 819-483-0456; *Fax:* 819-483-0450
Toll-Free: 877-770-6556
ski@csm-mcs.com
www.csm-mcs.com
www.facebook.com/csmmcs
twitter.com/csmmcs
www.youtube.com/user/csmmcs
Overview: A medium-sized national charitable organization founded in 1967
Mission: The Canadian Ski Marathon is an historic cross-county ski tour for people of all ages in celebration of Canadian winter. Their mission is to organize an annual & fully supported weekend in the wilderness, the Canadian Ski Marathon provides a uniquely Canadian cross-country skiing event with a broad appeal.
Affiliation(s): Tourisme Outaouais; Tourisme Laurentides
Finances: *Annual Operating Budget:* $250,000-$500,000; *Funding Sources:* Sponsors; participants
Staff Member(s): 3; 500 volunteer(s)
Membership: 2,000; *Fees:* Schedule available
Activities: Cross-Country Ski Tour; *Internships:* Yes
Chief Officer(s):
Paul "Boomer" Throop, President
pthroop@magma.ca
Frédéric Ménard, Director, Events

Canadian Ski Patrol (CSP) / Patrouille canadienne de ski (PCS)
4531 Southclark Pl., Ottawa ON K1T 3V2
Tel: 613-822-2245; *Fax:* 613-822-1088
Toll-Free: 900-565-2777
info@skipatrol.ca
www.csps.ca
www.facebook.com/CSP.PCS
twitter.com/CdnSkiPatrol
Overview: A medium-sized national charitable organization founded in 1940
Mission: To provide first aid & safety programs throughout Canada
Member of: Fédération Internationale des Patrouilles de Ski (FIPS) / International Federation of Ski Patrollers
Finances: *Funding Sources:* Sponsorships; Donations
Membership: 5,450; *Member Profile:* Volunteer patrollers, over the age of eighteen, who have undergone training sessions in first aid & rescue; *Committees:* Communications; Fund Development; Education; Finance & Administration; Operations
Activities: Patrolling over 200 resorts across Canada on alpine, Nordic, & tele-mark skis, as well as on snow boards; Providing year-round safety & rescue services by volunteering at non-skiing events during the summer; Presenting awards; Providing first aid training; *Awareness Events:* National First Aid Competition
Chief Officer(s):
Colin Saravanamuttoo, President & CEO, 613-822-2245 Ext. 224
csaravan@skipatrol.ca
Renée Thivierge, Office Manager, 613-822-2245 Ext. 231
manager@skipatrol.ca
Publications:
• 5/5 [a publication of the Canadian Ski Patrol]
Type: Newsletter
Pacific South Division (PSD)
BC
Chief Officer(s):
Ian Bowen, President
Atlantic East Division
NS
www.scotiazone.com
www.facebook.com/SkiPatrolNS
Chief Officer(s):

Bernie Robichau, President, Scotia Zone
president@scotiazone.com
• CSPS [Canadian Ski Patrol System] Scotia Zone Newsletter
Type: Newsletter
Drayton Valley - Mountain Division
3513 - 49 Ave., Drayton Valley AB T7A 1E3
www.skipatrol.ca/mountain
www.facebook.com/CanadianSkiPatrolMountainDivision
Chief Officer(s):
Dave Swindlehurst, President
dave.swindlehurst@weyerhaeuser.com
• Mountain Peaks: Newsletter of the Canadian Ski Patrol System, Mountain Division
Type: Newsletter
Profile: Upcoming events & division updates
• The Probe: The Voice of CSPS Calgary Zone
Type: Newsletter; *Frequency:* Monthly
Profile: Zone reports & forthcoming events
Atlantic West Division (CSP - AWD)
Mission: To promote safety & injury prevention; To provide high standards of education, certification, & delivery in first aid & rescue services
Chief Officer(s):
Doug Couture, Contact
doug.couture@skipatrol.ca
Manitoba Division
MB
info@cspsmanitoba.ca
www.cspsmanitoba.ca
Ontario Division
www.skipatrol.on.ca
Mission: To support the Canadian Ski Patrol System system through training & leadership
Chief Officer(s):
Bruce Boynton, President
Pacific North Division
Chief Officer(s):
Bill Hellyer, Contact
bill.hellyer@skipatrol.ca
Québec Division (PCSQ)
CP 536, Saint-Jérôme QC J7Z 5V3
Tél: 514-906-7099
Ligne sans frais: 866-747-8899
www.skipatrol.ca/quebec
Chief Officer(s):
Jean-Francois Bourk, President, Lanaudière
Serge Côté, President, Abitibi
Daniel Côté, President, Bois-Francs
Serge Laprise, President, Baie-Comeau
Serge Paradis, President, Est du Québec
Peter Patterson, President, Gaspé
Richard Eaton, President, Gatineau
Jean-Luc Sauvé, President, Laurentienne
Jean-Luc Lamarche, President, Mauricie
Marcel Lauzon, President, Québec
Gaëtan Girard, President, Saguenay-Lac-St-Jean
Nicolas Thisdel, President, Sept-Iles
Jean Côté, President, Cantons de l'Est
• Le Câble: Newsletter of the Canadian Ski Patrol System, Eastern Townships Zone
Type: Newsletter
Profile: Information about education, ski swaps, meetings, & operations in the zone
• Snow Squall: Newsletter of the Canadian Ski Patrol System, Gatineau Zone
Type: Newsletter; *Frequency:* Biweekly
Profile: Activities in the Gatineau Zone, including special events, instructor information, & awards
Saskatchewan Division
Saskatoon SK
saskdivision@skipatrol.ca
www.skipatrol.ca/saskatchewan

Canadian Skin Patient Alliance (CSPA)
#383, 136-2446 Bank St., Ottawa ON K1V 1A8
Tel: 613-440-4260; *Fax:* 877-294-1525
Toll-Free: 877-505-2772
info@canadianskin.ca
www.canadianskin.ca
www.facebook.com/CanadianSkin
twitter.com/canadianskin
Overview: A large national organization founded in 2007
Mission: To educate the public about skin health & to help patients experience skin health concerns
Affiliation(s): AboutFace; Alberta Society of Melanoma; Alliance

Québécoise du Psoriasis; BCCNS Life Support Network; British Columbia Lymphedema Association; Canadian Alopecia Areata Foundation; Canadian Burn Survivors Community; Canadian Pemphigus & Pemphigoid Foundation; Canadian Psoriasis Network; Canadian Skin Cancer Foundation; Cutaneous Lymphoma Foundation; DEBRA Canada, Epidermolysis Bullosa; Eczema Society of Canada; Neurofibromatosis Society of Ontario; Save Your Skin; Scleroderma Association of British Columbia; Scleroderma Society of Ontario; Canadian Association of Psoriasis Patients
Membership: *Committees:* Website; Advocacy; Affiliates; SKIN Conference Planning
Chief Officer(s):
Kathryn Andrews-Clay, Executive Director
kathrynclay@canadianskin.ca
Helen Crawford, Manager, CAPP Programs, Social Media & Governance
helencrawford@canadianskin.ca
• Canadian Skin Magazine
Type: Magazine; *Frequency:* 4 times a year; *Editor:* Sheri Pilon; *ISSN:* 1923-0729
Profile: The magazine publishes articles regarding skin health

Canadian Skipping Association See Canadian Rope Skipping Federation

Canadian Sleep Society (CSS) / Société Canadienne du Sommeil (SCS)
c/o Reut Gruber, McGill University, Douglas Institute, 6875, boul LaSalle, Montréal QC H4H 1R3
Fax: 877-659-0760
Toll-Free: 866-239-2176
Other Communication: media@canadiansleepsociety.ca
info@canadiansleepsociety.ca
www.canadiansleepsociety.ca
Overview: A small national charitable organization founded in 1986
Mission: To further the advancement & understanding of sleep & its disorders through scientific study & public awareness
Membership: 100-499; *Fees:* $100; $40 technologist; $25 student; $1000 corporate
Chief Officer(s):
Shelly K. Weiss, President
president@canadiansleepsociety.ca

Canadian Slovak League
#6, 259 Traders Blvd. East, Mississauga ON L4Z 2E5
Tel: 905-507-8004
administrator@kanadskyslovak.ca
www.ksliga.com
Overview: A small national organization founded in 1932

Canadian Slovenian Chamber of Commerce (CSCC)
747 Browns Line, Toronto ON M8W 3V7
Tel: 416-251-8456; *Fax:* 416-252-2092
info@canslo.com
www.canslo.com
www.linkedin.com/company/canadian-slovenian-chamber-of-commerce
www.facebook.com/CanadianSlovenianChamberofCommerce
Overview: A small international organization founded in 1990
Mission: To promote Canadian Slovenian business and enterprise, communication between people in business & to create opportunities for business investment in Canada and abroad.
Membership: *Fees:* $250 medium/large businesss; $100 small businesses/professionals/individuals; $0 non-profit organizations/students
Activities: CSCC Business Directory (online)
Chief Officer(s):
Simon Pribac, Executive Director

Canadian Snack Food Association (CSFA) / Association canadienne des fabricants des grignotines
c/o Ileana Lima, PO Box 42252, 128 Queen St. South, Mississauga ON L5M 4Z0
Tel: 289-997-1379
www.canadiansnack.com
Overview: A medium-sized national organization founded in 1957
Mission: To provide the leadership required for sustained growth & competitiveness of the industry; To influence policy formulation, legislation & regulations at all levels of government in the best interests of the industry; To encourage high standards for the protection of public health
Affiliation(s): Canadian Horticultural Council
Finances: *Annual Operating Budget:* Less than $50,000
Membership: 31 corporate; *Fees:* $4,000 business; $600 associate; *Member Profile:* Snack food manufacturers & suppliers
Chief Officer(s):
Kent Hawkins, President
Ileana Lima, Executive Vice-President
ileanal@4reflections.com
Meetings/Conferences:
• Canadian Snack Food Association 2018 62nd Annual Conference, 2018
Scope: National

Canadian Snowbird Association (CSA) / Association canadienne des Snowbirds
180 Lesmill Rd., Toronto ON M3B 2T5
Tel: 416-391-9000; *Fax:* 416-441-7007
Toll-Free: 800-265-3200
csastaff@snowbirds.org
www.snowbirds.org
Overview: A small national organization founded in 1992
Mission: Dedicated to actively defending & improving the rights & privileges of travelling Canadians
Finances: *Annual Operating Budget:* $500,000-$1,5 Million; *Funding Sources:* Membership fees; special donations
Staff Member(s): 6; 9 volunteer(s)
Membership: 70,000; *Fees:* $25 one year; $325 lifetime;
Committees: Membership; Promotion; Government Relations; Finance
Activities: Lifestyle presentations, Fall in Canada; Extravaganzas; Winter information meetings (Spring in the USA)
Chief Officer(s):
Michael MacKenzien, Executive Director
Michael.MacKenzie@snowbirds.org
Robert Slack, President
Publications:
• CSA [Canadian Snowbird Association] News / Nouvelles CSA
Type: Magazine; *Frequency:* Quarterly; *Accepts Advertising*; *Editor:* J. Ross Quigley; *ISSN:* 1195-2393; *Price:* Free with CSA membership; $20 Canada non-members; $30 International non-members
Profile: Government information, articles, CSA activities, insurance updates, health information, advice, events, awards, book reviews &benefits
• CSA [Canadian Snowbird Association] Information Booklets
Profile: Topics include the following: The CSA Member Handbook; The CSA Travel Information Guide; & The CSA Travellers' Checklist

Canadian Snowboard Federation
#301, 333 Terminal Ave., Vancouver BC V6A 4C1
Tel: 604-568-1135; *Fax:* 604-568-1639
info@canadasnowboard.ca
www.canadasnowboard.ca
www.facebook.com/canadasnowboard
twitter.com/CanadaSnowboard
www.youtube.com/user/CanadaSnowboardVideo
Also Known As: Canada~Snowboard
Overview: A medium-sized national organization
Mission: To be the national governing body of competitive snowboarding in Canada.
Activities: Freestyle; alpine; snowboardcross; para-snowboard
Chief Officer(s):
Patrick Jarvis, Executive Director
patrick.jarvis@canadasnowboard.ca
Robert Joncas, Director, High Performance
lebob@canadasnowboard.ca
Brendan Matthews, Manager, Business Operations
Brendan@canadasnowboard.ca

Canadian Snowsports Association (CSA) / L'Association canadienne des sports d'hiver (ACSH)
#202, 1451 West Broadway, Vancouver BC V6H 1H6
Tel: 604-734-6800; *Fax:* 604-669-7954
info@canadiansnowsports.com
www.canadiansnowsports.com
Previous Name: Canadian Ski & Snowboard Association; Canadian Ski Association
Overview: A large national organization founded in 1920
Mission: To develop elite amateur athletes; To pursue excellence at national & international level competition
Membership: 700+ ski clubs + 97,000 members
Chief Officer(s):
David Pym, Managing Director
dpym@isrm.com
Lillian Alderton, Administrator
lillianalderton@hotmail.com
Awards:
• John Semmelink Memorial Award
• Dee Road Memorial Award
• Patricia Ramage Volunteer of the Year Award

Canadian Soccer Association (CSA) / Association canadienne de soccer
237 Metcalfe St., Ottawa ON K2P 1R2
Tel: 613-237-7678; *Fax:* 613-237-1516
info@soccercan.ca
www.canadasoccer.com
www.facebook.com/canadasoccer
twitter.com/CanadaSoccerEN
www.youtube.com/CanadaSoccerTV
Overview: A large national organization founded in 1912
Mission: To promote the growth & development of soccer for all Canadians at all levels; To provide leadership & good governance for the sport
Affiliation(s): Féderation Internationale de Football Association, FIFA; Football Confederation; Canadian Olympic Association
Staff Member(s): 56
Membership: 850,000 registered players
Chief Officer(s):
Peter Montopoli, General Secretary
Sean Hefferman, CFO
Sandra Gage, CMO
Jason DeVos, Director, Development
jdevos@canadasoccer.com
Cathy Breda, Manager, Administration
cbreda@canadasoccer.com
  Technical Office
  BMO Field, 170 Princes' Blvd., Toronto ON M6K 3C3
  Tel: 416-263-5890; *Fax:* 416-263-5891

Canadian Social Work Foundation (CSWF) / Fondation canadienne du service social
#402, 383 Parkdale Ave., Ottawa ON K1Y 4R4
Tel: 613-729-6668; *Fax:* 613-729-9608
Toll-Free: 855-729-2279
casw@casw-acts.ca
www.casw-acts.ca
www.facebook.com/Canadian.Association.of.Social.Workers
Overview: A small national charitable organization
Mission: To edit & publish books, papers, journals & other forms of literature respecting social work in order to disseminate information to the public; to encourage studies; to promote, develop & sponsor activities strengthening social work
Finances: *Funding Sources:* Donations
Staff Member(s): 4
Membership: *Fees:* $50 affiliate; $0 students
Chief Officer(s):
Morel Caissie, President
Fred Phelps, Executive Director

Canadian Society for Aesthetic (Cosmetic) Plastic Surgery See Canadian Society for Aesthetic Plastic Surgery

Canadian Society for Aesthetic Plastic Surgery (CSAPS) / Société canadienne de chirurgie plastique et esthétique
70 Carson Ave., Whitby ON L1M 1J5
Tel: 905-665-9889; *Fax:* 905-665-7319
info@csaps.ca
www.csaps.ca
www.facebook.com/csaps
Previous Name: Canadian Society for Aesthetic (Cosmetic) Plastic Surgery
Overview: A small national organization founded in 1972
Mission: To improve cosmetic surgery outcomes; To maintain high surgical standards of clinical practice
Membership: 160+; *Fees:* Schedule available; *Member Profile:* Certified specialists in plastic surgery, with a special focus on aesthetic surgery; *Committees:* Ethics; Judicial; Constitution / Bylaws; Public Relations; Nominating; Educational; CMPA Ad Hoc; Public Education Ad Hoc
Activities: Supporting research; Providing education
Chief Officer(s):
Eric Bensimon, President
Tara Hewitt, Executive Administrator
csapsoffice@gmail.com
Meetings/Conferences:
• 2018 Canadian Society for Aesthetic Plastic Surgery 45th Annual Meeting, September, 2018, Westin Montréal, Montréal,

QC
Scope: National

Canadian Society for Aesthetics (CSA) / Société canadienne d'esthétique (SCE)
c/o Dawson College, 4729, av de Maisonneuve, Westmount QC H3Z 1M3
www.csa-sce.ca
Overview: A small national organization founded in 1984
Mission: To keep aesthetic theorists in close touch with the creative & critical practices that are the basis of their discipline; to increase awareness of aesthetic issues among Canadian citizens & develop the intellectual & conceptual resources for dealing with them.
Member of: Humanities & Social Sciences Federation of Canada
Finances: *Funding Sources:* Membership dues; HSSFC
Chief Officer(s):
Ira Newman, Anglophone President
inewman@mansfield.edu
Carl Simpson, Secretary, Membership
msimpson@wlu.ca

Canadian Society for Analytical Sciences & Spectroscopy
PO Box 46122, 2339 Ogilvie Rd., Ottawa ON K1J 9M7
Tel: 613-933-3719; *Fax:* 613-954-5984
www.csass.org
Previous Name: Spectroscopy Society of Canada
Overview: A medium-sized national organization founded in 1957
Mission: To organize programs of scientific & general interest for the educational benefit of members & the public; to organize annual scientific conferences & workshops on various aspects of pure & applied spectroscopy in the chemical, biological, geochemical & metallurgical sciences
Affiliation(s): Society for Applied Spectroscopy - USA; Colloquium Spectroscopicum Internationale; Chemical Institute of Canada; Canadian Society of Forensic Science
Membership: *Fees:* Schedule available
Chief Officer(s):
Graeme Spiers, President
gspiers@mirarco.org
Ana Delgado, Treasurer
ana.delgado@nrc.gc.ca

Canadian Society for Bioengineering (CSBE) / Société canadienne de génie agroalimentaire et de bioingénierie (SCGAB)
2028 Calico Crescent, Orléans ON K4A 4L7
Tel: 613-590-0975
bioeng@csbe-scgab.ca
csbe-scgab.ca
Previous Name: Canadian Society for Engineering in Agricultural, Food & Biological Systems
Overview: A medium-sized national organization founded in 1958
Mission: To provide expertise in the areas of farm power & machinery, structures & environment, soil & water & electrical power & processing
Affiliation(s): American Society of Agricultural & Biological Engineers
Finances: *Annual Operating Budget:* $100,000-$250,000; *Funding Sources:* Annual dues
Staff Member(s): 1; 17 volunteer(s)
Membership: 500 full + 200 students; *Fees:* Schedule available
Activities: Canadian Society for Bioengineering Foundation
Chief Officer(s):
Greg Clark, President
president@csbe-scgab.ca
John Feddes, Society Manager
manager@csbe-scgab.ca
Awards:
• John Turnbull Award
• John Clark Award
• Glenn Downing Award
• Jim Beamish Award
• Maple Leaf Award
• Industrial Award
• CSBE Fellow Award
• Young Engineer of the Year Award
Meetings/Conferences:
• CSBE/SCGAB 2018 AGM & Technical Conference, July, 2018, Guelph, ON
Scope: National
Publications:
• Canadian Biosystems Engineering Journal / Le Journal de la Société Canadienne de Génie Agroalimentaire et de Bioingénierie
Type: Journal; *Editor:* Ranjan Sri Ranjan; *Price:* $50 Canada non-members; $30 Canada CSBE / SCGAB members
Profile: Peer-reviewed papers
• Canadian Society for Bioengineering Annual Meeting Papers
Frequency: Annually
Profile: Presentations from conferences
• Perspectives: The Newsletter of CSBE [Canadian Society for Bioengineering] / Les Nouvelles de SCGAB
Type: Newsletter
Profile: Canadian Society for Bioengineering / Société canadienne de génie agroalimentaire et de bioingénierie activities, awards, chapter news, job opportunities, & events
• Resource [a publication of the Canadian Society for Bioengineering]
Type: Magazine; *Accepts Advertising*
Profile: Industry news & trends

Canadian Society for Brain, Behaviour & Cognitive Science (CSBBCS) / Société Canadienne des Sciences du Cerveau, du Comportement et de la Cognition
c/o Dept. of Psychology, University of British Columbia, Vancouver BC V6T 1Z4
secretary@csbbcs.org
www.csbbcs.org
Overview: A small national organization
Mission: To advance Canadian research in experimental psychology & behavioral neuroscience
Member of: National Consortium of Scientific & Educational Societies
Membership: 400+; *Fees:* $70 regular; $40 associate/student; *Member Profile:* Students & people with PhDs in psychology & related fields
Chief Officer(s):
Penny Pexman, President
Peter Graf, Secretary-Treasurer
Meetings/Conferences:
• Canadian Society for Brain, Behaviour & Cognitive Science 2018 Annual Meeting, July, 2018, Memorial University, St. John's, NL

Canadian Society for Chemical Engineering (CSChE) / Société canadienne de génie chimique (SCGC)
c/o The Chemical Institute of Canada (CIC), #550, 130 Slater St., Ottawa ON K1P 6E2
Tel: 613-232-6252; *Fax:* 613-232-5862
Toll-Free: 888-542-2242
www.cheminst.ca
Overview: A medium-sized national organization overseen by Chemical Institute of Canada
Mission: To advance the principles & practice of chemical engineering throughout Canada; To ensure excellence in chemical engineering; To act as the national voice of chemical engineering professionals on issues related to chemical engineering, such as regulatory affairs & research funding
Finances: *Funding Sources:* Membership fees
Membership: *Fees:* Schedule available; *Member Profile:* Chemical engineering professionals employed in academia, government, & industry
Activities: Promoting ethics & responsibility among members; Engaging in lobbying activities on behalf of members; Providing professional development activities; Organizing networking events; Increasing public awareness & understanding of chemical engineering
Chief Officer(s):
David Guss, President
david_guss@nexeninc.com
Roland Andersson, Executive Director
randersson@cheminst.ca
Amarjett Bassi, Vice-President
abassi@uwo.ca
Nicolas Abatzoglou, Director, Awards
Handan Tezel, Director, Conferences & Symposia
Madjid Mohseni, Director, Publications & Continuing Education
Francois Bertrand, Treasurer
Publications:
• The Canadian Journal of Chemical Engineering
Type: Journal; *Frequency:* Bimonthly

Canadian Society for Chemical Technology (CSCT) / Société canadienne de technologie chimique (SCTC)
#550, 130 Slater St., Ottawa ON K1P 6E2
Tel: 613-232-6252; *Fax:* 613-232-5862
Toll-Free: 888-542-2242
www.cheminst.ca
Overview: A small national organization overseen by Chemical Institute of Canada
Mission: To establish & maintain high standards in the profession of chemical technology throughout Canada
Finances: *Annual Operating Budget:* Less than $50,000; *Funding Sources:* Membership fees; Constituent fees; Certificates; Symposiums & courses
Membership: *Fees:* Schedule available; *Member Profile:* Chemical technology professionals, from academia, government, & industry; Students
Activities: Providing professional development opportunities; Certifying members Offering networking among technologists from industry, government, & academia; Increasing the public awareness of chemical technology
Chief Officer(s):
Donna McMahon, President
dmcmahon@suncor.com
Samantha Waytowich, Vice-President
swaytowich@leanscn.com
Roland Andersson, Executive Director
randersson@cheminst.ca
Kevin Ferris, Director, Certification
kferris@ferrischemicals.com

Canadian Society for Chemistry (CSC) / Société canadienne de chimie
#550, 130 Slater St., Ottawa ON K1P 6E2
Tel: 613-232-6252; *Fax:* 613-232-5862
Toll-Free: 888-542-2242
info@cheminst.ca
www.cheminst.ca
Overview: A small national organization overseen by Chemical Institute Of Canada
Mission: To represent the field of chemistry & the interests of chemists in industry, academia, & government; To advance the principles & practices of the chemical sciences for the betterment of society
Membership: *Member Profile:* Chemists
Activities: Holding four regional undergraduate student conferences annually in the Atlantic region, Québec, Southwestern Ontario, & Westen Canada; Advancing the public's understanding & appreciation of chemistry; Recommending standards of education in chemistry
Chief Officer(s):
Roland Andersson, Executive Director, 613-232-6252 Ext. 222
randersson@cheminst.ca
Joan Kingston, Director, 613-232-6252 Ext. 225
jkingston@cheminst.ca
Lucie Frigon, Manager, 613-232-6252 Ext. 240
lfrigon@cheminst.ca
Gale Thirlwall, Manager, Awards & Local Sections, 613-232-6252 Ext. 223
gthirlwall@cheminst.ca
Angie Moulton, Coordinator, Membership Services, 613-232-6252 Ext. 230
amoulton@cheminst.ca
Meetings/Conferences:
• Chemical Institute of Canada 101st Canadian Chemistry Conference & Exhibition 2018, May, 2018, Edmonton, AB
Scope: National
Contact Information: www.csc2018.ca
Publications:
• Canadian Chemical News / L'Actualité chimique canadienne
Type: Magazine; *Frequency:* 10 pa; *Accepts Advertising*; *Editor:* Terri Pavelic; *Price:* Free with membership in The Chemical Institute Of Canada
Profile: News about the Canadian & international chemical scene, for chemical professionals
• Canadian Journal of Chemistry
Type: Journal; *Frequency:* Monthly; *Editor:* Dr. Robert H. Lipson; *ISSN:* 1480-3291
Profile: Current research findings & articles, plus comprehensive reviews in all branches of chemistry

Canadian Society for Civil Engineering (CSCE) / Société canadienne de génie civil
4877, rue Sherbrooke ouest, Montréal QC H3Z 1G9
Tel: 514-933-2634; *Fax:* 514-933-3504
Other Communication: membership@csce.ca

Canadian Associations / Canadian Society for Clinical Investigation (CSCI) / Société canadienne de recherches cliniques (SCRC)

info@csce.ca
www.csce.ca
Overview: A medium-sized national organization founded in 1887 overseen by The Engineering Institute of Canada
Mission: To develop & maintain high standard of civil engineering practice in Canada; To enhance the public image of the civil engineering profession
Membership: *Fees:* Schedule available; *Committees:* Infrastructure Renewal; Innovations & IT; International Affairs; Sustainable Development; Career Development; Honours & Fellowships; History
Activities: Offering continuing education & networking opportunities; Working with sister organizations; Promoting civil engineering
Chief Officer(s):
Doug Salloum, Executive Director
doug.salloum@csce.ca
Mahmoud Lardjane, Manager, Programs
mahmoud@csce.ca
Louise Newman, Manager, Communications
louise@csce.ca
Andrea Grimaud, Officer, Membership Liaison
membership@csce.ca
Meetings/Conferences:
• 2018 Canadian Society for Civil Engineering Annual Conference & Annual General Meeting, 2018
Scope: National
Publications:
• Canadian Civil Engineer (CCE)
Type: Magazine; *Frequency:* 5 pa; *Accepts Advertising*; *Editor:* Louise Newman; *ISSN:* 9825-7515; *Price:* $35 Canada & U.S.A.; $45 other countries
Profile: Technical activity reports, technical articles, corporate & personal achievement items, & networking news
• Canadian Journal of Civil Engineering (CJCE)
Type: Journal
Profile: Technical journal featuring scholarly papers devoted to civil engineering
• Canadian Society for Civil Engineering Annual Report
Type: Yearbook; *Frequency:* Annually
Profile: Reports from executives such as the president, the president-elect, the executive director, vice-president, committees, & the CSCE Foundation, in addition to the auditor's report & financial statements
• Canadian Society for Civil Engineering E-Bulletin
Type: Newsletter; *Frequency:* Monthly; *Accepts Advertising*
Profile: Featuring current industry & society news, trends, & forthcoming events of interest to over 7,000 subscribers
• Canadian Society for Civil Engineering President's E-Letter
Type: Newsletter; *Frequency:* Monthly
Profile: Information for members of the Canadian Society for Civil Engineering, including forthcoming programs & conferences
• Canadian Society for Civil Engineering Conference Proceedings
Type: Yearbook; *Frequency:* Annually
Profile: Proceedings usually include an abstract book & CD-ROM with details of the society's annual conference
• A Civil Society - A brief personal history of the CSCE [Canadian Society for Civil Engineering]

Canadian Society for Clinical Investigation (CSCI) / Société canadienne de recherches cliniques (SCRC)
114 Cheyenne Way, Ottawa ON K2J 0E9
Fax: 613-491-0073
Toll-Free: 877-968-9449
info@csci-scrc.ca
www.csci-scrc.ca
Overview: A medium-sized national organization founded in 1951
Mission: To promote research in the field of human health throughout Canada; to lobby for research funding; to support Canadian researchers in their endeavours & at all stages of their careers by supporting knowledge translation & fostering communities of health science researchers
Finances: *Funding Sources:* Membership dues; grants
Membership: *Fees:* $200; $50 Associate; $0 Emeritus; *Member Profile:* General - person with an active interest in research; associate - person who holds a doctoral level degree & is still in training; *Committees:* Awards; Program & Education; Membership; Science Policy; Publications & Communications; Nominating
Chief Officer(s):
Norman Rosenblum, President
Awards:
• Distinguished Scientist Award

• CSCI/CAPM Core Medical Residents Research Award
• CSCI/CIHR Resident Research Prize
• CSCI/RCPSC/PAIRO Specialty Resident Research Awards
• Joe Doupe Young Investigator's Award
• Distinguished Service Award
• CSCI/RCPSC/CFBS G. Malcolm Brown Lecture
• CSCI/RCPSC Henry Friesen Award
Publications:
• Clinical & Investigative Medicine (CIM)
Type: Journal; *Frequency:* Bimonthly; *Editor:* David R. Bevan
Profile: Original research, policy changes that affect biological & medical science research, issues related to medical research funding, information for clinician-scientisttrainees

Canadian Society for Continental Philosophy (CSCP)
c/o Dept. of Philosophy, University of Calgary, 2500 University Dr. NW, Calgary AB T2N 1N4
www.c-scp.org
Previous Name: Canadian Society for Hermeneutics & Postmodern Thought
Overview: A small national organization
Mission: To be dedicated to the pursuit & exchange of philosophical ideas inspired by Continental European traditions; to provide a forum for scholarly interests in such fields as hermeneutics, existentialism, phenomenology, deconstruction, critical theory & poststructuralism
Membership: *Fees:* $35 student/unwaged; $55 regular
Activities: Annual meetings
Chief Officer(s):
Shannon Hoff, President
Lorraine Markotic, Treasurer

Canadian Society for Education through Art (CSEA) / Société canadienne d'éducation par l'art (SCEA)
PO Box 1700, Stn. CSC, University of Victoria, Victoria BC V8W 3N4
Tel: 250-721-7896; *Fax:* 250-721-7598
office.csea@gmail.com
www.csea-scea.ca
twitter.com/CSEA_SCEA
Overview: A medium-sized national organization founded in 1955
Mission: The Canadian Society for Education through Art, is a voluntary association and is the only Canadian national organization that brings together art educators, gallery educators, and others wtih simialr intersts and concerns.
Affiliation(s): British Columbia Art Teachers' Association; Fine Arts Council, Alberta Teachers' Association; Saskatchewan Society for Education through Art; Manitoba Association of Art Educators; Ontario Society for Education through Art; Provincial Association of Art Teachers; Association québécoise des éducateurs spécialisés en arts plastiques; New Brunswick Arts Education Council; Nova Scotia Art Teachers' Association; PEI Art Teachers' Association; Art Council of the Newfoundland Teachers' Association; Canadian Art Gallery Educators
Finances: *Annual Operating Budget:* Less than $50,000; *Funding Sources:* Membership fees
12 volunteer(s)
Membership: 350; *Fees:* $65; *Member Profile:* Represents all levels of education: elementary, secondary, college/university, ministries of education, art galleries/museums, and community education.
Activities: Canadian Children's Art Collection; archives; *Awareness Events:* Art Education Month, May; Library
Chief Officer(s):
Miriam Cooley, President, 780-492-0902
miriam.cooley@ualberta.ca
Awards:
• CSEA/Crayola Awards
Awarded to teachers of quality art programs in grades 3-6
• Student Scholarships
Awarded to Canadian high school graduates planning to continue their art education

Canadian Society for Eighteenth-Century Studies (CSECS) / Société canadienne d'étude du dix-huitième siècle (SCEDS)
c/o Department of French, University of Manitoba, 427 Fletcher Argue Bldg., Winnipeg MB R3T 2N2
Tel: 204-474-9206
www.csecs.ca
Overview: A small national charitable organization founded in 1971
Mission: To sustain, in Canada, interest in eighteenth-century civilization in Europe & the New World; to encourage, from a wide interdisciplinary base, research on the eighteenth-century; to make known to eighteenth-century specialists the work done in this area in Canada.
Member of: Canadian Federation for the Humanities
Affiliation(s): International Society for Eighteenth-Century Studies
Finances: *Funding Sources:* Membership fees; Social Science & Humanities Federation of Canada
Chief Officer(s):
Armelle St-Martin, President
armelle.stmartin@umanitoba.ca
Isabelle Tremblay, Secretary
Isabelle.Tremblay@rmc.ca
Julie Murray, Treasurer
julie_murray@carleton.ca
Awards:
• Mark Madoff Prize
For best graduate paper read at the conference
• D.W. Smith Eighteenth-Century Research Fellowship
; *Amount:* $2,000 *Contact:* Betty A. Schellenberg, schellen@sfu.ca
Meetings/Conferences:
• Canadian Society for Eighteenth-Century Studies 2018 Conference, October, 2018, Niagara Falls, ON
Publications:
• The Canadian Society for Eighteenth-Century Studies Bulletin
Type: Journal; *Frequency:* Semiannually; *Editor:* Stéphanie Massé; K. James-Cavan
• Lumen
Type: Journal; *Frequency:* Annually; *Editor:* Barbara K. Seeber; Ugo Dionne; *ISSN:* 0824-3298; *Price:* $29.95 Canada & U.S.A.; $50 international
Profile: Formerly known as Man and Nature / L'homme et la nature; Based on annual conference

Canadian Society for Engineering in Agricultural, Food & Biological Systems *See* Canadian Society for Bioengineering

Canadian Society for Engineering Management (CSEM) / Société canadienne de gestion en ingénierie
1295 Hwy. 2 East, Kingston ON K7L 4V1
Tel: 613-547-5989
louisem@cogeco.ca
www.csem-scgi.org
www.linkedin.com/groups/Canadian-Engineering-Management-4865922
Previous Name: EIC General Members Society
Overview: A medium-sized national organization founded in 1981 overseen by The Engineering Institute of Canada
Mission: To represent the interests & enhance the capabilities of engineers in management in order to promote & advance efficient management of commerce, industry & public affairs.
Finances: *Annual Operating Budget:* Less than $50,000; *Funding Sources:* Membership fees
Staff Member(s): 1; 8 volunteer(s)
Membership: 365; *Fees:* $85
Chief Officer(s):
Aidan Gordon, President
Dominique Janssens, Sec.-Treas.

Canadian Society for Epidemiology & Biostatistics (CESB) / Société canadienne d'épidémiologie et de biostatistique (SCEB)
c/o Pamela Wilson, The Willow Group, 1485 Laperriere Ave., Ottawa ON K1Z 7S8
Tel: 613-722-8796; *Fax:* 613-729-6206
secretariat@cseb.ca
cseb.ca
www.facebook.com/109122749151677
twitter.com/csebsceb
www.youtube.com/user/CSEBSCEB
Overview: A small national organization founded in 1990
Mission: To foster epidemiology & biostatistics research in Canada; To improve training in the disciplines of epidemiology & biostatistics in Canada
Membership: *Fees:* $50 students; $100 full membership; *Member Profile:* Epidemiologists; Health care professionals; Researchers; Biostatisticians; Statisticians; Students
Activities: Facilitating communication among epidemiologists & biostatisticians
Chief Officer(s):
Susan Jaglal, President
Paul Arora, Secretary
Meetings/Conferences:
• Canadian Society for Epidemiology & Biostatistics 2019

Biennial Conference, 2019
Scope: National
Publications:
• Canadian Society for Epidemiology & Biostatistics Newsletter
Type: Newsletter
Profile: Information of interest to members of the Society

Canadian Society for Exercise Physiology (CSEP) / Société canadienne de physiologie de l'exercice (SCPE)
#370, 18 Louisa St., Ottawa ON K1R 6Y6
Tel: 613-234-3755; *Fax:* 613-234-3565
Toll-Free: 877-651-3755
info@csep.ca
www.csep.ca
www.linkedin.com/company/csep-scpe
www.facebook.com/520719817945510
twitter.com/CSEPdotCA
Previous Name: Canadian Association of Sport Sciences
Overview: A medium-sized national organization founded in 1967
Mission: To promote the generation, synthesis, transfer, & application of knowledge & research related to exercise physiology, encompassing physical activity, fitness, health, nutrition, epidemiology & human performance; To act as the voice for exercise physiology in Canada
Membership: 5,400; *Fees:* $20 first-time sponsored students; $50 students; $175 active & affiliate members; *Member Profile:* Active members with the graduate degree, PhD, MD, or MSc; Affiliate members with a BSc, BA, BPE, BKin, or no degree; Organizations; Students currently enrolled full-time in university studies; Retired active members; *Committees:* Annual General Meeting Program; Applied Physiology, Nutrition, & Metabolism (APNM) Editorial; Finance; Graduate Student; CSEP Health & Fitness Program National Advisory; Knowledge Transfer; Physical Activity Measurement & Guidelines (PAMG) Steering; Expert Advisory (Scientific Advisors); CSEP Health & Fitness Program Executive; CSEP Certified Exercise Physiologist Technical; CSEP Certified Personal Trainer Technical; Strategic Health & Fitness Program Initiatives; CSEP Health & Fitness Program Marketing; Research Subcommittees (Existing & New Guidelines)
Activities: Offering the National Health & Fitness Program; Engaging in advocacy activities; Advertising job postings; Facilitating national communication through committees & networks; Providing networking opportunities
Chief Officer(s):
Phil Chilibeck, President/Chair
Awards:
• CSEP Young Investigator Award
• CSEP Honour Award
• Graduate Student Award
• CSEP / SCPE Undergraduate Student Award
• Health & Fitness Program Recognition Award
Meetings/Conferences:
• Canadian Society for Exercise Physiology 2018 AGM, October, 2018, Brock University, Niagara Falls, ON
Scope: National
• Canadian Society for Exercise Physiology 2019 AGM, October, 2019
Scope: National
Publications:
• Active Living During Pregnancy: Physical Activitiy Guidelines for Mother & Baby
Type: Manual; *Number of Pages:* 40; *ISBN:* 978-1-896900-06-3; *Price:* $11.95
Profile: A resource for pregnant women who want to maintain activity during pregnancy
• Applied Physiology, Nutrition & Metabolism (APNM)
Type: Journal; *Editor:* Terry Graham, PhD; *Price:* Free with membership in the Canadian Society for Exercise Physiology
Profile: Original research articles, reviews, & commentaries on the application of physiology, nutrition, & metabolism to the study of humanhealth, physical activity, & fitness
• Canada's Physical Activity Guide to Healthy Active Living (Adults 20-55): PA Guide Handbook
Type: Handbook; *Number of Pages:* 32
Profile: Detailed advice & case studies about becoming more active, produced by the Public Health Agency of Canada (PHAC) & theCanadian Society for Exercise Physiology (CSEP)
• The Canadian Physical Activity, Fitness & Lifestyle Approach (CPAFLA)
Type: Manual; *Number of Pages:* 300; *ISBN:* 978-1-896900-16-2; *Price:* $70

Profile: CSEP Health & Fitness Program's health-related appraisal & counselling strategy
• Communiqué [a publication of the Canadian Society for Exercise Physiology]
Type: Newsletter; *Frequency:* Monthly; *Accepts Advertising*; *Price:* Free withmembership in the Canadian Society for Exercise Physiology
Profile: A member newsletter of the Canadian Society for Exercise Physiology, with job postings & information about forthcoming conferences
• CSEP [Canadian Society for Exercise Physiology] Member Directory
Type: Directory
Profile: A listing of the more 4,500 members of the Canadian Society for Exercise Physiology, to help users locate CSEP Certified Personal Trainers or CSEPCertified Exercise Physiologists
• The CSEP [Canadian Society for Exercise Physiology] Certified Exercise Physiologist Certification Guide
Type: Guide; *Number of Pages:* 144; *ISBN:* 978-1-896900-26-1; *Price:* $39.95
Profile: For candidates preparing for the theory & practical examination process to be recognized as CSEPCertified Exercise Physiologist
• CSEP [Canadian Society for Exercise Physiology] Certified Personal Trainer Study Guide
Type: Guide; *Number of Pages:* 52; *ISBN:* 978-1-896900-28-5; *Price:* $29.95
Profile: For candidates preparing to obtain the professional personal training certificate in Canada
• Inclusive Fitness & Lifestyle Services for all (dis)Abilities
Type: Manual; *Number of Pages:* 300; *ISBN:* 978-1-896900-10-0; *Price:* $55
Profile: Resources to provide fitness assessment & active living counselling services
• Physical Activity Guide for Children (6-9 Years of Age): Family Guide to Physical Activity for Children
Type: Guide; *Number of Pages:* 12
Profile: Advice about how children can be active, produced by the Public Health Agency of Canada (PHAC) & the CanadianSociety for Exercise Physiology (CSEP)
• Physical Activity Guide for Children (6-9 Years of Age): Teacher's Guide to Physical Activity for Children
Type: Guide; *Number of Pages:* 8
Profile: Advice for teachers about how children can be active, produced by the Public Health Agency of Canada (PHAC) & theCanadian Society for Exercise Physiology (CSEP)
• Physical Activity Guide for Older Adults (Over 55): PA Guide Handbook for Older Adults
Type: Handbook; *Number of Pages:* 32
Profile: Detailed advice with tips on increasing physical activity, produced by the Public Health Agency of Canada (PHAC) & the CanadianSociety for Exercise Physiology (CSEP)
• Physical Activity Guide for Youth (10-14 Years of Age): Family Guide to Physical Activity for Youth
Type: Guide; *Number of Pages:* 12
Profile: A support resource for families, produced by the Public Health Agency of Canada (PHAC) & the Canadian Society forExercise Physiology (CSEP)
• Physical Activity Guide for Youth (10-14 Years of Age): Teacher's Guide to Physical Activity for Youth
Type: Guide; *Number of Pages:* 8
Profile: A support resource for teachers, produced by the Public Health Agency of Canada (PHAC) & the Canadian Society forExercise Physiology (CSEP)
• Professional Fitness & Lifestyle Consultant (PFLC) Resource Manual
Type: Manual; *Number of Pages:* 250; *ISBN:* 978-1-896900-04-9; *Price:* $55
Profile: The practical requirements for certification as a CSEP Certified Exercise Physiologist

Canadian Society for Hermeneutics & Postmodern Thought
See Canadian Society for Continental Philosophy

Canadian Society for Horticultural Science (CSHS) / Société canadienne de science horticole (SCSH)
c/o Dept. of Plant & Animal Sciences, Nova Scotia Agricultural College, PO Box 550, Truro NS B2N 5E3
Tel: 902-893-6032; *Fax:* 902-897-9762
www.cshs.ca
Overview: A small national organization founded in 1956
Mission: To advance research, teaching, information, & technology related to all horticultural crops
Membership: *Member Profile:* Scientists; Educators; Extension agents; Industry personnel; Students

Activities: Providing professional development opportunities; Organizing an annual conference & scientific meeting
Chief Officer(s):
Samir C. Debnath, President
samir.debnath@agr.gc.ca
Kris Pruski, Ph.D., Secretary-Treasurer
kpruski@nsac.ca
Publications:
• Canadian Journal of Plant Science (CJPS)
Type: Journal; *Frequency:* Quarterly; *Editor:* Vaino Poysa
Profile: Shared with the Canadian Society of Agronomy (CSA)
• CSHS [Canadian Society for Horticultural Science] Newsletter
Type: Newsletter; *Frequency:* Quarterly
Profile: Society activities, issues, & events
• CSHS [Canadian Society for Horticultural Science] Membership Directory
Type: Directory; *Frequency:* Annually
Profile: Listings of Society members, plus information about governance, committees, & awards
• Program & Abstracts of the CSHS [Canadian Society for Horticultural Science] Annual Conference
Type: Yearbook; *Frequency:* Annually
Profile: The latest horticultural research

Canadian Society for Immunology (CSI)
c/o Dept. of Veterinary Microbiology, Univ. of Saskatchewan, 52 Campus Dr., Saskatoon SK S7N 5B4
Tel: 306-966-7214; *Fax:* 306-966-7244
Other Communication: membership@csi-sci.ca
info@csi-sci.ca
www.csi-sci.ca
Overview: A small national charitable organization founded in 1966
Mission: To foster & support immunology research & education across Canada
Member of: Research Canada
Membership: 250+; *Fees:* $30 students; $50 postdoctoral fellows, research associates, technicians of CSI members; $80 educational faculty & professionals; *Member Profile:* Members from hospitals, research institutes, & universities across Canada
Activities: Lobbying for immunology research funding; Liaising between membership & national funding agencies; Presenting awards
Chief Officer(s):
Hanne Ostergaard, President
hanne.ostergaard@ualberta.ca
Lori Coulthurst, Society Administrator
Meetings/Conferences:
• 31st Annual Canadian Society for Immunology Meeting, June, 2018, Western University, London, ON
Scope: National

Canadian Society for International Health (CSIH) / Société canadienne de la santé internationale
#726, 1 Nicholas St., Ottawa ON K1N 7B7
Tel: 613-241-5785
csih@csih.org
www.csih.org
www.linkedin.com/groups/CSIH-Global-Health-Forum-3671985
www.facebook.com/CSIH.org
twitter.com/globalsante
Previous Name: Canadian Society for Tropical Medicine & International Health
Overview: A medium-sized international charitable organization founded in 1977
Mission: To promote international health & development through mobilization of Canadian resources; To advocate & facilitate research, education, & service activities in international health; To further Canadian strengths of progressive health policy & programming in all fields where global & domestic health concerns meet; To contribute to the evolving global understanding of health & development
Member of: Canadian Coalition for Global Health Research
Finances: *Funding Sources:* Membership fees; Contracts; CIDA; Competitive bids
Staff Member(s): 5
Membership: *Fees:* $50 regular; $25 student/retired/non-wage-earner; $250 organization; *Member Profile:* Persons with interest in health development, tropical medicine, health systems strengthening, & capacity building
Activities: *Internships:* Yes; *Library*
Chief Officer(s):
Kate Dickson, Co-Chair
L. Duncan Saunders, Co-Chair
Eva Slawecki, Acting Director, 613-241-5785 Ext. 325

Canadian Associations / Canadian Society for Italian Studies (CSIS) / Société canadienne pour les études italiennes

Meetings/Conferences:
• Canadian Society for International Health 24th Canadian Conference on Global Health 2018, November, 2018, Toronto, ON
Scope: National
Description: The conference is the largest meeting of researchers, academics, decision makers, NGOs, policy makers, students & health care providers involved with global health in Canada.
Publications:
• Synergy Online
Type: Newsletter; *Frequency:* Monthly
Profile: International health & development information, news bulletins, awards, conference information, & job listings

Canadian Society for Italian Studies (CSIS) / Société canadienne pour les études italiennes
c/o Sandra Parmegiani, School of Languages & Literatures, U of Guelph, 50 Stone Rd. East, Guelph ON N1G 2W1
Tel: 519-824-4120; *Fax:* 519-763-9572
sparmegi@uoguelph.ca
www.canadiansocietyforitalianstudies.camp7.org
Overview: A small national charitable organization
Mission: To foster & advance Italian studies in Canada & abroad
Finances: *Funding Sources:* Donations; Social Sciences & Humanities Research Council of Canada
Membership: *Fees:* $35 students, retired persons, & PhDs without full-time employment; $60 institutions; $85 sustaining members; $100 couples; $120 patrons; *Member Profile:* Teachers of Italian Studies; Researchers who deal with Italian material
Activities: Facilitating the exchange of ideas; Disseminating information
Chief Officer(s):
Roberto Perin, President, 416-736-2100 Ext. 88249, Fax: 416-487-6852
RPerin@glendon.yorku.ca
Paola Basile, Vice-President, 440-375-7542, Fax: 440-375-7005
pbasile@lec.edu
Sandra Parmegiani, Secretary-Treasurer, 519-824-4120 Ext. 54989, Fax: 519-763-9572
sparmegi@uoguelph.ca
Meetings/Conferences:
• Canadian Society for Italian Studies 2018 Annual Conference, May, 2018, University of Ottawa, Ottawa, ON
Scope: International
Publications:
• Biblioteca di Quaderni d'italianistica
Editor: Dr. Giuliana Katz
Profile: Translations & studies in linguistics, literary criticism, & pedagogy related to Italian culture
• Quaderni d'Italianistica
Type: Journal; *Frequency:* Semiannually; *Editor:* Konrad Eisenbichler; *Price:* $30 Canada individuals; $35 USA individuals; $40 international individuals
Profile: Peer-reviewed articles, published in English, French, & Italian

Canadian Society for Jewish Studies (CSJS) / Société Canadienne des études juives (SCEJ)
c/o Dr. Ira Robinson, Department of Religion, Concordia University, 1455, boul de Maisonneuve ouest, Montréal QC H3G 1M8
www.csjs.ca
Overview: A small national organization founded in 2004
Mission: To provide a venue for the presentation of Jewish studies research & information, primarily for faculty members, graduate students, & independent scholars in Canada
Membership: 37; *Fees:* $30 individual; $15 retired & students; *Member Profile:* Individuals with active scholarly interest in Canadian Jewish studies
Activities: Holding an annual conference; Disseminating information & publications
Chief Officer(s):
Ira Robinson, President, 514-848-2424 Ext. 2074, Fax: 514-848-4541
ira.robinson@sympatico.ca
Meetings/Conferences:
• Canadian Society for Jewish Studies 14th Annual Conference 2018, 2018
Scope: National

Canadian Society for Mechanical Engineering (CSME) / Société canadienne de génie mécanique (SCGM)
1295 Hwy. 2 East, Kingston ON K7L 4V1
Tel: 613-547-5989; *Fax:* 613-547-0195
csme@cogeco.ca
www.csme-scgm.ca
Overview: A medium-sized national charitable organization founded in 1970 overseen by The Engineering Institute of Canada
Mission: To benefit Canada & the world by fostering excellence in the practice of mechanical engineering; To support members
Affiliation(s): Engineering Institute of Canada
Membership: *Fees:* $15 students; $45 retired members; $85 first year membership; $115 professional affiliate; $125 full membership; *Member Profile:* Mechnical engineering personnel; Engineers in other disciplines who are interested in mechanical engineering; *Committees:* Executive; Regional Vice Presidents; Chairs Special; Chairs Standing; Chairs Technical
Activities: Providing continuing education; Arranging networking opportunities
Chief Officer(s):
Rama B. Bhat, President
Meetings/Conferences:
• Canadian Society for Mechanical Engineering International Congress 2018, May, 2018, York University, Toronto, ON
Scope: International
• 27th Canadian Congress of Applied Mechanics 2019, 2019
Scope: National
Description: Tech tracks at past conferences have included civil engineering, computational mechanics, dynamics & vibration, education in applied mechanics, fluid mechanics, manufacturing, mechatronics, micro-electro-mechanical systems, solid mechanics & materials, & thermodynamics & heat transfer
Publications:
• CSME [Canadian Society for Mechanical Engineering] Bulletin
Type: Newsletter; *Frequency:* 3 pa; *Editor:* Kamran Siddiqui, PhD; *Price:* Free with membership in theCanadian Society for Mechanical Engineering
Profile: News & articles of a general technical nature, covering all aspects of the practice of mechanical engineering
• From Steam to Space. . . Contributions of Mechanical Engineering to Canadian Development
Number of Pages: 400; *Editor:* Andrew H. Wilson; *Price:* $25 softcover; $50 hardcover
Profile: Essays, memoirs, & photographs
• Transactions of the Canadian Society for Mechanical Engineering
Type: Journal; *Frequency:* Quarterly; *Editor:* Paul J. Zsombor-Murray; *ISSN:* 0315-8977; *Price:* $40 / yearfor members of the Canadian Society for Mechanical Engineering
Profile: Scholarly papers of a reference or archival nature in the field of mechanical engineering or related disciplines

Canadian Society for Medical Laboratory Science (CSMLS) / Société canadienne de science de laboratoire médical (SCSLM)
33 Wellington St. North, Hamilton ON L8R 1M7
Tel: 905-528-8642; *Fax:* 905-528-4968
Toll-Free: 800-263-8277
info@csmls.org
www.csmls.org
www.facebook.com/csmls
twitter.com/csmls
www.youtube.com/user/csmls
Previous Name: Canadian Society of Laboratory Technologists
Overview: A large national licensing organization founded in 1937
Mission: To promote & maintain a nationally accepted standard of medical laboratory technology; To promote, maintain, & protect professional identity & interests of medical laboratory technologists
Member of: International Federation of Biomedical Laboratory Science
Affiliation(s): International Association of Medical Laboratory Technologists; Intersociety Council of Laboratory Medicine; Conjoint Council on Accreditation of Allied Programs in Health Care
Finances: *Annual Operating Budget:* Greater than $5 Million; *Funding Sources:* Membership dues
Membership: 14,000+; *Fees:* $142 active & affiliate; $85 inactive; $62 certified retired; $112 laboratory assistant; $78-$102 student; *Member Profile:* Certified medical laboratory technologists; *Committees:* Marketing & Communications; Professional Development; Council on National Certification; National Advocacy Council; National Regulatory Council
Activities: Developing competency profiles; Conducting examinations across Canada & issues certificates of qualification; Offering certification in general medical laboratory technology, cytology & clinical genetics; *Awareness Events:* National Medical Laboratory Week, 3rd week of April
Chief Officer(s):
Chris Hirtle, President
Christine Nielsen, Chief Executive Officer
Awards:
• CSMLS Student Scholarship Program
Awarded to the best students who are enrolled in general medical laboratory technology, cytotechnology, or cytogenetics studies *Deadline:* November; *Amount:* Five scholarships of $500 each
• E.V. Booth Scholarship Award
Awarded to certified medical laboratory technologists who are enrolled in studies leading to a degree in medical laboratory science; *Amount:* Two awards of $500
• Honorary Awards & Fellowship Awards
• Distinguished Fellowship Award
• The A.R. Shearer Pride of the Profession Award
• The David Ball Community Service Award
• Siemens Healthcare Diagnostics Student Scholarship
• Founders' Fund & International Founders' Fund Awards
• Barbara Santalab-Rickey Memorial Award
• Leaders of Tomorrow National Congress Grant
Meetings/Conferences:
• Canadian Society for Medical Laboratory Science LABCON2018, May, 2018, Caesars Windsor, Windsor, ON
Scope: National
Publications:
• Canadian Journal of Medical Laboratory Science
Type: Journal; *Frequency:* Quarterly
Profile: Articles on trends in medical laboratory science & other professional issues, book reviews, & a regular column on laboratory safety

The Canadian Society for Mesopotamian Studies (CSMS) / La Société canadienne des études mésopotamiennes
c/o RIM Project, University of Toronto, 4 Bancroft Ave., 4th Fl., Toronto ON M5S 1C1
Tel: 416-978-4531; *Fax:* 416-978-3305
csms@chass.utoronto.ca
www.chass.utoronto.ca/csms
Previous Name: Society for Mesopotamian Studies
Overview: A small international charitable organization founded in 1980
Mission: To stimulate interest among the general public in the culture, history & archaeology of Mesopotamia, in particular the civilizations of Sumer, Babylon & Assyria, as well as neighbouring ancient civilizations
Affiliation(s): Royal Inscriptions of Mesopotamia Project
Finances: *Annual Operating Budget:* Less than $50,000; *Funding Sources:* Membership dues; donations; grant
3 volunteer(s)
Membership: 2 institutional + 35 student + 5 senior/lifetime + 96 individual + 17 family + 49 regular subscriber + 26 exchange subscriber; *Fees:* Schedule available
Activities: Public lectures; films & music; travel; exhibitions; research; archaeology; evening courses; *Library:* Not open to public
Chief Officer(s):
Pail-Alain Beaulieu, President
Roy Thomas, Secretary-Treasurer
N.J. Johnson, Administrator
Publications:
• The Journal
Frequency: Annual; *Editor:* Dr. Douglas R. Frayne

Canadian Society for Molecular Biosciences (CSBM) / Société Canadienne pour Biosciences Moléculaires
c/o Rofail Conference & Management Services, 17 Dossetter Way, Ottawa ON K1G 4S3
Tel: 613-421-7229; *Fax:* 613-421-9811
contact@csmb-scbm.ca
www.csmb-scbm.ca
Previous Name: Canadian Biochemical Society
Merged from: Canadian Society for Biochemistry & Molecular & Cellular Biology; Genetics Society of Canada
Overview: A medium-sized national organization founded in 1958 overseen by Canadian Federation of Biological Societies
Finances: *Funding Sources:* Membership fees

Membership: *Member Profile:* Demonstrated interest in biochemistry research
Activities: *Internships:* Yes; *Rents Mailing List:* Yes
Chief Officer(s):
Christian Baron, President
Kristin Baetz, Vice-President
Publications:
• CSBMCB [The Canadian Society of Biochemistry, Molecular & Cellular Biology] Bulletin
Type: Newsletter
Profile: CSBMCB activites, meeting minutes, lectures, awards, & news from member departments

Canadian Society for Mucopolysaccharide & Related Diseases Inc.
PO Box 30034, RPO Parkgate, North Vancouver BC V7H 2Y8
Tel: 604-924-5130; *Fax:* 604-924-5131
Toll-Free: 800-667-1846
info@mpssociety.ca
www.mpssociety.ca
www.facebook.com/208787789156391
twitter.com/canmpssociety
Also Known As: The Canadian MPS Society
Overview: A small national charitable organization founded in 1984
Mission: To support families affected with MPS & related diseases
Member of: Canadian Organization for Rare Disorders
Finances: *Funding Sources:* Donations; Fundraising
Membership: *Member Profile:* Affected families; Professionals; Individuals interested in supporting MPS
Activities: Offering education to medical professionals & the public about MPS & related diseases; Raising funds for research; Referring families; Offering financial aid to affected families; Engaging in advocacy activities; Offering bereavement support; *Awareness Events:* Canadian MPS Jeans Days; The MPS CUP
Chief Officer(s):
Bernie Geiss, Chair
Jamie Myrah, Executive Director
Publications:
• The Canadian MPS Society Annual Report
Type: Yearbook; *Frequency:* Annually; *Price:* Free with Canadian MPS Society membership
• The Canadian MPS Society Family Referral Directory
Type: Directory; *Frequency:* Annually; *Price:* Free with Canadian MPS Society membership
• The Connection
Type: Newsletter; *Frequency:* Quarterly; *Price:* Free with Canadian MPS Society membership
Profile: A resource for families affected with MPS & related diseases, featuring MPS news, care options, new treatment updates, clinical trials, medical updates, current research, events, fundraising, & familynews

Canadian Society for Pharmaceutical Sciences (CSPS) / Société canadienne des sciences pharmaceutiques (SCSP)
Katz Group Centre, University of Alberta, #2-020L, 11361 - 87 Ave., Edmonton AB T6G 2E1
Tel: 780-492-0950; *Fax:* 780-492-0951
www.cspscanada.org
twitter.com/canadacsps
Overview: A medium-sized national organization founded in 1997
Mission: To advance pharmaceutical R&D & education; To provide a forum for researchers, industry & government to advance pharmaceutical sciences & increase drug discovery & development in Canada
Staff Member(s): 2
Membership: 400; *Fees:* $100 individual; $25 trainee; corporate varies
Chief Officer(s):
Frank Abbott, President
Bev Berekoff, Administrator
bberekoff@cspscanada.org
Meetings/Conferences:
• Canadian Society for Pharmaceutical Sciences 2018 Annual Symposium, May, 2018, Chelsea Hotel, Toronto, ON
Scope: National
Description: Educational sessions, networking opportunities, & the presentation of awards
Publications:
• Canadian Society for Pharmaceutical Sciences Newsletter
Type: Newsletter

Profile: Information about pharmaceutical events & society happenings
• Journal of Pharmacy & Pharmaceutical Sciences
Type: Journal; *Editor:* Dr. Fakhreddin Jamali; *ISSN:* 1482-1826
Profile: A peer-reviewed journal presenting review & original articles

Canadian Society for Psychomotor Learning & Sport Psychology (CSPLSP) / Société canadienne d'apprentissage psychomoteur et de psychologie du sport (SCAPPS)
#360, 125 University Private, Ottawa ON K1N 6N5
www.scapps.org
Overview: A small national organization founded in 1977
Mission: To promote the study of motor development, motor learning, motor control, & sport psychology
Activities: Facilitating the exchange of scientific information related to psychomotor learning & sport psychology
Chief Officer(s):
Chris Shields, President
Erin Cressman, Secretary, Communications
Awards:
• Franklin Henry Young Scientist Award
Presented annually to an outstanding student scholar
Meetings/Conferences:
• SCAPPS [Canadian Society for Psychomotor Learning & Sport Psychology] Conference 2018, October, 2018, Toronto, ON
Scope: National
Publications:
• Journal of Exercise, Movement, and Sport [a publication of the Canadian Society for Psychomotor Learning & Sport Psychology]
Type: Journal; *Editor:* Joel Barnes

Canadian Society for Quality (CSQ)
c/o Dr. Madhav Sinha, Winnipeg MB
Tel: 204-261-6606
csq@shaw.ca
canadianqualitycongress.com
www.facebook.com/pages/Canadian-Society-for-Quality/118131451687238
twitter.com/csq9
Overview: A medium-sized national organization
Meetings/Conferences:
• 10th Canadian Society for Quality Congress, September, 2018, Vancouver, BC
Scope: National
Description: Theme: "Innovation & Transformation to Embrace Change"

Canadian Society for Surgical Oncology (CSSO) / Société canadienne d'oncologie chirurgicale
c/o Jane Hanes, Princess Margaret Hospital, #3-130, 610 University Ave., Toronto ON M5G 2M9
Tel: 416-946-6583; *Fax:* 416-946-6590
www.cos.ca/csso
Overview: A small national organization founded in 1986
Mission: To encourage optimum cancer patient care through a multi-disciplinary treatment approach; To promote surgical oncology training programs in Canadian universities
Affiliation(s): Royal College of Physicians & Surgeons of Canada (RCPSC); Canadian Oncology Societies
Finances: *Funding Sources:* Membership dues
Membership: *Fees:* $150; *Member Profile:* Oncologists of all disciplines
Activities: Facilitating communication between surgeons; Encouraging research in oncologic surgery
Chief Officer(s):
Andy McFadden, President
Jane Hanes, Executive Coordinator

Canadian Society for the History & Philosophy of Science (CSHPS) / Société Canadienne d'Histoire et Philosophie des Sciences (SCHPS)
c/o Dr. Conor Burns, Department of History, Ryerson University, 350 Victoria St., Toronto ON M5C 2K3
www.yorku.ca/cshps1
Overview: A small national organization founded in 1959
Mission: To explore all aspects of science, past & present
Affiliation(s): Canadian Society for the History & Philosophy of Mathematics (CSHPM)
Membership: *Fees:* $25 students, retirees, & partially employed persons; $40 regular members; *Member Profile:* Interdisciplinary scholars, such as philosophers, historians, & sociologists; Persons interested in the history & philosophy of science; Students; Retirees; *Committees:* Programme; Nominating; Local Arrangements

Chief Officer(s):
Lesley Cormack, President
Conor Burns, Secretary-Treasurer
conor.burns@ryerson.ca
Awards:
• Richard Hadden Award
Awarded for the best student paper presented at the annual meeting
Publications:
• Communiqué: Newsletter of the Canadian Society for the History & Philosophy of Science
Type: Newsletter; *Frequency:* 3 pa; *Editor:* S. Lachapelle (slachap@uoguelph.ca); *Price:* Free with Canadian Society for the History & Philosophy of Science membership
Profile: Information for members about the society's activities, such as membership news, congressevents, & announcements

Canadian Society for the History of Medicine (CSHM) / Société canadienne d'histoire de la médecine (SCHM)
c/o University of Ottawa, #14022, 120 University, Ottawa ON K1N 6N5
Tel: 613-562-5700
www.cshm-schm.ca
Overview: A small national organization founded in 1950
Mission: To promote the study & communication of the history of health & medicine
Finances: *Funding Sources:* Social Sciences & Humanities Research Council (SSHRC); Associated Medical Services (AMS)
Membership: *Fees:* $30 student/retired/postdoctoral; $60 regular; $75 corporate; *Member Profile:* Individuals interested in a range of fields in the humanities & health sciences
Activities: Promoting research in all facets of the history of health & medicine
Chief Officer(s):
Sasha Mullally, President
Peter Twohig, Vice-President
Isabelle Perreault, Secretary-Treasurer & Coordinator, Membership
Meetings/Conferences:
• Canadian Society for the History of Medicine 2018 Annual Conference, May, 2018, University of Regina, Regina, SK
Scope: National
Description: Theme: "Gathering Diversities"
Publications:
• Canadian Bulletin of Medical History / Bulletin canadien d'histoire de la médecine
Type: Journal; *Frequency:* Semiannually; *Editor:* Cheryl Krasnick Warsh; *ISSN:* 0823-2105
Profile: Peer-reviewed original papers on all aspects of the history of medicine, health care, & relateddisciplines

Canadian Society for the Investigation of Child Abuse *See* Canadian Child Abuse Association

Canadian Society for the Prevention of Cruelty to Children (CSPCC)
PO Box 700, 362 Midland Ave., Midland ON L4R 4P4
Tel: 705-526-5647; *Fax:* 705-526-0214
cspcc@bellnet.ca
www.empathicparenting.org
Overview: A medium-sized national charitable organization founded in 1975
Mission: To increase public awareness of the long-term consequences of child abuse & neglect; to encourage primary prevention initiatives for improved nurturing of children in their earliest years of life
Member of: Canadian Coalition for the Rights of Children
Affiliation(s): EPOCH Worldwide; The Infant-Parent Institute, USA; Attachmente Parenting International; Center for Parent Education, USA
Finances: *Annual Operating Budget:* Less than $50,000; *Funding Sources:* Membership fees; donations
14 volunteer(s)
Activities: *Library:* Not open to public
Chief Officer(s):
E.T. Barker, President

Canadian Society for the Protection of Nature in Israel / La société canadienne pour la protection la nature en israél
#200, 25 Imperial St., Toronto ON M5P 1B9
Tel: 416-224-2318
cspnicanada@gmail.com
cspni.org

Canadian Associations / Canadian Society for the Study of Education (CSSE) / Société canadienne pour l'étude de l'éducation (SCÉÉ)

Overview: A small national charitable organization founded in 2011
Mission: A group of Canadian citizens with a desire to help protect Israel's treasured and threatened natural features.
Affiliation(s): Society for the Protection of Nature in Israel; American Society for the Protection of Nature in Israel (ASPNI)

Canadian Society for the Study of Allergy; Canadian Academy of Allergy See Canadian Society of Allergy & Clinical Immunology

Canadian Society for the Study of Education (CSSE) / Société canadienne pour l'étude de l'éducation (SCÉÉ)
#204, 260 Dalhousie St., Ottawa ON K1N 7E4
Tel: 613-241-0018; Fax: 613-241-0019
csse-scee@csse.ca
www.csse-scee.ca
www.facebook.com/csse.scee
twitter.com/CSSESCEE
Overview: A medium-sized national charitable organization founded in 1972
Mission: To advance knowledge & inform practice in educational settings; to promote the advancement of Canadian research & scholarship in education; to provide for the discussion of studies, issues & trends in education, & for the dissemination of research findings; to promote exchange among members & other educational researchers in Canada & internationally; to foster partnerships &, through educational research, influence public policy & help determine the nature, structure & funding of the research agenda
Member of: Canadian Education Association; Canadian Federation for the Humanities & Social Sciences
Finances: *Annual Operating Budget:* $100,000-$250,000; *Funding Sources:* Membership fees; publications; conference
Staff Member(s): 1; 30 volunteer(s)
Membership: 28 institutional + 343 student + 19 senior/lifetime + 535 individual + 20 international associate; *Fees:* $100 regular; $60 international; $50 student/retired/low income; *Committees:* Government & External Relations; R&D; Professional Enhancement & Collaboration; Conference
Chief Officer(s):
Nicholas Ng-A-Fook, President
Meetings/Conferences:
• Canadian Society for the Study of Education 2018 Annual Conference, May, 2018, University of Regina, Regina, SK
Scope: National
Description: Held in conjunction with the Congress of the Humanities & Social Sciences
Publications:
• The Canadian Journal of Education (CJE) / Revue canadienne de l'éducation
Type: Journal; *Frequency:* Quarterly; *Editor:* Katy Ellsworth
Profile: Educational scholarship in Canada
• Canadian Society for the Study of Education Membership Directory
Type: Directory
Profile: Electronic directory featuring general contact information & descriptions of completed & ongoing researh
• CSSE [Canadian Society for the Study of Education] News
Type: Newsletter; *Frequency:* Monthly; *Price:* Free with CSSE membership
Profile: Educational issues, CSSE activities; bilingual

Canadian Society for the Study of Fertility See Canadian Fertility & Andrology Society

Canadian Society for the Study of Higher Education (CSSHE) / La Société canadienne pour l'étude de l'enseignement supérieur (SCEES)
#204, 260 Dalhousie St., Ottawa ON K1N 7E4
Tel: 613-241-0018; Fax: 613-241-0019
csshe-scees@csse.ca
www.csshe-scees.ca
twitter.com/csshescees
Overview: A medium-sized national charitable organization founded in 1970
Mission: To advance the knowledge of post-secondary education through the promotion of research & its dissemination through publications & learned meetings
Finances: *Funding Sources:* Membership fees; publication sales
Membership: *Fees:* $110; $50 students/retired; *Member Profile:* Faculty & students in universities, community colleges, administrators & trustees, professionals in government departments & agencies, others with an interest in Canadian post-secondary education; *Committees:* Awards; Nominating; Publications

Chief Officer(s):
Kathleen Matheos, Treasurer
Walter Archer, President
walter.archer@ualberta.ca
Awards:
• Distinguished Member Award
For outstanding contribution to the CSSHE
• Research Award
For excellence in postsecondary education research
• Sheffield Award
For superior scholarly publication in the Journal
• George L. Geis Dissertation Award
For excellence in doctoral research on postsecondary education
• Masters Award
Publications:
• Canadian Journal of Higher Education (CJHE)
Type: Journal; *Editor:* Lesley Andres
Profile: Peer-reviewed articles about Canadian higher education for persons directly involved in higher education in Canada or very interested in the field
• Complete directory of CSSHE members / Bottin complet des membres de la SCÉES
Type: Directory
Profile: Listing of members by function or title

Canadian Society for the Study of Names (CSSN) / Société canadienne d'onomastique (SCO)
PO Box 2164, Stn. Hull, Gatineau QC J8X 3Z4
www.csj.ualberta.ca/sco
Overview: A small national charitable organization founded in 1967
Mission: CSSN promotes the study of all aspects of names & naming in Canada & elsewhere.
Member of: Canadian Federation for the Humanities & Social Sciences
Finances: *Funding Sources:* Membership dues
Membership: *Fees:* $25 regular; $20 retired; $15 student; $37.50 family; $30 retired family; $400 life membership; *Member Profile:* Persons who share the objectives of the Society
Activities: Facilitating exchange of ideas among onomatologists, toponymists, & scholars in the related fields of literary onomastics & linguistic aspects of names
Chief Officer(s):
Carol J. Léonard, Chair
carol.leonard@ualberta.ca
Léo La Brie, Secretary-Treasurer
Leo.Labrie@laposte.net
Publications:
• The Name Gleaner
Type: Newsletter; *Frequency:* 3 pa; *Editor:* William Davey; *Price:* Free with membership dues
• Onomastica Canadiana
Type: Journal; *Frequency:* Semiannually; *Number of Pages:* 56; *Editor:* Benoît Leblanc; *Price:* $20 libraries

Canadian Society for the Study of Practical Ethics (CSSPE) / Société canadienne pour l'étude de l'éthique appliquée (SCEEA)
c/o Dept. of Philosophy, #618, Jorgenson Hall, Ryerson Univ., 350 Victoria St., Toronto ON M5B 2K3
Tel: 416-979-5000; Fax: 416-979-5362
www.csspe.ca
Overview: A small national organization founded in 1987
Mission: To study all areas of practical ethics, including environmental ethics, health care ethics, bioethics, & business ethics
Membership: *Fees:* $20 student; $35 Contract Faculty/Post doc/ Retired; $50 Full Time Faulty/Professional; $75 Contributing Membership; *Member Profile:* Persons interested in practical ethics, from a variety of fields, such as academia, business, & the civil service
Activities: Addressing ethical issues which arise in areas of learning & activitiy, such as the social sciences & professions
Chief Officer(s):
Sandra Tomsons, President
stomsons@mts.net
Melany Banks, Secretary-Treasurer
mebanks@wlu.ca
Meetings/Conferences:
• Canadian Society for the Study of Practical Ethics 2018 Annual Conference, 2018
Scope: National

Canadian Society for the Study of Religion (CSSR) / Société canadienne pour l'étude de la religion (SCÉR)
c/o Richard Mann, 2A51 Paterson Hall, Dept. of Religion, Carleton U., 1125 Colonel By Dr., Ottawa ON K1S 5B6
www.cssrscer.ca
Overview: A small national organization founded in 1966
Mission: To promote research in the study of religion, with particular reference to Canada; To encourage a critical examination of the teaching of the discipline
Member of: International Association for the History of Religions (IAHR)
Affiliation(s): Canadian Federation for the Humanities & Social Sciences (CFHSS)
Membership: *Fees:* $50 students; $60 part-time & retired persons; $90 regular; *Member Profile:* Scholars engaged in various academic approaches to the study of religion
Chief Officer(s):
Rubina Ramji, President
ruby_ramji@cbu.ca
Arlene Macdonald, Membership Secretary
almacdon@utmb.edu
Richard Mann, Treasurer
Richard_mann@carleton.ca
Meetings/Conferences:
• Canadian Society for the Study of Religion 2018 Annual Meeting, May, 2018, University of Regina, Regina, SK
Scope: Provincial
Publications:
• Canadian Society for the Study of Religion Bulletin
Type: Newsletter; *Frequency:* Semiannually; *Editor:* Mark Chapman; *ISSN:* 0708-952X; *Price:* Free with CSSR membership
Profile: CSSR activies, member news, departmental news, & conference information
• Studies in Religion / Sciences Religieuses
Type: Journal; *Price:* Free with CSSR membership

Canadian Society for the Study of the Aging Male (CSSAM) / Société canadienne pour l'Étude de l'Homme Vieillissant (SCEHV)
71 Dewlane Dr., Toronto ON M2R 2P9
Tel: 416-480-0010; Fax: 416-480-0010
secretariat@cssam.com
www.cssam.com
Previous Name: Canadian Andropause Society
Overview: A small national organization founded in 1998
Mission: To support research on the physical, medical, sociological, & psychological changes in aging men
Membership: *Fees:* $65-$125
Chief Officer(s):
David Greenberg, President

The Canadian Society for the Weizmann Institute of Science (CSWIS)
#235, 4823, rue Sherbrooke ouest, Montréal ON H3Z 1G7
Tel: 514-342-0777
Toll-Free: 855-337-9611
www.weizmann.ca
www.linkedin.com/company/weizmann-canada
www.facebook.com/weizmanncanada
twitter.com/WeizmannCanada
youtube.com/user/WeizmannCanada;
flickr.com/photos/40652884@N07
Also Known As: Weizmann Canada
Overview: A medium-sized international charitable organization founded in 1964
Mission: To marshal Canadian support for the Weizmann Institute of Science in Rehovot, Israel; to help build & maintain scientific facilities; to acquire costly up-to-date research equipment & instrumentation; to set up endowments for research centres; to establish professional chairs & scholarships
Finances: *Annual Operating Budget:* $500,000-$1.5 Million; *Funding Sources:* Donations
Staff Member(s): 11
Membership: 7,000
Chief Officer(s):
Jeffrey I. Cohen, Chair
Susan Stern, National Executive Director & CEO, 514-342-0777 Ext. 101
susan@weizmann.ca
Lorie Blumer, National Manager, Communications, 514-342-0777 Ext. 102
lorie@weizmann.ca
Publications:
• Weizmann News [a publication of The Canadian Society for the

Weizmann Institute of Science]
Type: Newsletter; *Frequency:* Quarterly
Profile: Information on news, events, awards, programs, & initiatives related to Weizmann Canada.

Calgary Office
#506, 5920 - 1A St. SW, Calgary AB T2H 0G3
Tel: 587-774-7215
Toll-Free: 877-734-5948

Toronto Office
#603, 55 Eglinton Ave. East, Toronto ON M4P 1G8
Tel: 416-733-9220
Toll-Free: 800-387-3894
Chief Officer(s):
Claire Howard, Vice-President, 416-733-9220 Ext. 21
claire@weizmann.ca
Ilana Hirt, National Manager, 416-733-9220 Ext. 27
ilana@weizmann.ca

Vancouver Office
PO Box 38015, Stn. King Edward, Vancouver BC V5Z 4L9
Tel: 604-260-8506
Toll-Free: 877-734-5948
vancouver@weizmann.ca

Canadian Society for Traditional Music (CSTM) / Société canadienne pour les traditions musicales (SCTM)
c/o Cape Breton University, PO Box 5300, 1250 Grand Lake Rd., Sydney NS B1P 6L2
www.yorku.ca/cstm
www.facebook.com/CSTM.SCTM
twitter.com/CSTM_SCTM
Also Known As: Canadian Folk Music Society
Overview: A medium-sized national charitable organization founded in 1956
Mission: To study & promote musical traditions of all cultures; To reflect the interests of members of the music community
Member of: International Council for Traditional Music
Finances: *Annual Operating Budget:* Less than $50,000; *Funding Sources:* Membership dues; government & foundation grants
30 volunteer(s)
Membership: 200 individual + 100 institutional; *Fees:* $125 organization; $70 individual; $35 underemployed; *Member Profile:* Open
Activities: Offering mail order service of records, books, cassettes on Canadian folk music; Providing acts in consultative/teaching capacity to teachers, performers, etc.;
Rents Mailing List: Yes
Chief Officer(s):
Kaley Mason, President
kmason@lclark.edu
Monique Giroux, Treasurer
monique.c.giroux@gmail.com
Meghan Forsyth, Secretary

Canadian Society for Training & Development *See* Institute for Performance & Learning

Canadian Society for Transfusion Medicine (CSTM) / Société canadienne de médecine transfusionnelle
#6, 20 Crown Steel Dr., Markham ON L3R 9X9
Tel: 905-415-3917; *Fax:* 905-415-0071
Toll-Free: 855-415-3917
Other Communication: Toll-Free Fax: 866-882-7093
office@transfusion.ca
www.transfusion.ca
www.facebook.com/290163767690083
twitter.com/CanSocTransMed
Previous Name: Canadian Association of Immunohematologists
Overview: A medium-sized national organization founded in 1989
Mission: To promulgate throughout Canada a high level of ethics & professional standards; To create national & regional opportunities for the presentation & discussion of research & developments in these & allied fields; To initiate & maintain a program of continuing education; To promote good laboratory & good manufacturing practices; To establish mutually beneficial working relationships with relevant national & international societies & organizations; To be the primary voice for transfusion medicine in Canada
Finances: *Annual Operating Budget:* Less than $50,000; *Funding Sources:* Membership fees
Membership: 450; *Committees:* Communication; Membership; Standards; Translation
Chief Officer(s):
Darlene Mueller, President
president@transfusion.ca
Awards:
• Honorary Membership
• Ortho Award
• Blum Award
Meetings/Conferences:
• Canadian Society for Transfusion Medicine Conference 2018, June, 2018, Toronto, ON
Scope: National
Description: In conjunction with the 35th International Congress of the ISBT

Canadian Society for Tropical Medicine & International Health *See* Canadian Society for International Health

Canadian Society for Vascular Surgery (CSVS) / Société canadienne de chirurgie vasculaire
PO Box 58062, Ottawa ON K1C 7H4
Tel: 613-286-7583
info@canadianvascular.ca
canadianvascular.ca
twitter.com/canadianvascul1
Overview: A small national organization
Mission: To promote vascular health for Canadians
Finances: *Funding Sources:* Membership fees; Sponsorships
Activities: Promoting research; Providing continuing medical education; Engaging in advocacy activities; Facilitating the exchange of ideas & information
Chief Officer(s):
Kent MacKenzie, President
kent.mackenzie@muhc.mcgill.ca
Awards:
• National Student Research Awards Program
• Cook Research Award for Endovascular Therapy Research
• Gore Research Award
• John L. Provan Education Award
• Josephus Luke Award
• Sigvaris President's Award
Meetings/Conferences:
• Canadian Society for Vascular Surgery 2018 40th Annual Meeting, September, 2018, Montréal, QC
Scope: National
Description: The annual general meeting of the society, plus continuing education sessions, lectures, exhibits, & social events
Publications:
• Canadian Society for Vascular Surgery e-Newsletter
Type: Newsletter

Canadian Society for Yad Vashem
#218, 265 Rimrock Rd., Toronto ON M3J 3C6
Tel: 416-785-1333; *Fax:* 416-785-4536
Toll-Free: 888-494-7999
info@yadvashem.ca
www.yadvashem.ca
www.facebook.com/yadvashem
www.youtube.com/user/YadVashem
Overview: A medium-sized national charitable organization founded in 1986
Mission: To help support & finance the Canadian Pavilion for Holocaust Studies
Finances: *Funding Sources:* Donations
Activities: *Speaker Service:* Yes
Chief Officer(s):
Fran Sonshine, National Chair
Yaron Ashkenazi, Executive Director

Canadian Society of Addiction Medicine (CSAM) / La Société Medicale Canadienne sur l'Addiction (SMCA)
1444 40th St. NW, Calgary AB T3C 1W7
Tel: 403-246-9393
admin@csam-smca.org
www.csam-smca.org
www.linkedin.com/in/csam-smca
www.facebook.com/canadiansocietyofaddictionmedicine
twitter.com/csam_smca
Overview: A small national organization founded in 1989
Mission: To foster & promote medical sciences & clinical practice in the field of substance use disorders in Canada; To establish & promote standards of clinical practice
Affiliation(s): The International Society of Addiction Medicine
Finances: *Funding Sources:* Corporate sponsorship
Membership: 370; *Fees:* $200 MD & PhD; $50 associate; $25 retired; $5 student/intern/resident; *Member Profile:* MD members; Associate members; PhD members; Honorary members; Medical students, interns, & residents; Retired members; *Committees:* Journal; Education; Membership; By-Laws; Standards; Website; Sponsorship; Nominations; Economics; Conference; Bilingual; Executive; Advocacy
Activities: Offering scientific & medical information about addiction; Providing networking opportunities; Promoting research & medical education; Increasing public awareness
Chief Officer(s):
Paul Sobey, President
Publications:
• The Canadian Journal of Addiction [a publication of the Canadian Society of Addiction Medicine]
Type: Journal; *Editor:* Marilyn Dorozio
Profile: Information & scientific materials pertaining to the addiction medicine field
• CSAM [Canadian Society of Addiction Medicine] Bulletin
Type: Newsletter; *Frequency:* 3 pa
Profile: CSAM conferences, reports, membership information, research updates, clinical experiences, & continuing education opportunities related to addiction medicine

Canadian Society of Agronomy
S.C. Sheppard, PO Box 637, Pinawa MB R0E 1L0
Tel: 204-753-2747; *Fax:* 204-753-8478
www.agronomycanada.com
Overview: A medium-sized national organization
Mission: The mission of The Canadian Society of Agronomy is dedicated to enhancing cooperation and cooriindation among agronomists, to recognizing significant achievements in agronomy and to providing the oppourtunity to report and evaluate information pertinent to agronomy in Canada. The goals and objects include networking; external relations and awareness; and internal communications and coordination.
Member of: Agricultural Institute of Canada
Membership: 300
Chief Officer(s):
Steve Sheppard, PhD, Executive Director
sheppards@ecomatters.com

Canadian Society of Air Safety Investigators (CSASI)
139 West 13th Ave., Vancouver BC V5Y 1V8
avsafe@shaw.ca
www.beyondriskmgmt.com/csasi.htm
Overview: A small international organization founded in 1975
Mission: To improve air safety through investigation
Affiliation(s): International Society of Air Safety Investigators
3 volunteer(s)
Membership: *Fees:* $110 annual fee; $65 one time initiation fee; $25 student annual fee; $20 student one time initiation fee; *Member Profile:* Canadian aircraft accident investigators; Students
Chief Officer(s):
Barbara M. Dunn, President
avsafe@shaw.ca
Barry Wiszniowski, Vice-President
aviationsafety@rogers.com
Elaine Parker, Secretary-Treasurer
info@beyondriskmgmt.com
Publications:
• Canadian Society of Air Safety Investigators Proceedings
Price: Free with CSASI membership
Profile: Papers presented at each seminar
• Canadian Society of Air Safety Investigators Newsletter
Type: Newsletter; *Price:* Free with CSASI membership
• ISASI Forum
Frequency: Quarterly; *Price:* Free with CSASI membership

Canadian Society of Allergy & Clinical Immunology (CSACI) / Société canadienne d'allergie et d'immunologie clinique
PO Box 51045, Orléans ON K1E 3W4
Tel: 613-986-5869; *Fax:* 866-839-7501
info@csaci.ca
www.csaci.ca
www.facebook.com/471713226291440
twitter.com/csacimeeting
Previous Name: Canadian Society for the Study of Allergy; Canadian Academy of Allergy
Overview: A small national organization founded in 1945
Mission: To ensure optimal patient care by advancing the knowledge & practice of allergy, clinical immunology, & asthma
Finances: *Funding Sources:* Donations; Sponsorships
Membership: *Member Profile:* Clinical immunologists; Allergists; Asthma specialists; Allied health professionals; Medical students; Persons interested in the research & treatment of allergic diseases; *Committees:* Annual Scientific Program; CPD

Canadian Associations / Canadian Society of Animal Science (CSAS) / Société canadienne de science animale

Activities: Conducting research; Engaging in advocacy activities; Offering continuing professional development; Providing education to the public
Chief Officer(s):
Sandy Kapur, President
David Fischer, Vice-President
Harold Kim, Secretary-Treasurer
Publications:
• Allergy, Asthma & Clinical Immunology: Official Journal of the Canadian Society of Allergy & Clinical Immunology
Type: Journal; *Frequency:* Quarterly; *Editor:* Richard Warrington
Profile: Articles to further the understanding & treatment of allergic &immunologic disease
• CSACI [Canadian Society of Allergy & Clinical Immunology] Newsletter / Bulletin CSAIC
Type: Newsletter; *Frequency:* Bimonthly
Profile: CSACI activities, events, & awards

Canadian Society of Animal Science (CSAS) / Société canadienne de science animale
c/o Eveline Ibeagha-Awemu, Agriculture & Agri-Food Canada, 2000, rue College, Sherbrooke QC J1M 0C8
Tel: 819-780-7249; *Fax:* 819-564-5507
www.asas.org/CSAS
Overview: A medium-sized national organization founded in 1951
Mission: To provide opportunities to discuss the problems of the Canadian animal & poultry industries, with the objective of furthering advancements in these industries; To assist in the coordination of research, teaching & technology transfer related to the animal & poultry industries; To encourage publication of scientific information; To provide an annual forum for professionals in the agricultural industry to meet & discuss the most recent technological advancements in the field of animal & poultry science
Member of: Agricultural Institute of Canada
Membership: *Fees:* $110 regular; $65 new graduate; $45 retired; $15 student; *Member Profile:* Membership is open to persons currently or previously employed in research, teaching, administration, extension, production, marketing, or otherwise interested in any field pertaining to the animal industry. There are three categories for membership; regular, retired, or student members (undergraduate or graduate).; *Committees:* Awards; Membership
Chief Officer(s):
Miglior Filippo, President
miglior@cdn.ca
Awards:
• Canadian Society of Animal Science Fellowship
Awarded to a CSAS member for outstanding contributions in any field of animal agriculture; *Amount:* $1,000
• Excellence in Nutrition and Meat Sciences Award
Awarded to a CSAS member to recognize excellence in teaching & research in the fields of nutrition & meat science at the provincial, federal or international level; *Amount:* $1,000
• Technical Innovation in Enhancing Production of Safe Affordable Food Award
Awarded to a CSAS member to recognize outstanding service to the animal industries of Canada in technology, leadership & education; *Amount:* $1,000
• Young Scientist Award
Awarded to a CSAS member that has demonstrated excellence in research in any area of animal science & has held their PhD for a period not greater than seven years; *Amount:* $1,000
• Graduate Student Travel Bursaries
Awarded each year upon confirmation of attendance at CSAS annual meeting; *Amount:* $500
• Graduate Student Poster Presentations Awards
Awarded to recognize the top three poster presentations during the Graduate Student Competition at the annual meeting; *Amount:* $250 first place; $150 second place; $100 third place
• Graduate Student Oral Presentations Awards
Awarded to recognize the top three oral presentations during the Graduate Student Competition at the annual meeting; *Amount:* $250 first place; $150 second place; $100 third place
• Undergraduate Student Award of Academic Excellence
Awarded in recognition of superior academic achievement during the first three years of study within the Faculties of Agriculture at each Canadian university: UBC, U of Alberta, U of Saskatchewan, U of Manitoba, U of Guelph, McGill University (MacDonald Campus), Dalhousie University & Université Laval; *Amount:* $100
Meetings/Conferences:
• 2018 American Society of Animal Science & Canadian Society of Animal Science Annual Meeting & Trade Show, July, 2018
Scope: National
Publications:
• Animal Frontiers [a publication of the Canadian Society of Animal Science]
Type: Magazine; *Frequency:* q.; *Accepts Advertising*
Profile: Co-published with the American Society of Animal Science, American Meat Science Association & the European Association for Animal Production;peer-reviewed articles on animal agriculture
• Canadian Journal of Animal Science [a publication of the Canadian Society of Animal Science]
Type: Journal; *Frequency:* q.

Canadian Society of Association Executives (CSAE) / Société canadienne des directeurs d'association (SCDA)
#1100, 10 King St. East, Toronto ON M5C 1C3
Tel: 416-363-3555; *Fax:* 416-363-3630
Toll-Free: 800-461-3608
www.csae.com
www.linkedin.com/company/csae-canadian-society-of-association-executives
www.facebook.com/AssociationExecutives
twitter.com/csaeconnect
Previous Name: Institute of Association Executives
Overview: A large national organization founded in 1951
Mission: To provide members with the environment, knowledge, & resources to develop excellence in not-for-profit leadership through networking, education, advocacy, information, & research
Affiliation(s): European Society of Association Executives; American Society of Association Executives; 7 Canadian Chapters of Society of Association Executives: British Columbia, Edmonton, Manitoba, Trillium, Ottawa-Gatineau, Quebec, Nova Scotia
Finances: *Funding Sources:* Education & service offerings; Membership dues
Staff Member(s): 15
Membership: 600 corporate + 1,650 individual; *Fees:* Schedule available; *Member Profile:* Association executives & businesses
Activities: *Rents Mailing List:* Yes
Chief Officer(s):
Tracy Folkes Hanson, President & CEO, 416-363-3555 Ext. 234
tracy@csae.com
Michele Haché, Director, 416-363-3555 Ext. 223
Danielle Lamothe, Director, Education, 416-363-3555 Ext. 240
danielle@csae.com
Stewart Laszlo, Director, Marketing, 416-363-3555 Ext. 235
stewart@csae.com
Geeta Prashad, Director, Conferences & Events, 416-363-3555 Ext. 236
geeta@csae.com
Awards:
• Pinnacle Award
Awarded to recognize exceptional leadership
• Griner Award
Awarded to honour significant contributions made by business members to the association
• Honorary Award of Excellence
Awarded to recognize a member's sustained commitment & outstanding contribution to CSAE on a national basis or at the local chapter level
• Donna Mary Shaw Award
Awarded to encourage & enable individuals to pursue careers in the not-for-profit sector
• Associations Make a Better Canada Award
Recognizes CSAE member organizations that have initiated & implemented successful projects in the fields of public education, public affairs, government relations, professional development, or ethical, technical, or professional standards
• Communications Awards of Excellence
Acknowledges outstanding examples of successful communications vehicles created by CSAE member organizations
• Long-Term Service Award
Recognizes CSAE individuals who have been members for a period of 20 years or more
Meetings/Conferences:
• Canadian Society of Association Executives / Société canadienne d'association 2018 Conference & Showcase, October, 2018, Ottawa, ON
Scope: National
• Canadian Society of Association Executives / Société canadienne d'association 2019 Conference & Showcase, October, 2019, Vancouver, BC
Scope: National
• Canadian Society of Association Executives / Société canadienne d'association 2020 Conference & Showcase, November, 2020, Halifax, NS
Scope: National
Publications:
• Association Magazine [a publication of the Canadian Society of Association Executives]
Type: Magazine; *Accepts Advertising; Editor:* Sandi L. Humphrey; *ISSN:* 1189-9794
Profile: Practical advice regarding association management & governance membershiprecruitment, retention, lobbying & advocacy updates, revenue generation, data management, and necessary sector information

British Columbia Chapter
BC
Tel: 604-385-3396
bc@csae.com
www.csae.com/Networks/British-Columbia
www.linkedin.com/groups/4139578
twitter.com/csaebc
Chief Officer(s):
Rhian Williams, Chair, 250-851-0026
rhian.williams@hilton.com

Edmonton Chapter
c/o Jackie Bennett, PO Box 25562, Edmonton AB T5T 7E7
Tel: 780-803-3243
www.csae.com/Networks/Edmonton
Chief Officer(s):
Carmen Wyton, President
carmen@ripple-enterprises.ca
Daniel García, Vice-President
dan@knowprincipia.com

Manitoba Chapter
c/o Kalynn Spain, 699 Garfield St. North, Winnipeg MB R3G 2M4
Tel: 204-333-7537
manitoba@csae.com
www.csae.com/Networks/Manitoba
Chief Officer(s):
Ted Eastley, President, 204-254-5983
eastleyt@yahoo.ca
Patrick Hauta, 1st Vice-President, 204-957-4527
patrickh@wcc.mb.ca

Nova Scotia Chapter
PO Box 22057, 7071 Bayers Rd., Halifax NS B3L 4T7
Tel: 902-292-3839
atlantic@csae.com
www.csae.com/Networks/Nova-Scotia
Chief Officer(s):
Lyle Goldberg, President
lgoldberg@unsm.ca
Paula Goulding, Chapter Administrator

Ontario (Trillium) Chapter
PO Box 51165, #1, 70 Eglinton Square, Toronto ON M1L 4T2
Tel: 647-346-2723
admin@csae-trillium.com
www.csae.com/Networks/Trillium
Chief Officer(s):
Constance Wrigley-Thomas, Chair
Tracy Blyth, Executive Director
tracy@csae-trillium.com

Ottawa-Gatineau Chapter
Ottawa ON
Tel: 613-271-1476
csae.ottawa-gatineau@rogers.com
www.csae.com/Networks/Ottawa-Gatineau
Chief Officer(s):
Adele Fifield, Chair

Section du Québec
QC
Tél: 514-282-2739
www.csae.com/Networks/Quebec
www.facebook.com/ScdaQuebec
twitter.com/scdaquebec
Chief Officer(s):
François Gravel, Coordinateur
fgravel@gestias.qc.ca

Canadian Society of Atherosclerosis, Thrombosis & Vascular Biology (CSATVB) / Société canadienne

d'Athérosclérose, de Thrombose et de Biologie Vasculaire (SCATBV)
c/o Laurence Boudreault, Centre de recherche du CHU de Quebec, 2705, boul Laurier, #TR-93, Québec QC G1V 4G2
Tel: 418-656-4141; Fax: 418-654-2145
www.csatvb.ca
Previous Name: Canadian Atherosclerosis Society
Overview: A medium-sized national charitable organization founded in 1983
Mission: To provide a means of communication between Canadian professionals interested in atherosclerosis & cardiovascular disease; To promote research & education
Affiliation(s): International Atherosclerosis Society
Membership: 309; Fees: $100; Member Profile: Scientists, physicians, lipidologists, pathologists; Committees: Communication; Education; Finance; Long-Term Planning; Nominating; Trainee Advisory
Chief Officer(s):
Peter Julien, Treasurer
Laurence Boudreault, Contact
laurence.boudreault@crchuq.ulaval.ca
Awards:
• Young Investigator Awards
• Scientific Excellence Award
• TraineeTravel Subsidy

Canadian Society of Biblical Studies (CSBS) / Société canadienne des études bibliques (SCEB)
c/o Prof. Robert A. Derrenbacker, Jr., Regent College, 5800 University Blvd., Vancouver BC V6T 2E4
www.ccsr.ca
Overview: A small national organization founded in 1933
Mission: To stimulate the critical investigation of the classical biblical literature & related literature
Membership: Fees: $35 students & retired & unemployed persons; $72 full membership; Member Profile: Individuals interested in all aspects of the academic study of the Bible
Chief Officer(s):
Robert A. Derrenbacker, Jr., Treasurer & Membership Secretary
rderrenbacker@laurentian.ca
Meetings/Conferences:
• Canadian Society of Biblical Studies 2018 Annual Meeting (in conjunction with the 2018 Congress of the Humanities & Social Sciences), May, 2018, University of Regina, Regina, SK
Scope: National
Publications:
• Canadian Society of Biblical Studies Membership Directory
Type: Directory
• The CSBS [Canadian Society of Biblical Studies] / SCÉB [Société canadienne des études bibliques] Bulletin
Type: Yearbook; Frequency: Annually; Editor: Richard S. Ascough; Price: Free withCSBS membership
Profile: CSBS membership news, events, annual general meeting minutes, & financial statements
• Studies in Religion / Sciences Religieuses
Type: Journal; Price: Free with CSBS membership
Profile: Refereed articles

Canadian Society of Cardiac Surgeons / Société des chirurgiens cardiaques
#1403, 222 Queen St., Ottawa ON K1P 5V9
Tel: 613-569-3407; Fax: 613-569-6574
Toll-Free: 877-569-3407
www.ccs.ca
www.facebook.com/SCC.CCS.ca
twitter.com/SCC_CCS
Previous Name: Canadian Society of Cardiovascular & Thoracic Surgeons
Overview: A small national organization
Mission: To represent cardiovascular clinicians & scientists in Canada
Membership: Fees: $505; Member Profile: Canadian cardiovascular & thoracic surgeons
Chief Officer(s):
Catherine Kells, President
Anne Ferguson, Chief Executive Officer
ferguson@ccs.ca
Linda Palmer, Director, Membership & CCS Affiliate Services
palmer@ccs.ca
Susan Oliver, Director, Strategic Initiatives
oliver@ccs.ca
Melissa Keown, Director, Professional Development
keown@ccs.ca
Erin McGeachie, Manager, Health Policy
mcgeachie@ccs.ca

Julie Graves, Coordinator, Marketing & Communications
graves@ccs.ca
Carol DeHaros, Coordinator, Finance & Administration
deharos@ccs.ca

Canadian Society of Cardiology Technologists Inc. (CSCT) / Société canadienne des technologues en cardiologie inc.
PO Box 3121, Winnipeg MB R3C 4E6
Other Communication: education@csct.ca
info@csct.ca
www.csct.ca
Overview: A medium-sized national organization
Mission: To ensure a standard of excellence in the practice of cardiology technology in Canada
Affiliation(s): Canadian Cardiovascular Society (CCS)
Membership: 1,000+; Member Profile: Individuals employed in the field of cardiology
Activities: Providing continuing education
Chief Officer(s):
Shauna Ryall, President

Canadian Society of Cardiovascular & Thoracic Surgeons
See Canadian Society of Cardiac Surgeons

Canadian Society of Children's Authors, Illustrators & Performers (CANSCAIP) / La société canadienne des auteurs, illustrateurs et artistes pour enfants
#501, 720 Bathurst St., Toronto ON M5S 2R4
Tel: 416-515-1559
office@canscaip.org
www.canscaip.org
www.facebook.com/CANSCAIP.org
twitter.com/CANSCAIP
Overview: A medium-sized national organization founded in 1977
Mission: To promote the growth of children's literature by establishing the rapport with teachers, librarians & children; to establish communication between publishers & society; to encourage the development of new writers, illustrators & performers
Member of: Canadian Children's Book Centre
Finances: Funding Sources: Membership fees; workshops; travelling art collection
16 volunteer(s)
Membership: 400 professional + 650 associates; Fees: $75 professional; $35 associate; Member Profile: Professional - must be published; Associate - any interested person
Activities: Speaker Service: Yes
Chief Officer(s):
Bill Swan, President
Publications:
• CANSCAIP [Canadian Society of Children's Authors, Illustrators & Performers] News
Type: Newsletter; Frequency: Quarterly; Price: Free with CANSCAIP membership
Profile: Articles, interviews, new CANSCAIP members, awards, new books, publishers, & projects
• CANSCAIP [Canadian Society of Children's Authors, Illustrators & Performers] Monographs
Price: Free with CANSCAIP membership
Profile: Topics include How to Do a School Presentation & How to Negotiate an Illustrator Contract

Canadian Society of Chinese Medicine & Acupuncture (CSCMA)
#402, 245 Fairview Mall Dr., Toronto ON M2J 4T1
Tel: 416-597-6769; Fax: 416-597-9928
office@tcmcanada.org
www.tcmcanada.org
Overview: A small national organization founded in 1994
Mission: To unite traditional Chinese medicine (TCM) & acupuncture practitioners, & to advocate for legal recognition & regulation of TCM in Canada
Membership: 2,300; Fees: $100
Chief Officer(s):
Zhao Cheng, President
Gengmin Tang, Secretary General
Publications:
• The Canadian Society of Chinese Medicine & Acupuncture Publication
Type: Journal

Canadian Society of Church History (CSCH) / Société canadienne d'histoire de l'Église
c/o Robynne R. Healey, Dept. of History, Trinity Western University, 7600 Glover Rd., Langley BC V2Y 1Y1

csch-sche.ca
Overview: A small national organization founded in 1960
Mission: To encourage research in the history of Christianity, especially the history of Christianity in Canada
Member of: Canadian Corporation for Studies in Religion; Congress of Social Sciences & Humanities
Membership: Fees: $15 students; $30 retired academics; $33 individuals; Member Profile: Historians of Christianity in Canada & the United States
Chief Officer(s):
Scott McLaren, President
Lucille Marr, Vice-President & Program Chair
Robynne Rogers Healey, Administrative Secretary
robynne.healey@twu.ca
John H. Young, Treasurer
john.young@queensu.ca
Meetings/Conferences:
• Canadian Society of Church History 2018 Annual Meeting, May, 2018, Regina, SK
Scope: National
Publications:
• Historical Papers: Canadian Society of Church History
Type: Journal; Frequency: Annually; Editor: Robynne Rogers Healey; Price: Free with CSCH membership
Profile: A selection of papers delivered at the CSCH annual meeting

Canadian Society of Cinematographers (CSC)
#131, 3085 Kingston Rd., Toronto ON M1M 1P1
Tel: 416-266-0591; Fax: 416-266-3996
admin@csc.ca
www.csc.ca
Overview: A small national organization founded in 1957
Mission: To promote the art & craft of cinematography
Finances: Funding Sources: Sponsorships
Membership: 600; Member Profile: Canadian film & video professionals involved in the production of feature films, documentaries, television series, specials, & commercials
Activities: Providing professional education for members; Disseminating technical & product information
Chief Officer(s):
George Willis, President
Joan Hutton, Past President
joanhuttondesign@gmail.com
Susan Saranchuk, Executive Officer
Awards:
• Canadian Society of Cinematography Awards
18 awards given annually for various genres & contributions
Publications:
• Cinematographer [a publication of the Canadian Society of Cinematographers]
Type: Magazine; Frequency: 10 pa; Accepts Advertising
Profile: Personal & corporate profiles, awards, illustrated production & technical features, industry news & informative columns
• CSC [Canadian Society of Cinematographers] Directory
Type: Directory; Frequency: Semiannually; Accepts Advertising
Profile: Register of members, & a list of sponsors

Canadian Society of Clinical Chemists (CSCC) / Société canadienne des clinico-chimistes
PO Box 1570, #310, 4 Cataraqui St., Kingston ON K7K 1Z7
Tel: 613-531-8899; Fax: 866-303-0626
office@cscc.ca
www.cscc.ca
Overview: A medium-sized national organization founded in 1965
Mission: To establish standards for diagnostic services in the practice of clinical biochemistry & clinical laboratory medicine
Membership: Fees: $185 full; $180 associate; $75 affiliate; $55 student; Member Profile: Clinical biochemists throughout Canada; Committees: Credentials; Certification; Accreditation of Training Programs; Maintenance of Competence; Nominations & Awards
Activities: Providing leadership, education, & research in the practice of clinical biochemistry & clinical laboratory medicine; Liaising with goverment, industry, & healthcare associations; Engaging in advocacy activities
Chief Officer(s):
David Kinniburgh, President
Elizabeth Hooper, Executive Director
Ivan Blasutig, Treasurer
Meetings/Conferences:
• 2018 Canadian Society of Clinical Chemists Conference, 2018
Scope: National

Publications:
- Canadian Society of Clinical Chemists Member Handbook
Type: Yearbook; *Frequency:* Annually
- Clinical Biochemistry
Type: Journal; *Editor:* Edgard E. Delvin; *ISSN:* 0009-9120
Profile: Analytical & clinical investigative articles related to molecular biology, chemistry, biochemistry, immunology, clinical investigation, diagnosis, therapy, & monitoring humandisease, for chemists, immunologists, biologists, & biochemists
- The CSCC [Canadian Society of Clinical Chemists] News
Type: Newsletter
Profile: Society activities & information for CSCC members

Canadian Society of Clinical Neurophysiologists (CSCN) / Société canadienne de neurophysiologistes cliniques
#709, 7015 Macleod Trail SW, Calgary AB T2H 2K6
Tel: 403-229-9544; *Fax:* 403-229-1661
www.cnsfederation.org
Overview: A small national organization founded in 1990 overseen by Canadian Neurological Sciences Federation
Mission: To promote & encourage all aspects of neurophysiology, including research & education, in addition to assessment & accreditation in the field
Member of: Canadian Neurological Sciences Federation
Affiliation(s): Cdn. Brain Tumour Consortium; Cdn. Epilepsy Consortium; Cdn. Stroke Consortium; Cdn. League Against Epilepsy; Cdn. Headache Society; Cdn. Movement Disorders Group; Cdn. Network of MS Clinics; Cdn. Neurocritical Care Group; Amyotrophic Lateral Sclerosis Research Foundation; Consortium of Canadian Centres for Clinical Cognitive Research; Associate Societies: Assn. of Electromyography Technologists of Canada; Canadian Assn. of Electroneurophysiology Technologists; Canadian Assn. of Neuroscience; Canadian Assn. of Neuroscience Nurses; Canadian Assn. of Physical Medicine & Rehabilitation
Membership: 275; *Member Profile:* Individuals who pass the EEG or EMG exam; Other persons require the names & signatures of two active CSCN members in support of their application for membership; Junior members need the signature of either an active member or their training program director
Activities: Providing annual scientific sessions to promote the knowledge & practice of clinical neurophysiology; Providing physicians the opportunity to take exams in EEG &/or EMG
Chief Officer(s):
Dan Morin, CNSF CEO
dan-morin@cnsfederation.org
Awards:
- Herbert Jasper Prize
Awarded annually for the best submitted paper in clinical or basic neurophysiology by a resident or fellow in training; others also eligible; *Amount:* honorarium, fees to attend the annual meeting of the CNS
Publications:
- Canadian Journal of Neurological Sciences
Type: Journal; *Frequency:* Bimonthly; *Accepts Advertising*; *Editor:* G. Bryan Young
Profile: Peer-reviewed original articles

Canadian Society of Clinical Perfusion (CSCP) / Société Canadienne de Perfusion Clinique (SCPC)
914 Adirondack Rd., London ON N6K 4W7
Fax: 866-648-2763
Toll-Free: 888-496-2727
www.cscp.ca
www.facebook.com/CSCP-Online-1523661604524664
twitter.com/cscp_online
instagram.com/cscp_online
Overview: A medium-sized national organization
Mission: To encourage & foster the development of the profession of clinical perfusion, through education & certification
Membership: 257 + 10 corporate + 4 student + 2 honourary + 1 retired + 1 incorporated; *Fees:* $300 certified; $225 associate; $50 student; $240 institutional; $300 inactive (on approval of board of directors); $530-1200 corporate
Chief Officer(s):
Roger Stanzel, President
Cyril Serrick, Vice-President
Naresh Tinani, Executive Secretary
Bill Gibb, Treasurer
Meetings/Conferences:
- The Canadian Society of Clinical Perfusion 2018 National Meeting, October, 2018, Toronto, ON
Scope: National
Description: Continuing education sessions on product development involving the society's corporate members, a business meeting, Canadian Society of Clinical Perfusion cerification examinations held off site from the convention centre, the presentation of awards, & networking opportunities
Publications:
- The Perfusionist: The Official Publication of the Canadian Society of Clinical Perfusion
Type: Journal; *Frequency:* 3 pa; *Accepts Advertising*; *Editor:* Andrew Beney, MSc, CPC, CCP
Profile: Approximately 350 issues are distributed to Canadian certified perfusionists, subscribingstudents, American perfusionists, & corporate members

Canadian Society of Club Managers (CSCM) / La Société canadienne des directeurs de club
2943B Bloor St. West, Toronto ON M8X 1B3
Tel: 416-979-0640; *Fax:* 416-979-1144
Toll-Free: 877-376-2726
national@cscm.org
www.cscm.org
Overview: A small national organization
Mission: To provide managers with the tools necessary to manage their clubs
Finances: *Annual Operating Budget:* $250,000-$500,000
Staff Member(s): 5; 25 volunteer(s)
Membership: 560; *Fees:* Based on region; *Member Profile:* Managers of private or semi-private clubs in Canada; *Committees:* Executive; Editorial Advisory; Education; Technology; Certification
Chief Officer(s):
Elizabeth Di Chiara, Executive Director
elizabeth@cscm.org

Canadian Society of Consultant Pharmacists (CSCP)
info@cscpharm.com
www.cscpharm.com
www.linkedin.com/groups/4331158
twitter.com/ASCPharm
Overview: A small national organization
Mission: To improve quality of care for older persons by supporting & advancing pharmacists working in assisted living or long term care settings
Affiliation(s): American Society of Consultant Pharmacists
Finances: *Annual Operating Budget:* Less than $50,000
Membership: 150; *Fees:* Schedule available; *Member Profile:* Consultant pharmacists, long-term care providers
Activities: Supporting optimal pharmeceutical care of seniors & long term care residents
Chief Officer(s):
Neemet McDowell, President

Canadian Society of Corporate Secretaries See Governance Professionals of Canada

Canadian Society of Customs Brokers (CSCB) / Société canadienne des courtiers en douane
#320, 55 Murray St., Ottawa ON K1N 5M3
Tel: 613-562-3543; *Fax:* 613-562-3548
cscb@cscb.ca
www.cscb.ca
Previous Name: Canadian Association of Customs Brokers
Overview: A medium-sized international organization founded in 1921
Mission: To act as voice of the industry to all levels of government; To provide information to members on all matters affecting customs brokerage
Affiliation(s): International Federation of Customs Brokers Associations
Finances: *Funding Sources:* Membership dues
Membership: 160 customs brokers + 210 Certified Trade Compliance Specialists + 4,300 Certified Customs Specialists; *Fees:* Schedule available; *Member Profile:* Licensed customs brokers; Certified customs specialists; Firms engaged in international trade
Activities: Offering education & professional development programs about customs & international trade; Providing networking opportunities & advertising services; *Speaker Service:* Yes; *Library:* Not open to public
Chief Officer(s):
Angela Collins, Chair

Canadian Society of Cytology (CSC) / Société canadienne de cytologie
c/o Canadian Association of Pathologists, #310, 4 Cataraqui St., Kingston ON K7K 1Z7
Tel: 613-507-8528; *Fax:* 866-531-0626
www.cap-acp.org/cytology.php
Previous Name: Canadian Cytology Council
Overview: A small national charitable organization founded in 1961
Mission: To promote & support education in cytology; To maintain a high standard of practice within the discipline of cytopathology; To foster the development of cytopathology in Canada
Member of: Canadian Association of Pathologists / Association canadienne des pathologistes
Membership: *Member Profile:* Pathologists; Cytotechnologists with an interest in cytopathology
Activities: Conducting regular cytology surveys; Contributing to the development of the Guide for Training in General Pathology & cytotechnology training programs across Canada; Presenting awards; Facilitating the exchange of knowledge in cytopathology; Organizing educational programs; Developing guidelines for quality assurance programs in cytopathology
Chief Officer(s):
Janine Benoit, Chair
benoitj@shaw.ca
Publications:
- CSC [Canadian Society of Cytology] Bulletin
Type: Newsletter; *Frequency:* 3 pa

Canadian Society of Endocrinology & Metabolism (CSEM) / Société canadienne d'endocrinologie et métabolisme (SCEM)
#1403, 222 Queen St., Ottawa ON K1P 5V9
Tel: 613-594-0005; *Fax:* 613-569-6574
info@endo-metab.ca
www.endo-metab.ca
Overview: A small national organization founded in 1972
Mission: To advance the endocrinology & metabolism field in Canada
Membership: *Fees:* $100 active members; *Member Profile:* Clinical endocrinologists, educators, & researchers who provide health care, training, research in endocrinology; Graduate students, residents, & research fellows; emertius members; *Committees:* Awards; Continuing Professional Development; Program Planning; Residents Council/Review Course Planning; Guidelines; Quality Improvement; Nominating
Activities: Advocating for excellence in endocrinology research, education, & patient care; Promoting research in endocrinology & metabolism; Providing continuing professional development opportunities
Chief Officer(s):
Connie Chik, President
Alice Cheng, Secretary-Treasurer
Meetings/Conferences:
- Canadian Society of Endocrinology & Metabolism & Diabetes Canada Professional Conference & Annual Meetings, October, 2018, Halifax Convention Centre, Halifax, NS
Scope: National
Description: Interactive workshops, oral abstract sessions, poster presentations, speakers addressing current diagnosis & treatment issues, a trade show, social activities, & networking opportunities

Canadian Society of Environmental Biologists (CSEB) / Société canadienne des biologistes de l'environnement
PO Box 962, Stn. F, Toronto ON M4Y 2N9
www.cseb-scbe.org
Overview: A medium-sized national charitable organization founded in 1943
Mission: To further the conservation of natural resources of Canada & to promote the prudent management of these resources so as to minimize adverse environmental effects; to ensure high professional standards in education, research & management related to resources & environment; to advance the education of the public & to protect public interest on matters pertaining to the use of natural resources & the protection & management of the environment; to undertake environmental research & education programs; to assess & evaluate administrative & legislative policies having ecological significance in terms of conservation of resources & quality of the environment; to develop & promote policies that seek to achieve balance among resource management & utilization, protection of the environment & quality of life; to foster liaison among environmental biologists working within governmental, industrial & educational frameworks across Canada
Finances: *Annual Operating Budget:* Less than $50,000; *Funding Sources:* Membership dues
Staff Member(s): 2; 30 volunteer(s)
Membership: 500; *Fees:* $35; *Member Profile:* Regular - graduate from college or university in discipline of biological sciences, professionally engaged in teaching, management or

research related to natural resources & the environment; Student - persons enrolled in accredited college or university in discipline of biological sciences & preparing themselves for professional work in teaching, management or research related to natural resources; Associate - supporters in general
Activities: *Speaker Service:* Yes; *Rents Mailing List:* Yes
Chief Officer(s):
Robert Stedwill, President, 306-585-1854
rstedwill@live.ca
Publications:
• CSEB [Canadian Society of Environmental Biologists] National Newsletter / Bulletin
Type: Newsletter; *Frequency:* Quarterly; *Accepts Advertising*; *Editor:* Gary Ash; *ISSN:* 0318-5133; *Price:* Free with Canadian Society of Environmental Biologistsmembership
Profile: CSEB activities, & national & regional news, for members

Canadian Society of Exploration Geophysicists (CSEG)
#600, 640 - 8th Ave. SW, Calgary AB T2P 1G7
Tel: 403-262-0015
cseg.office@shaw.ca
www.cseg.ca
Overview: A medium-sized national organization founded in 1949
Mission: To promote the science of geophysics
Affiliation(s): Society of Exploration Geophysicists (USA); European Association of Geoscientists & Engineers
Finances: *Funding Sources:* Membership fees
Membership: 1,800; *Member Profile:* Geophysicists involved in hydrocarbon exploration; Geologists; Field specialists; Technical specialists; Academics; Interested industry personnel; Corporate members
Activities: Offering a mentorship program; Exchanging technical information; Providing networking activities
Chief Officer(s):
John Townsley, President
jtownsley@arcresources.com
Larry Herd, Vice-President
larryh@boydpetro.com
Jim Racette, Managing Director, 403-262-0015, Fax: 403-262-7383
jimra@shaw.ca
John Fernando, Director, Educational Services
john.fernando@sait.ca
Kelly Jamison, Director, Finance
kelly.jamison@divestco.com
Kristy Manchul, Director, Communications
kristy.manchul@cggveritas.com
Dave Nordin, Director, Member Service
denordin@telusplanet.net
Publications:
• Canadian Society of Exploration Geophysicists Annual Report
Type: Yearbook; *Frequency:* Annually
• The CSEG / CSPG Geophysical Atlas of Western Canadian Hydrocarbon Pools
Type: Atlas; *Editor:* Leonard V. Hills
• Recorder
Type: Magazine; *Frequency:* Monthly; *Accepts Advertising*
Profile: Canadian Society of Exploration Geophysicists membership news, & events, plus articles related to geophysics

Canadian Society of Forensic Science (CSFS)
PO Box 37040, 3332 McCarthy Rd., Ottawa ON K1V 0W0
Tel: 613-738-0001; *Fax:* 613-738-1987
csfs@bellnet.ca
www.csfs.ca
facebook.com/csfscanada/
Overview: A small national organization founded in 1953
Mission: To promote the study of forensic science; To maintain professional standards in the discipline of forensic science
Membership: *Fees:* $30; *Member Profile:* Professionals with an interest in forensic science; *Committees:* Awards; Finance; Membership; Nominating; Publication; Informatics & Education; Drugs & Driving; Constitution; Alcohol Test; Accreditation
Activities: Addressing educational, scientific, & legal issues within forensic science
Chief Officer(s):
G. Anderson, President
G. Verret, Secretary
D. Camellato, Treasurer
Publications:
• The Canadian Society of Forensic Science Journal
Type: Journal; *Frequency:* Quarterly; *Accepts Advertising*; *Price:* $115 Canada; $130 International

Profile: Original papers, & comments & reviews on the various aspects of forensic science, such as forensic chemistry, forensic odontology, forensic toxicology, forensic pathology,firearms examination, forensic biology, & forensic anthropology

Canadian Society of Forest Engineers *See* Canadian Institute of Forestry

Canadian Society of Gastroenterology Nurses & Associates (CSGNA)
#224, 1540 Cornwall Rd., Oakville ON L6J 7W5
Tel: 905-829-8794; *Fax:* 905-829-0242
Toll-Free: 866-544-8794
csgnaexecutiveassistant@csgna.com
www.csgna.com
Overview: A small national organization founded in 1984
Mission: To enhance the educational & professional growth of the membership within the resources available.
Member of: SIGNEA - the International Society of Gastroenterology Nurses & Associates
Affiliation(s): Canadian Nurses Association
Finances: *Funding Sources:* Membership fees; donations; fundraising
Membership: 467 members + 19 local chapters; *Fees:* $100 active/affiliate; *Member Profile:* Work in field of gastroenterology
Chief Officer(s):
Lisa Westin, President
Jacqui Ho, Treasurer
treasurer@csgna.com
Calgary Chapter
South Health Campus Endoscopy Unit, 4448 Front St. SE, Calgary AB T3M 1M4
Chief Officer(s):
Bobbi Sheppy, President
sheppyfamily@shaw.ca
Edmonton Chapter
c/o Endoscopy Unit, Misericordia Community Hospital, 16940 - 87 Ave., Edmonton AB T5R 4H5
Chief Officer(s):
Yvonne Verklan, President
yvohver@gmail.com
Golden Horseshoe Chapter
ON
Chief Officer(s):
Jody Hannah, President
jhanah@stjosham.on.ca
Greater Toronto Chapter
c/o St. Joseph's Healthcentre, 30 The Queensway, Toronto ON M6R 1B5
Tel: 416-530-6000
Chief Officer(s):
Daysi Sandino, President
daysisandino@yahoo.ca
London & Area Chapter
London ON
Chief Officer(s):
Donna Pratt, President
Donna.Pratt@lhsc.on.ca
London Chapter
London ON
Chief Officer(s):
Donna Pratt, President
Donna.Pratt@lhsc.on.ca
Manitoba Chapter
MB
Chief Officer(s):
Carol Reidy, President
creidy@sbgh.mb.ca
New Brunswick/PEI Chapter
NB
Chief Officer(s):
Cathy Arnold Cormier, President
cathy.arnoldcormier@horizonnb.ca
Newfoundland Chapter
NL
Chief Officer(s):
June Peckham, President
j.peckham@nf.sympatico.ca
Nova Scotia Chapter
NS
Chief Officer(s):
Marleen Spencer, President
marleen.spencer@cdha.nshealth.ca

Okanagan Chapter
Kelowna General Hospital, Gastroenterology Unit, 2268 Pandosy St., Kelowna BC V1Y 1T2
Tel: 250-868-8465
Chief Officer(s):
Bethany Rode, President
behl@shaw.ca
Ottawa Chapter
Ottawa ON
Chief Officer(s):
Joanne Bertrand, President
joanne.l.bertrand@gmail.com
Regina Chapter
Regina SK
Chief Officer(s):
Jennifer McIntyre, President
Jennifer.Mcintyre@rqhealth.ca
Vancouver Regional Chapter
Vancouver BC

Canadian Society of Geriatric Medicine *See* Canadian Geriatrics Society

Canadian Society of Hand Therapists (CSHT) / Societe canadienne des therapeutes de la main (SCTM)
#101, 10277 154 St., Surrey BC V3R 4J7
secretary@csht.org
www.csht.org
www.facebook.com/324550384259629
twitter.com/handtherapists
Overview: A medium-sized national organization
Mission: To provide education, information, & enhanced care for the improvement of upper extremity rehabilitation
Membership: *Fees:* $30; *Member Profile:* Occupational & physical therapists; *Committees:* Executive
Chief Officer(s):
Trevor Fraser, President
president@csht.org
Meetings/Conferences:
• Canadian Society of Hand Therapists Annual Conference 2018, April, 2018, Westin Ottawa, Ottawa, ON
Scope: National

Canadian Society of Hospital Pharmacists (CSHP) / Société canadienne des pharmaciens d'hôpitaux
#3, 30 Concourse Gate, Ottawa ON K2E 7V7
Tel: 613-736-9733; *Fax:* 613-736-5660
info@cshp.ca
www.cshp.ca
www.facebook.com/cshp-ca
twitter.com/CSHP_SCPH
Overview: A medium-sized national organization founded in 1947
Mission: To advance safe, effective medication use & patient care in hospitals & related health care settings throughout Canada; To act as an influential voice for hospital pharmacy; To encourage professional growth & practice excellence
Member of: Canadian Council on Continuing Education in Pharmacy
Finances: *Funding Sources:* Membership fees; Sponsorships
Membership: *Member Profile:* Hospital pharmacists across Canada; Residents & students; Hospital & industry corporate members; *Committees:* Advocacy; Bylaws; CSHP 2015 Steering; Educational Services; Finance & Audit; Government & Health Policy Planning; Membership; National Awards; Nominating; Pharmacy Specialty Networks Coordinating; Practice Standards Steering; Research
Activities: Developing standards; Facilitating research; Advocating for hospital pharmacy; Providing education, mentorship, & information; *Awareness Events:* Pharmacy Awareness Week
Chief Officer(s):
Myrella Roy, Executive Director
mroy@cshp.ca
Desarae Davidson, Interim Manager, Operations
ddavidson@cshp.ca
Amanda Iannaccio, Administrator, Publications
aiannaccio@cshp.ca
Anna Dudek, Administrator, Finance
adudek@cshp.ca
Robyn Rockwell, Administrator, Membership & Awards
rrockwell@cshp.ca
Meetings/Conferences:
• Canadian Society of Hospital Pharmacists 49th Professional Practice Conference 2018, February, 2018, Beanfield Centre,

Toronto, ON
Scope: National
Description: Informative sessions to educate & motivate participants
• Canadian Society of Hospital Pharmacists 2018 Annual General Meeting, October, 2018, Winnipeg, MB
Scope: National
Description: The annual general meeting of the society & educational workshops held each year in partnership with one of the society's branches
Publications:
• Canadian Journal of Hospital Pharmacy
Type: Journal; *Frequency:* Bimonthly; *Accepts Advertising*; *Editor:* Stephen Shalansky; *ISSN:* 0008-4123; *Price:* Free with Canadian Society of Hospital Pharmacistsmembership
Profile: A peer-reviewed scientific journal, featuring original research, case reports, & clinical reviews
• CSHP [Canadian Society of Hospital Pharmacists] eBulletin
Type: Newsletter; *Frequency:* Semimonthly; *Accepts Advertising*; *Price:* Free with Canadian Society of Hospital Pharmacists membership
Profile: Society news & career opportunities

Alberta
Edmonton AB
www.cshp-ab.ca
Chief Officer(s):
Sheri Koshman, President
Joshua Torrance, Treasurer

British Columbia
#200, 1765 West 8th Ave., Vancouver BC V6J 1V8
cshpbc@gmail.com
www.cshp-bc.ca
www.facebook.com/cshpbc
twitter.com/CSHPBCBranch
Chief Officer(s):
Michael Legal, President
Ivy Chow, Treasurer

Manitoba
200 Tache Ave., Winnipeg MB R3H 1A7
info4@cshp-mb.ca
www.cshp-mb.ca
Chief Officer(s):
Patrick Fitch, President
Alyn Stavness, Treasurer

New Brunswick
NB
webmaster@cshp-nb.ca
www.cshp-nb.ca
Chief Officer(s):
Leslie Manuel, President
Leslie.Manuel@horizonnb.ca
Rochelle Johnston, Director, Communication
Rochelle.Johnston@HorizonNB.ca

Newfoundland & Labrador
c/o PANL, 85 Thorburn Rd., St. John's NL A1E 1C1
admin@cshp-nl.com
www.cshp-nl.com
Chief Officer(s):
Tiffany Lee, President
tiffany.lee@mun.ca
Angie Payne, Treasurer
Angie.Payne@easternhealth.ca
• Branch Out: The Newsletter of the Newfoundland & Labrador Branch Canadian Society of Hospital Pharmacists
Type: Newsletter
Profile: Membership, awards, advocacy, & professional development updates, as well as upcoming events

Nova Scotia
Halifax NS
www.cshp-ns.com
Chief Officer(s):
Lisa Nodwell, President
Lisa.Nodwell@cdha.nshealth.ca
Heather MacKeen, Treasurer
heather.mackeen@cdha.nshealth.ca

Ontario
#3, 30 Concourse Gate, Ottawa ON K2V 7V7
Tel: 613-736-9733; *Fax:* 613-736-5660
www.cshpontario.ca
Chief Officer(s):
Dawn Jennings, President
Helen Briggs, Treasurer

Prince Edward Island
Charlottetown PE
Chief Officer(s):
Wendy Cooke, President
wpcooke@gov.pe.ca
Kelly Herget, Treasurer
kcherget@ihis.org

Québec
Association des pharmaciens des établissements de santé, #320, 4050, rue Molson, Montréal QC H1Y 3N1
Tel: 514-286-0776; *Fax:* 514-286-1081
info@apesquebec.org
www.apesquebec.org
Chief Officer(s):
Linda Vaillant, Directrice générale
France Boucher, Directrice générale adjointe

Saskatchewan
c/o Saskatoon Health Region, Saskatoon SK
www.cshp-sk.org
Chief Officer(s):
Jaris Swidrovich, President
president@cshp-sk.org
Leslie Dagg, Treasurer
treasurer@cshp-sk.org
• The PostScript
Type: Newsletter; *Editor:* Z. Dumont (postscript@cshp-sk.org)
Profile: Canadian Society of Hospital Pharmacists, Saskatchewan Branch highlights, membership news, professional development information, & upcoming events

Canadian Society of Internal Medicine (CSIM) / Société canadienne de médecine interne (SCMI)
#300, 421 Gilmour St., Ottawa ON K2P 0R5
Tel: 613-422-5977; *Fax:* 613-249-3326
Toll-Free: 855-893-2746
info@csim.ca
csim.ca
www.facebook.com/canadiansocietyofinternalmedicine
twitter.com/CSIMSCMI
Overview: A medium-sized national organization founded in 1984
Mission: To promote healthy living among Canadians; to provide leadership for physicians; to conduct research & education.
Affiliation(s): Canadian Medical Association
Finances: *Funding Sources:* Membership dues; grants
Membership: *Fees:* $250 full; $100 physician associate; $50 allied health professional associate; $0 senior/resident/medical student; *Member Profile:* General internal medicine physicians/residents; *Committees:* Education; Health Promotion; Research & Awards; Specialty Committee in Internal Medicine; Annual Meeting
Chief Officer(s):
Benjamin Chen, President
Awards:
• Canadian Society of Internal Medicine's Education & Research Fund
Support research and education for members of CSIM *Eligibility:* Resident & member of association *Deadline:* November
Publications:
• CJGIM (Canadian Journal of General Internal Medicine)
Type: Journal; *Frequency:* Quarterly
Profile: CSIM news, book reviews, articles, case reviews, history of medicine, & medical education

Canadian Society of Laboratory Technologists *See* Canadian Society for Medical Laboratory Science

Canadian Society of Landscape Architects (CSLA) / Association des architectes paysagistes du Canada (AAPC)
12 Forillon Cres., Ottawa ON K2M 2S5
Tel: 866-781-9799; *Fax:* 866-871-1419
info@csla.ca
www.csla.ca
www.linkedin.com/groups/4849978/profile
www.facebook.com/177312791600
twitter.com/CSLA_AAPC
Overview: A medium-sized national organization founded in 1934
Mission: To support the improvement &/or conservation of the natural, cultural, social & built environment; to promote visibility, recognition, acceptance & understanding of the profession by communicating its value in relation to that of the public good
Affiliation(s): International Federation of Landscape Architects; Landscape Alliance
Finances: *Annual Operating Budget:* $100,000-$250,000; *Funding Sources:* Membership dues
40 volunteer(s)
Membership: 1,900+; *Fees:* $115; *Member Profile:* Qualified & experienced landscape architects who practise their profession by providing a variety of services ranging from advice, consultation & design to preparing working drawings, contract documents & supervising the implementation of various size construction projects
Chief Officer(s):
Elizabeth A. Sharpe, Executive Director
executive-director@csla.ca
Meetings/Conferences:
• 2018 Canadian Society of Landscape Architects Congress, April, 2018, Westin Harbour Castle, Toronto, ON
Scope: National
Attendance: 4,500+
Publications:
• CSLA [Canadian Society of Landscape Architects] Bulletin
Type: Newsletter; *Frequency:* Monthly
Profile: News & events related to landscape architecture in Canada
• CSLA [Canadian Society of Landscape Architects] Membership Directory
Type: Directory
• CSLA [Canadian Society of Landscape Architects] Annual Report
Type: Yearbook; *Frequency:* Annually
• Landscapes / Paysages
Type: Journal; *Frequency:* Quarterly; *Accepts Advertising*
Profile: Articles about the professional practice of landscape architecture in Canada, related to culture, design, & the environment

Canadian Society of Mayflower Descendants
c/o Lynne Webb, 2927 Highfield Cres., Ottawa ON K2B 6G4
administrator@csmd.org
csmd.org
www.facebook.com/canadiansocietyofmayflowerdescendants
twitter.com/CanMayflower
Overview: A small national organization founded in 1980
Mission: To promote the memory of the Mayflower pilgrims & to inform the public of this era of Canadian history
Affiliation(s): General Society of Mayflower Descendants - USA
Finances: *Funding Sources:* Membership dues; donations
Membership: 577; *Fees:* $45; *Member Profile:* Direct descendants of Mayflower passengers; *Committees:* Governance; Nominating; Publicity
Activities: *Internships:* Yes; *Speaker Service:* Yes; *Library:* Collection at North York Public Library; Open to public
Chief Officer(s):
Joyce Cutler, Governor
governor@csmd.org
Publications:
• Canadian Pilgrim
Type: Newsletter; *Frequency:* Semiannually; *Price:* Free with Canadian Society of Mayflower Descendants membership
Profile: Society news, & genealogical & historical information
• The Mayflower Quarterly
Type: Journal; *Frequency:* Quarterly; *Price:* Free with Society membership
Profile: Genealogical information

Canadian Society of Medical Evaluators (CSME)
#301, 250 Consumers Rd., Toronto ON M2J 4V6
Tel: 416-487-4040; *Fax:* 416-495-8723
Toll-Free: 888-672-9999
info@csme.org
www.csme.org
www.facebook.com/101574806684190
Overview: A small national organization
Mission: To serve Canadian physicians who perform medical & medicolegal evaluations for patients or as a professional service to the legal profession, employers, the workplace safety & insurance board & the insurance industry
Membership: *Fees:* $295 associate; $450 general; *Committees:* Communications; Ethics; Education Programs; Guidelines; Membership
Chief Officer(s):
Renee Levine, Executive Director
rlevine@csme.org

Canadian Society of Medievalists (CSM)
104 Mount Aubrun St., 5th Fl., Cambridge MA 02138 USA
Tel: 617-491-1622; *Fax:* 617-492-3303
csmtreasurer@gmail.com
www.canadianmedievalists.ca

Overview: A small national organization founded in 1958
Mission: To promote the teaching & public awareness of plant physiology in Canada
Membership: Fees: $40 full; 25 post-doctoral; $15 student/emeritus & emerita/corresponding; Member Profile: Plant scientists in Canada; Retired members; Students; Persons who live outside Canada are eligible for corresponding membership; Committees: Society (Gold) Medal Award; C.D. Nelson Award; David J. Gifford Tree Physiology Award; Gleb Krotkov Award; Ann Oaks Scholarship; Ragai Ibrahim Award; Communications; Education; Meeting Site; Nominating; Auditors
Activities: Facilitating the exchange of information; Promoting the importance of research in plant sciences; Liaising with other educational, non-profit or governmental agencies or organizations to develop the science of plant physiology
Chief Officer(s):
Jean-Benoit Charron, Senior Director
seniordirector@cspb-scbv.ca
Anja Geitmann, President
cspb-vp@cspb-scbv.ca
Awards:
• C.D. Nelson Award
To honour outstanding research contributions to plant physiology
• Gleb Krotkov Award of the CSPP
To honour outstanding service to the Society
• The Gold Medal Award (The CSPP Medal)
To recognize either outstanding published contributions or distinguished service to plant physiology
• David J. Gifford Award in Tree Physiology
To recognize outstanding research contributions in tree physiology
• The President's Awards
To recognize the best student oral & poster presentations at the Annual General Meeting
• The Regional Directors' Awards
To recognize the best student oral & poster presentations at the Eastern and Western Regional Meetings
• Ragai Ibrahim Award
To recognize the best student paper
Meetings/Conferences:
• Canadian Society of Plant Biologists/Société canadienne de biologie végétale Annual General Meeting 2018, July, 2018, Montréal, QC
Scope: National
Description: Held in conjunction with the American Society of Plant Biologists & the International Society of Photosynthesis Research
Contact Information: URL: plantbiology.aspb.org
Publications:
• Canadian Society of Plant Physiologists Membership List
• CSPP [Canadian Society of Plant Physiologists] / SCPV [Société canadienne de physiologie végétale] Bulletin
Type: Newsletter; Frequency: Semiannually; Editor: Goeffrey Wasteneys; ISSN: 1183-9597
Profile: Issues related to plant biology, & CSPP / SCPV events, activites, awards, &financial information, of interest to society members

Canadian Society of Plant Physiologists See Canadian Society of Plant Biologists

Canadian Society of Plastic Surgeons (CSPS) / Société canadienne des chirurgiens plasticiens
PO Box 60192, Stn. Saint-Denis, Montréal QC H2J 4E1
Tel: 514-843-5415; Fax: 514-843-7005
csps_sccp@bellnet.ca
www.plasticsurgery.ca
Overview: A medium-sized national organization founded in 1947
Mission: To represent, promote & provide leadership for the descipline of plastic surgery across Canada
Affiliation(s): Canadian Medical Association
Finances: Annual Operating Budget: $100,000-$250,000; Funding Sources: Membership dues
Staff Member(s): 1
Membership: 400; Fees: $500; Member Profile: Active members are specialists in plastic surgery who practise in Canada & are certified by the Royal College of Physicians & Surgeons of Canada, the American Board of Plastic Surgery &/or the Collège des médecins du Québec; Associate members are plastic surgeons who practise outside Canada, who in the past have attended one of the meetings of the Canadian Society of Plastic Surgeons, & who are known to the membership; Senior associate members are exempt from annual dues and must be 60+ yrs. of age; Junior members are registered in a plastic surgery training program, with membership proposed by their director; Honorary members are nominated by the Board to recognize their contribution of services; Committees: Ethics; RCPSC Plastic Surgery Specialty; Young Plastic Surgeons; Canadian Journal of Plastic Surgery; Annual Meeting Local Host
Chief Officer(s):
Peter Lennox, President
Gorman Louie, Vice-President
Bing Gan, Secretary-Treasurer
Karyn Wagner, Executive Director
Meetings/Conferences:
• Canadian Society of Plastic Surgeons 2018 72nd Annual Meeting, June, 2018, Jasper, AB
Scope: National
Description: An opportunity for participants to learn during the scientific program & to view exhibits
Publications:
• CSPS News: The Newsletter of the Canadian Society of Plastic Surgeons
Type: Newsletter; Frequency: Semiannually; Editor: Karyn Wagner
Profile: Message from the president, meeting highlights, upcoming workshops, member news
• Plastic Surgery
Type: Journal; Editor: Dr. Edward Buchel

Canadian Society of Presbyterian History
c/o Burns Presbyterian Church, 765 Myrtle Rd. West, Ashburn ON L0B 1A0
Tel: 905-655-8509
www.csph.ca
Overview: A small local organization founded in 1975
Mission: To study Presbyterian & Reformed history
Chief Officer(s):
A. Donald MacLeod, President
adonaldmacleod@gmail.com

Canadian Society of Professional Event Planners (CanSPEP)
19270 Conc. #4, Alexandria ON K0C 1A0
Tel: 613-288-4539
Toll-Free: 866-467-2299
infoc@canspep.ca
www.canspep.ca
www.facebook.com/192650557472891
twitter.com/canspep
Previous Name: Independent Meeting Planners Association of Canada, Inc.
Overview: A small national organization founded in 1996
Mission: To promote, support & provide education to independent meeting & event planners & create public awareness around the profession of meeting & event planning
Finances: Annual Operating Budget: $100,000-$250,000; Funding Sources: Membership dues
Membership: 110; Fees: $295 full; $147.50 associate; $75 student; Member Profile: Self-employed meeting & event planners; Owners of an event management firm with 15 or fewer employees
Activities: Speaker Service: Yes
Chief Officer(s):
Bettyanne Sherrer, President
bettyanne@proplan.ca
Jeff Chabot, Association Coordinator
Meetings/Conferences:
• The Canadian Society of Professional Event Planners Annual Conference 2018, July, 2018, Sudbury, ON
Scope: National
Publications:
• Canadian Society of Professional Event Planners eNewsletter
Type: Newsletter
Profile: News & important dates for members

Canadian Society of Professionals in Disability Management (CSPDM)
c/o Pacific Coast University for Workplace Health Sciences, 4755 Cherry Creek Rd., Port Alberni BC V9Y 0A7
Tel: 778-421-0821; Fax: 778-421-0823
www.cspdm.ca
Overview: A small national organization founded in 2006
Mission: To minimize the socio-economic impact of disabling injuries & illnesses on employees & employers by establishing & supporting the practice of consensus based disability management through professional standards of quality innovation & leadership in the field
Member of: International Association of Professionals in Disability Management
Membership: 500
Activities: Library: Not open to public
Chief Officer(s):
Sheena Cook, Coordinator, Membership Services, 778-421-0821 Ext. 210
sheena@cspdm.ca
Publications:
• CSPDM [Canadian Society of Professionals in Disability Management] Connections
Type: Newsletter; Frequency: Quarterly
Profile: Information & resources relevant to disability management

Canadian Society of Public Health Dentists See Canadian Association of Public Health Dentistry

Canadian Society of Questers
PO Box 1465, Salmon Arm BC V1E 4P6
pinkrose4233@gmail.com
www.questers.ca
Overview: A small national organization founded in 1979
Mission: To promote the ancient art of divining in its many forms, including: dowsing for water, minerals, ley lines, & ancient ruins; questing/seeking for lost or stolen goods, missing persons, & answers to personal queries; radiesthesia to assist in good health by identifying allergies, determining supplements such as vitamins & minerals, & locating sources of disease; PSI to understand & develop the power of the mind
Membership: 25; Fees: $35 individual; $45 family
Chief Officer(s):
Carol Heywood, President, 541-846-6835
Meetings/Conferences:
• Canadian Society of Questers Spring Conference 2018, 2018
Scope: National
• Canadian Society of Questers Fall Conference 2018, 2018
Scope: National

Canadian Society of Respiratory Therapists (CSRT) / La Société canadienne des thérapeutes respiratoires (SCTR)
#201, 2460 Lancaster Rd., Ottawa ON K1B 4S5
Tel: 613-731-3164; Fax: 613-521-4314
Toll-Free: 800-267-3422
www.csrt.com
www.facebook.com/csrt.sctr
twitter.com/@CSRT_tweets
Overview: A medium-sized national organization founded in 1964
Mission: To provide leadership toward the advancement of cardiorespiratory care; To achieve excellence through the definition of roles, standards, & scope of clinical practice
Finances: Annual Operating Budget: $500,000-$1.5 Million
Staff Member(s): 5; 100 volunteer(s)
Membership: 3,000; Fees: $180
Activities: Providing education; Conducting research
Chief Officer(s):
Jeff Dionne, President
Adam Buettner, Treasurer
Christiane Ménard, Executive Director, 800-267-3422 Ext. 222
cmenard@csrt.com
Meetings/Conferences:
• Canadian Society of Respiratory Therapists 2018 Annual Education Conference, May, 2018, Vancouver, BC
Scope: National
Attendance: 400+
Description: Featuring internationally renowned speakers, workshops, & presentations for respiratory therapists
Contact Information: conference.csrt.com

Canadian Society of Safety Engineering, Inc. (CSSE) / Société canadienne de la santé et de la sécurité, inc.
468 Queen St. East, LL-02, Toronto ON M5A 1T7
Tel: 416-646-1600; Fax: 416-646-9460
Toll-Free: 877-446-2674
www.csse.org
www.linkedin.com/groups?gid=1558517
www.facebook.com/39373429711
twitter.com/csse
Previous Name: Ontario Society of Safety Engineering
Overview: A medium-sized national organization founded in 1949
Mission: To be the voice of safety in Canada
Affiliation(s): American Society of Safety Engineers
Finances: Annual Operating Budget: $250,000-$500,000; Funding Sources: Membership dues; educational programs
Staff Member(s): 7; 50 volunteer(s)

Membership: 30 associate + 100 student + 45 senior/lifetime + 2,000 individual; *Fees:* $150; *Member Profile:* Open to those employed full-time in occupational health, safety & environment work
Activities: Certification program for Health & Safety Consultant; *Awareness Events:* Canadian Occupational Health & Safety Week, 1st week of June; *Speaker Service:* Yes; *Rents Mailing List:* Yes
Chief Officer(s):
Wayne Glover, Executive Director
wglover@csse.org
Jim B. Hopkins, President
president@csse.org
Meetings/Conferences:
• Canadian Society of Safety Engineering 2018 Professional Development Conference, September, 2018, Niagara Falls, ON
Scope: National
Description: Theme: "People, Purpose & Passion: The Pathway to OHS Success"
Publications:
• CSSE [Canadian Society of Safety Engineering, Inc.] Contact
Type: Newsletter; *Frequency:* Quarterly; *Price:* Free with CSSE membership; $100 non-members

Canadian Society of Soil Science (CSSS) / Société canadienne de la science du sol (SCSS)
Business Office, PO Box 637, Pinawa MB R0E 1L0
Tel: 204-282-9486; *Fax:* 204-753-8478
sheppards@ecomatters.com
www.csss.ca
Overview: A medium-sized national charitable organization
Mission: To be actively engaged in land use, soils research, & classification
Member of: Agricultural Institute of Canada
Affiliation(s): International Union of Soil Science
Finances: *Funding Sources:* Membership dues
Membership: 100-499; *Member Profile:* Open to those concerned with farming practices as they affect soil quality & the development of soil conserving cropping practices, or those concerned with non-agricultural uses of soils, including forestry, engineering, & reclamation
Activities: *Speaker Service:* Yes
Chief Officer(s):
Maja Krzic, PhD, President
Amanda Dichon, PhD, Secretary
Kent Watson, Treasurer
Meetings/Conferences:
• 2018 Canadian Society of Soil Science Annual Meeting, June, 2018, Niagara Falls, ON
Description: Joint meeting with Canadian Geophysical Union (CGU) & Computational Infrastructure in Geodynamics (CIG)
Publications:
• Canadian Journal of Soil Science
Type: Journal; *Frequency:* Quarterly; *Editor:* Dr. F.J. Larney
Profile: International peer-reviewed original research related to the development, structure, use, & management of soils
• CSSS [Canadian Society of Soil Science] Newsletter
Type: Newsletter; *Frequency:* 3 pa; *Price:* Free with CSSS membership
Profile: CSSS activities, awards, events, & reports

Canadian Society of Sugar Artistry (CSSA)
35 - 19th St., Toronto ON M8V 3L4
Tel: 416-252-1294
www.cssainc.ca
www.facebook.com/101567256639834
Overview: A small national organization founded in 1983
Mission: Professional & non-professional society for those interested in sugar artistry
Member of: Arts Etobicoke
Staff Member(s): 10
Membership: 200 individual; *Fees:* $25; *Committees:* Newsletter
Activities: Two workshops annually; one Cake Show & Fall Competition
Chief Officer(s):
Ann Hetram, President
ann@cssainc.ca

Canadian Society of Teachers of the Alexander Technique (CANSTAT)
53 Bowden St., Toronto ON M4K 2X3
Toll-Free: 877-598-8879
info@CanSTAT.ca
www.canstat.ca
Overview: A small national organization
Mission: To establish & maintain standards for the certification of teachers and teacher training courses; to provide services to its members; to educate the public about the F. M. Alexander Technique.

Canadian Society of Technical Analysts (CSTA)
#436, 157 Adelaide St. West, Toronto ON M5H 4E7
Tel: 519-807-9178
toronto@csta.org
www.csta.org
Overview: A large national organization
Mission: To provide a forum for those interested in & working in technical analysis; To promote technical analysis within the financial community
Membership: *Fees:* Schedule available; *Member Profile:* People working in the technical analysis field; people interested in technical analysis; *Committees:* Education; Finance
Chief Officer(s):
Reagan Yuke, Business Manager
bm@csta.org

Canadian Society of Transplantation (CST) / Société canadienne de transplantation
114 Cheyenne Way, Ottawa ON K2J 0E9
Toll-Free: 877-968-9449
admin@cst-transplant.ca
www.cst-transplant.ca
Previous Name: Canadian Transplantation Society
Overview: A small national charitable organization
Mission: To provide leadership for the advancement of educational, scientific, & clinical aspects of transplantation in Canada
Finances: *Funding Sources:* Membership dues; Sponsorships
Membership: *Fees:* $25 associate member & trainee; $150 full member; $200 corporate; *Member Profile:* Medical doctor or scientist in the field of transplantation or an associated field; Person in a training program accredited by the Royal College of Physicians & Surgeons of Canada (or equivalent) in a field related to transplantation; Individual actively involved in transplantation clinical practice or research, such as a nurse practitioner or social worker; Person employed by an organization with corporate interests that are compatible with the interests & ethical standards of the Society; *Committees:* Education; Ethics; Governance & Nominations; Grants & Awards; Leading Clinical Practice; Public Policy; Research; Scientific Meetings; Standards
Activities: Implementing national strategies & policies; Promoting ethical practice in organ donation, clinical studies, & research; Encouraging research; Promoting high standards for education; Maintaining a national forum for scientists, surgeons, & physicians; Collaborating with related organizations
Chief Officer(s):
Atul Humar, President
Kathryn Tinckam, Secretary
Michael Mengel, Treasurer
Meetings/Conferences:
• Canadian Transplant Summit 2018, October, 2018, The Westin Ottawa, Ottawa, ON
Scope: National
Description: Hosted by the Canadian Society of Transplantation (CST), Canadian Blood Services (CBS), Canadian Blood & Marrow Transplant Group (CBMTG), & Canadian National Transplant Research Program (CNTRP)
Publications:
• CST [Canadian Society of Transplantation] News
Type: Newsletter; *Frequency:* 3 pa
Profile: Feature articles, plus information about the Canadian Society of Transplantation sent to all members

Canadian Society of Zoologists (CSZ) / Société canadienne de zoologie (SCZ)
c/o Département de biologie, Université Laval, Québec QC G1V 0A6
Tel: 902-820-2979
www.csz-scz.ca
Overview: A medium-sized national organization founded in 1961
Mission: To promote advancement & public awareness of zoology; To facilitate sharing of knowledge & ideas among all persons interested in science & practice of zoology; To organize discussions & debates of general interest
Affiliation(s): Canadian Council on Animal Care; Canadian Federation of Biological Societies
Finances: *Funding Sources:* Membership fees
Membership: 373; *Fees:* $80 regular; $20 student, associate, & emeritus; *Member Profile:* Working in zoology; *Committees:* Membership; Recognition; Science Policy; Biodiversity; Animal Care Advisory; Collections Advisory; Outstanding Ph.D. Thesis; Communications; Nominating
Chief Officer(s):
Helga Guderley, Secretary
helga.guderley@bio.ulaval.ca
Keith B. Tierney, Treasurer
ktierney@ualberta.ca
Awards:
• CSZ Public Awarensss Award - Public Education Prize
Intended to recognize excellent in public education about zoology; *Amount:* $300
• Helen Battle Award
Cash prize & scroll, given for the best student poster at the Annual Conference; *Amount:* $200
• Leo Margolis Scholarship
Presented to a Canadian who is registered in a graduate studies program at a Canadian university, whose research is in the field of fisheries biology; *Amount:* $500
• CSZ Student Research Grant
To assist students & post-doctoral fellows from Canadian Universities to conduct zoological research; *Amount:* Up to $500
• CSZ Public Awareness Award; Best issue driven popular press article
Cash prize & scroll, intended to encourage & stimulate members to increase public awarenss of zoology through articles in the popular press; *Amount:* $500
• Fry Award - Outstanding Biologist of the Year
Receives the Fry Medal, delivers the Fry Lecture at the AGM, full travel expenses are reimbursed
• Fry Award & Medal - Outstanding Zoologist of the Year
Recipient receives the Fry Medal, delivers the Fry Lecture at the Annual Meeting
• CSZ Distinguished Service Medal
Scroll & medal, presented at the AGM; recoziging members who have contributed to the well being of zoology in Canada, by working hard for the CSZ
• T.W.M. Cameron Outstanding Ph.D. Thesis Award
Recipient is invited to present a lecture of their dissertation to the AGM
• Hoar Award
Cash prize & scroll given for the best student paper presented orally at the Annual Conference; *Amount:* $500
• CSZ New Investigator Award
Scroll & cash award to an individual, who since professional appointment, has made a significant contribution to zoology & may be considered a 'rising star' in their field; *Amount:* Up to $500
Meetings/Conferences:
• Canadian Society of Zoologists 2018 57th Annual Meeting, May, 2018, Memorial University, St. John's, NL
Scope: National
Publications:
• Canadian Society of Zoologists / Société canadienne de zoologie Bulletin
Type: Newsletter; *Frequency:* 3 pa; *ISSN:* 0319-6674; *Price:* Free with CSZ / SCZ membership
Profile: CSZ / SCZ reports, events, articles, & interviews

Canadian Sociological Association (CSA) / Société canadienne de sociologie
PO Box 98014, 2126 Burnhamthorpe Rd. West, Mississauga ON L5L 5V4
Tel: 416-660-4378
office@csa-scs.ca
www.csa-scs.ca
www.linkedin.com/groups?mostPopular=&gid=3188569
www.facebook.com/134213209935255
twitter.com/csa_sociology
Overview: A medium-sized national licensing organization founded in 1964
Mission: To promote research, publication & teaching of sociology in Canada
Member of: Humanities & Social Science Federation of Canada; International Sociological Association
Finances: *Annual Operating Budget:* $50,000-$100,000; *Funding Sources:* Membership fees; grants
Staff Member(s): 2; 50 volunteer(s)
Membership: 850; *Fees:* Schedule available; *Member Profile:* Membership includes sociologists in education, government & business, students & individuals from other disciplines or affiliations who share a concern for sociology; *Committees:* Equity; Policy, Ethics & Professional Concerns; Research Advisory; Student Concerns

Activities: Conducting research; Organizing conference; Publishing journal; Offering awards; *Rents Mailing List:* Yes
Chief Officer(s):
Sherry Fox, Executive Administrator
Awards:
• Outstanding Services Awards
• Outstanding Contribution Awards
Given to recognize the work of eminent sociologists & anthropologists
• John Porter Award
Recognizes the best sociology book published in Canada in the past three years
Meetings/Conferences:
• Canadian Sociological Association 2019 Annual Conference, June, 2019, University of British Columbia, Vancouver, BC
Scope: National
Publications:
• Canadian Review of Sociology / Revue canadienne de sociologie
Type: Journal; *Frequency:* Quarterly; *Editor:* Dr. François Dépelteau; *ISSN:* 1755-618X; *Price:* Freewith CSA membership; $120 non-members
Profile: Formerly known as the Canadian Review of Sociology & Anthropology, the professional journal features articles & reviews
• CSA [Canadian Sociological Association] Newsletter
Type: Newsletter
Profile: News & events involving members

Canadian Solar Industries Association
#605, 150 Isabella St., Ottawa ON K1S 1V7
Fax: 613-736-8939
Toll-Free: 866-522-6742
info@cansia.ca
www.cansia.ca
www.linkedin.com/company/canadian-solar-industries-association-cansia
www.facebook.com/cansia
twitter.com/CanadianSIA
Also Known As: CanSIA
Overview: A medium-sized national organization founded in 1992
Mission: To develop a strong Canadian solar energy industry; To act as the voice for the solar energy industry in Canada
Member of: CanCORE
Finances: *Annual Operating Budget:* $500,000-$1.5 Million; *Funding Sources:* Membership fees
Staff Member(s): 8
Membership: 250; *Fees:* $100-$10,000; *Member Profile:* Solar energy companies across Canada; *Committees:* Policy & Market Development; Utilities & Regulatory Affairs; Communications
Activities: Offering education & networking events for members; Liaising with federal & provincial governments; *Speaker Service:* Yes
Chief Officer(s):
John A. Gorman, President & CEO
jgorman@cansia.ca
Wes Johnston, Vice President
wjohnston@cansia.ca
Meetings/Conferences:
• Canadian Solar Industries Association 2018 Solar Canada Annual Conference & Exposition, June, 2018, BMO Centre, Calgary, AB
Scope: National
Attendance: 4000+
Description: The presentation of timely topics for solar industry professionals from across Canada, featuring more than 60 speakers & 225 exhibitors
Contact Information: www.solarcanadaconference.ca
Publications:
• Solar Beat Newsletter
Type: Newsletter; *Frequency:* Bimonthly
Profile: News from the solar industry
• SOLutions Magazine [a publication of the Canadian Solar Industries Association]
Type: Magazine; *Frequency:* Semiannually; *Accepts Advertising*
Profile: Information from the Canadian Solar Industries Association

Canadian South Devon Association (CSDA)
PO Box 68, Lipton SK
Tel: 306-336-2666; *Fax:* 306-646-4460
info@southdevon.ca
www.southdevon.ca
Overview: A small national organization founded in 1975
Member of: Canadian Beef Breeds Council
Membership: *Member Profile:* Breeders of South Devon cattle in Canada
Chief Officer(s):
Gloria Bigalky, Secretary-Treasurer

Canadian Soybean Council
#201, 100 Stone Rd. West, Guelph ON N1G 5L3
Tel: 519-767-4124
info@soybeancouncil.ca
www.soybeancouncil.ca
Previous Name: Soyfoods Canada
Overview: A small national organization founded in 2005
Mission: To encourage growth, integrity, & sustainability in the Canadian soyfoods industry by promoting soyfoods, including soy-based foods & ingredients, to consumers
Membership: *Member Profile:* Soybean growers & suppliers; soyfood processors & distributors; marketing firms
Chief Officer(s):
John Johnston, Treasurer

Canadian Space Society (CSS) / Société spatiale canadienne
Bldg. E, PO Box 70009, Stn. Rimrock Plaza, 1115 Lodestar Rd., Toronto ON M3J 0H3
www.css.ca
ca.linkedin.com/company/canadian-space-society
www.facebook.com/CanadianSpaceSociety
twitter.com/cdnspacesociety
Overview: A small national organization founded in 1983
Mission: To conduct technical & outreach projects; To promote the involvement of Canadians in human exploration and space development
Membership: *Fees:* $75 regular; $40 students; *Member Profile:* Professionals & individuals interested in the exploration of the solar system
Activities: Increasing knowledge of space & space-related technologies among members & the public; Providing feedback to the government on legislation that impacts Canadian space development
Chief Officer(s):
Kevin Shortt, President
president@css.ca
Marc Fricker, Vice-President
vp@css.ca
Gary McQueen, Treasurer
treasurer@css.ca
Publications:
• Canadian Space Gazette
Frequency: Quarterly; *Accepts Advertising*
Profile: Current affairs in space development & exploration of interest to the Canadian space community

Canadian Special Crops Association (CSCA)
#1215, 220 Portage Ave., Winnipeg MB R3C 0A5
Tel: 204-925-3780; *Fax:* 204-925-4454
www.specialcrops.mb.ca
Overview: A medium-sized national organization founded in 1987
Mission: To encourage sustainable growth in the pulse industry by facilitating relations with growers
Membership: 110+; *Fees:* Schedule available; *Member Profile:* Companies involved in the merchandising of Canadian pulse & special crops
Chief Officer(s):
Colin Topham, President

Canadian Special Olympics Inc. *See* Special Olympics Canada

Canadian Speckle Park Association (CSPA)
PO Box 773, Crossfield AB T0M 0S0
Tel: 403-946-4635; *Fax:* 403-946-4635
info@canadianspecklepark.ca
www.canadianspecklepark.ca
Overview: A small national organization founded in 1993
Mission: To register Speckle Park cattle; To issue certificates of registration & transfer ownership of Speckle Park cattle; To implement mandates for the improvement of the Speckle Park breed; To promote Speckle Park cattle
Member of: Canadian Beef Breeds Council
Affiliation(s): Canadian Livestock Records Corporation
Membership: 1-99; *Fees:* $25 / year active membership; $10 junior membership; $100 associate membership; *Member Profile:* Breeders of Speckle Park cattle in Canada
Activities: Developing markets for Speckle Park cattle
Chief Officer(s):
Rod Remin, Business Manager, 403-946-4635, Fax: 403-946-4635
Debbie Spencer, President, 306-957-2010, Fax: 306-957-2019
redneckfarrier@sasktel.net

Canadian Sphagnum Peat Moss Association (CSPMA) / Association canadienne Tourbe de Sphaigne
#2208, 13 Mission Ave., St Albert AB T8N 1H6
Tel: 780-460-8280; *Fax:* 780-459-0939
cspma@peatmoss.com
www.peatmoss.com
www.facebook.com/peatmoss.canada
Also Known As: Peat and Peatlands
Overview: A medium-sized national organization founded in 1988
Mission: To promote the benefits of peat moss to horticulturists & home gardeners throughout North America
Member of: Canadian Society of Association Executives
Finances: *Annual Operating Budget:* $250,000-$500,000; *Funding Sources:* Membership dues
Staff Member(s): 2
Membership: 34 producers; *Member Profile:* Producers & brokers of Canadian peat moss; Suppliers to the industry
Chief Officer(s):
Paul Short, President

Canadian Spice Association (CSA) / Association canadienne des épices
PO Box 88059, 7235 Bellshire Gate, Mississauga ON L5N 8A0
contact@canadianspiceassociation.com
www.canadianspiceassociation.com
Overview: A medium-sized national organization founded in 1942
Mission: To foster & promote fellowship & goodwill among members; to advance the welfare of the Spice Trade & its commonly associated lines in Canada
Member of: American Spice Trade Association; Saskatchewan Herb & Seed Association
Affiliation(s): American Spice Trade Association; The Saskatchewan Herb and Spice Association; European Spice Association
Finances: *Funding Sources:* Membership dues
Membership: 36 corporate; *Member Profile:* Organizations involved in the spice industry
Chief Officer(s):
Tiina Henkusens, President

Canadian Spinal Research Organization (CSRO)
#2, 120 Newkirk Rd., Richmond Hill ON L4C 9S7
Tel: 905-508-4000; *Fax:* 905-508-4002
Toll-Free: 800-361-4004
www.csro.com
www.facebook.com/196341387063476
www.youtube.com/user/CSROVideos
Overview: A medium-sized national organization founded in 1984
Mission: To improve the physical quality of life for people with spinal injuries; to reduce the incidence of spinal cord injuries through awareness programs for the public & prevention programs with targeted groups
Member of: Charities First
Finances: *Funding Sources:* Corporate; individual; donations
Staff Member(s): 4
Membership: *Member Profile:* Anyone who is interested in supporting the search for a cure for spinal injuries & who submits the membership fee
Activities: Research work; prevention; awareness projects; *Internships:* Yes; *Speaker Service:* Yes
Chief Officer(s):
Kent Bassett-Spiers, Executive Director
Barry Munro, President
Publications:
• CSRO [Canadian Spinal Research Organization] Quarterly
Type: Magazine; *Frequency:* Quarterly

Canadian Sport Horse Association (CSHA)
PO Box 970, 7904 Franktown Rd., Richmond ON K0A 2Z0
Tel: 613-686-6161; *Fax:* 613-686-6170
csha@canadian-sport-horse.org
www.c-s-h-a.org
www.facebook.com/138540009572125
twitter.com/cdnsporthorse
Overview: A small national organization founded in 1933
Mission: To ensure the production & promotion of a sound, solid horse, with a good disposition, capable of competing successfully in the Olympic Disciplines at all levels of

Canadian Associations / Canadian Sport Massage Therapists Association (CSMTA) / Association canadienne des massothérapeutes du sport

competition.
Member of: World Breeding Federation
Staff Member(s): 1; 15 volunteer(s)
Membership: 718; *Fees:* $35 associate/youth; $85 individual; $850 life
Activities: Sport horse inspections; shows
Chief Officer(s):
Soo Olafsen, President
hefka13@gmail.com
Joanna Fast, Vice-President
wrenwoodfarm@gmail.com
Publications:
• Canadian Sport Horse Association Newsletter
Type: Newsletter; *Frequency:* Monthly
Profile: News & updates for members
• Canadian Sport Horse Association Stallion Directory
Type: Director
Profile: List of active stallions for each year, including age, breed & owner contact information

Canadian Sport Massage Therapists Association (CSMTA) / Association canadienne des massothérapeutes du sport
#236, 229 St. Clair St., Chatham ON N7L 3J4
Tel: 519-800-7134
natoffice@csmta.ca
www.csmta.ca
Overview: A medium-sized national licensing organization founded in 1987
Mission: To provide leadership in the field of sport massage therapy & education in Canada through the establishment of professional standards & qualifications of its members, as a certifying body
Affiliation(s): Canadian Olympic Committee; Expert Provider Group
Finances: *Annual Operating Budget:* Less than $50,000; *Funding Sources:* Membership fee; workshop
Staff Member(s): 1; 5 volunteer(s)
Membership: 70; *Member Profile:* 2,200-hr massage school or member of provincial association affiliated with CSMTA; *Committees:* Bylaws; Education; Certification & Examinations; Public Relations; Selections
Activities: Providing the National Sport Massage Certification Program (NSMCP); Promoting a professional climate for the growth of sport massage therapy in Canada
Chief Officer(s):
Jessica Sears, President
Monty Churchman, Vice-President
Mike Grafstein, Secretary
Jeanette Dobmeier, Treasurer
Brenda Caley, National Office Coordinator
Awards:
• Award of Excellence
Meetings/Conferences:
• Canadian Sport Massage Therapists Association 2018 Conference & AGM, 2018
Scope: National

Canadian Sport Parachuting Association (CSPA) / Association canadienne du parachutisme sportif (ACPS)
#204, 1468 Laurier St., Rockland ON K4K 1C7
Tel: 613-419-0908; *Fax:* 613-916-6008
office@cspa.ca
www.cspa.ca
Overview: A medium-sized national charitable organization founded in 1956
Member of: Aero Club of Canada
Membership: 2,000 + 48 member groups; *Committees:* Coaching Working; Technical Safety; Competition & National Teams; Web / Information Technology
Activities: *Library:* Not open to public
Chief Officer(s):
Michelle Matte-Stotyn, Executive Director, 613-419-0908 Ext. 2
michelle.matte-stotyn@cspa.ca
Publications:
• Canadian Sport Parachuting Association Technical Bulletins
Type: Guide

Canadian Sport Tourism Alliance (CSTA)
#600, 116 Lisgar St., Ottawa ON K2P 0C2
Tel: 613-688-5843; *Fax:* 613-238-3878
info@canadiansporttourism.com
www.canadiansporttourism.com
Overview: A small national organization founded in 2000
Mission: To market Canada internationally as a preferred sport tourism destination
Staff Member(s): 6
Membership: 200; *Committees:* Membership; Marketing & Communications; Research; Training & Education; Government Relations
Chief Officer(s):
Greg Stremlaw, Chair
gstremlaw@curling.ca
Rick Traer, CEO
rtraer@canadiansporttourism.com

Canadian Sporting Goods Association (CSGA) / Association canadienne d'articles de sport (ACAS)
#1272, 10 - 225 The East Mall, Toronto ON M9B 0A9
Toll-Free: 844-350-9902
info@csga.ca
www.csga.ca
www.linkedin.com/company/canadian-sporting-goods-association
www.facebook.com/211952635634448
twitter.com/CSGAhub
www.instagram.com/csgahub
Overview: A large national organization founded in 1945
Mission: To conduct quality trade shows; To provide forum responsive to the professional needs of its members; To initiate programs designed to stimulate sports activity participation as considered feasible
Affiliation(s): World Federation of the Sporting Goods Industry
Finances: *Funding Sources:* Membership dues; Trade shows
Membership: 2,000+ organizations; *Fees:* $500 supplier; $200 service provider/multi-line agency/sports association; $250 retailer; *Member Profile:* Bona fide members of the sporting goods industry
Chief Officer(s):
Kelly Falls, Coordinator, Membership & Advertising: North America, 905-842-2626
kelly@csga.ca

Canadian Square & Round Dance Society (CSRDS)
c/o Lorraine Kozera, 24 Aspen Villa Dr., Oak Bank MB R0E 1J2
Toll-Free: 866-206-6696
info@squaredance.ca
www.csrds.ca
Overview: A medium-sized national organization
Mission: To link information about Canadian square & round dancing associations together in order to promote awareness, inspire activity, & to offer information
Chief Officer(s):
Eric McCormack, President
ericmcc@gmail.com
Lorraine Kozera, Secretary
lkozera@mymts.net
John Kozera, Director, Manitoba

Canadian Squash Racquets Association *See* Squash Canada

The Canadian Stage Company
26 Berkeley St., Toronto ON M5A 2W3
Tel: 416-367-8243; *Fax:* 416-367-1768
www.canadianstage.com
www.facebook.com/cdnstage
twitter.com/canadianstage
www.youtube.com/user/canadianstage
Also Known As: CanStage
Overview: A medium-sized national charitable organization
Mission: To develop, produce & export the best in Canadian & international contemporary theatre
Member of: Professional Association of Canadian Theatres; Toronto Theatre Alliance
Staff Member(s): 48
Activities: Producing over 300 performances in four venues each year
Chief Officer(s):
Matthew Jocelyn, Artistic & General Director

Canadian Stamp Dealers' Association (CSDA) / Association canadienne des négociants en timbres-poste (ACNTP)
PO Box 81, Stn. Lambeth, London ON N6P 1P9
director@csdaonline.com
www.csdaonline.com
www.facebook.com/214870458990
Overview: A small national organization founded in 1942
Membership: *Member Profile:* Established full or part-time stamp dealers; Dealers from outside Canada must be a member of their country's trade association
Activities: Partnering with other major philatelic organizations
Chief Officer(s):
John Sheffield, Executive Director
director@csdaonline.com
Rick Day, President
medallionstamps@cogeco.ca
Ian Kimmerly, Vice-President
ian@iankimmerly.com
Publications:
• Beaver Tales [a publication of the Canadian Stamp Dealers' Association]
Type: Newsletter; *Price:* Free with CSDA membership
Profile: Industry news with current information
• Canadian Stamp Dealers' Association Membership Directory
Type: Directory; *Frequency:* Annually; *Price:* Free for collectors throughout the world

Canadian Standards Association (CSA)
178 Rexdale Blvd., Toronto ON M9W 1R3
Tel: 416-747-4000; *Fax:* 416-747-2473
Toll-Free: 800-463-6727
member@csagroup.org
www.csagroup.org
www.linkedin.com/company/459949
www.facebook.com/CSA-Group-113511338721494
twitter.com/CSA_Group
www.youtube.com/user/csastandards
Also Known As: CSA Group
Overview: A medium-sized national organization
Mission: To develop new standards & codes to meet needs, such as public health & safety & the facilitation of trade; To contribute to the global harmonization of standards; To serve government, industry, business, & consumers in Canada & the worldwide marketplace
Member of: CSA Group
Finances: *Funding Sources:* Sponsorships
Membership: 7,800
Activities: Presenting e-learning, seminars, & training opportunities, through the CSA Learning Centre, to assist people to understand standards; Reviewing & considering adopted & adapted standards from other organizations & countries
Chief Officer(s):
David Weinstein, President & CEO
Robert J. Falconi, VP, Gen. Counsel & Corp. Secretary
Esteban De Bernardis, Executive Vice-President
Vikki Dunn, Executive Vice-President, Strategic Marketing & Communications
Meetings/Conferences:
• Canadian Standards Association 2018 Annual Conference & Committee Week, June, 2018, Shaw Conference Centre, Edmonton, AB
Scope: National
Attendance: 700+
Description: Educational presentations & committee meetings
Publications:
• Canadian Standards Association Annual Report
Type: Yearbook; *Frequency:* Annually
Profile: A review of the association's activities for the past year
• Perspectives [a publication of the Canadian Standards Association]
Type: Newsletter; *Editor:* James Harrison
Profile: Current information about standards development initiatives for members

Eastern Region
865, rue Ellingham, Pointe-Claire QC H9R 5E8
Tel: 514-694-8110; *Fax:* 514-694-5001
Pacific Region
13799 Commerce Pkwy., Richmond BC V6V 2N9
Tel: 604-273-4581; *Fax:* 604-244-6600
Western Region
1707 - 94 St. NW, Edmonton AB T6N 1E6
Tel: 780-450-2111; *Fax:* 780-461-5322

Canadian Steel Construction Council (CSCC) / Conseil canadien de la construction en acier
#200, 3760 - 14th Ave., Markham ON L3R 3T7
Previous Name: Canadian Steel Industries Construction Council
Overview: A medium-sized national organization founded in 1960
Mission: To represent the manufacturers of steel products, including: open-web steel joists, steel platework, corrugated steel pipe, sheet steel, & steel fasteners; to promote the use of steel in construction through research & engineering

Affiliation(s): Canadian Institute of Steel Construction; Steel Structures Education Foundation
Membership: 1-99

Canadian Steel Door & Frame Manufacturers Association
See Canadian Steel Door Manufacturers Association

Canadian Steel Door Manufacturers Association (CSDMA)
#1801, 1 Yonge St., Toronto ON M5E 1W7
Tel: 416-363-7845; *Fax:* 416-369-0515
info@csdma.ca
www.csdma.org
Previous Name: Canadian Steel Door & Frame Manufacturers Association
Overview: A medium-sized national organization
Mission: To deliver standards and specifications regarding the manufacture and installation of steel doors, frames and related items, for the guidance of specifiers, end users, AEC professionals, and those interested in the construction trades at large.
Staff Member(s): 1
Membership: 13
Chief Officer(s):
Lois Marsh, Executive Director

Canadian Steel Industries Construction Council See Canadian Steel Construction Council

Canadian Steel Producers Association (CSPA) / Association canadienne des producteurs d'acier (ACPA)
#1220, 350 Albert St., Ottawa ON K1R 1A4
Tel: 613-238-6049; *Fax:* 613-238-1832
www.canadiansteel.ca
www.linkedin.com/company/breakwater-communications-and-government-affairs
www.facebook.com/220022834730294
twitter.com/CSPA_ACPA
Overview: A medium-sized national organization founded in 1986
Mission: To represent the steel producers that melt & pour steel in Canada
Finances: *Annual Operating Budget:* $500,000-$1.5 Million; *Funding Sources:* Membership dues
Staff Member(s): 4
Membership: 17; *Committees:* Communications; Environment; Climate Change; Statistics; Trade; Research & Development
Chief Officer(s):
Joseph Galimberti, President
j.galimberti@canadiansteel.ca

Canadian Steel Trade & Employment Congress
#800, 234 Eglinton Ave. East, Toronto ON M4P 1K7
Tel: 416-480-1797; *Fax:* 416-480-2986
general@cstec.ca
www.cstec.ca
www.linkedin.com/company/canadian-steel-trade-and-employment-congress
twitter.com/SteelSkills
www.vimeo.com/user8234365
Overview: A medium-sized national organization
Mission: To provide a forum for communication among steel companies, steelworkers, & governments to work for the betterment of the industry & its workforce
Staff Member(s): 5
Membership: *Committees:* Sector Study Steering
Chief Officer(s):
Ken Delaney, Executive Director
kdelaney@cstec.ca

Canadian Student Leadership Association (CSLA)
2460 Tanner Rd., Victoria BC V8Z 5R1
studentleadership.ca
www.facebook.com/CanadianStudentLeadershipAssociation
twitter.com/CSLA_Leaders
Overview: A small national charitable organization founded in 1983
Membership: *Fees:* $90
Activities: Distributes leadership resources, materials; scholarships; organizes programs and events for its member schools
Chief Officer(s):
Don Homan, Chair
dhoman@studentleadership.ca
Bill Conconi, Executive Director
bconconi@studentleadership.ca

Meetings/Conferences:
• Canadian Student Leadership Conference 2018, September, 2018, Edmonton, AB
Scope: National

Canadian Stuttering Association (CSA) / Association canadienne des bègues
PO Box 69001, Stn. St. Clair Centre, Toronto ON M4T 3A1
Tel: 416-840-5169
Toll-Free: 866-840-5169
csa-info@stutter.ca
www.stutter.ca
www.facebook.com/111972052148483
twitter.com/CSAStuttering
www.youtube.com/user/canstuttering
Previous Name: Canadian Association for People Who Stutter (CAPS)
Overview: A small national charitable organization founded in 1991
Mission: To support Canadians afflicted with the disorder of stuttering; To increase awareness of stuttering
Membership: *Member Profile:* Individuals who stutter; Families & friends of people who stutter; Professionals who work with people who stutter
Activities: Providing education & resources about stuttering; Offering self-help groups; Engaging in advocacy activities for people who stutter
Chief Officer(s):
Andrew Harding, National Coordinator
Meetings/Conferences:
• Canadian Stuttering Association 2018 Annual General Meeting, 2018
Scope: National
Publications:
• CSA [Canadian Stuttering Association] Newsletter
Type: Newsletter; *Frequency:* Quarterly
Profile: Developments in research & therapy, personal stories, news from CSA members, & CSA events

Canadian Sugar Institute (CSI) / Institut canadien du sucre
Water Park Pl., #620, 10 Bay St., Toronto ON M5J 2R8
Tel: 416-368-8091; *Fax:* 416-368-6426
info@sugar.ca
www.sugar.ca
Overview: A medium-sized national organization founded in 1966
Mission: To collect, analyze, & provide nutrition information on sugars, carbohydrates, & health
Member of: World Sugar Research Organization
Finances: *Annual Operating Budget:* $500,000-$1.5 Million; *Funding Sources:* Member companies
Staff Member(s): 5
Membership: 3 corporate; *Member Profile:* Sugar refining companies in Canada; *Committees:* Technical; Trade; Communications
Activities: *Library:* by appointment
Chief Officer(s):
Sandra Marsden, President
Flora Wang, Manager, Nutrition & Scientific Affairs
flora.wang@sugar.ca
Publications:
• Carbohydrate News
Type: Newsletter; *Frequency:* Annually
Profile: Recent scientific information on carbohydrate for health & education professionals
• Consumer Materials
Profile: Topics include practical information about sugar, such as understanding the Glycemic Index, & from plant to food, The CSI Recipe Collection, & testing your sugar IQ
• Nature's Sweet Mystery
Profile: Teaching resource for grades four to six with background information, activity sheets, & resource suggestions

Canadian Supply Chain Food Safety Coalition / Coalition canadienne de la filière alimentaire pour la salubrité des aliments
19 Elm St., Ottawa ON K1R 6M9
Tel: 613-233-7175
cscfsc@monachus.com
foodsafetycoalition.ca
Overview: A medium-sized national organization founded in 2000
Mission: To initiate a national standard for food safety
Membership: 37; *Fees:* $750 national organization/allied member; $300 provincial/local organization

Chief Officer(s):
Albert Chambers, Executive Director

Canadian Supply Chain Sector Council
136 Fredrick St., Bracebridge ON P1L 0A1
Tel: 705-645-4097
www.supplychaincanada.org
www.linkedin.com/groups/8153923
twitter.com/CSCSC_CCSCA
www.youtube.com/user/supplychaincanada
Overview: A small national organization
Mission: To work with supply chain partners to address & develop solutions to the sector's human resource challenges; To enhance the skills of individuals working in the supply chain; To create & strengthen connections with business & labour organizations, industry, governments, & the education community
Membership: *Member Profile:* Employees, academics, students, or career counsellors involved in a supply chain company or supply chain-related organization
Activities: Offering supply chain resources, products, & career information; Organizing projects; *Speaker Service:* Yes
Chief Officer(s):
Pat Campbell, Executive Director
pcampbell@supplychaincanada.org

Canadian Swine Breeders' Association (CSBA) / L'Association canadienne des éleveurs de porcs
#2, 408 Dundas St., Woodstock ON N4S 1B9
Tel: 519-421-2354; *Fax:* 519-421-0887
info@canswine.ca
www.canswine.ca
Previous Name: Purebred Swine Breeders' Association of Canada
Overview: A medium-sized national organization founded in 1889
Mission: To improve & promote Canadian purebred swine; to lobby on behalf of purebred swine breeders in Canada; to direct & regulate purebred swine industry; to be involved in registration & transfer of following breeds: Berkshire, British Saddleback, Chester White, Duroc, Hampshire, Large Black, Pietrain, Poland China, Spotted, Tamworth, Welsh, Yorkshire, Landrace, Lacombe, Red Wattle (registration forms can be obtained from Canadian Livestock Records Corporation).
Finances: *Annual Operating Budget:* $100,000-$250,000
Staff Member(s): 3
Membership: 120; *Fees:* Schedule available; *Member Profile:* Four classes: honorary, life, annual, non-resident; *Committees:* Promotion
Chief Officer(s):
Rosemary Smart, General Manager

Canadian Swine Council See Canadian Pork Council

Canadian Swine Exporters Association (CSEA)
#2, 408 Dundas St., Woodstock ON N4S 1B9
Tel: 519-421-0997; *Fax:* 519-421-0887
csea@rogers.com
www.canadianswine.com
Overview: A small national organization
Mission: To assist the Canadian swine industry promote & market swine genetics worldwide
Membership: 13; *Member Profile:* Represents the top exporters from Canada
Chief Officer(s):
Nancy F. Weicker, Executive Director

Canadian Swiss Cultural Association (CSCA)
Toronto ON
www.swissbiz.ca/csca.php
Overview: A small provincial organization founded in 1969
Mission: To promote & preserve Swiss-Canadian culture in Ontario
Membership: *Fees:* $30 individual; $50 family
Activities: Supporting & attending Swiss & Canadian art & cultural events
Chief Officer(s):
Sonja Evans-Good, President
gordonandsonja@rogers.com
Donna Lurz, Secretary
marklurz@sympatico.ca

Canadian Syringomyelia Network (CSN)
c/o The Forrestall Group, #4, 201 Whitehall Dr., Markham ON L3R 9Y3
Fax: 905-944-4844
www.csn.ca

Overview: A small national charitable organization founded in 1993
Mission: To provide information & support for persons with Syringomyelia & related conditions, plus their caregivers & families
Activities: Increasing public awareness of the effects of Syringomyelia; Organizing fundraising
Publications:
• The CSN News
Type: Newsletter; *Frequency:* Quarterly
Profile: Information & updates from the Canadian Syringomyelia Network

Canadian Table Soccer Association See Canadian Table Soccer Federation

Canadian Table Soccer Federation
Previous Name: Canadian Table Soccer Association
Overview: A small national organization
Mission: To oversee & monitor the growth of foosball in Canada.

Canadian Table Tennis Association See Table Tennis Canada

Canadian Tamil Congress
#513, 10 Milner Business Ct., Toronto ON M1B 3C6
Tel: 416-240-0078; *Fax:* 416-240-1601
info@canadiantamilcongress.ca
www.canadiantamilcongress.ca
Overview: A small national organization
Mission: To represent Tamil-Canadians; To promote the inclusion of Tamil-Canadians in local, regional, provincial, & national activities; To address issues affecting Tamil-Canadians; To work with Canadian & international organizations to provide aid to Tamils throughout the world; To promote the study & usage of Tamil language & culture; To advocate for equal rights for all diverse groups; To foster relationships with other ethnocultural groups in Canada
Activities: Organizing events & awareness campaigns;
Awareness Events: Tamil Fest
Chief Officer(s):
Vadivelu Santhakumar, President

Canadian Tamil Medical Association (CTMA)
#208, 31 Progress Ave., Toronto ON M1P 4S6
ctmacharity@gmail.com
www.ctmainfo.com
www.facebook.com/CTMACharity
Overview: A medium-sized national charitable organization founded in 1998
Mission: To support medical & dental projects & provide humanitarian assistance to communities impacted by natural disaster & civil disturbances in Sri Lanka
Activities: Funding health care projects in Toronto; Promoting health forums, community wellness programs, & health care education
Chief Officer(s):
Shan Shanmugavadivel, President

Canadian Tamil Professionals Association
#1140, 3280 Bloor St. West, Toronto ON M8X 2X3
info@tamilprofessional.ca
www.tamilprofessional.ca
www.linkedin.com/company/9369871
www.facebook.com/tamilprofessionals
twitter.com/CTPA_
www.instagram.com/ctpa_
Overview: A medium-sized national organization
Mission: To foster the advancement & development of Tamil professionals through the provision of tools, training, resources, & programs
Membership: *Fees:* $35
Activities: Offering the Paalam mentorship program; Organizing educational workshops & seminars, as well as networking events
Chief Officer(s):
Sagaana Mahendramohan, Chair

Canadian Tamil Youth Development Centre (CanTYD)
#40, 705 Progress Ave., Toronto ON M1H 2X1
Tel: 416-431-4100
info@cantyd.org
www.cantyd.org
twitter.com/cantyd
www.instagram.com/cantyd
Overview: A small local organization founded in 1998
Mission: To empower Tamil youth in Toronto through research, education, advocacy, & assistance; To provide young people with opportunities to develop professionally & personally; To promote a positive image of Tamil-Canadian youth
Activities: Developing educational programs for youth, parents, school boards, & community partners; Conducting research; Working with school boards & organizations to offer services to youth; Providing outreach services; Raising awareness on issues affecting Tamil youth
Chief Officer(s):
Vathanan Jegatheesan, Manager, Operations
Thamia Senthilnathan, Coordinator, Programs
Varoun Maharaj, Coordinator, Capacity Development
Awards:
• Academic Achievement, Awards of Excellence
• Athletic Achievement, Awards of Excellence
• Most Improved Student, Awards of Excellence
• Multimedia, Awards of Excellence
• Outstanding Community Contribution, Awards of Excellence
• Performing/Visual Arts, Awards of Excellence
• Young Entrepreneur, Awards of Excellence

Canadian Tamils' Chamber of Commerce
#209, 5200 Finch Ave. East, Toronto ON M1S 4Z4
Tel: 416-335-9791
info@ctcc.ca
www.ctcc.ca
www.facebook.com/CTCC25
twitter.com/CANTAMILChamber
www.instagram.com/cantamilchamber
Overview: A medium-sized national organization founded in 1991
Mission: To enhance entrepreneurship & socioeconomic development within the Tamil-Canadian community
Membership: *Fees:* $100 individual; $500 corporate
Activities: Organizing seminars, workshops, & conference to promote emerging entrepreneurs & businesses; Providing opportunities for members in the field of trade & commerce; Offering members a forum for networking
Chief Officer(s):
Dilani Gunarajah, President

Canadian Tarentaise Association (CTA)
c/p Rosalyn Harris, PO Box 1156, Shellbrook SK S0J 2E0
Toll-Free: 800-450-4181
canadiantarentaise@sasktel.net
www.canadiantarentaise.com
Overview: A small national organization founded in 1974
Mission: To develop, register & promote Tarentaise cattle in Canada.
Affiliation(s): American Tarentaise Association; SOPEXA - Cambery, France
Finances: *Funding Sources:* Membership & registration fees
Staff Member(s): 1
Membership: 7; *Fees:* $25 junior; $60 active; $100 associate lifetime; $200 active lifetime; *Committees:* Advertising & Promotion; Nominating; Breed Improvement & Memberships; Show & Sale; Advisory
Chief Officer(s):
Wayne Collette, President, 303-452-1820
keyholekg@aol.com
Rosalyn Harris, Secretary

Canadian Tax Foundation (CTF) / Foundation canadienne de fiscalité (FCF)
#1200, 595 Bay St., Toronto ON M5G 2N5
Tel: 416-599-0283; *Fax:* 416-599-9283
Toll-Free: 877-733-0283
www.ctf.ca
www.linkedin.com/groups?home=&gid=4000744
twitter.com/cdntaxfdn
Overview: A medium-sized national charitable organization founded in 1945
Mission: To create a greater understanding of the Canadian tax system; To improve the Canadian tax system
Membership: 11,000+; *Fees:* $29.75 student; $55 outside Canada; $115.50 retired; $175 academic & young practitioner; $350 individuals; *Member Profile:* Individuals & corporations from Canada & abroad
Activities: Providing tax information; Supporting members in their daily work in the taxation field; Conducting research projects; Contributing to tax & fiscal policy; *Library:* Douglas J. Sherbaniuk Research Centre
Chief Officer(s):
Penny Woolford, Chair
Gabrielle Richards, Vice-Chair
Debbie Selley, CGA, Treasurer
dselley@ctf.ca
Larry Chapman, FCPA, FCA, Executive Director & CEO
lchapman@ctf.ca
Judy Singh, Librarian
jisngh@ctf.ca
Awards:
• Douglas J. Sherbaniuk Distinguished Writing Award
• Student - Paper Award Competition
Meetings/Conferences:
• Canadian Tax Foundation 70th Annual Tax Conference, November, 2018, Vancouver, BC
Scope: National
Publications:
• Canadian Tax Foundation Conference Reports
Frequency: Annually; *Price:* Free with Canadian Tax Foundation membership
Profile: Proceedings & papers presented at conferences
• Canadian Tax Highlights / Faits saillants en fiscalité canadienne [a publication of the Canadian Tax Foundation]
Type: Newsletter; *Frequency:* Monthly; *Price:* Free with Canadian Tax Foundationmembership
Profile: Analyses of current topics & developments in the taxation field
• Canadian Tax Journal [a publication of the Canadian Tax Foundation]
Type: Journal; *Frequency:* Quarterly; *Accepts Advertising*;
Editor: Alan Macnaughton; Brian Carr; *Price:* Free with Canadian Tax Foundation membership
Profile: Scholarly articles on tax topics, analyses of changes in tax law, summaries of provincial budget figures, & reviews of taxliterature
• Tax for the Owner-Manager [a publication of the Canadian Tax Foundation]
Type: Newsletter; *Frequency:* Quarterly; *Price:* Free with Canadian Tax Foundation membership
Profile: Reports on tax developments, of interest to private corporations & their advisers
  Québec Office
  #2935, 1250, boul René-Lévesque ouest, Montréal QC H3B 4W8
  Tel: 514-939-6323; *Fax:* 514-939-7353
  Chief Officer(s):
  Jane Meagher, Director, Québec Office
  jmeagher@ctf.ca

Canadian Taxpayers Federation (CTF)
#265, 438 Victoria Ave. East, Regina SK S4N 0N7
Tel: 306-352-7199; *Fax:* 306-205-8339
Toll-Free: 800-667-7933
Other Communication: vimeo.com/taxpayerdotcom
admin@taxpayer.com
taxpayer.com
www.facebook.com/TaxpayerDOTcom
twitter.com/taxpayerdotcom
www.youtube.com/taxpayerdotcom
Previous Name: Association of Saskatchewan Taxpayers; Resolution One Association of Alberta
Overview: A large national organization founded in 1990
Mission: To advocate for the common interest of taxpayers; To effect public policy change
Finances: *Funding Sources:* Donations
Membership: 117,000 supporters; *Fees:* Free; *Member Profile:* Canadian citizens dedicated to lower taxes, less waste, & government accountability
Activities: Updating members about issues & actions; Conducting research; Issuing news releases & conducting media interviews; Making presentations to government; Organizing campaigns & petition drives; *Speaker Service:* Yes
Chief Officer(s):
Adam Daifallah, Chair
Troy Lanigan, President & CEO
tlanigan@shaw.ca
Melanie Harvie, Executive Vice-President
mharvie@taxpayer.com
Shannon Morrison, Vice-President, Operations
smorrison@taxpayer.com
Aaron Gunn, Director, Special Projects
agunn@taxpayer.com
Awards:
• The Federal Teddy, The Ted Weatherill Awards (The Teddies)
• The Provincial/Municipal Teddy, The Ted Weatherill Awards (The Teddies)
• The Lifetime Achievement Teddy, The Ted Weatherill Awards (The Teddies)

- TaxFighter of the Year
Publications:
- Let's Talk Taxes [a publication of the Canadian Taxpayers Federation]
Frequency: Weekly
Profile: Commentaries for media outlets across Canada
- Municipal Ratepayers Guide [a publication of the Canadian Taxpayers Federation]
- TaxFacts [a publication of the Canadian Taxpayers Federation]
Profile: Issues of taxation & government spending at the provincial & federal levels
- The Taxpayer [a publication of the Canadian Taxpayers Federation]
Type: Magazine; *Frequency:* Quarterly; *Accepts Advertising*; *Price:* Available to financial supporters
Profile: Canadian Taxpayers Federation national happenings, campaign updates, articles by CTF researchers, & guest commentaries

Alberta
#406, 1500 - 14th St. SW, Calgary AB T3C 1C9
Tel: 403-475-6207
www.taxpayer.com
twitter.com/paigemacp
Chief Officer(s):
Paige MacPherson, Director, Alberta
pmacpherson@taxpayer.com

Atlantic Canada
PO Box 34077, Stn. Scotia Square, 5201 Duke St., Halifax NS B3J 1N0
Tel: 902-407-5757
Toll-Free: 877-909-5757
atlantic.director@taxpayer.com
www.taxpayer.com
Chief Officer(s):
Kevin Lacey, Director

British Columbia
PO Box 20539, Stn. Howe St., Vancouver BC V6Z 2N8
Tel: 604-999-3319
www.taxpayer.com
twitter.com/jordanbateman
Chief Officer(s):
Jordan Bateman, Director, British Columbia
jbateman@taxpayer.com

Ontario
PO Box 38, 260 Adelaide St. East, Toronto ON M5A 1N1
Tel: 647-343-4150
on.director@taxpayer.com
www.taxpayer.com
twitter.com/cvangeyn
Chief Officer(s):
Christine Van Geyn, Director, Ontario

Prairies (Saskatchewan & Manitoba)
#265, 438 Victoria Ave. East, Regina SK S4N 0N7
Toll-Free: 800-667-7933
prairie@taxpayer.com
www.taxpayer.com
twitter.com/toddamackay
Chief Officer(s):
Todd MacKay, Director, Prairies, 306-582-7717

Canadian Teachers' Federation (CTF) / Fédération canadienne des enseignantes et des enseignants (FCE)
2490 Don Reid Dr., Ottawa ON K1H 1E1
Tel: 613-232-1505; *Fax:* 613-232-1886
Toll-Free: 866-283-1505
info@ctf-fce.ca
www.ctf-fce.ca
www.facebook.com/CTF.FCE
twitter.com/CanTeachersFed
www.youtube.com/user/canadianteachers
Overview: A large national organization founded in 1920
Mission: To promotes a strong publicly funded education system for Canada, one that enhances the country's competitiveness in a knowledge based global economy & gives children the opportunity to become active, engaged citizens
Member of: Education International
Finances: *Annual Operating Budget:* $3 Million-$5 Million
Staff Member(s): 45
Membership: 16 provincial & territorial teacher organizations representing 240,000+ teachers; *Fees:* $21.80 per teacher/per year; *Committees:* Aboriginal Education; Diversity and Human Rights; French as a First Language; Status of Women; Nominations; Resolutions; Constitution and By-laws; Finance; Retirement
Activities: *Awareness Events:* National Media Education Week
Library: George A. Croskery Memorial Library
Chief Officer(s):
Heather Smith, President
Cassandra Hallett DaSilva, Secretary General
Awards:
- CTF Special Recognition Awards
- CTF Public Education Advocacy Award
- CTF Outstanding Aboriginal Educator Award
Meetings/Conferences:
- Canadian Teachers' Federation 2018 Annual General Meeting, 2018
Scope: National
Description: Approval of a budget for the upcoming year, a discussion & determination of policy priorities, & an election of directors
Publications:
- CTF [Canadian Teachers' Federation] Annual Report
Type: Yearbook; *Frequency:* Annually
Profile: The work of the federation as directed by policy & priorities under the leadership of the Board of Directors
- The CTF [Canadian Teachers' Federation] Handbook
Type: Handbook
Profile: A compilation of the constitution, by-laws, policy, & regulations
- Perspectives [a publication of the Canadian Teachers' Federation]
Type: Newsletter; *Price:* Free
Profile: A forum for diverse perspectives on current education issues
- Sexual & Gender Minorities in Canadian Education & Society 1969-2013 [a publication of the Canadian Teachers' Federation]
Type: Guide; *Price:* $39
Profile: A handbook for K-12 educators containing ideas, resources & practices regarding sexual & genderminorities in education

Canadian Team Handball Federation (CTHF) / Fédération canadienne de handball olympique (FCHO)
453, rue Jacob-Nicol, Sherbrooke QC J1J 4E5
Tel: 819-563-7937; *Fax:* 819-563-5352
handballcanada.ca
Overview: A medium-sized national charitable organization founded in 1966
Affiliation(s): International Handball Federation; Pan American Team Handball Federation; Commonwealth Handball Federation
Finances: *Annual Operating Budget:* $500,000-$1.5 Million; *Funding Sources:* Sport Canada; COO; CAC
Staff Member(s): 1; 1 volunteer(s)
Membership: 15,000; *Fees:* $5; *Committees:* Management; Officials; Coaches; National Teams
Activities: Canadian Championship; Canada Cup; Pan-American Championships & Games; *Speaker Service:* Yes
Chief Officer(s):
Raquel Marinho, President
raquelpedercini@hotmail.com
François LeBeau, Chief Operating Officer
f.leleau@videotron.ca

Canadian Technical Asphalt Association (CTAA) / Association technique canadienne du bitume
#300, 895 Fort St., Victoria BC V8W 1H7
Tel: 250-361-9187; *Fax:* 250-361-9187
admin@ctaa.ca
www.ctaa.ca
www.linkedin.com/groups/3266673/profile
www.facebook.com/254383501294589
Overview: A medium-sized national organization founded in 1955
Mission: To organize efforts of membership on a non-profit, public service basis; To assemble, correlate & disseminate technical information on characteristics & uses of bituminous materials; To encourage research on uses of asphaltic materials; To encourage colleges to teach students to study asphalt technology
Finances: *Funding Sources:* Membership fees
Staff Member(s): 3
Membership: 700; *Fees:* $185; $400 sustaining; $0 student; *Member Profile:* Consultants; Contractors; Academia; Government
Activities: Organizing annual conference
Chief Officer(s):
Chuck McMillan, Secretary-Treasurer
Awards:
- Elaine Thompson Award, CTAA Annual Awards
Awarded to an author to recognize excellence in the written presentation of a submitted paper
- Norman W. McLeod Award, CTAA Annual Awards
Awarded to a presenter for their excellence in oral presentation
- Earl Kee Award, CTAA Annual Awards
Awarded to honour the best paper presented by a new author making their first oral presentation at the annual CTAA Conference
- Graduate Scholarship, CTAA Annual Scholarships
Presented to a student who has been admitted to or is enrolled in a Canadian university program leading to a post-graduate degree relating to asphalt technology; possible fields of study include chemistry, chemical engineering, & construction or civil engineering; *Amount:* $2,000
- Undergraduate Scholarship, CTAA Annual Scholarships
Presented to a student who has been admitted to or is enrolled in a Canadian university program leading to an undergraduate degree relating to asphalt technology; fields of study include chemistry, chemical engineering, & construction or civil engineering; *Amount:* $2,000
- Applied Technology Scholarship, CTAA Annual Scholarships
Presented to a student who has been admitted to or is enrolled in a Canadian college program leading to a diploma relating to asphalt technology; fields of study include chemistry, chemical engineering, & construction or civil engineering; *Amount:* $2,000
Meetings/Conferences:
- Canadian Technical Asphalt Association 63rd Annual Conference 2018, 2018
Scope: National
Publications:
- CTAA Newsletter
Type: Newsletter
Profile: CTAA conferences, scholarships, financial information, awards, & membership information

Canadian Technion Society *See* Technion Canada

Canadian Technology Human Resources Board (CTHRB) / Bureau canadien des ressources humaines en technologie
#2, 285 McLeod St., Ottawa ON K2P 1A1
Tel: 613-233-1955
info@cthrb.ca
www.cthrb.ca
Overview: A small national organization founded in 1995
Mission: To promote the use & continuous revision of national technician & technologist standards across Canada; to lead Canadian industrial & occupational technology organizations in identifying & resolving human resource issues that are challenging the industry
Finances: *Annual Operating Budget:* $250,000-$500,000
Staff Member(s): 5; 15 volunteer(s)
Activities: *Internships:* Yes; *Speaker Service:* Yes; *Library:* Resource Centre; by appointment
Chief Officer(s):
Barry Gander, Director, Communications
Publications:
- TechNews
Type: Newsletter; *Frequency:* Monthly
Profile: Activities affecting human resources & technology

Canadian Telecommunication Carriers Association *See* Frequency Co-ordination System Association

Canadian Television Series Development Foundation *See* Independent Production Fund

Canadian Tennis Association *See* Tennis Canada

Canadian Tenpin Federation, Inc. (CTF) / Fédération canadienne des dix-quilles, inc.
152 Cowichan Ct. West, Lethbridge AB T1K 7T7
Toll-Free: 833-381-2830
ctf@gotenpinbowling.ca
www.gotenpinbowling.ca
www.facebook.com/CanadianTenpinFederationInc
Overview: A large national organization founded in 1964
Mission: To promote & foster the sport of tenpin bowling in Canada by maintaining active membership in the world's appropriate affiliated tenpin organizations, providing competitive opportunities for all skill levels, culminating in the selection of a National Team; To encourage the development of skills through a national coaching certification program
Affiliation(s): Fédération internationale des quilleurs
20 volunteer(s)
Membership: 80,000 + 74 clubs; *Committees:* Awards; Coaching Development; Governance; High Performance Unit;

Membership/Association Services; Regulatory; Special Achievement Awards; Youth
Activities: *Awareness Events:* National Team Trials, every even year, May long weekend
Chief Officer(s):
Brian McMaster, President
brianmcmaster@gotenpinbowling.ca
Cathy Innes, Executive Director
cathyinnes@gotenpinbowling.ca
Awards:
• Honour Score Award
• Special Achievement Awards
• Purchasable Awards
Youth & tournament awards may be purchased from the Federation
• Sport Bowling Awards
Meetings/Conferences:
• Canadian Tenpin Federation 2018 AGM, 2018
Scope: National
Publications:
• CTF Connection
Type: Newsletter; *Frequency:* 5 pa; *Editor:* Curtis Kruschel; Dan Tereck
Profile: CTF events, tournaments, member news, & provincial news

Canadian Test Centre Inc. (CTC) / Services d'évaluation pédagogique
#10, 80 Citizen Ct., Markham ON L6G 1A7
Tel: 905-513-6636; *Fax:* 905-513-6639
Toll-Free: 800-668-1006
info@canadiantestcentre.com
www.canadiantestcentre.com
www.youtube.com/user/CanadianTestCentre
Overview: A medium-sized national organization founded in 1980
Mission: To publish & distribute test products; to support teachers to make their testing programs work; to invest in research & development projects which aim to improve the measurement & evaluation of student ability & achievement.
Finances: *Annual Operating Budget:* $500,000-$1.5 Million
Staff Member(s): 14
Chief Officer(s):
Ernest W. Cheng, Managing Director
ernest.cheng@canadiantestcentre.com

Canadian Textile Association (CTA) / La Fédération canadienne du textile
13 Interlacken Dr., Brampton ON L6X 0Y1
Tel: 647-821-4649
www.cdntexassoc.com
Previous Name: Textile Federation of Canada
Merged from: Canadian Association of Textile Chemists & Colourists; Textile Society of Canada
Overview: A medium-sized national charitable organization founded in 2003
Mission: To advance & disseminate knowledge of textiles; to promote sound procedures of textile processing; to encourage & sponsor textile research & investigation; to assist in the establishment of standards in the textile industry; to promote & encourage schools, classes & libraries for the study of textile technology; to collaborate with international groups in advancing the foregoing objectives
Finances: *Funding Sources:* Social activities
Membership: *Fees:* $50-$800; *Member Profile:* Textile graduates; textile related workers, industry
Activities: The promotion of the textile industry & textile education
Chief Officer(s):
John Secondi, President

Canadian Theatre Critics Association (CTCA) / Association des critiques de théâtre du Canada
c/o Anton Wagner, #2306, 201 Sherbourne St., Toronto ON M5A 3X2
www.canadiantheatrecritics.ca
Overview: A small national organization founded in 1979
Mission: To promote excellence in theatre criticism; to encourage the dissemination of information on theatre on a national level; to encourage the awareness & development of Canadian theatre nationally & internationally through theatre criticism in all the media; to promote & encourage excellence in Canadian theatre through national awards; to improve the status & working conditions of theatre critics
Member of: International Association of Theatre Critics

Affiliation(s): Capital Critics Association; Association québécoise des critiques de théâtre
Membership: 30; *Fees:* $45 regular; $25 associate; $10 student; *Member Profile:* Full - minimum three years professional theatre reviewing, feature writing or broadcasting within the entertainment field; associate - minimum one year of professional regular theatre reviewing, feature writing or broadcasting within the entertainment field
Chief Officer(s):
Martin Morrow, President
martinmorrow1@gmail.com
Anton Wagner, Coordinator, Awards & Membership
awagner@yorku.ca
Awards:
• The Herbert Whittaker Award for Outstanding Contribution to Canadian Theatre
Presented every other year to Canadian citizen or permanent resident working in any theatrical discipline who has demonstrated distinguished contribution in playwriting, performance, direction or design; named after Herbert Whittaker Founding Chairman of the Canadian Theatre Critics Assoc.
• Nathan Cohen Award for Excellence in Critical Writing
Publications:
• Critically Speaking [a publication of the Canadian Theatre Critics Association]
Type: Newsletter; *Editor:* Stephen Hunt
Profile: Provides coverage on issues related to theatre criticism, interviews with critics & reviews fromvarious national & international productions

Canadian Theological Society (CTS) / Société théologique canadienne
c/o M. Beavis, St. Thomas More College, 1437 College Dr., Saskatoon SK S7N 0W6
secretary@cts-stc.ca
cts-stc.ca
www.facebook.com/canadiantheologicalsociety
Overview: A small national organization founded in 1955
Mission: To promote theological reflection & writing in Canada
Member of: Canadian Corporation for the Study of Religion (CCSR)
Affiliation(s): Canadian Congress of the Humanities & Social Sciences
Membership: *Fees:* $70-$100 regular; $22-$45 student, part-time professor & unwaged; $25-$50 retired; *Member Profile:* Theologians, clergy, scholars & students from universities, seminaries & churches
Activities: *Awareness Events:* Annual Student Essay Contest
Chief Officer(s):
Jeremy Bergen, President
jbergen@uwaterloo.ca
Timothy Harvie, Vice President
timothy.harvie@stmu.ca
Nick Olkovich, Secretary
nick.olkovich@mail.utoronto.ca

Canadian Theosophical Association
89, promenade Riverside, Saint-Lambert QC J4R 1A3
Toll-Free: 866-277-0074
www.theosophical.ca
Previous Name: Canadian Federation of the Theosophical Society
Overview: A small national organization founded in 1924
Mission: To form a nucleus of the universal Brotherhood of Humanity without distinction of race, creed, sex, caste or colour; to encourage the study of comparative religion, philosophy & science; to investigate the unexplained laws of nature & the powers latent in man
Finances: *Annual Operating Budget:* Less than $50,000
Membership: 150 institutional; *Fees:* $25
Chief Officer(s):
Medardo Martinez Cruz, President

Canadian Therapeutic Riding Association / Association canadienne d'équitation thérapeutique
5420 Hwy. 6 North, RR#5, Guelph ON N1H 6J2
Tel: 519-767-0700; *Fax:* 519-767-0435
ctra@golden.net
www.cantra.ca
twitter.com/CanTRA_ACET
Also Known As: CanTRA
Overview: A large national charitable organization founded in 1980
Mission: To foster therapeutic riding for persons with disabilities by establishing riding standards in collaboration with the medical profession; To accredit programs, certify instructors & promote

research; To promote equestian sport & competition for persons with disabilities
Member of: Riding for Disabled International; Canadian Paralympic Committee; Canadian Equestrian Federation
Finances: *Funding Sources:* Donations; Membership fees; Fund-raising
5.00 volunteer(s)
Membership: 80+ member centres & 4,000 riders; *Fees:* $40 voting; $20 supporting
Activities: Offering the Certification Program for Therapeutic Riding Instructors (CTRI); *Speaker Service:* Yes
Chief Officer(s):
Eliane Trempe, President
Awards:
• Rhonda Davies Award for Outstanding Volunteer
• Andrea Gillies Award for Outstanding CanTRA Instructor
• Jetty Chapman Award for Outstanding Administrator
• CanTRA Therapy Horse
Publications:
• CanTRA [Canadian Therapeutic Riding Association] Caller / L'Appel ACET
Type: Newsletter; *Frequency:* q.; *Price:* free with membership
Profile: CanTRA conferences, articles, events, bylaws changes, & clinics
• Communiqué [a publication of the Canadian Therapeutic Riding Association]
Type: Newsletter; *Price:* free with membership
Profile: Information for CanTRA members, published between CanTRA Caller newsletters

Canadian Thoracic Society (CTS) / Société canadienne de thoracologie (SCT)
c/o National Office, The Lung Association, #300, 1750 Courtwood Cres., Ottawa ON K2C 2B5
Tel: 613-569-6411; *Fax:* 613-569-8860
ctsinfo@lung.ca
cts.lung.ca
Overview: A medium-sized international charitable organization founded in 1958 overseen by Canadian Lung Association
Mission: To enhance the prevention & treatment of respiratory diseases
Affiliation(s): AllerGen; American College of Chest Physicians; American Thoracic Society; Canadian COPD Alliance; Canadian Respiratory Health Professionals; Canadian Society of Allergy & Clinical Immunology; European Respiratory Society; Guidelines International Network
Finances: *Funding Sources:* Donations; Sponsorships
Membership: *Member Profile:* Canadian & international physicians & scientists; *Committees:* Canadian Respiratory Guidelines; Education; Long-term Planning; Membership & Communications; Research
Activities: Developing & implementing clinical practice guidelines; Advising the Canadian Lung Association on medical matters & programs; Promoting lung health & the best respiratory practices; Providing educational & clinical practice resources; Organizing professional development opportunities, as an accredited continuing professional development (CPD) provider, under the Royal College of Physicians & Surgeons of Canada's Maintenance of Certification program; Engaging in advocacy activities; Funding research
Chief Officer(s):
Andrew Halayko, President
John Granton, Secretary
Catherine Lemière, Treasurer
Janet Sutherland, Executive Director
Publications:
• Canadian Thoracic Society Annual Report
Type: Yearbook; *Frequency:* Annually
• Canadian Thoracic Society E-Bulletin
Type: Newsletter
Profile: Updates for all members of the Society

Canadian Thoroughbred Horse Society (CTHS) / Société canadienne du cheval Thoroughbred
PO Box 172, Toronto ON M9W 5L1
Tel: 416-675-1370; *Fax:* 416-675-9525
info@cthsnational.com
www.cthsnational.com
www.facebook.com/CanadianThoroughbredHorseSocietyNationalDivision
Overview: A medium-sized national organization founded in 1906
Mission: To assist & afford a means for promotion of interests of those engaged in breeding of thoroughbreds; to protect members against unbusinesslike methods; to diffuse information among members & others; to secure uniformity in usage &

business conditions; to determine requirements of horses as thoroughbreds by the Society; to promote, encourage & assist in livestock & agricultural exhibitions, fairs & racing; to sponsor, assist & conduct sales of thoroughbred stock; to compile statistics of the industry; to maintain efficient supervision of breeders of thoroughbred horses; to prevent, detect & punish fraud (ie. in registration of throughbreds).
Finances: *Annual Operating Budget:* $100,000-$250,000; *Funding Sources:* Membership dues; registration fees
Staff Member(s): 2
Membership: 1,421; *Fees:* Schedule available; *Member Profile:* Annual - owners of thoroughbreds for purpose of breeding in current year in Canada, registered in Stud Book recognized by the Society; associate annual - to be approved by National Board; *Committees:* Pedigree; Membership; Registration; Publications/Communications; Internal Committees (Constitution, Regional Sales)
Activities: *Library:* Documentation Centre; Open to public
Chief Officer(s):
Grant Watson, President
Fran Okihiro, Manager
fokihiro@cthsnational.com

Alberta Division
#218, 1935 - 32nd Ave. NE, Calgary AB T2E 7C8
Tel: 403-229-3609; *Fax:* 403-224-6909
cthsalta@telusplanet.net
www.cthsalta.com
www.facebook.com/cths.alberta
twitter.com/CTHSALTA
Mission: To promote the purchase of Alberta Thoroughbreds, keep records, organize sales, disseminate information, compile statistics and assist our membership with registration.
Chief Officer(s):
Jean Kruse, Manager

British Columbia Division
#7, 5492 Production Blvd., Surrey BC V3S 8P5
Tel: 604-534-0145; *Fax:* 604-534-2847
cthsbc@cthsbc.org
www.cthsbc.org
Mission: To assist in the promotion & development of those engaged in the breeding of Thoroughbreds; To protect members from unbusinesslike methods & maintain uniform standards in business conditions; To determine the requirements for the registration of horses as Thoroughbreds; To sponsor, assist & conduct Thoroughbred sales
Chief Officer(s):
Bette-Jean (B-J) Davidson, General Manager

Manitoba Division
PO Box 46152, Stn. Westdale, Winnipeg MB R3R 3S3
Tel: 204-832-1702; *Fax:* 204-831-6735
cthsmb@mts.net
www.cthsmb.ca
Mission: To assist breeders of Thoroughbred horses in Manitoba by aiding them with provincial bonus and incentive programs, the operation of auctions, and providing other services to members.
Chief Officer(s):
Jill Withers, Regional Secretary

Ontario Division
PO Box 172, Toronto ON M9W 5L1
Tel: 416-675-3602; *Fax:* 416-675-9405
cthsont@idirect.com
www.cthsont.com
Mission: To aim to ensure a viable future for its members by providing assistance and representation within the thoroughbred breeding industry
Chief Officer(s):
R. Glenn Sikura, President

Québec Division
c/o CTHS National Office, CP 172, Toronto ON M9W 5L1
Tél: 416-675-1370; *Téléc:* 416-675-9525
Mission: To assist breeders of Thoroughbred horses in Quebec, by aiding them with provincial bonus and incentive programs, the operation of auctions, and providing other services to members.

Saskatchewan Division
PO Box 1137, Saskatoon SK S7K 3N2
Mission: To assist breeders of Thoroughbred horses in Saskatchewan by aiding them with provincial bonus and incentive programs, the operation of auctions, and providing other services to members.

Canadian Tibetan Association of Ontario (CTAO)
40 Titan Rd., Toronto ON M8Z 2J8
Tel: 416-410-5606; *Fax:* 416-410-5606
www.ctao.org
Overview: A small provincial organization founded in 1980
Mission: To represent Tibetans in Ontario; To serve the needs of the Tibetan community in the province; To promote cross-cultural understanding
Activities: Assisting newcomers to Canada; Promoting the rights of all individuals; Encouraging Tibetan Canadians to participate in Candian society; Providing regular cultural programs to help community members keep their traditions alive; Fostering tolerance, through education & awareness activities
Chief Officer(s):
Tsering Tsomo, President
Ngawang Diki, Coordinator, Cultural

Canadian Tinnitus Foundation
#404, 1688 - 152 St., Surrey BC V4A 4N2
Tel: 604-317-2952
info@findthecurenow.org
www.findthecurenow.org
www.facebook.com/CanadianTinnitusFoundation
Overview: A medium-sized national organization
Mission: A not-for-profit organization working to expand awareness & generate funding for tinnitus research
Finances: *Funding Sources:* Donations
Chief Officer(s):
Nathan Nowak, President
John Jabat, Vice-President
Brian Cassidy, Treasurer
Elizabeth Eayrs, Secretary

Canadian Tire Coupon Collectors Club (CTCCC) / Club de collectionneurs de coupons Canadian Tire
1120, Place Charron, Blainville QC J7C 2T2
Tel: 450-419-7914; *Fax:* 450-430-7233
adamsdoug@rogers.com
www.ctccc.ca
Overview: A small national organization founded in 1990
Mission: To research, study & catalogue all merchant scrip issued by the Canadian Tire Corporation; to promote the collecting & trading of such scrip in numismatic circles; to archive a collection of the scrip with a major Canadian University
Member of: Canadian Numismatic Association
Affiliation(s): Canadian Paper Money Society
Finances: *Annual Operating Budget:* Less than $50,000; *Funding Sources:* Membership fees; auction premiums
8 volunteer(s)
Membership: 450; *Fees:* $15; *Committees:* Audio-visual; Archive; Publishing
Activities: Displaying collections; *Library:* by appointment
Chief Officer(s):
Thayer Bouck, President
mgiammarco@sympatico.ca
Publications:
• Bilodeau Guide
Price: $23.99 volume 1; $34 volume 2; $57.99 both volumes
Profile: Guide to Canadian Tire "money" in two volumes
• The Collector: The Canadian Tire Coupon Collectors Club Newsletter
Type: Newsletter; *Accepts Advertising*; *Price:* Free with CTCCC regular membership
Profile: Advertisement of wants of collectors, or items for sale to other collectors, & articles of interest to members

Canadian Tire Dealers Association
#5, 171 Ambassador Dr., Mississauga ON L5T 2J1
Tel: 905-795-3329; *Fax:* 905-795-3330
ctdaoffice@ctdealers.com
newsite.ctdealers.com
Overview: A small national organization founded in 1968
Mission: To provide an organization to promote the welfare of Canadian Tire (CT) Associate Dealers
Staff Member(s): 14
Chief Officer(s):
Terry Connoy, Executive Director

Canadian Titanic Society (CTS)
73 Austin Cres., Simcoe ON N3Y 5K7
Tel: 519-426-2330
canadiantitanicsociety@yahoo.ca
www.canadian-titanic-society.com
Also Known As: Titanic Historical Society of Canada
Overview: A small national organization founded in 1998
Mission: To preserve the history of the Titanic tragedy
Finances: *Funding Sources:* Sponsors
Membership: *Member Profile:* National & international members
Chief Officer(s):
Norm Lewis, President & CEO

Canadian Tooling & Machining Association (CTMA)
#3, 140 McGovern Dr., Cambridge ON N3H 4R7
Tel: 519-653-7265; *Fax:* 519-653-6764
info@ctma.com
www.ctma.com
Overview: A medium-sized national organization founded in 1963
Mission: To be an effective, broad-based, respected organization, representing the Canadian tooling & machining industry, nationally & internationally
Member of: International Special Tooling & Machining Association (ISTMA)
Affiliation(s): Auto Parts; Canadian Foundry Association; Canadian Plastics Institute; GTMA England; PMPTB - Ohio, USA; SPI - Toronto; CAMM - Windsor
Finances: *Annual Operating Budget:* $100,000-$250,000; *Funding Sources:* Membership dues
Staff Member(s): 3; 12 volunteer(s)
Membership: 160 corporate + 15 associate + 6 senior/lifetime; *Fees:* Schedule available; *Member Profile:* Corporate only; *Committees:* AGM & Dinner; Communications; Executive; Finance/Budget; Golf Tournament; Government Relations; Skills Training & Education; Survey
Activities: Annual Apprenticeship Competition
Chief Officer(s):
Robert Cattle, Executive Director
rcattle@ctma.com
Julie McFarlane, Office Manager
Publications:
• CTMA Buyers Guide
• CTMA Membership List
• CTMA View
Type: Newsletter; *Frequency:* Quarterly; *Accepts Advertising*

Canadian Tour Guide Association of British Columbia
PO Box 18515, 710 Granville St., Vancouver BC V6Z 0B3
info@ctgaofbc.com
www.ctgaofbc.com
Previous Name: Canadian Tourist Guide Association of BC
Overview: A medium-sized provincial organization founded in 1989
Mission: To develop a professional standard of tour guiding for members; to encourage tourist guide certification; to be a voice for tourist guides; to provide a place to exchange information
Member of: World Federation of Tourist Guide Associations
Membership: *Fees:* $65 professional; $50 associate/alumni; $35 student/educator; *Member Profile:* Tour guides, directors & greeters
Chief Officer(s):
Cheryl Lou Ornburn, President
president@ctgaofbc.com

Canadian Tourist Guide Association of BC *See* Canadian Tour Guide Association of British Columbia

Canadian Tourism Human Resource Council (CTHRC) / Conseil canadien des ressources humaines en tourisme (CCHRT)
#608, 151 Slater St., Ottawa ON K1J 7W9
Tel: 613-231-6949; *Fax:* 613-231-6853
info@cthrc.ca
www.cthrc.ca
www.linkedin.com/company/canadian-tourism-human-resource-council
www.facebook.com/CTHRC
twitter.com/cthrc
www.youtube.com/user/TourismHRCouncil
Overview: A medium-sized national organization founded in 1993
Mission: An organization whose overall goal is to improve the quality of the Canadian labour force, and to assist businesses to be more flexible in meeting changing competitive demands.
Finances: *Annual Operating Budget:* $100,000-$250,000
Staff Member(s): 25
Membership: 86; *Member Profile:* Business; labour; education; national associations; prov./territorial associations; individuals
Chief Officer(s):
Wendy Swedlove, President

Canadian Tourism Research Institute
255 Smyth Rd., Ottawa ON K1H 8M7
Tel: 613-526-3280; *Fax:* 613-526-4857
Toll-Free: 866-711-2262

Canadian Associations / Canadian Toy Association / Canadian Toy & Hobby Fair (CTA) / L'Association canadienne du Jouet

ctri@conferenceboard.ca
www.conferenceboard.ca
Overview: A medium-sized national organization
Mission: To provide data & economic models for the travel & tourism industry in Canada
Chief Officer(s):
Gregory Hermus, Associate Director
hermus@conferenceboard.ca

Canadian Toy Association / Canadian Toy & Hobby Fair (CTA) / L'Association canadienne du Jouet
PO Box 218, #2219, 160 Tycos Dr., Toronto ON M6B 1W8
Tel: 416-596-0671; Fax: 416-596-1808
info@cdntoyassn.com
www.cdntoyassn.com
www.linkedin.com/groups/2795252
twitter.com/CdnToy
Overview: A medium-sized national organization founded in 1932
Mission: To represent the toy industry in Canada
Member of: International Council of Toy Industries
Finances: Annual Operating Budget: $500,000-$1.5 Million
Staff Member(s): 2; 13 volunteer(s)
Membership: 155; Member Profile: Manufacturers, importers or distributors of toys, games, seasonal decorations & hobby products
Chief Officer(s):
Serge Micheli, Executive Director
Publications:
• Canadian Toy Association Newsletter
Type: Newsletter

Canadian Toy Collectors' Society Inc. (CTCS) / Société canadienne des collectionneurs de jouets
#245, 91 Rylander Blvd., Unit 7, Toronto ON M1B 5M5
ctcsweb@hotmail.com
www.ctcs.org
www.facebook.com/468396576552495
Overview: A medium-sized national organization founded in 1970
Mission: To promote interest in the collection & display of all types of toys, childhood memorabilia & literature; To acquire, maintain & house a collection of toys & to restore & preserve Canadian toys of historic significance
Affiliation(s): Dufferin County Museum & Archives
Finances: Annual Operating Budget: Less than $50,000; Funding Sources: Membership dues; model sales; toy show
12 volunteer(s)
Membership: 130; Fees: $55; Committees: Collections; Newsletter/Magazine; Publicity; Toy Show; Virtual Museum; Website & Facebook
Activities: Monthly membership meetings with identified display themes; Monthly newsletter & biannual magazine The Toy Collector; Maintaining a Virtual Toy Museum (www.ctcs.on.ca/vtm); Awareness Events: Annual Canada's Greatest Collector's Toy Show; Library: Not open to public
Chief Officer(s):
David Tozer, President

Canadian Toy Testing Council (CTTC) / Conseil canadien d'évaluation des jouets
1973 Baseline Rd., Ottawa ON K2C 0C7
Tel: 613-228-3155; Fax: 613-228-3242
cttc@toy-testing.org
www.toy-testing.org
www.facebook.com/CdnToyTesting
twitter.com/CdnToyTesting
Overview: A small national charitable organization founded in 1952
Mission: To encourage the design, manufacture & distribution of toys sensitive to children's needs through independent evaluation
Finances: Annual Operating Budget: $100,000-$250,000
400 volunteer(s)
Membership: 400; Fees: $30; Member Profile: Educators, parents
Activities: National Media Conference on the "Best" toys, annual
Chief Officer(s):
Liliane Benoît, Executive Director
Publications:
• Canadian Toy Testing Council Newsletter
Type: Newsletter; Frequency: Semiannually; Editor: Janet Hetherington; Price: Free with CTTC membership
Profile: Information about recent toys, & creative recommendations for children

• Toy Report
Type: Yearbook; Frequency: Annually; Editor: Judy Andrew Piel
Profile: Rating & a review of each toy tested

Canadian Track & Field Association See Athletics Canada

Canadian Trail & Mountain Running Association (CTMRA)
BC
www.mountainrunning.ca
www.facebook.com/groups/2229398616
twitter.com/CTMRA
Overview: A small national organization
Mission: To oversee the sport of mountain running in Canada.
Activities: Championship series
Chief Officer(s):
Adrian Lambert, Contact
adrian.lambert@mountainrunning.ca

Canadian Training Institute (CTI) / Institut canadien de formation
#400, 901 King St. West, Toronto ON M5V 3H5
Tel: 416-778-7056; Fax: 416-645-7041
www.canadiantraininginstitute.com
www.facebook.com/386480171436391
Overview: A small national charitable organization founded in 1983
Mission: To contribute to the effectiveness of services delivered by criminal justice & related human service agencies in Canada
Affiliation(s): Canadian Traumatic Stress Network; National Associations Active in Criminal Justice (NAACJ/ANIJC); American Probation & Parole Association (APPA); International Community & Corrections Association (ICCA)
Finances: Funding Sources: Donations; Sponsorships
Activities: Liaising with government; Offering courses & workshops; Disseminating information; Training; Consulting; Conducting research; Breaking the Cycle program for youth involved in gangs
Chief Officer(s):
Duncan Gillespie, Executive Director
dgillespie@cantraining.org
Publications:
• Canadian Training Institute Annual Report
Type: Yearbook; Frequency: Annually
• Community Corrections & Criminal Justice Work in Canada
• A Literature Review on Youth Violence: From Risk to Resiliency Utilizing a Developmental Perspective
Number of Pages: 128; ISBN: 0-921465-18-1; Price: $20
• Youth Justice in Canada: A Resource Manual
Type: Manual; Number of Pages: 310; ISBN: 0-921465-15-7; Price: $39 book; $45 binder

Canadian Trakehner Horse Society (CTHS)
PO Box 6009, New Hamburg ON N3A 2K6
Tel: 519-662-3209
cantrakhsivh@golden.net
www.cantrak.on.ca
www.facebook.com/203491652994222
Overview: A small national organization founded in 1974
Mission: To maintain a public registry of Trakehner horses under the Canadian Livestock Records Corporation; To promote & preserve Trakehner horses in Canada
Membership: Fees: $30 associate members; $45 single memberships; $80 families; $400 life memberships; Member Profile: Breeders, owners & friends of Trakehner horses
Activities: Providing information & support to members
Chief Officer(s):
Judy Kirkby, President, 306-931-8028
judlenn@sasktel.net
Herbert Boettcher, Vice President, 519-887-6040
Ingrid von Hausen, Registrar & Secretary, 516-662-3209
cantrakhsivh@golden.net
Laurel Glanfield, Treasurer, 604-534-4849
lglanfield@telus.net
Publications:
• Canadian Trakehner
Type: Magazine; Accepts Advertising; Price: Free with CTHS membership
• Canadian Trakehner News
Type: Newsletter; Frequency: Quarterly; Accepts Advertising; Price: Free with CTHS membership

Canadian Translators & Interpreters Council See Canadian Translators, Terminologists & Interpreters Council

Canadian Translators, Terminologists & Interpreters Council (CTTIC) / Conseil des traducteurs, terminologues et interprètes du Canada (CTTIC)
#1202, One Nicholas St., Ottawa ON K1N 7B7
Tel: 613-562-0379; Fax: 613-241-4098
info@cttic.org
www.cttic.org
Previous Name: Canadian Translators & Interpreters Council
Overview: A medium-sized national charitable organization founded in 1956
Mission: To ensure uniform standards for the practice of the profession; To make available to the public a body of reliable professionals in translation, terminology & interpretation
Finances: Annual Operating Budget: $50,000-$100,000
Staff Member(s): 1; 4 volunteer(s)
Membership: 3,500 in 10 societies
Activities: Programs in translation, terminology, interpretation; certification examinations
Chief Officer(s):
Golnaz Aliyarzadeh, President
golnaz.aliyarzadeh@cttic.org
Alain Otis, Secretary
alain.otis@cttic.org
Publications:
• CTTIC By-laws
• Symposium on Translation, Terminology & Interpretation in Cuba & Canada
Frequency: Biennially

Canadian Transplant Association (CTA) / Association canadienne des greffes
PO Box 74, Tavistock ON N0B 2R0
Toll-Free: 877-779-5991
cta@txworks.ca
www.organ-donation-works.org
www.linkedin.com/company/5165307
www.facebook.com/CanadianTransplantAssociationandGames
twitter.com/CTACanada
Previous Name: Canadian Transplant Games Association
Overview: A medium-sized national charitable organization founded in 1989
Mission: To promote a healthy lifestyle for transplant recipients
Finances: Funding Sources: Membership fees; Donations; Fundraising
Membership: Fees: $30 individual members; $150 family membership; $300 lifetime individual membership; Member Profile: Transplant recipients; Persons committed to removing barriers to organ donation
Activities: Supporting organ & tissue donation awareness activities; Offering education about transplantation; Providing information about the National & World Transplant Games; Organizing social activities; Speaker Service: Yes
Chief Officer(s):
Dave Smith, President
davidsmith@txworks.ca
Jennifer Holman, Vice-President, West
jenniferholman@txworks.ca
Bianca Segatto, Vice-President, East
bsegatto@txworks.ca
Robert Sallows, Secretary
rsallows@txworks.ca
Michael Sullivan, Treasurer
msullivan@txworks.ca
Neil Folkins, Director, Membership Development
neilfolkins@txworks.ca
Awards:
• Gloria Santini Memorial Award
To honour dedication & perseverance in supporting the mission of the Canadian Transplant Association
Publications:
• The Living Proof [a publication of the Canadian Transplant Association]
Type: Newsletter; Frequency: Quarterly; Editor: Jennifer Holman; Price: Free with membership in the Canadian Transplant Association
Profile: Canadian Transplant Association news, including event information, awards & inspiring stories

Alberta Region
AB
www.organ-donation-works.org

British Columbia Region
BC
www.organ-donation-works.org
Mission: To promote organ donation & transplantation throughout British Columbia

Chief Officer(s):
Margaret Benson, Regional Director, British Columbia
mmbenson@txworks.ca
New Brunswick (Eastern Provinces) Region
NB
www.organ-donation-works.org
Mission: Increasing awareness of organ & tissue donation in Newfoundland, Prince Edward Island, Nova Scotia, & New Brunswick
Chief Officer(s):
Mark Black, Regional Director, Eastern Provinces
markblack@txworks.ca
Ontario Region
ON
www.organ-donation-works.org
Mission: To encourage a healthy lifestyle for transplant recipients throughout Ontario
Chief Officer(s):
Sandra Holdsworth, Director, Ontario Region
sandraholdsworth@txworks.ca
Québec Region
c/o Gaston Martin, 101, rue Lavigne, Repentigny QC J6A 6B6
Tel: 450-654-3786
www.organ-donation-works.org
Chief Officer(s):
Gaston Martin, Director, Québec Region
gaston@txworks.ca
Saskatchewan Region
SK
www.organ-donation-works.org
Chief Officer(s):
Phil Gleim, Regional Director
philgleim@txworks.ca

Canadian Transplant Games Association *See* Canadian Transplant Association

Canadian Transplantation Society *See* Canadian Society of Transplantation

Canadian Transport Lawyers Association (CTLA)
c/o Heather Devine, Isaacs & Co., 11 King St. West, 11th Fl., Toronto ON M5H 4C7
www.ctla.ca
Overview: A small national organization
Mission: To provide a professional & social forum for lawyers engaged or otherwise interested in transportation law, regulatory policy, procedure & related legal interests
Membership: *Fees:* $100-125/US$100-$125 new member; $100-$195/US$100-$195 renewing member; *Member Profile:* Lawyers engaged in transportation law, regulatory policy & procedures & other related legal interests
Chief Officer(s):
Rabin Myer, President, 506-857-3591
myer@rabinlaw.ca
Pierre-Olivier Menard Dumas, Vice-President & Secretary, 418-640-4441
pierre-olivier.dumas@steinmonast.ca
Awards:
• C. Douglas MacLeod Memorial Scholarship
Awarded annually to a student, or students, completing the second year of the LLB program at Queen's University School of Law on the basis of outstanding academic performance, with an emphasis on achievements in constitutional & administrative law
Publications:
• The Transportation Lawyer
Type: Journal; *Price:* Subscription included with Canadian Transport Lawyers Association membership fees

Canadian Transport Tariff Bureau Association *See* Freight Carriers Association of Canada

Canadian Transportation Equipment Association (CTEA) / Association d'équipement de transport du canada (AETC)
#505, 4510 Rhodes Dr., Windsor ON N8W 5K5
Tel: 226-620-0779; *Fax:* 519-944-4912
don.moore@atminc.on.ca
www.ctea.ca
ca.linkedin.com/groups?gid=6508608
Overview: A medium-sized national organization founded in 1963
Mission: To promote excellence in commercial vehicle manufacturing; To effectively lobby all levels of government on the industry's behalf and bring together stakeholders to participate in generic cooperative testing & other mutually beneficial activities
Staff Member(s): 4
Membership: 520; *Fees:* $825; *Member Profile:* Commercial vehicle & component manufacturers; Dealers & distributors; Service providers
Activities: Lobbying; Providing access to technical & regulatory information; Offering networking opportunities; Encouraging research; *Speaker Service:* Yes
Chief Officer(s):
Don Moore, Executive Director
don.moore@atminc.on.ca
Meetings/Conferences:
• Canadian Transportation Equipment Association 55th Annual Conference, October, 2018, Westin Prince, Toronto, ON
Publications:
• Buyer's Guide to Members' Products & Services
Profile: Equipment, products, & services offered by companies, for CTEA / AETC members & potential customers
• CTEA Membership Directory
Type: Directory; *Frequency:* Monthly
Profile: Contact information for CTEA's members
• CTEA Today
Type: Magazine; *Frequency:* Bimonthly; *Price:* Free with CTEA membership
Profile: CTEA activities & events, industry news, & articles on issues
• Xpress Newsletter
Type: Newsletter; *Price:* Free with CTEA / AETC membership
Profile: Membership information, industry news, employment referrals, technical papers, new products, & surveys

Canadian Transportation Research Forum (CTRF) / Groupe de recherches sur les transports au Canada
PO Box 23033, Woodstock ON N4T 1R9
Tel: 519-421-9701; *Fax:* 519-421-9319
www.ctrf.ca
www.linkedin.com/groups/8205076/profile
twitter.com/ForCtrf
Overview: A medium-sized national charitable organization founded in 1965
Mission: To promote the development of research in transportation & related fields; to publish research papers through media & through national & regional forum meetings.
Membership: *Fees:* $148 individual; $32 student; $89 senior (65+); *Member Profile:* Open to anyone interested in any aspect of transportation; membership is currently comprised of professionals in the railway, trucking, airline, port, airport, shipping line, terminal operator, transit operator and pipline industries; shippers; employees of Transport Canada, the Canadian Transport Agency, Statistics Canads, Industry Canada & other federal agencies; consultants; unversities & colleges
Chief Officer(s):
Dan Lynch, President, 902-494-6248
dan.lynch@dal.ca
Carole Ann Woudsma, Secretary, 519-421-9701, Fax: 519-421-9319
cawoudsma@ctrf.ca
Malcolm Cairns, Executive Vice President, 613-692-2764
malcolmbcairns@gmail.com
Mario Iacobacci, Vice President, External Affairs, 514-287-8500 Ext. 8271
mario.iacobacci@aecom.com
Gerry Kolaitis, Vice President, Finance & Treasurer, 514-871-6169
gerry_kolaitis@viarail.ca
Barry Prentice, Vice President, Program, 204-261-5666
barry_pretice@umanitoba.ca
Gordo Tufts, Vice President, Meetings, 204-945-1557
gtufts@gov.mb.ca
Kalinga Jagoda, Vice President, Awards
kjagoda@uoguelp.ca
Awards:
• Scholarships for Graduate Study in Transportation
In cooperation with several other organizations, offers up to five scholarships; field of study may be in business administration, civil engineering, economics, geography, law, planning, or other fields *Eligibility:* Canadian citizen or permanent resident; full-time student at a Canadian university *Deadline:* January 31; *Amount:* $4,000-$6,000
• Student Research Paper Competition
Prizes awarded annually for student papers dealing with transportation; prizes are awarded for the best undergraduate papers, the best papers at the master's level, & the best papers at the doctorate level
Meetings/Conferences:
• Canadian Transportation Research Forum 53rd Annual Conference, 2018
Scope: National
Publications:
• FORUMation [a publication of the Canadian Transportation Research Forum]
Type: Newsletter; *Frequency:* 3 pa; *Number of Pages:* 11; *Price:* Free download
Profile: Provides highlights and information about the Canadian transport sectors

Canadian Transverse Myelitis Association (CTMA) / Association Canadienne de myélite transverse
263, Malcolm Circle, Dorval QC H9S 1T6
Tel: 514-636-9337
info@mytm.ca
www.mytm.ca
twitter.com/CTMAssociation
Overview: A medium-sized national organization
Mission: To help patients with transverse myelitis & their families build a network of support; To inform patients & families of new research & treatment that has been discovered; To raise awareness about the disorder
Chief Officer(s):
Kimberley Kotar, President & Founder

Canadian Trapshooting Association (CTA)
Saskatoon SK
www.shootcanada.ca
Overview: A medium-sized national organization founded in 1950
Mission: To promote clay target shooting as a recreational sport among shooters of every age, both sexes, & at every level of ability, the ultimate objective being to compete in the world championships held each year in Ohio
Member of: Amateur Trapshooting Association
Finances: *Annual Operating Budget:* Less than $50,000; *Funding Sources:* Fees collected at the national championships 150 volunteer(s)
Membership: 1,800
Chief Officer(s):
Dwight Smith, President

Canadian Tribute to Human Rights (CTHR) / Monument canadien pour les droits de la personne (MCDP)
#170, 99 - 5th Ave., Ottawa ON K1P 5P5
info@cthr-mcdp.com
www.cthr-mcdp.com
Also Known As: The Human Rights Monument
Overview: A small national charitable organization founded in 1984
Mission: To ensure public awareness of the presence in Ottawa of the Tribute monument as a symbol of Canadians' commitment to preserving & fostering human rights; To promote use of the site as a focal point for all groups working for human rights in Canada & internationally; To spread the concept of public places dedicated to human rights in other capital cities of countries that have affirmed the UN Universal Declaration of Human Rights.
Finances: *Annual Operating Budget:* Less than $50,000; *Funding Sources:* Donations; grants
Activities: *Speaker Service:* Yes

Canadian Trucking Alliance (CTA) / L'Alliance canadienne du camionnage (ACC)
555 Dixon Rd., Toronto ON M9W 1H8
Tel: 416-249-7401; *Fax:* 866-713-4188
publicaffairs@cantruck.ca
www.cantruck.ca
twitter.com/CanTruck
Overview: A large national organization founded in 1937
Mission: To promote business excellence in trucking; to participate in the development of public policy which supports the economic growth, safety & prosperity of the industry; to provide services, including research, development, products & information to meet the needs of the industry
Staff Member(s): 5
Membership: 4,000; *Member Profile:* Represented by a cross-section of the trucking industry, including carriers, owner-operators and industry suppliers
Activities: *Speaker Service:* Yes

Canadian Turkey Marketing Agency *See* Turkey Farmers of Canada

Canadian Associations / Canadian Ukrainian Immigrant Aid Society (CUIAS)

Canadian Ukrainian Immigrant Aid Society (CUIAS)
2383 Bloor St. West, 2nd Fl., Toronto ON M6S 1P9
Tel: 416-767-4595; *Fax:* 416-767-2658
www.cuias.org
Overview: A small international organization founded in 1977.
Mission: To sponsor & aid in settlement of Ukrainian refugees.
Member of: Ontario Council of Agencies Serving Immigrants
Affiliation(s): Ukrainian Canadian Congress
Finances: *Funding Sources:* Federal & provincial grants; donations; fees
Staff Member(s): 10
Chief Officer(s):
Ludmila Kolesnichenko, Executive Director
lkolesnichenko@cuias.org

Canadian Ultimate Players Association *See* Ultimate Canada

Canadian Underwater Games Association (CUGA)
c/o Melanie Johnson, Secretary, #2002, 535 Nicola St., Vancouver BC V6G 3G3
info@cuga.org
www.cuga.org
www.facebook.com/cuga.org
Overview: A small national organization founded in 1984.
Mission: To oversee underwater sports in Canada.
Affiliation(s): World Underwater Federation
Activities: Underwater hockey & underwater rugby
Chief Officer(s):
Adam Jocksch, President

Canadian Union of Brewery & General Workers, Local 325
1 Carlingview Dr., Toronto ON M9W 5E5
Tel: 416-675-2648; *Fax:* 416-675-6694
component325.ca
Overview: A small provincial organization founded in 1959.
Member of: National Union of Public and General Employees
Membership: *Member Profile:* Canadian Brewery Workers
Chief Officer(s):
Glen Hamilton, President

Canadian Union of Postal Workers (CUPW) / Syndicat des travailleurs et travailleuses des postes (STTP)
377 Bank St., Ottawa ON K2P 1Y3
Tel: 613-236-7238; *Fax:* 613-563-7861; *TTY:* 613-236-9753
feedback@cupw-sttp.org
www.cupw-sttp.org
www.linkedin.com/company/canadian-union-of-postal-workers
www.facebook.com/cupwsttp
twitter.com/cupw
www.youtube.com/user/cupwsttp
Overview: A large national organization
Mission: To be involved with various campaigns and activities which help support their members
Member of: Canadian Labour Congress
Membership: 54,000; *Member Profile:* Rural and suburban mail carriers, letter carriers, mail service couriers, postal clerks, mail handlers, mail despatchers, technicians, mechanics, electricians and electronic technicians; *Committees:* Human Rights; Women's; Work Measurement
Chief Officer(s):
Mike Palecek, National President
Bev Collins, National Sec.-Treas.
Meetings/Conferences:
• Canadian Union of Postal Workers National Convention 2018, 2018
Scope: National

Canadian Union of Public Employees (CUPE) / Syndicat canadien de la fonction publique (SCFP)
1375 St. Laurent Blvd., Ottawa ON K1G 0Z7
Tel: 613-237-1590; *Fax:* 613-237-5508
Toll-Free: 844-237-1590
www.cupe.ca
www.facebook.com/cupescfp
twitter.com/cupenat
www.linkedin.com/company/canadian-union-of-public-employees
Overview: A large national organization founded in 1963.
Mission: To advance the social, economic, & general welfare of both active & retired employees; To promote required legislation
Affiliation(s): Canadian Labour Congress; Public Services International; International Confederation of Free Trade Unions
Membership: 600,000+; *Member Profile:* Workers in the public service of Canada; *Committees:* National Advisory Committee on Pensions; National Global Justice; National Contracting Out & Privatization Coordinating; National Environment; National Health & Safety; National Health Care Issues; National Pink Triangle; National Women's; National Working Committee on Racism, Discrimination, & Employment Equity (National Rainbow Committee); National Child Care Working Group; Persons With Disabilities National Working Group; National Young Workers; National Literacy Working Group; National Political Action
Activities: Improving wages, working conditions, hours of work, & job security; Eliminating harassment & discrimination; Providing educational programs
Chief Officer(s):
Mark Hancock, National President
Charles Fleury, National Secretary-Treasurer
Meetings/Conferences:
• Canadian Union of Public Employees 2018 National Convention, 2018
Scope: National
Publications:
• The Canary [a publication of the Canadian Union of Public Employees]
Type: Newsletter; *Frequency:* s-a.; *Editor:* Wes Payne & Troy Winters
Profile: Features the latest news & developments in the health & safety world
• Counterpoint [a publication of the Canadian Union of Public Employees]
Type: Newsletter; *Frequency:* Quarterly; *Editor:* Catherine Louli; *ISSN:* 1920-2857
Profile: Available in print & online (1920-2865)
• CUPE Celebrates: Annual Report [a publication of the Canadian Union of Public Employees]
Type: Report; *Frequency:* Annually
Profile: Articles & facts about CUPE in Canada during the recent year
• CUPE International Solidarity Report [a publication of the Canadian Union of Public Employees]
Type: Report; *Author:* Catherine Louli
• Economy at Work [a publication of the Canadian Union of Public Employees]
Type: Newsletter; *Frequency:* 4 pa.; *Author:* Toby Sanger; *Editor:* Toby Sanger
Profile: National & provincial economic outlooks
• Global Justice [a publication of the Canadian Union of Public Employees]
Type: Newsletter; *Frequency:* s-a.; *Editor:* Kelti Cameron
Profile: Articles from around the world
• Tabletalk [a publication of the Canadian Union of Public Employees]
Type: Newsletter; *Frequency:* Quarterly; *Editor:* Margot Young
Profile: A bargaining resource, for CUPE local bargaining committees, elected officers, & servicing representatives

Alberta Division (CUPE AB)
c/o Alberta Regional Office, #300, 10235 - 124 St., Edmonton AB T5N 1P9
Tel: 780-484-7644; *Fax:* 780-489-2202
Toll-Free: 877-937-2873
larab@cupe.ca
alberta.cupe.ca
www.facebook.com/CupeAlberta
twitter.com/cupeab
Mission: To work together for improved working conditions, better wages, & strong public services in Alberta
Chief Officer(s):
Marle Roberts, President
cupeabpresident@gmail.com
Glynnis Lieb, Secretary-Treasurer
cupeabtreasurer@gmail.com

British Columbia Division (CUPE BC)
British Columbia Regional Office, #500, 4940 Canada Way, Burnaby BC V5G 4T3
Tel: 604-291-9119; *Fax:* 604-291-9043
info@cupe.bc.ca
www.cupe.bc.ca
www.facebook.com/CUPEBC
Chief Officer(s):
Paul Faoro, President
pfaoro@cupe.bc.ca
Trevor Davies, Secretary-Treasurer
tdavies@cupe.bc.ca

Manitoba Division (CUPE MB)
Manitoba Regional Office, #703, 275 Broadway, Winnipeg MB R3C 4M6
Tel: 204-942-0343; *Fax:* 204-956-7071
cupemb@cupe.mb.ca
www.cupe.mb.ca
www.facebook.com/CUPEManitoba
www.youtube.com/user/cupescfp
Chief Officer(s):
Kelly Moist, President
Mike Davidson, Vice-President
Phil Dembicki, Secretary-Treasurer
Ric McAlpine, Recording Secretary

New Brunswick Division (CUPE NB)
Maritime Regional Office, 91 Woodside Lane, Fredericton NB E3C 0C5
Tel: 506-458-8059; *Fax:* 506-452-1702
www.nb.cupe.ca
www.facebook.com/cupeNBscfp
twitter.com/cupemaritimes
Mission: To advance the efficiency of public employees in New Brunswick; To promote legislation in New Brunswick that furthers the interests of member unions
Chief Officer(s):
Daniel Légère, President
dlegere@cupe.ca

Newfoundland & Labrador Division (CUPE NL)
St. John's Area Office, PO Box 8745, Stn. A, 36 Austin St., St. John's NL A1B 3T2
Tel: 709-753-0732; *Fax:* 709-753-2313
Toll-Free: 866-771-2873
www.nl.cupe.ca
Chief Officer(s):
Wayne Lucas, President
wlucas@nl.rogers.com
Dawn Lahey, Vice-President
dlahey@nlpl.ca
Ed Whelan, Secretary-Treasurer
ewhelan@mun.ca
Derrick Barrett, Executive Officer
derrickbarrett@nl.rogers.com

Nova Scotia Division (CUPE NS)
c/o President, Nan McFadgen, PO Box 1794, Pictou NS B0K 1H0
Tel: 902-759-3231
www.novascotia.cupe.ca
www.facebook.com/CUPENovaScotia
twitter.com/cupenovascotia
Mission: To work for equitable treatment for all members
Chief Officer(s):
Nan McFadgen, President
nmcfadgen@cupe.ca
• CUPE Nova Scotia Newsletter
Type: Newsletter; *Frequency:* q.

Ontario Division (CUPE ON)
Ontario Regional Office, #1, 80 Commerce Valley Dr. East, Markham ON L3T 0B2
Tel: 905-739-9739; *Fax:* 905-739-9740
info@cupe.on.ca
www.cupe.on.ca
www.facebook.com/CUPEOntario
twitter.com/CUPEOntario
www.youtube.com/CUPEOntario
Mission: To act as a political voice for affiliated locals throughout Ontario; To campaign for legislative, policy, & political change on issues affecting public services
Chief Officer(s):
Fred Hahn, President
Candace Rennick, Secretary-Treasurer
Michael Hurley, First Vice-President
• Canadian Union of Public Employees Ontario Division Newsletter
Type: Newsletter; *Frequency:* Biweekly
Profile: Developments in CUPE Ontario sectors, campaign updates, & upcoming events

Prince Edward Island Division (CUPE PEI)
Charlottetown Area Office, 26 Paramount Dr., Charlottetown PE C1E 0C7
Tel: 902-566-4006; *Fax:* 902-892-0452
cupepei@gmail.com
www.cupepei.ca
www.facebook.com/465650880124770
twitter.com/cupepei
Mission: To advance the efficiency of public employees & the labour movement in Prince Edward Island; To assist in the organization of unorganized workers
Chief Officer(s):
Lori Mackay, President
lmackay@cupe.ca

Leonard Crawford, Vice-President
leonardjcrawford@hotmail.com
Debbie Wervers, Recording Secretary
Linda Jones, Secretary-Treasurer
lmjones@edu.pe.ca

Québec Division (CUPE QC)
Québec Regional Office, #7100, 565, boul Crémazie, Montréal QC H2M 2V9
Tél: 514-384-9681; *Téléc:* 514-384-9680
scfp.qc.ca
www.facebook.com/scfpquebec
twitter.com/SCFPQuebecInfos
www.youtube.com/user/SCFPQuebecInfos
Chief Officer(s):
Michel Bibeault, Regional Director

Saskatchewan Division (CUPE SK)
Saskatchewan Regional Office, 3275 East Eastgate Dr., Regina SK S4Z 1A5
Tel: 306-757-1009; *Fax:* 306-757-0102
cupesask@sasktel.net
www.sk.cupe.ca
www.facebook.com/cupesask
twitter.com/CUPEsask
Mission: To present positions of the union to government & media
Chief Officer(s):
Tom Graham, President
Jackie Christianson, Vice-President
Judy Henley, Secretary-Treasurer
Marcia Ray, Recording Secretary
Andrew Loewen, Executive Assistant
loewen.cupe@sasktel.net

Canadian Unitarian Council (CUC) / Conseil unitarien du Canada
#400, 215 Spadina Ave., Toronto ON M5T 2C7
Tel: 416-489-4121
Toll-Free: 888-568-5723
info@cuc.ca
www.cuc.ca
www.linkedin.com/company/canadian-unitarian-council
www.facebook.com/CanadianUnitarianCouncil
twitter.com/uucanada
www.youtube.com/channel/UCJ25IMWQwrxSnry11bdBS-g
Also Known As: Unitarian Church
Overview: A medium-sized national charitable organization founded in 1961
Mission: To enhance, nurture & promote Unitarian & Universalist religion in Canada; To provide support for religious exploration, spiritual growth & social responsibility
Affiliation(s): International Association for Religious Freedom; International Council of Unitarians & Universalists; Untarian Universalist Minsters of Canada
Finances: *Annual Operating Budget:* $250,000-$500,000; *Funding Sources:* Donations; Membership dues
Staff Member(s): 9; 20 volunteer(s)
Membership: 50 institutional; *Fees:* Schedule available; *Committees:* Lay & Chaplaincy; Social Responsibility; Congregational Development
Activities: *Library:* CUC Library; by appointment
Chief Officer(s):
Vyda Ng, Executive Director
vyda@cuc.ca
Keith Wilkinson, President
president@cuc.ca
Jane Ebbern, Vice President
vice.president@cuc.ca
Tanya Cothran, Treasurer
treasurer@cuc.ca
Carol Cummings Speirs, Secretary
secretary@cuc.ca
Meetings/Conferences:
• Canadian Unitarian Council National Conference & AGM 2018, May, 2018, McMaster University, Hamilton, ON
Scope: National
Publications:
• The Canadian Unitarian
Type: Newsletter; *Frequency:* Biannually; *Accepts Advertising;* *ISSN:* 0527-9860; *Price:* Free for members of CUC congregations; $9 without membership
• Canadian Unitarian Council eNews
Type: Newsletter; *Frequency:* bimonthly

Canadian Unitarians for Social Justice (CUJS)
Stn. 40011, Ottawa ON K1V 0W8
membership@cusj.org
cusj.org
Overview: A medium-sized national organization founded in 1996
Mission: A national, liberal religious organization, founded to actively promote Unitarian values through social action
Affiliation(s): Canadian Unitarian Council
Finances: *Annual Operating Budget:* Less than $50,000
Chief Officer(s):
Frances Deverell, President
president@cusj.org
Publications:
• JUSTnews
Type: Newsletter; *Editor:* Philip Symons

Canadian University & College Conference Officers Association *See* Canadian University & College Conference Organizers Association

Canadian University & College Conference Organizers Association (CUCCOA) / Association des coordonnateurs de congrès des universités et des collèges du Canada (ACCUCC)
312 Oakwood Ct., Newmarket ON L3Y 3C8
Tel: 905-954-0102; *Fax:* 905-895-1630
inquiries@cuccoa.org
www.cuccoa.org
Previous Name: Canadian University & College Conference Officers Association
Overview: A small national organization founded in 1978
Mission: Exists for the purpose of information sharing, professional development & group marketing
Finances: *Annual Operating Budget:* $50,000-$100,000
8 volunteer(s)
Membership: 75 institutions; *Fees:* $375; *Member Profile:* Normally restricted to universities & colleges in Canada
Chief Officer(s):
Carol Ford, Manager

Canadian University & College Counselling Association (CUCCA) / Association canadienne de counseling universitaire et collégial
c/o Canadian Association of College & University Student Services, #310, 4 Cataraqui St., Kingston ON K7K 1Z7
Tel: 613-531-9210; *Fax:* 866-303-0626
contact@cacuss.ca
www.eventsmgt.com
Previous Name: University Counselling & Placement Association
Overview: A small national organization founded in 1963
Membership: *Member Profile:* Individuals employed as counsellors & counselling psychologists, at Canadian post-secondary institutions, who counsel educators & graduate students in counselling-related programs
Activities: Providing professional development activities
Chief Officer(s):
Chris Mercer, President
Erin Bradford, Secretary/Treasurer
Awards:
• CUCCA Student Award
To recognize student innovations in counselling or applied research
• CUCCA Professional Development Award
One award is available in counselling & another in applied research
• CUCCA Award of Service
Publications:
• Coast to Coast
Type: Newsletter

Canadian University Football Coaches Association (CUFCA)
Overview: A small national organization founded in 1977
Mission: To improve the coaching of Canadian Interuniversity Athletic Union (CIAU) football teams; to improve the technical aspects of play in CIAU football
Affiliation(s): Canadian Interuniversity Athletic Union
Membership: 60 individuals + 24 teams; *Fees:* $40

Canadian University Music Society (CUMS) / Société de musique des universités canadiennes (SMUC)
#202, 10 Morrow Ave., Toronto ON M6R 2J1
Tel: 416-538-1650; *Fax:* 416-489-1713
office@muscan.org
www.muscan.org
Previous Name: Canadian Association of University Schools of Music
Overview: A medium-sized national charitable organization founded in 1979
Mission: To stimulate research, musical performance & composition; To improve instructional methods in university teaching; To provide a forum to exchange views on common problems, scholarly research in music & other matters of professional concern; To advise on new university programs & monitor existing programs
Member of: Humanities & Social Science Federation of Canada
Affiliation(s): Social Sciences & Humanities Research Council of Canada
Finances: *Annual Operating Budget:* Less than $50,000; *Funding Sources:* Social Sciences & Humanities Research Council of Canada; membership fees
Staff Member(s): 1
Membership: 45 institutional + 224 faculty & independent scholars + 48 students; *Fees:* $40-$70; *Member Profile:* Active interest in delivery & practice of music at post-secondary level in Canada; *Committees:* Standing Committee of Institutional Members
Chief Officer(s):
Glenn Colton, President
Awards:
• George Proctor Prize
Best paper presented by a graduate student at the CUMS annual conference
Meetings/Conferences:
• Canadian University Music Society Annual Conference 2018, May, 2018, MacEwan University, Edmonton, AB
Scope: National
Description: Theme: "MusEcologies"

Canadian University Nursing Students' Association *See* Canadian Nursing Students' Association

Canadian University Press (CUP) / Presse universitaire canadienne
c/o Canadian Media Guild, #810, 310 Front St. West, Toronto ON M5V 3B5
Tel: 416-962-2287
Toll-Free: 866-250-5595
www.cup.ca
www.facebook.com/canadianuniversitypress
twitter.com/canunipress
www.youtube.com/user/CUPonline
Overview: A medium-sized national organization founded in 1938
Mission: To elevate the standard of post-secondary student journalism; to foster communication among post-secondary student newspapers; to provide a national press service for post-secondary student newspapers; to provide facilities for the dissemination of news of importance to post-secondary students
Finances: *Annual Operating Budget:* $100,000-$250,000; *Funding Sources:* Membership fees; donations; grants
Membership: 30+ organizations; *Fees:* $300-$7,000; *Member Profile:* Democratically run post-secondary student newspapers
Activities: *Internships:* Yes; *Speaker Service:* Yes; *Rents Mailing List:* Yes; *Library:* CUP Resource Centre; by appointment
Chief Officer(s):
Nicolas Brown, President
president@cup.ca
Katherine Lapointe, Coordinator, Membership & Mentorship
cwa@cup.ca

Canadian Urban Institute (CUI)
#500, 30 Patrick St., Toronto ON M5T 3A3
Tel: 416-365-0816; *Fax:* 416-365-0650
cui@canurb.org
www.canurb.org
www.facebook.com/canurb
twitter.com/canurb
Overview: A medium-sized national organization founded in 1990
Mission: To achieve healthy urban development
Membership: *Fees:* $50-$2,500
Chief Officer(s):
Peter Halsall, Executive Director, 416-365-0816 Ext. 233
phalsall@canurb.org
Ariana Cancelli, Planner & Researcher, 416-365-0816 Ext. 280
acancelli@canurb.org
Lisa Cavicchia, Program Director, 416-365-0816 Ext. 223
lcavicchia@canurb.org
Navf Dhaliwal, Director, Fiance, 416-365-0816 Ext. 230
ndhaliwal@canurb.org

Canadian Associations / Canadian Urban Libraries Council (CULC)

Awards:
- Brownie Awards
- Urban Leadership Awards

Publications:
- The Urban Century
Type: Newsletter; *Frequency:* Annually; *Editor:* Philippa Campsi; *ISSN:* 1206-4599

Canadian Urban Libraries Council (CULC)
349 Main St., Bloomfield ON K0K 1G0
Tel: 416-699-1938; *Fax:* 866-211-2999
www.culc.ca
Previous Name: Council of Administrators of Large Urban Public Libraries
Overview: A medium-sized national organization founded in 1978
Mission: To identify the issues & choices available in developing urban public library services; To explore the philosophy & principles that govern public library service in urban areas; To comment on the state of public library service in Canada; To facilitate the exchange of ideas & information between member libraries; To influence legislation & financing of urban public libraries; To promote & work in conjunction with other library organizations in Canada to achieve an urban public library service which is comprehensive, economic & efficient; To provide the means for communication & information sharing between members of the public library community; To promote formal & informal cooperation with organizations & institutions in Canada & outside Canada whose goals & objectives are relevant to large urban public library service
Member of: International Federation of Library Associations
Finances: *Funding Sources:* Membership fees
Staff Member(s): 2
Membership: 45; *Fees:* Schedule available; *Member Profile:* Any single municipal urban public library system or urban library districts serving more than 100,000 population directly interested in aims & objectives of CULC
Activities: *Rents Mailing List:* Yes
Chief Officer(s):
Jefferson Gilbert, Executive Director
jgilbert@culc.ca
Paul Takala, Chair
Publications:
- Social Inclusion Audit & Toolkit [a publication of the Canadian Urban Libraries Council]
Type: Report; *Number of Pages:* 128; *ISBN:* 0-9865562-0-3; *Price:* $79 with CULC membership; $109 without membership
Profile: A study on social inclusion & the institution of the public library
- Trend Report [a publication of the Canadian Urban Libraries Council]
Type: Report
Profile: A commissioned study analyzing Key Performance Indicator Data; intended to assist libraries in gaining an understanding of their operating environment

Canadian Urban Transit Association (CUTA) / Association canadienne du transport urbain (ACTU)
#1401, 55 York St., Toronto ON M5J 1R7
Tel: 416-365-9800; *Fax:* 416-365-1295
www.cutaactu.ca
www.linkedin.com/company/canadian-urban-transit-association
www.facebook.com/CanadianTransit
twitter.com/canadiantransit
Overview: A large national organization founded in 1904
Mission: To provide value to its members and contribute to the success of public transit in Canada
Staff Member(s): 20
Membership: 488; *Fees:* Schedule available; *Member Profile:* Transit systems; Manufacturers & suppliers of transit equipment, proprietors & operating/management companies; Federal, provincial & municipal government agencies; Affiliated individuals & companies; *Committees:* Business Members; Communications & Public Affairs; Human Resources; Technical Services; Transit Board Members; Regional Committees
Activities: Conducting research & preparing statistics; Providing technical & operational information; Liaising with government; Partnering with other transportation associations & community development stakeholders; Engaging in advocacy activities; Raising public awareness of transit contributions to communities; *Library:* Canadian Urban Transit Association Library; Not open to public
Chief Officer(s):
Patrick Leclerc, President & Chief Executive Officer, 613-788-7982
leclerc@cutaactu.ca
Becky Benaissa, Director, Finance & Administration, 416-365-9800 Ext. 108
benaissa@cutaactu.ca
Jeff Mackey, Coordinator, Public Policy, 613-782-2454
mackey@cutaactu.ca
Lauren Rudko, Manager, Research & Technical Services, 416-365-9800 Ext. 113
rudko@cutaactu.ca
Sarah Ingram, Coordinator, Training, 416-365-9800 Ext. 115
ingram@cutaactu.ca
Johanne Palermo, Content Strategist, Publications, 416-365-9800 Ext. 120
palermo@cutaactu.ca
Awards:
- CUTA Corporate Leadership Awards
Presented in the categories of Environment, Innovation, Marketing & Cmmunciations, & Safety & Security
- CUTA Individual Leadership Awards
Presented in the categories of Excellence, Distinguished Service & Heroism; W.G Ross Lifetime Achievement Award presented to an individual with exceptional involvement in the promotion and practice of public transit in Canada
Meetings/Conferences:
- Canadian Urban Transit Association 2018 Fall Conference & Transit Show, November, 2018, Metro Toronto Convention Centre, Toronto, ON
Scope: National
Description: A yearly technical conference, which also includes the presentation of Employee Awards based on accomplishments in areas such as attendance, safety, & acts of heroism
- Canadian Urban Transit Association 2018 Annual Conference, 2018
Scope: National
Description: Professional development sessions & the presentation of Corporate Awards, held in May or June each year
Publications:
- Canadian Urban Transit Association's Online Buyer's Guide
Type: Guide
Profile: Online database of products & services organized by categories
- CUTA Membership Directory
Type: Directory; *Frequency:* Annually; *Accepts Advertising*; *Price:* $50
Profile: Specific contact details for transit systems, suppliers, government agencies, consultants & affiliate members
- EXPRESSions
Type: Newsletter; *Frequency:* s-m.; *Number of Pages:* 2; *Price:* Free download
Profile: Association activities & forthcoming events
- Transit Vision 2040
Type: Report; *Number of Pages:* 67
Profile: Report focused on the Transit Vision 2040: An industry vision of the role of public transit in Canada
- Urban Mobility Forum
Type: Magazine; *Frequency:* a.; *Accepts Advertising*; *Number of Pages:* 42; *Editor:* Johanne Palermo; *Price:* Free download
Profile: Candaadian transit industry news & information; special conference issues in May/June & November/December

Ottawa Office
#200, 440 Laurier Ave. West, Ottawa ON K1R 7X6
Tel: 613-690-5138; *Fax:* 613-248-7965

Canadian Urethane Foam Contractors Association (CUFCA) / Association canadienne des entrepreneurs en mousse de polyuréthane
3200 Wharton Way, Mississauga ON L4X 2C1
Fax: 877-416-3626
Toll-Free: 866-467-7729
cufca@cufca.ca
www.cufca.ca
Overview: A small national licensing organization founded in 1985
Mission: To champion the polyurethane foam industry in Canada; To maintain high standards in the industry; to ensure the professionalism & profitability of the industry
Membership: *Fees:* $500 general membership & contractors; $3,500 manufacturers; *Member Profile:* Manufacturers; Contractors
Activities: Liaising with government agencies; Encouraging professional development; Providing a quality assurance program; Promoting use of ray polyurethane foam; Facilitating research; Publishing; Implementing standards for materials
Chief Officer(s):
Ryan Dalgleish, Executive Director
Andrew B. Cole, Chair
Jean Doucet, Secretary-Treasurer, 418-679-0497

Canadian Urologic Oncology Group (CUOG)
c/o Dr. Fred Saad, CUOG Chairman, 1560, rue Sherbrooke est, Montréal QC H2L 4M1
Tel: 514-890-8000
fred.saad.chum@ssss.gouv.qc.ca
www.cuog.org
Overview: A small national organization
Mission: Clinical research investigator network committed to furthering urology research in Canada
Affiliation(s): Canadian Urological Association
Finances: *Funding Sources:* Investigator agreements; review charges; consultancy fees
Chief Officer(s):
Neil Fleshner, Chair

Canadian Urological Association (CUA) / Association des urologues du Canada
#401, 185, av Dorval, Dorval QC H9S 5J9
Tel: 514-395-0376; *Fax:* 514-395-1664
cua@cua.org
www.cua.org
www.linkedin.com/company/canadian-urological-association-journal-cuaj-
www.facebook.com/CanadianUrologyAssociation
twitter.com/CanUrolAssoc
Overview: A medium-sized national organization founded in 1945
Mission: To advance the urology field; To promote high standards of urologic care in Canada
Affiliation(s): Canadian Medical Association
Finances: *Annual Operating Budget:* $250,000-$500,000; *Funding Sources:* Annual dues; Annual Meeting; commercial donations
Staff Member(s): 5; 6 volunteer(s)
Membership: 600; *Fees:* $120; *Committees:* Interprovincial socioeconomic & manpower; Guidelines; Research
Activities: Supporting CUA Scholarship Foundation to financially aid young researchers in urology
Chief Officer(s):
Tiffany Pizioli, Executive Director
tiffany.pizioli@cua.org
Nadia Pace, Director, Communications
nadia.pace@cua.org
Denise Toner, Manager, Advertising & Membership
denise.toner@cua.org
Meetings/Conferences:
- Canadian Urological Association 2018 73rd Annual Meeting, June, 2018, Halifax Convention Centre, Halifax, NS
Scope: National
Attendance: 600
Publications:
- Canadian Urological Association Journal (CUAJ) / Journal de l'Association des urologues du Canada (JAUC)
Type: Journal; *Frequency:* Bimonthly; *Editor:* Adriana Modica
Profile: Peer-reviewd original scientific research, reviews, resident studies, & casereports
- CUA News: Newsletter of the Canadian Urological Association
Type: Newsletter; *Frequency:* Semiannually
Profile: CUA activities, programs, events, awards, professional development, & committee reports

Canadian Utilities & Northland Utilities Employees' Association; Alberta Power Employees' Association See Canadian Energy Workers' Association

Canadian Vaping Association
Bldg. 1, #401, 5025 Orbiter Dr., Mississauga ON L4W 4Y5
Toll-Free: 800-826-7146
info@thecva.org
www.canadianvapingassociation.org
www.facebook.com/thecanadianvapingassociationorg
Overview: A medium-sized national organization founded in 2014
Mission: To protect the interests of Canada's vaping industry; To liaison with provincial & federal governments on legislative & regulatory issues regarding vaping
Membership: 300; *Committees:* Communications; Government Relations; Membership
Activities: Offering resources; Lobbying
Chief Officer(s):
Stan Pijl, President
Publications:
- Canadian Vaping Association Newsletter

Type: Newsletter; *Accepts Advertising*
Profile: News about the association & vaping industry

Canadian Vascular Access Association (CVAA) / Association canadienne d'Accès Vasculaire
PO Box 68030, 753 Main St. East, Hamilton ON L8M 3M7
Fax: 888-243-9307
Toll-Free: 888-243-9307
cvaa@cvaa.info
www.cvaa.info
www.facebook.com/165776480198722
twitter.com/CVAACanada
Previous Name: Canadian Intravenous Nurses Association
Overview: A medium-sized national organization founded in 1975
Mission: To establish & promote standards of intravenous therapy to enhance patient care & safety
Membership: *Fees:* $110 regular/international; $80 retired; $15,000 platinum company; $10,000 gold company; $6,000 silver company; $3,000 bronze company; *Member Profile:* IV nurses & others involved in IV therapy; *Committees:* Professional Practice; Conference; Chapters & Membership; Constitution & Governance
Activities: *Library:* Documentation Centre
Chief Officer(s):
Sheryl McDiarmid, President
Melissa McQueen, Executive Director
Awards:
• Maisie Townend Scholarship Award
; *Amount:* Two $500 each
• Medex Canada Inc. Medical Products Editorial Award
; *Amount:* $1,000
• Poster Presentations Award
; *Amount:* $250 first prize; $150 second prize; $75 third prize
• Barbara Hill Award
• Certification Award
; *Amount:* $100 & a plaque
• CINA Award
Publications:
• CVAA [Canadian Vascular Access Association] Journal
Type: Journal; *Price:* $120 annual subscription; $40 individual issue; $30 individual article
Profile: Information regarding aspects of vascular access therapy
• The CVAA [Canadian Vascular Access Association] Link
Type: Newsletter; *Frequency:* Quarterly; *Price:* Free for CVAA members
Profile: Up-to-date information about happenings in the association, health care system, & industry

Winnipeg Chapter
Winnipeg MB
Chief Officer(s):
Belinda Waylett, President
bwaylett@exchange.hsc.mb.ca

Canadian Vehicle Manufacturers' Association (CVMA) / Association canadienne des constructeurs de véhicules
#400, 170 Attwell Dr., Toronto ON M9W 5Z5
Tel: 416-364-9333; *Fax:* 416-367-3221
Toll-Free: 800-758-7122
info@cvma.ca
www.cvma.ca
Previous Name: Canadian Automobile Chamber of Commerce
Overview: A medium-sized national organization founded in 1926
Mission: To create a framework within which member companies work together to achieve shared industry objectives on a range of important issues such as consumer protection, the environment, and vehicle safety
Member of: Canadian Society of Association Executives; Canadian Tax Foundation; Society of Automotive Engineers.
Finances: *Funding Sources:* Membership fees
Staff Member(s): 5
Membership: 4; *Member Profile:* Chrysler Canada Inc.; Ford Motor Company of Canada, Limited; General Motors of Canada Limited; Navistar Canada, Inc.
Activities: Canadian Motor Vehicle Arbitration Plan; *Speaker Service:* Yes; *Library:* by appointment Not open to public
Chief Officer(s):
Mark A. Nantais, President

Canadian Venture Capital Association See Canada's Venture Capital & Private Equity Association

Canadian Veterinary Medical Association (CVMA) / Association canadienne des médecins vétérinaires (ACMV)
339 Booth St., Ottawa ON K1R 7K1
Tel: 613-236-1162; *Fax:* 613-236-9681
Toll-Free: 800-567-2862
admin@cvma-acmv.org
www.canadianveterinarians.net
www.facebook.com/CanadianVeterinaryMedicalAssociation
twitter.com/CanVetMedAssoc
www.youtube.com/user/CVMAACMV
Overview: A medium-sized national organization founded in 1948
Mission: To represent the interests of the veterinary profession in Canada; To commit to excellence within the profession & to the well-being of animals; To promote public awareness of the contribution of animals & veterinarians to society
Finances: *Annual Operating Budget:* $1.5 Million-$3 Million
Staff Member(s): 17
Membership: *Member Profile:* Graduates in veterinary medicine; *Committees:* AHT/VTP Accreditation Program; Animal Welfare; Business Management Advisory Group; Canadian Veterinary Reserve Advisory Board; Communications Advisory Group; Editorial; Environmental Advisory Group; Executive; National Examining Board; National Issues; Professional Development; Student Liaison Advisory Group; Students of the CVMA; Veterinary Stewardship Pharmaceutical Advisory Group; Veterinary Wellness Advisory Group
Activities: *Awareness Events:* Animal Health Week, Oct.
Chief Officer(s):
Jost Am Rhyn, Chief Executive Officer, 613-236-1162 Ext. 114
Tanya Frye, Manager, Communications & Public Relations, 613-236-1162 Ext. 128
tfrye@cvma-acmv.org
Awards:
• CVMA Industry Award
• CVMA President's Award
• CVMA Award
Established 1966; awarded annually to a veterinary student in the third year at each of the four Canadian veterinary colleges; the recipient is selected by his/her classmates on the basis of achievement & leadership in student affairs
• R.V.L. Walker Award
Established 1986; awarded to an undergraduate student in one of the four veterinary colleges in Canada who has made the greatest contribution in promoting student interest in the Association; the recipient should have demonstrated active interest in student & college affairs & have a satisfactory student record
• The Merck Veterinary Award
Established 1985; award made to veterinarian whose work in food animal production practice, clinical research or basic sciences has contributed to the advancement of food animal medicine & surgery; *Amount:* $1,000
• CVMA Practice of the Year Award
• The Small Animal Practitioner Award
Established 1987 to encourage progress in the field of small animal medicine & surgery; awarded to a veterinarian whose work in small animal practice, clinical research or basic sciences is judged to have contributed significantly to the advancement of small animal medicine, surgery, or the management of small animal practice, including the advancement of the public's knowledge of the responsibilities of pet ownership; $1,000 & a plaque awarded
• The CVMA Humane Award
Established 1986 to encourage care & well-being of animals; awarded to an individual (veterinarian or non-veterinarian) whose work is judged to have contributed significantly to the welfare & well-being of animals; $1,000 & a plaque awarded
Meetings/Conferences:
• 2018 Canadian Veterinary Medical Association Convention, July, 2018, Vancouver, BC
Scope: National
Publications:
• Canadian Journal of Veterinary Research
Type: Journal; *Frequency:* Quarterly
• Canadian Veterinary Journal
Type: Journal; *Frequency:* Monthly

Canadian Vintage Motorcycle Group (CVMG)
c/o Dale Prisley, Membership Secretary, 467 Thorn Ridge Cres., Amherstburg ON N9V 3X4
www.cvmg.ca
Overview: A medium-sized national organization founded in 1968
Mission: To promote the use, restoration & interest in older motorcycles & those of historic interest
Membership: 1,700; *Fees:* $40
Chief Officer(s):
Jim Briggs, President
president@cvmg.ca
Bill Hoar, Correspondence Secretary
secretary@cvmg.ca
Dale Prisley, Membership Secretary
membership@cvmg.ca

Canadian Vintners Association (CVA) / L'Association des vignerons du Canada
#200, 440 Laurier Ave. West, Ottawa ON K1R 7X6
Tel: 613-782-2283; *Fax:* 613-782-2239
info@canadianvintners.com
www.canadianvintners.com
www.facebook.com/CVAwine
twitter.com/cvawine
Previous Name: Canadian Wine Institute
Overview: A medium-sized national organization founded in 2001
Mission: To formulate & promote policies that will advance the interests & goals of the Canadian wine sector.
Member of: International Federation of Wine & Spirits; Alberta Liquor Industry RoundTable; World Wine Trade Group; Alcohol in Moderation
Affiliation(s): Wine Council of Ontario; British Columbia Wine Institute, Winery Association of Nova Scotia
Staff Member(s): 4
Membership: 60 corporate; *Member Profile:* Licenced wineries & regional winery associations
Chief Officer(s):
Dan Paszkowski, President & CEO

Canadian Viola Society
c/o Ann Frederking, 2030 Woodglen Cres., Ottawa ON K1J 6G4
www.viola.ca
Overview: A small national organization
Mission: To improve communication among violists & enthusiasts both in Canada & worldwide
Affiliation(s): International Viola Society
Membership: *Fees:* $24 student/emeritus; $40 active; *Member Profile:* Musicians, amateurs & professionals
Chief Officer(s):
Jutta Puchhammer-Sédillot, President
president@viola.ca

Canadian Vocational Association (CAV) / Association canadienne de la formation professionnelle (ACFP)
c/o Ms Jane Louks, PO Box 816, Ottawa ON K0A 2Z0
Tel: 613-838-3244; *Fax:* 613-838-5930
cva-acfp.org
www.linkedin.com/groups/Canadian-Vocational-Association-Association-canadienne-3603028?trk=my_groups-b-grp-v
twitter.com/CVA_ACFP
Overview: A small national organization founded in 1960
Mission: A non-profit organization to promote and foster education and training which leads to occupational competence.
Membership: *Member Profile:* Post-secondary and secondary educational institutions, the business community and government officials from across Canada as well as internationally.
Chief Officer(s):
Pierre Morin, President, 450-812-7510
pmforminc@gmail.com
Publications:
• CVA Journal
Type: Journal; *Frequency:* Quarterly

Canadian Volkssport Federation (CVF) / Fédération canadienne volkssport (FCV)
PO Box 2668, Stn. D, Ottawa ON K1P 5W7
Tel: 613-234-7333
cvffcv@rogers.com
www.walks.ca
Overview: A medium-sized national organization founded in 1987
Mission: To promote non-competitive participation in walking & other recreational activities for fun, fitness & friendship
Member of: International Federation of Popular Sports
Finances: *Annual Operating Budget:* Less than $50,000; *Funding Sources:* Sanctioning fees
Staff Member(s): 1; 150 volunteer(s)

Canadian Associations / Canadian Warmblood Horse Breeders Association (CWHBA)

Membership: 51 clubs; *Fees:* $150 individual; $50 affiliate; *Member Profile:* Mostly ages 35-70; *Committees:* Board of Directors; Executive
Activities: Walking; swimming; skating; skiing - all non-competitively; *Speaker Service:* Yes
Chief Officer(s):
Beverley Cattrall, President
bevpop@telus.net
Awards:
• IVV's Individual Achievement Awards Program
Publications:
• Volkssport Canada [a publication of the Canadian Volkssport Federation]

Canadian Warmblood Horse Breeders Association (CWHBA)
PO Box 21100, 2105 - 8th St. East, Saskatoon SK S7H 5N9
Tel: 306-373-6620; *Fax:* 306-374-0646
office@canadianwarmbloods.com
www.canadianwarmbloods.com
www.facebook.com/CanadianWarmblood
Overview: A small national organization founded in 1991
Mission: To further warmblood horse breeding in Canada through the provision of information to breeders & the maintenance of a uniform breeding program
Membership: *Member Profile:* Breeders, owners, & friends of warmblood horses in Canada
Activities: Maintaining the Stud Book of Canadian Warmblood horses; Providing stallion & provincial mare inspections; Uniting warmblood horse breeders; Offering educational opportunities; Promoting breed shows & exhibitions; Increasing public understanding of Canadian warmblood horses
Chief Officer(s):
Chris Gould, President
Chairman@canadianwarmbloods.com
Charmaine Bergman, Secretary-Treasurer
Secretary@canadianwarmbloods.com
Awards:
• CWHBA Year-end High-point Awards
• CWHBA Ogilvy Equestrian Summer Circuit Awards
• CWHBA Achievement Award
• CWHBA Lifetime Performance Award
Publications:
• Breeder's Digest
Type: Newsletter; *Accepts Advertising*
• Stallion Directory
Type: Directory; *Frequency:* Annually

Canadian Warplane Heritage (CWH)
9280 Airport Rd., Mount Hope ON L0R 1W0
Tel: 905-679-4183; *Fax:* 905-679-4186
Toll-Free: 877-347-3359
museum@warplane.com
www.warplane.com
www.facebook.com/CanadianWarplaneHeritageMuseum
twitter.com/CWHM
www.flickr.com/groups/canadianwarplaneheritage
Also Known As: Canada's Flying Museum
Overview: A medium-sized national charitable organization founded in 1971
Mission: To acquire, document, preserve & maintain a complete collection of aircraft that were flown by Canadians & the Canadian military from the beginning of WWII to the present; To preserve the artifacts, books, periodicals & manuals relating to this mandate
Finances: *Annual Operating Budget:* $3 Million-$5 Million; *Funding Sources:* Membership fees; Grants; Donations
Staff Member(s): 20; 300 volunteer(s)
Membership: 33,000; *Fees:* $125 adult; $100 senior; $30 student; $175 family; *Member Profile:* Interest in Canadian aviation/history
Activities: *Awareness Events:* Remembrance Day; *Internships:* Yes; *Speaker Service:* Yes; *Library:* by appointment
Chief Officer(s):
Pamela Rickards, Vice President of Operations, 905-679-4183 Ext. 230
pam@warplane.com
Al Mickeloff, Manager, Marketing, 905-679-4183 Ext. 233
amickeloff@warplane.com

Canadian Water & Wastewater Association (CWWA) / Association canadienne des eaux potables et usées (ACEPU)
#11, 1010 Polytek St., Ottawa ON K1J 9H9
Tel: 613-747-0524; *Fax:* 613-747-0523
admin@cwwa.ca
www.cwwa.ca
www.linkedin.com/company/canadian-water-and-wastewater-association
www.facebook.com/CanadianWaterAndWastewaterAssociation
twitter.com/CWWACEPU
Overview: A medium-sized national organization founded in 1986
Mission: To represent the common interests of Canadian municipal water & wastewater systems to federal & interprovincial bodies; To serve as the voice of the water & wastewater services sector in Canada
Member of: American Water Works Association; Canadian Water Network
Finances: *Annual Operating Budget:* $500,000-$1.5 Million; *Funding Sources:* Membership; Events; Advertisement sales
Staff Member(s): 6; 100 volunteer(s)
Membership: 400 corporate; *Fees:* Schedule available; *Member Profile:* Owners or operators of municipal infrastructure or services; Individuals from the private sector & academics; Federal, provincial, or territorial government departments or agencies; *Committees:* Biosolids; Climate Change; Drinking Water Quality; Energy & Water Efficiency; Security & Emergency Management; Wastewater & Stormwater
Activities: Monitoring policies, legislation & standards; Liaising with federal & interprovincial organizations; Hosting workshops; Facilitating networking opportunities; Increasing & improving public awareness; Cooperating with regional water & wastewater associations; Organizing national conferences; *Awareness Events:* Window on Ottawa, June
Chief Officer(s):
Robert Haller, Executive Director
rhaller@cwwa.ca
Louisa Spina, Coordinator, Accounts & Membership
lspina@cwwa.ca
Anita Wilson, Coordinator, Event & Sponsorship
awilson@cwwa.ca
Adrian Toth, Director, Government Relations
atoth@cwwa.ca
Kara Parisien, Manager, Communication
kparisien@cwwa.ca
Awards:
• Steve Bonk Scholarship
To provide educational assistance to persons embarking on careers associated with municipal water supply or wastewater
Eligibility: University students studying water or wastewater
Deadline: June 1; *Amount:* $500
• Utility Excellence Awards
Awards for utility programs & initiatives in the areas of community outreach & risk taking
Meetings/Conferences:
• Canadian Water & Wastewater Association 2018 National Conference, 2018
Scope: National
Description: An exchange of news & views from Canadian utility conservation specialists
Publications:
• Canadian Municipal Water News & Review / Journal et faits sur l'eau municipale canadienne
Type: Magazine; *Frequency:* Semiannually; *Accepts Advertising*; *Editor:* Kara Parisien
Profile: National & international news & events
• CWWA [Canadian Water & Wastewater Association] Membership Directory
Type: Directory; *Accepts Advertising*
Profile: Directory acts as association information as well as a buyers' guide
• CWWA [Canadian Water & Wastewater Association] Bulletin
Type: Newsletter; *Frequency:* 10 pa; *Accepts Advertising*; *Editor:* Kara Parisien
Profile: National information on water & wastewater developments, for CWWA members
• CWWA Members' Briefing Book: Current National Issues & Topics Concerning Water & Wastewater Management in Canada
Frequency: Quarterly
Profile: Briefing notes on current management topics that are national in nature, to assist managers & operators
• Directory of Sources of Contaminants Entering Municipal Sewer Systems
Type: Directory
Profile: Aid in identifying industrial, commercial, & institutional sources of contaminants entering municipal sewage treatment plants
• Guideline on Sampling, Handling, Transporting & Analyzing Legal Wastewater Samples
• Meters Made Easy: A Guide to the Economic Appraisal of Alternative Metering Investment Strategies
Type: Guidebook
Profile: A tool to assist system owners & operators determine whether the introduction of meters will produce long-term savings intheir community
• Municipal Water & Wastewater Rate Manual
Type: Manual
Profile: New & alternative approaches to traditional & current rate setting methods
• Municipal Water & Wastewater Rates Primer
Type: Monograph
Profile: An overview of topics on rate setting
• National Water Works Operator Training Manuals
Type: Manual
• Survey on Chloramine in Drinking Water Disinfection
• Water Safety Plans for Municipal Drinking Water Systems
Profile: Hazard Analysis & Critical Control Points (HACCP) plan for the source, treatment, & distribution of drinking water in Canada

Canadian Water Network (CWN) / Réseau canadien de l'eau
University of Waterloo, 200 University Ave. West, Waterloo ON N2L 3G1
Tel: 519-888-4567; *Fax:* 519-883-7574
info@cwn-rce.ca
www.cwn-rce.ca
www.linkedin.com/company/canadian-water-network
www.facebook.com/CanadianWaterNetwork
twitter.com/CdnWaterNetwork
Overview: A medium-sized national organization founded in 2001
Mission: To create a national partnership in innovation that promotes environmentally responsible stewardship & opportunities with respect to Canada's water resources resulting in sustained prosperity & improved quality of life for Canadians.
Member of: Networks of Centres of Excellence
Finances: *Annual Operating Budget:* $3 Million-$5 Million
Staff Member(s): 8
Membership: 48 industrial, 65 government, 120 researchers, 200 students; *Fees:* None
Activities: Research funding, student development, national networking; *Internships:* Yes
Chief Officer(s):
Bernadette Conant, Executive Director, 519-888-4567
bconant@cwn-rce.ca
Mark Servos, Scientific Director, 519-888-4567 Ext. 36034
mservos@uwaterloo.ca

Canadian Water Quality Association (CWQA)
#504, 295 The West Mall, Toronto ON M9C 4Z4
Tel: 416-695-3068; *Fax:* 416-695-2945
Toll-Free: 866-383-7617
info@cwqa.com
www.cwqa.com
www.linkedin.com/groups/Canadian-Water-Quality-Association-3948494
twitter.com/cwqanews
Overview: A medium-sized national organization founded in 1956
Mission: To train, educate & certify water quality professionals; To serve as a unified & credible voice to members, government & the public; To be the resource for industry information & statistics
Staff Member(s): 5
Membership: 106 dealers/distributors + 16 manufacturers/suppliers + 10 associates; *Fees:* Schedule available; *Member Profile:* Companies that sell, service, supply, manufacture or distribute water treatment systems for residential, commerical or small system applications
Chief Officer(s):
Kevin Wong, Executive Director, 416-695-3068 Ext. 311
k.wong@cwqa.com
Aysha Muzaffar, Program Manager, 416-695-3068 Ext. 317
a.muzaffar@cwqa.com
Meetings/Conferences:
• Canadian Water Quality Association 2018 Annual General Meeting, 2018
Scope: National
Publications:
• Canadian Water Quality Association Membership Directory
Type: Directory
Profile: A listing of members by their head office or main facility, for use by Canadian Water Quality Association members only

• Communiqué [a publication of the Canadian Water Quality Association]
Frequency: 11 pa

Canadian Water Resources Association (CWRA) / Association canadienne des ressources hydriques (ACRH)
1401 - 14th St. North, Lethbridge AB T1H 2W6
Tel: 403-317-0017
services@aic.ca
www.cwra.org
www.linkedin.com/groups/CWRA-2294668
twitter.com/CWRA_Flows
Overview: A large national charitable organization founded in 1947
Mission: To encourage recognition of the high priority & value of water
Affiliation(s): Canadian Water & Wasterwater Association; International Water Resources Association; American Water Resources Association; British Hydological Society; American Institute of Hydrology
Finances: *Annual Operating Budget:* $100,000-$250,000; *Funding Sources:* Membership dues; Donations
Staff Member(s): 3; 50 volunteer(s)
Membership: 1,000; *Fees:* $5 - $1,750; *Member Profile:* Individuals & organizations interested in the management of Canada's water resources, including private & public sector water resource managers, administrators, scientists, academics, students & users; *Committees:* Finance; Publications; Fundraising; Scholarship; Communications; Website
Activities: Increasing awareness & understanding of Canada's water resources; Providing a forum for the exchange of information; Participating with appropriate agencies in international water management activities; *Internships:* Yes; *Speaker Service:* Yes
Chief Officer(s):
Dave Murray, President
Rick Ross, Executive Director
Awards:
• Ken Thompson Scholarship
; *Amount:* $2,000
• Dillon Scholarship
; *Amount:* $5,000
• The Hoskin Scientific Award
• Bill Stolte Student Paper Award
Awarded annually to the best student paper on water resources
• CWRA National Distinguished Achievement Award
Awarded to a CWRA member or past member who has provided distinguished service to or in the Canadian water resource community
Meetings/Conferences:
• Canadian Water Resources Association 2018 Conference, May, 2018, Victoria, BC
Scope: National
Description: Theme: "Our Common Water Future: Building Resilience Through Innovation"
Contact Information: URL: conference.cwra.org
Publications:
• Canadian Water Resources Journal
Type: Journal; *Frequency:* Quarterly; *Editor:* Diana M. Allen & James M. Buttle; *ISSN:* 0701-1784
Profile: Research articles, technical notes, & review papers
• CWRA [Canadian Water Resources Association] Water News
Type: Newsletter; *Frequency:* Quarterly; *Editor:* F.A. (Rick) Ross
Profile: National & branch activities, international water resource information, a technical supplement, & a profile article

Canadian Water Ski Association *See* Water Ski & Wakeboard Canada

Canadian Welding Bureau (CWB)
8260 Parkhill Dr., Milton ON L9T 5V7
Fax: 905-542-1318
Toll-Free: 800-844-6790
info@cwbgroup.org
www.cwbgroup.org
www.facebook.com/134949822909
twitter.com/cwbgroupandcwa
www.youtube.com/user/cwbgroup
Overview: A medium-sized national organization founded in 1947
Mission: To administrator certification programs for CSA Standards W47.1, W47.2, W186, W178.1 & W48 series; to provide support for welding-based programs in schools, education institutions, welding professionals & companies employing welding technology.
Membership: 7,600 clients
Activities: *Speaker Service:* Yes; *Library:* Gooderham Centre for Industrial Learning
Chief Officer(s):
Douglas Luciano, President
Alberta Region
#206, 2528 Ellwood Dr., Edmonton AB T6X 0A9
Toll-Free: 800-844-6790
info@cwbgroup.org
Chief Officer(s):
Bill Boyko, Regional Manager, Western Operations
Atlantic Region
#304, 73 Tacoma Dr., Dartmouth NS B2W 3Y6
Toll-Free: 800-844-6790
info@cwbgroup.org
Chief Officer(s):
Yvon Sénéchal, Regional Manager, Eastern Operations
Ontario Region
8260 Parkhill Dr., Milton ON L9T 5V7
Toll-Free: 800-844-6790
info@cwbgroup.org
Chief Officer(s):
Luis Romero, Regional Manager, Ontario
Québec Region
4321, Autoroute des Laurentides, Laval QC H7L 5W5
Toll-Free: 800-844-6790
info@cwbgroup.org
Chief Officer(s):
Yvon Sénéchal, Regional Manager, Eastern Operations
Western Region
#203, 1555 St. James St., Winnipeg MB R3H 1B5
Toll-Free: 800-844-6790
info@cwbgroup.org
Chief Officer(s):
Darcy Yantz, Regional Manager, Western Operations

Canadian Welfare Council *See* Canadian Council on Social Development

Canadian Well Logging Society (CWLS)
Scotia Centre, #2200, 700 - 2nd St. SW, Calgary AB T2P 2W1
Tel: 403-269-9366; *Fax:* 403-269-2787
www.cwls.org
www.linkedin.com/groups/4852822
Overview: A medium-sized national organization founded in 1957
Mission: To provide resources & support for those interested in log analysis & petrophysics
Finances: *Annual Operating Budget:* Less than $50,000; *Funding Sources:* Membership fees; corporate sponsors
Membership: 600; *Fees:* $40; *Member Profile:* Oil industry petrophysical interests
Chief Officer(s):
Manuel Aboud, President
maboud@slb.com
Publications:
• CWLS [Canadian Well Logging Society] Journal
Type: Journal; *Frequency:* Biennially; *Price:* Free with CWLS membership
Profile: Formal papers for people interested in formation evaluation
• CWLS [Canadian Well Logging Society] Annual Report
Type: Yearbook; *Frequency:* Annually; *Price:* Free with Canadian Well Logging Society membership
• InSite [a publication of the Canadian Well Logging Society]
Type: Magazine; *Frequency:* Quarterly; *Accepts Advertising*; *Editor:* Doug Kozak; Manuel Aboud; *Price:* Free with CWLS membership
Profile: Short articles, & upcoming events to inform CWLS members

Canadian Welsh Black Cattle Society (CWBCS) / Société Canadienne des bovins Welsh Black
c/o Canadian Livestock Records Corporation, 2417 Holly Lane, Ottawa ON K1V 0M7
Tel: 613-731-7110; *Fax:* 613-731-0704
www.clrc.ca/welshblack.shtml
Overview: A small national organization founded in 1971
Membership: *Fees:* $25; $150 lifetime; *Committees:* Bulletin; Website; Advertising & Promotions
Activities: Providing information about the Canadian Welsh black cattle breed
Chief Officer(s):
Randy Scott, President, 403-854-2135, Fax: 403-854-2135
Randy Kaiser, Vice-President
Arlin Strohschein, Secretary-Treasurer, 403-442-4372

Publications:
• Breeders Directory
Type: Directory
Profile: Contact information for breeders of Canadian Welsh black cattle
• The Welsh Black Bulletin
Type: Newsletter; *Accepts Advertising*; *Editor:* Randy Scott

Canadian Western Agribition Association (CWA)
PO Box 3535, Regina SK S4P 3J8
Tel: 306-565-0565; *Fax:* 306-757-9963
cwaquestions@agribition.com
www.agribition.com
www.facebook.com/Agribition
twitter.com/agribition
www.instagram.com/agribition
Overview: A medium-sized local organization founded in 1971
Mission: To create an atmosphere to promote Canadian agricultural products & their development; To host the annual Canadian Western Agribition to increase interest in agriculture
Finances: *Funding Sources:* Sponsorships
Membership: *Fees:* $100 corporate; $25 friends
Activities: Providing educational information to the agricultural industry & the public; Encouraging competition; Promoting urban-rural relations; *Awareness Events:* Canadian Western Agribition, November
Chief Officer(s):
Chris Lane, CEO, 306-924-9600
clane@agribition.com
Brady Kapovic, Manager, Business Development, 306-631-2854
sponsorship@agribition.com
Sarah Novak, Manager, Marketing & Brand, 306-924-9781
snovak@agribition.com
Corey Sentes, Manager, Finance, 306-924-9583
csentes@agribition.com
Publications:
• Agribition Insider
Type: Newsletter; *Frequency:* 3 pa
Profile: Agribition programs, shows, sponsors, awards, & livestock

Canadian Wheelchair Basketball Association (CWBA) / Association canadienne de basketball en fauteuil roulant (ACBFR)
#8, 6 Antares Dr., Phase 1, Ottawa ON K2E 8A9
Tel: 613-260-1296; *Fax:* 613-260-1456
Toll-Free: 877-843-2922
info@wheelchairbasketball.ca
www.wheelchairbasketball.ca
www.facebook.com/wheelchairbasketball
twitter.com/WCBballCanada
www.youtube.com/WheelchairBball
Also Known As: Wheelchair Basketball Canada
Overview: A medium-sized national charitable organization founded in 1994
Mission: To act as the governing body for wheelchair basketball in Canada
Member of: Canadian Paralympic Committee; International Wheelchair Basketball Federation
Affiliation(s): Canada Basketball
Staff Member(s): 11
Membership: 2,500
Chief Officer(s):
Wendy Gittens, Executive Director
wgittens@wheelchairbasketball.ca
Jeff Dunbrack, Director, High Performance
jdunbrack@wheelchairbasketball.ca
Courtney Pollock, Manager, Communications & Marketing
cpollock@wheelchairbasketball.ca
Ryan Lauzon, Coordinator, Programs
rlauzon@wheelchairbasketball.ca
Lindsay Crone, Coordinator, Communications
lcrone@wheelchairbasketball.ca
Publications:
• Around The Rim [a publication of the Canadian Wheelchair Basketball Association]
Type: Newsletter
• CWBA [Canadian Wheelchair Basketball Association] Annual Report
Type: Yearbook; *Frequency:* Annually

Canadian Wheelchair Sports Association (CWSA) / Association canadienne des sports en fauteuil roulant (ACSFR)
#108, 2255 St. Laurent Blvd., Ottawa ON K1G 4K3

Canadian Associations / Canadian Wild Turkey Federation (CWTF)

Tel: 613-523-0004; *Fax:* 613-523-0149
info@cwsa.ca
www.cwsa.ca
www.facebook.com/wheelchairrugbycanada
twitter.com/wcrugbycanada
www.youtube.com/wheelsportscanada
Overview: A large national charitable organization founded in 1967
Mission: To promote excellence & develop opportunities for Canadians in wheelchair sport
Affiliation(s): International Stoke Mandeville Wheelchair Sports Federation
Finances: *Funding Sources:* Federal government; Independent corporations; General public; Man in Motion Foundation
Staff Member(s): 7
Membership: *Member Profile:* Wheelchair athletes
Activities: Offering high performance sport programs for rugby; Engaging in advocacy activities
Chief Officer(s):
Donald Royer, President
Cathy Cadieux, Executive Director
ccadieux@cwsa.ca
Duncan Campbell, Director, National Development, 604-333-3539, Fax: 604-333-3450
duncancampbell@cwsa.ca
Andy Van Neutegem, Director, High Performance, Fax: 250-220-2501
andy@cwsa.ca
Nancy Wong, Program Coordinator, 604-333-3539, Fax: 604-333-3450
nancywong@cwsa.ca
Marnie McRoberts, Lead Medical Officer, 416-529-7731
marnie@cwsa.ca

Canadian Wholesale Drug Association *See* Canadian Association for Pharmacy Distribution Management

Canadian Wild Turkey Federation (CWTF)
RR#1, 215 Detroit Line, Wheatley ON N0P 2P0
Tel: 902-497-1611
www.cwtf.ca
www.facebook.com/canadianwildturkeyfederation
twitter.com/cwtffederation
www.instagram.com/canadianwildturkey
Overview: A medium-sized national organization
Mission: To preserve, restore, & manage wild turkeys as well as other wildlife & habitat in Canada; To collaborate with government agencies, organizations, & the public to create wildlife habitat conservation & education projects; To promote responsible fishing & hunting, & other activities related to wildlife & the outdoors
Membership: *Fees:* $35; $10 youth; $250 sponsor
Activities: Supporting & promoting educational & social events
Chief Officer(s):
Steve Nicholson, Director, Operations
snicholson@cwtf.ca
Publications:
• Canadian Strutter
Type: Magazine
Profile: Magazine for CWTF members

Canadian Wildflower Society *See* North American Native Plant Society

Canadian Wildlife Federation (CWF) / Fédération canadienne de la faune
350 Michael Cowpland Dr., Ottawa ON K2M 2W1
Tel: 613-599-9594; *Fax:* 613-599-4428
Toll-Free: 800-563-9453
info@cwf-fcf.org
www.cwf-fcf.org
ca.linkedin.com/company/canadian-wildlife-federation
www.facebook.com/CanadianWildlifeFederation
twitter.com/CWF_FCF
www.youtube.com/user/CanadianWildlifeFed
Overview: A large national charitable organization founded in 1961
Mission: To promote the conservation of fish & wildlife, wildlife habitat & quality aquatic environments; To foster an understanding of natural processes; To ensure adequate stocks of wildlife for the use & enjoyment of all Canadians; To sponsor research; To cooperate with legislators, government & non-government agencies in achieving conservation objectives
Member of: World Conservation Union
Finances: *Funding Sources:* Membership fees; Sales of merchandise; Donations
Membership: 300,000; *Fees:* $25; *Committees:* Affiliate; Associate Member; Audit; Awards; Constitution; Credentials; Energy; Environment; Fisheries; Forestry; Native Affairs; Nominating; Parks; Resolutions; Wildlife
Activities: Offering educational programs; Engaging in advocacy activities concerning national & international conservation & environmental issues; *Awareness Events:* National Wildlife Week, April; Canadian Rivers Day, June; *Speaker Service:* Yes; *Rents Mailing List:* Yes; *Library:* Open to public by appointment
Chief Officer(s):
Bates Rick, Acting Executive Vice-President & CEO
Awards:
• Conservation Awards Program
Presented annually to Canadian conservationists for their efforts in service, volunteerism, or advocacy
Publications:
• Canadian Wildlife [a publication of the Canadian Wildlife Federation]
Type: Magazine; *Frequency:* Bimonthly
Profile: Stories about Canadian & international wildlife, plus CWF news & reports, for young adults & adults
• Wild [a publication of the Canadian Wildlife Federation]
Type: Magazine; *Frequency:* 8 pa
Profile: Educational information & games, for children between the ages of 6 & 12

Canadian Wind Energy Association (CanWEA) / Association canadienne d'énergie éolienne
#710, 1600 Carling Ave., Ottawa ON K1Z 1G3
Tel: 613-234-8716; *Fax:* 613-234-5642
Toll-Free: 800-922-6932
info@canwea.ca
www.canwea.ca
www.linkedin.com/company/canadian-wind-energy-association
www.facebook.com/canadianwindenergyassociation
twitter.com/canwindenergy
www.youtube.com/canwea
Overview: A medium-sized national organization founded in 1984
Mission: To promote the social, economic, & environmental benefits of wind energy in Canada; To encourage the appropriate development & application of wind energy; To create suitable environmental policy
Finances: *Funding Sources:* Membership fees; Conference & workshop fees
Membership: 420; *Fees:* $100 individual; $550 associate; $2,900-$60,000 corporate; *Member Profile:* Organizations & individuals who are involved in the development & application of wind energy technology, products & services in Canada
Activities: Providing information about wind energy; Offering networking opportunities for all stakeholders; Facilitating research; Forming strategic alliances; *Library:* Canadian Wind Energy Association Library; by appointment
Chief Officer(s):
Cory Basil, Chair
Rochelle Pancoast, Vice-Chair
Peter Clibbon, Secretary
Colin Edwards, Treasurer
Awards:
• Individual Leadership Award
Awarded to an individual who has significantly advanced the wind energy industry in Canada.
• Group Leadership Award
Awarded to the government, corporation or non-profit organization that has contributed significantly to the advancement of wind energy in Canada.
• R.J. Templin Award
Awarded to any individual or organization who has undertaken scientific, technical, engineering or policy work that has significantly advanced the wind energy industry in Canada.
• Friend of Wind Award
Awarded in recognition of outstanding contributions made by individuals or groups in advancing awareness of the benefits of wind energy at the community level.
• The Matt Holder Community Connection Award
Awarded to an organization or individual who embodies the mandate of responsible development through a commitment to understand and build meaningful relationships with host communities.
• Wind Energy Project Award
Awarded to an organization or individual who embodies the mandate of responsible development through a commitment to understand and build meaningful relationships with host communities.
Meetings/Conferences:
• Canadian Wind Energy Association (CanWEA) 34th Annual Conference and Exhibition, October, 2018, BMO Centre, Calgary, AB
Scope: National
Description: To discuss the opportunities and latest developments in the wind energy industry.
Contact Information: www.windenergyevent.ca
Publications:
• CanWEA [Canadian Wind Energy Association] Members Directory
Type: Directory
Profile: Contact information & a profile of each CanWEA member
• WindLink [a publication of the Canadian Wind Energy Association]
Type: Newsletter; *Frequency:* Semimonthly
Profile: Issues & events that affect the Canadian wind energy for CanWEA members, policymakers, & the public
• WindSight [a publication of the Canadian Wind Energy Association]
Type: Magazine; *Frequency:* Quarterly
Profile: Detailed articles on Canadian wind energy projects & policy

Canadian Window & Door Manufacturers Association *See* Fenestration Canada

Canadian Wine Institute *See* Canadian Vintners Association

Canadian Wire Service Guild *See* Canadian Media Guild

Canadian Wireless Telecommunications Association (CWTA) / Association canadienne des télécommunications sans fil (ACTS)
#300, 80 Elgin St., Ottawa ON K1P 6R2
Tel: 613-233-4888; *Fax:* 613-233-2032
info@cwta.ca
www.cwta.ca
twitter.com/CWTAwireless
Previous Name: Radiocomm Association of Canada
Overview: A medium-sized national licensing charitable organization founded in 1970
Mission: The authority on wireless issues, trends & developments in Canada; represents cellular, PCS, messaging, mobile radio, fixed wireless & mobile satellite service providers as well as companies that develop & produce products & services for the industry.
Finances: *Funding Sources:* Membership fees; seminars; conferences; publications
Staff Member(s): 18
Membership: 182; *Fees:* Schedule available; *Committees:* 5G Canada Council; Government Relations & Regulatory Affairs Committee; Handset Security Committee; Health Committee; Mobile Content Council; Public Safety Committee; Recycling Committee; Research Working Group; SMS Short Code Council; Structure, Tower & Antenna Council (STAC); Taxation Committee; Wireless Accessibility Committee; Wireless Number Portability Council
Activities: *Rents Mailing List:* Yes
Chief Officer(s):
Robert Ghiz, President & CEO
Ursula Grant, Director, Industry Affairs, 613-233-4888 Ext. 208
ugrant@cwta.ca
Chris Jones, Director, Regulatory Affairs, Policy & Research, 613-233-4888 Ext. 213
cjones@cwta.ca

Canadian Women for Women in Afghanistan
PO Box 86016, Stn. Marda Loop, Calgary AB T2T 6B7
Tel: 403-244-5625
info@cw4wafghan.ca
www.cw4wafghan.ca
www.facebook.com/cw4wafghan
twitter.com/CW4WAfghan
Overview: A small national organization founded in 1996
Mission: CWWA is a volunteer, not-for-profit organization committed to supporting the empowerment of Afghan women and girls, with a network of chapters across Canada. It is registered charity, BN: 887718203RR0001.
Activities: Breaking Bread, a do-it-yourself potluck fundraiser, breakingbread@cw4wafghan.ca
Chief Officer(s):
Madeliene Tarasick, President
President@CW4WAfghan.ca
Janice Eisenhauer, Executive Director
ExecutiveDirector@CW4WAfghan.ca

Canadian Women in Communications (CWC) / Association canadienne des femmes en communication (AFC)
#300, 116 Lisgar St., Ottawa ON K2P 0C2
Tel: 613-706-0607; Fax: 613-706-0612
Toll-Free: 800-361-2978
cwcafc@cwc-afc.com
www.cwc-afc.com
Previous Name: Canadian Women in Radio & Television
Overview: A medium-sized national organization founded in 1991
Mission: To advance the role of women in the communications sector
Member of: The International Alliance for Women
Finances: Annual Operating Budget: $500,000-$1.5 Million; Funding Sources: Corporate
Staff Member(s): 5; 150 volunteer(s)
Membership: 1,500; Fees: $132.50 professional; $42.40 student; $99.38 Diamond; $112.63 Platinum; $119.25 Gold; Committees: Women on Boards; Strategic Review; Nominations & Governance; Communications & Membership; Chapter Liaison; Jeanne Sauvé; Annual Awards; Treasurer; Fundraising
Activities: Hosting an annual awards gala & chapter events
Chief Officer(s):
Joanne Stanley, Executive Director, 613-706-0607 Ext. 102
jstanley@cwc-afc.com
Awards:
• CWC Annual Awards
• Jeanne Sauvé Professional Development Program
• Career Accelerator Programs
• CWC/CBC Transformer Award

Canadian Women in Radio & Television See Canadian Women in Communications

Canadian Women Voters Congress
303 - 15041 Prospect Ave., White Rock BC V4B 2B5
info@womenvoters.ca
www.womenvoters.ca
www.facebook.com/womenvoters
twitter.com/womenvotersca
Previous Name: Congress of Canadian Women-British Columbia
Overview: A small provincial charitable organization
Mission: To ensure women have equal opportunities in the elctoral process
Activities: Operating the Women's Campaign School in Vancouver, British Columbia; holding workshops, talks & events
Chief Officer(s):
Paula Larson, Administrator

Canadian Women's Foundation / Fondation canadienne des femmes
#504, 133 Richmond St. West, Toronto ON M5H 2L3
Tel: 416-365-1444; Fax: 416-365-1745
Toll-Free: 866-293-4483; TTY: 416-365-1732
info@canadianwomen.org
www.canadianwomen.org
www.linkedin.com/company/the-canadian-women%27s-foundation
www.facebook.com/CanadianWomensFoundation
www.twitter.com/cdnwomenfdn
www.youtube.com/user/CanadianWomenFdn
Overview: A medium-sized national organization founded in 1989
Mission: To raise money to research, fund & share the best approaches to ending violence against women, to transition low-income women out of poverty
Finances: Annual Operating Budget: Less than $50,000
Staff Member(s): 24; 500 volunteer(s)
Activities: Violence prevention grants; CWF Economic Development Fund; Girls Program
Chief Officer(s):
Sheherazade Hirji, President & CEO
Awards:
• Violence Prevention grants
• Economic Development grants
• Girls' Fund grants
Publications:
• CWF [Canadian Women's Foundation] Annual Report
Type: Yearbook; Frequency: Annually
• Initiatives [a publicaton of the Canadian Women's Foundation]
Type: Newsletter
Profile: CWF information
• SHE [Canadian Women's Foundation] Magazine
Type: Magazine; Frequency: Quarterly

Calgary Office
#503, 5920 Macleod Trail SW, Calgary AB T2H 0K2
Tel: 403-984-2523

Canadian Women's Studies Association / L'association canadienne des études sur les femmes (CWSA / ACÉF) See Women's & Gender Studies et Recherches Féministes

Canadian Wood Council (CWC) / Conseil canadien du bois (CCB)
#400, 99 Bank St., Ottawa ON K1P 6B9
Tel: 613-747-5544; Fax: 613-747-6264
www.cwc.ca
twitter.com/CdnWoodFacts
Overview: A large national organization founded in 1959
Mission: To represent Canadian manufacturers of wood products; To ensure market access for wood products; To communicate technical information; To organize educational programs for students & construction professionals
Membership: 15 corporate; Fees: Schedule available; Member Profile: Manufacturers of Canadian wood products used in construction; Committees: Management: Audit, Finance & Risk Management; Membership; HR; Nominating. Operations: U.S. Affairs; Lumber Properties Steering Committee; Market Development; Fire & Structural Design; Canadian Wood Industries Forum on Market Access; Canadian Sustainable Building Partnership. Other: WoodWORKS!; Advisory Groups; Chairmen's Club
Activities: Awareness Events: Annual Wood WORKS! Awards Gala; Wood Solutions Fairs; Library: by appointment
Chief Officer(s):
Michael Giroux, President
Wanda Thompson, Chief Financial Officer
Natalie Tarini, Manager, Communications
Awards:
• Wood Design & Building Awards
Contact: Iona Lazea & Natalie Tarini, Coordinators, Phone: 613-747-5544, ext. 225/227
• WoodWORKS! Awards Program
Publications:
• Canadian Wood Council Technical Publications
Profile: Topics include the Wood Design Manual, Span Books, & Engineering Guides
• Wood Design & Building [a publication of the Canadian Wood Council]
Type: Magazine; Frequency: Quarterly; Accepts Advertising; Editor: Theresa Rogers; ISSN: 1206-677X; Price: $19.95
Profile: An information resource about wood use in architecture & construction
• Wood Design & Building Awards Book [a publication of the Canadian Wood Council]
Type: Yearbook; Frequency: Annually; Price: $39.95
Profile: Compilation of best projects submitted to the Wood Design Awards program

Canadian Wood Pallet & Container Association (CWPCA) / Association canadienne des manufacturiers de palettes et contenants (ACMPC)
#11, 1884 Merivale Rd., Ottawa ON K2G 1E6
Tel: 613-521-6468; Fax: 613-521-1835
Toll-Free: 877-224-3555
info@canadianpallets.com
www.canadianpallets.com
twitter.com/canadianpallets
Overview: A small national organization founded in 1967
Mission: To promote the general welfare of the wooden pallet & container manufacturing industry; to improve services directly or otherwise; to cooperate with officers of government & business in any program considered essential to the national welfare or economy; to engage in any other lawful activities & enjoy powers, rights & privileges granted or conferred upon associations of a similar nature.
Member of: Partners in Protection
Affiliation(s): National Wooden Pallet & Container Association; Western Pallet Association
Finances: Annual Operating Budget: $500,000-$1.5 Million
Staff Member(s): 4
Membership: 550; Fees: $595 manufacturer; $525 associate/supplier; Member Profile: Active manufacturers & suppliers within wood pallet & container industry
Activities: Speaker Service: Yes; Library: Open to public
Chief Officer(s):
Brian Isard, General Manager
brian.isard@canadianpallets.com
Scott Geffros, Assistant General Manager
scott.geffros@canadianpallets.com

Lori Devlin, Office Manager
lori.devlin@canadianpallets.com
Stephanie Poirier, Program Coordinator, CWPCP
stephanie.poirier@woodpackaging.ca
Publications:
• Bark Bits [a publication of the Canadian Wood Pallet & Container Association]
Type: Newsletter; Frequency: Monthly; Accepts Advertising

Canadian Wood Preservers Bureau See Wood Preservation Canada

Canadian Wood Truss Association (CWTA) / Association canadienne des fabricants de fermes de bois
527 Queensland Circle SE, Calgary AB T2J 4P7
Tel: 403-271-0520; Fax: 403-271-0520
cwta@telus.net
www.cwta.net
Overview: A small national organization founded in 1998
Mission: To act as the voice of the truss manufacturing industry; To develop & maintain uniform performance standards; To promote high standards of excellence for structural wood component manufacturers & distributors
Member of: Canadian Wood Council
Finances: Annual Operating Budget: Less than $50,000; Funding Sources: Membership fees
Staff Member(s): 1
Membership: 15; Member Profile: Metal plate connected wood truss manufacturers; Structural wood component manufacturers
Activities: Providing educational activities; Fostering training for members; Representing the industry; Internships: Yes
Chief Officer(s):
Daniel Després, President, 506-826-2154
ddespres@leonchouinard.com
Mike Fox, Vice-President, 613-544-8952
mark@terranovatruss.com
Publications:
• CWTA [Canadian Wood Truss Association] Training Manual
Type: Manual
• Truss Design Procedures & Specifications [a publication of the Canadian Wood Truss Association]
Profile: Outlines procedures & specifications for light metal plate connected wood trusses

The Canadian Woodlands Forum (CWF) / Forum canadien des opérations forestières
20 Coupar Terrace, Truro NS B2N 5L3
Tel: 902-897-6961; Fax: 902-897-6976
info@cwfcof.org
www.cwfcof.org
Overview: A medium-sized national organization founded in 1995
Mission: To support technology transfer & information sharing activities focusing on improving the competitiveness of forest operations
Finances: Funding Sources: Membership dues
Staff Member(s): 2
Membership: Fees: Schedule available
Chief Officer(s):
Peter Robichaud, Executive Director, 902-899-6420
probichaud@cwfcof.org

Sudbury
PO Box 22034, Sudbury ON P3A 3T0
Tel: 705-671-2444; Fax: 705-671-2446
Toll-Free: 877-671-2444

Canadian Worker Co-operative Federation (CWCF) / Fédération canadienne des coopératives de travail
#104, 402 - 30 Ave. NE, Calgary AB T2E 2E3
Tel: 403-276-8250; Fax: 403-338-0226
www.canadianworker.coop
www.facebook.com/canadianworkercoop
twitter.com/workercoop
www.youtube.com/channel/UCTpJxRLUgdmz7hVBodlLPQA
Overview: A medium-sized national organization founded in 1991
Mission: To be a growing & cohesive network of democratically-operated worker co-ops; To support & sustain the development of healthy local economies, based on co-operative values; To support the development of new worker co-opers; To represent the Canadian worker co-op movement in Canada & abroad
Member of: Co-operatives & Mutuals Canada (CMC); International Organisation of Industrial & Service Cooperatives (CICOPA)

Canadian Associations / Canadian Writers' Foundation Inc. (CWF) / La Fondation des écrivains canadiens inc.

Finances: Funding Sources: Membership dues; Fees for service contracts; Donations from supporting organizations
Staff Member(s): 4
Membership: Fees: $500 associate; $350 regional federation; schedule based on wages for worker co-operative members; *Member Profile:* Co-operatives across Canada
Activities: Representing the general interests of worker co-ops to various levels of government & other organizations; Creating & offering resources for worker co-ops; Facilitating conferences & workshops to foster networking & development; *Library:* Worker Co-op Resource Guide; Open to public
Chief Officer(s):
Hazel Corcoran, Executive Director
hazel@canadianworker.coop
Publications:
• Canadian Worker Co-operative Federation Newsletter
Type: Newsletter; *Frequency:* 6 pa
Profile: An information resource for members; includes federation news & important event dates

Canadian Writers' Foundation Inc. (CWF) / La Fondation des écrivains canadiens inc.
PO Box 13281, Stn. Kanata, Ottawa ON K2K 1X4
Tel: 613-256-6937; *Fax:* 613-256-5457
info@canadianwritersfoundation.org
www.canadianwritersfoundation.org
Overview: A small national charitable organization founded in 1931
Mission: Strives to continue building the capital fund through donations
Finances: Annual Operating Budget: $50,000-$100,000; *Funding Sources:* Donations; bequests; royalties; investment income
Staff Member(s): 1
Membership: 8; *Fees:* Annual donations; *Committees:* Executive; Advisory
Activities: Grants continued financial assistance to distinguished, senior Canadian writers in times of financial distress
Chief Officer(s):
Marianne Scott, President, 613-733-4223, Fax: 613-733-8752
Suzanne Williams, Executive Secretary

Canadian Yachting Association *See* Sail Canada

Canadian Young Judaea
788 Marlee Ave., Toronto ON M6B 3K1
Tel: 416-781-5156; *Fax:* 416-787-3100
www.youngjudaea.ca
www.facebook.com/youngjudaea
twitter.com/CdnYoungJudaea
Overview: A medium-sized national organization
Mission: To empower its members through their Jewish indentity
Staff Member(s): 8
Membership: Committees: Educational; Fundraising; National Camp Board; Marketing & Communications
Activities: Israel trips
Chief Officer(s):
Risa Epstein, National Executive Director
risa@youngjudaea.ca

Canadian Youth Business Foundation *See* Futurpreneur Canada

The Canadian Zionist Cultural Association (CZCA)
#201, 788 Marlee Ave., Toronto ON M6B 3K1
Tel: 416-783-3063; *Fax:* 416-787-7496
czcacanada@gmail.com
Overview: A small international charitable organization
Mission: To support humanitarian & educational programs in Israel
Activities: Providing scholarships; Operating camps for soldiers' orphans
Chief Officer(s):
Talia Klein Leighton, Administrator
talia.klein@czca.org

Canadian Zionist Federation (CZF) / La fédération sioniste canadienne
4600 Bathurst St., 4th Fl., Toronto ON M2R 3V2
Tel: 416-633-3988; *Fax:* 416-633-2758
czf@jazo.org.il
Overview: A large international organization founded in 1967
Mission: To promote the Zionist ideal among the Jewish population in Canada; To assist in strengthening the Jewish State of Israel; To enrich Canadian Jewish life through the provision of Jewish education & information on Israel & Zionism, through the promotion of Aliyah & activities among Jewish youth in Canada
Member of: World Zionist Organization
Affiliation(s): World Zionist Organization; Jewish Agency
Finances: Annual Operating Budget: $50,000-$100,000
Staff Member(s): 5; 30 volunteer(s)
Membership: 1,000-4,999; *Fees:* Schedule available
Activities: Speaker Service: Yes; *Library*
Chief Officer(s):
Florence Simon, National Executive Director
Central Region
4600 Bathurst St., 4th Fl., Toronto ON M2R 3V2
Tel: 416-633-3988; *Fax:* 416-635-2758
czf@jazo.org.il
Chief Officer(s):
Norman Stern, President
snstern@sympatico.ca
Eastern Region
5151, ch de la Cote-Saint-Luc, Montréal QC H3W 2H5
Tel: 514-739-7300; *Fax:* 514-739-9412
Midwest Region
#C300, 123 Doncaster St., Winnipeg MB R3N 2B2
Tel: 204-477-7400

Canadiana
#200, 440 Laurier Ave. West, Ottawa ON K1R 7X6
Tel: 613-235-2628; *Fax:* 613-235-9752
info@canadiana.ca
www.canadiana.ca
www.facebook.com/CanadianaCA
twitter.com/CanadianaCA
www.flickr.com/photos/canadiana_org
Previous Name: Canadian Institute for Historical Microreproductions
Overview: A medium-sized national charitable organization founded in 1978
Mission: To specialize in the digitization of, preservation of, & access to documentary heritage
Member of: Association for Canadian Studies; Canadian Historical Association; Canadian Initiative on Digital Libraries
Finances: Funding Sources: Subscriptions; Sales; National Library
Chief Officer(s):
William Wueppelmann, Interim Executive Director, 613-235-2628 Ext. 226
Daniel Velarde, Officer, Communications, 613-235-2628 Ext. 227
Awards:
• Digital History Essay Prize
Awarded to a student who demonstrates the most compelling use of Canadiana.org digitized historical content in their research
Eligibility: Students registered at a Canadian university & enrolled full-time at the undergraduate or graduate level in history or a related discipline *Deadline:* April; *Amount:* 4 at $300
Publications:
• Bulletin [a publication of Canadiana]
Type: Newsletter; *Frequency:* Bimonthly
Profile: News & updates on Canadiana.org projects & policies

Canadian-Arab Business Council *See* Canada-Arab Business Council

Canadian-Croatian Chamber of Commerce
630 The East Mall, Toronto ON M9B 4B1
Tel: 416-641-2829; *Fax:* 416-641-2700
contactus@croat.ca
www.croat.ca
www.linkedin.com/company/the-canadian-croatian-chamber-of-commerce
www.facebook.com/CanadianCroatianChamberofCommerce
twitter.com/CroatChamber
Overview: A medium-sized national organization founded in 1995
Mission: To represent Croatian-Canadian business in Canada
Staff Member(s): 1
Membership: Committees: Business Excellence Awards; Construction Liaison; Education, Culture & Heritage; Golf; Government Relations; Membership; Website & Technology; Youth Mentorship
Activities: Awareness Events: Taste of Croatia Golf Tournament; Annual Business Excellence Awards
Chief Officer(s):
Wanita Kelava, Manager

Canadian-Cuban Friendship Association Toronto (CCFA)
PO Box 99051, 1245 Dupont St., Toronto ON M6H 2A0
Tel: 416-410-8254; *Fax:* 905-951-7629
info@ccfatoronto.ca
www.ccfatoronto.ca
twitter.com/ccfatoronto
Also Known As: CCFA Toronto
Overview: A small international charitable organization founded in 1977
Mission: To promote cooperation & understanding between the people of Canada & Cuba; to fundraise to send material goods to Cuba, provide for Cubans passing through Toronto; to hold activities that help protect Canada's & Cuba's sovereignty
Member of: Canadian Network on Cuba
Finances: Annual Operating Budget: Less than $50,000
12 volunteer(s)
Membership: 100-499; *Fees:* $5-$25
Activities: Cultural & informational public meetings; *Speaker Service:* Yes
Chief Officer(s):
Elizabeth Hill, President
Publications:
• Amistad
Type: Newsletter; *Frequency:* Bimonthy
Profile: Articles pertaining to Cuban issues
• Amistad
Type: Newsletter; *Frequency:* Bimonthly
Profile: CCFA activities, events, & developments in Cuba

Canadian-Filipino Association of Yukon (CFAY)
Whitehorse YT
Tel: 867-336-4443
www.facebook.com/YukonFilipino
Overview: A small provincial organization
Mission: To assist Filipinos in Canada; to promote understanding between Filipinos and Canadians; to provide education & training opportunities to members of the Association; to organize recreational & cultural activities for members & others.
Chief Officer(s):
Mike Buensuceso, President

Canadian-Palestinian Education Exchange
612 Markham St., Toronto ON M6G 2L8
info@cepal.ca
www.cepal.ca
Overview: A medium-sized national organization
Mission: To educate Palestinian refugees in Lebanon and raise awareness to Canadians about Palestinian refugees difficult conditions in Lebanon.
Chief Officer(s):
Alexandra Conliffe, President

Canadians Concerned About Violence in Entertainment (C-CAVE)
167 Glen Rd., Toronto ON M4W 2W8
info@c-cave.com
www.c-cave.com
Overview: A small national organization founded in 1983
Mission: To provide public education on research findings related to media violence through popular culture, commodities marketed primarily to children, adolescents & adults.
Member of: Cultural Environment Movement
Affiliation(s): Coalition for Responsible Television (CRTV)
Finances: Funding Sources: Membership fees; private donations
Membership: Fees: $35 individual; $80 institution
Activities: Speaker Service: Yes; *Library:* Resource Centre; by appointment
Chief Officer(s):
Rose Anne Dyson, Media Contact
rose.dyson@c-cave.com

Canadians for Clean Prosperity
#503, 460 Richmond St. West, Toronto ON M5V 1Y1
Tel: 416-777-2327; *Fax:* 416-777-2524
Other Communication: Calgary, Phone/Fax: 587-316-7444
info@cleanprosperity.ca
www.cleanprosperity.ca
www.facebook.com/cleanprosperity
twitter.com/CleanProsperity
Overview: A small national organization
Mission: To build a strong economy using pollution fees to cut taxes
Finances: Funding Sources: Donations
Activities: Campaigns & advocacy

Chief Officer(s):
Mark Cameron, Executive Director
mcameron@cleanprosperity.ca
Tom Chervinsky, Acting Executive Director & Vice-President, Campaigns
tchervinsky@cleanprosperity.ca
Mollie Anderson, Coordinator, Engagement
manderson@cleanprosperity.ca

Canadians for Ethical Treatment of Food Animals (CETFA)
PO Box 18024, 2225 - 41 Ave. West, Vancouver BC V6M 4L3
care@cetfa.com
www.cetfa.com
www.facebook.com/cetfa.news
Overview: A medium-sized national organization founded in 1990
Mission: CETFA is an investigation-based, farm animal advocacy organization that promotes the humane treatment of animals raised for food. It works to educate the public about Canada's food industry by providing information on factory farming practices.
Membership: *Fees:* $10
Chief Officer(s):
Patricia Oswald, President
Twyla Francois, Head, Investigation, 204-296-1375
twyla.1@mts.net

Canadians for Health Research (CHR) / Les Canadiens pour la recherche médicale
PO Box 126, Westmount QC H3Z 2T1
Tel: 514-398-7478; *Fax:* 514-398-8361
www.chrcrm.org
www.facebook.com/300688209959308
twitter.com/chr_news
Overview: A medium-sized national charitable organization founded in 1976
Mission: To further understanding & communication among the public, the scientific community & government; To promote stability & quality in Canadian health research; to meet goals through the direct provision of information on request, & development & circulation of literature & special programming; To sponsor periodic conferences, workshops, a journalism award, & a student essay competition
Chief Officer(s):
Tim Lougheed, Chair
Publications:
• 30 Years of Health Research [a publication of Canadians for Health Research]
Type: Report
Profile: Series of monographs that report on 30 years of progress in scientific research
• The Diary [a publication of Canadians for Health Research]
Type: Newsletter; *Frequency:* Quarterly; *Price:* $250
Profile: Monitors animal-related issues nationally and internationally
• Future Health [a publication of Canadians for Health Research]
Type: Magazine; *Frequency:* Quarterly; *Price:* $25; $15 for schools and libraries
Profile: Contains highlights of Canadian health research
• Road to Discovery [a publication of Canadians for Health Research]
Type: Report
Profile: Published in conjunction with the Medical Research Council of Canada to promote student awareness of research in healthcare
• Salute to Excellence [a publication of Canadians for Health Research]
Type: Report
Profile: An outline of achievements of Canadian medical research from the 20th century
• A True Story [a publication of Canadians for Health Research]
Type: Report
Profile: Illustrated monograph that provides information on animals and medical research

Canadians of Bangladeshi Origin
84 Westhumber Blvd., Toronto ON M9W 3A4
Tel: 416-742-9818
Overview: A small national organization founded in 1972
Mission: To support persons of Banglasdeshi origin who live in Canada

Canadians' Choice Party (CCP)
#1, 927 Danforth Ave., Toronto ON M4J 1L8
Tel: 416-925-8858
canadianschoice@gmail.com
www.canadianschoice.ca
www.facebook.com/canadians.choice
twitter.com/CanadiansChoice
www.youtube.com/CanadiansChoiceParty
Overview: A small provincial organization
Chief Officer(s):
Bahman Yazdanfar, Party Leader

Canadian-Scandinavian Foundation (CSF) / Fondation Canada-Scandinavie
1438, rue Fullum, Montréal QC H2K 3M1
www.thecsfoundation.com
Overview: A small international charitable organization founded in 1950
Mission: To raise funds to distribute to Canadian students who wish to travel to Denmark, Finland, Iceland, Norway or Sweden, to undertake studies at a Scandinavian institution; to promote study/research projects by offering travel bursaries.
Membership: *Fees:* $25 friend; $50 donor; $75 benefactor; $100 patron/corporate
Activities: Research funding; dinners; *Speaker Service:* Yes
Chief Officer(s):
Noami Kramer, President
Awards:
• Brucebo Scholarships
2 scholarships given each year to young Canadian artists and a grant to 1 Swedish artist
• Special Purpose Grants
Travel grants in the range of $600 to $1,000, to help defray travel costs in connection with study visits

Canadienne de la Chèvre de Boucherie *See* Canadian Meat Goat Association

Les Canadiens pour la recherche médicale *See* Canadians for Health Research

CanAm Indian Friendship Centre of Windsor (CAIFC)
2929 Howard Ave., Windsor ON N8X 4W4
Tel: 519-253-3243; *Fax:* 519-253-7876
admin@caifc.ca
www.caifc.ca
Overview: A small local charitable organization founded in 1981
Mission: To advocate on behalf of Aboriginal people in Windsor; To improve the quality of life of community members
Affiliation(s): Ontario Federation of Indian Friendship Centres
Activities: Developing programs & services to meet community needs

Canards Illimités Canada *See* Ducks Unlimited Canada

Cancer Advocacy Coalition of Canada (CACC)
#1902, 2 Bloor St. West, Toronto ON M4W 3R1
Tel: 416-642-6472; *Fax:* 416-538-4874
Toll-Free: 855-572-3436
cacc@canceradvocacy.ca
www.canceradvocacy.ca
www.facebook.com/CancerAdvocacy
twitter.com/CancerAdvocacy1
canceradvocacy.tumblr.com
Overview: A medium-sized national organization
Mission: To ensure that Canadians receive the best cancer services; To benefit cancer survivors; To assist in shaping constructive change in the Canadian cancer system
Finances: *Funding Sources:* Donations; Fundraising; Sponsorships
Activities: Evaluating cancer system performance in Canada; Engaging in advocacy activities, related to patient, survivor, & family issues; Promoting positive cancer policies; Encouraging public funding for the control & prevention of cancer; Publishing assessments of the cancer system; Preparing positions papers, such as a position statement on isotopes
Chief Officer(s):
Dauna Crooks, Chair
Larry Broadfield, Vice-Chair
Publications:
• Report Card on Cancer in Canada
Frequency: Annually
Profile: Articles about the effectiveness of the cancer system in Canada

Cancer Care Ontario (CCO)
620 University Ave., Toronto ON M5G 2L7
Tel: 416-971-9800; *Fax:* 416-971-6888
info@cis.cancer.ca
www.cancercare.on.ca
www.linkedin.com/company/cancer-care-ontario
www.facebook.com/CCO.Ontario
twitter.com/CancerCare_ON
Overview: A medium-sized provincial organization
Mission: To advise the Ontario government on all aspects of provincial cancer care; To provide information to health care providers & decision makers; To motivate better cancer system performance
Finances: *Funding Sources:* Donations; provincial & federal funding
Membership: *Committees:* Audit & Finance; Corporate Governance/Nominating; Human Resources & Compensation; IM/IT; Strategic Planning, Performance & Risk Management
Chief Officer(s):
Ratan Ralliaram, Chair
Michael Sherar, President & CEO

Cancer de l'ovaire Canada *See* Ovarian Cancer Canada

Cancer de la vessie Canada *See* Bladder Cancer Canada

Cancer du Colon Canada *See* Colon Cancer Canada

Cancer Patient Education Network Canada (CPEN - Canada)
info@cancerpatienteducation.org
www.cancerpatienteducation.org
www.linkedin.com/groups?mostPopular=&gid=3300283
www.facebook.com/JoinCPEN
twitter.com/CPEN2014
Overview: A small national organization
Mission: To support cancer care providers in Canada, in the provision of effective, accurate, & comprehensive patient education; To empower cancer patients & their families to participate effectively in their care; To improve health outcomes, through cancer patient, family, & community education; To develop national standards for best practice in cancer patient education programs at cancer centres, hospitals, & community organizations
Membership: *Member Profile:* Health care professionals interested in cancer patient education at hospitals, cancer centers, & community organizations throughout Canada; Volunteers who participate in cancer patient education
Activities: Facilitating collaboration among leaders in cancer patient education; Promoting research in cancer patient education; Supporting the implementation & management of high quality patient education programs & resources; Providing educational information to cancer patients & families; Mentoring health care professionals & care providers to educate others; Advocating for institutional allocation of funding for cancer patient education programs
Chief Officer(s):
Susan Boyko, Chair, CPEN Canada Steering Committee
sboyko@hsnsudbury.ca

Cancer Research Society / Société de recherche sur le cancer
#402, 625, av Président-Kennedy, Montréal QC H3A 3S5
Tel: 514-861-9227; *Fax:* 514-861-9220
Toll-Free: 888-766-2262
info@src-crs.ca
www.crs-src.ca
www.linkedin.com/company/cancer-research-society-soci-t-de-recherche-sur-le-cancer
www.facebook.com/cancerresearchsociety
Overview: A large national charitable organization founded in 1945
Mission: To support basic cancer research through funding & seed money; To allocate grants & fellowships to universities & hospitals involved in research across Canada
Finances: *Annual Operating Budget:* Greater than $5 Million; *Funding Sources:* Donations
Staff Member(s): 24; 1000 volunteer(s)
Membership: 1,000; *Committees:* Audit; Communications & Web; Development; Executive; Investment; Governance; Human Resources & Recruitment; Major & Planned Gifts; Scientific Advisory
Chief Officer(s):
Andy Chabot, Executive Director
achabot@src-crs.ca
Nathalie Giroux, Vice-President & Chief Operating Officer
ngiroux@crs-src.ca
Ottawa
#305, 200 Isabella St., Ottawa ON K1S 1V7
Fax: 613-233-1030
Toll-Free: 888-766-2262
ottawa@src-crs.ca

Tel: 902-567-7752
foundation@cbdha.nshealth.ca
www.becauseyoucare.ca
www.facebook.com/CapeBretonCares
twitter.com/BecauseUCare
instagram.com/becauseucare
Overview: A small local charitable organization
Mission: To raise money on behalf of the Cape Breton Regional Hospital in order to improve the services provided to patients & to fund research
Staff Member(s): 6
Chief Officer(s):
Brad Jacobs, CEO, 902-567-8186
brad.jacobs@nshealth.ca

Cape Breton Tourist Association See Tourism Cape Breton

Cape Breton University Centre for International Studies (CIS) / Centre d'études internationales
Cape Breton University, PO Box 5300, Sydney NS B1P 6L2
Tel: 902-563-1274
cbu-cis.ca
Overview: A small local organization founded in 1978
Mission: To develop greater general awareness of the relevance & importance of international affairs to Canadians; To carry out extensive public educational programs on development, multiculturalism, human rights, environmental issues & peace; To encourage research & publications, sponsor guest speakers, workshops & seminars; To seek linkages with other universities & institutions both in Canada & elsewhere; To negotiate international exchange agreements & coordinate technical assistance projects
Member of: Canadian Council for International Cooperation
Finances: *Funding Sources:* University; government; projects
Activities: Lectures; seminars; youth conference; cultural events; *Speaker Service:* Yes; *Library:* Open to public
Chief Officer(s):
Garry Leech, Director
garry_leech@cbu.ca

Cape Breton University Faculty Association / Association des faculty du universitaire du Cap-Breton
Cape Breton University, PO Box 351, Stn. A, Sydney NS B1S 6H2
Tel: 902-563-1623; Fax: 902-563-1881
president@cbufa.ca
www.cbufa.ca
www.facebook.com/100307433386250?sk=wall
twitter.com/CBUFA
Previous Name: University College of Cape Breton Faculty Association of University Teachers
Overview: A small local organization founded in 1974
Affiliation(s): Canadian Association of University Teachers
Finances: *Annual Operating Budget:* Less than $50,000; *Funding Sources:* Membership dues
Membership: 110
Chief Officer(s):
Chester Pyne, President

Cape Sable Historical Society
The Old Courthouse, PO Box 67, 2401 Hwy. 3, RR#1, Barrington NS B0W 1E0
Tel: 902-637-2185
barmuseumcomplex@eastlink.ca
www.capesablehistoricalsociety.com
www.facebook.com/209904499063299
Overview: A small local organization founded in 1932
Mission: To preserve the archives & genealogy of Cape Sable Island & the surrounding region, including Shelburne County & the Municipality of Barrington; To provide information about family history & the local history of the Cape Sable area; To act as the custodian of the Seal Island Light Museum, the Old Meeting House, the Western Counties Military Museum, & the Barrington Woolen Mill
Finances: *Funding Sources:* Membership fees; Research fees; Admission fees
Membership: *Fees:* $10
Activities: Offering research facilities, resources, & staff to assist visitors with genealogical research; *Library:* Genealogical Research Centre; Open to public

Capilano College Faculty Association See Capilano University Faculty Association

Capilano University Faculty Association (CFA)
2055 Purcell Way, North Vancouver BC V7J 3H5

Tel: 604-984-4948
cfa@capilanou.ca
www.capilanofaculty.ca
www.facebook.com/CapUFaculty
twitter.com/CapUFaculty
Previous Name: Capilano College Faculty Association
Overview: A small local organization founded in 1969
Mission: To represent the faculty of Capilano University, by addressing issues of the faculty, such as professional development, workload, access to benefit plans, & appointments
Membership: 500+; *Member Profile:* Instructors from Capilano University; *Committees:* Audit; Benefits Review; Cap College Naming Opportunities; Disability Rehabilitation; Dispute Resolution; Education Policy; Employee & Family Assistance; Equivalent Workload; Faculty Professional Development; Food Services; Harassment; Human Rights & International Solidarity; Joint Occupational Health & Safety; Mediation; Non Regular Faculty; Paid Ed Leave; Parking; Pension Liaison; Physical Environment; Placement Review; Social; Status of Women; Student Appeals; Trade Union Practices & Ethics; Transportation; Washroom Advertising
Chief Officer(s):
Brent Calvert, President
cfa@capilanou.ca
Publications:
• Capilano University Faculty Association Newsletter
Type: Newsletter
Profile: Union issues

The Capital Commission of Prince Edward Island Inc. / La Commission de la Capitale de l'Ile-du-Prince-Édouard
#302, 52 Water St., Charlottetown PE C1A 7M4
Tel: 902-629-1864; Fax: 902-892-5486
Also Known As: Capital Commission
Overview: A medium-sized local organization founded in 1995
Mission: To promote & develop Charlottetown in its role as the Birthplace of Confederation in an authentic & accurate manner, resulting in diverse cultural & business opportunities for private enterprise
Member of: Tourism Industry Association of PEI; International Festivals & Events Association; PEI Convention Bureau; PEI Museum & Heritage Foundation, Greater Charlottetown Area Chamber of Commerce
Chief Officer(s):
Kim Green, Executive Director

Capital Region Beekeepers Association
c/o Alanya Smith, 2930 Prior St., Victoria BC V8T 3Y5
192.197.97.9/~vicbeekeepers/
Overview: A small local organization
Mission: To assist & educate member beekeepers
Membership: 100+; *Fees:* $25; *Member Profile:* Interested apiarists, as well as non-beekeepers, in the capital region area of British Columbia
Activities: Offering monthly meetings featuring a speaker, questions, & beekeeping information; Organizing a field day; Testing bees for nosema; Removing honey bees from yards; *Speaker Service:* Yes; *Library:* Capital Region Beekeepers Association Library
Publications:
• Beeline Newsletter
Type: Newsletter; *Frequency:* Monthly; *Price:* Free with Capital Region Beekeepers Association membership

Carberry & District Chamber of Commerce
PO Box 101, Carberry MB R0K 0H0
Tel: 204-834-6616
www.townofcarberry.ca
Overview: A small local organization
Membership: *Fees:* $50
Chief Officer(s):
Stuart Olmstead, President

Carberry Plains Arts Council
PO Box 130, 122 Main St., Carberry MB R0K 0H0
Tel: 204-834-6617; Fax: 204-834-6619
crbyarts@westman.wave.ca
home.westman.wave.ca/~crbyarts
Overview: A small local organization
Mission: To promote & encourage use of the arts as an integral part of the community
Member of: Manitoba Association of Community Arts Councils Inc.
Staff Member(s): 1
Chief Officer(s):
Sherry Howard, Administrative Director

Carcinoid NeuroEndocrine Tumour Society Canada
#4103, 3219 Yonge St., Toronto ON M4N 3S1
Tel: 416-628-3189
Toll-Free: 844-628-6788
Other Communication: support@cnetscanada.org
info@cnetscanada.org
www.cnetscanada.org
www.facebook.com/cnetscanada
twitter.com/CNETSCanada
www.youtube.com/user/cnetscanada
Also Known As: CNETS Canada
Overview: A large national charitable organization founded in 2007
Mission: To raise awareness about neuroendocrine tumours; to provide help & support to those suffering from this type of cancer; to fund research that treats neuroendocrine tumours
Staff Member(s): 2
Activities: *Awareness Events:* NET Cancer Awareness Day, November
Chief Officer(s):
Jacqueline Herman, President & Director, Treatment, Access & Health Policy
jackie.herman@cnetscanada.org

Cardiac Care Network of Ontario
#502, 4100 Yonge St., Toronto ON M2P 2B5
Tel: 416-512-7472; Fax: 416-512-6425
mail@ccn.on.ca
www.ccn.on.ca
Overview: A small provincial organization
Mission: To work as an advisory body to the Ministry of Health & Long-Term Care; To improve the quality of cardiovascular care in Ontario
Finances: *Funding Sources:* Ministry of Health & Long-Term Care
Staff Member(s): 16
Membership: 18; *Member Profile:* Cardiac centres in Ontario; *Committees:* Research & Publications
Activities: Collecting & reporting information on surgery, catheterization, angioplasty, eps & ablations & ICDs
Chief Officer(s):
Kori Kingsbury, Chief Executive Officer

Cardiac Health Foundation of Canada
#306, 901 Lawrence Ave. West, Toronto ON M6A 1C3
Tel: 416-730-8299; Fax: 416-730-0421
info@cardiachealth.ca
www.cardiachealth.ca
www.facebook.com/CardiacHealth
twitter.com/CardiacHealth
Previous Name: Canadian Cardiac Rehabilitation Foundation
Overview: A medium-sized national charitable organization
Mission: To lower instances of, & support recovery from, cardiovascular disease; To aid in the development of cardiovascular rehabilitation & education services & initiatives in Canada
Membership: *Committees:* Medical Advisory
Activities: Raising funds for the development of cardiovascular rehabilitation programs & services; Offering educational programs & resources designed to increase awareness of cardiovascular disease; Supporting research on cardiovascular disease management; Advocating for Canadians with cardiovascular disease; *Awareness Events:* Walk of Life, May
Chief Officer(s):
Barbara Kennedy, Executive Director
bkennedy@cardiachealth.ca
Christina Mellos, Manager, Operations
cmellos@cardiachealth.ca

Cardiac Rehabilitation Network of Ontario (CRNO)
347 Rumsey Rd., Toronto ON M4G 1R7
Tel: 416-597-3422; Fax: 416-597-7027
www.crno.ca
Overview: A small provincial organization founded in 2002 overseen by Canadian Association of Cardiovascular Prevention & Rehabilitation
Mission: Dedicated to the rehabilitation of individuals with cardiac disease, as well as the prevention of cardiac disease; advocacy on behalf of the patient through the advancement of health care services in Ontario
Finances: *Funding Sources:* Membership dues
Membership: *Fees:* $25 regular; $100-$250 institutional dependant on number of members; *Member Profile:* Anyone involved in some capacity with an Ontario cardiac rehabilitation program
Chief Officer(s):

Terry Fair, Chair, 905-895-4521 Ext. 2805
TFair@southlakeregional.org
Andrew Lotto, Treasurer/Registrar, 905-895-4521 Ext. 6896
alotto@southlakeregional.org

Cardiology Technologists' Association of British Columbia (CTABC)
PO Box 2575, 349 West Georgia St., Vancouver BC V6B 3W8
Toll-Free: 866-280-6535
info@ctabc.ca
www.ctabc.ca
Overview: A small provincial organization founded in 1975
Mission: To raise standards of practice & of patient care provided by cardiology technologists in British Columbia
Member of: Canadian Society of Cardiology Technologists (CSCT)
Affiliation(s): Canadian Cardiovascular Society (CCS)
Membership: 400+; *Fees:* $145 registered cardiology technologists; $95 inactive; $75 students; *Member Profile:* Registered cardiology technologists; Students
Activities: Increasing the level of competence of cardiology technologists; Maintaining professional standards; Providing education; *Library:* Lending Library
Chief Officer(s):
Shauna Ryall, CTABC President
president@ctabc.ca
Cheryl West, CTABC / CSCT Registrar
registrar@ctabc.ca
Jiannan Yu, Treasurer
treasurer@ctabc.ca
Awards:
• Marion Wright
Publications:
• Heart Copy: Cardiology Technologists' Association of BC Newsletter
Type: Newsletter
Profile: Association reports

Cardston & District Chamber of Commerce
PO Box 1212, 490 Main St., Cardston AB T0K 0K0
Tel: 403-795-1032; *Fax:* 403-653-2644
info@cardstonchamber.com
www.cardstonchamber.com
Overview: A small local organization
Mission: To promote & improve trade & commerce; To assist in providing economic growth, as well as civic & social being in the community & surrounding area
Chief Officer(s):
Michael Meeks, President
Angela Adams, Treasurer

Cardston Historical Society (CHS)
89 - 3 Ave. West, Cardston AB T0K 0K0
www.cardstonhistoricalsociety.org
www.facebook.com/1456999661242429
Overview: A small local charitable organization founded in 1975
Mission: To collect & arrange for display historical items from Cardston & district; To collect & store local newspapers & make them available for research; To collect history books from Southern Alberta for interest & research
Finances: *Funding Sources:* Municipality; government of Alberta
Activities: Operating both C.O. Card Home & Court House Museum, seasonal June 1 - Aug. 31; *Library:* by appointment
Chief Officer(s):
Daryl Hogenson, President

Cardus Institute
185 Young St., Hamilton ON L8N 1V9
Tel: 905-528-8866; *Fax:* 905-528-9433
Toll-Free: 888-339-8866
info@cardus.ca
www.cardus.ca
Also Known As: Cardus
Overview: A small national charitable organization
Mission: To renew & cultivate the institutions that affect social life in Canada; To challenge public debate about government, market, & civil society
Activities: Conducting original research on six aspects of North American public life (education, family, health, law, social cities, & work & economics)
Chief Officer(s):
Dan Postma, Director, Operations
dpostma@cardus.ca
Daniel Proussalidis, Director, Communications
dproussalidis@cardus.ca
Publications:
• Comment

Type: Magazine; *Frequency:* Quarterly; *Editor:* James K.A. Smith

CARE Canada
#100, 9 Gurdwara Rd., Ottawa ON K2E 7X6
Tel: 613-228-5600; *Fax:* 613-226-5777
Toll-Free: 800-267-5232
info@care.ca
www.care.ca
www.facebook.com/carecanada
twitter.com/CARE_CAN
www.youtube.com/carecanada
Overview: A large international charitable organization founded in 1946
Mission: To serve individuals & families in developing communities; To provide economic opportunity & emergency relief to those in need
Finances: *Annual Operating Budget:* Greater than $5 Million; *Funding Sources:* Federal government; Multinationals; Corporate & private donors
Staff Member(s): 102
Membership: 1-99
Activities: Delivering emergency relief; Liaising with policymakers to influence decisions; Strengthening economic opportunity by providing financial support; *Awareness Events:* Walk in Her Shoes, March; International Women's Day, March; Climb for CARE, January; *Internships:* Yes
Chief Officer(s):
Gillian Barth, President/CEO
Publications:
• CARE Canada Annual Report
Type: Report; *Frequency:* Annually

Care Institute of Safety & Health Inc.
1770 East 18th Ave., Vancouver BC V5N 5P6
Tel: 604-873-6018; *Fax:* 604-873-4443
Toll-Free: 800-923-4566
www.care-institute.com
Overview: A small local organization
Mission: To provide safety training for individuals & organizations
Activities: First aid training; transportation endorsement; WHMIS
Chief Officer(s):
Elaine Shigetomi, President & CEO

C.A.R.E. Jeunesse
Montréal QC
carejeunesse@gmail.com
carejeunesse.com
www.facebook.com/carejeunesse
twitter.com/care_jeunesse
Also Known As: Centre Amitié, Ressources et Entraide pour la Jeunesse
Overview: A medium-sized provincial organization overseen by Youth in Care Canada
Mission: • fournir des supports pour les jeunes placés et ancien(ne)s placés au Québec, y compris, mais sans s'y limiter: les foyers d'accueil, les foyers de groupe et une variété de centres résidentiels
Chief Officer(s):
Amanda Keller, Présidente et fondatrice
Jennifer Dupuis, Vice-Présidente

Career Colleges Ontario (CCO)
#2, 155 Lynden Rd., Brantford ON N3R 8A7
Tel: 519-752-2124; *Fax:* 519-752-3649
www.careercollegesontario.ca
www.linkedin.com/company/ontario-association-of-career-colleges
www.facebook.com/careercollegesontario
twitter.com/c_c_ontario
Previous Name: Private Career Educational Council; Ontario Association of Career Colleges
Overview: A medium-sized provincial organization founded in 1973
Mission: To act as the voice for the private career college sector in Ontario
Member of: National Association of Career Colleges
Finances: *Funding Sources:* Membership dues; Sponsorships
Membership: 250+; *Member Profile:* Private career colleges in Ontario; *Committees:* Membership; International Students; OACC Services; Ministry Liaison; Public Relations, Marketing, & Communications; Conference; Student Success; Program Standards; Private Career Colleges Act Review; Performance Accountability Measures; General Accreditation / Apprenticeship / Online; TCAF; Employment Ontario; Career College Quality; Finance & Budget; Nomination; Deputy Minister PCC Advisory; Governance; Private Career College Tours; RICC Focus Group
Activities: Providing a central clearing house; Promoting the interests of members; Advocating on behalf of members; Participating in negotiating regulations & legislation that impact the sector; Offering development workshops
Chief Officer(s):
Paul Kitchin, Executive Director, 519-752-2124 Ext. 103
paulkitchin@careercollegesontario.ca
Lorna Mills, Manager, Office & Financial Aid, 519-752-2124 Ext. 104
lornamills@careercollegesontario.ca
Meetings/Conferences:
• Career Colleges Ontario Annual Conference 2018, May, 2018, Niagara Falls, ON
Scope: Provincial
Contact Information: Assistant, Administration: April Chato, E-mail: aprilchato@careercollegesontario.ca, Phone: 519-752-2124, ext. 113; Assistant, Administration: Dena Stuart, E-mail: denastuart@careercollegesontario.ca, Phone: 519-752-2124, ext. 200
Publications:
• The OACC Voice [a publication of Career Colleges Ontario]
Type: Newsletter; *Frequency:* Monthly
Profile: Information for members

Career Management Association of BC; Labour Market & Career Information Association of British Columbia *See* British Columbia Career Development Association

Carefirst Seniors & Community Services Association
#501, 3601 Victoria Park Ave., Toronto ON M1W 3Y3
Tel: 416-502-2323; *Fax:* 416-502-2382
info@carefirstseniors.com
www.carefirstseniors.com
www.facebook.com/CarefirstSeniors
twitter.com/CarefirstSenior
Previous Name: Chinese Seniors Support Services Association
Overview: A small local charitable organization
Member of: United Way Greater Toronto, York Region, Peel Region
Finances: *Annual Operating Budget:* Greater than $5 Million; *Funding Sources:* Federal, provincial & municipal; membership dues; sales of goods & services
Staff Member(s): 350; 1200 volunteer(s)
Mississauga On-Site Drop-In Service
#81, 1177 Central Pkwy W., Mississauga ON L5C 4P3
Tel: 905-270-9988; *Fax:* 905-361-1082
mso@carefirstseniors.com
South Toronto Office, Helen Lam Community Service Centre
479 Dundas St. West, Toronto ON M5T 1H1
Tel: 416-585-2013; *Fax:* 416-585-2892
sto@carefirstseniors.com
www.carefirstseniors.com
Supportive Housing Services, Alexandra Park
#707, 91 Augusta Ave., Toronto ON M5T 2L2
Tel: 416-603-0909; *Fax:* 416-603-0436
shsa@carefirstseniors.com
Supportive Housing Services, Tam O'Shanter
#902, 3825 Sheppard Ave. East, Toronto ON M1T 3P6
Tel: 416-291-1800; *Fax:* 416-291-9586
shst@carefirstseniors.com
York Region Community Services Centre
#104A, 420 Hwy 7 East, Richmond Hill ON L4B 3K2
Tel: 905-771-3700; *Fax:* 905-763-3718
york@carefirstseniors.com

Carefree Society
2832 Queensway St., Prince George BC V2L 4M5
Tel: 250-562-1394; *Fax:* 250-562-1393
carefree_society@telus.net
www.carefreesociety.org
Also Known As: handyDART
Overview: A small local charitable organization founded in 1971
Mission: To provide transportation services for seniors and the disabled
Affiliation(s): BC Transit
Finances: *Annual Operating Budget:* $250,000-$500,000; *Funding Sources:* Provincial government; regional government
Staff Member(s): 12; 10 volunteer(s)
Membership: 15; *Fees:* $6; *Committees:* Accessible Transportation Awareness

Caregivers Alberta
c/o Fulton Place School, 10310 - 56th St. NW, Edmonton AB T6A 2J2
Tel: 780-453-5088; *Fax:* 780-465-5089
Toll-Free: 877-453-5088
office@caregiversalberta.ca
www.caregiversalberta.ca
www.linkedin.com/company/alberta-caregivers-association
www.facebook.com/AlbertaCaregivers
twitter.com/ABcaregivers
www.youtube.com/user/ABcaregivers
Also Known As: Alberta Caregivers Association
Overview: A small provincial charitable organization founded in 2001
Mission: To support family caregivers in Alberta, in order to ensure their well-being
Finances: *Funding Sources:* Membership fees; Donations; Fundraising
Membership: *Fees:* $20 individuals; $45 organizations; $150 corporations; *Member Profile:* Family caregivers in Alberta
Activities: Engaging in advocacy activities on behalf of family caregivers in Alberta; Providing educational actitivities, such as community caregiver workshops; Offering the COMPASS program (Caregiver Orientation for Mobilizing Personal Assets & Strengths through Self-care); Facilitating networking opportunities; Organizing information displays; *Speaker Service:* Yes
Chief Officer(s):
Arlene Baron, Office Manager
abaron@caregiversalberta.ca
Debbie Cameron-Laninga, Coordinator, Program
dcameron-laninga@caregiversalberta.ca
Andy King, Advisor, Communications
aking@caregiversalberta.ca
Publications:
• Caregivers Alberta Newsletter
Type: Newsletter
Profile: Information for family caregivers in Alberta, including articles, caregiver stories, training programs, & forthcoming activities

Caregivers Nova Scotia (CNS)
#2, 3433 Dutch Village Rd., Halifax NS B3N 2S7
Tel: 902-421-7390; *Fax:* 902-421-7338
Toll-Free: 877-488-7390
info@caregiversns.org
www.caregiversns.org
www.facebook.com/CaregiversNS
twitter.com/CaregiversNS
Also Known As: CaregiversNS
Previous Name: Family Caregivers Association of Nova Scotia
Overview: A small provincial organization founded in 1998
Mission: To support caregivers throughout Nova Scotia
Affiliation(s): Canadian Caregiver Coalition
Finances: *Annual Operating Budget:* $250,000-$500,000; *Funding Sources:* Nova Scotia Department of Health & Wellness - Continuing Care Branch; Sponsorships
Staff Member(s): 7
Membership: *Member Profile:* Individuals across Nova Scotia who care for & support family & friends who need assistance due to physical or mental disabilities
Activities: Providing education & information for caregivers across Nova Scotia; Offering assistance to caregivers by telephone & through peer support groups; Increasing public awareness of caregiver issues; Influencing public policy regarding caregivers, by participating in government task forces & working groups; Collaborating with other organizations to facilitate projects, such as the Working Together to Prevent Falling Among Seniors; *Awareness Events:* Caregivers' Awareness Week; *Internships:* Yes; *Speaker Service:* Yes; *Library:* Caregivers Nova Scotia Resources Library
Chief Officer(s):
Kathleen Rothwell, President
Angus Campbell, Executive Director
director@caregiversns.org
Jennifer Briand, Coordinator, Western Region Caregiver Support
western@caregiversns.org
Maggie Roach-Ganaway, Coordinator, Cape Breton Region Support
capebreton@caregiversns.org
Cindie Smith, Coordinator, Northern & Eastern Mainland Region Support
northern@Caregiversns.org
Publications:
• The Caregiver's Handbook [a publication of Caregivers Nova Scotia]
Type: Handbook; *Editor:* Angus Campbell
Profile: Information for unpaid family & friend caregivers in Nova Scotia
• Caregivers Nova Scotia News [a publication of Caregivers Nova Scotia]
Type: Newsletter; *Frequency:* Quarterly
Profile: Information about caregiving issues, forthcoming workshops, plus the experiences & concerns of caregivers

Carers ARK
924 Hollinrake Cres., Milton ON L9T 5T5
carers.ark@gmail.com
www.facebook.com/carersark
Overview: A small national charitable organization
Mission: To inform caregivers of their rights, privileges, & obligations; To protect caregivers when necessary; To develop caregivers' leadership skills; To assist caregivers in their spiritual & professional growth; To create a link between caregivers & outside agencies
Affiliation(s): Archdiocese of Toronto
Finances: *Funding Sources:* Donations; membership fees; corporate sponsorship
Membership: *Member Profile:* Caregivers
Activities: Training courses; presentations; seminars; retreats; workshops

Caribbean Community Council of Calgary
#357, 1500 - 14 St. SW, Calgary AB T3C 1C9
Tel: 403-774-1300
admin@carifestcalgary.com
www.carifestcalgary.com
twitter.com/thecarifest
www.youtube.com/user/TheCarifest
Also Known As: Carifest
Previous Name: Calgary Caribbean Cultural Association
Overview: A small local organization founded in 1981
Mission: To contribute to the vibrancy of Calgary by staging an ethnic festival that portrays the Caribbean's rich history & diverse peoples
Finances: *Annual Operating Budget:* $50,000-$100,000
Staff Member(s): 1; 250 volunteer(s)
Activities: *Awareness Events:* Carifest Week, June; *Library:* Open to public

Caribbean Students' Society of McGill University
#411, 3480, rue McTavish, Montréal QC H3A 0E7
Tel: 514-398-1519
Overview: A small local organization
Mission: To foster unity among people from the Caribbean at McGill & in Montréal; to promote the Caribbean culture & student interests on the McGill campus
Member of: Students' Society of McGill University
Finances: *Funding Sources:* Students' Society of McGill University
Activities: Parties & dinners; annual culture show; community service; trips; Roots-AfroCaribbean Explosion 2000

Cariboo Action Training Society
#130, 1460 - 6th Ave., Prince George BC V2L 3N2
Tel: 250-563-9159; *Fax:* 250-563-9154
camptrapping.com
Overview: A medium-sized provincial organization founded in 1971
Mission: To conduct a wilderness behaviour modification program for male young offenders, who attend as a condition of probation programs

Cariboo Chilcotin Child Development Centre Association (CDC)
690 - 2nd Ave. North, Williams Lake BC V2G 4C4
Tel: 250-392-4481; *Fax:* 250-392-4432
www.cccdca.org
Overview: A medium-sized local organization founded in 1975
Mission: To work in partnership with families & the community; To provide a comprehensive continuum of quality developmental support services for children & their families
Member of: BC Association for Child Development & Rehabilitation
Finances: *Annual Operating Budget:* $1.5 Million-$3 Million; *Funding Sources:* Government contracts; fees for service; donations
Staff Member(s): 35; 302 volunteer(s)
Membership: 12 institutional; 290 individual; *Fees:* $2
Activities: Child & Youth Care; Intensive Support & Supervision; FASD Key Worker & Parent Support Program; Infant Development; Occupational Therapy; Physiotherapy; Preschool; Speech & Language Therapy; Supported Child Development
Chief Officer(s):
Jerry Tickner, President

Cariboo Chilcotin Coast Tourism Association
#204, 350 Barnard St., Williams Lake BC V2G 4T9
Tel: 250-392-2226; *Fax:* 250-392-2838
Toll-Free: 800-663-5885
info@landwithoutlimits.com
www.landwithoutlimits.com
www.facebook.com/CaribooChilcotinCoast
twitter.com/CarChiCoa
www.youtube.com/user/TheCCCTA
Previous Name: Cariboo Tourism Association
Overview: A small local organization founded in 1961 overseen by Council of Tourism Associations of British Columbia
Mission: To promote tourism products of the Cariboo Chilcotin Coast region of BC. Products & services include, access to an extensive image bank, travel guide & DVD, familiarization tour assistance, itinerary planning assistance, property inspection/recommendations, regional knowledge.
Affiliation(s): Tourism BC; Council of Regional Tourist Associations; Cariboo Chilcotin Guide Outfitters Association; Guest Ranch Association of BC
Finances: *Funding Sources:* Membership fees; provincial/regional government
Staff Member(s): 4
Membership: *Member Profile:* Tourism product/service provider
Activities: *Speaker Service:* Yes; *Library:* CTA Library; by appointment
Chief Officer(s):
Amy Thacker, CEO
amy@landwithoutlimits.com

Cariboo Friendship Society
99 South 3rd Ave., Williams Lake BC V2G 1J1
Tel: 250-398-6831; *Fax:* 250-398-6115
admin@cfswl.ca
www.cariboofriendshipsociety.ca
Overview: A small local organization founded in 1969
Mission: To promote healthy lifestyles, & fostering fellowship & understanding between people by providing holistic programs & services to all.
Finances: *Funding Sources:* Provincial/federal governments; private donations; fundraising events
Activities: Chiwid Transition House; Little Moccasins Learning Centre; Children Who Witness Abuse Program; Pregnancy Outreach/Family Outreach Program; Emergency Shelter Services; Mental Health Program; Low-Income Urban Aboriginal Housing; Tenant Relations Coordinator
Chief Officer(s):
Rosanna McGregor, Executive Director
rmcgregor@cfswl.ca

Cariboo Tourism Association *See* Cariboo Chilcotin Coast Tourism Association

The Caritas Foundation *See* Covenant Foundation

Caritas Project Community Against Drugs *See* Caritas School of Life Therapeutic Community

Caritas School of Life Therapeutic Community
#1-2, 241 Hanlan Rd., Woodbridge ON L4L 3R7
Tel: 416-748-9988; *Fax:* 416-748-7341
Toll-Free: 800-201-8138
Other Communication: Alt. E-mails: help@caritas.ca; events@caritas.ca
info@caritas.ca
www.caritas.ca
www.facebook.com/468788439859031
twitter.com/Caritas4Life
www.youtube.com/user/CaritasFoundation
Also Known As: Caritas
Previous Name: Caritas Project Community Against Drugs
Overview: A small local organization founded in 1980
Mission: To prevent addiction through education & awareness; to provide a therapeutic community in order to rehabilitate those suffering from dependencies; to also aid people with mental health issues, behavioural problems, & family issues
Member of: Therapeutic Communities of America
Affiliation(s): Archdiocese of Toronto
Finances: *Funding Sources:* Central Local Health Integration Network; donations; fundraising
Staff Member(s): 14

Activities: Group sessions; day program; residential program; re-entry & transitional programs; aftercare; family support; public education
Chief Officer(s):
Gianni Carparelli, Founder
Franca Grilli, Coordinator, Human Resources & Administration
franca@caritas.ca

Carizon Family & Community Services
400 Queen St. South, Kitchener ON N2G 1W7
Tel: 519-743-6333; *Fax:* 519-743-3496
info@carizon.ca
www.carizon.ca
www.linkedin.com/company/carizon-family-and-community-services
www.facebook.com/carizonupdates
twitter.com/@carizon
Previous Name: kidsLINK; Mosaic Counselling & Family Services; Catholic Family Counselling Centre; Catholic Social Services; Catholic Welfare Bureau
Overview: A small local charitable organization founded in 1952 overseen by Ontario Association of Credit Counselling Services
Mission: To provide full-service professional counselling services in Kitchener & the surrounding region
Member of: Canadian Association of Credit Counselling Services; Ontario Association of Credit Counselling Services; United Way of Kitchener-Waterloo & Area; Family Service Ontario
Finances: *Annual Operating Budget:* $3 Million-$5 Million; *Funding Sources:* United Way; Government of Canada; Province of Ontario; Regional Municipality of Waterloo; Foundations, such as Pathways to Education Canada
Activities: Offering individual, group, & credit counselling; Providing workplace & employee assistance programs; Offering community outreach services
Chief Officer(s):
Stephen Swatridge, CEO
Lesley Barraball, Director, Children's Mental Health Services
Jennifer Berry, Director, Communications
Ted Conlin, Director, Business
Jean Davies, Director, Pathways to Education
Debbie Engel, Director, Community Services
Dale Gellatly, Director, Community Engagement
Awards:
• Leadership Award
For exceptional contribution to the well being of families in Canada
   St. Agatha Office
   PO Box 190, 1855 Notre Dame Dr., St Agatha ON N0B 2L0
   Tel: 519-746-5437

Carl Orff Canada Music for Children (COC)
PO Box 1, Grp 23 RR#1, East Selkirk MB R0E 0M0
www.orffcanada.ca
Overview: A medium-sized national organization founded in 1974
Mission: To encourage the development of a wholistic music education evolved from the pedagogical philosophy & approach of Carl Orff
Finances: *Annual Operating Budget:* $50,000-$100,000
17 volunteer(s)
Membership: 1,000; *Fees:* $100 institutional; $30 student; $60 individual
Chief Officer(s):
Liz Kristjanson, President
president@orffcanada.ca
Meetings/Conferences:
• Carl Orff Canada Music for Children 25th National Conference, April, 2018, Sheraton on the Falls, Niagara Falls, ON
Scope: National

Carleton County Historical Society, Inc. (CCHS)
128 Connell St., Woodstock NB E7M 1L5
Tel: 506-328-9706; *Fax:* 506-328-2942
cchs@nb.aibn.com
www.cchs-nb.ca
Overview: A small local organization founded in 1960
Mission: To research and document local history; to acquire and preserve historical documents and artefacts relating to the area; and to refurbish historical buildings.
Membership: *Fees:* $20 student; $25 individual; $300 life
Chief Officer(s):
John Thompson, President

Carleton County Law Association (CCLA) / Association du barreau du comté de Carleton (ABCC)
Law Library, Ottawa Courthouse, #2004, 161 Elgin St., Ottawa ON K2P 2K1
Tel: 613-233-7386; *Fax:* 613-238-3788
Toll-Free: 866-637-3888
www.ccla-abcc.ca
www.linkedin.com/company/county-of-carleton-law-association
www.facebook.com/CCLA.ABCC
twitter.com/ccla_abcc
Overview: A small local organization founded in 1888
Mission: To advance the interests of it members; To promote the administration of justice
Membership: *Fees:* Schedule available; *Member Profile:* Ottawa & Eastern Ontario lawyers
Activities: Offering continuing education programs; Providing networking opportunities; *Library:* County of Carleton Law Association Ottawa Courthouse Law Library
Chief Officer(s):
Rick Haga, Executive Director
rhaga@ccla-abcc.ca
Wanda Walters, Administrator, Finance
wwalters@ccla-abcc.ca
Jennifer Walker, BAH, BEd, MLIS, Head Librarian
jwalker@ccla-abcc.ca
Publications:
• CCLA [Carleton County Law Association] Newsletter
Type: Newsletter; *Frequency:* Weekly
Profile: Updated policies & procedures for CCLA members
• Ottawa & Eastern Ontario Lawyers' Directory
Type: Directory; *Frequency:* Annually; *Accepts Advertising*;
Price: $30-$50

Carleton Literacy Council
100 Broadway St., Woodstock NB E7M 5C5
Tel: 506-328-4779
Overview: A small local organization founded in 1987
Mission: To provide free, private tutoring to illiterate & functionally illiterate adults in the area, thereby increasing the rate of literacy & ensuring a brighter future for these people
Affiliation(s): Laubach Literacy of Canada
Finances: *Annual Operating Budget:* Less than $50,000
40 volunteer(s)
Membership: 50 individual
Chief Officer(s):
Angela Acott-Smith, Chair
angela.acottsmith@gnb.ca

Carleton Place & Beckwith Historical Society
267 Edmund St., Carleton Place ON K7C 3E8
Tel: 613-253-7013
www.cpbheritagemuseum.com
Overview: A small local charitable organization founded in 1984
Mission: To promote & educate on the subject of local history
Membership: *Fees:* $5 student; $7 senior; $10 individual; $15 family; $50 oraganization; $100 life
Activities: *Library:* Open to public by appointment

Carleton Place & District Chamber of Commerce & Visitor Centre
170 Bridge St., Carleton Place ON K7C 2V7
Tel: 613-257-1976; *Fax:* 613-257-4148
www.cpchamber.com
Overview: A small local charitable organization founded in 1916
Mission: To encourage & foster free enterprise & economic development; To support good government & create & maintain a positive business climate in Carleton Place & surrounding district
Member of: Ontario Chamber of Commerce; Lanark County Tourism Association
Finances: *Annual Operating Budget:* Less than $50,000; *Funding Sources:* Membership; fund-raising; town compensation
Staff Member(s): 1; 10 volunteer(s)
Membership: 205; *Fees:* Schedule available; *Committees:* Executive; Fiannce & Strategic Planning; Membership Value & Events
Activities: Offering insurance products, professional development training & seminars; Organizing networking meetings; Promoting businesses; Advocating on behalf of members; *Awareness Events:* Industrial Awareness Week
Chief Officer(s):
Donna MacDonald, Chair
Awards:
• Business Person of the Year

Carleton Road Industries Association (CRIA)
515 Carleton Rd., Lawrencetown NS B0S 1M0
Tel: 902-584-3332
admin@carleton515.ns.ca
www.carletonroadindustries.com
www.facebook.com/CarletonRoadIndustries
Overview: A small local charitable organization founded in 1977
Mission: To provide vocational & life skills training to adult residents of Annapolis & Kings Counties who have mental, intellectual, emotional &/or physical disabilities
Member of: DIRECTIONS Council for Vocational Services Society
Activities: Developmental services; employment programs; health & wellness program

Carleton University Academic Staff Association (CUASA) / Association du personnel enseignant de l'Université Carleton
Dunton Tower, Carleton University, #2004, 1125 Colonel By Dr., Ottawa ON K1S 5B6
Tel: 613-520-5607; *Fax:* 613-520-4426
cuasa@cuasa.ca
www.cuasa.ca
www.facebook.com/cuasaonline
twitter.com/cuasa
Overview: A medium-sized local organization founded in 1952
Mission: To serve as the collective bargaining agent for academic staff members at Ottawa's Carleton University; To promote the well-being of the academic community
Affiliation(s): Canadian Association of University Teachers (CAUT); National Union of the Canadian Association of University Teachers (NUCAUT); CAUT Defence Fund; Ontario Confederation of University Faculty Associations (OCUFA); Ontario Federation of Labour; Ottawa District Labour Council; Canadian Labour Congress
Staff Member(s): 6
Membership: 850+; *Member Profile:* Academic staff members at Carleton University in Ottawa; *Committees:* Collective Bargaining; Finance; Nominations & Elections; External Relations; Grievance Policy & Administration; Internal Affairs; Equity; Steering
Activities: Advising members; Providing grievance representation; *Library:* Carleton University Academic Staff Association Library
Chief Officer(s):
Daniel Draper, Interim Executive Director
daniel.draper@cuasa.ca
Pum van Veldhoven, President
Publications:
• CUASA Communiqué [a publication of the Carleton University Academic Staff Association]
Type: Newsletter

Carleton-Victoria Arts Council (CVAC)
c/o Pearl Black, 934 Route 590, Waterville NB E7P 1C4
Tel: 506-278-5154
carletonvictoriaarts@gmail.com
www.cvarts.ca
www.facebook.com/CVArtsC
twitter.com/CVArtsC
Overview: A small local organization founded in 1978
Mission: To provide Canadian entertainment & artists for a Canadian audience
Affiliation(s): New Brunswick Arts Council
Activities: To promote/sponsor performances by Canadian/Eastern Canadian performing artists (music, theatre & dance); 4-6 shows annually
Chief Officer(s):
Peter McLaughlin, Contact

Carleton-Victoria Forest Products Marketing Board & Wood Producers Association
151 Perkins Way, Florenceville NB E7L 3P6
Tel: 506-392-5584; *Fax:* 506-392-8290
info@cvwpa.ca
www.cvwpa.ca
Overview: A small local organization founded in 1975
Mission: To represent Private Woodlot Owners and Wood Producers from the counties of Carleton and Victoria (excluding the Parish of Drummond) in New Brunswick, Canada.
Member of: New Brunswick Federation of Woodlot Owners; Wood Products Group
Staff Member(s): 9
Membership: *Member Profile:* Private woodlot owners
Chief Officer(s):

Canadian Associations / Carman & Community Chamber of Commerce

Linda Bell, General Manager
linda.bell@cvwpa.ca

Carman & Community Chamber of Commerce
PO Box 249, Carman MB R0G 0J0
Tel: 204-750-3050
ccchamber@gmail.com
www.carmanchamber.ca
Overview: A small local organization founded in 1895
Mission: To provide services for members
Affiliation(s): Manitoba Chamber of Commerce
Finances: *Annual Operating Budget:* Less than $50,000; *Funding Sources:* Membership fees
Membership: 120+; *Fees:* $50-$100
Activities: Organizing & promoting events such as Fun & Value Days & Fair Parade & Pancake Breakfast; Offering training sessions; Promoting the area
Chief Officer(s):
Kate Petrie, President
Nikki Bartley, Executive Director

Carnaval de Québec / Québec Winter Carnival
205, boul des Cèdres, Québec QC G1L 1N8
Tél: 418-626-3716
Ligne sans frais: 866-422-7628
bonhomme@carnaval.qc.ca
www.carnaval.qc.ca
www.facebook.com/CarnavaldeQuebec
twitter.com/CarnavalQc
www.pinterest.com/carnavalquebec
Aperçu: *Dimension:* grande; *Envergure:* provinciale; Organisme sans but lucratif; fondée en 1954
Mission: Organiser annuellement une fête populaire hivernale dans le but de faire bénéficier à Québec une activité économique, touristique et sociale de première qualité dont les gens de la région seront fiers
Finances: *Budget de fonctionnement annuel:* Plus de $5 Million
Membre(s) du personnel: 70; 1400 bénévole(s)
Activités: *Stagiaires:* Oui; *Service de conférenciers:* Oui
Membre(s) du bureau directeur:
Alain April, Président

Caroline & District Chamber of Commerce
PO Box 90, Bay 2, 5040 - 49 Ave., Caroline AB T0M 0M0
Tel: 403-722-4066; *Fax:* 403-722-4002
ccoc@telus.net
www.carolinechamber.ca
www.facebook.com/160005550838372
Overview: A small local organization founded in 1980
Mission: To promote trade & commerce; To support community & tourism development; To encourage business growth; To voice local concerns to government
Member of: Alberta Chamber of Commerce
Membership: *Fees:* $10 individual; $50 business
Activities: Organizing & promoting events including Big Horn Rodeo Parade & Christmas Light-Up; *Library:* Caroline Municipal Library; Open to public
Chief Officer(s):
Shannon Fagnan, Manager

Carolinian Canada Coalition
Grosvenor Lodge, 1017 Western Rd., London ON N6G 1G5
Tel: 519-433-7077; *Fax:* 519-645-0981
info@carolinian.org
www.carolinian.org
www.facebook.com/caroliniancanada
twitter.com/caroliniancan
www.youtube.com/user/CarolinianCanada
Overview: A medium-sized local organization
Mission: To promote the protection and conservation of the Carolinian Life Zone of Southwestern Ontario.
Staff Member(s): 12
Membership: *Committees:* Management; Fundraising; Finance; Audit; Nominations
Chief Officer(s):
Michelle Kanter, Executive Director
admin@carolinian.org

Carousel Players
101 King St., 2nd Fl., St Catharines ON L2R 3H6
Tel: 905-682-8326; *Fax:* 905-682-9313
info@carouselplayers.com
www.facebook.com/carouselplayers
twitter.com/carouselplayers
Overview: A small local charitable organization founded in 1972
Mission: To use drama & theatre as a means of integrating & enlivening all aspects of the curriculum while developing the audience's awareness of & sensitivity to the experience of theatre
Member of: Professional Association of Canada Theatres; Theatre Ontario
Affiliation(s): Theatre for Young Audiences Association
Finances: *Funding Sources:* Canada Council; Ontario Arts Council
Staff Member(s): 4
Activities: *Speaker Service:* Yes
Chief Officer(s):
Pablo Felices-Luna, Artistic Director
pablo@carouselplayers.com
Jane Gardner, General Manager
jane@carouselplayers.com

CARP
70 Jefferson Ave., Toronto ON M6K 1Y4
Toll-Free: 888-363-2279
Other Communication: Advocacy e-mail: advocacy@carp.ca
support@carp.ca
www.carp.ca
www.facebook.com/CARP
twitter.com/carpnews
Previous Name: Canadian Association of Retired Persons
Overview: A large national organization founded in 1984
Mission: To promote the rights & quality of life of Canadians as they age through advocacy, education, information & CARP-recommended services & programs
Finances: *Funding Sources:* Membership fees
Membership: 300,000 in 50 chapters; *Fees:* Schedule available; *Member Profile:* No restrictions on membership
Activities: *Speaker Service:* Yes
Chief Officer(s):
Moses Znaimer, President
Laas Turnbull, Chief Operating Officer
Publications:
- CARP Action Online
Type: Newsletter
- CARP Health
Type: Newsletter
- CARP Lifestyle
Type: Newsletter
- CARP Promotions
Type: Newsletter
- CARP Savings
Type: Newsletter
- CARP Travel
Type: Newsletter

Ajax-Pickering Chapter
ajaxpickeringcarp@live.ca

Barrie Chapter
Tel: 705-252-4756
barrie@carp.ca
www.barriecarp.org
www.facebook.com/BarrieCARP36
Chief Officer(s):
Gwen Kavanagh, President

Brantford Chapter
Tel: 519-771-9287
brantford@carp.ca
www.facebook.com/BrantfordCARP
Chief Officer(s):
Ron Singer, President

Greater Bay of Quinte Area Chapter
Tel: 613-743-9365
bbq@carp.ca
www.facebook.com/CARP.BBQ
Chief Officer(s):
Bev Buchanan, President

Brockville & Thousand Islands Chapter
Tel: 613-802-0424

Calgary Chapter
Tel: 403-256-1181
calgary@carp.ca
www.facebook.com/CalgaryCARP
Chief Officer(s):
Greg McCaffrey, President

Chatham-Kent Chapter
carpchathamkent@gmail.com

Edmonton Chapter
carp.edmonton@gmail.com

Etobicoke Chapter
Tel: 416-607-2476
etobicoke@carp.ca
www.facebook.com/etobicokecarp
Chief Officer(s):
Anthony Quinn, President

Fort McMurray Chapter
fortmcmurraycarp@gmail.com

Fredericton Chapter
carp.fredericton@gmail.com

Georgian Bay Chapter
Tel: 705-888-9204
georgianbay@carp.ca
www.facebook.com/GeorgianBayCARP
Chief Officer(s):
Linda Flemington, President

Haliburton Chapter
Tel: 705-457-3919
haliburtonhighlands@carp.ca
www.facebook.com/haliburtonhighlandscarp
Chief Officer(s):
Bob Stinson, President

Halifax Chapter
Tel: 902-495-8284
anewvision@carpnovascotia.ca
www.carpnovascotia.ca

Halton Chapter
Tel: 905-319-7345
halton@carp.ca
www.facebook.com/HaltonCARP
Chief Officer(s):
Tom Carrothers, President

Hamilton Chapter
hamiltoncarp@gmail.com

Kingston Chapter
carpkingston@gmail.com

Waterloo Region Chapter
Tel: 519-267-5529
carpwaterlooregion@gmail.com
www.facebook.com/CarpWaterlooRegion

London Chapter
Tel: 519-679-3069
londonstthomas@carp.ca
www.facebook.com/LondonStThomasCARP
Chief Officer(s):
Pat Moauro, President

Mississauga Chapter
carpmississauga@gmail.com
Chief Officer(s):
Murray Etherington, Chapter President, 416-997-0919

Moncton Chapter
Tel: 506-854-5652
carpmonctonchapter@gmail.com

Montréal - Metro West Chapter
#209, 3484, boul des Sources, Dollard des Ormeaux QC H9B 1Z9
Toll-Free: 877-845-1054
montrealwest@carp.ca
www.carp.ca
www.facebook.com/WestIslandCARP
twitter.com/carpnews
Mission: To advocate for financial security & health care for aging Canadians
Chief Officer(s):
Lee Royko, President & Chapter Chair

Newmarket Aurora Chapter
newmarket.aurora.carp@gmail.com

Niagara Chapter
Tel: 905-931-3863
niagara@carp.ca
www.facebook.com/NiagaraRegionCARP
Chief Officer(s):
John Meguerian, President

North Bay Chapter
carpnorthbay@gmail.com

North Fraser Chapter
CARPnortfraserchapter@gmail.com
www.carp.ca
Chief Officer(s):
Tim Hicks, Chapter President, 604-522-9020
northfraser@carp.ca

North Shore Vancouver Chapter
carp.northshorevancouver@gmail.com

Chief Officer(s):
Elizabeth Dunbar, Chapter President, 604-926-8173
North York Chapter
carpnorthyork@gmail.com
Okanagan Valley Chapter
carpokanagan@hotmail.com
Chief Officer(s):
Mary Ann Murphy, Contact
Orillia Chapter
carporillia@gmail.com
Ottawa Chapter
Tel: 613-794-3060
ottawa@carp.ca
www.facebook.com/ottawaCARP
Chief Officer(s):
Rick Baker, President
Peterborough Chapter
Prince George Chapter
princegeorgecarp6@gmail.com
St. John's (Avalon) Chapter
Tel: 709-690-1238
st.johnsavalon@carp.ca
www.facebook.com/AvalonCARP
Chief Officer(s):
Sharron Callahan, President
Sault Ste. Marie Chapter
carpsaultstemarie@gmail.com
Scarborough Chapter
Tel: 416-282-9890
scarborough@carp.ca
www.facebook.com/ScarboroughCarp
Chief Officer(s):
Renate Crizzle, President
South Fraser Chapter
southfrasercarp@gmail.com
twitter.com/SouthFraserCARP
Sudbury Chapter
Tel: 705-618-9510
sudbury@carp.ca
www.facebook.com/SudburyCARP
Chief Officer(s):
Hugh Kruzel, President
Thunder Bay Chapter
Toronto (Downtown) Chapter
toronto@carp.ca
Chief Officer(s):
Anthony Quinn, Chapter President, 416-607-2476
Toronto (Pink) Chapter
Vancouver Central Chapter
Tel: 604-240-8085
www.facebook.com/CARPVancouverChapter45
Chief Officer(s):
Geoff Cowman, President
Vaughan Chapter
carp.vaughan@gmail.com
www.carpvaughan.com
Chief Officer(s):
George Mathew, Chapter Chair, 416-879-8470
Victoria Chapter
carpvictoriachapter@gmail.com
Whitby Oshawa Clarington Chapter
carpwoc@gmail.com
White Rock/Surrey Chapter
whiterocksurrey@carp.ca
Chief Officer(s):
Ramona Kaptyn, Chapter President, 778-294-0787
Windsor-Essex Chapter
Tel: 519-971-3713
windsoressex@carp.ca
www.facebook.com/WindsorEssexCARP
Chief Officer(s):
Larry Duffield, President
Winnipeg East Chapter
winnipegeastcarpchapter@gmail.com
Winnipeg West Chapter
carpwinnipegwest@gmail.com

Carp Agricultural Society
PO Box 188, Carp ON K0A 1L0
Tel: 613-839-2172; Fax: 613-839-1961
info@carpfair.ca
www.carpfair.ca

Overview: A medium-sized local charitable organization founded in 1863
Mission: To improve agriculture & the quality of life in the community by educating members & the community; To provide a community forum for discussing agricultural issues; To foster community development & community spirit; To help provide markets for Ontario products; To encourage conservation of natural resources, including soil conservation, reforestation, rural & urban beautification
Member of: Carp BIA
300 volunteer(s)
Membership: 500-999; *Committees:* Concessions; Light Horse; Heavy Horse; Gate; Parking; Dairy; Beef Cattle; Sheep; 4-H Club; Field Crops; Fruit & Vegetables; Grains & Seeds; Honey & Maple Syrup; Wine & Beer; Flowers; Domestic Science; Junior Department; Sewing, Needlework, & Crafts; Antiques; Story Book Farm
Chief Officer(s):
Joyce Trafford, General Manager
Paul Caldwell, President, Agriculture
Heather Johnston, President, Homecraft

Le Carré des Lombes
#401, 2022, rue Sherbrooke est, Montréal QC H2K 1B9
Tél: 514-287-9339
info@lecarredeslombes.com
www.lecarredeslombes.com
www.facebook.com/161816823394
vimeo.com/danieledesnoyers
Aperçu: *Dimension:* petite; *Envergure:* locale; Organisme sans but lucratif; fondée en 1989
Mission: Diffuser des spectacles de danse; promouvoir la danse comme discipline artistique
Membre(s) du personnel: 5
Membre(s) du bureau directeur:
Danièle Desnoyers, Directrice artistique et chorégraphe
danieledesnoyers@lecarredeslombes.com

Carrefour 50+ du Québec
#207, 148, av Belzile, Rimouski QC G5L 3E4
Tél: 418-722-6066; Téléc: 418-722-6077
Ligne sans frais: 855-722-6077
carrefour50@globetrotter.net
www.carrefour50.com
www.facebook.com/Carrefour50duQC
Nom précédent: Fédération des Clubs de l'Age d'Or de l'Est du Québec
Aperçu: *Dimension:* moyenne; *Envergure:* locale; Organisme sans but lucratif; fondée en 1972
Mission: Favoriser le bien-être collectif des membres; représenter et défendre les droits des aînés et des 50 ans et plus auprès des organismes locaux, régionaux et des instances provinciales et fédérales
Finances: *Budget de fonctionnement annuel:* $250,000-$500,000
Membre(s) du personnel: 4; 100 bénévole(s)
Membre: 25 000; *Montant de la cotisation:* 20$; *Critères d'admissibilite:* 50 ans et plus
Membre(s) du bureau directeur:
Denise Gagnon, Directrice générale

Carrefour canadien international *See* Canadian Crossroads International

Carrefour communautaire de Chibougamau
330, ch Merrill, Chibougamau QC G8P 2X4
Tél: 418-748-7266
carrefour_com@hotmail.com
Aperçu: *Dimension:* petite; *Envergure:* locale; fondée en 2001
Membre(s) du bureau directeur:
Brigitte Rosa, Responsable

Carrefour d'Actions Populaires
CP 426, Succ. Bureau-Chef, Saint-Jérôme QC J7Z 5V2
Tél: 450-432-8696; Téléc: 450-432-8696
www.carrefouractionspopulaire.com
Aperçu: *Dimension:* petite; *Envergure:* locale
Mission: Apporter aide et soutien aux personnes et aux familles moins fortunées
Membre(s) du bureau directeur:
Myriam Raymond, Coordonatrice
myriam@carrefouractionspopulaire.com

Carrefour d'entraide de Drummond (CEDI)
#308, 255, rue Brock, Drummondville QC J2C 1M5
Tél: 819-477-8105; Téléc: 819-477-7012
carrefourdentraide@cgocable.ca
www.cdcdrummond.com
Aperçu: *Dimension:* locale; Organisme sans but lucratif; fondée en 1978
Mission: Organisme de dépannage vital, de consultation budgétaire pour personnes à faibles revenus; Cuisines collectives
Finances: *Budget de fonctionnement annuel:* $100,000-$250,000
Membre(s) du personnel: 6; 10 bénévole(s)
Membre: 1-99
Membre(s) du bureau directeur:
Sylvain St-Onge, Directeur général

Carrefour de ressources en interculturel (CRIC)
#1, 1851, rue Defresne, Montréal QC H2K 2K2
Tél: 514-525-2778
info@criccentresud.org
www.criccentresud.org
Aperçu: *Dimension:* petite; *Envergure:* locale; fondée en 1999
Mission: Pour collecter des informations sur les cultures internationales afin de créer une meilleure compréhension entre les personnes d'origines culturelles différentes dans le centre-sud de Montréal
Membre(s) du bureau directeur:
Caroline Savard, Coordonnatrice
caroline@criccentresud.org
José Rebelo, Président, Conseil d'administration

Carrefour de solidarité internationale inc.
165, rue Moore, Sherbrooke QC J1H 1B8
Tél: 819-566-8595; Téléc: 819-566-8076
www.csisher.com
www.facebook.com/carrefour.solidarite.internationale
twitter.com/csisherbrooke
www.youtube.com/user/CSIsherbrooke
Également appelé: CSI - Sherbrooke
Aperçu: *Dimension:* petite; *Envergure:* internationale; Organisme sans but lucratif; fondée en 1976
Mission: Susciter la solidarité de la population de l'Estrie pour la justice sociale au plan international
Membre(s) du personnel: 9
Membre: *Montant de la cotisation:* Barème
Activités: Quinzaine du commerce équitable, mai; Festival de Cinéma Images du Sud, avril; *Stagiaires:* Oui; *Service de conférenciers:* Oui; *Bibliothèque:* Bibliothèque publique
Membre(s) du bureau directeur:
Jérémie Roberge, Président
Serge-Étienne Parent, Secrétaire
Marco Labrie, Directeur général
Publications:
• Carrefour de solidarité internationale rapport annuel
Type: Rapport; *Frequency:* Annuel

Carrefour jeunesse emploi de l'Outaouais (CJEO)
350, boul de la Gappe, Gatineau QC J8T 7T9
Tél: 819-561-7712; Téléc: 819-561-1455
info@cjeo.qc.ca
www.cjeo.qc.ca
www.linkedin.com/company/carrefour-jeunesse-emploi-de-l'outaouais
www.facebook.com/197339806961886
twitter.com/_cjeo
www.youtube.com/channel/UCTv0CrGXD-bjc03303Wj3MQ
Aperçu: *Dimension:* petite; *Envergure:* locale
Mission: Offrir des services qui visent à améliorer les conditions de vie des jeunes adultes de 16 à 35 ans en les accompagnant dans leur cheminement vers l'emploi, vers un retour aux études ou pour démarrer une entreprise.
Membre(s) du personnel: 36
Membre(s) du bureau directeur:
Martine Morissette, Directrice générale
direction@cjeo.qc.ca

Carrefour jeunesse emploi du Pontiac (CJEP)
CP 219, 80, rue Leslie, Campbell's Bay QC J0X 1K0
Tél: 819-648-5065
www.crep.qc.ca
Aperçu: *Dimension:* petite; *Envergure:* locale
Mission: Pour aider les jeunes à trouver des emplois et retournent à l'école
Membre(s) du personnel: 13
Membre: *Critères d'admissibilite:* Jeunes adultes
Membre(s) du bureau directeur:
Sylvie Landriault, Directrice générale

Carrefour Jeunesse Emploi Vallée-de-la-Gatineau (CJEVG)
217, rue Principale sud, Maniwaki QC J9E 2A3
Tél: 819-441-1165; *Téléc:* 819-441-1195
info@cjevg.qc.ca
www.cjevg.qc.ca
www.facebook.com/carrefour.emploi
Aperçu: *Dimension:* petite; *Envergure:* locale
Mission: Pour aider les jeunes à trouver des emplois et retournent à l'école
Membre: *Critères d'admissibilite:* Jeunes adultes

Carrefour jeunesse-emploi Papineau (CJEP)
112, rue MacLaren est, Gatineau QC J8L 1K1
Tél: 819-986-5248; *Téléc:* 819-986-9686
cjepapineau@cjepapineau.qc.ca
www.cjepapineau.qc.ca
Nom précédent: Action Emploi Papineau Inc.
Aperçu: *Dimension:* petite; *Envergure:* locale; fondée en 1986
Mission: Pour aider les jeunes à trouver des emplois et retournent à l'école
Membre(s) du personnel: 13
Membre: *Critères d'admissibilite:* Jeunes adultes
Membre(s) du bureau directeur:
Francine St-Jean, Directrice générale

Carrefour pour Elle
CP 21115, Succ. Jacques Cartier, Longueuil QC J4J 5J4
Tél: 450-651-5800
info@carrefourpourelle.org
www.carrefourpourelle.org
Aperçu: *Dimension:* petite; *Envergure:* locale
Mission: De fournir aux femmes et aux enfants qui sont victimes de violence un endroit sûr pour rester et pour leur offrir des compétences qui les aideront à surmonter les abus à l'avenir
Activités: Groupes de soutien; Recontres éclair; Groupes pour les enfants
Membre(s) du bureau directeur:
Sophie Boileau, Présidente, Conseil d'administration

Carrefour pour femmes inc. *See* Crossroads for Women Inc.

Carrefour Tiers-Monde (CTM)
365, boul Charest est, Québec QC G1K 3H3
Tél: 418-647-5853; *Téléc:* 418-647-5856
info@carrefour-tiers-monde.org
www.carrefour-tiers-monde.org
www.facebook.com/carrefourtiersmonde
Aperçu: *Dimension:* petite; *Envergure:* locale; fondée en 1969
Mission: Sensibiliser la population de la région de Québec aux problématiques de développement du Sud; offrir des occasions de formation pour ceux et celles qui veulent agir dans le domaine de la solidarité internationale; offrir un centre de ressources et de mobilisation aux individus et organismes de la région
Membre de: Association québécoise des organismes de coopérative internationale (AQOCI)
Finances: *Budget de fonctionnement annuel:* $100,000-$250,000; *Fonds:* Par projet
Membre(s) du personnel: 4; 70 bénévole(s)
Membre: 15 institutionnels (13 000 membres); 60 individus; *Montant de la cotisation:* 75$ institutionnel; 10$ individu; *Comités:* Recherche de financement
Activités: Journées québécoises de solidarité internationale; journée de solidarité Nord-Sud; Au Sud comme au Nord.... les enfants d'abord; *Evénements de sensibilisation:* Quinzaine du commerce équitable, mai; *Service de conférenciers:* Oui; *Bibliothèque:* Centre de documentation; Bibliothèque publique
Membre(s) du bureau directeur:
Nicole Piché, Agente, Communication
npiche@carrefour-tiers-monde.org

Boutique ÉquiMonde
365, boul Charest est, Québec QC G1K 3H3

Carrefour-Ressources
50, 1e rue ouest, Sainte-Anne-des-Monts QC G4V 2G5
Tél: 418-763-7707; *Téléc:* 418-763-7767
carrefourressources@globetrotter.net
www.facebook.com/carrefourressources
Nom précédent: Action Budget Denis Riverin Inc.
Aperçu: *Dimension:* petite; *Envergure:* locale; Organisme sans but lucratif; fondée en 1986
Mission: Développer et offrir des services aux familles et personnes à faible revenu ou vivant avec des difficultés pour qu'elles acquièrent et accroissent leur autonomie et leurs compétences personnelles, familiales et sociales
Activités: Ateliers de cuisine; ateliers manuels; ateliers sur la consommation; service de répit; cuisine communautaire

Carrot River & District Board of Trade
PO Box 340, Carrot River SK S0E 0L0
Tel: 306-768-2533; *Fax:* 306-768-3491
Overview: A small local organization

Carstairs & District Historical Society
PO Box 1067, Carstairs AB T0M 0N0
Tel: 403-337-3710
info@roulstonmuseum.ca
carstairsroulstonmuseum.ca
Also Known As: Roulston Museum
Overview: A small local charitable organization founded in 1986
Mission: To preserve the heritage of Carstairs & District; to record the history of pioneer & contemporary life in the Carstairs area; to administer the Roulston Museum by collecting, preserving, exhibiting & interpreting artifacts relevant to the area; to assemble accurate archives
Finances: *Funding Sources:* Town of Carstairs; Mountain View County; Carstairs 20/20 Partnership; Alberta Museums Association
Activities: Garden party; pioneer supper; *Library:* Roulston Museum Archives; Open to public
Awards:
• Bessie Pointen Appreciation Award
Presented to a person/group who has made outstanding contributions to the preservation of our history

Carstairs Chamber of Commerce
PO Box 968, Carstairs AB T0M 0N0
Tel: 403-337-3710
carstairschamber@gmail.com
www.carstairschamber.ca
www.facebook.com/carstairsonline
Overview: A small local organization
Mission: To promote the economic well-being of Carstairs & the surrounding community
Membership: *Member Profile:* Membership included in a Town of Carstairs business license

Carthy Foundation
PO Box 2554, Stn. M, Calgary AB T2P 2M7
Tel: 403-231-7922
coordinator@carthyfoundation.org
www.carthyfoundation.org
Overview: A small national charitable organization founded in 1965
Mission: To support Canadian charitable initiatives that focus on youth &/or environmental sustainability
Chief Officer(s):
Shelley Uytterhagen, President
Karen Wilkie, Program Director

Casa - Pueblito
#107A, 2238 Dundas St. West, Toronto ON M6R 3A9
Tel: 416-642-5781
info@casapueblito.org
www.casapueblito.org
www.facebook.com/CasaPueblito
twitter.com/CasaPueblito
instagram.com/casapueblito
Merged from: Pueblito Canada Incorporated; Casa Canadiense
Overview: A small international charitable organization founded in 1974
Mission: To work in partnership with Latin American organizations; To support the development of local programs for children in health care, childcare & education
Staff Member(s): 3; 28 volunteer(s)
Chief Officer(s):
Maria Paola Wong, Interim Executive Director
Publications:
• Casa - Pueblito Newsletter
Type: Newsletter; *Frequency:* Monthly
Profile: News & updates for members

Casa Cultural Peruana
#404, 20 Bergamot Ave., Toronto ON M9W 1V9
Tel: 416-206-2337
www.casaculturalperuana.com
www.facebook.com/185320361494606
Overview: A small local organization founded in 2001
Mission: To promote and defend Peruvian Cultural Heritage
Activities: Folk dances; Cultural exchanges; Parties

Casa do Benfica / Benfica House of Toronto
1 Robina Ave., Toronto ON M6C 3Y4
Tel: 416-653-6370
Overview: A small local organization founded in 1969
Affiliation(s): Sports Lisboa e Benfica (Lisbon, Portugal)
Finances: *Funding Sources:* Provincial government
Activities: Cultural centre whose activities include dances, folk dancing, karate, soccer, special dinners, pageants & other social events
Chief Officer(s):
Joe Loureiro, Manager

Casa do Ribatejo / Maison de Ribatejo
5979, rue Molson, Montréal QC H1Y 3C1
Tél: 514-729-7822
Également appelé: Ribatejo House
Aperçu: *Dimension:* petite; *Envergure:* locale

Casa dos Acores do Ontário / The Azorean House of Ontario
1136 College St., Toronto ON M6H 1B6
Tel: 416-603-2900; *Fax:* 416-603-0642
caosecretaria@gmail.com
www.facebook.com/cacores.ca
twitter.com/CasadosAcoresOn
Overview: A small local charitable organization founded in 1986
Affiliation(s): Association of Portuguese Clubs
Finances: *Annual Operating Budget:* $100,000-$250,000
40 volunteer(s)
Membership: 400 individual; *Fees:* $60 individual
Activities: Hosting & organizing cultural events; *Library:* Open to public
Chief Officer(s):
Suzanne Cunha, President

Casey House Hospice Inc.
9 Huntley St., Toronto ON M4Y 2K8
Tel: 416-962-7600; *Fax:* 416-962-5147
heart@caseyhouse.on.ca
www.caseyhouse.com
www.linkedin.com/company/casey-house-foundation
www.facebook.com/CaseyHouseTO
twitter.com/caseyhouseTO
www.youtube.com/caseyhousetv
Overview: A small local charitable organization founded in 1988 overseen by Canadian AIDS Society
Mission: To provide treatment, support & health services for people affected by HIV/AIDS
Member of: Ontario Hospital Association; Canadian Palliative Care Association
Affiliation(s): St. Michael's Hospital
Finances: *Funding Sources:* Ontario Ministry of Health; fundraising
200 volunteer(s)
Activities: Providing medical, palliative & supportive care for people with HIV/AIDS & their families & friends, provided in a 13-bed Hospice residence, & for up to 120 people at any one time through Home Hospice
Chief Officer(s):
Joanne Simons, Chief Executive Officer
Ann Stewart, Medical Director

Casting Directors Society of Canada (CDC)
info@castingsociety.ca
www.castingsociety.ca
Overview: A medium-sized national organization founded in 1981
Mission: An association that works to help the casting industry as a whole by representing professional casting directors working in every medium where professional actors are required.
Membership: *Member Profile:* Independent Canadian casting directors who have completed two full and consecutive years as a fully independent casting director.
Chief Officer(s):
Christine Poe, Secretary

Castle-Crown Wilderness Coalition (CCWC)
PO Box 2621, Pincher Creek AB T0K 1W0
Tel: 403-627-5059
office@ccwc.ab.ca
www.ccwc.ab.ca
www.facebook.com/castlecrownwildernesscoalition
Overview: A small local organization founded in 1989
Mission: To restore & maintain the Castle Wilderness within the Crown of the Continent Ecosystem
Finances: *Funding Sources:* Membership fees; Donations; Conservation organizations; Fisheries & Oceans Canada

Membership: 500+; *Fees:* $10
Activities: Sponsoring a stewardship program to monitor & restore the Castle Wilderness; Conducting hikes to raise awareness of the area; *Awareness Events:* Annual West Castle Wetland Ecological Reserve Weed Pull, July
Chief Officer(s):
Andrea Hlady, President
Publications:
• Bringing it Back: A Restoration Framework for the Castle Wilderness
• The Castle Wilderness Environmental Inventory
• Castle Wilderness News
Type: Newsletter
• The State of the Castle Wilderness: Annual Report
Type: Yearbook; *Frequency:* Annually

Castlegar & District Arts Council
PO Box 3501, Castlegar BC V1N 3W3
castlegararts@gmail.com
www.castlegarculture.com/culture-guide/castlegar-arts-council/
Overview: A small local organization
Mission: To promote the arts in Castlegar and the surrounding area
Member of: Assembly of BC Arts Councils
Staff Member(s): 1
Activities: Coordinating cultural programs & arts activities; Acting as a clearing house for information on cultural programs; Fostering & encouraging interest in the arts; Promoting public understanding & appreciation of community culture
Chief Officer(s):
Jacquie Hamilton, Treasurer, 250-365-8026

Castlegar & District Chamber of Commerce (CDCoC)
1995 - 6th Ave., Castlegar BC V1N 4B7
Tel: 250-365-6313; *Fax:* 250-365-5778
info@castlegar.com
www.castlegar.com
Overview: A medium-sized local organization founded in 1946
Mission: To encourage a business climate which enables our membership & community to prosper
Member of: BC Chamber of Commerce; Canadian Chamber of Commerce
Finances: *Funding Sources:* Membership dues; City of Castlegar; provincial government
Staff Member(s): 3
Membership: *Fees:* Schedule available based on number of employees
Activities: Golf tournament; member breakfasts & events; promotional materials; Christmas Light Up; 2010 Olympic Bid; Tourism Essentials; *Awareness Events:* Small Business Week; Chamber Week
Chief Officer(s):
Jane Charest, President

Castor Fish & Game Association
c/o Alberta Fish & Game Association, 6924 - 104th St., Edmonton AB T6H 2L7
Tel: 780-437-2342; *Fax:* 780-438-6872
office@afga.org
www.afga.org/html/content/clubandzones
Overview: A small local organization
Member of: Alberta Fish & Game Association
Chief Officer(s):
Wes Wagar, Director, Zone 3, Alberta Fish & Game Association

Catalyst Theatre Society of Alberta
9828 101A Ave., Edmonton AB T5J 3C6
Tel: 780-431-1750; *Fax:* 780-433-3060
info@catalysttheatre.ca
www.catalysttheatre.ca
www.facebook.com/catalysttheatreyeg
twitter.com/catalystyeg
Overview: A medium-sized provincial charitable organization founded in 1978
Mission: To create & present original Canadian work that explores new possibilities for theatre
Member of: Professional Association of Canadian Theatres (PACT); Canadian Conference for the Arts
Staff Member(s): 7
Membership: *Committees:* Youth Advisory
Chief Officer(s):
Jonathan Christenson, Artistic Director

Cataraqui Archaeological Research Foundation
611 Princess St., Kingston ON K7L 1E1
Tel: 613-542-3483
carf@carf.info
www.carf.info
www.facebook.com/Kingstonarchaeologicalcentre
twitter.com/carfkingston
Also Known As: Kingston Archaeological Centre
Overview: A small local charitable organization founded in 1983
Mission: To research & maintain archaeological resources in Ontario
Finances: *Funding Sources:* Private & public donations; Corporate support
Staff Member(s): 4
Activities: Sponsoring archaeological research; Providing public education; Offering activities for all ages, such as a summer camp called, "Can You Dig It?"; *Awareness Events:* Public Archaeology Day, July; Archaeology Week, June *Library:* Kingston Archaeological Centre Library; by appointment
Chief Officer(s):
Kip Parker, Executive Director
Publications:
• Subsoil
Type: Newsletter; *Frequency:* s-a.; *Price:* Free for members of the Cataraqui Archaeological Research Foundation
Profile: Recent activities, upcoming events, articles, fiction

Cathedral Bluffs Symphony Orchestra (CBSO)
PO Box 51074, 18 Eglinton Sq., Toronto ON M1L 2K2
Tel: 416-879-5566
info@cathedralbluffs.com
www.cathedralbluffs.com
www.facebook.com/1376703615900205
www.youtube.com/channel/UCjQ5dDliajV95HIIIbQKMUQ
Previous Name: Cathedral Bluffs Symphony Orchestra of Scarborough
Overview: A small local charitable organization founded in 1985 overseen by Orchestras Canada
Mission: To provide residents of Greater Toronto with an opportunity to hear classical symphonic music performed by a live orchestra; to provide both skilled and amateur musicians with an opportunity to perform
Member of: Scarborough Arts Council
Finances: *Funding Sources:* Box office; Donations; Government grants; Fund-raising
Staff Member(s): 6
Membership: *Member Profile:* Skilled musicians
Activities: 5 concert subscription series, annual Young Artists concert; *Library:* Not open to public
Chief Officer(s):
Peggy Wong, Orchestra Manager
Tim Hendrickson, President

Cathedral Bluffs Symphony Orchestra of Scarborough *See* Cathedral Bluffs Symphony Orchestra

Catherine Donnelly Foundation
12 Montcrest Blvd., Toronto ON M4K 1J7
Tel: 416-461-2996; *Fax:* 416-465-4193
info@catherinedonnellyfoundation.org
www.catherinedonnellyfoundation.org
www.facebook.com/catherinedonnellyfoundation
twitter.com/cdfoundation
Overview: A small national charitable organization founded in 2003
Mission: To support housing, adult education, & environmental initiatives that aim to improve the lives of marginalized persons &/or strengthen ecological justice
Activities: Advocating for climate justice & adult education; Collaborating with organizations to develop affordable housing solutions
Chief Officer(s):
Valerie Lemieux, General Director

Catholic Action Montreal / Action Catholique Montréal
#301, 1857, rue de Maisonneuve ouest, Montréal QC H3H 1J9
Tel: 514-937-2301
join@catholicaction.ca
www.catholicaction.ca
Overview: A small local charitable organization founded in 2015
Mission: To bring together members of Montreal's English-speaking Catholic community to help people in need
Finances: *Funding Sources:* Membership dues; Archdiocese of Montreal
Activities: Promoting educational, health, & social services
Chief Officer(s):
Anna Graham, Interim Chair

Catholic Association of Religious & Family Life Educators of Ontario (CARFLEO)
ON
contact@carfleo.org
www.carfleo.org
www.facebook.com/Carfleo
twitter.com/TWEETcarfleo
www.youtube.com/VIDEOCARFLEO
Merged from: Catholic Religious Education Consultants of Ontario; Ontario Catholic Family Life Educators Network
Overview: A medium-sized local charitable organization founded in 2005
Membership: *Member Profile:* Religious and Family Life Education in Ontario
Chief Officer(s):
Paul Beaudette, Chair
BeaudetteP@hwcdsb.ca
Awards:
• Archbishop Pocock Award for Excellence in Religious Education
• Fr. Angus MacDougall S.J. Award
Meetings/Conferences:
• Catholic Association of Religious and Family Life Educators of Ontario Conference & Annual General Meeting, March, 2018, Queen of Apostles, Mississauga, ON
Scope: Provincial

Catholic Bible Society *Voir* Société catholique de la Bible

Catholic Biblical Association of Canada (CBAC)
5650 Mavis Rd., Mississauga ON L5V 2N6
Tel: 905-568-4393
catholicbiblicalcanada@gmail.com
www.catholicbiblical.com
Previous Name: Canadian Catholic Biblical Association
Overview: A medium-sized national charitable organization founded in 1974
Mission: To build community within member parishes by energizing Catholics to embrace the Scriptures as a foundational source of spiritual nourishment
Affiliation(s): Archdiocese of Toronto; World Catholic Biblical Federation
Finances: *Annual Operating Budget:* $100,000-$250,000
Membership: *Fees:* $30
Activities: Workshops; Bible in My Life program; Children's summer programs; Pilgrimages; *Rents Mailing List:* Yes; *Library:* Catholic Biblical Association of Canada Resource Centre; Open to public
Chief Officer(s):
Jocelyn Monette, Executive Director

Catholic Centre for Immigrants - Ottawa + CIC Foundation / Centre Catholique pour Immigrants - Ottawa + Fondation du CCI
219 Argyle Ave., Ottawa ON K2P 2H4
Tel: 613-232-9634; *Fax:* 613-232-3660
cic@cic.ca
ccicottawa.ca
www.facebook.com/TheCommunityCup
Also Known As: CCI Ottawa
Previous Name: Catholic Immigration Centre + CIC Foundation
Overview: A medium-sized national organization founded in 1984
Membership: *Fees:* $10; *Member Profile:* All Canadian residents
Chief Officer(s):
Carl Nicolson, Executive Director, 613-232-9634 Ext. 335
carl@cic.ca

Catholic Charismatic Renewal Council, Toronto (CCRC)
830 Bathurst St., Toronto ON M5R 3G1
Tel: 416-466-0776; *Fax:* 905-454-0876
ccrctoronto@bellnet.ca
www.ccrctor.com
www.facebook.com/284998491631113
twitter.com/CCRCToronto
Also Known As: Catholic Charismatic Renewal
Overview: A small local organization
Mission: To stress the Lordship of Jesus through promoting baptism of the Holy Spirit
Affiliation(s): Archdiocese of Toronto
Activities: Life in The Spirit seminars; The Holy Eucharistic Devotions; Healing services; Evangelization; Devotional workshops; Special rallies & conferences
Chief Officer(s):

Matthias Yaw Kotoka Amuzu, Spiritual & Formation Institute Director
Pauline Susanto, Executive Secretary

Catholic Charities of The Archdiocese of Toronto
#400, 1155 Yonge St., Toronto ON M4T 1W2
Tel: 416-934-3401; *Fax:* 416-934-3402
info@catholiccharitiestor.org
www.catholiccharitiestor.org
twitter.com/charitiescares
Previous Name: Council of Catholic Charities
Overview: A medium-sized local licensing charitable organization founded in 1913
Mission: To ensure the provision of health & social sciences; To provide leadership & advocacy on behalf of member agencies & those in need; To serve people living & working throughout the Greater Toronto Area, as well as in Simcoe, Durham, Peel, & York
Affiliation(s): Catholic Family Services of Toronto & 26 member agencies
Finances: *Annual Operating Budget:* $250,000-$500,000
Staff Member(s): 1; 10 volunteer(s)
Membership: *Committees:* Allocations; Audit; Catholic Agencies; Communications; Employee Pension & Benefit; Human Resources; Membership Review; Nominating; Social Justice/Advocacy
Activities: *Speaker Service:* Yes
Chief Officer(s):
Thomas Cardinal Collins, Chair
Carmela Pallotto, President
Michael Fullan, Executive Director

Catholic Children's Aid Society of Hamilton (CCAS)
735 King St. East, Hamilton ON L8M 1A1
Tel: 905-525-2012; *Fax:* 905-525-5606
Other Communication: Emergency After Hours Phone: 905-525-5606
www.hamiltonccas.on.ca
www.facebook.com/hamiltonccas
twitter.com/HamiltonCCAS
www.youtube.com/channel/UCfl8rgJy4r8oMcepjfErppw/feed
Overview: A small local charitable organization founded in 1954
Mission: To provide child welfare & family services to the Hamilton community; To ensure that services are guided by Catholic values
Member of: Ontario Association of Children's Aid Societies
Affiliation(s): Council of Catholic Service Organziations
Finances: *Annual Operating Budget:* Greater than $5 Million; *Funding Sources:* Ontario Trillium Foundation; Donations
191 volunteer(s)
Membership: 100-499
Activities: Providing foster care & adoption services, Investigating possible instances of child abuse & neglect; *Awareness Events:* Serendipity Auction, Nov.; *Internships:* Yes; *Speaker Service:* Yes
Chief Officer(s):
Ersilia DiNardo, Executive Director

Catholic Children's Aid Society of Metropolitan Toronto *See* Catholic Children's Aid Society of Toronto

Catholic Children's Aid Society of Toronto (CCAS)
26 Maitland St., Toronto ON M4Y 1C6
Tel: 416-395-1500; *Fax:* 416-395-1581
communications@torontoccas.org
www.ccas.toronto.on.ca
Previous Name: Catholic Children's Aid Society of Metropolitan Toronto
Overview: A medium-sized local charitable organization founded in 1894
Mission: To provide social services that protect children, strengthen family life & are reflective of Catholic values
Member of: Catholic Charities of the Archdiocese of Toronto
Affiliation(s): Ministry of Children and Youth Services
Finances: *Funding Sources:* Provincial government; Private donations
Activities: Offering resources for individuals to report child abuse & neglect; Providing counselling services for children, adults, families, & immigrants; *Awareness Events:* Child Abuse Prevention Campaign
Chief Officer(s):
Janice Robinson, Executive Director
Publications:
• Catholic Children's Aid Society of Toronto Annual Report
Type: Report; *Frequency:* a.

• Connections [a publication of the Catholic Children's Aid Society of Toronto]
Type: Newsletter; *Frequency:* 3 pa
East Toronto Branch
1880 Birchmount Rd., Toronto ON M1P 2J7
Mission: On behalf of the Catholic community, this organization is committed to provide social services that protect children and strengthen family life.
Chief Officer(s):
Nancy DiNatale, Branch Manager
North West Toronto Branch
30 Drewry Ave., Toronto ON M2M 4C4
Chief Officer(s):
Nyron Sookraj, Branch Manager
Scarborough Branch
843 Kennedy Rd., Toronto ON M1K 2E3
Chief Officer(s):
Domenic Gratta, Branch Manager
South Toronto Branch
Dufferin Mall, #219, 900 Dufferin St., Toronto ON M6H 4B1
Chief Officer(s):
Renée Walsh, Branch Manager

Catholic Church Extension Society of Canada *See* Catholic Missions in Canada

Catholic Civil Rights League (CCRL)
2305 Bloor St. West, Toronto ON M6S 1P1
Tel: 416-466-8244; *Fax:* 416-466-0091
Toll-Free: 844-722-2275
www.ccrl.ca
www.youtube.com/user/CatholicCivilRights
Overview: A medium-sized national organization founded in 1985
Mission: To be witness for church teaching in public life; To combat anti-Catholic defamation in the media; To participate in debates on public policy
Affiliation(s): Archdiocese of Toronto
Finances: *Funding Sources:* Donations
Membership: *Fees:* $25 individuals; $15 students & seniors; $30 families; *Member Profile:* Catholics over the age of eighteen
Activities: Advocating with government & media
Chief Officer(s):
Christian D. Elia, Executive Director
celia@ccrl.ca
Awards:
• Archbishop Adam Exner Award for Catholic Excellence in Public Life
Contact: Phil Horgan
Publications:
• Civil Rights [a publication of the Catholic Civil Rights League]
Type: Newsletter; *Frequency:* Quarterly; *Price:* Free with Catholic Civil Rights League membership
Profile: Regional roundup, current issues, & media watch

Catholic Community Services Inc. *See* Foundation of Catholic Community Services Inc.

Catholic Cross Cultural Services (CCS)
#401, 55 Town Centre Ct., Toronto ON M1P 4X4
Tel: 416-757-7010; *Fax:* 416-757-7399
www.cathcrosscultural.org
Previous Name: Catholic Immigration Bureau
Overview: A medium-sized international charitable organization overseen by Ontario Council of Agencies Serving Immigrants
Mission: To promote the settlement & integration of immigrants & refugees facing linguistic & cultural barriers through the provision of community based services
Affiliation(s): Access for New Canadians
Finances: *Annual Operating Budget:* $3 Million-$5 Million
Staff Member(s): 98; 20 volunteer(s)
Membership: 60; *Fees:* $20 individual; $35 organization
Chief Officer(s):
Carolyn Davis, Executive Director
Brampton
#302, 8 Nelson St. West, Brampton ON L6X 4J2
Tel: 905-457-7740; *Fax:* 905-457-7769
Mississauga
3660 Hurontario St., 7th Fl., Mississauga ON L5B 3C4
Tel: 905-273-4140; *Fax:* 905-273-4176
Scarborough Region
#503, 1200 Markham Rd., Toronto ON M1H 3C3
Tel: 416-289-6766; *Fax:* 416-289-6198

Catholic Education Foundation of Ontario (CEFO)
80 Sheppard Ave. East, Toronto ON M2N 6E8

Tel: 416-229-5326; *Fax:* 416-229-5345
office@cefontario.ca
cefontario.ca
www.facebook.com/catholiceducationfoundationontario
Overview: A small provincial charitable organization founded in 1976
Mission: To foster & promote the principles of Catholic education; to support parents in their role as primary educators; to assist the Church in its pastoral responsibilities to the schools; to encourage the establishment of Catholic schools; to promote equity of educational funding in Ontario
Chief Officer(s):
Mary Eileen Donovan, President
president@cefontario.ca

Catholic Family Life Centre-Simcoe South; North Simcoe Catholic Family Life Centre *See* Catholic Family Services of Simcoe County

Catholic Family Service of Ottawa (CFS Ottawa) / Service familial catholique d'Ottawa (SFC Ottawa)
310 Olmstead St., Ottawa ON K1L 7K3
Tel: 613-233-8478; *Fax:* 613-233-9881
info@cfsottawa.ca
www.cfsottawa.ca
Previous Name: Catholic Family Service of Ottawa-Carleton
Overview: A small local charitable organization founded in 1940 overseen by Family Service Ontario
Mission: CFS Ottawa offers a range of social services in English & French to all residents of the Ottawa-Carleton area. Services include counselling, support to the victims or witnesses of family violence or sexual abuse, advocacy, community development. It is a registered charity, BN: 118841105RR0001.
Member of: Family Service Canada
Finances: *Annual Operating Budget:* $1.5 Million-$3 Million; *Funding Sources:* Provincial/municipal government; United Way; private donations
Staff Member(s): 34; 15 volunteer(s)
Membership: 50
Activities: *Internships:* Yes; *Library:* Not open to public
Chief Officer(s):
Isabelle Massip, President
Franca DiDiomete, Executive Director

Catholic Family Service of Ottawa-Carleton *See* Catholic Family Service of Ottawa

Catholic Family Services of Hamilton (CFS)
#201, 447 Main St. East, Hamilton ON L8N 1K1
Tel: 905-527-3823; *Fax:* 905-546-5779
Toll-Free: 877-527-3823
intake@cfshw.com
www.cfshw.com
www.linkedin.com/company/catholic-family-services-of-hamilton
www.facebook.com/Catholic.Family.Services.Hamilton
twitter.com/CFSHW
www.youtube.com/channel/UCeLsGYd3vHt5PGRkS8JJFjA
Previous Name: Catholic Family Services of Hamilton-Wentworth
Overview: A small local organization founded in 1944 overseen by Ontario Association of Credit Counselling Services
Mission: To provide individual, marriage, family, & credit counselling services in the Hamilton & Burlington communities
Member of: Ontario Association of Credit Counselling Service
Affiliation(s): Ontario Community Support Association; ONTCHILD; Family Services Ontario; Canadian Association for Community Care; Continuing Gerontological Education Cooperative; Older Persons' Mental Health & Addictions Network; Ontario Association on Developmental Disabilities; Ontario Case Managers Association; Ontario Gerontology Association; Ontario Partnership on Aging Development Disabilities
Finances: *Funding Sources:* Government of Canada; Province of Ontario; City of Hamilton; United Way of Burlington & Greater Hamilton; Foundations such as ON Trillium Foundation
Activities: Offering programs, such as the Employee Assistance Program, Debt Management Program, K.I.D.S. (Kids in Divorced / Separated Situations), Men's Anti-Violence & Abuse Program, & the Senior's Intervention & Support Program; Providing mediation services, in areas such as the workplace, credit, estates, & commerce; Offering consumer credit education to the general public; Offering money management coaching
Chief Officer(s):
Linda Dayler, Executive Director & Secretary
Paula Forbes, Associate Director

Catholic Family Services of Hamilton-Wentworth See Catholic Family Services of Hamilton

Catholic Family Services of Peel Dufferin (CFSPD)
Emerald Centre, #400, 10 Kingsbridge Garden Circle, Mississauga ON L5R 3K6
Tel: 905-450-1608; Fax: 905-897-2467
Other Communication: Services en Français 905-450-1608 ext 169
info@cfspd.com
www.cfspd.com
www.facebook.com/208938825992
Previous Name: Peel Dufferin Catholic Services
Overview: A small local charitable organization founded in 1981 overseen by Family Service Ontario
Mission: CFSPD is a multi-service counselling agency that supports families coping with difficulties, notably violence, trauma & abuse. Services are available in many languages to help people deal with such problems as depression, anxiety, grief, marital difficulties, parent-child conflict, developmental transitions & cutural adjustments. Offices in Mississauga & Brampton have walk-in clinics. The Society is a registered charity, BN: 119087823RR0001.
Member of: Catholic Charities; Archdiocese of Toronto; United Way of Peel Region
Finances: Annual Operating Budget: $500,000-$1.5 Million
Staff Member(s): 30; 85 volunteer(s)
Activities: Individual, couple & family therapy; support groups; workshops; Internships: Yes; Speaker Service: Yes
Chief Officer(s):
Ana Hill, Manager, Operations, 905-450-1608 Ext. 404
anahill@cfspd.com

Brampton Branch
#201, 60 West Dr., Brampton ON L6T 3T6
Tel: 905-450-1608; Fax: 905-450-8902

Caledon Branch
#D8, 18 King St. East, Bolton ON L7E 1E8
Tel: 905-450-1608; Fax: 905-450-8902

Orangeville Branch
Dufferin Child & Family Services, 655 Riddell Rd., Orangeville ON L9W 4Z5
Toll-Free: 888-940-0584

Catholic Family Services of Saskatoon (CFS)
#200, 506 25th St. East, Saskatoon SK S7K 4A7
Tel: 306-244-7773; Fax: 306-244-8537
staff@cfssaskatoon.sk.ca
www.cfssaskatoon.sk.ca
Overview: A small local charitable organization founded in 1940
Mission: To promote quality of life by developing & supporting the inherent strengths of individuals, families & the community
Member of: United Way of Saskatoon
Affiliation(s): Family Service Canada; Family Service Saskatchewan
Finances: Annual Operating Budget: $500,000-$1.5 Million; Funding Sources: Provincial & regional governments; United Way; Diocese of Saskatoon; community grants & donations 50 volunteer(s)
Membership: 1-99
Activities: Counselling; family & children's services; teen parent program; family to family ties program; families & schools together program; employee & family assistance prgrams, marriage preparation, work & family wellness presentations; event speakers; workshop presentations & consultations; Library: Not open to public
Chief Officer(s):
Trish St. Onge, Executive Director

Catholic Family Services of Simcoe County (CFSSC)
20 Anne St. S, Barrie ON L4N 2C6
Tel: 705-726-2503; Fax: 705-726-2570
info@cfssc.ca
www.cfssc.ca
www.facebook.com/CFSSC
twitter.com/CounselorSimcoe
Previous Name: Catholic Family Life Centre-Simcoe South; North Simcoe Catholic Family Life Centre
Overview: A small local charitable organization founded in 1979 overseen by Family Service Ontario
Mission: To offer professional social services to all residents of Simcoe South; services will be directed to the treatment of troubled families & individuals, as well as to strengthening & enriching family life & individual functioning in all their dimensions & contexts
Finances: Annual Operating Budget: $250,000-$500,000; Funding Sources: Charities; United Way
Staff Member(s): 20
Membership: 1-99
Activities: Family, individual & group counselling; family life education
Chief Officer(s):
Michelle Bergin, Executive Director
mbergin@cfssc.ca

Catholic Family Services of Toronto (CFS Toronto) / Services familiaux catholiques de Toronto
Catholic Pastoral Centre, #200, 1155 Yonge St., Toronto ON M4T 1W2
Tel: 416-921-1163; Fax: 416-921-1579
info@cfstoronto.com
www.cfstoronto.com
Previous Name: Catholic Welfare Bureau
Overview: A medium-sized local charitable organization founded in 1922
Mission: To help individuals & families develop their potential by providing wellness programs & treatment services
Member of: Catholic Charities of the Archdiocese of Toronto
Affiliation(s): Family Service Canada; Family Service Ontario
Finances: Annual Operating Budget: $1.5 Million-$3 Million
Staff Member(s): 35; 18 volunteer(s)
Activities: Library:
Chief Officer(s):
Ivana Zanardo, President
Denis Costello, Executive Director & Secretary

North Toronto Office
#300, 5799 Yonge St., Toronto ON M2M 3V3
Tel: 416-222-0048; Fax: 416-222-3321

The Catholic Foundation of Manitoba / Fondation catholique du Manitoba
622 Taché Ave., Winnipeg MB R2H 2B4
Tel: 204-233-4268
cfmb@mts.net
catholicfoundation.mb.ca
Overview: A medium-sized provincial organization founded in 1964
Mission: The vision of the Catholic Foundation is to provide for the needy, better the situation of the underprivileged, promote cultural advancement and scientific research, and promote the cultural life of the Catholic community of Manitoba by encouraging the funding of endowments and by providing prudent management of funds and responsible distribution of the derived revenue
Staff Member(s): 1; 18 volunteer(s)
Chief Officer(s):
Tom Lussier, President
Awards:
• Catholic Foundation of Manitoba Grants
Eligibility: Religious, educational or social agency

Catholic Health Alliance of Canada / Alliance catholique canadienne de la santé
Annex C, Saint-Vincent Hospital, 60 Cambridge St. North, Ottawa ON K1R 7A5
Tel: 613-562-6262; Fax: 613-782-2857
www.chac.ca
Previous Name: Catholic Health Association of Canada; Catholic Hospital Association of Canada
Overview: A large national charitable organization founded in 1939
Mission: To strengthen & support the ministry of Catholic health care organizations & providers, through advocacy & governance
Finances: Annual Operating Budget: $1.5 Million-$3 Million; Funding Sources: Membership dues
Membership: 7 provincial associations + 12 sponsor organizations + 100 hospitals, community health centres, nursing homes & long-term care facilities; Fees: Schedule available; Member Profile: Sponsor organizations of Catholic health care in Canada
Chief Officer(s):
Michael Shea, President & CEO, 780-781-4075
shea.chac@gmail.com
Awards:
• Midcareer Leadership Award
Eligibility: Nominees must be 45 years of age or younger & work in a Catholic health care organization
• Lifetime Achievement Award
Eligibility: Nominees must have sent the majority of their careers in Catholic health care
Meetings/Conferences:
• Catholic Health Alliance of Canada 2018 Annual Conference, May, 2018, Marriott Gateway on the Falls, Niagara Falls, ON
Scope: National
Publications:
• Catholic Health Alliance of Canada Annual Report
Type: Yearbook; Frequency: Annually
Profile: Financial & executive reports
• Facing Death, Discovering Life
Number of Pages: 78; Author: James Roche; ISBN: 9780920705360; Price: $10.95
• Forming Health Care Leaders: A Guide
Number of Pages: 143; ISBN: 9780920705421; Price: $12.50
• Health Ethics Guide
Number of Pages: 122; ISBN: 9780920705018; Price: $20
• Lift Up Your Hearts to the Lord
Number of Pages: 104; ISBN: 9780920705056; Price: $4
• Living With Hope in Times of Illness
Number of Pages: 30; Editor: Barry McGrorry; Greg J. Humbert; ISBN: 9780920705407; Price: $2
• Spirituality & Health: What's Good for the Soul Can Be Good for the Body, Too
Number of Pages: 74; Author: James Roche; ISBN: 9780920705247; Price: $9.95

Catholic Health Association of British Columbia (CHABC)
9387 Holmes St., Burnaby BC V3N 4C3
Tel: 604-524-3427; Fax: 604-524-3428
smhouse@shawlink.ca
chabc.bc.ca
Overview: A medium-sized provincial organization founded in 1940 overseen by Catholic Health Association of Canada
Mission: To witness to the healing ministry and abiding presence of Jesus. Inspired by the Gospel, this Association strives to have a universal concern for health as a condition for full human development.
Member of: Catholic Health Alliance of Canada; Health Employers Association of British Columbia
Affiliation(s): Euthanasia Prevention Coalition; Canadian Association of Parish Nurse Ministries
Staff Member(s): 2
Membership: 114; Committees: Mission Intergration; Pastral Care; Ethics
Chief Officer(s):
Dianne Doyle, President
Meetings/Conferences:
• Catholic Health Association of BC 78th Annual General Meeting and Conference, 2018, BC
Scope: Provincial

Catholic Health Association of Canada; Catholic Hospital Association of Canada See Catholic Health Alliance of Canada

Catholic Health Association of Manitoba (CHAM) / Association catholique manitobaine de la santé (ACMS)
SBGH Education Bldg., 409 Taché Ave., #N5067, Winnipeg MB R2H 2A6
Tel: 204-235-3136; Fax: 204-235-3811
www.cham.mb.ca
Overview: A medium-sized provincial charitable organization founded in 1943 overseen by Catholic Health Alliance of Canada
Mission: To carry out the healing ministry of the Catholic Church in the delivery of both health & social services in Manitoba; To treat the people of Manitoba with compassion & respect for all; To recognize the spiritual dimension integral to health & healing
Member of: Catholic Health Alliance of Canada
Affiliation(s): Bishops of Manitoba; Diocese of Churchill-Hudson Bay, Northwest Territories
Membership: Fees: $20 personal members; $100 associate members; Member Profile: Organizations; Health care facilities; Individuals
Activities: Promoting collaboration in health care services; Providing education to health care professionals, parish workers, & volunteers; Engaging in advocacy activities for the needs of the vulnerable & disadvantaged; Promoting the dignity & sacredness of each person; Awareness Events: CHAC World Day of the Sick
Chief Officer(s):
Wilmar Chopyk, Executive Director
wchopyk@cham.mb.ca
Publications:
• CHAM [Catholic Health Association of Manitoba] Newsletter
Type: Newsletter
Profile: Educational information for members & CHAM activities

Catholic Health Association of New Brunswick (CHANB) / L'Association catholique de la santé du Nouveau-Brunswick
1773 Water St., Miramichi NB E1N 1B2
Tel: 506-778-5302; *Fax:* 506-778-5303
nbcha@nb.aibn.com
www.chanb.com
Overview: A small provincial organization founded in 1986 overseen by Catholic Health Association of Canada
Mission: The Catholic Health Association of New Brunswick is a provincial Christian organization promoting health care in the tradition of the Catholic Church. The Association fosters healing in all its aspects: Physical, psychological, social and spiritual
Member of: Catholic Health Alliance of Canada
Membership: 300
Chief Officer(s):
Robert Stewart, Executive Director
rstewart@health.nb.ca

Catholic Health Association of Saskatchewan (CHAS)
1702 - 20 St. West, Saskatoon SK S7M 0Z9
Tel: 306-655-5330; *Fax:* 306-655-5333
cath.health@chassk.ca
www.chassk.ca
Overview: A medium-sized provincial charitable organization founded in 1943 overseen by Catholic Health Association of Canada
Mission: To provide leadership in mission, ethics, spiritual care, & social justice in Saskatchewan; To promote the sanctity of life & the dignity of all
Member of: Catholic Health Alliance of Canada
Membership: *Fees:* $25 person members; $75 associations; *Member Profile:* Institutions, groups, & individuals who are interested in Catholic health care & support the work of the association
Activities: Providing education & resources to members; Offering programs, such as the Parish Home Ministry of Care Program & the Catholic Health Leadership Program; Engaging in advocacy activities with the government; Providing both provincial & national networking opportunities; *Awareness Events:* Mission Week; World Day of the Sick *Library:* Catholic Health Association of Saskatchewan Resource Library
Chief Officer(s):
Chris Donald, President
Sandra Kary, Executive Director
sandra@chassk.ca
Terrie Michaud, Vice-President
Anne Reddekopp, Secretary-Treasurer
Sandy Normand, Coordinator, Mission Education
snormand@chassk.ca
Awards:
• Moola-Freer Scholarship & Award, Committee of the Board of Directors
Eligibility: Scholarship funds available to persons who have registered or are planning to register in a Palliative Care home study or certificate program. *Deadline:* June 30

Catholic Health Care Conference of Alberta *See* Christian Health Association of Alberta

Catholic Health of Alberta *See* Covenant Health

Catholic Health Sponsors of Ontario
#1801, 1 Yonge St., Toronto ON M5E 1W7
Tel: 416-740-0444
chco@chco.ca
www.chco.ca
Overview: A medium-sized provincial organization overseen by Catholic Health Association of Canada
Mission: To sponsor member institutions & strengthen Catholic health care in Ontario
Chief Officer(s):
John P. Ruetz, President & CEO
john.ruetz@chco.ca
Sarah Quackenbush, Consultant, Mission Education
squackenbush@csjssm.ca

Catholic Immigration Bureau *See* Catholic Cross Cultural Services

Catholic Immigration Centre + CIC Foundation *See* Catholic Centre for Immigrants - Ottawa + CIC Foundation

Catholic Missions in Canada (CMIC) / Missions catholiques au Canada
#201, 1155 Yonge St., Toronto ON M4T 1W2
Tel: 416-934-3424; *Fax:* 416-934-3425
Toll-Free: 866-937-2642
Other Communication: Alt. E-mail: faithfulstewards@cmic.info
info@cmic.info
www.cmic.info
www.facebook.com/catholicmissions
twitter.com/canadamissions
www.youtube.com/missioncanada;
catholicmissionsincanada.tumblr.com
Also Known As: Catholic Missions
Previous Name: Catholic Church Extension Society of Canada
Overview: A large national charitable organization founded in 1908
Mission: To keep the Catholic faith in remote & poor communities throughout Canada; To raise awareness of the needs of Canadian missions
Member of: Association of Fundraising Professionals (Toronto); Canadian Association of Gift Planners
Finances: *Annual Operating Budget:* $3 Million-$5 Million; *Funding Sources:* Donations; Fundraising
Staff Member(s): 11
Membership: 26 mission dioceses; *Committees:* Executive; Allocations; Finance; Nominating
Activities: Supporting over 600 missionaries who serve in home mission communities throughout Canada; Raising funds for religious education programs, leadership programs, church repair, & evangelization efforts; *Speaker Service:* Yes
Chief Officer(s):
Thomas C. Collins, Apostolic Chancellor
David Reilander, President
presidentdr@cmic.info
James Milway, Secretary
Awards:
• St. Joseph Award
Eligibility: Catholic missionary workers in Canada
Publications:
• Catholic Missions in Canada
Type: Magazine; *Frequency:* Quarterly; *Editor:* Patria C. Rivera
Profile: Information about missionaries who serve in home mission communities across Canada
• Catholic Missions in Canada Annual Report
Type: Yearbook; *Frequency:* Annually
Profile: Featuring information on CMIC's expenses & distributions
• Catholic Missions in Canada E-Newsletter
Type: Newsletter
• John & Emily Visit Catholic Missions in Canada [a publication of Catholic Missions in Canada]
Type: Book
Profile: A soft-cover activity book for children 12 & under

Catholic Near East Welfare Association Canada
1247 Kilborn Place, Ottawa ON K1H 6K9
Tel: 613-738-9666; *Fax:* 613-738-7666
Toll-Free: 866-322-4441
canada@cnewa.org
www.cnewa.ca
www.facebook.com/cnewacanada
twitter.com/CNEWA
www.youtube.com/thecnewa
Also Known As: CNEWA Canada
Overview: A small international organization founded in 1926
Mission: To work with Eastern Catholic churches to identify needs & implement necessary measures
Finances: *Funding Sources:* Donations
Activities: Serving the poor throughout the Middle East, Northeast Africa, India & Eastern Europe
Chief Officer(s):
Carl Hétu, National Director
Melodie Gabriel, Development Officer
Antin Sloboda, Project Officer
Publications:
• ONE [a publication of the Catholic Near East Welfare Association Canada]
Type: Magazine; *Frequency:* Quarterly; *Editor:* Msgr. John E. Kozar
Profile: Presents the heritage & culture of the Middle East, Northeast Africa, India & Eastern Europe

The Catholic Principals' Council of Ontario (CPCO)
PO Box 2325, #3030, 2300 Yonge St., Toronto ON M4P 1E4
Tel: 416-483-1556; *Fax:* 416-483-2554
Toll-Free: 888-621-9190
info@cpco.on.ca
www.cpco.on.ca
www.linkedin.com/company/1206013
twitter.com/CPCO2012
www.youtube.com/cpcotoronto
Overview: A small provincial organization
Mission: CPCO is a voluntary, professional association that serves more than 2,100 principals and vice-principals in twenty-nine Catholic school boards across Ontario
Finances: *Annual Operating Budget:* $1.5 Million-$3 Million
Staff Member(s): 6; 6 volunteer(s)
Membership: 2,000 members who are principals & vice-principals in more than 1,300 elementary & secondary separate schools across Ontario; *Committees:* Communications; Member Security; Professional Development; Finance; Issues in Catholic Education
Activities: Advocacy, professional development; legal services; *Speaker Service:* Yes
Chief Officer(s):
Paul Lacalamita, Executive Director
placalamita@cpco.on.ca
Randy Bissonnette, President
president@cpco.on.ca

Catholic Teachers Guild
80 Sackville St., Toronto ON M5A 3E5
Tel: 416-393-5204; *Fax:* 416-397-6586
catholicteachersguild.ca
Overview: A small national organization founded in 2000
Mission: To support & strengthen the vocation of teaching in the tradition of the Catholic
Affiliation(s): Archdiocese of Toronto
Finances: *Funding Sources:* Donations
Membership: *Fees:* $20 initial fee; $10 renewal fee; *Member Profile:* Active or retired Catholics involved in education at any level, including pre-school & post-secondary, who support the mission of the Guild; Catholic lay educators & volunteers who work in Catholic schools, public schools, private schools, & other educational institutions
Activities: Holding an Annual Education Mass & Lenten Retreat; Presenting lectures & workshops; Conducting book club meetings
Chief Officer(s):
Barry White, President
president@catholicteachersguild.ca
Mark Woermke, Vice President
vicepresident@catholicteachersguild.ca
Sean Adams, Secretary
secretary@catholicteachersguild.ca
Jordan O'Brien, Treasurer
treasurer@catholicteachersguild.ca

Catholic Welfare Bureau *See* Catholic Family Services of Toronto

Catholic Women's League of Canada (CWL)
702C Scotland Ave., Winnipeg MB R3M 1X5
Tel: 204-927-2310; *Fax:* 888-831-9507
Toll-Free: 888-656-4040
info@cwl.ca
www.cwl.ca
www.facebook.com/374698529280233
twitter.com/CWLNational
Overview: A large national organization
Mission: To help members live holier lives; To grow in relationship with Christ & the church; To carry out the work of Christ in the community & in the world; To serve the people of God; To ensure local leagues within Archdiocesan Parishes report to regional & provincial councils, & follow the constitution & bylaws of the CWL
Finances: *Funding Sources:* Donations
Membership: Over 50,000; *Member Profile:* Catholic women over sixteen years of age who wish to serve within their communities
Chief Officer(s):
Kim Scammell, Executive Director
executivedirector@cwl.ca
Diane Kelln, Coordinator, Convention & Events
correspondingsecretary@cwl.ca
Amanda McCormick, Coordinator, Membership
membership@cwl.ca
Meetings/Conferences:
• Catholic Women's League of Canada 2018 National Convention, August, 2018, Winnipeg, MB
Scope: National
• Catholic Women's League of Canada 2019 National Convention, August, 2019, Calgary, AB
Scope: National

- Catholic Women's League of Canada 2020 National Convention, August, 2020, Montréal, QC
Scope: National
- Catholic Women's League of Canada 2021 National Convention, August, 2021, Toronto, ON
Scope: National
Publications:
- The Canadian League [a publication of the Catholic Women's League of Canada]
Type: Newsletter; *Frequency:* 3 pa; *Price:* Free for Catholic Women's League of Canada members
Profile: Executive reports, meeting highlights, spiritual development, Christian family life, community, education, health, communications, laws, international relations, & provincial reports
- Catholic Women's League of Canada Annual Report
Type: Yearbook; *Frequency:* Annually
- Catholic Women's League of Canada Executive Handbook

Catholic Youth Studio - KSM Inc. (KSM)
183 Roncesvalles Ave., 2nd Fl., Toronto ON M6R 2L5
Tel: 416-588-0555; *Fax:* 416-588-9995
radio@catholicradio.ca
www.catholicradio.ca
www.facebook.com/KSMRADIO
twitter.com/KSMRADIO
Also Known As: Catholic Radio Toronto
Overview: A small local charitable organization founded in 1994
Mission: To reach those who have not yet experienced their "springtime of faith", by means of evangelization through modern forms of mass media; to broadcast a daily radio program, eleven hours per week in Polish, & to publish a magazine, in order to provide services to families
Affiliation(s): Archdiocese of Toronto
Finances: *Funding Sources:* Donations
Staff Member(s): 4; 50 volunteer(s)
Membership: *Member Profile:* Individuals who donate their talents & time at Catholic Youth Studio - KSM Inc., a media corporation for evangelization, in order to promote the Christian faith; Members are both youth & adults who share the Catholic Youth Studio's charism
Activities: Programming for youth, couples, & seniors; Providing faith instruction; *Awareness Events:* International Festival of Religious Song
Chief Officer(s):
Marcin Serwin, Director
Publications:
- Rodzina (Family)
Type: Magazine

CAUSE Canada
#150, 301 14 St. NW, Calgary AB T2N 2A1
Tel: 403-678-3332
Toll-Free: 888-552-2873
www.cause.ca
www.facebook.com/causecanada
twitter.com/causecanada
Also Known As: Christian Aid for Under-Assisted Societies Everywhere
Overview: A small international charitable organization founded in 1984
Mission: To support sustainable development projects in geographical regions where there is an under-representation of international aid organizations
Member of: Canadian Council for Christian Charities
Finances: *Annual Operating Budget:* $500,000-$1.5 Million
Staff Member(s): 7; 55 volunteer(s)
Membership: 40
Activities: Primary health care; water & sanitation restoration; gender-specific development initiatives; microenterprine project; *Speaker Service:* Yes
Chief Officer(s):
Wendy Fehr, Executive Director
Publications:
- CAUSE Canada Newsletter
Type: Newsletter

Cavalier Riding Club Ltd. (CRC)
705 Pine Glen Rd., Pine Glen NB E1J 1S1
Tel: 506-386-7652
cavalierridingclub.weebly.com
Also Known As: Greater Moncton Riding for the Disabled; CRC Therapeutic Horseback Riding for the Disabled
Overview: A small local organization
Mission: To use hippotherapy in order to treat certain physical and emotional conditions of individuals with a disability
Member of: Canadian Therapeutic Riding Association

Cavelier de Lasalle Historical Society *Voir* Société historique Cavelier-de-LaSalle

Cayuga & District Chamber of Commerce
PO Box 118, Cayuga ON N0A 1E0
Tel: 905-772-5954
info@cayugachamber.ca
cayugachamber.ca
www.facebook.com/CayugaChamber
Overview: A small local organization founded in 1992
Mission: To enhance the quality of life for area residents; To promote members
Membership: 86
Chief Officer(s):
John Edelman, President

CBC French Network Technicians' Union (Ind.) *Voir* Syndicat des technicien(ne)s et artisan(e)s du réseau français de Radio-Canada (ind.)

CCCC Relief & Development Group (R&D Group). *See* Canadian Christian Relief & Development Association

CCI-Ottawa Chapter *See* Canadian Condominium Institute

C.D. Howe Institute / Institut C.D. Howe
#300, 67 Yonge St., Toronto ON M5E 1J8
Tel: 416-865-1904; *Fax:* 416-865-1866
cdhowe@cdhowe.org
www.cdhowe.org
www.linkedin.com/company/c.d.-howe-institute
www.facebook.com/cdhoweinstitute
twitter.com/cdhoweinstitute
Overview: A medium-sized international organization founded in 1973
Mission: To identify current & emerging economic & social policy issues facing Canadians; to recommend particular policy options; to communicate conclusions of research to domestic & international audiences.
Finances: *Annual Operating Budget:* $3 Million-$5 Million; *Funding Sources:* Membership dues
Staff Member(s): 29
Membership: *Fees:* Schedule available; *Member Profile:* Participation in & support of its activities from business, organized labor, associations, professions & interested individuals
Activities: *Speaker Service:* Yes; *Library:* by appointment
Chief Officer(s):
William B.P. Robson, President & CEO
Daniel Schwanen, Vice-President, Research

CDC Centre-Sud
2187, rue Larivière, Montréal QC H2K 1P5
Tél: 514-521-0467; *Téléc:* 514-521-6923
info@cdccentresud.org
www.cdccentresud.org
www.facebook.com/222302597781803
Aperçu: *Dimension:* petite; *Envergure:* locale
Mission: Pour aider au développement socio-économique du centre-sud de Montréal
Membre: 60; *Critères d'admissibilite:* Les organismes communautaires; Les entreprises d'économie sociale
Activités: Assemblées communautaires
Membre(s) du bureau directeur:
François Bergeron, Directeur général

Cecebe Waterways Association (CWA)
c/o President, 332B Chapman Dr., Burks Falls ON P0A 1C0
Tel: 705-573-5090
www.cecebewaterways.ca
Overview: A medium-sized local organization
Mission: To represent families who are residents and/or landowners on Lake Cecebe.
Membership: *Fees:* $30
Chief Officer(s):
Peggy Frederikse, President
pfrederikse@sympatico.ca

Cedar Crest Society for Community Living
PO Box 1197, 410 Cedar Ave., 100 Mile House BC V0K 2E0
Tel: 250-395-4643; *Fax:* 250-395-4686
cedar_crest@bcinternet.net
www.cedarcrestsociety.com
Overview: A small local organization founded in 1973
Mission: To promote ongoing growth & development of any person with a mental handicap
Member of: British Columbia Association for Community Living

Finances: *Funding Sources:* Community donations, income from the Thrift Shop, contracts with the Ministry of Children & Family Services

The Celtic Way / La Route Celtique
324, rue Gosford sud, Inverness QC G0S 1K0
Tel: 418-453-3434; *Fax:* 418-453-3434
info@larouteceltique.org
www.larouteceltique.org
Overview: A small local organization founded in 2001
Mission: To promote the heritage of the Megantic region, Inverness in particular; to conduct historical & genealogical research, & communicate the results of that research to the public

Cement Association of Canada (CAC) / Association canadienne du ciment
#1105, 350 Sparks St., Ottawa ON K1R 7S8
Tel: 613-236-9471; *Fax:* 613-563-4498
www.cement.ca
twitter.com/rediscoverconc
Previous Name: Canadian Portland Cement Association
Overview: A medium-sized national organization overseen by Canadian Ready Mixed Cement Assocation
Mission: To represent all of Canada's cement producers; To improve & extend the uses of cement & concrete through market development, engineering, research, education, & public affairs work
Member of: Canadian Ready Mixed Cement Association; Concrete Council of Canada
Staff Member(s): 10
Membership: 7 companies; *Member Profile:* Companies with cement manufacturing facilities, granulating facilities, grinding facilities, or cement terminals in Canada
Chief Officer(s):
Michael McSweeney, President & Chief Executive Officer, 613-236-9471 Ext. 206
mmcsweeney@cement.ca

Ontario Region
#709, 44 Victoria St., Toronto ON M5C 1Y2
Tel: 416-449-3708
www.cement.ca
Mission: To engage the cement industry in a wide range of public policy issues, including sustainable infrastructure, climate change, clean air, & clean water
Chief Officer(s):
Adam Hayashi, Director, Market Intelligence & Economic Policy
ahayashi@cement.ca
Martha Murray, Director, Public Affairs, Sustainability, & Stakeholder Relations
mmurray@cement.ca
Sherry Sullivan, Director, Transportation & Built Environment
ssullivan@cement.ca

Québec & Atlantic Region
Tel: 438-863-9561
www.cement.ca
Mission: To engage the cement industry in a wide range of public policy issues - from sustainable infrastructure and climate change, to clean air and clean water.
Chief Officer(s):
Guillaume Lemieux, Director, Markets & Technical Affairs
glemieux@cement.ca

Western Region (Vancouver & Calgary)
900 - 1188 West Georgia St., Vancouver BC V6E 4A2
Mission: To serve as the voice of Canada's cement industry
Chief Officer(s):
Ken Carrusca, Vice-President, Environment & Marketing - Vancouver
kcarrusca@cement.ca
Shane Mulligan, Director, Technical Affairs & Stakeholder Relations - Calgary
smulligan@cement.ca

Western Region (Vancouver)
#820, 1200 West 73rd Ave., Vancouver BC V6P 6G5
Tel: 604-269-0582; *Fax:* 604-269-0585
www.cement.ca
Mission: To engage the cement industry in a wide range of public policy issues - from sustainable infrastructure and climate change, to clean air and clean water.
Chief Officer(s):
Andy Vizer, Director, Markets & Technical Affairs
avizer@cement.ca

Canadian Associations / Center for Research-Action on Race Relations (CRARR)

Center for Research-Action on Race Relations (CRARR)
#610, 460, rue Sainte-Catherine ouest, Montréal QC H3B 1A7
Tel: 514-939-3342; Fax: 514-939-9763
crarr@primus.ca
www.crarr.org
www.facebook.com/258996297500425?sk=wall
Overview: A medium-sized national organization founded in 1983
Mission: An independent, non-profit civil rights organization with the mandate to promote racial equality and combat racism in Canada.
Member of: Court Challenges Program of Canada
Finances: *Funding Sources:* Public and private institutions, unions, educational institutions and individual donors
Activities: Conferences, consultations and seminars on different race relations and civil rights issues; Awards; Training; Research-action projects; Charter research and litigation; *Rents Mailing List:* Yes
Chief Officer(s):
Fo Niemi, Executive Director

Centraide Abitibi Témiscamingue et Nord-du-Québec
1009, 6e rue, Val-d'Or QC J9P 3W4
Tél: 819-825-7139; Téléc: 819-825-7155
courrier@centraide-atnq.qc.ca
www.centraide-atnq.qc.ca
www.facebook.com/Centraide.ATNQ
Aperçu: *Dimension:* moyenne; *Envergure:* provinciale; Organisme sans but lucratif; fondée en 1983 surveillé par United Way of Canada - Centraide Canada
Affiliation(s): Chambre de Commerce; Comité prévention des crimes
Membre(s) du personnel: 5
Membre: *Comités:* Attribution
Activités: *Service de conférenciers:* Oui
Membre(s) du bureau directeur:
Huguette Boucher, Directrice générale

Centraide Bas St-Laurent
#303, 1555, boul Jacques Cartier, Mont-Joli QC G5H 2W1
Tél: 418-775-5555; Téléc: 418-775-5525
www.centraidebsl.org
www.facebook.com/centraidebsl
Aperçu: *Dimension:* petite; *Envergure:* locale; Organisme sans but lucratif; fondée en 1982 surveillé par United Way of Canada - Centraide Canada
Mission: Organisme sans but lucratif de lutte à la pauvreté et de soutien aux personnes démunies
Finances: *Budget de fonctionnement annuel:* $500,000-$1.5 Million
Membre(s) du personnel: 3; 100 bénévole(s)
Membre: 40; *Critères d'admissibilité:* Organismes communautaires; *Comités:* Comité des priorités; Comité d'allocations
Membre(s) du bureau directeur:
Eve Lavoie, Directrice générale

Centraide Centre du Québec
154, rue Dunkin, Drummondville QC J2B 5V1
Tél: 819-477-0505; Téléc: 819-477-6719
Ligne sans frais: 888-477-0505
bureau@centraide-cdq.ca
www.centraide-cdq.ca
www.facebook.com/CentraideCentreDuQuebec
twitter.com/centraide_cdq
Nom précédent: Centraide Coeur du Québec
Aperçu: *Dimension:* petite; *Envergure:* locale; Organisme sans but lucratif; fondée en 1979 surveillé par United Way of Canada - Centraide Canada
Mission: Rassembler les personnes et les ressources du Centre-du-Québec afin de contribuer au développement social de la communauté et d'améliorer la qualité de vie de ses membres les plus vulnérables et ce, en lien avec les organismes communautaires.
Membre(s) du personnel: 5
Membre: 1-99
Activités: Campagne annuelle de financement
Membre(s) du bureau directeur:
Isabelle Dionne, Directrice générale
idionne@centraide-cdq.ca

Centraide Coeur du Québec *Voir* Centraide Centre du Québec

Centraide Côte-Nord/Secteur ouest *Voir* Centraide Haute-Côte-Nord/Manicouagan

Centraide de l'ouest québécois *Voir* Centraide Outaouais

Centraide de la région du Grand Moncton et du Sud-Est du NB Inc. *See* United Way of Greater Moncton & Southeastern New Brunswick

Centraide de Niagara Sud *See* United Way South Niagara

Centraide de Stormont, Dundas & Glengarry *See* United Way of Stormont, Dundas & Glengarry

Centraide du Grand Montréal / Centraide of Greater Montréal
493, rue Sherbrooke ouest, Montréal QC H3A 1B6
Tél: 514-288-1261; Téléc: 514-350-7282
info@centraide-mtl.org
www.centraide-mtl.org
www.facebook.com/centraide.du.grand.montreal
twitter.com/centraidemtl
www.youtube.com/user/CentraideMtl
Aperçu: *Dimension:* grande; *Envergure:* locale; fondée en 1975 surveillé par United Way of Canada - Centraide Canada
Mission: To maximize financial & volunteer resources in order to promote mutual aid, social commitment, & self-reliance as effective means of improving the quality of life of the community, & especially of its neediest members
Activités:: *Bibliothèque:* rendez-vous
Membre(s) du bureau directeur:
Lili-Anna Peresa, Présidente et directrice générale

Centraide Duplessis
#101, 185, rue Napoléon, Sept-Iles QC G4R 4R7
Tél: 418-962-2011
administration@centraideduplessis.org
www.centraideduplessis.org
www.facebook.com/centraide.duplessis
Aperçu: *Dimension:* petite; *Envergure:* locale surveillé par United Way of Canada - Centraide Canada
Membre(s) du bureau directeur:
Denis Miousse, Directeur général
direction@centraideduplessis.org

Centraide Estrie
1150, rue Belvédère sud, Sherbrooke QC J1H 4C7
Tél: 819-569-9281; Téléc: 819-569-5195
reception.centraide@qc.aibn.com
www.centraideestrie.com
www.facebook.com/Centraide-Estrie-177152949010458
www.youtube.com/channel/UCM2Tm-5MS5gAIJ4UWEfg5jA
Aperçu: *Dimension:* petite; *Envergure:* locale; Organisme sans but lucratif; fondée en 1975 surveillé par United Way of Canada - Centraide Canada
Mission: Vise à soutenir les organismes bénévoles et communautaires engagés directement auprès des clientèles les plus démunies et vulnérables
Finances: *Budget de fonctionnement annuel:* $500,000-$1.5 Million
Membre(s) du personnel: 3; 1 bénévole(s)
Membre: 150
Membre(s) du bureau directeur:
Claude Forgues, Directeur général
centraide_estrie@qc.aibn.com

Centraide Gaspésie Îles-de-la-Madeleine
#216, 230, rte du Parc, Sainte-Anne-des-Monts QC G4V 2C4
Tél: 418-763-2171
mejcentraide@globetrotter.net
www.centraidegim.ca
www.facebook.com/centraide.gaspesie
Aperçu: *Dimension:* petite; *Envergure:* locale; fondée en 1988 surveillé par United Way of Canada - Centraide Canada
Mission: Soulager la misère et la souffrance humaine
Finances: *Budget de fonctionnement annuel:* $250,000-$500,000
400 bénévole(s)
Membre: *Montant de la cotisation:* 20$
Membre(s) du bureau directeur:
Stéphan Boucher, Directeur général

Centraide Gatineau-Labelle-Hautes-Laurentides
CP 154, 343, rue de la Madone, Mont-Laurier QC J9L 3G9
Tél: 819-623-4090; Téléc: 819-623-7646
bureau@centraideglhl.ca
www.maregioncentraide.com
www.facebook.com/Centraide.Gatineau.Labelle.Hautes.Laurentides
Aperçu: *Dimension:* moyenne; *Envergure:* locale; fondée en 1985 surveillé par United Way of Canada - Centraide Canada
Finances: *Budget de fonctionnement annuel:* $50,000-$100,000
Membre(s) du bureau directeur:
Laure Voilquin, Directrice générale

Centraide Haute-Côte-Nord/Manicouagan
#301, 858, rue de Puyjalon, Baie-Comeau QC G5C 1N1
Tél: 418-589-5567; Téléc: 418-295-2567
www.centraidehcnmanicouagan.ca
Nom précédent: Centraide Côte-Nord/Secteur ouest
Aperçu: *Dimension:* moyenne; *Envergure:* locale; Organisme sans but lucratif surveillé par United Way of Canada - Centraide Canada
Membre(s) du bureau directeur:
Carole Lemieux, Directrice générale

Centraide KRTB-Côte-du-Sud
100, 4e av, La Pocatière QC G0R 1Z0
Tél: 418-856-5105; Téléc: 418-856-4385
centraideportage@bellnet.ca
www.facebook.com/CentraideKrtbCoteDuSud
Nom précédent: Centraide Portage-Taché
Aperçu: *Dimension:* petite; *Envergure:* locale surveillé par United Way of Canada - Centraide Canada
Mission: D'aider les gens, d'affecter les ressources en fonction des besoins, d'améliorer la qualité de vie de chacun et de renforcer le soutien communautaire
Membre(s) du bureau directeur:
Sylvain Roy, Directeur général

Centraide Lanaudière
674, rue St-Louis, Joliette QC J6E 2Z6
Tél: 450-752-1999
www.centraide-lanaudiere.com
www.facebook.com/275362692481275
Aperçu: *Dimension:* moyenne; *Envergure:* locale; Organisme sans but lucratif; fondée en 1977 surveillé par United Way of Canada - Centraide Canada
Mission: Promouvoir l'entraide, le partage et l'engagement bénévole et communautaire
Membre de: Centraide Canada
Membre(s) du personnel: 5; 100+ bénévole(s)
Membre: *Critères d'admissibilite:* Etre résident de Lanaudière ou avoir sa place d'affaires ou son lieu de travail sur le territoire de Centraide Lanaudière
Activités: *Stagiaires:* Oui
Membre(s) du bureau directeur:
Nicole Campeau, Directrice générale

Centraide Laurentides
#107, 880, boul Michèle-Bohec, Blainville QC J7C 5E2
Tél: 450-436-1584; Téléc: 450-951-2772
www.centraidelaurentides.org
www.facebook.com/CentraideLaurentides
twitter.com/CentraideLauren
www.youtube.com/user/centraidelaurentides
Aperçu: *Dimension:* petite; *Envergure:* locale; Organisme sans but lucratif; fondée en 1962 surveillé par United Way of Canada - Centraide Canada
Mission: Contribuer, par la promotion du partage et de l'engagement bénévole et communautaire, à la construction d'une société d'entraide vouée à l'amélioration de la qualité de vie des personnes en difficulté
Finances: *Budget de fonctionnement annuel:* $1.5 Million-$3 Million
Membre(s) du personnel: 21; 1500 bénévole(s)
Activités: Mène une campagne de sollicitation à l'automne et soutient 75 organismes communautaires qui viennent en aide aux personnes dans le besoin, sur le territoire des Laurentides; opère trois comptoirs d'entraide; *Service de conférenciers:* Oui
Membre(s) du bureau directeur:
Suzanne M. Piché, Directrice générale, 450-436-1584 Ext. 225
spiche@centraidelaurentides.org

Centraide Mauricie
90, rue Des Casernes, Trois-Rivières QC G9A 1X2
Tél: 819-374-6207; Téléc: 819-374-6857
centraide.mauricie@centraidemauricie.ca
www.centraidemauricie.ca
www.linkedin.com/company/centraide-mauricie
www.facebook.com/centraide.mauricie
twitter.com/centraidem
Aperçu: *Dimension:* petite; *Envergure:* locale; Organisme sans but lucratif; fondée en 1956 surveillé par United Way of Canada - Centraide Canada
Mission: Travailler à un changement social pour une société plus juste, plus humaine et plus démocratique à travers la promotion de l'entraide, la solidarité et l'engagement bénévole

150 volunteer(s)
Membership: *Fees:* $20
Chief Officer(s):
Lenetta Parry, Executive Director
Helen Holton, President

Central Okanagan Foundation (COF)
Landmark 1, 306 - 1726 Dolphin Ave., Kelowna BC V1Y 9R9
Tel: 250-861-6160
info@centralokanaganfoundation.org
www.centralokanaganfoundation.org
www.facebook.com/centralokanaganfoundation
twitter.com/centralokanagan
Overview: A small national charitable organization founded in 1977
Mission: To enhance quality of life in the community through the stewardship of entrusted funds, grant making, & community leadership; To encourage all citizens to participate through the establishment of or contributions to endowment funds
Member of: Community Foundations of Canada
Affiliation(s): Association of Canadian Foundations
Finances: *Annual Operating Budget:* $100,000-$250,000
Staff Member(s): 3; 30 volunteer(s)
Membership: 140; *Committees:* Capital Development; Communication; Investment; Grants
Chief Officer(s):
Bruce Davies, Executive Director
bruce@centralokanaganfoundation.org

Central Okanagan Indian Friendship Society *See* Ki-Low-Na Friendship Society

Central Okanagan Naturalists Club (CONC)
PO Box 21128, Stn. Orchard Park, Kelowna BC V1Y 9N8
www.okanagannature.org
Overview: A small local charitable organization founded in 1962
Mission: To promote the enjoyment of nature through environmental appreciation & conservation; To encourage wise use & conservation of natural resources & environmental protection
Member of: Federation of BC Naturalists
Membership: *Fees:* $14 student; $30 single; $42 family
Activities: Hiking; skiing; botany; ornithology; participating with City of Kelowna in environmental events; conservation; *Library:* CONC Library; Not open to public
Publications:
• Central Okanagan Naturalist Newsletter
Type: Newsletter; *Frequency:* 10 pa; *Editor:* Teresa Smith

Central Ontario Beekeepers' Association
c/o Brent Cole, Herb Guy's Honey House, 3807 County Rd. 36, Buckhorn ON K0L 1J0
Tel: 705-657-9971
registrar@centralontariobeekeepers.ca
www.centralontariobeekeepers.ca
Overview: A small local organization
Mission: To develop the beekeeping skills of local beekeepers; To promote beekeeping in central Ontario, including Peterborough, Peterborough County, Northumberland County, Haliburton County, & the City of Kawartha Lakes
Member of: Ontario Beekeepers' Association
Affiliation(s): Canadian Association Insurance Program (CAP)
Membership: *Member Profile:* Commercial beekeepers & hobbyists from the central Ontario region
Activities: Conducting meetings for members; Organizing field days; Preparing informative displays about beekeeping; Providing information & networking oopportunities for beekeepers; Assisting members with problems encountered by beekeepers
Chief Officer(s):
Glen McMullen, President
president@centralontariobeekeepers.ca

Central Ontario Developmental Riding Program (CODRP)
Pride Stables, 584 Pioneer Tower Rd., Kitchener ON N2P 2H9
Tel: 519-653-4686; *Fax:* 519-653-5565
info@pridestables.com
www.pridestables.com
www.facebook.com/PrideStables
Also Known As: Pride Stables
Overview: A small local charitable organization founded in 1973
Mission: To provide a safe, high-quality riding program for persons with disabilities; to foster personal growth & improvement through the use of horses as a medium for development & therapy with the assistance of volunteers
Member of: Ontario Equestrian Federation; Association of Riding Establishments of Ontario
Affiliation(s): Ontario Therapeutic Riding Association (ONTRA)
Finances: *Funding Sources:* Service clubs; company & individual donations; municipal grants; special events
Staff Member(s): 8; 250 volunteer(s)
Membership: 350+ riders; *Member Profile:* Physical, mental & behavioral challenges
Activities: Integrated summer camp; therapeutic horseback riding; *Speaker Service:* Yes; *Library:* by appointment
Chief Officer(s):
Heather Mackneson, Executive Director

Central Ontario Industrial Relations Institute (COIRI)
350 Bay St., 10th Fl., Toronto ON M5H 2S6
Tel: 905-373-1761; *Fax:* 905-373-0190
www.coiri.com
Overview: A medium-sized local organization founded in 1943
Mission: To represent organizations in labour relations, employment law, human rights, workers compensation, pay equity and other related employment issues.
Membership: *Fees:* $625
Chief Officer(s):
Jane Stewart, Director, Publications
jane@coiri.com

Central Ontario Musicians' Association (COMA)
100 Ahrens St. West, Kitchener ON N2H 4C3
Tel: 519-744-4891; *Fax:* 519-744-2279
info@centralontariomusicians.org
www.centralontariomusicians.org
Overview: A small local organization founded in 1906
Mission: To help develop musical skill
Member of: American Federation of Musicians (Local 226)
Membership: 400; *Fees:* $139
Activities: *Library:* by appointment
Chief Officer(s):
Paul Mitchell, President
mitchgroup@rogers.com

Central Ontario Network for Black History
203 Rykert St., St Catharines ON L2R 7C2
Tel: 905-685-5222
Overview: A small local organization

Central Ontario Orchid Society (COOS)
41 Woodside Rd., Guelph ON N1G 2H1
personal.uwaterloo.ca/jerry/coos
Overview: A small local organization founded in 1985
Mission: To promote & train people about growing orchids
Finances: *Annual Operating Budget:* Less than $50,000
Membership: 100+; *Fees:* $15 individual; $20 family; $5 student
Activities: *Speaker Service:* Yes; *Library:* Not open to public
Chief Officer(s):
Gerhard Kompter, Interim President, 519-745-3815
Mary Ann Lang, Secretary, 519-747-1019
dalang@bell.net
Publications:
• The COOS [Central Ontario Orchid Society] Newsletter
Type: Newsletter; *Editor:* Cathy Ralston

Central Ontario Standardbred Association (COSA)
PO Box 297, 36 Main St. North, Campbellville ON L0P 1B0
Tel: 905-854-2672; *Fax:* 905-854-2644
cosaonline.com
Previous Name: Ontario Harness Horse Association
Overview: A small local organization founded in 2009 overseen by Standardbred Canada
Mission: To represent the interests of horsepeople racing at Woodbine & Mohawk Racetracks in central Ontario
Membership: 1500; *Fees:* Free; *Member Profile:* Horse owners, breeders, caretakers, trainers, & drivers in central Ontario
Chief Officer(s):
Bill O'Donnell, President
bill.o'donnell@cosaonline.com

Central St. Lawrence Real Estate Board *See* Rideau-St. Lawrence Real Estate Board

Central Service Association of Ontario *See* Medical Device Reprocessing Association of Ontario

Central Seven Association for Community Living *See* Community Living Durham North

Central Valley Naturalists *See* Abbotsford-Mission Nature Club

Central Vancouver Island Multicultural Society (CVIMS)
#101, 319 Selby St., Nanaimo BC V9R 2R4
Tel: 250-753-6911; *Fax:* 250-753-4250
www.cvims.org
www.facebook.com/immigrant.welcome.centre.nanaimobc
twitter.com/CVIMS
www.youtube.com/user/ImmigrantWelcomeCtr
Overview: A small local charitable organization
Mission: To offer immigrants such services as English language classes, employment & settlement assistance.
Member of: Affiliation of Multicultural Societies & Service Agencies of BC
Staff Member(s): 25
Membership: *Fees:* $10 individual; $20 group/family; $5 student; $50 corporate
Activities: Information Centre; interpreting & translation; assistance with governmental applications; cultural counselling
Chief Officer(s):
Graham Pike, President
president@cvims.org
Jennifer Fowler, Executive Director
jfowler@cvims.org

Central Vancouver Island Orchid Society
PO Box 1061, Nanaimo BC V9R 5Z2
www.cvios.com
Overview: A small local organization
Mission: To promote an interest in orchids & support research in the study of orchids
Membership: *Fees:* $25
Activities: *Library:*
Chief Officer(s):
Shelley Rattink, President

Centrale de l'enseignement du Québec *Voir* Centrale des syndicats du Québec

Centrale des professionnelles et professionnels de la santé *Voir* Alliance du personnel professionnel et technique de la santé et des services sociaux

Centrale des syndicats démocratiques (CSD)
#600, 900, av de Bourgogne, Québec QC G1X 3E3
Tél: 514-899-1070
Ligne sans frais: 866-651-0050
www.csd.qc.ca
www.facebook.com/CSDCentrale
twitter.com/CSDCentrale
Aperçu: *Dimension:* grande; *Envergure:* provinciale; fondée en 1972
Affiliation(s): Fédération démocratique de la métallurgie, des mines et des produits chimiques; Fédération des syndicats du textile et du vêtement inc.
Membre(s) du personnel: 78
Membre: 61 000; *Critères d'admissibilite:* Un syndicat affilié qui croit à la CSD
Activités:; *Bibliothèque:* rendez-vous
Membre(s) du bureau directeur:
François Vaudreuil, Président

Beauce
#11, 720 - 1e av, Saint-Georges QC G5Y 2C8
Tél: 418-228-9577; *Téléc:* 418-228-9558

Centre du Québec
66, boul Labbé sud, Victoriaville QC G6S 1B5
Tél: 819-758-3174; *Téléc:* 819-758-7105

Estrie
1009, rue Galt ouest, Sherbrooke QC J1H 1Z9
Tél: 819-569-9377; *Téléc:* 819-569-9370

Mauricie
141, rue Beauchemin, Trois-Rivières QC G8T 7L4
Tél: 819-376-3339; *Téléc:* 819-376-3475

Montmagny - Bas St-Laurent
119, av Collin, Montmagny QC G5V 2S7
Tél: 418-248-5766; *Téléc:* 418-248-5799

Montréal
#2000, 9405, rue Sherbrooke est, Montréal QC H1L 6P3
Tél: 514-899-1070; *Téléc:* 514-899-1216
www.csd.qc.ca

Richelieu - Yamaska
11, rue Chapleau, Granby QC J2G 6K1
Tél: 450-375-1122; *Téléc:* 450-375-1125

Saguenay - Lac St-Jean
3310, boul St-François, Jonquière QC G7X 2W9
Tél: 418-547-2622; *Téléc:* 418-547-2623

Centrale des syndicats du Québec (CSQ)
9405, rue Sherbrooke est, Montréal QC H1L 6P3

Canadian Associations / Centre Afrika

Tél: 514-356-8888; *Téléc:* 514-356-9999
Ligne sans frais: 800-465-0897
www.lacsq.org
www.facebook.com/lacsq
twitter.com/csq_centrale
www.youtube.com/user/csqvideos
Nom précédent: Centrale de l'enseignement du Québec
Aperçu: *Dimension:* grande; *Envergure:* provinciale; fondée en 1946
Mission: De regrouper dans un même mouvement des personnels salariés ayant des aspirations et des intérêts communs et de promouvoir leurs intérêts professionnels, sociaux, et économiques; dans cette perspective, elle travaille à établir un environnement syndical et professionnel exempt de harcèlement sexuel et favorise la vie syndicale par le partage des ressources; elle intervient au soutien direct de ses affiliés et assure différents services liés aux relations de travail et à la vie professionnelle (recherche dans le domaine de l'éducation, etc.)
Affiliation(s): Internationale de l'Éducation; Confédération des éducateurs d'Amérique
Finances: *Budget de fonctionnement annuel:* Plus de $5 Million
Membre(s) du personnel: 200
Membre: 180 000; *Critères d'admissibilité:* Personnel de l'éducation, de la santé et services sociaux de la petite enfance, des loisirs et des communications; *Comités:* Comité d'action sociopolitique; Comité en éducation pour un avenir viable; Comité en santé et sécurité du travail; Comité de la condition des femmes; Comité des jeunes; Comité pour la diversité sexuelle et l'identité de genre
Activités:; *Bibliothèque:* Centre de documentation; rendez-vous Not open to public
Membre(s) du bureau directeur:
Louise Chabot, Présidente
Publications:
• Nouvelles CSQ [publication Centrale des syndicats du Québec]
Type: Magazine; *Frequency:* 4 pa

   Bureau de Québec
   #100, 320, rue Saint-Joseph est, Québec QC G1K 9E7
   Tél: 418-649-8888; *Téléc:* 418-649-8800
   Ligne sans frais: 877-850-0897
   www.lacsq.org

Centre Afrika
1644, rue St-Hubert, Montréal QC H2L 3Z3
Tél: 514-843-4019; *Téléc:* 514-849-4323
centreafrika@centreafrika.com
www.centreafrika.com
www.facebook.com/centreafrika
www.youtube.com/channel/UCh07u7KOPIF43d_Qg-DPjQA
Aperçu: *Dimension:* petite; *Envergure:* locale; fondée en 1988
Mission: Activités sociales & culturelles et activités spirituelles/religieuses

Centre Anti-Poison du Québec
1270, ch Sainte-Foy, 4e étage, Québec QC G1S 2M4
Tél: 418-654-2731; *Téléc:* 418-654-2747
Ligne sans frais: 800-463-5060
Aperçu: *Dimension:* petite; *Envergure:* provinciale
Membre de: Canadian Association of Poison Control Centres
Membre(s) du bureau directeur:
Hélène Levasseur, Chef de service

Centre canadien d'arbitrage commercial (CCAC) / Canadian Commercial Arbitration Centre (CCAC)
Place du Canada, #905, 1010, rue de la Gauchetière ouest, Montréal QC H3B 2N2
Tél: 514-448-5980; *Téléc:* 514-448-5948
www.ccac-adr.org
www.linkedin.com/company/centre-canadien-d-arbitrage-commercial
Nom précédent: Centre d'arbitrage commercial national et international du Québec
Aperçu: *Dimension:* moyenne; *Envergure:* provinciale; Organisme sans but lucratif; fondée en 1986
Mission: Fournir des services de conciliation, de médiation et d'arbitrage pour les activités commerciales et de consommation; offrir des activités de formation aux arbitres et médiateurs; analyse de dossiers litigieux et études pour des organismes privés et publics
Membre de: International Federation of Commercial Arbitration Institutions
Finances: *Budget de fonctionnement annuel:* $250,000-$500,000
Membre(s) du personnel: 6
Membre: 100; *Montant de la cotisation:* Barème; *Comités:* Conseil des Experts; Comité de gestion des dossiers

Activités: Colloques; séminaires; *Bibliothèque* Not open to public
Membre(s) du bureau directeur:
Julie Houle, Coordonnatrice

Centre Canadien d'Architecture *See* Canadian Centre for Architecture

Centre canadien d'étude et de coopération internationale (CECI) / Canadian Centre for International Studies & Cooperation
3000, rue Omer-Lavallée, Montréal QC H1Y 3R8
Tél: 514-875-9911; *Téléc:* 514-875-6469
Ligne sans frais: 877-875-2324
info@ceci.ca
www.ceci.ca
www.facebook.com/cecicooperation
twitter.com/CECI_Canada
www.youtube.com/commceci
Aperçu: *Dimension:* grande; *Envergure:* internationale; Organisme sans but lucratif; fondée en 1958
Mission: Le CECI combat la pauvreté et l'exclusion; renforce les capacités de développment des communautés défavorisées; appuie des initiatives de paix, de droits humains et d'équité; mobilise des ressources et favorise l'échange de savoir-faire.
Membre de: Conseil canadien pour la coopération internationale/Canadian Council for International Cooperation; Association québécoise des organismes de coopération internationale
Membre: *Comités:* Advisory
Activités: Cours de formation; initiation de jeunes adultes à la coopération internationale; publications thématiques; sensibilisation du public et collecte de fonds pour l'aide au développement; *Stagiaires:* Oui; *Service de conférenciers:* Oui; *Bibliothèque:* Centre de documentation; rendez-vous
Membre(s) du bureau directeur:
Claudia Black, Directrice générale, 514-875-9911 Ext. 251
Publications:
• CECI [Centre canadien d'étude et de coopération internationale] Infolettre
Type: Newsletter

Centre canadien d'hygiène et de sécurité au travail *See* Canadian Centre for Occupational Health & Safety

Centre canadien d'innovations des pêches *See* Canadian Centre for Fisheries Innovation

Centre canadien de leadership en éducation (CLÉ)
#B120, 2445 boul. St-Laurent, Ottawa ON K1G 6C3
Tél: 613-747-7021; *Téléc:* 613-747-7277
Ligne sans frais: 800-372-5508
info@leCLE.com
www.lecle.com
Aperçu: *Dimension:* petite; *Envergure:* nationale
Mission: Un organisme pancanadien sans but lucratif voué au développement et à l'épanouissement de la Francophonie canadienne.
Membre(s) du bureau directeur:
Louis Claude Tremblay, Directeur général
lctremblay@lecle.com

Centre canadien de politique alternative *See* Canadian Centre for Policy Alternatives

Centre canadien du film *See* Canadian Film Centre

Centre canadien pour l'éthique dans le sport *See* Canadian Centre for Ethics in Sport

Centre canadien sur les dépendances et l'usage de substances *See* Canadian Centre on Substance Use & Addiction

Centre canadien-ukrainien de recherches et de documentation *See* Ukrainian Canadian Research & Documentation Centre

Centre Catholique pour Immigrants - Ottawa + Fondation du CCI *See* Catholic Centre for Immigrants - Ottawa + CIC Foundation

Le Centre commémoratif de l'Holocauste à Montréal *See* The Montréal Holocaust Memorial Centre

Centre Communautaire Bon Courage De Place Benoît / Place Benoît Bon Courage Community Centre
#2, 155, Place Benoît, Montréal QC H4N 2H4

Tél: 514-744-0897; *Téléc:* 514-744-6205
info@centreboncourage.org
www.centreboncourage.org
twitter.com/CCBonCourage
Aperçu: *Dimension:* petite; *Envergure:* locale; fondée en 1991
Membre de: ROCAJQ, ROCQLD, ACCESSS, TCRI, ImagineCanada
Finances: *Budget de fonctionnement annuel:* $500,000-$1.5 Million
Membre(s) du personnel: 16; 107 bénévole(s)
Membre: 323 familles
Activités: Jeunesse, famille, petite enfance; *Bibliothèque:* Bibliothèque; Bibliothèque publique
Membre(s) du bureau directeur:
Mame Moussa Sy, Directeur
mm.sy@centreboncourage.org
Nafissatova Duquenoy, Adjointe Directeur
n.duquenoy@centreboncourage.org

Centre communautaire de counselling du Nipissing *See* Community Counselling Centre of Nipissing

Centre communautaire des gais et lesbiennes de Montréal (CCGLM)
CP 476, Succ. C, Montréal QC H2L 4K4
Tél: 514-528-8424; *Téléc:* 514-528-9708
info@ccglm.org
www.ccglm.org
www.facebook.com/ccglm
Aperçu: *Dimension:* petite; *Envergure:* locale; fondée en 1988
Mission: Organisme sans but lucratif qui agit pour améliorer la condition des membres de nos communautés - lesbiennes, gais, bisexuel(les), transexuel(les), transgenres, et allosexuel(les); bibliothèque
Membre(s) du personnel: 3; 3 bénévole(s)
Membre: *Montant de la cotisation:* 10$ individu; 25$ groupe
Membre(s) du bureau directeur:
Christian Tanguay, Director-General

Centre Communautaire Esprit Saint *Voir* Centro Comunitàrio Divino Espìrito Santo

Centre Communautaire Tyndale St-Georges *See* Tyndale St-Georges Community Centre

Centre culturel franco-manitobain (CCFM)
340, boul Provencher, Winnipeg MB R2H 0G7
Tél: 204-233-8972; *Téléc:* 204-233-3324
reception@ccfm.mb.ca
www.ccfm.mb.ca
www.facebook.com/CCFManitobain
twitter.com/CCFManitobain
Aperçu: *Dimension:* petite; *Envergure:* provinciale; Organisme sans but lucratif; fondée en 1972 surveillé par Fédération des communautés francophones et acadienne du Canada
Mission: De maintenir, d'encourager, de favoriser et de patronner, par tous les moyens possibles, toutes les formes d'activités culturelles de langue française, et de rendre la culture canadienne-française accessible à tous les résidents de la province
Membre de: Federation Culturelle Canadienne Française; Association culturelle franco-manitobaine
Membre(s) du bureau directeur:
Ginette Lavack, Directrice générale, 204-233-8972 Ext. 428
glavack@ccfm.mb.ca

Le Centre culturel francophone de Vancouver (CCFV) / Vancouver Francophone Cultural Centre
1551 - 7 Ave. West, Vancouver BC V6J 1S1
Tél: 604-736-9806; *Téléc:* 604-736-4661
info@lecentreculturel.com
www.lecentreculturel.com
www.facebook.com/lecentreculturel
twitter.com/CCFV
Aperçu: *Dimension:* moyenne; *Envergure:* locale; Organisme sans but lucratif; fondée en 1975
Mission: Présenter des spectacles en langue française et expositions d'artistes francophones et francophiles, dans le but de rehausser l'appréciation artistique de l'ensemble de la population du Vancouver métropolitain; promouvoir l'éducation au moyen de services et de programmes éducatifs en langue française à l'ensemble de la population du Vancouver métropolitain
Membre de: Fédération des francophones de la Colombie-Britannique
Affiliation(s): Conférence canadienne des arts; Réseau

international pour la diversité culturelle; Réseau indépendant des diffuseurs d'événements artistiques unis (RIDEAU)
Finances: *Budget de fonctionnement annuel:* $500,000-$1.5 Million
Membre(s) du personnel: 6; 150 bénévole(s)
Membre: 1 000; *Montant de la cotisation:* Barème
Activités: Café-restaurant; des camps d'été pour les enfants; des ateliers récréatifs ou éducatifs; des expositions d'oeuvres d'art; vidéothèque; spectacles divers; bibliothèque; *Evénements de sensibilisation:* Festival d'Été; Coup de Coeur Francophone; *Bibliothèque:* LeCentre Library; Bibliothèque publique
Membre(s) du bureau directeur:
Pierre Rivard, Directeur général
pierre.rivard@lecentreculturel.com
Prix, Bourses:
• Prix Mercure
Remis à un individu qui a contribué à l'essor de la chanson d'expression française dans l'Ouest, que ce soit en tant qu'administrateur, musicien, promoteur, artiste de la scène ou autre artisan

Centre d'action bénévole de Montréal (CABM) / Volunteer Bureau of Montreal (VBM)
#300, 2015, rue Drummond, Montréal QC H3G 1W7
Tél: 514-842-3351; *Téléc:* 514-842-8977
info@cabm.net
www.cabm.net
www.facebook.com/benevolat
twitter.com/benevolat
www.youtube.com/user/cabmvbm1
Aperçu: *Dimension:* moyenne; *Envergure:* locale; fondée en 1937
Mission: Promotion de l'action bénévole
Membre de: Fédération des centres d'action bénévole du Québec; Bénévoles Canada
Affiliation(s): International Association for Volunteer Effort
Finances: *Budget de fonctionnement annuel:* $250,000-$500,000; *Fonds:* Centraide du Grand Montréal; Agence de la santé et des services sociaux de Montréal
Membre(s) du personnel: 9
Membre: 100; *Critères d'admissibilite:* Organisme communautaire ou association à but non lucratif
Activités: Services alimentaires; *Evénements de sensibilisation:* Semaine de l'action bénévole/Volunteer Week, 3e semaine d'avril; *Service de conférenciers:* Oui; *Bibliothèque:* Centre de documentation; Bibliothèque publique
Membre(s) du bureau directeur:
Pierre Morrissette, Directeur général

Centre d'action sida Montréal (Femmes) (CASMF) / Centre for AIDS Services of Montréal (Women)
1750, rue Saint-André, 3e étage, Montréal QC H2L 3T8
Tél: 514-495-0990; *Téléc:* 514-495-8087
casm@netrover.net
www.netrover.com/~casm
Aperçu: *Dimension:* petite; *Envergure:* locale
Mission: Offrir des services aux femmes affectées et infectées par le VIH/SIDA ainsi qu'aux membres de leur famille; ces actions, priorisant les besoins particuliers des femmes, ont pour but d'augmenter leur pouvoir à déterminer la qualité de leur propre vie
Membre de: Canadian AIDS Society; Fédération des femmes du Québec; Conseil des femmes de Montréal; Coalition des organismes communautaires québécois de lutte contre le sida
Membre: *Critères d'admissibilite:* Groupes des femmes séropositives, bénévoles, proches
Activités: Sessions d'informations sur le VIH/SIDA; ateliers sur la sexualité, l'estime de soi, les VIH/SIDA et les MTS; kiosques; projets ponctuels; ligne d'information, d'écoute et de références; intervention individuelle; accompagnement; fonds de dépannage; service de gardiennage; café-rencontre; diverses activités sociales; lobbying; levée de fonds

Centre d'adaptation de la main-d'oeuvre aérospatiale du Québec (CAMAQ)
5300, rue Chauveau, Montréal QC H1N 3V7
Tél: 514-596-3311; *Téléc:* 514-596-3388
info@camaq.org
www.camaq.org
twitter.com/CAMAQ_aero
Également appelé: Comité sectoriel de main-d'ouvre en aérospatiale
Aperçu: *Dimension:* petite; *Envergure:* provinciale; Organisme sans but lucratif; fondée en 1983

Mission: Susciter et d'appuyer la concertation des partenaires de l'industrie aérospatiale dans leurs efforts d'adaptation et de développement de la main-d'oeuvre.
Finances: *Fonds:* Emploi Québec
Membre(s) du bureau directeur:
Nathalie Paré, Directrice générale

Centre d'aide et de lutte contre les agressions à caractère sexuel de Châteauguay / Châteauguay Sexual Assault Center
CP 47030, Châteauguay QC J6K 5B7
Tél: 450-699-8258; *Téléc:* 450-699-7295
info@calacs-chateauguay.ca
calacs-chateauguay.ca
Également appelé: CALACS Châteauguay
Nom précédent: Centre d'aide et de prévention d'assauts sexuels de Châteauguay
Aperçu: *Dimension:* petite; *Envergure:* locale; Organisme sans but lucratif; fondée en 1979
Mission: Cet organisme offre les services suivants: aide aux femmes âgées de 14 ans et plus ayant vécu une agression à caractère sexuel, sans discrimination en raison de l'appartenance ethnique, culturelle, religieuse ou de l'orientation sexuelle; informe la population et la sensibilise à la problématique des agressions à caractère sexuel; suscite des réflexions afin de favoriser des changements sociaux et politiques
Membre de: Regroupement québécois des centres d'Aide et de Lutte contre les agressions à caractère sexuel
Finances: *Budget de fonctionnement annuel:* $250,000-$500,000; *Fonds:* Gouvernement provincial
Membre(s) du personnel: 6
Membre: 1-99
Activités: *Stagiaires:* Oui; *Bibliothèque:* rendez-vous

Centre d'aide et de lutte contre les agressions à caractère sexuel de Granby
CP 63, Granby QC J2G 8E2
Tél: 450-375-3338; *Téléc:* 450-375-0802
info@calacs-granby.qc.ca
www.calacs-granby.qc.ca
www.facebook.com/#!/calacs.degranby?fref=ts
Également appelé: CALACS-Granby
Aperçu: *Dimension:* petite; *Envergure:* locale; Organisme sans but lucratif; fondée en 1986
Mission: Le CALACS de Granby est un organisme féministe à but non lucratif qui lutte contre les agressions sexuelles et toute autre forme de violence sexuelle.
Membre de: Centre d,aide et de lutte contre les agressions à caractère sexuel (CALACS) de Granby
Affiliation(s): Regroupement québécois des CALACS
Finances: *Budget de fonctionnement annuel:* $100,000-$250,000; *Fonds:* Programme de soutien aux organismes communautaires (PSOC)
Membre(s) du personnel: 4; 15 bénévole(s)
Membre: 60; *Montant de la cotisation:* Don volontaire; *Critères d'admissibilite:* Femmes 18 ans et plus; *Comités:* Journal; Action vigilance; membership
Activités: Récréactives; formation en autodéfense pour femmes et adolescentes; mobilisation ponctuelle; *Evénements de sensibilisation:* Journée d'action contre la violence sexuelle faite aux femmes, sep..; *Stagiaires:* Oui; *Service de conférenciers:* Oui
Membre(s) du bureau directeur:
Carole Thériault, Contact
caroletheriault@calacs-granby.qc.ca

Centre d'aide et de lutte contre les agressions à caractère sexuel de la Rive-Sud
CP 13, LéVis QC G6V 6N6
Tél: 418-835-8342; *Téléc:* 418-835-8345
Ligne sans frais: 866-835-8342
info@calacsrivesud.org
www.calacsrivesud.org
www.facebook.com/calacs.rivesud
Également appelé: CALACS - Rive-Sud
Aperçu: *Dimension:* petite; *Envergure:* locale; Organisme sans but lucratif; fondée en 2001
Membre(s) du bureau directeur:
Pascale Brosseau, Coordonnatrice

Centre d'aide et de prévention d'assauts sexuels de Châteauguay *Voir* Centre d'aide et de lutte contre les agressions à caractère sexuel de Châteauguay

Centre d'aide personnes traumatisées crâniennes et handicapées physiques Laurentides (CAPTCHPL)
CP 11, Saint-Jérôme QC J7Z 5T7
Tél: 450-431-2860; *Téléc:* 450-431-7955
Ligne sans frais: 888-431-3437
lecaptchpl@sympatico.ca
www.captchpl.org
twitter.com/Captchpl
Aperçu: *Dimension:* petite; *Envergure:* locale
Mission: Pour aider les personnes souffrant de lésions cérébrales et physiquement handicapées dans la région des Laurentides du Québec; Pour favoriser l'intégration sociale des personnes handicapées physiques et de lésions cérébrales
Membre de: Regroupement des associations de personnes traumatisées craniocérébrales du Québec / Coalition of Associations of Craniocerebral Trauma in Quebec
Membre(s) du personnel: 9
Membre: *Critères d'admissibilite:* Les personnes atteintes de lésions cérébrales ou de handicaps physiques, et leurs familles, dans la région des Laurentides du Québec; *Comités:* Journal; Maison Matte Laurentides; Négociations SAAQ
Activités: Promouvoir les intérêts de cerveau blessés et handicapés physiques; Accroître la sensibilisation de lésion cérébrale et handicaps physiques dans la région des Laurentides; Promotion de la prévention; Fournir des services de soutien et d'information aux familles et amis de personnes qui sont victimes de traumatismes crâniens ou handicapés physiques; Offrir une éducation; Se référant personnes vers les ressources appropriées
Membre(s) du bureau directeur:
Michel Lajeunesse, Directeur général

Centre d'amitié autochtone de Montréal Inc. *See* Native Friendship Centre of Montréal Inc.

Centre d'amitié autochtone de Val-d'Or / Val-d'Or Native Friendship Centre
1272, 7e rue, Val-d'Or QC J9P 6W6
Tél: 819-825-6857; *Téléc:* 819-825-7515
info@caavd.ca
www.caavd.ca
www.facebook.com/caavd
www.youtube.com/user/caavd1
Aperçu: *Dimension:* petite; *Envergure:* locale; fondée en 1974
Mission: Offrir des services de qualité en milieu urbain, adaptés aux besoins des Autochtones; améliorer la qualité de vie et le mieux-être des Autochtones; respecter et diffuser la culture autochtone; faciliter les relations harmonieuses avec la communauté non-autochtone; contribuer à l'augmentation de la richesse collective.
Membre(s) du personnel: 44
Membre(s) du bureau directeur:
Oscar Kistabish, Président
Édith Cloutier, Directrice générale

Centre d'amitié autochtone du Québec (CAAQ) / Friendship Centre of Québec
234, rue Louis-IX, Québec QC G2B 1L4
Tél: 418-843-5818; *Téléc:* 418-843-8960
info.caaq@videotron.ca
www.caaq.net
Aperçu: *Dimension:* petite; *Envergure:* locale; Organisme sans but lucratif; fondée en 1979
Mission: Maintenir à Québec un lieu de rencontre afin de satisfaire les besoins culturels, matériels et sociaux des autochtones; fournir des installations centrales, convenables et appropriées; sensibiliser le public en général, aux besoins spécifiques des autochtones qui migrent en milieu urbain et faciliter leur acceptation; offrir des facilités d'hébergement à court et moyen terme aux autochtones de passage à Québec, venant y chercher différents services; améliorer la qualité de vie des autochtones en milieu urbain en leur prêtant assistance
Membre de: Association d'affaires des Premiers Peuples - Régie régionale de la Santé & Services sociaux; Regroupement des centres d'amitié autochtone du Québec
Affiliation(s): Association nationale des centres d'amitié
Finances: *Budget de fonctionnement annuel:* $500,000-$1.5 Million
Membre(s) du personnel: 1; 75 bénévole(s)
Membre: 250; *Montant de la cotisation:* 3$
Activités: Activités socioculturelles; communautaires; formation; services sociaux; service d'hébergement; garderie, service de garde à contribution réduite, de 7$/jour; centre de jour; Café Roreke; souper traditionnel pour les autochtones; *Evénements de sensibilisation:* Journée nationale des Autochtones; Journée mondiale du diable; *Bibliothèque:* Bibliothèque publique

Canadian Associations / Centre d'animation de développement et de recherche en éducation (CADRÉ)

Membre(s) du bureau directeur:
Jocelyne Gros-Louis, Directrice générale

Centre d'animation de développement et de recherche en éducation (CADRÉ)
1940, boul Henri-Bourassa est, Montréal QC H2B 1S2
Tél: 514-381-8891
Ligne sans frais: 888-381-8891
www.cadre21.org
twitter.com/LeCADRE21
Aperçu: *Dimension*: moyenne; *Envergure*: provinciale; Organisme sans but lucratif; fondée en 1968
Mission: Accompagner les intervenants francophones du monde de l'éducation dans leur réflexion, leur développement professionnel et leur veille sur les grands enjeux de l'éducation
Finances: *Budget de fonctionnement annuel*: $500,000-$1.5 Million
Activités:; *Bibliothèque*: Bibliothèque publique
Membre(s) du bureau directeur:
Jacques Cool, Directeur
jacques.cool@cadre21.org

Centre d'arbitrage commercial national et international du Québec *Voir* Centre canadien d'arbitrage commercial

Centre d'écoute Montérégie
1702, av Bourgogne, Chambly QC J3L 1Z2
Tél: 450-658-8509
Ligne sans frais: 877-658-8509
info@ecoutemonteregie.org
www.ecoutemonteregie.org
Aperçu: *Dimension*: petite; *Envergure*: locale; fondée en 2006
Mission: Soutient, écoute et aide les personnes de 50 ans et plus de la Montérégie
Membre(s) du bureau directeur:
Nathalie Barrette, Directrice
Nathalie Francoeur, Coordonnatrice

Centre d'éducation et d'action des femmes de Montréal (CÉAF)
2422, boul de Maisonneuve est, Montréal QC H2K 2E9
Tél: 514-524-3901; Téléc: 514-524-2183
www.ceaf-montreal.qc.ca
www.facebook.com/329404080465297
Aperçu: *Dimension*: petite; *Envergure*: locale; fondée en 1972
Mission: D'offrir des consultations à court terme, des références et informations; De proposer un programme d'activités sur 3 sessions: cafés-rencontres, autodéfense, groupe de soutien, comité journal et d'action, une chorale, etc.
Activités: *Service de conférenciers*: Oui; *Bibliothèque*

Centre d'entraide et de ralliement familial (CERF)
#101, 105, rue Ontario est, Montréal QC H2X 1G9
Tél: 514-288-8314; Téléc: 514-288-4176
info@cerf-montreal.org
www.cerf-montreal.org
twitter.com/C_E_R_F
Aperçu: *Dimension*: petite; *Envergure*: locale; fondée en 1995
Mission: Améliorer la qualité de vie des familles

Centre d'entrepreneuriat et PME (CEPME) / Centre for Entrepreneurship & Small Business
Université Laval, Pavillon Palasis-Prince, 2325, rue de la Terrasse, Québec QC G1V 0A6
Tél: 418-656-2131
entrepreneuriat.fsa.ulaval.ca
Aperçu: *Dimension*: petite; *Envergure*: internationale; fondée en 1993
Mission: Initier et coordonner des études sur l'entrepreneuriat et la PME; promouvoir l'apprentissage; développer des activités de formation et de perfectionnement; élaborer du matériel pédagogique et didactique; favoriser le partenariat et la participation des entrepreneurs; susciter les échanges d'expertise aux niveaux régional, national et international
Affiliation(s): Fondation de l'entrepreneurship du Québec; Canadian Council for Small Business & Entrepreneurship; Canadian Foundation for Economic Education; International Council for Small Business; International Small Business Congress; Centre SAHEL
Finances: *Budget de fonctionnement annuel*: $50,000-$100,000; *Fonds*: Projets; contrats
Membre(s) du personnel: 4
Membre: 7; *Critères d'admissibilité*: Universitaires; *Comités*: Orientation; Consultation
Activités: Recherches; conférences; séminaires; *Service de conférenciers*: Oui; *Bibliothèque*: rendez-vous
Membre(s) du bureau directeur:

Simon Chartier, Directeur
simon.chartier@fsa.ulaval.ca

Centre d'entreprise des femmes du Manitoba *See* Women's Enterprise Centre of Manitoba

Centre d'étude de la pratique d'assurance *See* Centre for Study of Insurance Operations

Centre d'étude des niveaux de vie *See* Centre for the Study of Living Standards

Centre d'études internationales *See* Cape Breton University Centre for International Studies

Centre d'études sur l'apprentissage et la performance *See* Centre for the Study of Learning & Performance

Centre d'Histoire de Saint-Hyacinthe
650, rue Girouard est, Saint-Hyacinthe QC J2S 2Y2
Tél: 450-774-0203; Téléc: 450-250-8127
infos@chsth.com
www.chsth.com
www.facebook.com/histoiremaskoutaine
twitter.com/histoiredemaska
Aperçu: *Dimension*: petite; *Envergure*: locale
Mission: Promouvoir et encourager l'étude de l'histoire. Le Centre d'histoire de Saint-Hyacinthe est né de la fusion du Centre d'archives du Séminaire de Saint-Hyacinthe et de la Société d'histoire régionale de Saint-Hyacinthe
Membre(s) du personnel: 4
Activités: Service de recherches en généalogie; consultation d'archives; vente de matériel généalogique; cours de généalogie; conférences
Membre(s) du bureau directeur:
Luc Cordeau, Directeur général
Marie-Marthe Bélisle, Responsable de la généalogie

Centre d'information canadien sur les diplômes internationaux *See* Canadian Information Centre for International Credentials

Centre d'information communautaire d'Ottawa *See* Community Information Centre of Ottawa

Centre d'information communautaure et de dépannage Ste-Marie (CICD)
2766, rue de Rouen, Montréal QC H2K 1N3
Tél: 514-526-4908; Téléc: 514-526-9050
cicdsm@cam.org
www.cam.org/~cicdsm
Aperçu: *Dimension*: petite; *Envergure*: locale; fondée en 1972
Mission: Pour aider les moins fortunés sur Saint Marie et Saint Jacques région en offrant des services sociaux gratuits et abordable
Membre(s) du bureau directeur:
Pierrette Malépart, Présidente, Conseil d'administration

Centre d'information et de recherche en consommation de Charlevoix-Ouest (CIRCCO)
#3, 3, rue Clarence Gagnon, Baie-Saint-Paul QC G3Z 1K5
Tél: 418-435-2884; Téléc: 418-435-3991
circco@bellnet.ca
www.circco.com
www.facebook.com/234716819950836
Aperçu: *Dimension*: petite; *Envergure*: locale; Organisme sans but lucratif; fondée en 1985 surveillé par Coalition des associations de consommateurs du Québec
Mission: Planifier, faire fonctionner un centre en information aux consommateurs et la protection collective des droits.
Membre de: Coalition des associations de consommateurs du Québec (CACQ)
Membre(s) du personnel: 2
Membre: *Montant de la cotisation*: Membre du CIRCCO 2$; 50$ de la Coalition
Activités: Information, protection du consommateur; cours en consommation, concours "Endettement-Predence"
Membre(s) du bureau directeur:
Christine Arbour, Coordonnatrice

Centre d'intervention budgétaire et sociale de la Mauricie
274, rue Bureau, Trois-Rivières QC G9A 2M7
Tél: 819-379-7888; Téléc: 819-376-6351
info@cibes-mauricie.ca
www.cibes-mauricie.ca
Également appelé: CIBES de la Mauricie
Nom précédent: Association coopérative d'économie familiale - Mauricie

Aperçu: *Dimension*: petite; *Envergure*: locale
Mission: Consacre ses actions à aider les familles et individus vivant des difficultés liées à l'endettement et aussi à lutter contre les injustices sociales
Membre: *Montant de la cotisation*: 10$
Membre(s) du bureau directeur:
Isabelle Bombardier, Présidente

Centre d'intervention et de prévention en toxicomanie de l'Outaouais (CIPTO)
92, rue Saint-Jacques, Gatineau QC J8X 2Z2
Tél: 819-770-7249; Téléc: 819-770-9199
Ligne sans frais: 866-778-4372
toxico@cipto.qc.ca
www.cipto.qc.ca
Aperçu: *Dimension*: petite; *Envergure*: locale; fondée en 1982
Mission: De développer des actions communautaires et d'offrir des services d'intervention et de prévention en toxicomanie à la population des secteurs Hull/ Grande-Rivière et une partie du Pontiac (Luskville et Quyon).
Membre(s) du bureau directeur:
Yves Séguin, Directeur général
yves.seguin@cipto.org

Centre d'organisation mauricien de services et d'éducation populaire (COMSEP)
#250, 1060, rue Saint-François-Xavier, Trois-Rivières QC G9A 1R8
Tél: 819-378-6963; Téléc: 819-378-0628
Autres numéros: Autre téléphone: 819-652-2285
comsep@comsep.qc.ca
www.comsep.qc.ca
Aperçu: *Dimension*: petite; *Envergure*: locale; fondée en 1986
Mission: D'améliorer la qualité de vie des plus démunis en leur fournissant l'orientation scolaire
Membre(s) du personnel: 17; 125 bénévole(s)
Membre: *Montant de la cotisation*: 1$; *Critères d'admissibilite*: Gens moins fortunés; *Comités*: Appui

Centre d'orientation sexuelle de l'université McGill (COSUM) / McGill University Sexual Identity Centre (MUSIC)
Dép. de psychiatrie, Hôpital général de Montréal, #A2-160, 1650, av Cedar, Montréal QC H3G 1A4
Tél: 514-934-1934; Téléc: 514-934-8471
music-cosum@mcgill.ca
www.mcgill.ca/cosum
Aperçu: *Dimension*: petite; *Envergure*: locale
Mission: Offre des psychothérapies individuelles à court terme, psychothérapies de groupe & de couple ou familiales
Membre(s) du bureau directeur:
Karine J. Igartua, Psychiatre

Centre de Bénévolat de la Péninsule Acadienne Inc. (CBPA)
#100, 220, boul St-Pierre ouest, Caraquet NB E1W 1A5
Tél: 506-727-1860; Téléc: 506-727-1862
centbene@nbnet.nb.ca
cbpa.ca
Aperçu: *Dimension*: petite; *Envergure*: locale
Membre(s) du bureau directeur:
Roger Boudreau, Président

Centre de caractérisation microscopique des matériaux / Centre for Characterization & Microscopy of Materials
CP 6079, Succ. Centre Ville, Montréal QC H3C 3A7
Tél: 514-340-4788; Téléc: 514-340-4468
cm2@polymtl.ca
www.cm2.polymtl.ca
Aperçu: *Dimension*: moyenne; *Envergure*: locale; Organisme sans but lucratif; fondée en 1988
Mission: Caractérisation microscopique; développement de nouveaux matériaux; formation de personnel hautement qualifié
Finances: *Budget de fonctionnement annuel*: $500,000-$1.5 Million
Membre(s) du personnel: 7
Membre: 1-99
Activités: *Stagiaires*: Oui; *Bibliothèque*: École Polytechnique Bibliothèque
Membre(s) du bureau directeur:
Gilles L'Espérance, Directeur

Centre de Conseil Communautaire *See* K3C Community Counselling Centres

Centre de counselling familial de Cornwall et Comtés unis *See* Counselling & Support Services of S.D. & G.

Centre de Counselling Familial de Timmins inc. *See* Timmins Family Counselling Centre, Inc.

Centre de détresse d'Ottawa et la région *See* Distress Centre of Ottawa & Region

Centre de documentation sur l'éducation des adultes et la condition féminine (CDEACF)
#101, 110, rue Ste-Thérèse, Montréal QC H2Y 1E6
Tél: 514-876-1180; *Téléc:* 514-876-1325
Ligne sans frais: 866-972-1180
info@cdeacf.ca
www.cdeacf.ca
www.facebook.com/CDEACF
twitter.com/alpha_cdeacf
Aperçu: Dimension: moyenne; *Envergure:* provinciale; fondée en 1983
Mission: Spécialiste de la documentation et de l'information, le CDÉACF est la référence francophone pour trouver, s'outiller et partager en alphabétisation et compétences essentielles;condition des femmes;en éducation des adultes.e d'expression qui a pour mission de collecter, diffuser et promouvoir et rendre accessibles, en français, les savoir-faire des milieux de l'éducation des adultes, de l'alphabétisation et de la condition féminine du Québec et des communautés francophones du Canada
Membre de: Groupe des 13; Institut de coopération pour l'éducation des adultes; Canadian Association of Prior Learning Assessment; Communautique; Association pour l'avancement des sciences et des techniques de la documentation; Relais-femmes
Affiliation(s): Coalition du thésaurus canadien d'alpahbétisation; Groupe des treize; Women Action; Association pour l'avancement des sciences et des techniques de la documentation; Institut canadien d'éducation des adultes
Finances: Budget de fonctionnement annuel: $500,000-$1.5 Million
Membre(s) du personnel: 14
Membre: 366; *Montant de la cotisation:* 25-40; *Critères d'admissibilite:* Déposant, structurant, sympatisant corporatif ou individuel
Activités: Formations; Veille informationnelle / bulletins; Prêt; Référence; *Service de conférenciers:* Oui; *Listes de destinataires:* Oui; *Bibliothèque:* Bibliothèque virtuelle - bv.cdeacf.ca; catalogue.cdeacf.ca; Bibliothèque publique
Membre(s) du bureau directeur:
Daniel Baril, Président
Mona Audet, Vice-Présidente
Geneviève Dorais-Beauregard, Directrice générale

Centre de Femmes Les Elles du Nord
#2, 570, 3e rue, Chibougamau QC G8P 1N9
Tél: 418-748-7171
ccfc@tlb.sympatico.ca
Aperçu: Dimension: petite; *Envergure:* locale
Membre(s) du bureau directeur:
Linda Boulanger, Responsable

Centre de formation à la coopération interculturelle du Québec (CFCI)
80, rue Frontenac, Rivière-du-Loup QC G5R 1R1
Tél: 418-862-6903
cfciaccueil@cegep-rdl.qc.ca
cfci.cegep-rdl.qc.ca
vimeo.com/cfci/videos
Aperçu: Dimension: petite; *Envergure:* internationale; fondée en 1985
Mission: Former des jeunes professionnels ou techniciens canadiens désireux de travailler à titre de coopérants ou voluntaires dans les PVD; réaliser des projets de DRH avec des institutions de formation dans les pays en voie de développement; interventions principalement en Afrique de l'Ouest (Mali, Burkina Faso) et en Amérique du Sud
Finances: Budget de fonctionnement annuel: $500,000-$1.5 Million
Membre(s) du personnel: 3
Membre: 10
Activités: Stagiaires: Oui; *Bibliothèque:* rendez-vous Not open to public
Membre(s) du bureau directeur:
Roselyne Leclerc, Coordonnatrice

Centre de formation en entreprise et récupération Normand-Maurice
605, rue Notre-Dame est, Victoriaville QC G6P 6Y9
Tél: 819-758-4789; *Téléc:* 819-752-3488
cfer@csbf.qc.ca
Aperçu: Dimension: moyenne; *Envergure:* provinciale
Mission: Offrir aux jeunes en difficultés une formation préparatoire au marché du travail; initier les enfants du primaire aux grandes problématiques environnementales; développer une conscience environnementale chez les jeunes
Membre(s) du bureau directeur:
Martin Verville, Président
Guy Martel, Directeur

Centre de formation et de consultation en métiers d'art / Arts & Crafts Training & Consultation Center
299, 3e av, Québec QC G1L 2V7
Tél: 418-647-0567; *Téléc:* 418-647-4880
infos@metierdart.com
www.metierdart.com
Aperçu: Dimension: petite; *Envergure:* locale
Mission: Assurer les futurs artisans d'une formation de qualité par le programme 'Techniques de métiers d'art au collégial' ainsi que diverses attestations d'études collégiales; offrir aux artisans professionnels des activités de perfectionnement; fournir une aide technique aux entreprises de métiers d'art; opérer un centre de documentation spécialisé en métiers d'art; stimuler la recherche et la diffusion des métiers d'art
Finances: Fonds: National Government
Membre(s) du bureau directeur:
François Bibeau, Directeur exécutif
fbibeau@metierdart.com

Centre de jour Guigues *Voir* Centre de services Guigues

Centre de la Communauté sourde du Montréal métropolitain (CCSMM)
#203, 2200, boul Crémazie est, Montréal QC H2E 2Z8
Tél: 514-903-2200; *Téléc:* 514-279-5373; *TTY:* 514-279-7609
ccsmm@videotron.ca
www.ccsmm.net
www.facebook.com/ccsmm.centrecommunautesourde
Aperçu: Dimension: petite; *Envergure:* locale; Organisme sans but lucratif; fondée en 1978
Mission: Promouvoir les droits et intérêts des personnes sourdes; offrir des activités d'information afin de renseigner notre clientèle; offrir de l'assistance pour la résolution de conflits d'ordre juridique ou autre
Affiliation(s): Regroupement de l'Organisme de Sourds du Québec, ROPMM, COPHAN, CDEC, RIOCm, RUTA
Finances: Budget de fonctionnement annuel: $100,000-$250,000; *Fonds:* Agence de la santé et des services sociaux
Membre(s) du personnel: 5; 40 bénévole(s)
Membre: 605; *Montant de la cotisation:* 10$ membre; 5$ âge d'or; *Critères d'admissibilite:* Personnes sourdes
Activités: Information et activités récréatives; *Stagiaires:* Oui; *Service de conférenciers:* Oui
Membre(s) du bureau directeur:
Gilles Read, Directeur général
Jeanne d'Arc Paradis, Adjointe
ccsmm.membres@videotron.ca
Marc-André Saucier, Agent des services communautaires et sociaux
ccsmm.service@videotron.ca
Yann Lacroix, Service de développement de l'employabilité
ccsmm.acces@videotron.ca

Centre de musique canadienne *See* Canadian Music Centre

Centre de plein air du Mont Chalco
CP 173, 264, rte 167, Chibougamau QC G8P 2K6
Tél: 418-748-7162; *Téléc:* 418-748-4685
info@montchalco.ca
www.montchalco.ca
Aperçu: Dimension: petite; *Envergure:* locale

Centre de prévention de la radicalisation menant à la violence (CPRMV)
#602, 800, boul de Maisonneuve est, Montréal QC H2L 4L8
Tél: 514-687-7141
Ligne sans frais: 877-687-7141
info@info-radical.org
www.info-radical.org
Aperçu: Dimension: petite; *Envergure:* provinciale; fondée en 2015
Mission: Prévenir la radicalisation menant à la violence; Contrer le discours violent; Définir les zones de prévention de la violence au Québec
Membre(s) du personnel: 10
Activités: Présentation des mesures concrètes pour prévenir la violence; Fournir un soutien psychosocial aux individus radicalisés; Mener des études; Diffusion de l'information;
Stagiaires: Oui
Membre(s) du bureau directeur:
Herman Okomba-Deparice, Directeur général
Marian Misdrahi, Coordinatrice, Programs

Centre de promotion du logiciel québécois; Réseau inter logiQ *Voir* Association québécoise des technologies

Centre de protection de l'enfance et de la jeunesse (CJMIU)
Montréal QC
www.ciusss-centresudmtl.gouv.qc.ca
www.youtube.com/user/centrejeunessemtl
Nom précédent: Le Centre jeunesse de Montréal - Institut universitaire; Le Centre jeunesse de Montréal; Les Centres jeunesse de Montréal; Centre Marie-Vincent
Aperçu: Dimension: petite; *Envergure:* locale; fondée en 1993
Membre(s) du personnel: 3

Centre de réadaptation Constance-Lethbridge (CRCL) / Constance Lethbridge Rehabilitation Centre
7005, boul de Maisonneuve ouest, Montréal QC H4B 1T3
Tél: 514-487-1770
Ligne sans frais: 866-487-1891
www.constance-lethbridge.qc.ca
www.linkedin.com/company/centre-de-readaptation-constance-lethbridge-rehabilitation-centre
www.facebook.com/ConstanceLethbridge
Aperçu: Dimension: moyenne; *Envergure:* locale; fondée en 1945 surveillé par Easter Seals Canada
Mission: Offrir des services spécialisés et ultraspécialisés à des adultes ayant une déficience motrice, en externe ou à domicile, de réadaptation, d'adaptation, de préparation et de support à l'intégration sociale ou professionnelle aux clientèles ayant des problèmes orthopédiques, neurologiques et rhumatologiques; offrir aussi une expertise d'évaluation de la conduite automobile, d'évaluation et d'orientation des capacités de travail de la personne handicapée
Affiliation(s): Confédération québécoise des centres d'hébergement et de réadaptation
Membre: Comités: Exécutif; Gouvernance et d'éthique; Vérification; Vigilance et de la qualité; Gestion des risques; Révision; Médecins, dentistes et pharmaciens; Multidisciplinaire; Usagers
Activités: Stagiaires: Oui; *Bibliothèque:* Bibliothèque médicale
Publications:
• Centre de réadaptation Constance-Lethbridge rapport annuel
Type: Rapport; *Frequency:* Annuel

Centre de réadaptation et dépendance le virage
5110, boul Cousineau, Saint-Hubert QC J3Y 7G5
Tél: 450-443-2100
Ligne sans frais: 800-363-9434
www.levirage.qc.ca
Nom précédent: Centre de réadaption Montérégie
Aperçu: Dimension: petite; *Envergure:* locale; fondée en 1995
Mission: Pour réhabiliter les personnes qui souffrent d'addictions diverses, de sorte qu'ils sont capables de se réinsérer dans la société
Finances: Budget de fonctionnement annuel: Plus de $5 Million
Membre(s) du personnel: 125
Membre: Montant de la cotisation: Gratuit

Centre de réadaption Montérégie *Voir* Centre de réadaptation et dépendance le virage

Centre de recherche des cantons de l'est *See* Eastern Townships Resource Centre

Centre de recherche et d'enseignement sur les droits de la personne *See* Human Rights Research & Education Centre

Centre de recherche et d'information en consommation de Port-Cartier
CP 204, #2, 1, rue Wood, Port-Cartier QC G5B 2G8
Tél: 418-766-3203; *Téléc:* 418-766-3312
cricportcartier@globetrotter.net
www.criccn.ca
Également appelé: CRIC de Port-Cartier
Aperçu: Dimension: petite; *Envergure:* locale; fondée en 1980 surveillé par Coalition des associations de consommateurs du Québec
Membre de: Coalition des associations de consommateurs du Québec (CACQ)
Membre(s) du bureau directeur:
Colette Girard Riffou, Directrice

Havre-Saint-Pierre
1158, rue Boréale, Havre-Saint-Pierre QC G0G 1P0
Sept-Iles
263, rue Papineau, Sept-Iles QC G4R 4J2

Centre de recherche et d'intervention interuniversitaire sur l'éducation et la vie au travail (CRIEVAT)
Pavillon des sciences de l'éducation, Université Laval, #658, 2320, rue des Bibliothèques, Québec QC G1V 0A6
Tél: 418-656-2131
crievat@fse.ulaval.ca
www.crievat.fse.ulaval.ca
Aperçu: *Dimension:* petite; *Envergure:* internationale; fondée en 1990
Mission: Développer de nouvelles connaissances et de nouvelles approches dans le domaine de l'éducation au travail; participer à la formation d'étudiants de 2e et 3e cycles et promouvoir l'éducation au travail dans la formation de futurs éducateurs; sensibiliser et impliquer les représentants du monde de l'éducation et du travail dans le développement de nouvelles stratégies d'éducation à la vie de travail; offrir aux chercheurs du Centre des services efficaces afin d'accroître leur productivité; aider au démarrage de nouveaux chercheurs universitaires dans le domaine de l'éducation au travail
Finances: *Budget de fonctionnement annuel:* Moins de $50,000; *Fonds:* Université Laval, Budget de developpement de la recherche
Membre(s) du personnel: 3
Membre: 1-99
Membre(s) du bureau directeur:
France Picard, Directrice

Centre de recherche et développement en économique *Voir* Centre interuniversitaire de recherche en économie quantitative

Centre de recherche interdisciplinaire sur la violence familiale et la violence faite aux femmes (CRI-VIFF)
Univ. de Montréal, CP 6128, Succ. Centre-Ville, Montréal QC H3C 3J7
Tél: 514-343-5708
cri-viff@umontreal.ca
www.criviff.qc.ca
Aperçu: *Dimension:* petite; *Envergure:* provinciale
Membre(s) du bureau directeur:
Marie-Marthe Cousineau, Directrice
mm.cousineau@umontreal.ca

Centre de recherche sur la vie marine de Grand Manan *See* Grand Manan Whale & Seabird Research Station

Centre de recherches pour le développement international *See* International Development Research Centre

Centre de ressources communautaires Olde Forge *See* The Olde Forge Community Resource Centre

Centre de ressources et d'intervention pour hommes abusés sexuellement dans leur enfance (CRIPHASE) / Resource and Intervention Center for Men Sexually Abused during their Childhood
#100, 8105, rue de Gaspé, Montréal QC H2P 2J9
Tél: 514-529-5567; *Téléc:* 514-529-0571
info@criphase.org
www.criphase.org
www.facebook.com/168619389848314
Aperçu: *Dimension:* petite; *Envergure:* locale; fondée en 1997
Mission: Services et ressources pour hommes abusés sexuellement dans leur enfance; groupes, activités/ateliers
Finances: *Budget de fonctionnement annuel:* $100,000-$250,000
Membre(s) du personnel: 8; 3 bénévole(s)
Membre: 350
Activités: Groupes de soutien; *Evénements de sensibilisation:* Marche de mobilisation et de soutien aux victimes d'agression sexuelle, avril; *Stagiaires:* Oui; *Service de conférenciers:* Oui; *Bibliothèque:* Bibtèque de CRIPHASE; rendez-vous
Membre(s) du bureau directeur:
Alice Charasse, Coordinatrice, 514-529-5567, Fax: 514-529-0571
direction.acharasse@criphase.org
Publications:
• Le Journal du CRIPHASE
Type: Journal; *Frequency:* 3 pa

Centre de ressources et transition pour danseurs *See* Dancer Transition Resource Centre

Centre de service familial d'Ottawa-Carleton *See* Family Service Centre of Ottawa-Carleton

Centre de services aux entreprises Canada-Yukon *See* Canada-Yukon Business Service Centre

Centre de services communautaires de Sudbury *See* Sudbury Community Service Centre Inc.

Centre de services Guigues
159 Murray St., Ottawa ON K1N 5M7
Tél: 613-241-1266; *Téléc:* 613-562-3021
info@centresg.ca
www.centresg.ca
Également appelé: Centre de jour polyvalent pour aînés francophones d'Ottawa-Carleton
Nom précédent: Centre de jour Guigues
Aperçu: *Dimension:* petite; *Envergure:* locale; Organisme sans but lucratif; fondée en 1981
Mission: Le centre est un organisme à but non-lucratif de la collectivité francophone de la région d'Ottawa qui assure des services de soutien communautaires et des services socio-récréatifs en français aux personnes aînées de même qu'aux adultes ayant un handicap physique
Membre de: Centraide
Finances: *Budget de fonctionnement annuel:* $250,000-$500,000; *Fonds:* Ministère de la Santé; Centraide; Ville d'Ottawa
Membre(s) du personnel: 20; 50 bénévole(s)
Membre: 100-499; *Montant de la cotisation:* 15$; *Critères d'admissibilite:* 50 ans et plus
Activités: Programme social et récréatif; Programme de soutien communautaire; Programme de soutien a domicile; Programme de jour; *Stagiaires:* Oui; *Bibliothèque* Not open to public
Membre(s) du bureau directeur:
Charles Simard, Directeur général par intérim

Centre de solidarité lesbienne
#301, 4126, rue Saint-Denis, Montréal QC H2W 2M5
Tél: 514-526-2452; *Téléc:* 514-526-3570
info@solidaritelesbienne.qc.ca
www.solidaritelesbienne.qc.ca
Aperçu: *Dimension:* petite; *Envergure:* provinciale
Mission: Le Centre est accessible aux personnes à mobilité réduite; organisme sans but lucratif qui a pour mission d'améliorer les conditions de vie des lesbiennes en leur offrant des services et des interventions adaptés à leur réalité et ce, dans les domaines de la violence conjugales, du bien-être et de la santé.

Le Centre de soutien en santé mentale - Montérégie (CSSM-M)
2510, rue Sainte-Hélène, Longueuil QC J4K 3V2
Tél: 450-677-4347; *Téléc:* 450-748-0503
www.schizophrenie-monteregie.com
schizomonteregie.blogspot.ca
Nom précédent: Société de Schizophrénie de la Montérégie
Aperçu: *Dimension:* petite; *Envergure:* locale
Mission: Aider toute personne atteintes de schizophrénie et leurs familles d'améliorer leur qualité de vie et de sensibiliser aux problèmes de schizophrénie provoque
Activités: *Evénements de sensibilisation:* Cyclothon Écile-Nelligan (août)
Membre(s) du bureau directeur:
Lucie Couillard, Dierctrice générale

Centre de soutien entr'Aidants (AFSAS)
1688, rue Gustave-Désourdy, Saint-Hubert QC J4T 1Y6
Tél: 450-465-2520; *Téléc:* 250-465-2290
info@centredesoutienentraidants.com
www.centredesoutienentraidants.com
Aperçu: *Dimension:* petite; *Envergure:* locale; fondée en 1990
Activités:; *Bibliothèque:* Centre de documentation
Membre(s) du bureau directeur:
Anyela Vergara, Directrice générale, 450-465-2520 Ext. 205
avergara@centredesoutienentraidants.com

Centre de toxicomanie et de santé mentale *See* Centre for Addiction & Mental Health

Centre de valorisation du patrimoine vivant (CVPV)
CP 123, Succ. B, 5, rue Cul-de-Sac, Québec QC G1K 7A1
Tél: 418-647-1598; *Téléc:* 418-647-4439
estrad@cvpv.net
cvpv.net
www.facebook.com/134434686579001
www.flickr.com/photos/cvpv
Également appelé: Es TRAD

Aperçu: *Dimension:* moyenne; *Envergure:* provinciale; fondée en 1981
Mission: Développer la compréhension, l'appréciation et la conservation de la culture traditionnelle (la musique, la danse, le chant, le conte, les coutumes, les arts et les métiers traditionnels) en la rendant visible et accessible dans tous les milieux de la société contemporaine
Membre: *Montant de la cotisation:* 20$ individuel; 30$ famille; 35$ organisme
Activités: Danses traditionnelles; location de matériel sonore; location des voûtes de la Maison Chevalier; expositions; *Bibliothèque:* Centre de documentation et audiothèque; Bibliothèque publique
Membre(s) du bureau directeur:
Jean-Pierre Chenard, Directeur

Centre des arts Saidye Bronfman *See* Segal Centre for the Performing Arts at the Saidye

Centre des auteurs dramatiques (CEAD)
#200, 261, rue du Saint-Sacrement, Montréal QC H2Y 3V2
Tél: 514-288-3384; *Téléc:* 514-288-7043
cead@cead.qc.ca
www.cead.qc.ca
www.facebook.com/178312752996
twitter.com/LeCEAD
www.youtube.com/user/CommunicationsCEAD
Aperçu: *Dimension:* petite; *Envergure:* nationale; Organisme sans but lucratif; fondée en 1965
Mission: Promotion et diffusion ici et à l'étranger des textes d'auteurs québécois et d'auteurs franco-canadiens; développement dramaturgique
Membre de: Conseil québécois du théâtre (CQT)
Membre(s) du personnel: 10
Membre: *Critères d'admissibilite:* Auteurs de fiction
Activités: La Semaine de la dramaturgie (lectures publiques); *Bibliothèque:* Centre de documentation; Bibliothèque publique
Membre(s) du bureau directeur:
Nicole Doucet, Directrice générale
doucet@cead.qc.ca
Lise Vaillancourt, Présidente

Centre des Femmes de Longueuil
1529, boul Lafayette, Longueuil QC J4K 3B6
Tél: 450-670-0002; *Téléc:* 450-670-9749
info@centredefemmeslongueuil.org
www.centredefemmeslongueuil.org
Aperçu: *Dimension:* petite; *Envergure:* locale
Mission: Pour donner aux femmes défavorisées un endroit où ils éprouvent un sentiment d'appartenance et de sécurité

Centre des femmes de Montréal *See* Women's Centre of Montréal

Centre des femmes de Montréal / Women's Centre of Montréal
3585, rue Saint-Urbain, Montréal QC H2X 2N6
Tél: 514-842-1066; *Téléc:* 514-842-1067
cfmwcm@centredesfemmes.com
www.centredesfemmesdemtl.org
Aperçu: *Dimension:* moyenne; *Envergure:* locale; fondée en 1973
Mission: D'offrir des services à caractère professionnel et éducatif, de même que des services de conseil et d'orientation pour aider les femmes à s'aider elles-mêmes
300 bénévole(s)
Membre(s) du bureau directeur:
Johanne Bélisle, Directrice générale

Centre des niveaux de compétence linguistique canadiens *See* Centre for Canadian Language Benchmarks

Centre des ressources sur la non-violence inc (CRNV) / Resource Centre on Non-Violence
#160, 1945, rue Mullins, Montréal QC H3K 1N9
Tél: 514-272-5012; *Téléc:* 514-272-5163
crnv@nonviolence.ca
www.nonviolence.ca
Aperçu: *Dimension:* petite; *Envergure:* locale; Organisme sans but lucratif; fondée en 1988
Mission: Le Centre vise à promouvoir une société qui s'inspire des principes et pratiques de la non-violence par le moyen de la recherche, de l'éducation, de l'information et d'interventions spécifiques
Membre de: Outils de Paix
Affiliation(s): Aboriginal Rights Coalition; Alliance Canadienne pour la paix; Maison St-Charles
Finances: *Budget de fonctionnement annuel:* $50,000-$100,000

Membre(s) du personnel: 2; 40 bénévole(s)
Membre: 15; *Montant de la cotisation:* 25$ membre associé
Activités: Volets: autochtone; paix et désarmement; résolution de conflicts; solidarité internationale; *Bibliothèque:* Bibliothèque publique
Membre(s) du bureau directeur:
Normand Beaudet, Directeur Général
Gerald Pascal, Administrateur
gpascal@nonviolence.ca
Shimbi Katchelewa, Coordonnateur

Centre des services sida secours du Québec *Voir* SIDALYS

Centre femmes de Rimouski
CP 36, Rimouski QC G5L 7B7
Tél: 418-723-0333; *Téléc:* 418-723-1889
accueil.femmes@globetrotter.net
www.centrefemmesrimouski.org
www.facebook.com/pages/Centre-Femmes-de-Rimouski/230583500412426
Aperçu: *Dimension:* petite; *Envergure:* locale; Organisme sans but lucratif
Mission: De favoriser l'amélioration des conditions de vie des femmes.
Affiliation(s): L'R des Centres de Femmes
Finances: *Fonds:* Gouvernement
Membre(s) du personnel: 5
Membre: *Montant de la cotisation:* 3$; 15$ membre sympathisante; 50$ membre groupe de soutien
Membre(s) du bureau directeur:
Louise Dionne, Coordonnatrice

Le Centre Financier International - Montréal *See* International Financial Centre of Montréal

LA Centre for Active Living
55 Rankin Cres., Toronto ON M6P 4E4
Tel: 416-452-4875
www.loyolaarrupecentre.com
www.facebook.com/LACentreforActiveLiving
twitter.com/lacseniors
Previous Name: Loyola Arrupe Centre for Seniors
Overview: A small local charitable organization founded in 2000
Mission: To serve the emotional & physical needs of people 55+; To provide & promote independent community living in an inclusive fashion; To allow seniors to live actively with dignity & confidence
Finances: *Funding Sources:* Ministry of Health & Long-Term Care; Municipal government; Donations; Fundraising
Staff Member(s): 2
Membership: *Fees:* $20; *Member Profile:* Seniors in the Toronto area
Activities: Offering recreational & spiritual programs; Organizing trips & outings; Facilitating Fall Flu Clinics & Income Tax Return Clinics
Chief Officer(s):
Sandra Cardillo, Executive Director

Centre for Addiction & Mental Health (CAMH) / Centre de toxicomanie et de santé mentale
250 College St., Toronto ON M5T 1R8
Tel: 416-535-8501
Toll-Free: 800-463-6273
www.camh.ca
www.linkedin.com/company/camh
www.facebook.com/CentreforAddictionandMentalHealth
twitter.com/CAMHnews
www.youtube.com/camhtv
Previous Name: Addiction Research Foundation
Overview: A large provincial charitable organization founded in 1998
Mission: To provide treatment for & research into substance abuse & mental health issues. Clinical & research sites in Toronto & across Ontario
Affiliation(s): University of Toronto; University of Western Ontario; WHO
Finances: *Annual Operating Budget:* Greater than $5 Million; *Funding Sources:* Ontario Ministry of Health; local government; foundations; contracts; donations
Staff Member(s): 3052; 1505 volunteer(s)
Membership: *Committees:* Audit, Finance & Resources; Clinical Quality; Governance; Property; Research
Activities: *Awareness Events:* National Drug Awareness Week, 3rd week of Nov.; National Mental Health Week, 1st week of May; Mental Illness Week, 2nd week of Oct.
Chief Officer(s):
Catherine Zahn, President & CEO

Centre for ADHD Awareness, Canada (CADDAC)
#604, 3950 - 14th Ave., Markham ON L3R 0A9
Tel: 416-637-8584; *Fax:* 905-475-3232
www.caddac.ca
www.facebook.com/CADDAC
twitter.com/CentreforADHD
Overview: A small national organization
Mission: The Centre for ADHD Awareness Canada, is a national, non profit, umbrella organization providing leadership in education and advocacy for ADHD organizations and individuals across Canada.
Chief Officer(s):
Heidi Bernhardt, President & Executive Director

Centre for Adults in Progressive Employment Society
40 Lower McLean St., Glace Bay NS B1A 2K7
Tel: 902-849-8187
www.capesociety.ca
Also Known As: CAPE Society
Overview: A small local organization founded in 1980
Mission: To provide clients with life skills training & employment programs
Member of: DIRECTIONS Council for Vocational Services Society
Affiliation(s): United Way of Canada; Sydney & Area Chamber of Commerce; Cape Breton Chamber of Voluntary Organizations; Literacy Nova Scotia
Activities: Operating a furniture & refinishing business & thrift store; vocational programs; community employment programs; school-to-work transitioning programs

---

Centre for AIDS Services of Montréal (Women) *Voir* Centre d'action sida Montréal (Femmes)

Centre for Applied Ethics *See* W. Maurice Young Centre for Applied Ethics

Centre for Canadian Language Benchmarks (CCLB) / Centre des niveaux de compétence linguistique canadiens (CNCLC)
#400, 294 Albert St., Ottawa ON K1P 6E6
Tel: 613-230-7729; *Fax:* 613-230-9305
info@language.ca
www.language.ca
Overview: A small national organization founded in 1998
Mission: To support the Canadian Language Benchmarks & Niveaux de compétence linguistique canadiens through policy, guidelines, research & development; To promote their recognition & use as practical, fair & reliable national standards of second language proficiency, in educational, training, community & workplace settings
Member of: Canadian Society of Association Executives (CSAE)
Finances: *Annual Operating Budget:* $3 Million-$5 Million; *Funding Sources:* Government
Staff Member(s): 12; 12 volunteer(s)
Membership: 12; *Committees:* Audit Risk Management; Board Evaluation; Nominating
Activities: Supporting individuals who teach & learn English & French as second languages
Chief Officer(s):
François Bélisle, Executive Director
fbelisle@language.ca
Publications:
• Inside Language [a publication of the Centre for Canadian Language Benchmarks]
Type: Newsletter

Centre for Characterization & Microscopy of Materials *Voir* Centre de caractérisation microscopique des matériaux

Centre for Child Development
9460 - 140th St., Surrey BC V3V 5Z4
Tel: 604-584-1361; *Fax:* 604-583-5113
info@centreforchilddevelopment.ca
www.the-centre.org
www.facebook.com/thecentreforchilddevelopment
twitter.com/Centreforchild
www.youtube.com/user/Centreforchild
Previous Name: South Fraser Child Development Centre; Lower Fraser Valley Cerebral Palsy Association
Overview: A medium-sized local charitable organization founded in 1953
Mission: To provide services for children with special needs & their families
Affiliation(s): BC Association of Child Development & Rehabilitation; Cerebral Palsy Association of BC; Commission on the Accreditation of Rehabilitation Facilities Canada (CARF)
Finances: *Funding Sources:* 60% government funding; 40% donations
Staff Member(s): 140
Activities: *Awareness Events:* Run, Walk & Roll, April; Gala of Hope, Nov.
Chief Officer(s):
Joe Hall, Chair
Gerard Bremault, Chief Executive Officer
gerard@the-centre.org
Amber Robinson, Vice-President, Marketing Communications
amber@the-centre.org

Centre for Community Based Research
190 Westmount Rd. North, Waterloo ON N2L 3G5
Tel: 519-885-1460; *Fax:* 519-885-6364
general@communitybasedresearch.ca
www.communitybasedresearch.ca
Previous Name: Centre for Research & Education in Human Services
Overview: A small national organization founded in 1982
Mission: To strengthen communities through social research
Activities: Community research projects in Ontario & across Canada
Chief Officer(s):
Joanna Ochocka, Executive Director
joanna@communitybasedresearch.ca
Rich Janzen, Executive Director
rich@communitybasedresearch.ca
Publications:
• Evaluation Handbook
Number of Pages: 215; *Author:* Andrew Taylor & Janos Botschner; *Price:* $69
• Pathways to Inclusion
Number of Pages: 276; *Author:* John Lord & Peggy Hutchison; *Price:* $29.50
• Shifting the Paradigm in Community Mental Health
Number of Pages: 295; *Author:* Geoff Nelson, John Lord et al.; *Price:* $25

Centre for Community Learning & Development (CCL&D)
Parliament Library, 269 Gerrard St. East, 2nd Fl., Toronto ON M5A 2G3
Tel: 416-968-6989; *Fax:* 416-968-0597
info@tccld.org
www.tccld.org
www.facebook.com/torontoccld
twitter.com/TorontoCCLD
Previous Name: East End Literacy
Overview: A small local organization founded in 1979
Mission: To build equality through community-based literay; to be the most integrated progressive literacy organization in Toronto, with the highest quality of teaching; to build the capacity of the people who live within our area through our work
Affiliation(s): Ontario Literacy Coalition
Finances: *Funding Sources:* Provincial Government; City of Toronto; United Way
Staff Member(s): 10
Activities: *Library:* Not open to public
Chief Officer(s):
Alfred Jean-Baptiste, Executive Director
alfred@tccld.org
Eusis Dougan-McKenzie, President

Centre for Comparative Literature
c/o Isabel Bader Theatre, 93 Charles St. West, 3rd Fl., Toronto ON M5S 1K9
Tel: 416-813-4041; *Fax:* 416-813-4040
www.complit.utoronto.ca
Overview: A small national organization
Mission: To offer M.A. & Ph.D programs in major areas from medieval to contemporary literature
Chief Officer(s):
Neil ten Kortenaar, Director, 416-813-4042
neil.kortenaar@utoronto.ca
Bao Nguyen, Graduate Administrator, 416-813-4041
banguyen@chass.utoronto.ca
Awards:
• Rutherford Memorial Medals
For graduates of exceptional promise & ability who are under 26; for outstanding research in physics or chemistry. *Eligibility:* To be eligible for an RSC award, candidates shall be Canadian citizens or persons having permanent resident status, and who have lived in Canada during the three years preceding the date

of nomination. *Deadline:* December 1; *Amount:* $2500, plus a gold plated silver medal *Contact:* Jeanne Salo, Fellowship and Awards Officer, 613/991-9007; jsalo@rsc.ca
• Miroslaw Romanowski Medal
For scientific work relating to environmental problems. *Eligibility:* To be eligible for an RSC award, candidates shall be Canadian citizens or persons having permanent resident status, and who have lived in Canada during the three years preceding the date of nomination. *Deadline:* December 1; *Amount:* Bronze medal & $3,000 *Contact:* Jeanne Salo, Fellowship and Awards Officer, 613/991-9007; jsalo@rsc.ca
• Thomas W. Eadie Medal
For contributions in Engineering & Applied Science *Eligibility:* To be eligible for an RSC award, candidates shall be Canadian citizens or persons having permanent resident status, & who have lived in Canada during the three years preceding the date of nomination *Deadline:* December 1; *Amount:* Bronze Medal & $3,000 *Contact:* Jeanne Salo, Fellowship & Awards Officer, 613/991-9007; E-mail: jsalo@rsc.ca
Meetings/Conferences:
• 28th Annual Conference of the Centre for Comparative Literature, February, 2018, University of Toronto, Toronto, ON
Scope: National
Description: Theme: "The Ocean & the Seas"

Centre for Effective Practice Inc.
#402, 203 College St., Toronto ON M5T 1P9
Tel: 647-260-7880
info@effectivepractice.org
www.effectivepractice.org
www.linkedin.com/company/centre-for-effective-practice
www.facebook.com/cephealth
twitter.com/cephealth
Overview: A medium-sized national organization founded in 2004
Mission: To provide support for healthcare providers; To create solutions for health systems & local practices through various initiatives; To improve healthcare outcomes for patients
Activities: Disseminating clinical tools, resources, programs, & other knowledge products; Offering academic detailing services; Providing guidance development & appraisal training; Maintaining TheWell, a site that gives providers access to clinical tools & resources
Chief Officer(s):
Tupper Bean, Executive Director
Jay Graydon, Director, Finance

Centre for Entrepreneurship & Small Business *Voir* Centre d'entrepreneuriat et PME

Centre for Entrepreneurship Education & Development Inc. (CEED)
Bayers Road Centre, #225, 7071 Bayers Rd., Halifax NS B3L 2C2
Tel: 902-421-2333; *Fax:* 902-482-0291
Toll-Free: 800-590-8481
info@ceed.ca
www.ceed.ca
www.linkedin.com/company-beta/314065
www.facebook.com/ceed.ca
twitter.com/ceed_halifax
www.youtube.com/ceedhalifax
Overview: A small provincial organization founded in 1993
Mission: To build entrepreneurial awareness & capacity throughout Atlantic Canada
Affiliation(s): Acadia Centre for Social & Business Entrepreneurship; Black Business Initiative; Canada Business Service Centre; Canada Business Development Corperations; Canadian Youth Business Foundation; Centre for Women in Business; Entrepreneurs with Disabilities Network; Halifax Chamber of Commerce
Finances: *Funding Sources:* Provincial & federal government
Activities: Workshops; Youth development; Programming for priority youth; Small business programs
Chief Officer(s):
Craig MacMullin, President & CEO, 902-421-2333 Ext. 7395
cmacmullin@ceed.ca

Centre for Equality Rights in Accommodation (CERA) / Centre pour les droits à l'égalité au logement
PO Box 23, #215, 340 College St., Toronto ON M5T 3A9
Tel: 416-944-0087; *Fax:* 416-944-1803
Toll-Free: 800-263-1139
cera@equalityrights.org
www.equalityrights.org/cera
Overview: A small provincial organization founded in 1987
Mission: To promote the knowledge & enforcement of human rights in accommodation through public education, provision of advice, assistance, representation & referral to victims of discrimination; To acquire adequate & affordable housing through enforcing their human rights
Finances: *Funding Sources:* Foundations; government; individuals; United Way
Staff Member(s): 8
Activities: National Anti-Poverty Organization; Anti-Racist Action Centre; Anti-Racist Response Network; Ontario Human Rights Working Group; Centre for Housing Rights & Evictions; Habitat International Coalition; *Library:* Resource Centre
Chief Officer(s):
Megan Evans Maxwell, Executive Director
megan@equalityrights.org

Centre for Excellence in Emergency Preparedness (CEEP)
PO Box 65504, Dundas ON L9H 6Y6
admin@ceep.ca
www.ceep.ca
www.facebook.com/150602708300341
twitter.com/EmergPrep
Overview: A small national organization founded in 1993
Mission: To develop a disaster resilient Canada; To prepare small businesses, non-profit organizations, & disaster management professionals; To foster the establishment & maintenance of professional standards & certification for the disaster management community
Finances: *Funding Sources:* Grants
Membership: *Member Profile:* Experts in emergency medicine, public health, infectious diseases, toxicology, and emergency medical services.
Activities: Advocating for disaster resilient communities; Liaising with all levels of government; Providing information & emergency preparedness programs; Sharing knowledge with international disaster management organizations
Publications:
• CCEP [Canadian Centre for Emergency Preparedness] Newsletter
Type: Newsletter; *Frequency:* Quarterly; *Price:* Free
• Disaster Management Canada (DMC)
Type: Magazine; *Frequency:* Quarterly; *Accepts Advertising*; *Price:* Free to qualified disaster management professionals withCanadian addresses
Profile: Timely, practical information from across the disaster management spectrum for emergency management & business continuity readers

Centre for Family Business (CFFB)
140 Westmount Rd. North, Waterloo ON N2L 3G6
Tel: 519-749-1441
info@cffb.ca
www.cffb.ca
Overview: A small local organization
Affiliation(s): University of Waterloo; Conrad Grebel College
Membership: 500; *Fees:* $1,400; *Committees:* Affilliation; Human Resources; Sponsorship; Membership; Program; Marketing
Activities: Monthly events for members; professional development workshops; family farm conferences
Chief Officer(s):
Dave Schnarr, Executive Director
Awards:
• Peter Hallman Mentor Award
• Milestone Achievement Award
• Anniversary Award
• Completed Succession Award

Centre for Fisheries Innovation *See* Canadian Centre for Fisheries Innovation

Centre for Immigrant & Community Services (CICS)
c/o Immigrant Resource Centre, 2330 Midland Ave., Toronto ON M1S 5G5
Tel: 416-292-7510; *Fax:* 416-292-7579; *Crisis Hot-Line:* 416-292-2832
info@cicscanada.com
www.cicscanada.com
www.facebook.com/cicscanada
twitter.com/cicscanada
Previous Name: Chinese Interpreter & Information Services; Chinese Information & Community Services of Greater Toronto; Centre for Information & Community Services
Overview: A medium-sized local charitable organization founded in 1974
Mission: To provide a wide range of cost-effective, culturally-sensitive & professional services; to empower newcomers to settle & integrate into Canadian society; to promote active citizenship in the community; committed to excellence & to be a leading agency in settlement, education & social services
Member of: Ontario Council of Agencies Serving Immigrants
Finances: *Annual Operating Budget:* $3 Million-$5 Million; *Funding Sources:* Government; United Way of Greater Toronto & United Way of York Region
Staff Member(s): 130; 1200 volunteer(s)
Membership: 2,500; *Fees:* $20
Activities: Newcomers Orientation Days; *Internships:* Yes
Library: Employment Resource Centre; Open to public
Chief Officer(s):
Moy Wong-Tam, Executive Director
Suba Satgunaraj, Director, Finance & Operations
LINC Centre
#501, 4002 Sheppard Ave. East, Toronto ON M1S 4R5
Tel: 416-299-8118; *Fax:* 416-299-7898
info@cicscanada.com
Markham South Welcome Centre
7220 Kennedy Rd., Markham ON L3R 7P2
Tel: 905-479-7926; *Fax:* 905-479-2603
info@welcomecentre.ca
North York Office
1761 Sheppard Ave. East, 1st Fl., Toronto ON M2J 0A5
Tel: 416-493-7510; *Fax:* 416-292-7579
info@cicscanada.com
Toronto Integrated Service Centre
#403, 3850 Finch Ave. East, Toronto ON M1T 3T6
Tel: 416-293-4565; *Fax:* 416-293-5692
info@cicscanada.com
Woodside Square LINC Centre
#202, 1571 Sandhurst Circle, Toronto ON M1V 1V2
Tel: 416-292-6558; *Fax:* 416-335-7293
info@cicscanada.com
York Region Immigrant Youth Centre
#2, 5284 Hwy. 7 East, Markham ON L3P 1B9
Tel: 905-294-8868; *Fax:* 905-294-8802
info@cicscanada.com

Centre for Immunization & Respiratory Infectious Diseases (CIRID)
c/o Public Health Agency of Canada, 130 Colonnade Rd., Ottawa ON K1A 0K9
www.phac-aspc.gc.ca/irid-diir
Overview: A small national organization
Mission: To decrease & eradicate instances of vaccine-preventable & infectious respiratory diseases; To lessen the negative impact of respiratory infections
Activities: Promoting Canadian immunization programs; Implementing the National Immunization Strategy; Collaborating internationally on disease prevention & control & immunization programs
Chief Officer(s):
Rhonda Kropp, Director General, 613-960-2893

Centre for Independent Living in Toronto (CILT)
#902, 365 Bloor St. East, Toronto ON M4W 3L4
Tel: 416-599-2458; *Fax:* 416-599-3555; *TTY:* 416-599-5077
cilt@cilt.ca
www.cilt.ca
Overview: A small local charitable organization
Mission: To help people with disabilities learn independent living skills & integrate into the community
Member of: Canadian Association of Independent Living Centers (CAILC); United Way of Greater Toronto
Chief Officer(s):
Meenu Sikand, President

Centre for Indigenous Environmental Resources, Inc. (CIER)
PO Box 26092, Stn. Maryland, Winnipeg MB R3G 3R3
Tel: 204-956-0660; *Fax:* 866-288-3919
earth@yourcier.org
www.yourcier.org
Overview: A small national organization
Mission: To protect & build sustainable indigenous communities
Chief Officer(s):
Merrell-Ann Phare, Executive Director
Kathy Johnson, Manager, Finance & Administration

Centre for Indigenous Sovereignty (CFIS)
14528 River Line Rd., RR#3, Thamesville ON N0P 2K0
Tel: 519-692-4141; *Fax:* 519-692-5633

Overview: A small national organization
Mission: To create an avenue to assist First Nation peoples in developing & implementing initiatives for the positive rebuilding of Indigenous communities, nations, governments & organizations

Centre for Inquiry Canada
#604, 55 Eglinton Ave. East, Toronto ON M4P 1G8
Tel: 647-391-2342
www.centreforinquiry.ca
www.facebook.com/CFICanada
twitter.com/cficanada
Overview: A medium-sized national charitable organization
Mission: To serve as the voice of science & secularism in Canada
Finances: Funding Sources: Donations; membership fees
Membership: Fees: $30; Member Profile: Individuals who are a part of or interested in the secular & humanistic community of Canada; Committees: Edcuation; Human Rights; Science
Activities: Organizing educational events; Library: Open to public
Chief Officer(s):
Eric Adriaans, National Executive Director

Centre for International Business Studies (CIBS)
University of Alberta, 3-23 Business Bldg., Edmonton AB T6G 2R6
Tel: 780-492-7676; Fax: 780-492-4631
cibs@ualberta.ca
www.business.ualberta.ca/cibs
Overview: A small international organization founded in 1989
Mission: To prepare students for a globally competitive environment & to provide corresponding information to the business community
Affiliation(s): University of Alberta, School of Business
Finances: Annual Operating Budget: $500,000-$1.5 Million; Funding Sources: Department of Foreign Affairs & International Trade; foundations; businesses
Staff Member(s): 3
Activities: Organize & present for international managers; host speakers; publish research papers; Speaker Service: Yes
Chief Officer(s):
Edy Wong, Director, 780-492-8137, Fax: 780-492-0280
edy@ualberta.ca

Centre for Investigative Journalism See Canadian Association of Journalists

The Centre for Israel & Jewish Affairs (CIJA)
PO Box 19514, Stn. Manulife Centre, 55 Bloor St. West, Toronto ON M4W 3T9
Tel: 416-925-7499
info@cija.ca
www.cija.ca
www.facebook.com/cijainfo
twitter.com/cijainfo
www.instagram.com/cijainfo
Previous Name: Canadian Jewish Congress
Overview: A medium-sized national charitable organization founded in 1919
Mission: To act as decision-making body of the Jewish community in Canada; To act on behalf of Canadian Jewish community on issues & concerns affecting Jews in Canada & around the world; To foster interaction between interests & needs of Jewish community in Canada & Canadian society at large on a broad range of political, charitable & social justice issues
Member of: Canadian Coalition for Genetic Fairness
Affiliation(s): World Jewish Congress; Conference on Jewish Material Claims Against Germany, Inc.; Memorial Foundation for Jewish Culture
Staff Member(s): 25; 125 volunteer(s)
Membership: 1,000-4,999; Committees: Archives; Community Relations; Holocaust Remembrance; Legal Advisory; Religious & Interreligious Affairs; Social Action
Activities: Library: National Jewish Archives; Open to public by appointment
Chief Officer(s):
David J. Cape, Chair

Calgary Jewish Federation
1607 - 90 Ave. SW, Calgary AB T2V 4V7
Tel: 403-253-8600
www.jewishcalgary.org
www.facebook.com/CalgaryJewishFederation
twitter.com/jewishcalgary
Member of: Canadian Jewish Congress
Affiliation(s): Akiva Academy; Calgary Jewish Academy; Camp BB Riback; Jewish Family Services Calgary; The Calgary Jewish Community Centre; Calgary Community Kollel
Chief Officer(s):
Adam Silver, Chief Executive Officer, 403-444-3151
asilver@jewishcalgary.org
• Pomegranate [a publication of the Calgary Jewish Federation]
Type: Newsletter
Profile: News & updates from the Calgary Jewish community

Jewish Federation of Edmonton
#200, 10220 - 156 St., Edmonton AB T5P 2R1
Tel: 780-487-0585
info@edjfed.org
www.jewishedmonton.org
www.facebook.com/jewishedmonton
twitter.com/jewishedmonton
www.instagram.com/jewishedmonton
Member of: Canadian Jewish Congress
Chief Officer(s):
Debby Shoctor, Chief Executive Officer, 780-487-0585 Ext. 203
debbys@edjfed.org

Jewish Federation of Ottawa
21 Nadolny Sachs Private, Ottawa ON K2A 1R9
Tel: 613-798-4696; Fax: 613-798-4695
jewishottawa.com
www.facebook.com/JFedOttawa
twitter.com/JewishOttawa
Chief Officer(s):
Andrea Freedman, President & CEO
afreedman@jewishottawa.com

Jewish Federation of Winnipeg
#300C, 123 Doncaster St., Winnipeg MB R3N 2B2
Tel: 204-477-7400
info@jewishwinnipeg.org
www.jewishwinnipeg.org
www.facebook.com/jewishwinnipeg
twitter.com/jewishwinnipeg
Chief Officer(s):
Elaine Goldstine, Chief Executive Officer, 204-477-7402
egoldstine@jewishwinnipeg.org

Québec Region
1, carré Cummings, Montréal QC H3W 1M6
Tel: 514-735-3541
fcja@federationcja.org
www.federationcja.org
www.linkedin.com/company/federation-cja
www.facebook.com/FEDERATIONCJA
twitter.com/FederationCJA
Chief Officer(s):
Deborah Corber, Chief Executive Officer

Centre for Jewish Education (CJE)
The Koschitzky Centre for Jewish Education, Sherman Campus, 4600 Bathurst St., 5th Fl., Toronto ON M2R 3V2
Tel: 416-635-2883; Fax: 416-633-7535
cjetoronto.com
Also Known As: The Julia and Henry Koschitzky Centre for Jewish Education
Previous Name: Ontario Association of Jewish Dayschools; Ontario Jewish Association for Equity in Education
Overview: A medium-sized provincial organization founded in 1984
Mission: To act as an educational pillar for UJA Federation of Greater Toronto; To strengthen, enrich & promote the quality of Jewish education in schools
Affiliation(s): UJA Federation of Greater Toronto
Membership: 1-99
Chief Officer(s):
Daniel Held, Executive Director

Centre for Newcomers Society of Calgary (CFN)
#1010, 999 - 36 St. NE, Calgary AB T2A 7X6
Tel: 403-569-3325
info@centrefornewcomers.ca
www.centrefornewcomers.ca
www.linkedin.com/company/centre-for-newcomers-society-of-calgary
www.facebook.com/centrefornewcomers
twitter.com/YYCNewcomers
cfnyyc.blogspot.ca
Previous Name: Calgary Mennonite Centre for Newcomers Society
Overview: A small local organization founded in 1988
Mission: To assist refugees & immigrants arriving in Calgary to meet their settlement needs; To provide services & initiatives that promote a welcoming environment for newcomers in Calgary
Member of: Alberta Association of Immigrant Serving Agencies; Calgary Chamber of Voluntary Organizations
Affiliation(s): Canadian Red Cross
Finances: Annual Operating Budget: Greater than $5 Million; Funding Sources: Government
Staff Member(s): 150; 560 volunteer(s)
Membership: Member Profile: Members beyond the Mennonite constituency is enoucraged.
Activities: Offering English language programs, as well as family, children & youth programs; settlement & integration services; career development & job search resources; work experience opportunities, including EthniCity Catering & accounting training; multicultural peer mentorship & volunteer development; Speaker Service: Yes; Library
Chief Officer(s):
Anila Lee Yuen, MBA, Chief Executive Officer
a.leeyuen@centrefornewcomers.ca
David Hohol, Manager, Communications & Community Relations
d.hohol@centrefornewcomers.ca

The Centre for Peace in the Balkans
PO Box 1500-1292, Toronto ON M9C 4V5
Tel: 416-201-9729; Fax: 416-201-7397
scontact@balkanpeace.org
www.balkanpeace.org
Overview: A small international organization
Mission: To advocate a balanced & accurate presentation of the current socio-political situation on the Balkan Peninsula through peaceful means & the presentation of pertinent materials

Centre for Research & Education in Human Services See Centre for Community Based Research

Centre for Research on Latin America & The Caribbean (CERLAC)
8th Fl., York Research Tower, York University, 4700 Keele St., Toronto ON M3J 1P3
Tel: 416-736-5237; Fax: 416-736-5688
cerlac@yorku.ca
www.yorku.ca/cerlac
Overview: A medium-sized international organization founded in 1978
Mission: To offer an interdisciplinary research unit concerned with economic development, political & social organization & cultural contributions of Latin America & the Caribbean; to build academic & cultural links between these regions & Canada; informs researchers, policy advisors & public on matters concerning the regions; to assist in development of research & teaching institutions that directly benefit people of the regions
Affiliation(s): Canadian Association for Latin American & Caribbean Studies; Development Education Centre; OXFAM-Canada; Centre for Spanish Speaking People; CCIC; AFG: KAIROS
Staff Member(s): 6
Activities: Research & conferences on the Americas; Migration & Refugee Flows/Population & Development Projects; Rural Development Project; Religions Project; Human Rights Project; Speaker Service: Yes; Rents Mailing List: Yes; Library: CERLAC Documentation Centre; by appointment
Chief Officer(s):
Eduardo Canel, Director
ecanel@yorku.ca

Centre for Research on Violence Against Women & Children
Faculty of Educ. Bldg., Western University, #1158, 1137 Western Rd., London ON N6G 1G7
Tel: 519-661-4040; Fax: 519-850-2464
www.crvawc.ca
Overview: A small provincial organization
Mission: To promote the development of community-centred, action research on violence against women & children; To facilitate the cooperation of individuals, groups, & institutions representing the diversity of the community to pursue research questions & training opportunities to understand & prevent abuse
Chief Officer(s):
Maly Bun-Lebert, Centre Manager
mbun@uwo.ca

Centre for Spanish Speaking Peoples
2141 Jane St., 2nd Fl., Toronto ON M3M 1A2
Tel: 416-533-8545; Fax: 416-533-5731
info@spanishservices.org

www.spanishservices.org
www.facebook.com/CPGHH
twitter.com/CSSPToronto
www.youtube.com/user/CSSPtoronto
Overview: A small local organization founded in 1973 overseen by Ontario Council of Agencies Serving Immigrants
Mission: To assist the Spanish speaking community in Metro Toronto
Finances: *Annual Operating Budget:* $1.5 Million-$3 Million
120 volunteer(s)
Activities: *Library:* Spanish Language Library; Open to public by appointment
Chief Officer(s):
Raul Burbano, President

Centre for Study of Insurance Operations (CSIO) / Centre d'étude de la pratique d'assurance
#500, 110 Yonge St., Toronto ON M5C 1T4
Tel: 416-360-1773; *Fax:* 416-364-1482
Toll-Free: 800-463-2746
helpdesk@csio.com
www.csio.com
www.linkedin.com/company/csio
twitter.com/csio
Overview: A medium-sized national organization
Mission: To act as the national standards association for property & casualty insurance by representing property & casualty industry initiatives; to provide a competitive advantage for the independent broker distribution channel
Membership: 100-499; *Member Profile:* Broker associations; Insurance companies; Insurance vendors
Activities: Developing & maintaining XML Standards, Electronic Data Interchange (EDI) Standards, Terminology Standards, Form Standards, Web Screen Standards, Industry owned & managed CSIOnet, & Forums for Implementations of Standards; Participating in ACORD Standards Plenary & Working Groups & the Insurance Global Standards Working Group; Developing & designing property & casualty industry application forms; Providing members with access to forms & standards; Offering educational sessions & networking opportunities
Chief Officer(s):
Steve Whitelaw, Chair
Catherine Smola, President & CEO

Montréal Office
#1305, 1155, rue University, Montréal QC H3B 3A7
Tel: 514-393-8200; *Fax:* 514-393-3625
Toll-Free: 877-393-2372

Centre for Suicide Prevention (CSP)
#320, 105 - 12 Ave. SE, Calgary AB T2G 1A1
Tel: 403-245-3900; *Fax:* 403-245-0299; *Crisis Hot-Line:* 403-266-4357
www.suicideinfo.ca
www.linkedin.com/company/centre-for-suicide-prevention
www.facebook.com/centreforsuicideprevention
twitter.com/cspyyc
suicideinfo.tumblr.com
Previous Name: Suicide Information & Education Centre
Overview: A medium-sized provincial charitable organization founded in 1982
Mission: To educate people about the risk of suicide & suicide prevention
Member of: Canadian Association for Suicide Prevention
Affiliation(s): Canadian Mental Health Association - Alberta Division
Finances: *Funding Sources:* User fees, government contracts, community grants, special events, memorial and individual donations
Staff Member(s): 11
Activities: Training workshops; online courses; webinars; literature scans & reviews; library database access; lending library & knowledge translation publications; *Library:* Resource Centre; Open to public
Chief Officer(s):
Mara Grunau, Executive Director
mara@suicideinfo.ca
Hilary Sirman, Director, Impact & Engagement
hilary@suicideinfo.ca
Crystal Walker, Coordinator, Communications
crystal@suicideinfo.ca

Centre for the Study of Classroom Processes *See* Centre for the Study of Learning & Performance

Centre for the Study of Learning & Performance (CSLP) / Centre d'études sur l'apprentissage et la performance (CEAP)
Université Concordia, #LB581, 1450, boul de Maisonneuve ouest, Montréal QC H3G 2V8
Tel: 514-848-2424; *Fax:* 514-848-4520
cslp@education.concordia.ca
doe.concordia.ca/cslp
Previous Name: Centre for the Study of Classroom Processes
Overview: A small national organization founded in 1988
Mission: The objectives of the CSLP are fourfold: to increase the theoretical and practical understanding of the factors that promote and hinder the learning and performance of complex skills; to provide training and support to educators and administrators; to provide the educational community with material and intellectual resources regarding new ideas in education; and to train students who have an interest in learning and performance and who are enrolled in graduate studies within the departments with which the centre and its members are affiliated.
Finances: *Funding Sources:* National government; provincial government; foundations; internal grants
Membership: 70
Activities: Research & training, Bi-annual Research Fair; *Internships:* Yes; *Speaker Service:* Yes; *Library:* CSLP Information Resource Centre; Open to public
Chief Officer(s):
Philip C. Abrami, Director
abrami@education.concordia.ca
Anne Wade, Manager & Information Specialist
wada@education.concordia.ca

Centre for the Study of Living Standards (CSLS) / Centre d'étude des niveaux de vie
#710, 151 Slater St., Ottawa ON K1P 5H3
Tel: 613-233-8891; *Fax:* 613-233-8250
www.csls.ca
Overview: A medium-sized national charitable organization founded in 1995
Mission: To gain a better understanding of trends in living standards & factors determining trends through research; to develop & advocate specific policies through expert consensus
Finances: *Funding Sources:* Federation & provincial governments; Foundations
Staff Member(s): 3
Activities: Conducting research on living standards, productivity, & economical well-being issues
Chief Officer(s):
Andrew Sharpe, Executive Director
andrew.sharpe@csls.ca
Publications:
• The International Productivity Monitor [a publication of the Centre for the Study of Living Standards]
Type: Journal; *Frequency:* 2 pa; *Editor:* Andrew Sharpe

Centre for Transportation Engineering & Planning (C-TEP)
c/o Stantec, Transportation, #200, 325 - 25 St. SE, Calgary AB T2A 7H8
Tel: 403-607-4482; *Fax:* 403-716-8129
www.c-tep.com
twitter.com/ctep_canada
Overview: A medium-sized national organization
Mission: To provide professional development & research related to Canadian transportation engineering & planning; To provide a forum for collaboration between institutions & various levels of government; To act as a resource centre for transportation engineers & planners
Membership: 33 organizations; *Fees:* Schedule available
Chief Officer(s):
Gerard Kennedy, President
Neil Little, Executive Director
nlittle@c-tep.com
Meetings/Conferences:
• 2018 Centre for Transportation Engineering & Planning Annual General Meeting, 2018

Centre for Women in Business (CWB)
c/o Mount Saint Vincent University, Margaret Norrie McCain Centre, #411, 166 Bedford Hwy, Halifax NS B3M 2J6
Tel: 902-457-6449; *Fax:* 902-443-4687
Toll-Free: 888-776-9022
cwb@msvu.ca
www.centreforwomeninbusiness.ca
www.linkedin.com/company/1539340
www.facebook.com/centreforwomeninbusiness
twitter.com/cwb_ns
www.youtube.com/user/CentreWomenBusiness
Overview: A medium-sized local organization
Mission: To help women entrepreneurs begin, develop & advance their businesses
Affiliation(s): Centre for Entrepreneurship Education & Development Inc.
Membership: *Fees:* $99-$125 individual; $499+ corporate
Activities: Conferences; Networking events
Chief Officer(s):
Tanya Priske, Executive Director, 902-457-6474
tanya.priske@msvu.ca
Publications:
• BizBeat [a publication of the Centre for Women in Business]
Type: Newsletter

Centre franco-ontarien de folklore (CFOF)
935, ch du Lac Ramsey, Sudbury ON P3E 2C6
Tél: 705-675-8986; *Téléc:* 705-675-5809
cfof@cfof.on.ca
www.cfof.on.ca
fr-fr.facebook.com/126335660730527
Aperçu: *Dimension:* petite; *Envergure:* provinciale; Organisme sans but lucratif; fondée en 1972
Mission: Cueillette, conservation et diffusion du partimoine franco-ontarien, en particulier, le patrimoine oral
Membre de: Association études canadiennes
Activités: *Bibliothèque:* Bibliothèque du CFOF et Bibliothèque de généalogie; rendez-vous
Membre(s) du bureau directeur:
Janik Aubin-Robert, Présidente

Centre franco-ontarien de ressources pédagogiques (CFORP)
435, rue Donald, Ottawa ON K1K 4X5
Tél: 613-747-8000; *Téléc:* 613-747-2808
Ligne sans frais: 877-742-3677
cforp@cforp.ca
www.cforp.ca
www.linkedin.com/company/cforp
www.facebook.com/cforp
twitter.com/CFORP
www.instagram.com/cforp
Aperçu: *Dimension:* moyenne; *Envergure:* provinciale; Organisme sans but lucratif; fondée en 1974
Mission: Produit et diffuse des ressources pédagogiques et offrir des services destinés à soutenir l'éducation en langue française
Membre de: Association canadienne d'éducation de langue française (ACELF); Association nationale des éditeurs de livres (ANEL)
Affiliation(s): Librairie du Centre
Finances: *Budget de fonctionnement annuel:* $3 Million-$5 Million
Membre(s) du personnel: 140
Membre: 1-99
Activités: *Stagiaires:* Oui; *Bibliothèque:* Librairie du Centre; Bibliothèque publique
Membre(s) du bureau directeur:
Claude Deschamps, Directeur général, 613-747-8000 Ext. 253
claude.deschamps@cforp.ca
Penny Bell, Directrice exécutive, Administration, Finances et Ressources humaines, 613-747-8000 Ext. 234
penny.bell@cforp.ca
HUbert Lalande, Directeur, Communications et marketing
Hubert.lalande@cforp.ca
Teresa Duénez, Chargée de projet, Communications, Marketing et Librairie
teresa.duenez@cforp.ca
Publications:
• La Minute [un publication de la Centre franco-ontarien de ressources pédagogiques]
Type: Bulletin

Centre francophone d'informatisation des organisations (CEFRIO)
#575, 888, rue Saint-Jean, Québec QC G1R 5H6
Tél: 418-523-3746; *Téléc:* 418-523-2329
www.cefrio.qc.ca
www.linkedin.com/groups?gid=3697317
www.facebook.com/CEFRIOTIC
twitter.com/cefrio
Nom précédent: Centre francophone de recherche en informatisation des organisations
Aperçu: *Dimension:* petite; *Envergure:* provinciale; Organisme sans but lucratif; fondée en 1987

Mission: Aider les organisations québécoises à utiliser les techniques de l'information de manière à être plus performantes, plus productives et plus innovatrices
Membre(s) du personnel: 24
Membre: 150; *Montant de la cotisation:* Variable, selon le nombre d'employés
Activités:; *Bibliothèque:* Centre de documentation; Not open to public
Membre(s) du bureau directeur:
Jacqueline Dubé, Présidente-directrice générale
  Bureau à Montréal
  #471, 550, rue Sherbrooke ouest, Montréal QC H3A 1B9
  Tél: 514-840-1245; *Téléc:* 514-840-1275

Centre francophone de recherche en informatisation des organisations *Voir* Centre francophone d'informatisation des organisations

Centre francophone de Toronto (CFT)
#303, 555, rue Richmond ouest, Toronto ON M5V 3B1
Tél: 416-922-2672; *Téléc:* 416-203-1165
infos@centrefranco.org
www.centrefranco.org
www.facebook.com/Centre.francophone.de.Toronto
twitter.com/CentrefrancoT
www.youtube.com/channel/UCK-ySdR14i29fBcm-xBVFYw
Nom précédent: Conseil des organismes francophones du Toronto Métropolitain; Centre francophones du Toronto Métropolitain
Aperçu: *Dimension:* moyenne; *Envergure:* locale; Organisme sans but lucratif; fondée en 1977
Mission: Permettre à la population francophone du grand Toronto d'avoir accès à des services d'information, d'orientation et d'encadrement susceptibles de promouvoir la dimension humaine, culturelle et communautaire des multiples visages de la francophonie
Affiliation(s): Assemblée des centres culturels de l'Ontario; Centraide
Finances: *Budget de fonctionnement annuel:* $500,000-$1.5 Million
Membre(s) du personnel: 12; 50 bénévole(s)
Membre: 20 individu; 5 institutionnel; *Montant de la cotisation:* 30$ institutionnel; 10$ individu
Activités: Consultation personnalisée dans les domaines de l'établissement; service de conseils d'emploi; accès à des offres d'emploi; *Bibliothèque* Not open to public
Membre(s) du bureau directeur:
Lise Marie Baudry, Directrice générale

Centre historique de St-Armand
166, rue Quinn, St-Armand QC J0J 1N0
Tél: 450-248-3393
Aperçu: *Dimension:* petite; *Envergure:* locale; fondée en 2002

Centre indien cri de Chibougamau
95, rue Jaculet, Chibougamau QC G8P 2G1
Tél: 418-748-7667
cicc@lino.com
Aperçu: *Dimension:* petite; *Envergure:* locale; fondée en 1969
Mission: Centre social pour les Autochtones de la région; centre d'exposition pour les artisans cri
Membre(s) du bureau directeur:
Jo-Ann Toulouse, Directice générale

Centre intégré d'employabilité locale des Collines-de-l'Outaouais (CIEL)
1694, Montée de la Source, Cantley QC J8V 3H6
Tél: 819-457-4480; *Téléc:* 819-457-1024
Ligne sans frais: 877-770-2435
info@cielcollines.org
www.cielcollines.org
www.facebook.com/160819140628575
Aperçu: *Dimension:* petite; *Envergure:* locale
Mission: Pour aider les jeunes à trouver des emplois et retournent à l'école
Membre: *Critères d'admissibilite:* Jeunes adultes
Membre(s) du bureau directeur:
Josiane Groulx, Directrice éxecutive
jgroulx@cielcollines.org

Centre interdisciplinaire de recherches sur les activités langagières (CIRAL)
Pavillon Charles-de-Koninck, Université Laval, #2260-A, Faculté des lettres, Québec QC G1V 0A6
Tél: 418-656-2131; *Téléc:* 418-656-2622
www.lli.ulaval.ca/recherche/groupes-et-laboratoires
Nom précédent: Centre international de recherche en aménagement linguistique
Aperçu: *Dimension:* petite; *Envergure:* internationale; fondée en 1967
Mission: Le Centre interdisciplinaire de recherches sur la activités langagières (CIRAL) regroupe cinq équipes régulières, une vingtaine de chercheurs et quelque soixante-dix étudiants de deuxième et troisième cycles. Tous partagent la même conception des questions linguistiques : la langue est indissociable de l'histoire et de la culture des groupes qui la parlent, et elle évolue en fonction des contacts interethniques et des pressions socioculturelles qui s'exercent sur elle.
Finances: *Fonds:* Subventions; Université Laval
Membre: 100-499; *Critères d'admissibilite:* Chercheur
Activités: Recherches en aménagement du corpus de la langue; recherches en aménagement du statut des langues; diffusion des travaux de recherches; formation des chercheur-e-s; collaboration avec d'autres centres ou universités et service au milieu; *Bibliothèque:* Bibliothèque publique
Membre(s) du bureau directeur:
Aline Francoeur, Directrice
aline.francoeur@lli.ulaval.ca

Centre international de criminologie comparée (CICC) / International Centre for Comparative Criminology
CP 6128, Succ. Downtown, Montréal QC H3C 3J7
Tél: 514-343-7065; *Téléc:* 514-343-2269
cicc@umontreal.ca
www.cicc.umontreal.ca
www.facebook.com/CICCUdeM
twitter.com/ciccTweet
www.youtube.com/cicctv
Aperçu: *Dimension:* petite; *Envergure:* internationale; fondée en 1969
Mission: Travaux de recherche en criminologie sur le comportement criminel ou déviant de la personne qui le pose ou le subit, et la réaction sociale au crime
Affiliation(s): Université de Montréal et Université du Québec à Trois-Rivières
Finances: *Budget de fonctionnement annuel:* $3 Million-$5 Million; *Fonds:* FQRSC, Université de Montréal
Membre(s) du personnel: 5
Membre: 38; *Critères d'admissibilite:* Chercheur; professeur
Activités: Colloques; séminaires; débats; conférences; *Evénements de sensibilisation:* Bourses de rédaction, de cueillette de données, de colloque, recherche et societé, entente de collaboration chercheur du milieu de pratique
Membre(s) du bureau directeur:
Carlo Morselli, Directeur
Publications:
• Bulletin CICC-Hebdo
Frequency: hebdomadaire
Profile: Un plateforme d'échange sur l'actualité criminologique
• CICC INFO
Frequency: semi-annuel
Profile: Le bulletin d'information du CICC

Centre international de documentation et d'échanges de la francophonie (CIDEF)
Pavillon Louis-Jacques Casault, Université Laval, #6411, 1055 av du Séminaire, Québec QC G1V 0A6
Tél: 418-656-2131
afi@com.ulaval.ca
www.afi.com.ulaval.ca
Aperçu: *Dimension:* moyenne; *Envergure:* internationale; fondée en 1984
Mission: Constituer et diffuser une documentation internationale de la francophonie.
Membre(s) du personnel: 2
Activités: Francophonie internationale; *Stagiaires:* Oui
Membre(s) du bureau directeur:
Charles Moumouni, Directeur de publication
Charles.Moumouni@com.ulaval.ca

Centre international de recherche en aménagement linguistique *Voir* Centre interdisciplinaire de recherches sur les activités langagières

Centre international de solidarité ouvrière (CISO)
#3500, 565, Crémazie est, Montréal QC H2M 2V6
Tél: 514-383-2266; *Téléc:* 514-383-1143
ciso@ciso.qc.ca
www.ciso.qc.ca
www.facebook.com/cqcam.ciso
twitter.com/CISO_Qc

Aperçu: *Dimension:* petite; *Envergure:* internationale; Organisme sans but lucratif; fondée en 1975
Membre de: Association québécoise des organismes coopération internationale
Finances: *Budget de fonctionnement annuel:* $500,000-$1.5 Million
Membre(s) du personnel: 3; 30 bénévole(s)
Membre: *Montant de la cotisation:* 5-35 individuel; 50-400 organisationnel
Membre(s) du bureau directeur:
Denise Gagnon, Présidente

Centre international pour la prévention de la criminalité (CIPC) / International Centre for the Prevention of Crime (ICPC)
#803, 465, rue St-Jean, Montréal QC H2Y 2R6
Tél: 514-288-6731; *Téléc:* 514-288-8763
cipc@cipc-icpc.org
www.crime-prevention-intl.org
www.linkedin.com/company/international-centre-for-the-prevention-of-crime-icpc-
www.facebook.com/PreventionofCrime
twitter.com/ICPC_CIPC
Aperçu: *Dimension:* moyenne; *Envergure:* internationale; Organisme sans but lucratif; fondée en 1994
Mission: Aider les pays et les villes à améliorer la sécurité des collectivités et à réduire la criminalité et la violence grâce à une prévention efficace
Finances: *Fonds:* Gouvernement
Membre(s) du personnel: 11
Membre: 99; *Montant de la cotisation:* Barème; *Comités:* Comité consultatif et d'orientation; Comité scientifique
Activités: *Stagiaires:* Oui; *Service de conférenciers:* Oui; *Bibliothèque:* Centre de documentation; Bibliothèque publique rendez-vous
Membre(s) du bureau directeur:
Daniel Cauchy, Directeur général
Publications:
• 100 Pratiques prometteuses pour des villes plus sûres [publication de CIPC]
Type: Rapport
• 4e Rapport international sur la prévention de la criminalité et la sécurité quotidienne [publication de CIPC]
Type: Rapport
• Étude sur la violence domestique - Gouvernement de la Norvège [publication de CIPC]
Type: Rapport
• Prévention de la criminalité associée aux drogues [publication de Centre international pour la prévention de la criminalité]
Type: Rapport
• Rapport sur la prévention de la criminalité liée à la consommation de drogue [publication de CIPC]
Type: Rapport
• Sécurité dans les institutions publiques [publication de Centre international pour la prévention de la criminalité]
Type: Rapport
• Les violences faites aux femmes dans les transports collectifs terrestres [publication de CIPC]
Type: Rapport

Centre interuniversitaire de recherche en économie quantitative (CIREQ)
Pavillon Lionel-Groulx, Université de Montréal, CP 6128, Succ. Centre-Ville, 3150, rue Jean-Brillant, #C-6088, Montréal QC H3C 3J7
Tél: 514-343-6557; *Téléc:* 514-343-5831
www.cireqmontreal.com
Nom précédent: Centre de recherche et développement en économique
Aperçu: *Dimension:* moyenne; *Envergure:* internationale; fondée en 2002
Mission: Recherches dans les domaines de l'économétrie théorique et appliquée, de l'économie financière et de la théorie économique
Finances: *Fonds:* FQRSC; Université de Montréal; Université McGill et Université Concordia
Membre(s) du personnel: 4
Membre: 50; *Critères d'admissibilite:* Chercheurs
Activités: Colloques; ateliers; conférences spéciales; séminaires; *Stagiaires:* Oui; *Service de conférenciers:* Oui; *Bibliothèque:* Centre de documentation; Bibliothèque publique
Membre(s) du bureau directeur:
Emanuela Cardia, Dirctrice, 514-343-6111 Ext. 2449
emanuela.cardia@umontreal.ca

Centre Jean-Claude Malépart
2633, rue Ontario est, Montréal QC H2K 1W8
Tél: 514-521-6884; Téléc: 514-521-6760
info@cjcm.ca
cjcm.ca
www.facebook.com/centrejcm
www.youtube.com/centrejcm
Aperçu: *Dimension:* petite; *Envergure:* locale
Mission: Pour améliorer la qualité de vie des résidents de la région en offrant des activités de loisirs abordables
Activités: Sport, Arts; Artisanat; Activités informatiques
Membre(s) du bureau directeur:
Adrien Michaud, Directeur
amichaud@cjcm.ca

Le Centre jeunesse de la Montérégie
575, rue Adoncour, Longueuil QC J4G 2M6
Tél: 450-928-5125
Ligne sans frais: 800-641-4315
www.centrejeunessemonteregie.qc.ca
Aperçu: *Dimension:* moyenne; *Envergure:* locale; fondée en 1995
Mission: Offrir aux enfants et aux adolescents en difficulté de même qu'à leurs parents, des services d'aide spécialisée qui visent leur sécurité, leur protection, leur responsabilisation et leur autonomie
Membre(s) du personnel: 1000
Membre: 1,000-4,999
Activités: La protection de l'enfance et de la jeunesse et l'aide aux parents de ces enfants et adolescents; l'aide et la responsabilisation des jeunes contrevenants et le support aux parents; l'adaptation, la réadaptation et l'intégration sociale des enfants et des adolescents en difficulté; l'aide aux jeunes mères (pères) en difficulté d'adaptation; le placement d'enfants et d'adolescents en milieu substitut; l'urgence D.P.J. (24 heures/7 jours par semaine); *Stagiaires:* Oui; *Bibliothèque:* Centre de documentation
Membre(s) du bureau directeur:
Catherine Lemay, Secrétaire

Le Centre jeunesse de Montréal - Institut universitaire; Le Centre jeunesse de Montréal; Les Centres jeunesse de Montréal; Centre Marie-Vincent *Voir* Centre de protection de l'enfance et de la jeunesse

Le centre jeunesse de Québec (CJQ)
2915, av du Bourg-Royal, Beauport QC G1C 3S2
Tél: 418-661-6951; Téléc: 418-661-2845
communication.cjq3@ssss.gouv.qc.ca
www.centrejeunessedequebec.qc.ca
Aperçu: *Dimension:* moyenne; *Envergure:* locale
Mission: Dispense des services psychosociaux, des services d'adaptation, des services de réadaptation et des services d'intégration sociale aux jeunes et aux mères en difficulté de la région de Québec ainsi qu'à leur famille
Membre(s) du bureau directeur:
Jacques Laforest, Directeur général

Centre local de développement Rouyn-Noranda (CLD R-N)
161, av Murdoch, Rouyn-Noranda QC J9X 1E3
Tél: 819-792-0142; Téléc: 819-762-7139
info@cldrn.ca
www.cldrn.ca
www.facebook.com/pages/CLD-Rouyn-Noranda/359012320874266
twitter.com/cldrouynnoranda
Aperçu: *Dimension:* petite; *Envergure:* locale; Organisme sans but lucratif; fondée en 1998
Mission: De soutenir et de promouvoir les entreprises locales afin de les aider à prospérer
Membre(s) du personnel: 17
Activités: Développement économique
Membre(s) du bureau directeur:
André Rouleau, Directeur général

Centre Montérégien de réadaptation (CMR)
5300, ch de Chambly, Saint-Hubert QC J3Y 3N7
Tél: 450-676-7447; Téléc: 450-676-0047
Ligne sans frais: 800-667-4369; TTY: 450-676-9841
Autres numéros: ATME sans frais: 1-866-676-1411
16cmr@ssss.gouv.qc.ca
www.cmrmonteregie.ca
Aperçu: *Dimension:* petite; *Envergure:* locale; fondée en 1991
Mission: Pour aider à la réhabilitation des personnes handicapées physiques et les troubles du langage
Membre: *Critères d'admissibilite:* Les personnes handicapées physiques et les troubles du langage
Membre(s) du bureau directeur:
Eve Morrisette, Présidente
Hélène Duval, Directrice générale, 450-676-7447 Ext. 2400

Centre multiethnique de Québec (CMQ)
200, rue Dorchester, Québec QC G1K 5Z1
Tél: 418-687-9771; Téléc: 418-687-9063
info@centremultiethnique.com
www.centremultiethnique.com
www.facebook.com/371879376223670
Également appelé: Fraternité multiculturelle
Aperçu: *Dimension:* moyenne; *Envergure:* locale; Organisme sans but lucratif; fondée en 1960
Mission: D'accueillir les immigrantes et immigrants de toutes catégories afin de faciliter leur établissement en Canada; De soutenir leur adaptation et leur intégration à la société québécoise et de favoriser leurs accès à de meilleures conditions socio-économiques
Membre de: Table de concertation pour les réfugiés et immigrants
Finances: *Budget de fonctionnement annuel:* $250,000-$500,000; *Fonds:* gouvernement provincial et fédéral
Membre(s) du personnel: 11; 50 bénévole(s)
Membre: 10 institutionnel; 300 individus; *Critères d'admissibilite:* Intérêt pour la cause des immigrants
Activités: *Stagiaires:* Oui
Membre(s) du bureau directeur:
Karine Verreault, Directrice

Le Centre parlementaire *See* Parliamentary Centre

Centre patronal de santé et sécurité du travail du Québec (CPSSTQ) / Employers Center for Occupational Health & Safety of Quebec
#1000, 500, rue Sherbrooke ouest, Montréal QC H3A 3C6
Tél: 514-842-8401; Téléc: 514-842-9375
www.centrepatronalsst.qc.ca
Aperçu: *Dimension:* grande; *Envergure:* provinciale; Organisme sans but lucratif; fondée en 1983
Mission: Fournir de l'information et de la formation en SST aux entreprises regroupées par les associations patronales membres du Centre patronal
Membre de: Société canadienne des directeurs d'associations
Finances: *Budget de fonctionnement annuel:* $3 Million-$5 Million
Membre(s) du personnel: 24; 7 bénévole(s)
Membre: 90+; *Montant de la cotisation:* 25$; *Critères d'admissibilité:* Associations d'employeurs
Activités: Cours; colloques; *Stagiaires:* Oui; *Service de conférenciers:* Oui; *Bibliothèque:* Centre de documentation; Not open to public
Membre(s) du bureau directeur:
Nadim Hanna, Président
Daniel Zizian, Président-directeur général
Publications:
• Convergence [a publication of the Centre patronal de santé et sécurité du travail du Québec]
Type: Journal
• SST Bonjour ! [a publication of the Centre patronal de santé et sécurité du travail du Québec]
Type: Newsletter

Centre pour la défense de l'intérêt public *See* The Public Interest Advocacy Centre

Centre pour les droits à l'égalité au logement *See* Centre for Equality Rights in Accommodation

Centre pour les victimes d'agression sexuelle de Fredericton *See* Fredericton Sexual Assault Crisis Centre

Centre Psycho-Pédagogique de Québec Inc.
École Saint-François, 1000, rue du Joli-Bois, Québec QC G1V 3Z6
Tél: 418-650-1171; Téléc: 418-650-1145
www.cppq.qc.ca
Aperçu: *Dimension:* petite; *Envergure:* provinciale
Membre: *Critères d'admissibilite:* L'école Saint-François aide les enfants, les parents et les écoles en fournissant une ressource appropriée à l'intérieur d'un enseignement personnalisé, dispensé de la troisième année du primaire à la troisième année du secondaire dans le but de favoriser l'intégration sociale de filles et garçons présentant des difficultés d'adaptation scolaire.
Activités: Classe nature; sortie thématiques et culturelles en groupe; ateliersss; service d'orientation; clinique juridique; *Stagiaires:* Oui

Membre(s) du bureau directeur:
Donald Gilbert, Président

Centre québécois de la déficience auditive *Voir* Réseau québécois pour l'inclusion social des personnnes sourdes et malentendantes

Centre québécois du droit de l'environnement (CQDE) / Québec Environmental Law Centre
454, av Laurier est, Montréal QC H2J 1E7
Tél: 514-272-2666; Téléc: 514-447-9455
info@cqde.org
www.cqde.org
www.facebook.com/DroitEnvironnementQC
Aperçu: *Dimension:* petite; *Envergure:* provinciale; Organisme sans but lucratif; fondée en 1989
Mission: Promouvoir le droit de l'environnement comme outil de protection de la santé publique et du patrimoine collectif
Finances: *Budget de fonctionnement annuel:* $100,000-$250,000
Membre: 120; *Montant de la cotisation:* 10$ étudiant; 20$ membre individuel; 50$ entreprise
Activités: *Service de conférenciers:* Oui; *Bibliothèque:* Bibliothèque publique rendez-vous
Membre(s) du bureau directeur:
Cédric Gagnon-Ducharme, Président
Marie-Josée Caya, Trésorière
Karine Péloffy, Secrétaire

Centre sida amitié (CSA)
527, rue St-Georges, Saint-Jérôme QC J7Z 5B6
Tél: 450-431-7432; Téléc: 450-431-6536
csa1@qc.aira.com
twitter.com/Sidaamitie
Aperçu: *Dimension:* petite; *Envergure:* locale; Organisme sans but lucratif; fondée en 1989 surveillé par Canadian AIDS Society
Activités: soutien; éducation/prévention; ligne info-sida; *Stagiaires:* Oui; *Service de conférenciers:* Oui

Centre Sportif de la Petite Bourgogne / Little Burgundy Sports Centre
1825, rue Notre-Dame ouest, Montréal QC H3J 1M5
Tél: 514-932-0800
centresportifdelapetitebourgogne.com
Aperçu: *Dimension:* petite; *Envergure:* locale; fondée en 1997
Membre(s) du bureau directeur:
Dickens Mathurin, Director General, 514-932-0800 Ext. 24
serviceclient@centresportif-cspb.com

Centre St-Pierre
1212, rue Panet, Montréal QC H2L 2Y7
Tél: 514-524-3561; Téléc: 514-524-5663
csp@centrestpierre.org
www.centrestpierre.org
Aperçu: *Dimension:* petite; *Envergure:* locale
Mission: Pour offrir une organisation communautaire avec les valeurs chrétiennes incorporés dans ses services
Activités: Animation; pstchothérapie; service d'accompagnement psycho-spirituel; dynamique du couple et mariage chrétien
Membre(s) du bureau directeur:
Lise Roy, Directrice générale

Centre Wellington Chamber of Commerce
400 Tower St. South, Fergus ON N1M 2P7
Tel: 519-843-5140; Fax: 519-787-0983
chamber@cwchamber.ca
www.cwchamber.ca
www.linkedin.com/company/centre-wellington-chamber-of-commerce
www.facebook.com/cwchamber
twitter.com/CW_Chamber
plus.google.com/107434428701192264584
Overview: A small local organization founded in 1999
Mission: To promote the social, civic & economic development of our community & serve as the voice of business
Member of: Canadian Chamber of Commerce; Ontario Chamber of Commerce
Staff Member(s): 2
Membership: *Fees:* Schedule available; *Committees:* Communications; Member Services; Nominations; Special Events
Activities: Golf Tournament; AGM; education sessions
Chief Officer(s):
Roberta Scarrow, General Manager
Awards:
• Citizen of the Year Award

Les Centres jeunesse de l'Outaouais (CJO)
105, boul Sacré-Coeur, Gatineau QC J8X 1C5
Tél: 819-771-6631
www.cjoutaouais.qc.ca
Merged from: Centre de services sociaux de l'Outaouais; Centre de réadaptation les jeunes de l'Outaouais
Aperçu: Dimension: petite; *Envergure:* locale; Organisme sans but lucratif; fondée en 1942
Mission: Nous assurons la protection des jeunes; nous amenons les jeunes à assumer leurs responsabilités et à se réadapter à la société en les aidant à retrouver un équilibre personnel et social; nous aidons enfants et adultes à se préparer à une adoption; nous aidons les enfants adoptés et parents naturels à reprendre contact; nous offrons notre expertise dans certaines causes de divorce; nous assurons aux jeunes un éventail de ressources d'hébergement
Membre de: Association des Centres jeunesse du Québec
Membre: *Critères d'admissibilite:* Membre du CA Collèges électoraux
Activités: Services psychosociaux; services de réadaptation; urgence sociale 24 heures par jour, 7 jours par semaine; *Stagiaires:* Oui; *Bibliothèque* Not open to public
Membre(s) du bureau directeur:
Luc Cadieux, Directeur général
Luc_Cadieux@ssss.gouv.qc.ca

Les Centres jeunesse de la Mauricie et du Centre de Québec
1455, boul du Carmel, Trois-Rivières QC G8Z 3R7
Ligne sans frais: 800-567-8520
www.ciusssmcq.ca
Nom précédent: Les Centres jeunesse Mauricie-Bois-Francs
Aperçu: Dimension: petite; *Envergure:* locale; fondée en 1996
Mission: Assurer la sécurité et le développement; assurer la responsabilisation des jeunes; aider les enfants, les jeunes, leurs parents et les jeunes mSres vivant des difficultés majeures au plan de leur fonctionnement; intervenir dans leur démarche de changement de leur situation personnelle, familiale et sociale

Les Centres jeunesse Mauricie-Bois-Francs *Voir* Les Centres jeunesse de la Mauricie et du Centre de Québec

Centreville Chamber of Commerce
836 Central St., Centreville NB E7K 2E7
Tel: 506-276-3674; *Fax:* 506-276-9891
Overview: A small local organization founded in 1985
Membership: 23
Chief Officer(s):
Robert Taylor, President

Centro Comunitàrio Divino Espìrito Santo / Centre Communautaire Esprit Saint
86872, rue de Forbin-Janson, Montréal QC H1K 2J9
Tél: 514-353-1550
Également appelé: Saint Esprit Community Centre
Aperçu: Dimension: petite; *Envergure:* locale

Cercle canadien de Toronto *Voir* Club canadien de Toronto

Cercle d'expression artistique Nyata Nyata
4374, boul St-Laurent, 2e étage, Montréal QC H2W 1Z5
Tél: 514-849-9781
Ligne sans frais: 877-692-8208
info@nyata-nyata.org
www.nyata-nyata.org
www.facebook.com/153132964772900
www.youtube.com/user/nyatanyata
Également appelé: Nyata Nyata
Aperçu: Dimension: petite; *Envergure:* locale; Organisme sans but lucratif
Mission: Pour créer musical et l'art chorégraphique dans le but de développer l'art de la danse et les compétences des artistes.
Membre(s) du personnel: 5; 3 bénévole(s)
Membre(s) du bureau directeur:
Zab Maboungou, Directrice artistique

Cercle de la finance internationale de Montréal / International Finance Club of Montréal
CP 63123, 38, Place du Commerce, Montréal QC H3E 1V6
Tél: 514-933-1451; *Téléc:* 514-933-1508
cfim@cercledelafinance.qc.ca
www.cercledelafinance.qc.ca
Nom précédent: Cercle des banquiers internationaux de Montréal
Aperçu: Dimension: petite; *Envergure:* internationale; fondée en 1984
Mission: Promouvoir au sein de la communauté financière les activités et les services de ses membres

1 bénévole(s)
Membre: 150; *Montant de la cotisation:* 500$ corporatifs; 125$ individuels; *Critères d'admissibilite:* Dirigeants d'institutions et d'organismes financiers à orientation internationale
Activités: *Stagiaires:* Oui; *Listes de destinataires:* Oui
Membre(s) du bureau directeur:
Luc St-Arnault, Président
Gérard Mournier, Trésorier
gerard.mounier@ccd.desjardins.com

Cercle des banquiers internationaux de Montréal *Voir* Cercle de la finance internationale de Montréal

Cercle des bénévoles du Musée des beaux-arts du Canada *See* Volunteer Circle of the National Gallery of Canada

Cercle des Fermières - Chibougamau
CP 417, Chibougamau QC G8P 2X7
Tél: 418-672-4877
www.cfq.qc.ca
Aperçu: Dimension: petite; *Envergure:* locale surveillé par Cercles de Fermières du Québec
Membre(s) du bureau directeur:
Colombe Bergeron, Responsable
colombeberge@hotmail.com

Cercle Esperanto d'Ottawa *See* Esperanto Rondo de Otavo

Le Cercle Molière
340, boul Provencher, Winnipeg MB R2H 0G7
Tél: 204-233-8053; *Téléc:* 204-233-2373
info@cerclemoliere.com
www.cerclemoliere.com
www.facebook.com/cerclemoliere
twitter.com/CercleMoliere
Aperçu: Dimension: moyenne; *Envergure:* provinciale; Organisme sans but lucratif; fondée en 1925
Mission: Présenter des spectacles de théâtre en français au Manitoba
Membre de: Association des compagnies de théâtre de l'Ouest; Association des théâtres francophones du Canada; Conférence canadienne des arts
Finances: *Fonds:* Conseil des arts du Manitoba; Conseil des arts du Canada; Patrimoine Canadien
Membre(s) du personnel: 7
Activités: Spectacles (grand public et jeunes publics), lectures, école de théâtre, festival de théâtre adolescent, grande soirée de levée de fonds; *Stagiaires:* Oui; *Service de conférenciers:* Oui
Membre(s) du bureau directeur:
Geneviève Pelletier, Directrice artistique et générale
genevieve@cerclemoliere.com

Cercle national des joualnistes du Canada *See* National Press Club of Canada Foundation

Le Cercle Saint-François *See* The Kindness Club

Cercles de fermières du Québec (CFQ)
1043, rue Tiffin, Longueuil QC J4P 3G7
Tél: 450-442-3983; *Téléc:* 450-442-4363
cerfer@cfq.qc.ca
www.cfq.qc.ca
www.facebook.com/283417910957
Aperçu: Dimension: moyenne; *Envergure:* provinciale; Organisme sans but lucratif; fondée en 1915
Mission: Association apolitique de femmes vouées à l'amélioration des conditions de vie de la femme et de la famille et à la transmission du patrimoine artisanal et culturel
Finances: *Budget de fonctionnement annuel:* $100,000-$250,000
Membre(s) du personnel: 3
Membre: 34 000; *Montant de la cotisation:* 25$; *Critères d'admissibilite:* Femme 14+; *Comités:* Art Textiles; Communications; Dossiers; Spécial Recrutement
Membre(s) du bureau directeur:
Suzanne Duchesneau, Présidente
Publications:
• L'Actuelle
Profile: Magazine

Cercles des jeunes naturalistes (CJN)
Jardin botanique de Montréal, #262, 4101, rue Sherbrooke est, Montréal QC H1X 2B2
Tél: 514-252-3023; *Téléc:* 514-254-8744
jeunesnaturalistes@gmail.com
www.jeunesnaturalistes.org
Aperçu: Dimension: grande; *Envergure:* nationale; Organisme sans but lucratif; fondée en 1931

Mission: Nous initions les jeunes à l'étude des sciences de la nature et à la protection de l'environnement
Membre de: Regroupement Loisir Québec
Finances: *Budget de fonctionnement annuel:* $50,000-$100,000; *Fonds:* Gouvernement provincial pour la gestion du Siège social; OSBL
Membre(s) du personnel: 3; 15 bénévole(s)
Membre: 2 000; *Montant de la cotisation:* 45$ individuel; 55-84 famille; *Comités:* Voir notre site internet
Activités: Camps nature; animations dans les cercles avec les Jeunes Naturalistes sur les sciences de la nature; activités parascolaires et dans les écoles; formation pour animateurs; trousses d'animations; festival provincial annuel; *Bibliothèque* Not open to public
Membre(s) du bureau directeur:
André St-Arnaud, Directeur général
Publications:
• Les Naturalistes [publication de Cercles des jeunes naturalistes]
Type: Revue

Cerebral Palsy Association in Alberta (CPAA)
12001 - 44 St. SE, Calgary AB T2Z 4G9
Tel: 403-543-1161; *Fax:* 403-543-1168
Toll-Free: 800-363-2807
admin@cpalberta.com
www.cpalberta.com
www.linkedin.com/in/cerebral-palsy-association-in-alberta-b9aa6562
www.facebook.com/CerebralPalsyAlberta
twitter.com/CPAlberta
www.instagram.com/cpalberta
Also Known As: CP Alberta
Overview: A medium-sized provincial organization founded in 1976
Mission: To improve the quality of life of persons with cerebral palsy through a broad range of programs, education, support of research, & the delivery of needed services to people with cerebral palsy & their families; To encourage persons with cerebral palsy to develop & pursue meaningful goals & achievements in life; To raise awareness in society of the abilities of individuals with cerebral palsy
Finances: *Annual Operating Budget:* $250,000-$500,000; *Funding Sources:* Fundraising; United Way; Donations; Grants; Sales of used clothing; Bottle recycling
Staff Member(s): 40; 300 volunteer(s)
Membership: 2,800; *Fees:* Free
Activities: Increasing public awareness; Engaging in advocacy activities; Researching; Recreation & sports; Youth transitions program; Support services; *Internships:* Yes; *Speaker Service:* Yes
Chief Officer(s):
Janice Bushfield, Executive Director
Mezaun Lakha-Evin, Associate Executive Director
mezaun@cpalberta.com
Joanne Dorn, Director, Development
jdorn@cpalberta.com
Mariana Nimara, Director, Administration
mariana@cpalberta.com
Shyam Poudyal, Manager, Finance
shyam@cpalberta.com

Cerebral Palsy Association of British Columbia (CPABC)
#330, 409 Granville St., Vancouver BC V6C 1T2
Tel: 604-408-9484; *Fax:* 604-408-9489
Toll-Free: 800-663-0004
info@bccerebralpalsy.com
www.bccerebralpalsy.com
www.facebook.com/cerebral.palsy.39
Also Known As: CP Association of BC
Overview: A medium-sized provincial organization founded in 1954
Mission: To raise awareness of cerebral palsy in the community; To assist those living with cerebral palsy to reach to maximum; To work to see those living with cerebral palsy realize their place as equals within a diverse society; To provide support & services that facilitate these needs; To make a Life Without Limits for people with disabilities
Member of: Better Business Bureau
Finances: *Annual Operating Budget:* $100,000-$250,000
Staff Member(s): 8; 30 volunteer(s)
Membership: 1,500; *Fees:* Free; *Committees:* Charitable Funders Network
Activities: Dance, yoga, art, & martial arts program; youth & senior support groups; camperships; educational bursaries;

Jason & Rand Fund (equipment subsidy); Movement Without Limits (Alinker); disability awareness presentations; individual & family support; navigator for youth transitioning to youth; *Awareness Events:* Cerebral Palsy Week, June *Library:* Resource Library; Open to public
Chief Officer(s):
Feri Dehdar, Executive Director
feri@bccerebralpalsy.com
Awards:
• Tanabe Bursary

Cerebral Palsy Association of Manitoba Inc. (CPAM)
#105, 500 Portage Ave., Winnipeg MB R3C 3X1
Tel: 204-982-4842; *Fax:* 204-982-4844
Toll-Free: 800-416-6166
office@cerebralpalsy.mb.ca
www.cerebralpalsy.mb.ca
www.facebook.com/CerebralPalsyAssociationOfMb
twitter.com/CerebralPalsyMB
Overview: A medium-sized provincial charitable organization founded in 1974
Mission: To enrich the lives of individuals affected by cerebral palsy through services, advocacy, education & peer support
Membership: *Fees:* $10 family & individual; $25 institution
Activities: *Speaker Service:* Yes; *Library:* Cerebral Palsy Library; Open to public
Chief Officer(s):
David Kron, Director, Membership & Programs
davidk@cerebralpalsy.mb.ca

Cerebral Palsy Association of Newfoundland & Labrador (CPNL)
PO Box 23059, Stn. Churchill Square, St. John's NL A1B 4J9
Tel: 709-753-9922
www.cerebralpalsynl.com
www.facebook.com/cerebralpalsynl
Previous Name: Newfoundland Cerebral Palsy Association Inc.
Overview: A small provincial charitable organization founded in 1961
Mission: To improve the quality of life of persons with cerebral palsy through programs, education, support of research & the delivery of needed services to people with cerebral palsy & their families
Member of: Atlantic Cerebral Palsy Association
Finances: *Funding Sources:* Donations; grants
Activities: Social events; meetings; Disability Awareness Project; *Library:* by appointment
Chief Officer(s):
Cindy Bishop, Secretary

Cerebral Palsy Foundation (St. John) Inc.
PO Box 2152, Saint John NB E2L 3V1
Tel: 506-648-0322
mail@cpfsj.ca
www.cpfsj.ca
Overview: A small local organization
Awards:
• Gertrude Aarela Memorial Scholarship
Eligibility: New Brunswick high school student with cerebral palsy planning on attending a post-secondary institution *Deadline:* May 15; *Amount:* $1000

Cerebral Palsy Sports Association of British Columbia See SportAbility BC

Certification Council of Early Childhood Educators of Nova Scotia (CCECENS)
#102, 3845 Joseph Howe Dr., Halifax NS B3L 4H9
Tel: 902-423-8199
ccecens@nschildcareassociation.org
www.ccecens.ca
Overview: A small provincial organization
Mission: To develop a high quality, professional, certified body of Early Childhood Educators
Affiliation(s): Canadian Child Care Federation
Finances: *Annual Operating Budget:* Less than $50,000
Membership: 52; *Fees:* $35; *Member Profile:* Early childhood educators & administrators
Chief Officer(s):
Elizabeth Hessian, Chair
Miriam Forbes, Registrar

Certified Dental Assistants of BC (CDABC)
#102, 211 Columbia St., Vancouver BC V6A 2R5
Tel: 604-714-1766; *Fax:* 604-714-1767
Toll-Free: 800-579-4440
info@cdabc.org
www.cdabc.org
www.linkedin.com/company/certified-dental-assistants-of-bc-cdabc-
www.facebook.com/76934117515
twitter.com/CDABC
Overview: A small provincial organization overseen by Canadian Dental Assistants Association
Mission: To promote the dental assisting profession in British Columbia; To protect the interests of members
Finances: *Funding Sources:* Grant
Staff Member(s): 5; 50 volunteer(s)
Membership: 5,700; *Fees:* $25 student; $125 active/associate
Activities: *Awareness Events:* Dental Assistants Recognition Week, March
Chief Officer(s):
Chelsie Trask-Soltesz, President

Certified General Accountants Association of the Northwest Territories & Nunavut
PO Box 128, 5016 - 50th Ave., Yellowknife NT X1A 2N1
Tel: 867-873-5620; *Fax:* 867-873-4469
Also Known As: CGA NWT/Nunavut
Overview: A medium-sized provincial charitable organization founded in 1977 overseen by Chartered Professional Accountants Canada
Mission: To provide training & professional support services to accountants in the Northwest Territories & Nunavut; To grant the exclusive rights to the CGA designation; To advance the interests of members; To protect the public; To advocate for the public interest
Membership: *Member Profile:* Certified General Accountants in the Northwest Territories & Nunavut, who have completed the CGA Program of Professional Studies, the CGA national exams, an approved degree, & the practical experience requirement; Certified General Accountants students
Activities: Enforcing professional standards & discipline members; Promoting the profession of accountancy in the north; Liaising with governments, regulatory authorities, & the community; Offering professional development opportunities (note that CGA NWT/Nunavut will integrate under the CPA banner once legislation is approved)
Chief Officer(s):
Biswanath Chakrabarty, CGA, President

Certified Organic Associations of British Columbia (COABC)
#202, 3002 - 32nd Ave., Vernon BC V1T 2L7
Tel: 250-260-4429; *Fax:* 250-260-4436
office@certifiedorganic.bc.ca
www.certifiedorganic.bc.ca
Overview: A medium-sized provincial organization founded in 1994
Mission: To maintain a credible set of organic production & processing standards
Staff Member(s): 3
Activities: Cyber-Help; Canadian Organic Initiative; Organic Environmental Farm Program; Organic Harvest Awards; Organic Sector Development Program; Standards
Chief Officer(s):
Jen Gamble, Administrator
admin@certifiedorganic.bc.ca
Meetings/Conferences:
• Certified Organic Associations of BC Conference 2018, 2018, BC
Scope: Provincial
Publications:
• BC Organic Grower
Frequency: Quarterly

Certified Professional Trainers Network (CPTN)
122 D'Arcy St., Toronto ON M5T 1K3
Tel: 416-979-1654
info@cptn.com
www.cptn.com
www.facebook.com/600340323384521
Previous Name: Canadian Personal Trainers Network
Overview: A small national organization founded in 1991
Mission: The organization integrates current research and practical applications for education, communication, professional development and marketing opportunities for Personal Trainers to maintain a leading edge on professional training developments.
Membership: *Fees:* $64.41
Activities: Offers certification for professional trainers
Chief Officer(s):
Susan Lee, President

Certified Technicians & Technologists Association of Manitoba (CTTAM)
#602, 1661 Portage Ave., Winnipeg MB R3J 3T7
Tel: 204-784-1088; *Fax:* 204-784-1084
Other Communication: Registration: 204-784-1082
admin@cttam.com
www.cttam.com
Previous Name: Manitoba Society of Certified Engineering Technicians & Technologists Inc.
Overview: A medium-sized provincial organization founded in 1965 overseen by Canadian Council of Technicians & Technologists
Mission: To advance the professional recognition & development of certified applied science technicians & technologists in a manner that serves the public interest
Member of: Science & Technology Awareness Network
Finances: *Funding Sources:* Membership fees
Staff Member(s): 4
Membership: 3,000+; *Fees:* $155; *Member Profile:* Open to those employed in all aspects of engineering technology (civil, mechanical, electrical, electronic, computer, instrumentation, surveying, design & drafting, structural, construction) provided they meet the academic requirements
Activities: *Internships:* Yes
Chief Officer(s):
Neil Klassen, CET, President
president@cttam.com
Terry Gifford, CAE, Executive Director, 204-784-1080
Robert D. Okabe, CET, IntET, Registrar, 204-784-1081
Awards:
• Scholarships
; *Amount:* Three $600 scholarships

Ceta-Research Inc.
PO Box 10, Trinity NL A0C 2S0
Tel: 709-464-3269; *Fax:* 709-464-3700
Overview: A medium-sized local organization founded in 1990
Mission: To undertake the rescue of entrapped whales & dolphins; to conduct research on whales; To organize a discovery in animal communication using Rhythm Bases Communication
Finances: *Annual Operating Budget:* $100,000-$250,000
Staff Member(s): 30
Membership: 5,000 individual
Chief Officer(s):
Peter Beamish, Director

CFA Society Calgary (CFASC)
PO Box 118, #100, 111 - 5th Ave. SW, Calgary AB T2P 3Y6
Tel: 403-249-2009; *Fax:* 403-206-0650
membership@cfacalgary.com
www.cfacalgary.com
www.linkedin.com/in/calgarycfasociety
www.facebook.com/CalgaryCFA
twitter.com/CFACalgary
Also Known As: CFA Calgary
Overview: A small local organization founded in 1976
Mission: To establish & maintain a standard level of ethics to benefit the organization & the community
Member of: CFA Institute
Finances: *Funding Sources:* Events registration; Sponsorship; Member dues
Staff Member(s): 2
Membership: 135,000; *Fees:* US$275 Regular/Affiliate; US$100 Retired; *Member Profile:* Investment professionals; *Committees:* Professional Development; Employer Outreach
Activities: Professional development; Candidate support; Networking events; Career development
Chief Officer(s):
Debbie Kunert, Executive Director
Jade Piraux, Coordinator, Communications/Events, 403-454-0773
events@cfacalgary.com
Awards:
• Access Scholarship
Eligibility: Interest in CFA Program with plans for enrollment
Deadline: September 15
Meetings/Conferences:
• CFA Society Calgary 41st Annual Forecast Dinner, January, 2018, Calgary, AB
Scope: Local

CFA Society Toronto
#701, 120 Adelaide St. West, Toronto ON M5H 1T1
Tel: 416-366-5755; *Fax:* 416-366-6716
www.cfatoronto.ca

www.linkedin.com/company/cfa-society-toronto?trk=fc_badge
twitter.com/cfatoronto
Also Known As: Toronto Chartered Financial Analyst Society
Previous Name: Toronto CFA Society; Toronto Society of Financial Analysts
Overview: A small local organization
Mission: To lead the investment profession in our local community by setting the highest standards of education, integrity & professional excellence
Affiliation(s): CFA Institute
Staff Member(s): 3
Membership: 7,000; *Committees:* Programming; Continuing Education; Corporate Finance; Equity; Fixed Income; Portfolio Management; Private Client; Risk Management & Alternative Investments; Career Management; External Relations & Advocacy; Kitchener-Waterloo; Awards & University Relations; Finance; Member Communications; Membership; Mentorship
Chief Officer(s):
Sue Lemon, Chief Executive Officer & Director

CFA Society Vancouver
PO Box 54080, Vancouver BC V7M 3L5
Tel: 604-435-9889; *Fax:* 888-635-0265
info@cfavancouver.com
www.cfasociety.org/vancouver
twitter.com/cfavancouver
Previous Name: Vancouver Society of Financial Analysts
Overview: A small local organization
Member of: Association for Investment Management & Research
Membership: 1054; *Fees:* US$225
Chief Officer(s):
Daren Atkinson, President
Virginia Coles, Executive Administrator

CFA Society Winnipeg
PO Box 2684, Winnipeg MB R3C 4B3
Tel: 204-471-3640
info@cfawinnipeg.ca
www.cfasociety.org/winnipeg/
Previous Name: Winnipeg Society of Financial Analysts
Overview: A small local organization
Member of: Association for Investment Management & Research
Chief Officer(s):
Graeme Hay, President
Meetings/Conferences:
• CFA Society Winnipeg 53rd Annual Forecast Dinner, January, 2018, RBC Convention Centre, Winnipeg, MB
Scope: Local

C.G. Jung Foundation of Ontario
14 Elm St., Toronto ON M5G 157
Tel: 416-961-9767; *Fax:* 416-961-6659
info@cgjungontario.com
www.cgjungontario.com
Also Known As: Ontario Association of Jungian Analysts
Overview: A small local charitable organization founded in 1971
Mission: To disseminate information about the psychological teachings of Carl Gustav Jung through lectures, seminars, workshops, a library & a bookstore; a list of Jungian analysts is available for referral
Member of: International Association of Jungian Analysts
Activities: Word & Image Bookshop; training institute since 2000; *Speaker Service:* Yes; *Library:* Fraser Boa Library; Not open to public
Chief Officer(s):
Catherine Johnson, Administrator
Publications:
• Chiron [a publication of the C.G. Jung Foundation of Ontario]
Type: Newsletter; *Editor:* Robert Black; *ISSN:* 1918-6142

Chabad Lubavitch Youth Organization
3429, rue Peel, Montréal QC H3A 1W7
Tel: 514-842-6616; *Fax:* 514-731-9303
www.chabad.org/centers
Overview: A medium-sized local organization
Affiliation(s): Chabad Project PRIDE; Jewish Business Network
Staff Member(s): 15; 300 volunteer(s)
Membership: 500 student; 3,000 individual
Chief Officer(s):
Berel Mochkin, Director

Chaeo Chow Association of Eastern Canada
568 Dundas St. West, Toronto ON M5T 1H5
Tel: 416-340-0839; *Fax:* 416-340-6386
Also Known As: CCA Youth Group
Previous Name: Chao Chow Association Of Ontario
Overview: A small local organization
Mission: CCA promotes Chinese Chaeo Chow culture & provides programs for seniors & activities for young people.

Chai-Tikvah The Life & Hope Foundation
#313, 4600 Bathurst St., Toronto ON M2R 3V2
Tel: 416-634-3050
info@lifeandhope.ca
www.lifeandhope.ca
Overview: A small local charitable organization
Mission: To support individuals with mental illness by providing secure housing options & services, & promoting their inclusion in society
Finances: *Funding Sources:* Donations
Activities: Providing residential services (group home facility & semi-independent living facility); Offering outreach & support group programs, educational resources, & a help line; Developing public awareness events & activities; Advocating on behalf of people with mental illness & their families; *Awareness Events:* Dinner Gala & Auction
Chief Officer(s):
David Drutz, Chair
Rochelle Goldman-Brown, Executive Director

Chamber of Commerce Niagara Falls, Canada
4056 Dorchester Rd., Niagara Falls ON L2E 6M9
Tel: 905-374-3666; *Fax:* 905-374-2972
info@niagarafallschamber.com
www.niagarafallschamber.com
www.linkedin.com/company/chamber-of-commerce-niagara-falls-canada
www.facebook.com/368306856223
twitter.com/NFChamber
www.youtube.com/user/NFChamber
Previous Name: Niagara Falls Chamber of Commerce
Overview: A small local organization founded in 1889
Mission: To maintain & improve trade & commerce; To promote the economic, civic & social welfare of the Municipality
Member of: Canadian Chamber of Commerce
Finances: *Funding Sources:* Membership fees
Staff Member(s): 5
Membership: *Fees:* Schedule available
Chief Officer(s):
Anna Pierce, Chair
Dolores Fabiano, Executive Director

Chamber of Commerce of Brantford & Brant (BRCC)
77 Charlotte St., Brantford ON N3T 2W8
Tel: 519-753-2617; *Fax:* 519-753-0921
www.brantfordbrantchamber.com
www.facebook.com/197455726976322
twitter.com/BtfdBrantChambr
Previous Name: Brantford Regional Chamber of Commerce
Overview: A small local organization founded in 1866
Mission: To promote the free enterprise system through improved trade & commerce; to advance the economic, civic & social welfare of the City of Brantford & its surrounding region; to assist & or cooperate with those organizations embodying similar objectives.
Finances: *Funding Sources:* Membership dues; programs
Staff Member(s): 5
Membership: *Fees:* Schedule available based on number of employees; *Committees:* Advocacy; Building & Grounds; Business Excellence; Education; Golf Tournament; Marketing; Membership/Ambassador; Technology; Women in Business
Activities: *Speaker Service:* Yes; *Library:* Open to public
Chief Officer(s):
Allan Lovett, President
Charlene Nicholson, CEO
charlene@brcc.ca
Awards:
• Business Excellence Awards

Chamber of Commerce of Metropolitan Montréal *Voir* Chambre de commerce du Montréal métropolitain

Chamber of Commerce of the City of Grand Forks, Grand Forks Board of Trade *See* Boundary Country Regional Chamber of Commerce

Chamber of Commerce Serving Coquitlam, Port Coquitlam, Port Moody *See* Tri-Cities Chamber of Commerce Serving Coquitlam, Port Coquitlam & Port Moody

Chamber of Marine Commerce (CMC) / Chambre du commerce maritime (CCM)
#700, 350 Sparks St., Ottawa ON K1R 7S8
Tel: 613-233-8779; *Fax:* 613-233-3743
email@cmc-ccm.com
www.marinedelivers.com
twitter.com/MarineDelivers
www.flickr.com/photos/marinecommerce/sets/
Previous Name: Great Lakes Waterways Development Association
Merged from: Canadian Shipowners Association (CSA)
Overview: A large national organization founded in 1959
Mission: To represent the bi-national Great Lakes-St. Lawrence commercial marine industry; To bring together all sectors of the economy that rely on a cost efficient & safe marine transportation system
Finances: *Funding Sources:* Membership dues
Membership: 130+ companies; *Member Profile:* Domestic & international ship owners & operators; Canadian & US ports; International shippers; The St. Lawrence Seaway; Terminals, elevators & logistics companies; Marine-related service providers
Chief Officer(s):
Bruce Burrows, President
bburrows@cmc-ccm.com
Robert Turner, Vice President, Operations
rturner@cmc-ccm.com
Julia Fields, Director, Communications
jfields@cmc-ccm.com
Publications:
• Marine Delivers Magazine [a publication of the Chamber of Marine Commerce]
Type: Magazine; *Frequency:* a.; *Accepts Advertising*; *Number of Pages:* 46; *Editor:* Julia Fields & Leo Ryan
Profile: Provides news & updates about the Chamber of Marine Commerce & the marine trade industry

Chamber of Mines of Eastern British Columbia
215 Hall St., Nelson BC V1L 5X4
Tel: 250-352-5242
chamberofmines@netidea.com
cmebc.com
www.facebook.com/ChamberOfMinesEasternBC
Overview: A medium-sized provincial organization founded in 1921
Mission: To act as advocate for the mining industry in British Columbia; to provide a collective voice on behalf of prospectors & miners; to provide information on exploration & mining; to educate the public through accessibility to mineral museum & library.
Member of: BC Mining Association; BC/Yukon Chamber of Mines
Membership: *Fees:* $40 individual; $100 2-10 employees; $200 11-30 employees; $300 31-50 employees; $500 51+ employees
Activities: *Library:*

Chambre d'immeuble d'Ottawa *See* Ottawa Real Estate Board

Chambre d'immeubles de Québec *Voir* Chambre immobilière de Québec

Chambre de commerce acadienne et francophone de l'Ile-du-Prince-Édouard
CP 7, Wellington PE C0B 2E0
Tél: 902-854-3439; *Téléc:* 902-854-3099
www.rdeeipe.net/ccaflipe
Aperçu: *Dimension:* petite; *Envergure:* locale
Membre: 40; *Montant de la cotisation:* 25$
Membre(s) du bureau directeur:
Raymond Arsenault, Coordonnateur

Chambre de commerce au Coeur de la Montérégie (CCCM)
319, ch de Chambly, Marieville QC J3M 1N9
Tél: 450-460-4019; *Téléc:* 450-460-2362
info@coeurmonteregie.com
www.coeurmonteregie.com
Nom précédent: Chambre de Commerce de Marieville
Aperçu: *Dimension:* petite; *Envergure:* locale; fondée en 1930
Mission: Regroupement volontaire de personnes du milieu dans un but de développement économique, civique et social des membres
Membre de: Chambre de Commerce de Québec; Chambre de Commerce du Canada
Finances: *Budget de fonctionnement annuel:* Moins de $50,000; *Fonds:* Dons; Profit des activités
Membre(s) du personnel: 2

Membre: 100+; *Montant de la cotisation:* Barème
Activités: Tournois de golf; déjeuners; causeries; rencontres de réseautage
Membre(s) du bureau directeur:
Véronique Côté, Directrice générale
vcote@coeurmonteregie.com

Chambre de commerce Baie-des-Chaleurs
114-B, av Grand-Pré, Bonaventure QC G0C 1E0
Tél: 418-534-0050; *Téléc:* 418-534-4747
www.ccbdc.ca
www.facebook.com/ccbaiedeschaleurs
twitter.com/CCBaieChaleurs
Nom précédent: Chambre de commerce de Bonaventure/St-Siméon/St-Élzear
Aperçu: Dimension: petite; *Envergure:* locale
Mission: Mobiliser la communauté d'affaires afin de créer une vitalité économique
Membre: *Montant de la cotisation:* Barème
Membre(s) du bureau directeur:
Maurice Quesnel, Directeur général
maurice@ccbdc.ca

Chambre de commerce Bellechasse-Etchemins
159-B, boul Bégin, Sainte-Clare QC G0R 2V0
Tél: 418-563-1131
ccb-e.ca
www.facebook.com/381810975165087
Aperçu: Dimension: petite; *Envergure:* locale
Membre: 350; *Comités:* TAM; Agro-forestiers; Industriel; Détails-services; Professional; OBNL
Membre(s) du bureau directeur:
Yvon Laflamme, Président
laflamme.yvon@rcgt.com

Chambre de Commerce Bois-des-Filion - Lorraine
CP 72012, Bois-des-Filion QC J6Z 4N9
Tél: 450-818-3481
info@ccbdfl.com
www.ccbdfl.com
www.facebook.com/155697847806886
Aperçu: Dimension: petite; *Envergure:* locale
Membre: 84; *Montant de la cotisation:* 160$ entreprise; 90$ individuel; *Comités:* Recrutement; Finances; Politique-Action; Clinique de Sang; Accueil et déjeuners; Conférences & Thématiques; Programme d'achat Local; Personnalité de l'année; Informatique & Média; Omnium de Golf
Membre(s) du bureau directeur:
Michel Bourgeois, Co-Président
Michel Limoges, Co-Président

Chambre de commerce Canada-Pologne
5570, rue Waverly, Montréal QC H2T 2Y1
Aperçu: Dimension: moyenne; *Envergure:* internationale

Chambre de commerce Canado-Suisse (Québec) Inc. (SCCCQ) / Swiss Canadian Chamber of Commerce (Québec) Inc.
#152, 3450, rue Drummond, Montréal QC H3G 1Y4
Tél: 514-937-5822
www.cccsqc.ca
Aperçu: Dimension: moyenne; *Envergure:* internationale; fondée en 1970
Mission: D'assumer un rôle de premier plan dans la promotion des relations commerciales, industrielles et financières entre la Suisse et le Canada, tout en se concentrant sur l'est du Canada
Membre(s) du bureau directeur:
Christian G. Dubois, Président

Chambre de commerce Canado-Tunisienne (CCCT) / Tunisian Canadian Chamber of Commerce
#810, 276, rue Saint-Jacques, Montréal QC H2Y 1N3
Tél: 514-847-1281
info@cccantun.com
www.cccantun.ca
www.facebook.com/cccantun
twitter.com/cccantun
Aperçu: Dimension: petite; *Envergure:* internationale; fondée en 1996
Mission: Le fer de lance du partenariat canado-tunisien; fournir des informations privilégiées sur les spécificités du marché tunisien; soutenir dans votre recherche de partenaires d'affaires tunisiens; appuyer dans la démarche de mise en marché de vos produits et services en Tunisie
Membre de: Chambre de commerce du Québec
Membre: *Critères d'admissibilité:* Tous les secteurs orientés à l'export/Tunisie

Activités: Événements, conférences, réception délégation tunisienne; mission Maghreb (Tunisie, Algerie, Maroc, Lybie)
Membre(s) du bureau directeur:
Abdeljelil Ouanès, Président

Chambre de commerce d'Amos-région *Voir* Chambre de Commerce et d'Industrie du Centre-Abitibi

Chambre de commerce d'industrie Les Moulins
2500, boul des Enterprises, Terrebonne QC J6X 4J8
Tél: 450-966-1536
info@ccimoulins.com
www.ccimoulins.com
www.linkedin.com/company/chambre-de-commerce-et-d%27industrie-les-moulins
twitter.com/CcMoulins
Aperçu: Dimension: petite; *Envergure:* locale; fondée en 1935
Mission: Le développement économique, touristique, civique et social du territoire de Terrebonne
Affiliation(s): Chambre de commerce du Canada; Chambre de commerce du Québec; Chambre de commerce régionale de Lanaudière; Réseau canadien de centres de services aux entreprises; Centre local de développement économique des Moulins (CLDEM); Centre local d'emploi de Terrebonne; Société de développement touristique des Moulins; Conseil de développement bioalimentaire de Lanaudière.
Membre(s) du personnel: 4
Membre: 800; *Montant de la cotisation:* 100$ OBNL; 150$ régulier
Membre(s) du bureau directeur:
Lucie Lecours, Directrice générale
lucie@ccimoulins.com

Chambre de commerce d'Orléans *See* Orléans Chamber of Commerce

Chambre de Commerce de Baie-Comeau *Voir* Chambre de commerce de Manicouagan

Chambre de commerce de Beauceville
CP 5142, Beauceville QC G5X 2P5
Tél: 418-774-1020
info@chambredecommercedebeauceville.com
www.chambredecommercedebeauceville.com
Aperçu: Dimension: petite; *Envergure:* locale; Organisme sans but lucratif; fondée en 1925
Mission: Participer au développement économique de la ville de Beauceville
Affiliation(s): Chambre de commerce du Québec; Chambre du commerce du Canada
Membre: *Montant de la cotisation:* Barème
Activités: *Service de conférenciers:* Oui
Membre(s) du bureau directeur:
François Veilleux, Président

Chambre de commerce de Bonaventure/St-Siméon/St-Élzear *Voir* Chambre de commerce Baie-des-Chaleurs

Chambre de commerce de Bouctouche *See* Bouctouche Chamber of Commerce

Chambre de commerce de Brandon
151, rue Saint-Gabriel, Saint-Gabriel QC J0K 2N0
Tél: 450-835-2105; *Téléc:* 450-835-2991
info@cc-brandon.com
cc-brandon.com
Aperçu: Dimension: petite; *Envergure:* locale; fondée en 1926
Mission: Développement commercial, industriel et touristique de la région
Affiliation(s): Chambre de commerce du Québec
Finances: *Budget de fonctionnement annuel:* Moins de $50,000
14 bénévole(s)
Membre: 120; *Montant de la cotisation:* 63-127
Membre(s) du bureau directeur:
Marc-André Forest, Président

Chambre de Commerce de Cap-des-Rosiers
1127, boul de Cap-des-Rosiers, Cap-des-Rosiers QC G4X 6G3
Aperçu: Dimension: petite; *Envergure:* locale

Chambre de commerce de Carleton
629, boul Perron, Carleton QC G0C 1J0
Tél: 418-364-1004
Aperçu: Dimension: petite; *Envergure:* locale

Chambre de commerce de Charlevoix
#209, 11, rue Saint-Jean-Baptiste, Baie-Saint-Paul QC G3Z 1M1

Tél: 418-760-8648
info@creezdesliens.com
www.creezdesliens.com
Nom précédent: Chambre de Commerce de Charlevoix-Ouest
Aperçu: Dimension: petite; *Envergure:* locale; Organisme sans but lucratif; fondée en 1940
Mission: De promouvoir les intérêts de ses membres afin de les aider à prospérer
Membre de: Chambre de Commerce de Québec
Membre(s) du personnel: 2
Membre: *Montant de la cotisation:* Barème
Activités: *Service de conférenciers:* Oui
Membre(s) du bureau directeur:
Johanne Côté, Directrice générale
johanne.cote@creezdesliens.com

Chambre de Commerce de Charlevoix-Ouest *Voir* Chambre de commerce de Charlevoix

Chambre de commerce de Chibougamau
#4, 600 - 3e rue, Chibougamau QC G8P 1P1
Tél: 418-748-4827; *Téléc:* 418-748-6179
info@ccchibougamau.com
www.chibougamauchapais.com
www.facebook.com/chibougamauchapais
Aperçu: Dimension: petite; *Envergure:* locale; Organisme sans but lucratif; fondée en 1954
Affiliation(s): Chambre de Commerce du Québec et du Canada
Finances: *Budget de fonctionnement annuel:* Moins de $50,000
Membre(s) du personnel: 1; 8 bénévole(s)
Membre: 400; *Montant de la cotisation:* 50$, 100$, 150$, 200$, 250$; *Critères d'admissibilité:* Commerçants et particuliers; *Comités:* Membres, interne, économique et politique
Activités: Gala des lauréats; dégustations vins et fromages; grandes virées; *Stagiaires:* Oui; *Service de conférenciers:* Oui; *Bibliothèque:* Bibliothèque de Chibougamau; Bibliothèque publique
Membre(s) du bureau directeur:
Mélanie Hébert, Coordonnatrice

Chambre de commerce de Chicoutimi *Voir* Chambre de commerce du Saguenay-Le Fjord

Chambre de commerce de Clare / Clare Chamber of Commerce
CP 35, Pointe-de-l'Église NS B0W 1M0
Tél: 902-769-5312; *Téléc:* 902-769-5500
contact@commercedeclare.ca
www.commercedeclare.ca
Aperçu: Dimension: petite; *Envergure:* locale; fondée en 1949
Mission: La Chambre de commerce de Clare représente les intérêts de la région au travers des défis économiques et sociaux; première Chambre française de la Nouvelle-Écosse
Membre: 100; *Montant de la cotisation:* 50$
Activités: *Listes de destinataires:* Oui
Membre(s) du bureau directeur:
Marcel Saulnier, Président

Chambre de commerce de Cocagne, Notre-Dame et Grande-Digue *Voir* Chambre de commerce Kent-Sud

Chambre de commerce de Collette
60, rue des Arbres, Collette NB E4Y 1G4
Tél: 506-775-2898; *Téléc:* 506-622-0477
Aperçu: Dimension: petite; *Envergure:* locale
Membre(s) du bureau directeur:
Maurice Desroches, Président

Chambre de commerce de Cowansville et région
#100-B, 104, rue du Sud, Cowansville QC J2K 2X2
Tél: 450-266-1665; *Téléc:* 450-266-4117
info@cccr.quebec
cccr.quebec
www.facebook.com/cowansville
Aperçu: Dimension: petite; *Envergure:* locale; fondée en 1968
Mission: Participe activement au développement économique de la ville tout en lui assurant une fenêtre ouverte sur le monde
Membre: 175; *Comités:* Communication; Financement et recrutement; Nouveaux membres
Membre(s) du bureau directeur:
Hélène Paquette, Présidente
Hélène Sactouris, Directrice générale

Chambre de commerce de Disraéli
CP 5008, Disraéli QC G0N 1E0
Courriel: chambrecommercedisraeli@gmail.com
chambrecommercedisraeli.com
www.facebook.com/ChambreCommerceDisraeli

Aperçu: *Dimension:* petite; *Envergure:* locale; fondée en 1952
Membre de: Québec Chamber of Commerce
Membre: 70
Membre(s) du bureau directeur:
Catherine Morency, Présidente

Chambre de commerce de East Angus et Région *Voir*
Chambre de commerce du Haut-Saint-François

Chambre de commerce de Ferme-Neuve
125, 12e rue, Ferme-Neuve QC J0W 1C0
Tél: 819-587-3882
ch.comm.fn@tlb.sympatico.ca
www.municipalite.ferme-neuve.qc.ca/Chambre_de_commerce.asp
www.facebook.com/CCFermeNeuve
Aperçu: *Dimension:* petite; *Envergure:* locale; Organisme sans but lucratif; fondée en 1959
Membre de: Chambre de commerce du Québec
Finances: *Budget de fonctionnement annuel:* Moins de $50,000
Membre: 93; *Montant de la cotisation:* 114,98$-172,46$;
Critères d'admissibilite: Commerce vente au détail

Chambre de Commerce de Fermont
CP 419, #6C, 299, Le Carrefour, Fermont QC G0G 1J0
Tél: 418-287-3000
Aperçu: *Dimension:* petite; *Envergure:* locale; Organisme sans but lucratif; fondée en 1998
Mission: Regrouper les gens d'affaires; soutenir l'intérêt des membres; favoriser les liens régionaux; promouvoir l'achat local; intervenir dans différents dossiers soci-économiques
Membre de: Chambre de commerce du Québec

Chambre de commerce de Fleurimont *Voir* Organisme de développement d'affaires commerciales et économiques

Chambre de commerce de Forestville
40, rte 138 ouest, Forestville QC G0T 1E0
Tél: 418-587-1585
chcommforestville@cgocable.ca
www.facebook.com/501570453233107
Aperçu: *Dimension:* petite; *Envergure:* locale
Membre: 70

La Chambre de Commerce de Fredericton *See* Fredericton Chamber of Commerce

Chambre de commerce de Gatineau
#100, 45, rue de Villebois, Gatineau QC J8T 8J7
Tél: 819-243-2246; *Téléc:* 819-243-3346
ccgatineau@ccgatineau.ca
www.ccgatineau.ca
www.facebook.com/ccgatineau
Aperçu: *Dimension:* petite; *Envergure:* locale
Mission: Stimuler la vitalité économique
Membre: *Montant de la cotisation:* Entreprise 900$, regulier 275$, jeune personne 137.50$
Membre(s) du bureau directeur:
Anne-Marie Proulx, Directrice générale

Chambre de Commerce de Hawkesbury et région *See* Hawkesbury & Region Chamber of Commerce

Chambre de commerce de l'Atlantique *See* Atlantic Chamber of Commerce

Chambre de commerce de l'Est de la Beauce
Saint-Prosper QC
Tél: 418-594-1219
ccest.beauce@hotmail.com
www.facebook.com/329086843866173
Nom précédent: Chambre de Commerce de St-Prosper
Aperçu: *Dimension:* petite; *Envergure:* locale; Organisme sans but lucratif; fondée en 1960
Mission: Rassembler et représenter les gens d'affaires du territoire afin de contribuer efficacement au développement socio-économique
Membre de: Fédération des chambres de commerce du Québec
Membre: *Critères d'admissibilite:* Travailleur autonome, entreprises, etc.
Activités: *Service de conférenciers:* Oui

Chambre de commerce de l'Est de Montréal
#100, 5600, rue Hochelaga, Montréal QC H1N 3L7
Tél: 514-354-5378; *Téléc:* 514-354-5340
info@ccemontreal.ca
www.ccemontreal.ca
www.linkedin.com/company/1099577
www.facebook.com/CCEMontreal
twitter.com/CCEMontreal
Aperçu: *Dimension:* petite; *Envergure:* locale
Mission: Défendre et de promouvoir les intérêts économiques et sociaux des 30 000 entreprises qui composent son territoire
Membre(s) du personnel: 10
Membre: *Montant de la cotisation:* Barème; *Comités:* Audit; Développment des affairs; Enjeux socioéconomiques; ESTim; Exportation; Golf; Gouvernance et ressources humaines; Jeunes leaders; Nomination; Plantification stratégique
Membre(s) du bureau directeur:
Carl Poulin, Président-directeur général par intérim
cpoulin@ccemontreal.ca

Chambre de commerce de l'Est de Portneuf
CP 4031, #2, rue de la Fabrique, Pont-Rouge QC G3H 3R4
Tél: 418-873-4085; *Téléc:* 418-873-4599
ccep@portneufest.com
www.portneufest.com
Aperçu: *Dimension:* petite; *Envergure:* locale
Mission: Pour promouvoir ses membres et de contribuer à leur succès commericial
Membre: *Montant de la cotisation:* Barème
Membre(s) du bureau directeur:
Karine Lacroix, Directrice

Chambre de commerce de l'Ile d'Orléans (CCIO)
490, côte du Pont, Saint-Pierre-Ile-d'Orléans QC G0A 4E0
Tél: 418-828-0880; *Téléc:* 418-828-2335
ccio@videotron.ca
cciledorleans.com
Aperçu: *Dimension:* petite; *Envergure:* locale
Mission: Organisme à but non lucratif et apolitique, la CCIO dessert plus de 220 membres répartis sur l'île d'Orléans, Beauport, Côte-de-Beaupré et Québec
Affiliation(s): Chambre de commerce du Québec
Finances: *Budget de fonctionnement annuel:* $100,000-$250,000
Membre(s) du personnel: 2; 13 bénévole(s)
Membre: 220; *Montant de la cotisation:* Barème; *Critères d'admissibilite:* Affaire-tourisme-conjoint
Membre(s) du bureau directeur:
Sylvie Ann Tremblay, Directrice générale

Chambre de commerce de l'Ouest-de-l'Ile de Montréal / West Island Chamber of Commerce
#106, 1870, boul des Sources, Pointe-Claire QC H9R 5N4
Tél: 514-697-4228; *Téléc:* 514-697-2562
info@ccoim.ca
www.ccoim.ca
www.facebook.com/CCOIM.WIMCC
twitter.com/chambrewest
Aperçu: *Dimension:* petite; *Envergure:* locale; fondée en 1979
Mission: D'assurer le bien-être économique de ses membres et de sa communauté d'affaires
Membre de: Chambre de commerce du Québec; Chambre de commerce du Canada
Membre(s) du personnel: 2
Membre: 850; *Montant de la cotisation:* Barème; *Comités:* Accueil-recrutement; Communication; Conseil des gouverneurs; Avantages commerciaux
Membre(s) du bureau directeur:
Joseph Huza, Directeur exécutif
jhuza@wimcc.ca

Chambre de Commerce de la Baie Georgienne Sud *See* Southern Georgian Bay Chamber of Commerce

Chambre de commerce de la grande région de Saint-Hyacinthe
780, av de L'Hôtel-de-ville, Saint-Hyacinthe QC J2S 5B2
Tél: 450-773-3474; *Téléc:* 450-773-9339
chambre@chambrecommerce.ca
www.chambrecommerce.ca
www.facebook.com/cclesmaskoutains
twitter.com/CCILM_1892
Aperçu: *Dimension:* petite; *Envergure:* locale; Organisme sans but lucratif; fondée en 1983
Mission: Vise, par le regroupement représentatif des forces de son milieu, à élaborer, développer et/ou parrainer toutes actions favorisant l'épanouissement du développement économique et social de la région tout en assurant la promotion et la défense des intérêts de ses membres
Membre de: Chambre de Commerce du Québec; Chambre de Commerce du Canada
Membre(s) du personnel: 2
Membre: 511; *Montant de la cotisation:* 75$ étudiant; 100$ particulier/travailleur autonome/communautaire; 125$ additionnel; 180$ entreprise; 250$ soutien; *Comités:* Agriculture et agroalimentaire; Formation Passion détail; Vision stratégique; Train de banlieue; Réseau RH
Membre(s) du bureau directeur:
Pierre Rhéaume, Directeur général
prheaume@chambrecommerce.ca

Chambre de commerce de la Haute-Gaspésie
96, boul Sainte-Anne ouest, Sainte-Anne-des-Monts QC G4V 1R3
Tél: 418-763-2200
info@cchautegaspesie.com
www.cchg.qc.ca
www.facebook.com/cchautegaspesie
twitter.com/cchautegaspesie
Aperçu: *Dimension:* petite; *Envergure:* locale
Mission: Intéressés au développement socio-économique de la Haute-Gaspésie
Membre(s) du bureau directeur:
Steve Ouimet, Président

Chambre de commerce de la Haute-Matawinie
521, rue Brassard, Saint-Michel-des-Saints QC J0K 3B0
Tél: 450-833-1334; *Téléc:* 450-833-1334
infocchm@satelcom.qc.ca
www.haute-matawinie.com
Aperçu: *Dimension:* petite; *Envergure:* locale
Mission: Regrouper les leaders de tout son territoire intéressés à travailler au bien-être économique, civique et social du milieu et au développement de ses ressources
Membre: *Critères d'admissibilite:* Entreprises locales
Membre(s) du bureau directeur:
France Chapdelaine, Directrice générale
chamhm@satelcom.qc.ca

Chambre de Commerce de la Jacques-Cartier
4517, rte de Fossambault, RR#3, Ste-Catherine-de-la-J-Cartier QC G0A 3M0
Tél: 418-875-4103
Aperçu: *Dimension:* petite; *Envergure:* locale

Chambre de commerce de la MRC de L'Assomption
#635, boul Iberville, Repentigny QC J6A 2C5
Tél: 450-581-3010; *Téléc:* 450-581-5069
info@ccmla.ca
www.ccmrclassomption.ca
Nom précédent: Chambre de commerce Pierre-Le Gardeur De Repentigny
Aperçu: *Dimension:* petite; *Envergure:* locale; fondée en 2012
Mission: La Chambre de commerce est un réseau de gens d'affaires qui a pour mission de favoriser le développement économique et social de la région, dans un esprit de concertation
Membre de: Chambre de Commerce du Québec
Finances: *Budget de fonctionnement annuel:* $100,000-$250,000
Membre(s) du personnel: 2; 15 bénévole(s)
Membre: 536; *Montant de la cotisation:* Barème; *Critères d'admissibilite:* Commercial; institutionnel; industriel; service
Activités: Dîners; conférences; golf; petits-déjeuner formation; *Service de conférenciers:* Oui
Membre(s) du bureau directeur:
Benoit Delisle, Président
Alain Bienvenu, Directeur général
dg@ccmla.ca

Chambre de commerce de la MRC de la Matapédia
#403, 123, rue Desbiens, Amqui QC G5J 3P9
Tél: 418-629-5765; *Téléc:* 418-629-5530
information@ccmrcmatapedia.qc.ca
www.ccmrcmatapedia.qc.ca
www.facebook.com/CCMRCM
plus.google.com/107383797735234822116
Aperçu: *Dimension:* petite; *Envergure:* locale; Organisme sans but lucratif; fondée en 2006
Mission: Travaille au bien-être économique, civique et social de la région et au développement de ses ressources; a pour but de traduire en actes les aspirations collectives de sa circonscription territoriale
Affiliation(s): Fédération des Chambres de commerce du Québec
Membre(s) du personnel: 1
Membre: 200+; *Montant de la cotisation:* Barème; *Comités:* Achat matapédien; Organisateur du Gala; Projets spéciaux
Activités: *Stagiaires:* Oui

Membre(s) du bureau directeur:
Pierre Langlois, Directeur général
direction@ccmrcmatapedia.qc.ca

Chambre de commerce de la MRC de Rivière-du-Loup
298, boul Armand-Thériault, Rivière-du-Loup QC G5R 4C2
Tél: 418-862-5243; *Téléc:* 418-862-5136
info@monreseaurdl.com
www.ccmrcrdl.com
www.facebook.com/CCMRCRDL
twitter.com/monreseaurdl
Nom précédent: Chambre de Commerce de Rivière-du-Loup
Aperçu: *Dimension:* petite; *Envergure:* locale; Organisme sans but lucratif; fondée en 1889
Mission: Favoriser le développement socio-économique de la région de Rivière-du-Loup; défendre les intérêts de ses membres auprès des différentes instances politiques; favoriser le réseautage entre ses membres
Membre de: Fédération des chambres de commerce du Québec
Membre(s) du personnel: 3
Membre: 400 entreprises; *Montant de la cotisation:* Barème
Activités: *Listes de destinataires:* Oui
Membre(s) du bureau directeur:
Karine Malenfant, Directrice générale
direction@monreseaurdl.com

Chambre de commerce de la région d'Acton
Édifice de la Gare, 980, rue Boulay, Acton Vale QC J0H 1A0
Tél: 450-546-0123; *Téléc:* 450-546-2709
ccracton@cooptel.qc.ca
www.chambredecommerce.info
Aperçu: *Dimension:* petite; *Envergure:* locale
Mission: Promouvoir l'action commerciale, sociale et communautaire
Membre de: Chambre de commerce du Québec
Membre: 115; *Montant de la cotisation:* Barème
Membre(s) du bureau directeur:
Alain Giguère, Président

Chambre de commerce de la région d'Edmundston
1, ch Canada, Edmundston NB E3V 1T6
Tél: 506-737-1866; *Téléc:* 506-737-1862
info@ccedmundston.com
www.ccedmundston.com
www.facebook.com/ChambredecommerceEdmundston
twitter.com/CCEdmundston
www.flickr.com/photos/ccedmundston
Aperçu: *Dimension:* petite; *Envergure:* locale; fondée en 1907
Affiliation(s): Chambre de commerce du Nouveau-Brunswick; Chambre de commerce des Provinces Atlantiques; Chambre de commerce du Canada; Chambre de commerce Internationale
Membre: *Montant de la cotisation:* Barème
Membre(s) du bureau directeur:
Marc Long, Directeur général
marclong@ccedmundston.com

Chambre de commerce de la région de Cap-Pelé
CP 1219, Cap-Pelé NB E4N 3B1
Tél: 506-332-0118
chambre_de_commerce@rogers.com
www.cap-pele.com
Aperçu: *Dimension:* petite; *Envergure:* locale; fondée en 1994
Membre(s) du bureau directeur:
Albert E. LeBlanc, Président
Gilles Haché, Secrétaire

Chambre de commerce de la région de Weedon
280, 9e av, Weedon QC J0B 3J0
Tél: 819-560-8555
Aperçu: *Dimension:* petite; *Envergure:* locale; Organisme sans but lucratif; fondée en 1957
Mission: Favoriser le développement économique par le réseautage et la concertation
Affiliation(s): Chambre de commerce du Québec
Membre: 55

Chambre de Commerce de la Rive-Sud de Québec *Voir* Chambre de commerce de Lévis

Chambre de commerce de la Vallée *See* Valley Chamber of Commerce

Chambre de Commerce de la Vallée de St-Sauveur *Voir* Chambre de commerce et de tourisme de la Vallée de Saint-Sauveur/Piedmont

Chambre de commerce de Lac-Brome
CP 3654, #316, 1, rue Knowlton, Lac-Brome QC J0E 1V0
Tél: 450-242-2870
info@cclacbrome.com
www.cclacbrome.com
Aperçu: *Dimension:* petite; *Envergure:* locale
Mission: Pour promouvoir le commerce dans la ville et d'offrir à ses membres des services pour aider à développer leur entreprise
Membre(s) du personnel: 1
Membre: 44
Membre(s) du bureau directeur:
Suzanne Gregory, Directrice générale

Chambre de commerce de Lévis
#225, 5700, rue J.B.-Michaud, Lévis QC G6V 0B1
Tél: 418-837-3411; *Téléc:* 418-837-8497
cclevis@cclevis.ca
www.cclevis.com
www.linkedin.com/groups?home=&gid=2918725
www.facebook.com/cclevis?sk=wall
twitter.com/cclevis
Nom précédent: Chambre de Commerce de la Rive-Sud de Québec
Aperçu: *Dimension:* petite; *Envergure:* locale; fondée en 1872
Mission: La Chambre de commerce de Lévis est le leader et le rassembleur de la communauté des affaires. Elle contribue activement au développement de sa région dans un esprit de concertation
Membre de: Chambre de commerce du Québec
Membre(s) du personnel: 7
Membre: 1 200; *Montant de la cotisation:* 145$; *Comités:* Recrutement; Gestion des Ressources Humaines; 5 à 7; organisateur des Pléiades; concours du Gala les Pléiades; Tournoi de golf; Programme Prêt à entreprendre; financement; Activités au féminin; Gouvernance; Coquetel Dînatoire; Tournoi de hockey des entreprises de la CCL; Conférences
Membre(s) du bureau directeur:
Stéphane Thériault, Directeur général

Chambre de commerce de Manicouagan
22, Place la Salle, 2e étage, Baie-Comeau QC G4Z 1K3
Tél: 418-296-2010; *Téléc:* 418-296-5397
info@ccmanic.qc.ca
www.ccmanic.qc.ca
www.linkedin.com/company/chambre-de-commerce-de-manicouagan
www.facebook.com/ChambrecommerceManicouagan
Nom précédent: Chambre de Commerce de Baie-Comeau
Aperçu: *Dimension:* petite; *Envergure:* locale
Mission: Favoriser le progrès de l'entreprise privée en encourageant l'entrepreneuriat et en jouant un rôle de catalyseur dans le développement économique, social et régional
Membre: *Montant de la cotisation:* Barème
Membre(s) du bureau directeur:
Dave Prévéreault, Directeur général

Chambre de Commerce de Maniwaki *Voir* Chambre de commerce et d'industrie de Maniwaki & Vallée de la Gatineau

Chambre de Commerce de Marieville *Voir* Chambre de commerce au Coeur de la Montérégie

Chambre de commerce de Mont-Laurier
CP 64, Mont-Laurier QC J9L 3G9
Tél: 819-623-3642; *Téléc:* 819-623-5220
Ligne sans frais: 855-623-3642
info@ccmont-laurier.com
www.ccmont-laurier.com
www.facebook.com/ChambreCommerceML
Aperçu: *Dimension:* petite; *Envergure:* locale; fondée en 1931
Mission: Développement des affaires
Membre de: Fédération des chambre de commerce du Québec; Chambre de commerce du Canada
Membre: *Montant de la cotisation:* Barème; *Comités:* Avantages; Golf; Gala des Draveurs; Enjeux
Activités: *Stagiaires:* Oui; *Service de conférenciers:* Oui
Membre(s) du bureau directeur:
Éric Tourangeau, Président
Jocelyn Girouard, Vice-Présidente
Audrey Lebel, Directrice générale

Chambre de commerce de Montmagny
#121, 6, rue St-Jean-Baptiste est, Montmagny QC G5V 1J7
Tél: 418-248-3111; *Téléc:* 418-241-5779
www.ccmontmagny.com
www.facebook.com/ccmontmagny
twitter.com/ccmontmagny
Aperçu: *Dimension:* petite; *Envergure:* locale; fondée en 1912

Chambre de commerce de Mont-Tremblant
#205, local 101, rue Lacasse, Mont-Tremblant QC J8E 3G6
Tél: 819-425-8441; *Téléc:* 819-425-7949
ccmt@ccm-t.ca
www.ccm-t.ca
www.facebook.com/ccmtremblant
Aperçu: *Dimension:* petite; *Envergure:* locale; fondée en 1983
Mission: La Chambre assure le maintien de conditions socio-économiques propices à la croissance des affaires et la promotion des intérêts de ses membres
Finances: *Budget de fonctionnement annuel:* Moins de $50,000
Membre: 610; *Montant de la cotisation:* Barème; *Comités:* Développement durable; Finances; Membership; Rayonnement
Membre(s) du bureau directeur:
France Paré, Présidente
Isabelle Plouffe, Directrice générale
isabelle.plouffe@ccm-t.ca

Chambre de commerce de Nipissing Ouest *See* West Nipissing Chamber of Commerce

Chambre de commerce de Notre Dame
PO Box 107, Notre Dame de Lourdes MB R0G 1M0
Tel: 204-248-2073; *Fax:* 204-248-2847
Overview: A small local organization
Chief Officer(s):
Lise Deleurme, President
deleurme@mymts.net

Chambre de commerce de Port-Cartier
CP 82, Port-Cartier QC G5B 2G7
Tél: 418-766-3110; *Téléc:* 418-766-6367
ccportcartier@globetrotter.net
www.ccportcartier.ca
Aperçu: *Dimension:* petite; *Envergure:* locale; fondée en 1979
Mission: Contribue au développement économique de sa région
Membre de: Chambre de Commerce du Québec; Chambre de Commerce du Canada
Membre: 140; *Comités:* Municipal; Industriel; Commercial; Touristique; Recrutement
Membre(s) du bureau directeur:
Danielle Beaupré, Présidente

Chambre de commerce de Rawdon
3874, rue Queen, Rawdon QC J0K 1S0
Tél: 450-834-2282; *Téléc:* 450-834-3084
ccdrawdon@gmail.com
www.chambrecommercerawdon.ca
www.linkedin.com/in/chambrecommercerawdon
www.facebook.com/chambrecommercerawdon
Aperçu: *Dimension:* petite; *Envergure:* locale; fondée en 1934
Mission: Contribuer à l'essor de la municipalité en assurant l'avancement du commerce, de l'industrie et du tourisme
Membre: 120
Membre(s) du bureau directeur:
Francis Martin, Président

Chambre de Commerce de Rivière-du-Loup *Voir* Chambre de commerce de la MRC de Rivière-du-Loup

Chambre de commerce de Rogersville / Rogersville Chamber of Commerce
#5, 11101, rue Principale, Rogersville NB E4Y 2N2
Tél: 506-775-0823; *Téléc:* 506-775-0826
Aperçu: *Dimension:* petite; *Envergure:* locale
Membre de: Chambre de commerce des provinces atlantiques
50 bénévole(s)
Membre: 75; *Montant de la cotisation:* 20$ institutionnel, 10$ individu

Chambre de Commerce de Saint Louis de Kent
83A rue Beauséjour, Saint-Louis-de-Kent NB E4X 1A6
Tel: 506-876-3475; *Fax:* 506-876-3477
Overview: A small local organization

Chambre de commerce de Saint-Bruno *Voir* Chambre de commerce Mont-Saint-Bruno

Chambre de commerce de Saint-Côme
1661A, rue Principale, Saint-Côme QC J0K 2B0
Tél: 450-883-2730
tourisme@stcomelanaudiere.ca
www.stcomelanaudiere.com
Aperçu: *Dimension:* petite; *Envergure:* locale; Organisme sans but lucratif; fondée en 1976

Mission: Promouvoir les ressources axées sur le développement économique local en stimulant le commerce, l'industrie et le tourisme
Membre: *Critères d'admissibilite:* Entreprises locales
Activités: Tournoi de golf en juillet
Membre(s) du bureau directeur:
Marie-Marthe Venne, Présidente par intérim

Chambre de commerce de Sainte-Adèle
1370, boul de Sainte-Adèle, Sainte-Adèle QC J8B 2N5
Tél: 450-229-2644; *Téléc:* 450-229-1436
chambredecommerce@sainte-adele.net
www.sainte-adele.net
www.facebook.com/sainteadele
twitter.com/sainteadele
Aperçu: *Dimension:* petite; *Envergure:* locale
Mission: Pour promouvoir le commerce et à aider leurs membres à prospérer
Membre(s) du personnel: 2
Membre: 472
Membre(s) du bureau directeur:
Guy Goyer, Directeur général
guy.goyer@sainte-adele.net

Chambre de commerce de Saint-Georges
#310, 8585, boul Lacroix, Saint-Georges QC G5Y 5L6
Tél: 418-228-7879; *Téléc:* 418-228-8074
reception@ccstgeorges.com
www.ccstgeorges.com
www.facebook.com/ccstgeorges
Aperçu: *Dimension:* petite; *Envergure:* locale; fondée en 1931
Mission: Rassembler et représenter les gens d'affaires de Saint-Georges et la région, afin de contribuer efficacement au développement socio-économique de notre communauté
Membre de: Conseil Économique de Beauce; Office de Tourisme de Beauce
Affiliation(s): Chambre de commerce du Québec; Chambre de commerce du Canada
Membre(s) du personnel: 3
Membre: *Montant de la cotisation:* Barème
Membre(s) du bureau directeur:
Nathalie Roy, Directrice générale
roy.nathalie@ccstgeorges.com

Chambre de commerce de Ste-Julienne
1799, rte 125, Sainte-Julienne QC J0K 2T0
Tél: 819-831-3551; *Téléc:* 819-831-3551
Aperçu: *Dimension:* petite; *Envergure:* locale; Organisme sans but lucratif; fondée en 1979
Membre(s) du bureau directeur:
Nicole Bourgie, Secrétaire

Chambre de commerce de Ste-Justine
167, rte 204, Sainte-Justine QC G0R 1Y0
Tél: 418-383-3207; *Téléc:* 418-383-3223
chambredecommercestejustine@sogetel.net
www.ccstejustine.ca
Aperçu: *Dimension:* petite; *Envergure:* locale
Mission: Pour maintenir une économie saine à Saint-Justine
Membre: 80+; *Montant de la cotisation:* Barème
Membre(s) du bureau directeur:
Bruno Turcotte, Président

La chambre de commerce de Saint-Malo & District
CP 328, Saint-Malo MB R0A 1T0
www.iadorestmalo.ca
Aperçu: *Dimension:* petite; *Envergure:* locale
Membre(s) du bureau directeur:
Aggie Gosselin, Présidente, 204-347-5493

Chambre de commerce de Saint-Quentin Inc.
144D, rue Canada, Saint-Quentin NB E8A 1G7
Tél: 506-235-3666; *Téléc:* 506-235-1804
www.saintquentinnb.com
www.facebook.com/ChambreDeCommerceDeStQuentin
Aperçu: *Dimension:* petite; *Envergure:* locale; fondée en 1946
Mission: Réunir ceux et celles qui veulent promouvoir et protéger les intérêts de la ville de Saint-Quentin et de sa région immédiate; encourager tous les citoyens à participer à la prospérité et croissance de la communauté; favoriser et améliorer l'industrie, le commerce et le bien-être économique, civique et de la communauté
Activités: Expositions commerciales et industrielles; journal pour membres; conférences lors de la semaine de la P.M.E.; projets d'été pour étudiants; réunions des membres tous les 3 mois; réunion annuelle en janvier; *Service de conférenciers:* Oui
Membre(s) du bureau directeur:

Pascale Bellavance, Présidente
Sandra Aubut, Secrétaire

Chambre de commerce de Sept-Îles
#237, 700, boul Laure, Sept-Iles QC G4R 1Y1
Tél: 418-968-3488; *Téléc:* 418-968-3432
ccsi@globetrotter.net
www.ccseptiles.com
Aperçu: *Dimension:* moyenne; *Envergure:* locale; Organisme sans but lucratif; fondée en 1952
Membre(s) du personnel: 2
Membre: 460; *Montant de la cotisation:* Barème
Membre(s) du bureau directeur:
Emilie Paquet, Directrice générale

Chambre de commerce de Sherbrooke
#202, 9, rue Wellington sud, Sherbrooke QC J1H 5C8
Tél: 819-822-6151; *Téléc:* 819-822-6156
info@ccsherbrooke.ca
www.ccsherbrooke.ca
www.facebook.com/ccsherbrooke
Aperçu: *Dimension:* petite; *Envergure:* locale
Mission: De favoriser et promouvoir le développement socio-économique de l'entreprise privée, défendre les intérêts de ses membres grâce à l'exercice de son leadership et assurer le maintien de conditions propices à la croissance des affaires de sa communauté
Affiliation(s): La jeune chambre de commerce de Sherbrooke
Membre(s) du personnel: 5
Membre: 1,413; *Montant de la cotisation:* 200$ association; *Comités:* Finance; Activités, Marketing, Recrutement et Service aux Membres; Gold; Opinion; Gala Reconnaissance Estrie; Grand Estrien; Achat Local; Économie Interculturelle
Membre(s) du bureau directeur:
Louise Bourgault, Directrice générale
lbourgault@ccsherbrooke.ca

Chambre de commerce de Shippagan inc.
227, boul J.D. Gauthier, Shippagan NB E8S 1N2
Tél: 506-336-3347
info@cdcshippagan.com
www.shippagan.ca
www.facebook.com/cdcshippagan
Aperçu: *Dimension:* petite; *Envergure:* locale
Membre(s) du bureau directeur:
Marie-Lou Noël, Présidente

Chambre de commerce de St-Côme-Linière (CCSCL)
1614, 6e rue, Saint-Côme-Linière QC G0M 1J0
Tél: 418-685-2630; *Téléc:* 418-685-2630
chambredecommerce@stcomeliniere.com
www.stcomeliniere.com/c_ccommerce.php
www.facebook.com/CCSCL
Aperçu: *Dimension:* petite; *Envergure:* locale; fondée en 1993
Mission: Sa mission est de défendre d'abord et avant tout, les membres qui la composent et de faire valoir leurs points de vue, leurs objectifs et leurs attentes
Membre: 50 organisations; 8 individu; *Montant de la cotisation:* Barème

Chambre de commerce de St-Donat
536A, rue Principale, Saint-Donat-de-Montcalm QC J0T 2C0
Tél: 819-216-2273
ccgsdonat@gmail.com
www.facebook.com/540807032764100
Aperçu: *Dimension:* petite; *Envergure:* locale; Organisme sans but lucratif; fondée en 1949
Mission: Promouvoir le mieux-être économique, civique et social de Saint-Donat
Finances: *Budget de fonctionnement annuel:* $50,000-$100,000
Membre: 147; *Montant de la cotisation:* 100$
Membre(s) du bureau directeur:
Karinne Poirier, Directrice générale

Chambre de commerce de St-Frédéric
850, rue de l'Hôtel-de-Ville, Saint-Frédéric QC G0N 1P0
Courriel: commerce@st-frederic.com
www.saint-frederic.com
Aperçu: *Dimension:* petite; *Envergure:* locale; Organisme sans but lucratif; fondée en 1971
Mission: Promouvoir le développement commercial, industriel et résidentiel de la Municipalité de St-Frédéric; remplir le parc industriel existant; attirer de nouveaux investisseurs et de nouveau résidents
Membre(s) du personnel: 5
Membre: *Montant de la cotisation:* 205$

Activités: *Evénements de sensibilisation:* Souper-bénéfice; *Bibliothèque:* Rayon de Soleil
Membre(s) du bureau directeur:
Cathy Poulin, Directrice générale

Chambre de commerce de St-Jean-de-Dieu
32, rue Principale sud, Saint-Jean-de-Dieu QC G0L 3M0
Tél: 418-963-3529
chambredecommercestjean@outlook.com
Aperçu: *Dimension:* petite; *Envergure:* locale
Membre(s) du bureau directeur:
Émilie Lebel, Directrice générale

Chambre de commerce de St-Jules-de-Beauce
169, Rang 3, Saint-Jules QC G0N 1R0
Tél: 418-397-1870
www.facebook.com/Chambre-de-commerce-de-St-Jules-226086874070046
Aperçu: *Dimension:* petite; *Envergure:* locale
Membre(s) du bureau directeur:
Dominic Paré, Présidente

Chambre de commerce de St-Léonard
8370, boul Lacordaire, Saint-Léonard QC H1R 3Y6
Tél: 514-325-4232; *Téléc:* 514-955-8544
info@saintleonardenaffaires.com
saintleonardenaffaires.com
fr-ca.facebook.com/207992709237477
twitter.com/chambrestleo
Aperçu: *Dimension:* petite; *Envergure:* locale; fondée en 1979
Mission: Défendre des intérêts de ses membres et de la communauté d'affaires de son territoire
Membre: *Montant de la cotisation:* 175$
Membre(s) du bureau directeur:
Salvatore Andricciola, Président

Chambre de Commerce de St-Prosper *Voir* Chambre de commerce de l'Est de la Beauce

Chambre de Commerce de St-Raymond *Voir* Chambre de commerce régionale de St-Raymond

Chambre de commerce de Timmins *See* Timmins Chamber of Commerce

Chambre de commerce de Tring-Jonction
CP 1012, Tring-Jonction QC G0N 1X0
Tél: 418-426-2135
c_de_commerce_tring@hotmail.com
www.tringjonction.qc.ca
Aperçu: *Dimension:* petite; *Envergure:* locale
Membre(s) du bureau directeur:
Richard Lagueux, Vice-président

Chambre de commerce de Valcourt et Région
980, rue St-Joseph, Valcourt QC J0E 2L0
Tél: 450-532-3263; *Téléc:* 450-532-5855
info@valcourtregion.com
www.valcourtregion.com
www.facebook.com/ccirv
twitter.com/valcourtregion
Aperçu: *Dimension:* petite; *Envergure:* locale; fondée en 1987
Mission: D'améliorer les activités économiques, sociales et civiques de la région de vacourt
Membre de: Chambre de commerce du Québec
Affiliation(s): Chambre de commerce régionale de l'Estrie
Membre: 55; *Montant de la cotisation:* 100$
Activités: *Listes de destinataires:* Oui
Membre(s) du bureau directeur:
Pierre Bonneau, Président

Chambre de commerce de Val-d'Or (CCVD)
#200, 921 - 3e av, Val-d'Or QC J9P 1T4
Tél: 819-825-3703; *Téléc:* 819-825-8599
info@ccvd.qc.ca
www.ccvd.qc.ca
www.linkedin.com/company/chambre-de-commerce-de-val-d'or
www.facebook.com/232034766863790
twitter.com/CCVDcom
www.youtube.com/user/CCVDCom
Aperçu: *Dimension:* petite; *Envergure:* locale
Mission: Etre partenaire du développement économique et social de la communauté valdorienne et à cette fin, mobiliser, appuyer et représenter ses membres, défendre leurs intérêts.
Membre(s) du personnel: 4
Membre: *Montant de la cotisation:* 114,98$
Membre(s) du bureau directeur:
Marcel H. Jolicoeur, Président

Canadian Associations / Chambre de commerce des Iles Lamèque et Miscou inc.

Hélène Paradis, Directrice générale
hparadis@ccvd.qc.ca

La Chambre de commerce de Welland/Pelham *See* The Welland/Pelham Chamber of Commerce

Chambre de commerce de Winnipeg *See* Winnipeg Chamber of Commerce

Chambre de commerce des Bois-Francs *Voir* Chambre de commerce et d'industrie des Bois-Francs et de l'Érable

Chambre de commerce des Iles Lamèque et Miscou inc.
CP 2075, Lamèque NB E8T 3N5
Tél: 506-344-3222; *Téléc:* 506-344-3266
www.cclamequemiscou.ca
www.facebook.com/cdclamequemiscou
Aperçu: Dimension: petite; *Envergure:* locale
Mission: De promouvoir les intérêts si ses membres afin de les aider à prospérer
Membre: 88; *Montant de la cotisation:* Barème
Membre(s) du bureau directeur:
Eugène Chiasson, Président

Chambre de commerce des Jardins de Napierville
780, rue Notre-Dame, Saint-Rémi QC J0L 2L0
Tél: 450-615-0512
Ligne sans frais: 844-467-6734
info@ccjdn.com
www.ccjdn.com
Nom précédent: Chambre de commerce Hemmingford—Napierville—Saint-Rémi
Aperçu: Dimension: petite; *Envergure:* locale; Organisme sans but lucratif
Mission: Participer à l'essor de l'économie du territoire; soutenir ses membres
Membre: 107
Membre(s) du bureau directeur:
Daniel Dagenais, Président

Chambre de commerce des Îles-de-la-Madeleine (CCIM)
Édifice Fernand Cyr, #103, 735, ch Principal, Cap-aux-Meules QC G4T 1G8
Tél: 418-986-4111; *Téléc:* 418-986-4112
info@ccim.qc.ca
www.ilesdelamadeleine.com
Aperçu: Dimension: petite; *Envergure:* locale; Organisme sans but lucratif; fondée en 1962
Mission: De veiller à la mise en place et au respect de conditions et d'infrastructures propices à la prospérité madelinienne
Membre de: Chambre du commerce du Québec; Chambre du commerce du Canada
Finances: Budget de fonctionnement annuel: $100,000-$250,000
Membre(s) du personnel: 3; 15 bénévole(s)
Membre: 250; *Montant de la cotisation:* 100-320; *Critères d'admissibilité:* PHE
Activités: Gala des Eloizes; *Evénements de sensibilisation:* Forum économique; *Service de conférenciers:* Oui; *Listes de destinataires:* Oui; *Bibliothèque:* rendez-vous
Membre(s) du bureau directeur:
Marius Arseneault, Président

La Chambre de commerce du Canada *See* The Canadian Chamber of Commerce

Chambre de commerce du Centre-de-la-Mauricie *Voir* Chambre de commerce et d'industrie de Shawinigan

Chambre de commerce du district de Granby-Bromont *Voir* Chambre de commerce Haute-Yamaska et Région

Chambre de Commerce du district de Trois-Rivières *Voir* Chambre de commerce et d'industries de Trois-Rivières

Chambre de commerce du Grand Bathurst *See* Greater Bathurst Chamber of Commerce

Chambre de commerce du grand de Châteauguay
#100, 15, boul Maple, Châteauguay QC J6J 3P7
Tél: 450-698-0027; *Téléc:* 450-698-0088
info@ccgchateauguay.ca
www.ccgchateauguay.ca
www.facebook.com/ChambreDeCommerceChateauguay
Aperçu: Dimension: petite; *Envergure:* locale
Mission: Agit comme un catalyseur à la promotion des forces économiques présentes sur son territoire
Membre: Montant de la cotisation: 110-200; *Critères d'admissibilite:* Entreprises de Grand Châteauguay
Membre(s) du bureau directeur:
Isabelle Poirier, Directrice générale
ipoirier@ccgchateauguay.ca

Chambre de commerce du Grand Joliette
500, boul Dollard, Joliette QC J6E 4M4
Tél: 450-759-6363; *Téléc:* 450-759-5012
info@ccgj.qc.ca
www.ccgj.qc.ca
www.facebook.com/CCGJoliette
twitter.com/CCGJoliette
www.youtube.com/user/CCGJoliette
Aperçu: Dimension: petite; *Envergure:* locale
Membre: Montant de la cotisation: 60$ membre junior/sénior; 135$ membre individuel; 160$ membre corporatif
Membre(s) du bureau directeur:
Pascale Lapointe-Manseau, Directrice générale
plapointe@ccgj.qc.ca
Meetings/Conferences:
• Chambre de Commerce du Grand Joliette Assemblée générale annuelle 2018, 2018, QC
Scope: Local

Chambre de commerce du Grand Moncton *See* Greater Moncton Chamber of Commerce

Chambre de commerce du Grand Shediac *See* Greater Shediac Chamber of Commerce

Chambre de commerce du Grand Sudbury *See* Greater Sudbury Chamber of Commerce

Chambre de commerce du Grand Tracadie-Sheila
#4104, rue Principale, Tracadie-Sheila NB E1X 1B8
Tél: 506-394-4028
www.ccgts.ca
www.facebook.com/111012852315372
twitter.com/CCG_TracadieS
Aperçu: Dimension: petite; *Envergure:* locale; fondée en 2009
Mission: De promouvoir et de développer le commerce dans la région
Membre de: Canadian Chamber of Commerce
Membre(s) du bureau directeur:
Rebecca Preston, Directrice générale

Chambre de commerce du Haut St-Maurice *Voir* Chambre de commerce et d'industrie du Haut St-Maurice

Chambre de commerce du Haut-Richelieu
Centre Ernest-Thuot, 75, 5e av, Saint-Jean-sur-Richelieu QC J2X 1T1
Tél: 450-346-2544; *Téléc:* 450-346-3812
info@ccihr.ca
www.ccihr.ca
www.linkedin.com/company/chambre-de-commerce-du-haut-richelieu
Aperçu: Dimension: petite; *Envergure:* locale; fondée en 1894
Mission: Pour aider à développer l'économie de la région et aider à développer le commerce
Membre: 575; *Montant de la cotisation:* 75$ individuel; 50$ jeunesse; 140$ 1 à 25 employés; 210$ 26 à 99 employés; 315$ 100+ employés; *Comités:* Agroalimentaire; Aile jeunesse; Exécutif; Gala de l'excellence; Golf; Industriel
Membre(s) du bureau directeur:
Stéphane Legrand, Directeur général

Chambre de commerce du Haut-Saint-François
221, St-Jean ouest, East Angus QC J0B 1R0
Tél: 819-832-4950; *Téléc:* 819-832-4950
info@chambredecommercehsf.com
www.chambredecommercehsf.com
Nom précédent: Chambre de commerce de East Angus et Région
Aperçu: Dimension: petite; *Envergure:* locale; Organisme sans but lucratif; fondée en 2010
Mission: Promouvoir le commerce et les industries dans la région
Membre de: Chambre de Commerce du Québec; Chambre de Commerce Régionale de l'Estrie
Finances: Budget de fonctionnement annuel: $50,000-$100,000
Membre(s) du personnel: 1; 17 bénévole(s)
Membre: 1-99; *Montant de la cotisation:* 113,95$
Membre(s) du bureau directeur:
Guy Boulanger, Président
Nancy Grenier, Directrice générale

Chambre de commerce du Montréal métropolitain / Chamber of Commerce of Metropolitan Montréal
#6000, 380, rue Saint-Antoine ouest, Montréal QC H2Y 3X7
Tél: 514-871-4000; *Téléc:* 514-871-1255
info@ccmm.ca
www.ccmm.ca
www.linkedin.com/groups/1835201
twitter.com/chambremontreal
Merged from: Montréal Board of Trade; Chambre de commerce de Montréal
Aperçu: Dimension: moyenne; *Envergure:* locale; Organisme sans but lucratif
Mission: Est le porte-parole du milieu des affaires et de la communauté en matière de croissance et de réussite économique; agit comme rassembleur et catalyseur des forces vives de l'économie métropolitaine; s'engage dans des secteurs clés du développement économique; favorise le développement d'un membership représentatif, fort, fier et engagé; offre des services adaptés aux besoins; prône une philosophie d'action axée sur la crédibilité, la pro-activité et l'impact
Finances: Budget de fonctionnement annuel: $3 Million-$5 Million
Membre(s) du personnel: 85
Membre: 5,000-14,999
Activités:; Bibliothèque: Info Entrepreneurs; Bibliothèque publique
Membre(s) du bureau directeur:
Michel Leblanc, Président et chef de la direction

Chambre de Commerce du Rouyn-Noranda régional *Voir* Chambre de commerce et d'industrie de Rouyn-Noranda

Chambre de commerce du Saguenay-Le Fjord
194, rue Price ouest, Chicoutimi QC G7J 1H1
Tél: 418-543-5941; *Téléc:* 418-543-5576
info@ccisf.ca
www.ccisf.ca
www.linkedin.com/company/chambre-de-commerce-du-saguenay
www.facebook.com/ccsaguenay
twitter.com/CCSaguenay
Nom précédent: Chambre de commerce de Chicoutimi
Aperçu: Dimension: petite; *Envergure:* locale
Membre(s) du bureau directeur:
Marie-Josée Morency, Directrice générale
mjmorency@ccisf.ca

Chambre de commerce du Témiscouata
CP 1726, #201, 3, rue de l'Hôtel-de-Ville, Témiscouata-sur-le-Lac QC G0L 1X0
Tél: 418-714-2263
info@cctemiscouata.com
www.cctemiscouata.com
Aperçu: Dimension: petite; *Envergure:* locale
Membre(s) du bureau directeur:
Martine Lemieux, Directrice générale

Chambre de commerce du Transcontinental
CP 2004, Rivière-Bleue QC G0L 2B0
Tél: 418-893-5504; *Téléc:* 418-893-2889
cctrans@sympatico.ca
pages.globetrotter.net/cctrans
Aperçu: Dimension: petite; *Envergure:* locale; fondée en 1950
Mission: La mission première de la Chambre de commerce est de stimuler le développement socio-économique des gens d'affaires et des citoyens du Transcontinental
Membre(s) du bureau directeur:
Sylvain Lafrance, Président

Chambre de commerce Duparquet
CP 369, Duparquet QC J0Z 1W0
Tél: 819-948-2030
Aperçu: Dimension: petite; *Envergure:* locale
Membre de: Chambre de Commerce du Québec
Membre(s) du bureau directeur:
Jasmine Therrien, Secrétaire

Chambre de commerce East Broughton
CP 916, East Broughton QC G0N 1G0
Tél: 418-351-0143
Aperçu: Dimension: petite; *Envergure:* locale
Membre: 65

Chambre de commerce et d'entrepreneuriat des Sources (CCES)
CP 599, Danville QC J0A 1A0
Tél: 819-839-2742; *Téléc:* 819-839-2347
www.facebook.com/ChambreCommerceEntrepreneuriatSources

Merged from: Chambre de commerce de Danville; Chambre de commerce et d'industrie des Sources
Aperçu: *Dimension:* petite; *Envergure:* locale; fondée en 1957
Mission: Favorise le développement des affaires dans sa collectivité
11 bénévole(s)
Membre: 75
Membre(s) du bureau directeur:
Isabelle Lodge, Présidente
Kathy Breton, Secrétaire

Chambre de commerce et d'industrie Beauharnois-Valleyfield-Haut Saint-Laurent
#400, 100, rue Sainte-Cécile, Salaberry-de-Valleyfield QC J6T 1M1
Tél: 450-373-8789; *Téléc:* 450-373-8642
info@ccibvhsl.ca
www.ccibv.ca
www.facebook.com/ccibv
Aperçu: *Dimension:* petite; *Envergure:* locale
Mission: De miser sur pied d'activités et de services propres à aider les gens d'affaires; de promouvoir des intérêts économiques régionaux face aux décideurs politiques et cela sous forme d'études, de consultations, d'expertises, de propositions et de représentations et enfin promotion du commerce local et régional
Membre: 550; *Montant de la cotisation:* 201,21$ régulier; 432,16$ corporatif; *Comités:* Tourisme; Relations municipales/intermunicipales et intergouvernementales; Dossiers économiques; Événements; Marketing et communication; Recrutement, renouvellement et intégration dans le milieu
Membre(s) du bureau directeur:
Sylvie Villemure, Directrice générale

Chambre de commerce et d'industrie Berthier-D'Autray
557, rue de Montcalm, Berthierville QC J0K 1A0
Tél: 450-836-4689; *Téléc:* 450-836-6483
info@cciba.org
www.cciba.org
www.facebook.com/cci.Berthier.Autray
Aperçu: *Dimension:* petite; *Envergure:* locale
Mission: L'organisme travaille au développement économique de ses membres et de sa communauté et intervient, au besoin, dans divers dossiers
Finances: *Budget de fonctionnement annuel:* $50,000-$100,000
Membre: 150; *Montant de la cotisation:* Barème
Membre(s) du bureau directeur:
Jean-François Laporte, Président

Chambre de commerce et d'industrie d'Abitibi-Ouest (CCAO)
364-A, rue Principale, La Sarre QC J9Z 1Z5
Tél: 819-333-9836; *Téléc:* 819-333-5737
ccao@ccao.qc.ca
www.ccao.qc.ca
www.facebook.com/CCIAbitibi.Ouest
Aperçu: *Dimension:* petite; *Envergure:* locale; fondée en 1953
Mission: La Chambre de commerce d'Abitibi-Ouest est une organisation sans but lucratif composée d'entreprises oeuvrant dans tous les secteurs d'activités, qui contribuent au développement économique en défendant la liberté d'entreprendre par l'exercice de son leadership, de son pouvoir de représentation et d'action.
Membre(s) du personnel: 3
Membre: 350; *Montant de la cotisation:* Barème; *Comités:* Gala excell'or; Golf
Membre(s) du bureau directeur:
Stéphanie Bédard, Directrice générale

Chambre de commerce et d'industrie d'Argenteuil
540, rue Berry, Lachute QC J8H 1S5
Tél: 450-562-1947; *Téléc:* 450-562-1896
info@cciargenteuil.com
www.cciargenteuil.com
www.facebook.com/cciargenteuil
Aperçu: *Dimension:* petite; *Envergure:* locale
Mission: Regroupement de gens d'affaires d'Argenteuil
Membre(s) du bureau directeur:
Marguerite Varin, Présidente

Chambre de commerce et d'industrie de Bécancour; Chambre de commerce de Bécancour *Voir* Chambre de commerce et d'industrie du Coeur-du-Québec

Chambre de commerce et d'industrie de Dolbeau-Mistassini
#110, 1201, rues des Érables, Dolbeau-Mistassini QC G8L 1C2
Tél: 418-276-6638; *Téléc:* 418-276-9518
info@ccidm.ca
www.ccidm.ca
Aperçu: *Dimension:* petite; *Envergure:* locale; Organisme sans but lucratif; fondée en 1946
Mission: Promouvoir le développement économique de sa région
Finances: *Budget de fonctionnement annuel:* Moins de $50,000
Membre: 155; *Montant de la cotisation:* 100$
Activités: *Service de conférenciers:* Oui
Membre(s) du bureau directeur:
Audrey Jobin, Directrice générale

Chambre de commerce et d'industrie de Drummond (CCID)
CP 188, 234, rue Saint-Marcel, Drummondville QC J2B 6V7
Tél: 819-477-7822
info@ccid.qc.ca
www.ccid.qc.ca
www.linkedin.com/company/4993229
www.facebook.com/273570949083
twitter.com/_CCID_
www.youtube.com/channel/UCoFAl0FERsHBU6CITMR1_Ug
Aperçu: *Dimension:* petite; *Envergure:* locale; fondée en 1902
Mission: La Chambre de commerce et d'industrie de Drummond est vouée au développement d'une économie solide et viable. Elle constitue une voix privilégiée de la communauté d'affaires drummondvilloise
Membre(s) du personnel: 4
Membre: *Montant de la cotisation:* Barème; *Comités:* Affaires commerciales; Affaires publiques; Affaires au féminin; Affaires Publiques; Golf et vélo; Manufacturier; Réseau et recrutement; Gala des Napoléon; Gouvernance et accréditation
Membre(s) du bureau directeur:
Alain Côté, Directeur général
acote@ccid.qc.ca

Chambre de commerce et d'industrie de la MRC de Maskinongé
396, av Ste-Élisabeth, Louiseville QC J5V 1M8
Tél: 819-228-8582; *Téléc:* 819-498-8323
Ligne sans frais: 866-900-8582
info@ccimm.ca
www.ccimm.ca
www.facebook.com/CCIMMaskinonge
Aperçu: *Dimension:* petite; *Envergure:* locale
Mission: Promouvoir le développement économique, social et culturel de la MRC de Maskinongé
Membre: 400
Membre(s) du bureau directeur:
Geneviève Scott Lafontaine, Directrice générale
dg@ccimm.ca

Chambre de commerce et d'Industrie de la région de Coaticook (CCIRC)
#22, 150, rue Child, Coaticook QC J1A 2B3
Tél: 819-849-4733; *Téléc:* 819-849-9683
info@ccircoaticook.ca
www.ccircoaticook.ca
Aperçu: *Dimension:* petite; *Envergure:* locale; Organisme sans but lucratif; fondée en 1899
Mission: Promouvoir et défendre le bien-être économique, civique et social des municipalités faisant partie de son territoire; stimuler le développement des ressources
Finances: *Budget de fonctionnement annuel:* Moins de $50,000
Membre: 250; *Montant de la cotisation:* Barème
Membre(s) du bureau directeur:
Caroline Thibeault, Présidente

Chambre de commerce et d'industrie de la région de Richmond
CP 3119, Richmond QC J0B 2H0
Tél: 819-826-5854
info@ccrichmond.com
www.ccrichmond.com
Aperçu: *Dimension:* petite; *Envergure:* locale; Organisme sans but lucratif; fondée en 1894
Mission: De travailler au bien être économique, civique, et social de la région de Richmond, et au développement de ses ressources en stimulant le commerce, l'industrie et le tourisme
Membre de: Fédération des chambres de commerce du Québec; Chambre de commerce du Canada
Membre: 53
Activités: Soupers, conférences mensuelles

Membre(s) du bureau directeur:
Hélène Tousignant, Présidente
Ginette Coutu-Poirier, Trésorière

Chambre de commerce et d'industrie de la Rive-Sud
#101, 85, rue Saint-Charles ouest, Longueuil QC J4H 1C5
Tél: 450-463-2121; *Téléc:* 450-463-1858
info@ccirs.qc.ca
www.ccirs.qc.ca
www.linkedin.com/groups/1621977
www.facebook.com/ccirsrivesud
twitter.com/CCIRS2010
Aperçu: *Dimension:* petite; *Envergure:* locale; fondée en 1974
Mission: De représenter les entreprises agissant sur son territoire; De prendre position sur les grands enjeux; D'offrir des services en lien avec leurs objectifs de réussite; en développant des partenariats et des occasions de maillage
Membre(s) du personnel: 10
Membre: 1 900; *Montant de la cotisation:* Barème; *Comités:* Accueil industriel; Développment durable; Femmes; Golf; Main-d'oeuvre; Aile jeunesse nouvelle génération d'affaires; Prix excellence; Relève; Rendez-vous; Transport
Membre(s) du bureau directeur:
Hélène Bergeron, Codirectrice générale
hbergeron@ccirs.qc.ca
Stéphanie Brodeur, Codirectrice générale

Chambre de commerce et d'industrie de la Rivière-Du-Nord
Voir Chambre de commerce et d'industrie St-Jérôme

Chambre de commerce et d'industrie de la Vallée-du-Richelieu
#203, 230, rue Brébeuf, Beloeil QC J3G 5P3
Tél: 450-464-3733; *Téléc:* 450-446-4163
www.ccivr.com
www.linkedin.com/groups/4077118
www.facebook.com/CCIVR
twitter.com/CCIVR
Nom précédent: Chambre de Commerce Vallée du Richelieu
Aperçu: *Dimension:* petite; *Envergure:* locale
Mission: De développer continuellement de nouveaux services pour ses membres, des services et des activités qui peuvent contribuer à faire connaître leur entreprise
Membre(s) du personnel: 3
Membre: 777; *Montant de la cotisation:* Barème
Membre(s) du bureau directeur:
Julie La Rochelle, Directrice générale
jlarochelle@ccivr.com

Chambre de commerce et d'industrie de Laval (CCIL)
#200, 1555, boul Chomedey, Laval QC H7V 3Z1
Tél: 450-682-5255; *Téléc:* 450-682-5735
info@ccilaval.qc.ca
www.ccilaval.qc.ca
www.linkedin.com/company/ccilaval---chambre-de-commerce-et-d%27industrie-de-laval
www.facebook.com/CCILaval
twitter.com/CCILaval
Aperçu: *Dimension:* petite; *Envergure:* locale; Organisme sans but lucratif; fondée en 1967
Mission: Assumer un leadership au sein des affaires à Laval par l'organisation d'activités de sensibilisation, d'information et de formation; défendre et promouvoir les intérêts des entreprises membres auprès de toute instance décisionnelle sur le plan des règles, des lois et du climat des affaires
Membre de: Chambre de Commerce du Québec; Chambre de Commerce du Canada
Finances: *Budget de fonctionnement annuel:* $1.5 Million-$3 Million
Membre(s) du personnel: 15; 150 bénévole(s)
Membre: 2 000; *Montant de la cotisation:* Barème; *Critères d'admissibilité:* Propriétaires, cadres supérieurs et professionnels d'entreprises diverses; *Comités:* Jeunes; Science et technologie; Ressources humaines; Transports
Activités: *Stagiaires:* Oui; *Service de conférenciers:* Oui; *Listes de destinataires:* Oui; *Bibliothèque:* Centre de documentation CCIL; rendez-vous
Membre(s) du bureau directeur:
Chantal Provost, Présidente-directrice générale
cprovost@ccilaval.qc.ca

Chambre de commerce et d'industrie de Malartic (CCIM)
#160, 866, rue Royale, Malartic QC J0Y 1Z0
Tél: 819-757-3338
info@ccimalartic.com

Canadian Associations / Chambre de commerce et d'industrie de Maniwaki & Vallée de la Gatineau (CCIM)

www.ccimalartic.com
fr-ca.facebook.com/cdcmalartic
Aperçu: Dimension: petite; *Envergure:* locale
Membre(s) du personnel: 1
Membre(s) du bureau directeur:
Claudette Jolin, Directrice
claudette@ccimalartic.com

Chambre de commerce et d'industrie de Maniwaki & Vallée de la Gatineau (CCIM)
186, rue King, Maniwaki QC J9E 3N6
Tél: 819-449-6627; *Téléc:* 819-449-7667
Ligne sans frais: 866-449-6728
info@ccmvg.com
www.ccmvg.com
Nom précédent: Chambre de Commerce de Maniwaki
Aperçu: Dimension: petite; *Envergure:* locale; Organisme sans but lucratif; fondée en 1983
Mission: Rassembler les gens d'affaires et intervenants du milieu des affaires pour contribuer au développement du mieux-être économique des entreprises et promouvoir le développement socio-économique de l'entreprise privée, défendre les intérêts de ses membres grâce à l'exercice de son leadership et assurer le maintien de conditions propices à la croissance des affaires de sa communauté
Membre de: Chambre de Commerce du Québec; Association touristique de l'Outaouais
Finances: *Budget de fonctionnement annuel:* $100,000-$250,000
Membre(s) du personnel: 1; 25 bénévole(s)
Membre: 200; *Montant de la cotisation:* Barème
Activités: Salon du Commerce; Gala PME; Tournoi de golf de la CCIM
Membre(s) du bureau directeur:
Kim Lafond, Administratrice

Chambre de commerce et d'industrie de Mirabel
#300, 11700, de L'Avenir, Mirabel QC J7J 0G7
Tél: 450-433-1944
www.ccimirabel.com
www.linkedin.com/company/2279237
twitter.com/CCIMirabel
Aperçu: Dimension: petite; *Envergure:* locale
Mission: Contribue au développement économique de la région
Membre(s) du bureau directeur:
Steve Raymond, Président

Chambre de commerce et d'industrie de Montréal-Nord (CRIMN)
#207, 5835, boul Léger, Montréal QC H1G 6E1
Tél: 514-329-4453; *Téléc:* 514-329-5318
www.ccimn.qc.ca
www.linkedin.com/company/3070769
www.facebook.com/ChambreCommerceMontrealNord
Aperçu: Dimension: petite; *Envergure:* locale; Organisme sans but lucratif; fondée en 1947
Mission: Promouvoir le progrès civique, commercial et industriel de la communauté
Membre de: Chambre de Commerce du Québec
Finances: *Budget de fonctionnement annuel:* $50,000-$100,000
Membre: 200; *Montant de la cotisation:* Barème
Membre(s) du bureau directeur:
Palmina Panichella, Directrice générale
palmina.panichella@ccimn.qc.ca

Chambre de commerce et d'industrie de Québec
#600, 900, boul René-Lévesque est, Québec QC G1R 2B5
Tél: 418-692-3853; *Téléc:* 418-694-2286
info@cciquebec.ca
www.cciquebec.ca
www.linkedin.com/company/chambre-de-commerce-et-d%27industrie-de-qu-bec
www.facebook.com/cciquebec
twitter.com/cciquebec
www.youtube.com/channel/UC6knYpzSAWYkHtfTqnIV6SA
Nom précédent: Chambre de Commerce et d'industrie du Québec métropolitain
Aperçu: Dimension: moyenne; *Envergure:* locale; fondée en 1809
Mission: Pour représenter les entreprises au Québec
Affiliation(s): Chambre de commerce du Canada
Membre(s) du personnel: 16
Membre: 4 600; *Montant de la cotisation:* 190$+; *Comités:* Action tourisme; Actions femmes et leadership; Entrepreneuriat; Fiscalité et finances publiques; Innovation; Réseautage
Activités: *Service de conférenciers:* Oui; *Listes de destinataires:* Oui

Membre(s) du bureau directeur:
Alain Aubut, Président et chef de la direction

Chambre de commerce et d'industrie de Roberval
CP 115, Roberval QC G8H 2N4
Tél: 418-275-3504; *Téléc:* 418-275-6895
info@ccroberval.ca
www.ccroberval.ca
www.facebook.com/ChambreCommerceRoberval
twitter.com/CCRoberval
Nom précédent: Chambre de commerce et d'industrie du secteur Roberval
Aperçu: Dimension: petite; *Envergure:* locale; Organisme sans but lucratif; fondée en 1921
Mission: Assurer le développement économique de son milieu en représentant les intérêts de ses membres auprès des intervenants socio-économiques et politiques
Affiliation(s): Chambre de Commerce du Québec; Chambre de Commerce du Canada
Finances: *Budget de fonctionnement annuel:* Moins de $50,000
Membre(s) du personnel: 1; 16 bénévole(s)
Membre: 180; *Montant de la cotisation:* 175-200; *Critères d'admissibilité:* Commerçant, professionnel, fonctionnaire
Activités: Tournois de golf sur glace du Lac St-Jean; dégustation de vin/fromage, mois de novembre; gala méritas; *Stagiaires:* Oui; *Service de conférenciers:* Oui
Membre(s) du bureau directeur:
Serge Taillon, Président
Jeannot Tremblay, Coordonnateur

Chambre de commerce et d'industrie de Rouyn-Noranda (CCIRN)
70, av du Lac, Rouyn-Noranda QC J9X 4N4
Tél: 819-797-2000; *Téléc:* 819-762-3091
reseau@ccirn.qc.ca
www.ccirn.qc.ca
www.linkedin.com/company/chambre-de-commerce-et-d'industrie-de-rouyn-noranda
www.facebook.com/ChambreRN
twitter.com/CCIRN
Nom précédent: Chambre de Commerce du Rouyn-Noranda régional
Aperçu: Dimension: moyenne; *Envergure:* locale; fondée en 1927
Membre de: Chambre de commerce du Canada; Corporation des Cadres des Chambres de commerce du Québec; Fédération des chambres de commerce du Québec
Finances: *Budget de fonctionnement annuel:* $100,000-$250,000
Membre(s) du personnel: 7; 15 bénévole(s)
Membre: 1,100; *Montant de la cotisation:* Barème; *Critères d'admissibilité:* Gens d'affaires et professionnels; *Comités:* ComaXAT
Activités: Gala; causeries; formation; promotion des membres; *Service de conférenciers:* Oui
Membre(s) du bureau directeur:
Julie Bouchard, Vice-présidente exéc. & Directrice générale, 819-797-2000 Ext. 222
julie.bouchard@ccirn.qc.ca
Publications:
• Bullxpress [publication de la Chambre de commerce et d'industrie de Rouyn-Noranda]

Chambre de commerce et d'industrie de Shawinigan
1635, 105e av, Shawinigan QC G9P 1M8
Tél: 819-536-0777; *Téléc:* 819-536-0039
info@ccishawinigan.ca
www.ccishawinigan.ca
www.linkedin.com/company/3266947
twitter.com/CCIShawinigan
Nom précédent: Chambre de commerce du Centre-de-la-Mauricie
Aperçu: Dimension: petite; *Envergure:* locale
Mission: Promouvoir et développer la région économique du Centre-de-la-Mauricie
Finances: *Budget de fonctionnement annuel:* Moins de $50,000
Membre: 100-499; *Montant de la cotisation:* 125-815; *Comités:* Programmation
Activités: *Stagiaires:* Oui
Membre(s) du bureau directeur:
Mario Lamontagne, Président
Martin St-Pierre, Directeur général
martin@ccishawinigan.ca

Chambre de commerce et d'industrie de Sorel-Tracy
67, rue George, Sorel-Tracy QC J3P 1C2

Tél: 450-742-0018; *Téléc:* 450-742-7442
www.ccstm.qc.ca
www.linkedin.com/groups/4147723
www.youtube.com/channel/UC2_SG-MoqKsusKJulFD6m5w
Aperçu: Dimension: petite; *Envergure:* locale
Mission: Promouvoir la liberté d'entreprendre; favorisant ainsi un environnement d'affaires innovant et concurrentiel
Membre: 400
Membre(s) du bureau directeur:
Sylvain Dupuis, Directeur général
sylvain.dupuis@ccist.ca

Chambre de commerce et d'industrie de St-Félicien *Voir* Chambre de commerce et d'industrie secteur Saint-Félicien inc.

Chambre de commerce et d'industrie de St-Joseph-de-Beauce
CP 5042, Saint-Joseph-de-Beauce QC G0S 2V0
Tél: 418-397-5980
admin@ccstjoseph.com
ccstjoseph.com
www.facebook.com/ccstjoseph
Aperçu: Dimension: petite; *Envergure:* locale
Membre: *Montant de la cotisation:* 80,48$
Membre(s) du bureau directeur:
Annie Thibeault, Coordonnatrice

Chambre de commerce et d'industrie de St-Laurent-Mont-Royal
#101, 5255, boul Henri-Bourassa, Montréal QC H4R 2M6
Tél: 514-333-5222; *Téléc:* 514-333-0937
info@ccsl-mr.com
www.ccsl-mr.com
Aperçu: Dimension: petite; *Envergure:* locale; Organisme sans but lucratif; fondée en 1981
Mission: De rassembler, informer et défendre les intérêts de ses membres
Membre de: Fédération des Chambres de Commerce du Québec
Membre(s) du personnel: 4
Membre: 385; *Montant de la cotisation:* Barème
Membre(s) du bureau directeur:
Sylvie Séguin, Directrice générale
seguins@ccsl-mr.com

Chambre de commerce et d'industrie de Thetford Mines (CCITM)
81, rue Notre-Dame ouest, Thetford Mines QC G6G 1J4
Tél: 418-338-4551; *Téléc:* 418-335-2066
www.ccitm.com
www.facebook.com/130888156958697
Également appelé: Chambre de commerce et d'industrie de l'Amiante
Aperçu: Dimension: petite; *Envergure:* locale
Mission: Promotion des intérêts des membres; Offre et analyse de services collectifs; susciter des initiatives bénéfiques à l'ensemble par la communication, l'information et la formation
Finances: *Budget de fonctionnement annuel:* $100,000-$250,000
Membre: *Montant de la cotisation:* Barème
Membre(s) du bureau directeur:
Louis Thivierge, Directeur général
dg.ccitm@bellnet.ca

Chambre de commerce et d'industrie de Varennes (CCIV)
2102, Marie-Victorin, #B, Varennes QC J3X 1R4
Tél: 450-652-4209; *Téléc:* 450-652-4244
info@cciv.ca
www.cciv.ca
Aperçu: Dimension: petite; *Envergure:* locale; fondée en 1952
Mission: De défendre les intérêts de ses membres afin de faire prospérer leur entreprise
Membre(s) du personnel: 1
Membre: 191; *Montant de la cotisation:* Barème
Membre(s) du bureau directeur:
Marie-Claude Lévesque, Directrice générale

Chambre de commerce et d'industrie des Bois-Francs et de l'Érable
122, rue de l'Acqueduc, Victoriaville QC G6P 1M3
Tél: 819-758-6371; *Téléc:* 819-758-4604
ccibf@ccibf.ca
www.ccibf.qc.ca
www.facebook.com/CCIBFE
twitter.com/ccibfe
www.youtube.com/ChambreCCIBFE

Nom précédent: Chambre de commerce des Bois-Francs
Aperçu: *Dimension:* petite; *Envergure:* locale; fondée en 1903
Mission: La Chambre de commerce et d'industrie des Bois-Francs et de l'Érable est, depuis 1903, un rassemblement volontaire et dynamique de dirigeant(e)s d'entreprise provenant de tous secteurs d'activité économique et de toute personne qui partage sa mission et sa vision. ®Ses membres ont pour mission commune d'initier, sous l'entité ®Chambre de commerce et d'industrie¯, des actions concertées favorisant le développement économique et social du groupe et de travailler ensemble à l'avancement des 35 municipalités des MRC d'Arthabaska et de l'Érable.
Membre(s) du personnel: 6
Membre: 1,464; *Montant de la cotisation:* Barème
Membre(s) du bureau directeur:
Josée Desharnais, Directrice générale
j.desharnais@ccibfe.com

Chambre de commerce et d'industrie du bassin de Chambly (CCIB)
929, boul de Périgny, Chambly QC J3L 5H5
Tél: 450-658-7598; *Téléc:* 450-658-3569
info@ccibc.qc.ca
www.ccibc.qc.ca
Aperçu: *Dimension:* petite; *Envergure:* locale
Mission: Développer, promouvoir et stimuler l'esprit commercial entre les membres, les villes et la collectivité
Finances: *Budget de fonctionnement annuel:* Moins de $50,000
Membre(s) du personnel: 1
Membre: 300
Membre(s) du bureau directeur:
Serge Gélinas, Directeur général

Chambre de Commerce et d'Industrie du Centre-Abitibi
644, 1e av ouest, Amos QC J9T 1V3
Tél: 819-732-8100; *Téléc:* 819-732-8131
info@ccica.ca
ccica.ca
www.linkedin.com/company/chambre-de-commerce-et-d%27ind ustrie-du-centre-abitibi
www.facebook.com/CCICentreAbitibi
twitter.com/ccicabitibi
Nom précédent: Chambre de commerce d'Amos-région
Aperçu: *Dimension:* petite; *Envergure:* locale
Mission: Chambre de commerce et d'industrie du Centre-Abitibi est la plus important rassemblement des gens d'affaires de la MRC Abitibi. En effet, la CCAR est un organisme regroupant 400 membres actifs en provenance de tous les milieux d'affaires: commerces, industries, professionnels, travailleurs autonomes et plus.
Membre(s) du personnel: 4
Membre: 398; *Montant de la cotisation:* Barème
Membre(s) du bureau directeur:
Joanne Breton, Directrice générale, 819-732-8100 Ext. 203
direction@ccica.ca

Chambre de commerce et d'industrie du Coeur-du-Québec
17905, boul des Acadiens, Bécancour QC G9H 1M4
Tél: 819-294-6010; *Téléc:* 819-294-6020
Ligne sans frais: 877-994-6010
info@ccicq.ca
www.ccicq.ca
Nom précédent: Chambre de commerce et d'industrie de Bécancour; Chambre de commerce de Bécancour
Aperçu: *Dimension:* petite; *Envergure:* locale; fondée en 1973
Mission: Favorise le développement d'un réseau d'affaires; la voix du milieu des affaires et de la communauté en matière de croissance et de réussite économiques; agit comme rassembleur et catalyseur des forces vives de l'économie locale
Membre(s) du bureau directeur:
Chantal Lafond, Présidente

Chambre de commerce et d'industrie du Haut St-Maurice
547-C, rue Commerciale, La Tuque QC G9X 3A7
Tél: 819-523-9933; *Téléc:* 819-523-9939
cchsm@lino.com
www.ccihsm.ca
Nom précédent: Chambre de commerce du Haut St-Maurice
Aperçu: *Dimension:* petite; *Envergure:* locale
Mission: Travaille au bien-être économique, civique et social du Haut-Saint-Maurice
Membre(s) du bureau directeur:
Mélanie Ricard, Présidente
Manon Côté, Directrice générale

Chambre de Commerce et d'industrie du Québec métropolitain *Voir* Chambre de commerce et d'industrie de Québec

Chambre de commerce et d'industrie du secteur Normandin
1048, rue St-Cyrille, Normandin QC G8M 4R9
Tél: 418-274-2004; *Téléc:* 418-274-7171
ccinormandin@hotmail.com
Aperçu: *Dimension:* petite; *Envergure:* locale
Membre: 70; *Critères d'admissibilité:* Commerçants; Entrepreneurs; Professionnels
Activités: *Evénements de sensibilisation:* Foire commerciale, aux années impaires
Membre(s) du bureau directeur:
Nicole Bilodeau, Directrice générale
ccinormandin@hotmail.com

Chambre de commerce et d'industrie du secteur Roberval
Voir Chambre de commerce et d'industrie de Roberval

Chambre de commerce et d'industrie du Sud-Ouest de Montréal
#32, 410, av Lafleur, Montréal QC H8R 3H6
Tél: 514-365-4575; *Téléc:* 514-365-0487
info@ccisom.ca
www.ccisom.ca
www.facebook.com/chambresudouest
Aperçu: *Dimension:* petite; *Envergure:* locale; fondée en 1952
Mission: Contribuer à la croissance économique de ses membres
Affiliation(s): Chambre de commerce du Canada; Fédération des Chambres de commerce du Québec
Membre(s) du personnel: 2
Membre: 397
Membre(s) du bureau directeur:
Bernard Blanchet, Directeur général

Chambre de commerce et d'industrie française au canada (CCIFC) / French Chamber of Commerce
#2B, 1455, rue Drummond, Montréal QC H3G 1W3
Tél: 514-281-1246; *Téléc:* 514-289-9594
info@ccifcmtl.ca
www.ccifcmtl.ca
www.linkedin.com/company/chambre-de-commerce-et-d%27ind ustrie-française-au-canada
www.facebook.com/147358495336342
twitter.com/CCIFCcanada
Aperçu: *Dimension:* moyenne; *Envergure:* internationale; Organisme sans but lucratif; fondée en 1886
Mission: Favoriser les échanges entre la France et le Canada; aider à trouver des partenaires
Membre de: Chambre de commerce du Québec
Membre(s) du personnel: 7
Membre: *Montant de la cotisation:* Barème; *Comités:* Membership; Ressources Humaines; Service d'Appui aux Entreprises; Convention d'affaires Canada-France; Publications; Déjeuners-Conférences; Tournoi de Golf; Grand Bal; Jeunes de la CCFC
Membre(s) du bureau directeur:
Véronique Loiseau, Directrice générale

Chambre de commerce et d'industrie Lac-Saint-Jean-Est
640, rue Côté-Ouest, Alma QC G8B 7S8
Tél: 418-662-2734; *Téléc:* 418-669-2220
cci@ccilacsaintjeanest.com
www.ccilacsaintjeanest.com
Aperçu: *Dimension:* petite; *Envergure:* locale; fondée en 1933
Membre(s) du personnel: 3
Membre: *Montant de la cotisation:* Barème
Membre(s) du bureau directeur:
Kathleen Voyer, Directrice générale
kvoyer@ccilacsaintjeanest.com

Chambre de commerce et d'industrie Magog-Orford
355, rue Principale ouest, Magog QC J1X 2B1
Tél: 819-843-3494; *Téléc:* 819-769-0292
info@ccimo.qc.ca
www.ccimagogorford.com
Aperçu: *Dimension:* petite; *Envergure:* locale
Mission: Promouvoir le développement de la communauté entrepreneuriale
Membre: *Montant de la cotisation:* Barème
Membre(s) du bureau directeur:
Louise Côté, Coprésidente
Éric Graveson, Coprésident

Chambre de commerce et d'industrie MRC de Deux-Montagne (CCI2M)
67A, boul Industriel, Saint-Eustache QC J7R 5B9
Tél: 450-491-1991; *Téléc:* 450-491-1648
info@chambrecommerce.com
www.chambrecommerce.com
www.linkedin.com/groups/3250810
twitter.com/CCI2M
Aperçu: *Dimension:* petite; *Envergure:* locale; Organisme sans but lucratif; fondée en 2014
Membre de: Association touristique des Basses Laurentides
Affiliation(s): Chambre de Commerce du Québec
Membre(s) du personnel: 6
Membre: 650; *Montant de la cotisation:* Barème; *Comités:* Évaluation de rendement des administrateurs et du directeur général; Financement; Mise en nomination des administrateurs; Offre de services; Recrutement de nouveaux membres; Relève; Vérification des politiques; Veille des intérêts d'affaires; Du verre à la fourchette 3e édition; La Classique des Gouverneurs 55e édition; Saveurs d'Oktobre; Soirée Encan; Projet IMPACC
Membre(s) du bureau directeur:
Mélanie Laroche, Directrice générale
mlaroche@cci2m.com

Chambre de commerce et d'industrie Nouvelle-Beauce (CCINB)
700, rue Notre-Dame nord, #C, Sainte-Marie QC G6E 2K9
Tél: 418-387-2006
Ligne sans frais: 866-387-2006
info@ccinb.ca
www.ccinb.ca
www.linkedin.com/company/chambre-de-commerce-et-d'industri e-nouvelle-beauce
www.facebook.com/ccinb
Aperçu: *Dimension:* petite; *Envergure:* locale; Organisme sans but lucratif; fondée en 1930
Mission: Réseautage d'entreprises, organisation d'activités pour les contacts commerciaux
Membre de: Fédération des Chambres de Commerce
Finances: *Budget de fonctionnement annuel:* $50,000-$100,000
Membre(s) du personnel: 2
Membre: 225; *Montant de la cotisation:* Barème; *Critères d'admissibilite:* Industriel et commerce
Activités: Business café; dîner conférence; activités de formation en entreprises; gala de reconnaissance
Membre(s) du bureau directeur:
Nancy Labbé, Directrice générale
nancy.labbe@ccinb.ca

Chambre de commerce et d'industrie Rimouski-Neigette
#101, 125, rue de l'Évêché ouest, Rimouski QC G5L 4H4
Tél: 418-722-4494; *Téléc:* 418-722-4494
info@ccrimouski.com
www.ccrimouski.com
www.facebook.com/233406713347742
Aperçu: *Dimension:* petite; *Envergure:* locale; Organisme sans but lucratif; fondée en 1908
Mission: Représenter les gens d'affaires rimouskois auprès des décideurs locaux, régionaux, provinciaux et nationaux; favoriser l'élaboration de nouvelles orientations de développement pour la région; favoriser les échanges fructueux entre nos membres
Membre: *Montant de la cotisation:* Brème; *Critères d'admissibilite:* Commerces, entreprises, travailleurs automnes, institutions; *Comités:* Table des Travailleurs autonomes; Table sur la relève entrepreneuriale; Table Affaire-Culture; Actions femmes et leadership
Membre(s) du bureau directeur:
Chantal Pilon, Présidente

Chambre de commerce et d'industrie secteur Saint-Félicien inc.
CP 34, 1209, boul Sacré-Coeur, Saint-Félicien QC G8K 2P8
Tél: 418-679-2097
fr-ca.facebook.com/chambredecommerce.saintfelicien
Nom précédent: Chambre de commerce et d'industrie de St-Félicien
Aperçu: *Dimension:* petite; *Envergure:* locale; Organisme sans but lucratif; fondée en 1950
Mission: Travailler au bien-être économique, civique et social de la ville de Saint-Félicien et au développement de ses ressources
Membre de: Fédération des chambres de commerce du Québec
Finances: *Budget de fonctionnement annuel:* $50,000-$100,000
Membre(s) du personnel: 2; 12 bénévole(s)

Membre: 125; *Montant de la cotisation:* Barème; *Critères d'admissibilité:* Commerces, industries, professionnels; *Comités:* Marketing; Communication; Développement; Finance
Activités: Colloque, formation, conférence, dîner; *Stagiaires:* Oui; *Service de conférenciers:* Oui; *Listes de destinataires:* Oui
Membre(s) du bureau directeur:
Marco Dallaire, Vice-président

Chambre de commerce et d'industrie St-Jérôme (CCISJ)
#20, 236, rue de Parent, Saint-Jérôme QC J7Z 1Z7
Tél: 450-431-4339; *Téléc:* 450-431-1677
www.ccisj.qc.ca
www.facebook.com/CCISJ
twitter.com/ccisj
Nom précédent: Chambre de commerce et d'industrie de la Rivière-Du-Nord
Aperçu: *Dimension:* petite; *Envergure:* locale; fondée en 1898
Mission: Voué à la promotion et à la prospérité du milieu des affaires; favorise la réussite des entreprises
Membre: *Montant de la cotisation:* Barème
Membre(s) du bureau directeur:
Michel Métivier, Directeur général
michel.metivier@ccisj.qc.ca

Chambre de commerce et d'industrie Thérèse-De Blainville (CCITB)
#202, 141, rue St-Charles, Sainte-Thérèse QC J7E 2A9
Tél: 450-435-8228; *Téléc:* 450-435-0820
info@ccitb.ca
www.ccitb.ca
www.linkedin.com/company/chambre-de-commerce-et-d-industrie-th-r-se-de-blainville
www.facebook.com/CCITB
twitter.com/laccitb
www.youtube.com/user/CCITB85
Aperçu: *Dimension:* petite; *Envergure:* locale
Membre de: Canadian Chamber of Commerce; Ontario Chamber of Commerce
Membre: 750; *Montant de la cotisation:* Barème; *Comités:* Affaires publiques; Gala Stellar; Golf; Gouvernance; Huîtres; Midis d'affaires; Perspectives; Vérification
Membre(s) du bureau directeur:
Cynthia Kabis, Directrice générale

Chambre de commerce et d'industrie Vaudreuil-Soulanges
450, rue Aimé-Vincent, 2e étage, Vaudreuil-Dorion QC J7V 5V5
Tél: 450-424-6886; *Téléc:* 450-424-4989
info@ccivs.ca
www.ccivs.ca
Aperçu: *Dimension:* petite; *Envergure:* locale
Mission: Favoriser le développement d'un réseau d'affaires représentatif, fort et engagé
Membre(s) du personnel: 1
Membre: 370+; *Montant de la cotisation:* Barème; *Comités:* Aménagement du territoire; Commandite; Budget-Comptabilité; Service aux membres/Développement des affaires/Industriel/Logement abordable; Gala; Golf; Jeunesse; Rayonnement régional/Grands dossiers régionaux; S.A.A.Q.; Hôpital; Vaudreuil-Dorion; Informatique; Tourisme, Culture et Art
Membre(s) du bureau directeur:
Nadine Lachance, Directrice générale

Chambre de commerce et d'industries de Trois-Rivières
CP 1045, #200, 225, rue des Forges, Trois-Rivières QC G9A 5K4
Tél: 819-375-9628; *Téléc:* 819-375-9083
info@ccitr.net
www.ccitr.net
www.facebook.com/158875090821998
Nom précédent: Chambre de Commerce du district de Trois-Rivières
Aperçu: *Dimension:* petite; *Envergure:* locale; fondée en 1881
Mission: Défendre les entreprises privées et d'améliorer la communauté
Membre de: Chambre de Commerce du Québec
Membre(s) du personnel: 6
Membre: 900; *Montant de la cotisation:* Barème; *Critères d'admissibilité:* Gens d'affaires; *Comités:* Stratégie Vigie; Soirée de dégustation Les vins du monde; Gala Radisson; Cocktail du Nouvel An; Séduction; Entrepreneuriat; Tournoi de golf
Activités: Déjeuner P.M.E.; Midi Causerie; formation; colloque; *Service de conférenciers:* Oui; *Bibliothèque:* Bibliothèque publique
Membre(s) du bureau directeur:

Marie-Pier Matteau, Directrice générale
mpmatteau@ccitr.net

Chambre de commerce et de tourisme de Gaspé
27, boul de York est, Gaspé QC G4X 2K9
Tél: 418-368-8525
info@cctgaspe.org
cctgaspe.org
www.facebook.com/chambredecommerceetdetourismedegaspe
Aperçu: *Dimension:* petite; *Envergure:* locale; Organisme sans but lucratif
Mission: Défendre les intérêts des membres et promouvoir l'activité économique
Membre de: Fédération des chambres de commerce du Québec
Membre(s) du personnel: 3
Membre: *Critères d'admissibilité:* Gens d'affaires; *Comités:* Label Qualité; Achat local - Gaspé; Affaires municipales; élève entrepreneuriale de La Côte-de-Gaspé; Local d'emploi et de main-d'ouvre (CLEMO); Revitalisation de Rivière-au-Renard; Pilotage des forums sur les hydrocarbures; Tourisme de la Fédération des Chambres de commerce du Québec (FCCQ)
Membre(s) du bureau directeur:
Olivier Nolleau, Directeur général
direction@cctgaspe.org

Chambre de commerce et de tourisme de la Vallée de Saint-Sauveur/Piedmont
30, rue Filion, Saint-Sauveur QC J0R 1R0
Tél: 450-227-2564; *Téléc:* 450-227-6480
Ligne sans frais: 877-528-2553
info@valleesaintsauveur.com
www.valleesaintsauveur.com
Nom précédent: Chambre de Commerce de la Vallée de St-Sauveur
Aperçu: *Dimension:* petite; *Envergure:* locale
Mission: Promouvoir la Vallée de Saint-Sauveur auprès des visiteurs
Membre(s) du bureau directeur:
Pierre Urquhart, Directeur général

Chambre de commerce et de tourisme de St-Adolphe-d'Howard
c/o Imagine Coiffure, #201, 1937, ch du Village, Saint-Adolphe-d'Howard QC J0T 2B0
Tél: 819-327-3845
www.st-adolphe.com
Aperçu: *Dimension:* petite; *Envergure:* locale
Mission: Promouvoir l'intérêt socio-économique de nos commerçants et travailleurs autonomes
Membre(s) du bureau directeur:
Michèle Nihoul, Présidente

Chambre de commerce et du tourisme du Grand Caraquet
1-39, boul St-Pierre ouest, Caraquet NB E1W 1B6
Tél: 506-727-2931; *Téléc:* 506-727-3191
info@chambregrandcaraquet.com
www.chambregrandcaraquet.com
Aperçu: *Dimension:* petite; *Envergure:* locale; fondée en 1937
Mission: La Chambre de commerce du Grand Caraquet a comme mission de participer au développement économique de toute la région et donc de favoriser la prospérité de gens d'affaires et l'essor de leurs entreprises
Membre(s) du personnel: 1
Membre: *Montant de la cotisation:* Barème
Membre(s) du bureau directeur:
Claude L'Espérance, Président
Véronique Savoie, Directrice générale

Chambre de commerce et industrie Mont-Joli-Mitis
CP 183, 1553, boul Jacques-Cartier, Mont-Joli QC G5H 3K9
Tél: 418-775-4366
info@ccimontjolimitis.com
www.ccimontjolimitis.com
Aperçu: *Dimension:* petite; *Envergure:* locale; fondée en 1930
Membre(s) du bureau directeur:
Pierre-Luc Harrison, Président
presidence@ccimontjolimitis.com

Chambre de commerce française au Canada - Section Québec
#400, 1020, rue Bouvier, Québec QC G2K 0K9
Tél: 418-522-3434; *Téléc:* 418-522-0045
info@ccfcquebec.ca
www.ccifcquebec.ca
www.linkedin.com/groups?trk=myg_ugrp_ovr&gid=2412719
facebook.com/147358495336342
twitter.com/ccifcquebec
ccfcquebec.wordpress.com
Aperçu: *Dimension:* petite; *Envergure:* provinciale
Mission: A pour mandat le développement des relations économiques entre la France et le Canada
Membre: *Montant de la cotisation:* Barème
Membre(s) du bureau directeur:
Jonathan Decherf, Président

Chambre de commerce francophone de Saint-Boniface (CCFSB) / St-Boniface Chamber of Commerce
CP 204, Saint-Boniface MB R2H 3B4
Tél: 204-235-1406; *Téléc:* 204-237-4618
info@ccfsb.mb.ca
www.ccfsb.mb.ca
www.facebook.com/ccfsb.saintboniface
twitter.com/ccfsbstboniface
Aperçu: *Dimension:* petite; *Envergure:* locale; Organisme sans but lucratif
Mission: Favoriser, d'améliorer et de promouvoir l'industrie, le développement, le commerce et le bien-être civique, social et économique régional
Membre(s) du personnel: 1; 11 bénévole(s)
Membre: 150; *Montant de la cotisation:* Barème
Membre(s) du bureau directeur:
Paulette Desaulniers, Executive Director

Chambre de commerce francophone de Vancouver (CCFC)
1555, 7e av ouest, Vancouver BC V6J 1S1
Tél: 604-601-2124
info@ccfvancouver.com
ccfvancouver.com
www.linkedin.com/company/chambre-de-commerce-francophone-de-vancouver
www.facebook.com/ccfvancouver
twitter.com/ccfvancouver
Aperçu: *Dimension:* petite; *Envergure:* locale; fondée en 1983
Mission: Organisme à but non-lucratif dont le mandat est de développer et d'améliorer les rapports commerciaux entre gens d'affaires d'expression française en Colombie-Britannique
Membre: *Montant de la cotisation:* 95-350
Membre(s) du bureau directeur:
Daniel Wang, Président
daniel_wang@cooperators.ca

Chambre de commerce Haute-Yamaska et Région (CCHYR)
650, rue Principale, Granby QC J2G 8L4
Tél: 450-372-6100; *Téléc:* 450-696-1119
info@cchyr.com
www.cchyr.ca
www.facebook.com/ChambreCommerceHauteYamaskaEtRegion
Nom précédent: Chambre de commerce du district de Granby-Bromont
Aperçu: *Dimension:* petite; *Envergure:* locale; fondée en 1900
Membre de: FCCQ
Membre: 700; *Montant de la cotisation:* Barème
Activités: *Service de conférenciers:* Oui; *Bibliothèque* Not open to public
Membre(s) du bureau directeur:
Sylvain Perron, Président

Chambre de commerce Hemmingford—Napierville—Saint-Rémi *Voir* Chambre de commerce des Jardins de Napierville

Chambre de commerce Indo-Canada *See* Indo-Canada Chamber of Commerce

Chambre de commerce juive *See* Jewish Chamber of Commerce

Chambre de commerce Kamouraska-L'Islet (CCKL)
#208, 1000 - 6e av, La Pocatière QC G0R 1Z0
Tél: 418-856-6227; *Téléc:* 418-856-6462
Ligne sans frais: 877-856-6227
cckl@qc.aira.com
www.cckl.org
Nom précédent: Chambre de Commerce la Pocatière
Aperçu: *Dimension:* petite; *Envergure:* locale; fondée en 1959
Mission: Regrouper des gens d'affaires ou des gens concernés par des activités commerciales sur son territoire; les représenter, leur assurer des services de liaison et faire le suivi des dossiers que lui confie l'assemblée de ses membres et/ou le conseil

d'administration; faire des représentations nécessaires auprès de toutes instances afin de défendre et promouvoir les points de vue de la Chambre, tout en respectant les priorités d'intervention que lui dicte l'assemblée des membres.
Membre de: Fédération des Chambres de commerce du Québec
Finances: *Budget de fonctionnement annuel:* $100,000-$250,000
Membre(s) du personnel: 2
Membre: 384; *Montant de la cotisation:* Barème; *Critères d'admissibilite:* Gens d'affaires
Activités: Déjeuners, dîners et soupers conférence; vins et fromages; tournois de golf; galas; colloques
Membre(s) du bureau directeur:
Élizabeth Hudon, Présidente

Chambre de commerce Kent-Sud
27, ch Michel, Grand-Digue NB E4R 4V9
Tél: 506-861-1454
www.kentsud.ca
Nom précédent: Chambre de commerce de Cocagne, Notre-Dame et Grande-Digue
Aperçu: *Dimension:* petite; *Envergure:* locale
Membre: 36
Membre(s) du bureau directeur:
Jacques Robichaud, Président

Chambre de Commerce la Pocatière *Voir* Chambre de commerce Kamouraska-L'Islet

Chambre de commerce Latino-américaine du Québec (CCLAQ)
#102, 5333, av Casgrain, Montréal QC H2T 1X3
Tél: 514-400-8969
info@cclaq.ca
www.cclaq.ca
ca.linkedin.com/in/cclaq
www.facebook.com/CCLAQ.CA
twitter.com/CCLAQ
plus.google.com/113923936639158701998/posts
Aperçu: *Dimension:* petite; *Envergure:* provinciale
Mission: Favoriser le développement socio-économique de la communauté latino-américaine du Québec
Membre: *Critères d'admissibilité:* Des personnes issus de la communauté latino-américaine et québécoises qui oeuvrent au sein d'entreprises établies au Québec
Membre(s) du bureau directeur:
Oscar Ramirez, Président

Chambre de commerce LGBT du Québec (CCLGBTQ) / The Québec LGBT Chamber of Commerce
#303.3, 372, rue Sainte-Catherine ouest, Montréal QC H3B 1A2
Tél: 514-522-1885
info@cclgbtq.org
www.cclgbtq.org
Aperçu: *Dimension:* petite; *Envergure:* locale; fondée en 1997
Mission: Défendre et promouvoir les intérêts de la communauté lesbienne et gaie d'affaires du Québec et favoriser le rayonnement de ses membres
Membre de: Fédération chambres de commerce du Québec
Finances: *Fonds:* Variées
Membre(s) du personnel: 2
Membre: 600+; *Montant de la cotisation:* Barème; *Critères d'admissibilite:* Professionnel; commerçant
Activités: Activités de réseautage; Conférence déjeuner; *Service de conférenciers:* Oui
Membre(s) du bureau directeur:
Steve Foster, Président
Prix, Bourses:
• Prix Phenicia

Chambre de commerce Mont-Saint-Bruno (CCMSB)
CP 123, Saint-Bruno QC J3V 4P8
Tél: 450-653-0585; *Téléc:* 450-653-6967
info@ccstbruno.ca
www.ccstbruno.ca
Nom précédent: Chambre de commerce de Saint-Bruno
Aperçu: *Dimension:* petite; *Envergure:* locale; fondée en 1956
Mission: Promouvoir et développer l'économie locale; représenter les membres devant les instances gouvernementales, municipales et commerciales; participer au bien-être économique, civique et social
Affiliation(s): Chambre de commerce du Québec; Chambre de commerce du Canada
Finances: *Budget de fonctionnement annuel:* Moins de $50,000

Membre: 200; *Montant de la cotisation:* 145$; *Critères d'admissibilite:* Autonomes; industries; commerces; professionnels
Activités: Conférences; tournoi de golf; gala du mérite économique, critérium cycliste
Membre(s) du bureau directeur:
Daniel Tousignant, CGA, Président
dan.tousignant@videotron.ca
Denis Lamothe, Directeur général

Chambre de commerce MRC du Rocher-Percé
#121-2, 129, boul René-Levesque ouest, Chandler QC G0C 1K0
Tél: 418-689-6998
ccrocherperce@gmail.com
www.ccrocherperce.org
www.facebook.com/ccrrocherperce
Aperçu: *Dimension:* petite; *Envergure:* locale; fondée en 1960
Mission: Représente les gens d'affaires du territoire de la MRC Rocher-Percé
Membre(s) du personnel: 1
Membre: 1-99; *Montant de la cotisation:* Barème
Membre(s) du bureau directeur:
Sandrine Rampeneaux, Présidente

Chambre de commerce Notre-Dame-du-Nord
3, rue Principale sud, Notre-Dame-du-Nord QC J0Z 3B0
Tél: 819-723-2586
Aperçu: *Dimension:* petite; *Envergure:* locale; fondée en 1949

Chambre de commerce Pierre-Le Gardeur De Repentigny
Voir Chambre de commerce de la MRC de L'Assomption

Chambre de commerce région de Matane
CP 518, Matane QC G4W 3P5
Tél: 418-562-9344
info@ccmatane.com
www.ccmatane.com
www.facebook.com/ccmatane
Aperçu: *Dimension:* petite; *Envergure:* locale
Mission: La Chambre de commerce - région de Matane est un groupe de personnes qui ont l'habilité de planifier, l'intelligence d'initier, le courage d'énoncer et l'énergie d'exécuter tout ce qui est susceptible d'améliorer la santé, le bien-être, la culture et le développement économique des gens d'affaires et des citoyens de la MRC
Membre(s) du personnel: 1
Membre: 239; *Montant de la cotisation:* Barème
Membre(s) du bureau directeur:
Marc Charest, Président

Chambre de commerce région de Mégantic
4336, rue Laval, Lac-Mégantic QC G6B 1B8
Tél: 819-583-5392
info@ccrmeg.com
www.ccrmeg.com
Aperçu: *Dimension:* petite; *Envergure:* locale; fondée en 1909
Mission: Contribuer au développement de la région du Granit en faisant la promotion de l'entrepreneuriat en en supportant son essor et son dynamisme
Membre de: Chambre de Commerce du Canada; Fédération des Chambres de Commerce du Québec; Chambre de Commerce Régional de l'Estrie
Membre: 249; *Critères d'admissibilite:* Entreprises locales
Membre(s) du bureau directeur:
Marc-Olivier Gagnon, Président

Chambre de commerce régional de Campbellton *See* Campbellton Regional Chamber of Commerce

Chambre de commerce régionale de St-Raymond (CCRSR)
#100, 1, av St-Jacques, Saint-Raymond QC G3L 3Y1
Tél: 418-337-4049; *Téléc:* 418-337-8017
ccrsr@cite.net
www.ccrsr.qc.ca
Nom précédent: Chambre de Commerce de St-Raymond
Aperçu: *Dimension:* petite; *Envergure:* locale; fondée en 1967
Mission: De soutenir et appuyer ses membres commerçants, entrepreneurs, gens d'affaires et individus évoluant dans le milieu des affaires de Saint-Raymond, Saint-Léonard et de Rivière-à-Pierre
Membre: 171
Membre(s) du bureau directeur:
Jean-François Drolet, Président

Chambre de commerce régionale de Windsor
CP 115, Windsor QC J1S 2L7

Tél: 819-434-5936
info@ccrwindsor.com
www.ccrwindsor.com
Aperçu: *Dimension:* petite; *Envergure:* locale
Mission: Pour aider à développer le commerce dans la région de Windsor afin que leurs membres sont en mesure de prospérer
Membre: 100; *Montant de la cotisation:* 103,48$
Membre(s) du bureau directeur:
Serge Ranger, Président

Chambre de commerce Ste-Émélie-de-l'Énergie
400, rue St-Michel, Sainte-Émélie-de-l'Énergie QC J0K 2K0
Tél: 450-886-1658
Aperçu: *Dimension:* petite; *Envergure:* locale

Chambre de commerce Saint-Lin-Laurentides
#101, 704, rue St-Isidore, Saint-Lin-Laurentides QC J5M 2V2
Tél: 450-439-3704; *Téléc:* 450-439-2066
Aperçu: *Dimension:* petite; *Envergure:* locale
Membre(s) du bureau directeur:
André Corbeil, Président

Chambre de commerce secteur ouest de Portneuf
150, rue Joseph, Saint-Marc-des-Carrières QC G0A 4B0
Tél: 418-268-5447
ccsop@portneufouest.com
www.portneufouest.com
Aperçu: *Dimension:* petite; *Envergure:* locale
Mission: De promouvoir et de soutenir ses membres
Membre(s) du personnel: 3
Membre: 132; *Montant de la cotisation:* Barème
Membre(s) du bureau directeur:
Pascal Lemercier, Communication et services aux membres

Chambre de commerce St-Félix de Valois
5306, rue Principale, Saint-Félix-de-Valois QC J0K 2M0
Tél: 450-889-8161; *Téléc:* 450-889-1590
ccst-flx@stfelixdevalois.qc.ca
www.stfelixdevalois.qc.ca
Aperçu: *Dimension:* petite; *Envergure:* locale; Organisme sans but lucratif; fondée en 1969
Mission: Travailler au bien-être économique, civique et social de Saint-Félix-de-Valois
Membre(s) du personnel: 2
Membre: 167; *Critères d'admissibilite:* Entrepreneurs; industrie; aviculteurs; agriculteurs
Activités: Souper des fêtes et membres honorifiques; conférences-causeries, amicale de golf; *Stagiaires:* Oui; *Service de conférenciers:* Oui; *Bibliothèque*
Membre(s) du bureau directeur:
Johanne Dufresne, Directrice générale

Chambre de commerce St-Jean-de-Matha
185, rue Laurent, Saint-Jean-de-Matha QC J0K 2S0
Tél: 450-886-0599; *Téléc:* 450-886-3123
info@chambrematha.com
www.chambrematha.com
Aperçu: *Dimension:* petite; *Envergure:* locale; fondée en 1973
Mission: Travailler à la promotion de ses membres, ainsi qu'au développement commercial, culturel et social de son village
Membre de: Fédération des Chambres de Commerce du Québec
Membre: 108
Membre(s) du bureau directeur:
Steve Adam, Président par intérim
Mélanie Paquin, Directrice
melanie.paquin@chambrematha.com

Chambre de commerce St-Martin de Beauce
CP 2022, 131, 1e av est, Saint-Martin QC G0M 1B0
Tél: 418-382-5549
chambre@st-martin.qc.ca
www.st-martin.qc.ca
Aperçu: *Dimension:* petite; *Envergure:* locale; Organisme sans but lucratif; fondée en 1985
Mission: Travailler au développement économique civique et social de la localité de St-Martin-De-Beauce
Affiliation(s): Chambre de commerce du Québec; Chambre de commerce du Canada
Activités: *Listes de destinataires:* Oui
Membre(s) du bureau directeur:
Pascal Bergeron, Président

Chambre de commerce Témis-Accord
1E, rue Notre-Dame, Ville-Marie QC J9V 1W3
Tél: 819-629-2918
dg@temis-accord.com

www.temis-accord.com
www.facebook.com/chambredecommerce.temisaccord
Aperçu: *Dimension:* petite; *Envergure:* locale; Organisme sans but lucratif; fondée en 1908
Mission: Est un groupe de personnes qui ont l'habilité de planifier, l'intelligence d'initier, le courage de dénoncer et d'exécuter tout ce qui est susceptible d'améliorer la santé, le bien-être, la culture et le développement économique des citoyens et des gens d'affaires du Témiscamingue
Membre(s) du bureau directeur:
Véronic Girard, Co-Présidente
Alexandre Touzin, Co-Président

Chambre de commerce Témiscaming-Kipawa (CCTK)
CP 442, 15, rue Principale, Kipawa QC J0Z 2H0
Tél: 819-627-6160
cctk.info@gmail.com
www.temiscaming.net
Aperçu: *Dimension:* petite; *Envergure:* locale
Mission: Promouvoir et encourager le développement économique
Membre de: Chambre de commerce du Québec
Membre(s) du bureau directeur:
Guylaine Létourneau, Présidente

Chambre de commerce Vallée de la Missisquoi
Rte 245, Bolton Centre QC J0E 1G0
Tél: 450-292-4217; *Téléc:* 450-292-4224
Aperçu: *Dimension:* petite; *Envergure:* locale; fondée en 1989
Mission: Promouvoir la région et ses commerces; encourager la venue de nouveaux commerces; encourager et accueillir les jeunes entrepreneurs
Membre de: Chambre de commerce du Québec
Finances: *Budget de fonctionnement annuel:* $50,000-$100,000

Chambre de commerce Vallée de la Petite-Nation
185, rue Henri-Bourassa, Papineauville QC J0V 1R0
Tél: 819-427-8450
direction.ccvpn@videotron.ca
www.ccvpn.org
Aperçu: *Dimension:* petite; *Envergure:* locale
Mission: Pour stimuler l'économie et la croissance des entreprises locales à travers des projets d'intérêt commun
Membre(s) du personnel: 2
Membre: 150; *Montant de la cotisation:* 100$ travailleur autonome/entreprise de moins de 3 ans d'existenc; 180$ entreprise de plus de 3 ans d'existence
Membre(s) du bureau directeur:
Jean Careau, Directeur général

Chambre de Commerce Vallée du Richelieu *Voir* Chambre de commerce et d'industrie de la Vallée-du-Richelieu

Chambre de l'assurance de dommages (CHAD)
#1200, 999, boul de Maisonneuve ouest, Montréal QC H3A 3L4
Tél: 514-842-2591; *Téléc:* 514-842-3138
Ligne sans frais: 800-361-7288
info@chad.qc.ca
www.chad.ca
www.linkedin.com/company/2579212
Nom précédent: Association des courtiers d'assurances de la Province de Québec
Aperçu: *Dimension:* grande; *Envergure:* provinciale; Organisme de réglementation; fondée en 1999
Mission: Assurer la protection du public en matière d'assurance de dommages et d'expertise en règlement de sinistres; encadrer de façon préventive et disciplinaire la pratique professionnelle des individus et des organisations oeuvrant dans ces domaines
Finances: *Budget de fonctionnement annuel:* $1.5 Million-$3 Million
Membre(s) du personnel: 34
Membre: 14 500+; *Critères d'admissibilité:* Agents; courtiers; experts en sinistre; *Comités:* Déontologie et de règles de pratique; Discipline; Gouvernance et d'éthique; Nomination; Vérification; Développement professionnel; Affaires de régulation
Activités: *Service de conférenciers:* Oui
Membre(s) du bureau directeur:
Diane Beaudry, CPA, CA, ICD.D., Chair
Maya Raic, MBA, M. Sc. pol, Présidente-directrice générale
Prix, Bourses:
• Le prix Marcel-Tassé

Chambre de la sécurité financière (CSF)
300, rue Léo-Pariseau, 26e étage, Montréal QC H2X 4B8
Tél: 514-282-5777; *Téléc:* 514-282-2225
Ligne sans frais: 800-361-9989

renseignements@chambresf.com
www.chambresf.com
www.linkedin.com/company/1004475
www.facebook.com/ChambreSF
twitter.com/ChambreSF
www.youtube.com/chambresf
Nom précédent: Association des intermédiaires en assurance de personnes du Québec
Aperçu: *Dimension:* moyenne; *Envergure:* provinciale; Organisme sans but lucratif; fondée en 1999
Mission: Assurer la protection du public en maintenant la discipline et en veillant à la formation et à la déontologie de ses membres
Finances: *Budget de fonctionnement annuel:* Plus de $5 Million
Membre(s) du personnel: 50; 320 bénévole(s)
Membre: 32 000; *Montant de la cotisation:* 275$; *Critères d'admissibilite:* Exerçant dans les disciplines suivantes: l'assurance de personnes; l'assurance collective de personnes; la planification financière; le courtage en épargne collective; le courtage en plans de bourses d'études; *Comités:* Discipline; Réglementation; Gouvernance; Sections; Vérification et finances; Formation et développement professionnel; Relève
Activités: Assemblée générale annuelle; camp de formation
Membre(s) du bureau directeur:
Luc Labelle, Président et chef de la direction

Chambre des huissiers de justice du Québec (CHJQ)
#970, 507, Place-d'Armes, Montréal QC H2Y 2W8
Tél: 514-721-1100; *Téléc:* 514-721-7878
Ligne sans frais: 800-500-7022
chjq@chjq.ca
www.huissiersquebec.qc.ca
Aperçu: *Dimension:* petite; *Envergure:* provinciale
Mission: La Chambre a pour principale fonction d'assurer la protection du public. A cette fin, elle doit notamment contrôler l'exercice de la profession par ses membres
Finances: *Budget de fonctionnement annuel:* $500,000-$1.5 Million
Membre(s) du personnel: 9
Membre: *Comités:* La formation professionnelle et la formation continue obligatoire; Les normes d'équivalence pour la délivrance d'un permis; Conciliation et arbitrage des comptes d'honoraires; Conseil de discipline; Inspection professionnelle; Révision; La réforme du tarif
Membre(s) du bureau directeur:
André Bizier, Président/Directeur général par intérim
president@chjq.ca

Chambre des notaires du Québec
#600, 1801, av McGill College, Montréal QC H3A 0A7
Tél: 514-879-1793; *Téléc:* 514-879-1923
Ligne sans frais: 800-263-1793
www.cnq.org
www.youtube.com/user/ChambreDesNotaires
Également appelé: Ordre des notaires du Québec
Aperçu: *Dimension:* moyenne; *Envergure:* provinciale; Organisme de réglementation; fondée en 1847
Mission: D'assurer principalement la protection du public utilisateur des services professionnels de notaire
Membre de: Union internationale du notariat latin
Affiliation(s): Fédération des professions juridiques
Membre: *Critères d'admissibilité:* Stage de la CNQ; *Comités:* Consultatif du Centre d'expertise en droit immobilier; Consultatif en droit des personnes, de la famille et des successions; D'arbitrage des comptes d'honoraires des notaires; Gouvernance et d'éthique de la Chambre des notaires du Québec; Formation continue; Formation des notaires; Législation; Placements; Réglementation; Révision; Sélection pour le programme de bourses d'études supérieures; Vérification et prospectives financières; Communications; Inspection professionnelle; Fonds d'études notariales; Fonds d'indemnisation; Régime de retraite; Exercice illégal de la profession de notaire
Activités: *Stagiaires:* Oui; *Service de conférenciers:* Oui; *Bibliothèque* Not open to public
Membre(s) du bureau directeur:
Christian Tremblay, Directeur général

Chambre du commerce maritime *See* Chamber of Marine Commerce

Chambre immobilière Centre du Québec Inc.
445, rue Brock, Drummondville QC J2B 1E2
Tél: 819-477-1033; *Téléc:* 819-474-7913
Ligne sans frais: 877-546-8320

chambre@cgocable.ca
www.immobiliercentreduquebec.com
Aperçu: *Dimension:* moyenne; *Envergure:* locale surveillé par Fédération des Chambres immobilières du Québec
Membre de: The Canadian Real Estate Association
Membre(s) du bureau directeur:
Nathalie Bisson, Présidente

Chambre immobilière de l'Abitibi-Témiscamingue Inc. (CIAT)
#203, 33, av Horne, Rouyn-Noranda QC J9X 4S1
Tél: 819-762-1777; *Téléc:* 819-762-4030
ciat@cablevision.qc.ca
www.ciat.qc.ca
Aperçu: *Dimension:* petite; *Envergure:* locale; Organisme sans but lucratif; fondée en 1985 surveillé par Fédération des Chambres immobilières du Québec
Membre de: The Canadian Real Estate Association
Membre: 58 courtiers
Membre(s) du bureau directeur:
Robert Brière, Président
robertbbriere@royallepage.ca
Gilles Langlais, Directeur général

Chambre immobilière de l'Estrie inc.
19, rue King ouest, Sherbrooke QC J1H 1N4
Tél: 819-566-7616; *Téléc:* 819-566-7688
info@mon-toit.net
www.mon-toit.net
Aperçu: *Dimension:* moyenne; *Envergure:* locale surveillé par Fédération des Chambres immobilières du Québec
Mission: Promouvoir et protéger les intérêts de l'industrie immobilière du Québec afin que les Chambres et les membres accomplissent avec succès leurs objectifs d'affaires.
Membre de: The Canadian Real Estate Association
Membre(s) du bureau directeur:
Lucien Choquette, Président

Chambre immobilière de l'Outaouais
106, boul Sacré-Coeur, Gatineau QC J8X 1E1
Tél: 819-771-5221; *Téléc:* 819-771-8715
info@avecunagent.com
www.avecunagent.com
www.facebook.com/104740336281495
twitter.com/avecuncourtier
Aperçu: *Dimension:* petite; *Envergure:* locale surveillé par Fédération des Chambres immobilières du Québec
Mission: De fournir à ses membres les outils nécessaires pour réussir
Membre de: The Canadian Real Estate Association
Membre: 500; *Comités:* Activités récréatives; Formation; Révision des Règlements et Politiques; Action politique; Communication et visibilité
Membre(s) du bureau directeur:
Chantal Legault, Directrice générale

Chambre immobilière de la Haute Yamaska Inc. (CIHY) / Haute Yamaska Real Estate Board
#3, 45, rue Centre, Granby QC J2G 5B4
Tél: 450-378-6702; *Téléc:* 450-375-5268
administration.cihy@videotron.ca
Aperçu: *Dimension:* petite; *Envergure:* locale; fondée en 1984 surveillé par Fédération des Chambres immobilières du Québec
Mission: Offrir des services de formation et d'information pour les agents immobiliers.
Membre de: The Canadian Real Estate Association
Membre(s) du bureau directeur:
Lise Desrochers, Directrice générale

Chambre immobilière de la Mauricie Inc. / Trois-Rivières Real Estate Board
1275, boul des Forges, Trois-Rivières QC G8Z 1T7
Tél: 819-379-9081; *Téléc:* 819-379-9262
info@cimauricie.com
www.cimauricie.com
Aperçu: *Dimension:* moyenne; *Envergure:* locale; Organisme sans but lucratif; fondée en 1962 surveillé par Fédération des Chambres immobilières du Québec
Membre de: The Canadian Real Estate Association
Membre(s) du personnel: 2
Membre: 1,200; *Critères d'admissibilite:* Détenir un certificat d'agent ou de courtier immobilier
Activités: *Service de conférenciers:* Oui
Membre(s) du bureau directeur:
Lise Girardeau, Directrice générale
cimauricie@cgocable.ca

Chambre immobilière de Lanaudière Inc.
765, boul Manseau, Joliette QC J6E 3E8
Tél: 450-759-8511; *Téléc:* 450-759-6557
cil@immobilierlanaudiere.com
www.immobilierlanaudiere.com
Aperçu: Dimension: moyenne; *Envergure:* locale; fondée en 1982 surveillé par Fédération des Chambres immobilières du Québec
Membre de: The Canadian Real Estate Association
Membre(s) du personnel: 1
Membre: 160
Membre(s) du bureau directeur:
Louise Renaud, Directrice générale

Chambre immobilière de Québec
600, ch du Golf, Ile-des-Soeurs QC H3E 1A8
Tél: 514-762-0212; *Téléc:* 514-762-0365
Ligne sans frais: 866-882-0212
info@fciq.ca
www.fciq.ca
twitter.com/fciq_eco
Nom précédent: Chambre d'immeubles de Québec
Aperçu: Dimension: moyenne; *Envergure:* locale surveillé par Fédération des Chambres immobilières du Québec
Mission: Promouvoir et protéger les intérêts de l'industrie immobilière du Québec afin que les Chambres et les membres accomplissent avec succès leurs objectifs d'affaires.
Membre de: The Canadian Real Estate Association
Membre: 12 chambres immobilières; *Critères d'admissibilite:* Chambres immobilières
Membre(s) du bureau directeur:
Gina Gaudreault, Président

Chambre immobilière de Saint-Hyacinthe Inc.
CP 667, Saint-Hyacinthe QC J2S 7P5
Tél: 450-799-2210; *Téléc:* 450-799-2230
chimmob@cgocable.ca
www.chambreimmobilieresthyacinthe.com
Aperçu: Dimension: petite; *Envergure:* locale; fondée en 1984 surveillé par Fédération des Chambres immobilières du Québec
Mission: Promouvoir et protéger les intérêts de l'industrie immobilière du Québec afin que les Chambres et les membres accomplissent avec succès leurs objectifs d'affaires.
Membre de: The Canadian Real Estate Association
Membre: 100
Membre(s) du bureau directeur:
Pierre Tanguay, Président

Chambre immobilière des Laurentides (CIL)
570, boul des Laurentides, Piedmont QC J0R 1K0
Tél: 450-240-0006
Ligne sans frais: 800-263-3511
info@cilaurentides.ca
www.cilaurentides.ca
www.facebook.com/OptionLaurentides
Également appelé: Un PRO du Nord
Aperçu: Dimension: petite; *Envergure:* locale; Organisme sans but lucratif; fondée en 1982 surveillé par Fédération des Chambres immobilières du Québec
Mission: De promouvoir et à développer des intérêts professionnels, économiques et sociaux de ses membres
Membre de: The Canadian Real Estate Association
Membre: 600 courtiers et agents immobiliers; *Critères d'admissibilite:* Courtiers et agents immobiliers de la région
Membre(s) du bureau directeur:
Francine Soucy, Présidente
fsoucy@immobilierlaurentien.com
Daniel Vandal, Directrice générale

Chambre immobilière du Grand Montréal / Greater Montréal Real Estate Board
600, ch du Golf, Ile-des-Soeurs QC H3E 1A8
Tél: 514-762-2440; *Téléc:* 514-762-1854
Ligne sans frais: 888-762-2440
cigm@cigm.qc.ca
www.cigm.qc.ca
Aperçu: Dimension: moyenne; *Envergure:* locale surveillé par Fédération des Chambres immobilières du Québec
Mission: De protéger les intérêts commerciaux de ses membres afin de développer leur succès
Membre de: The Canadian Real Estate Association
Membre: 10,000+
Membre(s) du bureau directeur:
Éric Charbonneau, Directeur général

Chambre immobilière du Saguenay-Lac St-Jean Inc. (CISL)
#140, 2655, boul du Royaume, Jonquière QC G7S 4S9
Tél: 418-548-8808; *Téléc:* 418-548-2588
info@immobiliersaguenay.com
www.immobiliersaguenay.com
www.facebook.com/immobilier.saguenay
Aperçu: Dimension: moyenne; *Envergure:* locale; Organisme sans but lucratif; fondée en 1954 surveillée par Fédération des Chambres immobilières du Québec
Mission: Regrouper les membres afin de leur fournir des services, assurer la qualité de leur travail, défendre et promouvoir leurs intérêts; protéger et promouvoir le commerce de l'immobilier et encourager l'accès à la propriété; offrir de la formation et du perfectionnement dans le domaine immobilier afin d'assurer et de garantir le professionnalisme de l'industrie; faciliter au public en général l'accès à l'information dans le domaine immobilier
Membre de: The Canadian Real Estate Association
Finances: *Budget de fonctionnement annuel:* $100,000-$250,000
Membre(s) du personnel: 2; 7 bénévole(s)
Membre: 150; *Montant de la cotisation:* 225$; *Critères d'admissibilite:* Courtiers, agents et professionnels de l'immobilier
Activités: Cours de perfectionnement
Membre(s) du bureau directeur:
Carlos Cordeiro, Directeur général
cisl@immobiliersaguenay.com

Champlain Coin Club
Orillia ON
Tel: 705-327-1789
ChamplainCoinClub@gmail.com
Overview: A small local organization
Chief Officer(s):
Doug McGarvey, Secretary

The Champlain Society
University of Toronto Press, 5201 Dufferin St., Toronto ON M3H 5T8
Tel: 416-667-7777; *Fax:* 416-667-7881
info@champlainsociety.ca
www.champlainsociety.ca
www.facebook.com/ChamplainSoc
twitter.com/ChamplainSoc
Overview: A medium-sized national charitable organization founded in 1905
Mission: To preserve & promote the eye-witness accounts of Canada's past, including journals, diaries, books, letters & documents
Finances: *Annual Operating Budget:* $50,000-$100,000; *Funding Sources:* Membership fees; donations
6 volunteer(s)
Membership: 750; *Fees:* $110 individual; $55 student; $150 library; *Member Profile:* Readers of Canadian history; libraries; *Committees:* Executive; Publications; Special Events; Membership; Funding; Nominations
Activities: Administers Chalmers Award for best book in Ontario history; Publish an annual volume of edited documentary history
Chief Officer(s):
Lauren Naus, Contact, 416-667-7777 Ext. 7869
lnaus@utpress.utoronto.ca
Awards:
• The Floyd S. Chalmers Award in Ontario History
Awarded annually to the best book on Ontario history published in the preceeding year; *Amount:* $2000
Publications:
• General Series
Type: Book
Profile: Documents on the Canadian experience, described by an expert in the field

Change for Children Association (CFCA)
10808 - 124 St., 2nd Fl., Edmonton AB T5M 0H3
Tel: 780-448-1505; *Fax:* 780-448-1507
cfca@changeforchildren.org
www.changeforchildren.org
www.facebook.com/change4children
twitter.com/change4justice
www.youtube.com/user/cfca100/videos
Also Known As: Change for Children
Overview: A small international charitable organization founded in 1976
Mission: To support local projects in various parts of the Global South; To identify the root causes of poverty & provide assistance to find solutions; To ensure that all donor dollars go directly to the people; To educate Canadians about the Global South through literature, lectures, & discussions; To raise awareness of global interdependence & gather support for greater justice & equality
Member of: Alberta Council for Global Cooperation
Finances: *Annual Operating Budget:* $500,000-$1.5 Million
Staff Member(s): 4; 72 volunteer(s)
Membership: 3,000; *Fees:* Donations of $10 & over; *Committees:* Executive; Finance; Development
Activities: International development; global education; development cafe; development dinner; *Internships:* Yes; *Speaker Service:* Yes; *Library:* Open to public
Chief Officer(s):
Lorraine Swift, Executive Director
lorena@changeforchildren.org
Nicole Farn, Coordinator, Communications
nicole@changeforchildren.org

The Change Foundation
PO Box 42, #2501, 200 Front St. West, Toronto ON M5V 3M1
Tel: 416-205-1579
info@changefoundation.com
www.changefoundation.ca
www.linkedin.com/company/the-change-foundation
twitter.com/TheChangeFdn
www.youtube.com/user/thechangefoundation
Overview: A large provincial organization founded in 1996
Mission: To promote, support & improve health & health care delivery through four activity areas: applied research, grants for Change Initiatives, & knowledge transfer through development & education programs
Staff Member(s): 11
Chief Officer(s):
Cathy Fooks, President & CEO
cfooks@changefoundation.com
Carol Bullock, Manager, Corporate Support
cbullock@changefoundation.com
Christa Haanstra, Executive Lead, Strategic Communications
chaanstra@changefoundation.com

Channel Port Aux Basques & Area Chamber of Commerce
PO Box 1389, Channel-Port-aux-Basques NL A0M 1C0
Tel: 709-695-3688
pabchamber@nf.aibn.com
www.facebook.com/232588160087117
Overview: A small local organization

Chantiers jeunesse
4545, av Pierre-de Coubertin, Montréal QC H1V 3R2
Tél: 514-252-3015; *Téléc:* 514-251-8719
Ligne sans frais: 800-361-2055
cj@cj.qc.ca
www.cj.qc.ca
www.facebook.com/Chantiersjeunesse
Nom précédent: Mouvement québécois des chantiers jeunesse
Aperçu: Dimension: moyenne; *Envergure:* provinciale; Organisme sans but lucratif; fondée en 1980
Mission: Favoriser le développement de jeunes citoyens actifs et engagés, à appuyer le développement d'une communauté et du plein potentiel des personnes en offrant des lieux d'apprentissages et de formation en collaboration avec des partenaires d'ici et d'ailleurs et ce dans un esprit de solidarité et de respect des différences
Membre de: Regroupement loisir Québec; Conseil Québébcois du Loisir; Alliance européenne des organismes des organisations de service volontaire
Affiliation(s): Secrétariat au loisir et au sport; Ministère de santé et services sociaux
Finances: *Fonds:* Provincial Government
Membre(s) du personnel: 5
Membre: *Montant de la cotisation:* 10$ indiviuel; 25$ organisme; *Critères d'admissibilite:* Jeunes de 16 - 30 ans
Activités: Projects de travail volontaire au Québec et à l'étranger; *Stagiaires:* Oui
Membre(s) du bureau directeur:
Stéphanie Fey, Président

Chants Libres, compagnie lyrique de création
#303, 1908, rue Panet, Montréal QC H2L 3A2
Tél: 514-841-2642
creation@chantslibres.org
www.chantslibres.org
www.facebook.com/ChantsLibres
twitter.com/ChantsLibres
www.youtube.com/user/chantslibres

Aperçu: *Dimension:* petite; *Envergure:* locale; fondée en 1990
Mission: Réunir des créateurs de toutes les disciplines (musique, théâtre, arts plastiques, arts électroniques, vidéo etc.) autour d'un point commun: la voix
Membre(s) du personnel: 4
Membre(s) du bureau directeur:
Martin Boisjoly, Directeur général
Pauline Vaillancourt, Directrice artistique
pauline@chantslibres.org

Chao Chow Association Of Ontario *See* Chaeo Chow Association of Eastern Canada

Chapel Hill Historical Society
PO Box 46, Shag Harbour NS B0W 3B0
Tel: 902-723-2949
chapelhillns@gmail.com
www.chapelhillmuseumns.com
Overview: A small local charitable organization founded in 1980
Mission: To promote heritage & history of the area
Member of: Federation of the Nova Scotian Heritage; Nova Scotia Lighthouse Preservation Society
Activities: Operates Chapel Hill Museum June 1 - Sept. 15; *Library:* Chapel Hill Museum; Open to public

Chapitre de Québec *Voir* Sign Association of Canada

CHARGE Syndrome Canada
PO Box 61509, Stn. Fennell, Hamilton ON L8T 5A1
Tel: 519-752-4685; *Fax:* 519-758-9919
admin@chargesyndrome.ca
www.chargesyndrome.ca
Overview: A small national charitable organization founded in 2003
Mission: To raise money for the sufferers of CHARGE Syndrome, as well as CHARGE Syndrome research

Charlotte Seafood Employees Association / Association des employés de Charlotte Seafood
c/o 669 Main St., Blacks Harbour NB E5H 1K1
Tel: 506-456-3391; *Fax:* 506-456-1569
Overview: A medium-sized local organization
Membership: 744
Chief Officer(s):
William Beney, President

Charlottetown Area Baseball Association (CABA)
c/o Baseball PEI, 40 Enman Cres., Charlottetown PE C1E 1E6
Tel: 902-368-4203; *Fax:* 902-368-4548
baseball@sportpei.pe.ca
baseballpei.ca/page/show/1703665-charlottetown-all-seasons
Overview: A medium-sized local organization
Member of: Baseball PEI

Charlottetown Board of Trade *See* Greater Charlottetown & Area Chamber of Commerce

Charlottetown Downtown Residents Association (CDRA)
cdrainpei@gmail.com
www.facebook.com/185367578171566?sk=notes
Overview: A medium-sized local organization
Mission: To create a vibrant and safe downtown community and to offer a forum for discussion, deliberation and consensus on matters affecting the downtown City Area and the Waterfront.
Membership: *Fees:* $10; *Member Profile:* Open to any person residing in the downtown Charlottetown City Area bounded by Euston Street and inclusively between West Street and Esher Street.

CharterAbility
PO Box 60024, Oakville ON L6J 6G4
Tel: 905-466-2016
info@charterability.com
www.charterability.com
Overview: A small local organization
Mission: To promote accessible boating & provide a barrier-free, fully accessible, charter boat service on Lake Ontario for groups of people of all ages with disabilities or mobility impairments
Chief Officer(s):
Stephen Cull, Founder & President

Chartered Accountants' Education Foundation of Alberta (CAEF)
c/o Manulife Place, Institute of Chartered Accountants of Alberta, #580, 10180 - 101st St., Edmonton AB T5J 4R2
Toll-Free: 800-232-9406
www.albertacas.ca/CAEducationFoundation.aspx
Previous Name: Alberta CA Profession's Non-Profit Foundation
Overview: A small provincial organization founded in 1982
Mission: To support accounting & business education in Alberta; To promote the excellence of the CA profession
Finances: *Funding Sources:* Member's annual $60 contribution; Donations
Activities: Supporting post-secondary institutions, accounting educators, & students, through university operational funding, a Teaching Prize, student conferences & career information events, plus scholarships, awards, & bursaries
Chief Officer(s):
Alex Tutschek, Chair
Publications:
• Chartered Accountants' Education Foundation Report to the Community
Type: Report
• Chartered Accountants' Education Foundation Annual Report
Type: Yearbook; *Frequency:* Annually

The Chartered Institute of Logistics & Transport in North America (CILT) / Institut agréé de la logistique et des transports Amérique du Nord
#205, 1435 Sandford Fleming Ave., Ottawa ON K1G 3H3
Tel: 613-738-3003; *Fax:* 613-738-3033
requestinfo@ciltna.com
www.ciltna.com
Also Known As: CILT in North America
Previous Name: Chartered Institute of Transport Canadian Division
Overview: A medium-sized international organization founded in 1919
Mission: To enable growth, professional development, reputation & membership within the profession of Supply Chain Logistics
Member of: Chartered Institute of Transport
Finances: *Funding Sources:* Membership fees, conferences, workshop revenue
Staff Member(s): 1; 15 volunteer(s)
Membership: 250; *Fees:* Schedule available; *Member Profile:* Individuals with experience, interest & education in the transportation field.; *Committees:* Regional
Chief Officer(s):
Bob Armstrong, President, 416-418-3990
armstrong@ciltna.com
David Collenette, Chair
david.collenette@hillandknowlton.ca
  Manitoba Region
  73 Nassena Cres., Winnipeg MB R2P 0K8
  Tel: 204-633-4956
  Chief Officer(s):
  David Bibby, Regional Chair
  Pacific Region
  c/o CILTNA, #900, 275 Slater St., Ottawa ON K1P 5H9
  Tel: 613-688-1438; *Fax:* 613-688-0966
  www.linkedin.com/groups/CILTNA-Pacific-Chapter-4942351
  Chief Officer(s):
  Marian Robson, Regional Chair

Chartered Institute of Secretaries *See* Institute of Chartered Secretaries & Administrators - Canadian Division

Chartered Institute of Transport Canadian Division *See* The Chartered Institute of Logistics & Transport in North America

Chartered Professional Accountants Canada (CPA) / Comptables professionnels agréés du Canada
277 Wellington St. West, Toronto ON M5V 3H2
Tel: 416-977-3222; *Fax:* 416-977-8585
Toll-Free: 800-268-3793
member.services@cpacanada.ca
www.cpacanada.ca
www.linkedin.com/company/cpa-canada
www.facebook.com/CPAcanada
twitter.com/CPAcanada
www.youtube.com/cpacanada
Also Known As: CPA Canada
Merged from: Canadian Institute of Chartered Accountants; Certified Management Accountants of Canada; CGA-Canada
Overview: A large national licensing organization founded in 1902
Mission: To foster public confidence in the chartered accountant profession; To assist members to excel; To oversee a single, unified professional accounting designation known as CPA (note that some provinces/regions will be represented by a merged CPA body, while others will be represented by the legacy bodies until integration is complete)
Membership: 200,000+
Activities: Providing continuing education opportunities
Chief Officer(s):
Joy Thomas, MBA, FCPA, FCMA, President & CEO
Stephen Anisman, CPA, CMA, Chief Financial Officer
Tashia Batstone, MBA, FCPA, FCA, Senior Vice-President, External Relations & Business Development
Lou Ragagnin, BBA, CPA, CA, Senior Vice-President, Operations
Gord Beal, CPA, CA, M.Ed., Vice-President, Research, Guidance & Support
Gale Evans, CPA, CMA, C.Dir, Vice-President, Administration
Nancy Foran, FCPA, FCMA, C.D, Vice-President, International
Stephenie Fox, CPA, CA, Vice-President, Financial Reporting & Assurance Standards
Gabe Hayos, FCPA, FCA, Vice-President, Taxation
Andrew (Sandy) Hilton, MA, Ph.D., FCPA, Vice-President, Pre-Certification Education
Heather Whyte, MBA, APR, Vice-President, Strategic Communications, Branding & Public Affairs
Cairine Wilson, MBA, CAE, Vice-President, Corporate Citizenship
Michele Wood-Tweel, FCPA, FCA, Vice-President, Regulatory Affairs
Awards:
• Awards of Excellence in Corporate Reporting
National awards for corporate reporting, recognizing the best in the country.
Meetings/Conferences:
• Chartered Professional Accountants Canada 2018 ONE National Conference, October, 2018, Halifax, NS
Scope: National
Publications:
• CPA Magazine [a publication of the Chartered Professional Accountants]
Type: Magazine; *Frequency:* 10 pa; *Accepts Advertising*; *Editor:* Okey Chigbo; *ISSN:* 0317-6878; *Price:* $32 members, $55non-members; $45 students; $5.50 single issue
Profile: An information resource for Canadian chartered accountants & financial executives
  Burnaby Office
  #100, 4200 North Fraser Way, Burnaby BC V5J 5K7
  Tel: 604-669-3555; *Fax:* 604-689-5845
  Toll-Free: 800-663-1529
  Montréal Office
  680, rue Sherbrooke ouest, 17e étage, Montréal QC H3A 2M7
  Ottawa Office
  #1201, 350 Sparks St., Ottawa ON K1R 7S8
  Tel: 613-789-7771; *Fax:* 613-789-7772

Chartered Professional Accountants of Alberta
#800, 4440 - 7th Ave. SW, Calgary AB T2P 0X8
Tel: 403-299-1300; *Fax:* 403-299-1339
Toll-Free: 800-232-9406
Other Communication: Member Registrations:
registrations@cpaalberta.ca
info@cpaalberta.ca
www.cpaalberta.ca
www.facebook.com/CPAalberta
twitter.com/cpa_ab
Also Known As: CPA Alberta
Merged from: CGA - AB; CMA Canada - Alberta; Institute of Chartered Accountants of Alberta
Overview: A large provincial licensing organization overseen by Chartered Professional Accountants Canada
Mission: To bring together the former Canadian accounting programs (Certified Management Accountants, Certified General Accountants & Chartered Accountants) in Alberta; to be the primary, internationally recognized Canadian accounting designation
Membership: 28,000+; *Fees:* Schedule available
Activities: Providing professional development opportunities
Chief Officer(s):
Rachel Miller, FCA, FCPA, Chief Executive Officer
Gordon Turtle, Senior Vice-President, Communications
  Edmonton Office
  Manulife Place, #580, 10180 - 101 St., Edmonton AB T5J 4R2
  Tel: 780-424-7391; *Fax:* 780-425-8766
  Toll-Free: 800-232-9406

Chartered Professional Accountants of British Columbia (CPABC)
#800, 555 West Hastings St., Vancouver BC V6B 4N6
Tel: 604-872-7222
Toll-Free: 800-663-2677
www.bccpa.ca
www.linkedin.com/company/cpabritishcolumbia
www.facebook.com/cpabc
twitter.com/cpa_bc
www.youtube.com/user/cpabritishcolumbia
Also Known As: CPA British Columbia
Merged from: Institute of Chartered Accountants of BC; CGA - BC; CMA Canada - BC
Overview: A large provincial licensing organization overseen by Chartered Professional Accountants Canada
Mission: To administer the CPA designation in BC; To train & certify CPA students
Membership: 34,000+ members & 5,200 students & candidates
Activities: Providing professional development opportunities
Chief Officer(s):
Richard Rees, FCPA, FCA, Chief Executive Officer
Amy Lam, FCPA, FCA, CFO & Executive Vice-President, Operations
James (Jamie) Midgley, FCPA, FCA, Executive Vice-President, Regulation & Registrar
Vinetta Peek, FCPA, FCMA, Executive Vice-President, Marketing & Business Development
Jan Sampson, FCPA, FCA, Executive Vice-President, Education & Member Engagement
Meetings/Conferences:
• Chartered Professional Accountants of British Columbia Spring Pacific Summit 2018, May, 2018, Vancouver Convention Centre West, Vancouver, BC
Scope: Provincial
Publications:
• CPABC In Focus [a publication of the Chartered Professional Accountants of British Columbia]
Type: Journal; *Frequency:* 6 pa.; *Editor:* Michelle McRae
Profile: Contains news on professional matters & challenges facing the accounting profession on a wide range of topical subjects

Chartered Professional Accountants of Manitoba (CPAMB)
#1675, 1 Lombard Place, Winnipeg MB R3B 0X3
Tel: 204-943-1538; *Fax:* 204-943-7119
Toll-Free: 800-841-7148
cpamb@cpamb.ca
www.cpamb.ca
www.linkedin.com/groups/CPA-Manitoba-6573960
www.facebook.com/CPAmanitoba
twitter.com/CPAManitoba
Also Known As: CPA Manitoba
Merged from: Institute of Chartered Accountants of Manitoba; CGA - Manitoba; CMA Canada - Manitoba
Overview: A large provincial licensing organization founded in 2014 overseen by Chartered Professional Accountants Canada
Mission: To oversee the integration of the Institute of Chartered Accountants of Manitoba (CA Manitoba), the Certified General Accountants Association of Manitoba (CGA Manitoba), & the Certified Management Accountants of Manitoba (CGA Manitoba) under the Chartered Professional Accountants (CPA) banner; To administer the CPA designation in MB
Membership: 9,000+
Activities: Providing professional development opportunities
Chief Officer(s):
Todd Scaletta, FCPA, FCMA, President & CEO, 204-943-1530
tscaletta@cpamb.ca
Grant Christensen, FCPA, FCGA, Chief Operating Officer, 204-594-9025
gchristensen@cpamb.ca
Kathy Zaplitny, CPA, CA, Senior Director, Regulatory Affairs & Member Services, 204-924-4411
kzaplitny@cpamb.ca
Awards:
• CPA Manitoba Lifetime Achievement Award
• CPA Manitoba Early Achievement Award
• CPA Manitoba Community Service Award
• CPA Manitoba Meritorious Service Award
Meetings/Conferences:
• CPA Manitoba Annual General Meeting 2018, 2018, MB
Scope: Provincial
Publications:
• CPA Manitoba eNews [a publication of the Chartered Professional Accountants of Manitoba]
Type: Newsletter; *Frequency:* m.
Profile: Contains news, upcoming events, & other pertinent information for Association members, candidates, & accounting students

Chartered Professional Accountants of New Brunswick (CPANB) / Comptables professionnels agréés Nouveau-Brunswick
#602, 860 Main St., Moncton NB E1C 1G2
Tel: 506-830-3300; *Fax:* 506-830-3310
info@cpanewbrunswick.ca
www.cpanewbrunswick.ca
twitter.com/CPAnewbrunswick
Also Known As: CPA New Brunswick
Merged from: New Brunswick Institute of Chartered Accountants; CGA - New Brunswick; CMA - New Brunswick
Overview: A large provincial licensing organization founded in 2014 overseen by Chartered Professional Accountants Canada
Mission: To train & certify CPA candidates/students; To regulate professional development of members; To protect the public through ethical standards & discipline
Membership: 2,200+
Activities: Providing professional development opportunities
Chief Officer(s):
Nancy Whipp, CPA, CA, Chief Executive Officer, 506-830-3300 Ext. 107
nwhipp@cpanewbrunswick.ca
Danielle Pieroni, Manager, Communications & Public Relations, 506-830-3300 Ext. 103
dpieroni@cpanewbrunswick.ca
Mylène Lapierre, CPA, CA, CFE, Senior Manager, Practice Inspection & Professional Standards, 506-830-3300 Ext. 105
mlapierre@cpanewbrunswick.ca
Kristen Steeves, CPA, CGA, Senior Manager, Operations, 506-830-3300 Ext. 102
ksteeves@cpanewbrunswick.ca
Murielle Cormier, Coordinator, Member Services
mcormier@cpanewbrunswick.ca
Meetings/Conferences:
• Chartered Professional Accountants of New Brunswick Spring CPD Conference 2018, 2018, NB
Scope: Provincial

Chartered Professional Accountants of Newfoundland & Labrador (CPA NL)
#500, 95 Bonaventure Ave., St. John's NL A1B 2X5
Tel: 709-753-3090; *Fax:* 709-753-3609
Other Communication: CPA Atlantic School of Business, URL: cpaatlantic.ca
www.cpanl.ca
www.linkedin.com/company/5268250
twitter.com/CPANL
Merged from: CA Newfoundland & Labrador; CMA Newfoundland & Labrador; CGA Newfoundland & Labrador
Overview: A large provincial licensing organization founded in 2014 overseen by Chartered Professional Accountants Canada
Mission: To enhance the influence, relevance & value of the Canadian CPA profession through the protection of the public & support to its members & students
Membership: 1,777
Activities: Providing professional development opportunities
Chief Officer(s):
Jason Hillyard, CPA, CGA, Chief Executive Officer
jhillyard@cpanl.ca
Kim Mayo, CPA, CA, Director, Professional Services & Operations
kmayo@cpanl.ca
Meetings/Conferences:
• Chartered Professional Accountants of Newfoundland & Labrador 2018 Fall Professional Development Conference, 2018, NL
Scope: Provincial

Chartered Professional Accountants of Nova Scotia
#300, 1871 Hollis St., Halifax NS B3J 0C3
Tel: 902-425-7273
info@cpans.ca
www.cpans.ca
Also Known As: CPA Nova Scotia
Merged from: CMA Nova Scotia; General Accountants of NS; Chartered Accountants of NS
Overview: A medium-sized provincial licensing organization founded in 1900 overseen by Chartered Professional Accountants Canada
Mission: To protect & serve the public & members by providing exceptional services & resources within a well-regulated CPA profession
Finances: *Annual Operating Budget:* $500,000-$1.5 Million
Activities: Providing professional development opportunities
Chief Officer(s):
Patricia (Patti) Towler, BA, JD, LLM, CI, CEO
ptowler@cpans.ca

Chartered Professional Accountants of Ontario
69 Bloor St. East, Toronto ON M4W 1B3
Tel: 416-962-1841; *Fax:* 416-962-8900
Toll-Free: 800-387-0735
Other Communication: Legacy Sites: www.cga-ontario.org;
www.cmaontario.org
customerservice@cpaontario.ca
www.cpaontario.ca
www.linkedin.com/company/cpa-ontario
www.facebook.com/CPAOntario
twitter.com/CPA_Ontario
Also Known As: CPA Ontario
Merged from: Institute of Chartered Accountants of Ontario; CGA Ontario; CMA Ontario
Overview: A medium-sized provincial licensing organization founded in 1879 overseen by Chartered Professional Accountants Canada
Mission: To foster public confidence in the Chartered Professional Accountant profession, by acting in the public interest & helping members excel. CPA Ontario sets & enforces high standards of practice, qualification & education; promotes professional excellence & ethical conduct; encourages continuous improvement of capabilities among members; promotes the profession while serving as its primary voice in Ontario
Member of: Ontario Chamber of Commerce; Metro Toronto Board of Trade
Finances: *Annual Operating Budget:* Greater than $5 Million; *Funding Sources:* Membership fees; CA education & professional development programs
Membership: 80,000 chartered accountants + 20,000 CA students
Activities: Conferences, meetings, awards, continuing education, speakers, tax clinics, children's charities & other community initiatives
Chief Officer(s):
Carol Wilding, FCPA, FCA, President & CEO
Publications:
• D&A Magazine [a publication of Chartered Professional Accountants of Ontario]
Type: Magazine; *Frequency:* Quarterly

Chartered Professional Accountants of Prince Edward Island (CPA PEI)
PO Box 301, #600, 97 Queen St., Charlottetown PE C1A 7K7
Tel: 902-894-4290; *Fax:* 902-894-4791
Other Communication: Legacy Site: www.cma-pei.com
info@cpapei.ca
www.cpapei.ca
Merged from: Institute of Chartered Accountants of PEI; CGA-PEI; CMA-PEI
Overview: A large provincial licensing organization founded in 2014 overseen by Chartered Professional Accountants Canada
Mission: To foster the growth & evolution of the accounting profession in Prince Edward Island
Membership: 600+
Activities: Providing professional development opportunities
Chief Officer(s):
Tanya O'Brien, CPA, CA, Chief Executive Officer
tobrien@cpapei.ca
Publications:
• CPAPEI [Chartered Professional Accountants of Prince Edward Island] Newsletter
Type: Newsletter; *Frequency:* q.
Profile: Contains news & Association updates

Chartered Professional Accountants of Saskatchewan (CPA SK)
#101, 4581 Parliament Ave., Regina SK S4W 0G3
Tel: 306-359-0272; *Fax:* 306-347-8580
Toll-Free: 800-667-3535
info@cpask.ca
www.cpask.ca
Also Known As: CPA Saskatchewan
Merged from: Institute of Chartered Accountants of Saskatchewan; CMA Saskatchewan; CGA Saskatchewan

Overview: A large provincial licensing organization founded in 2014 overseen by Chartered Professional Accountants Canada
Mission: To administer the CPA designation in Saskatchewan
Membership: 5,000+
Activities: Providing professional development opportunities
Chief Officer(s):
Shelley Thiel, FCPA, FCA, Chief Executive Officer
sthiel@cpask.ca
Meetings/Conferences:
• Chartered Professional Accountants of Saskatchewan Conference 2018, 2018, SK
Scope: Provincial
Publications:
• CPA SK [Chartered Professional Accountants of Saskatchewan] Connect
Type: Newsletter

Chartered Professional Accountants of the Yukon (CPAYT)
c/o Chartered Professional Accountants of British Columbia, #800, 555 West Hastings St., Vancouver BC V6B 4N6
Tel: 604-872-7222
Toll-Free: 800-663-2677
Other Communication: Legacy Sites:
www.cga.org/canada/yukon; www.icayt.ca
www.bccpa.ca/yukon
linkedin.com/company/cpabritishcolumbia
www.facebook.com/cpabc
twitter.com/cpa_bc
www.youtube.com/user/cpabritishcolumbia
Merged from: Institute of Chartered Accountants of the Yukon; CGA - Yukon; CMA Canada - Yukon
Overview: A large provincial licensing organization founded in 2014 overseen by Chartered Professional Accountants Canada
Mission: To administer the CPA designation in the Yukon
Activities: Providing professional development opportunities
Chief Officer(s):
Richard Rees, FCPA, FCA, President & CEO

Chartered Professionals in Human Resources (CPHR) / Conseillers en ressources humaines agréés (CRHA)
#603, 150 Metcalfe St., Ottawa ON K2P 1P1
Tel: 613-567-2477; *Fax:* 613-567-2478
Toll-Free: 866-560-1288
info@cchra-ccarh.ca
www.cchra-ccarh.ca
Previous Name: Canadian Council of Human Resources Associations
Overview: A medium-sized national organization founded in 1994
Mission: To protect the public & advance the economic & social success of Canadian workplaces through strategic HR leadership
Member of: North American Human Resource Management Association; World Federation of Personnel Management Associations
Staff Member(s): 1
Membership: 27,000; *Committees:* Chief Staff Officers Council; Governance; Finance & Audit; Standards; Executive
Activities: Certified Human Resources Professional (CHRP) designation; *Awareness Events:* National Human Resources Forum, fall
Chief Officer(s):
Anthony Ariganello, Chief Executive Officer

Chartered Professionals in Human Resources Manitoba
#1810, 275 Portage Ave., Winnipeg MB R3B 2B3
Tel: 204-943-2836; *Fax:* 204-943-1109
hrmam@hrmam.org
www.hrmam.org
twitter.com/CPHRMB
Also Known As: CPHR Manitoba
Previous Name: Human Resource Management Association of Manitoba; Personnel Association of Greater Winnipeg
Merged from: Manitoba Association of Learning Facilitators
Overview: A small provincial organization founded in 1943
Mission: To enhance & promote the value of the human resource profession & practices across Manitoba
Member of: Canadian Council of Human Resource Associations; North American Human Resource Management Association; World Federation of Personnel Management Association
Affiliation(s): Society for Human Resource Management
Finances: *Annual Operating Budget:* $100,000-$250,000
Staff Member(s): 2
Membership: 1,200; *Fees:* $65-$367
Activities: *Internships:* Yes; *Speaker Service:* Yes
Chief Officer(s):
Ron Gauthier, CEO & Registrar, 204-943-0884
ron@cphrmb.ca
Lori Brûlé, Manager, 204-943-3624
lori@cphrmb.ca
Awards:
• Life Member Award
• HR Excellence Awards
Includes Business Excellence Awards & Professional Excellence Awards
Meetings/Conferences:
• Chartered Professionals in Human Resources Manitoba Human Resources & Leadership Conference 2018, October, 2018, RBC Convention Centre Winnipeg, Winnipeg, MB
Scope: Provincial
Publications:
• HRmatters [a publication of Chartered Professionals in Human Resources Manitoba]
Type: Magazine; *Frequency:* Fall & spring; *Editor:* Lindsay Barnett
• Weekly HRmatters [a publication of Chartered Professionals in Human Resources Manitoba]
Type: E-Newsletter; *Frequency:* Weekly

Chartered Professionals in Human Resources of Alberta
#990, 105 - 12 Ave. SE, Calgary AB T2G 1A1
Tel: 403-209-2420; *Fax:* 403-209-2401
Toll-Free: 800-668-6125
info@cphrab.ca
www.cphrab.ca
www.linkedin.com/company/18064075
twitter.com/CPHRab
Also Known As: CPHR Alberta
Previous Name: Human Resources Institute of Alberta
Overview: A small provincial organization founded in 1984
Mission: To promote & encourage maintenance of the professional standards in the field of human resources management & to set out the standard & process for certification as a Certified Human Resources Professional
Member of: Canadian Council of Human Resources Associations
Finances: *Funding Sources:* Membership fees
Membership: 3,000+; *Fees:* $60 + GST student; $200 + GST associate, general; $225 CHRP candidate; $350 + GST certified; *Member Profile:* Certified professionals
Activities: Annual conference
Chief Officer(s):
Diane Dutton, Manager, Professional Development
ddutton@cphrab.ca
Lynda Bergeron, Coordinator, Member Services
lbergeron@cphrab.ca
Meetings/Conferences:
• Chartered Professionals in Human Resources of Alberta 2018 Conference, April, 2018, Telus Convention Centre, Calgary, AB
Scope: Provincial
Description: Theme: "HR Undefined"

Chartered Professionals in Human Resources of British Columbia & Yukon
#1101, 1111 West Hastings St., Vancouver BC V6E 2J3
Tel: 604-684-7228; *Fax:* 604-684-3225
Toll-Free: 800-665-1961
info@cphrbc.ca
www.cphrbc.ca
www.linkedin.com/company/17984002
www.facebook.com/CPHRBC
twitter.com/cphrbc
www.youtube.com/user/BCHRMA
Also Known As: CPHR BC & Yukon
Previous Name: Human Resources Management Association
Overview: A medium-sized provincial organization founded in 1942
Mission: To uphold industry standards; To advance professional people practices
Member of: Canadian Council of Human Resource Associations
Staff Member(s): 26
Membership: 4,000+; *Fees:* $400 general; $60 student; $750 corporate; *Member Profile:* Members include CEOs, directors of human resources, consultants, educators, students, human resources generalists, & small-business owners; *Committees:* Awards; CHRP Audit; Recertification; Conference Steering
Activities: Providing human resources information & services; Partnering with post-secondary academic institutions & education providers; Providing networking opportunities
Chief Officer(s):
Anthony Ariganello, President & CEO
aariganello@cphrbc.ca
Trish Andrea, CHPR Registrar
tandrea@cphrbc.ca
Kelly Aslanowicz, Senior Manager, Business Development
kaslanowicz@cphrbc.ca
Vicki Bauman, Coordinator, Member Services
v.bauman@cphrbc.ca
Erin Breden, Specialist, Communications
ebreden@cphrbc.ca
Awards:
• Rising Star Award
For HR practitioners within the first five years of their career
• HR Professional of the Year
• CEO Award
Meetings/Conferences:
• Chartered Professionals in Human Resources of British Columbia & Yukon 2018 Conference & Tradeshow, May, 2018, Vancouver, BC
Scope: Provincial
Description: A human resources professional development event, with guest speakers, educational sessions, exhibits, the presentation of awards, & networking events
Publications:
• PeopleTalk [a publication of the Chartered Professionals in Human Resources of British Columbia & Yukon]
Type: Magazine; *Frequency:* Weekly; *Accepts Advertising*
Profile: Each issue focuses on a topical human resources theme, plus labour relations, books & websites, health & wellness, CHRP certification, international news, & technology services for human resources

Chartered Professionals in Human Resources Saskatchewan
2106 Lorne St., Regina SK S4P 2M5
Tel: 306-522-0184; *Fax:* 306-522-1783
info@cphrsk.ca
www.cphrsk.ca
www.linkedin.com/company/saskatchewan-association-of-human-resource-professionals
www.facebook.com/cphrsk
twitter.com/CPHRSK
Also Known As: CPHR Saskatchewan
Previous Name: Saskatchewan Association of Human Resource Professionals; Saskatchewan Council of Human Resource Associations
Overview: A small provincial organization
Mission: To promote & encourage leadership & expertise within human resource practitioners in all functional areas of human resource management through provincial networks & developmental opportunities while supporting professional standards to influence organizational excellence
Member of: Canadian Council of Human Resources Associations
Finances: *Funding Sources:* Membership dues
Staff Member(s): 4; 75 volunteer(s)
Membership: 1,500; *Fees:* $0 student members; $160 regular & associate members; *Member Profile:* Human resources students & professionals living in Saskatchewan; *Committees:* Recertification; Communications; Conference; Mentorship; Programming; Investigation & Discipline
Chief Officer(s):
Nicole Norton Scott, Executive Director & Registrar, 306-522-0184
nnortonscott@cphrsk.ca
Britany Hamilton, Administrative Coordinator
bhamilton@cphrsk.ca
Meetings/Conferences:
• Chartered Professionals in Human Resources Saskatchewan 2018 Conference, 2018, SK
• HR Saskatchewan
Type: Magazine; *Frequency:* Biannually; *Accepts Advertising*; *Price:* Included with membership

Chartered Shorthand Reporters' Association of Ontario (CSRAO)
#425, 157 Adelaide St. West, Toronto ON M5H 4E7
www.csrao.net
Overview: A small provincial licensing organization founded in 1891
Mission: To qualify & maintain qualifications of verbatim court reporters; To offer training & education to prospective reporters;

To liaise with governments to ensure use of new technology
Affiliation(s): National Court Reporters Association
9 volunteer(s)
Membership: 100 associate + 50 student + 200 senior/lifetime + 50 other; *Fees:* $30 student/affiliate/retired fellow/retired associate; $100 fellows; *Member Profile:* Fellow - by examination; associate - by occupation; student - by attendance at recognized school; *Committees:* Training & Education; Official Reporters; Technology
Chief Officer(s):
Angela Gunn, President
president@csrao.net

Chase & District Chamber of Commerce
PO Box 592, 400 Shuswap Ave., Chase BC V0E 1M0
Tel: 250-679-8432; *Fax:* 250-679-3120
admin@chasechamber.com
www.chasechamber.com
www.facebook.com/ChaseChamber1
Also Known As: Chase Info Centre
Overview: A small local organization founded in 1954
Mission: To promote & improve trade, commerce, economic, civic & social welfare of the district
Member of: BC Chamber of Commerce; Canadian Chamber of Commerce
Finances: *Funding Sources:* Membership dues; government grants
Staff Member(s): 1
Membership: *Fees:* Schedule available
Chief Officer(s):
Carmen Miller, President

Châteauguay Sexual Assault Center *Voir* Centre d'aide et de lutte contre les agressions à caractère sexuel de Châteauguay

Chatham & District Association for Community Living See Community Living Chatham-Kent

Chatham & District Chamber of Commerce See Chatham-Kent Chamber of Commerce

Chatham & District Labour Council See Chatham-Kent Labour Council

Chatham Outreach for Hunger
PO Box 953, Chatham ON N7M 5L3
Tel: 519-351-8381
bjl@ciaccess.com
www.outreachforhunger.com
Also Known As: Food Bank
Overview: A small local charitable organization founded in 1988
Mission: To provide food to low income families on an emergency basis
Member of: Ontario Association of Food Banks; Food Banks Canada
Finances: *Funding Sources:* Community supported
Activities: *Speaker Service:* Yes

Chatham Railroad Museum Society
PO Box 434, 2 McLean St., Chatham ON N7M 5K5
Tel: 519-352-3097
crms@mnsi.net
www.chathamrailroadmuseum.ca
www.facebook.com/pages/Chatham-Railroad-Museum-CRMS/195849387130379
Overview: A small local charitable organization founded in 1989
Mission: To commemorate railway and local history by educating the public through the use of interactive displays & railway artefacts
Staff Member(s): 3; 10 volunteer(s)
Membership: 1-99
Activities: *Awareness Events:* William Glassco Railroad Fun Day

Chatham-Kent Big Sisters Association Inc. See Big Brothers Big Sisters of Ontario

Chatham-Kent Chamber of Commerce
54 - 4th St., Chatham ON N7M 2G2
Tel: 519-352-7540
www.chatham-kentchamber.ca
www.linkedin.com/company/chatham-kent-chamber-of-commerce
www.facebook.com/ChathamKentChamberofCommerce
twitter.com/CKChamber
Previous Name: Chatham & District Chamber of Commerce
Overview: A medium-sized local organization
Staff Member(s): 2

Chief Officer(s):
G.A. (Gail) Antaya, President & CEO, 519-352-7540 Ext. 22
gail@chatham-kentchamber.ca

Chatham-Kent Labour Council
280 Merritt Ave., Chatham ON N7M 3G1
Tel: 519-351-6621; *Fax:* 519-351-9403
cklc@kent.net
www.kent.net/cklc
Previous Name: Chatham & District Labour Council
Overview: A small local organization founded in 1958 overseen by Ontario Federation of Labour
Mission: To group together local labour councils and unions
Chief Officer(s):
Jeff McFadden, President
jeff_mcfadden@hotmail.com
Elizabeth Cannon, Secretary
ecannon@cogeco.ca

Chatham-Kent Multiple Birth Association
Chatham ON
Tel: 519-825-9075
chatham@multiplebirthscanada.org
www.multiplebirthscanada.org/~chatham
Overview: A small local organization founded in 1987 overseen by Multiple Births Canada
Membership: *Fees:* $30

Chatham-Kent Real Estate Board
252 Wellington St. W., Chatham ON N7M 1K1
Tel: 519-352-4351
ckreb@mnsi.net
boards.mls.ca/chatham
www.facebook.com/153823918039312
Overview: A small local organization overseen by Ontario Real Estate Association
Finances: *Funding Sources:* Membership fees
Activities: *Library:*
Chief Officer(s):
Jamie Winkler, President

Chawkers Foundation
506 Clinton St., Toronto ON M6G 2Z4
information@thechawkersfoundation.org
www.thechawkersfoundation.org
Overview: A small national charitable organization founded in 1988
Mission: To support registered Canadian charities working in the areas of education & environmental research & protection, as well as non-fiction writing
Activities: Contributing to educational enterprises & programs
Chief Officer(s):
Jim O'Reilly, President
Duncan Alexander, Vice-President & Treasurer
Jerry Lazare, Secretary

Chebucto Community Net (CCN) / Réseau communautaire Chebucto (RCC)
#006, Chase Bldg., Dalhousie University, Halifax NS B3H 4R2
Tel: 902-494-2449; *Fax:* 902-494-1242
office@chebucto.ns.ca
www.chebucto.ns.ca
www.facebook.com/pages/Chebucto-Community-Net/191676037573945
twitter.com/ChebuctoCommNet
Overview: A small local charitable organization founded in 1994
Mission: To provide the technology, infrastructure & training to enable all people in the Greater Halifax Region to participate in an electronic public space
Membership: *Fees:* Schedule available

Chebucto Symphony Orchestra
PO Box 27024, 5595 Fenwick St., Halifax NS B3H 4M8
Tel: 902-431-7654
info@chebuctosymphony.ca
www.chebuctosymphony.ca
www.facebook.com/ChebuctoSymphony
Also Known As: Chebucto Orchestral Society of Nova Scotia
Overview: A small local charitable organization founded in 1976 overseen by Orchestras Canada
Mission: To provide an opportunity for amateur musicians to perform the great symphonic works & to bring classical music to local audiences
Member of: Orchestras Canada
Finances: *Funding Sources:* Donations; Ticket revenue

Membership: 1-99; *Fees:* $150 regular; $50 students; *Member Profile:* Talented amateur musicians from the Halifax Regional Municipality
Activities: Performing a minimum of four public concerts per year; Performing charity concerts; Commissioning original compositions from Atlantic region musicians; Providing soloist opportunities for young musicians; *Library:* Music Library; Open to public
Chief Officer(s):
Christopher Palmer, Musical Director

Chedoke Numismatic Society
ON
Overview: A small local organization
Member of: Royal Canadian Numismatic Association

Cheer Canada
c/o Alberta Cheerleading Association, PO Box 31006, Edmonton AB T5Z 3P3
Tel: 780-417-0050; *Fax:* 780-417-0093
Toll-Free: 888-756-9220
Other Communication: Funding, E-mail: funding@cheercanada.net
info@cheerleadingcanadainc.com
www.cheerleadingcanadainc.com
www.facebook.com/CheerleadingCanada
twitter.com/cheercanada
Overview: A medium-sized national organization founded in 2011
Mission: To provide opportunities to all recreational & competitive members, while workig in partnership with its members to lead, support & promote cheerleading in Canada
Affiliation(s): International All Star Federation Worlds; US All Star Federation
Membership: 9 associations; *Member Profile:* Provincial cheerleading associations
Chief Officer(s):
Jim Greenough, President & Pacific Regional Director
Krista Gerlich-Fitzgerald, Vice-President

Cheer Nova Scotia
NS
www.cheerns.com
Overview: A small provincial organization overseen by Cheer Canada
Mission: To promote cheerleading in Nova Scotia.
Member of: Cheer Canada
Membre(s) du bureau directeur:
Megan Spencer, President
president@nscheer.com
Monique Johnson, Treasurer
communicator@nscheer.com

Chemainus & District Chamber of Commerce
PO Box 575, #102, 9799 Waterwheel Cres., Chemainus BC V0R 1K0
Tel: 250-246-3944; *Fax:* 250-246-3251
chamber@chemainus.bc.ca
www.chemainus.bc.ca
www.facebook.com/ChemainusVisitorCentreAndChamberOfCommerce
twitter.com/ChemainusCOC
Overview: A small local organization founded in 1949
Member of: BC Chamber of Commerce; Canadian Chamber of Commerce; Tourism BC; Tourism Association of Vancouver Island; Tourism Victoria
Finances: *Funding Sources:* Municipality of North Cowichan; BC Tourism; Service Canada
Staff Member(s): 2
Membership: *Member Profile:* Businesses
Activities: Participating in the Chemainus Giant Street Market & the Chemainus Wednesday Market; *Awareness Events:* Golden Brush Awards & Silent Auction
Chief Officer(s):
Jeanne Ross, Chamber Coordinator
Amy Fieldon, Coordinator, Visitor Centre
visitorcentre@chemainus.bc.ca

Chemainus Harvest House Society Food Bank
PO Box 188, 9814 Willow St., Chemainus BC V0R 1K0
Tel: 250-246-3455
harvesthouse@shaw.ca
www.chemainusharvesthouse.com
Overview: A small local charitable organization overseen by Food Banks British Columbia
Member of: Food Banks British Columbia; Food Banks Canada
Finances: *Annual Operating Budget:* $50,000-$100,000

25 volunteer(s)
Membership: 25; *Fees:* $5
Chief Officer(s):
Sylvia Massey, Chair of the Board, 250-246-4816
sylviamassey@shaw.ca

Chemical Institute of Canada (CIC) / Institut de chimie du Canada
#400, 222 Queen St., Ottawa ON K1P 5V9
Tel: 613-232-6252; *Fax:* 613-232-5862
Toll-Free: 888-542-2242
info@cheminst.ca
www.cheminst.ca
www.linkedin.com/company/chemical-institute-of-canada
www.facebook.com/ChemicalInstituteOfCanada
fr.twitter.com/CIC_ChemInst
www.flickr.com/photos/61234653@N08
Overview: A large national organization founded in 1945
Mission: To maintain all branches of the professions of chemical sciences & chemical engineering in their proper status among other learned & scientific professions; To encourage original research & develop & maintain high standards in profession; To enhance usefulness of profession to the public
Affiliation(s): Canadian Society for Chemical Engineering; Canadian Society for Chemical Technology; Canadian Society for Chemistry
Finances: *Funding Sources:* Membership fees
Membership: 6,000; *Fees:* Schedule available; *Member Profile:* Open to those interested in chemistry & chemical technology & engineering with appropriate background; *Committees:* Finance; Fellowship
Activities: *Awareness Events:* National Chemistry Week; *Speaker Service:* Yes; *Rents Mailing List:* Yes
Chief Officer(s):
Roland Andersson, Executive Director, 613-232-6252 Ext. 222
randersson@cheminst.ca
Joan Kingston, Director, Finance & Administration, 613-232-6252 Ext. 225
jkingston@cheminst.ca
Gale Thirlwall, Manager, Awards & Local Sections, 613-232-6252 Ext. 223
gthirlwall@cheminst.ca
Bernadette Dacey, Director, Communications & Marketing, 613-232-6252 Ext. 228
bdacey@cheminst.ca
Lyndsay Burman, Leader, Membership Communications, 613-232-6252 Ext. 227
lburman@cheminst.ca
Awards:
• The Chemical Institute of Canada Award for Environmental Improvement
A plaque & certificate & up to $500 travel assistance awarded to a company, individual, team or organization in Canada for a significant achievement in pollution prevention, treatment or remediation in Canada *Contact:* Awards Manager, E-mail: awards@cheminst.ca
• The Catalysis Award
Awarded biennially to an individual who has made a distinguished contribution to the field of catalysis; sponsored by the Canadian Catalysis Foundation; *Amount:* A rhodium-plated silver medal & travel expense to present the award lecture
• Chemical Institute of Canada Awards
The institute administers several awards & scholarships in chemistry, chemical engineering, & macromolecular science or engineering
• The Macromolecular Science & Engineering Lecture Award
Established 1989; awarded annually to an individual who has made a distinguished contribution to macromolecular science & engineering; *Amount:* $1,500 & a framed scroll provided by Novacor Chemicals Ltd.
• Pestcon Graduate Scholarship
For M.Sc. or Ph.D. students for research into alternate pest control strategies *Deadline:* March; *Amount:* $3,000
• Union Carbide Award for Chemical Education
Established 1961; awarded annually to recognize an individual who has made outstanding contributions in Canada to education at any level in the field of chemistry or chemical engineering; *Amount:* $1,000, a scroll & up to $400 in travel expenses if required
• Polysar Awards of the CIC for High School Chemistry Teachers
Two awards a year recognizing excellence in the teaching of chemistry at the secondary level in Canada; *Amount:* $500, a scroll & membership in the CIC
• Sarnia Chemical Engineering Community Scholarship
Awarded to an undergraduate student about to enter the final year of studies at a Canadian university in chemical engineering; based on academic excellence & demonstrated contributions to the Canadian Society for Chemical Engineering; *Amount:* $1,000
• The Chemical Institute of Canada Medal
Established 1951; a palladium medal is awarded as a mark of distinction & recognition to a person who has made an outstanding contribution to the science of chemistry or chemical engineering in Canada
• The Montreal Medal
Established 1956; awarded annually as a mark of distinction & honour to a resident of Canada who has shown significant leadership in or has made an outstanding contribution to the profession of chemistry or chemical engineering in Canada; *Amount:* A medal & up to $300 travel expenses if required
Meetings/Conferences:
• 101st Canadian Chemistry Conference & Exhibition, May, 2018, Edmonton, AB
Scope: National
• 68th Canadian Chemical Engineering Conference, October, 2018, Toronto, ON
Scope: National
Contact Information: www.csche2018.ca
• 102nd Canadian Chemistry Conference & Exhibition, June, 2019, Québec, QC
Scope: National
• 103rd Canadian Chemistry Conference & Exhibition, May, 2020, Winnipeg, MB
Scope: National
Publications:
• Canadian Chemical News
Type: Magazine; *Frequency:* Bimonthly
• The Canadian Journal of Chemical Engineering
Type: Journal

Chemins du soleil
1155, rue Alexandre de Sève, Montréal QC H2L 2T7
Tél: 514-528-9991
admin@cheminsdusoleil.org
cheminsdusoleil.org
www.facebook.com/leschemins
Aperçu: *Dimension:* petite; *Envergure:* locale
Mission: Pour offrir des activités récréatives, culturelles, sportives et éducatives pour les jeunes vivant dans le centre-sud de Montréal
Membre(s) du personnel: 5
Activités: *Evénements de sensibilisation:* Magasin-Partage de la Rentrée Scolaire (août); Magasin-Partage de Noël (décembre)
Membre(s) du bureau directeur:
Daniel Lauzon, Directeur
daniel.lauzon@cheminsdusoleil.org

Chemistry Industry Association of Canada (CIAC)
#805, 350 Sparks St., Ottawa ON K1R 7S8
Tel: 613-237-6215; *Fax:* 613-237-4061
info@canadianchemistry.ca
www.canadianchemistry.ca
www.linkedin.com/company/chemistry-industry-association-of-canada/
www.facebook.com/ChemistryCanada
twitter.com/ChemistryCanada
Previous Name: Canadian Chemical Producers' Association
Overview: A medium-sized national organization founded in 1962
Mission: To represent the interests of chemical manufacturers; To promote the ethic, "Responsible Care"; To act responsibly, with accountability & openness
Membership: 60+; *Member Profile:* Companies that manufacture or formulate chemicals, with a commitment to ethics & codes; Companies that directly manage chemicals; Companies that supply goods or services to the chemical industry; Responsible care partnership associations & responsible care supporting associations
Activities: Communicating values & concerns of the chemcial producing industry to member companies, governments, & the public; Supporting & sharing successful practices; Promoting improved safety & environmental performance; *Library*
Chief Officer(s):
Richard Paton, President & CEO, 613-237-6215 Ext. 231
Pierre Gauthier, Vice-President, Public Affairs, 613-237-6215 Ext. 225
David Podruzny, Vice-President, Business & Economics, 613-237-6215 Ext. 229
Gordon Lloyd, Vice-President, Technical Affairs, 613-237-6215 Ext. 243
Bob Masterson, Vice-President, Responsible Care, 613-237-6215 Ext. 234
Publications:
• Catalyst
Frequency: Quarterly; *Accepts Advertising*; *Editor:* Michael Bourque
Profile: Feature articles & departments about the management of chemicals throughout their life cycle
Alberta Regional Office
#223, 97 - 53017 Range Rd., Ardrossan AB T8E 2M3
Tel: 780-922-5902
Chief Officer(s):
Al Schulz, Regional Director
alschulz@telusplanet.net
British Columbia Regional Office
#13, 1238 Cardero St., Vancouver BC V6G 2H6
Tel: 778-888-6461
Chief Officer(s):
Lorna Young, Regional Director
lyoung@canadianchemistry.ca
Ontario Regional Office
41 Cornerbrook Dr., Toronto ON M3A 1H5
Tel: 416-445-9353
Chief Officer(s):
Norm Huebel, Regional Director
nhuebel@sympatico.ca
Québec Regional Office
8910, rue Deschambault, Saint-Léonard QC H1R 2C4
Tel: 514-324-1308
Chief Officer(s):
Jules Lauzon, Regional Director
jlauzon@videotron.ca

Chesley & District Chamber of Commerce
PO Box 406, 106 - 1st Ave. South, Chesley ON N0G 1L0
Tel: 519-363-9837
Overview: A small local organization
Membership: 60; *Fees:* $85; *Member Profile:* Business owners

Chess Federation of Canada / Fédération canadienne des échecs
#356, 17A-218 Silvercreek Pkwy. North, Guelph ON N1H 8E8
Tel: 519-265-1789
info@chess.ca
www.chess.ca
www.linkedin.com/groups?home=&gid=3949499
www.facebook.com/163031117086480
twitter.com/ChessCanada
www.youtube.com/ChessCanada
Overview: A medium-sized national charitable organization founded in 1872
Mission: To coordinate chess play across Canada
Affiliation(s): Fédération internationale des échecs
Staff Member(s): 2
Membership: 1,866; *Fees:* Schedule available; *Committees:* Kalev Pugi Fund; National Appeals; Tournament Director & Organizer; Olympic; Olympic Fundraising; Youth
Chief Officer(s):
Vlad Drkulec, President
president@chess.ca
Michael von Keitz, Executive Director

Chess'n Math Association (CMA) / Association échecs et maths (AEM)
3423, rue Saint-Denis, Montréal QC H2X 3L2
Tel: 514-845-8352; *Fax:* 514-845-8810
montreal@echecs.org
www.chess-math.org
Overview: A medium-sized national organization founded in 1985
Mission: To promote chess in schools across Canada
Finances: *Annual Operating Budget:* $1.5 Million-$3 Million
Staff Member(s): 20; 25 volunteer(s)
Membership: 10,000
Chief Officer(s):
Larry Bevand, Executive Director
Ottawa Branch
250 Bank St., Ottawa ON K2P 1X4
Tel: 613-565-3662; *Fax:* 613-565-5190
ottawa@chess-math.org
Toronto Branch
701 Mount Pleasant Rd., Toronto ON M4S 2N4
Tel: 416-488-5506; *Fax:* 416-486-4637
toronto@chess-math.org

Chester Municipal Chamber of Commerce
4171 Hwy. 3, RR#2, Chester NS B0J 1J0

Tel: 902-275-4709; *Fax:* 902-275-4629
Admin@ChesterAreaNS.ca
www.chesterns.com
www.facebook.com/138252302853117
twitter.com/chestermunchamb
Overview: A small local organization founded in 1935
Finances: *Funding Sources:* Membership dues; fundraising
Membership: *Fees:* $125 associate; $110 full; $55 retired/non-profit; *Committees:* Executive; Finance; Visitor Centre Information; Marketing & Communications; Memberships; Economic Development; Events
Chief Officer(s):
Anthony Smith, Chair

Chester Municipal Heritage Society (CMHS)
PO Box 628, 133 Central St., Chester NS B0J 1J0
Tel: 902-275-3826
lordlyhouse@ns.aliantzinc.ca
chester-municipal-heritage-society.ca
www.facebook.com/180126828677505
www.youtube.com/user/lordlymuseum
Overview: A small local charitable organization founded in 1981
Mission: To encourage & promote interest in & preservation of local heritage & our built heritage
Member of: Federation of the Nova Scotian Heritage
Affiliation(s): South Shore Tourism Association; Chester Chamber of Commerce
Finances: *Funding Sources:* Fundraising; donations
Membership: *Fees:* $15 individual; $25 family; $100 supporter; $250 contributer; $500 patron; $1000 benefactor; *Committees:* Fundraising; Newsletter/Parkbookings; Art Show/Christmas Show; Membership; Auction; Nominating; Acquisitions/Research/Program; Building
Activities: Ooperates Lordly House Museum; House & Harbour Tour
Chief Officer(s):
Carol Nauss, Chair

Cheticamp Association for Community Living (CACL)
PO Box 550, Cheticamp NS B0E 1H0
Tel: 902-224-2195; *Fax:* 902-224-1673
www.cheticampcacl.ca
Overview: A small local organization overseen by Nova Scotia Association for Community Living
Mission: To help each client to reach his or her potential; to encourage & facilitate the growth of each client; to integrate clients into the community
Member of: DIRECTIONS Council for Vocational Services Society; Nova Scotia Association for Community Living
Activities: Green Door workshop; woodworking studio; residential services; L'Attique second hand clothing store
Chief Officer(s):
Bill Barnet, President

Chetwynd & District Chamber of Commerce
PO Box 870, 5217 North Access Rd., Chetwynd BC V0C 1J0
Tel: 250-788-3345; *Fax:* 250-788-3655
manager@chetwyndchamber.ca
www.chetwyndchamber.ca
www.facebook.com/Chetwynd-Chamber-of-Commerce-272995369408697
Overview: A small local organization
Member of: BC Chamber of Commerce
Finances: *Funding Sources:* Fees for service; fundraising
Chief Officer(s):
Tonia Richter, Executive Director
Carmen Westgate, President

Les Chevaliers de Colomb du Québec / Knights of Columbus of Québec
670, av Chambly, Saint-Hyacinthe QC J2S 6V4
Tél: 450-768-0616; *Téléc:* 450-768-1660
Ligne sans frais: 866-893-3681
conact@chevaliersdecolomb.com
www.chevaliersdecolomb.com
Aperçu: *Dimension:* moyenne; *Envergure:* provinciale
Mission: Un groupe d'entraide et une société fraternelle, qui unit des hommes de foi; l'ordre n'est pas rattaché à la structure juridique de l'Église catholique mais c'est un ordre de laïcs catholiques et exclusivement masculin
Membre: 104 000 individuals
Membre(s) du bureau directeur:
Fernand Rochon, Directeur général
fernand.rochon@chevaliersdecolomb.com

Les Chevaliers de Colomb du Québec, District No 37, Conseil 5198
124, rue des Forces Armées, Chibougamau QC G8P 2K5
Tél: 418-748-2411
dd37cc@hotmail.com
www.chevaliersdecolomb.com
Aperçu: *Dimension:* petite; *Envergure:* locale
Membre(s) du bureau directeur:
Danny Bouchard, Député de district, 418-748-6482
Gaston Deroy, Grand Chevalier

Chez Doris
1430, Chomedey, Montréal QC H3H 2A7
Tél: 514-937-2341; *Téléc:* 514-937-2417
information@chezdoris.org
www.chezdoris.org
www.facebook.com/ChezDorisRefuge
Aperçu: *Dimension:* petite; *Envergure:* locale; Organisme sans but lucratif
Mission: Offre un refuge de jour, sept jours sur sept, pour les femmes en difficulté
Finances: *Fonds:* Donations
Activités: Services et programmes: des repas; santé physique et mentale; assistance aux femmes inuit et autochtones; des vêtements; des activités sociaux-récréatives; des services pratique
Membre(s) du bureau directeur:
Marina Boulos-Winton, Directrice générale

Chez les français de L'Anse-à-Canards inc.
CP 337, RR#1, L'Anse-à-Canards NL A0N 1R0
Tél: 709-642-5498; *Téléc:* 709-642-5294
cfac_bdb@hotmail.com
www.francotnl.ca/CFAC
Aperçu: *Dimension:* petite; *Envergure:* locale; fondée en 1972
Mission: S'engage à préserver et à promouvoir la langue et la culture française des communautés de L'Anse-à-Canards et de Maison d'Hiver.
Affiliation(s): La Fédération des francophones de Terre-Neuve et du Labrador; L'Association francophone du Labrador.
Activités: Le Jour de l'Armistice; La Chandeleur; festival folklorique
Membre(s) du bureau directeur:
Bernard Félix, Président
Robert Félix, Agent culturel

Chezzetcook Historical Society
PO Box 7, Head Chezzetcook NS B0J 1N0
Tel: 902-827-4177
www.rootsweb.ancestry.com/~nschezhs
Overview: A small local organization founded in 1974
Mission: To preserve articles or information of historical value from East Chezzetcook, Porter's Lake, West Chezzetcook & Seaforth areas
Member of: Federation of the Nova Scotian Heritage

Chicken Farmers of Canada (CFC) / Les Producteurs de poulet du Canada
#1007, 350 Sparks St., Ottawa ON K1R 7S8
Tel: 613-241-2800; *Fax:* 613-241-5999
cfc@chicken.ca
www.chickenfarmers.ca
www.facebook.com/chickenfarmers
twitter.com/chickenfarmers
www.pinterest.com/chickendotca
Previous Name: Canadian Chicken Marketing Agency
Overview: A large national organization founded in 1978
Mission: To build an evidence-based, consumer driven Canadian chicken industry that provides opportunities for profitable growth for all stakeholders
Member of: Canadian Federation of Agriculture
Finances: *Annual Operating Budget:* $500,000-$1.5 Million
Staff Member(s): 22
Membership: 2,700 Canadian chicken producers; *Committees:* Executive; Finance; Policy; Production; Consumer Relations; Representatives
Chief Officer(s):
Mike Dungate, Executive Director
mdungate@chicken.ca
Lisa Bishop-Spencer, Manager, Communications
lbishop@chicken.ca
Publications:
• Allocation Calendar [a publication of Chicken Farmers of Canada]
Type: Calendar; *Frequency:* Annually
Profile: Information on the chicken industry
• Chicken Farmer Newsletter [a publication of Chicken Farmers of Canada]
Type: Newsletter; *Frequency:* Monthly
• Chicken Farmers of Canada 5-year Strategic Plan
Type: Report
• Chicken Farmers of Canada Annual Report
Type: Yearbook; *Frequency:* Annually
• Chicken Fax/Repères [a publication of Chicken Farmers of Canada]
Type: Newsletter; *Frequency:* Monthly
Profile: Canadian chicken market trends
• Data Booklet [a publication of Chicken Farmers of Canada]
Type: Booklet; *Frequency:* Annually
Profile: Yearly overview of the Canadian chicken industry
• Geneva Watch [a publication of Chicken Farmers of Canada]
Type: Newsletter; *Frequency:* Weekly; *Editor:* Charles Akande
Profile: Information on World Trade Organization negoiations involving agriculture; published by Dairy Farmers of Canada, Chicken Farmers of Canada, EggFarmers of Canada, Turkey Farmers of Canada and Canadian Hatching Egg Producers
• Good Business, Great Chicken [a publication of Chicken Farmers of Canada]
Type: Guide
Profile: Information on the chicken industry
• Storage Stocks [a publication of Chicken Farmers of Canada]
Type: Report; *Frequency:* Monthly
Profile: Information on Canadian chicken storage stocks

Chicken Farmers of New Brunswick / Les Éleveurs de poulets du Nouveau-Brunswick
#103, 277 Main St., Fredericton NB E3A 1E1
Tel: 506-452-8085; *Fax:* 506-451-2121
Overview: A medium-sized provincial organization overseen by Chicken Farmers of Canada
Mission: To control the marketing of chickens in the area within its jurisdiction; To cooperate with similar boards in other areas; To stimulate & increase the demand for chickens produced in New Brunswick; To improve the process of marketing
5 volunteer(s)

Chicken Farmers of Newfoundland & Labrador
PO Box 8098, St. John's NL A1B 3M9
Tel: 709-747-1493; *Fax:* 709-747-0544
www.nlchicken.com
Previous Name: Newfoundland Chicken Marketing Board
Overview: A medium-sized provincial organization overseen by Chicken Farmers of Canada
Member of: Chicken Farmers of Canada
Finances: *Annual Operating Budget:* $250,000-$500,000
Chief Officer(s):
Ron Walsh, Executive Director

Chicken Farmers of Nova Scotia
531 Main St., Kentville NS B4N 1L4
Tel: 902-681-7400; *Fax:* 902-681-7401
chicken@nschicken.com
www.nschicken.com
www.facebook.com/Chicken.Farmers.of.Nova.Scotia
Overview: A medium-sized provincial organization founded in 1966 overseen by Chicken Farmers of Canada
Finances: *Funding Sources:* Levy system for chicken farmers
Membership: 84; *Member Profile:* Chicken farmers in Nova Scotia

Chicken Farmers of Prince Edward Island
4701 Baldwin Rd., RR#6, Cardigan PE C0A 1G0
Tel: 902-838-4108; *Fax:* 902-838-4108
peipoultry@pei.sympatico.ca
Previous Name: Prince Edward Island Poultry Meat Commodity Marketing Board
Overview: A medium-sized provincial organization founded in 1973
Member of: Chicken Farmers of Canada; Nationa CFC Finance Committee; Canadian Broiler Council
Chief Officer(s):
Janet Murphy Hilliard, General Manager

Chicken Farmers of Saskatchewan (CFS)
Rumley Building, #201, 224 Pacific Ave., Saskatoon SK S7K 1N9
Tel: 306-242-3611; *Fax:* 306-242-3286
www.saskatchewanchicken.ca
Overview: A medium-sized provincial organization founded in 1966 overseen by Chicken Farmers of Canada
Mission: To advance the chicken industry in Saskatchewan, based on consumer needs & built on innovation, profitability &

the ability of stakeholders to work together
Affiliation(s): Chicken Farmers of Canada
Finances: *Funding Sources:* Levy system for chicken producers
Staff Member(s): 5
Membership: 70
Chief Officer(s):
Kari Tosczak, Executive Director
kari@saskatchewanchicken.ca
Colleen Kohlruss, Executive Assistant & Promotions
cfos@sasktel.net

Chiefs of Ontario
#804, 111 Peter St., Toronto ON M5V 2H1
Tel: 416-597-1266; *Fax:* 416-597-8365
Toll-Free: 877-517-6527
www.chiefs-of-ontario.org
twitter.com/chiefsofontario
vimeo.com/chiefsofontario;
www.flickr.com/photos/chiefsofontario
Overview: A medium-sized provincial organization
Mission: To enable the political leadership to discuss regional, provincial & national priorities affecting First Nation people in Ontario & to provide a unified voice on these issues.
Affiliation(s): Assembly of First Nations
Staff Member(s): 33
Chief Officer(s):
Pam Montour, Executive Director
executive.director@coo.org

Child & Family Services of Timmins & District *See* North Eastern Ontario Family & Children's Services

Child & Family Services of Western Manitoba (C&FS Western)
800 McTavish Ave., Brandon MB R7A 7L4
Tel: 204-726-6030; *Fax:* 204-726-6775
Toll-Free: 800-483-8980
info@cfswestern.mb.ca
www.cfswestern.mb.ca
Previous Name: Children's Aid Society of Western Manitoba
Overview: A medium-sized local charitable organization founded in 1899
Mission: To ensure children are safe in strong loving families within caring communities
Member of: Child Welfare League of Canada
Finances: *Annual Operating Budget:* Less than $50,000; *Funding Sources:* Government; United Way; private donations; rural campaigns; service clubs; foundations
Staff Member(s): 160; 46 volunteer(s)
Membership: 120; *Fees:* $10/1 yr.; $25/3 yrs.
Activities: Child protection services; family counselling; family support worker program; Family Resource Centre; family aid program; shared service programs; summer programs; parent-child home program; preschool enrichment; Victoria Day Care; unmarried parent service; sexual abuse treatment; adoption; post-adoption; foster care; *Library:* Not open to public
Chief Officer(s):
Phil Shaman, President
Candace Kowalchuk, Specialist, Human Resources
hr@cfswestern.mb.ca
Susan Cable, Coordinator, Community Education
commed@cfswestern.mb.ca

Child & Parent Resource Institute (CPRI)
600 Sanatorium Rd., London ON N6H 3W7
Tel: 519-858-2774; *Fax:* 519-858-3913
Toll-Free: 877-494-2774; *TTY:* 519-858-0257
www.cpri.ca
Previous Name: Children's Psychiatric Research Institute
Overview: A medium-sized local organization founded in 1960
Mission: To enhance the quality of life of children & youth with complex mental health or developmental challenges; to assist their families so these children & youth can reach their full potential
Member of: Ontario Association of Children's Mental Health Centres
Membership: *Committees:* Regional Advisory
Activities: *Speaker Service:* Yes; *Library:* Dr. Joseph Pozsonyi Memorial Library; Open to public

Child & Youth Care Association of Alberta (CYCAA)
255 Bonnie Doon Mall, 8330 - 82nd Ave., Edmonton AB T6C 4E3
Tel: 780-809-0890; *Fax:* 780-428-3844
info@cycaa.com
www.cycaa.com
www.facebook.com/ChildAndYouthCareAssociationOfAlberta
twitter.com/CYCAA1
Overview: A small provincial organization founded in 1972
Mission: To promote, improve & maintain progressive standards of child/youth care services; To encourage an active public interest in child/youth care services
Member of: Alberta Association of Services for Children & Families
Affiliation(s): Council of Canadian Child & Youth Care Associations
Finances: *Annual Operating Budget:* Less than $50,000
Staff Member(s): 3; 20 volunteer(s)
Membership: 750; *Fees:* $100 full member/agency/educational member; $125 out of province full member; $35 student; *Member Profile:* Child & youth care workers, not daycare workers
Activities: Certification program for child & youth care workers; *Library:* Not open to public
Chief Officer(s):
Catherine Hedlin, President
Awards:
• Child & Youth Care Counsellor of the Year

Child & Youth Care Association of Newfoundland & Labrador (CYCANL)
PO Box 632, St. John's NL A1C 5K8
Fax: 709-739-1857
cycassociation@cycanl.ca
www.cycanl.ca
Overview: A small provincial organization
Mission: To advocate for child & youth in general &, specifically, those in care; To provide members with up-to-date information on developments in the field of Child & Youth Care through newsletters & journals; To promote the field of Child & Youth Care as a profession through the development of standards & ethics for those working in the field; To provide members with a forum to network with others in the field
Membership: *Fees:* $40 full membership; $20 student membership; *Committees:* Finance; Membership; Newsletter; Public Relations/Fundraising; Standards; Steering & Program
Chief Officer(s):
Jaime Lundrigan, President

The Child Abuse Survivor Monument Project (CASMP)
274 Rhodes Ave., Toronto ON M4L 3A3
Tel: 416-469-4764; *Fax:* 416-963-8892
mci@irvingstudios.com
www.irvingstudios.com/child_abuse_survivor_monument
www.facebook.com/ChildAbuseMonument
twitter.com/ChildAbuseMnumt
www.youtube.com/user/ChildAbuseMonument
Also Known As: Survivor Monument Project
Overview: A small local charitable organization founded in 1995
Mission: To build a memorial monument for & by survivors of child abuse to assist with the personal & social healing of the ravages of child abuse
Affiliation(s): Children's Aid Foundation
Finances: *Funding Sources:* Private donations; government grants
Activities: *Speaker Service:* Yes; *Library:* CASMP Library; by appointment
Chief Officer(s):
Michael C. Irving, Artistic Director

Child Care Advocacy Association of Canada (CCAAC) / Association canadienne pour la promotion des services de garde à l'enfance (ACPSGE)
225 Brunswick Ave., Toronto ON M5S 2M6
Tel: 416-926-8859
www.ccaac.ca
www.facebook.com/childcareadvocacyassociationofcanada
twitter.com/CCAAC_ACPSGE
Previous Name: Canadian Day Care Advocacy Association
Overview: A medium-sized national licensing organization founded in 1982
Mission: To work toward expanding the child care system & improving its quality; To advocate for the development of an affordable, comprehensive, high-quality, not-for-profit child care system that is supported by public funds & accessible to every Canadian family who wishes to use it
Member of: National Action Committee on the Status of Women
Affiliation(s): Canadian Labour Congress; Public Service Alliance; Canadian Union of Public Employees
Finances: *Funding Sources:* Donations; Government
Membership: 1,000; *Fees:* $15 individual/family; $50 organization/group; $5 full-time student
Activities: *Speaker Service:* Yes

Child Care Connection Nova Scotia (CCCNS)
#100, 1200 Tower Rd., Halifax NS B3H 4K6
Tel: 902-423-8199; *Fax:* 902-492-8106
Toll-Free: 800-565-8199
Other Communication: resource@cccns.org
info@cccns.org
www.cccns.org
Overview: A small provincial organization founded in 1989
Mission: To provide resources & support to early childhood practitioners throughout Nova Scotia
Finances: *Funding Sources:* Nova Scotia Department of Community Services; Advertising, publication, & product sales; Income from events
Staff Member(s): 2
Membership: *Member Profile:* Early childhood practitioners in Nova Scotia
Activities: Providing professional development activities; Raising the public image of early childhood practice; Engaging in advocacy activities; Producing fact sheets; *Library:* Child Care Connection Resource Library
Chief Officer(s):
Barb Bigelow, Co-Chair
Donna Stapleton, Co-Chair
Elaine Ferguson, Executive Director
Pat McCormack, Coordinator, Office & Resources
Publications:
• A Best Practices Approach to Regulated Child Care within a Framework that Supports Good Outcomes for Children
Author: E. Ferguson; K. Flanagan Rochon
• Child Care Administrator Credentialing In Canada, A Work In Progress Appendix A; Appendix B; & Appendix C
Author: T. McCormick Ferguson; E. Ferguson
• Child Care Centre Directory
Type: Directory
Profile: Listings of licensed centres in Nova Scotia, including information such as address, capacity, children's age range, number of staff, & type of program
• Child Care Connection Nova Scotia Report to Stakeholders
Type: Yearbook; *Frequency:* Annually
• ConnectioNS [a publication of Child Care Connection Nova Scotia]
Type: Journal; *Frequency:* 2-3 pa; *Accepts Advertising*; *Editor:* E. Elaine Ferguson; *ISSN:* 0843-6304
Profile: Distributed to Nova Scotia's child care centres & other organizations & individuals
• Maximizing Child Care Services: The Role of Owners & Boards
Author: T. McCormick Ferguson; E. Ferguson
• Retention & Recruitment Challenges in Canadian Child Care
Author: Elaine Ferguson; Connie Miller
• Toward a Best Practices Framework for Licensing Child Care Facilities in Canada
Author: E. Ferguson; K. Flanagan Rochon

Child Care Providers Resource Network of Ottawa-Carleton
#275, 30 Colonnade Rd., Ottawa ON K2E 7J6
Tel: 613-749-5211; *Fax:* 613-749-6650
info@ccprn.com
www.ccprn.com
www.facebook.com/234504449898448?ref=ts
www.youtube.com/childcareproviders/
Overview: A small provincial organization
Mission: The Child Care Providers Resource Network of Ottawa-Carleton, is a non-profit, charitable organization committed to providing support, information, training and resources to individuals who offer child care in a home setting.
Activities: Workshops; Children's events; Bi-monthly newsletter; *Library:* Resource Library
Chief Officer(s):
Doreen Cowin, Executive Director
doreen@ccprn.com

Child Development Centre Society of Fort St. John & District
10417 - 106th Ave., Fort St John BC V1J 2M8
Tel: 250-785-3200; *Fax:* 250-785-3202
info@cdcfsj.ca
www.cdcfsj.ca
Overview: A small local charitable organization founded in 1973
Mission: To promote the treatment & education of children with special needs, to ensure that they & their families are effectively & locally served with dignity & respect.

Member of: BC Association for Child Development & Intervention
Affiliation(s): Cerebral Palsy Association of British Columbia
Finances: *Funding Sources:* Regional government; private & corporate donors
Activities: Operation of the Child Development Centre (CDC) with programs including physiotherapy, speech therapy, occupational therapy, Early Learning Program
Chief Officer(s):
Andy Ackerman, President
Penny Gagnon, Executive Director

Child Development Institute (CDI)
197 Euclid Ave., Toronto ON M6J 2J8
Tel: 416-603-1827; *Fax:* 416-603-6655
info@childdevelop.ca
www.childdevelop.ca
ca.linkedin.com/company/child-development-institute
www.facebook.com/childdevelop
twitter.com/officialcdi
www.youtube.com/user/CDICanada
Overview: A medium-sized international charitable organization
Mission: An accredited children's mental health agency that develops innovative programming for children ages 0-12 and youth ages 13-18 and their families in the areas of Early Intervention Services, Family Violence Services and Healthy Child Development.
Finances: *Funding Sources:* Donations
Membership: *Fees:* $40 active; $125 associate
Chief Officer(s):
Tony Diniz, Chief Executive Officer
tdiniz@childdevelop.ca
Shauna Klein, Director, Fund Development, Marketing and Communications
sklein@childdevelop.ca

Child Evangelism Fellowship of Canada
PO Box 165, Stn. Main, 337 Henderson Hwy., Winnipeg MB R3C 2G9
Tel: 204-943-2774; *Fax:* 204-943-9967
Toll-Free: 866-943-2774
info@cefcanada.org
www.cefcanada.org
Also Known As: CEF Canada
Overview: A medium-sized national charitable organization founded in 1937
Mission: CEF Canada is a bible-centred organization of born-again believers whose purpose is to evangelize & disciple children with the gospel of Jesus Christ.
Member of: Canadian Council of Christian Charities
Affiliation(s): Child Evangelism Fellowship Inc.; CEF of Nations
Finances: *Annual Operating Budget:* $500,000-$1.5 Million; *Funding Sources:* Individual, corporate & church donations
Staff Member(s): 45; 200 volunteer(s)
Membership: 1-99
Activities: Children's Ministries Institute; offers courses/programs, materials & training for Christian education among children
Chief Officer(s):
Jerry Hanson, National Director
jhanson@cefcanada.org
Brenda Hanson, Director, Education
bhanson@cefcanada.org

Child Evangelism Fellowship - Atlantic
PO Box 134, Moncton NB E1C 8R9
Tel: 506-378-4775
Chief Officer(s):
Ron Wiebe, Provincial Director
rwiebe@cefcanada.org

Child Evangelism Fellowship of Alberta (CEF Alberta)
2115 - 5 Ave. NW, Calgary AB T2N 0S6
Fax: 800-561-0686
Toll-Free: 800-561-5315
info@cefalberta.org
www.cefalberta.org
www.facebook.com/cefalberta
Chief Officer(s):
Jerry Durston, Provincial Director
jerry.durston@cefministries.org

Child Evangelism Fellowship of British Columbia
#204, 18515 - 53 Ave., Surrey BC V3S 7A4
Tel: 604-576-7796; *Fax:* 604-582-0491
Toll-Free: 855-576-7796
info@cefbc.com
www.cefbc.com

Chief Officer(s):
Dennis Quin, Provincial Director
dennisq@cefbc.com

Child Evangelism Fellowship of Manitoba (CEF Manitoba)
179 Henderson Hwy., Winnipeg MB R2L 1L5
Tel: 204-663-3300; *Fax:* 204-667-1026
cefmb@mts.net
cefmanitoba.org
Chief Officer(s):
Matthew Maniate, Provincial Director

Child Evangelism Fellowship of Ontario (CEFOntario)
335 Robinson Rd., RR #4, Brantford ON N3T 5L7
Tel: 519-751-1233; *Fax:* 519-751-2233
info@cefontario.org
www.cefontario.org
www.facebook.com/139808322733114
Chief Officer(s):
Rob Lukings, Provincial Director
rlukings@cefontario.org

Child Evangelism Fellowship of Saskatchewan
74 Marquis Cres., Regina SK S4S 6J9
Tel: 306-584-9622; *Fax:* 306-584-1308
info@cefsask.org
www.cefsask.org
www.facebook.com/cefsask
twitter.com/cefsask
Chief Officer(s):
Jerry Durston, Provincial Director
jdurston@cefsask.org

Québec - Association Évangile & Enfance
2225, rue Mistral, Brossard QC J4Y 2T3
Tél: 450-926-3357
info@aeecefquebec.org
aeecefquebec.org
Chief Officer(s):
Mary Porter, Directrice
Jenne Phillips, Directrice

Child Find British Columbia
#208, 2722 Fifth St., Victoria BC V8T 4B2
Tel: 250-382-7311; *Fax:* 250-382-0227
Toll-Free: 888-689-3463
childvicbc@shaw.ca
childfindbc.com
Overview: A small provincial charitable organization founded in 1984 overseen by Child Find Canada Inc.
Mission: To assist in the search & location of missing children, providing support to law enforcement & families; To educate & prevent the abduction & exploitation of children & provide awareness
Member of: Association of Missing & Exploited Children's Organizations
Finances: *Annual Operating Budget:* $100,000-$250,000; *Funding Sources:* Fundraising; sponsorships; grants & foundations
Staff Member(s): 2; 500 volunteer(s)
Activities: *Awareness Events:* National Missing Children's Day, May 25; Green Ribbon of Hope Campaign, May; *Speaker Service:* Yes
Chief Officer(s):
Steve Orcherton, Executive Director

Child Find Canada Inc. (CFC)
PO Box 237, Oakville MB R0H 0Y0
Tel: 204-870-1298
childcan@aol.com
www.childfind.ca
Also Known As: ChildFind Canada
Overview: A small national charitable organization founded in 1988
Mission: Supports provincial Child Find organizations in the location of & education in the prevention of missing children; increases national awareness of issues relating to missing children; advocates for the protection & rights of children.
Finances: *Funding Sources:* Corporate & individual donations
Membership: 9 provincial offices; *Member Profile:* Over 18 years of age; police security clearance; references; application; personal suitability
Activities: Prevention & education material; child & baby identification kits

Child Find Newfoundland & Labrador
PO Box 13232, St. John's NL A1B 4A5
Tel: 709-738-4400
childfindnl@bellaliant.com
www.childfind.ca

Overview: A medium-sized provincial organization overseen by Child Find Canada Inc.
Mission: To prevent missing children; To support the search for missing children
Activities: *Awareness Events:* National Missing Children's Day, May 25; Green Ribbon of Hope Campaign, May

Child Find Nova Scotia
PO Box 31302, Halifax NS B3K 5Y5
Tel: 902-454-2030; *Fax:* 902-429-6749
Toll-Free: 800-682-9006
childns@aol.com
Overview: A medium-sized provincial organization overseen by Child Find Canada Inc.
Activities: *Awareness Events:* National Missing Children's Day, May 25; Green Ribbon of Hope Campaign, May

Child Find Ontario
#303B, 75 Front St. East, Toronto ON M5E 1V9
Tel: 416-987-9684
Toll-Free: 866-543-8477
Other Communication: Alt. URL: www.missingkids.ca
mail@childfindontario.ca
www.childfindontario.ca
Overview: A small provincial charitable organization founded in 1983 overseen by Child Find Canada Inc.
Mission: To assist in the search & recovery process of missing children
Affiliation(s): Canadian Centre for Child Protection Inc.
Finances: *Funding Sources:* Donations
Activities: Fingerprinting events; information booths; abduction education; assistance in search for missing children; *Awareness Events:* National Missing Children's Day, May 25; Green Ribbon of Hope Campaign, May; *Speaker Service:* Yes

Northern Ontario Office
303 York St., Sudbury ON P3E 2A5
Tel: 705-671-9888

Child Find PEI Inc.
39 Riverbank Dr., Johnston's River PE C1B 3E7
Tel: 902-566-5935; *Fax:* 902-368-1389
Toll-Free: 800-387-7962
childfindpei@gmail.com
www.childfindpei.com
www.facebook.com/459667334088816
Overview: A small provincial charitable organization founded in 1988 overseen by Child Find Canada Inc.
Mission: To assist in the location of missing children; to increase awareness of the problem of missing children; to teache ways to prevent abduction; to provide assistance & support to families of a missing child.
Member of: Association of Missing & Exploited Children's Organizations
Affiliation(s): PEI Amber Alert
Staff Member(s): 1; 50 volunteer(s)
Activities: "All About Me ID" (fingerprinting clinics); Teen Runaway; Case Management; educational videos; distribution of brochures & pamphlets; public displays at community events; distribution of missing children posters; *Awareness Events:* National Missing Children's Day, May 25; Green Ribbon of Hope Campaign, May; *Speaker Service:* Yes; *Library:* Open to public
Chief Officer(s):
Megan DeCoste, President

Child Find Saskatchewan Inc.
#202, 3502 Taylor St. East, Saskatoon SK S7H 5H9
Tel: 306-955-0070; *Fax:* 306-373-1311
Toll-Free: 800-513-3463
childfind@childfind.sk.ca
www.childfind.sk.ca
Overview: A small provincial charitable organization founded in 1984 overseen by Child Find Canada Inc.
Mission: To locate missing & abducted children & reunite them with their lawful parent or guardian; To increase public awareness of the need to protect children; To educate both parents & child on street proofing technology & to support families of missing children
Affiliation(s): Federation of Saskatchewan Indian Nations; Saskatoon Indian & Metis Friendship Centre; Saskatchewan Association of Chiefs of Police; Saskatchewan Federation of Police Officers
Finances: *Annual Operating Budget:* $100,000-$250,000; *Funding Sources:* Private & corporate donations
Membership: 1-99
Activities: All About Me ID; ID clinics; ALERT Youth; education programs on child personal safety, streetproofing, runaways &

prevention of abductions; national picture distribution; poster distribution; *Awareness Events:* National Missing Children's Day, May 25; Green Ribbon of Hope Campaign, May; *Speaker Service:* Yes; *Library:* Open to public by appointment
Chief Officer(s):
Phyllis Hallatt, President
Publications:
• Alert Magazine [a publication of Child Find Saskatchewan Inc.]
Type: Magazine; *Frequency:* Quarterly

CHILD Foundation (CHILD)
U.B.C. Campus, #201, 2150 Western Parkway, Vancouver BC V6T 1V6
Tel: 604-736-0645; *Fax:* 604-228-0066
info@child.ca
www.child.ca
www.facebook.com/pages/The-CHILD-Foundation/141407274 8840373
Also Known As: Children with Intestinal & Liver Disorders
Overview: A small provincial charitable organization founded in 1995
Mission: To help an almost forgotten group of youngsters who suffer from incurable digestive disorders such as Crohn's Disease, Ulcerative Colitis & related IBD (intestinal & bowel disorders) & liver disorders; To find a cure through research for these diseases
Member of: Vancouver Board of Trade
Affiliation(s): CHILD Foundation USA
Membership: *Member Profile:* Business leaders & members of families of Crohn's or Colitis patients
Activities: *Awareness Events:* Fashion for CHILD; Snowbirds Fly for CHILD; Doormen's Dinner for CHILD; Golf for CHILD; *Speaker Service:* Yes
Chief Officer(s):
Grace M. McCarthy, Chair
Mary Parsons, President & CEO

Child Welfare League of Canada (CWLC) / Ligue pour le bien-être de l'enfance du Canada (LBEC)
226 Argyle Ave., Ottawa ON K2P 1B9
Tel: 613-235-4412; *Fax:* 613-235-7616
info@cwlc.ca
www.cwlc.ca
www.facebook.com/CWLC.LBEC
Overview: A large national charitable organization founded in 1994
Mission: To provide public education on the needs of all children, youth & their families through research, information & other services directed toward enhancing & improving public awareness; To facilitate the development of standards in services to children, youth & their families; To encourage excellence in the delivery of these services
Member of: Canadian Coalition for the Rights of Children
Affiliation(s): Child Welfare League of America
Finances: *Annual Operating Budget:* $250,000-$500,000; *Funding Sources:* Membership dues; Consultation fees; Projects; Conference income; Sustaining grant
Staff Member(s): 8
Membership: 135 organizations; *Fees:* Schedule available; *Member Profile:* Professionals who support the welfare & protection of children
Activities: Training programs for professional staff, caregivers, volunteers; Information resources for the public & organizations; Program reviews; Looking after children program; Centre of Excellence for Child Welfare; *Awareness Events:* Atlantic Canada Child Welfare Forum; *Internships:* Yes; *Speaker Service:* Yes; *Rents Mailing List:* Yes; *Library:* Canadian Resource Centre on Children & Youth; Open to public
Chief Officer(s):
Andrew Koster, Board Chair
Gordon Phaneuf, MSW, RSW, Chief Executive Officer
gord@cwlc.ca
Awards:
• Youth Achievement Award
Honours a young person (under 21) who is either in care or has left care, & has demonstrated commitment to self-improvement & contributed to the positive image of youth
• Advocacy Award
Awarded to an individual or organization that has made a positive impact on public opinion regarding child welfare in Canada
• Research & Program Excellence Award
Honours excellence in child welfare research
• Children's Services Award
Awarded to a staff member or team that has shown commitment, creativity & dedication in their work in the child welfare sector
• Foster Parent Award
Awarded to a foster parent or foster family that has provided outstanding care to the children &/or youth placed in his or her care
Publications:
• The Child Welfare League of Canada Newsletter
Type: Newsletter

Childcare Resource & Research Unit
225 Brunswick Ave., Toronto ON M5S 2M6
Tel: 416-926-9264; *Fax:* 416-964-8239
contactus@childcarecanada.org
www.childcarecanada.org
www.facebook.com/1120886888724 63?sk=wall
twitter.com/childcarepolicy
Overview: A small national organization
Chief Officer(s):
Martha Friendly, Coordinator
mfriendly@childcarecanada.org

Childhood Cancer Canada Foundation
#801, 21 St. Clair Ave. East, Toronto ON M4T 1L9
Tel: 416-489-6440; *Fax:* 416-489-9812
Toll-Free: 800-363-1062
info@childhoodcancer.ca
www.childhoodcancer.ca
www.facebook.com/ChildhoodCancerCanada
twitter.com/chldhdcancercan
Overview: A large national organization founded in 1987
Mission: To help improve the lives of children suffering from cancer through family support programs; to fund cancer research
Finances: *Annual Operating Budget:* $1.5 Million-$3 Million
Staff Member(s): 7
Chief Officer(s):
Glenn Fraser, Chair

British Columbia Childhood Cancer Parent's Association
British Columbia Children's Hospital, #A127A, 4480 Oak St., Vancouver BC V6H 3B8
Tel: 604-875-2345

Candlelighters Newfoundland & Labrador
PO Box 5846, St. John's NL A1C 5X3
Tel: 709-745-4448
Toll-Free: 866-745-4448
info@Candlelightersnl.ca
www.candlelightersnl.ca
www.facebook.com/CandlelightersNL
twitter.com/CandlelighterNL
Chief Officer(s):
Amananda Kinsman, Coordinator, Provincial Family Program
coordinator@candlelightersnl.ca

Manitoba - Candlelighters Childhood Cancer Support Group (CCCSG)
PO Box 350, RR#1, Winkler MB R6W 4A1
support@manitobacandlelighters.ca
www.manitobacandlelighters.ca
Chief Officer(s):
Denis Foidart, Chair, 204-737-2684
denlis@wiband.ca

SK - Candlelighters - Prince Albert
350 - 30th St. East, Prince Albert SK S6V 1Z4
Tel: 306-763-7356

SK - Regina Candlelighters
100 cardinal Cres., Regina SK S4S 4Y7
Tel: 306-529-3292
sask.candlelighters@sasktel.net
Chief Officer(s):
David Achter, Contact
Tangy Achter, Contact

Childhood Obesity Foundation (COF)
Robert H.N. Ho Research Centre, VGH Hospital Campus, 771A - 2635 Laurel St., Vancouver BC V5Z 1M9
Tel: 604-251-2229
info@childhoodobesityfoundation.ca
www.childhoodobesityfoundation.ca
www.facebook.com/childhoodobesityfoundation
twitter.com/COF_5210
Overview: A small national charitable organization founded in 2004
Mission: Aims to reduce the prevalence of childhood obesity in Canada.
Chief Officer(s):
Tom Warshawski, Chair

Children & Family Services for York Region See York Region Children's Aid Society

Children and Youth in Challenging Contexts Network (CYCC)
PO Box 15000, 6420 Coburg Rd., Halifax ON B3H 4R2
Tel: 902-494-4087
cyccnetwork.org
www.facebook.com/CYCCNetwork
twitter.com/CYCCNetwork
www.youtube.com/user/cyccnetwork
Overview: A medium-sized national organization
Mission: The CYCC Network is a knowledge mobilization network that was created to improve mental health and well-being for vulnerable and at-risk children and youth in Canada.
Chief Officer(s):
Lisa Lachance, Executive Director
lisa.lachance@dal.ca

Children of the World Adoption Society Inc. / Société d'adoption enfants du monde inc.
815 rue Lippmann, 2e étage, Laval QC H7S 1G3
Tel: 514-332-6332; *Fax:* 514-688-9339
Toll-Free: 800-381-3588
info@enfantsdumonde.org
www.enfantsdumonde.org
Overview: A small international organization founded in 1989
Mission: To help parents adopt children from foreign countries in compliance with the laws & traditions of those countries, in a spirit of humanitarian co-operation.
Affiliation(s): Secrétariat à l'Adoption Internationale (SAI); Quebec Association of Youth Centres
Activities: International adoption
Chief Officer(s):
Hélène Duval, President

Lower St. Lawrence - Gaspé Office
PO Box 417, 7, rue Bossé, Saint-Antonin QC G0L 2J0
Tel: 418-868-1889; *Fax:* 418-868-1889
Chief Officer(s):
Martin Desrosiers, Regional Coordinator
mdesros@videotron.ca

Saguenay - Lac-St-Jean Office
238, rue Olier, Chicoutimi QC G7G 4J3
Tel: 418-545-8536; *Fax:* 418-543-8211
Chief Officer(s):
Sylvie Tremblay, Regional Coordinator
boivinsylvieguy@videotron.ca

The Children's Aid Foundation of York Region
#19, 201 Millway Ave., Vaughan ON L4K 5K8
Tel: 905-738-8675
www.cafyr.org
www.facebook.com/184207384932619
Overview: A small local organization
Mission: To improve the lives of abused children through enrichment, education, & prevention; To raise funds to support the children & families served by Children's Aid Societies
Activities: Raising money; Allocating & disbursing funds to programs & agencies; *Awareness Events:* Children's Aid Foundation Bike Ride; Children's Aid Foundation Annual Golf Classic
Chief Officer(s):
Attilio Lio, President

Children's Aid Society of Algoma / Société de l'aide à l'enfance d'Algoma
191 Northern Ave. East, Sault Ste Marie ON P6B 4H8
Tel: 705-949-0162; *Fax:* 705-949-4747
Toll-Free: 888-414-3571
www.algomacas.org
Overview: A small local organization founded in 1902
Mission: To protect the children of Algoma; to promote their well-being in a manner that reflects community standards & the spirit or legislation, while making efficient use of community & society resources
Member of: Ontario Association of Children's Aid Societies
Finances: *Annual Operating Budget:* Greater than $5 Million; *Funding Sources:* Ministry of Children and Youth Services
Activities: Providing children & family services, adoption services, & foster care; Offering guidelines for reporting child abuse
Chief Officer(s):
Kim Streich-Poser, Executive Director

Blind River Office
9 Lawton St., Blind River ON P0R 1B0

Tel: 705-356-1464; Fax: 705-356-0773
Elliot Lake Office
29 Manitoba Rd., Elliot Lake ON P5A 2A7
Tel: 705-848-8000; Fax: 705-848-5145
Hornepayne Office
#7, 8 - 2nd St., Hornepayne ON P0M 1Z0
Tel: 807-868-2624
Wawa Office
31 Algoma St., Wawa ON P0S 1K0
Tel: 705-856-2960; Fax: 705-856-7379

Children's Aid Society of Brant See Brant Family & Children's Services

Children's Aid Society of Metropolitan Toronto See Children's Aid Society of Toronto

Children's Aid Society of Ottawa (CASO) / La Société de l'aide à l'enfance d'Ottawa
1602 Telesat Ct., Gloucester ON K1B 1B1
Tel: 613-747-7800; Fax: 613-747-4456; TTY: 613-742-1617
yourcasquestion@casott.on.ca
www.casott.on.ca
www.facebook.com/ottawacas
twitter.com/OttawaCas
www.youtube.com/user/casott123
Previous Name: Ottawa-Carleton Children's Aid Society
Overview: A small local charitable organization founded in 1893
Mission: To protect the children & youth of the Ottawa area from abuse & neglect, as regulated by Ontario's Ministry of Children & Youth Services & as governed by the Child & Family Services Act
Finances: Funding Sources: Government of Ontario
Activities: Offering information sessions about foster care & adoption; Awareness Events: Child Abuse Prevention Month, October; Foster Family Week, October
Chief Officer(s):
Tess Porter, Executive Director
Publications:
• Children's Aid Society of Ottawa Annual Report
Type: Report; Frequency: a.

Children's Aid Society of Oxford County
712 Peel St., Woodstock ON N4S 0B4
Tel: 519-539-6176; Fax: 519-421-0123
Toll-Free: 800-250-7010
info@casoxford.on.ca
www.casoxford.on.ca
Also Known As: CAS Oxford
Previous Name: Oxford Family & Child Services
Overview: A small local organization founded in 1895
Mission: To serve & promote the best interests, protection & well-being of children, while supporting the autonomy, integrity & cultural diversity of families and communities
Member of: Ontario Association of Children's Aid Societies
Finances: Annual Operating Budget: $1.5 Million-$3 Million; Funding Sources: Provincial government
Staff Member(s): 100; 75 volunteer(s)
Activities: Screening/training/counseling foster & adoptive parents; Offering guidance to families for protecting children; Investigating instances of possible child abuse or neglect; Internships: Yes; Speaker Service: Yes
Chief Officer(s):
Bruce Burbank, Executive Director

Children's Aid Society of the District of Nipissing & Parry Sound / La Société d'aide à l'enfance Nipissing & Parry Sound
433 McIntyre St. West, North Bay ON P1B 2Z3
Tel: 705-472-0910; Fax: 705-472-9743
Toll-Free: 877-303-0910
www.parnipcas.org
Previous Name: Nipissing Children's Aid Society for the District of Nipissing & Parry Sound
Overview: A small local licensing charitable organization founded in 1907
Mission: To promote the well-being & protection of children & youth, and advocates for their fundamental rights
Member of: Ontario Association of Children's Aid Societies
Finances: Funding Sources: Ontario Ministry of Children & Youth Services; donations
Activities: Screening/training of foster parents; Assisting young mothers; Providing adoption & counselling services; Establishing partnerships with other community services
Chief Officer(s):
Joe Rogers, President

Children's Aid Society of the Districts of Sudbury & Manitoulin (CAS) / La Société d'aide à l'enfance des districts de Sudbury et de Manitoulin
#3, 319 Lasalle Blvd., Sudbury ON P3A 1W7
Tel: 705-566-3113; Fax: 705-521-7372
Toll-Free: 800-272-4334
www.casdsm.on.ca
Merged from: Sudbury Children's Aid Society; Manitoulin Children's Aid Society
Overview: A medium-sized local charitable organization founded in 1971
Mission: To protect the well-being of children in the community
Member of: Ontario Association of Children's Aid Societies
Finances: Funding Sources: Provincial government
Activities: Providing adoption & foster placement services; Investigating possible instances of child abuse & neglect; Speaker Service: Yes
Chief Officer(s):
Elaina Groves, Executive Director
Chapleau Office
34 Birch St. East, Chapleau ON P0M 1K0
Tel: 705-864-0329; Fax: 705-864-2133

Children's Aid Society of the Region of Peel
West Tower, 6860 Century Ave., Mississauga ON L5N 2W5
Tel: 905-363-6131; Fax: 905-363-6133
Toll-Free: 888-700-0996
mail@peelcas.org
www.peelcas.org
www.youtube.com/user/PeelChildrensAid
Also Known As: Peel Children's Aid
Overview: A medium-sized local charitable organization founded in 1944
Mission: To protect children & strengthen families & communities through partnership
Membership: Member Profile: Must work or live in the region of Peel
Activities: Awareness Events: Use Your Voice Campaign, Oct.; Speaker Service: Yes
Chief Officer(s):
Rav Bains, Executive Director

Children's Aid Society of Toronto
30 Isabella St., Toronto ON M4Y 1N1
Tel: 416-924-4640
www.torontocas.ca
www.linkedin.com/company/children's-aid-society-of-toronto
twitter.com/TorontoCAS
Also Known As: Toronto CAS
Previous Name: Children's Aid Society of Metropolitan Toronto
Overview: A large local organization founded in 1891
Mission: To protect children from emotional, sexual & physical harm by working with individual children & their families; To provide a high standard & continuity of substitute parental care for those children who cannot remain at home; To develop prevention programs
Member of: Ontario Association of Children's Aid Societies; Child Welfare League of Canada; Child Welfare League of America
Finances: Annual Operating Budget: Greater than $5 Million; Funding Sources: Provincial government; federal government; Children's Aid Foundation; sundry
Staff Member(s): 798
Activities: Internships: Yes; Speaker Service: Yes
Chief Officer(s):
David Rivard, CEO
Mahesh Prajapat, Chief Operating Officer
Anthony Battista, Chief Financial Officer
Marnie Lynn, Chief Human Resources Officer
Publications:
• Communicate [a publication of the Children's Aid Society of Toronto]
Type: Newsletter

Children's Aid Society of Western Manitoba See Child & Family Services of Western Manitoba

Children's Arts Umbrella Association
1286 Cartwright St., Vancouver BC V6H 3R8
Tel: 604-681-5268; Fax: 604-681-5272
info@artsumbrella.com
www.artsumbrella.com
www.facebook.com/artsumbrella
twitter.com/artsumbrella
www.youtube.com/artsumbrellabc
Also Known As: Arts Umbrella
Overview: A small local charitable organization founded in 1979
Mission: Canada's visual & performing arts institute for young people of ages 2 to 19
Finances: Annual Operating Budget: $3 Million-$5 Million; Funding Sources: Government; fundraising; private sector corporations
300 volunteer(s)
Chief Officer(s):
Jamie Pitblado, Chair
Lucille Pacey, President & CEO

The Children's Broadcast Institute See Youth Media Alliance

Children's Cottage Society
845 McDougall Rd. NE, Calgary AB T2E 5A5
Tel: 403-283-4200; Fax: 403-283-4393; Crisis Hot-Line: 403-233-2273
www.childrenscottage.ab.ca
www.facebook.com/childrenscottagecalgary
twitter.com/childrnscottage
www.youtube.com/user/ChildrensCottage
Overview: A small local charitable organization
Mission: To prevent violence towards children & ensure a safe environment for them
Finances: Annual Operating Budget: $100,000-$250,000; Funding Sources: Provincial & municipal governments; foundation grants; donations; fundraising
Staff Member(s): 16; 1670 volunteer(s)
Chief Officer(s):
Patty Kilgallon, Executive Director
pkilgallon@childrenscottage.ab.ca

Children's Education Funds Inc. (CEFI)
3221 North Service Rd., Burlington ON L7N 3G2
Tel: 905-331-8377; Fax: 905-331-9977
Toll-Free: 800-246-1203
www.cefi.ca
Overview: A medium-sized national organization founded in 1990
Mission: To help build a better society through the education of children.

Children's Health Foundation of Vancouver Island
2390 Arbutus Rd., Victoria BC V8N 1V7
Tel: 250-519-6977; Fax: 250-519-6715
childrenshealthvi.org
www.linkedin.com/company/2291213
twitter.com/childrensvi
www.youtube.com/user/QAFoundation
Overview: A small local charitable organization founded in 1922
Mission: To support children in need by raising funds towards improving their health and well being
Staff Member(s): 10
Activities: Fundraising
Chief Officer(s):
Veronica Carroll, Chief Executive Officer
veronica.carroll@viha.ca
Frances Melville, Director, Operations
frances.melville@viha.ca

Children's Health Foundations
345 Westminster Ave., London ON N6C 4V3
Tel: 519-432-8564; Fax: 519-432-5907
Toll-Free: 888-834-2696
info@childhealth.ca
childhealth.ca
www.facebook.com/CHFHope
twitter.com/CHFHope
www.youtube.com/user/ChildrensRaisingHope
Overview: A small local charitable organization founded in 1922
Mission: To help raise funds for children's hospitals in order to provide patients with improved health care services & to fund research
Staff Member(s): 17
Activities: Fundraising
Chief Officer(s):
Sherri Bocchini, Chief Development Officer
sbocchini@childhealth.ca
Tracy Loosemore, Chief Operating Officer
tloosemore@childhealth.ca

Children's Heart Association for Support & Education (CHASE)
Tel: 416-410-2427
kidheart@angelfire.com
www.angelfire.com/on/chase
Overview: A small national organization founded in 1984

Mission: Organization committed to promoting awareness about congenital heart disease; to provide encouragement to families affected by CHD; driven to become the leading provider of resoures to education & support those who seek an understanding of the disease.
Finances: *Annual Operating Budget:* Less than $50,000
Membership: 527; *Member Profile:* Families & professionals dealing with congenital heart disease.; *Committees:* Awarenes; Fundraising; Social
Activities: *Awareness Events:* Feb. 14 CHD Day *Library:* CHIP; Open to public

Children's Heart Society
#128, 9920 63 Ave., Edmonton AB T6E 0G9
Tel: 780-454-7665
childrensheart@shaw.ca
www.childrensheart.ca
www.facebook.com/childrenshearts
twitter.com/childrenshearts
Overview: A small local organization
Mission: To support children with heart disease & their families
Membership: *Fees:* $30
Chief Officer(s):
Andrea Luft, President
chsgalaedmonton@gmail.com
Danielle Tailleur, Director, Membership
dtailleur@ellisdon.com

Children's Hospital Foundation of Manitoba
#CE501, 840 Sherbrook St., Winnipeg MB R3A 1S1
Tel: 204-787-4000; *Fax:* 204-787-4114
Toll-Free: 866-953-5437
Other Communication: Donations 204-953-5437
goodbear.mb.ca
www.facebook.com/childrenshospitalfoundation
twitter.com/chfmanitoba
www.youtube.com/user/DRGoodbear1
Overview: A large provincial charitable organization founded in 1971
Mission: To help raise funds for the Winnipeg Children's Hospital & the Manitoba Institute of Child Health in order to provide patients with improved health care services & to fund research
Finances: *Annual Operating Budget:* Greater than $5 Million
Staff Member(s): 20
Membership: *Committees:* Advisory Council; Child Health Advisory Council; Development; Finance; Human Resources; Investment; Marketing & Communications; Nominating/Governance
Activities: Fundraising
Chief Officer(s):
Lawrence Prout, President & CEO
lprout@hsc.mb.ca

Children's Hospital Foundation of Saskatchewan
#1, 345 - 3 Ave. South, Saskatoon SK S7K 1M6
Tel: 306-931-4887
Toll-Free: 888-808-5437
info@chfsask.ca
www.childrenshospitalsask.ca
www.facebook.com/CHFSask
twitter.com/childhospitalsk
www.youtube.com/user/ChildHospitalSK
Overview: A small provincial charitable organization
Mission: To help raise funds for the Children's Hospital of Saskatchewan in order to provide patients with improved health care services & to fund research
Activities: Fundraising
Chief Officer(s):
Brynn Boback-Lane, President & CEO

Children's Hospital of Eastern Ontario Foundation
415 Smyth Rd., Ottawa ON K1H 8M8
Tel: 613-737-2780; *Fax:* 613-738-4818
Toll-Free: 800-561-5638
www.cheofoundation.com
www.facebook.com/CHEOkids
twitter.com/cheohospital
www.youtube.com/user/CHEOvideos
Also Known As: Children's Hospital Foundation
Overview: A medium-sized local charitable organization founded in 1974
Mission: To advance the physical, mental, & social well-being of children & their families in Eastern Ontario & Western Quebec by raising, managing, & disbursing funds; To support the Children's Hospital of Eastern Ontario
Member of: Children's Miracle Network Telethon

Finances: *Funding Sources:* Fundraising
Activities: *Speaker Service:* Yes
Chief Officer(s):
Mahesh Mani, Chair
Len Hanes, Director, Communications
lhanes@cheofoundation.com

Children's International Summer Villages (Canada) Inc. (CISV) / Villages internationaux d'enfants
233 Chaplin Cres., Toronto ON M5P 1B1
canada@cisv.org
www.ca.cisv.org
Overview: A medium-sized national organization founded in 1957
Mission: To promote cross-cultural friendship, through educational programs for youth & adults in 60 countries; To prepare indivduals to become active & contributing members of a peaceful society; To stimulate the life-long development of amicable relationships & effective & appropriate leadership towards a fair & just world
Member of: Canadian Council for International Cooperation

Children's Mental Health Ontario (CMHO) / Santé Mentale pour Enfants Ontario (SMEO)
#309, 40 St. Clair Ave. East, Toronto ON M4T 1M9
Tel: 416-921-2109; *Fax:* 416-921-7600
info@cmho.org
www.cmho.org
www.linkedin.com/company/747188
www.facebook.com/kidsmentalhealth
twitter.com/kidsmentalhlth
www.youtube.com/user/ChangeTheView2016
Also Known As: Ontario Association of Children's Mental Health Centres
Overview: A medium-sized provincial charitable organization founded in 1972
Mission: To promote, support & strengthen a sustainable system of mental health services for children, youth & their families
Member of: Child Welfare League of Canada
Finances: *Annual Operating Budget:* $1.5 Million-$3 Million; *Funding Sources:* Membership dues
Staff Member(s): 15
Membership: 85; *Fees:* 0.3% of annual operating budget for cmh services + $585; *Member Profile:* Children's mental health centres
Activities: Annual conference; Webinars; *Awareness Events:* Children's Mental Health Week, May
Chief Officer(s):
Kimberly Moran, Chief Executive Officer
kmoran@cmho.org
Meetings/Conferences:
• Children's Mental Health Ontario Annual Conference 2018, 2018, ON
Scope: National

Children's Miracle Network
#200, 8001 Weston Rd., Vaughan ON L4L 9C8
Tel: 905-265-9750; *Fax:* 905-265-9749
childrensmiraclenetwork.ca
www.facebook.com/cmnhospitals
twitter.com/cmncanada
www.youtube.com/cmnhospitals
Overview: A large international charitable organization
Mission: To raise funds for children's hospitals
Finances: *Funding Sources:* Fundraising
Membership: 170 hospitals, 14 of which are in Canada
Chief Officer(s):
John Bozard, Chair
Nana Mensah, Vice Chair
Rick Merrill, Treasurer
Barbara Walczyk, Secretary

Children's Oncology Care of Ontario Inc. *See* Ronald McDonald House Toronto

Children's Psychiatric Research Institute *See* Child & Parent Resource Institute

Children's Rehabilitation & Cerebral Palsy Association; Children's Centre for Ability *See* British Columbia Centre for Ability Association

Children's Resource & Consultation Centre of Ontario
100 St. Clair Ave. West, Toronto ON M4V 1N3
Tel: 416-923-7771
www.ontarioadoptions.com

Overview: A small provincial organization
Mission: The Centre is an adoption agency licensed both domestically and internationally in Bangladesh, Hong Kong, India, Jamaica, Lebanon, Pakistan, Philippines, Thailand, Trinidad & U.S.
Activities: Consultation on adoptive planning
Chief Officer(s):
Michael Blugerman, Executive Director

Children's Safety Association of Canada
PO Box 551, 2110 Kipling Ave. North, Toronto ON M9W 4K0
Toll-Free: 888-499-4444
info@safekid.org
www.safekid.org
www.facebook.com/388063844595114
twitter.com/CHASAorg
Overview: A small national organization founded in 1992
Mission: The Association provides information on child safety.
Membership: *Member Profile:* Parents of children 0-5
Activities: Free window blind repair kits; free identification & print kits; free 32 page safety info kit; free scalding prevention stickers
Chief Officer(s):
Andre Brisebois, President
Publications:
• Child Safety
Type: magazine

Children's Wish Foundation of Canada / Fondation canadienne rêves d'enfants
#350, 1101 Kingston Rd., Pickering ON L1V 1B5
Tel: 905-839-8882; *Fax:* 905-839-3745
Toll-Free: 800-700-4437
nat@childrenswish.ca
www.childrenswish.ca
www.linkedin.com/company/children's-wish-foundation-of-canada
www.facebook.com/ChildrensWish
twitter.com/Childrens_wish
www.instagram.com/childrenswishfoundation
Overview: A large national charitable organization founded in 1984
Mission: The Foundation grants wishes to children suffering from a high risk, life-threatening illnesses
Finances: *Annual Operating Budget:* Greater than $5 Million; *Funding Sources:* Donations
Staff Member(s): 90
Activities: *Awareness Events:* Wishmaker Parade, Oct. 14
Chief Officer(s):
Chris Kotsopoulos, CEO
chris.kotsopoulos@childrenswish.ca
Rea Ganesh, National Director, Development
rea.ganesh@childrenswish.ca
Lyanne Goulin, National Director, Wish Granting
lyanne.goulin@childrenswish.ca

Alberta & N.W.T. Chapter - Calgary
#270, 2323 - 32 Ave. NE, Calgary AB T2E 6Z3
Tel: 403-265-9039; *Fax:* 403-265-1704
Toll-Free: 800-267-9474
ab@childrenswish.ca
www.facebook.com/ChildrensWishAB
twitter.com/ChildrensWishAB
Chief Officer(s):
Kyla Martin, Provincial Director
kyla.martin@childrenswish.ca

Alberta & N.W.T. Chapter - Edmonton
#200, 9750 - 51 Ave. NW, Edmonton AB T6E 0A6
Tel: 780-340-9039; *Fax:* 587-881-0064
Toll-Free: 800-267-9474
ab@childrenswish.ca
www.facebook.com/ChildrensWishAB
twitter.com/ChildrensWishAB
Chief Officer(s):
Kyla Martin, Provincial Director
kyla.martin@childrenswish.ca

British Columbia & Yukon Chapter
#450, 319 West Pender St., Vancouver BC V6B 1T3
Tel: 604-299-2241; *Fax:* 604-299-1228
Toll-Free: 800-267-9474
bc@childrenswish.ca
www.facebook.com/ChildrensWishBC
twitter.com/cwfbc
Chief Officer(s):
Jennifer Petersen, Provincial Director
jennifer.petersen@childrenswish.ca

Bureau de Montréal
#904, 4200, boul St-Laurent, Montréal QC H2W 2R2
Tél: 514-289-1777; *Téléc:* 514-298-8504
Ligne sans frais: 800-267-9474
qo@revesdenfants.ca
www.facebook.com/revesenfants
twitter.com/Reves_denfants
Chief Officer(s):
Juli Meilleur, Directrice générale
juli.meilleur@childrenswish.ca
Bureau de Québec
Halles Fleur de Lys, #904, 245, rue Soumande, Québec QC G1M 3H6
Tél: 418-650-2111; *Téléc:* 418-650-3466
Ligne sans frais: 800-267-9474
qe@revesdenfants.ca
www.facebook.com/revesenfants
twitter.com/Reves_denfants
Chief Officer(s):
Pierre-Luc Berthiaume, Directeur régional, Est-du-Québec
pierre-luc.berthiaume@revesdenfants.ca
Manitoba & Nunavut Chapter
350 St. Mary Ave., Winnipeg MB R3C 3J2
Tel: 204-945-9474; *Fax:* 204-945-9479
Toll-Free: 800-267-9474
mb@childrenswish.ca
www.facebook.com/ChildrensWishMB
twitter.com/ChildrensWishMB
Chief Officer(s):
Maria Toscano, Provincial Director
maria.toscano@childrenswish.ca
National Capital Region
#206, 1800 Bank St., Ottawa ON K1V 0W3
Tel: 613-221-9474; *Fax:* 613-221-9441
Toll-Free: 800-267-9474
ncr@childrenswish.ca
www.facebook.com/ChildrensWishNatCap
twitter.com/ChildrensWishNC
Chief Officer(s):
Leanne Brown, Regional Director
Leanne.Brown@childrenswish.ca
New Brunswick Chapter
#C202, 600 Main St., Saint John NB E2K 1J5
Tel: 506-632-0099; *Fax:* 506-635-6924
Toll-Free: 800-267-9474
nb@childrenswish.ca
www.facebook.com/ChildrensWishFoundationNB
twitter.com/NBChildrensWish
Chief Officer(s):
Kelly Hare, Chapter Director
kelly.hare@childrenswish.ca
Newfoundland & Labrador Chapter
#211 - 31 Peet St., St. John's NL A1B 3W8
Tel: 709-739-9474; *Fax:* 709- 72-6947
Toll-Free: 800-267-9474
nl@childrenswish.ca
www.facebook.com/ChildrensWishNL
twitter.com/cwfnl
Chief Officer(s):
Edie Newton, Provincial Director
edie.newton@childrenswish.ca
Nova Scotia Chapter
#105, 238 Brownlow Ave., Dartmouth NS B3B 2B4
Tel: 902-492-1984; *Fax:* 902-492-1908
Toll-Free: 800-267-9474
ns@childrenswish.ca
www.facebook.com/ChildrensWishNS
twitter.com/ChildrensWishNS
Chief Officer(s):
Cheryl Matthews, Provincial Director
cheryl.matthews@childrenswish.ca
Ontario Chapter
#360, 1101 Kingston Rd., Pickering ON L1V 1B5
Tel: 905-427-5353; *Fax:* 905-427-0536
Toll-Free: 800-267-9474
on@childrenswish.ca
www.facebook.com/ChildrensWishON
twitter.com/ChildrensWishON
Chief Officer(s):
Tiffany MacDonald, Provincial Director
tiffany.macdonald@childrenswish.ca
Prince Edward Island Chapter
Midtown Plaza, #7, 375 University Ave., Charlottetown PE C1A 2S2
Tel: 902-566-5526; *Fax:* 902-894-8412
Toll-Free: 800-267-9474
pei@childrenswish.ca
www.facebook.com/ChildrensWishPE
twitter.com/ChildrensWishPE
Chief Officer(s):
Beth Corney Gauthier, Provincial Director
beth.corneygauthier@childrenswish.ca
Saskatchewan Chapter
3602 Millar Ave., Saskatoon SK S7K 3L3
Tel: 306-955-0511; *Fax:* 306-653-9474
Toll-Free: 800-267-9474
sk@childrenswish.ca
Chief Officer(s):
Gay Anderson, Provincial Director
gay.anderson@childrenswish.ca

Children's Writers & Illustrators of British Columbia Society (CWILL BC)
c/o Mary Jane Muir, #406, 2938 Laurel St., Vancouver BC V5Z 3T3
membership@cwill.bc.ca
www.cwill.bc.ca
www.facebook.com/CWILLBC
cwillbc.wordpress.com
Overview: A small provincial organization founded in 1994
Mission: To publicize & promote members' books; to provide support & allows for information exchange about creating books for young people; to communicate with other arts groups in BC & Canada.
Member of: Vancouver Cultural Alliance
Finances: *Funding Sources:* Membership fees
Membership: 150; *Fees:* $55; *Member Profile:* Published writers & illustrators
Activities: *Speaker Service:* Yes; *Library:* Collection of books at UBC Education Library; Not open to public
Chief Officer(s):
Lori Sherritt-Fleming, President

Chilliwack & District Real Estate Board
#1, 8433 Harvard Pl., Chilliwack BC V2P 7Z5
Tel: 604-792-0912; *Fax:* 604-792-6795
cadreb@telus.net
cadreb.com
twitter.com/ChilliwackREB
Overview: A medium-sized local organization overseen by British Columbia Real Estate Association
Mission: To serve the real estate needs of Chilliwack, Agassiz, Hope, Boston Bar and Harrison.
Member of: The Canadian Real Estate Association
Staff Member(s): 4
Chief Officer(s):
Steve Lerigny, Executive Officer

Chilliwack Chamber of Commerce
#201, 46093 Yale Rd., Chilliwack BC V2P 2L8
Tel: 604-793-4323
info@chilliwackchamber.com
www.chilliwackchamber.com
www.linkedin.com/company/chilliwack-chamber-of-commerce
www.facebook.com/140662687837
twitter.com/chwkchamber
www.youtube.com/user/ChilliwackChamber?ob=0
Overview: A small local organization founded in 1903
Mission: To promote economic growth & development for the benefit of the commercial, agricultural, industrial, civic & social well-being of the district
Member of: Canadian Chamber of Commerce; Better Business Bureau; BC Chamber of Commerce; Vancouver Coast & Mountains Tourism Region
Finances: *Funding Sources:* Provincial & municipal government; fundraising
Membership: *Fees:* Schedule available
Activities: Forestry Task Force; Shop Local Program; *Speaker Service:* Yes; *Library:* Business Information Centre; Open to public
Chief Officer(s):
Kirk Dzaman, President
Fieny van den Boom, Executive Director

Chilliwack Community Arts Council
#20, 5725 Vedder Rd., Chilliwack BC V2R 3N4
Tel: 604-769-2787; *Fax:* 604-769-2788
info@chilliwackartscouncil.com
chilliwackartscouncil.com
www.facebook.com/ChilliwackArts
twitter.com/ChilliwackArts
www.youtube.com/user/ChwkArtsCouncil?feature=mhum
Overview: A small local organization founded in 1960
Mission: To enrich the quality of life for the residents of Chilliwack by the effective use of resources & volunteers to encourage education & participation in the arts
Member of: Assembly of BC Arts Councils; BC Touring Council; BC Bluegrass Association
Finances: *Annual Operating Budget:* $500,000-$1.5 Million
Staff Member(s): 12; 100 volunteer(s)
Membership: 350; *Fees:* $15 individual; $25 family/group; $100 corporation
Activities: Concerts, Bluegrass Festival, craft market, film screenings
Chief Officer(s):
Patti Lawn, Executive Director
Awards:
• Community Arts Council Fine Arts Awards
Eligibility: A full-time, post-secondary student in the Fine Arts field, past or present resident of Chilliwack *Deadline:* April 1; *Amount:* $500
• Mary Elizabeth Allan Memorial Award
Eligibility: A full-time, post-secondary student in the Theatre field, past or present resident of Chilliwack *Deadline:* April 1; *Amount:* $500
• Jenny Child Memorial Award
Eligibility: A full-time, post-secondary student in a Fine Arts field, past or present resident of Chilliwack *Deadline:* April 1; *Amount:* $500
• Robert (Bob) Forsythe Memorial Award
Eligibility: A full-time, post-secondary student in the Theatre field, past or present resident of Chilliwack *Deadline:* April 1; *Amount:* $500

Chilliwack Field Naturalists
45365 Labelle Ave., Chilliwack BC V2P 6Z3
Tel: 604-792-8062
postmaster@chilliwackfieldnaturalists.freeservers.com
www.chilliwackfieldnaturalists.com
www.facebook.com/ChilliwackFieldNats
Overview: A small local organization founded in 1970
Mission: To promote the enjoyment of nature through environmental appreciation & conservation; To encourage wise use & conservation of natural resources & environmental protection
Member of: Federation of BC Naturalists
Membership: 60 individual; *Fees:* $28 individual; $38 family; *Committees:* Conservation; Education
Activities: Field trips; meetings & speakers; education; *Awareness Events:* Christmas Bird Count, December; *Library:* Not open to public
Chief Officer(s):
Janne Perrin, President
djperrin@uniserve.com

Chilliwack Society for Community Living (CSCL)
9353 Mary St., Chilliwack BC V2P 4G9
Tel: 604-792-7726; *Fax:* 604-792-7962
administration@cscl.org
www.cscl.org
www.facebook.com/cscl.org
twitter.com/CSCLtweets
Overview: A small local charitable organization founded in 1954
Mission: CSCL is an accredited, non-profit, charitable organization that seeks to promote & enhance the quality of life for people with developmental disabilities.
Membership: 100
Activities: Adult day services; adult community services; community housing coordination; children's services; short-term respite care services
Chief Officer(s):
Helen Tolmie, President
Brenda Gillette, Executive Director
brenda.gillette@cscl.org

Chilliwack Symphony Orchestra & Chorus (CSO)
PO Box 521, Stn. Main, Chilliwack BC V2P 7V5
Tel: 604-795-0521
chilliwacksymphony@gmail.com
www.chilliwacksymphony.com
www.facebook.com/Chiliwack.Symphony.Orchestra.and.Chorus
twitter.com/chwksymphony
Overview: A small local charitable organization founded in 1999 overseen by Orchestras Canada
Mission: To perform orchestral music to the residents of Chilliwack and surrounding communities.

Finances: *Funding Sources:* Ticket sales; Individual & corporate donations; Fundraising
Membership: 147
Activities: Performing concert series; Facilitating youth outreach & education programs
Chief Officer(s):
Paula Dewit, Music Director

China Canada Investment Association (CCIA)
#503, 3601 Hwy #7 East, Markham ON L3R 0M3
Tel: 905-305-6865
ccia2002@gmail.com
cciacanada.com
Also Known As: Canadian Chinese Investment Association
Overview: A small national organization founded in 2010
Mission: To advocate for cultural & economic exchanges between China & Canada
Membership: *Member Profile:* Representitives from sectors such as financial services, real estate, legal services, manufacturing, construction, transportation, mining & energy, information & communication technology, high-tech & education
Chief Officer(s):
Sophia Ming Sun, President

China Council for the Promotion of International Trade - Canadian Office (CCPIT)
#908, 150 York St., Toronto ON M5H 3S5
Tel: 416-363-8561; *Fax:* 416-363-0152
ccpitcanada@gmail.com
overseas.ccpit.org/ca
Overview: A medium-sized international organization founded in 1952
Staff Member(s): 3

China Inland Mission *See* OMF International - Canada

China Native Evangelistic Crusade *See* Partners International

Chinese Benevolent Association of Vancouver (CBA)
108 East Pender St., Vancouver BC V6A 1T3
Tel: 604-681-1923; *Fax:* 604-682-0073
info@cbavancouver.ca
www.cbavancouver.ca
Also Known As: Shanghai Alley & Canton Alley
Overview: A small local organization founded in 1906
Mission: To provide support and leadership within the Chinese Canadian community.
Member of: Chinese Canadian National Council
Activities: Establishment of an affliated society to provide low cost housing; fund-raising campaigns to aid victims of natual disasters; Spring Festival Parade

Chinese Canadian Association of Prince Edward Island (CCAPEI)
36 Massey Dr., Charlottetown PE C1E 1R6
Overview: A small provincial organization

Chinese Canadian Chiropractic Society (CCCS)
c/o Federation of Chinese Canadian Professionals, 55 Glenn Hawthorne Blvd., Mississauga ON L5R 3S6
Tel: 905-890-3235; *Fax:* 905-568-5293
fccpontario.com/professional-sections/chiropractic
Overview: A small national organization founded in 2001
Mission: Created in order to educate the Chinese community about the benefits of chiropractic care
Membership: 1-99
Chief Officer(s):
Frank Nhan, Representative

Chinese Canadian National Council (CCNC) / Conseil national des canadiens chinois
#507, 302 Spadina Ave., Toronto ON M5T 2E7
Tel: 416-977-9871; *Fax:* 416-977-1630
national@ccnc.ca
www.ccnc.ca
Overview: A medium-sized national organization founded in 1980
Mission: To promote the rights of all individuals, in particular, those of Chinese Canadians & to encourage their full & equal participation in Canadian society; to create an environment in Canada in which the rights of all individuals are fully recognized & protected; to promote understanding & cooperation between Chinese Canadians & all other ethnic, cultural, & racial groups in Canada; to encourage & develop in persons of Chinese descent, a desire to know & respect their historical & cultural heritage, & to educate them in adopting a creative & positive attitude towards the Chinese Canadian contribution to society & the Chinese Canadian heritage
Member of: Canadian Ethnocultural Council; National Organization of Immigrants of Visible Minority Women; National Action Committee of Status of Women
Affiliation(s): Canadian Council for Refugees; Coalition for a Just Immigration Refugee Policy
Activities: *Speaker Service:* Yes; *Library:* by appointment
Chief Officer(s):
Victor Wong, Executive Director
  AB - Calgary Chinese Community Service Association
  #108, 197 - 1 St. SW, Calgary AB T2P 4M4
  Tel: 403-265-8446; *Fax:* 403-233-0070
  cccsa@cadvision.com
  Chief Officer(s):
  Lloyd Wong, Co-Chair
  Edith Chan, Co-Chair
  British Columbia - United Chinese Community Enrichment Service Society
  302 Spadina Ave., Toronto ON M5T 2C7
  Tel: 416-596-0833
  www.facebook.com/CCNCTO
  Nfld. - Chinese Association of Newfoundland & Labrador (CANL)
  PO Box 7311, St. John's NL A1E 3Y5
  Tel: 709-754-1470
  Chief Officer(s):
  Betty Wong, President
  bwong@mun.ca
  NS - Chinese Society of Nova Scotia
  PO Box 29055, Stn. Halifax Shopping Centre, Halifax NS B3L 4T8
  csnsca@gmail.com
  www.cs-ns.com
  Chief Officer(s):
  Yonggan Zhao, President
  ON - CCNC London
  1701 Trafalgar St., London ON N5W 1X2
  Tel: 519-451-0760
  info@londonccnc.ca
  www.londonccnc.ca
  Chief Officer(s):
  Joan Lee, President
  ON - CCNC Ottawa
  391 Bank St., 2nd Fl., Ottawa ON K2P 1Y3
  Tel: 613-996-8139
  Chief Officer(s):
  Jonas Ma, President
  ON - CCNC Toronto
  #123, 215 Spadina Ave., Toronto ON M5T 2C7
  Tel: 416-596-0833
  info@ccnctoronto.ca
  www.facebook.com/CCNCTO
  Chief Officer(s):
  Kristyn Wong-Tam, President
  ON - Central Ontario Chinese Cultural Centre (COCCC)
  #9, 100 Campbell Ave., Kitchener ON N2H 4X8
  Tel: 519-576-6168
  info@coccc.net
  www.coccc.net
  www.facebook.com/COCCC
  Chief Officer(s):
  Shu Hing Man, President
  president@coccc.net
  ON - Chinese Canadians for Equity in York Region
  PO Box 51, #97C2, 4350 Steeles Ave., Markham ON L3R 9V4
  Chief Officer(s):
  Amy Lam, President
  ON - Lambton Chinese Canadian Association
  PO Box 301, Sarnia ON N7T 7J2
  Chief Officer(s):
  Song Choo, President
  ksyinc@ebtech.net

Chinese Canadian Table Tennis Federation
11751 Voyageur Way, Richmond BC V6X 3J4
Tel: 604-278-0033; *Fax:* 604-273-9217
ccttf@teamgroup.bc.ca
www.ccttf.org
Overview: A medium-sized national organization founded in 2000
Mission: To promote table tennis; To assist in the development of future Canadian athletes; To provide the public with information on the health benefits of table tennis
Membership: *Fees:* $10 voting members/members; $50 affiliated members; *Member Profile:* Voting members: Canadians residents over the age of 19; Affiliated members: local groups, including clubs, leagues, schools, & zones; Members: any individual interested in the activities of the federation
Activities: Supporting & organizing table tennis events

Chinese Canadian Writers' Association
PO Box 44122, Burnaby BC V5B 4Y2
Tel: 604-818-0831
www.ccwriters.ca
Overview: A small national organization founded in 1987
Mission: To promote the work of Chinese Canadian writers; To facilitate the exchange of literature among Chinese Canadian writers
Activities: Organizing book launches

Chinese Cultural Association of Saint John (CCASJ)
PO Box 2661, Saint John NB E2L 4Z1
Tel: 506-645-1910
info@ccasj.org
www.ccasj.org
www.facebook.com/534026059992706
Overview: A small local organization founded in 1984
Mission: CCASJ provides public education of Chinese culture & heritage; promotes understanding & goodwill among all Canadians
Member of: Chinese Canadian National Council
Finances: *Funding Sources:* Saint John Community Arts Funding Program
Membership: 150; *Fees:* $10 individual; $15 family
Activities: Dragonboat racing; fund-raising for local charities; Chinese language classes; Asian Heritage Gala; Canada Day People's Parade

Chinese Cultural Centre (CCC)
50 East Pender St., Vancouver BC V6A 3V6
Tel: 604-658-8850; *Fax:* 604-687-6260
www.cccvan.com
www.facebook.com/cccvan
Also Known As: Chinese Cultural Centre of Greater Vancouver
Overview: A small local charitable organization founded in 1973
Mission: To preserve & promote Chinese cultural heritage; to foster better understanding among cultural groups; to facilitate cultural exchange.
Member of: Vancouver Cultural Alliance
Affiliation(s): Chinese Benevolent Association of Vancouver; Vancouver Multicultural Society; Cultural Human Resources Council
Finances: *Funding Sources:* Provincial government; facility rental; telethons, radiothons & raffles
Membership: 1,200; *Fees:* $15 individual; $30 family; $10 seniors/students; $2,000 life membership
Activities: Chinatown Arts & Cultural Festival; Chinese Language School & educational classes for adults & childeren; exhibition of visual arts; museum programs; concerts; film festivals & other community events; summer camp; museum & archives; *Internships:* Yes; *Speaker Service:* Yes
Chief Officer(s):
Daisey Yau, Executive Director
Mike Jang, Chair
  Richmond Office
  #860, 4400 Hazelbridge Way, Richmond BC V6X 3R8
  Tel: 604-658-8875; *Fax:* 604-658-8854

Chinese Cultural Centre of Greater Toronto (CCC)
5183 Sheppard Ave. East, Toronto ON M1B 5Z5
Tel: 416-292-9293; *Fax:* 416-292-9215
info@cccgt.org
www.cccgt.org
www.facebook.com/171784883266
Overview: A medium-sized local charitable organization founded in 1989
Mission: To promote Chinese culture within the multicultural context of Canadian society; to facilitate communication & understanding between Canada & Southeast Asian countries in culture, education & trade
Membership: *Fees:* $22 individual; $11 student/senior; $33 family; *Committees:* Operations; Programs; Special Events; Building & Facilities; Finance; Culture & Education; Marketing & Sponsorship; IT; Legal Consultant; Outreach
Activities: *Library:* Richard Charles Lee Resource Centre
Chief Officer(s):
Ming-Tat Cheung, President & Chair

Chinese Family Life Services Project *See* Chinese Family Services of Ontario

Chinese Family Service of Greater Montréal *Voir* Service à la famille chinoise du Grand Montréal

Chinese Family Services of Ontario
#229, 3330 Midland Ave., Toronto ON M1V 5E7
Tel: 416-979-8299; *Fax:* 416-979-2743
Toll-Free: 866-979-8298; *TTY:* 416-979-5898
info@chinesefamilyso.com
www.chinesefamilyso.com
Previous Name: Chinese Family Life Services Project
Overview: A small local charitable organization founded in 1988 overseen by Ontario Council of Agencies Serving Immigrants
Mission: To offer service that help Chinese immigrants settle in Canada
Finances: *Annual Operating Budget:* $1.5 Million-$3 Million; *Funding Sources:* Government levels; United Way Toronto & York; donations
Staff Member(s): 25
Activities: Family life education programs; group counseling; domestic violence intervention program; addiction therapy; youth services; sexual orientation counseling; employment assistance program; internships; *Speaker Service:* Yes
Chief Officer(s):
Patrick Au, Executive Director

Chinese Federation of Commerce of Canada
#218, 2688 Shell Rd., Richmond BC V6X 4E1
Tel: 604-273-1655; *Fax:* 604-248-2388
info@cfccanada.org
www.cfccanada.org
Overview: A small national organization founded in 1989
Mission: To provide business development assistance to members; To promote integration of members into Canadian society
Membership: 24 organizations
Activities: Organizing networking & skill development programs, public affairs programs, & membership & annual events
Chief Officer(s):
Pius Chan, President

Chinese Interpreter & Information Services; Chinese Information & Community Services of Greater Toronto; Centre for Information & Community Servi *See* Centre for Immigrant & Community Services

Chinese Medicine & Acupuncture Association of Canada (CMAAC)
154 Wellington St., London ON N6B 2K8
Tel: 519-642-1970; *Fax:* 519-642-2932
headoffice@cmaac.ca
www.cmaac.ca
Overview: A medium-sized national organization founded in 1983
Mission: To unite practitioners of Eastern & Western Medicine; To develop & establish high standards of education & training for practitioners; To promote & attend international conferences; To assist in the exchange of scientific research; To act as an educational vehicle for the public
Member of: World Federation of Acupuncture
Affiliation(s): World Wildlife Fund Canada; Canadian Health Care Anti-Fraud Association
Membership: 756; *Fees:* $100; *Member Profile:* Practitioners of acupuncture & Chinese medicine
Chief Officer(s):
Cedric Cheung, President

  Alberta Chapter
  414 Lee Ridge Rd., Edmonton AB T6K 0N7
  Tel: 780-497-4610; *Fax:* 780-461-6366
  Chief Officer(s):
  King Sang Wong, President
  British Columbia Chapter
  BC

  Manitoba Chapter
  1036 Portage Ave., Winnipeg MB R3G 0S2
  Tel: 204-284-4047; *Fax:* 204-284-5755
  Chief Officer(s):
  Lin Liu, President
  liulin1036@hotmail.com
  New Brunswick Chapter
  NB
  Tel: 506-382-1288
  Chief Officer(s):
  Hui Zhang, President
  zhanghuiacu@hotmail.com
  Newfoundland Chapter
  16 Dan's Rd., Portugal Cove-St. Philips NL A1M 1H3

  Tel: 709-895-2907; *Fax:* 709-754-5802
  Chief Officer(s):
  Michelle Collett, President
  collettmichele@hotmail.com
  Nova Scotia Chapter
  6066 Quinpool Rd., Halifax NS B3L 1A1
  Tel: 902-832-0688; *Fax:* 902-835-3298
  acup@eastlink.ca
  Chief Officer(s):
  Diana Tong Li, President
  Ontario Office
  117 King St. East, Oshawa ON L1H 1B9
  Tel: 905-721-4917; *Fax:* 905-721-4336
  Chief Officer(s):
  Jane Cheung, Chair, TCM Policy Development & Communications Committee
  Québec Chapter
  1312, rue Jean-Charles Catin, Cap Rouge QC G1Y 2X3
  Tel: 613-569-8947; *Fax:* 613-569-8947
  Chief Officer(s):
  Gasan Askerow, President
  askerow@bell.net
  Saskatchewan Chapter
  3829B Albert St. South, Regina SK S4S 3R4
  Tel: 306-584-9888; *Fax:* 306-584-9888
  saskatchewanacupuncture@gmail.com
  Chief Officer(s):
  Diana Dong Yue Zhang, President

Chinese Neighbourhood Society of Montréal / Amitié Chinoise de Montréal
15, rue Viger ouest, 3e étage, Montréal QC H2Z 1E6
Tel: 514-866-7133; *Fax:* 514-866-8636
Overview: A small local organization
Member of: Chinese Canadian National Council
Chief Officer(s):
Kenneth Cheung, President

Chinese Professionals Association of Canada (CPAC)
4150 Finch Ave. East, Toronto ON M1S 3T9
Tel: 416-298-7885; *Fax:* 416-298-0068
office@cpac-canada.ca
www.cpac-canada.ca
www.linkedin.com/company/chinese-professionals-association-of-canada-cpac-
Overview: A large national organization founded in 1992
Mission: To advocate for the interests of association members & the Chinese Canadian community
Finances: *Funding Sources:* Corporate sponsorships
Membership: 20,000+; *Fees:* $130; *Member Profile:* Chinese Canadian professionals; *Committees:* Executive; International Exchange; Finance; Membership; Program; Recreation, Culture & Entrepreneurship; Resources Development
Activities: Facilitating professional development; Providing networking opportunities; Assisting association members with settlement & integration in Canadian society; Offering training & education to internationally trained professionals & families
Chief Officer(s):
Margaret Yang, President
Andi Shi, Executive Director

Chinese Real Estate Professionals Association of British Columbia (CREPA)
PO Box 27555, Stn. Oakridge, 650 West 41st Ave., Vancouver BC V5Z 4M4
info2@crepa.ca
www.crepa.ca
Overview: A small provincial organization founded in 1997
Mission: To promote the interests of Chinese real estate professionals; To encourage professionalism, partnership, & support among members
Membership: *Fees:* $100
Chief Officer(s):
David Tam, President

Chinese Seniors Support Services Association *See* Carefirst Seniors & Community Services Association

Chinook Applied Research Association (CARA)
PO Box 690, Oyen AB T0J 2J0
Tel: 403-664-3777; *Fax:* 403-664-3007
cara-1@telus.net
www.chinookappliedresearch.ca
www.facebook.com/CARAresearch
twitter.com/CARAresearch

Overview: A small local organization overseen by Agricultural Research & Extension Council of Alberta
Mission: To expand agricultural research
Member of: Agricultural Research & Extension Council of Alberta
Membership: *Fees:* $20 (annual); $80 (5 years)
Chief Officer(s):
Dianne Westerlund, Manager
cara-dw@telus.net
Shelley Norris, Office Manager
Publications:
• Grain, Grass & Growth [a publication of Chinook Applied Research Association]
Type: Newsletter

Chinook Musical Society
159 Lake Adams Cres. SE, Calgary AB T2J 3N2
Tel: 403-271-3719
general@saturdaynightspecial.ca
www.saturdaynightspecial.ca
Overview: A small local organization founded in 1976
Activities: Presents between 9 and 10 Saturday evening concerts per year
Chief Officer(s):
David McIntyre, President

Chinook Regional Hospital Foundation (CRHF)
960 - 19th St. South, Lethbridge AB T1J 1W5
Tel: 403-388-6001; *Fax:* 403-388-6604
info@crhfoundation.com
www.crhfoundation.ca
www.facebook.com/crhfoundation.ca
twitter.com/crh_foundation
Also Known As: CRH Foundation
Overview: A small local charitable organization
Mission: To raise, receive & distribute funds for equipment & programs in order to enhance patient services at Chinook Regional Hospital; Primarily fund the purchase & maintenance of equipment that will enhance care & attract medical specialists
Finances: *Funding Sources:* Donations; Fundraising
Activities: *Awareness Events:* Care from the Heart Radiothon, Feb.; Truck Raffle, Sept.; Christmas Tree Festival & Lights of Hope, Dec.
Chief Officer(s):
Jason Vanden Hoek, Executive Director

Chipman Community Care Inc.
PO Box 435, Chipman NB E4A 3N4
Tel: 506-339-5565; *Fax:* 506-339-6823
communitycareinc@hotmail.com
Overview: A small local charitable organization founded in 1987
Mission: To promote total community wellness among youth to seniors
Member of: Association of Food Banks & C.V.A.'s for New Brunswick; Atlantic Alliance of Food Banks & C.V.A.'s
Finances: *Funding Sources:* Federal & Provincial grants; NB Protestant Orphanage; Village of Chipman; Fundraising
Activities: Food, Clothing bank; low-income housing; youth centre
Chief Officer(s):
Mary West, President

Chiropractic Awareness Council *See* Alliance for Chiropractic

Chiropractic Foundation for Spinal Research *See* Canadian Chiropractic Research Foundation

Chiropractors' Association of Saskatchewan (CAS)
3420A Hill Ave., Regina SK S4S 0W9
Tel: 306-585-1411; *Fax:* 306-585-0685
admin@saskchiropractic.ca
www.saskchiropractic.ca
www.youtube.com/user/SaskChiro
Overview: A medium-sized provincial organization founded in 1943 overseen by Canadian Chiropractic Association
Mission: To standardize & elevate chiropractic methods
Finances: *Annual Operating Budget:* $500,000-$1.5 Million; *Funding Sources:* Membership dies
Staff Member(s): 3; 50 volunteer(s)
Membership: 200; *Committees:* Bylaws & Resolutions; Chiropractic Compensation Review; Continuing Education; Discipline; Examination; Finance; Insurance Relations; Investigation; Modes of Care; Nominations; Public Relations; Quality Assurance; Vocational Guidance
Activities: Regulating chiropractic care in Saskatchewan; Promoting chiropractic profession; *Internships:* Yes
Chief Officer(s):

Kevin Henbid, President
Denise Gerein, Registrar
dgerein@saskchiropractic.ca

Chisholm Services for Children
5724 South St., Halifax NS B3H 1S4
Tel: 902-423-9871; *Fax:* 902-422-3725
info@chisholm4children.ca
www.chisholm4children.ca
twitter.com/chisholm4c
Overview: A medium-sized local charitable organization founded in 2004
Mission: To offer residential care, support, & early intervention programs for children in need; To provide resources, education, & advocacy to meet the needs of children
Chief Officer(s):
Wade Johnston, Executive Director
wjohnston@chisholm4children.ca
Daniel Abar, Director, Clinical Services
dabar@chisholm4children.ca
Geoff Hurst, Director, Business Development
ghurst@chisholm4children.ca

Chiu Chow Benevolent Association of BC Canada
#1265, 3779 Sexsmith Rd., Richmond BC V6X 3Z9
Tel: 604-270-1008; *Fax:* 604-270-1898
chiuchow1265bc@gmail.com
www.chiuchow.bc.ca
Overview: A small national organization
Mission: To unite Chiu Chow people in British Columbia; To provide assistance to new Chiu Chow immigrants to British Columbia; To promote Chiu Chow talent; To develop education & commerce
Membership: *Fees:* $50-$350

Choiceland & District Chamber of Commerce
c/o Town of Choiceland, PO Box 279, 115 - 1st St. East, Choiceland SK S0J 0M0
Tel: 306-428-2070; *Fax:* 306-428-2071
Overview: A small local organization
Mission: Supporting business and community in the town of Choiceland.

Choir Alberta (ACF)
#103, 10612 - 124 St., Edmonton AB T5N 1S4
Tel: 780-488-7464; *Fax:* 780-488-6403
info@albertachoralfederation.ca
www.albertachoralfederation.ca
www.facebook.com/158600474208014
Previous Name: Alberta Choir Federation
Overview: A medium-sized provincial charitable organization founded in 1972
Mission: To promote choral music within the communities of Alberta; to gain support for choral music through public policy
Member of: Music Alberta; Association of Canadian Choral Conductors; Canadian Conference for the Arts
Finances: *Annual Operating Budget:* $250,000-$500,000; *Funding Sources:* Membership fees; Alberta Foundation for the Arts
Staff Member(s): 3; 125 volunteer(s)
Membership: 450; *Fees:* $25 adult/student; $150 choir/institution/corporate; $95 conductor/educator; *Member Profile:* Interest in choral music; *Committees:* Programs & Services; Finance; Personnel; Advocacy
Activities: Concerts; Conferences, Festivals & Workshops; *Library:* Choral Lending Library; Open to public
Chief Officer(s):
Brendan Lord, Executive Director
brendan@albertachoralfederation.ca

Choirs Ontario
1422 Bayview Ave., #A, Toronto ON M4G 3A7
Tel: 416-923-1144; *Fax:* 416-929-0415
Toll-Free: 866-935-1144
info@choirsontario.org
www.choirsontario.org
Also Known As: Ontario Choral Federation
Overview: A medium-sized provincial organization
Mission: To promote choral singing in communities, schools, universities, & places of worship throughout Ontario
Staff Member(s): 2
Membership: *Fees:* Schedule available
Chief Officer(s):
Elena Koneva, Office Manager
Awards:
• The Ruth Watson Henderson Choral Composition Prize

• The Leslie Bell Prize for Choral Conducting
Offered every two years and administered by the Ontario Arts Council

Chorale Les Voix de la Vallée du Cuivre de Chibougamau inc.
CP 129, Chibougamau QC G8P 2K6
Tél: 418-748-6892
Aperçu: *Dimension:* petite; *Envergure:* locale
Membre(s) du bureau directeur:
Bruno Marceau, Président

Chosen People Ministries (Canada) (CPM)
PO Box 58103, Stn. Dufferin-Lawrence, 225 Bridgeland Ave., Toronto ON M6A 3C8
Tel: 416-250-0177; *Fax:* 416-250-9235
Toll-Free: 888-442-5535
info@chosenpeople.ca
www.chosenpeople.ca
Also Known As: Beth Sar Shalom Mission
Overview: A medium-sized national charitable organization founded in 1894
Mission: To pray for, evangelize, disciple & serve Jewish people everywhere
Finances: *Annual Operating Budget:* $500,000-$1.5 Million; *Funding Sources:* Donations
Staff Member(s): 14
Activities: *Speaker Service:* Yes
Chief Officer(s):
Jorge Sedaca, National Director

Chown Adult Day Care Centre
Taoist Building, 94 East 15th Ave., Vancouver BC V5T 2R5
Tel: 604-879-0947; *Fax:* 604-879-0121
chownadc@shaw.ca
chownadc.com
www.facebook.com/pages/Chown-Adult-Day-Centre/236969846432675
Overview: A small local charitable organization
Mission: The Centre serves frail elders, disabled older & younger adults who need support to maintain health, & live in their community as independently as possible.
Member of: British Columbia Association of Community Care; Health Employers Association of British Columbia
Finances: *Funding Sources:* Provincial Government; Donations
Staff Member(s): 9
Activities: fitness & creative arts programs; chat groups; health services

Chris Spencer Foundation
Bentall Centre, PO Box 48284, Vancouver BC V7X 1A1
Tel: 604-608-2560
Overview: A small local charitable organization founded in 1949
Mission: To provide grants to charitable organizations supporting boys & girls in Canada in the Greater Vancouver & Lower Fraser Valley area of B.C.

The Christian & Missionary Alliance in Canada (C&MA) / L'Alliance chrétienne et missionnaire au Canada
#100, 30 Carrier Dr., Toronto ON M9W 5T7
Tel: 416-674-7878; *Fax:* 416-674-0808
Other Communication: vimeo.com/cmaincanada
info@cmacan.org
www.cmacan.org/home
www.facebook.com/CMAllianceinCanada
twitter.com/CMAinCanada
www.youtube.com/user/cmacan
Also Known As: The Alliance Church
Overview: A medium-sized national charitable organization founded in 1981
Mission: To be committed to Jesus & his mission by being Christ-centred, Spirit-empowered & Mission-focused in everything they do
Member of: Canadian Council of Christian Charities; Alliance World Fellowship
Affiliation(s): Alliance Life Magazine; Al Hayat Ministries; Evangelical Fellowship of Canada
Finances: *Annual Operating Budget:* Greater than $5 Million; *Funding Sources:* Donations
Staff Member(s): 1642
Membership: 440 churches + 48,922 baptized + 132,323 inclusive members + 205 Canadian International Workers
Activities: Missions, locally & globally
Chief Officer(s):
David Hearn, President

Canadian Midwest District (CMD) Office
2950 Arens Rd., Regina SK S4V 1N8
Tel: 306-586-3549
office@cma-cmd.ca
www.cma-cmd.ca
www.facebook.com/260082770709468
Chief Officer(s):
Al Fedorak, District Superintendent, 306-586-3549

Canadian Pacific District (CPD) Office
#101 - 17660 65A Ave., Surrey BC V3S 5N4
Tel: 604-372-1922; *Fax:* 604-372-1923
cpdoffice@pacificdistrict.ca
pacificdistrict.ca
www.facebook.com/123480364431374
twitter.com/PacificDistrict
www.youtube.com/user/PacificDistrict
Chief Officer(s):
Errol Rempel, District Superintendent, 604-372-1922

Central Canadian District (CCD) Office
155 Panin Rd., Burlington ON L7P 5A6
Tel: 905-639-9615; *Fax:* 905-634-7044
www.cmaccd.com
Chief Officer(s):
Brian Thom, District Superintendent, 902-639-9615 Ext. 215
thomb@cmaccd.com

Eastern Canadian District (ECD) Office
#12, 11 Stanley Ct., Whitby ON L1N 8P9
Tel: 905-430-0955; *Fax:* 905-430-0779
www.easterndistrict.ca
www.facebook.com/ECDCMA
twitter.com/ECDCMA
Chief Officer(s):
John Healey, District Superintendent

St. Lawrence District (SLD) Office
#215, 5473, av Royalmount, Mont-Royal QC H4P 1J3
Tel: 514-733-0343; *Fax:* 514-733-0683
acmpq@bellnet.ca
www.acmqc.org/en/
Chief Officer(s):
Yvan Fournier, District Superintendent

Western Canadian District (WCD) Office
#333, 30 Springborough Blvd. SW, Calgary AB T3H 0N9
Tel: 403-265-7900; *Fax:* 403-265-4599
office@transformcma.ca
www.cmawdo.org
www.youtube.com/user/WesternCanDistrict
Chief Officer(s):
Brent Trask, District Superintendent

Christian Aid Mission *See* Intercede International

Christian Blind Mission International (CBMI)
PO Box 800, 3844 Stouffville Rd., Stouffville ON L4A 7Z9
Tel: 905-640-6464; *Fax:* 905-640-4332
Toll-Free: 800-567-2264
cbm@cbmcanada.org
www.cbmcanada.org
www.facebook.com/101857609865125
twitter.com/cbmCanada
www.youtube.com/user/cbmcanada; pinterest.com/cbmcanada
Overview: A medium-sized international charitable organization founded in 1978
Mission: With core values based on Christian faith, CBMI serves the blind & disabled in the developing world, irrespective of nationality, race, sex, or religion; prevents & treats blindness & other disabilities through medical care, rehabilitation training & integration programs; helps people to help themselves.
Member of: Canadian Council of Christian Charities
Finances: *Annual Operating Budget:* Greater than $5 Million
Staff Member(s): 28; 45 volunteer(s)
Activities: Talking Book Library; Craft Store; works with nearly 600 mission agencies, local churches, Christian relief organizations & self-help groups overseas; *Rents Mailing List:* Yes; *Library:* Talking Book Library; Open to public
Chief Officer(s):
Jonathan Liteplo, Chair
Ed Epp, Executive Director

Christian Catholic Church Canada (CCRCC) / Église catholique-chrétien Canada
PO Box 2043, Stn. Hull, Gatineau QC J8X 3Z2
Tel: 613-738-2942; *Fax:* 613-738-7835
info@ccrcc.ca
www.ccrcc.ca
Previous Name: Canadian Chapter of the International Council of Community Churches

Dennis Perrin, Director, Prairies
Fort McMurray Regional Office
#1, 400 Taiga Nova Cres., Fort McMurray AB T9K 0T4
Tel: 780-792-5292; *Fax:* 780-791-9711
Toll-Free: 877-792-5292
Chief Officer(s):
Jayson Bueckert, Regional Director
Fort St. John/Northeastern BC Regional Office
PO Box 2, #210, 10504 - 100th Ave., Fort St. John BC V1J 1Z2
Tel: 250-785-5005; *Fax:* 250-785-5006
Toll-Free: 800-331-2522
Chief Officer(s):
David Prentice, Director, British Columbia
GTA/Central/Northern Ontario Regional Office
#1, 2555 Meadowpine Blvd., Mississauga ON L5N 6C3
Tel: 905-812-2855; *Fax:* 905-812-5556
Toll-Free: 800-268-5281
Chief Officer(s):
J.D. Alkema, Regional Director
Kelowna/Southern Interior, BC Regional Office
#105, 2040 Springfield Rd., Kelowna BC V1Y 9N7
Tel: 250-868-9111; *Fax:* 250-868-9192
Toll-Free: 866-757-2522
Chief Officer(s):
Jim Oostenbrink, Regional Director
Kitchener/Cambridge/Waterloo Regional Office
45 Commerce Ct., Cambridge ON N3C 4P7
Tel: 519-653-3002; *Fax:* 519-653-3004
Toll-Free: 877-701-2522
Chief Officer(s):
Ian DeWaard, Director, Ontario
Niagara/Hamilton/Brant Regional Office
PO Box 219, 89 South Service Rd., Grimsby ON L3M 4G3
Tel: 905-945-1500; *Fax:* 905-945-7200
Toll-Free: 800-463-2522
Chief Officer(s):
Ian DeWaard, Director, Ontario
Ottawa/Eastern Ontario Regional Office
#100, 38 Antares Dr., Ottawa ON K2E 7V2
Tel: 613-238-2522; *Fax:* 613-238-9255
Toll-Free: 888-279-2522
Chief Officer(s):
Ian DeWaard, Director, Ontario
Saskatoon Regional Office
3634 Millar Ave., Saskatoon SK S7P 0B1
Tel: 306-649-2522; *Fax:* 306-649-2526
Toll-Free: 877-649-2522
Chief Officer(s):
Dennis Perrin, Regional Director, Prairies
Southwestern Ontario Regional Office
455 Keil Dr. South, Chatham ON N7M 6M4
Tel: 519-354-4831; *Fax:* 519-354-3723
Toll-Free: 800-561-2522
Chief Officer(s):
Trish Douma, Regional Director
Vancouver/Lower Mainland Regional Office
19955 - 81A Ave., Langley BC V2Y 0C7
Tel: 604-888-7220; *Fax:* 604-455-1565
Toll-Free: 800-331-2522
Chief Officer(s):
David Prentice, Director, British Columbia
Winnipeg Regional Office
#100, 185 Provencher Blvd., Winnipeg MB R2H 0G4
Tel: 204-989-0198; *Fax:* 204-942-6967
Toll-Free: 877-989-2522
Chief Officer(s):
Geoff Dueck Thiessen, Regional Director
gdueckthiessen@clac.ca

Christian Medical & Dental Society of Canada (CMDS)
9A - 1000 Windmill Rd, Dartmouth NS B3B 1L7
Tel: 902-406-2955
Toll-Free: 888-256-8653
office@cmdscanada.org
www.cmdscanada.org
www.facebook.com/CMDSCanada
twitter.com/CMDSCanada
www.youtube.com/channel/UCOB5Hpx1ERDs2anDNy6fYuA
Overview: A medium-sized national organization founded in 1971
Mission: To uphold a Christian view of medicine & dentistry; to understand & minister to the spiritual needs of colleagues; to create educational materials about public policy & health; to develop programs that promote a Christian view of medical ethics; & to support local group activities, plan conferences, & locate mentorship & other opportunities.
Member of: International Christian Medical & Dental Association
Finances: *Funding Sources:* Dues; Donations
Membership: *Fees:* $365 Full-time Medical & Dental Practitioners; $180 Part-time Practitioners; $55 Residents; $25 Medical or Dental Students or Missionaries; *Member Profile:* Christian physicians, dentists, & students who wish to integrate faith with professional practice
Activities: Offers workshops & conferences; supports a toll-free helpline for medical & dental trainees; publishes a Members Directory & other literature; offers mission opportunities
Chief Officer(s):
Larry Worthen, Executive Director
lworthen@cmdscanada.org
Stephanie Potter, Manager, Communications
sjpotter@cmdscanada.org

Christian Reformed Church in North America (CRCNA)
PO Box 5070, Stn. LCD 1, 3475 Mainway, Burlington ON L7R 3Y8
Tel: 905-336-2920; *Fax:* 905-336-8344
Toll-Free: 800-730-3490
crcna@crcna.ca
www.crcna.org
www.facebook.com/crcna
twitter.com/crcna
Overview: A large international organization founded in 1857
Mission: To be a diverse family of congregations, assemblies & ministries expressing the good news of God's kingdom
Affiliation(s): National Association of Evangelicals; Reformed Ecumenical Council; World Alliance of Reformed Churches; Canadian Council of Churches; Evangelical Fellowship of Canada
Finances: *Annual Operating Budget:* Greater than $5 Million; *Funding Sources:* Gifts & donations
Staff Member(s): 225
Membership: In US & Canada: 245,217 members in more than 1,000 congregations; *Committees:* Abuse Prevention; Back to God Hour; Calvin College; Calvin Theological Seminary; CRC Publications; Home Missions; World Missions; World Relief; Chaplaincy Ministries; CRC Loan Fund; Disability Concerns; Fund for Smaller Churches; Pastor-Church Relations; Pensions & Insurance; Race Relations; Historical; Interchurch Relations; Sermons for Reading Services
Activities: *Awareness Events:* Sea to Sea Celebration Rally; *Speaker Service:* Yes
Chief Officer(s):
Steven Timmermans, Executive Director
executive-director@crcna.org
Publications:
• The Banner
Type: Magazine; *Frequency:* Monthly; *Editor:* Rev Bob De Moor

Christian Reformed World Relief Committee *See* World Renew

Christian Stewardship Services (CSS)
#214A, 500 Alden Rd., Markham ON L3R 5H5
Fax: 905-947-9263
Toll-Free: 800-267-8890
info@csservices.ca
www.csservices.ca
Overview: A medium-sized national charitable organization founded in 1976
Mission: To connect families, faith, & finances for efficient estate & gift planning; To promote Biblical stewardship
Member of: Canadian Council of Christian Charities
Affiliation(s): Diaconal Ministries of the Christian Reformed Church
Finances: *Funding Sources:* Christian charities, including churches & schools; Social service organizations
Activities: Providing advice about will & estate planning; Offering the Growing & Giving program, featuring presentations & workshops
Chief Officer(s):
Maynard Wiersma, CFP, Executive Director
maynardw@csservices.ca
Rob Vandebelt, Manager, Fund
robv@csservices.ca
Mary Benn, Administrator, Finance
finance@csservices.ca
Publications:
• Advancing Stewardship [a publication of Christian Stewardship Services]
Type: Newsletter; *Frequency:* Semiannually
Profile: Information about the organization & its work
• Christian Stewardship Services Annual Report
Type: Yearbook; *Frequency:* Annually

Christie-Ossington Neighbourhood Centre (CONC)
854 Bloor St. West, Toronto ON M6G 1M2
Tel: 416-534-8941; *Fax:* 416-534-8704
www.conccommunity.org
Overview: A medium-sized local charitable organization founded in 1994
Mission: To improve the quality of life in the Christie Ossington community by working in collaboration with residents, community institutions, agencies, local businesses and stakeholders to create a safe and healthy community.
Finances: *Funding Sources:* Government, United Way, Donations
Staff Member(s): 43
Chief Officer(s):
Lynn Daly, Executive Director
lynn@conc.ca

Christina Lake Chamber of Commerce
1675 Hwy. 3, Christina Lake BC V0H 1E2
Tel: 250-447-6161; *Fax:* 250-447-6161
tourism@christinalake.com
www.christinalake.com
Overview: A small local organization
Member of: BC Chamber of Commerce
Finances: *Funding Sources:* Membership dues
7 volunteer(s)
Membership: 52; *Fees:* Schedule available
Activities: Fishing derby; winter fest; trail & park development

Christmas Tree Farmers of Ontario (CFTO)
9251 County Rd. 1, Palgrave ON L0N 1P0
Fax: 905-729-0548
Toll-Free: 800-661-3530
www.christmastrees.on.ca
Overview: A small provincial organization founded in 1950
Member of: Canadian Christmas Tree Growers Association
Membership: *Fees:* Member $195; Senior member $250; Plus member $360; Associate member $130; Subscriber $80; *Member Profile:* Christmas tree farmers
Chief Officer(s):
Shirley Brennan, Executive Director

Chronic Pain Association of Canada (CPAC)
PO Box 66017, Stn. Heritage, Edmonton AB T6J 6T4
Tel: 780-482-6727; *Fax:* 780-433-3128
cpac@chronicpaincanada.com
www.chronicpaincanada.com
Previous Name: North American Chronic Pain Association of Canada
Overview: A medium-sized national charitable organization founded in 1986
Mission: To advance the treatment & management of chronic intractable pain; to develop research projects to promote the discovery of a cure for this disease; to educate both the health care community & the public
Finances: *Funding Sources:* Donations
Membership: *Fees:* $15; *Member Profile:* Individuals interested in chronic pain; 26 self-help groups
Activities: Self-help groups; education & research; networking with organizations of contiguous purpose; *Awareness Events:* Chronic Pain Awareness Week, 2nd week of Nov.; *Speaker Service:* Yes; *Library:* by appointment
Chief Officer(s):
Terry Bremner, President
Barry Ulmer, Executive Director

Chrysotile Institute / Instit du Chrysotile
#1640, 1200, av McGill College, Montréal QC H3B 4G7
Tel: 514-877-9797; *Fax:* 514-877-9717
info@chrysotile.com
www.chrysotile.com
Overview: A medium-sized national organization founded in 1984
Mission: To promote the implementation & enforcement of effective regulations, standards, work practices & techniques for the safe use of asbestos
Membership: *Member Profile:* Industry, labour & government representatives

Overview: A large international charitable organization founded in 1858
Mission: To advance the kingdom of God through worship, pastoral work & fellowship
Affiliation(s): International Council of Community Churches (ICCC), ICCC Canada, World Council of Churches
Finances: *Annual Operating Budget:* Less than $50,000; *Funding Sources:* Clergy; churches; benefactors
Staff Member(s): 15; 25 volunteer(s)
Membership: 1,000-4,999; *Fees:* $200 church; $50 clergy; *Committees:* Order of the Crown of Thorns
Activities: Church ministry; Seminary program; Counselling & mediation services; *Library:* Christian Catholic Church Canada Archives; Open to public by appointment
Chief Officer(s):
Serge A. Thériault, Évêque et président
sergeatheriault@hotmail.com

Christian Children's Fund of Canada (CCFC)
1200 Denison St., Markham ON L3R 8G6
Tel: 905-754-1001; *Fax:* 905-754-1002
Toll-Free: 800-263-5437
Other Communication: media@ccfcanada.ca
donor-relations@ccfcanada.ca
www.ccfcanada.ca
www.facebook.com/CCFC
twitter.com/CCFCanada
www.youtube.com/c/ccfcanada
Overview: A large international charitable organization founded in 1960
Mission: To focus upon community development ministry, starting with basic assistance & leading to programs stressing self-help & eventual independence; To work with colleagues & partners in developing countries; To reach out to children & families of all faiths
Member of: Canadian Council of Christian Charities; Better Business Bureau; ChildFund Alliance; Imagine Canada
Affiliation(s): Canadian Marketing Association; Association of Fundraising Professionals
Finances: *Funding Sources:* Donations
200 volunteer(s)
Membership: 30,000+; *Fees:* $39/month suggested donation
Activities: Working to help those affected by HIV/AIDS; Providng water & sanitation; Offering education; *Internships:* Yes; *Speaker Service:* Yes
Chief Officer(s):
Douglas Ellenor, Chair
Terrance M Slobodian, Vice-President, Fund Development & Communications
Jim Carrie, Vice-President, Global Operations
Jeff Hogan, CPA; CA; CSR-P, Vice-President, Finance & Corporate Services
Publications:
• Child Essentials Newsletter
Type: Newsletter; *Frequency:* Monthly
• ChildVoice
Type: Magazine; *Frequency:* s-a.; *Editor:* Vicki Quigley
Profile: Magazine for donors featuring stories of sponsored children

Christian Church (Disciples of Christ) in Canada (DISCAN) / Église chrétienne (Disciples du Christ) au Canada
ON
www.canadadisciples.org
Previous Name: All-Canada Committee of the Christian Church (Disciples of Christ)
Overview: A small national charitable organization founded in 1922
Member of: The Canadian Council of Churches
Affiliation(s): The Christian Church (Disciples of Christ) in USA
Finances: *Annual Operating Budget:* $100,000-$250,000; *Funding Sources:* Donations
Staff Member(s): 2
Membership: 4,000 + 30 churches; *Committees:* Archives; Biennial Convention; Christian Nurture, Service, Witness; Church Development; College; Ministry
Activities: *Internships:* Yes; *Speaker Service:* Yes; *Library:* Resource Centre
Chief Officer(s):
Richard E. (Rick) Hamilton, Interim Regional Minister

The Christian Episcopal Church of Canada (CECC)
9280 #2 Rd., Richmond BC V7E 2C8
Tel: 604-275-7422
xnec1662@gmail.com
www.xnec.ca
Also Known As: Traditional Anglican Church in Canada
Overview: A small national charitable organization founded in 1991
Mission: To be a national Catholic & Apostolic Church of the Anglican tradition in Canada
Member of: Anglican Communion
Affiliation(s): Christian Episcopal Church in the USA
Finances: *Annual Operating Budget:* $100,000-$250,000; *Funding Sources:* Donations
Staff Member(s): 12; 40 volunteer(s)
Membership: 450; *Fees:* Free-will offerings; *Member Profile:* Baptised & confirmed Anglican Christians; *Committees:* Parochial Church Council, Assembly & Consistory; Diocesan Synod & Diocesan Council
Activities: Traditional Anglican faith & worship according to the Book of Common Prayer
Chief Officer(s):
Robert D. Redmile

Christian Farmers Federation of Ontario (CFFO)
642 Woolwich St., Guelph ON N1H 3Y2
Tel: 519-837-1620; *Fax:* 519-824-1835
Toll-Free: 855-800-0306
cffomail@christianfarmers.org
www.christianfarmers.org
www.facebook.com/CFFOnt
twitter.com/CFFOnt
www.youtube.com/user/ChristianFarmers
Overview: A large provincial organization founded in 1954
Mission: To enable members as producers, marketers, & citizens by developing both the entrepreneurial & community leadership of members; To promote a family farm & stewardship perspective; To be upfront about the Christian value system that motivates members, in order to make the wisdom of the Christian faith available to farm practice & farm policy
Affiliation(s): AG Care; Christian Farmers Federation of Alberta; Christian Environmental Council; Rural Development Advisory Committee
Finances: *Annual Operating Budget:* $500,000-$1.5 Million; *Funding Sources:* Membership fees
Staff Member(s): 4
Membership: *Fees:* $195; *Member Profile:* Full-time commercial family farm entrepreneurs; part-time, hobby & lifestyle farmers; all those who have directed their farm organization fee to CFFO when they register with the Ontario Ministry of Agriculture, Food & Rural Affairs as part of the farm business registration process; *Committees:* Stewardship & Policy East; Stewardship & Policy West
Activities: Our Farm Environmental Agenda (drafted by a coalition of Christian Farmers Federation of Ontario, AGCare, Ontario Federation of Agriculture, & the Ontario Farm Animal Council) outlines the strong commitment of farmers, through farm plans, to document present environmental conditions on their farms, develop a strategy for making appropriate changes, document actual farm practices & use that data for the development of new farm environmental initiatives; *Speaker Service:* Yes; *Library*
Chief Officer(s):
Clarence Nywening, President
Suzanne Armstrong, Director, Research & Policy

Christian Health Association of Alberta (CHAA)
PO Box 4173, 132 Warwick Rd., Edmonton AB T6E 4P8
Tel: 780-488-8074; *Fax:* 780-475-7968
chaaa@compusmart.ab.ca
www.chaaa.ab.ca
Also Known As: Catholic Health Association of Alberta & Affiliates
Previous Name: Catholic Health Care Conference of Alberta
Overview: A medium-sized provincial charitable organization founded in 1943 overseen by Catholic Health Association of Canada
Mission: Represents the shared vision & values of those seeking to make visible Jesus the Healer; provides support & leadership to members & the community through education, advocacy & collaboration
Member of: Catholic Health Association of Canada
Finances: *Annual Operating Budget:* $50,000-$100,000
Staff Member(s): 1; 13 volunteer(s)
Membership: 22 health facilities + 29 associate + 48 personal + 10 life; *Fees:* $25 individual; $75 associate
Chief Officer(s):
Glyn J. Smith, Administrator

Christian Heritage Party of British Columbia
PO Box 724, Telkwa BC V0J 2X0
Tel: 250-846-5432
info@chpbc.ca
www.chpbc.ca
Also Known As: CHP British Columbia
Previous Name: British Columbia Heritage Party
Overview: A small provincial organization founded in 2010
Mission: To advocate in favour of establishing a constitution to govern the province of British Columbia
Chief Officer(s):
Rod Taylor, Party Leader

Christian Heritage Party of Canada (CHP) / Parti de l'héritage du Canada
PO Box 4958, Stn. E, Ottawa ON K1S 5J1
Fax: 819-281-7174
Toll-Free: 888-868-3247
info@chp.ca
www.chp.ca
www.facebook.com/CHP.ca.Canada
twitter.com/CHPCanada
www.youtube.com/user/christianheritage
Also Known As: Canada's Responsible Alternative
Overview: A large national organization founded in 1986
Mission: To provide true Christian leadership & uphold biblical principles in federal legislation; To attain the leadership of the federal government of Canada through the existing democratic process
Affiliation(s): CHP New Zealand; Christian Heritage International Political Society
Finances: *Annual Operating Budget:* $250,000-$500,000; *Funding Sources:* Membership fees & donations
Staff Member(s): 3
Membership: 6,000+; *Fees:* $25 individual; $40 family; $200 individual lifetime; $300 husband & wife
Activities: *Speaker Service:* Yes; *Library:* Not open to public
Chief Officer(s):
Rod Taylor, National Leader
leader@chp.ca
Dave Bylsma, President
nationalpres@chp.ca

Christian Labour Association of Canada (CLAC) / Association chrétienne du travail du Canada
2335 Argentia Rd., Mississauga ON L5N 5N3
Tel: 905-812-2855; *Fax:* 905-812-5556
Toll-Free: 800-268-5281
headoffice@clac.ca
www.clac.ca
www.facebook.com/clacunion
twitter.com/clacunion
www.youtube.com/user/CLACunion
Overview: A medium-sized national organization founded in 1952
Mission: To promote labour relations based on the social principles of justice, respect & dignity; To stand up for fair wages, reasonable work hours, good benefits, a dependable retirement savings plan, job security, professional development & opportunities for advancement
Member of: World Organization of Workers
Staff Member(s): 250
Membership: 55,000
Activities: Training programs; *Speaker Service:* Yes; *Library:* by appointment
Chief Officer(s):
Dick Heinen, Executive Director
dheinen@clac.ca
Hank Beekhuis, Ontario Provincial Director
Dennis Perrin, Prairies Director
David Prentice, BC Director
Wayne Prins, Alberta Director
Awards:
• Frank Kooger Award
• Christian Labour Association of Canada Scholarships
   Calgary Regional Office
   3617 - 63 Ave. NE, Calgary AB T3J 5K1
   Tel: 403-686-0288; *Fax:* 403-686-0357
   Toll-Free: 866-686-0288
   Chief Officer(s):
   Dennis Perrin, Regional Director, Prairies
   Edmonton Regional Office
   14920 - 118 Ave., Edmonton AB T5V 1B8
   Fax: 780-451-3976
   Toll-Free: 877-863-5154
   Chief Officer(s):

Activities: Creation of national industrial associations; Training workshops & courses; Regulatory activities; Publications; *Library:* by appointment
Chief Officer(s):
Denis Hamel, Director General

CHUM Charitable Foundation; CHUM's Kid's Crusade Foundation See CP24 CHUM Christmas Wish

Church Council on Justice & Corrections (CCJC) / Conseil des églises pour la justice et la criminologie (CÉJC)
#303, 200 Isabella St., Ottawa ON K1S 1V7
Tel: 613-563-1688; *Fax:* 613-237-6129
ccjc@ccjc.ca
www.ccjc.ca
www.linkedin.com/company/the-church-council-on-justice-and-corrections
www.facebook.com/180318678672186
twitter.com/CCJCCanada
www.youtube.com/channel/UCbL3WH8MfWbUp-31s9gPjoQ
Overview: A medium-sized national charitable organization founded in 1972
Mission: To strengthen churches' ministry in fields of crime prevention, justice & corrections; to initiate, encourage & support programs which sensitize congregations & educate volunteer groups to participate in development of community responses to crime, justice & corrections; to promote a healing justice; to examine & respond to policy concerns with assistance of churches; to call on churches to address issues; to provide resources to churches & other related organizations.
Member of: National Associations Active in Criminal Justice
Affiliation(s): The Network - Interaction for Conflict Resolution
Finances: *Annual Operating Budget:* $250,000-$500,000
Staff Member(s): 3
Membership: 46 directors + 292 supporting; *Fees:* $40 individuals; $200 organizations
Activities: *Internships:* Yes; *Speaker Service:* Yes; *Library*
Chief Officer(s):
Schuyler Playford, Manager, Operations & Project Development, 613-563-1688 Ext. 105
splayford@ccjc.ca
Kathryn Bliss, Manager, Education & Community Engagement, 613-563-1688 Ext. 101
kbliss@ccjc.ca

> **Le Conseil Des Églises Pour La Justice Et La Criminologie (CEJC) Québec**
> #322, 2715, ch de la Côte-Sainte-Catherine, Montréal QC H3T 1B6
> *Tél:* 514-738-5075; *Téléc:* 514-735-2935
> cejcq-provincial@sympatico.ca

The Church Lads' Brigade (CLB)
PO Box 28126, 82 Harvey Rd., St. John's NL A1B 4J8
Tel: 709-722-1737; *Fax:* 709-722-1734
info@theclb.ca
www.theclb.ca
www.facebook.com/TheCLB
twitter.com/TheCLB_NL
www.youtube.com/channel/UCEfcL5pd1b6z5iOgPlJqr5Q
Also Known As: The CLB
Overview: A medium-sized provincial organization founded in 1892
Mission: To help youth develop the necessary skills to become future leaders through ecuation, recreational & social activities
Affiliation(s): The Church Lads' & Church Girls' Brigade (UK)
Finances: *Annual Operating Budget:* $50,000-$100,000; *Funding Sources:* Donations; building rentals; fundraising
Staff Member(s): 1; 200 volunteer(s)
Membership: 600 individuals + 16 companies; *Fees:* $20; *Member Profile:* All youth
Activities: Youth activities; Courses in badge work; Leadership training; Duke of Edinburgh's Award; Sports, camps & other activities; *Internships:* Yes *Library:* CLB Archives; Open to public by appointment
Chief Officer(s):
Derek White, Executive Director
derek@theclb.ca

Church Library Association of British Columbia (CLABC)
c/o Membership Secretary, 1732 - 10 St. East, Courtenay BC V9N 7H7
clabc.ca@gmail.com
www.clabc.ca
www.facebook.com/ca.clabc
Overview: A small provincial organization founded in 1971
Mission: To help church libraries in British Columbia make the most of their resources
Membership: *Member Profile:* Churches & church librarians in British Columbia
Activities: Helping churches create proactive, engaging libraries
Meetings/Conferences:
• Church Library Association of British Columbia (CLABC) Conference 2018, 2018, BC
Scope: Provincial
Publications:
• Church Library Association of British Columbia Newsletter
Type: Newsletter; *Frequency:* Quarterly; *ISSN:* 0380-2566
Profile: A forum for exchange of news & ideas among members; Newsletter also includes book reviews & news articles

Church Library Association of Ontario (CLAO)
c/o Alice Meems, Treasurer, 112 Bristol St., Guelph ON N1H 3L6
treasurer@clao.ca
www.clao.ca
www.facebook.com/churchlibraryassociationofontario
Overview: A small provincial organization founded in 1969
Mission: To help church libraries in Ontario make the most of their resources
Membership: *Fees:* $20; *Member Profile:* Churches & church librarians in Ontario
Activities: Helping churches create pro-active, engaging libraries
Chief Officer(s):
Medda Burnett, President
president@clao.ca
Laurie Lee Sproule, Coordinator, Communications & Outreach
communications@clao.ca
Alice Meems, Treasurer
treasurer@clao.ca
Awards:
• Anita Dalton Awards
Awarded for service to the CLAO
• Emma Austin Award
Awarded to recognize excellence in Ministry in individual church libraries
• Jean Van Esch Awards
Awarded to recognize excellence in service
• Elsie Riva Awards
Awarded to recognize outstanding publicity/marketing in a church library
• Nettie Friesen Awards
Awarded to recognize outstanding church library-related publications
Meetings/Conferences:
• Church Library Association of Ontario 2018 Spring Conference, 2018, ON
Scope: Provincial
Description: Workshops, speakers, exhibitors, vendors & a book swap.
Contact Information: conference@clao.ca
Publications:
• Library Lines [a publication of the Church Library Association of Ontario]
Type: Newsletter; *Frequency:* Quarterly
Profile: Articles, book reviews, & practical information for church libraries

Church of England in Canada See The Anglican Church of Canada

Church of God of Prophecy in Canada
Eastern Canada Head Office, 5145 Tomken Rd., Mississauga ON L4W 1P1
Tel: 905-625-1278; *Fax:* 905-625-1316
info@cogop.ca
www.cogop.ca
Overview: A medium-sized national charitable organization
Mission: The Church of God of Prophecy has its roots in the Holiness/Pentecostal tradition and has felt a special burden to call attention to the principle of unity in the body of Christ, while faithfully proclaiming the gospel of Jesus Christ before a watching world.
Finances: *Annual Operating Budget:* $100,000-$250,000
Staff Member(s): 3
Membership: 28 churches
Activities: *Internships:* Yes; *Speaker Service:* Yes
Chief Officer(s):
Woodroe Thompson, Bishop
revt@cogoop.ca

Church of Jesus Christ of Latter-day Saints - Canada
c/o Toronto Ontario Temple, 10060 Bramalea Rd., Brampton ON L6R 1A1
Tel: 905-799-1122; *Fax:* 905-799-1140
canada@ldschurch.org
canada.lds.org
www.facebook.com/LDSinCanada
twitter.com/ldsincanada
www.youtube.com/user/MormonMessages
Overview: A large national organization founded in 1830
Membership: 190,265 members + 479 congregations in Canada
Activities: *Speaker Service:* Yes; *Library:* Family History Library; by appointment

Church of Scientology of Toronto
2 College St., Toronto ON M5G 1K3
Tel: 416-925-2145; *Fax:* 416-925-1685
toronto@scientology.net
www.scientology-toronto.org
Overview: A medium-sized local organization
Mission: To disseminiate the ideologies of scientology
Member of: Church of Scientology

Church of the Good Shepherd (CoGS)
116 Queen St. North, Kitchener ON N2H 2H7
Tel: 519-743-3845; *Fax:* 519-743-3375
office@shepherdsway.ca
www.shepherdsway.ca
Also Known As: Swedenborgian Church
Overview: A small local organization
Mission: To welcome all on a spiritual journey based on love, a deeper understanding og the Bible's teachings & a new passion for Creation
Affiliation(s): Swedenborg Church Youth League; Marigold Whole Life Centre; Gathering Leaves
Staff Member(s): 2
Membership: 140 individual
Activities: Kidspace; Sunday School; Children's Services
Chief Officer(s):
Dave Rogalsky, Minister

Churchill Chamber of Commerce
PO Box 176, Churchill MB R0B 0E0
Tel: 204-675-2022; *Fax:* 204-675-2021
Toll-Free: 888-389-2327
churchillchamber@mts.net
churchillchamberofcommerce.ca
Overview: A small local organization
Membership: 43

Churchill Park Family Care Society
3311 Centre St. NW, Calgary AB T2E 2X7
Tel: 403-266-4656; *Fax:* 403-264-5657
cpfirst@churchillpark.ca
www.churchillpark.ca
www.facebook.com/133191603370805
Overview: A small local organization founded in 1970
Mission: To offer quality child care; To help families & caregivers access support & emergency assistance
Activities: Sharing resources to help with child rearing; Accommodating children with special needs
Chief Officer(s):
Sharon Reib, Executive Director
Dionne Maier, Senior Director, Human Resources
Don Ballance, Director, Finance
Christie Scarlett, Director, Operations

La cinémathèque québécoise
335, boul de Maisonneuve est, Montréal QC H2X 1K1
Tél: 514-842-9763; *Téléc:* 514-842-1816
info@cinematheque.qc.ca
www.cinematheque.qc.ca
www.facebook.com/cinematheque.quebecoise
twitter.com/cinemathequeqc
www.instagram.com/cinemathequeqc
Également appelé: Musée de l'image en mouvement
Aperçu: *Dimension:* moyenne; *Envergure:* provinciale; Organisme sans but lucratif; fondée en 1963
Mission: Conservation et mise en valeur du patrimoine cinématographique et télévisuel; promouvoir la culture cinématographique; créer des archives de cinéma; acquérir et conserver des films ainsi que toute la documentation qui s'y rattache; projeter ces films et exposer ces documents de facon non commerciale à des fins historique, pédagogique et

artistique.
Membre de: Fédération internationale des archives du film
Finances: *Budget de fonctionnement annuel:* $1.5 Million-$3 Million; *Fonds:* Ministère de la Culture et des communications du Québec; Patrimoine canadien, Conseil des arts du Canada
Membre(s) du personnel: 54; 2 bénévole(s)
Membre: 500; *Montant de la cotisation:* 120$; *Critères d'admissibilite:* Tous ceux qui s'intéressent à l'histoire, l'actualité et l'avenir du cinéma, de la télévision et des nouveaux médias
Activités:; *Bibliothèque:* Médiathèque Guy-L.-Coté; Bibliothèque publique
Membre(s) du bureau directeur:
Louis-Philippe Rochon, Président
Dominique Dugas, Vice Président
Christian Pitchen, Vice Président
Frédérick Pelletier, Secrétaire
Normand Grégoire, Trésorier

CIO Association of Canada (CIOCAN)
National Office, #305, 7270 Woodbine Ave., Markham ON L3R 4B9
Tel: 905-752-1899; *Fax:* 905-513-1248
Toll-Free: 877-865-9009
www.ciocan.ca
www.linkedin.com/company/cio-association-of-canada
twitter.com/CIO_CAN
Overview: A large national organization founded in 2004
Mission: To facilitate networking, sharing of best practices & executive development, & to drive advocacy on issues facing IT Executives/CIOs. Chapters: Calgary, Edmonton, Manitoba, Ottawa, Toronto & Vancouver
Membership: *Fees:* $375 academic; $600 associate; $750 full; *Member Profile:* IT executives; Chief Information Officers
Activities: Networking events; seminars; outreach; advocacy; research; scholarships; leadership development
Chief Officer(s):
Tracy Blyth, Executive Director, 905-752-1899 Ext. 255
Alison Toscano, Director, Operations, 905-752-1899 Ext. 257
Meetings/Conferences:
• CIO Peer Forum 2018, April, 2018, Vancouver Marriott Pinnacle Downtown, Vancouver, BC
Scope: National

Calgary Chapter
www.ciocan.ca/Chapters/Calgary
Chief Officer(s):
John Vince, President

Edmonton Chapter
www.ciocan.ca/Chapters/Edmonton
Chief Officer(s):
Shaun Guthrie, President

Toronto Chapter
www.ciocan.ca/Chapters/Toronto
Chief Officer(s):
Sherif Sheta, President

Vancouver Chapter
admin@ciocan-vancouver.ca
www.ciocan.ca/Chapters/Vancouver
Chief Officer(s):
Gary Munro, President
Lisa Bateman, Contact

Ottawa Chapter
www.ciocan.ca/Chapters/Ottawa
Chief Officer(s):
Philippe Johnston, President

CIRANO
2020, rue University, 25e étage, Montréal QC H3A 2A5
Tel: 514-985-4000; *Fax:* 514-985-4039
webmaster@cirano.qc.ca
www.cirano.qc.ca
Also Known As: Center for Interuniversity Research & Analysis of Organizations
Overview: A medium-sized provincial organization founded in 1998
Mission: To bolster firms' efficiency & competitive edge through the rapid transfer of new knowledge generated by its research; to encourage the integration of organizations' knowledge & preoccupations & practitioners' experience into teaching & research programs; to develop & keep in Québec world-class research teams who perform scientific analyses of organizations & strategic behaviour; to contribute to training a new generation of top-tier scientists & professionals in Québec

Circle of Eagles Lodge
1470 East Broadway, Vancouver BC V5N 1V6
Tel: 604-874-9610; *Fax:* 604-874-3858
Toll-Free: 888-332-6357
www.circleofeagles.com
Overview: A medium-sized local organization founded in 1970
Mission: To provide services to incarcerated Native men; to assist Native ex-offenders in becoming productive, contributing members of society
Finances: *Annual Operating Budget:* $250,000-$500,000
Activities: Post-release residential house; hands-on job development & lifeskills program; individual counselling; temporary financial assistance; social orientation; shelter & food services; liaison between inmates, corrections & the community; assisting Native clubs within the institutions
Chief Officer(s):
Ken Clement, President

Circulation Management Association of Canada (CMC) / Association canadienne des chefs de tirage
c/o Target Audience Management Inc., #6, 50 Main St. East, Beeton ON L0G 1A0
Tel: 905-729-1046; *Fax:* 905-729-4432
admin@thecmc.ca
thecmc.ca
www.facebook.com/180627152014026
twitter.com/CircCanada
Previous Name: Canadian Circulation Management Association
Overview: A small national organization founded in 1981
Mission: To provide professional development, promotes fellowship within the circulation profession & raises the profile of circulation professionals by rewarding outstanding achievement.
Affiliation(s): Newspaper Association of America
Membership: *Fees:* $139; *Member Profile:* Circulation professionals of the Canadian magazine industry
Activities: *Rents Mailing List:* Yes; *Library*
Chief Officer(s):
Tony Danas, President
tony.danas@gmail.com
Ron Sellwood, Director, Communications, 416-754-3900 Ext. 285
rons@ctcmagazines.com
Brian Gillet, Administrator
Awards:
• ACE Awards
Eligibility: Demonstration of excellent circulation work in Cdn. publishing industry
• Magazine Marketer of the Year Award
Eligibility: Having produced a body of work or notable achievement/contribution in the Cdn. magazine marketing field
Publications:
• The Circulator

Cities of New Brunswick Association (CNBA)
PO Box 1421, Stn. A, Fredericton NB E3B 5E3
Tel: 506-452-9292; *Fax:* 506-452-9898
info@8citiesnb.com
www.8citiesnb.com
twitter.com/CNBA_ACNB
Overview: A medium-sized provincial organization
Mission: To promote the exchange of information among members; To co-operate & liaise with other agencies & associations having a municipal interest; To strive for a united front in all matters pertaining to the realization of municipal goals
Finances: *Funding Sources:* Membership dues
Membership: 8; *Member Profile:* The communities of Bathurst, Campbellton, Dieppe, Edmundston, Frederickton, Miramichi, Moncton & Saint John
Chief Officer(s):
Eric Megarity, President
Charline McCoy, Acting Executive Director

Citizen Advocacy Montreal *Voir* Parrainage civique Montréal

Citizen Scientists
1749 Meadowvale Rd., Toronto ON M1B 5W8
info@citizenscientists.ca
www.citizenscientists.ca
Overview: A medium-sized local organization founded in 2001
Mission: To monitor local watersheds, foster local environmental stewardship, and educate volunteers and the public.

Citizens Concerned About Free Trade (CCAFT)
PO Box 8052, Saskatoon SK S7K 4R7
Tel: 306-244-5757; *Fax:* 306-244-3790
ccaftnat@sk.sympatico.ca
www.davidorchard.com/ccaft
Overview: A small national organization
Mission: To provide information & mobilize those opposed to the Free Trade Agreements & the loss of Canadian sovereignty; to have Canada exercise the termination clauses of both the FTA & NAFTA so that the country can protect its resources & play an independent role in world affairs
Membership: 5,000
Toronto Office
#202, 9 Bloor St. East, Toronto ON M4W 1A9
Tel: 416-922-7867; *Fax:* 416-922-7883
ccafttor@sympatico.ca
Vancouver Office
PO Box 4185, #210, 207 West Hastings, Vancouver BC V6B 3Z6
Tel: 604-683-3733; *Fax:* 604-683-3749
ccaftvan@telus.net

Citizens for a Safe Environment (CSE)
Tel: 416-461-1092
info@csetoronto.org
www.csetoronto.org
Overview: A medium-sized local organization founded in 1983
Mission: To promomote waste management practices that protect the health of Toronto citizens, their communities and the environment.
Member of: Ontario Environmental Network
Activities: *Awareness Events:* Green Tea Parties; *Speaker Service:* Yes

Citizens for an Oak Ridges Trail *See* Oak Ridges Trail Association

Citizens for Public Justice *See* CPJ Corp.

Citizens for Safe Cycling *See* Bike Ottawa

Citizens Opposed to Paving the Escarpment (COPE)
PO Box 20014, 2211 Brant St., Burlington ON L7P 0A4
mail@cope-nomph.org
www.cope-nomph.org
www.facebook.com/nohighway
twitter.com/StopHwy
Overview: A large local organization
Mission: To preserve the Niagara Escarpment, by ensuring that no new highway corridors are paved across the Niagara Escarpment & that all viable alternatives to the proposed Mid-Peninsula Highway are fully considered
Affiliation(s): Coalition on the Niagara Escarpment; Sierra Club
Membership: 1000+; *Fees:* Donations of $10 or more

Citizens' Environment Alliance (CEA)
1950 Ottawa St., Windsor ON N8Y 1R7
Tel: 519-973-1116; *Fax:* 519-973-8360
ceaadmin@cogeco.net
www.citizensenvironmentalliance.org
Previous Name: Citizens' Environment Alliance of Southwestern Ontario
Overview: A small local charitable organization founded in 1985
Mission: CEA is a non-profit, grass-roots, international, education & research organization that aims to protect, restore & enhance the quality of the local environment in the Detroit-St. Clair Rivers corridor & in the Essex-Kent regions of the Great Lakes Basin; educate the public about environmental problems & solutions as they relate to the Great Lakes ecosystems & in particular to Southwestern Ontario. It is a registered charity, BN: 899837850RR0001.
Member of: Canadian Environmental Network; Ontario Environment Network; Environmental Action Ontario
Affiliation(s): Canadian Environmental Network (RCEN); Ontario Environmental Network (OEN); Lake Erie Millennium Network (LEMN); Ontario Water Conservation Alliance
Finances: *Annual Operating Budget:* $50,000-$100,000 20 volunteer(s)
Membership: 100-499; *Fees:* Donations; *Committees:* Endangered Species; Toxic Trackers; Air Quality; Area Clean-up Team
Activities: "State of the Detroit River" boat tour; annual "Weenie Award" night; endangered natural spaces; toxic trackers; air quality; Detroit River clean-up; waste management; *Speaker Service:* Yes; *Rents Mailing List:* Yes; *Library:* Environmental & Resource Library; Open to public

Citizens' Environment Alliance of Southwestern Ontario *See* Citizens' Environment Alliance

Citizens' Environment Watch (CEW)
#380, 401 Richmond St. West, Toronto ON M5V 3A8

Tel: 647-258-3280; *Fax:* 416-979-3155
info@citizensenvironmentwatch.org
www.citizensenvironmentwatch.org
Overview: A medium-sized national organization founded in 1996
Mission: To provide communities the tools for education, monitoring and influencing positive change and to encourage people to take an active role in restoring and sustaining nature.
Finances: *Annual Operating Budget:* $250,000-$500,000; *Funding Sources:* Government, Foundations
Staff Member(s): 4
Chief Officer(s):
Meredith Cochrane, Executive Director

Citizenship Council of Manitoba Inc. *See* Immigrant Centre Manitoba Inc.

Citroën Autoclub Canada
49 Alabaster Dr., Brampton ON L6V 4G9
citroenvie.com
Overview: A medium-sized national organization
Mission: To promote preservation, restoration & recognition of all Citroëns
Membership: *Fees:* US$20 basic; US$30 full; US$40 overseas
Activities: Meetings; rallies & tours; special tool-lending service
Chief Officer(s):
George Dyke, President, 647-896-3202
gdyke@sympatico.ca

City Clerks & Election Officers Association *See* Alberta Municipal Clerks Association

City Farmer - Canada's Office of Urban Agriculture
PO Box 74567, Stn. Kitsilano, Vancouver BC V6K 4P4
Tel: 604-685-5832
cityfarmer@gmail.com
www.cityfarmer.org
Overview: A small national organization founded in 1978
Mission: To encourage gardening in an urban environment
Activities: Research Garden functions as the City of Vancouver's Compost Demonstration Garden & site of the Compost Hotline: 604-736-2250
Chief Officer(s):
Michael Levenston, Executive Director

City Index Referral Association *See* Community Food Sharing Association

The City of Greater Sudbury Developmental Services
245 Mountain St., Sudbury ON P3B 2T8
Tel: 705-674-1451
www.cgsds.ca
Previous Name: Sudbury & District Association for Community Living
Overview: A small local organization
Member of: Ontario Agencies Supporting Individuals with Special Needs (OASIS)
Chief Officer(s):
Pascal Joseph, President
Mila Wong, Executive Director
mwong@vianet.ca

City of Waterloo Staff Association
Waterloo City Hall, PO Box 337, 100 Regina St. South, Waterloo ON N2J 4A8
Tel: 519-886-1550; *Fax:* 519-747-8760
www.city.waterloo.on.ca
Overview: A small local organization
Mission: The Association is a labour group that represents inside workers who provide administrative, program management & supervisory support for the City's operations.
Membership: 220

Civic Institute of Professional Personnel (CIPP) / L'Institut professionnel du personnel municipal (IPPM)
#270, 117 Centrepointe Dr., Ottawa ON K2G 5X3
Tel: 613-241-3730; *Fax:* 613-241-4461
admin@cipp.on.ca
www.cipp.on.ca
www.facebook.com/CIPPOttawa
twitter.com/CIPPOttawa
Overview: A small local organization
Mission: CIPP represents members in the negotiation and administration of their rights under their respective collective agreements.
Staff Member(s): 5

Membership: *Member Profile:* Professional public sector employees; *Committees:* City Negotiating; OCHC Negotiating; Grievance Arbitration Approval; Policy & Education
Chief Officer(s):
Doug Laviolette, President
Sheila Stansislawski, Executive Director
sheilas@cipp.on.ca

Civil Air Search & Rescue Association (CASARA)
Tel: 204-953-2290
www.casara.ca
Overview: A large national organization founded in 1984
Mission: To promote aviation safety; To support Canada's Search & Rescue (SAR) program
Membership: 2,000+ pilots, navigators, & spotters
Chief Officer(s):
Frank Schuurmans, President
Awards:
• Volunteer Award
Recognizes the exceptional service of a volunteer
• Continuation Pilot Training Award
Presented annually to one of the top graduates of the power pilot training program
• CASARA Scholarship Program
; *Amount:* $300-$5,000

Civil Constables Association of Nova Scotia (CCANS)
8 Evergreen Dr., Truro NS B2N 5J1
www.nsbailiff.ca
Overview: A small provincial organization founded in 2002
Mission: To represent bailiffs & process servers from Nova Scotia
Membership: *Fees:* $60 civil constables; $45 associate/corporate members; *Member Profile:* Appointed civil constable individuals in Nova Scotia; Corporations or individuals who have a direct involvement in the civil enforcement industry in Nova Scotia may be associate members
Chief Officer(s):
Michael Lutes, President

Civil Service Association of Ontario *See* Ontario Public Service Employees Union

Clan Donald Canada
PO Box 417, Trenton NS B0K 1X0
Tel: 902-752-6616
ebmac@ns.sympatico.ca
www.clandonaldcanada.ca
Overview: A medium-sized national organization founded in 1996
Mission: To maintain contact with members of Clan Donald around Canada
Chief Officer(s):
Priscilla Sharkey, Secretary
thesharkeys@eastlink.ca
Glenda McDonell, High Commissioner
glendamgm@sympatico.ca

Clan Farquharson Association of Canada
#2, 76 Hatherly Rd., Toronto ON M6E 1W2
Overview: A small national organization founded in 1984
Mission: To promote & preserve the heritage & interests of the Scottish clan of Farquharson through history, genealogy, social events, literature & language (Gaelic).
Member of: Nova Scotia Scottish Clans Association
Finances: *Funding Sources:* Membership fees
Membership: *Fees:* $20 individual; $25 family; $20 associate member; *Member Profile:* Persons of Scottish descent related to Clan Farquharson
Chief Officer(s):
David E. Coutts, President, 647-693-3710
dcouttsca2012@hotmail.com

Clan Fraser Society of Canada (CFSC)
c/o W. Neil Fraser, #1101, 71 Charles St. East, Toronto ON M4Y 2T3
Tel: 416-920-6851
enquiry@clanfraser.ca
www.clanfraser.ca
Previous Name: Clan Fraser Society of North America, Canadian Region
Overview: A small national organization founded in 1868
Mission: To collect & disseminate information on history & the exploits of Frasers in Canada & Scotland; To act as liaison with clan chiefs
Affiliation(s): Clan Fraser Society of Australia; Clan Fraser

Society of New Zealand; Clan Fraser Society of Scotland & the UK
Finances: *Annual Operating Budget:* Less than $50,000
5 volunteer(s)
Membership: 650 individual; *Fees:* $25; *Member Profile:* People with the surname of Fraser or septs of Clan Fraser
Activities: Fraser history & genealogy in Canada & Scotland
Chief Officer(s):
W. Neil Fraser, Chair
Publications:
• Clan Fraser: A History
Author: Flora Marjory Fraser; *Price:* $28 hardcover; $22 paperback

Clan Fraser Society of North America, Canadian Region *See* Clan Fraser Society of Canada

Clan Gunn Society of North America - Eastern Canada Branch
c/o Edward Gunn, 10485, rue Vanier, Québec QC G2B 3N4
Tel: 418-842-6563
www.clangunn.com
Overview: A small provincial organization founded in 2001
Mission: To unite all family members; to renew pride in family & clan by fostering kinship & increasing knowledge & understanding of Scottish history through cultural activities.
Finances: *Annual Operating Budget:* Less than $50,000; *Funding Sources:* Membership fees; donations
Chief Officer(s):
Ted Gunn, Co-Commissioner
gunn@upc.qc.ca
Louise Gunn, Co-Commissioner
Publications:
• Gunnsmoke
Type: newsletter

Clan Lamont Society of Canada
485 Cobequid Rd., Sackville NS B4C 3Y7
info@clanlamont.ca
www.clanlamont.ca
Also Known As: Clan MacEaracher
Overview: A small international charitable organization founded in 1986
Mission: To promote the Gaelic language in Nova Scotia; to help with cost of restoration of Kilfinnan Church in Scotland; To promote Celtic music & customs
Member of: Federation of Scottish Clans in Nova Scotia; Canadian Association of Scottish Societies of Canada
Affiliation(s): Clan Lamont Scotland, Australia, USA
Finances: *Annual Operating Budget:* Less than $50,000; *Funding Sources:* Membership dues; fundraising
6 volunteer(s)
Membership: 100; *Fees:* $15 individual; $20 family; *Member Profile:* All persons interested in Scottish culture; *Committees:* History Research
Activities: Meetings; outings; Highland games; Tartan Day; Lamont Memorial Day; Robbie Burns Day; *Awareness Events:* Tartan Day in Canada, April 6; Lamont Memorial Days, June 1-3
Chief Officer(s):
Jean Watson, President
Elsie Turner, Treasurer

Clan MacKenzie Society in the Americas, Canadian Chapter *See* Clan Mackenzie Society of Canada

Clan Mackenzie Society of Canada
580 Rebecca St., Oakville ON L6K 3N9
www.clanmackenziecanada.ca
www.facebook.com/clanmackenzieca
Previous Name: Clan MacKenzie Society in the Americas, Canadian Chapter
Overview: A small national charitable organization founded in 1986
Mission: To support history, culture & education of MacKenzies & Clan in Canada, Scotland & worldwide
Affiliation(s): Clan MacKenzie Societies in Scotland, USA, Australia, New Zealand
Finances: *Annual Operating Budget:* Less than $50,000; *Funding Sources:* Membership dues; sales; lotteries; donations
12 volunteer(s)
Membership: 400+; *Fees:* $20
Activities: Tent at Highland Games across Canada; annual dinner & picnic; *Awareness Events:* Highland Games *Library:* Private Collection; Not open to public
Chief Officer(s):
Sharie Northey Argue, President

Canadian Associations / Clan MacLeod Societies of Canada (CMSC)

Alan McKenzie, Treasurer
alan@mkz.com

Clan MacLeod Societies of Canada (CMSC)
6 Peace Ct., Caledon ON L7E 3R7
www.clanmacleod-canada.com
Overview: A medium-sized national organization founded in 1935
Mission: The Societies aim to strengthen bonds of clan fellowship across Canada; to advance knowledge about the history in Canada of the MacLeods & septs; to maintain & procure documents & genealogical records for the National Archives; to encourage appreciation & performance of Celtic Arts (music, piping & dancing); to assist in the restoration & repair of places & objects of historical interest.
Member of: World Associate Clan MacLeod Societies
Chief Officer(s):
Judy McLeod Tipple, President

Southern Alberta Branch
#224, 16 Midlake Blvd. SE, Calgary AB T2X 3P2
Tel: 403-869-8144; Fax: 403-201-3303
clanmacleod.ca

British Columbia Interior Branch
c/o J. McLeod, PO Box 1835, Merritt BC V1K 1B8

Central Ontario Branch
211 Dixon Dr., Milton ON L9T 6C5

Glengarry Ontario Branch
PO Box 192, 5 Maxwell St., Ingleside ON K0C 1M0
www.clanmacleod-canada.com
Chief Officer(s):
Joan MacEwan, President

Manitoba Branch
MB

Ottawa Branch
c/o I.M. Johnston, 1102 - 1285 Cahill Dr. East, Ottawa ON K1V 9A7

Vancouver Branch
c/o Edie Kernighan, 855 Grover Ave., Coquitlam BC V3J 3E4
clanmacleodsocietygv.blogspot.ca
www.facebook.com/385314628266032

Vancouver Island Branch
c/o Malcolm MacLeod, 1068 Islay St., Duncan BC V9L 2E1
Tel: 250-746-3997

Clan Matheson Society of Nova Scotia
88 Beaumont Dr., Lower Sackville NS B4C 1V6
Tel: 902-865-5735
Overview: A small provincial organization founded in 1985
Finances: *Funding Sources:* Fundraising events
Chief Officer(s):
Albert Matheson, President
albert.matheson@clanmatheson.org

Clans & Scottish Societies of Canada (CASSOC)
c/o Secretary, #78, 24 Fundy Bay Blvd., Toronto ON M1W 3A4
Tel: 416-492-1623
editor@cassoc.ca
www.cassoc.ca
Overview: A medium-sized national charitable organization founded in 1976
Mission: To foster the organization of & cooperation between Scottish associations, federations, clans, societies & groups through initiation & coordination of projects & undertakings; To advance Scottish cultural heritage in Canada
Finances: *Annual Operating Budget:* Less than $50,000; *Funding Sources:* Membership fees
75 volunteer(s)
Membership: 64 organizations; *Fees:* $50
Activities: Booth at Scottish events (Highland Games, etc.); newsletter; telephone service; *Speaker Service:* Yes
Chief Officer(s):
Karen McCrimmon, Chair
chairperson@cassoc.ca
Jo Ann M. Tuskin, Secretary
secretary@cassoc.ca

Clare Chamber of Commerce *Voir* Chambre de commerce de Clare

Clarenville Area Chamber of Commerce
#203, 293 Memorial Dr., Clarenville NL A5A 1R5
Tel: 709-466-5800; Fax: 709-466-5803
Toll-Free: 866-466-5800
info@clarenvilleareachamber.com
www.clarenvilleareachamber.com
www.facebook.com/clarenvillearea.chamberofcommerce
twitter.com/chamber_cville
Overview: A small local organization
Mission: To promote Clarenville as a tourist destination & to improve economic development
Staff Member(s): 1
Membership: 140; *Fees:* Schedule available based on number of employees; *Committees:* Public Relations Membership; Events; Profit; Finance; Strategic Planning
Chief Officer(s):
Jason Strickland, President
Ina Marsh, Office Manager

Claresholm & District Chamber of Commerce
PO Box 1092, Claresholm AB T0L 0T0
Tel: 403-625-3395
www.claresholmchamber.ca
www.facebook.com/claresholmchamber
Overview: A small local organization
Mission: To promote Claresholm as a strong, united community; To encourage new business; To help existing business grow & prosper
Membership: 105
Chief Officer(s):
Russell Sawatzky, President
president@claresholmchamber.ca

Classical & Medieval Numismatic Society (CMNS)
3329 Queen St. East, Toronto ON M4E 1E8
cmns.info@gmail.com
www.cmns.ca
Overview: A small international organization founded in 1991
Mission: To promote & encourage study & research in the field of numismatics & history as they relate to ancient & medieval coinage & related subjects; to publish the writings that are the result of such activity.
Member of: Royal Canadian Numismatic Association; Numismatic Network Canada; American Numismatic Society; American Numismatic Association
Finances: *Funding Sources:* Membership dues; donations; grants
Membership: *Member Profile:* Collectors, historians, students; those interested in ancient & medieval coinage & history
Activities: Publish quarterly journal; hold educations meeting & programs; *Speaker Service:* Yes; *Library:* by appointment Not open to public

Classical Accordion Society of Canada
3296 Cindy Cr., Mississauga ON L4Y 3J6
Tel: 905-625-0422
Overview: A small national organization founded in 1979
Finances: *Annual Operating Budget:* $50,000-$100,000
6 volunteer(s)
Membership: 26 individual; 15 associate
Activities: *Rents Mailing List:* Yes
Chief Officer(s):
Joseph Macerollo, President

Classical Association of Canada (CAC) / Société canadienne des études classiques (SCEC)
c/o Guy Chamberland, Thornloe College at Laurentian University, Laurentian University, Sudbury ON P3E 2C6
www.cac-scec.ca
Overview: A small national charitable organization founded in 1947
Mission: To advance the study of the civilizations of the Roman & Greek worlds; To promote teaching of classical civilizations & languages in Canadian schools; To encourage research in classical studies
Affiliation(s): Canadian Federation for the Humanities & Social Sciences; Fédération Internationale des Études Classiques; Canadian Institute in Greece
Finances: *Funding Sources:* Donations
Activities: Increasing public awareness of the importance of classical studies; Promoting the study of women, gender, & sexuality in the ancient world, through the Women's Network; Liaising with other Canadian & international scholarly associations; *Speaker Service:* Yes
Chief Officer(s):
Guy Chamberland, Secretary
secretary@cac-scec.ca
Awards:
• Desmond Conacher Scholarship
Eligibility: Students entering graduate studies in classics or a related discipline; *Amount:* $2,500
• Undergraduate Essay Contest
Eligibility: Undergraduate students taking Classics courses at Canadian universities
• National Greek & Latin Sight Translation Competitions
Eligibility: Canadian students at the high school & university level
Deadline: January
• Grace Irwin Award for Classics
Eligibility: Secondary school teachers of Latin, Ancient Greek, or Classical Civilization who is seeking to upgrade abilities; *Amount:* $500
• Graduate Student Presentation Prize
To honour a graduate student who delivers the best paper at the annual meeting of The Classical Association of Canada
• Award of Merit
To recognize oustanding service to the discipline
Meetings/Conferences:
• Classical Association of Canada Annual Conference 2018, May, 2018, University of Calgary, Calgary, AB
Scope: National
Contact Information: URL: cacscec2018.wordpress.com
Publications:
• Canadian Classical Electronic Bulletin [a publication of the Classical Association of Canada]
Type: Newsletter; *Frequency:* Monthly; *Editor:* Guy Chamberland
• Mouseion [a publication of the Classical Association of Canada]
Type: Journal; *Frequency:* 3 pa; *Editor:* Brad Levett et al.; *ISSN:* 1913-5416
Profile: A scholarly publication published by the University of Calgary Press for the Classical Association of Canada
• Phoenix [a publication of the Classical Association of Canada]
Type: Journal; *Accepts Advertising*; *Editor:* Michele George; *ISSN:* 0031-8299
Profile: An international scholarly publication published by the University of Toronto Press for the Classical Associationof Canada

Clay Tree Society for People with Developmental Disabilities
838 Old Victoria Rd., Nanaimo BC V9R 6A1
Tel: 250-753-5322; Fax: 250-753-2749
claytree@shaw.ca
www.claytree.org
www.facebook.com/ClayTreeSociety
Overview: A small local organization founded in 1957
Mission: To provide support to individuals with developmental disabilities with programs focusing on community inclusion & recreation, life skills, volunteer opportunities, artistic exploration, personal empowerment & independence
Chief Officer(s):
Glenys Patmore, Executive Director, 250-753-5322 Ext. 1, Fax: 250-753-2749
glenys.claytree@shaw.ca

La Clé d'la Baie en Huronie - Association culturelle francophone
#5, 2, promenade Marsellus, Barrie ON L4N 0Y4
Tél: 705-725-9755; Téléc: 705-725-1955
Autres numéros: Penetanguishene Tél: 705-549-3116; Télé: 705-549-6463
lacle@lacle.ca
www.lacle.ca
Également appelé: La Clé d'la Baie
Aperçu: *Dimension:* petite; *Envergure:* locale; Organisme sans but lucratif; fondée en 1996
Mission: La Clé d'la Baie est un organisme catalyseur au service de la communauté francophone du comté de Simcoe; promouvoir la participation active des membres de la communauté; rechercher l'épanouissement et le développement harmonieux de la communauté francophone, tout en lui permettant de vivre sa langue, sa culture, son identité et son héritage
Finances: *Budget de fonctionnement annuel:* $500,000-$1.5 Million; *Fonds:* Gouvernement fédéral et provincial; autofinancement
Membre(s) du personnel: 40; 150 bénévole(s)
Membre: 100-499; *Critères d'admissibilite:* francophones; *Comités:* Exécutif; Socioculturel; Radio; Actions politiques
Activités: Spectacles, camps d'été, radio communautaire, développement communautaire; *Service de conférenciers:* Oui
Membre(s) du bureau directeur:
Pierre Casault, Directeur général
pcasault@lacle.ca

Clean Air Strategic Alliance (CASA)
10035 - 108 St., 10th Fl., Edmonton AB T5J 3E1

Tel: 780-427-9793; Fax: 780-422-3127
casa@casahome.org
www.casahome.org
www.facebook.com/419768864745652
twitter.com/CleanAirSA
www.flickr.com/photos/81460374@N02
Overview: A medium-sized provincial organization founded in 1994
Mission: To manage strategic issues of air quality in Alberta; To represent three levels of government, as well as industry & NGOs; To plan for, organize, & commit resources related to air quality in Alberta
Finances: *Funding Sources:* Industry; Government; Donations
Staff Member(s): 5
Chief Officer(s):
Norman MacLeod, Executive Director

Clean Annapolis River Project (CARP)
PO Box 395, 314 St. George St., Annapolis Royal NS B0S 1A0
Tel: 902-532-7533; *Fax:* 902-532-3038
Toll-Free: 888-547-4344
carp@annapolisriver.ca
www.annapolisriver.ca
www.facebook.com/CleanAnnapolisRiverProject
twitter.com/CARPAnnapolis
www.youtube.com/user/CARPAnnapolis
Overview: A medium-sized local charitable organization founded in 1990
Mission: To promote, encourage & assist with the wise use of the resources of the Annapolis Watershed; water quality monitoring program
Finances: *Annual Operating Budget:* $250,000-$500,000; *Funding Sources:* Private & public
Staff Member(s): 12; 60 volunteer(s)
Membership: 100; *Fees:* $15 student; $25 individual; $50 family/institutional; $100 lifetime
Activities: Environment monitoring; habitat restoration; climate change issues; water quality issues; public awareness; *Internships:* Yes; *Speaker Service:* Yes; *Library:* by appointment
Chief Officer(s):
Levi Cliche, Executive Director
levicliche@annapolisriver.ca

Clean Calgary Association *See* Green Calgary

Clean Energy British Columbia (CEBC)
#354, 409 Granville St., Vancouver BC V6C 1T2
Tel: 604-568-4778; *Fax:* 604-568-4724
Toll-Free: 855-568-4778
www.cleanenergybc.org
www.linkedin.com/groups/4767428/profile
www.facebook.com/CleanEnergyBC
twitter.com/CleanEnergyBC
Also Known As: Clean Energy BC
Previous Name: Independent Power Association of BC
Overview: A small provincial organization founded in 1992
Mission: To develop a viable power generation & power management industry in British Columbia that serves the public interest by providing cost-effective electricity through the efficient & environmentally responsible development of the province's generation & transmission resources & facilitites
Membership: *Fees:* $75-$10,000; *Committees:* Conference; First Nations; Hydro; Market Development; Market Issues; Operational Safety; Thermal; Wind; Solar
Activities: Engaging in policy implementation
Chief Officer(s):
Bryan MacLeod, Manager, Development & Operations
bryan.macleod@cleanenergybc.org
Lisa Bateman, Manager, Office & Events
lisa.bateman@cleanenergybc.org
Meetings/Conferences:
• Clean Energy BC 28th AGM & Industry Outlook, 2018, BC
Scope: Provincial

Clean North
736A Queen St. East, Sault Ste Marie ON P6A 2A9
Tel: 705-945-1573
info@cleannorth.org
www.cleannorth.org
Also Known As: The Sault & District Recycling Association
Overview: A small provincial organization founded in 1989
Mission: This citizens' group promotes environmental protection through reduction, reuse & recycling of residential & industrial waste in Sault Ste. Marie & the Algoma District.
Member of: Northwatch; Ontario Environmental Network
Affiliation(s): Ontario Environment Network; Northwatch

Finances: *Annual Operating Budget:* $50,000-$100,000; *Funding Sources:* Membership dues; fundraising; foundations; grants
210 volunteer(s)
Membership: 350; *Fees:* $10 & $15
Activities: Recycling phone books; dry cells; Christmas trees; *Internships:* Yes; *Speaker Service:* Yes; *Library:* Environmental Resource Room; Open to public
Chief Officer(s):
David Trowbridge, Chair

The Clean Nova Scotia Foundation *See* Clean Nova Scotia Foundation

Clean Nova Scotia Foundation (CNS)
126 Portland St., Dartmouth NS B2Y 1H8
Tel: 902-420-3474; *Fax:* 902-982-6768
Toll-Free: 855-736-3474
info@clean.ns.ca
www.clean.ns.ca
www.facebook.com/CleanFoundation
twitter.com/CleanFoundation
www.youtube.com/CleanFoundation
Also Known As: Clean Foundation
Previous Name: The Clean Nova Scotia Foundation
Overview: A medium-sized provincial charitable organization founded in 1988
Mission: To inspire positive environmental change in Nova Scotia; To support clean leaders; To work towards achieving a clean environment & clean water
Finances: *Annual Operating Budget:* Greater than $5 Million; *Funding Sources:* Donations; Sponsorships
Staff Member(s): 40
Membership: *Member Profile:* Persons & businesses committed to the creation of a sustainable & healthy environment in Nova Scotia
Activities: Providing environmental education & information; program areas include energy & climate change, clean water, waste reduction, youth engagement (including the Nova Scotia Youth Corps) & sustainable transportation; *Awareness Events:* Commuter Challenge; Clean Across Nova Scotia; *Internships:* Yes; *Speaker Service:* Yes
Chief Officer(s):
Scott Skinner, Executive Director, 902-420-3476
sskinner@clean.ns.ca
Gina Patterson, Director, Policy & Strategic Relations, 902-420-6593
patterson@clean.ns.ca
Geoff McCain, Senior Manager, Finance & Administration, 902-420-7943
gmccain@clean.ns.ca
Erin Burbridge, Director, Programs & Regulatory Affairs, 902-420-8832
eburbidge@clean.ns.ca
Charlynne Robertson, Coordinator, Waste Programs, 902-420-7937
crobertson@clean.ns.ca
Camilla Melrose, Coordinator, Water Programs, 902-420-7933
water@clean.ns.ca
Awards:
• Clean Nova Scotia Scholarship Award
Eligibility: A Nova Scotia graduate student (Masters or PhD) conducting research in environmental studies *Deadline:* February
Publications:
• A Carbon Offsetting Primer
Author: Gina Patterson
• Clean Nova Scotia Annual Report
Type: Yearbook; *Frequency:* Annually
• Clean Nova Scotia Strategic Plan
Profile: A direction for the organization's activities during the next three to five years
• A Guide to Energy Efficiency for Religious Buildings in Nova Scotia
Type: Guide; *Number of Pages:* 50
Profile: Sections of the guide include getting started, the walk-through audit, how to do a greenhouse gas inventory, youth group engagement, energy efficiencyimprovements, a case study, a master checklist, resources for churches, & references

Clearwater & District Chamber of Commerce
209 Dutch Lake Rd., Clearwater BC V0E 1N2
Tel: 250-674-2646; *Fax:* 250-674-3693
www.clearwaterbcchamber.com
Overview: A small local organization founded in 1956
Finances: *Funding Sources:* Membership dues

Membership: *Fees:* Schedule available; *Member Profile:* Business
Activities: *Library:* Business Information Centre; Not open to public
Awards:
• Annual Awards
Annual award, given to Citizen, Youth, Employee, Retail/Service and Tourism Business of the Year

Clearwater & District Food Bank *See* Clearwater & District Food Bank Society

Clearwater & District Food Bank Society
741 Clearwater Village Rd., Clearwater BC V0E 1N0
Tel: 250-674-3697; *Fax:* 250-674-3402
Previous Name: Clearwater & District Food Bank
Overview: A small local organization overseen by Food Banks British Columbia
Member of: Food Banks British Columbia
Chief Officer(s):
Heather Stanley, Contact
pandhlc@telus.net

Les Clefs d'Or Canada
c/o Oak Bay Beach Hotel, 1175 Beach Dr., Victoria BC V8S 2N2
Tel: 250-598-4556
www.lesclefsdorcanada.org
Overview: A small national organization founded in 1976
Mission: To grow & promote Les Clefs d'Or & the concierge profession
Finances: *Funding Sources:* Corporate sponsorship
Membership: 55 individual; 19 professional affiliate; *Fees:* $300 and up; *Member Profile:* Hotel concierge
Chief Officer(s):
Carolina Avaria, President
president@lesclefsdorcanada.org
Dillon Carfoot, National Secretary
secretary@lesclefsdorcanada.org

Clements Centre Society
5856 Clements St., Duncan BC V9L 3W3
Tel: 250-746-4135; *Fax:* 250-746-1636
clementscentre.org
www.facebook.com/214754818591076
twitter.com/ClementsCentre
Previous Name: Cowichan Valley Association for Community Living
Overview: A small local charitable organization founded in 1957
Mission: To provide support & services to individuals with developmental disabilities & their families in the Cowichan Valley, promoting the acceptance & inclusion of all people
Member of: British Columbia Association for Community Living; Canadian Association for Community Living
Affiliation(s): Commission on Accreditation of Rehabilitation Facilities (CARF); Thrifty Foods
Finances: *Funding Sources:* Ministry for Children & Families; United Way; Duncan Volunteer Fire Department; BC Gaming Commission
Activities: Child development services; residential services; adult day programs; *Speaker Service:* Yes; *Library:* Toy Resource Lending Library; by appointment
Chief Officer(s):
Leslie Welin, President

Climate Action Network - Canada
#305, 75 Albert St., Ottawa ON K1P 5E7
Toll-Free: 855-254-6638
info@climateactionnetwork.ca
www.climateactionnetwork.ca
www.facebook.com/climate.action.network.canada
twitter.com/CANRACCanada
www.youtube.com/user/CANRACCanada
Overview: A small national organization
Mission: To support & empower Canada's governments, private sector, labour & civil society by designing, developing & implementing effective strategies to reduce greenhouse gas emissions at international, national & local levels; To prevent dangerous levels of human interference with the global climate system
Membership: *Fees:* Schedule available
Chief Officer(s):
Catherine Abreu, Executive Director
catherineabreu@climateactionnetwork.ca

Climb Yukon Association
YT

Canadian Associations / Clinical Nurse Specialist Association of Ontario (CNS)

info@climbyukon.net
www.climbyukon.net
Overview: A small provincial organization
Mission: To develop to the climbing community in the Yukon as a recreational opportunity for adults & youth, to raise awareness of & address access & safety concerns.

Clinical Nurse Specialist Association of Ontario (CNS)
c/o Registered Nurses' Association of Ontario, 158 Pearl St., Toronto ON M5H 1L3
Tel: 416-599-1925
cns-ontario.rnao.ca
www.facebook.com/113210988761198?fref=ts
twitter.com/cnsig
youtube.com/cnsig
Overview: A small provincial organization founded in 1977
Mission: To support the role of advanced nursing practice in Ontario; To address issues that affect clinical nursing practice
Member of: Registered Nurses' Association of Ontario
Membership: *Fees:* $40 / year (including membership in the Canadian Association of Advanced Practice Nurses); *Member Profile:* Registered Nurses' Association of Ontario members or affiliates who are committed to advanced nursing practice
Activities: Promoting & clarifying the role of advanced nursing practice throughout Ontario; Presenting educational events, such as workshops; Supporting research in nursing; Providing professional networking opportunities; Engaging in lobbying activities
Chief Officer(s):
Paul-André Gauthier, Co-President & Director of Finance
Awards:
• Clinical Nurse Specialist of the Year Award
To recognize outstanding professional achievement as a clinical nurse specialist in the domains of advanced nursing practice
Contact: Mitzi G. Mitchell, E-mail: mitzi.mitchell@rogers.com or mitzim@yorku.ca
• CNSIG Education Award
; *Amount:* $1,000 *Contact:* Mitzi G. Mitchell, E-mail: mitzim@yorku.ca or Mitzi.mitchell@rogers.com
Publications:
• Clinical Nurse Specialist Newsletter
Type: Newsletter; *Frequency:* Quarterly; *Editor:* Dania Versailles
Profile: Group activities, articles, plus event reviews & announcements

Cloverdale & District Chamber of Commerce
5748 - 176 St., Cloverdale BC V3S 4C8
Tel: 604-574-9802; *Fax:* 604-574-9122
info@cloverdalechamber.ca
www.cloverdalechamber.ca
www.facebook.com/CloverdaleChamber
twitter.com/cloverdalecoc
Overview: A small local organization founded in 1949
Mission: To promote & improve trade, commerce, economic, civic & social welfare in the district of Cloverdale Surrey
Member of: Surrey Regional Chamber of Commerce
Staff Member(s): 2; 11 volunteer(s)
Membership: 130; *Fees:* $120
Chief Officer(s):
John Gibeau, President
Publications:
• Chamber Voice [a publication of the Cloverdale & District Chamber of Commerce]
Type: Newsletter

Club 'Les Pongistes d'Ungava'
129, 4e av, Chibougamau QC G8P 3C4
Aperçu: Dimension: petite; *Envergure:* locale
Membre(s) du bureau directeur:
David Pichette, Président

Club alpin du Canada *See* Alpine Club of Canada

Le Club BMW du Canada *See* BMW Clubs Canada

Club canadien de Toronto
#66030, 1116 ave Wilson, Toronto ON M3M 3G1
Tél: 416-243-0662; *Téléc:* 416-243-9655
info@clubcanadien.ca
www.clubcanadien.ca
www.facebook.com/clubcanadien
twitter.com/clubcanadienTO
Nom précédent: Cercle canadien de Toronto
Aperçu: Dimension: petite; *Envergure:* locale; Organisme sans but lucratif; fondée en 1986

Mission: Donner l'occasion aux francophones et francophiles à Toronto d'échanger, de s'enrichir et d'établir des contacts. Le Club agit comme un élément catalyseur et rassembleur de la grande communauté francophone des milieux d'affaires, académiques, culturels et gouvernementaux
Finances: *Budget de fonctionnement annuel:* $100,000-$250,000; *Fonds:* Privé
Membre(s) du personnel: 1; 30 bénévole(s)
Membre: 350; *Montant de la cotisation:* 30$ étudiant; 70$ individuelle; 120$ couple; 215$ (pour 4 délégué(s) d'une même entreprise); *Critères d'admissibilite:* Gens d'affaires de Bay St.
Activités: Déjeuners d'affaires mensuels; *Service de conférenciers:* Oui
Membre(s) du bureau directeur:
Yannick Rose, Président
Jean-C. Martin, Directeur général

Club canin canadien *See* Canadian Kennel Club

Club cycliste de la Montérégie
#201, 1204, rue Sentier, Longueuil QC J4N 1S4
Tél: 450-647-2012
admin@clubcyclistemonteregie.qc.ca
clubcyclistemonteregie.qc.ca
Aperçu: Dimension: petite; *Envergure:* locale
Mission: De donner à ses membres la possibilité de rester en forme grâce à vélo
Membre(s) du bureau directeur:
André Desjardins, Président, Conseil d'administration

Club d'astronomie Quasar de Chibougamau
783, 6e rue, Chibougamau QC G8P 2W4
Tél: 418-748-4642
www.faaq.org/clubs/quasar
Aperçu: Dimension: petite; *Envergure:* locale
Membre: *Montant de la cotisation:* 7,50$ étudiant; 10$ personnes âgées; 15$ adulte; 20$ famille
Membre(s) du bureau directeur:
Pierre Bureau, Président
pbureau@hotmail.com

Club d'auto-neige Chibougamau inc.
CP 43, Chibougamau QC G8P 2K5
Tél: 418-748-3065
www.motoneigechibougamau.ca
Aperçu: Dimension: petite; *Envergure:* locale

Club d'électricité du Québec inc. *Voir* Association de l'industrie électrique du Québec

Club d'observateurs d'oiseaux de Laval (COOL)
Pavillon du Bois Papineau, #214, 3235, boul St-Martin est, Laval QC H7E 5G8
Tél: 450-664-4718
lavalcool2@hotmail.com
www.lavalcool.com
Aperçu: Dimension: petite; *Envergure:* locale; Organisme sans but lucratif; fondée en 1993
Mission: Étude et observation des oiseaux sauvages et la protection de leurs habitats.
Affiliation(s): Association québécoise des groupes d'ornithologues
Membre: *Montant de la cotisation:* 35$ familial; 25$ individu; 40$ corporatif

Club d'Ornithologie de Longueuil
CP 21099, Succ. Jacques Cartier, Longueuil QC J4J 5J4
Courriel: ornitho_longueuil@hotmail.com
clubornithologielongueuil.blogspot.ca
www.facebook.com/315821868435402
Aperçu: Dimension: petite; *Envergure:* locale; fondée en 1988
Mission: Promouvoir l'observation des oiseaux, amener la population à s'intéresser aux oiseaux; contribuer à la protection des oiseaux et de leurs habitats
Membre de: QuébecOiseaux
145 bénévole(s)
Membre: 300+; *Montant de la cotisation:* 25$ Individuelle; 30$ Famille
Activités: Excursion observation d'oiseaux; Conférences
Membre(s) du bureau directeur:
Paul Fortin, Président, Conseil d'administration
Publications:
• Le Chardonneret
Type: Bulletin; *Frequency:* 3 fois par ans
Profile: Les articles qui contiennent nouvelles sur le club, écrits par ses membres

Club d'ornithologie de Mirabel (COMIR)
CP 3418, 9009, Rte Arthur-Sauvé, Mirabel QC J7N 2T8
Tél: 450-258-4924
admin@comirabel.org
comirabel.org
Aperçu: Dimension: petite; *Envergure:* locale; fondée en 1999
Mission: Le territoire couvert part le COMIR s'étend de la rivière des Mille-Iles au Sud, Prévost au Nord, la rivière des Outaouais (Rivière Rouge) à l'Ouest et la route 117 à l'Est.
Affiliation(s): Regroupement QuébecOiseaux
Membre: 165 familles
Activités: Rencontre d'initiation à l'ornithologie; présentations; conférences, sorites & observations d'oiseaux; observations nocturnes; recontres sociales & pique-niques
Membre(s) du bureau directeur:
Normande Lapensée, Présidente
Denis Lauzon, Vice-président

Club de collectionneurs de coupons Canadian Tire *See* Canadian Tire Coupon Collectors Club

Club de curling Mont-Bruno
1390, rue Goyer, Saint-Bruno QC J3V 3Z3
Tél: 450-653-6913
Info2@CurlingMontBruno.com
www.curlingmontbruno.com
Aperçu: Dimension: moyenne; *Envergure:* locale; fondée en 1960
Affiliation(s): Association Canadienne de curling; Curling Québec; Association régionale curling Montréal
Membre: *Montant de la cotisation:* 80$ - 1,015$
Activités: Tournoi de curling
Membre(s) du bureau directeur:
Alain Beaumier, Président, Conseil d'adminitration

Le Club de gemmologie et de minérlogie de Montréal *See* Montréal Gem & Mineral Club

Club de généalogie de Sainte-Julie *Voir* Société de généalogie de la Jemmerais

Club de golf Chibougamau-Chapais inc.
CP 81, 130, rue des Forces-Armées, Chibougamau QC G8P 3A1
Tél: 418-748-4709; *Téléc:* 418-748-2471
golfchibougamau@hotmail.com
Nom précédent: Club de golf de Chibougamau inc.
Aperçu: Dimension: petite; *Envergure:* locale
Membre(s) du personnel: 12; 10 bénévole(s)

Club de golf de Chibougamau inc. *Voir* Club de golf Chibougamau-Chapais inc.

Club de karaté Shotokan Chibougamau
576, Bordeleau, Chibougamau QC G8P 1A6
Tél: 418-748-4048
ville.chibougamau.qc.ca
Aperçu: Dimension: petite; *Envergure:* locale; fondée en 1972
Membre(s) du bureau directeur:
Claude Bédard, Instructeur chef, 418-770-6933
cbedard@karatechibougamau.com

Club de l'âge d'or Les intrépides de Chibougamau
126, rue des Forces-Armées, Chibougamau QC G8P 3A1
Tél: 418-748-6703
Aperçu: Dimension: petite; *Envergure:* locale
Membre(s) du bureau directeur:
Darquise St-Georges, Présidente, 418-748-2400

Club de marche de Québec
15, rue Jean de Brébeuf, Québec QC G2A 2V7
www.clubdemarche.net
Aperçu: Dimension: petite; *Envergure:* locale
Mission: Pour engager la communauté dans les activités de l'ordre
Membre: *Montant de la cotisation:* 20$
Activités: Marches en ville; Randonnées pédestres; Activitées sociales
Membre(s) du bureau directeur:
Nicole Thivierge, Présidente, Conseil d'administration, 418-842-7950

Club de marche de Rimouski
CP 444, Succ. A, Rimouski QC G5L 7C3
Tél: 514-725-3696
CMR1994@hotmail.com
www.rimouskiweb.com
Aperçu: Dimension: petite; *Envergure:* locale

Mission: Pour organiser des randonnées de groupe et l'exploration scénique du Québec
Membre: *Montant de la cotisation:* 15$

Club de marche moi mes souliers
3155, rue Fortin, Trois-Rivières QC G8Z 2C3
Tél: 819-373-1109
www.moimessouliers.com
Aperçu: *Dimension:* petite; *Envergure:* locale; fondée en 1993
Mission: Pour pouvoir promenades au Canada et aux États-Unis pour ses membres
Membre: 100; *Montant de la cotisation:* 20$ individuelle; 30$ Famille
Membre(s) du bureau directeur:
Louis Giroux, Président, Conseil d'administration
louis.giroux13@cgocable.cam

Club de natation Natchib inc.
CP 213, Chibougamau QC G8P 2K7
Tél: 418-748-8038
Aperçu: *Dimension:* petite; *Envergure:* locale
Membre(s) du bureau directeur:
Stéphanie McKenzie, Président

Club de naturalistes de Prince George *See* Prince George Naturalists Club

Club de Numismates du Bas St-Laurent (CNBSL)
CP 1475, Rimouski QC G5L 8M3
Tél: 418-723-8586
www.cnbsl.org
Aperçu: *Dimension:* petite; *Envergure:* locale; fondée en 1979
Mission: De fournir un lieu de rencontre pour ceux qui s'intéressent à la collecte de pièces de monnaie
Membre: *Montant de la cotisation:* Barème
Membre(s) du bureau directeur:
Gaétan Aubin, Président
gaubin@globetrotter.net

Club de patinage artistique Les lames givrées inc.
CP 453, Chibougamau QC G8P 2X9
Tél: 418-748-2671
leslamesgivrees@hotmail.com
Aperçu: *Dimension:* petite; *Envergure:* locale
Membre(s) du bureau directeur:
Joline Bélanger, Présidente, 418-748-2339

Club de photo de Boucherville
Centre Mgr Poissant, Café Belle-Lurette, 566, boul Marie-Victorian, Boucherville QC J4B 1X1
Tél: 450-449-1649
clubphotoboucherville.org
Aperçu: *Dimension:* petite; *Envergure:* locale
Mission: De créer un réseau de photographes qui sont capables d'encourager et d'aider les uns les autres
Membre(s) du bureau directeur:
Nicole Boucher, Présidente, Conseil d'administration

Club de photographie L'Oeil qui voit de Saint-Hubert
2060, rue Holmes, #A2-A3, Saint-Hubert QC J4T 1R8
Tél: 514-686-3633
info@oeilquivoit.com
oeilquivoit.com
www.facebook.com/oeilquivoit
Aperçu: *Dimension:* petite; *Envergure:* locale; fondée en 1986
Mission: Pour partager une passion pour la photographie parmi ses membres
Activités: Ateliers techniques; conférences
Membre(s) du bureau directeur:
Nathalie Madore, Présidente, Conseil d'administration

Club de plein air Les Aventuriers
4545, av Pierre-de-Coubertin, Montréal QC H1V 0B2
Tél: 514-374-6078
info@aventuriers.qc.ca
www.aventuriers.qc.ca
Aperçu: *Dimension:* petite; *Envergure:* locale; fondée en 1976
Mission: Pour rassembler les gens afin de réaliser des activités de plein air
Membre: *Montant de la cotisation:* 30$ individual; 30$ monoparental; 50$ familial
Activités: Canot; Vélo; Randonnée pédestre et raquette; Kayak de mer; Ski de randonnée
Publications:
• L'Écope
Type: Journal
Profile: Articles et photos des membres du club

Club de trafic de Québec (CTQ)
CP 44521, Lévis QC G7A 4X5
Courriel: info@clubtraficqc.com
www.clubtraficqc.com
Aperçu: *Dimension:* moyenne; *Envergure:* provinciale; Organisme sans but lucratif; fondée en 1960
Mission: Regrouper les représentants oeuvrant dans le domaine du transport de la grande région de Québec
Finances: *Budget de fonctionnement annuel:* $100,000-$250,000
Membre: 137; *Montant de la cotisation:* 85$
Membre(s) du bureau directeur:
Benoit Latour, Président
b.latour@pmtroy.com

Club de vol à voile de Québec
CP 9276, Sainte-Foy QC G1V 4B1
Tél: 418-337-4905
www.cvvq.net
www.facebook.com/CVVQPlaneur
twitter.com/Planeur_Quebec
Aperçu: *Dimension:* petite; *Envergure:* locale; fondée en 1954
Mission: Les principaux objectifs de notre association sont de fournir une plate-forme d'opération sécuritaire pour la pratique de notre sport et d'offrir une formation de qualité à de nouveaux adeptes qui se joignent à nous.
Membre: *Montant de la cotisation:* Barème; *Comités:* Aménagement; Planification de la flotte; Recrutement
Membre(s) du bureau directeur:
Pierre Beaulieu, Président

Club de Vol à Voile MSC *See* Montréal Soaring Council

Club des collectionneurs d'épinglettes Inc. (CCE) / Pin Collectors' Club
Courriel: clubepinglettes@hotmail.com
pincollectors.unblog.fr
Aperçu: *Dimension:* petite; *Envergure:* nationale; Organisme sans but lucratif; fondée en 1984
Mission: Regrouper les collectionneurs d'épinglettes intéressés
Finances: *Budget de fonctionnement annuel:* Moins de $50,000
12 bénévole(s)
Membre: 200; *Montant de la cotisation:* Selon la formule d'adhésion, renouvellement: 24$
Activités: Rencontres mensuelles des membres par région; expositions régionales; Festival d'épinglettes

Club des débrouillards
4475, rue Frontenac, Montréal QC H2H 2S2
Tél: 514-844-2111; *Téléc:* 514-278-3030
scientifix@lesdebrouillards.com
www.lesdebrouillards.qc.ca
Aperçu: *Dimension:* grande; *Envergure:* provinciale
Mission: Pour faire découvrir aux jeunes le bonheur de la lecture et développer leur goût de la découverte et de la science
Membre: 24,000; *Critères d'admissibilite:* Jeunes intéressées à la science
Membre(s) du bureau directeur:
Martin Laverdure, Représentant publicitaire, 514-239-3629
martin@laverdure-marketing.com
Publications:
• Les Débrouillards [a publication of the Club des débrouillards]
Type: Magazine; *ISSN:* 1187-8681

Club des Garçons et Filles d'Ottawa *See* Boys & Girls Clubs of Ontario

Club des ornithologues de Québec inc. (COQ)
Domaine de Maizerets, 2000, boul Montmorency, Québec QC G1J 5E7
Tél: 418-661-3544
coq@coq.qc.ca
www.coq.qc.ca
Aperçu: *Dimension:* petite; *Envergure:* provinciale; fondée en 1955
Mission: Faire connaître les oiseaux, loisir, protection de l'avifaune et des habitats, participation à des activités scientifiques.
Membre de: Regroupement QuébecOiseaux
Finances: *Budget de fonctionnement annuel:* Moins de $50,000; *Fonds:* Cotisations des membres, support de la Ville de Québec pour les espaces de rangement et les locaux
75 bénévole(s)
Membre: 700; *Montant de la cotisation:* 25 $ / année; *Comités:* Conseil d'administration; Plusieurs autres comités

Activités: Publication du Bulletin ornithologique; Excursions, conférences, cours, compilation de données d'observation; *Service de conférenciers:* Oui
Membre(s) du bureau directeur:
Norbert Lacroix, Président
norbert.lacroix@mat.ulaval.ca
Marguerite Larouche, Vice-président
marlarou@sympatico.ca
Louis Messely, Secrétaire
lmessely@mediom.qc.ca
Meetings/Conferences:
• Club des ornithologues de Québec 2018 Assemblée générale annuelle, February, 2018
Scope: Provincial
Publications:
• Bulletin ornithologique
Editor: Pierre Otis

Club des sports moteur d'Ottawa *See* Motorsport Club of Ottawa

Club export agro-alimentaire du Québec *Voir* Groupe export agroalimentaire Québec - Canada

Club Garçons et Filles de Dieppe *See* Boys & Girls Clubs of New Brunswick

Club garçons et filles de LaSalle *See* Boys & Girls Clubs of Québec

Club informatique de Brossard (RIB)
Centre Georges-Henri Brossard, #111, 3205, boul Rome, Brossard QC J4Y 1R2
Tél: 450-656-3348; *Téléc:* 450-678-4801
ribnathaliecroteau@videotron.ca
clubrib.org
Aperçu: *Dimension:* petite; *Envergure:* locale; fondée en 2005
Mission: de partager les connaissances et aider les membres à apprendre à utiliser les ordinateurs, les téléphones cellulaires intelligents et les tablettes
Membre: *Montant de la cotisation:* 35$

Club informatique de Longueuil (CIL)
930, rue Saint-Jacques, Longueuil QC J4H 3E2
Tél: 450-670-5268
admin@clubinfolongueuil.qc.ca
clubinfolongueuil.qc.ca
twitter.com/clubCIL
Aperçu: *Dimension:* petite; *Envergure:* locale
Mission: Pour partager des informations utiles sur la façon d'utiliser un ordinateur
Membre(s) du personnel: 7
Membre: *Montant de la cotisation:* 25$; *Critères d'admissibilite:* Gens de la Rive-Sud de Montréal
Membre(s) du bureau directeur:
Fernand Laurin, Président, Conseil d'administration

Club informatique Mont-Bruno
1585, rue Montarville, Saint-Bruno-sur-Richelieu QC J3V 3T8
Tél: 450-653-3755
cimbcc@cimbcc.org
cimbcc.org
Aperçu: *Dimension:* petite; *Envergure:* locale
Mission: De partager les connaissances et aider les membres à apprendre à utiliser un ordinateur
60+ bénévole(s)
Membre(s) du bureau directeur:
Réjean Côté, Président, Conseil d'administration

Club Kiwanis Chibougamau
CP 61, Chibougamau QC G8P 2K5
Tél: 418-770-8303
Aperçu: *Dimension:* petite; *Envergure:* locale
Membre(s) du bureau directeur:
Yves Lachaine, Président

Club Lions de Chibougamau
CP 11, Chibougamau QC G8P 2K5
Tél: 418-770-9366
lionschibougamau@hotmail.com
lionschibougamau.icr.qc.ca
Aperçu: *Dimension:* petite; *Envergure:* locale
Membre(s) du bureau directeur:
Mario Asselin, Président

Club nautique de Chibougamau inc.
CP 395, Chibougamau QC G8P 2X8
Tél: 418-748-6180
Aperçu: *Dimension:* petite; *Envergure:* locale

Canadian Associations / Club Optimiste de Rivière-du-Loup inc.

Club Optimiste de Rivière-du-Loup inc.
CP 1344, Rivière-du-Loup QC G5R 4L9
Tél: 418-862-8454; *Téléc:* 418-862-3366
service@optimiste.org
www.optimiste.org
Aperçu: Dimension: petite; *Envergure:* locale
Mission: Les clubs Optimistes inspirent le meilleur chez les jeunes depuis 1919 en rencontrant les besoins des jeunes de toutes les collectivités du monde. Ils organisent des projets de service communautaire positifs qui visent à tendre la main à la jeunesse.
Membre(s) du bureau directeur:
Jean-Louis Dorval, Trésorier

Club photo Évasion
1540, rue Montarville, Saint-Bruno QC J3V 3T7
Tél: 438-274-9424
clubphotoevasion@gmail.com
clubphotoevasion.com
Aperçu: Dimension: petite; *Envergure:* locale; fondée en 1985
Mission: D'aider ses membres partagent leurs connaissances et leur amour de la photographie et de développer leurs compétences
Membre: *Montant de la cotisation:* 75$
Membre(s) du bureau directeur:
Suzanne Tremblay, Présidente, Conseil d'administration

Club portugais de Montréal *Voir* Clube Portugal de Montreal

Club progrès du Canada *See* Canadian Progress Club

Club Richelieu Boréal de Chibougamau
CP 522, Chibougamau QC G8P 2X9
Tél: 418-748-2398
Aperçu: Dimension: petite; *Envergure:* locale
Membre(s) du bureau directeur:
Julie Poirier, Responsable

Club Shorthorn du Québec *See* Québec Shorthorn Association

Club timbres et monnaies de Sorel inc.
CP 542, Succ. Bureau-Chef, Sorel-Tracy QC J3P 5N9
Tél: 450-855-1648
Aperçu: Dimension: petite; *Envergure:* locale
Membre de: Fédération québécoise de philatélie - Montréal
Membre(s) du bureau directeur:
Éric Forest, Président
ricky.itg@gmail.com

Club violettes Longueuil
CP 5000, 1, boul Curé Poirier est, Longueuil QC J4K 4Y7
Tél: 450-628-4791
club_violettes_longueuil@hotmail.com
club-violettes-longueuil.org
Aperçu: Dimension: petite; *Envergure:* locale; fondée en 1991
Mission: Encourager la culture de la violette africaine pour les personnes vivant à Longueuil
Membre: *Montant de la cotisation:* 20$ individu; 25$ couple
Membre(s) du bureau directeur:
Pierre Laforest, Président, Conseil d'administration

Clube Oriental Português de Montreal / Est club portugais de Montréal
4000, rue Courtai, Montréal QC H3S 1C2
Tél: 514-342-4373
Également appelé: Montreal Portuguese Oriental Club
Aperçu: Dimension: petite; *Envergure:* locale

Clube Portugal de Montreal / Club portugais de Montréal
4397, boul St-Laurent, Montréal QC H7H 1G7
Tél: 514-844-1406
Également appelé: Montreal Portuguese Club
Aperçu: Dimension: petite; *Envergure:* locale

Les Clubs 4-H du Québec
#202, 6500 boul Arthur-Sauvé, Laval QC H7R 3X7
Tél: 450-314-1942; *Téléc:* 450-314-1952
Autres numéros: Sherbrooke location: 819-562-9413
info@clubs4h.qc.ca
www.clubs4h.qc.ca
www.facebook.com/LesClubs4HDuQuebec
Également appelé: Québec 4-H
Nom précédent: Québec Young Farmers
Aperçu: Dimension: moyenne; *Envergure:* provinciale; fondée en 1942
Mission: Développer l'intérêt et les compétences des jeunes relativement à la nature, la forêt et l'environnement par des activités éducatives et de loisir
Membre de: Canadian 4-H Council; Conseil québécois du Loisir; Regroupement du Loisir et du sport du Québec; Conseil régional de l'environnement de Laval
Finances: *Budget de fonctionnement annuel:* $500,000-$1.5 Million; *Fonds:* Ministères; villes et autres
Membre(s) du personnel: 6; 200 bénévole(s)
Membre: 2 870; *Montant de la cotisation:* 100$ par club; *Critères d'admissibilité:* Must be 6-21 years of age & member of Québec 4-H; *Comités:* Lifestock Management Tour; Provincial Rally
Activités: Clubs; ateliers éducatifs; activités de sensibilisation; outils pédagogiques; *Stagiaires:* Oui
Membre(s) du bureau directeur:
Andrée Gignac, Directrice
agignac@clubs4h.qc.ca
Publications:
• Les Clubs 4-H du Québec Brochure
Type: Brochure
• Les Clubs 4-H du Québec Infolettre
Type: Newsletter

Clubs 4-H du Québec
#202, 6500, boul Arthur-Sauvé, Laval QC H7R 3X7
Tél: 450-314-1942; *Téléc:* 450-314-1952
info@clubs4h.qc.ca
www.clubs4h.qc.ca
Aperçu: Dimension: moyenne; *Envergure:* provinciale; fondée en 1942
Mission: Susciter et développer, chez le jeune, une préoccupation active pour la conservation de l'arbre, du milieu forestier et de l'environnement; développer le sens des autres, le sens des responsabilités, l'esprit d'initiative, la créativité, le sens de l'émerveillement et le respect pour tout ce qui vit; contribuer à répandre dans le public une mentalité de conservation envers l'environnement, en posant des gestes concrets pour l'amélioration de la qualité de la vie
Membre de: Regroupement Loisir Québec; Conseil québecois du loisir
Finances: *Budget de fonctionnement annuel:* $100,000-$250,000; *Fonds:* Financement municipal, provincial, et fédéral; les frais d'adhésion; collecte de fonds
Membre(s) du personnel: 4; 300 bénévole(s)
Membre: 30 institutionnel; 1 000 individu; *Montant de la cotisation:* $100/club
Activités: *Evénements de sensibilisation:* Mois de l'arbre et des forêts, mai
Membre(s) du bureau directeur:
Andrée Gignac, Directrice
agignac@clubs4h.qc.ca

Clubs garçons & filles du Canada *See* Boys & Girls Clubs of Canada

Clydesdale Horse Association of Canada
c/o Marlene Langille, 395 Foxbrook Rd., RR#2, Hopewell NS B0K 1C0
Tel: 902-923-2600
mlangille@auracom.com
www.canadianclydesdales.ca
Overview: A small national organization founded in 1886
Mission: To establish standards of breeding; To develop & regulate the breeding of Clydesdale horses in Canada; To enhance the image, usability, & marketability of the Clydesdale horse
Affiliation(s): Canadian Livestock Records Corporation
Membership: *Fees:* $37.66 NB, ON, NL; $38 PEI; $38.33 NS; $35 all other provinces; *Member Profile:* Any person who is interested in the well-being & advancement of purebred Clydesdale horses
Activities: Collecting & preserving the breeding & orign of Clydesdale horses; Compiling statistics of the industry; Educating the public about Clydesdale horses; Protecting & assisting breeders; Supervising breeders
Chief Officer(s):
Marlene Langille, Secretary
Publications:
• Canadian Clydesdale Contact
Type: Magazine; *Frequency:* Annually; *Price:* Free with membership in the Clydesdale Horse Association of Canada
Profile: News & results of Clydesdale shows from throughout Canada

CMA Canada - Northwest Territories & Nunavut (CMA NWT&NU)
PO Box 512, Yellowknife NT X1A 2N4
Tel: 867-876-1290; *Fax:* 867-920-2503
Overview: A small provincial organization overseen by Chartered Professional Accountants Canada
Membership: *Member Profile:* Certified Management Accountants (CMAs) in the Northwest Territories & Nunavut
Activities: Providing professional development opportunities (note that CMA NWT&NU will integrate under the CPA banner once legislation is approved)

CNBC
100 Convention Way, Cochrane AB T4C 2G2
Tel: 403-932-5688; *Fax:* 403-932-4937
Toll-Free: 888-442-2272
office@ccsb.ca
www.ccsb.ca
Previous Name: Canadian Convention of Southern Baptists
Overview: A medium-sized national charitable organization founded in 1985
Mission: To network churches with each other to see God add New Believers, New Disciplemarkers & New Communitites of Faith to the family of congregations
Affiliation(s): Southern Baptist Convention
Finances: *Funding Sources:* Member churches
Staff Member(s): 8; 4 volunteer(s)
Membership: 300 churches
Activities: *Library:* CNBC Resource Centre; Open to public
Chief Officer(s):
Gerry Taillon, National Ministry Leader
gtaillon@cnbc.ca
Publications:
• The Baptist Horizon
Type: Journal; *Frequency:* Bimonthly; *Editor:* Debbie Shelton; *ISSN:* 1195-4744
Profile: CCSB news

CNTU Federation - Construction (CNTU) *Voir* Fédération CSN - Construction (CSN)

COACH - Canada's Health Informatics Association *See* Digital Health Canada

Coaches Association of British Columbia *See* ViaSport

Coaches Association of Ontario (CAO)
#200A, 1 Concorde Gate, Toronto ON M3C 3N6
Tel: 416-426-7086; *Fax:* 416-426-7331
www.coachesontario.ca
www.linkedin.com/company/coaches-association-of-ontario
www.facebook.com/coachesontario
twitter.com/coaches_ont
www.youtube.com/user/CoachesOntario
Overview: A medium-sized provincial organization founded in 2002
Mission: To represent coaches in Ontario; To promote coaching ethics; To provide resources for coaches; To foster an appreciation for coaches in the wider community
Member of: Ontario Not for Profit Network
Affiliation(s): National Coaching Certification Program (NCCP)
Finances: *Annual Operating Budget:* $500,000-$1.5 Million; *Funding Sources:* Federal & provincial government; Fundraising; Events
Staff Member(s): 8; 12 volunteer(s)
Membership: 25,000; *Fees:* Schedule available
Activities: Conducting sport workshops; Providing support & education for sport coaches in all levels; Advocating for community leadership & sport programming; *Internships:* Yes
Chief Officer(s):
Susan Kitchen, Executive Director, 416-426-7088
susan@coachesontario.ca
Jeremy Cross, Director, 416-426-7056
jeremy@coachesontario.ca
Awards:
• Coaches Helping Coaches
Eligibility: Mentor coach & apprentice coach pairing *Deadline:* October; *Amount:* $500
Meetings/Conferences:
• 2018 Ontario Coaches Conference, April, 2018, London, ON
Scope: Provincial
Publications:
• Coach 2 Coach [a publication of the Coaches Association of Ontario]
Type: Newsletter
Profile: Discussion of coaching topics

Coaches Association of PEI (CAPEI)
40 Enman Cres., Charlottetown PE C1E 1E6
Tel: 902-368-4110; *Fax:* 902-368-4548
Toll-Free: 800-247-6712

Other Communication: Toll free fax: 800-235-5687
sports@sportpei.pe.ca
www.sportpei.pe.ca
www.facebook.com/SportPEI
twitter.com/SportPEI
Overview: A small provincial organization founded in 1992 overseen by Sport PEI Inc.
Mission: To educate, develop & promote coaching & coaches for the benefit of athletes, sport & the community in general; To encourage fair play, integrity & the pursuit of excellence
Member of: Coaching Association of Canada
Finances: *Funding Sources:* Membership fees; fundraising
Staff Member(s): 8
Membership: 50 organizations
Chief Officer(s):
Gemma Koughan, Executive Director
gkoughan@sportpei.pe.ca

Coaching Association of Canada (CAC) / Association canadienne des entraîneurs
2451 Riverside Dr., Ottawa ON K1H 7X7
Tel: 613-235-5000; *Fax:* 613-235-9500
www.coach.ca
www.facebook.com/coach.ca
twitter.com/CAC_ACE
www.youtube.com/CDNcoach2010
Overview: A large national charitable organization founded in 1971
Mission: To improve implementation & delivery of National Coaching Certification Program; To establish coaching as viable career within the Canadian sports system; To increase the number of qualified full-time & part-time remunerated coaches at various levels within the sport system
Affiliation(s): Professional Arm: Canadian Professional Coaches Association
Finances: *Funding Sources:* Sport Canada; Corporations; Foundations
Activities: Offering the following programs: National Coaching Certification Program (NCCP); Sport Nutrition; Petro-Canada Sport Leadership sportif; Investors Group Community Coaching Conferences; *Speaker Service:* Yes
Chief Officer(s):
Lorraine Lafrenière, Chief Executive Officer, 613-235-5000 Ext. 2363
llafreniere@coach.ca
Keira Torkko, Chief Operating Officer, 613-235-5000 Ext. 2365
ktorkko@coach.ca
Natalie Rumscheidt, Director, Marketing & Communications, 613-235-5000 Ext. 2051
nrumscheidt@coach.ca
Awards:
- Petro-Canada Coaching Excellence Awards
- Geoff Gowan Award
- Investors Group NCCP Coach Developer Awards
- Jack Donohue Award
- Sheila Robertson Award

Meetings/Conferences:
- Coaching Association of Canada 2018 Petro-Canada Sport Leadership sportif Conference, November, 2018, Westin Ottawa, Ottawa, ON
Scope: National
Description: An inpiring event for coaches, featuring guest speakers & the presentation of sport leadership awards

Coaching Manitoba
145 Pacific Ave., Winnipeg MB R2B 2Z6
Tel: 204-925-5692; *Fax:* 204-925-5624
Toll-Free: 888-887-7307
coaching@sportmanitoba.ca
www.coachingmanitoba.ca
Overview: A small provincial organization
Mission: To train coaches in Manitoba
Member of: Sport Manitoba
Staff Member(s): 4
Chief Officer(s):
Susan Lamboo, Coaching Manager, 204-925-5669
susan.lamboo@sportmanitoba.ca

Coady International Institute (CII)
St. Francis Xavier University, PO Box 5000, 4780 Tompkins Lane, Antigonish NS B2G 2W5
Tel: 902-867-3960; *Fax:* 902-867-3907
Toll-Free: 866-820-7835
coadycom@stfx.ca
www.coady.stfx.ca
twitter.com/coadystfx
www.youtube.com/user/CoadyInstitute
Overview: A large international charitable organization founded in 1959
Mission: To promote learning in individuals & organizations engaged in community-driven action to achieve wellbeing, global justice, peace & participating democracy
Member of: Canadian Council for International Cooperation
Finances: *Annual Operating Budget:* $1.5 Million-$3 Million
Staff Member(s): 28
Membership: *Committees:* University Advisory
Activities: Conferences & presentations; publishes occasional papers; *Awareness Events:* Coady Celebrates, Nov 1; *Internships:* Yes *Library:* Marie Michael Library; Open to public
Chief Officer(s):
June Webber, Director

Coal Association of Canada (CAC)
#150, 205 - 9th Ave. SE, Calgary AB T2G 0R3
Tel: 403-262-1544; *Fax:* 403-265-7604
Toll-Free: 800-910-2625
info@coal.ca
www.coal.ca
twitter.com/coalcanada
Overview: A medium-sized national organization
Mission: To promote coal as a vital energy source that is abundant, safe, reliable, environmentally and economically acceptable.
Membership: 78 corporate
Chief Officer(s):
Ann Marie Hann, President
hann@coal.ca
Michelle Mondeville, Director, Communications and Stakeholder Relations
mondeville@coal.ca
Meetings/Conferences:
- Coal Association of Canada 2018 Conference, September, 2018, Westin Bayshore, Vancouver, BC
Scope: National

Coaldale & District Chamber of Commerce
PO Box 1117, 1401 - 20 Ave., Coaldale AB T1M 1M9
Tel: 403-345-2358; *Fax:* 403-345-2339
info@coaldalechamber.com
www.coaldalechamber.com
Overview: A small local organization
Mission: To serve as the voice of the business community; To address issues of the community, as well as provincial & federal concerns; To help business members grow by providing networking opportunities & events
Member of: Alberta Chamber of Commerce; Canadian Chamber of Commerce
Finances: *Annual Operating Budget:* Less than $50,000; *Funding Sources:* Membership fees; grants
20 volunteer(s)
Membership: 150; *Fees:* Schedule available
Chief Officer(s):
Everett Duerksen, President

Coalition Avenir Québec
#50, 1260 rue Mill, Montréal QC H3K 2B4
Tél: 514-800-6000; *Téléc:* 514-800-0081
Ligne sans frais: 866-416-2960
info@lacaq.org
coalitionavenirquebec.org
www.facebook.com/coalitionavenir
twitter.com/coalitionavenir
www.youtube.com/user/AvenirCoalition
Aperçu: *Dimension:* petite; *Envergure:* provinciale; fondée en 2011
Membre(s) du bureau directeur:
François Legault, Chef
Stéphane Le Bouyonnec, Président

Coalition canadien contre la peine de mort *See* Canadian Coalition Against the Death Penalty

Coalition canadienne de l'énergie géothermique *See* Canadian GeoExchange Coalition

Coalition canadienne de la filière alimentaire pour la salubrité des aliments *See* Canadian Supply Chain Food Safety Coalition

Coalition canadienne de la santé *See* Canadian Health Coalition

Coalition canadienne des aidants et aidantes naturels *See* Canadian Caregiver Coalition

Coalition canadienne des organismes bénévoles en santé *See* Health Charities Coalition of Canada

Coalition canadienne des politiques sur les drogues *See* Canadian Drug Policy Coalition

Coalition Canadienne pour L'Équité Génétique *See* Canadian Coalition for Genetic Fairness

Coalition Canadienne pour la Protection des Animaux de Ferme *See* Canadian Coalition for Farm Animals

Coalition canadienne pour un accès équitable à la technologie digitale *See* Canadian Coalition for Fair Digital Access

Coalition d'une vie active pour les ainé(e)s *See* Active Living Coalition for Older Adults

Coalition des associations de consommateurs du Québec (CACQ)
#393, 1600, av de Lorimier, Montréal QC H2K 3W5
Tél: 514-362-8623; *Téléc:* 514-521-7081
Ligne sans frais: 877-962-2227
info@cacq.ca
defensedesconsommateurs.org
www.facebook.com/PageCACQ
Aperçu: *Dimension:* moyenne; *Envergure:* provinciale
Membre: *Critères d'admissibilite:* Associations de consommateurs
Membre(s) du bureau directeur:
Élisabeth Circé Côté, Coordonnatrice
coordo@cacq.ca
Jennifer Vales, Agente de communication
communications@cacq.ca

Coalition des centres anti-viol de l'Ontario *See* Ontario Coalition of Rape Crisis Centres

Coalition des communautés en santé de l'Ontario *See* Ontario Healthy Communities Coalition

Coalition des familles homoparentales *Voir* Coalition des familles LGBT

Coalition des familles LGBT / LGBT Family Coalition
Montréal QC
Tél: 514-846-7600
info@familleslgbt.org
www.familleslgbt.org
Nom précédent: Coalition des familles homoparentales
Aperçu: *Dimension:* petite; *Envergure:* locale; fondée en 1998
Mission: Milite pour la reconnaissance légale et sociale des familles homoparentales; groupe bilingue de parents lesbiens, gais, bisexuels et transgenres. Québec: 418-523-5572
Membre: *Montant de la cotisation:* 40$ par famille
Membre(s) du bureau directeur:
Mona Greenbaum, Directrice générale
mona@familleslgbt.org

Coalition des femmes de l'Alberta
Bldg. 2, #300, 8627, rue Marie-Anne-Gaboury, Edmonton AB T6C 3N1
Tél: 780-468-2288; *Téléc:* 780-468-2210
femmes@coalitionfemmes.ab.ca
www.coalitionfemmes.ab.ca
Nom précédent: Coalition des femmes francophones de l'Alberta; Association des groupes de femmes francophones de l'Alberta
Aperçu: *Dimension:* petite; *Envergure:* provinciale; Organisme sans but lucratif; fondée en 2002
Mission: Développer et favoriser des activités variées de sensibilisation, d'animation, de revendication et de formation qui répondent aux besoins des femmes francophones de l'Alberta
Affiliation(s): Alliance des femmes de la francophonie canadienne; Conseil de développement économique de l'Alberta; Institut Guy-Lacombe de la famille; Réseau canadien de santé des femmes
Membre(s) du personnel: 1
Membre: *Critères d'admissibilite:* Femme francophone de l'Alberta
Activités: Ateliers; conférences; sensibilisation aux dossiers socio-politiques touchant les femmes, développement personnel, leadership, estime de soi, confiance en soi, gestion du temps, l'art de parler en public; consultations provinciales; *Service de conférenciers:* Oui
Membre(s) du bureau directeur:

Canadian Associations / Coalition des organismes communautaires québécois de lutte contre le sida (COCQ-SIDA)

Gioia Sallustio-Jarvis, Présidente
Vicky Choquette, Vice-présidente
Geneviève Labrie, Trésorière
Fabienne Bühl, Agente de développement
Publications:
• Bulletin de la Coalition [a publication of Coalition des femmes de l'Alberta]
Type: Bulletin

Coalition des femmes francophones de l'Alberta; Association des groupes de femmes francophones de l'Alberta *Voir* Coalition des femmes de l'Alberta

Coalition des organismes communautaires québécois de lutte contre le sida (COCQ-SIDA)
1, rue Sherbrooke est, Montréal QC H2X 3V8
Tél: 514-844-2477; *Téléc:* 514-844-2498
Ligne sans frais: 866-535-0481
info@cocqsida.com
www.cocqsida.com
www.facebook.com/COCQSIDA
twitter.com/COCQSIDA
Aperçu: *Dimension:* moyenne; *Envergure:* provinciale; Organisme sans but lucratif; fondée en 1990
Mission: Représenter les membres afin de favoriser l'émergence et le soutien d'une action concertée dans les dossiers d'intérêt commun; faire reconnaître l'expertise et l'apport des organismes communautaires et non-gouvernementaux dans la lutte contre le sida.
Membre(s) du personnel: 10
Membre: 38 organismes; *Critères d'admissibilite:* Groupes communautaires; *Comités:* Qualité de vie des PVVIH; Femmes; Hommes gais et comités ayant des relations sexuelles avec d'autres hommes (HARSAH); Communautés ethnoculturelles; Droits et VIH; Communications; Recherche communautaire; Suivi de l'AGA et du Forum; Rédaction Remaides
Activités: *Service de conférenciers:* Oui; *Bibliothèque:* rendez-vous
Membre(s) du bureau directeur:
Hélène Légaré, Présidente
Ken Monteith, Directeur général
ken.monteith@cocqsida.com

Coalition for a Smoke-Free Nova Scotia
PO Box 822, Lower Sackville NS B4V 3V3
Tel: 902-864-9633; *Fax:* 902-484-6946
Toll-Free: 866-777-7374
carivanlingen@smokefreens.ca
www.smokefreens.ca
Also Known As: Smoke-Free Nova Scotia
Previous Name: Nova Scotia Council on Smoking & Health
Overview: A small provincial organization
Mission: Committed to the achievement of a tobacco-free Nova Scotia
Member of: Canadian Council on Smoking & Health
Finances: *Funding Sources:* Provincial government grants; Membership fees
Membership: 31; *Fees:* $20-200; *Member Profile:* Health professionals; Health agencies; Individuals
Activities: Media strategies; Public presentaions; Educational material; Consultations with government; *Awareness Events:* National Non-Smoking Week

Coalition for Active Living (CAL)
#301, 2197 Riverside Dr., Ottawa ON K1H 7X3
Tel: 613-277-9979
info@activeliving.ca
www.activeliving.ca
Overview: A small national organization
Mission: To ensure that environments in which people live support regular physical activity.
Finances: *Funding Sources:* Physical Activity Contribution Program of Health Canada
Staff Member(s): 1
Membership: 100+ organiations
Chief Officer(s):
Christa Costas-Bradstreet, Co-Chair
Nancy Dubois, Co-Chair

Coalition for Gun Control / Coalition pour le contrôle des armes
PO Box 90062, 1488 Queen St. West, Toronto ON M6K 3K3
Tel: 416-604-0209
coalitionforguncontrol@gmail.com
www.guncontrol.ca
twitter.com/CGCguncontrol
Overview: A small local organization founded in 1990
Mission: To reduce gun crimes; to promote strict laws on gun control
Bureau de Montréal
1301, rue Sherbrooke, Montréal QC H2L 1M3
Tél: 514-528-2360
cgc.montreal@gmail.com
twitter.com/CGCmontreal

Coalition for Lesbian & Gay Rights in Ontario; Coalition for Gay Rights in Ontario *See* Queer Ontario

Coalition for Music Education in British Columbia (CME)
BC
www.cmebc.org
www.facebook.com/cmebc
twitter.com/cmebc
Overview: A small provincial organization
Mission: To protect & promote public school music education in British Columbia
Affiliation(s): Coalition for Music Education in Canada
Membership: *Fees:* $25 individual; $15 student/senior; $50 parent advisory council; $150 not-for-profit; $250 corporate

Coalition for Music Education in Canada (CMEC)
PO Box 556, Agincourt ON M1S 3C5
Tel: 416-298-2871; *Fax:* 416-298-5730
cmec.convio.net
www.facebook.com/MusicMakesUs.ca
twitter.com/musicmakesus_ca
youtube.com/musicmondaycanada
Overview: A small national organization
Mission: To raise the awareness & understanding of the role that music plays in Canadian culture; To advocate for the contribution that music education makes in the lives of all Canadians
Staff Member(s): 2
Chief Officer(s):
Holly Nimmons, Executive Director
Publications:
• Coalition for Music Education in Canada Newsletter
Type: Newsletter; *Frequency:* Irregular; *Editor:* Norman Mould

Coalition for the Protection of Human Life *See* Campaign Life Coalition

Coalition Jeunesse Sierra *See* Sierra Youth Coalition

Coalition nationale des citoyens inc. *See* The National Citizens Coalition

Coalition of Associations of Craniocerebral Trauma in Quebec *Voir* Regroupement des associations de personnes traumatisées craniocérébrales du Québec

Coalition of BC Businesses (COBCB)
PO Box 12125, #2410, 555 West Hastings St., Vancouver BC V6B 4N6
Tel: 604-682-8366
info@coalitionbcbusiness.ca
www.coalitionbcbusiness.ca
twitter.com/CoalitionBC
Overview: A small provincial organization founded in 1992
Mission: To represent the interests of businesses, with an aim to help foster a positive relationship between employers & employees in labour & employment policy.
Membership: *Member Profile:* Associations who represent small- & medium-sized businesses in various sectors in BC

Coalition of Black Trade Unionists
CBTU Ontario/Canada Chapter, c/o Yolanda McClean, #200, 1482 Bathurst St., Toronto ON M5P 3H1
cbtuontario@gmail.com
www.cbtu.ca
www.facebook.com/CBTUCanada
twitter.com/CBTU_Canada
Also Known As: CBTU Canada
Overview: A medium-sized national organization
Mission: To promote access & to open doors for Black workers & workers of color within the labour movement; To promote minority rights within unions, to the benefit of all workers within unions; To organize to maximize our political influence within the labour movement; To encourage & support the full participation of black workers & workers of colour in their unions
Member of: Coalition of Black Trade Unionists International
Membership: *Committees:* Resolutions/Constitution/Bylaws; Scholarship; Political Action; Men's; Women's; Social/Fundraising; Young Workers Under 40; Retiree
Chief Officer(s):
Yolanda McClean, President
yolanda.mcclean@cupe4400.org
Awards:
• Ann Newman Scholarship
; *Amount:* $1,000
• Young Women's Post Secondary Scholarship
; *Amount:* $500

Coalition of Rail Shippers (CRS)
c/o Canadian Industrial Transportation Association, #405, 580 Terry Fox Dr., Ottawa ON K2L 4C2
Tel: 613-599-3283; *Fax:* 613-599-1295
Overview: A medium-sized national organization founded in 2005
Mission: To provide input to government on matters affecting Canadian, rail freight transportation.
Membership: *Member Profile:* Shipping industry associations
Chief Officer(s):
Robert H. Ballantyne, Chair, 613-599-8993 Ext. 223, Fax: 613-294-4569
ballantyne@bellnet.ca

Coalition on the Niagara Escarpment (CONE)
193 James St. South, Hamilton ON L8P 3A8
Tel: 905-529-4955; *Fax:* 905-529-9503
cone@niagaraescarpment.org
www.niagaraescarpment.org
Overview: A small local organization founded in 1978
Mission: CONE is a non-profit alliance of environmental groups, conservation organizations, and concerned citizens and businesses dedicated to the protection of Ontario's Niagara Escarpment.
Affiliation(s): The Greenbelt Foundation, Niagara Escarpment Foundation
Membership: 26 organizations; *Fees:* $35 individual; $60-$120 corporate
Chief Officer(s):
Robert Patrick, President

Coalition Ontarienne pour de meilleurs services éducatifs à l'enfance *See* Ontario Coalition for Better Child Care

Coalition pour l'alphabétisme du Nouveau-Brunswick *See* Literacy Coalition of New Brunswick

Coalition pour le contrôle des armes *See* Coalition for Gun Control

Coalition québécoise pour le contrôle du tabac (CQCT)
#200, 4126, rue Saint-Denis, Montréal QC H2W 2M5
Tél: 514-598-5533; *Téléc:* 514-598-5283
coalition@cqct.qc.ca
www.cqct.qc.ca
Aperçu: *Dimension:* petite; *Envergure:* provinciale
Membre(s) du personnel: 5
Membre(s) du bureau directeur:
Flory Doucas, Codirectrice
Louis Gauvin, Cofondateur & Codirecteur
Heidi Rathjen, Cofondatrice & Codirectrice

Coalition sida des sourds du Québec (CSSQ)
Edifice Plessis, #320, 2075, rue Plessis, Montréal QC H2L 2Y4
Ligne sans frais: 877-535-5556
info@cssq.org
www.cssq.org
Aperçu: *Dimension:* petite; *Envergure:* provinciale; Organisme sans but lucratif; fondée en 1992 surveillé par Canadian AIDS Society
Mission: Informer et mettre en garde la communauté sourde du Québec contre les risques de contracter le Sida et les ITSS (Infections transmissibles sexuellement par le sang); dispenser des services et activités aux personnes sourdes et malentendantes atteintes du VIH/Sida et de l'ITSS
Affiliation(s): Coalition des organismes communautaires québécois de lutte contre le sida
Membre: *Critères d'admissibilite:* Clientèle - population sourde et malentendante du Québec; personnes sourdes vivant avec le VIH/SIDA; personnes sourdes proches; aucune limite d'âge; *Comités:* Prévention et de l'éducation; Usagers; Agentes multiplicateurs; Rédaction du bulletin La CSSQ vous informe; Membres
Activités: Activités d'éducation/prévention; groupe de support pour personnes atteintes et leurs proches; accompagnement et soutien des pairs; ligne d'écoute (TTY); rencontres individuelles; counselling; services psychosociaux (en collaboration avec l'institut Raymond Dewar); information; orientation; références;

vidéo: le Sida frappe aussi les Sourds; un manuel illustré pour l'éducation et la prévention du VIH/Sida; un répertoire de signes LSQ pertinents au VIH/Sida; *Stagiaires:* Oui; *Service de conférenciers:* Oui
Membre(s) du bureau directeur:
Darren Saunders, Président
Michel Turgeon, Directeur général
direction@cssq.org

Coalition to Oppose the Arms Trade (COAT)
541 McLeod St., Ottawa ON K1R 5R2
Tel: 613-231-3076
overcoat@rogers.com
coat.ncf.ca
Overview: A medium-sized national organization
Mission: To actively oppose the arms trade and support the anti-war movement.
Chief Officer(s):
Richard Sanders, Coordinator
Publications:
• Press for Conversion
Frequency: 3 pa; *Price:* $8 per issue; $25 annual subscription

Coalition to Save the Elms *See* Trees Winnipeg

Coast Forest & Lumber Association *See* Coast Forest Products Association

Coast Forest Products Association (CFPA)
#1200, 1090 West Pender St., Vancouver BC V6E 2N7
Tel: 604-891-1237; *Fax:* 604-682-8641
info@coastforest.org
www.coastforest.org
twitter.com/CoastForest
www.youtube.com/user/CoastForest
Also Known As: Coast Forest
Previous Name: Coast Forest & Lumber Association
Overview: A medium-sized international organization founded in 1994
Mission: To promote the interests & protect the rights of those engaged in the coast forest industry in BC
Member of: Canadian Wood Council; Business Council of BC; Vancouver Board of Trade
Finances: *Funding Sources:* Coast Forest Industry; Partnership funding for lumber promotion in Japan & China
Staff Member(s): 6
Membership: 19; *Member Profile:* Logging companies &/or lumber manufacturing companies
Activities: User-pay menu programs; log security; Japan & China lumber promotion
Chief Officer(s):
Rick Jeffrey, President/CEO

Coast Foundation Society (CFS)
293 East 11 Ave., Vancouver BC V5T 2C4
Tel: 604-872-3502; *Fax:* 604-879-2363
Toll-Free: 877-602-6278
info@coastmentalhealth.com
www.coastmentalhealth.com
www.facebook.com/coastmentalhealth
twitter.com/CoastMH
Overview: A medium-sized provincial charitable organization founded in 1974
Mission: To promote recovery of persons with mental illness
Member of: Canadian Council of Health Services Association
Finances: *Funding Sources:* Donations; government grants; membership fees; BC Housing
Activities: AGM; Courage to Come Back; Endeavour; Christmas crafts fair; picnic; *Awareness Events:* Mental Health Week, May *Library:* Resource Centre; Open to public
Chief Officer(s):
Isabela Zabava, Executive Director
isabelaz@coastmentalhealth.com

Coast Waste Management Association (CWMA)
1185 Rolmar Cres., Cobble Hill BC V0R 1L4
Tel: 250-733-2213; *Fax:* 250-733-2214
Toll-Free: 886-386-2962
info@cwma.bc.ca
www.cwma.bc.ca
Overview: A small local organization
Mission: To facilitate communication between members; to provide networking & educational opportunities
Membership: 136; *Member Profile:* Members of the solid waste industry on Vancouver Island, the Gulf Islands & the Sunshine Coast
Chief Officer(s):

Malcolm Harvey, Chair, 604-831-7203
malcolm_harvey@telus.net
Will Burrows, Executive Director
info@cwma.bc.ca
Publications:
• CWMA [Coast Waste Management Association] News
Type: Newsletter; *Frequency:* q.
• CWMA [Coast Waste Management Association] E-bulletins
Type: Bulletin

Coastal Ecosystems Research Foundation
BC
Overview: A small local organization founded in 1995
Mission: To fund ecological research through eco-tourism
Finances: *Annual Operating Budget:* $50,000-$100,000;
Funding Sources: Provincial & national government
Staff Member(s): 4
Membership: 120
Chief Officer(s):
William Megill, Ph.D., Research Director

Coastal First Nations
#1660, 409 Granville St., Vancouver BC V6C 1T2
Tel: 604-696-9889; *Fax:* 604-696-9887
info@coastalfirstnations.ca
www.coastalfirstnations.ca
www.facebook.com/coastalfirstnations
twitter.com/cfngbi
Overview: A small provincial organization founded in 2000
Mission: To protect the Great Bear Rainforest; To promote sustainable economic development on Haida Gwaii & the North & Central Coasts of British Columbia; To develop a conservation-based economy that protects ecosystems & First Nations culture
Staff Member(s): 7
Membership: 9 member nations; *Member Profile:* Wuikinuxv Nation; Heiltsuk Nation; Kitasoo/Xaixais Nation; Nuxalk Nation; Gitga'at Nation; Metlakatla Nation; Old Massett; Skidegate; Council of the Haida Nation; *Committees:* Executive
Activities: Managing & planning for marine & land resources in the Great Bear region; Developing & supporting sustainable economic initiatives; Advocating for environmental protection & conservation
Chief Officer(s):
Gary Wilson, General Manager
gwilson@coastalfirstnations.ca
Bess Brown, Manager, Communications
bbrown@coastalfirstnations.ca
Johanna Helbig, Administrator, Projects
jhelbig@coastalfirstnations.ca
Publications:
• Coastal First Nations Newsletter
Type: Newsletter

Coastal Jazz & Blues Society (CJBS)
295 - 7th Ave. West, 2nd Fl., Vancouver BC V5Y 1L9
Tel: 604-872-5200; *Fax:* 604-872-5250
Toll-Free: 888-438-5200
cjbs@coastaljazz.ca
www.coastaljazz.ca
www.facebook.com/profile.php?id=100000842108783
twitter.com/vanjazzfest
Also Known As: TD Vancouver International Jazz Festival
Overview: A small local charitable organization founded in 1986
Mission: To produce concerts, festivals & events featuring a comprehensive & diverse range of artists representing jazz, blues & improvised music
Member of: Vancouver Cultural Alliance
Affiliation(s): Westcan Jazz Association; Jazz Festivals Canada
Finances: *Annual Operating Budget:* $3 Million-$5 Million;
Funding Sources: Earned income; sponsorship; grant; donations; memberships
Staff Member(s): 10; 750 volunteer(s)
Membership: 170; *Fees:* $50; *Member Profile:* Producer & presenter of concerts, festivals & workshops
Activities: TD Vancouver International Jazz Festival;
Internships: Yes
Chief Officer(s):
Fatima Amarshi, Executive Director
Ken Pickering, Artistic Director
John Orysik, Media Director

Coastal Zone Canada Association (CZCA)
c/o Jennifer Barr, Dalhousie University, PO Box 15000, 6414 Coburg Rd., Halifax NS B3H 4R2

Tel: 902-494-4650; *Fax:* 902-494-1334
czcadmin@dal.ca
www.czca-azcc.org
Overview: A small local organization founded in 1993
Mission: A society of coastal zone management professionals and others interested in and supportive of Integrated Coastal Zone Management goals in Canada and abroad.
Membership: *Fees:* $20-$40
Meetings/Conferences:
• Coastal Zone Canada 2018, 2018
Scope: National
Contact Information: Peter Zuzek; Email: pzuzek@baird.com

The Coaster Enthusiasts of Canada
cec@chebucto.org
www.cec.chebucto.org
Overview: A small national organization
Membership: *Member Profile:* Group of persons whose primary interest is robots, amusement parks, rides, fairs & exhibitions
Chief Officer(s):
Richard Bonner, Contact

Cobequid Arts Council
605 Prince St., Truro NS B2N 1G2
Tel: 902-897-4004
marigold@downtowntruro.ca
www.marigoldcentre.ca
www.facebook.com/MarigoldCentre
twitter.com/MarigoldCentre
marigoldcentre.tumblr.com
Also Known As: Marigold Culture Centre
Overview: A small local organization founded in 1978
Mission: To direct, coordinate & advise on arts & cultural activities in Colchester area, Nova Scotia; To act as liaison between arts organizations in the region
Member of: Performing Arts Sponsors Organization of Nova Scotia
Finances: *Funding Sources:* Government; fundraising
Staff Member(s): 4
Membership: *Fees:* $25 deck hand; $75 captain; $150 admiral; *Member Profile:* Interest in arts & culture
Activities: Fundraising; Performance
Chief Officer(s):
Al Rosen, Executive director, 902-893-2718, Fax: 902-895-9712
al.rosen@marigoldcentre.ca

Cobourg & District Chamber of Commerce *See* Northumberland Central Chamber of Commerce

Cobourg & District Historical Society (CDHS)
200 Ontario St., Cobourg ON K9A 5P4
Tel: 905-377-0413
archivist@cdhsarchives.org
Overview: A small local charitable organization founded in 1980
Mission: To preserve & understand the history of Cobourg & surrounding area of Hamilton & Haldimand Townships, with a primary focus being the conservation of the Archives, a collection of historical documents & photographs.
Member of: Ontario Historical Society; Archives Associations
Finances: *Funding Sources:* Membership dues; government grants
Activities: Exhibits; open houses; tours; monthly meetings with guest speakers; *Library:* The Cobourg & District Historical Society Archives; Open to public
Publications:
• Historical Review
Type: Journal; *Frequency:* Annually
• Historically Speaking
Type: Newsletter; *Frequency:* Monthly

Cobourg Community Information Centre Inc. *See* Info Northumberland

Cobourg-Port Hope District Real Estate Board *See* Northumberland Hills Association of Realtors

Cochrane & District Chamber of Commerce
PO Box 996, Cochrane AB T4C 1B1
Tel: 403-932-0320; *Fax:* 403-541-0915
c.business@cochranechamber.ca
www.cochranechamber.ca
Overview: A small local organization founded in 1978
Mission: To promote community businesses & drive economic development in the area
Finances: *Annual Operating Budget:* $50,000-$100,000
Staff Member(s): 1; 12 volunteer(s)
Membership: 268; *Fees:* $140-$350 based on number of employees; $140 associate

Canadian Associations / CODE

Chief Officer(s):
Bill Popplewell, President

CODE
321 Chapel St., Ottawa ON K1N 7Z2
Tel: 613-232-3569; *Fax:* 613-232-7435
Toll-Free: 800-661-2633
Other Communication: donor.donateur@codecan.org
codehq@codecan.org
www.codecan.org
www.facebook.com/code.org
twitter.com/codecan_org
www.youtube.com/user/TheCodecan
Also Known As: Canadian Organization for Development through Education
Overview: A large international charitable organization founded in 1959
Mission: To enable people to learn by developing partnerships that provide resources for learning, to promote awareness & understanding & to encourage self-reliance; To support training for teachers & librarians; To coordinate book donations from North American publishers to schools & libraries in the developing world
Member of: Canadian Council for International Cooperation
Affiliation(s): International Book Bank; CODE Europe; CODE Inc.; CODE Foundation
Finances: *Annual Operating Budget:* $1.5 Million-$3 Million; *Funding Sources:* Individual; Corporate donations
Activities: Organizing Adopt a Library to support a community library in Tanzania, Ethiopia or Malawi
Chief Officer(s):
Scott Walter, Executive Director
swalter@codecan.org
Marc Molnar, Director, Finance & Administration
mmolnar@codecan.org
Allen LeBlanc, Director, Fund Development & Marketing
aleblanc@codecan.org
Geneviève Spicer, Manager, Integrated Marketing Communications
gspicer@codecan.org

Co-Dependents Recovery Society
PO Box 306, Stn. Main, Surrey BC V3T 5B6
Tel: 604-239-1042; *Fax:* 888-675-8325
board@cdrs.ca
www.cdrs.ca
Overview: A small local organization
Mission: To translate & distribute material to Co-dependents Annoymous groups at a reduced cost, and to help promote Co-dependents Annoymous across Canada
Membership: *Member Profile:* Adults seeking healthy relationships

CoDevelopment Canada (CODEV)
#260, 2747 East Hastings St., Vancouver BC V5K 1Z8
Tel: 604-708-1495; *Fax:* 604-708-1497
codev@codev.org
www.codev.org
www.facebook.com/CoDevCanada
twitter.com/CoDevCanada
Overview: A small international charitable organization founded in 1985
Mission: To initiate social change in Latin American, facilitating relationships between Northern & Southern organizations that share a commitment to workers' rights, community development & women's rights.
Member of: BC Council for International Cooperation
Affiliation(s): CUPE Global Justice; Hospital Employees' Union (HEU); World Community Development Education Society (WCDES)
Finances: *Funding Sources:* Canadian International Development Agency; Global Development Fund; private donors
Staff Member(s): 7
Membership: *Fees:* $10 student/retired/low income; $25 individual; $40 family; $50-$500+ organization
Activities: Solidarity work in Latin America; workshops; film festivals; concerts; *Internships:* Yes
Chief Officer(s):
Joey Hartman, President
Barbara Wood, Executive Director
bwood@codev.org

A Coeur d'Homme
#135, 947, av Royale, Québec QC G1E 1Z9
Tél: 418-660-7799; *Téléc:* 418-660-8053
Ligne sans frais: 877-660-7799
acoeurdhomme@videotron.ca
www.acoeurdhomme.com
Également appelé: Réseau d'aide aux hommes pour une société sans violence
Nom précédent: Association des ressources intervenant auprès des hommes ayant des comportement violent
Aperçu: *Dimension:* moyenne; *Envergure:* provinciale
Mission: Association qui a pour mission d'agir comme ambassadeur de ses membres afin de promouvoir, au niveau socio-politique, un réseau oeuvrant en transformation sociale visant des rapports égalitaires et sans violence
Membre(s) du personnel: 2
Membre: 29 organismes communautaires répartis dans 15 régions du Québec
Membre(s) du bureau directeur:
Rémi Bilodeau, Directeur général
dgacdh@videotron.ca

A coeur joie Nouveau-Brunswick Inc. (ACJ)
1, rue des Arts, Saint-Antoine-de-Kent NB E0A 2X0
Tél: 506-525-2707
Aperçu: *Dimension:* petite; *Envergure:* provinciale; fondée en 1971
Mission: Promotion du chant chorale par des stages de formation, des rencontres, des semaines chantantes; permettre l'accès à tous à la documentation chorale, (des milliers de titres et des nouveautés annuelles)
Membre de: Conseil international à coeur joie
Finances: *Budget de fonctionnement annuel:* Moins de $50,000; *Fonds:* Gouvernement régional
12 bénévole(s)
Membre: 16; *Montant de la cotisation:* 50$ par chorale, plus 2$ par choriste; *Critères d'admissibilite:* Présidents et directeurs généraux d'associations et chefs de choeur
Activités: Les Arcadiades; *Stagiaires:* Oui; *Service de conférenciers:* Oui; *Bibliothèque:* Centre de Documentation; Bibliothèque publique

Coffee Association of Canada (CAC) / Association du café du Canada
#1100, 120 Eglinton Ave. East, Toronto ON M4P 1E2
Tel: 416-510-8032; *Fax:* 416-320-5075
info@coffeeassoc.com
www.coffeeassoc.com
Overview: A medium-sized national organization founded in 1991
Mission: To address industry-wide issues on behalf of members, keeping them fully informed, & allowing them to focus on the proprietary concerns of building their businesses
Staff Member(s): 2
Membership: 23; *Fees:* Schedule available; *Member Profile:* Coffee industry members involved in importing, processing, distributing or individuals involved in the foodservice hospitality sector
Chief Officer(s):
Sandy McAlpine, President
sandym@coffeeassoc.com

Colchester Community Workshops Foundation
PO Box 314, 168 Arthur Street, Truro NS B2N 5C5
Tel: 902-893-7228
www.colchestercommunityworkshops.com
www.facebook.com/495880690505429
Overview: A small local organization founded in 1999
Mission: To create & manage funds for the exclusive benefit of the Colchester Community Workshops by providing a facility & resources to support its clients who seek to earn an independent lifestyle
Activities: Golf tournament
Chief Officer(s):
Don Hoadley, Executive Director
hoadley@ns.sympatico.ca

Colchester Highland Games & Gathering Society (CHGG)
60 Eastmount Ct., East Mountain NS B6L 2E8
Tel: 902-897-4712
events@colchesterhighlandgames.com
www.colchesterhighlandgames.com
www.facebook.com/colchesterhighlandgames
twitter.com/cchighlandgames
Also Known As: The Colchester Games
Overview: A small local organization founded in 2016
Mission: To promote sportsmanship, music, dance, the arts, volunteerism, youth & community
Affiliation(s): The Scots Society of Colchester
Finances: *Annual Operating Budget:* $50,000-$100,000; *Funding Sources:* Donations; Fundraising; Grants; Ticket sales
25 volunteer(s)
Membership: 25; *Committees:* Funding; Heavyweights; Highland Dance; Music Stage; Piping; Planning; Steering
Activities: Organizing Highland Games, including Heavyweights, Highland Dance, Pipes & Drums, Solo Piper, Tug 'o' War, Live Music & Dance Stage, Bike Race, Kids Races, Obstacle Courses, Dog Agility, Historical Re-enactment; Supporting local community & businesses
Meetings/Conferences:
• Highland Games & Gathering 2018, September, 2018, Bible Hill, NS
Scope: Local

Colchester Historical Society
PO Box 412, Truro NS B2N 5C5
Tel: 902-895-6284; *Fax:* 902-895-9530
colchesterhistoreum.ca
Also Known As: Colchester Historical Museum
Overview: A small local charitable organization founded in 1954
Mission: To gather, compile & preserve artifacts & printed documents of historic value & interest; To gather & record stories until now unwritten, which exist only in the memory of older people; To promote the marking of historic sites within the county by suitable plaques, etc.; To cooperate with civic officials in civic celebrations of a historic nature
Member of: Heritage Canada; Federation of the Nova Scotian Heritage; Canadian Museums Association; Council of Canadian Archives; Council of Nova Scotia Archives
Finances: *Funding Sources:* Provincial government; membership fees; municipal government; corporate; private donors
Membership: *Fees:* $20 individual; $25 family; $30 institution; $200 life; *Committees:* Archives; Core Exhibit; Marketing; Fundraising; Heritage; Human Resources
Activities: Maintains a museum & Archives/Research Library; exhibits 6 times a year; *Library:* Colchester Historical Society Archives; Open to public
Chief Officer(s):
Joe Ballard, President
Awards:
• Heritage Awards Program

Colchester-East Hants Public Library Foundation
754 Prince St., Truro NS B2N 1G9
Tel: 902-957-4438; *Fax:* 902-895-7149
Toll-Free: 888-632-9088
lovemylibrary.ca/foundation
www.facebook.com/GiftMyLibrary
twitter.com/GiftMyLibrary
Overview: A small local charitable organization
Mission: To maintain & enhance the library system
Activities: Books by Mail; Home Reader Service; Satellite Library Service; Annual Library Giving Campaign
Chief Officer(s):
Mary Brown, Chair

Cold Lake Native Friendship Centre
PO Box 1978, 5015 - 55 St., Cold Lake AB T9M 1P4
Tel: 780-594-7526; *Fax:* 780-594-1599
cold1@telus.net
clnfc.ca/index.php/home/cold-lake-friendship-centre
www.facebook.com/ColdLakeFriendshipCentre
Previous Name: Grand Centre Canadian Native Friendship Centre
Overview: A small local charitable organization overseen by Alberta Native Friendship Centres Association
Mission: The Centre aims to facilitate the advancement of cultural, social, recreation between Natives & non-Native people of Cold Lake area.
Member of: Alberta Native Friendship Centres Association (ANFCA)
Finances: *Annual Operating Budget:* $50,000-$100,000
Staff Member(s): 14; 50 volunteer(s)
Membership: 213; *Fees:* $1
Activities: Youth Centre Drop-in; Friday Hot Lunch; AES Workers; Probation; Youth Justice; Referrals
Chief Officer(s):
Agnes Gendron, Executive Director

Cold Lake Regional Chamber of Commerce
4009 50th St., Cold Lake AB T9M 1P1
Tel: 780-594-4747
www.coldlakechamber.ca
www.facebook.com/120651524644643
twitter.com/ColdLakeChamber

Overview: A small local organization
Mission: To act as the unified business organization of choice; To promote progression & professionalism; To provide support to members
Member of: Alberta Chamber of Commerce
Finances: *Funding Sources:* Membership dues; Projects
Staff Member(s): 3
Membership: 320; *Fees:* Schedule available; *Member Profile:* Local businesses
Activities: Organizing a Sports Show, a Community Fish Fry, & the Business of the Year Awards; Producing a community guide; *Internships:* Yes
Chief Officer(s):
Trevor Benoit, President
Sherri Bohme, Executive Director

Cole Foundation / Fondation Cole
c/o Barry Cole, 407 Clarke Ave., Montréal QC H3Y 3C3
www.colefoundation.ca
Overview: A small local charitable organization founded in 1980
Mission: To promote research & child care in pediatric & young adult pre-leukemia, leukemia, & lymphoma; To support non-medical community initiatives in Montreal
Activities: Offering fellowships to Clinical Fellows, postdoctoral residents, & graduate students conducting clinical, translational, & fundamental research activities; Fostering intercultural dialogue through the Intercultural Conversations theatre program
Chief Officer(s):
Barry Cole, President
John Moran, Secretary-Treasurer

Cole Harbour Ringette Association (CHRA)
NS
Overview: A small local organization overseen by Ringette Nova Scotia
Member of: Ringette Nova Scotia
Membership: 1-99; *Fees:* schedule

Cole Harbour Rural Heritage Society (CHRHS)
471 Poplar Dr., Cole Harbour NS B2W 4L2
Tel: 902-434-0222
farm.museum@ns.aliantzinc.ca
www.coleharbourfarmmuseum.ca
Overview: A small local charitable organization founded in 1973
Mission: To protect & increase awareness of the natural history & cultural resources of Cole Harbour & the surrounding area; To foster appreciation & respect for the resources of the Cole Harbour region
Finances: *Funding Sources:* Community support
Membership: *Fees:* $20 individuals; $30 families
Activities: Administering the Cole Harbour Rural Heritage Farm Museum, a community museum that preserves & interprets the agricultural history of Cole Harbour; Preserving the former Methodist Chapel, now known as the Cole Harbour Meeting House; Advocating for the protection of natural history in the Cole Harbour area; Providing education about the ecosystem of the region; Promoting careful use of sensitive lands around Cole Harbour

Colin B. Glassco Charitable Foundation for Children
64 New St. SE, Calgary AB T2G 3Y1
Tel: 403-266-3536
glasscocb@shaw.ca
www.glasscofoundation.org
Overview: A small international charitable organization
Mission: To address children's issues in Canada & Zambia through the provision of financial & organizational assistance & on-site support
Activities: Building community schools & water wells in Zambia; Holding up to 30 eye clinics per year for children with eye-related issues; Providing homes, education, & other necessities for orphans through the Chishawasha Orphanage Project; Providing a breakfast program for children in the Lutsel K'e community in the Northwest Territories; Supporting Canuck Place Children's Hospice in Vancouver
Chief Officer(s):
Colin B. Glassco, Founder

Collaboration Santé Internationale (CSI)
1001, ch de la Canardière, Québec QC G1J 5G5
Tél: 418-522-6065; *Téléc:* 418-522-5530
csi@csiquebec.org
www.facebook.com/csiquebec
Aperçu: *Dimension:* grande; *Envergure:* internationale; Organisme sans but lucratif; fondée en 1968
Mission: Soutenir nos Canadiens impliqués dans les dispensaires et les hôpitaux des pays en voie de développement en leur fournissant le matériel de travail; recueillir, sélectionner, et expédier dans les pays du tiers-monde, par l'intermédiaire de Canadiens qui oeuvrent dans le domaine de la santé, des médicaments et de l'équipement médical et hospitalier; parrainer des projets de construction et d'aménagement de dispensaires et d'hôpitaux et soutenir des équipes de médecins et de techniciens spécialisés dans le domaine de la santé publique
Membre de: Association Québecoise des Organismes de Coopération Internationale; Conseil Canadien pour la Coopération Internationale; Canadian International Development Agency
Finances: *Budget de fonctionnement annuel:* $500,000-$1.5 Million
Membre(s) du personnel: 23; 210 bénévole(s)
Membre: 14,000
Activités: *Evénements de sensibilisation:* Soupers bénéfices; Rencontres en écoles et universités; *Service de conférenciers:* Oui
Membre(s) du bureau directeur:
Stéphane Galibois, Président
Publications:
• Bulletin de Collaboration Santé Internationale
Type: Bulletin; *Frequency:* semi-annuel; *Price:* Free

Collaborative Centre for Justice & Safety
3737 Wascana Pkwy., Regina SK S4S 0A2
Tel: 306-337-2570
www.justiceandsafety.ca
Overview: A small provincial organization
Staff Member(s): 2
Chief Officer(s):
Steve Palmer, Executive Director
steve.palmer@uregina.ca

Collectif action alternative en obésité *Voir* ÉquiLibre - Groupe d'action sur le poids

Collectif des femmes immigrantes du Québec (CFIQ)
7124, rue Boyer, Montréal QC H2S 2J8
Tél: 514-279-4246; *Téléc:* 514-279-8536
info@cfiq.ca
www.cfiq.ca
Aperçu: *Dimension:* moyenne; *Envergure:* provinciale; Organisme sans but lucratif; fondée en 1983
Mission: Préparation à l'emploi des immigrants, formation, placement à Montréal et en région
Affiliation(s): Relais femmes
Finances: *Budget de fonctionnement annuel:* $500,000-$1.5 Million; *Fonds:* Subventions
Membre(s) du personnel: 10; 7 bénévole(s)
Membre: 45; *Montant de la cotisation:* 5 $; *Critères d'admissibilite:* Individus ou groupes de femmes immigrantes
Activités: Ateliers en employabilité, café rencontre, coaching, atelier de français, atelier d'anglais et atelier pour les mères immigrantes; *Stagiaires:* Oui; *Service de conférenciers:* Oui; *Bibliothèque:* Cyber Emploi
Membre(s) du bureau directeur:
Aoura Bizzarri, Directrice générale
aoura@cfiq.ca
Marie-Josée Duplessis, Adjointe à la direction
marie-josee@cfiq.ca

Collectif féministe Rouyn-Noranda/Centre de femmes "Entre-Femmes"
CP 1051, 60, rue du Terminus ouest, Rouyn-Noranda QC J9X 5C8
Tél: 819-764-4714; *Téléc:* 819-764-4715
entrefemmes@sympatico.ca
centreentrefemmes.abitemis.info
www.facebook.com/centreentrefemmes.rouynnoranda
Aperçu: *Dimension:* moyenne; *Envergure:* locale; fondée en 1973
Mission: Alternative à l'isolement psycho-social des femmes; réseau d'entraide et d'action; permettre à des femmes isolées, souvent démunies, d'entreprendre avec d'autres femmes, un processus d'autonomie sur des plans économiques, affectifs, sociaux
Membre de: L'R des centres de femmes du Québec
Affiliation(s): Fédération du Québec pour le planning des naissances; Regroupement des centres des femmes du Québec
Finances: *Budget de fonctionnement annuel:* $50,000-$100,000; *Fonds:* Gouvernement provincial
Membre(s) du personnel: 3; 15 bénévole(s)
Activités: *Stagiaires:* Oui

Collectif pour un Québec sans pauvreté
#309, 165, rue Carillon, Québec QC G1K 9E9
Tél: 418-525-0040; *Téléc:* 418-525-0740
collectif@pauvrete.qc.ca
www.pauvrete.qc.ca
www.facebook.com/collectif.quebecsanspauvrete
twitter.com/QcSansPauvrete
www.youtube.com/user/Quebecsanspauvrete
Aperçu: *Dimension:* petite; *Envergure:* provinciale
Mission: Est à la fois un mouvement et un espace citoyen qui vise à générer de façon pluraliste et non partisane, avec les personnes en situation de pauvreté et toute personne ou organisation qui veut y contribuer, les conditions nécessaires pour établir les bases permanentes d'un Québec sans pauvreté
Membre(s) du bureau directeur:
Claude Goulet, Adjoint administratif

The College & Association of Registered Nurses of Alberta (CARNA)
11620 - 168 St., Edmonton AB T5M 4A6
Tel: 780-451-0043; *Fax:* 780-452-3276
Toll-Free: 800-252-9392
carna@nurses.ab.ca
www.nurses.ab.ca
www.facebook.com/albertarns
twitter.com/albertarns
www.youtube.com/carnavideo
Previous Name: Alberta Association of Registered Nurses
Overview: A large provincial licensing organization founded in 1916 overseen by Canadian Nurses Association
Mission: To set nursing practice standards & to ensure Albertans receive safe, competent, & ethical nursing services
Finances: *Funding Sources:* Membership fees
Membership: *Committees:* Appeals; Appointments; Competence; Complaint Review; Finance, Audit & Pension; Leadership Review; Nominations; Provincial Executive; Registration; Registration Review
Activities: Registers, disciplines & provides professional development activities; *Awareness Events:* National Nursing Week, May *Library:* Museum & Archives; Open to public by appointment
Chief Officer(s):
Jerry Macdonald, President
Publications:
• Alberta RN [a publication of The College & Association of Registered Nurses of Alberta]
Type: Magazine; *Frequency:* Quarterly

College & Association of Respiratory Therapists of Alberta (CARTA)
#218, 6715 - 8 St. NE, Calgary AB T2E 7H7
Tel: 403-274-1828; *Fax:* 403-274-9703
Toll-Free: 800-205-2778
www.carta.ca
Previous Name: Alberta College & Association of Respiratory Therapy
Overview: A medium-sized provincial licensing organization founded in 1971
Mission: To serve & protect the public interest by regulating the respiratory therapy profession; To provide professional services to members
Member of: Federation of Regulated Health Professions of Alberta
Affiliation(s): Respiratory Therapy Labour Mobility Consortium
Staff Member(s): 2; 20 volunteer(s)
Membership: 867; *Fees:* $333; *Committees:* Competency; Registration
Activities: Education forum & tradeshow; annual meetings
Chief Officer(s):
Irina Charania, President
Bryan Buell, Executive Director
bryan.buell@carta.ca

College & University Retiree Associations of Canada (CURAC) / Associations de retraités des universités et collèges du Canada (ARUCC)
255 Morrison Rd., Kitchener ON N2A 2W6
curac@curac.ca
www.curac.ca
www.facebook.com/CURAC.ARUCC
Overview: A medium-sized national organization
Mission: To facilitate communication among college & university retirees in all parts of Canada; To collect & disseminate information about retirement policies, pensions, & benefits; To continue relationships of retirees with their colleges & universities; To address other matters of mutual interest

Membership: *Fees:* Schedule available
Chief Officer(s):
David Swayne, President
president@curac.ca
Mary Johnston, Secretary
secretary@curac.ca
Meetings/Conferences:
• CURAC/ARUCC 2018, May, 2018, Dalhousie University, Halifax, NS
Scope: National
Description: Hosted by the Association of Dalhousie Retirees & Pensioners
Contact Information: E-mail: adrp@dal.ca
Publications:
• Newsletter/Bulletin [a publication of College & University Retiree Associations of Canada]
Type: Newsletter; *Frequency:* 2 pa
Profile: CURAC also releases a blog version

Collège canadien de généticiens médicaux *See* Canadian College of Medical Geneticists

Collège canadien des leaders en santé *See* Canadian College of Health Leaders

Collège canadien des physiciens en médecine *See* Canadian College of Physicists in Medicine

Collège des médecins de famille du Canada *See* College of Family Physicians of Canada

Collège des médecins du Québec (CMQ)
2170, boul René-Lévesque ouest, Montréal QC H3H 2T8
Tél: 514-933-4441; *Téléc:* 514-933-3112
Ligne sans frais: 888-633-3246
info@cmq.org
www.cmq.org
www.facebook.com/257741694238490
twitter.com/CMQ_org
Aperçu: *Dimension:* moyenne; *Envergure:* provinciale; Organisme sans but lucratif; fondée en 1847
Mission: Promouvoir une médecine de qualité pour protéger le public et contribuer à l'amélioration de la santé des Québécois
Membre de: Conseil interprofessionnel du Québec
Affiliation(s): Federation of Medical Licensing Authorities of Canada
Membre: *Critères d'admissibilite:* Médecine; *Comités:* Admission à l'excercie; Inspection professionelle; Développement professionel continu; Dévlopement professionnel continu; Études médicales et agrément; Finances et vérification; Révision; Discipline; Transplantation; Périnatalité et mortalité maternelle
Activités: Direction générale, direction de l'amélioration de l'exercice; direction des études médicales; direction des enquêtes; *Listes de destinataires:* Oui; *Bibliothèque:* Centre du documentation; Not open to public
Membre(s) du bureau directeur:
Charles Bernard, Président-directeur général
Yves Robert, Secrétaire
Prix, Bourses:
• Grand prix du Collège
annuel dépuis 1997
Meetings/Conferences:
• Collège des médecins du Québec Colloque et assemblée génerale annuelle 2018, 2018
Scope: Provincial

Collège des médecins et chirurgiens du Nouveau-Brunswick *See* College of Physicians & Surgeons of New Brunswick

Collège des psychologues du Nouveau-Brunswick *See* College of Psychologists of New Brunswick

Le Collège du Savoir
20, rue Nelson ouest, Brampton ON L6X 2M5
Tél: 905-457-7884
www.lecollegedusavoir.com
www.linkedin.com/in/le-collège-du-savoir-040077b0
Aperçu: *Dimension:* petite; *Envergure:* locale; fondée en 1992
Mission: Assurer l'éducation et la formation de l'emploi aux francophones de la région de Peel; Préparer les adultes pour obtenir une équivalence d'études secondaires
Activités: Offrant des ateliers d'alphabétisation et de numératie; Offrir de la formation des compétences relatives à l'employabilité; Préparation pour l'acquisition des notion nécessaires à l'obtention du GED (équivalence du secondaire)
Membre(s) du bureau directeur:

Anna Veltri, Directrice
collegeanna@on.aibn.com

College of Alberta Denturists (CAD)
Sun Life Place, #270, 10123 - 99th St., Edmonton AB T5J 3H1
Tel: 780-429-2330; *Fax:* 780-429-2336
Toll-Free: 800-260-2742
reception@collegeofabdenturists.ca
www.collegeofabdenturists.ca
Overview: A medium-sized provincial organization founded in 2002
Mission: To govern the denturism profession in the province of Alberta; To ensure that Albertans receive ethical, professional & safe denturist services
Membership: *Member Profile:* Regulated Members have approval to provide independent denturist services as indicated in the Denturists Profession Regulation. Provisional Regulated Members have graduated from a three-year denturist training program & are in the process of completing the College's registration examinations. Some Provsisional Regulated Members are authorized to provide denturist services while under direct supervision of a College approved Regulated Member. Intern members have graduated from a denturist training program & are in the process of completing their required internship & challenging licensure examinations. Honorary members are appointed by the Council of the College of Alberta Denturists. These individuals are not provided with a practice permit & cannot legally provide any denturist services.; *Committees:* Examination; Fee Guide Development & Negotiation; Registration; Standards
Chief Officer(s):
Rodney Laliberte, President
John Burnham, Vice-President
Carol Stewart, Registrar
registrar@collegeofabdenturists.ca
Publications:
• Wild Rose Denturist [a publication of the College of Alberta Denturists]
Type: Newsletter; *Frequency:* 3 pa

College of Alberta Professional Foresters
#200, 10544 - 106 St., Edmonton AB T5H 2X6
Tel: 780-432-1177; *Fax:* 780-432-7046
office@capf.ca
www.capf.ca
Previous Name: Alberta Registered Professional Foresters Association
Overview: A medium-sized provincial licensing organization founded in 1988
Mission: To maintain an accurate register of registered professional foresters in Alberta; To set standards of professional conduct & competence for members; To administer the title, Registered Professional Forester (RPF)
Member of: Canadian Federation of Professional Foresters Associations
Affiliation(s): Alberta Forest Technologists Association; Canadian Institute of Forestry
Finances: *Funding Sources:* Membership fees
Staff Member(s): 2
Membership: *Member Profile:* B.Sc. in Forestry + professional examination + 2 yr. Forester-in-Training period; *Committees:* Executive; Competence; Registration; Policy, Act, Regulation & Bylaws; Finance; Nominating; Program; Transformation Steering
Chief Officer(s):
Noel St. Jean, President
ngjstjean@shaw.ca
Doug Krystofiak, Executive Director & Registrar
registrar@capf.ca
Awards:
• Frank Appleby Professional Award

College of Alberta Psychologists
Sun Life Place, #2100, 10123 - 99th St. NW, Edmonton AB T5J 3H1
Tel: 780-424-5070
Toll-Free: 800-659-0857
psych@cap.ab.ca
www.cap.ab.ca
Overview: A small provincial organization
Mission: To develop ethical & practice standards for the profession of psychology in Alberta
Membership: *Committees:* Oral Examinations; Hearing Tribunals/Complaint Review; Registration Advisory; Practice Advisory
Chief Officer(s):
Lorraine Stewart, President

Richard Spelliscy, Registrar

College of Applied Biology British Columbia
#205, 733 Johnson St., Victoria BC V8W 3C7
Tel: 250-383-3306; *Fax:* 250-383-2400
cab@cab-bc.org
www.cab-bc.org
www.linkedin.com/company/college-of-applied-biology
www.facebook.com/CollegeofAppliedBiology
twitter.com/CABiology
Overview: A small provincial licensing organization
Mission: To uphold & protect the public interest by: preserving & protecting the scientific methods & principles that are the foundation of the applied bilogical sciences; To uphold the principles of stewardship of aquatic & terrestrial ecosystems & biological resources; To ensure the integrity, objectivity & expertise of its members
Staff Member(s): 6
Membership: *Fees:* $15 student; $80 trainee; $125 technologist; $175 professional; *Committees:* Executive; Finance; Audit & Practice Review; Scholarship; Governance; Nominations; Professional Liaison; Credentials; Discipline; Communications; Biologists Canada; Ethics; National Conference; Right-to-Practice
Chief Officer(s):
Vanessa Craig, President
Pierre Lachetti, Executive Director

College of Audiologists & Speech-Language Pathologists of Ontario (CASLPO) / Ordre des audiologistes et des orthophonistes de l'Ontario (OAOO)
PO Box 71, #5060, 3080 Yonge St., Toronto ON M4N 3N1
Tel: 416-975-5347; *Fax:* 416-975-8394
Toll-Free: 800-993-9459
caslpo@caslpo.com
www.caslpo.com
Overview: A medium-sized provincial licensing organization
Mission: To regulate the practice of the professions & govern the members; To develop, establish & maintain standards of qualification; To assure the quality of the practice of the professions; Develop & maintain a code of ethics & standards
Finances: *Funding Sources:* Membership dues & services; investment income
Staff Member(s): 14
Membership: 3,700; *Fees:* $700 general/academic; $350 initial/non-practising; $70; *Member Profile:* Speech-Language Pathologists & Audiologists; *Committees:* Executive; ICRC; Discipline; Fitness to Practice; Patient Relations; Quality Asssurance; Registration; Finance; Audiology Practice; SLP Practice
Chief Officer(s):
Scott Whyte, President
Brian O'Riordan, Registrar, 416-975-5347 Ext. 215
boriordan@caslpo.com

College of Audiologists and Speech-Language Pathologists of Manitoba (CASLPM) / Association des orthophonistes et des audiologistes du Manitoba
#1, 333 Vaughan St., Winnipeg MB R3B 3J9
Tel: 204-453-4539; *Fax:* 204-477-1881
office@caslpm.ca
www.caslpm.ca
Previous Name: Manitoba Speech & Hearing Association
Overview: A small provincial licensing organization founded in 1958
Mission: To ensure that members of the association provide high quality speech-language pathology & audiology services to persons with commmunication disorders & their families
Membership: *Fees:* Schedule available; *Member Profile:* Speech-language pathologists & audiologists who work in Manitoba; Individuals who practice in another regulated province in Canada who apply for membership under the Labour Mobility Act & Chapter 7 (Labour Mobility) of the Agreement on Internal Trade; Affiliate members who are interested in speech-language pathology/audiology; Students studying speech-language pathology/audiology
Activities: *Awareness Events:* Speech & Hearing Month, May
Chief Officer(s):
Caroline Wilson, Director, Professional Practice
carolinewilson@caslpm.ca
Lori McKietiuk, Registrar
lorimckietiuk@caslpm.ca
Leitta Taylor, Administrator

Meetings/Conferences:
• College of Audiologists and Speech-Language Pathologists of Manitoba AGM 2018, May, 2018
Scope: Provincial
• College of Audiologists and Speech-Language Pathologists of Manitoba Annual Educational Conference 2018, 2018
Scope: Provincial

College of Chiropodists of Ontario (COCOO)
#2102, 180 Dundas St. West, Toronto ON M5G 1Z8
Tel: 416-542-1333; *Fax:* 416-542-1666
Toll-Free: 877-232-7653
www.cocoo.on.ca
Overview: A small provincial licensing organization
Mission: To protect public interest by ensuring competent care is given by chiropodists & podiatrists in Ontario
Membership: 500; *Fees:* $950; *Member Profile:* Practicing Chiropodists & Podiatrists in Ontario; *Committees:* Discipline; Executive; Fitness to Practice; Inquiries, Complaints & Reports; Patient Relations; Quality Assurance; Registration
Chief Officer(s):
Sohail Mall, President

College of Chiropractors of Alberta; Alberta Chiropractic Association See Alberta College & Association of Chiropractors

College of Chiropractors of British Columbia (CCBC)
#125, 3751 Shell Rd., Richmond BC V6X 2W2
Tel: 604-270-1332; *Fax:* 604-278-0093
Toll-Free: 866-256-1474
www.chirobc.com
Previous Name: British Columbia College of Chiropractors
Overview: A medium-sized provincial organization
Mission: To deal with concerns from the public or practitioners regarding BC chiropractic doctors
Affiliation(s): British Columbia Chiropractic Association
Membership: *Committees:* Registration; Inquiry (Bylaw 16); Discipline (Bylaw 17); Quality Assurance (Bylaw 18); Patient Relations (Bylaw 19)
Chief Officer(s):
David Olson, Chair
Avtar Jassal, Vice-Chair
Awards:
• College of Chiropractors of British Columbia Research Awards
To honour College of Chiropractors of British Columbia members for their research papers
Meetings/Conferences:
• BC Chiropractic Association 2018 Annual General Meeting, 2018, BC
Scope: Provincial
Publications:
• College of Chiropractors of British Columbia Annual Report
Type: Yearbook; *Frequency:* Annually
Profile: Reports from the chair, the registrar, & committee chairs
• College of Chiropractors of British Columbia Professional Conduct Handbook
Type: Handbook; *Number of Pages:* 36
Profile: Contents include the code of ethics plus the standards, limits, & conditions of practice

College of Chiropractors of Ontario
#902, 130 Bloor St. West, Toronto ON M5S 1N5
Tel: 416-922-6355; *Fax:* 416-925-9610
Toll-Free: 877-577-4772
cco.info@cco.on.ca
www.cco.on.ca
Overview: A small provincial organization
Mission: To develop admission, conduct, & practice standards
Membership: *Committees:* Executive; Inquiries, Complaints & Reports; Discipline; Fitness to Practise; Patient Relations; Quality Assurance; Registration; Advertising
Activities: Offering skill development programs to members
Chief Officer(s):
Jo-Ann Willson, Registrar
jpwillson@cco.on.ca

College of Dental Hygienists of British Columbia (CDHBC)
#600, 3795 Carey Rd., Victoria BC V8Z 6T8
Tel: 250-383-4101; *Fax:* 250-383-4144
Toll-Free: 800-778-8277
cdhbc@cdhbc.com
www.cdhbc.com
Overview: A small provincial licensing organization founded in 1995
Mission: Responsible for establishing, monitoring & enforcing standards that assures the public of safe, ethical & competent dental hygiene care
Finances: *Funding Sources:* Membership dues
Staff Member(s): 6
Membership: 2500; *Fees:* $400 practicing; $200 non-practicing; *Committees:* Registration; Quality Assurance; Inquiry; Discipline
Chief Officer(s):
Jennifer Lawrence, Registrar

College of Dental Hygienists of Nova Scotia (CDHNS)
Armdale Professional Centre, #11, 2625 Joseph Howe Dr., Halifax NS B3L 4G4
Tel: 902-444-7241; *Fax:* 902-444-7242
info@cdhns.ca
www.cdhns.ca
Overview: A small provincial organization founded in 2009 overseen by Canadian Dental Hygienists Association
Mission: To advance the profession & contribute to the health of the public
Finances: *Annual Operating Budget:* Less than $50,000
Staff Member(s): 2; 40 volunteer(s)
Membership: 550+; *Committees:* Continuing Competency (Education); Credentials; Executive; Hearing; Investigations; Member Services; Ownership Linkage
Activities: Public health education; *Awareness Events:* National Dental Hygienists' Week, April; *Speaker Service:* Yes; *Library:* CDHNS Resource Centre
Chief Officer(s):
Patricia Grant, Registrar
Publications:
• The Unison [a publication of the College of Dental Hygienists of Nova Scotia]
Type: Newsletter; *Frequency:* Quarterly; *Editor:* Rosemary Bourque
Profile: Available to members of the CDHNS and to other provincial Dental Hygiene Associations across Canada

College of Dental Surgeons of British Columbia (CDSBC)
#500, 1765 West 8th Ave., Vancouver BC V6J 5C6
Tel: 604-736-3621; *Fax:* 604-734-9448
Toll-Free: 800-663-9169
info@cdsbc.org
www.cdsbc.org
Overview: A large provincial licensing organization founded in 1908
Mission: To register, license & regulate dentists & certified dental assistants; To assure British Columbians of professional standards of health care, ethics, & competence by regulating dentistry in a fair & reasonable manner; To administer the Dentists Act
Finances: *Funding Sources:* Membership fees
Staff Member(s): 37
Membership: 3,400 dentists + 6,400 certified dental assistants + 8 dental therapists; *Member Profile:* Dentist or certified dental assistant; *Committees:* Audit; CDA Advisory; CDA Certification; Continuing Education Subcommittee; Discipline; Ethics; Governance; Inquiry; Nominations; Quality Assurance; Registration; Sedation & General Anaesthetic Services
Activities: *Internships:* Yes; *Rents Mailing List:* Yes
Chief Officer(s):
Jerome Marburg, Registrar & CEO
registrarsoffice@cdsbc.org
Awards:
• Honoured Member Award
• Distinguished Service Award
• Award of Merit
Meetings/Conferences:
• 2018 College of Dental Surgeons of British Columbia Annual General Meeting, 2018, BC
Scope: Provincial

College of Dental Surgeons of Saskatchewan
Tower at Midtown, #1202, 201 - 1 Ave. South, Saskatoon SK S7K 1J5
Tel: 306-244-5072; *Fax:* 306-244-2476
cdss@saskdentists.com
www.saskdentists.com
Overview: A medium-sized provincial licensing organization founded in 1906 overseen by Canadian Dental Association
Mission: To operate as a provincial licensing body
Member of: Canadian Dental Association
Chief Officer(s):
Brent Dergousoff, Chair
Mike Prestie, President
Louie Kriel, Vice-President

College of Dental Technicians of British Columbia (CDT)
#N208, 5811 Cooney Rd., Richmond BC V6X 3M1
Tel: 604-278-8324; *Fax:* 604-278-8325
Toll-Free: 877-666-8324
info@cdt.bc.ca
www.cdt.bc.ca
Overview: A small provincial organization founded in 1995
Mission: To serve and protect the public by regulating the profession of dental technology.

College of Dental Technologists of Alberta (CDTA)
#7, 9343 - 50 St. NW, Edmonton AB T6B 2L5
Tel: 780-469-0615; *Fax:* 780-469-1340
membersinfo@cdta.ca
www.cdta.ca
Overview: A medium-sized provincial organization founded in 1990
Mission: To regulate the profession of Dental Technology in the province of Alberta
Staff Member(s): 6
Chief Officer(s):
Gary Wakelam, President
Jason Lohr, Vice-President
Clarence Spring, Treasurer
Bob Westlake, Executive Director
Tara Trembley, Registrar & Office Manager

College of Dental Technologists of Ontario
#300, 2100 Ellesmere Rd., Toronto ON M1H 3B7
Tel: 416-438-5003; *Fax:* 416-438-5004
Toll-Free: 877-391-2386
info@cdto.ca
www.cdto.ca
Previous Name: Governing Board of Dental Technicians of Ontario
Overview: A small provincial licensing organization
Mission: To serve & protect the public interest by regulating & guiding the dental technology profession
Finances: *Funding Sources:* Membership registration
Staff Member(s): 5
Membership: *Member Profile:* Must pass registration examination; *Committees:* Executive; Registration; Inquiries, Complaints & Reports; Discipline; Quality Assurance; Patient Relations; Fitness to Practice
Activities: *Speaker Service:* Yes
Chief Officer(s):
Judy Rigby, Registrar
jrigby@cdto.ca

College of Denturists of British Columbia (CDBC)
#101, 309 - 6th St., New Westminster BC V3L 3A7
Tel: 604-515-0533; *Fax:* 604-515-0534
registrar@cd.bc.ca
www.cd.bc.ca
Overview: A small provincial organization
Mission: To serve & protect the public; To exercise its powers & discharge its responsibilities under all enactments in the public interest
Membership: *Committees:* Discipline; Executive; Finance & Audit; Inquiry; Nominations; Patient Relations; Quality Assurance; Registration
Chief Officer(s):
Paul McKivett, Chair
Publications:
• College of Denturists of British Columbia Newsletter
Type: Newsletter; *Frequency:* Irregular

College of Denturists of Ontario (CDO)
#903, 180 Bloor St. West, Toronto ON M5S 2V6
Tel: 416-925-6331; *Fax:* 416-925-6332
Toll-Free: 888-236-4326
info@denturists-cdo.com
www.denturists-cdo.com
www.linkedin.com/company/college-of-denturists-of-ontario
Overview: A small provincial licensing organization founded in 1973
Mission: To regulate, govern & develop the profession while serving the public interest
Affiliation(s): Benard & Associates; Robin Bigglestone (Robin's Ready Inc.); Shannon Hawkshaw, John Seychuck, & Ivy Tse (Adams & Miles LLP)
Finances: *Funding Sources:* License, examination, incorporation, & membership fees

Canadian Associations / College of Dietitians of Alberta

Staff Member(s): 7
Membership: *Fees:* $2,147; *Committees:* Executive; Inquiries, Complaints & Reports; Registration; Discipline; Fitness; Patient Relations; Quality Assurance; Qualifying Examination; Professional Practice; Qualifying Examinations Appeals; Nominating
Chief Officer(s):
Abena Buahene, Registrar
abuahene@denturists-cdo.com

College of Dietitians of Alberta
#740, 10707 - 100 Ave., Edmonton AB T5J 3M1
Tel: 780-448-0059; *Fax:* 780-489-7759
Toll-Free: 866-493-4348
office@collegeofdietitians.ab.ca
www.collegeofdietitians.ab.ca
Overview: A small provincial licensing organization overseen by Dietitians of Canada
Mission: The College is the regulatory body of registered dieticians/nutritionists in Alberta, setting entry requirements, standards of practice. It is accountable to both the government & the public.
Membership: 900
Chief Officer(s):
Doug Cook, Executive Director & Registrar

College of Dietitians of British Columbia (CDBC)
#409, 1367 West Broadway, Vancouver BC V6H 4A7
Tel: 604-736-2016; *Fax:* 604-736-2018
Toll-Free: 877-736-2016
info@collegeofdietitiansbc.org
www.collegeofdietitiansbc.org
Overview: A medium-sized provincial licensing organization founded in 2004 overseen by Dietitians of Canada
Mission: To serve & protect the nutritional health of the public through quality dietetic practice
Finances: *Annual Operating Budget:* $500,000-$1.5 Million
Staff Member(s): 4; 21 volunteer(s)
Membership: 1,189; *Fees:* $830 registration fee; *Committees:* Inquiry; Quality Assurance; Registration; Discipline
Chief Officer(s):
Fern Hubbard, Registrar
Mélanie Journoud, Deputy Registrar, Quality Assurance
Chi Cejalvo, Deputy Registrar, Registration & Communication

College of Dietitians of Manitoba
#36, 1313 Border St., Winnipeg MB R3H 0X4
Tel: 204-694-0532; *Fax:* 204-889-1755
Toll-Free: 866-283-2823
office.cdm@mts.net
www.manitobadietitians.ca
Overview: A small provincial organization overseen by Dietitians of Canada
Mission: To act as the regulating body within the province for dietitians & the profession of dietetics; To set education standards; To ensure competency of members
Member of: Alliance of Dietetic Regulatory Bodies
Finances: *Funding Sources:* Membership fees
Membership: *Fees:* $525; *Member Profile:* B.Sc. & accredited dietetic internship; *Committees:* Complaints; Executive; Board of Assessors; Screening; Audit; Finance
Chief Officer(s):
Michelle Hagglund, Registrar

College of Dietitians of Ontario (CDO) / L'Ordre des diététistes de l'Ontario
PO Box 30, #1810, 5775 Yonge St., Toronto ON M2M 4J1
Tel: 416-598-1725; *Fax:* 416-598-0274
Toll-Free: 800-668-4990
information@collegeofdietitians.org
www.collegeofdietitians.org
www.facebook.com/CollegeDietitiansOntario
twitter.com/CDOntario
Also Known As: CDO
Overview: A medium-sized provincial licensing charitable organization founded in 1993 overseen by Dietitians of Canada
Mission: To promote awareness of & access to competent, high quality nutritional care for Ontarians
Member of: The Federation of Health Regulatory Bodies of Ontario; Alliance of Canadian Dietetic Regulatory Bodies; Council of Licensure, Enforcement and Regulation
Finances: *Funding Sources:* Membership dues
Staff Member(s): 12
Membership: *Member Profile:* Registered dietitians in Ontario; *Committees:* Registration; Quality Assurance; Inquiries, Complaints and Reports; Patient Relations; Discipline; Fitness to Practice; Legislative Issues; Executive; Elections

Activities: *Speaker Service:* Yes
Chief Officer(s):
Melisse L. Willems, Registrar & Executive Director, 416-598-1725 Ext. 228
melisse.willems@collegeofdietitians.org

College of Family Physicians of Canada (CFPC) / Collège des médecins de famille du Canada
2630 Skymark Ave., Mississauga ON L4W 5A4
Tel: 905-629-0900; *Fax:* 888-843-2372
Toll-Free: 800-387-6197
info@cfpc.ca
www.cfpc.ca
twitter.com/FamPhysCan
www.youtube.com/user/CFPCMedia
Overview: A large national organization founded in 1954
Mission: To improve the health of Canadians by promoting high standards of medical education & care in family practice, by contributing to public understanding of healthful living, by supporting ready access to family physician services, & by encouraging research & disseminating knowledge about family medicine
Finances: *Annual Operating Budget:* Greater than $5 Million; *Funding Sources:* Membership & examination fees
Staff Member(s): 84
Membership: 28,623 physicians; *Fees:* Schedule available; *Member Profile:* Licensed physicians in good standing & engaged in the practice of family medicine; residents & medical students; specialists; *Committees:* Accreditation; Advancing Rural Family Medicine; Family Practice; Advances in Labour & Risk Management; Bylaws; Examinations; Ethics; Faculty Development Education; Family Medicine Forum Advisory; Finance & Audit; First Five Years; Global Health; Governance Advisory; History & Humanities in Family Medicine; Honours & Awards; Membership Advisory; Continuing Professional Development; Nominating; Patient Education; Patient's Medical Home Steering; Postgraduate Education; Prevention in Hand Development & Steering; Self Learning; Undergraduate Education; Working Group on Certification Process
Activities: Administers a Research & Education Foundation; *Library:* Canadian Library of Family Medicine; Not open to public
Chief Officer(s):
David White, MD, CCFP, FCFP, President
Guillaume Charbonneau, MD, CCFP, President-Elect
Francine Lemire, MD CM, CCFP, FC, Executive Director & CEO
Awards:
• Leadership Awards for Residents & Medical Students
• W. Victor Johnston Award
• Ian McWhinney Award
• Irwin Bean Award
• Family Physician Research Grants
• Family Physician Study Grants
• Janus Scholarships
• Hollister King Study Grant
• Nadine St-Pierre Award
• Bob Robertson Award
• Research Awards for Residents
• D.I. Rice Merit Award
Awarded annually to a renowned leader in family medicine to allow travel for a period of approximately one month in order to engage in educational activities; *Amount:* $10,000 plus travel expenses
• D.M. Robb Research Award
Awarded annually to a community-based family physician to conduct research in family medicine; *Amount:* $2,500
• CFP Research Award
Sponsored by Canadian Family Physician; awarded to the author of the best article of original research published in the Canadian Family Physician during the previous year; *Amount:* $1,000
• Ortho French & English Literary Award
Sponsored by Ortho Pharmaceutical (Canada) Ltd.; awarded to the best article written in French & published in Canadian Family Physician during the current year; *Amount:* $1,000 & certificate
• Family Physician of the Year Award
Sponsored by Janseen Ortho; awarded to physicians who have been in family practice for a minimum of 15 years & members of the college for at least 10 years, & who have made outstanding contributions to family medicine, to their communities & to the college
Meetings/Conferences:
• College of Family Physicians of Canada / Collège des médecins de famille du Canada 2018 Annual General Meeting, 2018
Scope: Provincial

Publications:
• Canadian Family Physician [a publication of the College of Family Physicians of Canada]
Type: Journal
Profile: Current issues & developments in family medicine
• eNews [a publication of the College of Family Physicians of Canada]
Type: Newsletter; *Frequency:* Monthly
• Kaléidoscope [a publication of the College of Family Physicians of Canada]
Type: Newsletter
Profile: Developments in family medicine research
• Section of Residents Newsletter [a publication of the College of Family Physicians of Canada]
Type: Newsletter
Profile: Information for family medicine residents

Alberta College of Family Physicians
Centre 170, #370, 10403 - 172 St., Edmonton AB T5S 1K9
Tel: 780-488-2395; *Fax:* 780-488-2396
Toll-Free: 800-361-0607
info@acfp.ca
www.acfp.ca
twitter.com/ABFamDocs
Mission: To act as a respected voice for family practice in Alberta; To advance excellence in family practice
Chief Officer(s):
John Chmelicek, President
acfppres@acfp.ca
Terri Potter, Executive Director
terri.potter@acfp.ca

British Columbia College of Family Physicians (BCCFP)
#330, 1665 West Broadway, Vancouver BC V6J 1X1
Tel: 604-736-1877; *Fax:* 604-736-4675
office@bccfp.bc.ca
www.bccfp.bc.ca
Mission: To represent family physicians/general practitioners in the discipline of Family Medicine
Chief Officer(s):
Christie Newton, President
Toby Kirshin, Executive Director
Ian Tang, Project Manager

Collège québécois des médecins de famille
#202, 3210, av Jacques-Bureau, Laval QC H7P 0A9
Tél: 450-973-2228; *Téléc:* 450-973-4329
Ligne sans frais: 800-481-5962
adjointe@cqmf.qc.ca
www.cqmf.qc.ca
Mission: D'améliorer la santé des Québécois et la qualité des soins de première ligne
Chief Officer(s):
Maxine Dumas Pilon, Présidente
Nicole Cloutier, Directrice générale

Manitoba College of Family Physicians
#240, 1695 Henderson Hwy., Winnipeg MB R2G 1P1
Tel: 204-668-3667; *Fax:* 204-668-3663
Toll-Free: 844-668-3667
www.mcfp.mb.ca
Mission: To improve the health of Canadians; To promote high standards of medical education & care in family practice; To contribute to public understanding of healthy living; To support ready access to family physician services; To encourage research & disseminate knowledge about family medicine
Chief Officer(s):
Deirdre O'Flaherty, President
Tamara Buchel, Executive Director
tamarabuchel@mcfp.mb.ca
Amanda Woodard, Administrator & Office Manager
amandaw@cfpc.ca

New Brunswick College of Family Physicians
950 Picot Ave., Bathurst NB E2A 4Z9
Tel: 506-548-4707; *Fax:* 506-548-4761
nbcfp@cfpc.ca
www.nbcfp.ca
www.facebook.com/Nbcfp
twitter.com/nbcfp_cmfnb
Mission: To provide support for family physicians; To help family physicians offer high quality care to their patients
Chief Officer(s):
Melissa McQuaid, President
Ghislain Lavoie, Secretary-Treasurer

Newfoundland & Labrador Chapter
#2713A, 300 Prince Philip Dr., St. John's NL A1B 3V6

Tel: 709-864-6566
nl.cfpc.ca
Mission: To promote & support family physicians in Newfoundland & Labrador
Member of: The College of Family Physicians of Canada
Chief Officer(s):
Dave Thomas, President
Debbie Rideout, Administrator
debbierideout@cfpc.ca

Nova Scotia College of Family Physicians
Mill Cove Plaza, #207, 967 Bedford Hwy., Bedford NS B4A 1A9
Tel: 902-499-0303; *Fax:* 902-832-1193
admin@nsfamdocs.com
www.nsfamdocs.com
Mission: To encourage high standards of medical education & care; To promote & support family physicians & related services
Chief Officer(s):
Peter Brennan, President
Cathie W. Carroll, Executive Director

Ontario College of Family Physicians
#2100, 400 University Ave., Toronto ON M5G 1S5
Tel: 416-867-9646; *Fax:* 416-867-9990
Toll-Free: 800-670-6237
ocfp@cfpc.ca
www.ocfp.on.ca
twitter.com/OntarioCollege
Mission: To provide education & continuing professional development opportunities for members; To maintain high standards of medical care & education in family practice; To advocate for family physicians
Chief Officer(s):
Jessica Hill, Chief Executive Officer
Glenn Brown, President

Prince Edward Island Chapter
253 King St., Charlottetown PE C1A 1C4
Tel: 902-894-2605; *Fax:* 902-894-3975
pei.cfp@pei.aibn.com
pei.cfpc.ca
Mission: To improve the health of Canadians by offering knowledge about healthy living & family medicine, supporting research & access to services, & promoting high standards of medical care & education
Chief Officer(s):
Shannon Curtis, President
Rosemary Burke-Perry, Administrator

Saskatchewan College of Family Physicians
105-2174 Airport Dr., Saskatoon SK S7L 6M6
Tel: 306-665-7714; *Fax:* 306-665-0047
scfp@cfpc.ca
sk.cfpc.ca
twitter.com/SKChapterCFPC
Chief Officer(s):
Danielle Cutts, President
C. James Stewart, Executive Director
jstewart@cfpc.ca

College of Hearing Aid Practitioners of Alberta (CHAPA)
4017 - 63 St., Camrose AB T4V 2X2
Tel: 403-510-1863; *Fax:* 780-678-3282
Toll-Free: 866-990-4327
registrar@chapa.ca
www.chapa.ca
Overview: A medium-sized provincial organization founded in 2002
Mission: To regulate the hearing aid practitioner profession; To ensure clients receive the best possible treatment & equipment so that they are able to hear to the best of their ability
Membership: *Fees:* $625 hearing aid practitioner & registered hearing aid practitioner; $50 student; $250 associate or out-of-province/inactive; $150 interim; *Committees:* Advertising; Awards; Complaints; Continuing Competence; Exam; Finance; Hearings; Negotiations; Nominations; Registration; Symposium
Chief Officer(s):
Allen Kirkham, Executive Director
Holly Barry, Registrar

College of Licensed Practical Nurses of Alberta (CLPNA)
13163 - 146 St., Edmonton AB T5L 4S8
Tel: 780-484-8886; *Fax:* 780-484-9069
Toll-Free: 800-661-5877
info@clpna.com

www.clpna.com
www.linkedin.com/company/college-of-licensed-practical-nurses-of-alberta-clpna-
www.facebook.com/CLPNA
twitter.com/clpna
www.youtube.com/clpna
Previous Name: Professional Council of Licensed Practical Nurses
Overview: A medium-sized provincial licensing organization founded in 1985 overseen by Canadian Council of Practical Nurse Regulators
Mission: To regulate & lead the profession in a manner that protects & serves the public through excellence in Practical Nursing
Finances: *Funding Sources:* Membership dues
Staff Member(s): 21
Membership: 10,623; *Fees:* $400; $50 associate; *Member Profile:* Licensed Practical Nurses; *Committees:* Complaint Review; Competence; Education Standards Advisory
Activities: *Library:* Not open to public
Chief Officer(s):
Linda L. Stanger, Chief Executive Officer
lstanger@clpna.com

College of Licensed Practical Nurses of BC (CLPNBC)
#260, 3480 Gilmore Way, Burnaby BC V5G 4Y1
Tel: 778-373-3101; *Fax:* 778-373-3102
Toll-Free: 877-373-2201
info@clpnbc.org
www.clpnbc.org
Overview: A medium-sized provincial licensing organization founded in 1965 overseen by Canadian Council of Practical Nurse Regulators
Mission: To regulate practical nursing in the public interest
Finances: *Annual Operating Budget:* $3 Million-$5 Million; *Funding Sources:* Membership dues 88%; other 12%
Membership: *Fees:* $270; *Member Profile:* Licensed practical nurses; *Committees:* Discipline; Finance & Audit; Inquiry; Quality Assurance; Registration; Standards & Education
Activities: *Speaker Service:* Yes
Awards:
• John MacKay Financial Bursary for Student PN in Need

College of Licensed Practical Nurses of Manitoba (CLPNM)
463 St. Anne's Rd., Winnipeg MB R2M 3C9
Tel: 204-663-1212; *Fax:* 204-663-1207
Toll-Free: 877-663-1212
www.clpnm.ca
Overview: A small provincial organization overseen by Canadian Council of Practical Nurse Regulators
Mission: The governing body for the Licensed Practical Nurses in Manitoba. The College's duty is to carry out its activities and govern its members in a manner that serves and protects the public interest. The College establishes requirements to enter the profession and assures the quality of the practice of LPNs through the development and enforcement of standards and practice and continuing competence programs.
Staff Member(s): 11
Chief Officer(s):
Jennifer Breton, LPN, RN, BN, Executive Director
jbreton@clpnm.ca
Barb Palz, Business Manager
bpalz@clpnm.ca

College of Licensed Practical Nurses of Newfoundland & Labrador (CLPNNL)
9 Paton St., St. John's NL A1B 4S8
Tel: 709-579-3843; *Fax:* 709-579-8268
Toll-Free: 888-579-2576
info@clpnnl.ca
www.clpnnl.ca
Previous Name: Newfoundland Council for Nursing Assistants
Overview: A small provincial licensing organization overseen by Canadian Council of Practical Nurse Regulators
Mission: To regulate the practice of Licensed Practical Nurses in Newfound & Labrador; to promote safety and protection of the general public through the provision of safe, competent and ethical nursing care.
Finances: *Annual Operating Budget:* $500,000-$1.5 Million
Staff Member(s): 4
Membership: *Committees:* Complaints Authorization; Discipline Panel; Education; Finance
Chief Officer(s):

Paul D. Fisher, Executive Director/Registrar
pfisher@clpnnl.ca

College of Licensed Practical Nurses of Nova Scotia (CLPNNS)
Starlite Gallery, #302, 7071 Bayers Rd., Halifax NS B3L 2C2
Tel: 902-423-8517; *Fax:* 902-425-6811
Toll-Free: 800-718-8517
www.clpnns.ca
Previous Name: Licensed Practical Nurses Association of Nova Scotia; Nova Scotia Certified Nursing Assistants Association
Overview: A medium-sized provincial organization founded in 1956 overseen by Canadian Council of Practical Nurse Regulators
Mission: To represent licensed practical nurses within the health care system; To protect the public by providing safe, competent nursing care
Finances: *Funding Sources:* Membership fees
Staff Member(s): 8
Membership: *Fees:* $280; *Committees:* Complaints; Continuing Competence Program; Document Reviewers; Education; Professional Conduct
Activities: *Internships:* Yes; *Speaker Service:* Yes; *Library:* Video Library; Not open to public
Chief Officer(s):
Ann Mann, Executive Director
ann@clpnns.ca
Awards:
• Best Bedside Nurse Award

College of Licensed Practical Nurses of PEI
#204, 155 Belvedere Ave., Charlottetown PE C1A 2Y9
Tel: 902-566-1512
www.clpnpei.ca
Previous Name: Licensed Practical Nurses Association & Regulatory Board of PEI
Overview: A medium-sized provincial organization overseen by Canadian Council of Practical Nurse Regulators
Mission: To represent practical nurses within the health care system
Chief Officer(s):
Dawn Rix-Moore, Executive Director
drix-moore@lpna.ca
Kimberley Jay, Registrar
kjay@lpna.ca

College of Massage Therapists of British Columbia (CMTBC)
#304, 1212 West Broadway, Vancouver BC V6H 3V1
Tel: 604-736-3404; *Fax:* 604-736-6500
Toll-Free: 877-321-3404
info@cmtbc.ca
www.cmtbc.ca
Overview: A medium-sized provincial organization founded in 1994
Mission: To regulate the message therapy profession in order to protect the public
Finances: *Funding Sources:* Membership dues
Staff Member(s): 7
Membership: *Member Profile:* Massage therapists; *Committees:* Discipline; Finance & Audit; Governance & Human Resources; Inquiry; Patient Relations; Quality Assurance; Registration
Chief Officer(s):
Susan Addario, Registrar & CEO
registrar@cmtbc.ca

College of Massage Therapists of Ontario (CMTO) / L'Ordre des massothérapeutes de l'Ontario
#810, 1867 Yonge St., Toronto ON M4S 1Y5
Tel: 416-489-2626; *Fax:* 416-489-2625
Toll-Free: 800-465-1933
cmto@cmto.com
www.cmto.com
Overview: A medium-sized provincial licensing organization founded in 1919
Mission: To promote the highest possible quality of massage therapy practice; To protect the public by providing massage therapy in a safe & ethical manner; To serve its members
Member of: Federation of Health Regulatory Colleges of Ontario
Finances: *Annual Operating Budget:* Greater than $5 Million; *Funding Sources:* Membership dues; examination fees; investment income
Staff Member(s): 24
Membership: 11,200; *Fees:* $571 regular; $173 inactive; *Member Profile:* Massage therapist - MT or Registered Massage Therapist - RMT designation; *Committees:* Appeals; Client

Canadian Associations / College of Medical Laboratory Technologists of Alberta (CMLTA)

Relations; Discipline; Executive; Fitness to Practise; Inquiries, Complaints & Reports; Quality Assurance; Registration
Chief Officer(s):
Corinne Flitton, Registrar & CEO

College of Medical Laboratory Technologists of Alberta (CMLTA)
#301, 9426 - 51 Ave. NW, Edmonton AB T6E 5A6
Tel: 780-435-5452; Fax: 780-437-1442
Toll-Free: 800-265-9351
info@cmlta.org
www.cmlta.org
Previous Name: Alberta College of Medical Laboratory Technologists
Overview: A medium-sized provincial licensing charitable organization founded in 1981 overseen by Canadian Society for Medical Laboratory Science
Mission: To ensure excellence in medical laboratory science in Alberta
Staff Member(s): 5
Membership: *Committees:* Legislation Sub-Committee
Activities: Setting entrance to practice requirements; Maintaining a Continuing Competence Program; Adjudicating complaints of unprofessional conduct
Chief Officer(s):
Lori Kmet, Executive Director & Registrar
registrar@cmlta.org
Larissa Fadish, Deputy Registrar & Manager, Professional Practice
deputyregistrar@cmlta.org
Sharon Semeniuk, Manager, Finance
finance@cmlta.org
Awards:
• Award of Merit
• Member Bursary Awards
• Award of Distinction

College of Medical Radiation Technologists of Ontario / Ordre des technologues en radiation médicale de l'Ontario
#300, 375 University Ave., Toronto ON M5G 2J5
Tel: 416-975-4353; Fax: 416-975-4355
Toll-Free: 800-563-5847
info@cmrto.org
www.cmrto.org
www.facebook.com/CMRTO
Overview: A medium-sized provincial organization
Mission: To serve & protect the people of Ontario through self-regulation of the profession
Membership: *Committees:* Executive; Inquiries, Complaints & Reports; Discipline; Fitness to Practice; Patient Relations; Quality Assurance; Registration; Finance & Audit; Staff Relations; Nominating; Privacy
Chief Officer(s):
Linda Gough, Registrar & CEO
lgough@cmrto.org

College of Midwives of British Columbia (CMBC)
#603, 601 West Broadway, Vancouver BC V5Z 4C2
Tel: 604-742-2230; Fax: 604-730-8908
information@cmbc.bc.ca
www.cmbc.bc.ca
Overview: A small provincial licensing organization founded in 1995
Mission: To serve & protect the public interest by registering competent midwives who will practise safely & ethically in British Columbia
Finances: *Annual Operating Budget:* $500,000-$1.5 Million; *Funding Sources:* Membership fees
Staff Member(s): 5; 9 volunteer(s)
Membership: 110; *Fees:* $1,800; *Member Profile:* Registered midwives; *Committees:* Executive; Registration; Quality Assurance; Inquiry; Client Relations; Discipline; Aboriginal
Activities: Regulation of the profession; set education & registration requirements & standards of practice
Chief Officer(s):
Louise Aerts, Registrar & Executive Director, 604-742-2234
registr@cmbc.bc.ca

College of Midwives of Manitoba
#230, 500 Portage Ave., Winnipeg MB R3C 3X1
Tel: 204-783-4520; Fax: 204-779-1490
admin@midwives.mb.ca
www.midwives.mb.ca
Overview: A medium-sized provincial organization founded in 1997
Mission: To justify public trust and confidence, to uphold and enhance the good standing and reputation of the profession, to serve the interests of society and, above all, to safeguard the interests of individual clients.
Finances: *Funding Sources:* Provincial funding; membership dues; sales of goods & services; pension plan
Staff Member(s): 3
Membership: *Fees:* $1600
Chief Officer(s):
Patty Eadie, Executive Director
director@midwives.mb.ca

College of Midwives of Ontario / Ordre des Sages-Femmes de l'Ontario
#303, 21 St. Clair Ave. East, Toronto ON M4T 1L9
Tel: 416-640-2252; Fax: 416-640-2257
admin@cmo.on.ca
www.cmo.on.ca
Overview: A medium-sized provincial licensing organization founded in 1993
Mission: Ensures that its members provide competent & ethical care to the clients they serve; Establishes standards that ensure its members are responsive to individual & community needs; Promotes a model of care for the profession that encourages informed choice for the client and participation of women by providing standards
Finances: *Funding Sources:* Membership fees
Staff Member(s): 11
Chief Officer(s):
Kelly Dobbin, Registrar-CEO, 416-640-2252 Ext. 226
registrar@cmo.on.ca
Barbara Borland, President
Wendy Murko, Vice-President
Publications:
• College of Midwives of Ontario Member Communiqué
Type: Newsletter; *Frequency:* Quarterly
Profile: Practice notes, news, & updates

College of Naturopathic Doctors of Alberta (CNDA)
813 - 14th St. NW, Calgary AB T2N 2A4
Tel: 403-266-2446; Fax: 403-226-2433
secretary@cnda.net
www.cnda.net
twitter.com/CollegeNDAB
Previous Name: Alberta Association of Naturopathic Practitioners
Overview: A small provincial organization overseen by The Canadian Association of Naturopathic Doctors
Mission: To maintain a high standard of practice among naturopathic doctors.
Finances: *Funding Sources:* Membership dues
Membership: *Member Profile:* Naturopathic professionals; *Committees:* Complaints; Competence; Registration
Chief Officer(s):
Alissa Gaul, President

College of Naturopathic Physicians of British Columbia (CNPBC)
#840, 605 Robson St., Vancouver BC V6B 5J3
Tel: 604-688-8236; Fax: 604-688-8476
Toll-Free: 877-611-8236
office@cnpbc.bc.ca
www.cnpbc.bc.ca
Previous Name: Association of Naturopathic Physicians of British Columbia
Overview: A small provincial licensing organization founded in 1936
Mission: To set standards of professional practice amongst naturopathic physicians in BC.
Staff Member(s): 5
Membership: *Fees:* $1,650 active; $200 associate; *Member Profile:* All licensed & registered naturopathic physicians; *Committees:* Discipline; Examination; Finance & Administration; Inquiry; Patient Relations; Pharmacopoeia & Diagnostics Referral; Registration; Quality Assurance
Chief Officer(s):
Howard Greenstein, CEO & Registrar
registrar@cnpbc.bc.ca

The College of Naturopaths of Ontario
150 John St., 10th Fl., Toronto ON M5V 3E3
Tel: 416-583-6010; Fax: 416-583-6011
info@collegeofnaturopaths.on.ca
www.collegeofnaturopaths.on.ca
Previous Name: Board of Directors of Drugless Therapy, Naturopathy (Ontario)
Overview: A small provincial licensing organization founded in 1925
Mission: To register & regulate naturopathic doctors in Ontario; To investigate complaints from patients & the public
Member of: Federation of Health Regulatory Colleges of Ontario
Affiliation(s): North American Board of Naturopathic Examiners; Ontario Association of Naturopathic Doctors
Membership: 500-999; *Fees:* $490 inactive; $575 general; *Committees:* Audit; Discipline; Examination Appeals; Executive; Fitness to Practice; Inquiry, Complaints & Reports; Inspection; Nominations & Elections; Patient Relations; Quality Assurance; Registration; Schedule Substance Review
Chief Officer(s):
Andrew Parr, Registrar & CEO
registrar@collegeofnaturopaths.on.ca
Syed Mehdi, Officer, Finance & Administration
Erica Laugalys, Manager, Examinations & Entry to Practise
Anna Jeremian, Manager, Membership

College of Nurses of Ontario (CNO) / Ordre des infirmières et infirmiers de l'Ontario
101 Davenport Rd., Toronto ON M5R 3P1
Tel: 416-928-0900; Fax: 416-928-6507
Toll-Free: 800-387-5526
www.cno.org
www.linkedin.com/company/college-of-nurses-of-ontario
www.facebook.com/collegeofnurses
www.youtube.com/user/cnometrics
Overview: A large provincial licensing organization founded in 1963 overseen by Canadian Council of Practical Nurse Regulators
Mission: To protect the public's right to quality nursing services by providing leadership to the nursing profession in self-regulation
Finances: *Funding Sources:* Membership fees
Membership: *Committees:* Disipline; Executive; Finance; Fitness to Practice; Inquiries, Complaints & Reports; Quality Assurance; Registration
Activities: *Library:* Not open to public
Chief Officer(s):
Anne Coghlan, Executive Director
ed@cnomail.org

College of Occupational Therapists of British Columbia (COTBC)
#402, 3795 Carey Rd., Victoria BC V8Z 6T8
Tel: 250-386-6822; Fax: 250-386-6824
Toll-Free: 866-386-6822
info@cotbc.org
www.cotbc.org
www.linkedin.com/company/college-of-occupational-therapists-of-british-columbia
www.facebook.com/OTCollegeBC
twitter.com/OTCollegeBC
Overview: A small provincial licensing organization
Mission: To establish standards of practice & conduct; To enhance quality assurance; To monitor quality of practice & continuing competence; To improve competence of occupational therapists; To investigate complaints; To enforce standards
Finances: *Annual Operating Budget:* $500,000-$1.5 Million; *Funding Sources:* Application fees; Registration fees
Staff Member(s): 4
Membership: 1,600; *Fees:* $350 practicing; $75 non-practicing
Chief Officer(s):
Kathy Corbett, Registrar
kcorbett@cotbc.org
Cindy McLean, Deputy Registrar
cmclean@cotbc.org
Mary Clark, Director, Quality Assurance Program & Communications
mclark@cotbc.org

College of Occupational Therapists of Manitoba (COTM) / L'Ordre des ergothérapeutes du Manitoba
#7, 120 Maryland St., Winnipeg MB R3G 1L1
Tel: 204-957-1214; Fax: 204-775-2340
Toll-Free: 866-957-1214
otinfo@cotm.ca
www.cotm.ca
Previous Name: Association of Occupational Therapists of Manitoba
Overview: A small provincial licensing organization founded in 1971
Mission: To register occupational therapists in Manitoba; to investigate complaints; to administer The Occupational Therapists Act

Affiliation(s): Association of Canadian Occupational Therapy Regulatory Organizations
Finances: *Funding Sources:* Membership fees
Staff Member(s): 3
Membership: *Fees:* Schedule available; *Committees:* Executive; Practice Issues; Investigation; Inquiry; Communications; Continuing Competence; Legislation
Chief Officer(s):
Sharon Kathleen Eadie, Executive Director
sharon.eadie@cotm.ca

College of Occupational Therapists of Nova Scotia (COTNS)
Mumford Professional Centre, #2132B, 6960 Mumford Rd., Halifax NS B3L 4P1
Tel: 902-455-0556; *Fax:* 902-455-0621
admin@cotns.ca
www.cotns.ca
Overview: A medium-sized provincial organization
Mission: Regulates the practice of occupational therapists by ensuring safe and ethical services that will protect the public it serves.
Membership: 483; *Fees:* $375 annual fee; *Committees:* Continuing competency; Nominations; Advisory Committee for the College Complains Process; Practice; Credentials
Chief Officer(s):
Pauline Cousins, Chair
Allanna Jost, Treasurer
Gayle Salsman, Registrar

College of Occupational Therapists of Ontario (COTO) / Ordre des ergothérapeutes de l'Ontario
PO Box 78, #900, 20 Bay St., Toronto ON M5J 2N8
Tel: 416-214-1177; *Fax:* 416-214-1173
Toll-Free: 800-890-6570
info@coto.org
www.coto.org
www.linkedin.com/company/college-of-occupational-therapists-of-ontario
Overview: A medium-sized provincial licensing organization
Mission: Self-governing body that protects the public interest & improves their health & well-being by registering, regulating & supporting the ongoing competency of Occupational Therapists
Finances: *Annual Operating Budget:* $3 Million-$5 Million; *Funding Sources:* Registration & application fees
Staff Member(s): 17
Membership: *Fees:* $657.55 + HST: annual renewal; $200 + HST: new application fee; $40 + HST: re-instatement fee; *Committees:* Inquiries, Complaints & Reports; Discipline; Fitness to Practice; Patient Relations; Quality Assurance; Registration
Chief Officer(s):
Jane Cox, President
Elinor Larney, Registrar
elarney@coto.org

College of Opticians of Alberta (COA)
#201, 2528 Ellwood Dr. SW, Edmonton AB T6X 0A9
Tel: 780-429-2694; *Fax:* 780-426-5576
Toll-Free: 800-263-6026
www.opticians.ab.ca
www.facebook.com/pages/Opticians-of-Alberta/301105265172
twitter.com/CO_alberta
Previous Name: Alberta Opticians Association; Alberta Guild of Opthalmic Dispensers
Overview: A medium-sized provincial organization founded in 1965
Mission: To promote the advancement of knowledge, skills & competence of members & encourage education & training programs while representing members on all issues affecting the profession; to act as a regulatory body; to provide opportunities for opticians to improve their skills while advancing competency through education & cooperation with other eye care professions
Member of: Opticians Association of Canada
Affiliation(s): National Accreditation Committee of Opticians
Finances: *Funding Sources:* Membership dues
Membership: *Fees:* $732.91 opticians; $910.23 contact lens practitioners; $295.53 non-practicing; *Committees:* Regulatory; Hearing Tribunal; Examination; Field Supervision; Finance & Audit; Association; Negotiations
Activities: *Internships:* Yes
Chief Officer(s):
Maureen Hussey, Executive Director & Registrar
mhussey@opticians.ab.ca

College of Opticians of British Columbia (COBC)
#403, 1505 West 2nd Ave., Vancouver BC V6H 3Y4
Tel: 604-278-7510; *Fax:* 604-278-7594
Toll-Free: 888-771-6755
reception@cobc.ca
www.cobc.ca
www.facebook.com/CollegeofOpticiansBC
twitter.com/CO_BritishC
www.youtube.com/user/LicensedOptician
Overview: A small provincial licensing organization founded in 1994
Mission: To govern the practice of opticianry in BC.
Finances: *Funding Sources:* Licensing fees
Staff Member(s): 4
Membership: 1,118; *Fees:* Schedule available; *Committees:* Discipline; Executive; Inquiry; Quality Assurance; Registration; Patient Relations
Activities: Assessment, registration & licensing of all opticians & contact lens fitters; handle complaints & inquiries
Chief Officer(s):
Raheem Savja, Chair
Connie Chong, Registrar & Executive Director
cchong@cobc.ca

College of Opticians of Ontario (COO)
#902, 85 Richmond St. West, Toronto ON M5H 2C9
Tel: 416-368-3616; *Fax:* 416-368-2713
Toll-Free: 800-990-9793
mail@coptont.org
www.coptont.org
Overview: A medium-sized provincial organization
Mission: To regulate & improve the practice of opticians in Ontario
Affiliation(s): Federation of Health Regulatory Colleges of Ontario
Staff Member(s): 8
Membership: *Fees:* $120 student; $835 individual; *Committees:* Executive; Inquiries, Complaints & Reports; Patient Relations; Quality Assurance; Registration; Fitness to Practise; Discipline; Governance; Professional Misconduct Regulation
Chief Officer(s):
Fazal Khan, Registrar
fkhan@coptont.org

College of Optometrists of BC
#906, 938 Howe St., Vancouver BC V6Z 1N9
Tel: 604-623-3464; *Fax:* 604-623-3465
Toll-Free: 866-910-3464
college@optometrybc.ca
www.optometrybc.com
Previous Name: Board of Examiners in Optometry in B.C.
Overview: A medium-sized provincial organization
Mission: To serve & protect the public interest by guiding the profession of optometry in British Columbia
Membership: *Committees:* Discipline; Inquiry; Patient Relations; Pharmaceutical Advisory; Quality Assurance; Registration
Chief Officer(s):
Dale Dergousoff, Chair
Robin Simpson, Registrar
Stanka Jovicevic, Chief Administrative Officer
Meetings/Conferences:
• College of Optometrists of BC 2018 Annual General Meeting, 2018, BC
Scope: Provincial
Description: The presentation of financial statements, as well as reports from the chair, the registrar, the deputy registrar, & college board members
Publications:
• College of Optometrists of BC Annual Report
Type: Yearbook; *Frequency:* Annually
Profile: A year end summary
• College of Optometrists of BC Registrant Directory
Type: Directory
Profile: Public information in the Register includes a registrant's name, class, registration number, business address, & business telephone number
• The Examiner: The Official Newsletter of The College of Optometrists of BC
Type: Newsletter
Profile: Messages from the Chair & the Registrar, plus information about fees, bylaws, & new registrants

College of Optometrists of Ontario / Ordre des optométristes de l'Ontario
#900, 65 St. Clair Ave. East, Toronto ON M4T 2Y3
Tel: 416-962-4071; *Fax:* 416-962-4073
Toll-Free: 888-825-2554
info@collegeoptom.on.ca
www.collegeoptom.on.ca
www.facebook.com/collegeoptom
twitter.com/collegeoptom
Overview: A medium-sized provincial licensing organization founded in 1919
Mission: To serve the public interest by guiding the optometry profession; To ensure that safe, ethical & quality eye care is delivered; To maintain high standards within the field
Staff Member(s): 11
Membership: *Fees:* $945; *Member Profile:* Professional optometrists; *Committees:* Executive; Registration; Inquiries, Complaints & Reports; Quality Assurance; Discipline; Patient Relations; Fitness to Practise; Optometry Review; Clinical Practice Panel
Activities: Registering & governing optometrists in Ontario; *Rents Mailing List:* Yes
Chief Officer(s):
Thomas Noël, President
Paula Garshowitz, Registrar
Louise Kassabian, Manager, Membership & Office Administration
lkassabian@collegeoptom.on.ca

College of Pharmacists of British Columbia
#200, 1765 West 8 Ave., Vancouver BC V6J 5C6
Tel: 604-733-2440; *Fax:* 604-733-2493
Toll-Free: 800-663-1940
info@bcpharmacists.org
www.bcpharmacists.org
twitter.com/BCPharmacists
Overview: A medium-sized provincial licensing organization founded in 1891 overseen by National Association of Pharmacy Regulatory Authorities
Mission: Safe & effective pharmacy practice outcomes for the people of British Columbia.
Member of: Canadian Council on Continuing Education in Pharmacy
Finances: *Funding Sources:* License & registration fees
Staff Member(s): 39
Membership: *Member Profile:* Pharmacists licensed to practice in BC; *Committees:* Audit & Finance; Communications & Engagement Advisory; Community Pharmacy Advisory Committee; Discipline; Ethics Advisory; Hospital Pharmacy; Injection Drug Administration; Inquiry; Jurisprudence; Legislation; Practice Review; Quality Assurance; Registration; Residential Care Advisory
Activities: *Internships:* Yes
Chief Officer(s):
Anar Dossa, Chair
anar.dossa@bcpharmacists.org
Bob Nakagawa, Registrar
Ashifa Keshavji, Director, Practice Reviews & Competency
Awards:
• Past President's Award
• Certificate of Merit
• Certificate of Honour
• Certificate of Recognition
• Bowl of Hygeia

College of Pharmacists of Manitoba
200 Tache Ave., Winnipeg MB R2H 1A7
Tel: 204-233-1411; *Fax:* 204-237-3468
info@cphm.ca
mpha.in1touch.org
Previous Name: Manitoba Pharmaceutical Association
Overview: A small provincial organization founded in 1878 overseen by National Association of Pharmacy Regulatory Authorities
Mission: To administer the Manitoba Pharmaceutical Act; to give license to & monitors pharmacists in the province, setingt standards of practice & investigating complaints.
Member of: Canadian Council on Continuing Education in Pharmacy; National Assn. of Pharmacy Regulatory Authorities (NAPRA); District 5, National Assn. of Boards of Pharmacy
Membership: *Committees:* Awards & Nominating; Executive; Finance & Risk Management; Governance; Professional Development; Standards of Practice
Chief Officer(s):
Glenda Marsh, President
Ronald Guse, Registrar

College of Physical Therapists of Alberta See Physiotherapy Alberta - College + Association

College of Physical Therapists of British Columbia (CPTBC)
#1420, 1200 West 73rd Ave., Vancouver BC V6P 6G5

Canadian Associations / College of Physicians & Surgeons of Alberta (CPSA)

Tel: 604-730-9193; Fax: 604-730-9273
Toll-Free: 877-576-6744
info@cptbc.org
www.cptbc.org
Overview: A medium-sized provincial organization founded in 1994 overseen by Canadian Alliance of Physiotherapy Regulators
Mission: To serve and protect the public by ensuring that Physical Therapists provide high quality, competent and ethical services.
Member of: Canadian Alliance of Physiotherapy Regulators
Finances: *Annual Operating Budget:* $1.5 Million-$3 Million; *Funding Sources:* Registration fees; application fees; interest income; permit fees; cost recovery/fines; corporation fees
Staff Member(s): 8
Membership: *Committees:* Registration; Quality Assurance; Patient Relations; Inquiry; Discipline; Legislative; Finance; Nominations Working
Chief Officer(s):
Brenda Hudson, Registrar
brenda_hudson@cptbc.org

College of Physicians & Surgeons of Alberta (CPSA)
#2700, 10020 - 100 St. NW, Edmonton AB T5J 0N3
Tel: 780-423-4764; Fax: 780-420-0651
Toll-Free: 800-561-3899
publicinquiries@cpsa.ab.ca
www.cpsa.ca
Overview: A medium-sized provincial licensing organization founded in 1905 overseen by Federation of Regulatory Authorities of Canada
Mission: To serve the public & guide the medical profession; To identify factors affecting competent medical practice; To promote quality improvement in medical practice; To ensure practitioners meet our registration standards; To resolve complaints involving practitioners fairly & effectively
Finances: *Funding Sources:* Membership fees
Staff Member(s): 48
Membership: 9,014 individual; *Fees:* $800 physcian; $500 professional corporation; *Member Profile:* Physicians practicing medicine in Alberta; *Committees:* Competence; Medical Informatics; Finance & Audit; Infection Prevention and Control; Physician Health Monitoring; Physician Prescribing Practices; Medical Facility Accreditation; Physician Performance; Executive; Complaint Review; Nominating; TPP Steering
Activities: Licensing & disciplinary body for the physicians & surgeons of Alberta
Chief Officer(s):
James Stone, President

College of Physicians & Surgeons of British Columbia (CPSBC)
#300, 699 Howe St., Vancouver BC V6C 0B4
Tel: 604-733-7758; Fax: 604-733-3503
Toll-Free: 800-461-3008
www.cpsbc.ca
www.linkedin.com/company/2905395
twitter.com/cpsbc_ca
Overview: A medium-sized provincial licensing organization founded in 1886 overseen by Federation of Regulatory Authorities of Canada
Finances: *Funding Sources:* Licensure fees
Membership: *Committees:* Executive; Finance & Audit; Registration; Inquiry; Discipline; Ethics; Patient Relations; Quality Assurance; Blood Borne Communicable Diseases; Medical Practice Assessment; Methadone Maintenance; Prescription Review; Non-Hospital Medical & Surgical Facilities Program; Diagnostic Accreditation Program; Library
Activities: *Library:* Medical Library Service; Not open to public
Chief Officer(s):
L.C. Jewett, President
Heidi Oetter, Registrar

College of Physicians & Surgeons of Manitoba (CPSM)
#1000, 1661 Portage Ave., Winnipeg MB R3J 3T7
Tel: 204-774-4344; Fax: 204-774-0750
Toll-Free: 877-774-4344
cpsm@cpsm.mb.ca
cpsm.mb.ca
Also Known As: CPS Manitoba
Overview: A medium-sized provincial licensing organization founded in 1871 overseen by Federation of Regulatory Authorities of Canada
Membership: *Committees:* Executive; Audit; Nominating; Central Standards; Complaints; Investigation; Inquiry; Appeals; Program Review
Chief Officer(s):
Brent Kvern, President
Anna Ziomek, Registrar
theregistrar@cpsm.mb.ca

College of Physicians & Surgeons of New Brunswick / Collège des médecins et chirurgiens du Nouveau-Brunswick
#300, 1 Hampton Rd., Rothesay NB E2E 5K8
Tel: 506-849-5050; Fax: 506-849-5069
Toll-Free: 800-667-4641
info@cpsnb.org
www.cpsnb.org
Overview: A medium-sized provincial licensing organization founded in 1981 overseen by Federation of Regulatory Authorities of Canada
Activities: *Rents Mailing List:* Yes
Chief Officer(s):
Lisa Jean Sutherland, President

College of Physicians & Surgeons of Newfoundland & Labrador
#W100, 120 Torbay Rd., St. John's NL A1A 2G8
Tel: 709-726-8546; Fax: 709-726-4725
cpsnl@cpsnl.ca
www.cpsnl.ca
Previous Name: Newfoundland Medical Board
Overview: A medium-sized provincial licensing organization founded in 1893 overseen by Federation of Regulatory Authorities of Canada
Mission: To protect the public; to regulate the practice of medicine & medical practitioners
Chief Officer(s):
Linda Inkpen, Registrar
Arthur Rideout, Chair
Publications:
• College of Physicians & Surgeons of Newfoundland & Labrador Annual Report
Type: Yearbook; *Frequency:* Annually
• Practice Dialogue [a publication of the College of Physicians & Surgeons of Newfoundland & Labrador]
Type: Newsletter
Profile: Published under authority of the Registrar

College of Physicians & Surgeons of Nova Scotia (CPSNS)
#5005, 7071 Bayers Rd., Halifax NS B3L 2C2
Tel: 902-422-5823; Fax: 902-422-7476
Toll-Free: 877-282-7767
info@cpsns.ns.ca
www.cpsns.ns.ca
www.linkedin.com/company/2497006
www.facebook.com/291670920671
Previous Name: Provincial Medical Board of Nova Scotia
Overview: A medium-sized provincial licensing organization founded in 1872 overseen by Federation of Regulatory Authorities of Canada
Mission: To govern the practice of medicine in the public interest
Finances: *Annual Operating Budget:* Greater than $5 Million; *Funding Sources:* Licensing fees
Membership: 3,258; *Member Profile:* Physicians
Chief Officer(s):
James MacLachlan, President

College of Physicians & Surgeons of Ontario (CPSO)
80 College St., Toronto ON M5G 2E2
Tel: 416-967-2600; Fax: 416-961-3330
Toll-Free: 800-268-7096
feedback@cpso.on.ca
www.cpso.on.ca
www.linkedin.com/groups/4760466
www.facebook.com/thecpso
twitter.com/cpso_ca
www.youtube.com/user/theCpso
Overview: A large provincial licensing organization founded in 1866 overseen by Federation of Regulatory Authorities of Canada
Mission: To ensure the best quality care for the people of Ontario by the doctors of Ontario
Finances: *Funding Sources:* Membership dues
Membership: *Fees:* $1,625; *Member Profile:* Physicians; *Committees:* Discipline; Education; Executive; Finance; Fitness to Practice; Governance; Inquiries, Complaints & Reports; Methadone; Outreach; Patient Relations; Premises Inspection; Quality Assurance; Registration
Chief Officer(s):
Steven Bodley, President
Rocco Gerace, Registrar
Awards:
• The Council Award
Eligibility: Ontario physicians
Publications:
• Dialogue [a publication of the College of the Physicians & Surgeons of Ontario]
Type: Magazine; *Frequency:* Quarterly
• Methadone News [a publication of the College of Physicians & Surgeons of Ontario]
Type: Newsletter

College of Physicians & Surgeons of Prince Edward Island
14 Paramount Dr., Charlottetown PE C1E 0C7
Tel: 902-566-3861; Fax: 902-566-3986
cpspei.ca
Previous Name: Medical Council of Prince Edward Island
Overview: A small provincial licensing organization founded in 1988 overseen by Federation of Regulatory Authorities of Canada
Mission: To act as the regulatory body for physicians in the province, responsible for licensing all medical doctors, maintaining medical standards, handling complaints from the public, & delivering disciplinary action
Staff Member(s): 4
Membership: *Member Profile:* Licensed physician in PEI
Activities: *Rents Mailing List:* Yes; *Library:* Not open to public
Chief Officer(s):
Cyril Moyse, Registrar
cmoyse@cpspei.ca
Melissa MacDonald, Office Manager
mmacdonald@cpspei.ca

College of Physicians & Surgeons of Saskatchewan (CPSS)
#101, 2174 Airport Dr., Saskatoon SK S7L 6M6
Tel: 306-244-7355; Fax: 306-244-0090
Toll-Free: 800-667-1668
cpssinfo@cps.sk.ca
www.cps.sk.ca
Overview: A medium-sized provincial organization founded in 1905 overseen by Federation of Regulatory Authorities of Canada
Mission: To be responsible for licensing properly qualified medical practitioners, developing & ensuring the standards of practice in all fields of medicine, investigating & disciplining of all doctors whose standards of medical care, ethical or professional conduct are questioned
Finances: *Funding Sources:* Membership fees
Membership: *Committees:* Competency Assessment & Maintenance; Complaints Resolution; Discipline; Health Care Facilities Credentialing; Medical Imaging; Practice Enhancement Program
Activities: *Rents Mailing List:* Yes
Chief Officer(s):
Karen Shaw, Registar & Chief Executive Officer
karen.shaw@cps.sk.ca
Micheal Howard-Tripp, Deputy Registrar & Medical Manager
micheal.howard-tripp@cps.sk.ca
Barb Porter, Director, Physician Registration
cpssreg@cps.sk.ca

College of Physiotherapists of Manitoba (CPM)
#211, 675 Pembina Hwy., Winnipeg MB R3M 2L6
Tel: 204-287-8502; Fax: 204-474-2506
info@manitobaphysio.com
www.manitobaphysio.com
Overview: A small provincial licensing organization founded in 1957 overseen by Canadian Alliance of Physiotherapy Regulators
Mission: To protect the public by ensuring quality physiotherapy is provided to the public
Member of: Canadian Alliance of Physiotherapy Regulators
Staff Member(s): 6
Membership: *Committees:* Complaints; Continuing Competency; Ethics; Inquiry; Legislative; Governance & Nominating; Physiotherpay Standards
Chief Officer(s):
Tanya Kozera, Chair
cpmchair@manitobaphysio.com

Brenda McKechnie, Registrar/Executive Director
Publications:
• In Touch Newsletter [a publication of the College of Physiotherapists of Manitoba]
Type: Newsletter

College of Physiotherapists of Ontario (CPO) / Ordre des physiothérapeutes de l'Ontario
#901, 375 University Ave., Toronto ON M5G 2J5
Tel: 416-591-3828; *Fax:* 416-591-3834
Toll-Free: 800-583-5885
info@collegept.org
www.collegept.org
twitter.com/CollegeofPTs
www.youtube.com/user/CollegeofPts
Overview: A medium-sized provincial organization founded in 1994 overseen by Canadian Alliance of Physiotherapy Regulators
Mission: To protect & serve the public interest by ensuring that physiotherapists provide high quality, competent & ethical services
Member of: Canadian Alliance of Physiotherapy Regulators
Affiliation(s): Federation of Health Regulatory Colleges of Ontario; Canadian Physiotherapy Association; Ontario Physiotherapy Association; Federation of State Boards of Physical Therapy; World Confederation of Physical Therapy
Finances: *Annual Operating Budget:* Greater than $5 Million; *Funding Sources:* Membership fees
Staff Member(s): 24
Membership: 7,792; *Member Profile:* Physiotherapists registered to practice in Ontario; *Committees:* Executive; Inquiries, Complaints & Reports; Discipline & Fitness; Patient Relations; Registration; Quality Management; Finance
Activities: Registering physiotherapists for practice in Ontario; dealing with concerns about members' practices from the public; annual meeting, June; *Speaker Service:* Yes
Chief Officer(s):
Rod Hamilton, Associate Registrar, Policy Ext. 232
rhamilton@collegept.org
Shenda Tanchak, Registrar & CEO
Lisa Pretty, Communications Director
Awards:
• Award of Distinction

College of Podiatric Physicians of Alberta (CPPA)
#2020, 61 Broadway Blvd., Sherwood Park AB T8H 2C1
Tel: 780-922-7609
www.albertapodiatry.com
Overview: A small provincial organization founded in 1932
Mission: To act in accordance with the Podiatry Act, under the Statutes of Alberta; To advance the profession of podiatry in Alberta
Member of: American Podiatric Medical Association, Inc., Region 7
Membership: *Member Profile:* Medical doctors in Alberta who specialize in treating ailments of the feet & ankles; Members must act in accordance with the Code of Conduct of the College of Podiatric Physicians of Alberta
Activities: Disciplining members; Registering candidates who qualify under The Podiatry Act
Chief Officer(s):
Jayne Jeneroux, Executive Director
Bradley Sonnema, President
president@albertapodiatry.com

College of Podiatrists of Manitoba (COPOM)
#512, 428 Portage Ave., Winnipeg MB R3C 0E2
Tel: 204-942-3256
www.copom.org
Overview: A small provincial licensing organization
Mission: The College is a provincial regulatory body that protects the public by ensuring podiatrists in Mantioba follow the standards of practice defined in The Podiatry Act, 2001.
Membership: *Member Profile:* Provincially registered podiatrists
Chief Officer(s):
Iain Palmer, Chair
Martin Colledge, Registrar
Registrar@copom.org

College of Psychologists of British Columbia (CPBC)
#404, 1755 West Broadway, Vancouver BC V6J 4S5
Tel: 604-736-6164; *Fax:* 604-736-6133
Toll-Free: 800-665-0979
www.collegeofpsychologists.bc.ca
Overview: A medium-sized provincial organization

Mission: To regulate the profession of psychology in British Columbia by establishing practice standards & taking action when standards are not met
Staff Member(s): 3
Membership: *Fees:* $1200 active register; $600 limited register (non-practicing or out-of-province); $150 limited register (retired); *Committees:* Registration; Quality Assurance; Inquiry; Discipline; Patient Relations
Chief Officer(s):
Andrea Kowaz, Registrar & CEO
Amy Janeck, Deputy Registrar
Susan Turnbull, Director, Practice Support
David Perry, Director, Policy & External Relations
Publications:
• The Chronicle [a publication of the College of Psychologists of British Columbia]
Type: Newsletter

College of Psychologists of New Brunswick (CPNB) / Collège des psychologues du Nouveau-Brunswick
PO Box 201, Stn. A, Fredericton NB E3B 4Y9
Tel: 506-382-1994; *Fax:* 506-857-9813
Other Communication: Address: #435, 236 St. George St., Moncton, NB E1C 1W1
admin@cpnb.ca
www.cpnb.ca
www.facebook.com/1869589116588642
twitter.com/CPNBPsychology
Overview: A small provincial licensing organization founded in 1965
Mission: To regulate the practice of psychology; to represent the interests of its members
Staff Member(s): 3
Chief Officer(s):
Douglas French, L.Psych., President
Mandy McLean, Executive Director
mandy.mclean@cpnb.ca

The College of Psychologists of Ontario (CPO)
#500, 110 Eglinton Ave. West, Toronto ON M4R 1A3
Tel: 416-961-8817; *Fax:* 416-961-2635
Toll-Free: 800-489-8388
cpo@cpo.on.ca
www.cpo.on.ca
Overview: A large provincial licensing organization
Mission: To monitor & regulate the practice of psychology in Ontario
Finances: *Funding Sources:* Registration & application fees
Membership: *Member Profile:* Psychologists & Psychological Associates; *Committees:* Executive; Client Relations; Discipline; Finance & Audit; Fitness to Practice; Inquiries, Complaints & Reports; Jurisprudence & Ethics; Nominations & Leadership Development; Quality Assurance; Registration
Chief Officer(s):
Rick Morris, Registrar & Executive Director
Publications:
• The College of Psychologists of Ontario Standards of Professional Conduct
Type: Manual; *Number of Pages:* 22
Profile: Members of the College of Psychologists must adhere to the standards while practicing the profession
• e-Bulletin [a publication of the College of Psychologists of Ontario]
Type: Newsletter
Profile: Articles, discipline proceedings, by-law amendments, & committee & council news

College of Registered Dental Hygienists of Alberta (CRDHA)
#302, 8657 - 51 Ave., Edmonton AB T6E 6A8
Tel: 780-465-1756; *Fax:* 780-440-0544
Toll-Free: 877-465-1756
info@crdha.ca
www.crdha.ca
Overview: A small provincial licensing organization
Mission: To regulate the practice of dental hygiene for the public; To advance the profession of dental hygiene
Finances: *Annual Operating Budget:* $3 Million-$5 Million
Membership: *Member Profile:* Registered dental hygienists in Alberta; *Committees:* Registration; Competence
Chief Officer(s):
Brenda Walker, CEO & Registrar

College of Registered Nurses of British Columbia (CRNBC)
2855 Arbutus St., Vancouver BC V6J 3Y8

Tel: 604-736-7331; *Fax:* 604-738-2272
Toll-Free: 800-565-6505
info@crnbc.ca
www.crnbc.ca
www.facebook.com/CRNBC
twitter.com/CRNBC
Previous Name: Registered Nurses Association of British Columbia
Overview: A large provincial licensing organization founded in 1912 overseen by Canadian Nurses Association
Mission: To provide safe & appropriate nursing practice regulated by nurses in the public interest; To promote good practice, prevent poor practice & intervene when practice is unacceptable
Finances: *Funding Sources:* Membership fees; grants; sales
Membership: *Member Profile:* Registered nurses; *Committees:* Certified Practices Approval; Disipline; Education Program Review; Finance & Audit; Inquiry; Nominations; Nurse Practitioner Examination; Nurse Practitioner Standards; Quality Assurance; Registration
Activities: *Speaker Service:* Yes; *Library:* by appointment
Chief Officer(s):
Cynthia Johansen, CEO/Registrar
ceo@crnbc.ca
Meetings/Conferences:
• Association of Registered Nurses of British Columbia 2018 Annual General Meeting, 2018, BC
Scope: Provincial
Publications:
• Nursing Matters [a publication of the College of Registered Nurses of British Columbia]
Type: Newsletter; *Frequency:* 10-11 times pa

College of Registered Nurses of Manitoba (CRNM)
890 Pembina Hwy., Winnipeg MB R3M 2M8
Tel: 204-774-3477; *Fax:* 204-775-6052
Toll-Free: 800-665-2027
registration@crnm.mb.ca
www.crnm.mb.ca
www.facebook.com/collegeofrnsmb
Previous Name: Manitoba Association of Registered Nurses
Overview: A medium-sized provincial licensing organization founded in 1913 overseen by Canadian Nurses Association
Mission: To regulate the practice of registered nurses; To advance the quality of nursing to protect the public interest
Staff Member(s): 30
Chief Officer(s):
Katherine Stansfield, Executive Director, 204-784-5188
kstansfield@crnm.mb.ca
Tammy Murdoch, Manager, Registration Services, 204-784-6460
tmurdoch@crnm.mb.ca
Kristin Hancock, Manager, Communications, 204-789-0662
khancock@crnm.mb.ca

College of Registered Nurses of Nova Scotia (CRNNS)
#4005, 7071 Bayers Rd., Halifax NS B3L 2C2
Tel: 902-491-9744; *Fax:* 902-491-9510
Toll-Free: 800-565-9744
info@crnns.ca
www.crnns.ca
Previous Name: Registered Nurses Association of Nova Scotia
Overview: A medium-sized provincial licensing organization founded in 1910 overseen by Canadian Nurses Association
Mission: Registered nurses regulating their profession to promote excellence in nursing practice.
Finances: *Funding Sources:* Membership fees
Staff Member(s): 29
Membership: 10,303; *Member Profile:* Registered nurses; *Committees:* Complaints; Professional Conduct; Education Advisory; Registration Appeal; Reinstatement; Nurse Practitioner; Interdisciplinary Nurse Practitioner Practice Review; Fitness to Practise; Nominations; Awards Selections
Chief Officer(s):
Sue Smith, CEO & Registrar, 902-491-9744 Ext. 223
ssmith@crnns.ca

College of Registered Psychiatric Nurses of Alberta
#201, 9711 - 45 Ave., Edmonton AB T6E 5V8
Tel: 780-434-7666; *Fax:* 780-436-4165
Toll-Free: 877-234-7666
crpna@crpna.ab.ca
www.crpna.ab.ca
Previous Name: Registered Psychiatric Nurses Association of Alberta

Overview: A medium-sized provincial organization
Mission: To protect & serve the public interest by ensuring members provide safe, competent & ethical practice; To address the needs of members & the public through education, regulation, & advocacy
Membership: *Committees:* Finance; Education; Continuing Competence; Personnel; Recognition & Awards; Education Fund Selection
Chief Officer(s):
Mary Haase, President
Barbara Lowe, Executive Director
barbara.lowe@crpna.ab.ca

College of Registered Psychiatric Nurses of B.C. (CRPNBC)
#307, 2502 St. Johns St., Port Moody BC V3H 2B4
Tel: 604-931-5200; *Fax:* 604-931-5277
Toll-Free: 800-565-2505
crpnbc@crpnbc.ca
www.crpnbc.ca
Overview: A small provincial organization
Mission: To serve & protect the public through self-regulation, assuring a safe, accountable, & ethical level of psychiatric nursing practice
Staff Member(s): 4
Membership: *Fees:* $357 practicing Members; $63 non-practicing members; *Committees:* Inquiry; Patient Relations & Professional Practice; Quality Assurance; Registration
Chief Officer(s):
Kyong-ae Kim, CEO
kkim@crpnbc.ca
Fiona Ramsay, Registrar & Director, Operations
framsay@crpnbc.ca
Publications:
• College of Registered Psychiatric Nurses of BC Annual Report
Type: Yearbook; *Frequency:* Annually

College of Registered Psychiatric Nurses of British Columbia
#307, 2502 St. Johns St., Port Moody BC V3H 2B4
Tel: 604-931-5200; *Fax:* 604-931-5277
Toll-Free: 800-565-2505
www.crpnbc.ca
Previous Name: Registered Psychiatric Nurses Association of British Columbia
Overview: A medium-sized provincial organization founded in 1974
Mission: To serve & protect the public; to assure a safe, accountable & ethical level of psychiatric nursing practice
Membership: *Committees:* Registration; Quality Assurance; Patient Relations & Professional Practice; Inquiry
Chief Officer(s):
Dorothy Jennings, Chair
Kyong-ae Kim, Executive Director & Registrar
Publications:
• The Communicator
Type: Magazine; *Frequency:* Quarterly; *Accepts Advertising;*
Editor: Dr. Jacqollyne Keath

College of Registered Psychiatric Nurses of Manitoba (CRPNM)
1854 Portage Ave., Winnipeg MB R3J 0G9
Tel: 204-888-4841; *Fax:* 204-888-8638
www.crpnm.mb.ca
Previous Name: Registered Psychiatric Nurses Association of Manitoba
Overview: A medium-sized provincial licensing organization founded in 1960
Mission: To ensure that members of the profession provide safe & effective psychiatric nursing services to the public of Manitoba, in accordance with the Registered Psychiatric Nurses Act
Staff Member(s): 4
Membership: *Fees:* $515.14 practicing; $105 non-practicing; *Committees:* Investigations; Discipline; Psychiatric Nursing Education; Governance; Quality Assurance
Activities: *Library:*
Chief Officer(s):
Laura Panteluk, Executive Director
Publications:
• Annual Report of The College of Registered Psychiatric Nurses of Manitoba
Type: Yearbook; *Frequency:* Annually
• CRPNM [College of Registered Psychiatric Nurses of Manitoba] Advisor

College of Registered Psychotherapists of Ontario (CRPO)
163 Queen St. East, 4th Fl., Toronto ON M5A 1S21
Tel: 416-862-4801; *Fax:* 416-974-4079
Toll-Free: 888-661-4801
info@crpo.ca
www.crpo.ca
Overview: A small provincial licensing organization
Mission: To regulate the profession of psychotherapy & to maintain professional, ethical standards.
Membership: *Committees:* Client Relations; Discipline; Examination; Executive; Fitness to Practise; Inquiries, Complaints & Reports; Nominations & Elections; Quality Assurance; Registration
Chief Officer(s):
Joyce Rowlands, Registrar

College of Respiratory Therapists of Ontario (CRTO)
#2103, 180 Dundas St. West, Toronto ON M5G 1Z8
Tel: 416-591-7800; *Fax:* 416-591-7890
Toll-Free: 800-261-0528
questions@crto.on.ca
www.crto.on.ca
twitter.com/theCRTO
www.youtube.com/user/TheCRTO
Overview: A medium-sized provincial licensing organization
Mission: To regulate the profession of respiratory care in Ontario
Staff Member(s): 8
Membership: *Fees:* $500; *Committees:* Discipline; Executive; Fitness to Practice; ICRC; Patient Relations; Quality Assurance; Registration
Chief Officer(s):
David Jones, President

College of the Rockies Faculty Association (CORFA)
PO Box 8500, 2700 College Way, Cranbrook BC V1C 5L7
Tel: 250-489-8251
www.corfa.org
www.facebook.com/CollegeOftheRockiesFA
Previous Name: East Kootenay Community College Faculty Association
Overview: A small local organization founded in 1976
Mission: To bargain a collective agreement on behalf of the College of the Rockies faculty members
Member of: College & Institutes Educators Association (CIEA)
Affiliation(s): Canadian Association of University Teachers; East Kootenay District Labour Council; Federation of Post-Secondary Educators of BC
Finances: *Annual Operating Budget:* $50,000-$100,000
Membership: 150; *Committees:* Awards; College Diversity; College Policy; Disability Management; Education Council; Employee Family Assistance Program; Executive; Faculty Development; Faculty Labour Management; Occupational Health & Safety; Program Review Oversight; Student Affairs Policy; Sustainability; Wellness
Chief Officer(s):
Joan Kaun, President

College of Traditional Chinese Medicine Practitioners & Acupuncturists of British Columbia (CTCMABC)
1664 - West 8th Ave., Vancouver BC V6J 1V4
Tel: 604-738-7100; *Fax:* 604-738-7171
info@ctcma.bc.ca
www.ctcma.bc.ca
Overview: A small provincial organization founded in 1996
Mission: To protect the public by establishing a system of mandatory registration in which practitioners have to meet & maintain standards in TCM & acupuncture care established by the College
Chief Officer(s):
Mary S. Watterson, Registrar & CEO
Publications:
• Balance [a publication of the College of Traditional Chinese Medicine Practitioners & Acupuncturists of British Columbia]
Type: Newsletter; *Frequency:* 4 pa

College of Veterinarians of British Columbia (CVBC)
#107, 828 Harbourside Dr., North Vancouver BC V7P 3R9
Tel: 604-929-7090; *Fax:* 604-929-7095
Toll-Free: 800-463-5399
reception@cvbc.ca
www.cvbc.ca
Previous Name: British Columbia Veterinary Medical Association

Overview: A medium-sized provincial licensing organization founded in 1907 overseen by Canadian Veterinary Medical Association
Mission: To serve members by promoting their professional image, providing a forum for addressing issues of importance to the profession, offering continuing education & protecting their interests & rights; to protect & serve animals & animal custodians through evaluation of veterinary competence & facility quality & by enforcing the Veterinarians Act & Bylaws
Finances: *Funding Sources:* Membership dues
Staff Member(s): 8
Membership: 2,445; *Fees:* Schedule available; *Member Profile:* Veterinarians
Chief Officer(s):
Larry W. Odegard, Registrar & CEO
John Brocklebank, Deputy Registrar

College of Veterinarians of Ontario (CVO)
2106 Gordon St., Guelph ON N1L 1G6
Tel: 519-824-5600; *Fax:* 519-824-6497
Toll-Free: 800-424-2856
inquiries@cvo.org
www.cvo.org
www.linkedin.com/company/the-college-of-veterinarians-of-ontario
twitter.com/cvo_org
Overview: A medium-sized provincial licensing organization founded in 1872
Mission: To protect the public by regulating & enhancing the veterinary profession in Ontario
Membership: *Committees:* Accreditation; Complaints; Discipline; Executive; Quality Assurance; Registration
Activities: *Rents Mailing List:* Yes
Chief Officer(s):
Marc Marin, President
president@cvo.org
Jan Robinson, Registrar & Chief Executive Officer
registrarsinbox@cvo.org
Publications:
• College of Veterinarians of Ontario Update
; *ISSN:* 0821-6320
Profile: Comprehensive, accurate & defensible information about regulatory issues for members

Collège royal canadien des organistes *See* Royal Canadian College of Organists

Collège Royal des Chirurgiens Dentistes du Canada *See* Royal College of Dentists of Canada

Le Collège royal des médecins et chirurgiens du Canada *See* The Royal College of Physicians & Surgeons of Canada

Colleges and Institutes Canada (CICan) / Collèges et instituts Canada
#701, 1 Rideau St., Ottawa ON K1N 8S7
Tel: 613-746-2222; *Fax:* 613-746-6721
info@collegesinstitutes.ca
www.collegesinstitutes.ca
www.facebook.com/collegesinstitutes
twitter.com/CollegeCan
www.instagram.com/College_can
Previous Name: Association des collèges communautaires du Canada
Overview: A large national organization
Mission: To represent publicly supported colleges, institutes, cégeps, & polytechnics in Canada & Internationally
Finances: *Annual Operating Budget:* Greater than $5 Million; *Funding Sources:* Membership fees
Staff Member(s): 55
Membership: 150 colleges, institutes & groups; *Fees:* Based on overall operating revenue of each institution; *Member Profile:* Regular (publicly-funded institutions); Associates (privately-funded institutions & educational organizations); *Committees:* Canadian Program Advisory & International Program Advisory Committees; Program Review
Activities: Awards Program; Canadian College Partnership Program; Student Mobility Program
Chief Officer(s):
Denise Amyot, President & CEO, 613-746-2222 Ext. 6492
damyot@collegesinstitutes.ca
Leah Jurkovic, Director, 613-746-2222 Ext. 3119
ljurkovic@collegesinstitutes.ca
Awards:
• Indigenous Education Excellence
• Applied Research & Innovation Excellence
• Internationalization Excellence

- Leadership Excellence
- Program Excellence
- Staff Excellence
- Student Leadership Excellence
- Faculty Leadership Excellence

Meetings/Conferences:
• Colleges and Institutes Canada 2018 Conference, April, 2018, Victoria, BC
Scope: National
Attendance: 800

Collèges et instituts Canada *See* Colleges and Institutes Canada

Colleges Ontario
PO Box 88, #1600, 20 Bay St., Toronto ON M5J 2N8
Tel: 647-258-7670; *Fax:* 647-258-7699
www.collegesontario.org
www.linkedin.com/company/network-for-innovation-and-entrepreneurship
www.facebook.com/CollegesOntario
twitter.com/CollegesOntario
www.youtube.com/user/CollegesOntario1?feature=mhee
Previous Name: Association of Colleges of Applied Arts & Technology of Ontario
Overview: A medium-sized provincial organization
Mission: To represent Ontario colleges; To advocate on provincial & national issues on behalf of its membership
Membership: Ontario's 24 colleges of applied arts & technology; *Fees:* Schedule available
Activities: *Speaker Service:* Yes
Chief Officer(s):
Linda Franklin, President & CEO, 647-258-7676
franklin@collegesontario.org
Rob Savage, Director, Communications, 647-258-7687
savage@collegesontario.org
Caroline Donkin, Director, Member Services & Special Projects, 647-258-7673
donkin@collegesontario.org
Bill Summers, Vice-President, Research & Policy, 647-258-7689
summers@collegesontario.org
Awards:
• Premier's Awards
The Premier's Awards recognize outstanding college graduates from Ontario's 24 public colleges. Presented annually in six categories: Business, Community Services, Creative Arts and Design, Health Sciences, Recent Graduate and Technology.
Contact: Specialist, Events: Yvonne Leoveras,
leoveras@collegesontario.org
• Minister's Lifetime Achievement Award
Recognizes success in advancing Ontario college education.
Contact: Specialist, Events: Yvonne Leoveras,
leoveras@collegesontario.org

Heads, Libraries and Learning Resources (HLLR)
c/o Karla Van Kessel, Fanshawe College, 1001 Fanshawe College Blvd., London ON N5Y 5R6
www.hllr.org
Mission: To advocate on behalf of students for the best possible college library services & resources; To provide a forum for the discussion of issues, trends, & concerns related to the field of learning resources in Ontario colleges.
Chief Officer(s):
Karla Van Kessel, Vice-Chair, HLLR Executive, 519-452-4430 Ext. 4351, Fax: 519-452-4473
kvankessel@fanshawec.ca

Collingwood & District Historical Society
PO Box 181, Collingwood ON L9Y 3Z5
Tel: 705-446-1820
www.historicallyspeakingcdhs.ca
www.facebook.com/collingwoodhistoricalsociety
www.youtube.com/channel/UC9SzLj34EcxEVN8LsAlUJGQ
Overview: A small local organization founded in 1976
Mission: To research, record, preserve & promotoe public interest in the history of the Collingwood district; to identify structures of historical & architectural merit in the district & promotes their preservation.
Member of: Heritage Canada, Ontario Historical Society; Simcoe County Historical Association
Finances: *Funding Sources:* Membership fees
Membership: *Fees:* $20 individual; $30 couple/corporate
Activities: Tours of historic homes; regular meetings with speakers
Chief Officer(s):
Bruce Mackison, President
Joan Miller, Secretary

Publications:
• Historically Speaking
Type: newsletter

Collingwood Chamber of Commerce
#102, 115 Hurontario St., Collingwood ON L9Y 2L9
Tel: 705-445-0221
info@collingwoodchamber.com
www.collingwoodchamber.com
www.facebook.com/Collingwood-Chamber-of-Commerce-172645832762961
twitter.com/CwoodChamber
Overview: A small local organization founded in 1880
Mission: To act as the recognized voice of business committed to the enhancement of economic prosperity in the Collingwood area
Affiliation(s): Canadian Chamber of Commerce; Ontario Chamber of Commerce
Staff Member(s): 2
Membership: *Fees:* Schedule available; *Member Profile:* Business; non-profit organizations; individuals; *Committees:* Government; Marketing
Activities: Training seminars; social; networking events
Chief Officer(s):
John Alsop, President
Trish Irwin, General Manager & CEO
tirwin@collingwoodchamber.com

Collingwood Community Living *See* E3 Community Services

Colon Cancer Canada / Cancer du Colon Canada
#204A, 5915 Leslie St., Toronto ON M2H 1J8
Tel: 416-785-0449; *Fax:* 416-785-0450
Toll-Free: 888-571-8547
info@coloncancercanada.ca
www.coloncancercanada.ca
www.facebook.com/coloncancercda
twitter.com/ColonCancerCda
Previous Name: National Colorectal Cancer Campaign
Overview: A small national organization founded in 1996
Mission: To raise public awareness for the disease of colorectal cancer & to raise money for vital research
Staff Member(s): 5
Activities: Charity golf tournament; fundraisers; *Awareness Events:* Colon Cancer Awareness Month, March
Chief Officer(s):
Bunnie Schwartz, President/Co-Founder
hmschwartz@rogers.com
Amy Lerman-Elmaleh, Executive Director/Co-Founder
amy@coloncancercanada.ca

Colorectal Cancer Association of Canada (CCAC)
#204, 60 St. Clair Ave. East, Toronto ON M4T 1N5
Tel: 416-920-4333; *Fax:* 416-920-3004
information@colorectal-cancer.ca
www.colorectal-cancer.ca
www.facebook.com/Colorectal
twitter.com/coloncanada
www.youtube.com/user/ccac1230
Overview: A small national organization
Mission: To support people with colorectal cancer, their families & caregivers; to improve the quality of life of patients & increase awareness of the disease
Activities: *Awareness Events:* Colorectal Cancer Awareness Month, March
Chief Officer(s):
Barry D. Stein, President
barrys@colorectal-cancer.ca

Columbia Valley Chamber of Commerce (CVCC)
PO Box 1019, 651 Hwy. 93/85, Invermere BC V0A 1K0
Tel: 250-342-2844; *Fax:* 250-342-3261
info@cvchamber.ca
www.cvchamber.ca
www.facebook.com/ColumbiaValleyChamber
twitter.com/cv_chamber
Overview: A small local organization founded in 1991
Mission: To promote the economic prosperity of the area & its residents
Affiliation(s): British Columbia Chamber of Commerce
Finances: *Annual Operating Budget:* $100,000-$250,000; *Funding Sources:* British Columbia Ministry of Small Business, Tourism, & Culture; District of Invermere; Membership dues; Fundraising
Staff Member(s): 1
Membership: 320; *Fees:* Schedule available; *Member Profile:* Business; professionals & individuals

Activities: *Awareness Events:* Chamber Week, Feb.; Small Business Week, Oct.; *Library:* Open to public
Chief Officer(s):
Susan E. Clovechok, Executive Director

Columbia Valley Chamber of Commerce; Invermere Business Committee; Fairmont Business Association; Windermere Board of Trade *See* Radium Hot Springs Chamber of Commerce

Comité canadien d'action sur le statut de la femme *See* National Action Committee on the Status of Women

Comité canadien de catalogage *See* Canadian Committee on Cataloguing

Comité canadien des étudiants et étudiantes aux cycles supérieurs en éducation *See* Canadian Committee of Graduate Students in Education

Comité canadien du MARC *See* Canadian Committee on MARC

Comité canadien sur l'histoire du travail *See* Canadian Committee on Labour History

Comité condition féminine Baie-James
#203, 552 - 3e rue, Chibougamau QC G8P 1N9
Tél: 418-748-4408; *Téléc:* 418-748-2486
ccfbj@tlb.sympatico.ca
ccfbj.com
Aperçu: *Dimension:* moyenne; *Envergure:* locale; fondée en 2001
Mission: A pour mission l'amélioration des conditions de vie des Jamésiennes
Membre: 5 membres individuelles; 13 associations
Membre(s) du bureau directeur:
Gérald Lemoine, Présidente

Comité culturel "La Chaussée"
Cap-Pelé NB
Aperçu: *Dimension:* petite; *Envergure:* locale; Organisme sans but lucratif; fondée en 1979
Mission: Le Comité culturel La Chaussée oeuvre en collaboration avec la municipalité, les écoles et autres organismes communautaires, pour promouvoir la fierté communautaire à travers la création et l'expression dans divers domaines culturels: théâtre, musique populaire et traditionnelle, spectacles, littérature et beaux-arts
Membre de: Conseil de promotion et de diffusion de la culture
Finances: *Budget de fonctionnement annuel:* Moins de $50,000
6 bénévole(s)
Membre: 1-99; *Critères d'admissibilite:* Oeuvre en collaboration avec la municipalité, les écoles et autres organismes communautaires, pour promouvoir la fierté communautaire à travers la création et l'expression dans divers domaines culturels: théâtre, musique populaire et traditionnelle, spectacles, littérature et beaux-arts

Comité d'action des citoyennes et citoyens de Verdun
3972, rue de Verdun, Verdun QC H4G 1K9
Tél: 514-769-2228; *Téléc:* 514-769-0825
www.cacv-verdun.org
Aperçu: *Dimension:* petite; *Envergure:* locale; fondée en 1975
Mission: Le CACV soutien les personnes les plus démunies afin qu'elles améliorent leurs conditions de vie dans une optique de prise en charge
Membre(s) du personnel: 4
Membre(s) du bureau directeur:
Chantal Lamarre, Directrice

Comité d'action Parc Extension (CAPE)
#03, 419, rue St-Roch, Montréal QC H3N 1K2
Tél: 514-278-6028; *Téléc:* 514-278-0900
Aperçu: *Dimension:* petite; *Envergure:* locale; fondée en 1986
Mission: A pour mission d'améliorer les conditions de vie de tous les citoyens/citoyennes du quartier Parc Extension
Membre(s) du bureau directeur:
Denis Giraldeau, Coordonnateur

Comité de bénévolat de Rogersville
#12, 11133, rue Principale, Rogersville NB E4Y 2N4
Tél: 506-775-2811
Aperçu: *Dimension:* petite; *Envergure:* locale
Mission: Aider les familles démunies en leur fournissant une boîte de nourriture
Membre de: Association of Food Banks & C.V.A. for New Brunswick; Atlantic Alliance of Food Banks & C.V.A.

Finances: *Budget de fonctionnement annuel:* Moins de $50,000
Membre: 1-99; *Montant de la cotisation:* 25$

Comité de parents du Nouveau-Brunswick *Voir* Association francophone des parents du Nouveau-Brunswick

Comité de solidarité tiers-monde/Trois-Rivières *Voir* Comité de solidarité/Trois-Rivières

Comité de solidarité/Trois-Rivières
942, rue Ste-Geneviève, Trois-Rivières QC G9A 3X6
Tél: 819-373-2598; *Téléc:* 819-373-7892
www.cs3r.org
www.facebook.com/comitedesolidarite
Nom précédent: Comité de solidarité tiers-monde/Trois-Rivières
Aperçu: *Dimension:* petite; *Envergure:* internationale; Organisme sans but lucratif; fondée en 1973
Mission: De contribuer à l'édification d'un monde plus juste et plus harmonieux où l'ensemble des peuples et des citoyens et citoyennes qui en font partie se partageraient équitablement les ressources et les richesses de la planète; promouvoir la solidarité avec les peuples de l'Afrique, de l'Amérique latine, du Moyen-Orient; se concrétise par des activités d'information, d'éducation, et des campagnes publiques que le Comité organise dans les écoles, les médias, les organisations populaires et syndicales et dans le grand public
Membre de: Solidarité Canada Sahel; Solidarité Populaire Québec; Corporation développement communautaire
Affiliation(s): Association québécoise des organismes de coopération internationale
Finances: *Budget de fonctionnement annuel:* $500,000-$1.5 Million
Membre(s) du personnel: 8; 50 bénévole(s)
Membre: 2 500; *Comités:* Action solidaire; Jeunesse; Femme et développement; Réseau d'urgence; Communication
Activités: Rendez-vous ethnique; animation Tiers Monde; stages à l'étranger; campagnes de solidarité; *Stagiaires:* Oui; *Bibliothèque:* Bibliothèque publique
Membre(s) du bureau directeur:
Jean-Marc Lord, Directeur général
jean.marc.lord@cs3r.org

Comité des citoyens et citoyennes du quartier Saint-Sauveur
301, rue Carillon, Québec QC G1K 5B3
Tél: 418-529-6158; *Téléc:* 418-529-9455
cccqss@bellnet.ca
www.cccqss.org
www.facebook.com/CCCQSS
Aperçu: *Dimension:* petite; *Envergure:* locale
Membre: *Montant de la cotisation:* 3$ les personnes sans emploi; 5$ ceux qui travaillent

Comité des orphelins victimes d'abus (COVA)
1710, rue Beaudry, Montréal QC H2L E37
Tél: 514-523-3843
Aperçu: *Dimension:* petite; *Envergure:* locale
Mission: De faire respecter les droits des orphelins qui ont été abusés physiquement et sexuellement

Comité des personnes atteintes du VIH du Québec (CPAVIH)
#310, 2075, rue Plessis, Montréal QC H2L 2Y4
Tél: 514-521-8720; *Téléc:* 514-521-9633
Ligne sans frais: 800-927-2844
cpavih@cpavih.qc.ca
Aperçu: *Dimension:* moyenne; *Envergure:* provinciale; Organisme sans but lucratif; fondée en 1987
Mission: Informer les personnes vivant avec le VIH/SIDA; promouvoir leurs droits afin d'améliorer leur qualité de vie
Membre de: Canadian AIDS Society
Finances: *Fonds:* Gouvernemental; corporatif; privé
Membre: *Critères d'admissibilite:* Personnes atteintes du VIH/SIDA
Activités: Info-traitements; info juridique; activités socio-culturelles; centre de documentation; *Bibliothèque:* Centre de documentation; rendez-vous

Comité du patrimoine paysager estrien (CPPE)
#300, 230, rue King ouest, Sherbrooke QC J1H 1P9
Tél: 819-563-1911
info@paysagesestriens.qc.ca
www.paysagesestriens.qc.ca
Aperçu: *Dimension:* petite; *Envergure:* locale; fondée en 2001
Mission: Sensibiliser, informer et promouvoir la préservation et la valorisation du patrimoine paysager estrien auprès de la collectivité régionale.

Activités: Campagne de sensibilisation et d'information; causerie-conférence; affiche promotionnelle; rédaction d'une Charte du patrimoine paysager estrien

Comité du SIDA d'Ottawa *See* AIDS Committee of Ottawa

Comité du sida de North Bay et de la région *See* AIDS Committee of North Bay & Area

Comité logement de Lacine-Lasalle
426, rue St-Jacques ouest, Lachine QC H8R 1E8
Tél: 514-544-4294; *Téléc:* 514-366-0505
logement.lachine-lasalle@videotron.ca
Aperçu: *Dimension:* petite; *Envergure:* locale
Membre(s) du bureau directeur:
Daniel Chainey, Responsable

Comité logement du Plateau Mont-Royal
#328, 4450, rue St-Hubert, Montréal QC H2J 2W9
Tél: 514-527-3495; *Téléc:* 514-527-6653
clplateau@yahoo.ca
sites.google.com/site/comitelogementplateau
Aperçu: *Dimension:* petite; *Envergure:* locale; fondée en 1975

Comité logement Rosemont
#R-145, 5350, rue Lafond, Montréal QC H1X 2X2
Tél: 514-597-2581; *Téléc:* 514-524-9813
info@comitelogement.org
www.comitelogement.org
www.facebook.com/comitelogement
Aperçu: *Dimension:* petite; *Envergure:* locale; fondée en 1977
Mission: Défendre et promouvoir les droits des locataires du quartier Rosemont
Membre(s) du personnel: 4
Membre: 500-600; *Montant de la cotisation:* 3$
Membre(s) du bureau directeur:
Martine Poitras, Coordonnatrice

Comité olympique canadien *See* Canadian Olympic Committee

Comité paralympique canadien *See* Canadian Paralympic Committee

Comité pour la justice sociale *See* Social Justice Committee

Comité québécois femmes et développement (CQFD)
#540, 1001, rue Sherbrooke est, Montréal QC H2L 1L3
Tél: 514-871-1086; *Téléc:* 514-871-9866
Aperçu: *Dimension:* petite; *Envergure:* provinciale; fondée en 1984 surveillé par Association Québécoise des organismes de coopération internationale
Mission: Le CQFD est un regroupement de femmes du milieu des organismes de coopération internationale, du milieu universitaire, syndical et groupes de femmes du Québec. Ses objectifs sont de favoriser la concertation, la réflexion et le partenariat entre groupes de femmes du Nord et du Sud

Comité régional d'éducation pour le développement international de Lanaudière (CRÉDIL)
200, rue de Salaberry, Joliette QC J6E 4G1
Tél: 450-756-0011; *Téléc:* 450-759-8749
info@credil.qc.ca
www.credil.qc.ca
www.facebook.com/credil.joliette
Aperçu: *Dimension:* petite; *Envergure:* locale; Organisme sans but lucratif; fondée en 1976
Mission: Promouvoir l'éducation au développement international dans la région de Lanaudière, la solidarité avec des organisations populaires d'ici et celles d'autres pays pour appuyer les initiatives de partenariat, l'initiation et support d'engagements concrets en appui aux efforts de justice dans le monde; accueil de nouveaux arrivants dans la région de Lanaudière.
Affiliation(s): Association québécoise d'organismes de coopération internationale; Emploi Québec
Finances: *Fonds:* Ministère de l'Immigration et des Communautés culturelles; Ministère des Relations internationales
Membre(s) du personnel: 6
Membre: *Montant de la cotisation:* 10$ individuel; 50$ organisationnel; *Critères d'admissibilité:* Individuel et corporatif
Activités: Journées québécoises de la solidarité internationale; stages de coopération internationale; kiosque de produits équitables; aide aux devoirs; jumelage; logement; *Événements de sensibilisation:* Journées québécoises de la solidarité internationale, nov.; *Stagiaires:* Oui
Membre(s) du bureau directeur:

Daniel Tessier, Coordonnateur par intérim
coordination@credil.qc.ca

Comité régional des associations pour la déficience intellectuelle (CRADI)
#100, 5095 - 9e av, Montréal QC H1Y 2J3
Tél: 514-255-8111; *Téléc:* 514-255-3444
cradi@cradi.com
www.cradi.com
Aperçu: *Dimension:* petite; *Envergure:* locale
Membre: 31
Membre(s) du bureau directeur:
Djamila Benabdelkader, Présidente

Comité Social Centre-Sud (CSCS)
1710, rue Beaudry, Montréal QC H2L 3E7
Tél: 514-596-7092; *Téléc:* 514-596-7093
webmestre@comitesocialcentresud.org
www.comitesocialcentresud.org
Aperçu: *Dimension:* petite; *Envergure:* locale; fondée en 1971
Mission: Pour aider les membres de la communauté à faire face aux injustices sociales qu'ils peuvent faire face et leur offrir une éducation dans divers domaines
Membre: *Montant de la cotisation:* 5$
Activités: Événements; sorties; cours; atelier de couture
Membre(s) du bureau directeur:
Loriane Séguin, Directrice générale
cscs.direction@comitesocialcentresud.org

Comité UNICEF Canada *See* UNICEF Canada

Commercial & Press Photographers Association of Canada (CAPPAC) *See* Professional Photographers of Canada

Commercial Seed Analysts Association of Canada Inc. (CSAAC)
5788 L&A Rd., Vernon BC V1B 3PG
Tel: 204-720-0052
www.seedanalysts.ca
Overview: A medium-sized national licensing organization founded in 1944
Mission: To help determine the future of the seed industry; to enhance professionalism through ongoing education; to provide customers with seed analysis services & information
Membership: 100+; *Fees:* $66-$386; *Committees:* Ethics; Membership; Methods & Procedures; Research & Review; Seed Analyst Accreditation; CSAAC By-law Review; CSGA Standard & Stock Seed; CSI; Germination Magazine; Grant; Historical; Nomination; Seed Sector; Vigour; Webinar;Proficiency Testing
Activities: Exams & accreditation
Chief Officer(s):
Morgan Webb, President
morgan@seedcheck.net
Krista Erickson, Executive Director
csaacexecutivedirector@gmail.com
Awards:
• The Marie Greeniaus Award
Meetings/Conferences:
• Commercial Seed Analysts Association of Canada Annual Convention 2018, May, 2018, Saskatoon, SK
• Commercial Seed Analysts Association of Canada Annual Convention 2019, May, 2019, London, ON
Publications:
• Breaking Dormancy [a publication of the Commercial Seed Analysts Association of Canada Inc.]
Type: Newsletter; *Frequency:* Monthly

Commission canadienne d'histoire militaire (CCHM) / Canadian Commission of Military History (CCMH)
Quartier général de la Défense nationale, 101 Colonel By Dr., Ottawa ON K1A 0K2
Téléc: 613-990-8579
Aperçu: *Dimension:* petite; *Envergure:* nationale; fondée en 1973
Mission: La CCHM est une organisation bénévole, ne comptant qu'un Conseil de direction, sans membres, collaborant à la Commission internationale d'histoire militaire (CIHM) du Comité international des Sciences historiques (CISH) de Genève, Suisse; La Commission canadienne cherche à servir de lien entre les historiens militaires canadiens et la communauté internationale des chercheurs et écrivains en histoire militaire; La Commission canadienne travaille aussi à mieux faire connaître l'histoire militaire canadienne au Canada et à l'étranger
Affiliation(s): Canadian Historical Association; Commission internationale d'histoire militaire
Finances: *Budget de fonctionnement annuel:* Moins de $50,000
3 bénévole(s)

Activités: Représentations canadiennes auprès de la Commission internationale pour l'histoire militaire (CIHM); participation à l'organisation du congrès international annuel de la CIHM; liaisons diverses avec les autres commissions nationales participantes de la CIHM; participation à la préparation de la bibliographie international annuelle du Comité de bibliographie de la CIHM; financement d'activités canadiennes dans le domaine de l'histoire militaire

Commission canadienne du lait *See* Canadian Dairy Commission

Commission canadienne pour l'UNESCO *See* Canadian Commission for UNESCO

Commission canadienne pour la théorie des machines et des mécanismes (CCToMM) / Canadian Committee for the Theory of Machines & Mechanisms
Faculté de génie mécanique, Université du Nouveau Brunswick, CP 4400, Fredericton NB E3B 5A3
Tél: 506-458-7454; *Téléc:* 506-453-5025
www.cctomm.mae.carleton.ca
Aperçu: *Dimension:* petite; *Envergure:* nationale; fondée en 1993
Mission: Promouvoir le développement dans le domaine des machines et des mécanismes par la recherche théorique et expérimentale et leurs applications pratiques.
Membre de: International Federation for the Theory of Machines & Mechanisms (IFToMM)
Membre: *Montant de la cotisation:* 50$
Membre(s) du bureau directeur:
Marc Arsenault, Secrétaire général
marc.arsenault@laurentian.ca
Scott Nokleby, Responsable des communications
scott.nokleby@uoit.ca

Commission Coopération Environnementale *See* Commission for Environmental Cooperation

La Commission Crie-Naskapie *See* Cree-Naskapi Commission

Commission culturelle fransaskoise *Voir* Conseil culturel fransaskois

Commission d'enseignement spécial des provinces de l'Atlantique *See* Atlantic Provinces Special Education Authority

La Commission de la Capitale de l'Ile-du-Prince-Édouard *See* The Capital Commission of Prince Edward Island Inc.

Commission de la Médiathèque Père-Louis-Lamontagne
300 Beaverbrook Rd., Miramichi NB E1V 1A1
Tél: 506-627-4084; *Téléc:* 506-627-4592
mediathequep@gnb.ca
www.mpll.nb.ca
Aperçu: *Dimension:* petite; *Envergure:* locale; Organisme sans but lucratif; fondée en 1986
Mission: Travailler à l'amélioration constante des services offerts par la Médiathèque Père-Louis-Lamontagne
Finances: *Budget de fonctionnement annuel:* Moins de $50,000
Membre: 7
Activités: *Service de conférenciers:* Oui; *Bibliothèque:* Médiathèque Père-Louis-Lamontagne; Bibliothèque publique
Membre(s) du bureau directeur:
Geneviève Thériault McGraw, Directrice

Commission de Ski pour Personnes Handicapées du Québec (CSPHQ)
QC
Aperçu: *Dimension:* petite; *Envergure:* provinciale surveillé par Canadian Association for Disabled Skiing
Mission: Promouvoir et pratiquer le ski alpin
Membre de: Ski Québec; Canadian Association for Disabled Skiing
Membre: *Critères d'admissibilite:* Adolescent et adulte ayant une déficience physique
Activités: Cours de ski alpin adapté (luge, bi-ski)

Commission des sépultures de guerre du Commonwealth - Agence canadienne *See* Commonwealth War Graves Commission - Canadian Agency

Commission des services financiers de l'Ontario *See* Financial Services Commission of Ontario

Commission des services financiers et des services aux consommateurs *See* Financial & Consumer Services Commission

Commission Électrotechnique Internationale - Comité National du Canada *See* International Electrotechnical Commission - Canadian National Committee

Commission for Environmental Cooperation (CEC) / Commission Coopération Environnementale
Secretariat, #200, 393, rue St-Jacques ouest, Montréal QC H2Y 1N9
Tel: 514-350-4300; *Fax:* 514-350-4314
info@cec.org
www.cec.org
www.linkedin.com/company/commission-for-environmental-cooperation-of-north-america
www.facebook.com/CECconnect
twitter.com/CECweb
www.youtube.com/CECweb
Mission: The Commission for Environmental Cooperation (CEC) is an international organization created by Canada, Mexico & the United States under the North American Agreement on Environmental Cooperation (NAAEC). The CEC was established to address regional environmental concerns, help prevent potential trade & environmental conflicts & to promote the effective enforcement of environmental law. The Agreement complements the environmental provisions of the North American Free Trade Agreement (NAFTA).
Chief Officer(s):
César Rafael Chávez, Executive Director, 514-350-4317
crchavez@cec.org
Nathalie Daoust, Council Liaison, 514-350-4310
ndaoust@cec.org
 Mexico Liaison Office
 Progreso #3, Viveros de Coyoacán, Mexico DF 04110 Mexico
 Tel: 52-555 659 5021; *Fax:* 52-555-659 5023

La Commission internationale de juristes (section canadienne) *See* International Commission of Jurists (Canadian Section)

Commission nationale des parents francophones (CNPF)
#300, 450 rue Rideau, Ottawa ON K1N 5T4
Tél: 613-288-0958; *Téléc:* 613-688-1367
Ligne sans frais: 800-665-5148
info@cnpf.ca
cnpf.ca
www.facebook.com/LaCNPF
twitter.com/LaCNPF
www.vimeo.com/cnpf
Aperçu: *Dimension:* moyenne; *Envergure:* nationale; fondée en 1979 surveillé par Fédération des communautés francophones et acadienne du Canada
Mission: Pour soutenir les branches provinciales de l'organisation et les aider à fournir de l'aide aux parents
Affiliation(s): Association canadienne d'éducation de langue française; Fédération nationale des conseils scolaires francophones; Ministère du Patrimoine canadien; Ministère de l'Emploi et du Développement social Canada; Commissariat aux langues officielles; Secrétariat aux affaires intergouvernementales canadiennes
Membre(s) du personnel: 3
Membre: 12 organisations
Membre(s) du bureau directeur:
Véronique Legault, Présidente

Committee of Presidents of Universities of Ontario *See* Council of Ontario Universities

Committee on Canadian Labour History *See* Canadian Committee on Labour History

Committee on Learning Resources (CLR) *See* Colleges Ontario

Commonwealth Association for Public Administration & Management (CAPAM)
#202, 291 Dalhousie St., Ottawa ON K1N 7E5
Tel: 819-956-7961; *Fax:* 613-701-4236
capam@capam.org
www.capam.org
www.linkedin.com/company/commonwealth-association-for-public-administration-and-management
www.facebook.com/CAPAMorg
twitter.com/CAPAM_
Overview: A small international organization founded in 1994
Mission: To provide a forum to exchange information, innovations & experiences of public service management; to enhance Commonwealth cooperation, to improve managerial competence & organizational excellence in governance.
Affiliation(s): African Association for Public Administration and Management (AAPAM); Arab Urban Development Institute; Association of Management Development Institutions in South Asia (AMDISA); Caribbean Centre for Development Administration (CARICAD); Institute of Public Administration Australia (IPAA); Public Management and Policy Association - United Kingdom (PMPA)
Finances: *Funding Sources:* Membership dues; government agencies internationally
Staff Member(s): 4
Membership: 1,100; *Fees:* US$180 individual; US$3900 institutional; *Member Profile:* Individuals, institutions & professional organizations, representatives of all levels of government, both elected & appointed officials, the academic community & the private sector
Activities: *Library:* Practice Knowledge Centre; by appointment
Chief Officer(s):
Ali Hamsa, President
Gay Hamilton, Executive Director & CEO
ghamilton@capam.org

Commonwealth Association of Museums (CAM)
c/o Catherine C. Cole, 10023 - 93rd St., Edmonton AB T5H 1W6
Tel: 780-424-2229
www.maltwood.uvic.ca/cam
Overview: A small international organization founded in 1974
Mission: To improve museums & their societies in the Commonwealth & around the world; To high standards of museum activity throughout the Commonwealth; To create & strengthen links between museums & persons in the museum profession; To involve children & youth in museum development & activities
Affiliation(s): International Council of Museums
Finances: *Funding Sources:* Membership fees; Commonwealth Foundation
Membership: *Member Profile:* Individuals, associations, & institutions from Commonwealth nations; Associate members from outside the Commonwealth
Activities: Collaborating with Commonwealth governments, non-governmental organizations, & other museum organizations; Offering professional development activities, such as a distance learning program, seminars, & workshops; Disseminating information, such as occasional papers & conference, workshop, & symposia proceedings & reports; Facilitating networking opportunities
Chief Officer(s):
Catherine C. Cole, MA, FCMA, Secretary General, 780-424-2229
CatherineC.Cole@telus.net
Publications:
• CAM [Commonwealth Association of Museums] Bulletin
Frequency: Irregular; *ISSN:* 1026-5155
Profile: Updates for association members; including recent & forthcoming meetings
• The Commonwealth Association of Museums On-Line International Journal
Type: Journal; *Editor:* L. Irvine; M. Segger; B. Winters
Profile: A compilation of papers presented at conferences & meetings

Commonwealth Forestry Association - Canadian Chapter (CFA)
c/o Prof. Shashi Kant, Faculty of Forestry, University of Toronto, 33 Willcocks St., Toronto ON M5S 3B3
www.cfa-international.org
twitter.com/CFAforestry
Overview: A small international organization founded in 1921
Mission: To promote the conservation and sustainable management of the world's forests and the contribution they make to peoples' livelihoods
Member of: Commonwealth Forestry Association, UK
Finances: *Annual Operating Budget:* Less than $50,000
1 volunteer(s)
Membership: 60; *Fees:* $108; *Member Profile:* Professional foresters
Chief Officer(s):
Shashi Kant, Regional Director, The Americas
shashi.kant@utoronto.ca

The Commonwealth Games Association of Canada Inc. *See* Commonwealth Games Canada

Commonwealth Games Canada (CGC) / Jeux du Commonwealth Canada
#201, 2255 St. Laurent Blvd., Ottawa ON K1G 4K3
Tel: 613-244-6868; *Fax:* 613-244-6826
info@commonwealthgames.ca

www.commonwealthgames.ca
www.facebook.com/265526150138420
twitter.com/cgc_jcc
www.youtube.com/user/cgcTVjcc
Previous Name: The Commonwealth Games Association of Canada Inc.
Overview: A small international organization founded in 1977
Affiliation(s): Commonwealth Games Federation - London, England
Finances: *Annual Operating Budget:* $100,000-$250,000
Staff Member(s): 2; 60 volunteer(s)
Membership: 60 individual
Activities: *Internships:* Yes; *Library:* Open to public
Chief Officer(s):
Brian MacPherson, Chief Executive Officer, 613-244-6868 Ext. 226
brian@commonwealthgames.ca
Kelly Laframboise, Manager, Administration & Operations, 613-244-6868 Ext. 222
kelly@commonwealthgames.ca

The Commonwealth of Learning (COL)
#2500, 4710 Kingsway, Burnaby BC V5H 4M2
Tel: 604-775-8200; *Fax:* 604-775-8210
info@col.org
www.col.org
www.linkedin.com/company/commonwealth-of-learning
www.facebook.com/COL4D
twitter.com/COL4D
www.youtube.com/user/comlearn
Overview: A large international organization founded in 1988
Mission: To create & widen access to education & to improve its quality, utilising distance education techniques & associated communications technologies to meet the particular requirements of member countries
Affiliation(s): Commonwealth Educational Media Centre for Asia (CEMCA); Commonwealth Secretariat; Commonwealth Foundation; Commonwealth Connects
Finances: *Annual Operating Budget:* Greater than $5 Million; *Funding Sources:* Voluntary pledges; strategic partnerships
Staff Member(s): 40
Membership: 54 commonwealth governments; *Fees:* Voluntary contributions; *Member Profile:* Commonwealth Member Governments
Activities: *Awareness Events:* Commonwealth Day, second Monday of March; *Internships:* Yes *Library:* Information Resource Centre; by appointment
Chief Officer(s):
Asha S. Kanwar, President & CEO

Commonwealth War Graves Commission - Canadian Agency (CWGC) / Commission des sépultures de guerre du Commonwealth - Agence canadienne (CSGC)
#1707, 66 Slater St., Ottawa ON K1A 0P4
Tel: 613-992-3224; *Fax:* 613-995-0431
cwgc-canada@vac-acc.gc.ca
www.cwgc-canadianagency.ca
Overview: A medium-sized international organization founded in 1917
Mission: To ensure Commonwealth War Burials in the Americas (including the Caribbean) are marked & maintained; To ensure maintenance of memorials to the missing; To keep records & registers; To discharge Commission duties for Commonwealth war graves in the Americas (comprising some 3,350 cemeteries & over 20,000 commemorations)
Affiliation(s): Commonwealth War Graves Commission
Finances: *Funding Sources:* Governments of Canada, Australia, India, New Zealand, South Africa, & United Kingdom
Staff Member(s): 9
Activities: *Speaker Service:* Yes
Chief Officer(s):
David Kettle, Canandian Agency Director

La communauté bahá'íe du Canada *See* The Bahá'í Community of Canada

La communauté coréenne du grand Montréal *See* Korean Community of Greater Montréal

Communauté Laotienne du Québec (CLQ) / Lao Community of Québec
#400, 6555, ch de la Côte-des-Neiges, Montréal QC H3S 2A6
Tél: 514-341-1057; *Téléc:* 514-341-8404
information@romel-montreal.org
www.romel-montreal.ca

Aperçu: Dimension: petite; *Envergure:* provinciale; fondée en 1982
Mission: La Communauté Laotienne du Québec est un des organismes fondateurs du Regroupement des organismes du Montréal ethnique pour le logement (ROMEL); ROMEL centralise toute l'information sur l'habitation et informe les membres des communautés culturelles sur les programmes et services en matière d'habitation.
Membre de: Regroupement des organismes du Montréal ethnique pour le logement
Affiliation(s): Federation des Associations Lao du Canada
Membre(s) du personnel: 13
Activités: Donne des services d'interprète et d'accompagnement; information sur l'habitation
Membre(s) du bureau directeur:
Mazen Houdeib, Directeur général

La Communauté lithuanienne du Canada *See* The Lithuanian Canadian Community

Communauté musulmane du Québec *See* Muslim Community of Québec

Communauté sépharade unifiée du Québec (CSUQ)
#216, 5151 Cote-Ste-Catherine, Montréal QC H3W 1M6
Tél: 514-733-4998; *Téléc:* 514-733-3158
info@csuq.org
www.csuq.org
www.facebook.com/lacsuq
Également appelé: La Voix sépharade
Nom précédent: Association Sépharade Francophone
Aperçu: Dimension: moyenne; *Envergure:* provinciale; Organisme sans but lucratif; fondée en 1966
Mission: Préserver la culture et le patrimoine sépharade; défendre les intérêts de la population sépharade et la représenter auprès des divers paliers gouvernementaux ainsi que d'autres associations communautaires
Membre de: Fédération - CJA
Finances: *Budget de fonctionnement annuel:* $500,000-$1.5 Million
Membre(s) du personnel: 10; 200 bénévole(s)
Membre: 25 000; *Comités:* Administration; Affaires religieuses; Affaires sociales; Éducation et Culture; Financement; Information; Planification communautaire; Relations publiques; Ressources humaines
Activités: La Commission de l'Information, un comité permanent, informe toute la population sépharade des réalisations et projets de la communauté ainsi qu' une information culturelle, religieuse et générale; *Bibliothèque:* rendez-vous

Communauté vietnamienne au Canada, région de Montréal
#495, 6767, ch Côte-des-Neiges, Montréal QC H2E 2T6
Tél: 514-340-9630; *Téléc:* 514-340-1926
communaute.viet.montreal@gmail.com
vietnam.ca
twitter.com/cdnvqgvm
Aperçu: Dimension: petite; *Envergure:* locale; fondée en 1954
Membre de: Vietnamese Canadian Federation
Activités: Immigration et Intégration; Cours et formation
Membre(s) du bureau directeur:
Lê Minh Thinh, Directeur exécutif

Communication & Natural Logic International Society
90, av Vincent d'Indy, #B430, Montréal QC H3C 3J7
www.communalis.ca
Also Known As: Communalis
Overview: A medium-sized international organization
Mission: To disseminate information & research issues surrounding communication, argumentation, logic & social representation from an interdisciplinary perspective
Membership: *Fees:* $30-$90 regular; $15-$60 associate
Chief Officer(s):
Milton Campos, Chief Executive Officer

Communicative Disorders Assistant Association of Canada (CDAAC)
PO Box 55009, 1800 Sheppard Ave. East, Toronto ON M2J 3Z6
info@cdaac.ca
www.cdaac.ca
www.linkedin.com/groups/Communicative-Disorders-Assistant-Association-Canada-8174736
www.facebook.com/106123889530114
twitter.com/CDAAC
Overview: A small national organization

Mission: To unite members of the profession & protect the character & status of the profession; To maintain & improve the qualifications & standards of the profession; to represent the members in their relationships with other associations, government, colleges, & other national & international organizations; To promote & achieve statutory regulations for members; To provide the public with information regarding our profession & membership; To provide support & share information for the mutual benefit of members
Membership: *Fees:* $75; $30 student; *Member Profile:* Communicative Disorders Assistants
Activities: *Library:* Resource Library

Communion & Liberation Canada
#314, 1857, boul de Maisonneuve ouest, Montréal QC H3H 1J9
Tel: 514-667-5709
clonline.ca
Also Known As: CL Canada
Previous Name: Gioventù Studentesca (Student Youth)
Overview: A small national organization founded in 1954
Mission: To educate to Christian maturity; to collaborate in the mission of the Church in all facets of contemporary life
Finances: *Funding Sources:* Donations
Membership: *Member Profile:* Male & female adults & children who wish to participate in the ecclesial movement
Activities: Providing a weekly catechesis, known as a School of Community, for adults to meet in order to read, meditate, & discuss; Offering "Little School" meetings for children
Chief Officer(s):
Julian Carron, President, Fraternity of CL
Filomena Vecchio-Scandinavo, Contact, 416-746-2015
mena_vecchio@yahoo.ca
Publications:
• Traces
Type: Magazine; *Frequency:* Monthly; *Editor:* Davide Perillo; *Price:* $45
Profile: International magazine of the Movement of Communion & Liberation, with testimonies from around the world, articles on the life of the Church, & cultural, social, & politicaltopics

Communist Party of BC (CPCBC)
706 Clark Dr., Vancouver BC V5L 3J1
Tel: 604-254-9836
cpbc@telus.net
Overview: A small provincial organization overseen by Communist Party Of Canada
Chief Officer(s):
Timothy Gidora, Party Leader

Communist Party of Canada (CPC) / Parti Communiste du Canada
Central Committee, 290A Danforth Ave., Toronto ON M4K 1N6
Tel: 416-469-2446
info@cpc-pcc.ca
www.communist-party.ca
www.facebook.com/CommunistPartyOfCanada
twitter.com/compartycanada
flickr.com/photos/communist-party-of-canada
Overview: A small national organization founded in 1921
Mission: To establish a socialist society in Canada, in which the principal means of producing & distributing wealth will be the common property of society as a whole
Finances: *Funding Sources:* Membership dues
Membership: *Committees:* Alberta; British Columbia; Saskatechewan; Manitoba; Ontario; Atlantic
Activities: *Library:* CPC Resource Centre
Chief Officer(s):
Liz Rowley, Party Leader
Publications:
• People's Voice
Type: Newspaper; *Frequency:* Monthly

Communist Party of Canada (Alberta) (CPC-A)
PO Box 68112, Stn. Bonnie Doon, Edmonton AB T6C 4N6
Tel: 780-934-7893
office@communistparty-alberta.ca
www.communistparty-alberta.ca
Overview: A small provincial organization overseen by Communist Party Of Canada
Chief Officer(s):
Naomi Rankin, Party Leader

Communist Party of Canada (Manitoba) (CPC-M)
387 Selkirk Ave., Winnipeg MB R2W 2M3
Tel: 204-586-7824
cpc-mb@changetheworldmb.ca

Overview: A small provincial organization overseen by Communist Party Of Canada
Chief Officer(s):
Darrell Rankin, Party Leader

Communist Party of Canada (Marxist-Leninist) (CPC(ML)) / Parti communiste du Canada (marxiste-léniniste)
National Headquarters, PO Box 666, Stn. C, Montréal QC H2L 4L5
Tel: 514-522-1373; *Fax:* 514-522-1373
office@cpcml.ca
www.cpcml.ca
Also Known As: The Marxist-Leninist Party of Canada
Overview: A small national organization founded in 1970
Mission: To attain communism & the complete emancipation of the working class; To ensure that all people have claims on the society by virtue of being human
Chief Officer(s):
Anna Di Carlo, Party Leader
leader@mlpc.ca

Communist Party of Canada (Ontario) (CPCO)
290A Danforth Ave., Toronto ON M4K 1N6
Tel: 416-469-2446
info@communistpartyontario.ca
www.communistpartyontario.ca
twitter.com/oncommunists
Overview: A small provincial organization overseen by Communist Party Of Canada
Chief Officer(s):
Dave McKee, Party Leader

Communitas Supportive Care Society
#103, 2776 Bourquin Cres. West, Abbotsford BC V2S 6A4
Tel: 604-850-6608; *Fax:* 604-850-2634
Toll-Free: 800-622-5455
office@communitascare.com
www.communitascare.com
www.linkedin.com/company/communitas-supportive-care-society
www.facebook.com/CommunitasCare
twitter.com/CommunitasCare
Previous Name: Mennonite Central Committee Supportive Care Services Society
Overview: A small local organization
Mission: Provide various resources to persons living & dealing with mental, physical &/or emotional disabilities.
Member of: Association for Community Living; Community Social Services Employers Association; Psychosocial Rehabilitation Canada; BC Association for Child Development & Intervention; Denominational Health Association; Fraser Valley Brain Injury Association
Affiliation(s): Jean Vanier; Henri Nouwen; Copeland Centre for Wellness & Recovery; International Initiative for Mental Health; Living Room; Mental Health Commission of Canada; STEP Enterprises; Mennonite Central Committee (British Columbia & Canada); Mennonite Disaster Service; Ten Thousand Villages
Finances: *Annual Operating Budget:* Greater than $5 Million
Activities: *Awareness Events:* Curl for Care, Jan.
Chief Officer(s):
Karyn Santiago, Chief Executive Officer
Gary Falk, Chair
Jacquie Lepp, CPA, Treasurer

Communitech
#100, 151 Charles St. West, Kitchener ON N2G 1H6
Tel: 519-888-9944; *Fax:* 519-804-2225
www.communitech.ca
www.linkedin.com/groups/Communitech-2071521
www.facebook.com/communitechpage
twitter.com/communitech
Previous Name: Communitech Technology Association
Overview: A small local organization founded in 1997
Mission: to support technology companies in the Kitchener-Waterloo Region; to promote networking among professionals & a sharing of ideas; to foster the creation of new companies & coaches them through early stages.
Staff Member(s): 24
Membership: *Fees:* Schedule available based on number of employees; *Member Profile:* Technology companies; service providers; educational institutions; municipal entities
Activities: Canadian Digital Media Network (CDMN); monthly lunch & breakfast; Annual Spring Conference
Chief Officer(s):
Iain Klugman, President & CEO
iain.klugman@communitech.ca

Communitech Technology Association *See* Communitech

Community & Family Services of Chatham *See* Family Service Kent

Community & Hospital Infection Control Association Canada *See* Infection & Prevention Control Canada

Community Action Resource Centre (CARC)
1652 Keele St., Toronto ON M6M 3W3
Tel: 416-652-2273; *Fax:* 416-652-8992
www.communityarc.ca
www.facebook.com/CommunityActionResourceCentre
twitter.com/communityarc
Merged from: Community Information Centre for the City of York & Connect Information Post
Overview: A small local charitable organization founded in 2004 overseen by InformOntario
Mission: Mobilizing resources and providing supportive social services for the empowerment of individuals and groups.
Finances: *Funding Sources:* Provincial governemt; United Way Toronto; Industry Canada
Activities: Clothing bank; individual & family support; voicemail; income tax clinics; access to computers

Community Action Resource Centre (CARC)
1652 Keele St., Toronto ON M6M 3W3
Tel: 416-652-2273; *Fax:* 416-652-8992
www.communityarc.ca
www.facebook.com/CommunityActionResourceCentre
twitter.com/communityarc
Merged from: Connect Information Post; Community Information Centre For The City Of York
Overview: A medium-sized local charitable organization founded in 2004
Mission: To build the capacity of communities by mobilizing resources & providing supportive social services, for the empowerment of individuals & groups with a focus on serving the most vulnerable and disadvantaged.
Finances: *Funding Sources:* Government, United Way, Donations
Membership: *Fees:* Free

Community AIDS Treatment Information Exchange *See* Canadian AIDS Treatment Information Exchange

Community Arts Council of Fort St. James
PO Box 846, Fort St James BC V0J 1P0
Tel: 250-996-8233
www.facebook.com/FortArts
Overview: A small local organization
Mission: To bring amateur theatre & film to the Fort St. James community
Member of: Assembly of BC Arts Councils
Finances: *Funding Sources:* Municipal & provincial government

Community Arts Council of Greater Victoria (CACGV)
3220 Cedar Hil Rd., Victoria BC V8P 3Y3
Tel: 250-475-7123
info@cacgv.ca
www.cacgv.ca
www.facebook.com/145619592158880
twitter.com/CACGV
Overview: A small local charitable organization founded in 1965
Mission: To promote public awareness of & opportunities in arts & culture activities; to ensure that the arts remain a priority in government budget planning.
Member of: BC Assembly of Arts Councils
Finances: *Annual Operating Budget:* $100,000-$250,000; *Funding Sources:* Provincial & CRD government; donations; BCAC
150 volunteer(s)
Membership: *Fees:* $10 student; $30 individual; $150 patron; *Member Profile:* Individuals & groups; artists of all disciplines; instructors; *Committees:* Nomination; Performance; Visual Arts; Literary
Activities: Resource & Information Centre; Members Art Gallery; arts in education; community development; group grants; *Internships:* Yes *Library:* CACGV Resource Centre; Open to public
Chief Officer(s):
Judy Moore, President
Awards:
• Michael Blake Watercolour Award
• Erika Kurth Scholarship/Bursary Award

Community Arts Council of Prince George & District
2820 - 15 Ave., Prince George BC V2M 1T1
Tel: 250-562-6935; *Fax:* 250-562-0436
info@studio2880.com
www.studio2880.com
Also Known As: Studio 2880 Arts Center
Overview: A small local organization founded in 1969
Mission: To support, encourage & promote all arts in Prince George and District, providing a creative climate to nurture artistic talent.
Member of: Assembly of BC Arts Councils; Prince George Chamber of Commerce; CIRAC; Canadian Conference of the Arts
Staff Member(s): 9
Membership: 180 individual + 57 member groups; *Fees:* $20 individual; $50 guild or club; *Member Profile:* Arts groups & artistic individuals
Activities: Studio Fair; Arts Gallery of Honour; Spring Arts Bazaar; Try Us Out Festival; Summer Day Camp of the Arts
Chief Officer(s):
Wendy Young, Executive Director
executive@studio2880.com
Awards:
• Scholarship Fund
Eligibility: Local high school students interested in visual, performing or literary arts; *Amount:* $500

Community Arts Council of Richmond (CACR)
PO Box 36546, Stn. Seafair, Richmond BC V7C 5M4
richmondartscouncil@gmail.com
www.richmondartscouncil.org
www.facebook.com/227503713954030
twitter.com/RichmondBCArts
Overview: A medium-sized local charitable organization founded in 1970
Mission: To promote the arts & artisans in Richmond, British Columbia; To advocate for the arts & artists; To support emerging & disabled artists
Affiliation(s): Arts BC; Alliance for Arts; BC Arts Council; Richmond Chamber of COmmerice; Heritage Canada
Finances: *Funding Sources:* Donations; Fundraising
Membership: 29; *Fees:* $10 associate; $15 student; $20 supprting; $35 participating artists; $100 group; $100 individual lifetime; $500 group lifetime; *Member Profile:* Artists from the Richmond, British Columbia area, such as painters, jewellers, sculptors, musicians, potters, wood turners, weavers; Supporting members, such as non-artists who support the work of the council
Activities: Operating the Artisans' Galleria & gift shop in Steveston, British Columbia; Presenting art exhibitions, such as the annual Indian Summer Art Show; Offering grants; Providing publicity for members; Assisting members with the sale of their work; Working with other non-profit community groups
Chief Officer(s):
Natasha Lozovsky-Burns, President
Klaas Focker, Vice-President
Lee Beaudry, Secretary
Margaret Stephens, Treasurer & Administrator
Publications:
• Community Arts Council of Richmond Newsletter
Type: Newsletter
Profile: Information about forthcoming exhibitions & events
• Community Arts Council of Richmond Member Directory
Type: Directory
Profile: Listings of artists & their artistic medium

Community Arts Council of T'Lagunna *See* Maple Ridge Pitt Meadows Arts Council

Community Arts Council of the Alberni Valley
3061 - 8 Ave., Port Alberni BC V9Y 2K5
Tel: 250-724-3412
communityarts@shawcable.com
www.portalberniarts.com
www.facebook.com/CommunityArtsCouncilOfTheAlberniValley
Also Known As: Rollin Art Centre
Overview: A small local charitable organization
Mission: To enrich life in the community through the promotion of arts, with a focus on collecting, protecting, conserving & presenting work by local artists.
Member of: Assembly of BC Arts Councils
Finances: *Funding Sources:* Civic; provincial grants; gallery & gift shop sales; box office; fundraising
Activities: Public gardens; visual arts gallery & programs; performing arts series; special events; art programs & classes

Community Association for Riding for the Disabled (CARD)
4777 Dufferin St., Toronto ON M3H 5T3
Tel: 416-667-8600; *Fax:* 416-739-7520
info@card.ca
www.card.ca
Overview: A medium-sized local charitable organization founded in 1969
Mission: To improve the lives of children & adults with disabilities through therapeutic riding programs
Member of: Canadian Therapeutic Riding Association
Affiliation(s): Ontario Therapeutic Riding Association
Finances: *Funding Sources:* Government; fundraising; special events; corporate donations; private donations
Staff Member(s): 9; 350 volunteer(s)
Membership: 600; *Fees:* $25
Activities: Summer program; Ride-a-thon; dinner; auction
Chief Officer(s):
Penny Smith, Executive Director
penny@card.ca
Seana Waldon, Director, Therapeutic Riding Services
seana@card.ca
Judy Wanless, Director, Volunteer Services
judy@card.ca
Bonnie Hartley, Coordinator, Fundraising & Events
bonnie@card.ca

Community Care Belleville *See* Community Care for South Hastings

Community Care for South Hastings
#63, 470 Dundas St. East, Belleville ON K8N 1G1
Tel: 613-969-0130; *Fax:* 613-969-1719
www.ccsh.ca
www.facebook.com/241358299396920
twitter.com/CCSouthHastings
Previous Name: Community Care Belleville
Overview: A small local charitable organization founded in 1980
Mission: To provide programs & services for physically disabled individuals
Member of: Ontario Community Support Association; SEO Community Support Services Network
Affiliation(s): Pensioners Concerned
Finances: *Funding Sources:* United Way Quinte; Donations; Local Health Integration Network, Parrot Foundation
Membership: *Fees:* $5
Activities: Meals On Wheels (hot and frozen); Escorted Transportation; House Care; Crisis Intervention & Support; Reassurance and Safety, Congregate Dining, Therapeutic Activity, Service Arrangement and Coordination, 55 Alive Drive Refresher, Footcare; *Speaker Service:* Yes
Chief Officer(s):
Shell-Lee Wert, Executive Director

Deseronto Office
293 Main St., Deseronto ON K0K 1X0
Tel: 613-396-6591; *Fax:* 613-396-6592
Chief Officer(s):
Lisa Murray, Manager, Program

Community Care Peterborough
185 Hunter St. East, Peterborough ON K9H 0H1
Tel: 705-742-7067; *Fax:* 705-745-6011; *TTY:* 705-742-2075
centofc@commcareptbo.org
www.commcareptbo.org
www.facebook.com/149883285049420
twitter.com/CommCarePtbo
www.youtube.com/user/CommunityCarePtbo
Overview: A small local charitable organization founded in 1984 overseen by InformOntario
Mission: The association is a network of community offices that provides essential services to seniors & disabled, so they may remain living at home.
Member of: United Way
Finances: *Funding Sources:* Provincial; foundations; private donations
Activities: Caremobile; Meals on Wheels; Diner's Club; reassurance phone calls; arranging brokered workers for home maintenance; *Awareness Events:* Kilometres for Care, Apr.; Half-Marathon, Nov.; *Rents Mailing List:* Yes
Chief Officer(s):
Doug Downer, President
Danielle Belair, Executive Director
Publications:
• The Thread
Type: Newsletter

Apsley Office
PO Box 303, 168 Burleigh St., Apsley ON K0L 1A0
Tel: 705-656-4589; *Fax:* 705-656-2542
apsley@commcareptbo.org
Chief Officer(s):
Amanda Smith, Program Support

Chemung Office
549 Ennis Rd., Ennismore ON K0L 1T0
Tel: 705-292-8708; *Fax:* 705-292-8750
chemung@commcareptbo.org
Chief Officer(s):
Denise Gould, Coordinator

Harvey Office
PO Box 12, 1937 Lakehurst Rd., Buckhorn ON K0L 1J0
Tel: 705-657-2171; *Fax:* 705-657-3457
harvofc@commcareptbo.org
Chief Officer(s):
Lynda McKerr, Coordinator

Havelock Office
107 Concession St. North, Havelock ON K0L 1Z0
Tel: 705-778-7831; *Fax:* 705-778-7924
havelock@commcareptbo.org
Chief Officer(s):
Tammy Ross, Coordinator

Lakefield Office
PO Box 001, 40 Rabbit St., Lakefield ON K0L 2H0
Tel: 705-652-8655; *Fax:* 705-652-7332
lakfield@commcareptbo.org
Chief Officer(s):
Lorri Rork, Coordinator

Millbrook Office
PO Box 257, 22 King St. East, Millbrook ON L0A 1G0
Tel: 705-932-2011; *Fax:* 705-932-4058
millofc@commcareptbo.org
Chief Officer(s):
Karen Morton, Coordinator

Norwood Office
PO Box 436, 2281 Hwy. 45, Norwood ON K0L 2V0
Tel: 705-639-5631; *Fax:* 705-639-2511
norwood@commcareptbo.org
Chief Officer(s):
Tammy Ross, Coordinator

Community Connection (CDIC)
PO Box 683, 275 - 1st St., Collingwood ON L9Y 4E8
Tel: 705-444-0040; *Fax:* 705-445-1516
info@communityconnection.ca
www.communityconnection.ca
Also Known As: Collingwood & District Information Centre
Overview: A medium-sized local charitable organization founded in 1969 overseen by InformOntario
Mission: To offer free & confidential information & referral services to anyone needing help
Member of: InformCanada; Alliance of Information & Referral Systems; Volunteer Canada; InformOntario; Community Information Online Consortium; Child Youth and Family Services Coalition of Simcoe County
Affiliation(s): United Way
Finances: *Funding Sources:* Municipal government; United Way; fundraising
Activities: Free legal advice clinic; *Rents Mailing List:* Yes
Awards:
• ACICO Accreditation

Community Counselling & Resource Centre (CCRC)
540 George St. North, Peterborough ON K9H 3S2
Tel: 705-743-2272; *Fax:* 705-742-3015
ccrc@ccrc-ptbo.com
www.ccrc-ptbo.com
www.facebook.com/CCRC.Peterborough
twitter.com/CCRC_Ptbo
Overview: A small local charitable organization overseen by Ontario Association of Credit Counselling Services
Mission: To provide professional & confidential counselling, support, & resources related to financial management in Peterborough, Haliburton, Kawartha Lakes, & Northumberland Counties in Ontario
Member of: Ontario Association of Credit Counselling Services; United Way of Peterborough & District
Affiliation(s): Family Services Canada
Finances: *Funding Sources:* Donations
Activities: Offering money management, budgeting, debt, & bankruptcy counselling; Establishing community partnerships; Providing preventative education; Offering debt repayment programs

Chief Officer(s):
Mike Burger, President

Community Counselling Centre of Nipissing / Centre communautaire de counselling du Nipissing
361 McIntyre St. East, North Bay ON P1B 1C9
Tel: 705-472-6515; *Fax:* 705-472-4582; *Crisis Hot-Line:* 866-887-0015
info@cccnip.com
www.cccnip.com
Previous Name: Family Life Centre
Overview: A small local charitable organization founded in 1972 overseen by Ontario Association of Credit Counselling Services
Mission: To provide professional community & credit counselling services, plus developmental, addiction, & sexual assault services, to individuals, couples, & families in North Bay & the surrounding community
Member of: Ontario Association of Credit Counselling Services
Finances: *Funding Sources:* Donations
Activities: Arranging groups such as The Overcoming Abuse Group, The Women's Assertiveness Group, & the Dawn Youth Group for youth experiencing problems related to the use of substances; Offering employee & family assistance programs; Providing education to the public; Offering consulting services to community organizations & industries
Chief Officer(s):
Alan McQuarrie, Executive Director
amcquarrie@cccnip.com

Community Development Council Durham (CDCD)
#4, 458 Fairall St., Ajax ON L1S 1R6
Tel: 905-686-2661; *Fax:* 905-686-4157
Toll-Free: 866-746-3696
info@cdcd.org
www.cdcd.org
www.facebook.com/cdcdurham
twitter.com/CDCDurham
Previous Name: Social Development Council Ajax-Pickering; Ajax/Pickering Social Development Council
Overview: A small local charitable organization founded in 1970
Mission: To create, to advocate & to support policies, attitudes & actions which enhance individual, family & community growth
Member of: Social Planning Network of Ontario; Canadian Council of Social Development
Finances: *Annual Operating Budget:* $250,000-$500,000; *Funding Sources:* United Way; Region of Durham; Federal government
Staff Member(s): 11; 100 volunteer(s)
Membership: 100+; *Fees:* $15 student/senior; $25 individual; $50 non-profit; $75 corporate
Activities: Social research; community planning; information centre; rent bank; housing; immigration & settlement services; breakfast program; annual meeting, April
Chief Officer(s):
Keith Hernandez, President

Community Development Council of Belleville & District *See* Community Development Council of Quinte

Community Development Council of Quinte
65 Station St., Belleville ON K8N 2S6
Tel: 613-968-2466; *Fax:* 613-968-2251
www.cdcquinte.co
www.facebook.com/214450471935888
twitter.com/cdcquinte
Also Known As: CDC Quinte
Previous Name: Community Development Council of Belleville & District
Overview: A small local charitable organization founded in 1989
Mission: To promote the planning & provision of health & social services to ensure area residents are provided with the necessities of life & an opportunity to improve their quality of living.
Member of: Social Planning Network of Ontario
Activities: Task Force on Hunger; Hungry for Action; Anti-Poverty Research Projects; Good Food Box Program; Good Lunch Box Program; Collective Kitchens; Planting Seeds for Change; Second Helping; NEXUS; Non-Dinner Dinner; Quality of Life Index Project; Healthy Community Week; How to Start Your Own Food Co-op; *Speaker Service:* Yes; *Library:* Open to public
Chief Officer(s):
Ruth Ingersoll, Executive Director

Community Development Halton (CDH)
860 Harrington Ct., Burlington ON L7N 3N4

Tel: 905-632-1975; *Fax:* 905-632-0778
Toll-Free: 855-395-8807
office@cdhalton.ca
www.cdhalton.ca
www.facebook.com/ComDevHalton
twitter.com/ComDevHalton
www.youtube.com/user/cdhweb
Previous Name: Halton Social Planning Council & Volunteer Centre
Overview: A small local charitable organization founded in 1970
Mission: To improve the quality of life for community residents, focusing on research, community planning & promotion of volunteerism.
Member of: Community Information Online Consortium (CIOC); Ontario Volunteer Centre Network
Finances: *Annual Operating Budget:* $500,000-$1.5 Million; *Funding Sources:* United Ways of Burlington, Greater Hamilton & Oakville; Ontario Trillium Foundation; Municipal government
Staff Member(s): 10
Membership: *Fees:* $5 unemployed; $25 adult; $50 small organization; $100 medium organization; $150 large organization
Activities: Workshops, seminars
Chief Officer(s):
John Searles, President
Joey Edwardh, Executive Director

Community Energy Association (CEA)
#326, 638 - 7th Ave. West, Vancouver BC V5Z 1B5
Tel: 604-628-7076; *Fax:* 778-786-1613
info@communityenergy.bc.ca
www.communityenergy.bc.ca
Overview: A medium-sized provincial charitable organization founded in 1993
Mission: To support local governments in British Columbia in energy conservation & climate change activities
Finances: *Funding Sources:* Membership revenues; Fundraising
Membership: *Fees:* $2,500 local government associate; $5,000 corporate energetic supporter
Activities: Communicating with elected officials, municipal & regional district staff, & First Nations in British Columbia; Offering advisory services to local governments regarding energy innovations; Promoting energy efficiency & renewable energy for infrastructure; Encouraging local governments to consider energy in land planning & development; Conducting research on energy related topics; *Speaker Service:* Yes
Chief Officer(s):
Dale Littlejohn, Executive Director, 604-628-7076 Ext. 700
dlittlejohn@communityenergy.bc.ca
Patricia Bell, Head of Planning & Director of Education, 604-936-0470 Ext. 706
pbell@communityenergy.bc.ca
Peter Robinson, Chief Technology Officer, 604-628-7076 Ext. 704
probinson@communityenergy.bc.ca
Publications:
• Community Energy Association Directory
Type: Directory
Profile: Listings of association members
• Energy Brief for Elected Officials
Type: Guide
Profile: Information for local government leaders
• Heating Our Communities
Type: Guide
Profile: A renewable energy guide produced for local government leaders

Community Enhancement & Economic Development Society (CEEDS)
6810 Horse Lake Rd., Lone Butte BC V0K 1X3
Tel: 250-395-3580
ceeds@bcinternet.net
www.horselakefarmcoop.ca/ceeds
Overview: A small local organization founded in 1971
Mission: To promote small scale organic farming & to provide food, fuel & shelter to the memebers of the group
Member of: International WWOOF Association
Activities: Organic farming; animal husbandry; bee-keeping; *Speaker Service:* Yes

Community Enhancement Association
105B Walker St., Truro NS B2N 4B1
Tel: 902-893-1911; *Fax:* 902-893-4474
Overview: A small local organization

Mission: The Association acts as a vehicle for continuing cultivation & development of the African Nova Scotian community of Colchester County.
Finances: *Funding Sources:* federal government
Activities: Training youth for employment

Community Financial Counselling Services (CFCS)
#516, 238 Portage Ave., Winnipeg MB R3C 0B9
Tel: 204-989-1900; *Fax:* 204-989-1908
Toll-Free: 888-573-2383
www.debthelpmanitoba.com
www.facebook.com/204965096269852
twitter.com/debthelpmb
Previous Name: Credit Counselling Canada - Manitoba
Overview: A small provincial charitable organization founded in 1974
Mission: To offer respectful & effective debt management services to vulnerable & high risk populations, in Manitoba, for no cost or minimal cost
Member of: Credit Counselling Canada; United Way of Winnipeg
Finances: *Funding Sources:* United Way; Department of Finance, Province of Manitoba; Manitoba Lotteries Commission; Private donations
Activities: Providing financial counselling; Assisting persons to develop decision-making skills & self-management abilities; Offering community education & information to increase knowledge of financial counselling; Collaborating with other helpful organizations, such as The Workers Compensation Board, to offer an integrated service; Offering the Gambling Project, funded by the Manitoba Lotteries Corporation, in partnership with the Addictions Foundation of Manitoba; Providing income tax preparation for social assistance recipient
Chief Officer(s):
John Silver, Executive Director

Community Folk Art Council of Toronto (CFAC)
173B Front St. East, Toronto ON M5A 3Z4
Tel: 416-986-5310
cfactoronto@gmail.com
www.cfactoronto.com
www.facebook.com/CFACToronto
Overview: A medium-sized local charitable organization founded in 1968
Mission: To preserve, uphold, develop, & advance the cultural & artistic heritage of the people of Toronto through performances & the provision of educational resources
Member of: Folklore Canada International
Finances: *Annual Operating Budget:* $50,000-$100,000
Staff Member(s): 1
Membership: 95 groups; *Fees:* $75 individual; $125 group; *Member Profile:* Arts groups & individuals preserving & promoting heritage & traditions
Activities: Organizing festivals that showcase the various ethnic communities of Toronto; Offering educational programs & teaching multiculturalism; Publishing resources on the preservation of traditional culture; Promoting initiatives that celebrate diversity; Representing multicultural performers; *Awareness Events:* Multicultural Canada Day Festival, July
Chief Officer(s):
Wendy Limbertie, Executive Director

Community Food Sharing Association
PO Box 6291, 21 Mews Pl., St. John's NL A1C 6J9
Tel: 709-722-0130
cfsa.nf.net
Previous Name: City Index Referral Association
Overview: A small local organization
Mission: To act as a central collection & distribution point for member agencies throughout the province, with a goal to eliminate chronic hunger & alleviate poverty.
Member of: Newfoundland & Labrador Association of Food Distribution & Voluntary Action; Atlantic Alliance of Food Banks & C.V.A.'s; Food Banks Canada
Chief Officer(s):
Wanda Drodge, Chair

Community Foundation for Greater Toronto *See* Toronto Community Foundation

Community Foundation for Kingston & Area
#6, 165 Ontario St., Kingston ON K7L 2Y6
Tel: 613-546-9696; *Fax:* 613-531-9238
www.cfka.org
www.linkedin.com/company/community-foundation-for-kingston-&-area
www.facebook.com/CFKingstonArea

twitter.com/CFKingstonArea
www.youtube.com/user/cfkaed
Previous Name: The Martello Tower Society
Overview: A small local charitable organization founded in 1995
Mission: To raise funds for enhancing the quality of life of the community
Member of: Community Foundations of Canada
Finances: *Annual Operating Budget:* $100,000-$250,000; *Funding Sources:* Donations; corporations; grants
Staff Member(s): 3; 60 volunteer(s)
Membership: *Committees:* Community Engagement; Executive; Finance; First Capital Challenge Loan Review; Fundraising; Governance; Grants; Investment; Marketing & Communications; Nominations Advisory; Personnel; Regina Rosen Food First Fund; Resource Development; Vital Signs
Activities: Grant making
Chief Officer(s):
Tina Bailey, Executive Director
tina@cfka.org
Mora Chatterson, Coordinator, Finance & Operations
mora@cfka.org
Becky Cowan, Coordinator, Administration
becky@cfka.org
Awards:
• The Community Foundation for Kingston & Area Grant

The Community Foundation of Durham Region
PO Box 322, 701 Rossland Rd. East, Whitby ON L1N 9K3
Tel: 905-430-6507
info@durhamcommunityfoundation.ca
www.durhamcommunityfoundation.ca
ca.linkedin.com/in/durhamcf
www.facebook.com/Durhamcf
Overview: A small local charitable organization founded in 1995
Mission: To provide & administer charitable capital endowment funds & donations for the benefit of the citizens of the region
Member of: Community Foundations of Canada
Finances: *Annual Operating Budget:* $250,000-$500,000; *Funding Sources:* Donations
Staff Member(s): 1
Membership: *Committees:* Asset Development; Odyssey Ball; Grants; Hole in Won Golf; Investment; Marketing
Chief Officer(s):
Vivian Curl, Executive Director
vivian@durhamcommunityfoundation.ca

Community Foundation of Greater Québec *Voir* Fondation communautaire du Grand-Québec

Community Foundation of Lethbridge & Southwestern Alberta
404 - 8 St. South, Lethbridge AB T1J 2J7
Tel: 403-328-5297; *Fax:* 403-328-6061
office@cflsa.ca
cflsa.ca
www.facebook.com/cflsa
twitter.com/LethFoundation
Overview: A small local charitable organization founded in 1966
Mission: To receive & administer donations in trust for charitable, educational & cultural purposes
Member of: Community Foundations of Canada
Staff Member(s): 2
Membership: *Committees:* Executive; Development; Audit; Governance; Grants; Investment; Nomination; Vital Signs
Chief Officer(s):
George Hall, Executive Director
ghall@cflsa.ca

Community Foundation of Nova Scotia
#806, 1888 Brunswick St., Halifax NS B3J 3J8
Tel: 902-490-5907; *Fax:* 902-490-5917
Toll-Free: 877-999-5907
infocfns@cfns.ca
www.cfns-fcne.ca
www.facebook.com/CommunityFoundationofNovaScotia
twitter.com/communityns
Overview: A small provincial charitable organization
Mission: To accumulate financial & social capital for communities in Nova Scotia
Chief Officer(s):
Angela Bishop, Executive Director

Community Foundation of Ottawa (CFO) / Fondation communautaire d'Ottawa
#301, 75 Albert St., Ottawa ON K1P 5E7
Tel: 613-236-1616; *Fax:* 613-236-1621
info@cfo-fco.ca

Canadian Associations / Community Foundation of Prince Edward Island

communityfoundationottawa.ca
www.facebook.com/229469483746057
twitter.com/Ottawa_Gives
www.youtube.com/user/cfottawagives
Previous Name: Community Foundation of Ottawa-Carleton
Overview: A small national charitable organization founded in 1987
Mission: To accumulate funds from bequests, endowments, memorials & other charitable gifts to be held in trust in order to generate income, which in turn is used for a range of charitable interests & needs; to give grants to not-for-profit organizations in all sectors that are recognized as registered charities.
Affiliation(s): Community Foundations of Canada; Council on Foundations - USA
Finances: *Annual Operating Budget:* $250,000-$500,000; *Funding Sources:* United Way; donors
Staff Member(s): 13
Membership: *Committees:* Grants; Nominating; Inventestment; Governance; Finance & Audit; Impact Investing
Activities: Annual celebration; *Internships:* Yes; *Speaker Service:* Yes
Chief Officer(s):
Brian Toller, Chair
Marco Pagani, President & CEO

Community Foundation of Ottawa-Carleton See Community Foundation of Ottawa

Community Foundation of Prince Edward Island
119 Queen St., Charlottetown PE C1A 4B3
Tel: 902-892-3440; *Fax:* 902-892-0880
Toll-Free: 800-566-7307
cfpei@pei.aibn.com
www.cfpei.ca
Overview: A small provincial charitable organization founded in 1993
Mission: To provide leadership & financial support to initiatives that aim to enhance communities in PEI
Activities: Working with donors to create endowment funds; Distributing grants & scholarships; Offering resources & expertise
Chief Officer(s):
Marla Gidney, Officer, Finance
Kent Hudson, Officer, Fund Development
Publications:
• Community Foundation of Prince Edward Island Annual Report
Type: Yearbook; *Frequency:* Annually

Community Foundations of Canada
#600, 123 Slater St., Ottawa ON K1P 5H2
Tel: 613-236-2664
www.communityfoundations.ca
www.facebook.com/CommunityFdnsCanadaHome
twitter.com/CommFdnsCanada
www.youtube.com/user/cfcteam
Overview: A medium-sized national charitable organization
Mission: To help Canadians improve their communities; To support community foundations across Canada
Membership: 191 foundations
Activities: Supporting local initiatives & youth programs; Promoting food programs & advocating for healthy food access; Impact investing; Organizing community sports events; Strengthening community knowledge by collecting data & publishing Vital Signs reports
Chief Officer(s):
Ian Bird, President
ibird@communityfoundations.ca
Andrew Chunilall, CEO
achunilall@communityfoundations.ca
Andrea Dicks, COO
adicks@communityfoundations.ca
Lesley Inglis, Director, Corporate Services
linglis@communityfoundations.ca
Cindy Lindsay, Director, Member Services
clindsay@communityfoundations.ca
Lee Rose, Director, Community Knowledge
lrose@communityfoundations.ca
David Venn, Director, Communications
dvenn@communityfoundations.ca

Community Futures Development Association of British Columbia (CFBC)
7871 Stave Lake St., #C230, Mission BC V2V 0C5
Tel: 604-289-4222
info@communityfutures.ca
www.communityfutures.ca
www.linkedin.com/company/community-futures-british-columbia
www.facebook.com/CommunityFuturesBC
twitter.com/Comm_FuturesBC
plus.google.com/+communityfutures
Also Known As: Community Futures British Columbia
Overview: A medium-sized provincial organization founded in 1993
Mission: To coordinate community economic development initiatives in British Columbia; To encourage economic diversification in rural communities; To improve economic conditions in British Columbia; To promote long-term community economic sustainability; To enhance regional competitiveness; To help with the growth of members
Member of: BC Chamber of Commerce; Economic Development Association of BC
Finances: *Annual Operating Budget:* $250,000-$500,000
Staff Member(s): 5; 20 volunteer(s)
Membership: 34 organizations; *Fees:* $1,000; *Member Profile:* Community Futures offices throughout British Columbia, such as Community Futures Central Kootenay, Community Futures North Okanagan, & Community Futures Sunshine Coast
Activities: Supporting community economic development strategies; Engaging in advocacy activities; Providing resources on topics such as starting a business, financing a business, & accessing government programs & services; Funding projects submitted by affiliated Community Futures locations, as part of the Rural Economic Diversification Initiative of British Columbia project, which is a joint initiative between Community Futures British Columbia & the Western Economic Diversification Canada
Chief Officer(s):
Robert Annis, Chair
Marie Gallant, Executive Director
mgallant@communityfutures.ca
Garry Angus, Provincial Coordinator, Entrepreneurs with Disabilities Program (EDP)
gangus@communityfutures.ca
Vanessa Tveitane, Administrator, Communications & Office
vtveitane@communityfutures.ca

Community Futures Manitoba Inc. (CFM)
#559, 167 Lombard Ave., Winnipeg MB R3B 0V3
Tel: 204-943-2905; *Fax:* 204-956-9363
info@cfmanitoba.ca
www.cfmanitoba.ca
www.facebook.com/cfmanitoba
Overview: A medium-sized provincial organization
Mission: To strengthen rural economies in Manitoba; To promote the rural & northern region of Manitoba & its economic opportunities
Affiliation(s): Western Economic Diversification Canada
Finances: *Funding Sources:* Government of Canada, through Western Economic Diversification Canada
Membership: 16 Community Future organizations; *Member Profile:* Community Future organizations throughout rural & northern Manitoba
Activities: Assisting in community economic development, through the development of long-term plans; Enabling entrepreneurship across rural & northern Manitoba; Providing business counselling, training, & resources; Offering access to business loans
Meetings/Conferences:
• 22nd Vision Quest Conference & Trade Show 2018, May, 2018, RBC Convention Centre, Winnipeg, MB
Scope: Provincial
Attendance: 1,000+
Description: An annual event for business leaders, innovators, & entrepreneurs, from Manitoba, Saskatchewan, Alberta, northern Ontario, Nunavut, Northwest Territories, & the United States, to discuss & promote Aboriginal business & community development, featuring interactive workshops, motivational keynote presentations from business leaders, a trade show with more than 80 booths, & social & networking events
Contact Information: www.vqconference.com
• Community Futures Manitoba 2018 Annual Provincial Conference, 2018, MB
Scope: Provincial
Attendance: 150
Description: A yearly event to explore economic development issues in Manitoba, featuring keynote addresses
Contact Information: info@cfmanitoba.ca
Publications:
• Community Futures Manitoba Inc. Annual Report
Type: Yearbook; *Frequency:* Annually
Profile: An overview of the organization's activities, plus goals & strategies

• Futurescape [a publication of Community Futures Manitoba]
Type: Newsletter
Profile: Updates on ways the Community Futures Program assists rural Manitobans to diversify & grow their communities

Community Futures Network Society of Alberta (CFNA)
Bldg. B, PO Box 184, #3209, 101 Sunset Dr., Cochrane AB T4C 0B4
Tel: 403-851-9995; *Fax:* 403-851-9905
Toll-Free: 877-482-3672
cfna.albertacf.com
Overview: A medium-sized provincial organization
Mission: To work towards an economically strong & diversified rural Alberta; To support Community Futures organizations throughout rural Alberta; To facilitate the sustainability of the Community Futures program
Finances: *Funding Sources:* Western Economic Diversification Canada
Membership: 27 organizations; *Member Profile:* Alberta Community Futures organizations
Activities: Supporting the delivery of Community Futures initiatives; Developing & implementing community-based economic development & diversification strategies; Offering small business loans; Delivering the Self Employment Program; Providing the Entrepreneurs with Disabilities Program
Chief Officer(s):
Shane Stewart, Chair
Jon Close, Executive Director, 403-851-9995 Ext. 2
Judy McMillan-Evans, Manager, Projects & Capacity Building

Community Futures Saskatchewan
c/o Vickie Newmeyer, PO Box 2167, 125 - 1st Ave. East, Kindersley SK S0L 1S0
Tel: 306-463-1850; *Fax:* 306-463-1855
Toll-Free: 888-919-3800
cfsask.ca
www.facebook.com/cfsask
twitter.com/cfsaskatoon
Overview: A small provincial organization founded in 1985
Mission: To work as a grassroots economic renewal initiative, through local entrepreneur development & community & social economic development in rural & northern Saskatchewan; To support & guide persons who are interested in setting up a small business
Finances: *Funding Sources:* Western Economic Diversification Canada
Membership: *Member Profile:* Local Community Futures Development Corporations in Saskatchewan
Activities: Assisting persons in Saskatchewan who wish to establish or expand a small business; Providing business skills training; Offering business loans; Delivering the Entrepreneurs with Disabilities program
Chief Officer(s):
Lori Ries, Chair
Jason Denbow, Executive Director
Publications:
• I Am an Entrepreneur
Type: Workbook; *Number of Pages:* 98
Profile: A self assessment guide about starting a business

Community Futures West Yellowhead
221 Pembina Ave., Hinton AB T7E 2B3
Tel: 780-865-1224
Toll-Free: 800-263-1716
www.cfwestyellowhead.com
Overview: A small local organization
Mission: To diversify the economy of the West Yellowhead region through entrepreneurship & community development
Finances: *Funding Sources:* Federal government
Activities: Business training & development; business loans
Chief Officer(s):
Johannes Zwart, Chair
Nancy Robbins, General Manager

Community Futures Wild Rose
PO Box 2159, #101, 331 - 3 Ave., Strathmore AB T1P 1K2
Tel: 403-934-8888; *Fax:* 403-934-6492
Toll-Free: 888-881-9675
wildrose.albertacf.com
Previous Name: Wild Rose Economic Development Corporation
Overview: A small local organization founded in 1929
Mission: To maintain, improve & expand existing businesses & to attract new ones to Three Hills
Affiliation(s): Economic Development Association of Alberta
Finances: *Funding Sources:* Regional Government
8 volunteer(s)

Membership: 1-99
Chief Officer(s):
Alice Booth, Chair
Ron Cox, General Manager

Community Futures Yellowhead East
PO Box 2185, #1, 5023 - 50 Ave., Whitecourt AB T7S 1P8
Tel: 780-706-3500
Toll-Free: 877-706-3500
yellowheadeast.albertacf.com
facebook.com/communityfuturesye
youtube.com/communityfuturesye
Overview: A small local organization founded in 1986
Mission: To provide a single window of opportunity through which businesses & other entities can access information, resources, financial assistance & training in order to foster economic development, resulting in job creation
Finances: Funding Sources: National government
Staff Member(s): 40; 14 volunteer(s)
Chief Officer(s):
Roxanne Harper, Manager

Community Health Nurses of Canada (CHNC) / Infirmières et infirmiers en santé communautaire au Canada (IISCC)
632 Hugel Ave., Midland ON L4R 1W7
Tel: 705-527-1014
info@chnc.ca
www.chnc.ca
www.facebook.com/250569078355380
Overview: A medium-sized national organization founded in 1987
Mission: To act as the voice of community health nurses across Canada; To advocate for the role of community health nurses; To identify & address social & environmental determinants of health by promoting healthy public policy; To encourage a publicly funded, universal health system; To respond to issues which affect community health nurses; To advance practice excellence; To strengthen leadership in community health nursing
Member of: Canadian Nurses Association (CNA)
Affiliation(s): Registered Nurses Association Community Health Nurses Initiatives Group
Membership: 400; Fees: $75; Member Profile: Community health nurses throughout Canada; Provincial & territorial community health nursing interest groups; Committees: Certification; Communications; Governance; Membership; National Conference; Research & Health Policy; Standards & Competencies
Activities: Facilitating communication among community health nurses throughout Canada; Developing standards of practice & a community health nursing certification process; Library
Chief Officer(s):
Joyce Fox, Executive Director
ed.chnc@gmail.com
Awards:
• Award of Merit
• Barbara Mildon Community Health Nursing Certification Bursary
; Amount: $500
Meetings/Conferences:
• Community Health Nurses of Canada 2018 National Community Health Nursing Conference, June, 2018, The Double Tree Hotel & Conference Centre, Regina, SK
Scope: National
Description: Theme: "Caring, Connecting & Leading for a Healthy Canada"
Publications:
• Community Health Nursing Certification Guidebook [a publication of the Community Health Nurses of Canada]
Price: $50
• Community Health Nursing Standards of Practice [a publication of the Community Health Nurses of Canada]
Price: $17
• Community Health Nursing Standards of Practice Toolkit [a publication of the Community Health Nurses of Canada]
Profile: A resource to facilitate use of standards
• Community Health Nursing Vision 2020: Shaping the Future [a publication of the Community Health Nurses of Canada]
• Great Big News [a publication of Community Health Nurses of Canada]
Type: Newsletter
Profile: Member newsletter
• Public Health Nursing Discipline Specific Competencies [a publication of the Community Health Nurses of Canada]
Price: $12

• Public Health Nursing Practice in Canada: A Review of the Literature [a publication of the Community Health Nurses of Canada]

Community Heritage Federation See Community Museums Association of Prince Edward Island

Community Heritage Ontario (CHO)
24 Conlins Rd., Toronto ON M1C 1C3
Tel: 416-282-2710; Fax: 416-282-9482
info@communityheritageontario.ca
www.communityheritageontario.ca
www.facebook.com/215682445171022
twitter.com/CHOntario
Overview: A medium-sized provincial charitable organization founded in 1991
Mission: Umbrella organization to the volunteer, municipally-appointed heritage advisory committees (LACACs); encourages the development of same & furthers the identification, preservation, interpretation & wise use of community heritage
Member of: Heritage Canada
Finances: Funding Sources: Membership fees; grants
Membership: Fees: $75 group; $35 individual; $35 school/student; $100 corporate; Member Profile: Heritage associations in Ontario
Activities: Speaker Service: Yes
Chief Officer(s):
Wayne Morgan, President
waynemorgan@communityheritageontario.ca
Rick Schofield, Secretary & Treasurer
rickschofield@communityheritageontario.ca
Meetings/Conferences:
• Community Heritage Ontario 2018 Ontario Heritage Conference, June, 2018, Sault Ste Marie, ON
Scope: Provincial

Community Information - Essex See Essex Community Services

Community Information Centre Belle River See Lakeshore Community Services

Community Information Centre of Ottawa (CIC) / Centre d'information communautaire d'Ottawa
PO Box 41146, 1910 St-Laurent Blvd., Ottawa ON K1G 1A4
Tel: 613-761-9076; Fax: 613-761-9077
Toll-Free: 877-761-9076; TTY: 888-340-1001
info@cominfo-ottawa.org
www.cominfo-ottawa.org
www.facebook.com/211EasternOntario
twitter.com/211EasternON
Overview: A medium-sized local charitable organization founded in 1974
Mission: To provide a link between individuals & organizations in Ottawa & the community resources or services they need through information & referral services in both official languages
Member of: InformOntario; InformCanada
Finances: Annual Operating Budget: $100,000-$250,000; Funding Sources: City of Ottawa; United Way of Ottawa; directory sales
Staff Member(s): 4; 6 volunteer(s)
Activities: Providing information on community & social services; Referring clients to agencies that offer health & social programs; Maintaining databases & directories; Rents Mailing List: Yes; Library: Open to public
Chief Officer(s):
Marie-Andrée Carrière, Executive Director
MA.Carriere@cominfo-ottawa.org

Community Information Fairview (CIF)
PO Box 210, 1800 Sheppard Ave. East, Toronto ON M2J 5A7
Tel: 416-493-0752; Fax: 416-493-0823
communityinfofairview@rogers.com
Overview: A small local organization founded in 1971
Mission: To provide accessible space within Fairview Mall to better serve the community; To assure equality of access to CIF services to the best of our abilities; To provide full access to people with physical & mental impairments; to improve & build partnerships with other community organizations & the private sector; To assist community development activities; To assist other community organizations to attain their goals; To promote the development of a Community Resource Centre
Member of: Federation of Community Information Centres of Toronto; Inform Canada
Membership: Member Profile: Volunteers with 50 hrs of community service

Activities: Information; legal clinic

Community Information Hamilton (CIH)
Hamilton Public Library, PO Box 2700, 55 York Blvd., 5th Fl., Hamilton ON L8N 4E4
Tel: 905-528-0104; Fax: 905-528-7764
informationhamilton.ca
www.facebook.com/Inform.Hamilton
twitter.com/informhamilton
Also Known As: Inform Hamilton
Previous Name: Community Information Service Hamilton-Wentworth
Overview: A small local charitable organization founded in 1971
Mission: To connect people with community & government services; To provide individuals, organizations, business & governments with information on resources available in Hamilton-Wentworth
Member of: Inform Ontario; ACICO/Inform Canada
Finances: Annual Operating Budget: $100,000-$250,000; Funding Sources: City of Hamilton; United Way; publication sales
Staff Member(s): 6; 14 volunteer(s)
Membership: 30; Fees: $5
Activities: Library: Open to public

Community Information Service Hamilton-Wentworth See Community Information Hamilton

Community Integration Services Society (CISS)
2175 Mary Hill Rd., Port Coquitlam BC V3C 3A2
Tel: 604-461-2131; Fax: 778-285-5520
oadmin@gociss.org
www.gociss.org
Overview: A small local organization
Mission: To help people with disabilities become active members of society
Chief Officer(s):
Shari Mahar, Executive Director
smahar@gociss.org

Community Involvement of the Disabled (CID)
#5, 28 Hillview Ave., Sydney NS B1P 2H4
Tel: 902-564-9817; Fax: 902-564-5758
Overview: A small local charitable organization founded in 1977
Mission: Advocacy for persons with disabilities
Member of: Nova Scotia League for Equal Opportunities
Activities: Library: Open to public

Community Kitchen Program of Calgary
3751 - 21 St. NE, Calgary AB T2E 6T5
Tel: 403-275-0258
www.ckpcalgary.ca
www.facebook.com/community.kitchen.program
twitter.com/ckpcalgary
Overview: A small local charitable organization overseen by Food Banks Alberta Association
Mission: To work with individuals, families & communities to facilitate &/or enable initiatives that reduce hunger
Member of: Food Banks Alberta Association
Chief Officer(s):
Sundae Nordin, CEO

Community Legal Assistance Society
#300, 1140 West Pender St., Vancouver BC V6E 4G1
Tel: 604-685-3425; Fax: 604-685-7611
Toll-Free: 888-685-6222
www.clasbc.net
www.facebook.com/204399496259131
twitter.com/clasbc
Overview: A large local organization founded in 1971
Mission: To provide legal assistance to persons who are physically, mentally, socially, economically or otherwise disadvantaged, through litigation, test cases, public education & law reform endeavours
Affiliation(s): Legal Services Society; Law Foundation of British Columbia
Finances: Annual Operating Budget: $1.5 Million-$3 Million; Funding Sources: Provincial government
Staff Member(s): 35; 17 volunteer(s)
Membership: 27 individual
Chief Officer(s):
Aleem Bharmal, Executive Director
abharmal@clasbc.net
Publications:
• Community Legal Assistance Society Annual Report
Type: Report; Frequency: Annually

British Columbia Human Rights Clinic
#300, 1140 West Pender St., Vancouver BC V6E 4G1
Tel: 604-622-1100; *Fax:* 604-685-7611
Toll-Free: 855-685-6222
infobchrc@clasbc.net
www.bchrc.net
twitter.com/bchrc
Mission: To provide legal assistance, mediation services, & representation to complainants who have cases before the BC Human Rights Tribunal; To strengthen understandings of human rights through education & training

Community Legal Education Association (Manitoba) Inc. (CLEA) / Association d'éducation juridique communautaire (Manitoba) inc.
#205, 414 Graham Ave., Winnipeg MB R3C 0L8
Tel: 204-943-2382; *Fax:* 204-943-3600
mctroszko@communitylegal.mb.ca
www.communitylegal.mb.ca
www.facebook.com/339159352882635
Overview: A medium-sized provincial charitable organization founded in 1984
Mission: To provide legal education & information programs to Manitobans
Finances: *Funding Sources:* Law Society of Manitoba; The Manitoba Law Foundation; Justice Canada; Youth Justice Policy; The Winnipeg Foundation; Investors Group; Legal Aid MB
Membership: *Fees:* $2 low income; $25 individual; $40 organization
Activities: Provision of school programs plus workshops & classes in the community; Law Phone-In & Lawyer Referral Program; Publication of pamphlets, booklets & education kits; *Speaker Service:* Yes; *Library:* Open to public
Chief Officer(s):
Mary Troszko, Executive Director
Geof Langen, President
Publications:
• CLEA [Community Legal Education Association (Manitoba) Inc.] Newsletter
Type: Newsletter; *Frequency:* Semiannually
• Manitoba Legal Services Directory
Type: Directory; *Price:* $20

Community Legal Education Ontario (CLEO)
#506, 180 Dundas St. West, Toronto ON M5G 1Z8
Tel: 416-408-4420; *Fax:* 416-408-4424
info@cleo.on.ca
www.cleo.on.ca
Overview: A medium-sized provincial charitable organization founded in 1974
Mission: To provide public legal education services & programs that benefit the low income community, disadvantaged persons, such as immigrants & refugees, seniors, women, & injured workers in Ontario
Finances: *Funding Sources:* Legal Aid Ontario; Department of Justice Canada
Activities: Provision of CLEONet, a web site for community workers & advocates; Publication of information on various legal topics; Six Languages Text & Audio Project to improve access to legal information by low-income people in the Chinese, Arabic, Tamil, Urdu, Spanish, & Somali linguistic communities; Research
Chief Officer(s):
Julie Mathews, Executive Director
Jane Withey, Director, Clinic Operations

Community Legal Information Association of Prince Edward Island (CLIA PEI)
Royalty Centre, #11, 40 Enman Cres., Charlottetown PE C1A 7K4
Tel: 902-892-0853
Toll-Free: 800-240-9798
clia@cliapei.ca
www.cliapei.ca
www.facebook.com/CLIAPEI
twitter.com/cliapei
www.youtube.com/CLIAPEI
Overview: A medium-sized provincial charitable organization founded in 1985
Mission: To provide Islanders with understandable, useful information about the Canadian laws & the justice system
Member of: Prince Edward Island Literacy Alliance Inc.; Public Legal Education Association of Canada

Finances: *Annual Operating Budget:* $100,000-$250,000;
Funding Sources: Justice Canada; provincial government; Law Foundation of PEI
Staff Member(s): 3; 100 volunteer(s)
Membership: 50; *Fees:* $2
Activities: *Speaker Service:* Yes; *Library:* Open to public
Chief Officer(s):
Warren Banks, President
David Daughton, Executive Director

Community Living Ajax-Pickering & Whitby
36 Emperor St., Ajax ON L1S 1M7
Tel: 905-427-3300; *Fax:* 905-427-3310
info@apwcommunityliving.org
www.cl-apw.org
Previous Name: Ajax, Pickering & Whitby Association for Community Living
Overview: A small local charitable organization founded in 1957 overseen by Community Living Ontario
Member of: Community Living Ontario
Staff Member(s): 140
Membership: 300; *Fees:* $10
Chief Officer(s):
Barbara Andrews, Executive Director
Chris Cook, President

Community Living Algoma
99 Northern Ave. East, Sault Ste Marie ON P6B 4H5
Tel: 705-253-1700; *Fax:* 705-253-1777
Toll-Free: 800-448-8097
www.communitylivingalgoma.org
Overview: A large local charitable organization founded in 1954 overseen by Community Living Ontario
Mission: To help all people live in a state of dignity in their community, where they can access the support needed to ensure full inclusion
Member of: Community Living Ontario
Membership: *Fees:* $15 individual & affiliate; $50 corporate; *Committees:* Planning Development & Advocacy; Education; Finance; Human Resources & French Language Services; Quality Enhancement
Activities: Residential, support & vocation services; day programs; *Library:* by appointment
Chief Officer(s):
John Policicchio, Executive Director
Publications:
• News & Views [a publication of Community Living Algoma]
Type: Newsletter

Community Living Alternatives Society (CLAS)
46B Chipman Dr., Kentville NS B4N 3V7
Tel: 902-681-8920; *Fax:* 902-681-2850
clas@ns.sympatico.ca
www.clasnovascotia.com
Overview: A small local charitable organization founded in 1976
Mission: Provides quality community living opportunities for individuals with intellectual challenges; promotes & facilitates the exercise of individual rights, the fulfillment of responsibilities & the participation of individuals within their community
Staff Member(s): 130
Chief Officer(s):
Brian Wolfe, Executive Director

Community Living Association (Lanark County) (CLA (LC))
178 Town Line East, Carleton Place ON K7C 2C2
Tel: 613-257-8040; *Fax:* 613-257-5679
inquiries@clalanark.ca
www.clalanark.ca
Overview: A small local charitable organization founded in 1965 overseen by Community Living Ontario
Mission: To help all persons live in a state of dignity, share all elements of living in the community & have the opportunity to participate effectively
Member of: Community Living Ontario
Finances: *Annual Operating Budget:* $1.5 Million-$3 Million
Staff Member(s): 87; 20 volunteer(s)
Membership: 50; *Fees:* $10; *Committees:* Fundraising, Association Well-Being; Health & Safety
Activities: Providing individual day & resident support in Larnark County, focused in Almonte, Carleton Place, Smiths Falls & Perth; *Speaker Service:* Yes; *Library:* Open to public
Chief Officer(s):
Tony Pacheco, Executive Director, 613-257-8040 Ext. 40
tony@clalanark.ca

Community Living Association for South Simcoe (CLASS)
125 Dufferin St. South, Alliston ON L9R 1E9
Tel: 705-435-4792; *Fax:* 705-435-2766
www.class.on.ca
www.facebook.com/400120446712712?ref=hl
twitter.com/CLASS_Community
Overview: A small local organization founded in 1962 overseen by Community Living Ontario
Mission: To advocate that persons with developmental disabilities live in a state of dignity, have equal opportunity to maximize individual potential for personal growth & participate in all elements of life in the community
Member of: Ontario Agencies Supporting Individuals with Special Needs
Staff Member(s): 109
Membership: 70; *Fees:* $15
Activities: *Internships:* Yes
Chief Officer(s):
Vito Facciolo, Executive Director, 705-435-4792 Ext. 224
vito@class.on.ca

Community Living Association for the Little Divide; Lac La Biche & District Association for the Handicapped *See* Lac La Biche Disability Services

Community Living Association for York South; York South Association for Community Living *See* Community Living York South

Community Living Atikokan (CLA)
PO Box 2054, 114 Gorrie St., Atikokan ON P0T 1C0
Tel: 807-597-2259; *Fax:* 807-597-1495
www.cl-atikokan.ca
Previous Name: Atikokan & District Association for the Developmental Services
Overview: A small local charitable organization founded in 1969
Member of: Community Living Ontario
Finances: *Funding Sources:* Ministry of Community & Social Services; fundraising
Activities: Group living; supported independent living; training & leisure centre; & transition program. Services include: yard maintenance; auto detailing; catering services; laundry services; janitorial services; Chips R' Us; wedding decoration; mail pick-up & delivery; collating; paper shredding; & promotional buttons.
Chief Officer(s):
Jim Turner, Executive Director, 807-597-2020
jim.turner@cl-atikokan.ca

Community Living Brantford
366 Dalhousie St., Brantford ON N3S 1K9
Tel: 519-756-2662; *Fax:* 519-756-7668
communitylivingbrant@clbrant.com
www.clbrant.com
Previous Name: Brantford & District Association for Community Living
Overview: A small local charitable organization founded in 1952 overseen by Community Living Ontario
Mission: To promote full citizenship & respect for all people, through education, support, & services designed to meet the diverse developmental needs of children, adults, & their families
Member of: Ontario Agencies Supporting Individuals with Special Needs (OASIS); Community Living Ontario
Finances: *Annual Operating Budget:* Greater than $5 Million; *Funding Sources:* Ontario Ministry of Community & Social Services; Contract revenue; Membership fees; Fundraising
Staff Member(s): 250; 20 volunteer(s)
Membership: 300; *Fees:* $10 family; $15 family; $5 associate; *Member Profile:* Parents, interested citizens; *Committees:* Public Education; Resource Management; Quality Enhancement
Activities: Operates 12 group homes, a Day Program for 100 adults & a Day Program for 45 adults with multiple challenges; provides support for over 70 individuals who live on their own; provides peer support groups for teens; adult literacy program; provides advocacy & support to parents & family members; *Speaker Service:* Yes
Chief Officer(s):
Wendy Matthews, Administrator
Awards:
• Leo Mahon Memorial Scholarship
Awarded to a student entering post-secondary education who would benefit the field of Developmental Handicaps; *Amount:* $1,000

Community Living Cambridge
160 Hespeler Rd., Cambridge ON N1R 6V7

Tel: 519-623-7490; Fax: 519-740-8073
www.communitylivingcambridge.ca
www.facebook.com/CommunityLivingCambridge
twitter.com/clcambridgeON
Previous Name: Cambridge Association for the Mentally Handicapped
Overview: A small local charitable organization founded in 1954
Mission: To ensure that all people who have a mental handicap live in a state of dignity & are provided with the opportunity to become self-sufficient & to realize their individual potential
Member of: Community Living Ontario
Affiliation(s): Ontario Association For Community Living
Finances: *Funding Sources:* Provincial government; legacies & bequests; private donations; memberships; fees for services; fundraising
Membership: *Fees:* $10 individual; $15 family
Activities: Preschool resources; recreation; family services; residential services; vocational & adult day services; supported employment services & community options
Chief Officer(s):
Terry Lake, President
Denise Gruber, Executive Director, 519-623-7490 Ext. 2226

Community Living Campbellford/Brighton (CLCB)
PO Box 1360, 65 Bridge St. East, Campbellford ON K0L 1L0
Tel: 705-653-1821; *Fax:* 705-653-5738
Toll-Free: 866-528-0825
admin@communitylivingcampbellford.com
www.communitylivingcampbellford.com
www.linkedin.com/company/community-living-campbellford-brighton
www.facebook.com/CLCfordBrighton
twitter.com/clcfordbrighton
Previous Name: Campbellford & District Association for Community Living
Overview: A small local organization founded in 1960 overseen by Community Living Ontario
Mission: To provide support & services to people; To promote opportunities for personal growth within their community
Member of: Community Living Ontario
Finances: *Annual Operating Budget:* Greater than $5 Million; *Funding Sources:* Government grants
Staff Member(s): 122; 25 volunteer(s)
Membership: 75; *Fees:* $15
Chief Officer(s):
Nancy Brown, Executive Director, 705-653-1821 Ext. 211
nbrown@communitylivingcampbellford.com
Publications:
• Community Living Campbellford/Brighton Annual Report
Type: Report; *Frequency:* Annually

Community Living Chatham-Kent
PO Box 967, Chatham ON N7M 5L3
Tel: 519-352-1174; *Fax:* 519-352-5459
www.clc-k.ca
www.facebook.com/communitylivingchathamkent
Previous Name: Chatham & District Association for Community Living
Overview: A small local organization founded in 1955 overseen by Community Living Ontario
Mission: To support individuals with intellectual disabilities & their families so that they are able to participate fully in their community
Member of: Community Living Ontario
Staff Member(s): 260
Membership: *Fees:* $10 single/family
Chief Officer(s):
Ron Coristine, Executive Director, 519-352-1174 Ext. 242
rcoristine@clc-k.ca

Community Living Dryden-Sioux Lookout (CLDSL)
280 Arthur St., Dryden ON P8N 1K8
Tel: 807-223-3364; *Fax:* 807-223-5784
www.cldsl.ca
www.facebook.com/96367942643
Previous Name: Dryden & District Association for Community Living
Overview: A small local charitable organization founded in 1968
Mission: To provide support programs to individuals with developmental & intellectual disabilities in the Dryden, Sioux Lookout, & Hudson area; To help disabled individuals become participating citizens in society
Member of: Community Living Ontario
Finances: *Funding Sources:* Membership fees; fundraising
Membership: 27; *Fees:* $15 single; $20 family; $100 coporate; $200 corporate gold
Activities: Offering programs & services, including residential services, supported independent living, clinical video conferencing, employment services, Community Inclusion Hub, & family support programs
Chief Officer(s):
Sherry Baum, Executive Director
sherry.baum@cldsl.ca
Lynda Menard-Penner, Director, Services
lynda.menard-penner@cldsl.ca
Barb Kirouac, Director, Human Resources, Quality Assurance & Administration
barbara.kirouac@cldsl.ca
Shauna Spalding, Director, Finance & Assets
shauna.spalding@cldsl.ca

Community Living Dufferin
065371 County Rd. 3, East Garafraxa ON L9W 7J8
Tel: 519-941-8971; *Fax:* 519-941-9121
info@communitylivingdufferin.ca
www.communitylivingdufferin.ca
www.facebook.com/communitylivingdufferin
twitter.com/cldufferin
www.youtube.com/user/CLDufferin
Previous Name: Dufferin Association for Community Living
Overview: A small local charitable organization founded in 1954 overseen by Community Living Ontario
Mission: To encourage people with developmental disabilities & their families to pursue enriched connections within their community
Member of: Community Living Ontario; Canadian Association for Community Living
Finances: *Funding Sources:* Ministry of Community & Social Services; Dufferin County; Foundations; fundraising
Membership: 1-99; *Fees:* $10
Activities: Offering community outreach & employment services
Chief Officer(s):
Sheryl Chandler, Executive Director, 519-941-8971 Ext. 136
sheryl@communitylivingdufferin.ca

Community Living Dundas County (CLDC)
PO Box 678, 55 Allison Ave., Morrisburg ON K0C 1X0
Tel: 613-543-3737; *Fax:* 613-543-4432
cldc@cldc.ca
www.cldc.ca
Previous Name: Dundas County Community Living Inc.
Overview: A small local organization
Mission: To advocate for the inclusion of people with an intellectual disability in their communities, promoting opportunities for their personal growth, providing training & resources for them & their families
Member of: Community Living Ontario
Finances: *Funding Sources:* Provincial government, donations
Activities: Social, leisure-based day support; transitional support from school to community; support for securing employment
Chief Officer(s):
Marja Smellink, President
Debbie Boardman, Executive Director
dbcardman@cldc.ca
Brenda Laviolette, Director, Supports & Services
blaviolette@cldc.ca
Sandra O'Neil, Manager, Human Resources
soneil@cldc.ca
Nancy Cassell, Manager, Finance
ncassell@cldc.ca

Community Living Durham North
#2, 60 Vanedward Dr., Port Perry ON L9L 1G3
Tel: 905-985-8511; *Fax:* 905-985-0799
cldn.ca
www.facebook.com/communitylivingdurhamnorth
twitter.com/CLDurhamNorth
Previous Name: Central Seven Association for Community Living
Overview: A small local charitable organization founded in 1967 overseen by Community Living Ontario
Mission: To provide services to people with developmental disabilities in the northern portion of Durham Region - Brock, Scugog & Uxbridge townships; to promote the idea that all people live in a state of dignity, share in all elements of living in the community & have the opportunity to participate effectively
Affiliation(s): Canadian Association for Community Living; Ontario Association for Community Living
Finances: *Annual Operating Budget:* $3 Million-$5 Million; *Funding Sources:* Donations
Staff Member(s): 135; 35 volunteer(s)
Membership: 70; *Fees:* $10
Chief Officer(s):
Glenn Taylor, Executive Director
glenn@cldn.ca

Community Living Elgin (CLE)
400 Talbot St., St Thomas ON N5P 1B8
Tel: 519-631-9222; *Fax:* 519-633-4392
info@communitylivingelgin.com
www.communitylivingelgin.com
Previous Name: Elgin Association for Community Living
Overview: A small local charitable organization founded in 1958
Mission: To provide support & services, primarily to people with developmental disabilities & their families to enable them to participate at full potential within the community
Member of: Community Living Ontario
Finances: *Funding Sources:* Provincial government; United Way; fundraising
Activities: Adult Development Centre; Friendco, a workshop providing contract work to manufacturing companies; Family Enrichment Centre; Parent-Child Place; toy lending library; *Speaker Service:* Yes
Chief Officer(s):
Bob Ashcroft, President
Michelle Palmer, Interim Executive Director
m.palmer@communitylivingelgin.com

Community Living Espanola
345 Centre St., Espanola ON P5E 1E4
Tel: 705-869-0442; *Fax:* 705-869-0446
www.clespanola.ca
www.facebook.com/506858389367383
twitter.com/clespanola
Previous Name: Espanola & District Association for Community Living
Overview: A small local charitable organization
Mission: To provide services to individuals with intellectual challenges, fostering meaningful living for those with developmental disabilities
Member of: Community Living Ontario
Membership: 36; *Fees:* $3
Chief Officer(s):
Louise Laplante, Executive Director
louise.laplante@clespanola.ca

Community Living Essex County
Essex Centre, 372 Talbot St. North, Essex ON N8M 2W4
Tel: 519-776-6483; *Fax:* 519-776-6972
communitylivingessex.org
www.linkedin.com/company/community-living-essex-county
www.facebook.com/clessexcounty
twitter.com/clessexcounty
www.youtube.com/user/clessexcounty
Overview: A large local charitable organization founded in 1961 overseen by Community Living Ontario
Mission: To provide programs & support for people with a developmental disability & their families; To ensure that all people have the right to live in a state of dignity & share in all elements of living in the community with the opportunity to participate effectively
Member of: Community Living Ontario
Finances: *Funding Sources:* Ontario Ministry of Community & Social Services; donations; fundraising
Staff Member(s): 600
Membership: *Fees:* $10 individual & affiliate; $150 corporate
Activities: *Awareness Events:* Ruthven Apple Festival, Sept.; Jingle Bell Run/Walk & Wheel, Nov.; *Speaker Service:* Yes; *Library:* Open to public
Chief Officer(s):
Nancy Wallace-Gero, Executive Director
nancywallacegero@communitylivingessex.org
Publications:
• The Profile [a publication of Community Living Essex County]
Type: Newsletter; *Frequency:* Quarterly

Amherstburg - Channel Office
260 Bathurst St., Amherstburg ON N9V 1Y9
Tel: 519-736-5077; *Fax:* 519-736-9982
Chief Officer(s):
Anne Garrod, Director, Supports & Services, West Area, 519-776-6483 Ext. 262
annegarrod@communitylivingessex.org

Leamington - Southshore Office
245 Talbot St. West, Leamington ON N8H 1N8
Tel: 519-326-4311; *Fax:* 519-326-7794
Chief Officer(s):

Canadian Associations / Community Living Fort Erie (CLFE)

Lee-Anne Dupuis, Director, Supports & Services, South Area,
519-776-6483 Ext. 263
leeannedupuis@communitylivingessex.org

Tecumseh - Northshore Office
13158 Tecumseh Rd. East, Tecumseh ON N8N 3T6
Tel: 519-979-0057; *Fax:* 519-979-2881
Chief Officer(s):
Sue Grando, Director, Supports & Services, North Area,
519-776-6483 Ext. 236
suegrando@communitylivingessex.org

Community Living Fort Erie (CLFE)
PO Box 520, 615 Industrial Dr., Fort Erie ON L2A 5Y1
Tel: 905-871-6770; *Fax:* 905-871-3339
www.clfe.ca
www.facebook.com/CommunityLivingFortErie
twitter.com/LivingFortErie
www.youtube.com/user/CLFortErie
Overview: A small local charitable organization founded in 1958 overseen by Community Living Ontario
Mission: To help all people with developmental disability live in a state of dignity, share in all elements of living in the community & have the opportunity to participate effectively
Member of: Community Living Ontario
Finances: *Funding Sources:* Ministry of Community & Social Services; fundraising
Membership: *Fees:* $2 associate/self advocate; $10 individual; $50 corporate
Activities: Accommodation services; employment services; supported independent living; parent resource centre; friendship camp; inclusion community camps for children; volunteer services; *Awareness Events:* Community Living Month, May; *Library:* by appointment
Chief Officer(s):
Maureen Brown, Executive Director

Community Living Fort Frances & District (CLFFD)
PO Box 147, 340 Scott St., Fort Frances ON P9A 3M5
Tel: 807-274-5556; *Fax:* 807-274-5009
www.communitylivingfortfrances.com
www.facebook.com/233045073492780
Also Known As: Community Living Fort Frances
Overview: A small local charitable organization founded in 1965
Mission: To ensure that all people live in a state of dignity, sharing & participating in all elements of living in the community
Member of: Community Living Ontario
Finances: *Annual Operating Budget:* Greater than $5 Million; *Funding Sources:* Provincial government
Staff Member(s): 102; 12 volunteer(s)
Membership: 35; *Fees:* $5; *Member Profile:* Individuals living with a disabling condition produces an impairment of motor, cognitive, or sensory function skills & which limits his or her ability to live independently; *Committees:* Special Projects
Activities: Providing 24 hour support for the intellectually disabled; Providing supported independent living; Offering supported employment opportunities; Organizing transitional services; *Internships:* Yes
Chief Officer(s):
Alanna J. Barr, Executive Director
ajbarrclffd@vianet.ca

Community Living Glengarry (CLG)
332 MacDonald Blvd., Alexandria ON K0C 1A0
Tel: 613-525-4357; *Fax:* 613-525-4360
info@clglen.on.ca
clglen.on.ca
www.facebook.com/114656748615866
Previous Name: Glengarry Association for Community Living
Overview: A small local organization
Mission: To support individuals who are intellectually challenged by creating an inclusive community where everyone can reach their full potential
Member of: Community Living Ontario
Membership: *Fees:* $9 family; $6 single
Activities: Skills training; employment assistance; foster home program
Chief Officer(s):
Dan Giroux, Chair
Publications:
• The Informer / Le Bulletin
Type: Newsletter; *Frequency:* Quarterly
Profile: Promotes the agency & highlights success stories of individuals

Community Living Greater Sudbury (CLGS) / Integration Communautaire Grand Sudbury
303 York St., Sudbury ON P3E 2A5
Tel: 705-671-7181
generalemail@clgs.ca
www.communitylivinggreatersudbury.ca
www.facebook.com/124688977552028
Previous Name: Greater Sudbury Association for Community Living
Overview: A large local charitable organization founded in 1963 overseen by Community Living Ontario
Mission: To provide support to people with developmental disabilities to help them lead full lives
Member of: Community Living Ontario
Staff Member(s): 250
Activities: Home Program for Adults & Children; Group Homes with a Behavioral Service Component; Vocational Alternatives; Day Programs; Advocates Group; Annual General Meeting held in June of each year
Chief Officer(s):
Paul De Luisa, President
Leighton Roslyn, Executive Director
Publications:
• CLGS [Community Living Greater Sudbury] Newsletter
Type: Newsletter

Community Living Grimsby, Lincoln & West Lincoln
PO Box 220, Beamsville ON L0R 1B0
Tel: 905-563-4115; *Fax:* 905-563-8887
info@cl-grimsbylincoln.ca
www.cl-grimsbylincoln.ca
Previous Name: Grimsby/Lincoln & District Association for Community Living Inc.
Overview: A large local organization founded in 1965 overseen by Community Living Ontario
Mission: To support & provide services for individuals with a developmental disability & their families
Member of: Community Living Ontario
Finances: *Annual Operating Budget:* $3 Million-$5 Million; *Funding Sources:* Membership fees; Donations
Staff Member(s): 160
Membership: *Fees:* $5 basic; $10 family
Activities: *Awareness Events:* Grimsby Festival of Art, Sept.; Walkathon/Bike-a-thon, May
Chief Officer(s):
Sarina Labonté, Executive Director
Meetings/Conferences:
• Community Living Grimsby, Lincoln & West Lincoln 53rd Annual General Meeting, 2018
Scope: Local

Beamsville - C.D. Hopkins Centre
4330 Lincoln Ave., Beamsville ON L0R 1B2
Tel: 905-563-4115; *Fax:* 905-563-8616
info@cl-grimsbylincoln.ca

Grimsby - Employment Services
183B South Service Rd., Grimsby ON L3M 4H6
Tel: 905-563-4115; *Fax:* 905-945-0239
info@cl-grimsbylincoln.ca

Grimsby - Livingston Resource Centre
41 Livingston Ave., Grimsby ON L3M 1L2
Tel: 905-309-0530
info@cl-grimsbylincoln.ca

Community Living Guelph Wellington
8 Royal Rd., Guelph ON N1H 1G3
Tel: 519-824-2480; *Fax:* 519-821-6174
Admin@clgw.ca
www.clgw.ca
www.instagram.com/CLGuelphWell
www.facebook.com/157729250963604
twitter.com/CLGuelphWell
Overview: A small local charitable organization founded in 1955 overseen by Community Living Ontario
Mission: To advocate for people who have an intellectual disability & their families, promoting & facilitating their full participation in the community
Member of: Ontario Agencies Supporting People with Special Needs; Community Living Ontario
Finances: *Annual Operating Budget:* Greater than $5 Million; *Funding Sources:* Community fundraising, Ministry of Community, Family & Children's Services
Staff Member(s): 360; 100 volunteer(s)
Membership: 120; *Fees:* $10
Chief Officer(s):
Laura Hanley, Interim Executive Director
lHanley@clgw.ca

Community Living Haldimand
PO Box 396, 2256 River Rd., Cayuga ON N0A 1E0
Tel: 905-772-3344
www.clhaldimand.com
Previous Name: Haldimand Association for the Developmentally Challenged
Overview: A small local charitable organization founded in 1957 overseen by Community Living Ontario
Mission: To ensure that all people live in a state of dignity, share in all elements of living in the community & have equal opportunity to participate effectively
Member of: Community Living Ontario
Staff Member(s): 120
Membership: *Fees:* $10; *Member Profile:* Community & family members
Activities: *Library:* Open to public by appointment
Chief Officer(s):
Susan Wavell, Executive Director

Community Living Haliburton County
PO Box 90, 14 South St., Haliburton ON K0M 1S0
Tel: 705-457-2626; *Fax:* 705-457-9287
www.communitylivinghaliburtoncounty.com
www.facebook.com/CommunityLivingHaliburtonCounty
Previous Name: Haliburton County Association for Community Living
Overview: A small local organization overseen by Community Living Ontario
Mission: To advocate for people with intellectual disabliities & their families, so they may participate & live fully in in all aspects of the community
Member of: Community Living Ontario
Chief Officer(s):
Teresa Jordan, Executive Director, 705-457-2626 Ext. 25
tjordan@communitylivingkl.ca

Community Living Hamilton
William H. Tallman Administrative Centre, 191 York Blvd., Hamilton ON L8R 1Y6
Tel: 905-528-0281; *Fax:* 905-528-5156
info@clham.com
www.communitylivinghamilton.com
Previous Name: Hamilton Association for Community Living
Overview: A small local organization overseen by Community Living Ontario
Mission: To support individuals with intellectual disabilities, so they may have an equal opportunity to participate fully in community life
Member of: Community Living Ontario
Membership: *Fees:* $15 regular/associate; $20 family; $25 agency
Chief Officer(s):
Sherry Parsley, Executive Director

Community Living Huntsville (CLH)
99 West Rd, Huntsville ON P1H 1M1
Tel: 705-789-4543; *Fax:* 705-789-0752
clh@clhuntsville.ca
www.clhuntsville.ca
twitter.com/clhuntsville
Previous Name: Huntsville & District Association for the Mentally Retarded
Overview: A medium-sized local charitable organization founded in 1962 overseen by Community Living Ontario
Mission: To develop an inclusive community in North Muskoka; To support people with special needs to live with dignity, share in all elements of living in the community; To participate as fully as they choose
Member of: Community Living Ontario
Affiliation(s): Ontario Agencies supporting individuals with special needs
Activities: *Speaker Service:* Yes

Community Living Huronia (CLH)
339 Olive St., Midland ON L4R 2R4
Tel: 705-526-4253; *Fax:* 705-526-8299
www.clhmidland.on.ca
Overview: A medium-sized local charitable organization founded in 1960 overseen by Community Living Ontario
Mission: To ensure that people with developmental handicaps can live in a state of dignity, with opportunities to participate as effectively as possible in all community activities
Affiliation(s): OASIS

Finances: *Funding Sources:* Ministry of Community & Social Services; Ministry of Municipal Affairs & Housing; County of Simcoe
Staff Member(s): 230
Membership: *Member Profile:* Local residents
Activities: Gala Event, Nov.
Chief Officer(s):
Paul Hamelin, President

Community Living Kawartha Lakes (CLKL)
#200, 205 McLaughlin Rd., Lindsay ON K9V 0K7
Tel: 705-328-0464; *Fax:* 705-328-0495
www.communitylivingkl.ca
www.facebook.com/339996636039284
twitter.com/CLKLTeresa
Previous Name: Victoria County Association for Community Living
Overview: A small local charitable organization founded in 1960 overseen by Community Living Ontario
Mission: To support people with developmental challenges & their families to achieve personal goals; To participate in the development of healthy, inclusive communities
Member of: Community Living Ontario
Membership: *Fees:* $10 individual; $15 family; $500 lifetime
Activities: *Awareness Events:* Community Living Month, May; *Speaker Service:* Yes; *Library:* by appointment
Chief Officer(s):
Teresa Jordan, Executive Director
TJordan@communitylivingkl.ca

Community Living Kincardine & District
PO Box 9000, 286 Lambton St., Kincardine ON N2Z 2Z3
Tel: 519-396-9434
www.clkd.ca
www.facebook.com/CommunityLivingKD
twitter.com/CL_Kincardine
www.youtube.com/user/CommLivingKincardine
Overview: A small local organization founded in 1964 overseen by Community Living Ontario
Mission: To help all persons live in a state of dignity, share in all elements of living in the community & have the opportunity to participate fully
Finances: *Funding Sources:* Ministry of Community & Social Services
Membership: *Fees:* $10 individual; $100 corporate
Chief Officer(s):
Andy Swan, Executive Director
aswan.clkd@tnt21.com

Community Living Kingston / Intégration Communautaire Kingston
1412 Princess St., Kingston ON K7M 3E5
Tel: 613-546-6613; *Fax:* 613-546-0436
www.communitylivingkingston.org
www.facebook.com/communitylivingkingston
Previous Name: Kingston & District Association for Community Living
Overview: A large local charitable organization founded in 1953 overseen by Community Living Ontario
Mission: To help persons who live with a mental disability have full access to the full range of experiences offered by their community; To ensure all persons live in a state of dignity, share in all elements of living in the community & have the opportunity to participate effectively
Member of: Community Living Ontario; Canadian Association for Community Living
Finances: *Funding Sources:* Provincial government; user fees; United Way; fundraising; City of Kingston
Membership: *Member Profile:* People with developmental disabilities, their families & friends; concerned citizens
Activities: Family support; residential, vocational & leisure services; *Library*
Chief Officer(s):
Peter Sproul, Executive Director
peter.sproul@clkingston.ca
Sheri Scott, Director, Operations
sheri.scott@clkingston.ca
Matt Luck, Director, Finance & Administration
matthew.luck@clkingston.ca

Community Living London (CLL)
190 Adelaide St. South, London ON N5Z 3L1
Tel: 519-686-3000
info@cll.on.ca
www.cll.on.ca
www.facebook.com/communitylivinglondon
twitter.com/CommLivLondon

Overview: A medium-sized local charitable organization founded in 1952 overseen by Community Living Ontario
Mission: To empower people with intellectual disabilities & their families to reach their goals
Member of: Community Living Ontario
Finances: *Annual Operating Budget:* Greater than $5 Million; *Funding Sources:* Ontario Ministry of Community, Family & Children's Services; United Way of Greater London
Staff Member(s): 433; 218 volunteer(s)
Membership: 169; *Fees:* $15; *Member Profile:* Parents/friends of people with an intellectual disability; *Committees:* Advocacy; Child and Youth Network, Liaison; Intake Coordinators
Activities: *Internships:* Yes; *Speaker Service:* Yes
Chief Officer(s):
Michelle Palmer, Executive Director, 519-686-3000 Ext. 330
michelle.palmer@cll.on.ca

Community Living Manitoba
#6, 120 Maryland St., Winnipeg MB R3G 1L1
Tel: 204-786-1607; *Fax:* 204-789-9850
aclmb@aclmb.ca
www.aclmb.ca
www.facebook.com/370890112967949
twitter.com/aclmanitoba
Also Known As: Community Living - MB
Previous Name: Association for Community Living - Manitoba
Overview: A medium-sized provincial organization overseen by Canadian Association for Community Living
Mission: To promote the welfare of people with handicaps & their families; To speak on behalf of people with developmental disabilities in Manitoba; To ensure that every person in Manitoba has access to supports necessary to live with dignity & to participate fully in the community of his/her choice
Member of: Canadian Association for Community Living
Chief Officer(s):
Sean Michaels, President
Meghan Menzies, Vice-President
Tracy Holod, Secretary

Community Living Manitoulin
PO Box 152, 6062 Hwy. 542, Mindemoya ON P0P 1S0
Tel: 705-377-6699; *Fax:* 705-377-7175
www.clmanitoulin.ca
www.facebook.com/clmanitoulin
Previous Name: Manitoulin District Association for Community Living
Overview: A small local charitable organization overseen by Community Living Ontario
Mission: To offer residential, vocational & community services to adults with intellectual disabilities
Member of: Community Living Ontario
Staff Member(s): 60
Membership: *Fees:* $5
Chief Officer(s):
Tammie Molenaar, Executive Director, 705-377-6699 Ext. 22
tmolenaar@clmanitoulin.com

Community Living Mississauga (CLM)
#1, 6695 Millcreek Dr., Mississauga ON L5N 5R8
Tel: 905-542-2694; *Fax:* 905-542-0987
www.clmiss.ca
www.facebook.com/communitylivingmississauga
twitter.com/CLMississauga
Overview: A small local charitable organization founded in 1955 overseen by Community Living Ontario
Mission: To assist people who have an intellectual disability to achieve their goals & advocates for their participation within the community
Member of: Community Living Ontario
Finances: *Funding Sources:* Government; United Way; Private donations
Membership: 235; *Fees:* $15
Activities: *Awareness Events:* Community Living Month, May; *Speaker Service:* Yes; *Rents Mailing List:* Yes; *Library:* Knowledge Network, Mississauga Central Library; Open to public
Chief Officer(s):
Eugene Nolin, President
Keith Tansley, Executive Director
keitht@clmiss.ca

Community Living Newmarket/Aurora District (CLNAD)
195 Harry Walker Pkwy., Newmarket ON L3Y 7B3
Tel: 905-898-3000; *Fax:* 905-898-6441
info@clnad.com
www.clnad.com

www.linkedin.com/company/community-living-central-york
www.facebook.com/communitylivingcentralyork
twitter.com/CLCentralYork
Previous Name: Newmarket & District Association for Community Living
Overview: A large local charitable organization founded in 1954 overseen by Community Living Ontario
Mission: To help all persons who are developmentally disabled live in a state of dignity, share in all elements of living in community & have the opportunity to participate effectively
Member of: Community Living Ontario
Affiliation(s): Canadian Association for Community Living
Finances: *Funding Sources:* Ministry of Community & Social Services; United Way of York Region
Membership: *Fees:* $10 single; $25 family; $5 senior; $100 business; $150 lifetime
Activities: Art show; fundraising events; *Speaker Service:* Yes; *Library:* Open to public
Chief Officer(s):
Karen Richards, President
Colleen Zakoor, Executive Director
colleen.zakoor@clnad.com

Community Living North Bay / Intégration Communautaire North Bay
161 Main St. East, North Bay ON P1B 1A9
Tel: 705-476-3288; *Fax:* 705-476-4788
info@communitylivingnorthbay.org
www.communitylivingnorthbay.org
Overview: A small local charitable organization founded in 1954 overseen by Community Living Ontario
Mission: To help all persons in need of developmental support live in the community in a state of dignity & have the opportunity to share & participate effectively
Finances: *Funding Sources:* Fundraising
Membership: *Fees:* $5; $100 lifetime
Activities: *Library:* Eleanor Broydell Literacy Library; Open to public
Chief Officer(s):
Hélène Morin-Chain, Chair
Jennifer Valenti, Executive Director, 705-476-3288 Ext. 225

Community Living North Frontenac
PO Box 76, Sharbot Lake ON K0H 2P0
Tel: 613-279-3731; *Fax:* 613-279-3732
Other Communication: After Hours Phone: 613-279-2120
edicintio@clnf.ca
www.communitylivingnorthfrontenac.com
Overview: A small local organization overseen by Community Living Ontario
Mission: To help children & adults with an intellectual disability in the North Frontenac area have an equal opportunity to participate & share in all facets of community life
Membership: 11
Chief Officer(s):
Dean Walsh, Executive Director
dwalsh@vclnf.ca

Community Living North Halton (CLNH)
917B Nipissing Rd., Milton ON L9T 5E3
Tel: 905-878-2337; *Fax:* 905-878-5413
info@clnh.on.ca
www.clnh.on.ca
www.facebook.com/clnhalton
twitter.com/CLNorthHalton
Overview: A large local charitable organization founded in 1955 overseen by Community Living Ontario
Mission: To provide support & services to individuals with developmental disabilities; To enhance their personal growth & inclusion in the community
Member of: Community Living Ontario
Affiliation(s): Ontario Agencies Supporting Individuals with Special Needs
Finances: *Funding Sources:* Ministry of Community & Social Services; United Way of Milton & of Halton Hills; Region of Halton
Membership: *Fees:* $25 individual; $35 family; $50 corporate
Activities: Day; Residential; Supported Independent Living & Adult Development/Life Skills; *Awareness Events:* Walk-A-Thon fundraiser, May; Golf Tournament, Sept.; *Internships:* Yes; *Speaker Service:* Yes; *Library:* Open to public
Chief Officer(s):
Greg Edmiston, Executive Director
gedmiston@clnh.on.ca
Publications:
• The Link [a publication of Community Living North Halton]
Type: Newsletter

Canadian Associations / Community Living Oakville (CLO)

Community Living Oakville (CLO)
301 Wyecroft Rd., Oakville ON L6K 2H2
Tel: 905-844-0146; Fax: 905-339-1541
www.oakcl.org
www.linkedin.com/company/community-living-oakville-on
www.facebook.com/OakvilleCL
twitter.com/OakvilleCL
Overview: A large local charitable organization founded in 1955 overseen by Community Living Ontario
Mission: To support developmentally disabled adults through sheltered workshops, residential homes, day programs & independent living
Member of: Community Living Ontario; Oakville United Way
Finances: Funding Sources: United Way; Halton Region; fees; donations
Activities: Awareness Events: Annual Golf Tournament
Chief Officer(s):
Janet Lorimer, Executive Director
janet.lorimer@oakcl.org
Publications:
• Community Living Oakville Newsletter
Type: Newsletter

Community Living Ontario (CLO) / Intégration communautaire Ontario
#201, 1 Valleybrook Dr., Toronto ON M3B 2S7
Tel: 416-447-4348; Fax: 416-447-8974
Toll-Free: 800-278-8025
info@communitylivingontario.ca
www.communitylivingontario.ca
www.facebook.com/communitylivingontario
twitter.com/CLOntario
www.youtube.com/user/comlivon
Also Known As: The Ontario Association for Community Living
Overview: A large provincial charitable organization founded in 1954 overseen by Canadian Association for Community Living
Mission: To lobby on behalf of people with intellectual disablilities in Ontario; To ensure that every person in Ontario has access to supports to live with dignity & to participate in the community of his/her choice
Member of: Canadian Association for Community Living
Finances: Funding Sources: Local associations; Fundraising
Staff Member(s): 15
Membership: 12,000+ individuals + 117 local associations; Member Profile: Individuals; Local Community Living associations; Committees: Awards; By-Laws/Resolutions; Communications Strategies; Community Living Inclusion Project Committee; Conference; Council of Community Living Ontario; Executive; Federation Well Being Committee; Finance; Government Relations; Nominations; Social Policy
Chief Officer(s):
Chris Beesley, CEO, 416-447-4348 Ext. 227
chris@communitylivngontario.ca
Ron Laroche, Director, Communications, Marketing & Fund Development, 416-447-4348 Ext. 223
rlaroche@communitylivingontario.ca
Keith Dee, Director, Membership Services, 416-447-4348 Ext. 242
kdee@communitylivingontario.ca
Gordon Kyle, Director, Policy Analysis, Planning & Accountability, 416-447-4348 Ext. 230
gkyle@communitylivingontario.ca

Community Living Oshawa / Clarington
39 Wellington St. East, Oshawa ON L1H 3Y1
Tel: 905-576-3011; Fax: 905-576-9754
www.communitylivingoc.ca
www.facebook.com/CommunityLivingOshawaClarington
Previous Name: Oshawa / Clarington Association for Community Living
Overview: A large local charitable organization founded in 1954 overseen by Community Living Ontario
Mission: To enable the community to welcome & support citizens with developmental handicaps as valued, participating & contributing members
Member of: Community Living Ontario
Affiliation(s): Developmental Services Ontario
Finances: Annual Operating Budget: $3 Million-$5 Million; Funding Sources: Donations; Membership dues; Government funding
Staff Member(s): 200; 40 volunteer(s)
Chief Officer(s):
Terri Gray, Executive Director, 905-576-3011 Ext. 323
tgray@communitylivingoc.ca
Meetings/Conferences:
• Community Living Oshawa / Clarington 2018 Annual General Meeting, 2018, ON
Scope: Local
Publications:
• News & Views [a publication of Community Living Oshawa / Clarington]
Type: Newsletter; Frequency: Quarterly; Price: Free with membership in Community Living Oshawa / Clarington
Profile: Information for Community Living members

Community Living Owen Sound & District
769 - 4 Ave. East, Owen Sound ON N4K 2N5
Tel: 519-371-9251; Fax: 519-371-5168
www.communitylivingowensound.ca
Previous Name: Owen Sound & District Association for the Mentally Retarded
Overview: A medium-sized local organization founded in 1954 overseen by Community Living Ontario
Mission: To assist people with developmental needs to live, work, & participate in the community as equal & valued partners
Member of: Community Living Ontario
Finances: Funding Sources: Ministry of Community & Social Services; donations
Activities: Library:

Community Living Parry Sound (CLPS)
38 Joseph St., Parry Sound ON P2A 2G5
Tel: 705-746-9330; Fax: 705-746-6151
www.clps.ca
www.facebook.com/communitylivingparrysound
twitter.com/CLParrySound
Overview: A small local charitable organization founded in 1962 overseen by Community Living Ontario
Mission: To provide services & opportunities that enable individuals with intellectual disabilities to effectively participate in their community according to their interests & abilities
Member of: Community Living Ontario; Ontario Agencies Supporting Individuals with Special Needs
Finances: Funding Sources: Provincial government; Fundraising
Membership: Fees: $10; $100 lifetime
Activities: Library: Open to public by appointment
Chief Officer(s):
Jo-Anne Demick, Executive Director
  Addie St. Residence
  15 Addie St., Parry Sound ON P2A 2K2
  Tel: 705-746-7300

Community Living Peterborough (CLP)
223 Aylmer St., Peterborough ON K9J 3K3
Tel: 705-743-2411; Fax: 705-743-3722
www.communitylivingpeterborough.ca
www.facebook.com/CommunityLivingPtbo
twitter.com/CLPeterborough
www.youtube.com/user/CommunityLivingPtbo
Overview: A small local charitable organization founded in 1953 overseen by Community Living Ontario
Mission: To inspire respect & equality for people living with an intellectual disability in Peterborough, Ontario
Member of: Community Living Ontario
Finances: Funding Sources: Donations; Fundraising
Staff Member(s): 13
Activities: Offering job training; Providing a workforce to Peterborough companies, through the Small Business Resource Centre; Facilitating suitable living options for adults over the age of 21; Supporting families; Increasing community knowledge; Coordinating educational workshops for parents; Providing school & employment advocacy
Chief Officer(s):
Jack Gillan, Chief Executive Officer, 705-743-2412 Ext. 516
jgillan@communitylivingpeterborough.ca
Barb Hiland, Director, Operations, 705-743-2412 Ext. 544
bhiland@communitylivingpeterborough.ca
Cindy Hobbins, Manager, Community Development, Communications, & Quality Enhancement, 705-743-2412 Ext. 525
chobbins@communitylivingpeterborough.ca
Publications:
• Opening Doors . . . to Building Inclusive Communities
Type: Newsletter
Profile: Community Living Peterborough activities & campaign updates

Community Living Port Colborne-Wainfleet
100 MacRae Ave., Port Colborne ON L3K 2A8
Tel: 905-835-8941; Fax: 905-835-5515
admin@cplcw.ca
www.portcolbornecommunityliving.com
Previous Name: Port Colborne District Association for Community Living, Inc.
Overview: A medium-sized local organization founded in 1962 overseen by Community Living Ontario
Mission: To promote the idea that all people should live in a state of dignity, share in all elements of living in the community & have equal opportunity to participate effectively
Member of: Community Living Ontario
Membership: Fees: $5
Chief Officer(s):
Vickie Moreland, Executive Director, 905-835-8941 Ext. 102
vmoreland@clpcw.com

Community Living Prince Edward (County)
#1, 67 King St., Picton ON K0K 2T0
Tel: 613-476-6038; Fax: 613-476-2868
info@clpe.on.ca
www.clpe.on.ca
Previous Name: Prince Edward Association for Community Living
Overview: A small local charitable organization founded in 1965 overseen by Community Living Ontario
Mission: To provide services to facilitate the participation of people with developmental disabilities into community life
Member of: Community Living Ontario
Finances: Funding Sources: Ontario government; Client fees; Donations
Membership: Fees: $5
Chief Officer(s):
Susan Treverton, Executive Director
susan.treverton@clpe.on.ca

Community Living Quinte West (CLQW)
11 Canal St., Trenton ON K8V 4K3
Tel: 613-394-2222; Fax: 613-394-0381
communitylivingquintewest@clqw.com
clqw.ca
www.facebook.com/communitylivingquintewest
Previous Name: Trenton & District Association for Community Living
Overview: A small local charitable organization founded in 1959 overseen by Community Living Ontario
Mission: To provide services to persons with intellectual disabilities & their families so they may participate fully in their community
Member of: Community Living Ontario
Finances: Funding Sources: Fundraising
Chief Officer(s):
Starr Olsen, Executive Director
starr@clqw.ca

Community Living Renfrew County South
PO Box 683, 326 Raglan St. South, Renfrew ON K7V 4E7
Tel: 613-432-6763; Fax: 613-432-9465
commliving@clrcs.com
www.clrcs.com
Previous Name: Renfrew & District Association for the Mentally Retarded
Overview: A small local organization founded in 1965 overseen by Community Living Ontario
Mission: To achieve state of existence in which all persons live in dignity, share in all elements of living in the community & have the opportunity to participate effectively
Member of: Community Living Ontario; Canadian Association for Community Living
Finances: Annual Operating Budget: $1.5 Million-$3 Million
Staff Member(s): 38; 20 volunteer(s)
Membership: 100; Fees: $5; Committees: Finance; Personnel; planning & Priorities
Chief Officer(s):
Jennifer Creeden, Executive Director, 613-432-6763 Ext. 106
jcreeden@clrcs.com

Community Living St. Marys & Area Association
PO Box 1618, 300 Elgin St. East, St Marys ON N4X 1B9
Tel: 519-284-1400; Fax: 519-284-3120
info@clstmarys.ca
www.communitylivingstmarys.ca
www.facebook.com/158281517682083
Overview: A small local organization founded in 1962
Mission: To encourage members of the community to welcome & support all people as valued citizens; To promote a fully integrated community
Member of: Community Living Ontario

Finances: *Annual Operating Budget:* $500,000-$1.5 Million; *Funding Sources:* Fundraising
Staff Member(s): 50
Membership: 75; *Fees:* $5
Activities: Advocating for individualized disability supports funding; *Library:* Open to public
Chief Officer(s):
Marg McLean, Executive Director
mmclean@clstmarys.ca
Jennifer Leslie, Director, Planning & Facilitation Services
jleslie@clstmarys.ca
Kim Monden, Director, Community Involvement & Support Services
kmonden@clstmarys.ca
Vickie Logan, Manager, Finance
vlogan@clstmarys.ca

Community Living Sarnia & District *See* Community Living Sarnia-Lambton

Community Living Sarnia-Lambton (CLSL)
#202, 551 Exmouth St., Sarnia ON N7T 7J4
Tel: 519-332-0560; *Fax:* 519-332-3446
clsd@communitylivingsarnia.org
www.communitylivingsarnia.org
Previous Name: Community Living Sarnia & District
Overview: A small local charitable organization founded in 1955 overseen by Community Living Ontario
Mission: To ensure persons with developmental disabilities & their families live & share in all aspects of the community & that they have opportunites to participate fully
Member of: Community Living Ontario; Ontario Agencies Supporting Individuals with Special Needs (OASIS)
Finances: *Annual Operating Budget:* Greater than $5 Million; *Funding Sources:* Federal & provincial governments; United Way; Corporate & private donations
Staff Member(s): 210; 100 volunteer(s)
Membership: *Committees:* Executive; Resource; Resource Development; Fund Raising
Chief Officer(s):
John Hagens, Executive Director

Community Living Society (CLS)
713 Columbia St., 7th Fl., New Westminster BC V3M 1B2
Tel: 604-523-0303; *Fax:* 604-523-9399
contactus@communitylivingsociety.ca
www.communitylivingsociety.ca
Overview: A medium-sized local charitable organization founded in 1978
Mission: To support each individual to live with dignity & to thrive as a fully participating citizen within their community; To offer personalized & flexible home & community opportunities to individuals with a disability
Member of: British Columbia Association for Community Living
Finances: *Funding Sources:* Government
Staff Member(s): 9
Membership: *Fees:* $5 single; $10 family; $100 life; *Committees:* Finance; Branding; Executive; Fund Development; Aging with Dignity; Orientation; Governance
Chief Officer(s):
Ross Chilton, Executive Director, 604-523-0303 Ext. 314
rchilton@communitylivingsociety.com
Publications:
• Communicator Newsletter [a publication of the Community Living Society]
Type: Newsletter
• Community Living Society Annual Report
Type: Report

Community Living South Huron
146 Main St., Dashwood ON N0M 1N0
Tel: 519-237-3637; *Fax:* 519-237-3190
clsh@hay.net
www.clsh.ca
Overview: A small local charitable organization founded in 1968 overseen by Community Living Ontario
Mission: To provide support to individuals with developmental challenges to participate in & contribute to all aspects of family & community life
Member of: Community Living Ontario
Finances: *Funding Sources:* Community & social services
Membership: *Fees:* $20 family
Activities: *Rents Mailing List:* Yes
Chief Officer(s):
Bruce Shaw, Executive Director
Judy Mallette, President

Community Living South Muskoka
15 Depot Dr., Bracebridge ON P1L 0A1
Tel: 705-645-5494; *Fax:* 705-645-4621
info@clsm.on.ca
www.clsm.on.ca
Overview: A medium-sized local organization founded in 1960 overseen by Community Living Ontario
Mission: To promote that all persons should live in a state of dignity, share in all elements of living in the community, & have the opportunity to participate effectively
Chief Officer(s):
Gord Haugh, Chair
Krista Haiduk-Collier, Chief Executive Officer

Community Living Stormont County (CLSC) / Intégration communautaire comté de Stormont
280 - 9 St. West, Cornwall ON K6H 5J6
Tel: 613-938-9550; *Fax:* 613-938-2033
info@clstormont.ca
www.communitylivingstormontcounty.ca
www.facebook.com/201683936572529
Overview: A medium-sized local charitable organization founded in 1958 overseen by Community Living Ontario
Mission: To help all people live in a state of dignity, share in all elements of living in the community & have the opportunity to participate effectively
Member of: Community Living Ontario
Finances: *Funding Sources:* Ministry of Community & Social Services; Ministry of Housing; fundraising; donations
Activities: Supporting pre-school children through the Early Childhood Integration Support Service; Facilitating residential, recreational & work services for adults; Networking; *Library:* Resource Room; by appointment
Chief Officer(s):
Linda Lister, President

Community Living Stratford & Area
112 Frederick St., Stratford ON N5A 3V7
Tel: 519-273-1000
info@clsa.ca
www.clsa.ca
www.facebook.com/107173169314101
twitter.com/commliving
www.youtube.com/user/CommLivingStratford
Previous Name: Stratford Area Association for Community Living
Overview: A small local charitable organization founded in 1957 overseen by Community Living Ontario
Mission: To provide support to adults with developmental disabilities in order to help them live full lives.
Member of: Community Living Ontario
Finances: *Funding Sources:* Provincial government; fundraising
Membership: *Member Profile:* Parents; community members; agencies
Activities: *Awareness Events:* Swing into Spring, May; *Library*
Chief Officer(s):
Trevor McGregor, Executive Director
Pat White, President

Community Living Temiskaming South
PO Box 1149, 513 Amwell St., Haileybury ON P0J 1K0
Tel: 705-672-2000; *Fax:* 705-672-2722
www.clts.ca
Overview: A small local organization
Mission: To ensure the inclusion of all persons in all aspects of living in the community
Member of: Community Living Ontario
Chief Officer(s):
Tony Rachwalski, Executive Director

Community Living Thunder Bay (CLTB)
1501 Dease St., Thunder Bay ON P7C 5H3
Tel: 807-622-1099; *Fax:* 807-622-8528
www.cltb.ca
www.facebook.com/communitylivingtb
Previous Name: Lakehead Association for Community Living
Overview: A small local charitable organization founded in 1954 overseen by Community Living Ontario
Mission: To advocate for the rights & quality of life of people served; To educate & support the community to share the vision of the association; To provide services & supports to people served & to their families; To be accountable to people servee, their families, the membership of CLTB, & the community
Member of: Community Living Ontario
Finances: *Funding Sources:* The Ministry of Community and Social Services; United Way; fundraising; donations

Membership: *Fees:* $5 individual; $10 family; $40 agency; *Member Profile:* Family & friends of people with a developmental disability
Activities: Support & advocacy services for people with a developmental disability & their families; *Speaker Service:* Yes; *Library*
Chief Officer(s):
Lisa Ellacott, President
Lisa Foster, Executive Director
lisa.foster@cltb.ca
Publications:
• The Advocate
Type: Newsletter; *Frequency:* Bi-annually

Community Living Timmins Intégration Communautaire
166 Brousseau Ave., Timmins ON P4N 5Y4
Tel: 705-268-8811; *Fax:* 705-267-2011
admin@cltic.ca
www.communitylivingtimmins.com
Overview: A medium-sized local organization founded in 1955 overseen by Community Living Ontario
Mission: To help all persons to live in a state of dignity, share in all elements of living in the community & have the opportunity to participate effectively
Member of: Community Living Ontario
Finances: *Funding Sources:* Government; United Way; Fundraising
Membership: *Committees:* Management-Finance; Parents Advisory; Support Services; Public Education; Housing; Nominations; Health & Safety; Employer/Employee Relations
Activities: *Awareness Events:* Community Living Month, May; *Internships:* Yes *Library:* Resource Centre
Chief Officer(s):
Johanne Rondeau-Bernier, Executive Director
jrondeau@cltic.ca

Community Living Toronto
20 Spadina Rd., Toronto ON M5R 2S7
Tel: 416-968-0650
cltoronto.ca
www.facebook.com/CLToronto
twitter.com/cltoronto
Previous Name: Toronto Association for Community Living
Overview: A medium-sized local charitable organization founded in 1951 overseen by Community Living Ontario
Mission: To ensure that persons with an intellectual disability live in a state of dignity, share in all elements of living in their community & have equal opportunity to participate effectively
Member of: Community Living Ontario; United Way of Greater Toronto
Affiliation(s): Canadian Association for Community Living
Membership: *Member Profile:* Families & supporters of people with an intellectual disability
Activities: *Speaker Service:* Yes
Chief Officer(s):
Brad Saunders, Chief Executive Officer
brad.saunders@cltoronto.ca

Community Living Upper Ottawa Valley
PO Box 1030, 894 Pembroke St. West, Pembroke ON K8A 6Y6
Tel: 613-735-0659; *Fax:* 613-735-1373
info@communitylivingupperottawavalley.ca
www.communitylivingupperottawavalley.ca
Previous Name: Pembroke & District Association for Community Living
Overview: A medium-sized local charitable organization founded in 1958 overseen by Community Living Ontario
Mission: To foster the development of communities by: offering support & services based on each person's uniqueness; developing community capacity & partnerships; offering opportunities for stakeholders to learn & take leadership; promoting inclusion, community living, & diversity; engaging in human rights advocacy; & eliminating physical, attitudinal, & societal barriers to full citizenship
Member of: Community Living Ontario; OASIS
Finances: *Funding Sources:* Ministry of Community & Social Services
Staff Member(s): 100; 15 volunteer(s)
Membership: *Fees:* $10 individual; $50 corporate; $100 lifetime
Activities: Support to families; community respite; supported independent living; LifeShare program; group living; community options; employment services
Chief Officer(s):
Chris Grayson, Executive Director
cgrayson@cluov.ca

Canadian Associations / Community Living Victoria

Community Living Victoria
3861 Cedar Hill Cross Rd., Victoria BC V8P 2M7
Tel: 250-477-7231; *Fax:* 250-477-6944
communitylivingvictoria.ca
www.facebook.com/CommunityLivingVictoria
Previous Name: Victoria Association for Community Living
Overview: A small local charitable organization founded in 1955
Mission: To support people with developmental disabilities by nurturing their ability to choose, promoting inclusion in the community & creating a sense of belonging
Member of: British Columbia Association for Community Living
Affiliation(s): Canadian Association for Community Living
Finances: *Funding Sources:* United Way; government; private donations
Membership: *Fees:* $20 single; $35 family/organization; *Member Profile:* General public
Activities: *Awareness Events:* Community Living Day; *Library:* by appointment
Chief Officer(s):
Ellen Tarshis, Executive Director, 250-477-7231 Ext. 226
etarshis@clvic.ca

Community Living Walkerton & District (CLWD)
PO Box 999, 19 Durham St. East, Walkerton ON N0G 2V0
Tel: 519-881-3713; *Fax:* 519-881-0531
info@clwalkerton.org
www.clwalkerton.org
www.facebook.com/clwalkerton
Previous Name: Walkerton & District Community Support Services
Overview: A small local charitable organization founded in 1956 overseen by Community Living Ontario
Mission: To ensure that persons with developmental disabilities & their families have the opportunity to live & effectively participate in their community
Member of: Community Living Ontario
Chief Officer(s):
Rick Hill, Executive Director, 519-881-3713 Ext. 103

Community Living Wallaceburg (CLW)
1100 Dufferin Ave., Wallaceburg ON N8A 2W1
Tel: 519-627-0777; *Fax:* 519-627-8905
www.getintocommunityliving.com
www.facebook.com/CLWallaceburg
twitter.com/clwallaceburg
www.youtube.com/CLWallaceburg
Previous Name: Wallaceburg & Sydenham District Association for Community Living
Overview: A small local charitable organization founded in 1956 overseen by Community Living Ontario
Mission: To provide a range of accommodation, community & employment services to enable people with intellectual disabilities to realize their potential within inclusive communities
Member of: Community Living Ontario; Ontario Agencies Supporting Individuals with Special Needs; Ontario Association on Developmental Disabilities; Integration Action for Inclusion in Education & Community; National Conference of Executives of the Arc
Membership: *Fees:* $5 single; $10 family
Chief Officer(s):
Derek McGiven, President

Community Living Welland Pelham
535 Sutherland Ave., Welland ON L3B 5A4
Tel: 905-735-0081; *Fax:* 905-735-9431
communityliving@cl-wellandpelham.ca
www.cl-wellandpelham.ca
www.facebook.com/CLWellandPelham
twitter.com/CLWellandPelham
www.youtube.com/CLWellandPelham
Previous Name: Welland District Association for Community Living
Overview: A small local organization
Mission: To promote the inclusion of intellectually disabled individuals
Member of: Community Living Ontario
Chief Officer(s):
Heather Schneider, President
Barbara Vyrostko, Executive Director
barbvyrostko@cl-wellandpelham.ca
Leslie Monger, Director, Adult Services
lesliemonger@cl-wellandpelham.ca
Theresa Terrebery, Manager, Administration
theresaterreberry@cl-wellandpelham.ca
Dianne Bewzak, Manager, Finance
diannebewzak@cl-wellandpelham.ca

Community Living West Nipissing (CLWN) / Intégration communautaire de Nipissing ouest
75 Railway St., Sturgeon Falls ON P2B 3A1
Tel: 705-753-1665; *Fax:* 705-753-2482
communitylivingwestnipissing.com
Previous Name: West Nipissing Association for Community Living
Overview: A small local charitable organization founded in 1968 overseen by Community Living Ontario
Mission: To build a community where everyone belongs, one person at a time; To bea welcoming community that respects all its members in their diversity, their contributions, & their aspirations
Member of: Community Living Ontario
Finances: *Funding Sources:* Government; Fundraising; Sale of goods & services
Activities: *Library:*

Community Living West Northumberland
275 Cottesmore Ave., Cobourg ON K9A 4E3
Tel: 905-372-4455; *Fax:* 905-372-2783
info@communitylivingwestnorthumberland.ca
www.communitylivingwestnorthumberland.ca
Previous Name: Port Hope/Cobourg & District Association for Community Living
Overview: A small local charitable organization founded in 1959 overseen by Community Living Ontario
Mission: To provide support to individuals with an intellectual disability, helping them to particpate fully in the community
Member of: United Way; Ontario Association for Community Living
Finances: *Funding Sources:* Ministry of Community & Social Services
Staff Member(s): 8
Activities: Offering skills training, vocational employment, & recreational support for individuals with intellectual disabilities
Chief Officer(s):
Cathy Timlin, Executive Director
ctimlin@communitylivingwestnorthumberland.ca

Community Living Wiarton & District *See* Bruce Peninsula Association for Community Living

Community Living Windsor (CLW)
7025 Enterprise Way, Windsor ON N8T 3N6
Tel: 519-974-4221; *Fax:* 519-974-4157
info@clwindsor.org
www.clwindsor.org
Previous Name: Windsor Community Living Support Services
Overview: A medium-sized local organization founded in 1953 overseen by Community Living Ontario
Mission: To provide support to people with developmental disabilities to help them lead a full life.
Member of: Community Living Ontario; Canadian Association for Community Living; OASIS
Finances: *Funding Sources:* Government; foundation; donations; fees
Membership: *Fees:* $11 individuals; $14 families
Activities: *Speaker Service:* Yes; *Library:* Open to public
Chief Officer(s):
John Fairley, President
Xavier Noordermeer, Executive Director

Community Living York South (CLYS)
101 Edward Ave., Richmond Hill ON L4C 5E5
Tel: 905-884-9110; *Fax:* 905-737-3284
Toll-Free: 877-737-3475
info@communitylivingyorksouth.ca
www.communitylivingyorksouth.ca
www.linkedin.com/company/community-living-york-south
www.facebook.com/clyorksouth
twitter.com/CLYorkSouth
Previous Name: Community Living Association for York South; York South Association for Community Living
Overview: A large local charitable organization founded in 1954 overseen by Community Living Ontario
Mission: To assist all individuals with a developmental disability to choose & access those aspects of daily living which enhance their quality of life in the community
Member of: Community Living Ontario
Affiliation(s): United Way
Finances: *Funding Sources:* United Way; donations; provincial government
Membership: *Committees:* External Rights Review; *Task Forces:* Aging; Business; Staff/Communication/Information; Community Outreach; Financial/Investment/Foundation
Chief Officer(s):
Don Wilkinson, Executive Director
Publications:
• Access [a publication of Community Living York South] *Type:* Newsletter

Markham Office
#13, 5694 Hwy. 7, Markham ON L3P 1B4
Tel: 905-294-4971; *Fax:* 905-472-5409
Vaughan Office
#6, 136 Winges Rd., Woodbridge ON L4L 6C3
Tel: 905-264-7262; *Fax:* 905-264-7850

Community Microskills Development Centre
1 Vulcan St., Toronto ON M9W 1L3
Tel: 416-247-7181; *Fax:* 416-247-1877
Toll-Free: 877-979-3999
admin@microskills.ca
www.microskills.ca
www.linkedin.com/company/93300
www.facebook.com/MicroSkillsBetterFuture
twitter.com/MicroSkills
www.youtube.com/user/MicroSkillsCentre
Previous Name: Rexdale Community Microskills Development Centre
Overview: A small local charitable organization founded in 1984 overseen by Ontario Council of Agencies Serving Immigrants
Mission: To assist the unemployed, with a focus on immigrants, racial minorities, youth & women, to acquire skills needed for economic, social & political equality in society.
Member of: Onestep, CED Learning Network
Affiliation(s): Teachers of English as a Second Language Ontario
Finances: *Annual Operating Budget:* Greater than $5 Million; *Funding Sources:* All levels of government; foundations; corporate donors
Staff Member(s): 103; 200 volunteer(s)
Membership: *Fees:* $10 Microskills graduate/unemployed; $25 employed; $50 non-profit organization; $150 coporation
Activities: Settlement & after-school programs; employment counselling; *Speaker Service:* Yes; *Library:* MicroSkills Employment Resource Centre
Chief Officer(s):
Karen Webb, Chair
Kay Blair, Executive Director
kblair@microskills.ca

Community Museums Association of Prince Edward Island
PO Box 22002, Charlottetown PE C1A 9J2
Tel: 902-892-8837; *Fax:* 902-892-1459
info@museumspei.ca
www.museumspei.ca
wwww.facebook.com/116764358400112
Previous Name: Community Heritage Federation
Overview: A medium-sized provincial organization founded in 1983
Mission: To foster & support museums, historical societies & other non-profit organizations concerned with heritage of PEI.
Member of: Heritage Canada; Canadian Museums Association
Finances: *Funding Sources:* Membership fees; federal & provincial grants
Staff Member(s): 1
Membership: 37 museums; *Fees:* $15 individual; $30 organization/associate; $100 patron; *Member Profile:* Community museums; educational institutions; individuals
Chief Officer(s):
David Panton, President
Barry King, Executive Director

Community of Christ - Canada East Mission
#129, 355 Elmira Rd. North, Guelph ON N1K 1S5
Tel: 519-822-4150; *Fax:* 519-822-1236
Toll-Free: 888-411-7537
www.communityofchrist.ca/index.php/cem
Also Known As: Saints' Church
Previous Name: Reorganized Church of Jesus Christ of Latter Day Saints (Canada)
Overview: A medium-sized local charitable organization founded in 1830
Mission: To proclaim Jesus Christ & promote communitites of joy, hope, love & peace
Membership: 45 congregations; *Member Profile:* Individuals & congregations in Ontario, Quebec, New Brunswick, Prince Edward Island & Nova Scotia
Chief Officer(s):
Kerry Richards, President, 519-822-4150 Ext. 28
kerry@communityofchrist.com

Dar Shepherdson, Financial Officer, 519-822-4150 Ext. 34
dar@communityofchrist.ca

Community of Christ - Canada West Mission (CWM)
PO Box 345, #224, 6655 - 178th St. NW, Edmonton AB T5T 4J5
Tel: 877-411-2632
www.communityofchrist.ca/index.php/cwm
Overview: A small local organization
Mission: To proclaim Jesus Christ & promote communities of joy, hope, love, & peace
Membership: 15 congregations and missions; Member Profile: Individuals & congregations in Western Canada (Manitoba - British Columbia)
Chief Officer(s):
Stephen Thompson, President & Financial Officer, Mission Centre, 877-411-2632 Ext. 1
steve@communityofchrist.ca
Publications:
• Family Camps, Youth Camps, Retreats
Type: Directory
Profile: Dates, directors & registrars of upcoming camps & retreats
• The Mission Messenger
Type: Newsletter
Profile: Articles & events to inform members & friends of the church

Community One Foundation
PO Box 760, Stn. F, Toronto ON M4Y 2N6
Tel: 416-920-5422
info@communityone.ca
www.communityone.ca
www.facebook.com/CommunityOneFoundation
twitter.com/C1Foundation
instagram.com/c1foundation
Previous Name: Lesbian & Gay Community Appeal Foundation
Overview: A medium-sized local charitable organization founded in 1980
Mission: To raise & disburse funds for the advancement of lesbian, gay, bisexual & transgender projects, artists & organizations; To fund projects in the areas of health & social services, arts & culture, research & education, political & legal
Member of: Canadian Centre for Philanthropy
Finances: Annual Operating Budget: $50,000-$100,000
20 volunteer(s)
Membership: 1,000 individual
Activities: Speaker Service: Yes
Chief Officer(s):
Terrance Greene, Co-Chair
Kevin Ormsby, Co-Chair

Community Planning Association of Alberta (CPAA)
#205, 10940 - 166A St., Edmonton AB T5P 3V5
Tel: 780-432-6387; Fax: 780-452-7718
cpaa@cpaa.biz
www.cpaa.biz
Overview: A small provincial organization
Mission: The Community Planning Association of Alberta is an organization dedicated to the promotion of community planning in the Province of Alberta.
Finances: Annual Operating Budget: $100,000-$250,000
Staff Member(s): 3; 100 volunteer(s)
Membership: Fees: $25 student; $100 individual; $250 group
Chief Officer(s):
Gloria Wilkinson, Chair
Awards:
• Community Planning of Association Scholarship
; Amount: $1000
Meetings/Conferences:
• 2018 Community Planning Association of Alberta Annual Planning Conference, April, 2018, Black Knight Inn, Red Deer, AB
Scope: Provincial

Community Resource Centre (Killaloe) Inc. (CRC)
PO Box 59, Killaloe ON K0J 2A0
Tel: 613-757-3108; Fax: 613-757-0208
Toll-Free: 888-757-3108
director@crc-renfrewcounty.com
www.crc-renfrewcounty.com
Also Known As: The Resource Centre
Overview: A small local charitable organization founded in 1987 overseen by InformOntario
Mission: To improve the quality of life in the community by supporting and encouraging improved family life, cooperation, right livelihood and social development.
Member of: Ontario Association of Family Resource Programs;
FRP Canada
Affiliation(s): Ontario Community Action Program for Children; Canada Prenatal Nutrition Coation
Membership: Member Profile: Citizens of rural Renfrew County
Activities: Information & referral; prenatal nutrition; second hand clothing store; mobile toy & book lending library; mobile information centre for rural communities in southwest Renfrew County; programs for pre-school children accompanied by an adult; Awareness Events: Toy Bus Day in the Park Library: Toy & Book Library

Community Sector Council, Newfoundland & Labrador (CSC NL)
25 Anderson Ave., St. John's NL A1B 3E4
Tel: 709-753-9860; Fax: 709-753-6112
Toll-Free: 866-753-9860
csc@cscnl.ca
communitysector.nl.ca
www.facebook.com/cscnl
twitter.com/CSCNL
Also Known As: CSC
Previous Name: Community Services Council, Newfoundland & Labrador
Overview: A small local charitable organization founded in 1976
Mission: To work towards an inclusive society that supports individuals, families, & communities; To promote citizen engagement & the integration of social & economic development; To take a leadership role in shaping public policies
Member of: Canadian Federation of Voluntary Sector Networks; Volunteer Canada; Cities Reducing Poverty - Tamarack Institute; Imagine Canada; St. John's Board of Trade
Finances: Annual Operating Budget: $500,000-$1.5 Million; Funding Sources: Government; Corporations; Foundations
Staff Member(s): 10; 15 volunteer(s)
Membership: Committees: Annual Volunteer Week; Community Sector Pulse Panel; Community Sector Working; Vibrant Communities - Citizens Voice Network
Activities: Research & development; Training; Volunteer Week celebrations; Volunteer Week luncheon; Awareness Events: Volunteer Week; National Child Day; Internships: Yes; Speaker Service: Yes; Library: Open to public by appointment
Chief Officer(s):
Penelope M. Rowe, CEO
pennyrowe@cscnl.ca
Awards:
• Annual Volunteer Week Grants
Offered each year in partnership with other organizations; offered to organizations and/or communities to host events that celebrate volunteerism; Amount: $100
Publications:
• NL Community Sector News
Type: Newsletter; Frequency: Monthly; Editor: Josh Smee
Profile: Information on training opportunities, policy discussions, & ideas relevant to community organizations in Newfoundland & Labrador

Community Services Council, Newfoundland & Labrador
See Community Sector Council, Newfoundland & Labrador

Community Social Services Employers' Association (CSSEA)
Two Bentall Centre, PO Box 232, #800, 555 Burrard St., Vancouver BC V7X 1M8
Tel: 604-687-7220; Fax: 604-687-7266
Toll-Free: 800-377-3340
cssea@cssea.bc.ca
www.cssea.bc.ca
Overview: A medium-sized provincial organization founded in 1994
Mission: To strive for excellence & innovation in human resources & labour relations
Finances: Annual Operating Budget: $3 Million-$5 Million
Staff Member(s): 21
Membership: 202
Chief Officer(s):
Gentil Mateus, Chief Executive Officer
gmateus@cssea.bc.ca
Thomas Marshall, Director, Communications
tmarshall@cssea.bc.ca

Community Support Centre Haldimand-Norfolk (CSCHN)
103 Inverness St., Caledonia ON N3W 1B1
Tel: 905-765-4408; Fax: 289-284-0571
info@cschn.org
www.cschn.org
www.facebook.com/CommunitySupportCentreHN
twitter.com/cschaldnor
Previous Name: Haldimand Community Support Centre
Overview: A small local charitable organization founded in 1986
Mission: To provide comprehensive client-driven community support/services to individuals & families within Haldimand-Norfolk
Member of: United Way of Haldimand-Norfolk
Finances: Annual Operating Budget: $50,000-$100,000
Staff Member(s): 7; 15 volunteer(s)
Membership: 1-99; Fees: $5-$100 individual; $25-150 organizations/businesses
Activities: Library: Open to public
Chief Officer(s):
Andrea Gee, Executive Director
agee@cschn.org

Community Torchlight Guelph/Wellington/Dufferin
PO Box 1027, Guelph ON N1H 6N1
Tel: 519-821-3761; Fax: 519-821-8190; Crisis Hot-Line: 888-821-3760
info@communitytorchlight.com
www.communitytorchlight.com
www.linkedin.com/pub/community-torchlight/23/2a2/236
twitter.com/CommunityTorch
Previous Name: Distress Centre Wellington/Dufferin; Guelph Distress Centre
Overview: A small local charitable organization founded in 1969 overseen by Distress Centres Ontario
Mission: To provide a free, 24-hour listening, referral & crisis assistance telephone service to Guelph & rural Wellington & Dufferin counties
Finances: Funding Sources: United Way of Guelph & Wellington; Ontario Ministry of Health & Long-Term Care
Staff Member(s): 5
Activities: Operating Distress line 519-821-3760; TeleCheck 519-415-3764; Youth support line 519-821-5469; Emergency shelter line 519-767-6594
Chief Officer(s):
Katherine Johnson, Manager, Services
kjohnson@communitytorchlight.com
Judith Rosenberg, Coordinator, Community Development & Recruitment
jrosenberg@communitytorchlight.com

Comox Valley Chamber of Commerce (CVCC)
2040 Cliffe Ave., Courtenay BC V9N 2L3
Tel: 250-334-3234; Fax: 250-334-4908
Toll-Free: 888-357-4471
events@comoxvalleychamber.com
www.comoxvalleychamber.com
www.facebook.com/ComoxValleyChamber
twitter.com/cxValleyChamber
Overview: A medium-sized local organization founded in 1919
Mission: To support, promote & represent the interests of members in municipal, provincial & national issues
Member of: BC Chamber of Commerce
Finances: Funding Sources: Membership dues
Staff Member(s): 5
Membership: Fees: Schedule available
Chief Officer(s):
Kevin East, Chair
Dianne Hawkins, CEO
dhawkins@comoxvalleychamber.com

Comox Valley Child Development Association
237 - 3rd St., Courtenay BC V9N 1E1
Tel: 250-338-4288; Fax: 250-338-9326
info@cvcda.ca
www.cvcda.ca
www.facebook.com/157683204244728
www.youtube.com/watch?v=asJV-7FIeJo
Overview: A small local organization
Mission: Serves children in the Comox Valley region who need extra support
Activities: Annual Telethon; Library: Lending Library
Chief Officer(s):
Heather McFetridge, Executive Director
Publications:
• Oasis
Type: Newsletter; Frequency: Quarterly

Comox Valley Community Arts Council (CVCAC)
c/o Comox Valley Centre for the Arts, #202, 580 Duncan St., Courtenay BC V9N 2M7
Tel: 250-338-4417
info@comoxvalleyarts.org

www.comoxvalleyarts.org
www.facebook.com/ComoxValleyArts
twitter.com/CVCartscouncil
Overview: A small local charitable organization founded in 1965
Mission: To promote & foster cultural, educational & artistic activities in the Comox Valley
Affiliation(s): Canadian Conference of the Arts; Assembly of BC Arts Councils; Pacific Regional Arts Council; Courtenay Recreational Association; Tourism Comox Valley; Comox Valley Chamber of Commerce
Finances: *Funding Sources:* Provincial & municipal governments; private & individual donations; fundraising
Staff Member(s): 2
Membership: *Fees:* $20 individual; $35 group
Activities: Trumpeter Swan Festival juried art show; Annual Community Juried Show; community art project; Art in the Park children's art program; banner project; Endowment Fund; concert series; exhibitions; *Library:* Resource Room; Open to public
Chief Officer(s):
Dallas Stevenson, Executive Director

Comox Valley Food Bank Society
PO Box 3028, 1491 McPhee St., Courtenay BC V9N 5N3
Tel: 250-338-0615
comoxvfbsociety@shaw.ca
Overview: A small local charitable organization overseen by Food Banks British Columbia
Mission: To provide food to the needy in Comox Valley.
Member of: Food Banks British Columbia
Chief Officer(s):
Jeff Hampton, President
jeffandsusan@shaw.ca

Comox Valley Therapeutic Riding Society (CVTRS)
PO Box 3666, Courtenay BC V9N 7P1
Tel: 250-338-1968; *Fax:* 250-338-4137
cvtrs@telus.net
www.cvtrs.org
Also Known As: Therapeutic Riding
Overview: A small local charitable organization founded in 1986
Mission: To provide a therapeutic riding program for physically, mentally & emotionally disabled, hearing & visually impaired children & adults
Member of: Canadian Therapeutic Riding Association
Affiliation(s): North American Handicapped Riding Association
Finances: *Funding Sources:* United Way; donations; fundraising
Staff Member(s): 10; 175 volunteer(s)
Membership: 130; *Fees:* $20 individual; $30 group/family
Activities: Therapy with the use of a horse
Chief Officer(s):
Nancy King, Executive Director

Comox Valley United Way
PO Box 3097, Stn. Main, Courtenay BC V9N 5N3
Tel: 250-338-1151
www.uwcnvi.ca
Overview: A small local organization overseen by United Way of Canada - Centraide Canada

Compagnie d'opéra canadienne *See* Canadian Opera Company

Compagnie de Danse ethnique Migrations *Voir* Compagnie de danse Migrations

Compagnie de danse Migrations
880, av Pére-Marquette, Québec QC G1S 24A
Tél: 581-983-8092
migrationsdanse@gmail.com
www.migrationsdanse.com
Nom précédent: Compagnie de Danse ethnique Migrations
Aperçu: *Dimension:* petite; *Envergure:* locale; Organisme sans but lucratif; fondée en 1981
Mission: Création, formation, production et diffusion de la danse et musique traditionnelle québécoise et des cultures du monde
Membre de: Office du Tourisme et des Congrès de la Communauté Urbaine de Québec
Affiliation(s): Folklore Canada International
Finances: *Fonds:* Conseil des Arts et Lettres du Québec; Ville de Québec
Activités: Spectacles - Galas Danse et Musique du Monde; *Stagiaires:* Oui; *Service de conférenciers:* Oui

La Compagnie des philosophes
100, rue St-Laurent ouest, Montréal QC J4H 1M1
Tél: 450-670-8775
philosophes@me.com
cdesphilosophes.org
Aperçu: *Dimension:* petite; *Envergure:* locale
Mission: Promouvoir la pensée et les théories philosophique des choses qui peuvent être utilisés dans la vie quotidienne
Membre: *Montant de la cotisation:* 25$
Activités: Les dimanches philo; journées thématiques et fins de semaines philosophiques; ciné-clubs philosophiques; cafés-philo
Membre(s) du bureau directeur:
Jacques Perron, Directeur général
jacquesjperron@me.com

Compagnie Marie Chouinard
4499, av de l'esplanade, Montréal QC H2W 1T2
Tél: 514-843-9036; *Téléc:* 514-843-7616
info@mariechouinard.com
www.mariechouinard.com
www.facebook.com/ciemariechouinard
twitter.com/mariechouinard
www.youtube.com/user/MarieChouinard
Aperçu: *Dimension:* petite; *Envergure:* locale
Mission: Pour être dédié à des interprétations modernes et uniques de la danse, nouvelle chorégraphie artistique, et l'expression à travers les mouvements du corps humain
Membre(s) du bureau directeur:
Marie Chouinard, Directrice générale et artistique

Compagnie vox théâtre
#202, 112, rue Nelson, Ottawa ON K1N 7R5
Tél: 613-241-1090; *Téléc:* 613-241-0250
info@voxtheatre.ca
www.voxtheatre.ca
www.facebook.com/220424964644192
Également appelé: Vox Théâtre
Aperçu: *Dimension:* petite; *Envergure:* locale; Organisme sans but lucratif; fondée en 1979
Mission: Avec son travail de création, ses productions de théâtre chanté, ses accueils de spectacle pluridisciplinaires et ses tournées, la compagnie Vox Théâtre présente une programation complète pour les enfants et leur propose aussi des activités de formation
Membre de: Association des théâtres francophones du Canada; Théâtre Action
Finances: *Fonds:* Conseil des Arts du Canada; Patrimoine canadien; Conseil des arts de l'Ontario, Ville d'Ottawa
Membre(s) du personnel: 2
Activités: Théâtre de création francophone pour les enfants; services d'ateliers en théâtre et d'autres formes des arts de la scène
Membre(s) du bureau directeur:
Pier Rodier, Direction artistique et générale
prodier@voxtheatre.ca

Company of Women
1353 Cleaver Dr., Oakville ON L6J 1W5
Tel: 905-338-1771; *Fax:* 905-338-3018
www.companyofwomen.ca
www.facebook.com/companyofwomen
twitter.com/companyofwomen
Overview: A small local organization
Membership: *Fees:* $195 full; $115 social; $285 corporate; $95 youth
Chief Officer(s):
Anne Day, Founder
anne@companyofwomen.ca
Publications:
• Company
Profile: Quarterly magazine

The Comparative & International Education Society of Canada (CIESC) / La Société canadienne d'éducation comparée et internationale (SCECI)
c/o Canadian Society for the Study of Education, #204, 260 Dalhousie St., Ottawa ON K1N 7E4
Tel: 613-241-0018; *Fax:* 613-241-0019
ciescanada.ca
www.facebook.com/ciescsceci
Overview: A small international charitable organization founded in 1967 overseen by Canadian Society for the Study of Education
Mission: To promote international knowledge & understanding in education; To examine educational systems in international & comparative framework
Member of: Canadian Society for the Study of Education
Affiliation(s): World Congress of Comparative Education Societies
Finances: *Annual Operating Budget:* Less than $50,000
Membership: 150 Canada & abroad
Chief Officer(s):
Kumari Beck, President, 778-782-8599
kumari_beck@sfu.ca
Awards:
• Michel LaFerrière Award
• Douglas Ray Award
• David Wilson Award
• Graduate Conference Travel Grant
• Conference Travel Subsidy Grant
Meetings/Conferences:
• The Comparative & International Education Society of Canada 2018 Conference, May, 2018, University of Regina, Regina, SK
Scope: National
Publications:
• Comparative & International Education / Éducation comparée et internationale
Type: Journal; *Frequency:* 2 pa
Profile: Articles deal with education in a comparative & international perspective

Compass Centre for Sexual Wellness
#50, 9912 - 106 St., Edmonton AB T5K 1C5
Tel: 780-423-3737; *Fax:* 780-425-1782
info@compasscentre.ca
www.compasscentre.ca
www.facebook.com/64347076574
twitter.com/CompassCentre
Previous Name: OPTIONS Sexual Health Association; Planned Parenthood Association of Edmonton
Overview: A small local charitable organization founded in 1964
Mission: To promote healthy sexuality for all, through education, counselling, advocacy, in partnership with the community
Member of: Canadian Federation for Sexual Health; International Planned Parenthood
Affiliation(s): Planned Parenthood Alberta
Finances: *Funding Sources:* Municipal government; United Way; foundations; fundraising; donors
Membership: *Fees:* $50 supporting agency; $30 individual; $20 student
Activities: Educational presentations of accurate, comprehensive & holistic information on all aspects of sexuality; counselling services with regard to sexuality, pregnancy options & contraception; advocacy; annual auction; community events; summer programs for teens; *Awareness Events:* Edmonton's Pride Parade, June

Compassion Canada
PO Box 5591, London ON N6A 5G8
Tel: 519-668-0224; *Fax:* 866-685-1107
Toll-Free: 800-563-5437
info@compassion.ca
www.compassion.ca
Overview: A medium-sized international charitable organization founded in 1963
Mission: To provide sponsors for children in Third World countries; To aid community development projects in cooperation with Canadian International Development Agency; To be an advocate for children, to release them from their spiritual, economic, social & physical poverty & to enable them to become responsible & fulfilled Christian adults
Member of: Better Business Bureau; Canadian Council of Christian Charities; Association of Evangelical Relief & Development Organizations; Evangelical Fellowship of Canada
Finances: *Funding Sources:* Donations; government grants
Activities: *Speaker Service:* Yes
Chief Officer(s):
Barry Slauenwhite, President & CEO
Jim Bartholomew, Vice-President, Strategy & Marketing
Tim DeWeerd, Vice-President, Business Services
Deb Wilkins, Vice-President, Engagement

Compensation Employees' Union (Ind.) (CEU) / Syndicat des employés d'indemnisation (ind.)
#120, 13775 Commerce Pkwy., Richmond BC V6V 2V4
Tel: 604-278-4050; *Fax:* 604-278-5002
www.ceu.bc.ca
www.facebook.com/313873122023339
twitter.com/CEUOurUnion
Overview: A medium-sized provincial organization founded in 1974
Mission: The Compensation Employees' Union was certified in 1974. The CEU is an all inclusive bargaining unit representing all workers at the Workers' Compensation Board that are not excluded by law. The membership ranges from cleaners,

support positions, technicial positions, officer level positions, physiologists, and lawyers.
Member of: National Union of Public and General Employees
Finances: *Annual Operating Budget:* $500,000-$1.5 Million
Staff Member(s): 5
Membership: 2,100
Activities: *Library:* Not open to public
Chief Officer(s):
Sandra Wright, President
Candace Philpitt, Secretary

Compétences Canada *See* Skills Canada

Compost Council of Canada / Conseil canadien du compost
16 Northumberland St., Toronto ON M6H 1P7
Tel: 416-535-0240; *Fax:* 416-536-9892
Toll-Free: 877-571-4769
info@compost.org
www.compost.org
www.facebook.com/people/Compost-Council/100001137258465
Overview: A medium-sized national organization founded in 1991
Mission: To advance organics residuals recycling & compost use; To contribute to environmental sustainability
Activities: Providing resources for the Canadian compost industry; *Awareness Events:* Compost Week, May
Chief Officer(s):
Susan Antler, Executive Director
Meetings/Conferences:
• Compost Council of Canada 2018 28th Annual National Compost Conference, 2018
Scope: National
Description: Current developments in the composting industry, such as research, processing improvements, & community developments
Publications:
• Compost Matters
Type: Newsletter
Profile: Information for members of the Compost Council of Canada, such as regulations, members, grants, workshops, conferences, & awareness events

Comptables professionnels agréés du Canada *See* Chartered Professional Accountants Canada

Comptables professionnels agréés Nouveau-Brunswick *See* Chartered Professional Accountants of New Brunswick

Compton County Historical Museum Society (CCHMS) / Société du Musée historique du Comté de Compton
Eaton COrner Museum, 374, rte 253, Cookshire-Eaton QC J0B 1M0
Tel: 819-875-5256
info@eatoncorner.ca
www.eatoncorner.ca
Overview: A small local charitable organization founded in 1959 overseen by Fédération des sociétés d'histoire du Québec
Mission: To operate the county museum; to promote the study & appreciation of the history of Eaton Corner & Compton County; to erect monuments, memorials & plaques; to maintain archives
Member of: Quebec Anglophone Heritage Network
Finances: *Funding Sources:* Fundraising; membership fees
Membership: *Fees:* $10 individual; $15 family; $75 lifetime; *Committees:* Activities; Collections & Archives; Exhibition Development; Museum Administration; Buildings & Grounds; Heritage Gardens & Landscaping; Fundraising
Activities: Irish Variety Evening; Heritage Costume Dance; Hymn Sings at the Museum (music by a treadle-powered harmonium); Foliage & Heritge Tour; *Library:* Compton County Historical Museum Society Resource Centre; Open to public
Chief Officer(s):
Marc Nault, President

Compton Historical Society / Société d'histoire de Compton
6280, rte Louis St-Laurent, Compton QC J0B 1L0
Tel: 819-835-9117
Overview: A small local organization founded in 1993
Finances: *Annual Operating Budget:* Less than $50,000
4 volunteer(s)
Membership: *Fees:* $5 individual; $10 family
Activities: Publishing books on local history; restoration of abandoned cemeteries
Chief Officer(s):
Russell Nichols, President

Computer Learning & Information Centre Society of Calgary *See* CanLearn Society for Persons with Learning Difficulties

Computer Modelling Group (CMG)
#200, 1824 Crowchild Trail NW, Calgary AB T2M 3Y7
Tel: 403-531-1300; *Fax:* 403-289-8502
cmgl@cmgl.ca
www.cmgroup.com
Overview: A small international organization founded in 1978
Mission: To develop technology transfer of oil & gas reservoir simulation software; To provide practical solutions for reservoir modelling & simulation, advanced software, advanced oil recovery (EOR/IOR) processes, reservoir engineering, consulting, training & technical support.
Chief Officer(s):
Ken M. Dedeluk, President & CEO
ken.dedeluk@cmgl.ca
David Hicks, Vice-President, Eastern Hemisphere
James C. Erdle, Vice-President, USA & Latin America
jim.erdle@cmgl.ca
  Europe Office
  Howbery Park, #4, Isis Building, Wallingford OX10 8ba United Kingdom
  Tel: 44-1491-832447
  CMG-sales-Europe@cmgl.ca
  Chief Officer(s):
  Steve Webb, General Manager
  Middle East Office
  Building 12, PO Box 500 446, #320, Dubai Internet City, Dubai United Arab Emirates
  Tel: 971-4-434-5190; *Fax:* 971-4-423-0740
  CMG-sales-ME@cmgl.ca
  Chief Officer(s):
  David Hicks, Vice President, Eastern Hemisphere
  South America Office
  Centro Empresarial Eurobuilding, Calle La Guarita, #2-A, Caracas Venezuela
  Tel: 58-212-993-0463; *Fax:* 58-212-993-0315
  CMG-sales-LA@cmgl.ca
  Chief Officer(s):
  Carlos Granado, Manager, Venezuela & Trinidad
  USA office
  #860, 450 Gears Rd., Houston TX 77067 USA
  Tel: 281-872-8500; *Fax:* 281-872-8577
  CMG-sales-USA@cmgl.ca
  Chief Officer(s):
  Jim Erdle, Vice-President, USA & Latin America

Computer-Using Educators of BC
c/o BC Teachers Federation, #100, 550 West 6 Ave., Vancouver BC V5Z 4P2
Tel: 604-871-1848
Toll-Free: 800-663-9163
cuebc.ca
twitter.com/cuebc
Overview: A small provincial organization
Mission: To promote the educational uses of computer technology in British Columbia schools
Member of: BC Teachers' Federation
Activities: Conferences; newsletter
Chief Officer(s):
Mike Silverton, President
msilverton@cuebc.ca

Conayt Friendship Society
PO Box 1989, Merritt BC V1K 1B8
Tel: 250-378-5107; *Fax:* 250-378-6676
Other Communication: Alternate Phone: 250-378-8501
conayt.com
Overview: A small local organization founded in 1968
Mission: To holistically improve the quality of life, cultural distinctiveness, & cooperation between Aboriginal & non-Aboriginal members of the community
Staff Member(s): 14
Membership: *Fees:* $5
Activities: Providing housing & counselling services; Operating day camps; Offering prenatal nutrition programs
Chief Officer(s):
Teressa Nahanee, Executive Director, 250-378-5107 Ext. 8510
tnahanee@conayt.com

Conception Bay Area Chamber of Commerce
105 Church Rd., #A, Conception Bay South NL A1X 6K6
Tel: 709-834-5670; *Fax:* 709-834-5760
info@cbachamber.com
www.cbachamber.com
www.facebook.com/cbachamber
twitter.com/cbachamber
Overview: A small local organization
Mission: To protect the interests of businesses in the Conception Bay Area
Member of: Newfoundland & Labrador Chamber of Commerce
Membership: 145
Chief Officer(s):
Margo Murphy, President
Awards:
• Business Recognition Awards
Awards to Entrepreneur of the Year, Best New Business of the Year, and Best Established Business of the Year

Concerned Children's Advertisers
#200, 10 Alcorn Ave., Toronto ON M4V 3A9
Tel: 416-484-0871; *Fax:* 416-484-6564
info@cca-arpe.ca
cca-arpe.ca
Overview: A medium-sized national organization founded in 1990
Mission: To produce campaigns such as public service announcements, curricula & advice for families, in order to responsibly handle issues such as drug abuse, child abuse, child safety, self-esteem, bullying, media literacy & healthy lifestyles.
Affiliation(s): Canadian Association of Principals; Canadian Teachers' Federation; The Canadian Home & School Federation; Dietitians of Canada; Active Living Alliance
Membership: *Member Profile:* Canadian companies who produce responsible marketing & advertising campaigns aimed at children & their families
Chief Officer(s):
Craig Hutchison, Chair
Sherry MacLauchlan, Vice-Chair
Russ Ward, Treasurer

Concerned Friends of Ontario Citizens in Care Facilities (CFOCCF)
140 Merton St., 2nd Fl., Toronto ON M4S 1A1
Tel: 416-489-0146
Toll-Free: 855-489-0146
info@concernedfriends.ca
www.concernedfriends.ca
Overview: A small provincial charitable organization founded in 1980
Mission: To address the issues involving the care & conditions surrounding residents of long-term care facilities; To increase awareness of issues & concerns among the general public & provincial government; To provide information about the rights & responsibilities of residents of long-term care facilities under government legislation
Affiliation(s): Self Help Resource Centre of Greater Toronto
Finances: *Funding Sources:* Ontario Trillium Foundation; membership dues; donations; sale of publications
Membership: *Fees:* $25; *Member Profile:* Associate or employee of a long-term care facility; *Committees:* Advocacy; Volunteer
Chief Officer(s):
Jordanne Holland, President

Concordia Caribbean Students' Union (CCSU)
Concordia University, Hall Building, #H-733-3, 1455, boul de Maisonneuve ouest, Montréal QC H3G 1M8
Tel: 514-848-2424
concordia.caribbean@gmail.com
ccsu.concordia.ca
Overview: A small local organization
Mission: The mission of CCSU is to educate and promote Caribbean culture to the entire student body, including those of non-caribbean descent. We also help facilitate the transition of the new Carribean students to Concordia and Montreal's social scene.

Concordia University Faculty Association (CUFA) / Association des professeurs de l'Université Concordia
7141, rue Sherbrooke ouest, #HB-109, Montréal QC H4B 1R6
Tel: 514-848-2424; *Fax:* 514-848-3997
cufa@alcor.concordia.ca
www.cufa.net
Overview: A medium-sized local organization
Mission: To represent its members at Concordia University, which includes full-time faculty, including those on limited and extended term and professional librarians

Staff Member(s): 2
Chief Officer(s):
Lucie Lequin, President
Lucie.Lequin@concordia.ca

Concordia University Part-time Faculty Association (CUPFA) / Association des professeures et professeurs à temps partiel de l'Université Concordia (APTPUC)
Sir George Williams Campus, 1455, boul de Maisonneuve ouest, #K-340, Montréal QC H3G 1M8
Tel: 514-848-3691; *Fax:* 514-848-3648
cupfa@alcor.concordia.ca
www.cupfa.org
Overview: A small local organization
Mission: CUPFA is a certified, non-affliated labour organization aiming to improve the working conditions of the part-time faculty & maintain harmonious relations between them & Concordia University.
Staff Member(s): 2
Membership: *Committees:* Finance; Grievance; Professional Development; Negotiating
Chief Officer(s):
Dave Douglas, President

Concours de musique du Canada inc. (CMC) / Canadian Music Competitions Inc.
69, rue Sherbrooke ouest, Montréal QC H2X 1X2
Tél: 514-284-5398; *Téléc:* 514-284-6828
Ligne sans frais: 877-879-1959
info@cmcnational.com
www.cmcnational.com
www.facebook.com/CMCnational
Aperçu: *Dimension:* moyenne; *Envergure:* nationale; Organisme sans but lucratif; fondée en 1958
Mission: Faire participer a une véritable expérience nationale de musique, en étroite collaboration avec les institutions et les professeurs de musique du pays, les plus doués de nos jeunes musiciennes et musiciens canadiens; réunir les jeunes interprètes canadiens, de les soutenir dans leur apprentissage de la musique classique et d'encourager le dépassement de soi, la discipline et la persévérance
Finances: *Budget de fonctionnement annuel:* $250,000-$500,000
Membre(s) du personnel: 4; 50 bénévole(s)
Membre: 1 000; *Comités:* 14 sections bénévoles: Vancouver; Calgary; Edmonton; Winnipeg; Toronto; Oakville; Ottawa; Montréal; Sherbrooke; Trois-Rivières; Saguenay; Québec; Rimouski; Halifax
Activités: Musique classique; *Stagiaires:* Oui
Membre(s) du bureau directeur:
Marie-Claude Matton, Directrice générale
Prix, Bourses:
- CMC Scholarship

Concrete B.C. (BCRMCA)
26162 - 30A Ave., Langley BC V4W 2W5
Tel: 604-626-4141; *Fax:* 604-626-4143
concrete@concretebc.ca
www.concretebc.ca
Previous Name: British Columbia Ready Mixed Concrete Association
Overview: A medium-sized provincial organization overseen by Canadian Ready Mixed Concrete Association
Mission: To work cooperatively with all levels of government to ensure the ready-mix concrete industry operates with a focus on B.C.'s communities & the environment
Member of: Canadian Ready Mixed Concrete Association
Staff Member(s): 2
Membership: 266; *Fees:* Schedule available; *Member Profile:* Ready-mix concrete producers & suppliers in B.C.
Chief Officer(s):
Charles Kelly, President, 604-760-4696, Fax: 604-626-4143
ckelly@concretebc.ca
Carolyn Campbell, Vice-President, Operations & Membership, 250-859-3532, Fax: 604-626-4143
ccampbell@concretebc.ca

Concrete Forming Association of Ontario (CFAO)
ON
Overview: A small provincial organization founded in 1971
Mission: Contractors are engaged in highrise formwork within the ICI (industrial, commercial, institutional) sectors of the construction industry in Ontario
Member of: Toronto Construction Association
Finances: *Annual Operating Budget:* Less than $50,000; *Funding Sources:* Membership dues; industry funds

10 volunteer(s)
Membership: 10; *Fees:* $200
Awards:
- Civil Engineering Award
The Scholarship Committee of the Department of Civil Engineering takes into consideration the following factors: work experience, interest, career aspirations in the construction industry; family affiliations in any respect of the industry; financial need; academic proficiency; priority consideration to first-time applicants, however, a previous award winner may be considered given extenuating circumstances (i.e. financial need) *Eligibility:* Ryerson Polytechnic University students who have completed their first or second year of the Civil Engineering program & who are continuing on into the second or third year on a full-time basis in the immediate year following; *Amount:* $500

Concrete Manitoba (MRMCA)
PO Box 1787, Stn. Main, Winnipeg MB R3C 2Z9
Tel: 204-667-8539; *Fax:* 204-661-8489
info@concretemanitoba.ca
www.concretemanitoba.ca
twitter.com/concretemb
Previous Name: Manitoba Ready Mixed Concrete Association
Overview: A small provincial organization founded in 1971 overseen by Canadian Ready Mixed Concrete Association
Mission: To market & promote concrete, while advocating for its use in the development of Manitoba's infrastructure
Member of: Canadian Ready Mixed Concrete Association
Finances: *Funding Sources:* Membership
Membership: 100 companies; *Fees:* $200 + $22.50 per truck to a maximum of $800, for concrete producers; $300 associate members; $200 cement suppliers; *Member Profile:* Producers; Associates; Cement Supplies; & Honourary Members
Activities: Engaging in lobbying activities; Promoting the use of concrete; Providing networking opportunities; Offering eduational programs, such as safety & technical seminars & concrete workshops; Awarding scholarships; *Library:* MRMCA Technical Information Library
Chief Officer(s):
Fred Kennell, Chair
Hubert Boulet, Vice-Chair
Publications:
- Manitoba Ready-Mixed Concrete Association Inc. Membership Directory
Type: Directory
- Manitoba Ready-Mixed Concrete Association Inc. Newsletter
Type: Newsletter

Concrete Ontario (RMCAO)
#102B, 1 Prologis Blvd., Mississauga ON L5w 0G2
Tel: 905-564-2726; *Fax:* 905-564-5680
www.rmcao.org
www.facebook.com/ConcreteOntario
twitter.com/ConcreteOntario
www.youtube.com/concreteontario
Also Known As: Ready Mixed Concrete Association of Ontario
Overview: A medium-sized provincial organization founded in 1959 overseen by Canadian Ready Mixed Concrete Association
Mission: To promote & further the business, technology & use of quality concrete through partnership between producers & the construction & specifying industriesin Ontario
Member of: Canadian Ready Mixed Concrete Association
Finances: *Funding Sources:* Membership dues; Events
Membership: 100-499; *Fees:* Schedule available; *Member Profile:* Active: Any person, firm or corporation engaged in the supply or sale of ready mixed concrete in Ontario; Associate: Any person, firm or corporation engaged in the manufacture or sale of machinery. equipment, supplies or services used in the ready mixed concrete industry; *Committees:* Associate Members; Environment; Health & Safety; Technical; Transportation
Chief Officer(s):
Bart Kanters, Vice President, 905-564-6932
bkanters@concreteontario.org
Sylvia Benevides, Director, Meetings & Industry Event Planner, 905-564-6878
sbenevides@concreteontario.org
Alen Keri, Engineer, Technical Services, 905-564-4772
akeri@concreteontario.org
Awards:
- Ontario Concrete Awards
Meetings/Conferences:
- RMCAO [Ready Mixed Concrete Association of Ontario] 58th Annual General Meeting & Convention, 2018, ON
Scope: Provincial

Publications:
- FLASH
Type: Newsletter; *Frequency:* Bimonthly

Concrete Precasters Association of Ontario (CPA)
5001 Dufferin Ave., Wallaceburg ON N8A 4M9
Tel: 866-853-0310; *Fax:* 866-853-0311
info@cpaontario.com
www.cpaontario.com
Overview: A small provincial organization founded in 1991
Mission: To unite, improve & represent the interests of the precast concrete manufacturers in Ontario
Staff Member(s): 2
Membership: 80; *Committees:* Membership; Technical; Marketing; Convention; Safety
Chief Officer(s):
Jason Schoenfeld, President
Brian Hoffman, Administrator

Concrete Sask (SRMCA)
#101, 1102 - 8th Ave., Regina SK S4R 1C9
Tel: 306-757-2788; *Fax:* 306-546-3477
acampbell@concretesask.org
www.concretesask.org
www.facebook.com/ConcreteSask
twitter.com/srmcaconcrete
Previous Name: Saskatchewan Ready Mixed Concrete Association Inc.; Prairie Ready Mixed Concrete Association
Overview: A small provincial organization founded in 1963 overseen by Canadian Ready Mixed Concrete Association
Mission: To promote the highest quality of concrete produced by its members; To improve the industry in all aspects & represent its members in relation to governments, environmental agencies & other industry-related associations
Member of: Canadian Ready Mixed Concrete Association
Membership: 60 concrete plants; *Member Profile:* Producers & Associates
Chief Officer(s):
Rod Smith, President, 306-545-3200
Garth Sanders, Executive Director, Finance
gsanders@accesscomm.ca

Conditionnement physique Noueau-Brunswick *See* Fitness New Brunswick

Condominium Home Owners' Association of British Columbia (CHOA)
#200, 65 Richmond St., New Westminster BC V3L 5P5
Tel: 604-584-2462; *Fax:* 604-515-9643
Toll-Free: 877-353-2462
info@choa.bc.ca
www.choa.bc.ca
Overview: A medium-sized provincial organization founded in 1976
Mission: To promote the understanding of strata property living & the interests of strata property owners by providing advisory services, education, advocacy, resources, & support for its members
Chief Officer(s):
Tony Gioventu, Executive Director
tony@choa.bc.ca

Confederacy of Mainland Mi'kmaq (CMM)
PO Box 1590, 57 Martin Cresc., Truro NS B2N 6N7
Tel: 902-895-6385; *Fax:* 902-893-1520
Toll-Free: 877-892-2424
www.cmmns.com
Overview: A medium-sized provincial organization founded in 1986
Mission: To proactively promote and assist Mi'kmaw communities' initiatives toward self determination and enhancement of community.
Membership: 6 communities
Chief Officer(s):
Donald M. Julien, Executive Director

Confederation College Aboriginal Student Association *See* Oshki Anishnawbeg Student Association

Confédération des associations d'étudiants et étudiantes de l'Université Laval (CADÉUL)
Pavillon Maurice-Pollack, Université Laval, #2265, 2305 rue de l'Université, Québec QC G1V 1A6
Tél: 418-656-7931; *Téléc:* 418-656-3328
cadeul@cadeul.ulaval.ca
www.cadeul.ulaval.ca
www.facebook.com/CADEUL

twitter.com/cadeul
www.youtube.com/user/CADEUL
Aperçu: *Dimension:* moyenne; *Envergure:* locale
Mission: La Confédération des associations d'étudiants et étudiantes de l'Université Laval est l'association étudiante qui représente tous les étudiants inscrits au premier cycle à l'Université Laval.
Membre(s) du personnel: 19
Membre(s) du bureau directeur:
Caroline Aubry-Abel, Présidente
presidence@cadeul.ulaval.ca
Thierry Bouchard-Vincent, Vice-président, L'enseignement et à la recherche
enseignement@cadeul.ulaval.ca
Dominique Caron Bélanger, Vice-présidente, Affaires internes
interne@cadeul.ulaval.ca
Florence Côté, Vice-présidente, Affaires externes
externes@cadeul.ulaval.ca
Thomas Pouliot, Directeur, Services
directeur@cadeul.ulaval.ca

Confédération des Éducateurs physiques du Québec *Voir* Fédération des éducateurs et éducatrices physiques enseignants du Québec

Confédération des Organismes de Personnes Handicapées du Québec (COPHAN)
#300, 2030, boul Pie-IX, Montréal QC H1V 2C8
Tél: 514-284-0155; *Téléc:* 514-284-0775
info@cophan.org
www.cophan.org
Nom précédent: Confédération des organismes provinciaux de personnes handicapées du Québec
Aperçu: *Dimension:* moyenne; *Envergure:* provinciale; Organisme sans but lucratif; fondée en 1985
Mission: Milite pour la défense des droits et la promotion des intérêts des personnes ayant des limitations fonctionnelles, de tous âges
Membre de: Conseil de canadiens avec déficiences
Membre(s) du personnel: 4
Membre: *Critères d'admissibilite:* Association qui promeut les intérêts et défend les droits des personnes handicapées
Membre(s) du bureau directeur:
Richard Lavigne, Directeur général
direction@cophan.org
Véronique Vézina, Présidente

Confédération des organismes familiaux du Québec (COFAQ)
4657, rue Papineau, Montréal QC H2H 1V4
Tél: 514-521-4777; *Téléc:* 514-521-6272
www.cofaq.qc.ca
www.facebook.com/CofaqFamille
twitter.com/CofaqFamille
Aperçu: *Dimension:* grande; *Envergure:* provinciale; Organisme sans but lucratif; fondée en 1972
Mission: Représenter les familles et revendiquer leurs droits auprès des diverses instances publiques et privées; Promouvoir des projets innovateurs et le développement d'expertises satisfaisant aux besoins des familles et leurs organisations; Réaliser des activités de soutien auprès des membres
Membre de: Institut Vanier de la famille; Réseau pour un Québec famille; Carrefour action municipal et famille
Membre(s) du personnel: 10
Membre: 40 organismes; *Montant de la cotisation:* 75$ fédératif; 40$ associatif; *Critères d'admissibilite:* Organismes familiaux ou regroupement d'organismes
Membre(s) du bureau directeur:
Jean-Christophe Filosa, Présidente
Robert Rodrigue, Trésorière
Meetings/Conferences:
• Confédération des organismes familiaux du Québec Assemblée générale 2018, 2018, QC
Scope: Provincial
Publications:
• Confédération des organismes familiaux du Québec rapport annuel
Type: Rapport
• Info-Contact [publication Confédération des organismes familiaux du Québec]
Type: Bulletin

Confédération des organismes provinciaux de personnes handicapées du Québec *Voir* Confédération des Organismes de Personnes Handicapées du Québec

Confédération des peuples autochtones du Québec (CPAQ) / Confederation of Aboriginal People of Québec (CAPQ)
QC
Courriel: info@cpaq.ca
www.cpaq.ca
Aperçu: *Dimension:* moyenne; *Envergure:* provinciale
Mission: Organisation provinciale qui représente les intérêts des Autochtones du Québec qui sont membres d'une de leurs communautés affiliées
Membre: *Montant de la cotisation:* $30

Confédération des syndicats nationaux (CSN) / Confederation of National Trade Unions
1601, av De Lorimier, Montréal QC H2K 4M5
Tél: 514-598-2271; *Téléc:* 514-598-2052
sesyndiquer@csn.qc.ca
www.csn.qc.ca
www.facebook.com/LaCSN
twitter.com/laCSN
Aperçu: *Dimension:* grande; *Envergure:* nationale; Organisme sans but lucratif; fondée en 1921
Mission: La Confédération limite ses activités principalement au Québec, quoique certains locaux soient établis hors de la province; comprend 9 fédérations, 13 conseils centraux et 2 800 syndicats
Affiliation(s): Confédération internationale des syndicats libres
Finances: *Budget de fonctionnement annuel:* Plus de $5 Million
Membre(s) du personnel: 450
Membre: 280 000; *Comités:* Le comité confédéral de santé et sécurité; Le comité national de la condition féminine; Le comité confédéral sur les relations interculturelles; Le comité national des jeunes; Le comité confédéral des LGBT
Activités: Réunion du conseil confédéral, 4 fois par an, à Montréal et Québec; *Stagiaires:* Oui; *Bibliothèque:* Service de documentation
Membre(s) du bureau directeur:
Pierre Patry, Trésorier
Jacques Létourneau, Présidente
Jean Lortie, Secrétaire générale

Confederation of Aboriginal People of Québec *Voir* Confederation des peuples autochtones du Québec

Confederation of Alberta Faculty Associations (CAFA)
Univ. of Alberta, 11043 - 90 Ave., Edmonton AB T6G 2E1
Tel: 780-492-5630; *Fax:* 780-436-0516
www.ualberta.ca/~cafa/
twitter.com/cafaab
Overview: A medium-sized provincial organization overseen by Canadian Association of University Teachers
Mission: CAFA is a professional organization of faculty and faculty association in Alberta Universities. The objects of the Confderation are to promote the quality of education in the province and to promote the well-being of Alberta Universities and their academic staff. Comprised of four associations: The Association of Academic Staff University of Alberta, Athabasca University Faculty Association, The Faculty Association of the University of Calgary and The University of Lethbridge Faculty Association.
Membership: 3,511 individuals + 6 organizations
Chief Officer(s):
John Nicholls, Executive Director, 780-492-5630
john.nicholls@ualberta.ca
Lori Morinville, Administrative Officer, 780-492-5630
lori.morinville@ualberta.ca
Awards:
• CAFA Distinguished Academic Awards
Recognizes members, who through their research and/or other scholarly, creative or professional activities, have made outstanding contributions to the community beyond the university. *Eligibility:* Current member of one of the academic staff associations within CAFA

Confederation of Canadian Wushu Organizations *See* WushuCanada

Confederation of National Trade Unions *Voir* Confédération des syndicats nationaux

Confederation of Ontario University Staff Associations & Unions (COUSA)
ON
www.cousa.on.ca
Overview: A medium-sized local organization founded in 1974
Mission: To provide support and advocacy for the non-academic staff of Ontario's universities.
Membership: 5 unions

Confederation of Resident & Ratepayer Associations (CORRA)
63 The South Kingsway, Toronto ON M6S 3T4
corratoronto@gmail.com
Overview: A small local organization
Mission: The association coordinates the activities of & lobbies for member associations to promote better urban life & beneficial legislation. It acts as watchdog to protect city neighbourhoods, parks & waterfront.
Finances: *Annual Operating Budget:* Less than $50,000; *Funding Sources:* Membership dues
8 volunteer(s)
Membership: *Fees:* $50; *Member Profile:* Resident & ratepayer associations
Chief Officer(s):
William Roberts, Chair, 416-769-3162
willadvocate@aol.com

Confederation of University Faculty Associations of British Columbia (CUFA BC)
#315, 207 West Hastings St., Vancouver BC V6B 1H7
Tel: 604-646-4677; *Fax:* 604-646-4676
www.cufa.bc.ca
Overview: A medium-sized provincial organization overseen by Canadian Association of University Teachers
Membership: 5,400
Chief Officer(s):
Jim Johnson, President
Michael Conlon, Executive Director
execdir@cufa.bc.ca
Haida Antolick, Resource Coordinator
coordinator@cufa.bc.ca
Awards:
• CUFA/BC Distinguished Academics Awards

Confédération québécoise des coopératives d'habitation (CQCH)
#202, 840, rue Raoul-Jobin, Québec QC G1N 1S7
Tél: 418-648-6758; *Téléc:* 418-648-8580
Ligne sans frais: 800-667-9386
info@cqch.qc.ca
www.cooperativehabitation.coop
Aperçu: *Dimension:* moyenne; *Envergure:* provinciale; Organisme sans but lucratif; fondée en 1987
Finances: *Budget de fonctionnement annuel:* $500,000-$1.5 Million
Membre(s) du personnel: 10
Membre: 7; *Critères d'admissibilite:* Fédérations des coopératives d'habitation
Membre(s) du bureau directeur:
Guillaume Brien, Directrice générale
guillaume.brien@reseaucoop.com
Michèle La Haye, Présidente, Conseil d'administration

Confédération québécoise des coopératives d'habitation en Outaouais
#106, 178, boul Greber, Gatineau QC J8T 6Z6
Tél: 819-243-3717; *Téléc:* 819-243-5356
cooperativehabition.coop
Aperçu: *Dimension:* petite; *Envergure:* locale; fondée en 1985
Mission: Pour promouvoir le logement coopératif au Québec
Membre de: Confédération québécoise des coopératives d'habitation
Finances: *Budget de fonctionnement annuel:* $250,000-$500,000
Membre: 1-99
Activités: Services aux membres; développement de nouvelles coopératives; gestion de coopératives d'habitation et d'organismes sans but lucratif
Membre(s) du bureau directeur:
Nathalie Mercier, Coordonnatrice
nmercier@logeaction.com

Le Conference Board du Canada *See* The Conference Board of Canada

The Conference Board of Canada / Le Conference Board du Canada
255 Smyth Rd., Ottawa ON K1H 8M7
Tel: 613-526-3280; *Fax:* 613-526-4857
Toll-Free: 866-711-2262
contactcboc@conferenceboard.ca
www.conferenceboard.ca

Canadian Associations / Conférence des recteurs et des principaux des universités du Québec (CREPUQ) / Conference of Rectors & Principals of Quebec Universities

www.linkedin.com/company/the-conference-board-of-canada
www.facebook.com/ConferenceBoardofCanada
twitter.com/ConfBoardofCda
Overview: A medium-sized national organization founded in 1954
Mission: To be dedicated to applied research, notably in public policy, economic trends, & organizational performance
Finances: *Funding Sources:* Fees for service to the public & private sectors
Activities: The Business & Environment Research Program provides research & networking facilities for business & government in the economics, business management & public policy aspects of environmental issues. Other activities include conferences, publishing & disseminating research, & facilitating networking & training for leadership; *Library:* Information Centre; by appointment
Chief Officer(s):
Daniel Muzyka, President & CEO
Craig Alexander, Senior Vice-President & Chief Economist
Michael Bloom, Vice-President, Industry & Business Strategy
Awards:
• National Awards in Governance
Awarded to boards of directors that have demonstrated excellence in governance & have implemented successful innovations in their governance practices; overall award for innovation & sector specific awards for public, private & not for profit sectors
• National Awards for Excellence in Business-Education Partnership
Awarded to partnerships that have a demonstrated record of success in promoting the importance of science, technology &/or mathematics; linking education & the world of work, promoting teacher development, encouraging students to stay in school, expanding vocational &/or apprenticeship training

Conférence canadienne des arts *See* Canadian Conference of the Arts

Conférence des associations de la défense *See* Conference of Defence Associations

Conférence des coopératives forestières du Québec *Voir* Fédération québécoise des coopératives forestières

Conférence des évêques catholiques du Canada *See* Canadian Conference of Catholic Bishops

Conférence des recteurs et des principaux des universités du Québec (CREPUQ) / Conference of Rectors & Principals of Quebec Universities
c/o Conférence des recteurs et des principaux, #200, 500, rue Sherbrooke ouest, Montréal QC H3A 3C6
Tél: 514-288-8524; *Télec:* 514-288-0554
info@crepuq.qc.ca
www.crepuq.qc.ca
Aperçu: *Dimension:* moyenne; *Envergure:* provinciale; fondée en 1963
Mission: Est un organisme privé qui regroupe, sur une base volontaire, tous les établissements universitaires québécois; sert de forum permanent d'échanges et de concertation qui permet aux gestionnaires de partager leurs expériences en vue d'améliorer l'efficacité générale du système universitaire québécois.
Finances: *Fonds:* Les cotisations annuelles des membres
Membre(s) du personnel: 33
Membre: 7 établissements universitaires québécois
Activités: *Bibliothèque;*
Membre(s) du bureau directeur:
Daniel Zizian, Directeur général, 514-288-8524 Ext. 201
daniel.zizian@crepuq.qc.ca

Conference ferroviaire de Teamsters Canada *See* Teamsters Canada Rail Conference

Conférence générale des assemblées de dieu canadiennes *See* General Conference of the Canadian Assemblies of God

Conference of Defence Associations (CDA) / Conférence des associations de la défense
#412A, 151 Slater St., Ottawa ON K1P 5H3
Tel: 613-236-1252; *Fax:* 613-236-8191
cda@cda-cdai.ca
www.cdacanada.ca
twitter.com/CDAInstitute
Overview: A medium-sized national charitable organization founded in 1932
Mission: To place before people of Canada problems of defence & the well-being of Canada's Armed Forces
Affiliation(s): Conference of Defence Associations Institute
Finances: *Funding Sources:* Individual subscriptions; Vimy Award dinner
Staff Member(s): 4
Membership: 52 associations; *Member Profile:* Associate - The Air Cadet League of Canada; Army, Navy, Air Force Veterans in Canada; Atlantic Chief & P.O.'s Association; The Army Cadet League of Canada; Canadian NATO Defence College Association; The Canadian Airborne Forces Association; The Canadian Defence Industries Association; The Canadian Institute of Strategic Studies; The Canadian War Museum; The Dominion of Canada Rifle Association; The Federation of Military & United Services Institutes of Canada; Military Engineering Institute of Canada; The Military Public Affairs Association of Canada; The Navy League of Canada; Organization of Military Museums of Canada; Reserves 2000; Royal Military Colleges Club of Canada; *Committees:* Executive
Activities: Seminars & symposiums; *Internships:* Yes; *Speaker Service:* Yes
Chief Officer(s):
Alain Pellerin, Executive Director
director@cda-cdai.ca
Peter Forsberg, Officer, Public Affairs
pao@cda-cdai.ca
Awards:
• The Vimy Award
To recognize one Canadian who has made a significant contribution to the defence & security of our nation & the preservation of our democratic values

Conference of Independent Schools (Ontario) (CIS)
PO Box 27, Whitby ON L1N 5R7
Tel: 905-665-8622; *Fax:* 905-665-8635
admin@cisontario.ca
www.cisontario.ca
twitter.com/CISOntario
Overview: A small provincial organization founded in 1983 overseen by Canadian Accredited Independent Schools
Mission: To provide a collegial forum to promote excellence in education among its member schools
Member of: Canadian Accredited Independent Schools
Affiliation(s): National Association of Independent Schools
Finances: *Annual Operating Budget:* $100,000-$250,000; *Funding Sources:* Membership dues
Staff Member(s): 2
Membership: 45 Member schools; *Member Profile:* Not-for-profit independent schools
Chief Officer(s):
Sarah Craig, Executive Director
scraig@cisontario.ca

Conference of New England Governors & Eastern Canadian Premiers
Council Secretariat, PO Box 2044, #1006, 5161 George St., Halifax NS B3J 2Z1
Tel: 902-424-7590; *Fax:* 902-424-8976
info@cap-cpma.ca
www.cap-cpma.ca
Mission: To expand economic ties among the Atlantic provinces, Québec, & six New England states; To foster energy exchanges; To coordinate numerous policies & programs, in areas such as transportation, forest management, tourism, small-scale agriculture & fisheries; To enact policy resolutions that call on actions by the state & provincial governments, as well as by the two national governments; To promote natural gas, resource & infrastructure development
Membership: *Member Profile:* Premiers of the Atlantic provinces & Québec; Governors of six New England States
Activities: Hosting conferences of the Premiers & Governors to discuss issues of common interest; Convening meetings of state & provincial officials; Organizing workshops & roundtables; Preparing reports & studies; Monitoring & acting on common issues in the northeast region, such as electric restructuring
Chief Officer(s):
Tim Porter, Secretary to Council, 902-424-7600
tporter@cap-cpma.ca

Conference of Rectors & Principals of Quebec Universities *Voir* Conférence des recteurs et des principaux des universités du Québec

Conference of Representatives of the Governing Bodies of the Legal Profession in the Provinces of Canada *See* Federation of Law Societies of Canada

Conference pour l'harmonisation des lois au Canada *See* Uniform Law Conference of Canada

Conflict Resolution Saskatchewan
PO Box 3765, Regina SK S4P 3N8
Tel: 306-565-3939; *Fax:* 306-586-6711
Toll-Free: 866-565-3938
admin@conflictresolutionsk.ca
www.conflictresolutionsk.ca
Previous Name: Mediation Saskatchewan
Overview: A small provincial organization
Affiliation(s): Family Mediation Canada
Membership: Fees: $25 introductory; $250 organizational/sponsor
Activities: Provide a directory of mediators

Confrérie de la librairie ancienne du Québec (CLAQ)
CP 1056, Succ. C, Montréal QC H2L 4V3
Tél: 514-273-4963
Autres numéros: cote@bibliopolis.net
claqsec@bibliopolis.net
www.bibliopolis.net/claq
Aperçu: *Dimension:* petite; *Envergure:* provinciale; fondée en 1987
Mission: Promouvoir l'intérêt pour le livre ancien

Congregation Beth Israel - British Columbia
989 West 28th Ave., Vancouver BC V5Z 0E8
Tel: 604-731-4161; *Fax:* 604-731-4989
info@bethisrael.ca
www.bethisrael.ca
www.youtube.com/channel/UCV32q1muJX33op5rSZA7FTQ
Overview: A small local organization founded in 1932
Mission: The congregation is dedicated to the strengthening of all aspects of Jewish life, including worship & Torah study, religious, educational & social activities for all ages, & the observance of life cycle events.
Member of: United Synagogue of Conservative Judaism
Activities: Youth programs; Hebrew school; facility rental; Rabbi Wilfred & Phyllis Solomon Museum; *Library:* Moe Cohen Library; Not open to public
Chief Officer(s):
Gary Miller, President
Jonathan Infeld, Klei Kodesh
rabbiinfeld@bethisrael.ca
Shannon Etkin, Executive Director
shannon@bethisrael.ca

Congrégation de Sainte-Croix - Les Frères de Sainte-Croix / Congregation of Holy Cross
4901, rue du Piedmont, Montréal QC H3V 1E3
Tél: 514-731-7828; *Télec:* 514-731-7820
saintecroixcsc@yahoo.ca
www.ste-croix.qc.ca
Aperçu: *Dimension:* petite; *Envergure:* locale
Mission: Congrégation religieuse catholique qui oeuvre en éducation, en milieu paroissial et dans divers autres secteurs de la société

Congrégation des Soeurs de Sainte-Anne / Congregation of Sisters of Saint Anne
1950, rue Provost, Lachine QC H8S 1P7
Tél: 514-637-3783; *Télec:* 514-637-5400
accueil@ssacong.org
www.ssacong.org
Aperçu: *Dimension:* petite; *Envergure:* internationale; Organisme sans but lucratif; fondée en 1850
Mission: Impliquée dans l'éducation, les soins de santé, l'animation pastorale et sociale en divers milieux
Finances: *Budget de fonctionnement annuel:* $100,000-$250,000
Membre(s) du bureau directeur:
Marie Ellen King, Supérieure générale
Madeleine Lanoue, Secrétaire générale

Congrégation des Soeurs de Saint-Joseph de Saint-Vallier (SSJ)
860, av Louis-Fréchette, Québec QC G1S 3N3
Tél: 418-683-9653; *Télec:* 418-681-8781
Nom précédent: Soeurs de Saint-Joseph de Saint-Vallier
Aperçu: *Dimension:* petite; *Envergure:* locale; fondée en 1683
Membre: 165
Membre(s) du bureau directeur:
Jeanne d'Arc Auclair, Supérieure générale

Congregation of Holy Cross *Voir* Congrégation de Sainte-Croix - Les Frères de Sainte-Croix

Congregation of Missionaries of the Precious Blood, Atlantic Province
100 Pelmo Cres., Toronto ON M9N 2Y1
Tel: 416-531-4423
preciousbloodatlantic.org
Overview: A small provincial charitable organization founded in 1987
Mission: To be rooted in the word of God & reach out to the marginalized
Chief Officer(s):
Mario Cafarelli, Provincial Director

Congregation of St. Basil (CSB)
95 St. Joseph St., Toronto ON M5S 3C2
Tel: 416-921-6674
vocation@basilian.org
www.basilian.org
www.facebook.com/TheBasilians
twitter.com/TheBasilians
www.youtube.com/user/cavalka124
Also Known As: Basilian Fathers
Overview: A small international organization founded in 1822
Mission: Roman Catholic congregation of priests whose primary apostolate is education, parishes & Hispanic ministry in Canada, USA, Mexico, Colombia & France
Member of: RC Church
Finances: *Annual Operating Budget:* Less than $50,000
3 volunteer(s)
Membership: 325; *Member Profile:* Priests; Students for the priesthood
Activities: *Library:* Congregation of St. Basil Library; by appointment
Chief Officer(s):
George Smith, Superior General
David Katulski, Vicar General

Congregation of Sisters of Saint Anne *Voir* Congrégation des Soeurs de Sainte-Anne

Congregational Christian Churches in Canada (CCCC)
442 Grey St., Brantford ON N3S 7N3
Tel: 519-751-0606
4cnational@gmail.com
www.cccc.ca
www.facebook.com/4CChurches
twitter.com/CanadaCongr
Overview: A medium-sized national charitable organization founded in 1821
Mission: To celebrate & serve Jesus Christ in the 21st century through shared concern for others
Finances: *Annual Operating Budget:* $100,000-$250,000
Staff Member(s): 2
Membership: 8,000 + 100 churches across Canada; *Fees:* $50; *Member Profile:* Churches or individuals in accord with CCCC's Statement of Faith and Founding Principles as set out in their By-Law and Supplementary Letters Patent
Activities: *Internships:* Yes
Chief Officer(s):
David Schrader, National Pastor
nationalpastor@bellnet.ca
Phillip Noll, Chair of the Board
Kathleen Horwood, Executive Assistant to National Pastor
Meetings/Conferences:
• Congregational Christian Churches in Canada National Conference 2018, 2018

Congrès canadien polonais *See* Canadian Polish Congress

Congrès des Peuples Autochtones *See* Congress of Aboriginal Peoples

Congrès des ukrainiens canadiens *See* Ukrainian Canadian Congress

Congrès du travail du Canada *See* Canadian Labour Congress

Congrès mondial des ukrainiens *See* Ukrainian World Congress

Congrès national des italo-canadiens *See* National Congress of Italian-Canadians

Congress of Aboriginal Peoples (CAP) / Congrès des Peuples Autochtones
867 St. Laurent Blvd., Ottawa ON K1K 3B1
Tel: 613-747-6022; *Fax:* 613-747-8834
Toll-Free: 888-997-9927
reception@abo-peoples.org
www.abo-peoples.org
www.facebook.com/178584242154616
twitter.com/CAPChief
www.youtube.com/user/TheCAPOttawa
Previous Name: Native Council of Canada
Overview: A large national organization
Mission: To represent approximately 3/4 million Aboriginal people living off-reserve in Canada
Finances: *Annual Operating Budget:* $3 Million-$5 Million; *Funding Sources:* Heritage Canada; Health Canada; Privy Council Office
Membership: Over 50,000
Activities: *Internships:* Yes
Chief Officer(s):
Dwight Dorey, National Chief
Jim Devoe, Chief Executive Officer
j.devoe@abo-peoples.org

Congress of Black Lawyers & Jurists of Québec
445, boul St-Laurent, 5e étage, Montréal QC H3S 2B8
Tel: 514-954-3471
Overview: A medium-sized provincial organization
Mission: Please call prior to visit

Congress of Canadian Women-British Columbia *See* Canadian Women Voters Congress

Congress of Union Retirees Canada (CURC) / Association des syndicalistes retraités du Canada (ASRC)
2841 Riverside Dr., Ottawa ON K1V 8X7
Tel: 613-526-7422; *Fax:* 613-521-4655
unionretiree.ca
www.facebook.com/315702295180775
twitter.com/UnionRetirees
Overview: A large national organization founded in 1991
Mission: To ensure that the concerns of senior citizens & union retirees are heard across Canada
Affiliation(s): Canadian Labour Congress
Membership: *Fees:* Schedule available; *Member Profile:* Individual union retirees; Spouses of union retiree; Current unionmembers, over 50 years of age
Chief Officer(s):
Len Hope, President
Doug MacPherson, First Vice-President
Louisette Hinton, Second Vice-President
Maureen King, Secretary
Lucienne Bahuaud, Treasurer

Connect Society - D.E.A.F. Services
6240 - 113 St., Edmonton AB T6H 3L2
Tel: 780-454-9581; *Fax:* 780-447-5820; *TTY:* 780-454-9581
info@connectsociety.org
www.connectsociety.org
www.facebook.com/connectsocietyedmonton
www.youtube.com/user/ConnectSociety50
Previous Name: Association for the Hearing Handicapped
Overview: A small local charitable organization founded in 1963
Mission: To bring about the full participation in society of deaf & hard of hearing individuals & their families
Staff Member(s): 8
Activities: Early Intervention Program; Early Childhood Services; Family Support Program; Stay & Study; Community Living Support Services; *Speaker Service:* Yes
Chief Officer(s):
Cheryl Rehead, CEO
redhead@connectsociety.org

Connexions Information Sharing Services
#201, 812A Bloor St. West, Toronto ON M6G 1L9
Tel: 416-964-7799
mailroom@connexions.org
www.connexions.org
www.facebook.com/ConnexionsOnline
twitter.com/connexi0ns
Overview: A small national organization founded in 1975
Mission: To connect people working for social justice with information, ideas, groups & the history of social change movements.
Finances: *Annual Operating Budget:* Less than $50,000
Staff Member(s): 3; 20 volunteer(s)
Activities: *Rents Mailing List:* Yes; *Library:* Open to public by appointment
Chief Officer(s):
Ulli Diemer, Coordinator

Conseil atlantique des ministres de l'Éducation et de la Formation *See* Council of Atlantic Ministers of Education & Training

Conseil atlantique du Canada *See* Atlantic Council of Canada

Conseil canadien d'évaluation des jouets *See* Canadian Toy Testing Council

Conseil canadien d'orthoptique *See* Canadian Orthoptic Council

Conseil canadien de certification en architecture *See* Canadian Architectural Certification Board

Conseil canadien de développement social *See* Canadian Council on Social Development

Conseil canadien de droit international *See* Canadian Council on International Law

Le Conseil canadien de l'agrément des programmes de pharmacie *See* The Canadian Council for Accreditation of Pharmacy Programs

Conseil canadien de l'aviation et de l'aérospatiale *See* Canadian Council for Aviation & Aerospace

Le conseil canadien de l'éducation permanente en pharmacie *See* The Canadian Council on Continuing Education in Pharmacy

Conseil canadien de l'énergie *See* Energy Council of Canada

Conseil canadien de l'horticulture *See* Canadian Horticultural Council

Conseil canadien de la construction en acier *See* Canadian Steel Construction Council

Conseil Canadien de la Coopération *Voir* Conseil canadien de la coopération et de la mutualité

Conseil canadien de la coopération et de la mutualité (CCCM)
#400, 275, rue Bank, Ottawa ON K2P 2L6
Tél: 613-238-6712; *Téléc:* 613-567-0658
info@coopscanada.coop
canada.coop
www.facebook.com/792260167456516
twitter.com/CoopFrancoCan
Nom précédent: Conseil Canadien de la Coopération
Aperçu: *Dimension:* petite; *Envergure:* nationale; Organisme sans but lucratif; fondée en 1946
Mission: Le Conseil vise à promouvoir la coopération en vue du développement socio-économique des communautés francophones du Canada.
Affiliation(s): Alliance coopérative internationale
Finances: *Fonds:* Gouvernement fédéral
Membre(s) du personnel: 8
Membre: 61; *Critères d'admissibilite:* Conseils provinciaux de la coopération
Activités: Initiative de développement coopératif; adaptation agricole: une approche coopérative; séminaire de perfectionnement en leadership coopératif; chroniques "Culture action"; conférence de santé; programme "Jeune dirigeant stagiaire"; *Événements de sensibilisation:* Semaine de la coopération; *Bibliothèque:* C.C.C.; rendez-vous
Membre(s) du bureau directeur:
Denyse Guy, Directrice générale
dguy@canada.coop
Prix, Bourses:
• Ordre du Mérite Coopératif Canadien

Conseil canadien de la fourrure *See* The Fur Council of Canada

Le Conseil canadien de la réadaptation et du travail *See* Canadian Council on Rehabilitation & Work

Conseil canadien de la sécurité *See* Canada Safety Council

Conseil Canadien de la sécurité du levage et du gréage *See* Canadian Hoisting & Rigging Safety Council

Conseil canadien de la sécurité nautique *See* Canadian Safe Boating Council

Conseil canadien de protection des animaux *See* Canadian Council on Animal Care

Conseil canadien des administrateurs en transport motorisé *See* Canadian Council of Motor Transport Administrators

Canadian Associations / Conseil central de l'Estrie (CSN) (CCSNE)

Conseil canadien des administrateurs universitaires en éducation physique et kinésiologie *See* Canadian Council of University Physical Education & Kinesiology Administrators

Conseil canadien des affaires *See* Business Council of Canada

Conseil canadien des archives *See* Canadian Council of Archives

Le Conseil canadien des aveugles *See* The Canadian Council of the Blind

Conseil canadien des directeurs provinciaux et des commissaires des incendies *See* Council of Canadian Fire Marshals & Fire Commissioners

Le conseil Canadien des églises *See* The Canadian Council of Churches

Conseil canadien des examens chiropratiques *See* Canadian Chiropractic Examining Board

Le Conseil canadien des Examinateurs pour les Arpenteurs-géomètres *See* Canadian Board of Examiners for Professional Surveyors

Conseil canadien des femmes musulmanes *See* Canadian Council of Muslim Women

Conseil Canadien des Géoscientifiques Professionnels *See* Canadian Council of Professional Geoscientists

Conseil canadien des infirmières et infirmiers en nursing cardiovasculaire *See* Canadian Council of Cardiovascular Nurses

Conseil canadien des laboratoires indépendants *See* Canadian Council of Independent Laboratories

Conseil canadien des ministres de l'environnement *See* Canadian Council of Ministers of the Environment

Conseil canadien des ministres des forêts *See* Canadian Council of Forest Ministers

Conseil canadien des normes de la radiotélévision *See* Canadian Broadcast Standards Council

Conseil canadien des organismes de motoneige *See* Canadian Council of Snowmobile Organizations

Conseil Canadien des Pêches *See* Fisheries Council of Canada

Conseil canadien des pêcheurs professionnels *See* Canadian Council of Professional Fish Harvesters

Conseil canadien des piscines et spas *See* Pool & Hot Tub Council of Canada

Conseil canadien des PME et de l'entrepreneuriat *See* Canadian Council for Small Business & Entrepreneurship

Conseil canadien des professionnels en securité agréés *See* Board of Canadian Registered Safety Professionals

Conseil canadien des responsables de la réglementation d'assurance *See* Canadian Council of Insurance Regulators

Conseil canadien des ressources humaines en tourisme *See* Canadian Tourism Human Resource Council

Le Conseil canadien des soins respiratoires inc. *See* Canadian Board for Respiratory Care Inc.

Conseil canadien des techniciens et technologues *See* Canadian Council of Technicians & Technologists

Conseil canadien du bois *See* Canadian Wood Council

Conseil canadien du commerce de détail *See* Retail Council of Canada

Conseil canadien du compost *See* Compost Council of Canada

Conseil canadien du miel *See* Canadian Honey Council

Conseil canadien du porc *See* Canadian Pork Council

Conseil canadien du ski *See* Canadian Ski Council

Conseil canadien du transport de passages *See* Motor Carrier Passenger Council of Canada

Le Conseil canadien pour l'avancement de l'éducation *See* Canadian Council for the Advancement of Education

Conseil canadien pour la coopération internationale *See* Canadian Council for International Co-operation

Conseil canadien pour la diversité administrative *See* Canadian Board Diversity Council

Conseil canadien pour le commerce autochtone *See* Canadian Council for Aboriginal Business

Conseil canadien pour le contrôle du tabac *See* Canadian Council for Tobacco Control

Conseil Canadien pour les Amériques *See* Canadian Council for the Americas

Le Conseil canadien pour les partenariats public-privé *See* The Canadian Council for Public-Private Partnerships

Conseil canadien sur la reddition de comptes *See* Canadian Public Accountability Board

Conseil central de l'Estrie (CSN) (CCSNE)
180, rue de l'Acadie, Sherbrooke QC J1H 2T3
Tél: 819-563-6515; *Téléc:* 819-563-4242
Également appelé: Conseil central des syndicats nationaux de l'Estrie (CSN)
Aperçu: *Dimension:* petite; *Envergure:* locale; Organisme sans but lucratif; fondée en 1925
Mission: Promouvoir et défendre les intérêts professionels, économiques, sociaux, culturels et moraux des travailleuses et travailleurs et de leur syndicats affiliés; parmi ses objectifs immediats, le conseil général s'interesse à l'expansion du syndicalisme et au plein exercise du droit d'association dans la région
Membre de: Confédération des syndicats nationaux

Conseil central du Montréal métropolitain (CCMM-CSN)
1601, av De Lorimier, Montréal QC H2K 4M5
Tél: 514-598-2021; *Téléc:* 514-598-2020
receptionccmm@csn.qc.ca
www.ccmm-csn.qc.ca
www.facebook.com/Conseil.Central.Montreal.Metropolitain.CSN
Aperçu: *Dimension:* petite; *Envergure:* locale
Membre(s) du personnel: 15
Membre(s) du bureau directeur:
Mireille Bénard, Coordonnatrice
mireille.benard@csn.qc.ca

Conseil Commercial Canada - Albanie *See* Canada - Albania Business Council

Conseil commercial Canada Chine *See* Canada China Business Council

Conseil commercial canadien-arménien inc. *See* Canadian Armenian Business Council Inc.

Conseil communautaire Beausoleil
300, ch Beaverbrook, Miramichi NB E1V 1A1
Tél: 506-627-4135; *Téléc:* 506-627-4592
contact@carrefourbeausoleil.ca
www.ccbmiramichi.com
www.facebook.com/carrefourbeausoleil
twitter.com/CCBInc
www.youtube.com/carrefourbeausoleil
Aperçu: *Dimension:* petite; *Envergure:* locale
Mission: Assurer l'épanouissement de la communauté francophone de la Miramichi par la promotion de la langue et de la culture françaises en offrant des programmes et des services qui répondent aux besoins de cette communauté
Membre de: Conseil de promotion et de diffusion de la culture
Membre(s) du bureau directeur:
Sylvain Melançon, Directeur général
sylvain.melancon@carrefourbeausoleil.ca

Conseil communautaire Notre-Dame-de-Grâce / Notre-Dame-de-Grâce Community Council
#204, 5964, av Notre-Dame-de-Grâce, Montréal QC H4A 1N1
Tél: 514-484-1471
ndgcc@ndg.ca
www.ndg.ca
Aperçu: *Dimension:* petite; *Envergure:* locale
Membre(s) du personnel: 14; 3 bénévole(s)
Membre(s) du bureau directeur:
Halah Al-Ubaidi, Directrice générale
admin@ndg.ca

Conseil communautaire Samuel-de-Champlain *Voir* Association régionale de la communauté francophone de Saint-Jean inc.

Conseil communauté en santé du Manitoba (CCS)
#400, 400, av Taché, Saint-Boniface MB R2H 3C3
Tél: 204-235-3293; *Téléc:* 204-237-0984
santeenfrancais@santeenfrancais.com
www.santeenfrancais.com
Aperçu: *Dimension:* petite; *Envergure:* provinciale; fondée en 2004 surveillée par Société santé en français
Mission: Promouvoir l'accès à des services de qualité en français
Membre(s) du personnel: 5
Membre(s) du bureau directeur:
Annie Bédard, Directrice générale
abedard2@santeenfrancais.com

Conseil consultatif canadien de la radio *See* Radio Advisory Board of Canada

Conseil consultatif mixte de l'industrie des animaux de compagnie *See* PIJAC Canada

Conseil consultatif sur la condition féminine de la Nouvelle-Écosse *See* Nova Scotia Advisory Council on the Status of Women

Conseil coopératif acadien de la Nouvelle-Écosse (CCANE)
CP 667, Chéticamp NS B0E 1H0
Tél: 902-224-2205
coopacadien@ns.sympatico.ca
www.conseilcoopne.ca
www.facebook.com/162273307127445
Aperçu: *Dimension:* petite; *Envergure:* locale; Organisme sans but lucratif; fondée en 1980
Mission: Le Conseil coopératif acadien de la Nouvelle-Écosse a pour mission de promouvoir le développement coopératif acadien de la Nouvelle-Écosse.
Membre de: Le Conseil canadien de la coopération
Affiliation(s): Le magasin coopératif de Chéticamp; La Caisse Populaire Acadienne; La Coopérative Radio Chéticamp Ltée; The Co-operators; La coopérative La Résidence Acadienne; St. Joseph's Credit Union; La Caisse populaire de Clare Ltée
Membre: 7
Membre(s) du bureau directeur:
Angus Lefort, Président

Conseil culturel de la Montérégie inc *Voir* Conseil montérégien de la culture et des communications

Conseil culturel fransaskois (CCF) / Fransaskois Cultural Council
#216, 1440 - 9e av Nord, Regina SK S4R 8B1
Tél: 306-565-8916; *Téléc:* 306-565-2922
Ligne sans frais: 877-463-6223
ccf@culturel.sk.ca
www.culturel.sk.ca
www.facebook.com/Fransaskois
Nom précédent: Commission culturelle fransaskoise
Aperçu: *Dimension:* petite; *Envergure:* provinciale; Organisme sans but lucratif; fondée en 1974
Mission: Faire une plus grande place à la culture francophone et fransaskoise dans les écoles fransaskoises et d'immersion; renforcer les "systèmes" de diffusion en mettant en place différents moyens d'appuyer le travail des diffuseurs (ex: appui organisationnel, tournées d'artistes, outils de promotion); favoriser le cheminement professionnel des artistes en leur donnant les outils nécessaires dans les cinq domaines suivants: formation, création, production, diffusion, promotion; faire reconnaître l'importance du secteur culturel et artistique francophone par la communauté de la Saskatchewan et par les organismes fransaskois
Membre de: Fédération culturelle canadienne-française; SaskCulture
Finances: *Fonds:* Patrimoine canadien; Sasklotteries; BMLO (Bureau de la minorité de langue officielle)
Membre(s) du personnel: 6
Membre: *Critères d'admissibilite:* Association porte-parole des arts et de la culture des francophones en Saskatchewan
Activités: Ateliers InPA; programmation annuelle culturelle, scolaire, artistique; Gala fransaskois de la chanson
Membre(s) du bureau directeur:
Suzanne Compagne, Directrice générale
direction@culturel.ca
Prix, Bourses:
• Le lys d'art

Conseil d'Adoption du Canada *See* Adoption Council of Canada

Conseil d'alphabétisation de l'ouest du Québec *See* Western Québec Literacy Council

Conseil d'alphabétisation de Yamaska *Voir* Yamaska Literacy Council

Conseil d'artisanat du Nouveau-Brunswick *See* New Brunswick Crafts Council

Conseil d'information et éducation sexuelles du Canada *See* Sex Information & Education Council of Canada

Conseil d'initiatives des ressources de construction *See* Construction Resource Initiatives Council

Conseil d'intervention pour l'accès des femmes au travail (CIAFT)
#403, 110, rue Ste-Thérèse, Montréal QC H2Y 1E6
Tél: 514-954-0220; *Téléc:* 514-954-1230
info@ciaft.qc.ca
www.femmesautravail.qc.ca
www.facebook.com/CIAFT
Aperçu: Dimension: petite; *Envergure:* provinciale; Organisme sans but lucratif; fondée en 1982
Mission: Oeuvrer à la défense, la promotion et le développement de services, de politiques et de mesures favorisant la réponse aux besoins spécifiques des femmes en matière de travail; faire reconnaître les droits des femmes au travail et obtenir l'égalité professionnelle des femmes
Affiliation(s): Fédération des femmes du Québec
Membre(s) du personnel: 2
Membre: 41 groupes; *Montant de la cotisation:* 40$ individuelle; 100$ organisme
Membre(s) du bureau directeur:
Nathalie Goulet, Présidente
ngoulet@ciaft.qc.ca

Conseil de arts AOE *See* Arts Ottawa East-Est

Conseil de commerce Canada-Inde *See* Canada-India Business Council

Conseil de commerce canado-arabe *See* Canada-Arab Business Council

Conseil de conservation de l'Ontario *See* Conservation Council of Ontario

Conseil de coopération de l'Ontario (CCO)
#201, 435, boul St-Laurent, Ottawa ON K1K 2Z8
Tél: 613-745-8619; *Téléc:* 613-745-4649
Ligne sans frais: 866-290-1168
info@cco.coop
www.cco.coop
www.linkedin.com/company/conseil-de-la-coop-ration-de-l-ontario
www.facebook.com/LeConseildelacooperationdelOntario
twitter.com/ccocoop
www.youtube.com/user/conseilcoopontario
Aperçu: Dimension: moyenne; *Envergure:* provinciale; fondée en 1964
Mission: Favoriser la prise en charge socio-économique de la communauté francophone de l'Ontario par le biais de la coopération
Membre de: Conseil canadien de la coopération
Affiliation(s): Association canadienne française de l'Ontario
Finances: Fonds: Office des affaires francophones; Patrimoine canadien; Secrétariat aux affaires intergouvernementale
Membre(s) du personnel: 5
Membre: Montant de la cotisation: 25$ + 1$ par membre pour les coopératives; 10$ individuel; *Critères d'admissibilite:* Etre une coopérative francophone de l'Ontario ou un projet de coopérative en développement
Activités: Consultation; formation; information; développement; ateliers; appui technique (étude de faisabilité, incorporation, plan d'affaire); *Stagiaires:* Oui; *Service de conférenciers:* Oui
Membre(s) du bureau directeur:
Luc Morin, Directeur général
luc.morin@cco.coop

Conseil de développement du loisir scientifique *Voir* Réseau Technoscience

Conseil de développement économique des municipalités bilingues du Manitoba (CDEM)
#200, 614, rue Des Meurons, Winnipeg MB R2H 2P9
Tél: 204-925-2320; *Téléc:* 204-237-4618
Ligne sans frais: 800-990-2332
www.cdem.com
Nom précédent: Association des municipalités bilingues du Manitoba
Aperçu: Dimension: petite; *Envergure:* provinciale; fondée en 1996
Mission: Encourager, stimuler et organiser le développement économique dans les municipalités bilingues
Membre(s) du bureau directeur:
Louis Allain, Directeur général, 204-925-2322
lallain@cdem.com

Conseil de formation pharmaceutique continue *See* Council for Continuing Pharmaceutical Education

Conseil de l'enveloppe du bâtiment du Québec (CEBQ) / Québec Building Envelope Council (QBEC)
12465, 94e av, Montréal QC H1C 1H6
Tél: 514-943-0251; *Téléc:* 514-943-0300
www.cebq.org
Aperçu: Dimension: moyenne; *Envergure:* provinciale; fondée en 1989
Mission: Organiser des forums afin de faciliter la discussion et le transfert de technologies auprès de l'industrie de la construction
Membre de: National Building Envelope Council
Finances: Budget de fonctionnement annuel: Moins de $50,000
2 bénévole(s)
Membre: 500; *Montant de la cotisation:* 120$ individuel; 360$ corporatif; *Critères d'admissibilite:* Professionnel de la construction
Activités: Conférences mensuelles; cours sur l'enveloppe du bâtiment; Envol: banque de données d'articles et publications sur l'enveloppe du bâtiment; *Service de conférenciers:* Oui; *Bibliothèque*
Membre(s) du bureau directeur:
Mario D. Gonçalves, Président
m.goncalves@cebq.org
Nathalie Martin, CPA, CGA, Directrice
n.martin@cebq.org

Le Conseil de l'industrie de la motocyclette et du cyclomoteur *See* Motorcycle & Moped Industry Council

Conseil de l'industrie forestière du Québec (CIFQ) / Québec Forestry Industry Council (QFIC)
#200, 1175, av Lavigerie, Sainte-Foy QC G1V 4P1
Tél: 418-657-7916; *Téléc:* 418-657-7971
info@cifq.qc.ca
www.cifq.qc.ca
www.linkedin.com/company/conseil-de-l-industrie-foresti-re-du-quebec
twitter.com/CIFQ
Nom précédent: Association des manufacturiers de bois de sciage du Québec
Aperçu: Dimension: grande; *Envergure:* provinciale
Mission: Représente la très grande majorité des entreprises de sciage résineux, de pâtes, papiers, cartons et panneaux oeuvrant au Québec; Consacre à la défense des intérêts de ces entreprsies, à la promotion de leur contribution au développement socio-économique, à la gestion intégrée et à l'aménagement durable des forêts, de même qu'à l'utilisation optimale des ressources naturelles; Oeuvre auprès des instances gouvernementales, des organismes publics et parapublics, des organisations et de la population; Encourage un comportement responsable de ses membres en regard des dimensions environnementales, économiques et sociales de leurs activités
Membre(s) du personnel: 40
Membre: 200 compagnies; *Critères d'admissibilite:* Membres réguliers - compagnies possédant une ou des usines de sciage ou de rabotage ou papetière; membres remanufacturiers - compagnies dont la fonction consiste à transformer le bois en provenance d'une scierie; membres associés - grossistes, manufacturiers d'équipements, consultants, sociétés financières dont les activités sont reliées à celles des membres réguliers
Activités: Listes de destinataires: Oui
Membre(s) du bureau directeur:
André Tremblay, Président-CEO
Mario St-Laurent, Directeur, Communications
Pierre Vézina, Directeur, Energy & Environment
Prix, Bourses:
• Bourses académiques de l'Université Laval
• Bourses d'excellence attribuées aux Centres de formation professionnelle en foresterie

Conseil de l'industrie laitière du Québec inc. *Voir* Conseil des industriels laitiers du Québec inc.

Conseil de l'Ontario pour la coopération internationale *See* Ontario Council for International Cooperation

Conseil de la conservation du Nouveau-Brunswick *See* Conservation Council of New Brunswick

Conseil de la coopération de L'Ile-du-Prince-Édouard
CP 124, RR#1, Wellington Station PE C0B 2E0
Tél: 902-854-2667; *Téléc:* 902-854-2981
Aperçu: Dimension: moyenne; *Envergure:* provinciale

Conseil de la Coopération de la Saskatchewan (CCS)
#205, 1440, 9e av, Regina SK S4R 8B1
Tél: 306-566-6000
Ligne sans frais: 800-670-0879
info@ccs-sk.ca
www.ccs-sk.ca
www.facebook.com/conseilcoopsk
twitter.com/ccs_sk_ca
www.youtube.com/user/conseilcoopsk
Aperçu: Dimension: petite; *Envergure:* provinciale; Organisme sans but lucratif; fondée en 1947
Mission: Le CCS s'engage à trouver les moyens et les ressources nécessaires afin d'offire des programmes et des services qui: permettent la mise en oeuvre d'une stratégie de développement diversifiée à l'intérieur de la communauté fransaskoise; assurent un support aux projets de développement économique communautaire; appuient la création et l'épanouissement d'entreprises fransaskoises
Affiliation(s): Conseil Canadien de la Coopération; Réseau de développement économique et d'employabilité
Membre(s) du personnel: 14
Membre: Montant de la cotisation: 5$; *Critères d'admissibilite:* Entreprise; caisse populaire; association économique; individu; coopérative
Membre(s) du bureau directeur:
Robert Therrien, Directeur général
robert.therrien@ccs-sk.ca

Conseil de la coopération du Québec *Voir* Conseil québécois de la coopération et de la mutualité

Conseil de la culture de L'Abitibi-Témiscamingue (CRCAT)
150, av du Lac, Rouyn-Noranda QC J9X 4N5
Tél: 819-764-9511; *Téléc:* 819-764-6375
Ligne sans frais: 877-764-9511
info@ccat.qc.ca
www.ccat.qc.ca
www.facebook.com/290070211341
twitter.com/CultureAT
Aperçu: Dimension: petite; *Envergure:* locale; Organisme sans but lucratif; fondée en 1977
Mission: Unir tous les agences, corporations, corps publics et municipaux, associations et organismes, entreprises et personnes oeuvrant dans le domaine culturel de la région; contribuer à la définition des orientations et au développement de l'activité culturelle dans le meilleur intérêt régional; faire connaître la réalité et les particularités de la culture en Abitibi-Témiscamingue à l'extérieur de la région
Finances: Fonds: Ministère de la Culture et des Communications du Québec
Membre(s) du personnel: 5
Membre: 780; *Montant de la cotisation:* 25$ individu; 60$ organisme; *Critères d'admissibilite:* S'intéresser à la vie culturelle; demeurer en Abitibi-Témiscamingue
Activités: Cours de formation et perfectionnement; *Listes de destinataires:* Oui; *Bibliothèque:* Bibliothèque publique
Membre(s) du bureau directeur:
Madeleine Perron, Directrice générale
madeleine.perron@ccat.qc.ca

Conseil de la culture de la Gaspésie (CCG)
169, av Grand Pré, Bonaventure QC G0C 1E0
Tél: 418-534-4139; *Téléc:* 418-534-4113
Ligne sans frais: 800-820-0883
info@culturegaspesie.org
www.zonegaspesie.qc.ca
www.facebook.com/culturegaspesie
www.youtube.com/user/joelgauthier
Aperçu: Dimension: petite; *Envergure:* locale; Organisme sans but lucratif; fondée en 1992

Mission: Promouvoir et défendre les intérêts du milieu culturel tout en travaillant à favoriser une meilleure visibilité des produits culturels gaspésiens
Membre de: Les arts et la ville; ATR Gaspésie
Membre(s) du personnel: 5
Membre: 200+; *Montant de la cotisation:* 25$ individu; 60$ organisme; 75$ entreprise; *Critères d'admissibilite:* Artistes; organismes culturels; municipalités
Membre(s) du bureau directeur:
Anick Loisel, Directrice générale
aloisel@culturegaspesie.org

Conseil de la culture de la région de Québec/Chaudière-Appalaches *Voir* Conseil de la culture des régions de Québec et de Chaudière-Appalaches

Conseil de la culture de la région Saguenay/Lac-St-Jean/Chibougamau/Chapais *Voir* Conseil régional de la culture Saguenay-Lac-Saint-Jean

Conseil de la culture de Lanaudière
165, rue Lajoie sud, Joliette QC J6E 5K9
Tél: 450-753-7444; *Téléc:* 450-753-9047
Ligne sans frais: 866-334-7444
info@culturelanaudiere.qc.ca
www.culturelanaudiere.qc.ca
Aperçu: *Dimension:* petite; *Envergure:* locale; Organisme sans but lucratif; fondée en 1978
Mission: Voir au développement culturel régional
Membre(s) du personnel: 3
Membre: 392; *Montant de la cotisation:* Barème
Activités: *Listes de destinataires:* Oui
Membre(s) du bureau directeur:
Jean-Pierre Corneault, Président
Andrée Saint-Georges, Directrice générale, 450-753-7444 Ext. 25

Conseil de la culture des Laurentides (CCL)
#400, 223, rue St-Georges, Saint-Jérôme QC J7Z 5A1
Tél: 450-432-2425; *Téléc:* 450-432-8434
Ligne sans frais: 866-432-2680
ccl@culturelaurentides.com
www.culturelaurentides.com
fr-ca.facebook.com/culturelaurentides
twitter.com/cclaurentides
Nom précédent: Conseil de la culture et des communications des Laurentides
Aperçu: *Dimension:* moyenne; *Envergure:* locale; Organisme sans but lucratif; fondée en 1978
Mission: Appuyer le développement des arts et de la culture sur son territoire; regrouper, représenter et offrir des services aux intervenants de l'ensemble des domaines artistiques et culturels des Laurentides; mener des actions de sensibilisation, de représentation, de promotion et de développement auprès des principaux acteurs du milieu culturel régional; jouer un rôle conseil auprès des différents partenaires
Affiliation(s): Conférence régionale des élus (CRÉ)
Finances: *Budget de fonctionnement annuel:* $250,000-$500,000
Membre(s) du personnel: 5; 15 bénévole(s)
Membre: 400; *Montant de la cotisation:* 20-250; *Critères d'admissibilite:* Membre individuel (artiste, artisan et intervenant); membre associé (hors région); organisme sans but lucratif, organisme municipal ou parapublic; entreprise privée; milieu municipal et MRC (Municipalité régionale de comté); *Comités:* Communications et nouvelles technologies de communications; Grands Prix; Métiers d'art
Activités: Contribuer au développement culturel régional; inventorier les ressources et organismes culturels de la région; agir comme agent de décentralisation des services culturels; être représentatif du milieu culturel régional; faire des recommandations auprès du ministère de la Culture et des Communications et du Conseil des arts et des lettres du Québec dans les secteurs d'activité professionnelle suivant les arts et les lettres, l'histoire, la conservation et la mise en valeur de notre patrimoine, et le design; *Bibliothèque:* Centre de documentation; Bibliothèque publique
Membre(s) du bureau directeur:
Mélanie Gosselin, Directrice générale
direction@culturelaurentides.com
Prix, Bourses:
• Colloque sur la culture
• Grands prix de la culture des Laurentides

Conseil de la culture des régions de Québec et de Chaudière-Appalaches
#120, 310, boul Langelier, Québec QC G1K 5N3
Tél: 418-523-1333; *Téléc:* 418-523-9944
ccr@culture-quebec.qc.ca
www.culture-quebec.qc.ca
www.facebook.com/conseilculture
twitter.com/conseilquebec
www.youtube.com/user/conseilcultureqc
Nom précédent: Conseil de la culture de la région de Québec/Chaudière-Appalaches
Aperçu: *Dimension:* petite; *Envergure:* locale
Mission: Favoriser le développement des arts et de la culture sur son territoire
Finances: *Fonds:* Ministère de la Culture et des Communications; Emploi-Québec; Conseil des arts et des lettres du Québec
Activités: Programmes de formation; services-conseils et accompagnement; gestion de projets; recherche
Membre(s) du bureau directeur:
Philippe Sauvageau, Président
Manon Laliberté, Directrice générale
Prix, Bourses:
• Prix d'excellence des arts et de la culture
Eligibility: Décernés à ceux et celles qui contribuent à l'excellence de l'activité artistique et culturelle de la grande région de la Capitale Nationale
• Prix du patrimoine
Eligibility: Reconnaître les réalisation et actions en conservation et mise en valeur du patrimoine

Conseil de la culture du Bas-Saint-Laurent (CRCBSL)
CP 873, 88, Saint-Germain ouest, Rimouski QC G5L 7C9
Tél: 418-722-6246; *Téléc:* 418-724-2216
info@crcbsl.org
crcbsl.org
www.facebook.com/113141962078442
twitter.com/CultureBSL
www.youtube.com/user/ConseildelacultureBS
Aperçu: *Dimension:* moyenne; *Envergure:* locale; Organisme sans but lucratif; fondée en 1976
Mission: Contribuer au développement culturel de la région; être un agent de décentralisation des services culturels; identifier, analyser les besoins et les points de vue de la région et promouvoir la défense des intérêts culturels des membres; assurer une planification au niveau de la région en collaboration avec ses membres
Membre de: Conférence canadienne des arts
Membre(s) du personnel: 6
Membre: *Montant de la cotisation:* 60$ institutionnel; 25$ individu; *Critères d'admissibilite:* Etre un artiste ou un organisme culturel
Activités: *Listes de destinataires:* Oui; *Bibliothèque:* rendez-vous
Membre(s) du bureau directeur:
Ginette Lepage, Directrice générale
ginette.lepage@crcbsl.org

Conseil de la culture du Coeur-du-Québec; Conseil de la culture et des communications de la Mauricie *Voir* Culture Mauricie

Conseil de la culture et des communications des Laurentides *Voir* Conseil de la culture des Laurentides

Conseil de la Saskatchewan pour la co-opération internationale *See* Saskatchewan Council for International Co-operation

Conseil de la sécurité en fertilisation *See* Fertilizer Safety & Security Council

Conseil de la souveraineté du Québec (CSQ)
49, rue Archambault, Repentigny QC J6A 1A2
Tél: 514-303-6561
unis@souverainete.info
www.souverainete.info
www.facebook.com/Conseildelasouverainete
twitter.com/ConseilSouvQc
www.youtube.com/channel/UCuGyZrxvZFB2F0miMYm6EaA
Aperçu: *Dimension:* petite; *Envergure:* provinciale
Mission: A toute latitude pour stimuler dans la population québécoise l'idéal de souveraineté, faire valoir la nécessité de celle-ci pour l'avenir de la nation québécoise, être à l'origine d'initiatives originales pour garder la souveraineté à l'ordre du jour et appuyer toute initiative en ce sens
Membre(s) du bureau directeur:
Gilbert Paquette, Président

Conseil de la transformation agroalimentaire et des produits de consommation (CTAC) / Council of Food Processing & Consumer Products
216, rue Denison est, Granby QC J2H 2R6
Tél: 450-349-1521; *Téléc:* 450-349-6923
info@conseiltac.com
www.conseiltac.com
www.linkedin.com/company/1237456
Nom précédent: Association des manufacturiers de produits alimentaires du Québec
Merged from: Conseil de la boulangerie du Québec; Association des abattoirs avicoles du Québec
Aperçu: *Dimension:* moyenne; *Envergure:* provinciale; Organisme sans but lucratif; fondée en 1954
Mission: Le porte-parole officiel des manufacturiers de produits alimentaires du Québec qui s'y regroupent à titre de membres fabricants; canalise les représentations des manufacturiers, en particulier auprès des gouvernements; coordonne l'action des membres en vue de promouvoir leurs intérêts économiques, sociaux et professionnels; suscite l'éducation des consommateurs sur les valeurs d'une bonne alimentation; favorise la promotion des produits fabriqués par les membres; établit des liaisons entre les manufacturiers, les producteurs, les fournisseurs, les distributeurs, les consommateurs et les autres maillons de la chaîne alimentaire; encourage la recherche dans les domaines de l'agriculture, de l'alimentation et du marketing
Finances: *Budget de fonctionnement annuel:* $500,000-$1.5 Million
Membre(s) du personnel: 5
Membre: 450; *Critères d'admissibilite:* Fabricants; fournisseurs; distributeurs; *Comités:* Activités sociales; Agriculture; Environnement; Mise en marché; Négociations; Nomination; Recrutement; Santé et securité du travail; Travail
Membre(s) du bureau directeur:
Sylvie Cloutier, Présidente-directrice générale
sylviecloutier@conseiltaq.com

Conseil de planification sociale d'Ottawa *See* Social Planning Council of Ottawa

Conseil de planification sociale Region de Sudbury *See* Social Planning Council of Sudbury Region

Conseil de presse du Québec (CPQ) / Québec Press Council
#A208, 1000, rue Fullum, Montréal QC H2K 3L7
Tél: 514-529-2818; *Téléc:* 514-873-4434
Ligne sans frais: 877-250-3060
info@conseildepresse.qc.ca
conseildepresse.qc.ca
twitter.com/MagazineCPQ
Aperçu: *Dimension:* petite; *Envergure:* provinciale; Organisme sans but lucratif; fondée en 1973
Mission: Le Conseil de presse du Québec est un organisme privé, à but non lucratif, qui ouvre depuis près de quarante ans à la protection de la liberté de la presse et à la défense du droit du public à une information de qualité. Son action s'étend à tous les médias d'information distribués ou diffusés au Québec, qu'ils soient membres ou non du Conseil, qu'ils appartiennent à la presse écrite ou électronique.
Finances: *Budget de fonctionnement annuel:* $500,000-$1.5 Million
Membre(s) du personnel: 5; 22 bénévole(s)
Membre: 22; *Montant de la cotisation:* barème; *Critères d'admissibilite:* Médias; Journalistes; Public; *Comités:* Comité des plaintes; Comité d'appel
Activités: Ombudsman de la presse au Québec; *Stagiaires:* Oui; *Service de conférenciers:* Oui; *Bibliothèque:* Centre de documentation
Membre(s) du bureau directeur:
Guy Amyot, Secrétaire général
guy.amyot@conseildepresse.qc.ca
Julien Acosta, Directeur des communications
julien.acosta@conseildepresse.qc.ca

Conseil de recherche en réassurance *See* Reinsurance Research Council

Conseil de recherches en sciences naturelles et en génie du Canada *See* Natural Sciences & Engineering Research Council of Canada

Conseil de sécurité d'Ottawa *See* Ottawa Safety Council

Conseil des 4-H du Canada *See* Canadian 4-H Council

Conseil des académies canadiennes *See* Council of Canadian Academies

Le conseil des aéroports du Canada *See* Canadian Airports Council

Conseil des archives du Nouveau-Brunswick *See* Council of Archives New Brunswick

Conseil des arts d'Ottawa *See* Ottawa Arts Council

Conseil des arts de Hearst (CAH)
75, 9e rue, Hearst ON P0L 1N0
Tél: 705-362-4900; *Téléc:* 705-362-4600
www.conseildesartsdehearst.ca
Aperçu: *Dimension:* petite; *Envergure:* locale; fondée en 1978
Mission: Le Conseil des Arts de Hearst développe auprès de sa communauté un intérêt pour les arts et la culture francophone. Il offre des expériences artistiques et culturelles de qualité qui sont mémorables et signifiantes. Il encourage le rayonnement d'artistes de langue française par le biais d'une programmation variée
Finances: *Budget de fonctionnement annuel:* $250,000-$500,000
Membre(s) du personnel: 3; 60 bénévole(s)
Membre: 400; *Montant de la cotisation:* 20 $ individuelle; 35 $ familiale; 40 $ entreprise ou organisme
Activités: Le Festival de musique (mars); bingo (mars & novembre); Soirée Dégustation (juin); Le Festival National de L'Humour (septembre)
Membre(s) du bureau directeur:
Shana Vernier, Président
Valérie Picard, Directrice générale
dg@conseildesartsdehearst.ca

Conseil des arts de l'Ontario *See* Ontario Arts Council

Conseil des arts de la communauté urbaine de Montréal *Voir* Conseil des arts de Montréal

Conseil des arts de Montréal (CAM)
Édifice Gaston Miron, 1210, rue Sherbrooke est, Montréal QC H2L 1L9
Tél: 514-280-3580; *Téléc:* 514-280-3784
artsmontreal@ville.montreal.qc.ca
www.artsmontreal.org
www.facebook.com/ArtsMontreal
twitter.com/ConseilArtsMtl
Nom précédent: Conseil des arts de la communauté urbaine de Montréal
Aperçu: *Dimension:* moyenne; *Envergure:* locale; fondée en 1956
Mission: Soutenir, encourager et harmoniser les initiatives d'ordre artistique et culturel sur le territoire de la ville de Montréal.
Membre de: Chambre de commerce du Montréal métropolitain; Conférence canadienne des arts; Conseil régional de développement de l'Ile de Montréal; Les arts et la ville; Corporation du Faubourg St-Laurent
Finances: *Budget de fonctionnement annuel:* Plus de $5 Million
Membre(s) du personnel: 15
Membre: 21; *Critères d'admissibilite:* Organismes professionnels oeuvrant dans les disciplines des arts visuels, du cinéma et des arts médiatiques, de la danse, de la littérature, des nouvelles pratiques artistiques, de la musique et du théâtre;
Comités: Arts visuels et littérature; Danse, cinéma et arts multidisciplinaires; Musique; Théâtre; Jeunes publics; Arts et arrondissements
Activités: Programme général d'aide financière; Jouer dans l'île; Art et communauté; Jeunes publics - public de demain; Grand Prix du Conseil des art; Programme d'échanges culturels; Services et expertise; Maison du Conseil des arts
Membre(s) du bureau directeur:
Nathalie Maillé, Directrice générale et sec. conseil
nmaille.p@ville.montreal.qc.ca
France Laroche, Directrice de l'administration
france.laroche@ville.montreal.qc.ca
Prix, Bourses:
• Grand Prix annuel du Conseil des arts
Reconnaît annuellement l'excellence d'une production ou d'un événement réalisé sur le territoire de la Ville de Montréal dans l'une des disciplines suivantes : arts visuels, arts médiatiques, cinéma et vidéo, danse, littérature, musique et théâtre; *Amount:* Bourse de 25 000$ + prix de reconnaissance

Conseil des arts de Sudbury *See* Sudbury Arts Council

Conseil des arts des TNO *See* Northwest Territories Arts Council

Conseil des arts du Manitoba *See* Manitoba Arts Council

Conseil des arts et des lettres du Québec
79, boul René Lévesque est, 3e étage, Québec QC G1R 5N5
Tél: 418-643-1707; *Téléc:* 418-643-4558
Ligne sans frais: 800-897-1707
info@calq.gouv.qc.ca
www.calq.gouv.qc.ca
www.facebook.com/12468994038
twitter.com/LeCALQ
www.youtube.com/user/LeCALQ
Également appelé: CALQ
Aperçu: *Dimension:* moyenne; *Envergure:* provinciale; fondée en 1993
Mission: Soutenir dans toutes les régions du Québec la création, l'expérimentation, la production et la diffusion dans les domaines des arts de la scène (théâtre, danse, musique, chanson, arts du cirque), des arts médiatiques (arts numériques, cinéma et vidéo), des arts multidisciplinaires, des arts visuels, de la littérature et du conte, des métiers d'art et de la recherche architecturale et d'en favoriser la reconnaissance et le rayonnement au Québec, au Canada et à l'étranger.
Membre(s) du personnel: 72
Activités:; *Bibliothèque:* Centre de documentation; Not open to public
Membre(s) du bureau directeur:
Marie DuPont, Président du conseil d'administration, 514-864-3350
marie.dupont@calq.gouv.qc.ca
Stéphan La Roche, Président & Directeur général, 514-864-4333
micheline.bahl-levasseur@calq.gouv.qc.ca

Conseil des bio-industries du Québec; Association québécoise des bio-industries *Voir* BIOQuébec

Le Conseil des Canadiens *See* The Council of Canadians

Conseil des Canadiens avec déficiences *See* Council of Canadians with Disabilities

Conseil des directeurs médias du Québec (CDMQ)
#925, 2015, rue Peel, Montréal QC H3A 1T8
Tél: 514-990-1899
www.cdmq.org
www.facebook.com/170319683021723
Aperçu: *Dimension:* petite; *Envergure:* provinciale; Organisme sans but lucratif
Mission: Etre un point de convergence d'opinions et d'information, un instrument de défense des intérêts des clients/agences et un outil de promotion et de stimulation de la fonction média
Affiliation(s): Association canadienne des annonceurs; Association des agences de publicitéu Québec; Canadian Media Directors' Council; Publicité Club de Montréal
Membre(s) du bureau directeur:
Michèle Savard, Présidente
michele.savard@carat.com

Conseil des doyens et des doyennes des facultés de droit du Canada *See* Council of Canadian Law Deans

Conseil des églises pour la justice et la criminologie *See* Church Council on Justice & Corrections

Conseil des entrepreneurs agricoles (CEA)
CP 163, 2020, rue Girourard ouest, Saint-Hyacinthe QC J2S 340
Tél: 450-278-5562
info@leconseil.net
www.leconseil.ca
Aperçu: *Dimension:* moyenne; *Envergure:* provinciale
Mission: Vise à donner aux producteurs agricoles toute la latitude pour prendre les décisions importantes en matière de gestion, de mise en marché et de représentation syndicale
Membre: de 5 organisations; *Critères d'admissibilite:* Membre de l'une d'organisations affiliées de CEA
Membre(s) du bureau directeur:
Jacques Cartier, Président
jcartier@leconseil.net

Conseil des experts-comptables de la province de l'Ontario *See* Public Accountants Council for the Province of Ontario

Conseil des fabricants de bois *See* Wood Manufacturing Council

Le Conseil des femmes de Montréal *See* Montréal Council of Women

Conseil des industriels laitiers du Québec inc. (CILQ) / Québec Dairy Council Inc.
#307, 2035, av Victoria, Saint-Lambert QC J4S 1H1
Tél: 450-486-7331; *Téléc:* 450-486-7017
cilq@cilq.ca
cilq.ca
Nom précédent: Conseil de l'industrie laitière du Québec inc.
Aperçu: *Dimension:* grande; *Envergure:* provinciale; fondée en 1963
Mission: Regrouper les entreprises laitières industrielles du Québec qui s'occupent des différentes phases de la transformation, distribution et commercialisation du lait et des produits laitiers; promotion, protection et développement de leurs intérêts économiques, sociaux et professionnels
Membre(s) du personnel: 5
Membre(s) du bureau directeur:
Charles Langlois, Président-directeur général
charles.langlois@cilq.ca
Youenn Soumahoro, Économiste
youenn.soumahoro@cilq.ca
Yolaine Villeneuve, Directrice, Affaires publiques & corporatives
yolaine.villeneuve@cilq.ca
Prix, Bourses:
• Prix Donat-Roy

Conseil des jeux du Canada *See* Canada Games Council

Conseil des métiers d'art du Québec (ind.) (CMA) / Québec Crafts Council (Ind.)
Marché Bonsecours, #400, 390, rue St-Paul est, Montréal QC H2Y 1H2
Tél: 514-861-2787; *Téléc:* 514-861-9191
Ligne sans frais: 855-515-2787
info@metiersdart.ca
www.metiers-d-art.qc.ca
Nom précédent: Société de mise en marché des métiers d'art inc.
Aperçu: *Dimension:* moyenne; *Envergure:* provinciale; fondée en 1985
Mission: Pour distribuer les créations métiers d'art auprès des grossistes canadiens et étrangers.
Membre(s) du personnel: 19
Membre: 900; *Montant de la cotisation:* Barème
Membre(s) du bureau directeur:
Patrice Bolduc, Adjoint du directeur général
patrice.bolduc@metiersdart.ca

Conseil des ministres de l'éducation (Canada) *See* Council of Ministers of Education, Canada

Conseil des normes de la publicité *Voir* Les normes canadiennes de la publicité

Conseil des organismes francophones de la région de Durham (COFRD)
#2D, 57 Simcoe St. South, Oshawa ON L1H 4G4
Tél: 905-434-7676; *Téléc:* 905-434-7260
www.cofrd.org
www.facebook.com/cofrd.cofrd.9
twitter.com/COFRD_oshawa
Aperçu: *Dimension:* petite; *Envergure:* locale; Organisme sans but lucratif; fondée en 1984
Mission: Oeuvrer au développement, à l'épanouissement et à la vitalité de la population francophone de la région de Durham; offrir grammation et des services accessibles qui répondent aux besoins de l'ensemble de la communauté d'expression française
Membre de: Réseau Ontario; AFO; Théâtre Action
Finances: *Budget de fonctionnement annuel:* $100,000-$250,000; *Fonds:* Patrimoine canadien
Membre(s) du personnel: 9; 60 bénévole(s)
Membre: 23 organismes francophones de la région de Durham; *Comités:* Finances; prélèvements de fonds
Activités: Culturelles, socio-économiques, sociales; *Bibliothèque:* Librarie du centre; Bibliothèque publique
Membre(s) du bureau directeur:
Elaine Legault, Directrice générale
elegault@cofrd.org

Conseil des organismes francophones du Toronto Métropolitain; Centre francophones du Toronto Métropolitain *Voir* Centre francophone de Toronto

Le Conseil Des Personnes Agées De La Communauté Noire De Montréal *See* Council for Black Aging

Conseil des relations internationales de Montréal (CORIM)
#1424, 1550, rue Metcalfe, Montréal QC H3A 1X6
Tél: 514-340-9622; *Téléc:* 514-340-9904
courrier@corim.qc.ca
www.corim.qc.ca/home

Canadian Associations / Conseil du bâtiment durable du Canada - Québec

Aperçu: *Dimension:* petite; *Envergure:* locale; fondée en 1985
Mission: Le CORIM a pour mission de favoriser une plus grande connaissance des affaires internationales et susciter par ses événements et ses partenariats une collaboration plus étroite entre les divers milieux montréalais intéressés aux questions internationales
Membre: *Montant de la cotisation:* $25 étudiant; 100$ individuel; 395$ organisme sans but lucratif; 850$ corporatif; 1 850$ membre gouverneur; 5 000$+ membre gouverneur émérite
Membre(s) du bureau directeur:
Pierre Lemonde, Président-directeur général
plemonde@corim.qc.ca

Conseil des ressources humaines de l'industrie du vêtement *See* Apparel Human Resources Council

Conseil des ressources humaines de l'industrie minière *See* Mining Industry Human Resources Council

Conseil des Sentiers de l'Ontario *See* Ontario Trails Council

Conseil des Soins Palliatifs *See* Council on Palliative Care

Conseil des technologies de l'information et des communications du Canada *See* Information & Communications Technology Council of Canada

Conseil des traducteurs, terminologues et interprètes du Canada *See* Canadian Translators, Terminologists & Interpreters Council

Conseil des travailleurs de Sept-Îles et du Golfe *Voir* Conseil régional FTQ Sept-Îles et Côte-Nord - Bureau régional FTQ Côte Nord

Conseil des universités de l'Ontario *See* Council of Ontario Universities

Conseil des viandes du Canada *See* Canadian Meat Council

Conseil du bâtiment durable du Canada *See* Canada Green Building Council

Conseil du bâtiment durable du Canada - Québec
6418, rue St-Hubert, Montréal QC H2S 2M2
Tél: 514-563-2001
Ligne sans frais: 855-825-6558
info@batimentdurable.ca
www.batimentdurable.ca
www.linkedin.com/groups/4654185
www.facebook.com/SQCBDCa
twitter.com/Quebec_CBDCa
Aperçu: *Dimension:* petite; *Envergure:* provinciale
Mission: Créer des bâtiments et des collectivités écologiques, rentables et offrant des lieux de vie, de travail et de loisirs sains
Membre: *Montant de la cotisation:* 20-150
Membre(s) du bureau directeur:
Geneviève Pepin, Directrice générale
genevieve.pepin@batimentdurable.ca

Conseil du loisir scientifique de l'Estrie *Voir* Technoscience Estrie

Conseil du loisir scientifique de Québec *Voir* Boîte à science - Conseil du loisir scientifique du Québec

Conseil du Manitoba pour la coopération internationale *See* Manitoba Council for International Cooperation

Conseil du patronat du Québec (CPQ) / Québec Employers Council
#510, 1010, rue Sherbrooke ouest, Montréal QC H3A 2R7
Tél: 514-288-5161; *Téléc:* 514-288-5165
Ligne sans frais: 877-288-5161
www.cpq.qc.ca
www.linkedin.com/groups/Conseil-patronat-Québec-2908454
www.facebook.com/conseilpatronat
twitter.com/conseilpatronat
www.youtube.com/user/CPQ2010
Aperçu: *Dimension:* moyenne; *Envergure:* provinciale; fondée en 1969
Mission: Le Conseil du patronat du Québec a pour mission de s'assurer que les entreprises puissent disposer au Québec des meilleures conditions possibles- notamment en matière de capital humain- afin de prosperer de fason durable dans un contexte de concurrence mondiale.
Finances: *Budget de fonctionnement annuel:* $500,000-$1.5 Million
Membre(s) du personnel: 18
Membre: 53 associations + 200 entreprises; *Comités:* Rémunération et avantages sociaux; éducation et adéquation formation-emploi; relations du travail; santé et la sécurité du travail; fiscalité et finances publiques; affaires publiques; spéciaux de veille stratégique
Activités: *Service de conférenciers:* Oui; *Bibliothèque:* rendez-vous Not open to public
Membre(s) du bureau directeur:
Yves-Thomas Dorval, Président
president@cpq.qc.ca
Camilla Sironi, Conseillère principale, Communications
csironi@cpq.qc.ca

Conseil du peuplier du Canada *See* Poplar Council of Canada

Conseil du recyclage de l'Ontario *See* Recycling Council of Ontario

Conseil du travail d'Ottawa et du district *See* Ottawa & District Labour Council

Conseil du travail de Montréal *Voir* Conseil régional FTQ Montréal Métropolitain

Conseil du travail de Saguenay-Lac-St-Jean *Voir* Conseil régional FTQ Saguenay-Lac-St-Jean-Chibougamau-Chapais

Conseil du troisième âge de Saint-Lambert / St. Lambert Council for Seniors
Maison Desaulniers, 574, av Notre-Dame, Saint-Lambert QC J4P 2K9
Tél: 450-671-1757; *Téléc:* 450-923-6608
stlambertseniors@sympatico.ca
stlambertseniors.ca
Aperçu: *Dimension:* petite; *Envergure:* locale; fondée en 1973
Mission: Pour aider les aînés à participer à des activités de groupe
Membre: *Montant de la cotisation:* 30$; *Critères d'admissibilite:* Toute gens qui habite sur la Ville de St-Lambert, ou toute gens qui va à l'église à St-Lambert qui a 55 ans et plus.
Activités: Album souvenir; Artisanat; Bridge; Club de courtepointes; Club de moélisme de chemin de fer; Club d'informatique; Scrabble; Billard; Voyages
Membre(s) du bureau directeur:
Elwyn Llewelyn, Président, Conseil d'administration

Conseil économique des provinces de l'Atlantique *See* Atlantic Provinces Economic Council

Conseil économique du Nouveau-Brunswick inc. (CÉNB)
#314, 236, rue St-Georges, Moncton NB E1C 1W1
Tél: 506-857-3143; *Téléc:* 506-857-9906
Ligne sans frais: 800-561-4446
cenb@cenb.com
www.cenb.com
www.facebook.com/cenbinc
Aperçu: *Dimension:* petite; *Envergure:* provinciale; Organisme sans but lucratif; fondée en 1979
Mission: Être le porte-parole de la communauté d'affaires francophone du NB
Membre(s) du personnel: 10
Membre: 1 000; *Montant de la cotisation:* Barème; *Critères d'admissibilite:* Entreprises et francophones du monde des affaires
Membre(s) du bureau directeur:
Robert Moreau, Président
president@cenb.com
Anne Hébert, Directrice générale
anne@cenb.com

Conseil en crédit du Canada *See* Credit Counselling Canada

Conseil ethnoculturel du Canada *See* Canadian Ethnocultural Council

Conseil francophone de la chanson (CFC)
2190, ch Hamel, Sherbrooke QC J1R 0P8
Tél: 819-820-0589
sg@conseilfrancophone.org
www.chanson.ca
Aperçu: *Dimension:* petite; *Envergure:* internationale; fondée en 1986
Mission: Promouvoir la chanson et les musiques de l'espace francophone
Finances: *Fonds:* Ministère de la Culture et des Communications (Québec)
Membre(s) du bureau directeur:
Jacques Labrecque, Vice-président, Amérique du nord
jacques.labrecque@usherbrooke.ca

Conseil FTQ Drummondville
175, rue Saint-Marcel, Drummondville QC J2B 2E1
Tél: 819-475-1320
syndicat_metallos_7885@hotmail.com
Aperçu: *Dimension:* petite; *Envergure:* locale surveillé par Fédération des travailleurs et travailleuses du Québec

Conseil international d'études canadiennes *See* International Council for Canadian Studies

Conseil international des associations de design graphique *See* International Council of Design

Le Conseil international des organisations de lutte contre le SIDA *See* International Council of AIDS Service Organizations

Conseil international du Canada *See* Canadian International Council

Conseil interprofessionnel du Québec (CIQ) / Québec Interprofessional Council
Tour ouest, #890, 550, rue Sherbrooke ouest, Montréal QC H3A 1B9
Tél: 514-288-3574; *Téléc:* 514-288-3580
courrier@professions-quebec.org
www.professions-quebec.org
www.linkedin.com/company/conseil-interprofessionnel-du-qu-be-c
www.facebook.com/ciq.ordres
twitter.com/Professions_QC
www.youtube.com/channel/UCQW3nF-ym1d1Sv6lyTnbevA
Aperçu: *Dimension:* grande; *Envergure:* provinciale; fondée en 1965
Mission: Forum d'échange et de concertation de même que la voix collective des ordres professionnels; mandat d'organisme conseil auprès de l'autorité publique
Finances: *Budget de fonctionnement annuel:* $500,000-$1.5 Million
Membre(s) du personnel: 5; 200 bénévole(s)
Membre: 46 ordres professionnels; *Comités:* Communications; Directions générales; Formation; Inspection professionnelle; Secrétaires de comité de discipline; Syndics

Conseil jeunesse francophone de la Colombie-Britannique (CJFCB) / British Columbian Francophone Youth Council
#229B, 1555, 7e av Ouest, Vancouver BC V6J 1S1
Tél: 604-736-6970; *Téléc:* 604-732-3236
information@cjfcb.com
www.cjfcb.com
www.facebook.com/CJFCB
twitter.com/cjfcb
instagram.com/conseiljeunessecb
Aperçu: *Dimension:* petite; *Envergure:* provinciale; Organisme sans but lucratif; fondée en 1989
Mission: Promouvoir, encourager et offrir des opportunités de formation aux jeunes francophones de la Colombie-Britannique afin de développer leur plein potentiel; encourager le développement de regroupements de la jeunesse francophone, au niveau local et régional; faire vivre les avantages de garder et de développer la langue et la culture francophone aux jeunes francophones de la C-B; assurer le développement et l'accroissement de partenariats avec la communauté globale; offrir des opportunités de regroupement aux jeunes francophones de la C-B, et ce au niveau provincial, interprovincial et national; offrir aux jeunes francophones de la C-B des renseignements sur les activités, services et programmes disponibles à la jeunesse francophone
Membre de: Fédération de la jeunesse canadienne-française inc.; Fédération des francophones de la Colombie-Britannique
Affiliation(s): Conseil scolaire-francophone de la C-B
Finances: *Fonds:* Patrimoine Canadien; Ministère de l'Éducation en CB; Développement des ressources humaines Canada
Membre(s) du personnel: 4
Membre: *Critères d'admissibilite:* Jeunes francophones et francophiles 12 à 25 ans
Activités: Parlement jeunesse francophone de la C-B; parlement franco-canadien du Nord et de l'Ouest; jeux francophone de la C-B, du Nord et de l'Ouest; jeux de la francophonie canadienne; camp de leadership, animation culturelle; formation diverses
Membre(s) du bureau directeur:
Shadie Bourget, Présidente
Rémi Marien, Directeur général
direction@cjfcb.com

Conseil jeunesse provincial (Manitoba) (CJP) / Provincial Youth Council
340, boul Provencher, Saint-Boniface MB R2H 0G7
Tél: 204-237-8947; *Téléc:* 204-237-5076
direction@conseil-jeunesse.mb.ca
www.conseil-jeunesse.mb.ca
www.facebook.com/conseil.jeunesse.provincial
twitter.com/CjpManitoba
www.youtube.com/CjpManitoba
Aperçu: Dimension: petite; *Envergure:* provinciale; Organisme sans but lucratif; fondée en 1974
Mission: Sensibiliser les jeunes à leur identité franco-manitobaine et de promouvoir le regroupement et le développement des jeunes au point de vue politique, éducatif, culturel et économique
Membre de: Fédération de la jeunesse canadienne-française inc.
Membre(s) du personnel: 6
Membre: Critères d'admissibilite: Jeunes francophones du Manitoba de 14 à 25 ans
Activités: Pleine lune; Stage de leadership; Projet étudiants animateurs; Rassemblement Intense des Francophones Rigolos Adolescents et l'Fun; programme d'animation culturelle
Membre(s) du bureau directeur:
Roxane Dupuis, Directrice générale
direction@conseil-jeunesse.mb.ca

Le Conseil médical du Canada *See* Medical Council of Canada

Conseil montérégien de la culture et des communications (CMCC)
#130, 80, rue Saint-Laurent ouest, Longueuil QC J4H 1L8
Tél: 450-651-0694; *Téléc:* 450-651-6020
Ligne sans frais: 877-651-0694
info@culturemonteregie.qc.ca
www.culturemonteregie.qc.ca
fr.facebook.com/179952732502
twitter.com/conseilculture
Nom précédent: Conseil culturel de la Montérégie inc
Aperçu: Dimension: petite; *Envergure:* provinciale; Organisme sans but lucratif; fondée en 1978
Mission: Assurer le rassemblement et la concertation des intervenants culturels de la Montérégie; contribuer à établir les priorités de développement culturel de ce territoire; conseiller la Ministre de la culture et des communications
Membre de: Table de concertation des conseils régionaux de la culture
Affiliation(s): Conseil régional de développement de la Montérégie
Membre(s) du personnel: 7
Membre: 310; *Montant de la cotisation:* Barème; *Critères d'admissibilite:* Regroupe toute personne majeure ayant sa résidence ou sa place d'affaires sur le territoire et tout organisme (corporation ou groupement volontaire) qui a son siège social ou son principal établissement sur le territoire de la Montérégie
Activités:; *Bibliothèque:* Bibliothèque publique rendez-vous
Membre(s) du bureau directeur:
Dominic Trudel, Directeur général
dtrudel@culturemonteregie.qc.ca

Conseil multiculturel du Nouveau-Brunswick *See* New Brunswick Multicultural Council

Conseil national d'éthique en recherche chez l'humain *See* National Council on Ethics in Human Research

Conseil National de l'Enveloppe du Bâtiment *See* National Building Envelope Council

Conseil national des associations barbadiennes au Canada *See* National Council of Barbadian Associations in Canada

Conseil national des associations canadiennes des Philippines *See* National Council of Canadian Filipino Associations

Conseil national des associations d'anciens combattants au Canada *See* National Council of Veteran Associations

Conseil national des canadiens chinois *See* Chinese Canadian National Council

Le Conseil national des femmes du Canada *See* The National Council of Women of Canada

Conseil national des femmes métisses, inc. *See* Métis National Council of Women

Conseil National des Relations Canado-Arabes *See* National Council on Canada-Arab Relations

Conseil national du meuble
4360, rue Tanguay, Laval QC H7R 5Z5
Tél: 450-962-5757
Nom précédent: Corporation des marchands de meubles du Québec
Aperçu: Dimension: moyenne; *Envergure:* nationale
Membre(s) du bureau directeur:
Denis Bourgault, Directeur général

Le conseil national du secteur des produits de la mer *See* National Seafood Sector Council

Conseil national Société de Saint-Vincent de Paul (SSVP) / Society of Saint Vincent de Paul
2463, rue Innes, Ottawa ON K1B 3K3
Tél: 613-837-4363; *Téléc:* 613-837-7375
Ligne sans frais: 866-997-7787
national@ssvp.ca
www.ssvp.ca
Aperçu: Dimension: grande; *Envergure:* nationale; Organisme sans but lucratif; fondée en 1846
Mission: To live the Gospel message through personal contact with those in need & helping in all possible ways
Finances: Budget de fonctionnement annuel: $100,000-$250,000; *Fonds:* Donations
Membre: 5,000-14,999
Membre(s) du bureau directeur:
Jean-Noël Cormier, President
president@ssvp.ca
Madelaine Soulière, Secretary
Solange Fortin, Treasurer
Publications:
• National President's Newsletter [a publication of the Society of Saint Vincent de Paul]
Type: Newsletter
• VincentPaul Canada: The Magazine of The Society of St. Vincent de Paul
Type: Magazine; *Frequency:* Quarterly; *Editor:* Jean-Noël Cormier; *ISSN:* O703 6477
Edmonton
PO Box 11532, Stn. Main, Edmonton AB T5J 3K7
Tel: 780-471-5577
ssvpedmonton@gmail.com
www.ssvpedmonton.ca
Halifax Particular Council
2170 Barrington St., Halifax NS B3K 2W4
Tel: 902-422-2049
Ottawa Central Council
#303, 207 Bank St., Ottawa ON K2P 2N2
Tel: 613-241-1225
bernie-on-ca-ssvp@rogers.com
Toronto Central Council
240 Church St., Toronto ON M5B 1Z2
Tel: 416-364-5577; *Fax:* 416-364-2055
info@ssvptoronto.cam
www.ssvptoronto.ca
Membre(s) du bureau directeur:
Robert Ossowski, President
Vancouver Central Council
Vancouver BC
Tel: 604-873-1306
www.ssvp-vancouver.ca
Vancouver Island
4349 West Saanich Rd., Victoria BC V8Z 3E8
Tel: 250-727-0007; *Fax:* 250-727-0771
info@svdpvictoria.com
www.svdpvictoria.com
www.facebook.com/ssvpvancouver
Membre(s) du bureau directeur:
Angela Hudson, Executive Director
Joe Rigby, President
Western Regional Council
c/o St. Basil's Church, 604 – 13th St. North, Lethbridge AB T1H 2S7
Tel: 403-328-5493
www.ssvpwrc.ca
Membre(s) du bureau directeur:
Peter Ouellette, President

Conseil oecuménique des chrétiennes du Canada *See* Women's Inter-Church Council of Canada

Le Conseil ontarien d'évaluation des qualifications *See* Qualifications Evaluation Council of Ontario

Conseil ontarien de commerce des véhicules automobiles *See* Ontario Motor Vehicle Industry Council

Conseil Ontarien de Recherche en Loisir *See* Ontario Research Council on Leisure

Conseil ontarien des études supérieures *See* Ontario Council on Graduate Studies

Le Conseil ontarien pour le jeu responsable *See* Responsible Gambling Council (Ontario)

Conseil patronal de l'environnement du Québec (CPEQ)
#504, 640, rue Saint-Paul ouest, Montréal QC H3C 1L9
Tél: 514-393-1122; *Téléc:* 514-393-1146
info@cpeq.qc.ca
www.cpeq.qc.ca
Aperçu: Dimension: moyenne; *Envergure:* provinciale
Mission: De promouvoir les intérêts de l'industrie et l'entreprise en matière d'environnement
Membre(s) du personnel: 8
Membre: 212 enterprises + 32 associations; *Montant de la cotisation:* Barème
Membre(s) du bureau directeur:
Hélène Lauzon, Présidente

Conseil pédagogique interdisciplinaire du Québec (CPIQ)
#202, 1319, ch de Chambly, Longueuil QC J4J 3X1
Tél: 450-928-8770; *Téléc:* 450-928-8771
secretariat@conseil-cpiq.qc.ca
www.conseil-cpiq.qc.ca
Aperçu: Dimension: moyenne; *Envergure:* provinciale; fondée en 1968
Mission: Regroupement des associations professionnelles d'enseignants pour la promotion de la pédagogie et la qualité de l'enseignement au Québec
Membre: 21 associations; *Montant de la cotisation:* 2,30$ par membres d'associations pour membres actifs; 150$ membres associés; *Critères d'admissibilite:* Associations professionnelles d'enseignants; *Comités:* Vérification et finances; Gouvernance; Promotion du CPIQ et de ses associations et de recrutement; *Publications;* L'insertion professionnelle du personnel enseignant
Activités: Liste des publications sur le site web
Membre(s) du bureau directeur:
Louise Trudel, Directrice générale

Conseil pour l'enseignement de la lecture aux analphabètes de Montréal *See* Reading Council for Literacy Advance in Montréal

Conseil pour le développement de l'alphabétisme et des compétences des adultes du Nouveau-Brunswick (CODACNB)
#314, 236, rue Saint-Georges, Moncton NB E1C 1W1
Tél: 506-869-9926; *Téléc:* 506-857-3143
Ligne sans frais: 866-473-4404
www.codacnb.ca
www.facebook.com/alphabetisationNB
twitter.com/CODACNB
Aperçu: Dimension: petite; *Envergure:* provinciale; Organisme sans but lucratif; fondée en 1989
Mission: Promouvoir l'alphabétisation en français au Nouveau-Brunswick; assurer une concertation des intervenants en alphabétisation en français au Nouveau-Brunswick
Membre de: Fédération canadienne pour l'alphabétisation en français
Membre(s) du personnel: 6
Membre: 13; *Critères d'admissibilite:* Conseils d'alphabétisation
Activités:; *Bibliothèque:* Centre de ressources; rendez-vous
Membre(s) du bureau directeur:
Anne-Lise Blin, Directrice générale
Prix, Bourses:
• Bourse Denise Poirier
Pour rendre hommage à une personne qui a réussi le programme d'alphabétisation et qui a pour but de continuer ses études et qui a contribué à l'avancement de l'alphabétisation dans sa communauté

Conseil provincial du soutien scolaire
#7100, 565 boul Crémazie est, Montréal QC H2M 2V9
Tél: 514-384-9681; *Téléc:* 514-384-9680
www.cpss.qc.ca
Aperçu: Dimension: moyenne; *Envergure:* provinciale

Canadian Associations / Conseil québécois de la coopération et de la mutualité (CCQ)

Mission: Négocier la convention collective; de voir à son application et de promouvoir la qualité de vie de ses membres
Membre: 7,500; Comités: Sous-Traitance; Santé/Sécurité; Équité salariale; Mobilisation; Négociation
Membre(s) du bureau directeur:
Pierre Degray, Président

Conseil provincial et territorial des bibliotheques See Provincial & Territorial Public Library Council

Conseil québécois de la coopération et de la mutualité (CCQ)
#204, 5955, rue Saint-Laurent, Lévis QC G6V 3P5
Tél: 418-835-3710; Téléc: 418-835-6322
info@coopquebec.coop
www.coopquebec.qc.ca
www.facebook.com/quebec.coop
twitter.com/CQCMCOOP
Nom précédent: Conseil de la coopération du Québec
Aperçu: Dimension: moyenne; Envergure: provinciale; fondée en 1939
Mission: Pour unir des organisations coopératives du Québec pour favoriser l'action concertée de ses membres, promouvoir l'authenticité coopérative, défendre les intérêts de ses membres
Affiliation(s): Conseil canadien de la coopération; Alliance coopérative internationale
Membre(s) du personnel: 21
Membre: 43; Critères d'admissibilite: Toute organisation appliquant les règles d'action coopérative énoncées par l'Alliance coopérative internationale peut être représentée
Activités: Bibliothèque;
Membre(s) du bureau directeur:
Gaston Bédard, Directeur général intérimaire
gastonbedard@coopquebec.coop

Conseil québécois de la franchise (CQF)
2115, boul des Laurentides, Laval QC H7M 4M2
Tél: 514-340-6018; Téléc: 450-967-2749
info@cqf.ca
www.cqf.ca
www.linkedin.com/groups/Franchise-Entrepreneurship-3934413
www.facebook.com/ConseilQuebecoisDeLaFranchise
twitter.com/info_cqf
www.youtube.com/user/lecqf
Aperçu: Dimension: petite; Envergure: provinciale; fondée en 1984
Mission: Promouvoir la franchise entre les entreprises au Québec
Membre: 325; Montant de la cotisation: Barème; Critères d'admissibilite: Franchiseurs et fournisseurs; Comités: Exécutif; Affaires légales; Communications; Formation; Gala et Temple de la renommée; Tournoi de golf; Jury Prix Maillon d'or; Mises en candidature Prix Maillon d'or; Prix Hommage; Relations publiques et Collège des experts; Semaine de l'entrepreneurship en franchise
Membre(s) du bureau directeur:
Pieere Garceau, Président-directeur général
pierregarceau@cqf.ca

Conseil québécois de la musique (CQM)
#302, 1908, rue Panet, Montréal QC H2L 3A2
Tél: 514-524-1310; Téléc: 514-524-2219
Ligne sans frais: 866-999-1310
info@cqm.qc.ca
www.cqm.qc.ca
www.facebook.com/conseilquebecoisdelamusique
twitter.com/CQMOpus
Aperçu: Dimension: moyenne; Envergure: provinciale; Organisme sans but lucratif; fondée en 1987
Mission: Rassembler les professionels du secteur de la musique de concert (musiques ancienne médiévale, baroque, de la Renaissance, classique, romantique, moderne, contemporaine, Jazz, électronacqoustique, du monde); promouvoir la discipline et soutenir son rayonnement
Membre de: Conseil international de la musique; Les Arts et la Ville
Affiliation(s): Conseil international de la musique
Finances: Budget de fonctionnement annuel: $250,000-$500,000
Membre(s) du personnel: 4
Membre: 300; Montant de la cotisation: Barème; Critères d'admissibilite: Organismes et individus oeuvrant professionnellement en musique de concert
Activités: Divers colloques; conférences; ateliers de formation; Événements de sensibilisation: Journée internationale de la musique
Membre(s) du bureau directeur:

Dominic Trudel, Directeur général
direction@cqm.qc.ca
Prix, Bourses:
• Prix Opus
Eligibility: Souligne l'excellence de la musique de concert au Québec dans différents répertoires musicaux

Conseil québécois des arts médiatiques (CQAM)
3995, rue Berri, Montréal QC H2L 4H2
Tél: 514-527-5116
Ligne sans frais: 888-527-5116
www.cqam.org
Aperçu: Dimension: moyenne; Envergure: provinciale
Membre(s) du bureau directeur:
Robin Dupuis, Président
Isabelle L'Italien, Directrice générale
dg@cqam.org

Conseil québécois des gais et lesbiennes du Québec (CQGL)
CP 182, Succ. C, Montréal QC H2L 4K1
Tél: 514-759-6844
info@conseil-lgbt.ca
www.cqgl.ca
www.facebook.com/CQLGBT
twitter.com/cqlgbt
Aperçu: Dimension: petite; Envergure: provinciale
Mission: A pour mission concrétiser notre leitmotive 'S'engager pour l'égalité sociale'. Adresse civique: #100, 1307, rue Sainte-Catherine Est, Montréal, QC.
Membre: Montant de la cotisation: 20$ étudiants; 40$ individus; 50$ organismes à but non lucratif
Membre(s) du bureau directeur:
Steve Foster, Directeur général
dg@conseil-lgbt.ca

Le Conseil Québécois du Chardon Inc. See Québec Thistle Council Inc.

Conseil québécois du commerce de détail (CQCD) / Retail Council of Québec
#910, 630, rue Sherbrooke ouest, Montréal QC H3A 1E4
Tél: 514-842-6681; Téléc: 514-842-7627
Ligne sans frais: 800-364-6766
cqcd@cqcd.org
www.cqcd.org
Aperçu: Dimension: moyenne; Envergure: provinciale; Organisme sans but lucratif; fondée en 1978
Mission: Promouvoir, représenter et valoriser le secteur du commerce de détail au Québec et les détaillants qui en font partie afin d'assurer le sain développement et la prospérité du secteur
Finances: Budget de fonctionnement annuel: $500,000-$1.5 Million
Membre(s) du personnel: 12; 75 bénévole(s)
Membre: 5,000 établissements commerciaux; Montant de la cotisation: Barème
Membre(s) du bureau directeur:
Léopold Turgeon, Président
Chantale Bélanger, Directrice, Comptabilité et administration
cbelanger@cqcd.org

Conseil québécois du théâtre (CQT)
#808, 460, rue Sainte-Catherine ouest, Montréal QC H3B 1A7
Tél: 514-954-0270; Téléc: 514-954-0165
Ligne sans frais: 866-954-0270
cqt@cqt.qc.ca
www.cqt.ca
www.facebook.com/ConseilQuebecoisDuTheatre
twitter.com/cqt_theatre
www.youtube.com/user/ChaineCQT
Aperçu: Dimension: moyenne; Envergure: provinciale; fondée en 1983
Mission: Promouvoir et défendre les intérêts du milieu théâtral et le représenter auprès de diverses instances; concerter, animer et informer la communauté théâtrale sur toutes les questions qui touchent la pratique théâtrale; promouvoir et développer le théâtre
Membre de: L'institut internationale du théâtre
Membre(s) du personnel: 7
Membre: 216; Comités: Actions politiques; Animation du milieu; Avenir du théâtre; Balises de succession; Conditions socioéconomiques; Formation continue; Formation professionnelle; Nouveaux modèles de gestion; Promotion collective du théâtre; Théâtre jeune public
Activités: Événements de sensibilisation: Journée mondiale du théâtre; Bibliothèque

Membre(s) du bureau directeur:
Sylvie Meste, Directrice générale
dge@cqt.qc.ca
Pier DuFour, Responsable administratif

Conseil québécois sur le tabac et la santé / Québec Council on Tobacco & Health
#302, 4126, rue Saint-Denis, Montréal QC H2W 2M5
Tél: 514-948-5317; Téléc: 514-948-4582
info@cqts.qc.ca
www.cqts.qc.ca
twitter.com/cqts
Aperçu: Dimension: moyenne; Envergure: provinciale; Organisme sans but lucratif; fondée en 1976
Mission: Promouvoir la santé du fumeur et du non-fumeur; faire le lien entre les associations, groupes bénévoles et autres intéressés à la santé publique; trouver des approches et des moyens pour améliorer l'éducation face à l'usage du tabac
Membre de: Conseil canadien pour le contrôle du tabac
Finances: Budget de fonctionnement annuel: $250,000-$500,000
Membre: 600
Activités: Événements de sensibilisation: Semaine québécoise sans tabac
Membre(s) du bureau directeur:
Mario Bujold, Directeur général
Claire Harvey, Agente, Communications et relations médias

Conseil régional de Baie Comeau (Manicouagan) - Bureau régional FTQ Côte Nord
#309, 1041, rue de Mingan, Baie-Comeau QC G5C 3W1
Tél: 418-295-3551; Téléc: 418-589-7620
crhcnmanicouagan@cgocable.ca
www.cotenord.ftq.qc.ca
Aperçu: Dimension: petite; Envergure: locale surveillé par Fédération des travailleurs et travailleuses du Québec

Conseil régional de l'environnement de la Gaspésie et des Îles-de-la-Madeleine (CREGIM)
#103, 106-A, Port Royal, Bonaventure QC G0C 1E0
Tél: 418-534-4498
Ligne sans frais: 877-534-4498
cregim@globetrotter.net
www.cregim.org
www.facebook.com/269353189800151?ref=hl
twitter.com/CREGIM1
Aperçu: Dimension: petite; Envergure: locale; fondée en 1995
Mission: Regrouper et représenter des organismes proenvironnementaux et des individus voués à la protection et la mise en valeur de l'environnement, auprès de toutes les instances concernées; favoriser la concertation et assurer l'établissement de priorités et de suivi en matière d'environnement; favoriser et promouvoir des stratégies d'actions concertées; agir à titre d'organisme ressource aux services des intervenants régionaux
Affiliation(s): Regroupement national des Conseils régionaux en environnement
Finances: Budget de fonctionnement annuel: $50,000-$100,000; Fonds: Gouvernement provincial; gouvernement régional; gouvernement municipal
Membre(s) du personnel: 4; 9 bénévole(s)
Membre: 119; Montant de la cotisation: 100$ institutionnel; 10$ individu; 30$ associé
Membre(s) du bureau directeur:
Caroline Duchesne, Directrice
caroline.cregim@globetrotter.net
Steve Pronovost, Présidente
Monette Bujold, Secrétaire adjointe-administrative
monette.cregim@globetrotter.net

Conseil régional de la culture de l'Outaouais
432, boul Alexandre-Taché, Gatineau QC J9A 1M7
Tél: 819-595-2601; Téléc: 819-595-9088
Ligne sans frais: 855-595-2601
info@crco.org
www.crco.org
www.linkedin.com/in/communicationcrco
www.facebook.com/275021145886146
twitter.com/Culture07
Aperçu: Dimension: petite; Envergure: locale; fondée en 1976
Mission: Conseiller, concerter, consulter et représenter le milieu culturel et artistique de la région de l'Outaouais, en ayant comme objectif principal le développement du secteur.
Membre(s) du personnel: 4
Membre: Montant de la cotisation: 15$ étudiant; 20$ ami; 30$ titulaire; 50-75 organisme sans but lucratif; 85$ entreprise; 100$ institutionnel; 125-1000 municipal; 250$ MRC

Membre(s) du bureau directeur:
Julie Martineau, Directrice Générale
direction@crco.org

Conseil régional de la culture et des communications de la Côte-Nord (CRCCCN)
22, Place La Salle, 1e étage, Baie-Comeau QC G4Z 1K3
Tél: 418-296-1450; *Téléc:* 418-296-1457
Ligne sans frais: 866-295-6744
secretariat@culturecotenord.com
www.culturecotenord.com
www.facebook.com/crcccn
Aperçu: *Dimension:* petite; *Envergure:* locale; Organisme sans but lucratif; fondée en 1973
Mission: Développer les arts et lettres, la culture et les communications dans la région; offrir des services de qualité à ses membres
Membre(s) du personnel: 3
Membre: 257; *Montant de la cotisation:* 20$ individu; 35$ organisme; 50-100 municipalité; *Critères d'admissibilite:* Organismes culturels et artistes
Activités: Forums; formation; remise de prix; promotion du tourisme; développement des médias communautaires et autochtones; services de secrétariat; *Listes de destinataires:* Oui; *Bibliothèque*
Membre(s) du bureau directeur:
Marie-France Lévesque, Directrice générale
dg@culturecotenord.com
Prix, Bourses:
• Prix d'Excellence Culture et Communications Côte-Nord

Conseil régional de la culture Saguenay-Lac-Saint-Jean (CRC)
1640, av Hamilton est, Alma QC G8B 4Z1
Tél: 418-662-6623; *Téléc:* 418-662-1071
secretariat@crc02.qc.ca
www.ccr-sl.qc.ca
Nom précédent: Conseil de la culture de la région Saguenay/Lac-St-Jean/Chibougamau/Chapais
Aperçu: *Dimension:* petite; *Envergure:* locale; Organisme sans but lucratif; fondée en 1977
Mission: Développer les arts, la culture et la communication au Saguenay-Lac-Saint-Jean en exerçant les rôles de concertation, représentation, information, consultation de promotion de services aux membres et au milieu culturel
Finances: *Budget de fonctionnement annuel:* $100,000-$250,000
Membre(s) du personnel: 5
Membre: 200; *Montant de la cotisation:* Barème; *Critères d'admissibilité:* Organismes culturels et scolaires; individus; municipalités; *Comités:* Conseil d'administration; Comité exécutif
Activités:; *Bibliothèque:* rendez-vous Not open to public
Membre(s) du bureau directeur:
Lucien Frenette, Directeur général
direction@crc02.qc.ca
Lyne L'Italien, Présidente
lyne@theatrelarubrique.com

Conseil régional des personnes âgées italo-canadiennes de Montréal
671, rue Ogilvy, Montréal QC H3N 1N4
Tél: 514-273-6588; *Téléc:* 514-273-6636
craic@securenet.net
www.craic.ca
Aperçu: *Dimension:* moyenne; *Envergure:* locale; Organisme sans but lucratif; fondée en 1974
Mission: Favoriser le maintien à domicile des personnes âgées et leur autonomie physique et intellectuelle; améliorer la qualité de vie des personnes âgées dans leur environnement naturel le plus longtemps possible
Membre: 13,000
Activités: Popote roulante; traduction; accompagnement; repas communautaires; cours et activités éducatives, récréatives, culturelles; assistance aux immigrants
Membre(s) du bureau directeur:
Franco Rocchi, Contact

Conseil régional FTQ Abitibi-Témiscamingue - Nord-du-Québec
#3100, 201, rue du Terminus ouest, Rouyn-Noranda QC J9X 2P7
Tél: 819-762-1354; *Téléc:* 819-762-1411
crftq-atndq@ftq.qc.ca
www.abitibi-nordqc.ftq.qc.ca
Aperçu: *Dimension:* petite; *Envergure:* locale surveillé par Fédération des travailleurs et travailleuses du Québec

Conseil régional FTQ Bas St-Laurent - Gaspésie-Îles-de-la-Madeleine
#608, 2, rue Saint-Germain est, Rimouski QC G5L 8T7
Tél: 418-722-8232; *Téléc:* 418-722-8380
crftq-bslgi@ftq.qc.ca
www.bsl-gaspesie.ftq.qc.ca
Aperçu: *Dimension:* petite; *Envergure:* locale surveillé par Fédération des travailleurs et travailleuses du Québec

Conseil régional FTQ de l'Ouatouais
#311, 259, boul Saint-Joseph, Gatineau QC J8V 2R1
Tél: 819-777-4473; *Téléc:* 819-777-1973
ftq07@bellnet.ca
www.outaouais.ftq.qc.ca
Aperçu: *Dimension:* petite; *Envergure:* locale surveillé par Fédération des travailleurs et travailleuses du Québec

Conseil régional FTQ de la Haute-Yamaska - Bureau régional FTQ - Montérégie
CP 244, 370, rue Principale, Granby QC J2G 8E5
Tél: 450-378-3557; *Téléc:* 450-378-4172
conseilregionalf.t.q.h.y@qc.aira.com
www.monteregie.ftq.qc.ca
Aperçu: *Dimension:* petite; *Envergure:* locale surveillé par Fédération des travailleurs et travailleuses du Québec

Conseil régional FTQ de la Mauricie et du Centre-du-Québec - Bureau régional FTQ - Maurice et Centre du Québec
#101, 7080, rue Marion, Trois-Rivières QC G9A 6G4
Tél: 819-378-4049; *Téléc:* 819-378-4362
CRFTQMCQ@ftq.qc.ca
www.mauriciecentreqc.ftq.qc.ca
Aperçu: *Dimension:* petite; *Envergure:* locale surveillé par Fédération des travailleurs et travailleuses du Québec

Conseil régional FTQ du Richelieu - Bureau régional FTQ - Montérégie
#6200, 4805, boul Lapinière, Brossard QC J4Z 0G2
Tél: 450-926-6200; *Téléc:* 450-926-6204
sgirard@ftq.qc.ca
www.monteregie.ftq.qc.ca
Aperçu: *Dimension:* petite; *Envergure:* locale surveillé par Fédération des travailleurs et travailleuses du Québec

Conseil régional FTQ du Suroît - Bureau régional FTQ - Montérégie
3, rue Bay, Salaberry-de-Valleyfield QC J6S 1X3
Tél: 450-567-0170
danielmallette@cgocable.ca
www.monteregie.ftq.qc.ca
Aperçu: *Dimension:* petite; *Envergure:* locale surveillé par Fédération des travailleurs et travailleuses du Québec

Conseil régional FTQ Estrie
2100, rue King ouest, Sherbrooke QC J1J 2E8
Tél: 819-562-3922; *Téléc:* 819-563-6916
crftqestrie@ftq.qc.ca
www.estrie.ftq.qc.ca
Aperçu: *Dimension:* petite; *Envergure:* locale; Organisme sans but lucratif surveillé par Fédération des travailleurs et travailleuses du Québec
Affiliation(s): Fédération des travailleurs et travailleuses du Québec
Membre(s) du bureau directeur:
Harold Arseneault, Président

Conseil régional FTQ Montréal Métropolitain
#2500, 565, boul Crémazie est, Montréal QC H2M 2V6
Tél: 514-387-3666; *Téléc:* 514-387-4393
crftqmm@ftq.qc.ca
www.montrealmetro.ftq.qc.ca
Nom précédent: Conseil du travail de Montréal
Aperçu: *Dimension:* moyenne; *Envergure:* locale; fondée en 1886 surveillé par Fédération des travailleurs et travailleuses du Québec
Affiliation(s): Fédération des travailleurs et travailleuses du Québec
Activités: *Stagiaires:* Oui
Membre(s) du bureau directeur:
Danielle Casara, Présidente
dcasara@ftq.qc.ca

Conseil régional FTQ Québec et Chaudière-Appalaches (CRQCA)
#120, 5000, boul des Gradins, Québec QC G2J 1N3
Tél: 418-622-4941; *Téléc:* 418-623-9932
crqca@videotron.ca
www.quebec-chaudiereappalaches.ftq.qc.ca
Aperçu: *Dimension:* petite; *Envergure:* locale surveillé par Fédération des travailleurs et travailleuses du Québec
Affiliation(s): Fédération des travailleurs et travailleuses du Québec
Membre(s) du bureau directeur:
Sébastien Boies, Président, 416-622-4941, Fax: 416-623-9932
crqca@videotron.ca
Yves Marcoux, Vice-Président
Louise Lemieux, Secrétaire archiviste
Roch Lessard, Trésorier

Conseil régional FTQ Saguenay-Lac-St-Jean-Chibougamau-Chapais (CRFTQSLSJ)
#100, 2679, boul du Royaume, Jonquière QC G7S 5T1
Tél: 418-699-0199; *Téléc:* 418-699-7179
ftqsaglac@ftq.qc.ca
www.saglac-chibougamauchapais.ftq.qc.ca
Nom précédent: Conseil du travail de Saguenay-Lac-St-Jean
Aperçu: *Dimension:* petite; *Envergure:* locale; Organisme sans but lucratif; fondée en 1965 surveillé par Fédération des travailleurs et travailleuses du Québec
Membre de: Fédération des travailleurs et travailleuses du Québec; Congrès du travail du Canada
Affiliation(s): Fédération des travailleurs et travailleuses du Québec
Finances: *Budget de fonctionnement annuel:* $50,000-$100,000
Membre(s) du personnel: 2; 50 bénévole(s)
Membre: 16,000
Membre(s) du bureau directeur:
Michel Routhier, Président

Conseil régional FTQ Sept-Îles et Côte-Nord - Bureau régional FTQ Côte Nord
#203, 737, boul Laure, Sept-Iles QC G4R 1Y2
Tél: 418-962-3551
bmethot@ftq.qc.ca
www.cotenord.ftq.qc.ca
Nom précédent: Conseil des travailleurs de Sept-îles et du Golfe
Aperçu: *Dimension:* petite; *Envergure:* locale surveillé par Fédération des travailleurs et travailleuses du Québec
Affiliation(s): Fédération des travailleurs et travailleuses du Québec

Conseil sectoriel de la police *See* Police Sector Council

Le Conseil sur le vieillissement d'Ottawa *See* The Council on Aging of Ottawa

Conseil unitarien du Canada *See* Canadian Unitarian Council

Les Conseillers en développement de l'employabilité (CODEM)
#2, 1951, boul de Maisonneuve est, Montréal QC H2K 2C9
Tél: 514-522-9151; *Téléc:* 514-522-5547
sae@codem.qc.ca
www.codem.qc.ca
www.linkedin.com/company/codem-—-les-conseillers-en-d-velopement-de-l%27employabilit-
www.facebook.com/services.codem
Aperçu: *Dimension:* petite; *Envergure:* provinciale; fondée en 1984
Mission: Favoriser le développement de l'employabilité des personnes qui rencontrent des difficultés d'intégration
Membre(s) du bureau directeur:
Rachel Guidet, Directrice

Conseillers en ressources humaines agréés *See* Chartered Professionals in Human Resources

Conservation Council of New Brunswick (CCNB) / Conseil de la conservation du Nouveau-Brunswick
180 St. John St., Fredericton NB E3B 4A9
Tel: 506-458-8747; *Fax:* 506-458-1047
info@conservationcouncil.ca
www.conservationcouncil.ca
www.facebook.com/ccnbaction
twitter.com/cc_nb
www.youtube.com/user/ccnbactiontv
Overview: A medium-sized provincial charitable organization founded in 1969
Mission: To generate awareness of the ecological foundations of our quality of life; To promote public policies with respect to the integrity of natural systems & to contribute to a sustainable

society; To advocate appropriate remedies to pressing environmental problems such as ground water contamination & hazardous wastes
Member of: New Brunswick Environmental Network; Canadian Environmental Networks
Affiliation(s): Friends of the Earth Canada
Finances: *Funding Sources:* Enterprise activities; Special events; Contracts for special projects
Staff Member(s): 6
Activities: *Rents Mailing List:* Yes; Library
Chief Officer(s):
Céline Delacroix, Executive Director
Stephanie Coburn, President

Conservation Council of Ontario (CCO) / Conseil de conservation de l'Ontario
c/o Hardy Stevenson & Associates, 364 Davenport Rd., Toronto ON M5R 1K6
Tel: 416-533-1635; *Fax:* 416-979-3936
conserveontario.ca
www.linkedin.com/company-beta/2458603
www.facebook.com/ontarioconserves
twitter.com/ccoweconserve
www.instagram.com/weconserve
Overview: A medium-sized provincial charitable organization founded in 1952
Mission: To build a strong conservation movement across Ontario
100 volunteer(s)
Membership: *Member Profile:* Municipalities, businesses, organizations, & individuals dedicated to conservation & a healthy environment
Activities: Increasing public awareness of conservation; Developing a provincial fund to support conservation efforts throughout Ontario

Conservation de la faune au Canada *See* Wildlife Preservation Canada

Conservation Enforcement Officers Association of Nova Scotia
PO Box 190, Windsor NS B0N 2T0
Overview: A small provincial charitable organization founded in 1985
Mission: To represent working & retired Conservation Officers in Nova Scotia
Membership: 30; *Member Profile:* Conservation Officers; Park Wardens; Fisheries Officers; Fisheries Inspectors; Environment Inspectors; Municipal Police Officers; RCMP Officers
Activities: Organizing conservation programs; Donating funds to schools, centers, & other organizations; Supporting members & newly trained hunters

Conservation Foundation of Greater Toronto
1000 Murray Ross Pkwy., Toronto ON M3J 2P3
Tel: 416-667-6279; *Fax:* 416-667-6275
fdn@thelivingcity.org
www.thelivingcity.org
www.facebook.com/TheLivingCity
twitter.com/LivingCityFDN
www.instagram.com/livingcityfdn
Also Known As: The Living City Foundation
Previous Name: The Metropolitan Toronto & Region Conservation Foundation; The Conservation Foundation of Greater Toronto
Overview: A small local charitable organization founded in 1961
Mission: To acquire & manage regional greenspace & watershed conservation lands; To support watershed management, reforestation, wildlife habitats, public access & recreation, historic sites, & environmental rehabilitation of natural spaces
Affiliation(s): The Toronto & Region Conservation Authority
Finances: *Annual Operating Budget:* $250,000-$500,000; *Funding Sources:* Donors include businesses, industries, other foundations, estates, conservation organizations & individuals
20 volunteer(s)
Membership: 20; *Committees:* Board; Campaign; Executive; Members
Activities: Tree For Life Program; Kortright Centre for Conservation; Conservation Education Field Centres (conservation education schools at Albion Hills, Cold Creek & Claremont Conservation Areas); conservation libraries & scholarships; Don River; Greenspace Strategy (the authority's conservation vision for the 21st century - urges greater cooperation between the authority, the province & the municipalities in managing the regional watershed; advocates protection of the Oak Ridges Moraine complex

Chief Officer(s):
Derek Edwards, Interim Executive Director
dedwards@trca.on.ca
Awards:
• The Living City Leaders Scholarships
Eligibility: Students enrolled in post-secondary conservation-related studies; *Amount:* $1,500

Conservation Halton Foundation
2596 Britannia Rd. West, Burlington ON L7P 0G3
Tel: 905-336-1158; *Fax:* 905-336-7014
Other Communication: Planning E-mail: envserv@hrca.on.ca
foundation@hrca.on.ca
www.conservationhalton.ca/foundation
www.facebook.com/ConservationHalton
twitter.com/CH_Comm
www.instagram.com/conservationhalton
Previous Name: Halton Foundation
Overview: A small local charitable organization founded in 1974
Mission: To raise funds for Conservation Halton projects & programs that protect & enhance the natural environment
Finances: *Annual Operating Budget:* $100,000-$250,000
Chief Officer(s):
Jim A. Sweetlove, Chair, Conservation Halton Foundation
Gerry Smallegange, Chair, Conservation Halton

Conservation Ontario
PO Box 11, 120 Bayview Pkwy., Newmarket ON L3R 4W3
Tel: 905-895-0716; *Fax:* 905-895-0751
info@conservationontario.ca
www.conservation-ontario.on.ca
www.facebook.com/126861190733330
twitter.com/conont
instagram.com/con_ont
Also Known As: Association of Conservation Authorities of Ontario
Overview: A medium-sized provincial organization founded in 1946
Mission: To represent & support a network of community-based environmental organizations; To ensure conservation, restoration, & responsible management of Ontario's wetlands, woodlands, & natural habitat
Finances: *Funding Sources:* Levies provided by the conservation authorities
Staff Member(s): 13
Membership: 36 organizations; *Member Profile:* Ontario's conservation authorities; Community-based watershed management agencies
Activities: Developing programs to protect life & property from natural hazards, such as erosion & flooding; Encouraging watershed stewardship practices; Promoting teh expertise of conservation authorities in managing Ontario's environment
Chief Officer(s):
Dick Hibma, Chair
chair@conservationontario.ca
Kim Gavine, General Manager, 905-895-0716 Ext. 231
kgavine@conservationontario.ca
Bonnie Fox, Manager, Policy & Planning, 905-896-0716 Ext. 223
bfox@conservationontario.ca
Jane Lewington, Specialist, Marketing & Communications, 905-895-0716 Ext. 222
jlewington@conservationontario.ca
Publications:
• Adaptive Management of Stream Corridors in Ontario
Type: Report
Profile: A planning & design guide
• An Evaluation of Water Resource Monitoring Efforts in Support of Agricultural Stewardship in Watersheds of the Great Lakes
Type: Report
Profile: Produced by Conservation Ontario in partnership with the Ontario Ministry of Agriculture, Food &Rural Affairs
• Conservation Ontario Annual Report
Type: Yearbook; *Frequency:* Annually
• Conservation Ontario E-Bulletin
Type: Newsletter
Profile: Information & updates on issues about conservation authorities
• Cost Benefit Analysis of Agricultural Source Water Protection Beneficial Management Practices
Type: Report
Profile: Agricultural beneficial management practices such as plant buffers, soile testing, crop covers, & crop rotation to protect thequality & supply of water
• Guide to Conservation Areas
Type: Guide; *Number of Pages:* 64

Profile: A guide to 261 conservation areas among 36 conservation authorities in Ontario
• Innovations in Water Management
Type: Report
Profile: Place-based environmental management approaches
• Navigating Ontario's Future: A Water Budget Overview for Ontario
Type: Report; *Number of Pages:* 36
• Navigating Ontario's Future: Overview of Integrated Watershed Management in Ontario
Type: Report; *Number of Pages:* 122
• Navigating Ontario's Future: Water Management Framework
Type: Report; *Number of Pages:* 32
Profile: Contents include the need for a framework, developing the water management framework, the use of the framework in Ontario, & next steps
• Ontario Drinking Water Stewardship Program Outreach & Education Toolkit
Type: Kit
Profile: A communication toolkit for each Source Protection Region & Source Protection Area in Ontario
• Protecting People & Property: A Business Case for Investing in Flood Prevention & Control
Type: Report; *Number of Pages:* 56; *Author:* M. Fortin
Profile: Subjects addressed include the evolution of flood management, accomplishments, flood frequency & severity, responding tofuture risks, & costs & benefitis of improvements
• Sensitivity Mapping & Local Watershed Assessments for Climate Change Detection & Adaptation Monitoring
Type: Report; *Number of Pages:* 77
Profile: Topics include Ontario sensitivity assessment using GIS mapping, climate change detection monitoring, & climatechange adaptation monitoring
• Walkerton Inquiry
Type: Report
Profile: A summary of Conservation Ontario's participation in part II of the Walkerton Inquiry, including a position paper entitled "The Importance of Watershed Management in Protecting Ontario's Drinking WaterSupplies"
• Water Resources Information Project
Type: Report
Profile: The current state of water information in Ontario

Conservative Party of Canada / Parti conservateur du Canada
#1720, 130 Albert St., Ottawa ON K1P 5G4
Toll-Free: 866-808-8407
www.conservative.ca
www.facebook.com/cpcpcc
twitter.com/CPC_HQ
www.youtube.com/cpcpcc
Previous Name: Progressive Conservative Party of Canada; Canadian Alliance Party; Canadian Conservative Reform Alliance
Overview: A large national organization founded in 2003
Mission: To provide Canadians with an alternative to the Liberal government; To develop innovative & practical new policy ideas such as the Federal Accountability Act, the Public Transit Tax Credit & the Apprenticeship Incentive Grant
Chief Officer(s):
Andrew Scheer, Leader

Conservatory Canada
201 Queens Ave., London ON N6A 1J1
Tel: 519-433-3147; *Fax:* 519-433-7404
Toll-Free: 800-461-5367
officeadmin@conservatorycanada.ca
www.conservatorycanada.ca
www.facebook.com/ConservatoryCanada
twitter.com/conservatorycan
www.youtube.com/user/ConservatoryCanada
Previous Name: Western Board of Music
Overview: A medium-sized local licensing charitable organization founded in 1934
Mission: To promote achievement in music through a comprehensive program of study, evaluation & recognition for teachers & students; To foster the development of musical talent & potential
Staff Member(s): 3
Activities: Providing a standardized system of music examinations & education to students in Canada; Offering resources
Chief Officer(s):
Derek Oger, Executive Director

Conserver Society of Hamilton & District Inc.
c/o EcoHouse, 22 Veevers Dr., Hamilton ON L8K 5P5
contact@conserversociety.ca
www.conserversociety.ca
Overview: A small local charitable organization founded in 1969
Mission: To promote a healthy, sustainable environment in Hamilton, Ontario & the surrounding area; To provide public education about environmental issues
Finances: *Funding Sources:* Donations; Membership fees; Sponsorships
Membership: *Fees:* $10 individuals; $20 families; $40 organizations
Activities: Partnering with like-minded organizations
Chief Officer(s):
Don McLean, Chair
Publications:
• Environmental Advocate
Type: Newsletter; *Price:* Free with membership in the Conserver Society of Hamilton & District Inc.
Profile: Information related to envrionmental issues

Consolidated Credit Counseling Services of Canada, Inc.
#400, 505 Consumers Rd., Toronto ON M2J 4V8
Tel: 416-915-5200; *Fax:* 800-656-4187
Toll-Free: 888-287-8506
counsellor@consolidatedcredit.ca
www.consolidatedcredit.ca
www.linkedin.com/company/consolidated-credit-counseling-services-of-canada
www.facebook.com/consolidatedcreditcanada
twitter.com/debt_free_2day
plus.google.com/107802209722404534513
Overview: A medium-sized national charitable organization overseen by Ontario Association of Credit Counselling Services
Mission: To provide professional, unbiased counselling & educational services to people distressed about debts; To encourage personal financial literacy
Member of: Ontario Association of Credit Counselling Services
Activities: Providing education to consumers on topics such as budgeting, managing credit, cutting costs, & surviving layoffs; Offering consumer debt strategies
Chief Officer(s):
Jeffrey Schwartz, Executive Director
jschwartz@consolidatedcredit.ca
Publications:
• All About Credit [a publication of Consolidated Credit Counseling Services of Canada, Inc.]
Type: Booklet; *Number of Pages:* 20; *Price:* Free
• Avoiding Foreclosure [a publication of the Consolidated Credit Counseling Services of Canada, Inc.]
Type: Booklet; *Number of Pages:* 14; *Price:* Free
• Budgeting 101 [a publication of the Consolidated Credit Counseling Services of Canada, Inc.]
Type: Booklet; *Number of Pages:* 24; *Price:* Free
Profile: Practical information for students
• Budgeting Made Easy [a publication of the Consolidated Credit Counseling Services of Canada, Inc.]
Type: Booklet; *Number of Pages:* 20; *Price:* Free
• Coping with Financial Stress [a publication of Consolidated Credit Counseling Services of Canada, Inc.]
Type: Booklet; *Number of Pages:* 16; *Price:* Free
• Credit in a New Country [a publication of Consolidated Credit Counseling Services of Canada, Inc.]
Type: Booklet; *Number of Pages:* 16; *Price:* Free
• Cutting Car Costs [a publication of the Consolidated Credit Counseling Services of Canada, Inc.]
Type: Booklet; *Number of Pages:* 16; *Price:* Free
• Divorce & Your Credit [a publication of the Consolidated Credit Counseling Services of Canada, Inc.]
Type: Booklet; *Number of Pages:* 16; *Price:* Free
• Holiday Survival Guide [a publication of the Consolidated Credit Counseling Services of Canada, Inc.]
Type: Booklet; *Number of Pages:* 18; *Price:* Free
• Identity Theft [a publication of Consolidated Credit Counseling Services of Canada, Inc.]
Type: Booklet; *Number of Pages:* 16; *Price:* Free
• Make the Most of Your Credit Score [a publication of the Consolidated Credit Counseling Services of Canada, Inc.]
Type: Booklet; *Number of Pages:* 12; *Price:* Free
• Managing Your Money [a publication of the Consolidated Credit Counseling Services of Canada, Inc.]
Type: Booklet; *Number of Pages:* 7; *Price:* Free
• Money Savers for New Parents [a publication of the Consolidated Credit Counseling Services of Canada, Inc.]
Type: Booklet; *Number of Pages:* 14; *Price:* Free
• Planning your Golden Years: A Retirement Guide [a publication of the Consolidated Credit Counseling Services of Canada, Inc.]
Type: Booklet; *Number of Pages:* 16; *Price:* Free
• Repair Your Credit [a publication of the Consolidated Credit Counseling Services of Canada, Inc.]
Type: Booklet; *Number of Pages:* 16; *Price:* Free
• Save Energy, Save Money [a publication of the Consolidated Credit Counseling Services of Canada, Inc.]
Type: Booklet; *Number of Pages:* 6; *Price:* Free
• Savings & Chequing [a publication of the Consolidated Credit Counseling Services of Canada, Inc.]
Type: Booklet; *Number of Pages:* 14; *Price:* Free
• Shop Smart & Save [a publication of the Consolidated Credit Counseling Services of Canada, Inc.]
Type: Booklet; *Number of Pages:* 16; *Price:* Free
• Surviving a Layoff [publication of Consolidated Credit Counseling Services of Canada, Inc.]
Type: Booklet; *Number of Pages:* 16; *Price:* Free
• Talking Money with Your Kids [a publication of the Consolidated Credit Counseling Services of Canada, Inc.]
Type: Booklet; *Number of Pages:* 16; *Price:* Free
• Taxes: Save Money, Solve Problems [a publication of the Consolidated Credit Counseling Services of Canada, Inc.]
Type: Booklet; *Number of Pages:* 6; *Price:* Free
• Vacation Budgeting [a publication of the Consolidated Credit Counseling Services of Canada, Inc.]
Type: Booklet; *Number of Pages:* 16; *Price:* Free
• The Wedding Planner [a publication of the Consolidated Credit Counseling Services of Canada, Inc.]
Type: Booklet; *Number of Pages:* 16; *Price:* Free
• When Love, Marriage, & Money Come Together [a publication of the Consolidated Credit Counseling Services of Canada, Inc.]
Type: Booklet; *Number of Pages:* 6; *Price:* Free
• Women & Money [a publication of Consolidated Credit Counseling Services of Canada, Inc.]
Type: Booklet; *Number of Pages:* 6; *Price:* Free

Consort & District Chamber of Commerce
PO Box 335, Consort AB T0C 1B0
Tel: 403-577-3644
www.facebook.com/699661170102456
Overview: A small local organization
Mission: To promote business & tourism in the area
Chief Officer(s):
Donna Ward, President

Consortium canadien des ordres des sages-femmes *See* Canadian Midwifery Regulators Consortium

Consortium de bibliothèques du Manitoba *See* Manitoba Library Consortium Inc.

Consortium photonique de l'industrie canadienne *See* Canadian Photonic Industry Consortium

Constance Lethbridge Rehabilitation Centre *Voir* Centre de réadaptation Constance-Lethbridge

Constructeurs mondiaux d'automobiles du Canada *See* Global Automakers of Canada

Construction Association of New Brunswick (CANB) / Association de la construction du nouveau-brunswick
59 Avonlea Ct., Fredericton NB E3C 1N8
Tel: 506-459-5770; *Fax:* 506-457-1913
canb4@nbnet.nb.ca
www.constructnb.ca
Overview: A medium-sized provincial organization founded in 1971 overseen by Canadian Construction Association
Mission: To co-ordinate a consensus to effectively present the Industry's collective views to various client groups, particularly to relevant departments & agencies of the provincial government
Membership: 13 associations; *Member Profile:* Construction related associations
Chief Officer(s):
Rob Carvell, President
John Landry, Executive Director

Fredericton Northwest Construction Association (FNWCA)
59 Avonlea Ct., Fredericton NB E3C 1N8
Tel: 506-458-1086; *Fax:* 506-453-1958
fnwca@nbnet.nb.ca
www.fnwca.ca
twitter.com/FNWCA1
Chief Officer(s):
Trevor Tomilson, President
Susan McDonald, Office Manager

Moncton Northeast Construction Association (MNECA)
297 Collishaw St., Moncton NB E1C 9R2
Tel: 506-857-4038; *Fax:* 506-857-8861
info@mneca.ca
mneca.ca
Chief Officer(s):
Nadine Fullarton, President, 506-857-4128
nfullerton@mneca.ca

Saint John
263 Germain St., Saint John NB E2L 2G7
Tel: 506-633-1101; *Fax:* 506-633-1265
sjcic@nb.aibn.com
www.sjcic.ca
www.facebook.com/CANBSJ
twitter.com/CANBSJ

Construction Association of Nova Scotia
#103, 134 Eileen Stubbs Ave., Dartmouth NS B3B 0A9
Tel: 902-468-2267; *Fax:* 902-468-2470
cans@cans.ns.ca
www.cans.ns.ca
Overview: A medium-sized provincial organization overseen by Canadian Construction Association
Mission: To represent the interests of its members
Staff Member(s): 13
Membership: 760+; *Fees:* $1,507 full; $660 associate; *Member Profile:* Companies involved in construction work
Chief Officer(s):
Duncan Williams, President
dwilliams@cans.ns.ca

Construction Association of Prince Edward Island (CAPEI)
PO Box 728, #223, 40 Enman Cres., Charlottetown PE C1A 7L3
Tel: 902-368-3303; *Fax:* 902-894-9757
admin@capei.ca
www.capei.ca
Overview: A medium-sized provincial organization overseen by Canadian Construction Association
Mission: To foster, promote & advance the interests & efficiency of Prince Edward Island's construction industry
Staff Member(s): 3
Membership: 148; *Fees:* schedule; *Member Profile:* Construction related enterprises
Chief Officer(s):
Stanley (Sam) Sanderson, General Manager
sam@capei.ca
Grant MacPherson, President
gmacpherson@macleanconstruction.com
Publications:
• CAPEI [Construction Association of Prince Edward Island] Project Newsletter
Type: Newsletter; *Frequency:* Weekly
• Construction Association of Prince Edward Island Membership Directory
Type: Directory
Profile: Guide for public of CAPEI members' company information
• Working for You [a publication of the Construction Association of Prince Edward Island]
Type: Newsletter

Construction Association of Québec *Voir* Association de la construction du Québec

Construction Association of Rural Manitoba Inc. (CARM)
950B - 10th St., Brandon MB R7A 6B5
Tel: 204-727-4567; *Fax:* 204-727-1048
Toll-Free: 800-798-7483
carm@carm.ca
www.carm.ca
Overview: A small provincial charitable organization founded in 1913
Mission: To provide services & representation to members; To act as a liaison between members & consumers of construction services & other interested groups for the betterment of the industry
Finances: *Annual Operating Budget:* $100,000-$250,000
Staff Member(s): 3
Membership: 190; *Fees:* $250+
Activities: *Library:* Not open to public
Chief Officer(s):

Karen Roe, Executive Director, 204-571-0041
executive.director@carm.ca
Publications:
- Construction Association of Rural Manitoba Inc. Directory & Buyers' Guide

Type: Guide; *Frequency:* Annually; *Accepts Advertising*; *Editor:* Cindy Chan

Construction Employers Coordinating Council of Ontario (CECCO)
#708, 6299 Airport Rd., Mississauga ON L4V 1N3
Tel: 905-677-6200; *Fax:* 905-677-7634
admin@cecco.org
www.cecco.org
Overview: A small provincial organization founded in 1979
Mission: To coordinate collective bargaining on behalf of designated Employer Bargaining Agencies responsible for the negotiation of province-wide, single-trade agreements applicable to the ICI sectors of the construction industry
Staff Member(s): 2; 6 volunteer(s)
Membership: 20; *Member Profile:* Construction employer bargaining agencies
Chief Officer(s):
Wayne Peterson, Executive Director
wpeterson@cecco.org

Construction Labour Relations - An Alberta Association (CLRA)
Calgary Office, #207, 2725 - 12 St. NE, Calgary AB T2E 7J2
Tel: 403-250-7390; *Fax:* 403-250-5516
Toll-Free: 800-450-7204
www.clra.org
Previous Name: Alberta Construction Labour Relations Association
Overview: A medium-sized provincial organization founded in 1971
Mission: To represent construction employers in collective bargaining, collective agreement administration, administrative labour law, lobbying.
Member of: Canadian Construction Association
Finances: *Funding Sources:* Membership fees
Membership: *Member Profile:* General construction union contractor
Activities: *Library:* Catalogue; Open to public
Edmonton Office (CLR-A)
#904, 10050 - 112 St., Edmonton AB T5K 2J1
Tel: 780-451-5444; *Fax:* 780-451-5447
Toll-Free: 800-450-7204
www.clra.org
Mission: To provide industrial, commercial and institutional construction employers assistance in bargaining, developing public policy, training, dealing with unions, administration and collective bargaining.

Construction Labour Relations Association of British Columbia
97 - 6 St., New Westminster BC V3L 5H8
Tel: 604-524-4911; *Fax:* 604-524-3925
www.clra-bc.com
Overview: A small provincial organization founded in 1969
Mission: To represent members & building trades-signatory contractors in matters of labour relations & human resources
Chief Officer(s):
Clyde Scollan, President
Dave Earle, Vice-President, Government Relations & HR Services
Gregg Sewell, Vice-President, Labour Relations

Construction Labour Relations Association of Newfoundland & Labrador (CLRA)
69 Mews Pl., St. John's NL A1B 4N2
Tel: 709-753-5770; *Fax:* 709-753-5771
lrideout@clranl.com
www.clranl.com
Overview: A small provincial organization founded in 1973
Mission: To be the sole & exclusive bargaining agent for all unionized employers employing unionized trades persons in the commercial & industrial sectors of Newfoundland & Labrador's construction industry
Membership: *Member Profile:* Any individual engaged in the construction industry in Newfoundland & Labrador
Chief Officer(s):
Neil Chaplin, President

Construction Maintenance & Allied Workers Canada (CMAW)
1450 Kootenay St., Vancouver BC V5K 4R1
Tel: 604-437-0471; *Fax:* 604-437-1110
Toll-Free: 855-616-3555
reception@cmaw.ca
www.cmaw.ca
twitter.com/CMAWunion
Previous Name: British Columbia Carpenters Union
Overview: A medium-sized national organization founded in 2004
Mission: To organize workers & encourage an apprenticeship system & higher standard of skill; To develop, improve & enforce the program & standards of occupational safety & health; To develop good public relations with the community; To assist each other to secure employment & to reduce the hours of daily labour
Finances: *Annual Operating Budget:* $500,000-$1.5 Million
Membership: 7,000+; *Member Profile:* Carpenters; Carpenter apprentices; Lathers; Millwrights; Floorlayers; Industrial workers; Other construction trades & school board employees
Chief Officer(s):
Jan Noster, President
jan.noster@cmaw.ca
Paul Nedelec, Secretary-Treasurer
pnedelec@cmaw.ca

Construction Management Bureau Limited *See* Nova Scotia Construction Labour Relations Association Limited

Construction Owners Association of Alberta (COAA)
Sun Life Place, #800, 10123 - 99 St. NW, Edmonton AB T5J 3H1
Tel: 780-420-1145; *Fax:* 780-425-4623
coaa.admin@coaa.ab.ca
www.coaa.ab.ca
Overview: A medium-sized provincial organization
Mission: To provide leadership enabling the Alberta heavy industrial construction & industrial maintenance industries to be successful in a drive for safe, effective, timely & productive project execution
Membership: *Member Profile:* Companies & other organizations that construct & use major built assets in the course of their operations; Companies that are suppliers & performers of construction services for the Alberta heavy industrial construction sector; *Committees:* Construction & Performance; Contracting; Safety; Workforce & Development
Chief Officer(s):
Neil Shelly, P.Eng., Executive Director, 780-420-1145 Ext. 224
neil@coaa.ab.ca
Amanda Rose, Comminications Officer, 780-420-1145 Ext. 226
amanda@coaa.ab.ca
Meetings/Conferences:
- Construction Owners Association of Alberta Best Practices Conference 2018, May, 2018, Shaw Conference Centre, Edmonton, AB

Scope: Provincial

Construction Resource Initiatives Council (CRI) / Conseil d'initiatives des ressources de construction
#609 Donald B. Munro Dr., Carp ON K0A 1L0
Tel: 613-795-4632; *Fax:* 613-839-0704
info@cricouncil.com
www.cricouncil.com
www.linkedin.com/groups/Construction-Resource-Initiatives-Council-3819158
www.facebook.com/330962370266752
twitter.com/CRICouncil
Overview: A small national organization
Mission: To develop strategies that help the building industry achieve the goal of zero waste production.
Membership: 137; *Fees:* Schedule available; *Member Profile:* Those who sipport the council & its goals
Chief Officer(s):
Renée L. Gratton, President & CEO
renee.gratton@cricouncil.com

Construction Safety Association of Manitoba (CSAM)
1447 Waverly St., Winnipeg MB R3T 0P7
Tel: 204-775-3171; *Fax:* 204-779-3505
safety@constructionsafety.ca
www.constructionsafety.ca
Overview: A small provincial organization founded in 1989
Mission: To promote safe work practices & procedures throughout Manitoba's construction industry; To provide news about changes to health & safety regulations; To offer information about accident prevention methods
Member of: Canadian Federation of Construction Safety Associations
Finances: *Funding Sources:* Manitoba contractors, through a surchrge on a percentage of their assessment premiums collected by the Workers Compensation Baord
Activities: Developing training programs; Working with the Workers Compensation Board of Manitoba & the Workplace Saftey & Health Branch
Chief Officer(s):
Sean Scott, Executive Director
sean@constructionsafety.ca
Derek Pott, Manager, Client Services
derek@constructionsafety.ca
Tara Zukewich, Program Manager
tara@constructionsafety.ca
Mitch Calvert, Coordinator, Marketing & Innovations
mitch@constructionsafety.ca
Marla Fillion, Coordinator, Training & Program
marla@constructionsafety.ca
Meetings/Conferences:
- Construction Safety Association of Manitoba - The Safety Conference 2018, February, 2018, RBC Convention Centre, Winnipeg, MB

Scope: Provincial
Description: A safety & health conference for construction owners, supervisors, foremen, safety committees, workers, & students, featuring workshops & a trade show with more than 100 exhibitors
Publications:
- Construction Safety Association of Manitoba Newsletter

Type: Newsletter; *Price:* Free, as part of themandate to assist construction employers in safety matters
Profile: Information & education about safety regulatory matters & accident prevention methods for building construction employers throughout Manitoba

Construction Safety Association of Ontario *See* Infrastructure Health & Safety Association

Construction Safety Network *See* BC Construction Safety Alliance

Construction Sector Council *See* BuildForce Canada

Construction Specifications Canada (CSC) / Devis de construction Canada
#312, 120 Carlton St., Toronto ON M5A 4K2
Tel: 416-777-2198; *Fax:* 416-777-2197
Other Communication: Toll Free Fax: 800-668-5684
www.csc-dcc.ca
www.linkedin.com/company/construction-specifications-canada
www.facebook.com/120516191352386?ref=ts
Previous Name: Specification Writers Association of Canada
Overview: A large national organization founded in 1954
Mission: To improve communication, contract documentation, & technical information in the construction industry
Affiliation(s): Construction Specification Foundation; Construction Specifications Canada/Alberta Section Training Trust Fund; Construction Specifications Institute; Canadian Standards Assoc.; Mechanical Contractors Assoc. of Canada; Ontario Bid Depository Council; Alberta Building Envelope Council; Alberta Roofing Contractor's Assoc.; Canadian Institute of Plumbing & Heating; Assoc. of Professional Engineers of Canada; Royal Architectural Institute of Canada; Canadian Construction Assoc.; Toronto Construction Assoc.; Society of the Plastics Industry of Canada; Thermal Insulation Assoc. of Canada
Finances: *Annual Operating Budget:* $500,000-$1.5 Million; *Funding Sources:* Sale of technical documents; Membership fees
Staff Member(s): 4
Membership: 650 specifier architects & engineers + 750 industrial manufacturers, suppliers & contractors; *Fees:* $250; $50 student; *Member Profile:* Specifiers, architects, engineers, construction product manufacturers & distributors, general & trade contractors; *Committees:* Awards; Conferences; Executive; Finance; French Language Publications; Legislative; Professional Development & Education; Technical Studies
Activities: Offering national education programs & courses; *Speaker Service:* Yes; *Rents Mailing List:* Yes
Chief Officer(s):
Peter S. Emmett, President
pemmett@whwarchitects.com
Nick Franjic, Executive Director
nfranjic@on.aibn.com
Awards:
- Chapter Award of Merit
- Program Directors' Awards
- The Technical Studies Committee Award

- National Award of Merit
- Honorary Membership
- Life Membership Award
- Chapter of the Year
- Construction Canada's Article of the Year Award
- Russell W. Cornell Award

Meetings/Conferences:
• Construction Specifications Canada 2018 Conference, May, 2018
Scope: National
Contact Information: Executive Director: Nick Franjic, E-mail: nfranjic@csc-dcc.ca
Publications:
• Construction Contact Administration (CCA) Manual [a publication of Construction Specifications Canada]
Type: Book; *Price:* $175
• Manual of Practice [a publication of Construction Specifications Canada]
Type: Book; *Price:* $350
• Master Specifications [a publication of Construction Specifications Canada]
Type: Book
• Principles of Construction Documentation (PCD) Manual [a publication of Construction Specifications Canada]
Type: Book; *Price:* $100
• Technical Representative Manual [a publication of Construction Specifications Canada]
Type: Book; *Price:* $175

Construction Technology Centre Atlantic (CTCA)
#229, 15 Dineen Dr., Fredericton NB E3B 5A3
Tel: 506-453-4789; *Fax:* 506-453-4819
CTCA@unb.ca
Overview: A small local organization founded in 1988
Mission: To assist industry in increasing awareness & access to the latest technological advances in construction management, for both the office and the job site.
Member of: Canadian Construction Research Board (CCRB); Canadian Technology Network (CTN)
Affiliation(s): National Research Council (NRC); Industrial Research Assistance Program (IRAP)
Finances: *Funding Sources:* Consulting & training
Activities: Distribution of new technologies & information to the architectural, engineering & construction industries

Consulting Engineers of Alberta (CEA)
Phipps-McKinnon Building, #870, 10020 - 101A Ave., Edmonton AB T5J 3G2
Tel: 780-421-1852; *Fax:* 780-424-5225
info@cea.ca
www.cea.ca
www.linkedin.com/company/consulting-engineers-of-alberta
www.facebook.com/749479441765790
twitter.com/ConsultingEngAB
Overview: A medium-sized provincial organization founded in 1978 overseen by Association of Consulting Engineering Companies - Canada
Mission: To provide leadership to foster a positive business environment for the consulting engineering firms in Alberta; To promote the engineering industry; To enhance interests & opportunities of CEA members; To provide society with high standards of engineering design & safety
Finances: *Funding Sources:* Membership fees; Sponsorships
Membership: *Committees:* Board of Directors; BIM; Buildings; City of Calgary Liaison; City of Edmonton Liaison; Environmental; Industrial; Municipal Liaison; Transportation; Young Professionals' Group
Activities: Protecting legislative & regulatory interests; Offering a forum to exchange ideas; Providing training programs & information; *Speaker Service:* Yes
Chief Officer(s):
Matt Brassard, President
mbrassard@urbansystems.ca
Ken Pilip, CEO & Registrar
kpilip@cea.ca
Lisa Krewda, Director, Operations
lkrewda@cea.ca
Chantal Sargent, Manager, Events
csargent@cea.ca
Meetings/Conferences:
• Consulting Engineers of Alberta 40th Annual General Meeting, 2018, AB
Scope: Provincial
Attendance: 700+
Publications:
• Bullet [a publication of the Consulting Engineers of Alberta]
Type: Newsletter
Profile: Information for Consulting Engineers of Alberta, such as forthcoming meetings, sponsorship opportunities, & social events
• CEA [Consulting Engineers of Alberta] Progress Report on Salaries
Frequency: Annually
Profile: Salary recommendations
• CEA [Consulting Engineers of Alberta] Annual Report
Type: Yearbook; *Frequency:* Annually
• Consulting Engineers of Alberta Directory of Members
Type: Directory
Profile: Listing of members, including location & size of firms
• Consulting Engineers Rate Guidelines
Profile: Standard hourly rates for engineers, technicians, & technologists in Alberta

Consulting Engineers of British Columbia *See* Association of Consulting Engineering Companies - British Columbia

Consulting Engineers of Manitoba Inc. *See* Association of Consulting Engineering Companies - Manitoba

Consulting Engineers of Newfoundland & Labrador (CENL)
PO Box 1236, St. John's NL A1C 5M9
Tel: 709-726-3468
www.consultingengineersofnl.ca
Overview: A small provincial organization overseen by Association of Consulting Engineering Companies - Canada
Mission: To unite the local industry; to promote & advocate common business interests; to support the development & successs of member firms.
Membership: *Member Profile:* Firms in Newfoundland & Labrador that provide professional engineering servies to the public & private sectors
Chief Officer(s):
Mike Brady, P.Eng., PMP, President

Consulting Engineers of Nova Scotia (CENS)
PO Box 613, Stn. M, Halifax NS B3J 2R7
Tel: 902-461-1325; *Fax:* 902-461-1321
cens@eastlink.ca
www.cens.org
Previous Name: Nova Scotia Consulting Engineers Association
Overview: A medium-sized provincial organization founded in 1973 overseen by Association of Consulting Engineering Companies - Canada
Mission: To enable the consulting engineering industry in Nova Scotia to capitalize on opportunities to grow; To promote employment of member firms
Membership: 61 companies; *Member Profile:* Nova Scotia based companies in the business of engineering & related services
Activities: Maintaining high professional standards in the industry; Increasing awareness about the work & employment of consulting engineers
Chief Officer(s):
Scott Kyle, President, 902-450-4000
skyle@dillon.ca
Skit Ferguson, Executive Director
Meetings/Conferences:
• Consulting Engineers of Nova Scotia 2018 Annual General Meeting, 2018, NS
Scope: Provincial

Consulting Engineers of Ontario (CEO)
#405, 10 Four Seasons Pl., Toronto ON M9B 6H7
Tel: 416-620-1400; *Fax:* 416-620-5803
www.ceo.on.ca
www.linkedin.com/company/consulting-engineers-of-ontario
www.facebook.com/ConsultingEngON
twitter.com/ConsultingEngON
www.youtube.com/user/CEOYT
Overview: A medium-sized provincial organization founded in 1975 overseen by Association of Consulting Engineering Companies - Canada
Mission: To further the maintenance of high professional standards in consulting engineering profession; to promote cordial relations among various consulting firms in Ontario; to foster interchange of professional management & business experience & information among consulting engineers; to develop regional representation & participation in affairs of the association
Finances: *Annual Operating Budget:* $250,000-$500,000
Staff Member(s): 5
Membership: 250 firms; *Committees:* Audit & Finance; Business Risk; City of Toronto Liaison; Communication; Government Relations; Membership Services; Metrolinx Liaison; Ministry of Transportation of Ontario Liaison; Municipal Engineers Association Liaison; Toronto Transit Commission (TTC) Liaison; York Region Liaison; Young Professionals Group
Activities: *Speaker Service:* Yes
Chief Officer(s):
Bruce Potter, Chair
Barry Steinburg, Chief Executive Officer, 416-620-1400 Ext. 221
bsteinberg@ceo.on.ca
Jennifer Parent, Manager, Events & Member Services, 416-620-1400 Ext. 223
jparent@ceo.on.ca
Diane Lee, Coordinator, Communications, 416-620-1400 Ext. 227
dlee@ceo.on.ca
Meetings/Conferences:
• Consulting Engineers of Ontario 2018 Annual General Meeting, 2018, ON
Scope: Provincial

Consulting Engineers of Saskatchewan; Association of Consulting Engineers of Saskatchewan *See* Association of Consulting Engineering Companies - Saskatchewan

Consulting Engineers of the Northwest Territories (CENT)
c/o NAPEG, Bowling Green Bldg., #201, 4817 - 49th St., Yellowknife NT X1A 3S7
info@cent-nt.ca
www.cent-nt.ca
Overview: A small provincial organization overseen by Association of Consulting Engineering Companies - Canada
Mission: To promote positive business relationships between member firms & clients; to promote members' business interests.
Member of: Association of Canadian Engineering Companies (ACEC)
Membership: *Member Profile:* Independent engineering consulting firms located in the NWT & Nunavut
Chief Officer(s):
Carlos Philipovsky, President
president@cent-nt.ca

Consulting Engineers of Yukon (CEY)
c/o EBA Engineering Consultants Ltd., #6, 151 Industrial Rd., Whitehorse YT Y1A 2V3
Tel: 867-668-3068; *Fax:* 867-668-4349
cey@eba.ca
www.cey.ca
Overview: A small provincial organization founded in 1983 overseen by Association of Consulting Engineering Companies - Canada
Mission: To maintain high professional standards in the consulting engineering profession; To promote cordial relations among various consulting firms in the Yukon; to foster interchange of professional management & business experience & information among consulting engineers; To develop regional representation & participation in affairs of the association
Membership: 21 firms (13 members & 8 associate)

Consumer Electronics Marketers of Canada: A Division of Electro-Federation Canada (CEMC)
#300, 180 Attwell Dr., Mississauga ON M9W 6A9
Tel: 905-602-8877; *Fax:* 416-679-9234
info@electrofed.com
www.electrofed.com/cemc
Overview: A medium-sized national organization overseen by Electro-Federation Canada Inc.
Mission: To represent the consumer electronic marketing industry; To provide information for CEMC members to help them make good business decisions; To report on the status of the consumer electronics market
Membership: *Member Profile:* Manufacturers, importers, & distributors of consumer electronic products in Canada
Activities: Harmonizing standards; Addressing regulatory issues; Collecting statistical information
Chief Officer(s):
John Henderson, Chair
Susan Winter, Vice-President
swinter@electrofed.com

Consumer Health Organization of Canada (CHOC)
#1901, 355 St. Clair Ave. West, Toronto ON M5P 1N5

Canadian Associations / Consumer Health Products Canada

Tel: 416-924-9800; *Fax:* 416-924-6404
info@consumerhealth.org
www.consumerhealth.org
Overview: A medium-sized national organization founded in 1973
Mission: To encourage the prevention of all kinds of illness through knowledge; To help the individual, the family & the community to enjoy the benefits of a more wholesome lifestyle; To promote harmony & cooperation between like-minded groups
Affiliation(s): National Health Federation in US
Membership: *Fees:* $45
Activities: *Speaker Service:* Yes
Chief Officer(s):
Libby Gardon, President
Meetings/Conferences:
• Total Health '18 Convention & Exhibition, May, 2018, Metro Toronto Convention Centre, Toronto, ON
Scope: International
Description: Speakers will focus on creating good health and preventing disease using natural methods: energy medicine, organic gardening, traditional farming, agricultural biodiversity, healthy homes, ecologically based communities, renewable energy source and preserving a healthy environment for our children. We as consumers must choose foods and medicines which do no harm to people, animals or our planet.

Consumer Health Products Canada
Constitution Square, Tower III, #240, 340 Albert St., Ottawa ON K1R 7Y6
Tel: 613-723-0777; *Fax:* 613-723-0779
general@chpcanada.ca
www.chpcanada.ca
www.linkedin.com/company/consumer-health-products-canada
twitter.com/chp_can
www.youtube.com/CHPCanada0
Also Known As: CHP Canada
Previous Name: Nonprescription Drug Manufacturers Association of Canada; NDMAC, Advancing Canadian Self-Care
Overview: A medium-sized national organization founded in 1896
Mission: To contribute to quality of life & cost-effective health care for Canadians by creating & maintaining an environment for the growth of responsible self-medication
Member of: World Self-Medication Industry
Finances: *Annual Operating Budget:* $500,000-$1.5 Million
Staff Member(s): 9; 70 volunteer(s)
Membership: 45; *Fees:* $1,000 - $2,000; *Member Profile:* Manufacturers of over-the-counter medicines; associate - suppliers of goods & services to manufacturers; *Committees:* Associates; Product Authorization; Product Information; Product Quality; Strategies
Chief Officer(s):
Karen Proud, President
karen.proud@chpcanada.ca
Adam Kingsley, Vice-President, Operations
adam.kingsley@chpcanada.ca
Gerry Harrington, Vice-President, Policy & Regulatory Affairs
gerry.harrington@chpcanada.ca
Clarke Cross, Director, Government Relations
clarke.cross@chpcanada.ca
Kristin Willemsen, Director, Scientific & Regulatory Affairs
kristin.willemsen@chpcanada.ca
Marie-France MacKinnon, Manager, Communications
mf.mackinnon@chpcanada.ca
Sherri Sheney, Manager, Member Services
sherri.sheney@chpcanada.ca

Consumer Policy Institute (CPI)
225 Brunswick Ave., Toronto ON M5S 2M6
Tel: 416-964-9223; *Fax:* 416-964-8239
cpi@eprf.ca
www.c-p-i.org/cpi
Overview: A small local organization founded in 1980
Mission: A project of the Energy Probe Research Foundation (EPRF), CPI focuses on the force of the individual consumer, the empowerment of the general public brought about by the communications revolution & trade liberalization, circumstances that are eroding the power of traditional authorities in society. CPI understands this individual empowerment must be rooted in a sense of responsibility to other people & to the environment. The Institute is activly involved in a number of campaigns, covering a wide range of such fields as health care, tranportation, economic policy, automobile insurance & airports.
Chief Officer(s):
Lawrence Solomon, Executive Director
lawrence.solomon@nextcity.com

Consumer Protection BC
PO Box 9244, Victoria BC V8W 9J2
Tel: 604-320-1667; *Fax:* 250-920-7181
Toll-Free: 888-564-9963
www.consumerprotectionbc.ca
www.facebook.com/ConsumerProtectionBC
twitter.com/consumerprobc
www.youtube.com/user/ConsumerProBC
Previous Name: Business Practices & Consumer Protection Authority of British Columbia
Overview: A small provincial organization founded in 2004
Mission: To deliver consumer protection services throughout British Columbia; promote fairness and understanding in the marketplace; and enforce consumer protection laws in BC.
Chief Officer(s):
Robert Gialloreto, President & CEO

Consumers Council of Canada (CCC)
Commercial Bldg., #201, 1920 Yonge St., Toronto ON M4S 3E2
Tel: 416-483-2696
www.consumerscouncil.com
Overview: A small national organization
Mission: To enhance the marketplace in Canada
Membership: *Fees:* $50 individual
Chief Officer(s):
Don Mercer, President
Ken Whitehurst, Executive Director

Consumers' Association of Canada (CAC) / Association des consommateurs du Canada
Ottawa ON
Tel: 604-418-8359
consumer@rogers.com
www.consumer.ca
www.facebook.com/consumercanada
twitter.com/ConsumerCanada
Overview: A large national organization founded in 1947
Mission: To represent & articulate the best interests of Canadian consumers to all levels of government & to all sectors of society by continually earning recognition as the trusted voice of the consumer on a national basis; to inform & educate consumers on marketplace issues; To work with government & industry to solve marketplace problems; To focus its work in the areas of food, health, trade, standards, financial services, communications industries & other marketplace issues as they emerge
Finances: *Funding Sources:* Membership fees; project grants; donations
Membership: *Member Profile:* Open; *Committees:* Health; Economics & Finance
Activities: Consumer literacy program; consumer referral, information, education, consumer representation - standards development & implementation, multi-stakeholder working groups & advisory committees, special purpose task forces; *Speaker Service:* Yes
Chief Officer(s):
Bruce Cran, President & Director
Trevor Todd, Director

Contact Centre Canada
Toronto ON
canadacontact.ca
www.linkedin.com/groups/Canada-Contact-Centre-Association-5119908
www.facebook.com/CanadaContact
twitter.com/canadacontact
Overview: A medium-sized national organization
Mission: To contribute to the health & prosperity of the customer contact centre industry & of its workforce
Membership: *Member Profile:* Contact centre organizations; labour representatives; provincial industry associations; educational institutions; vendors & consultants that provide services to the Canadian contact centre industry
Chief Officer(s):
Robert Campbell, Contact

Contact Point
#200, 18 Spadina Rd., Toronto ON M5R 2S7
Tel: 416-929-2510; *Fax:* 416-923-2536
contactpoint@ceric.ca
www.contactpoint.ca
Overview: A small national organization
Mission: A practitioner-driven, Canadian website dedicated to providing multi-sectoral career development practitioners and career counsellors with career resources, learning and networking.
Affiliation(s): The Counselling Foundation of Canada
Chief Officer(s):
Jennifer Browne, President
Publications:
• Canadian Journal of Career Development
Type: Journal; *Editor:* Rob Shea
• Contact Point Bulletin
Type: Newsletter; *Frequency:* Quarterly

Contagious Mountain Bike Club (CMBC)
4061 - 4th Ave., Whitehorse YT Y1A 1H1
Tel: 867-668-4990
Other Communication: CMBC URL: cmbcyukon.ca
info@cmbcyukon.ca
sportyukon.com/member/cycling-association-of-yukon
Overview: A small provincial organization
Mission: To promote off-road cycling in the Yukon.
Chief Officer(s):
Sue Richards, President
susanlearichards@gmail.com

Contemporary Dancers Canada *See* Winnipeg's Contemporary Dancers

Conteurs du Canada *See* Storytellers of Canada

Continental Automated Buildings Association (CABA) / Association continentale pour l'automatisation des bâtiments
#210, 1173 Cyrville Rd., Ottawa ON K1J 7S6
Tel: 613-686-1814; *Fax:* 613-744-7833
Toll-Free: 888-798-2222
caba@caba.org
www.caba.org
www.linkedin.com/company/continental-automated-buildings-association-caba-
www.facebook.com/108759039149175?fref=ts
twitter.com/caba_news
www.youtube.com/cabaconf
Also Known As: North America's Home & Building Automation Association
Previous Name: Canadian Automated Buildings Association
Overview: A medium-sized national organization founded in 1988
Mission: To promote advanced technologies for the automation of homes & buildings in North America; To create opportunities for members
Activities: Providing information, education, & networking opportunities related to home & building automation; Encouraging research & development in the use of technology & integrated systems; *Library:* Research Library
Chief Officer(s):
Ronald J. Zimmer, President & Chief Executive Officer, 613-686-1814 Ext. 230
zimmer@caba.org
Noranda Haasper, Financial Administrator, 613-686-1814 Ext. 221
haasper@caba.org
Greg Walker, Director, Research, 613-686-1814 Ext. 227
walker@caba.org
Rawlson O'Neil King, Director, Communications, 613-686-1814 Ext. 225
king@caba.org
Publications:
• CABA [Continental Automated Buildings Association] eBulletin
Type: Newsletter; *Accepts Advertising*
Profile: Industry & membership developments
• CABA [Continental Automated Buildings Association] Information Series
Profile: Industry intelligence for the home & large building automation & integrated systems sector
• CABA [Continental Automated Buildings Association] Event Reports
Profile: Information about industry-related conferences & events
• iHomes & Buildings
Type: Magazine; *Accepts Advertising*
Profile: Up-to-date information on trends & products in the industry

Continuing Care Association of Nova Scotia (CCANS)
c/o Sunshine Personal Home Care, 38A Withrod Dr., Halifax NS B3N 1B1
Tel: 902-446-3140
ccans@eastlink.ca
www.ccans.info
Previous Name: Association of Licensed Nursing Homes (ALNH); Associated Homes for Special Care (AHSC)

Overview: A small provincial organization founded in 1964
Mission: To represent continuing care facilities throughout Nova Scotia
Finances: *Funding Sources:* Membership fees
Membership: 51 organizations; *Fees:* $365; *Member Profile:* Organizations across Nova Scotia, such as nursing homes, adult residential centres, regional rehabilitation centres, residential care facilities, licensed group homes, small option homes for persons with disabilities or seniors, & supported apartments
Activities: Engaging in advocacy activities; Liaising with Nova Scotia's Department of Community Services & Department of Health; Supporting caregivers; Offering educational opportunities; Providing a supportive network
Chief Officer(s):
Michael Walsh, President
Meetings/Conferences:
• Continuing Care Association of Nova Scotia 2018 AGM, 2018
Scope: Provincial

Continuing Legal Education Society of BC
#500, 1155 West Pender St., Vancouver BC V6E 2P4
Tel: 604-669-3544; *Fax:* 604-669-9260
Toll-Free: 800-663-0437
custserv@cle.bc.ca
www.cle.bc.ca
www.linkedin.com/company/continuing-legal-education-society-of-bc
www.facebook.com/clebc
www.twitter.com/clebc
www.youtube.com/user/TheCLEBC
Overview: A medium-sized provincial organization founded in 1965
Mission: To meet the present & future educational needs of the legal profession in British Columbia
Finances: *Funding Sources:* Course registrations; Publication sales
Membership: *Member Profile:* British Columbia lawyers & their support staff
Activities: Provision of courses on a great range of topics; Publication of practice-oriented books
Chief Officer(s):
Gwendoline C. Allison, Chair
Ronald G. Friesen, Chief Executive Officer, 604-893-2114
rfriesen@cle.bc.ca
Publications:
• Case Digest Connection
Profile: Timely digest of cases decided by the British Columbia superior courts, selected Provincial Court decisions, & Supreme Court of Canada cases which originated in British Columbia

Convention & Visitors Bureau of Sarnia/Lambton *See* Tourism Sarnia Lambton

Convention & Visitors Bureau of Windsor, Essex County & Pelee Island *See* Tourism Windsor Essex Pelee Island

Convention des Églises Baptistes de l'Atlantique *See* Convention of Atlantic Baptist Churches

Convention of Atlantic Baptist Churches (CABC) / Convention des Églises Baptistes de l'Atlantique
1655 Manawagonish Rd., Saint John NB E2M 3Y2
Tel: 506-635-1922; *Fax:* 506-635-0366
cabc@baptist-atlantic.ca
www.baptist-atlantic.ca
www.linkedin.com/company/2498898
www.facebook.com/atlanticbaptist
twitter.com/atlanticbaptist
plus.google.com/101053298635931681383
Also Known As: Atlantic Baptist Convention
Previous Name: United Baptist Convention of the Maritime Provinces
Overview: A medium-sized local charitable organization founded in 1905 overseen by Canadian Baptist Ministries
Mission: To resource pastors, churches, & people; To facilitate a shared mission on behalf of churches; To establish & maintain professional standards & ethics for clergy
Finances: *Annual Operating Budget:* $1.5 Million-$3 Million
Staff Member(s): 18
Membership: *Committees:* Acadia Divinity College; Acadia University; Atlantic Baptist Mission Board; Atlantic Baptist Senior Citizen's Homes Inc.; Atlantic Baptist University; Atlantic Baptist Foundation; Baptist Bookroom; Nominating; Historical; Pension & Insurance Board; Board of Ministerial Standards & Education
Activities: Providing seminars, conferences, stewardship education, & retreats; *Speaker Service:* Yes
Chief Officer(s):
Peter Reid, Executive Minister
peter.reid@baptist-atlantic.ca
Kevin Vincent, Associate Executive Minister, New Congregations
kevin.vincent@baptist-atlantic.ca
Meetings/Conferences:
• Oasis 2018, August, 2018, Acadia University, Wolfville, NS
Scope: Provincial
Publications:
• Convention Update
Type: Newsletter; *Frequency:* Monthly
• Youth & Family Update
Type: Newsletter; *Frequency:* Monthly

Conway Workshop Association
PO Box 568, 63 Shreve St., Digby NS B0V 1A0
Tel: 902-245-5391; *Fax:* 902-245-5539
conwayworkshop@ns.sympatico.ca
www.conwayworkshop.com
Overview: A small local organization
Mission: To help people with disabilities develop life skills so that they may live as independently as possible
Member of: DIRECTIONS Council for Vocational Services Society
Chief Officer(s):
Jill Baxter, Executive Director

Coop des Producteurs d'arbres de Noël du N.-B. *See* New Brunswick Christmas Tree Growers Co-op Ltd.

La Coop Fédérée
#200, 9001, boul de l'Acadie, Montréal QC H4N 3H7
Tél: 514-384-6450; *Téléc:* 514-384-7176
information@lacoop.coop
www.lacoop.coop
www.linkedin.com/company/55527
twitter.com/LaCoop_federee
www.youtube.com/user/LaCoopfederee
Nom précédent: Coopérative fédérée du Québec
Aperçu: *Dimension:* grande; *Envergure:* provinciale; fondée en 1922 surveillé par Canadian Federation of Agriculture
Mission: Fournit aux agriculteurs, directement ou par l'entremise de ses coopératives sociétaires, une vaste gamme de biens et de services nécessaires à l'exploitation de leur entreprise, y compris des produits pétroliers; de plus, elle transforme et commercialise sur les marchés locaux et internationaux divers produits agricoles: viande porcine, volaille, etc.
Finances: *Budget de fonctionnement annuel:* Plus de $5 Million
Membre(s) du personnel: 7
Membre: 95 coopératives
Activités: *Stagiaires:* Oui
Membre(s) du bureau directeur:
Denis Richard, Président

Coop kayak des îles
60, av du Parc, Trois-Pistoles QC G0L 4K0
Tél: 418-851-4637
info@kayaksdesiles.com
www.kayaksdesiles.com
www.facebook.com/124709937578452
Aperçu: *Dimension:* petite; *Envergure:* locale; fondée en 1999
Mission: Pour faire du kayak de mer plus accessible
Membre(s) du personnel: 6
Membre: *Montant de la cotisation:* 350$ par deux places; 150$ par une place
Membre(s) du bureau directeur:
Mikaël Rioux, Chef-guide

Cooper Institute / L'Institut Cooper
81 Prince St., Charlottetown PE C1A 4R3
Tel: 902-894-4573; *Fax:* 902-368-7180
www.cooperinstitute.ca
www.facebook.com/pages/Cooper-Institute/156027014448502
Overview: A small provincial organization founded in 1984
Mission: To promote programs that are focussed on livable income for all, food sovereignty & cultural diversity & inclusion; to conduct research & popular education projects on provincial, national & international level.
Staff Member(s): 3
Membership: 14
Chief Officer(s):
Joe Byrne, President
Awards:
• The Reverend Vincent Murnghan Memorial Scholarship
Offered to a qualified refugee or foreign student displaying commitment to working for social justice and to improving the living conditions in the community and on the planet, and academic achievement or evidence of academic potential. It is hoped that this scholarship will further Father Murnaghan's vision of justice and capacity-building by enabling a qualified refugee or foreign student to proceed with his/her studies.; *Amount:* $1000

La coopérative de Solidarité de Répit et d'Etraide (COOP SORE)
170, rue des Épinettes, Morin-Heights QC J0R 1H0
Tél: 450-226-2466; *Téléc:* 450-226-2211
sore@cgocable.ca
coopsore.org
Aperçu: *Dimension:* petite; *Envergure:* locale; Organisme sans but lucratif
Mission: De créer une communauté de soignants où les idées et les informations sont fournies afin d'apporter de nouveaux éléments à leur emploi en aidant les personnes âgées
Membre(s) du personnel: 5
Membre: *Montant de la cotisation:* 10$ pour les membres; *Critères d'admissibilite:* Personnes qui sonts des proches aidant, ou personne qui désire soutenir l'organisation
Membre(s) du bureau directeur:
Nicole Poirier, Présidente
Claire Lefebvre, Coordonnatrice

Co-operative Education & Work-Integrated Learning Canada (CEWIL)
#200, 411 Richmond St. East, Toronto ON M5A 3S5
Fax: 416-929-5256
cewil@cewilcanada.ca
www.cewilcanada.ca
Previous Name: Canadian Association for Co-operative Education
Overview: A medium-sized national organization founded in 1973
Mission: To act as the voice for post-secondary co-operative education in Canada; To advance post-secondary co-operative education throughout the country; To establish national standards
Affiliation(s): World Association for Cooperative Education (WACE)
Finances: *Funding Sources:* Membership fees; Sponsorships
Membership: *Fees:* Schedule available; *Member Profile:* Organizations & persons with a professional interest in co-operative education; *Committees:* Co-op Student of the Year; Communication; International; Co-op Week; Membership; Nomination & Awards; Professional Development; Research
Activities: Promoting co-operative education & accreditation; Offering mentorship for institutions considering accreditation; Providing opportunities for professional development; Offering networking opportunities for sharing best practices; Increasing national & government awareness; Presenting annual awards; *Awareness Events:* National Co-operative Education Week, March
Chief Officer(s):
Rachel King, Director, Operations, 416-483-3311 Ext. 230
Awards:
• Albert S. Barber Award
Recognizes outstanding contributions to the advancement of the philosophy and practice of Co-operative Education in Canada *Eligibility:* Member of CAFCE; must have made an outstanding contribution to the association *Deadline:* August
• Dr. Graham Branton Research Award
Recognizes outstanding contributions to the advancement of the philosophy and practice of Co-operative Education in Canada *Eligibility:* Member of CAFCE; must have made an outstanding contribution to the association *Deadline:* August
• Co-op Student of the Year Awards
This award recognizes a wide variety of achievements — job performance, academic performance and responsibility, and particular contributions to their co-op employer, to Co-operative Education, and the community-at-large *Eligibility:* One college co-op student & one university co-op student *Deadline:* January; *Amount:* $500
• Emery-Dufault Award
• Service Award
Awarded to recognize meritorious service to the CAFCE
Deadline: August
Meetings/Conferences:
• Co-operative Education & Work-Integrated Learning Canada 2018 National Conference, July, 2018, Concordia University, Montréal, QC
Scope: National
Publications:
• CAFCE [Canadian Association for Co-operative Education]

News
Type: Newletter
• Canadian Association for Co-operative Education Annual Report
Type: Yearbook; *Frequency:* Annually
• Co-operative Education Directory
Type: Directory
Profile: Listings of post-secondary co-operative education programs offered by CAFCE member institutions
• Co-operative Education Manual
Type: Manual; *Number of Pages:* 62
Profile: A guide to planning & implementing co-operative education programs in post-secondary institutions
• National Co-op Statistics

Coopérative fédérée du Québec *Voir* La Coop Fédérée

Cooperative Housing Federation of British Columbia (CHFBC)
#220, 1651 Commercial Dr., Vancouver BC V5L 3Y3
Tel: 604-879-5111; *Fax:* 604-879-4611
Toll-Free: 866-879-5111
info@chf.bc.ca
www.chf.bc.ca
www.facebook.com/coophousingbc
twitter.com/chfbc
www.youtube.com/user/coopsbc
www.flickr.com/photos/bchousingcoops
Overview: A medium-sized provincial organization founded in 1982
Mission: To unit, represent & serve members in a thriving cooperative housing movement
Affiliation(s): Cooperative Housing Federation Canada: Vancouver Office
Membership: *Committees:* Education; Finance; Aging in Place
Chief Officer(s):
Thom Armstrong, Executive Director
tarmstrong@chf.bc.ca
Awards:
• Mary Flynn Award of Cooperation

Cooperative Housing Federation of Canada (CHF Canada) / Fédération de l'habitation coopérative du Canada (FHCC)
#311, 225 Metcalfe St., Ottawa ON K2P 1P9
Tel: 613-230-2201; *Fax:* 613-230-2231
Toll-Free: 800-465-2752
info@chfcanada.coop
www.chfca.ca
www.facebook.com/chfcanada
twitter.com/CHFCanada
www.youtube.com/user/coophousing
Overview: A large national organization founded in 1968
Mission: To unite, represent & serve the co-op housing community across Canada
Membership: *Committees:* Federations; Diversity; Finance & Audit; Risk Underwriting Fund Administration
Chief Officer(s):
Nicholas Gazzard, Executive Director, 613-230-2201 Ext. 230
ngazzard@chfcanada.coop
Publications:
• Newsbriefs [a publication of the Cooperative Housing Federation of Canada]
Type: Newsletter; *Frequency:* Quarterly; *Editor:* Scott Jackson
Profile: News, issues, & events that affect Ontario housing co-operatives

British Columbia Region
#220, 1651 Commercial Dr., Vancouver BC V5L 3Y3
Tel: 604-879-4116; *Fax:* 604-879-4116
Toll-Free: 877-533-2667
chfcanada.coop/your-region/british-columbia

Prairie Region
PO Box 124, #13B, 30 - 360 Main St., Winnipeg MB R3C 3Z8
Tel: 204-947-5411; *Fax:* 204-947-5412
Toll-Free: 888-591-3301
chfcanada.coop/your-region/prairies
Chief Officer(s):
Blair Hamilton, Program Manager
bhamilton@chfcanada.coop
• Newsbriefs, Manitoba Edition [a publication of the Cooperative Housing Federation of Canada]
Type: Newsletter; *Frequency:* Quarterly; *Editor:* Tammy Robinson
Profile: News, issues & events that affect Manitoba housing co-operatives

Atlantic Region
Tower 1, #405, 202 Brownlow Ave., Halifax NS B3B 1T5
Tel: 902-423-7119; *Fax:* 902-423-7058
Toll-Free: 866-213-2667
chfcanada.coop/your-region/atlantic-region
Chief Officer(s):
Karen Brodeur, Program Manager, Cooperative Services
kbrodeur@chfcanada.coop
Cathy Volans, Coordinator, Cooperative Services
cvolans@chfcanada.coop

Ontario Region
#313, 720 Spadina Ave., Toronto ON M5S 2T9
Tel: 416-366-1711; *Fax:* 416-366-3876
Toll-Free: 800-268-2537
info@chfcanada.coop
chfcanada.coop/your-region/ontario-region
Chief Officer(s):
Patrick Newman, Regional Director, Ontario
pnewman@chfcanada.coop
• Bulletin for Ontario-program Co-ops
Profile: Information about work at provincial & municipal levels for co-ops
• Newsbriefs, Ontario Edition [a publication of the Cooperative Housing Federation of Canada]
Type: Newsletter; *Editor:* Keith Moyer
Profile: News, issues, & events that affect Ontario housing co-operatives
• SHRA [Social Housing Reform Act] Details
Profile: Educational series about the Social Housing Reform Act for Ontario-program co-ops

Co-operative Housing Federation of Toronto (CHFT)
#306, 658 Danforth Ave., Toronto ON M4J 5B9
Tel: 416-465-8688; *Fax:* 416-465-8337
info@coophousing.com
chft.coop
Overview: A medium-sized local organization founded in 1974
Mission: To promote the development of new co-ops & to provide the education & assistance needed by the co-operative housing sector; Serves Durham, Toronto & York region
Staff Member(s): 8
Membership: 45,000 individuals
Chief Officer(s):
Tom Clement, Executive Director
tom@coophousing.com

Co-operatives & Mutuals Canada (CMC) / Coopératives et mutuelles Canada
#400, 275 Bank St., Ottawa ON K2P 2L6
Tel: 613-238-6712; *Fax:* 613-567-0658
info@canada.coop
www.canada.coop
www.facebook.com/coopscanada
twitter.com/CoopsCanada
Overview: A large national organization founded in 2014
Mission: To unite co-operatives & mutuals from various industry sectors & regions of Canada
Affiliation(s): International Co-operative Alliance
Membership: 60 Co-operatives & Mutuals; *Member Profile:* Co-operatives & mutuals in Canada
Activities: Assisting developing organizations; providing relevant news & data to members; educational programs; lobbying; providing a forum for members; *Awareness Events:* Co-op Week, Oct.
Chief Officer(s):
Doug Potentier, President
Denyse Guy, Executive Director
dguy@canada.coop
Madeleine Brillant, Director, Corporate Affairs
mbrillant@canada.coop

Coopératives et mutuelles Canada *See* Co-operatives & Mutuals Canada

Copian
Sterling House, 767 Brunswick St., Fredericton NB E3B 1H8
Tel: 506-457-6900; *Fax:* 506-457-6910
Toll-Free: 800-720-6253
contact@copian.ca
www.copian.ca
twitter.com/Copian_E
Previous Name: National Adult Literacy Database
Overview: A small national charitable organization founded in 1989
Mission: To provide an information network, in both official languages; to support the Canadian literacy community: adult learners, practitioners, organizations & governments
Finances: *Annual Operating Budget:* $500,000-$1.5 Million
Staff Member(s): 15; 1 volunteer(s)
Activities: *Awareness Events:* Family Literacy Day, January 27
Chief Officer(s):
Bill Stirling, CEO
bill.stirling@copian.ca

The Coptic Orthodox Church (Canada)
St. Mark's Coptic Orthodox Church, 41 Glendinning Ave., Toronto ON M1W 3E2
Tel: 416-494-4449; *Fax:* 416-494-4196
mail@coptorthodox.ca
stmarkstoronto.ca
Overview: A small national organization
Member of: The Canadian Council of Churches; Coptic Orthodox Patriarchate
Chief Officer(s):
M.A. Marcos, Priest
FrMarcos@coptorthodox.ca

Copyright Visual Arts / Droits d'auteur Arts Visuels
214 Barclay Rd., Ottawa ON K1K 3C2
Tel: 613-232-3818; *Fax:* 613-232-8384
carcc@carcc.ca
www.carcc.ca
Previous Name: Canadian Artists Representation Copyright Collective Inc.
Overview: A medium-sized national organization founded in 1990
Mission: To negotiate and issue licenses that allow the legal use of its members' works, collect royalties and fairly pay artists
Affiliation(s): Canadian Arts Representation/Le Front des artistes canadiens
Staff Member(s): 1
Membership: 1000; *Fees:* Schedule available; *Member Profile:* Artists living in Canada & Canadian artists living outside Canada
Chief Officer(s):
Deborah Carruthers, Co-Chair
Patrick Lamb, Co-Chair

Coquitlam Area Fine Arts Council; ARC Arts Council *See* ArtsConnect - Tri-Cities Regional Arts Council

Corbrook Awakening Abilities
581 Trethewey Dr., Toronto ON M6M 4B8
Tel: 416-245-5565
info@corbrook.com
www.corbrook.com
www.facebook.com/CorbrookOfficial
twitter.com/corbrookcanada
Overview: A small local organization
Mission: To provide personal development & meaningful work opportunities for people with varying ability levels
Membership: *Member Profile:* Persons 18 years of age or older with a development disability; *Committees:* Finance; Human Resources; Governance; Business Resources
Activities: Employment services; personalized services; REVEL program; Youth Centred Day Respite Services; Learning & Literacy programs
Chief Officer(s):
Judy Cooper, President

Corner Brook & District Labour Council
Corner Brook NL
cbdistrictlabourcouncil@gmail.com
Overview: A small local organization
Member of: Newfoundland & Labrador Federation of Labour

Corner Brook Chamber of Commerce *See* Greater Corner Brook Board of Trade

Cornerstone Counselling Society of Edmonton
#302, 10140 - 117 St., Edmonton AB T5K 1X3
Tel: 780-482-6215; *Fax:* 780-482-7199
office@cornerstonecounselling.com
www.cornerstonecounselling.com
Overview: A small local charitable organization founded in 1977
Mission: To provide professional psychological services aimed at promoting wholeness of life through counselling education, assessment & training; services provided to individuals, families & couples in need regardless of income & sensitivity to individual physical, emotional, cultural & spiritual dimensions
Staff Member(s): 29

Activities: Individual, marital & family therapy; psycho/educational programs; Ryan Smyth Golf Tournament; annual banquet; *Speaker Service:* Yes
Chief Officer(s):
Sheila Stauffer, Executive Director

Cornwall & Area Chamber of Commerce
#100, 113 - 2nd St. East, Cornwall ON K6J 1Y5
Tel: 613-933-4004
info@cornwallchamber.com
www.cornwallchamber.com
www.facebook.com/ChamberCornwall
twitter.com/chambercornwall
Previous Name: Cornwall Chamber of Commerce
Overview: A small local organization founded in 1890
Mission: To promote the commercial, agricultural, industrial & communal interests of the city of Cornwall & area; To maintain just & equitable principles in business & professional usage
Member of: Canadian Chamber of Commerce; Ontario Chamber of Commerce
Activities: *Speaker Service:* Yes
Chief Officer(s):
Denis Carr, President
Lezlie Strasser, Executive Manager

Cornwall & District Labour Council
21 Water St. West, Cornwall ON K6J 1A1
Tel: 613-933-8670
info@cornwalllabour.ca
www.cornwalllabour.ca
Overview: A small local organization overseen by Ontario Federation of Labour
Membership: 10,000

Cornwall & District Real Estate Board
407B Pitt St., Cornwall ON K6J 3R3
Tel: 613-932-6457; *Fax:* 613-932-1687
www.mls-cornwall.com
Overview: A small local organization overseen by Ontario Real Estate Association
Member of: The Canadian Real Estate Association
Membership: 176
Chief Officer(s):
Dani Tedesco-Derouchie, Executive Officer, 613-932-6457

Cornwall Chamber of Commerce *See* Cornwall & Area Chamber of Commerce

Cornwall Police Association (CPA) / Association de la police de Cornwall
340 Pitt St., Cornwall ON K6J 3P9
cpa@cornwallpoliceassociation.ca
www.cornwallpoliceassociation.ca
Overview: A small local organization founded in 1954
Membership: 128
Chief Officer(s):
Dave MacLean, President
maclean.d@cornwallpoliceassociation.ca

Cornwall Township Historical Society
17109 Valade Rd., St Andrews ON K0C 2A0
Tel: 613-932-4390
info@cornwalltwphistorical.ca
www.cornwalltwphistorical.ca
Overview: A small local charitable organization founded in 1977
Mission: To preserve & promote local history
Finances: *Annual Operating Budget:* Less than $50,000; *Funding Sources:* Heritage grant; raffles; fundraisers
Membership: 108; *Fees:* $5 single; $8 family; $35 life
Activities: Operating local museum
Chief Officer(s):
Maureen McAlear, Director
Don McIntosh, Director

Coronach Community Chamber of Commerce
PO Box 577, Coronach SK S0H 0Z0
Tel: 306-267-2077; *Fax:* 306-267-2047
Overview: A small local organization
Affiliation(s): Saskatchewan Chamber of Commerce
Finances: *Annual Operating Budget:* Less than $50,000
Staff Member(s): 4
Membership: 1-99; *Fees:* $50
Activities: Agricultural Fair
Chief Officer(s):
J. Marshall, President
S. Nelson, Secretary

Coronation Chamber of Commerce
PO Box 960, Coronation AB T0C 1C0
Tel: 403-578-4580
Overview: A small local organization
Mission: To promote & drive economic & community development in the area
Member of: Alberta Chamber of Commerce
Finances: *Annual Operating Budget:* Less than $50,000
Membership: 1-99; *Fees:* $50
Activities: Organizing trade shows
Chief Officer(s):
Jodi Shipton, President

Corporate Art Collectors Association *Voir* Association des collections d'entreprises

Corporation culturelle Latino-Américaine de l'Amitié (COCLA)
1357, rue Saint-Louis, Montréal QC H4L 2P4
Tél: 514-748-0796; *Téléc:* 514-748-7210
cocla.mtl@gmail.com
www.coclamontreal.org
twitter.com/cocla_montreal
Aperçu: *Dimension:* petite; *Envergure:* internationale; fondée en 1984
Mission: Accueillir les nouveaux-arrivants d'origine latino-américaine et d'autres ethnies culturelles; soutenir les besoins vitaux de ceux-ci tels que la nourriture, le logement, le vêtement, le transport et la communication; réaliser les programmes d'éducation permettant à ces nouveaux-arrivants leur adaptation à la société québécoise et canadienne
Membre de: L'Église Unie du Canada/The United Church of Canada
Affiliation(s): Moisson Montréal; Renaissance Montréal
Membre(s) du personnel: 3
Activités: Groupe de femmes; service d'interprètes; conférences; cours de langue; camp d'été; ateliers
Membre(s) du bureau directeur:
Julio Rivera-Gamarra, Directeur général
Julio.cocla@gmail.com

Corporation de développement économique communautaire Centre-Sud/Plateau Mont-Royal (CDEC-CSPMR)
#11, 425, rue Sherbrooke est, Montréal QC H2L 1J9
Tél: 514-845-2332; *Téléc:* 514-845-7244
info@cdec-cspmr.org
www.cdec-cspmr.org
www.facebook.com/CDECCSPMR
twitter.com/CDECCSPMR
Aperçu: *Dimension:* petite; *Envergure:* locale; fondée en 1986
Mission: Pour améliorer la situation économique et sociale des personnes vivant dans Centre-Sud, Plateau Mont-Royal, Saint-Louis et Mile-End
Membre: 90; *Montant de la cotisation:* 10$ individuelle; 25$ organisme

Corporation des agronomes du Québec *Voir* Ordre des agronomes du Québec

Corporation des approvisionneurs du Québec (CAQ)
Complexe Tassé, #302, 895, boul Séminaire nord, Saint-Jean-sur-Richelieu QC J3A 1J2
Tél: 450-357-0033; *Téléc:* 450-357-0044
Ligne sans frais: 800-977-1877
info@caq.qc.ca
www.caq.qc.ca
www.facebook.com/CorpoAppQc
Nom précédent: Purchasing Management Association of Canada - Québec Institute
Aperçu: *Dimension:* petite; *Envergure:* provinciale; Organisme sans but lucratif; Organisme de réglementation surveillé par Supply Chain Management Association
Mission: La Corporation des approvisionneurs du Québec assure le développement professionnel de ses membres et veille à promouvoir et favoriser l'implantation des meilleures pratiques en matière de gestion de la chaîne d'approvisionnement au sein des entreprises québécoises afin que la valeur stratégique de l'approvisionnement puisse contribuer pleinement à l'essor des entreprises et à la société québécoise.
Membre: 1,100+
Membre(s) du bureau directeur:
Pierre St-Jean, Président

Corporation des associations de détaillants d'automobiles *See* Canadian Automobile Dealers' Association

Corporation des bibliothécaires professionnels du Québec (CBPQ) / Corporation of Professional Librarians of Québec
#215, 1453 rue Beaubien est, Montréal QC H2G 3C6
Tél: 514-845-3327; *Téléc:* 514-845-1618
info@cbpq.qc.ca
www.cbpq.qc.ca
www.facebook.com/cbpq.qc.ca
twitter.com/CBPQ_QC
Aperçu: *Dimension:* moyenne; *Envergure:* provinciale; fondée en 1969
Mission: Développer les services de bibliothèques; établir des normes de compétence; encourager et stimuler la recherche en bibliothéconomie; promouvoir et développer les intérêts professionnels de ses membres
Finances: *Fonds:* Frais de cotisation; Revenus de formation
Membre(s) du personnel: 3
Membre: *Critères d'admissibilite:* Maîtrise de bibliothéconomie/sciences de l'information; *Comités:* Activités sociales; Argus; Communications; Corpoclic; Élections; Formation continue; Mentorat; Mise en candidature; Prise de position; Règlements, résolutions, discipline et de l'admission
Activités: Congrès; Mentorat; Formation; Activités rencontre; Campagne de communication; *Stagiaires:* Oui; *Service de conférenciers:* Oui
Membre(s) du bureau directeur:
Catherine Mongeau, Directrice générale
Prix, Bourses:
• Prix bibliothécaire de l'année
Stimuler et reconnaître l'excellence parmi les membres; attirer l'attention des médias sur les récipiendaires de cette distinction honorifique et sur la nature des réalisations primées; orienter des perceptions; le prix comporte les volets suivants: distinction honorifique, remise d'une épinglette en or, publicité entourant l'événement
Publications:
• Argus [publication de Corporation des bibliothécaires professionnels du Québec]
Type: Revue; *Frequency:* 3 fois par ans; *Accepts Advertising*; *Price:* 35$ individuel; 43$institutionnel; 52$ États-Unis; 25$ Étudiants
Profile: Un revue contenant des articles et des nouvelles se rapportant aux bibliothécaires et de l'industrie de la bibliothèque
• Corpoclic [publication de Corporation des bibliothécaires professionnels du Québec]
Type: Bulletin; *Frequency:* 4 fois par ans
Profile: Un bulletin de nouvelles de la corporation à l'intérêt des membres

Corporation des bijoutiers du Québec (CBQ) / Québec Jewellers' Corporation
868, rue Brissette, Sainte-Julie QC J3E 2B1
Tél: 514-485-3333; *Téléc:* 450-649-8984
info@cbq.qc.ca
www.cbq.qc.ca
Aperçu: *Dimension:* moyenne; *Envergure:* provinciale; Organisme sans but lucratif; fondée en 1952
Mission: La promotion des membres, la défence de leurs intérêts économiques et sociaux et le développement du professionnalisme chez nos membres; garantir au public un meilleur service et l'intégrité des bijoutiers membres; accroître la compétence des gens du métier; favoriser l'exercise du métier selon l'art et la science
Membre de: Association des professionels en exposition du Québec (APEQ)
Finances: *Budget de fonctionnement annuel:* $250,000-$500,000
Membre(s) du personnel: 2; 20 bénévole(s)
Membre: 550; *Montant de la cotisation:* 190$ - 350$
Activités: *Bibliothèque:* Not open to public
Membre(s) du bureau directeur:
André Marchand, Président
Lise Petitpas, Directrice générale
lisepetitpas@cbq.qc.ca

Corporation des Chemins Craig et Gosford
2600, boul Frontenac ouest, Thetford Mines QC G6H 2C6
Tél: 418-423-3333; *Téléc:* 418-423-3331
Ligne sans frais: 877-335-7141
www.craig-gosford.ca
Aperçu: *Dimension:* petite; *Envergure:* locale; fondée en 2000
Mission: Mettre en valeur l'histoire et le patrimoine religieux des vieux axes routiers Craig et Gosford.
Membre(s) du bureau directeur:
Cindy White, Vice-présidente

Corporation des concessionnaires d'automobiles du Québec inc. (CCAQ)
#750, 140, Grande-Allée est, Québec QC G1R 5M8
Tél: 418-523-2991; *Téléc:* 418-523-3725
Ligne sans frais: 800-463-5189
info@ccaq.com
www.ccaq.com
www.facebook.com/LaCCAQ
twitter.com/CCAQ
plus.google.com/114145954123226218123
Aperçu: *Dimension:* grande; *Envergure:* nationale; Organisme sans but lucratif; fondée en 1945
Mission: Offre une multitude de services aux membres; représenter ses membres
Membre de: Canadian Automobile Dealers Association
Affiliation(s): CarrXpert; Occasion en On; ULTRA
Membre: *Critères d'admissibilite:* Détenir une franchise d'un constructeur
Activités: *Service de conférenciers:* Oui
Membre(s) du bureau directeur:
Jacques Béchard, Président-directeur général
j.bechard@ccaq.com

Corporation des entrepreneurs généraux du Québec (CEGQ)
6800, boul Pie-IX, Montréal QC H1X 2C8
Tél: 514-325-8454; *Téléc:* 514-325-0612
Ligne sans frais: 877-425-8454
www.cegq.com
www.linkedin.com/company/1828006
twitter.com/la_cegq
Aperçu: *Dimension:* petite; *Envergure:* provinciale; fondée en 1996
Mission: Voué exclusivement à la défense des intérêts collectifs et des droits des entrepreneurs généraux, oeuvrant principalement dans le secteur ICI (industriel, commercial et institutionnel)
Membre(s) du bureau directeur:
Eric Côté, Vice président exécutif
ecote@cegq.com

Corporation des entrepreneurs spécialisés du Grand Montréal inc. (CESGM)
#500, 5181, rue d'Amiens, Montréal QC H1G 6N9
Tél: 514-955-3548; *Téléc:* 514-955-6623
Ligne sans frais: 800-772-3746
www.cesgm.com
Aperçu: *Dimension:* moyenne; *Envergure:* locale; Organisme sans but lucratif; fondée en 1988
Mission: Aider les entreprises en construction à réussir leurs examens de compétence à la régie du bâtiment; à faire démarrer leur entreprise et à rester en affaires
Membre de: Fédération des Associations et Corporations en Construction du Québec inc.
Membre: *Critères d'admissibilite:* Tous les domaines en construction
Activités: Offrir des cours de perfectionnement; cours en administration; lecture de plan; estimation; gestion de travaux, sécurité, etc.; *Stagiaires:* Oui; *Bibliothèque:* Biblio CESGM
Membre(s) du bureau directeur:
Loraine Groulx, Vice présidente, Opérations
lgroulx@cesgm.com

Corporation des entreprises de traitement de l'air et du froid (CETAF) / Corporation of Air Treatment & Cold Processing Enterprises
#203, 6555, boul Métropolitain est, Montréal QC H1P 3H3
Tél: 514-735-1131; *Téléc:* 514-735-3509
Ligne sans frais: 866-402-3823
cetaf@cetaf.qc.ca
www.cetaf.qc.ca
Aperçu: *Dimension:* moyenne; *Envergure:* provinciale; Organisme sans but lucratif; fondée en 1964
Mission: Représenter et défendre les intérêts de ses membres; règlementer leur discipline et leur conduite professionnelle; favoriser et encourager la formation permanente
Membre(s) du personnel: 4
Membre: 320 entreprises; *Critères d'admissibilite:* Détenir une licence de la RBQ #4230.1, 4230.2, 4230.3, 4234, 4250.4 ou 4509; *Comités:* Arénas; Bureau de l'efficacité et de l'innovation énergétiques; Discipline; Formation et perfectionnement; Événements spéciaux; Gaz métro; HRAI; Hydro-Québec/Énercible; MCEE; Recrutement et services aux membres; Rédaction du climapresse et revenus publicitaires
Activités: Mecanex-Climatex: Exposition commerciale - le carrefour annuel des professionnels de l'installation, de la vente et du service, dans l'industrie du traitement de l'air et du froid; séminaires; programme de formation et de perfectionnement; tournoi de golf annuel; *Bibliothèque:* rendez-vous
Membre(s) du bureau directeur:
Claudette Carrier, Directrice générale
claudette.carrier@cetaf.qc.ca
Publications:
• ClimaPresse
Profile: Une revue technique et professionnelle d'expression française, publiée 6 fois l'an

Corporation des infirmières et infirmiers de salle d'opération du Québec (CIISOQ)
CP 63, 10, Place du Commerce, Brossard QC J4W 3L7
Courriel: info@ciisoq.ca
www.ciisoq.ca
www.facebook.com/ciisoq
Aperçu: *Dimension:* moyenne; *Envergure:* provinciale surveillé par Operating Room Nurses Association of Canada
Mission: Promotion de l'excellence des soins dispensés par l'infirmière en soins périopératoires
Membre(s) du bureau directeur:
Mireille Bélanger, Présidente
presidence@ciisoq.ca

Corporation des maîtres électriciens du Québec (CMEQ) / Corporation of Master Electricians of Québec
5925, boul Décarie, Montréal QC H3W 3C9
Tél: 514-738-2184; *Téléc:* 514-738-2192
Ligne sans frais: 800-361-9061
info@cmeq.org
www.cmeq.org
www.facebook.com/CMEQ.org
twitter.com/cmeq_
Aperçu: *Dimension:* moyenne; *Envergure:* provinciale; Organisme de réglementation; fondée en 1950 surveillé par Canadian Electrical Contractors Association
Mission: Augmenter la compétence des membres; règlementer la conduite des membres et de la profession; faciliter et encourager les membres à se familiariser avec des nouvelles techniques; chercher des solutions pratiques aux problèmes communs de l'industrie électrique
Membre: *Critères d'admissibilite:* Titulaire d'une licence d'entrepreneur en électricité
Activités: *Service de conférenciers:* Oui; *Listes de destinataires:* Oui
Membre(s) du bureau directeur:
Simon Bussière, Directeur général et vice-président exécutif
simon.bussiere@cmeq.org

Corporation des maîtres mécaniciens en tuyauterie du Québec (CMMTQ) / Corporation of Master Pipe Mechanics of Québec
8175, boul St-Laurent, Montréal QC H2P 2M1
Tél: 514-382-2668; *Téléc:* 514-382-1566
Ligne sans frais: 800-465-2668
www.cmmtq.org
Aperçu: *Dimension:* moyenne; *Envergure:* provinciale; Organisme sans but lucratif; fondée en 1949
Mission: Augmenter la compétence et l'habilité de ses membres en vue d'assurer au public une plus grande sécurité et protection au point de vue de l'hygiène et de la santé
Membre de: Heating, Refrigeration & Air Conditioning Institute of Canada
Finances: *Budget de fonctionnement annuel:* $500,000-$1.5 Million
Membre(s) du personnel: 21
Membre: 2 200; *Montant de la cotisation:* 660$; *Critères d'admissibilite:* Entrepreneur en mécanique du bâtiment
Activités: Mécanex
Membre(s) du bureau directeur:
André Bergeron, Directeur général
Alain Daigle, Président
Publications:
• L'Entre-Presse
Type: Newsletter; *Frequency:* Biweekly

Corporation des marchands de meubles du Québec *Voir* Conseil national du meuble

Corporation des officiers municipaux agréés du Québec (COMAQ) / Corporation of Chartered Municipal Officers of Québec
Édifice Lomer-Gouin, 575, rue Saint-Amable, #R02, Québec QC G1R 2G4
Tél: 418-527-1231; *Téléc:* 418-527-4462
Ligne sans frais: 800-305-1031
info@comaq.qc.ca
www.comaq.qc.ca
Aperçu: *Dimension:* moyenne; *Envergure:* provinciale; fondée en 1968
Mission: Regrouper les cadres municipaux des cités et villes du Québec; promouvoir la formation professionnelle par l'organisation de cours; protéger les intérêts sociaux-économiques des membres.
Membre: 650 officiers municipaux; *Critères d'admissibilite:* Gestionnaires municipaux; *Comités:* Formation professionnelle; Technologies de l'information; Législation; Finances et fiscalité municipales; Carrefour; Congrès; Recrutement; Scrutins; TPS-TVQ
Activités: Cours aménagement et urbanisme; scrutins municipaux; rédaction d'articles - information; étude des lois municipales des cités et villes; *Listes de destinataires:* Oui
Membre(s) du bureau directeur:
Julie Faucher, Diretrice générale
julie.faucher@comaq.qc.ca

Corporation des praticiens en médecine douce du Canada (CPMDQ)
CP 51071, 101, boul Cardinal-Léger, Pincourt QC J7V 9T3
Tél: 514-221-3740
Ligne sans frais: 800-624-6627
info@cpmdq.com
www.cpmdq.com
Aperçu: *Dimension:* petite; *Envergure:* nationale; fondée en 1991
Mission: De contribuer à l'essor d'une société où les individus, leurs familles et leurs communautés seraient responsables et capables d'assurer le développement et l'amélioration de leur santé physique, psychologique, spirituelle et sociale, grâce à des solutions globales, novatrices et durables.
Membre: *Montant de la cotisation:* Barème; *Critères d'admissibilite:* Thérapeute en médecine paramédical

Corporation des propriétaires immobiliers du Québec (CORPIQ)
#131, 750, boul Marcel-Laurin, Montréal QC H4M 2M4
Tél: 514-748-1921; *Téléc:* 514-748-2473
Ligne sans frais: 800-548-1921
www.corpiq.com
www.linkedin.com/company/corpiq
www.facebook.com/corpiq
Aperçu: *Dimension:* moyenne; *Envergure:* provinciale; fondée en 1980
Membre de: Canadian Federation of Appartment Association
Finances: *Budget de fonctionnement annuel:* $1.5 Million-$3 Million
Membre(s) du personnel: 15; 12 bénévole(s)
Membre: 25 000; *Montant de la cotisation:* 135-475
Activités: Information; représentation; regroupement et achats

Corporation des services d'ambulance du Québec
#205, 455, rue Marais, Québec QC G1M 3A2
Tél: 418-681-4448; *Téléc:* 418-681-4667
Ligne sans frais: 800-463-6773
www.csaq.org
Aperçu: *Dimension:* petite; *Envergure:* provinciale; fondée en 1972
Mission: Pour offrir une gamme de services et d'avantages à ses membres et à défendre les intérêts de ces derniers auprès des différentes instances gouvernementales, auprès de ses membres au Québec.
Affiliation(s): Association des hôpitaux du Québec
Membre(s) du bureau directeur:
Denis Perrault, Directeur général
denis.perrault@csaq.org

Corporation des thanatologues du Québec (CTQ)
#115, 4600, boul Henri-Bourassa, Québec QC G1H 3A5
Tél: 418-622-1717; *Téléc:* 418-622-5557
Ligne sans frais: 800-463-4935
info@corpothanato.com
www.domainefuneraire.com
www.facebook.com/corporation.thanatologues.quebec
twitter.com/corpothanato
Aperçu: *Dimension:* moyenne; *Envergure:* provinciale; fondée en 1956
Mission: Représenter le domaine funéraire, supporter son évolution promouvoir l'excellence et contribuer au développement d'affaire de ses membres pour le mieux être de la population

Finances: *Budget de fonctionnement annuel:* $500,000-$1.5 Million
Membre(s) du personnel: 2; 20 bénévole(s)
Membre: 400
Activités: *Listes de destinataires:* Oui
Membre(s) du bureau directeur:
René Goyer, Président

Corporation des thérapeutes du sport du Québec (CTSQ)
7141, rue Sherbrooke ouest, #SP165, Montréal QC H4B 1R6
Tél: 514-848-2424
admin@ctsq.qc.ca
www.ctsq.qc.ca
www.facebook.com/therapeutesdusport
twitter.com/therapiedusport
Aperçu: *Dimension:* petite; *Envergure:* provinciale; Organisme sans but lucratif; Organisme de réglementation
Membre de: Canadian Athletic Therapists Association
Finances: *Budget de fonctionnement annuel:* Moins de $50,000
Membre: 100-499
Activités: Développement professionnel ainsi que réglementation et attribution de licences professionnelles
Membre(s) du bureau directeur:
Fayez Abdulrahman, President
president@ctsq.qc.ca
Eric Grenier-Denis, Executive Director
Prix, Bourses:
• Hall of Fame Award
• Special Recognition Award
• Outstanding Internship Supervisor Award
• Merit Award
Meetings/Conferences:
• Corporation des thérapeutes du sport du Québec Annual Athletic Therapy Conference 2018, April, 2018, Montréal, QC
Scope: Provincial

Corporation des traducteurs, traductrices, terminologues et interprètes du Nouveau-Brunswick (CTINB) / Corporation of Translators, Terminologists & Interpreters of New Brunswick
CP 427, Fredericton NB E3B 4Z9
Tél: 506-458-1519
ctinb@nbnet.nb.ca
www.ctinb.nb.ca
Aperçu: *Dimension:* moyenne; *Envergure:* provinciale; Organisme sans but lucratif; fondée en 1970 surveillé par Canadian Translators, Terminologists & Interpreters Council
Mission: Donner à ses membres une voix collective; promouvoir le perfectionnement professionnel de ses membres; veiller à ce que ses membres respectent son Code de déontologie; faire connaître le rôle professionnel de ses membres dans la société; protéger l'intérêt public en faisant subir des examens d'admission à la CTINB et d'agrément des membres ainsi qu'en examinant les plaintes reçues à l'égard des membres; entretenir des liens avec les organismes semblables et avec les établissements de formation universitaire dans les domaines de la traduction, de la terminologie et de l'interprétation
Affiliation(s): Fédération internationale des traducteurs
Finances: *Budget de fonctionnement annuel:* Moins de $50,000
Membre(s) du personnel: 1; 5 bénévole(s)
Membre: 150 agréés + 60 associés; *Montant de la cotisation:* 150$ agréés; 75$ associés; *Comités:* Agrément; adhésion; discipline
Activités: Ateliers de perfectionnement professionnel; *Evénements de sensibilisation:* Journée nationale et internationale de la traduction

Corporation du patrimoine et du tourisme religieux de Québec
20, rue de Buade, Québec QC G1R 4A1
Tél: 418-694-0665; *Téléc:* 418-692-5860
info@patrimoine-religieux.com
www.patrimoine-religieux.com
Aperçu: *Dimension:* moyenne; *Envergure:* provinciale
Mission: La Corporation veille à l'animation, à l'interprétation et à la mise en valeur du patrimoine religieux de Québec.
Activités: Visites thématiques et pèlerinages, programmation, activités éducatives, service d'animation, service de documentation et d'information

Corporation l'Espoir
#511, 55, rue Dupras, LaSalle QC H8R 4A8
Tél: 514-367-3757; *Téléc:* 514-367-0444
info@corporationespoir.org
www.corporationespoir.org
www.facebook.com/296348483713938

Aperçu: *Dimension:* petite; *Envergure:* locale; Organisme sans but lucratif; fondée en 1976
Mission: Regroupe des parents de personnes qui présentent une déficience intellectuelle; maintien dans le milieu familial, l'intégration et la participation sociale de toutes les personnes handicapées
Affiliation(s): Association du Québec pour l'intégration sociale
Membre(s) du personnel: 12
Membre(s) du bureau directeur:
Martine Rainville, Directrice générale par interim
martine@corporationespoir.org
Publications:
• Défi [a publication of Corporation l'Espoir]
Type: Journal

Corporation of Air Treatment & Cold Processing Enterprises *Voir* Corporation des entreprises de traitement de l'air et du froid

Corporation of BC Land Surveyors *See* Association of British Columbia Land Surveyors

Corporation of Chartered Municipal Officers of Québec *Voir* Corporation des officiers municipaux agréés du Québec

Corporation of Master Electricians of Québec *Voir* Corporation des maîtres électriciens du Québec

Corporation of Master Pipe Mechanics of Québec *Voir* Corporation des maîtres mécaniciens en tuyauterie du Québec

Corporation of Professional Librarians of Québec *Voir* Corporation des bibliothécaires professionnels du Québec

Corporation of Translators, Terminologists & Interpreters of New Brunswick *Voir* Corporation des traducteurs, traductrices, terminologues et interprètes du Nouveau-Brunswick

Corporation pour la formation et le développement ERS *See* ERS Training & Development Corporation

Corporation professionnelle des audioprothésistes du Québec *Voir* Ordre des audioprothésistes du Québec

Corporation professionnelle des conseillers et conseillères d'orientation du Québec *Voir* Ordre des conseillers et conseillères d'orientation du Québec

Corporation professionnelle des infirmières et infirmiers auxiliaires du Québec *Voir* Ordre des infirmières et infirmiers auxiliaires du Québec

Corporation professionnelle des technologistes médicaux du Québec *Voir* Ordre professionnel des technologistes médicaux du Québec

Corporation professionnelle des technologues professionnelles du Québec *Voir* Ordre des technologues professionnels du Québec

Corporations des assureurs directs de dommage (CADD)
c/o La Capitale assurances générales inc., 625, rue St-Amable, Québec QC G1R 2G5
Tél: 418-266-9762
secretariat@cadd.ca
www.cadd.ca
Aperçu: *Dimension:* petite; *Envergure:* provinciale
Membre(s) du bureau directeur:
Henry Blumenthal, Président
Jean Mathieu Potvin, Secrétaire Trésorier

Le Corps Canadien des Commissionnaires *See* The Canadian Corps of Commissionaires

Corridor Community Options for Adults (CCOA)
21 Convent Rd., Enfield NS B2T 1C9
Tel: 902-883-9404; *Fax:* 902-883-1251
Overview: A small local organization
Member of: DIRECTIONS Council for Vocational Services Society
Chief Officer(s):
Ross Young, Manager
ccoa.manager@gmail.com

Corrugated Steel Pipe Institute (CSPI) / Institut pour tuyaux de tôle ondulée
#2A, 652 Bishop St. North, Cambridge ON N3H 4V6
Tel: 519-650-8080; *Fax:* 519-650-8081
info@cspi.ca
www.cspi.ca
Overview: A medium-sized national organization

Mission: To promote & encourage general & wider use of corrugated steel pipe for drainage & other uses across Canada; to initiate & support research, marketing, promotion, public relations & advertising programs designed to broaden the markets for CSP products; to cooperate with public & private agencies engaged in the formulation of specifications & designs for drainage & other underground structures; to provide the industry & the public with documented experience & up-to-date technical information on CSP products & their proper use & application; to enhance, through responsible public relations practices, the reputation & image of the Canadian CSP industry; to cooperate with allied industry & government authorities; to encourage & participate in educational endeavours in colleges & universities.
Activities: *Library:* Open to public
Chief Officer(s):
David J. Penny, Marketing Manager
djpenny@cspi.ca

Corsa Ontario
401 Beechwood Cres., Burlington ON L7L 3P7
www.corsaontario.com
Overview: A small provincial organization founded in 1969
Mission: To preserve Corvairs
Member of: Corvair Society of America
Finances: *Annual Operating Budget:* Less than $50,000
10 volunteer(s)
Membership: 65; *Fees:* $25
Chief Officer(s):
Ed Bartlett, President
malibusled@hotmail.com

Cosmetologists' Association of British Columbia; Cosmetology Industry Association of British Columbia *See* BeautyCouncil

Cosmetology Association of Nova Scotia (CANS)
126 Chain Link Dr., Halifax NS B3S 1A2
Tel: 902-468-6477; *Fax:* 902-468-7147
Toll-Free: 800-765-8757
www.nscosmetology.ca
Overview: A medium-sized provincial licensing organization founded in 1962
Mission: To apply standards ensuring the safety of the public & practitioners
Finances: *Annual Operating Budget:* $250,000-$500,000; *Funding Sources:* Membership fees
Staff Member(s): 3; 11 volunteer(s)
Membership: 5,000; *Fees:* $35 - $45
Chief Officer(s):
Lloyd Petrie, Chair

Cosmopolitan Music Society
8426 Gateway Blvd. NW, Edmonton AB T6E 4B4
Tel: 780-432-9333; *Fax:* 780-439-2595
info@cosmopolitanmusic.org
cosmopolitanmusic.org
www.facebook.com/CosmopolitanMusicSociety
twitter.com/CosmoYEG
Overview: A small local charitable organization founded in 1963
Staff Member(s): 2; 50+ volunteer(s)
Membership: 250
Chief Officer(s):
Cheryl Balay, General Manager
generalmanager@cosmopolitanmusic.org

COSTI Immigrant Services
Education Centre, 1710 Dufferin St., Toronto ON M6E 3P2
Tel: 416-658-1600; *Fax:* 416-658-8537
info@costi.org
www.costi.org
Overview: A small local organization founded in 1981
Mission: To provide educational, social & employment support to help immigrants in the greater Toronto area attain self-sufficiency in Canadian society. Services are provided in over 60 languages.
Finances: *Funding Sources:* Federal, provincial, municipal governments; United Way; private charitable foundations
Membership: *Fees:* $10 voting/individual associate; $25 ornganizational associate; *Committees:* Finance; Human Resources; Women's Services; Public Relations; Development Council
Activities: Referrals; work placement; language training; translation/interpretation; settlement services; family counselling; service for seniors
Chief Officer(s):
Bruno M. Suppa, President

Mario J. Calla, Executive Director
Brampton - Language, Employment & Settlement Services
Centennial Mall, #3, 227 Vodden St. East, Brampton ON L6V 1N2
Tel: 905-459-6700; *Fax:* 905-459-3626
Brampton & Caledon Employment Centre
#300, 10 Gillingham Dr., Brampton ON L6X 5A5
Tel: 905-459-8855; *Fax:* 905-459-9015
bramptonemployment@costi.org
Caledonia Centre
700 Caledonia Rd., Toronto ON M6B 3X7
Tel: 416-789-7925; *Fax:* 416-789-3499
employ@costi.org
Corvetti Education Centre
760 College St., Toronto ON M6G 1C4
Tel: 416-534-7400; *Fax:* 416-534-2482
edu@costi.org
Jane St. Hub
1541 Jane St., Toronto ON M9N 2R3
Tel: 416-645-7575; *Fax:* 416-645-7580
Markham - Enhanced Language Training Services
7220 Kennedy Fields Plaza, Markham ON L3P 7P2
Tel: 905-479-7926; *Fax:* 905-479-7425
Markham North - Language, Settlement & Skills Training Services
#102-103, 8400 Woodbine Ave., Markham ON L3R 4N7
Tel: 289-846-3645; *Fax:* 905-477-6478
esltmarkham@costi.org
Mississauga Centre
6750 Winston Churchill Blvd., #8A, Mississauga ON L5N 4C4
Tel: 905-567-0482; *Fax:* 905-567-0144
mississaugaemployment@costi.org
North York Centre
Sheridan Mall, #114, 1700 Wilson Ave., Toronto ON M3L 1B2
Tel: 416-244-0480; *Fax:* 416-244-0379
nyork@costi.org
Reception Centre
100 Lippincott St., Toronto ON M5S 2P1
Tel: 416-922-6688; *Fax:* 416-922-6668
reception@costi.org
Richmond Hill - Language, Settlement & Skills Training Services
9325 Yonge St., Richmond Hill ON L4C 0A8
Tel: 289-842-3124; *Fax:* 905-884-3163
Toronto - Employment Services
Weston Square, 35 King St., Toronto ON M9N 3R8
Tel: 416-588-2240; *Fax:* 416-244-2583
westonemployment@costi.org
Chief Officer(s):
Joe MacDonald, President
Vaughan - Language, Settlement & Skills Training Services
9100 Jane St., Bldg. H, Vaughan ON L4K 0A4
Tel: 905-761-1155; *Fax:* 905-761-2080
Vaughan Centre
#102, 3100 Rutherford Rd., Vaughan ON L4K 4R6
Tel: 905-669-5627; *Fax:* 905-669-1127
vaughanemployment@costi.org
Chief Officer(s):
Julie Darboh, General Manager, 905-669-5627 Ext. 3242
Samantha Timbers, Manager, 905-669-5627 Ext. 3243

Costume Society of Ontario (CSO)
PO Box 981, Stn. F, Toronto ON M4Y 2N9
costumesocietyontario@gmail.com
www.costumesociety.ca
www.facebook.com/CostumeSocietyofOntario
Overview: A small provincial organization founded in 1970
Mission: To promote education in dress throughout the ages to individuals who share an interest in costume or textile history, theatrical costuming, or fashion design; to encourage the preservation of historic costume & related source material
Activities: Regular program of lectures, seminars, workshops, & field trips

Côte-des-Neiges Black Community Association Inc. *Voir* Association de le communauté noire de Côte-des-Neiges inc.

Couchiching Institute on Public Affairs (CIPA)
#301, 250 Consumers Rd., Toronto ON M2J 4V6
Tel: 416-642-6374; *Fax:* 416-495-8723
Toll-Free: 866-647-6374
couch@couchichinginstitute.ca
www.couchichinginstitute.ca
www.facebook.com/couchichinginstitute
twitter.com/couchiching
couchichinginstitute.tumblr.com
Overview: A small international charitable organization founded in 1932
Mission: To bring together interested Canadians to discuss important public policy issues with experts & other members of the general public
Finances: *Annual Operating Budget:* $100,000-$250,000; *Funding Sources:* Charitable, corporate, personal & government donations; membership & conference fees
Staff Member(s): 6
Membership: *Fees:* $2500 Coporate; $75 individual; $25 student; *Member Profile:* Individuals interested in public affairs; *Committees:* Program; Marketing & Communications; Conversations & Roundtables; Fundraising; Big Picture; Partnerships; Youth & Young Professionals
Chief Officer(s):
Amanuel Melles, President
Shannon Bott, Executive Director, 416-494-1440 Ext. 229
sbott@couchichinginstitute.ca
Awards:
• Couchiching Award for Public Policy Leadership
• The Aczel Fund
• The Fresh Minds Fund
• Kurt Swinton Fund

Council Fire Native Cultural Centre *See* Toronto Council Fire Native Cultural Centre

Council for a Tobacco-Free Manitoba *See* Manitoba Tobacco Reduction Alliance

Council for Advancement of Native Development Officers (CANDO)
9635 - 45 Ave., Edmonton AB T6E 5Z8
Tel: 780-990-0303; *Fax:* 780-429-7487
Toll-Free: 800-463-9300
cando@edo.ca
www.edo.ca
www.facebook.com/CandoEDO
twitter.com/CandoEDO
Overview: A medium-sized national organization
Mission: To build capacity to strengthen Aboriginal economies
Chief Officer(s):
Keith Matthew, President, 250-828-9833
Ray Wanuch, PAED, Executive Director
ray.wanuch@edo.ca
Paul Macedo, Communications Officer
paul.macedo@edo.ca

Council for Automotive Human Resources (CAHR)
#801, 10 Four Seasons Pl., Toronto ON M9B 6H7
Tel: 416-621-2614; *Fax:* 416-621-5926
Toll-Free: 866-242-2078
info@cahr-crha.ca
www.linkedin.com/company/council-for-automotive-human-resources
Overview: A medium-sized national organization
Mission: To develop leadership in building skills & driving innovation, fundamental skills required for the industry today & in the future, & the continual drive to improve through innovation

Council for Black Aging / Le Conseil Des Personnes Agées De La Communauté Noire De Montréal
8606, rue Centrale, Montréal QC H4C 1M8
Tel: 514-935-4951
Overview: A medium-sized local organization
Mission: The Council for Black Aging works as an advocate for the needs of Black seniors, undertaking activities designed to advance the interests of Black elders, keeping Black seniors better informed of issues relating to the availability of health and social services, and developing a unique day centre and a nursing home for Black elders.

Council for Continuing Pharmaceutical Education (CCPE) / Conseil de formation pharmaceutique continue (CFPC)
#350, 3333 boul de la Côte-Vertu, Montréal QC H4R 2N1
Tel: 514-333-8362; *Fax:* 514-333-1119
Toll-Free: 888-333-8362
www.ccpe-cfpc.com
Previous Name: Council for the Accreditation of Pharmaceutical Manufacturers Representatives of Canada
Overview: A small national organization founded in 1969
Mission: To provide educational programs to establish improved professional standards within the Canadian pharmaceutical industry; To better meet the needs & expectations of our internal & external stakeholders in the healthcare industry
Staff Member(s): 6
Membership: 17 companies; *Member Profile:* Representatives associated with member companies who by their functions interface with other partners in the Canadian Health Care system
Chief Officer(s):
Jim Shea, General Manager
jshea@ccpe-cfpc.org

Council for the Accreditation of Pharmaceutical Manufacturers Representatives of Canada *See* Council for Continuing Pharmaceutical Education

Council for the Arts in Ottawa *See* Ottawa Arts Council

Council of Administrators of Large Urban Public Libraries *See* Canadian Urban Libraries Council

Council of Agencies Serving South Asians (CASSA)
#301A, 5200 Finch Ave. East, Toronto ON M1K 2N8
Tel: 416-932-1359; *Fax:* 416-932-9305
cassa@cassa.on.ca
www.cassa.on.ca
www.facebook.com/CASSAOnline
twitter.com/CASSACanada
Overview: A small local organization
Mission: To advocate for & support existing as well as emerging agencies; To ensure that the social service needs of the community are met; To play an active role in eliminating all forms of discrimination in society
Membership: *Fees:* $10 individual; $20 organization
Chief Officer(s):
Neethan Shan, Executive Director
Farhat Hasan, Administrator, Finance & Office

Council of Archives New Brunswick (CANB) / Conseil des archives du Nouveau-Brunswick
PO Box 1204, Stn. A, Fredericton NB E3B 5C8
Tel: 506-453-4327; *Fax:* 506-453-3288
archives.advisor@gnb.ca
www.canbarchives.ca
www.facebook.com/CANBarchives
twitter.com/CANBarchives
Overview: A small provincial organization founded in 1985 overseen by Canadian Council of Archives
Mission: To address the needs of the archival institutions in New Brunswick; To provide training & information on developments in the profession; To encourage information sharing & cooperation in educational opportunities with Maritime sister provinces & national associations
Finances: *Funding Sources:* Subventions; government grants
Membership: 49; *Fees:* $45; *Member Profile:* Institutions; communities; museums
Chief Officer(s):
David Mawhinney, President
dmawhinney@mta.ca
Awards:
• CANB-NB Provincial Grant Program
Deadline: September
Meetings/Conferences:
• Council of Archives New Brunswick Annual General Meeting 2018, 2018, NB
Scope: Provincial

Council of Atlantic Ministers of Education & Training (CAMET) / Conseil atlantique des ministres de l'Éducation et de la Formation (CAMEF)
PO Box 2044, Halifax NS B3J 2Z1
Tel: 902-424-3295; *Fax:* 902-424-8976
camet-camef@cap-cpma.ca
www.camet-camef.ca
Previous Name: Atlantic Provinces Education Foundation
Overview: A medium-sized local organization founded in 1982
Mission: To allow the ministers responsible for education & training in the Atlantic provinces to collaborate & respond to needs identified in public & post-secondary education; To enhance cooperation in public & post-secondary education to improve learning for Atlantic Canadians
Chief Officer(s):
Rhéal Poirier, Secretary, 902-424-3295
rpoirier@cap-cpma.ca
Sylvie Martin, Regional Coordinator, 902-424-8906
smartin@cap-cpma.ca

Council of Atlantic Premiers (CAP)
Council Secretariat, PO Box 2044, #1006, 5161 George St., Halifax NS B3J 2Z1
Tel: 902-424-7590; *Fax:* 902-424-8976
info@cap-cpma.ca
www.cap-cpma.ca
Mission: The mandate of the Council is to promote Atlantic Canadian interests on national issues. To accomplish this, the Council seeks to establish common views & positions to ensure that Atlantic Canadians & their interests are well represented in national debates. The work of the Council of Atlantic Premiers builds on the ongoing work of the Council of Maritime Premiers & the Conference of Atlantic Premiers. The premiers are committed to work together on behalf of Atlantic Canadians to strengthen the economic competitiveness of the region, improve the quality of public services to Atlantic Canadians and/or improve the cost-effectiveness of delivering public services to Atlantic Canadians.
Membership: *Member Profile:* Premiers of New Brunswick, Newfoundland & Labrador, Nova Scotia & Prince Edward Island
Activities: Specific areas of focus include: Energy & the Environment (including climate change mitigation & adaptation); Innovation & Economic Progress (including research & development); Population & Immigration (including workforce growth & retention); & Trade & Procurement.
Chief Officer(s):
Tim Porter, Secretary to Council, 902-424-7600
tporter@cap-cpma.ca

Council of Canadian Academies / Conseil des académies canadiennes
#1401, 180 Elgin St., Ottawa ON K2P 2K3
Tel: 613-567-5000; *Fax:* 613-567-5060
info@scienceadvice.ca
www.scienceadvice.ca
twitter.com/Scienceadvice
Previous Name: Canadian Academies of Science
Overview: A small national organization founded in 2005
Mission: To support independent, expert assessment of the science underlying issues of public concern.
Finances: *Funding Sources:* Federal government
Staff Member(s): 28
Membership: 3; *Member Profile:* Royal Society of Canada; Canadian Academy of Engineering; Canadian Academy of Health Sciences; *Committees:* Scientific Advisor; Executive; Audit & Finance; Investment; Nominations, Selection & Governance; Human Resources & Compensation
Chief Officer(s):
Margaret Bloodworth, Chair
Janet Bax, Interim President, 613-567-5000 Ext. 267
janet.bax@scienceadvice.ca
Tom Bursey, Vice-President, Corporate Services & CFO, 613-567-5000 Ext. 224
tom.bursey@scienceadvice.ca

Council of Canadian Fire Marshals & Fire Commissioners (CCFMFC) / Conseil canadien des directeurs provinciaux et des commissaires des incendies
c/o 491 McLeod Hill Rd., Fredericton NB E3A 6H6
Tel: 506-453-1208; *Fax:* 506-457-0793
CCFMFC@rogers.com
www.ccfmfc.ca
Overview: A medium-sized national organization founded in 1921
Mission: To contribute to a reduction in the number of fire deaths
Activities: Advising on & promoting legislation, policies, & procedures; Participating in the development of standards & codes; Arranging national fire loss statistics; Supporting professional development of the Canadian fire service; Identifying trends related to the causes of fire; Providing a forum for the exchange of information on fire safety matters; Offering advice to accredited agencies involved in the testing & certification of fire protection equipment
Chief Officer(s):
Duane McKay, President
Harold Pothier, Vice-President
Philippa Gourley, Secretary-Treasurer

Council of Canadian Law Deans (CCLD) / Conseil des doyens et des doyennes des facultés de droit du Canada (CDFDC)
c/o Brigitte Pilon, Executive Director, 57 Louis Pasteur, Ottawa ON K1N 6N5
Tel: 613-824-9233; *Fax:* 613-824-9233
brigitteccld@rogers.com
www.ccld-cdfdc.ca
Overview: A small national organization overseen by Universities Canada
Mission: To consult on matters of mutual concern, including legal education in Canada, legal research, cooperation among law schools & relations with law teachers, accreditation bodies, the legal profession & others
Member of: Universities Canada
Finances: *Annual Operating Budget:* Less than $50,000
Staff Member(s): 1
Membership: 23; *Member Profile:* Heads of various law schools & departments across Canada
Activities: Two meetings per year; sponsorship of law teaching forum
Chief Officer(s):
Brigitte Pilon, Executive Director

The Council of Canadians (COC) / Le Conseil des Canadiens
#300, 251 Bank St., Ottawa ON K2P 1X3
Tel: 613-233-2773; *Fax:* 613-233-6776
Toll-Free: 800-387-7177
inquiries@canadians.org
www.canadians.org
www.facebook.com/CouncilofCDNS?rf=105965852767091
twitter.com/councilofcdns
www.youtube.com/councilofcanadians
Overview: A medium-sized national organization founded in 1985
Mission: With chapters across the country, The Council of Canadians is Canada's largest citizens' organization, working to protect Canadian independence in areas such as energy & environment, health care & fair trade. The Council provides a critical voice on key national issues: safeguarding our social programs, promoting economic justice, renewing Canada's democracy, asserting Canadian sovereignty, promoting alternatives to corporate-style free trade & preserving the environment
Finances: *Funding Sources:* Membership dues; donations
Activities: Campaigns: Deep Integration (the increasing harmonisation of Canadian policies in key areas with those of the U.S.); Health Care; Trade; Water; Energy; Food; Peace; Blue Planet Project; *Rents Mailing List:* Yes; *Library:* Open to public by appointment
Chief Officer(s):
Maude Barlow, National Chairperson

Atlantic
#211, 2099 Gottigen St., Halifax NS B3K 3B2
Tel: 902-422-7811
Toll-Free: 877-772-7811
atlantic@canadians.org
Chief Officer(s):
Angela Giles, Regional Organizer

British Columbia & Yukon
#700, 207 West Hastings St., Vancouver BC V6B 1H7
Tel: 604-688-8846
Toll-Free: 888-566-3888
bc-yukon@canadians.org
Chief Officer(s):
Harjap Grewal, Regional Organizer

Ontario, Québec, Nunavut
#210, 116 Spadina Ave., Toronto ON M5V 2K6
Tel: 416-979-5554
Toll-Free: 800-208-7156
ontario-quebec@canadians.org
Chief Officer(s):
Stuart Trew, Regional Organizer

Prairies
#34, 9912 - 106 St., Edmonton AB T5K 1C5
Tel: 780-429-4500
Toll-Free: 877-729-4500
prairies@canadians.org
Chief Officer(s):
Sheila Muxlow, Regional Organizer

Council of Canadians with Disabilities (CCD) / Conseil des Canadiens avec déficiences
#909, 294 Portage Ave., Winnipeg MB R3C 0B9
Tel: 204-947-0303; *Fax:* 204-942-4625; *TTY:* 204-943-4757
ccd@ccdonline.ca
www.ccdonline.ca
www.facebook.com/ccdonline
twitter.com/ccdonline
www.youtube.com/ccdonline
Overview: A medium-sized national organization founded in 1976
Mission: To improve the status of disabled citizens in Canadian society; To promote self-help for persons with disabilities; To provide a democratic structure for disabled citizens to voice concerns; To monitor federal legislation; To share information & cooperate with disabled persons' organizations in Canada & in other countries; To establish a positive image of disabled Canadians
Member of: Disabled Peoples International
Affiliation(s): Consumer Organization of Disabled People of Newfoundland & Labrador; PEI Council of the Disabled; Nova Scotia League for Equal Opportunities; PUSH-Ontario; Manitoba League of the Physically Handicapped; Saskatchewan Voice of the Handicapped; Alberta Committee of Disabled Citizens; British Columbia Coalition of the Disabled; Association canadienne des sourds; DAWN Canada; National Network on Mental Health; Thalidomide Victims of Canada; National Education Association of Disabled Students; People First of Canada
Finances: *Funding Sources:* Human Resources Development
Membership: 17 organizations; *Member Profile:* Consumer controlled advocacy associations; *Committees:* Human Rights; International Development; Social Policy; Transportation
Activities: *Speaker Service:* Yes; *Library:* by appointment Not open to public
Chief Officer(s):
Jewelles Smith, Chair
Carmela Hutchison, Secretary
Kory Earle, Treasurer

Council of Catholic Charities *See* Catholic Charities of The Archdiocese of Toronto

Council of Catholic School Superintendents of Alberta (CCSSA)
21 Walters Place, Leduc AB T9E 8S7
Tel: 780-913-0194
www.ccssa.ca
www.facebook.com/NCRegister
twitter.com/acstanews
Overview: A small provincial organization
Mission: Provides a forum for discussion regarding the direction & development of Catholic Education in Alberta
Membership: 35
Chief Officer(s):
Jamie McNamara, Executive Director, 780-913-0194

Council of Federal Libraries / Conseil des bibliothèques du gouvernement fédéral *See* Federal Libraries Coordination Secretariat

Council of Food Processing & Consumer Products *Voir* Conseil de la transformation agroalimentaire et des produits de consommation

Council of Forest Industries (COFI)
Pender Place I Business Building, #1501, 700 Pender St. West, Vancouver BC V6C 1G8
Tel: 604-684-0211; *Fax:* 604-687-4930
info@cofi.org
www.cofi.org
Also Known As: Canadian Forest Industries Council
Overview: A medium-sized provincial organization
Mission: To be the voice of the British Columbia interior forest industry; To offer member companies services in areas such as international market & trade development, community relations, public affairs, quality control, & forest policy
Membership: *Member Profile:* Companies that operate production facilities in forest dependent communities in the interior of British Columbia
Activities: Advocating for British Columbia's forest industry; Liaising with government about the development & implementation of policies related to British Columbia's forest sector; Increasing public awareness about the importance of the forest sector
Chief Officer(s):
Ken Higginbotham, Chair
John Allan, President & Chief Executive Officer
Paul J. Newman, Executive Director, Market Access & Trade
newman@cofi.org
Doug Routledge, Vice-President, Forestry & Northern Operations
routledge@cofi.org

Anne Mauch, Director, Regulatory Issues
mauch@cofi.org
Meetings/Conferences:
• Council of Forest Industries 2018 Annual Convention, April, 2018, Kelowna, BC
Scope: National
Attendance: 500-900
Description: A meeting about issues affecting the forestry industries of British Columbia.
Contact Information: Phone: 604-684-0211; Fax: 604-687-4930
• Council of Forest Industries 2019 Annual Convention, April, 2019, Prince George, BC
Scope: National
Attendance: 500-900
Description: A meeting about issues affecting the forestry industries of British Columbia.
Contact Information: Phone: 604-684-0211; Fax: 604-687-4930
Publications:
• British Columbia Forest Industry Fact Book
Type: Book
Profile: Sections include the world's forests & forest industry; Canada's forests & forest industry; competitiveness; land use, forest management, & the environment; & British Columbiaforest industry statistical tables
• COFI [Council of Forest Industries] News: Month in Review
Type: Newsletter
Profile: Council of Forest Industries events & British Columbia forest industry news
• Council of Forest Industries Annual Report
Type: Yearbook; Frequency: Annually
Profile: A review of operations & the financial report
• Quarterly Stumpage Update [a publication of the Council of Forest Industries]
Profile: Including British Columbia stumpage parameters & average stumpage prices

Council of Marine Carriers
#215, 3989 Henning Dr., Burnaby BC V5C 6P8
Tel: 604-687-9677; Fax: 604-687-1788
cmc@comc.cc
www.comc.cc
Overview: A small national organization founded in 1972
Staff Member(s): 3
Chief Officer(s):
Leo Stradiotti, President
ole@dccnet.com

Council of Ministers of Education, Canada (CMEC) / Conseil des ministres de l'éducation (Canada)
#1106, 95 St. Clair Ave. West, Toronto ON M4V 1N6
Tel: 416-962-8100; Fax: 416-962-2800
information@cmec.ca
www.cmec.ca
www.linkedin.com/company/cmec
twitter.com/ccmec
Overview: A medium-sized national organization founded in 1967
Mission: To act as a forum to discuss policy issues; to consult & cooperate with national education organizations & the federal government; to represent the education interests of the provinces & territories internationally
Finances: Funding Sources: Membership dues
Membership: 13 institutional; Member Profile: Provincial & territorial departments responsible for education

Council of Nova Scotia Archives (CNSA)
6016 University Ave., Halifax NS B3H 1W4
Tel: 902-424-7093
advisor@councilofnsarchives.ca
www.councilofnsarchives.ca
www.facebook.com/536190566445902
Overview: A medium-sized provincial charitable organization founded in 1983 overseen by Canadian Council of Archives
Mission: To foster education of archival standards & practices to preserve Nova Scotia's documentary heritage; To promote archival standards, procedures, & practices
Staff Member(s): 1
Membership: Fees: $55 General; $50 Individual; $25 Student; Schedule for institutions; Member Profile: Archivists & archives in Nova Scotia, such as university archives, religious archives, community archives, museums, provincial archives, corporations, & heritage associations; Committees: Executive; Education; Awards; Preservation; Renewal & Sustainability; MemoryNS
Activities: Advocating for the importance of archives, preservation, & public access; Liaising with the Canadian Council of Archives; Providing training & advisory services; Establishing the CNSA Acquisition Strategy for cooperative acquisisition practices in Nova Scotian archives; Library: CNSA Lending Library; by appointment
Chief Officer(s):
Jamie Serran, Advisor, Archives
advisor@councilofnsarchives.ca
Awards:
• Carman V. Carroll Award for Outstanding Achievement in Archival Preservation
• Anna Hamilton Award for Outstanding Voluntary Service to the Nova Scotian Archival Community
• Dr. Phyllis R. Blakeley Award for Archival Excellence
Meetings/Conferences:
• Council of Nova Scotia Archives Annual General Meeting 2018, 2018, NS
Scope: Provincial

Council of Ontario Construction Associations (COCA)
#2001, 180 Dundas St. West, Toronto ON M5G 1Z8
Tel: 416-968-7200; Fax: 416-968-0362
info@coca.on.ca
www.coca.on.ca
www.linkedin.com/company/2397076
www.facebook.com/172643879452017
twitter.com/ICIconstruction
Overview: A large provincial organization founded in 1974
Mission: To contribute to the long-term growth & profitability of the construction industry in Ontario; To speak with a unified voice to government, the industry & the public
Staff Member(s): 4
Membership: 32 organizations; Committees: Executive; Chief Operating Officers; Construction Lien Act; WSIB/Occupational Health & Safety; Infrastructure Task Force
Activities: Speaker Service: Yes
Chief Officer(s):
Ian Cunningham, President, 416-968-7200 Ext. 224
icunningham@coca.on.ca
Martin Benson, Manager, Operations & Member Services, 416-968-7200 Ext. 222
mbenson@coca.on.ca
Awards:
• Cliff Bulmer Award
• Chair's Award
• President's Award
Meetings/Conferences:
• Council of Ontario Construction Associations Annual General Meeting 2018, 2018, ON
Scope: Provincial
Contact Information: Manager, Operations & Member Services: Martin Benson, E-mail: mbenson@coca.on.ca; Phone: 416-968-7200, ext. 222
Publications:
• Council of Ontario Construction Associations Member Directory

Barrie Construction Association (BCA)
200 Brock St., Barrie ON L4N 2M4
Tel: 705-726-5864; Fax: 705-726-4649
admin@gvca.org
www.gvca.org
www.facebook.com/barrieconstructionassociation
twitter.com/barrieconstruct
Chief Officer(s):
Robert Stiemer, President
Alison Smith, Executive Director

Construction Association of Thunder Bay (CATB)
857 North May St., Thunder Bay ON P7C 3S2
Tel: 807-622-9645; Fax: 807-623-2296
information@catb.on.ca
www.catb.on.ca

Grand Valley Construction Association (GVCA)
25 Sheldon Dr., Cambridge ON N1R 6R8
Tel: 519-622-4822; Fax: 519-621-3289
Toll-Free: 800-265-7847
admin@gvca.org
www.gvca.org
twitter.com/GVCANews
Chief Officer(s):
Martha George, President
mgeorge@gvca.org

Hamilton-Halton Construction Association (HHCA)
#100, 370 York Blvd., Hamilton ON L8R 3L1
Tel: 905-522-5220; Fax: 905-572-9166
www.hhca.ca
twitter.com/HHCA_1920
Chief Officer(s):
Sue Ramsay, General Manager
sue@hhca.ca

London & District Construction Association
331 Aberdeen Dr., London ON N5V 4S4
Tel: 519-453-5322; Fax: 519-453-5335
info@ldca.on.ca
www.ldca.on.ca
Chief Officer(s):
Jim Sheffield, President
Mike Carter, Executive Director
m.carter@ldca.on.ca

Niagara Construction Association
34 Scott St. West, St Catharines ON L2R 1C9
Tel: 905-682-6661; Fax: 905-688-5029
office@niagaraconstruction.org
niagaraconstruction.org
www.facebook.com/ncaconstructniagara
twitter.com/construct_nca
Chief Officer(s):
Karin Sheldrick, General Manager
karin@niagaraconstruction.org

Northeastern Ontario Construction Association (NOCA)
257 Beatty St., Sudbury ON P3C 4G1
Tel: 705-673-5619; Fax: 705-673-7910
nocabuild.com
twitter.com/nocabuild
Chief Officer(s):
Denis Shank, Executive Director
dshank@sudburyca.com

Peterborough Construction Association (PCA)
#2, 494 The Parkway, Peterborough ON K9J 7L9
Tel: 705-745-3581; Fax: 705-745-9234
office@peterboroughconstructionassociation.ca
www.peterboroughconstructionassociation.ca
www.facebook.com/barrieconstructionassociation
twitter.com/barrieconstruct
Chief Officer(s):
Melinda Brown, Contact

Sarnia Construction Association
PO Box 545, 954 Upper Canada Dr., Sarnia ON N7T 7J4
Tel: 519-344-7441; Fax: 519-344-7501
sca@bellnet.ca
sarniaconstructionassociation.ca
Chief Officer(s):
Scott Saunders, President

Sault Ste Marie Construction Association (SSMCA)
117 White Oak Dr. East, Sault Ste Marie ON P6B 4J7
Tel: 705-759-8830; Fax: 705-759-6783
ssmca.com
www.facebook.com/ssmconstructionassociation
Chief Officer(s):
Adam Pinder, Manager
adam@ssmca.com

Toronto Construction Association
70 Leek Cres., Richmond Hill ON L4B 1H1
Tel: 416-499-4000; Fax: 416-499-8752
www.tcaconnect.com
www.facebook.com/YCLToronto
twitter.com/tca_connect
Chief Officer(s):
Craig Lesurf, Chair
John G. Mollenhauer, President & CEO
jmollenhauer@tcaconnect.com

Windsor Construction Association (WCA)
#100, 2880 Temple Dr., Windsor ON N8W 5J5
Tel: 519-974-9680; Fax: 519-974-3854
construction@wca.on.ca
www.wca.on.ca
Chief Officer(s):
Davide Petretta, President, 519-737-1292

Council of Ontario Drama & Dance Educators (CODE)
ON
code.on.ca
Overview: A small provincial organization founded in 1970
Mission: To promote strong arts education in schools and communities across Ontario; Provide a forum for the exchange of ideas among those involved in drama and dance in education; Provide professional development in those involved in drama and dance in education; and Provide leadership and advocacy in drama and dance in education.
Membership: Fees: $50

Chief Officer(s):
Sarah Papoff, President
president@code.on.ca

Council of Ontario Universities (COU) / Conseil des universités de l'Ontario
#1800, 180 Dundas St. West, Toronto ON M5G 1Z8
Tel: 416-979-2165; *Fax:* 416-979-8635
cou@cou.on.ca
www.cou.on.ca
www.linkedin.com/company/council-of-ontario-universities
www.facebook.com/CouncilofOntarioUniversities
twitter.com/OntUniv
Also Known As: COU Holding Association Inc.
Previous Name: Committee of Presidents of Universities of Ontario
Overview: A medium-sized provincial charitable organization founded in 1962
Mission: To work with & on behalf of members to meet public policy expectations related to accountability, diversity of educational opportunity, financial self-reliance, & responsiveness to educational & marketplace needs
Finances: *Annual Operating Budget:* Greater than $5 Million
40 volunteer(s)
Membership: 20; *Committees:* Budget & Audit; Executive; Government & Community Relations; Nominations; Relationships with Other Post-Secondary Institutions
Activities: Advocating; Researching; Communicating to public; Processing university applications
Chief Officer(s):
Patrick Deane, Chair
David Lindsay, President & CEO
dlindsay@cou.on.ca
Marina Piao, Executive Director, Corporate Services
mpiao@cou.on.ca
Brian Timney, Executive Director, Quality Assurance
btimney@cou.on.ca
Barbara Hauser, Secretary to Council
bhauser@cou.on.ca

Council of Outdoor Educators of Ontario (COEO)
c/o Sport Alliance Ontario, 3 Concorde Gate, Toronto ON M3C 3N7
info@coeo.org
www.coeo.org
www.facebook.com/coeo
Overview: A medium-sized provincial charitable organization founded in 1969
Mission: To promote outdoor education in a safe manner; to develop environmental awareness of the outdoors; to act as a professional body for outdoor educators in Ontario
Member of: North American Association of Environmental Educators
Finances: *Annual Operating Budget:* Less than $50,000
20 volunteer(s)
Membership: 30 student + 10 senior/lifetime + 200 individual; *Fees:* $35 student; $50 individual; $60 family
Activities: *Speaker Service:* Yes
Meetings/Conferences:
• Council of Outdoor Educators of Ontario Make Peace With Winter 2018, January, 2018, ON
Scope: National
Publications:
• Pathways: The Ontario Journal of Outdoor Education
Type: Journal; *Frequency:* Quarterly

Council of Parent Participation Preschools in British Columbia (CPPPBC)
PO Box 704, 4974 Kingsway, Burnaby BC V5H 4M9
Tel: 604-435-4430
cnclbc@telus.net
www.cpppreschools.bc.ca
www.facebook.com/CouncilOfPPPsInBc
twitter.com/CPPPBC
Overview: A medium-sized provincial organization founded in 1945
Mission: To provide a high standard of education for pre-schoolers (3 & 4 year-olds) & also a planned adult education program, through the co-operative efforts of parents & supervisors
Affiliation(s): Parent Cooperative Preschools International
Staff Member(s): 3; 1500 volunteer(s)
Membership: 39 institutional + 1,500 individual; *Fees:* $60 family metro; $45 family provincial
Chief Officer(s):
Roberta Stuart, Executive Director

Council of Post Secondary Library Directors, British Columbia (CPSLD)
c/o Patricia Cia, Langara College, 100 West 49th Ave., Vancouver BC V5Y 2Z6
Tel: 604-323-5243
www.cpsld.ca
Overview: A small provincial organization
Mission: To represent library directors from British Columbia's post secondary education institutions; To strengthen the post secondary library system in British Columbia to benefit both students & stakeholders
Membership: 27; *Member Profile:* Library directors or chief librarians from not-for-profit post secondary education institutions in British Columbia
Activities: Engaging in advocacy activities; Facilitating communication on issues of common concern
Chief Officer(s):
Patricia Cia, President
pcia@langara.ca
Meetings/Conferences:
• Council of Post Secondary Library Directors, British Columbia Spring 2018 Meeting, May, 2018, Emily Carr University of Art & Design, Vancouver, BC
Scope: Provincial
Description: A meeting held with a program of interest to library directors & chief librarians from not-for-profit post secondary education institutions in British Columbia
Publications:
• CPSLD [Council of Post Secondary Library Directors, British Columbia] Newsletter
Type: Newsletter; *Frequency:* Semiannually; *Editor:* Katherine Plett
Profile: Reports from British Columbia's post secondary institutions

Council of Prairie & Pacific University Libraries (COPPUL)
University of British Columbia, #219, 1958 Main Mall, Vancouver BC V6T 1Z2
Fax: 604-822-9122
www.coppul.ca
twitter.com/coppul
Previous Name: Council of Prairie University Libraries
Overview: A small provincial organization founded in 1968
Mission: To work together to leverage members' collective expertise, resources, & influence; To increase capacity & infrastructure; To enhance learning, teaching, student experiences, & research at member institutions
Finances: *Annual Operating Budget:* $250,000-$500,000; *Funding Sources:* Membership fees
Membership: 22 university libraries + 15 affiliate members; *Fees:* Pro-rated on basis of university operating budget; *Member Profile:* Western university libraries & other university libraries (affiliate member) which support the goals of the Council; *Committees:* Collections; Digital Preservation Working Group; Scholarly Communications Working Group
Chief Officer(s):
Kristina McDavid, Executive Director
execdir@coppul.ca
Awards:
• COPPUL Outstanding Contribution Award
Awarded to honour exemplary contributions to the consortium
Eligibility: Individuals employed by COPPUL member institutions

Council of Prairie University Libraries *See* Council of Prairie & Pacific University Libraries

Council of Private Investigators - Ontario (CPIO)
#300, 10 Milner Business Court, Toronto ON M1B 3C6
Tel: 647-777-8418; *Fax:* 647-777-8301
info@cpiontario.ca
www.cpi-ontario.com
www.facebook.com/1469094056636753
twitter.com/CPIO2014
Previous Name: Association of Investigators & Guard Agencies of Ontario Inc.
Overview: A small provincial organization
Mission: To represent the interests of private investigators in Ontario
Finances: *Annual Operating Budget:* $50,000-$100,000; *Funding Sources:* Membership dues
Membership: 100-499; *Fees:* $70 graduate; $85 individual; $100 associate; $250 agency
Activities: Educational meetings & seminars; industry training; advocacy of professional standards; *Speaker Service:* Yes
Chief Officer(s):
Brian Sartorelli, President
Lloyd Vaughan, Chief Executive Vice-President
Penny Hill, Administrator

The Council of Senior Citizens Organization of British Columbia (COSCO)
c/o Ernie Bayer, Membership Secretary, 6079 - 184A St., Surrey BC V0N 2W5
Tel: 604-576-9734
coscobc.ca
www.facebook.com/317963575008774
Overview: A medium-sized provincial organization
Mission: To co-ordinate and advance issues concerned with the welfare of elder citizens in BC.
Affiliation(s): National Pension Federation
Membership: 85 seniors groups; *Member Profile:* Seniors over 50 years of age
Activities: Workshops
Chief Officer(s):
Lorraine Logan, President, 604-916-5151
president@coscobc.ca

Council of the Haida Nation - Haida Fisheries Program (HFP)
PO Box 589, Stn. Masset, Old Masset BC V0T 1M0
Tel: 250-626-5252; *Fax:* 250-626-3403
Toll-Free: 888-638-7778
www.haidanation.ca/Pages/programs/fisheries.html
Overview: A small local organization
Mission: The Program provides advice to the Council of the Haida Nation about actions, political or otherwise, on the marine habitat & environment. It assesses all commerical/recreational fisheries & any plans affecting marine resources. Its priority is the protection of Aboriginal rights & title of the Haida people.
Activities: Pallant Creek hatchery; Integrated Marine Use Plan; abalone stewardship
Chief Officer(s):
Robert Davis, Treasurer

Council of Ukrainian Credit Unions of Canada
145 Evans Ave., Toronto ON M8Z 5X8
Tel: 416-323-3495; *Fax:* 416-923-7904
info@cucuc.ca
www.cucuc.ca
Also Known As: CUCUC
Overview: A small national organization founded in 1971
Mission: To unite & promote Ukrainian member credit unions in Canada; To assist with the development of credit unions in Ukraine
Membership: 6 credit unions; *Member Profile:* Ukrainian Canadian credit unions
Chief Officer(s):
Olya Sheweli, President

Council of Yukon First Nations (CYFN)
2166 - 2nd Ave., Whitehorse YT Y1A 4P1
Tel: 867-393-9200; *Fax:* 867-668-6577
reception@cyfn.net
www.cyfn.ca
Overview: A small provincial organization
Mission: The Council of Yukon First Nations is the central political organization for the First Nation people of the Yukon. It's mission is to serve the needs of First Nations within the Yukon and the MacKenzie delta.
Membership: 11 Yukon First Nations; *Committees:* Education; Finance & Administration; Circumpolar Relations; Natural Resources & Environment; Self-Government Secretariat; Justice Program; Health & Social; Yukon Native Language Centre; Training Policy; Yukon Aboriginal Sports Circle
Chief Officer(s):
Ruth Massie, Grand Chief
ruth.massie@cyfn.net
Michelle Kolla, Executive Director
michelle.kolla@cyfn.net

The Council on Aging of Ottawa (COA) / Le Conseil sur le vieillissement d'Ottawa (CSV)
#101, 1247 Kilborn Pl., Ottawa ON K1H 6K9
Tel: 613-789-3577; *Fax:* 613-789-4406
coa@coaottawa.ca
www.coaottawa.ca
www.facebook.com/coaottawa
Previous Name: Ottawa-Carleton Council on Aging
Overview: A small local charitable organization founded in 1975
Mission: To enhance the qualilty of life of all seniors in Ottawa; To work with & for seniors in the community to voice issues & concerns to all levels of government & the general public

Finances: Annual Operating Budget: $100,000-$250,000; *Funding Sources:* City of Ottawa; United Way/Centraide Ottawa; Ministry of Health & LTC
Staff Member(s): 5
Membership: 380; *Fees:* $30 individual; $75 organization/agency; $250 corporate; *Member Profile:* Seniors; individuals; community organizations & professionals; *Committees:* Seven standing committees, working groups & projects
Activities: Senior Accessible Health Care Forum; COA Spring Luncheon; AGM; projects & various forums; *Library:* COA Library; Open to public
Chief Officer(s):
John E. Johnson, President

Council on Aging, Windsor - Essex County (COA)
c/o Centres for Seniors Windsor, 635 McEwan Ave., Windsor ON N9B 2E9
Tel: 519-254-9342; *Fax:* 519-254-1869
information@councilonaging.ca
www.councilonaging.ca
Overview: A small local charitable organization founded in 1988
Mission: To enhance the quality of life of seniors in Windsor - Essex County in Ontario; To assist in the development & coordination of services for local seniors
Member of: Provincial Network of Councils
Finances: Funding Sources: Ontario Trillum Foundation; Sponsorships; Fundraising
Activities: Advocating on behalf of seniors; Increasing public awareness about issues related to aging; Conducting research & needs assessments; Providing education; Offering information & referral services; *Speaker Service:* Yes
Chief Officer(s):
Deana Johnson, Executive Director

Council on American-Islamic Relations Canada See National Council of Canadian Muslims

Council on Drug Abuse (CODA)
#120, 215 Spadina Ave., Toronto ON M5T 2C7
Tel: 416-763-1491
info@drugabuse.ca
www.drugabuse.ca
twitter.com/yacers
Overview: A small national charitable organization founded in 1969
Mission: To prevent & reduce substance abuse, primarily among youth, by sponsoring education programs in schools
Finances: Funding Sources: Federal government; foundations; corporations; individual donors
Activities: Speaker Service: Yes; *Library:* by appointment
Chief Officer(s):
Lorraine Patterson, Chair

Council on Palliative Care / Conseil des Soins Palliatifs
3605, rue de la Montagne, Montréal QC H3G 2M1
Tel: 514-845-0795
fmpa202@gmail.com
www.mcgill.ca/council-on-palliative-care
www.facebook.com/CouncilOnPalliativeCare
twitter.com/PalliativeCares
Overview: A small national organization founded in 1994
Mission: To work in association with McGill University to raise public awareness & support of palliative care; To increase the availability of palliative care
Activities: Liaising with healthcare planners, educators, practitioners, & the community; Providing information about palliative care
Chief Officer(s):
Suzanne O'Brien, Co-Chair
John Sanford, Co-Chair
Publications:
• Council on Palliative Care Newsletter
Type: Newsletter
Profile: Council news, articles about palliative care, meeting highlights, & upcoming events

Counselling & Support Services of S.D. & G. / Centre de counselling familial de Cornwall et Comtés unis
26 Montreal Rd., Cornwall ON K6H 1B1
Tel: 613-932-4610; *Fax:* 613-932-5765
admin@css-sdg.ca
www.css-sdg.ca
Previous Name: Family Counselling Centre of Cornwall & United Counties
Overview: A small local organization founded in 1938 overseen by Ontario Association of Credit Counselling Services
Mission: To offer professional credit & family counselling as well as support services to persons in Cornwall & the United Counties; To support adults with a developmental disability to live within the community & to achieve their potential
Member of: United Way; Family Service Ontario
Finances: Funding Sources: Sponsorships; Ministry of Community & Social Services
Activities: Providing educational services; Offering community integration services; Engaging in advocacy activities; Offering counselling in areas such as personal, couple, & family issues; Providing programs, such as the Employee Assistance Program, Creative Coping for Kids & Changing Directions
Chief Officer(s):
Raymond Houde, Executive Director

The Counselling Foundation of Canada
#300, 2 St. Clair Ave. East, Toronto ON M4T 2T5
Tel: 416-923-8953; *Fax:* 416-923-2536
info@counselling.net
www.counselling.net
Overview: A small national organization founded in 1959
Mission: To engage in charitable & educational activities for the benefit of people, thus enabling them to improve their lifestyles & make a more effective contribution to their communities
Affiliation(s): Contact Point
Chief Officer(s):
Donald G. Lawson, Chair
Bruce Lawson, President
blawson@counselling.net
Diana Castro, Office Administrator
diana@counselling.net

Counselling Services of Belleville & District (CSBD)
12 Moira St. East, Belleville ON K8P 2R9
Tel: 613-966-7413; *Fax:* 613-966-2357
csbd@csbd.on.ca
www.csbd.on.ca
Overview: A small local charitable organization founded in 1978 overseen by Family Service Ontario
Mission: To offer behavioural assessment & counselling, advocacy & support to families & individuals.
Affiliation(s): YMCA, for summer camps
Finances: Funding Sources: Government; county; United Way of Quinte; fees, donations
Activities: Adult Protective Services; Autism Intervention Program; Family Court Clinic; Infant & Child Development Program

Counterpoint Community Orchestra
PO Box 41, 552 Church St., Toronto ON M4Y 2E3
Tel: 416-654-9806
info@ccorchestra.org
www.ccorchestra.org
www.facebook.com/CounterpointCommunityOrchestra
twitter.com/CounterpointCCO
Overview: A small local charitable organization founded in 1984 overseen by Orchestras Canada
Mission: To foster pride as a LGBT positive orchestra; to perform for the community & promote equality within Toronto
Member of: Orchestras Canada
Finances: Funding Sources: Toronto Arts Council; Corporate & individual donations
Membership: Committees: Bylaws/Board Development; Concert; Fundraising; Program; Marketing & Promotion; Publishing
Chief Officer(s):
Terry Kowalczuk, Music Director

The County & District Law Presidents' Association See Federation of Ontario Law Associations

County of Perth Law Association
Perth Courthouse, 1 Huron St., Stratford ON N5A 5S4
Tel: 519-271-1871; *Fax:* 519-271-3522
Toll-Free: 866-365-0218
perthlaw@on.aibn.com
www.libraryco.ca/library/county-of-perth-law-association
Overview: A small local organization founded in 1883
Membership: 50; *Member Profile:* Lawyers
Activities: Library: Law Library
Chief Officer(s):
Wendy Hearder-Moan, Library Manager

Couples for Christ Canada (CFC)
#3, 418 Hanlan Rd., Vaughan ON L4L 4Z1
Tel: 905-851-2119
couplesforchrist.ca
www.facebook.com/cfchristcanada
Overview: A small national organization
Mission: To renew & strengthen Christian family life
Affiliation(s): Archdiocese of Toronto
Activities: Conferences; summits; concerts; CFC Youth program; *Awareness Events:* Live Loud, Dec.

Couples for Christ Edmonton
11030 - 127 St., Edmonton AB T5M 3K7
Tel: 780-222-8467
cfc-edmonton.ca

Couples for Christ Montréal

Couples for Christ Vancouver
#250, 2981 Simpson Rd., Richmond BC V6X 2R2
Tel: 604-270-9463; *Fax:* 604-270-6855

Couples for Christ Winnipeg
404 Notre Dame Ave., Winnipeg MB R3B 1R1
Tel: 204-775-7503
www.facebook.com/cfcwinnipeg

Couples For Christ Foundation for Family & Life (CFCFFL)
#7, 2250 Midland Ave., Toronto ON M1P 4R9
Tel: 416-335-3358; *Fax:* 416-335-0051
cfcffl@cfcfflcanada.org
www.cfcfflcanada.org
Overview: A small national charitable organization founded in 2007
Mission: To engage in activities & services which focus on evangelization, family life renewal, & defense of the culture of life; To provide ministries, such as Missions & Evangelization, Social Ministries (work for justice & the poor), Pastoral Support (formation & work for life), & Communities Support (financial, legal, music, & commuications support)
Affiliation(s): Archdiocese of Toronto
Finances: Funding Sources: Donations
Membership: Member Profile: Couples, & single people must attend & complete the Christian Life Seminar (CLS) given by CFCFFL; Youth must attend & complete a Christian Youth Camp given by the Family Ministry of CFCFFL
Activities: Offering prayer groups for youth, singles, & couples; Presenting retreats, seminars, & conferences
Chief Officer(s):
Eden Ben, Country Coordinator
Vuoleen Ben, Country Coordinator

Couples For Christ (CFC)
156 Shorting Rd., Toronto ON M1S 3S6
Tel: 416-321-1937; *Fax:* 416-321-8498
cfctoronto@cfc-canada.org
couplesforchristcanada.ca
Overview: A small national charitable organization founded in 1981
Mission: To provide services, such as evangelization for adults & youth, & family renewal; to offer CFC family ministries, such as CFC Kids For Christ, CFC Youth For Christ, CFC Singles For Christ, CFC Handmaids of the Lord (a community of Christian women helping other women renew & live their Christian faith), & CFC Servants of the Lord (community of men who are either bachelors, married, separated, divorced or widowers); to work with the poor; to ensure governance by the CFC Council in Manila in each country where CFC exists
Affiliation(s): Archdiocese of Toronto
Finances: Funding Sources: Donations
Membership: Member Profile: Couples & single people who desire to join the CFC ministries must attend a Christian Life Program, which focuses on lay & family viewpoints; Graduates of the Christian Life Program apply for membership & must be approved by the area council; For teens & young children, weekend camps are held; CFC members are part of an association recognized by the Council of the Pontifical Laity as an International Association of the Lay Faithful
Activities: Counselling; Providing faith instruction & prayer groups; Offering marriage preparation & family planning services; Assisting immigrants & refugees through Immigrant & Refugee Centres; Offering religious goods & books; Helping the separated, divorced, & widowed; Providing study centres; Hosting monthly assemblies; Assisting the parish in any capacity given by the parish priest; Conducting RCIA & prolife activities; Presenting Christian Life Programs & pastoral formation teachings
Chief Officer(s):
Fulgencio (Sonny) Bautista, Contact

Courtenay & District Historical Society
207 - 4th St., Courtenay BC V9N 1G7
Tel: 250-334-0686; *Fax:* 250-338-0619
museum@island.net
www.courtenaymuseum.ca
www.facebook.com/courtenaymuseum
twitter.com/courtenaymuseum
www.youtube.com/user/courtenaymuseum
Also Known As: Courtenay & District Museum & Archives
Overview: A small local charitable organization founded in 1953
Mission: To maintain the museum of local historic & palaeontological artifacts.
Member of: Canadian Museums Association; BC Museums Association
Affiliation(s): British Columbia Paleontological Alliance; Comox Valley Naturalists Society; Royal Tyrrell Museum; Comox Valley Family History Group; Comox Valley Tourism; Downtown Courtenay
Membership: *Fees:* $21 single; $31.50 family; $52.50 corporate; $210 life
Activities: Capes Escape, the museum's 1930s style home; *Library:* Research Centre; Open to public by appointment

Courtenay Gem & Mineral Club
2616 Mabley Rd., Courtenay BC V9N 9K2
Tel: 250-703-3444
Overview: A small local organization
Member of: British Columbia Lapidary Society
Activities: Meetings 3rd Tues. of every month
Chief Officer(s):
Russell Ball, Contact
dj_fossil@hotmail.com

Courtiers indépendants en sécurité financière du Canada
See Independent Financial Brokers of Canada

Covenant Foundation
3C60 - 11111 Jasper Ave. NW, Edmonton AB T5K 0L4
Tel: 780-342-8126
Toll-Free: 866-342-8126
info@caritasfoundation.ca
covenantfoundation.ca
Previous Name: The Caritas Foundation
Overview: A small local charitable organization founded in 1994
Mission: To raise funds to support 15 Covenant Health facilities across the province of Alberta
Affiliation(s): Covenant Health
Finances: *Funding Sources:* Donations; fundraising
Chief Officer(s):
Tracy Sopkow, Chief Executive Officer, 780-342-8038, Fax: 780-342-8195
tracy.sopkow@covenanthealth.ca
Laura Ruddock, Director, Philanthropy, 780-342-8303
laura.ruddock@covenanthealth.ca
Andrea Donini, Senior Manager, Communications, 780-342-8978
Andrea.Donini@covenanthealth.ca

Covenant Health (ACHC)
3033 - 66 St. NW, Edmonton AB T6K 4B2
Tel: 780-735-9000
www.covenanthealth.ca
Previous Name: Catholic Health of Alberta
Overview: A small provincial organization
Mission: To be a part of the healing mission of Jesus by serving with compassion
Membership: 12 Catholic health care facilities
Chief Officer(s):
Patrick Dumelie, CEO
Owen Heisler, Vice President & Chief Medical Officer, Medicine
Rosa Rudelich, Vice President & Chief Operating Officer
Karen Galenzoski, Vice President & Human Resources Officer
Gordon Self, Vice President, Mission, Ethics & Spirituality

Covenant House Toronto
20 Gerrard St. East, Toronto ON M5B 2P3
Tel: 416-598-4898; *Fax:* 416-204-7030
Toll-Free: 800-435-7308
www.covenanthousetoronto.ca
www.linkedin.com/company/covenant-house-toronto
www.facebook.com/covenanthousetoronto
twitter.com/covenanthouseto
www.youtube.com/user/covenanthousetoronto
Overview: A large local charitable organization founded in 1982
Mission: To provide a crisis shelter for homeless & runaway youth who are 16 to 21 years of age; To offer assessment, counselling, & referral services
Affiliation(s): Covenant House International
Finances: *Annual Operating Budget:* Greater than $5 Million; *Funding Sources:* Donations; Municipal funding; ShareLife
Activities: *Awareness Events:* Covenant House Month, Feb.; GMP Capital Inc. Wine & Dine Gala, June; Sleep Out for Street Kids; *Speaker Service:* Yes
Chief Officer(s):
Bruce Rivers, Executive Director
Tracie LeBlanc, Contact, Communications
tleblanc@covenanthouse.ca
Publications:
• Good Samaritan News [a publication of Covenant House Toronto]
Type: Newsletter

Coverdale Centre for Women Inc.
10 Culloden Court, Saint John NB E2L 3B9
Tel: 506-634-1649; *Fax:* 506-634-1647
coverdaleprograms@gmail.ca
www.coverdalecenterforwomen.com
Overview: A small local organization
Mission: Coverdale Center for Women Inc. provides programs and services for women including self-development programs in groups and individual counseling. It is a drop-in center where women can find support, referrals to community services, general counseling, addiction counselling, positive recreation, and self-improvement courses.
Activities: *Awareness Events:* International Women's Month; Purple Ribbon Campaign
Chief Officer(s):
Mary Saulnier-Taylor, Executive Director, 506-634-0840
mary@coverdalecenterforwomen.ca

Cowichan Intercultural Society
#205, 394 Duncan St., Duncan BC V9L 3W4
Tel: 250-748-3112
office@cis-iwc.org
www.cisduncan.ca
www.facebook.com/177342358949472
twitter.com/CISiwc
www.youtube.com/user/interculturalsociety
Previous Name: Cowichan Valley Intercultural & Immigrant Aid Society
Overview: A small local organization founded in 1981
Mission: To provide services & support to new Canadians to help them integrate into the Cowichan Valley communities.
Member of: Affiliation of Multicultural Societies & Service Agencies of BC
Finances: *Annual Operating Budget:* $500,000-$1.5 Million; *Funding Sources:* Federal, provincial governments; donations; special events; affinitive progams
Staff Member(s): 18; 167 volunteer(s)
Membership: *Fees:* $10 individual; $15 family; $30 corporate
Activities: ESL classes; employment assistance; children's summer programs
Chief Officer(s):
Lynn Weaver, Executive Director
lynn@cis-iwc.org

Cowichan Lake District Chamber of Commerce
PO Box 824, 125C South Shore Rd., Lake Cowichan BC V0R 2G0
Tel: 250-749-3244; *Fax:* 250-749-0187
info@cowichanlake.ca
www.cowichanlake.ca
Overview: A small local organization founded in 1946
Affiliation(s): Canadian Chamber of Commerce
Finances: *Annual Operating Budget:* Less than $50,000; *Funding Sources:* Donations; membership dues
Staff Member(s): 1
Membership: 62; *Fees:* $80-$180; *Committees:* Breakfast on the Town; Heritage Days; Shop Talk; Sunshine; Tourist Information
Activities: Daffy Daze, Apr.; Heritage Dayz, May; Lake Days, June; December Madness & Santa Parade

Cowichan Therapeutic Riding Association (CRTA)
c/o Providence Farm, 1843 Tzouhalem Rd., Duncan BC V9L 5L6
Tel: 250-746-1028; *Fax:* 250-746-1033
info@ctra.ca
www.ctra.ca
www.facebook.com/cowichantherapeuticridingassociation
instagram.com/cowichantherapeuticriding
Overview: A small local charitable organization founded in 1985
Mission: To use horses to help persons with various disabilities in the Cowichan area of British Columbia achieve physical & mental health, behavioral, communication, cognitive, & social goals; To provide therapeutic or sporting activities in a safe environment with qualified instruction in order to improve the quality of life for persons with disabilities
Staff Member(s): 16; 85 volunteer(s)
Activities: Receiving referrals from doctors, psychologists, physiotherapists, schools, & other health care organizations; Offering individualized riding programs; Providing a training program & workplace for persons with barriers to employment; Educating the public to see the contributions of persons with disabilities
Publications:
• The Leading Rein
Type: Newsletter; *Accepts Advertising*
Profile: Updates from the association, including a calendar of events, & information on upcoming riding programs

Cowichan United Way
1 Kenneth Place, Duncan BC V9L 5G3
Tel: 250-748-1312; *Fax:* 250-748-7652
Toll-Free: 877-748-1312
office@cowichan.unitedway.ca
www.cowichan.unitedway.ca
www.facebook.com/UnitedWayCowichan
twitter.com/uwcowichan
Overview: A small local charitable organization founded in 1976 overseen by United Way of Canada - Centraide Canada
Mission: To fundraise for charities; To provide guidance & counsel to charitable organization; To take leadership role in raising awareness of community needs
Staff Member(s): 3
Activities: Fundraises for 21 local community organizations; *Speaker Service:* Yes
Chief Officer(s):
Mike Murphy, President
Heather Gardiner, Interim Advisor
hgardiner@cowichan.unitedway.ca

Cowichan Valley Arts Council
2687 James St., 2nd Fl., Duncan BC V9L 2X5
Tel: 250-746-1633
cvartscouncil@shaw.ca
www.cowichanvalleyartscouncil.ca
www.facebook.com/cowichanvalleyartscouncil.ca
Overview: A small local organization founded in 1971
Mission: The Council is a non-profit organization that promotes the understanding & appreciation of art among local residents, & encourages the community to participate in artistic activities. It is a registered charity, BN: 867654022RR0001.
Member of: Assembly of BC Arts Councils
Finances: *Funding Sources:* British Columbia Arts Council
Staff Member(s): 2; 130 volunteer(s)
Membership: 250; *Fees:* $20 individual; $10 student; $35 family; $40 group; $50 business
Activities: Cowichan Valley Arts Centre
Chief Officer(s):
Gail Robertson, President

Cowichan Valley Association for Community Living *See* Clements Centre Society

Cowichan Valley Basket Society
5810 Garden St., Duncan BC V9L 3V9
Tel: 250-746-1566
cvbs@shaw.ca
www.cvbs.ca
www.facebook.com/285894211554071
Overview: A small local charitable organization founded in 1988 overseen by Food Banks British Columbia
Mission: To provide food to the needy in the Cowichan Valley.
Member of: Food Banks British Columbia
Affiliation(s): Food Banks Canada
Finances: *Funding Sources:* Donations
Chief Officer(s):
Colleen Fuller, Manager

Cowichan Valley Intercultural & Immigrant Aid Society *See* Cowichan Intercultural Society

Cowichan Valley Naturalists' Society (CVNS)
#6, 55 Station St., Duncan BC V9L 1M2
Tel: 250-746-6141
cvns@naturecowichan.net
www.naturecowichan.net/CVNS
Overview: A small local organization founded in 1962

Affiliation(s): BC Nature: The Federation of British Columbia Naturalists
Membership: *Fees:* $30 individuals; $35 families of Young Naturalists Club members; $45 families; *Member Profile:* Naturalists in the Cowichan Valley of British Columbia
Activities: Providing educational programs; Organizing nature hikes
Chief Officer(s):
John Scull, Contact
Publications:
• Valley Naturalist [a publication of the Cowichan Valley Naturalists' Society]
Type: Newsletter; *Price:* Free with memberships in the Cowichan Valley Naturalists' Society
Profile: Information & events for naturalists in the Cowichan Valley

CP24 CHUM Christmas Wish
Bell Media, 299 Queen St. West, Toronto ON M5V 2Z5
Tel: 416-384-4199
thewish@bellmedia.ca
www.ctv.ca/TheWish
Previous Name: CHUM Charitable Foundation; CHUM's Kid's Crusade Foundation
Overview: A small local charitable organization founded in 1966
Mission: To provide financial assistance to charitable organizations and social service agencies
Activities: CP24/CHUM Christmas Wish

CPE du Carrefour
2355, rue Provençale, Montréal QC H2K 4P9
Tél: 514-526-8444
www.cpeducarrefour.qc.ca
Nom précédent: Garderie du Carrefour
Aperçu: *Dimension:* petite; *Envergure:* locale; fondée en 1979
Mission: De fournir des soins de qualité et une éducation aux enfants
Membre(s) du bureau directeur:
André Rémillard, Directeur général

CPJ Corp. (CPJ)
#501, 309 Cooper St., Ottawa ON K2P 0G5
Tel: 613-232-0275; *Fax:* 613-232-1275
Toll-Free: 800-667-8046
cpj@cpj.ca
www.cpj.ca
www.facebook.com/citizensforpublicjustice
twitter.com/publicjustice
www.youtube.com/user/c4pj
Previous Name: Citizens for Public Justice
Overview: A medium-sized national charitable organization founded in 1963
Mission: To promote public justice in Canada byshaping key public policy debates through research & analysis, publishing & public dialogue; CPJ encourages citizens, leaders in society & governments to support policies & practices which reflect God's call for love, justice & stewardship
Finances: *Funding Sources:* Membership dues; donations; grants
Staff Member(s): 10
Membership: *Fees:* $50 regular; $25 low income; $10 students
Activities: *Internships:* Yes; *Speaker Service:* Yes; *Library:* by appointment
Chief Officer(s):
Joe Gunn, Executive Director
joe@cpj.ca

The CPR Stockholder's Society
6084 Millwoods Rd. South, Edmonton AB T6L 1N5
Overview: A small local organization founded in 1980
Mission: To perpetuate the memory of fictional detective Sherlock Holmes of Baker St.; to study & discuss detective fiction & (English) Victorian Age in general; to enjoy social activities related to foregoing; Society's name taken from a reference to Canadian Pacific Railroad in a Sherlock Holmes story
Affiliation(s): The Baker Street Irregulars of New York; The Bootmakers of Toronto; The Sherlock Holmes Society of London - UK
Finances: *Annual Operating Budget:* Less than $50,000
4 volunteer(s)
Membership: 20 individual; *Fees:* $10; *Member Profile:* Interest in Sherlock Holmes, other writings of Arthur Conan Doyle & the Victorian period in England
Activities: *Three dinner meetings; three occasional meetings annually*
Chief Officer(s):
David Graves, Contact

Craft Council of British Columbia (CCBC)
Granville Island, 1386 Cartwright St., Vancouver BC V6H 3R8
Tel: 604-687-6511
contact_us@craftcouncilbc.ca
www.cabc.net
www.linkedin.com/company/craft-council-of-bc
www.facebook.com/craftcouncilbc
twitter.com/CraftCouncilBC
pinterest.com/craftcouncilbc; www.instagram.com/craftcouncilbc
Previous Name: Craftsmen's Association of British Columbia
Overview: A small provincial charitable organization founded in 1973
Mission: To develop excellence in crafts
Affiliation(s): British Columbia Arts Council; Canada Council for the Arts; Canadian Crafts Federation; Granville Island Business & Community Association
Finances: *Annual Operating Budget:* $250,000-$500,000; *Funding Sources:* Donations; Programs; Supporting Organizations
Staff Member(s): 4; 30 volunteer(s)
Membership: 500 individual + 50 organizations; *Fees:* Schedule available; *Member Profile:* Crafts people; Supporters; Guilds
Activities: Organizing exhibitions & lectures; *Internships:* Yes
Library: Resource Centre
Chief Officer(s):
Raine McKay, Executive Director
Awards:
• Grace Cameron Rogers Scholarship
• Hilde Gerson Award
• Filberg Professional Development Bursary

Craft Council of Newfoundland & Labrador
Devon House, 59 Duckworth St., St. John's NL A1C 1E6
Tel: 709-753-2749; *Fax:* 709-753-2766
info@craftcouncil.nl.ca
www.craftcouncil.nl.ca
www.facebook.com/CraftCouncilNL
twitter.com/CraftCouncilNL
www.flickr.com/photos/craftcouncilnl
Previous Name: Newfoundland & Labrador Crafts Development Association
Overview: A small provincial organization founded in 1972
Mission: To produce high quality work; To assist & advise members in wide variety of craft-related areas
Member of: Canadian Crafts Federation
Finances: *Annual Operating Budget:* $500,000-$1.5 Million
Staff Member(s): 9; 100 volunteer(s)
Membership: 300; *Fees:* $30 student; $80 general; $95 marketing; *Committees:* Standards; Clay; Awards
Activities: *Speaker Service:* Yes; *Library*
Chief Officer(s):
Rowena House, Executive Director
rhouse@craftcouncil.nl.ca
Publications:
• Craft Council [a publication of the Craft Council of Newfoundland & Labrador]
Type: Newsletter; *Frequency:* bi-monthly

Craftsmen's Association of British Columbia *See* Craft Council of British Columbia

Cranbrook & District Arts Council (CDAC)
#104, 135 - 10 Ave. South, Cranbrook BC V1C 2N1
Tel: 250-426-4223; *Fax:* 250-426-4223
cdac@shaw.ca
www.cranbrookanddistrictartscouncil.com
www.facebook.com/CranbrookArtsCouncil
Overview: A small local charitable organization founded in 1973
Mission: To provide arts education through exhibitions, gallery shows & festivals, theatre performances & literary work
Member of: Assembly of BC Arts Councils
Staff Member(s): 1
Membership: *Fees:* $5; *Member Profile:* Artists of all disciplines; arts organizations & individuals
Activities: VisArts; Y-ART, Youth-Art (Young Artist Revealing Talent); Art Walk; Literary Arts; Performing Arts; Arts Education; Visual Arts & Special Events; *Speaker Service:* Yes; *Library:* Resource Library; Open to public
Chief Officer(s):
Mitchell Pocha, President

Cranbrook & District Chamber of Commerce
Cranbrook & District Chamber of Commerce, PO Box 84, Cranbrook BC V1C 4H6
Tel: 250-426-5914; *Fax:* 250-426-3873
Toll-Free: 800-222-6174
info@cranbrookchamber.com
www.cranbrookchamber.com
www.facebook.com/cranbrookchamber
twitter.com/cranbrookchambr
Overview: A medium-sized local organization founded in 1910
Mission: To promote the community & its businessess; To protect the interests of businesses; To attract new businesses to the area
Member of: British Columbia Chamber of Commerce; Canadian Chamber of Commerce
Staff Member(s): 4
Membership: 500; *Fees:* Schedule available
Chief Officer(s):
David Struthers, President
David Hull, Executive Director

Cranbrook Archives, Museum & Landmark Foundation (CMRT)
PO Box 400, Cranbrook BC V1C 4H9
Tel: 250-489-3918; *Fax:* 250-489-5744
mail@trainsdeluxe.com
www.trainsdeluxe.com
Also Known As: The Canadian Museum of Rail Travel
Overview: A medium-sized local charitable organization founded in 1976
Mission: To restore & preserve Canada's Railway Heritage through the collection, restoration & exhibition of vintage CPR passenger train sets, interpretive & Royal Cars of State currrently totaling 28 cars & the three-storey high restored Cafe from the former CPR "Royal Alexandra Hotel" of Winnipeg, Manitoba (1906), presently displayed at new larger site on Hwy. 3/95
Member of: BC Museums Association; Canadian Museum Association; BC Heritage Association; Canadian Council for Rail Heritage
Finances: *Funding Sources:* Federal, provincial, municipal, individual & corporate donations; fundraising; tour ticket & gift shop sales
Staff Member(s): 3
Activities: Guided tours restored luxury trains & the Royal Alexandra Hall (1906); annual gala fundraising gourmet dinner, Nov.; gift shop; special events annually; Heritage Dinner, early Sept.; *Library:* Cranbrook Historical Archives & Library; Open to public
Chief Officer(s):
Garry W. Anderson, Executive Director/CEO

Cranbrook Food Bank Society
104 - 8th Ave. South, Cranbrook BC V1C 2K5
Tel: 250-426-7664
Overview: A small local organization overseen by Food Banks British Columbia
Mission: To distribute food to the needy in the local area.
Member of: Food Banks British Columbia; Food Banks Canada

Cranbrook Society for Community Living (CSCL)
Cranbrook Community Living Center, 22 - 14th Ave. South, Cranbrook BC V1C 2W8
Tel: 250-426-7588; *Fax:* 250-426-7990
info@cranbrookscl.ca
www.cranbrookscl.ca
www.facebook.com/cranbrooksociety
Overview: A small local charitable organization founded in 1956
Mission: CSCL is a non-profit society that supports individuals with developmental delays & their families, helping them to live & participate in the community. It is CARF-accredited.
Member of: Kootenay Society for Community Living
Affiliation(s): Community Living BC; Interior Health Authority; College of the Rockies
Staff Member(s): 100
Activities: *Library:* Open to public
Chief Officer(s):
Margaret Laidlaw, Executive Director

Crane Rental Association of Canada
PO Box 26, Regina SK S4P 2Z5
Tel: 306-585-2722; *Fax:* 306-584-3566
Toll-Free: 855-680-2722
info@crac-canada.com
www.crac-canada.com
Overview: A small national organization
Mission: The Crane Rental Association of Canada is dedicated to providing a social and educational forum to advance safety and professional expertise to the Canadian Industry.
Chief Officer(s):

Jean-Louis Lapointe, Chair
Meetings/Conferences:
• Crane Rental Association of Canada 2018 Conference, June, 2018, Fort Garry Hotel, Winnipeg, MB
Scope: National

Creation Science Association of British Columbia
PO Box 39577, RPO White Rock, Surrey BC V4A 0A9
Tel: 604-535-0019
info@creationbc.org
www.creationbc.org
Overview: A small provincial charitable organization founded in 1968
Mission: To compile scientific as well as Biblical evidence that supports creation & contradicts evolution; To communicate this information to schools, churches & the general public
Finances: *Annual Operating Budget:* Less than $50,000
25 volunteer(s)
Membership: 125 individual; *Fees:* $15 individual
Activities: *Speaker Service:* Yes; *Library:* DVD Lending Library; by appointment
Chief Officer(s):
George Pearce, President

Creation Science of Saskatchewan Inc. (CSSI)
PO Box 26, Kenaston SK S0G 2N0
Tel: 306-252-2842; *Fax:* 306-252-2842
www.creation-science.sk.ca
Overview: A small provincial charitable organization founded in 1978
Mission: To collect, organize & distribute information on Creation; To develop a better public understanding of Creation; To prepare & promote resource material on scientific creation for educational use & to be used in school curricula
Finances: *Annual Operating Budget:* Less than $50,000; *Funding Sources:* Donations
13 volunteer(s)
Membership: 15 institutional + 140 individual; *Fees:* $10
Activities: Meetings; Speakers; Book tables; Tours; Summer camp; *Speaker Service:* Yes; *Library:* Creation Science of Saskatchewan Library; by appointment
Chief Officer(s):
Keith Miller, President

Creative BC (CRBC)
2225 West Broadway, Vancouver BC V6K 2E4
Tel: 604-736-7997; *Fax:* 604-736-7290
info@creativebc.com
www.creativebc.com
www.facebook.com/creativebcs
twitter.com/creativebcs
Merged from: BC Film Commission; BC Film + Media
Overview: A small provincial organization founded in 2013
Mission: To promote the creative industries in British Columbia, including film, music, publishing & digital
Staff Member(s): 18
Activities: *Internships:* Yes
Chief Officer(s):
Prem Gill, Chief Executive Officer
pgill@creativebc.com
Robert Wong, Vice-President
bwong@creativebc.com
Karin Watson, Director, Business Operations
kwatson@creativebc.com
Awards:
• MPPIA Short Film Award
Eligibility: Emerging BC filmmaker; *Amount:* $15,000, + production services of $100,000

Creative Jewellers Guild of BC (CJG)
Richmond Cultural Centre, 7700 Minoru Gate, Richmond BC V6Y 1R9
info@creativejewellersguild.com
creativejewellersguild.com
Overview: A small provincial organization founded in 1957
Mission: To encourage & teach members in the design & creation of jewellery, keeping them abreast of new techniques & products.
Member of: Lapidary Society of BC; Metal Arts Guild of Canada
Affiliation(s): Gem & Mineral Federation of Canada
Membership: *Fees:* $35; $50 couple; *Member Profile:* People related to creating traditional & contemporary jewlery
Activities: BC Rock & Mineral Show; meetings on 3rd Sun. every month; *Internships:* Yes; *Library:* Not open to public

Credit Association of Greater Toronto (CAGT)
c/o Equifax Canada Co., 5700 Yonge St., 15th Fl., Toronto ON M2M 4K2
Tel: 416-227-5242; *Fax:* 416-227-8661
kerina@cagt.ca
www.cagt.ca
Overview: A small national organization founded in 1944
Mission: To offer members a forum for sharing information & expertise
Membership: 69 companies; *Fees:* $375 corporate; $150 small business; *Committees:* Membership; Logistics; Communications; Professional Development; Program; Marketing; Sponsorship
Activities: Networking/educational sessions; dinner meetings
Chief Officer(s):
Jeff Schwartz, President
jeff@consolidatedcredit.ca
Kerina Cumming, Executive Assistant
kerina@cagt.ca
Publications:
• News & Views [a publication of the Credit Association of Greater Toronto]
Type: Newsletter

Credit Canada Debt Solutions, Inc.
#810, 45 Sheppard Ave. East, Toronto ON M2N 5W9
Tel: 416-228-3328
Toll-Free: 800-267-2272
info@creditcanada.com
creditcanada.com
www.facebook.com/creditcanada
twitter.com/creditcanada
www.youtube.com/creditcanada
Also Known As: Credit Canada
Previous Name: Credit Counselling Service of Toronto
Overview: A medium-sized national charitable organization founded in 1966
Mission: To help people get out of debt; To provide professional money management & credit management counselling, personal debt consolidation & resolutions, preventative counselling, educational services, & tools & resources in the areas of budgeting, financial goal-setting, & everyday money management; Serves nationally across Canada
Member of: Credit Counselling Canada
Staff Member(s): 40
Activities: Debt consolidation & credit building, & free credit & debt counselling; Money management, budgeting, & educational seminars; *Awareness Events:* Credit Education Week; *Speaker Service:* Yes
Chief Officer(s):
Keith Emery, Director, Operations, 416-228-2541
kemery@creditcanada.com
Adriana Molina, Manager, Marketing, 416-228-3328 Ext. 8085
amolina@creditcanada.com
Philip Brown, Contact, Client Services, 416-228-2517
pbrown@creditcanada.com
Publications:
• Credit Canada Newsletter [a publication of Credit Canada Debt Solutions, Inc.]
Type: Newsletter; *Price:* Free
Profile: Practical money management tips, plus current information about Credit Canada & the credit industry

> **SOS Dettes - Solutions à l'endettement**
> 1547 Merivale Rd., Nepean ON K2G 4V3
> *Tél:* 514-375-0138
> Ligne sans frais: 866-615-1226
> info@sosdettes.ca
> www.sosdettes.ca

Credit Counselling Canada (CCC) / Conseil en crédit du Canada
#1600, 401 Bay St., Toronto ON M5H 2Y4
Toll-Free: 866-398-5999
contact@creditcounsellingcanada.ca
www.creditcounsellingcanada.ca
twitter.com/Creditcc
www.youtube.com/channel/UCj1dgARyEE1aya5RtJxvuUw
Overview: A medium-sized national organization founded in 2000
Mission: To ensure all Canadians have access to not-for-profit credit counselling; to ensure a quality of service is provided to Canadians by member agencies; to advocate on issues relevant to money management & the wise use of credit along with public policy & legislative issues around these; to promote awareness of the existence & availability of non-profit credit counselling; to cultivate positive working relationships with stakeholders
Membership: *Member Profile:* Not-for-profit credit counselling agencies & Orderly Payment of Debt programs from all across Canada

Credit Counselling Canada - Manitoba *See* Community Financial Counselling Services

Credit Counselling of Regional Niagara (CCRN)
264 Welland Ave., St Catharines ON L2R 2P8
Tel: 905-684-9401; *Fax:* 905-687-9904
Toll-Free: 800-663-3973
info@ccrn.ca
www.ccrn.ca
Overview: A small local charitable organization founded in 1975 overseen by Ontario Association of Credit Counselling Services
Mission: To provide confidential financial, credit, & bankruptcy counselling to persons throughout Ontario's Niagara Region
Member of: Ontario Association of Credit Counselling Services; Credit Counselling Canada; United Way
Finances: *Funding Sources:* United Way; Client fees; Creditors
Activities: Arranging debt repayment programs with creditors; Assisting with rent arrears through the Rent Bank Program; Helping clients with budget development; Offering consumer education & community outreach; Operating Project Share in Niagara Falls & Employment Help Centres in Welland & Grimsby
Chief Officer(s):
Bob Lawler, Executive Director
Birgit Bedesky, Administrator & Counsellor, Rent Bank
Marni Dubiel, Administrator, Trust
Kathleen Batstone, Coordinator, Education

Credit Counselling Service of Sault Ste. Marie & District
298 Queen St. East, Sault Ste Marie ON P6A 1Y7
Tel: 705-254-1424; *Fax:* 705-254-2541
info@creditcounsellingssm.ca
www.creditcounsellingssm.ca
Overview: A small local charitable organization founded in 1969 overseen by Ontario Association of Credit Counselling Services
Mission: To provide confidential financial counselling to persons in Sault Ste Marie & the surrounding area
Member of: Ontario Association of Credit Counselling Services (OACCS); Canadian Association of Credit Counselling Services; United Way of Sault Ste. Marie
Finances: *Funding Sources:* Ontario Trillium Foundation
Activities: Offering alternatives to bankruptcy; Liaising with creditors; Creating debt repayment plans; Assisting with budget planning; Providing consumer education
Publications:
• Common Cents
Type: Newsletter; *Frequency:* Quarterly
Profile: Practical information about financial concerns

Credit Counselling Service of Toronto *See* Credit Canada Debt Solutions, Inc.

Credit Counselling Services of Alberta *See* Money Mentors

Credit Counselling Services of Atlantic Canada, Inc. (CCSAC)
Saint John Office, 20 Alma St., Saint John NB E2L 5G6
Tel: 506-652-1613; *Fax:* 506-633-6057
Toll-Free: 888-753-2227
ccsinfo@solveyourdebts.com
www.solveyourdebts.com
www.facebook.com/solveyourdebts
twitter.com/SolveYourDebts
www.youtube.com/user/SolveYourDebts
Also Known As: CCS of Atlantic Canada, Inc.
Overview: A medium-sized local organization founded in 1994
Member of: Credit Counselling Canada
Chief Officer(s):
John D. Eisner, President, 888-753-2227 Ext. 204
john@solveyourdebts.com

> **New Brunswick - Fredericton**
> #115, 535 Beaverbrook Crt., Fredericton NB E3B 1X6
> *Fax:* 506-453-0564
> *Toll-Free:* 888-753-2227
> ccsinfo@solveyourdebts.com
>
> **New Brunswick - Moncton**
> #103, 1010 St. George Blvd., Moncton NB E2L 5G6
> *Fax:* 506-382-5910
> *Toll-Free:* 888-753-2227
> ccsinfo@solveyourdebts.com
>
> **Nova Scotia - Dartmouth**
> Metropolitan Place, #102, 99 Wyse Rd., Dartmouth NS B3A 4S5

Canadian Associations / Credit Counselling Services of Cochrane District

Fax: 902-455-0947
Toll-Free: 888-753-2227
ccsinfo@solveyourdebts.com

Nova Scotia - New Glasgow
Aberdeen Mall, #235, 610 East River Rd., New Glasgow NS B2H 3S2
Fax: 902-752-8153
Toll-Free: 888-753-2227
ccsinfo@solveyourdebts.com

Nova Scotia - Sydney
Medical Arts Building, #112, 336 King's Rd., Sydney NS B1S 1A9
Fax: 902-564-0448
Toll-Free: 888-753-2227
ccsinfo@solveyourdebts.com

Nova Scotia - Truro
Bank of Montreal Building, #312, 35 Commercial St., Truro NS B2N 3H9
Fax: 902-895-0334
Toll-Free: 888-753-2227
ccsinfo@solveyourdebts.com

Prince Edward Island - Charlottetown
#203, 342 Grafton St., Charlottetown PE C1A 1L8
Fax: 902-892-1477
Toll-Free: 888-753-2227
ccsinfo@solveyourdebts.com

Credit Counselling Services of Cochrane District
#310, 60 Wilson Ave., Timmins ON P4N 2S7
Tel: 705-267-5817
Toll-Free: 866-267-5817
creditcanada.com/credit-counselling-in-timmins
Overview: A small local charitable organization founded in 1977 overseen by Ontario Association of Credit Counselling Services
Mission: To assist persons in Timmins & the surrounding region with their financial difficulties
Member of: Ontario Association of Credit Counselling Service (OACCS); Porcupine United Way
Finances: Funding Sources: Ontario Trillium Foundation
Activities: Helping persons find solutions to their financial problems; Providing creditor intervention services; Offering debt management programs; Providing money management education to students, from elementary to post-secondary; Offering seminars to local businesses, community groups, & the public
Chief Officer(s):
Mitch Gauthier, Executive Director
ccsmitch@ntl.sympatico.ca

Credit Counselling Services of Newfoundland & Labrador
22 Queen's Rd., St. John's NL A1C 2A5
Tel: 709-753-5812; Fax: 709-753-3390
Toll-Free: 888-738-3328
info@ccsnl.ca
www.ccsnl.ca
www.facebook.com/CreditCounsellingServicesNL
twitter.com/CCSNLTweets
Also Known As: Credit & Debt Solutions
Overview: A small provincial organization founded in 1983
Mission: To help spread financial well being through counselling & education
Member of: Credit Counselling Canada
Affiliation(s): Ontario Association of Credit Counselling Services
Finances: Funding Sources: Credit Grantors
Staff Member(s): 4
Chief Officer(s):
Al Antle, Executive Director
aantle@ccsnl.ca
Awards:
• Fifield/Halley Memorial Award
Eligibility: First year college & university students Deadline: November 30; Amount: $300; $400; $500

Corner Brook Office
#407, 9 Main St., Corner Brook NL A0H 6G7
Tel: 709-634-7772; Fax: 709-634-7790
Chief Officer(s):
Karen Milley, Contact
kmilley@ccsnl.ca

Credit Counselling Services of Southwestern Ontario See Financial Fitness Centre

Credit Counselling Society
#440, 88 - 6th St., New Westminster BC V3L 5B3
Tel: 604-527-8999; Fax: b04-527-8008
Toll-Free: 888-527-8999
info@nomoredebts.org
www.nomoredebts.org
www.facebook.com/nomoredebts
twitter.com/nomoredebts_org
www.youtube.com/user/CreditCounsellingSoc
Overview: A small provincial organization overseen by Credit Counselling Canada
Mission: To help consumers resolve debt & money problems & gain control over their finances
Member of: Credit Counselling Canada
Activities: For services in Nanaimo: 201 Selby St.; and in Victoria: 547 Michigan St. For both locations call 1-888-527-8999
Chief Officer(s):
Scott Hannah, President & CEO

Abbotsford
#209, 2316 McCallum Rd., Abbotsford BC V2S 3P4
Tel: 604-859-5757
Toll-Free: 888-527-8999

Burnaby
Central Park Business Centre, #300, 3665 Kingsway, Vancouver BC V5R 5W2
Tel: 604-527-8999

Calgary
#210, 1935 - 32 Ave. NE, Calgary AB T2E 7C8
Tel: 403-263-9905
Toll-Free: 888-527-8999

Delta - Surrey
#228, 7164 - 120th St., Surrey BC V3W 3M8
Tel: 604-527-8999

Edmonton
#610, 10216 - 124 St. NW, Edmonton AB T5N 4A3
Tel: 780-701-0083
Toll-Free: 888-527-8999

Hamilton
#906, 20 Hughson St. South, Hamilton ON L8N 2A1
Tel: 905-538-5035
Toll-Free: 888-527-8999

Kelowna
Stewart Centre Building, #230, 1855 Kirschner Rd., Kelowna BC V1Y 4N7
Tel: 250-860-3000
Toll-Free: 888-527-8999

London
City Centre Building, Tower B, 6th Floor, #651, 380 Wellington St., London ON N6A 5B5
Tel: 519-286-0801
Toll-Free: 888-527-8999

Nanaimo
Oceanview Executive Centre, #203, 335 Wesley St., Nanaimo BC V9R 2T5
Tel: 250-741-8558
Toll-Free: 888-527-8999

Ottawa
#514, 130 Albert St., Ottawa ON K1P 5G4
Tel: 613-234-0505

Port Coquitlam
Tri-City Business Centre, #2300, 2850 Shaughnessy St., Port Coquitlam BC V3C 6K5
Tel: 604-527-8999

Regina
Broad Street Business Centre, #322, 845 Broad St., Regina SK S4R 8G9
Tel: 306-525-6999
Toll-Free: 888-527-8999

Surrey - Guildford
#201, 15399 - 102A Ave., Surrey BC V3R 7K1
Tel: 604-527-8999
Toll-Free: 888-527-8999

Toronto
#250, 425 Bloor St. East, Toronto ON M4W 3R4
Tel: 647-776-0485
Toll-Free: 888-527-8999

Vancouver
#495, 1140 West Pender St., Vancouver BC V6E 4G1
Tel: 604-527-8999
Toll-Free: 888-527-8999

Victoria
Cook Medical Building, #214, 1175 Cook St., Victoria BC V8V 4A1
Tel: 250-382-9559
Toll-Free: 888-527-8999

Winnipeg
Power Building, #611, 428 Portage Ave., Winnipeg MB R3C 0E2
Tel: 204-942-8789
Toll-Free: 888-527-8999

Credit Counselling Thames Valley; Family Service London
See Family Service Thames Valley

Credit Institute of Canada (CIC) / L'Institut canadien du crédit
#216C, 219 Dufferin St., Toronto ON M6K 3J1
Tel: 416-572-2615; Fax: 416-572-2619
Toll-Free: 888-447-3324
geninfo@creditedu.org
www.creditedu.org
www.linkedin.com/groups/2370374
www.facebook.com/creditedu
twitter.com/creditinstitute
www.youtube.com/user/creditinstitute
Previous Name: Canadian Institute of Credit & Financial Management
Overview: A medium-sized national charitable organization founded in 1928
Mission: To provide credit education for credit & financial professionals in Canada
Finances: Funding Sources: Membership fees; CIC Store
Staff Member(s): 8
Membership: Fees: $150; Member Profile: Credit & financial professionals; Committees: Audit
Activities: Offering credit & financial management training; Providing credit management resources; Granting designations in credit management, such as CCP (formerly FCI) & ACI; Awarding academic achievements through a national awards program; Offering networking opportunities; Providing the Credit Institute Employment Referral Program; Monitoring & reacting to legislative issues relevant to the industry; Library: Credit Reference Library; by appointment Not open to public
Chief Officer(s):
Nawshad Khadaroo, General Manager, 416-572-2615 Ext. 224
mgredu@creditedu.org
Publications:
• Bankruptcy & Insolvency Act - A Creditor's Perspective [a publication of the Credit Institute of Canada]
Price: $45 + GST members; $55 + GST non-members
Profile: Topics include an overview of the Bankruptcy & Insolvency Act, effects of bankruptcy on creditors, & effects of bankruptcyon debtors
• Credit Institute of Canada Handbook, Volume 1
Type: Handbook; Price: $149 + GST members; $169+ GST non-members
Profile: Topics include credit investigations, financial statement analysis, securities, bankruptcy & insolvency, & credit department organization & reporting
• Credit Institute of Canada Handbook, Volume 2
Type: Handbook; Price: $149 + GST members; $169 + GST non-members
Profile: Topics include international credit management, credit fraud, & an introduction to e-commerce
• Credit Institute of Canada Membership Directory
Type: Directory
Profile: A listing of current members by individual & company name
• Credit Institute of Canada Student Handbook
Type: Yearbook; Frequency: Annually
• Debtor-Creditor Law and Procedure [a publication of the Credit Institute of Canada]
Price: $76 + GST members;$96 + GST non-members
Profile: Topics include an introduction to the debt collection process, small claims court proceedings, & tenancy rights & remedies
• To Your Credit [a publication of the Credit Institute of Canada]
Type: Newsletter; Frequency: Quarterly
Profile: Available to members

Atlantic Chapter
atlantic@creditedu.org
atlantic.creditedu.org
Chief Officer(s):
Roger McCaie, President
mccaie.roger@midlandtransport.com

British Columbia Chapter
#79, 16995 - 64th Ave., Cloverdale BC V3S 0V9
Tel: 604-576-7611; Fax: 604-576-7612
info@cicbcchapter.org
cicbcchapter.org
Chief Officer(s):

Laureen Carroll, President
Calgary Chapter
PO Box 4651, Calgary AB T2T 5P1
calgary@creditedu.org
calgary.creditedu.org
Chief Officer(s):
Ken Spurr, President, 403-291-1013 Ext. 231
kspurr@shoemakerdrywall.com
Conestoga Chapter
Conestoga ON
conestoga@creditedu.org
conestoga.creditedu.org
Chief Officer(s):
Wilma Potter, President, 905-595-3234
wpotter@colortech.com
Edmonton Chapter
Edmonton AB
edmonton@creditedu.org
edmonton.creditedu.org
Chief Officer(s):
David Hopkyns, President, 888-797-7727 Ext. 2380, Fax: 877-425-1522
dhopkyns@metcredit.com
Hamilton & District Chapter
1239 Baldwin Dr., Oakville ON L6J 2W4
cichamilton@gmail.com
hamilton.creditedu.org
Chief Officer(s):
Frank Morson, President, 905-816-5156, Fax: 905-819-7358
fmorson@russelmetals.com
Manitoba Chapter
PO Box 476, Winnipeg MB R3C 2J3
manitoba@creditedu.org
manitoba.creditedu.org
Chief Officer(s):
Debbie Baines, President
debbie.baines@standardaero.com
Montréal/Québec City Chapter
CP 11006, 1484 Mgr. Langlois, Valleyfield QC J6S 1E3
Tél: 514-990-8533
Ligne sans frais: 866-990-8533
montreal-quebec@creditedu.org
www.creditedu.org/chapters/chapters/montreal_quebec
Chief Officer(s):
Simi Silber, Président
Ottawa Chapter
Ottawa ON
ottawa@creditedu.org
ottawa.creditedu.org
Saskatchewan Chapter
PO Box 7884, Saskatoon SK S7K 4R6
Tel: 306-931-9682
cicsaskchapter@sasktel.net
creditedu.org
Chief Officer(s):
Geri Meyer, President
geri@chfsask.ca
South Western Ontario Chapter
ON
swo@creditedu.org
swo.creditedu.org
Chief Officer(s):
Christine Chase, President, 519-681-3264 Ext. 111, Fax: 519-658-1204
christine_chase@ryder.com
Toronto Chapter
13 Mullord Ave., Ajax ON L1Z 1K7
Tel: 905-426-7929; *Fax:* 905-426-2344
toronto@creditedu.org
www.cictoronto.org
Chief Officer(s):
Gail Maguire, President
gail.maguire@kellogg.com
Erin Marcelino, Executive Administrator

Credit Union Central of Alberta *See* Alberta Central

Credit Union Central of British Columbia; Ontario Credit Union League Ltd. *See* Central 1 Credit Union

Credit Union Central of Canada; Canadian Cooperative Credit Society *See* Canadian Credit Union Association

Credit Union Central of Manitoba (CUCM)
#400, 317 Donald St., Winnipeg MB R3B 2H6
Tel: 204-985-4700; *Fax:* 204-949-0217
cuinfo@cucm.org
www.creditunion.mb.ca
Overview: A small provincial organization overseen by Canadian Credit Union Association
Mission: To act as the trade association for credit unions in Manitoba; To represent Manitoba's 41 credit unions
Member of: Canadian Credit Union Association
Activities: Engaging in advocacy activities; Providing services, such as product & service research & development, consulting, banking services, & financial & capital management
Chief Officer(s):
Russell Fast, Chair
Garth Manness, Chief Executive Officer
Awards:
• Order of Merit Award
Meetings/Conferences:
• Manitoba's Credit Unions Conference and AGM 2018, 2018
Scope: Provincial
Publications:
• Credit Union Central of Manitoba Annual Report
Type: Yearbook; *Frequency:* Annually

Credit Union Central of Newfoundland & Labrador *See* Newfoundland & Labrador Credit Union

Credit Union Central of Nova Scotia; Credit Union Central of New Brunswick; Credit Union Central of Prince Edward Island *See* Credit Unions Atlantic Canada

Credit Unions Atlantic Canada
PO Box 9200, 6074 Lady Hammond Rd., Halifax NS B3K 5N3
Tel: 902-453-0680; *Fax:* 902-455-2437
Toll-Free: 800-668-2879
atlanticcreditunions.ca
twitter.com/AtlCreditUnions
Also Known As: Atlantic Credit Unions; Atlantic Central
Previous Name: Credit Union Central of Nova Scotia; Credit Union Central of New Brunswick; Credit Union Central of Prince Edward Island
Overview: A small provincial organization founded in 1934 overseen by Canadian Credit Union Association
Mission: To represent & support the credit unions of Nova Scotia, New Brunswick, Newfoundland & Labrador, & Prince Edward Island; To manage the system's liquidity reserve requirements
Member of: Canadian Credit Union Association
Activities: Providing financial services, such as investment banking services; offering trade association & support services, such as human resources, legal advice, consulting, & provincial marketing & communication; raising awareness of the work of credit unions; *Awareness Events:* Credit Union Day, October
Chief Officer(s):
Michael Leonard, President & CEO
Sharon Arnold, Chief Risk Officer & Senior Vice-President, Finance
Publications:
• Credit Union Central of Nova Scotia Yearbook
Type: Yearbook; *Frequency:* Annually
  Charlottetown Office
  281 University Ave., Charlottetown PE C1A 7M4
  Tel: 902-566-3350; *Fax:* 902-368-3534
  Riverview Office
  663 Pinewood Rd., Riverview NB E1B 5R6
  Tel: 506-857-8184; *Fax:* 506-857-9431

Credit Valley Conservation Foundation
1255 Old Derry Rd., Mississauga ON L5N 6R4
Tel: 905-670-1615; *Fax:* 905-670-2210
Toll-Free: 800-668-5557
cvc@creditvalleyca.ca
www.creditvalleyca.ca
www.facebook.com/creditvalleyconservation
twitter.com/cvc_ca
www.youtube.com/user/CreditValleyCA;
www.flickr.com/photos/cvca
Overview: A small local organization founded in 1954
Mission: To raise funds & awareness in support of Credit Valley Conservation's goal of an environmentally healthy river for economically & socially healthy communities
Finances: *Funding Sources:* Member municipalities; funds also generated by Credit Valley Conservation Foundation
Activities: Publishing a coffee table book; Raising funds for the development of the Elora Cataract Trailway & Glassford Arboretum Trail; Providing an annual bursary to a student at the University of Guelph & University of Toronto; *Library:* Resource Library
Chief Officer(s):
Nando Iannicca, Chair
Publications:
• Credit Cascades [a publication of the Credit Valley Conservation Foundation]
Frequency: Quarterly
Profile: Updates on work being done by the CVC.
• Currents [a publication of the Credit Valley Conservation Foundation]
Frequency: s-a.
Profile: A means of connecting the public to the Credit River Watershed.
• The Source [a publication of the Credit Valley Conservation Foundation]
Frequency: Monthly
Profile: Credit River Watershed news, profiles, tips, & opportunities.

Creelman Agricultural Society
PO Box 46, Creelman SK S0G 0X0
Tel: 306-722-3735; *Fax:* 306-722-3740
CreelmanKid@gmail.com
www.creelmanagsociety.ca
www.facebook.com/CreelmanAgSociety
twitter.com/CreelmanAg
Overview: A small local organization
Mission: To improve agriculture & the quality of life in the community by educating members & the community; To provide a community forum for discussion of agricultural issues; To encourage conservation of natural resources
Member of: Saskatchewan Association of Agricultural Societies & Exhibitions
Activities: *Awareness Events:* Creelman Fair, July
Chief Officer(s):
Christine Procyk, Secretary
cmprocyk@yahoo.ca

Cree-Naskapi Commission / La Commission Crie-Naskapie
#305, 222 Queen St., Ottawa ON K1P 5V9
Tel: 613-234-4288; *Fax:* 613-234-8102
Toll-Free: 888-236-6603
www.creenaskapicommission.net
Overview: A small local organization founded in 1984
Mission: To monitor the implementation of the Cree-Naskapi (of Quebec) Act.
Staff Member(s): 5
Activities: *Library:* by appointment
Chief Officer(s):
Richard Saunders, Chair
saunders'943@sympatico.ca
Brian Shawana, Director General
brian@creenaskapicommission.net

Cremona Water Valley & District Chamber of Commerce
PO Box 356, Cremona AB T0M 0R0
Tel: 403-637-2030
info@cremonawatervalley.com
www.cremonawatervalley.com
www.facebook.com/CremonaWaterValley
Overview: A small local organization
Mission: To support & promote local businesses & the community
Member of: Alberta chambers Commerce
Membership: 9
Chief Officer(s):
Linda Newsome, President

Crescent Beach *See* Association of Neighbourhood Houses BC

Creston & District Historical & Museum Society (CDHMS)
219 Devon St., Creston BC V0B 1G3
Tel: 250-428-9262; *Fax:* 250-428-9262
mail@creston.museum.bc.ca
www.creston.museum.bc.ca
www.facebook.com/CrestonMuseum
twitter.com/CrestonMuseum
Also Known As: Creston Museum
Overview: A small local charitable organization founded in 1971
Mission: To collect, preserve & exhibit the human & natural history of the Creston Valley for the education & entertainment of the local & visiting public
Member of: British Columbia Museums Association; Archives

Association of BC; Creston Chamber of Commerce; Community of Creston Arts Council
Finances: *Funding Sources:* Rental fees; tax money; admission revenues
Membership: *Fees:* $10 individual; $25 family; $100 patron
Activities: Guided tours; special exhibits; school programs; public outreach programs; research facilities; special events; *Library:* Creston Archives; Open to public
Chief Officer(s):
Ian Currie, President

Creston Valley Chamber of Commerce
PO Box 268, 121 Northwest Blvd. (Hwy. 3), Creston BC V0B 1G0
Tel: 250-428-4342; *Fax:* 250-428-9411
Toll-Free: 866-528-4342
info@crestonvalleychamber.com
www.crestonvalleychamber.com
twitter.com/CrestonVC
Overview: A small local organization founded in 1910
Mission: To be a catalyst for sustainable economic growth by providing education, networking & advocacy to government
Member of: BC Chamber of Commerce; Canadian Chamber of Commerce; International Selkirk Loop
Finances: *Funding Sources:* Town of Creston; Regional District; fundraising; membership fees
Staff Member(s): 2
Membership: *Fees:* Schedule available
Activities: *Library:* Business Information Resource Desk
Chief Officer(s):
Rob Schepers, President, 250-428-9388
Jim Jacobsen, Executive Director, 250-428-4342

Creston Valley Prospectors & Lapidary Club
c/o 1114 Adler St., Creston BC V0B 1G4
Tel: 250-428-0236
Overview: A small local organization
Affiliation(s): British Columbia Lapidary Society; Gem & Mineral Federation of Canada
Membership: *Member Profile:* Persons in the Creston Vally area of British Columbia who are interested in collecting & polishing rocks & stones to make jewelry
Activities: Hosting monthly meetings; Offering summer camps; Teaching lapidary
Chief Officer(s):
Gerry Rehwald, Contact

La Crete & Area Chamber of Commerce
PO Box 1088, #1, 10500 - 100 St., La Crete AB T0H 2H0
Tel: 780-928-2278; *Fax:* 780-928-2234
admin@lacretechamber.com
lacretechamber.com
www.facebook.com/LaCreteAreaChamber
twitter.com/LaCreteChamber
Overview: A small local charitable organization
Mission: To contribute to economic prosperity in La Crete & area; To improve quality of life
Finances: *Annual Operating Budget:* $50,000-$100,000; *Funding Sources:* Membership fees; Fund raising; Municipality
Staff Member(s): 3
Membership: 119; *Fees:* Schedule available; *Member Profile:* Businesses
Activities: Organizing Spring Trade Show; Holding monthly membership meetings; Offering business programs, services & information; *Library:* Open to public
Chief Officer(s):
Larry Neufeld, Manager

Cricket Alberta (ACA)
#222, 7 Westwinds CR NE, Calgary AB T3J 5H2
cricket@cricketalberta.ca
www.cricketalberta.ca
www.facebook.com/155440747942009
twitter.com/CricketAlberta
Previous Name: Alberta Cricket Association
Overview: A small provincial organization founded in 1975 overseen by Cricket Canada
Member of: Cricket Canada
Finances: *Annual Operating Budget:* $50,000-$100,000; *Funding Sources:* Government; casino; membership fees
30 volunteer(s)
Membership: 500; *Fees:* $500 team; *Member Profile:* 10 to 55 years of age; *Committees:* Executive; By-Laws; Juniors
Activities: Competitions; school cricket; coaching; training camps
Chief Officer(s):
Manzoor Choudhary, President, 403-605-4843
manzoor@cricketalberta.ca

Cricket Canada
#3, 120 Woodstream Blvd., Woodbridge ON L4L 7Z1
Tel: 647-632-4218
info@cricketcanada.org
www.gocricketgocanada.com
twitter.com/canadiancricket
Also Known As: Canadian Cricket Association
Overview: A large national organization founded in 1892
Mission: To foster growth & development of cricket in Canada
Affiliation(s): International Cricket Council; Kanga Ball Canada
Finances: *Funding Sources:* Ministry of Heritage; International Cricket Council Volunteer Donations
130 volunteer(s)
Membership: 30 senior/lifetime + 400 teams + 15,500 players; *Fees:* $85 per team
Activities: *Internships:* Yes; *Speaker Service:* Yes
Chief Officer(s):
Ranjit Saini, President & Chair

Cricket Council of Ontario (CCO)
25 Pacific Wind Cres., Brampton ON L6R 2B1
Tel: 905-230-9392
www.cricketcouncilofontario.ca
www.facebook.com/CricketOntario
twitter.com/cricketontario
Previous Name: Ontario Cricket Association Inc.
Overview: A medium-sized provincial organization founded in 2009 overseen by Cricket Canada
Mission: To be the provincial governing body of the sport of cricket in Ontario.
Member of: Cricket Canada
Membership: 9 associations/leagues
Activities: *Rents Mailing List:* Yes
Chief Officer(s):
Praim Persaud, President, 416-621-2020
praimp@yahoo.com
Tan Qureshi, Manager, Public Relations
tqureshi@cricketcouncilofontario.ca

Cricket New Brunswick (CNB)
Fredericton NB
info@cricketnb.org
cricketnb.org
www.facebook.com/CNB.Fredericton
Also Known As: Cricket NB
Previous Name: New Brunswick Cricket Association
Overview: A small provincial organization overseen by Cricket Canada
Mission: To facilitate the development & growth of the sport of cricket; To establish cricket as a competitite sport in New Brunswick; To promote participation in schools
Member of: Cricket Canada
6 volunteer(s)
Membership: 1-99; *Fees:* $75 full
Activities: Awareness lessons; Cricket camps
Chief Officer(s):
Aditya Aggarwal, President
aditya.aggarwal@cricketnb.org
Devansh Bhavishi, Secretary
dbhavishi@cricketnb.org

The Crime Writers of Canada (CWC)
#4C, 240 Westwood Rd., Guelph ON N1H 7W9
info@crimewriterscanada.com
www.crimewriterscanada.com
Overview: A small national organization founded in 1982
Mission: To promote Canadian crime writing
Finances: *Funding Sources:* Membership fees; grant from Canadian Heritage; sponsorships by Canadian publishers
Membership: *Fees:* $85 associate; $125 professional; *Member Profile:* Authors of crime fiction, true crime & genre/reference criticism & promoters thereof: agents, editors, publishers, specialty booksellers & teachers of post-secondary courses on the genre
Activities: *Speaker Service:* Yes
Chief Officer(s):
Vicki Delany, Chair
Awards:
• The Arthur Ellis Awards
Established 1984; awarded annually in the following categories: best crime novel (by a previously published novelist), best crime non-fiction, best first crime novel (by a previously unpublished novelist), best crime short story, best juvenile crime book, & best crime writing in French

Criminal Lawyers' Association (CLA)
#1, 189 Queen St. East, Toronto ON M5A 1S2
Tel: 416-214-9875; *Fax:* 416-968-6818
www.criminallawyers.ca
Overview: A medium-sized national organization founded in 1971
Mission: To be the voice for criminal justice & civil liberties in Canada
Affiliation(s): US National Association of Criminal Defence Lawyers; The Canadian Counsel of Criminal Defence Lawyers (CCCDL); The County & District Law President's Association (CDLPA)
Membership: 1,000+; *Member Profile:* Criminal law practitioners; *Committees:* Executive
Activities: Advising all levels of government & the judiciary on issues relating to legislation & the administration of criminal justice; Assisting members in practice of criminal litigation; Developing continuing education programs for criminal law practitioners; Hosting an annual criminal defence law conference
Chief Officer(s):
Anthony Moustacalis, President
Anthony Laycock, Executive Director
anthony@criminallawyers.ca
Awards:
• G. Arthur Martin Criminal Justice Medal
For an outstanding contribution to criminal justice

Crisis Centre North Bay
PO Box 1407, North Bay ON P1B 8K6
Tel: 705-472-6204; *Fax:* 705-472-6236
info@crisiscentre-nb.on.ca
www.crisiscentre-nb.on.ca
Overview: A small local charitable organization founded in 1972 overseen by Distress Centres Ontario
Mission: To help people in crises by providing temporary room & board as well as rehabilitation services
Staff Member(s): 70

Crohn's & Colitis Canada / Crohn's et Colitis Canada
#600, 60 St. Clair Ave. East, Toronto ON M4T 1N5
Tel: 416-920-5035; *Fax:* 416-929-0364
Toll-Free: 800-387-1479
support@crohnsandcolitis.ca
www.crohnsandcolitis.ca
www.linkedin.com/company/crohn's-and-colitis-foundation-of-canada
www.facebook.com/crohnsandcolitis.ca
twitter.com/getgutsyCanada
www.youtube.com/user/getgutsy
Previous Name: Crohn's & Colitis Foundation of Canada; Canadian Foundation for Ileitis & Colitis
Overview: A medium-sized national charitable organization founded in 1974
Mission: To find a cure for Crohn's disease & ulcerative colitis; To raise funds for medical research; To educate individuals with inflammatory bowel disease, their families, health professionals, & the public
Activities: *Awareness Events:* M&M Meat Shops Charity BBQ Day, May; Gutsy Walk, June; All That Glitters Gala, November
Chief Officer(s):
Mina Mawani, President & CEO
Tim Berry, Vice-President, Finance
Angie Specic, Vice-President, Marketing & Communications
Alberta/NWT Region
#3100, 246 Stewart Green SW, Calgary AB T3H 3C8
Toll-Free: 888-884-2232
Chief Officer(s):
Patricia Glenn, Regional Director
pglenn@crohnsandcolitis.ca
Atlantic Canada Region
PO Box 173, Lower Sackville NS B4C 2S9
Tel: 902-297-1649; *Fax:* 902-422-6552
Toll-Free: 800-265-1101
Chief Officer(s):
Edna Mendelson, Regional Director
emendelson@crohnsandcolitis.ca
British Columbia/Yukon Region
PO Box 47147, Stn. City Square, Vancouver BC V5Z 4L6
Toll-Free: 800-513-8202
britishcolumbia@crohnsandcolitis.ca
Chief Officer(s):
Colleen Hauck, Regional Director
chauck@crohnsandcolitis.ca
Bureau du Québec
#420, 1980, rue Sherbrooke ouest, Montréal QC H3H 1E8

Tél: 514-342-0666; *Téléc:* 514-342-1011
Ligne sans frais: 800-461-4683
Chief Officer(s):
Edna Mendelson, Directrice régionale
emendelson@crohnsandcolitis.ca
Manitoba/Saskatchewan/Nunavut Region
PO Box 20009, 3310 Portage Ave., Winnipeg MB R3K 2E5
Tel: 204-231-2115; *Fax:* 204-237-8214
Toll-Free: 866-856-8551
centralcanada@ccfc.ca
Chief Officer(s):
Shair Wolsey, Regional Director
swolsey@crohnsandcolitis.ca
Ontario Region
#600, 60 St. Clair Ave. East, Toronto ON M4T 1N5
Tel: 613-806-7956; *Fax:* 416-929-0364
Toll-Free: 800-387-1479
Chief Officer(s):
Jacqueline Alvarez, Regional Director
jalvarez@crohnsandcolitis.ca

Crohn's & Colitis Foundation of Canada; Canadian Foundation for Ileitis & Colitis *See* Crohn's & Colitis Canada

Crohn's et Colitis Canada *See* Crohn's & Colitis Canada

Crop Protection Institute of Canada *See* CropLife Canada

CropLife Canada
#612, 350 Sparks St., Ottawa ON K1R 7S8
Tel: 613-230-9881
www.croplife.ca
twitter.com/croplifecanada
www.youtube.com/croplifecanada
Previous Name: Crop Protection Institute of Canada
Overview: A medium-sized national organization founded in 1952
Mission: To represent Canada's plant science industry; To foster the developmment of the industry; To build Canadians' trust & appreciation for plant science innovations
Member of: CropLife International
Finances: *Funding Sources:* Sponsorships
Staff Member(s): 16
Membership: 36; *Member Profile:* Developers, manufacturers, & distributors of plant science innovations
Activities: Conducting research; Promoting the code of conduct
Chief Officer(s):
Lorne Hepworth, President, 613-230-9881 Ext. 3225
hepworth@croplife.ca
Maria Trainer, Managing Director, Regulatory Affairs
trainer@croplife.ca
Nadine Sisk, Vice President, Communications & Member Services
siskn@croplife.ca
Russel Hurst, Executive Director, Stewardship & Sustainability
hurstr@croplife.ca
Annie Hsu, Vice-President, Finance & Administration
hsua@croplife.ca
Pierre Petelle, Vice-President, Chemistry
petellep@croplife.ca
Dennis Prouse, Vice-President, Government Affairs
proused@croplife.ca
Janice Tranberg, Vice-President, Western Canada, 306-373-4052
tranbergj@croplife.ca
Meetings/Conferences:
• GrowCanada 2018, 2018
Scope: National

Croquet Canada
24 Deloraine Ave., Toronto ON M5M 2A7
croquet@sympatico.ca
www.croquet.ca
Overview: A large national organization
Mission: To promote & develop croquet in Canada
Membership: *Fees:* $20 individual; $75 clubs; *Committees:* Communications; Finance; Nominating & Governance; Selection
Chief Officer(s):
Ian MacGregor, President

Cross Country Alberta (CCA)
Percy Page Centre, 11759 Groat Rd., Edmonton AB T5M 3K6
Tel: 780-415-1738; *Fax:* 780-427-0524
manager@xcountryab.net
www.xcountryab.net
www.facebook.com/CrossCountryAlberta
twitter.com/xcountryab

Overview: A medium-sized provincial organization overseen by Cross Country Canada
Mission: To lead, develop, & promote the sport of cross-country skiing througout Alberta
Member of: Cross Country Canada
Staff Member(s): 2
Membership: 3,890; *Fees:* $11 child; $13 youth; $18 adult; $100 club
Activities: Quality service; leadership & skier development; management & education
Chief Officer(s):
Jo Wolach, Chair
jo@xsitra.com
Michael Neary, Manager, Sport
Laura Filipow, Coordinator, Programs
cca@xcountryab.net
Awards:
• Coach of the Year Award
• Outstanding Retailer of the Year Award
• Outstanding Ski Area Operations Award
• Race Organizer of the Year Award
• Official of the Year Award
• Leadership Grant

Cross Country British Columbia (CCBC)
#106, 3003 - 30th St., Vernon BC V1T 9J5
Tel: 250-545-9600; *Fax:* 250-545-9614
office@crosscountrybc.ca
www.crosscountrybc.ca
www.facebook.com/Cross-Country-BC-829014633823512
instagram.com/crosscountrybc
Also Known As: Cross Country BC
Overview: A small provincial organization overseen by Cross Country Canada
Mission: The association is the governing body for the sport of cross country skiing in BC.
Member of: Cross Country Canada
Membership: 14,000
Chief Officer(s):
Wannes Luppens, Executive Director
wannes@crosscountrybc.ca
Dennis Wu, Coordinator, Administration & Communications

Cross Country Canada (CCC) / Ski de fond Canada (SFC)
Bill Warren Training Centre, #100, 1995 Olympic Way, Canmore AB T1W 2T6
Tel: 403-678-6791; *Fax:* 403-678-3885
Toll-Free: 877-609-3215
info@cccski.com
www.cccski.com
www.facebook.com/138553616175807
twitter.com/cccski
www.youtube.com/user/xccanada
Overview: A medium-sized national charitable organization
Mission: To develop & deliver programs designed to achieve international excellence in cross-country skiing; to provide national programs for continuous development of cross-country skiing from introductory experience to international excellence, for participants of all ages & abilities, fostering the principles of ethical conduct & fair play
Member of: True Sport
Affiliation(s): Canadian Ski & Snowboard Association
Finances: *Annual Operating Budget:* $500,000-$1.5 Million
Staff Member(s): 25
Membership: 55,000; *Committees:* Women's; Events; High Performance; Coach & Athlete Development; Fundraising; Communications
Activities: *Internships:* Yes
Chief Officer(s):
Jamie Coatsworth, Chair, 416-486-0825
jamie.coatsworth@gmail.com
Davin MacIntosh, Chief Executive Officer, 403-678-6791 Ext. 38
dmacintosh@cccski.com
Mike Edwards, Director, High Performance Para-Nordic, 403-678-6791 Ext. 35
medwards@cccski.com
Thomas Holland, Director, High Performance, 403-678-6791 Ext. 37
tholland@cccski.com
Awards:
• Dave Rees Award
• The Firth Award
• Volunteer of the Year
• Sponsor of the Year
• Media Award

• Sofie Manarin Award
• Ski to School Scholarship

Cross Country New Brunswick / Ski de fond Nouveau-Brunswick
c/o Manon Losier, 1482, ch Saulnier ouest, Benoit NB E1X 2A8
Tel: 506-395-0020
xcskinb@bellaliant.net
www.xcski-nb.ca
www.facebook.com/nbskiteam
Overview: A medium-sized provincial organization overseen by Cross Country Canada
Mission: To promote cross country skiing among the general population of New Brunswick; To provide a sense of leadership; To offer a variety of programs & services
Member of: Cross Country Canada
Chief Officer(s):
Dave Moore, Chair
moored@bellaliant.net
Arthur Austin, Treasurer
arthur.austin@gmail.com

Cross Country Newfoundland & Labrador
c/o Gerry Rideout, 301 Curtis Cres., Labrador City NL A2V 2B8
Tel: 709-944-5842
www.crosscountrynl.com
Overview: A medium-sized provincial organization overseen by Cross Country Canada
Chief Officer(s):
Gerry Rideout, President
rideoutg@crrstv.net

Cross Country Northwest Territories *See* Northwest Territories Ski Division

Cross Country Nova Scotia (CCSNS)
5516 Spring Garden Rd., 4th Fl., Halifax NS B3J 1G6
Tel: 902-425-5454; *Fax:* 902-425-5606
ccns@sportnovascotia.ca
crosscountryns.ca
www.facebook.com/114825378670589
Previous Name: Nordic Ski Nova Scotia
Overview: A medium-sized provincial organization founded in 1968 overseen by Cross Country Canada
Mission: To promote & encourage the sport/recreation of cross-country skiing; To provide & maintain rules & regulations in the province; To encourage & foster general public support of the activities & programs of CCSNS; To provide a resource centre for the membership & the general public; To select & train members of the provincial team to represent the province
Member of: Cross Country Canada
8 volunteer(s)
Membership: 200; *Fees:* Schedule available

Cross Country PEI
PO Box 532, Souris PE C0A 2B0
srobrien@eastlink.ca
www.cccski.com/Contacts/Division-Offices.aspx
Overview: A small provincial organization overseen by Cross Country Canada
Mission: The association is the governing body for the sport of cross country skiing in PEI.
Member of: Cross Country Canada
Chief Officer(s):
Steve O'Brien, Contact
srobrien@eastlink.ca

Cross Country Saskatchewan (CCS)
1860 Lorne St., Regina SK S4P 2L7
Tel: 306-780-9240; *Fax:* 306-780-9462
ccs@sasktel.net
crosscountrysask.ca
www.facebook.com/431140886944432
twitter.com/XCSask
Overview: A small provincial organization overseen by Cross Country Canada
Mission: CCS is a non-profit, volunteer-directed organization of skiing clubs. It develops & supports competitive & recreational cross country skiing programs throughout Saskatchewan.
Member of: Sask Ski Association; Sask Sport; Cross Country Canada
Finances: *Annual Operating Budget:* $100,000-$250,000
Staff Member(s): 1
Membership: 26 clubs; *Fees:* Schedule available; *Member Profile:* Skiing clubs with at least 10 members
Chief Officer(s):

Canadian Associations / Cross Country Ski Association of Manitoba (CCSAM)

Dan Brisbin, President
danbrisbin@sasktel.net
Alana Ottenbreit, Executive Director
Awards:
- Event Grant
- Loppet Funding
- Sask Cup Race Funding
- Professional Services Access Grant
- Facility Grants
- MAP Grants

Publications:
- Nordic News [a publication of Cross Country Saskatchewan]
Type: Newsletter

Cross Country Ski Association of Manitoba (CCSAM)
Sport for Life Centre, 145 Pacific Ave., Winnipeg MB R3B 2Z6
Tel: 204-925-5639
info@ccsam.ca
www.ccsam.ca
www.facebook.com/ccski
twitter.com/xcountryskimb
www.youtube.com/xcountryskimb
Overview: A small provincial organization overseen by Cross Country Canada
Mission: CCSAM is a volunteer-based organization that provides leadership and direction towards broad participation in the sport of cross country skiing.
Member of: Cross Country Canada
Affiliation(s): Sport Manitoba
Membership: *Member Profile:* Any member of a cross country ski club in MB may join.
Chief Officer(s):
Richard Huybers, Chairperson
richard.huybers@grainscanada.gc.ca
Karin McSherry, Executive Director

Cross Country Ski Ontario
c/o Liz Inkila, 738 River St., Thunder Bay ON P7A 3S8
Tel: 807-768-4617
admin@xco.org
www.xco.org
twitter.com/xcoorg
Overview: A medium-sized provincial organization overseen by Cross Country Canada
Mission: To govern the sport of cross country skiing in Ontario.
Member of: Cross Country Canada
Chief Officer(s):
Liz Inkila, Director, Administration
Meetings/Conferences:
- Cross Country Ski Ontario 2018 Annual General Meeting, 2018, ON
Scope: Provincial
Description: Board meetings are held each month by telephone, & the annual general meeting takes place each May

Cross Country Yukon (CCY)
4061 - 4th Ave., Whitehorse YT Y1A 1H1
Tel: 867-334-9220
www.crosscountryyukon.com
Previous Name: Yukon Ski Division
Overview: A medium-sized provincial organization founded in 1985 overseen by Cross Country Canada
Mission: To develop cross country skiing in the Yukon
Member of: Cross Country Canada
Finances: *Annual Operating Budget:* $100,000-$250,000;
Funding Sources: Yukon territorial government; Yukon Lotteries; fundraising
Staff Member(s): 2; 200 volunteer(s)
Membership: 900 + 17 clubs; *Fees:* Schedule available;
Committees: Events & Technical; High Performance; Leadership Development; Youth Development
Activities: Clinic courses include: coaching; ski trail design; trail grooming; avalanche awareness; jackrabbit leader course; backcountry; ski patrol
Chief Officer(s):
Alain Masson, Sport Coordinator & Head Coach
xcyukon@gmail.com

The Cross-Cultural Community Services Association (TCCSA)
#206, 302 Spadina Ave., Toronto ON M5T 2E7
Tel: 416-977-4026; *Fax:* 416-351-0510
www.tccsa.on.ca
Overview: A medium-sized local organization overseen by Ontario Council of Agencies Serving Immigrants
Mission: To provide social services to enhance the well-being of diversified communities
Staff Member(s): 7
Activities: Offering settlement services, community & youth services, & education & language training
Chief Officer(s):
Isa Lee, Executive Director

Crossfield Chamber of Commerce
PO Box 1490, 1005 Ross St., Crossfield AB T0M 0S0
Tel: 403-813-5133; *Fax:* 403-946-0157
info@crossfieldchamber.org
www.crossfieldchamber.org
Overview: A small local organization founded in 2003
Mission: To serve the business, economic, & social communities of Crossfield, Alberta & the surrounding area; To help the community continue to grow & prosper
Chief Officer(s):
Karen Postill, President
president@crossfieldchamber.org

Crossreach Adult Day Centre
3348 West Broadway, Vancouver BC V6R 2B2
Tel: 604-732-1477; *Fax:* 604-732-1430
info@crossreachseniors.com
www.crossreachseniors.com
Previous Name: Crossreach Project of Vancouver
Overview: A small local charitable organization founded in 1972
Mission: To provide services to seniors in Vancouver; To support independent living for seniors
Finances: *Funding Sources:* Membership & client fees; Vancouver Coastal Health Authority; Donations; Legacies; Fundraising; Rental of premises; Partnerships with businesses
Membership: *Fees:* Schedule available
Activities: Operating an adult day centre; Providing respite for caregivers; Offering social interaction & other engaging activities for seniors; Arranging continuing education & special training programs for staff; Raising awareness in the community
Chief Officer(s):
Jessica Malkoske, Executive Director

Crossreach Project of Vancouver *See* Crossreach Adult Day Centre

Crossroads for Women Inc. / Carrefour pour femmes inc.
PO Box 1247, Moncton NB E1C 8P9
Fax: 506-853-4159; *Crisis Hot-Line:* 506-853-0811
crossroads@nb.aibn.com
www.crossroadsforwomen.ca
Overview: A small local charitable organization founded in 1981
Mission: Transition house for women & their children, victims of family violence
Member of: United Way
Affiliation(s): New Brunswick Coalition of Transition Houses
Finances: *Annual Operating Budget:* $250,000-$500,000;
Funding Sources: Provincial government; United Way; corporate & individual donations
Staff Member(s): 13; 18 volunteer(s)
Membership: 140; *Fees:* $50; *Committees:* Coalition Against Abuse in Relationships; Communications; Chamber of Commerce; Community Advisory; Mental Health
Activities: Fundraising; public awareness; speakers; transition shelter; second stage housing; *Speaker Service:* Yes; *Library*
Chief Officer(s):
Tina Thibodeau, Executive Director

CrossTrainers Canada
PO Box 1426, Bradford ON L3Z 2B7
Tel: 416-697-0147
Other Communication: crosstrainersblog.wordpress.com
ct@ctministries.ca
www.ctministries.ca
www.facebook.com/crosstrainerscanada
twitter.com/CT_Canada
www.instagram.com/ctcanada
Overview: A small local organization founded in 2001
Mission: The association is a Christian ministry organization with members from several local churches serving the Bradford community.
Finances: *Funding Sources:* Corporate sponsors
Staff Member(s): 5
Activities: Connections Centre with True Vibe program, Playzone, cafe & special events; The Hub Youth Centre with A Hand Up Clothing Room; Mercy House, a women's shelter
Chief Officer(s):
Jodi Greenstreet, Executive Director

Patti LaRose, Director, Operations
Jenna Wickens, Director, Youth

The Crow's Nest Military Artifacts Association (CNMAA)
PO Box 23161, St. John's NL A1B 4J9
Tel: 709-753-6927
crowsnoc@nf.aibn.com
crowsnestnl.ca
Overview: A small provincial organization founded in 1987
Mission: The Artifacts Association has framed, maintained, and photographed the artifacts, as well as performed other functions, using government grants and volunteer labour.
Affiliation(s): The Crow's Nest
Membership: *Fees:* $15
Chief Officer(s):
Gary Green, President

Crowsnest Community Support Society
PO Box 507, Stn. Coleman, 8102 - 19 Ave., Crowsnest Pass AB T0K 0M0
Tel: 403-563-5265; *Fax:* 403-563-3144
Also Known As: Mountain View Industries
Previous Name: Crowsnest Pass Mentally Handicapped Society
Overview: A small local charitable organization founded in 1964
Mission: To provide support & assistance to individuals with developmental disabilities, so they may participate & live as independently as possible within the community.
Member of: Alberta Association of Rehabilitation Centres
Finances: *Funding Sources:* Government; donations; production revenue
Membership: *Member Profile:* Volunteer board members
Activities: Day programs; employment & housing services

Crowsnest Pass Allied Arts Association
PO Box 1469, Blairmore AB T0K 0E3
Tel: 403-562-2218; *Fax:* 403-562-2218
cnpaaa@shaw.ca
Overview: A small local charitable organization founded in 1985
Mission: To offer art courses in the community & operate the Crowsnest Pass Public Art Gallery
Finances: *Funding Sources:* Municipal government; fundraising; Alberta Foundation for the Arts; sponsorship
Membership: *Member Profile:* Interest in the arts
Activities: Art exhibitions; art education; performing & literary arts

Crowsnest Pass Boys & Girls Club *See* Boys & Girls Clubs of Alberta

Crowsnest Pass Chamber of Commerce
PO Box 706, 12707 - 20th Ave., Blairmore AB T0K 0E0
Tel: 403-562-7108; *Fax:* 403-562-7493
Toll-Free: 888-562-7108
office@crowsnestpasschamber.ca
www.crowsnestpasschamber.ca
www.linkedin.com/in/crowsnest-pass-chamber-of-commerce-45ab946a
www.facebook.com/CrowsnestPassChamber
Previous Name: Blairmore Board of Trade
Overview: A small local organization founded in 1946
Mission: To act as a link for business, marketing, & tourism for the Crowsnest Pass area of Alberta
Member of: The Alberta Chamber of Commerce
Affiliation(s): Alberta Chamber of Commerce
Finances: *Annual Operating Budget:* $50,000-$100,000;
Funding Sources: Membership dues; Grants; Fundraising
Staff Member(s): 1; 10 volunteer(s)
Membership: 118; *Fees:* Schedule available, based upon number of employees
Chief Officer(s):
Sacha Anderson, President
president@crowsnestpasschamber.ca
Tim May, Treasurer
treasurer@crowsnestpasschamber.ca
Claire Rogers, Secretary
secretary@crowsnestpasschamber.ca
Publications:
- Chamber Chatter [a publication of Crowsnest Pass Chamber of Commerce]
Type: Newsletter

Crowsnest Pass Mentally Handicapped Society *See* Crowsnest Community Support Society

Crowsnest Pass Society for the Prevention of Cruelty to Animals
PO Box 725, Blairmore AB T0K 0E0
Tel: 403-564-4859
Also Known As: Crowsnest Pass SPCA
Overview: A small local organization founded in 1975
Member of: Alberta Society for the Prevention of Cruelty to Animals
Chief Officer(s):
Lee Potts, President

Crowsnest Pass Symphony
PO Box 416, Blairmore AB T0K 0E0
Tel: 403-562-2405; *Fax:* 403-562-7501
Overview: A small local organization founded in 1925 overseen by Orchestras Canada
Mission: To provide a vehicle for young people to learn & perform music; to give amateur adult musicians the opportunity to play classical music recreationally
Member of: Orchestras Canada
Membership: *Member Profile:* Orchestra members
Activities: Presents 2 concerts per year; *Library:* by appointment
Chief Officer(s):
Jerry Lonsbury, Conductor
sjlons@shaw.ca

Cryonics Society of Canada (CSC)
PO Box 11514, 600 The East Mall, Toronto ON M9B 4B0
csc4@cryocdn.org
www.cryocdn.org
Overview: A small national organization founded in 1988
Mission: To promote & provide information to the public about cryonics; To assist individuals in making cryonic suspension arrangements; To encourage research in cryonics & other life-extension sciences
Finances: *Funding Sources:* Membership fees; subscriptions
Activities: *Speaker Service:* Yes; *Library:* by appointment

Crystal City & District Chamber of Commerce
PO Box 56, Crystal City MB R0K 0N0
Tel: 204-873-2427; *Fax:* 204-873-2656
chamberofcommerce@crystalcitymb.ca
www.crystalcitymb.ca
Overview: A small local organization
Mission: To stimulate business growth in Crystal City & surrounding area
Member of: Manitoba Chamber of Commerce
Finances: *Annual Operating Budget:* Less than $50,000
Staff Member(s): 1; 20 volunteer(s)
Membership: 36; *Fees:* $20; *Member Profile:* Retail merchants; *Committees:* Business Promotion; Community Development
Activities: *Awareness Events:* Annual Fall Supper, Oct.
Chief Officer(s):
Doug Treble, Contact, 204-873-2523
Mike Webber, Contact, 204-873-2374

CTT Group Centre for Textile & Geosynthetic Technologies
Voir Groupe CTT Group

Cu Nim Gliding Club
PO Box 17, #11, RR#1, Okotoks AB T1S 1A1
Tel: 403-938-2796
www.cunim.org
Overview: A small local organization
Member of: Soaring Association of Canada
Affiliation(s): Alberta Soaring Council
Finances: *Annual Operating Budget:* $50,000-$100,000
6 volunteer(s)
Membership: 60; *Fees:* $450
Chief Officer(s):
Pablo Wainstein, President

The Cultch (VECC)
1895 Venables St., Vancouver BC V5L 2H6
Tel: 604-251-1766; *Fax:* 604-251-1730
info@thecultch.com
www.thecultch.com
www.facebook.com/TheCultch
twitter.com/thecultch
www.youtube.com/user/thecultchvideos
Previous Name: Vancouver East Cultural Centre
Overview: A medium-sized local organization founded in 1973
Mission: To present, produce, co-present & support innovative & contemporary performing & visual artists
Member of: CanDance; Tourism Vancouver; Alliance for Arts + Culture; Greater Vancouver Professional Theatre Alliance (GVPTA); Canadian Arts Presenting Association (CAPACOA); Western Arts Alliance (WAA); BC Touring Council (BCTC)
Finances: *Funding Sources:* 3 levels of government; corporate; private
Staff Member(s): 55
Membership: 1,200 +
Activities: *Internships:* Yes
Chief Officer(s):
Heather Redfern, Executive Director
heather@thecultch.com
Reid Cindy, Managing Director
cindy@thecultch.com

Cultivons Biologique Canada *See* Canadian Organic Growers Inc.

Cultural Human Resources Council (CHRC)
#606, 151 Slater St., Ottawa ON K1N 9J6
Tel: 613-562-1535; *Fax:* 613-562-2982
Toll-Free: 866-562-1535
info@culturalhrc.ca
www.culturalhrc.ca
www.facebook.com/CHRC.CRHSC
twitter.com/CulturalHRC
Overview: A small national organization founded in 1995
Mission: To address the training & career development needs of employers & cultural workers including artists, technical staff, managers & all others engaged professionally in the arts. It aims to strengthen the Canadian cultural workforce.
Finances: *Funding Sources:* Federal government
Staff Member(s): 4
Membership: *Fees:* $35 individual; $100-500 organization based on type/budget; *Member Profile:* Employers & workers in the cultural sector, including live performing arts, writing & publishing, visuals arts & crafts, film & television, broadcasting, digital media, music & sound recording, & heritage
Activities: CultureWorks job & resume database; *Internships:* Yes
Chief Officer(s):
Richard Hornsby, Chair
Susan Annis, Executive Director
sannis@culturalhrc.ca

Cultural Industries Ontario North (CION)
#103, 40 Larch St., Sudbury ON P3E 5M7
Tel: 705-885-9889; *Fax:* 705-688-1351
info@cionorth.ca
cionorth.ca
Also Known As: Music and Film in Motion
Overview: A medium-sized national organization
Mission: A pan Northern Ontario cultural organization serving the needs of everyone working in music, film, television and digital media across Northern Ontario.
Membership: *Committees:* Northern Ontario Film & Television Advisory Committee
Chief Officer(s):
Jen McKerral, Music Outreach Officer;
jmckerral@cionorth.ca

Culture Mauricie (CCCM)
#102, 25, rue des Forges, Trois-Rivières QC G9A 6A7
Tél: 819-374-3242; *Téléc:* 819-374-2649
info@culturemauricie.ca
www.culturemauricie.ca
www.facebook.com/culturemauricie
www.youtube.com/culturemauricie
Nom précédent: Conseil de la culture du Coeur-du-Québec; Conseil de la culture et des communications de la Mauricie
Aperçu: *Dimension:* petite; *Envergure:* locale; Organisme sans but lucratif; fondée en 1978
Mission: Rassembler et représenter les artistes professionnels, les diffuseurs et les organismes culturels de la Mauricie; assurer la promotion et la reconnaissance des intérêts artistiques et culturels auprès des instances régionales et nationales
Finances: *Budget de fonctionnement annuel:* $100,000-$250,000
9 bénévole(s)
Membre: 200 individu; 100 corporatif; *Montant de la cotisation:* Barème; *Critères d'admissibilite:* Toute personne ou organisme concerné par le développement culturel régional; *Comités:* Arts visuels; Métiers d'art; Musique; Théâtre; Danse; Lettres; Histoire; Musée; Archives; Patrimoine; Salles de spectacles; Événements majeurs; Municipalités
Activités: Programmes de formation
Membre(s) du bureau directeur:
Éric Lord, Directeur général
direction@culturemauricie.ca

Culture Regeneration Research Society
#2/F, 5069 Beresford St., Burnaby BC V5J 1H8
Tel: 604-435-5486; *Fax:* 604-435-9344
Toll-Free: 866-435-2777
info@crrs.org
www.crrs.org
Overview: A medium-sized national organization founded in 1994
Mission: To promote & regenerate Chinese culture through the exchange of western & Chinese values & philosophies; To increase western society's understanding of Chinese history, culture, & social development
Finances: *Funding Sources:* Donations
Activities: Engaging with Chinese government officials & submitting recommendations; Offering leadership training workshops; Providing academic seminars & conferences; Providing education funding to students; Working with academic institutions to develop academic & educational projects; Raising awareness of social issues relating to China; Participating in outreach services such as poverty relief
Chief Officer(s):
Thomas In-Sing Leung, President
Publications:
• Cultural China
Type: Journal; *Frequency:* Quarterly
Profile: Publishes scholars' research on literature, history, & philosophy

Cumberland Chamber of Commerce *See* Orléans Chamber of Commerce

Cumberland Chamber of Commerce
PO Box 250, 2680 Dunsmuir Ave., Cumberland BC V0R 1S0
Tel: 250-336-8313
Toll-Free: 866-301-4636
chamber@cumberlandbc.org
cumberlandbc.org
Overview: A small local organization founded in 1994
Member of: British Columbia Chamber of Commerce
Affiliation(s): North By Northwest Tourism Association of BC
Finances: *Annual Operating Budget:* Less than $50,000; *Funding Sources:* Membership fees; government
2 volunteer(s)
Membership: 1-99

Cumberland County Family Planning Association *See* Sexual Health Centre for Cumberland County

Cumberland County Genealogical Society (CCGS)
PO Box 1071, 16 Church St., Amherst NS B4H 4E2
Tel: 902-661-7278
archives@ccgsns.com
www.ccgsns.com
www.facebook.com/CCGSAmherst
twitter.com/ccgsns
Overview: A small local organization
Mission: To promote the study of genealogy & to collect genealogical information
Membership: *Fees:* $15 single; $20 family
Chief Officer(s):
Don Tabor, President
don.tabor@eastlink.ca

Cumberland Equal Rights for the Disabled (CERD)
PO Box 75, Maccan NS B0L 1B0
Tel: 902-545-2065
Overview: A small local organization
Affiliation(s): Nova Scotia League for Equal Opportunities; Disabled Individuals Alliance
Chief Officer(s):
Linda Styles, Contact

Cumberland Museum Society
c/o Cumberland County Museum & Archives, 150 Church St., Amherst NS B4H 3C4
Tel: 902-667-2561; *Fax:* 902-667-0996
ccma@cumberlandcountymuseum.com
www.cumberlandcountymuseum.com
Previous Name: Amherst Township Historical Society
Overview: A small local charitable organization founded in 1973
Mission: To operate a museum; to collect, preserve & display the material & documentary culture of Cumberland for the education & enjoyment of present & future generations
Member of: Council of Nova Scotia Archives; Association of Nova Scotia Museums

Finances: Annual Operating Budget: $50,000-$100,000; *Funding Sources:* Provincial, federal & municipal government; fundraising
Staff Member(s): 2; 12 volunteer(s)
Membership: 130; *Fees:* $15; *Committees:* Fundraising; Garden; Membership; Special Events; Program; Communications; Exhibits
Activities: Public & school programs; dinners.; *Awareness Events:* International Museum Day, May 18; Annual Four Fathers Dinner, September; Museums Across the Marsh, June
Library: Genealogical Archives; Open to public by appointment
Chief Officer(s):
Brian Trenholm, Chair
Shelley Rector, Treasurer

Cumulative Environmental Management Association (CEMA)
Morrison Center, #214, 9914 Morrison St., Fort McMurray AB T9H 4A4
Tel: 780-799-3947; *Fax:* 780-714-3081
info@cemaonline.ca
www.cemaonline.ca
www.facebook.com/111309945551863
twitter.com/cemacomms
Overview: A medium-sized national organization founded in 2000
Mission: To study the cumulative environmental effects of industrial development in the region and produce guidelines and management frameworks.
Membership: 44 institutional
Chief Officer(s):
Glen Semenchuk, Executive Director
glen.semenchuk@cemaonline.ca

Curl BC
#2001A, 3713 Kensington Ave., Burnaby BC V5B 0A7
Tel: 604-333-3616; *Fax:* 604-333-3615
Toll-Free: 800-667-2875
www.curlbc.ca
www.facebook.com/curlbc.ca
twitter.com/curlbc
www.youtube.com/user/CurlBC
Merged from: Pacific Coast Curling Association; BC Ladies' Curling Association; BC Interior Curling Association
Overview: A medium-sized provincial organization founded in 2004 overseen by Canadian Curling Association
Mission: To deliver all curling programs & services in British Columbia
Affiliation(s): BC Interior Masters Curling Association; Pacific Coast Masters Curling Association
Staff Member(s): 6
Chief Officer(s):
Scott Braley, Executive Director & CEO, 604-333-3621
sbraley@curlbc.ca

Curling Québec
4545, av Pierre-de Coubertin, Montréal QC H1V 0B2
Tél: 514-252-3088; *Téléc:* 514-252-3342
Ligne sans frais: 888-292-2875
info@curling-quebec.qc.ca
www.curling-quebec.qc.ca
www.facebook.com/CurlingQuebec
twitter.com/curlingquebec
Également appelé: Fédération québécoise de curling
Aperçu: Dimension: moyenne; *Envergure:* provinciale; Organisme sans but lucratif; fondée en 1976 surveillé par Canadian Curling Association
Mission: Offrir aux amateurs de curling, et à tous ceux désirant le devenir, la possibilité de jouer au curling à l'intérieur d'une structure organisée appuyée par divers services
Membre de: Fédération mondiale de curling
Membre: 10 000; *Comités:* Excellence; Championnats; Junior
Membre(s) du bureau directeur:
Marco Berthelot, Directeur général
mferraro@curling-quebec.qc.ca

CurlManitoba Inc.
#309, 145 Pacific Ave., Winnipeg MB R3B 2Z6
Tel: 204-925-5723; *Fax:* 204-925-5720
mca@curlmanitoba.org
www.curlmanitoba.org
www.facebook.com/323935420031
twitter.com/curlmanitoba
Merged from: Manitoba Ladies Curling Association
Overview: A medium-sized provincial organization founded in 2000 overseen by Canadian Curling Association
Mission: To promote the sport of curling in Manitoba.
Affiliation(s): Canadian Curling Association
Staff Member(s): 7
Membership: Fees: Schedule available; *Committees:* Finance; Board Development; Executive
Activities: Learn to curl clinics; coaching courses; ice technician courses; business of curling courses; club ice & rock consultation; game promotion; competition organization; establishment & governance of competition rules & regulations
Chief Officer(s):
Craig Baker, Executive Director
cbaker@curlmanitoba.org
Rob Van Kommer, President
president@curlmanitoba.org
Awards:
• Outstanding Achievements
• Scholarships
• Honourary Life Memberships

Curriculum Services Canada (CSC) / Service des programmes d'études Canada
#1450, 439 University Ave., Toronto ON M5G 1Y8
Tel: 416-591-1576; *Fax:* 416-591-1578
Toll-Free: 800-837-3048
csc@curriculum.org
www.curriculum.org
www.facebook.com/cservicescanada
twitter.com/CSCorganization
Overview: A medium-sized national organization
Mission: The Pan-Canadian standards agency for quality assurance in learning products and programs. It is a not-for-profit and provides services including development, implementation, evaluation, and accreditation of teaching and/or learning resources, and the delivery of web-based professional learning opportunities across Canada and internationally.
Affiliation(s): The Curriculum Foundation
Chief Officer(s):
Amy Coupal, Executive Director
Ardeth Staz, Chair

Cursillo Movement of the Archdiocese of Toronto
PO Box 58021, 500 Rossland Rd. West, Oshawa ON L1J 8L6
www.cursillotoronto.org
Overview: A small local charitable organization
Mission: To discover & understand, in a profound & intense way, God's deep love; To share this belief in the everyday environment, particularly with those who are distant from the Christian faith & the Church
Affiliation(s): Archdiocese of Toronto
Membership: Member Profile: Men & women who desire to encounter themselves, Christ, & others, & to transform this encounter into friendship with Christ & others
Activities: Spreading faith in all environments; Offering Linguistic Cursillo Groups (Chinese, French, Hungarian, Korean, Spanish, & Vietnamese) in the Archdiocese of Toronto; Providing faith instruction & renewal programs; Sharing prayer life & apostolic activities
Chief Officer(s):
Terrence McKenna, Spiritual Director
Publications:
• The Fourth Day
Type: Newsletter

CUSO International
#200, 44 Eccles St., Ottawa ON K1R 6S4
Tel: 613-829-7445; *Fax:* 613-829-7996
Toll-Free: 888-434-2876
questions@cusointernational.org
www.cusointernational.org
www.linkedin.com/company/cuso-international
www.facebook.com/CusoInternational
twitter.com/CusoIntl
www.youtube.com/cusointernational
Previous Name: CUSO-VSO; Canadian University Service Overseas
Overview: A large international charitable organization founded in 1961
Mission: To work through skilled volunteers to aid global social justice; To address poverty, human rights violations, HIV/AIDS, inequity & environmental degradation; To give Canadians information, the experiences & the tools they need to become active global citizens
Member of: VSO International; Canadian Council for International Cooperation; Global Campaign for Education (GCE); Global Citizens for Change Coalition; Canadian Make Poverty History Campaign
Affiliation(s): CJEO Youth Avenue Internationale; El Salvador Cultural Partnership; International Model Forest Partnership; Canadian Community Economic Development Network (CCEDNet); Marbek Resource Consultants
Finances: Annual Operating Budget: Greater than $5 Million; *Funding Sources:* Grants; Donations
Staff Member(s): 58; 576 volunteer(s)
Activities: Developing community projects & programs; Supporting health initiatives; *Internships:* Yes; *Speaker Service:* Yes
Chief Officer(s):
Glenn Mifflin, CEO
   Atlantic Regional Office
   #500, 1001, rue Sherbrooke est, Montréal QC H2L 1L3
   Tel: 514-276-8528
   atlanticconnect@cusointernational.org
   Mission: To promote policies for developing global sustainability.
   Québec Regional Office
   #500, 1001, rue Sherbrooke est, Montréal QC H2L 1L3
   Tel: 514-276-8528
   quebecconnect@cusointernational.org
   Chief Officer(s):
   Christine Messier, Public Engagement Officer
   christine.messier@cusointernational.org
   Toronto Office
   #166, 215 Spadina Ave., Toronto ON M5T 2C7
   Tel: 647-478-4089
   outreach@cusointernational.org
   Mission: To support alliances for global social justice; to work with people striving for freedom, gender & racial equality, self-determination & cultural survival; to share information, human & material resources; to promote policies for developing global sustainability.
   Chief Officer(s):
   Jessica Dubelaar, Public Engagement Officer

CUSO-VSO; Canadian University Service Overseas *See* CUSO International

Customer Service Professionals Network (CSPN)
#5, 25 Royal Crest Ct., Markham ON L3R 9X4
Tel: 905-477-5544; *Fax:* 905-940-1278
mycspn.com
www.linkedin.com/groups?gid=7487566&trk
www.facebook.com/myCSPN
twitter.com/myCSPN
instagram.com/myCSPN
Overview: A medium-sized provincial organization founded in 1981
Mission: To provide educational presentations & networking to assist customer service professionals with the information they need to increase productivity & profit for their organizations
Finances: Annual Operating Budget: Less than $50,000; *Funding Sources:* Membership dues; special events
Membership: 2,500; *Fees:* $150 individual; $495 corporate; $600 vendor; *Member Profile:* Customer service professionals; vendors; consultants; *Committees:* Executive Council; Welcoming
Activities: Speakers & workshops; panel & discussion; social events; Day on the Green; Education Day; *Awareness Events:* Professional Education Day; Customer Service Week
Chief Officer(s):
Dolly Konzelmann, President, 905-477-5544

Customs & Immigration Union (CIU) / Syndicat des douanes et de l'immigration (SDI)
1741 Woodward Dr., Ottawa ON K2C 0P9
Tel: 613-723-8008; *Fax:* 613-723-7895
web@ciu-sdi.ca
www.ciu-sdi.ca
www.facebook.com/ciu-sdi
twitter.com/ciusdi_en
Previous Name: Customs Excise Union Douanes Accise (CEUDA)
Overview: A medium-sized national organization founded in 1968 overseen by Public Service Alliance of Canada
Mission: To address CIU-SDI members' concerns on a timely basis
Affiliation(s): Canadian Professional Police Association (CPPA); Child Find Canada; Mother Against Drunk Driving (MADD Canada); Canadian Federation of Students (CFS); Canadian American Border Trade Alliance (CABTA); Canadian Labour Congress (CLC); Canadian Manufacturers and Exporters (CME); Fédération des travailleurs et travailleuses du Québec; Federation of Canadian Municipalities (FCM); Labour College of

Canada; National Treasury Employees Union (NTEU), U.S.; Public Service Alliance of Canada (PSAC)
Staff Member(s): 11
Membership: *Committees:* CIU-SDI Standing Finance; By-Laws; Union/Management Relations; Component Collective Bargaining; National Occupational Safety & Health; Honours & Awards; Human Resources Working; Border Security; Joint Union/Management Employment Equity; CIU-SDI Standing Equal Opportunities; Immigration Transition Advisory
Activities: Hosting a national convention; Appearing as a witness before Parliamentary Committees, House of Commons & Senate; Conducting national lobbying campaigns
Chief Officer(s):
Jean-Pierre Fortin, National President
jp.fortin@ciu-sdi.ca
Mark Weber, First National Vice President
mark.weber@ciu-sdi.ca

Customs Excise Union Douanes Accise (CEUDA) *See* Customs & Immigration Union

Cut Knife Chamber of Commerce
PO Box 629, Cut Knife SK S0M 0N0
Tel: 306-398-2060; *Fax:* 306-398-2062
Overview: A small local organization

Cycle Toronto
#307, 720 Bathurst St., Toronto ON M5S 2R4
Tel: 416-644-7188
www.cycleto.ca
www.facebook.com/cycletoronto
twitter.com/cycletoronto
Previous Name: Toronto Cyclists Union
Overview: A small local organization
Mission: Cycle Toronto is a member-supported organization that advocates for a healthy, safe, cycling-friendly city for all.
Finances: *Annual Operating Budget:* $250,000-$500,000
Membership: 2,865; *Fees:* $20-$150
Activities: *Awareness Events:* Bike Month, May
Chief Officer(s):
Jared Kolb, Executive Director
jared.kolb@cycleto.ca

Cycling Association of the Yukon
4061 - 4th Ave., Whitehorse YT Y1A 1H1
info@yukoncycling.com
yukoncycling.com
Overview: A small provincial organization overseen by Cycling Canada Cyclisme
Member of: Cycling Canada Cyclisme; Sport Yukon
Chief Officer(s):
Marc LaPointe, President

Cycling British Columbia (CBC)
#201, 210 West Broadway, Vancouver BC V5Y 3W2
Tel: 604-737-3034; *Fax:* 604-737-3141
membership@cyclingbc.net
cyclingbc.net
www.facebook.com/122018951154516
twitter.com/raceinbc
www.youtube.com/user/cyclingbc
Also Known As: Cycling BC
Previous Name: Bicycling Association of BC
Overview: A medium-sized provincial organization founded in 1974 overseen by Cycling Canada Cyclisme
Mission: To enable, enhance, & encourage cycling in British Columbia
Member of: Cycling Canada Cyclisme
Staff Member(s): 7
Membership: *Fees:* Schedule available; *Committees:* Governance Review; Female Program Development
Activities: *Rents Mailing List:* Yes; *Library:* Not open to public
Chief Officer(s):
Richard Wooles, Executive Director
richard@cyclingbc.net
Diana Hardie, Director, Finance & Administration
diana@cyclingbc.net
Tara Mowat, Coordinator, High Performance
tara@cyclingbc.net
Awards:
• BC Cup Champions
• Club, Coach, Organizer, Commissaire of the Year Awards

Cycling Canada Cyclisme
#203, 2197 Riverside Dr., Ottawa ON K1H 7X3
Tel: 613-248-1353; *Fax:* 613-248-9311
general@cyclingcanada.ca
www.cyclingcanada.ca
www.facebook.com/CyclingCanada
twitter.com/CyclingCanada
www.youtube.com/user/CanadianCycling
Previous Name: Canadian Cycling Association
Overview: A medium-sized national organization founded in 1882
Mission: To organize & promote cycling in Canada, including BMX, road racing, track, & mountain biking, for sport & fitness.
Chief Officer(s):
Greg Mathieu, CEO & Secretary General
greg.mathieu@cyclingcanada.ca
Jacques Landry, Head Coach & Director, High Performance
jacques.landry@cyclingcanada.ca
Mathieu Boucher, Director, Performance Development
mathieu.boucher@cyclingcanada.ca
Brett Stewart, Director, Finance & Administration
brett.stewart@cyclingcanada.ca
Matthew Jeffries, Director, Marketing & Communications
matthew.jeffries@cyclingcanada.ca
Publications:
• Athlete Bios [a publication of the Canadian Cycling Association]
• Canadian Cycling Association / Association cycliste canadienne Directory
Type: Directory
• CCA [Canadian Cycling Association] Annual Report
Frequency: Annually
• Cycling Long Term Athlete Development Model

Cycling PEI (CPEI)
Sport PEI, PO Box 302, 40 Enman Cresent, Charlottetown PE C1A 7K7
Tel: 902-368-4985; *Fax:* 902-368-4548
www.cpei.ca
twitter.com/cyclingpei
Overview: A small provincial organization overseen by Cycling Canada Cyclisme
Mission: To develop cycling in PEI
Member of: Cycling Canada Cyclisme
Membership: *Fees:* $20 youth general; $30 senior general; $30 youth citizen; $40 senior citizen; $50 youth UCI racing license; $90 senior UCI racing license
Activities: *Awareness Events:* Red Mud Mountain Mayhem, Aug.
Chief Officer(s):
David Sims, President
sims@cpei.ca
Mike Connolly, Executive Director
mconnolly@sportpei.pe.ca

Cyclo-Nature
4693, rue de Lanaudière, Montréal QC H2L 3P6
Courriel: info@cyclonature.org
www.cyclonature.org
Aperçu: *Dimension:* petite; *Envergure:* locale; fondée en 1974
Mission: Pour réunir des gens qui sont enthousiastes au sujet des activités de plein air et de vélo

Cypress Hills Ability Centres, Inc. (CHACI)
PO Box 579, 395 7th St. West, Shaunavon SK S0N 2M0
Tel: 306-297-2776; *Fax:* 306-297-2574
information@chaci.com
www.chaci.com
Previous Name: Shaunawan Ability Centre
Merged from: Cypress Hills Developmental Association & Shaunawan Ability Centre
Overview: A small local organization founded in 1974
Mission: To help individuals with disabilities reach their fullest potential by providing support & rehabilitation services
Affiliation(s): Saskatchewan Association of Rehabilitation Centres
Finances: *Annual Operating Budget:* $500,000-$1.5 Million; *Funding Sources:* Provincial government
Staff Member(s): 40; 2 volunteer(s)
Membership: 7 individual; *Fees:* $1 individual
Activities: Accreditation through Saskatchewan Association of Rehabilitation Centres; *Awareness Events:* Bowlathon, Feb.
Chief Officer(s):
Phyllis Edgington, Chief Executive Officer
chaciceo@sasktel.net

Cypress Hills Registered Horse Breeders' Association
c/o William & Donna Beierbach, PO Box 416, Maple Creek SK S0N 1N0
Tel: 306-299-2073
1yquarterhorses@gmail.com
www.cypresshorsebreeders.com
Overview: A small local organization
Membership: 23; *Member Profile:* Registered horse breeders in the Cypress Hills region of southwestern Saskatchewan & southeastern Alberta
Activities: Hosting The Annual Cypress Hills Registered Horse Breeders Production Sale each September; Providing information about members' ranch histories, breedings programs, & sales

Cypress River Chamber of Commerce
PO Box 261, Cypress River MB R0K 0P0
Tel: 204-743-2119; *Fax:* 204-743-2339
www.cypressriver.ca
Overview: A small local organization
Mission: To promote & support local businesses
Chief Officer(s):
Jim Cassels, President
cypressmotorinnone@hotmail.com

Cypriot Federation of Canada / Fédération chypriote du Canada
6 Thorncliff Park Dr., Toronto ON M4H 1H1
Tel: 416-696-7400; *Fax:* 416-696-9465
cypriotfederation@rogers.com
cypriotfederation.ca
Overview: A small national organization
Mission: To co-ordinate activities relating to ethnicity, community, education & culture
Member of: Canadian Ethnocultural Council
Chief Officer(s):
Christine Amygdalidis, President
Petros Mina, General Secretary

Cystic Fibrosis Canada / Fibrose Kystique Canada
National Office, #800, 2323 Yonge St., Toronto ON M4P 2C9
Tel: 416-485-9149; *Fax:* 416-485-0960
Toll-Free: 800-378-2233
info@cysticfibrosis.ca
www.cysticfibrosis.ca
www.facebook.com/CysticFibrosisCanada
twitter.com/CFCanada
www.youtube.com/CysticFibrosisCanada
Previous Name: Canadian Cystic Fibrosis Foundation
Overview: A large national charitable organization founded in 1960
Mission: To help people with Cystic Fibrosis through funding research towards a cure or control; To support high quality care; To promote public awareness; To raise & allocate funds
Member of: Canadian Centre for Philanthropy; Canadian Coalition for Genetic Fairness
Affiliation(s): Cystic Fibrosis Worldwide
Finances: *Funding Sources:* Donations; Fundraising
Staff Member(s): 18
Membership: 50 chapters; *Committees:* Scientific Advisory
Activities: Many scientific grants & awards; research programs; *Awareness Events:* Cystic Fibrosis Month, May; *Speaker Service:* Yes
Chief Officer(s):
Martha Beaumont, Chief Financial & Operations Officer
mbeaumont@cysticfibrosis.ca
Publications:
• Breathe - Final Report [a publication of Cystic Fibrosis Canada]
Type: Report
• Canadian Patient Data Registry Report [a publication of Cystic Fibrosis Canada]
Type: Report
• Candid Facts [a publication of Cystic Fibrosis Canada]
Type: Newsletter; *Frequency:* Quarterly; *ISSN:* 0226-2347
Profile: News about events, research, & treatments for CFC members, donors, partners, & friends
• CFC [Cystic Fibrosis Canada] Annual Report
Type: Yearbook; *Frequency:* Annually
• Circle of Friends [a publication of Cystic Fibrosis Canada]
Frequency: Semiannually; *Price:* Free for adults with CF & other interested persons
Profile: National newsletter for Canadian adults with cystic fibrosis
• Cystic Fibrosis Canada Grants & Awards Guide [a publication of Cystic Fibrosis Canada]
Type: Guide
• The Guide: Resources for the CF Community [a publication of Cystic Fibrosis Canada]
Type: Guide

Canadian Associations / Czech & Slovak Association of Canada

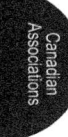

• Insights [a publication of Cystic Fibrosis Canada]
Type: Newsletter
Profile: For the CF community, support groups, & other interested persons

Cystic Fibrosis Québec *Voir* Fibrose kystique Québec

Czech & Slovak Association of Canada
PO Box 564, 3044 Bloor St. West, Toronto ON M8X 2Y8
Tel: 416-925-2241; *Fax:* 416-925-1940
ustredi@cssk.ca
www.cssk.ca
Previous Name: Czechoslovak Association of Canada
Overview: A medium-sized national organization founded in 1939
Mission: To develop the highest standards of citizenship in Canadians of Czech or Slovak origin by encouraging, carrying on & participating in activities of national, patriotic, cultural & humanitarian nature; to act in matters affecting status rights & welfare of Canadians of Czech or Slovak origin; to cultivate in members appreciation of their mother tongue, cultural heritage & historical traditions; to promote growth of spirit in toleration, understanding & goodwill between all ethnic elements in Canada; to conduct research & encourage studies.
Member of: Canadian Ethnocultural Council; OCASI
Activities: *Library:* by appointment Not open to public
Chief Officer(s):
Marie Fuchsová, President

Czech Cultural Club *See* Edmonton Czech Language Society

Czechoslovak Association of Canada *See* Czech & Slovak Association of Canada

Dads Can
c/o St. Joseph's Health Care, PO Box 34, 268 Grosvenor St., London ON N6A 4V2
Tel: 519-646-6095
Toll-Free: 888-323-7226
www.dadscan.ca
Overview: A small national charitable organization
Mission: To "re-enculture" a fatherhood ideal by promoting responsible & involved fathering through the support of men's personal development into fatherhood & healthy fathering patterns
Finances: *Annual Operating Budget:* Less than $50,000
Membership: 1-99
Activities: *Speaker Service:* Yes
Chief Officer(s):
Neil R. Campbell, President/Executive Director

Daily Bread Food Bank
191 New Toronto St., Toronto ON M8V 2E7
Tel: 416-203-0050; *Fax:* 416-203-0049
info@dailybread.ca
www.dailybread.ca
www.facebook.com/DailyBreadFoodBank
twitter.com/DailyBreadTO
www.instagram.com/DailyBreadTO
Overview: A small local organization
Mission: To end poverty & hunger through research, education, & advocacy; To help member agencies provide support & food to people struggling with hunger
Member of: Food Banks Canada
Finances: *Annual Operating Budget:* $3 Million-$5 Million
Staff Member(s): 40; 160 volunteer(s)
Membership: 129; *Fees:* $25; *Member Profile:* Food agencies in the Greater Toronto Area who distribute food to people in need
Activities: Annual Spring, Fall & Winter food drives; *Awareness Events:* Holiday Drive, December *Library:* Learning Centre
Chief Officer(s):
Gail Nyberg, Executive Director, 416-203-0050 Ext. 230
gail@dailybread.ca
Laurie Snyder, Director, Operations
Nancy Bennett, Director, Philanthropy & Private-Sector Partnerships
Tammy Davey-Wiebe, Director, Finance & Information Technology
Richard Matern, Director, Research & Communicatons
Charles Jergl, Director, Agency Relations
Beth Sorichetti, Director, Human Resources

Dairy Farmers of Canada (DFC) / Les Producteurs laitiers du Canada (PLC)
21 Florence St., Ottawa ON K2P 0W6
Tel: 613-236-9997; *Fax:* 613-236-0905
info.policy@dfc-plc.ca
www.dairyfarmers.ca
twitter.com/dfc_plc
Overview: A medium-sized national organization founded in 1934 overseen by Canadian Federation of Agriculture
Mission: To coordinate action of dairy producer organizations on all issues of national scope; To collaborate with relevant agencies in elaboration of national policies of interest to Canadian dairy industry
Member of: International Dairy Federation
Finances: *Funding Sources:* Agriculture & Agri-Food Canada; the National Science & Engineering Research Council
Membership: *Member Profile:* Dairy producers; organizations; breed-related organizations; milk recording; *Committees:* Promotion
Activities: Promoting & marketing dairy products such as cheese & butter as well as nutrition communications directed to health officials & consumers; *Library:* Not open to public
Chief Officer(s):
Wally Smith, President

Montréal Office
#700, 1801, av McGill College, Montréal QC H3A 2N4
Tel: 514-284-1092; *Fax:* 514-284-0449
Toll-Free: 800-361-4632
info@dfc-plc.ca

Dairy Farmers of Manitoba (DFM) / Producteurs Laitiers du Manitoba
4055 Portage Ave., Winnipeg MB R3K 2E8
Tel: 204-488-6455; *Fax:* 204-488-4772
Toll-Free: 800-567-1671
general@milk.mb.ca
www.milk.mb.ca
Previous Name: Manitoba Milk Producers
Overview: A small provincial organization founded in 1974
Mission: To represent the interests of dairy farmers of Manitoba at the provincial & national levels; To produce milk according to the highest standards; To sell milk from Manitoba's dairy farmers to processors
Finances: *Funding Sources:* Manitoba's dairy farmers
Membership: *Member Profile:* Dairy farmers in Manitoba
Activities: Developing advertising programs

Dairy Farmers of New Brunswick (DFNB) / Producteurs laitiers du Nouveau-Brunswick
PO Box 5034, Sussex NB E4E 5L2
Tel: 506-432-4330; *Fax:* 506-432-4333
nbmilk@nbmilk.org
www.nbmilk.org
Overview: A small provincial organization
Mission: To represent the interests of dairy farmers in New Brunswick; To produce high quality milk
Finances: *Funding Sources:* Dairy farmers of New Brunswick
Membership: *Member Profile:* New Brunswick's dairy farmers
Activities: Marketing raw milk
Chief Officer(s):
Steve Michaud, General Manager, 506-432-0357
stevem@nbmilk.org

Dairy Farmers of Newfoundland & Labrador (DFNL)
Building 5A, 308 Brookfield Rd., St. John's NL A1E 0B2
Tel: 709-364-6634; *Fax:* 709-364-8364
milk@dfnl.nf.net
Overview: A small provincial organization founded in 1983
Mission: To regulate milk production in Newfoundland & Labrador
Member of: Dairy Farmers of Canada
Staff Member(s): 4
Membership: 34

Dairy Farmers of Nova Scotia (DFNS)
#100, 4060 Hwy. 236, Lower Truro NS B6L 1J9
Tel: 902-893-6455; *Fax:* 902-897-9768
www.dfns.ca
Overview: A medium-sized provincial organization founded in 2001
Mission: To provide a regulatory & administrative service to Nova Scotia's dairy producers
Membership: 250
Chief Officer(s):
Brian Cameron, General Manager, 902-893-6455 Ext. 1
bcameron@dfns.ca

Dairy Farmers of Ontario (DFO)
6780 Campobello Rd., Mississauga ON L5N 2L8
Tel: 905-821-8970; *Fax:* 905-821-3160
questions@milk.org
www.milk.org
www.facebook.com/OntarioDairy
twitter.com/DairyOntario
Overview: A small provincial organization founded in 1995
Mission: To provide leadership and excellence in the production and marketing of Canadian milk
Staff Member(s): 74
Membership: *Member Profile:* Dairy farmers in Ontario
Activities: Developing advertising programs
Chief Officer(s):
Peter Gould, General Manager & CEO
peter.gould@milk.org
Meetings/Conferences:
• Dairy Farmers of Ontario Annual Meeting 2018, 2018, ON
Scope: Provincial

Dairy Nutrition Council of Alberta *See* Alberta Milk

Dalhousie Faculty Association / Association des professeurs de Dalhousie
PO Box 15000, 6280 South St., Halifax NS B3H 4R2
Tel: 902-494-3722; *Fax:* 902-494-6740
dfa@dal.ca
dfa.ns.ca
twitter.com/dalfacultyassoc
Overview: A medium-sized local organization
Mission: To represent the interests of all Dalhousie University staff & faculty members in employment relations matters
Staff Member(s): 4
Membership: 870; *Committees:* Executive; Grievance
Chief Officer(s):
Kevin Grundy, President
Kevin.Grundy@dal.ca
Lynn Purves, Administrative Officer

Dalhousie Medical Research Foundation
PO Box 15000, Halifax NS B3H 4R2
Tel: 902-494-3502; *Fax:* 902-494-1372
Toll-Free: 888-866-6559
dmrf@dal.ca
www.dmrf.ca
Overview: A small local charitable organization
Mission: To provide funds to the research department of the Dalhousie Medical school & other affiliated health care facilities
Affiliation(s): Dalhousie Medical School
Staff Member(s): 5
Membership: *Committees:* Scientific Advisory
Chief Officer(s):
Jyl MacKinnon, Executive Director
Jyl.MacKinnon@Dal.ca

Dalhousie University School of Information Management Associated Alumni
Kenneth C. Rowe Management Bldg., #4010, 6100 University Ave., Halifax NS B3H 4R2
Tel: 902-494-3656
sim@dal.ca
sim.management.dal.ca
www.linkedin.com/groups?gid=2360751
www.facebook.com/SIMDalhousie
twitter.com/dalsimnews
blogs.dal.ca/sim
Overview: A small local organization founded in 1974
Mission: To advance the interests of information professionals, particularly their education; To promote the objectives & best interests of the Dalhousie School of Information Management & the professional objectives & interests of the individual members of the Associated Alumni.
Chief Officer(s):
Sandra Toze, Director
stoze@dal.ca

Dance Centre
Scotiabank Dance Centre, 677 Davie St., Level 6, Vancouver BC V6B 2G6
Tel: 604-606-6400; *Fax:* 604-606-6401
info@thedancecentre.ca
www.thedancecentre.ca
www.facebook.com/thedancecentre
twitter.com/dancecentre
Overview: A small local charitable organization founded in 1986
Mission: To raise the profile of dance in BC; to serve as a focal point & advocate for issues & concerns affecting the entire dance community; to coordinate the resources & activities of this wide ranging community
Member of: Alliance for Arts and Culture; CanDance Network; Canadian Dance Assembly; World Dance Alliance Americas

Finances: *Annual Operating Budget:* $250,000-$500,000; *Funding Sources:* Government; private; earned
Staff Member(s): 7; 30 volunteer(s)
Membership: 220; *Fees:* $50-75 individual; $90-315 corporate; *Member Profile:* Dance companies; independent artists; educators; dance enthusiasts & supporters; *Committees:* Artistic Advisory; Fundraising
Activities: Administration; video production; consultation; presentation; advocacy; operation of Scotiabank Dance Centre facility; *Awareness Events:* International Dance Day, April 29; *Internships:* Yes *Library:* Dr. Yosef Wosk Video Library; Not open to public
Chief Officer(s):
Heather Bray, Marketing Manager
Mirna Zagar, Executive Director
executivedirector@thedancecentre.ca
Awards:
• The Isadora Award
Awarded for excellence in dance & significant contribution to the dance community & to the art form
• Dance Central
Type: Online Publication; *Frequency:* Bimonthly; *Accepts Advertising*; *Editor:* Andreas Kahre
Profile: The publication features interviews with people in the dance community

The Dance Centre (TDC)
Scotiabank Dance Centre, 677 Davie St., 6th Fl., Vancouver BC V6B 2G6
Tel: 604-606-6400; *Fax:* 604-606-6401
info@thedancecentre.ca
www.thedancecentre.ca
www.facebook.com/thedancecentre
twitter.com/dancecentre
www.youtube.com/thedancecentrebc
Overview: A small local charitable organization founded in 1986
Mission: To increase the exposure of performing arts through the presentation of interdisciplinary performances & workshops; to present contemporary dance work & interdisciplinary dance/theatre/music performances of the highest quality; to act as a catalyst & animator for dance & associated arts in the community & to offer infrastructure & presentation support of that activity
Staff Member(s): 27
Membership: *Fees:* $25 student; $50 associate; $75 full; $90 emerging company; schedule for companies dependant on annual budget; *Member Profile:* Dancers, choreographers, teachers & companies
Chief Officer(s):
Mima Zagar, Executive Director
executivedirector@thedancecentre.ca
Awards:
• The Isadora Award
Awarded to recognize professionals who have made an outstanding contribution to dance in British Columbia *Deadline:* January
• The Iris Garland Emerging Choreographer Award
Awarded every two years to a senior dance student between the ages of 19 and 35 who demonstrates outstanding choreographic ability & professional potential*Deadline:* January; *Amount:* $5,000
• The Lola Award
Awarded to encourage the work of senior or mid-career choreographers *Deadline:* January

Dance Manitoba Inc.
Pantages Playhouse Theatre, #204, 180 Market Ave. East, Winnipeg MB R3B 0P7
Tel: 204-989-5260; *Fax:* 204-989-5268
info@dancemanitoba.org
www.dancemanitoba.org
www.facebook.com/210968142294814
Overview: A small provincial organization
Mission: To promote the development of dance through festivals, workshops, & showcases
Membership: 146; *Fees:* $25 adult; $15 youth/student; $35 organization
Chief Officer(s):
Nicole Owens, Executive Director

Dance Nova Scotia
1113 Marginal Rd., Halifax NS B3H 4P7
Tel: 902-422-1749; *Fax:* 902-422-0881
office@dancens.ca
www.dancens.ca
www.facebook.com/DanceNovaScotia
twitter.com/dancenovascotia
Also Known As: DANS
Overview: A medium-sized provincial charitable organization founded in 1974
Mission: To promote, stimulate, & encourage the development of dance as a cultural, educational, healthy, & social activity for all ages, abilities, & backgrounds
Member of: Cultural Federations of Nova Scotia
Finances: *Annual Operating Budget:* $100,000-$250,000; *Funding Sources:* Government; program revenue
Staff Member(s): 6; 20 volunteer(s)
Membership: 125; *Fees:* $25 individual; $50 organization; *Member Profile:* Dance teachers; dance organizations; *Committees:* Dance for Health: Seniors; Education; Membership
Activities: Programs (Dance for Health; Seniors, Dare to Dance School challenge, Breakspace); dance workshops; yearly young choreographer's competition; member's services; studio services for emerging choreographers; *Awareness Events:* International Day of Dance; Dance for Health; *Library:* Open to public by appointment
Chief Officer(s):
Cliff Le Jeune, Executive Director
director@dancens.ca
Bonny Lee, Administrative Officer
office@dancens.ca

Dance Ontario Association / Association Ontario Danse
The Distillery District, #304, 15 Case Goods Lane, Toronto ON M5A 3C4
Tel: 416-204-1083; *Fax:* 416-204-1085
contact@danceontario.ca
www.danceontario.ca
Overview: A small provincial organization founded in 1976
Mission: To support the advancement of all forms of dance; To offer a unified voice on dance issues
Finances: *Funding Sources:* Donations; Fundraising
Membership: 600+; *Fees:* $10 students; $25 affiliates & associates; $30 individuals; $60 groups; *Member Profile:* Persons who make their careers in dance professions; Persons who are interested in dance; Persons affiliated with a member group of Dance Ontario; Students; Groups, such as schools, studios, & associations, in the field of dance
Activities: Promoting all forms of dance & the development of performance facilities; Producing dance programs; Giving advice & industry information; Facilitating communication amongst the dance community; Offering referrals to dance services; Providing networking opportunities; Training management; Organizing workshops in areas such as kinetics & choreography
Chief Officer(s):
Samara Thompson, Chair
Jennifer Watkins, Vice-Chair
Rosslyn Jacob Edwards, Executive Director
Sashar Zarif, Secretary
Cynthia Lickers-Sage, Treasurer
Publications:
• Dance Ontario Directory
Type: Directory
Profile: Listings of members, their professions, & services
• Dance Ontario Newsletter
Type: Newsletter
Profile: Information about member performance & events

Dance Oremus Danse (DOD)
PO Box 322, 8023 Palmer Rd., Combermere ON K0J 1L0
Tel: 613-756-3284
www.danceoremusdanse.org
Overview: A small local charitable organization founded in 1983
Mission: To increase the public's appreciation of the aesthetic arts by promoting & encouraging the philosophy, movement practices & dance forms of Isadora Duncan (1877-1927) & European neo-classical dance, via seminars, workshops, courses on dance, performance, publishing & other media
Finances: *Annual Operating Budget:* $100,000-$250,000; *Funding Sources:* Private; Corporate; Government
Staff Member(s): 4
Activities: Performing; Providing classes, conferences & symposiums; Lecturing; Touring; Conducting research; Conserving Duncan Dance; *Speaker Service:* Yes; *Library:* Dance OREMUS Danse Library; Open to public by appointment
Chief Officer(s):
Peter M. Stadnyk, President, 416-536-9002
peterstadnyk@rogers.com
Paul-James Dwyer, Executive Director
pauljamesdwyer@yahoo.ca

Dance Saskatchewan Inc.
205A Pacific Ave., Saskatoon SK S7K 1N9
Tel: 306-931-8480; *Fax:* 306-244-1520
Toll-Free: 800-667-8480
dancesask@sasktel.net
www.dancesask.com
www.facebook.com/dance.saskatchewan
twitter.com/DanceSask
www.youtube.com/user/Dancesaskatchewan
Overview: A medium-sized provincial charitable organization founded in 1979
Mission: To support & enhance the development of all dance forms; To promote dance in Saskatchewan; To represent & educate about dance; To encourage a passion for dance; To create a viable, unified organization which represents & advocates dance interests; To foster free expression of cultural identity through dance; To establish an active environment which focuses on job creation, performance & cultural diversity within a central dance facility
Member of: World Dance Alliance; Dance & Child International; SaskCulture Inc.
Affiliation(s): Canadian Association of Professional Dance Organizations
Finances: *Funding Sources:* Saskatchewan Lotteries; charitable donations
Staff Member(s): 9
Membership: *Fees:* Schedule available; *Member Profile:* Professional dancers & dance companies; Non-professional individuals, families & groups interested in dance
Activities: Dance flooring; Offering workshops & community assistance in the development of social/ethnic dance forms; Providing scholarships & grants; *Speaker Service:* Yes; *Library:* Open to public
Chief Officer(s):
Linda Coe-Kirkham, Executive Director

Dance Umbrella of Ontario (DUO)
476 Parliament St., 2nd Fl., Toronto ON M4X 1P2
Tel: 416-504-6429; *Fax:* 416-504-8702
duo@danceumbrella.net
www.danceumbrella.net
www.facebook.com/DanceUmbrellaofOntario
twitter.com/danceumbrella
Overview: A small provincial organization founded in 1988
Mission: To assist & support professional dance creators in Ontario dance centres
Member of: Canadian Conference for the Arts
Affiliation(s): Arts Vote; Dance Ontario
Finances: *Funding Sources:* Canada Council of the Arts; Ontario Arts Council; Toronto Arts Council; Ontario government
Staff Member(s): 5
Membership: *Member Profile:* Dance professionals
Activities: *Library:* The Dance Plant; by appointment
Chief Officer(s):
Robert Sauvey, Executive Director

Dancemakers
#301, 15 Case Goods Ln., Toronto ON M5A 3C4
Tel: 416-367-1800
info@dancemakers.org
dancemakers.org
www.linkedin.com/company/dancemakers-school-of-dance
www.facebook.com/dancemakersTO
twitter.com/DancemakersTO
www.youtube.com/user/dancemakerstoronto
Overview: A small local charitable organization founded in 1974
Mission: To bring dance of challenging physicality & emotional impact to audiences by drawing on the diverse talents & individual strengths of its artists; To develop & support works which both provoke & entertain
Member of: Canadian Dance Assembly; Dance Ontario
Finances: *Funding Sources:* Government & private sector
Staff Member(s): 5
Activities: Collaborating with resident artists; Organizing performances; Offering open class & training programs; Renting out studio space
Chief Officer(s):
Amelia Ehrhardt, Artistic Director, 416-367-1800 Ext. 202
amelia@dancemakers.org

Dancer Transition Resource Centre (DTRC) / Centre de ressources et transition pour danseurs (CRTD)
The Lynda Hamilton Centre, #303, 1000 Yonge St., Toronto ON M4W 2K2
Tel: 416-595-5655; *Fax:* 416-595-0009
Toll-Free: 800-667-0851

Canadian Associations / DanceSport Alberta (DSAB)

nationaloffice@dtrc.ca
www.dtrc.ca
www.facebook.com/dtrcnews
twitter.com/dancetransition
www.youtube.com/user/DancerTransition
Overview: A medium-sized national charitable organization founded in 1985
Mission: TO help dancers make necessary transitions into, within & from professional performing; To provide resources for the dance community & the public, offering seminars, education materials & other information
Member of: Dance Ontario; Association of Dance in Universities & Colleges in Canada; International Organization for the Transition of Professional Dancers; Ontario Coalition of Arts Service Organizations; Canadian Conference of the Arts
Affiliation(s): Alberta Canada; Ballet BC; Danse Montréal; Ballet Kelowna; Compagnoe Marie Chouinard; Les Grands Ballets; National Ballet of Canada; O Vertigo; Toronto Dance Theatre; Winnipeg Contemporary Dancers; Dancemakers & the Centre for Creation; Danny Grossman Dance; Decidedly Jazz Danceworks; Canada's Royal Winnipeg Ballet
Finances: *Funding Sources:* Government; Private; Corporations; Foundations; Donations; Special events; Membership dues
Staff Member(s): 11
Membership: *Fees:* $75-$250; *Member Profile:* Open to dancers who are at least 18 years old, have at least one professional performance on their resume & agree to contribute 1% of their salary equally matched by their companies; Dancers may also join on individual basis
Activities: Counselling Referral Program to assist dancers find employment within & outside dance profession; Dancer Awareness Program; Public Awareness Program; Dancer Award Fund; Annual conference "on the MOVE"; *Library:* Open to public
Chief Officer(s):
Monique Rabideau, Chair
Amanda Hancox, Executive Director
ahancox@dtrc.ca
Awards:
- Anne M. Delicaet Bursary
To help fund tuition, books &/or supplies for applicant in their third year of full-time retraining/grants received from the DTRC; *Amount:* Award amount is discretionary
- Sara Symons Bursary
Open to all recipients of at least one year of funding under type C grant who are continuing their studies; *Amount:* Amount is discretionary
- Lynda Hamilton Award
Awarded annually to a dancer in transition who has completed two years of study & requires a third to complete or continue the proposed course of study; *Amount:* $18,000 subsistence & $4,000 for tuition & supplies
- Peter F. Bronfman Memorial Award
It is earmarked for a second or third year of retraining & subsistence & may be only awarded for the full amount; *Amount:* $18,000 subsistence & $4,000 for tuition & supplies
- Karen Kain Award
Given to a dancer entering a second or subsequent year of full-time retraining; *Amount:* Award is discretionary
- Grants for Retraining & Subsistence
- Erik Bruhn Memorial Award
Awarded yearly to a dancer who has completed stream 1 & requires a second year to complete or continue proposed course of study; *Amount:* $18,000 for subsistence & $4,000 for tuition & supplies
- Zella Wolofsky/Doug Wright Bursary
Awarded to a dancer with a degree from a recognized university & who is in second or subsequent year of professional program or doing graduate studies or second degree; *Amount:* $2,000 for any purpose

British Columbia
#712, 402 West Pender St., Vancouver BC V6B 1T6
Tel: 604-899-0755; *Fax:* 604-899-0752
bcoffice@dtrc.ca
Chief Officer(s):
Nina Jane Patel, BC Manager

Québec
#313, 3680, rue Jeanne-Mance, Montréal QC H2X 2K5
Tel: 514-284-1515
bureauqc@crtd.ca
Chief Officer(s):
Parise Mongrain, Program Officer

DanceSport Alberta (DSAB)
AB
president@dancesportalberta.org
www.dancesportalberta.org
Overview: A small provincial organization founded in 1989 overseen by Canada DanceSport
Chief Officer(s):
Wayne Backer, President
wbacker@shaw.ca
Debi Bowman, Vice President
debi@dancesportalberta.org

DanceSport Atlantic (DAA)
3273 Beaver Bank Rd., Lower Sackville NS B4C 2S6
Tel: 902-865-9914
www.dancesport.ca/page11.php
Overview: A small provincial organization overseen by Canada DanceSport
Chief Officer(s):
Heather Fairbairn, President
hfairbairn@live.ca
Mai Miyano, Vice President
maimiyano@hotmail.com

DanceSport Québec (DSQ)
4545, av Pierre-De Coubertin, Montréal QC H1V 0B2
Tél: 514-418-8264
Ligne sans frais: 800-474-5746
info@dansesportquebec.com
dansesportquebec.com
Aperçu: *Dimension:* petite; *Envergure:* provinciale surveillé par Canada DanceSport
Membre(s) du bureau directeur:
Marjolaine Lagace, President
marjolaine.lagace@dansesportquebec.com
Simone Di Tomasso, Vice President
simone.ditomasso@dansesportquebec.com

Dania Home Society
4279 Norland Ave., Burnaby BC V5G 3Z6
Tel: 604-299-2414; *Fax:* 604-299-7775
info@dania.bc.ca
www.dania.bc.ca
Overview: A small local charitable organization founded in 1941
Mission: To operate housing & care facilities for the elderly, maintaining a distinctly Danish style in keeping with the heritage & wishes of the founders
Member of: Federation of Danish Associations in Canada
Affiliation(s): Fraser Health Authority
Membership: *Fees:* $15 annual; $150 life
Activities: Dania Home; Dania Manor; Carl Mortensen Manor
Chief Officer(s):
Kjeld Christensen, President
Margaret Douglas-Matthews, Executive Director

Danish Canadian Chamber of Commerce (DCCC)
Tel: 416-923-1811; *Fax:* 416-962-3668
Overview: A small international organization founded in 1992
Mission: To help promote business relations between Denmark & Canada; to be a forum for discussions concerning Danish-Canadian trade; to be an advisory & consultative body available to Canadian & Danish governmental representatives
Member of: The European Union Chamber of Commerce
Finances: *Annual Operating Budget:* Less than $50,000; *Funding Sources:* Membership fees
Membership: 100; *Fees:* $95 individual; $400 corporate; $750 sponsor
Activities: Luncheon meetings; corporate presentations; conferences & seminars; social events

Danish Canadian Club of Calgary
727 - 11 Ave. SW, Calgary AB T2R 0E3
Tel: 403-261-9774; *Fax:* 403-261-6631
dcc@danishclubcalgary.com
www.danishclubcalgary.com
www.facebook.com/TheDanishCanadianClub
Overview: A small local licensing organization founded in 1933
Member of: Federation of Danish Associations in Canada
Finances: *Funding Sources:* Membership dues; fundraising; banquets
Membership: *Fees:* $30
Chief Officer(s):
Ben Kromand, President
Peter Christensen, General Manager
peter.christensen@danishclubcalgary.com

Danish Canadian National Museum Society (DCNMS)
PO Box 92, Spruce View AB T0M 1V0
Tel: 403-728-0019; *Fax:* 403-728-0020
Toll-Free: 888-443-4114
info@stepintothesaga.com
thedanishcanadianmuseum.com
www.facebook.com/theDanishCanadianMuseum
twitter.com/danishcanadians
Also Known As: Danish Canadian National Museum & Gardens
Overview: A small national charitable organization founded in 1992
Mission: To enrich Canada through the Danish Canadian National Museum, located in Dickson, Alberta; To preserve & promote the culture & history of the Danes in Canada for a greater understanding & celebration of all humanity
Affiliation(s): Federation of Danish Associations in Canada
Finances: *Annual Operating Budget:* $100,000-$250,000; *Funding Sources:* Dontations; fundraising; government grants; on-site operations
Staff Member(s): 1; 100 volunteer(s)
Membership: 700+; *Fees:* $25 individual; $30 family; $100 organization
Activities: *Awareness Events:* St. Hans Fest, June; *Library*
Chief Officer(s):
Svend E. Nielsen, President
viking1@airenet.com
Brian Desjardins, Executive Director
executive@stepintothesaga.com
Faye Kjearsgaard, Curator
curator@danishcanadians.com

Danish Canadian Society of Saint John
112 Birch Cres. East, Rothesay NB E2H 1S6
Tel: 506-847-1021
Overview: A small local organization founded in 1987
Member of: Federation of Danish Associations in Canada
Affiliation(s): Multicultural Association of Saint John
Finances: *Funding Sources:* Membership fees
Membership: *Member Profile:* Danish descent or interest

The Danish Club of Ottawa
PO Box 55032, 240 Sparks St., Ottawa ON K1P 1A1
info@danishclubottawa.com
www.danishclubottawa.com
www.facebook.com/DanishClubofOttawa
Overview: A small local organization founded in 1975
Mission: To promote customs, traditions & other matters peculiar to Danish culture; to foster good relations between Canada & Denmark
Member of: Federation of Danish Associations in Canada
Finances: *Funding Sources:* Membership fees; activities; bazaar
10 volunteer(s)
Membership: 270 individual; *Fees:* $25 family; $15 single; $17 senior couple; $10 senior single; *Committees:* Bazaar; Church
Activities: *Speaker Service:* Yes
Chief Officer(s):
Ted Hansen, President

Danish Heritage Society of Dickson *See* Dickson Store Museum Society

Danse-Cité inc
#426, 3680, rue Jeanne-Mance, Montréal QC H2X 2K5
Tél: 514-525-3595
info@danse-cite.org
www.danse-cite.org
www.facebook.com/dansecite
twitter.com/dansecite
www.youtube.com/user/DANSECITE
Aperçu: *Dimension:* petite; *Envergure:* locale; fondée en 1982
Mission: Création et production de spectacles de danse contemporain
Membre de: Regroupement québécois de la danse
Membre(s) du personnel: 8
Membre(s) du bureau directeur:
Daniel Soulières, Directeur artistique

Dartmouth Adult Services Centre (DASC)
59 Dorey Ave., Dartmouth NS B3B 0B2
Tel: 902-468-6606; *Fax:* 902-468-5359
info@dasc-ns.ca
www.dasc-ns.ca
www.facebook.com/DASCIndustries
twitter.com/dasc_info

Overview: A small local organization founded in 1966
Mission: To provide a vocational day program for adults with intellectual disabilities
Member of: DIRECTIONS Council for Vocational Services Society
Staff Member(s): 40
Activities: Services include: Promotional Button Manufacturing, Mailing Services; & Packaging & Assembly, Boardroom Rentals
Chief Officer(s):
Cathy Deagle-Gammon, Executive Director, 902-468-6606 Ext. 224
director@dasc-ns.ca
Publications:
• DASC [Dartmouth Adult Services Centre] Newsletter
Type: Newsletter; Frequency: q.

Dartmouth Historical Association
Tel: 902-469-2018
www.dartmouthheritagemuseum.ns.ca/dhmDartmouthHistAssoc.html
Overview: A small local charitable organization founded in 1993
Mission: To administer the Leighton Dillman Scholarship Fund; To encourage research & to discuss policies affecting Dartmouth's heritage; To study future plans of Dartmouth; To publish books on local history; To place plaques in public buildings that have been named for people
Affiliation(s): Federation of Nova Scotian Heritage
Finances: Annual Operating Budget: Less than $50,000; Funding Sources: Membership fees; Book sale
10 volunteer(s)
Membership: 200 individual; Fees: $8 individual
Activities: Awareness Events: Halifax Explosion Remembrance, Dec. 6; Speaker Service: Yes
Chief Officer(s):
Harry Chapman, President
hechapman@eastlink.ca

Dartmouth N.S. Family History Centre
44 Cumberland Dr., Dartmouth NS B2V 2C7
Tel: 902-462-0628
ns_dartmouth@ldsmail.net
nsgna.ednet.ns.ca/fhc
Overview: A small local organization
Mission: To do genealogical research
Member of: The Church of Jesus Christ Latter-Day Saints
Finances: Annual Operating Budget: Less than $50,000
Staff Member(s): 13; 12 volunteer(s)
Activities: Library: Open to public

Dartmouth Ringette Association
NS
harbourcitylakers@gmail.com
dartmouthringette.com
Overview: A small local organization overseen by Ringette Nova Scotia
Mission: To operate the Harbour City Lakers League.
Member of: Ringette Nova Scotia
Membership: 11 teams
Chief Officer(s):
Susan Graham, President

Darts Alberta
c/o Sandi Orr, PO Box 163, #14, 9977 - 178 St. NW, Edmonton AB T5T 6J6
Tel: 780-908-0475
administrator@dartsalberta.com
www.dartsalberta.com
Overview: A small provincial organization overseen by National Darts Federation of Canada
Mission: To provide recreational & competitive opportunities for darts players of all levels in Alberta
Member of: National Darts Federation of Canada
Membership: Fees: $40 individual
Activities: Sport programs; educational opportunities for coaches & officials; recognition programs
Chief Officer(s):
Dean Lawson, President, 403-527-0847
president@dartsalberta.com
Sandi Orr, Administrator
administrator@dartsalberta.com

Darts British Columbia Association (DBCA)
c/o Donna Bisaro, #901, 668 Columbia St., New Westminster BC V3M 1A9
executive@dartsbc.ca
www.dartsbc.ca
www.facebook.com/BcDarts

Overview: A small provincial organization overseen by National Darts Federation of Canada
Mission: To provide recreational & competitive opportunities for darts players of all levels in British Columbia
Member of: National Darts Federation of Canada
Membership: 8 leagues/associations; Fees: $5
Chief Officer(s):
Ray Bode, Provincial Director
raybode@shaw.ca
Suzie Letude, Vice President
suzie_letrud1@hotmail.com

Darts Ontario
ON
Tel: 905-426-7493; Fax: 905-426-8270
provincialdirector@dartsontario.com
www.dartsontario.com
Overview: A small provincial organization overseen by National Darts Federation of Canada
Mission: To provide recreational & competitive opportunities for darts players of all levels in Ontario
Member of: National Darts Federation of Canada
Membership: Fees: $18 affiliate; $20 youth; $23 adult
Chief Officer(s):
Susan Hine, President & Provincial Director, 905-426-7493, Fax: 905-426-8270
president@dartsontario.com
Stuart Rutten, Secretary, 416-951-6503
secretary@dartsontario.com

Darts Prince Edward Island
PE
dartspei.ca
Also Known As: Darts PEI
Overview: A small provincial organization overseen by National Darts Federation of Canada
Mission: To provide recreational & competitive opportunities for darts players of all levels in Prince Edward Island
Member of: National Darts Federation of Canada
Chief Officer(s):
Heidi Duchesne, Provincial Director
director@dartspei.com
Darren MacNevin, President
president@dartspei.com
Joey Gallant, Vice President
vice-president@dartspei.com

Daughters of Isabella
40 Bashford Rd., Ajax ON L1S 3Y2
info@daughtersofisabella.org
www.daughtersofisabella.org
Overview: A small local charitable organization
Mission: To unite Catholic women; To uphold the teachings of the Catholic Church & high ideals of life & morals; To extend the circle of friends for Catholic women & to establish bonds among Catholic women throughout the world; To pursue good in society; To foster growth of Catholic women in every aspect of life, including spiritual, social, & charitable; To ensure governance by The International Circle of the Daughters of Isabella; To implement programs & projects consistent with the laws & rules of the organization's constitution
Membership: Member Profile: Catholic women over the age of sixteen
Activities: Conducting monthly business & social meetings; Acting upon the sponsorship of charitable, spiritual, civic, & social programs; Holding ceremonies for the installation of officers & the conferral of degrees for new members
Chief Officer(s):
Monique Kelly, Contact
moniquehkelly@gmail.com

Dauphin & District Allied Arts Council Inc. (DDAAC)
104 - 1st Ave. NW, Dauphin MB R7N 1G9
Tel: 204-638-6231
info@watsonartcentre.com
www.watsonartcentre.com
Overview: A small local charitable organization founded in 1972
Mission: To promote the arts in Dauphin & district through ongoing programs in visual & performing arts, workshops & arts-related activities.
Member of: Manitoba Arts Network
Finances: Funding Sources: Provincial government; City of Dauphin; rentals
Membership: Fees: $12 Senior; $15 Single; $20 Family; $30 Affiliate; $50 Corporate; $100 Associate
Activities: Arts programming; gallery; art in library; Speaker Service: Yes

Chief Officer(s):
Michelle Nyquist, President
Susan Kowalski, Administrator

Dauphin & District Chamber of Commerce
100 Main St. South, Dauphin MB R7N 1K3
Tel: 204-622-3140; Fax: 204-622-3141
coordinator@dauphinchamber.ca
www.dauphinchamber.ca
Overview: A small local organization founded in 1903
Member of: Manitoba Chamber of Commerce
Finances: Funding Sources: Membership dues; group insurance administration fees; grants
Staff Member(s): 1
Membership: Fees: Schedule available; Committees: Membership; Education; Street Fair
Chief Officer(s):
Joanne Vandepoele, President
Awards:
• Community Appreciation Award
• Don Persson Memorial Award

Dauphin Friendship Centre (DFC)
210 - 1st Ave. NE, Dauphin MB R7N 1A7
Tel: 204-638-5707; Fax: 204-638-4799
dfcexec@mts.net
www.dauphinfriendshipcentre.com
www.facebook.com/DauphinFriendshipCenter
Overview: A small local charitable organization founded in 1974
Mission: To enhance the quality of life for Aboriginal and Non-Aboriginal people in the community by working together to provide services and programs to meet the needs of its membership and community.
Affiliation(s): Manitoba Association of Friendship Centres; National Association of Friendship Centres
Membership: Fees: $1
Activities: Children's Christmas Party; Adult Christmas Dinner & Dance; Halloween Howl; Annual Aboriginal Festival; Youth program; Craft/Sewing club; volunteer appreciation luncheon; quarterly networking luncheon; annual youth Christmas dance; Annual National Aboriginal Solidarity Day activities; bingos; Library: Not open to public
Awards:
• DFC Scholarships/Bursaries

Davenport-Perth Neighbourhood & Community Health Centre (DPNCHC)
1900 Davenport Rd., Toronto ON M6N 1B7
Tel: 416-656-8025; Fax: 416-656-1264
info@dpnchc.ca
dpnchc.com
Overview: A medium-sized local charitable organization founded in 1984
Mission: The Davenport-Perth Neighbourhood Centre (DPNC) is a multi-service agency located in the west end of Toronto dedicated to encouraging people to work together and take action to improve the political, social, economic, spiritual and cultural life of the whole community.
Finances: Annual Operating Budget: Greater than $5 Million; Funding Sources: Federal, provincial & municipal governments; foundations; donations; United Way; fundraising
Chief Officer(s):
Wade Hilier, President

David Foster Foundation
212 Henry St., Victoria BC V9A 3H9
Tel: 250-475-1223; Fax: 250-475-1193
Toll-Free: 877-777-7675
info@davidfosterfoundation.com
www.davidfosterfoundation.com
www.linkedin.com/company/david-foster-foundation
www.facebook.com/DavidFosterFoundation
twitter.com/davidfosterfdn
Overview: A small local charitable organization founded in 1986
Mission: To provide financial assistance to families of children undergoing transplant surgery; To raise public awareness regarding organ donation
Chief Officer(s):
Michael Ravenhill, CEO
mravenhill@davidfosterfoundation.com

David Suzuki Foundation (DSF)
#219, 2211 West 4 Ave., Vancouver BC V6K 4S2
Tel: 604-732-4228
Toll-Free: 800-453-1533
contact@davidsuzuki.org
www.davidsuzuki.org

www.facebook.com/DavidSuzuki
twitter.com/DavidSuzukiFDN
www.youtube.com/user/DavidSuzukiFDN
Overview: A small national charitable organization founded in 1991
Mission: To seek out & commission the best, most up-to-date research to help reveal ways we can live in balance with nature; to support the implementation of ecologically sustainable models - from local projects, such as habitat restoration, to international initiatives, such as better frameworks for economic decisions; to ensure the solutions developed through research & application to reach the widest possible audience, & help mobilize broadly supported change; to urge decision makers to adopt policies which encourage & guide individuals & businesses, so their daily decisions reflect the need to act within nature's constraints
Member of: Canadian Renewable Energy Alliance
Staff Member(s): 69
Membership: *Committees:* Governance; Quebec Orientation; Finance & Audit; Investment; Program; Development
Chief Officer(s):
Tara Cullis, President
James Hoggan, Chair
Peter Robinson, CEO

Dawson City Chamber of Commerce
PO Box 1006, 1102 Front St., Dawson City YT Y0B 1G0
Tel: 867-993-5274; *Fax:* 867-993-6817
office@dawsoncitychamberofcommerce.ca
www.dawsoncitychamberofcommerce.ca
Overview: A small local organization
Mission: To grow businesses & promote economic development in Dawson City & the surrounding area
Activities: Advocating; Offering networking & marketing opportunities; Providing information on business issues
Chief Officer(s):
Dick Van Nostrand, President

Dawson Creek & District Chamber of Commerce
10201 - 10th St., Dawson Creek BC V1G 3T5
Tel: 250-782-4868; *Fax:* 250-782-2371
info@dawsoncreekchamber.ca
www.dawsoncreekchamber.ca
www.facebook.com/184324961604326
Overview: A small local organization founded in 1944
Mission: To lead, promote & protect the economic & social prosperity of Dawson Creek & District
Affiliation(s): BC Chamber of Commerce
Finances: *Funding Sources:* Membership dues; service fees
Staff Member(s): 1
Membership: *Fees:* Schedule available
Activities: *Rents Mailing List:* Yes
Chief Officer(s):
Anjula Benjamin, President
Kathleen Connolly, Executive Director
Kathleen@dawsoncreekchamber.ca

Dawson Creek Construction Association
1000 - 102 Ave., Dawson Creek BC V1G 2C1
Tel: 250-782-4704; *Fax:* 250-782-2524
Overview: A small local organization
Chief Officer(s):
Tom van Spronsen, President

Dawson Creek Society for Community Living
1334 - 102 Ave., Dawson Creek BC V1G 2C6
Tel: 250-782-2611; *Fax:* 250-782-2662
www.dcscl.org
Overview: A small local organization founded in 1958
Mission: To assist people with disabilities to become full community participants through training, education, support & advocacy
Member of: British Columbia Association for Community Living
Finances: *Funding Sources:* BC Housing Management Commission; Central Mortgage & Housing Corp.; Community Living BC; Northern Health Authority
Activities: Semi-Independent Living program; Opportunity Centre; Aurora Housing; Southview Housing Project, a seniors apartment complex
Chief Officer(s):
Marla Reed, Executive Director

Daybreak *See* L'Arche Ontario

Deaf Children's Society of B.C. (DCS)
#200, 7355 Canada Way, Burnaby BC V3N 4Z6
Tel: 604-525-6056; *Fax:* 604-525-7307; *TTY:* 604-525-9390
www.deafchildren.bc.ca
www.facebook.com/pages/Deaf-Childrens-Society-of-BC/146576198745766
Previous Name: Deaf Children's Society of British Columbia
Overview: A small provincial charitable organization founded in 1975
Mission: To help deaf children and their families in the province
Finances: *Funding Sources:* Provincial government; fundraisers
Staff Member(s): 11
Membership: *Fees:* $30
Activities: Early Literacy, preschool, speech-language & sign-language programs; summer playgroup; *Library:* DCS Library; Open to public
Chief Officer(s):
Janice Springfield, Executive Director

Deaf Children's Society of British Columbia *See* Deaf Children's Society of B.C.

Deafness Advocacy Association Nova Scotia (DAANS)
Halifax NS
Tel: 902-425-0240; *TTY:* 902-425-0119
daans@ns.sympatico.ca
www.facebook.com/109727935783155
Overview: A small provincial charitable organization founded in 1979
Mission: The Association promotes the rights & needs of the deaf, hard-of-hearing, late-deafened & deafblind in the province.
Member of: Canadian Association of the Deaf
Activities: Support; advocacy; special projects; education; human rights; *Speaker Service:* Yes; *Library:* Open to public

Dease Lake & District Chamber of Commerce
PO Box 338, Dease Lake BC V0C 1L0
Tel: 250-771-3900; *Fax:* 250-771-3900
Overview: A small local organization
Member of: BC Chamber of Commerce
5 volunteer(s)

Debden & District Chamber of Commerce
PO Box 91, Debden SK S0J 0S0
Tel: 306-724-4414; *Fax:* 306-724-2220
www.debden.net
Overview: A small local organization
Mission: To promote business development & tourism in the area
Activities: Conducting historical research; Promoting tourism development & business
Chief Officer(s):
Rhonda Peterson, President
Amelie Patrick, Secretary

DeBolt & District Pioneer Museum Society
PO Box 447, DeBolt AB T0H 1B0
Tel: 780-957-3957; *Fax:* 780-957-2934
deboltmuseum@gmail.com
Overview: A small local charitable organization founded in 1975
Mission: To preserve the history of the rural pioneer in DeBolt & district; To research & publish books on history of the area
Member of: Alberta Museum Association
Affiliation(s): Spirit of the Peace
Finances: *Annual Operating Budget:* Less than $50,000; *Funding Sources:* Donations; book sales; municipal & provincial grants; lottery funds; quilt raffles; hall rental
25 volunteer(s)
Membership: 50; *Fees:* $1; *Member Profile:* Retired & homemakers; *Committees:* Exhibits; Legion Hall
Activities: Thursday morning workshops; published four local history books; *Awareness Events:* Heritage Day, mid-August; *Library:* by appointment
Chief Officer(s):
Fran Moore, Curator & President

DEBRA Canada
PO Box 76035, #3, 1500 Upper Middle Rd., Oakville ON L6M 3H5
Toll-Free: 800-313-3012
Other Communication: French Phone: 866-433-0676
debra@debracanada.org
www.debracanada.org
www.facebook.com/groups/18951212616
twitter.com/DEBRACanada
Overview: A medium-sized national charitable organization
Mission: To support patients of Epidermolysis Bullosa & their families & provide funding for the medical needs of patients
Activities: *Awareness Events:* Epidermolysis Bullosa Awareness Week, Oct.
Chief Officer(s):
Tina Boileau, President
tina@debracanada.org

Decidedly Jazz Danceworks
111 12 Ave. SE, Calgary AB T2G 0Z9
Tel: 403-245-3533; *Fax:* 403-245-3584
djd@decidedlyjazz.com
www.decidedlyjazz.com
www.facebook.com/162890170398000
twitter.com/DecidedlyJazz
www.youtube.com/user/decidedlyjazz
Overview: A small local organization founded in 1984
Mission: To create concert jazz dance that sustains the spirit & traditions of jazz; To mix groove, African roots, rhythm, improvisation, interplay with musicians, & soul; To offer a season of performances, touring, & jazz classes
Staff Member(s): 12
Chief Officer(s):
Kimberley Cooper, Artistic Director
Kathi Sundstrom, Executive Director

Deep River Symphony Orchestra (DRSO)
PO Box 398, Deep River ON K0J 1P0
Tel: 613-584-4264
drsoemail@gmail.com
www.drso.ca
Overview: A small local organization founded in 1952 overseen by Orchestras Canada
Mission: To promote the development & enjoyment of music in the Upper Ottawa Valley
Member of: Ontario Federation of Symphony Orchestras; Deep River Community Association; Valley Arts Council
Finances: *Funding Sources:* Subscriptions; Donations; Fund-raising; Ontario Arts Council; Town of Deep River
Staff Member(s): 7
Activities: 10 public concerts each season; *Library:* Open to public
Chief Officer(s):
Peter Morris, Music Director
Jane Craig, President
drsoemail@gmail.com

Deep Roots Music Cooperative
466A Main St., Wolfville NS B4P 1E2
Tel: 902-542-7668
office@deeprootsmusic.ca
www.deeprootsmusic.ca
www.facebook.com/DeepRoots
twitter.com/DeepRootsM
Overview: A small national organization
Mission: To develop year-round musical programs culminating in an annual festival; To encourage meaningful connections between cultures, community groups, artists & audiences
100 volunteer(s)
Membership: *Fees:* $10 or 15 hours volunteer time
Activities: Organizing the Deep Roots Music Festival
Chief Officer(s):
Peter Mowat, President

Deer Lake Chamber of Commerce
#3, 44 Trans Canada Hwy., Deer Lake NL A8A 2E4
Tel: 709-635-3260; *Fax:* 709-635-4077
info@deerlakechamber.com
www.deerlakechamber.com
Overview: A small local organization founded in 1960
Member of: Atlantic Provinces Chamber of Commerce
Affiliation(s): Newfoundland Chambers of Commerce
Membership: 180; *Fees:* Schedule available
Activities: *Awareness Events:* Small Business Week, October
Chief Officer(s):
Tina Barry-Keith, Treasurer
Roseann White, President

Defense environmentale *See* Environmental Defence

Dejinta Beesha Multi-Service Centre
8 Taber Rd., Toronto ON M9W 3A4
Tel: 416-743-1286; *Fax:* 416-743-1233
info@dejinta.org
dejinta.org
Overview: A medium-sized local charitable organization founded in 1994
Mission: To provide settlement, integration, recreation, health, employment, education, & social services to the community; Offering services in English, French, Italian, Arabic, Somali, & Kiswahili

Finances: *Funding Sources:* Government; Donations
Staff Member(s): 9
Chief Officer(s):
Mohamed Gilao, Executive Director
mgilao@dejinta.org

Delburne & District Chamber of Commerce
PO Box 254, Delburne AB T0M 0V0
Tel: 403-749-3606; *Fax:* 403-749-2800
www.delburne.ca
Overview: A small local organization
Mission: To promote & support business in the area
Chief Officer(s):
Shelly Nicholson, Director

Deloraine & District Chamber of Commerce
c/o Town of Deloraine, PO Box 387, Deloraine MB R0M 0M0
Tel: 204-747-2572; *Fax:* 204-747-2927
deloraine.org/business/chamber-of-commerce
Overview: A small local organization
Mission: To support & promote business in the area
Member of: Manitoba Chamber of Commerce
Finances: *Annual Operating Budget:* Less than $50,000; *Funding Sources:* Municipal governments; membership fees
20 volunteer(s)
Membership: 75; *Fees:* $50
Chief Officer(s):
Shirley Bell, President

Delta Arts Council (DAC)
11489 - 84 Ave., Delta BC V4C 2L9
Tel: 604-596-1025
deltaartscouncil@gmail.com
www.deltaartscouncil.ca
www.facebook.com/197425190124
twitter.com/DeltaArtCouncil
Overview: A small local charitable organization founded in 1969
Mission: To foster cultural & artistic activities within the community, by encouraging amateur, emergent and professional artists
Member of: Assembly of BC Arts Councils
Finances: *Funding Sources:* Municipal, provincial & federal government; fundraising
Membership: *Fees:* $10 student; $25 individual; $40 family/non-profit; $50 artists group; $100 corporate
Activities: Tsawwassen Arts Centre; Firehall Centre for the Arts; Gallery North; Arts Alive; juried exhibitions; monthly TV shows; Maddfest; Xmas Craft Fair; ongoing art classes; summer art camp; garden party; monthly performances; 4 Arts resource centres: Arts & Coffee Corner; *Library:* Resource Centre; Open to public
Chief Officer(s):
Janet Law, President
Awards:
• Scholarships

Delta Chamber of Commerce
6201 - 60 Ave., Delta BC V4K 4E2
Tel: 604-946-4232; *Fax:* 604-946-5285
admin@deltachamber.ca
www.deltachamber.ca
www.linkedin.com/pub/delta-chamber-of-commerce/22/541/89
www.facebook.com/169103131415
twitter.com/deltachamber
www.youtube.com/user/DeltaChamber
Overview: A small local charitable organization founded in 1910
Mission: To create & maintain a prosperous environment for business, industry, tourism & commerce in our community
Member of: BC Chamber of Commerce
Finances: *Funding Sources:* Membership dues; municipal
Staff Member(s): 4
Membership: *Fees:* Schedule available
Activities: Monthly networking lunches; business trade show; Tour de Delta; *Speaker Service:* Yes; *Library:* Business Centre; Open to public
Chief Officer(s):
Ian Tait, Executive Director
ian@deltachamber.ca
Dave Hamilton, Chair
Awards:
• Citizen & Business of the Year Awards

Delta Community Career & Living Society *See* Delta Community Living Society

Delta Community Living Society (DCLS)
#1, 3800 - 72 St., Delta BC V4K 3N2
Tel: 604-946-9508; *Fax:* 604-940-9683
dcls@dcls.ca
dcls.ca
www.facebook.com/dcls.ca
Previous Name: Delta Community Career & Living Society
Overview: A small local charitable organization founded in 1963
Mission: To support adults who have a developmental disability & their families; To seek to improve their quality of life by assisting in personal goals & developing life skills to become valued citizens
Member of: British Columbia Association for Community Living
Membership: *Fees:* Schedule available
Activities: *Library:* by appointment
Chief Officer(s):
Paul Brooks, President
Publications:
• Delta Community Living Society Connections Newsletter
Type: Newsletter; *Frequency:* q.

Delta Family Resource Centre
#5, 2972 Islington Ave., Toronto ON M9L 2K6
Tel: 416-747-1172; *Fax:* 416-747-7415
contactus@dfrc.ca
www.dfrc.ca
www.facebook.com/deltafamilycentre
twitter.com/DeltaFamilyRC
Overview: A medium-sized local charitable organization
Mission: To support the needs of families & children within the community; Offering services in English, Spanish, Italian, Hindi, Punjabi, Laotian, Gujarati, Somali, Cantonese, Tamil, Mandarin, Thi, Ewe, Twi, Urdu, Dari, & Ga
Finances: *Funding Sources:* Government; Foundations; Donations; United Way
Membership: *Fees:* $2 regular member; $20 associate member/organization/group
Chief Officer(s):
Rosalyn Miller, Executive Director

Delta Rockhound Gem & Mineral Club
5457 - 4A Ave., Delta BC V4M 1H6
Tel: 604-943-5518
Overview: A small local organization founded in 1968
Member of: British Columbia Lapidary Society
Finances: *Funding Sources:* Membership fees
Activities: Field trips; meetings 3rd Mon. every month
Chief Officer(s):
Mary Cool, Contact
coolgirl@dccnet.com

Delta Symphony Society *See* Richmond Delta Youth Orchestra

Demeter Canada
14 Simcoe Blvd., Simcoe ON N3Y 3L5
Tel: 519-426-9021
www.demetercanada.ca
Overview: A medium-sized national organization
Mission: To coordinate biodynamic agriculture certification in Canada
Member of: Demeter International
Membership: *Member Profile:* Farms in Canada that adhere to Demeter International's Standards for Certification; *Committees:* Certification

Democracy Watch
PO Box 821, Stn. B, #412, 1 Nicholas St., Ottawa ON K1P 5P9
Tel: 613-241-5179; *Fax:* 613-241-4758
info@democracywatch.ca
democracywatch.ca
www.facebook.com/DemocracyWatch
twitter.com/democracywatchr
www.youtube.com/dwatchcda
Overview: A medium-sized national organization
Mission: To advocate for democratic reform, government accountability, and corporate responsibility.
Finances: *Funding Sources:* Donations
Chief Officer(s):
Duff Conacher, Coordinator

Denesoline Corporation Ltd.
PO Box 72, Lutsel K'e NT X0E 1A0
Tel: 867-370-3095; *Fax:* 867-370-3976
Previous Name: Lutsel K'E Development Corporation
Overview: A small local organization founded in 1990
Mission: Owned by the Lutsel K'e Dene Band, the corporation is a business development company which administers contracts for firefighting, ice road maintenance, survey stake production, hunting & outfitting, residential constuction & general contracting. It also has formed joint ventures with & has investment equity in other industry corporations.
Affiliation(s): Ta'egera Corporation; Great Slave Helicopters Ltd.
Chief Officer(s):
Roy Shields, CEO

Dental Association of Prince Edward Island (DAPEI)
184 Belvedere Ave., Charlottetown PE C1A 2Z1
Tel: 902-892-4470; *Fax:* 902-892-0234
www.dapei.ca
Overview: A small provincial licensing organization founded in 1931 overseen by Canadian Dental Association
Mission: To stimulate professional growth in dentistry; To regulate dentistry in Prince Edward Island
Member of: Canadian Dental Association
Staff Member(s): 2
Membership: 76; *Member Profile:* Dentists; dental specialists
Activities: *Awareness Events:* Dental Health Month, April; *Speaker Service:* Yes; *Rents Mailing List:* Yes
Chief Officer(s):
Paul McNab, President
Brian Barrett, Executive Director
Ray Wenn, Registrar

Dental Council of Prince Edward Island
184 Belvedere Ave., Charlottetown PE C1A 2Z1
Tel: 902-892-4470; *Fax:* 902-892-4470
Overview: A small provincial licensing organization

Dental Technicians Association of Saskatchewan
PO Box 8035, Saskatoon SK S7K 4R7
Tel: 306-764-5525
sask.dtas@hotmail.com
Overview: A small provincial organization
Mission: To represent & regulate the dental technicians of Saskatchewan.

Denturist Association of British Columbia
PO Box 1802, Gibsons BC V0N 1V0
Tel: 604-886-1705
info@denturist.bc.ca
www.denturist.bc.ca
Overview: A small provincial organization overseen by Denturist Association of Canada
Chief Officer(s):
Kore Connolly, President

Denturist Association of Canada (DAC) / Association des denturologistes du Canada (ADC)
66 Dundas St. East, Belleville ON K8N 1C1
Tel: 613-968-9467
Toll-Free: 877-538-3123
dacdenturist@bellnet.ca
www.denturist.org
Previous Name: Interprovincial Denturist Societies
Overview: A medium-sized national organization founded in 1971
Mission: To promote oral health in Canada through the profession of denturism
Member of: International Federation of Denturists
Membership: 12 associations; *Member Profile:* Provincial denturist associations
Activities: *Speaker Service:* Yes; *Rents Mailing List:* Yes; *Library*
Chief Officer(s):
Steve Sailer, Vice-President, Administration
Awards:
• Robert Perreault Memorial Award
• George Connolly Denturist of the Year Award

Denturist Association of Manitoba
PO Box 69012, RPO Tuxedo Park, Winnipeg MB R3P 2G9
Tel: 204-897-1087; *Fax:* 204-488-2872
administrator@denturistmb.org
www.denturistmb.org
Overview: A small provincial licensing organization founded in 1970 overseen by Denturist Association of Canada
Mission: To represent Manitoba denturists & ensure high quality, low cost delivery of dentures direct to the public
Member of: International Federation of Denturists
Finances: *Funding Sources:* Membership fees
Membership: *Member Profile:* Licensed denturist
Activities: *Internships:* Yes

Denturist Association of Newfoundland & Labrador
323 Freshwater Rd., St. John's NL A1B 1C3

Tel: 709-364-4813
info@denturistassociationnl.ca
www.denturistassociationnl.ca
Overview: A small provincial organization overseen by Denturist Association of Canada
Mission: To promote denturism as a profession & provide services for its members
Member of: The Denturist Associationg of Canada; International Federation of Denturists
Membership: 23
Chief Officer(s):
Steve Browne, President

Denturist Association of Northwest Territories
PO Box 1506, Yellowknife NT X1A 2P2
Tel: 867-766-3666; *Fax:* 867-669-0103
Overview: A small provincial organization overseen by Denturist Association of Canada

Denturist Association of Ontario (DAO)
#106, 5780 Timberlea Blvd., Mississauga ON L4W 4W8
Tel: 905-238-6090; *Fax:* 905-238-7090
Toll-Free: 800-284-7311
info@denturistassociation.ca
denturistassociation.ca
Overview: A small provincial organization overseen by Denturist Association of Canada
Mission: To develop services & tools that help denturists in their practices as well as address denturist needs & concerns
Member of: The Denturist Association of Canada
Membership: 500+
Activities: Fabrication & repair of dentures; visitation services;
Library: Not open to public
Chief Officer(s):
Frank Odorico, President

Denturist Society of Nova Scotia
c/o Diane Carrigan-Weir, 3951 South River Rd., Antigonish NS B2G 2H6
Tel: 902-863-3131; *Fax:* 902-863-3131
info@nsdenturistsociety.ca
www.nsdenturistsociety.ca
Overview: A small provincial licensing organization overseen by Denturist Association of Canada
Mission: To promote denturists in Nova Scotia
Member of: Denturist Association of Canada
Chief Officer(s):
Diane Carrigan-Weir, President

Denturist Society of Prince Edward Island
Down East Mall, PO Box 1589, 500 Main St., Montague PE C0A 1R0
Tel: 902-569-5511; *Fax:* 902-692-2607
Overview: A small provincial organization overseen by Denturist Association of Canada
Chief Officer(s):
David Murphy, Registrar
davidmurphy@pei.sympatico.ca

Design Exchange (DX)
Toronto Dominion Centre, PO Box 18, 234 Bay St., Toronto ON M5K 1B2
Tel: 416-363-6121; *Fax:* 416-368-0684
Other Communication: membership@dx.org
info@dx.org
www.dx.org
www.facebook.com/DesignExchange
twitter.com/designexchange
www.instagram.com/designexchange
Also Known As: The Group for the Creation of a Design Centre in Toronto
Overview: A medium-sized national organization founded in 1987
Mission: To provide a design museum & centre for design research & education; To raise awareness & understanding of design
Finances: *Funding Sources:* Donations; Sponsorships
Membership: *Member Profile:* Designers, students & business professionals
Activities: Offering programs to promote the value of Canadian design; Showcasing good Canadian design; Organizing competitions; Presenting awards; Fundraising
Chief Officer(s):
Alex James, Chief Financial Officer, 647-278-8436
alex@dx.org
Shauna Levy, President & CEO, 416-216-2145
shauna@dx.org

Designers d'intérieur du Canada *See* Interior Designers of Canada

Desta Black Youth Network
Padua Centre, 1950, rue St-Antoine ouest, Montréal QC H3J 1A5
Tel: 514-932-7597; *Fax:* 514-932-9468
friendsofdesta@gmail.com
www.destanetwork.ca
www.facebook.com/destabyn
Overview: A small local organization
Mission: To provide an outreach initiative to young adults, from ages 18 to 25, within the Black community; To mentor marginalized youth in the areas of education, employment, & personal growth; To empower vision, strengthen authentic identity, & promote excellence
Staff Member(s): 4
Chief Officer(s):
Frances Waithe, Executive Director

Destination Eastern & Northumberland Shores (DEANS)
PO Box 55, 115 MacLean St., New Glasgow NS B2H 5E1
Tel: 902-752-6383
Toll-Free: 877-816-2326
www.visitdeans.ca
Merged from: Antigonish-Eastern Shore Tourist Association; Pictou County Tourist Association
Overview: A small local organization founded in 2011
Mission: To promote tourism in the counties of Antigonish, Guysborough, Pictou, & Eastern Halifax Regional Municipality
Finances: *Funding Sources:* Regional government
Chief Officer(s):
Cindy MacKinnon, Managing Director
cindy@visitdeans.ca
Publications:
• Destination Eastern & Northumberland Shores Newsletter
Type: Newsletter

Destination Halifax
#802, 1800 Argyle St., Halifax NS B3J 3N8
Tel: 902-422-9334; *Fax:* 902-492-3175
Toll-Free: 877-422-9334
info@discoverhalifaxns.com
www.destinationhalifax.com
twitter.com/HfxNovaScotia
www.youtube.com/user/destinationhalifax
Also Known As: Discover Halifax
Previous Name: Greater Halifax Conventions & Meetings Bureau
Overview: A small local organization founded in 2002
Mission: To increase Greater Halifax's market share of the meetings & conventions market by promoting the region as a destination for meetings, conventions, exhibitions & special events; To provide meeting planners with a full range of services which will promote & build attendance at their Halifax meetings; To create business opportunities for bureau members & to develop pre- & post- conference travel opportunities
Finances: *Annual Operating Budget:* $500,000-$1.5 Million
Staff Member(s): 12
Membership: 142; *Fees:* Schedule available; *Member Profile:* An organization company that books & services meetings & conventions
Activities: *Speaker Service:* Yes
Chief Officer(s):
Ross Jefferson, President & CEO

Destination Sherbrooke
785, rue King ouest, Sherbrooke QC J1H 1R8
Tél: 819-821-1919
Ligne sans frais: 800-561-8331
info@destinationsherbrooke.com
www.destinationsherbrooke.com
www.facebook.com/destinationsherbrooke
twitter.com/DSherbrooke
www.youtube.com/user/destinationsherb
Nom précédent: Tourisme Sherbrooke; Société de développement économique de la région sherbrookoise - Tourisme
Aperçu: *Dimension:* petite; *Envergure:* locale
Mission: Créer, animer, obtenir et administrer les activités touristiques pour la ville de Sherbrook; favoriser la recherche et le développement des dossiers touristiques; assurer la promotion du secteur touristique; agir comme expert conseil dans le domaine touristique auprès de la Société de développement économique de Sherbrooke
Membre(s) du personnel: 6
Membre(s) du bureau directeur:
Denis Bernier, Directeur général
denis.bernier@destinationsherbrooke.com

Deutsch-Kanadische Industrie- und Handelskammer *See* Canadian German Chamber of Industry & Commerce Inc.

A deux mains *See* Head & Hands

Deux/Dix *See* Two/Ten Charity Trust of Canada Inc.

Developing Countries Farm Radio Network *See* Farm Radio International

Development & Peace / Développement et paix
1425, boul René-Lévesque ouest, 3e étage, Montréal QC H3G 1T7
Tel: 514-257-8711; *Fax:* 514-257-8497
Toll-Free: 888-234-8533
info@devp.org
www.devp.org
www.facebook.com/devpeace
twitter.com/DevPeace
www.youtube.com/devpeacetv;
www.flickr.com/photos/devpedu/sets
Also Known As: Canadian Catholic Organization for Development & Peace
Overview: A large international charitable organization founded in 1967
Mission: To support partners in the Global South who promote alternatives to unfair social, political & economic structures
Member of: Caritas Internationalis; Conseil canadien pour la coopération internationale / Canadian Council for International Cooperation
Affiliation(s): Coopération internationale pour le développement et la solidarité
Finances: *Funding Sources:* Donations; Canadian International Development Agency (provision of grants for projects & programs)
Staff Member(s): 61; 5,00 volunteer(s)
Membership: 10,000; *Fees:* 5$
Activities: Providing financial support for projects in the developing world; Contributing to emergency relief; Engaging in advocacy activities related to crises & issues in developing countries
Chief Officer(s):
G. Gagnon, Contact
Publications:
• Development & Peace Annual Report
Frequency: Annually
• Global Village Voice [a publication of Development & Peace]
Type: Newsletter; *Frequency:* 3 pa; *ISSN:* 0383-6703

Alberta/Mackenzie
8421 - 101st Ave., Edmonton AB T6A 0L1
Tel: 587-224-9017
Chief Officer(s):
Sara Farid, Contact
sfarid@devp.org

British Columbia & Yukon
John Paul II Pastoral Centre, 4885 Saint John Paul II Way, Vancouver BC V5Z 0G3
Tel: 604-683-0281
Chief Officer(s):
Jeremy Laurie, Contact
jlaurie@devp.org

Manitoba
622 Tache Ave., Saint-Boniface MB R2H 2B4
Tel: 204-231-2848; *Fax:* 204-231-7471
ccodpmb@gmail.com
Chief Officer(s):
Janelle Delorme, Contact

Nouveau-Brunswick
576, rue Centrale, Memramcook NB E4K 3S7
Tél: 506-758-2586
Chief Officer(s):
Tina Ruest, Contact
truest@devp.org

Nova Scotia/New Brunswick/PEI/Newfoundland & Labrador
#205, 59 Inglis Pl., Antigonish NS B2N 4B5
Tel: 902-897-0469; *Fax:* 902-897-2852
Chief Officer(s):
Tara Hurford, Contact
thurford@devp.org

Ontario - Central
#400, 80 Hayden St., Toronto ON M4Y 3G2

Tel: 416-922-1592; Fax: 416-922-0957
Chief Officer(s):
Luke Stocking, Contact
lstocking@devp.org
Ontario - Eastern
1247 Kilborn Pl., Ottawa ON K1H 6K9
Tel: 613-738-9644; Fax: 613-738-0130
Chief Officer(s):
Genevieve Gallant, Contact
ggallant@devp.org
Ontario - Southwestern
698 King St. West, Hamilton ON L8P 1C7
Tel: 905-521-5632
Chief Officer(s):
Nana Kojo Damptey, Contact
nkdamptey@devp.org
Québec - Gatineau/Ottawa (French)
180, boul Mont-Bleu, Gatineau QC J8Z 3J5
Tél: 819-771-8391; Téléc: 819-778-8969
Chief Officer(s):
Jean-François Langlais, Contact
jflanglais@devp.org
Québec - Montréal
1425, boul René-Lévesque ouest, 3e étage, Montréal QC H3G 1T7
Tél: 514-257-8711; Téléc: 514-257-8497
Chief Officer(s):
Jean-Paul St-Germain, Contact
jpstgermain@devp.org
Marie-Sophie Villeneuve, Contact
msvilleneuve@devp.org
Québec - Québec
1073, boul René-Lévesque ouest, Québec QC G1S 4R5
Tél: 418-683-9901; Téléc: 418-683-9331
Chief Officer(s):
Elisabeth Desgranges, Contact
edesgranges@devp.org
Pascal André Charlebois, Contact
pcharlebois@devp.org
Saskatchewan
PO Box 1838, Battleford SK S0M 0E0
Tel: 306-937-7675
Chief Officer(s):
Armella Sonntag, Contact
asonntag@devp.org

Developmental Disabilities Resource Centre of Calgary (DDRC)
4631 Richardson Way SW, Calgary AB T3E 7B7
Tel: 403-240-3111; Fax: 403-240-3230
info@ddrc.com
www.ddrc.ca
www.linkedin.com/company/ddrc_2
www.facebook.com/DDRCCalgary
twitter.com/DDRC_Calgary
instagram.com/ddrc_calgary
Overview: A medium-sized local charitable organization founded in 1952
Mission: To facilitate personal choice & build the community's capacity to include person's with developmental disabilities
Member of: Alberta Association for Community Living
Finances: Funding Sources: Government contracts; fees for service; private fundraising; commercial ventures
Membership: Fees: Schedule available
Activities: Awards of Distinction; Speaker Service: Yes
Chief Officer(s):
Helen Cowie, Chief Executive Officer
Awards:
• Inclusion Awards
Honour people and organizations that create and foster inclusive communities
Publications:
• Connection [a publication of the Developmental Disabilities Resource Centre of Calgary]
Type: Newsletter; Frequency: Biannually
• Developmental Disabilities Resource Centre of Calgary Annual Report
Type: Report; Frequency: Annually

Développement et paix See Development & Peace

Devis de construction Canada See Construction Specifications Canada

Devon & District Chamber of Commerce
#401, 32 Athabasca Ave., Devon AB T9G 1G2
Tel: 780-987-5177; Fax: 780-987-3303
devoncc@telus.net
www.devon.ca/Business/ChamberofCommerce.aspx
Overview: A small local organization
Member of: Alberta Chamber of Commerce
Finances: Annual Operating Budget: Less than $50,000; Funding Sources: Memberships & Fundraising Events
Staff Member(s): 1; 20 volunteer(s)
Membership: 82; Fees: $125; Member Profile: Businesses in & near Devon, Alberta
Chief Officer(s):
Jeff Millar, President
Barry Breau, Manager

Diabète Québec (ADQ) / Diabetes Quebec
#300, 8550, boul Pie-IX, Montréal QC H1Z 4G2
Tél: 514-259-3422; Téléc: 514-259-9286
Ligne sans frais: 800-361-3504
info@diabete.qc.ca
www.diabete.qc.ca
www.facebook.com/diabetequebec
twitter.com/DiabeteQuebec
Également appelé: Association Diabète Québec
Nom précédent: Association du Diabète du Québec
Aperçu: Dimension: moyenne; Envergure: provinciale; fondée en 1954
Mission: Regrouper les diabétiques et favoriser l'entraide; les renseigner sur les façons de faire face à la maladie; informer le grand public et le sensibiliser à la condition de personnes souffrant du diabète; ouvrir de nouvelles voies dans le domaine de la recherche pour en venir à triompher du diabète
Membre de: Fédération Internationale du Diabète
Finances: Budget de fonctionnement annuel: $1.5 Million-$3 Million
Membre(s) du personnel: 16; 2 bénévole(s)
Membre: 25 000; Montant de la cotisation: 20$ membre régulier; Comités: Conseil d'administration; Conseil d'administration; Conseil professionnel de Diabète Québec
Activités: Congrès scientifique; service téléphonique InfoDiabète; formation; concours; publications; Evénements de sensibilisation: Mois du diabète nov.; Service de conférenciers: Oui
Membre(s) du bureau directeur:
Sylvie Lauzon, Présidente
direction@diabete.qc.ca
Marcelle Paquette, Directeur, Finances et administration
paquette@diabete.qc.ca
Prix, Bourses:
• Bourses d'été et Subvention de démarrage
Eligibility: Étudiants niveaux Bac, M.Sc. et Ph.D.; Médecins chercheurs Deadline: Mars; Amount: 3000$ à 25,000$
Publications:
• Plein Soleil
Type: Magazine; Editor: Louise Bouchard
Profile: Traite des sujets en relation avec le diabète : alimentation, traitement, activité physique, recherche, vivre avec le diabète, etc.

Diabetes Canada (CDA) / Association canadienne du diabète
#1400, 522 University Ave., Toronto ON M5G 2R5
Tel: 416-363-3373; Fax: 416-363-7465
Toll-Free: 800-226-8464
info@diabetes.ca
www.diabetes.ca
www.linkedin.com/company/diabetescanada
www.facebook.com/DiabetesCanada
twitter.com/DiabetesCanada
instagram.com/DiabetesCanada
Previous Name: Canadian Diabetes Association
Overview: A large national charitable organization founded in 1953
Mission: To advance the welfare of Canadians with diabetes; to support research into the causes, complications, treatment, & cure of diabetes; To promote & strengthen services for people affected by diabetes & their families; To work with health professionals to improve standards in care the & treatment of diabetes; To develop guidelines for diabetes education in Canada; To promote the rights of Canadians affected by diabetes in an effort to bring about positive change in the areas of public awareness, government policy, health policy issues, & employment
Member of: International Diabetes Federation
Finances: Funding Sources: Donations; Government; Services; Support from charities; National Diabetes Trust
2000 volunteer(s)
Membership: Fees: $100 professional; $50 associate; $50 student; basic membership is free; Member Profile: Regular membership open to anyone; Professional members come from educational, research & clinical care fields
Activities: Awareness Events: Diabetes Month, November; Speaker Service: Yes; Library: Resource Centre; Open to public by appointment
Chief Officer(s):
Jim Newton, Chair
Rick Blickstead, President & CEO
John Reidy, Chief Financial Officer
Russell Williams, Vice President, Government Relations & Public Policy
Janelle Robertson, Vice President, National Diabetes Trust, 709-747-4598
Jovita Sundaramoorthy, Vice President, Research & Education, 416-408-7090
Meetings/Conferences:
• Canadian Diabetes Association Professional Conference 2018, October, 2018, Halifax Convention Centre, Halifax, NS
Scope: National
Contact Information: professional.conference@diabetes.ca
Publications:
• Canadian Diabetes Clinical & Scientific Section (C&SS) Connect [a publication of Diabetes Canada]
Type: Newsletter; Frequency: q.; Price: free with C&SS membership to Diabetes Canada
• Canadian Journal of Diabetes (CJD) [a publication of Diabetes Canada]
Type: Journal; Frequency: bi-m.
Profile: Peer-reviewed, interdisciplinary journal for diabetes healthcare professionals, including articles, news from the Clinical & Scientific Section & theDiabetes Educators Section of Diabetes Canada, & resource reviews
• Diabetes Canada Advocacy Reports
Type: Report; Price: Free
Profile: Series of reports on diabetes that aims to inform & educate decision makers, governments, & the general public on issues surrounding diabetes today
• Diabetes Canada Annual Report
Frequency: a.
• The Diabetes Communicator [a publication of Diabetes Canada]
Type: Newsletter; Editor: Colleen Rand; Price: free with DES membership to Diabetes Canada
Profile: Information on the Diabetes Educator Section (DES)
• Diabetes Current [a publication of Diabetes Canada]
Type: Newsletter; Frequency: Monthly; Price: Free
Profile: Electronic newsletter containing information on association news, research, medical breakthroughs & more
• Diabetes Dialogue [a publication of Diabetes Canada]
Type: Magazine; Frequency: q.
Profile: Information about research, medical updates, nutrition, exercise, lifestyle management, & resources
• Pacesetter [a publication of Diabetes Canada]
Type: Newsletter; Frequency: Monthly; Price: Free
Profile: E-newsletter for Team Diabetes members, featuring information about upcoming marathon events, news, training & fundraising tips, & human interest stories

Calgary & District Branch
#204, 2323 - 32 Ave. NE, Calgary AB T2E 6Z3
Tel: 403-266-0620; Fax: 403-269-8927
Edmonton & District Branch
#104, 12220 Stony Plain Rd., Edmonton AB T5N 3Y4
Tel: 780-423-1232; Fax: 780-423-3322
GTA Regional Leadership Centre
#1400, 522 University Ave., Toronto ON M5G 2R5
Tel: 416-363-3373; Fax: 416-363-7465
Chief Officer(s):
Kerry Bruder, Regional Director
Manitoba & Nunavut Regional Leadership Centre
#200, 310 Broadway, Winnipeg MB R3C 0S6
Tel: 204-925-3800; Fax: 204-949-0266
Chief Officer(s):
Andrea Kwasnicki, Regional Director
andrea.kwasnicki@diabetes.ca
New Brunswick Region
730 McLeod Ave., Fredericton NB E3B 1V5
Tel: 506-452-9009; Fax: 506-455-4728
Toll-Free: 800-884-4232
Chief Officer(s):
Lisa Matte, Regional Director, Martimes
lisa.matte@diabetes.ca

Canadian Associations / Dial-a-Tutor

Newfoundland & Labrador Regional Leadership Centre
#2007, 29-31 Pippy Pl., St. John's NL A1B 3X2
Tel: 709-754-0953; *Fax:* 709-754-0734
Chief Officer(s):
Felicia Chapman, Contact
felicia.chapman@diabetes.ca

North Saskatchewan Regional Leadership Centre
#104, 2301 Ave. C North, Saskatoon SK S7L 5Z5
Tel: 306-933-1238; *Fax:* 306-244-2012
Toll-Free: 800-996-4446

Nova Scotia Leadership Centre
#101, 137 Chain Lake Dr., Halifax NS B3S 1B3
Tel: 902-453-4232; *Fax:* 902-453-4440
Toll-Free: 800-326-7712
Chief Officer(s):
Lisa Matte, Regional Director, Maritimes
lisa.matte@diabetes.ca

Ottawa & District Branch
45 Montreal Rd., Ottawa ON K1L 6E8
Tel: 613-521-1902; *Fax:* 613-521-3667

Prince Edward Island Region
Sherwood Business Centre, 161 St. Peter's Rd., Charlottetown PE C1A 5P7
Tel: 902-894-3195; *Fax:* 902-368-1928
Chief Officer(s):
Terry Lewis, Manager, Community Engagement
terry.lewis@diabetes.ca

Diabetes Quebec *Voir* Diabète Québec

Diabetes Research Foundation *See* Juvenile Diabetes Research Foundation Canada

Dial-a-Tutor
#4-5074, 5845 Yonge St., Toronto ON M2M 4K3
Tel: 416-607-6401
dialatutor.ca
twitter.com/tutorsforless
Also Known As: Tutors For Less
Overview: A small local organization founded in 1996
Mission: To provide individualized, in-home tutoring sessions.
Finances: *Funding Sources:* Hourly service fees

Diamond Valley & District Boys & Girls Club *See* Boys & Girls Clubs of Alberta

Diamond Valley Chamber of Commerce
PO Box 61, Turner Valley AB T0L 2A0
Tel: 403-819-4994
info@diamondvalleychamber.ca
diamondvalleychamber.ca
www.facebook.com/diamondvalleychamber
Overview: A small local organization
Mission: To work with local municipal councils, business associations & local organizations to promote trade & commerce
Member of: Alberta Chamber of Commerce
Finances: *Annual Operating Budget:* Less than $50,000
5 volunteer(s)
Membership: 28; *Fees:* $95
Chief Officer(s):
Bev Geier, President

Dickson Store Museum Society
PO Box 146, Spruce View AB T0M 1V0
Tel: 403-728-3355; *Fax:* 403-728-3351
dicksonstoremuseum@gmail.com
www.dicksonstoremuseum.com
Previous Name: Danish Heritage Society of Dickson
Overview: A small local charitable organization founded in 1985
Mission: TO manage the Dickson Store Museum; To preserve the history of Dickson & area pioneers
Member of: Federation of Danish Associations in Canada; Museums Alberta; Central Alberta Regional Museums Network
Finances: *Funding Sources:* Grants; donations; sales; membership dues; fundraising events
Membership: *Fees:* $10 single or family; $100 life
Activities: Home On the Range project; maintaining Dickson Store Museum, open to the public, tour & school groups; the museum contains hardware, dry goods & groceries which were available in the 1930s; the second floor is furnished as a typical 1930s home; the original post-office serves as a gift-shop; officially opened by Queen Margrethe II; *Awareness Events:* Dickson Harvest Festival, Oct.; Scandinavian Julestue, Nov.
Library: Archives; by appointment

Didsbury & District Historical Society
PO Box 1175, 2110 - 21 Ave., Didsbury AB T0M 0W0
Tel: 403-335-9295
ddhs@telusplanet.net
www.didsburymuseum.com
Overview: A small local charitable organization founded in 1978
Mission: To preserve, research, display, & interpret items about the founding, settlement, & development of the Town of Didsbury, Alberta
Finances: *Funding Sources:* Donations; Fundraising; Grants
Membership: *Fees:* $5 single; $10 family
Activities: Providing education about local history
Chief Officer(s):
Rick Astle, President

Didsbury Chamber of Commerce
1811 - 20 St., Didsbury AB T0M 0W0
Tel: 403-335-3265; *Fax:* 403-335-4399
www.didsburychamber.ca
www.facebook.com/DidsburyChamber
twitter.com/didsburychamber
Overview: A small local organization founded in 1962
Mission: To increase communication within the business community & beyond; To keep their members informed on Chamber activities
Membership: 75; *Committees:* Member Services; Marketing; Didsbury Art, Travel & Trade Expo; Special Event; Small Business Week; Policy/Issues; Strategic Plan
Chief Officer(s):
Margo Ward, President

Les diététistes du Canada *See* Dietitians of Canada

Dietitians of Canada (DC) / Les diététistes du Canada
#604, 480 University Ave., Toronto ON M5G 1V2
Tel: 416-596-0857; *Fax:* 416-596-0603
contactus@dietitians.ca
www.dietitians.ca
Previous Name: Canadian Dietetic Association
Overview: A medium-sized national organization founded in 1935
Mission: To advance health, through food & nutrition; To act as the voice of the dietitian profession in Canada
Finances: *Funding Sources:* Membership fees; Sponsorships
Membership: *Member Profile:* Registered & registration eligible dietitians; Internationally educated dietitians; Retired dietitians; Academics; Students in accredited undergraduate dietetics & internship programs
Activities: Engaging in advocacy activities; Developing standards; Offering workshops, webinars, & podcasts; Providing nutrition information; Facilitating access to counselling, consultations, & media interviews; Organizing networking opportunities; *Awareness Events:* Nutrition Month, March; National Dietitians' Day, March
Chief Officer(s):
Marsha Sharp, Chief Executive Officer
Corinne Eisenbraun, Director, Professional Development & Support
Janice Macdonald, Director, Communications
Meetings/Conferences:
• Dietitians of Canada National Conference 2018, June, 2018, Westin Bayshore, Vancouver, BC
Scope: National
Description: Theme: "Elevate Influence Inspire"
Publications:
• Canadian Journal of Dietetic Research & Practice
Type: Journal; *Frequency:* Quarterly; *Editor:* Dawna Royall; *ISSN:* 1486-3847
Profile: A peer-reviewed publication, featuring manuscripts of original research, professional practice, & reviews
• Dietitians of Canada Annual Report
Type: Yearbook; *Frequency:* Annually

Digby & Area Board of Trade (DABT)
PO Box 641, Digby NS B0V 1A0
Tel: 902-245-2553
info@digbytrade.ca
www.digbytrade.ca
www.facebook.com/digbytrade
twitter.com/digbytrade
Overview: A small local organization
Membership: *Fees:* $30 individual; $75 business
Chief Officer(s):
Karen Enright, President

Digital Health Canada
#110, 151 Yonge St., Toronto ON M5C 2W7
Tel: 647-775-8555
info@digitalhealthcanada.com
digitalhealthcanada.com
www.linkedin.com/company/415342
www.facebook.com/digitalhealthcdn
twitter.com/COACH_HI
Previous Name: COACH - Canada's Health Informatics Association
Overview: A large national organization founded in 1975
Mission: To improve the health of Canadians & enhance the management of Canada's health system by advancing the practice of health information management & effective utilization of associated technologies
Member of: International Medical Informatics Association
Finances: *Funding Sources:* Membership fees; workshops; conferences
Membership: 1,800; *Fees:* Schedule available; *Member Profile:* Interest in health informatics
Chief Officer(s):
Mark Casselman, Chief Executive Officer
mark.casselman@digitalhealthcanada.com
Shannon Bott, Executive Director, Operations
sbott@digitalhealthcanada.com
Awards:
• Canadian Health Informatics Award
• Women Leaders in Digital Health Award
• Steven Huesing Scholarship
Meetings/Conferences:
• e-Health 2018, May, 2018, Vancouver, BC
Scope: National
Attendance: 1,500+

Digital Imaging Association (DIA)
#300, 1370 Don Mills Rd., Toronto ON M3B 3N7
Tel: 416-482-2223
www.digitalimagingassoc.ca
Previous Name: Ontario Prepress Association
Overview: A small provincial organization founded in 1987
Mission: To provide educational & networking opportunities for members
Finances: *Annual Operating Budget:* Less than $50,000; *Funding Sources:* Membership; Sponsorships
Staff Member(s): 1; 17 volunteer(s)
Membership: 60+ companies; *Fees:* $100 individual; $200-$850 corporate; *Member Profile:* Suppliers & manufacturers of equipment & consumables used in the pre-press, printing & finishing industries; *Committees:* Technical & Member Services
Activities: Organizing educational meetings & other events; *Awareness Events:* Golf Tournament, June; Christmas Luncheon; *Speaker Service:* Yes
Chief Officer(s):
Marg Macleod, Administrator
marg@digitalimagingassoc.ca

Digital Nova Scotia (ITANS)
Technology Innovation Centre, 1 Research Dr., Dartmouth NS B2Y 4M9
Tel: 902-423-5332; *Fax:* 877-282-9506
info@digitalnovascotia.com
www.digitalnovascotia.com
www.linkedin.com/groups/Digital-Nova-Scotia-1801099/about
twitter.com/digitalns
www.youtube.com/user/digitalnovascotia
Previous Name: Information Technology Industry Alliance of Nova Scotia; Software Industry Association of Nova Scotia
Overview: A medium-sized provincial organization founded in 1989
Mission: To be dedicated to the development & growth of the digital technologies industry in Nova Scotia
Member of: CATAAtlantic
Chief Officer(s):
Ulrike Bahr-Gedalia, President & CEO
ulrike@digitalnovascotia.com
Bruce MacDougall, Chair
Bruce.MacDougall@Internetworking-Atlantic.com
Emily Boucher, Director, Marketing & Research
emily.boucher@digitalnovascotia.com

Dignitas International
#35, 550 Queen St. East, Toronto ON M5A 1V2
Tel: 416-260-3100
Toll-Free: 866-576-3100
info@dignitasinternational.org
dignitasinternational.org
www.linkedin.com/company/dignitas-international
www.facebook.com/DignitasInternational

twitter.com/dignitasintl
www.instagram.com/dignitasintl;
www.youtube.com/dignitasonline
Overview: A large international charitable organization founded in 2004
Mission: To improve access to quality health care for people facing a high burden of disease & unequal access to services; To educate health care workers in remote areas on ways to treat HIV, TB, & malaria; To work towards the eradication of the AIDS epidemic in Malawi
Finances: *Funding Sources:* Donations
Staff Member(s): 12
Activities: Establishing & operating treatment centres; Training health care workers on how to deliver effective treatment regimens; Developing a research program; Launching Aboriginal Health Partners Program to use knowledge gained in Malawi to strengthen health care delivery in Northern Ontario
Chief Officer(s):
Heather Johnston, President & Chief Executive Officer
Emmay Mah, Director, Programs & Policy
e.mah@dignitasinternational.org
Joep Van Oosterhout, Director, Medical & Research
j.vanoosterhout@dignitasinternational.org

Malawi Branch
PO Box 1071, Zomba Malawi
Tel: 265 (0)1 525 420
Chief Officer(s):
Vanessa Van Schoor, Country Director
v.vanschoor@dignitasinternational.org
Daniela Garone, Manager, Medical
d.garone@dignitasinternational.org

USA Office
#1350, 8333 Douglas Ave., Dallas TX 75225-5860 USA

Dignity Canada Dignité
PO Box 2102, Stn. D, Ottawa ON K1P 5W3
Tel: 613-746-7281
Other Communication: Newsletter subscription:
subscribe@dignitycanada.org
info@dignitycanada.org
www.dignitycanada.org
www.facebook.com/groups/253558468022157
Overview: A medium-sized national organization
Mission: To voice the concerns of Roman Catholic sexual minorities; To promote the development of sexual theology, justice, & acceptance of the lesbian & gay community; To reinforce a sense of dignity & to encourage gay men & lesbian women to become more active members in the Church & society
Finances: *Funding Sources:* Donations
Activities: Encouraging spiritual development, education, & social involvement
Chief Officer(s):
Frank Testin, President
president@dignitycanada.org
Norman Prince, Secretary

Dignity Toronto Dignité
175 Windermere Ave., Toronto ON M6S 3J8
Tel: 416-925-9872
toronto@dignitycanada.org
dignitycanada.org/toronto.html
www.facebook.com/dignitytoronto
Overview: A small local organization founded in 1974 overseen by Dignity Canada Dignité
Mission: To support & affirm gay & lesbian Roman Catholics through spiritual development, education, social involvement, equity issues, & social events
Member of: Dignity Canada Dignité
Finances: *Annual Operating Budget:* Less than $50,000
Membership: 20; *Fees:* $30
Activities: Monthly liturgical meeting to support gay & lesbian Roman Catholics; social gatherings
Chief Officer(s):
Frank Testin, President
president@dignitycanada.org

Dignity Vancouver Dignité
PO Box 3016, Stn. Terminal, Vancouver BC V6B 3X5
vancouver@dignitycanada.org
dignitycanada.org/vancouver.html
Overview: A small local organization founded in 1977 overseen by Dignity Canada Dignité
Mission: The organization works within the Catholic Church & with other Catholic groups to reform the church's theological stance pertaining to sexual minorities. It supports gay & lesbian Catholics & their friends, encouraging participation in educational, spiritual, & social activities.
Member of: Dignity Canada Dignité
Finances: *Annual Operating Budget:* Less than $50,000
Membership: 12; *Fees:* $35 individual; *Member Profile:* Roman Catholic gays, lesbians, friends
Chief Officer(s):
Kevin Simpson, Treasurer, 604-874-3428
treasurer@dignitycanada.org

Dignity Winnipeg Dignité
PO Box 1912, Winnipeg MB R3C 3R2
Tel: 204-779-6446
winnipeg@dignitycanada.org
www.dignitycanada.org
Overview: A small provincial organization founded in 1970 overseen by Dignity Canada Dignité
Mission: To bring together gay & lesbian Catholics & their friends; To encourage a process of self-understanding & personal integration with respect to issues, including spirituality & sexuality
Member of: Dignity Canada Dignité
Finances: *Annual Operating Budget:* Less than $50,000
3 volunteer(s)
Membership: 20; *Fees:* $25 (optional); *Member Profile:* LGBT community; non-gay men & women, encompassing a broad spectrum of professions, political beliefs, ethnic & linguistic backgrounds & economic levels
Activities: Regular liturgies/discussion groups; annual retreat; social events; brochures; *Speaker Service:* Yes
Chief Officer(s):
Thomas Novak, National Chaplain, 204-287-8583

Diman Association Canada (Lebanese) (DAC)
c/o Diman Lebanese Centre, 345 Kearney Lake Rd., Bedford NS B4B 1H6
Tel: 902-457-3221
dimanassociation@gmail.com
Overview: A small national organization founded in 1973
Member of: Multicultural Association of Nova Scotia
Affiliation(s): Diman Association Australia; Diman Association Lebanon (NADEE)
Finances: *Funding Sources:* Private donations
Membership: *Member Profile:* Over 15 years of age & from Diman
Chief Officer(s):
Samir Metlej, President

Direct Sellers Association of Canada (DSA) / Association de ventes directes du Canada
#250, 180 Attwell Dr., Toronto ON M9W 6A9
Tel: 416-679-8555; *Fax:* 416-679-1568
info@dsa.ca
www.dsa.ca
www.facebook.com/322698510777
twitter.com/dsacanada
Overview: A small national organization founded in 1954
Mission: To represent companies that manufacture & distribute goods & services through independent sales contractors, away from a fixed retail location; To encourage strong consumer protection, through Codes of Ethics & Business Practices; To engage in discussion with government & industry; To act as the voice of the direct selling industry to government in pursuit of better business opportunities for Canadian entrepreneurs.
Membership: 48
Chief Officer(s):
Angela Abdallah, Chair
Ross Creber, President & Secretary

Direction Chrétienne
#520, 1450, rue City Councillors, Montréal QC H3A 2E6
Tél: 514-878-3035; *Téléc:* 514-878-8048
info@direction.ca
www.direction.ca
Également appelé: Christian Direction
Aperçu: *Dimension:* petite; *Envergure:* provinciale; Organisme sans but lucratif; fondée en 1964
Mission: Rendre visite aux communautés chrétiennes locales et particulièrement celles des grands centres urbains afin de se faire connaître et partager son mandat
Finances: *Budget de fonctionnement annuel:* $500,000-$1.5 Million
Membre(s) du personnel: 13; 3 bénévole(s)
Membre: 1-99
Membre(s) du bureau directeur:
Glenn Smith, Executive Director

DIRECTIONS Council for Vocational Services Society
#920, 99 Wyse Rd., Dartmouth NS B3A 4S5
Tel: 902-466-2220; *Fax:* 902-461-2220
www.directionscouncil.org
Previous Name: Workshop Council of Nova Scotia
Overview: A medium-sized provincial organization
Mission: To promote the abilities & inclusion of persons with disabilities in the every day activities of their community
Membership: 29 agencies
Chief Officer(s):
Bob Bennett, President

Directors Guild of Canada (DGC) / La Guilde canadienne des réalisateurs
#600, 111 Peter St., Toronto ON M5V 2H1
Tel: 416-925-8200; *Fax:* 416-925-8400
Toll-Free: 888-972-0098
mail@dgc.ca
www.dgc.ca
twitter.com/DGCnational
vimeo.com/dgcnational; www.flickr.com/photos/dgcnational
Overview: A medium-sized national organization founded in 1962
Mission: To represent key creative & logistical personnel in the film & television industry; to promote & advance the quality & vitality of Canadian feature film
Staff Member(s): 16
Membership: 3,800+; *Member Profile:* Directors; Assistant Directors; Unit Directors; Art Directors; Assistant Art Directors; Set Designers; Production Designers; Assistant Production Managers; Location Managers; Assistant Location Managers; Unit Managers; Supervising Picture Editors; Picture Editors; Post Production Supervisors; Supervising Sound Editors; Sound Editors; Music Editors; Documentary Editors; Commercial Editors; Assistant Picture Editors; Assistant Sound Editors; Production Secretaries; Production Coordinators; Technical Coordinators; Post Production Coordinators; Production Assistants; Production Accountants; Art Department Trainees; Trainee Assistant Editors & any trainee, apprentice or other assistant of each category above
Activities: *Internships:* Yes; *Speaker Service:* Yes
Chief Officer(s):
Tim Southam, President
Brian Baker, National Executive Director, 416-482-3811 Ext. 232

Alberta District Council
#133, 2526 Battleford Ave. SW, Calgary AB T3Z 7J4
Tel: 403-217-8672; *Fax:* 403-217-8678
dgc@dgcalberta.ca
www.dgc.ca/alberta
Chief Officer(s):
Hudson Cooley, Chair
Carol Romanow, Business Agent

Atlantic Regional District Council
#501B, 1496 Lower Water St., Halifax NS B3J 1R9
Tel: 902-492-3424; *Fax:* 902-492-2678
info@dgcatlantic.ca
www.dgc.ca/atlanticregion
Chief Officer(s):
Shauna Hatt, Chair
James B. Nicholson, Business Agent
jamesbn@dgcatlantic.ca

British Columbia District Council
#430, 1152 Mainland St., Vancouver BC V6B 2X4
Tel: 604-688-2976; *Fax:* 604-688-2610
info@dgcbc.com
www.dgc.ca/bc
www.facebook.com/257912354261860
twitter.com/DGCBC
Chief Officer(s):
Allan Harmon, Chair
Crawford Hawkins, Executive Director
chawkins@dgcbc.com

Conseil du Québec
#708, 4200, boul Saint-Laurent, Montréal QC H2W 2R2
Tél: 514-844-4084; *Téléc:* 514-844-1067
action@dgc.ca
www.dgc.ca/quebec
Chief Officer(s):
Anne Sirois, Présidente
Chantal Barrette, Agente d'affaires
cbarrette@dgc.ca

Manitoba District Council
c/o DGC National Office, #600, 111 Peter St., Toronto ON M5V 2H1

Canadian Associations / Disability Alliance British Columbia (DABC)

Fax: 416-925-8400
Toll-Free: 888-972-0098
www.dgc.ca/manitoba
Chief Officer(s):
Cathie Edgar, President
Catherine Middleton, Business Agent
cmiddleton@dgc.ca

Ontario District Council
#600, 111 Peter St., Toronto ON M5V 2H1
Tel: 416-925-8200; Fax: 416-925-8400
Toll-Free: 888-972-0098; Crisis Hot-Line: 416-557-6223
cjohn@dgc.ca
www.dgc.ca/ontario
Chief Officer(s):
Alan Goluboff, Chair
Bill Skolnik, Executive Director & CEO
bskolnik@dgcontario.ca

Saskatchewan District Council
c/o DGC National Office, #600, 111 Peter St., Toronto ON M5V 2H1
Toll-Free: 888-972-0098
sdc@dgc.ca
www.dgcsask.com
Chief Officer(s):
Phil Doersken, Chair
Catherine Middleton, Business Agent
cmiddleton@dgc.ca

Disability Alliance British Columbia (DABC)
#204, 456 West Broadway, Vancouver BC V5Y 1R3
Tel: 604-875-0188; Fax: 604-875-9227
Toll-Free: 800-663-1278; TTY: 604-875-8835
feedback@disabilityalliancebc.org
www.disabilityalliancebc.org
www.linkedin.com/company/4863769
www.facebook.com/DisabilityAllianceBC
twitter.com/DisabAllianceBC
www.youtube.com/user/TheBCCPD
Previous Name: British Columbia Coalition of People with Disabilities
Overview: A medium-sized provincial charitable organization founded in 1977
Mission: To raise public & political awareness of issues concerning people with disabilities; To facilitate full participation of disabled people in society by promoting independence & the self-help model; To lobby government on policies & attitudes which affect people with disabilities
Affiliation(s): Council of Canadians with Disabilities
Staff Member(s): 14; 12 volunteer(s)
Membership: 1,200 groups/individual; *Fees:* $15; *Committees:* Transportation; Physical Access
Activities: Advocacy Access Program; AIDS & Disability Action Program; Individualized Funding Community Development Project; Community & Residents Mentors Associatin Project; Wellness & Disability Initiative; *Speaker Service:* Yes; *Library:* BCCPD Library; Open to public
Chief Officer(s):
Jane Dyson, Executive Director, 604-875-0188
jwd@disabilityalliancebc.org
Sam Turcott, Director, Advocacy Access Program, 604-872-1278
sam@disabilityalliancebc.org
Justina Loh, Administrative Director, 604-875-0188
jloh@disabilityalliancebc.org

Disability Awareness Consultants (DAC)
146 Haslam St., Toronto ON M1N 3N7
Tel: 416-267-5939
disabilityawarenessconsultants.com
Previous Name: Handidactis
Overview: A small local organization founded in 2006
Mission: To offer training & awareness programs to company employees so they can work comfortably with clients & coworkers who have disabilities; To help companies comply with the Accessibility for Ontarians with Disabilities Act; To conduct site audits in order to build barrier-free environments
Finances: *Annual Operating Budget:* Less than $50,000; *Funding Sources:* Private; Fee-based services
Staff Member(s): 1
Activities: *Speaker Service:* Yes
Chief Officer(s):
Lauri Sue Robertson, President & Owner
laurisue@bell.net
William F. Robertson, Vice-President, Operations

Disabled Individuals Alliance (DIAL)
Bethune Bldg., #262, 1278 Tower Rd., Halifax NS B3H 2Y9
Tel: 902-422-6888; Fax: 902-425-0766
MAJ@ns.sympatico.ca
www.nsnet.org/dial
Overview: A small local organization founded in 1978
Mission: DIAL (Disabled Individuals Alliance) is a cross-disability consumer group formed to bring together persons with varying disabilities and interested non-disabled individuals, enabling the disabled as a whole to speak out with a unified voice as to their common needs and goals.
Member of: Nova Scotia League for Equal Opportunities
Membership: *Member Profile:* People with disabilities; families of people with disabilities; supporters of people with disabilities

Disabled Peoples' International (DPI) / Organisation mondiale des personnes handicapées
PO Box 70073, Stn. Place Bell, 160 Elgin St., Ottawa ON K2P 2M3
www.dpi.org
Overview: A small international charitable organization founded in 1981
Mission: To promote the human rights of disabled people through full participation, equalization of opportunity & development
Affiliation(s): United Nations; International Labour Organization
Finances: *Annual Operating Budget:* $500,000-$1.5 Million
Staff Member(s): 5; 3 volunteer(s)
Membership: 135 National Assemblies; 1,300 e-news members; *Fees:* Schedule available; *Committees:* Human Rights; Francophone; Peace; Women's Independent Living; Education; Constitutional
Activities: *Internships:* Yes; *Library*
Chief Officer(s):
Rachel Kachaje, Chair
rachel.kachaje@dpi.org

Disabled Sailing Association of B.C. (DSA)
#318, 425 Carrall St., Vancouver BC V6B 6E3
Tel: 604-688-6464; Fax: 604-688-6463
dsa@disabilityfoundation.org
www.disabledsailingbc.org
www.facebook.com/DisabledSailingAssociation
twitter.com/DisabilityFdn
Overview: A small provincial licensing charitable organization founded in 1989
Mission: To help people with disabilities live independent lives
Member of: AbleSail Network; BC Sailing
Affiliation(s): BC Sport & Fitness Council for the Disabled; Sam Sullivan Disability Foundation
Staff Member(s): 5; 35 volunteer(s)
Membership: *Fees:* $10 per sail
Activities: Offer sailors with physical disabilities a chance to sail solo or with a companion; Approximately 1000 sails completed each summer
Chief Officer(s):
Stephen Hunter, Contact, 604-688-6464
shunter@disabilityfoundation.org

Disabled Skiers Association of BC *See* BC Adaptive Snowsports

DisAbled Women's Network of Canada / Réseau d'Action des Femmes Handicapées du Canada
#505, 110, rue St-Thérèse, Montréal QC H2Y 1E6
Tel: 514-396-0009; Fax: 514-396-6585
Toll-Free: 866-396-0074
www.dawncanada.net
www.facebook.com/dawnrafhcanada
twitter.com/DAWNRAFHCanada
www.youtube.com/user/DAWNRAFHCanada
Also Known As: DAWN-RAFH Canada
Overview: A small national organization founded in 1985
Mission: To end the poverty, isolation, discrimination & violence experienced by women with disabilities; To ensure the accessibility of services to women with disabilities; To address key issues concerning women with disabilities
Member of: National Action Committee on the Status of Women
Affiliation(s): Council of Canadians with Disabilities
Finances: *Annual Operating Budget:* $100,000-$250,000
Staff Member(s): 5; 200 volunteer(s)
Membership: 300-400; *Fees:* Free; *Member Profile:* Women with disAbilities; *Committees:* Women's Partnership; Equality Rights; Health; Technology
Chief Officer(s):
Bonnie Brayton, National Executive Director
Selma Kouidri, Coordinator, Inclusion
inclusion@dawncanada.net
Hanane Khales, Coordinator, Communications
communications@dawncanada.net

Disaster Recovery Institute Canada (DRIC)
468 Queen St. East, #LL-02, Toronto ON M5A 1T7
Tel: 416-646-2750; Fax: 416-646-9460
Toll-Free: 844-228-8135
info@dri.ca
www.dri.ca
www.linkedin.com/groups/4111512
www.facebook.com/762001333828346
twitter.com/DRICInfo
Also Known As: DRI CANADA
Overview: A small national organization founded in 1996
Mission: To provide the leadership & best practices that serve as a base of common knowledge for all business continuity/disaster recovery planners & organizations throughout the industry
Affiliation(s): DRI International; Canadian Centre for Emergency Preparedness
Finances: *Annual Operating Budget:* $250,000-$500,000; *Funding Sources:* Training courses; application fees; membership fees
Staff Member(s): 5; 20 volunteer(s)
Membership: 750; *Member Profile:* Passing of exam, review by committee; *Committees:* Awards; Certification; Education
Activities: Education & training; professional certification; promotion of the business continuity/disaster recovery field; major business continuity/emergency preparedness conferences throughout North America
Chief Officer(s):
Perry Ruehlen, Executive Director
Awards:
• Award of Excellence

Discalced Carmelite Secular Order - Canada (OCDS)
11 Tangle Briarway, Toronto ON M2J 2M5
Tel: 416-223-2830; Fax: 416-223-9418
ocds.secretariat.ca@sympatico.ca
www.ocds.ca
Overview: A small national organization
Mission: To live in alliegiance to Jesus Christ; To meditate on the law of the Lord; To engage in spiritual reading; To live an intense life of faith, hope, & charity
Affiliation(s): Order of Our Lady of Mount Carmel; St. Teresa of Jesus; Archdiocese of Toronto
Finances: *Funding Sources:* Fundraising
Membership: *Member Profile:* Men & women, over the age of eighteen, who are constant in professing the Catholic faith; Members may not be professed members of another Order
Activities: Engaging in Daily Mass, morning & evening prayer from the Liturgy of the Hours, night, & mental prayer, & monthly formation meetings
Publications:
• Carmel-Lights
Type: Newsletter

Discovery Islands Chamber of Commerce
PO Box 790, Quathiaski Cove BC V0P 1N0
chamber@discoveryislands.ca
www.discoveryislands.ca/chamber
twitter.com/DiscoveryIsles
Overview: A small local organization
Membership: *Fees:* $30 individual/society; $50 small business; $100 business
Chief Officer(s):
Michael Lynch, President

Distance Riders of Manitoba Association (DRMA)
MB
Tel: 204-330-1773
www.distanceridersofmanitoba.ca
Overview: A small provincial organization founded in 1993 overseen by Canadian Long Distance Riding Association
Mission: DRMA promotes endurance riding in the province of Manitoba & brings together equestrians interested in the sport.
Member of: Manitoba Horse Council; Canadian Long Distance Riding Association
Affiliation(s): American Endurance Ride Conference
Membership: 30; *Fees:* $25 single; $40 family; *Member Profile:* Manitoba equestrians
Activities: Supervised rides; competitions
Chief Officer(s):
Jessica Manness, Secretary
northranch@hotmail.com

Maura Leahy, Treasurer & Membership Contact
Maura.Leahy@live.ca

Distress Centre Niagara Inc.
PO Box 25014, Stn. Pen Centre-Glendale Ave., St Catharines ON L2T 2C4
Fax: 905-682-7959; *Crisis Hot-Line:* 905-688-3711
dcniagara@distresscentreniagara.com
distresscentreniagara.com
Overview: A small local organization founded in 1970 overseen by Distress Centres Ontario
Mission: To provide a no-cost confidential telephone support service by trained volunteers to assist anyone in need in the Niagara area
Finances: *Funding Sources:* United Way; Donations
Activities: *Speaker Service:* Yes

Distress Centre North Halton
PO Box 85, Georgetown ON L7G 4T1
Tel: 905-877-0655; *Fax:* 905-877-0655; *Crisis Hot-Line:* 905-877-1211
dcnhalton@bellnet.ca
www.dchalton.ca
Overview: A small local organization founded in 1973 overseen by Distress Centres Ontario
Mission: To provide confidential listening, emotional support, referrals & information, & crisis intervention
Finances: *Funding Sources:* United Way; donations
Activities: Bereavement Support Program

Distress Centre of Durham Region (DCD)
306 Brock St. North, Whitby ON L1N 4H7
Tel: 905-430-3511; *Crisis Hot-Line:* 800-452-0688
dcd@distresscentredurham.com
www.distresscentredurham.com
www.facebook.com/DurhamDistress
twitter.com/DurhamDistress
Overview: A small local charitable organization founded in 1970
Mission: To help people in distress to cope, by providing emotional support, crisis/suicide management & community education
Member of: Distress Centres Ontario; Canadian Association of Suicide Prevention
Finances: *Annual Operating Budget:* $100,000-$250,000; *Funding Sources:* United Way; public donors; fundraising events
Staff Member(s): 4
Activities: Free, confidential 24-hr telephone helpline; crisis intervention; community education; suicide & homicide survivor support groups; adolescent suicide awareness program; *Speaker Service:* Yes
Chief Officer(s):
Victoria Kehoe, Executive Director
victoria@distresscentredurham.com

Distress Centre of Ottawa & Region (DCOR) / Centre de détresse d'Ottawa et la région
PO Box 3457, Stn. C, Ottawa ON K1Y 4J6
Tel: 613-238-1089; *Fax:* 613-722-5217
www.dcottawa.on.ca
www.facebook.com/DistressCentreOR
twitter.com/DistressCentreO
Also Known As: Distress Centre Ottawa
Previous Name: Distress Centre Ottawa/Carleton
Overview: A small local charitable organization founded in 1969 overseen by Distress Centres Ontario
Mission: The Distress Centre is a non-profit organization that provides 24/7 confidential telephone services for emotional support, suicide prevention/intervention, postvention, crisis intervention, information referral & education services. It is a registered charity, BN: 108079815RR0001
Affiliation(s): American Association of Suicidology; Canadian Association for Suicide Prevention; International Association for Suicide Prevention
55 volunteer(s)
Activities: *Awareness Events:* Festival of Chocolate, Feb.; Leadercast Leadership Event, May; *Internships:* Yes; *Speaker Service:* Yes

Distress Centre Ottawa/Carleton *See* Distress Centre of Ottawa & Region

Distress Centre Wellington/Dufferin; Guelph Distress Centre *See* Community Torchlight Guelph/Wellington/Dufferin

Distress Centres of Toronto
PO Box 243, Stn. Adelaide, Toronto ON M5C 2J4
Tel: 416-598-0166; *TTY:* 416-408-0007; *Crisis Hot-Line:* 416-408-4357
info@torontodistresscentre.com
www.torontodistresscentre.com
www.facebook.com/1536691786591642
twitter.com/DC_TO
Overview: A small local organization founded in 1967
Mission: To assist emotionally distressed individuals deal with those issues they are currently unable to manage
Affiliation(s): Ontario Association of Distress Centres
Staff Member(s): 11
Activities: *Speaker Service:* Yes; *Rents Mailing List:* Yes
Chief Officer(s):
Karen Letofsky, Executive Director, 416-598-0168
karen@torontodistresscentre.com

Distress Centres Ontario (DCO)
#1016, 30 Duke St. West, Kitchener ON N2H 3W5
Tel: 416-486-2242; *Fax:* 519-342-0970
info@dcontario.org
www.dcontario.org
Previous Name: Ontario Association of Distress Centres
Overview: A medium-sized provincial charitable organization founded in 1971
Mission: To transfer best practices between member centres; To promote, support & sustain member agencies
Membership: 15; *Member Profile:* Distress centres in Ontario
Activities: Hosting an annual meeting; Offering networking opportunities for member centres; Providing educational forums & training; Forming partnerships to assist in offering support, referral, & mental health services; Increasing public awareness; Liaising with funding bodies, government, & the public; *Awareness Events:* World Suicide Prevention Day, September
Chief Officer(s):
Karen Letofsky, Chair
Elizabeth Fisk, Executive Director

Distress Line Sarnia
Bldg. 1030, 1086 Modeland Rd., Sarnia ON N7S 6L2
Tel: 519-336-0120; *Fax:* 519-336-8517
Toll-Free: 800-831-3031; *Crisis Hot-Line:* 888-347-8737
www.familycounsellingctr.com
Also Known As: Family Counselling Centre
Overview: A small local charitable organization founded in 1973 overseen by Distress Centres Ontario
Mission: To help strengthen people & their relationships with others
Member of: Distress Centres Ontario
Finances: *Funding Sources:* United Way
85 volunteer(s)
Activities: Conferences; resources; meetings; *Awareness Events:* Suicide Awareness Week; *Internships:* Yes; *Speaker Service:* Yes
Chief Officer(s):
Don Pitt, Executive Director
don.pitt@familycounsellingctr.com

District 69 Association for the Disabled *See* Parksville & District Association for Community Living

District 69 Community Arts Council *See* Oceanside Community Arts Council

District Indian Youth Club *See* Red Lake Indian Friendship Centre

District of Mission Arts Council
33529 - 1st Ave., Mission BC V2V 1H1
Tel: 604-826-0029; *Fax:* 604-826-0090
info@missionartscouncil.ca
www.missionartscouncil.ca
www.facebook.com/MissionArtsCentre
twitter.com/missionartscncl
Also Known As: Mission Arts Council
Overview: A small local charitable organization founded in 1972
Mission: To foster the development & appreciation of the arts by providing cultural & educational activities for the community of the District of Mission
Member of: Assembly of BC Arts Councils; South West Regional Arts Council
Finances: *Annual Operating Budget:* $50,000-$100,000; *Funding Sources:* Membership dues; grants; donations
Staff Member(s): 1; 60 volunteer(s)
Membership: *Fees:* $30 individual; $45 family; $75 group; $20 seniors; $5 MYAC student; $10 non-voting; *Member Profile:* Interest in the arts; *Committees:* Volunteer; Gallery; ArteScapes; Children's Festival; Christmas Craft Fair; Envision Twilight Concerts; Events; Fundraising; Gift Shop; Halloween Haunted Mansion; Home Routes; Art Shows; Website
Activities: Art related workshops & festivals; Studio Tour; Children's Art Fest; Banner Festival; Gallery; *Awareness Events:* Children's Festival, June; Christmas Market, Nov.
Chief Officer(s):
Nancy Arcand, Executive Director
nancy@missionartscouncil.ca

Dive B.C. *See* British Columbia Diving

Dive Ontario
216 Gilwood Park Dr., Penetanguishene ON L9M 1Z6
Tel: 705-355-3483; *Fax:* 705-355-4663
contactus@diveontario.com
www.diveontario.com
www.facebook.com/DiveOntario
Overview: A small provincial organization
Mission: To provide programs & services to its members
Affiliation(s): Community & recreation centres around the province; Dive Plongeon Canada
Membership: 11 clubs; *Member Profile:* Diving clubs in Ontario; *Committees:* HP Implementation; Sport Development; Media & Marketing
Chief Officer(s):
Bernie Olanski, President
bernie@lexcor.ca

DIVERSEcity Community Resources Society
13455 - 76 Ave., Surrey BC V3W 2W3
Tel: 604-597-0205; *Fax:* 604-597-4299
info@dcrs.ca
www.dcrs.ca
Also Known As: DIVERSEcity
Previous Name: Surrey-Delta Immigrant Services Society
Overview: A small local charitable organization founded in 1978
Mission: To promote the independence of immigrants & to build strong culturally diverse communities
Member of: Affiliation of Multicultural Societies & Service Agencies of BC
Finances: *Annual Operating Budget:* $3 Million-$5 Million; *Funding Sources:* Federal, provincial & service fees; United Way
Staff Member(s): 85; 150 volunteer(s)
Membership: 200; *Member Profile:* Any resident who supports the mission
Activities: Settlement services; community development; language training; interpretation & translation; job search services; *Internships:* Yes; *Speaker Service:* Yes
Chief Officer(s):
Neelam Sahota, CEO
ceo@dcrs.ca
Tahzeem Kassam, COO
tkassam@dcrs.ca
Awards:
• Cultural DIVERSEcity Awards for Business

Diving Plongeon Canada (DPC) / Association canadienne du plongeon amateur Inc.
#312, 700 Industrial Ave., Ottawa ON K1G 0Y9
Tel: 613-736-5238; *Fax:* 613-736-0409
cada@diving.ca
www.diving.ca
www.facebook.com/DivingPCanada
twitter.com/DivingPlongeon
Also Known As: Canadian Amateur Diving Association Inc.
Overview: A medium-sized national charitable organization founded in 1967
Mission: To promote the growth & awareness of diving in Canada; To contribute to the development of globally accepted standards of diving; To support the rules & regulations of international competition
Member of: FINA
Affiliation(s): Aquatics Federation of Canada; Swimming Natation Canada; Synchronized Swimming; Water Polo Canada
Finances: *Funding Sources:* Government; Self Funding; Donations; Sponsorships
Staff Member(s): 10
Membership: 67 local diving clubs + 4,000 high performance athletes; *Member Profile:* Diving associations; Local diving clubs; High performance athletes; *Committees:* Athlete; Technical; Officials; Rules & Regulations
Activities: Providing programs & services for participants to achieve excellence & self-fulfillment; Obtaining media coverage & increasing spectators at events; Developing elite athletes; Communicating with members; Hosting an annual general meeting; Presenting DPC awards
Chief Officer(s):
Penny Joyce, Chief Operating Officer
penny@diving.ca

Mitch Geller, Chief Technical Officer
mitch@diving.ca
Scott Cranham, Director, Talent Management
scott@diving.ca
Jeff Feeney, Manager, Events & Communications
jeff@diving.ca

Division de l'Atlantique de l'association Canadienne des Géographes See Canadian Association of Geographers

Dixon Hall
58 Sumach St., Toronto ON M5A 3J7
Tel: 416-863-0499; Fax: 416-863-9981
info@dixonhall.org
www.dixonhall.org
www.facebook.com/DixonHallToronto
twitter.com/dixon_hall
Overview: A medium-sized local charitable organization founded in 1929
Mission: To create opportunities for people of all ages to dream, to achieve and to live full and rewarding lives.
Finances: Funding Sources: Government, Foundations, Donations, United Way
Membership: Committees: Strategic Planning; Finance & Audit; Fundraising, Development & Communications; Governance; Programs
Chief Officer(s):
Kate Stark, Executive Director

Doctors Manitoba
20 Desjardins Dr., Winnipeg MB R3X 0E8
Tel: 204-985-5888; Fax: 204-985-5844
Toll-Free: 888-322-4242
general@docsmb.org
www.docsmb.org
Previous Name: Manitoba Medical Association
Overview: A medium-sized provincial organization founded in 1908 overseen by Canadian Medical Association
Mission: To unite & advocate for Manitoba physicians; To encourage the highest standards of health care for the people of Manitoba
Finances: Funding Sources: Membership dues
Staff Member(s): 17
Membership: 2,272; Member Profile: Manitoba physicians, medical students & residents
Activities: Operating physician support hotlines; Acting as the sole bargaining agent for member physicians & physician groups
Chief Officer(s):
Robert Cram, Chief Executive Officer, 204-985-5843
rcram@docsmb.org
Rick Sawyer, Chief Administrative Officer, 204-985-5842
rsawyer@docsmb.org
Meetings/Conferences:
• Doctors Manitoba 2018 Annual General Meeting, 2018
Scope: Provincial
Publications:
• Rounds [a publication of Doctors Manitoba]
Type: Magazine; Frequency: 4 pa.; Accepts Advertising
Profile: Features member profiles & industry news

Doctors Nova Scotia
25 Spectacle Lake Dr., Dartmouth NS B3B 1X7
Tel: 902-468-1866; Fax: 902-468-6578
Toll-Free: 800-563-3427
info@doctorsns.com
www.doctorsns.com
twitter.com/Doctors_NS
Previous Name: Medical Society of Nova Scotia
Overview: A medium-sized provincial organization founded in 1861 overseen by Canadian Medical Association
Mission: To maintain the integrity of the medical profession; To represent members; To promote high quality health care & disease prevention in Nova Scotia
Member of: Canadian Medical Association
Staff Member(s): 32
Membership: 3,500 physicians; Member Profile: Doctors, medical students, & residents in Nova Scotia; Committees: Audit; Governance; IT Steering; Policy & Health Issues
Activities: Educating the public on healthy lifestyle choices; Partnering with organizations; Offering the Youth Running for Fun Program; Voicing physician concerns with the health-care system; Advising on health-related policies & legislation
Chief Officer(s):
Nancy MacCready-Williams, CEO
John Sullivan, President
Meetings/Conferences:
• Doctors Nova Scotia 2018 Annual Conference, June, 2018, Membertou Convention Centre, Sydney, NS
Scope: Provincial

Doctors of BC
#115, 1665 West Broadway, Vancouver BC V6J 5A4
Tel: 604-736-5551; Fax: 604-638-2917
Toll-Free: 800-665-2262
communications@doctorsofbc.ca
www.doctorsofbc.ca
ca.linkedin.com/company/1154933
www.facebook.com/bcsdoctors
twitter.com/doctorsofbc
Previous Name: British Columbia Medical Association
Overview: A medium-sized provincial organization founded in 1900 overseen by Canadian Medical Association
Mission: To promote a social, economic, & political climate in which members can provide the citizens of British Columbia with the highest standard of health care while achieving maximum professional satisfaction & fair economic reward
Activities: Offering programs to explore & articulate concerns regarding environmental health issues in a fashion which will best enable an informed public to participate in an open, valid, scientifically based analysis of issues involved; Assisting society in development of policies dealing with environmental health issues; Enhancing public health & harmony between humans & nature; Waste Management; Water Quality; Air Quality;
Internships: Yes; Speaker Service: Yes; Rents Mailing List: Yes; Library
Chief Officer(s):
Allan Seckel, Chief Executive Officer
Alan Ruddiman, President
president@doctorsofbc.ca
Awards:
• Dr David M. Bachop Gold Medal for Distinguished Medical Service
• Dr. Cam Coady Medal of Excellence
• Dr Don Rix Award for Physician Leadership (D.B. Rix Award)
• Doctors of BC Silver Medal of Service Award
Publications:
• BC Medical Journal
Type: Journal; Editor: D.R. Richardson, MD

Doctors without Borders Canada (MSF) / Médecins sans frontières Canada (MSF-C)
#402, 720 Spadina Ave., Toronto ON M5S 2T9
Tel: 416-964-0619; Fax: 416-963-8707
Toll-Free: 800-982-7903
msfcan@msf.ca
www.msf.ca
www.linkedin.com/company/6952
www.facebook.com/msf.english
twitter.com/MSF_Canada
www.youtube.com/user/MSFCanada
Also Known As: MSF Canada
Overview: A small national charitable organization founded in 1991
Mission: To offer assistance to populations in distress, to victims of natural or man-made disasters & to victims of armed conflict, without discrimination & irrespective of race, religion, creed or political affiliation.
Finances: Annual Operating Budget: Greater than $5 Million
Staff Member(s): 67
Activities: Sending medical & non-medical volunteers overseas to provide humanitarian relief during conflicts, epidemics & natural disasters; Internships: Yes; Speaker Service: Yes; Rents Mailing List: Yes; Library: by appointment
Chief Officer(s):
Heather Culbert, President
Stephen Cornish, Executive Director
Québec Office
#220, 1470, rue Peel, Montréal QC H3A 1T1
Tél: 514-845-5621; Téléc: 514-845-3707
Ligne sans frais: 866-878-5621
msfqc@msf.ca

Documentaristes du Canada See Documentary Organization of Canada

Documentary Organization of Canada (DOC) / Documentaristes du Canada
Centre for Social Innovation, #126, 215 Spadina Ave., Toronto ON M5T 2C7
Tel: 416-599-3844; Fax: 416-979-3836
Toll-Free: 877-467-4485
info@docorg.ca
www.docorg.ca
Previous Name: Canadian Independent Film Caucus
Overview: A small national organization founded in 1983
Mission: To support the art of independent documentary filmmaking & filmmakers in Canada
Member of: Observatoire du Documentaire; Canadian Conference of the Arts
Staff Member(s): 2
Membership: 650; Fees: $157.50 individual; $52.50 student; $525 associate; Member Profile: Directors; producers; craftspeople
Activities: Toronto, Ottawa-Gatineau, British Columbia, Atlantic, Québec, Newfoundland Chapters
Chief Officer(s):
Pepita Ferrari, Chair
Publications:
• POV Magazine
Frequency: Quarterly

Dog Guides Canada
152 Wilson St., Oakville ON L6K 0G6
Tel: 905-842-2891; Fax: 905-842-3373
Toll-Free: 800-768-3030; TTY: 905-842-1585
info@dogguides.com
www.dogguides.com
www.facebook.com/LFCDogGuides
twitter.com/LFCDogGuides
Also Known As: Lions Foundation of Canada Dog Guides and Sibtech Creations
Previous Name: Canine Vision Canada
Overview: A medium-sized national organization founded in 1985
Mission: To provide Dog Guides to Canadians through various programs, including Canine Vision Canada, Hearing Ear Dogs of Canada, & Service Dog Guides
Member of: Lions Foundation of Canada
Finances: Annual Operating Budget: $3 Million-$5 Million
Staff Member(s): 35; 2000 volunteer(s)
Activities: Speaker Service: Yes
Chief Officer(s):
Sandy Turney, Executive Director
sandyturney@dogguides.com
Julie Jelinek, Director, Development
jjelinek@dogguides.com
Alex Ivic, Director, Programs
aivic@dogguides.com
Sarah Miller, Manager, Communications
smiller@dogguides.com

Doggone Safe
2295 Mohawk Trail, Campbellville ON L0P 1B0
Tel: 905-854-3232; Fax: 905-854-3271
Toll-Free: 877-350-3232
www.doggonesafe.com
www.facebook.com/DoggoneSafe
www.youtube.com/clickerpuppytrainer
Overview: A small national organization
Mission: To prevent dog bites; To help children & families learn how to be safe around familiar & unfamiliar dogs; To support victims of dog bites
Membership: Fees: $20
Activities: Offering Be a Tree, Be Doggone Smart, & Be Doggone Smart at Home seminars for children, workers, & parents
Chief Officer(s):
Joan Orr, President
joanorr@doggonesafe.com

Dominion Automobile Association Limited
PO Box 5817, London ON N6A 4T3
Toll-Free: 877-322-1033; Crisis Hot-Line: 519-434-2185
www.daa.ca
Overview: A small national organization
Mission: To provide road assistance to members.
Affiliation(s): MADD Canada
Membership: Member Profile: Automobile owners
Activities: Battery boost; locked car service; tire change; fuel delivery, towing
Chief Officer(s):
Jackie McTaggart, Chief Operating Officer

Dominion of Canada Rifle Association (DCRA) / L'Association de tir dominion du canada
45 Shirley Blvd., Ottawa ON K2K 2W6
Tel: 613-829-8281; Fax: 613-829-0099
office@dcra.ca
www.dcra.ca

Overview: A small national charitable organization founded in 1868
Finances: *Annual Operating Budget:* $100,000-$250,000
Staff Member(s): 3; 60 volunteer(s)
Membership: 1,000; *Member Profile:* 10 provincial rifle associations; Yukon Rifle Association; National Capital Region Rifle Association
Activities: Annual Canadian Fullbore Rifle Championships
Chief Officer(s):
Jim Thompson, Executive Director
Stan E. Frost, Executive Vice-President
T.F. deFaye, President

Dominion Rabbit & Cavy Breeders Association (DR&CBA)
c/o Maureen Dyke, 243099 - 5th Side Rd., Amaranth ON L9W 0V4
www.drcba.ca
Overview: A small national organization founded in 1909
Mission: To promote & encourage the hobby of raising purebred rabbits & cavies for market, for show & for pleasure
Membership: 100+; *Fees:* $20 family; $15 individual; $10 youth; *Member Profile:* Rabbit & cavy enthusiasts
Activities: Shows; sweepstakes awards program; workshops; youth member program; licensing of judges; publishes standards
Chief Officer(s):
Brian Dart, President
Maureen Dyke, Secretary-Treasurer
maureendyke@sympatico.ca
Awards:
• Sweepstakes Awards

The Donkey Sanctuary of Canada (DSC)
PO Box 27063, Stn. Clair, Guelph ON N1L 0C1
Tel: 519-836-1697; *Fax:* 519-821-0698
info@thedonkeysanctuary.ca
www.thedonkeysanctuary.ca
www.facebook.com/TheDonkeySanctuary
twitter.com/DonkeySancCa
www.youtube.com/user/DonkeySanctuary001
Overview: A small national charitable organization founded in 1992
Mission: To provide a lifelong home to unwanted, neglected or abused donkeys & mules; To offer animal welfare education; To offer a life skills & companion animal program to people with unique needs
Finances: *Annual Operating Budget:* $500,000-$1.5 Million; *Funding Sources:* Private donations & foundation grants
Staff Member(s): 9; 35 volunteer(s)
Activities: *Awareness Events:* Donkey Day, 2nd Sunday in June; *Internships:* Yes; *Speaker Service:* Yes
Chief Officer(s):
Katharine Harkins, Executive Director

Donner Canadian Foundation / Fondation canadienne Donner
8 Prince Arthur Ave., 3rd Fl., Toronto ON M5R 1A9
Tel: 416-920-6400; *Fax:* 416-920-5577
www.donnerfoundation.org
Overview: A small national organization founded in 1950
Mission: In addition to ongoing funding of public policy research, the Foundation supports environmental, international development, and social service projects.
Chief Officer(s):
Helen McLean, Executive Director
mclean@donner.ca
Amy Buskirk, Senior Program Officer
buskirk@donner.ca
Awards:
• The Donner Prize
Award of $35,000 for the best book on Canadian public policy; five runners-up prizes of $5,000 each

Door & Hardware Institute in Canada
#310, 2175 Sheppard Ave. East, Toronto ON M2J 1W8
Tel: 416-492-6502; *Fax:* 416-491-1670
www.dhicanada.ca
twitter.com/dhicanada
Overview: A small international organization founded in 1977
Mission: To serve Canadian members as the professional development, information, advocate & certification resource for the total distribution process in the architectural openings industry.
Staff Member(s): 6
Membership: 700 Canadian + 5,000 international; *Fees:* Schedule available; *Committees:* Strategic Planning; Finance; Education; Membership; Marketing & Communications; Codes; Program
Chief Officer(s):
Lawrence Beatty, President
lawrence.beatty@shanahans.com
Carolyne Vigon, Executive Director, 416-492-6502 Ext. 251
carolyne@taylorenterprises.com

Doorsteps Neighbourhood Services
#106, 200 Chalkfarm Dr., Toronto ON M3L 2H7
Tel: 416-243-5480; *Fax:* 416-243-7406
www.doorsteps.ca
Overview: A medium-sized local charitable organization
Mission: To focus on community education, prevention, & the enhancement of resiliency of individuals & communities
Finances: *Annual Operating Budget:* $500,000-$1.5 Million; *Funding Sources:* Government; United Way
Staff Member(s): 12
Chief Officer(s):
Carol Thames, Executive Director
cthames@doorsteps.ca

Dorchester & Westmorland Literacy Council
c/o 132 Lockhart Ave., Moncton NB E1C 6R7
Tel: 506-379-4064; *Fax:* 506-379-4204
Overview: A small local charitable organization
Mission: The Council provides educational opportunities to inmates at Dorchester & Westmorland institutions.
Affiliation(s): Laubach Literacy New Brunswick
Chief Officer(s):
Bill Cairns, Contact
William.Cairns@CSC-SCC.gc.ca

Dorval Historical Society *Voir* Société historique de Dorval

Douglas College Faculty Association (DCFA) / Association des professeurs du Collège Douglas
PO Box 2503, New Westminster BC V3L 5B2
Tel: 604-527-5166; *Fax:* 604-520-1496
www.dcfa.ca
Overview: A small local organization
Mission: To act as the bargaining agent for faculty at Douglas College in New Westminster & Coquitlam, BC; to negotiate wages, benefits and working conditions for its members; to ensure the representation of faculty interests; to represent faculty facing complaints; to liaise with other labour groups.
Membership: *Committees:* Contract; Occupational Health & Safety; Rehabilitation
Chief Officer(s):
Erin Rozman, President
rozmane@douglascollege.ca
Lil Mairs, Administrative Assistant
mairsl@douglas.bc.ca

Down Syndrome Association of Ontario (DSAO)
300 Sunset Blvd., Peterborough ON K9H 5L3
Tel: 905-439-6644
Toll-Free: 855-921-3726
www.dsao.ca
www.facebook.com/DSAOntario
twitter.com/DSAOntario
Overview: A small provincial charitable organization
Mission: To ensure equality for people with Down Syndrome
Meetings/Conferences:
• 2018 Down Syndrome Association of Ontario Conference, 2018, ON
Scope: Provincial

Down Syndrome Association of Toronto (DSAT)
PO Box 40039, Stn. Liberty Village, Toronto ON M5V 0K7
Tel: 416-966-0990
info@dsat.ca
www.dsat.ca
www.facebook.com/dsatoronto
twitter.com/DSAToronto
www.youtube.com/user/DSAToronto
Overview: A small local charitable organization founded in 1987
Mission: To pursue civil & human rights, equality of opportunity & the full integration of persons with Down syndrome; To ensure that all students with Down syndrome are welcomed in regular classes in neighbourhood schools with appropriate support services
Activities: Social & information network; educational seminars & family-centered social events; *Awareness Events:* Down Syndrome Awareness Week, Nov.; *Rents Mailing List:* Yes; *Library:* Open to public by appointment
Chief Officer(s):
Bhaskar Thiagarajan, President
Publications:
• Down Syndrome Association of Toronto Newsletter
Type: Newsletter

Down Syndrome Research Foundation (DSRF)
1409 Sperling Ave., Burnaby BC V5B 4J8
Tel: 604-444-3773; *Fax:* 604-431-9248
info@dsrf.org
www.dsrf.org
www.linkedin.com/company/down-syndrome-research-foundation
www.facebook.com/DSRFCanada
twitter.com/DSRFcanada
www.instagram.com/dsrfcanada
Overview: A small national charitable organization founded in 1995
Mission: To maximize the ability of people with Down Syndrome to lead independent lives & to participate in the community in which they live; To provide educational programs & services that are guided by foundational research; To collaborate with researchers, professionals & families to empower people with Down Syndrome
Member of: Down Syndrome International
Finances: *Annual Operating Budget:* $1.5 Million-$3 Million; *Funding Sources:* Donations; Grants; User fees
Staff Member(s): 20; 100 volunteer(s)
Membership: *Fees:* $40; *Member Profile:* Parents, educators, general public
Activities: Offering educational programs & services; Providing research; Disseminating information; *Internships:* Yes; *Speaker Service:* Yes; *Library:* Open to public
Chief Officer(s):
Geoff Griffiths, Chair
Dawn McKenna, Executive Director
dawn@dsrf.org
Publications:
• Hand in Hand [a publication of the Down Syndrome Research Foundation]
Type: Newsletter; *Frequency:* Quarterly; *Editor:* Glen Hoos

Downtown Business Association of Edmonton (DBA)
10121 Jasper Ave., Edmonton AB T5J 4X6
Tel: 780-424-4085
info@edmontondowntown.com
www.edmontondowntown.com
www.facebook.com/190749960939389
twitter.com/DBAyeg
Overview: A medium-sized local organization founded in 1985
Mission: To promote downtown as the preferred place to work, shop, live & enjoy
Finances: *Funding Sources:* Municipal levy & sponsorships
Membership: 1,831; *Member Profile:* Downtown businesses; *Committees:* Business Recruitment; Operations; Marketing; Executive
Activities: Family Day; Light-Up Downtown; Indoor Santa Parade; Chili Cook-Off
Chief Officer(s):
Penny Omell, Chair
Jim Taylor, Executive Director

The Downtown Churchworkers' Association *See* Moorelands Community Services

Downtown Legal Services (DLS)
Fasken Martineau DuMoulin Centre for Legal Services, 655 Spadina Ave., Toronto ON M5S 2H9
Tel: 416-934-4535; *Fax:* 416-934-4536
law.dls@utoronto.ca
downtownlegalservices.ca
Also Known As: University of Toronto Community Legal Clinic
Overview: A small local organization founded in 1972
Mission: To provide legal assistance to those who cannot afford other legal services.
Member of: Association of Student Legal Aid Societies of Ontario
Affiliation(s): University of Toronto Faculty of Law; Out of the Cold, for homeless clients; MealTrans, for transgendered clients; Red Door, a shelter for abused women and their children
Finances: *Funding Sources:* Legal Aid Ontario
Staff Member(s): 6
Membership: *Member Profile:* Students at faculty of law
Activities: Legal assistance in summary conviction, criminal, academic, landlord/tenant, employment & immigration; Public Interest Advocacy clinical education programs; *Internships:* Yes; *Speaker Service:* Yes; *Library:* DLS Library; Not open to public

Canadian Associations / Downtown Truro Partnership (DTP)

Chief Officer(s):
Lisa Cirillo, Executive Director
Martha Turner, Office Manager

Downtown Truro Partnership (DTP)
PO Box 912, 605 Prince St., Truro NS B2N 5G7
Tel: 902-895-9258; *Fax:* 902-895-9712
contactus@downtowntruro.ca
www.downtowntruro.ca
www.facebook.com/downtowntruro
Overview: A small local organization founded in 1979
Chief Officer(s):
Debbie Elliott, Executive Director

Downtown Vancouver Association (DVA)
PO Box 11, 555 Seymour St., Vancouver BC V6B 3H6
Tel: 604-921-7400
info@thedva.com
www.thedva.com
www.facebook.com/Downtown-Vancouver-Association-751192691594154
twitter.com/DVA_metrocore
Overview: A medium-sized local organization founded in 1946
Mission: To promote downtown Vancouver as the focus of urban activities in the Lower Mainland & the Province of British Columbia; To enhance the economic, commercial & social welfare of Downtown Vancouver; To study & advance any project, plan or improvement designed to benefit the City as a whole, & Downtown Vancouver in particular; To provide cooperation & aid to individuals or groups in projects designed to benefit the City & Downtown Vancouver; To regularly communicate to the public concerning the health & welfare of the whole City & the downtown; To commit to action on all matters that benefit the City & Downtown Vancouver
Member of: International Downtown Association
Affiliation(s): Downtown Vancouver Business Improvement Association
Finances: *Annual Operating Budget:* $50,000-$100,000; *Funding Sources:* Membership fees
Staff Member(s): 1
Membership: 200 corporate + 10 institutional + 10 associate + 100 individual; *Fees:* $120-$1,400; *Committees:* Arts & Culture; Planning & Development; Retail; Taxation & Assessment; Tourism; Transportation & Communications
Activities: Networking monthly speaker series
Chief Officer(s):
Herman Mah, Executive Director

Dr. H. Bliss Murphy Cancer Care Foundation
Dr. H. Bliss Murphy Cancer Centre, 300 Prince Philip Dr., St. John's NL A1B 3V6
Tel: 709-777-7589; *Fax:* 709-777-2372
cancercarefoundation.nl.ca
www.facebook.com/cancercarefoundation
twitter.com/Cancercarefdn
www.youtube.com/user/Cstarz76
Overview: A small local charitable organization
Mission: To raise money on behalf of the Dr. H. Bliss Murphy Cancer Centre in order to improve the services offered to patients & to fund research
Staff Member(s): 6
Chief Officer(s):
Lynette Hillier, Executive Director, 709-777-7590, Fax: 797-772-372
lynette.hillier@easternhealth.ca

Dr. James Naismith Basketball Foundation / La fondation de basketball Dr James Naismith
2729 Draper Ave., Ottawa ON K2H 7A1
Tel: 613-256-3610
www.naismithbasketball.ca
Also Known As: Naismith Foundation; Naismith Museum & Hall of Fame
Overview: A medium-sized national charitable organization founded in 1989
Mission: To establish & operate the Naismith International Basketball Centre which will reflect the remarkable heritage & development of Naismith's game in Canada & around the world.
Affiliation(s): Basketball Canada
Finances: *Funding Sources:* Fundraising; merchandise sales; special events
Activities: To preserve, conserve & promote the life & times of Dr. James Naismith & his gift to mankind - basketball, through the museum & related programs; *Library:* Naismith Basketball Resource Collection; by appointment

Dragon Boat Canada (DBC) / Bateau-Dragon Canada (BDC)
#331, 2255B Queen St. East, Toronto ON M4E 1G3
Tel: 613-482-1377
dragonboat.ca
www.facebook.com/DBC.BDC
twitter.com/DragonBoatCda
Overview: A medium-sized national organization
Mission: To be the official governing of dragon boat racing in Canada.
Member of: International Dragon Boat Federation
Membership: *Fees:* Schedule available
Chief Officer(s):
Chloe Greenhalgh, Executive Director
director@dragonboat.ca

Dragon Boat Festival Society *See* Canadian International Dragon Boat Festival Society

Drainage Superintendents Association of Ontario (DSAO)
PO Box 100, Bradford ON L3Z 2A7
Tel: 905-778-4321
dsao@dsao.net
www.dsao.net
Overview: A medium-sized provincial organization founded in 1984
Mission: To improve the knowledge of drainage through the exchange of ideas & information; to consider & deal with construction, maintenance of, & improvement to drainage works; to unite the drainage superintendents & commissioners for the promotion of better maintenance, repair & improvement of drainage works in Ontario.
Finances: *Funding Sources:* Membership fees
Membership: *Fees:* $175
Chief Officer(s):
Eric Westerberg, President
ericw@chatham-kent.ca
Sarah Murray, Executive Secretary
smurray@townofbwg.com
  Bluewater
  Woolwich ON
  Tel: 519-880-2708; *Fax:* 519-880-2709
  Chief Officer(s):
  Greg Nancekivell, Board Director
  greg@dietricheng.com
  Central Region
  Bradford West Gwillimbury ON
  Tel: 905-778-4321; *Fax:* 905-775-0153
  dsao@dsao.net
  Chief Officer(s):
  Frank Jonkman, Past President, DSAO
  fjonkman@townofbwg.com
  Eastern Region
  Ottawa ON
  Tel: 613-580-2424; *Fax:* 613-489-2880
  dsao@dsao.net
  Chief Officer(s):
  Eric Cryderman, Board Director
  eric.cryderman@ottawa.ca
  Elgin/Lambton/Middlesex
  Sarnia ON
  Tel: 519-332-0330; *Fax:* 519-332-0776
  dsao@dsao.net
  Chief Officer(s):
  David Moores, Board Director
  david.moores@sarnia.ca
  Essex/Chatham/Kent
  Chatham-Kent ON
  Tel: 519-360-1998; *Fax:* 519-436-3240
  dsao@dsao.net
  Chief Officer(s):
  Eric Westerberg, President, DSAO
  ericw@chatham-kent.ca
  Niagara Region
  Norfolk County ON
  Tel: 519-582-2100; *Fax:* 519-582-4571
  dsao@dsao.net
  Chief Officer(s):
  Bill Mayes, Vice-President, DSAO
  bill.mayes@norfolkcounty.ca

Drayton Valley & District Chamber of Commerce (DVDCC)
PO Box 5318, #112, 4302 50 St., Drayton Valley AB T7A 1R5

Tel: 780-542-7578; *Fax:* 780-542-2688
www.draytonvalley.ca/chamber-of-commerce/
Overview: A small local organization founded in 1961
Mission: To promote & enhance free enterprise & the economy of Drayton Valley & district
Member of: Alberta Chamber Executives; Alberta Chamber of Commerce; Canadian Chamber of Commerce
Finances: *Annual Operating Budget:* $100,000-$250,000
Staff Member(s): 2; 12 volunteer(s)
Membership: 130+; *Fees:* $65-$295; *Committees:* Agriculture; Advisory; Business Development; Natural Resources; Policy Development & Review; Retail Merchants; Tourism; Trade Show; AGM; Membership
Activities: Organizing Spring Trade Show & Sale, Fall Trade Show, Junior Achievement, & Parade Entries; Providing host seminars & speakers; *Library:* Tourism Information Centre; Open to public
Chief Officer(s):
Heather Yakimchuk, President
Awards:
• Best Business Award
• Chamber Spirit Award

Drayton Valley Association for Community Living *See* Beehive Support Services Association

The Dream Factory
#303, 1 Wesley Ave., Winnipeg MB R3C 4C6
Tel: 204-989-4010; *Fax:* 204-944-9549
Toll-Free: 866-989-4010
dream@thedreamfactory.ca
www.thedreamfactory.ca
www.facebook.com/TheDreamFactoryMB
twitter.com/DreamFactoryMB
www.youtube.com/user/TheDreamFactoryMB
Previous Name: The Rainbow Society
Overview: A small provincial charitable organization founded in 1983
Mission: To provide the opportunity for children (ages 3 to 18) who are suffering from life-threatening illness to fulfill their dreams
Affiliation(s): Rainbow Society of Alberta
Finances: *Annual Operating Budget:* $250,000-$500,000
Staff Member(s): 3; 100 volunteer(s)
Membership: 1-99
Chief Officer(s):
Leilani Kagan, President
Howard Koks, Executive Director
howard@thedreamfactory.ca
Alyssa Slike, Officer, Development
alyssa@thedreamfactory.ca
Cindy Titus, Coordinator, Communications & Fundraising
cindy@thedreamfactory.ca
Isaura Clark, Coordinator, Volunteer
isaura@thedreamfactory.ca

Dreams Take Flight
PO Box 7000, Stn. Airport, Dorval QC H4Y 1J2
Tel: 204-479-5267
canada@dreamstakeflight.ca
www.dreamstakeflight.ca
www.facebook.com/DreamsTakeFlightCanada
twitter.com/DreamsTakeFlght
Overview: A small national charitable organization founded in 1989
Mission: To provide Disney vacations to children with mental & physical disabilities
Chief Officer(s):
Bev Watson, President
ntl.president@dreamstakeflight.ca

Dress for Success
2016 Gottingen St., Halifax NS B3K 3A9
Tel: 902-493-7377
halifax@dressforsuccess.org
halifax.dressforsuccess.org
www.facebook.com/halifaxdressforsuccess
twitter.com/DFSHalifax
Overview: A small local charitable organization founded in 2001
Mission: To provide free interview appropriate clothing & job development skills to low-income women who are making a permanent transition to the workforce
Finances: *Annual Operating Budget:* $50,000-$100,000
Staff Member(s): 1; 40 volunteer(s)
Activities: Career Centre; Suiting for Confidence program; *Awareness Events:* Totally Suitable Tea Party, every summer; *Speaker Service:* Yes

Activities: *Library:*
Chief Officer(s):
Jacquie Blackburn, Treasurer
jacquies.parrots@sympatico.ca
Awards:
- Canadian Parrot Conference Aviculturist Service Award
- DAS Patron Award

Durham Chamber Orchestra
Whitby ON
info@durhamchamberorchestra.com
www.durhamchamberorchestra.com
www.facebook.com/DurhamChamberOrchestra
Previous Name: Ajax-Pickering Chamber Orchestra
Overview: A small local organization overseen by Orchestras Canada
Member of: Orchestras Canada
Membership: 30
Chief Officer(s):
Andrew Uranowski, Music Director

Durham Deaf Services (DDS)
750 King St. East, Oshawa ON L1H 1G9
Tel: 905-579-3328; *Fax:* 905-728-1183; *TTY:* 905-579-6495
info@durhamdeaf.org
www.durhamdeaf.org
www.facebook.com/durhamdeafservices
www.youtube.com/user/DurhamDeafServices
Overview: A small local charitable organization founded in 1982
Mission: To offer services & educational programs to promote self-reliance within the deaf, deafened & hard-of-hearing community; to increase awareness of deaf culture.
Affiliation(s): Ontario Association of the Deaf, Canadian Association of the Deaf
Finances: *Funding Sources:* Federal & provincial government; United Way; William F. Hayball Foundation
Staff Member(s): 9
Membership: *Fees:* $15 senior/student; $20 senior couple; $25 individual; $35 family; $60 organization
Activities: Durham Deaf Club; *Speaker Service:* Yes; *Library:* Resource Centre; Open to public
Chief Officer(s):
Yvonne Brown, Executive Director

Durham Parents of Multiples (DPOM)
PO Box 70607, Whitby ON L1N 2K0
Toll-Free: 888-358-5145
Other Communication: durham@multiplebirthscanada.org
durhamparentsofmultiples@yahoo.ca
www.multiplebirthscanada.org/~durham
Overview: A small local organization overseen by Multiple Births Canada
Mission: Providing support services for parents of multiple birth children in Durham Region.
Membership: *Fees:* $35 single parent; $40 family

Durham Personal Computer Users' Club (DPCUC)
PMB #110, #27, 1300 King St. East, Oshawa ON L1H 8J4
Tel: 905-623-2787
www.durhampc-usersclub.on.ca
Overview: A small local organization founded in 1986
Membership: *Fees:* $40; *Member Profile:* Computer enthusiasts from Ontario's Durham Region
Activities: Hosting general monthly meetings; Establishing Special Interest Groups
Chief Officer(s):
John Sylvestervich, President, 905-723-6797
jsylvest@rogers.com
Anne Delong, Vice-President, 905-623-6975
annedelong@timetraces.com
Linda Netten, Director, Membership
linnetten@idirect.com
Publications:
- PC Monitor
Type: Newsletter; *Frequency:* Monthly; *Price:* Free with membership in the Durham Personal Coputer Users' Club
Profile: News & tips from the club

Durham Region Association of REALTORS (DRAR)
#14, 50 Richmond St. East, Oshawa ON L1G 7C7
Tel: 905-723-8184; *Fax:* 905-723-7531
Reception@DurhamRealEstate.org
www.durhamrealestate.org
twitter.com/DurhamRENews
Previous Name: Oshawa & District Real Estate Board
Overview: A small local organization founded in 1954 overseen by Ontario Real Estate Association
Mission: To pursue excellence & professionalism in real estate through commitment & service
Member of: The Canadian Real Estate Association
Finances: *Annual Operating Budget:* $500,000-$1.5 Million; *Funding Sources:* Membership dues
Staff Member(s): 8
Membership: 900+; *Committees:* Professional Standards; Political Action
Chief Officer(s):
Nancy Shaw, Executive Officer, 905-723-8184 Ext. 204
Nancy@DurhamRealEstate.org

Durham Region Beekeepers' Association
Sunderland ON
Tel: 905-852-0733
Overview: A small local organization
Mission: To share beekeeping techniques in Durham Region
Member of: Ontario Beekeepers' Association
Membership: *Member Profile:* Beekeepers in Durham Region, Ontario
Activities: Providing a forum for networking; Organizing meetings at the Scugog Christian School in Prince Albert; Offering support services to the region's beekeepers
Chief Officer(s):
Toni Beckmann, President
tbeckmann@andrewswireless.net

Durham Region Law Association (DRLA)
150 Bond St. East, Oshawa ON L1G 0A2
Tel: 905-579-9554; *Fax:* 905-579-1801
Toll-Free: 866-742-4316
drlalaw@bellnet.ca
www.durhamregionlawassociation.com
Overview: A small local organization founded in 1879
Staff Member(s): 1
Activities: Golf Tournament; *Library:* Terence V. Kelly Law Library
Chief Officer(s):
Deborah Hastings, President

Durham Regional Labour Council (DRLC)
115 Albert St., Oshawa ON L1H 4R3
Tel: 905-579-5188
durhamlc@durhamlabour.ca
www.durhamlabour.com
Previous Name: Oshawa & District Labour Council
Overview: A large local organization founded in 1942 overseen by Ontario Federation of Labour
Mission: To advocate workers' rights & to better the quality of life for workers, their families, & their communities
Member of: Ontario Federation of Labour
Affiliation(s): Canadian Labour Congress
Finances: *Annual Operating Budget:* $50,000-$100,000
Staff Member(s): 1
Membership: 50,000+; *Fees:* $.20 per member per month; *Committees:* Women's; Education; Human Rights; Union Label & Labour Day; Community Outreach; Membership; Strike Support
Activities: *Awareness Events:* Labour Day, Sept.; *Speaker Service:* Yes
Chief Officer(s):
Bill Stratton, Secretary-Treasurer

Durham Regional Police Association
725 Conlin Rd., Whitby ON L1R 2W8
Tel: 905-655-5566; *Fax:* 905-655-5066
info@drpa.ca
www.drpa.ca
Overview: A small local organization
Mission: The Association is the negotiating body for employees, both uniform & civilian, of the Durham Regional Police Services.
Affiliation(s): Police Association of Ontario; Canadian Police Association
Staff Member(s): 5
Membership: 800 uniform members + 300 civilian members; *Member Profile:* Employees of the Durham Regional Police Services
Activities: Child Safety Handbook
Chief Officer(s):
Randy Henning, President

Durham Youth Orchestra (DYO)
c/o John Beaton, 168 Gladstone Ave., Oshawa ON L1J 4E7
Tel: 905-579-2401
www.dyomusic.com
www.facebook.com/DurhamYouthOrchestra
Overview: A small local charitable organization founded in 1993 overseen by Orchestras Canada
Mission: To nurture the artistic growth of young musicians through orchestral performance; To positively contribute to the musical landscape of Durham Region
Member of: Orchestras Canada
Finances: *Funding Sources:* Individual & corporate sponsors; Provincial government
Membership: *Fees:* $350; *Member Profile:* Young musicians with a passion for classical music who want to develop their musical skills in an orchestral setting
Activities: Performing public concerts; Visiting local schools to perform educational outreach concerts
Chief Officer(s):
John Beaton, Music Director
jbeaton@dyomusic.com

Dutch Canadian Association of Greater Toronto Inc.
207 Newton Dr., Toronto ON M2M 2P2
Tel: 416-229-1753
Overview: A small local organization founded in 1960

Dutch Canadian Business Club of Calgary (DCBC)
Calgary AB
www.dcbc.ca
www.linkedin.com/pub/gijs-van-rooijen/5/36a/51
Overview: A small local organization
Mission: To bring together entrepreneurs of Dutch heritage for the purpose of networking, business seminars, business promotion & celebrating Dutch tradition
Membership: 160
Activities: Spring business market; Stampede Barbeque; an Indonesian evening; Christmas dinner; Business Excursion; Computer Clinic; Dutch Movie Night; Business Exchange; Experience Exchange
Chief Officer(s):
Gijs van Rooijen, President

Dutch-Canadian Association Ottawa Valley/Outaouais
PO Box 78061, Stn. Meriline, Ottawa ON K2E 1B1
info@dutchinottawa.ca
www.dutchinottawa.ca
Overview: A small local organization founded in 1990
Mission: To provide Dutch Canadians with a home feeling of gezelligheid by organizing events
Finances: *Annual Operating Budget:* Less than $50,000
40 volunteer(s)
Membership: 220; *Fees:* $15 single; $25 couple
Activities: Sinterklaas, Koninginnedag, Koek en Zepie, Tulip festival
Chief Officer(s):
Anouk Hoedeman, President

Dying with Dignity (DWD) / Mourir dans la dignité
#802, 55 Eglinton Ave. East, Toronto ON M4P 1G8
Tel: 416-486-3998; *Fax:* 416-486-5562
Toll-Free: 800-495-6156
www.dyingwithdignity.ca
www.facebook.com/DWDCanada
twitter.com/DWDCanada
www.youtube.com/user/DWDCanada
Overview: A medium-sized national charitable organization founded in 1980
Mission: To improve the quality of dying for all Canadians in accordance with their own wishes, values & beliefs
Affiliation(s): World Federation of Right to Die Societies
Finances: *Annual Operating Budget:* $50,000-$100,000; *Funding Sources:* Membership fees; Donations; Fundraising
Staff Member(s): 4; 20 volunteer(s)
Membership: 7,000; *Fees:* $40-$75; *Committees:* Membership; Social Action; Counselling
Activities: Counselling & advocacy; *Speaker Service:* Yes; *Library:* Open to public by appointment
Chief Officer(s):
Shanaaz Gokool, Chief Executive Officer
Valerie Fernandes, Director, Operations & Programs
Anya Colangelo, Coordinator, Membership & Office
Kelsey Goforth, Coordinator, National Volunteer & Events
Cory Ruf, Coordinator, Communications
Nino Sekopet, Manager, Personal Support & Advocacy

Dystonia Medical Research Foundation Canada / Fondation de recherches médicales sur la dystonie
#305, 121 Richmond St. West, Toronto ON M5H 2K1
Tel: 416-488-6974; *Fax:* 416-488-5878
Toll-Free: 800-361-8061

info@dystoniacanada.org
www.dystoniacanada.org
www.facebook.com/DMRFC
Also Known As: DMRF Canada
Overview: A small international charitable organization founded in 1976
Mission: To advance & support research relating to dystonia; To build awareness about the illness in order to educate both medical & lay communities; To sponsor patient & family support groups & programs
Member of: Dystonia Medical Research Foundation
Finances: *Funding Sources:* Contributions
Staff Member(s): 2
Activities: Organizing support group meetings; Engaging in grassroots & national awareness & advocacy; Providing education through regional symposiums; Funding research; *Library:* Not open to public
Chief Officer(s):
Stefanie Ince, Executive Director
stefanieince@dystoniacanada.org

Alberta - Calgary Support Group
c/o Developmental Disabilities Resource Centre, 4631 Richardson Way SW, Calgary AB T3E 7B7
Toll-Free: 800-361-8061
Chief Officer(s):
Margaret Roy, Contact, 403-271-4438
roymg@telusplanet.net

British Columbia - Kelowna Area Support Group
Kelowna BC
Tel: 250-763-7739
Chief Officer(s):
Anne Skomedal, Contact
rskomedal@shaw.ca

Manitoba - Winnipeg Support Group
Winnipeg MB

New Brunswick - Moncton Support Group
Moncton NB
Chief Officer(s):
Shirley Sharkey, Contact, 506-204-2722
j.s.sharkey@rogers.com

Nova Scotia - Port Hawesbury Area Contact
Port Hawkesbury NS
Chief Officer(s):
Marcellin Chiasson, Contact, 902-625-1811
marcellin.chiasson@ns.sympatico.ca

Nunavut - Iqaluit Area Contact
Iqaluit NU
Tel: 867-979-3791
info@dystoniacanada.org
Chief Officer(s):
Sharon Gee, Contact
sharon_gee@hotmail.com

Ontario - Golden Triangle Support Group
ON
Mission: Servicing the Waterloo-Kitchener, Cambridge & Guelph area

Ontario - Hamilton Support Group
Hamilton ON
Chief Officer(s):
Laurie Bell, Contact, 905-774-4111
landbell@rogers.com

Ontario - London Support Group
London ON
Chief Officer(s):
Michelle & Bruce Goodhue, Contacts, 519-455-7457
bgood137@sympatico.ca

Ontario - Ottawa Support Group
Ottawa ON
Tel: 613-224-6888
Toll-Free: 800-361-8061
Chief Officer(s):
John Heney, Contact
jjheney@netrover.com

Ontario - Sudbury Support Group
Sudbury ON
Chief Officer(s):
Mary Guy, Contact, 705-524-0606
maryguy@personainternet.com

Ontario - Toronto Support Group
Toronto ON
Chief Officer(s):
Wendy Paul, Contact, Membership co-ordinator & support, 416-789-0154
dmrft@rogers.com

Québec - Montréal Support Group
Montréal QC
Chief Officer(s):
Chloe Belisle, Contact, 514-696-0949

Saskatchewan - Saskatoon Support Group
SK
Chief Officer(s):
Diane Haugen, Contact, 306-477-0577
dystonia@sasktel.net

Dystrophie musculaire Canada *See* Muscular Dystrophy Canada

Dze L K'ant Friendship Centre Society
PO Box 2920, 1188 Main St., Smithers BC V0J 2N0
Tel: 250-847-5211; *Fax:* 250-847-5144
dzelkant@gmail.com
www.dzelkant.com
Previous Name: Dze L K'ant Indian Friendship Centre Society
Overview: A small local charitable organization founded in 1974 overseen by British Columbia Association of Aboriginal Friendship Centres
Mission: The Centre is a community-based organization providing programs & services to enhance self-reliance, self-efficiency & self-awareness among Aboriginal people.
Member of: BC Association of Aboriginal Friendship Centres
Staff Member(s): 16
Activities: A variety of programs, including: family support; legal support; mental health/HIV/AIDS workshops; addiction counselling; hospital liaison; community action for children; pregnancy outreach; youth after-school activities
Chief Officer(s):
Annette Morgan, Executive Director
Genevieve Poirier, Program Director

Dease Lake Location
PO Box 328, 71 Stikine, Dease Lake BC V0C 1L0
Tel: 250-771-3147
deasepop@gmail.com

Houston Location
3383 - 11 St., Houston BC V0J 1Z0
Tel: 250-845-2131; *Fax:* 250-845-2136
aecdhouston@gmail.com

Dze L K'ant Indian Friendship Centre Society *See* Dze L K'ant Friendship Centre Society

E3 Community Services (E3)
100 Pretty River Pkwy. North, Collingwood ON L9Y 4X2
Tel: 705-445-6351
e3@e3.ca
www.e3.ca
Previous Name: Collingwood Community Living
Overview: A medium-sized local charitable organization founded in 1962
Mission: To educate, enable & enrich clients, staff & community
Member of: Ontario Agencies Supporting Individuals with Special Needs (OASIS)
Membership: *Member Profile:* Parents & other interested community members
Activities: *Library:* Open to public
Chief Officer(s):
Gordon Anton, CEO
Farel Anderson, President

Eagle Valley Arts Council (EVAC)
Red Barn Arts Centre, PO Box 686, 1226 Riverside Rd., Sicamous BC V0E 2V0
Tel: 250-836-2220
www.eaglevalleyartscouncil.com
Overview: A small local organization founded in 1980
Mission: To encourage & coordinate arts & culture in the community by developing programs & services, primarily at the Red Barn Arts Centre, which it owns & operates.
Member of: Assembly of BC Arts Councils; Thompson Okanagan Network of Arts Councils
Affiliation(s): Heritage Canada
Finances: *Funding Sources:* Grants; functions; rentals; programs
Membership: 9; *Member Profile:* Arts groups
Activities: Art exhibitions, concerts & plays
Chief Officer(s):
Carla Krens, President

Eaglesland Albanian Society of BC
#220, 102 - 15910 Fraser Hwy., Surrey BC V4N 0X9

Tel: 604-507-8334
info@eaglesland.org
www.eaglesland.org
Overview: A small local organization
Mission: To promote & provide education as well as recreational events for the Albanian community living in Vancouver
Activities: Parties; National Celebrations; Picnics; Sporting events; Youth & student meeting
Chief Officer(s):
Estref Resuli, President, Board of Directors

Early Childhood Care & Education New Brunswick (ECCENB) / Soins et éducation à la petite enfance Nouveau-Brunswick
#300, 56 Avonlea Ct., Fredericton NB E3C 1N8
Tel: 506-454-4765; *Fax:* 506-854-8333
Toll-Free: 888-834-7070
eccenb.sepenb@nb.aibn.com
Overview: A medium-sized provincial organization founded in 1999
Mission: To support early childhood educators in New Brunswick
Affiliation(s): Canadian Child Care Federation
Finances: *Funding Sources:* Membership fees
Membership: *Fees:* $40 students, parents, & seniors; $60 early childhood educators; $300 corporations; *Member Profile:* Individuals employed in a child care facility; Seniors; Parents; Students; Corporations
Chief Officer(s):
Marjolaine St-Pierre, Executive Director, 506-454-4765 Ext. 4
marjolaine.stpierre@nb.aibn.com
Publications:
• Early Childhood Care & Education New Brunswick Newsletter
Type: Newsletter; *Price:* Free with Early Childhood Care & Education New Brunswick membership

Early Childhood Development Association of Prince Edward Island (ECDA)
PO Box 223, #115, 3 Brighton Rd., Charlottetown PE C1A 7K4
Tel: 902-368-1866
info@ecdaofpei.ca
www.ecdaofpei.ca
www.facebook.com/ECDAofPEI
twitter.com/ECDAofPEI
Overview: A small provincial organization founded in 1974
Mission: To promote & support early childhood development programs & services throughout Prince Edward Island
Member of: Prince Edward Island Literacy Alliance Inc.
Affiliation(s): Canadian Child Care Federation
Membership: *Fees:* $39 student; $65 associate; $130 professional; $390 corporate; *Member Profile:* Persons certified as an early childhood educators; Early childhood assistants; Licensed child care facilities; Corporate members that provide services to child care facilities; Associate members who support the association's mission; Students
Activities: Encouraging research; Providing resources about early childhood development; Offering professional development opportunities for early childhood educators; Liaising with government; Providing networking activities; *Awareness Events:* Early Childhood Education Week *Library:* Early Childhood Development Association of PEI Resource Library
Chief Officer(s):
Sonya Hooper, Executive Director
s.hooper@earlychildhooddevelopment.ca
Publications:
• Week at a Glance [a publication of Early Childhood Development Association of Prince Edward Island]
Type: Newsletter; *Frequency:* Weekly; *Price:* Free with membership in the Early Childhood Development Association of PEI

Early Childhood Educators of British Columbia (ECEBC)
2774 East Broadway, Vancouver BC V5M 1Y8
Tel: 604-709-6063; *Fax:* 604-709-6077
Toll-Free: 800-797-5602
membership@ecebc.ca
www.ecebc.ca
twitter.com/ECEBC1
Overview: A small provincial organization founded in 1969
Mission: To provide a network of support & services for members through a regional branch network; To promote professional development & high standards of practice; advocates for child care practitioners, young children & families; To participate in the development of child care training &

professional development opportunities; To liaise with other early childhood provincial & national organizations.
Member of: Canadian Child Care Federation
Affiliation(s): Westcoast Child Care Resource Centre; Child Care Advocacy Forum
Finances: *Funding Sources:* Membership dues
Staff Member(s): 3
Membership: *Fees:* $50; *Member Profile:* ECE qualified or ECE student; associate membership available for those in a related field
Chief Officer(s):
Taya Whitehouse, President
tayawhitehead@hotmail.com
Emily Mlieczko, Executive Director
executive.director@ecebc.ca

Early Childhood Intervention Program (ECIP) Sask. Inc.
2220 College Ave., 2nd Fl., Regina SK S4P 4V9
Fax: 306-787-0277
www.saskatchewan.ca/residents/family-and-social-support
Overview: A small local charitable organization founded in 1981
Mission: To provide a link between families & other professionals, working collaboratively with child care providers, speech & language pathologists, phyiotherapists, occupational therapists, nurses, physicians, teachers & school administrators to build trust & achieve mutually identified goals for the children & families
Finances: *Funding Sources:* United Way
Activities: Consultation; Liaising with the Government of Saskatchewan & other organizations; Developing training programs for staff; *Awareness Events:* Early Childhood Intervention Program (ECIP) Week, April

Kindersley - West Central ECIP Inc.
PO Box 775, 125 - 1st Ave. East, Kindersley SK S0L 1S0
Tel: 306-463-6822; *Fax:* 306-463-6898
westcentralecip@sasktel.net

La Ronge - Children North ECIP Inc. (CNECIP)
#106, 708 La Ronge Ave., La Ronge SK S0J 1L0
Tel: 306-425-6600; *Fax:* 306-425-6667
ChildrenNorthECIP@mcrrha.sk.ca
Chief Officer(s):
Daina Lapworth, Contact
daina.lapworth@mcrrha.sk.ca

Lloydminster - Midwest Family Connections
Co-op Plaza, #103, 4910 - 50th St., Lower Level, Lloydminster SK S9V 0Y5
Tel: 306-825-5911; *Fax:* 306-825-5912
Toll-Free: 866-651-5911
info@midwestfamilyconnections.ca
www.midwestfamilyconnections.ca
Chief Officer(s):
Sherri Husch Foote, Executive Director
sherri@midwestfamilyconnections.ca

Meadow Lake - Meadow Lake & Area Early Childhood Services Inc.
PO Box 2368, 201 - 4th Ave. East, Meadow Lake SK S0M 1V0
Tel: 306-236-4247; *Fax:* 306-236-1479
meadowlake.ecip@sasktel.net

Moose Jaw - South Central ECIP Inc.
#37, 1322 - 11th Ave. NW, Moose Jaw SK S9H 4L9
Tel: 306-692-2616; *Fax:* 306-692-2377
southcentral.ecip@sasktel.net

North Battleford - Battlefords ECIP Inc. (BECIP)
PO Box 1297, North Battleford SK S9A 3L8
Tel: 306-446-4545; *Fax:* 306-446-0575
becip@sasktel.net
www.becip.org
www.facebook.com/saskatchewan.ecip
Chief Officer(s):
Colleen Sabraw, Executive Director

Prince Albert - Prince Albert ECIP Inc. (PAECIP)
3041 Sheman Dr., Prince Albert SK S6V 7B7
Tel: 306-922-3247; *Fax:* 306-763-5244
paecip@sasktel.net
Member of: Saskatchewan Early Childhood Intervention Program

Regina - Regina Region ECIP
#305, 1102 - 8th Ave., Regina SK S4R 1C9
Tel: 306-374-5021
ecip.rr@sasktel.net

Saskatoon - Prairie Hills ECIP Inc. (PHECIP)
Kinsmen Children's Centre, 1319 Colony St., Saskatoon SK S7N 2Z1
Tel: 306-655-1083; *Fax:* 306-655-1449
Chief Officer(s):
Arlene Trask, Contact

Swift Current - Swift Current ECIP Inc.
El Wood Bldg., PO Box 486, 350 Cheadle St. West, 3rd Fl., Swift Current SK S9H 3W3
Tel: 306-773-3600; *Fax:* 306-778-6633
swiftcurrentecip@sasktel.net
Chief Officer(s):
Wayne Cormier, Executive Director

Tisdale - North East ECIP Inc.
PO Box 1675, 610 - 100A St., Tisdale SK S0E 1T0
Tel: 306-873-3411; *Fax:* 306-873-3452
neecip@sasktel.net

Weyburn - Holy Family RCSSD 140
110 Souris Ave., Weyburn SK S4H 2Z8
Tel: 306-842-7025; *Fax:* 306-842-7033
wec.ecip@sasktel.net
Chief Officer(s):
Lynn Colquhoun, Contact
lynn.colquhoun@holyfamilyrcssd.ca

Weyburn - Weyburn & Area ECIP Inc.
405 Coteau Ave., Weyburn SK S4H 1H2
Tel: 306-842-2686; *Fax:* 306-842-0723
wecip@sasktel.net

Yorkton - Parkland ECIP Inc. (PECIP)
83 North St., Yorkton SK S3N 0G9
Tel: 306-786-6988; *Fax:* 306-786-7116
parklandecip@sasktel.net
Chief Officer(s):
Michelle Yaschuk, Executive Director

Early Music Vancouver (EMV)
1254 - 7 Ave. West, Vancouver BC V6H 1B6
Tel: 604-732-1610; *Fax:* 604-732-1602
www.earlymusic.bc.ca
www.facebook.com/earlymusicvancouver
twitter.com/earlymusicvan
Also Known As: Vancouver Society for Early Music
Overview: A small local charitable organization founded in 1970
Mission: To foster increased understanding & appreciation of early music by providing educational programs, high quality concerts at reasonable prices featuring both local & internationally acclaimed musicians & by providing informative publications
Member of: Alliance for Arts & Culture
Finances: *Annual Operating Budget:* $500,000-$1.5 Million; *Funding Sources:* Individual & corporate donations
Staff Member(s): 5; 100 volunteer(s)
Membership: 100-499; *Fees:* $35
Activities: Performing concert series; Facilitating workshops for musicians of all levels
Chief Officer(s):
Tim Rendell, Managing Director, 604-732-1610 Ext. 2006
tim@earlymusic.bc.ca
Matthew White, Artistic Director, 604-732-1610 Ext. 2005
matthew@earlymusic.bc.ca

Earth Day Canada (EDC) / Jour de la terre Canada
276 Roncesvalles Ave., Toronto ON M6R 2M2
Tel: 416-599-1991; *Fax:* 416-599-3100
Toll-Free: 888-283-2784
info@earthday.ca
www.earthday.ca
www.facebook.com/EarthDayCanada
twitter.com/earthdaycanada
www.youtube.com/user/EarthDayCanada
Overview: A medium-sized national charitable organization founded in 1991
Mission: To inspire & support Canadians to connect with nature & build resilient communities
Affiliation(s): Earth Day Network; 3,500 community-based organizations
Finances: *Funding Sources:* Sponsorships; Donations
Membership: 5,000 organizations
Activities: Coordinating & promoting Earth Day; Circulating educational materials; Initiating & coordinating environmental projects; Offering programs, such as EcoKids; *Awareness Events:* Earth Day, April; Earth Month
Chief Officer(s):
Deb Doncaster, President

Earth Energy Society of Canada (EESC) / Société canadienne de l'énergie du sol (SCES)
7885 Jock Trail, Richmond ON K0A 2Z0
Tel: 343-882-7900; *Fax:* 613-822-4987
info@earthenergy.ca
www.earthenergy.ca
Also Known As: International Ground Source Heat Pump Association - Canadian Chapter
Overview: A medium-sized national organization founded in 1985
Mission: To represent the ground-source & geothermal heat pump industry by promoting quality installations & earth energy technology
Member of: International Ground Source Heat Pump Association - International
Finances: *Funding Sources:* Membership dues
Staff Member(s): 1; 8 volunteer(s)
Activities: Dealer training
Chief Officer(s):
Bill Eggertson, Consultant, 343-882-7900
Eggertson@EarthEnergy.ca

Earthroots
#410, 401 Richmond St. West, Toronto ON M5V 3A8
Tel: 416-599-0152; *Fax:* 416-340-2429
Other Communication: www.wolvesontario.org
info@earthroots.org
www.earthroots.org
www.facebook.com/Earthroots.Coalition
twitter.com/Earthroots
Previous Name: Earthroots Coalition; Temagami Wilderness Society
Overview: A medium-sized local organization founded in 1986
Mission: To preserve Ontario's ancient forests & other threatened ecosystems
Affiliation(s): Temagami Wilderness Society
Finances: *Annual Operating Budget:* $250,000-$500,000; *Funding Sources:* Individual donors
Staff Member(s): 5; 40 volunteer(s)
Membership: 12,000
Activities: Working to protect wilderness, wildlife & watersheds through research, education & action
Chief Officer(s):
Amber Ellis, Executive Director
amber@earthroots.org

Earthroots Coalition; Temagami Wilderness Society *See* Earthroots

Earthsave Canada (ESC) / SauveTerre
#170 - 422 Richards St., Vancouver BC V6B 2Z4
Tel: 604-731-5885; *Fax:* 604-731-5805
office@earthsave.ca
www.earthsave.ca
www.facebook.com/EarthsaveCanada
twitter.com/earthsavecanada
www.youtube.com/user/earthsavecanada
Overview: A small national charitable organization founded in 1990
Mission: To promote awareness of the health, ethical & environmental consequences of our food choices; To advocate transition to a plant-based diet for better health, a cleaner environment & a more compassionate world
Affiliation(s): EarthSave International
Finances: *Annual Operating Budget:* $100,000-$250,000; *Funding Sources:* BC Gaming; Individual donations; Memberships; Retail sales
Staff Member(s): 2; 250 volunteer(s)
Membership: 500; *Fees:* $24 senior; $36 individual; $48 family; $96 corporate; $12 youth/student
Activities: Wellness Show; Healthy Living Expo; monthly potlucks; monthly dine-outs; Healthy School Lunch Program; Taste of Health, Vegeterian Food Festival; *Awareness Events:* Taste of Health, Vegetarian Food Festival, Oct.; World Veg Week Fundraiser, Nov.; Vegstock; *Library:* Open to public
Chief Officer(s):
David Steele, President
Darrel Yurychuk, Secretary
Publications:
- Canada Earthsaver [a publication of Earthsave Canada]
 Type: Newsletter; *Frequency:* Quarterly

Earthsave Whistler
whistler@earthsave.ca
earthsavewhistler.com
www.facebook.com/EarthsaveWhistler

Earthwise Society
twitter.com/earthsavewhstlr
pinterest.com/earthsavewhstlr

Earthwise Society
6400 - 3rd Ave., Delta BC V4L 1B1
Tel: 604-946-9828
info@earthwisesociety.bc.ca
www.earthwisesociety.bc.ca
www.facebook.com/earthwisebc
twitter.com/EarthwiseBC
Previous Name: DRS Earthwise Society; Delta Recycling Society
Overview: A small local organization
Mission: To create & foster sustainable communities through education & community initiatives
Activities: Market Day; Root to Rise: Yoga Event; Music in the Garden; Family Harvest Box; workshops; Ecotours; education resources
Chief Officer(s):
Patricia Fleming, Executive Director

East Coast Aquarium Society (ECAS)
c/o 91 Deerbrooke Dr., Dartmouth NS B2V 1X2
ECAS.ca
www.facebook.com/eastcoastaquariumsociety
Overview: A medium-sized local organization founded in 2004
Mission: To further the aquarium hobby and promote the practice of keeping tropical fish.
Member of: Canadian Association of Aquarium Clubs; Federation of American Aquarium Societies
Chief Officer(s):
Kathryn Purdy, President
kat@eastcoastaquariumsociety.ca
Kelly Lively Jones, Director, Membership
klivelyjones@eastlink.ca

East Coast Music Association (ECMA) / Association de la musique de la côte est
PO Box 31237, Halifax NS B3K 5Y1
Tel: 902-423-6770; *Fax:* 888-519-0346
Toll-Free: 800-513-4953
ecma@ecma.com
www.ecma.com
Also Known As: East Coast Music Awards
Overview: A medium-sized local organization founded in 1989
Mission: To develop, foster, promote & celebrate East Coast music locally & globally
Affiliation(s): Music Industry Associations; Canadian Academy of Recording Arts & Science; FACTOR
Staff Member(s): 6
Membership: *Fees:* $60 individual; $500 lifetime; $25 student; *Member Profile:* Music industry professionals, musicians, fans
Chief Officer(s):
Andy McLean, Executive Director
andy@ecma.com
Awards:
• East Coast Music Awards
General Categories: Male Artist of the Year, Female Artist of the Year, Group of the Year, Songwriter of the Year, Single of the Year, Video of the Year, Album of the Year, New Artist(s) of the Year, Entertainer of the Year; Genre Specific Categories: Country Recording of the Year, Pop Recording of the Year, Rock Recording of the Year, Instrumental Recording of the Year, Alternative Recording of the Year, Jazz Recording of the Year, Blues Recording of the Year, Gospel Recording of the Year, Children's Recording of the Year, Bluegrass Recording of the Year, Urban Recording of the Year, Classical Recording of the Year, Roots/Traditional Recording of the Year, Folk Recording of the Year; Cultural Categories: Francophone Recording of the Year

East Coast Trail Association
PO Box 8034, 50 Pippy Place, 2nd Fl., St. John's NL A1B 3M7
Tel: 709-738-4453; *Fax:* 709-738-1122
information@eastcoasttrail.com
www.eastcoasttrail.com
www.facebook.com/EastCoastTrail
twitter.com/eastcoasttrail
www.instagram.com/eastcoasttrail
Overview: A small local charitable organization
Mission: To develop, maintain & protect the East Coast Trail
150 volunteer(s)
Membership: *Fees:* $25 regular; $100 community or organization; $500 life; *Committees:* Finance & Administration; Fundraising & Revenue; Land & Legal; Marketing & Communications; Membership & Volunteers; Trail Management
Activities: Operating the East Coast Trail Shop, which sells guide books, maps, t-shirts & other merchandise; *Awareness Events:* Annual Fundraising Hike, June
Chief Officer(s):
Randy Murphy, President
Ed Delaney, Manager, Trail Operations
delaneyecta@yahoo.com
Karla Fuglem, Manager, Business
karla.fuglem@eastcoasttrail.com

East Durham Historical Society *See* Municipality of Port Hope Historical Society

East End Literacy *See* Centre for Community Learning & Development

East End Literacy *See* Toronto Centre for Community Learning & Development

East European Genealogical Society, Inc. (EEGS)
PO Box 2536, Winnipeg MB R3C 4A7
Tel: 204-989-3292
info@eegsociety.org
www.eegsociety.org
www.facebook.com/eegsociety
Overview: A small national charitable organization founded in 1996
Finances: *Annual Operating Budget:* Less than $50,000
12 volunteer(s)
Membership: 450; *Fees:* $38
Activities: Monthly meetings; workshops; lectures; *Library*
Chief Officer(s):
Marni Domolewski, President

East Georgian Bay Historical Foundation
8 Queen St. East, Elmvale ON L0L 1P0
Tel: 705-322-3000; *Fax:* 705-322-0771
Overview: A small local charitable organization founded in 1981
Mission: The Society aims to preserve the heritage of the Districts of Muskoka, Parry Sound, & the County of Simcoe & has published several titles on the history of the region.
Finances: *Annual Operating Budget:* Less than $50,000
4 volunteer(s)
Membership: 1-99
Activities: Local history publishing; heritage conservation advocacy; *Library*
Chief Officer(s):
Gary E. French, President
french@bellnet.ca

East Gwillimbury Chamber of Commerce (EGCOC)
PO Box 1099, #100, 19027 Leslie St., Sharon ON L0G 1V0
Tel: 905-478-8447
egcoc@egcoc.org
www.egcoc.org
www.linkedin.com/in/east-gwillimbury-chamber-of-commerce-0812a288
www.facebook.com/East-Gwillimbury-Chamber-of-Commerce-346448468797672
twitter.com/EGChamber
Overview: A small local organization
Membership: *Fees:* Schedule available
Activities: Networking events

East Hants & District Chamber of Commerce (EHDCC)
Parker Place Mall, Upper Level, 8 Old Enfield Rd., Enfield NS B2T 1C9
Tel: 902-883-1010; *Fax:* 902-883-7862
info@ehcc.ca
www.ehcc.ca
www.linkedin.com/groups?gid=4076625&trk=hb_side_g
www.facebook.com/171077252957659
twitter.com/easthantschambr
Overview: A small local organization founded in 1986
Mission: To influence any major issues which are deemed to have an impact on the economic strength, prosperity & interests of communities; To provide members with services designed to improve their business opportunities
Member of: Atlantic Provinces Chamber of Commerce; Nova Scotia Chamber of Commerce
Finances: *Funding Sources:* Membership dues
Membership: *Fees:* Schedule available; *Committees:* Advocacy; Communications; Education; Events; Membership; Finance; Executive
Activities: Trade shows; travel bureau; maps; *Awareness Events:* Showcase of East Hants, May
Chief Officer(s):
Pat Mills, President
Awards:
• Student Entrepreneurship
• Business Entrepreneurship

East Hants Historical Society
8488 Hwy. 215, Maitland NS B0N 1T0
hantshistorical@gmail.com
www.ehhs.weebly.com
www.facebook.com/EastHantsHistoricalSociety
Overview: A small local charitable organization founded in 1967
Mission: To preserve & promote the history of East Hants, Nova Scotia; To provide genealogical resources
Finances: *Funding Sources:* Donations
Membership: *Fees:* $5/year
Activities: Maintaining & operating a museum in the former Lower Selma United Church; *Library:* East Hants Historical Society Research Library; Open to public
Chief Officer(s):
Nancy Doane, Co-Chair, Museum Committee, 902-632-2504
Doug Lynch, Co-Chair, Museum Committee, 902-957-2057

East Kootenay Chamber of Mines
#201, 12 - 11th Ave. South, Cranbrook BC V1C 2P1
Tel: 250-489-2255; *Fax:* 250-426-8755
www.ekcm.org/chamber2
www.facebook.com/EastKootenayChamberOfMines
Overview: A small local organization founded in 1992
Mission: To promote mining iterests in south-eastern British Columbia
Membership: *Member Profile:* Representatives from the general public, prospectors, geoscientists, resource companies & mine personnel
Activities: *Library:* Resource Library; Drill Library
Chief Officer(s):
Jason Jacob, President, 250-464-9559

East Kootenay Community College Faculty Association *See* College of the Rockies Faculty Association

East Kootenay District Labour Council
#104, 105 - 9th Ave. South, Cranbrook BC V1C 2M1
Tel: 250-426-2670
www.facebook.com/187439044629035
Overview: A small local organization overseen by British Columbia Federation of Labour
Mission: To advance the economic & social welfare of workers in the East Kootenay region of British Columbia
Affiliation(s): Canadian Labour Congress (CLC)
Activities: Promoting interests of affiliates; Raising awareness of workers' rights; Sponsoring community events, such as the East Kootenay Labour Day Picnic; Hosting events to mark the Day of Mourning
Chief Officer(s):
Jackie Spain, President

East Prince Youth Development Centre (EPYDC)
98 Water St., Summerside PE C1N 4N6
Tel: 902-436-2815
epydc@epydc.org
www.epydc.org
www.facebook.com/262790347085606
Overview: A small local organization
Mission: Dedicated to helping youth with health, education, & employment problems to achieve their goals
Staff Member(s): 6
Chief Officer(s):
Barb Broome, Acting Manager
barbbroome@epydc.org

East Shore Internet Society
Crawford Bay Motel, PO Box 145, #10, 16210 Hwy. 3A, Crawford Bay BC V0B 1E0
Toll-Free: 844-776-1075
www.eastshoreinternet.ca
www.facebook.com/eastshoreinternetsociety
Overview: A medium-sized provincial organization founded in 2005
Mission: To provide Crawford Bay & the surrounding central Kootenay Lake area with affordable & reliable high-speed internet service
Chief Officer(s):
Fraser Robb, President

East Toronto Community Legal Services
1320 Gerrard St. East, Toronto ON M4L 3X1
Tel: 416-461-8102; *Fax:* 416-461-7497
www.etcls.ca

Overview: A small local organization
Mission: To provide legal advice & representation in the areas of: Landlord/Tenant; Immigration; Employment Insurance & Employment Law; Canada Pension; Criminal Injuries Compensation; Consumer Law; Small Claims Court matters; Ontario Works/Ontario Disability Support Program (ODSP).
Finances: *Funding Sources:* Legal Aid Ontario
Staff Member(s): 7
Activities: Chinese-speaking lawyer on Tues. afternoons; *Speaker Service:* Yes

East Wellington Advisory Group for Family Services *See* East Wellington Community Services

East Wellington Community Services (EWCS)
PO Box 786, 45 Main St., Erin ON N0B 1T0
Tel: 519-833-9696; *Fax:* 519-833-7563
www.eastwellingtoncommunityservices.com
www.facebook.com/east.wellington
Previous Name: East Wellington Advisory Group for Family Services
Overview: A small local charitable organization founded in 1984
Mission: To provide essential services to the community in order to support families, individuals, children, & seniors
Member of: Inform Ontario; Community Support Association
Finances: *Funding Sources:* Guelph/Wellington United Way; public donations; fundraising events & activities; Ministry of Health
Staff Member(s): 15
Activities: Employment services; Human Resources Job Bank; Foodshare; volunteer transportation program; income tax clinics; public access terminal to the internet; information & referrals; child care resource centre; seniors centre; seniors day program
Chief Officer(s):
Rebeca Greco, President
Kari Simpson, Chief Executive Officer
kari.s@ew-cs.com

East York - Scarborough Reading Association
#309, 1315 Lawrence Ave. East, Toronto ON M3A 3R3
Tel: 416-444-7473; *Fax:* 416-444-9282
eys@readingfortheloveofit.com
www.readingfortheloveofit.com
twitter.com/eysreading
www.youtube.com/user/EYSReadingAssn
Overview: A small local organization
Mission: Committed to improving the quality of literacy instruction and encouraging the development of a lifelong interest in reading.
Chief Officer(s):
Kathy Lazarovits, Président

East York Historical Society (EYHS)
107 Cambridge Ave., Toronto ON M4K 2L7
eyhs@eastyork.org
www.eastyork.org/eyhs.html
Overview: A small local organization founded in 1980
Mission: To disseminate historical information; To arouse an interest in the past; To encourage the preservation of the historical, archaeological & architectural heritage of East York by publishing or printing material, by marking buildings, sites or other features of the historical landscapes, by holding public meetings, lectures & exhibitions, & by undertaking a variety of information sharing, publicity & public education programs
Member of: Ontario Historical Society; Toronto Historical Association
Finances: *Annual Operating Budget:* Less than $50,000; *Funding Sources:* Membership fees; sale of desktop flags; provincial government; Toronto Public Library
10 volunteer(s)
Membership: 133; *Fees:* $15 individual; $20 family; $7 student; $50 organization
Activities: Lectures; trips to historical sites; erecting historical plaques in East York community; discussion group meetings
Publications:
• East York Inklings [a publication of the East York Historical Society]
Type: Newsletter; *Frequency:* 5 pa

East York Learning Experience (EYLE)
266 Donlands Ave., Toronto ON M4J 5B1
Tel: 416-425-2666; *Fax:* 416-425-0682
eyle@idirect.com
www.eastyorklearningexperience.ca
Overview: A small local organization founded in 1986
Mission: A literacy program serving East York, parts of East Toronto and west Scarborough.

Affiliation(s): Metro Toronto Movement for Literacy; Ontario Literacy Coalition; Community Literacy of Ontario; Community Social Planning Council
Finances: *Annual Operating Budget:* $100,000-$250,000
Staff Member(s): 3; 90 volunteer(s)
Membership: 100; *Member Profile:* Adults 18+; *Committees:* Fundraising; Program; Newsletter; Learners'
Activities: Computer-based learning services; tutoring; *Awareness Events:* Word on the Street; *Library:* Not open to public
Chief Officer(s):
Gail McCullough, Director

Eastend & District Chamber of Commerce
PO Box 534, Eastend SK S0N 0T0
Tel: 306-295-4070; *Fax:* 306-295-3883
Overview: A small local organization
Member of: Saskatoon Chamber of Commerce

Eastend Arts Council
PO Box 415, Eastend SK S0N 0T0
Tel: 306-295-3281
admin@stegnerhouse.ca
www.stegnerhouse.ca
Overview: A small local charitable organization founded in 1978
Mission: The Council is a non-profit organization that operates the Wallace Stegner House as an artists' retreat.
Finances: *Funding Sources:* Federal & provinicial governments; foundations; trusts; private donors
Activities: Missoula Children's Theatre; biannual art show & local events that involve the arts; Stegner House Dinner
Chief Officer(s):
Anne Davis, President
Awards:
• Wallace Stegner Grant for the Arts
Eligibility: Graduating student at Eastend High School whose submitted composition is chosen by the committee; *Amount:* $500, plus 1-yr. free residence at retreat

Easter Seals Canada / Timbres de Pâques Canada
#401, 40 Holly St., Toronto ON M4S 3C3
Tel: 416-932-8382; *Fax:* 416-932-9844
Toll-Free: 877-376-6362
info@easterseals.ca
www.easterseals.ca
www.facebook.com/eastersealscanada
twitter.com/easterseals
Also Known As: Canadian Rehabilitation Council for the Disabled
Previous Name: Easter Seals/March of Dimes National Council
Overview: A medium-sized national charitable organization founded in 1962
Mission: To enhance the quality of life, self-esteem, & self-determination of Canadians with physical disabilities; To support the social & economic integration of people with disabilities
Member of: Imagine Canada's Ethical Code Program
Finances: *Funding Sources:* Corporate sponsorships; Donations; Fundraising
Staff Member(s): 9
Membership: *Committees:* Executive; Governance & Nominations; Audit; Licensee Relations & Intellectual Property; Public Affairs; CEO
Activities: Delivering programs & services; Raising awareness of disability issues; *Awareness Events:* Easter Seals Month, March
Chief Officer(s):
Dave Starrett, Chief Executive Officer, 416-932-8382 Ext. 250
Alex Krievins, National Director, Programs & Development, 416-932-8382 Ext. 228
Frank Williamson, Director, Finance, 416-932-8382 Ext. 222
Publications:
• Easter Seals Canada Annual Report
Type: Yearbook; *Frequency:* Annually
Profile: Messages from the Chair of the Board & the Chief Executive Officer, information about the organization's programs & fundraising efforts, & the treasurer's report

Easter Seals New Brunswick (ESNB) / Les Timbres de Pâques N.-B.
65 Brunswick St., Fredericton NB E3B 1G5
Tel: 506-458-8739; *Fax:* 506-457-2863
info@easterseals.nb.ca
www.easterseals.nb.ca
www.facebook.com/246795441998452
twitter.com/EasterSealsNB

Also Known As: Canadian Rehabilitation Council for the Disabled (New Brunswick)
Overview: A medium-sized provincial charitable organization founded in 1966 overseen by Easter Seals Canada
Mission: To provide rehabilitation services & programs to persons with disabilities in New Brunswick; To improve public attitudes towards disabled persons; To provide disabled persons with new opportunities; to provide orthopedic appliances, rehabilitative equipment, technical aids & computers; To advocate on behalf of disabled persons; To serve as information resource centre for disabled persons, students, the public & health professionals; To hold the franchise for the Easter Seals campaign; To provide interprovincial transportation assistance to treatment & diagnostic centres
Finances: *Annual Operating Budget:* $500,000-$1.5 Million; *Funding Sources:* Public donations; Fee for service
Staff Member(s): 11; 25 volunteer(s)
Membership: 500; *Committees:* Executive; Finance; Governance & Nominating; Resource Development; Equipment Program; Camp Rotary; Technology; Transportation
Activities: *Speaker Service:* Yes
Chief Officer(s):
Julia Latham, Executive Director
Awards:
• Easter Seals New Brunswick Awards of Merit Program
Publications:
• Easter Seals New Brunswick Annual Report
Type: Report; *Frequency:* Annually

Easter Seals Newfoundland & Labrador
Husky Energy Easter Seals House, 206 Mount Scio Rd., St. John's NL A1B 4L5
Tel: 709-754-1399; *Fax:* 709-754-1398
info@easterseals.nf.ca
www.easterseals.nf.ca
www.linkedin.com/company/easter-seals-newfoundland-and-labrador
www.facebook.com/EasterSealsNL
twitter.com/eastersealsnl
Previous Name: Newfoundland Society for the Physically Disabled Inc.
Overview: A medium-sized provincial organization founded in 1950 overseen by Easter Seals Canada
Mission: To maximize the abilities & enhancing the lives of children & youth with physical disabilities through recreational, social & other therapeutic programs, direct assistance, education & advocacy
Staff Member(s): 10
Activities: Providing services for individuals with disabilities; Fundraising
Chief Officer(s):
Mark Bradbury, Chief Executive Officer, 709-754-1399 Ext. 222
markb@eastersealsnl.ca

Easter Seals Nova Scotia (AFNS)
3670 Kempt Rd., Halifax NS B3K 4X8
Tel: 902-453-6000
mailing@easterseals.ns.ca
www.easterseals.ns.ca
www.facebook.com/ESnovascotia
twitter.com/Eastersealsns
www.youtube.com/user/eastersealsns
Previous Name: Abilities Foundation of Nova Scotia
Overview: A medium-sized provincial charitable organization founded in 1931 overseen by Easter Seals Canada
Mission: To enable Nova Scotians with physical disabilities to enhance their quality of life by realizing their individual potential
Finances: *Funding Sources:* Mail campaign; Special events; Donations
Membership: *Committees:* Program; Development; Nominating
Activities: Providing services that promote mobility, inclusion, & independence; *Awareness Events:* Easter Seals 24-Hour Relay, July; *Library:* Open to public
Chief Officer(s):
Henk van Leeuwen, President & CEO, 902-453-6000 Ext. 222
henk@easterseals.ns.ca
Publications:
• Easter Seals Nova Scotia Annual Report
Type: Report; *Frequency:* Annually

Easter Seals Ontario (TESS) / Société du timbre de Pâques de l'Ontario
#700, 1 Concorde Gate, Toronto ON M3C 3C6
Tel: 416-421-8377; *Fax:* 416-696-1035
Toll-Free: 800-668-6252
info@easterseals.org

www.easterseals.org
www.linkedin.com/company/107859
www.facebook.com/EasterSealsON
twitter.com/eastersealson
www.youtube.com/user/Eastersealsont
Overview: A large provincial charitable organization founded in 1922 overseen by Easter Seals Canada
Mission: To help children with physical disabilities achieve their full individual potential & future independence
Member of: Canadian Centre for Philanthropy
Affiliation(s): BC Lions Society for Children with Disabilities; Newfoundland Society for the Physically Disabled; Québec Easter Seal Society; Easter Seal Ability Council - Alberta; Saskatchewan Abilities Council; Society for Manitobans with Disabilities; Rotary Club of Charlottetown; Abilities Foundation of Nova Scotia; CRCD New Brunswick branch; National Easter Seal Society, USA
Finances: *Annual Operating Budget:* Greater than $5 Million; *Funding Sources:* 94% public + 1% investment income + 1% government grants + 3% fees for services + 1% other
Membership: *Member Profile:* Board members; past employees; past ambassadors; key supporters & volunteers; parents; *Committees:* Scholarships; Ambassadors; Public Awareness
Activities: Directing services to physically disabled children, usually up to age 19 & their families; Providing programs, research, advocacy & public education; *Speaker Service:* Yes; *Library:* Easter Seal Resource Centre & Archives; Open to public
Chief Officer(s):
John M. Herhalt, Chair
Kevin J. Collins, President & CEO
Awards:
• Beatrice Drinnan Spence Scholarship Fund
Eligibility: Youth & young adults with physical disabilities *Deadline:* May
• Rose Brodie Provincial Ambassador Scholarship Fund
Eligibility: Former Provincial or Local Ambassadors *Deadline:* May
• Hira Scholarship Fund
• TD Scholarship for Easter Seals Youth
• Truelove Dell Scholarship Fund
Eligibility: Easter Seals youth who demonstrate outstanding community service in the Greater Toronto Area *Deadline:* May
• Sal Iacono Family Bursary Endowment Fund
Eligibility: Youth & young adults pursuing post secondary education at Algonquin College *Deadline:* May
• Agnes McIntosh Scholarship Fund
Eligibility: Youth & young adults with physical disabilities *Deadline:* May

Eastern Region - Kingston
#111, 993 Princess St., Kingston ON K7L 1H3
Tel: 613-547-4126
Toll-Free: 888-667-0043

Eastern Region - Ottawa
#350, 1101 Prince of Wales Dr., Ottawa ON K2C 3W7
Tel: 613-226-3051
Toll-Free: 800-561-4313

Northern Region - Sault Ste. Marie
364 Queen St. East, Sault Ste Marie ON P6A 1Z1
Tel: 705-945-1279
Chief Officer(s):
Carolyn O'Connor, Contact
coconnor@easterseals.org

Northern Region - Sudbury
887 Notre Dame Ave., #F, Sudbury ON P3A 2T2
Tel: 705-566-8858
Toll-Free: 800-316-5730
Chief Officer(s):
Carmen Bazinet, Contact
cbazinet@easterseals.org

Northern Region - Thunder Bay
#201, 91 Cumberland St. South, Thunder Bay ON P7B 6A7
Tel: 807-345-7622
Toll-Free: 800-267-3778

Western Region - Burlington / Mississauga / Oakville
PO Box 209, 4035 Fairview St., Burlington ON L7L 6E8
Tel: 289-208-1040
Chief Officer(s):
Susan Smith, Regional Manager
ssmith@easterseals.org

Western Region - London
#1, 2265 Oxford St. West, London ON N6K 4P1
Tel: 519-432-9669
Toll-Free: 888-278-7797

Western Region - Windsor / Sarnia
2117 Pelissier St., Windsor ON N8X 1N3
Tel: 519-944-0044
Toll-Free: 888-535-5623

Easter Seals/March of Dimes National Council *See* Easter Seals Canada

Eastern Canada Orchid Society (ECOS)
12, rue Dephoure, Dollard des Ormeaux QC H9B 1C2
Tel: 514-684-3904
info@ecosorchids.ca
www.ecosorchids.ca
www.facebook.com/ECOSorchids
Overview: A small national organization founded in 1953
Mission: ECOS is a non-profit group of orchid hobbyists dedicated to promoting the art, science & culture of raising orchids in the Montréal area.
Affiliation(s): Canadian Orchid Congress; American Orchid Society
Membership: *Fees:* $30 individual; $35 couple
Activities: Orchidfête; *Library:* Not open to public
Chief Officer(s):
Brian Dunbar, President

Eastern Canadian Galloway Association
1001 Hwy. 97, RR#3, Puslinch ON N0B 2J0
Tel: 905-659-2311; *Fax:* 905-659-2670
www.galloway.ca/ecga
Overview: A small local licensing organization founded in 1967
Mission: To promote the breeding of Galloway cattle in Ontario, Québec & Atlantic Provinces.
Member of: Canadian Galloway Association
Membership: 21
Chief Officer(s):
Marie Blake, President, 519-291-2797
Ciaran McIlwraith, Secretary
msciaran@aol.com

Eastern Charlotte Chamber of Commerce (ECCC)
#2, 21 Main St., St George NB E5C 3H9
Tel: 506-456-3951; *Fax:* 506-755-6174
Overview: A small local organization
Member of: Atlantic Provinces Chamber of Commerce; Canadian Chamber of Commerce
Finances: *Funding Sources:* Membership fees; insurance
Chief Officer(s):
Dorothy Gaudet, President
Irene Wright, Secretary

Eastern Fishermen's Federation
PO Box 907, Grand Manan NB E5G 4M1
Tel: 506-662-8416; *Fax:* 506-662-8336
eff@nb.aibn.com
www.easternfishermensfederation.ca
Overview: A small local organization founded in 1979
Mission: To unite & inform member fishing organizations on issues of common interest.
Membership: 22 organizations; *Member Profile:* Fishermen's associations in Eastern Canada
Chief Officer(s):
Eugene O'Leary, President
eugeneol@yahoo.com

Eastern Kings Health Foundation Inc.
17 Knight's Lane, Souris PE C0A 2B0
Tel: 902-687-7150
info@ekhf.ca
www.ekhf.ca
www.facebook.com/887373407990219
twitter.com/EKHF_PEI
Overview: A small local charitable organization founded in 1988
Mission: To maintain & strengthen the health of citizens in the Eastern Kings area of PEI by providing funding for medical equipment & resources; To support the Souris Hospital, Colville Manor, & healthcare programs & services
Finances: *Funding Sources:* Donations
Activities: Fundraising
Chief Officer(s):
Gertie Campbell, President

Eastern Ontario Archivists Association *See* Archives Association of Ontario

Eastern Ontario Beekeepers' Association (EOBA)
c/o David Gray, PO Box 375, 1222 Bankfield Rd., Manotick ON K4M 1A4
Tel: 613-692-3363
info@all-things.com
www.all-things.com/eoba
Overview: A small local organization
Mission: To assist persons interested in bees & beekeeping in eastern Ontario; To promote improvement in eastern Ontario's beekeeping industry
Member of: Ontario Beekeepers' Association
Membership: 87; *Member Profile:* Any individual residing in eastern Ontario who is interested in beekeeping
Activities: Helping members with problems associated with beekeeping; Disseminating timely information about beekeeping; Liaising with the Ontario Ministry of Agriculture & Food; Educating the public; Exchanging ideas about beekeeping amongst members
Chief Officer(s):
Noel Peter, Director
ve3dpn@rac.ca
Juliet Bancroft, Director
jetpets@hotmail.com
Martin Damus, Director
Damusm@inspection.gc.ca
David Gray, Director, 613-692-3363
Joanne Levac, Director
mark.lauterbach@sympatico.ca
Craig McCaffrey, Director, 613-692-4020
Publications:
• Eastern Ontario Beekeepers Association Newsletter
Type: Newsletter
Profile: Information about association business, plus forthcoming meetings & events

Eastern Ontario Concert Orchestra *See* Quinte Symphony

Eastern Ontario Model Forest
PO Box 2111, 10 Campus Dr., Kemptville ON K0G 1J0
Tel: 613-258-8241; *Fax:* 613-258-8363
modelforest@eomf.on.ca
www.eomf.on.ca
Overview: A small local organization
Mission: To demonstrate how partners, representing a diversity of forest values, can work together to achieve sustainable forest management using innovative, region-specific approaches
Member of: Canadian Model Forest Network
Chief Officer(s):
Jim McCready, President
Elizabeth Holmes, General Manager
eholmes@eomf.on.ca

Eastern Ontario Travel Association *See* Ontario East Tourism Association

Eastern Prince Edward Island Chamber of Commerce
PO Box 1593, Montague PE C0A 1R0
Tel: 902-838-3131
info@epeicc.ca
www.epeicc.ca
www.facebook.com/epeicc
twitter.com/epeicc
Previous Name: Southern Kings & Queens Chamber of Commerce
Overview: A small local organization founded in 2002
Mission: To provide an economic advantage to business members by providing them with priority customer referrals; To represent them in community endeavours; To provide them with networking capabilities unavailable to non-members
Membership: *Fees:* Schedule available
Chief Officer(s):
Marie LaVie, Managing Director

Eastern Shore Fisherman's Protective Association
9042 Hwy. 7, Head Jeddore NS B0J 2P0
Tel: 902-889-3185
esfpa@esfpa.ca
www.facebook.com/973736219388516
Overview: A small local organization
Mission: To develop opportunities to protect & maintain the interests of fishermen along the Eastern shore
Member of: Eastern Fisherman's Federation
Finances: *Funding Sources:* Membership dues
Staff Member(s): 3; 150 volunteer(s)
Membership: 200; *Fees:* $100
Chief Officer(s):
Peter Connors, President

Eastern Shore Ringette Association (ESRA)
NS
esringette.goalline.ca
Overview: A small local organization overseen by Ringette Nova Scotia
Member of: Ringette Nova Scotia
Membership: 3 teams; *Member Profile:* Teams with players 4-10; Teams with players 18+
Chief Officer(s):
Mary Stienburg, President
presidentESRA@gmail.com

Eastern Shore Volunteer Food Bank
Lakehill Dr., Musquodoboit Harbour NS B3E 1L6
Tel: 902-889-9243
Overview: A small local organization
Member of: Nova Scotia Food Bank Association; Atlantic Alliance of Food Banks & C.V.A.'s; Food Banks Canada

Eastern Shores Independent Association for Support Personnel (ESIASP)
c/o Eastern Shores School Board, 40, rue Mountsorrel, New Carlisle QC G0C 1Z0
Tel: 418-752-2247; *Fax:* 418-752-6447
esiasp@navigue.com
Overview: A small local organization
Chief Officer(s):
Louise C. Jones, President

Eastern Townships Association of Teachers *See* Appalachian Teachers' Association

Eastern Townships Resource Centre (ETRC) / Centre de recherche des cantons de l'est
Bishop's University, 2600, rue College, Sherbrooke QC J1M 1Z7
Tel: 819-822-9600
etrc@ubishops.ca
www.etrc.ca
www.facebook.com/easterntownshipresourcecentre
Overview: A small local organization founded in 1982
Mission: To promote the study of the history, culture & society of the Eastern Townships of Québec, with a special focus on the English-speaking communities; to preserve the region's living & archival heritage.
Staff Member(s): 3
Activities: Funding regional & community-based research projects; holding conferences & forums; exhibitions; preserving archival collections; *Internships:* Yes *Library:* Old Library, Bishop's University; Open to public
Chief Officer(s):
Fabian Will, Executive Director, 819-822-9600 Ext. 2647
Publications:
• Journal of the Eastern Townships Studies/Revue d'études des Cantons-de-l'Est
Type: journal
Profile: JETS is a bilingual, interdisciplinary dissemination of research, articles, notes, criticism, personal accounts & descriptions of archival fondsrelevant to the Eastern Townships.

Eastern Veterinary Technician Association (EVTA)
146 East St., Port Hood NS B0E 2W0
Tel: 902-787-2437
www.evta.ca
Overview: A small local organization founded in 1988
Member of: Canadian Association of Animal Health Technologists & Technicians
Affiliation(s): Canadian Veterinary Medical Association
Finances: *Funding Sources:* Donations; membership fees
Membership: *Fees:* $20 student; $150 regular; *Member Profile:* Registered Veterinary Technicians; those who have passed the Veterinary Technician National Examination
Activities: *Awareness Events:* Veterinary Technician Week, Oct.
Chief Officer(s):
Joye Sears, President
Beverly MacDonald, Executive Director
bev@evta.ca
Awards:
• Veterinary Technician of the Year Award
• EVTA Bursary
For students; *Amount:* $100

EastGen
7660 Mill Rd., Guelph ON N1H 6J1
Tel: 519-821-2150; *Fax:* 519-763-6582
Toll-Free: 888-821-2150
info@eastgen.ca
www.eastgen.ca
www.facebook.com/EastGen
twitter.com/EastGenGenetics
Merged from: Eastern Breeders Inc. & Gencor
Overview: A large local organization founded in 2011
Mission: To act as a farmer-directed AI cooperative & offer services to members in Ontario, New Brunswick, PEI, & Newfoundland & Labrador
Finances: *Annual Operating Budget:* $3 Million-$5 Million
Staff Member(s): 305
Membership: 8,500
Chief Officer(s):
Alan Brown, President

Eastview Neighbourhood Community Centre
86 Blake St., Toronto ON M4J 3C9
Tel: 416-392-1750; *Fax:* 416-392-1175
contact@eastviewcentre.com
www.eastviewcentre.com
www.facebook.com/EastviewNeighbourhoodCommunityCentre
twitter.com/eastviewcentre
Overview: A small local charitable organization
Mission: To provide programs for children, adults, seniors & immigrants.
Member of: Boys & Girls Clubs of Canada
Affiliation(s): Toronto-Danforth Early Years Centre; Toronto District School Board; Daily Bread Food Bank
Finances: *Funding Sources:* All 3 levels of government; corporations; foundations; private donations
Staff Member(s): 16
Membership: *Fees:* $5 child/youth; $10 adult/senior; $20 family
Activities: A variety of recreational programs for each age group; ESL & Mandarin classes; immigrant support group; food bank
Chief Officer(s):
Bev Wolfus, Chair & President
Kerry Bowser, Executive Director

Eating Disorder Association of Canada (EDAC) / Association des Troubles Alimentaires du Canada (ATAC)
ON
edacatac@gmail.com
www.edac-atac.ca
twitter.com/EDACATAC
Overview: A small national organization
Mission: EDAC-ATAC aims to serve the needs of those whose lives are impacted by eating disorders.
Chief Officer(s):
Jadine Cairns, President
Meetings/Conferences:
• Eating Disorder Association of Canada 6th Biennial Conference, 2018
Scope: National

Eatonia & District Chamber of Commerce
PO Box 370, Eatonia SK S0L 0Y0
Tel: 306-967-2582; *Fax:* 306-967-2267
Overview: A small local organization
Member of: Saskatchewan Chamber of Commerce
Membership: 40; *Fees:* $25

Eatonia Arts Council
PO Box 39, Eatonia SK S0L 0Y0
Tel: 204-967-2550
Overview: A small local organization founded in 1988
Mission: To encourage people in the community, especially the youth, to become involved in the arts, drawing, painting, taking photos or doing crafts.
Member of: Organization of Saskatchewan Arts Councils
Activities: Annual Adjudicated Art Show

Eau Vive *See* WaterCan

Echo-Edson Cultural Heritage Organization
4818 - 7 Ave., Edson AB T7E 1K8
Tel: 780-723-3582
echored@telus.net
www.redbrickartscentre.com
Also Known As: Red Brick Arts Centre & Museum
Overview: A small local organization founded in 1985
Mission: To restore & maintain the Red Brick School built in 1913 & to operate it as an arts centre & museum
Member of: Alberta Museums Association
Finances: *Annual Operating Budget:* $50,000-$100,000; *Funding Sources:* Provincial, federal & municipal government; donations; rentals
Staff Member(s): 2; 15 volunteer(s)
Membership: 1-99
Activities: Art classes & shows; tours; theatre & dance
Chief Officer(s):
Betty Stiltzenberger, President

Échographie Canada *See* Sonography Canada

The Eckhardt-Gramatté Foundation
54 Harrow St., Winnipeg MB R3M 2Y7
Tel: 204-452-9750; *Fax:* 204-477-6511
egf@egre.mb.ca
www.egre.mb.ca
Overview: A small national organization founded in 1982
Mission: Established in honour of Sonia & Walter Gramatté; to advance public appreciation, understanding & knowledge of the music & artistic works of these two individuals
Finances: *Annual Operating Budget:* $50,000-$100,000
Staff Member(s): 3
Activities: *Library:* by appointment
Chief Officer(s):
Lynda Hiebert, Executive Director

Eckville & District Chamber of Commerce
PO Box 609, Eckville AB T0M 0X0
Overview: A small local organization

L'Écluse des Laurentides
22A, rue Goyer, Saint-Sauveur QC J0R 1R0
Tél: 450-744-1393; *Téléc:* 450-744-1335
ecluse@cgocable.ca
www.ecluse.org
Aperçu: *Dimension:* petite; *Envergure:* locale; fondée en 1991
Membre(s) du bureau directeur:
Émilie Rouleau, Directrice

Éco Entreprises Québec (EEQ)
#600, 1600, boul René-Lévesque ouest, Montréal QC H3H 1P9
Tél: 514-987-1491; *Téléc:* 514-987-1598
service@ecoentreprises.qc.ca
www.ecoentreprises.qc.ca
www.linkedin.com/company/éco-entreprises-québec
www.facebook.com/ecoentreprisesqc
Aperçu: *Dimension:* petite; *Envergure:* provinciale; fondée en 2003
Mission: Organisme privé sans but lucratif; représenter les entreprises assujetties à la Loi sur la qualité de l'environnement qui mettent sur le marché québécois des contenants et emballages et des imprimés.
Membre de: Chambre de commerce du Montréal métropolitain; Conseil patronal de l'environnement du Québec; EXPRA
Membre(s) du personnel: 6
Membre: 3 000
Membre(s) du bureau directeur:
Maryse Vermette, Présidente-directrice générale
mvermette@ecoentreprises.qc.ca
Virginie Bussières, Directrice, Affaires corporatives, relations externes et communications
vbussieres@ecoentreprises.qc.ca
Prix, Bourses:
• Prix Phénix

Ecoforestry Institute Society (EIS)
PO Box 5070, Stn. B, Victoria BC V8R 6N3
Tel: 604-595-0655
ecoforestry@gmail.com
www.ecoforestry.ca
www.facebook.com/wildwoodecoforest
Overview: A small national charitable organization founded in 1992
Mission: To provide ecologically sound alternatives to current ruinous industrial forestry practices; To support preservation of ancient & natural forests; to encourage restoration of plantation tree farms to natural forest status
Member of: BC Environmental Network; Forest Stewardship Council
Finances: *Annual Operating Budget:* $50,000-$100,000; *Funding Sources:* Foundations; Donations; Subscriptions
Staff Member(s): 1; 12 volunteer(s)
Membership: 250; *Fees:* $10
Activities: Providing community outreach services through conferences, videos, & publications; Helping community watershed & land trusts organize ecoforestry programs; *Speaker Service:* Yes
Chief Officer(s):
Kathy Code, Director, Communications

Canadian Associations / Ecojustice Canada Society

Ecojustice Canada Society
#390, 425 Carrall St., Vancouver BC V6B 6E3
Tel: 604-685-5618; *Fax:* 604-685-7813
Toll-Free: 800-926-7744
info@ecojustice.ca
www.ecojustice.ca
www.facebook.com/ecojustice
twitter.com/ecojustice_ca
Also Known As: Ecojustice
Previous Name: Sierra Legal Defence Fund
Overview: A medium-sized national charitable organization founded in 1990
Mission: To provide legal representation to environmental groups that cannot afford to go to court against large institutions when important wilderness values are at stake; to bring selected cases with the ultimate goal of establishing an aggregate of strong legal precedents that recognize environmental values; to provide professional advice on the development of environmental legislation
Finances: *Annual Operating Budget:* $1.5 Million-$3 Million; *Funding Sources:* Individual donors; private foundations
Staff Member(s): 49; 10 volunteer(s)
Membership: 5,000-14,999
Activities: Free legal services; litigation; *Internships:* Yes
Chief Officer(s):
Devon Page, Executive Director
Marion Greene, Chief Financial Officer
Andrea Gutierrez, Director, Operations
Huda Al-Saedy, Director, Philanthropy
Kimberly Shearon, Director, Strategic Communications

Alberta Office
#800, 744 4th Ave. SW, Calgary AB T2P 3T4
Tel: 403-705-0202; *Fax:* 403-452-6574

Ecojustice Environmental Law Clinic at the University of Ottawa
c/o University of Ottawa, Faculty of Law, #216, 1 Stewart St., Ottawa ON K1N 7M9
Tel: 613-562-5800; *Fax:* 613-562-5319

Toronto Office
PO Box 106, #1910, 777 Bay St., Toronto ON M5G 2C8
Tel: 416-368-7533; *Fax:* 416-363-2746

École internationale de français (EIF)
CP 500, Trois-Rivières QC G9A 5H7
Tél: 819-376-5124; *Téléc:* 819-376-5166
Ligne sans frais: 888-343-8645
eif@uqtr.ca
www.uqtr.ca/eif
www.facebook.com/EIF.UQTR
twitter.com/eif_uqtr
Aperçu: *Dimension:* petite; *Envergure:* internationale; fondée en 1974
Mission: Offre des programmes intensifs d'immersion en français
Affiliation(s): Conseil des Ministres de l'Éducation du Canada
Finances: *Budget de fonctionnement annuel:* $50,000-$100,000
Membre(s) du personnel: 50
Membre: 11 institutionnel; *Critères d'admissibilite:* Apprenants de 18 ans et plus
Activités: Excursions, soirées; *Stagiaires:* Oui; *Service de conférenciers:* Oui
Membre(s) du bureau directeur:
Daniel Lavoie, Directeur
daniel.lavoie@uqtr.ca

Ecological Agriculture Projects (EAP) / Projets pour une agriculture écologique (PAE)
Macdonald Campus of McGill University, Sainte-Anne-de-Bellevue QC H9X 3V9
Tel: 514-398-7771; *Fax:* 514-398-7621
ecological.agriculture@mcgill.ca
eap.mcgill.ca
Overview: A small national organization founded in 1974
Mission: To facilitate the establishment of nutritional, just, & sustainable food systems worldwide
Affiliation(s): International Federation of Organic Agriculture Movements
Finances: *Annual Operating Budget:* $100,000-$250,000
Staff Member(s): 1
Membership: *Fees:* $40 individual; $60 organization; $500 sustaining; $1,250 organization
Activities: *Speaker Service:* Yes; *Library:* Open to public by appointment
Meetings/Conferences:
• 2018 Guelph Organic Conference & Trade Show, January, 2018, Guelph, ON
Scope: Local
Attendance: 1800-2000
Contact Information: www.guelphorganicconf.ca

Ecological Farmers of Ontario (EFO)
5420 Hwy. 6 North, RR#5, Guelph ON N1H 6J2
Tel: 519-822-8606; *Fax:* 519-822-5681
Toll-Free: 877-822-8606
info@efao.ca
www.efao.ca
Overview: A medium-sized provincial charitable organization founded in 1979
Mission: To provide information about ecological farming practices in Ontario
Finances: *Funding Sources:* George Cedric Metcalf Foundation; Ontario Trillium Foundation; Friends of Greenbelt Foundation
Membership: *Member Profile:* Ontario farmers; *Committees:* Energy & farming; Peak oil; Soil & carbon
Activities: Providing access to advice; Organizing farm tours
Chief Officer(s):
Chris Litster, President
Shauna Bloom, Manager, Programs
programs@efao.ca
Caitlin Hill, Coordinator, Communications & Outreach
outreach@efao.ca
Karen Maitland, Coordinator, Membership Services
Smith Dave, Treasurer
Publications:
• Ecological Farmers of Ontario Newsletter
Type: Newsletter; *Editor:* Fiona Wagner

Ecology Action Centre (EAC)
2705 Fern Lane, Halifax NS B3K 4L3
Tel: 902-429-2202; *Fax:* 902-405-3716
info@ecologyaction.ca
www.ecologyaction.ca
www.facebook.com/EcologyActionCentre
twitter.com/ecologyaction
Overview: A medium-sized provincial organization founded in 1971
Mission: To act as a voice for Nova Scotia's environment; To build a healthier, more sustainable Nova Scotia
Member of: Canadian Renewable Energy Alliance
Finances: *Funding Sources:* Membership dues; Donations
Membership: 2,400; *Fees:* $20 student/senior; $40 organizational/regular; $60 family; $120 supporting; *Committees:* Coastal & Water; Marine; Wilderness Issues; Transportation; Energy Issues; Food Action; Built Environment
Activities: Communication; Education and Programming; Research; Advocacy; *Internships:* Yes; *Speaker Service:* Yes; *Library:* Open to public
Chief Officer(s):
Maggy Burns, Managing Director, 902-429-5287
centre@ecologyaction.ca
Rochelle Owen, Co-Chair

Ecology North
5016 - 50 Ave., Yellowknife NT X1A 2P3
Tel: 867-873-6019
admin@ecologynorth.ca
www.ecologynorth.ca
www.facebook.com/ecologynorth
twitter.com/ecologynorth
Overview: A small local organization founded in 1971
Mission: To promote appreciation & protection of the natural environment of the Northwest Territories; To foster public awareness through seminars & outdoor activities; To provide a forum for communication of ideas on environmental issues between the scientific community, government & the peoples of the Northwest Territories
Member of: Canadian Environmental Network
Finances: *Annual Operating Budget:* $50,000-$100,000
Staff Member(s): 2
Membership: 200; *Fees:* $10 individual; $20 family; *Committees:* Recycling; Botanical Gardens/Volunteer Development; Endangered Species
Activities: Participates in environmental hearings; reviews legislation & policy; sponsors a wide range of activities such as bird walks & nature hikes; public education seminars on various aspects of the northern environment; community recycling programs such as Rent-a-Plate; *Awareness Events:* Earth Week, April; Folk on the Rocks *Library:* Recycling Resource Centre
Chief Officer(s):
Craig Scott, Executive Director

Écomusée de l'Au-Delà
CP 365, Succ. C, Montréal QC H2L 4K3
Tél: 514-528-8826
courriel@ecomuseedelaudela.net
www.ecomuseedelau-dela.net
Aperçu: *Dimension:* petite; *Envergure:* locale
Mission: Promouvoir la sauvegarde, la conservation, la restauration et la connaissance des cimetières
Membre(s) du bureau directeur:
Alain Tremblay, Directeur exécutif

Economic Developers Alberta (EDA)
Suite 127, #406, 917 - 85 St. SW, Calgary AB T3H 5Z9
Tel: 403-214-0224; *Fax:* 403-214-0224
Toll-Free: 866-671-8182
www.edaalberta.ca
www.linkedin.com/groups/Economic-Developers-Alberta-1448077
www.facebook.com/518610924817696
twitter.com/edaalberta
Previous Name: Economic Developers Association of Alberta
Overview: A small provincial organization founded in 1974
Mission: To enhance the economic development profession in Alberta, providing a network of communication, information & education
Affiliation(s): Economic Developers Association of Canada; Canadian Association of Petroleum Producers
Finances: *Annual Operating Budget:* $100,000-$250,000; *Funding Sources:* Membership fees
Staff Member(s): 4
Membership: 100-499; *Fees:* $68 student; $137 associate/corporate individual & elected official; $205 regular
Activities: *Speaker Service:* Yes
Chief Officer(s):
Jeff Penney, President
Leann Hackman-Carty, Chief Executive Officer
leann@edaalberta.ca
Awards:
• Economic Developer of the Year Award
• Alex Metcalf Awards
• Marketing Awards
• President's Award
Meetings/Conferences:
• Economic Developers Alberta 2018 Annual Professional Conference & AGM, March, 2018, Banff Centre, Banff, AB
Scope: Provincial
Description: Theme: "Diverse. Determined. Driven."

Economic Developers Association of Alberta *See* Economic Developers Alberta

Economic Developers Association of Canada (EDAC) / Association canadienne de développement économique (ACDE)
#200, 7 Innovation Dr., Hamilton ON L9H 7H9
Tel: 905-689-8771
info@edac.ca
www.edac.ca
twitter.com/E_D_A_C
Previous Name: Industrial Developers Association of Canada
Overview: A medium-sized national organization founded in 1968
Mission: To contribute to Canada's economic, social, & environmental well-being by advancing economic development; To enhance professional competence & ethical service
Affiliation(s): Provincial partners: APDEQ, EDA, EDABC, IEDC, EDCO, SEDA, Economic Developers Association of MB; Federal Economic Development Initiative in Northern ON; NS Association of Regional Development Authorities; Enterprise Network. Federal partners: Agriculture & Agri-Food Canada; Atlantic Canada Opportunities Agency; Canadian Commercial Corporation, Dept. of Environment, Dept. of Finance, Export Development Corp., Industry Canada, Invest in Canada, National Research Council, Public Works & Government Services, Revenue Can., Smart Communities 'Empowering Canadians', Statistics Can., CIDA, ICCI, HRSDC
Membership: *Fees:* Schedule available; *Member Profile:* Economic development practitioners; Students
Activities: Liaising internationally, federally, provincially, & municipally; Providing professional development opportunities; Ensuring members follow the association's "Code of Ethics"; *Rents Mailing List:* Yes
Chief Officer(s):
Penny A. Gardiner, Chief Executive Officer
gardiner@edac.ca

Greg Borduas, President
greg.borduas@gmail.com
David Emerson, 1st Vice-President
emerson@unb.ca
Kevin Rose, 2nd Vice-President
krose@waubetek.com
Gerry Gabinet, Treasurer
gabinet@strathcona.ab.ca
Awards:
• Marketing Canada Awards
• EDAC / RBC Financial Group Economic Development Achievement of The Year Award
Meetings/Conferences:
• Economic Developers Association of Canada 50th Annual Conference, September, 2018, Fredericton, NB
Scope: National
Publications:
• Communique [a publication of the Economic Developers Association of Canada]
Type: Newsletter; *Editor:* Susan Touchette

Economic Developers Association of Manitoba (EDAM)
#700, 177 Lombard Ave., Winnipeg MB R3B 0W5
Tel: 204-795-2000; *Fax:* 204-925-8000
info@edamonline.ca
www.edamonline.ca
www.linkedin.com/groups/Economic-Developers-Association-Manitoba-3202078
www.facebook.com/160988724423
Overview: A small provincial organization founded in 1993
Mission: EDAM is an independent, non-profit, incorporated association aiming to improve communication within the economic development profession.
Affiliation(s): Economic Development Association of Canada; similar provincial associations
Membership: *Fees:* $150 individual; $325 organization; $400 associate/corporate; $50 student; *Member Profile:* Anyone engaged in economic development in Manitoba; *Committees:* Executive; Communications; Forum
Chief Officer(s):
Colleen Engel, Chair
Shelley Morris, Manager

Economic Developers Council of Ontario Inc. (EDCO)
6506 Marlene Ave., Cornwall ON K6H 7H9
Tel: 613-931-9827; *Fax:* 613-931-9828
edco@edco.on.ca
www.edco.on.ca
www.linkedin.com/company/economic-developers-council-of-ontario
twitter.com/edco1edco
Previous Name: Ontario Industrial Development Council Inc.
Overview: A medium-sized provincial organization founded in 1957
Mission: To provide a forum for economic development related educational activities; to increase the profile of EDCO & the profession; to encourage & create an awareness of economic development issues with relevant government agencies; to promote & develop Ontario as a premier location for economic activity by increasing employment & prosperity, & enhancing the quality of life within the Ontario municipalities.
Member of: Economic Developers Association of Canada; International Economic Development Council; Ontario East Economic Development Commission; Northwestern Ontario Development Network
Finances: *Funding Sources:* Membership dues; corporate sponsors
Membership: *Fees:* Schedule available; *Member Profile:* Persons directly or indirectly engaged in business & economic development for benefit of Ontario
Activities: *Speaker Service:* Yes
Chief Officer(s):
Jennifer Patterson, President
Heather Lalonde, Executive Director
Awards:
• Ontario Economic Development Awards
• Economic Development Achievement Award
Meetings/Conferences:
• Economic Developers Council of Ontario 61st Annual Conference & Showcase 2018, February, 2018, Sheraton Centre Toronto Hotel, Toronto, ON
Scope: Provincial
Description: Theme: "Mission Possible: Agents of Change"
Contact Information: www.edcoconference.com

Economic Development Association of British Columbia
See British Columbia Economic Development Association

Economic Development Brandon (EDB)
City of Brandon, 410 - 9th St., Brandon MB R7A 6A2
Tel: 204-729-2132; *Fax:* 204-729-8244
Toll-Free: 866-729-2132
econdev@brandon.ca
www.economicdevelopmentbrandon.com
www.facebook.com/EconomicDevelopmentBrandon
twitter.com/EconDevBrandon
Previous Name: Brandon Economic Development Board
Overview: A small local organization founded in 1982
Mission: To promote economic & population growth in Brandon, MB
Member of: Brandon Chamber of Commerce; Economic Developers Association of Canada (EDAC); International Economic Development Council (IEDC)
Finances: *Annual Operating Budget:* $250,000-$500,000; *Funding Sources:* City of Brandon
Staff Member(s): 3
Activities: Providing relocation & business assistance; *Speaker Service:* Yes
Chief Officer(s):
Sandy Trudel, Director, Economic Development, 204-729-2131
s.trudel@brandon.ca
Dan Fontaine, Specialist, Business Development, 204-729-2133
d.fontaine@brandon.ca

Economic Development Professionals Association of Québec *Voir* Association des professionnels en développement économique du Québec

Economic Development Winnipeg Inc. (EDW)
#300, 259 Portage Ave., Winnipeg MB R3B 2A9
Tel: 204-954-1997
www.economicdevelopmentwinnipeg.com
www.linkedin.com/company/economic-development-winnipeg-inc.
twitter.com/EDWinnipeg
www.youtube.com/user/EDWinnipeg
Overview: A medium-sized local organization founded in 2002
Mission: To act as Winnipeg's economic development & tourism services agency, by marketing the city & providing related economic development & tourism services
Activities: Providing information, statistics, & resources about Winnipeg; Assisting in meeting & event plans; Promoting travel to Winnipeg; Developing partnerships; Supporting the attraction, expansion, & retention of business in Winnipeg; Leveraging investment in targeted projects & sectors
Chief Officer(s):
Marina R. James, President & CEO
Greg Dandewich, Senior Vice-President, 204-954-1982
greg@economicdevelopmentwinnipeg.com
Chantal Sturk-Nadeau, Senior Vice-President, Tourism, 204-954-1987
chantal@tourismwinnipeg.com

Economics Society of Northern Alberta (ESNA)
PO Box 1434, Edmonton AB T5J 2N6
www.esna.ca
www.linkedin.com/groups/Economics-Society-Northern-Alberta-6612956
Overview: A small local organization founded in 1965
Mission: To bring together individuals interested in the field of economics & provides regular meetings for discussion & exchange of ideas relating to applied economics; to promote public awareness & understanding of current economic problems, issues & achievements.
Finances: *Funding Sources:* Membership dues; event fees; individual donations
Activities: Annual conferences; luncheons with speakers; *Speaker Service:* Yes
Chief Officer(s):
Mark Parsons, President

Economists', Sociologists' & Statisticians' Association *See* Canadian Association of Professional Employees

EcoPerth
2196 Old Brooke Rd., RR#2, Maberly ON K0H 2B0
Tel: 613-267-6463; *Fax:* 613-268-2907
info@ecoperth.on.ca
www.ecoperth.on.ca
Overview: A small local organization
Mission: To promote local projects that are environmentally sustainable and economically efficient in the Perth, Ontario area.
Chief Officer(s):
Bob Argue, Executive Director
bob@ecoperth.on.ca

Éco-Quartier Sainte-Marie
2151, rue Parthenais, Montréal QC H2K 3T3
Tél: 514-523-9220; *Téléc:* 514-523-2653
eqsm@qc.aira.com
www.eco-quartiersm.ca
Aperçu: *Dimension:* petite; *Envergure:* locale
Mission: Pour aider financièrement les organismes communautaires qui travaillent dans le domaine de l'environnement et de créer une ville plus écologique
Membre(s) du bureau directeur:
Marie-Noëlle Foschini, Directrice générale
André Gagnon, Président, Conseil d'administration

EcoSource Mississauga
Meadowvale South Recreation Centre, 6600 Falconer Dr., 2nd Fl., Mississauga ON L5N 1M2
Tel: 905-274-6222; *Fax:* 905-858-8927
info@ecosource.ca
www.ecosource.ca
www.facebook.com/EcosourceGreen
twitter.com/EcoSourceGreen
Overview: A small local charitable organization founded in 1979
Mission: To offer education & programs related to the environment
Finances: *Funding Sources:* Donations; Foundations; Municipal government agencies; Corporations
Staff Member(s): 14
Chief Officer(s):
Andrea Dawber, Acting Executive Director
adawber@ecosource.ca
Anita Wong, Manager, Community Gardens Program
awong@ecosource.ca
Publications:
• Ecosource Quarterly Newsletter
Type: Newsletter; *Frequency:* q.
Profile: Provides information on organization-wide events, news, & updates from Ecosource; discusses overarching themes & issues
• Peel Environmental Youth Alliance [a publication of Ecosource]
Type: Newsletter; *Frequency:* Semimonthly; *Editor:* Rahul Mehta
Profile: Environmental events & opportunities for students in the Region of Peel
• Trailblazers [a publication of Ecosource]
Type: Newsletter
Profile: Information for Region of Peel educators about environmental teaching resources & events

Ecotrust Canada
#90, 425 Carrall St., Vancouver BC V6B 6E3
Tel: 604-682-4141; *Fax:* 604-862-1944
info@ecotrust.ca
ecotrust.ca
www.facebook.com/ecotrust.ca
twitter.com/ecotrustcanada
www.youtube.com/user/EcotrustCanada
Overview: A small provincial charitable organization
Mission: To improve environmental sustainability in British Columbia
Affiliation(s): Ecotrust; Ecotrust Australia; Forest Stewardship Council; Heiltsuk Nation; Na' Na' kila Institute; Qqs Projects Society; Raincoast Conservation Society; West Coast Aquatic Management Board; Shorebank Enterprise Group; ShoreBank Pacific; Tsleil-Waututh Nation; Vancity
Staff Member(s): 31
Chief Officer(s):
Brenda Reid-Kuecks, President

EcoWatch Canada (EWC)
seeds@telusplanet.net
www.ecowatchcanada.org
www.linkedin.com/company/ecowatch-canada
www.facebook.com/ecowatchcanada
twitter.com/ecowatchcanada
ecowatchcanada.wordpress.com
Overview: A medium-sized national charitable organization founded in 2008
Mission: To improve the environmental quality, to educate our future generations, and to raise awareness among our community by partnering with local businesses, community leaders, government officials, schools and neighbors.
Chief Officer(s):
Carmen Ng, Executive Director

L'Écrit Tôt de Saint-Hubert
4050, rue Grande Allée, Saint-Hubert QC J4T 2W2
Tél: 450-443-1411; Téléc: 450-443-3772
ecritot@bellnet.ca
www.ecritot.ca
Aperçu: *Dimension:* petite; *Envergure:* locale; fondée en 1991
Mission: Accompagne des adultes et des familles dans l'apprentissage des connaissances de base en lecture, écriture et calcul; travaille à la prévention de l'analphabétisme ainsi qu'à la sensibilisation de la population aux réalités sociales et économiques que vivent les personnes qui éprouvent des difficultés à lire et à écrire
Membre: *Montant de la cotisation:* 15$; *Critères d'admissibilite:* Adultes analphabètes ou peu scolarisés
Activités: Ateliers d'alphabétisation; programmes Lecteurs à domicile; L'École des parents
Membre(s) du bureau directeur:
Joanne Côté, Directrice générale

Écrivains Francophones d'Amérique
1995, rue Sherbrooke ouest, Montréal QC H3A 1H9
Tél: 514-318-2590
lesecrivainsfrancophones@yahoo.ca
ecrivainsfrancophones.com
www.facebook.com/111361458891464
Nom précédent: Société des écrivains canadiens
Aperçu: *Dimension:* petite; *Envergure:* nationale; fondée en 1936
Mission: Grouper en association les écrivains de langue française, de nationalité canadienne, domiciliés ou non au Canada, auteurs d'un ou de plusieurs livres publiés au Canada ou ailleurs par des éditeurs homologués; servir et défendre les intérêts de la littérature canadienne; prendre toutes les mesures nécessaires ou opportunes pour assurer le respect de la propriété littéraire de ses membres.
Membre: *Critères d'admissibilite:* Écrivains
Activités: Participation aux Salons du livre; conférences; lectures publiques; dîners-causeries; rencontres auteur-lecteurs, etc.; *Service de conférenciers:* Oui
Membre(s) du bureau directeur:
Gino Levesque, Responsable
Prix, Bourses:
• Prix de la SEC
Attribué chaque année à un roman, à un essai ou à un recueil de poèmes, chacun de ces trois genres littéraires revenant une année sur trois. Le Prix n'est attribué qu'à des ouvrages publiés en français au Canada

Les écrivains indépendants d'Ottawa *See* Ottawa Independent Writers

Ecumenical Coalition for Economic Justice; GATT-Fly *See* KAIROS: Canadian Ecumenical Justice Initiatives

Ecumenical Committee of Manitoba *See* Association of Christian Churches in Manitoba

Ecumenical Forum of Canada; The Canadian Churches' Forum for Global Ministries *See* Forum for Intercultural Leadership & Learning

Eczema Society of Canada / Société d'Eczéma du Canada
PO Box 25009, 417 The Queensway South, Keswick ON L4P 2C7
Toll-Free: 966-329-3621
www.eczemahelp.ca
www.facebook.com/EczemaSocietyofCanada
www.youtube.com/user/EczemaHelp
Previous Name: Canadian Eczema Society for Education & Research
Overview: A small national charitable organization founded in 1997
Mission: To disseminate information about eczema & its treatment to both patients, families & their doctors; To encourage & fund basic research on eczema; To increase public awareness of eczema in society in general
Membership: *Member Profile:* Patients; parents of patients; doctors
Chief Officer(s):
Amanda Cresswell-Melville, President-Executive Director
director@eczemahelp.ca

Edam & District Board of Trade
PO Box 430, Edam SK S0M 0V0
Tel: 306-397-2297; *Fax:* 306-397-2555
Overview: A small local organization founded in 1940
Membership: 60
Activities: *Rents Mailing List:* Yes
Chief Officer(s):
Angela Blanchette, Secretary

EDAM Performing Arts Society (EDAM)
303 East 8th Ave., Vancouver BC V5T 1S1
Tel: 604-876-9559
info@edamdance.org
www.edamdance.org
www.facebook.com/159929590739220
twitter.com/edamdance
Overview: A small local charitable organization founded in 1982
Mission: To explore new directions in dance & the performing arts
Member of: The Dance Centre; Alliance for Arts & Culture
Finances: *Funding Sources:* Canada Council; BC Arts Council; City of Vancouver; Vancouver Foundation; BC Gaming Branch
Chief Officer(s):
Peter Bingham, Artistic Director
Mona Hamill, General Manager

Eden Community Food Bank (ECFB)
#2, 3185 Unity Dr., Mississauga ON L5L 4L5
Tel: 905-785-3651
info@edenfoodbank.org
edenfoodbank.org
www.facebook.com/edencommunityfoodbank
twitter.com/edenfoodbank
Overview: A small local organization founded in 1990
Mission: To provide food to the less fortunate & promote healthy eating
Staff Member(s): 7
Membership: *Committees:* Finance; Fundraising; HR; Marketing; Events
Chief Officer(s):
Bill Crawford, Executive Director
bill.crawford@edenfoodbank.org

Edgerton & District Chamber of Commerce
PO Box 337, Edgerton AB T0B 1K0
Tel: 780-755-3006
Overview: A small local organization

Edgerton & District Historical Society
PO Box 174, Edgerton AB T0B 1K0
Tel: 780-755-2189; *Fax:* 780-755-2181
Overview: A small local charitable organization
Mission: To present artifacts that depict the history of Edgerton, Alberta & the surrounding region at the six buildings that make up the Edgerton Museum
Finances: *Funding Sources:* Donations; Fundraising
Activities: Maintaining the original Grand Trunk Pacific Station, the Battle Valley School, & the Egerton Methodist Church

Edith Lando Charitable Foundation
1499 Angus Dr., Vancouver BC V6H 1V2
rbeiser4@gmail.com
www.edithlando.com
Overview: A small local charitable organization founded in 1973
Mission: To support programs that nurture self-esteem of young children
Finances: *Annual Operating Budget:* $50,000-$100,000
2 volunteer(s)
Activities: Grants for operating, capital projects, conferences, deficit financing, endowments; grants for special projects, seed money, matching funds, programs, research
Chief Officer(s):
Roberta Beiser, Director

Editors' Association of Canada (EAC) / Association canadienne des réviseurs (ACR)
#505, 27 Carlton St., Toronto ON M5B 1L2
Tel: 416-975-1379; *Fax:* 416-975-1637
Toll-Free: 866-226-3348
info@editors.ca
www.editors.ca
twitter.com/eac_acr
Also Known As: Editors Canada
Previous Name: Freelance Editors' Association of Canada
Overview: A medium-sized national organization founded in 1979
Mission: To promote & maintain standards of professional editing & publishing; to set guidelines to help editors secure fair pay & good working conditions, fosters networking among editors & cooperates with other publishing associations in areas of common concern.
Member of: Book & Periodical Council; Canadian Conference of the Arts; Cultural Human Resources Council
Affiliation(s): Canadian Conference of the Arts
Finances: *Funding Sources:* Membership dues; conference fees
Membership: 1,500; *Fees:* $260 voting & qualifying members; $130 student & emeritus; *Member Profile:* Membership categories include students, qualifying members, voting members, emeritus members, & honorary life members. Voting members have completed at least 500 hours of editorial work over the 12 months preceding application for membership. Qualifying membership is open to anyone with an interest in editing.; *Committees:* Certification Steering; Conference; Newsletter; Francophone Affairs; Marketing & Public Affairs; Member Communications; Member Services; Professional Standards; Publications; Training & Development; Volunteer Management; External Liaison; Human Resources; Nominating
Activities: Sponsoring professional development seminars; establishing guidelines to help editors secure fair working conditions; facilitating networking
Chief Officer(s):
Anne Louise Mahoney, President
president@editors.ca
Patrick Banville, Executive Director
executivedirector@editors.ca
Awards:
• Tom Fairley Award for Editorial Excellence
Eligibility: Open to all editors, both freelance & in-house, for any editorial work published in Canada in English or French; *Amount:* $2,000
• Claudette Upton Scholarship
Eligibility: Current member of EAC; *Amount:* $1,000 to attend national conference, association workshops or purchase EAC publications
Meetings/Conferences:
• Editors' Association of Canada Conference 2018, May, 2018, Radisson Hotel Saskatoon, Saskatoon, SK
Scope: National
Publications:
• Active Voice / La Voix active
Type: Newsletter; *Frequency:* Quarterly; *Editor:* Wilf Popoff; Michelle Boulton
• Editing Canadian English
Number of Pages: 258; *ISBN:* 1-55199-045-8
• Editors' Association of Canada Certification: Study Guide and Exemplars
Profile: Guides for editors through the certification process
• Meeting Editorial Standards
ISBN: 1-55322-003-X
• Professional Editorial Standards
Profile: Skills & knowledge needed for editing in English-language media in Canada
British Columbia
PO Box 1688, Stn. Bentall Centre, Vancouver BC V6C 2P7
bc@editors.ca
www.facebook.com/EAC.BC
twitter.com/EditorsBC
Chief Officer(s):
Micheline Brodeur, Chair
bcchair@editors.ca
National Capital Region
PO Box 62035, Stn. E, Ottawa ON K1C 7H8
ncr@editors.ca
www.linkedin.com/groups?gid=1858228
twitter.com/EditorsNCR
Chief Officer(s):
Maureen Moyes, Executive Director
Prairie Provinces
Edmonton AB
Chief Officer(s):
Emily Staniland, Branch Contact
Volunteer-with-PPB@editors.ca
Québec/Région de l'Atlantique
CP 46042, Pointe-Claire QC H9R 5R4
Courriel: rqa-qac@editors.ca
www.facebook.com/326039037428133
twitter.com/RQA_QAC
Chief Officer(s):
Karen Schell, Administratrice
Toronto
PO Box 5833, Stn. A, Toronto ON M5W 1P2
Tel: 416-975-5528; *Fax:* 416-492-1719
toronto@editors.ca
www.facebook.com/EACToronto
twitter.com/EACToronto
Chief Officer(s):

Lisa Jemison, Chair
toronto_br_chair@editors.ca

Edmonton & District Council of Churches (EDCC)
c/o St. Patrick's Anglican Church, 334 Knottwood Rd. North, Edmonton AB T6K 2Z7
Tel: 780-463-5452
admin@EDCCunity.org
www.edccunity.org
Overview: A small local organization founded in 1942
Mission: To express the essential unity of the body of Christ through worship, fellowship, dialogue, cooperation, service & prayer
Affiliation(s): Canadian Council of Churches
Finances: Annual Operating Budget: Less than $50,000
Staff Member(s): 1; 7 volunteer(s)
Membership: 22; Fees: $60 denominational member; $30 individual member; Member Profile: Any churches, Christian Organizations or individuals who accept Jesus Christ as Lord & Saviour; Committees: Ecumenical Coordinators; Week of Prayer for Christian Unity Service Planning Committee; Way of the Cross Planning Committee; No Room in the Inn Planning Committee
Activities: Organization of events; Distribution of information; Participation in interdenominational projects; Awareness Events: Week of Prayer for Christian Unity, Jan.; Good Friday Way of the Cross; No Room in the Inn Fundraising for Low Income Housing, Dec.
Chief Officer(s):
Kevin Kraglund, President
president.edcc@telus.net
Awards:
• Rev. Marilyn McClung Memorial Award for Ecumenism
Eligibility: Individuals who have made outstanding or specific contributions to the Edmonton & District Council of Churches' ecumenical efforts

Edmonton & District Labour Council (EDLC)
10212 - 112 St. NW, Edmonton AB T5K 1M4
Tel: 780-474-4747; Fax: 780-477-1064
office@edlc.ca
www.edlc.ca
www.facebook.com/edmlabour
twitter.com/edmlabour
Overview: A medium-sized local organization founded in 1906 overseen by Alberta Federation of Labour
Mission: To advocate rights of workers through City Hall & school boards; To provide monthly forum for exchanging information on developments in unions; To facilitate unity in labour; To support & organize rallies; To offer strike support; To maintain involvement in civic boards & committees
Member of: Canadian Labour Congress; Alberta Federation of Labour
Affiliation(s): Alliance of Canadian Cinema, Television & Radio Artists Alberta; Amalgamated Transit Union; Bakery, Confectionery, Tobacco Workers & Grain Millers' International Union; Health Sciences Association of Alberta; International Association of Machinists & Aerospace Workers; International Alliance of Theatrical Stage Employees; International Union of Painters & Allied Trades; Public Service Alliance of Canada; Service Employees International Union; United Food & Commercial Workers; United Nurses of Alberta; United Steel Workers
Finances: Annual Operating Budget: $100,000-$250,000
Staff Member(s): 1; 140 volunteer(s)
Membership: 45,000 local unions; Fees: $5; Member Profile: Any organization already affiliated to the Canadian Labour Congress; Committees: Education; Political Action; Community Services; Strike Support; Peace; Finance
Activities: Organizing Labour Day BBQs for the unemployed & labour appreciation events; Speaker Service: Yes; Library: by appointment
Chief Officer(s):
Bruce Fafard, President
Publications:
• EDLC [Edmonton & District Labour Council] Labour Reporter
Type: Newsletter

Edmonton (Alberta) Nerve Pain Association (EANPA)
14016 - 91 A Ave., Edmonton AB T5R 5A7
Tel: 780-217-9306
neuropathy_nervepain@hotmail.com
www.edmontonnervepain.ca
Overview: A medium-sized provincial charitable organization
Mission: To support people suffering from neuropathic pain

Chief Officer(s):
Claude M. Roberto, President

Edmonton Aboriginal Senior Centre (NSC)
Cottage E, 10107 - 134 Ave., Edmonton AB T5E 1J2
Tel: 780-476-6595
manager@easc.ca
www.easc.ca
Previous Name: Métis Women's Council of Edmonton
Overview: A small local charitable organization founded in 1986
Mission: To promote welfare, education & interests of Aboriginal seniors within the Edmonton area
Finances: Funding Sources: City of Edmonton community services; Alberta Municipal Affairs
Staff Member(s): 4
Activities: Native Seniors Drop-in Centre; Outreach Program; Urban Native Housing Registry; Speaker Service: Yes; Library

Edmonton Arts Council (EAC)
Prince of Wales Armouries, 10440 - 108 Ave., 2nd Fl., Edmonton AB T5H 3Z9
Tel: 780-424-2787; Fax: 780-425-7620
www.edmontonarts.ab.ca
www.facebook.com/edmontonarts
twitter.com/artsedmonton
Overview: A small local organization
Mission: To support & promote the arts community in Edmonton; to provide support to festivals, arts organizations & individual artists
Affiliation(s): Arts Habitat Association of Edmonton
Staff Member(s): 18
Membership: 298; Fees: $25 individual full/associate; $50 organization full/associate; free - students; Member Profile: Artists, arts & festival organizations; individuals, businesses, government members, corporations & media supporting the arts in Edmonton; Committees: Equity
Activities: Public Art Conservation project; Graffiti Zones program; transitory public art; community public art; Percent for Art acquisition program
Chief Officer(s):
Brian Webb, Chair
Paul Moulton, Executive Director
pmoulton@edmontonarts.ca
Awards:
• Lee Fund for the Arts Grant
Eligibility: 18 years of age or older; resident of greater Edmonton region; Canadian citizen or landed immigrant; Amount: $10,000 max.
• Project Grant for Individual Artists
Eligibility: Emerging or established professional artist; resides in City of Edmonton; has peer recognition; has received public exposure Deadline: July 1; Amount: $25,000 maximum
• Cultural Diversity in the Arts Awards
Eligibility: From ethnically diverse cultural background; Edmonton resident; 18 yrs. or older; working in any artistic medium, including but not limited to, dance, theatre, music, literary arts, storytelling & other oral traditions, fine craft, media arts or visual arts Deadline: October; Amount: 12 awards, $7,500 each

Edmonton Association of the Deaf (EAD)
#203, 11404 - 142 St., Edmonton AB T5M 1V1
Overview: A small local charitable organization
Affiliation(s): Alberta Association of the Deaf; Alberta Cultural Society Deaf; Alberta Deaf Sports Association
Activities: Deaf social night; deaf summer camp; senior citizens
Chief Officer(s):
Matthew Kuntz, President
02mathewkuntz@gmail.com

Edmonton Bicycle & Touring Club (EBTC)
PO Box 52017, Stn. Garneau, Edmonton AB T6G 2T5
Tel: 780-424-2453
www.bikeclub.ca
www.facebook.com/groups/21002145481
twitter.com/EBTCbikeclub
Overview: A small local organization founded in 1978
Affiliation(s): Alberta Bicycle Association
Finances: Annual Operating Budget: $50,000-$100,000
7 volunteer(s)
Membership: 301; Fees: $33 single; $18 for additional family member (18 years & older); Member Profile: Single, married, families, all ages & walks of life
Activities: Day & overnight cycling trips; cross-country skiing; social events; Awareness Events: Tour de l'Alberta; Library: Not open to public
Chief Officer(s):

Charles World, President
president@bikeclub.ca

Edmonton Boxing & Wrestling Commission See Edmonton Combative Sports Commission

Edmonton Centre for Equal Justice See Edmonton Community Legal Centre

Edmonton CFA Society
Standard Life Centre, PO Box 479, #21, 10405 Jasper Ave., Edmonton AB T5J 3N4
Toll-Free: 866-494-3732
info@edmontoncfa.ca
www.edmontoncfa.ca
Also Known As: Edmonton Society of Financial Analysts
Overview: A small local charitable organization founded in 1976
Mission: To promote professional & ethical standards in Edmonton, Alberta's investment industry; To advance the interests of members
Member of: CFA Institute
Finances: Funding Sources: Sponsorships
Membership: Member Profile: Individuals in the investment community in Edmonton, such as pension fund managers, security analysts, stockbrokers, & investment counsellors; Committees: CFA Prep Courses; Membership; Programs
Activities: Encouraging professional development through the CFA Program in Edmonton; Presenting programs, with speakers on topics related to the investment industry; Facilitating the exchange of information between members, Edmonton's financial community, the international investment community, & the general public; Raising awareness of the investment industry & the CFA designation
Chief Officer(s):
Chris Turchansky, President
cturchansky@atb.com
Brett Kimak, Vice-President
brett.kimak@aimco.alberta.ca
Rodney Lance Babineau, Secretary
rod.babineau@gov.ab.ca
Theresa Walton, Treasurer
theresa.walton@telus.com
Publications:
• Edmonton CFA Society Annual Report
Type: Yearbook; Frequency: Annually
• News & Views [a publication of the Edmonton CFA Society]
Type: Newsletter
Profile: Society activities & forthcoming events

Edmonton Chamber Music Society
PO Box 60354, Stn. U of Alberta, Edmonton AB T6G 2S6
Tel: 780-433-4532
ecms@edmontonchambermusic.org
www.edmontonchambermusic.org
www.facebook.com/edmonton.chambermusicsociety
twitter.com/ECMS4
www.youtube.com/user/ViolaChambers
Overview: A small local organization founded in 1954
Mission: To present a series of six to eight chamber music concerts each season
Finances: Funding Sources: Municipal government, provincial government; donations; ticket sales
Chief Officer(s):
Verna Quon, Contact
vquon@telusplanet.net

Edmonton Chamber of Commerce
World Trade Centre, Sun Life Place, #600, 9990 Jasper Ave., Edmonton AB T5J 1P7
Tel: 780-426-4620; Fax: 780-424-7946
info@edmontonchamber.com
www.edmontonchamber.com
ca.linkedin.com/company/edmonton-chamber-of-commerce
www.facebook.com/EdmontonChamber
twitter.com/edmontonchamber
www.youtube.com/edmontonchamber
Overview: A medium-sized local organization founded in 1889
Mission: To facilitate economic growth by providing information, business opportunities, educational programs & services to members; To positively influence Edmonton's business environment
Member of: World Trade Centre Association
Finances: Funding Sources: Membership fees
Membership: Fees: Schedule available; Committees: Policy; Executive

Canadian Associations / Edmonton Chamber of Voluntary Organizations

Activities: Organizing advocacy, education, & networking events; Providing information & resources; *Internships:* Yes; *Speaker Service:* Yes; *Library:* World Trade Centre Library
Chief Officer(s):
Janet M. Riopel, President & CEO
Awards:
• Centennial Scholarship

Edmonton Chamber of Voluntary Organizations
Bonnie Doon Professional Centre, #255, 8330 - 82 Ave., Edmonton AB T6C 4E3
Tel: 780-428-5487
info@ecvo.ca
www.ecvo.ca
www.facebook.com/EdmCVO
twitter.com/Edmcvo
Overview: A small local organization
Mission: To provide leadership & mobilize the collective resources of the voluntary sector; To enhance programs, services, operations & governance of not-for-profit organizations in the Edmonton region
Chief Officer(s):
Russ Dahms, Executive Director
director@ecvo.ca

Edmonton Classical Guitar Society
14104 Vallerview Dr., Edmonton AB T5R 5T8
Tel: 587-708-2044; *Fax:* 780-489-9583
www.edmontonclassicalguitarsociety.org
Overview: A small local organization founded in 1995
Mission: To foster an appreciation for the classical guitar by providing a forum for listening, learning, performing & teaching.
Membership: *Fees:* $30 regular; $60 partner; $100 sustaining
Activities: Regular concerts
Chief Officer(s):
David Grainger Brown, President

Edmonton Combative Sports Commission (ECSC)
c/o Community Standards/Community Services, CN Tower, PO Box 2359, 10004 - 104 Ave., 12th Fl., Edmonton AB T5J 2R7
Tel: 780-495-0382; *Fax:* 780-429-6976
ecsc.ca
Previous Name: Edmonton Boxing & Wrestling Commission
Overview: A small local licensing organization founded in 1938 overseen by Canadian Professional Boxing Council
Mission: The ECSC regulates, governs & controls boxing, wrestling & full-contact karate bouts & contests within Edmonton; enforces the CPBF safety code.
Member of: Canadian Professional Boxing Federation
Affiliation(s): Association of Boxing Commissions
Finances: *Annual Operating Budget:* $50,000-$100,000; *Funding Sources:* Permit fees
24 volunteer(s)
Membership: 8; *Member Profile:* By City Council appointment
Chief Officer(s):
Pat Reid, Executive Director
pat.reid@edmonton.ca

Edmonton Community Foundation
9910 103 St. NW, Edmonton AB T5K 2V7
Tel: 780-426-0015; *Fax:* 780-425-0121
Toll-Free: 866-626-0015
info@ecfoundation.org
www.ecfoundation.org
Overview: A small local charitable organization
Mission: To promote philanthropy; To fund charitable activities that aim to improve quality of life in Edmonton
Membership: *Committees:* Audit; Endowment Development; Governance; Granting Programs; Investment
Activities: Organizing Willpower Wills Week; Offering training & coaching services through the Endowment Sustainability Program
Chief Officer(s):
Martin Garber-Conrad, CEO
martin@ecfoundation.org
Kathy Hawkesworth, Director, Donor Services
khawkesworth@ecfoundation.org
Chris Quinn, Director, Finance & Operations
Craig Stumpf-Allen, Director, Grants & Community Engagement
craig@ecfoundation.org
Carol Watson, Director, Communications
cwatson@ecfoundation.org
Awards:
• Belcourt Brosseau Métis Awards, Student Awards
Eligibility: Métis students who live in Alberta *Deadline:* March 31; *Amount:* $2,000-$10,000

• Winspear Fund Scholarships for Advanced Classical Music, Student Awards
Eligibility: Students from the Edmonton area who will study classical music outside Alberta *Deadline:* March 31; *Amount:* $1,000-$8,000
• Ranald & Vera Shean Memorial Scholarships, Student Awards
Eligibility: Students from Edmonton or Northern Alberta who are studying classical music (violin or piano) *Deadline:* March 31; *Amount:* $1,000-$5,000
• Rose Margaret King Merit Awards, Student Awards
Eligibility: Students experiencing financial need who have attended school in Edmonton at some point between kindergarten & Grade 12 *Deadline:* May 15; *Amount:* $2,000-$5,000
• Don Howden & Jane Squire Howden Awards, Student Awards
Eligibility: Students experiencing financial need who have attended school in Edmonton at some point between kindergarten & Grade 12 *Deadline:* May 15; *Amount:* $2,000-$5,000
• Teri Taylor-Tunski Awards, Student Awards
Eligibility: Students experiencing financial need who have attended school in Edmonton at some point between kindergarten & Grade 12 *Deadline:* May 15; *Amount:* $2,000-$5,000
• Alexandra M. Munn Scholarships, Student Awards
Eligibility: Students from the Edmonton area aged 11-15 who demonstrate talent in classical music *Deadline:* May 15
• John & Andrea Wallin Awards, Student Awards
Eligibility: Students from the Edmonton area aged 11-15 who demonstrate talent in classical music *Deadline:* May 15
• Edmonton Refugee & Emerging Communities Awards, Student Awards
Deadline: May 15
• Nancy Fairley Scholarship, Student Awards
Eligibility: Edmonton public or Catholic students in an International Baccalaureate (IB) program; must be nominated by their IB English 30 teacher *Deadline:* May 31; *Amount:* $3,000
• Don and Norine Lowry Awards for Women of Excellence, Student Awards
Eligibility: Women of all ages studying water, power, finance, energy, accounting, healthcare, safety, &/or community relations *Deadline:* May 31; *Amount:* $1,000-$5,000
• Community Scholarships, Student Awards
Eligibility: Students from Edmonton &/or Northern Alberta who have a history of community involvement & who are experiencing financial need *Deadline:* June 15; *Amount:* $1,000-$4,000
• Al Maurer Awards
Eligibility: Public service employees working in Edmonton *Deadline:* August 31; *Amount:* $500-$2,500
• Charmaine Letourneau Scholarships, Student Awards
Eligibility: Deaf or hard of hearing students living in Alberta *Deadline:* August 31

Edmonton Community Legal Centre (ECLC)
10020 - 100 St., Edmonton AB T5J 0N3
Tel: 780-702-1725; *Fax:* 780-702-1726
intake@eclc.ca
www.eclc.ca
www.linkedin.com/company/561962
www.facebook.com/669360153096072
twitter.com/ECLCLaw
Previous Name: Edmonton Centre for Equal Justice
Overview: A small local organization
Mission: To provide free legal advice, representation, referral & legal education to low-income Edmontonians
Staff Member(s): 7; 62 volunteer(s)
Chief Officer(s):
Debbie Klein, Executive Director

Edmonton Community Networks (ECN)
c/o Tera-Byte Dot Com Inc., Terminal Level, 10004 - 104 Ave., Edmonton AB T5J 0K1
Tel: 780-413-1868; *Fax:* 780-413-1869
Toll-Free: 877-837-2298
support@ecn.ab.ca
www.ecn.ab.ca
Also Known As: Edmonton FreeNet
Overview: A small local charitable organization founded in 1994
Mission: To promote internet literacy by providing low cost internet access & training classes. It has installed access terminals in libraries & other public locations for free internet usage by the Edmonton community.
Member of: Edmonton Chamber of Commerce
Activities: Internet access; training & education; community building

Edmonton Composers' Concert Society (ECCS) / L'association des compositeurs d'Edmonton
#302, 11124 - 68th Ave., Edmonton AB T6H 2C2
Tel: 780-432-1618
Overview: A small local charitable organization founded in 1985
Mission: To sponsor concerts which feature Canadian composers
Member of: Alberta Motion Picture Industries Association
Finances: *Annual Operating Budget:* Less than $50,000; *Funding Sources:* The Canada Council for the Arts; Winspear Fund; SOCAN Foundation; Alberta Foundation for the Arts
Membership: 90; *Fees:* $25 full; $10 associate; *Member Profile:* Interest in contemporary music: composer, performer, auditor
Activities: Annual New Music Festival; "New Music Alberta" concert series; CD releases; *Library*
Chief Officer(s):
Piotr Grella-Mozejko, Artistic Director & General Manager

Edmonton Construction Association
10215 - 176 St., Edmonton AB T5S 1M1
Tel: 780-483-1130; *Fax:* 780-484-0299
www.edmca.com
www.linkedin.com/company/the-edmonton-construction-association
www.facebook.com/ECABuildsYEG
twitter.com/ECAbuildsYEG
Overview: A small local organization
Mission: To strengthen & advance the construction industry in Edmonton & Western Canada; To serve member firms
Membership: 1,047; *Fees:* $1,975 full; $650 associate; *Member Profile:* General contractors, trade contractors, manufacturers, suppliers, & other firms involved in the construction industry; *Committees:* Education; Finance & Risk Management; Governance & HR; Procurement; Stakeholder Strategies & Engagement; Trade Definitions
Activities: Providing education & networking opportunities
Chief Officer(s):
John McNicoll, Executive Director
Caroline Bowen, Director, Membership
Faizal Jessani, Director, Finance & Corporate Services
Matt Schellenberger, Director, Corporate Development
Jay Summach, Director, Education & Communications
Publications:
• Breaking Ground [a publication of the Edmonton Construction Association]
Type: Magazine
• On the Level [a publication of the Edmonton Construction Association]
Type: Newsletter
Profile: Association information, events, & courses; industry news

Edmonton Czech Language Society
8623 - 33 Ave., Edmonton AB T6K 2X9
Tel: 780-462-5817
Previous Name: Czech Cultural Club
Overview: A small local organization
Mission: To provide cultural & support services for the Czech community
Activities: Sports, cultural & social activities
Chief Officer(s):
Milos Hajek, President
Stanya Kresta, Secretary/Alternative

Edmonton Dental Assistants Association (EDAA)
4 Elbow Dr., Devon AB T9G 1M5
Tel: 780-987-2022; *Fax:* 780-987-2022
edaa@interbaun.com
www.edaa.ab.ca
www.facebook.com/431730580181670
Overview: A small local organization founded in 1972
Mission: To support & promote members; To address issues & concerns of the dental assisting profession
Membership: *Member Profile:* Dental assistants in Edmonton; *Committees:* Awards; Budget; Bylaws Review; CE Review; Conference; Dental Assistants Week; Dental Health Promotions; Member Services; Nominations
Activities: *Awareness Events:* National Dental Assistants Week, March
Chief Officer(s):
Debbie Hartt, President
Cynthia Clark, Director, Finance
Tara Jeethan, Director, Education
Sarah Nitz, Director, Social
Lisa Mueller, Director, Dental Health Promotions

Edmonton District Soccer Association (EDSA)
17415 - 106A Ave., Edmonton AB T5S 1M7
Tel: 780-413-0140; Fax: 780-481-4619
www.edsa.org
www.facebook.com/99060275311
twitter.com/EdmontonSoccer
Overview: A small local organization overseen by Alberta Soccer Association
Staff Member(s): 6
Chief Officer(s):
Mike Thome, Executive Director, 780-413-0140 Ext. 8

Edmonton Economic Development Corporation (EEDC)
World Trade Centre Edmonton, 9990 Jasper Ave. 3rd Fl., Edmonton AB T5J 1P7
Tel: 780-424-9191
Toll-Free: 800-661-6965
www.eedc.ca
www.linkedin.com/company/edmonton-economic-development-corp
www.facebook.com/EdmontonEconomicDevelopmentCorp
twitter.com/eedc
www.youtube.com/eedcedmonton
Overview: A small local organization
Mission: To foster entrepreneurship & economic growth in Edmonton
Activities: Overseeing the following divisions: Edmonton Tourism, Enterprise Edmonton, the Shaw Conference Centre & the Edmonton Research Park
Chief Officer(s):
Brad Ferguson, President & CEO
BFerguson@edmonton.com
Derek Hudson, Chief Operating Officer, 780-401-7681
dhudson@edmonton.com
Kevin Weidlich, Vice-President, Marketing & Communications, 780-917-7890
kweidlich@edmonton.com

Edmonton Tourism
c/o Edmonton Economic Development Corporation, World Trade Centre, 9990 Jasper Ave. 3rd Fl., Edmonton AB T5J 1P7
Tel: 780-424-9191
Toll-Free: 800-463-4667
info@exploreedmonton.com
exploreedmonton.com
www.facebook.com/EdmontonTourism
twitter.com/edmontontourism
instagram.com/exploreedmonton
Mission: Edmonton Tourism creates, implements, & evaluates tourism marketing initiatives for Greater Edmonton, working with both public & private tourism industry partners. It is a division of the Edmonton Economic Development Corporation (EEDC), an independent corporate entity established by the City to promote economic growth & development.
Chief Officer(s):
Maggie Davison, Vice-President, Edmonton Tourism, EEDC, 780-917-7623
mdavison@edmonton.com

Edmonton Epilepsy Association (EEA)
11215 Groat Rd. NW, Edmonton AB T5M 3K2
Tel: 780-488-9600; Fax: 780-447-5486
Toll-Free: 866-374-5377
info@edmontonepilepsy.org
www.edmontonepilepsy.org
Overview: A small local charitable organization founded in 1961
Mission: To ensure the well-being of persons with epilepsy through increased public awareness & education to further to address specific concerns both personal & social that these individuals experience
Member of: United Way
Affiliation(s): Canadian Epilepsy Alliance; Epilepsy Canada
Staff Member(s): 5
Membership: Fees: $15; Member Profile: Persons with epilepsy; caregivers; health/educational professionals
Activities: Awareness; Education; Support; Awareness Events: Epilepsy Month, Mar.; Speaker Service: Yes; Library: Open to public
Chief Officer(s):
Gary Sampley, Executive Director/COO
gary@edmontonepilepsy.org
Awards:
• Continuing Education Scholarships
Eligibility: Individuals who are entering or continuing in college or university studies & who are under a Canadian physician's care for epilepsy; Amount: 2 at $1000
• Employer of the Year
• Achiever of the Year
Publications:
• Focus on Epilepsy [a publication of the Edmonton Epilepsy Association]
Type: Newsletter; Frequency: s-a.
Profile: Association news, stories from members

Edmonton Executives Association
PO Box 4044, Edmonton AB T6E 4S8
Tel: 780-413-1979; Fax: 780-413-1975
director@eea.org
www.eea.org
Overview: A small local organization
Mission: To help business leaders in Edmonton by providing direct business, referrals & information.
Member of: International Executives Association
Membership: 179; Fees: $375 + GST initiation; $1366 + GST annual dues; Member Profile: Business owners, executives; membership is limited to one firm per business or professional sector

Edmonton Federation of Community Leagues (EFCL)
7103 - 105 St. NW, Edmonton AB T6E 4G8
Tel: 780-437-2913; Fax: 780-437-4710
www.efcl.org
www.facebook.com/yegCLs
twitter.com/efcl
www.instagram.com/yegcls
Overview: A medium-sized local organization founded in 1921
Mission: To serve as the parent body of 157 community leagues in Edmonton; To represent & promote community leagues
Finances: Annual Operating Budget: $100,000-$250,000; Funding Sources: Regional government
Staff Member(s): 10; 40 volunteer(s)
Membership: 148 institutional; 50,000+ individual; Fees: $425 institutional; Member Profile: Community leagues; Committees: Performing Arts; Planning & Development
Activities: Organizing events, projects, seminars, & workshops
Chief Officer(s):
Debra Jakubec, Executive Director
debra.jakubec@efcl.org
Joanne Booth, Senior Director, Operations & Membership
joanne.booth@efcl.org

Edmonton Fire Fighters Union
#200, 7024 - 101 Ave., Edmonton AB T6A 0H7
Tel: 780-429-9020; Fax: 780-420-1667
effu@edmontonfirefighters.com
www.edmontonfirefighters.com
Overview: A small local organization founded in 1917
Mission: EFFU is the offical lobbying & negotiating body for its members. Its designation is IAFF Local 209.
Member of: Canadian Association of Fire Fighters
Affiliation(s): International Association of Fire Fighters; Muscular Dystrophy Canada
Membership: 1000; Member Profile: Uniformed dispatchers, fire fighters, inspectors, investigators, mechanics, & support personnel in Edmonton
Activities: Firefighters Burn Treatment Society, Edmonton Chapter; fundraising events for various charities
Chief Officer(s):
Greg Holubowich, President
gregholubowich@edmontonfirefighters.com
Bud McCarthy, Treasurer
budmccarthy@edmontonfirefighters.com

Edmonton Folk Music Festival
PO Box 4130, 10115 - 97A Ave., Edmonton AB T6E 4T2
Tel: 780-429-1899; Fax: 780-424-1132
admin@efmf.ab.ca
www.edmontonfolkfest.org
www.facebook.com/EdmontonFolkMusicFestival
twitter.com/edmfolkfest
www.youtube.com/EdmontonFolkFest
Overview: A small international charitable organization founded in 1980
Mission: The festival in a not-for-profit society dedicated to bringing in the best of folk music from around the world.
Finances: Annual Operating Budget: $1.5 Million-$3 Million
Staff Member(s): 14; 2000 volunteer(s)
Membership: Member Profile: Must be a volunteer in good standing
Activities: Edmonton Folk Music Festival, August

Edmonton Health Care Citizenship Society See Action for Healthy Communities

Edmonton Heritage Festival Association (EHFA)
10125 - 157 St., Edmonton AB T5P 2T9
Tel: 780-488-3378; Fax: 780-455-9097
info@heritage-festival.com
www.heritage-festival.com
www.facebook.com/EdmontonHeritageFestivalAssociation
twitter.com/EdmHeritageFest
Overview: A small local charitable organization founded in 1976
Mission: To present an annual family oriented Multicultural Festival to raise public awareness, understanding & appreciation for the cultural diversity which characterizes our unique international community
Member of: Northwest Festivals Association; National Tour Association
Finances: Annual Operating Budget: $250,000-$500,000
Staff Member(s): 2; 1200 volunteer(s)
Activities: Internships: Yes; Speaker Service: Yes; Library: by appointment
Chief Officer(s):
Jack Little, Executive Director
jacklittle@heritage-festival.com
Wendy Carter, Volunteer Coordinator
wendy@heritage-festival.com

Edmonton Humane Society for the Prevention of Cruelty to Animals (EHSPCA)
13620 - 163 St. NW, Edmonton AB T5V 0B2
Tel: 780-471-1774; Fax: 780-479-8946
ehs@edmontonhumanesociety.com
www.edmontonhumanesociety.com
www.facebook.com/EdmontonHumaneSociety
twitter.com/edmontonhumane
www.youtube.com/user/EdmontonHumane
Also Known As: Edmonton Humane SPCA
Previous Name: Edmonton Society for the Prevention of Cruelty to Animals
Overview: A small local charitable organization founded in 1910
Mission: To protect animals from suffering; To promote life long committment to animal welfare & dignity
Member of: Canadian Federation of Humane Societies; Canadian Association of Animal Welfare Administrators
Affiliation(s): World Society for the Protection of Animals
Finances: Funding Sources: Fee for service contracts with the municipality of Edmonton & outlying municipalities
Membership: Fees: $5 senior; $20 individual; $25 family; $100 corporate; $5 junior
Activities: Adopts animals out to new homes; Lost & Found animal registry; Rural registry; investigates animal abuse; Awareness Events: Pets in the Park, July; Speaker Service: Yes; Rents Mailing List: Yes; Library: Open to public
Chief Officer(s):
Stephanie McDonald, Chief Executive Officer

Edmonton Immigrant Services Association (EISA)
#201, 10720 - 113 St., Edmonton AB T5H 3H8
Tel: 780-474-8445; Fax: 780-477-0883
www.eisa-edmonton.org
www.facebook.com/edmontonEISA
twitter.com/EISA_Edmonton
Overview: A small local charitable organization founded in 1976
Mission: To help immigrants & refugees adapt & fully integrate in Canadian society; to promote cross-cultural understanding; to initiate programs & services to bridge cultural gaps.
Member of: Alberta Association of Immigrant Serving Agencies
Affiliation(s): Northern Alberta Alliance on Race Relations
Finances: Funding Sources: Federal, provincial, municipal, individual donors
Activities: Interpretation/translation services; ESL classes; human rights education classes; school settlement support; summer camp; mentorship & host services
Chief Officer(s):
Rajiv Sinha, Chair
Janette De Cordova, Treasurer

Edmonton Inner City Housing Society (EICHS)
9430 - 111 Ave., Edmonton AB T5G 0A4
Tel: 780-423-1339; Fax: 780-423-1166
offmngr@telusplanet.net
www.eichs.org
Also Known As: The Intermet Housing Society of Edmonton
Overview: A small local charitable organization founded in 1983

Mission: To provide affordable housing to low-income & disadvantaged people of Edmonton's inner city & to facilitate tenant involvement in the management of their housing & society
Finances: *Annual Operating Budget:* $500,000-$1.5 Million; *Funding Sources:* Provincial government; city grants; donations; rental income
Staff Member(s): 14; 60 volunteer(s)
Membership: 100-499
Chief Officer(s):
Cecilia Blasetti, President
Cameron McDonald, Executive Director

Edmonton Insurance Association (EIA)
c/o Economical Ins. Group, #1600, 10250 - 101 St. NW, Edmonton AB T5J 3P4
Tel: 780-426-1234
www.edmontoninsuranceassociation.com
www.linkedin.com/groups?gid=4330904
Previous Name: Insurance Women of Edmonton
Overview: A small local organization founded in 1981
Mission: Non-profit, voluntary association dedicated to promoting education, fellowship and loyalty
Member of: Canadian Association of Insurance Women
Membership: *Fees:* $50
Chief Officer(s):
Candace Martin, President
Candace.Martin@economical.com

Edmonton Interdistrict Youth Soccer Association (EIYSA)
#307, 8925 - 51 Ave., Edmonton AB T5E 5J3
Tel: 780-462-3537; *Fax:* 780-444-4321
admin@eiysa.com
www.eiysa.com
Overview: A small local organization overseen by Alberta Soccer Association
Member of: Alberta Soccer Association
Staff Member(s): 6
Membership: 11 teams
Chief Officer(s):
Barrie White, President & COO
exdir@eiysa.com

Edmonton International Baseball Foundation (EIBF)
12314 - 76 St. NW, Edmonton AB T5B 2E4
Tel: 780-474-0795
webmaster@baseballeibf.ca
baseballeibf.ca
Overview: A small international organization founded in 1979
Mission: To help develop amateur baseball through financial assistance; to host international amateur baseball events
Affiliation(s): Baseball Canada; International Baseball Federation
Activities: Championships & world cups; four scholarships awarded annually
Chief Officer(s):
Ron Hayter, Chair

Edmonton International Film Festival Society (EIFFS)
#201, 10816A - 82nd Ave., Edmonton AB T6E 2B3
Tel: 780-423-0844
info@edmontonfilmfest.com
www.edmontonfilmfest.com
www.facebook.com/edmontonfilmfest
twitter.com/edmfilmfest
www.youtube.com/user/Edmontonfilmfest
Overview: A small international charitable organization founded in 2004
Mission: To produce a film festival for 9 days each autumn showing international, independent films in categories that include contemporary, world cinema, Canadian, documentary, alternative, shorts.
Staff Member(s): 15
Chief Officer(s):
Kerrie Long, Festival Producer

Edmonton Japanese Community Association
6750 - 88 St., Edmonton AB T6E 5H6
Tel: 780-466-8166; *Fax:* 780-465-0376
office@ejca.org
www.ejca.org
Overview: A small local organization
Mission: To help incorporate people of Japanese origin into Canadian society & ro preserve Japanese culture in Canada
Member of: National Association of Japanese Canadians
Membership: *Fees:* $20 single; $35 family
Activities: Cultural programs; Japanese language classes; clubs & groups; *Awareness Events:* Fall Bazaar, Nov. *Library:* Gordon Hirabashi Library
Chief Officer(s):
Stephanie Bozzer, President
Publications:
• Moshi Moshi [a publication of the Edmonton Japanese Community Association]
Type: Newsletter; *Frequency:* bi-m.

Edmonton Jazz Society (EJS)
11 Tommy Banks Way, Edmonton AB T6E 2M2
Tel: 780-432-0428; *Fax:* 780-433-3773
www.yardbirdsuite.com
www.facebook.com/YardbirdSuite
twitter.com/yardbirdsuite
Also Known As: Yardbird Suite
Overview: A small local organization founded in 1973
Mission: To present, promote & develop the performance of live jazz music in the city of Edmonton
Member of: Western Jazz Association
Membership: *Fees:* $30 student/senior; $50 regular; $300 silver; $500 gold
Activities: Presenting concerts & events, including the Littlebirds Educational Band Project
Chief Officer(s):
Francis Remedios, President

Edmonton Kiwanis Music Festival
14205 109 Ave., Edmonton AB T5N 1H5
Tel: 780-488-3498; *Fax:* 780-488-6925
musicfest@edmontonkiwanis.com
www.edmontonkiwanis.com
www.facebook.com/EdmontonKiwanisMusicFestival
Overview: A small local organization
Mission: To create opportunities for music students, musicians, actors, & music lovers
Activities: Organizing an annual music festival
Chief Officer(s):
Heather Bedford-Clooney, Executive Director, 780-488-3498
hbedford@shaw.ca

Edmonton Law Librarians Association *See* Edmonton Law Libraries Association

Edmonton Law Libraries Association (ELLA)
PO Box 47093, 62 Edmonton City Centre, Edmonton AB T5J 4N1
secretary@edmontonlawlibraries.ca
www.edmontonlawlibraries.ca
Previous Name: Edmonton Law Librarians Association
Overview: A small local organization
Mission: To provide professional services & to create networks between professionals in the law library field.
Membership: *Fees:* $25 active/affiliate; free for students; *Committees:* Head Start
Chief Officer(s):
Megan Siu, Chair
chair@edmontonlawlibraries.ca
Meetings/Conferences:
• Edmonton Law Libraries Association Annual General Meeting 2018, 2018
Scope: Provincial

Edmonton Library Association *See* Greater Edmonton Library Association

Edmonton Minor Soccer Association (EMSA)
Edmonton South Soccer Centre, 6520 Roper Rd., Edmonton AB T6B 3K8
Tel: 780-413-3672; *Fax:* 780-490-1652
edmontonsoccer.com
www.facebook.com/254791561239153
twitter.com/EMSAmain
instagram.com/emsamain
Overview: A small local organization overseen by Alberta Soccer Association
Member of: Alberta Soccer Association
Staff Member(s): 6
Membership: 89 teams

Edmonton Motor Dealers' Association (EMDA)
#200, 11729 - 105 Ave., Edmonton AB T5H 0L9
www.emdacars.com
Overview: A small local organization founded in 1953
Mission: To promote cooperation, discussion & the exchange of ideas & business methods between members of the association; To encourage the participation of members in industry & PR events, such as the Edmonton Motor Show, that enhance the image of industry in Edmonton; To represent the industry to government; To collect & disseminate information relative to the industry; To regulate the industry; to support educative initiatives
Member of: Motor Dealers Association of Alberta
Finances: *Annual Operating Budget:* $50,000-$100,000; *Funding Sources:* Auto show
Membership: 78; *Fees:* $120

Edmonton Musicians' Association (EMA)
#302, 10765 - 98 St., Edmonton AB T5H 2P2
Tel: 780-422-2449; *Fax:* 780-423-4212
info@afmedmonton.ca
www.afmedmonton.ca
Also Known As: Local 390, American Federation of Musicians
Overview: A small local organization founded in 1907
Mission: To provide services which protect their members, facilitate networking & allow them access to a pension plan & other resources, such as instrument/gear insurance
Member of: American Federation of Musicians
Membership: *Fees:* $150
Activities: Assistance in applying for P2 visa to work in the U.S.
Chief Officer(s):
E. Eddy Bayens, President
Edith Stacey, Office Manager

Edmonton Numismatic Society
PO Box 78057, Stn. Collingwood, Edmonton AB T5T 6A1
Tel: 780-270-6312
www.edmontoncoinclub.com
www.facebook.com/EdmontonNumismaticSociety
twitter.com/ENSCoinClub
Overview: A small local organization founded in 1954
Membership: *Fees:* $15-$40 regular; $5-$20 junior; $15-$40 family
Chief Officer(s):
Marc Bink, President
Mitch Goudreau, Secretary
secretary_ens@yahoo.ca
Publications:
• The Planchet [a publication of the Edmonton Numismatic Society]
Type: Newsletter; *Frequency:* 10 pa; *Editor:* Joe Kennedy

Edmonton Opera Association
15230 - 128 Ave., Edmonton AB T5V 1A8
Tel: 780-424-4040; *Fax:* 780-429-0600
edmopera@edmontonopera.com
www.edmontonopera.com
www.facebook.com/EdmontonOpera
twitter.com/edmontonopera
Overview: A small local charitable organization founded in 1963
Mission: To develop & promote opera as a dynamic & progressive art form; To attract & challenge audiences & artists through a creative program of opera production & education
Member of: Opera Canada; Opera America; Canadian Actors' Equity Association
Finances: *Funding Sources:* Grants; fundraising; sponsorship; box office; individual & corporate donations
Staff Member(s): 15
Activities: Producing four operas produced per season; Giving lectures prior to each performance to educate the audience about opera; Organizing four opera brunches per season at local hotel with brief performances by each opera's principals; Offering four opera overtures per season which include a chance for the public to meet each opera's creative team; *Library:* Not open to public
Chief Officer(s):
Tim Yakimec, General Director
tim.yakimec@edmontonopera.com

Edmonton Persons Living with HIV Society *See* Living Positive

Edmonton Police Association (EPA) / Association de la police d'Edmonton
c/o Alberta Federation of Police Associations, 10150 - 97 Ave., Edmonton AB T5K 2T5
Tel: 780-496-8600; *Fax:* 780-428-0374
www.albertapolice.ca
Overview: A small local organization founded in 1972
Member of: Canadian Police Association
Affiliation(s): Alberta Federation of Police Associations
Finances: *Annual Operating Budget:* $500,000-$1.5 Million
Staff Member(s): 5
Membership: 1,100; *Member Profile:* Serving officers up to rank of staff sergeant

Activities: Labour relations; disciplinary representations; charity & welfare obligations

Edmonton Radial Railway Society (ERRS)
PO Box 76057, Stn. Southgate, Edmonton AB T6H 5Y7
Tel: 780-437-7721; Fax: 780-437-3095
info@edmonton-radial-railway.ab.ca
www.edmonton-radial-railway.ab.ca
www.facebook.com/edmontonstreetcar
twitter.com/yegstreetcar
Overview: A small national charitable organization founded in 1980
Mission: To collect, preserve & interpret the history & technology of street railways with particular emphasis on Edmonton's streetcar system
Member of: Canadian Museum Association
Affiliation(s): Association of Tourist Railroads and Railway Museums; Alberta Museums Association; Virtual Museum of Canada
Finances: Annual Operating Budget: $100,000-$250,000; Funding Sources: Municipal, provincial & federal governments; donations
60 volunteer(s)
Membership: 130; Fees: $20
Activities: Operating 2 historic street railway lines within Edmonton from May to Oct.; streetcar museum; streetcar chartering service; restoration, maintenance & operation of historic streetcars; Library: Edmonton Radial Railway Society Library
Chief Officer(s):
Hans Ryffel, President
president@edmonton-radial-railway.ab.ca

Edmonton Reptile & Amphibian Society (ERAS)
PO Box 52128, 10907 - 82 Ave., Edmonton AB T6G 1C0
Tel: 780-429-0934
www.edmontonreptiles.com
www.facebook.com/EdmontonREPTILES
twitter.com/EdmontonREPTILE
Overview: A small local organization
Membership: Fees: $36
Chief Officer(s):
Kelly Moffatt, Coordinator, Membership
memberships@edmontonreptiles.com
Awards:
• Annual ERAS Legacy Award
Recognizes outstanding efforts of a society member each year.

Edmonton Soaring Club (ESC)
Chipman AB
Tel: 780-363-3860
info@edmontonsoaringclub.com
www.edmontonsoaringclub.com
Overview: A small local organization founded in 1957
Mission: To promote soaring & provide enthusiasts with the means to practice soaring
Member of: Soaring Association of Canada
Affiliation(s): Alberta Soaring Council; other soaring clubs
Membership: Fees: Schedule available
Activities: Flying gliders; teaching how to fly; expeditions; social events

Edmonton Social Planning Council (ESPC)
#37, 9912 - 106 St., Edmonton AB T5K 1C5
Tel: 780-423-2031; Fax: 780-425-6244
edmontonspc@gmail.com
www.edmontonsocialplanning.ca
www.facebook.com/edmontonspc
twitter.com/edmontonspc
Overview: A medium-sized provincial charitable organization founded in 1940
Mission: To provide leadership within the community by addressing & researching social issues, informing public discussion & influencing social policy
Finances: Annual Operating Budget: $250,000-$500,000; Funding Sources: United Way of the Alberta Capital Region; Edmonton Community Foundation; Edmonton Community Investment Operating Grant; AB Gaming & Liquor Commission
Staff Member(s): 5; 54 volunteer(s)
Membership: Fees: Limited Income/Student $5; Associate $15; Individual $25; Corporate (Small) $50; Corporate (Large) $75; Committees: Finance; Policy; Advocacy; Board Development; Casino
Activities: Monitoring social issues & trends; Producing publications on a variety of social issues; Conducting surveys & presenting reports; Researching & analyzing policies; Partnering with other organizations to meet community needs; Providing public education; Advocating; Awareness Events: Lunch & Learn; Internships: Yes; Speaker Service: Yes; Library: ESPC Resource Library
Chief Officer(s):
Susan Morrissey, Executive Director, 780-423-2031 Ext. 353
Vasant Chotai, President

Edmonton Society for the Prevention of Cruelty to Animals
See Edmonton Humane Society for the Prevention of Cruelty to Animals

Edmonton Space & Science Foundation (ESSF)
11211 - 142 St., Edmonton AB T5M 4A1
Tel: 780-452-9100; Fax: 780-455-5882
info@telusworldofscienceedmonton.com
www.telusworldofscienceedmonton.com
www.facebook.com/EdmontonScience
twitter.com/twosedm
Also Known As: Telus World of Science - Edmonton
Overview: A small local organization founded in 1978
Mission: To inspire & motivate people to learn about & contribute to science & technology advances that strengthen themselves, their family & community
Finances: Annual Operating Budget: $3 Million-$5 Million; Funding Sources: Revenue; donations; grants
Staff Member(s): 82; 265 volunteer(s)
Membership: 5,000-14,999; Fees: Schedule available
Activities: Community courses; Mobile Astronomy program; Challenger Missions; Summer camps; IMAX films; full-dome shows; observatory; Library: by appointment
Chief Officer(s):
Alan Nursall, President & CEO

Edmonton Stamp Club (ESC)
PO Box 399, Edmonton AB T5J 2J6
Tel: 780-437-1787
www.edmontonstampclub.com
Overview: A small local organization founded in 1912
Mission: To promote & encourage all aspects of philately for the benefit of all members
Member of: Royal Philatelic Society of Canada; American Philatelic Society
Finances: Annual Operating Budget: Less than $50,000; Funding Sources: Membership dues; shows
Staff Member(s): 12; 10 volunteer(s)
Membership: 300; Fees: $30 individual; $40 family; Member Profile: Interest in stamp collecting
Activities: Meetings held twice a month; Junior Club; auctions; seminars; Awareness Events: National Show, 3rd weekend in March; Library
Chief Officer(s):
Fred Tauber, Secretary, Membership, 780-469-3034
Publications:
• ESC [Edmonton Stamp Club] Bulletin
Type: Newsletter; Frequency: Monthly
Profile: Online newsletter

Edmonton Symphony Orchestra (ESO)
9720 - 102 Ave. NW, Edmonton AB T5J 4B2
Tel: 780-428-1108
info@winspearcentre.com
www.edmontonsymphony.com
www.facebook.com/edmontonsymphony
twitter.com/edmsymphony
www.youtube.com/edmontonsymphony
Overview: A small local charitable organization founded in 1952 overseen by Orchestras Canada
Mission: To foster appreciation & enjoyment of live, professional orchestral music through presenting concert performances, educational & community programs
Member of: Edmonton Arts Council
Affiliation(s): International Alliance of Theatrical Stage Employees, Moving Picture Technicians, Artists & Allied Crafts of the US & Canada
Finances: Funding Sources: Government; Corporate & individual donations; Performance revenue
Staff Member(s): 48
Membership: Committees: Patron development; Community Relations; Educational Outreach
Activities: Education Concerts; Adopt-A-Player Program; Symphony Under the Sky festival; Library: Not open to public
Chief Officer(s):
Annemarie Petrov, Executive Director, 780-401-2500
annemarie.petrov@winspearcentre.com
Rob McAlear, Artistic Administrator, 780-401-2510
rob.mcalear@winspearcentre.com

Edmonton Telephone Historical Information Centre Foundation
See Telephone Historical Centre

Edmonton Trout Fishing Club
Edmonton AB
info@edmontontrout.ca
www.edmontontrout.ca
www.facebook.com/EdmontonTroutFishingClub
Overview: A small local charitable organization founded in 1953
Mission: To foster, instruct & promote the art of fly tying, fly casting, & the betterment of trout fishing among its members
Member of: Alberta Fish & Game Association
Finances: Funding Sources: Membership fees; auction
Membership: Fees: $40
Activities: Shares stream enhancement projects with Trout Unlimited

Edmonton Tumblewood Lapidary Club (ETLC)
11B St. Anne St., St Albert AB T8N 1E8
edmontonlapidary@gmail.com
www.edmontonlapidary.ca
www.facebook.com/EdmontonTumblewoodLapidaryClub
Overview: A small local charitable organization
Mission: To promote the lapidary hobby in Edmonton & surrounding areas.
Member of: Alberta Federation of Rock Clubs
Affiliation(s): Gem & Mineral Federation of Canada
Membership: Fees: $25 single; $35 family
Activities: Collecting, cutting, polishing & displaying rocks, gems & minerals; Speaker Service: Yes; Library: Not open to public

Edmonton Twin & Triplet Club (ETTC)
PO Box 809, Edmonton AB T5J 2L8
Tel: 780-455-5520
edmonton@multiplebirthscanada.org
www.ettc.ca
www.facebook.com/pages/Edmonton-Twin-and-Triplet-Club/103081349749564
twitter.com/EdmTwin_Triplet
Overview: A small local organization overseen by Multiple Births Canada
Mission: To provide moral support and guidance for parents, to promote an interest in, and supply information about multiple births.
Activities: Library:
Awards:
• The Edmonton Twin and Triplet Club Scholarship
Eligibility: Edmonton or area resident; full-time postsecondary student Deadline: December 31; Amount: $1,000 (8) or $500 (16)
Publications:
• The Twindow
Type: Newsletter; Frequency: 9 pa

Edmonton Weavers' Guild (EWG)
10139 - 87 Ave. NW, Edmonton AB T6E 2P3
Tel: 780-425-9280
www.edmontonweavers.org
www.facebook.com/156971051010759
Overview: A small local organization founded in 1953
Mission: To provide an opportunity for local weavers, spinners & dyers to meet, exchange ideas & learn; To foster inspiration & growth; To enhance public awareness of fibre arts through regular study groups, public classes, sales & demonstrations
Affiliation(s): Handweavers, Spinners & Dyers of Alberta; Guild of Canadian Weavers; Handweavers Guild of America
Finances: Annual Operating Budget: Less than $50,000; Funding Sources: Annual sale; provincial & city grants
Membership: 130; Fees: $50; Member Profile: Anyone with knowledge of or interest in spinning, weaving, dyeing
Activities: Classes; workshops; demonstrations; displays; Awareness Events: Annual Sale, 1st Sat. in Nov. Library: Guild Library
Publications:
• Webs & Wheels [a publication of the Edmonton Weavers' Guild]
Type: Newsletter; Frequency: 5 pa.

Edmonton Youth Orchestra Association (EYO)
PO Box 66041, Stn. Heritage, Edmonton AB T6J 6T4
Tel: 780-436-7932; Fax: 780-436-7932
eyo@shaw.ca
www.eyso.com
Overview: A small local charitable organization founded in 1952 overseen by Orchestras Canada

Mission: To provide young musicians with the opportunity to develop their orchestral skills & increase their knowledge & appreciation of music, while enriching the cultural life of the community through concerts & benefit performances
Member of: Orchestras Canada
Finances: *Funding Sources:* Government grants; Corporate sponsorship; Individual donors
Staff Member(s): 4
Chief Officer(s):
Michael Massey, Music Director

Edmonton Zone Medical Staff Association (EZMSA)
Edmonton AB
Tel: 780-735-2924; *Fax:* 780-735-9091
Overview: A small local organization
Mission: Represents physicians working in the Capital Region of Alberta (Edmonton) in a number of forums including the Regional Medical Advisory Committee, Physician's Liason Committee & the Minister of Health for Alberta
Finances: *Funding Sources:* Membership dues
Membership: *Member Profile:* Physicians; Oral Surgeons; Clinical doctoral laboratory scientists
Activities: Continuing education; Edmonton Zone Medical Staff Association Golf Tournament; Edmonton Doctor's Curling League; Annual banquet
Chief Officer(s):
Robert Broad, President, 780-735-2924
Laurie Wear, Administrator
laurie.wear@covenanthealth.ca

Edmonton's Food Bank
PO Box 62061, 11508 - 120 St. NW, Edmonton AB T5M 4B5
Tel: 780-425-2133; *Fax:* 780-426-1590
info@edmontonsfoodbank.com
www.edmontonsfoodbank.com
www.facebook.com/Yegfoodbank
twitter.com/yegfoodbank
www.instagram.com/yegfoodbank
Overview: A medium-sized local charitable organization overseen by Food Banks Alberta Association
Mission: To collect surplus & donated food for effective distribution, free of charge, to people in need in the community; To seek solutions to the causes of hunger
Member of: Food Banks Alberta Association; Food Banks Canada
Chief Officer(s):
Marjorie Bencz, Executive Director
Mark Doram, Director, Operations
dir.ops@edmontonsfoodbank.com
Suedelle Baudais, Coordinator, Administration

Edson & District Chamber of Commerce
221-55 St, Edson AB T7E 1L5
Tel: 780-723-4918; *Fax:* 780-723-5545
edsonchamber@gmail.com
www.edsonchamber.com
www.facebook.com/228445173932496
Overview: A small local organization founded in 1912
Mission: To be the voice of the business community, dedicated to the enhancement of trade & commerce in Edson.
Member of: Alberta Chamber of Commerce; Canadian Chamber of Commerce; Yellowhead Highway Association
Finances: *Funding Sources:* Membership fees; special events; annual campaign; government employment grants
Staff Member(s): 1
Membership: *Fees:* Schedule available based on number of staff; *Member Profile:* Financial; industry; retail; manufacturing; educational; service; hospitality; fitness, etc.
Activities: *Library:* Open to public
Chief Officer(s):
Wendy Holuboch, Executive Director
Awards:
• Small Business of the Year Award
• Volunteer of the Year Award
• Employee of the Year Award
• Best Service Award
• Corporate Citizen Award
• Parade Awards
• Trade Show Awards

Edson Association for the Developmentally Handicapped
See Supporting Choices of People Edson

Edson Friendship Centre
#13, 5023 - 3rd Ave., Edson AB T7E 1X7
Tel: 780-723-5494; *Fax:* 780-723-4359
efc99@telus.net
www.facebook.com/110865509072047
Overview: A small local charitable organization founded in 1986 overseen by Alberta Native Friendship Centres Association
Member of: National Association of Friendship Centre; Alberta Native Friendship Centres Association
Finances: *Annual Operating Budget:* $250,000-$500,000
Staff Member(s): 15; 30 volunteer(s)
Membership: 110; *Fees:* $3
Activities: *Library:* Resource Library; Open to public

Éduc'alcool
#1000, 606, rue Cathcart, Montréal QC H3B 1K9
Tél: 514-875-7454; *Téléc:* 514-875-5990
Ligne sans frais: 888-252-6651
info@educalcool.qc.ca
www.educalcool.qc.ca
www.facebook.com/279669212081870
twitter.com/educalcool
www.youtube.com/user/deuxtroisquatrezero
Aperçu: *Dimension:* moyenne; *Envergure:* provinciale; Organisme sans but lucratif; fondée en 1989
Mission: Promouvoir la consommation équilibrée et responsable de l'alcool par des activités d'éducation, de sensibilisation et de communication; coordonner les actions de différents organismes nationaux oeuvrant dans le même but
Affiliation(s): Conseil international sur les problemes de l'alcoolisme et des toxicomanies
Membre: *Critères d'admissibilite:* Associations professionnelles, organismes parapublics, individus interessés aux objectifs de l'organisme
Activités: Campagnes d'éducation, de prévention et d'information sur l'alcool
Membre(s) du bureau directeur:
Hubert Sacy, Directeur général
Prix, Bourses:
• Bourse Marie-Soleil Tougas

Education Assistants Association of the Waterloo Region District School Board (EAA)
465 Philip St., Waterloo ON N2L 6C7
Tel: 519-745-4221
Overview: A small local organization
Chief Officer(s):
Kiki Bamberger, President

Éducation physique et santé Canada *See* Physical & Health Education Canada

Education Safety Association of Ontario; Municipal Health & Safety Assn; Ontario Safety Assn. for Community & Healthcare *See* Public Services Health & Safety Association

Education Support Staff of the Ontario Secondary School Teachers' Federation - District 24 - Waterloo (ESS/OSSTF)
225 Centennial Ct., Kitchener ON N2B 3X2
Tel: 519-571-0331; *Fax:* 519-571-9288
www.d24.osstf.ca
Previous Name: Educational Support Staff Association
Overview: A small provincial organization
Mission: To represent education workers in the Waterloo region
Membership: 2,700+; *Member Profile:* Office, clerical & technical support staff for Waterloo Region District School Board; *Committees:* Political Action; Education Services; Status of Women; Human Rights
Activities: *Speaker Service:* Yes
Chief Officer(s):
Sherry Freund, President
sfreund@bellnet.ca

Education to Spread Compassion
Toronto ON
ariellasings@sympatico.ca
www.educationtospreadcompassion.weebly.com
www.facebook.com/educationtospreadcompassion
Overview: A small provincial organization
Mission: To use education to teach students to have compassion for animals; To convince the Ontario Ministry of Education to bring the Meatless Mondays initiative to all secondary & elementary public schools, as well as to develop & implement a compassionate all-inclusive curriculum

Education Wife Assault *See* Springtide Resources

Educational Computing Organization of Ontario (ECOO) / Organisation ontarienne pour la cybernétique en éducation
ON
communications@ecoo.org
www.ecoo.org
twitter.com/ecooWeb
Overview: A small provincial organization founded in 1979
Mission: To disseminate information to computer using teachers across the curriculum, from kindergarten to post-secondary education
Membership: 1,000-4,999; *Fees:* Schedule available
Chief Officer(s):
Mark Carbone, President
ecoopresident@ecoo.org

Educational Support Staff Association *See* Education Support Staff of the Ontario Secondary School Teachers' Federation - District 24 - Waterloo

Educators for Distributed Learning PSA (British Columbia) (EDLPSA)
c/o BC Teachers' Federation, #100, 550 West 6 Ave., Vancouver BC V5Z 4P2
Tel: 604-592-4263
bcedlpsa@gmail.com
bcedl.ca
Previous Name: British Columbia Educators for Distributed Learning Provincial Specialist Association
Overview: A small provincial organization
Mission: To promote distributed learning, as well as hospital-homebound instruction, to the public
Member of: BC Teachers' Federation
Chief Officer(s):
David Comrie, President
dcomrie@sd73.bc.ca

EduNova
#300, 1533 Barrington St., Halifax NS B3J 1Z4
Tel: 902-424-8274; *Fax:* 902-424-8134
info@edunova.ca
studynovascotia.ca
www.facebook.com/212866282085259
twitter.com/edunova_news
www.youtube.com/edun0va
Overview: A small provincial organization
Mission: To raise the profile of education & training expertise in Nova Scotia
Membership: 30+; *Member Profile:* Universities; Community college campuses; English-language school boards; Private language schools; Independent schools; Consultants & training partners
Chief Officer(s):
Wendy Luther, President & CEO, 902-424-4058
wendy@edunova.ca
Michael Hennigar, Director, Recruitment & Marketing, 902-424-8189
michael@edunova.ca
Natasha McNeil, Manager, Operations & Accounts, 902-424-8178
natasha@edunova.ca

effect:hope
#200, 90 Allstate Pkwy., Markham ON L3R 6H3
Tel: 905-886-2885; *Fax:* 905-886-2887
Toll-Free: 888-537-7679
info@effecthope.org
effecthope.org
www.linkedin.com/company/3068053
www.facebook.com/effecthope
twitter.com/effecthope
www.youtube.com/user/effecthope
Also Known As: The Leprosy Mission Canada
Previous Name: The Mission to Lepers
Overview: A medium-sized international organization founded in 1892
Mission: To provide care & support to leprosy patients in many parts of the world including India, Bangladesh, & Nigeria
Member of: Canadian Council of Christian Charities
Affiliation(s): The Leprosy Mission International
Finances: *Annual Operating Budget:* Greater than $5 Million; *Funding Sources:* Federal & provincial funding agencies; individual contributions
Membership: *Committees:* Audit
Activities: *Speaker Service:* Yes; *Library:* Open to public by appointment
Chief Officer(s):

Peter Derrick, Executive Director

Efile Agents & Tax Preparers Association of Canada *See* EFILE Association of Canada

EFILE Association of Canada (EAC) / Association de TED du Canada (ATC)
PO Box 20040, Kelowna BC V1Y 9H2
Fax: 866-511-6879
Toll-Free: 866-384-4066
swatson@efile.ca
www.efile.ca
Previous Name: Efile Agents & Tax Preparers Association of Canada
Overview: A medium-sized national organization founded in 1993
Mission: To facilitate the operation of tax practices; To communicate the concerns of members to the Canada Revenue Agency, federal & provincial ministries of revenue, & tax software providers; To request remediation; To promote the electronic filing of personal & corporate tax returns
Membership: *Fees:* $140 plus GST / HST; *Member Profile:* Tax practitioners, throughout Canada, from sole proprietors to large national firms
Activities: Meeting with senior managers of Canada Revenue Agency to discuss tax policies & administrative issues that affect tax practitioners; Lobbying for changes to facilitate the operation of tax practitioners; Encouraging member proficiency; Offering resources to members
Chief Officer(s):
Steve Watson, Executive Director
swatson@efile.ca
Publications:
• CRA (Canada Revenue Agency) Tax Centre Directory [a publication of the EFILE Association of Canada]
Type: Directory
• EAC / ATC Annual Submission to the CRA [a publication of the EFILE Association of Canada]
Frequency: Annually; *Price:* Free to EFILE Association of Canadamembers
Profile: Results of a survey of EFILE Association of Canada members to learn the issues that hinder their work
• Impact [a publication of the EFILE Association of Canada]
Type: Newsletter; *Frequency:* 3 pa; *Price:* Free to EFILE Association of Canada members
Profile: Association information updates plus issues in the tax & EFILE service industry

Egale Canada
185 Carlton St., Toronto ON M5A 2K7
Tel: 416-964-7887; *Fax:* 416-963-5665
Toll-Free: 888-204-7777
egale.canada@egale.ca
www.egale.ca
www.facebook.com/EgaleCanada
twitter.com/egalecanada
Overview: A medium-sized national organization founded in 1986
Mission: To advance equality & justice for lesbian, gay, bisexual & transgendered persons, & their families in Canada
Finances: *Funding Sources:* Donations
Membership: *Committees:* Executive; Legal Issues; Political Action; Fundraising; Equal Marriage; Intersections; Trans Caucus; Two-Spirited & People-of-Colour Caucus; International Affairs; Adopt-an-MP; Planned Giving; Finance; Bylaws & Policies; Nominations; Elections
Activities: Implementing the Safe Schools Campaign; Intervening before the Supreme Court of Canada; Appearing before federal Parliamentary Committees; Providing public education; Hosting an annual general meeting; Conducting surveys
Chief Officer(s):
Helen Kennedy, Executive Director

Egg Farmers of Canada (EFC) / Producteurs d'oufs du Canada
21 Florence St., Ottawa ON K2P 0W6
www.eggfarmers.ca
twitter.com/eggsoeufs
Previous Name: Canadian Egg Marketing Agency
Overview: A large national organization founded in 1972 overseen by Canadian Federation of Agriculture
Mission: To forcast demand for eggs; To promote eggs nationally; To develop national standards for egg farming
Member of: Canadian Federation of Agriculture
Affiliation(s): World Trade Organization (WTO)
Membership: 1,000 farm families

Chief Officer(s):
Peter Clarke, Chair
Tim Lambert, CEO

Église adventiste du septième jour au Canada *See* Seventh-day Adventist Church in Canada

L'Église anglicane du Canada *See* The Anglican Church of Canada

Église apostolique de Pentecôte du Canada inc. *See* Apostolic Church of Pentecost of Canada Inc.

Église catholique-chrétien Canada *See* Christian Catholic Church Canada

Église chrétienne (Disciples du Christ) au Canada *See* Christian Church (Disciples of Christ) in Canada

Église Luthérienne du Canada *See* Lutheran Church - Canada

Église méthodiste libre du Canada *See* Free Methodist Church in Canada

L'Église orthodoxe ukrainienne du Canada *See* Ukrainian Orthodox Church of Canada

Église presbytérienne au Canada *See* Presbyterian Church in Canada

L'Église Réformée du Québec (ERQ) / The Reformed Church of Québec. (RCQ)
1355 boul René-Lévesque ouest, Montréal QC H3G 1T3
Tél: 514-767-3165
info@erq.qc.ca
erq.qc.ca
www.facebook.com/jeunesse.erq
Nom précédent: Église Réformée St-Jean
Aperçu: *Dimension:* moyenne; *Envergure:* provinciale
Affiliation(s): Christian Reformed Church; Presbyterian Church of North America
Membre(s) du bureau directeur:
Jean Zoellner, Pastor

Église Réformée St-Jean *Voir* L'Église Réformée du Québec

L'Église Unie du Canada *See* United Church of Canada

Église Unie du Canada *See* United Church of Canada Foundation

EIC General Members Society *See* Canadian Society for Engineering Management

The EJLB Foundation
#1050, 1350, rue Sherbrooke ouest, Montréal QC H3G 1J1
Fax: 514-843-4080
general@fondationecho.ca
www.ejlb.qc.ca
Overview: A small local organization founded in 1983
Mission: Provides grants to organizations with areas of interest in mental health and the environment
Chief Officer(s):
Kevin Leonard, Executive Director
Awards:
• The EJLB Foundation Grant

Elbert Chartrand Friendship Centre
PO Box 1448, 1413 Main St. East, Swan River MB R0L 1Z0
Tel: 204-734-9301; *Fax:* 204-734-3090
Overview: A small local organization
Mission: To promote continuous public relations aimed at creating and developing mutual understanding and to improve relations between people of Indian descent and others

Eldee Foundation
c/o Bloomfield & Associates, #1720, 1080, Côte du Beaver Hill, Montréal QC H2Z 1S8
Tel: 514-871-9571; *Fax:* 514-397-0816
www.eldeefoundation.ca
Overview: A small local charitable organization founded in 1961
Mission: To provides grants mostly for education & medical research to organizations primarily for the benefit of persons of the Jewish faith
Chief Officer(s):
Harry J.F. Bloomfield, President

Elder Abuse Ontario
#306, 2 Billingham Rd., Toronto ON M9B 6E1
Tel: 416-916-6728
Other Communication: Senior Safety Line: 1-866-299-1011
info@elderabuseontario.com

www.elderabuseontario.com
ca.linkedin.com/pub/elder-abuse-ontario/98/b57/a21
www.facebook.com/ElderAbuseOntario
twitter.com/ElderAbuseOnt
www.youtube.com/ElderAbuseOntario
Previous Name: Ontario Network for the Prevention of Elder Abuse
Overview: A small provincial charitable organization founded in 1989
Mission: To carry out The Ontario Strategy to Combat Elder Abuse, as mandated by the Government of Ontario; to create an Ontario that is free from abuse for all seniors
Finances: *Annual Operating Budget:* $500,000-$1.5 Million; *Funding Sources:* Ontario Trillium Foundation
Staff Member(s): 12
Membership: *Member Profile:* Individuals interested in, or working in, the field of elder abuse
Activities: Raising awareness about the neglect & abuse of older adults in Ontario; Engaging in advocacy activities; Providing educational & training opportunities; Disseminating information; Collaborating with other organizations; Providing a network of regional consultants; Supporting research in elder abuse; Establishing the Vibrancy campaign, featuring a touring exhibition & spokesperson; Providing networking opportunities; operating the Senior Safety Line, which operates 24/7, 365 days a year, in over 150 languages; *Awareness Events:* Elder Abuse Awareness Day; *Speaker Service:* Yes
Chief Officer(s):
Joe Bornstein, Chair
Maureen Etkin, Executive Director
maureenetkin@elderabuseontario.com
Mary Mead, Office Manager
admin@elderabuseontario.com
Publications:
• Elder Abuse Newsletter
Type: Newsletter; *Price:* Free with membership in the Ontario Network for the Prevention of Elder Abuse
• Ontario Network for the Prevention of Elder Abuse Annual Report
Type: Yearbook; *Frequency:* Annually

Elder Active Recreation Association (ERA)
4061 - 4th Ave., Whitehorse YT Y1A 1H1
Tel: 867-456-8252
office@elderactive.ca
www.elderactive.ca
Overview: A medium-sized provincial organization
Mission: To enhance the quality of life of Yukon seniors & elders by supporting them in living healthy lives with independence & dignity; to support seniors & elders in helping other seniors & elders to live full, active & healthy lives, & to develop active communities throughout the Yukon where seniors & elders can make positive lifestyle choices, exchange wisdom & connect with others in friendship, recreation & creativity. Physical office address: #302, 309 Strickland St., Whitehorse, YT Y1A 2J9.
Membership: *Fees:* $10; *Member Profile:* Yukoners 55 years of age and over
Chief Officer(s):
Glen Doumont, Office Coordinator
Jennifer Massie, Program Coordinator
programs@elderactive.ca

Elder Mediation Canada (EMC)
www.eldermediation.ca
Overview: A medium-sized national organization
Mission: To advance the practice of elder mediation in Canada; to improve the qualifications & effectiveness of mediators
Affiliation(s): Elder Mediation International Network; Family Mediation Canada
Membership: *Fees:* $60

Electric Mobility Canada (EMC) / Mobilité Électrique Canada
#11-530, 38, Place du Commerce, Iles de Soeurs QC H3E 1T8
Fax: 514-769-1286
info@emc-mec.ca
www.emc-mec.ca
www.linkedin.com/pub/al-cormier/15/985/559
www.facebook.com/240477292643669?ref=ts
twitter.com/EMC_MEC
www.youtube.com/user/ElectricMobilityCA
Overview: A small national organization
Mission: To promote electric mobility as a readily available and important solution to Canada's emerging energy & environmental issues

Canadian Associations / Electric Vehicle Council of Ottawa (EVCO)

Membership: 125; *Fees:* Schedule available; *Member Profile:* Manufacturers or industry personnel; Energy providers; Fleet managers; Not-for-Profit Organizations & Academics; Supporters; Associate Members; *Committees:* Government Relations; Working Group on PEV Readiness; Electric Bus
Activities: Annual conference, newsletter, webinars; *Awareness Events:* National Drive Electric Week
Chief Officer(s):
Chantal Guimont, President & CEO, 514-916-4165
chantal.guimont@emc-mec.ca
Marie-Andrée Émond, Coordinator, Member Services, 514-916-0553
m.a.emond@emc-mec.ca
Meetings/Conferences:
• 10th Annual Electric Vehicles Conference & Trade Show 2018, April, 2018, Westin Ottawa, Ottawa, ON
Scope: National
• Electric Mobility Canada 2018 Annual General Meeting, 2018
Scope: National

Electric Vehicle Council of Ottawa (EVCO)
PO Box 4044, Stn. E, Ottawa ON K1S 5B1
info@evco.ca
www.evco.ca
www.youtube.com/EVCOdotCA
Overview: A small local organization founded in 1980
Mission: To promote the use of electric vehicles as a viable transportation alternative
Membership: *Fees:* $20 regular; $5 student/academic/associate
Activities: Offering technical literature; Organizing displays, demonstrations, talks & competitions; Hosting monthly meetings; Participating in advocacy projects; *Library:* Electric Vehicle Council of Ottawa Print & Video Library
Chief Officer(s):
Gérard Gavrel, President
president@evco.ca
Darren Robinchaud, Board Secretary
drobichaud@evco.ca
David French, Treasurer
dfrench@evco.ca
Publications:
• EV Circuit
Type: Newsletter
Profile: Information for members of the Electric Vehicle Council of Ottawa

Electric Vehicle Society (EVS)
c/o #40, 55 Kelfield St., Toronto ON M9W 5A3
Tel: 416-788-7438
info@evsociety.ca
www.evsociety.ca
www.linkedin.com/company/electric-vehicle-society-of-canada
www.facebook.com/EVSociety
Overview: A medium-sized national organization founded in 1991
Mission: To investigate & promote clean transportation technologies
Membership: *Fees:* $20 students, spouses, & seniors; $30 adults; $50 families; $100 corporations; *Member Profile:* Engineers; Environmentalists; Enthusiasts for electric energy for propulsion
Activities: Providing a forum for member discussions; Examining modes of electric transportation
Chief Officer(s):
Emile Stevens, President
president@evsociety.ca
Publications:
• Electric Vehicle Conversion Manual: A Workshop Guide for High Schools
Type: Manual; *Number of Pages:* 85; *Author:* Neil Gover et al.
Profile: Contents include the move to sustainable transportation, getting started, basics of electrical energy & electricity, starting theconversion, & EV performance & evaluation
• EVSurge [a publication of the Electric Vehicle Society of Canada]
Type: Newsletter; *Frequency:* Bimonthly; *Editor:* Robert Weekley; *Price:* Free with Electric VehicleSociety of Canada membership
Profile: Electric Vehicle Society of Canada events, membership information, & articles about activities in the EV world

Electrical & Mechanical Engineering Association (EMEA) / Association du génie électronique et mécanique
PO Box 1000, Stn. Main, Borden ON L0M 1C0
Tel: 705-423-2598
EMEBranchGEM@forces.gc.ca
Www.emebranchgem.ca
www.facebook.com/eme.branchgem
twitter.com/emebranchgem
Overview: A small national organization founded in 1945
Mission: To uphold the EME Branch of the Canadian Forces; to represent the interests of the Branch to defense associations & the federal government
Member of: Conference of Defence Associations
Membership: *Member Profile:* Retired or active members of the EME Branch of the Canadian Armed Forces
Activities: Annual general meeting; seminars; regular meetings with guest speakers

Electrical Association of Manitoba Inc. (EAM)
#104, 1780 Wellington Ave., Winnipeg MB R3H 1B3
Tel: 204-783-4125; *Fax:* 204-783-4216
www.eamanitoba.ca
www.facebook.com/electricalassociationofmanitoba
twitter.com/eam1_eam
Previous Name: Manitoba Electrical League Inc.
Merged from: Electrical Service League; Manitoba Electrical Association
Overview: A medium-sized provincial organization founded in 1957 overseen by Canadian Electrical Contractors Association
Mission: To advise & inform all people of Manitoba on effective use of electricity toward maintenance & betterment of standards of living; to encourage cooperation of various branches of electrical industry in developing programs in support of common marketing objectives.
Membership: 211 corporate; *Fees:* Schedule available
Activities: *Rents Mailing List:* Yes
Chief Officer(s):
Gord Macpherson, Executive Director
Publications:
• Power Up [a publication of the Electrical Association of Manitoba]
Type: Newsletter

Electrical Construction Association of Hamilton (ECA Hamilton)
#102, 370 York Blvd., Hamilton ON L8R 3L1
Tel: 905-522-1070; *Fax:* 905-522-2199
ecah@on.aibn.com
www.ecahamilton.ca
Overview: A small local organization founded in 1946
Affiliation(s): Electrical Contractors Association of Ontario; International Brotherhood of Electrical Workers, Local 105
Finances: *Funding Sources:* Membership fees
Membership: 56; *Member Profile:* Electrical contractors
Activities: Apprenticeship training; negotiating collective agreements
Chief Officer(s):
Mark Lloyd, President

Electrical Contractors Association of Alberta (ECAA)
17725 - 103 Ave., Edmonton AB T5S 1N8
Tel: 780-451-2412; *Fax:* 780-455-9815
Toll-Free: 800-252-9375
ecaa@ecaa.ab.ca
www.ecaa.ab.ca
www.facebook.com/ECAAlberta
twitter.com/ECA_AB
Also Known As: ECA Alberta
Overview: A medium-sized provincial organization overseen by Canadian Electrical Contractors Association
Mission: To work towards increased contractors knowledge & efficiency; improved communication between industry sections; government liaison for training qualifications & regulations; overall improvement of the electrical industry
Membership: 500; *Fees:* Schedule available; *Member Profile:* Electrical contractors; *Committees:* Apprenticeship; Associate Liaison; Convention; Communications (Internal & External); ECAA Industry Appointment; Finance (Ways & Means); Fire Technical Council; Labour Relations; Labour Relations Union; Legislation; Membership; Nominations; PEC Discipline; PEC Education; PEC Marketing; PEC Practice Review; PEC Registration; Safety Codes - Electrical Technical Council
Chief Officer(s):
Sheri McLean, CAE, Executive Director
smclean@ecaa.ab.ca

Electrical Contractors Association of BC (ECABC)
#201, 3989 Henning Dr., Burnaby BC V5C 6N5
Tel: 604-294-4123; *Fax:* 604-294-4120
www.eca.bc.ca
www.youtube.com/ecabctv
Overview: A medium-sized provincial organization founded in 1952 overseen by Canadian Electrical Contractors Association
Mission: To promote use of electricity; to strengthen, encourage & promote electrical contracting industry; to promote functions assisting businessmen to become more efficient & profitable.
Affiliation(s): National Electrical Contractors Association
Finances: *Funding Sources:* Membership dues
Staff Member(s): 4
Membership: 225; *Fees:* Schedule available; *Member Profile:* Electrical contractors in the province of British Columbia; *Committees:* Education & Training; Electrical Heritage Society of BC; Governance; New Membership; Subcontract Program
Activities: *Internships:* Yes; *Speaker Service:* Yes; *Rents Mailing List:* Yes; *Library:* Not open to public
Chief Officer(s):
Deborah Cahill, President
Melissa Cornwell, Office Manager & Coordinator, Education

Electrical Contractors Association of London (ECAL)
4140 Gore Rd., RR#1, Dorchester ON N0L 1G4
Tel: 519-268-1060; *Fax:* 519-268-1061
Overview: A small local organization founded in 1961
Member of: Electrical Contractors of Ontario
Chief Officer(s):
Wayne Crockett, Manager
w.crockett@bell.net

Electrical Contractors Association of New Brunswick, Inc. (ECANB)
62 Durelle St., Fredericton NB E3C 0G2
Tel: 506-452-7627
eca.nb.ca
Overview: A small provincial organization founded in 1964 overseen by Canadian Electrical Contractors Association
Affiliation(s): Construction Association of New Brunswick Inc.; Canadian Construction Association; Construction Information Network; Fredericton Northwest Construction Association; IBEW Canada/International; Moncton Northeast Construction Association; New Brunswick Construction Safety Association; National Electrical Contractors Association; National Trade Contractors Coalition of Canada
Finances: *Annual Operating Budget:* $50,000-$100,000
Staff Member(s): 2
Membership: 21 corporate; *Fees:* Schedule available
Chief Officer(s):
David Ellis, Executive Director

Electrical Contractors Association of Ontario (ECAO)
#702, 10 Carlson Court, Toronto ON M9W 6L2
Tel: 416-675-3226; *Fax:* 416-675-7736
Toll-Free: 800-387-3226
ecao@ecao.org
www.ecao.org
www.linkedin.com/company/electrical-contractors-association-of-ontario
www.facebook.com/141086522621754
twitter.com/ecaontario
Also Known As: ECA Ontario
Overview: A medium-sized provincial organization founded in 1948 overseen by Canadian Electrical Contractors Association
Mission: To serve & represent the interests of the electrical contracting industry
Member of: Canadian Electrical Contractors Association; Ontario Joint Standard Practices Committee; Construction Bid Depository of Ontario
Affiliation(s): 13 Area Electrical Contractors Associations (ECAs); Council of Ontario Construction Associations; Provincial Advisory Committee for the Construction & Maintenance Electrician; Electrical Contractor Registration Agency (ECRA) for Master Electrician & Electrical Contractor Licensing
Staff Member(s): 6
Membership: *Fees:* $621.50 associate; schedule for direct; *Member Profile:* Electrical contractors with a contractual relationship with the International Brotherhood of Electrical Workers (IBEW); *Committees:* Standard Practices; Codes & Standards; Electrical Trade Bargaining Agency; Human Resources; Member Services; Power & Utility Sector; Public Relations & Communications
Activities: Making representations on behalf of the industry to government; Developing standard practices
Chief Officer(s):

Jodi Travers, Manager, Labour Relations, 800-387-3226 Ext. 3140
jtravers@ecao.org
Awards:
• ECAO Scholarships
To recognize the importance of post-secondary education; To encourage a high level of academic achievement *Eligibility:* Children or wards of salaried employees of ECAO member companies
• Douglas J. B. Wright Award
Awarded to honour individuals who demonstrate dedication & commitment to the electrical contracting industry
• R. H. (Hugh) Carroll Award
Awarded to honour member firms who best demonstrate a commitment to safety in the electrical contracting industry
Meetings/Conferences:
• Electrical Contractors Association of Ontario Annual Industry Conference 2018, 2018, ON
Scope: Provincial
Publications:
• Electrical Contractors Association of Ontario Calendar
Type: Yearbook; *Frequency:* Annually; *Accepts Advertising*
Profile: Contains important dates & member event listings
• Electrical Contractors Association of Ontario eNewsletter
Type: Magazine; *Frequency:* Monthly
Profile: Contains important updates for members
• Ontario Electrical Contractor [a publication of the Electrical Contractors Association of Ontario]
Type: Magazine; *Frequency:* 3 pa; *Accepts Advertising*
Profile: Contains important dates, member news, event listings, & articles

Electrical Contractors Association of Quinte-St. Lawrence
#2, 1575 John Counter Blvd., Kingston ON K7M 3L5
Tel: 613-541-0633; *Fax:* 613-541-0863
Overview: A small local organization
Affiliation(s): Electrical Contractors Association of Ontario
Chief Officer(s):
Jeff Green, Manager
greenj@bellnet.ca

Electrical Contractors Association of Saskatchewan (ECAS)
PO Box 21077, Regina SK 34V 1J4
Tel: 306-537-0982
www.ecasask.ca
Overview: A medium-sized provincial organization founded in 1958 overseen by Canadian Electrical Contractors Association
Mission: To voice the concerns of electrical contractors in Saskatchewan; To improve the electrical industry
Affiliation(s): Canadian Electrical Contractors Association; National Electrical Contractors Association; Saskatoon Electrical Contractors Association; Saskatchewan Construction Association; Electrical Contractors Association of BC; Saskatchewan Construction Safety Association; Electrical Contractors Association of Alberta; Electrical Contractors Association of Ontario
Membership: *Member Profile:* Companies that have a current Saskatchewan electrical contractors license; Suppliers, manufacturers, engineers, or affiliates that support the electrical industry; *Committees:* Apprenticeship & Training; Membership; Code Revisions; Standard Contract Practices; Public Relations; Annual Meeting & Convention
Activities: Communicating with members; Increasing contractors' knowledge & efficiency; Promoting exchange of ideas between all electrical contracting industry sections; Liaising with government for qualifications, training, & regulations
Chief Officer(s):
Doug Folk, Executive Director
dfolk@ecasask.ca
Awards:
• Electrical Contractors Association of Saskatchewan Scholarship
Eligibility: Individuals who are employees of a member company & have completed their third or fourth year apprenticeship
Deadline: December; *Amount:* $500
Publications:
• The Conduit [a publication of the Electrical Contractors Association of Saskatchewan]
Type: Newsletter

Electrical Contractors Association of Thunder Bay (ECATB)
910 Cobalt Cres., Thunder Bay ON P7B 5W3
Tel: 807-623-4174; *Fax:* 807-623-4572
ecatb@tbaytel.net
Overview: A small local organization
Member of: Electrical Contractors Association of Ontario
Chief Officer(s):
Karyn Sundell, Executive Vice-President

Electricity Distributors Association (EDA)
#1100, 3700 Steeles Ave. West, Vaughan ON L4L 8K8
Tel: 905-265-5300; *Fax:* 905-265-5301
Toll-Free: 800-668-9979
email@eda-on.ca
www.eda-on.ca
www.facebook.com/EDAMembersAssistSandy
twitter.com/EDA_ONT
Previous Name: Municipal Electric Association
Overview: A medium-sized provincial organization founded in 1986
Mission: To provide local electricity distribution companies with the valued industry knowledge, networking opportunities & collective action vital to members' business success
Finances: *Annual Operating Budget:* Greater than $5 Million; *Funding Sources:* Membership dues
Staff Member(s): 18; 100 volunteer(s)
Membership: 256; *Member Profile:* Public & privately owned electricity distributors in Ontario
Chief Officer(s):
Teresa Sarkesian, President & CEO, 905-265-5313
tsarkesian@eda-on.ca
Ted Wigdor, Vice President, Corporate & Member Affairs, 905-265-5362
twigdor@eda-on.ca
Justin Rangooni, Vice President, Policy & Government Affairs, 905-265-5325
jrangooni@eda-on.ca
Meetings/Conferences:
• Electricity Distributors Association 2018 Annual General Meeting, 2018
Scope: Provincial

Electricity Human Resources Canada (EHRC)
#405, 2197 Riverside Dr., Ottawa ON K1H 7X3
Tel: 613-235-5540; *Fax:* 613-235-6922
info@electricityhr.ca
electricityhr.ca
www.facebook.com/ElectricityHR
twitter.com/electricityHR
Previous Name: Electricity Sector Council
Overview: A medium-sized national organization
Mission: To work to strengthen the ability of the Canadian electricity industry to meet current & future needs for their workforce
Staff Member(s): 6
Membership: *Fees:* $1,000-$6,000
Chief Officer(s):
Michelle Branigan, Chief Executive Officer
Julie Aitken, Project Manager, Diversity & Inclusion

Electricity Sector Council *See* Electricity Human Resources Canada

Électro-Fédération Canada *See* Electro-Federation Canada

Electro-Federation Canada (EFC) / Électro-Fédération Canada
#300, 180 Attwell Dr., Toronto ON M9W 6A9
Tel: 905-602-8877; *Fax:* 416-679-9234
Toll-Free: 866-602-8877
info@electrofed.com
www.electrofed.com
www.linkedin.com/groups/3236862/profile
twitter.com/EFC_Tweets
Overview: A medium-sized national organization founded in 1995
Mission: To represent members provincially, federally & internationally on issues affecting the electro-technical business; To advance the electrical market
Member of: Canadian Chamber of Commerce
Finances: *Annual Operating Budget:* $3 Million-$5 Million; *Funding Sources:* Self-funded by members
Staff Member(s): 17; 600 volunteer(s)
Membership: 260+; *Member Profile:* Companies that manufacture, distribute & service electrical, electronic & telecommunication products; *Committees:* National Advisory Council
Activities: Collecting & disseminating market data; Providing networking opportunities; Hosting annual conferences; Researching; Offering educational programs; Communicating with members; Promoting the industry, electrical safety, energy efficiency & sustainability; Conducting surveys; *Speaker Service:* Yes
Chief Officer(s):
Carol McGlogan, President & CEO, 647-260-3093
cmcglogan@electrofed.com
Susan Adler, Manager, Member Services, 647-258-7476
sadler@electrofed.com
Philip Lefrancq, Vice-President, Finance & Administration, 647-260-3086
plefrancq@electrofed.com
Awards:
• Industry Recognition Award (IRA)
Presented annually to an individual who has influenced the Canadian electrical and/or electronics industries, either as a current or retired industry delegate, or as an industry supporter.
• Annual Marketing Awards Program
This awards program is designed to recognize organizations demonstrating marketing excellence and innovation within the Canadian electrical manufacturing, distribution and electronics industry. *Eligibility:* Current EFC member
• Electro-Federation Canada Scholarship Program
This awards program is designed to recognize organizations demonstrating marketing excellence and innovation within the Canadian electrical manufacturing, distribution and electronics industry. *Eligibility:* College & university students in second year
Deadline: May; *Amount:* $140,000
Meetings/Conferences:
• Electro-Federation Canada Conference 2018, 2018
Scope: National
Publications:
• InfoElectro [a publication of Electro-Federation Canada]
Type: Newsletter; *Editor:* John Jefkins

Electronic Commerce Council of Canada *See* GS1 Canada

Electronic Frontier Canada Inc. (EFC) / Frontière électronique du Canada
20 Richmond Ave., Kitchener ON N2G 1Y9
Tel: 905-525-9140; *Fax:* 905-546-9995
www.efc.ca
Overview: A small national organization founded in 1994
Mission: To ensure that the principals embodied in the Canadian Charter of Rights & Freedoms are protected as new computing, communications & information technologies emerge.
Affiliation(s): Electronic Frontier Foundation, San Francisco
Finances: *Funding Sources:* Membership fees & donations
Membership: *Fees:* $20 student; $40 regular
Activities: Research & education on issues such as the impact of information, computing & communication technologies on Canadian society; email discussion list; *Speaker Service:* Yes
Chief Officer(s):
David Jones, President
djones@efc.ca
Jeffrey Shallit, Vice-President/Treasurer, 519-888-4804
shallit@efc.ca
Richard Rosenberg, Vice-President, 604-822-4142
rosen@efc.ca

Electronic Recycling Association (ERA)
1301 - 34 Ave. SE, Calgary AB T2G 1V8
Tel: 403-262-4488
Toll-Free: 877-939-2783
www.era.ca
www.linkedin.com/company/electronic-recycling-association
www.facebook.com/ElectronicRecyclingAssociation
twitter.com/DonateRecycleIT
Overview: A medium-sized national organization founded in 2004
Mission: To reduce the negative environmental impact caused by electronic waste by providing computer donation & recycling services
Membership: *Fees:* $50 personal; $100 business; $75 education & health care facilities/non-profit; $200 government
Activities: Offering responsible equipment disposal options; Reusing unwanted computers & electronic equipment through recovery, refurbishment, & computer donation programs
Chief Officer(s):
Bojan Paduh, President

Electronics Import Committee (EIC)
PO Box 189, Stn. Don Mills, Toronto ON M3C 2S2
Tel: 416-595-5333
info@iecanada.com
www.iecanada.com

Overview: A small national organization overseen by The Canadian Association of Importers & Exporters
Mission: To represent members' interests before government & regulatory bodies.
Staff Member(s): 6
Membership: *Fees:* $1,175 regular corporate; $1,995 leadership circle corporate; *Member Profile:* Canadian Importers Association membership; *Committees:* Food
Activities: *Speaker Service:* Yes
Chief Officer(s):
Joy Nott, President

Electronics Product Stewardship Canada (EPSC)
#403, 550 Bayview Ave., Toronto ON M4W 3X8
Tel: 647-351-7415
info@epsc.ca
www.epsc.ca
twitter.com/EPSC_Canada
Overview: A medium-sized national organization founded in 2003
Mission: To design, promote & implement sustainable solutions for electronics waste
Staff Member(s): 2
Membership: 16 leading electronics manufacturers
Chief Officer(s):
Shelagh Kerr, President/CEO
shelagh@epsc.ca
Nathan B. MacDonald, Director, Environmental Programs
nathan@epsc.ca

Elementary Teachers' Federation of Ontario (ETFO) / Fédération des enseignantes et des enseignants de l'élémentaire de l'Ontario (FEEO)
136 Isabella St., Toronto ON M4Y 1P6
Tel: 416-962-3836; Fax: 416-642-2424
Toll-Free: 888-838-3836
www.etfo.ca
www.facebook.com/ETFOprovincialoffice
twitter.com/etfonews
www.youtube.com/user/ETFOprovincial
Merged from: Federation of Women Teachers' Associations of Ontario; Ontario Public School Teachers' Federation
Overview: A large provincial organization founded in 1998
Mission: To regulate relations between employees & employer; To advance the cause of education & the status of teachers & educational workers; To promote a high standard of professional ethics & a high standard of professional competence; To foster a climate of social justice in Ontario & continue a leadership role in such areas as anti-poverty, non-violence & equity; To promote & protect the interests of all members of the Federation & the students in their care; To cooperate with other organizations in Ontario, Canada & elsewhere
Member of: Ontario Teachers' Federation; Ontario Federation of Labour; Canadian Labour Congress
Finances: *Annual Operating Budget:* Greater than $5 Million
Staff Member(s): 100
Membership: 73,000; *Fees:* Statutory members 1.6% earnings; Associate membership $100; Retired members as an associate $15; *Member Profile:* Teachers; Occasional teachers; Educational workers; *Committees:* Aboriginal Education; Annual Meeting; Anti-Racist Education; Arts; Awards; Collective Bargaining; Disability Issues; Early Years; Education Support Personnel; English as a Second Language; Environmental; French as a Second Language; Gender Issues; Human Rights; Intermediate Division; International Assistance; Labour; Lesbian, Gay, Bi-sexual & Transgender Members; Men's Focus; New Members; Occasional Teacher; Occupational Health & Safety; Pension; Political Action; Professional Development/Curriculum; Professional Relations; Special Education; Status of Women; Teacher Education/Faculty Liaison
Chief Officer(s):
Sam Hammond, President
shammond@etfo.org
Karen Campbell, Vice-President
kcampbell@etfo.org
Susan Swackhammer, Vice-President
sswackhammer@etfo.org
Nancy Lawler, Vice-President
nlawler@etfo.org
Awards:
- Doctoral Scholarship
- Honorary Life Membership
- Rainbow Visions Award
Honorary life membership award
- Bursaries for Sons & Daughters of ETFO Members Entering a Faculty of Education
- Master's Scholarship - Women's Program
- Outstanding Role Model for Women Award - Women's Program
- Women Working in Social Activism on behalf of Women & Children - Women's Program
- Women Who Develop Special Projects in Science & Technology - Women's Program
- Aboriginal Women in Education Bursaries - Women's Program
- Doctoral Scholarship - Women's Program
- Master's Scholarship
- Women's Studies Scholarship
- Children's Literature Award
- Humanitarian Award for an ETFO Member
- Humanitarian Award for Non-ETFO Member
- Health & Safety Activist Award
- Member Service & Engagement Award
- New Member Award
- Native as a Second Language Qualification Bursary
- Writer's Award
- Writer's Award - Women's Program
- Anti-Bias Curriculum Development Award
- ETFO Bursaries (Designated Groups)
- ETFO Bursaries - Women's Program (Designated Persons)
- Arts & Culture Award
- Curriculum Development Award - Women's Program
- Curriculum Development Award
- Bev Saskoley Anti-Racism Scholarship
- Bev Saskoley Anti-Racism Scholarship - Women's Program
Meetings/Conferences:
- Elementary Teachers' Federation of Ontario 2018...And Still We Rise, February, 2018, Fairmont Royal York Hotel, Toronto, ON
Scope: Provincial
Description: Annual women's leadership conference
Contact Information: Conference Contact: Kelly Hayes, E-mail: khayes@etfo.org
- Elementary Teachers' Federation of Ontario 2018 Annual Meeting, August, 2018, Sheraton Centre Toronto Hotel, Toronto, ON
Scope: Provincial
Publications:
- @ETFO [Elementary Teachers' Federation of Ontario] eNewsletter
Type: Newsletter
- ETFO [Elementary Teachers' Federation of Ontario] Voice
Type: Magazine; *Accepts Advertising*; *Editor:* Izida Zorde
- ETFO [Elementary Teachers' Federation of Ontario] Stewards' Mailing
Type: Newsletter

Elevate NWO (ATB)
574 Memorial Ave., Thunder Bay ON P7B 3Z2
Tel: 807-345-1516; Fax: 807-345-2505
Toll-Free: 800-488-5840
info@elevatenwo.org
www.elevatenwo.org
www.facebook.com/169997633037453
twitter.com/elevatenwo
Previous Name: AIDS Thunder Bay
Overview: A small local charitable organization founded in 1985
Mission: To confront HIV/AIDS infection through prevention, support, education, & advocacy
Member of: Canadian AIDS Society; Ontario AIDS Network
Finances: *Funding Sources:* Government; Donations; Fundraising
Staff Member(s): 16
Membership: *Fees:* $10 basic; $25 supporting
Activities: Offering education, outreach, & harm reduction programs; Funding research; *Awareness Events:* World Hepatitis Day, July; Opening Doors HIV/AIDS Counselling Conference, Oct.; BINGO; *Speaker Service:* Yes; *Library:* Gabe Kakeeway Memorial HIV/AIDS Library; Open to public
Chief Officer(s):
Dennis Eeles, President
Holly Gauvin, Executive Director
hgauvin@elevatenwo.org
Publications:
- Front Line
Type: Newsletter; *Editor:* Selly Pajamaki
Profile: Contains association news & important event dates

Élèves ontariens contre l'ivresse au volant *See* Ontario Students Against Impaired Driving

Les éleveurs de dindon du Canada *See* Turkey Farmers of Canada

Les Éleveurs de dindons du Nouveau-Brunswick *See* Turkey Farmers of New Brunswick

Éleveurs de porcs du Québec
#120, 555, boul Roland-Therrien, Longueuil QC J4H 4E9
Tél: 450-679-0540; Téléc: 450-679-0102
leseleveursdeporcs@upa.qc.ca
www.leseleveursdeporcsduquebec.com
www.facebook.com/Porcduquebec
twitter.com/PorcQc
www.youtube.com/user/leporcduquebec
Nom précédent: Fédération des producteurs de porcs du Québec
Aperçu: *Dimension:* moyenne; *Envergure:* provinciale; fondée en 1966
Mission: A l'ordre du jour du Plan agroenvironnemental de la production porcine on trouve; l'application de plans de fertilisation sur toutes les fermes; la diminution des rejets de phosphore et d'azote pour éviter la surfertilisation; la réduction des odeurs; l'utilisation du lisier comme matière fertilisante; mise en place d'actions collectives.
Membre de: Canadian Pork Council
Affiliation(s): Union des producteurs agricoles du Québec
Membre: 3,560; *Comités:* Naisseurs; Finisseurs
Membre(s) du bureau directeur:
David Boissonneault, Président

Les Éleveurs de poulets du Nouveau-Brunswick *See* Chicken Farmers of New Brunswick

Éleveurs de volailles du Québec
#250, 555, boul Roland-Therrien, Longueuil QC J4H 4G1
Tél: 450-679-0530; Téléc: 450-679-5375
evq@upa.qc.ca
volaillesduquebec.qc.ca
Nom précédent: Fédération des producteurs de volailles du Québec
Aperçu: *Dimension:* moyenne; *Envergure:* provinciale; Organisme sans but lucratif; fondée en 1970
Mission: A pour mission l'étude, la défense et le développement des intérêts économiques, sociaux et moraux de ses membres; Favorise et stimule la mobilisation et la participation de ses membres tout en les consultant et en les informant; Développe et renforce la mise en marché collective des poulets et des dindons produits au Québec, en mettant en place des services garantissant le fonctionnement optimal du plan conjoint et des autres outils de mise en marché
Membre de: Union des producteurs agricoles; Producteurs de poulet du Canada; Office canadien de commercialisation du dindon
Finances: *Budget de fonctionnement annuel:* Plus de $5 Million
Membre(s) du personnel: 26
Membre: 800; *Critères d'admissibilté:* Producteurs de poulets ou de dindons
Membre(s) du bureau directeur:
Pierre-Luc Leblanc, Président

Elgin Association for Community Living *See* Community Living Elgin

Elgin Baptist Association
ON
elginbaptist@gmail.com
elginbaptist.wordpress.com
Overview: A small local organization founded in 1874 overseen by Canadian Baptists of Ontario and Quebec
Mission: To bring together Baptist churches & to promote the interests of the members
Member of: Canadian Baptists of Ontario & Quebec; Canadian Baptist Ministries; Baptist World Alliance
Membership: 8 churches; *Member Profile:* Baptist churches in Elgin County
Chief Officer(s):
Margaret Bell, Moderator

Elgin-St.Thomas United Way Services *See* United Way Elgin-St. Thomas

Eli Bay Relaxation Response Institute
226 Wychwood Ave., Toronto ON M6C 2T3
Tel: 416-932-2784
Other Communication: Presentation & Workshop e-mail: info@kmprod.com
www.elibay.com
Also Known As: The Relaxation Response Ltd.
Overview: A small local organization founded in 1978

Mission: To empower individuals & organizations with mind-body skills proven to effectively release stress anywhere & anytime
Finances: *Annual Operating Budget:* $250,000-$500,000
Activities: Training, keynotes & A/V resources for stress control & change management; *Speaker Service:* Yes
Chief Officer(s):
Eli Bay, Founder

Elie Chamber of Commerce
PO Box 175, Elie MB R0H 0H0
Tel: 204-353-2392; *Fax:* 204-353-2286
Overview: A small local organization

Elizabeth Fry Society of BC *See* Canadian Association of Elizabeth Fry Societies

Elizabeth Fry Society of Québec *Voir* Canadian Association of Elizabeth Fry Societies

Elizabeth House / Maison Elizabeth
2131, av Marlowe, Montréal QC H4A 3L4
Tel: 514-482-2488; *Fax:* 514-482-9467
questions@maisonelizabethhouse.com
www.maisonelizabethhouse.com
Overview: A small provincial charitable organization founded in 1968
Mission: To provide a continuum of specialized services to pregnant adolescents & women, mothers & babies, fathers, & families experiencing significant difficulty in adjusting to pregnancy & to their new roles as parents & caregivers; To support clients as they make choices & are directed to appropriate resources either in-house or in the community; To serve the anglophone community throughout the province of Quebec
Activities: Rehabilitation Services; Pre-Natal and Mother-Baby Programs; Semi-Supervised and Transitional Apartment ProgramsSupported independent Living; Family Assistance Program; Education Programs; Child Stimulation Program; Summer Day Camp
Chief Officer(s):
Linda Schachtler, Executive Director
linda.schachtler.elizabeth@ssss.gouv.qc.ca

Elk Point Chamber of Commerce
PO Box 639, Elk Point AB T0A 1A0
Tel: 780-724-3810; *Fax:* 780-724-2762
www.elkpoint.ca/chamber-of-commerce
Overview: A small local organization
Mission: To promote the business sector of Elk Point
Membership: 41
Chief Officer(s):
Vicki Brooker, Secretary

Elk Valley Society for Community Living (EVSCL)
PO Box 1464, Fernie BC V0B 1M0
Tel: 250-423-7635
cmp@telus.net
Previous Name: Elk Valley Society for the Handicapped
Overview: A small local charitable organization
Member of: Kootenay Regional Society for Community Living
Affiliation(s): B.C. Association for Community Living
Membership: 17; *Member Profile:* People with special needs, their families & advocates; *Committees:* Housing; Education; Fundraising; Summer Program
Activities: Summer program for children with special needs; advocate for integration of special needs into schools, community activities

Elk Valley Society for the Handicapped *See* Elk Valley Society for Community Living

Elkford Chamber of Commerce
PO Box 220, 4A Front St., Elkford BC V0B 1H0
Tel: 250-425-5725
info@elkfordchamberofcommerce.com
www.elkfordchamberofcommerce.com
Overview: A small local charitable organization founded in 1981
Member of: Canadian Chamber of Commerce; BC Chamber of Commerce; Tourism Rockies
Finances: *Funding Sources:* Membership dues; grants
Membership: *Fees:* Schedule available; *Member Profile:* Interest in the promotion & development of the community of Elkford
Activities: Two annual festivals; Wilderness Classic Sled Dog Derby; Visitor Info Centre; Business Info Centre; Summer Job Bank; *Awareness Events:* Chamber Week; Small Business Week; Mining Week *Library:* Business Library; Open to public

Elkhorn Chamber of Commerce
PO Box 141, Elkhorn MB R0M 0N0
www.elkhornchamberofcommerce.ca
www.facebook.com/ElkhornChamber
Overview: A small local organization founded in 1899
Mission: To promote area businesses & the community
Membership: 39
Chief Officer(s):
Mark Humphries, President

Elliot Lake & District Chamber of Commerce
PO Box 81, Elliot Lake ON P5A 2J6
Tel: 705-848-3974; *Fax:* 705-848-7121
www.elliotlakechamber.com
Overview: A small local organization founded in 1958
Mission: To promote & improve trade & the economic, civic & social welfare of the Elliot Lake District
Member of: Ontario Chamber of Commerce; Algoma Kinniwabi Travel Association
Finances: *Funding Sources:* Membership fees
Activities: Business development; Small Business Awards; Fall Extravaganza; Spring Trade Show
Chief Officer(s):
Todd Stencill, General Manager

Elora Arts Council (EAC)
PO Box 3084, Elora ON N0B 1S0
Tel: 519-846-9638
eloraartscouncil@gmail.com
www.artscouncil.elora.on.ca
Overview: A small local organization founded in 1985
Mission: To support the arts in all displines, including visual art, music, writing, theatre & film, giving particular encouragement to emerging artists in the community.
Affiliation(s): Puppets Elora; Elora Poetry Centre; Elora Community Theatre; Gallery Music Group; Elora Centre for the Arts; Guelph Arts Council; Wellington County; Township of Centre Wellington; Ontario Trillium Foundation
Finances: *Funding Sources:* Ontario Trillium Foundation
Membership: *Fees:* $15 individual; $25 family/group; *Committees:* Art In Public Places
Activities: Juried art shows; Elora Writers' Festival; concerts
Chief Officer(s):
Barbara Lee, Chair
Melanie Morel, Treasurer

Elora Centre for Environmental Excellence *See* Elora Environment Centre

Elora Environment Centre
PO Box 1100; 75 Melville St., 2nd Fl., Elora ON N0B 1S0
Tel: 519-846-8464; *Fax:* 519-846-8464
Toll-Free: 866-865-7337
info@eloraenvironmentcentre.ca
www.ecee.on.ca
Previous Name: Elora Centre for Environmental Excellence
Overview: A small local charitable organization founded in 1993
Mission: The Centre a not-for-profit organization focused on providing leadership in community-based environmental initiatives for both urban & rural communities. Areas of experience include: energy efficiency, greenhouse gas reduction, water efficiency, sustainable transportation, environmental education. It is a registered charity, BN: 138373196RR0001.
Member of: Green Communities Canada
Affiliation(s): Ontario Environmental Network; Centre for Applied Renewable Energy; GreenPathways; several municipal governments & hydro-electric companies
Finances: *Annual Operating Budget:* $50,000-$100,000; *Funding Sources:* Fees from clients; Natural Resources Canada
Staff Member(s): 7
Activities: Home energy evaluations; NeighbourWoods tree steward program; *Speaker Service:* Yes
Chief Officer(s):
Jennifer McLellan, Chair
Matt Vermeulen, Acting General Manager
manager@eloraenvironmentcentre.ca

Elsa Wild Animal Appeal of Canada
PO Box 45051, 2482 Yonge St., Toronto ON M4P 3E3
Tel: 416-489-8862
info@elsacanada.com
www.elsacanada.com
Also Known As: Elsa Canada
Overview: A small national charitable organization founded in 1972
Mission: To help save endangered wildlife species in Canada

Finances: *Funding Sources:* Donations; membership fees; fundraising
Chief Officer(s):
Betty Henderson, President

Embalmers' Association *See* Ontario Funeral Service Association

Embroiderers' Association of Canada, Inc. (EAC)
c/o Membership Director, 168 Kroeker Ave., Steinbach MB R5G 0L8
www.eac.ca
Overview: A medium-sized national charitable organization founded in 1973
Mission: To preserve traditional techniques & promote new challenges in embroidery through education & networking; to offer courses in embroidery & certifies teachers.
Member of: International Council of Needlework Associations
Finances: *Funding Sources:* Membership dues; seminars fees
Membership: 1,500; *Fees:* Schedule available
Activities: Correspondence courses; exhibitions; competitions; awards; online store; *Speaker Service:* Yes; *Library:* Leonida Leatherdale Needle Arts Library; by appointment Not open to public
Chief Officer(s):
Beryl Burnett, President
president@eac.ca
Dianna Thorne, Treasurer
treasurer@eac.ca

Alberta - Calgary Guild of Needle & Fibre Arts
739 - 20 Ave. NW, Calgary AB T2M 1E1
www.cgnfa.ca
Chief Officer(s):
Anne Joy, President

Alberta - Edmonton Needlecraft Guild
PO Box 76027, Stn. Southgate, Edmonton AB T6H 5Y7
contacts@edmneedlecraftguild.org
www.edmneedlecraftguild.org
www.facebook.com/pages/Edmonton-Needlecraft-Guild/107443652618019

Alberta - Lakeland Needle Art Guild
Cold Lake AB
Tel: 780-594-5608

British Columbia - Arrowsmith Needle Arts
c/o Qualicum Beach Civic Centre, 747 Jones St., Qualicum Beach BC V9K 1S4
1waddell@telus.net

British Columbia - Campbell River Needlearts Guild
Campbell River BC

British Columbia - Comox Valley Needlearts Guild
c/o Berwick House, 1700 Comox Ave., Comox BC V9M 4H4
cvnaginfo@shaw.ca

British Columbia - Embroiderers' Guild of Victoria
Victoria BC
Tel: 250-386-7933
www.embroiderersguildvictoria.ca
www.facebook.com/embroiderersguildofvictoria

British Columbia - Island Stitchery Guild
Nanaimo BC
islandstitcheryguild.org

British Columbia - North Peace Needle Arts Guild
Fort St John BC

British Columbia - Okanagan Guild of Needlearts
PO Box 266, #101, 1865 Dilworth Dr., Kelowna BC V1V 9T1
www.ogna.org
Chief Officer(s):
Heather Fedick, President

British Columbia - Semiahmoo Guild of Needlearts
White Rock BC

British Columbia - Shuswap NeedleArts Guild (SNAG)
Tappen BC
Tel: 250-832-0972
shuswapneedlearts@gmail.com

British Columbia - Vancouver Guild of Embroiderers
Vancouver BC
vge.information@gmail.com
www.vgeweb.ca

Manitoba - Winnipeg Embroiderers' Guild
St. Mary's Rd. United Church, 613 St. Mary's Rd., Winnipeg MB R2M 3L8
wpgembguild@gmail.com
www.winnipegembroiderersguild.ca
Chief Officer(s):

Patty Hawkins, President
wegpres@gmail.com
N.B. - Chickadee Chapter of Needle Arts
Dieppe NB
N.B. - Embroiderers' Guild of Fredericton
c/o Stepping Stone Senior Centre, 15 Saunders St., Fredericton NB E3B 1M9
N.B. - Kingston Peninsula Stitchers' Guild
Kingston NB
Tel: 506-763-2470
Chief Officer(s):
Anne Titus, Contact
N.B. - Pleasant Valley Stitchers
c/o Belleisle Community Centre, 1648 Rte. 124, Springfield NB E5T 2J8
Tel: 506-839-2474
Chief Officer(s):
Mary McConchie, Contact
kmmcco@nb.aibn.com
NL - St. John's Guild of Embroiderers
St. John's NL
N.S. - Alderney Needlearts Guild
Dartmouth NS
N.S. - Marigold Guild of Needle Arts
c/o Cheryl Kienzle, 168 Teviot Pl., Valley NS B6L 4K8
marigoldguildofneedlearts.ca
Chief Officer(s):
Kim Fielding, President
N.S. - Stitchery Guild of Bedford
Bedford NS
N.S. - Town Clock Stitchers
Halifax NS
www.townclockstitchers.ca
Member of: Embroiderers' Association of Canada
Ontario - Cataraqui Guild of Needle Arts
#802, 829 Norwest Rd., Kingston ON K7P 2N3
cgna@quiltskingston.org
quiltskingston.org/cgna
Chief Officer(s):
Diane Dukoff, President
Ontario - Embroiderers' Guild of Peterborough
Peterborough ON
Tel: 705-742-2201
Ontario - Norfolk's Own Needle Arts Guild
c/o Jane Hunter, 374 - 13 St., RR#4, Simcoe ON N3Y 4K3
Chief Officer(s):
Jane Hunter, Contact, 519-426-6238
Ontario - Ottawa Valley Guild of Stitchery
c/o 6 Epworth Dr., Ottawa ON K2G 2L5
ovgs@hotmail.com
www.ovgs.ca
Ontario - Quinte Needlearts Guild
Belleville ON
Tel: 613-967-7917
Chief Officer(s):
Marg Whittleton, President, 613-476-7723
Ontario - Simcoe County Embroidery Guild
c/o Midhurst Community Centre, 24 Doran Rd., Midhurst ON L0L 1X0
Ontario - Toronto Guild of Stitchery
#1087, 7B Pleasant Blvd., Toronto ON M4T 1K2
tgsinfo@tgsweb.ca
tgsweb.ca
www.facebook.com/374104039360534
Member of: Embroiderers' Association of Canada, Inc.
Ontario - Tulip Tree Needlearts
Chatham-Kent ON
P.E.I. - Island Treasures Needleart Guild
55 Hillside Dr., Summerside PE C1N 6C2
Tel: 902-436-1525
Chief Officer(s):
Judy Bowser, President
judybowser@hotmail.com
P.E.I. - Lady's Slipper Needle Arts Guild
PE
Québec - Lakeshore Creative Stitchery Guild/La Guilde des Travaux á l'Aiguille du Lakeshore
c/o Stewart Hall, 176, ch du Bord-du-Lac, Pointe-Claire QC H9S 4J7
info@lcsg-gtal.ca
lcsg-gtal.ca
Chief Officer(s):
Rosemary Sookman, President

Saskatchewan - Bridge City Needlearts Guild
Saskatoon SK
info@bcng.ca
bcng.ca
www.facebook.com/pages/Bridge-City-NeedleArts-Guild/158192510870267
Chief Officer(s):
Maggie Sim, President
president@bcng.ca
Saskatchewan - Pine Needle Arts Guild
Nipawin SK
Saskatchewan - Regina Stitchery Guild
PO Box 785, Regina SK S4P 3A8
mail@reginastitcheryguild.ca
www.reginastitcheryguild.ca
www.facebook.com/pages/Regina-Stitchery-Guild/223276807685622
Yukon Guild of Needlearts
Whitehorse YT

Emil Skarin Fund
c/o The Senate, 150 Assiniboia Hall, University of Alberta, Edmonton AB T6G 2E7
Tel: 780-492-2268; *Fax:* 780-492-2448
www.senate.ualberta.ca/en/EmilSkarinFund.aspx
Overview: A small provincial charitable organization founded in 1976
Mission: To support humanities & arts projects of value to the public as well as to the University of Alberta (proposals originating outside Alberta will not be considered)
Finances: *Funding Sources:* Endowment
Chief Officer(s):
Derek Roy-Brenneis, Senate Director
derek.roy-brenneis@ualberta.ca

Emily Carr University of Art & Design Faculty Association (ECUADFA)
c/o Emily Carr University of Art + Design, 1399 Johnston St., Vancouver BC V6H 3R9
Tel: 604-844-3866; *Fax:* 604-844-3801
www.ecuadfa.org
www.facebook.com/ECUADFA
Overview: A small local organization
Mission: TO act as the bargaining agent for the faculty members of Emily Carr University of Art & Design (including sessional instructors, lecturers, adjunct faculty, regular faculty, & non-teaching faculty, such as counselors, librarians).
Member of: Federation of Post-Secondary Educators of British Columbia (FPSE)
Affiliation(s): Canadian Association of University Teachers (CAUT)
Chief Officer(s):
Rita Wong, President

Emmanuel International Canada (EIC)
PO Box 1179, 3967 Stouffville Rd., Stouffville ON L4A 8A2
Tel: 905-640-2111; *Fax:* 905-640-2186
Toll-Free: 866-269-6312
info@eicanada.org
www.eicanada.org
www.linkedin.com/company/emmanuel-international-canada
www.facebook.com/239293974881
twitter.com/EIC_stouffville
Previous Name: Emmanuel Relief & Rehabilitation International (Canada)
Overview: A large national charitable organization founded in 1983
Mission: To link caring Canadians with churches worldwide to transform lives in the most desperate places; To bring assistance to communities, families & individuals in needs
Member of: Canadian Council of Christian Charities
Finances: *Annual Operating Budget:* $1.5 Million-$3 Million; *Funding Sources:* Government; Donations
Staff Member(s): 14; 3 volunteer(s)
Membership: 1-99; *Member Profile:* Seven National Affiliates: Australia, Brazil, Canada, Malawi, The Philippines, The United Kingdom & The United States
Activities: Development, relief, rehabilitation & spiritual outreach programs; *Internships:* Yes
Chief Officer(s):
Richard McGowan, Executive Director, Canada
Publications:
• Emmanuel Relief & Rehabilitation International Annual Report
Type: Yearbook

Emmanuel Relief & Rehabilitation International (Canada)
See Emmanuel International Canada

Emmaus Canada
emmauscanada@sympatico.ca
www3.sympatico.ca/pcmax
Overview: A small national organization
Mission: To deepen & nurture members' faith
Affiliation(s): Archdiocese of Toronto
Chief Officer(s):
Claude Sam-Foh, Chair
Loretta Liu, Treasurer
Paul McAuley, Spiritual Director

Emo Chamber of Commerce
c/o Township of Emo, PO Box 520, 39 Roy St., Emo ON P0W 1E0
Tel: 807-482-2580; *Fax:* 807-482-2741
www.emo.ca
www.facebook.com/EmoChamber
Overview: A small local organization
Mission: To protect the interests of the business community
Member of: Northwestern Ontario Associated Chambers of Commerce
Membership: 30
Activities: *Awareness Events:* Spring Fever Days; Holly Daze
Chief Officer(s):
Dave Goodman, Vice-President
Mary Goodman, Treasurer

EMPHASE Mauricie-Centre-du-Québec
Trois-Rivières QC
Tél: 819-519-4273
Ligne sans frais: 855-519-4273
emphase.mauricie@gmail.com
www.emphase-mauricie-cq.org
www.facebook.com/wix
www.twitter.com/wix
Aperçu: *Dimension:* petite; *Envergure:* locale; Organisme sans but lucratif
Mission: EMPHASE est un organisme sans but lucratif qui vise à améliorer le bien-être personnel et social des hommes ayant subi des agressions sexuelles grâce à la réalisation d'activités et à la mise en place de services.

Empire Club of Canada
Fairmont Royal York Hotel, 100 Front St. West, Level H, Toronto ON M5J 1E3
Tel: 416-364-2878; *Fax:* 416-364-7271
info@empireclub.org
www.empireclub.org
www.linkedin.com/groups/Empire-Club-Canada-2488065
www.facebook.com/169851787973
twitter.com/Empire_Club
www.flickr.com/photos/empire_club
Overview: A small national organization founded in 1903
Mission: To present prominent speakers from professions such as businesses, labour, education, government & cultural organizations.
Membership: *Fees:* $75 adult; $40 senior student; $200 corporate
Chief Officer(s):
Noble Chummar, President

EmployAbilities
10909 Jasper Ave., 4th Fl., Edmonton AB T5J 3L9
Tel: 780-423-4106
employ@employabilities.ab.ca
www.employabilities.ab.ca
www.facebook.com/EmployAbilities
twitter.com/employabilities
Overview: A medium-sized provincial charitable organization
Mission: To promote & enhance employment & learning opportunities for persons with disabilities
Finances: *Funding Sources:* All levels of government; fundraising; donations
Chief Officer(s):
Ollie Triska, President

Employees Association of Milltronics - CNFIU Local 3005 / Association des employés de Milltronics (FCNSI)
PO Box 4225, Peterborough ON K9J 7B1
Tel: 705-745-2431; *Fax:* 705-741-0466
Overview: A small local organization founded in 1977
Chief Officer(s):
Baswick Al, President

Employees' Association Hammond Manufacturing Company Ltd.
c/o Hammond Manufacturing Co. Ltd., 394 Edinburgh Rd. North, Guelph ON N1H 1E5
Tel: 519-822-2962; *Fax:* 519-822-0715
Overview: A small local organization
Membership: 270; *Member Profile:* Employees of Hammond Manufacturing
Chief Officer(s):
Bill Robinson, President

Employees' Union of St. Mary's of the Lake Hospital - CNFIU Local 3001 / Association des employés, l'Hôpital Saint Mary's of the Lake (FCNSI)
340 Union St., Kingston ON K7L 5A2
Tel: 613-544-5220; *Fax:* 613-544-8527
Overview: A small local organization

Employers Center for Occupational Health & Safety of Quebec *Voir* Centre patronal de santé et sécurité du travail du Québec

Employers' Council of BC *See* Business Council of British Columbia

Employment & Education Centre (EEC)
PO Box 191, 105 Strowger Blvd., Brockville ON K6V 5V2
Tel: 613-498-2111; *Fax:* 613-498-2116
Toll-Free: 800-926-0777; *TTY:* 613-498-1610
info@eecentre.ca
eecentre.com/ticcs.php
Also Known As: 1000 Islands Credit Counselling Services
Overview: A small local organization founded in 1996 overseen by Ontario Association of Credit Counselling Services
Mission: To offer employment, debt, credit, & student loan counselling services to persons in Brockville & the 1,000 Islands region of Ontario; To provide resources about life skills, job searches, & financial management
Member of: Ontario Association of Credit Counselling Services
Finances: *Funding Sources:* Government of Canada
Activities: Helping persons find solutions to their money management issues, through debt repayment programs; Presenting workshops, such as budget planning courses; Offering cash flow analysis; *Library:* Employment & Education Centre Resource Centre; Open to public
Chief Officer(s):
Sherri Simzer, Executive Director
Deborah Alarie, Manager, Employment Services
deborah@eecentre.com
Blake McKim, Officer, Communications & Public Relations
blake@eecentre.com

Emunah Women of Canada
#18, 7005, rue Kildare, Côte Saint-Luc QC H4W 1C1
Tel: 514-485-2397; *Fax:* 514-483-3624
Toll-Free: 877-485-2397
emunahcanada@emunahcanada.org
www.emunahcanada.org
Also Known As: Mizrachi Hapoel Hamizrachi Women's Organization of Canada
Overview: A small local charitable organization founded in 1943
Mission: To provide social welfare services to cildren
Member of: World Emunah; Canadian Jewish Congress; Canadian Zionist Organization
Membership: *Fees:* $36
Activities: *Speaker Service:* Yes
Chief Officer(s):
Aryella Weisz, President
aryella@emunahcanada.org

Toronto Chapter
#300, 333 Wilson Ave., Toronto ON M3H 1T2
Tel: 416-636-0036; *Fax:* 416-636-0039
toronto@emunahcanada.org
Mission: To strengthen religious consciousness, provide social care & religious & secular education for children & youth, with selective vocational & academic training; provides care for approximately 8,000 children in over 127 day care centres & nurseries across Israel; educates more than 2,000 girls in 6 high schools & supports 5 children's homes & youth villages for more than 600 children
Chief Officer(s):
Roberta Newman, Co-President
Alina Mayer, Co-President

En ligne directe *See* Ability Online Support Network

Enactus Canada
#800, 920 Yonge St., Toronto ON M4W 3C7
Tel: 416-304-1566; *Fax:* 416-864-0514
Toll-Free: 800-766-8169
info@acecanada.ca
www.acecanada.ca
www.linkedin.com/groups/ACE-Advancing-Canadian-Entrepreneurship-1180307
www.facebook.com/EnactusCanada
twitter.com/Enactus_Canada
www.youtube.com/user/EnactusCanada
Previous Name: Advancing Canadian Entrepreneurship Inc.; Canada's Future Entrepreneurial Leaders
Overview: A small national organization
Mission: Enactus is a national charitable organization that is teaching and igniting young Canadians to create brighter futures for themselves and their communities.
Staff Member(s): 10
Chief Officer(s):
Ian Aitken, Chair
Nicole Almond, President

Enasco - Institute of Social Service for Workers of Italian Origin *See* 50 & Piu Enasco

End Legislated Poverty (ELP)
#211, 456 West Broadway, Vancouver BC V5Y 1R3
Tel: 604-879-1209
Toll-Free: 866-879-1209
elp@vcn.bc.ca
www.vcn.bc.ca/~elp
www.facebook.com/127936363907270
Overview: A small local organization founded in 1985
Mission: To organize low income people; To educate on the need to end poverty; To encourage unity & cooperation between unpaid & paid working people; To include low income people from marginalized communities
Staff Member(s): 3; 250 volunteer(s)
Membership: 34; *Fees:* $1
Activities: *Library:* Resource Centre; by appointment

Enderby & District Arts Council (EDAC)
PO Box 757, Enderby BC V0E 1V0
contact@enderbyartscouncil.com
www.enderbyartscouncil.com
www.facebook.com/1455855661326469
Overview: A small local charitable organization founded in 1991
Mission: To organize & provide grants for such cultural activities as workshops, public art (such as murals and sculpture), lectures & entertainment in the Enderby area.
Member of: Okanagan Mainline Arts Council
Finances: *Funding Sources:* municpal support; BC Arts Council; donations
Membership: *Fees:* $10 adult; $3 youth; $18 community organization; $20 corporate

Enderby & District Chamber of Commerce
702 Railway St., Enderby BC V0E 1V0
Tel: 250-838-6727; *Fax:* 250-838-0123
Toll-Free: 877-213-6509
www.enderbychamber.com
www.facebook.com/EnderbyChamber
twitter.com/EnderbyChamber
Overview: A small local organization
Mission: To encourage, promote & develop the interest of business for the prosperity of the whole community
Member of: BC Chamber of Commerce
Finances: *Funding Sources:* Government; membership fees
Staff Member(s): 3
Chief Officer(s):
Corinne Van De Crommenacker, General Manager
corinne@enderbychamber.com
Lynne Holmes, President

Enderby & District Museum Society
PO Box 367, 901 George St., Enderby BC V0E 1V0
Tel: 250-838-7170
enderbymuseum@shaw.ca
www.enderbymuseum.ca
www.facebook.com/enderbymuseum
twitter.com/enderbymuseum
Overview: A small local charitable organization founded in 1973
Mission: To collect, preserve, research, exhibit & interpret a collection of representative objects & supporting archival material relevant to the human & natural history of Enderby & district
Affiliation(s): BC Museums Association; Archives Association of BC
Finances: *Annual Operating Budget:* Less than $50,000; *Funding Sources:* City & regional district; donations
Staff Member(s): 1; 14 volunteer(s)
Membership: 105; *Fees:* $10 individual; $15 family
Activities: Guest speakers; Teas; Displays for special events; Research facility; *Library:* Open to public

Ending Violence Association of British Columbia (EVA BC)
#1404, 510 West Hastings St., Vancouver BC V6B 1L8
Tel: 604-633-2506; *Fax:* 604-633-2507
evabc@endingviolence.org
www.endingviolence.org
www.facebook.com/EndingViolence.org
twitter.com/EndViolenceBC
Previous Name: British Columbia Association of Specialized Victim Assistance & Counselling Programs
Overview: A medium-sized provincial organization
Mission: To work as a provincial coordinating & networking organization for sexual assault centres, specialized victim assistance, & stopping the violence counselling programs; To assist those providing front line service
Finances: *Funding Sources:* Provincial Government
Staff Member(s): 13
Membership: 193 member programs; *Fees:* Schedule available
Chief Officer(s):
Tracy Porteous, Executive Director
porteous@endingviolence.org
Jennifer Woods, Co-chair
Bally Bassi, Co-chair

The Endometriosis Network
790 Bay St., 8th Fl., Toronto ON M5G 1N8
Tel: 416-591-3963
support@endometriosisnetwork.ca
www.endometriosisnetwork.ca
www.facebook.com/TheEndoNetwork
twitter.com/theendonetwork
Previous Name: Toronto Endometriosis Network
Overview: A small national organization founded in 1987
Mission: To increase public & professional awareness of endometriosis; To encourage professional medical research toward early diagnosis & cure of endometriosis; To provide support & education to sufferers & their families
Affiliation(s): Endometriosis Sisterhood
Finances: *Annual Operating Budget:* Less than $50,000; *Funding Sources:* Membership dues; donations
Membership: *Fees:* $30; *Committees:* Education; Finance; Fundraising
Activities: Offering support groups & information packages; Giving referrals; Holding public meetings
Chief Officer(s):
Katie McLeod, Director, Support
katie@endometriosisnetwork.ca

Endurance Riders Association of British Columbia (ERABC)
5068 - 47A Ave., Delta BC V4K 1T8
Tel: 604-940-6958
tobytrot@telus.net
www.erabc.com
Overview: A small provincial organization founded in 1989
Mission: ERABC fosters interest in the equestrian sport of endurance riding & promotes training & competition opportunities for beginning & advanced riders. It also assists in the development & preservation of courses or terrain suitable for endurance competitions.
Affiliation(s): Endurance Canada
Finances: *Annual Operating Budget:* Less than $50,000
Membership: 1-99; *Fees:* $30 adult; $60 family; $20 youth
Activities: *Awareness Events:* Ride Over the Rainbow
Chief Officer(s):
Murray Mackenzie, President
macheli@telus.net

Endurance Riders of Alberta (ERA)
AB
Tel: 780-797-5404
enduranceridersofalberta.com
www.facebook.com/269711222453
Overview: A small provincial organization founded in 1981
Mission: To promote education & good horsemanship through endurance riding
Member of: Alberta Equestrian Federation; Canadian Long Distance Riding Association
Affiliation(s): Canadian Long Distance Riding Association
Membership: *Fees:* $30 individual; $60 family; $25 junior

Canadian Associations / Énergie Solaire Québec

Activities: Host clinics; sanctions endurance events in Alberta
Chief Officer(s):
Owen Fulcher, President
erapresident@live.ca
Awards:
- High Points & Mileage Awards
- Darlene Keys Family Award
- Elaine Delbeke Memorial Partners Award
- Ron Janzen Memorial Sportsmanship Award

Énergie Solaire Québec
CP 540, Succ. St-Laurent, Montréal QC H4L 4V7
Tél: 514-392-0095
www.esq.qc.ca
Aperçu: Dimension: petite; *Envergure:* provinciale
Mission: Promouvoir l'utilisation de l'énergie solaire au Québec
Membre: *Montant de la cotisation:* 40$ individuel
Activités: Souper solaire; clinique solaire; concours Cocktail Transport

Energy Action Council of Toronto (EnerACT)
51 Wolseley St., 5th Fl., Toronto ON M5T 1A4
Tel: 416-488-3966; Fax: 416-203-3121
Overview: A small local organization
Mission: To accelerate the change in society's usage of energy away from environmentally inappropriate forms towards conservation & renewable energy; To encourage the further application of technologies which contribute to energy conservation & the wider use of renewable energy; To broaden society's understanding of the relationship between energy & the environment & the potential for meeting society's energy needs through conservation & renewable energy technologies; To assist in the development of public policies which encourage energy conservation & the use of renewable energy
Membership: *Fees:* Schedule available
Chief Officer(s):
Mark Fernandez, Project Coordinator
Fraser Stewart, Executive Director

Energy Council of Canada / Conseil canadien de l'énergie
#608, 350 Sparks St., Ottawa ON K1R 7S8
Tel: 613-232-8239; Fax: 613-232-1079
www.energy.ca
twitter.com/EnergyCouncilCA
Previous Name: World Energy Council - Canadian Member Committee
Overview: A medium-sized national organization founded in 1924
Mission: To foster a greater understanding of energy issues; To enhance the effectiveness of the Canadian energy strategy
Member of: World Energy Council
Staff Member(s): 3
Membership: 75+; *Member Profile:* Representatives from all facets of Canada's energy sector, including energy producers, energy users, equipment manufacturers, engineering firms, energy associations, financial organizations, legal firms, educational institutions & government department & agencies
Activities: Providing networking opportunities; Sponsoring forums & conferences; Disseminating current energy reports & information; Contributing to the development of the Canadian energy policy
Chief Officer(s):
Graham Campbell, President, 613-232-8239 Ext. 601
graham.campbell@energy.ca
Brigitte Svarich, Director, Operations, 613-232-8239 Ext. 602
brigitte.svarich@energy.ca
Max Arsenault, Coordinator, Administration & Activities, 613-232-8239 Ext. 603
max.arsenault@energy.ca
Meetings/Conferences:
- Energy Council of Canada 2018 Canadian Energy Industry: Updates & Insights, 2018
Scope: National

Energy Probe Research Foundation (EPRF)
225 Brunswick Ave., Toronto ON M5S 2M6
Tel: 416-964-9223; Fax: 416-964-8239
webadmin@eprf.ca
epresearchfoundation.wordpress.com
www.facebook.com/EnergyProbeResearchFoundation
Overview: A medium-sized national charitable organization founded in 1980
Mission: To educate Canadians about the benefits of conservation & renewable energy; To provide businesses, the government & the public with information on energy & energy-related issues; To help Canada secure long-term energy self-sufficiency
Affiliation(s): Energy Probe; Probe International; Environment Probe; Consumer Policy Institute; Urban Renaissance Institute; Environmental Bureau of Investigation; Three Gorges Probe; Canadian Environmental News Network
Finances: *Annual Operating Budget:* $1.5 Million-$3 Million; *Funding Sources:* Foundation grants; Donations; Publication sales & fees
Staff Member(s): 15; 10 volunteer(s)
Membership: 50,000 supporters
Activities: Policy research & education; *Internships:* Yes; *Speaker Service:* Yes; *Library:* Energy Probe Research Foundation Library; Open to public
Chief Officer(s):
Patricia Adams, President
Elizabeth Brubaker, Executive Director, Environment Probe
Awards:
- The Margaret Laurence Fund
Grants & scholarships are made to foster an understanding of peace & the environment upon which the fate of the planet rests
Eligibility: Recipients of the grants & scholarships are limited to students, authors, researchers, & publishers, working with the foundation in collaborative projects approved by the directors

Enfant-Retour Québec / Missing Children Quebec
#420, 6830, av du Parc, Montréal QC H3N 1W7
Tél: 514-843-4333; Téléc: 514-843-8211
Ligne sans frais: 888-692-4673
info@enfant-retourquebec.ca
www.enfant-retourquebec.ca
www.facebook.com/182144014082
twitter.com/enfantretourqc
Nom précédent: Réseau Enfants Retour Canada
Aperçu: Dimension: moyenne; *Envergure:* provinciale; Organisme sans but lucratif; fondée en 1985
Mission: Assister les parents à la recherche de leurs enfants portés disparus; aider également les professionnels, avocats, policiers, travailleurs sociaux impliqués dans une situation de disparition d'enfant ou de prévention contre une disparition; réseau international de communication et d'aide qui oeuvre également à sensibiliser la population au problème des enfants disparus et exploités par des affiches, émissions, documents
Membre de: Association of Missing & Exploited Children's Organizations (AMECO)
Finances: *Budget de fonctionnement annuel:* $250,000-$500,000
Membre(s) du personnel: 7; 230 bénévole(s)
Membre: *Montant de la cotisation:* Dor voluntaire
Activités: Défi annuel Bateaux-Dragons; Classique de golf; *Evénements de sensibilisation:* Journée nationale des enfants disparus, 25 mai; Journée provinciale d'identification d'enfants; *Stagiaires:* Oui; *Service de conférenciers:* Oui; *Bibliothèque:* Bibliothèque publique rendez-vous
Membre(s) du bureau directeur:
Yves J. Beauchesne, Président
Pina Arcamone, Directrice générale
Nancy Duncan, Directrice, Progreammes d'assistance aux familles

Enform
Head Office, 5055 - 11th St. NE, Calgary AB T2E 8N4
Tel: 403-516-8000; Fax: 403-516-8166
Toll-Free: 800-667-5557
customerservice@enform.ca
www.enform.ca
www.linkedin.com/company-beta/1035924
www.facebook.com/EnformSafety
twitter.com/enformsafety
www.youtube.com/user/EnformSafety
Also Known As: The Safety Association for the Upstream Oil & Gas Industry
Previous Name: Petroleum Industry Training Service
Overview: A large national licensing charitable organization founded in 2005
Mission: To improve the Canadian upstream oil & gas industry's safety performance; To prevent work-related injuries in the upstream oil & gas industry in Canada
Affiliation(s): Canadian Association of Geophysical Contractors (CAGC); Canadian Association of Oilwell Drilling Contractors (CAODC); Canadian Association of Petroleum Producers (CAPP); Canadian Energy Pipeline Association (CEPA); Petroleum Services Association of Canada (PSAC); Small Explorers & Producers Association of Canada (SEPAC); Petroleum Human Resources Council of Canada; Western Canadian Spill Services
Activities: Providing training courses; Offering saftey information; Promoting shared safety practices in the Canadian oil & gas industry; Providing the Small Employers Certificate of Recognition (SECOR), the Certificate of Recognition (COR) & the Petroleum Competency Program
Chief Officer(s):
Duane Mather, Chair
Cameron MacGillivray, President & CEO
Jeff Rose, Chief Operating Officer
Paula Campkin, Vice-President & Chief Safety Officer, Industry Development
Rick Shatosky, Vice-President, Accounting & Planning
Meetings/Conferences:
- Petroleum Safety Conference 2018, May, 2018, Fairmont Banff Springs, Banff, AB
Scope: National
Publications:
- Enform Insider
Type: Newsletter
British Columbia Office
#1240, 9600 - 93rd Ave., Fort St. John BC V1J 5Z2
Tel: 250-794-0100; Fax: 250-785-6013
Toll-Free: 855-436-3676
Genesee - Enform Ignition Training Facility
Genesee AB
Tel: 780-955-7770; Fax: 800-667-5557
Toll-Free: 800-667-5557
Nisku Training Facility
1803 - 11 St., Nisku AB T9E 1A8
Tel: 780-955-7770; Fax: 780-955-2454
Toll-Free: 800-667-5557
Saskatchewan Office
#208, 117 - 3rd St. NE, Weyburn SK S4H 0W3
Tel: 306-842-9822
Toll-Free: 877-336-3676

The Engineering Institute of Canada (EIC) / L'Institut canadien des ingénieurs (ICI)
PO Box 40140, Ottawa ON K1V 0W8
www.eic-ici.ca
www.linkedin.com/company/the-engineering-institute-of-canada
Overview: A large national charitable organization founded in 1887
Mission: To further the development of engineering in Canada; To stimulate the advancement of the quality & scope of Canadian engineering; To meet regularly with other engineering organizations & industries to promote understanding & improvement of the profession, the diffusion of engineering information & to provide Canadian representation in specialized engineering fields; To interact with government agencies & departments for the purpose of influencing decision making on matters relating to engineering & technology; To cooperate with the provincial engineering licensing bodies, The Canadian Council of Professional Engineering, The Association of Consulting Engineers of Canada, The Canadian Academy of Engineering & other engineering organizations in matters of common interest; To promote interaction with specific interest groups; To collaborate with universities & educational institutions
Affiliation(s): Engineers Canada; Association of Canadian Engineering Companies; Canadian Academy of Engineering; International Association for Continuing Education & Training (IACET); International Association for Continuing Engineering Education (IACEE)
Finances: *Annual Operating Budget:* $100,000-$250,000; *Funding Sources:* Membership fees; Con Ed quality, Assurance program, Career Site
Staff Member(s): 2; 20 volunteer(s)
Membership: 12 member societies; *Fees:* $2.50 per regular member of the member society; *Committees:* Executives, Council, Honours & Awards; History & Archives; Life Members Organization
Activities: Promoting the creation, exchange & dissemination of technical information; Organizing conferences & symposia & promoting continuing education for engineers; Supporting engineering student advancement; Maintaining an official Registry of Continuing Education Units & Professional Development Activities; *Library:* Archives at University of Ontario Inst.; Open to public
Chief Officer(s):
Guy Gosselin, Executive Director, 613-796-4750
ggosselin.eic@gmail.com
Mohammud Emamally, Administrative Officer
admin.officer@eic-ici.ca
Awards:
- EIC Fellows & Medals (Kennedy, Smith, Lo, Stirling & CPR)

- The Julian C. Smith Medal
- The John B. Stirling Medal
Established in 1987 in honour of Dr. John B. Stirling, a past president of the EIC & an outstanding engineer; medal is awarded in recognition of leadership & distinguished service at the national level within the institute &/or its member societies
- Canadian Pacific Rail Engineering Medal
Established 1987 in appreciation of CP Rail's contribution to the development of Canada; awarded in recognition of leadership & distinguished service at the local level within the institute &/or its member societies
- The Sir John Kennedy Medal
Established in 1927 in commemoration of the great services rendered in the field of engineering by Sir John Kennedy, a past president of the EIC; medal is awarded every two years by the council in recognition of outstanding merit in the profession or of noteworthy contributions to the science of engineering or to the benefit of the institute

Engineers Canada / Ingénieurs Canada
#300, Metcalfe St., Ottawa ON K1P 6L5
Tel: 613-232-2474; *Fax:* 613-230-5759
Toll-Free: 877-408-9273
Other Communication: Executive e-mail:
executive.office@engineerscanada.ca
info@engineerscanada.ca
www.engineerscanada.ca
www.linkedin.com/company/engineers-canada
www.facebook.com/EngineersCanada
twitter.com/engineerscanada
www.youtube.com/user/EngineersCanada
Previous Name: Canadian Council of Professional Engineers
Overview: A large national organization founded in 1936
Mission: To establish & maintain a common bond between constituent associations; To assist constituent associations to meet their common needs & those of their members by coordinating standards, procedures, & programs across Canada; To represent the engineering profession with respect to national & international affairs; To increase the profile & prestige of the engineering profession
Affiliation(s): World Federation of Engineering Organizations
Finances: *Funding Sources:* Membership dues
Membership: 10 provincial + 2 territorial associations representing 280,000 professional engineers; *Committees:* Board: Audit; Accreditation Board & Sub Committees; Qualifications Board; Compensation; Executive; Governance; Linkages. Operational: Affinity & Insurance Programs Advisory; Awards; Bridging Government & Engineers; Globalization; Public Affairs Advisory; Public Infrastructure Engineering Vulnerability; Equitable Participation in Engineering. National Coordination Groups: CEO Group; Environmental Officials; Admissions Officials; Practice Officials; Presidents Group; Discipline & Enforcement Officials; Communications Officials
Activities: Awards & Scholarhips; *Awareness Events:* National Engineering Month, March
Chief Officer(s):
Russ Kinghorn, MBA, FEC, P.Eng, President
Stephanie Price, P.Eng., CAE, Interim Cheif Executive Officer
stephanie.price@engineerscanada.ca
Colin Brown, PMP, CPC, ELI-M, Vice-President, Operations
colin.brown@engineerscanada.ca
Jeanette M. Southwood, M.A.Sc., P.Eng., Vice-President, Strategy & Partnerships
jeanette.southwood@engineerscanada.ca
Awards:
- Meritorious Service Award for Professional Service
For outstanding contribution to a professional, consulting or technical engineering association or society in Canada
- Gold Medal Award
- Meritorious Service Award for Community Service
Awarded for exemplary voluntary contribution to a community organization or humanitarian endeavour
- Young Engineer Achievement Award
Awarded for outstanding contribution in a field of engineering by an engineer 35 years of age or younger
- Medal for Distinction in Engineering Education
Awarded for exemplary contribution to engineering teaching at a Canadian University
- Gold Medal Award
Awarded for exceptional individual achievement & distinction in a field of engineering
- Gold Medal Student Award
- National Award for an Engineering Project or Achievement
- Engineers Canada Fellowship

Meetings/Conferences:
- Engineers Canada Board, Annual & Executive Committee Meetings 2018, May, 2018, Saskatoon, SK
Scope: National
Publications:
- Engineers Canada Newsletter
Type: Newsletter

Engineers Canada (EC) / Ingénieurs Canada (IC)
#1100, 180 Elgin St., Ottawa ON K2P 2K3
Tel: 613-232-2474; *Fax:* 613-230-5759
Other Communication: communications@engineerscanada.ca
info@engineerscanada.ca
www.engineerscanada.ca
www.linkedin.com/company/engineers-canada
www.facebook.com/EngineersCanada
twitter.com/engineerscanada
www.youtube.com/user/EngineersCanada
Overview: A small national organization founded in 1936
Mission: Regulates the practice of engineering in Canada and license the country's more than 160,000 professional engineers.
Member of: Canadian Network of National Associations of Regulators
Activities: *Awareness Events:* National Engineering Month, March
Chief Officer(s):
Kim Allen, Chief Executive Officer
Kim.allen@engineerscanada.ca
Marc Bourgeois, Director, Communications & Public Affairs
marc.bourgeois@engineerscanada.ca
Publications:
- Engineering on the Hill
Type: Newlsetter; *Frequency:* Semiannually
Profile: Reports on issues on Parliament Hill of interest to the engineering profession.

Engineers Nova Scotia
1355 Barrington St., Halifax NS B3J 1Y9
Tel: 902-429-2250; *Fax:* 902-423-9769
Toll-Free: 888-802-7367
info@engineersnovascotia.ca
www.engineersnovascotia.ca
Overview: A medium-sized provincial licensing organization founded in 1920 overseen by Engineers Canada
Mission: To establish, maintain & develop standards of knowledge & skill; qualification & practice; & professional ethics; To promote pthe value & proficiency of the Engineering profession
Member of: Engineers Canada
Finances: *Funding Sources:* Membership dues
230 volunteer(s)
Membership: 6,500; *Committees:* Executive; Professional Practice; Sustainability; National Engineering Week; Student Affairs; Professonal Development; Young Professionals; Annual General Meeting; Public Health & Safety; Women in Engineering; Complaints; Discipline; Finance; Awards; Nominations; Scrutineers; Lt. Gov Award Jury Panel
Activities: *Awareness Events:* National Engineering Week, March
Chief Officer(s):
Len White, P.Eng., Chief Executive Officer & Registrar
lwhite@engineersnovascotia.ca
Katherine MacLeod, P.Eng., President
Meetings/Conferences:
- Engineers Nova Scotia Conference & AGM 2018, 2018, NS
Scope: Provincial
Description: A business meeting with guest speakers for professional engineers & engineers-in-training in Nova Scotia

Engineers Without Borders (EWB) / Ingénieurs sans Frontières (ISF)
#601, 366 Adelaide St. West, Toronto ON M5V 1R9
Tel: 416-481-3696; *Fax:* 416-352-5360
Toll-Free: 866-481-3696
info@ewb.ca
www.ewb.ca
www.facebook.com/ewbcanada
twitter.com/ewb
www.youtube.com/user/ewbcanada
Overview: A small international organization
Mission: To promote human development through access to technology
Staff Member(s): 13
Chief Officer(s):
George Roter, CEO & Co-Founder
george@ewb.ca

Alex Conliffe, VP of Operations

Engineers Without Borders Quebec *Voir* Ingénieurs Sans Frontières Québec

Englehart & District Chamber of Commerce
PO Box 171, Englehart ON P0J 1H0
englehartchamber.weebly.com
Overview: A small local organization
Mission: To promote member businesses & the community
Membership: 50
Chief Officer(s):
Wayne Stratton, President

English Additional Language Learners Provincial Specialist Association
c/o BC Teachers Federation, #100, 550 West 6 Ave., Vancouver BC V5Z 4P2
Tel: 604-871-2283; *Fax:* 205-871-2286
Toll-Free: 800-663-9163
ellpsa.ca
twitter.com/ESLPSA
Overview: A small provincial organization founded in 1989
Mission: To improve & promote English as a second language learning
Member of: BC Teachers' Federation
Chief Officer(s):
Marc Tremblay, President
mtremblay@sd45.bc.ca

English Speaking Catholic Council (ESCC)
2005, rue St-Marc, Montréal QC H3H 2G8
Tel: 514-937-2301; *Fax:* 514-907-5010
escc@bellnet.ca
www.catholiccouncil.ca
Overview: A small local charitable organization founded in 1981
Mission: To represent Montréal's English-speaking Catholic community
Membership: *Committees:* Advisory; Communications; Community Animation; Education; Executive; Finance; Health & Social Services; Seniors; Social Issues; Young Adults
Activities: Organizing community events; Promoting research; Offering education
Chief Officer(s):
Anna Farrow, Executive Director
Suzanne Brown, Executive Secretary
Awards:
- Bishop Crowley Memorial Award
Awarded to a person, group, or organization that has contributed to or influenced Montreal's English-speaking Catholic community
Publications:
- English Speaking Catholic Council Annual Report
Type: Yearbook; *Frequency:* Annually

English-Language Arts Network (ELAN)
#708, 460, Sainte-Catherine ouest, Montréal QC H3B 1A7
Tel: 514-935-3312
admin@quebec-elan.org
www.quebec-elan.org
www.facebook.com/QCELAN
twitter.com/elanquebec
Overview: A medium-sized provincial organization founded in 2005
Mission: Québec-wide network of English-speaking artists from all disciplines to promote the sharing of expertise, ideas & resources
Affiliation(s): Québec Drama Federation; Québec Writers' Federation; Association of English Language Publishers of Québec
Staff Member(s): 4; 1 volunteer(s)
Membership: 800; *Fees:* $10-$50; *Member Profile:* Anglophone artists who work in Québec, including writers, visual artists, actors, musicians, filmmakers, playwrights, dancers, etc.; *Committees:* Professional Development Group; Outreach Group; Social Events Group
Activities: Resource sharing; collective promotion; professional development; arts advocacy; *Internships:* Yes
Chief Officer(s):
Guy Rodgers, Executive Director

Enokhok Development Corporation Ltd.
#200, 9405 - 45 Ave. NW, Edmonton AB T6E 6B9
Tel: 780-452-5784; *Fax:* 780-482-2267
Toll-Free: 866-452-5623
info@enokhok.com
www.enokhok.com
Overview: A small local organization founded in 1984

Mission: The company is a general contractor that also owns & manages rental property in Cambridge Bay, Kugluktuk and Gjoa Haven.

Enokhok Inn & Suits - Campbridge Bay
PO Box 103, Cambridge Bay NU X0B 0C0
Tel: 867-983-2532; *Fax:* 867-983-2271
info@enokhok.com

Les Enseignants et enseignantes retraités de l'Ontario *See* The Retired Teachers of Ontario

Ensemble contemporain de Montréal (ECM+)
3890, rue Clark, Montréal QC H2W 1W6
Tél: 514-524-0173; *Téléc:* 514-524-0179
info@ecm.qc.ca
www.ecm.qc.ca
www.facebook.com/135587246763
Aperçu: *Dimension:* petite; *Envergure:* locale; Organisme sans but lucratif surveillé par Orchestras Canada
Mission: Promouvoir la création de la musique canadienne par la performance, la formation et le recherche multidisciplinaire
Membre de: Orchestres Canada
Membre(s) du personnel: 7
Activités: *Listes de destinataires:* Oui
Membre(s) du bureau directeur:
Natalie Watanabe, Directrice générale
Véronique Lacroix, Directrice artistique

Ensemble vocal Ganymède
CP 476, Succ. C, Montréal QC H2L 4K4
Tél: 514-528-6302
contacter@evganymede.com
www.evganymede.com
Aperçu: *Dimension:* petite; *Envergure:* locale; fondée en 1991
Mission: Présenter le répertoire classique de la voix masculine; D'introduire dans l'imagerie populaire une autre vision de la communauté gaie
Membre(s) du bureau directeur:
Yvan Sabourin, Directeur

Entertainment Software Association of Canada (ESAC)
#408, 130 Spadina Ave., Toronto ON M5V 2L4
Tel: 416-620-7171; *Fax:* 416-620-7085
theesa.ca
www.facebook.com/EntertainmentSoftwareAssociationofCanada
twitter.com/ESACanada
www.youtube.com/TheESACanada
Overview: A small national organization
Mission: To advocate on behalf of its members before government committees; to provide research services to its members
Staff Member(s): 4
Membership: 21 companies
Chief Officer(s):
Jayson Hilchie, President & CEO

Entomological Society of Alberta (ESA)
Great West Life Bldg., Alberta Agriculture & Forestry, 9920 - 108 St., 8th Fl., Edmonton AB T5K 2M4
www.entsocalberta.ca/esa.htm
Overview: A small provincial organization founded in 1952
Mission: To foster the advancement, exchange & dissemination of the knowledge of insects in relation to their importance in agriculture, forestry, public health & industry
Member of: Entomological Society of Canada
Finances: *Annual Operating Budget:* Less than $50,000
Membership: 108; *Fees:* $20; $10 student/retired
Chief Officer(s):
Caroline Whitehouse, Treasurer
caroline.whitehouse@gov.ab.ca

Entomological Society of British Columbia (ESBC)
c/o Bob Lalonde, UBC Okanagan, Science Bldg., 1177 Research Rd., Kelowna BC V1V 1V7
entsocbc.ca
www.linkedin.com/groups/4760901/profile
www.facebook.com/groups/135038946598013
twitter.com/EntSocBC
Overview: A small provincial organization founded in 1902
Member of: Entomological Society of Canada
15 volunteer(s)
Membership: 230; *Fees:* $20 regular; $10 students; *Member Profile:* Professional; amateur; student entomologists
Activities: *Library:* Pacific Forestry Centre
Chief Officer(s):
Bob Lalonde, President
president@entsocbc.ca
Awards:
• Student Oral Presentation Awards
• Graduate Student Scholarship Competition
; *Amount:* 2 at $400
Meetings/Conferences:
• Entomological Society of British Columbia Annual General Meeting & Symposium 2018, 2018, BC
Scope: Provincial
Publications:
• Boreus [a publication of the Entomological Society of British Columbia]
Type: Newsletter

Entomological Society of Canada (ESC)
393 Winston Ave., Ottawa ON K2A 1Y8
Tel: 613-725-2619
entsoc.can@bellnet.ca
www.esc-sec.ca
twitter.com/CanEntomologist
Overview: A small national organization founded in 1863
Mission: The Society promotes research, disseminating knowledge of insects, and encourages the continued participation of all "students and lovers of Entomology".
Membership: *Member Profile:* Amateurs & professionals; *Committees:* Youth and Amateur Encouragement; Awards; Microscope; Newsletter Editor; Regional Director to ESC
Chief Officer(s):
Rebecca Hallett, President, 519-824-4120 Ext. 54488, Fax: 519-837-0442
rhallett@uoguelph.ca
Meetings/Conferences:
• 2018 Entomological Society of Canada Annual Meeting, November, 2018, Vancouver, BC
Scope: National
Description: Joint meeting with Entomological Society of America (ESA) & Entomological Society of British Columbia (ESBC)
Publications:
• The Canadian Entomologist
Type: Journal; *Frequency:* 6 pa; *Editor:* Dr. Christopher Buddle
Profile: Publishes original research papers and scientific notes dealing with all facets of entomology.

Entomological Society of Manitoba Inc. (ESM)
Department of Entomology, University of Manitoba, #214, 12 Dafoe Rd., Winnipeg MB R3T 2N2
home.cc.umanitoba.ca/~fieldspg
Overview: A small provincial charitable organization founded in 1945
Mission: To encourage & promote the field of entomology; To provide a forum to enable individuals with an interest in entomology to acquire & share information
Affiliation(s): Entomological Society of Canada
Finances: *Annual Operating Budget:* Less than $50,000; *Funding Sources:* Donations; membership fees; interest income; fundraising
25 volunteer(s)
Membership: 100+; *Fees:* $25; $10 student; *Member Profile:* Professional & amateur entomologists; *Committees:* Common Names of Insects; Endowment Fund; Finance; Fundraising; Newsletter; Nomination; Scholarships & Awards; Scientific Program; Scrutineers; Social; Web Page; Youth Encouragement & Public Education
Activities: Scientific paper symposia; public education presentations on entomology; *Library:* Agriculture & Agrifood Canada Resource Centre; Not open to public
Chief Officer(s):
Sarah Semmler, Secretary
ssemmler@winnipeg.ca
Awards:
• ESM Scholarship
• ESM Student Achievement Award
• ORKIN/SWAT Award

Entomological Society of Ontario (ESO)
c/o Vista Centre, PO Box 83025, 1830 Bank St., Ottawa ON K1V 1A3
Tel: 603-736-3393
www.entsocont.ca
Overview: A small provincial organization founded in 1863
Mission: To foster interest in entomology
Finances: *Annual Operating Budget:* Less than $50,000
Membership: 100-499; *Member Profile:* Amateurs & professionals
Activities: *Library:*
Chief Officer(s):
Bruce Gill, President, 613-759-1842, Fax: 613-759-6938
bruce.gill@inspection.gc.ca
Nicole McKenzie, Secretary
nicole_mckenzie@hc-sc.gc.ca
Meetings/Conferences:
• Entomological Society of Ontario 155th Annual General Meeting 2018, 2018
Scope: Provincial
Description: A gathering of entomologists of all disciplines
Publications:
• Journal of the Entomological Society of Ontario
Type: Journal; *Frequency:* Annually

Entomological Society of Saskatchewan (ESS)
c/o Agriculture & Agri-Food Canada, 107 Science Pl., Saskatoon SK S7N 0X2
Tel: 306-956-7287; *Fax:* 306-956-7247
www.entsocsask.ca
Overview: A small provincial organization founded in 1952
Mission: The Society promotes the significance of entomology to the general public & provides a forum for those interested in the field to communicate. It also works in conjunction with other similar societies.
Member of: Entomological Society of Canada
Finances: *Annual Operating Budget:* Less than $50,000
Membership: *Fees:* $20; $5 student; *Member Profile:* Amateurs & professionals; *Committees:* Youth and Amateur Encouragement; Awards; Microscope; Newsletter Editor; Regional Director to ESC
Activities: North American butterfly count; insect inventory of endangered/protected ecosystems; talks & presentations; displays at schools; *Speaker Service:* Yes; *Rents Mailing List:* Yes; *Library*
Chief Officer(s):
Margaret Gruber, President
margaret.gruber@agr.gc.ca

Entraide - femmes de Gatineau inc. *Voir* Entraide familiale de l'Outaouais inc.

Entraide familiale de l'Outaouais inc.
310-B, rue Notre-Dame, Gatineau QC J8P 1L1
Tél: 819-669-0686
entraidefamiliale.wordpress.com
www.facebook.com/EntraideFamilialeOutaouais
twitter.com/EFOutaouais
www.youtube.com/user/EntraideFamiliale
Nom précédent: Entraide - femmes de Gatineau inc.
Aperçu: *Dimension:* petite; *Envergure:* locale; Organisme sans but lucratif; fondée en 1990
Mission: Pour fournir des services essentiels à ceux qui en ont besoin mais ne peut pas se le permettre
Membre(s) du personnel: 5
Membre: 1 873; *Critères d'admissibilite:* Être prestataire d'aide sociale, ou avoir un revenu de moins de 20 000 par année pour 1 famille de 4 personnes
Activités:; *Bibliothèque:* Bibliothèque publique
Membre(s) du bureau directeur:
Diane Tremblay, Directrice générale
dtremblay@entraidefamiliale.com

Entraide Léo-Théorêt
2000B, rue Alaxandre-de-Sève, Montréal QC H2L 2W4
Tél: 514-521-0095
entraideleotheoret@hotmail.com
Aperçu: *Dimension:* petite; *Envergure:* locale
Mission: Pour aider les moins fortunés en leur offrant des services sociaux abordables
Affiliation(s): Corporateion de dévelopment communautaire centre-sud; Table de concertation et d'intervention po9ur une garantie alimentaire

Entraide universitaire mondiale du Canada *See* World University Service of Canada

Entre Nous Femmes Housing Society
#21, 3550 SE Marine Dr., Vancouver BC V5S 4R3
Tel: 604-451-4412; *Fax:* 604-451-4415
enf@telus.net
www.enfhs.org
Also Known As: ENF Housing
Overview: A small local charitable organization founded in 1985
Mission: To provide & manage safe, affordable community homes & townhouses for female-led, single parent families in the

Greater Vancouver Area; to operate 345 housing units.
Member of: British Columbia Non-Profit Housing Association
Membership: *Fees:* $2
Chief Officer(s):
Tracy McCullough, Executive Director
Publications:
• ENF Newsletter
Type: Newsletter; *Frequency:* Semiannually

Entre-amis Lavallois inc
4490, 10e rue, Laval QC H7R 6A9
Tél: 450-962-4058
Aperçu: *Dimension:* petite; *Envergure:* provinciale
Mission: Offrir une activité culturelle et de rencontre aux personnes atteintes de déficience intellectuelle
Membre: *Critères d'admissibilité:* Personnes vivant avec une déficience intellectuelle
Activités: Soirées de danse

Entrepreneurs with Disabilities Network (EDN)
PO Box 44, #504, 5475 Spring Garden Rd., Halifax NS B3J 3T2
ednns.ca
www.facebook.com/EntrepreneurswithDisabilitiesNetwork
twitter.com/EDNns
Overview: A small provincial organization founded in 2004
Mission: To encourage entrepreneurship to people with disabilities; to understand the needs of entrepreneurs with disabilities & to represent them; to work on behalf of entrepreneurs with disabilities to advise government, business service providers & others on how best to serve them
Affiliation(s): Centre for Entrepreneurship Education & Development Inc.
Staff Member(s): 3
Chief Officer(s):
Brian Aird, Executive Director
Awards:
• Entrepreneur of the Year Awards
Publications:
• EDN [Entrepreneurs with Disabilities Network] Newsletter
Type: Newsletter; *Frequency:* q.

Enviro-Accès Inc.
#150, 85, rue Belvédère nord, Sherbrooke QC J1H 4A7
Tél: 819-823-2230; *Téléc:* 819-823-6632
enviro@enviroaccess.ca
www.enviroaccess.ca
Également appelé: Centre pour l'avancement des technologies environnementales
Aperçu: *Dimension:* moyenne; *Envergure:* provinciale; fondée en 1993
Mission: Supporter les petites et moyennes entreprises qui oeuvrent dans le domaine de l'environnement en leur offrant les services professionnels nécessaires au développement de leurs projets et de leurs affaires.
Membre(s) du personnel: 9
Membre: 1-99
Membre(s) du bureau directeur:
Manon Laporte, Présidente-directrice générale
mlaporte@enviroaccess.ca
  Montréal
  #440, 50, rue Sainte-Catherine ouest, Montréal QC H2X 3V4
  Tél: 514-284-5794; *Téléc:* 514-284-6034
  Membre(s) du bureau directeur:
  Maude Lauzon-Gosselin, Directrice de projets
  mlauzongosselin@enviroaccess.ca

Environment Resources Managament Association
PO Box 857, Grand Falls-Windsor NL A2A 2P7
Tel: 709-489-7350
info@exploitsriver.ca
www.exploitsriver.ca/association.php
Overview: A medium-sized national organization founded in 1984
Mission: To promote the development of the Exploits River as a major Atlantic Salmon producing river.
Staff Member(s): 50

Environmental & Outdoor Education Council of Alberta *See*
Global, Environmental & Outdoor Education Council

Environmental Abatement Council of Ontario (EACO)
70 Leek Cres., Richmond Hill ON L4B 1H1
Tel: 416-499-4000; *Fax:* 416-499-8752
info@eacoontario.com
www.eacoontario.com
www.linkedin.com/company/environmental-abatement-council-of-ontario
twitter.com/eacoontario
Previous Name: Ontario Asbestos Removal Contractors Association
Overview: A medium-sized provincial organization founded in 1992
Mission: To collect, generate & disseminate information concerning environmental abatement & other hazardous environmental health issues
Finances: *Annual Operating Budget:* Less than $50,000; *Funding Sources:* Membership dues
Staff Member(s): 10; 30 volunteer(s)
Membership: 1-99; *Fees:* Schedule available
Chief Officer(s):
Mark Reinhardt, Secretary-Treasurer

Environmental Action Barrie - Living Green
Barrie ON
www.livinggreenbarrie.com
twitter.com/livinggreenbarr
Overview: A small local charitable organization founded in 1990
Mission: To provide education & awareness about environmental issues for the people of Barrie, Ontario & neighbouring communities; To promote environmentally friendly practices
Finances: *Funding Sources:* Donations
Activities: Carrying out eco-projects; Providing articles related to environmental issues; Offering environmental information & activities through a website, as a website based organization; *Speaker Service:* Yes
Chief Officer(s):
Meghan Rafferty, Chair

Environmental Careers Organization of Canada / L'Organisation pour les carrières en environnement du Canada
#200, 308 - 11th Ave. SE, Calgary AB T2G 0Y2
Tel: 403-233-0748; *Fax:* 403-269-9544
Toll-Free: 800-890-1924
info@eco.ca
www.eco.ca
www.facebook.com/ecocanada
twitter.com/ecocanada
Also Known As: ECO Canada
Previous Name: Canadian Council for Human Resources in the Environment Industry
Overview: A medium-sized national organization founded in 1992
Mission: To provide services to all participants in the environmental sector, including educators, students, practitioners & employers
Finances: *Funding Sources:* Government of Canada's Sector Council Program
Activities: Providing career information & job boards; Recruiting; Offering ECO Canada internships; Providing professional development opportunities to practitioners; Offering employee retention strategies to employers; Providing tools for career change & career development; Disseminating human resource statistics & trends; Increasing Aboriginal employment in the environment sector through career awareness, training & employment resources
Chief Officer(s):
Faramarz Bogzaran, Chair
John Wiebe, Secretary-Treasurer
Kevin Nilson, President/CEO

Environmental Coalition of Prince Edward Island (ECO-PEI)
c/o Voluntary Resource Centre, 81 Prince St., Charlottetown PE C1A 4R3
Tel: 902-651-2575
mail@ecopei.ca
www.ecopei.ca
Overview: A small provincial organization founded in 1988
Mission: To work in partnership in order to understand & improve the Island's environment
Member of: Canadian Renewable Energy Alliance
Membership: *Fees:* $10 basic; $25 supporting; $100 corporate
Chief Officer(s):
Gary Schneider, Co-Chair
Publications:
• ECO-NEWS [a publication of the Environmental Coalition of Prince Edward Island]
Type: Newsletter

Environmental Defence / Defense environmentale
#300, 116 Spadina Ave., Toronto ON M5V 2K6
Tel: 416-323-9521; *Fax:* 416-323-9301
Toll-Free: 877-399-2333
info@environmentaldefence.ca
www.environmentaldefence.ca
www.linkedin.com/company/environmental-defence
www.facebook.com/EnvironmentalDefenceCanada
twitter.com/envirodefence
Previous Name: Canadian Environmental Defence Fund
Overview: A medium-sized national charitable organization founded in 1984
Mission: To protect the environment & human health; To research, educate, & initiate action in the courts when necessary
Member of: Canadian Environmental Network
Finances: *Annual Operating Budget:* $500,000-$1.5 Million
25 volunteer(s)
Chief Officer(s):
Tim Gray, Executive Director, 416-323-9521 Ext. 288
Suzanne Karajaberlian, Managing Director

Environmental Education Association of the Yukon (EEAY)
Whitehorse YT
eeyukon@gmail.com
taiga.net/YukonEE
Overview: A small provincial organization
Mission: To promote environmental education in the Yukon and foster communication between individuals and groups with and interest in environmental education.
Member of: EENorth; Canada's Arctic Environmental Education Network

Environmental Education Ontario (EEON)
32 Springdale Dr., Kitchener ON N2K 1P9
Tel: 519-579-3097
admin@eeon.org
www.eeon.org
twitter.com/GREENINGONTARIO
Overview: A small local charitable organization founded in 2000
Mission: To promote the facilitation, development & implementation of education on sustainable environments in Ontario
Member of: Education Alliance for a Sustainable Ontario
Finances: *Funding Sources:* Federal & provincial governments; foundations
Membership: *Member Profile:* Environmental & ecological educators, concerned citizens, parents, & representatives from non-governmental organizations & government agencies
Activities: Listserv; meetings; representations; *Speaker Service:* Yes
Meetings/Conferences:
• Environmental Education Ontario AGM 2018, 2018, ON
Scope: Provincial

Environmental Educators' Provincial Specialist Association (EEPSA)
c/o British Columbia Teachers' Federation, #100, 550 - 6th Ave. West, Vancouver BC V5Z 4P2
Tel: 604-871-2283
eepsa.org
www.facebook.com/eepsa.bc
twitter.com/EEPSA
Overview: A medium-sized provincial organization founded in 1972
Mission: To promote, through public education, greater awareness, understanding & appreciation of the environment & to encourage global citizenship through the development of active decision making
Member of: BC Teachers' Federation
Finances: *Funding Sources:* Membership dues
Membership: 200; *Fees:* $15 student; $25 BCTF members; $45.68 associate
Chief Officer(s):
Selina Metcalfe, President
selmet@shaw.ca

Environmental Health Association of British Columbia (EHABC)
PO Box 30033, RPO Reyolds, Victoria BC V8X 5E1
Tel: 250-658-2027
Other Communication: ehabc.wordpress.com
info@ehabc.org
www.ehabc.org
www.facebook.com/353025931439290
Overview: A medium-sized provincial charitable organization founded in 1993
Mission: To raise awareness within the medical community, educational institutions, & the general public to prevent further

Canadian Associations / Environmental Health Association of Nova Scotia (EHANS)

cases of environmental sensitivity from occurring
Affiliation(s): EHA Nova Scotia; EHA Québec; EHA Ontario; EHA Alberta
Membership: *Fees:* $25

Environmental Health Association of Nova Scotia (EHANS)
PO Box 31323, Halifax NS B3K 5Y5
Toll-Free: 800-449-1995
ehans@environmentalhealth.ca
www.environmentalhealth.ca
www.facebook.com/165405756830794
Previous Name: Nova Scotia Allergy & Environmental Health Association
Overview: A small provincial organization founded in 1985
Mission: To offer assistance to individuals affected by environmental health issues; To prevent illness caused by environmental factors through the promotion of health policies & practices
Membership: *Fees:* $25 individual; $35 family; $75 supporting
Chief Officer(s):
Eric Slone, President

Environmental Health Association of Ontario (EHA Ontario)
PO Box 33023, Ottawa ON K2C 3Y9
Tel: 613-860-2342
helpline@ehaontario.ca
www.ehaontario.ca
Previous Name: Allergy & Environmental Health Association
Overview: A small provincial charitable organization founded in 1975
Mission: To promote awareness of environmental conditions that may be harmful to human health, & advocates less-contaminated sources of food, water, clothing, personal & home care products, home furnishings & building materials
Member of: Human Ecology Foundation of Canada
Affiliation(s): EHA Nova Scotia; EHA Québec; EHA Alberta; EHA BC
Finances: *Funding Sources:* Donations; Membership fees
Membership: *Fees:* $28; *Member Profile:* Individuals with environmental sensitivities & their families
Activities: *Library:* AEHA-Ottawa Library; Not open to public

Environmental Health Association of Québec *Voir*
Association pour la santé environnementale du Québec

Environmental Health Foundation of Canada (EHFC)
c/o Tim Roark, 3301 - 164A St., Surrey BC V3S 0G5
Tel: 778-574-1188
www.ehfc.ca
Overview: A small national charitable organization founded in 1989 overseen by Canadian Institute of Public Health Inspectors
Mission: To advance environmental health in Canada through the development & implementation of education & research initiatives
Membership: *Member Profile:* Members of the environmental public health profession; industry representatives; educational institutions; government
Chief Officer(s):
Tim Roark, Treasurer
trustees@ehfc.ca

The Environmental Law Centre (Alberta) Society (ELC)
#410, 10115 - 100A St., Edmonton AB T5J 2W2
Tel: 780-424-5099; *Fax:* 780-424-5133
Toll-Free: 800-661-4238
elc@elc.ab.ca
www.elc.ab.ca
www.facebook.com/environmentallawcentre
twitter.com/ELC_Alberta
www.youtube.com/ELCAlberta
Also Known As: Environmental Law Centre
Overview: A small provincial charitable organization founded in 1982
Mission: To conduct research in environmental & natural resources law, policy & procedure; To educate the public on environmental law; To operate an environmental law information & referral service for the benefit of the public; To monitor relevant municipal, provincial & federal environmental laws, policies & procedures, & make recommendations for reform
Member of: Alberta Environmental Network
Finances: *Annual Operating Budget:* $500,000-$1.5 Million; *Funding Sources:* Alberta Law Foundation; Public support
Staff Member(s): 7
Activities: *Speaker Service:* Yes; *Rents Mailing List:* Yes

Chief Officer(s):
Jason Unger, Acting Executive Director

Environmental Managers Association of British Columbia (EMABC)
PO Box 3741, Vancouver BC V6B 3Z8
Tel: 604-998-2226; *Fax:* 604-998-2226
info@emaofbc.com
www.emaofbc.com
www.linkedin.com/groups/1856767
twitter.com/emaofbc
Also Known As: EMA of BC
Overview: A medium-sized provincial organization
Mission: To encourage education, share knowledge among members and create a forum for environmental management issues in the industrial, commercial and institutional sectors, serve as a key resource of environmental information for members and explore existing and emerging environmental issues.
Membership: 67 corporate; *Fees:* $250 NGO/Not for Profit; $375 Sole Proprietorship; $500 Corporate
Chief Officer(s):
Leanne Harris, B.Sc., President
lharris@emaofbc.com
Don Bryant, MBA, P.Eng, P.E, Executive Director
dbryant@emaofbc.com
Awards:
• Environmental Management Awards
Meetings/Conferences:
• 2018 Environmental Managers Association of British Columbia Workshop, 2018, BC
Scope: Provincial

Environmental Services Association of Alberta (ESAA)
#102, 2528 Ellwood Dr. SW, Edmonton AB T6X 0A9
Tel: 780-429-6363; *Fax:* 780-429-4249
Toll-Free: 800-661-9278
info@esaa.org
www.esaa.org
Previous Name: Alberta Special Waste Services Association
Overview: A medium-sized provincial organization founded in 1987
Mission: To act as the voice of Alberta's environment industry
Membership: 200+ organizations; *Fees:* $475
Activities: Communicating with all levels of government; Providing networking opportunities; Offering market & industry information
Chief Officer(s):
Craig Robertson, President
Randy Neumann, Secretary
Skip Kerr, Treasurer
Joe Barraclough, Director, Industry & Government Relations, 780-429-6363 Ext. 224
Joe Chowaniec, Director, Program & Event Development, 780-429-6363 Ext. 223
chowaniec@esaa.org
Meetings/Conferences:
• Environmental Services Association of Alberta EnviroTech 2018, April, 2018, Hyatt Regency Calgary, Calgary, AB
Scope: Provincial
Contact Information: Director, Program & Event Development: Joe Chowaniec, Phone: 780-429-6363, ext. 223, E-mail: chowaniec@esaa.org
• Environmental Services Association of Alberta RemTech 2018, October, 2018, Fairmont Banff Springs, Banff, AB
Scope: Provincial
Description: Remediation technology information for environmental professionals, such as engineering firms, pipeline companies, drill companies, energy marketers, natural gas producers, oil & gase services companies, environmental consulting firms, & mining companies
Contact Information: Director, Program & Event Development: Joe Chowaniec, Phone: 780-429-6363, ext. 223, E-mail: chowaniec@esaa.org
Publications:
• B.I.D.S. (Business Initiative Development Service)
Type: Newsletter; *Frequency:* Weekly
Profile: Environmental business opportunities, news, & marketing information for the buyers & sellers of environmental goods & services
• Environmental Association of Alberta Annual Report
Type: Yearbook; *Frequency:* Annually
• The ESAA [Environmental Services Association of Alberta] Weekly News
Type: Newsletter; *Frequency:* Weekly; *Accepts Advertising*

Profile: Association happenings, such as conferences & job opportunities, for Environmental Services Association of Alberta members
• The Regulatory Review [a publication of the Environmental Services Association of Alberta]
Frequency: Monthly
Profile: Current information on environmental policies & law, produced by the Environmental Services Association of Alberta & the EnvironmentalLaw Center

Environmental Services Association of Nova Scotia (ESANS)
Woodside Industrial Park, #211-2, 1 Research Dr., Dartmouth NS B2Y 4M9
Tel: 902-463-3538; *Fax:* 902-466-6889
contact@esans.ca
www.esans.ca
Also Known As: Nova Scotia Environmental Business Network
Overview: A medium-sized provincial organization founded in 1994
Mission: ESANS is a province-wide business organization dedicated to the promotion of environmental products, services & organizations within the environmental industry.
Finances: *Annual Operating Budget:* $100,000-$250,000; *Funding Sources:* Membership; projects; government
Staff Member(s): 1
Membership: 100-499; *Fees:* Schedule available; *Member Profile:* Individuals & companies/organizations involved in the environmental industry; *Committees:* Communications; Membership; Finance
Activities: *Awareness Events:* Membership Appreciation Social; *Internships:* Yes; *Rents Mailing List:* Yes
Chief Officer(s):
Norval Collins, President
ncollins@cefconsultants.ns.ca
Sandra Lynch, Operations Manager
sandra@esans.ca

Environmental Studies Association of Canada (ESAC) / Association canadienne d'études environnementales
c/o Dean's Office, Faculty of Environmental Studies, Univ. of Waterloo, Waterloo ON N2L 3G1
Tel: 519-888-4442; *Fax:* 519-746-0292
Toll-Free: 866-437-2587
www.esac.ca
www.facebook.com/218543575398
twitter.com/esaccanada
Overview: A small national organization founded in 1993
Mission: To to advance research & teaching activities in areas related to environmental studies in Canada
Membership: *Fees:* $45 student & unwaged & small NGO; $95 faculty & professional; $125 institutional; *Member Profile:* Members include individuals, who are interested in social science & humanities approaches to environmental issues, from educational institutions, government agencies, & private sector & non-profit organizations.
Chief Officer(s):
Chris Ling, Co-President
chris.ling@royalroads.ca
Shirley Thompson, Co-President
s.thompson@ad.umanitoba.ca
Meetings/Conferences:
• Environmental Studies Association of Canada 2018 Annual Conference & AGM, May, 2018
Scope: National
Attendance: 8,000+
Publications:
• Directory of ESAC [Environmental Studies Association of Canada] Members
Type: Directory; *Frequency:* Annually
Profile: Listing of ESAC members, with their areas of interest & research
• Rhizome [a publication of the Environmental Studies Association of Canada]
Type: Newsletter; *Editor:* Angela Waldie
Profile: Information about conferences, research projects, events, new publications, & teaching materials

Environmental Youth Alliance (EYA)
#517, 119 Pender St. West, Vancouver BC V6B 1S5
Tel: 604-689-4446
info@eya.ca
www.eya.ca
www.facebook.com/EnvironmentalYouthAlliance

twitter.com/EnviroYA
www.youtube.com/user/EnviroYouthAlliance
Overview: A small local organization founded in 1989
Mission: To save the earth through non-violent means; To promote change by educating people on our interconnectedness with Nature & involving youth in action projects; To create a youth movement that is activist-oriented & works towards environmental respect & protection.
Finances: *Annual Operating Budget:* $100,000-$250,000; *Funding Sources:* Federal, provincial & municipal government; foundations
Staff Member(s): 2; 25 volunteer(s)
Membership: 10,000
Activities: Stewardship of urban sites; *Speaker Service:* Yes; *Library:* by appointment
Chief Officer(s):
Hartley Rosen, Managing Director
hartley@eya.ca

Environnement jeunesse
Maison du développement durable, #400, 50, rue Sainte-Catherine ouest, Montréal QC H2X 3V4
Tél: 514-252-3016; *Téléc:* 514-254-5873
Ligne sans frais: 866-377-3016
infoenjeu@enjeu.qc.ca
enjeu.qc.ca
www.facebook.com/environnement.jeunesse
twitter.com/ENJEUquebec
vimeo.com/channels/enjeu
Également appelé: ENJEU
Aperçu: *Dimension:* moyenne; *Envergure:* provinciale; fondée en 1979
Mission: Promouvoir la conservation et l'amélioration de la qualité de l'environnement; développer chez les jeunes les qualités favorisant leur implication sociale.
Affiliation(s): Réseau québécois des groupes écologistes; Association québécoise pour la promotion de l'éducation relative à l'environnement
Membre(s) du personnel: 12
Membre: 1027 individuel + 167 collectif; *Montant de la cotisation:* 10$ étudiant; 20$ individuel; 50$ collectif; 35$ famille; 100$ souien; 1000$ donateur
Activités: Tient une assemblée générale annuelle; organise un colloque annuel, La Bise D'Automne; tient des comités inter-groupes; réalise L'Écologie en Action, un vaste projet d'éducation et d'action relatifs à l'environnement; offre un Service d'Activités en Formation et en Éducation Relatives à l'Environnement; produit une panoplie d'outils de qualité visant à soutenir l'action des groupes membres; participe à des processus de consultation publique; *Service de conférenciers:* Oui
Membre(s) du bureau directeur:
Jérôme Normand, Directeur général
jnormand@enjeu.qc.ca

Envol SRT
#302, 92, boul St-Raymond, Gatineau QC J8Y 1S7
Tél: 819-770-1622; *Téléc:* 819-771-5566
envoladmin@videotron.ca
www.envolsrt.org
Aperçu: *Dimension:* petite; *Envergure:* locale
Mission: Pour aider les jeunes qui ont un problème persistant de santé mentale à trouver un emploi
Membre: *Critères d'admissibilite:* Jeunes adultes qui ont un problème persistant de santé mentale

Ephemera Society of Canada
36 Macauley Dr., Thornhill ON L3T 5S5
ephemera@tht.net
www.ephemerasociety.org/news/news-canada.html
Overview: A small national organization founded in 1987
Mission: The Society preserves, studies & exhibits Canada's cultural heritage in the medium of printing.
Membership: *Member Profile:* Researchers, dealers, collectors, historians
Activities: Regular membership meetings; lectures
Chief Officer(s):
E. Richard McKinstry, President

Épilepsie Canada See Epilepsy Canada

Épilepsie Ontario See Epilepsy Ontario

Epilepsy & Seizure Association of Manitoba
#4, 1805 Main St., Winnipeg MB R2V 2A2
Tel: 204-783-0466; *Fax:* 204-784-9689
esam@manitobaepilepsy.org
www.manitobaepilepsy.org
Also Known As: Manitoba Epilepsy Association
Overview: A small provincial charitable organization founded in 1975
Mission: To improve the quality of life of persons with epilepsy by providing programs & education, & supporting research & services
Member of: Canadian Epilepsy Alliance
Finances: *Funding Sources:* Donations & fundraisers
Activities: Offering library loans, information & referrals, support groups & community education; *Speaker Service:* Yes; *Library:* Resource Centre; Open to public
Chief Officer(s):
Diane Wall, President
Chris Kullman, Vice-President
Krys Kirton, Secretary

Epilepsy Association of Calgary / Association d'épilepsie de Calgary
4112 - 4th St. NW, Calgary AB T2K 1A2
Tel: 403-230-2764; *Fax:* 403-230-5766
Toll-Free: 866-374-5377
info@epilepsycalgary.com
www.epilepsycalgary.com
www.facebook.com/EpilepgyCalgary
twitter.com/epilepsycalgary
Overview: A small local charitable organization founded in 1955
Mission: To address community needs related to epilepsy; to improve the quality of life of persons with epilepsy through a broad range of programs, education, advocacy, support
Affiliation(s): Canadian Epilepsy Alliance/Alliance Canadienne d'Epilepsié
Finances: *Annual Operating Budget:* $250,000-$500,000; *Funding Sources:* Memberships; donations; fundraising activities; United Way; Rotary Club
Staff Member(s): 4
Membership: *Fees:* $20 annual; $200 life
Activities: *Awareness Events:* Epilepsy Education Month, Nov.; Purple Day for Epilepsy Awareness, March 26; *Speaker Service:* Yes
Chief Officer(s):
Kathy Fyfe, Executive Director
kathyf@epilepsycalgary.com
Publications:
• Epigram [a publication of Epilepsy Association of Calgary]
Type: Newsletter; *Frequency:* Irregular
Profile: News, updates, & important dates
Central Alberta Office
4811 - 48th St., Red Deer AB T4N 1S6
Tel: 403-358-3358; *Fax:* 403-358-3595
Chief Officer(s):
Norma Jaskela, Program Coordinator
centralabinfo@epilepsycalgary.com

Epilepsy Association of Nova Scotia (EANS)
#306, 5880 Spring Garden Rd., Halifax NS B3H 1Y1
Tel: 902-429-2633; *Fax:* 902-425-0821
Toll-Free: 866-374-5377
www.epilepsyns.com
www.facebook.com/epilepsyns.org
twitter.com/epilepsy_ns
www.instagram.com/epilepsy_ns
Overview: A small provincial charitable organization founded in 1980
Mission: To provide support for people with epilepsy; To promote awareness & public understanding of epilepsy; To encourage research into the causes, treatment & prevention of epilepsy
Member of: Epilepsy Foundation of America; Canadian Epilepsy Alliance
Finances: *Funding Sources:* Donations; fundraising activities; grants
Membership: *Fees:* $15; *Committees:* Fundraising; Human Resources & Finance; Education; Nominations
Activities: Workshops; seminars; support groups; counselling & referral; education programs to schools, employers, institutions, mall displays; interviews with the media; newspaper ads; door-to-door campaign; *Speaker Service:* Yes; *Library:* Resource Library; Open to public by appointment
Chief Officer(s):
Debbi Tobin, Executive Director
Publications:
• Epicure [a publication of the Epilepsy Association of Nova Scotia]
Type: Newsletter; *Frequency:* 3 pa

Epilepsy Canada (EC) / Épilepsie Canada
#2B, 2900 John St., Markham ON L3R 5G3
Fax: 905-764-1231
Toll-Free: 877-734-0873
epilepsy@epilepsy.ca
www.epilepsy.ca
Overview: A medium-sized national charitable organization founded in 1966
Mission: To enhance the quality of life for persons affected by epilepsy; To promote & support research into all aspects of epilepsy; To facilitate educational initiatives; To increase public & professional awareness of epilepsy; To fund research; To encourage governments to address the needs of people with epilepsy
Member of: International Bureau for Epilepsy (IBE); Canadian League Against Epilepsy
Finances: *Funding Sources:* Donations; Corporate support
Chief Officer(s):
Jacques Brunelle, National President
jbrunelle@tennistremblant.com
Gary N. Collins, Executive Director
garycollins@4growth.ca
Awards:
• Epilepsy Scholarship Awards

Epilepsy Ontario / Épilepsie Ontario
#803, 3100 Steeles Ave. East, Toronto ON L3R 8T3
Tel: 905-474-9696; *Fax:* 905-474-3663
Toll-Free: 800-463-1119
info@epilepsyontario.org
www.epilepsyontario.org
www.facebook.com/epilepsy.ontario
twitter.com/EpilepsyOntario
Overview: A medium-sized provincial charitable organization founded in 1956
Mission: To promote optimal quality of life for people living with seizure disorders; To advocate for awareness, support services & research into these disorders & maintains a network of local agencies, contacts & associates to provide services, counselling & referrals
Affiliation(s): Canadian Epilepsy Alliance; Epilepsy Canada
Finances: *Funding Sources:* Gaming; public donations; special events
Membership: 17 chapters; *Fees:* Schedule available; *Member Profile:* Provincial/local chapters; *Committees:* Executive
Activities: Conferences; children's camp; chapter development; education; youth camps; *Speaker Service:* Yes; *Library:* Resource Centre; Open to public by appointment
Chief Officer(s):
Paul Raymond, Executive Director
paul@epilepsyontario.org
Durham Region
#3, 310 Byron St. South, Whitby ON L1N 4P8
Tel: 905-430-3090; *Fax:* 905-430-3080
support@epilepsydurham.com
www.epilepsydurham.com
www.facebook.com/EpilepsyDurham
twitter.com/Epilepsy_Durham
www.youtube.com/user/DurhamEpilepsy
Chief Officer(s):
Dianne McKenzie, Executive Director
dianne.mckenzie@epilepsydurham.com
Halton Peel Hamilton Region
#4, 2160 Dunwin Dr., Mississauga ON L5L 5M8
Tel: 905-450-1900
Toll-Free: 855-734-2111
info@epilepsyco.org
ehph.ca
www.youtube.com/channel/UCMs-90IDVPBUXoUi4tUv0Zw
Chief Officer(s):
Cynthia Milburn, Executive Director
cynthia@epilepsyco.org
London & Area
690 Hale St., London ON N5W 1H4
Tel: 519-433-4073; *Fax:* 519-433-4079
Toll-Free: 866-374-5377
support@epilepsysupport.ca
www.epilepsysupportcentre.com
www.facebook.com/epilepsysupport
twitter.com/EpilepsySWO
www.youtube.com/user/EpilepsyLondon
Chief Officer(s):

Canadian Associations / Epilepsy Saskatoon

Michelle Franklin, Executive Director
michelle@epilepsysupport.ca
Ottawa-Carleton
#207, 211 Bronson Ave., Ottawa ON K1R 6H5
Tel: 613-594-9255; *Fax:* 613-594-5189
Toll-Free: 866-374-5377
info@epilepsyottawa.ca
www.epilepsyottawa.ca
www.facebook.com/EpilepsyOttawa
twitter.com/Epilepsy_Ottawa
www.youtube.com/channel/UCkeb41QGDCVAVSiyUAIVNKA
Chief Officer(s):
Peter Andrews, President
Peterborough & Area
Unit 6, Charlotte Mews, PO Box 2453, 203 Simcoe St., Peterborough ON K9J 7Y8
Tel: 705-874-1897
Toll-Free: 800-463-1119
epilepsyptbo@yahoo.ca
epilepsyontario.org/agency/epilepsy-peterborough-and-area
Chief Officer(s):
Tom Appleby, Executive Director
Simcoe County
Victoria Village, #7, 72 Ross St., Barrie ON L4N 1G3
Tel: 705-737-3132; *Fax:* 705-737-5045
Toll-Free: 866-374-5377
epilepsysimcoecounty@rogers.com
www.epilepsysimcoecounty.ca
www.facebook.com/epilepsysimcoecountybarrie
twitter.com/simcoeepilepsy
Chief Officer(s):
Sue Donovan, Executive Director
Southeastern Ontario
#205, 920 Princess St., Kingston ON K7L 1H1
Tel: 613-542-6222; *Fax:* 613-548-4162
Toll-Free: 866-374-5377
admin@epilepsyresource.org
www.epilepsyresource.org
www.facebook.com/EpilepsyResourceCentre
twitter.com/EpilepsyResourc
Chief Officer(s):
Tom Coke, Executive Director
tcoke@epilepsyresource.org
Timmins
733 Ross Ave. East, Timmins ON P4N 8S8
Tel: 705-264-2933; *Fax:* 705-264-0350
Toll-Free: 866-374-5377
info@seizurebraininjurycentre.com
www.seizurebraininjurycentre.com
www.facebook.com/seizurebraininjurycentre
twitter.com/letstalkbrain
Mission: To provide programs in Public Education and Family Support surrounding seizures and acquired brain injuries
Chief Officer(s):
Rhonda Latendresse, Executive Director
rhondal@seizurebraininjurycentre.com
Jacques Arbic, President
Toronto
#210, 468 Queen St. East, Toronto ON M5A 1T7
Tel: 416-964-9095; *Fax:* 416-964-2492
info@epilepsytoronto.org
www.epilepsytoronto.org
www.facebook.com/epilepsytoronto
twitter.com/epilepsytoronto
www.youtube.com/channel/UCTZiK0J7kSc1LR4blViMcyA
Chief Officer(s):
Geoff Bobb, Executive Director, 416-964-9095 Ext. 214
gbobb@epilepsytoronto.org
Waterloo/Wellington
#5, 165 Hollinger Cres., Kitchener ON N2K 2Z2
Tel: 519-745-2112; *Fax:* 519-745-2435
epilepsy@epilww.com
www.epilww.com
www.facebook.com/epilww
Chief Officer(s):
Jennifer Lyon, Executive Director
Windsor/Essex County
Epilepsy Support Centre, 690 Hale St., London ON N5W 1H4
Tel: 519-890-6614
communications@epilepsysupport.ca
epilepsysupport.ca
www.facebook.com/epilepsysupport

twitter.com/EpilepsySC
www.youtube.com/user/EpilepsyLondon
Chief Officer(s):
Mary Secco, Director, Strategic Initiatives
mary@epilepsysupport.ca
York Region
11181 Yonge St., Richmond Hill ON L4S 1L2
Tel: 905-508-5404; *Fax:* 905-508-0920
info@epilepsyyork.org
www.epilepsyyork.org
www.facebook.com/epilepsyyorkregion
twitter.com/epilepsyyork
Chief Officer(s):
Claudia Cozza, Executive Director
ccozza@epilepsyyork.org

Epilepsy Saskatoon
PO Box 1792, Saskatoon SK S7K 4J1
Tel: 306-665-1939
www.facebook.com/EpilepsySaskatoon
Overview: A small local charitable organization founded in 1978
Mission: To improve the quality of life of persons with epilepsy through a broad range of programs, education, support of research & the delivery of needed services to people with epilepsy & their families
Member of: Canadian Epilepsy Alliance
Finances: *Funding Sources:* Membership fees; United Way
Activities: *Awareness Events:* Epilepsy Month, Mar.; *Speaker Service:* Yes; *Rents Mailing List:* Yes; *Library:* ES Resource Centre

Equestrian Association for the Disabled
8360 Leeming Rd., RR#3, Mount Hope ON L0R 1W0
Tel: 905-679-8323; *Fax:* 905-679-1705
info@tead.on.ca
www.tead.on.ca
www.facebook.com/TEADStables
Also Known As: TEAD
Overview: A small local charitable organization founded in 1978
Mission: To enhance the life of children & adults with physical, mental, & emotional handicaps, through equestrian therapy
Finances: *Funding Sources:* Donations; Grants; Fundraising
Membership: *Fees:* Schedule available
Activities: Offering riding therapy, rehabilitation, & recreation to children & adults with disabilities
Chief Officer(s):
Hilary Webb, Manager, Programs, 905-679-8323 Ext. 224
hilary@tead.on.ca
Helen Clayton, Manager, Farm, 905-679-8323 Ext. 230
helen@tead.on.ca

Equestrian Canada (EC)
#100, 308 Legget Dr., Ottawa ON K2K 1Y6
Tel: 613-287-1515; *Fax:* 613-248-3484
Toll-Free: 866-282-8395
inquiries@equestrian.ca
www.equestrian.ca
www.facebook.com/equestriancan
twitter.com/Equestrian_Can
Previous Name: Equine Canada; Canadian Equestrian Federation
Overview: A large national licensing charitable organization founded in 1977
Mission: To promote & develop a unified Canadian Equine Community, an economically viable horse industry, & access to the use of horses for leisure, sport & commerce
Affiliation(s): Provincial Partners: Horse Council of B.C., Alberta Equestrian Federation, Saskatchewan Horse Federation, Manitoba Horse Council, Ontario Equestrian Federation, Fédération Équestre du Quebec, New Brunswick Equestrian Association, PEI Horse Council, Nova Scotia Equestrian Federation, Newfoundland Equestrian Association, Canadian Pony Club
Finances: *Funding Sources:* Government of Canada; Donations; Memberships
Membership: 56 corporate + 1,165 associate + 4,897 senior + 183 lifetime + 1,736 junior + 436 junior associate; *Fees:* $250 corporate-syndicate; $35 associate; $78 senior; $700 lifetime; $58 junior; $25 junior associate; *Member Profile:* License Profile: Senior Competitive License Holder - owner, lessee, agent, trainer, or EC certified coach; Junior Competitive License Holder - under 18 with the same qualifications; Lifetime - senior license holder level with the same qualifications; Corporate-syndicate - corporations, business enterprises & syndicates which own a horse or horses; Associate - wishes to compete in EC Provincial Circuit shows, or a member of a breed association competing at

EC member shows in that breed's classes only; *Committees:* Audit; Governance; Human Resource; Ethics; Finance; Health & Welfare; Nominations; Joint Steering; Recognition & Awards; LTED Competitions Review
Activities: Coaching program; Rider preparation program; *Awareness Events:* Horse Week; *Rents Mailing List:* Yes; *Library*
Chief Officer(s):
Jorge Bernhard, President
Eva Havaris, Chief Executive Officer
ceo@equestrian.ca
Mike Mouat, Director, Finance & Administration
mmouat@equestrian.ca
Awards:
- Canadian Bred Horse of the Year
- Canadian Breeder of the Year
- Equestrian of the Year - The Doctor George Jacobsen Trophy
- Junior Equestrian of the Year - The Gillian Wilson Trophy
- Volunteer of the Year
Presented by BFL Canada
- Media Award - The Susan Jane Anstey Trophy
Presented by BFL Canada
- Just Add Horses Environmental Award
Presented by BFL Canada
- Lifetime Achievement Award
Presented by BFL Canada
Meetings/Conferences:
- 2018 Equestrian Canada Convention, April, 2018, Ottawa, ON
Scope: National
Publications:
- Horse Life
Type: Magazine
Profile: Updates for dressage, driving, endurance, eventing, hunter/jumper, paraequestian, reining, vaulting, breeds, industry news

ÉquiLibre - Groupe d'action sur le poids
#304, 7200, rue Hutchison, Montréal QC H3N 1Z2
Tél: 514-270-3779; *Téléc:* 514-270-1974
Ligne sans frais: 877-270-3779
info@equilibre.ca
www.equilibre.ca
www.facebook.com/GroupeEquiLibre
twitter.com/groupeequilibre
www.youtube.com/user/groupeequilibre
Nom précédent: Collectif action alternative en obésité
Aperçu: *Dimension:* petite; *Envergure:* locale; Organisme sans but lucratif
Mission: Favoriser la prévention et la diminution des problèmes reliés au poids et à l'image corporelle par l'élaboration d'actions de sensibilisation, et la conception de programmes et d'outils éducatifs à l'intention de la population et des professionnels de la santé
Membre(s) du personnel: 16
Membre: *Montant de la cotisation:* 20$ étudiant; 65$ professionel; 125$ corporatif
Membre(s) du bureau directeur:
Roxanne Léonard, Directrice générale
roxanne.leonard@equilibre.ca

Equine Association of Yukon (EAY)
PO Box 30011, Whitehorse YT Y1A 5M2
equineyukon@gmail.com
equineyukon.weebly.com
Overview: A small provincial organization
Mission: To be the governing body for equine sports in the Yukon.
Membership: *Fees:* $20 junior; $30 senior; $70 family

Equine Canada; Canadian Equestrian Federation *See* Equestrian Canada

Equine Guelph
University of Guelph, 50 McGilvray St., Guelph ON N1G 2W1
Tel: 519-824-4120
www.equineguelph.ca
Overview: A small local organization founded in 2003
Mission: To provide support for horses & the horse industry; To enhance the health & well-being of horses
Finances: *Funding Sources:* Donations
Activities: Offering educational resources, workshops, & courses on equine welfare & science; Presenting EquiMania!, an interactive exhibit for youth; Conducting & disseminating research; Promoting healthcare & industry development
Chief Officer(s):
Gayle Ecker, Director, 519-824-4120 Ext. 56678
gecker@uoguelph.ca

Susan Raymond, Officer, Communications & Programs,
519-824-4120 Ext. 54230
slraymon@uoguelph.ca

Equitas - Centre international d'éducation aux droits humains See Equitas - International Centre for Human Rights Education

Equitas - International Centre for Human Rights Education / Equitas - Centre international d'éducation aux droits humains
#1100, 666, rue Sherbrooke ouest, Montréal QC H3A 1E7
Tel: 514-954-0382; *Fax:* 514-954-0659
info@equitas.org
www.equitas.org
www.linkedin.com/groups/Equitas-International-Centre-Human-Rights-1828397
twitter.com/equitasintl
www.youtube.com/user/EquitasHRE
Previous Name: Canadian Human Rights Foundation
Overview: A medium-sized national charitable organization founded in 1967
Mission: To provide human rights education in Canada & abroad, based on the principles elaborated in the Universal Declaration of Human Rights
Staff Member(s): 23
Activities: *Internships:* Yes; *Speaker Service:* Yes
Chief Officer(s):
Rob Yalden, President
Ian Hamilton, Executive Director
ihamilton@equitas.org

Eriksdale & District Chamber of Commerce
PO Box 434, Eriksdale MB R0C 0W0
Tel: 204-739-2606
www.eriksdale.com
Overview: A small local organization
Chief Officer(s):
Keith Lundale, President
klundale@mts.net

Erin Soaring Society
ON
Overview: A small local organization overseen by Soaring Association of Canada

Eritrean Canadian Community Centre of Metropolitan Toronto (ECCC)
579 St. Clair Ave. West, Toronto ON M6C 1A3
Tel: 416-658-8580; *Fax:* 416-658-7442
info@eccctoronto.ca
www.eccctoronto.ca
Overview: A small local organization founded in 1985
Mission: To provide immigrant & refugee settlement services & create an environment for building capacity in the Eritrean community of Toronto.

Ernest C. Manning Awards Foundation / Fondation des Prix Ernest C. Manning
#267, 3553 - 31 St. NW, Calgary AB T2L 2K7
Tel: 403-930-4332; *Fax:* 403-930-4329
info@manningawards.ca
www.manningawards.ca
www.linkedin.com/company/ernest-c-manning-awards-foundation
www.facebook.com/ManningAwards
twitter.com/manningawardsca
www.youtube.com/user/TheManningAwards
Overview: A small national organization
Mission: To recognize & encourage innovation in Canada. An independent committee of expert evaluators chooses the award winners from a selection of nominees & their decision is final.
Membership: *Committees:* Selection
Chief Officer(s):
John K. Read, Chair
Awards:
• The Manning Awards
Given annually to Canadian innovators who have conceived & developed new concepts, procedures, processes or products of benefit to Canada; awards may be in any area of activity
Deadline: February; *Amount:* One $100,000 Principal Award; one $25,000 Award of Distinction; two $10,000 Innovation prizes
• Young Canadian Innovation Awards
; *Amount:* $4,000 ea./8 recipients

Errington Therapeutic Riding Association (ETRA)
Pyramid Stables, PO Box 462, 7581 Harby Rd., Lantzville, Parksville BC V9P 2G6
etrainfo@shaw.ca
www.etra.ca
www.facebook.com/ETRAPledgeRide2016
Overview: A small local organization founded in 1989
Mission: ETRA is an independent, non-profit association that gives people with disabilities the chance to ride a horse, to improve their physical and/or mental well-being, & enhance their sense of achievement & self-worth.
Member of: CanTRA; B.C. Therapeutic Riding Association
Affiliation(s): BC Therapeutic Riding Association; Canadian Therapeutic Riding Association
Finances: *Annual Operating Budget:* Less than $50,000; *Funding Sources:* Provincial government; rider fees; donations; community organizations
40 volunteer(s)
Membership: 112; *Fees:* $5
Activities: *Speaker Service:* Yes
Chief Officer(s):
Regine Eder, President
regine.eder@shaw.ca

ERS Training & Development Corporation (ERS) / Corporation pour la formation et le développement ERS
#810, 5250, rue Ferrier, Montréal QC H4P 1L4
Tel: 514-731-3419; *Fax:* 514-731-4999
ers@erstraining.ca
www.erstraining.ca
Overview: A medium-sized national charitable organization founded in 1986
Mission: To promote development & training; to identify the needs of youth; to develop & promote training skills & employment readiness; to seek out & put in place programs for the improvement of youth circumstances; to implement programs so that all may achieve full potential
Finances: *Annual Operating Budget:* $250,000-$500,000
Staff Member(s): 8; 7 volunteer(s)
Membership: 15; *Fees:* $25 annually
Activities: *Internships:* Yes
Chief Officer(s):
Peter L. Clément, Président et directeur général
peterclement@erstraining.ca

Est club portugais de Montréal *Voir* Clube Oriental Português de Montreal

Escadrilles canadiennes de plaisance See Canadian Power & Sail Squadrons (Canadian Headquarters)

Eskasoni Fish & Wildlife Commission (EFWC)
4115 Shore Rd., Eskasoni NS B1W 1M4
Tel: 902-379-2024; *Fax:* 902-379-2159
info@efwc.ca
www.efwc.ca
www.facebook.com/EFWC01
twitter.com/ESKFISHWILDLIFE
Overview: A small local organization founded in 1991
Mission: To facilitate the Aboriginal Fisheries Strategy agreement; To create partnerships with other agencies & organizations dealing with fish & wildlife
Chief Officer(s):
Thomas J. Johnson, Executive Director
tom@efwc.ca

The ESOP (Employee Share Ownership Plan) Association See ESOP Association Canada

ESOP Association Canada (ESOP)
www.esop-canada.com
Previous Name: The ESOP (Employee Share Ownership Plan) Association
Overview: A small national organization founded in 1990
Mission: To promote & assist the implementation of employee share ownership through education, networking & lobbying
Member of: Canadian Advanced Technology Alliance
Affiliation(s): National Centre for Employee Ownership
Staff Member(s): 1; 12 volunteer(s)
Membership: *Fees:* $240

Espanola & District Association for Community Living See Community Living Espanola

Espanola & District Chamber of Commerce See LaCloche Foothills Chamber of Commerce

Esperanto Association of Canada (KEA) / Association canadienne d'esperanto
277, rue Regina, Montréal QC H4G 2G6
www.esperanto.ca/en/kea
Also Known As: Kanada Esperanto-Asocio
Overview: A small national charitable organization founded in 1958
Mission: To promote & teach the neutral international language of Esperanto
Affiliation(s): Universal Esperanto Association - Rotterdam
Finances: *Annual Operating Budget:* Less than $50,000; *Funding Sources:* Membership fees; donations
Staff Member(s): 1; 9 volunteer(s)
Membership: 40 lifetime + 150 individual; *Fees:* $25 individual; $400 life; free for youth 18 & under; *Member Profile:* Interest in international language; *Committees:* Esperanto Book Service; Publications; Nominations
Activities: Offering correspondence courses & examination services; Disseminating information in & on the language Esperanto; *Awareness Events:* Week of International Friendship, last full week of Feb.; Zamenhof Day, Dec. 15; *Internships:* Yes; *Speaker Service:* Yes; *Rents Mailing List:* Yes; *Library:* Libraro Ludovika; by appointment
Chief Officer(s):
Paul Hopkins, President
Tamara Anna Kozeij, Director

Esperanto Rondo de Otavo (ERO) / Cercle Esperanto d'Ottawa
Ottawa ON
Tel: 613-996-8216
esperanto.ca/ottawa
Also Known As: Esperanto Circle of Ottawa
Previous Name: Ontario Esperanto-Asocio
Overview: A medium-sized local organization founded in 1989
Mission: To provide a forum where Ontario speakers of Esperanto may find & become acquainted with each other, practise the language, exchange expertise about the Esperanto movement & language, & generally enjoy themselves together; To inform & educate Ontarians about the Esperanto language, movement & the community, & how these can provide the most efficient communication channel between speakers of different mother tongues; To establish relations with the Ontario government & provincial-level enterprises & other Ontario associations potentially showing some common goal or interest with the association, & linking the association with other organizations at the local, provincial, national, & international levels in the worldwide Esperanto movement
Finances: *Annual Operating Budget:* Less than $50,000; *Funding Sources:* Membership fees; donations
Membership: 1-99
Activities: *Speaker Service:* Yes

Esperanto-Toronto
Toronto ON
esperanto.toronto@gmail.com
esperanto.ca/toronto
twitter.com/torontanoj
Previous Name: Toronto Esperanto-Klubo
Overview: A small local organization founded in 1950
Mission: To provide a social home base for individuals wishing to learn & practise the international language, Esperanto; To provide the necessary information & courses about Esperanto
Affiliation(s): Canadian Esperanto Association
Finances: *Annual Operating Budget:* Less than $50,000
Membership: 190
Activities: Weekly meetings; *Speaker Service:* Yes; *Library:* by appointment Not open to public
Chief Officer(s):
Matthew Chisholm, President
Jed Meltzer, Vice-President
Detlef Karthaus, Treasurer
Publications:
• La Torontano [a publication of Esperanto-Toronto]
Type: Newsletter

Esprit Orchestra
#511, 174 Spadina Ave., Toronto ON M5T 2C2
Tel: 416-815-7887; *Fax:* 416-815-7337
info@espritorchestra.com
www.espritorchestra.com
www.linkedin.com/company/esprit-orchestra
www.facebook.com/EspritOrchestra
twitter.com/espritorchestra
www.youtube.com/EspritOrchestra
Overview: A small local charitable organization founded in 1983 overseen by Orchestras Canada
Mission: To present "new music" programs & collaborative arts events; to act as an example for new music groups to develop

similar programs which strengthen the new music community as a whole
Finances: *Funding Sources:* Government; Private foundations; Individual donations
Staff Member(s): 5
Activities: Performing concerts; facilitating education & outreach programs; Recording for film
Chief Officer(s):
Rachel Gauntlett, Manager, Operations
Alex Pauk, Music Director

Esquimalt Chamber of Commerce
#103, 1249 Esquimalt Rd., Victoria BC V9A 3P2
Tel: 250-590-2125; *Fax:* 250-590-1843
admin@esquimaltchamber.ca
esquimaltchamber.ca
www.facebook.com/EsquimaltChamber
twitter.com/esqchamber
Overview: A small local organization founded in 1947
Finances: *Funding Sources:* Membership dues
Membership: *Fees:* $198 businesses with under 100 employees; $182 home-based businesses; $160 non profit organizations; *Member Profile:* Business licence to operate within municipality of Esquimalt
Activities: *Speaker Service:* Yes
Chief Officer(s):
Bill Lang, President, 250-386-3456

Essa & District Agricultural Society
7505 - 10th Line, Thornton ON L0L 2N0
Tel: 705-726-1200; *Fax:* 705-726-1250
info@essaagriplex.ca
essaagriplex.ca
www.facebook.com/essaagriplex.ca
twitter.com/essaagriplex
Previous Name: Barrie Agricultural Society
Overview: A small local charitable organization founded in 1853
Mission: To encourage an awareness of agriculture; To promote improvements in the quality of life for persons living in our community, rural & urban; To organize & operate the Barrie Fair & other similar events; To provide a venue where exhibitors can showcase, compete & market their products, crops or livestock
Finances: *Annual Operating Budget:* $250,000-$500,000; *Funding Sources:* Sponsors; Rental revenue; Barrie Fair
Staff Member(s): 4; 150 volunteer(s)
Membership: 1,000-4,999; *Fees:* $5
Chief Officer(s):
Henry VanderWielen, President
Wayne Hawke, Executive Director
Cindy Vecchiarelli, Administrator
cindy@essaagriplex.ca

Essa Historical Society
c/o Olive Lee, 20 Henry St., Thornton ON L0L 2N0
Tel: 705-458-9971
Overview: A small local organization founded in 1979
Mission: To update the history of Essa Township; to promote the preservation of historical buildings & landmarks.
Member of: Ontario Historical Society
Affiliation(s): Simcoe County Historical Society
Membership: *Fees:* $10 single; $20 couple
Activities: Undertakes historical research & identifies historical landmarks in Essa Township
Chief Officer(s):
Arnold Banting, President, 705-719-6535
Olive Lee, Secretary
teddylee1@rogers.com
Publications:
• Early History of Ivy
Type: book
Profile: A collection of photos & information on the hamlet of Ivy

Essential Skills Ontario (OLC)
#503, 65 Wellesley St. East, Toronto ON M4Y 1G7
Tel: 416-963-5787; *Fax:* 416-963-8102
info@essentialskillsontario.ca
www.essentialskillsontario.ca
www.linkedin.com/company/essential-skills-ontario
www.facebook.com/EssentialSkillsOntario
twitter.com/ES_Ontario
www.youtube.com/user/SpotlightonLearning
Previous Name: Ontario Literacy Coalition
Overview: A medium-sized provincial organization founded in 1986
Mission: To help provide adults with *essential skills* that allow them to grow in their lives, careers, & communities
Finances: *Annual Operating Budget:* $250,000-$500,000
Staff Member(s): 2
Membership: 250+
Activities: Partnering with stakeholders to research & implement effective skills training; Informing policy through evidence-based research studies; Supporting & strengthening practitioners to allow them to deliver high quality training; Offering professional development opportunities; *Speaker Service:* Yes
Chief Officer(s):
Lesley Brown, Executive Director
lesley@essentialskillsontario.ca
Susanne Smith, Director, Finance & Administration
susanne@essentialskillsontario.ca
Meetings/Conferences:
• Essential Skills Ontario Annual General Meeting 2018, 2018, ON
Scope: Provincial
Contact Information: Director, Finance & Administration: Susanne Smith, E-mail: susanne@essentialskillsontario.ca
Publications:
• E-ssential News [a publication of Essential Skills Ontario]
Type: Newsletter; *Frequency:* Monthly
Profile: Contains news & updates for members

Les EssentiElles
Centre de la francophonie, 302, rue Strickland, Whitehorse YT Y1A 2K1
Tél: 867-668-2636; *Téléc:* 867-668-3511
elles@lesessentielles.ca
lesessentielles.ca
www.facebook.com/lesessentiellesyukon
twitter.com/elles_yukon
Aperçu: *Dimension:* moyenne; *Envergure:* provinciale
Mission: De représenter les intérêts des femmes francophones du Yukon
Membre de: Fédération nationale des femmes canadiennes françaises; Réseau canadien pour la santé des femmes; Nouveau Départ; Assemblée des aînées et aînés francophones du Canada; Association franco-yukonnaise; Partenariat communauté en santé; Partenariat communauté en éducation
Membre(s) du personnel: 3
Activités: Projet: Le Partenariat communauté en santé
Membre(s) du bureau directeur:
Paige Galette, Présidente
Elaine Michaud, Directrice

Essex Community Services (ECS)
#7, 35 Victoria Ave., Essex ON N8M 1M4
Tel: 519-776-4231; *Fax:* 519-776-4966
ecs@essexcs.on.ca
www.essexcs.on.ca
Previous Name: Community Information - Essex
Overview: A small local charitable organization founded in 1975 overseen by InformOntario
Mission: The organization provides a number of services to members of the community, including door-to-door transporation assistance for seniors, coat collection for children, income tax clinic, job bank, community resource library.
Affiliation(s): Inform Canada
Staff Member(s): 4
Activities: "Share the Warmth"; job kiosk; fundraising; community crisis centre; children's crisis centre; Hiatus House; counselling; housing info services; Care-A-Van; Foot Care Clinic; Income Tax Clinic; Coats for Kids; Letter Carrier's Alert; Security Reassurance; *Library:* Resource
Chief Officer(s):
Kelly Stack, Executive Director
director@essexcs.on.ca

Essex County Cattlemen's Association
#310, 5568 Lakeshore Rd., RR#2, Essex ON N0P 1J0
Tel: 519-687-2530; *Fax:* 519-687-3792
Overview: A small local organization
Affiliation(s): Ontario Cattlemen's Association
Chief Officer(s):
Shawn Morris, President
shawn@jackmorrisauctions.com

Essex County Orchid Society
280 Howards Ave., Windsor ON N0R 1L0
essexcountyorchidsociety.webs.com
www.facebook.com/EssexCountyOrchidSociety
Overview: A small local organization founded in 2009
Mission: To provide knowledge & information to its members
Member of: Canadian Orchid Congress; American Orchid Society; Mid-America Orchid Congress
Membership: *Fees:* $20 single; $25 family
Chief Officer(s):
Barb Morden, President
barbmorden@cogeco.ca

Essex County Stamp Club (Windsor)
Windsor ON
Tel: 519-966-2276
www.essexcountystampclub.com
Overview: A small local organization founded in 1978
Mission: To promote stamp collecting to all ages; To learn by collecting & taking care of a collection
Affiliation(s): American Philatelic Society; Royal Philatelic Society of Canada
Finances: *Annual Operating Budget:* Less than $50,000; *Funding Sources:* Membership fees; annual show
Staff Member(s): 5
Membership: 62; *Fees:* $15; *Member Profile:* All ages 18+; *Committees:* Executive
Activities: Slide shows; guest speakers; auction; youth program; *Awareness Events:* WINPEX Annual Show, 1st Sat. in March; *Library:* Not open to public
Chief Officer(s):
Brian Cutler, President
cutler@mnsi.net

Essex Law Association
245 Windsor Ave., Windsor ON N9A 1J2
Tel: 519-252-8418; *Fax:* 519-252-9686
www.essexlaw.ca
Overview: A small local organization founded in 1884
Staff Member(s): 2
Membership: 600+; *Fees:* $105
Activities: *Library:* County Courthouse Library
Chief Officer(s):
Philip S. Chandler, President
Awards:
• Essex Law Association Centennial Scholarship
Eligibility: Students in the law program at the University of Windsor
Publications:
• Caveat
Type: Newsletter

Essex-Kent Cage Bird Society
1647 Jefferson Blvd., Windsor ON N8T 2V6
Tel: 519-948-6398
www.essexkentcbs.com
Overview: A small local organization founded in 1976
Mission: To promote the caring, breeding, & keeping of cage birds; To educate members & the general public on the proper care of cage birds; To gather & disseminate scientific knowledge on the breeding & care of cage birds
Member of: Avicultural Advancement Council of Canada
Affiliation(s): Avian Preservation Foundation; National Finch & Softbill Society; National Cockatiel Society; African Lovebird Society; North American Parrot Society
Finances: *Annual Operating Budget:* Less than $50,000; *Funding Sources:* Donations; exhibitions
Membership: 165; *Fees:* $30 family or single; $20 junior; *Member Profile:* Bird keepers & breeders, exhibitors & pets
Activities: Presenting 2 shows per year - Young Feather Show (Summer) & Annual Show (Fall); Organizing monthly meetings with occasional guest speakers
Chief Officer(s):
Alfred Mion, President, 519-948-6398
julianne@mnsi.net

Esterhazy & District Chamber of Commerce
PO Box 490, Esterhazy SK S0A 0X0
Tel: 306-745-5405; *Fax:* 306-745-6797
Overview: A small local organization
Mission: To contribute to the development & growth of the business environment in Esterhazy Saskatchewan & the surrounding area
Member of: Saskatchewan Chamber of Commerce

Estevan & District Labour Committee
270 Duncan Rd., Estevan SK S4A 4A6
Overview: A small local organization overseen by Saskatchewan Federation of Labour
Mission: To promote the interests of affiliates in Estevan, Saskatchewan & the surrounding region; To advance the economic & social welfare of workers
Affiliation(s): Canadian Labour Congress (CLC)
Activities: Presenting educational opportunities; Raising awareness of occupational health & safety; Organizing a

ceremony to mark the annual Day of Mourning for Workers Killed & Injured on the Job
Chief Officer(s):
Sammy Dryden, Acting President, 306-634-3292
s.g.dryden@sasktel.net

Estevan Arts Council
Souris Valley Aquatic & Leisure Centre, 701 Souris Ave., Estevan SK S4A 2T1
Tel: 306-634-3942
estevanartscouncil@sasktel.net
www.estevanartscouncil.com
Overview: A small local charitable organization founded in 1967
Mission: To promote the arts & culture in Estevan & area
Member of: Organization of Saskatchewan Arts Councils
Finances: *Annual Operating Budget:* $50,000-$100,000; *Funding Sources:* Grants; donations; workshop fees; ticket sales
Staff Member(s): 1; 15 volunteer(s)
Membership: 15; *Committees:* Stars for Saskatchewan; Koncerts for Kids; Visual Arts
Activities: Art, painting, drawing, ceramics & pottery classes; "koncerts for kids"; Stars for Saskatchewan Concert Series

Estevan Chamber of Commerce
#2, 322 - 4th St., Estevan SK S4A 0T8
Tel: 306-634-2828; *Fax:* 306-634-6729
admin@estevanchamber.ca
www.estevanchamber.ca
www.linkedin.com/company/estevan-chamber-of-commerce
www.facebook.com/EstevanChamberofCommerce
twitter.com/EstevanChamber
Also Known As: Estevan Chamber
Overview: A small local organization founded in 1904
Mission: To improve the business climate and community well being
Member of: Saskatchewan Chamber of Commerce; Canadian Chamber of Commerce; Canada North America Trade Corridor; SKEconomic Developers Association, Economic Developers Association of Canada, Tourism Saskatchewan
Finances: *Funding Sources:* Membership fundraising; business directory sales, events, contracted services
Staff Member(s): 4
Membership: 343; *Fees:* Schedule available; *Member Profile:* Any reputable person, directly or indirectly engaged or interested in trade, commerce or the economic & social welfare of the district; *Committees:* Economic Development & Tourism
Activities: Organizing political forums, community-wide customer service evaluations, trade shows & events, & educational & leadership seminars; Advocating for business community, economic, & tourism development; *Awareness Events:* Farmer Appreciation, Feb.; Leadership Seminar, Estevan Business Excellence Awards, Showcase; Pure Energy Weekend, Kickoff to Christmas; *Library*
Chief Officer(s):
Jackie Wall, Executive Director
executivedirector@estevanchamber.ca
Awards:
• Estevan Comprehensive High School Bursary; *Amount:* $1,000

Estevan Exhibition Association
PO Box 100, 811 Souris Ave., Estevan SK S4A 2A2
Tel: 306-634-5595; *Fax:* 306-634-8833
eea@sasktel.net
Overview: A small local organization founded in 1905
Mission: To promotes agriculture, recreation & the development of community spirit.
Member of: Western Canada Fairs; CAFE; Saskatchewan Southeast Tourism Association; Estevan Chamber of Commerce; Saskatchewan Association of Agricultural Societies & Exhibitions (SAASE)
Activities: Annual Estevan Fair; Annual Rodeo; Rumble in the Dirt Cabaret
Chief Officer(s):
Dallas Spencer, President

Eston Arts Council
PO Box 327, Eston SK S0L 1A0
Overview: A small local charitable organization
Member of: Organization of Saskatchewan Arts Councils
Finances: *Annual Operating Budget:* Less than $50,000; *Funding Sources:* Fundraising; grants
25 volunteer(s)
Membership: 1-99
Activities: Art shows; drama presentations

Estonian Central Council in Canada (EKN)
310 Bloor St. West, Toronto ON M5S 1W4
estoniancentralcouncil@gmail.com
www.estoniancouncil.ca
www.facebook.com/estoniancouncil
Overview: A medium-sized national organization founded in 1951 overseen by Baltic Federation in Canada
Mission: To help further the interests & development of the Estonian community in Canada
Member of: Estonian World Congress; Baltic Federation of Canada; Central & Eastern European Council of Canada
Chief Officer(s):
Marcus Kolga, President

Estonian Evangelical Lutheran Church Consistory (EELC)
383 Jarvis St., Toronto ON M5B 2C7
Tel: 416-925-5465; *Fax:* 416-925-5688
e.e.l.k@eelk.ee
www.eelk.ee/eng_EELCabroad.html
www.facebook.com/EestiKirik
Overview: A medium-sized national organization founded in 1950
Mission: EELC is an independent, self-governing church which functions on democratic grounds, calls together congregations, ordains pastors, holds services & carries out religious ceremonies according to the Service Book, the Statutes & the established order. The Consistory is the government of the EELC.
Affiliation(s): Lutheran World Federation; World Council of Churches
Staff Member(s): 4; 10 volunteer(s)
Membership: 15,700 + 63 congregations

ETC Group
ETC Headquarters, #206, 180 Metcalfe St., Ottawa ON K2P 1P5
Tel: 613-241-2267; *Fax:* 613-241-2506
etc@etcgroup.org
www.etcgroup.org
www.linkedin.com/company/2587794
www.facebook.com/theetcgroup
Also Known As: Action Group on Erosion, Technology & Concentration
Previous Name: Rural Advancement Foundation International
Overview: A small international organization founded in 1985
Staff Member(s): 8; 2 volunteer(s)
Activities: *Library:* ETC Group Resource Library; by appointment
Chief Officer(s):
Neth Daño, Co-Executive Director
Jim Thomas, Co-Executive Director

Ethics Practitioners' Association of Canada (EPAC) / Association des praticiens en éthique du Canada (APEC)
c/o Secretariat, 1485 Laperriere Ave., Ottawa ON K1Z 7S8
Tel: 613-722-2273; *Fax:* 613-729-6206
service@epac-apec.ca
www.epac-apec.ca
Overview: A small national organization
Mission: To enable individuals to work successfully in the field of ethics in organizations by enhancing the quality & availability of ethics advice & services across Canada
Membership: *Fees:* $75 individual; $25 student; *Committees:* Membership; Revenue Generation; Communications; Education; Governance & Planning; Audit & Risk Management; Workshop Task Force; Privacy
Activities: *Internships:* Yes
Chief Officer(s):
Robert Czerny, Chair

Ethiopiaid
#900, 275 Slater St., Ottawa ON K1P 5H9
Tel: 613-238-4481
info@ethiopiaid.ca
www.ethiopiaid.ca
www.facebook.com/EthiopiaidCanada
twitter.com/EthiopiaidCAN
Overview: A medium-sized international charitable organization founded in 1989
Mission: To create lasting & positive change in Ethiopia by tackling the problems of poverty, ill health & poor education; To donate to local community projects in Ethiopia
Chief Officer(s):
Olivier Bonnet, Executive Director
Jennifer Naidoo, Officer, Development & Communications

Ethiopian Association in the Greater Toronto Area & Surrounding Regions
1950 Danforth Ave., Toronto ON M4C 1J4
Tel: 416-649-1522
office@ethiocommun.org
www.ethiocommun.org
Overview: A small local charitable organization founded in 1981 overseen by Ontario Council of Agencies Serving Immigrants
Mission: To assist Ethiopians & other newcomers in the GTA & surrounding regions in settlement & integration processes; To preserve & promote Ethiopian heritage; To ensure the inclusion of persons of Ethiopian origin in all aspects of social, cultural, & civic life in Canada
Staff Member(s): 18
Membership: 1,500; *Fees:* $60; *Committees:* Executive; Budget & Finance; Nominations; Research & Education; Seniors; Social & Cultural; Women; Youth
Activities: Offering newcomers settlement services; crisis counselling; seniors programs; *Awareness Events:* Ethiopian-Canadian Day, September
Chief Officer(s):
Yeshihareg Worku, President

Etobicoke Historical Society
c/o Montgomery's Inn, 4709 Dundas St. West, Toronto ON M9A 1A8
www.etobicokehistorical.com
www.facebook.com/etobicokehistory
twitter.com/EtobHistory
Overview: A small local charitable organization founded in 1958
Mission: To engage in the collection, preservation & publication of material relevant to the history & heritage of Etobicoke; to support the preservation & restoration of historically significant properties in the community; to collect & catalogue a panorama of photographs of Etobicoke
Member of: Ontario Historical Society
Finances: *Funding Sources:* Provincial government; membership fees
Membership: *Fees:* $20 institution; $25 individual; $35 couple; $200 individual life; $250 couple life
Chief Officer(s):
James Geneau, President
james@united-thinking.com

Etobicoke Humane Society (EHS)
67 Six Point Rd., Toronto ON M8Z 2X3
Tel: 416-249-6100; *Fax:* 416-249-6100
info@etobicokehumanesociety.com
www.etobicokehumanesociety.com
www.linkedin.com/company/2992106
www.facebook.com/etobicokehumanesociety
twitter.com/EtobHumaneSoc
www.instagram.com/etobicokehumanesociety
Overview: A medium-sized local charitable organization founded in 1987
Mission: To protect, care for, & advance the welfare of animals
Member of: Canadian Federation of Humane Societies
Affiliation(s): Ontario Society for the Prevention of Cruelty to Animals (OSPCA)
Finances: *Annual Operating Budget:* $50,000-$100,000; *Funding Sources:* Public donations; bequests; special events
40 volunteer(s)
Membership: 2,500; *Fees:* $50; $40 senior; *Committees:* Cat Adoption; Dog Adoption; Executive; Finance; Administration; Education; Fundraising; Animal Protection Services; PR; Membership/Volunteers; Shelter
Activities: Annual Dog Walk-a-Thon; Tag Day; Paws & Claws; Petsmart Santa Photos; *Library:* Pet Care Library; Open to public
Chief Officer(s):
Cristina Scassa, President

Etobicoke North Community Information Centre *See* Albion Neighbourhood Services

Etobicoke Philharmonic Orchestra (EPO)
PO Box 60002, 1500 Islington Ave, Toronto ON M9A 5G2
Tel: 416-239-5665
info@eporchestra.ca
www.eporchestra.ca
www.facebook.com/eporchestra
twitter.com/eporchestra
Overview: A small local charitable organization founded in 1960 overseen by Orchestras Canada
Mission: To provide an opportunity for trained amateur musicians to perform together & become acquainted with an orchestral repertoire; to provide the community with symphonic

music, competently performed in a local setting; to assist serious music students in their studies through performance experience & a scholarship program
Member of: Arts Etobicoke; Orchestras Ontario; Orchestras Canada
Finances: *Funding Sources:* Government grants; Fundraising projects; Box office; Corporate & individual donations
Staff Member(s): 8; 36 volunteer(s)
Membership: 68 individual
Chief Officer(s):
Judy Allan, President
Judy Gargaro, General Manager
manager@eporchestra.ca
Awards:
• Etobicoke Philarhmonic Orchestra Student Scholarship
Eligibility: Students studying music privately with intentions of entering a career in music

Eucharistic Apostles of the Divine Mercy (EADM)
c/o Rolando & Susan Dela Rosa, 49 Parsons Pl., Thornhill ON L4J 7Y4
Tel: 647-239-9350
www.thedivinemercy.org
Also Known As: EADM Cenacle Prayer Group of Toronto
Overview: A small local organization
Mission: To encourage members to care for the rejected, the lonely, the disabled, the elderly, & the dying
Affiliation(s): Archdiocese of Toronto
Activities: Meetings; youth retreat
Chief Officer(s):
Mario Salvadori, Spiritual Director

European Evangelistic Crusade, Inc. *See* Global Outreach Mission

European Union Chamber of Commerce in Toronto (EUCOCIT)
#1500, 480 University Ave., Toronto ON M5G 1V2
Tel: 416-598-7087; *Fax:* 416-598-1840
info@eucocit.com
www.eucocit.com
www.linkedin.com/groups/2924006
Overview: A large international organization founded in 1995
Mission: To strengthen economic ties between Canada & Europe; To act as the business voice of & the point of contact for European business interests in Canada
Finances: *Funding Sources:* Membership fees; event revenue; sponsorships
Membership: 27; *Fees:* $250
Chief Officer(s):
Thomas Beck, President

Eva's Initiatives for Homeless Youth
#245, 401 Richmond St. West, Toronto ON M5V 3A8
Tel: 416-977-4497
info@evas.ca
www.evas.ca
www.linkedin.com/company/eva%27s-initiatives
www.facebook.com/evasinitiatives
twitter.com/evasinitiatives
www.instagram.com/evasinitiatives
Also Known As: Eva's Initiatives
Overview: A small local organization founded in 1992
Mission: To create opportunities for homeless youth
Finances: *Funding Sources:* Donations
Staff Member(s): 110; 75 volunteer(s)
Activities: Providing harm reduction; training, & employment resources; Teaching youth life skills; Facilitating the Family Reconnect Program to reunite homeless youth & their families
Chief Officer(s):
Beth Gebreab, Manager, Administrative Services
bgebreab@evas.ca

Evangel Hall Mission (EHM)
552 Adelaide St. West, Toronto ON M5V 3W8
Tel: 416-504-3563; *Fax:* 416-504-8056
information@evangelhall.ca
www.evangelhall.ca
www.facebook.com/evangelhallmission
twitter.com/ehm_1913
Overview: A small local charitable organization founded in 1913
Mission: To deliver programs that deal with poverty and homelessness; To offer a continuum of care from emergency food, clothing & shelter to transitional & long-term housing
Affiliation(s): Presbyterian Church in Canada

Activities: Offering support, housing assistance, & services, including Out of the Cold Program, community dinners, dental clinic, & youth programs
Publications:
• Faith, Hope and Love
Type: Book; *Price:* $50
Profile: A special commemorative book to celebrate 100 years of service to the community.

Evangelical Covenant Church of Canada (ECCC)
PO Box 23117, RPO McGillvray, Winnipeg MB R3R 5S3
Tel: 204-269-3437; *Fax:* 204-269-3584
office@covchurch.ca
www.covchurch.ca
Overview: A medium-sized national charitable organization founded in 1904
Mission: To make & deepend disciples, start & strengthen churches, develop leaders, love justice & do mercy
Member of: World Relief Canada; The Evangelical Fellowship of Canada; The Canadian Council of Christian Charities
Finances: *Funding Sources:* Donations
Membership: *Member Profile:* Evangelical Covenant Churches in Canada
Chief Officer(s):
Jeff Anderson, Superintendent/President
ccc1@mts.net

Evangelical Fellowship of Canada (EFC) / Alliance évangélique du Canada
PO Box 5885, Stn. Beaver Creek, #103, 9821 Leslie St., Richmond Hill ON L4B 0B8
Tel: 905-479-4742
Toll-Free: 866-302-3362
efc@evangelicalfellowship.ca
www.evangelicalfellowship.ca
www.facebook.com/theefc
twitter.com/theefc
www.youtube.com/user/theEFCca
Overview: A medium-sized national charitable organization founded in 1964
Mission: EFC is the national association of evangelical Christians in Canada. Its aims are to be a public advocate of the gospel of Jesus Christ; to provide an evangelical identity which unites Canadian Christians of diverse backgrounds; to express biblical views on current issues; to assist individuals & groups in proclaiming the gospel & advancing Christian values.
Member of: World Evangelical Fellowship
Finances: *Annual Operating Budget:* $1.5 Million-$3 Million; *Funding Sources:* General & corporate donations; member & subscriber fees
Staff Member(s): 20; 90 volunteer(s)
Membership: 42 evangelical denominations + 64 organizations + 37 educational institutions + 1,000 churches
Activities: Task forces: Evangelism; Women in Ministry; Aboriginal; Global Mission; Commissions: Education; Religious Liberty; Social Action; *Internships:* Yes; *Speaker Service:* Yes
Chief Officer(s):
Bill Fietje, Chair
Bruce J. Clemenger, President
Awards:
• Brian Stiller Leadership Award
  Centre for Faith & Public Life
  #1410, 130 Albert St., Ottawa ON K1P 5G4
  Tel: 613-233-9868; *Fax:* 613-233-0301
  ottawa@evangelicalfellowship.ca

Evangelical Lutheran Church in Canada (ELCIC)
#600, 177 Lombard Ave., Winnipeg MB R3B 0W5
Tel: 204-984-9173; *Fax:* 204-984-9185
Toll-Free: 888-786-6707
www.elcic.ca
www.facebook.com/CanadianLutherans
twitter.com/elcicinfo
Overview: A medium-sized national charitable organization founded in 1986
Mission: The Church shares the gospel of Jesus Christ with people in Canada & around the world through the proclamation of the Word, celebration of the sacraments, & through service in Christ's name. It functions through three major entities: nationally as the ELCIC, regionally as synods, & locally as congregations.
Member of: Canadian Council of Churches; Lutheran Council in Canada; Lutheran World Federation; World Council of Churches
Affiliation(s): Anglican Church of Canada
Finances: *Annual Operating Budget:* $1.5 Million-$3 Million; *Funding Sources:* Donations

Staff Member(s): 20
Membership: 145,376 individuals; approx. 600 congregations; *Member Profile:* Current members in a congregation
Chief Officer(s):
Susan Johnson, National Bishop, 204-984-9157
Trina Gallop, Director, Communications & Stewardship, 204-984-9172
Gloria McNabb, Director, Finance & Administration, 204-984-9178
Publications:
• Canada Lutheran [a publication of the Evangelical Lutheran Church in Canada]
Type: Magazine; *Frequency:* Monthly; *Editor:* Kenn Ward
Profile: To engage the Evangelical Lutheran Church in Canada in a dynamic dialogue in which information, inspiration and ideasare shared in a thoughtful and stimulating way.

  British Columbia Synod
  80 - 10th Ave. East, New Westminster BC V3L 4R5
  Tel: 604-524-1318; *Fax:* 604-524-9255
  bcsynod@elcic.ca
  www.bcsynod.org
  Chief Officer(s):
  Gregory Mohr, Bishop
  gmohr@elcic.ca

  Eastern Synod
  74 Weber St. West, Kitchener ON N2H 3Z3
  Tel: 519-743-1461; *Fax:* 519-743-4291
  www.easternsynod.org
  www.facebook.com/ESynodELCIC
  twitter.com/ESynodELCIC
  Chief Officer(s):
  Michael J. Pryse, Bishop
  mpryse@elcic.ca

  Manitoba/Northwestern Ontario Synod
  935 Nesbitt Bay, Winnipeg MB R3T 1X5
  Tel: 204-889-3760; *Fax:* 204-896-0272
  mnosynod@elcic.ca
  www.mnosynod.org
  www.facebook.com/123283781082392
  Chief Officer(s):
  Elaine Sauer, Bishop
  esauer@elcic.ca

  Saskatchewan Synod
  714 Preston Ave., Saskatoon SK S7H 2V2
  Tel: 306-244-2474
  sksynod@elcic.ca
  sasksynod.ca
  www.facebook.com/sasksynod
  twitter.com/sasksynod
  Chief Officer(s):
  Sid Haugen, Bishop
  shaugen@elcic.ca

  Synod of Alberta & the Territories
  10014 - 81 Ave. NW, Edmonton AB T6E 1W8
  Tel: 780-439-2636; *Fax:* 780-433-6623
  Toll-Free: 866-430-2636
  info@albertasynod.ca
  www.albertasynod.ca
  Chief Officer(s):
  Larry Kochendorfer, Bishop
  lkochendorfer@elcic.ca

Evangelical Medical Aid Society Canada (EMAS)
1295 North Service Rd., Burlington ON L7R 4M2
Tel: 905-319-3415
Toll-Free: 866-648-0664
info@emascanada.org
www.emascanada.org
www.facebook.com/EMASCANADA
twitter.com/emascanada
Overview: A medium-sized international charitable organization founded in 1948
Mission: To provide medical care for those in need in a Christlike manner
Finances: *Annual Operating Budget:* $500,000-$1.5 Million; *Funding Sources:* Private donations
Staff Member(s): 2; 200 volunteer(s)
Membership: 30
Activities: Providing healthcare-related programs with a spiritual component
Chief Officer(s):
Peter Agwa, Executive Director
Ellen Watson, Director, Administration
ellen@emascanada.org

Publications:
• EMASsary [a publication of Evangelical Medical Aid Society Canada]
Type: Newsletter; *Editor:* Ellen Watson

Evangelical Mennonite Conference (EMC)
440 Main St., Steinbach MB R5G 1Z5
Tel: 204-326-6401; *Fax:* 204-326-1613
www.emconf.ca
www.facebook.com/emconference
Overview: A medium-sized national charitable organization founded in 1812
Mission: To advance Chirst's kingdom culture as members live, reach, gather & teach
Finances: *Annual Operating Budget:* $1.5 Million-$3 Million; *Funding Sources:* Donations
Membership: 7,200
Activities: *Library:* Evangelical Mennonite Conference Archives
Chief Officer(s):
Tim Dyck, General Secretary
Publications:
• The Messenger
Type: Magazine; *Frequency:* Monthly; *Editor:* Terry Smith; *ISSN:* 0701-3299
Profile: The Messenger's purpose is to inform the general public about activities and events in the denomination and provide instruction on godliness and victorious living.

Evangelical Order of Certified Pastoral Counsellors of America (EOCPCA)
#210, 3350 Fairview St., Burlington ON L7N 3L5
Tel: 905-639-0137; *Fax:* 905-333-8901
eocpc@cogeco.ca
www.eocpc.com
Previous Name: Order of Certified Pastoral Counsellors of America
Overview: A medium-sized national organization founded in 1982
Mission: To promote a Christian-oriented order; To certify & accredit pastoral counsellors by federal charter
Member of: Canadian Christian Counsellors Association; Canadian Christian Clinical Counsellors College
Affiliation(s): California State Christian University
Finances: *Annual Operating Budget:* $500,000-$1.5 Million
Staff Member(s): 3
Membership: 1,200 individual; *Fees:* $100-400
Activities: Courses, certifications & workshops
Chief Officer(s):
Stephen Hambly, Contact

Evangelical Tract Distributors (EDT)
PO Box 146, Edmonton AB T5J 2G9
Tel: 780-477-1538; *Fax:* 780-477-3795
www.evangelicaltract.com
Overview: A small national organization founded in 1935
Mission: EDT is a non-profit organization that prints & distributes Christian gospel tracts free of charge. It is a registered charity, BN: 130522659RR0001.
Chief Officer(s):
John Harder, President/Managing Director
Publications:
• The Evangelist
Type: Newsletter; *Frequency:* Monthly

Evansburg & Entwistle Chamber of Commerce
PO Box 598, Evansburg AB T0E 0T0
Tel: 780-727-3526; *Fax:* 780-727-3526
info@partnersonthepembina.com
www.partnersonthepembina.com
Overview: A small local charitable organization
Mission: To facilitate community & economic development in the area
Member of: Alberta Chambers of Commerce
20 volunteer(s)
Membership: 53; *Fees:* $60 business; $30 individual
Chief Officer(s):
Eric Karlzen, President
Al Hagman, Vice-President

Eventing Canada [!]
59 Hillside Dr., Toronto ON M4K 2M1
Tel: 416-429-1415
www.eventingcanada.com
www.facebook.com/EventingCanada
twitter.com/Eventing_Canada
Overview: A small national organization founded in 1996
Mission: To independently promote the sport of eventing

Chief Officer(s):
Sue Grocott, Contact
sgrocott@eventingcanada.com

Evergreen
Evergreen Brick Works, #300, 550 Bayview Ave, Toronto ON M4W 3X8
Tel: 416-596-1495; *Fax:* 416-596-1443
Toll-Free: 888-426-3138
info@evergreen.ca
www.evergreen.ca
www.facebook.com/EvergreenCanada
twitter.com/EvergreenCanada
www.instagram.com/EvergreenCanada
Previous Name: The Evergreen Foundation
Overview: A medium-sized national charitable organization founded in 1991
Mission: To bring communities & nature together for the benefit of both; To create sustaining, healthy, dynamic outdoor spaces by engaging people & encouraging local stewardship
Finances: *Funding Sources:* Donations; Sponsorships
Activities: Creating innovative resources; Transforming school grounds & home landscapes; Conserving publicly accessible land; Hosting conferences; *Library*
Chief Officer(s):
Geoff Cape, Executive Director
gcape@evergreen.ca
Seana Irvine, Chief Strategy officer
seana@evergreen.ca
Hamilton Office
294 James St. North, Hamilton ON L8R 2L3
Chief Officer(s):
Jay Carter, Contact
jcarter@evergreen.ca
Vancouver Office
#90, 425 Carrall St., Vancouver BC V6B 6E3
Tel: 604-689-0766
infobc@evergreen.ca

The Evergreen Foundation *See* Evergreen

Evergreen Party of Alberta; Vision 2012; Alberta Greens *See* The Green Party of Alberta

Evergreen Theatre Society
#2, 1709 8th Ave. SE, Calgary AB T2E 0S9
Tel: 403-228-1384; *Fax:* 403-229-1385
Toll-Free: 877-840-9746
info@evergreentheatre.com
www.evergreentheatre.com
www.facebook.com/229733167114546
twitter.com/evergreen_th
Overview: A small local charitable organization founded in 1991
Mission: To create innovative, entertaining, accessible, & educational theatre for a healthy & sustainable future
Staff Member(s): 6
Activities: *Internships:* Yes
Chief Officer(s):
Valmai Goggin, Artistic Producer
valmai@evergreentheatre.com
Sean Fraser, Executive Director
sean@evergreentheatre.com

Ex Libris Association
c/o Faculty of Information Studies, University of Toronto, 140 St. George St., Toronto ON M5S 3G6
Tel: 416-978-7079
www.exlibris.ca
www.linkedin.com/groups/4628613/profile
www.facebook.com/ExLibrisAssociation
Overview: A small national charitable organization founded in 1986
Mission: To encourage the publication of the history of Canadian libraries & librarianship & the identification & preservation of materials relating to library history in Canada which are not at present collected, organized or preserved by any other organization; To serve as a voice for retired librarians on important library-related issues
Finances: *Annual Operating Budget:* Less than $50,000; *Funding Sources:* Membership dues; Donations
15 volunteer(s)
Membership: 200+; *Fees:* $35 regular; *Member Profile:* Retired librarians & others interested in association's objectives
Chief Officer(s):
Rick Ficek, President
Jean Weihs, Recording & Correspondence Secretary

Awards:
• W. Kaye Lamb Award for Service to Seniors
Publications:
• Biographies of Librarians & Information Professionals in Canada [a publication of the Ex Libris Association]
Profile: A database of individuals who have been influential in library & information science in Canada
• ELAN [a publication of the Ex Libris Association]
Type: Newsletter; *Frequency:* s-a.; *ISSN:* 1709-1179
• A History of Education for Library & Information Studies in Canada [a publication of the Ex Libris Association]
Type: Report; *Price:* $7
• The Morton Years [a publication of the Ex Libris Association]
Type: Book; *Number of Pages:* 141; *Author:* Elizabeth Hulse; *ISBN:* 0-9699645-0-1; *Price:* $7
Profile: An account of the Canadian Library Association from 1946-1971

Examinateurs canadiens en optométrie *See* Canadian Examiners in Optometry

Excellence Canada
#402, 154 University Ave., Toronto ON M5H 3Y9
Tel: 416-251-7600; *Fax:* 416-251-9131
Toll-Free: 800-263-9648
info@excellence.ca
www.excellence.ca
www.linkedin.com/company/excellence-canada
www.facebook.com/82765064279
twitter.com/excellencecan
Previous Name: National Quality Institute
Overview: A medium-sized national organization founded in 1992
Mission: To inspire & foster excellence in Canadian organizations; to enhance Canada's national well-being & global leadership through the incorporation of quality principles in business, government, education & health care; to promote, encourage & support the understanding & adoption of total quality principles & practices in all sectors of the economy across Canada; & to recognize outstanding achievement through the Canada Awards for Excellence
Member of: World Quality Council; International Auditor Training & Certification Association (IATCA); Board of Trade of Metropolitan Toronto; World Trade Centre
Finances: *Annual Operating Budget:* $1.5 Million-$3 Million; *Funding Sources:* Membership fees; products & services
Membership: 1-99; *Fees:* Schedule available; *Committees:* Operations
Activities: Providing tools & training on quality & Excellence Canada's Excellence Innovation & Wellness Standard; Conducting site assessments & registration; Administering Canada's recognition program for innovation, entrepreneurship & quality; *Awareness Events:* Canada's Healthy Workplace Week, Oct.; *Speaker Service:* Yes
Chief Officer(s):
Allan Ebedes, President & CEO
Awards:
• Canada Awards for Excellence
Previously called the Canada Awards for Business Excellence & established by the Government of Canada in 1984, the awards recognize outstanding continuous achievement in three categories: Excellence, Innovation & Wellness; Healthy Workplace & Mental Health at Work
• Canadian Business Excellence Awards for Private Businesses
Meetings/Conferences:
• Excellence Canada 2018 Performance Excellence Summit & Canada Awards for Excellence, 2018
Scope: National

Exempt Market Dealers Association of Canada; Limited Markets Dealers Association of Canada *See* Private Capital Markets Association of Canada

Exhibitions Association of Nova Scotia (EANS)
40 Gateway Rd., Halifax NS B3M 1M9
Tel: 902-443-2039
www.eans.ca
Overview: A small provincial organization
Mission: To promote such events as fairs & exhibitions across the province
Chief Officer(s):
Glen E. Jefferson, Executive Director

Experiences Canada
#201, 1150 Morrison Dr., Ottawa ON K2H 8S9
Tel: 613-727-3832; *Fax:* 613-727-3831
Toll-Free: 800-387-3832

communications@experiencescanada.ca
www.experiencescanada.ca
www.linkedin.com/company/society-for-educational-visits-and-exchanges-in-canada
www.youtube.com/user/SEVECanada
Previous Name: Society for Educational Visits & Exchanges in Canada; Bilingual Exchange Secretariat & Visites interprovinciales
Overview: A large national charitable organization founded in 1936
Mission: To create, facilitate & promote enriching educational opportunities within Canada for the development of mutual respect & understanding through programs of exploration in language & culture
Member of: Canadian Education Association
Finances: *Annual Operating Budget:* Greater than $5 Million; *Funding Sources:* Canadian Heritage (Exchanges Canada); membership dues; individual corporate donations; cost recovery
Staff Member(s): 10; 50 volunteer(s)
Membership: 500; *Fees:* $50; *Committees:* Youth Advisory
Activities: *Speaker Service:* Yes
Chief Officer(s):
Deborah Morrison, President & CEO
dmorrison@experiencescanada.ca
Ellen Glouchkow, Director, Finance & Administration
eglouchkow@experiencescanada.ca
Jamie McCullough, Director, Programs
jmccullough@experiencescanada.ca
Awards:
• Experiences Canada Award

Experimental Aircraft Association of Canada *See* Recreational Aircraft Association

Exploits Regional Chamber of Commerce
PO Box 272, 2B Mill Rd., Grand Falls-Windsor NL A2A 2J7
Tel: 709-489-7512; *Fax:* 709-489-7532
info@exploitschamber.com
www.exploitschamber.com
Previous Name: Grand Falls-Windsor Chamber of Commerce
Overview: A small local organization
Member of: Newfoundland & Labrador Chamber of Commerce; Atlantic Provinces Chamber of Commerce; Canadian Chamber of Commerce
Membership: 184; *Fees:* Schedule available; *Member Profile:* Businesses
Chief Officer(s):
Kris Spurrell, President

Exploits Valley Society for the Prevention of Cruelty to Animals
13A Duggan St., Grand Falls-Windsor NL A2A 2P7
Tel: 709-489-3604
evspca@yahoo.com
www.envision.ca/webs/exploitsvalleyspca
www.facebook.com/EVSPCA
Also Known As: Exploits Valley SPCA
Overview: A small local organization founded in 1971
Mission: To care for animals humanely through sheltering & public education.
Member of: Canadian Federation of Humane Societies
Chief Officer(s):
Sheila Baird, Manager

Explorer's Club (Canadian Chapter)
BC
www.explorersclub.ca
Overview: A medium-sized national organization founded in 1979
Mission: To promote field sciences & exploration of land, sea, air & space
Affiliation(s): Explorer's Club (New York)
Finances: *Annual Operating Budget:* Less than $50,000
Membership: 110; 3,000 worldwide; *Fees:* Schedule available; *Member Profile:* Field scientists
Activities: *Speaker Service:* Yes
Chief Officer(s):
Ray Hyland, Chair
chapterchair@explorersclub.ca
Maeva Gauthier, Communications Director
communications@explorersclub.ca
Publications:
• Far Afield [a publication of the Explorer's Club (Canadian Chapter)]
Type: Newsletter; *Frequency:* bi-annually

Explorers & Producers Association of Canada (EPAC)
#1060, 717 - 7th Ave. SW, Calgary AB T2P 0Z3
Tel: 403-269-3454; *Fax:* 403-269-3636
info@explorersandproducers.ca
www.explorersandproducers.ca
Previous Name: Small Explorers & Producers Association of Canada
Overview: A medium-sized national organization founded in 1986
Mission: To advocate to governments, policy makers & regulators on behalf of members to ensure that member interests are reflected in a fiscal & regulatory framework that encourages investment & supports a prosperous oil & gas industy
Staff Member(s): 3; 24 volunteer(s)
Membership: 387 corporate; *Fees:* $590-$10,000
Chief Officer(s):
Gary Leach, President
Awards:
• EPAC Awards
The EPAC Awards will promote and celebrate Canadian oil and gas achievement, business success and entrepreneurship. The awards aim to recognize, motivate and inspire Canadians to continue innovating and advancing our nation's energy industry.
Eligibility: Award categories this year include Top Emerging, Top Junior, Top Intermediate/Senior and Top International.
• CAPP-EPAC Scholarship Fund for Alberta Post-Secondary Students
Eligibility: Alberta post-secondary students enrolled in qualifying fields of study

Expo agricole de Chicoutimi
CP 8222, 350, boul de l'Université, Chicoutimi QC G7H 5B7
Tél: 418-545-8597; *Téléc:* 418-545-9243
www.expoagricoledechicoutimi.com
Nom précédent: Société d'agriculture de Chicoutimi
Aperçu: *Dimension:* petite; *Envergure:* locale
Affiliation(s): Association des expositions agricoles du Québec
Finances: *Fonds:* Gouvernement régional
Membre(s) du personnel: 1; 6 bénévole(s)
Membre: 70 individu; 5 associé; *Montant de la cotisation:* 10$ individu; 100$ associé
Activités: Exposition agricole
Membre(s) du bureau directeur:
Louis-Joseph Jean, Directeur général
expoagricole@qc.aira.com

Exposition nationale canadienne *See* Canadian National Exhibition Association

Eye Bank of BC (EBBC)
Jim Pattison Pavilion North - B205, 855 West 12th Ave, Vancouver BC V5Z 1M9
Tel: 604-875-4567; *Fax:* 604-875-5316
Toll-Free: 800-667-2060
eyebankofbc@vch.ca
www.eyebankofbc.ca
www.facebook.com/EyeBankBC
twitter.com/VCHEyeBankBC
Overview: A medium-sized provincial charitable organization founded in 1983
Mission: To acquire human donor eye tissue for the purposes of corneal transplant, sclera grafts & medical research
Member of: Eye Bank Association of America
Affiliation(s): Canadian National Institute for the Blind; Eye Bank Association of America; Canadian Ophthalmological Society
Finances: *Annual Operating Budget:* $100,000-$250,000; *Funding Sources:* BC government, Health Care Division
Staff Member(s): 10
Activities: *Awareness Events:* Organ Donor Awareness, last week in Apr.; *Speaker Service:* Yes; *Library:* by appointment
Chief Officer(s):
Linda Wong, Manager
Sonia Yeung, Medical Director

Eye Bank of Canada - Ontario Division
Dept. of Ophthalmology, University of Toronto, 1929 Bayview Ave., Toronto ON M4G 0A1
Tel: 416-978-7355; *Fax:* 416-978-1522
eye.bank@utoronto.ca
www.eyebank.utoronto.ca
Also Known As: Ontario Eye Bank
Overview: A small provincial charitable organization founded in 1955
Mission: To provide donated eye tissue for surgical use in those whose vision can be restored or improved through corneal transplantation or other eye surgery
Affiliation(s): Canadian National Institute for the Blind; University of Toronto
Finances: *Funding Sources:* Ontario Ministry of Health
Activities: *Speaker Service:* Yes
Chief Officer(s):
Fides Coloma, Manager
Awards:
• Certificates of Merit to Top Donor Hospitals, individuals & organizations who volunteer time & service

Fabricants de produits alimentaires du Canada *See* Food Processors of Canada

Facility Association
PO Box 121, #2400, 777 Bay St., Toronto ON M5G 2C8
Tel: 416-863-1750; *Fax:* 416-868-0894
Toll-Free: 800-268-9572
mail@facilityassociation.com
www.facilityassociation.com
Overview: A medium-sized national organization founded in 1979
Mission: To ensure the availability of automobile insurance for owners & licensed drivers of motor vehicles who may otherwise have difficulty obtaining such insurance.
Membership: *Member Profile:* All property & casualty companies writing automobile business in all provinces & territories except BC, Manitoba, Québec & Saskatchewan.
Chief Officer(s):
David J. Simpson, President & CEO

The Factory: Hamilton Media Arts Centre
228 James St. North, Hamilton ON L8R 2L3
Tel: 905-577-9191
info@hamiltonmediaarts.org
www.hamiltonmediaarts.com
www.facebook.com/factorymedia
twitter.com/FactoryMediaArt
www.youtube.com/user/tfhmac
Also Known As: The Factory
Overview: A small local organization
Mission: To support an artist-driven resource center dedicated to the production and promotion of creatively diverse forms of independent film, video, and time-based multimedia arts in Hamilton and the surrounding region.
Finances: *Funding Sources:* Canada Council for the Arts; Ontario Arts Council; City of Hamilton
Membership: *Fees:* $25 associate/student/senior; $45 full; $175 organizational
Chief Officer(s):
Ernest Gibson, Chair

Facultés d'agriculture et de médecine vétérinaire du Canada *See* Canadian Faculties of Agriculture & Veterinary Medicine

Faculty Association of Medicine Hat College / Association des professeurs du Collège de Medicine Hat
c/o Medicine Hat College, 299 College Dr. SE, Medicine Hat AB T1A 3Y6
Tel: 403-504-3616; *Fax:* 403-504-3666
facultyassoc@mhc.ab.ca
www.mhc.ab.ca/Employees/FacultyAssociation.aspx
Overview: A small local organization
Mission: To represent the interests of its members in all contractual matters
Member of: Alberta Colleges & Institutes Faculties Association (ACIFA)
Membership: *Committees:* Health & Safety; Bylaws; Worload Review; Social; Short Term Leave Review; Negotiations; Negotiations Advisory; Faculty Evluation; Professional Development
Chief Officer(s):
Elizabeth Pennefather-O'Brien, President
eobrien@mhc.ab.ca
Monika Farmer, Contact

Faculty Association of Red Deer College (FARDC) / Association des professeurs du Collège Red Deer
c/o Red Deer College, PO Box 5005, 100 College Blvd., Red Deer AB T4N 5H5
Tel: 403-343-4092
extension.rdc.ab.ca/portal/fardc
Overview: A small local organization founded in 1968

Mission: To encourage its members to pursue professional & personal growth through teaching
Affiliation(s): Alberta College & Institute Faculties Association
Finances: *Funding Sources:* Membership dues
Membership: 400 individual; *Member Profile:* Academic staff members are designated by the Board of Governors at Red Deer College; *Committees:* Academic Council; Faculty Performance; Negotiations; Professional Development; Academic Policy; Awards Advisory; Benefits Advisory; CAT Fund; Curriculum; Dispute Resolution; Employee Award & Recognition; Faculty Scholarship Recognition; Faculty Workload; Occupational Health & Safety; Research & Scholarship; Students Awards Selection; Student Dispute, Appeal & Misconduct
Chief Officer(s):
Ken Heather, President
ken.heather@rdc.ab.ca

Faculty Association of the College of New Caledonia (FACNC) / Association des professeurs du Collège de New Caledonia
3477 - 15th Ave., Prince George BC V2N 3Z3
Tel: 250-564-7880; *Fax:* 250-563-2776
facnc_local3@telus.net
www.cnc.bc.ca
Overview: A small local organization
Mission: To represent the College of New Caledonia's faculty members
Finances: *Annual Operating Budget:* $100,000-$250,000
Membership: 400; *Committees:* Community Outreach; Disability Management; Education Leave; Human Rights; Non-Regular Faculty; Occupational Health & Safety; Political Action; Professional Development; Social; Status of Women
Activities: Supporting students through 20 annual scholarships; Lobbying for publicly-funded post-secondary education; Raising awareness of current issues
Chief Officer(s):
Bill Deutch, President
facnc_president@telus.net

Faculty Association of the Open Learning Agency See
Thompson Rivers University Open Learning Faculty Association

Faculty Association of University of Saint Thomas (FAUST) / Association des professeurs de l'Université Saint-Thomas
St. Thomas University, Edmund Casey, #211, 51 Dineen Dr., Fredericton NB E3B 5G3
Tel: 506-452-9667
faust@stu.ca
www.faustnb.ca
Overview: A small local organization
Mission: To promote the welfare & interests of the association & its members
Member of: Federation of New Brunswick Faculty Associations; Canadian Association of University Teachers
Membership: *Committees:* Communications; Benefits; Equity; Health & Safety; Part-time Issues; SoOcial; Grievance; Joint; Harassment Policy; Bargaining
Chief Officer(s):
Mary Lou Babineau, President
maryloub@stu.ca
Bonnie Huskins, Professional Officer, 506-452-9667

FADOQ - Mouvement des Ainés du Quebec *Voir* FADOQ

The Fair Rental Policy Organization of Ontario (FRPO)
#105, 20 Upjohn Rd., Toronto ON M3B 2V9
Tel: 416-385-1100; *Fax:* 416-385-7112
Toll-Free: 877-688-1960
info@frpo.org
www.frpo.org
www.facebook.com/117940918260439
www.youtube.com/user/FRPO2011
Overview: A small provincial organization
Chief Officer(s):
Vince Brescia, President & CEO
vbrescia@frpo.org

Fair Vote Canada (FVC)
#408, 283 Danforth Ave., Toronto ON M4K 1N2
Tel: 416-410-4034
office@fairvote.ca
www.fairvotecanada.org
www.facebook.com/fairvotecanada
twitter.com/FairVoteCanada
www.youtube.com/user/FairVoteCanada
Overview: A small national organization
Mission: FVC is a national, multi-partisan citizens' campaign to promote voting system reform, specifically for proportional elections. It advocates for a national process that enables Canadian voters to choose which voting system shall be used to elect their representatives.
Staff Member(s): 2
Chief Officer(s):
Kelly Carmichael, Executive Director

Fairview & District Chamber of Commerce
Lancaster Place, #111, 10316 - 109 St., Fairview AB T0H 0L0
Tel: 780-835-5999; *Fax:* 780-835-5991
director@fairviewchamber.com
www.fairviewchamber.com
www.facebook.com/257844710942600
twitter.com/fairviewAbChamb
Overview: A small local licensing organization
Mission: To provide leadership to ensure a stable business base & networking system
Member of: Alberta Chamber of Commerce; Canadian Chamber of Commerce; Mighty Peace Tourism
Finances: *Annual Operating Budget:* $50,000-$100,000; *Funding Sources:* Membership dues; events
10 volunteer(s)
Membership: 106; *Fees:* $80.25-$214; *Committees:* Commercial Highway Signs; Finances; Membership; Policy & Bylaws; Visitor Information Centre; Website & Technology
Chief Officer(s):
Debie Knudsen, Executive Director
director@fairviewchamber.com

Fais-Un-Voeu Canada See Make-A-Wish Canada

Falcon, West Hawk & Caddy Lakes Chamber of Commerce (FWHLCC)
PO Box 187, Falcon Beach MB R0E 0N0
Tel: 204-349-3134; *Fax:* 204-349-3134
falconwesthawkchamber.com
Overview: A small local organization
Mission: To promote the communities of Falcon Lake, West Hawk Lake & surrounding areas
Member of: Manitoba Chamber of Commerce
Affiliation(s): Canadian Chamber of Commerce
Finances: *Annual Operating Budget:* Less than $50,000; *Funding Sources:* Membership fees
Membership: 55; *Fees:* Schedule available; *Committees:* Architectural; Tourism

Falher Chamber of Commerce
PO Box 814, 11 Central Ave. SW, Falher AB T0H 1M0
Tel: 780-837-2364
Overview: A small local organization founded in 1940
Mission: To promote the area's economy & encourage business & industrial development, broaden the tax base & provide employment opportunities in Falher & area
Affiliation(s): Falher & Area Economic Development & Tourism
Staff Member(s): 1
Membership: 45; *Fees:* Based on number of employees

Falher Friendship Corner Association (FFCA)
PO Box 453, Falher AB T0H 1M0
Tel: 780-837-2153; *Fax:* 780-837-2254
Overview: A small local organization
Mission: To promote the welfare of people with handicaps & their families
Member of: Alberta Association for Community Living

Falkland Chamber of Commerce
PO Box 92, Hwy. 97, Falkland BC V0E 1W0
Tel: 250-379-2780
Overview: A small local organization
Finances: *Funding Sources:* Membership dues
Membership: 8

Falls Brook Centre
476 West Glassville Rd., Glassville NB E7L 1W4
Tel: 506-246-1114; *Fax:* 506-246-1116
admin@fallsbrookcentre.ca
www.fallsbrookcentre.ca
Overview: A small local organization
Mission: Situated on 400 acres of rural forest and farmland, the Centre is a sustainable community demonstration and training centre. On-site activities and features include solar and wind energy systems, organic gardening, forest trails, herbariums and tree nurseries, and a conference centre. The Centre promotes sustainability and collaborates with the community to provide alternatives.
Member of: Canadian Renewable Energy Alliance
Affiliation(s): Canadian Coalition for Biodiversity
Staff Member(s): 6
Activities: Education and Outreach; Community Development; International Work; workshops and workbees
Chief Officer(s):
Marc Gionet, Executive Director

Falun Dafa Canada
Toronto ON
Tel: 416-731-6000
Toll-Free: 866-325-8622
toronto-1@falundafa.ca
falundafa.ca
Also Known As: Falun Gong
Overview: A medium-sized national organization
Mission: To improve body, mind & spirit; The ancient practice was introduced to the public by Mr. Li Hongzhi in 1992 in China; There are now more than 100 million practitioners around the world; The ultimate objective is to assimilate to the supreme principle: Truthfulness, Compassion, & Tolerance (Zhen, Shan, Ren)

Familial GI Cancer Registry See Zane Cohen Centre for Digestive Diseases Familial Gastrointestinal Cancer Registry

Families for a Secure Future
16 Roncesvalles Ave., Toronto ON M6R 2K3
Tel: 647-693-9397
www.familiesforasecurefuture.ca
Overview: A small local charitable organization
Mission: To support & assist adults with developmental disabilities; To help families by providing resources & support networks
Finances: *Funding Sources:* Donations
Chief Officer(s):
Nancy Friday, Executive Assistant

Family & Children's Services Niagara (FACS)
PO Box 24028, St Catharines ON L2R 7P7
Tel: 905-937-7731; *Fax:* 905-646-7085
Toll-Free: 888-937-7731
info@facsniagara.on.ca
www.facsniagara.on.ca
www.facebook.com/familyandchildrensservicesniagara
twitter.com/FACSNiagara
Also Known As: FACS Niagara
Overview: A large local charitable organization founded in 1898
Mission: To protect children & support those in need of safe homes; To provide guidance & counselling services to families; To investigate all reports of possible child abuse or neglect
Member of: Ontario Association of Children's Aid Societies
Finances: *Annual Operating Budget:* Greater than $5 Million; *Funding Sources:* 100% Province of Ontario (core services); donations
Staff Member(s): 360; 240 volunteer(s)
Membership: 50; *Fees:* $25; *Member Profile:* Reside or work in Niagara, 18 years old; *Committees:* Standing Board
Activities: Child protection & family services; adoption services; nursery school-parent enrichment program; family counselling centre; regional adolescent centre; mobile toy lending library; Ontario Early Years Program (Niagara South); *Awareness Events:* Child Abuse & Neglect Prevention Month, Oct.; *Internships:* Yes; *Speaker Service:* Yes
Chief Officer(s):
Chris Steven, Executive Director

Niagara Falls Branch
7900 Canadian Dr., Niagara Falls ON L2E 6S5
Welland Branch
654 South Pelham St., Welland ON L3C 3C8

Family & Children's Services of Frontenac, Lennox & Addington
817 Division St., Kingston ON K7K 4C2
Tel: 613-545-3227; *Fax:* 613-542-4428
Toll-Free: 855-445-3227
info@facsfla.ca
www.facsfla.ca
www.facebook.com/facsfla
twitter.com/FACSFLA
www.youtube.com/user/FACSFLA
Merged from: Children's Aid Society of the City of Kingston and County of Frontenac; Lennox & Addington CAS
Overview: A small local charitable organization founded in 1994

Canadian Associations / Family & Children's Services of Guelph & Wellington County (F&CS)

Mission: To provide professional child protection services which safeguard children, support nurturing environments & strengthen families
Member of: Ontario Association of Children's Aid Societies
Affiliation(s): Community Living Kingston; Kingston Interval House; Northern Frontenac Community Services; Frontenac Community Mental Health Services; Pathways for Children & Youth; Youth Diversion Program
Activities: Coordinating of foster care & adoption; Investigating possible child abuse or neglect; Counselling; *Speaker Service:* Yes
Chief Officer(s):
Steve Woodman, Executive Director

Family & Children's Services of Guelph & Wellington County (F&CS)
PO Box 1088, 275 Eramosa Rd., Guelph ON N1H 6N3
Tel: 519-824-2410; *Fax:* 519-763-9628
Toll-Free: 800-265-8300
info@fcsgw.org
www.fcsgw.org
www.facebook.com/371460589598793
twitter.com/fcsgw
Also Known As: Children's Aid Society of Guelph & Wellington County
Overview: A small local charitable organization founded in 1934
Mission: To provide help & support services for families to ensure that children are protected from physical & emotional abuse or neglect
Member of: Ontario Association of Children's Aid Societies
Finances: *Annual Operating Budget:* Greater than $5 Million
Staff Member(s): 140; 160 volunteer(s)
Membership: *Fees:* $5
Chief Officer(s):
Daniel Moore, Executive Director

County Office
PO Box 29, 6484 Wellington Rd. 7, Elora ON N0B 1S0
Fax: 519-846-1005
Toll-Free: 800-265-8300
Mission: To advocate & provide for the protection of children, to support & strengthen families, & promote the well-being of children in our communities.

Shelldale Centre Branch
PO Box 1088, 20 Shelldale Cres., Guelph ON N1H 6N3
Fax: 519-766-4537
Toll-Free: 800-265-8300

Family & Children's Services of Lanark, Leeds & Grenville
438 Laurier Blvd., Brockville ON K6V 6C5
Tel: 613-498-2100; *Fax:* 613-498-2108
Toll-Free: 800-481-7834
www.casbrock.com
Merged from: Children's Aid Society of Lanark & Smiths Falls; Family & Children's Services of Leeds & Grenville
Overview: A small local organization overseen by Family Service Ontario
Mission: To protect children & ensure the safety of those in need; to provide care for those children under concern, as well as guidance & counselling to families to prevent circumstances requiring the protection of children.

Gananoque Office
#300, 375 William St., Gananoque ON K7G 1T2
Tel: 613-382-8220; *Fax:* 613-382-3579

Kemptville Office
PO Box 1299, 5 Clothier St. East, Kemptville ON K0G 1J0
Tel: 613-258-1460; *Fax:* 613-258-4459

Family & Children's Services of Renfrew County
#100, 77 Mary St., Pembroke ON K8A 5V4
Tel: 613-735-6866; *Fax:* 613-735-6641
Toll-Free: 800-267-5878
inquiries@fcsrenfrew.on.ca
www.fcsrenfrew.on.ca
Previous Name: Renfrew Family & Child Services
Overview: A medium-sized local charitable organization founded in 1935
Mission: To support & enhance the lives of children, youth, & families in Ontario's County of Renfrew by providing essential, mandated, & volutary services; To improve the quality of life for children, youth, & adults with developmental disabilities
Member of: Ontario Association of Children's Aid Societies
Membership: *Fees:* $10; *Member Profile:* Board members; Volunteers; Community; *Committees:* Executive; Personnel; Services
Activities: Providing crisis intervention services; Investigating cases of neglect; Providing child protection services; Arranging financial assistance & safe shelter; Counselling individuals & families; Organizing foster care & adoption services; Providing developmental services, such as infant development, behaviour, & speech programs, as well as service coordination; Offering educational programs; Arranging family visitations & exchanges; Providing after school tutorial services, such as The Kumon Method; *Awareness Events:* Purple Ribbon - Child Abuse Prevention Month, October
Chief Officer(s):
Arijana Haramincic, Executive Director
Awards:
• Service Awards to Foster Parents
• Staff Recognition

Renfrew Office
331 Martin St., Renfrew ON K7V 1A1
Tel: 613-432-4821; *Fax:* 613-432-9278
Toll-Free: 800-267-5878

Family & Children's Services of the District of Rainy River (FACS)
820 Lakeview Dr., Kenora ON P9N 3P7
Tel: 807-467-5437; *Fax:* 807-467-5539; *Crisis Hot-Line:* 800-465-1100
www.krrcfs.ca
Also Known As: Kenora-Patricia Child & Family Services
Overview: A small local charitable organization founded in 1935
Mission: To ensure the safety of children & youth; to provide a variety of services to protect them; to investigate any concerns of their abuse or neglect.
Member of: Ontario Association of Children's Aid Societies; Children's Mental Health Associations of Ontario
Finances: *Funding Sources:* Provincial
Activities: Child welfare; children's mental health; child development; supervised access; family relief; *Speaker Service:* Yes; *Library:* FACS Library; Open to public
Chief Officer(s):
Bill Leonard, Executive Director
Publications:
• Developmental Services Newsletter [a publication of the Family & Children's Services of the District of Rainy River]
Type: Newsletter; *Frequency:* Bimonthly
• Family & Children's Services of the District of Rainy River Newsletter
Type: Newsletter; *Frequency:* 7 pa

Atikokan Office
211 Main St. West, Atikokan ON P0T 1C0
Tel: 807-597-2700; *Fax:* 807-597-6920

Dryden Office
175 West River Rd., Dryden ON P8N 2Z4
Tel: 807-223-5325; *Fax:* 807-223-5324

Fort Frances Office
240 - 1st St. East, Fort Frances ON P9A 1K5
Tel: 807-274-7787; *Fax:* 807-274-6646

Red Lake Office
201 Howey St., Red Lake ON P0V 2M0
Tel: 807-727-2165; *Fax:* 807-727-2645

Sioux Lookout Office
41 King St., Sioux Lookout ON P8T 1B7
Tel: 807-737-3250; *Fax:* 807-737-2611

Family & Community Support Services Association of Alberta (FCSSAA)
Belmead Professional Bldg., #106, 8944 - 182 St., Edmonton AB T5T 2E3
Tel: 780-415-4790; *Fax:* 780-415-4793
assistant@fcssaa.org
www.fcssaa.org
Previous Name: Preventative Social Services Association
Overview: A medium-sized provincial organization founded in 1981
Mission: To advocate on behalf of local communities & programs to the general public, municipal governments, regional services, provincial & national agencies, & authorities; To educate individuals, communities, boards, & staff
Membership: 100-499; *Fees:* Schedule available; *Member Profile:* FCSS programs in Alberta representing municipalities & Métis settlements
Activities: Hosting conferences; Sharing information about FCSS programs; Developing resources; *Library:* FCSSAA Resource Library
Chief Officer(s):
Arnold Hanson, President
Deb Teed, Executive Director, 780-422-0133
director@fcssaa.org
Judy Macknee, Executive Assistant

Family Caregivers Association of Nova Scotia *See* Caregivers Nova Scotia

Family Caregivers of British Columbia
#6, 3318 Oak St., Victoria BC V8X 1R1
Tel: 250-384-0408; *Fax:* 250-361-2660
Toll-Free: 877-520-3267
www.familycaregiversbc.ca
www.facebook.com/FamilyCaregiversBC
twitter.com/caringbc
Previous Name: Family Caregivers' Network Society
Overview: A small provincial charitable organization founded in 1989
Mission: To provide support, education, & information for family caregivers in British Columbia
Finances: *Funding Sources:* Membership fees; Donations; Fundraising
Membership: *Fees:* $20 individuals; $30 non-profit organizations; $100 corporate members
Activities: Hosting workshops for family caregivers; Organizing regular family caregiver support groups; Offering telephone or in-person support; Providing information & referrals; *Library:* Family Caregivers' Network Society Resource Lending Library; Open to public
Chief Officer(s):
Barb MacLean, Executive Director
Alyshia Vogt, President
Publications:
• Caregiver Connection [a publication of the Family Caregivers of British Columbia]
Type: Newsletter; *Frequency:* Quarterly
Profile: Articles about family caregiving issues
• Facilitator's Manual: Educational Activities to Support Family Caregivers
Price: $75
Profile: Featuring facilitation techniques, outlines for workshops, & learning activities for healthcare provider training programs
• Medical Information Package
Price: Free with membership in theFamily Caregivers of British Columbia; $3 non-members
Profile: Including a medical information record, information about incapacity planning, plus information from the British Columbia Transplant Society & the Heart & Stroke Foundation
• Network News [a publication of the Family Caregivers of British Columbia]
Type: Newsletter; *Frequency:* Bimonthly; *Price:* Free with membership in the Family Caregivers of British Columbia
Profile: Informative articles about caregiving issues & notices of upcoming events
• Resource Guide for Family Caregivers
Type: Handbook; *Number of Pages:* 160; *Price:* $15 members; $20 non-members
Profile: Practical information to help caregivers make decisions

Family Caregivers' Network Society *See* Family Caregivers of British Columbia

Family Counselling & Support Services for Guelph-Wellington (FCSS)
109 Surrey St. East, Guelph ON N1H 3P7
Tel: 519-824-2431
Toll-Free: 800-307-7078
info@familyserviceguelph.on.ca
www.familyserviceguelph.on.ca
Previous Name: Guelph-Wellington Counselling Centre
Overview: A small local charitable organization founded in 1987 overseen by Ontario Association of Credit Counselling Services
Mission: To provide professional counselling, support, educational, & advocacy services for the citizens of the Guelph-Wellington region
Member of: Credit Counselling Canada; Ontario Association of Credit Counselling Services
Affiliation(s): Family Service Ontario; Family Service Canada
Finances: *Funding Sources:* Donations; Local institutions
Activities: Providing counselling in areas such as relationships, family violence, credit & debt, & addictions & gambling; Engaging in advocacy activities; Offering groups, such as the separation & divorce recovery group, building peaceful families, anger management for men, & healing the trauma of early childhood incest & sexual abuse issues; Providing programs, such as the Employee Assistance Program, Debt Management Program, & the Case Management Services Program for individuals with developmental disabilities

Publications:
• Family Counselling & Support Services for Guelph-Wellington Annual Report
Type: Yearbook; *Frequency:* Annually

Family Counselling Centre of Brant, Inc.
54 Brant Ave., Brantford ON N3T 3G8
Tel: 519-753-4173; *Fax:* 519-753-9287
office@fccb.ca
www.fccb.ca
Previous Name: Family Service Bureau of Brantford & Brant County, Inc.
Overview: A small local organization founded in 1914 overseen by Ontario Association of Credit Counselling Services
Mission: To offer professional & ethical counselling services to persons in need in Brantford & the Brant County Region of Ontario
Member of: Ontario Association of Credit Counselling Services
Activities: Providing individual, couple, family, group, & credit counselling; Engaging in advocacy activities; Providing creditor mediation services; Offering an employee assistance program; Providing family relief services; Assisting with community integration; Offering behaviour therapy consultation to nurseries, preschools, schools, community agencies, caregivers, individuals, & families; Operating early learning & parenting centres; Increasing community awareness of individual & family issues; Providing informative resources
Publications:
• Family Matters [a publication of the Family Counselling Centre of Brant, Inc.]
Type: Newsletter
Profile: Issue topics include aging parents, fostering self, & working through depression
• Solutions [a publication of the Family Counselling Centre of Brant, Inc.]
Type: Newsletter
Profile: A newsletter from the Family Services Employee Assistance Program

Family Counselling Centre of Cambridge & North Dumfries
18 Walnut St., Cambridge ON N1R 2E7
Tel: 519-621-5090; *Fax:* 519-622-9394
www.fcccnd.com
www.facebook.com/FamilyCounsellingCentreCND
Previous Name: Family Services Cambridge & North Dumfries
Overview: A small local charitable organization founded in 1940
Mission: To offer counselling & outreach to members of the community
Member of: Family Services Canada; Family Services Ontario
Staff Member(s): 20
Chief Officer(s):
Bobbye Goldenberg, Executive Director

Family Counselling Centre of Cornwall & United Counties
See Counselling & Support Services of S.D. & G.

Family Day Care Services (Toronto)
#400, 155 Gordon Baker Rd., Toronto ON M2H 3N5
Tel: 416-922-9556; *Fax:* 416-922-5335
www.familydaycare.com
www.facebook.com/FamilyDayCareServices
twitter.com/familydaygta
Previous Name: Protestant Children's Home
Overview: A large local charitable organization founded in 1851 overseen by Family Service Ontario
Mission: To meet the needs of children & families; To aid in optimum development of the child, be it physical care, social, emotional or cognitive development; To assist & support the family unit to function more effectively economically, socially & emotionally
Member of: Home Child Care Association of Ontario
Finances: *Annual Operating Budget:* Greater than $5 Million; *Funding Sources:* United Way; provincial government; fundraising
Activities: *Speaker Service:* Yes
Chief Officer(s):
Joan Arruda, CEO
jarruda@familydaycare.com

Family Enterprise Xchange (FEX)
#135, 690 Dorval Dr., Oakville ON L6K 3W7
Tel: 905-337-8375; *Fax:* 905-337-0572
Toll-Free: 866-849-0099
www.family-enterprise-xchange.com
www.linkedin.com/groups/1883375
www.facebook.com/FamilyEnterpriseXchange
twitter.com/FEXcanada
www.youtube.com/user/CAFECanada1
Previous Name: Canadian Association of Family Enterprise
Overview: A medium-sized national licensing organization
Mission: To help business families across Canada succeed
Finances: *Annual Operating Budget:* $500,000-$1.5 Million; *Funding Sources:* Corporate sponsorship; Membership fees
Staff Member(s): 11; 100+ volunteer(s)
Membership: 800+; *Fees:* Schedule available based on chapter; *Member Profile:* Family businesses; Professionals that provide consulting & services to family businesses
Activities: Holding workshops, seminars, & networking events in chapters across Canada; *Speaker Service:* Yes; *Library:* Family Enterprise Xchange E-Learning Centre; Not open to public
Chief Officer(s):
Bill Brushett, President & CEO, 905-337-8375 Ext. 230
bbrushett@family-enterprise-xchange.com
Paul MacDonald, COO, 905-337-8375 Ext. 223
pmacdonald@family-enterprise-xchange.com
Lorraine Bauer, National Director, 905-337-8375 Ext. 224
lorraine@family-enterprise-xchange.com
Russel Baskin, Director, Education & Programs, 905-337-8375 Ext. 264
rbaskin@family-enterprise-xchange.com
Beverly Hardy, Manager, Office & Accounting, 905-337-8375 Ext. 225
Peter Cotterill, Manager, Business Development, 778-991-3365
pcotterill@family-enterprise-xchange.com
Jessica Pavkovic, Manager, Marketing & Communications, 905-337-8375 Ext. 227
jpavkovic@family-enterprise-xchange.com
Awards:
• FEX Family Enterprise of the Year Award
Established to recognize the importance of family enterprise; looks at: job creation, technological advancement, environment, innovation & entrepeneurial success; open to any family enterprise, private or publicly owned
Meetings/Conferences:
• Family Enterprise Xchange 2018 Symposium, September, 2018, Niagara-on-the-Lake, ON

FEX Calgary
PO Box 16055, Stn. Lower Mount Royal, Calgary AB T2T 1A0
Tel: 587-284-2233
calgary@family-enterprise-xchange.com
family-enterprise-xchange.com/chapters/calgary
Chief Officer(s):
Todd Coleman, President
Debbie Van Camp, Manager, Membership & Community Engagement

FEX Central Ontario
#135, 690 Dorval Dr., Oakville ON L6K 3W7
Tel: 905-337-8375; *Fax:* 905-337-0572
Toll-Free: 866-849-0099
centralontario@family-enterprise-xchange.com
family-enterprise-xchange.com/chapters/central-ontario
Chief Officer(s):
Ashleigh Blackmore, Manager, Membership & Community Engagement

FEX Edmonton
Edmonton AB
Toll-Free: 866-849-0099
edmonton@family-enterprise-xchange.com
family-enterprise-xchange.com/chapters/edmonton
Chief Officer(s):
C.J. Zvanitajs, Contact

FEX Nova Scotia
NS
info@family-enterprise-xchange.com
family-enterprise-xchange.com/chapters/nova-scotia
Chief Officer(s):
Rebecca Holmes, Office Coordinator

FEX Okanagan
#200, 3200 Richter St., Kelowna BC V1W 5K9
Tel: 250-215-2969
okanagan@family-enterprise-xchange.com
family-enterprise-xchange.com/chapters/okanagan
Chief Officer(s):
Carolyn Reimer, Manager, Membership & Community Engagement

FEX Ottawa
PO Box 8096, Stn. T, Ottawa ON K1G 3H6
Tel: 613-232-2233
ottawa@family-enterprise-xchange.com
family-enterprise-xchange.com/chapters/ottawa
Chief Officer(s):
Richard Plummer, Manager, Membership & Community Engagement

FEX Regina
PO Box 37228, Regina SK S4S 7K4
Toll-Free: 866-578-0978
regina@family-enterprise-xchange.com
family-enterprise-xchange.com/chapters/regina
Chief Officer(s):
Petra Coutts, Manager, Membership & Community Engagement

FEX Saskatoon
Norplex Business Centre, 2366 Ave. C North, Saskatoon SK S7L 5X5
Tel: 306-292-7838
saskatoon@family-enterprise-xchange.com
family-enterprise-xchange.com/chapters/saskatoon
Chief Officer(s):
Paula Simon, Manager, Membership & Community Engagement

FEX Southwestern Ontario
PO Box 20086, 431 Boler Rd., London ON N6K 2K0
Tel: 519-642-4349; *Fax:* 519-642-2873
swo@family-enterprise-xchange.com
family-enterprise-xchange.com/chapters/southwestern-ontario
Chief Officer(s):
Tamelynda Lux, Manager, Membership & Community Engagement

FEX Vancouver Island
Victoria BC
vancouverisland@family-enterprise-xchange.com
family-enterprise-xchange.com/chapters/vancouver-island

FEX Vancouver Region
Vancouver BC V6Z 3B7
Tel: 604-721-1241
vancouver@family-enterprise-xchange.com
family-enterprise-xchange.com/chapters/vancouver-region
Chief Officer(s):
Colleen Fitzpatrick, Manager, Membership & Community Engagement

Family History Society of Newfoundland & Labrador
PO Box 8008, #101A, 66 Kenmount Rd., St. John's NL A1B 3V7
Tel: 709-754-9525; *Fax:* 709-754-6430
fhs@fhsnl.ca
www.fhsnl.ca
www.facebook.com/144749998869923
twitter.com/fhsnl
Previous Name: Newfoundland & Labrador Genealogical Society Inc.
Overview: A medium-sized provincial organization founded in 1984
Mission: To encourage & promote the study of family history in Newfoundland & Labrador; To collect & preserve local genealogical & historical records & materials; to foster education in genealogical research
Finances: *Funding Sources:* Membership fees
Membership: *Fees:* $42/yr; $700/life; *Member Profile:* All individuals, groups, & institutions
Activities: *Library:* The Family History Resource Centre; Open to public
Chief Officer(s):
Smith Frederick, President
Dunne Paul, Secretary
Publications:
• The Newfoundland Ancestor [a publication of the Family History Society of Newfoundland & Labrador]
Type: Journal; *Frequency:* Quarterly; *Editor:* Ethel Dempsey et al.

Family Life Centre *See* Community Counselling Centre of Nipissing

Family Mediation Canada (FMC) / Médiation Familiale Canada
#180, 55 Northfield Dr. East, Waterloo ON N2K 3T6
Tel: 519-585-3118; *Fax:* 416-849-0643
Toll-Free: 877-362-2005
fmc@fmc.ca
www.fmc.ca
Overview: A medium-sized national charitable organization founded in 1985

Mission: To improve the provision for cooperative conflict resolution in areas such as separation & divorce, child welfare, adoption, parent & teen counselling, age-related issues, & wills & estates
Affiliation(s): Mediate BC Society; Alberta Family Mediation Society; Conflict Resolution Saskatchewan Inc.; Family Mediation Manitoba Inc.; Ontario Association for Family Mediation; Association de médiation familiale du Québec; Family Mediation Nova Scotia; Mediation PEI Inc.; Mediation Yukon Society
Membership: *Fees:* $25 student; $50 supporting; $125 individual; $145 Nova Scotia individual; $150 PEI individual; *Member Profile:* Lawyers; Human services professionals; Social workers; Health care professionals
Activities: Providing information; Referring families to family mediators throughout Canada; Promoting mediation & other forms of conflict resolution; Hosting an annual general meeting; Posting jobs; *Library*
Chief Officer(s):
Tamara Bodnaruk-Wide, President
tamara@axisfamilymediation.com
Carrie Cekerevac, Manager, Operations
carrie@fmc.ca
Awards:
• Daniel L. Hamoline Bursary
• Family Mediation Achievement Awards

Family Mediation Manitoba (FMM)
PO Box 2369, Winnipeg MB R3C 4A6
Tel: 204-989-5330; *Fax:* 204-694-7555
contact@familymediationmanitoba.ca
www.familymediationmanitoba.ca
Overview: A small provincial organization founded in 1986
Mission: To promote the use of mediation as a preferred method of dispute resolution in family matters
Affiliation(s): Family Mediation Canada
Finances: *Funding Sources:* Membership fees
Membership: *Fees:* $50-$125; *Member Profile:* Private & court-based mediators, lawyers, social workers, judges, human services workers & students
Activities: Seminars; Educational material; Networking
Chief Officer(s):
Karen Burwash, President
president@familymediationmanitoba.ca
Publications:
• Directory of Mediators [a publication of Family Mediation Manitoba Inc.]
Type: Directory

Family of the Immaculate Heart of Mary
368 Melville Ave., Maple ON L6A 2N8
Tel: 905-832-1893; *Fax:* 905-832-3954
Overview: A small local organization founded in 2007
Mission: To serve God & promote the Roman Catholic Faith
Affiliation(s): Archdiocese of Toronto
Activities: Parish missions; spiritual exercises; worship
Chief Officer(s):
Solidea Didonato, Contact

Family Prayer Mission (Ontario) (FPM)
2478 Callum Ave., Mississauga ON L5B 2H9
Tel: 905-896-2854
familyprayer@sympatico.ca
www.familyprayermission.org
Overview: A small local charitable organization founded in 1989
Mission: To strengthen family bonds through prayer & worship
Affiliation(s): Archdiocese of Toronto
Membership: *Fees:* $15
Activities: Retreats
Chief Officer(s):
Rappai Nedumpara, President

Family Service Association of Halifax
West End Mall, #S14, 6960 Mumford Rd., Halifax NS B3L 4P1
Tel: 902-420-1980; *Fax:* 902-423-9830
Toll-Free: 888-886-5552
admin@fshalifax.com
www.fshalifax.com
Overview: A medium-sized local organization
Mission: To offer professional, confidential counselling and education services to enable people to function more effectively at home, in the community and in their work environment.
Chief Officer(s):
Mary Clancy, Chair
Valerie Bobyk, Executive Director

Family Service Association of Toronto *See* Family Service Toronto

Family Service Bureau of Brantford & Brant County, Inc. *See* Family Counselling Centre of Brant, Inc.

Family Service Canada (FSC) / Services à la famille - Canada
c/o 312 Parkdale Ave., Ottawa ON K1Y 4X45
Toll-Free: 877-451-1055
www.familyservicecanada.org
Overview: A medium-sized national organization founded in 1982
Mission: To promote families as the primary source of nurturing & development of individuals, their relationship in families & communities, through promoting & ensuring the best policies & services for families in Canada.
Member of: Coalition of National Voluntary Organizations
Finances: *Funding Sources:* Membership fees; grants
Membership: 33 agencies; *Fees:* Schedule available; *Member Profile:* Family service agencies, corporations, national & provincial organizations, government agencies & interested individuals
Chief Officer(s):
Heather Underhill, Manager, Operations
heatherp@familyservicecanada.org
Awards:
• Leadership Award

Family Service Centre of Ottawa-Carleton / Centre de service familial d'Ottawa-Carleton
312 Parkdale Ave., Ottawa ON K1Y 4X5
Tel: 613-725-3601; *Fax:* 613-725-5651; *TTY:* 613-725-6175
fsfo@familyservicesottawa.org
www.familyservicesottawa.org
www.facebook.com/familyservicesottawa
Overview: A medium-sized local organization founded in 1914 overseen by Family Service Ontario
Mission: To strengthen all aspects of family & community living through the provision of family focused, professional social services in the areas of counselling, family life education, social planning & advocacy
Affiliation(s): Family Service Canada
Finances: *Annual Operating Budget:* $3 Million-$5 Million; *Funding Sources:* United Way; Government; Fees; Donations; Fundraising; Grants; Interest
Staff Member(s): 90; 130 volunteer(s)
Activities: *Speaker Service:* Yes
Chief Officer(s):
Kathryn Ann Hill, Executive Director

Family Service Kent / Services à la Famille - Kent
50 Adelaide St., Chatham ON N7M 6K7
Tel: 519-354-6221; *Fax:* 519-354-5152
Toll-Free: 855-437-5368
familyservicekent.com
Previous Name: Community & Family Services of Chatham
Overview: A small local charitable organization founded in 1969 overseen by Ontario Association of Credit Counselling Services
Mission: To provide confidential counselling services by extensively trained & experienced persons to individuals & groups in Chatham-Kent communities
Member of: Ontario Association of Credit Counselling Services
Affiliation(s): Canadian Family Services Accreditation Program; Association of Credit Counselling Services
Finances: *Funding Sources:* United Way; Ministry of Community & Social Services; Ministry of Children & Youth Services; Ministry of Health & Long Term Care; Employee Assistance
Activities: Providing counselling services, in areas such as credit & sexual assault; Offering programs, such as the Credit Counselling Program, Employee Assistance Program, CHAP (Community Home Support Assisting People), APSW (Advocacy & Protective Service Worker), & the KIDS Team (Kent Inter-Disciplinary Support)
Chief Officer(s):
Brad Davis, Executive Director

Family Service Moncton Inc. / Services à la famille - Moncton, Inc
#T410, 22 Church St., Moncton NB E1C 0P7
Tel: 506-857-3258; *Fax:* 506-858-8315
Toll-Free: 800-390-3258
fsmoncton@rogers.com
www.fsmoncton.com
Overview: A small local organization founded in 1986
Affiliation(s): Family Service Canada
Finances: *Annual Operating Budget:* $500,000-$1.5 Million

Staff Member(s): 15; 10 volunteer(s)
Chief Officer(s):
Brenda Robinson, Chair
Maurice D. LeBlanc, RSW, MPA, CEO

Family Service Ontario / Services à la famille - Ontario
#630, 190 Attwell Dr., Toronto ON M9W 6H8
Tel: 416-231-6003; *Fax:* 416-231-2405
www.familyserviceontario.org
www.facebook.com/familyserviceontario
twitter.com/FamServOntario
Overview: A medium-sized provincial charitable organization founded in 1974
Mission: To support & assist member family service agencies
Affiliation(s): Ontario Association of Credit Counselling Services; Family Services Canada; Catholic Charities; United Way; Canadian Council of Social Development
Staff Member(s): 3
Membership: 42 agencies
Chief Officer(s):
John Ellis, Executive Director

Family Service Thames Valley (FSTV)
125 Woodward Ave., London ON N6J 2H1
Tel: 519-433-0159
fstv@familyservicethamesvalley.com
www.familyservicethamesvalley.com
Previous Name: Credit Counselling Thames Valley; Family Service London
Overview: A small local organization founded in 1967 overseen by Ontario Association of Credit Counselling Services
Mission: To provide counselling & support services for individuals, families, & organizations in London & its surrounding communities; To promote wise money management by consumers
Activities: Offering a credit & bankruptcy counselling program to provide solutions to debt problems; Intervening with creditors; Providing educational seminars for groups; Offering organization & employee care programs; *Speaker Service:* Yes
Chief Officer(s):
Louise Pitre, Executive Director

Family Service Toronto (FST)
#202, 128A Sterling Rd., Toronto ON M6R 2B7
Tel: 416-595-9618
www.familyservicetoronto.org
www.linkedin.com/company/family-service-toronto
www.facebook.com/FamilyServiceToronto
twitter.com/FamilyServiceTO
www.youtube.com/user/FamilyServiceToronto
Previous Name: Family Service Association of Toronto
Overview: A small local charitable organization founded in 1914
Mission: To help individuals & families affected by socio-economic circumstances or mental health issues
Member of: Family Service Ontario; United Way
Affiliation(s): Family Service Canada
Membership: *Fees:* Free; *Committees:* Financial Affairs; Governance
Activities: Counselling for individuals, couples & families; support for lesbians & gay men; support for people affected by HIV/AIDS; community development; counselling for battered women & abusive men; counselling, family life education & mediation for families undergoing separation, divorce & remarriage; promoting physical & emotional well-being for seniors & their caregivers; support for children & adults with developmental disabilities & their families; Bolton Camp; advocating for social policy; *Internships:* Yes; *Speaker Service:* Yes; *Library:* Open to public
Chief Officer(s):
Ted Betts, President
Margaret Hancock, Executive Director

Family Services Cambridge & North Dumfries *See* Family Counselling Centre of Cambridge & North Dumfries

Family Services of Greater Vancouver (FSGV)
#201, 1638 East Broadway, Vancouver BC V5N 1W1
Tel: 604-731-4951; *Fax:* 604-733-7009
www.fsgv.ca
www.linkedin.com/company/family-services-of-greater-vancouver
www.facebook.com/FamilyServicesGreaterVancouver
twitter.com/VanFamServices
Overview: A medium-sized local charitable organization founded in 1928

Mission: To strengthen people, families, & communities; To provide a diverse range of professional support & counselling services to those who are experiencing challenges in their lives
Member of: Family Service Canada; Alliance for Children & Families; Child Welfare League of Canada
Affiliation(s): Commission of Accreditation & Rehabilitation Facilities
151 volunteer(s)
Membership: 35
Activities: Offering professional counselling, consultation, education, & other supportive programs for people of all ages & income levels; *Library:* Not open to public
Chief Officer(s):
Karin Kirkpatrick, Chief Executive Officer
Jessica Denholm, Vice-President
Lara Barley, Director, Human Resources
Lise Beauchesne, Director, Trauma, Counselling & Victim Services
J. Christian le Nobel, Director, Finance
Calum Scott, Director, Community Engagement & Marketing
Karen Dickenson Smith, Director, Specialized Family Supports
Publications:
• Family Services of Greater Vancouver Newsletter
Type: Newsletter
Profile: Association happenings & supporter stories

Family Services Perth-Huron (FSPH)
142 Waterloo St., Stratford ON N5A 4B4
Tel: 519-273-1020; *Fax:* 519-273-6993
Toll-Free: 800-268-0903
office@debtontario.com
www.debtontario.com
Also Known As: Grey Bruce Credit Counselling
Overview: A small local charitable organization founded in 1975 overseen by Ontario Association of Credit Counselling Services
Mission: To provide professional, confidential counselling & family support services to individuals & families in Bruce, Grey, Huron, & Perth Counties
Member of: Credit Counselling Canada; Ontario Association of Credit Counselling Services; United Way
Activities: Coordinating respite care; Teaching literacy & numeracy skills; Providing programs, such as the Debt Management Program, Employee Assistance Program; Family Home Program, & the Familiy Violence Program for Men; Offering mediation services; Promoting consumer credit education
Chief Officer(s):
Susan Melkert, Executive Director

Family Services Thunder Bay See Thunder Bay Counselling Centre

Family Services Windsor-Essex Counselling & Advocacy Centre
1770 Langlois Ave., Windsor ON N8X 4M5
Tel: 519-966-5010; *Fax:* 519-256-5258
Toll-Free: 888-933-1831
info@fswe.ca
www.familyserviceswe.ca
Previous Name: Windsor Catholic Family Service Bureau
Overview: A small local charitable organization
Mission: To strengthen the ability of individuals, families & communities to reach their potential
Finances: *Funding Sources:* United Way; government; fees
Activities: *Speaker Service:* Yes

Family Services York Region (Georgina)
PO Box 8, 25202 Warden Ave., Sutton West ON L0E 1R0
Tel: 905-476-3611; *Fax:* 905-476-6601
Previous Name: Georgina Family Life Centre
Overview: A small local charitable organization founded in 1972 overseen by Family Service Ontario
Mission: To counsel families & individuals through times of stress; to enrich the quality of life in individuals, marriage & family relationships; to help family members develop life skills which will enable them to live fuller & happier lives; to provide grief counselling
Member of: United Way
Finances: *Funding Sources:* United Way; client fees; Trillium Foundation
Activities: *Internships:* Yes

Family Supports Institute Ontario
#206, 489 College St., Toronto ON M6G 1A5
Tel: 416-538-0628
program.manager@fsio.ca
www.fsio.ca

Overview: A small provincial organization
Mission: The Family Supports Institute Ontario exists to advance the well-being of families.
Member of: Canadian Association of Family Resource Programs (FRP Canada)
Chief Officer(s):
Karen Vallée, Contact

Family YMCA of Windsor - Essex County See YMCA Canada

Fanshawe Community Orchestra See London Community Orchestra

The Farha Foundation / La Fondation Farha
#100, 576, rue Sainte-Catherine est, Montréal QC H2L 2E1
Tel: 514-270-4900; *Fax:* 514-270-5363
farha@farha.qc.ca
www.farha.qc.ca
www.facebook.com/FondationFARHAFoundation
twitter.com/FarhaFoundation
www.youtube.com/user/farhafondation
Overview: A medium-sized provincial charitable organization founded in 1992
Mission: To raise funds to improve the quality of life for persons living with HIV & AIDS throughout Québec
Finances: *Funding Sources:* Private donations
Membership: *Committees:* Grant; Executive
Activities: *Awareness Events:* Ça Marche - AIDS Fundraising Walk; *Speaker Service:* Yes
Chief Officer(s):
Nancy Farha, Executive Director Ext. 223
n.farha@farha.qc.ca

Farm & Food Care Canada
#202, 100 Stone Rd. West, Guelph ON N1G 5L3
Tel: 519-837-1326
info@farmfoodcare.org
www.farmfoodcare.org
www.facebook.com/FarmFoodCare
twitter.com/farmfoodcare
www.youtube.com/user/FarmandFoodCare
Overview: A small national charitable organization founded in 2011
Mission: To develop & support programs to communicate with Canadians helping to build confidence & trust in Canadian food & farming
Chief Officer(s):
Crystal Mackay, Chief Executive Officer

Farm & Food Care Ontario
#106, 100 Stone Rd. West, Guelph ON N1G 5L3
Tel: 519-837-1326; *Fax:* 519-837-3209
www.farmfoodcare.org
www.facebook.com/FarmFoodCare
twitter.com/farmfoodcare
www.youtube.com/user/FarmandFoodCare
Merged from: Ontario Farm Animal Council; Agricultural Groups Concerned about Resources and the Environment
Overview: A medium-sized provincial organization founded in 2012
Mission: To support & promote the responsible production & marketing of livestock & poultry by Ontario farmers & through a variety of initiatives, to better inform the public of the excellence of animal agriculture
Finances: *Funding Sources:* Memberships; corporate sponsorships; grants
Staff Member(s): 3
Membership: *Fees:* $250-$30,000
Activities: Consumer & producer displays; public speaking; agri-food spokespeople training; media relations; industry representation & services; referral and research

Farm & Ranch Safety & Health Association (FARSHA)
#311, 9440 - 202 St., Langley BC V1M 4A6
Tel: 604-881-6078; *Fax:* 604-881-6079
Toll-Free: 877-533-1789
farmsafe@farsha.bc.ca
www.farsha.bc.ca
www.facebook.com/FARSHABC
twitter.com/FARSHA_OHS
www.youtube.com/farshavideos
Overview: A medium-sized provincial organization founded in 1993
Mission: To reduce the number of accidents on farms & ranches in British Columbia through an active program of education & training in all regions of the province

Staff Member(s): 4
Activities: *Library:* Open to public
Chief Officer(s):
Ralph McGinn, Chair
Bruce Johnson, Executive Director
bruce@farsha.bc.ca

Farm Management Canada
#300, 250 City Centre Ave., Ottawa ON K1R 6K7
Tel: 613-237-9060; *Fax:* 613-237-9330
Toll-Free: 888-232-3262
info@fmc-gac.com
www.fmc-gac.com
www.facebook.com/fmc.gac
twitter.com/FMC_GAC
www.youtube.com/user/fmcgac
Previous Name: Canadian Farm Business Management Council
Overview: A medium-sized national organization founded in 1992
Mission: To advance farm business management so that managers have access to the skills & tools for success
Finances: *Annual Operating Budget:* $1.5 Million-$3 Million
Staff Member(s): 8
Membership: 57 organizations; *Member Profile:* Associations; producers; governments; individuals; corporations
Activities: *Speaker Service:* Yes
Chief Officer(s):
Heather Watson, Executive Director, 613-237-9060 Ext. 31
heather.watson@fmc-gac.com.

Farm Radio International / Radios Rurales Internationales
1404 Scott St., Ottawa ON K1Y 4M8
Tel: 613-761-3650; *Fax:* 613-798-0990
Toll-Free: 888-773-7717
info@farmradio.org
www.farmradio.org
www.linkedin.com/company/farm-radio-international
www.facebook.com/farmradio
twitter.com/farmradio
www.youtube.com/farmradioint
Previous Name: Developing Countries Farm Radio Network
Overview: A medium-sized international charitable organization founded in 1979
Mission: To increase food supplies & to improve the nutrition, health & quality of life of small-scale farmers in developing countries through a coordinating network of broadcasters & others who exchange information about simple, practical sustainable farming techniques & health practices; To support broadcasters to strengthen small scale farmers & rural life
Member of: Canadian Centre for Philanthropy; Ontario Council for International Cooperation; Canadian Council for International Cooperation
Finances: *Annual Operating Budget:* $250,000-$500,000; *Funding Sources:* Private donations; government grants; CIDA
Staff Member(s): 6; 10 volunteer(s)
Membership: 500; *Fees:* Free to radio stations in developing countries; *Member Profile:* Rural radio broadcasters in developing countries
Activities: *Library:*
Chief Officer(s):
Kevin Perkins, Executive Director
kperkins@farmradio.org
Publications:
• Network News
Type: Newsletter
Profile: Provides information about the program and the people involved in the organization, as well as updates on Canada's international development program.

Farmers of North America (FNA)
320 - 22nd St. East, Saskatoon SK S7K 0H1
Tel: 306-665-2294; *Fax:* 306-651-0444
Toll-Free: 877-362-3276
www.fna.ca
www.linkedin.com/company/farmers-of-north-america
www.facebook.com/farmersofnorthamerica
Overview: A large national organization founded in 1998
Mission: To improve farm profitability across Canada
Membership: 10,000
Chief Officer(s):
James Mann, President & CEO

Farmers of North America Strategic Agriculture Institute (FNA-SAG)
320 - 22nd St. East, Saskatoon SK S7K 0H1

Canadian Associations / Farmers' Markets of Nova Scotia Cooperative Ltd. (FMNS)

Tel: 306-665-2294; *Fax:* 306-651-0444
www.fnastag.ca
Overview: A large national organization founded in 2008 overseen by Farmers of North America
Mission: To identify new methods for farm profitability; To identify policy & regulatory issues affecting profitability, & to help advocate for change; To identify areas of needed research
Member of: Canadian Federation of Agriculture
Chief Officer(s):
Bob Friesen, CEO
Ottawa Office
21 Florence St., Ottawa ON K2P 0W6
Tel: 613-230-2222; *Fax:* 613-230-2235

Farmers' Markets of Nova Scotia Cooperative Ltd. (FMNS)
1999 Millsville Rd., Scotsburn NS B0K 1R0
Tel: 902-485-9330
FMNS@farmersmarketsnovascotia.ca
farmersmarketsnovascotia.ca
www.facebook.com/FarmersMarketsNovaScotia
twitter.com/marketfreshns
Overview: A small provincial organization founded in 2004
Mission: To maintain & develop a network of farmers' markets throughout Nova Scotia
Chief Officer(s):
Keltie Butler, Executive Director
Publications:
• Farmers' Markets of Nova Scotia Newsletter
Type: Newsletter

Farmers' Markets Ontario (FMO)
54 Bayshore Rd., Brighton ON K0K 1H0
Tel: 613-475-4769; *Fax:* 613-475-2913
Toll-Free: 800-387-3276
fmo@farmersmarketsontario.com
www.farmersmarketsontario.com
www.facebook.com/111525108903511
twitter.com/FarmersMktsOnt
Overview: A large provincial organization founded in 1991
Mission: To promote & encourage farmers' markets in Ontario
Membership: *Fees:* Schedule available, based upon number of vendors
Chief Officer(s):
Robert T. Chorney, Executive Director
Publications:
• Market Matters [a publication of Farmers' Markets Ontario]
Type: Newsletter

FarmFolk CityFolk
#203, 1661 Duranleau St., Vancouver BC V6H 3S3
Tel: 604-730-0450
info@farmfolkcityfolk.ca
www.farmfolkcityfolk.ca
www.facebook.com/FarmFolkCityFolk
twitter.com/ffcf
Previous Name: FarmFolk/CityFolk Society
Overview: A small local charitable organization founded in 1993
Mission: To work with others for a local, sustainable food system; To make connection between farm & city, producer & consumer, grower & eater that creates sustainable communities; To protect foodlands, support farmers & food producers, & connect communities
Finances: *Annual Operating Budget:* $100,000-$250,000; *Funding Sources:* Foundations; memberships; donations
Staff Member(s): 4; 80 volunteer(s)
Membership: 15 institutional; 200 student; 200 individual; 20 associate; *Fees:* $500+ corporate; $100 farm; $50 family; $30 individual; *Member Profile:* Not-for-profit, charitable organization
Activities: Events; projects; education; *Awareness Events:* "Feast of Fields" Fundraiser, Sept. *Library:* FarmFolk/CityFolk Resource Library; Open to public
Chief Officer(s):
Nicholas Scapillati, Execxutive Director

FarmFolk/CityFolk Society See FarmFolk CityFolk

Farming Smarter
211034 Hwy. 512, Lethbridge AB T1J 5N9
Tel: 403-317-0022
www.farmingsmarter.com
www.facebook.com/farmingsmarter
twitter.com/farmingsmarter
www.youtube.com/farmingsmarter
Overview: A small local organization founded in 1994 overseen by Agricultural Research & Extension Council of Alberta
Mission: To improve sustainability & efficiency of farming methods throughout Southern Alberta
Member of: Agricultural Research & Extension Council of Alberta
Chief Officer(s):
Ken Coles, General Manager, 403-317-0757
ken@farmingsmarter.com
Claudette Lacombe, Manager, Communications, 403-317-0022
claudette@farmingsmarter.com
Publications:
• Farming Smarter Newsletter
Type: Newsletter

Faro Humane Society
PO Box 315, Faro YT Y0B 1K0
Tel: 867-994-2713; *Fax:* 867-994-3154
Overview: A small local organization
Mission: To protect dogs, cats, horses, birds, livestock, lab animals, wildlife & the environment.
Member of: Canadian Federation of Humane Societies

FAST (Fighting Antisemitism Together)
Toronto ON
Tel: 416-916-8366
www.fightingantisemitism.ca
Overview: A small local organization founded in 2005
Mission: To challenge antisemitism & intolerance through education
Membership: *Member Profile:* Non-Jewish Canadian business & community leaders
Activities: "Choose Your Voice: Antisemitism in Canada" - educational program for students in grades 6-8
Chief Officer(s):
Nicole Miller, Executive Director

F.A.S.T.
#7B, 2441 Lakeshore Rd. West, Oakville ON L6L 5V5
Tel: 905-469-6338
Toll-Free: 888-651-5186
www.familytalk.ca
Also Known As: Family Adolescent Straight Talk Inc.
Overview: A small local charitable organization
Mission: F.A.S.T. helps people to recover from substance abuse/addicitons, by providing a safe environment in to receive crisis counselling, reconcile with family, friends and employers, and participate in ongoing individual and group therapy.
Staff Member(s): 5
Chief Officer(s):
Jim Harkins, Executive Director/Senior Counselor

FaunENord
CP 422, 512, rte 167 sud, Chibougamau QC G8P 2X8
Tél: 418-748-4441; *Téléc:* 418-748-1110
faunenord@lino.com
www.faunenord.org
www.facebook.com/FaunENord
Aperçu: *Dimension:* petite; *Envergure:* locale
Mission: Une entreprise vouée à la promotion & à l'aménagement durable des ressources fauniques & des écosystèmes
Membre(s) du bureau directeur:
Isabelle Milord, Présidente

Federal Association of Security Officials (FASO) / Association fédérale des représentants de la sécurité
PO Box 2384, Stn. D, Ottawa ON K1P 5W5
Fax: 613-773-5787
Toll-Free: 888-330-3276
info@faso-afrs.ca
faso-afrs.ca
Overview: A medium-sized national organization founded in 1992
Mission: To enhance the performance & career development of federal security officers through enhancing the security function in government & improving the professionalism of security officers.
Membership: *Member Profile:* Federal government employees & employees of agencies who are subject to the Policy on Government Security
Chief Officer(s):
Claude J.G. Levesque, President

Federal Liberal Association of Nunavut
c/o Liberal Party of Canada, #920, 350 Albert St., Ottawa ON K1P 6M8
Toll-Free: 888-542-3725
assistance@liberal.ca
Overview: A small provincial organization
Mission: To represent the Liberal Party in Nunavut
Chief Officer(s):
Ranbir Hundal, President

Federal Libraries Coordination Secretariat
Place de la Cité, 550, boul de la Cité, Gatineau QC K1A 0N4
Tel: 613-410-9752; *Fax:* 819-934-7539
BAC.SCBGF-FLCS.LAC@canada.ca
Previous Name: Council of Federal Libraries / Conseil des bibliothèques du gouvernement fédéral
Overview: A medium-sized national organization founded in 1976
Mission: To coordinate federal libraries service reports to the Recordkeeping & Library Coordination Office of the Government Records Branch
Membership: *Member Profile:* All library and library-like entities within the federal government
Chief Officer(s):
Anne Chartrand, Resources Officer, Federal Libraries Consortium

Federal Superannuates National Association See National Association of Federal Retirees

Federated Women's Institutes of Canada (FWIC) / Fédération des instituts féminins du Canada
PO Box 209, 359 Blue Lake Rd., St George ON N0E 1N0
Tel: 519-448-3873; *Fax:* 519-448-3506
www.fwic.ca
www.facebook.com/WomensInstitutes
twitter.com/fwicanada
Overview: A large national charitable organization founded in 1919
Mission: To act as a united voice for Women's Institutes of Canada; To promote Canadian women, families, & community living
Finances: *Funding Sources:* Membership fees
Staff Member(s): 2
Membership: 18,000; *Member Profile:* Any member in good standing of any provincial unit, institute, or body of women
Activities: Providing resources; Intitiating programs; Providing inter-communication opportunities; Hosting conferences, workshops & meetings
Chief Officer(s):
Kate Belair, Executive Director
Awards:
• Peace Garden Scholarship Program
Awarded to allow one recipient to participate in a one-week educational program at the International Peace Garden, located on the Manitoba & North Dakota border *Eligibility:* Women between 17 & 20 years of age interested in leadership, marketing, social media, horticulture, public relations, inspiring others, & positive social change; community & volunteer experience are assets
• Erland Lee Award
Presented to a gentleman who has made an oustanding contribution to the Women's Institute movement *Deadline:* March 31
• Adelaide Hunter Hoodless Canadian Woman of the Year Award
Awarded to acknowledge outstanding community service & dedication *Deadline:* December 31
Publications:
• Federated News [a publication of the Federated Women's Institutes of Canada]
Type: Newsletter
• Federated Women's Institutes of Canada Triennial Report
Type: Report; *Frequency:* Triennal

Federated Women's Institutes of Ontario (FWIO)
552 Ridge Rd., Stoney Creek ON L8J 2Y6
Tel: 905-662-2691; *Fax:* 905-930-8631
www.fwio.on.ca
twitter.com/fwiontario
Overview: A medium-sized provincial charitable organization founded in 1897 overseen by Federated Women's Institutes of Canada
Mission: To assist & encourage women to become more knowledgeable & responsible citizens; To promote & develop good family life skills; To help discover, stimulate & develop leadership; To help identify & resolve need in the community
Member of: Associated Country Women of the World
Finances: *Annual Operating Budget:* $250,000-$500,000; *Funding Sources:* Membership dues; Fundraising; Gala events

Staff Member(s): 5; 1000 volunteer(s)
Membership: 10,500; *Fees:* $50; *Member Profile:* Persons 16 years of age & over; *Committees:* Membership; Convention; Education; Erland Lee Museum; Budget; Home & Country Editorial; Personnel; Resolutions; Scholarship
Chief Officer(s):
Kim Sauder, Executive Administrator
kim@fwio.on.ca
Andrea Morrison, Manager, Program & Communications
andream@fwio.on.ca
Awards:
• Woman of Excellence in Agriculture Award
  Eligibility: Women in Ontario who are currently involved in agriculture
• Woman of Excellence Fair Award
  Awarded to recognize significant contributions made by WI members working at local fairs
Meetings/Conferences:
• Federated Women's Institutes of Ontario Annual General Meeting 2018, 2018, ON
Scope: Provincial
Contact Information: Administrator: Kim Sauder, E-mail: kim@fwio.on.ca

Fédération acadienne de la Nouvelle-Écosse (FANE)
La Maison acadienne, 54, rue Queen, Dartmouth NS B2Y 1G3
Tél: 902-433-0065; *Téléc:* 902-433-0066
info@federationacadienne.ca
www.acadiene.ca
www.facebook.com/1FANE
twitter.com/faneacadie
Aperçu: Dimension: moyenne; *Envergure:* provinciale; fondée en 1968 surveillé par Fédération des communautés francophones et acadienne du Canada
Mission: Un regroupement d'organismes régionaux, provinciaux et institutionnels d'expression française qui s'engage à promouvoir l'épanouissement et le développement global de la communauté acadienne et francophone de la Nouvelle-Écosse
Membre de: Fédération canadienne pour l'alphabétisation en français; Société nationale des Acadiens
Membre(s) du personnel: 9
Membre: 28 associations
Activités:; *Bibliothèque:* Bibliothèque publique
Membre(s) du bureau directeur:
Marie-Claude Rioux, Directrice générale, 902-433-0064
dg@federationacadienne.ca

Centre communautaire La Picasse
CP 70, 3435 Rte 206, Petit de Grat NS B0E 2L0
Tél: 902-226-0149; *Téléc:* 902-226-0549
lapicasse@lapicasse.ca
www.lapicasse.ca
twitter.com/LaPicasse
Membre(s) du bureau directeur:
Yvon Samson, Directrice générale
direction@lapicasse.ca

Community education center Étoile de l'Acadie
15 Inglis St., Sydney NS B1P 7C6
Tél: 902-564-0432
etoile@eastlink.ca
www.etoiledelacadie.com
Membre(s) du bureau directeur:
Patrick DeLamirande, Président
president@etoiledelacadie.com

Conseil acadien de Par-en-Bas
CP 63, 4258, Rte 308, Tusket NS B0W 3M0
Tél: 902-648-2253; *Téléc:* 902-648-2340
www.capeb.ca
www.facebook.com/350741674069
Membre(s) du bureau directeur:
Clyde deViller, Directrice générale
cdeviller@capeb.ca

Conseil communautaire du Grand-Havre
201C du Portage Ave., Dartmouth NS B2X 3T4
Tél: 902-435-3244; *Téléc:* 902-435-1255
info@ccgh.ca
ccgh.ca
www.linkedin.com/in/conseilcommunautaire
www.facebook.com/126180694133823
twitter.com/ccghavre
www.youtube.com/user/conseilcommunautaire
Membre(s) du bureau directeur:
Claude Renaud, President

Société acadienne de Clare
CP 167, 795 Comeauville, Saulnierville NS B0W 2Z0
Tél: 902-769-0955; *Téléc:* 902-769-0979
sa.clare@ns.aliantzinc.ca
www.saclare.ca
Membre(s) du bureau directeur:
Diane Besner, Présidente

Société Acadienne Sainte-Croix
1154, chemin Pomquet Monks Head, Antigonish NS B2G 2L4
Tél: 902-386-2679; *Téléc:* 902-735-3069
societesaintecroix.ca
www.facebook.com/176029749128363
Membre(s) du bureau directeur:
Rollande Dubé, Directrice générale
dg@societesaintecroix.ca

Société Saint-Pierre
CP 430, 15584 Cabot Trail Hwy, Cheticamp NS B0E 1H0
Tél: 902-224-2642; *Téléc:* 902-224-1579
lestroispignons@ns.sympatico.ca
lestroispignons.com/ssp/en/index.php
www.facebook.com/lestroispignons
twitter.com/LesTroisPignons
Membre(s) du bureau directeur:
Lisette Aucoin-Bourgeois, Directrice générale
lisettebourgeois@ns.sympatico.ca

Fédération aquatique du Canada See Aquatic Federation of Canada

Fédération autonome du collégial (ind.) (FAC) / Autonomous Federation of Collegial Staff (Ind.)
#400, 1259, rue Berri, Montréal QC H2L 4C7
Tél: 514-848-9977; *Téléc:* 514-848-0166
Aperçu: Dimension: moyenne; *Envergure:* provinciale; fondée en 1988
Mission: Défendre et développer les intérêts économiques, sociaux, pédagogiques et professionnels du personnel enseignant des cégeps; défendre le droit d'association, la libre négociation et la liberté d'action syndicale; négocier et s'assurer de l'application des conventions collectives; de représenter ses syndicats affiliés partout où leurs intérêts sont débattus
Membre: 4 000 individus; 18 sections locales; *Critères d'admissibilité:* Syndicat d'enseignant-es de cégep; faire parvenir votre demande à la FAC; *Comités:* Négociation; Information; Affaires pédagogiques; Condition féminine; Pratiques syndicales; Application convention collective; Solidarité internationale

Fédération Auto-Québec *Voir* Auto Sport Québec

Fédération baton canadienne See Canadian Baton Twirling Federation

Fédération canadienne d'agrément des conseillers en toxicomanie See Canadian Addiction Counsellors Certification Federation

La fédération canadienne d'aromathérapistes See Canadian Federation of Aromatherapists

Fédération canadienne d'escrime See Canadian Fencing Federation

Fédération canadienne de baseball amateur See Baseball Canada

Fédération canadienne de course d'orientation See Canadian Orienteering Federation

Fédération canadienne de culturisme See Canadian Bodybuilding Federation

Fédération canadienne de handball olympique See Canadian Team Handball Federation

Fédération canadienne de kendo See Canadian Kendo Federation

Fédération canadienne de l'agriculture See Canadian Federation of Agriculture

Fédération canadienne de l'entreprise indépendante See Canadian Federation of Independent Business

Fédération canadienne de la faune See Canadian Wildlife Federation

Fédération canadienne des amis de musées See Canadian Federation of Friends of Museums

Fédération canadienne des associations de bibliothèques See Canadian Federation of Library Associations

Fédération canadienne des Associations de propriétaires immobiliers See Canadian Federation of Apartment Associations

Fédération Canadienne des associations de techniciens d'entrien d'aéronefs See Canadian Federation of Aircraft Maintenance Engineers Associations

Fédération canadienne des associations des professeurs de musique See Canadian Federation of Music Teachers' Associations

Fédération canadienne des associations foyer-école See Canadian Home & School Federation

Fédération canadienne des clubs des femmes de carrières commerciales et professionnelles See The Canadian Federation of Business & Professional Women's Clubs

Fédération canadienne des coopératives de travail See Canadian Worker Co-operative Federation

Fédération canadienne des dix-quilles, inc. See Canadian Tenpin Federation, Inc.

Fédération canadienne des doyens des écoles d'administration See Canadian Federation of Business School Deans

Fédération canadienne des échecs See Chess Federation of Canada

Fédération canadienne des enseignantes et des enseignants See Canadian Teachers' Federation

Fédération canadienne des épiciers indépendants See Canadian Federation of Independent Grocers

Fédération canadienne des étudiantes et étudiants See Canadian Federation of Students

Fédération canadienne des étudiants et étudiantes en génie See Canadian Federation of Engineering Students

Fédération canadienne des femmes diplômées des universités See Canadian Federation of University Women

La Fédération canadienne des festivals de musique See Federation of Canadian Music Festivals

Fédération canadienne des gemmes et des minéraux See Gem & Mineral Federation of Canada

Fédération canadienne des infirmières et infirmiers en santé mentale See Canadian Federation of Mental Health Nurses

Fédération canadienne des jeunes ligues See Canadian Federation of Junior Leagues

Fédération canadienne des métiers d'art See Canadian Crafts Federation

Fédération canadienne des municipalités See Federation of Canadian Municipalities

Fédération Canadienne des Orthothérapeutes See Canadian Federation of Orthotherapists

Fédération Canadienne des Retraités See Canadian Federation of Pensioners

Fédération canadienne des sciences de la Terre See Canadian Federation of Earth Sciences

Fédération Canadienne des Sciences Humaines See Canadian Federation for the Humanities & Social Sciences

Fédération canadienne des services de garde à l'enfance See Canadian Child Care Federation

La Fédération canadienne des syndicats d'infirmières/infirmiers See Canadian Federation of Nurses Unions

Fédération canadienne du mouton See Canadian Sheep Federation

La Fédération canadienne du textile See Canadian Textile Association

Fédération canadienne du vêtement See Canadian Apparel Federation

La Fédération canadienne incorporée de bridge See Canadian Bridge Federation

Canadian Associations / Fédération CSN - Construction (CSN) / CNTU Federation - Construction (CNTU)

Fédération canadienne nationale des syndicats indépendants See Canadian National Federation of Independent Unions

Fédération canadienne volkssport See Canadian Volkssport Federation

La Fédération Canado-Arabe See Canadian Arab Federation

Fédération chypriote du Canada See Cypriot Federation of Canada

Fédération CSN - Construction (CSN) / CNTU Federation - Construction (CNTU)
2100, boul de Maisonneuve est, 4e étage, Montréal QC H2K 4S1
Tél: 514-598-2044; Téléc: 514-598-2040
www.csnconstruction.qc.ca
www.facebook.com/csnconstruction
Aperçu: Dimension: moyenne; *Envergure:* provinciale
Mission: Pour défendre les droits de leurs membres et de leur assurer de bonnes conditions de travail
Membre(s) du personnel: 4
Membre: 18,000
Membre(s) du bureau directeur:
Pierre Brassard, Président
pierre.brassard@csnconstruction.qc.ca
Karyne Prégent, Secrétaire général
karyne.pregent@csn.qc.ca

Fédération Culinaire Canadienne See Canadian Culinary Federation

Fédération culturelle acadienne de la Nouvelle-Écosse (FECANE)
54, rue Queen, Dartmouth NS B2Y 1G3
Tél: 902-466-1610; Téléc: 902-466-7970
www.fecane.com
www.facebook.com/infofecane
twitter.com/InfoFecane
Nom précédent: Fédération des festivals acadiens de la Nouvelle-Écosse
Aperçu: Dimension: petite; *Envergure:* provinciale; Organisme sans but lucratif; fondée en 1990
Mission: Déveloper et de promouvoir les différents produits artistiques acadiens de la N.E. Nos activités se concentrent sur les différentes communautés acadiennes de la N.E. mais peuvent également se dérouler à l'extérieur de la province
Membre(s) du personnel: 3
Membre: Montant de la cotisation: Barème
Activités: Promotion et développement de la culture acadienne en Nouvelle Écosse
Membre(s) du bureau directeur:
Martin Théberge, Directeur général

Fédération culturelle canadienne-française (FCCF)
Place de la Francophonie, #405, 450, rue Rideau, Ottawa ON K1N 5Z4
Tél: 613-241-8770; Téléc: 613-241-6064
Ligne sans frais: 800-267-2005
info@fccf.ca
www.fccf.ca
www.facebook.com/infofccf
twitter.com/infofccf
Aperçu: Dimension: moyenne; *Envergure:* nationale; fondée en 1977
Mission: Défendre et promouvoir les arts et la culture de la francophonie canadienne hors-Québec.
Membre de: Conseil canadiens des arts; Conseil francophone de la chanson; Conseil des ressources humaines du secteur culturel
Finances: Budget de fonctionnement annuel: $500,000-$1.5 Million
Membre(s) du personnel: 3; 32 bénévole(s)
Membre: 14 associations culturelles provinciales; *Montant de la cotisation:* 800$
Membre(s) du bureau directeur:
Maggy Razafimbahiny, Directrice générale
mrazafimbahiny@fccf.ca

Fédération culturelle de L'Ile-du-Prince-Édouard inc. (FCIPE)
5, promenade Acadienne, Charlottetown PE C1C 1M2
Tél: 902-368-1895; Téléc: 902-370-7334
fcipe@ssta.org
www.fcipe.ca
www.facebook.com/federation.culturelle

Aperçu: Dimension: petite; *Envergure:* provinciale; fondée en 1990
Mission: Développement culturel de la communauté acadienne et francophone
Affiliation(s): Commission culturelle de l'Atlantique; Fédération culturelle canadienne-française
Membre: 13; *Montant de la cotisation:* 10$ individuel; 50$ organisme; *Critères d'admissibilite:* Comité culture; musée; centre d'art
Activités: Stagiaires: Oui; *Bibliothèque:* Bibliothèque publique
Membre(s) du bureau directeur:
Michelle Blanchard, Présidente

Fédération culturelle finno-canadienne See Finnish Canadian Cultural Federation

Fédération cycliste du Québec Voir Fédération québécoise des sports cyclistes

Fédération d'agriculture biologique du Québec Voir Table de développement de la production biologique

Fédération d'athlétisme du Québec Voir Fédération québécoise d'athlétisme

Fédération d'escrime du Québec
4545, av Pierre-de Coubertin, Montréal QC H1V 0B2
Tél: 514-252-3045; Téléc: 514-254-3451
info@escrimequebec.qc.ca
www.escrimequebec.qc.ca
www.facebook.com/280110325350969
Aperçu: Dimension: moyenne; *Envergure:* provinciale surveillé par Canadian Fencing Federation
Membre(s) du bureau directeur:
Marc Lavoie, Directeur
mlavoie@uottawa.ca

Fédération de balle au mur du Canada See Canadian Handball Association

Fédération de basketball du Québec (FBBQ) / Québec Basketball Federation
4545, av Pierre-de Coubertin, Montréal QC H1V 0B2
Tél: 514-252-3057; Téléc: 514-252-3357
www.basketball.qc.ca
www.facebook.com/BasketballQc
twitter.com/BasketballQc
www.youtube.com/user/BasketballQc
Également appelé: Basketball Québec
Aperçu: Dimension: grande; *Envergure:* provinciale; Organisme sans but lucratif; fondée en 1970 surveillé par Canada Basketball
Mission: Développement et promotion de la discipline; Formation de joueurs, entraîneurs et arbitres; organisation de compétitions provinciales; Programme Poursuite de l'Excellence (Équipes et Espoirs du Québec)
Membre(s) du personnel: 7
Membre: 35,000 personnes
Activités: Stagiaires: Oui; *Service de conférenciers:* Oui
Membre(s) du bureau directeur:
Daniel Grimard, Directeur général
dgrimard@basketball.qc.ca

Fédération de Boulingrin du Québec See Québec Lawn Bowling Federation

Fédération de cheerleading du Québec (FCQ)
4545, av Pierre-de Coubertin, Montréal QC H1V 0B2
Tél: 514-252-3145; Téléc: 514-252-3146
Ligne sans frais: 866-694-3145
info@cheerleadingquebec.com
www.cheerleadingquebec.com
www.facebook.com/252273871484094
Aperçu: Dimension: petite; *Envergure:* provinciale surveillé par Cheer Canada
Membre de: Cheer Canada
Membre(s) du bureau directeur:
Jocelyn Deslaurier, Président
president@cheerleadingquebec.com
Catherine Marois Blanchet, Directrice générale, 514-252-3000 Ext. 3465
cmblanchet@cheerleadingquebec.com

Fédération de crosse du Québec (FCQ)
CP 1000, Succ. M, 4545, av Pierre-de Coubertin, Montréal QC H1V 3R2
Courriel: crosse@crosse.qc.ca
www.crossequebec.com

Aperçu: Dimension: moyenne; *Envergure:* provinciale; fondée en 1971 surveillé par Canadian Lacrosse Association
Mission: Offrir des services et des programmes axés vers le développement du sport de la crosse sur un plan régional et international
Membre de: Fédération Internationale d'Inter-Crosse; Canadian Lacrosse Association
Affiliation(s): Sports Québec; Regroupement Loisir Québec
Finances: Budget de fonctionnement annuel: $100,000-$250,000
Membre(s) du personnel: 2; 45 bénévole(s)
Membre: Comités: Commission tecchnique; Commission de développement; Interventions stratégiques
Activités: Stages de formation, conférences, ligues d'inter-crosse, compétitions; *Stagiaires:* Oui; *Service de conférenciers:* Oui
Membre(s) du bureau directeur:
Pierre Filion, Directeur
pierrefilion@bell.net

Fédération de football amateur de Québec Voir Football Québec

Fédération de golf du Québec / Québec Golf Federation
4545, av Pierre-de Coubertin, Montréal QC H1V 0B2
Tél: 514-252-3345; Téléc: 514-252-3346
golfquebec@golfquebec.org
www.golfquebec.org
www.facebook.com/golfquebec
twitter.com/golf_quebec
www.youtube.com/user/GolfQuebecMedias
Également appelé: Golf Québec
Nom précédent: Association de golf du Québec
Aperçu: Dimension: moyenne; *Envergure:* provinciale; Organisme sans but lucratif; fondée en 1920 surveillé par Golf Canada
Mission: Assurer le leadership; Favoriser la croissance et le développement du golf amateur dans toute la province tout en préservant l'intégrité et les traditions du jeu
Membre(s) du personnel: 9; 250 bénévole(s)
Membre: 61 000; *Montant de la cotisation:* 29$ adultes; 15$ juniors
Membre(s) du bureau directeur:
Jean-Pierre Beaulieu, Directeur général, 514-252-3345 Ext. 3732
jpbeaulieu@golfquebec.org
Meetings/Conferences:
• Fédération de golf du Québec Assemblée générale annuelle 2018, 2018
Scope: Provincial

Fédération de gymnastique du Québec (FGQ) / Québec Gymnastics Federation
4545, av Pierre-de-Coubertin, Montréal QC H1V 0B2
Tél: 514-252-3043; Téléc: 514-252-3169
info@gymqc.ca
www.gymqc.ca
www.facebook.com/GymQc
www.instagram.com/gymqc
Aperçu: Dimension: grande; *Envergure:* provinciale; fondée en 1971
Mission: Promouvoir et assurer le développement de la gymnastique à travers tout le Québec; favoriser l'éclosion des talents en vue d'une participation aux plans national et international; unir et coordonner les efforts de toutes les personnes intéressées dans le sport de la gym
Membre de: Canadian Gymnastics Federation
Membre(s) du personnel: 11
Membre: Critères d'admissibilite: Athléthes, entraîneurs, membres
Activités: Evénements de sensibilisation: Semaine de la prévention; *Stagiaires:* Oui; *Bibliothèque:* Bibliothèque publique
Membre(s) du bureau directeur:
Serge Sabourin, Président
Helen Brossard, Vice-présidente

Fédération de l'âge d'or du Québec Voir Réseau FADOQ

Fédération de l'habitation coopérative du Canada See Cooperative Housing Federation of Canada

Fédération de l'industrie manufacturière (FIM-CSN)
#204, 2100, boul de Maisonneuve est, Montréal QC H2K 4S1
Tél: 514-529-4937; Téléc: 514-529-4935
Ligne sans frais: 877-529-4977
fim@csn.qc.ca

www.fim.csn.qc.ca
www.facebook.com/FIMCSN
Nom précédent: Fédération de la métallurgie
Aperçu: *Dimension:* grande; *Envergure:* provinciale; fondée en 2011
Membre de: Confédération des syndicats nationaux
Finances: *Budget de fonctionnement annuel:* $100,000-$250,000
Membre(s) du personnel: 10
Membre: 30 000 + 320 sections locales; *Critères d'admissibilite:* Ajusteurs, assembleurs, bobineurs, camionneurs, chimistes, commis, comptables, carrossiers, dessinateurs, électriciens, employé-es de soutien, fondeurs, journaliers, machinistes, magasiniers, mécaniciens, métallurgistes, mineurs, opérateurs, peintres, plombiers, secrétaires, soudeurs, techniciens, tuyauteurs; *Comités:* Surveillance; Santé sécurité et environnement; Formation; Jeunes; Condition féminine
Activités: Bibliothèque: Not open to public
Membre(s) du bureau directeur:
Alain Lampron, Président
Kathy Beaulieu, Secrétaire-Trésorier

Baie-Comeau
999, rue Comtois, Baie-Comeau QC G5C 2A5
Tél: 418-589-6353; *Téléc:* 418-589-6873
Ligne sans frais: 844-589-6353
fim.baie-comeau@csn.qc.ca
Membre(s) du bureau directeur:
Marie-Ellen Tremblay, Secrétaire

Joliette
190, rue Montcalm, 1e étage, Joliette QC J6E 5G4
Tél: 450-759-4142; *Téléc:* 450-759-3234
Ligne sans frais: 844-759-4142
fim.joliette@csn.qc.ca
Membre(s) du bureau directeur:
Michèle Côté, Secrétaire

Québec
#350, 155, boul Charest est, Québec QC G1K 3G6
Tél: 418-647-5845; *Téléc:* 418-647-5884
Ligne sans frais: 877-647-5778
fim.quebec@csn.qc.ca
Membre(s) du bureau directeur:
Johanne Verret, Secrétaire

Rouyn-Noranda
243, rue Murdoch, Rouyn-Noranda QC J9X 1E8
Tél: 819-764-9541; *Téléc:* 819-764-4405
Ligne sans frais: 844-764-9541
fim.abitibi@csn.qc.ca
Membre(s) du bureau directeur:
Sylvie Gaudet, Secrétaire

Saguenay
73, rue Arthur-Hamel, Saguenay QC G7H 3M9
Tél: 418-459-7702; *Téléc:* 418-459-2192
Ligne sans frais: 866-549-7786
fim.saguenay@csn.qc.ca

Sherbrooke
#220, 180, Côte de l'Acadie, Sherbrooke QC J1H 2T3
Tél: 819-563-5006; *Téléc:* 819-563-4242
Ligne sans frais: 888-331-3886
fim.sherbrooke@csn.qc.ca
Membre(s) du bureau directeur:
Micheline Asselin, Secrétaire

Sorel-Tracy
815, rte Marie-Victorin, Sorel-Tracy QC J3R 1L1
Tél: 450-743-5502; *Téléc:* 450-743-6127
Ligne sans frais: 844-743-5502
fim.sorel@csn.qc.ca
Membre(s) du bureau directeur:
Ginette Houle, Secrétaire

Fédération de l'informatique du Québec *Voir* Réseau ACTION TI

Fédération de l'Union des producteurs agricoles de la Beauce *Voir* Fédération de l'UPA de la Beauce

Fédération de l'UPA - Abitibi-Témiscamingue
970, av Larivière, Rouyn-Noranda QC J9X 4K5
Tél: 819-762-0833; *Téléc:* 819-762-0575
abitibi-temiscamingue@upa.qc.ca
Aperçu: *Dimension:* moyenne; *Envergure:* locale; fondée en 1976
Mission: L'étude, la défense et le développement des intérêts économiques, sociaux et moraux de ses membres, en l'occurrence les producteurs et productrices agricoles
Affiliation(s): Confédération de l'UPA
Finances: *Budget de fonctionnement annuel:* $500,000-$1.5 Million; *Fonds:* Gouvernement provincial
Membre(s) du personnel: 16
Membre: 720; *Critères d'admissibilite:* Producteurs et productrices agricoles
Membre(s) du bureau directeur:
Linda Lavoie, Coordonnatrice, Centre d'emploi agricole

Fédération de l'UPA - Bas-Saint-Laurent
284, rue Potvin, Rimouski QC G5L 7P5
Tél: 418-723-2424; *Téléc:* 418-723-6045
bas-saint-laurent@upa.qc.ca
www.bas-saint-laurent.upa.qc.ca
Aperçu: *Dimension:* moyenne; *Envergure:* locale
Membre: 2 500
Membre(s) du bureau directeur:
Gilbert Marquis, Président

Fédération de l'UPA - Mauricie
230, rue Vachon, Trois-Rivières QC G8T 8Y2
Tél: 819-378-4033; *Téléc:* 819-371-2712
mauricie@upa.qc.ca
www.mauricie.upa.qc.ca
Aperçu: *Dimension:* moyenne; *Envergure:* locale
Membre: 1 587
Membre(s) du bureau directeur:
Jean-Marie Giguère, Président

Fédération de l'UPA de la Beauce
2550, 127e rue est, Saint-Georges QC G5Y 5L1
Tél: 418-228-5588; *Téléc:* 418-228-3943
Nom précédent: Fédération de l'Union des producteurs agricoles de la Beauce
Aperçu: *Dimension:* petite; *Envergure:* locale
Mission: Oeuvrer à l'amélioration des conditions de vie des producteurs et productrices agricoles de la région, tant du point de vue économique, social que moral
Membre(s) du personnel: 33
Membre: 3 000
Activités: *Listes de destinataires:* Oui
Membre(s) du bureau directeur:
Paul Doyon, Président

Fédération de l'UPA de la Montérégie
3800, boul Casavant ouest, Saint-Hyacinthe QC J2S 8E3
Tél: 450-774-9154; *Téléc:* 450-778-3797
upamonteregie@upa.qc.ca
www.upamonteregie.ca
Merged from: Fédération de l'UPA de Saint-Hyacinthe; Fédération de l'UPA de Saint-Jean-Valleyfield
Aperçu: *Dimension:* moyenne; *Envergure:* locale; fondée en 1931
Mission: Défendre les droits des agriculteurs et leur fournir différents services
Affiliation(s): Confédération de l'UPA
Finances: *Budget de fonctionnement annuel:* $100,000-$250,000
Membre: 6 300; *Montant de la cotisation:* 490$ institutionnel; 245$ individu; *Critères d'admissibilite:* Agriculteurs; agricultrices; *Comités:* Alus; aménagement du territoire; environnement; finances; fiscalité municipale; producteurs anglophones; vie syndicale et des communications
Activités: Syndicalisme agricole et formation; comptabilité et fiscalité; centre agricole
Membre(s) du bureau directeur:
Robert Racine, Directeur régional
rracine@upa.qc.ca
Claire Pomerleau, Secrétaire de direction
cpomerleau@upa.qc.ca

Bureau de Saint-Rémi
6, rue du Moulin, Saint-Rémi QC J0L 2L0
Tél: 450-454-5115; *Téléc:* 877-414-7870
upamonteregie@upa.qc.ca

Fédération de la faune du Nouveau-Brunswick *See* New Brunswick Wildlife Federation

Fédération de la jeunesse canadienne-française Inc. (FJCF)
#403, 450 Rideau St., Ottawa ON K1N 5Z4
Tél: 613-562-4624; *Téléc:* 613-562-3995
Ligne sans frais: 800-267-5173
admim@fjcf.ca
www.fjcf.ca
www.facebook.com/fjcf.ca
twitter.com/FJCF_Canada
www.flickr.com/photos/fjcf_canada
Aperçu: *Dimension:* moyenne; *Envergure:* nationale; Organisme sans but lucratif; fondée en 1974 surveillé par Fédération des communautés francophones et acadienne du Canada
Mission: Etre le porte-parole national de la jeunesse canadienne-française et acadienne; assurer l'épanouissement de la jeunesse dans les secteurs de l'éducation, des arts et communications, des loisirs et de l'économie; augmenter la visibilité de la FJCF et de ses membres auprès de leurs différentes clientèles; augmenter les occasions pour les jeunes d'utiliser la langue française; renforcer le sentiment d'appartenance des jeunes, pour qu'ils soient des agents de changement dans leur communauté
Membre(s) du personnel: 8
Membre: 11
Activités: Jeux de la francophonie canadienne; Parlement jeunesse pancanadien; Réseau international de la jeunesse; *Stagiaires:* Oui; *Service de conférenciers:* Oui
Membre(s) du bureau directeur:
Justin Johnson, Président

Fédération de la jeunesse franco-ontarienne (FESFO)
#202, 135, rue Alice, Ottawa ON K1L 7X5
Tél: 613-260-8055; *Téléc:* 613-260-5346
Ligne sans frais: 877-260-8055
info@fesfo.ca
www.fesfo.ca
www.facebook.com/fesfo
twitter.com/laFESFO
www.youtube.com/user/LaFESFO
Nom précédent: Fédération des Élèves du secondaire franco-ontarien
Aperçu: *Dimension:* moyenne; *Envergure:* provinciale; Organisme sans but lucratif; fondée en 1975
Mission: S'assure que la jeunesse franco-ontarienne participe pleinement au développement de sa communauté
Affiliation(s): Fédération de la jeunesse canadienne-française
Membre(s) du personnel: 12
Membre: 25 000; *Critères d'admissibilite:* Agé entre 14 et 18 ans
Activités: Ateliers de formation; consultations auprès des membres; formation en leadership et estime de soi; activisme et lobbying politique; *Evénements de sensibilisation:* Jeux Franco-Ontariens; Forums "Organizzaction"; Parlement jeunesse francophone de l'Ontario; *Service de conférenciers:* Oui
Membre(s) du bureau directeur:
Andrée Newell, Directrice générale
anewell@fesfo.ca

Fédération de la métallurgie *Voir* Fédération de l'industrie manufacturière (FIM-CSN)

Fédération de la relève agricole du Québec (FRAQ)
#105, 555, boul Roland-Therrien, Longueuil QC J4H 4E7
Tél: 450-679-0530; *Téléc:* 450-679-2375
fraq@upa.qc.ca
www.fraq.qc.ca
www.facebook.com/fraqreleve
twitter.com/LaFraq
www.youtube.com/user/lesbobtrotteurs
Aperçu: *Dimension:* moyenne; *Envergure:* provinciale; fondée en 1982
Mission: Améliorer les conditions d'établissement en agriculture et travailler à une meilleure préparation des jeunes qui se destinent à une carrière en production agricole
Membre de: Union des producteurs agricoles
Membre(s) du personnel: 3
Membre: 2,000; *Montant de la cotisation:* Barème; *Critères d'admissibilite:* Jeunes âgés entre 16 et 35 ans intéressés à l'agriculture
Membre(s) du bureau directeur:
Yourianne Plante, Directrice générale par intérim
yplante@upa.qc.ca

Fédération de la santé du Québec - CSQ (FSQ-CSQ)
9405, rue Sherbrooke est, Montréal QC H1L 6P3
Tél: 514-356-8888; *Téléc:* 514-667-5590
fsq@csq.qc.net
www.fsq.lacsq.org
Nom précédent: Union québécoise des infirmières et infirmiers
Aperçu: *Dimension:* moyenne; *Envergure:* provinciale; Organisme sans but lucratif; fondée en 1988
Mission: La FSQ assure la représentation de ses membres, donne aux syndicats une structure politique et fournit, en collaboration avec la CSQ, des services aux membres en matière de relations de travail, de professionnel, de négociation et de formation

Canadian Associations / Fédération de la santé et des services sociaux (FSSS)

Affiliation(s): Centrale des syndicats du Québec (CSQ); Syndicat des infirmières, inhalothérapeutes, infirmières auxiliaires du Cour-du-Québec; Syndicat des infirmières et infirmiers de l'Est du Québec; Syndicat des infirmières, inhalothérapeutes et infirmières auxiliaires de Laval; Syndicat des intervenantes et intervenants de la santé du Nord-Est québécois; Syndicat des infirmières et infirmières auxiliaires de l'hôpital Marie-Clarac; Syndicat du personnel infirmier d'Héma-Québec
Membre: 7 000 infirmières; *Critères d'admissibilite:* Infirmières; infirmières auxiliaire; inhalothérapeutes; puéricultrices
Activités: Service de conférenciers: Oui
Membre(s) du bureau directeur:
Claire Montour, Présidente

Fédération de la santé et des services sociaux (FSSS)
1601, av de Lorimier, Montréal QC H2K 4M5
Tél: 514-598-2210; *Téléc:* 514-598-2223
www.fsss.qc.ca
www.facebook.com/FSSSCSN
twitter.com/FSSSCSN
www.youtube.com/user/f3scsn
Aperçu: Dimension: grande; *Envergure:* nationale
Mission: De promouvoir et sauvegarder la santé, la sécurité et les intérêts des personnes employées des établissements affiliés ou en voie d'affiliation; de représenter ses membres auprès de la Confédération des syndicats nationaux en lui soumettant toutes questions d'intérêt général; de représenter ses membres, de concert avec la CSN, partout où les intérêts généraux des travailleuses et travailleurs le justifient; d'aider à conclure, en faveur des syndicats affiliés, des conventions collectives de travail et en favoriser l'application; de collaborer à l'éducation des travailleuses et travailleurs et à la formation de responsables et militantes et militants syndicaux; d'assurer les services à ses syndicats affiliés; de favoriser et d'établir des liens inter-syndicaux avec les autres travailleuses et travailleurs dans le secteur public et para-public et dans le secteur privé du Québec et du Canada
Membre de: Confédération des syndicats nationaux
Membre: 110 000+; *Critères d'admissibilite:* Etre un sydicat affilié à la Confédération des syndicats nationaux et à la Fédération des affaires sociales
Activités: Bibliothèque:
Membre(s) du bureau directeur:
Jeff Begley, Président
jeff.begley@csn.qc.ca
Nadine Lambert, Secrétaire générale-trésorière
nadine.lambert@csn.qc.ca

Fédération de lutte olympique du Québec / Québec Wrestling Association
4545, av Pierre de Couberlin, Montréal QC H1V 3R2
Tél: 514-252-3044
www.quebecolympicwrestling.ca
Aperçu: Dimension: moyenne; *Envergure:* provinciale surveillé par Canadian Amateur Wrestling Association

Fédération de nage synchronisée *Voir* Synchro-Québec

Fédération de natation du Québec (FNQ)
CP 1000, Succ. M, 4545, av Pierre-de Coubertin, Montréal QC H1V 0B2
Tél: 514-252-3200; *Téléc:* 514-252-3232
fnq@fnq.qc.ca
www.fnq.qc.ca
www.facebook.com/163831313666941
twitter.com/fednatationqc
Aperçu: Dimension: moyenne; *Envergure:* provinciale surveillé par Swimming Canada
Membre de: Swimming Canada
Affiliation(s): Éducation, Loisir et Sport Québec; AQUAM Équipes; Groupe Hospitalité Westmont (Quality et Comfort Inn); Location Sauvageau; Trophies Dubois; Westjet; Financière Manuvie; McAuslan
Membre: *Comités:* Provincial des officiels; coordination et standardisation, tenue des championnats; maîtres-nageurs; révision du guide technique; suivi du programme d'assistance financière; soutien informatique; paranatation; Défi sportif; Temple de la renommée; budget; révision des règlements généraux et discipline; mise en candidature; Assemblée générale annuelle
Membre(s) du bureau directeur:
Isabelle Ducharme, Directrice générale
iducharme@fnq.qc.ca

Fédération de Netball du Québec / Québec Amateur Netball Federation (QANF)
CP 1000, Succ. M, 4545, av Pierre-de Coubertin, Montréal QC H1V 3R2
Tél: 514-486-2769
www.netballquebec.ca
www.facebook.com/QuebecNetball
Également appelé: Netball Québec
Aperçu: Dimension: moyenne; *Envergure:* provinciale; fondée en 1974 surveillé par Netball Canada
Mission: Promouvoir et développer le netball féminin au Québec
Membre de: Netball Canada
Affiliation(s): International Federation of Netball Associations
Membre: 750; *Comités:* Technique
Activités: Tournois; Ligues; Cliniques pour entraîneurs et arbitres
Membre(s) du bureau directeur:
Avice Roberts-Joseph, Présidente
Sheryl Stephens, Secrétaire

Fédération de Patinage de Vitesse du Québec
930, av Roland Beaudin, Sainte-Foy QC G1V 4H8
Tél: 418-651-1973; *Téléc:* 418-651-1977
Ligne sans frais: 877-651-1973
www.fpvq.org
www.facebook.com/FPVQ.org
twitter.com/PatinVitesseQc
Aperçu: Dimension: petite; *Envergure:* provinciale surveillé par Speed Skating Canada
Mission: Depuis un peu plus d'un mois déjà, les athlètes du Centre national courte piste sont en entraînement hors glace sous la surveillance des entraîneurs et avec la grande collaboration du groupe Actiforme.
Membre de: Speed Skating Canada
Membre(s) du personnel: 6

Fédération de pétanque du Québec
4545, av Pierre-de Coubertin, Montréal QC H1V 0B2
Tél: 514-252-3077
petanque@petanque.qc.ca
www.petanque.qc.ca
www.facebook.com/189251017803912
Aperçu: Dimension: moyenne; *Envergure:* provinciale
Mission: Développement du sport de pétanque
Membre: 4 000; 14 organismes régionaux
Membre(s) du bureau directeur:
Janick Provencher, Présidente

Fédération de rugby du Québec (FRQ) / Quebec Rugby Union
CP 1000, Succ. M, 4545, av Pierre-de Coubertin, Montréal QC H1V 3R2
Tél: 514-252-3189; *Téléc:* 514-252-3159
info@rugbyquebec.qc.ca
www.rugbyquebec.qc.ca
www.facebook.com/98779487768
twitter.com/RugbyQuebec
Aperçu: Dimension: moyenne; *Envergure:* provinciale surveillé par Rugby Canada
Mission: Promouvoir le sport et la santé physique en général, et sans limiter ce qui précède le sport du rugby; organiser des tournois de Rugby dans la province de Québec; regrouper les associations régionales et les clubs de Rugby du Québec
Membre de: Rugby Canada
Membre(s) du personnel: 3
Membre: 2 610
Membre(s) du bureau directeur:
Martin Cormier, Directeur général

Fédération de soccer du Québec (FDSDQ)
#210, 955, av Bois-de-Boulogne, Laval QC H7N 4G1
Tél: 450-975-3355
courriel@federation-soccer.qc.ca
www.federation-soccer.qc.ca
www.facebook.com/SoccerQuebec
twitter.com/SoccerQuebec
www.youtube.com/user/FederationSoccerQC
Également appelé: Soccer Québec
Nom précédent: Fédération québécoise de soccer football
Aperçu: Dimension: grande; *Envergure:* provinciale; fondée en 1911 surveillé par Canadian Soccer Association
Membre de: Canadian Soccer Association
Finances: *Fonds:* Société de Promotion du Soccer
Membre: 82 000; *Comités:* Exécutif; Compétitions; Provincial Arbitrage; Technique

Fédération de sociétés mutuelles d'assurance générale (Groupe promutuel)
#400, 2000, boul Lebourgneuf, Québec QC G2K 0B6
Ligne sans frais: 866-999-2433
federation@promutuel.ca
www.promutuel.ca
Aperçu: Dimension: petite; *Envergure:* provinciale; fondée en 1852
Mission: Promouvoir et offrir des produits d'assurance et des services financiers qui répondent aux attentes des membres-assurés et des clients et souvent les précèdent
Affiliation(s): Association canadienne des compagnies d'assurance mutuelles; Société de coopération pour le développement international
Membre(s) du personnel: 1800
Membre: 24 sociétés mutuelles d'assurance; *Critères d'admissibilite:* Client en assurance dommages
Activités: Assurance; services financiers
Membre(s) du bureau directeur:
Sylvain Fauchon, Chef de la direction

Fédération de tennis de table du Québec (FTTQ)
4545, av Pierre-de Coubertin, Montréal QC H1V 0B2
Tél: 514-252-3064; *Téléc:* 514-251-8038
www.tennisdetable.ca
www.facebook.com/tennisdetableQC
twitter.com/tennisdetableQC
www.youtube.com/user/TennisdetableQC
Aperçu: Dimension: moyenne; *Envergure:* provinciale surveillé par Table Tennis Canada
Membre de: Table Tennis Canada
Membre(s) du personnel: 3
Membre(s) du bureau directeur:
Yves Surprenant, Président

Fédération de tir à l'arc du Québec (FTAQ)
CP 1000, Succ. M, 4545, av Pierre-de Coubertin, Montréal QC H1V 3R2
Tél: 514-252-3054; *Téléc:* 514-252-3165
taq@tiralarcquebec.com
www.tiralarquebec.com
www.facebook.com/tiralarcquebec
Aperçu: Dimension: petite; *Envergure:* provinciale surveillé par Archery Canada Tir à l'Arc
Membre de: Archery Canada Tir à l'Arc
Membre(s) du personnel: 3
Membre: 3 000
Membre(s) du bureau directeur:
Glenn Gudgeon, Président
president@tiralarcquebec.com
Publications:
• Fédération de tir à l'arc du Québec bulletin
Type: Bulletin

Fédération de tir du Canada *See* Shooting Federation of Canada

Fédération de voile du Québec
4545, av Pierre-de Coubertin, Montréal QC H1V 0B2
Tél: 514-252-3097; *Téléc:* 514-252-3044
www.voile.qc.ca
www.facebook.com/voilequebec
Aperçu: Dimension: petite; *Envergure:* provinciale; fondée en 1970 surveillé par Sail Canada
Mission: Encourager et promouvoir la pratique de la voile, sous toutes ses formes au Québec
Membre: *Comités:* Voile adaptée; Élite; Circuit du Québec; Régie de course; Croisière et plaisance; Formation dériveur; Formation croisière
Membre(s) du bureau directeur:
Natalie Matthon, Directrice générale

Fédération de volleyball du Québec (FVBQ)
4545, av Pierre-de Coubertin, Montréal QC H1V 0B2
Tél: 514-252-3065; *Téléc:* 514-252-3176
info-fvbq@volleyball.qc.ca
www.volleyball.qc.ca
www.facebook.com/VolleyballQC
twitter.com/volleyballqc
www.youtube.com/volleyballquebec
Également appelé: Volleyball Québec
Aperçu: Dimension: moyenne; *Envergure:* provinciale; Organisme sans but lucratif; fondée en 1968 surveillé par Volleyball Canada
Mission: Régir le volleyball à l'intérieur et à l'extérieur du Québec; promouvoir le volleyball; former les intervenants impliqués dans l'encadrement du participant; offrir des services

aux membres
Affiliation(s): Sports Québec; Regroupement loisirs Québec
Finances: *Budget de fonctionnement annuel:* $500,000-$1.5 Million; *Fonds:* Gouvernement provincial
Membre(s) du personnel: 5; 100 bénévole(s)
Membre: 20,000; *Critères d'admissibilite:* Entraîneurs, athlètes, arbitres, adeptes, bénévoles; *Comités:* Entraîneurs; Arbitres; Élite; Techniques
Activités: Volleybal compétitif et récréatif; édition, publication et vente de documents techniques et pédagogiques; programme de formation des entraîneurs; vente de vidéos; *Stagiaires:* Oui; *Service de conférenciers:* Oui; *Bibliothèque:* rendez-vous
Membre(s) du bureau directeur:
Félix Dion, Président

Fédération de Water-Polo du Québec (FWPQ) / Water Polo Québec
4545, av Pierre-de Coubertin, Montréal QC H1V 0B2
Tél: 514-252-3098
Autres numéros: Alt. Phone: 514-621-0379
www.waterpolo-quebec.qc.ca
www.facebook.com/federationwaterpoloquebec
Aperçu: *Dimension:* petite; *Envergure:* provinciale; Organisme sans but lucratif surveillé par Water Polo Canada
Mission: Regrouper en association représentative, toute personne qui s'adonne à l'activité du water-polo; sensibiliser la population du Québec à cette activité de loisirs; favoriser le développement sous toutes ses formes
Membre de: Sports Québec; Regroupement Loisirs Québec; Water Polo Canada
Finances: *Fonds:* Ministère de l'Éducation.
Activités: Coordonne les programmes des équipes féminines et masculines du Québec; sanctionne les différents tournois provinciaux; organise les stages, cliniques et autres événements
Membre(s) du bureau directeur:
Ariane Clavet-Gaumont, Directrice générale

Fédération des Agricotours du Québec *Voir* Association de l'Agricotourism et du Tourisme Gourmand

Fédération des agriculteurs et agricultrices francophones du Nouveau-Brunswick (FAAFNB)
18, rue de l'École, Edmundston NB E3V 1X6
Tél: 506-735-4886; *Téléc:* 506-737-4070
faafnb@nbnet.nb.ca
Aperçu: *Dimension:* petite; *Envergure:* provinciale; Organisme sans but lucratif; fondée en 1985
Mission: Promouvoir et défendre les intérêts des agriculteurs et agricultrices francophones du Nouveau-Brunswick, sur le plan provincial et national; participer au développement de l'agriculture et l'épanouissement des producteurs et productrices agricoles francophones du Nouveau-Brunswick
Membre de: Conseil économique du Nouveau-Brunswick; Construction Association of New Brunswick
Finances: *Budget de fonctionnement annuel:* $50,000-$100,000
Membre(s) du personnel: 5
Membre: 200; *Critères d'admissibilite:* Producteur agricole
Membre(s) du bureau directeur:
Paul-Emile Soucy, Président
Diane Côté, Directrice executive

Fédération des agricultrices du Québec (FAQ)
555, boul Roland-Therrien, Longueuil QC J4H 4E7
Tél: 450-679-0540; *Téléc:* 450-463-5228
fed.agricultrices@upa.qc.ca
www.agricultrices.com
Aperçu: *Dimension:* moyenne; *Envergure:* provinciale; Organisme sans but lucratif; fondée en 1987
Mission: Valoriser la profession; créer un réseau entre les femmes; avoir une force politique capable de défendre les intérêts des agricultrices; prodiguer de la formation
Membre de: L'Union des producteurs agricoles
Membre: 1,000-4,999; *Critères d'admissibilite:* Agricultrice, membre de soutien

Fédération des aînées et aînés francophones du Canada (FAAFC)
#300, 450 rue Rideau, Ottawa ON K1N 5Z4
Tél: 613-564-0212; *Téléc:* 613-564-0212
info@faafc.ca
www.faafc.ca
www.youtube.com/user/LaFAAFC
Nom précédent: L'Assemblée des aînées et aînés francophones du Canada
Aperçu: *Dimension:* moyenne; *Envergure:* nationale; fondée en 1992

Mission: Défendre les droits des personnes à la retraite; Défendre les droits des préretraités; Programmes intergénérationnels; Protection de la langue et la culture française
Finances: *Budget de fonctionnement annuel:* $100,000-$250,000
Membre: *Montant de la cotisation:* Barème
Membre(s) du bureau directeur:
Roger Doiron, Président
Jean-Luc Racine, Directeur général
Michel Vézina, Premier vice-président, Saskatchewan
André Faubert, Deuxième vice-présidente, Québec
Richard Martin, Trésorier, Terre-Neuve & Labrador
Mélina Gallant, Secrétaire, Ile-du-Prince-Édouard
Marie-Christine Aubrey, Administratrice, Territoire du Nord-Ouest
Louis Bernardin, Administrateur, Manitoba
Roland Gallant, Administrateur, Nouveau-Brunswick
Charles Gaudet, Administrateur, Nouvelle-Écosse
Claire Grisé, Administratrice, Colombie-Britannique
Germaine Lehodey, Administratrice, Alberta
Francine Poirier, Administratrice, Ontario
Roxanne Thibaudeau, Administratrice, Yukon

Fédération des aînés et des retraités francophones de l'Ontario (FARFO)
1490, ch Star Top, Ottawa ON K1B 3W6
Ligne sans frais: 800-819-3236
administration@farfo.ca
www.farfo.ca
www.facebook.com/farfoprovinciale
twitter.com/lafarfoprov
Nom précédent: Fédération des aînés francophones de l'Ontario
Aperçu: *Dimension:* moyenne; *Envergure:* provinciale; Organisme sans but lucratif; fondée en 1978
Mission: Promouvoir les retraités et aînées francophones et francophiles de l'Ontario et être leur porte-parole officiel; améliorer la qualité de vie des retraités et aînés francophones de l'Ontario
Affiliation(s): Assemblée des retraités et des aînées francophones du Canada
Finances: *Budget de fonctionnement annuel:* $250,000-$500,000; *Fonds:* Patrimoine Canada; Ressources humaines Canada; Procureur général du Canada; Nouveaux horizons
Membre(s) du personnel: 5; 30 bénévole(s)
Membre: 10 500; *Montant de la cotisation:* 20$; *Comités:* Finances; congrès; logement
Activités: Journées santé; foires d'information; voyages internationaux
Membre(s) du bureau directeur:
Denise Lemire, Directrice générale
dg@farfo.ca

Fédération des aînés Franco-Albertains (FAFA)
#136, 8627, rue Marie-Anne-Gaboury, Edmonton AB T6C 3N1
Tél: 780-465-8965; *Téléc:* 780-468-6535
bureau@fafalta.ca
www.fafalta.ca
Aperçu: *Dimension:* petite; *Envergure:* provinciale; fondée en 1991
Mission: Protéger les droits des aînés francophones en Alberta et favoriser leur plein épanouissement
Membre de: La Société généalogique; Alberta Council on Aging
Membre(s) du personnel: 1
Membre: *Critères d'admissibilite:* Gens qui a 50+ ans et qui parle français
Activités: Conférences; ateliers; congrès; assemblée annuelle
Membre(s) du bureau directeur:
Yannick Freychet, Directeur général
yannick.freychet@fafalta.ca

Fédération des aînés franco-manitobains inc. (FAFM)
#107, 400, rue des Meurons, Saint-Boniface MB R2H 3H3
Tél: 204-235-0670; *Téléc:* 204-231-7071
Ligne sans frais: 855-235-0670
info@fafm.mb.ca
www.fafm.mb.ca
Aperçu: *Dimension:* moyenne; *Envergure:* provinciale; Organisme sans but lucratif; fondée en 1977
Mission: Revendique et représente les intérêts des francophones de 55 ans et plus
Membre: *Montant de la cotisation:* 15$

Activités: Activités en groupe; sessions d'information; tournois de golf; pièces de théâtre; service d'écoute
Membre(s) du bureau directeur:
Gérard Curé, Directeur général

Fédération des aînés francophones de l'Ontario *Voir* Fédération des aînés et des retraités francophones de l'Ontario

Fédération des aînés fransaskois (FAF)
#213, 308 - 4e av nord, Saskatoon SK S7K 2L7
Tél: 306-653-7442
aines@sasktel.net
www.fransaskois.info/federation-des-aines-fransaskois-n583.html
Aperçu: *Dimension:* petite; *Envergure:* provinciale; Organisme sans but lucratif; fondée en 1983
Mission: La FAF a pour but de favoriser le développement et l'épanouissement des personnes âgées et retraitées de 50 ans et plus francophones en Saskatchewan
Membre de: Assemblée des aînés et aînés francophones du Canada; Saskatchewan Seniors Mechanism; Provincial Advisory Comittee of Older Persons
Membre: *Critères d'admissibilite:* Personnes âgées et retraitées de 50 ans et plus
Activités: Épluchette de blé d'Inde; Fête de Noël; cours Internet; conférences; fête fransaskoise; ateliers divers (santé, formation); jeux des aînés

Fédération des apiculteurs du Québec
Maison de l'UPA, #225, 555, boul Roland-Therrien, Longueuil QC J4H 4E7
Tél: 450-679-0540; *Téléc:* 450-463-5226
apiculteur@upa.qc.ca
www.apiculteursduquebec.com
Nom précédent: Fédération des producteurs de miel du Québec
Aperçu: *Dimension:* petite; *Envergure:* provinciale; fondée en 1979
Mission: Défendre les intérêts des apiculteurs de Québec
Membre de: Conseil canadien du miel
Affiliation(s): Union des producteurs agricoles (UPA); Conseil canadien du miel
Finances: *Budget de fonctionnement annuel:* $100,000-$250,000
Membre(s) du personnel: 1
Membre: 150; *Montant de la cotisation:* Barème; *Critères d'admissibilite:* Apiculteur
Membre(s) du bureau directeur:
Léo Buteau, Président

Fédération des associations danoises du Canada *See* Federation of Danish Associations in Canada

Fédération des associations de familles du Québec (FAFQ)
650, rue Graham-Bell, Québec QC G1N 4H5
Tél: 418-653-2137; *Téléc:* 418-653-6387
info@fafq.org
fafq.org
Nom précédent: Fédération des familles-souches du Québec
Aperçu: *Dimension:* moyenne; *Envergure:* provinciale; Organisme sans but lucratif; fondée en 1983
Mission: Favoriser les regroupements en associations de familles; fournir différents services techniques et de l'aide-conseil
Membre de: Conseil Québecois de Loisir et Regroupement Loisir Québec
Membre(s) du personnel: 4
Membre: 218
Activités: Congrès annuel; Journées d'information à l'automne; Ateliers de formation; *Service de conférenciers:* Oui
Membre(s) du bureau directeur:
Claude Trudel, Président
trudelcl@globetrotter.net
Yves Boisvert, Directeur, 418-653-2137 Ext. 224
yboisvert@fafq.org
Meetings/Conferences:
• Fédération des associations de familles du Québec Congrès & assemblée générale 2018, 2018, QC
Scope: Provincial
Contact Information: Directeur: Yves Boisvert, Courriel: yboisvert@fafq.org

Fédération des associations de familles monoparentales et recomposées du Québec

Canadian Associations / Fédération des associations de familles monoparentales et recomposées du Québec (FAFMRQ) / Federation of Single-Parent Family Associations of Québec

(FAFMRQ) / Federation of Single-Parent Family Associations of Québec
584, rue Guizot est, Montréal QC H2P 1N3
Tél: 514-729-6666; Téléc: 514-729-6746
fafmrq.info@videotron.ca
www.fafmrq.org
twitter.com/FAFMRQ
Aperçu: Dimension: moyenne; Envergure: provinciale; Organisme sans but lucratif; fondée en 1974
Mission: Travailler à améliorer les conditions socio-économiques des familles monoparentales et recomposées du Québec.
Membre(s) du personnel: 3
Membre: 35 associations; Montant de la cotisation: Barème
Activités: Rencontres; colloques; Stagiaires: Oui
Membre(s) du bureau directeur:
Sylvie Lévesque, Directrice générale
fafmrq.sylvie@videotron.ca

Fédération des associations de juristes d'expression française de common law (FAJEF)
#1, 242, rue Goulet, Winnipeg MB R2H 0S2
Tél: 204-415-7551; Téléc: 204-415-4482
www.fajef.ca
Aperçu: Dimension: moyenne; Envergure: provinciale; fondée en 1992 surveillé par Fédération des communautés francophones et acadienne du Canada
Mission: Pour fournir un soutien et de représenter ses membres
Membre: Critères d'admissibilite: Associations de juristes francophones qui défendent les droits des francophones

Fédération des Associations de Musiciens-Éducateurs du Québec (FAMÉQ)
55, rue Greenfield, Longueuil QC J4V 2J6
Tél: 450-466-6799
info@fameq.org
www.fameq.org
www.facebook.com/204489629683586
Aperçu: Dimension: moyenne; Envergure: provinciale; fondée en 1967
Mission: Représentater les musiciens éducateurs; participer à la concertation et mobilisation des musiciens éducateurs; promouvoir l'éducation musicale
Membre: Montant de la cotisation: 90$ personnes en exercice; 60$ retraités; 30$ étudiants
Activités: Journée de la musique; concours; chorales; formation
Membre(s) du bureau directeur:
Maryse Forand, Directrice générale
dg@fameq.org

Fédération des associations de parents francophones de l'Ontario Voir Parents partenaires en éducation

Fédération des associations de professeures et professeurs d'université du Nouveau-Brunswick See Federation of New Brunswick Faculty Associations

Fédération des associations du sport scolaire de l'Ontario See Ontario Federation of School Athletic Associations

Fédération des Associations et Corporations en Construction du Québec
#500, 5181, rue d'Amiens, Montréal QC H1G 6N9
Tél: 514-955-8508; Téléc: 514-955-6623
info@faccq.org
www.faccq.org
Aperçu: Dimension: moyenne; Envergure: provinciale; fondée en 1993
Mission: Promouvoir les droits des entrepreneurs; défendre leurs intérêts; vulgariser les Lois et règlements régissant l'industrie de la construction
Membre(s) du bureau directeur:
Ronald Marin, Président
rmarin@faccq.org

Fédération des associations étudiantes du campus de l'université de Montréal (FAÉCUM)
3200, rue Jean-Brillant, #B1265, Montréal QC H3T 1N8
Tél: 514-343-5947
info@faecum.qc.ca
www.faecum.qc.ca
www.linkedin.com/company/fédération-des-associations-étudiantes-du-campus-de-l%27université-de-montréal
www.facebook.com/FAECUM
twitter.com/FAECUM
www.instagram.com/FAECUM;
www.youtube.com/user/faecumofficiel
Aperçu: Dimension: grande; Envergure: locale; fondée en 1976
Mission: Représenter les étudiants de l'Université par l'intermédiaire de leurs Associations; Défendre leurs droits et intérêts dans le domaine académique et au niveau social, économique, culturel et politique
Membre de: Fédération étudiante universitaire du Québec
Membre: 82 associations qui représentent 37 000 membres; Montant de la cotisation: Barème; Critères d'admissibilite: associations étudiantes
Membre(s) du bureau directeur:
Nicolas Lavallée, Secrétaire général
sg@faecum.qc.ca
Josée Ricard, Directrice générale
dg@faecum.qc.ca

Fédération des associations foyer-école du Québec Inc. See Québec Federation of Home & School Associations Inc.

Fédération des associations roumaines du Canada Voir Fondation roumaine de Montréal

Fédération des astronomes amateurs du Québec
4545, av Pierre-de Coubertin, Montréal QC H1V 3R2
Tél: 514-252-3038
info@faaq.org
www.faaq.org
Aperçu: Dimension: petite; Envergure: provinciale; Organisme sans but lucratif; fondée en 1976
Mission: Représenter et regrouper les individus, groupes (clubs) et institutions reliés à l'astronomie amateur au Québec
Affiliation(s): Conseil Québécois du Loisir; Regroupement Loisir Québec; Association Française d'Astronomie; International Dark-sky Association
Membre: Montant de la cotisation: 15$ individu; 75$ corporatifs éducationnels; 125$ corporatifs institutionnels; Critères d'admissibilite: Astronome amateur
Activités: Bibliothèque virtuelle
Membre(s) du bureau directeur:
Rémi Laccasse, Président

Fédération des aveugles du Québec inc. See Québec Federation of the Blind Inc.

Fédération des caisses Desjardins du Québec
100, av des Commandeurs, Lévis QC G6V 7N5
Tél: 418-835-8444
Ligne sans frais: 866-835-8444
www.desjardins.com
www.linkedin.com/company/desjardins
www.facebook.com/Desjardinsgroup
twitter.com/desjardinsgroup
www.youtube.com/user/desjardinsgroup
Aperçu: Dimension: grande; Envergure: provinciale
Mission: To support the Desjardins caisses in Québec.
Membre: 255 individuals in 17 councils
Membre(s) du bureau directeur:
Guy Cormier, Chair, President & CEO, Desjardins Group
Normand Desautels, Senior Vice-President & General Manager

Abitibi-Témiscamingue - Nord du Québec
602, 3e av, Val-d'Or QC J9P 1S5
Tél: 819-825-2843; Téléc: 819-825-7083
Ligne sans frais: 866-588-2843

Bas St-Laurent
CP 880, 100, rue Julien-Rehel, Rimouski QC G5L 7C9
Tél: 418-723-3368; Téléc: 418-723-7107
Ligne sans frais: 888-880-9824

Centre-du-Quebec
460, boul Saint-Joseph, Drummondville QC J2C 2A8
Tél: 819-474-2524; Téléc: 819-417-4212
Ligne sans frais: 855-474-2524

Chaudière-Appalaches
#300, 1017, boul Vachon nord, Sainte-Marie QC G6E 1M3
Tél: 418-386-1333; Téléc: 418-386-1330
Ligne sans frais: 877-707-1333

Estrie
#300, 1815, rue King ouest, Sherbrooke QC J1J 2E3
Tél: 819-821-2201; Téléc: 819-821-1077
Ligne sans frais: 866-821-2201

Gaspésie/Iles-de-la-Madeleine
CP 190, 554, boul Perron est, Maria QC G0C 1Y0
Tél: 418-759-3456; Téléc: 418-759-3801
Ligne sans frais: 866-381-3456

Lanaudière
820, montée Masson, Mascouche QC J7K 3B6
Tél: 450-474-2474; Téléc: 450-474-5774

Laval-Laurentides
#210, 2550, boul Daniel-Johnson, Laval QC H7T 2L1
Tél: 450-978-2212; Téléc: 450-978-1123

Mauricie
1200, rue Royale, Trois-Rivières QC G9A 4J2
Tél: 819-376-1200; Téléc: 819-375-5036
Ligne sans frais: 877-375-4987

Montérégie
850, boul Casavant ouest, Saint-Hyacinthe QC J2S 7S3
Tél: 450-261-8888; Téléc: 450-261-8886
Ligne sans frais: 866-465-8888

Montréal
Niveau Promenade, CP 244, Succ. Desjardins, #100, 52, complexe Desjardins, Montréal QC H5B 1B4
Tél: 514-281-7101; Téléc: 514-281-6232

Outaouais
655, boul Saint-René ouest, Gatineau QC J8T 8M4
Tél: 819-568-5368; Téléc: 819-568-9063
Ligne sans frais: 877-568-5368

Québec-Rive-Sud
#600, 1610, boul Alphonse-Desjardins, Lévis QC G6V 0H1
Tél: 418-834-4343; Téléc: 418-833-2098
Ligne sans frais: 866-771-4343

Rive-Sud de Montréal
#100, 1850, av Panama, Brossard QC J4W 3C6
Tél: 450-671-3720; Téléc: 450-671-2431

Saguenay-Lac-Saint-Jean-Charlevoix
#700, 1685, boul Talbot, Saguenay QC G7H 7Y4
Tél: 418-543-1700; Téléc: 418-549-7244

Fédération des caisses populaires acadiennes
Édifice Martin-J.-Légère, CP 5554, 295, boul St-Pierre ouest, Caraquet NB E1W 1B7
Tél: 506-726-4000; Téléc: 506-726-4001
www.acadie.com
www.facebook.com/caissespopulairesacadiennes
twitter.com/CPAcadiennes
Aperçu: Dimension: moyenne; Envergure: provinciale; fondée en 1945
Mission: Améliorer la qualité de vie de ceux et celles qui y adhèrent tout en contribuant à l'autosuffisance socio-économique de la collectivité acadienne du Nouveau-Brunswick, dans le respect de son identité linguistique et ses valeurs coopératives
Membre(s) du personnel: 1000
Membre: 155,000
Membre(s) du bureau directeur:
Camille H. Thériault, Président/Directeur général

Fédération des cégeps
500, boul Crémazie est, Montréal QC H2P 1E7
Tél: 514-381-8631; Téléc: 514-381-2263
comm@fedecegeps.qc.ca
www.fedecegeps.qc.ca
www.facebook.com/monretouraucegep
Aperçu: Dimension: moyenne; Envergure: provinciale; fondée en 1969
Mission: De promouvoir le développement de l'enseignement collégial; au nom de ses membres, la Fédération établit des contacts et étudie les dossiers communs avec différents partenaires gouvernementaux et privés, notamment en ce qui concerne les affaires pédagogiques, étudiantes, matérielles et financières, et les ressources humaines du réseau
Membre: 48 collèges publics du Québec
Activités:; Bibliothèque: rendez-vous
Membre(s) du bureau directeur:
Marie-France Bélanger, Présidente
Bernard Tremblay, Président-directeur général
bernard.tremblay@fedecegeps.qc.ca

Fédération des centres d'action bénévole du Québec (FCABQ)
1557, av Papineau, Montréal QC H2K 4H7
Tél: 514-843-6312; Téléc: 514-843-6485
Ligne sans frais: 800-715-7515
info@fcabq.org
www.fcabq.org
www.facebook.com/fcabq
Aperçu: Dimension: moyenne; Envergure: provinciale; Organisme sans but lucratif; fondée en 1972
Mission: Promouvoir l'action bénévole au Québec; former un centre d'action bénévole; organiser la semaine de l'action bénévole.
Membre de: Bénévoles Canada
Affiliation(s): International Association for Volunteer Effort
Membre(s) du personnel: 4
Membre: 111

Activités: *Stagiaires:* Oui; *Service de conférenciers:* Oui; *Bibliothèque*
Membre(s) du bureau directeur:
Fimba Tankoano, Directeur général
direction@fcabq.org

Fédération des centres de ressourcement Chrétien
CP 87127, Succ. Charlesbourg, 870, carré de Tracy est, Québec QC G1G 5E1
Tél: 418-623-5597
fcrc@ressourcementchretien.qc.ca
www.ressourcementchretien.qc.ca
Aperçu: *Dimension:* moyenne; *Envergure:* provinciale; fondée en 1960
Mission: Pour aider les centres chrétiens avec leurs buts
4 bénévole(s)
Membre(s) du bureau directeur:
Michel Paquet, Président, Conseil d'administration

Fédération des chambres de commerce du Québec (FCCQ)
#1100, 555, boul René-Lévesque ouest, Montréal QC H2Z 1B1
Tél: 514-844-9571; *Téléc:* 514-844-0226
Ligne sans frais: 800-361-5019
www.fccq.ca
twitter.com/FCCQ
Aperçu: *Dimension:* moyenne; *Envergure:* provinciale; fondée en 1909
Mission: Représenter les chambres de commerce et les entreprises du Québec
Membre: 140 chambres; *Critères d'admissibilite:* Chambres de commerce au Québec
Activités: Plaidoyer pour le compte des entreprises; Créer un solide réseau d'entreprises interconnecté; Favoriser l'esprit d'entreprise au Québec
Membre(s) du bureau directeur:
Stéphane Forget, Président-Directeur général, 514-844-9571 Ext. 3257
Jean-Guy Delorme, Vice-Président, Réseau et développmnt, 514-844-9571 Ext. 3229
David Laureti, Directeur, Stratégie et affaires économiques, 514-844-9571 Ext. 3244
Michel Philibert, Directeur, Communications, 514-844-9571 Ext. 3242
Publications:
• L'Exclusif [publication de la Fédération des chambres de commerce du Québec]
Type: Bulletin; *Frequency:* hebdomadaire
• Le FCCQeXpress [publication de la Fédération des chambres de commerce du Québec]
Type: Bulletin; *Frequency:* bi-mensuel
• Fédération des chambres de commerce du Québec rapport annuel
Type: Rapport; *Frequency:* annuel
• L'Indicateur FCCQ [Fédération des chambres de commerce du Québec]
Type: Rapport; *Frequency:* irrégulier

Fédération des chambres de commerce du Québec (FCCQ)
#1100, 555, boul René-Lévesque ouest, Montréal QC H2Z 1B1
Tél: 514-844-9571; *Téléc:* 514-844-0226
Ligne sans frais: 800-361-5019
info@fccq.ca
www.fccq.ca
www.linkedin.com/groups/Fédération-chambres-commerce-Québec-4659438
www.facebook.com/FCCQ.Reseau
twitter.com/FCCQ
Aperçu: *Dimension:* petite; *Envergure:* provinciale; fondée en 1909
Mission: Promouvoir la liberté d'entreprendre qui s'inspire de l'initiative et dela créativité afin de contribuer à la richesse collective en coordonnant l'apport du travail de tous; positionner la FCCQ comme le regroupement incontournable des intérêts d'affaires sur l'échiquier socio-économique et politique du Québec
Finances: *Budget de fonctionnement annuel:* $1.5 Million-$3 Million
Membre: 60 000 entreprises
Membre(s) du bureau directeur:
Stéphane Forget, Président-directeur général

Fédération des Chambres immobilières du Québec (FCIQ)
600, ch du Golf, Ile-des-Soeurs QC H3E 1A8
Tél: 514-762-0212; *Téléc:* 514-762-0365
Ligne sans frais: 866-882-0212
info@fciq.ca
www.fciq.ca
twitter.com/fciq_eco
Aperçu: *Dimension:* grande; *Envergure:* provinciale; Organisme sans but lucratif; fondée en 1991
Mission: Promouvoir et protéger les intérêts de l'industrie immobilière du Québec afin que les Chambres et les membres accomplissent avec succès leurs objectifs d'affaires
Membre de: The Canadian Real Estate Association
Membre: 8 500
Membre(s) du bureau directeur:
Normand Racine, Président du conseil d'administration
Chantal de Repentigny, Directrice adjointe, Communication et relations avec l'industrie, 514-762-0212 Ext. 130
chantal.derepentigny@fciq.ca

Fédération des chorales de la Nouvelle-Écosse *See* Nova Scotia Choral Federation

Fédération des chorales du Nouveau-Brunswick *See* New Brunswick Choral Federation

Fédération des citoyens aînés du Nouveau-Brunswick inc. *See* New Brunswick Senior Citizens Federation Inc.

Fédération des clubs de croquet du Québec (FCCQ)
CP 1000, Succ. M, 4545, av Pierre-de Coubertin, Montréal QC H1V 3R2
Tél: 514-252-3032
croquet@fqjr.qc.ca
croquet.quebecjeux.org
Aperçu: *Dimension:* petite; *Envergure:* provinciale; fondée en 1973
Membre: 635; *Montant de la cotisation:* 10$ individu
Membre(s) du bureau directeur:
Jacques Noël, Président, 819-379-8035

Fédération des clubs de fers du Québec
4545, av Pierre-de Coubertin, Montréal QC H1V 0B2
Tél: 514-252-3032
fers@fqjr.qc.ca
fers.quebecjeux.org
www.facebook.com/1433138876961682
Aperçu: *Dimension:* moyenne; *Envergure:* provinciale; fondée en 1961 surveillé par Horseshoe Canada
Mission: La FCFQ veut promouvoir la pratique du lancer de fers. Elle favorise les rencontres et les tournois qui contribuent au développement de la discipline. Elle distribue de l'information, donne des cours et des démonstrations
Membre de: Horseshoe Canada
Membre: *Montant de la cotisation:* 12$ individuel; 50$ club/ligue/ville
Membre(s) du bureau directeur:
Kenny Weightman, Président

Fédération des Clubs de l'Age d'Or de l'Est du Québec *Voir* Carrefour 50+ du Québec

Fédération des clubs de motoneigistes du Québec (FCMQ)
CP 1000, Succ. M, 4545, av Pierre-de Coubertin, Montréal QC H1V 3R2
Tél: 514-252-3076; *Téléc:* 514-254-2066
Ligne sans frais: 844-253-4343
info@fcmq.qc.ca
www.fcmq.qc.ca
www.facebook.com/FCMQ40
twitter.com/Fed_MotoneigeQc
Aperçu: *Dimension:* moyenne; *Envergure:* provinciale; Organisme sans but lucratif; fondée en 1974
Mission: La Fédération des clubs de motoneigistes du Québec est un organisme à but non lucratif, voué au développement et à la promotion de la pratique de la motoneige dans tout le Québec
Finances: *Budget de fonctionnement annuel:* $3 Million-$5 Million
Membre(s) du personnel: 10; 3000 bénévole(s)
Membre: 228; *Montant de la cotisation:* 250$/club
Membre(s) du bureau directeur:
Serge Ritcher, Président

Fédération des comités de parents de la Province de Québec inc *Voir* Fédération des comités de parents du Québec inc.

Fédération des comités de parents du Québec inc. (FCPQ)
2263, boul Louis-XIV, Québec QC G1C 1A4
Tél: 418-667-2432; *Téléc:* 418-667-6713
Ligne sans frais: 800-463-7268
courrier@fcpq.qc.ca
www.fcpq.qc.ca
www.facebook.com/fcpq.parents
twitter.com/fcpq
Nom précédent: Fédération des comités de parents de la Province de Québec inc
Aperçu: *Dimension:* petite; *Envergure:* provinciale
Mission: De défendre et de promouvoir les droits et les intérêts des parents des élèves des écoles publiques primaires et secondaires de façon à assurer la qualité de l'éducation offerte aux enfants
Membre: *Comités:* Exécutif; Éthique
Membre(s) du bureau directeur:
Gaston Rioux, Président
president@fcpq.qc.ca
Marc Charland, Directeur général
Jonatan Bérubé, Conseiller aux communications
communications@fcpq.qc.ca

La Fédération des commissions scolaires du Québec (FCSQ)
1001, av Bégon, Québec QC G1X 3M4
Tél: 418-651-3220; *Téléc:* 418-651-2574
Ligne sans frais: 800-463-3311
info@fcsq.qc.ca
www.fcsq.qc.ca
www.linkedin.com/company-beta/736250
www.facebook.com/LaFCSQ
twitter.com/fcsq
www.youtube.com/user/fcsq2011/videos
Aperçu: *Dimension:* moyenne; *Envergure:* provinciale; fondée en 1947
Mission: Tout en conservant ses tâches premières de coordination et d'unification, la mission de la Fédération s'est élargie, au fil des ans, pour rencontrer deux objectifs principaux : contribuer à promouvoir l'éducation ainsi que représenter et défendre avec détermination les intérêts des commissions scolaires.
Membre de: Association canadienne d'éducation de langue française
Finances: *Budget de fonctionnement annuel:* $3 Million-$5 Million
Membre(s) du personnel: 50
Membre: 61 commissions scolaires
Activités: *Evénements de sensibilisation:* Assemblée générale; *Bibliothèque* Not open to public
Membre(s) du bureau directeur:
Josée Bouchard, Présidente
Pâquerette Gagnon, Directrice générale
Publications:
• Commissaires [a publication of La Fédération des commissions scolaires du Québec]
Type: Bulletin
• Savoir [a publication of La Fédération des commissions scolaires du Québec]
Type: Magazine

Fédération des communautés francophones et acadienne du Canada (FCFAC)
#300,450, rue Rideau, Ottawa ON K1N 5Z4
Tél: 613-241-7600; *Téléc:* 613-241-6046
info@fcfa.ca
www.fcfa.ca
www.facebook.com/FCFACanada
twitter.com/fcfacanada
Nom précédent: Fédération des francophones hors Québec
Aperçu: *Dimension:* grande; *Envergure:* nationale; Organisme sans but lucratif; fondée en 1975
Mission: Défendre et promouvoir les droits et les intérêts des communautés francophones et acadiennes qu'elle représente
Membre: 22 corporations à but non-lucratif; *Montant de la cotisation:* 500$
Activités: *Stagiaires:* Oui; *Listes de destinataires:* Oui; *Bibliothèque:* Bibliothèque publique rendez-vous
Membre(s) du bureau directeur:
Suzanne Bossé, Directrice générale
bosse@fcfa.ca
Sylviane Lanthier, Présidente

Fédération des coopératives d'habitation de l'Estrie (FCHE)
548, rue Dufferin, Sherbrooke QC J1H 4N1
Tél: 819-566-6303; *Téléc:* 819-829-1593
fche@reseaucoop.com
Aperçu: Dimension: petite; *Envergure:* locale
Membre de: Confédération québécoise des coopératives d'habitation

Fédération des coopératives d'habitation de la Mauricie et du Centre-du-Québec (FECHMACQ)
#230, 235, rue Hénòt, Drummondville QC J2C 6X5
Tél: 819-477-6986; *Téléc:* 819-477-3827
Ligne sans frais: 888-477-6986
info@fechmacq.ca
www.cooperativehabitation.coop
Aperçu: Dimension: petite; *Envergure:* locale
Membre de: Confédération québécoise des coopératives d'habitation
Membre(s) du personnel: 3
Membre(s) du bureau directeur:
Mireille Pepin, Directrice générale
mpepin@fechmacq.ca
Michel Legault, Président

Fédération des coopératives d'habitation du Royaume Saguenay Lac-Saint-Jean
#110, 30, rue Racine est, Chicoutimi QC G7H 1P5
Tél: 418-543-6858; *Téléc:* 418-543-4698
fechas@qc.aira.com
www.cooperativehabitation.coop
Également appelé: FECHAS
Aperçu: Dimension: petite; *Envergure:* locale; Organisme sans but lucratif; fondée en 1990
Mission: Développer de nouvelles coopératives d'habitation; regrouper les coopératives d'habitation; offrir des services à ses membres COOP et OSBL en logement social
Membre de: Confédération québécoise des coopératives d'habitation (CQCH)
Finances: *Budget de fonctionnement annuel:* $100,000-$250,000; *Fonds:* Gouvernement provincial
Membre(s) du personnel: 3; 5 bénévole(s)
Membre: 33 coopératives; 12 OBNL; *Montant de la cotisation:* 40$
Membre(s) du bureau directeur:
Dennis Bolduc, Coordonnateur au dév. et affaires
Régine Lalancette, Coordonnatrice administrative
Marie-Andrée Turcotte, Présidente

Fédération des coopératives d'habitation intermunicipale du Montréal métropolitain (FECHIMM) / Montréal Federation of Housing Cooperatives
#202, 3155, rue Hochelaga, Montréal QC H1W 1G4
Tél: 514-843-6929; *Téléc:* 514-843-5241
info@fechimm.coop
www.fechimm.coop
www.facebook.com/146339935412999
twitter.com/FECHIMM
Aperçu: Dimension: petite; *Envergure:* locale
Mission: D'unir les coopératives de logement en leur fournissant des formations et des ateliers
Membre de: Confédération québécoise des coopératives d'habitation
Membre(s) du personnel: 32
Membre: 440 coopératives membres
Membre(s) du bureau directeur:
Francine Néméh, Directrice générale
fnemeh@fechimm.coop

Fédération des coopératives d'habitation Montérégiennes (FECHAM)
150, rue Grant, Longueuil QC J4H 3H6
Tél: 450-651-5520; *Téléc:* 450-651-5522
Ligne sans frais: 888-651-5520
Autres numéros: Télécopieur sans frais: 1-888-651-5522
info@fecham.coop
www.cooperativehabitation.coop
Aperçu: Dimension: petite; *Envergure:* locale; fondée en 1983
Mission: L'Association vise à regrouper les coops d'habitation en Montérégie; représenter et défendre les membres et leur offrir des services; promouvoir la formule coop sans but lucratif en habitation
Membre de: Confédération québécoise des coopératives d'habitation
Affiliation(s): Confédération québécoise des coopératives d'habitation; Fédération de l'habitation coopérative du Canada
Finances: *Budget de fonctionnement annuel:* $250,000-$500,000; *Fonds:* Gouvernement provincial et revenus autonomes
Membre(s) du personnel: 7; 7 bénévole(s)
Membre: 1-99; *Critères d'admissibilité:* Coopératives d'habitation situées sur le territoire de la Montérégie
Activités: *Stagiaires:* Oui
Membre(s) du bureau directeur:
Raymond Giguère, Agent de gestion financière
raymondgiguere@fecham.coop

Fédération des coopératives de Québec, Chaudière-Appalaches (FECHAQC)
#205A, 275, rue du Parvis, Québec QC G1K 6G7
Tél: 418-648-1354; *Téléc:* 418-648-9991
Ligne sans frais: 866-313-2667
info@fechaqc.qc.ca
Aperçu: Dimension: petite; *Envergure:* locale; fondée en 1981
Membre de: Confédération québécoise des coopératives d'habitation

Fédération des courtiers en fonds mutuels *See* Federation of Mutual Fund Dealers

Fédération des dames d'Acadie *Voir* Fédération des femmes acadiennes et francophones du Nouveau-Brunswick

Fédération des dentistes spécialistes du Québec (FDSQ) / Federation of dental specialists of Quebec
#302, 14, ch Bates, Outremont QC H2V 1A8
Tél: 514-737-4901
info@fdsq.qc.ca
www.fdsq.qc.ca
www.facebook.com/543154982403967
Aperçu: Dimension: petite; *Envergure:* provinciale; fondée en 1972
Mission: De promouvoir des intérêts professionnels de ses membres; de développer scientifique des spécialistes de la médecine dentaire
Membre(s) du bureau directeur:
Victor Legault, Président

Fédération des Écrivaines et Écrivains du Québec *See* Québec Writers' Federation

Fédération des éducateurs et éducatrices physiques enseignants du Québec (FEEPEQ)
2500, boul de l'Université, Sherbrooke QC J1K 2R1
Tél: 819-821-8000; *Téléc:* 819-821-7970
info@feepeq.com
www.feepeq.com
www.facebook.com/180360724546
twitter.com/feepeq
Nom précédent: Confédération des Éducateurs physiques du Québec
Aperçu: Dimension: moyenne; *Envergure:* provinciale; Organisme sans but lucratif; fondée en 1960
Mission: Représenter plus du tiers des éducateurs/trices physiques oeuvrant activement partout au Québec
Affiliation(s): Sports Québec; Fédération québécoise du sport étudiant
Finances: *Budget de fonctionnement annuel:* $100,000-$250,000
Membre(s) du personnel: 4; 40 bénévole(s)
Membre: 1 700; *Montant de la cotisation:* Barème; *Critères d'admissibilité:* Éducateur physique enseignant selon les régions d'appartenance; *Comités:* Exécutif; finances; partenariats; publications; pédagogie; professionnalisation; congrès; dossiers Internet
Activités: Formation; information; sensibilisation; congrès; Mouvement Pupilles de l'Enseignement Public; *Service de conférenciers:* Oui; *Listes de destinataires:* Oui; *Bibliothèque:* rendez-vous
Membre(s) du bureau directeur:
Patrick Parent, Président
Nathalie Morneau, Directrice, Opérations

Fédération des Élèves du secondaire franco-ontarien *Voir* Fédération de la jeunesse franco-ontarienne

Fédération des employées et employés de services publics inc. (CSN) (FEESP) / Federation of Public Service Employees Inc. (CNTU)
1601, av de Lorimier, Montréal QC H2K 4M5
Tél: 514-598-2231; *Téléc:* 514-598-2398
feesp.courrier@csn.qc.ca
www.feesp.csn.qc.ca
www.facebook.com/feespcsn
Aperçu: Dimension: moyenne; *Envergure:* nationale; Organisme sans but lucratif
Mission: Il est composé de quatre personnes élues, du coordonnateur ou coordonnatrice des services et de la personne déléguée syndicale.
Affiliation(s): Confédération des syndicats nationaux
Membre: 55 000 + 400 sections locales; *Comités:* Formation; Condition féminine; Santé-sécurité-environnement
Membre(s) du bureau directeur:
Nathalie Arguin, Secéraire-générale

Fédération des employés du préhospitaliers du Québec (FPHQ)
481, ch Grande-Côte, Rosemère QC J7A 1M1
Téléc: 888-728-2397
Ligne sans frais: 800-661-1556
www.fphq.ca
Aperçu: Dimension: petite; *Envergure:* provinciale
Mission: Veille à ce que le secteur préhospitalier puisse offrir des services de qualité aux citoyens
Membre: 49
Membre(s) du bureau directeur:
Daniel Chouinard, Président

Fédération des enseignantes et des enseignants de l'élémentaire de l'Ontario *See* Elementary Teachers' Federation of Ontario

Fédération des enseignantes et des enseignants de l'Ontario *See* Ontario Teachers' Federation

Fédération des enseignants de cégeps
9405, rue Sherbrooke est, Montréal QC H1L 6P3
Tél: 514-356-8888; *Téléc:* 514-354-8535
Ligne sans frais: 800-465-0897
fec@csq.qc.net
www.fec.csq.qc.net
www.facebook.com/feccsq
twitter.com/feccsq
Aperçu: Dimension: moyenne; *Envergure:* provinciale surveillé par Centrale des syndicats du Québec
Mission: De protéger les intérêts de ses membres
Affiliation(s): Centrale des syndicats du Québec
Membre: 13 sections locales; *Comités:* Négociation; D'information, de formation et d'application de la convention collective; Condition des femmes; Relève syndicale; Formation continue; Vigilance
Membre(s) du bureau directeur:
Mario Beauchemin, President
fec.beauchemin.mario@csq.qc.net

Fédération des enseignants de l'Ile-du-Prince-Édouard *See* Prince Edward Island Teachers' Federation

Fédération des enseignants de la Colombie-Britannique *See* British Columbia Teachers' Federation

Fédération des enseignants des écoles juives *See* Federation of Teachers of Jewish Schools

Fédération des enseignants des écoles secondaires de l'Ontario *See* Ontario Secondary School Teachers' Federation

Fédération des enseignants du Nouveau-Brunswick *See* New Brunswick Teachers' Association

Fédération des enseignants et des enseignantes de la Saskatchewan *See* Saskatchewan Teachers' Federation

Fédération des établissements d'enseignement privés (FEEP)
1940, boul Henri-Bourassa est, Montréal QC H2B 1S2
Tél: 514-381-8891; *Téléc:* 514-381-4086
Ligne sans frais: 888-381-8891
info@feep.qc.ca
www.feep.qc.ca
twitter.com/lafeep
Nom précédent: Association des institutions d'enseignement secondaire; Association québécoise des Écoles secondaires privées
Aperçu: Dimension: moyenne; *Envergure:* provinciale; Organisme sans but lucratif; fondée en 1968
Mission: Soutien des établissements membres sur les plans administratifs, pédagogiques et de la vie scolaire; représentation auprès du gouvernement
Membre: 181; *Critères d'admissibilite:* Établissements d'enseignement privés
Activités:; *Bibliothèque:* Centre de documentation; Bibliothèque publique rendez-vous

Membre(s) du bureau directeur:
Nancy Brosseau, Directrice générale, 514-381-8891 Ext. 232
brosseaun@feep.qc.ca

Fédération des étudiants en médecine du Canada *See* Canadian Federation of Medical Students

Fédération des familles et amis de la personne atteinte de maladie mentale (FFAPAMM) / Federation of Families & Friends of Persons with a Mental Illness
#203, 1990, rue Cyrille-Duquet, Québec QC G1N 4K8
Tél: 418-687-0474; *Téléc:* 418-687-0123
Ligne sans frais: 800-323-0474
info@ffapamm.com
www.ffapamm.com
Aperçu: Dimension: moyenne; *Envergure:* provinciale; Organisme sans but lucratif; fondée en 1986
Mission: Défendre et promouvoir les intérêts de ses membres; de les soutenir dans leur développement; de sensibiliser l'opinion publique aux problèmes reliés à la maladie mentale; de créer des programmes de communication et d'éducation
Membre(s) du personnel: 3
Membre: *Critères d'admissibilite:* Associations d'entraide pour familles et amis de la personne atteinte de maladie mentale
Membre(s) du bureau directeur:
Hélène Fradet, Directrice générale

Fédération des familles-souches du Québec *Voir* Fédération des associations de familles du Québec

La Fédération des femmes acadiennes de la Nouvelle-Écosse (FFANE)
54, rue Queen, Dartmouth NS B2Y 1G3
Tél: 902-433-2088; *Téléc:* 902-433-0066
Ligne sans frais: 877-433-2088
info@femmesacadiennes.ca
www.ffane.ca
Nom précédent: Association des femmes acadiennes en marche de la région de Richmond
Aperçu: Dimension: petite; *Envergure:* locale; Organisme sans but lucratif
Mission: Promouvoir le développement du plein potentiel de la femme acadienne du comté de Richmond
Membre de: Fédération des Acadiennes de la Nouvelle-Écosse
Affiliation(s): Association des acadiennes de la Nouvelle-Ecosse
Finances: *Fonds:* Gouvernement régional
Membre(s) du bureau directeur:
Micheline Gélinas, Directrice générale
dg@femmesacadiennes.ca

Fédération des femmes acadiennes et francophones du Nouveau-Brunswick (FFAFNB)
1309, Sunset, Bathurst NB E2A 3N8
Tél: 506-546-3033; *Téléc:* 506-546-6688
ffafnb@nb.aibn.com
www.ffafnb.org
Nom précédent: Fédération des dames d'Acadie
Aperçu: Dimension: petite; *Envergure:* locale; fondée en 1968
Mission: FDA regroupe les femmes francophones du N.-B. dans le but de promouvoir les intérêts et de défendre les droits des femmes et des francophones du N.-B; favorise toute action visant l'épanouissement des femmes et des francophones et leur plein accès à l'égalité et à la justice sociale
Membre de: La Fédération nationale des femmes canadiennes-françaises
Membre: *Montant de la cotisation:* Membre d'un cercle : 20 $; Membre individuelle : 25 $; Groupe membre : 50 $
Membre(s) du bureau directeur:
Lisette Surette, Présidente
Della Collette Lacenaire, Vice-présidente

Fédération des femmes du Québec (FFQ)
#309, 110, rue St-Thérèse, Montréal QC H2Y 1E6
Tél: 514-876-0166; *Téléc:* 514-876-0162
info@ffq.qc.ca
www.ffq.qc.ca
www.facebook.com/FFQMMF
twitter.com/LaFFQ
www.flickr.com/photos/laffq
Aperçu: Dimension: moyenne; *Envergure:* provinciale; fondée en 1966
Mission: Pour défendre les droits et intérêts des femmes
Membre(s) du personnel: 6

Membre: 197; *Critères d'admissibilité:* Toute association exclusivement ou majoritairement composée de femmes; *Comités:* Travail
Membre(s) du bureau directeur:
Alexa Conradi, Présidente
Eve-Marie Lacasse, Coordonnatrice, 514-876-0166 Ext. 1505
emlacasse@ffq.qc.ca

Fédération des femmes médecins du Canada *See* Federation of Medical Women of Canada

Fédération des festivals acadiens de la Nouvelle-Écosse *Voir* Fédération culturelle acadienne de la Nouvelle-Écosse

La Fédération des festivals de musique du Nouveau-Brunswick inc. *See* New Brunswick Federation of Music Festivals Inc.

La Fédération des francophones de la Colombie-Britannique (FFCB)
1575 - 7e av ouest, Vancouver BC V6J 1S1
Tél: 604-732-1420; *Téléc:* 604-732-3236
www.ffcb.ca
www.facebook.com/FederationFrancophoneCB
twitter.com/FedeFrancoCB
Aperçu: Dimension: moyenne; *Envergure:* provinciale; Organisme sans but lucratif; fondée en 1945
Mission: Promouvoir, représenter et défendre les droits et intérêts des francophones de la Colombie-Britannique et protéger leur patrimoine linguistique et culturel
Membre de: La Fédération des communauté@s francophones et acadienne au Canada
Finances: *Fonds:* Heritage Canada/Patrimoine canadien
Membre: 35 associations; *Montant de la cotisation:* 200$
Activités:; *Bibliothèque:* Centre de ressources francophones; Bibliothèque publique
Membre(s) du bureau directeur:
Robert Rothon, Directeur général
Prix, Bourses:
• Prix Napoléon Gareau
Prix de reconnaissance du dénouement des bénévoles de la Colombie-Britannique; décerné annuellement
• Prix Cornouiller d'or
En guise de reconnaissance au fonctionnement d'un ministère ou d'une institution fédéral(e) ou provincial(e), qui s'est distinguée en matière de francophonie; décerné annuellement

La Fédération des francophones de Terre-Neuve et du Labrador (FFTNL)
#233, 65, ch Ridge, St. John's NL A1B 4P5
Tél: 709-722-0627; *Téléc:* 709-722-9904
info@fftnl.ca
www.fftnl.ca
www.facebook.com/FrancoTnl
twitter.com/FrancoTnl
Nom précédent: Les Terre-Neuviens français
Aperçu: Dimension: petite; *Envergure:* provinciale; fondée en 1971
Mission: Organisme sans but lucratif qui travaille à la défense et à la promotion des droits et intérêts de la communauté francophone et acadienne de Terre-Neuve-et-Labrador
Activités: Carnaval d'hiver; bingos; marche de la St-Jean-Baptiste

Fédération des francophones hors Québec *Voir* Fédération des communautés francophones et acadienne du Canada

Fédération des harmonies du Québec *Voir* Fédération des harmonies et des orchestres symphoniques du Québec

Fédération des harmonies et des orchestres symphoniques du Québec (FHOSQ)
4545, av Pierre-de Coubertin, Montréal QC H1V 0B2
Tél: 514-252-3026; *Téléc:* 514-252-3115
info@fhosq.org
www.fhosq.org
www.facebook.com/162997715993
twitter.com/FHOSQ
Nom précédent: Fédération des harmonies du Québec
Aperçu: Dimension: moyenne; *Envergure:* provinciale; fondée en 1927 surveillé par Canadian Band Association
Mission: Contribuer au développement et à l'amélioration des harmonies en tant que loisir éducatif et culturel
Membre de: L'association Canadienne des Harmonies
Affiliation(s): Fédération des associations de musiciens éducateurs du Québec
Membre: 350 harmonies, orchestres et stage bands; *Montant de la cotisation:* 130$ ordinaires; 80$ affins

Activités: *Service de conférenciers:* Oui; *Bibliothèque*
Membre(s) du bureau directeur:
Chantal Isabelle, Directrice générale

Fédération des infirmières et infirmiers du Québec *Voir* Fédération interprofessionnelle de la santé du Québec

Fédération des instituts féminins du Canada *See* Federated Women's Institutes of Canada

Fédération des intervenantes en petite enfance du Québec (FIPEQ)
9405, rue Sherbrooke est, Montréal QC H1L 6P3
Tél: 514-356-8888; *Téléc:* 514-356-9999
Ligne sans frais: 800-465-0897
fipeq@csq.qc.net
Aperçu: Dimension: petite; *Envergure:* provinciale; fondée en 1985
Mission: La Fédération des intervenantes en petite enfance du Québec (FIPEQ) est vouée à la promotion de la profession, à la défense des droits et des intérêts ainsi qu'à l'amélioration des conditions de vie de toutes les intervenantes, tant travailleuses autonomes que salariées, oeuvrant au service des centres de la petite enfance.
Membre(s) du bureau directeur:
Kathleen Courville, Présidente

Fédération des jeunes francophones du Nouveau-Brunswick Inc. (FJFNB)
#101, 51, rue Highfield, Moncton NB E1C 5N2
Tél: 506-857-0926; *Téléc:* 506-388-1368
Ligne sans frais: 877-353-6200
fjfnb@fjfnb.nb.ca
www.fjfnb.nb.ca
www.facebook.com/299405679140
twitter.com/fjfnb
www.youtube.com/lafjfnb
Aperçu: Dimension: moyenne; *Envergure:* provinciale; Organisme sans but lucratif; fondée en 1971
Mission: Réunir les jeunes francophones, acadiens et acadiennes du N.-B. âgés de 14 à 21 ans afin d'assurer le développement et l'épanouissement de cette jeunesse
Finances: *Budget de fonctionnement annuel:* $500,000-$1.5 Million; *Fonds:* Gouvernemental
Membre(s) du personnel: 8
Membre: 8700; *Critères d'admissibilite:* Conseil des étudiants des écoles francophones du N.-B.
Activités: Conseil des présidents; colloque sur le leadership; programmes d'échanges internationaux; programmes d'échanges de jeunes travailleurs; programmes d'échanges en agriculture; camps musicaux; Échanges Jeunesse Canada; Forums Jeunesses Canada; *Stagiaires:* Oui
Membre(s) du bureau directeur:
Rémi Goupil, Directeur général
directeur@fjfnb.nb.ca

Fédération des loisirs-danse du Québec (FLDQ)
4545, av Pierre-de Coubertin, Montréal QC H1V 3R2
Tél: 514-252-3029; *Téléc:* 514-251-8038
Également appelé: Danse Québec
Aperçu: Dimension: petite; *Envergure:* provinciale
Mission: De promouvoir et développer la danse sous toutes ses formes
Membre(s) du bureau directeur:
France Dagenais, Présidente

Fédération des maisons d'hébergement pour femmes (FMHF)
CP 55036, Succ. Maisonneuve, Montréal QC H1W 0A1
Tél: 514-878-9757; *Téléc:* 514-878-9755
www.fede.qc.ca
Aperçu: Dimension: moyenne; *Envergure:* provinciale; Organisme sans but lucratif; fondée en 1987
Mission: La Fédération promouvoit et défend les intérêts des maisons d'hébergement pour femmes violentées et en difficulté membres en tenant compte de leur autonomie, de leurs particularités, de leurs similitudes et de leurs différences et ce, dans un esprit de partenariat et de concertation
Membre de: Relais Femmes; Fédération des Femmes du Québec; Table des Regroupements provinciaux d'organismes communautaires et bénévoles
Finances: *Budget de fonctionnement annuel:* $100,000-$250,000
Membre: 40; *Montant de la cotisation:* 1% subvention de base; *Critères d'admissibilite:* Maisons d'hébergement
Activités: Formation; representation; sensibilisation

Fédération des médecins omnipraticiens du Québec (FMOQ) / Québec Federation of General Practitioners
2, Place Alexis Nihon, 3500, boul de Maisonneuve ouest, 20e étage, Westmount QC H3Z 3C1
Tél: 514-878-1911
Ligne sans frais: 800-361-8499
info@fmoq.org
www.fmoq.org
twitter.com/FMOQ
Aperçu: *Dimension:* moyenne; *Envergure:* provinciale; fondée en 1963
Mission: Étude et défense des intérêts économiques, sociaux, moraux et scientifiques des associations et de leurs membres; promouvoir et développer le rôle de l'omnipraticien dans les sphères de la vie économique, sociale, scientifique et culturelle en définissant d'une façon objective le statut propre à l'omnipraticien
Membre de: World Organization of National Colleges; Academies & Academic Associations of General Practitioners/Family Physicians
Finances: *Budget de fonctionnement annuel:* Plus de $5 Million
Membre: 8 000; *Montant de la cotisation:* 1030$
Activités: *Service de conférenciers:* Oui; *Bibliothèque:* Centre de documentation; rendez-vous Not open to public
Membre(s) du bureau directeur:
Louis Godin, Président-directeur général
lgodin@fmoq.org

Fédération des médecins résidents du Québec inc. (ind.) (FMRQ) / Québec Federation of Residents (Ind.)
#510, 630, rue Sherbrooke ouest, Montréal QC H3A 1E4
Tél: 514-282-0256; *Téléc:* 514-282-0471
Ligne sans frais: 800-465-0215
fmrq@fmrq.qc.ca
www.fmrq.qc.ca
www.facebook.com/fmrqc
twitter.com/fmrq
Aperçu: *Dimension:* moyenne; *Envergure:* provinciale; fondée en 1966
Mission: D'étudier, de défendre et de développer des intérêts économiques, sociaux, moraux et scientifiques des syndicats et des leurs membres
Membre(s) du personnel: 16
Membre: 3 500
Membre(s) du bureau directeur:
Patrice Savignac Dufour, Executive Director
psavignacdufour@fmrq.qc.ca
Patrick Labelle, Director, Administrative Services
plabelle@fmrq.qc.ca

Fédération des médecins spécialistes du Québec (FMSQ)
CP 216, Succ. Desjardins, #3000, 2, Complexe Desjardins, Montréal QC H5B 1G8
Tél: 514-350-5000; *Téléc:* 514-350-5100
Ligne sans frais: 800-561-0703
www.fmsq.org
www.facebook.com/laFMSQ
twitter.com/FMSQ
Aperçu: *Dimension:* moyenne; *Envergure:* provinciale; fondée en 1965
Mission: Défendre et promouvoir les intérêts économiques, professionnels et scientifiques des médecins spécialistes
Membre(s) du personnel: 50
Membre: 10 000
Activités:; *Bibliothèque:* Centre de documentation
Membre(s) du bureau directeur:
Diane Francoeur, Présidente

Fédération des Métis du Manitoba *See* Manitoba Métis Federation

La fédération des mouvements personne d'abord du Québec
3958, rue Dandurand, #S-4, Montréal QC
Tél: 514-723-7507; *Téléc:* 514-723-2517
Ligne sans frais: 877-475-1617
fmpdaq@bellnet.ca
www.fmpdaq.org
Aperçu: *Dimension:* petite; *Envergure:* provinciale; fondée en 1991 surveillé par People First of Canada
Mission: Défendre les droits et intérêts des personnes ayant une déficience intellectuelle; Promouvoir l'auto-défense

Activités: Sensibilisation et les activités de plaidoyer; Communiquer avec le gouvernement; Plaidoyer pour l'accès au logement et la participation du public
Membre(s) du bureau directeur:
Françoise Charbonneau, Coordinatrice

Drummondville
#433, 255, rue Brock, Drummondville QC J2C 1M5
Tél: 819-478-3899; *Téléc:* 819-478-7533
mpda@mpda-drummond.qc.ca
www.mpda-drummond.qc.ca
www.facebook.com/mpda.drummondville
Membre(s) du bureau directeur:
Marcel Blais, Contact

Joliette
340, rue St-Viateur, Joliette QC J6E 3A7
Tél: 450-755-4171; *Téléc:* 450-755-3999
mpdaj@videotron.ca
Membre(s) du bureau directeur:
Diane Léveillé, Contact

Lachute
177, rue Béthanie, Lachute QC J8H 2M2
Tél: 450-562-5846; *Téléc:* 450-409-1425
mouvement_lachute1@outlook.com
Membre(s) du bureau directeur:
Holly Crooks, Présidente

Laval
Résidence Louise-Vachon, 4390, boul Saint-Martin ouest, #B5, Laval QC H7T 1C3
Tél: 450-687-2970
mpdalaval@hotmail.com
Membre(s) du bureau directeur:
Nathalie Ladouceur, Présidente

Mauricie
#22, 1322, rue Ste-Julie, Trois-Rivières QC G9A 1Y6
Tél: 819-370-2803; *Téléc:* 819-370-2803
mpdamauricie@gmail.com
Membre(s) du bureau directeur:
Vincent Langevin, Président

Québec Métropolitain
2101, 1e av, Québec QC G1L 3M6
Tél: 418-524-2404; *Téléc:* 418-524-2404
mpdaqm@videotron.ca
Membre(s) du bureau directeur:
Michel Aubut, Président

Sainte-Agathe
Sainte-Agathe-des-Monts QC
Membre(s) du bureau directeur:
Rachel Therrien, Contact

Sainte-Thérèse
CP 12, rue St-Joseph, Sainte-Thérèse QC J7E 3L6
Tél: 450-818-1883; *Téléc:* 450-818-1507
mpdatherese@videotron.ca
www.mpdatherese12.com
Membre(s) du bureau directeur:
Gabriel Laberge, Président

Saint-Eustache
CP 221, Succ. Saint-Eustache, Saint-Eustache QC J7R 4K6
Tél: 450-623-7792; *Téléc:* 450-472-3181
mpdasteustache@gmail.com
Membre(s) du bureau directeur:
Paul-André Raymond, Président

Saint-Jérôme
CP 445, Succ. Chef de Saint-Jérôme, Saint-Jérôme QC J7Z 5V2
Tél: 450-438-6256
mpdastjerome@hotmail.com
Membre(s) du bureau directeur:
Joé Vaillancourt, Président

Fédération des ordres des médecins du Canada *See* Federation of Medical Regulatory Authorities of Canada

Fédération des ordres des médecins du Canada *See* Federation of Medical Regulatory Authorities of Canada

Fédération des ordres professionnels de juristes du Canada *See* Federation of Law Societies of Canada

Fédération des OSBL d'habitation de Montréal
#105, 1650, rue St-Timothée, Montréal QC H2X 3P1
Tél: 514-527-6668; *Téléc:* 514-527-7388
fohm@videotron.ca
fohm.rqoh.com
Aperçu: *Dimension:* petite; *Envergure:* locale

Mission: Soutenir le développement de logements à but non lucratif et de fournir des logements abordables pour les locataires à faible revenu à Montréal
Affiliation(s): Réseau québécois des OSBL d'habitation
Membre: 216
Activités: Activités de formation; Des forums pour tennants et les personnes âgées; Réunions
Membre(s) du bureau directeur:
Claudine Laurin, Directrice générale

Fédération des ouvriers des chantiers navals de la Colombie-Britannique *See* Shipyard General Workers' Federation of British Columbia

Fédération des parents acadiens de la Nouvelle-Écosse (FPANE)
54, rue Queen, Dartmouth NS B2Y 1G3
Tél: 902-435-2060; *Téléc:* 902-433-0066
Ligne sans frais: 877-326-4553
fpane@fpane.ca
www.fpane.ca
Aperçu: *Dimension:* petite; *Envergure:* provinciale; Organisme sans but lucratif
Affiliation(s): Commission nationale des parents francophones
Finances: *Budget de fonctionnement annuel:* $50,000-$100,000
Membre(s) du personnel: 1; 15 bénévole(s)
Membre: 1-99
Membre(s) du bureau directeur:
Louise d'Entremont, Directrice générale par intérim

Fédération des parents de l'Ile-du-Prince-Édouard (FPIPE)
5 Maris Stella Ave., Summerside PE C1N 6M9
Tél: 902-888-1694; *Téléc:* 902-436-6936
fpipe.org
www.facebook.com/parentsipe
twitter.com/fpipeorg
Aperçu: *Dimension:* petite; *Envergure:* provinciale
Mission: Promouvoir l'éducation et la culture acadienne et française, en travaillant pour la mise sur pied et le développement d'institutions préscolaires et scolaires de français langue première à l'Ile-du-Prince-Édouard
Affiliation(s): Commission nationale des parents francophones
Membre(s) du personnel: 1
Membre: 10 comités DE PARENTS
Membre(s) du bureau directeur:
Anastasia DesRoches, Directrice générale

Fédération des parents du Manitoba (FPCP)
MB
www.lapfm.com
Nom précédent: Fédération provinciale des comités de parents du Manitoba
Aperçu: *Dimension:* moyenne; *Envergure:* provinciale; Organisme sans but lucratif; fondée en 1976
Mission: Appuyer les membres dans le développement des milieux, familial, éducatif (préscolaire et scolaire) et communautaire, propices à l'épanouissement des familles francophones
Membre de: Commission nationale des parents francophones
Finances: *Budget de fonctionnement annuel:* $250,000-$500,000
Membre: 80 regroupements membres
Activités: Formation; animation; ressources; représentation; soutien; *Bibliothèque:* Centre de ressources éducatives à l'enfance (CRÉE); Bibliothèque publique

Fédération des parents francophones de Colombie-Britannique (FPFCB)
#223, 1555 - 7e av Ouest, Vancouver BC V6J 1S1
Tél: 604-736-5056; *Téléc:* 604-736-1259
Ligne sans frais: 800-905-5056
info@fpfcb.bc.ca
www.fpfcb.bc.ca
www.facebook.com/FederationParentsCB
Nom précédent: Association des parents francophones de la Colombie-Britannique
Aperçu: *Dimension:* moyenne; *Envergure:* provinciale; Organisme sans but lucratif; fondée en 1980
Mission: Appuyer les parents de la Colombie Britannique dans leur rôle de premier éducateur de leurs enfants et de promouvoir leur participation à l'établissement d'un milieu éducatif et communautaire qui favorise le plein épanouissement français des enfants et des familles
Affiliation(s): Commission nationale des parents francophones
Finances: *Budget de fonctionnement annuel:* $250,000-$500,000

Membre(s) du personnel: 4
Membre: 1-99; *Montant de la cotisation:* 20$; *Critères d'admissibilité:* Association locale de parents
Activités: Semaine nationale de la francophonie; congrès annuel; *Stagiaires:* Oui; *Service de conférenciers:* Oui; *Bibliothèque:* Centre de ressources Tire-Lire
Membre(s) du bureau directeur:
Marie-Andrée Asselin, Directrice générale

Fédération des parents francophones de l'Alberta (FPFA)
#112, 8627 rue Marie-Anne-Gaboury nord-ouest, Edmonton AB T6C 3N1
Tél: 780-468-6934; *Téléc:* 780-469-4799
info@fpfa.ab.ca
www.fpfa.ab.ca
www.facebook.com/FPFAlberta
Nom précédent: Association albertaine des parents francophones
Aperçu: Dimension: moyenne; *Envergure:* provinciale; Organisme sans but lucratif; fondée en 1986
Mission: Favoriser la participation dynamique des parents à l'éducation francophone de leurs enfants, au foyer, à l'école et dans la communauté de l'Alberta
Membre de: La Commission nationale des parents francophones (CNPF)
Membre: 1-99
Membre(s) du bureau directeur:
Mireille Péloquin, Directrice générale
direction@fpfa.ab.ca
David Caron, Directeur adjoint
davidcaron@fpfa.ab.ca
Marie-Chantal Daval-Bérillon, Adjointe-administrative

Fédération des parents francophones de Terre-Neuve et du Labrador (FPFTNL)
65, ch Ridge, St. John's NL A1B 4P5
Tél: 709-722-7669; *Téléc:* 709-722-7696
Ligne sans frais: 888-749-7669
www.fpftnl.ca
Aperçu: Dimension: petite; *Envergure:* provinciale; fondée en 1989
Membre de: Association canadienne d'éducation de langue française; La Commission nationale des parents francophones; Association of Early Childhood Educators, Newfoundland and Labrador; Fédération des francophones de Terre-Neuve et du Labrador
Affiliation(s): Commission nationale des parents francophones
Membre: 6 comités parents
Activités: Concours littéraire provincial; visites d'écoles

Fédération des policiers du Québec (ind.) *Voir* Fédération des policiers et policières municipaux du Québec (ind.)

Fédération des policiers et policières municipaux du Québec (ind.) (FPMQ) / Québec Federation of Policemen (Ind.)
7955, boul Louis-Hippolyte-La Fontaine, Anjou QC H1K 4E4
Tél: 514-356-3321; *Téléc:* 514-356-1158
Ligne sans frais: 800-361-0321
info@fpmq.org
www.fpmq.org
www.facebook.com/policiersMun
twitter.com/policiersmun
Nom précédent: Fédération des policiers du Québec (ind.)
Aperçu: Dimension: moyenne; *Envergure:* provinciale; fondée en 1965
Mission: L'étude et la défense des intérêts économiques, professionnels, sociaux et moraux de ses associations-membres et de tous les policiers que celles-ci regroupent.
Membre(s) du personnel: 5
Membre: 3 685 + 30 sections locales; *Critères d'admissibilite:* Associations syndicales de policiers municipaux
Activités: Congrès, Tournois de golf, Gala du Ménite policier
Membre(s) du bureau directeur:
Denis Côté, Président
dcote@fpmq.org
Luc Lalonde, Directeur exécutif
llalonde@fpmq.org
Publications:
• La Voix policière [une publication de la Fédération des policiers et policières municipaux du Québec]
Type: Journal; *Frequency:* annuel
Profile: Comprend des articles sur la sécurité, la prévention du crime et la police communautaire

Fédération des producteurs acéricoles du Québec (FPAQ) / Québec Maple Syrup Producers Federation
#525, 555, boul Roland-Therrien, Longueuil QC J4H 4G5
Tél: 450-679-7021; *Téléc:* 450-679-3687
Ligne sans frais: 855-679-7021
www.fpaq.ca
Aperçu: Dimension: petite; *Envergure:* provinciale; fondée en 1966

Fédération des producteurs d'agneaux et moutons du Québec (FPAMQ)
CP 8484, #545, 555, boul Roland-Therrien, Longueuil QC J4H 4E7
Tél: 450-679-0540; *Téléc:* 450-674-4415
info@agneauduquebec.com
www.agneauduquebec.com
www.facebook.com/127544713953964
Aperçu: Dimension: moyenne; *Envergure:* provinciale; fondée en 1981
Mission: Défendre les droits économiques, sociaux et moraux des producteurs d'agneaux du Québec; organiser la mise en marché des produits
Affiliation(s): Union des producteurs agricoles
Finances: *Budget de fonctionnement annuel:* $250,000-$500,000
Membre(s) du personnel: 7
Membre: 12 syndicats; 960 adhérents; *Critères d'admissibilité:* Producteurs d'agneaux et de moutons
Membre(s) du bureau directeur:
Amina Baba-Khelil, Directrice générale

Fédération des producteurs d'oeufs de consommation du Québec (FPOCQ)
Maison de l'UPA, #320, 555, boul Roland-Therrien, Longueuil QC J4H 4E7
Tél: 450-679-0530; *Téléc:* 450-679-0855
www.oeuf.ca
www.facebook.com/lesoeufs
Aperçu: Dimension: moyenne; *Envergure:* provinciale; Organisme de réglementation; fondée en 1964
Mission: Favoriser le développement durable de l'industrie québécoise des oeufs et ce par: le respect de l'environnement et le bien-être des animaux; en procurant un revenu équitable aux intervenants du secteur; en répondant aux attentes des consommateurs avec des oeufs et produits de haute qualité
Membre de: L'Union des producteurs agricoles; L'Office canadien de commercialisation des oeufs
Finances: *Budget de fonctionnement annuel:* Plus de $5 Million
Membre(s) du personnel: 13
Membre: 103; *Critères d'admissibilité:* Détenir un quota de production et de mise en marché
Membre(s) du bureau directeur:
Serge Lefebvre, Président

La Fédération des producteurs de bois du Québec *Voir* Fédération des producteurs forestiers du Québec

Fédération des producteurs de bovins du Québec (FPBQ) / Federation of Québec Beef Producers
#305, 555, boul Roland-Therrien, Longueuil QC J4H 4G2
Tél: 450-679-0530; *Téléc:* 450-442-9348
www.bovin.qc.ca
Aperçu: Dimension: moyenne; *Envergure:* provinciale; Organisme sans but lucratif; fondée en 1974
Mission: Regrouper et défendre les intérêts professionnels et économiques des producteurs de bovins du Québec; administrer et appliquer le plan conjoint des producteurs de bovins du Québec
Affiliation(s): Union des producteurs agricoles
Finances: *Budget de fonctionnement annuel:* $1.5 Million-$3 Million; *Fonds:* Publicité et promotion du veau; fonds de recherche et développement
Membre(s) du personnel: 37
Membre: 12 000 entreprises agricoles; *Critères d'admissibilité:* Producteurs agricoles
Activités: *Listes de destinataires:* Oui
Membre(s) du bureau directeur:
Claude Viel, Président
Guy Gallant, Vice-président

Fédération des producteurs de cultures commerciales du Québec (FPCCQ)
#505, 555, boul Roland-Therrien, Longueuil QC J4H 3Y9
Tél: 450-679-0540; *Téléc:* 450-679-6372
fpccq@fpccq.qc.ca
www.fpccq.qc.ca
www.facebook.com/SIMFPCCQ

Aperçu: Dimension: petite; *Envergure:* provinciale; fondée en 1975
Affiliation(s): Union des producteurs agricoles (UPA)
Membre: 11 syndicats
Membre(s) du bureau directeur:
Christian Overbeek, Président

Fédération des producteurs de lait du Québec *Voir* Les producteurs de lait du Québec

Fédération des producteurs de miel du Québec *Voir* Fédération des apiculteurs du Québec

Fédération des producteurs de pommes de terre du Québec (FPPTQ)
#375, 555, boul Roland-Therrien, Longueuil QC J4H 4E7
Tél: 450-679-0530; *Téléc:* 450-679-5595
fpptq@upa.qc.ca
www.fpptq.qc.ca
Aperçu: Dimension: moyenne; *Envergure:* provinciale; fondée en 1966
Mission: Organisation de la mise en marché
Affiliation(s): L'union des producteurs agricoles
Membre(s) du personnel: 6
Membre(s) du bureau directeur:
Clément Lalancette, Directeur général
clementlalancette@upa.qc.ca

Fédération des producteurs de porcs du Québec *Voir* Éleveurs de porcs du Québec

Fédération des producteurs de volailles du Québec *Voir* Éleveurs de volailles du Québec

Fédération des producteurs forestiers du Québec
#565, 555, boul Roland-Therrien, Longueuil QC J4H 4E7
Tél: 450-679-0530; *Téléc:* 450-679-4300
bois@upa.qc.ca
www.foretprivee.ca
www.facebook.com/federationdesproducteursforestiers
Nom précédent: La Fédération des producteurs de bois du Québec
Aperçu: Dimension: moyenne; *Envergure:* provinciale; fondée en 1970
Mission: Défendre les intérêts de l'ensemble des propriétaires de boisés du Québec ainsi que l'élaboration et la promotion des politiques souhaitables et nécessaires pour atteindre cet objectif; Représenter les propriétaires de boisés privés auprès des pouvoirs publics et des autres groupes de la société au niveau provincial et national; Coordonner l'ensemble des activités des Syndicats et Offices de producteurs de bois ainsi que l'établissement, le maintien et le développement entre eux d'une étroite collaboration
Affiliation(s): Union des producteurs agricoles
Finances: *Budget de fonctionnement annuel:* $500,000-$1.5 Million
Membre(s) du personnel: 9
Membre(s) du bureau directeur:
Marc-André Côté, Directeur
macote@upa.qc.ca

Fédération des professionnèles (FPCSN) / Quebec Federation of Managers & Professional Salaried Workers (CNTU)
#150, 1601, av de Lorimier, Montréal QC H2K 4M5
Tél: 514-598-2143; *Téléc:* 514-598-2491
Ligne sans frais: 888-633-2143
www.fpcsn.qc.ca
Nom précédent: Fédération des professionnelles et professionnels salarié(e)s et des cadres du Québec
Aperçu: Dimension: moyenne; *Envergure:* provinciale; Organisme sans but lucratif; fondée en 1964
Mission: Regroupe plus de 7000 professionnèles oeuvrant dans différents secteurs d'activités: santé et services sociaux, organismes gouvernementaux, éducation, secteur municipal, médecines alternatives, secteur juridique, intégration à l'emploi, professionnelles autonomes, organismes communautaires, etc
Membre de: Confédération des syndicats nationaux
Membre(s) du personnel: 10
Membre: 7 142 + 28 sections locales; *Critères d'admissibilite:* Professionnel de travail social ou secteur communautaire, universitaire, aide juridique
Activités: Congrès au printemps; *Stagiaires:* Oui
Membre(s) du bureau directeur:
Ginette Langlois, Présidente
ginette.langlois@csn.qc.ca
Lucie Dufour, Secrétaire générale
lucie.dufour@csn.qc.ca

Canadian Associations / Fédération des professionnelles et professionnels de l'éducation du Québec (FPPE) / Québec Federation of Professional Employees in Education

Fédération des professionnelles et professionnels de l'éducation du Québec (FPPE) / Québec Federation of Professional Employees in Education
9405, rue Sherbrooke est, Montréal QC H1L 6P3
Tél: 514-356-0505; *Téléc:* 514-356-1324
infos@fppe.qc.ca
www.fppe.qc.ca
twitter.com/FPPECSQ
www.youtube.com/user/FPPECSQ
Nom précédent: Fédération des syndicats de professionnelles et professionnels de commissions scolaires du Québec
Aperçu: *Dimension:* grande; *Envergure:* provinciale; Organisme sans but lucratif; fondée en 1985 surveillé par Centrale des syndicats du Québec
Mission: De promouvoir et de développer les intérêts professionnels, sociaux et économiques des professionnelles et professionnels de l'éducation du Québec ainsi que de défendre les droits fondamentaux compris à l'intérieur des chartes, le droit d'association, le droit à la libre négociation et le droit à la liberté d'action syndicale; de représenter ses syndicats affiliés à un niveau national; d'orienter et de coordonner la représentation de ses syndicats affiliés auprès des instances de la Centrale; de diriger et de coordonner la négociation des conventions collectives; de concilier les conflits qui peuvent naître entre les syndicats affiliés; de mettre à la disposition des syndicats affiliés et de leurs membres des services de qualité en matière de négociation et d'application des conditions de travail et des droits sociaux, d'information et de formation syndicale
Finances: *Budget de fonctionnement annuel:* $3 Million-$5 Million
Membre(s) du personnel: 10
Membre: 6 500 + 20 syndicats; *Montant de la cotisation:* 0,74% du traitement; *Critères d'admissibilite:* Professionnels de l'éducation; *Comités:* Santé-Sécurité; Affaires Finiancières; Condition de Femmes; Jeunes; Statuts; Élections
Membre(s) du bureau directeur:
Johanne Pomerleau, Président
fppe.pomerleau.johanne@lacsq.org
Jean-Marie Comeau, Vice-présidente
fppe.comeau.jean-marie@lacsq.org

Syndicat des professionnelles et professionnels scolaires de la Gaspésie et des Iles-de-la-Madeleine (SPPGIM)
237, 9e rue, Paspébiac QC G0C 2K0
Tél: 418-408-0418
a01.gaspesie@lacsq.org
www.fppe.ca/sppgim
Membre(s) du bureau directeur:
Steeve Loisel, Président

Syndicat des professionnelles et professionnels de l'éducation du Bas St-Laurent (SPPEBSL)
150, rue Émile-Labbé, Amqui QC G5J 1J4
Tél: 418-629-6200
a02.bas.st.laurent@lacsq.org
www.sppebsl.org
Membre(s) du bureau directeur:
Diane Bélanger, Présidente

Syndicat des professionnelles et professionnels des commissions scolaires du Grand-Portage (SPGP)
CP 1353, Rivière-du-Loup QC G5R 4L9
Tél: 418-854-2370
a03.grand.portage@lacsq.org
www.fppe.ca/spgp
Membre(s) du bureau directeur:
Jonanne Gingras, Présidente
johannedulac@hotmail.com

Syndicat des professionnelles et professionnels des commissions scolaires de l'Estrie (SPPCSE)
257, rue Queen, Sherbrooke QC J1M 1K7
Tél: 819-212-3401
a07.estrie@lacsq.org
www.sppcse.qc.ca
Membre(s) du bureau directeur:
Martin Côté, Président

Syndicat des professionnelles et professionnels de Richelieu Yamaska (SPPRY)
CP 8000, 1111, rue Simonds sud, Granby QC J2G 9H7
Tél: 450-378-9981
a08.richelieu.yamaska@lacsq.org
www.fppe.ca/sppry
Membre(s) du bureau directeur:
Chantal Robitaille, Présidente
robitaic@csvdc.qc.ca

Syndicat des professionnelles et professionnels de la Montérégie (SPM)
7500, ch Chambly, Saint-Hubert QC J3Y 3S6
Tél: 450-462-2581
a30.monteregie@lacsq.org
www.sppmcsq.ca
Membre(s) du bureau directeur:
Jacques Landry, Président

Syndicat des professionnelles et professionnels du milieu de l'éducation de Montréal (SPPMÉM)
#101, 3205, boul Saint-Joseph est, Montréal QC H1Y 2B6
Tél: 514-254-6993; *Téléc:* 514-254-4744
info@sppmem.ca
www.sppmem.ca
Membre(s) du bureau directeur:
Michel Mayrand, Président
presidence@sppmem.ca

Syndicat des professionnelles et professionnels de l'Ouest de Montréal (SPPOM)
#204, 3300, boul de la Côte-Vertu, Ville Saint-Laurent QC H4R 2B7
Tél: 514-748-5983; *Téléc:* 514-748-5822
sppom@sppom.qc.ca
www.fppe.ca/sppom
Membre(s) du bureau directeur:
Carolane Desmarais, Présidente
carolane.desmarais@sppom.qc.ca

Syndicat des professionnelles et professionnels en milieu scolaire du Nord-Ouest (SPPMSNO)
230, rue Authier, Rivière-Héva QC J07 2H0
Tél: 819-735-2040; *Téléc:* 819-735-2018
a16.nord.ouest@lacsq.org
www.sppmsno.com
Membre(s) du bureau directeur:
Annie Chartier, Présidente

Syndicat des professionnelles et professionnels de l'éducation des Laurentides-Lanaudière (SPPÉLL)
#109, 995, rue Labelle, Saint-Jérôme QC J7Z 5N7
Tél: 450-438-3131
www.sppell.org
Membre(s) du bureau directeur:
Ghislaine Filion, Présidente
presidencesppell@gmail.com

Syndicat des professionnelles et professionnels de commissions scolaires du Lac St-Jean, Pays-des-Bleuets et Baie-James (SPPLPB)
795, 3e rue, Chibougamau QC G8P 1P7
Tél: 418-770-6217
a22.lac.st.jean@lacsq.org
www.fppe.ca/spplpb
Membre(s) du bureau directeur:
Marc Nolet, Président

Syndicat des professionnelles et professionnels de l'éducation du Saguenay (SPPÉS)
210, ch des Vacanciers, RR#2, Labrecque QC G0W 2W0
Tél: 418-548-3113
a23.saguenay@csq.qc.net
www.fppe.qc.ca/sppes
Membre(s) du bureau directeur:
Richard Brisson, Président
richard.brisson@csjonquiere.qc.ca

Syndicat des professionnelles et professionnels de la Haute Côte Nord (SPPHCN)
QC
Courriel: a24.haute.cote.nord@lacsq.org
Membre(s) du bureau directeur:
Renée Dufour, Présidente

Syndicat des professionnelles et professionnels du Nord-Est du Québec (SPPNEQ)
288 Holliday, Sept-Iles QC G4R 5G1
Courriel: a25.nord.est@csq.qc.net
www.fppe.ca/sppneq
Membre(s) du bureau directeur:
Éric Lavoie, Président
ericlavoie@csdufer.qc.ca

Syndicat du personnel professionnel de l'éducation du Coeur et du Centre du Québec (SPPECCQ)
CP 1414, 2057, av des Coopérants, Trois-Rivières QC G9A 5L2
Tél: 819-693-1442; *Téléc:* 819-693-3790
syndicat@sppeccq.org
www.sppeccq.org
Membre(s) du bureau directeur:
Jean Martineau, Président

Syndicat du personnel professionnel de l'éducation Chaudière-Appalaches (SPPÉCA)
#2C, 156, rte Marie-Victorin, Lévis QC G7A 2T4
Tél: 418-496-6196
sppeca29@gmail.com
www.fppe.ca/sppeca
Membre(s) du bureau directeur:
Line Thériault, Présidente

Syndicat du personnel professionnel des commissions scolaires de la Région de Québec (SPPRÉQ)
#320, rue St-Joseph est, Québec QC G1K 9E7
Tél: 418-649-7726; *Téléc:* 418-525-0772
a26.region.quebec@lacsq.org
sppreq.ca
Membre(s) du bureau directeur:
Pierre Bélanger, Président

Syndicat du personnel professionnel des commissions scolaires de l'Outaouais (SPPCSO)
CP 12006, Gatineau QC J8T 0C3
Courriel: a15.outaouais@lacsq.org
www.fppe.ca/sppcso
Membre(s) du bureau directeur:
Louise Coutu, Présidente

Fédération des professionnelles et professionnels salarié(e)s et des cadres du Québec *Voir* Fédération des professionnelles

Fédération des professionnels chinois canadiens (Québec) *See* Federation of Chinese Canadian Professionals (Québec)

Fédération des propriétaires de lots boisés du Nouveau-Brunswick inc. *See* New Brunswick Federation of Woodlot Owners Inc.

Fédération des quilles du Canada *See* Bowling Federation of Canada

Fédération des sciences neurologiques du Canada *See* Canadian Neurological Sciences Federation

Fédération des scouts de l'Atlantique
126, ch Gerard, Haut-Saint-Antoine NB E4V 3B1
Tél: 506-525-2093; *Téléc:* 506-525-9548
scoutatl@nb.sympatico.ca
Aperçu: *Dimension:* moyenne; *Envergure:* locale; Organisme sans but lucratif; fondée en 1975
Mission: Promotion et développement du scoutisme francophone dans les provinces de l'Atlantique; formation des adultes à l'animation scoute; faire vivre aux jeunes de 7 à 21 ans l'aventure et la philosophie du scoutisme en leur permettant de prendre une part active dans leur formation
Membre de: Association des Scouts du Canada
Membre: *Critères d'admissibilite:* Jeunes âgés de 7 à 21 ans
Activités: *Stagiaires:* Oui

District Boishébert
Fredericton NB

District d'Edmundston
Edmundston NB

District de Chéticamp
Chéticamp NS

District de Gloucester
Paquetville NB

Fédération des scouts de l'ouest
67, Berwick Cres. NO, Calgary AB T3K 1P7
Tél: 403-274-0463; *Téléc:* 403-275-3749
scouts.ouest@home.com
members.shaw.ca/scouts.ouest/
Aperçu: *Dimension:* petite; *Envergure:* locale
Membre de: Scouts du Canada
Membre(s) du bureau directeur:
Roseline Cyr, Secrétariat

Fédération des secrétaires professionnelles du Québec (FSPQ)
#390-1, 1173, boul Charest ouest, Québec QC G1N 2C9
Tél: 418-527-5041; *Téléc:* 418-527-2160
Ligne sans frais: 866-527-5041
info@fspq.qc.ca
www.fspq.qc.ca
www.linkedin.com/groups?gid=2340718
twitter.com/FSPQ
Aperçu: *Dimension:* moyenne; *Envergure:* provinciale
Mission: Travail à la valorisation de la profession.
Membre: *Montant de la cotisation:* 95$ agréée; 45$ étudiante; 387,35$ corporatif

Membre(s) du bureau directeur:
Anick Blouin, Présidente

Fédération des sociétés canadiennes d'assistance aux animaux See Canadian Federation of Humane Societies

Fédération des sociétés d'histoire du Québec
4545, av Pierre-de Coubertin, Montréal QC H1V 0B2
Tél: 514-252-3031; Téléc: 514-251-8038
Ligne sans frais: 866-691-7207
fshq@histoirequebec.qc.ca
www.histoirequebec.qc.ca
twitter.com/FederationHQ
Aperçu: *Dimension:* moyenne; *Envergure:* nationale; Organisme sans but lucratif; fondée en 1965
Mission: Regrouper les organisations historiques de Québec.
Membre de: Heritage Canada
Membre(s) du personnel: 2
Membre: *Montant de la cotisation:* 30$ indiviuel; 138$ institutionnel; *Critères d'admissibilite:* Société d'histoire, de généalogie, du patrimoine ou affinitaire; *Comités:* Patrimoine
Activités:; *Bibliothèque:* Centre de documentation; rendez-vous
Membre(s) du bureau directeur:
Richard M. Bégin, Président
beginrm@ca.intern.net
Prix, Bourses:
• Prix Léonidas-Bélanger
Eligibility: Reconnaît le travail de diffusion réalisé par un organisme
• Prix Rodolphe-Fournier
Eligibility: Prix décerné pour la promotion de la recherche en histoire du notariat
• Prix Honorius-Provost
Eligibility: Reconnaît le travail bénévole

Fédération des sociétés d'horticulture et d'écologie du Québec (FSHÉQ)
CP 1000, Succ. M, 4545, av Pierre-de Coubertin, Montréal QC H1V 3R2
Tél: 514-252-3010; Téléc: 514-251-8038
fsheq@fsheq.com
www.fsheq.com
www.facebook.com/305119346270307?fref=ts
Aperçu: *Dimension:* moyenne; *Envergure:* provinciale; Organisme sans but lucratif; fondée en 1978
Mission: Regrouper tous les organismes voués à l'horticulture; faire la promotion de l'horticulture.
Finances: *Budget de fonctionnement annuel:* $50,000-$100,000 3 bénévole(s)
Membre: 280; *Montant de la cotisation:* 90$; *Critères d'admissibilite:* Sociétés d'horticulture
Activités: *Service de conférenciers:* Oui
Membre(s) du bureau directeur:
Thérèse Tourigny, Directrice générale
ttourigny@fsheq.com

Fédération des syndicats de l'action collective (FSAC)
9405, rue Sherbrooke est, Montréal QC H1L 6P3
Tél: 514-606-8263
www.fsac-csq.org
Nom précédent: Fédération du personnel du loisir, de la culture et du communautaire
Aperçu: *Dimension:* moyenne; *Envergure:* provinciale; fondée en 1979 surveillé par Centrale des syndicats du Québec
Mission: Regroupe les syndicats qui représentent le personnel oeuvrant dans les secteurs du loisir, du sport, de la culture du tourisme, du communautaire, l'économie sociale, le tourisme social, les bibliothèques et les services d'intégration
Membre de: Centrale des syndicats du Québec
Finances: *Budget de fonctionnement annuel:* $50,000-$100,000
Membre: 612; *Critères d'admissibilite:* Salariés syndiqués
Membre(s) du bureau directeur:
Jacques Legault, Président
Richard Vennes, Secrétaire général
vennes.richard@lacsq.org

Fédération des Syndicats de l'Enseignement (FSE)
CP 100, 320, rue Saint-Joseph est, Québec QC G1K 9E7
Tél: 418-649-8888; Téléc: 418-649-1914
Ligne sans frais: 877-850-0897
fse@fse.lacsq.org
www.fse.qc.net
www.facebook.com/FSECSQ
twitter.com/FSECSQ
www.youtube.com/user/z00lantp

Aperçu: *Dimension:* grande; *Envergure:* provinciale; Organisme sans but lucratif; fondée en 1988 surveillé par Centrale des syndicats du Québec
Mission: Promouvoir les intérêts professionnels, sociaux et économiques du personnel enseignant des commissions scolaires; orienter et coordonner la représentation des syndicats affiliées auprès des instances de la Centrale et de représenter les syndicats affiliés là où leurs intérêts et leurs droits sont débattus; assumer prioritairement la responsabilité des négociations, les aspects sectoriels des relations du travail et de l'action juridique ainsi que les questions professionnelles à caractère sectoriel; favoriser la concertation entre les syndicats affiliés et concilier les divergences qui pourraient naître entre eux.
Membre(s) du personnel: 23
Membre: 60 000+; un regroupement de 35 syndicats; *Comités:* Élection; finances et de péréquation; statuts et règlements; formation générale des jeunes; formation professionnelle; éducation des adultes; interprétation et d'application de la convention collective
Membre(s) du bureau directeur:
Laurier Caron, Directeur général
caron.laurier@fse.lacsq.org

Fédération des syndicats de la santé et des services sociaux (F4S-CSQ)
9405, rue Sherbrooke est, Montréal QC H1L 6P3
Tél: 514-356-8888; Téléc: 514-356-2845
info@f4s.gs
www.f4s.gs
Aperçu: *Dimension:* petite; *Envergure:* provinciale
Mission: S'assurer que ses membres travaillent dans des conditions de sécurité; de représenter les intérêts de ses membres au cours des conventions collectives
Membre(s) du bureau directeur:
Claude Demontigny, Président
demontigny.claude@csq.qc.net

Fédération des syndicats de professionnelles et professionnels de commissions scolaires du Québec Voir Fédération des professionnelles et professionnels de l'éducation du Québec

Fédération des transporteurs par autobus / Bus Carriers Federation
#250, 5700, boul des Galeries, Québec QC G2K 0H5
Tél: 418-476-8181; Téléc: 418-476-8177
Ligne sans frais: 844-476-8181
www.federationautobus.com
Merged from: Association des propriétaires d'autobus du Québec; Association du transport écolier du Québec
Aperçu: *Dimension:* moyenne; *Envergure:* provinciale; fondée en 2014
Mission: La Fédération des transporteurs par autobus a pour mission de favoriser la mobilité efficace et sécuritaire des personnes et ainsi contribuer à l'image, la valorisation et la stabilité du transport collectif de personnes.
Membre: 700; *Critères d'admissibilité:* Transportateurs par autocars; Vendeurs de produits touristiques pour les groupes; *Comités:* Audit; Assurance; Sécurité; Urbain et interurbain; Transport scolaire; Nolisé-touristique; Transport spécialisé (adapté, aéroportuaire, médical, abonnement et collectif rural)
Membre(s) du bureau directeur:
Luc Lafrance, Président-Directeur Général, 418-476-8181 Ext. 214
llafrance@federationautobus.com
Meetings/Conferences:
• Fédération des transporteurs par autobus congrès annuel, June, 2018, Hilton Québec, Québec, QC
Description: Panel de discussion, atelier
Publications:
• Le Transporteur [Magazine de la Fédération des transporteurs par autobus]
Type: Magazine; *Frequency:* trimestriel; *Accepts Advertising*; *Number of Pages:* 30; *Author:* Martin Bureau; *Editor:* Mireille Bélanger

Fédération des trappeurs gestionnaires du Québec (FTGQ)
1737, rue de Champigny est, Québec QC G2G 1A6
Tél: 418-872-7644; Téléc: 418-872-6131
Ligne sans frais: 866-260-7644
ftgq@ftgq.qc.ca
www.ftgq.qc.ca
Aperçu: *Dimension:* moyenne; *Envergure:* provinciale; fondée en 1976
Affiliation(s): Association provinciale des trappeurs de l'Abitibi-Témiscamingue; Association des trappeurs du Bas Saint-Laurent; Association régionale des trappeurs de Chaudière-Appalaches; Regroupement des trappeurs de la Côte-Nord; Association provinciale des trappeurs indépendants, Conseil Estrie; Association provinciale des trappeurs indépendants, Conseil de la Gaspésie; Association des trappeurs du Haut-Saint-Maurice; Association régionale des trappeurs Laurentides/Labelle; Association régionale des trappeurs Mauricie/Bois-Francs; Association des trappeurs Mauricie/Bois-Francs
Membre(s) du bureau directeur:
Érick Tremblay, Président
tremblay-erick@hotmail.com

Fédération des travailleurs et travailleises du Québec (FTQ) / Québec Federation of Labour
#12100, 565, boul Crémazie est, Montréal QC H2M 2W3
Tél: 514-383-8000; Téléc: 514-383-8004
Ligne sans frais: 877-897-0057
www.ftq.qc.ca
www.facebook.com/laFTQ
twitter.com/FTQnouvelles
Aperçu: *Dimension:* moyenne; *Envergure:* provinciale surveillé par Canadian Labour Congress
Membre: 600 000+
Membre(s) du bureau directeur:
Michel Arsenault, Président

Fédération des travailleurs et travailleuses du Nouveau-Brunswick See New Brunswick Federation of Labour

Fédération des travailleurs et travailleuses du Québec - Construction
#201, 9671 boul Métropolitain est, Montréal QC H1J 3C1
Tél: 514-381-7300; Téléc: 514-381-5173
Ligne sans frais: 877-666-4060
www.ftqconstruction.org
www.facebook.com/ConstructionFTQ
twitter.com/FTQConstruction
www.youtube.com/user/FTQconstruction
Également appelé: FTQ-Construction
Aperçu: *Dimension:* grande; *Envergure:* provinciale surveillé par Fédération des travailleurs et travailleuses du Québec
Mission: On peut facilement affirmer que la mission d'une association syndicale est quasi sans limite. La FTQ-Construction a, bien entendu, de manière très précise le mandat de négocier les conventions collectives applicables dans les sous secteurs d'activités (industriel, commercial et institutionnel, génie civil et voirie, résidentiel) et de voir à leur application. Mais bien au-delà de ce mandat traditionnel, la FTQ-Construction veut s'assurer d'être présent dans l'ensemble des débats représentant un intérêt pour les travailleurs et les travailleuses qu'il représente.
Affiliation(s): Fraternité inter-provinciale des ouvriers en électricité; Fraternité provinciale des ouvriers en électricité; Fraternité nationale des charpentiers-menuisiers; Union des opérateurs de machinerie lourde; Assn. des manoeuvres interprovinciaux; Assn. nationale des travailleurs en réfrigération, climatisation & protection-incendie; Assn. canadienne des métiers de la truelle; Union nationale des poseurs de systèmes intérieurs & revêtements souples; Assn. nationale des ferblantiers & couvreurs; Assn. nationale des peintres & métiers connexes; Fraternité internationale des peintres & métiers connexes
Membre: 73 000
Membre(s) du bureau directeur:
Yves Ouellet, Directeur général

Fédération des unions de familles inc. Voir La Fédération québécoise des organismes communautaires Famille

Fédération dramatique du Québec See The Québec Drama Federation

Fédération du baseball amateur du Québec
CP 1000, Succ. M, 4545, av Pierre-de Coubertin, Montréal QC H1V 0B2
Tél: 514-252-3075; Téléc: 514-252-3134
Ligne sans frais: 800-361-2054
info@baseballquebec.qc.ca
www.baseballquebec.qc.ca
www.facebook.com/baseballquebec
twitter.com/baseballquebec
Également appelé: Baseball Québec
Aperçu: *Dimension:* moyenne; *Envergure:* provinciale surveillé par Baseball Canada
Mission: Donner un cadre général d'ordre et de discipline à tous les intervenants du baseball québécois; Reconnaître le droit pour tous les joueurs d'évoluer au baseball selon des normes et

Canadian Associations / Fédération du commerce (CSN)

critères précis; Donner un cadre pour l'application d'une réglementation uniforme dans tout le Québec; Fournir les moyens à chacun de s'amuser, de participer et de se perfectionner afin de donner un idéal à ceux qui aspirent à une carrière
Membre(s) du bureau directeur:
Maxime Lamarche, Directeur général
mlamarche@baseballquebec.qc.ca

Fédération du commerce (CSN)
1601, av De Lorimier, Montréal QC H2K 4M5
Tél: 514-598-2421; *Télec:* 514-598-2304
infofc@csn.qc.ca
www.fc-csn.ca
Aperçu: *Dimension:* moyenne; *Envergure:* provinciale
Membre: 28,500 + 360 sections locales; *Comités:* Santé sécurité environnement; Avantages sociaux; Femmes
Membre(s) du bureau directeur:
Serge Fournier, Président
serge.fournier@csn.qc.ca

Fédération du personnel de l'enseignement privé (FPEP)
9405, rue Sherbrooke est, Montréal QC H1L 6P3
Tél: 514-356-8888; *Télec:* 514-356-1866
fpep@csq.qc.net
www.fpep.csq.qc.net
Aperçu: *Dimension:* moyenne; *Envergure:* provinciale; Organisme sans but lucratif; fondée en 1986
Membre de: Centrale des syndicats du Québec
Finances: *Fonds:* Grille tarifaire
Membre(s) du personnel: 11
Membre: 2 800 individu; 43 unités; *Montant de la cotisation:* 0.576% du salaire; *Critères d'admissibilité:* Organisation syndicale; *Comités:* Élections; Élèves handicapés ou en difficulté d'adaptation ou d'apprentissage (HDAA); Comité du personnel professionnel et de soutien (CPPS); Environnement; Action professionnel
Activités: Relations du travail et d'action professionnelle
Membre(s) du bureau directeur:
Francine Lamoureux, Présidente, 514-356-8888 Ext. 2810
lamoureux.francine@csq.qc.net
Martine Dion, Première Vice-Présidente, 514-356-8888 Ext. 2813
dion.martine@csq.qc.net
Denis Benoit, Deuxième Vice-Président
fpep@csq.qc.net
Stéphane Lévis, Secrétaire
fpep@csq.qc.net
Marie-Josée Noël, Trésorerie
fpep@csq.qc.net

Fédération du personnel de soutien scolaire (CSQ) (FPSS) / Federation of Support Staff
9405, rue Sherbrooke est, Montréal QC H1L 6P3
Tél: 514-356-8888; *Télec:* 514-493-3697
Ligne sans frais: 800-465-0897
fpss@csq.qc.net
www.fpss.lacsq.org
www.facebook.com/fpss.csq
twitter.com/FPSSCSQ
Également appelé: FPSS-CSQ
Aperçu: *Dimension:* moyenne; *Envergure:* provinciale; Organisme sans but lucratif; fondée en 1998 surveillé par Centrale des syndicats du Québec
Mission: Le seul regroupement au Québec représentant du personnel de soutien scolaire des écoles et des centres
Membre de: Centrale des syndicats du Québec
Membre: 25 500, 17 syndicats, 22 commissions scolaires; *Comités:* Comités de vie professionnelle et les tables de travail; Comité d'interprétation, de formation et d'application de la convention collective
Activités: *Événements de sensibilisation:* Journée nationale du personnel de soutien scolaire CSQ, sept.
Membre(s) du bureau directeur:
Éric Pronovost, Présidente

Fédération du personnel du loisir, de la culture et du communautaire *Voir* Fédération des syndicats de l'action collective

Fédération du personnel professionnel des collèges (FPPC)
9405, rue Sherbrooke est, Montréal QC H1L 6P3
Tél: 514-356-8888; *Télec:* 514-356-3377
fppc@csq.qc.net
fppc.qc.ca
www.facebook.com/fppc.csq
twitter.com/fppc_csq
Aperçu: *Dimension:* moyenne; *Envergure:* provinciale; fondée en 1975 surveillé par Centrale des syndicats du Québec
Mission: Défendre et promouvoir la fonction professionnelle dans les collèges
Finances: *Budget de fonctionnement annuel:* $250,000-$500,000
Membre(s) du personnel: 2
Membre: 900
Activités: *Service de conférenciers:* Oui
Membre(s) du bureau directeur:
Bernard Bérubé, Président
berube.bernard@csq.qc.net

Fédération du personnel professionnel des universités et de la recherche (FPPU)
873, rue du Haut-Boc, Trois-Rivières QC G9A 4W7
Tél: 819-840-4544; *Télec:* 819-840-4294
info@fppu.ca
www.fppu.ca
www.facebook.com/518734318146156
Aperçu: *Dimension:* moyenne; *Envergure:* provinciale; fondée en 1978 surveillé par Centrale des syndicats du Québec
Mission: La FPPU est la seule organisation syndicale regroupant exclusivement le personnel professionnel des universités et de la recherche
Finances: *Budget de fonctionnement annuel:* $250,000-$500,000
Membre: 1,600 + 10 sections locales

Fédération du plongeon amateur du Québec (FPAQ)
4545, av Pierre-de Coubertin, Montréal QC H1V 0b2
Tél: 514-252-3096; *Télec:* 514-252-3094
info@plongeon.qc.ca
www.plongeon.qc.ca
twitter.com/PlongeonQuebec
Également appelé: Plongeon Québec
Aperçu: *Dimension:* moyenne; *Envergure:* provinciale; fondée en 1971
Mission: Régir le plongeon sur l'ensemble du territoire québécois; promouvoir le plongeon et sa pratique; tenir et organiser des stages de formation et des compétitions de plongeon; regrouper les associations de plongeon
Membre de: Diving Plongeon Canada; Sports-Québec; AQUM; Club de la médaille d'or; Institut national du sport-Montréal
Finances: *Budget de fonctionnement annuel:* $250,000-$500,000
Membre(s) du personnel: 3; 100+ bénévole(s)
Membre: 3,000; *Montant de la cotisation:* Barème; *Comités:* Entraîneurs; Officiels; L'élite
Activités: *Stagiaires:* Oui; *Service de conférenciers:* Oui
Membre(s) du bureau directeur:
Claudie Dumais, Directrice exécutive
cdumais@plongeon.qc.ca
Meetings/Conferences:
• Fédération du plongeon amateur du Québec assemblée générale annuelle 2018, 2018, QC
Scope: Provincial
Publications:
• La Vrille [publication de la Fédération du plongeon amateur du Québec]
Type: Newsletter

Fédération du Québec pour le planning des naissances (FQPN)
#405, 110, rue Ste-Thérèse, Montréal QC H2Y 1E6
Tél: 514-866-3721; *Télec:* 514-866-1100
info@fqpn.qc.ca
www.fqpn.qc.ca
Aperçu: *Dimension:* moyenne; *Envergure:* provinciale; fondée en 1972
Mission: Promouvoir les droits des femmes dans le domaine de la santé, particulièrement la reproduction et la sexualité; promouvoir l'accès à une information critique et fiable, la liberté de choix et le consentement des femmes face à leur propre corps.
Membre de: La Table des fédérations et des organismes nationaux pour l'éducation populaire autonome; Comité québécois femmes et développement; Women Global Network for Reproductive Rights; Réseau canadien pour la santé des femmes; Health Action International
Membre: 41; *Montant de la cotisation:* 5$ personnes à faible revenu; 30$ individuel; 75$ organismes et groupes communautaires; 150$ associations professionnelles
Activités: Information; éducation populaire; actions collectives; lobbying; *Service de conférenciers:* Oui; *Bibliothèque:* rendez-vous
Membre(s) du bureau directeur:
Judith Rouan, Présidente

Fédération du saumon atlantique *See* Atlantic Salmon Federation

Fédération du travail de l'Alberta *See* Alberta Federation of Labour

Fédération du travail de l'Ile-du-Prince-Édouard *See* Prince Edward Island Federation of Labour

Fédération du travail de l'Ontario *See* Ontario Federation of Labour

Fédération du travail de la Colombie-Britannique *See* British Columbia Federation of Labour

Fédération du travail de la Nouvelle-Écosse *See* Nova Scotia Federation of Labour

Fédération du travail de la Saskatchewan *See* Saskatchewan Federation of Labour

Fédération du travail de Terre-Neuve et du Labrador *See* Newfoundland & Labrador Federation of Labour

Fédération du travail des Territoires du Nord *See* Northern Territories Federation of Labour

Fédération du travail du Manitoba *See* Manitoba Federation of Labour

Fédération du travail du Yukon *See* Yukon Federation of Labour

Fédération équestre du Québec inc. (FEQ)
4545, av Pierre-de Coubertin, Montréal QC H1V 0B2
Tél: 514-252-3053; *Télec:* 514-252-3068
Ligne sans frais: 866-575-0515
infocheval@feq.qc.ca
www.feq.qc.ca
www.facebook.com/386728291214
www.youtube.com/EquestreQuebec
Aperçu: *Dimension:* moyenne; *Envergure:* provinciale; Organisme sans but lucratif; fondée en 1970
Mission: Promotion et développement de l'activité équestre au Québec
Membre de: Canadian Equestrian Federation
Membre: 12,000; *Montant de la cotisation:* 46$ junior; 56$ senior
Membre(s) du bureau directeur:
Richard Mongeau, Directeur général
rmongeau@feq.qc.ca

Fédération étudiante universitaire du Québec (FEUQ) / Québec University Students' Federation
15, rue Marie-Anne ouest, 2e étage, Montréal QC H2W 1B6
Tél: 514-396-3380; *Télec:* 514-396-7140
Ligne sans frais: 877-396-3380
feuq@feuq.qc.ca
www.feuq.qc.ca
www.facebook.com/page.FEUQ
twitter.com/feuq
www.flickr.com/photos/feuq
Aperçu: *Dimension:* grande; *Envergure:* provinciale; fondée en 1989
Mission: Défendre et promouvoir les droits des étudiantes et étudiants universitaires du Québec
Membre de: Union internationale étudiante
Finances: *Budget de fonctionnement annuel:* $500,000-$1.5 Million
Membre(s) du personnel: 8
Membre: 120 000 (15 associations étudiantes)
Membre(s) du bureau directeur:
Jonathan Bouchard, Président
Alex Goyer, Vice-président exécutive

Federation for Scottish Culture in Nova Scotia (FSCNS)
PO Box 811, Lower Sackville NS B4C 3V3
info@scotsns.ca
www.scotsns.ca
Overview: A medium-sized provincial organization founded in 1982
Mission: To act as the voice for Nova Scotia's clans, Scottish-cultural communities & cultural associations; To create

appreciation for Scottish culture, traditions & heritage
Affiliation(s): International Gathering of the Clans Nova Scotia
Finances: *Funding Sources:* Fundraising
Membership: *Fees:* $15 individuals; $30 clan societies, Scottish cultural organizations, family associations; *Member Profile:* Any individual interested in learning more about Scottish culture; Clan societies; Scottish-cultural organizations; *Committees:* Audit; By-laws; Media Relations; Membership; Newsletter; Nominating; President's Advisory Council; Scholarship; Finance & Fundraising
Activities: Building partnerships with the Scottish community & sister organizations; Preserving & promoting Scottish culture & heritage
Chief Officer(s):
Thomas (Tom) E.S. Wallace, President
Daniel G. Campbell, 1st Vice-President
Audrey Manzer, Secretary
Al Matheson, Treasurer
Awards:
• Federation of Scottish Clans in Nova Scotia Scholarship

Fédération franco-ténoise (FFT)
5016 - 48e rue, Yellowknife NT X1A 2N9
Tél: 867-920-2919; *Téléc:* 867-873-2458
info@franco-nord.com
www.federation-franco-tenoise.com
www.facebook.com/infolafft
twitter.com/La_FFT
Aperçu: *Dimension:* moyenne; *Envergure:* provinciale; fondée en 1978 surveillé par Fédération des communautés francophones et acadienne du Canada
Mission: Afin de promouvoir et de préserver la communauté francophone des Territoires du Nord-Ouest
Affiliation(s): Association des francophones du delta du Mackenzie; Association des francophones de Fort Smith; Association des parents ayants droit de Yellowknife; Association franco-culturelle de Hay River; Association franco-culturelle de Yellowknife; Azimut Communications
Membre(s) du personnel: 5
Membre(s) du bureau directeur:
Rachelle Francoeur, Président
president@franco-nord.com

Fédération indépendante des syndicats affiliés (ind.) *Voir* Fédération indépendante des syndicats autonomes

Fédération indépendante des syndicats autonomes (FISA) / Independent Federation of Autonomous Unions
#201, 1778, boul Wilfrid-Hamel, Québec QC G1N 3Y8
Tél: 418-529-4571; *Téléc:* 418-529-4695
Ligne sans frais: 800-407-3472
info@fisa.ca
www.fisa.ca
Nom précédent: Fédération indépendante des syndicats affiliés (ind.)
Aperçu: *Dimension:* moyenne; *Envergure:* provinciale; Organisme sans but lucratif; fondée en 1947
Mission: Fournir des services d'organisation, de conseils, de représentation et d'aide financière aux associations membres.
Activités: *Stagiaires:* Oui; *Service de conférenciers:* Oui
Membre(s) du bureau directeur:
Jean Gagnon, Président
  Montréal
  #220, 2220, boul Lapinière, Montréal QC J4W 1M2
  Tél: 514-736-2787; *Téléc:* 450-766-3473
  Ligne sans frais: 800-353-3472
  info.montreal@fisa.ca
  fisa.ca/contact/montreal
  Saguenay
  3798, rue du Roi-Georges, Jonquière QC G7X 1T3
  Tél: 418-547-9389; *Téléc:* 418-547-7143
  Ligne sans frais: 877-547-9389
  info.saguenay@fisa.ca
  fisa.ca/contact/saguenay

Fédération interdisciplinaire de l'horticulture ornementale du Québec (FIHOQ)
#300E, 3230, rue Sicotte ouest, Saint-Hyacinthe QC J2S 7B3
Tél: 450-774-2228; *Téléc:* 450-774-3556
fihoq@fihoq.qc.ca
www.fihoq.qc.ca
www.facebook.com/fihoq
Aperçu: *Dimension:* moyenne; *Envergure:* provinciale; fondée en 1977
Mission: Grouper en fédération les associations professionnelles qui s'occupent d'horticulture ornementale au Québec; étudier, promouvoir, protéger et développer de toutes manières les intérêts économiques, sociaux et professionnels de ses membres; imprimer, éditer des revues, journaux, périodiques et plus généralement, toutes publications du domaine de l'horticulture ornementale aux fins d'information, de culture professionnelle et de propagande; organiser et tenir des cours, conférences, congrès, assemblées, expositions et autres réunions pour la promotion, le développement et la vulgarisation de l'horticulture ornementale; promouvoir la protection du consommateur dans le domaine de l'horticulture ornementale; assurer une représentation tant sur le plan local et national, que sur le plan international des personnes oeuvrant dans le domaine de l'horticulture ornementale au Québec.
Affiliation(s): Association internationale des producteurs en horticulture; Conseil canadien de l'horticulture; Conseil québécois de l'horticulture
Membre(s) du personnel: 11
Membre: 10 associations
Activités: *Stagiaires:* Oui
Membre(s) du bureau directeur:
Luce Daigneault, Directrice générale
luce.daigneault@fihoq.qc.ca
Lise Gauthier, Président

Fédération internationale de football corporatif *See* International Federation of Corporate Football

Fédération internationale du vieillissement *See* International Federation on Aging

Fédération interprofessionnelle de la santé du Québec (FIQ)
1234, av Papineau, Montréal QC H2K 0A4
Tél: 514-987-1141; *Téléc:* 514-987-7273
Ligne sans frais: 877-987-7273
www.fiqsante.qc.ca
www.facebook.com/FIQSante
WWW.twitter.com/FIQSante
www.youtube.com/FIQSante
Nom précédent: Fédération des infirmières et infirmiers du Québec
Aperçu: *Dimension:* grande; *Envergure:* provinciale; fondée en 1987
Mission: Améliorer les conditions de travail des infirmières, infirmiers & cardiorespiratoires; s'associer aux luttes des femmes et être présente dans les débats concernant les orientations du système de santé
Finances: *Budget de fonctionnement annuel:* Plus de $5 Million
Membre(s) du personnel: 150
Membre: 57 000 + 61 syndicats; *Comités:* Condition féminine; éducation-animation; élection; fonds de défense syndicale; jeunes; évaluation des publications; santé & sécurité du travail; vérification interne; ad hoc Solidarité
Activités: *Bibliothèque:*
Membre(s) du bureau directeur:
Régine Laurent, Présidente
  FIQ - Abitibi-Témiscamingue
  #106, 170, av Principale, Rouyn-Noranda QC J9X 4P7
  Tél: 819-797-1748; *Téléc:* 819-797-1937
  Ligne sans frais: 800-567-6564
  FIQ - Estrie
  #110, 2630, rue King ouest, Sherbrooke QC J1J 2H1
  Tél: 819-346-4914; *Téléc:* 819-563-9825
  Ligne sans frais: 800-567-2776
  FIQ - Gaspésie Bas St-Laurent
  #219, 84, rue St-Germain est, Rimouski QC G5L 7K1
  Tél: 418-723-2251; *Téléc:* 418-723-7928
  Ligne sans frais: 800-463-0628
  FIQ - Mauricie Bois-Francs
  #305, 465, 5e rue, Shawinigan QC G9N 1E5
  Tél: 819-346-4914; *Téléc:* 819-563-9825
  Ligne sans frais: 800-567-2776
  FIQ - Outaouais
  #230, 370, boul Gréber, Gatineau QC J8T 5R6
  Tél: 819-568-4243; *Téléc:* 819-568-0493
  Ligne sans frais: 800-567-9651
  FIQ - Québec
  1260, rue du Blizzard, Québec QC G2K 0J1
  Tél: 418-626-2226; *Téléc:* 418-626-2111
  Ligne sans frais: 800-463-6770
  www.fiqsante.qc.ca/fr/contents/pages/accueil.html
  www.facebook.com/FIQSante
  twitter.com/FIQSante
  www.youtube.com/user/FIQSante
  FIQ - Saguenay/Lac St-Jean
  451, rue Racine est, Chicoutimi QC G7H 1T5
  Tél: 418-690-2252; *Téléc:* 418-690-3216
  Ligne sans frais: 800-567-8105

Fédération maritime du Canada *See* Shipping Federation of Canada

La Fédération mondiale de chiropratique *See* World Federation of Chiropractic

Fédération mondiale de l'hémophilie *See* World Federation of Hemophilia

Fédération motocycliste du Québec (FMQ) / Quebec Motorcyclist Federation
#460, 9675, av Papineau, Montréal QC H1R 3J2
Tél: 514-252-8121
fmq@fmq.qc.ca
www.fmq.qc.ca
www.facebook.com/FmqFederationMotocyclisteDuQuebec
Aperçu: *Dimension:* moyenne; *Envergure:* provinciale; fondée en 1974
Mission: La promotion du motocyclisme, de ses intérêts et la défense de ses droits; enseignement de la sécurité à motocyclette
Membre de: Motorcycle Alliance of Canada (MAC)
Membre: 5 000; *Montant de la cotisation:* 50$ individu; *Critères d'admissibilite:* Motocyclistes de tous les âges
Activités: Congrès annuel; Salon de la Moto à Montréal et Québec; table de concertation; cours Moto Pro FMQ; *Stagiaires:* Oui
Membre(s) du bureau directeur:
Gilles Dubois, Président
gillesdubois@fmq.qc.ca

Fédération nationale de dards du Canada *See* National Darts Federation of Canada

Fédération nationale des communications (CSN) (FNC) / National Federation of Communication Workers (CNTU)
1601, av de Lorimier, Montréal QC H2K 4M5
Tél: 514-598-2132; *Téléc:* 514-598-2431
fnc@fncom.org
www.fncom.org
Aperçu: *Dimension:* moyenne; *Envergure:* nationale; fondée en 1972
Mission: La défense des intérêts économiques, sociaux, politiques et professionnels des membres
Membre de: Confédération des syndicats nationaux
Finances: *Budget de fonctionnement annuel:* $500,000-$1.5 Million
Membre: 78 syndicats
Membre(s) du bureau directeur:
Pascale St-Onge, Présidente
pascale.st-onge@fnc.quebec
Francine Bousquet, Coordonnatrice
francine.bousquet@fnc.quebec

Fédération nationale des enseignants et des enseignantes du Québec (FNEEQ) / National Federation of Québec Teachers
1601, av de Lorimier, Montréal QC H2K 4M5
Tél: 514-598-2241; *Téléc:* 514-598-2190
Ligne sans frais: 877-312-2241
fneeq.reception@csn.qc.ca
www.fneeq.qc.ca
www.facebook.com/FneeqCSN
twitter.com/FneeqCSN
Aperçu: *Dimension:* moyenne; *Envergure:* provinciale; fondée en 1969
Mission: La Fédération nationale des enseignantes et des enseignants du Québec (FNEEQ) est une fédération de la CSN qui regroupe les syndicats de l'enseignement. La mission première de la FNEEQ est l'amélioration des conditions de travail par l'entremise de la négociation et de l'application d'une convention collective entre un employeur et le personnel enseignant et salarié
Finances: *Budget de fonctionnement annuel:* $1.5 Million-$3 Million
Membre(s) du personnel: 30
Membre: 34 000; 101 syndicats (46 syndicats de cégeps; 43 syndicats d'établissements d'enseignement privés; 13 syndicats d'établissements universitaires)
Membre(s) du bureau directeur:

Canadian Associations / Fédération nationale des services de préparation au mariage (FNSPM)

Caroline Senneville, Présidente
caroline.senneville@csn.qc.ca
Jean Murdock, Secrétaire général et trésorier
jean.murdock@csn.qc.ca

Fédération nationale des femmes canadiennes-françaises;
Fédération des femmes canadiennes-françaises *Voir*
Alliance des femmes de la francophonie canadienne

Fédération nationale des retraités *See* National Pensioners Federation

Fédération nationale des services de préparation au mariage (FNSPM)
CP 1480, Trois-Rivières QC G9A 5L6
Tél: 819-379-1432; *Téléc:* 819-379-2496
www.fnspm.ca
Également appelé: Fédération Nationale SFM
Aperçu: *Dimension:* moyenne; *Envergure:* nationale; Organisme sans but lucratif
Mission: Offrir en collaboration avec les diocèses un service d'accompagnement aux couples ayant choisi le mariage catholique; accompagner sur le plan humain et chrétien, les personnes ayant choisi de s'engager dans un projet de vie à deux
Membre(s) du personnel: 2
Activités: Formation; production d'outils pédagogiques; soutien technique aux équipes; *Stagiaires:* Oui
Membre(s) du bureau directeur:
Simon Bournival, Directeur général
directiongenerale@fnspm.ca

Fédération nationale du MFC - Mouvement des Femmes Chrétiennes *Voir* Mouvement des femmes Chrétiennes

Fédération nationale lettone au Canada *See* Latvian National Federation in Canada

Fédération nationale Ukrainienne au Canada *See* Ukrainian National Federation of Canada

Fédération nautique du Canada *See* Canadian Boating Federation

Federation of Aboriginal Foster Parents (FAFP)
3455 Kaslo St., Vancouver BC V3M 3H4
Tel: 604-291-7091; *Fax:* 604-291-7098
Toll-Free: 866-291-7091
info@fafp.ca
www.fafp.ca
Overview: A medium-sized provincial organization
Mission: The Federation of Aboriginal Foster Parents represents Foster Parents providing quality care for Aboriginal children in a nurturing, culturally appropriate environment
Finances: *Funding Sources:* provincial & federal funding
Membership: *Fees:* $10 5 yr. single; $20 5 yr. couple; $5 5 yr. associate; $50 1 yr. corporate
Chief Officer(s):
Stephen W. Kozey, Executive Director
skozey@fafp.ca
Faye Poirier, President
Rick Poitras, Vice-President

Federation of Asian Students (FAS) *See* University of Alberta South East Asian Students' Association

Federation of Automobile Dealer Associations of Canada *See* Canadian Automobile Dealers' Association

Federation of B.C. Youth in Care Networks (FBCYICN)
#500, 625 Agnes St., New Westminster BC V3M 5Y4
Tel: 604-527-7762; *Fax:* 604-527-7764
Toll-Free: 800-565-8055; *Crisis Hot-Line:* 866-872-0113
info@fbcyicn.ca
www.fbcyicn.ca
www.facebook.com/YouthInCareBC
twitter.com/fbcyicn
Overview: A medium-sized provincial organization founded in 1993 overseen by Youth in Care Canada
Mission: To improve the lives of young people in & from government care in BC
Staff Member(s): 7
Membership: *Member Profile:* Individuals between the ages of 14 & 24 who are in or from government care in BC
Activities: Providing programming, youth retreats, & bursaries; Offering volunteer & leadership training; *Awareness Events:* BC Child & Youth in Care Week, June
Chief Officer(s):
Jules Wilson, Executive Director, 778-389-9492
jules.wilson@fbcyicn.ca
Brittaney Andreychuk, Manager, Operations, 604-527-7762 Ext. 115
brittaney.andreychuk@fbcyicn.ca
Awards:
• Education Achievement Bursary
Eligibility: Youth in care or from care (either a continuing custody order or temporary custody order) who are enrolled or planning to enroll in a secondary, post-secondary academic, technical, or vocational program at an accredited instituion; *Amount:* up to $5,000 *Contact:* Steve Smith, Assistant Coordinator, Programs, E-mail: steve.smith@fbcyicn.ca
• Reach for Success Bursary
Eligibility: Youth in care or from care (either a continuing custody order or temporary custody order) who are enrolled or planning to enroll in a personal or professional development course or activity; *Amount:* $1,500 *Contact:* Steve Smith, Assistant Coordinator, Programs, E-mail: steve.smith@fbcyicn.ca

Federation of British Columbia Writers (FBCW)
#412, 1641 Lonsdale Ave., Vancouver BC V7M 2J5
Tel: 250-741-6514
membership@bcwriters.ca
www.bcwriters.ca
www.facebook.com/bcwriters
twitter.com/bcwriters
Also Known As: Federation of BC Writers
Overview: A medium-sized provincial charitable organization founded in 1976
Mission: To develop, support, inform, & promote writers in British Columbia; To foster a community for writing in British Columbia
Finances: *Funding Sources:* Membership dues; Fundraising; Corporate & private sponsorships; Province of British Columbia's BC Arts Council & Direct Access Program
Membership: 700+; *Fees:* $25 youth; $45 senior; $80 annual; *Member Profile:* Emerging & established writers; Persons interested in federation authors' works
Activities: Providing programs & resources; Organizing an annual writing contest; Arranging author visits to schools; Providing reading opportunities; Offering promotional services; Conducting workshops; Networking opportunities; *Library*
Chief Officer(s):
Ann Graham Walker, President
president@bcwriters.ca
Shaleeta Harrison, Executive Director
communications@bcwriters.ca
Publications:
• WordWorks [a publication of the Federation of British Columbia Writers]
Type: Journal; *Frequency:* Quarterly; *Accepts Advertising*; *Editor:* Shaleeta Harper
Profile: Literary magazine 'for writers, about writing'
• WriteOn eNews [a publication of the Federation of British Columbia Writers]
Type: E-Newsletter; *Frequency:* biweekly; *Accepts Advertising*

Federation of Broomball Associations of Ontario
c/o Gerry Wever, President, 515 Gascon St., Russell ON K4R 1C6
Tel: 613-445-0904; *Fax:* 613-445-9844
www.ontariobroomball.ca
Previous Name: Broomball Federation of Ontario
Overview: A medium-sized provincial organization overseen by Ballon sur glace Broomball Canada
Mission: To serve broomball players, coaches, & leagues in Ontario
Member of: Ballon sur glace Broomball Canada
Finances: *Annual Operating Budget:* $50,000-$100,000
20 volunteer(s)
Membership: 4,000; *Fees:* Schedule available; *Committees:* Officials; Coaching; Executive
Activities: Hosting high school tournaments, qualifier tournaments, junior provincials, & senior provincials; Conducting coaching clinics
Chief Officer(s):
Gerry Wever, President
gerry.wever@ontariobroomball.ca
Marilyn Squibb, Contact, Registration
marilyn.squibb@ontariobroomball.ca
Archie Wilson, Contact, Technical
archie.wilson@palmerstongrain.com
Awards:
• Junior Female Player of the Year
• Junior Male Player of the Year
• Female Player of the Year
• Male Player of the Year
• Coach of the Year
• Official of the Year

Federation of Calgary Communities (FCC)
#301, 1609 - 14 St. SW, Calgary AB T3C 1E4
Tel: 403-244-4111; *Fax:* 403-244-4129
fcc@calgarycommunities.com
www.calgarycommunities.com
www.facebook.com/FederationofCalgaryCommunities
twitter.com/FedYYC
www.youtube.com/user/FederationCalgary
Overview: A small local licensing organization founded in 1961
Mission: To enhance Calgary communities
Finances: *Annual Operating Budget:* $100,000-$250,000
Staff Member(s): 1; 25 volunteer(s)
Membership: 114
Activities: *Library:* Open to public
Chief Officer(s):
Leslie Evans, Executive Director
leslie.evans@calgarycommunities.com
Robin Elford, President

Federation of Canada-China Friendship Associations (FCCFA)
159 Oakmount Rd. SW, Calgary AB T2V 4X3
federation.tripod.com
www.facebook.com/fccfa1
Overview: A small international organization founded in 1980
Mission: To work with students from the Peoples' Republic of China studying in Canada; To take groups to China; To welcome delegations coming from China; To promote cultural exchanges
Affiliation(s): Chinese People's Association for Friendship With Foreign Countries
Membership: 1,800
Chief Officer(s):
Gary Levy, President

Federation of Canada-China Friendship Associations - Ottawa Chapter (CCFS-O)
PO Box 8461, Stn. Terminal, Ottawa ON K1G 3H9
www.ccfso.org
www.facebook.com/ccfs.ottawa
Also Known As: CCFS-Ottawa
Overview: A small international organization founded in 1976 overseen by Federation of Canada-China Friendship Associations
Mission: To help Canadians become better informed about China
Member of: Federation of Canada-China Friendship Associations
Membership: 250+
Activities: Chinese New Year's Banquet; conferences & tours in China
Chief Officer(s):
Roy Atkinson, Co-President
Gary Levy, Co-President

Federation of Canadian Archers Inc. *See* Archery Canada Tir à l'Arc

Federation of Canadian Artists (FCA)
1241 Cartwright St., Vancouver BC V6H 4B7
Tel: 604-681-2744; *Fax:* 604-681-2740
fcaadmin@artists.ca
artists.ca
Overview: A medium-sized national charitable organization founded in 1941
Mission: To share & promote the visual arts
Finances: *Funding Sources:* Membership fees; Government & foundation grants; Donations; Sponsorships; Fundraising; Revenue from education programs; Painting & other retail sales
Staff Member(s): 7
Membership: 2,500+; *Fees:* $50 supporting; $80 Active & Signature; *Member Profile:* Artists & art lovers from across Canada; *Committees:* Standards
Activities: Offering visual art exhibitions & education
Chief Officer(s):
Dene Croft, President
president@artists.ca
Charlie Easton, Vice-President
1stvp@artists.ca
Patrick E. Meyer, Executive Director, 604-681-2744
executivedirector@artists.ca
Helen Duckworth, Coordinator, Gallery, 604-681-8534
fcagallery@artists.ca

Alyssa Giddings, Coordinator, Education & Membership, 604-681-2744
Publications:
• Art Avenue [a publication of the Federation of Canadian Artists]
Type: Magazine; *Frequency:* Bimonthly; *Editor:* Carol Crenna; *Price:* Free with membership in theFederation of Canadian Artists
Profile: Articles, images of recently exhibited works, member news, forthcoming events, & painting tips

Federation of Canadian Electrolysis Associations (FCEA)
PO Box 1777, Pictou NS B0K 1H0
Tel: 902-485-4557
Toll-Free: 888-333-2783
fcea@fcea.org
www.fcea.org
Overview: A small national organization
Mission: Dedicated to promoting professionalism and education in permanent hair removal.
Affiliation(s): The Association of Professional Electrologists of BC; Electrolysis Society of Alberta; Saskatchewan Electrologists Association Incorporated; Manitoba Electrologists Association Inc.; Atlantic Association of Professional Electrologists; Federation of Canadian Electrolysis Associations Ontario Chapter
Chief Officer(s):
Gail MacDonald, President

Federation of Canadian Independent Deposit Brokers See Registered Deposit Brokers Association

Federation of Canadian Municipalities (FCM) / Fédération canadienne des municipalités
24 Clarence St., Ottawa ON K1N 5P3
Tel: 613-241-5221; *Fax:* 613-241-7440
info@fcm.ca
www.fcm.ca
www.linkedin.com/company/federation-of-canadian-municipalities
www.facebook.com/FederationofCanadianMunicipalities
twitter.com/FCM_online
www.youtube.com/user/FCMChannel
Previous Name: Canadian Federation of Mayors & Municipalities
Overview: A large national organization founded in 1901
Mission: FCM is the national voice of municipal government that represents the interests of municipalities on policy & program matters that fall within federal jurisdiction. Its goal in serving elected municipal officials is the improvement of the quality of life in all communities.
Finances: *Funding Sources:* Membership fees; advertising; trade show; market research
Membership: 2,000; *Fees:* Schedule available based on population; *Member Profile:* Members include Canada's cities, small urban & rural communities, & provincial & territorial municipal associations.; *Committees:* Standing Committees: Increasing Women's Participation in Municipal Government; Community Safety & Crime Prevention; Environmental Issues & Sustainable Development; International Relations; Municipal Finance & Intergovernmental Arrangements; Municipal Infrastructure & Transportation Policy; Northern Forum; Rural Forum; Social Economic Development
Activities: Promoting strong, effective, & accountable municipal government; *Rents Mailing List:* Yes
Chief Officer(s):
Clark Somerville, President
Jenny Gerbasi, First Vice-President
Awards:
• Race Relations Awards
• FCM/CH2M Hill Canada Awards
• The Roll of Honour
• Outstanding International Volunteer Contribution Awards
• Ann MacLean Award for Outstanding Service by a Woman in Municipal Politics
Recognizes retired women municipal politicians who have shown exemplary service to their community and constituents and to mentoring women who want to run for elected office.
• Canadian Women in Municipal Government Scholarship
Eligibility: The scholarship is open to female students enrolled in any year of study in secondary school and who are contributing to their school's leadership team or student council.; *Amount:* $500 (5)
• Mayor Andrée Boucher Memorial Scholarship
Eligibility: Female college or university student deemed to have submitted the best research paper on a topic related to women in politics.; *Amount:* $2,000
Meetings/Conferences:
• Federation of Canadian Municipalities 2018 Annual Conference & Trade Show, May, 2018, Halifax, NS
Scope: National
Publications:
• Federation of Canadian Municipalities Annual Report
Type: Yearbook; *Frequency:* Annually
• Forum: Canada's National Municipal Magazine
Type: Magazine; *Frequency:* Bimonthly; *Accepts Advertising;* *Editor:* Robert Ross
Profile: Recent municipal-sector developments

Federation of Canadian Music Festivals (FCMF) / La Fédération canadienne des festivals de musique
c/o Barbara Long, Executive Director, 11119 rte 130, Somerville NB E7P 2S4
Tel: 506-375-6752
Toll-Free: 866-245-1680
info@fcmf.org
www.fcmf.org
www.facebook.com/nationalmusicfestival
Overview: A large national organization founded in 1949
Mission: To act as an umbrella organization for 230+ local & provincial festivals; To develop & encourage Canadian talent in the performance & knowledge of classical music; To encourage the study & practice of the art of music alone or in conjunction with related arts; To organize the National Music Festival in which winners from each province participate
Affiliation(s): Canadian Conference of the Arts; provincial music festival organizations
Finances: *Annual Operating Budget:* Less than $50,000; *Funding Sources:* Affiliation & membership fees; donations
Membership: 230+ local festivals; *Fees:* $50 regular; $100 sustaining; $200 patron; $500 life; *Member Profile:* Competitors, volunteers, adjudicators, music lovers; *Committees:* Syllabus; History; Finance; Planning; Adjudicator Selection; Marketing & Communications; Musical Theatre
Activities: *Awareness Events:* National Music Festival; *Speaker Service:* Yes; *Rents Mailing List:* Yes
Chief Officer(s):
Joy McFarlane-Burton, President, 306-652-2960
president@fcmf.org
Barbara Long, Executive Director, 506-375-6752
Publications:
• Più Mosso [a publication of the Federation of Canadian Music Festivals]
Type: Newsletter

Federation of Canadian Naturists (FCN)
PO Box 186, Stn. D, Toronto ON M9A 4X2
Tel: 416-410-6833
Toll-Free: 888-512-6833
Other Communication: Membership E-mail: membership@fcn.ca
information@fcn.ca
www.fcn.ca
www.facebook.com/CanadianNaturists
twitter.com/FCNaturists
Overview: A small national organization founded in 1985
Mission: To promote naturism (social nudism) as a healthy, wholesome & completely natural lifestyle
Member of: International Naturist Federation
Affiliation(s): Fédération québécoise de naturisme
Finances: *Annual Operating Budget:* $50,000-$100,000; *Funding Sources:* Membership dues; subscribers fees 20 volunteer(s)
Membership: 2,400; *Fees:* $50 Canada; $55 USA; $60 international
Activities: *Speaker Service:* Yes
Chief Officer(s):
Ron Schout, President
president@fcn.ca
Publications:
• Going Natural/au Naturel [a publication of the Federation of Canadian Naturists]
Type: Magazine; *Frequency:* Quarterly

Federation of Canadian Turkish Associations (FCTA) / Kanada Türk Dernekleri Federasyonu
#15, 1170 Sheppard Ave. West, Toronto ON M3K 2A3
Tel: 647-955-1923; *Fax:* 647-776-3111
info@turkishfederation.ca
www.turkishfederation.ca
Overview: A large national organization founded in 1985
Mission: To support & encourage activities that deal with important cultural, economic, educational, historical, social & religious issues that relate to the Turkish Community in Canada
Member of: Canadian Ethnocultural Council
Finances: *Funding Sources:* Membership fees; Grants; Sponsorships
Membership: 17 associations + 50,000 members; *Committees:* General Assembly; External Relations; Community Relations; Executive; Audit; Honour
Activities: *Speaker Service:* Yes; *Rents Mailing List:* Yes

Federation of Chinese Canadian Professionals (Ontario) (FCCP)
Coral Place, 55 Glenn Hawthorne Blvd., Mississauga ON L5R 3S6
Tel: 905-890-3235; *Fax:* 905-568-5293
www.fccpontario.com
Overview: A small provincial charitable organization founded in 1975
Mission: Fosters the promotion, cooperation, & growth among Chinese Canadian Professionals from various disciplines, including: accounting, architecture, biomedical, chiropractic, dental, education, engineering, information technology, legal, medical, pharmacy, & physiotherapy
Membership: 1,200 individual + 12 professional subsections
Chief Officer(s):
Josephine Kiang, President

Federation of Chinese Canadian Professionals (Québec) (FCCP Québec) / Fédération des professionnels chinois canadiens (Québec)
PO Box 5388, Stn. B, Montréal QC H3B 3K5
Tel: 514-954-3160
Overview: A medium-sized provincial organization founded in 1993
Mission: To promote the well-being of Chinese Canadian professionals in Québec; To liaise & cooperate with Chinese Canadian professionals in other parts of Canada & throughout the world; To provide a strong voice for the group
Finances: *Funding Sources:* Sponsorships
Chief Officer(s):
Howard Tan, President
htan222@yahoo.ca
John Chen, Vice-President
Renee Chin, Treasurer

Federation of Dance Clubs of New Brunswick (FDCNB)
c/o President, 35 Berwick St., Fredericton NB E3A 4Y2
Tel: 506-472-1444
www.squaredancenb.ca
Previous Name: New Brunswick Federation of Dance Clubs
Overview: A medium-sized provincial organization overseen by Canadian Square & Round Dance Society
Mission: To serve as New Brunswick's family of dancers, expounding the virtues of dance-related recreational activity in every region of the province, actively involved with training, teaching, instructing, informing & assisting others to learn more about dance-related ideas
Member of: Canadian Square & Round Dance Society
Chief Officer(s):
Terry Hebert, President
sdcaller@nbnet.nb.ca

Federation of Danish Associations in Canada / Fédération des associations danoises du Canada
679 Eastvale Ct., Gloucester ON K1J 6Z7
Other Communication: Alt. URL: home.ca.inter.net/~robuch/dan-fed.htm
secretary@danishfederation.ca
www.danishfederation.ca
Also Known As: The Danish Federation
Overview: A medium-sized national organization founded in 1981
Mission: To promote cooperation among Danish Canadian organizations; To promote preservation & understanding of Danish tradition & heritage
Membership: 40 organizations
Activities: Exchanging ideas & experiences; Coordinating joint projects; Organizing heritage seminars & conferences; Building a national museum; Providing support & assistance to members
Chief Officer(s):
Rolf Buschardt Christensen, President
Gert Andersen, Vice-President
Aase Christensen, Secretary
Sune Overgaard, Treasurer

Meetings/Conferences:
• Federation of Danish Associations in Canada 2018 Danish Canadian Conference, May, 2018, Halifax, NS
Scope: National
Publications:
• Directory of Danish Organazitions in Canada [a publication of the Federation of Danish Associations in Canada]
Type: Directory
• Heritage Book [a publication of the Federation of Danish Associations in Canada]
Type: Book; *Frequency:* Annually; *Number of Pages:* 200; *Price:* $12
Alberta-Northwest Territories Region
AB
Ontario Region
ON
Chief Officer(s):
Eva Terp, President
Pacific Region
BC
Québec Region
QC

Federation of dental specialists of Quebec *Voir* Fédération des dentistes spécialistes du Québec

Federation of Families & Friends of Persons with a Mental Illness *Voir* Fédération des familles et amis de la personne atteinte de maladie mentale

Federation of Foster Families of Nova Scotia (FFFNS)
#350, 99 Wyse Rd., Dartmouth NS B3A 4S5
Tel: 902-424-3071; *Fax:* 902-424-5199
Toll-Free: 888-845-1555
www.fosterfamilies.ns.ca
twitter.com/Foster_Care_NS
Previous Name: Federation of Foster Family Associations of Nova Scotia
Overview: A medium-sized provincial charitable organization founded in 1976
Mission: To act as the voice for all foster parents in Nova Scotia; to ensure assistance & support for foster families & Foster Family Associations
Member of: Canadian Foster Family Association
Affiliation(s): NS Council for the Family; Child Welfare League of Canada; International Foster Care Organization
Finances: *Funding Sources:* Provincial government
Staff Member(s): 6
Membership: *Member Profile:* Foster parents; *Committees:* Provincial Foster Care Policy; P.R.I.D.E Provincial Education; Provincial Awareness & Recruitement
Activities: *Awareness Events:* Foster Family Week, Oct.
Library: Federation of Foster Families of Nova Scotia Library
Chief Officer(s):
Gary Landry, Executive Director
gary.landry@novascotia.ca
Debbie Thibault, Coordinator, Training
deborah.thibault@novascotia.ca
Awards:
• The Thelma Goodall Memorial Bursary
• The Jenny Cajolais Memorial Bursary
• Amanda's Gift Bursary Program
• Education Achievement Award
Meetings/Conferences:
• 2018 Annual General Meeting & Symposium of the Federation of Foster Families of Nova Scotia, 2018, NS
Scope: Provincial

Federation of Foster Family Associations of Nova Scotia *See* Federation of Foster Families of Nova Scotia

Federation of Health Regulatory Colleges of Ontario (FHRCO) / Ordres de réglementation des professionnels de la santé de l'Ontario (ORPSO)
PO Box 244, #301, 396 Osborne St., Beaverton ON L0K 1A0
Tel: 416-493-4076; *Fax:* 866-814-6456
info@regulatedhealthprofessions.on.ca
www.regulatedhealthprofessions.on.ca
Overview: A medium-sized provincial organization
Mission: To regulate health professionals in Ontario; To protect the public's right to safe, effective, & ethical health care
Membership: 26; *Member Profile:* Health regulatory colleges in Ontario
Chief Officer(s):
Shenda Tanchak, President

Beth Ann Kenny, Executive Coordinator

Federation of Independent School Associations of BC (FISA)
150 Robson St., Vancouver BC V6B 2A7
Tel: 604-684-6023; *Fax:* 604-684-3163
info@fisabc.ca
www.fisabc.ca
Overview: A medium-sized provincial organization founded in 1966 overseen by Federation of Independent Schools in Canada
Mission: To assist independent schools in maintaining their independence while seeking fair treatment for them in legislative & financial terms.
Finances: *Annual Operating Budget:* $100,000-$250,000; *Funding Sources:* Membership fees
Staff Member(s): 2
Membership: 200 schools + 4 associations
Activities: *Speaker Service:* Yes
Chief Officer(s):
Peter Froese, Executive Director
Doug Lauson, President

Federation of Junior Leagues of Canada *See* Canadian Federation of Junior Leagues

Federation of Korean Canadian Associations
Tel: 514-481-4008; *Fax:* 514-481-6860
federationkca@gmail.com
www.koreancanadian.org
Overview: A small local organization
Member of: Canadian Ethnocultural Council

Federation of Law Reform Agencies of Canada (FOLRAC)
c/o Manitoba Law Reform Commission, 405 Broadway, 12th Fl., Winnipeg MB R3C 3L6
Tel: 604-822-0142; *Fax:* 604-822-0144
folracanada@gmail.com
www.folrac.com
Overview: A medium-sized national organization founded in 1990
Mission: Collection of 8 law reform agencies, from various provinces, who meet yearly to exchange information.
Chief Officer(s):
Greg Steele, President

Fédération of Law Societies of Canada (FLSC) / Fédération des ordres professionnels de juristes du Canada
World Exchange Plaza, #1810, 45 O'Connor St., Ottawa ON K1P 1A4
Tel: 613-236-7272; *Fax:* 613-236-7233
info@flsc.ca
www.flsc.ca
Previous Name: Conference of Representatives of the Governing Bodies of the Legal Profession in the Provinces of Canada
Overview: A medium-sized national organization founded in 1926
Mission: To coordinate the law societies of Canada; To act as a voice for Canadian law societies
Affiliation(s): International Bar Association; Union Internationale des Avocats
Membership: 14 law societies; *Member Profile:* Law societies in Canada, which regulate notaries in Québec & lawyers in the remainder of Canada in the public interest
Activities: Assessing & certifying the qualifications of persons with international legal credentials, through the National Committee on Accreditation; Offering the National Criminal Law Program & the National Family Law Program; Sponsoring continuing legal education programs; Studying matters of concern to the legal profession in Canada; Offering a forum for the exchange of views & information; Operating CanLII, a publicly accessible & free online search engine; Improving public understanding of the legal profession in Canada
Chief Officer(s):
Jeff Hirsch, President, 204-934-2336
jbh@tdslaw.com
Jonathan G. Herman, Chief Executive Officer
jherman@flsc.ca
Bob Linney, Director, Communications
blinney@flsc.ca

Federation of Medical Regulatory Authorities of Canada (FMRAC) / Fédération des ordres des médecins du Canada
#103, 2283 St. Laurent Blvd., Ottawa ON K1G 5A2

Tel: 613-738-0372; *Fax:* 613-738-9169
info@fmrac.ca
www.fmrac.ca
Overview: A medium-sized national licensing organization founded in 1968
Mission: To provide a national structure for the provincial & territorial medical regulatory authorities; To present & pursue issues of common concern & interest; To share, consider, & develop positions on such matters
Finances: *Funding Sources:* Membership fees
Staff Member(s): 5
Membership: 13; *Member Profile:* Provincial & territorial regulatory authorities; *Committees:* Accreditation & Education Advisory; Executive; Risk Management
Chief Officer(s):
Fleur-Ange Lefebvre, Executive Director & CEO
falefebvre@fmrac.ca

Federation of Medical Regulatory Authorities of Canada (FMRAC) / Fédération des ordres des médecins du Canada (FOMC)
1021 Thomas Spratt Pl., Ottawa ON K1G 5L5
Tel: 613-738-0372; *Fax:* 613-738-9169
info@fmrac.ca
www.fmrac.ca
twitter.com/FMRAC_ca
Overview: A medium-sized national organization
Mission: To provide a national structure for the provincial & territorial medical regulatory authorities to present & pursue issues of common concerns & interest; To share, consider, & develop positions on such matters; To develop services & benefits for its members
Staff Member(s): 3
Membership: 13
Chief Officer(s):
Fleur-Ange Lefebvre, Executive Director & CEO
falefebvre@fmrac.ca
Louise Auger, Director, Professional Affairs
lauger@fmrac.ca
Kim MacDonald, Manager, Member Services
kmacdonald@fmrac.ca
Meetings/Conferences:
• Federation of Medical Regulatory Authorities of Canada 2018 Annual Meeting & Conference, June, 2018, Charlottetown, PE
Scope: National
• Federation of Medical Regulatory Authorities of Canada 2019 Annual Meeting & Conference, June, 2019, Whistler, BC
Scope: National

Federation of Medical Women of Canada (FMWC) / Fédération des femmes médecins du Canada
1021 Thomas Spratt Pl., Ottawa ON K1G 5L5
Tel: 613-569-5881; *Fax:* 613-249-3906
Toll-Free: 877-771-3777
fmwcmain@fmwc.ca
www.fmwc.ca
Overview: A large national organization founded in 1924
Mission: To ensure the professional, social, & personal advancement of women physicians; To promote the well-being of women in the medical profession & in society at large
Affiliation(s): Canadian Medical Association; Medical Women's International Association
Finances: *Funding Sources:* Membership fees; sponsors; corporate
Membership: *Fees:* Schedule available; *Member Profile:* Women medical students; women physicians; associate member - men or non-physician women committed to the advancement of women's health; *Committees:* Membership; National Pap Test Campaign; Finance; Maude Abbott Charitable Funds; Communications; Website; By-Law
Activities: 19 branches across Canada; *Awareness Events:* Women's Health Day; National Cervical Cancer Awareness Week, October; *Speaker Service:* Yes
Chief Officer(s):
Bev Johnson, President
Awards:
• Maude Abbott Loan
• May Cohen Award
• Margaret Owens-Waite Memorial Fund
• Enid Johnson MacLeod Award
• The Reproductive Health Award
• Student Leadership Award
• Jessie McGeachy Award
• Dr. Shelagh Lindsay Medical Award

Federation of Metro Tenants' Associations (FMTA)
PO Box 73102, Stn. Wood St., Toronto ON M4Y 2W5
Tel: 416-646-1772; *Crisis Hot-Line:* 416-921-9494
fmta@torontotenants.org
www.torontotenants.org
Previous Name: Federation of Metro Toronto Tenants' Associations
Overview: A medium-sized local organization founded in 1974
Mission: To inform & educate tenants; to encourage the organization of tenants; to lobby for tenant protection laws; to promote affordable housing
Membership: 3,000+; *Fees:* Schedule available
Activities: Offering the tenant hotline for referrals & information about tenant rights; helping tenants to challenge rent increases & to promote better maintenance in buildings, through the outreach & organizing team; publishing numerous guides, manuals, fact-sheets, sample letters & newsletters

Federation of Metro Toronto Tenants' Associations *See* Federation of Metro Tenants' Associations

Federation of Mountain Clubs of British Columbia (FMCBC)
Mountain Equipment Co-op Store, PO Box 18673, 130 West Broadway, 2nd Fl., Vancouver BC V5T 4E7
Tel: 604-873-6096; *Fax:* 604-873-6086
fmcbc@mountainclubs.org
www.mountainclubs.org
www.facebook.com/129423370477517
twitter.com/mountainclubs
Overview: A small provincial charitable organization founded in 1980
Mission: To promote hiking & mountaineering
Member of: Donations; Membership dues
Membership: 3500; *Fees:* Individual $25
Chief Officer(s):
Scott Webster, President
Jodi Appleton, Manager, Program and Administration
admin.manager@mountainclubs.org
Publications:
• Cloudburst
Type: Newsletter
• Training Manuals
Type: Manual
Profile: Training manuals to support courses in mountaineering, climbing, avalanche safety and other outdoor skills

Federation of Music Festivals of Nova Scotia
PO Box 31, Lunenburg NS B0J 2C0
Tel: 902-640-2448
www.musicfestivalsnovascotia.ca
Overview: A medium-sized provincial organization overseen by Federation of Canadian Music Festivals
Chief Officer(s):
Pamela Rogers, Secretary
pamelasrogers@gmail.com

Federation of Mutual Fund Dealers (FMFD) / Fédération des courtiers en fonds mutuels
c/o S. Kegie, Executive Director, 44 Faversham Cres., Toronto ON M9C 3X6
Tel: 416-621-8857
www.fmfd.ca
Overview: A medium-sized national organization founded in 1996
Mission: To be the representative voice of mutual fund distribution in Canada; to provide a forum for stakeholders; to advocate for members
Membership: 27 dealers + 25 affiliates; *Fees:* $550-$5,500 dealer; $175-$5,500 affiliate
Activities: Networking; education opportunities; meetings with trade associations, lobby groups, regulators & individuals in order to further the federation's mandate
Chief Officer(s):
Sandra Kegie, Executive Director, 647-409-8369
skegie@rogers.com

Federation of New Brunswick Faculty Associations (FNBFA) / Fédération des associations de professeures et professeurs d'université du Nouveau-Brunswick (FAPPUNB)
#204, 361 Victoria St., Fredericton NB E3B 1W5
Tel: 506-458-8977; *Fax:* 506-458-5620
www.fnbfa.ca
Overview: A small provincial organization founded in 1973 overseen by Canadian Association of University Teachers
Mission: To promote interests of teachers, librarians & researchers in universities & colleges of New Brunswick; To advance standards of professions & to seek to improve quality of higher education in the Province
Staff Member(s): 2
Membership: 6 organizations representing 1,800 members; *Member Profile:* University professor & librarian associations; *Committees:* Communications; Prix Nicole Raymond Award; Legal Assistance; Collective Bargaining; George P. Semeluk Scholarship
Activities: *Speaker Service:* Yes
Chief Officer(s):
Jean Sauvageau, President
jsauvageau@stu.ca
Elisabeth Hans, Executive Director
Awards:
• George P. Semezuk Scholarship
• Prix Nicole Raymond Award

Federation of Newfoundland & Labrador Square Dance
NL
Tel: 709-579-0980
Overview: A small provincial organization
Member of: Canadian Square & Round Dance Society
Chief Officer(s):
Jim Critch, President

Federation of North American Explorers (FNE)
c/o Paul Ritchi, 43 Bluesky Cres., Richmond Hill ON L4C 8J2
Tel: 416-435-6593
info@fneexplorers.com
www.fneexplorers.com
www.facebook.com/FNEExplorers
twitter.com/PaulRitchi
www.youtube.com/user/FNEExp
Also Known As: FN Explorers
Overview: A small local charitable organization founded in 1956
Mission: To deliver traditional values to youth, from a Catholic faith perspective
Member of: International Union of European FSE Guides & Scouts (Union Internationale des Guides et Scouts d'Europe)
Affiliation(s): Archdiocese of Toronto
Finances: *Funding Sources:* Donations
Membership: *Member Profile:* Baptized Christian youth & adults, or individuals who are preparing to be baptized
Activities: Camping weekends, outdoor survival activities & community service; Earning badges by successfully completing certain activities
Chief Officer(s):
Paul Ritchi, General Commissioner & Founder
paul.ritchi@gmail.com
Tony D'Avanzo, President & Chairman

Federation of Northern Ontario Municipalities (FONOM)
88 Riverside Dr., Kapuskasing ON P5N 1B3
Tel: 705-337-4454; *Fax:* 705-337-1741
fonom.info@gmail.com
www.fonom.org
Overview: A medium-sized local organization founded in 1960
Mission: To act as the voice for the people of northeastern Ontario communities; To work for the betterment of municipal government by striving for improved legislation respecting local government in northern Ontario
Member of: Association of Municipalities of Ontario
Finances: *Funding Sources:* Membership fees; Provincial grants; Sponsorships
Membership: 111; *Member Profile:* Municipal governments from the following districts: Cochrane, Algoma, Manitoulin, Nipissing, Parry Sound, Sudbury, & Timiskaming
Chief Officer(s):
Alan Spacek, President
Meetings/Conferences:
• Federation of Northern Ontario Municipalities 2018 58th Annual Conference, May, 2018, Parry Sound, ON
Scope: Local
Description: A meeting for northern Ontario's municipal decision makers, featuring exhibits by suppliers, vendors, & professionals who provide services to municipalities
• Federation of Northern Ontario Municipalities 2019 59th Annual Conference, May, 2019, Sudbury, ON
Scope: Local
Description: A meeting for northern Ontario's municipal decision makers, featuring exhibits by suppliers, vendors, & professionals who provide services to municipalities

Federation of Nova Scotia Naturalists *See* Nature Nova Scotia (Federation of Nova Scotia Naturalists)

Federation of Nova Scotian Heritage *See* Association of Nova Scotia Museums

Federation of Nunavut Teachers *See* Nunavut Teachers' Association

Federation of Ontario Bed & Breakfast Accommodation (FOBBA)
29 Albert St., Orillia ON L3V 5J9
Tel: 705-329-3242
talk2us@fobba.com
www.fobba.com
Overview: A small provincial organization founded in 1987
Mission: To represent the interests of independent bed & breakfast operators, country inns, bed & breakfast associations & registries, to the public & various governmental agencies
Finances: *Annual Operating Budget:* Less than $50,000; *Funding Sources:* Membership fees
12 volunteer(s)
Membership: 330; *Fees:* $150/year; *Member Profile:* Bed & breakfast owner/operators; *Committees:* Marketing; Membership
Activities: Advocating for members to government; Establishing & maintaining industry standards; Inspecting member properties; Providing education & marketing for members; *Library:* FOBBA Knowledge Bank
Chief Officer(s):
Doug Frost, President, 705-487-5723
president@fobba.com
Don Matthews, Vice-President, 613-382-4377
vp@fobba.com
Meetings/Conferences:
• Federation of Ontario Bed & Breakfast Accommodation 2018 Conference & Annual General Meeting, April, 2018, Deerhurst Resort, Huntsville, ON
Scope: Provincial
Publications:
• FOBBA [Federation of Ontario Bed & Breakfast Accommodation] Newsletter
Type: Newsletter
Profile: Information on board activities, advocacy, members & promotional opportunities

Federation of Ontario Cottagers' Associations (FOCA)
#201, 159 King St., Peterborough ON K9J 2R8
Tel: 705-749-3622; *Fax:* 705-749-6522
info@foca.on.ca
www.foca.on.ca
www.facebook.com/foca.on.ca
Overview: A medium-sized provincial organization founded in 1963
Mission: To ensure a healthy future for waterfront Ontario; To support the interests of Ontario's cottagers
Member of: Ontario Biodiversity Council; Ontario Onsite Wastewater Association
Finances: *Annual Operating Budget:* $250,000-$500,000; *Funding Sources:* Membership fees; Sponsorships; Donations
Staff Member(s): 4; 20 volunteer(s)
Membership: 50,000 families; *Fees:* Schedule available; *Member Profile:* Ontario cottagers' associations; Individuals, such as waterfront property owners
Activities: Providing information about issues that affect cottage properties; Offering networking opportunities
Chief Officer(s):
Terry Rees, Executive Director, 705-749-3622 Ext. 4
trees@foca.on.ca
Publications:
• Federation of Ontario Cottagers' Associations Report to Members
Type: Newsletter; *Price:* Free with Federation of Ontario Cottagers' Associations membership
Profile: Federation activities
• Lake Stewards Newsletter
Type: Newsletter; *Frequency:* Annually; *Price:* Free with Federation of Ontario Cottagers' Associations membership

Federation of Ontario Law Associations (FOLA)
731 - 9th St. West, Owen Sound ON N4K 3P5
Tel: 519-270-4283
info@fola.ca
www.fola.ca
twitter.com/ont_law_assoc
Previous Name: The County & District Law Presidents' Association

Overview: A small provincial organization
Mission: To advance & represent the interests of member associations throughout the province of Ontario; To serve the legal profession & the people of Ontario in pursuit of the continued delivery of excellent legal services in each county, district or region in Ontario; To preserve the independence of the Bar
Finances: Annual Operating Budget: $250,000-$500,000
Staff Member(s): 2; 11 volunteer(s)
Membership: 12,000; Member Profile: Private practice lawyers in Ontario firms; Committees: The County Law Library; Professional Governance; Court Resources; Judiciary and Government; Legal Services; Real Estate Law; Rules & Practice Issues; Legal Aid
Chief Officer(s):
Eldon Horner, Chair
Michael Ras, Executive Director, 647-228-2339
mike.ras@fola.ca
Kelly Lovell, Executive Assistant, 519-270-4283
Meetings/Conferences:
• Federation of Ontario Law Associations 2019 Bi-Annual Plenary, 2019, ON
Scope: Provincial

Federation of Ontario Memorial Societies - Funeral Consumers Alliance (FOOMS-FCA)
Toronto ON
fooms-fca.org/fms
Overview: A small provincial charitable organization
Mission: To coordinate all memorial societies in Ontario
Finances: Annual Operating Budget: Less than $50,000
20 volunteer(s)
Membership: 6 societies; 51,000 members; Committees: Publicity; Legislation
Activities: Annual meeting; Speaker Service: Yes
Chief Officer(s):
Pearl Davie, Contact

Federation of Ontario Naturalists See Ontario Nature

Federation of Ontario Public Libraries (FOPL)
c/o North York Central Library, 5120 Yonge St., Toronto ON M2N 5N9
Tel: 416-395-5638; Fax: 416-395-0743
admin@fopl.ca
www.fopl.ca
www.facebook.com/160173540675944
twitter.com/foplnews
Overview: A medium-sized provincial organization
Mission: To represent Ontario's public library systems; To advocate for support, programs, & resources that will contribute to the success of Ontario public libraries
Membership: 190+; Member Profile: Libraries in Ontario
Activities: Securing funding; Enhancing library programs
Chief Officer(s):
Stephen Abram, Executive Director, 416-395-0746
sabram@fopl.ca

Federation of Portuguese Canadian Business & Professionals Inc. (FPCBP)
1136 College St., Toronto ON M6H 1B6
Tel: 416-537-8874; Fax: 416-537-9706
info@fpcbp.com
www.fpcbp.com
www.facebook.com/143576472378864
Overview: A small national organization founded in 1981
Mission: To promote Portuguese culture & heritage; To foster business & community development in the Greater Toronto area
Finances: Funding Sources: Sponsorships; Grants
Activities: Advocating on behalf of members; Enhancing political visibility; Partnering with other community groups; Organizing events, such as monthly business forums & social activities; Promoting business interaction & developing networking opportunities; Encouraging & improving academic excellence amongst Portuguese-Canadians; Fostering professionalism; Engaging Portuguese youth & the community to recognize & celebrate Portuguese history & heritage
Chief Officer(s):
Isabel Christina Bento Martins, President
Francine Antonio, Vice-President
Josie Caldas, Secretary
Sergio Ruivo, Treasurer
Awards:
• FPCBP Scholarship
To recognize the outstanding academic achievements of our Luso Canadian youth

• FPCBP Business Excellence Awards
To recognize individuals in the business & professional community who demonstrate excellence in their field of work
Publications:
• FPCBP Directory
Type: Directory

Federation of Prince Edward Island Municipalities Inc. (FPEIM)
1 Kirkdale Rd., Charlottetown PE C1E 1R3
Tel: 902-566-1493; Fax: 902-566-2880
info@fpeim.ca
www.fpeim.ca
Overview: A large provincial organization founded in 1957
Mission: To represent the interests of the cities, towns & communities within PEI; To secure united action for the protection of individual municipalities & municipal interests as a whole; To act as a clearing house for the collection, exchange & dissemination of information of concern & interest to member municipalities; To provide training, education & development opportunities for elected & appointed municipal officials
Member of: Federation of Canadian Municipalities
Affiliation(s): Association of Municipal Administrators, PEI
Finances: Annual Operating Budget: $100,000-$250,000;
Funding Sources: Small government grant; Membership dues
Staff Member(s): 2; 13 volunteer(s)
Membership: 43 municipalities; Fees: Schedule available;
Member Profile: Incorporated municipalities; Committees: Membership; Constitution & Policy; Finance & Audit; Nominating; Resolutions; Urban
Activities: Liaising with provincial municipal associations across Canada as well as provincial & federal government departments;
Awareness Events: Municipal Government Week; Library: by appointment
Chief Officer(s):
John Dewey, Executive Director
jdewey@fpeim.ca
Bruce MacDougall, President
president@fpeim.ca
Awards:
• The Gilbert C. Bell Memorial Award
Presented annually to a full-time undergraduate student who exemplifies an interest in a career in Public Administration by obtaining the highest mark in Public Administration Course #311 - Public Policy & Administration 1, in that academic year
• Municipal Achievement Award
Awarded annually to a municipality that has demonstrated a commitment to improving the quality of life of its residents through innovative local projects & activities; two awards presented each year: one award to a municipality with a population of 1,500 & under; one award to a municipality with a population over 1,500; open to FPEI Municipalities members
• Bruce H. Yeo Award
Meetings/Conferences:
• Federation of Prince Edward Island Municipalities Inc. Annual General Meeting 2018, 2018
Scope: Provincial
Contact Information: Assistant, Administrative: Julie McMurrer, E-mail: jmcmurrer@fpeim.ca
Publications:
• FPEIM [Federation of Prince Edward Island Municipalities Inc.] News
Type: Newsletter

Federation of Public Service Employees Inc. (CNTU) Voir Fédération des employées et employés de services publics inc. (CSN)

Federation of Québec Alzheimer Societies Voir Fédération québécoise des sociétés Alzheimer

Federation of Québec Beef Producers Voir Fédération des producteurs de bovins du Québec

Federation of Saskatchewan Indian Nations
Asimakaniseekan Askiy Reserve, #100, 103A Packham Ave., Saskatoon SK S7N 4K4
Tel: 306-665-1215; Fax: 306-244-4413
www.fsin.com
Previous Name: Federation of Saskatchewan Indians
Overview: A small provincial organization overseen by Congress of Aboriginal Peoples
Mission: To honour the spirit & intent of the First Nations Treaties & their rights; to foster the economic, educational & social endeavours of the First Nation people & adherence to democratic procedure & civil law.
Membership: 74 First Nations

Activities: Education & Training Secretariat
Chief Officer(s):
Kim Jonathan, Interim Chief
Office of Treaty Governance Processes
#100, 130A Packham Ave., Saskatoon SK S7N 4K4
Tel: 306-665-1215; Fax: 306-244-4413

Federation of Saskatchewan Indians See Federation of Saskatchewan Indian Nations

Federation of Saskatchewan Surface Rights Association (FSSRA)
PO Box 53, Lone Rock SK S0M 1K0
Tel: 306-387-6650; Fax: 306-387-6650
Overview: A small provincial organization founded in 1982
Mission: To aid in reclamation concerns in land, gas lines, rail lines, compensation, environmental issues & legislation
Affiliation(s): Alberta Surface Rights Federation
Membership: 1-99; Member Profile: Farmers
Activities: Speaker Service: Yes
Chief Officer(s):
Terry Crush, Contact

Federation of Senior Citizens & Pensioners of Nova Scotia (FSCPNS)
c/o Bernie LaRusic, 21 Grandview St., Sydney NS B1P 3N4
Tel: 902-562-1901
Previous Name: Nova Scotia Federation of Senior Citizens & Pensioners
Overview: A medium-sized provincial organization founded in 1973
Mission: To help seniors maintain the health services & pension incomes that they now have
Member of: National Federation of Senior Citizens & Pensioners
Membership: Member Profile: A member of a senior citizens club
Chief Officer(s):
Bernie LaRusic, President
bernielarusic_392@hotmail.com

Federation of Single-Parent Family Associations of Québec Voir Fédération des associations de familles monoparentales et recomposées du Québec

Federation of Support Staff Voir Fédération du personnel de soutien scolaire (CSQ)

Federation of Teachers of Jewish Schools (FTJS) / Fédération des enseignants des écoles juives
#3265, 6900, boul Decarie, Montréal QC H3X 2T8
Tel: 514-738-6852; Fax: 514-738-9660
info@ftjs.org
www.ftjs.org
Overview: A medium-sized local organization founded in 1947
Mission: To promote the advancement of professional economic & social welfare of its members by securing collective agreements; to engage in activities conducive to the well-being & furthering of Jewish, Hebrew & secular education
Membership: Fees: Schedule available; Member Profile: Those teaching in Jewish schools in Montréal
Chief Officer(s):
Mordechai Antal, President

Federation of Temporary Help Services See Association of Canadian Search, Employment & Staffing Services

Fédération professionnelle des journalistes du Québec (FPJQ)
#105, 1012, av Mont Royal est, Montréal QC H2J 1X6
Tél: 514-522-6142; Téléc: 514-522-6071
info@fpjq.org
www.fpjq.org
www.facebook.com/pages/FPJQ/256594304445143
twitter.com/fpjq
www.youtube.com/channel/UCCxQxREz2d3ff-55-8sFqHg
Aperçu: Dimension: moyenne; Envergure: provinciale; fondée en 1969
Mission: Pour défendre la liberté d'expression pour la presse et le droit du public à la connaissance
Membre(s) du personnel: 3
Membre: Montant de la cotisation: 46$ étudiant; 82$ associé/membre professionnel gagnant moins de 25 000 $/an; 174$ professional
Activités: Congrès annuel des journalistes; Sessions de prfectionnement Defense de la liberté de la presse; Droit du public à l'information; Prix et bourses journalistiques; Emmission de la carte de presse

Membre(s) du bureau directeur:
Caroline Locher, Directrice générale
caroline.locher@fpjq.org

Fédération provinciale des comités de parents du Manitoba
Voir Fédération des parents du Manitoba

Fédération québécoise d'athlétisme (FQA)
4545, av Pierre-de Coubertin, Montréal QC H1V 0B2
Tél: 514-252-3041; *Téléc:* 514-252-3042
fqa@athletisme.qc.ca
www.athletisme.qc.ca
www.facebook.com/athletismequebec
twitter.com/Athl_FQA
www.youtube.com/athletismequebec
Nom précédent: Fédération d'athlétisme du Québec
Aperçu: *Dimension:* moyenne; *Envergure:* provinciale; Organisme sans but lucratif; fondée en 1968 surveillé par Athletics Canada
Mission: Promouvoir l'athlétisme au Québec
Membre de: Athletics Canada
Membre(s) du personnel: 6
Membre: *Montant de la cotisation:* Barème; *Critères d'admissibilite:* Coureurs sur route; athlètes; entraîneurs; officiels; membres associés; *Comités:* Technique provinciale; Officiels, règlements et organisations; Jeunes
Activités: *Service de conférenciers:* Oui
Membre(s) du bureau directeur:
Sylvain Proulx, Président
Laurent Godbout, Directeur général
lgodbout@athletisme.qc.ca

Fédération québécoise de ballon sur glace
4545, av Pierre-de Coubertin, Montréal QC H1V 3R2
Tél: 514-252-3078
fqbg.comm@gmail.com
www.fqbg.net
www.facebook.com/157977357723290
Aperçu: *Dimension:* moyenne; *Envergure:* provinciale
Mission: La Fédération Québécoise de Ballon sur Glace a pour but de promouvoir le sport du ballon sur glace dans la province de Québec
Membre de: Fédération canadienne de ballon sur glace
Membre(s) du bureau directeur:
Normand Perreault, Président
normandperreault8@gmail.com

Fédération québécoise de biathlon
CP 69023, Québec QC G2B 6C3
Courriel: info@fqb.quebec
www.fqb.quebec
www.facebook.com/acbq.qc.ca
Nom précédent: Association des clubs de biathlon du Québec
Aperçu: *Dimension:* petite; *Envergure:* provinciale; fondée en 2002 surveillé par Biathlon Canada
Membre de: Biathlon Canada
Membre(s) du bureau directeur:
Jean-Guy Lévesque, Président
president@fqb.quebec
Donald Villeneuve, Vice-Président, Administration
vpadministration@fqb.quebec

Fédération Québécoise de Boxe Olympique (FQBO)
4545, av Pierre-de Coubertin, Montréal QC H1V 0B2
Tél: 514-252-3047; *Téléc:* 514-254-2144
Ligne sans frais: 866-241-3779
info@fqbo.qc.ca
www.fqbo.qc.ca
www.facebook.com/groups/5136898117
www.youtube.com/channel/UCwrq3BlBvgb28mB6GIVsJaA
Également appelé: Boxe Québec
Aperçu: *Dimension:* moyenne; *Envergure:* provinciale surveillé par Canadian Amateur Boxing Association
Membre de: Canadian Amateur Boxing Association
Membre: 2 000

Fédération québécoise de camping et de caravaning inc. (FQCC)
CP 100, #100, 1560, rue Eiffel, Boucherville QC J4B 5Y1
Tél: 450-650-3722; *Téléc:* 450-650-3721
Ligne sans frais: 877-650-3722
info@fqcc.ca
www.fqcc.ca
www.facebook.com/LaFQCC
www.youtube.com/user/LaFQCC
Aperçu: *Dimension:* grande; *Envergure:* provinciale; fondée en 1967
Mission: Unir les adepts du camping et du caravaning; Entreprendre et coordonner des actions relatives au camping et au caravaning
Membre de: Fédération internationale de camping et de caravaning
Finances: *Budget de fonctionnement annuel:* $500,000-$1.5 Million
Membre(s) du personnel: 10
Membre: 45 000 familles membres; *Montant de la cotisation:* 45$
Activités: *Service de conférenciers:* Oui
Membre(s) du bureau directeur:
Yvan Lafontaine, Président
Michel Quintal, Trésorier

Fédération québécoise de canoë-kayak d'eau vives
4545, av Pierre-de Coubertin, Montréal QC H1V 0B2
Tél: 438-333-1913
www.federationkayak.qc.ca
www.facebook.com/fqckev
Aperçu: *Dimension:* petite; *Envergure:* provinciale; fondée en 1971 surveillé par CanoeKayak Canada
Mission: Promouvoir le sport et la pratique d'activités en eau vive au Québec
Membre de: CanoeKayak Canada

Fédération québécoise de course d'orientation *See* Orienteering Québec

Fédération Québécoise de Dynamophilie (FQD)
679, av du Parc, Sherbrooke QC J1N 3N5
Tél: 819-864-4810
www.fqd-quebec.com
www.facebook.com/dynamophilie
Aperçu: *Dimension:* petite; *Envergure:* provinciale surveillé par Canadian Powerlifting Union
Mission: Promouvoir, contrôler et développer la dynamophilie auprès de la population du Québec.
Affiliation(s): Canadian Powerlifting Union; International Powerlifting Federation
Membre: *Montant de la cotisation:* 55$; 45$ les moins de 18 ans
Membre(s) du bureau directeur:
Louis Lévesque, Président
louis.lvesque2@sympatico.ca

Fédération québécoise de handball olympique (FQHO)
CP 1000, Succ. M, 4545, av Pierre-de Coubertin, Montréal QC H1V 3R2
Tél: 514-252-3067; *Téléc:* 514-252-3176
handball@handball.qc.ca
www.handball.qc.ca
Aperçu: *Dimension:* petite; *Envergure:* locale
Mission: Handball Québec est le seul organisme reconnu par le Secrétariat au Loisir et au Sport du Gouvernement du Québec pour régir le handball au Québec.
Membre de: Canadian Team Handball Federation
Membre: *Comités:* Comité Technique d'Arbitrage; Comité de discipline
Membre(s) du bureau directeur:
Michelle Lortie, Directrice
mlortie@handball.qc.ca

Fédération québécoise de hockey sur glace *Voir* Hockey Québec

Fédération québécoise de l'autisme (FQA) / Québec Federation for Autism
#200, 7675, boul Saint-Laurent, Montréal QC H2R 1W9
Tél: 514-270-7386; *Téléc:* 514-270-9261
Ligne sans frais: 888-830-2833
info@autisme.qc.ca
www.autisme.qc.ca
www.facebook.com/autisme.qc.ca
Nom précédent: Société québécoise de l'autisme
Aperçu: *Dimension:* moyenne; *Envergure:* provinciale; Organisme sans but lucratif; fondée en 1976 surveillé par Autism Society Canada
Mission: Promouvoir et défendre les droits et les intérêts de la personne autiste ou ayant un trouble envahissant du développement afin qu'elle accède à une vie digne et à une meilleure autonomie sociale possible; mobiliser tous les acteurs concernés afin de promouvoir le bien-être des personnes, sensibiliser et informer la population sur le trouble du spectre de l'autisme ainsi que sur la situation des familles, et contribuer au développement des connaissances et à leur diffusion
Finances: *Fonds:* Gouvernement
Membre(s) du personnel: 3; 10 bénévole(s)
Membre: 18 organismes; *Montant de la cotisation:* 50$ organismes communautaires; 100$ autres organismes; *Critères d'admissibilité:* Organismes offrant des services aux personnes autistes ou ayant un trouble envahissant du développement
Activités: Défense des droits; représentations publiques et politiques; élaboration de mémoires et d'avis; participation à des comités et à des tables de concertation; information et formation; écoute et soutien; promotion des initiatives de nature à développer les capacités optimales des personnes autistes; vie associative; *Stagiaires:* Oui; *Bibliothèque:* Centre de documentation; Not open to public
Membre(s) du bureau directeur:
Jo-Ann Lauzon, Directrice générale
direction@autisme.qc.ca

Fédération québécoise de la faune *Voir* Fédération québécoise des chasseurs et pêcheurs

Fédération québécoise de la marche
4545, av Pierre-de Coubertin, Montréal QC H1V 0B2
Tél: 514-252-3157; *Téléc:* 514-252-5137
Ligne sans frais: 866-252-2065
infomarche@fqmarche.qc.ca
www.fqmarche.qc.ca
www.facebook.com/138582999548977
twitter.com/QuebecMarche
www.youtube.com/user/fqmarche
Aperçu: *Dimension:* moyenne; *Envergure:* provinciale; Organisme sans but lucratif; fondée en 1978
Mission: Promotion de la marche et de la randonnée pedestre; support au développement de lieux de marche
Membre de: Conseil québécois du loisir
Finances: *Budget de fonctionnement annuel:* $250,000-$500,000
Membre(s) du personnel: 5; 26 bénévole(s)
Membre: 3 000 individu; 100 clubs; *Montant de la cotisation:* 29,50$ individu; 35,50$ famille; *Comités:* Marches populaires; Raquette; Sentiers-Québec
Activités: Evénements de sensibilisation: Festival de la marche, oct.; Festival de la raquette, fév.; *Bibliothèque:* Bibliothèque publique
Membre(s) du bureau directeur:
Daniel Pouplot, Directeur général
dpouplot@fqmarche.qc.ca
Prix, Bourses:
• Prix sentiers Québec
• Certificat du Randonneur émerite québécois
• Padelima

Fédération québécoise de la montagne et de l'escalade (FQME)
4545, av Pierre-de Coubertin, Montréal QC H1V 0B2
Tél: 514-252-3004; *Téléc:* 514-252-3201
Ligne sans frais: 866-204-3763
operations@fqme.qc.ca
www.fqme.qc.ca
twitter.com/Escalade_FQME
www.facebook.com/FQMEescalade
Aperçu: *Dimension:* petite; *Envergure:* provinciale; Organisme sans but lucratif; fondée en 1969
Mission: Regrouper les adeptes de l'escalade et de l'alpinisme au Québec; promouvoir l'escalade (rocher et glace) et le ski de l'alpinisme et de randonnée en montagne; promouvoir une pratique sécuritaire de ces activités; protéger et rendre accessibles les différents sites d'escalade et de grande randonnée à skis au Québec
Membre de: Canadian Avalanche Association; Outdoor Recreation Coalition of America (ORCA)
Affiliation(s): Union internationale des associations d'alpinisme
Finances: *Budget de fonctionnement annuel:* $100,000-$250,000
Membre: 2 000; *Montant de la cotisation:* Barème; *Comités:* Formation; Site; Expédition
Activités: Amateur d'activités montagnes; *Stagiaires:* Oui; *Bibliothèque:* Centre de documentation; rendez-vous
Membre(s) du bureau directeur:
André St-Jacques, Directeur des opérations, 514-252-3000 Ext. 3406

Fédération québécoise de naturisme (FQN)
4545, av Pierre-de Coubertin, Montréal QC H1V 0B2
Tél: 514-252-3014
info@vivrenu.ca
www.fqn.qc.ca
www.facebook.com/fedquenat
twitter.com/fedquenat

Canadian Associations / Fédération québécoise de philatélie (FQP)

Aperçu: *Dimension:* moyenne; *Envergure:* provinciale; fondée en 1977
Mission: Regrouper les naturistes; promouvoir et favoriser le développement de la pratique du naturisme au Québec
Membre de: Fédération naturiste internationale
Affiliation(s): Federation of Canadian Naturists
Finances: *Budget de fonctionnement annuel:* Moins de $50,000; *Fonds:* Provincial government
9 bénévole(s)
Membre: 400 individus; 4 institutionels; *Montant de la cotisation:* $22 jeune; $42 régulier
Activités: Sports et loisirs naturistes organisés durant l'année
Membre(s) du bureau directeur:
François Lévesque, Président

Fédération québécoise de philatélie (FQP)
4545, av Pierre-de Coubertin, Montréal QC H1V 0B2
Tél: 514-252-3035
fqp@philatelie.qc.ca
www.philatelie.qc.ca
Également appelé: Philatélie Québec
Aperçu: *Dimension:* moyenne; *Envergure:* provinciale; fondée en 1971
Mission: Promouvoir la pratique de la philatélie
Affiliation(s): Regroupement Loisir-Québec
Finances: *Budget de fonctionnement annuel:* Moins de $50,000
50 bénévole(s)
Membre: 300 institutionnel; 5 000 individu; 100 associé; *Montant de la cotisation:* 20$ institutionnel; 8$ individu
Activités: Expositions; Salon Philatélique; Quoffilex; *Stagiaires:* Oui; *Bibliothèque:* rendez-vous
Membre(s) du bureau directeur:
Jacques Poitras, Président

Fédération québécoise de soccer football *Voir* Fédération de soccer du Québec

Fédération québécoise de tennis *Voir* Tennis Québec

Fédération québécoise de tir (FQT) / Québec Shooting Federation
6897, rue Jarry est, Montréal QC H1P 1W7
Tél: 514-252-3056; *Téléc:* 514-252-3060
Ligne sans frais: 888-514-7847
fqt@fqtir.qc.ca
www.fqtir.qc.ca
Aperçu: *Dimension:* petite; *Envergure:* provinciale; Organisme sans but lucratif; fondée en 1978
Mission: La FQT est un organisme à but non lucratif voué à la promotion du tir sportif sur tout le territoire de la province du Québec et qui est reconnue et subventionnée par l'intermédiaire du Secrétariat au loisir et au sport (Gouvernement du Québec)
Membre de: Fédération de tir du Canada; Shooting Federation of Canada
Affiliation(s): Regroupment Loisir Québec; Sports Québec
Finances: *Budget de fonctionnement annuel:* $250,000-$500,000; *Fonds:* Gouvernement du Québec
Membre(s) du personnel: 3; 400 bénévole(s)
Membre: 6,000; *Comités:* Carabine; pistolet; plateaux; chasse; moderne; poudre noire; pratique pour policiers et civils
Activités: Assemblée général annuelle; *Stagiaires:* Oui
Membre(s) du bureau directeur:
Gilles Bédard, Directeur exécutif, 514-252-3056 Ext. 3611
gbedard@fqtir.qc.ca
Gérald Tousignant, Président

Fédération québécoise des activités subaquatiques (FQAS)
4545, av Pierre-de Coubertin, Montréal QC H1V 0B2
Tél: 514-252-3009; *Téléc:* 514-254-1363
Ligne sans frais: 866-391-8835
info@fqas.qc.ca
www.fqas.qc.ca
www.facebook.com/FederationQuebecoisedesActivitesSubaquatiques
Aperçu: *Dimension:* moyenne; *Envergure:* provinciale; Organisme sans but lucratif; fondée en 1970
Mission: Regrouper les adeptes de la plongée et des activités subaquatiques; promouvoir la sécurité dans la pratique des activités subaquatiques; informer et renseigner ses membres et la population sur les bienfaits de la pratique; promouvoir ces activités comme moyen de formation et comme loisir
Affiliation(s): Confédération mondiale des activités subaquatiques
Finances: *Budget de fonctionnement annuel:* $250,000-$500,000; *Fonds:* Gouvernement provincial
Membre(s) du personnel: 2; 150 bénévole(s)
Membre: 100 institutionnel + 2 200 individu; *Montant de la cotisation:* $34.50 individu; $56 famille
Activités: *Stagiaires:* Oui; *Service de conférenciers:* Oui; *Bibliothèque:* Librairie FQAS; rendez-vous
Membre(s) du bureau directeur:
Alain Gauthier, Directeur général
direction@fqas.qc.ca

Fédération québécoise des centres communautaires de loisir inc. (FQCCL)
2301, 1e av, Québec QC G1L 3M9
Tél: 418-686-0012; *Téléc:* 418-686-0021
Ligne sans frais: 888-686-8356
fqccl@fqccl.org
www.fqccl.org
Aperçu: *Dimension:* petite; *Envergure:* locale; Organisme sans but lucratif; fondée en 1976
Mission: Regroupe les centres pour qu'ils s'entraident dans leur cheminement; veille à la formation des intervenants et des bénévoles; aide à améliorer le bien-être et le développement de leur communauté locale; promeut les initiatives nouvelles des centres, spécialement dans la prise en charge des milieux les plus démunis; aide les centres dans leur financement
Membre de: Conseil québécois du loisir
Finances: *Budget de fonctionnement annuel:* $250,000-$500,000; *Fonds:* Gouvernement provincial
Membre(s) du personnel: 12; 100 bénévole(s)
Membre: 58 institutionnel; *Critères d'admissibilite:* Centre communautaire de loisir
Activités: *Stagiaires:* Oui; *Service de conférenciers:* Oui
Membre(s) du bureau directeur:
Sylvain Turcotte, Président

Fédération québécoise des chasseurs et pêcheurs
162, rue du Brome, Québec QC G3A 2P5
Tél: 418-878-8901; *Téléc:* 418-878-8980
Ligne sans frais: 888-523-2863
info@fedecp.qc.ca
www.fedecp.qc.ca
www.facebook.com/116805682100
twitter.com/FederationCP
Nom précédent: Fédération québécoise de la faune
Aperçu: *Dimension:* moyenne; *Envergure:* provinciale; fondée en 1946 surveillé par Canadian Wildlife Federation
Mission: Contribuer, dans le respect de la faune et de ses habitats, à la gestion du développement et à la perpétuation de la chasse et de la pêche comme activités traditionnelles et sportives
Membre: 200 associations; *Montant de la cotisation:* 39,95$ membre individuel; *Critères d'admissibilite:* Chasseurs, pêcheurs
Membre(s) du bureau directeur:
Pierre Latraverse, Président

Fédération québécoise des coopératives en milieu scolaire (FQCMS)
#200, 3188, ch Sainte-Foy, Québec QC G1X 1R4
Tél: 418-650-3333; *Téléc:* 418-651-3860
www.fqcms.com
www.facebook.com/FQCMS
twitter.com/FQCMS
Aperçu: *Dimension:* grande; *Envergure:* provinciale; fondée en 1983
Mission: Regroupe 60 coopératives en milieu scolaire
Membre: 400 000 membres

Bureau d'Anjou
#501, 7333, Place des Roseraies, Anjou QC H1M 2X6
Tél: 514-352-1121; *Téléc:* 514-352-1764

Fédération québécoise des coopératives forestières (FQCF)
#350, 3375, ch Sainte-Foy, Québec QC G1X 1S7
Tél: 418-651-0388; *Téléc:* 418-651-3860
cathyg@fqcf.coop
www.fqcf.coop
www.linkedin.com/company-beta/2474726
www.facebook.com/laFQCF
twitter.com/@LaFQCF
Nom précédent: Conférence des coopératives forestières du Québec
Aperçu: *Dimension:* moyenne; *Envergure:* provinciale; fondée en 1985
Mission: La Fédération québécoise des coopératives forestières (FQCF) regroupe et représente dans des domaines d'intérêts communs l'ensemble des coopératives forestières de travailleurs, les coopératives de travailleurs actionnaires et les coopératives de solidarité actives dans le milieu forestier, et ce dans toutes les régions du Québec
Finances: *Budget de fonctionnement annuel:* $500,000-$1.5 Million
Membre(s) du personnel: 4
Membre: 44
Membre(s) du bureau directeur:
Jocelyn Lessard, Directeur général, 418-651-0388 Ext. 324
j.lessard@fqcf.coop
Cathy Gagnon, Adjointe administrative, 418-651-0388 Ext. 321
cathyg@fqcf.coop

Fédération québécoise des directions d'établissements d'enseignement (FQDE)
#100, 7855, boul Louis-H-Lafontaine, Anjou QC H1K 4E4
Tél: 514-353-7511; *Téléc:* 514-353-2064
www.fqde.qc.ca
www.facebook.com/FQDE1
twitter.com/fqde
Aperçu: *Dimension:* moyenne; *Envergure:* provinciale; Organisme sans but lucratif; fondée en 1961
Mission: Défendre les droits des directeurs, directrices, directeurs adjoints, directrices adjointes d'établissements d'enseignement, sans oublier de promouvoir l'excellence dans la direction des établissements d'enseignement au Québec: en supportant des associations de directions d'établissement d'enseignement; en faisant en sorte que les directions d'établissement d'enseignement aient un environnement de travail favorisant la réalisation du projet éducatif; en s'assurant que les directions d'établissement d'enseignement maintenant une compétence de gestionnaire de haute qualité.
Finances: *Budget de fonctionnement annuel:* $500,000-$1.5 Million
Membre(s) du personnel: 10
Membre: 23 associations (2300 membres) + 1 association de 2430 retraités; *Montant de la cotisation:* 1% du traitement
Activités: *Service de conférenciers:* Oui
Membre(s) du bureau directeur:
Lorraine Normand-Charbonneau, Présidente
Marie Boucher, Coordonnatrice, Affaires professionnelles
marie.boucher@fqde.qc.ca

Fédération québécoise des échecs (FQE) / Québec Chess Federation
4545, rue Pierre-de-Coubertin, Montréal QC H1V 0B2
Tél: 514-252-3034; *Téléc:* 514-251-8038
info@fqechecs.qc.ca
www.fqechecs.qc.ca
www.facebook.com/eqechecs
twitter.com/fqechecs
Aperçu: *Dimension:* moyenne; *Envergure:* provinciale; Organisme sans but lucratif; fondée en 1967
Mission: Promouvoir l'étude, l'enseignement et la pratique du jeu d'échecs au Québec
Membre de: Regroupement Loisir-Québec
Finances: *Budget de fonctionnement annuel:* $100,000-$250,000
Membre(s) du personnel: 3; 7 bénévole(s)
Membre: 2 000 individu; 45 clubs; *Montant de la cotisation:* 45$ adulte; 35$ junior; 25$ cadet
Activités: Publication du Magazine Bimestriel Echec+Championnats Nationaux D'Echecs; *Service de conférenciers:* Oui
Membre(s) du bureau directeur:
Richard Bérubé, Directeur Général
dirgen@fqechecs.qc.ca
Publications:
• Échec+ [a publication of Fédération québécoise des échecs]
Type: Magazine

Fédération Québécoise des Intervenants en Sécurité Incendie (FQISI)
CP 40025, Granby QC J2G 9SI
Tél: 514-990-1338; *Téléc:* 514-666-9119
info@fqisi.org
www.fqisi.org
www.linkedin.com/company/fqisi---f-d-ration-qu-b-coise-des-intervenants-en-s-curit-incendie
www.facebook.com/FQISI.org
Nom précédent: Association Québécoise des Pompiers Volontaires et Permanents
Aperçu: *Dimension:* moyenne; *Envergure:* provinciale; fondée en 1978
Mission: Aider à promouvoir la prévention des incendies; aider, soutenir et susciter des efforts en vue de réduire les pertes de vie; favoriser le perfectionnement en vue de combattre plus

efficacement les incendies; promouvoir l'éducation populaire en général sur la protection et la prévention des incendies; faire des recommandations auprès des corps politiques et gouvernementaux
Membre(s) du personnel: 4
Membre: 500-999; *Montant de la cotisation:* Barème; *Critères d'admissibilite:* Actif, oeuvrant dans le domaine de la protection contre les incendies et ayant acquitté sa cotisation; *Comités:* Consultatif
Activités: *Stagiaires:* Oui; *Service de conférenciers:* Oui
Membre(s) du bureau directeur:
Jocelyn Lussier, Président
president@fqisi.org
Alain Richard, Directeur Éxécutif
directeur.executif@fqisi.org

Fédération québécoise des jeux récréatifs (FQJR)
4545, av Pierre-de Coubertin, Montréal QC H1V 0B2
Tél: 514-252-3032
info@quebecjeux.org
www.quebecjeux.org
www.facebook.com/355560369062
www.youtube.com/user/FQJRJeux
Aperçu: *Dimension:* moyenne; *Envergure:* provinciale; fondée en 1975
Mission: De promouvoir les sports de loisirs et jeux
Membre: 23 organismes; *Montant de la cotisation:* Barème
Membre(s) du bureau directeur:
Dominic Robitaille, Président

Fédération québécoise des laryngectomisés / Quebec Federation of Laryngectomees
5565, rue Sherbrooke est, Montréal QC H1N 1A2
Tél: 514-259-5113; *Téléc:* 514-259-8946
fqlar@fqlar.qc.ca
www.fqlar.qc.ca
Nom précédent: Association des laryngectomisés de Montréal
Aperçu: *Dimension:* moyenne; *Envergure:* provinciale; Organisme sans but lucratif; fondée en 1979
Mission: Etre la voix de l'ensemble des personnes laryngectomisées, glossectomisées et trachéotomisées du Québec; assurer une meilleure connaissance des besoins particuliers de ces personnes et promouvoir la satisfaction de ces besoins
Affiliation(s): Société canadienne du Cancer; International Association of Laryngectomy
Membre: *Montant de la cotisation:* 5$; *Critères d'admissibilite:* Personne laryngectomisée, glossectomisée ou trachéotomisée; toute autre personne désireuse d'offrir son aide bénévole
Membre(s) du bureau directeur:
Chantal Blouet, Responsable

Fédération québécoise des massothérapeutes (FQM)
#400, 4428, boul St-Laurent, Montréal QC H2W 1Z5
Tél: 514-597-0505; *Téléc:* 514-597-0141
Ligne sans frais: 800-363-9609
administration@fqm.qc.ca
www.fqm.qc.ca
www.facebook.com/massotherapie.FQM
twitter.com/FederationFQM
www.youtube.com/user/FQMmassotherapie
Aperçu: *Dimension:* moyenne; *Envergure:* provinciale; Organisme sans but lucratif; Organisme de réglementation; fondée en 1979
Mission: Regrouper les massothérapeutes afin de promouvoir la massothérapie sous l'intérêt public et de valoriser la profession de la massothérapie
Membre(s) du personnel: 12
Membre(s) du bureau directeur:
Sylvie Bédard, Présidente directrice générale
sylvie.bedard@fqm.qc.ca

Fédération Québécoise des Municipalités (FQM)
#560, 2954, boul Laurier, Sainte-Foy QC G1V 4T2
Tél: 418-651-3343; *Téléc:* 418-651-1127
Ligne sans frais: 866-951-3343
info@fqm.ca
www.fqm.ca
www.facebook.com/FQMenligne
twitter.com/fqmenligne
Nom précédent: Union des municipalités régionales de comté et des municipalités locales du Québec
Aperçu: *Dimension:* moyenne; *Envergure:* provinciale; fondée en 1944
Mission: Etre la porte-parole des régions; défendre les intérêts de ses membres
Membre: 1000 municipalités et presque la totalité des MRC; *Critères d'admissibilite:* Municipalités
Activités: *Service de conférenciers:* Oui
Membre(s) du bureau directeur:
Bernard Généreux, Président
Ann Bourget, Directrice générale

La Fédération québécoise des organismes communautaires Famille (FQOCF)
222, av Victoria, Saint-Lambert QC J4P 2H6
Tél: 450-466-2538; *Téléc:* 450-466-4196
Ligne sans frais: 866-982-9990
accueil@fqocf.org
www.fqocf.org
Nom précédent: Fédération des unions de familles inc.
Aperçu: *Dimension:* moyenne; *Envergure:* provinciale; fondée en 1961
Mission: Contribuer au développement d'une politique familiale; promouvoir le mieux-être des familles et la compétence parentale; soutenir les familles dans leur quotidien, leur réflexion et leurs actions; aider les familles à se regrouper; informer, assister et stimuler les groupes membres dans leurs initiatives
Membre de: Union internationale des organismes familiaux
Affiliation(s): Institut Vanier de la Famille
Membre: 200; *Montant de la cotisation:* 200$; *Critères d'admissibilite:* Organismes communautaires famille
Activités: Représentation; animation; formation; carrefour d'échanges
Membre(s) du bureau directeur:
Louisane Côté, Directrice générale

Fédération québécoise des professeures et professeurs d'université (FQPPU) / Québec Federation of University Professors
#300, 666, rue Sherbrooke, Montréal QC H3A 1E7
Tél: 514-843-5953; *Téléc:* 514-843-6928
Ligne sans frais: 888-843-5953
federation@fqppu.org
www.fqppu.org
twitter.com/fqppu
Aperçu: *Dimension:* moyenne; *Envergure:* provinciale surveillé par Canadian Association of University Teachers
Mission: Ouvrer au maintien, à la défense, à la promotion et au développement de l'université comme service public; défendre une université accessible et de qualité
Membre de: Association canadienne des professeures et professeurs d'université (ACPPU); Fédération mondiale des travailleurs scientifiques (FMTS); Internationale de l'éducation (IE); Table des partenaires universitaires au Québec (TPU); Reseau canadien pour l'éducation publique (PEN/REP)
Membre(s) du personnel: 3
Membre(s) du bureau directeur:
Jean-Marie Lafortune, Président
Publications:
• Bulletin FQPPU [Fédération québécoise des professeures et professeurs d'université]
Type: Bulletin
Profile: Comprend des nouvelles et les priorités pour l'association
• La condition professorale dans les universités québécoises - La recherche et la création [publication de FQPPU]
Type: Communiqué; *Price:* 10$
• La condition professorale dans les universités québécoises - La collégialité et la gestion [publication de FQPPU]
Type: Communiqué; *Price:* 10$
• La condition professorale dans les universités québécoises - Le défi des conciliations [publication de FQPPU]
Type: Communiqué; *Price:* 10$
• Femmes et pouvoir dans les universités québécoises [publication de FQPPU]
Type: Communiqué; *Author:* Françoise Naudillon et al.
• Le financement des fonds de fonctionnement universitaire au Québec [publication de FQPPU]
Type: Rapport; *Author:* Françoise Naudillon et al.
• Le fonds des immobilisations des universités - Une nouvelle cohérence à trouver entre vocations, budgets et réalités
Type: Rapport; *Author:* Élaine Hémond
• L'impact des politiques de l'innovation sur la recherche universitaire: systèmes nationaux et réseaux mondiaux
Type: Étude; *Author:* Pierre Milot
• Rempart de la "cité universitaire" depuis vingt ans (1991-2011) [publication de FQPPU]
Type: Rapport; *Author:* Pierre Hébert; *ISBN:* 978-2-921002-17-2; *Price:* 15$
• L'université et ses professeures - Une relation paradoxale [publication de FQPPU]
Type: Rapport; *Author:* Françoise Naudillon; *ISBN:* 2-921002-20-5

Fédération québécoise des revêtements de sol (FQRS)
#410, 7400, boul Les Galeries d'Anjou, Anjou QC H1M 3M2
Tél: 514-355-8001; *Téléc:* 514-355-4159
fqrs@spg.qc.ca
www.fqrs.ca
Aperçu: *Dimension:* petite; *Envergure:* provinciale; Organisme sans but lucratif; fondée en 1960
Mission: Se consacrer en permanence et en exclusivité à la promotion et à la défense des intérêts professionnels et commerciaux se ses membres
Membre: *Montant de la cotisation:* Barème; *Critères d'admissibilite:* Entreprises dans le revêtement de sol
Activités: Tournois de golf; soirée Méritas; colloque; déjeuner-causerie; *Service de conférenciers:* Oui
Membre(s) du bureau directeur:
Jean-Marc Couture, Secrétaire-trésorier

Fédération québécoise des revêtements de sol (FQRS) / Québec Institute of Floor Covering
#403, 2030, boul Pie-IX, Montréal QC H1V 2C8
Tél: 514-355-8001; *Téléc:* 514-355-4159
fqrs@spg.qc.ca
www.fqrs.ca
Nom précédent: Institut québécois des revêtements de sol inc.
Aperçu: *Dimension:* moyenne; *Envergure:* provinciale; fondée en 1972
Mission: Regrouper les gens de l'industrie des revêtements de sol pour les aider dans les différents domaines
Membre de: National Floor Covering Association
Membre(s) du personnel: 2
Membre: *Critères d'admissibilite:* Opérer dans l'industrie du couvre-planchers ou dans un secteur connexe
Membre(s) du bureau directeur:
Pierre Hébert, Président

Fédération québécoise des sociétés Alzheimer (FQSA) / Federation of Québec Alzheimer Societies
#200, 5165, rue Sherbrooke ouest, Montréal QC H4A 1T6
Tél: 514-369-7891; *Téléc:* 514-369-7900
Ligne sans frais: 888-636-6473
www.alzheimerquebec.ca
www.facebook.com/LaFederationQuebecoiseDesSocietesAlzheimer
twitter.com/FqsaAlzh
www.youtube.com/user/FQSA1
Aperçu: *Dimension:* grande; *Envergure:* provinciale; Organisme sans but lucratif; fondée en 1985 surveillé par Alzheimer Society of Canada
Mission: Alléger les conséquences personnelles et sociales de la maladie d'Alzheimer; diffuser l'information auprès du public sur la maladie d'Alzheimer et sur les services offerts par notre réseau; soutenir les sociétés qui offrent aide et formation; promouvoir et encourager la recherche sur la maladie d'Alzheimer entre autres par la gestion d'un fonds provincial de la recherche; établir des relations et faire des représentations auprès des autorités concernées
Finances: *Budget de fonctionnement annuel:* $3 Million-$5 Million
Membre(s) du personnel: 4
Membre: 20 Sociétés Alzheimer régionales
Activités: *Evénements de sensibilisation:* Mois de sensibilisation, jan.; *Bibliothèque:* Centre d'information; rendez-vous
Membre(s) du bureau directeur:
Jean-François Lamarche, Directeur général

Bas St-Laurent
Légion canadienne, 114, av St-Jérôme, Matane QC G4W 3A2
Tél: 418-562-2144; *Téléc:* 418-562-7449
Ligne sans frais: 877-446-2144
info@alzheimer-bsl.com
www.alzheimer-bsl.com
www.facebook.com/societealzheimer.bassaintlaurent
Membre(s) du bureau directeur:
Denis Bond, Président

Centre du Québec
880, rue Côté, Saint-Charles-de-Drummond QC J2C 4Z7
Tél: 819-474-3666; *Téléc:* 819-474-3133
myosotis@aide-internet.org
www.alzheimer-centre-du-quebec.org
Membre(s) du bureau directeur:
Nagui Habashi, Directeur général

Canadian Associations / Fédération québécoise des sociétés de généalogie (FQSG)

Chaudière-Appalaches
CP 1, 440, boul Vachon sud, Sainte-Marie QC G6E 3B4
Tél: 418-387-1230; Téléc: 418-387-1360
Ligne sans frais: 888-387-1230
sachap@globetrotter.net
www.alzheimerchap.qc.ca
Membre(s) du bureau directeur:
Sonia Nadeau, Directrice générale

Côte-Nord
373, av Jolliet, Sept-Iles QC G4R 2B1
Tél: 418-968-4673; Téléc: 418-962-4161
Ligne sans frais: 866-366-4673
sacotenord@globetrotter.net

Estrie
#112, 740, rue Galt ouest, Sherbrooke QC J1H 1Z3
Tél: 819-821-5127; Téléc: 819-820-8649
info@alzheimerestrie.com
www.alzheimerestrie.com
www.facebook.com/saeestrie
twitter.com/AlzheimerEstrie
Membre(s) du bureau directeur:
Caroline Giguère, Directrice générale
carolinegiguere@alzheimerestrie.com

Gaspésie/Iles-De-La-Madeleine
114C, av Grand-Pré, Bonaventure QC G0C 1E0
Tél: 418-534-1313; Téléc: 418-534-1312
www.alzheimer.ca/fr/gim
Membre(s) du bureau directeur:
Bernard Babin, Directeur général
bernard.sagim@navigue.com

Granby et Région
#3, 356, rue Principale, Granby QC J2G 2W6
Tél: 450-777-3363; Téléc: 450-777-8677
sagrinfo@videotron.ca
www.alzheimergranby.ca

Haut-Richelieu
#2, 125, rue Jacques Cartier nord, Saint-Jean-sur-Richelieu QC J3B 8C9
Tél: 450-347-5500; Téléc: 450-347-7370
info@sahr.ca
www.sahr.ca

Lanaudière
190, rue Montcalm, Joliette QC J6E 5G4
Tél: 450-759-3057; Téléc: 450-760-2633
Ligne sans frais: 877-759-3077
info@sadl.org
www.sadl.org
www.facebook.com/alzheimerlanaudiere
Membre(s) du bureau directeur:
Janie Duval, Directrice générale

Laurentides
CP 276, #100, 31, rue Principale, Sainte-Agathe-des-Monts QC J8C 3A3
Tél: 819-326-7136; Téléc: 819-326-9664
Ligne sans frais: 800-978-7881
admin@salaurentides.ca
www.alzheimerlaurentides.com
www.facebook.com/361627480558344
Membre(s) du bureau directeur:
Catherine Vaudry, Directrice générale
direction@salaurentides.ca

Laval
2525, boul René-Laennec, Laval QC H7K 0B2
Tél: 450-629-0966; Téléc: 450-975-0517
info@alzheimerlaval.org
www.alzheimerlaval.ca
Membre(s) du bureau directeur:
Lise Lalande, Directrice générale
llalande@alzheimerlaval.org

Maskoutains-Vallée des Patriotes
650, rue Girouard est, Saint-Hyacinthe QC J2S 2Y2
Tél: 450-768-6616; Téléc: 450-768-3716
info@alzheimermvp.com
www.alzheimermvp.com
www.facebook.com/alzheimer.mvp
Membre(s) du bureau directeur:
Flore Barrière, Directrice générale

Outaouais québécois
380, boul St-Raymond, Gatineau QC J9A 1V9
Tél: 819-777-4232; Téléc: 819-777-0728
Ligne sans frais: 877-777-0888
saoq@saoq.org
www.saoq.org
www.linkedin.com/company/1079874
www.facebook.com/saoq.org
twitter.com/AlzOutaouais
www.youtube.com/channel/UC1rMYxu-ZqK6FTGwHRJ4ecQ
Membre(s) du bureau directeur:
Marie-Josée Williams, Directrice
mjwilliams@saoq.org

Québec
#201, 1040, av Belvédère, Québec QC G1S 3G3
Tél: 418-527-4294; Téléc: 418-527-9966
Ligne sans frais: 866-350-4294
info@societealzheimerdequebec.com
www.societealzheimerdequebec.com
www.facebook.com/311740120513
twitter.com/AlzheimerQc
Membre(s) du bureau directeur:
Hélène Thibault, Directrice générale
hthibault@societealzheimerdequebec.com

Rive-Sud
1160, boul Nobert, Longueuil QC J4K 2P1
Tél: 450-442-3333; Téléc: 450-442-9271
info@alzheimerrivesud.ca
www.alzheimerrivesud.ca
Membre(s) du bureau directeur:
Geneviève Grégoire, Directrice générale
ggregoire@alzheimerrivesud.ca

Rouyn-Noranda
CP 336, 58, rue Monseigneur Tessier est, Rouyn-Noranda QC J9X 5C3
Tél: 819-764-3554; Téléc: 819-764-3534
sam@cablevision.qc.ca

Sagamie
1657, av du Pont nord, Alma QC G8B 5G2
Tél: 418-668-0161; Téléc: 418-668-2639
alzheimersag@bellnet.ca
www.alzheimersagamie.com
www.facebook.com/595496990477731
twitter.com/FqsaAlzh
www.youtube.com/user/FQSA1
Membre(s) du bureau directeur:
Josée Pearson, Directrice générale

Société Alzheimer Society Montréal
#410, 5165, rue Sherbrooke ouest, Montréal QC H4A 1T6
Tél: 514-369-0800; Téléc: 514-369-4103
info@alzheimermontreal.ca
www.alzheimer.ca/montreal
www.facebook.com/Montreal.Alzheimer
twitter.com/AlzMtl
www.youtube.com/user/montrealalzheimer
Membre(s) du bureau directeur:
Gérald Hubert, Directeur général
ghubert@alzheimermontreal.ca

Suroît
#101, 340, boul du Havre, Salaberry-de-Valleyfield QC J6S 1S6
Tél: 450-373-0303; Téléc: 450-373-0388
Ligne sans frais: 877-773-0303
info@alzheimersuroit.com
www.alzheimersuroit.com
Membre(s) du bureau directeur:
Ian Worthington, Président

Val d'or
734, 4e av, Val-d'Or QC J9P 1J2
Tél: 819-825-7444; Téléc: 819-825-7448
sco.alz.valdor@tlb.sympatico.ca

Fédération québécoise des sociétés de généalogie (FQSG)
CP 9454, Succ. Sainte-Foy, 1055, av du Séminaire, Québec QC G1V 4B8
Tél: 418-653-3940; Téléc: 418-653-3940
www.federationgenealogie.qc.ca
Aperçu: Dimension: moyenne; *Envergure:* provinciale; Organisme sans but lucratif; fondée en 1984
Mission: Représenter les sociétés de généalogie locales et régionales; la promotion et l'épanouissement de la généalogie au Québec et son rayonnement à l'étranger sont les buts visés
Membre de: Confédération internationale de généalogie et d'héraldique
Finances: Budget de fonctionnement annuel: $50,000-$100,000; *Fonds:* Ministère de la Culture et des Communications
Membre(s) du personnel: 2; 9 bénévole(s)
Membre: 54 sociétés; *Montant de la cotisation:* Barème; *Critères d'admissibilite:* Tout organisme de généalogie sans but lucratif dont le siège social est situé sur le territoire du Québec ou à l'extérieur; *Comités:* Portail; Attestation de compétence
Membre(s) du bureau directeur:
Pierre Soucy, Directeur général
Prix, Bourses:
• Le prix Septentrion
• Le prix Cyprien-Tanguay
• Le prix Jeunéalogie
Publications:
• FQSG [Fédération québécoise des sociétés de généalogie] Infolettre
Type: Newsletter; *Frequency:* Mensuel
Profile: Courriel mensuel décrivant les activités et nouvelles relatives à FQSG, société de généalogie et les évènements spéciaux

Fédération québécoise des sports cyclistes (FQSC) / Québec Cycling Sports Federation
4545, av Pierre-de Coubertin, Montréal QC H1V 3R2
Tél: 514-252-3071; Téléc: 514-252-3165
info@fqsc.net
www.fqsc.net
www.facebook.com/176077399110320
twitter.com/FQSC
Nom précédent: Fédération cycliste du Québec
Aperçu: Dimension: moyenne; *Envergure:* provinciale; Organisme sans but lucratif; fondée en 1971 surveillé par Cycling Canada Cyclisme
Mission: Régie et promotion des sports cyclistes au Québec
Membre de: Cycling Canada Cyclisme
Affiliation(s): Union cycliste internationale; Sports-Québec; Regroupement loisir Québec
Finances: Budget de fonctionnement annuel: $500,000-$1.5 Million
Membre(s) du personnel: 5; 57 bénévole(s)
Membre: 5 000 individus; 150 clubs; *Montant de la cotisation:* Schedule available
Activités: Temple de la Renommée du Cyclisme Québécois; mérite cycliste québécois; *Bibliothèque* Not open to public
Membre(s) du bureau directeur:
Louis Barbeau, Directeur général, 514-252-3071 Ext. 3523
lbarbeau@fqsc.net

Fédération québécoise du canot camping inc *Voir*
Fédération québécoise du canot et du kayak

Fédération québécoise du canot et du kayak (FQCK)
CP 1000, Succ. M, 4545, av Pierre-de Coubertin, Montréal QC H1V 3R2
Tél: 514-252-3001; Téléc: 514-252-3091
info@canot-kayak.qc.ca
www.canot-kayak.qc.ca
www.facebook.com/254842564559812
Nom précédent: Fédération québécoise du canot camping inc
Aperçu: Dimension: moyenne; *Envergure:* provinciale; Organisme sans but lucratif; fondée en 1976
Mission: Regrouper les organismes et individus intéressés à la pratique du canotage récréatif et du canot-camping et de promouvoir la pratique de ces activités en utilisant le canot ouvert de type amérindien autrement appelé Canot Canadien
15 bénévole(s)
Membre: 4 000; *Montant de la cotisation:* 40$; *Comités:* Cartographie; Formation
Activités: Stagiaires: Oui; *Service de conférenciers:* Oui
Membre(s) du bureau directeur:
Philippe Pelland, Directeur général
ppelland@canot-kayak.qc.ca
Jean A. Plamondon, Président
Bernard Hugonnier, Directeur, Technique
bhugonnier@canot-kayak.qc.ca
Émilie Bisson, Agent, Information et aux communications
ebisson@canot-kayak.qc.ca

La Fédération Québécoise du Cricket Inc. / The Quebec Cricket Federation Inc. (QCF)
7037, boul Acadie, Montréal QC H3N 2V5
Tél: 514-279-6628
www.quebeccricket.com
Aperçu: Dimension: petite; *Envergure:* provinciale surveillé par Cricket Canada
Membre de: Cricket Canada
Membre: Comités: School Program; Umpiring Association; Disciplinary; Senior Selection; Junior Selection; Umpiring Co-ordinator; Statisticians; Development Co-ordinators; Publication; Woman Co-ordinator
Membre(s) du bureau directeur:

Charles Pais, President, 514-824-0370
charles_pais@hotmail.com
Dalip Kirpaul, Secretary
qcf1@hotmail.com

Fédération québécoise du loisir littéraire (FQLL)
4545, av Pierre-de Coubertin, Montréal QC H1V 0B2
Tél: 514-252-3033
Ligne sans frais: 866-533-3755
fqll.ca
Nom précédent: Loisir littéraire du Québec
Aperçu: Dimension: moyenne; *Envergure:* provinciale; Organisme sans but lucratif; fondée en 1962
Mission: Offre au grand public l'accès à toutes les formes de l'expression littéraire et artistique dans un contexte de loisir, d'éducation et de perfectionnement
Finances: Budget de fonctionnement annuel: Moins de $50,000
Membre(s) du personnel: 2; 5 bénévole(s)
Membre: 700; *Montant de la cotisation:* 40$ individuel, 25$ étudiant, 35$ âge d'or, 50$ corporatif
Activités: Ateliers pour lire, dire et écrire, concours littéraire annuel, soirées de lecture; Evénements de sensibilisation: Je vous entends écrire - spectacle littéraire annuel; *Service de conférenciers:* Oui
Membre(s) du bureau directeur:
Diane Robert, Présidente
Serge Larochelle, Vice Présidente
Lisa D'amico, Secrétaire-Trésorière

Fédération québécoise du scoutisme *Voir* Association des Scouts du Canada

Fédération québécoise du sport étudiant *Voir* Réseau du sport étudiant du Québec

Fédération québécoise du théâtre amateur (FQTA)
CP 211, Succ. Saint-Élie-d'Orford, Sherbrooke QC J1R 1A1
Tél: 819-571-9358
Ligne sans frais: 877-752-2501
info@fqta.ca
www.fqta.ca
Nom précédent: Association québécoise du théâtre amateur inc.
Aperçu: Dimension: petite; *Envergure:* provinciale; Organisme sans but lucratif; fondée en 1958
Mission: Promouvoir le théâtre amateur en réunissant tous les individus et les groupes de théâtre pour contribuer à l'éducation artistique, esthétique et sociale de la population; établir un contact permanent entre les individus; fournir des occasions d'échange, de travaux, de recherches, de méthodes, de matériel et d'information ayant trait au théâtre
Membre de: Association Internationale du Théâtre Amateur; Conseil québécois du loisir; Regroupement Loisir Québec; Théâtre Canada
Affiliation(s): Académie théâtrale l'Envol de Laval; AQAD; Art Neuf; Cabotins de Thetford Mines; Café-Théâtre de Chambly; Catherine Chevrot; CEAD - Centre des auteurs dramatiques; Frasqc Productions; Collège Notre-Dame-de-Lourdes; Commission Scolaire du Lac-Témiscamingue; Compagnie de théâtre Sauvageau; Corporation Les Amis de la musique de Richmond et Festival de Richmond; CQL - Conseil Québécois du loisir; Double Défi; École Nationale de théâtre du Canada; Festival de Richmond & Les Amis de la Musique de Richmond; Festival de théâtre amateur Esprit-Saint; Festival des Molières; Groupe de la Veillée
Membre: 86; *Critères d'admissibilite:* Troupe et individus
Activités: Concours création-production-théâtre; festival international de théâtre amateur; *Evénements de sensibilisation:* Concours Création-Production-Théâtre, juin; *Bibliothèque:* Bibliothèque publique
Membre(s) du bureau directeur:
Yoland Roy, Directeur général

Fédération québécoise pour le saumon atlantique (FQSA)
42B, rue Racine, Québec QC G2B 1C6
Tél: 418-847-9191; *Téléc:* 418-847-9279
Ligne sans frais: 888-847-9191
secretariat@saumon-fqsa.qc.ca
fqsa.ca
www.facebook.com/fqsa.saumon
twitter.com/SaumonFQSA
instagram.com/fqsa_saumon
Aperçu: Dimension: moyenne; *Envergure:* provinciale; fondée en 1984 surveillé par Atlantic Salmon Federation
Mission: Organisme à but non lucratif dont la raison d'être est d'unir et de représenter les intérêts de l'ensemble des saumoniers du Québec
Membre: 1 000; *Montant de la cotisation:* 40$
Activités: Service de conférenciers: Oui
Membre(s) du bureau directeur:
Frédéric Raymond, Directeur général
fraymond@fqsa.ca

La fédération sioniste canadienne *See* Canadian Zionist Federation

Fédération ski nautique et planche Québec
CP 1000, Succ. M, 4545, av Pierre-de Coubertin, Montréal QC H1V 3R2
Tél: 514-252-3092; *Téléc:* 514-252-3186
info@skinautiqueetplanchequebec.qc.ca
www.skinautiqueetplanchequebec.qc.ca
Aperçu: Dimension: petite; *Envergure:* provinciale
Membre: 600; *Montant de la cotisation:* 45$ individuelle; 70$ familiale
Membre(s) du bureau directeur:
Louis Simard, Président

Fédération sportive de ringuette du Québec
4545, av Pierre-de Coubertin, Montréal QC H1V 3R2
Tél: 514-252-3085; *Téléc:* 514-254-1069
ringuette@ringuette-quebec.qc.ca
www.ringuette-quebec.qc.ca
www.facebook.com/RinguetteQuebec-139856822762458
twitter.com/ringuetteqc
www.youtube.com/channel/UChlZmg35-zhVgGBkgru8k7g
Aperçu: Dimension: petite; *Envergure:* provinciale; fondée en 1973
Mission: Promouvoir le sport de la ringuette au Québec
Membre(s) du personnel: 3
Membre(s) du bureau directeur:
Louise Morin, Contact

Fédération vietnamienne du Canada *See* Vietnamese Canadian Federation

Fédérations de l'UPA de Lévis Bellechasse, Rive Nord, Lotbinière-Mégantic
5185, rue Rideau, Québec QC G2E 5H5
Tél: 418-872-0770; *Téléc:* 418-872-3386
Aperçu: Dimension: petite; *Envergure:* locale; fondée en 1924
Mission: Défendre l'intérêt des membres auprès des corps publics; négociation collective pour obtenir de meilleurs prix pour les produits; gestion d'organismes de producteurs
Affiliation(s): Confédération de l'U.P.A.
Finances: Budget de fonctionnement annuel: $3 Million-$5 Million
Membre(s) du personnel: 64
Membre: 6 500; *Montant de la cotisation:* 281,81$; *Critères d'admissibilite:* Productrice ou producteur agricole
Activités: Listes de destinataires: Oui
Membre(s) du bureau directeur:
Luce Bisson, Présidente

Feed Nova Scotia (FNS)
213 Bedford Hwy., Halifax NS B3M 2J9
Tel: 902-457-1900; *Fax:* 902-457-4500
communications@feednovascotia.ca
www.feednovascotia.ca
www.facebook.com/feednovascotia
twitter.com/feednovascotia
www.youtube.com/user/feednovascotia
Also Known As: Metro Food Bank Society-Nova Scotia
Previous Name: Metro Food Bank Society
Overview: A small provincial charitable organization founded in 1984
Mission: To help feed the hungry by collecting & distributing food.
Member of: Canadian Association of Food Banks
Membership: 150+; *Member Profile:* Food banks; shelters; soup kitchens
Activities: Client support services; food distribution; job training for the food industry; *Awareness Events:* Hunger Awareness Week, June; *Internships:* Yes; *Speaker Service:* Yes; *Library:* by appointment
Chief Officer(s):
Paul Kidston, Chair
Dianne Swinemar, Executive Director
dswinemar@feednovascotia.ca

Publications:
• Foodchain
Type: Newsletter; *Frequency:* Monthly

FEESA - An Environmental Education Society *See* Inside Education

Fellowship of Evangelical Baptist Churches
PO Box 457, 351 Elizabeth St., Guelph ON N1H 6K9
Tel: 519-821-4830; *Fax:* 519-821-9829
www.fellowship.ca
www.facebook.com/FellowshipNatl
twitter.com/FellowshipNatl
Also Known As: The Fellowship
Overview: A medium-sized national organization
Mission: To glorify God & to proclaim the good news of Jesus Christ, evangelizing the current generation & producing healthy, growing churches in Canada & around the world
Member of: The Evangelical Fellowship of Canada
Affiliation(s): Association d'églises baptistes évangéliques au québec
Finances: *Annual Operating Budget:* Greater than $5 Million
Staff Member(s): 16
Membership: 500+ churches
Activities: *Library:* Fellowship of Evangelical Baptist Churches Archives
Chief Officer(s):
Steven Jones, President, 519-821-4830 Ext. 231
sjones@fellowship.ca

FEB Central
175 Holiday Inn Dr., Cambridge ON N3C 3T2
Tel: 519-654-9555; *Fax:* 519-654-9991
admin@febcentral.ca
www.febcentral.ca
www.facebook.com/febcentral
Chief Officer(s):
Ed F. Fontaine, Chair, 905-887-5651
edfontaine@springvale.ca
Bob Flemming, Regional Director, 519-591-7756
bob@febcentral.ca

Fellowship Atlantic
39 Olive Ave., Bedford NS B4B 1C7
Tel: 902-482-4132; *Fax:* 902-482-4669
fellowshipatlantic@gmail.com
www.fellowshipatlantic.com
Chief Officer(s):
Glenn Goode, Regional Director
gagoode@gmail.com
• Fellowship Atlantic Newsletter
Type: Newsletter; *Frequency:* Weekly

Fellowship Pacific
PO Box 1107, 9111 Church St., Fort Langley BC V1M 2S4
Tel: 778-298-8887; *Fax:* 778-298-4594
fellowship@shaw.ca
www.bcfellowship.ca
Chief Officer(s):
Colin Van der Vuur, Church Planting Director
colin.fellowship@shaw.ca

Fellowship Prairies
Taylor College Seminary, PO Box 168, 11525 - 23 Ave., Benke Hall, #207-208, Edmonton AB T6J 4T3
Tel: 780-451-4878; *Fax:* 780-436-4871
www.fellowshipprairies.ca

Feminine Association for Education & Social Action *Voir* Association féminine d'éducation et d'action sociale

Feminist Alliance for International Action (FAFIA) / Alliance féministe pour l'action internationale (AFAI)
251 Bank St., 2nd Fl., Ottawa ON K1P 1X3
Tel: 613-232-9505
communications@fafia-afai.org
www.fafia-afai.org
www.facebook.com/fafia.afai
twitter.com/FAFIAAFAI
Overview: A medium-sized national organization
Mission: To advocate for women's rights policies; To address women's issues, including gender equality, violence, & economic & social rights; To support women
Activities: Providing training & resources
Chief Officer(s):
Jackie Neapole

Femmes autochtones du Québec inc. (FAQ) / Québec Native Women Inc.
CP 1989, Kahnawake QC J0L 1B0

Tél: 450-632-0088; *Téléc:* 450-632-9280
info@faq-qnw.org
www.faq-qnw.org
www.facebook.com/FAQQNW
twitter.com/FAQQNW
vimeo.com/user14258370
Aperçu: *Dimension:* moyenne; *Envergure:* provinciale; Organisme sans but lucratif; fondée en 1974 surveillé par Native Women's Association of Canada
Mission: Appuyer les efforts des femmes autochtones pour l'amélioration de leurs conditions de vie par la promotion de la non-violence, de la justice et de l'égalité des droits et de les soutenir dans leur engagement au sein de leur communauté
Activités:; *Bibliothèque:* Centre de Documentation; Bibliothèque publique rendez-vous
Membre(s) du bureau directeur:
Viviane Michel, Présidente

Les femmes sur les marchés financiers *See* Women in Capital Markets

Fencing - Escrime New Brunswick (FENB)
47 Sloat St., Hanwell NB E3C 1M4
fencingnb@gmail.com
www.fencingnb.ca
Previous Name: New Brunswick Fencing Association
Overview: A small provincial organization overseen by Canadian Fencing Federation
Mission: To promote & develop the sport of fencing in New Brunswick
Member of: Canadian Fencing Federation; Sport New Brunswick
Membership: *Fees:* $20 associate; $25 first-time member; $60 fencing member
Chief Officer(s):
Melodie Piercey, Contact

Fencing Association of Nova Scotia (FANS) / Association d'escrime de la Nouvelle-Écosse
c/o Sport Nova Scotia, 5516 Spring Garden Rd., 4th Fl., Halifax NS B3J 3G6
Fax: 902-425-5606
info@nsfencing.ca
www.nsfencing.ca
twitter.com/FencingNS
Overview: A small provincial organization overseen by Canadian Fencing Federation
Mission: To develop & promote the sport of fencing in Nova Scotia
Member of: Canadian Fencing Federation
Membership: *Member Profile:* National fencing competitors; Provincial fencing competitors; Recreational fencers; Persons who wish to promote fencing
Activities: Providing information about tournaments
Chief Officer(s):
Sean Brillant, Contact

Fenelon Falls & District Chamber of Commerce
PO Box 28, 15 Oak St., Fenelon Falls ON K0M 1N0
Tel: 705-887-3409; *Fax:* 705-887-6912
info@fenelonfallschamber.com
www.fenelonfallschamber.com
www.facebook.com/FenelonFallsDistrictChamberofCommerce
twitter.com/ffdchamber
www.youtube.com/channel/UCl3SxaMNk5V0hzAMYFuDIXg
Previous Name: Fenelon Falls North Kawartha District Chamber of Commerce
Overview: A small local organization founded in 1956
Mission: To promote economic confidence for the business community; To attract people to live & play in the area on a year-round basis by providing products, programs, events, & services for the benefit of members, visitors & residents
Member of: Ontario Chamber of Commerce
Finances: *Funding Sources:* Membership dues; home show
Staff Member(s): 2
Membership: *Fees:* $56.50 associate; $165 regular; *Committees:* Financial; Communication/Marketing; IT/Website; Country Living Show; Special Events; Santa Day; Waterfront Improvement; Administrative Staff; Fenelon Forward; New Member Welcome; Village Improvement; Tourism
Chief Officer(s):
Grant Allman, President

Fenelon Falls North Kawartha District Chamber of Commerce *See* Fenelon Falls & District Chamber of Commerce

Fenelon Falls Stamp Club
Fenelon Falls ON
Tel: 705-324-7577
Overview: A small local organization founded in 1985
Mission: To promote the study and interest in philately in Fenelon Falls.
Member of: Royal Philatelic Society of Canada
Activities: Meetings 2nd Monday, every month; *Speaker Service:* Yes
Chief Officer(s):
Lloyd McEwan, President
lmccewan@sympatico.ca

Fenestration Association of BC (FEN-BC)
#101, 20351 Duncan Way, Langley BC V3A 7N3
Tel: 778-571-0245; *Fax:* 866-253-9979
info@fen-bc.org
www.fen-bc.org
www.facebook.com/561853500522221
twitter.com/fenbc
www.youtube.com/user/FenBC?feature=mhee
Merged from: Glazing Contractors Association of BC (GCABC); Window and Door Manufacturers Association of BC
Overview: A medium-sized provincial organization
Mission: A nonprofit trade association representing the interests of businesses engaged in the fenestration industry in BC.
Membership: *Member Profile:* Western Canadian companies involved with the fenestration industry.; *Committees:* Marketing; Membership; Technical
Chief Officer(s):
Zana Gordon, Executive Director, 604-855-0245
zgordon@fen-bc.org
Meetings/Conferences:
• Fenestration Association of BC Technical Conference 2018, February, 2018, Surrey, BC
Scope: Provincial
Publications:
• Fenestration West Magazine
Type: Magazine; *Frequency:* Quarterly

Fenestration Canada
#1208, 130 Albert St., Ottawa ON K1P 5G4
Tel: 613-235-5511; *Fax:* 613-235-4664
info@fenestrationcanada.ca
www.fenestrationcanada.ca
Previous Name: Canadian Window & Door Manufacturers Association
Overview: A medium-sized national organization founded in 1967
Mission: To represents its members in all aspects of the window & door manufacturing industry, including formulating & promoting high standards of quality in manufacturing, design, marketing, distribution, sales, & application of all types of window & door products
Membership: 150+; *Fees:* Schedule available; *Member Profile:* Manufacturers of all types & classes of window & door products; Suppliers of raw materials & processing machinery; Research & testing facilities; *Committees:* Win-Door Show; Membership & Marketing; Meetings; Technical; Government Relations; Education
Activities: Representing industry views to the federal & provincial governments & crown corporations; Scheduling meetings, activities, plant tours, & discussions encouraging a healthy exchange of ideas on product & marketing strategies; Providing information on the industry, government regulations, building codes, & standards; Distributing newsletters, special bulletins & memos to keep members aware of the latest developments facing the industry & the association
Chief Officer(s):
Yvan Banman, President
yhoule@portesetfenetrepresident.com
Eva Ryterband, Treasurer
eva@screenco.ca
Meetings/Conferences:
• Fenestration Canada 2018 Annual General Meeting, 2018
Scope: National
Description: A business meeting to keep current with industry trends & opportunities
• Win-Door North America 2018 (an event owned & produced by Fenestration Canada), December, 2018, Québec City Convention Centre, Québec, QC
Scope: International
Description: Meetings, demonstrations, & seminars, plus an opportunity for suppliers to show their products & services to manufacturers & fabricators from across Canada, the United States, & international destinations

Fernie & District Arts Council (FDAC)
PO Box 1453, 601 - 1 Ave., Fernie BC V0B 1M0
Tel: 250-423-4842; *Fax:* 250-423-4842
info@theartsstation.com
www.theartsstation.com
www.facebook.com/110980688947549
twitter.com/artsstation
vimeo.com/ferniearts
Also Known As: The Arts Station
Overview: A small local charitable organization founded in 1973
Mission: To encourage appreciation of the arts & artistic expression throughout community
Member of: Arts BC; BC Arts Council; BC Touring Council; Heritage BC
Affiliation(s): Cultural Network of the Rockies; Columbia Kootenay Cultural Alliance
Finances: *Annual Operating Budget:* $100,000-$250,000; *Funding Sources:* Municipal, provincial & federal government; Private
Staff Member(s): 2; 100 volunteer(s)
Membership: 300+; *Fees:* $35 adult; $15 youth; $20 Senior; *Member Profile:* Artists; crafts people; businesses; *Committees:* Gallery; Concert; Garden; Film; Volunteer; Human Resources; Strategic Planning; Programming
Activities: Organizing creative workshops, concerts, plays, children's art camps, & film festivals; Offering rental spaces available; *Internships:* Yes
Chief Officer(s):
Erin Teeple, Administrator

Fernie & District Historical Society
PO Box 1527, Fernie BC V0B 1M0
Tel: 250-423-7016
www.ferniemuseum.com
Overview: A small local organization founded in 1964
Mission: To preserve & present the history of Fernie by collecting & displaying photographs, artifacts & documents relating to the town's development.
Membership: *Fees:* $10 individual; $15 family
Publications:
• Fernie, A Celebration of 100 Years
Type: book; *Price:* $31

Fernie Chamber of Commerce
102 Hwy. #3, Fernie BC V0B 1M5
Tel: 250-423-6868; *Fax:* 250-423-3811
Toll-Free: 877-433-7643
members@ferniechamber.com
www.ferniechamber.com
www.facebook.com/ferniechamberofcommerce
twitter.com/FernieChamber
Overview: A small local organization founded in 1902
Mission: To promote & improve the economy & the social quality of life in Fernie & area
Member of: Canadian Chamber of Commerce; BC Chamber of Commerce
Affiliation(s): Economic Development Association of BC
Finances: *Funding Sources:* Membership dues; fee-for-service contracts
Staff Member(s): 2
Membership: *Fees:* Schedule available
Activities: Visitor information centre; economic development centre; commercial info; marketing; tourism promotions; events coordination; *Library:* Business Information Centre; Open to public
Chief Officer(s):
Sheila Byers, President
Patty Vadnais, Executive Director

Fertilizer Canada
#907, 350 Sparks St., Ottawa ON K1R 7S8
Tel: 613-230-2600; *Fax:* 613-230-5142
info@fertilizercanada.ca
www.fertilizercanada.ca
www.linkedin.com/company/canadian-fertilizer-institute
twitter.com/FertilizerCA
Previous Name: Canadian Fertilizer Institute
Overview: A medium-sized national organization
Mission: To represent manufacturers, wholesale, & retail distributors of nitrogen, phosphate, & potash fertilizers
Membership: 70 organizations
Chief Officer(s):
Garth Whyte, President & CEO, 613-786-3030
gwhyte@fertilizercanada.ca

Clyde Graham, Senior Vice-President, 613-786-3033
cgraham@fertilizercanada.ca
Cassandra Cotton, Director, Sustainability, 613-786-3029
ccotton@fertilizercanada.ca
Catherine King, Director, Public Outreach, 613-786-3026
cking@fertilizercanada.ca
Emily Pearce Rayner, Director, Government Relations, 613-786-3034
epearce@fertilizercanada.ca
Elizabeth Smith, Manager, Communications, 613-786-3039
esmith@fertilizercanada.ca
Amanda Pach, Manager, Environment & Safety, 613-786-3040
apach@fertilizercanada.ca
Meetings/Conferences:
• Fertilizer Canada 2018 Annual Conference, August, 2018, Fairmont Le Château Frontenac, Québec, QC
Scope: National

Fertilizer Safety & Security Council (FSSC) / Conseil de la sécurité en fertilisation (CSF)
#907, 350 Sparks St., Ottawa ON K1N 7S8
Tel: 613-230-2600
info@fssc.ca
www.fssc.ca
Overview: A small national organization founded in 2003
Mission: To promote the safe and secure manufacturing, handling, storage, transportation and application of commercial fertilizers thereby protecting employees, transportation workers, first responders, farmers and the general public from risk due to accidental release, environmental emergency, or criminal misuse of fertilizer products.
Chief Officer(s):
Giulia Brutesco, Director, Scientific & Regulatory Affairs
gbrutesco@cfi.ca

Festival Chorus of Calgary
c/o Arts Commons, 205 - 8 Ave. SE, Calgary AB T2G 0K9
Tel: 403-294-7400
info@thefestivalchorus.com
www.thefestivalchorus.com
www.facebook.com/182865794560
Overview: A small local charitable organization founded in 1959
Mission: To present choral music & concert presentations for the community
Finances: *Funding Sources:* Private & corporate donations; ticket sales; membership fees; government grants
Membership: 80
Activities: *Internships:* Yes
Chief Officer(s):
Mel Kirby, Artistic Director
artisticdirector@thefestivalchorus.com

Festival d'été de Québec / Québec City Summer Festival
#150, 683, rue Saint-Joseph est, Québec QC G1K 3C1
Tél: 418-523-4540; *Téléc:* 418-523-0194
Ligne sans frais: 888-992-5200
infofestival@infofestival.com
www.infofestival.com
www.facebook.com/FestivaldetedeQuebec
twitter.com/FestivalEteQc
www.youtube.com/user/infofestival;
www.flickr.com/photos/infofestival
Aperçu: *Dimension:* petite; *Envergure:* locale; fondée en 1968
Membre(s) du bureau directeur:
Claude Doré, Directeur général par interim
Prix, Bourses:
• Prix Miroir

Festival de concours du Québec *See* Québec Competitive Festival of Music

Festivals & Events Ontario (FEO)
#301, 5 Graham St., Woodstock ON N4S 6J5
Tel: 519-537-2226; *Fax:* 519-537-2226
info@festivalsandeventsontario.ca
www.festivalsandeventsontario.ca
www.facebook.com/FestivalsandEventsOntario
twitter.com/FEOntario
Overview: A small provincial organization founded in 1987
Mission: Festivals & Events Ontario (FEO) is an association devoted to the growth and stability of the festival and event industry in Ontario. FEO provides festival and event organizers across the province with a networking forum offering professional development opportunities and resources aimed to encourage professionalism and excellence in the delivery of festivals and special events.

Staff Member(s): 4
Chief Officer(s):
Debbie Mann, Interim Executive Director
debbie@festivalsandeventsontario.ca
Martha Cookson, Administrative Coordinator
martha@festivalsandeventsontario.ca
Meetings/Conferences:
• Festivals & Events Ontario 2018 Conference, February, 2018, Hamilton Convention Centre, Hamilton, ON
Scope: Provincial
Contact Information: www.feo2018.com

Festivals et Événements Québec (FEQ)
4545, av Pierre-de Coubertin, Montréal QC H1V 0B2
Tél: 514-252-3037; *Téléc:* 514-254-1617
Ligne sans frais: 800-361-7688
info@satqfeq.com
www.attractionsevenements.com
twitter.com/SATQFEQ
Également appelé: Société des fêtes et festivals du Québec
Aperçu: *Dimension:* moyenne; *Envergure:* provinciale; fondée en 1976
Mission: Regrouper les fêtes, festivals et événements, de les promouvoir et de leur offrir des services qui favorisent leur développement
Membre de: Regroupement Loisir Québec
Affiliation(s): International Festivals Association
Finances: *Budget de fonctionnement annuel:* $500,000-$1.5 Million
Membre(s) du personnel: 28; 15 bénévole(s)
Membre: 248; *Montant de la cotisation:* 305-950
Activités: *Listes de destinataires:* Oui
Membre(s) du bureau directeur:
Pierre-Paul Leduc, Directeur général
pierre-paul.leduc@satqfeq.com
Luc Martineau, Directeur, Marketing
luc.martineau@satqfeq.com
Sylvain Martineau, Directeur-adjoint, Marketing et des ventes
sylvain.martineau@satqfeq.com
Sylvie Théberge, Directrice générale adjointe
sylvie.theberge@satqfeq.com
Mélanie Sigouin, Agente aux communications
msigouin@satqfeq.com

Fibromyalgia Association of Saskatchewan (FMAS)
PO Box 7525, Saskatoon SK S7K 4L4
Tel: 306-343-3627
Overview: A small provincial charitable organization founded in 1994
Mission: To improve the quality of life for those directly or indirectly affected by fibromyalgia syndrome (FMS) & chronic fatigue syndrome (CFS).
Affiliation(s): FM-CFS Canada
Activities: Annual fall seminar/conference; information sharing; public awareness; self-help groups

Fibromyalgia Support Group of Winnipeg, Inc.
c/o SMD Clearinghouse, 825 Sherbrook St., Winnipeg MB R3A 1M5
Tel: 204-975-3037
info@fmswinnipeg.com
www.fmswinnipeg.com
Also Known As: Fibromyalgia Syndrome Winnipeg
Overview: A small local charitable organization founded in 1992
Mission: To sponsor & promote educational services to all persons with fibromyalgia, as well as families, friends, health care professionals & the general public; To promote & sponsor scientific & clinical research relating to causes, treatments & cure of fibromyalgia
Member of: SMD Self-Help Clearinghouse
Finances: *Annual Operating Budget:* Less than $50,000
Staff Member(s): 6; 8 volunteer(s)
Membership: 120; *Fees:* $20 regular; $30 professional; *Member Profile:* People with fibromyalgia; *Committees:* Membership; Finance; Newsletter; Library; Education Course; Public Relations; Phoning
Activities: Monthly meetings; educational program; neighbourhood groups; *Library:* Lending Library; Not open to public

Fibrose Kystique Canada *See* Cystic Fibrosis Canada

Fibrose kystique Québec (FKQ) / Cystic Fibrosis Québec (CFQ)
#505, 625, av du Président-Kennedy, Montréal QC H3A 1K2
Tél: 514-877-6161; *Téléc:* 514-877-6116
Ligne sans frais: 800-363-7711

www.fibrosekystique.ca/quebec
www.facebook.com/FKQuebec
twitter.com/FKQuebec
plus.google.com/106908476349956061911
Nom précédent: Association québécoise de la fibrose kystique (AQFK)
Aperçu: *Dimension:* moyenne; *Envergure:* provinciale; Organisme sans but lucratif; fondée en 1981
Mission: Sensibiliser la population sur la fibrose kystique; amasser des fonds pour la recherche médicale; améliorer la qualité de vie des personnes atteintes de FK; découvrir un remède ou un moyen de contrôler la fibrose kystique
Membre de: Cystic Fibrosis Canada
Finances: *Budget de fonctionnement annuel:* $3 Million-$5 Million
Membre(s) du personnel: 9; 1000 bénévole(s)
Activités: Grand bal de la FK; spectacle bénéfice; tirage provincial; recueillir des fonds servant à financer un réseau de centres de recherche intensive et de thérapie à travers le Québec, où les personnes atteintes de fibrose kystique peuvent recevoir des soins appropriés; *Événements de sensibilisation:* Marchethon de Montréal, mai; Mois de la fibrose kystique, mai; *Stagiaires:* Oui; *Bibliothèque* Not open to public
Membre(s) du bureau directeur:
Neil Beaudette, Directeur général par intérim
nbeaudette@fkq.ca

Section Charlevoix-ouest
Baie-Saint-Paul QC
Membre(s) du bureau directeur:
Sylvian Lajoie, Président
lajoie300@hotmail.com

Section Côte-Nord
Baie-Comeau QC
Membre(s) du bureau directeur:
Sophie Girard, Présidente
pizzaroyale@globetrotter.net

Section Estrie
Sherbrooke QC
Membre(s) du bureau directeur:
Michael Roy, Président
michel.roy488@gmail.com

Section La Malbaie
La Malbaie QC
Membre(s) du bureau directeur:
Girard Dorothée, Présidente
dorothee.aurele@sympatico.ca

Section Mauricie/Centre-du-Québec
Trois-Rivières QC
Membre(s) du bureau directeur:
Lisette Tremblay, Présidente
sourislisette@hotmail.com

Section Montréal
Montréal QC
Membre(s) du bureau directeur:
Nicole Laberge, Présidente
labergenicole@gmail.com

Section Outaouais
Gatineau QC
Membre(s) du bureau directeur:
Mario Gagnon, Président
1mariogagnon@gmail.com

Section Québec
#227, 2750, ch Sainte-Foy, Québec QC G1V 1V6
Tél: 418-653-2086
Ligne sans frais: 877-653-2086
info@fkquebec.com
www.fkquebec.com
Membre(s) du bureau directeur:
Terry Hall, Président
terry.hall@hotmail.com

Section Saguenay
Chicoutimi QC
Membre(s) du bureau directeur:
Andrée-Anne Guay, Présidente
andree-anne.guay@csjonquiere.qc.ca

Fiducie du patrimoine ontarien *See* Ontario Heritage Trust

Fiducie foncière Vallée de Ruiter *See* Ruiter Valley Land Trust

Fiducie Nationale du Canada *See* National Trust for Canada

Field Botanists of Ontario (FBO)
c/o W.D. McIlveen, RR#1, Acton ON L7J 2L7
www.trentu.ca/fbo

Canadian Associations / Field Hockey Alberta (FHA)

Overview: A small provincial organization founded in 1983
Mission: To increase documentation of the flora of Ontario; To encourage interest in botany & conservation in the province of Ontario
Membership: *Fees:* $20 individuals; $25 families; $350 life memberships; *Member Profile:* Amateur & professional botanists of all ages
Activities: Offering field trips; Providing education & workshops; Offering botanical expertise; Encouraging the exchange of botanical information; Facilitating networking opportunities
Chief Officer(s):
Mike McMurtry, President
michael.mcmurtry@sympatico.ca
Bill Westerhof, Vice-President
dwesterhof@beaconenviro.com
Nancy Falkenberg, Secretary
falken@rogers.ca
Bill Draper, Treasurer
william.draper@sympatico.ca
Bill McIlveen, Chair, Membership
wmcilveen@sympatico.ca
Meetings/Conferences:
• Field Botanists of Ontario Annual General Meeting, 2018, ON
Scope: Provincial
Publications:
• Field Botanists of Ontario Newsletter
Type: Newsletter; *Frequency:* Quarterly; *Editor:* Cheryl Hendrickson
Profile: Articles, meeting information, & field trip reports

Field Hockey Alberta (FHA)
#1, 2135 Westmount Rd. NW, Calgary AB T2N 3N3
Tel: 403-670-0014; *Fax:* 403-670-0018
Toll-Free: 888-670-0018
info@fieldhockey.ab.ca
www.fieldhockey.ab.ca
www.facebook.com/105274359520461
Merged from: Alberta Field Hockey Association
Overview: A small provincial charitable organization founded in 1974 overseen by Field Hockey Canada
Mission: To develop field hockey for all in Alberta; To provide & facilitate provincial field hockey teams
Member of: Field Hockey Canada
Staff Member(s): 2; 50 volunteer(s)
Membership: 800; *Fees:* Schedule available; *Committees:* High Performance; Umpiring; South/North Alberta
Activities: School programs, clinics, festivals, equipment rentals; *Speaker Service:* Yes; *Library:* Open to public by appointment
Chief Officer(s):
Burgundy Biletski, Executive Director
burgundy@fieldhockey.ab.ca

Field Hockey BC (FHBC) / Hockey sur gazon C-B
#202, 210 West Broadway, Vancouver BC V5Y 3W2
Tel: 604-737-3046; *Fax:* 604-737-6488
info@fieldhockeybc.com
www.fieldhockeybc.com
www.facebook.com/fieldhockeybc
twitter.com/fieldhockeybc
www.youtube.com/user/fieldhockeybc
Merged from: British Columbia Field Hockey Association; British Columbia Women's Field Hockey Federation
Overview: A medium-sized provincial organization founded in 1992 overseen by Field Hockey Canada
Mission: To foster, promote & encourage the development & organization of field hockey in BC at all levels
Member of: Field Hockey Canada
Finances: *Annual Operating Budget:* $500,000-$1.5 Million; *Funding Sources:* Provincial government; membership fees
Staff Member(s): 5
Membership: 7,275; *Fees:* Schedule available; *Committees:* High Performance; Finance
Chief Officer(s):
Mark Saunders, Executive Director, 604-737-3045
mark@fieldhockeybc.com
Awards:
• Senior Female Player of the Year Award
• Senior Male Player of the Year Award
• Junior Female Player of the Year Award
Awarded in two categories: Under 15 & Under 18.
• Junior Male Player of the Year Award
Awarded in two categories: Under 15 & Under 18.
• Barbara Schrodt Award
Awarded in two categories: Under 15 & Under 18.
• Contribution to Men's Field Hockey Award
Awarded in two categories: Under 15 & Under 18.
• Coach of the Year Award
Awarded in two categories: Under 15 & Under 18.
• Umpire of the Year Award
Awarded in two categories: Under 15 & Under 18.
Publications:
• CornerShot [a publication of Field Hockey BC]
Type: Newsletter
Profile: News & updates for members

Field Hockey Canada (FHC) / Hockey sur gazon Canada
3800 Wesbrook Mall, Vancouver BC V6S 2L9
www.fieldhockey.ca
www.facebook.com/FHCanada
twitter.com/FieldHockeyCan
www.youtube.com/user/hockeysurgazoncanada
Previous Name: Canadian Field Hockey Association
Overview: A medium-sized national charitable organization founded in 1991
Mission: To promote the development & growth of field hockey in Canada; To provide coaching, training, & competitive opportunities to prepare Canada's national teams
Member of: International Hockey Federation (FIH); Pan American Hockey Federation (PAHF)
Finances: *Funding Sources:* Sponsorships; Donations
Membership: 7 provincial associations; *Fees:* $20; *Member Profile:* Members of Field Hockey Canada member clubs
Activities: Hosting world class field hockey events in Canada; Seeking partnerships with corporations; Offering technical programs
Chief Officer(s):
Jeff Sauvé, Chief Executive Officer
jsauve@fieldhockey.ca
Kevin Underhill, Manager, Communications
kunderhill@fieldhockey.ca

Field Hockey Manitoba (FHM)
MB
info@fieldhockeymb.org
www.fieldhockeymb.org
www.facebook.com/fieldhockey.manitoba
Overview: A small provincial organization overseen by Field Hockey Canada
Mission: The Association fosters growth & development of field hockey & indoor hockey in Manitoba.
Member of: Field Hockey Canada
Staff Member(s): 2
Membership: 100; *Fees:* Schedule available

Field Hockey Nova Scotia
5516 Spring Garden Rd., 4th Fl., Halifax NS B3J 1G6
Tel: 902-425-5450
info@fieldhockey.ns.ca
www.fieldhockey.ns.ca
Overview: A small provincial organization founded in 1971 overseen by Field Hockey Canada
Mission: The Association promotes the sport of field hockey for both men & women in the province of Nova Scotia.
Member of: Field Hockey Canada
Chief Officer(s):
Sharon Rajaraman, President
president@fieldhockey.ns.ca
Patrick Thompson, Administrative Coordinator
Awards:
• Nancy Tokaryk Memorial Trust Fund
Eligibility: A female student who participates in women's field hockey, is active in the sports community through volunteerism, maintains at least a 3.0 GPA & has been formally accepted to a program at a post-secondary institution *Deadline:* May 3; *Amount:* $1000 *Contact:* Sharon Rajaraman, President, 809 McLean St., Halifax, NS B3H 2T9
Publications:
• The Scoop [a publication of Field Hockey Nova Scotia]
Type: Newsletter; *Frequency:* Irregular
Profile: News & updates for members

Field Hockey Ontario (FHO)
PO Box 80030, Stn. Appleby, Burlington ON L7L 6B1
Tel: 905-492-1680
Other Communication: Development, E-mail: development@fieldhockeyontario.com
info@fieldhockeyontario.com
www.fieldhockeyontario.com
www.facebook.com/FieldHockeyOntario
twitter.com/FieldHockeyOnt
Merged from: Ontario Field Hockey Association; Women's Field Hockey Association
Overview: A medium-sized provincial organization founded in 1985 overseen by Field Hockey Canada
Mission: To promote the sport of field hockey for both men & women in the province of Ontario.
Member of: Field Hockey Canada
Finances: *Annual Operating Budget:* $100,000-$250,000; *Funding Sources:* Sponsorship; government grants; membership fees
Staff Member(s): 3; 180 volunteer(s)
Membership: 6,000; *Fees:* Schedule available
Activities: *Internships:* Yes
Chief Officer(s):
Ramandeep Brar, President
ramandeep.brar@fieldhockeyontario.com
Joseph Fernando, Coordinator, High Performance/Athlete & Coach Development
joseph.fernando@fieldhockeyontario.com
Bimal Jhass, Coordinator, Technical
bimal.jhass@fieldhockeyontario.com

Fife House
490 Sherburne St., 2nd Fl., Toronto ON M4X 1K9
Tel: 416-205-9888; *Fax:* 416-205-9919
www.fifehouse.org
www.facebook.com/FifeHouse
twitter.com/FifeHouse
Overview: A medium-sized local charitable organization founded in 1988 overseen by Canadian AIDS Society
Mission: To provide secure, affordable, supportive housing & support services to people living with HIV/AIDS
Member of: Ontario AIDS Network; Ontario Non-Profit Housing Association
Finances: *Annual Operating Budget:* $3 Million-$5 Million; *Funding Sources:* Federal, provincial & municipal government; Toronto Central Local Health Integration Network; Ontario HIV Treatment Network
Chief Officer(s):
Keith Hambly, Executive Director
khambly@fifehouse.org

15th Field Artillery Regiment Museum & Archives Society
Bessborough Armoury, 2025 West 11th Ave., Vancouver BC V6J 2C7
Tel: 604-666-4370; *Fax:* 604-666-4083
Overview: A small local charitable organization founded in 1983
Mission: To collect & preserve artifacts, photos, & documents related to artillery units in the Greater Vancouver region; To restore World War II Point Grey Battery
Member of: Canadian Museums Association; BC Museums Association; Organization of Military Museums of Canada
Finances: *Funding Sources:* Public donations; Government grants
Activities: *Library:* 15th Field Regiment Archives; Open to public by appointment

50 & Piu Enasco
#103, 3939 Hastings St., Burnaby BC V5C 2H8
Tel: 604-294-2023; *Fax:* 604-294-2118
Toll-Free: 800-269-0065
canada1@enasco.it
www.50epiucanadaenasco.com
Previous Name: Enasco - Institute of Social Service for Workers of Italian Origin
Overview: A small national organization founded in 1967
Mission: ENASCO is an agency assisting people free of charge in applying to receive social security benefits from Italy, Canada & other countries.
Chief Officer(s):
Leonara Perizzolo, Contact
l.perizzolo@enasco.it
Hamilton Office
#12, 1001 Rymal Rd. East, Hamilton ON L8W 3M2
Tel: 905-318-4488; *Fax:* 905-385-4823
canada1@enasco.it
Chief Officer(s):
Catia Squartecchia, Contact
c.squartecchia@enasco.it
St. Catharines Office
30 Facer St., St Catharines ON L2M 5H3
Tel: 905-646-6555; *Fax:* 905-935-1572
Chief Officer(s):
Vilma Vergalito, Contact
v.vergalito@enasco.it

Toronto Office
1337 St. Clair Ave. West, Toronto ON M6E 1C3
Tel: 416-652-3759; *Fax:* 888-888-2465
canada1@enasco.it
Chief Officer(s):
Diego Zuccarelli, Contact
d.zuccarelli@enasco.it
Woodbridge Office
Market Lane, #201, 140 Woodbridge Ave., Woodbridge ON L4L 4K9
Tel: 905-266-1866; *Fax:* 905-266-1867
Chief Officer(s):
Vincenzo Ghiandoni, Contact
v.ghiandoni@enasco.it

Filarmónica Portuguesa de Montreal / Philharmonique Portugais de Montréal
260, rue Rachel est, Montréal QC H2W 1E6
Tél: 514-982-0688; *Téléc:* 514-982-0607
www.filarmonicaportuguesa.com
Également appelé: Montreal Portuguese Philharmonic
Aperçu: *Dimension:* petite; *Envergure:* locale; fondée en 1972
Mission: Un orchestre avec des musiciens canadiens-portugais
Activités: Concerts; Festivals de musique
Membre(s) du bureau directeur:
Joao Balança, Président, 514-465-3230

Filipino Association of Nova Scotia (FANS)
NS
www.filipinonovascotia.org
www.facebook.com/FilipinoAssociationOfNovaScotia
twitter.com/FilipinoNS
www.instagram.com/filipinons
Overview: A small local organization founded in 1964
Mission: To promote understanding between Filipinos & people from all nations
Membership: *Member Profile:* Filipinos in Nova Scotia & the Atlantic Region
Activities: Participating in cultural events; Arranging social activities; *Awareness Events:* Fiesta Filipino
Chief Officer(s):
Gerald Bermundo, President
Erlinda Unite, Secretary
Alma Barnuevo Mackenzie, Treasurer

Filipino Canadian Association of London & District (FCALD)
London ON
fcald.wordpress.com
www.facebook.com/fcaldlondon
twitter.com/fcaldlondon
Overview: A small local organization
Mission: To promote Filipino heritage & culture in London, Ontario & the surrounding region
Membership: *Member Profile:* Filipino Canadian children & adults from the London, Ontario area
Activities: Organizing cultural, educational, & social activities
Publications:
• Filipino Canadian Association of London & District Newsletter
Type: Newsletter
Profile: Association activities available for members

Filipino Canadian Association of Vaughan (FCAV)
Vaughan ON
Tel: 905-881-4600
fcav@rogers.com
www.fcav.ca
www.facebook.com/fcaov
Overview: A small local organization founded in 1990
Mission: To assist Filipino Canadians in Vaughan, Ontario; To promote community spirit among Filipinos; To assimilate Filipino culture into Canadian society
Finances: *Funding Sources:* Membership fees; Grants; Fundraising
Membership: *Member Profile:* Filipino Canadians in Vaughan, Ontario
Activities: Helping new Filipino immigrants to Vaughan; Participating in civic & community events; Offering educational & recreational programs, such as English tutorials, heritage classes, & cultural dancing; Providing seminars on topics such as immigration & caregiving; Participating in a Friendship Agreement with Baguio City in the Philippines, to promote economic opportunities & cultural, social, & educational exchanges; *Awareness Events:* Philippine Independence Day Parade (Filipino Day)
Chief Officer(s):
Erlinda Insigne, Chair
Gloria Pasildo, Vice-President
Lily Miranda, Secretary, 647-886-8223
lilyleo2750@yahoo.com
Mina Benesa, Treasurer

Filipino Canadian Catholic Charismatic Prayer Communities (FCCCPC)
53 Belvedere Cres., Richmond Hill ON L4C 8VA
Tel: 416-903-3453
fcccpc@yahoo.com
www.fcccpc.com
Overview: A small national organization founded in 1992
Mission: To help Filipino charismatic communities & create a venue of consultation, discernment & counseling among community members
Affiliation(s): Archdiocese of Toronto
Membership: 10+ charismatic prayer communities; *Member Profile:* Individuals are members of a Catholic prayer community (majority of members are of Filipino heritage)
Activities: Counselling; Providing faith instruction & prayer groups; Offering renewal programs, general assemblies & fellowship; Presenting spiritual formation seminars
Chief Officer(s):
Ben Ebcas, Jr., Spiritual Director
Don Quilao, Head Servant
cbquilao@rogers.com
Evelyn Abutan, Secretary
Caring Labindao, Treasurer

Filipino Canadian Technical Professionals Association of Manitoba, Inc. (FCTPAM)
c/o CCI Cadpower Canada Inc., #3, 1680 Dublin Ave., Winnipeg MB R3H 1AB
Tel: 204-988-9100; *Fax:* 204-786-3033
directors@fctpam.net
www.fctpam.net
Previous Name: Filipino Technical Professionals Association of Manitoba, Inc.
Overview: A small provincial organization founded in 1992
Mission: To guide graduates of engineering, architecture, & other technical courses from the Philippines in the recognition & accreditation of foreign credentials
Finances: *Funding Sources:* Membership fees; Fundraising
Membership: *Member Profile:* Filipinos who reside in Canada, & Canadian born Filipinos, who are engineers, architects, technicians, or technologists & who are registered or practise in Manitoba
Activities: Assisting newly arrived immigrants to integrate to life in Canada; Organizing cultural, social, & recreational activities; Providing skills & technical development programs

Filipino Students' Association of Toronto (FSAT)
12 Hart House Circle, Toronto ON M5S 3J9
Tel: 289-200-3438
fsat.fsat@gmail.com
fsat.sa.utoronto.ca
twitter.com/FSAT
Overview: A small local organization
Mission: To encourage Filipino young people to further their education; To promote awareness of the Filipino community & the Filipino culture at the University of Toronto; To represent Filipino students & the Filipino culture at the University of Toronto's St. George Campus
Finances: *Funding Sources:* Fundraising; Sponsorships
Membership: *Member Profile:* Filipino students, faculty, alumni, & staff from the University of Toronto; Interested non-Filipino students, faculty, alumni, & staff from the University of Toronto
Activities: Liaising between the University of Toronto & the Filipino community; Speaking to high school students; Awarding scholarships to high school students; Offering mentorship programs; Providing academic events, featuring lectures by professors & Filipino speakers; Organizing cultural workshops; Participating in multicultual fairs; Offering social activities within the campus community; Sponsoring a child's tuition in the Philippines; Organizing a homework club at The Filipino Centre
Chief Officer(s):
Jannel Fontz, Coordinator, Internal & University Affairs
Liza Caringal, Coordinator, Internal & University Affairs

Filipino Technical Professionals Association of Manitoba, Inc. *See* Filipino Canadian Technical Professionals Association of Manitoba, Inc.

Film & Video Arts Society Alberta (FAVA)
Ortona Armoury Arts Building, 9722 - 102 St., 2nd Fl., Edmonton AB T5K 0X4
Tel: 780-429-1671; *Fax:* 780-429-3636
Other Communication: Rentals Phone: 780-424-4368
info@fava.ca
www.fava.ca
www.facebook.com/fava.love.75
twitter.com/FAVA_Love
Overview: A small provincial charitable organization founded in 1982
Mission: Independent artists willing to challenge & explore through their creativity; all members contribute through some combination of financial support, talents, skills & expertise; in return, FAVA provides an open atmosphere & access to resources - equipment, peer support & shared information
Member of: Independent Media Arts Alliance; Alberta Media Arts Alliance; Edmonton Arts Council
Affiliation(s): Independent Film & Video Alliance; Alberta Media Arts Alliance
Finances: *Annual Operating Budget:* $250,000-$500,000; *Funding Sources:* Grants; Classes & Workshops; Equipment Rental; Member Fees
Staff Member(s): 5; 200 volunteer(s)
Membership: 300; *Fees:* $42 producer; $68.25 general; $89.25 associate
Activities: Monthly screenings; participation in Global Visions; Edmonton International Film Festival; workshops; *Speaker Service:* Yes; *Library:* by appointment
Chief Officer(s):
Dylan Pearce, President
Dave Cunningham, Executive Director
ed@fava.ca

Film Studies Association of Canada (FSAC/ACÉC) / Association canadienne des études cinématographiques (ACEC)
c/o Peter Lester, Brock University, 500 Glenridge Ave., St Catharines ON L2S 3A1
fsac@filmstudies.ca
www.filmstudies.ca
www.facebook.com/FSAC.ACEC
twitter.com/_filmstudies
Overview: A small national organization founded in 1977 overseen by Canadian Federation for Humanities & Social Sciences
Mission: To foster & advance the study of the history & art of film & its related fields.
Affiliation(s): Association for the Study of Canadian Radio & Television; Association québécoise des études cinématographiques
Finances: *Funding Sources:* Membership fees; award from SSHRC
Membership: *Fees:* $110 regular; $50 associate; $40 retired; $30 student/contract instructors; $100 sustaining
Chief Officer(s):
Liz Czach, President
Peter Lester, Secretary
membership@filmstudies.ca
Awards:
• Gerald Pratley Award
Meetings/Conferences:
• Film Studies Association of Canada 2018 Annual Conference, May, 2018, University of Regina, Regina, SK
Scope: National
Publications:
• Canadian Journal of Film Studies
Type: Journal; *Frequency:* Quarterly; *Editor:* William C. Wees
• Continuity
Type: Newsletter; *Frequency:* Irregular; *Editor:* Jean Charles Bellemare

FilmOntario
625 Church St., 2nd Fl., Toronto ON M4Y 2G1
Tel: 416-642-6704
www.filmontario.ca
Overview: A large provincial organization
Mission: To market Ontario as a creator of film content & a location for film & television production
Membership: 30,000; *Member Profile:* Companies, producers, unions, guilds, financial services & organizations within Ontario
Chief Officer(s):
Cynthia Lynch, Managing Director & Counsel
clynch@filmontario.ca

Finance Montréal
#1600, 1130 rue Sherbrooke ouest, Montréal QC H3A 2M8
Tel: 514-287-1477; *Fax:* 514-287-1694
www.finance-montreal.com

www.linkedin.com/company/finance-montreal
twitter.com/FinanceMontreal
Overview: A small local organization founded in 2010
Mission: To enhance Montréal's financial industry; To drive financial growth in Montréal by promoting cooperation among various institutions; To generate awareness about financial specializations in Montréal; To promote fiscal incentives in order to strengthen the presence of foreign financial institutions in Québec; To develop financial entrepreneurship, global companies, a competitive financial information technology sector, & the influence of Montréal's financial services industry, both within Canada & internationally
Chief Officer(s):
Louis Lévesque, Chief Executive Officer

Financial & Consumer Affairs Authority of Saskatchewan (FCAA)
#601, 1919 Saskatchewan Dr., Regina SK S4P 4H2
Tel: 306-787-5645; *Fax:* 306-787-5899
Other Communication: Consumer Protection Inquiries: consumerprotection@gov.sk.ca
fcaa@gov.sk.ca
www.fcaa.gov.sk.ca
Overview: A medium-sized provincial organization overseen by Canadian Securities Administrators
Mission: To strengthen Saskatchewan's financial marketplace & protect consumers
Member of: Canadian Securities Administrators
Activities: Regulating providers of financial products & services
Chief Officer(s):
Roger Sobotkiewicz, Chair & CEO
Publications:
• FCAA [Financial & Consumer Affairs Authority of Saskatchewan] Annual Report
Type: Report; *Frequency:* Annually
• FCAA [Financial & Consumer Affairs Authority of Saskatchewan] Strategic Plan
Type: Report; *Frequency:* Annually
• Statistical Report of the Superintendent of Insurance [publication of Financial & Consumer Affairs Authority of Saskatchewan]
Type: Report; *Frequency:* Annually

Financial & Consumer Services Commission (FCNB) / Commission des services financiers et des services aux consommateurs
#300, 85 Charlotte St., Saint John NB E2L 2J2
Fax: 506-658-3059
Toll-Free: 866-933-2222
info@fcnb.ca
www.fcnb.ca
www.facebook.com/FCNB.ca
twitter.com/FCNB_
instagram.com/fcnb.ca
Previous Name: New Brunswick Securities Commission
Overview: A medium-sized provincial organization founded in 2013 overseen by Canadian Securities Administrators
Mission: To administer & enforce provincial legislation pertaining to the following sectors: securities, insurance, pensions, credit unions, caisses populaires, trust & loan companies, co-operatives, & other consumer legislation
Member of: Canadian Securities Administrators; Council of Securities Regulators of the Americas; North American Securities Administrators Association
Affiliation(s): International Forum for Investor Education (IFIE); International Organization of Securities Commissions; Securities & Exchange Commission (USA)
Finances: *Funding Sources:* By investors, through the securities industry
Activities: Developing securities regulation; Registering persons & companies operating in New Brunswick's securities industry; Providing educational resources to New Brunswick residents who are interested in the investing process; Reviewing prospectuses; Considering exemption applications; Taking enforcement action when securities laws have been contravened
Chief Officer(s):
Peter Klohn, Chair
Rick Hancox, Chief Executive Officer
Publications:
• Financial & Consumer Services Commission Annual Report
Type: Report; *Frequency:* Annually
• Financial & Consumer Services Commission Governance Policy
Profile: An outline of the governance policy of the Commission
  Fredericton
  #200, 225 King St., Fredericton NB E3B 1E1
  Fax: 506-658-3059
  Toll-Free: 866-933-2222
  info@fcnb.ca
  www.fcnb.ca

Financial Executives Institute Canada *See* Financial Executives International Canada

Financial Executives International Canada (FEIC)
#300, 116 Simcoe St., Toronto ON M5H 4E2
Tel: 416-366-3007
Toll-Free: 866-677-3007
membership@feicanada.org
www.feicanada.org
www.linkedin.com/company/fei-canada
www.facebook.com/financialexecs
twitter.com/FEICanada
Also Known As: FEI Canada
Previous Name: Financial Executives Institute Canada
Overview: A medium-sized national organization founded in 1931
Mission: To promote ethical conduct in the practice of financial management; To contribute to the legal & policy making process in Canada; To provide advocacy, leadership & professional development services to members
Finances: *Annual Operating Budget:* $1.5 Million-$3 Million; *Funding Sources:* Sponsorship
Staff Member(s): 9; 150 volunteer(s)
Membership: 1,500+; *Fees:* Schedule available; *Member Profile:* Senior financial officers of medium to large organizations
Activities: Providing seminars, conferences, professional development events, & networking opportunities; Offering advocacy services, programs, & research studies; Advocating; *Internships:* Yes
Chief Officer(s):
Pierre Pigott, CPA, CA, President & CEO
Marietjie Bower, CPA, CMA, Chief Financial Officer, 416-366-3007 Ext. 5115
mbower@feicanada.org
Laura Pacheco, MBA, CPA, CGA, Vice-President, Research, 416-366-3007 Ext. 5111
lpacheco@feicanada.org
Stephen Ilkiw, Director, Sales, 416-366-3007 Ext. 5108
silkiw@feicanada.org
Rita Plaskett, Director, Events, 416-366-3007 Ext. 5116
rplaskett@feicanada.org
Awards:
• Frank S. Capon Distinguished Service Award
Eligibility: Veteran & long-serving member of FEI Canada
Meetings/Conferences:
• Financial Executives International Canada Annual Conference
2018, June, 2018, Halifax Conference Centre, Halifax, NS
Scope: National
Contact Information: Rita Plaskett, Director of Events, 416-366-3007 x5116
Publications:
• Finance & Accounting Review [a publication of the Financial Executives International Canada]
Type: Journal; *Frequency:* Monthly; *Editor:* Laura Bobak; *Price:* Free to members of Financial ExecutivesInternational Canada
Profile: Domestic & international happenings in the industry
• Financial Executives International Canada Annual Report
Type: Yearbook; *Frequency:* Annually
• Xpress [a publication of the Financial Executives International Canada]
Type: Newsletter; *Frequency:* Monthly; *Editor:* Laura Bobak; *Price:* Free tomembers of Financial Executives International Canada
Profile: Happenings at FEI Canada plus forthcoming professional development activitie, new members, & job postings
  Atlantic Provinces Chapter
  Chief Officer(s):
  Anne-Marie Gammon, President, 902-835-6650
  agammon@ns.sympatico.ca
  Ray McCormick, Treasurer
  ray.mccormick@impgroup.com
  Calgary Chapter
  Calgary AB
  Chief Officer(s):
  Vic Fitch, President, 403-968-9460
  vfitch@feicanada.org
  Al Johnson, Treasurer
  • Calgary Newsletter [a publication of the Financial Executives International Canada - Calgary Chapter]
  Editor: Tariq Malik
  Profile: News & committee reports for members
  Edmonton Chapter
  Edmonton AB
  Chief Officer(s):
  Doug Woloshyn, President, 780-391-3528
  Doug.Woloshyn@apsc.ca
  Kevin Higa, Treasurer
  higak@telus.net
  National Capital Region Chapter
  Ottawa ON
  Chief Officer(s):
  Dean Cosman, President, 613-996-9043
  dcosman@cdic.ca
  Ernie Briard, Vice-President & Treasurer
  erniebriard@rogers.com
  Québec Chapter
  Montréal QC
  Tel: 514-695-9196
  quebec@financialexecutives.ca
  Chief Officer(s):
  Louis Marcotte, President
  Andrée Pinard, Treasurer
  Regina Chapter
  Regina SK
  Chief Officer(s):
  Gary Maystruck, President, 306-924-0367
  gwm@sasktel.net
  Christine Short, Treasurer
  cshort@saskenergy.com
  Southern Golden Horseshoe Chapter
  FEI.SGH@gmail.com
  Chief Officer(s):
  Stacey Sinclair, President, 905-399-9732
  Dan Bowes, Secretary-Treasurer
  dtbowes@cogeco.ca
  Southwestern Ontario Chapter
  Chief Officer(s):
  Maryann Moons, President, 519-457-8404
  maryannmoons@gmail.com
  Jim King, Treasurer
  jimking@teksavvy.com
  • Financial Executives International Southwestern Ontario Chapter Newsletter
  Type: Newsletter; *Frequency:* Annually
  Profile: Chapter news for members, including upcoming events & reviews of conferences & activities
  Toronto Chapter
  Toronto ON
  Tel: 905-330-5055
  Toronto.Chapter@feicanada.org
  Chief Officer(s):
  David Minas, President
  dminas@discountcar.com
  Elvira Rago, Administrative Director
  • Financial Executives International Canada Toronto Newsletter
  Type: Newsletter; *Frequency:* 3 pa
  Profile: Chapter news & committee reports
  Vancouver Chapter
  Vancouver BC
  Chief Officer(s):
  Liz Bowell, Chapter Administrator, 604-569-4119
  feicvancouver@shaw.ca
  Peter Ballachey, Treasurer
  ballachey@shaw.ca
  • Financial Executives International Canada Vancouver Chapter Newsletter
  Type: Newsletter; *Frequency:* 11 pa
  Profile: News, upcoming events, & committee reports for members
  Winnipeg Chapter
  Winnipeg MB
  Chief Officer(s):
  John Cole, President
  jcole@palliser.ca
  Dana Thiessen, Treasurer
  dana.thiessen@shaw.ca

Financial Executives International Canada Hamilton Chapter *See* Financial Executives International Canada

Financial Fitness Centre
1770 Langlois Ave., Windsor ON N8X 4M5
Tel: 519-258-2030
Toll-Free: 877-777-9218
info@financialfitnesswindsor.com
www.financialfitnesswindsor.com

www.linkedin.com/company/financial-fitness-windsor
www.facebook.com/FinancialFitnessWindsor
twitter.com/FinancialFitWin
Previous Name: Credit Counselling Services of Southwestern Ontario
Overview: A small local charitable organization overseen by Ontario Association of Credit Counselling Services
Mission: To assist persons in southwestern Ontario to solve their money problems; To provide confidential credit, debt, bankruptcy, & budget counselling
Member of: Credit Counselling Canada; Ontario Association of Credit Counselling Services
Affiliation(s): Family Services Credit Counselling Employee Assistance Programs
Finances: *Funding Sources:* United Way of Windsor / Essex; Creditors
Activities: Teaching budgeting & money management skills; Presenting workshops & community education; Contacting creditors to negotiate payment plans
Chief Officer(s):
Wendy Dupuis, Executive Director

 Sarnia Office
 420 East St. North, Sarnia ON N7T 6Y5
 Tel: 519-542-1130
 Toll-Free: 877-777-9218
 Chief Officer(s):
 Joanna Marks, Contact

Financial Management Institute of Canada (FMI) / Institut de la gestion financière (IFG)
#601, 200 Elgin St., Ottawa ON K2P 1L5
Tel: 613-569-1158; *Fax:* 613-569-4532
Other Communication: French URL: www.igf.ca
national@fmi.ca
www.fmi.ca
www.linkedin.com/groups/2350339
www.facebook.com/fmiigf
twitter.com/FMI_IGF
www.youtube.com/user/FMIIGF
Overview: A medium-sized national organization founded in 1962
Mission: To be the source for professional development on topical issues & best practices to public sector financial management stakeholders; To facilitate the dissemination of information on managing public sector resources
Finances: *Funding Sources:* Membership fees; Sponsorships
Membership: 2,240; *Member Profile:* Professionals in the finance field throughout Canada
Activities: Offering seminars & learning events for both members & non-members, as well as a Professional Development Week; Providing networking opportunities
Chief Officer(s):
Christopher Egan, Chief Executive Officer
chris@fmi.ca
Cheryl Elliott, Manager, Marketing & Communications
cheryl@fmi.ca
Meetings/Conferences:
• Financial Management Institute of Canada Professional Development Week 2018, November, 2018
Scope: National
Publications:
• Community Report [a publication of the Financial Management Institute of Canada]
Type: Report; *Frequency:* Annually
Profile: An overview of the Financial Management Institute of Canada
• Financial Management Institute of Canada Annual Report
Type: Yearbook; *Frequency:* Annually
• FMI / IGF Journal [a publication of the Financial Management Institute of Canada]
Type: Magazine; *Frequency:* 3 pa; *Accepts Advertising; Editor:* Rocky J. Dwyer, PhD, CMA
Profile: News, articles, & columns of interest to public sector professionals in the field of public sector financialmanagement

Financial Markets Association of Canada (FMAC) / Association des marchés financiers du Canada
#301, 250 Consumers Rd., Toronto ON M2J 4V6
Tel: 416-773-0584; *Fax:* 416-495-8723
fmac@fmac.ca
www.fmac.ca
Previous Name: Foreign Exchange Association of Canada
Overview: A medium-sized national organization founded in 1972
Mission: To promote the educational & professional interests of participants in the Canadian wholesale financial markets; To ensure members adhere to international principles of professional conduct
Affiliation(s): Association Cambiste Internationale (ACI); Canadian Foreign Exchange Committee; Canadian Committee for Professionalism
Membership: 350+; *Member Profile:* A professional who deals in money markets, foreign exchange, captital markets, & derivatives, & whose institution is registered with & regulated by at least one of the following authorities: Office of the Superintendent of Financial Institutions, Securities & Exchange Commission, Investment Dealers Association, Financial Services Commission of Ontario, & the Ontario Securities Commission
Activities: Hosting business functions with speakers; Providing networking opportunities
Chief Officer(s):
Jean-François Gratton, President
Maria Jones, Secretary
Blake Jsespersen, Treasurer & Past President
Publications:
• Market Maker [a publication of the Financial Markets Association of Canada]
Type: Newsletter; *Frequency:* Quarterly
Profile: Activities of the association

Financial Planners Standards Council *See* Financial Planning Standards Council

Financial Planning Standards Council (FPSC)
#902, 375 University Ave., Toronto ON M5G 2J5
Tel: 416-593-8587; *Fax:* 416-593-6903
Toll-Free: 800-305-9886
Other Communication: communications@fpsc.ca
inform@fpsc.ca
www.fpsc.ca
www.linkedin.com/company/100790
www.facebook.com/FPSC.Canada
twitter.com/FPSC_Canada
www.youtube.com/user/FPVision2020
Previous Name: Financial Planners Standards Council
Overview: A medium-sized national licensing organization founded in 1995
Mission: To develop, enforce, & promote competency & ethical standards in financial planning by those who have earned the designation of Certified Financial Planner (CFP)
Affiliation(s): The Financial Advisors Association of Canada; The Canadian Institute of Chartered Accountants; The Canadian Institute of Financial Planning; Certified General Accountants Association of Canada; Certified Management Accountants of Canada; Credit Union Institute of Canada
Membership: *Committees:* Recognition & Awards; Panel of Examiners; Governance; Compensation; Audit; Certification; Enforcement; Nominating
Activities: Increasing awareness of the importance of financial planning; Presenting honours & awards; Hosting financial planning seminars; Conducting surveys; Collecting statistics; *Awareness Events:* Financial Planning Week Canada
Chief Officer(s):
Lisa Pflieger, Chair
Dawn Hawley, Vice-Chair
Cary List, President & Chief Executive Officer
Kimberley Ney, Vice-President, Communications & Program Development
Stephen Rotstein, Vice-President, Policy & Regulatory Affairs
Heather Terrence, Vice-President, Operations
Joan Yudelson, Vice-President, Professional Practice
Isabelle Gonthier, Director, Certification Process & Examinations
Publications:
• CFP Code of Ethics [a publication of the Financial Planning Standards Council]
Type: Booklet; *Number of Pages:* 10
Profile: The Code of Ethics that Certified Financial Planner professionals must abide by to maintain their Certified Financial Planner license
• CFP Financial Planning Practice Standards [a publication of the Financial Planning Standards Council]
Type: Booklet; *Number of Pages:* 14
Profile: An outline of practice standards to which Certified Financial Planner professionals must adhere
• CFP Professional Competency Profile [a publication of the Financial Planning Standards Council]
Number of Pages: 54
Profile: An outline of the competencies that all Certified Financial Planner professionals must possess
• Do I need help with my financial planning? [a publication of the Financial Planning Standards Council]
Type: Booklet; *Number of Pages:* 4
Profile: Information for clients on working with a financial planner
• Financial Planning Standards Council Strategic Plan
Profile: A guide for the organization's future
• Financial Planning Standards Council Annual Report
Type: Yearbook; *Frequency:* Annually
• FPSC [Financial Planning Standards Council] Bulletin
Type: Newsletter; *Editor:* Tamara Smith
Profile: Information for Certified Financial Planner professionals & their clients, including a report on disciplinary action, interviews, & upcoming events
• What assurance do I have that financial planning is working for me? [a publication of Financial Planning Standards Council]
Type: Booklet; *Number of Pages:* 4
Profile: A guide for clients to understanding the Certified Financial Planner Code of Ethics & Standardsof Practice & Competency
• What makes CFP certification trustworthy? [a publication of the Financial Planning Standards Council]
Type: Booklet; *Number of Pages:* 8
Profile: An overview of Certified Financial Planner certification for consumers

Financial Services Commission of Ontario (FSCO) / Commission des services financiers de l'Ontario (CSFO)
PO Box 85, 5160 Yonge St., 17th Fl., Toronto ON M2N 6L9
Tel: 416-250-7250; *Fax:* 416-590-7070
Toll-Free: 800-668-0128; *TTY:* 800-387-0584
contactcentre@fsco.gov.on.ca
www.fsco.gov.on.ca
Previous Name: Canadian Council of Insurance Regulators
Overview: A small provincial organization founded in 1998
Mission: To regulate the following sectors in Ontario: insurance; pension plans; loan & trust companies; credit unions & caisses populaires; mortgage brokering; co-operative corporations in Ontario; & service providers who invoice auto insurers for statutory accident benefits claims.
Chief Officer(s):
Brian Mills, Interim Chief Executive Officer

Findhelp Information Services
PO Box 203, #125, 543 Richmond St. West, Toronto ON M5V 1Y6
Tel: 416-392-4605; *Fax:* 416-392-4404
Toll-Free: 800-836-3238; *TTY:* 888-340-1001
info@findhelp.ca
www.211toronto.ca
www.facebook.com/211Central
twitter.com/211Central
Also Known As: 211 Toronto
Overview: A small local charitable organization founded in 1952 overseen by InformOntario
Mission: To provide comprehensive information & referral services in English, French & other languages; resources for information & referral professionals; call centre; newcomer services; Possibilities online employment resource centre; training & outreach
Member of: Alliance of Information & Referral Systems
Affiliation(s): United Way of Greater Toronto
Finances: *Funding Sources:* United Way of Greater Toronto; provincial & city funding
Activities: Database of over 4,000 community services & programs; training & staff development programs for direct service providers working in information & referral environments; information & referral on a wide range of community, social services, health & government programs; *Rents Mailing List:* Yes

Finnish Canadian Cultural Federation / Fédération culturelle finno-canadienne
Toronto ON
Overview: A small international organization founded in 1971
Mission: To act as non-political coordinator between associations, congregations, clubs & other groups of Finnish ethnic background; To promote Finland & Canadians of Finnish origin; To promote Canada & its Finnish ethnic community in Finland; To support Annual Finnish Canadian Grand Festival
Member of: Canadian Ethnocultural Council
Affiliation(s): Finland Society, R.Y.; Finn Fest USA, Inc.
Finances: *Annual Operating Budget:* Less than $50,000; *Funding Sources:* Membership fees
12 volunteer(s)
Membership: 1-99; *Fees:* Schedule available; *Member Profile:* Canadian non-political organizations, clubs, congregations & other groups of Finnish ethnic origin; *Committees:* Finnish-Canadian Grand Festival; Archives

Canadian Associations / Finnish Canadian Rest Home Association

Finnish Canadian Rest Home Association
2288 Harrison Dr., Vancouver BC V5P 2P6
Tel: 604-325-8241; Fax: 604-325-2394
info@finncare.ca
finncare.ca
Overview: A small local organization founded in 1958
Mission: To represent a number of Finnish Canadian rest homes & seniors apartments in the Vancouver Area
Staff Member(s): 11
Membership: Fees: $20; $200 lifetime
Chief Officer(s):
Tanya Rautava, Administrator
finnishhome@telus.net

Fire Fighters Historical Society of Winnipeg, Inc.
56 Maple St., Winnipeg MB R3B 0Y8
Tel: 204-942-4817; Fax: 204-885-1306
firemuseum@gatewest.net
www.winnipegfiremuseum.ca
Overview: A small local charitable organization founded in 1982
Mission: To preserve & display equipment, historical records & photos related to the history of the Winnipeg Fire Department
Finances: Annual Operating Budget: Less than $50,000; Funding Sources: Membership dues; donations
11 volunteer(s)
Membership: 300; Fees: $15
Activities: Library: by appointment

Fire Prevention Canada (FPC)
PO Box 37009, 3332 McCarthy Rd., Ottawa ON K1V 0W0
Tel: 613-749-3844
info@fiprecan.ca
www.fiprecan.ca
Also Known As: Fiprecan
Overview: A medium-sized national charitable organization
Mission: To work with the public & private sectors to achieve fire safety through education.
Staff Member(s): 1
Chief Officer(s):
Peter Adamakos, National Manager
padamakos@fiprecan.ca

Firefighters Burn Fund Inc. (FFBF)
#303, 83 Garry St., Winnipeg MB R3C 4J9
Tel: 204-783-1733; Fax: 204-772-2531
inquiries@firefightersburnfund.mb.ca
www.firefightersburnfund.mb.ca
www.facebook.com/manitobafirefighters.burnfund?fref=ts
Overview: A medium-sized provincial charitable organization founded in 1978
Mission: To improve health care available to adults & children in Manitoba who suffer burn injuries; To develop & support fire/burn prevention initiatives so that needless injuries & deaths are prevented
Member of: American Burn Association, Canadian Association of Fire Chiefs
Finances: Annual Operating Budget: $100,000-$250,000; Funding Sources: Fundraising
6 volunteer(s)
Membership: 950; Fees: $1; Committees: Executive
Activities: Sponsors a burn camp for children who have been patients in the burn unit; promotes Learn Not To Burn curriculum throughout province; Speaker Service: Yes
Chief Officer(s):
Martin Johnson, Chairman

Firefly
820 Lakeview Dr., Kenora ON P9N 3P7
Tel: 807-467-5437; Fax: 807-467-5444
Toll-Free: 800-465-7203
www.fireflynw.ca
Merged from: Lake of the Woods Child Development Centre; Patricia Centre for Children and Youth
Overview: A small local organization founded in 2011
Mission: To provide services & programs that help children develop emotionally & physically
Activities: Assessment, counselling & training programs
Chief Officer(s):
Karen Ingebrigtson, Chief Executive Officer, 807-467-5440
kingebrigtson@fireflynw.ca

First Nation Lands Managers Association of Québec & Labrador (FNLMAQ&L)
c/o Gino Clement, 17, ch Riverside ouest, Listuguj First Nation QC E3E 1K3
Tel: 418-788-2136
Overview: A small provincial organization founded in 2002 overseen by National Aboriginal Lands Managers Association
Staff Member(s): 1
Chief Officer(s):
Gino Clement, Chair
gclement@listuguj.ca

First Nations Agricultural Lending Association (FNALA)
PO Box 1186, Stn. Main, 7410 Dallas Dr., Kamloops BC V2C 6H3
Tel: 250-314-6804; Fax: 250-314-6809
Toll-Free: 866-314-6804
Overview: A small provincial organization founded in 1988
Mission: To provide loans to Aboriginal agricultural & agri-food businesses (on & off-reserve projects)
Affiliation(s): First Nations Agricultural Association; Aboriginal Agricultural Education Society of British Columbia
Finances: Funding Sources: Government

First Nations Breast Cancer Society
#309, 1333 East 7th Ave., Vancouver BC V5N 1R6
Tel: 604-872-4390; Fax: 604-875-0779
echoes@fnbreastcancer.bc.ca
www.fnbreastcancer.bc.ca
Overview: A small national organization founded in 1995
Mission: Offers breast cancer education and support to First Nations women.
Finances: Funding Sources: Donations; member fees
Membership: Fees: $15 regualr; $0 for breast cancer survivors
Chief Officer(s):
Jacqueline Davis, President
jdavis@fnbreastcancer.bc.ca

First Nations Chiefs of Police Association (FNCPA)
c/o Akwesasne Mohawk Police, PO Box 579, 73 Sweetgrass Ln., Cornwall ON K6H 5T3
Tel: 613-575-2340; Fax: 613-575-2334
admin@fncpa.ca
www.fncpa.ca
Overview: A small national organization
Mission: To serve First Nation police services & First Nation territories across Canada by facilitating the highest level of professionalism & accountability in their police services, all in a manner that reflects the unique cultures, constitutional status, social circumstances, traditions, & aspirations of First Nations
Membership: 72; Fees: $150 active, associate, sustaining; Committees: Credentials; By-Laws; Training Assessment; S.I.U. Protocol; Recruitment & Retnetion; APD Evaluation
Chief Officer(s):
Dwayne Zacharie, President
president@fncpa.ca
Lennard Busch, Vice-President, West
vicepresidentwest@fncpa.ca
Rick Angeconeb, Vice-President, East
Jerry Swamp, Secretary-Treasurer
secretary-treasurer@fncpa.ca
Karen Haines, Executive Administrative Assistant
Awards:
• National Youth Justice Policing Award

First Nations Child & Family Caring Society of Canada
#401, 309 Cooper St., Ottawa ON K2P 0GS
Tel: 613-230-5885; Fax: 613-230-3080
info@fncaringsociety.com
www.fncaringsociety.com
www.facebook.com/CaringSociety
twitter.com/Caringsociety
www.youtube.com/user/fncaringsociety
Overview: A small national organization founded in 2003
Mission: To provide support in caring for First Nations children & families
Membership: Fees: $75 individual; $25 student; $350-$600 associate/agency
Chief Officer(s):
Cindy Blackstock, Executive Director

First Nations Confederacy of Cultural Education Centres
#302, 666 Kirkwood Ave., Ottawa ON K1Z 5X9
Tel: 613-728-5999; Fax: 613-728-2247
www.fnccec.com
Overview: A medium-sized provincial organization
Mission: To advocate for the recovery, maintenance, enhancement & preservation of First Nations languages, cultures & traditions
Membership: 87 First Nations cultural centres & programs; Member Profile: Canadian First Nations cultural centres & programs
Activities: Providing programs & technical support to member centres; Developing projects; Offering public education; Increasing cultural awarness; Liaising with government, museums, academic institutions, & professional groups; Establishing partnerships; Assisting in the establishment of First Nations cultural centres
Chief Officer(s):
Claudette Commanda, Executive Director
Donna Goodleaf, National President
Tiffany Sark-Carr, Vice-President
Dorothy Myo, Secretary-Treasurer

First Nations Education Council (FNEC)
95, rue De l'Ours, Wendake QC G0A 4V0
Tel: 418-842-7672; Fax: 418-842-9988
info@cepn-fnec.com
www.cepn-fnec.com
www.facebook.com/cepn.fnec
www.youtube.com/user/CEPNFNEC
Overview: A small national organization
Mission: To achieve full jurisdiction over education. This will be accomplished through mutual collaboration, in providing mandates to the Education Secretariat in Assembly, to support, promote, inform and defend the interests and actions of members in regards to all matters of education, while respecting our unique cultural identities and common beliefs, and promoting our languages, values and traditions.
Chief Officer(s):
Lise Bastien, Director
lbastien@cepn-fnec.com
Publications:
• The Journal
Type: Newsletter; Frequency: 2 pa

First Nations Environmental Network
PO Box 394, Tofino BC V0R 2Z0
Tel: 250-726-5265; Fax: 250-725-2357
councilfire@hotmail.com
www.fnen.org
Overview: A small national organization overseen by Canadian Environmental Network
Mission: The First Nations Environmental Network is a circle of First Nations people committed to protecting, defending, and restoring the balance of all life by honouring traditional Indigenous values and the path of our ancestors.
Membership: 20

First Nations Friendship Centre (FNFC)
2904 - 29th Ave., Vernon BC V1T 1Y7
Tel: 250-542-1247; Fax: 205-542-3707
fnfc@shawcable.com
Also Known As: First Nations Friendship Centre Society
Overview: A small local charitable organization founded in 1975
Mission: To improve the quality of life for Native People in a welcome environment, by supporting self-determined activities which encourage equal access to & participation in Canadian society & which respect Native cultural distinctiveness
Activities: Programs for children, youth & adults; health programs

First Nations SchoolNet (FNS)
Indian & Northern Affairs Canada, Education Program Directorate, 10, rue Wellington, Tour nord, Gatineau QC K1A 0H4
Toll-Free: 800-567-9604; TTY: 866-553-0554
pnr-fns@ainc-inac.gc.ca
www.ainc-inac.gc.ca/edu/ep/index1-eng.asp
Overview: A medium-sized national organization founded in 1996
Mission: Established by the federal government, FNS provides internet access, computer equipment & technical support to First Nations schools on reserves across the country. Students can connect with each other, develop new skills, & participate in national & international events. Six non-profit, regional management organizations deliver the program in their respective region, working with Indian & Northern Affairs Canada.
Membership: Member Profile: All First Nations schools
Atlantic Region
c/o Mi'kmaw Kina'matnewey, 47 Maillard St., Membertou NS B1S 2P5
Tel: 902-567-0842; Fax: 902-567-0337
Toll-Free: 877-484-7606

admin@firstnationhelp.com
www.firstnationhelp.com
www.facebook.com/firstnationhelp
twitter.com/firstnationhelp
Chief Officer(s):
Kevin Burton, Director
Jetta Denny, Communications & Youth Coordinator
jetta@firstnationhelp.com
British Columbia Region
c/o First Nations Education Steering Committee, #113, 100 Park Royal South, West Vancouver BC V7T 1A2
Tel: 604-925-6087; *Fax:* 604-925-6097
Toll-Free: 877-422-3672
info@fnesc.ca
www.fnesc.ca
twitter.com/FNESC
Chief Officer(s):
Deborah Jeffrey, Executive Director
djeffrey@fnesc.ca
Manitoba Region
c/o Keewatin Tribal Council, #26, 30 Fort St., Winnipeg MB R3C 1C4
Fax: 204-949-4015
Toll-Free: 866-397-5446
info@mfns.ca
www.mfns.ca
Ontario Region
PO Box 1439, Sioux Lookout ON P8T 1B9
Tel: 807-737-1135; *Fax:* 807-737-1720
Toll-Free: 877-737-5638
www.knet.ca
Québec Region
a/s Conseil en Éducation des Premières Nations, 95, rue de l'Ours, Wendake QC G0A 4V0
Tél: 418-842-7672; *Téléc:* 418-842-9988
info@cepn-fnec.com
www.cepn-fnec.com
www.facebook.com/people/cepn-fnec/100001611305347
www.youtube.com/user/CEPNFNEC
Chief Officer(s):
Lise Bastien, Directrice générale
lbastien@cepn-fnec.com
Josée Goulet, Directeur adjoint
jgoulet@cepn-fnec.com
Saskatchewan & Alberta Region
c/o Keewatin Career Development Corporation, 135 Finlayson St., La Ronge SK S0J 1L0
Tel: 306-425-4778; *Fax:* 306-425-4780
Toll-Free: 866-966-5232
office@kcdc.ca
www.kcdc.ca
• PRISM International
Price: $28 individual subscription; $46 library/institution subscription
Profile: Contemporary writing journal; published quarterly

First Pacific Theatre Society
1440 West 12 Ave., Vancouver BC V6H 1M8
Tel: 604-731-5483
info@pacifictheatre.org
www.pacifictheatre.org
www.facebook.com/pacifictheatre
twitter.com/pacifictheatre
Also Known As: Pacific Theatre
Overview: A small local charitable organization founded in 1984
Mission: To produce high quality theatre; To operate with artistic, spiritual, relational & financial integrity
Member of: Greater Vancouver Professional Theatre Alliance; Alliance for Arts & Culture
Affiliation(s): Professional Association of Canadian Theatres
Finances: *Funding Sources:* Private; corporate; government
Staff Member(s): 6
Activities: Producing theatre performances; Offering workshops & theatre rentals; *Internships:* Yes
Chief Officer(s):
Ron Reed, Artistic & Executive Director
ron@ronreed.com
Alison Chisholm, Co-General Manager
alison@pacifictheatre.org
Frank Nickel, Co-General Manager
frank@pacifictheatre.org
Andrea Loewen, Director
andrea@pacifictheatre.org

First Portuguese Canadian Cultural Centre
60 Caledonia Rd., Toronto ON M6E 4S3
Tel: 416-531-9971; *Fax:* 416-658-3553
fpccc@firstportuguese.com
www.firstportuguese.com
www.linkedin.com/company/first-portuguese-canadian-cultural-centre
www.facebook.com/212725188833941
Overview: A small national organization founded in 1956
Mission: To provide assistance to individuals, institutions, associations or any other type of organization so as to enhance health, welfare, education, knowledge & well-being of the Portuguese-speaking community & of the Canadian community as a whole; to provide theory & practice of the principles of good citizenship; to unite members in the bonds of friendship, good fellowship & mutual understanding; to provide facilities for education & instruction in the laws of Canada, the English language & the cultures of Portugal & Canada; to receive & maintain funds for charitable, educational or any other purposes beneficial to the community
Member of: Canadian Ethnocultural Council
Finances: *Funding Sources:* Citizenship & Immigration Canada; City of Toronto; Trillium Foundation
Membership: *Member Profile:* Portuguese-speaking
Activities: Portuguese Seniors' Centre offers social, cultural & educational programs; LINC - Language Instruction for Newcomers to Canada
Chief Officer(s):
Maria Tavares, Contact
mariatavares@firstportuguese.com

FIRST Robotics Canada
PO Box 518, Stn. Main, Pickering ON L1V 2R7
info@firstroboticscanada.org
www.firstroboticscanada.org
www.linkedin.com/groups/4554063
www.facebook.com/FIRSTRoboticsCanada
twitter.com/CANFIRST
www.youtube.com/user/FIRSTRoboticsCanada
Also Known As: For Inspiration & Recognition of Science & Technology
Previous Name: Canadian Association for Student Robotics
Overview: A small national organization
Mission: To encourage young people to enter the fields of science, technology, & engineering
Chief Officer(s):
Mark Breadner, President
mark.breadner@firstroboticscanada.org

First Unitarian Congregation of Toronto
175 St. Clair Ave. West, Toronto ON M4V 1P7
Tel: 416-924-9654; *Fax:* 416-924-9655
administrator@firstunitariantoronto.org
www.firstunitariantoronto.org
www.facebook.com/firstunitariantoronto
www.youtube.com/user/firstunitarianTO/videos
Overview: A small local charitable organization founded in 1845
Mission: To be committed to love & justice; To seek and understand the meaning of life, connect with others in a common purpose & serve life to build a better world
Member of: Canadian Unitarian Council
Finances: *Annual Operating Budget:* $250,000-$500,000
Staff Member(s): 7; 70 volunteer(s)
Membership: 306 individuals
Activities: Monthly newcomers' orientation; Weekly Sunday services; Social justice & community outreach; Refugee Sponsorship; Reconciliation Working Group; Art Exhibitions, publications & a dinner series; Courses & Programs on Diverse Faith matters; *Internships:* Yes; *Library:* by appointment
Chief Officer(s):
Shawn Newton, Minister, 416-924-9654 Ext. 222, *Fax:* 416-924-9655
ShawnNewton@FirstUnitarianToronto.org
Publications:
• First Light [a publication of the First Unitarian Congregation of Toronto]
Type: E-Newsletter; *Frequency:* Weekly
• Horizons
Type: Newsletter; *Frequency:* Monthly

First Vancouver Theatre Space Society (FVTS)
PO Box 203, 1398 Cartwright St., Vancouver BC V6H 3R8
Tel: 604-257-0350
info@vancouverfringe.com
www.vancouverfringe.com
www.facebook.com/VancouverFringeFestival
twitter.com/VancouverFringe
Also Known As: Theatre Space
Overview: A small local organization founded in 1983
Mission: To promoting interest in the arts in Vancouver; To nurture & support artists
Member of: CAFF
Staff Member(s): 14
Activities: Producing, promoting, & operating the Vancouver Fringe Festival; Managing the Festival Box Office; *Awareness Events:* Vancouver Fringe Festival, Sept.
Chief Officer(s):
David Jordan, Executive Director
executivedirector@vancouverfringe.com
Eduardo Ottoni, Production Manager
production@vancouverfringe.com

Fiscal & Financial Planning Association *Voir* Association de planification fiscale et financière

Fish Harvesters Resource Centres (FRC)
PO Box 1242, Stn. C, 368 Hamilton Ave., St. John's NL A1C 5M9
Tel: 709-576-0292; *Fax:* 709-576-0339
www.frc.nf.ca
Overview: A small provincial organization founded in 1993
Mission: The Centres assist & support the restructuring of the Newfoundland & Labrador fishing industry by providing information & resources to fish harvesters in the province. They offer business counselling & technical assistance to encourage entrepreneurship among harvesters.
Affiliation(s): FFAW/CAW Fish; Food & Allied Workers Union; Atlantic Canada Opportunities Agency (ACOA)
Staff Member(s): 7; 330 volunteer(s)
Chief Officer(s):
Liz Smith, Executive Director
lizsmith@frc.nf.ca

Fish, Food & Allied Workers (FFAW)
PO Box 10, Stn. C, 368 Hamilton Ave., 2nd. Fl., St. John's NL A1C 5H5
Tel: 709-576-7276; *Fax:* 709-576-1962
president@ffaw.net
www.ffaw.nf.ca
Overview: A medium-sized provincial organization
Mission: To represent employees in the fishing industry in Newfoundland and Labrador
Member of: Unifor
Affiliation(s): Canadian Council of Professional Fish Harvesters; National Seafood Sector Council
Staff Member(s): 7
Membership: 15,000; *Committees:* Community; Regional; Fleet; Fish Plants; Brewery; Metal Fabrication; Window Manufacturing; Hotel; Retail; Trawlers; Oil Tankers; Tug Boats
Chief Officer(s):
Keith Sullivan, President
president@ffaw.net
David Decker, Secretary-Treasurer
ddecker@ffaw.nfld.net

Fisher Branch & District Chamber of Commerce
PO Box 566, Fisher Branch MB R0C 0Z0
Tel: 204-372-8585
fisherchamber@gmail.com
www.fisherbranchchamber.com
Overview: A small local organization
Mission: To improve the business community of Fisher Branch & district
Membership: 35; *Fees:* $75
Chief Officer(s):
Wayne Smith, President

Fisheries Council of Canada (FCC) / Conseil Canadien des Pêches
#610, 170 Laurier Ave. West, Ottawa ON K1P 5V5
Tel: 613-727-7450; *Fax:* 613-727-7453
info@fisheriescouncil.org
www.fisheriescouncil.ca
Previous Name: Canadian Fisheries Association
Overview: A large national organization founded in 1915
Mission: To represent Canada's fish & seafood industry
Membership: 58; *Fees:* $600 associate members; $5000 special purpose associations; *Member Profile:* Enterprises & associations that harvest, handle, process, distribute, & market fish & seafood; Associate institutions & firms that provide a product or service to the fish & seafood industry

Canadian Associations / Fishermen & Scientists Research Society (FSRS)

Activities: Developing an economically sound & competitive industry; Liaising with government departments & agencies
Chief Officer(s):
Gilbert Linstead, Chair
Meetings/Conferences:
• 2018 Fisheries Council of Canada Annual Conference, 2018, Ottawa, ON
Scope: National
Description: Educational sessions, opportunities to network, & social programs
Publications:
• Building a Fishery that Works: Ottawa Update
Type: Newsletter; *Frequency:* Monthly
Profile: Updates on the Council's activities, environmental issues, Canadian & international fisheries issues, & market reports
• Fisheries Council of Canada Annual Fish & Seafood Products & Services Directory
Type: Directory; *Frequency:* Annually
Profile: Listings to promote members' products & services

Fishermen & Scientists Research Society (FSRS)
PO Box 25125, Halifax NS B3M 4H4
Tel: 902-876-1160; *Fax:* 902-876-1320
www.fsrs.ns.ca
Overview: A medium-sized provincial organization
Mission: To establish and maintain a network of fishermen and scientific personnel that are concerned with the long-term sustainability of the marine fishing industry in the Atlantic Region.
Membership: *Member Profile:* Fishermen; Research scientists; *Committees:* Communications; Scientific Program; Shellfish Working Group;Groundfish Working Group; Nearshore Temperature Monitoring Project Working Group
Chief Officer(s):
Patricia King, General Manager, 902-876-1160
pmdservices@bellaliant.net

Fitness New Brunswick (NBCFAL) / Conditionnement physique Noueau-Brunswick (CCPVANB)
Lady Beaverbrook Gym, University of New Brunswick, PO Box 4400, #A112A, 2 Peter Kelly Dr., Fredericton NB E3B 5A3
Tel: 506-453-1094; *Fax:* 506-453-1099
Toll-Free: 888-790-1411
membershipservices@fitnessnb.ca
www.fitnessnb.ca
www.facebook.com/Fitness.New.Brunswick
twitter.com/FitnessNB
Previous Name: New Brunswick Council for Fitness & Active Living (NBCFAL); New Brunswick Fitness Council
Overview: A small provincial organization founded in 1988
Mission: To certify fitness professionals in New Brunswick; to promote professionalism in the fitness industry; To offer standardization & consistency in training programs; To uphold professional ethics through the Code of Conduct for fitness service providers
Member of: Coalition for Active Living (CCAL)
Affiliation(s): Atlantic Canadian Society for Exercise Physiology (CSEP) Health & Fitness Program (H&FP); National Fitness Leadership Alliance (NFLA)
Membership: *Fees:* $62.15; *Committees:* Professional Development; Marketing & Communications; Human Resources; Translation; Conference
Activities: Providing fitness education in New Brunswick; Raising public awareness of safe & effective practices for fitness professionals
Chief Officer(s):
Marilynn Georgas, Executive Director
executivedirector@fitnessnb.ca
Erin Maranda, Coordinator, Projects
projectscoordinator@fitnessnb.ca
Meetings/Conferences:
• Fitness New Brunswick Annual General Meeting 2018, 2018
Scope: Provincial
• Fitness New Brunswick Annual Summit 2018, 2018
Scope: Provincial

The 519 Church St. Community Centre
519 Church St., Toronto ON M4Y 2C9
Tel: 416-392-6874; *Fax:* 416-392-0519
info@the519.org
www.the519.org
www.facebook.com/The519
twitter.com/The519
www.youtube.com/The519Toronto

Also Known As: The 519
Overview: A medium-sized local charitable organization founded in 1975
Mission: To act as a meeting place & focal point for the diverse downtown Toronto community; To respond to the needs of the local neighbourhood and the broader Lesbian, Gay, Bisexual, Transsexual, Transgender, and Queer community
Finances: *Annual Operating Budget:* $3 Million-$5 Million; *Funding Sources:* Federal, provincial & municipal governments; United Way; Individual & corporate donors
Chief Officer(s):
Maura Lawless, Executive Director
Awards:
• The Will Munro Fund for Queer & Trans People Living with Cancer
To help reduce financial hardship & improve the quality of life for LGBTQ people living with cancer, especially those who experience barriers in accessing health care (low-income individuals; Indigenous people; newcomers & refugees)
Eligibility: LGBTQ people of all ages who are living with cancer in Ontario*Location:* January 15; March 15; May 15; July 15; September 15; *Amount:* $5,000

Flamborough Chamber of Commerce (FCC)
#227, 7 innovation Dr., Flamborough ON L9H 7H9
Tel: 905-689-7650; *Fax:* 905-689-1313
admin@flamboroughchamber.ca
flamboroughchamber.ca
www.facebook.com/FlamboroughCofC
twitter.com/flamboroughcofc
Overview: A small local organization founded in 1982
Mission: To recognize & encourage good corporate citizenship, defending & promoting private enterprise; To contribute to the growth of a healthy local economy & continual improvement to the quality of life in Flamborough
Affiliation(s): Ontario & Canadian Chamber of Commerce
Finances: *Funding Sources:* Membership fees
Staff Member(s): 2
Membership: 180+; *Fees:* Schedule available
Chief Officer(s):
Arend Kersten, Executive Director
arend@flamboroughchamber.ca
Awards:
• Outstanding Business Achievement Awards
• Lifetime Achievement Award
Publications:
• Bottom Line [a publication of the Flamborough Chamber of Commerce]
Type: Newspaper; *Frequency:* Monthly
• Flamborough Community Guide & Business Directory
Type: Directory

Flamborough Information & Community Services (FICS)
857 Millgrove Side Rd., Waterdown ON L0R 2H0
Tel: 905-689-7880
fics@infoflam.on.ca
www.infoflam.on.ca
www.facebook.com/FlamboroughInformationAndCommunityServices
Overview: A small local charitable organization founded in 1977 overseen by InformOntario
Mission: To empower residents through information & referral services; to enhance quality of life by identifying unmet needs, liaising with the community & facilitating social services
Member of: Inform Hamilton
Chief Officer(s):
Shelley Scott, Executive Director

Flavour Manufacturers Association of Canada (FMAC) / Association canadienne de fabricants des arômes
#600, 100 Sheppard Ave. East, Toronto ON M2N 5N6
Tel: 416-510-8036; *Fax:* 416-510-8043
info@flavourcanada.ca
www.flavorcanada.com
Overview: A medium-sized national organization founded in 1990
Mission: To serve the needs of the Canadian flavour industry by providing a forum for the examination of industry problems, assisting in the implementation of solutions, & fostering a global perspective for creativity, innovation & competition.
Membership: *Member Profile:* Flavour manufacturers; flavour ingredient suppliers; others with interest in the Canadian flavour industry

Flax Council of Canada
#465, 167 Lombard Ave., Winnipeg MB R3B 0T6
Tel: 204-982-2115; *Fax:* 204-982-2128
flax@flaxcouncil.ca
www.flaxcouncil.ca
Overview: A medium-sized national organization founded in 1985
Mission: To provide a central focus for industry, producers, government, research institutions & marketing organizations; to promote flax worldwide through crop, market & product development.
Staff Member(s): 4
Membership: *Committees:* Communications; Market Development; Research & Technical; Member Relations; Value Added Processing; Finance
Activities: *Library:* Open to public
Chief Officer(s):
William Hill, President

Flemingdon Community Legal Services
#1, 1 Leaside Park Dr., Toronto ON M4H 1R1
Tel: 416-441-1764; *Fax:* 416-441-0269
www.flemingdonlegal.com
Overview: A small local organization founded in 1980
Mission: The agency provides free legal assistance to low income people who live within their geographical catchbasin. Cases taken involve: landlord/tenant law; employment & income; immigration matters. There is also a satellite office at 5 Massey Square Toronto, ON, M4C 5L3, 416-461-0969. Walk-ins are welcome.
Finances: *Funding Sources:* Legal Aid Ontario
Staff Member(s): 14
Chief Officer(s):
Marjorie Hiley, Executive Director

Flemingdon Neighbourhood Services
#104, 10 Gateway Blvd., Toronto ON M3C 3A1
Tel: 416-424-2900; *Fax:* 416-424-3455
info@fnservices.org
www.fnservices.org
Overview: A medium-sized local charitable organization
Mission: To enhance the over-all quality of life for residents of Flemingdon Park and the City of Toronto by increasing access to information and community resources for our clients through advocacy, empowerment and education.
Finances: *Annual Operating Budget:* $500,000-$1.5 Million; *Funding Sources:* Government, United Way
Staff Member(s): 21
Membership: *Fees:* Free
Chief Officer(s):
John Carey, Executive Director

A fleur de sein
313, 3e rue, Chibougamau QC G8P 1N4
Tél: 418-748-7914; *Téléc:* 418-748-4422
Aperçu: *Dimension:* petite; *Envergure:* locale; fondée en 1987
Mission: Offrir solidarité, présence, écoute & entraide à ceux & celles qui sont atteints d'un cancer, quel qu'il soit
Membre de: Regroupement Provincial des Organismes et Groupes d'entraide Communautaire en Oncologie; Vie Nouvelle
Affiliation(s): Réseau québécoise pour la santé du sein
Membre: 75 individus
Membre(s) du bureau directeur:
Suzanne Hamel Migneau, Présidente, A fleur de sein

Fleurs Canada *See* Flowers Canada

Flin Flon & District Chamber of Commerce
#235, 35 Main St., Flin Flon MB R8A 1J7
Tel: 204-687-4518
flinflonchamber@mymts.net
www.flinflondistrictchamber.com
www.facebook.com/flinflondistrictchamber
twitter.com/FlinFlonChamber
Overview: A medium-sized local organization founded in 1948
Mission: To promote & improve trade & commerce & the economic, civic & social welfare of the district; the Chamber represents the communities of Flin Flon, Creighton, Denare Beach, & Cranberry Portage.
Finances: *Funding Sources:* City Map; postcards; gala; membership
Membership: 110; *Fees:* Schedule available based on number of employees
Activities: *Speaker Service:* Yes
Chief Officer(s):
Dianne Russell, President
Karen MacKinnon, President Elect

Flin Flon Aboriginal Friendship Association Inc.
57 Church St., Flin Flon MB R8A 1K8
Tel: 204-687-3900
p.e.c@mymts.net
flinflonfriendshipcentre.ca
Previous Name: Flin Flon Indian & Metis Friendship Centre; Flin Flon Indian-Metis Friendship Association Inc.
Overview: A small local organization founded in 1966
Mission: To encourage active participation of Aboriginal people in Canadian society, promoting awareness of Aboriginal cultural; to provide culturally sensitive programs & services to members of the community.
Activities: Sweetgrass Aboriginal Head Start Initiative; Community Youth Resource Centre; Partners For Careers; Parent/Child Centred Initiative

Flin Flon Indian & Metis Friendship Centre; Flin Flon Indian-Metis Friendship Association Inc. *See* Flin Flon Aboriginal Friendship Association Inc.

Floorball Alberta
Edmonton AB
Tel: 780-999-5333
info@floorballalberta.com
www.floorballalberta.com
www.facebook.com/FloorballAlberta
twitter.com/Floorball_AB
Overview: A small provincial organization founded in 2010 overseen by Floorball Canada
Mission: To be the provincial governing body for the sport of floorball in Alberta
Member of: Floorball Canada
Membership: 6 regional associations

Floorball Canada
347 Brunswick Ave., Toronto ON M5R 2Z1
Tel: 416-970-2529
info@floorballcanada.org
www.floorballcanada.org
www.facebook.com/CanadaFloorball
twitter.com/CanadaFloorball
Overview: A medium-sized national organization
Mission: To be the official governing body of the sport of floorball in Canada
Member of: International Floorball Federation
Affiliation(s): Hockey Canada
Membership: *Fees:* $15 recreational; $30 competetive
Chief Officer(s):
Randy Sa'd, President

Floorball Nova Scotia
NS
floorballnovascotia.ca
www.linkedin.com/pub/floorball-nova-scotia/5a/831/b28
www.facebook.com/256739071063733
Overview: A small provincial organization overseen by Floorball Canada
Mission: To be the provincial governing body for the sport of floorball in Nova Scotia.
Member of: Floorball Canada
Membership: 5 provincial leagues
Activities: Learn to Play clincs; Birthday parties; Leagues; Tournaments; Recreational pick-up games

Floorball Québec
2105 rue Guerin, Laval QC H7E 1R7
Tel: 514-567-8449
info@floorballqc.ca
www.floorballqc.ca
www.facebook.com/floorballqc
twitter.com/floorballqc
www.youtube.com/user/iffchannel
Overview: A small provincial organization founded in 2014 overseen by Floorball Canada
Mission: To promote floorball in Quebec
Member of: Floorball Canada

FloraQuebeca
4101, rue Sherbrooke est, Montréal QC H1X 2B2
Tél: 450-258-0448
floraquebeca@hotmail.com
www.floraquebeca.qc.ca
Aperçu: *Dimension:* petite; *Envergure:* locale; Organisme sans but lucratif; fondée en 1996
Mission: Vouée à la connaissance, à la promotion et surtout à la protection de la flore et des paysages végétaux du Québec
Finances: *Budget de fonctionnement annuel:* Moins de $50,000

5 bénévole(s)
Membre: 105; *Montant de la cotisation:* 15$ individuel; 20$ familial; *Comités:* Bulletin; Flore québécoise; Bryologie; Flore photographique
Membre(s) du bureau directeur:
André Lapointe, Président

Florenceville-Bristol Chamber of Commerce
#1, 8696 Main St., Florenceville-Bristol NB E7L 1Y7
Tel: 506-392-0900; *Fax:* 506-392-5211
chamber@florencevillebristol.ca
www.florenceville.ca/html/chamber.html
Overview: A small local organization
Chief Officer(s):
Doug Thomson, Treasurer

Flowercart
9412 Commercial St., New Minas NS B4N 3E9
Tel: 902-681-0120; *Fax:* 902-681-0922
info@flowercart.ca
www.flowercart.ca
www.facebook.com/Flowercart
Overview: A small local charitable organization founded in 1970
Mission: To provide supported training & employment for adults with intellectual disabilities
Member of: DIRECTIONS Council for Vocational Services Society
Membership: *Committees:* Budget; Executive Director Evalution; Nominating
Chief Officer(s):
Marilyn Reeve, Chair
Jeff Kelly, Executive Director
jeffkelly@flowercart.ca
Publications:
• FlowercartNEWS
Type: Newsletter; *Frequency:* 3 pa

Flowers Canada (FC) / Fleurs Canada
Retail & Distribution Sector, #406, 150 Bank St., Ottawa ON K1H 1B8
Fax: 866-671-8091
Toll-Free: 800-447-5147
flowers@flowerscanada.org
www.flowerscanada.org
Also Known As: Association of the Canadian Floral Industry
Overview: A medium-sized national organization founded in 1897
Mission: To act as the voice of & help to improve the Canadian floriculture industry
Membership: 1,000; *Fees:* $200 associates; $265 retailers; $500 distributors & wholesalers; *Member Profile:* Flower growers; Distributors; Retailers; Educators; Associates
Activities: Establishing partnerships; Researching; Developing consumers; Taking legislative action; Encouraging professional accreditation; Providing education; Offering business services; Giving sales & marketing support; Organizing conferences; Communicating with members; Developing standards; Conducting research; Identifying & sharing best practices; Promoting e-business; Presenting awards; *Library:* Flowers Canada Library; Not open to public
Chief Officer(s):
Susan Clarke, Senator
James Fuller, Chairman
Jeff Walters, President

Flowers Canada Growers (FCA)
#7, 45 Speedvale Ave. East, Guelph ON N1H 1J2
Tel: 519-836-5495; *Fax:* 519-836-7529
Toll-Free: 800-698-0113
flowers@fco.on.ca
www.flowerscanadagrowers.com
Overview: A medium-sized national organization
Mission: To help members increase their exposure & sales by addressing issues pertaining to the industry
Staff Member(s): 12
Membership: 357
Chief Officer(s):
Dean Shoemaker, Executive Director

Foam Lake & District Chamber of Commerce
PO Box 238, Foam Lake SK S0A 1A0
Tel: 306-272-4191
Overview: A small local organization
Chief Officer(s):
Jim Kurtz, President

Focolare Movement - Canada / Mouvement des Focolari
PO Box 69523, 5845 Yonge St., Toronto ON M2M 4K3
Tel: 416-250-6606
toronto@focolare.ca
www.focolare.ca
www.facebook.com/focolare.org
twitter.com/Focolare_org
vimeo.com/focolareorg
Overview: A small national charitable organization founded in 1943
Mission: To fulfill Jesus' last will & testament: "That all may be one"; To strive for the Focolare spirituality to have an impact on family life, youth, & all areas of ecclesial & secular life; To promote the ideals of unity & universal brotherhood
Affiliation(s): Archdiocese of Toronto
Finances: *Funding Sources:* Donations
Membership: *Member Profile:* Individuals of all ages, walks of life, & vocations; Churches of religions & convictions that differ from Catholicism
Activities: Providing gatherings for families, youth, children, & various branches
Chief Officer(s):
Brigitte Sass, Contact, Women's Branch
Jacques Maillet, Contact, Men's Branch
Publications:
• Living World
Type: Magazine; *Frequency:* Monthly
Profile: Articles on religion & culture

FOCUS
4921 - 51 Ave., Vermilion AB T9X 1S8
Tel: 780-853-4121; *Fax:* 780-853-2840
admindesk@focusverm.ca
www.focusverm.ca
Previous Name: Vermilion Association for Persons with Disabilities
Overview: A small local charitable organization founded in 1959
Mission: To branch out in response to community needs; To empower people to meet their needs
Member of: Alberta Association for Community Living; Alberta Association of Rehabilitation Centers; Alberta Association for Services to Children & Families
Finances: *Annual Operating Budget:* $1.5 Million-$3 Million; *Funding Sources:* PDD Board; productive enterprise; donations; Children's Authority; HRDC
Staff Member(s): 58
Membership: 8; *Committees:* Finance; Advocacy; Resource; Program; Fundraising

Focus for Ethnic Women (FEW)
550 Parkside Dr., #A8, Waterloo ON N2L 5V4
Tel: 519-746-3411; *Fax:* 519-746-6799
info@few.on.ca
www.few.on.ca
www.facebook.com/Focusforethnicwomen
twitter.com/Focus4EthnicWmn
Overview: A small local organization founded in 1987
Mission: To enhance the participation of immigrant & visible minority women in Canadian society, through innovative & collaborative efforts among the board, staff, participants, funders & community partners
Staff Member(s): 13; 9 volunteer(s)
Membership: 19
Activities: Career exploration & counselling; Skills training; Job search assistance; Resume- & cover letter-building workshops; Industrial sewing training; Leadership & personal development workshops; Interview preparation; Computer training; *Awareness Events:* Focus on Friends Fundraising *Library:* Learner Resource Centre
Chief Officer(s):
Renu Bhandari, Executive Director

Focus Humanitarian Assistance Canada
#200, 49 Wynford Dr., Toronto ON M3C 1K1
Tel: 416-423-7988; *Fax:* 416-423-4216
Toll-Free: 800-423-7972
focuscanada@focushumanitarian.org
www.focus-canada.org
Overview: A small international charitable organization founded in 1994
Mission: To respond to international crises; To provide emergency relief & risk management services to communities affected by natural or man-made disasters
Finances: *Funding Sources:* Donations; Fundraising
Activities: Offering emergency assistance & relief

Canadian Associations / Focus on the Family Canada

Chief Officer(s):
Aysha Kaba, Senior Program Officer

Focus on the Family Canada
19946 - 80A Ave., Langley BC V2Y 0J8
Tel: 604-455-7900; *Fax:* 604-455-7999
Toll-Free: 800-661-9800
Other Communication: hr@fotf.ca
letters@fotf.ca
www.focusonthefamily.com
www.facebook.com/fotfcanada
twitter.com/fotfcanada
Overview: A large national charitable organization founded in 1982
Mission: To strengthen & encourage the Canadian family through education & support based on Christian principles
Member of: Canadian Council of Christian Charities
Finances: *Funding Sources:* Donations
250 volunteer(s)
Activities: Seminars & conferences; Resources; Personal counselling & prayer support; *Library:* Focus on the Family Canada Library
Chief Officer(s):
Terence Rolston, President
Publications:
• inFocus
Type: Newsletter
• Thriving Family
Type: Magazine

Fogo Island Folk Alliance
PO Box 146, Fogo NL A0G 2B0
Tel: 709-266-2403
Brimstonehead_festival@yahoo.ca
brimstoneheadfestival.com
www.facebook.com/BrimstoneHeadFolkFestival
Overview: A small local organization founded in 1985
Mission: To promote traditional Newfoundland & Irish music
Finances: *Funding Sources:* Provincial
Activities: The Brimstone Head Folk Festival

Fogolârs Federation of Canada
7065 Islington Ave., Woodbridge ON L4L 1V9
Tel: 905-851-7898
fog.fed@sympatico.ca
www.fogolarsfederation.com
Overview: A small national organization founded in 1974
Mission: To preserve Friulian language & culture by bringing together all Fruilian communities in Canada
Membership: 16 associations
Activities: Lobbying to governments in Italy & Canada; Collecting funds for philanthropic campaigns; Organizing a national congress
Chief Officer(s):
Giuseppe Toso, President
Publications:
• La Cisilute
Type: Magazine; *Frequency:* Biannually

FogQuest
448 Monarch Pl., Kamloops BC V2E 2B2
Tel: 250-374-1745; *Fax:* 250-374-1746
info@fogquest.org
www.fogquest.org
Overview: A small international charitable organization founded in 1987
Mission: To plan & implement water projects for rural communities located in developing countries
Finances: *Funding Sources:* Grants; donations; membership fees
Membership: *Fees:* $40 individuals; $35 students
Chief Officer(s):
Robert Schemenauer, Executive Director
Melissa Rosato, Associate Executive Director
Meetings/Conferences:
• 8th International Conference on Fog, Fog Collection and Dew, 2019, Taipei
Scope: International

Foire agricole royale d'hiver *See* Royal Agricultural Winter Fair Association

Folk Arts Council of St Catharines
85 Church St., St Catharines ON L2R 3C7
Tel: 905-685-6589; *Fax:* 905-685-8376
generalenquiries@folk-arts.ca
www.folk-arts.ca
www.facebook.com/niagarafolkartsmulticulturalcentre
twitter.com/niagarafolkarts
www.instagram.com/niagarafolkarts
Also Known As: Niagara Folk Arts Multicultural Centre
Overview: A small local charitable organization founded in 1970
Mission: To support the community of newcomers in the Niagara region
Member of: Regional Association of Volunteer Administrators; Festival & Event Ontario; Niagara North Community Legal Assistance; Ontario Council of Agencies Serving Immigrants; Community Development & Race Relations
Affiliation(s): Canadian Council of Refugees; St. Catharines & Area Arts Council
Finances: *Annual Operating Budget:* $500,000-$1.5 Million
Staff Member(s): 30; 100 volunteer(s)
Membership: 50+ associations, organizations & individuals; *Fees:* $75 ethnocultural groups; $25 community groups; $15 individuals
Activities: Youth services; skills training programs; settlement services; job search programs; English classes; Crossroads self-employment program; Community Connections for Newcomers to Canada; Childminding; *Library:* Resource Centre; Open to public
Chief Officer(s):
Jeff Burch, Executive Director
jburch@folk-arts.ca

Folk Arts Council of Winnipeg *See* Folklorama

Folk Festival Society of Calgary
1215 - 10 Ave. SE, Calgary AB T2G 0W6
Tel: 403-233-0904; *Fax:* 403-266-3373
www.calgaryfolkfest.com
www.facebook.com/calgaryfolkfest
Also Known As: Calgary Folk Music Festival
Overview: A medium-sized local charitable organization founded in 1989
Mission: Promotes folk music and folk artists from several genres including blues, Celtic, traditional music, roots, global grooves, cutting-edge sounds, dub, bluegrass, funk, country, hip-hop, R& B, old-timey, spoken word, and alternative.
Finances: *Funding Sources:* Municipal government; national government; provincial government
Staff Member(s): 11; 1350 volunteer(s)
Activities: *Speaker Service:* Yes; *Rents Mailing List:* Yes
Chief Officer(s):
Talia Potter, Acting General Manager
talia@calgaryfolkfest.com
Kerry Clarke, Artistic Director
kerry@calgaryfolkfest.com
Dean Warnock, Production Manager
dean@calgaryfolkfest.com

Folklorama
183 Kennedy St., 2nd Fl., Winnipeg MB R3C 1S6
Tel: 204-982-6210; *Fax:* 204-943-1956
Toll-Free: 800-665-0234
info@folklorama.ca
www.folklorama.ca
www.facebook.com/Folklorama
twitter.com/folklorama
Previous Name: Folk Arts Council of Winnipeg
Overview: A large local organization founded in 1970
Mission: To organize a two-week multicultural festival to celebrate diversity & to promote cultural understanding
Finances: *Annual Operating Budget:* $1.5 Million-$3 Million
Staff Member(s): 13; 2000 volunteer(s)
Membership: 200; *Fees:* Schedule available
Activities: *Library:* by appointment
Chief Officer(s):
Teresa Cotroneo, Acting Executive Director, 204-982-6216
tcotroneo@folklorama.ca
Christa Mariash, Director, Marketing & Communications, 204-982-6212
cmariash@folklorama.ca

Folklore Canada International (FCI)
2040, rue Alexandre-de-Sève, Montréal QC H2L 2W4
Tel: 514-524-8552; *Fax:* 514-524-0262
patrimoine@qc.aira.com
www.folklore-canada.org
Overview: A small international charitable organization founded in 1986
Mission: To promote folk arts; to organize cultural exhanges between groups at national & international levels; to organize international folk arts festivals.
Member of: Conseil international des organisations de festivals de folklore et d'arts traditionels.
Finances: *Funding Sources:* Membership dues; projects
Membership: *Member Profile:* Folk groups & festivals
Activities: Consultant expertise; training; international relations & invitations; *Speaker Service:* Yes; *Library:* by appointment

Folklore Studies Association of Canada (FSAC) / Association canadienne d'ethnologie et de folklore (ACEF)
CÉLAT - Faculté des lettres, Pavillon Charles-De-Koninck, 1030, av des Sciences humaines, Université Laval, Québec QC G1V 0A6
Tel: 418-656-2131
www.acef-fsac.ulaval.ca
Overview: A small national charitable organization founded in 1976
Mission: To increase education & research in the field of folklore studies
Affiliation(s): Humanities & Social Sciences Federation of Canada
Finances: *Annual Operating Budget:* Less than $50,000
Staff Member(s): 1; 50 volunteer(s)
Membership: 200; *Fees:* $60 individual; $30 student/underemployed; $80 institutional; $720 lifetime; *Member Profile:* University faculty, students, researchers, museum/archivist
Activities: *Speaker Service:* Yes; *Rents Mailing List:* Yes
Chief Officer(s):
Ian Hayes, Secretary-Treasurer
Awards:
• Luc Lacourcière Memorial Scholarship
• Marius Barbeau Medal
Publications:
• Ethnologies
Type: Journal

Fondation Alfred Dallaire
1111, av Laurier ouest, Montréal QC H2V 2L3
Tél: 514-277-7778
Ligne sans frais: 866-277-7778
info@memoria.ca
www.memoria.ca
Aperçu: *Dimension:* petite; *Envergure:* nationale; Organisme sans but lucratif

Fondation André Sénécal pour la recherche sur la moelle épinière *Voir* Fondation pour la recherche sur la moelle épinière

Fondation Asie Pacifique du Canada *See* Asia Pacific Foundation of Canada

Fondation autochtone nationale de partenariat pour la lutte contre les dépendances *See* National Native Addictions Partnership Foundation

Fondation Canada-Scandinavie *See* Canadian-Scandinavian Foundation

La Fondation canadienne d'ergothérapie *See* Canadian Occupational Therapy Foundation

La Fondation canadienne de l'ouïe *See* Hearing Foundation of Canada

Fondation canadienne de la maladie de lyme *See* Canadian Lyme Disease Foundation

La Fondation canadienne de la porphyrie *See* Canadian Porphyria Foundation Inc.

Fondation canadienne de la recherche dur l'alcoolisation foetale *See* Canadian Foundation on Fetal Alcohol Research

La Fondation canadienne de la Thyroïde *See* Thyroid Foundation of Canada

La fondation canadienne de pédiatrie *See* Canadian Pediatric Foundation

La Fondation canadienne de recherche de l'anémie de Fanconi *See* Canadian Fanconi Anemia Research Fund

Fondation canadienne de recherche sur le cancer de la prostate *See* Prostate Cancer Canada

Fondation canadienne de recherche sur le SIDA *See* Canadian Foundation for AIDS Research

Fondation Canadienne des 3c *See* The 3C Foundation of Canada

Fondation canadienne des echanges educatifs *See* Canadian Education Exchange Foundation

Fondation canadienne des études ukrainiennes *See* Canadian Foundation for Ukrainian Studies

Fondation canadienne des femmes *See* Canadian Women's Foundation

Fondation canadienne des maladies inflammatoires de l'intestin *Voir* Crohn's & Colitis Canada

Fondation canadienne des plantes ornementales *See* Canadian Ornamental Plant Foundation

Fondation canadienne des pompiers morts en service *See* Canadian Fallen Firefighters Foundation

Fondation canadienne Donner *See* Donner Canadian Foundation

Fondation canadienne du foie *See* Canadian Liver Foundation

Fondation canadienne du rein *See* Kidney Foundation of Canada

La Fondation canadienne du rein, section Chibougamau
CP 462, Chibougamau QC G8P 2Y8
Aperçu: Dimension: petite; *Envergure:* locale surveillé par The Kidney Foundation of Canada
Membre(s) du bureau directeur:
Hélène Ross-Arseneault

Fondation canadienne du service social *See* Canadian Social Work Foundation

La Fondation canadienne du syndrome de Tourette *See* Tourette Syndrome Foundation of Canada

Fondation canadienne for la promotion de la santé digestive *See* Canadian Digestive Health Foundation

Fondation canadienne MedicAlert *See* Canadian MedicAlert Foundation

Fondation canadienne pour l'amélioration des services de santé *See* Canadian Foundation for Healthcare Improvement

Fondation canadienne pour l'innovation *See* Canada Foundation for Innovation

Fondation canadienne pour la pharmacie *See* Canadian Foundation for Pharmacy

La Fondation canadienne pour la recherche en chiropratique *See* Canadian Chiropractic Research Foundation

Fondation canadienne pour le développement de carrière *See* Canadian Career Development Foundation

Fondation canadienne pour les sciences du climat et de l'atmosphère *See* Canadian Foundation for Climate & Atmospheric Sciences

Fondation canadienne rêves d'enfants *See* Children's Wish Foundation of Canada

La Fondation canadienne sur les tumeurs cérébrales *See* Brain Tumour Foundation of Canada

Fondation canadienne-polonaise *See* Canadian Polish Foundation

Fondation Cardio-Montérégienne (FOCAM)
#230, 1750, boul Marie-Victorin, Longueuil QC J4G 1A5
Tél: 450-468-3333; *Téléc:* 450-468-3334
www.fondationcardio-monteregienne.ca
Aperçu: Dimension: petite; *Envergure:* locale
Mission: Encourager et soutenir l'avancement de la science médicale au moyen de dons permettant l'acquisition d'équipements reliés à la médecine cardiaque.

Fondation Caritas-Sherbrooke inc.
110, rue Ozias-Leduc, Sherbrooke QC J1H 1M7
Tél: 819-566-6345; *Téléc:* 819-566-6181
Info@caritas-estrie.org
www.caritas-estrie.org/organismes-connexes/fondation-caritas
Également appelé: Caritas
Aperçu: Dimension: petite; *Envergure:* locale; Organisme sans but lucratif; fondée en 1969
Mission: Venir en aide à Caritas Sherbrooke qui supporte des services et des organismes qui viennent répondre aux besoins des défavorisés en Estrie

Finances: *Budget de fonctionnement annuel:* Moins de $50,000
Membre(s) du personnel: 1; 11 bénévole(s)
Membre: 10
Activités: Campagnes de financement
Membre(s) du bureau directeur:
Yvon Couture, Directeur général
yrcouture@caritas-estrie.org

Fondation catholique du Manitoba *See* The Catholic Foundation of Manitoba

Fondation Centre de cancérologie Charles-Bruneau
4515, rue de Rouen, Montréal QC H1V 1H1
Tél: 514-256-0404; *Téléc:* 514-256-2116
Ligne sans frais: 877-256-0404
fondation@charlesbruneau.qc.ca
charlesbruneau.qc.ca
www.facebook.com/fcharlesbruneau
twitter.com/fcharlesbruneau
www.youtube.com/fcharlesbruneau
Aperçu: Dimension: petite; *Envergure:* locale; Organisme sans but lucratif
Mission: Pour amasser des fonds qui finance la recherche sur le cancer pédiatrique
Membre(s) du personnel: 14
Membre(s) du bureau directeur:
Rébecca Dumont, Directrice générale
rdumont@charlesbruneau.qc.ca

Fondation Charles LeMoyne *Voir* Fondation Hôpital Charles-LeMoyne

Fondation CHU de Québec
Hôpital Saint-François d'Assise, 10, rue de l'Espinay, #E1-152, Québec QC G1L 3L5
Tél: 418-525-4385; *Téléc:* 418-525-4393
fondation.chuq@chuq.qc.ca
www.fondationduchuq.org
twitter.com/FCHUQ
Aperçu: Dimension: petite; *Envergure:* locale; Organisme sans but lucratif
Mission: Pour augmenter des fonds sur le compte de 5 hôpitaux pour améliorer les services offerts aux patients et à financer la recherche
Membre(s) du personnel: 22
Membre: *Comités:* Organisateur du Bal des Grands romantiques; Organisateur du Tournoi de golf; Organisateur du Loto-Voyages et cadeaux de rêve; Communications
Membre(s) du bureau directeur:
Marie-Claude Paré, Présidente et chef de la direction
marie-claude.pare@chudequebec.ca

Fondation CHU Dumont Foundation
330 University Ave., Moncton NB E1C 2Z3
Tel: 506-862-4285; *Fax:* 506-862-4474
Toll-Free: 800-862-6775
info@fondationdumont.ca
www.chudumont.ca
www.facebook.com/ChuDumont
Overview: A small local charitable organization
Mission: To raise money on behalf of the Dr. Georges L. Dumont Hospital to improve the services offered to patients & to fund research
Staff Member(s): 11
Chief Officer(s):
Jacques B. LeBlanc, President & CEO

Fondation CHU Sainte-Justine
#335, 5757, av Decelles, Montréal QC H3S 2C3
Tél: 514-345-4710; *Téléc:* 514-345-4718
Ligne sans frais: 888-235-3667
fondation@sainte-justine.org
www.fondation-sainte-justine.org
www.facebook.com/fondationsaintejustine
twitter.com/fondstejustine
www.youtube.com/user/FondationHSJ
Aperçu: Dimension: petite; *Envergure:* locale; Organisme sans but lucratif; fondée en 1987
Mission: Pour amasser des fonds pour le compte de le CHU Sainte-Justine que aident à améliorer les services offerts aux patients et à financer la recherche
Membre(s) du bureau directeur:
Maud Cohen, Présidente et directrice générale

Fondation Cole *See* Cole Foundation

Fondation communautaire d'Ottawa *See* Community Foundation of Ottawa

Fondation communautaire du Grand-Québec (FCG-Q) / Community Foundation of Greater Québec
#150, 3100, av Du Bourg Royal, Québec QC G1C 5S7
Tél: 418-521-6664; *Téléc:* 418-521-6668
info@fcommunautaire.com
www.fcommunautaire.com
www.facebook.com/FCdGQ
twitter.com/FCGQ
Aperçu: Dimension: petite; *Envergure:* locale; Organisme sans but lucratif; fondée en 1993
Mission: La mission de la Fondation est d'améliorer la qualité de vie de la communauté en offrant à ses donateurs la possibilité de créer des fonds qui constituent des capitaux perpétuels et inaliénables dont les revenus sont redistribués principalement selon les fins que poursuit chaque fonds; la FCGQ offre aux entreprises privées, aux organismes à but non lucratif, aux fondations caritatives, aux fiducies, aux individus et aux familles de l'aide et des ressources pour créer des fonds qui porteront leur nom ou celui d'êtres chers; les revenus découlant de la gestion des fonds sont répartis sous forme de subventions à toute une gamme d'organismes oeuvrant dans les domaines des services sociaux, de l'action communautaire, des arts et de la culture, de l'éducation, de l'aide internationale, de la santé et de l'environnement
Membre de: Fondation communautaire du Canada
Affiliation(s): Association canadienne des professionnels en dons planifiés; Un héritage à partager
Membre(s) du personnel: 5
Membre: *Critères d'admissibilité:* Les membres sont actifs dans le milieu et proviennent de sphères professionnelles variées pour assurer l'équilibre dans la représentation; *Comités:* Placement; Audit; Promotion et développement; Attribution d'aide financière; Gouvernance et ressources humaines
Activités: *Stagiaires:* Oui; *Service de conférenciers:* Oui
Membre(s) du bureau directeur:
Nataly Rae, Directrice générale
nrae@fcommunautaire.com
Robert Tanguay, Président
Daniel Doucet, 1er Vice-président
Diane Bélanger, 2e Vice-présidente

Fondation communautaire juive de Montréal *See* Jewish Community Foundation of Montréal

Fondation culturelle Canada-Israël *See* Canada-Israel Cultural Foundation

Fondation d'aide aux personnes incontinentes (Canada) *See* The Canadian Continence Foundation

Fondation d'art Inuit *See* Inuit Art Foundation

Fondation d'éducation économique *See* Canadian Foundation for Economic Education

La fondation de basketball Dr James Naismith *See* Dr. James Naismith Basketball Foundation

Fondation de danse Margie Gillis *See* Margie Gillis Dance Foundation

La Fondation de Jerusalem du Canada Inc *See* Jerusalem Foundation of Canada Inc

Fondation de l'Ataxie Charlevoix-Saguenay / Ataxia of Charlevoix-Saguenay Foundation
#2100, 1000, rue Sherbrooke ouest, Montréal QC H3A 3G4
Tél: 514-370-3625; *Téléc:* 514-370-3615
ataxia@arsacs.com
www.arsacs.com
Aperçu: Dimension: moyenne; *Envergure:* locale; fondée en 2006
Mission: Financer la recherche scientifique sur l'ataxie récessive spastique autosomique de Charlevoix-Saguenay
Membre(s) du bureau directeur:
Jean Groleau, Président

Fondation de l'entrepreneurship
65, rue Sainte-Anne, 10e étage, Québec QC G1R 3X5
Tél: 418-646-1994; *Téléc:* 418-646-2246
Ligne sans frais: 800-661-2160
info@reseaum.com
www.reseaum.com
www.linkedin.com/groups/135631
www.facebook.com/fondationdelentrepreneurship
twitter.com/entreprendreinc
www.youtube.com/FondEntrepreneurship
Nom précédent: Fondation de l'entrepreneurship du Québec

Canadian Associations / Fondation de l'Hôpital de Montréal pour enfants / Montréal Children's Hospital Foundation

Aperçu: Dimension: moyenne; *Envergure:* provinciale; Organisme sans but lucratif; fondée en 1980
Mission: Promouvoir la culture entrepreneuriale, dans toutes ses formes d'expression, comme moyen privilégié pour assurer le développement économique et social de toutes les régions
Finances: Budget de fonctionnement annuel: $1.5 Million-$3 Million; *Fonds:* Gouvernements fédéral et provincial et entreprises privées
Membre(s) du personnel: 20; 1200 bénévole(s)
Membre: 400 institutionnel; *Montant de la cotisation:* 100$
Activités: Stagiaires: Oui; *Listes de destinataires:* Oui
Membre(s) du bureau directeur:
Pierre Duhamel, Directeur général
pduhamel@entrepreneurship.qc.ca

Fondation de l'entrepreneurship du Québec *Voir* Fondation de l'entrepreneurship

Fondation de l'Hôpital de Montréal pour enfants / Montréal Children's Hospital Foundation
1, Place Alexis Nihon, #1420, 3400, boul de Maisonneuve ouest, Montréal QC H3Z 3B8
Tel: 514-934-4846; *Fax:* 514-939-3551
Toll-Free: 866-934-4846
info@fhme.ca
fondationduchildren.com
www.facebook.com/lechildren
twitter.com/hopitalchildren
www.youtube.com/montrealchildrens
Overview: A small local charitable organization
Mission: Pour amasser des fonds au nom de l'Hôpital de Montréal pour enfants afin de financer la recherche et améliorer les soins aux patients
Finances: Annual Operating Budget: Greater than $5 Million
Chief Officer(s):
Marie-Josée Gariépy, Présidente
mgar@fhme.com

Fondation de l'Hôpital du Sacré-Coeur de Montréal
5400, boul Gouin ouest, Montréal QC H4J 1C5
Tél: 514-338-2303; *Téléc:* 514-338-3153
Ligne sans frais: 866-453-3666
fondation.hsc@ssss.gouv.qc.ca
www.fhscm.com
www.linkedin.com/company/5323549
www.facebook.com/FondationHopitalSacreCoeur
twitter.com/fhscm
www.youtube.com/user/HSCM2009
Aperçu: Dimension: petite; *Envergure:* locale; Organisme sans but lucratif; fondée en 1976
Mission: Pour amasser des fonds au nom du Hôpital du Sacré-Coeur de Montréal afin de financer la recherche et améliorer les soins aux patients
Membre(s) du personnel: 10
Membre(s) du bureau directeur:
Paul Bergeron, Directeur général
paul.bergeron.cnmtl@ssss.gouv.qc.ca

Fondation de l'Hôpital Général de Montréal / Montréal General Hospital Foundation
1650, av Cedar, #E6-129, Montréal QC H3G 1A4
Tel: 514-934-8230; *Fax:* 514-937-7683
info@mghfoundation.com
www.mghfoundation.com
Overview: A small local charitable organization founded in 1973
Mission: Pour amasser des fonds au nom de l'Hôpital Général de Montréal afin de financer la recherche et améliorer les soins aux patients
Staff Member(s): 10
Chief Officer(s):
Jean-Guy Gourdeau, Président & directeur exécutif
jggourdeau@mghfoundation.com
Awards:
• Research Awards

Fondation de l'Hôpital Maisonneuve-Rosemont
#270, 5345, boul de L'Assomption, Montréal QC H1T 4B3
Tél: 514-252-3435; *Téléc:* 514-252-3943
info@fondationhmr.ca
fondationhmr.ca
www.linkedin.com/company-beta/10080977
www.facebook.com/fondationhmr
twitter.com/fondationhmr
www.youtube.com/user/FondationHMR
Aperçu: Dimension: petite; *Envergure:* locale; Organisme sans but lucratif
Mission: Pour amasser des fonds pour le compte de l'Hôpital Maisonneuve-Rosemont que contribuent à améliorer les services offerts aux patients et à financer la recherche
Membre(s) du personnel: 17; 122 bénévole(s)
Membre(s) du bureau directeur:
Lucie Drapeau, Directrice générale

Fondation de l'Ordre des infirmières et infirmiers du Québec
4200, rue Molson, Montréal QC H1Y 4V4
Tél: 514-935-2501; *Téléc:* 514-935-2055
Ligne sans frais: 800-363-6048
info@fondationoiiq.org
www.fondationoiiq.org
www.facebook.com/Ordre.infirmieres.infirmiers.Quebec
twitter.com/OIIQ
vimeo.com/oiiq
Nom précédent: Fondation de recherche en sciences infirmières du Québec
Aperçu: Dimension: petite; *Envergure:* provinciale; Organisme sans but lucratif; fondée en 1987
Mission: Promouvoir l'avancement des sciences infirmières et l'amélioration continue des soins infirmiers au Québec par le soutien à la recherche et le transfert de connaissances; son but ultime demeure l'amélioration de la santé et du bien-être des Québécoises et des Québécois
Finances: Budget de fonctionnement annuel: $250,000-$500,000
Membre: *Critères d'admissibilite:* Infirmière, infirmier ou personne intéressée à la recherche en soins infirmiers
Activités: Collecte de fonds; subventionner des projets cliniques soumis par des infirmières; Tournoi annuel de golf, sept.; Soirée Inspiration, mai
Membre(s) du bureau directeur:
Nancy Hammond, Présidente

Fondation de la banque d'yeux du Québec inc. / Québec Eye Bank Foundation
5415, boul de l'Assomption, Montréal QC H1T 2M4
Tél: 514-252-3886; *Téléc:* 514-252-3821
Aperçu: Dimension: petite; *Envergure:* provinciale; Organisme sans but lucratif; fondée en 1976
Mission: Financement de la recherche sur les maladies de l'oeil et plus particulièrement de la cornée (greffe)
Finances: Budget de fonctionnement annuel: $50,000-$100,000
Activités: Service de conférenciers: Oui

Fondation de la famille Birks *See* Birks Family Foundation

Fondation de la famille Brian Bronfman *See* Brian Bronfman Family Foundation

La fondation de la famille J.W. McConnell *See* The J.W. McConnell Family Foundation

Fondation de la faune du Québec (FFQ)
#420, 1175, av Lavigerie, Québec QC G1V 4P1
Tél: 418-644-7926; *Téléc:* 418-643-7655
Ligne sans frais: 877-639-0742
ffq@fondationdelafaune.qc.ca
www.fondationdelafaune.qc.ca
www.facebook.com/fondationdelafauneduquebec
Aperçu: Dimension: moyenne; *Envergure:* provinciale; Organisme sans but lucratif; fondée en 1987
Mission: Promouvoir la conservation et la mise en valeur de la faune et de son habitat
Finances: Budget de fonctionnement annuel: $3 Million-$5 Million
Membre(s) du personnel: 17
Membre: 4 500; *Montant de la cotisation:* 20$
Activités: Programmes de subvention: amélioration de la qualité des habitats aquatiques; faire connaître nos habitats fauniques; programme d'aide à la protection des habitats; pêche en herbe, faune en danger; programme de mise en valeur des cours d'eau en milieu agricole
Membre(s) du bureau directeur:
André Martin, Président-directeur général
direction@fondationdelafaune.qc.ca

Fondation de la greffe de moelle osseuse de l'Est du Québec (FGMOEQ)
1433, 4e av, Québec QC G1J 3B9
Tél: 418-529-5580; *Téléc:* 418-529-4004
Ligne sans frais: 877-520-3466
info@fondation-moelle-osseuse.org
www.fondation-moelle-osseuse.org
Aperçu: Dimension: petite; *Envergure:* locale; Organisme sans but lucratif; fondée en 1996
Mission: Venir en aide aux personnes greffées et à leurs proches en fournissant des services gratuits ou à coût modique
Activités: Service d'écoute; réseau d'entraide; service de consultation psychologique; facilités d'hébergement et service de transport; centre de documentation; *Service de conférenciers:* Oui; *Bibliothèque:* rendez-vous
Membre(s) du bureau directeur:
Pierre Drolet, Président

Fondation de la radio française en Saskatchewan *Voir* Fondation fransaskoise

Fondation de recherche de l'Institut canadien des valeurs mobilières *See* Canadian Securities Institute Research Foundation

Fondation de recherche en sciences infirmières du Québec *Voir* Fondation de l'Ordre des infirmières et infirmiers du Québec

Fondation de recherches médicales sur la dystonie *See* Dystonia Medical Research Foundation Canada

Fondation de recherches sur les blessures de la route *See* Traffic Injury Research Foundation

Fondation des amis de l'environnement TD *See* TD Friends of the Environment Foundation

La Fondation des Amis de la généalogie
QC
sgce.whc.ca/fondation
Aperçu: Dimension: petite; *Envergure:* locale; fondée en 1980
Membre(s) du bureau directeur:
Jacques Gagnon, Président

La Fondation des Auberges du coeur
Tour sud, #17, 4246, rue Juean-Talon est, Montréal QC H1S 1J8
Tél: 514-523-3659; *Téléc:* 514-523-2109
Ligne sans frais: 866-992-6387
info@aubergesducoeur.com
www.aubergesducoeur.com
www.facebook.com/LaFondationdesAubergesducoeur
www.instagram.com/fondationsaubergesducoeur
Nom précédent: Regroupement des Auberges du Coeur
Aperçu: Dimension: moyenne; *Envergure:* provinciale; fondée en 1987
Mission: Défendre l'existence & l'autonomie des ressources communautaires d'hébergement pour jeunes adolescents & jeunes adultes en difficulté ou sans abri; Agir comme porte-parole des jeunes sans abri; Favoriser entre les maisons, les jeunes & les partenaires des communautés d'appartenance de chacune des Auberges des échanges sur les besoins des jeunes
Membre(s) du bureau directeur:
Michèle Noël, Directeur général
michelle.noel@aubergesducoeur.org

Fondation des aveugles du Québec (FAQ)
5112, rue Bellechasse, Montréal QC H1T 2A4
Tél: 514-259-9470; *Téléc:* 514-254-5079
Ligne sans frais: 855-249-5112
www.aveugles.org
www.linkedin.com/company/2968845
www.facebook.com/aveugles
twitter.com/Aveugles_Qc
www.youtube.com/user/fondationaveuglesqc
Aperçu: Dimension: petite; *Envergure:* provinciale
Mission: Soutenir les personnes handicapées de la vue, les conseiller et les aider à mener une vie la plus autonome possible à la maison, au travail et dans les loisirs; informer le public sur l'importance de la prévention quotidienne afin de conserver une bonne vision
Membre(s) du personnel: 7
Activités: Sorties éducatives; camps d'été; ski alpin
Membre(s) du bureau directeur:
Ronald Beauregard, Directeur général

Fondation des Clubs Garçons et Filles du Canada *See* Boys & Girls Clubs of Canada Foundation

La Fondation des écrivains canadiens inc. *See* Canadian Writers' Foundation Inc.

Fondation des étoiles / Foundation of Stars
#205, 370, rue Guy, Montréal QC H3J 1S6
Tél: 514-595-5730; *Téléc:* 514-595-5745
Ligne sans frais: 800-665-2358
info@fondationdesetoiles.ca

www.fondationdesetoiles.ca
www.linkedin.com/in/fondation-des-%C3%A9toiles-77a55063
www.facebook.com/FondationDesEtoiles
twitter.com/EnfantsEtoiles
instagram.com/fondation_des_etoiles
Aperçu: Dimension: moyenne; *Envergure:* provinciale; Organisme sans but lucratif; fondée en 1977
Mission: Amasser des fonds pour la recherche sur les maladies infantiles au Québec; ces fonds sont distribués aux quatre centres de recherche suivants: Centre de recherche de l'Hôpital Ste-Justine, Institut de recherche de l'Hôpital de Montréal pour enfants, Centre Hospitalier Universitaire de Québec et Centre Hospitalier Universitaire de Sherbrooke
Finances: *Budget de fonctionnement annuel:* $1.5 Million-$3 Million; *Fonds:* Sources de financement publiques
Membre(s) du personnel: 7; 100 bénévole(s)
Activités: *Stagiaires:* Oui
Membre(s) du bureau directeur:
Josée Saint-Pierre, Présidente-directrice générale
jsaint-pierre@fondationdesetoiles.ca
Étienne Lalonde, Directeur, Développement
elalonde@fondationdesetoiles.ca

Fondation des infirmières et infirmiers du Canada See Canadian Nurses Foundation

Fondation des maladies du coeur de la Saskatchewan See Heart & Stroke Foundation of Saskatchewan

Fondation des maladies du coeur du Canada See Heart & Stroke Foundation of Canada

Fondation des maladies du coeur du Nouveau-Brunswick See Heart & Stroke Foundation of New Brunswick

Fondation des maladies du coeur du Québec (FMCQ) / Heart & Stroke Foundation of Québec
#500, 1434, rue Sainte-Catherine ouest, Montréal QC H3G 1R4
Tél: 514-871-1551; *Téléc:* 514-871-9385
Ligne sans frais: 800-567-8563
www.coeuretavc.ca
Nom précédent: Fondation du Québec des maladies du coeur
Aperçu: Dimension: grande; *Envergure:* provinciale; Organisme sans but lucratif; fondée en 1955 surveillé par Heart & Stroke Foundation of Canada
Mission: Forte de l'engagement de ses donateurs, de ses bénévoles et de ses employés, a pour mission de contribuer à l'avancement de la recherche et de promouvoir la santé du coeur, afin de réduire les invalidités et les décès dus aux maladies cardiovasculaires et aux accidents vasculaires cérébraux
Finances: *Budget de fonctionnement annuel:* Plus de $5 Million
Activités: *Stagiaires:* Oui; *Service de conférenciers:* Oui
Membre(s) du bureau directeur:
Ronald Davidson, Directeur, Développement communautaire, Québec

Bas St-Laurent et Gaspésie
33, boul René-Lepage est, Rimouski QC G5L 1N8
Tél: 418-869-1022; *Téléc:* 418-869-2748
Ligne sans frais: 888-473-4636
Membre(s) du bureau directeur:
Louiselle Bérubé, Directrice régionale

Côte-Nord
1, rue Arnaud, Les Escoumins QC G0T 1K0
Tél: 418-233-2119; *Téléc:* 418-233-3771
Membre(s) du bureau directeur:
Liliane Larouche, Personne responsable

Estrie
#100, 2630, rue King ouest, Sherbrooke QC J1J 2H1
Tél: 819-562-7942; *Téléc:* 819-564-0690
Membre(s) du bureau directeur:
Manon Thibodeau, Directrice régionale

La Capitale
#261, 4715, av des Replats, Québec QC G2J 1B8
Tél: 418-682-6387; *Téléc:* 418-682-8214
Membre(s) du bureau directeur:
Jocelyn Thémens, Directeur régional

Laval/Laurentides/Lanaudière
Tour A, #410, 1600, boul Saint-Martin est, Laval QC H7G 4R8
Tél: 450-669-6909; *Téléc:* 450-669-8987
Membre(s) du bureau directeur:
Carol Pincox, Directrice régionale

Mauricie/Centre du Québec
137, rue Radisson, Trois-Rivières QC G9A 2C5
Tél: 819-375-9565; *Téléc:* 819-375-0233

Ouest de Montréal
#18, 795, av Carson, Dorval QC H9S 1L7
Tél: 514-636-4599; *Téléc:* 514-636-8576
Membre(s) du bureau directeur:
Dalia Solo, Directrice régionale

Outaouais
#007, 109, rue Wright, Gatineau QC J8X 2G7
Tél: 819-771-8595; *Téléc:* 819-771-7070
Membre(s) du bureau directeur:
Gabrielle Ouzilleau, Directrice régionale

Rive-Sud/Montérégie
#200, 1194, ch de Chambly, Longueuil QC J4J 2W6
Tél: 450-442-6387; *Téléc:* 450-442-3329
Membre(s) du bureau directeur:
Hélène Gagné, Directrice régionale

Saguenay/Lac Saint-Jean
#251, 152, rue Racine est, Chicoutimi QC G7H 1R8
Tél: 418-543-8959; *Téléc:* 418-543-5872
Membre(s) du bureau directeur:
Martine Paradis, Directrice régionale

Fondation des maladies mentales / Mental Illness Foundation
#804, 55, av du Mont-Royal ouest, Montréal QC H2T 2S6
Tél: 514-529-5354; *Téléc:* 514-529-9877
Ligne sans frais: 888-529-5354
info@fondationdesmaladiesmentales.org
www.fondationdesmaladiesmentales.org
Nom précédent: Fondation québécoise des maladies mentales
Aperçu: Dimension: petite; *Envergure:* provinciale; fondée en 1980
Mission: Pour mettre des services cliniques en place et les maintenir; prévenir les maladies mentales
Membre(s) du personnel: 13
Activités: *Listes de destinataires:* Oui
Membre(s) du bureau directeur:
Isabelle Limoges, Directrice générale
ilimoges@fondationdesmaladiesmentales.org

Fondation des pompiers du Québec pour les grands brûlés
1050, ch Ste-Foy, Québec QC G1S 4L8
Tél: 418-682-7709; *Téléc:* 418-682-7800
Ligne sans frais: 877-682-7709
info@fondationdespompiers.ca
www.fondationdespompiers.ca
www.facebook.com/FondationDesPompiers
www.youtube.com/user/FondationPompiers
Aperçu: Dimension: petite; *Envergure:* provinciale; Organisme sans but lucratif
Mission: Venir en aide aux grands brûlés de la province en améliorant la qualité des soins dont ils doivent bénéficier, via les centres de traitement et de recherche du Québec
Finances: *Fonds:* Dons; Lotopompiers; Lotovoyages; calendriers des pompiers
Membre(s) du personnel: 4; 700+ bénévole(s)
Activités: Tournoi de golf; Soirée des bénévoles; Tombolas; Carting
Membre(s) du bureau directeur:
Sylvie Tremblay, Directrice générale

Montréal
#200, 2575, Place Chassé, Montréal QC H1Y 2C3
Tél: 514-523-5325; *Téléc:* 514-523-3348
Ligne sans frais: 888-523-5325
info@fondationdespompiers.ca
www.fondationdespompiers.ca

Fondation des Prix Ernest C. Manning See Ernest C. Manning Awards Foundation

La Fondation des services communautaires catholiques inc. See Foundation of Catholic Community Services Inc.

La fondation des soins avancés en urgence coronarienne du Canada See Advanced Coronary Treatment (ACT) Foundation of Canada

Fondation des sourds du Québec inc.
3348, boul Mgr-Gauthier, Beauport QC G1E 2W2
Tél: 418-660-6800; *Téléc:* 418-666-0123
Ligne sans frais: 800-463-5617
www.fondationdessourds.net
Aperçu: Dimension: petite; *Envergure:* provinciale; Organisme sans but lucratif; fondée en 1986
Mission: Aider les sourds dans leurs activités quotidiennes afin de contribuer à l'amélioration de la qualité de vie, dans une société d'entendants

Activités: Assistance dans la recherche d'emploi; financement d'equipement; cours de LSQ; *Stagiaires:* Oui
Membre(s) du bureau directeur:
Daniel Forgues, Président

Fondation Desjardins
1, Complexe Desjardins, CP 7, Succ. Desjardins, Montréal QC H5B 1B2
Tél: 514-281-7171; *Téléc:* 514-281-2391
Ligne sans frais: 800-443-8611
desjardins.foundation@desjardins.com
www.desjardins.com
Aperçu: Dimension: petite; *Envergure:* provinciale; Organisme sans but lucratif; fondée en 1970
Mission: Supporter l'éducation et la recherche en coopération, économie, administration, sciences humaines et arts
Membre(s) du personnel: 9
Membre: *Critères d'admissibilite:* Résidents du Québec
Activités: Bourses universitaires; *Stagiaires:* Oui
Membre(s) du bureau directeur:
Diane Derome, Directrice générale

Fondation Diane Hébert Inc
132, rue Blainville est, Sainte-Thérèse-de-Blainville QC J7E 1M2
Tél: 450-971-1112; *Téléc:* 450-971-1818
Ligne sans frais: 877-971-1110
fdh@macten.net
Aperçu: Dimension: moyenne; *Envergure:* nationale; Organisme sans but lucratif; fondée en 1987
Mission: Services directs offerts aux patients en attente de greffes, aux greffés et à leur famille autant sur le plan moral, physique ou financier; prêt d'équipements médicaux tels que chaises roulantes électriques; la Fondation vise aussi à sensibiliser la population au don d'organes
Membre de: Info Don D'Organes; Québec Transplant; Canadian Transplant Association
Activités: *Evénements de sensibilisation:* Semaine du don d'organes, dernière semaine d'avril (du L au V); *Service de conférenciers:* Oui

Fondation Drummond See Drummond Foundation

Fondation du barreau du Québec
Maison du Barreau, 445, boul Saint-Laurent, Montréal QC H2Y 3T8
Tél: 514-954-3400
Ligne sans frais: 800-361-8495
information@barreau.qc.ca
www.barreau.qc.ca
www.linkedin.com/groups?gid=2206718
www.facebook.com/barreauduquebec
twitter.com/BarreauduQuebec
plus.google.com/101349996276959545722
Aperçu: Dimension: petite; *Envergure:* provinciale; fondée en 1978
Mission: Subventionner, primer et supporter des travaux axés vers l'intérêt public et utiles à la pratique du droit.
Membre: *Comités:* Accès à la profession; Arbitrage des comptes d'honoraires des avocats; Discipline; Équivalences; Exécutif; Fonds d'études juridiques; Fonds d'indemnisation; Formation continue obligatoire; Formation des avocats; Formation professionnelle des avocats; Inspection professionnelle; Médiation civile et commerciale et aux petites créances; Médiation familiale; Requêtes; Révision des plaintes; Sténographie
Membre(s) du bureau directeur:
Bernard Synnott, Président

Fondation du bien-être animal du Canada See Animal Welfare Foundation of Canada

Fondation du CHUM
#800, 465, rue McGill, Montréal QC H2Y 2H1
Tél: 514-890-8077; *Téléc:* 514-412-7393
Ligne sans frais: 877-570-0797
info@fondationduchum.com
fondationduchum.com
www.linkedin.com/company/fondation-du-chum
www.facebook.com/FondationCHUM
twitter.com/FondationCHUM
www.youtube.com/user/fondationduchum
Aperçu: Dimension: petite; *Envergure:* locale; Organisme sans but lucratif
Mission: Pour amasser des fonds pour le compte de le Centre hospitalier de l'Université de Montréal pour améliorer les services offerts aux patients et à financer la recherche
Membre(s) du bureau directeur:

Canadian Associations / Fondation Dufresne et Gauthier

Luce Moreau, Présidente-directrice générale

Fondation du conseil des gouverneurs du centre de recherche et de développement sur les aliments inc *Voir* Fondation Initia

La fondation du droit de l'Ontario *See* Law Foundation of Ontario

Fondation du Grand Montréal *See* Foundation of Greater Montreal

Fondation du Québec des maladies du coeur *Voir* Fondation des maladies du coeur du Québec

Fondation du sentier transcanadian *See* Trans Canada Trail Foundation

Fondation Dufresne et Gauthier
#200, 2505 boul Laurier, Québec QC G1V 2L2
Tél: 418-650-5222
info@fdg.ca
www.fdg.ca
www.facebook.com/fondationdufresnegauthier
Aperçu: Dimension: petite; *Envergure:* locale; Organisme sans but lucratif; fondée en 2001
Mission: Venir en aide aux enfants de familles plus vulnérables et aux jeunes en situation de risque
Membre(s) du bureau directeur:
Johanne Beauvilliers, Directrice générale

Fondation Edward Assh
80, av du Collège, Beauport QC G1E 2Y1
Aperçu: Dimension: petite; *Envergure:* internationale; Organisme sans but lucratif; fondée en 1989
Mission: Fondation charitable pour venir en aide aux plus démunis, orphelins, personnes âgées, infirmes dans les pays du Tiers-monde

Fondation Émergence inc.
Centre Maisonneuve, CP 55510, Montréal QC H1W 0A1
Tél: 438-384-1058
courrier@fondationemergence.org
www.fondationemergence.org
www.facebook.com/fondationemergence
twitter.com/fondemergence
Aperçu: Dimension: moyenne; *Envergure:* provinciale
Mission: D'éduquer, d'informer et de sensibiliser la population aux réalités des personnes gaies, lesbiennes, bisexuelles et trans
Activités: Programme de défense des droits
Membre(s) du bureau directeur:
Claude Leblond, Président

La Fondation Émile-Nelligan
#202, 100, rue Sherbrooke est, Montréal QC H2X 1C3
Tél: 514-278-4657; *Téléc:* 514-278-1943
info@fondation-nelligan.org
www.fondation-nelligan.org
Aperçu: Dimension: petite; *Envergure:* provinciale; Organisme sans but lucratif; fondée en 1979
Membre(s) du bureau directeur:
Manon Gagnon, Directrice générale
Michel Dallaire, Président
Prix, Bourses:
• Prix Ozias-Leduc
Prix triennal en arts visuels (peinture, sculpture, gravure, installations, 'land art'). Décerné à un artiste citoyen du Canada né au Québec ou à un artiste citoyen du Canada ayant sa résidence principale au Québec depuis au moins dix ans; *Amount:* 25 000$
• Prix Serge-Garant
Prix triennal de composition musicale décerné à un compositeur citoyen du Canada né au Québec ou à un compositeur citoyen du Canada ayant sa résidence principale au Québec depuis au moins dix ans; *Amount:* 25 000$
• Prix Émile-Nelligan
Prix annuel. Il s'agit d'un prix de poésie décerné à un poète de moins de 35 ans, pour un recueil publié au cours de l'année; *Amount:* 7 500$ et une médaille en bronze frappée à l'effigie d'Émile Nelligan
• Prix Gilles-Corbeil
Prix triennal en littérature (poésie, roman, nouvelles, récits, théâtre ou essai littéraire). Décerné à un écrivain citoyen du Canada ou des États-Unis, pour une oeuvre écrite en langue française; *Amount:* 100 000$

Fondation Famille Molson *See* The Molson Family Foundation

La Fondation Farha *See* The Farha Foundation

Fondation fiduciaire canadienne de bourses d'études *See* Canadian Scholarship Trust Foundation

Fondation franco-ontarienne (FFO)
CP 7340, Ottawa ON K1L 8E4
Tél: 613-565-4720; *Téléc:* 613-565-8539
info@fondationfranco-ontarienne.ca
www.fondationfranco-ontarienne.ca
www.facebook.com/Fondationfranco
twitter.com/fondationfranco
Aperçu: Dimension: petite; *Envergure:* provinciale; Organisme sans but lucratif; fondée en 1986
Mission: La Fondation franco-ontarienne appuie financièrement la réalisation d'initiatives qui assurent la vitalité de la communauté franco-ontarienne
Membre(s) du personnel: 5
Membre: *Critères d'admissibilite:* Professionnels; commerçants
Activités: Vin et fromage; programme d'appuis financiers
Membre(s) du bureau directeur:
Martin Arseneau, Directeur général par intérim
marseneau@fondationfranco.ca

Fondation fransaskoise
#205, 1440, 9e av, Regina SK S4R 8B1
Tél: 306-566-6000
Ligne sans frais: 800-670-0879
fondationfransaskoise@ccs-sk.ca
www.fondationfransaskoise.ca
Nom précédent: Fondation de la radio française en Saskatchewan
Aperçu: Dimension: petite; *Envergure:* provinciale; Organisme sans but lucratif; fondée en 1998
Mission: Octroi de bourses d'études en français - enseignement ou communication - en plus de subventions de projets et de programmes susceptibles à faciliter la survivance de la langue française en Saskatchewan
Activités: L'octroi de subventions aux communautés locales francophones pour le financement d'activités susceptibles d'améliorer la qualité de vie en français dans ses communautés
Membre(s) du bureau directeur:
Roger Lepage, Président
Laurette Lefol, Vice-présidente
Michel Vézina, Secrétaire

Fondation Frontière *See* Frontiers Foundation

Fondation Graham Boeckh *See* Graham Boeckh Foundation

La fondation Gustav Levinschi *See* Gustav Levinschi Foundation

Fondation Harmonie du Canada *See* Harmony Foundation of Canada

Fondation Hôpital Charles-LeMoyne (FHCLM)
3120, boul Taschereau, Greenfield Park QC J4V 2H1
Tél: 450-466-5487; *Téléc:* 450-672-1716
www.fhclm.ca
www.facebook.com/FondationCharlesLeMoyne
Nom précédent: Fondation Charles LeMoyne
Aperçu: Dimension: petite; *Envergure:* locale; Organisme sans but lucratif; fondée en 1964
Mission: S'occuper de réunir les fonds pour que l'Hôpital Charles LeMoyne puisse acheter et remplacer de l'équipement spécialisé et pour permettre la recherche médicale
Finances: *Budget de fonctionnement annuel:* $3 Million-$5 Million
Membre(s) du personnel: 4; 100 bénévole(s)
Membre: 100-499
Activités: Tournoi de golf mixte et féminin; grand bal; bingo; tirage-voyages; dégustation homard
Membre(s) du bureau directeur:
Danièle J. Martin, Directrice générale

Fondation Hydro-Québec pour l'environnement / Hydro-Québec Foundation for the Environment
75, rue Notre-Dame ouest, 2e étage, Montréal QC H2Z 1A4
Tél: 514-289-5384; *Téléc:* 514-289-2840
fondation-environnement@hydro.qc.ca
www.hydroquebec.com/fondation-environnement
Aperçu: Dimension: petite; *Envergure:* provinciale
Mission: Promouvoir la conservation, la restauration et la mise en valeur de la faune, de la flore et des habitats naturels; soutenir les besoins locaux en matière de prise en charge de l'environnement; contribuer à l'utilisation responsable et durable des ressources naturelles

Membre(s) du bureau directeur:
Stella Leney, Présidente

Fondation Initia
3600, boul Casavant ouest, Saint-Hyacinthe QC J2S 8E3
Tél: 450-768-3340; *Téléc:* 450-773-8461
info@initia.org
www.initia.org
www.linkedin.com/groups/Professionnels-lagroalimentaire-4008965
twitter.com/initiaorg
vimeo.com/initia
Nom précédent: Fondation du conseil des gouverneurs du centre de recherche et de développement sur les aliments inc
Aperçu: Dimension: petite; *Envergure:* nationale; Organisme sans but lucratif; fondée en 1991
Mission: Les activités de la Fondation INITIA sont au service de tous les acteurs de la transformation des aliments et ont pour objectif de: favoriser le dialogue et l'échange; encourager l'innovation; transférer les connaissances; disséminer l'information; et faciliter la globalisation.
Membre(s) du personnel: 3
Membre: *Montant de la cotisation:* 100$ individu; 500$ institutionnel; *Critères d'admissibilite:* Secteur de la transformation des aliments
Activités: Transfert de connaissances scientifiques; *Bibliothèque:* CRDA
Membre(s) du bureau directeur:
Véronique Fournier, Directrice exécutive, Affaires scientifiques
veronique@initia.org
Prix, Bourses:
• Prix Innovation André-Latour
Souligner les efforts soutenus en recherche et développement des intervenants du milieu; *Amount:* 5 000$

Fondation Institut de Cardiologie de Montréal / Montréal Heart Institute Foundation
4100, rue Molson, Montréal QC N1Y 3N1
Tel: 514-593-2525; *Fax:* 514-376-5400
Toll-Free: 877-518-2525
ficmdon@icm-mhi.org
www.icm-mhi.org/fr/fondation
www.facebook.com/institutcardiologiemontreal
twitter.com/ICMtl
www.youtube.com/user/InstitutdeCardioMtl
Overview: A small local charitable organization founded in 1977
Mission: Pour amasser des fonds au nom de l'Institut de Cardiologie de Montréal afin de financer la recherche
Staff Member(s): 22
Chief Officer(s):
Mélanie La Couture, Directrice générale
melanie.lacouture@icm-mhi.org

Fondation J. Armand Bombardier *See* J. Armand Bombardier Foundation

Fondation Jeanne-Crevier
151, rue de Muy, Boucherville QC J4B 4W7
Tél: 450-655-8587; *Téléc:* 450-641-3082
info@fondationjeannecrevier.org
www.fondationjeannecrevier.org
Aperçu: Dimension: petite; *Envergure:* provinciale; Organisme sans but lucratif; fondée en 1987
Mission: Dédié au mieux-être des résidents et usagers du Centre d'hébergement Jeanne-Crevier de Boucherville
Membre(s) du bureau directeur:
Marjolaine Tessier, Présidente

La Fondation Jeux Canada Games Saint John, Inc. *See* Saint John Jeux Canada Games Foundation Inc.

Fondation Jules et Paul-Émile Léger
130, av de l'Épée, Montréal QC H2V 3T2
Tél: 514-495-2409
Ligne sans frais: 877-288-7383
Autres numéros: www.flickr.com/photos/72235893@N02
info@leger.org
www.leger.org
www.facebook.com/LOEUVRELEGER
twitter.com/LOEUVRELEGER
www.youtube.com/user/LOEUVRELEGER
Également appelé: L'Oeuvre Léger
Nom précédent: Institut Cardinal Léger contre la lèpre
Aperçu: Dimension: grande; *Envergure:* internationale; Organisme sans but lucratif; fondée en 1981
Mission: La Fondation Jules et Paul-Émile Léger est constituée de six filiales pour mener à bien les différents aspects de sa

mission. A l'international: Institut Cardinal Léger pour la santé (contre la lèpre et les grandes pendémies); La Croix d'or (enfants), le Cardinal Léger et ses oeuvres (développement durable). Les autres filiales sont au Canada: Secours aux aînés; les Partenaires contre la violence et la faim; Recours des sans-abris
Membre de: Chambre de commerce du Montréal Métropolitain
Affiliation(s): Anonyme; Intergénérations Québec; Centre d'action bénévole St-Siméon/Port-Daniel; Fondation de la Visite; Foyer des jeunes travailleurs et travailleuses de Montréal; Le regroupement communautaire L'itinéraire; Maison des enfants Marie-Rose; Présence Amie De La Montérégie; Programme d'aide aux jeunes mères célibataires en difficulté: l'envol
Finances: *Fonds:* Gouvernement international
Membre: *Comités:* Direction; Consultatif honoraire
Activités: Omnium de Golf; Concert Cardinal Léger; Nourrir un Enfant
Membre(s) du bureau directeur:
Richard Veenstra, Directeur général
Gary Béliveau, Directeur, Opérations
Esteban Bongiovanni, Directeur, Communications
Publications:
• Au présent [a publication of the Fondation Jules et Paul-Émile Léger]
Type: Bulletin

Fondation Les oiseleurs du Québec inc.
2044, ch Demers, Lévis QC G7A 2N3
Tél: 418-564-4513
oiseleurs@oiseleurs.ca
www.oiseleurs.ca
Aperçu: *Dimension:* moyenne; *Envergure:* provinciale; Organisme sans but lucratif; fondée en 1986
Mission: Promouvoir et développer les connaissances et les recherches permettant de mieux gérer les ressources naturelles dans un contexte de développement durable; renseigner et sensibiliser le public; le conscientiser sur l'importance de la préservation des ressources naturelles dans un contexte de développement durable
Membre de: Association canadienne-française pour l'avancement des sciences; Conseil régional de l'environnement Chaudière-Appalaches
5 bénévole(s)
Membre: 1-99; *Montant de la cotisation:* 50$
Activités: *Service de conférenciers:* Oui

Fondation Lionel-Groulx (FLG)
261, av Bloomfield, Montréal QC H2V 3R6
Tél: 514-271-4759; *Téléc:* 514-271-6369
www.fondationlionelgroulx.org
www.facebook.com/fondationlionelgroulx
twitter.com/fondlgroulx
Aperçu: *Dimension:* petite; *Envergure:* nationale; Organisme sans but lucratif; fondée en 1956
Mission: Encourager et soutenir la recherche et les publications en histoire de l'Amérique française; entretenir l'intérêt pour l'histoire nationale; et contribuer à développer l'enseignement de l'histoire
Affiliation(s): Centre de recherche Lionel-Groulx
Finances: *Budget de fonctionnement annuel:* $250,000-$500,000
Membre(s) du personnel: 6
Membre: 100-499
Activités: Concours Lionel-Groulx pour les écoles secondaires; *Stagiaires:* Oui
Membre(s) du bureau directeur:
Pierre Graveline, Directeur général, 514-271-4759 Ext. 222
Prix, Bourses:
• Prix Jean-Éthier-Blais de critique littéraire
• Prix Maxime-Raymond

Fondation Lucie et André Chagnon / Lucie & André Chagnon Foundation
#1000, 2001, av McGill College, Montréal QC H3A 1G1
Tél: 514-380-2001; *Téléc:* 514-340-8434
info@fondationchagnon.org
www.fondationchagnon.org
twitter.com/FondChagnon
www.youtube.com/user/FondationChagnon
Aperçu: *Dimension:* moyenne; *Envergure:* nationale
Mission: Contribuer au développement et à l'amélioration de la santé par la prévention de la pauvreté et de la maladie en agissant principalement auprès des enfants et de leurs parents
Membre: *Comités:* Gouverne; Vérification; Placements
Membre(s) du bureau directeur:
André Chagnon, Président du conseil

Fondation maman Dion
130A, rue Notre-Dame, Charlemagne QC J5Z 1H2
Tél: 450-585-3466; *Téléc:* 450-585-7636
Ligne sans frais: 866-430-3466
info@fondationmamandion.org
www.fondationmamandion.org
www.facebook.com/132517813484098
twitter.com/FMDion
Aperçu: *Dimension:* petite; *Envergure:* provinciale; fondée en 2006
Mission: Favoriser l'épanouissement, le développement de l'estime de soi et le désir de réussir à l'école des jeunes québécois issus de milieux défavorisés
Activités: Offrir un répit financier aux familles vulnérables
Membre(s) du bureau directeur:
Richard Laramée, Président

Fondation manitobaine de lutte contre les dépendances *See* Addictions Foundation of Manitoba

La Fondation manitobaine du droit *See* The Manitoba Law Foundation

Fondation Marie-Éve Saulnier
#102, 3925, Grande-Allée, Saint-Hubert QC J4T 2V8
Tél: 450-926-9000; *Téléc:* 450-766-8843
www.fondationmarieevesaulnier.qc.ca
www.facebook.com/Fondation.Marie.Eve.Saulnier2014
twitter.com/FondationMES
www.youtube.com/channel/UCKSL9-vwaPFPiHGDYXjLs_g
Aperçu: *Dimension:* petite; *Envergure:* provinciale; fondée en 1997
Mission: La Fondation Marie-Éve Saulnier améliore au jour le jour la qualité de vie des enfants atteints de cancer.
Membre(s) du bureau directeur:
Linda Langlois Saulnier, Directrice générale

Fondation Mario-Racine / Mario Racine Foundation
#110, 2075, rue Plessis, Montréal QC H2L 2Y4
Tél: 514-528-5940
fondationmarioracine99@gmail.com
www.algi.qc.ca/asso/fmr
Aperçu: *Dimension:* petite; *Envergure:* locale
Mission: A pour mission de favoriser le développement communautaire et culturel des gais et lesbiennes à Montréal; est engagée dans la réalisation du Centre communautaire des gais et lesbiennes de Montréal.
Membre(s) du bureau directeur:
Michel Durocher, Président

La Fondation médicale canadienne *See* Canadian Medical Foundation

Fondation Michaëlle Jean *See* Michaëlle Jean Foundation

Fondation Miriam *See* Miriam Foundation

Fondation nationale des prix du magazine canadien *See* National Magazine Awards Foundation

Fondation Optimiste des enfants canadiens *See* Canadian Children's Optimist Foundation

Fondation orthopédique du Canada *See* Canadian Orthopaedic Foundation

Fondation Père-Ménard
1195, rue Sauvé est, Montréal QC H2C 1Z8
Tél: 514-274-7645; *Téléc:* 514-274-7647
Ligne sans frais: 800-665-7645
info@fondationperemenard.org
www.fondationperemenard.org
www.facebook.com/145827832121166
Aperçu: *Dimension:* petite; *Envergure:* internationale; Organisme sans but lucratif; fondée en 1970
Mission: Améliorer de façon durable la qualité de vie des populations défavorisées des pays en développement, principalement en Amérique du sud, en encourageant et soutenant l'établissement et la gestion de projets communautaires en santé, éducation, eau et alimentation ainsi que la formation de leaders spirituels locaux
Finances: *Budget de fonctionnement annuel:* $1.5 Million-$3 Million
Membre(s) du personnel: 3; 10 bénévole(s)
Membre: 15 000+
Membre(s) du bureau directeur:
Miriam Castro Herrera, Directrice générale
mcastro@fondationperemenard.org

Fondation pour enfants diabétiques
#100, 306, rue Saint-Zotique est, Montréal QC H2S 1L6
Tél: 514-731-9683; *Téléc:* 514-731-2683
Ligne sans frais: 800-731-9683
info@diabete-enfants.ca
www.diabetes-children.ca
www.linkedin.com/company/la-fondation-pour-enfants-diabétiques
www.facebook.com/DiabeteEnfants
twitter.com/DiabeteEnfants
Aperçu: *Dimension:* moyenne; *Envergure:* provinciale; fondée en 1974
Mission: Subvenir au développement de camp spécialisé pour enfants et adolescents diabétiques; soutenir des projets d'enseignement et d'information sur les soins en diabète pédiatrique; faire la promotion de soins de santé optimaux pour les enfants diabétiques
Membre(s) du personnel: 9
Membre(s) du bureau directeur:
Danielle Brien, Directrice générale
dbrien@diabete-enfants.ca

Fondation pour l'aide aux travailleuses et travailleurs accidentés (FATA)
6839-A, rue Drolet, Montréal QC H2S 2T1
Tél: 514-271-0901; *Téléc:* 514-271-6078
fata@fata.qc.ca
www.fata.qc.ca
Aperçu: *Dimension:* petite; *Envergure:* provinciale
Mission: Promouvoir des intérêts de travailleuses et de travailleurs affectés par des accidents ou des maladies du travail

La Fondation pour l'avancement du droit au Nouveau-Brunswick *See* New Brunswick Law Foundation

Fondation pour la protection des sites naturels du Nouveau-Brunswick *See* Nature Trust of New Brunswick

Fondation pour la recherche sur la moelle épinière
#400, 6020, rue Jean-Talon est, Montréal QC H1S 3B1
Tél: 514-341-7272; *Téléc:* 514-341-8884
Ligne sans frais: 877-341-7272
info@moelleepiniere.com
www.moelleepiniere.com
www.facebook.com/MEMOQuebec
twitter.com/MEMOQuebec
Nom précédent: Fondation André Sénécal pour la recherche sur la moelle épinière
Aperçu: *Dimension:* moyenne; *Envergure:* provinciale; fondée en 1994
Mission: A pour but de récolter des fonds pour financer, principalement, la recherche scientifique et médicale sur les lésions médullaires
Membre(s) du personnel: 20
Membre(s) du bureau directeur:
Walter Zelaya, Directeur général
wzelaya@moelleepiniere.com

Fondation pour le développement de la jeunesse T.R.E.E. *See* T.R.E.E. Foundation for Youth Development

La Fondation pour le journalisme canadien *See* Canadian Journalism Foundation

Fondation Québec Labrador du (Canada) inc. *See* Québec-Labrador Foundation (Canada) Inc.

Fondation québécoise de la déficience intellectuelle (FQDI)
6275, boul des Grandes-Prairies, Montréal QC H1P 1A5
Tél: 514-725-9797; *Téléc:* 514-725-3530
www.fqdi.ca
www.facebook.com/LeSupportFondationDI
Aperçu: *Dimension:* petite; *Envergure:* provinciale; Organisme sans but lucratif; fondée en 1988
Mission: Amasse des fonds pour venir en aide aux organismes oeuvrant à l'intégration et à l'amélioration de la qualité de vie des personnes présentant une déficience intellectuelle
Affiliation(s): Association du Québec pour l'intégration sociale
Activités: Collecte d'articles et de vêtements usagés par le biais de boîtes; collectes à domicile; *Stagiaires:* Oui
Membre(s) du bureau directeur:
Philippe Siebes, Directeur général

Fondation québécoise de la maladie coeliaque (FQMC) / Québec Celiac Foundation
#230, 4837, rue Boyer, Montréal QC H2J 3E6

Tél: 514-529-8806; Téléc: 514-529-2046
info@fqmc.org
www.fqmc.org
Aperçu: *Dimension:* petite; *Envergure:* provinciale; Organisme sans but lucratif; fondée en 1983
Mission: Diffuser de l'information sur la maladie et le régime sans gluten; faciliter l'approvisionnement; encourager les initiatives des membres; supporter les membres et défendre leurs droits; favoriser la recherche; solliciter des fonds pour réaliser ses mandats
Finances: *Budget de fonctionnement annuel:* $100,000-$250,000
Membre(s) du personnel: 2; 60 bénévole(s)
Membre: 1 650; *Montant de la cotisation:* 75$ adhésion; 90$ professionnel de la santé; *Critères d'admissibilité:* Atteint de la maladie coeliaque; *Comités:* Club des 100 Gluten; Documentation; Communication; Financement; Info-Voyage; Médical; Support psychologique; Nutrition; Liaisons avec les régions; Colloque; Conseiller juridique; Siège social de la fondation
Activités:; *Bibliothèque:* Centre de documentation; rendez-vous
Membre(s) du bureau directeur:
Suzanne Laurencelle, Directrice Générale

Fondation québécoise des maladies mentales *Voir* Fondation des maladies mentales

Fondation québécoise du cancer
2075, rue de Champlain, Montréal QC H2L 2T1
Tél: 514-527-2194; Téléc: 514-527-1943
Ligne sans frais: 877-336-4443
cancerquebec.mtl@fqc.qc.ca
www.fqc.qc.ca
www.facebook.com/fqcancer
Aperçu: *Dimension:* petite; *Envergure:* provinciale; Organisme sans but lucratif; fondée en 1979
Mission: Vouée à l'amélioration de la condition de la personne atteinte de cancer et de ses proches; offrir des services d'hôtellerie, d'écoute et d'information pour gens atteints du cancer; améliorer la qualité de vie des patients et celle de leurs proches.
Finances: *Budget de fonctionnement annuel:* Plus de $5 Million*Fonds:* Dons individuels; Hôtelleries; Activités-bénéfice; Entreprises; Legs testamentaires; Dons In memoriam; Fondations
1600 bénévole(s)
Activités: *Stagiaires:* Oui; *Bibliothèque:* Bibliothèque publique
Membre(s) du bureau directeur:
Pierre-Yves Gagnon, Directeur général

Hôtellerie de l'Estrie
3001, 12e av nord, Sherbrooke QC J1H 5N4
Tél: 819-822-2125; Téléc: 819-822-1392
cancerquebec.she@fqc.qc.ca
www.fqc.qc.ca
Membre(s) du bureau directeur:
Marie Toupin, Directrice

Hôtellerie de l'Outaouais
Pavillon Michael J. MacGivney, 555, boul de l'Hôpital, Gatineau QC J8V 3T4
Tél: 819-561-2262; Téléc: 819-561-1727
cancerquebec.gat@fqc.qc.ca
www.fqc.qc.ca
Membre(s) du bureau directeur:
Corinne Lorman, Directrice

Hôtellerie de la Mauricie
3110, rue Louis-Pasteur, Trois-Rivières QC G8Z 4E3
Tél: 819-693-4242; Téléc: 819-693-4243
cancerquebec.trv@fqc.qc.ca
www.fqc.qc.ca
Membre(s) du bureau directeur:
Luce Girard, Directrice

Hôtellerie de Montréal
2075, rue de Champlain, Montréal QC H2L 2T1
Tél: 514-527-2194; Téléc: 514-527-1943
Ligne sans frais: 877-336-4443
cancerquebec.mtl@fqc.qc.ca
www.fqc.qc.ca
Membre(s) du bureau directeur:
Pierre-Yves Gagnon, Directeur

Fondation québécoise en environnement / Québec Environment Foundation
#203, av Christophe-Colomb, Montréal QC H2M 2E3
Tél: 514-849-3323
info@fqe.qc.ca
www.fqe.qc.ca
www.facebook.com/FQEnvironnement
twitter.com/fqe
Aperçu: *Dimension:* moyenne; *Envergure:* provinciale; Organisme sans but lucratif; fondée en 1987
Mission: Sensibiliser les Québécoises et les Québécois à l'égard de l'environnement par l'information et l'éducation; créer une synergie entre l'économie et l'écologie; favoriser la recherche et la mise en place de solutions concrètes et efficaces
Finances: *Budget de fonctionnement annuel:* $500,000-$1.5 Million
Membre(s) du personnel: 3; 35 bénévole(s)
Membre: 210 membres; 10 000 ami(e)s
Activités: Journées éducatives, Colloques, Conférences, Plantations d'arbres; *Service de conférenciers:* Oui
Membre(s) du bureau directeur:
Louis-Paul Allard, Président

Fondation québécoise pour l'alphabétisation
#200, 5420, boul Saint-Laurent, Montréal QC H2T 1S1
Tél: 514-289-1178; Téléc: 514-289-9286
Ligne sans frais: 800-361-9142
www.fondationalphabetisation.org
www.facebook.com/fondationalphabetisation
twitter.com/fondationalpha
Aperçu: *Dimension:* petite; *Envergure:* provinciale; Organisme sans but lucratif; fondée en 1989
Mission: Faire en sorte que tous, adultes et enfants, aient accès à la lecture et à l'écriture.
Membre(s) du personnel: 7
Activités: Campagnes médias; *Stagiaires:* Oui; *Service de conférenciers:* Oui
Membre(s) du bureau directeur:
Nancy Leggett-Bachand, Présidente-Directrice Générale

Fondation Ressources-Jeunesse (FRJ)
#300, 1001, boul de Maisonneuve ouest, Montréal QC H3A 3C8
Tél: 514-982-0577; Téléc: 514-286-7554
info@frj.qc.ca
www.frj.qc.ca
www.linkedin.com/company/fondation-ressources-jeunesse
www.facebook.com/480926321968659
twitter.com/FondationRJ
Aperçu: *Dimension:* petite; *Envergure:* provinciale; fondée en 1979
Mission: Intégration des jeunes (18-30 ans) sans emploi au marché du travail et la prise en main de leur carrière
Membre(s) du personnel: 14
Activités: *Stagiaires:* Oui
Membre(s) du bureau directeur:
Francine Giguère, Présidente-directrice générale
fgiguere@frj.qc.ca

Fondation Richelieu International (FRI)
#25, 1010 rue Polytek, Ottawa ON K1J 9J1
Tél: 613-742-6911; Téléc: 613-742-6916
Ligne sans frais: 800-267-6525
international@richelieu.org
www.fondationrichelieu.org
www.facebook.com/RichelieuInternational
Aperçu: *Dimension:* petite; *Envergure:* internationale; fondée en 1944
Mission: Recueillir des dons auprès de ses membres et du grand public en général afin d'appuyer des services, des projets et des programmes visant le mieux-être des jeunes
Membre(s) du personnel: 3
Membre: 250 clubs
Activités: Réseau Ado
Membre(s) du bureau directeur:
Mélanie Raymond, Directeur général

Fondation roumaine de Montréal / Tribuna Noastra
3550, ch Côte-des-Neiges, #RC90, Montréal QC H3H 1V4
Tél: 514-937-4473; Téléc: 514-937-0049
tribunanoastra@hotmail.com
www.fundatiaromana.org
Nom précédent: Fédération des associations roumaines du Canada
Aperçu: *Dimension:* petite; *Envergure:* locale; Organisme sans but lucratif; fondée en 2005
Mission: Service d'accueil et d'intégration des immigrants
Finances: *Budget de fonctionnement annuel:* $50,000-$100,000
Membre(s) du personnel: 16; 50 bénévole(s)
Membre: *Comités:* Mutuelles entre les gens d'affaires canadiens et roumains
Activités: Faciliter les liaisons; *Stagiaires:* Oui; *Service de conférenciers:* Oui; *Listes de destinataires:* Oui; *Bibliothèque:* Bibliothèque de langue roumaine

Membre(s) du bureau directeur:
Basile Gliga, Président

Fondation Santé Gatineau
Pavillon Desjardins, 116, boul Lionel-Émond, #B-202, Gatineau QC J8Y 1W7
Tél: 819-966-6108; Téléc: 819-966-6012
csssgatineau_info_fondation@ssss.gouv.qc.ca
www.fondationsantegatineau.ca
www.facebook.com/FondationSanteGatineau
twitter.com/FondSanteGat
Aperçu: *Dimension:* petite; *Envergure:* locale; Organisme sans but lucratif
Mission: Pour augmenter des fonds sur le compte du CSSS de Gatineau pour améliorer les services offerts aux patients et à financer la recherche
Membre: *Comités:* Dons Majeurs; Audit; Dons Planifiés; Activités Publiques; Communications; Ressources Humaines; Placement
Membre(s) du bureau directeur:
Jean Pigeon, Directeur général

Fondation Savoy inc. *Voir* Savoy Foundation Inc.

Fondation Sommeil: Association de personnes atteintes de déficiences reliées au sommeil
#380A, 1600, av de Lorimier, Montréal QC H2K 3W5
Tél: 514-522-3901
Ligne sans frais: 888-622-3901
info@fondationsommeil.com
www.fondationsommeil.com
www.linkedin.com/company/5240224
www.facebook.com/FondationSommeilQuebec
twitter.com/FondationSom
Également appelé: Fondation Sommeil
Aperçu: *Dimension:* moyenne; *Envergure:* provinciale; Organisme sans but lucratif; fondée en 1990
Mission: Rejoindre les gens touchés par des troubles du sommeil et les appuyer dans leur démarche
Membre de: Confédération des organismes de personnes handicapées du Québec
Affiliation(s): Regroupement des organismes de promotion du Montréal Métropolitain
Membre: *Montant de la cotisation:* 25$; *Critères d'admissibilite:* Adolescents 15 - adultes
Activités: Rencontres d'échange et d'information; congrès; *Bibliothèque:* Centre de documentation; rendez-vous
Membre(s) du bureau directeur:
Jacques Clairoux, Directeur

Fondation sport pur *See* True Sport Foundation

La Fondation Terry Fox *See* The Terry Fox Foundation

Fondation Tourisme Jeunesse / Youth Travel Foundation
3514, av Lacombe, Montréal QC H3T 1M1
Tél: 514-731-1015
Ligne sans frais: 866-754-1015
info@ftj-ytf.org
ftj-ytf.org
www.linkedin.com/company/fondation-tourisme-jeunesse
www.facebook.com/FTJYTF
Nom précédent: Organisation pour le tourisme étudiant au Québec et Fédération québécoise d'ajisme
Aperçu: *Dimension:* grande; *Envergure:* provinciale; Organisme sans but lucratif; fondée en 1989
Mission: Rendre accessible le tourisme aux jeunes, en développant divers outils et services, notamment par le biais des bureaux d'information voyages et des auberges de jeunesse du Québec
Membre de: Hostelling International - Canada
Affiliation(s): Fédération internationale des auberges de jeunesse; Regroupement loisir Québec; Bureau canadien de l'éducation internationale; Bureau international du tourisme social
Finances: *Fonds:* Gouvernement du Québec
Membre: *Critères d'admissibilite:* Détenir une carte de membre Hostelling International
Activités: Bureaux d'information sur les voyages; Auberges de jeunesse; Voyages Tourisme Jeunesse; Boutiques Tourisme Jeunesse; Conférences sur travail à l'étranger; Fondation Tourisme Jeunesse; *Stagiaires:* Oui; *Service de conférenciers:* Oui
Membre(s) du bureau directeur:
Jacques Perreault, Directeur général

La Fondation Trillium de l'Ontario *See* The Ontario Trillium Foundation

La Fondation Vimy *See* The Vimy Foundation

Fondation Wellspring pour les personnes atteintes de cancer *See* Wellspring Cancer Support Foundation

Fondations philanthropiques Canada *See* Philanthropic Foundations Canada

Fonds canadien de protection des épargnants *See* Canadian Investor Protection Fund

Fonds d'action et d'éducation juridiques pour les femmes *See* Women's Legal Education & Action Fund

Fonds d'études académiques pour les Noirs *See* Black Academic Scholarship Fund

Fonds des Athlètes Canadiens *See* Canadian Athletes Now Fund

Le fonds du Primat pour le secours et le développement mondial *See* The Primate's World Relief & Development Fund

Fonds du Souvenir *See* Last Post Fund

Fonds indépendant de production *See* Independent Production Fund

Fonds international pour la protection des animaux *See* International Fund for Animal Welfare Canada

Fonds mondial pour la nature *See* World Wildlife Fund - Canada

Food & Consumer Products of Canada (FCPC) / Produits alimentaires et de consommation du Canada (PACC)
#600, 100 Sheppard Ave. East, Toronto ON M2N 6N5
Tel: 416-510-8024; *Fax:* 416-510-8043
info@fcpc.ca
www.fcpc.ca
www.linkedin.com/company/food-&-consumer-products-of-canada
twitter.com/FCPC1
Previous Name: Grocery Products Manufacturers of Canada; Food & Consumer Products Manufacturers of Canada
Overview: A large national organization founded in 1959
Mission: To represent the food & consumer products industry, from small independently-owned companies to large multinationals
Staff Member(s): 12
Membership: *Member Profile:* Companies that make & market retailer & national brands; *Committees:* Board; Industry Affairs; Public Affairs; Networking
Activities: Offering educational opportunities; Engaging in advocacy activities; Advising members about government policy changes; Offering networking opportunities; *Awareness Events:* Annual Charity Golf Tournament, June
Chief Officer(s):
Nancy Croitoru, President & Chief Executive Officer
Paula Pergantis, Vice-President, Finance & Corporate Services, 416-510-8089
Rachel Kagan, Vice-President, Environment & Sustainability Policy, 416-510-8263
Tom Arnold, Director, Communications, 416-510-8088
Meetings/Conferences:
• Food & Consumer Products of Canada Annual Supply Chain Symposium 2018, 2018
Scope: National
• Food & Consumer Products of Canada National Sales Symposium 2018, 2018
Scope: National

Food Allergy Canada
#507, 505 Consumers Rd., Toronto ON M2J 4V8
Tel: 416-785-5666; *Fax:* 416-785-0458
Toll-Free: 866-785-5660
www.foodallergycanada.ca
www.facebook.com/FoodAllergyCanada
twitter.com/foodallergycan
www.youtube.com/foodallergycanada
Previous Name: Anaphylaxis Canada
Overview: A medium-sized national charitable organization
Mission: To inform, support, educate, & advocate for the needs of individuals & families living with food allergies & those who are at risk from anaphylaxis; To conduct & support research related to anaphylaxis

Affiliation(s): Dare Foods; Enjoy Life; Kellogg Canada; Loblaw Companies Ltd.; Mars Canada; Nestle Canada; Pepsico Canada; Pfizer Canada; Scotiabank Group; TD Securities; TELUS
Finances: *Funding Sources:* Membership dues; Donations; Grants; Sales of resources & services
Staff Member(s): 4
Chief Officer(s):
Jennifer Gerdts, Chair
Jeff Smith, Vice-Chair
Brian Brennan, Treasurer
Laurie Harada, Executive Director
Beatrice Povolo, Director, Advocacy & Media Relations
Ranjit Dhanjal, Director, Marketing
Tammy White, Office Manager
Publications:
• Food Allergy Canada Brochure
Type: Brochure
• Kids' Club Newsletter [a publication of Food Allergy Canada]
Type: Newsletter
Profile: Information & activities for children living with allergies & anaphylaxis
• The Ultimate Guidebook for Teens with Food Allergies [a publication of Food Allergy Canada]
Type: Book
Profile: Information & advice on food allergies for teenagers

Food Bank Moncton Inc. *See* Food Depot Alimentaire, Inc.

Food Bank of Waterloo Region (FBWR)
50 Alpine Ct., Kitchener ON N2E 2M7
Tel: 519-743-5576; *Fax:* 519-743-8965
www.thefoodbank.ca
www.facebook.com/10150145973860618
twitter.com/FoodBankWatReg
Overview: A small local charitable organization founded in 1984
Mission: To support the well-being of low-income persons
Member of: Ontario Association of Food Banks; Food Banks Canada
Affiliation(s): Dairy Farmers of Ontario
Staff Member(s): 17
Membership: 100+; *Member Profile:* Agencies that distribute food to the less fortunate in Waterloo Region
Activities: *Internships:* Yes; *Speaker Service:* Yes
Chief Officer(s):
Wendi Campbell, Executive Director

Food Banks Alberta Association
#30, 50 Bellerose Dr., St Albert AB T8N 3L5
Tel: 780-459-4598; *Fax:* 780-459-6347
Toll-Free: 866-251-2326
contact@foodbanksalberta.ca
www.foodbanksalberta.ca
www.linkedin.com/company/alberta-food-banks
www.facebook.com/FoodBanksAlberta
twitter.com/FoodBanksAB
www.instagram.com/foodbanksalberta
Previous Name: Alberta Food Bank Network Association
Overview: A medium-sized provincial charitable organization founded in 1998
Mission: To foster support, communication, & cooperation within the food bank community; To educate the public about hunger & poverty
Member of: Food Banks Canada
Affiliation(s): Community Kitchen Program of Calgary
Finances: *Funding Sources:* Corporate sponsors; private donors
Membership: 84; *Fees:* $50-$1,000; *Member Profile:* Small, medium & large food banks across the province
Activities: Coordinating product from Food Banks Canada; Coordinating provincial fundraising; Liaising between local food banks & national agency
Chief Officer(s):
Lori McRitchie, Chair
Awards:
• Fresh Food Fund
Eligibility: A member of Food Banks Alberta that operates in a community of less than 100,000 people; *Amount:* $2,000-$6,000

Food Banks British Columbia (FBBC)
13595 King George Blvd., Surrey BC V3T 2V1
Tel: 604-489-1798; *Fax:* 604-498-1795
info@foodbanksbc.com
www.foodbanksbc.ca
www.facebook.com/FoodBanksBC
twitter.com/RealFoodBanksBC
Overview: A small provincial charitable organization

Mission: To work to reduce hunger across BC
Member of: Food Banks Canada
Finances: *Funding Sources:* Corporate sponsors; private donors
Staff Member(s): 2
Membership: 93; *Member Profile:* Small, medium & large food banks across the province
Activities: Coordination of product from Food Bank Canada; coordination of provincial fundraising; liaising between local food banks & national agency
Chief Officer(s):
Laura Lansink, Executive Director
laura@foodbanksbc.com

Food Banks Canada / Banques alimentaires Canada
Bldg. 2, #400, 5025 Orbitor Dr., Mississauga ON L4W 4Y5
Tel: 905-602-5234; *Fax:* 905-602-5614
Toll-Free: 877-535-0958
www.foodbankscanada.ca
www.facebook.com/FoodBanksCanada
twitter.com/foodbankscanada
www.youtube.com/user/FoodBanksCanada1
Previous Name: Canadian Association of Food Banks
Overview: A medium-sized national charitable organization founded in 1988
Mission: To act as the voice for the hungry in Canada; To find short term & long term solutions for Canadians who are assisted by food banks
Member of: Global FoodBanking Network
Finances: *Funding Sources:* Donations; Sponsorships
Staff Member(s): 19
Membership: 10 provincial food bank associations + 450+ food banks; *Member Profile:* Provincial food bank associations; Food banks & their associated agencies
Activities: Collecting & sharing donations of food with members; Sharing donated funds; Collecting statistics about hunger in Canada; Raising awareness of hunger; Lobbying government to establish policies to reduce hunger; Promoting the dignity of food bank clients & the ethical stewardship of food donations; *Awareness Events:* National Hunger Awareness Day
Chief Officer(s):
Katharine Schmidt, Executive Director, 416-203-9241 Ext. 222
Brian Fraser, Chair
Marc Guay, Vice-Chair
Monica Donahue, Secretary
Allan Cosman, Treasurer
Publications:
• HungerCount
Type: Yearbook; *Frequency:* Annually
Profile: A national survey of emergency food programs in Canada
• Provisions
Type: Newsletter
Profile: Featuring statistics, advocacy efforts, & event results

Food Beverage Canada (FBC)
#201, 17914 - 105 Ave., Edmonton AB T5S 2H5
Tel: 780-486-9679; *Fax:* 780-484-0985
Toll-Free: 800-493-9767
www.foodbeveragecanada.com
Overview: A small national organization founded in 1994
Mission: To develop export strategies & programs that will strengthen & increase our members' share of global food & beverage markets

Food Depot Alimentaire, Inc.
330 MacNaughton Ave., Moncton NB E1H 2K1
Tel: 506-383-4281; *Fax:* 506-388-5822
info@fooddepot.ca
www.fooddepotalimentaire.ca
www.facebook.com/268995153176974
Previous Name: Food Bank Moncton Inc.
Overview: A small local charitable organization founded in 1986
Mission: To collect & supply food to food banks in the province
Member of: Association of Food Banks & C.V.A.s for New Brunswick; Canadian Association of Food Banks
Finances: *Annual Operating Budget:* $50,000-$100,000; *Funding Sources:* City; province; donations
20 volunteer(s)
Membership: 20 food banks

Food for Life Canada
2258 Mountainside Dr., Burlington ON L7P 1B7
Tel: 905-510-5724
info@foodforlife.ca
www.foodforlife.ca
Overview: A small local charitable organization

Canadian Associations / Food Processors of Canada (FPC) / Fabricants de produits alimentaires du Canada

Mission: To collect & distribute fresh food to people in need in the Halton region
Staff Member(s): 7; 800 volunteer(s)
Chief Officer(s):
Ian Gibbons, Director, Operations
ian@foodforlife.ca

Food Institute of Canada *See* Food Processors of Canada

Food Processors of Canada (FPC) / Fabricants de produits alimentaires du Canada
#900, 350 Sparks St., Ottawa ON K1R 7S8
Tel: 613-722-1000; *Fax:* 613-722-1404
Other Communication: conferences@foodprocessors.ca
fpc@foodprocessors.ca
www.foodprocessors.ca
Previous Name: Food Institute of Canada
Overview: A medium-sized national organization founded in 1989
Mission: To provide professional services & advice to members on matters such as manufacturing, trade, & commerce
Membership: *Member Profile:* Canadian food industry executives who own or manage food processing companies
Activities: Maintaining relationships with government departments to affect policies, programs, & regulations; Organizing conferences; Providing networking opportunities
Chief Officer(s):
Christopher J. Kyte, President
Mel Fruitman, Vice-President

Foodservice Consultants Society International - Canadian Chapter
c/o CRS Management Services Ltd., 524 Beresford Ave., Toronto ON M6S 3C1
Tel: 416-769-8097; *Fax:* 416-769-0217
canada@fcsi.org
www.fcsi.org
www.facebook.com/FCSI.Canadachapter
twitter.com/FCSIcdn
Overview: A small national organization founded in 1984
Mission: To maintain & advance a professional standard in the food service & hospitality industry
Member of: FCSI Worldwide
Activities: Fundraisers; Meetings; Educational Programs
Chief Officer(s):
Cathy Sommers, Administrator

Foodshare (Metro) Toronto *See* Foodshare Toronto

Foodshare Toronto
90 Croatia St., Toronto ON M6H 1K9
Tel: 416-363-6441; *Fax:* 416-363-0474
info@foodshare.net
www.foodshare.net
www.facebook.com/FoodShareTO
twitter.com/FoodShareTO
www.youtube.com/user/FoodShareTO
Previous Name: Foodshare (Metro) Toronto
Overview: A medium-sized local charitable organization founded in 1985
Mission: Working with communities to improve access to affordable & healthy food, from field to table
Finances: *Annual Operating Budget:* Greater than $5 Million; *Funding Sources:* Private donors; government; foundations
Staff Member(s): 49; 5133 volunteer(s)
Activities: Operates fresh fruit & vegetable distribution system, the Good Food Box; Toronto Kitchen Incubator, an industrial kitchen available for rent to entrepreneurs & community groups; Field to Table Catering Co., a CED project specializing in healthy, seasonal food; education & training on community kitchens & gardens; baby nutrition workshops; advocacy on hunger & food security; operates FoodLink Hotline: a food bank & alternative food project referral service
Chief Officer(s):
Debbie Field, Executive Director
debbie@foodshare.net

Foosball Québec
QC
Tél: 418-906-0977
foosballquebec@gmail.com
www.foosballquebec.com
www.facebook.com/foosballquebec
Aperçu: *Dimension:* petite; *Envergure:* provinciale
Membre(s) du bureau directeur:
Lévesque Olivier, Président

Foot Care Canada *See* Canadian Association of Foot Care Nurses

Football BC
#434, 6540 Hastings St., Burnaby BC V5B 4Z5
Tel: 604-677-1025
communications@playfootball.bc.ca
www.playfootball.bc.ca
www.facebook.com/footballbc
twitter.com/Football_BC
Also Known As: British Columbia Amateur Football Association
Overview: A medium-sized provincial organization
Mission: To operate as the governing body for amateur football in British Columbia. Office location: #222, 6939 Hastings St., Burnaby, BC, V5B 1S9
Staff Member(s): 3
Membership: 6 associations; *Member Profile:* Football leagues, coaches & officials
Activities: Clinics; Camp; Education sessions
Chief Officer(s):
Patrick Waslen, Executive Director

Football Canada
#205, 825 Exhibition Way, Ottawa ON K1S 5J3
Tel: 613-564-0003; *Fax:* 613-564-6309
info@footballcanada.com
footballcanada.com
www.facebook.com/FootballCanada
twitter.com/FootballCanada
www.youtube.com/user/FootballCanada1884
Also Known As: Canadian Amateur Football Association
Previous Name: Canadian Rugby Football Union
Overview: A medium-sized national charitable organization founded in 1884
Mission: Through its members, to initate, regulate, & manage the programs, services & activities that promote participation & excellence in Canadian Amateur Football.
Finances: *Annual Operating Budget:* $250,000-$500,000; *Funding Sources:* Membership fees; government; corporate sponsors
Membership: 110,000
Activities: Football Canada Cup; Touch Bowl
Chief Officer(s):
Kim Wudrick, President
Shannon Donovan, Executive Director
sdonovan@footballcanada.com
Aaron Geisler, Manager, Development
ageisler@footballcanada.com
Vanisha Mistry, Coordinator, Communications
vmistry@footballcanada.com
Jean-François Lefebvre, Coordinator, Program Development
jlefebvre@footballcanada.com

Football Nova Scotia Association
5516 Spring Garden Rd., Halifax NS B3J 1G6
Tel: 902-425-5450; *Fax:* 902-425-5606
footballns@ns.aliantzinc.ca
www.footballnovascotia.ca
www.facebook.com/footballnovascotia
twitter.com/footballns
Overview: A small provincial organization founded in 1974
Mission: To promote amateur football in Nova Scotia, at both the competitive & recreational levels, to assist members with their programs, & to develop the sport in new areas of the province
Affiliation(s): Canadian Amateur Football Association
Finances: *Funding Sources:* Provincial Government
Staff Member(s): 1; 14 volunteer(s)
Membership: 1,000 individual
Activities: *Rents Mailing List:* Yes
Chief Officer(s):
Richard MacLean, President
football@eastlink.ca
Rob Manson, Vice-President
rmanson@oceansecurities.com

Football Ontario *See* Ontario Football Alliance

Football PEI
PE
Tel: 902-368-4262; *Fax:* 902-368-4548
footballpeiexecutive@gmail.com
www.peifootball.ca
twitter.com/footballpei
Overview: A large provincial organization
Mission: To operate as the provincial sport governing body for amateur football in Prince Edward Island; To promote & further the development of the sport in its three forms - flag, tackle, & touch
Chief Officer(s):
Glen Flood, Executive Director
gflood@sportpei.pe.ca

Football Québec (FFAQ) / Fédération de football amateur de Québec
4545, av Pierre-de Coubertin, Montréal QC H1V 0B2
Tél: 514-252-3059; *Téléc:* 514-252-5216
footballquebec.com
www.facebook.com/footballquebec
twitter.com/footballquebec
Aperçu: *Dimension:* moyenne; *Envergure:* provinciale; fondée en 1882
Mission: Régir le développement du football au Québec, avec règlement de sécurité, formation des entraîneurs et des officiels, et les championnats provinciaux
Membre de: Sport Québec
Affiliation(s): National Football Federation of Canada
Finances: *Budget de fonctionnement annuel:* $250,000-$500,000; *Fonds:* Gouvernement provincial
Membre(s) du personnel: 3; 3000 bénévole(s)
Membre: 15 000
Membre(s) du bureau directeur:
Jean-Charles Meffe, Directeur général, 514-252-3059 Ext. 3514

Foothills Forage & Grazing Association (FFGA)
PO Box 458, Okotoks AB T1S 1A7
Tel: 403-995-9466
www.foothillsforage.com
www.facebook.com/166272723417016
twitter.com/FoothillsForage
Overview: A small local organization founded in 1972 overseen by Agricultural Research & Extension Council of Alberta
Mission: To provide forage & livestock information to producers; To partner with industry, government & the agricultural community; To help producers enhance their forages & regenerate their soils
Member of: Agricultural Research & Extension Council of Alberta; Canadian Roundtable for Sustainable Beef
Staff Member(s): 2; 11 volunteer(s)
Membership: 170; *Fees:* $30; *Member Profile:* Any individual or firm involved in the production of forage
Activities: Organizing workshops, conferences, tours & field days; *Speaker Service:* Yes
Chief Officer(s):
Laura Gibney, Manager
laura@foothillsforage.com
Rachel McLean, Coordinator, Environmental & Communication
rachel@foothillsforage.com
Publications:
• Grassroots News & Views [a publication of Foothills Forage & Grazing Association]
Type: Newsletter; *Editor:* Rachel McLean

Foothills Library Association (FLA)
PO Box 29, #101, 223 - 12th Ave. SW, Calgary AB T2R 0G9
www.fla.org
Overview: A small local organization founded in 1975
Mission: To share & promote the concerns of library & information professionals in the Calgary area
Membership: *Fees:* $30; *Member Profile:* People interested in the information professions in the Foothills region of Alberta; Institutions & organizations interested in the objectives of the association
Activities: Facilitating networking opportunities within the Calgary library community; Offering presentations & discussions on prominent issues in libraries in the region; Organizing seminars, lectures, & tours to contribute to the professional development of members
Chief Officer(s):
Donna Campbell, Secretary
secretary@fla.org
Awards:
• Rachel Chan Memorial Grant
Awarded to assist a member with limited or no access to funding in attending a library conference related to their work; *Amount:* up to $500
Publications:
• Foothills Library Association Gazette (FLAG)
Type: Newsletter; *Frequency:* Quarterly; *Price:* Free with membership in the Foothills Library Association
Profile: Foothills Library Association business & activities

- Foothills Library Association Membership Directory
Type: Directory; *Editor:* John Wright; Katie Edwards
Profile: Listings of members' names & affiations

Foothills Model Forest *See* Foothills Research Institute

Foothills Orchid Society
PO Box 22111, Stn. Bankers Hall, Calgary AB T2P 4J5
calgaryorchidsociety@shaw.ca
www.foothillsorchidsociety.com
Overview: A small local organization
Member of: Canadian Orchid Congress
Affiliation(s): American Orchid Society; Orchid Digest; Orchid Society of Alberta
Membership: *Fees:* $30

Foothills Research Institute
1176 Switzer Dr., Hinton AB T7V 1V3
Tel: 780-865-8330
friresearch.ca
Also Known As: fRI Research
Previous Name: Foothills Model Forest
Overview: A small local organization founded in 1992
Mission: To develop science-based tools for sustainable land & resource management
Member of: Canadian Model Forest Network
Finances: *Annual Operating Budget:* $3 Million-$5 Million
Membership: 1-99; *Member Profile:* Industry, government, environmental non-governmental offices, academics, aboriginals, researchers; *Committees:* Scientific Advisory
Chief Officer(s):
Ryan Tew, General Manager

Footprints Dance Project Society of Alberta
3935 Varsity Dr. SW, Calgary AB T3A 0Z3
Tel: 587-228-5440
calgaryfootprintsdance@gmail.com
www.footprintsdance.com
www.facebook.com/footprintsyyc
www.youtube.com/user/CalgaryFootprints
Overview: A small provincial organization founded in 1999
Mission: To ensure children and youth have opportunities to explore and express the creativities inside their hearts and minds, and to level the performing arts field for the disadvantaged and disabled, to build a caring community, and to democratize participation in the arts.
Chief Officer(s):
Andrea Pass, Artistic Producer

Force Jeunesse
#322, 1000, rue Saint-Antoine ouest, Montréal QC H3C 3R7
Tél: 514-384-8666; *Téléc:* 514-384-6442
info@forcejeunesse.qc.ca
www.forcejeunesse.qc.ca
www.facebook.com/ForceJeunesse
twitter.com/FORCEJEUNESSE
Aperçu: *Dimension:* moyenne; *Envergure:* provinciale; fondée en 1998
Mission: Force Jeunesse est un regroupement de jeunes travailleurs issus de différents milieux dont le principe fondateur est l'équité intergénérationnelle; agit concrètement en revendiquant des mesures qui améliorent la situation économique et sociale des jeunes.
Membre: 9 associations; *Montant de la cotisation:* 10$ membre individuel; 50$ membre associatif; *Critères d'admissibilite:* Associations et individus
Membre(s) du bureau directeur:
Jonathan Plamondon, Président

Foreign Agricultural Resource Management Services (FARMS)
#706, 5995 Avebury Rd., Mississauga ON L5R 3P9
Fax: 905-568-4175
Toll-Free: 866-271-0826
www.farmsontario.ca
Overview: A medium-sized international organization founded in 1987 overseen by Canadian Federation of Agriculture
Mission: To facilitate & coordinate requests for foreign seasonal agricultural workers
Member of: Canadian Federation of Agriculture
Membership: 6 countries; *Member Profile:* Participating countries: Barbados, Eastern Caribbean, Jamaica, Mexico & Trinidad & Tobago
Activities: Operating CanAg Travel Services; providing forms & information online
Chief Officer(s):
Ken Forth, President

Sue Williams, General Manager

Foreign Exchange Association of Canada *See* Financial Markets Association of Canada

Foremost & District Chamber of Commerce
PO Box 272, Foremost AB T0K 0X0
Tel: 403-867-3077; *Fax:* 403-867-2700
www.foremostalberta.com
Overview: A small local organization

Forest Engineering Research Institute of Canada, A Division of FPInnovations *See* FPInnovations

Forest Nova Scotia
PO Box 696, Truro NS B2N 5E5
Tel: 902-895-1179; *Fax:* 902-893-1197
forestns.ca
Previous Name: Forest Products Association of Nova Scotia
Overview: A medium-sized provincial organization founded in 1934
Mission: To act as the voice of the forest industry in Nova Scotia; To cooperate with industry, federal, provincial, & municipal governments, & other stakeholders to ensure adherence to forest management & stewardship policies; To promote sustainable management & viability of the forest industry
Membership: 500-999; *Fees:* Schedule available; *Member Profile:* Representatives from the logging sector of the trucking industry; Pulp & paper manufacturers; Sawmill operators; Forest equipment operators; Woodlot owners; Small & large landowners; Maple product producers; Silviculture & harvesting contractors; Christmas tree producers
Activities: Enhancing training standards; Providing educational programs in schools; *Awareness Events:* National Forest Week
Meetings/Conferences:
- Forest Nova Scotia 2018 84th Annual Meeting, 2018, NS
Scope: Provincial
Description: A yearly gathering of association members
Contact Information: Phone: 902-895-1179

Forest Products Association of Canada (FPAC) / Association des produits forestiers du Canada
#410, 99 Bank St., Ottawa ON K1P 6B9
Tel: 613-563-1441; *Fax:* 613-563-4720
ottawa@fpac.ca
www.fpac.ca
www.facebook.com/FPAC.APFC
twitter.com/FPAC_APFC
www.youtube.com/ForestProdsAssocCan
Previous Name: Canadian Pulp & Paper Association
Overview: A medium-sized national organization founded in 1913
Mission: To be the voice of Canada's wood, pulp & paper producers nationally & internationally in the areas of government, trade, & environmental affairs; To advance the Canadian forest products industry's global competitiveness & sustainable stewardship; To operate in a mannner which is economically viable, environmentally responsible, & socially desirable
Membership: *Member Profile:* Canadian producers of forest products, with third-party certification of member companies' forest practices
Activities: Liaising with governments, non-governmental organizations (NGOs), & multi-stakeholder groups; Conducting advertising campaigns; *Library:* Forest Products Association of Canada Resource Centre
Chief Officer(s):
David Lindsay, President & Chief Executive Officer
Susan Murray, Executive Director, Public Relations
smurray@fpac.ca
Publications:
- A Buyers' Guide to Canada's Sustainable Forest Products
Type: Guide; *Number of Pages:* 32
Profile: Contents include sustainable procurement, key issues related to sustainable procurement, sample forest products procurement, green building with Canada's forestproducts, FPAC member companies, a glossary, useful links, reference guides, & standards, & environmental performance data
- Canadian Wood, Renewable by Nature, Sustainable by Design
Type: Report; *Number of Pages:* 22
Profile: Information about sustainable forest management in Canada
- Forest Certification in Canada: The Programs, Similarities, & Achievements
Type: Report; *Number of Pages:* 26
Profile: Contents include an introduction to certification, Canada,

a world leader in forest certification, & key elements of certification programs
- Forest Products Association of Canada Annual Report
Type: Yearbook; *Frequency:* Annually
- FPAC [Forest Products Association of Canada] Sustainability Report
Type: Report; *Frequency:* Biennially
- The New Face of the Canadian Forest Industry: The Emerging Bio-revolution (The Bio-pathways Project)
Type: Report
Profile: An examination of the market potential of emerging bio-energy, bio-chemical, & bio-products
- Tackle Climate Change, Use Wood
Type: Report; *Number of Pages:* 22
Profile: Managing forests to mitigate climate change
- Transforming Canada's Forest Products Industry: Summary of Findings from the Future Bio-Pathways Project
Type: Report
Profile: Forest Products Association of Canada investigators & their partner, FPInnovations, examine traditional & emergingbio-industries to assess how wood fibre can create bio-products such as bio-energy & bio-chemicals
- Woodland Caribou Recovery: Audit of Operatinig Practices & Mitigation Measures Employed within Woodland Caribou Ranges
Type: Report; *Author:* Golder Associates
Profile: An audit commissioned by the Forest Products Association of Canada & the CaribouLandscape Management Association

Forest Products Association of Nova Scotia *See* Forest Nova Scotia

Foresters
ON
Tel: 416-429-3000; *Fax:* 416-467-2518
Toll-Free: 800-828-1540
service@foresters.com
www.foresters.com
www.facebook.com/Foresters
twitter.com/weareforesters
www.youtube.com/c/foresters; www.pinterest.com/foresters
Previous Name: The Independent Order of Foresters
Overview: A large national organization founded in 1874
Mission: A fraternal benefit society which provides life insurance & other financial products to its members
Affiliation(s): Children's Miracle Network; Barnardo's Children's Charity (U.K.)
Membership: 735,000+
Chief Officer(s):
Anthony M. (Tony) Garcia, President & Chief Executive Officer
Awards:
- Foresters Competitive Scholarships
Eligibility: Students of any age with a minimum 40 hours community service and a GPA of at least 2.8% or 70%; *Amount:* Up to $11,000 (250)
Burlington
#402, 3027 Harvester Rd., Burlington ON L7N 3G7
Tel: 905-637-5119
Edmonton
#100, 10637 - 124 St., Edmonton AB T5J 3G1
Tel: 780-425-2948; *Fax:* 780-425-9124
Markham
#401, 3000 Steeles Ave. East, Markham ON L3R 4T9
Tel: 905-474-3665

Forests Ontario
#700, 144 Front St. West, Toronto ON M5J 2L7
Tel: 416-646-1193; *Fax:* 416-493-4608
Toll-Free: 877-646-1193
info@treesontario.ca
www.forestsontario.ca
www.linkedin.com/company/1243400
www.facebook.com/Forests.Ontario
twitter.com/Forests_Ontario
www.youtube.com/user/ontforest
Merged from: Trees Ontario & Ontario Forestry Association
Overview: A medium-sized provincial charitable organization founded in 1949 overseen by Canadian Forestry Association
Mission: To promote sound land use & full development protection & utilization of Ontario's forest resources for maximum public advantage; to increase public awareness, school education & natural appreciation of forests; to bring about better understanding of forests to people of all ages & backgrounds
Finances: *Annual Operating Budget:* $250,000-$500,000
Staff Member(s): 4; 100 volunteer(s)

Membership: 1000; *Fees:* $50 individual, $25 student, $150 group, $85 educational institution, $1000 life
Activities: 50 Million Tree Program; Forest Recovery Canada; Workshops; Tree Planting; Landowner Resources; Educational Programs; *Speaker Service:* Yes
Chief Officer(s):
Rob Keen, CEO
Al Corlett, Director of Programs
Shelley McKay, Director of Communications & Development
Awards:
• James S. Miller Memorial Scholarship
Eligibility: Student in Northern Ontario in final year of high school entering first year of post-secondary education in natural resources or related field *Deadline:* February *Contact:* Tracey Cooke
• John Wesley Beaver Memorial Awards
Eligibility: Student of Native ancestry entering Ontario college or university for engineering, technology, environmental studies, forestry, biology, land use & environmental planning, or business; *Amount:* $4000
• Bentley Cropping Systems Fellowship
Eligibility: Student in graduate studies doing research related to agriculture, forestry or biology in developing countries; *Amount:* $30,000
• William Peyton Hubbard Award
Eligibility: African-Canadian student in 2nd, 3rd or 4th year in engineering, computer science, forestry or business; *Amount:* $2,000-4,000
Meetings/Conferences:
• Forests Ontario Conference 2018, 2018, ON
Scope: Provincial

Forever Chai Foundation of Canada
PO Box 49560, 80 Glen Shields Ave., Concord ON L4K 4P6
Tel: 416-695-8885; *Fax:* 416-765-0026
info@foreverchai.org
www.foreverchai.org
www.facebook.com/197167993646657
Overview: A small international charitable organization founded in 2009
Mission: To provide funds & assistance to mothers & children in crisis; To support the Shabtai Levi Home in Haifa, Israel
Chief Officer(s):
Ellen Goldstein, President
ellengoldstein@hotmail.com
Marya Grad, Treasurer
mgrad@rogers.com

Forever Young Seniors Society (FYSS)
Vancouver BC
Tel: 604-454-9907
contact@foreveryoungseniorssociety.com
www.foreveryoungseniorssociety.com
www.youtube.com/user/fysscanada
Overview: A small local organization
Mission: To preserve the Filipino heritage & cultural traditions; To serve Filipino Canadian seniors in the Vancouver area
Membership: *Fees:* $10 regular members; $8 associate members; *Member Profile:* Filipino Canadian seniors, over 50 years of age, in the Vancouver area; Associate members range in age from 20 to 49 years
Activities: Hosting Filipino traditional cultural events; Offering social & recreational activities for Filipino seniors in the Vancouver area; Organizing an annual general meeting; Raising public awareness of the Filipino community, through participation in community events; Offering assistance to members
Chief Officer(s):
Romeo Mercado, President
Juanita Lamothe, Vice-President
Adel Johanson, Secretary
Angie Jimenez, Treasurer
Publications:
• Forever Young Journal
Type: Newsletter
Profile: Society activities, membership news, & forthcoming events

Formation juridique permanente du Nouveau-Brunswick *See* New Brunswick Continuing Legal Education

Fort Calgary Society
PO Box 2100, Stn. M, Calgary AB T2P 2M5
Tel: 403-290-1875; *Fax:* 403-265-6534
info@fortcalgary.com
www.fortcalgary.com
www.facebook.com/fortcalgary
twitter.com/fortcalgary
www.instagram.com/fortcalgary
Overview: A small local organization founded in 1977
Mission: To preserve, interpret & promote the early history of the Mounted Police at Fort Calgary & to communicate Calgary's early cultural heritage & diversity through its interactive programs, services & exhibits.
Member of: Alberta Museums Association; Alliance for Historic Landscape Preservation; Old Forts Trail
Finances: *Annual Operating Budget:* $1.5 Million-$3 Million; *Funding Sources:* City of Calgary; province of Alberta; private
203 volunteer(s)
Activities: *Library:* Resource Centre
Chief Officer(s):
Cecilia Gossen, Chair
Sara-Jane Gruetzner, President & CEO

Fort Edmonton Foundation
PO Box 67112, Stn. Meadowlark, Edmonton AB T5R 5Y3
Tel: 780-496-6978
Other Communication: www.flickr.com/photos/fortedmontonpark
admin@fortedmontonfoundation.org
www.fortedmontonfoundation.org
www.facebook.com/fortedmontonpark
twitter.com/SupportTheFort
www.youtube.com/fortedmontonpark
Previous Name: Fort Edmonton Historical Foundation
Overview: A small local charitable organization founded in 1969
Mission: To raise capital funding for the ongoing development of Fort Edmonton Park; To recreate as historically accurate as possible the history of the city of Edmonton; To create & promote FEF as an internationally acclaimed living history experience
Member of: Museums Alberta; Alberta Association of Fundraising Executives
Finances: *Annual Operating Budget:* $100,000-$250,000; *Funding Sources:* Fundraising; donations
100 volunteer(s)
Membership: 100 individual
Activities: *Library:* Resource Centre; Not open to public
Chief Officer(s):
Michael Paull, President
Janet Tryhuba, Executive Director

Fort Edmonton Historical Foundation *See* Fort Edmonton Foundation

Fort Erie Business Success & Loan Centre (BSL)
45 Jarvis St., Fort Erie ON L2A 2S3
Tel: 905-871-7331; *Fax:* 905-871-5284
info@bslforterie.ca
www.bslft.com
Previous Name: Business Development Centre of Greater Fort Erie
Overview: A small provincial organization founded in 1985
Mission: To provide loans to small businesses & entrepreneurs to start & maintain businesses, or to finance growth for existing companies & start-up businesses; To administer the Ontario Self-Employment Benefit program for eligible individuals
Member of: Ontario Association of Community Development Corporations
Affiliation(s): Human Resources Development Canada; Ministry of Training, College, & Universities
Finances: *Annual Operating Budget:* $100,000-$250,000
Staff Member(s): 3; 11 volunteer(s)
Membership: 17
Activities: Assisting in the development of a business plan; Providing ongoing monitoring & training; Offering coaching & evaluation of progress during the first year of a new business; *Speaker Service:* Yes; *Library:* BSL Reference Library; Open to public
Chief Officer(s):
Steve Helwig, Office Manager

Fort Erie Native Friendship Centre
796 Buffalo Rd., Fort Erie ON L2A 5H2
Tel: 905-871-8931
reception@fenfc.org
www.fenfc.org
www.facebook.com/FortErieNFC
Overview: A small local organization
Mission: To enhance all aspects of Native life through such programs as day care services & the distribution of business attire & advice to those seeking employment.
Staff Member(s): 28
Membership: *Fees:* $2 organization/honourary/elder/senior; $3 adult; $5 family
Activities: Aboriginal Alcohol & Drug Worker Program (ADDWP)

Fort Frances & District Labour Council
140 - 4th St. West, Fort Frances ON P9A 3B8
Tel: 807-274-7411
Overview: A small local organization overseen by Ontario Federation of Labour

Fort Frances Chamber of Commerce (FFCC)
#102, 240 - 1st St. East, Fort Frances ON P9A 1K5
Tel: 807-274-5773; *Fax:* 807-274-8706
Toll-Free: 800-820-3678
thefort@fortfranceschamber.com
www.fortfranceschamber.com
www.facebook.com/300272150100708
Overview: A small local charitable organization founded in 1909
Mission: To improve trade & commerce & the economic, civic & social welfare of the district; To promote tourism, agriculture & labour
Member of: Ontario's Sunset Country Travel Association; Northwestern Ontario Tourism Association; Northwestern Ontario Associated Chambers of Commerce
Affiliation(s): Ontario Chamber of Commerce; Canadian Chamber of Commerce
Finances: *Funding Sources:* Membership dues; fundraising
Membership: *Fees:* Schedule available; *Committees:* By-Law Review; Events & Projects; Executive, Finance & Personnel; Government Relations; Membership & Marketing; Nominations; Young Entrepreneurs
Activities: Business Awards; Trade Show; Quest for the Best
Chief Officer(s):
Jennifer Greenhalgh, President
Awards:
• Two Scholarships for the Fort Frances High School
; *Amount:* $250
• Business of the Year Award
• Community Safety Award

Fort Macleod & District Chamber of Commerce
PO Box 178, Fort MacLeod AB T0L 0Z0
Tel: 587-220-5335
fmchamber1888@gmail.com
www.fort-macleod-chamber.com
www.facebook.com/FortMacleodChamber
Overview: A small local organization
Mission: To promote & assist local businesses; To strengthen economic development in the local community
Chief Officer(s):
Andrew Beusekom, Vice-President

Fort Macleod Historical Association
PO Box 776, 219 Jerry Potts Blvd., Fort MacLeod AB T0L 0Z0
Tel: 403-553-4703; *Fax:* 403-553-3451
Toll-Free: 866-273-6841
info@nwmpmuseum.com
www.nwmpmuseum.com
Also Known As: The Fort Museum
Overview: A small local charitable organization founded in 1957
Mission: To preserve, educate, inform & entertain visitors with collection of North West Mounted Police, Royal Canadian Mounted Police, Native & pioneer artifacts; To aim to keep North West Mounted Police tradition alive through musical ride by Fort Mounted Patrol
Member of: Alberta Museums Association
Finances: *Annual Operating Budget:* $100,000-$250,000; *Funding Sources:* Admission fees; gift shop sales; student grants
Staff Member(s): 40; 15 volunteer(s)
Membership: 100; *Fees:* $25 business; $5 senior; $10 single; $15 family; *Committees:* Finance; Programs; Archives; Personnel; Grounds; Mounted Patrol
Activities: *Awareness Events:* Museum's Day, July 1; Heritage Fest

Fort McMurray Association for Community Living (FMACL)
10010 Franklin Ave., Fort McMurray AB T9H 2K6
Tel: 780-791-3009; *Fax:* 780-791-7506
Overview: A small local charitable organization founded in 1969
Mission: To provide service to individuals with physical & mental challenges, to seniors & to newcomers
Member of: Alberta Association for Community Living
Activities: Career & employment counseling; training & skill enhancement programs; immigrant assessment services

Fort McMurray Chamber of Commerce
#105, 9912 Franklin Ave., Fort McMurray AB T9H 2K5
Tel: 780-743-3100; Fax: 780-790-9757
www.fortmcmurraychamber.ca
www.facebook.com/ymmchamber
Overview: A small local organization founded in 1914 overseen by Alberta Chambers of Commerce
Mission: To promote & strengthen the economy of Fort McMurray & region
Member of: Canadian Chamber of Commerce
Finances: Funding Sources: Membership dues; fundraising
Staff Member(s): 2
Membership: 650+; Fees: Schedule available; Member Profile: Interest in trade, commerce or the economic & social welfare of the district
Activities: Awareness Events: Small Business Week
Chief Officer(s):
Nick Sanders, President
Awards:
- Business of the Year
- Small Business of the Year
- Environmental Leadership of the Year
- Family Friendly Business Award of Distinction
- X-ceptional kidz
- Leader of Tomorrow Award
- Sustainable Communities Recognition Award
- Public Service Award of Excellence

Fort McMurray Food Bank See Wood Buffalo Food Bank

Fort McMurray Genealogical Study Group See Alberta Genealogical Society

Fort McMurray Historical Society
1 Tolen Dr., Fort McMurray AB T9H 1G7
Tel: 780-791-7575; Fax: 780-791-5180
info@fmheritage.com
www.fortmcmurrayheritage.com
www.facebook.com/260650299824
twitter.com/McMurrayHistory
Also Known As: Heritage Park
Previous Name: Historical Society of Fort McMurray
Overview: A small local charitable organization founded in 1974
Mission: To encourage & participate in collecting, preserving, researching & interpreting artifacts, documents, buildings & sites; To preserve & maintain an ongoing record of the history of the region; To inform & educate the public regarding the social & cultural history
Member of: Fort McMurray Tourism; Chamber of Commerce; Alberta Museums; Canadian Museums
Affiliation(s): Travel Alberta; Chevron Canada
Finances: Funding Sources: Donations; Federal, provincial, & municipal funding; Sale of goods & services
Staff Member(s): 10; 20+ volunteer(s)
Membership: 51+; Fees: $20
Activities: Informing & educating the public regarding social & cultural history, through school programs, summer camps, & special events such as Pioneer Days & Celtic Day in the Park; Providing photo reproduction; Supporting research projects; Awareness Events: National Indigenous Peoples Day, June; Heritage Day, August; Old Fashioned Christmas, November Library: Fort McMurray Historical Society Library; Open to public by appointment
Chief Officer(s):
Roseann Davidson, Executive Director
execdirector@fmheritage.com

Fort McMurray Realtors Association
9909 Sutherland St., Fort McMurray AB T9H 1V3
Tel: 780-791-1124; Fax: 780-743-4724
boards.mls.ca/fortmcmurray
Overview: A small local organization overseen by Alberta Real Estate Association
Member of: Alberta Real Estate Association; The Canadian Real Estate Association
Chief Officer(s):
Chris Moskalyk, Executive Officer
moskalykc@shaw.ca

Fort McMurray Society for the Prevention of Cruelty to Animals
155 MacAlpine Cres., Fort McMurray AB T9H 4A5
Tel: 780-743-8997
info@fortmcmurrayspca.ca
www.fortmcmurrayspca.ca
www.facebook.com/307296965992025
Also Known As: Fort McMurray SPCA
Overview: A small local charitable organization founded in 1978 overseen by Canadian Federation of Humane Societies
Mission: To ensure the humane treatment of all animals
Member of: Alberta Society for the Prevention of Cruelty to Animals; Canadian Federation of Humane Societies
Finances: Funding Sources: United Way; Fundraising
Staff Member(s): 19

Fort McMurray Youth Soccer Association (FMYSA)
PO Box 10, 8115 Franklin Ave., Fort McMurray AB T9H 2H7
Tel: 780-791-7090; Fax: 780-791-1446
fmysa@shaw.ca
www.fmyouthsoccer.com
Overview: A small local organization overseen by Alberta Soccer Association
Member of: Alberta Soccer Association
Chief Officer(s):
Ian Diaz, Technical Director
fmysatechnicaldirector@gmail.com
Bill Carr, President
president.fmysa@shaw.ca
Awards:
- Grey Kampala Scholarship
- Will Kristman Scholarship
- FMYSA Scholarship

Fort Nelson & District Chamber of Commerce
PO Box 196, 5500 Alaska Hwy., Fort Nelson BC V0C 1R0
Tel: 250-774-2956; Fax: 250-774-2958
info@fortnelsonchamber.com
www.fortnelsonchamber.com
www.facebook.com/fnchamber
twitter.com/FNchamber
Overview: A small local organization founded in 1959
Mission: To be the collective voice for businesses in the region; To promote & enhance trade & commerce for the benefit of the region
Member of: British Columbia Chamber of Commerce; Canadian Chamber of Commerce
Finances: Funding Sources: Fundraising activities
Staff Member(s): 2
Membership: Fees: Schedule available; Member Profile: Business leaders & companies
Activities: Organizing events & awards ceremonies; Awareness Events: Business & Community Excellence Awards Library: Business Information; Open to public
Chief Officer(s):
Kim Eglinski, President
Bev Vandersteen, Executive Director
bvandersteen@fortnelsonchamber.com

Fort Nelson Aboriginal Friendship Society
PO Box 1266, 5012 – 49th Ave., Fort Nelson BC V0C 1R0
Tel: 250-774-2993
friendshipecoviety@northwestel.net
Also Known As: Fort Nelson Friendship Centre
Previous Name: Fort Nelson-Liard Friendship Society
Overview: A small local charitable organization founded in 1975
Mission: Committed to assisting in the transition of Aboriginal people to the urban community; provides programs & events that enhance self-esteem & positive growth for Aboriginal & Non-Aboriginal
Activities: Youth activities; dances; elders luncheons; A&D counselling; fashion shows; fundraising

Fort Nelson-Liard Friendship Society See Fort Nelson Aboriginal Friendship Society

Fort Qu'Appelle & District Chamber of Commerce
PO Box 1273, Fort Qu'Appelle SK S0G 1S0
Tel: 306-332-7930
FQChamber@hotmail.com
www.facebook.com/1528285077467488
Overview: A small local organization
Mission: To act as the voice of business in Fort Qu-Appelle Saskatchewan & the surrounding area
Member of: Saskatchewan Chamber of Commerce

Fort St. James Chamber of Commerce
PO Box 1164, 115 Douglas Ave., Fort St. James BC V0J 1P0
Tel: 250-996-7023; Fax: 250-996-7047
fsjchamb@fsjames.com
www.fortstjameschamber.ca
Overview: A small local organization founded in 1985
Mission: To strengthen the business climate of Fort St. James
Member of: BC Chamber of Commerce
Finances: Annual Operating Budget: Less than $50,000; Funding Sources: Fishing Derby; Business Directory; Thunder On Ice
Staff Member(s): 2
Membership: 99; Fees: $45-$295
Activities: Organizing events such as Fishing Derby & Thunder On Ice; Awareness Events: Chamber Week; Library: Open to public

Fort St. John & District Chamber of Commerce
#100, 9907 - 99 Ave., Fort St John BC V1J 1V1
Tel: 250-785-6037; Fax: 250-785-6050
info@fsjchamber.com
www.fsjchamber.com
www.facebook.com/122497777819790
twitter.com/fsjchamber
Overview: A small local organization founded in 1961
Mission: To promote the economic & social well-being of the businesses & community within the Fort St. John District; To continue to provide & enhance services & information to the members of the Chamber of Commerce
Member of: BC Chamber of Commerce; Canadian Chamber of Commerce; Northern Rockies Alaska Highway Tourism Association
Finances: Funding Sources: Membership fees; fees for service
Staff Member(s): 2
Membership: Fees: Schedule available
Activities: Special Improvement project program; district enhancement programs for existing & new business opportunities; Library: Northpeace Business Resource Centre
Chief Officer(s):
Lilia Hansen, Executive Director
Tony Zabinsky, President

Fort St. John Association for Community Living (FSJACL)
10251 - 100 Ave., Fort St John BC V1J 1Y8
Tel: 250-787-9262; Fax: 250-787-9224
info@fsjacl.com
www.fsjacl.com
Overview: A small local charitable organization founded in 1960
Mission: To educate, advocate & provide quality services for those with mental disabilities to ensure opportunities in all areas of their lives
Member of: British Columbia Association for Community Living
Membership: Fees: $10; Member Profile: All who believe that all individuals with a developmental disability have the right to the same opportunities as other citizens to live in a manner consistent with their needs & capabilities
Activities: Residential Services include: a Street House - community living for adults; Dee Jay's Place - community living for adults; 10th Avenue House - community living for adults; apartment support program; Community Connections Program - support & skills development for handicapped adults in the community; Careers - pre-employment preparation, job training & support for people facing challenging circumstances; Awareness Events: Pay it Forward Day, June Library: Professional Resource Program
Chief Officer(s):
Cindy Mohr, Executive Director
cindy.mohr@fsjacl.com

Fort St. John Community Arts Council
PO Box 6474, Fort St John BC V1J 4H9
Tel: 250-787-2781; Fax: 250-787-9781
info@fsjarts.org
fsjarts.org
www.facebook.com/fsjarts.council
twitter.com/fsjarts
Overview: A small local organization founded in 1970
Mission: To increase & broaden the opportunities for Fort St. John & district citizens to enjoy & to participate in cultural activities; to help coordinate the work & programmes of cultural groups in the area; to stimulate & encourage the development of cultural project & to render service to all participating groups
Member of: BC Arts Council
Finances: Funding Sources: Provincial government; City of Fort St. John; BC Arts Council
Awards:
- The Lindsay Dumaine Memorial Music Scholarship Fund
Publications:
- The Reflection
Type: Newsletter; Frequency: Quarterly

Fort Saskatchewan Chamber of Commerce
PO Box 3072, 10030 - 99 Ave., Fort Saskatchewan AB T8L 2T1

Canadian Associations / Fort Saskatchewan Fish & Game Association

Tel: 780-998-4355; Fax: 780-998-1515
chamber@fortsaskchamber.com
www.fortsaskchamber.com
www.facebook.com/fortsaskchamber
twitter.com/FtSaskChamber
Overview: A small local organization founded in 1954
Mission: To stimulate business growth & engagement through memberships, networking & advocacy
Affiliation(s): Alberta Chamber of Commerce; Canadian Chamber of Commerce
Finances: Annual Operating Budget: $100,000-$250,000
Membership: 300+
Chief Officer(s):
Lisa Makin, President
Dione Chambers, Executive Director

Fort Saskatchewan Fish & Game Association
PO Box 3038, Fort Saskatchewan AB T8L 2T1
Tel: 780-998-0062
fortfishngame@hotmail.com
www.fsfga.com
Overview: A small local organization founded in 1958
Mission: To promote through education, lobbying & programs the conservation & utilization of fish & wildlife; protect & enhance the habitat they depend on
Member of: Alberta Fish & Game Association
Finances: Funding Sources: Fundraising
500 volunteer(s)
Membership: 500; Fees: $25
Activities: Monthly club meetings; various events for members & families; Awareness Events: Kid's Ice Fishing Derby, March; Fishing Derby, June; Family Fun Day & Fishing Derby, Dec.
Chief Officer(s):
Gord Blize, President

Fort Saskatchewan Historical Society
10006 - 100 Ave., Fort Saskatchewan AB T8L 1V9
Tel: 780-998-1783
fortsaskhistoricalsociety@gmail.com
www.facebook.com/522313361151571
Also Known As: Fort Saskatchewan Museum
Overview: A small local charitable organization founded in 1958
Mission: To collect, preserve, document & display artifacts pertaining to local history by means of operating a community museum
Member of: Alberta Museums Association; Canadian Museums Association
Activities: Library: Resource Centre; Open to public by appointment

Fort Saskatchewan Minor Sports Association (FSMSA)
Jubilee Recreation Center, PO Box 3071, Fort Saskatchewan AB T8L 2T1
Tel: 780-998-1835
fsmsa@telus.net
www.fsmsa.net
Overview: A small local organization
Mission: To govern minor sports in Fort Saskatchewan
Membership: Committees: Bylaw Review; Disciplinary; Minor Sport Executive
Chief Officer(s):
Vaughan McGrath, President, 780-992-1735
vmcgrath@telusplanet.net

Fort Simpson Chamber of Commerce
PO Box 244, Fort Simpson NT X0E 0N0
Tel: 867-695-6538; Fax: 867-695-3551
fscofc@gmail.com
www.fortsimpsonchamber.ca
Overview: A small local organization founded in 1970
Member of: Canadian Chamber of Commerce; NWT Chamber of Commerce
Finances: Annual Operating Budget: Less than $50,000
Membership: 60; Fees: Schedule available; Committees: Tourism; Mackenzie Hwy.
Chief Officer(s):
Kirby Groat, President

Fort Vermilion & Area Board of Trade
PO Box 456, Fort Vermilion AB T0H 1N0
Tel: 780-927-3505
www.fortvermilionboardoftrade.ca
Overview: A small local organization founded in 1914
Member of: Alberta Chamber of Commerce
Membership: 1-99
Activities: Speaker Service: Yes; Library: Resource Centre

Fort Whoop-up Interpretive Society
PO Box 1074, Lethbridge AB T1J 4A2
Tel: 403-329-0444; Fax: 403-329-0645
info@fortwhoopup.com
www.fortwhoopup.com
www.facebook.com/WhoopUp
twitter.com/FortWhoopUp
Overview: A small local charitable organization founded in 1973
Mission: To operate the Fort Whoop-Up National Historic Site
Finances: Funding Sources: Donations; Fundraising; Admission
Activities: Providing information about Blackfoot culture

Fort William Trades & Labour Council See Thunder Bay & District Labour Council

Fort York Food Bank (FYFB)
797 Dundas St. West, Toronto ON M6J 1V2
Tel: 416-203-3011; Fax: 416-203-3275
info@fyfb.com
www.fyfb.com
Overview: A small local charitable organization
Mission: To collect & distribute a 3 day supply of food to people in need in downton Toronto
Staff Member(s): 1
Membership: Committees: Steering
Chief Officer(s):
Mike Schoonheyt, Program Manager

Fortier Danse-Création
#301, 2022, rue Sherbrooke est, Montréal QC H2K 1B9
Tél: 514-529-8158; Téléc: 514-525-8575
admin@fortier-danse.com
www.fortier-danse.com
www.facebook.com/fortier.dansecreation
twitter.com/FortierDanse
vimeo.com/user8490850
Aperçu: Dimension: petite; Envergure: locale; Organisme sans but lucratif; fondée en 1981
Mission: Création et diffusion des oeuvres du chorégraphe Paul-André Fortier
Membre de: Regroupement québécois de la danse; Conférence canadienne des arts
Membre(s) du personnel: 10
Membre(s) du bureau directeur:
Paul-André Fortier, Directeur artistique
Gilles Savary, Directeur général

Fortress Louisbourg Association
265 Park Service Rd., Louisbourg NS B1C 2L2
Tel: 902-733-3548; Fax: 902-733-3046
Other Communication: Events & Programs Phone: 902-733-3548
info@fortressoflouisbourg.ca
www.fortressoflouisbourg.ca
www.facebook.com/216181515095381
twitter.com/FortressAssoc
www.youtube.com/FortressLouisbourg
Overview: A small local charitable organization
Mission: To foster an appreciation for the history of Canada in regards to the Fortress of Louisbourg
Activities: Operating the Fortress of Louisbourg
Chief Officer(s):
Paul Gartland, President
Mitch McNutt, General Manager
mmcnutt@fortressoflouisbourg.ca

FortWhyte Alive
1961 McCreary Rd., Winnipeg MB R3P 2K9
Tel: 204-989-8355; Fax: 204-895-4700
info@fortwhyte.org
www.fortwhyte.org
www.facebook.com/FortWhyteAlive
twitter.com/fortwhytealive
Previous Name: Wildlife Foundation of Manitoba; Fort Whyte Centre for Environmental Education
Overview: A small local organization founded in 1966
Mission: FortWhyte Alive is dedicated to providing programming, natural settings and facilities for environmental education and outdoor recreation. In so doing, FortWhyte promotes awareness and understanding of the natural world and actions leading to sustainable living.
Membership: 2,000; Fees: Schedule available
Chief Officer(s):
Bill Elliott, President/CEO

Forum canadien des opérations forestières See The Canadian Woodlands Forum

Forum canadien sur l'apprentissage See Canadian Apprenticeship Forum

Forum conjoint des autorités de réglementation du marché financier See Joint Forum of Financial Market Regulators

Forum des fédérations See Forum of Federations

Forum des politiques publiques du Canada See Canada's Public Policy Forum

Forum for Intercultural Leadership & Learning
The Canadian Churches' Forum for Global Ministries, 47 Queen's Park Cres. East, Toronto ON M5S 2C3
Tel: 416-924-9351; Fax: 416-978-7821
www.ccforum.ca
www.facebook.com/InterculturalLeadershipandLearning
Previous Name: Ecumenical Forum of Canada; The Canadian Churches' Forum for Global Ministries
Overview: A medium-sized international charitable organization founded in 1921
Mission: To provide ecumenical orientation & re-entry programs for mission personnel; To stimulate ecumenical dialogue on issues of mission, global concerns & social justice
Member of: International Association for Mission Studies; Forum on International Personnel
Affiliation(s): Canadian Council of Churches
Finances: Annual Operating Budget: $100,000-$250,000; Funding Sources: Churches; Religious orders; Individuals
Staff Member(s): 2; 30 volunteer(s)
Membership: 1-99
Activities: Mission Personnel Programs; Annual Katherine Hockin Award & Dinner; International visitors; Publications; Roundtables & guest speakers; Library: Forum for Intercultural Leadership & Learning Library; by appointment
Chief Officer(s):
Jonathan Schmidt, Director
Jolan Ready, Administrator
Awards:
• Katharine Hockin Award for Global Mission & Ministry
Publications:
• Forum Focus [a publication of the The Canadian Churches' Forum for Global Ministries]
Type: Newsletter; Frequency: Annually; Editor: Alice Schuda; Jonathan Schmidt
Profile: Letters from overseas, information about mission personnel programs, book reviews, articles byinternational visitors, articles related to global mission, & updates on Forum staff & board members

Forum for International Trade Training (FITT) / Forum pour la formation en commerce international
#300, 116 Lisgar St., Ottawa ON K2P 0C2
Tel: 613-230-3553; Fax: 613-230-6808
Toll-Free: 800-561-3488
info@fitt.ca
www.fitt.ca
www.linkedin.com/company/fitt-forum-for-international-trade-training-
www.facebook.com/FITTNews
twitter.com/FITTNews
Overview: A small international licensing organization founded in 1992
Mission: To provide quality programs' training & certification in international trade designed to prepare businesses & individuals to compete successfully in world markets.
Affiliation(s): Founding Partners: Canadian Manufacturers & Exporters Association; Canadian Chamber of Commerce; Rounding Partners: Canadian Association of Importers & Exporters; Canadian Professional Logistics Institute; World Trade Centres of Canada; Industry Canada; DFAIT; HRDC; Canadian Professional Sales Association; Canadian Federation of Labour
Membership: Fees: $40 student; $100 general; $695 corporate
Activities: Rents Mailing List: Yes
Chief Officer(s):
Caroline Tompkins, President

Forum francophone des affaires (FFA-CNC)
6256, av Henri-Julien, Montréal QC H2S 2T8
Tél: 514-717-5610
www.ffacnc.qc.ca
Aperçu: Dimension: moyenne; Envergure: internationale; Organisme sans but lucratif; fondée en 1987
Mission: Planifier, organiser et réaliser toutes formes d'activités (colloques, missions, réseautage, publications, etc.) susceptibles de permettre aux dirigeants francophones d'entreprises et

d'organisations canadiennes de faire plus et mieux sur les marchés du monde entier
Membre de: FFA International
Affiliation(s): FFA Atlantique
Membre: *Montant de la cotisation:* 10$ étudiant; 75$ individuel; 150$ ONBL; 350$ corporatif
Activités: Bourse de réseautage; déjeuners/causeries; tables rondes; missions commerciales; séances d'information

Forum of Federations / Forum des fédérations
#411, 75 Albert St., Ottawa ON K1P 5E7
Tel: 613-244-3360; *Fax:* 613-244-3372
forum@forumfed.org
www.forumfed.org
Also Known As: An International Network of Federalism
Overview: A medium-sized international charitable organization founded in 2000
Mission: To promote intergovernmental learning; To develop solutions to challenges related to multi-level governance; To help build democracy in fragile or post-conflict countries by focusing on local empowerment
Activities: *Internships:* Yes; *Library:* by appointment
Chief Officer(s):
Rupak Chattopadhyay, President & CEO
chattopadhyay@forumfed.org
Publications:
• Federations [a publication of Forum of Federations]
Type: Magazine; *Frequency:* 3 pa; *Price:* $25 subscription
Profile: Published in multiple languages

Forum pour la formation en commerce international *See* Forum for International Trade Training

Foster Parent Support Services Society (FPSS)
#145, 735 Goldstream Ave., Victoria BC V9B 2X4
Tel: 778-430-5459; *Fax:* 778-430-5463
Toll-Free: 888-922-8437
admin@fpsss.com
www.fpsss.com
www.facebook.com/fpsssociety
twitter.com/FPSSSociety
Overview: A small local charitable organization
Mission: To provide meaningful and accessible support, education and networking services which will continually enhance the skills and abilities of foster parents to deliver the best care possible to the children in their homes.
Chief Officer(s):
Dan Malone, Executive Director
execdirect@fpsss.com

Foster Parents Association of Ottawa
1602 Telesat Ct., Ottawa ON K1B 1B1
Tel: 613-747-7800
ottawafpa@casott.on.ca
Previous Name: Ottawa & District Foster Parent Association
Overview: A small local organization founded in 1975
Mission: A local organization providing mutual support to families caring for foster children. During monthly meetings, members share their concerns & information on parenting skills through discussions & guest speakers
Finances: *Funding Sources:* Children's Aid Society
Chief Officer(s):
Peter Fortier, President

Foster Parents Plan Canada *See* Plan Canada

Foundation Assisting Canadian Talent on Recordings (FACTOR)
247 Spadina Ave., 3rd Fl., Toronto ON M5T 3A8
Toll-Free: 877-696-2215
general.info@factor.ca
www.factor.ca
www.facebook.com/FACTORCanada
twitter.com/FACTORCanada
www.youtube.com/user/FACTORfunded
Previous Name: Foundation to Assist Canadian Talent on Records
Overview: A large national organization founded in 1982
Mission: To provide financial assistance for production of sound recordings, videos, syndicated radio programs & international tour support; English-language counterpart of Musicaction
Finances: *Annual Operating Budget:* $3 Million-$5 Million; *Funding Sources:* Dept. of Canadian Heritage; Private Radio Broadcasting
Staff Member(s): 19
Activities: *Speaker Service:* Yes; *Rents Mailing List:* Yes
Chief Officer(s):
Duncan McKie, President
duncan.mckie@factor.ca
Allison Outhit, Vice-President, Operations
allison.outhit@factor.ca
Awards:
• FACTOR Grants
Available to Artists for Sound Recordings, Marketing & Promotion, Videos, Touring and Showcasing. There are also programs supporting Record Labels, Distributors, Music Publishers, Artist Managers, Songwriters, Music Industry Associations, Music Industry events and Collective Digital Initiatives.

Foundation canadienne de fiscalité *See* Canadian Tax Foundation

The Foundation Fighting Blindness (FFB)
890 Yonge St., 12th Fl., Toronto ON M4W 3P4
Tel: 416-360-4200; *Fax:* 416-360-0060
Toll-Free: 800-461-3331
info@ffb.ca
www.ffb.ca
www.facebook.com/187447074652378
twitter.com/FFBCanada
www.youtube.com/user/FFBCanada
Previous Name: RP Research Foundation - Fighting Blindness
Overview: A medium-sized national charitable organization founded in 1974
Mission: To support & promote research directed to finding the causes, treatments & ultimately the cures for retinitis pigmentosa, macular degeneration & related retinal diseases
Member of: International RP Association; Canadian Coalition for Genetic Fairness
Affiliation(s): US RP Foundation
Finances: *Funding Sources:* Individual donations
Activities: *Awareness Events:* Ride for Sight; Forever Yonge Run; RP Golf Classic; *Speaker Service:* Yes; *Library:* Not open to public
Chief Officer(s):
Sharon M. Colle, President & CEO
scolle@ffb.ca
Rahn Dodick, Treasurer
Malcolm Hunter, Corporate Secretary

The Foundation for Active Healthy Kids *See* Active Healthy Kids Canada

Foundation for Advancing Family Medicine of the College of Family Physicians of Canada (FAFM)
2630 Skymark Ave., Mississauga ON L4W 5A4
Tel: 905-629-0900
Toll-Free: 800-387-6197
fafm.cfpc.ca
www.linkedin.com/company/991629
www.facebook.com/foundationforadvancingfamilymedicine
twitter.com/fafm_cfpc
www.flickr.com/photos/cfpc
Previous Name: Research & Education Foundation of the College of Family Physicians of Canada
Overview: A large national charitable organization founded in 1995
Mission: To raise funds in order to support family doctors
Finances: *Funding Sources:* Fundraisers; donations
Activities: Awarding over 200 awards, grants & scholarships; *Awareness Events:* Walk for Doctors of Tomorrow, Nov.
Chief Officer(s):
Sarah Delaney, Director, Awards & Development
Awards:
• Jean-Pierre Despins Award
To recognize an individual who has been an outstanding advocate & spokesperson for family medicine and/or physicians & their patients *Eligibility:* Must be a CFPC family physician member
• Hollister King Rural Family Practice Scholarship
To recognize continuing medical education/continuing professional development related to rural family practice *Eligibility:* Must be a practicing family doctor & CFPC member
• Ian McWhinney Family Medicine Education Award
To recognize an outstanding family medicine teacher
Publications:
• Partners [a publication of the Foundation for Advancing Family Medicine of the College of Family Physicians of Canada]
Type: Newsletter

Foundation for Education Perth Huron
62 Chalk St. North, Seaforth ON N0K 1W0
Tel: 519-527-0111; *Fax:* 519-527-0444
Toll-Free: 800-592-5437
foundationforeducation@gmail.com
www.foundationforeducation.ca
www.facebook.com/foundationforeducation
twitter.com/found4education
www.youtube.com/user/foundation4education
Previous Name: Foundation for Enriching Education Perth Huron; Perth Foundation for the Enrichment of Education
Overview: A small local charitable organization founded in 1988
Mission: To develop, support & encourage the integration of the rich & unique cultural, corporate, industrial & agricultural resources of Huron & Perth counties into the school system
Finances: *Annual Operating Budget:* $250,000-$500,000; *Funding Sources:* Government; foundations; corporate; community; special events
Staff Member(s): 6; 12 volunteer(s)
Membership: 50 corporate + 30 individual; *Fees:* $50 sustaining; $100 Founder's Club; $25 associate
Activities: Arts-based programs; fundraising; consultant to schools; life skill mentorship; *Awareness Events:* Charity Auction, Nov.
Chief Officer(s):
Wes MacVicar, Executive Director
wesmacv@fc.amdsb.ca
Lynda McGregor, Director, Development

Foundation for Educational Exchange Between Canada & the United States of America
#2015, 350 Albert St., Ottawa ON K1R 1A4
Tel: 613-688-5540; *Fax:* 613-237-2029
info@fulbright.ca
www.fulbright.ca
www.facebook.com/fulbright.canada
twitter.com/FulbrightPrgrm
www.youtube.com/user/FulbrightCanada
Also Known As: Fulbright Canada
Overview: A medium-sized international charitable organization founded in 1990
Mission: To support outstanding graduate students, faculty, professionals & independent researchers in order to enhance understanding between the people of Canada & the United States
Finances: *Funding Sources:* Department of Foreign Affairs and International Trade Canada; United States Department of State; Public sector partners; Private sector partners
Activities: Presenting grants & scholarships to Canadian & American scholars, post-doctoral researchers, experienced professionals, junior professionals, executives of the Government of Canada, & Canadian & American teachers; *Internships:* Yes
Chief Officer(s):
Michael K. Hawes, Executive Director
mhawes@fulbright.ca

Foundation for Enriching Education Perth Huron; Perth Foundation for the Enrichment of Education *See* Foundation for Education Perth Huron

Foundation for International Training (FIT)
#110, 7181 Woodbine Ave., Markham ON L3R 1A3
Tel: 416-305-8680; *Fax:* 905-305-8681
info@ffit.org
www.ffit.org
www.facebook.com/171697116212687
Overview: A large international charitable organization founded in 1976
Mission: To strengthen human & social capital in developing countries
Activities: Developing & implementing activities on project sites, in partnership with host countries; Offering a Youth Internship Program
Chief Officer(s):
Richard Beattie, Chair
Mirabelle Rodrigues, Executive Director

Foundation for Legal Research (FLR) / La foundation pour la recherche juridique
c/o Stephanie Elyea, Administrator, #500, 865 Carling Ave., Ottawa ON K1S 5S8
Toll-Free: 800-267-8860
foundationforlegalresearch.org
Overview: A small local charitable organization founded in 1959
Mission: To support & maintain scholarships, bursaries & prizes in the field of legal research
Affiliation(s): Canadian Bar Association
Finances: *Annual Operating Budget:* $100,000-$250,000

Membership: 500; *Fees:* $2,000 initial contribution fee
Chief Officer(s):
Nicholas Kasirer, Chair, 514-393-4862
nkasirer@judicom.ca
Francois Letourneaux, Secretary
Stephen Bresolin, Treasurer
stephenb@cba.org
Awards:
• Walter Owen Book Prize
; *Amount:* $10,000 *Contact:* John N. Davis, jdavis@osgoode.yorku.ca

Foundation for Prader-Willi Research in Canada (FPWR Canada)
#370, 19 - 13085 Yonge St., Richmond Hill ON L4E 0K2
Toll-Free: 866-993-7972
www.fpwr.ca
www.facebook.com/fpwr.org
www.youtube.com/user/fpwrcanada
Previous Name: Canadian Prader-Willi Syndrome Association
Overview: A small national charitable organization founded in 2006
Mission: To educate families & inform community services on behalf of individuals with Prader-Willi Syndrome, about the special needs of persons with this condition in Canada
Member of: International Prader-Willi Syndrome Organization
Affiliation(s): Ontario Prader-Willi Syndrome Association; British Columbia Prader-Willi Syndrome Association; Alberta Prader-Willi Association; Foundation for Prader Willi Research
Finances: *Annual Operating Budget:* Less than $50,000
Membership: *Member Profile:* People with a special interest in the syndrome
Activities: Provides counselling & up-to-date scientific information on PWS; *Library:* Research Centre; Open to public by appointment
Chief Officer(s):
Keegan Johnson, President & Chair
Carole Barron, Executive Director
carole.barron@fpwr.ca
Michelle Cordeiro, Director, Operations
michelle.cordeiro@fpwr.ca
Carole Elkhal, Director, Community
carole.elkhal@fpwr.ca

Foundation for the Study of Objective Art
80 Gerrard St. East, Toronto ON M5B 1G6
Tel: 416-977-1077
ob-art@arcturus.ca
www.arcturus.ca/about_us.php
www.facebook.com/GalleryArcturus
twitter.com/GalleryArcturus
www.youtube.com/user/GalleryArcturus
Also Known As: Gallery Arcturus
Overview: A small local organization founded in 1994
Mission: To acquire a permanent collection of works by contemporary North American artists; To make the collection available to the public; To further understanding of objective art by offering study materials & educational programs
Member of: Art Gallery of Ontario; Ontario Association of Art Galleries
Affiliation(s): Art Gallery of Ontario; Ontario Museum Association
Finances: *Funding Sources:* Private
Activities: *Library:*

Foundation of Catholic Community Services Inc. (FCCS) / La Fondation des services communautaires catholiques inc.
1857, boul de Maisonneuve ouest, Montréal QC H3H 1J9
Tel: 514-934-1326; *Fax:* 514-934-0453
Other Communication: 514-937-2301, Local 279
info@fccsmontreal.org
www.fccsmontreal.org
twitter.com/CCSMontreal
www.youtube.com/channel/UCSlZdslLG8cmtCqm_Es2ATQ
Previous Name: Catholic Community Services Inc.
Overview: A medium-sized local organization founded in 1974
Mission: To provide a broad spectrum of social services on behalf of the English-speaking Catholic community of the Diocese of Montréal
Finances: *Annual Operating Budget:* $1.5 Million-$3 Million
Staff Member(s): 33; 1104 volunteer(s)
Membership: 65; *Fees:* $10
Activities: Youth groups; Home sharing; Administrative & support services; Community organization & development; Family support programs; Personal development & support groups; Camping services; Almage Senior Centre; Teapot Senior Centre; Good Shepherd Community Centre; Home Support Program; Volunteer coordination; Home Day Care Program; *Speaker Service:* Yes
Chief Officer(s):
Andrea Bobkowicz, President

Foundation of Greater Montreal / Fondation du Grand Montréal
#1000, 505, boul René-Lévesque ouest, Montréal QC H2Z 1Y7
Tel: 514-866-0808; *Fax:* 514-866-4022
info@fgmtl.org
www.fgmtl.org
www.facebook.com/fondationdugrandmontreal
twitter.com/FondationGRMTL
www.youtube.com/user/fgmtlvideos
Overview: A small local charitable organization
Mission: To assist individuals, families, & organizations in creating philanthropic funds for causes in the areas of education, health, social development, arts & culture, & the environment
Membership: 190+; *Committees:* Audit; Community Engagement; Governance, Ethics & Nominations; Investment
Chief Officer(s):
Yvan Gauthier, President & CEO
yvan.gauthier@fgmtl.org
Corinne Adelakoun, Director, Communications
corinne.adelakoun@fgmtl.org
Diane Bertrand, Director, Community Engagement
diane.bertrand@fgmtl.org
Lise Charbonneau, Director, Administration & Finance
lise.charbonneau@fgmtl.org
Hélène Latreille, Director, Philanthropic Development
helene.latreille@fgmtl.org

Foundation of Stars *Voir* Fondation des étoiles

La foundation pour la recherche juridique *See* Foundation for Legal Research

Foundation to Assist Canadian Talent on Records *See* Foundation Assisting Canadian Talent on Recordings

Foundation to Underwrite New Drama for Pay Television (FUND) *See* The Harold Greenberg Fund

Fountain of Love & Life (FLL)
#9, 9033 Leslie St., Richmond Hill ON L4B 4K3
Tel: 905-707-7800; *Fax:* 888-606-4808
Toll-Free: 888-606-4808
info@fll.cc
www.fll.cc
Overview: A small local organization founded in 2004
Mission: To use the media to spread the Good Word of Christ, as taught by the Roman Catholic Church, to Chinese communities; FLL is the Chinese Programming Ministry of Salt + Light Television
Affiliation(s): Archdiocese of Toronto
Finances: *Funding Sources:* Donations
Activities: Television & radio programs
Chief Officer(s):
Paul Yeung, Contact
paulyeung@fll.cc
Publications:
• FLL [Fountain of Love & Life] Spotlight
Type: Newsletter; *Frequency:* 3 pa

4Cs Foundation
#104, 5663 Cornwallis St., Halifax NS B3K 1B6
Tel: 902-422-4805
info@4csfoundation.com
www.4csfoundation.com
Overview: A small local organization founded in 1999
Mission: To support meaningful relationships between children, youth, artists & other community members through engagement in collaborative, arts-based community development (community arts) projects
Staff Member(s): 1
Activities: Provides grants for arts-based community development in the Halifax Regional Municipality
Chief Officer(s):
Terri Whetstone, Executive Director

4Korners Family Resource Center (4K)
200, rue Henri-Dunant, Deux-Montagnes QC J7R 4W6
Tel: 450-974-3940
Toll-Free: 888-974-3940
info@4kornerscenter.org
www.4kornerscenter.org
www.facebook.com/4KornersCenter
twitter.com/4Kornerstweets
plus.google.com/u/0/b/117288266282386520155/+4kornerscenterOrgPage
Also Known As: 4Korners
Overview: A small local charitable organization founded in 2005
Mission: To provide day care support & services in English for the community in the Laurentian region
Member of: Regroupement des organismes communautaires des Laurentides
Finances: *Annual Operating Budget:* $250,000-$500,000; *Funding Sources:* Government; Memberships; Donations; Partner organizations
Staff Member(s): 11; 20 volunteer(s)
Membership: 120; *Fees:* $25 per member; *Committees:* English Communications; Kanesatake Health Partnership; Laurentian English Services Advisory Network; Proches aidants; Regroupement; Table de concertation; Table jeunesse Argenteuil
Activities: Organizing Tai Chi sessions, Senior Men's Coffee Group, Yoga for Seniors, Annual Health Caravan, & What's for Dinner program; Offering caregiver workshops & support groups, health information sessions, reassurance calls, & courses; *Internships:* Yes; *Speaker Service:* Yes; *Library*
Chief Officer(s):
Peter Andreozzi, President, Board of Directors
president@4kornerscenter.org
Lisa Agombar, Executive Director
lisa@4kornerscenter.org
Amanda Fougere, Executive Assistant
amanda@4kornerscenter.org
Publications:
• 4Korners Family Resource Center Newsletter
Type: Newsletter; *Frequency:* Monthly; *Editor:* Amanda Fougere

Foursquare Gospel Church of Canada
#307, 2099 Lougheed Hwy., Port Coquitlam BC V3B 1A8
Tel: 604-941-8414; *Fax:* 604-941-8415
Toll-Free: 866-941-8414
info@foursquare.ca
www.foursquare.ca
www.facebook.com/foursquarecanada
Overview: A medium-sized national charitable organization founded in 1981
Mission: To not just make converts, but to make disciples who not only believe, but live by the truths that Jesus is Saviour, Healer, Baptizer with the Holy Spirit & Soon-coming King
Member of: Evangelical Fellowship of Canada
Finances: *Annual Operating Budget:* $250,000-$500,000
Staff Member(s): 3
Membership: 67 churches
Chief Officer(s):
Steve Falkiner, President
president@foursquare.ca

Fox Creek Chamber of Commerce
PO Box 774, 105 Campground Rd., Fox Creek AB T0H 1P0
Tel: 780-622-2670; *Fax:* 780-622-2677
office@foxcreekchamber.ca
foxcreekchamber.ca
Overview: A small local organization
Finances: *Funding Sources:* Membership; advertising; donations
Membership: *Fees:* Schedule available based on employees.
Chief Officer(s):
Corbett Fertig, President

Fox Valley Chamber of Commerce
c/o Delia Hughes, PO Box 72, Fox Valley SK S0N 0V0
Overview: A small local organization
Chief Officer(s):
Delia E. Hughes, Contact

FPInnovations
570, boul Saint-Jean, Pointe-Claire QC H9R 3J9
Tel: 514-630-4100; *Fax:* 514-630-4134
info@fpinnovations.ca
fpinnovations.ca
twitter.com/fpinnovations
Previous Name: Forest Engineering Research Institute of Canada, A Division of FPInnovations
Overview: A medium-sized national organization founded in 1975
Mission: To develop & assist with the implementation of innovative & safe forest operational solutions, which encompass areas such as the engineering, environmental, & human aspects of forestry & wildland fire operations; To improve sustainable

forest operations in Canada; To provide members with knowledge & technology, based on research, to conduct cost-competitive, quality forest operations
Finances: *Funding Sources:* Forestry companies; Government of Canada; Provincial & territorial governments
Staff Member(s): 100
Membership: *Member Profile:* Forestry companies; Canadian forestry equipment manufacturers & distributors (CFEMD); *Committees:* Strategic Advisory; Advisory Committee on Forest Engineering Research; Advisory Committee on Wildland Fire Operations Research
Activities: Researching, in consultation with members & partners, which focuses on silvicultural operations, harvesting, wildland fire operations, transportation & roads, & precision forestry; Providing Feric workshops & seminars; *Library:* FERIC Library
Chief Officer(s):
Pierre Lapointe, President & CEO
Hervé Deschênes, Vice-President, Business Development
herve.deschenes@fpinnovations.ca
 Edmonton Division
 11810, Kingsway NW, Edmonton AB T5G 0X5
 Tel: 780-413-9031
 Québec Division
 319, rue Franquet, Québec QC G1P 4R4
 Tel: 418-659-2647
 Vancouver Division
 2601 East Mall, Vancouver BC V6T 1Z4
 Tel: 604-224-3221
 Chief Officer(s):
 John W. Mann, Vice-President, Western Region

Fragile X Research Foundation of Canada (FXRFC)
167 Queen St. West, Brampton ON L6Y 1M5
Tel: 905-453-9366
info@fragilexcanada.ca
www.fragilexcanada.ca
Overview: A small national charitable organization founded in 1997
Mission: To raise public awareness of Fragile X; to raise money for Fragile X research & support services; to establish a support system for those with & affected by Fragile X
Membership: *Committees:* National Fundraising and Volunteer; Marketing; Scientific
Chief Officer(s):
Carlo Paribello, President / Medical Director
medical@fragilexcanada.ca

Francofonds inc.
#101, 205, boul Provencher, Winnipeg MB R2H 0G4
Tél: 204-237-5852; *Téléc:* 204-233-6405
Ligne sans frais: 866-237-5852
info@francofonds.org
www.francofonds.org
Aperçu: *Dimension:* petite; *Envergure:* provinciale; Organisme sans but lucratif; fondée en 1978
Mission: Promouvoir et appuyer le développement de la communauté franco-manitobaine
Finances: *Budget de fonctionnement annuel:* $50,000-$100,000
Membre(s) du personnel: 2; 10 bénévole(s)
Membre: 1,000-4,999
Membre(s) du bureau directeur:
Madeleine Arbez, Directrice générale
marbez@francofonds.org

Franco-Jeunes de Terre-Neuve et du Labrador (FJTNL)
#233, 65, ch Ridge, St. John's NL A1B 4P5
Tél: 709-722-8302; *Téléc:* 709-722-9904
coord@fjtnl.ca
www.fjtnl.ca
Aperçu: *Dimension:* petite; *Envergure:* provinciale; fondée en 1988
Mission: Sauvegarder, promouvoir et assurer l'épanouissement de la langue et la culture française auprès des jeunes francophones et acadiens qui résident à Terre-Neuve et au Labrador; maximiser les expériences langagières chez la clientèle jeunesse qu'elle dessert
Membre de: Fédération de la jeunesse canadienne-française inc.; Sociéte nationale de l'Acadie, inc.
Affiliation(s): Fédération des francophones de Terre-Neuve et du Labrador
Finances: *Budget de fonctionnement annuel:* $50,000-$100,000
Membre(s) du personnel: 4

Membre: 80; *Montant de la cotisation:* 1$; *Critères d'admissibilite:* Jeunes de 13 ans à 21 ans résidant dans l'une des 3 régions francophone de TNL
Activités: Jeux de l'Acadie; Festival jeunesse de l'atlantique; formation; loisirs; arts; direction
Membre(s) du bureau directeur:
Jeffrey Young, Président
presidence@fjtnl.ca

Franco-Ontarian Teachers' Association *Voir* Association des enseignantes et des enseignants franco-ontariens

Francophone Association of Municipalities of Ontario *Voir* L'Association française des municipalités de l'Ontario

Francophonie jeunesse de l'Alberta (FJA) / French Youth Association of Alberta
#306, 8627 Marie-Anne Gaboury St., Edmonton AB T6C 3N1
Tél: 780-469-1344; *Téléc:* 780-469-0014
www.fja.ab.ca
www.facebook.com/fjalberta
twitter.com/FJAlberta
Aperçu: *Dimension:* petite; *Envergure:* provinciale; Organisme sans but lucratif; fondée en 1972
Mission: Stimuler la jeunesse albertaine d'expression française à se découvrir et à vivre son plein potentiel
Membre de: Fédération de la jeunesse canadienne-française inc.
Affiliation(s): Association canadienne-française de l'Alberta
Finances: *Budget de fonctionnement annuel:* $250,000-$500,000
Membre(s) du personnel: 3; 75 bénévole(s)
Membre: 700; *Critères d'admissibilite:* Jeunes d'expression française âgés de 14 à 25 ans résidant en Alberta
Activités: Stages de leadership, regroupements jeunesses; parlement jeunesse et formation aux conseils d'étudiants; fête franco-albertaine; congrès provincial; le RaJe; Jeux de la francophonie; Evénements de sensibilisation: Fête franco-albertaine, août; *Stagiaires:* Oui
Membre(s) du bureau directeur:
Casey Edmunds, Directeur général
c.edmunds@fja.ab.ca

Fransaskois Cultural Council *Voir* Conseil culturel fransaskois

Fransaskois Parents Association *Voir* Association des parents fransaskois

Fraser Basin Council (FBC)
Main Office, 470 Granville St., 1st Fl., Vancouver BC V6C 1V5
Tel: 604-488-5350; *Fax:* 604-488-5351
info@fraserbasin.bc.ca
www.fraserbasin.bc.ca
Overview: A medium-sized local organization founded in 1997
Mission: To advance sustainability in the Fraser River Basin & across British Columbia
Chief Officer(s):
David Marshall, Executive Director
dmarshall@fraserbasin.bc.ca
Charlotte Argue, Program Manager, Climate Change & Air Quality Program
cargue@fraserbasin.bc.ca
Awards:
• Sustainability Awards
Publications:
• Basin News [a publication of the Fraser Basin Council]
Type: Newsletter; *Frequency:* 2 pa
 Cariboo-Chilcotin Regional Office
 #104, 197 Second Ave. North, Williams Lake BC V2G 1Z5
 Tel: 250-392-1400
 Chief Officer(s):
 Erin Robinson, Regional Manager
 erobinson@fraserbasin.bc.ca
 Fraser Valley Regional Office
 BC
 Chief Officer(s):
 Christina Toth, Assistant Regional Manager
 ctoth@fraserbasin.bc.ca
 Greater Vancouver Sea to Sky Regional Office (GVSS)
 470 Granville St., 1st Fl., Vancouver BC V6C 1V5
 Tel: 604-488-5365; *Fax:* 604-488-5351
 Chief Officer(s):
 Theresa Fresco, Regional Manager
 tfresco@fraserbasin.bc.ca
 Thompson Regional Office
 #200A, 1383 McGill Rd., Kamloops BC V2C 6K7
 Tel: 250-314-9660

 Chief Officer(s):
 Mike Simpson, Senior Regional Manager
 msimpson@fraserbasin.bc.ca
 Upper Fraser Regional Office
 #207, 155 George St., Prince George BC V2L 1P8
 Tel: 250-612-0252; *Fax:* 250-564-6514
 Chief Officer(s):
 Terry Robert, Senior Regional Manager
 trobert@fraserbasin.bc.ca

The Fraser Institute
1770 Burrard St., 4th Fl., Vancouver BC V6J 3G7
Tel: 604-688-0221; *Fax:* 604-688-8539
info@fraserinstitute.ca
www.fraserinstitute.ca
www.linkedin.com/company/the-fraser-institute
www.facebook.com/fraserinstitute
twitter.com/FraserInstitute
www.youtube.com/FraserInstitute
Overview: A medium-sized national charitable organization founded in 1974
Mission: To redirect public attention to the role competitive markets play in the economic well-being of all Canadians
Affiliation(s): Organizations in 57 countries
Finances: *Funding Sources:* Donations; sale of publications; grants from foundations
Activities: *Internships:* Yes; *Library:* by appointment
Chief Officer(s):
Peter Brown, Chair
Niels Veldhuis, President
niels.veldhuis@fraserinstitute.org
Kenneth P. Green, Senior Director, Centre for Natural Resources
ken.green@fraserinstitute.org
 Calgary Office
 #403, 525 - 11th Ave. SW, Calgary AB T2R 0C9
 Tel: 403-216-7175; *Fax:* 403-234-9010
 Montréal Office
 #252, 1470, rue Peel, Montréal QC H3A 1T1
 Tél: 514-281-9550; *Téléc:* 514-281-9464
 Toronto Office
 #401, 1491 Yonge St., Toronto ON M4T 1Z4
 Tel: 416-363-6575; *Fax:* 416-934-1639

Fraser Lake Chamber of Commerce
c/o Village of Fraser Lake, PO Box 430, 210 Carrier Cres., Fraser Lake BC V0J 1S0
Tel: 250-699-6257; *Fax:* 250-699-6469
www.fraserlake.ca
www.facebook.com/fraserlake
Overview: A small local organization
Mission: To represent members; To promote economic prosperity & community development; To enhance quality of life
Finances: *Funding Sources:* Membership dues
Membership: 8
Chief Officer(s):
Teresa Findlay, President

Fraser Valley Egg Producers' Association
c/o Agir Labour Pool, #307, 34252 Marshall Rd., Abbotsford BC V2S 5E4
Tel: 604-853-3556; *Fax:* 604-853-7471
Overview: A small local organization
Chief Officer(s):
Garth Bean, Secretary
Dan Kampen, President

Fraser Valley Labour Council
#202, 9292 - 200th St., Langley BC V1M 3A6
Tel: 604-314-9867; *Fax:* 604-430-6762
bharder@usw.ca
www.fvlc.ca
Overview: A small local organization founded in 2007 overseen by British Columbia Federation of Labour
Mission: To advance the economic, social, & political life of persons in British Columbia's Fraser Valley; To act as the unified voice for workers to ensure workers' rights, such as fair wages & safe working conditions
Membership: 12,000; *Member Profile:* Members of unions from the Fraser Valley region of British Columbia, such as Chilliwack, Hope, Abbotsford, Mission, Lytton, & Harrison
Activities: Lobbying governments about worker's issues; Providing labour education; Conducting campaigns to support the issues of working families; Supporting local organizations, such as the United Way
Chief Officer(s):

Canadian Associations / Fraser Valley Real Estate Board

Brian Harder, President
bharder@usw.ca
Daniella Pohl, Secretary
Kathy Gowridge, Treasurer
Meetings/Conferences:
• Fraser Valley Labour Council 2018 Annual General Meeting, 2018, BC
Scope: Local

Fraser Valley Real Estate Board
15463 - 104 Ave., Surrey BC V3R 1N9
Tel: 604-930-7600; *Fax:* 604-588-0325
Toll-Free: 877-286-5685
mls@fvreb.bc.ca
www.fvreb.bc.ca
www.linkedin.com/company/fraser-valley-real-estate-board
www.facebook.com/FVREB
twitter.com/FVREB
Overview: A medium-sized local organization founded in 1955 overseen by British Columbia Real Estate Association
Mission: To provide the most efficient real estate marketing service.
Member of: The Canadian Real Estate Association
Finances: *Funding Sources:* Membership dues; service fees
Membership: 3,000; *Member Profile:* Licensed real estate sales
Activities: *Library:* Not open to public
Chief Officer(s):
Ron Todson, President
Rob Philipp, Chief Executive Officer

Fraser Valley Rock & Gem Club
#109, 22015 - 48 Ave., Langley BC V3A 8L3
Tel: 604-532-8734
Overview: A small local charitable organization founded in 1959
Mission: To promote & encourage the lapidary/rockhound hobby, which includes collecting minerals & other geological materials; to encourage camaraderie & cooperation within the club & with other lapidary clubs & organizations.
Member of: Lapidary Rock & Mineral Society of British Columbia; Gem & Mineral Federation of Canada
Activities: Rockhounding; lapidary; silversmithing; jewellery; fossils; field trips; monthly meetings; *Library:* Not open to public
Chief Officer(s):
Karen Archibald, Contact
karchiba@telus.net

Fraser Valley Square & Round Dance Association
BC
www.region2.squaredance.bc.ca
Overview: A small local organization founded in 1959
Mission: To promote square, round, clogging, & contra dancing
Member of: BC Square & Round Dance Federation
Affiliation(s): Canadian Square & Round Dance Society
45 volunteer(s)
Membership: 700; *Fees:* $1
Activities: *Speaker Service:* Yes; *Rents Mailing List:* Yes
Chief Officer(s):
Sylvia French, Secretary, 604-469-1661

Fraser Valley Symphony Society (FVS)
PO Box 122, Abbotsford BC V2S 4N8
Tel: 604-744-9110
info@fraservalleysymphony.org
www.fraservalleysymphony.org
Overview: A small local organization founded in 1984 overseen by Orchestras Canada
Activities: Concerts & rehearsals
Chief Officer(s):
Lindsay Mellor, Music Director

Fraserside Community Services Society
350 - 550 6th St. West, New Westminster BC V3L 3B7
Tel: 604-522-3722; *Fax:* 604-522-1116
info@fraserside.bc.ca
www.fraserside.bc.ca
Overview: A small local charitable organization founded in 1972
Mission: To provide a range of services assisting people to overcome challenging conditions; Maximize their quality of life; Offer programs that inform, motivate & facilitate self-help
Affiliation(s): British Columbia Association for Community Living; Federation of Child & Family Services
Membership: *Fees:* Schedule available
Chief Officer(s):
Linda Edmonds, Chief Executive Officer, 604-522-3722 Ext. 116
ledmonds@fraserside.bc.ca

Frasier Valley Orchid Society
George Preston Recreation Centre, 20699 - 42 Ave., Langley BC V3A 2G5
Tel: 604-530-1323
www.fraservalleyorchidsociety.com
www.facebook.com/FraserValleyOrchidSociety
twitter.com/wix
plus.google.com/117167403531518744294
Overview: A small local organization founded in 1978
Chief Officer(s):
Dianne Gillis, President

Fraternité des Indiens de la Colombie-Britannique *See* Native Brotherhood of British Columbia

Fraternité des Policiers et Policières de la Ville de Québec (FPPVQ)
#210, 600, boul Pierre-Bertrand, Québec QC G1M 3W5
Tél: 418-683-8558; *Téléc:* 418-683-4637
info@fppvq.qc.ca
www.fppvq.qc.ca
www.facebook.com/FPPVQ
twitter.com/fppvq
Nom précédent: Syndicat professionnel de la police municipale de Québec
Aperçu: Dimension: petite; *Envergure:* locale
Membre: 777
Membre(s) du bureau directeur:
Marc Richard, Président
president@fppvq.qc.ca

Fraternite des prisons du Canada *See* Prison Fellowship Canada

Fraternité interprovinciale des ouvriers en électricité (CTC) (FIPOE) / Interprovincial Brotherhood of Electrical Workers (CLC)
10200, boul Golf, Montréal QC H1J 2Y7
Tél: 514-385-3476; *Téléc:* 514-385-9298
Ligne sans frais: 855-453-4763
info@fipoe.org
www.fipoe.org
www.facebook.com/FIPOE
twitter.com/fipoeorg
www.youtube.com/fipoeorg
Aperçu: Dimension: grande; *Envergure:* provinciale
Mission: Regrouper des électriciens de construction, des installateurs de systèmes d'alarmes et des monteurs de ligne
Membre: 12 000 individus + 10 sections locales
Membre(s) du bureau directeur:
Styve Grenier, Président
styve.grenier@fipoe.org
Arnold Guérin, Directeur général
arnold.guerin@fipoe.org
Publications:
• La FIPOE [publication Fraternité interprovinciale des ouvriers en électricité]
Type: Journal

Fraternité nationale des forestiers et travailleurs d'usine (CTC) / National Brotherhood of Foresters & Industrial Workers (CLC)
Locale 9, #8, rue Père Divet, Sept-Iles QC G4R 3N2
Tél: 418-968-3008
Aperçu: Dimension: grande; *Envergure:* nationale; Organisme sans but lucratif; fondée en 1981
Mission: L'étude, la sauvegarde et le développement des intérêts économiques, et l'application de conventions collectives
Affiliation(s): Fédération des travailleurs et travailleuses de Québec
Membre(s) du personnel: 5
Membre: 5 000; *Critères d'admissibilite:* Doit être salarié qui a signé sa formule d'adhésion à la fraternité et qui a payé la cotisation requise durant six mois consécutifs
Activités: *Bibliothèque:*
Membre(s) du bureau directeur:
Yves Guérette, Président

Fred Victor Centre
59 Adelaide St. East, 6th Fl., Toronto ON M5C 1K6
Tel: 416-364-8228; *Fax:* 416-364-4728
www.fredvictor.org
Merged from: Community Resource Connections of Toronto; Fred Victor Centre
Overview: A medium-sized local charitable organization founded in 1894
Mission: To offer a continuum of community services, housing options and advocacy for adults who are experiencing homelessness, marginalization and poverty; over 150 beds and spaces are available across 6 sites and programs; in 2015, Community Resource Connections of Toronto integrated with Fred Victor
Finances: *Annual Operating Budget:* Greater than $5 Million; *Funding Sources:* Federal, provincial & municipal government; Toronto United Church Council; foundations; individual & corporate donations
Chief Officer(s):
Mark Aston, Executive Director
maston@fredvictor.org

The Freda Centre for Research on Violence Against Women & Children
Simon Fraser University, 515 West Hastings St., Vancouver BC V6B 5K3
Tel: 778-782-5197
freda@sfu.ca
fredacentre.com
twitter.com/FREDA_Centre
Overview: A small provincial organization founded in 1992
Mission: To facilitate & conduct research on violence against women & children, in order to raise awareness & effect policy
Staff Member(s): 8
Chief Officer(s):
Margaret A. Jackson, Director

Fredericton Anti-Poverty Association (FAPO)
242 Gibson St., Fredericton NB E3A 4E3
Tel: 506-458-9102
fapo@antipoverty.com
antipoverty.com
www.facebook.com/185812278109170
Overview: A small provincial charitable organization founded in 1991
Affiliation(s): National Anti-Poverty Organization
Membership: *Member Profile:* Must have received social assistance at one time
Activities: Presentations to municipal & provincial government; speakers panel; observer attendance at Civic Board & committees including police, hospital & city council; sponsors Anti-Poverty Legal Clinic; undertaking a study of operation of food banks

Fredericton Area Moms of Multiples (FAMOM)
Fredericton NB
Other Communication: fredericton@multiplebirthscanada.org
frederictonareamoms@gmail.com
www.multiplebirthscanada.org/~fredericton
Overview: A small local organization overseen by Multiple Births Canada

Fredericton Board of Trade *See* Fredericton Chamber of Commerce

Fredericton Chamber of Commerce / La Chambre de Commerce de Fredericton
PO Box 275, #200, 364 York St., Fredericton NB E3B 4Y9
Tel: 506-458-8006; *Fax:* 506-451-1119
fchamber@frederictonchamber.ca
www.frederictonchamber.ca
www.facebook.com/frederictonchamber
twitter.com/Fton_Chamber
Previous Name: Fredericton Board of Trade
Overview: A medium-sized local organization founded in 1874
Mission: To contribute to the economic development of the community by being the advocate of business in the Greater Fredericton area
Membership: 950; *Member Profile:* Small, medium & large businesses in the Fredericton area; *Committees:* Executive; Provincial/Federal Government Affairs; Municipal Government Affairs; Economic Development; Business Excellence Awards Selection; Distinguished Citizens Awards Selection; Policy; Physician Recruitment; Communications; New Member Welcome & Retention; Events & Networking; Professional Development; Business Excellence Awards Nomination; Business Excellence Award Criteria
Activities: Working with economic development organizations & government on behalf of Chamber members; Providing networking opportunities; Offering education sessions
Chief Officer(s):
Stephen Hill, President
Krista Ross, Chief Executive Officer
kristar@frederictonchamber.ca

Awards:
- Distinguished Citizen Awards
- Business Excellence Awards

Fredericton Community Services Inc.
686 Riverside Dr., Fredericton NB E3A 8R6
Tel: 506-459-7461
Overview: A small local organization founded in 1983
Mission: To provide food & clothing to those in need
Member of: Canadian Association of Food Banks
Staff Member(s): 4; 15 volunteer(s)
Chief Officer(s):
Elizabeth Thurber, Contact

Fredericton Fish & Game Association (FFGA)
461 Saint Marys St., Fredericton NB E3A 8H4
Tel: 506-458-5643
www.frederictonfishandgame.ca
www.facebook.com/165642576892091
Overview: A small local organization founded in 1924
Mission: To foster sound management & wise use of natural resources so that economic, recreational & aesthetic values may continue to benefit future generations
Member of: New Brunswick Wildlife Federation
Finances: *Annual Operating Budget:* Less than $50,000
30 volunteer(s)
Membership: 140; *Fees:* Schedule available; *Member Profile:* Individuals concerned about natural resources & willing to assist in conservation; *Committees:* Jr. Branch; Education; Environment; Conservation Lottery; Wildlife; Newsletter
Activities: Adopt-A-Stream; Youth Fishing Tournament; Fishing & Hunting Enhancement Project; education & speakers
Chief Officer(s):
Rod Currie, President

Fredericton Numismatic Society
89 Bellflower St., New Maryland NB E3C 1C2
Overview: A small local organization
Member of: Royal Canadian Numismatic Association

Fredericton Police Association / Association des policiers de Fredericton
311 Queen St., Fredericton NB E3B 1B1
Tel: 506-460-2300; *Fax:* 506-460-2316
Overview: A small local organization

Fredericton Rape Crisis Centre *See* Fredericton Sexual Assault Crisis Centre

Fredericton Sexual Assault Crisis Centre (FSACC) / Centre pour les victimes d'agression sexuelle de Fredericton
PO Box 174, Fredericton NB E3B 4Y9
Tel: 506-454-0460; *Fax:* 506-457-2780; *Crisis Hot-Line:* 506-454-0437
fsacc@nbnet.nb.ca
www.fsacc.ca
Previous Name: Fredericton Rape Crisis Centre
Overview: A small local charitable organization founded in 1975 overseen by Canadian Association of Sexual Assault Centres
Mission: To eradicate violence against women & children through public education & direct services to victims of incest, sexual assault, sexual harassment & dating violence
Member of: National Action Committee on the Status of Women
Finances: *Funding Sources:* United Way; Project Grants; Donations; Fundraising; Corporations
Membership: *Member Profile:* Women; 18 years & older
Activities: Crisis Line Program; Public Education Program; Dating Violence Program; Sexual Assault Counselling Program; Self-Protection Program; *Speaker Service:* Yes; *Library:* Open to public by appointment

Fredericton Society for the Prevention of Cruelty to Animals
165 Hilton Rd., Fredericton NB E3B 4Y9
Tel: 506-459-1555
info@frederictonspca.ca
www.frederictonspca.ca
www.facebook.com/frederictonspca
twitter.com/frederictonspca
www.youtube.com/user/frederictonspca
Also Known As: Fredericton SPCA
Overview: A small local charitable organization founded in 1914
Mission: To investigate allegations of cruelty to animals under the SPCA Act & the Criminal Code; to promote the welfare of animals
Member of: Canadian Federation of Humane Societies
Finances: *Funding Sources:* Donations; fundraising

Staff Member(s): 11
Membership: *Fees:* $15 individual; $30 family; $100 corporate
Chief Officer(s):
Scott Elliot, President
Annette James, Director, Operations

Fredericton Tourism
11 Carleton St., Fredericton NB E3B 3T1
Tel: 506-460-2041; *Fax:* 506-460-2474
Toll-Free: 888-888-4768
tourism@fredericton.ca
www.tourismfredericton.ca
www.facebook.com/FrederictonTourism
twitter.com/FredTourism
www.youtube.com/user/FrederictonTourism
Also Known As: Fredericton Visitor & Convention Bureau
Overview: A small local organization overseen by Tourism Industry Association of New Brunswick
Mission: To develop & run a variety of cultural programs largely focused in the Historic Garrison District; to operate 2 municipal Visitor Information Centres, Lighthouse on the Green, & River Valley Crafts retail shop.
Member of: Tourism Industry Association of Canada; Tourism Industry Association of New Brunswick
Affiliation(s): Canadian Association of Visitor & Convention Bureaux
Finances: *Funding Sources:* Municipal government
Staff Member(s): 10
Chief Officer(s):
Ken Forrest, Director, Growth & Community Planning, 506-460-2696

Free Methodist Church in Canada (FMCIC) / Église méthodiste libre du Canada
4315 Village Centre Ct., Mississauga ON L4Z 1S2
Tel: 905-848-2600; *Fax:* 905-848-2603
ministrycentre@fmc-canada.org
www.fmc-canada.org
www.facebook.com/137599632927885
twitter.com/FMCIC
vimeo.com/user18221796
Overview: A medium-sized national organization founded in 1880
Mission: To find ways to engage unreached people & unreached communitites with the gospel; To mature congregations through developing healthy pastoral & lay leaders; To commission prepared people to purposeful service; To interpret life theologically through intentional reflection; To invest human & financial resources strategically; To communicate & celebrate through listening to & inspiring one another
Member of: Free Methodist World Conference
Affiliation(s): Evangelical Fellowship of Canada; Canadian Council of Christian Charities; World Relief Canada
Finances: *Annual Operating Budget:* $1.5 Million-$3 Million
Staff Member(s): 11
Membership: 6,765 attendees at 146 churches
Activities: *Internships:* Yes; *Speaker Service:* Yes
Chief Officer(s):
Cliff Fletcher, Bishop
Marc McAlister, Director, Church Health
Mark Molczanski, Director, Administrative Services
Jared Siebert, Director, Church Planting

Free the Children *See* WE Charity

Free Vietnamese Association of Manitoba
#100, 458 Balmoral St., Winnipeg MB R3B 2P8
Tel: 204-774-3214
banguyen@hotmail.com
Overview: A medium-sized provincial organization
Member of: Vietnamese Canadian Federation

Freedom Party of Ontario (FPO)
240 Commissioners Rd. West, London ON N6J 1Y1
Tel: 519-681-3999; *Fax:* 519-681-2857
Toll-Free: 800-830-3301
feedback@freedomparty.on.ca
www.freedomparty.on.ca
twitter.com/fpontario
www.youtube.com/fpontario
Overview: A small provincial organization founded in 1984
Mission: To provide a capitalist political alternative in Ontario, & to form an elected government in Ontario, based on the principles of fundamental rights & freedoms
Finances: *Annual Operating Budget:* $50,000-$100,000
100 volunteer(s)
Membership: 500 individual; *Fees:* $10 individual

Activities: Political lobbying; fielding candidates in Ontario provincial elections; *Speaker Service:* Yes
Chief Officer(s):
Paul McKeever, Leader, 905-721-9772
pmckeever@freedomparty.on.ca

Freelance Editors' Association of Canada *See* Editors' Association of Canada

Freestyle Ski Nova Scotia (FSNS)
5516 Spring Garden Rd., 4th Fl., Halifax NS B3J 1G6
Tel: 902-425-5450; *Fax:* 902-425-5606
alpinens@sportnovascotia.ca
freestylenovascotia.ca
www.facebook.com/Freestyle-Ski-Nova-Scotia-1510479565896482
twitter.com/FreestyleNS
Overview: A small provincial organization overseen by Canadian Freestyle Ski Association
Mission: To govern the sport of freestyle skiing in Nova Scotia.
Member of: Canadian Freestyle Ski Association; Alpine Ski Nova Scotia
Membership: *Committees:* Competitions; Marketing & Communications; High Performance; Sport Development
Chief Officer(s):
Lorraine Burch, Executive Director
Meetings/Conferences:
- Freestyle Ski Nova Scotia Annual General Meeting 2018, 2018 *Scope:* Provincial

Freestyle Skiing Ontario (FSO)
134 Osler St., Toronto ON M6N 2Y8
Tel: 416-238-7604
Toll-Free: 877-578-6581
info@ontariofreestyle.com
www.ontariofreestyle.com
www.facebook.com/156749758280
twitter.com/FreestyleSkiOnt
instagram.com/freestyleskiingontario
Overview: A small provincial organization overseen by Canadian Freestyle Ski Association
Mission: To direct the sport of freestyle skiing in Ontario.
Member of: Canadian Freestyle Ski Association
Chief Officer(s):
Jeff Ord, Executive Director, 416-238-7604 Ext. 700
jefford@ontariofreestyle.com

Freight Carriers Association of Canada (FCA)
#3-4, 427 Garrison Rd., Fort Erie ON L2A 6E6
Fax: 905-994-0117
Toll-Free: 800-559-7421
info@fca-natc.org
www.fca-natc.org
Previous Name: Canadian Transport Tariff Bureau Association
Overview: A medium-sized national organization
Mission: To provide quality information, products & services to users, providers & third parties involved in motor carrier transportation
Affiliation(s): North American Transportation Council
Finances: *Annual Operating Budget:* $1.5 Million-$3 Million; *Funding Sources:* Membership fees; Sales of publications & software
Staff Member(s): 5
Membership: *Member Profile:* For-hire motor carriers engaged in the for-hire trucking industry in Canada
Activities: Holding carrier meetings & seminars; Disseminating information; *Speaker Service:* Yes
Chief Officer(s):
David J. Sirgey, President, 800-559-7421 Ext. 214
dsirgey@natc.com
Julie Gauthier, Administrative Assistant, 800-559-7421 Ext. 218
julieg@natc.com
Diane Sheppard, Accounting Supervisor, 800-559-7421 Ext. 207
dsheppard@natc.com
Jon Ainsworth, Manager, Information Technology & Development, 800-559-7421 Ext. 217
jda@natc.com
Mary Anne Vehrs, Sales & Marketing, 800-559-7421 Ext. 212
mvehrs@natc.com

Freight Management Association of Canada (FMA) / Association canadienne de gestion du fret (AGF)
#405, 580 Terry Fox Dr., Ottawa ON K2L 4B9
Tel: 613-599-3283; *Fax:* 613-599-1295
info@fma-agf.ca
www.fma-agf.ca
www.linkedin.com/company-beta/2326466

www.facebook.com/fma.agf
twitter.com/FMA_AGF
Previous Name: Canadian Industrial Transportation Association
Overview: A medium-sized national organization founded in 1916
Mission: To support the shipper community by advocating on behalf of Canadian industry to address complex concerns related to freight transportation & logistics issues
Finances: *Annual Operating Budget:* $100,000-$250,000; *Funding Sources:* Membership fees; Advertising; Seminars; Conferences
Staff Member(s): 3
Membership: 100+; *Fees:* $1,090-$5,895; *Member Profile:* Companies involved in the shipping industry; *Committees:* Air; Marine; Rail; Truck
Activities: Engaging in advocacy; Providing seminars, advertising, job postings, & networking opportunities; Offering information, directories, & publications; Organizing meetings & events; *Speaker Service:* Yes
Chief Officer(s):
Robert Ballantyne, P.Eng, President
ballantyne@fma-agf.ca
Awards:
• Supply Chain Executive of the Year Award
Eligibility: Individuals who have contributed to the transportation & logistics field, demonstrated innovation in transportation & logistics management, & promoted legislation that advances safe & efficient transportation services *Deadline:* August
Meetings/Conferences:
• Cargo Logistics Canada Expo & Conference 2018, February, 2018, Vancouver Convention Centre, Vancouver, BC
Scope: National
Contact Information: cargologisticscanada.com
Publications:
• The Shipper Advocate [a publication of the Freight Management Association of Canada]
Type: Magazine; *Frequency:* s-a.; *Number of Pages:* 22; *Author:* John Levi; *Editor:* Kim Biggar; *Price:* Free download
Profile: Information & news about Canada's shipper community

French Chamber of Commerce *Voir* Chambre de commerce et d'industrie française au canada

French Jurists Association of Saskatchewan *Voir* Association des juristes d'expression française de la Saskatchewan

French Youth Association of Alberta *Voir* Francophonie jeunesse de l'Alberta

Frequency Co-ordination System Association (FCSA) / Association pour la coordination des fréquences
#700, 1 Nicholas St., Ottawa ON K1N 7B7
Tel: 613-241-3080; *Fax:* 613-241-9632
www.fcsa.ca
Previous Name: Canadian Telecommunication Carriers Association
Overview: A medium-sized national organization founded in 1983
Mission: To operate & administer computerized Microwave Information & Coordination System (MICS); to provide cost-effective, timely & high quality centralized administrative & technical services to allow members to be able to effectively plan & coordinate frequencies for microwave communication systems on national basis.
Finances: *Funding Sources:* Member organizations
Staff Member(s): 5
Membership: 23 organizations; *Member Profile:* Telecommunications service providers; *Committees:* MICS Management; MICS Technical Group
Chief Officer(s):
Alejandro Moreno, General Manager/Secretary-Treasurer
amoreno.fcsa@sympatico.ca

Frères de Notre-Dame de la Miséricorde / Brothers of Our Lady of Mercy
1149, ch Tour du Lac nord, Lac-Sergent QC G0A 2J0
Courriel: fndm@cite.net
www.crc-canada.org/fr/node/412
Aperçu: *Dimension:* petite; *Envergure:* internationale; Organisme sans but lucratif; fondée en 1839
Mission: Rassembler des personnes en vue d'un travail apostolique auprès des jeunes et particulièrement auprès des personnes éprouvant des difficultés
Finances: *Budget de fonctionnement annuel:* Moins de $50,000
Membre(s) du personnel: 1; 6 bénévole(s)

Membre: 9
Membre(s) du bureau directeur:
Omer Beaulieu, Délégué du Supérieur général

Les Frères du Bon-Pasteur *See* The Brothers of the Good Shepherd

Fresh Outlook Foundation (FOF)
12510 Ponderosa Rd., Lake Country BC V4V 2G9
Tel: 250-766-1777; *Fax:* 250-766-1767
www.freshoutlookfoundation.org
www.facebook.com/FreshOutlookFoundation?ref=website
twitter.com/FreshOutlook
Overview: A small national charitable organization founded in 2007
Mission: The Fresh Outlook Foundation (FOF) builds sustainable communities through a focus on the social, cultural, environmental, and economic aspects of community sustainability.
Finances: *Funding Sources:* Donations (industry, business); government (federal/provincial, less than 5%); private foundations
Activities: Green School Program, environmental action program for elementary school students; Challenge Programs; Water & Clean Air; Writing & Bird challenges for elementary & junior high school students; Creating a Climate of Change Multimedia Program; Energy Literacy Series; Taking Action on Climate Change
Chief Officer(s):
Joanne de Vries, CEO
jo@freshoutlookfoundation.org

Freshwater Fisheries Society of British Columbia (FFSBC)
#101, 80 Regatta Landing, Victoria BC V9A 7S2
Tel: 250-414-4200; *Fax:* 250-414-4211
Toll-Free: 888-601-4200
fish@gofishbc.com
www.gofishbc.com
www.facebook.com/gofishbc
twitter.com/go_fish_bc
www.youtube.com/gofishbc
Overview: A medium-sized provincial organization
Mission: To stock eggs & fish into lakes & streams across British Columbia; To support sturgeon & steelhead recovery programs; To operate hatcheries & visitor's centres
Activities: Providing information related to freshwater fishing & freshwater ecosystems in British Columbia; Partnering with organizations such as the Ministry of Environment to offer the Go Fish program so that children can experience fishing & foster an appreciation for the environment
Chief Officer(s):
Don Peterson, President
Jonathan Pew, Chair
James Gordon, Secretary-Treasurer

The Friends of Algonquin Park
PO Box 248, Whitney ON K0J 2M0
Tel: 613-637-2828; *Fax:* 613-637-2138
www.algonquinpark.on.ca/friends
Overview: A small local charitable organization founded in 1983
Mission: To further the educational & interpretive programs in Algonquin Park
Affiliation(s): Canadian Parks Partnership; Ontario Parks
Finances: *Annual Operating Budget:* $500,000-$1.5 Million
Staff Member(s): 7; 197 volunteer(s)
Membership: 3,000; *Fees:* $7 student; $12 individual; $17 family
Activities: *Speaker Service:* Yes
Chief Officer(s):
Lee Pauzé, General Manager

The Friends of Awenda Park / Les Amis du Parc Awenda
c/o Awenda Provincial Park, PO Box 5004, Penetanguishene ON L9M 2G2
Tel: 705-549-6378
Other Communication: 705-549-2231 (Awenda Provincial Park)
awenda@csolve.net
www.awendapark.ca
Overview: A small local organization founded in 1991
Mission: Dedicated to the preservation, understanding & interpretation of Awenda's biological, geological & cultural treasurers

The Friends of Bon Echo Park
16151 Highway 41, RR#1, Cloyne ON K0H 1K0

Tel: 613-336-0830; *Fax:* 613-336-2712
logistics@bonechofriends.ca
www.bonechofriends.ca
www.facebook.com/bonechofriends
Overview: A small local charitable organization
Mission: To preserve the natural & cultural heritage of Bon Echo Provincial Park
Finances: *Annual Operating Budget:* $100,000-$250,000
90 volunteer(s)
Membership: 200; *Fees:* $15 individual; $25 family; $150 life
Activities: Annual Art Show & Sale, July
Chief Officer(s):
Ernest Lapchinski, President
Derek Maggs, Executive Director

The Friends of Bonnechere Parks
RR#5, 4024 Round Lake Rd., Killaloe ON K0J 2A0
Tel: 613-732-9273
friends@bonnecherepark.on.ca
www.bonnecherepark.on.ca
www.facebook.com/bonnecherepark
twitter.com/bonnechere
Overview: A small local organization founded in 1992
Mission: To encourage & support programs for interpretive, educational, scientific, historical, protection & preservation purposes related to the natural & historic resources of the Little Bonnechere River in the Ottawa Valley
Membership: *Fees:* $10 individual; $15 family

Friends of Canadian Broadcasting (FCB)
#200-238, 131 Bloor St. West, Toronto ON M5S 1R8
Tel: 416-968-7496; *Fax:* 416-968-7406
friends@friends.ca
www.friends.ca
www.facebook.com/friendscb
twitter.com/friendscb
www.youtube.com/user/FriendsCB
Overview: A large national organization founded in 1985
Mission: To defend & enhance the quality & quantity of Canadian programming in the Canadian audio-visual system
Finances: *Annual Operating Budget:* $1.5 Million-$3 Million; *Funding Sources:* Membership fees
Membership: 66,000 households
Chief Officer(s):
Ian Morrison, Spokesperson
Awards:
• The Dalton Camp Award
Award will go to the winner of an essay competition on the link between democracy and the media in Canada.

Friends of Chamber Music
PO Box 38046, Stn. King Edward Mall, Vancouver BC V5Z 4L9
Tel: 604-722-1264
www.friendsofchambermusic.ca
www.facebook.com/focm.org
twitter.com/fcmvancouver
www.youtube.com/user/FCMVancouver
Overview: A small local charitable organization founded in 1948
Mission: To present the best in chamber music
Member of: Alliance for Arts & Culture
Finances: *Annual Operating Budget:* $100,000-$250,000; *Funding Sources:* Donations; Subscriptions; Ticket sales
24 volunteer(s)
Membership: 350; *Fees:* Schedule available
Activities: Performing a series of ten concerts; *Awareness Events:* Young Musicians Competition
Chief Officer(s):
Eric Wilson, Contact, 604-266-6030
ericwilson@telus.net

The Friends of Charleston Lake Park
148 Woodvale Rd., RR#4, Lansdowne ON K0E 1L0
www.friendsofcharlestonlakepark.com
www.facebook.com/friendscharlestonlakepark
twitter.com/CharlestonLkPP
Overview: A small local charitable organization
Mission: To help people enjoy Charleston Lake Park
Chief Officer(s):
Gerry Gustar, Secretary

Friends of Clayoquot Sound (FOCS)
PO Box 489, Tofino BC V0R 2Z0
Tel: 250-725-4218
info@focs.ca
www.focs.ca
Overview: A medium-sized local charitable organization founded in 1979

Mission: To advocate for the earth, air & waters of Clayoquot Sound & all temperate rainforests; To reduce economic reliance upon raw resource extraction by developing sustainability in rural & urban cultures; To oppose logging on ancient temperate rainforests, as well as the export of raw (unprocessed) logs; To support ecoforestry in second growth forest; To promote reduced wood & paper consumption & support the use of ecologically sustainable, tree-free alternatives to wood & wood-fibre products; To advocate taking fish farms out of wild waters & putting them in on-land closed containment systems
Member of: BC Environmental Network; Coastal Alliance for Aquaculture Reform (CAAR)
Affiliation(s): Greenpeace; Sierra Club; Natural Resources Defence Council; Western Canada Wilderness Committee (WCWC)
Finances: *Annual Operating Budget:* $100,000-$250,000; *Funding Sources:* Individual donors; foundation grants
Staff Member(s): 4
Membership: 3,000; *Fees:* $25
Activities: *Speaker Service:* Yes; *Library:* FOCS Resource Centre
Chief Officer(s):
Jeh Custerra, Contact
jeh@focs.ca

Friends of Devonian Botanic Garden
PO Box 69227, Stn. skyview, 13040 - 137 Ave. NW, Edmonton AB T8N 2H2
Tel: 780-221-6467
info@friends-devonianbotanicgarden.org
www.friends-devonianbotanicgarden.org
www.facebook.com/FriendsOfTheDevonianBotanicGarden
twitter.com/FriendsofDBG
www.pinterest.com/devonianbotanic/pins
Overview: A small local charitable organization founded in 1971
Mission: To promote a wider educational use & public appreciation of the scientific & cultural values of the Devonian Botanic Garden by the larger Edmonton community & beyond
Finances: *Annual Operating Budget:* $50,000-$100,000; *Funding Sources:* Membership fees; donations; grants
Staff Member(s): 1; 15 volunteer(s)
Membership: 375; *Fees:* $75 families; $50 individuals; $40 seniors/students
Activities: Promote & finance construction of gardens, paths, signs, structures & other facilities; raise funds for projects of the society; promote volunteerism
Chief Officer(s):
Brenda Harvey, President
brendaharvey@telus.net

Friends of Dismas
PO Box 3005, 1730 Bur Oak Ave., Markham ON L6E 0J1
friendsofdismas@gmail.com
www.friendsofdismas.com
twitter.com/friendsofdismas
Overview: A small local organization
Mission: To help people affected by crime through the building of a creative & healing community
Affiliation(s): Archdiocese of Toronto
Finances: *Funding Sources:* Donations
Chief Officer(s):
Michael Walsh, Contact

Friends of Ecological Reserves (FER)
PO Box 8477, Stn. Central, Victoria BC V8W 3S1
Tel: 250-361-1694
ecoreserves@hotmail.com
www.ecoreserves.bc.ca
Overview: A small local charitable organization founded in 1982
Mission: To promote the interests of British Columbia's ecological reserves program
Finances: *Funding Sources:* Donations; Fundraising
Membership: *Fees:* $15 students & seniors; $20 individuals; $25 families & institutions
Activities: Supporting research in the area of ecological reserves; Organizing field trips
Chief Officer(s):
Michael Fenger, President
Stephen Ruttan, Vice-President
Publications:
• The Log [a publication of the Friends of Ecological Reserves]
Type: Newsletter; *Frequency:* Semiannually; *Editor:* Louise Beinhauer; *Price:* Free to members of Friends ofEcological Reserves
Profile: Information about the establishment, management, & maintenance of ecological reserves in British Columbia

Friends of Ferris Provincial Park
PO Box 504, Campbellford ON K0L 1L0
Tel: 705-653-3575
info@friendsofferris.ca
www.friendsofferris.ca
www.facebook.com/138273219576405
Overview: A small local organization founded in 1994
Mission: The Friends of Ferris is a non-profit group of volunteers who are hard at work, constantly bringing to Ferris special events and promotions unique to the Provincial Park.
Membership: *Fees:* $10 individual; $17 family
Chief Officer(s):
Doreen Sharpe, President

The Friends of Fort York & Garrison Common
PO Box 183, Toronto ON M5A 1N1
info@fortyork.ca
www.fortyork.ca
www.facebook.com/fortyork
twitter.com/fortyork
Overview: A small local charitable organization founded in 1994
Mission: To enhance the reputation & financial security of Historic Fort York
Affiliation(s): Heritage Toronto
Membership: *Fees:* $40 individual; $60 family; $100-$249 special friend of Fort York; $250 patron
Chief Officer(s):
Harriet De Koven, Co-Chair
Stephen Otto, Co-Chair

The Friends of Frontenac Park
PO Box 2237, Kingston ON K7L 5J8
frontenacpark@frontenacpark.ca
www.frontenacpark.ca
www.facebook.com/frontenacpark
twitter.com/frontenacpark
Overview: A small local organization

The Friends of Killarney Park
c/o Killarney Provincial Park, Killarney ON P0M 2A0
Tel: 705-287-2800; *Fax:* 705-287-2922
friendsofkillarneypark.ca
www.facebook.com/FriendsofKillarneyPark
www.youtube.com/user/friendsofkillarney
Overview: A small local organization founded in 1986
Mission: To enhance the interpretive, educational & recreational objectives of Killarney Park
Chief Officer(s):
Kris Puhvel, Executive Director

The Friends of Library & Archives Canada / Les Amis de Bibliothèque et archives Canada
395 Wellington St., Ottawa ON K1A 0N4
Tel: 613-943-1544; *Fax:* 613-943-2343
Other Communication: Alternate Phone: 613-992-8304
friends.amis@bac-lac.gc.ca
www.friendsoflibraryandarchivescanada.ca
Merged from: Friends of the National Archives of Canada; Friends of the National Library of Canada
Overview: A small national charitable organization founded in 2003
Mission: To promote & encourage public interest in & support for the work of Library & Archives Canada in fulfilling its role as a preserver of the national published & unpublished heritage; To provide interested persons & organizations with the opportunity to share in the activities of Library & Archives Canada; To attract collections of Canadiana as gifts to Library & Archives Canada; To organize fundraising events in support of a variety of its endeavours, including special acquisitions
Affiliation(s): Friends of Canadian Libraries
Finances: *Funding Sources:* Membership fees; Donations; Fundraising events
Activities: Offering cultural programs; Fundraising for the National Library
Chief Officer(s):
Marianne Scott, President
Kathleen Shaw, Vice-President
Michael Gnarowski, Treasurer

The Friends of MacGregor Point
c/o MacGregor Point Provincial Park, RR#1, Port Elgin ON N0H 2C5
Tel: 519-389-6232; *Fax:* 519-389-2444
fompp@bmts.com
www.friendsofmacgregor.org
www.facebook.com/101912730956
twitter.com/fompp

Friends of Mashkinonje Park
Site 8, Box 1, 99 Langs Landing, Monetville ON P0M 2K0
friendsofmashkinonje@yahoo.ca
www.mashkinonje.com
Overview: A small local organization founded in 2000
Mission: To maintain & share the beauty of this unique area of scenic shorelines & wonderful wetlands
Membership: *Fees:* $15 individual; $25 family; $50 organization
Chief Officer(s):
Angela Martin, President
Publications:
• The Wetlands Observer
Type: Newsletter; *Frequency:* Semiannually

Friends of Music Therapy / Association de Musicothérapie du Canada
#202, 4056 Dorchester Rd., Niagara Falls ON L2E 6M9
Tel: 905-374-8878; *Fax:* 888-665-1307
www.friendsofmusictherapy.com
www.youtube.com/user/norriswhitney
Overview: A medium-sized national organization founded in 2010
Mission: The Friends of Music Therapy Endowment Fund was established at SickKids Foundation to provide permanent financial support to the Music Therapy Program at The Hospital for Sick Children.
Finances: *Funding Sources:* Donations
Chief Officer(s):
Kevin Goranson, Co-Founder
kevin@friendsofmusictherapy.com
Jim Norris, Co-Founder
jnorris@nor.com

The Friends of Nancy Island Historic Site & Wasaga Beach Park
11 - 22nd St. North, Wasaga Beach ON L9Z 2V9
Tel: 705-429-2516
www.wasagabeachpark.com
Overview: A small local organization
Mission: To further the educational & interpretive programs of Wasaga Beach Provincial Park & Nancy Island Historic Site
Membership: *Fees:* $10 individual; $20 family; $50 corporate; $100 life (individual); $165 life (family)

Friends of Nature Conservation Society
PO Box 281, Chester NS B0J 1J0
Tel: 902-275-3361
info@friends-of-nature.ca
www.friends-of-nature.ca
www.facebook.com/friendsofnatureconservationsociety
Overview: A small local organization founded in 1954
Mission: To preserve the balance of nature for the mutual benefit of people & their plant & animal friends
Member of: Nova Scotia Environmental Network; Nova Scotia Public Lands Coalition
Affiliation(s): Nature Canada; Friends of Nature, Incorporated
Finances: *Annual Operating Budget:* Less than $50,000
Membership: 100-499; *Fees:* $10
Activities: *Library:* Friends of Nature: Environmental Library
Chief Officer(s):
Sydney Dumaresq, Chair

The Friends of Pinery Park
c/o The Visitor Centre, Pinery Provincial Park, Lambton Shores ON N0M 2L0
Tel: 519-243-1521
friends.pinery@gmail.com
www.pinerypark.on.ca
Overview: A small local organization founded in 1989
Mission: To develop interpretive, educational, historical, & scientific projects & programs to ensure that Pinery Provincial Park's natural legacy will remain for future generations

The Friends of Presqu'ile Park
PO Box 1442, Brighton ON K0K 1H0
Tel: 613-475-1688; *Fax:* 613-475-2209
info@friendsofpresquile.on.ca
www.friendsofpresquile.on.ca
Overview: A small local organization

Canadian Associations / Friends of Red Hill Valley

Mission: To enhance the educational, interpretive, & scientific research programs at Presqu'ile Provincial Park

Friends of Red Hill Valley
PO Box 61536, Hamilton ON L8T 5A1
Tel: 905-664-8796
redhill@hwcn.org
Overview: A medium-sized local organization founded in 1991
Mission: To protect & enhance the Red Hill Valley in Hamilton, Ontario
Membership: 800; *Fees:* $5
Chief Officer(s):
Don McLean, Chair
don.mclean@cogeco.ca

The Friends of Rondeau Park
RR#1, Morpeth ON N0P 1X0
Tel: 519-674-1750
info@rondeauprovincialpark.ca
www.rondeauprovincialpark.ca
Overview: A small local organization
Mission: To raise funds on a continuing basis in order to encourage & support programs for interpretive, educational, scientific, historical, protection, & preservation purposes related to the natural & historical resources of Rondeau Provincial Park & other Ontario Provincial Parks
Membership: *Fees:* $15 individual; $20 family

The Friends of Sandbanks Park
PO Box 20007, 97 Main St., Picton ON K0K 0A0
friends@friendsofsandbanks.org
friendsofsandbanks.org
Overview: A small local organization founded in 1993
Mission: To protect & preserve the natural & cultural history of provincial park through interpretation, education, & scientific & historic research
Publications:
• What's New at the Friends of Sandbanks
Type: Bulletin; *Frequency:* Monthly

Friends of Short Hills Park
PO Box 236, Fonthill ON L0S 1E0
shorthillspark@gmail.com
www.friendsofshorthillspark.ca
www.youtube.com/user/friendsofshorthills?feature=mhum
Overview: A small local organization
Mission: To preserve the cultural & natural integrity of Short Hills Provincial Park through liaison with Ontario Parks, volunteer work, public education & fundraising activities
Membership: *Fees:* $20

Friends of Simon Wiesenthal Centre for Holocaust Studies - Canada
#902, 5075 Yonge St., Toronto ON M2N 6C6
Tel: 416-864-9735; *Fax:* 416-864-1083
Toll-Free: 866-864-9735
swcmain@fswc.ca
www.friendsofsimonwiesenthalcenter.com
www.linkedin.com/pub/avi-benlolo/10/173/131
www.facebook.com/244499848933801
twitter.com/avibenlolo
www.youtube.com/profile?user=FSWC2009#g/u
Overview: A small national charitable organization founded in 1980
Mission: To carry out in Canada the work of the Wiesenthal Center in California, by bringing antisemitism, bigotry, racial hatred, & ethnic intolerance to the attention of the Canadian government, the public & media
Staff Member(s): 7
Activities: *Internships:* Yes; *Speaker Service:* Yes; *Library:* Open to public by appointment
Chief Officer(s):
Avi Benlolo, President & CEO
president@fswc.ca

The Friends of Sleeping Giant
267 Sherwood Dr., Thunder Bay ON P7B 6L2
Overview: A small local organization founded in 1993
Mission: To assist in conserving & fostering an appreciation for Sleeping Giant Provincial Park

Friends of SOS Children's Villages, Canada Inc. *See* SOS Children's Villages Canada

Friends of the Archibald
Archibald Library, Briercrest College and Seminary, 510 College Dr., Caronport SK S0H 0S0
Tel: 306-756-3252
library@briercrest.ca
www.briercrest.ca/library/databases/FAL
Overview: A small local organization
Mission: To promote the library as a place that supports & fosters the learning community
Membership: *Fees:* $15
Activities: Supporting fundraising efforts
Chief Officer(s):
Brad Doerksen, Library Director
bdoerksen@briercrest.ca

Friends of the Canadian Centre for Architecture *See* Les Amis du centre canadien d'architecture

Friends of The Canadian War Museum (FCWM) / Les Amis du Musée canadien de la guerre (AMCG)
1 Vimy Pl., Ottawa ON K1A 0M8
Tel: 819-776-8618; *Fax:* 819-776-8623
fcwm-amcg@magma.ca
www.friends-amis.ca
www.facebook.com/warmuseum
twitter.com/FCWMCanada
Overview: A medium-sized national organization founded in 1987
Mission: To promote & stimulate interest in & give support to the Canadian War Museum by promoting & organizing special events compatible with the approved themes & objectives of the Museum; to provide volunteers to the Museum, raise funds & promote understanding, communication & cooperation between the people of Canada & military museums of Canada.
Member of: Council of Heritage Organizations in Ottawa (CHOO)
Finances: *Funding Sources:* Membership and Donations
Membership: 600; *Fees:* $25 individual; *Committees:* Events, Research, Membership, Communications, Resources
Activities: Guides for the Canadian War Museum; silent auctions; book sales; fundraising; *Internships:* Yes; *Speaker Service:* Yes
Chief Officer(s):
Douglas C. Rowland, President
Linda Colwell, Vice President
Helen McKiernan, Secretary
David Parr, Treasurer
Publications:
• The Torch
Type: Newsletter; *Frequency:* Quarterly; *Editor:* Bon Margeson

Friends of the Central Experimental Farm (FCEF)
Building 72, Central Experimental Farm, Ottawa ON K1A 0C6
Tel: 613-230-3276; *Fax:* 613-230-1238
info@friendsofthefarm.ca
www.friendsofthefarm.ca
www.facebook.com/FCEFOttawa
twitter.com/FCEFOttawa
www.flickr.com/groups/aogcef
Overview: A small local charitable organization
Mission: To preserve, maintain, protect and enhance the Arboretum, the Ornamental Gardens and other public areas of the Central Experimental Farm in Ottawa, Ontario, Canada.
Finances: *Funding Sources:* Membership fees; Government grants
Membership: *Fees:* $25 adult; $45 family; $20 student/senior; $250 corporate
Chief Officer(s):
Eric Jones, President

Friends of the Coves Subwatershed Inc. (FOTCSI)
111 Elmwood Ave. East, London ON N6C 1J4
Tel: 519-640-5397; *Fax:* 519-640-5780
contact@thecoves.ca
www.thecoves.ca
Overview: A small local organization
Mission: To support the protection, conservation & stewardship of the Coves Subwatershed
Staff Member(s): 1
Membership: *Fees:* $25 individual; $35 family; $75 non-profit organization; $200 corporate
Activities: *Awareness Events:* Christmas Bird Count, December
Chief Officer(s):
Thom McClenaghan, President

Friends of the Earth Canada (FoE) / Les Ami(e)s de la Terre Canada
#200, 251 Bank St., Ottawa ON K2P 1X3
Tel: 613-241-0085; *Fax:* 613-566-3449
Toll-Free: 888-385-4444
foe@foecanada.org
www.foecanada.org
www.facebook.com/foe.canada
twitter.com/FoE_Canada
www.youtube.com/user/FOECanada
Overview: A large international charitable organization founded in 1978
Mission: To serve as a national voice for the environment, working with others to inspire the renewal of our communities & the earth, through research, education, advocacy & cooperation
Member of: Friends of the Earth International; Canadian Council for International Cooperation
Affiliation(s): Canadian Environmental Network
Finances: *Annual Operating Budget:* $250,000-$500,000; *Funding Sources:* Individual & corporate donations; Foundation; Government; Earned income/merchandise
Staff Member(s): 3; 10 volunteer(s)
Membership: 1,000-4,999
Activities: *Speaker Service:* Yes
Chief Officer(s):
Beatrice Olivastri, Chief Executive Officer
beatrice@foecanada.org
Stephen Barg, President

Friends of the Environment Foundation *See* TD Friends of the Environment Foundation

Friends of the Forestry Farm House Inc. (FFFH)
1903 Forestry Farm Dr., Saskatoon SK S7S 1G9
Tel: 306-249-1315
www.fffh.ca
Overview: A small local charitable organization founded in 1996
Mission: To restore the superintendent's residence of the Sutherland Forest Nursery Station which, from 1913 to 1965, distributed millions of trees to prairie farmers, who planted these trees on their land to create the miles of shelterbelts
Affiliation(s): Saskatoon Tourism; Saskatchewan Tourism
Finances: *Annual Operating Budget:* Less than $50,000; *Funding Sources:* Saskatchewan Heritage Foundation; City of Saskatoon Heritage Conservation Program
Staff Member(s): 3; 20 volunteer(s)
Membership: 1-99; *Fees:* $10
Activities: Historical walking tour brochure; Victoria Day High Tea; Haunted House Program; Old Fashioned Christmas Party; *Speaker Service:* Yes
Chief Officer(s):
Bernie Cruikshank, President

Friends of the Greater Sudbury Public Library
Greater Sudbury Public Library, 74 Mackenzie St., Sudbury ON P3C 4X8
Tel: 705-673-1155
www.sudburylibraries.ca/en/aboutus/Friends.asp
Overview: A small local charitable organization founded in 1997
Mission: To support the Greater Sudbury Public Library through fundraising & advocacy
Finances: *Annual Operating Budget:* Less than $50,000
12 volunteer(s)
Membership: 12; *Fees:* Schedule available
Chief Officer(s):
Jessica Watts, Coordinator, Outreach, Programs & Partnerships

Friends of the Greenbelt Foundation
#500, 661 Yonge St., Toronto ON M4Y 1Z9
Tel: 416-960-0001; *Fax:* 416-960-0030
info@greenbelt.ca
www.greenbelt.ca
www.linkedin.com/company/friends-of-the-greenbelt-foundation
www.facebook.com/ontariogreenbelt
twitter.com/greenbeltca
Overview: A large provincial organization
Mission: To help foster the Greenbelt's living countryside by nurturing & supporting activities that preserve its environmental & agricultural integrity
Finances: *Annual Operating Budget:* $3 Million-$5 Million
Chief Officer(s):
Burkhard Mausberg, CEO
Awards:
• Friends of the Greenbelt Foundation Grants Program

Friends of the Haileybury Heritage Museum
PO Box 911, 575 Main St., Haileybury ON P0J 1K0
Tel: 705-672-1922; *Fax:* 705-672-2551
hhmuseum@hotmail.com
www.haileyburyheritagemuseum.ca
Overview: A small local organization founded in 1983

Mission: To preserve & develop heritage tourism in Haileybury; to stimulate public interest in Haileybury's history; to disseminate heritage information; to provide support to the Museum's operations
Affiliation(s): Ontario Historical Society
Finances: *Annual Operating Budget:* $50,000-$100,000
Staff Member(s): 2; 20 volunteer(s)
Membership: 200; *Fees:* $15 individual; $25 family; $30 corporate
Activities: Operates Haileybury Heritage Museum; *Library:* Sehldon Dobbs Memorial Research Room; Open to public
Chief Officer(s):
Allan Bellaire, Coordinator, Museum Operations

Friends of the Land of the Wine *See* Amici dell'Enotria Toronto

Friends of the McCreary Centre Society *See* McCreary Centre Society

Friends of The Moncton Hospital Foundation
135 MacBeath Ave., Moncton NB E1C 6Z8
Tel: 506-857-5488; *Fax:* 506-857-5753
friends@horizonnb.org
www.friendsfoundation.ca
www.facebook.com/FriendsofTMH
twitter.com/FriendsofTMH
www.youtube.com/user/FriendsofTMH
Overview: A small local charitable organization founded in 1965
Mission: To raise money on behalf of the Moncton Hospital in order to improve the services offered to patients & fund research
Staff Member(s): 9
Chief Officer(s):
Linda Saunders, President & CEO
linda.saunders@horizonnb.ca

Friends of the Montréal Botanical Garden *Voir* Les Amis du Jardin botanique de Montréal

Friends of the Oldman River (FOR)
615 Deer Croft Way SE, Calgary AB T2J 5V4
Tel: 403-271-1408
Overview: A small local organization founded in 1987
Mission: To defend the Oldman River from environmentally destructive activities; to protect the Oldman River & decommission the Oldman Dam
Member of: Alberta Environmental Network
Affiliation(s): Canadian Environmental Network
Finances: *Annual Operating Budget:* Less than $50,000; *Funding Sources:* Membership dues; donations
8 volunteer(s)
Membership: 1,000; *Fees:* $5
Activities: Sustainable community/watershed project in Cameroon; legal actions on water issues; *Speaker Service:* Yes

Friends of the Orphans, Canada
470 Industrial Ave., Woodstock ON N4S 7L1
Tel: 519-421-1992; *Fax:* 519-421-7593
Toll-Free: 855-741-4033
info@fotocan.org
www.fotocan.org
Also Known As: Nuestros Pequeños Hermanos International
Overview: A medium-sized international charitable organization founded in 1977
Mission: To provide a home, education, shelter & nourishment for orphans in Mexico, Honduras, Haiti, Nicaragua, Guatemala & El Salvador
Affiliation(s): Nuestros Pequeños Hermanos
Finances: *Funding Sources:* Donations; sponsorship
Staff Member(s): 2
Chief Officer(s):
Margaret Blair, Executive Director

Friends of the Third World
6207 - 144 St., Edmonton AB T6H 4H8
Tel: 780-434-0671; *Fax:* 780-495-2201
Overview: A small international organization
Mission: To establish links with southern & northern NGOs working in the areas of environment & development; provides expertise in the fields of environment, natural resources, communication, women in development & education
Chief Officer(s):
Prem Kumar, Secretary

Friends of the Ukrainian Village Society
c/o 8820 - 112 St., Edmonton AB T6G 2P8
Tel: 780-662-3640; *Fax:* 780-662-3273
info@friendsukrainianvillage.com
www.friendsukrainianvillage.com
www.facebook.com/164545290238894
Overview: A small local organization
Chief Officer(s):
Nick Fedchyshyn, President

Ukrainian Museum & Village Society Inc.
5302 PR#209, Gardenton MB R0A 0M0
Tel: 204-425-3072
Mission: To provide the rural communities with activities & to preserve the history of the area; Museum includes exhibit of churches, Ukrainian clothing & artifacts of late 1800s & early 1900s; site includes museum, one room school, thatched roof house & a campground

The Friends of West Kootenay Parks Society (FWKP)
PO Box 212, Nelson BC V1L 5P9
fwkp@kics.bc.ca
www.fwkp.kics.bc.ca
Overview: A small local organization founded in 1988
Mission: To promote conservationist & recreational use of British Columbia parks in the West Kootenay area
Membership: *Fees:* $10
Activities: Kokanee Glacier Alpine Campaign; advocacy for parks; construction projects; fundraising; publicizing parks issues
Chief Officer(s):
Bill Bryce, Chair

Friendship Centre of Québec *Voir* Centre d'amitié autochtone du Québec

Friendship House Association of Prince Rupert
744 Fraser St., Prince Rupert BC V8J 1P9
Tel: 250-627-1717; *Fax:* 250-627-7533
reception@friendshiphouse.ca
www.friendshiphouse.ca
www.facebook.com/235609558272
Overview: A small local organization founded in 1958
Mission: To provide educational & cultural programs to the First Nations community in Prince Rupert

From Grief To Action (FGTA)
c/o St. Mary's Anglican Church, 2490 West 37th Ave., Vancouver BC V6M 1P5
www.fromgrieftoaction.com
Overview: A small local charitable organization founded in 1999
Mission: To serve as a support group for those affected by drug addiction in a family member or friend; To promote the recognition of drug addiction as a health issue; To support a comprehensive continuum of care for drug users, including harm reduction, detoxification, treatment & rehabilitation; To provide educational resources on drug abuse prevention
Finances: *Funding Sources:* United Way; Donations
Membership: *Fees:* $25 individual; $45 family; $100 organization
Chief Officer(s):
Bev Gutray, Director

Front commun des personnes assistées sociales du Québec
2000, boul St-Joseph est, Montréal QC H2H 1E4
Tél: 514-987-1989; *Téléc:* 514-987-1918
sol@fcpasq.qc.ca
www.fcpasq.qc.ca
Aperçu: *Dimension:* petite; *Envergure:* nationale; fondée en 1977
Mission: Défendre les droits des personnes assistées sociales; regrouper et mobiliser les personnes assistées sociales; informer les personnes assistées sociales; améliorer les conditions de vie des personnes assistées sociales
Finances: *Budget de fonctionnement annuel:* $100,000-$250,000; *Fonds:* Les Communautés religieuses du Québec; les groupes syndicaux du Québec
Membre: 34
Membre(s) du bureau directeur:
Nicole Jetté, Porte-parole

Front commun québécois pour une gestion écologique des déchets (FCQGED)
#107, 1431, rue Fullum, Montréal QC H2K 0B5
Tél: 514-396-2686
info@fcqged.org
www.fcqged.org
Aperçu: *Dimension:* petite; *Envergure:* provinciale
Mission: Mise sur pied d'alternatives aux méthodes traditionnelles de traitement des déchets
Membre(s) du bureau directeur:

Jérôme Normand, Président

Le Front des artistes canadiens *See* Canadian Artists Representatio

Le Front des artistes canadiens de l'Ontario *See* Canadian Artists' Representation Ontario

Le Front des artistes canadiens de Manitoba *See* Canadian Artists' Representation Manitoba

Frontenac County Schools Museum Association
PO Box 246, Kingston ON K7L 5J9
Tel: 613-544-9113
fcschoolsmuseum@gmail.com
www.fcsmuseum.com
www.facebook.com/SchoolsMuseum
Overview: A small local organization founded in 1977
Mission: To establish & run the Frontenac County Schools Museum; to research & compile the history of Frontenac County schools; to collect & preserve the artifacts & archival records from the schools & to present this material to the general public & the educational community
Member of: Ontario Museum Association; Canadian Museum Association; Kingston Association of Museums, Historic Sites & Galleries
Membership: *Fees:* $30
Activities: Exhibits; tours; education; archival assistance; *Library*

Frontenac Law Association
Frontenac County Courthouse, 5 Court St., Kingston ON K7L 2N4
Tel: 613-542-0034; *Fax:* 613-531-9764
library@cfla.on.ca
www.cfla.on.ca
Overview: A small local organization
Activities: *Library:* Frontenac Law Association Library
Chief Officer(s):
Leanne Wight, President
president@cfla.on.ca

Frontier Duty Free Association (FDFA) / Association Frontière Hors Taxes (AFHT)
#402, 116 Lisgar St., Ottawa ON K2P 0C2
Tel: 613-688-9788; *Fax:* 613-701-4289
www.fdfa.ca
www.facebook.com/dutyfreecanada
twitter.com/CanadaDutyFree
Overview: A small national organization founded in 1984
Mission: To promote the development of Canada's land border duty free industry by acting as a voice, advocate & business resource for member stores
Membership: 24 stores; *Member Profile:* Land Border duty free shops in Canada; Duty free shops in the U.S. & in Canadian Airports
Chief Officer(s):
Abe Taqtaq, President
Allison Boucher, Manager, Operations
aboucher@fdfa.ca

Frontière électronique du Canada *See* Electronic Frontier Canada Inc.

Frontiers Foundation (FF/OB) / Fondation Frontière
419 Coxwell Ave., Toronto ON M4L 3B9
Tel: 416-690-3930; *Fax:* 416-690-3934
www.frontiersfoundation.ca
www.facebook.com/pages/Frontiers-Foundation/66661443145
Also Known As: Operation Beaver
Overview: A medium-sized international charitable organization founded in 1968
Mission: To implement the enduring relief of human poverty throughout Canada & also abroad in tangible advancement projects.
Member of: Canadian Council for International Organization; Coordinating Committee for International Voluntary Service
Affiliation(s): Native Council of Canada
Activities: Housing projects in 30 communities annually + seven educational projects in Northern communities
Chief Officer(s):
Marco A. Guzman, Executive Director
marcoguzman@frontiersfoundation.ca
Lawrence Gladue, President
Awards:
• Volunteer of the Year

Manitoba Office
201 Portage Ave., 18th Fl., Winnipeg MB R3B 3K6

Canadian Associations / FTQ Laurentides-Lanaudière

Tel: 204-221-5209; Fax: 204-926-8501
admin@frontiersmb.ca
frontiersmb.ca

North Western Office
9781 - 127 St., Surrey BC V3V 5J1
Tel: 604-585-6646; Fax: 604-585-6647
fronwest@shaw.ca
northernfrontiers.org
Chief Officer(s):
Don Irving, Coordinator

Québec Office
11A, 5e av ouest, Cadillac QC J0Y 1C0
Tel: 819-760-3476
Chief Officer(s):
Lylas Polson, Coordinator
lylas.polson@hotmail.com

FTQ Laurentides-Lanaudière
330, rue Parent, 2e étage, Saint-Jérôme QC J7Z 2A2
Tél: 450-431-6659; Téléc: 450-438-0567
ftql-l@qc.aira.com
www.ftql-l.ftq.qc.ca
Aperçu: *Dimension:* petite; *Envergure:* locale surveillé par Fédération des travailleurs et travailleuses du Québec

Fujiwara Dance Inventions
509 Parliament St., 2nd Fl., Toronto ON M4X 1P3
Tel: 416-593-8455
info@fujiwaradance.com
www.fujiwaradance.com
www.facebook.com/fujiwaradance
twitter.com/fujiwaradance
www.youtube.com/user/fujiwaradance
Overview: A small local organization
Mission: To create, perform, & teach dance; To use dance to move & change people, as well as encounter the complexity of humanity
Chief Officer(s):
Denise Fujiwara, Artistic Director

Full Gospel Business Men's Fellowship in Canada (FGBMFI)
2891 Martin Rd., Blezard Valley ON P0M 1E0
Tel: 416-449-7272; Fax: 416-449-9743
Toll-Free: 877-296-1715
www.fgbmfi.ca
www.facebook.com/groups/5807578145
Overview: A medium-sized national charitable organization founded in 1964
Mission: To reach men at all levels of our modern society, calling them to God, & releasing them into their respective gifts & talents through the Holy Spirit
Member of: Full Gospel Business Men's Fellowship International
Finances: *Annual Operating Budget:* $100,000-$250,000
Staff Member(s): 2; 2 volunteer(s)
Membership: 1,000-4,999; *Fees:* $60 individual
Activities: National convention; *Internships:* Yes; *Speaker Service:* Yes
Chief Officer(s):
Ron Hutzal, President

Fundy Model Forest Network
13 Drury's Cover Rd., Lower Cove NB E4E 4E4
Tel: 506-432-7575; Fax: 506-432-7562
info@fundymodelforest.net
www.fundymodelforest.net
www.facebook.com/fundymodelforest
Overview: A small local organization
Member of: Canadian Model Forest Network
Membership: 30
Chief Officer(s):
Nairn Hay, General Manager
nairn@fundymodelforest.net

Fundy Stamp Collectors Club
c/o 34 Berwick St., Riverview NB E1B 5P4
info@fundystampclub.ca
www.fundystampclub.ca
Overview: A small provincial organization founded in 1997
Mission: To promote & foster stamp collecting
Membership: *Fees:* $20; *Member Profile:* Sponsored by current members
Chief Officer(s):
Art Gillard, President

Fundy Trail Beagle Club
540 Garnett Settlement Rd., Saint John NB E2S 1S6
Tel: 506-652-2272
Overview: A small local organization
Member of: New Brunswick Wildlife Federation
Chief Officer(s):
Michael Hicks, President

Funeral & Cremation Services Council of Saskatchewan (FCSCS)
3847C Albert St., Regina SK S4S 3R4
Tel: 306-584-1575; Fax: 306-584-1576
administration@funeralinfo.ca
www.fcscs.ca
Previous Name: Saskatchewan Funeral Service Association
Overview: A small provincial licensing organization founded in 2001
Mission: To outline standard practices for the funeral industry for the benefit of the public
Affiliation(s): Funeral Service Association of Canada
Finances: *Annual Operating Budget:* $250,000-$500,000; *Funding Sources:* Licenses; Regulatory fees
Staff Member(s): 4
Membership: *Committees:* Audit/Finance; Communications; Education & Professional development; Legislative & Governance; Licensing; Pandemic Planning; INvestigation Panel; Discipline Panel
Activities: *Internships:* Yes; *Library:* Open to public by appointment
Chief Officer(s):
Raymond Bailey, Chair
Sandy Mahon, Registrar
registrar@funeralinfo.ca

Funeral Advisory & Memorial Society (FAMS)
PO Box 65, Stn. F, 55 St. Phillips Rd., Toronto ON M9P 2N8
Tel: 416-241-6274
info@fams.ca
www.fams.ca
Also Known As: Toronto Memorial Society
Overview: A medium-sized local organization founded in 1957
Mission: To provide consumer advice on funeral planning
Member of: Federation of Ontario Memorial Societies - Funeral Consumers Alliance
Membership: *Fees:* $40 single; $35 additional family members over 18 years old; $15 persons of limited means; *Member Profile:* Individuals interested in funeral pre-arrangements
Activities: Assisting members with the pre-arrangement of simple & inexpensive funerals; Providing information about funeral planning
Chief Officer(s):
Margaret Adamson, Chair
Shirley Zinman, Vice Chair
Albert Tucker, Treasurer
Publications:
• FAMS [Funeral Advisory & Memorial Society] Newsletter *Type:* Newsletter; *Frequency:* Annually

Funeral Advisory & Memorial Society of Saskatchewan (FAMSS)
PO Box 1846, Saskatoon SK S7K 3S2
Tel: 306-374-5190
Toll-Free: 866-283-2677
info@famss.ca
www.famss.ca
Previous Name: Memorial Society of Saskatchewan
Overview: A small provincial organization founded in 1969
Mission: To provide simplicity in obtaining affordable funeral plans through membership from certified funeral service provider in the major urban areas of the province; to provide an information kit to guide a person to make an informed decision on pre-planning a funeral
Member of: Federation of Ontario Memorial Societies - Funeral Consumers Alliance
Membership: *Fees:* $25
Activities: *Speaker Service:* Yes

Funeral Consumers Advocacy of London & Windsor
PO Box 1729, London ON N6A 5H9
www.fcalw.org
www.facebook.com/fcalw
twitter.com/FCALW1963
Previous Name: Memorial Society of London; London Memorial Society; Memorial & Funeral Advisory Society of London
Overview: A small local organization founded in 1963
Member of: Federation of Ontario Memorial Societies - Funeral Consumers Alliance
Finances: *Annual Operating Budget:* Less than $50,000; *Funding Sources:* Member donations
Staff Member(s): 7; 7 volunteer(s)
Membership: 850; *Fees:* $20/member; *Member Profile:* Those interested in preplanning & simple funerals
Activities: Educational presentations; information service; *Speaker Service:* Yes
Chief Officer(s):
Amelia Wehlau, Secretary
afwehlau@astro.uwo.ca

Funeral Information & Memorial Society of Guelph
PO Box 1784, Guelph ON N1H 7A1
Tel: 519-835-9603
memorialsociety_guelph@hotmail.com
Also Known As: Memorial Society of Guelph
Overview: A small local organization founded in 1970
Mission: To assist people in planning & arranging simple, inexpensive & dignified funerals by providing information
Member of: Federation of Ontario Memorial Societies - Funeral Consumers Alliance
Finances: *Annual Operating Budget:* Less than $50,000
8 volunteer(s)
Membership: *Fees:* $15 life
Activities: *Speaker Service:* Yes
Chief Officer(s):
Kevin Mooney, Contact

Funeral Planning & Memorial Society of Manitoba
613 St. Mary's Rd., Winnipeg MB R2M 3L8
Tel: 204-452-7999
FPMSInfo@mts.net
www.funeralsocietymb.org
Overview: A small provincial organization
Mission: To help Manitobans when having to make funeral arrangements
Member of: Memorial Society Association of Canada
Membership: *Fees:* $15 lifetime; $25 family lifetime

Funeral Service Association of Canada (FSAC) / L'Association des services funéraires du Canada
#304, 555 Legget Dr., Ottawa ON K2K 2K3
Tel: 613-271-2107; Fax: 613-271-3737
Toll-Free: 866-841-7779
info@fsac.ca
www.fsac.ca
www.facebook.com/FuneralAssociation
Overview: A medium-sized national organization founded in 1921
Mission: To provide a collective voice for the Canadian funeral professional; To provide high quality professional services with dignity & competence; To ensure compliance with all provisions of the law; To provide information about services
Finances: *Funding Sources:* Membership fee
Membership: *Member Profile:* Canadian funeral professionals; Suppliers; *Committees:* Education; Government Relations; Health & Pandemic Planning; Communications; Membership Growth & Strategic Development; Executive; Coalition
Activities: Cooperating with related professions; Offering continuing education; Organizing conventions
Chief Officer(s):
Faye Doucette, President
belvederefh@eastlink.ca
Phil Fredette, Vice-President
pfredette@arbormemorial.com
Meetings/Conferences:
• Funeral Service Association of Canada 2018 Convention & Trade Show, June, 2018, Ottawa, ON
Scope: National

Fung Loy Kok Institute of Taoism (FLK)
134 D'Arcy St., Toronto ON M5T 1K3
Tel: 416-656-2110; Fax: 416-654-3937
fungloykok@taoist.org
www.taoist.org
Overview: A small international organization
Mission: Observes the unified teachings of the three religions of Confucianism, Buddhism & Taoism.
Affiliation(s): Taoist Tai Chi Society of Canada
Activities: Tai Chi arts; Taoist meditation
• FunTeam Mini Try-athlon Grant
• RecTeam Event Grant
• FunTeam Equipment & Facilities Grant
• FunTeam Membership Grant
• RBC Sereda Hockey Grant
• FunTeam Alberta Outstanding Participant Award
• Randy Gregg Volunteer Award

FunTeam Alberta
11759 Groat Rd., Edmonton AB T5M 3K6
Tel: 780-490-0242; *Fax:* 780-485-0262
admin@funteamalberta.com
www.funteamalberta.com
www.facebook.com/FunTeamAB
twitter.com/FunTeamAlberta
Overview: A small provincial organization founded in 1990
Mission: To provide the opportunity for children, youth & adults in Alberta to engage in sporting activities at low costs; To foster leadership skills
Finances: *Funding Sources:* Government of Alberta
Activities: FunTeam (12 & under); RecTeam (13+); Family Try-Athlon; Mini Try-Athlon; FunTeam Young Leaders; Awards & Grant programs; *Awareness Events:* FunTeam Family Field Day
Chief Officer(s):
Randy Gregg, President
Scott Kramble, Executive Director
info@funteamalberta.com
Gabriela Nef Ojeda, Special Projects Coordinator
admin@funteamalberta.com
Awards:
• FunTeam Family Try-athlon Grant

The Fur Council of Canada (FCC) / Conseil canadien de la fourrure
#1270, 1435, rue Saint-Alexandre, Montréal QC H3A 2G4
Tel: 514-844-1945; *Fax:* 514-844-8593
Other Communication: Alt. URLs: www.truthaboutfur.com; www.furisgreen.com
info@furcouncil.com
www.furcouncil.com
www.youtube.com/user/EcoFurs
Overview: A medium-sized national organization founded in 1964
Mission: To promote all aspects of the fur trade
Activities: Public education; fashion promotion & advertising; market development

Fur Institute of Canada (FIC) / Institut de la fourrure du Canada (IFC)
#701, 331 Cooper St., Ottawa ON K2P 0G5
Tel: 613-231-7099; *Fax:* 613-231-7940
www.fur.ca
www.facebook.com/FurInstituteOfCanada
twitter.com/furinstitute
Overview: A medium-sized national organization founded in 1983
Mission: To promote the sustainable & wise use of Canadian fur resources
Member of: International Fur Trade Federation; International Association of Fish & Wildlife Agencies; International Council for Game & Wildlife Conservation; International Union for Conservation of Nature
Finances: *Funding Sources:* Membership dues; Donations
Staff Member(s): 4
Membership: *Member Profile:* Trappers; Fur Farmers; Wholesale Fur Dealers; Fur Manufacturers & Processors; Fur Retailers; Aboriginal Organizations; Conservation Organizations; Animal Welfare Associations; Support Industries; Government of Canada; Provincial & Territorial Governments; *Committees:* Trap Research & Development; Communications; Sealing; Human-Wildlife
Activities: Coordinating the implementation of the Agreement on International Humane Trapping Standards in Canada; Presenting awards; Offering programs such as trap research & testing, conservation, international relations, communication, aboriginal communications & funding; Researching; Promoting conservation efforts
Chief Officer(s):
Dion Dakins, Chair
James Baker, Executive Director

Fur-Bearer Defenders (FBD)
179 West Broadway, Vancouver BC V5Y 1P4
Tel: 604-435-1850
fbd@furbearerdefenders.com
furbearerdefenders.com
ca.linkedin.com/pub/fur-bearer-s-assoc/20/52/587
www.facebook.com/FurFree
twitter.com/FurBearers
www.youtube.com/user/furbearerdefenders
Also Known As: The Association for the Protection of Fur-Bearing Animals
Previous Name: The Fur-Bearers
Overview: A medium-sized national charitable organization founded in 1944
Mission: To stop trapping cruelty & protect fur-bearing animals
Finances: *Funding Sources:* Donations; Membership dues
Staff Member(s): 5
Membership: *Fees:* $25
Activities: Providing information to government, media, activists, & the public; Launching campaigns to create awareness; *Awareness Events:* Living with Wildlife Webinar Series
Chief Officer(s):
Lesley Fox, Executive Director

The Fur-Bearers *See* Fur-Bearer Defenders

Furriers Guild of Canada
#211, 4174 Dundas St. West, Toronto ON M8X 1X3
Tel: 416-234-9494; *Fax:* 416-234-2244
furriersguildca@ica.net
Merged from: Fur Trade Association of Canada (Ontario) Inc.; Retail Furriers Guild of Canada
Overview: A medium-sized national organization
Mission: To promote Canadian fur retailers
Membership: *Member Profile:* Canadian fur retailers
Activities: Providing programs such as community outreach

Further Poultry Processors Association of Canada (FPPAC)
#206, 1545 Carling Ave., Ottawa ON K1Z 8P9
Tel: 613-738-1175
www.fppac.ca
Overview: A medium-sized national organization founded in 1984
Mission: To promote, foster, develop & represent the interests of corporations engaged in the further processing of poultry
Affiliation(s): Further Poultry Processors Association of Ontario
Finances: *Funding Sources:* Membership dues
Membership: 1-99; *Fees:* Sliding scale; *Member Profile:* Manufacturers of poultry products
Activities: *Library:* by appointment
Chief Officer(s):
Blair Shier, Chair
Ian Hesketh, Vice-Chair
Bruce McCullagh, Secretary-Treasurer

Fuse Collective
University of Calgary, 2500 University Dr. NW, Calgary AB T2N 1N4
info@fusecollective.org
fusecollective.org
www.facebook.com/FUSEYYC
twitter.com/fusecollective
Previous Name: Institute for Sustainable Energy, Economy & Environment Student's Association
Overview: A large provincial organization founded in 2006
Mission: To promote & create initiatives that reflect the growing movement to obtain a cleaner energy supply, healthy environment, & efficient economy
Chief Officer(s):
April Kargard, President

Fusion: The Ontario Clay & Glass Association
1444 Queen St. East, Toronto ON M4L 1E1
Tel: 416-438-8946; *Fax:* 416-438-0192
fusion@clayandglass.on.ca
www.clayandglass.on.ca
Previous Name: Ontario Potters Association
Overview: A medium-sized provincial charitable organization
Mission: To encourage & promote excellence & quality in clay & glass; to provide opportunities for fellowship & a sense of community involvement; to provide continuing education resources for members & people interested in clay & glass; to reach out, demonstrating tolerance, caring & acceptance for the diverse aspects of expression in clay & glass.
Affiliation(s): Ontario Crafts Council; Canadian Clay & Glass Gallery; National Council on Education for the Ceramic Art; Studio Potter Network
Finances: *Funding Sources:* Ontario Arts Council
Membership: *Fees:* Schedule available; *Member Profile:* People who enjoy handmade clay & glass objects
Activities: "Fireworks", biennial juried exhibition of the finest works of members; silent auction, annual fundraiser; conference, regional workshops & weekend demonstrations; permanent art collection at Burlington Arts Centre
Chief Officer(s):
Jenanne Longman, Office Administrator

FutureWatch Environment & Development Education Partners
3101 Dundas St. West, Toronto ON M6P 1Z9
Tel: 416-926-1985; *Fax:* 416-926-0618
info@futurewatch.net
www.futurewatch.net
Also Known As: FutureWatch
Overview: A small local charitable organization founded in 1993
Mission: To foster the creation of healthy & sustainable communities locally & internationally
Staff Member(s): 6
Chief Officer(s):
Lidia Ferreira, Executive Director
lidiaf@futurewatch.net

Futurpreneur Canada
#700, 133 Richmond St. West, Toronto ON M5H 2L3
Fax: 877-408-3234
Toll-Free: 866-646-2922
www.futurpreneur.ca
www.linkedin.com/company/futurpreneur-canada
www.facebook.com/futurpreneur
twitter.com/@Futurpreneur
www.youtube.com/user/CYBF
Previous Name: Canadian Youth Business Foundation
Overview: A medium-sized national organization founded in 1996
Mission: A national, non-profit organization that provides financing, mentoring and support tools to aspiring business owners aged 18-39.
Membership: 6,900
Activities: Pre-Launch Coaching; Online Resources; Financing; Mentoring
Chief Officer(s):
Julia Deans, CEO, 416-408-2923 Ext. 3001
jdeans@futurpreneur.ca
Rebecca Dew, CFO, 416-408-2923 Ext. 2102
rdew@futurpreneur.ca
Awards:
• BDC Mentorship Award
Alberta Office
Willow Park Centre, #418, 10325 Bonaventure Dr. SE, Calgary AB T2J 7E4
Tel: 403-265-2923; *Fax:* 403-265-2343
www.facebook.com/FuturpreneurAB
twitter.com/@FuturpreneurAB
Chief Officer(s):
Kathy McReynolds, Contact, 403-265-3228, Fax: 403-265-2343
kmcreynolds@cybf.ca
Atlantic Office
#204, 540 Southgate Dr., Bedford NS B4A 0C9
Tel: 902-407-7709
www.facebook.com/futurpreneurATL
twitter.com/@futurpreneurATL
Chief Officer(s):
Christian Perron
British Columbia Office
#580, 425 Carrall St., Vancouver BC V6B 6E3
Tel: 604-598-2923
www.facebook.com/FuturpreneurBC
twitter.com/@FuturpreneurBC
Manitoba Office
#500, 321 McDermot Ave., Winnipeg MB R3A 0A3
Tel: 204-480-8481
www.facebook.com/futurpreneurMB
twitter.com/@futurpreneurMB
Québec Office
#402, 5605, av De Gaspé, Montréal QC H2T 2A4
Tel: 514-225-7035
www.facebook.com/futurpreneurQC
twitter.com/@futurpreneurQC
Saskatchewan Office
#113, 220 - 20th St., Saskatoon SK S7M 0W9
Tel: 306-717-9216
www.facebook.com/futurpreneurSK
twitter.com/@futurpreneurSK

Gabriola Island Chamber of Commerce
PO Box 249, #6, 480 North Rd., Gabriola BC V0R 1X0
Tel: 250-247-9332
giccmanager@shaw.ca
www.adventuregabriola.ca
www.facebook.com/GabriolaIslandbc
Overview: A small local charitable organization founded in 1984

Mission: To promote & improve trade & commerce & the economic, civic & social welfare of Gabriola
Member of: BC Chamber of Commerce
Affiliation(s): Tourism Association of Vancouver Island
Membership: 115; *Fees:* Schedule available; *Member Profile:* Local businesses
Activities: *Library:* Not open to public
Chief Officer(s):
Gloria Hatfield, President
Tammie Hennigar, Manager

Gagetown & Area Chamber of Commerce
c/o Village Office, 68 Babbit St., Gagetown NB E5M 1C8
Tel: 506-488-3567
Overview: A small local organization founded in 1992
Mission: To promote local businesses & help them grow
Member of: Atlantic Chamber of Commerce; New Brunswick Chamber of Commerce
Finances: *Funding Sources:* Membership dues; provincial government
Membership: *Member Profile:* Small businesses; Crafts; Artists; Retailers; B&B

Gai Écoute inc.
CP 1006, Succ. C, Montréal QC H2L 4V2
Tél: 514-866-6788; *Téléc:* 514-866-8157
courrier@gaiecoute.org
www.gaiecoute.org
www.facebook.com/gaiecoute
twitter.com/gaiecoute
www.youtube.com/gaiecoute
Aperçu: *Dimension:* petite; *Envergure:* locale; Organisme sans but lucratif; fondée en 1980
Mission: Offrir un soutien aux personnes homosexuelles en difficulté, ainsi qu'à leurs proches; offrir une écoute attentive à ces personnes, ainsi qu'une information générale sur le milieu gai et lesbien; faciliter l'intégration des personnes homosexuelles dans leur communauté et dans la société et contribuer à leur bien-être; combattre les préjugés
Finances: *Budget de fonctionnement annuel:* $100,000-$250,000
Membre(s) du personnel: 3; 60 bénévole(s)
Membre: 1-99
Activités: *Service de conférenciers:* Oui; *Bibliothèque*
Membre(s) du bureau directeur:
Laurent McCutcheon, Président

Gainey Foundation
420, rue Guy, Montréal QC H3J 1S6
info@gaineyfoundation.com
www.gaineyfoundation.com
Overview: A small national charitable organization
Mission: To support charitable organizations that offer environmental or arts education programs for youth
Finances: *Funding Sources:* Donations
Activities: Organizing fundraising concerts
Chief Officer(s):
Anna Gainey, Executive Director
Awards:
• Gainey Foundation Grant
Eligibility: Federally registered charities

The Gairdner Foundation
MaRS Centre, South Tower, #407, 101 College St., Toronto ON M5G 1L7
Tel: 416-596-9996; *Fax:* 416-596-9992
thegairdner@gairdner.org
www.gairdner.org
www.facebook.com/263607420316593
twitter.com/GairdnerAwards
www.youtube.com/user/CanadaGairdnerAwards
Overview: A small national charitable organization founded in 1957
Mission: To recognize researchers who have made signifcant contributions to the medical science field
Finances: *Annual Operating Budget:* $50,000-$100,000
Staff Member(s): 1; 1 volunteer(s)
Membership: *Committees:* Board of Trustees; Medical Advisory Board; Medical Review Panel
Chief Officer(s):
Janet Rossant, President & Scientific Director
janet.rossant@gairdner.org
Penny Balberman, Financial Director
penny@gairdner.org
Nora Cox, Office Manager
nora@gairdner.org

Awards:
• Canada Gairdner International Awards
Awarded to biomedical scientists whose works have contributed to the understanding of human biology & disease
• Canada Gairdner Global Health Award
Awarded to a scientist whose work has contributed or will potentially contribute to health outcomes in the developing world
• Canada Gairdner Wightman Award
Awarded to a Canadian who has shown leadership in the medical science field

Galiano Island Chamber of Commerce
PO Box 73, Galiano Island BC V0N 1P0
Tel: 250-539-2233
www.galianoisland.com
Also Known As: Galiano Travel Infocentre
Overview: A small local organization
Mission: To strengthen the community & protect the environment by developing local business
Member of: BC Chamber of Commerce; Tourism Victoria
Finances: *Annual Operating Budget:* Less than $50,000
Staff Member(s): 1; 8 volunteer(s)
Membership: 104; *Fees:* $40; *Committees:* Brochure; Tourism; Booth; Communication; Social
Activities: Maintaining tourist booth; Offering services directory; Organizing chamber socials twice a year; *Internships:* Yes
Library: Infocentre; Open to public
Chief Officer(s):
Richard Dewinetz, President
president@galianoisland.com

Galiano Rod & Gun Club
#2, 594 Porlier Pass Rd., Galiano Island BC V0N 1P0
Tel: 250-539-2113
Overview: A small local organization

Galt and District Real Estate Board; Real Estate Board of Cambridge *See* Cambridge Association of Realtors Inc.

GAMA International Canada / GAMA International du Canada
#209, 390 Queens Quay West, Toronto ON M4V 3A2
Tel: 416-444-5251; *Fax:* 416-444-8031
Toll-Free: 800-563-5822
info@gamacanada.com
www.gamacanada.com
www.linkedin.com/groups/GAMA-International-Canada-1952201
twitter.com/Advocis
www.youtube.com/user/AdvocisTFAAC
Previous Name: Managers Association of Financial Advisors of Canada
Overview: A medium-sized national organization founded in 1974
Mission: To focus on professional development for leaders involved in the distribution of financial services
Finances: *Annual Operating Budget:* $250,000-$500,000; *Funding Sources:* Membership dues; corporate sponsorship
Staff Member(s): 1
Membership: 24 chapters; *Fees:* Schedule available; *Member Profile:* Leaders in distribution management in financial services; individuals in activities related to financial services with an interest in management; companies that wish to be sponsors or supporters
Activities: Teleconferences, newsletters & articles, annual awards
Chief Officer(s):
Rob Popazzi, President
robert.popazzi@sunflie.com
Celia Ciotola, Director
cciotola@advocis.ca
Awards:
• Agency Builder Award (ABA)
• Agency Achievement Award (AAA)
• National Management Award (NMA)

GAMA International du Canada *See* GAMA International Canada

Gananoque Food Bank
c/o Gananoque Legion, 55 King St. East, Gananoque ON K7G 1E8
Tel: 613-382-4434
ganfoodbank@gmail.com
Also Known As: Gananoque & District Food Bank
Overview: A small local charitable organization founded in 1987
Member of: Ontario Association of Food Banks
Staff Member(s): 1; 50 volunteer(s)

Membership: 1-99
Activities: Spring Appreciation Day for Volunteers; Annual Food Drive; Santa Claus parade
Chief Officer(s):
Cliff Weir, President
c_weir@sympatico.ca

Ganaraska Hiking Trail Association (GHTA)
PO Box 693, Orillia ON L3V 6K7
admin@ganaraska-hiking-trail.ca
www.ganaraska-hiking-trail.ca
Overview: A small local charitable organization founded in 1969
Mission: To construct & maintain a hiking trail from Port Hope to Glen Huron; to encourage recreational hiking & respect for the environment
Member of: Hike Ontario; Ontario Nature
Finances: *Funding Sources:* Membership dues; donations
Membership: *Fees:* $25
Activities: On the edge of the Laurentian Shield, within reach of Ontario's major cities, the trail forms a vital link in the National Trail network (500 km)
Chief Officer(s):
Bob Bowles, President
rbowles@rogers.com

Gander & Area Chamber of Commerce (GACC)
109 Trans Canada Hwy., Gander NL A1V 1P6
Tel: 709-256-7110; *Fax:* 709-256-4794
chambergeneral@ganderchamber.nf.ca
www.ganderchamber.nf.ca
Overview: A small local charitable organization founded in 1959
Mission: To promote & improve the economic climate of the area; To support the needs & concerns of the business community; To enhance the civic & social well-being of the community
Member of: Newfoundland & Labrador Chamber of Commerce; Atlantic Provinces Chamber of Commerce
Finances: *Annual Operating Budget:* $100,000-$250,000; *Funding Sources:* Membership fees
Staff Member(s): 2; 11 volunteer(s)
Membership: 200+ businesses; *Fees:* Schedule available
Activities: Organizing & supporting events; *Awareness Events:* Golf Tournament & Auction; Small Business Week; Joe & Clarice Goodyear Business Achievement Awards Gala *Library:* Business Library
Chief Officer(s):
Debby Yannakidis, Chair
Hazel Bishop, Executive Director

Gander & Area Society for the Prevention of Cruelty to Animals
36 McCurdy Dr., Gander NL A1V 1A2
Tel: 709-651-3002
ganderspca@hotmail.com
www.envision.ca/webs/ganderandareaspca
Also Known As: Gander & Area SPCA
Overview: A small local organization founded in 1985
Finances: *Annual Operating Budget:* Less than $50,000; *Funding Sources:* Fundraising
Membership: 30

The Garden Clubs of Ontario (GCO)
PO Box 399, Hamilton ON L8N 3H8
www.gardenclubsofontario.org
www.facebook.com/GardenClubsOfOntario
Overview: A small provincial organization founded in 1954
Mission: To stimulate knowledge & love of gardening amongst amateurs; to aid in the protection of native plants, trees, birds & soil; to encourage civic planning
Member of: Ontario Horticultural Association; World Association of Flower Arrangers
Finances: *Annual Operating Budget:* $50,000-$100,000
15 volunteer(s)
Membership: 1,500 individual; *Committees:* Archives; Judges; National & International Liaison
Activities: Coordinates activities of 12 Garden Clubs in Ontario; Tour of Summer Gardens
Chief Officer(s):
Janice Middleton, Contact
  Burlington
  PO Box 85185, Stn. Brant Plaza, Burlington ON L7R 4K4
  Tel: 905-632-0561
  Chief Officer(s):
  Heather Medley, President
  Dundas
  101 King St. East, Dundas ON L9H 1B9

Tel: 905-627-0884
dundas@gardenclubsofontario.ca
Chief Officer(s):
June Solntseff, President
Georgian Bay
Grey Sauble Conservation Authority, 237897 Inglis Falls Rd., RR #4, Owen Sound ON N4K 5N6
Tel: 519-414-4564
georgianbay@gardenclubsofontario.ca
georgianbaygardenclubowensound.com
Chief Officer(s):
Marsha Barrow, President
Hamilton
180 Dalewood Cres., Hamilton ON L8S 4C1
Tel: 905-528-7441
hamilton@gardenclubsofontario.ca
Chief Officer(s):
Wendy Downing, President
Kitchener-Waterloo
27 Autumn Ridge Trail, Kitchener ON N2P 2J6
Tel: 519-578-8682
kitchenerwaterloo@gardenclubsofontario.ca
Chief Officer(s):
Geri Laughlen, President
London
Civic Garden Complex, 625 Springbank Dr., London ON N6K 4T1
Tel: 519-471-6200
www.gardencluboflondon.ca
www.facebook.com/GardenClubOfLondon
Chief Officer(s):
Jeanne Anne Goldrick, President
Milne House
The Toronto Botanical Garden, 777 Lawrence Ave. East, Toronto ON M3C 1P2
milnehouse@gardenclubsofontario.ca
Chief Officer(s):
Patrisha Galiana, President
Niagara
565 Niagara Pkwy., Niagara Falls ON L2E 6T2
Tel: 905-937-1427
niagara@gardenclubsofontario.ca
Chief Officer(s):
Anne Lemon, President, 905-295-4228
Toronto
777 Lawrence Ave. East, Toronto ON M3C 1P2
Tel: 416-447-5218; *Fax:* 416-447-2154
gardencluboftoronto@on.aibn.com
www.thegardencluboftoronto.ca
Chief Officer(s):
Janet Kennish, President
Toronto Japanese Garden
1063 Pape Ave., Toronto ON M4K 3W4
Tel: 416-425-3161
tjgc@rogers.com
tjgc.awardspace.com
Chief Officer(s):
Toshi Oikawa, President

Garderie du Carrefour *Voir* CPE du Carrefour

Gardiner Centre
Business Administration Bldg., Memorial University of Newfoundland, St. John's NL A1B 3X5
Tel: 709-864-7977; *Fax:* 709-864-7999
gardinercentre@mun.ca
www.mun.ca/gardinercentre
www.linkedin.com/company/gardinercentrememorialuniversity
twitter.com/GardinerCentre
www.youtube.com/user/GardinerCentre
Merged from: P.J. Gardiner Institute (PJG); Centre for Management Development (CMD)
Overview: A small local organization
Mission: To connect Memorial University of Newfoundland's Faculty of Business with Newfoundland & Labrador's business community; To advance business knowledge & skills in the public & private sectors
Activities: Offering professional development programs & customized training
Chief Officer(s):
Leigh Puddester, Director
leigh.puddester@mun.ca
Valerie Howe, Manager, Operations
vhowe@mun.ca

Garrod Association
11797 rue Poincaré, Montréal QC H3L 3L6
www.garrod.ca
Also Known As: Canadian Association of Centres for the Management of Hereditary Metabolic Diseases
Overview: A small national organization
Mission: To coordinate the management of inherited metabolic disorders; To provide a forum for the exchange of information & develop guidelines for the investigation & treatment of the diseases
Affiliation(s): Western Group of Investigators of Inborn Errors of Metabolism; Canadian Paediatric Society; Canadian Dietetic Association; Canadian Society for Metabolic Diseases; CORD (Canadian Organization of Rare Disorders); Canadian College of Medical Geneticists (CCMG); SIMD; National Food Distribution Centre for the Treatment of Hereditary Metabolic Diseases
Membership: 16; *Fees:* $30; *Member Profile:* Hereditary metabolic disease centres in Canada
Chief Officer(s):
Pranesh Chakraborty, Chair
pchakraborty@cheo.on.ca
Pierre Allard, Secretary-Treasurer, 514-345-4931
pierre.allard.hsj@ssss.gouv.qc.ca
Meetings/Conferences:
• Garrod Association 2018 Garrod Symposium, 2018
Scope: National

Garth Homer Society
813 Darwin Ave, Victoria BC V8X 2X7
Tel: 250-475-2270; *Fax:* 250-475-2279
ghsinquiries@garthhomersociety.org
www.garthhomersociety.org
www.facebook.com/garthhomer
twitter.com/garthhomer1
Overview: A small local organization founded in 1979
Mission: To create opportunities for independance, growth & community participation for people who strive to overcome developmental & physical obstacles
Member of: B.C. Association for Community Living
Finances: *Annual Operating Budget:* $3 Million-$5 Million; *Funding Sources:* Provincial government
Staff Member(s): 52; 25 volunteer(s)
Membership: 110 individuals; *Fees:* $20 individual
Activities: Day program & supported employment services for adults with developmental disabilities
Chief Officer(s):
Bruce Homer, Chair
chair@garthhomersociety.org
Mitchell Temkin, Chief Executive Officer

Gas Processing Association Canada (GPAC)
#600, 900 - 6th Ave. SW, Calgary AB T2P 3K2
Tel: 403-244-4487; *Fax:* 403-244-2340
info@gpacanada.com
www.gpacanada.com
www.linkedin.com/groups/Gas-Processing-Association-Canada-4334615
twitter.com/GPACanada
Previous Name: Canadian Gas Processors Association
Overview: A medium-sized national organization founded in 1960
Mission: To promote the interaction & exchange of ideas & technology that will add value to those who are involved with or affected by the hydrocarbon processing industry
Affiliation(s): Gas Processors Association (USA)
Finances: *Funding Sources:* Membership dues
17 volunteer(s)
Membership: 750 individuals; *Fees:* $85 Regular, $9 Alumni; $20 student; *Member Profile:* Employees of companies that process gaseous & liquid hydrocarbons; *Committees:* Safety; Research; Environment; Membership; Publications; Northern
Activities: *Library:* Gas Processing Association of Canada Library
Chief Officer(s):
Greg Bury, President, 403-465-2998
president@gpacanada.com
Paul Naphin, Vice President, 403-589-1685
vp@gpacanada.com
Howard Smith, G.A.S. Liason, 403-874-5366
gasliason@gpacanada.com
Steven Summers, Director, Membership, 403-801-7253
membership@gpacanada.com
Awards:
• Safety Awards

Meetings/Conferences:
• GPAC/PJVA 25th Annual Joint Conference, 2018
Scope: National

Gateway Association
#201, 10941 - 120 St., Edmonton AB
Tel: 780-454-0701; *Fax:* 780-454-0843
info@gatewayassociation.ca
www.gatewayassociation.ca
twitter.com/GatewayAssocEdm
Overview: A small local charitable organization founded in 1975
Mission: To serve as a leader & influencer in community development; To break barriers for individuals with disabilities; To help the community to understand disabilities
Member of: Alberta Association for Community Living
Finances: *Funding Sources:* United Way; City of Edmonton; Alberta Lottery Fund; Grants
Staff Member(s): 17
Membership: *Member Profile:* Families; professionals; agencies; schools
Activities: Providing education, family support, mentorship, & inclusive employment; *Speaker Service:* Yes; *Library:* Family Resource Centre; Open to public
Chief Officer(s):
Christine Spottiswood, Executive Director, 780-454-0701 Ext. 107
christine@gatewayassociation.ca
Awards:
• Arbor Awards
Presented in 6 categories to honour members and other community leaders for promoting the values of the Association
Publications:
• Gateway Association for Community Living Newsletter
Type: Newsletter; *Frequency:* 3 pa.

GATEWAY Centre For Learning (GCFL)
488 Dominion Ave., Midland ON L4R 1P6
Tel: 705-527-1522; *Fax:* 705-527-0693
admin@gatewaycentreforlearning.ca
www.gatewaycentreforlearning.ca
www.facebook.com/GatewayCentreForLearningMidland
twitter.com/Gateway_Midland
Overview: A small local charitable organization founded in 1982
Mission: To train volunteers to work one-to-one with adults to help them acquire basic reading, writing, numeracy & computer skills; To offer small group classes; To raise awareness of literacy needs in local community; To promote a literate society
Member of: Community Literacy Ontario; Laubach Literacy Ontario; Simcoe Muskoka Literacy Network; Simcoe Muskoka Workforce Development Board
Affiliation(s): Laubach Literacy of Canada-Ontario
Finances: *Annual Operating Budget:* $100,000-$250,000; *Funding Sources:* Provincial government; Fundraising; United Way
Staff Member(s): 5; 60 volunteer(s)
Membership: 100; *Committees:* Executive; Finance; Fund Development; Human Resources; Nominating
Activities: Offering tutoring sessions for adults; Maintaining used bookstore, Bookmark; *Awareness Events:* Bruce Stanton Fundraiser, April; Art Show, April; *Speaker Service:* Yes; *Library:* Open to public
Chief Officer(s):
Kathy Banks, President
Jennifer Ellis, Executive Director
ed@gatewaycentreforlearning.ca

Gateway Research Organization (GRO)
PO Box 5865, 10336 - 106 St., Westlock AB T7P 2G1
Tel: 780-349-4546; *Fax:* 780-349-5399
Other Communication: Forage e-mail: groforage@telus.net
grohome@telus.net
www.areca.ab.ca/grohome.html
www.facebook.com/GatewayResearchOrganizationgro
twitter.com/gatewayresearch
Overview: A small local organization founded in 1979 overseen by Agricultural Research & Extension Council of Alberta
Mission: To meet the changing needs of the agriculture industry in Alberta by working with producers & industry stakeholders
Member of: Agricultural Research & Extension Council of Alberta
Staff Member(s): 1
Membership: *Fees:* $30
Chief Officer(s):
Keith Taylor, Chair
Michelle Holden, Manager, 780-349-4546, Fax: 780-349-5399
grocrops@telus.net

Publications:
• Hayshaker [a publication of the Gateway Research Organization]
Type: Newsletter; *Frequency:* 2 pa

The Gathering Place *See* Ma-Mow-We-Tak Friendship Centre Inc.

Gatineau Gliding Club (GGC)
PO Box 8145, Stn. T, Ottawa ON K1G 3H6
Tel: 613-673-5386
ggc@gatineauglidingclub.ca
www.gatineauglidingclub.ca
Overview: A small local organization
Member of: Soaring Association of Canada
Membership: 100

Gatineau Valley Historical Society (GVHS) / Société historique de la Vallée de la Gatineau
CP 1803, Chelsea QC J9B 1A1
Tél: 819-827-6224
info@gvhs.ca
www.gvhs.ca
Aperçu: *Dimension:* petite; *Envergure:* locale; Organisme sans but lucratif; fondée en 1962
Mission: To promote matters of historical significance in the Gatineau Valley region of Québec; To provide historical resources, such as newspapers, photographs, & oral histories
Finances: *Fonds:* Donations; Fundraising
Membre: 300
Activités: Maintaining the Chelsea Pioneer Cemetery; Hosting speakers who are experts on history & heritage subjects; Offering tours to points of historic interest; *Bibliothèque:* Gatineau Valley Historical Society Archives; Bibliothèque publique
Prix, Bourses:
• Arthur Davison Award for the Best Article
Publications:
• Gatineau Valley Historical Society Newsletter
Type: Newsletter; *Frequency:* Quarterly
Profile: Information about the society's forthcoming meetings & events
• Up the Gatineau
Type: Journal; *Frequency:* Annually
Profile: Local history articles

Gay & Lesbian Community Centre of Edmonton *See* Pride Centre of Edmonton

Gay Fathers of Montréal Inc. *Voir* Association des pères gais de Montréal inc.

Gay Fathers of Toronto
c/o The 519 Church St. Community Centre, 519 Church St., Toronto ON M4Y 2C9
info@gayfathers-toronto.com
www.gayfathers-toronto.com
Overview: A small local organization founded in 1987
Mission: To offer a supportive environment to fathers who are gay-oriented by providing assistance in building a positive self-image & by encouraging them to be loving & responsible
Finances: *Annual Operating Budget:* Less than $50,000
20 volunteer(s)
Membership: 50; *Fees:* $25
Activities: *Library:* Not open to public

Gay Line *See* CAEO Québec

Gays & Lesbians of the First Nations *See* 2-Spirited People of the First Nations

Les Gédéons - L'Association Internationale des Gédéons au Canada *See* Gideons International in Canada

Gelbvieh Association of Alberta/BC (GAA/BC)
PO Box 11, Tatla Lake BC V0L 1V0
Tel: 250-476-1221; *Fax:* 250-476-1280
halfwayranch2000@hotmail.com
Overview: A small provincial organization founded in 1974
Mission: To promote the Gelbvieh breed in Alberta & British Columbia through a newsletter & information booth displayed at livestock expositions
Member of: Canadian Gelbvieh Association
Finances: *Funding Sources:* Membership dues; fundraising; advertising
Membership: 64
Activities: National Gelbvieh Show & Sale; Annual Field Day
Chief Officer(s):
Romacordelia Cox, President
cordy_cox@hotmail.com

Gem & Mineral Club of Scarborough (GMCS)
PO Box 36048, Toronto ON M3B 0A3
scarbgemclub@gmail.com
www.scarbgemclub.ca
www.facebook.com/181294731911802
Overview: A small local organization founded in 1963
Mission: To promote collecting & studying rocks, minerals, fossils, & lapidary work
Member of: Central Canadian Federation of Mineralogical Societies (CCFMS)
Membership: *Fees:* $20 single members; $25 families; *Member Profile:* Collectors & mineral enthusiasts in Scarborough, Ontario
Activities: Hosting monthly meetings from September to June; Exchanging information about the hobby; Organizing exhibits; Presenting auctions; Planning mineral & fossil collecting field trips; Providing workshops; *Awareness Events:* Gem Show, September *Library:* Gem & Mineral Club of Scarborough Library
Publications:
• Strata Data: GMCS [Gem & Mineral Club of Scarborough] Newsletter
Type: Newsletter; *Frequency:* 10 pa
Profile: Upcoming events & articles about the hobby

Gem & Mineral Federation of Canada (GMFC) / Fédération canadienne des gemmes et des minéraux
PO Box 42015, RPO North, Winfield BC V4V 1Z8
Tel: 250-766-4353
president@gmfc.ca
www.gmfc.ca
Overview: A small national organization founded in 1977
Mission: To promote earth sciences; to protect collecting sites; to educate collectors; to foster good will, friendship & rapport among all
Membership: *Committees:* Communications; Education; Membership/Directory/Supplies; Public Relatiosn & Show Registry; Field Trips
Chief Officer(s):
Peter Hagar, President
madpete@accesscomm.ca

Alberta Federation of Rock Clubs (AFRC)
c/o Pauline Zeschuk, 2073 Blackmud Creek Dr. SW, Edmonton AB T6W 1G8
Tel: 780-430-6694
www.afrc.ca
Chief Officer(s):
Pauline Zeschuk, Secretary

British Columbia Lapidary Society (BCLS)
c/o Georgina Selinger, PO Box 10072, Abbotsford BC V4X 2M0
Tel: 604-852-1307
bcls10072@hotmail.com
www.lapidary.bc.ca
Chief Officer(s):
Georgina Selinger, Exec. Secretary

Mid Pro Rock & Gem Society
1010 Central Ave., Prince Albert SK S6V 4V5
Tel: 306-764-1049
Chief Officer(s):
Douglas Hodgins, Secretary

Nova Scotia Mineral & Gem Society
c/o Nova Scotia Museum of Natural History, 1747 Summer St., Halifax NS B3H 3A6
www.nsmgs.ca

Rock of Ages Lapidary Club
#142, 505 Chalmers Ave., Winnipeg MB R2L 0G4
Tel: 204-832-1109
Chief Officer(s):
Joan Turner, Secretary

Genealogical Association of Nova Scotia (GANS) / Association généalogique de la Nouvelle-Écosse
PO Box 333, 3045 Robie St., Halifax NS B3K 4P6
Tel: 902-454-0322
info@novascotiaancestors.ca
www.novascotiaancestors.ca
www.facebook.com/NovaScotiaAncestors
twitter.com/NSAncestors
Overview: A small provincial charitable organization founded in 1982
Mission: To encourage interest in & to raise standards of research in genealogy through workshops & publications; to acquaint members with research materials & methods to serve as medium of exchange for genealogical information; to support the collection & preservation of documents & other genealogical materials; to foster recognition of the value of genealogy to a proper study of the social sciences.
Member of: Federation of Nova Scotian Heritage; Canadian Federation of Genealogical & Family History Societies Inc.
Affiliation(s): Genealogical Institute of the Maritimes; Council of Nova Scotia Archives
Finances: *Funding Sources:* Membership fees; donations; sale of publications
Membership: 600; *Fees:* $30; $750 lifetime
Chief Officer(s):
Allan Marble, President

Genealogical Institute of The Maritimes (GIM) / Institut généalogique des Provinces Maritimes
PO Box 36022, 5675 Spring Garden Rd., Halifax NS B3J 1G0
nsgna.ednet.ns.ca/gim
Overview: A medium-sized provincial licensing organization founded in 1983
Mission: To pursue geneaology; to upgrade the quality of professional family history research in the Maritimes
Member of: Nova Scotia Genealogical Network Association
Finances: *Funding Sources:* Membership & accreditation fees
Membership: 23; *Fees:* $15
Activities: Professional accreditation of genealogical researchers
Chief Officer(s):
Allen Marble, Contact
allan.marble@ns.sympatico.ca

Généalogie Abitibi-Témiscamingue
CP 371, Rouyn-Noranda QC J9X 5C4
Courriel: genat@genat.org
www.genat.org
Aperçu: *Dimension:* petite; *Envergure:* locale; fondée en 1995
Membre: *Montant de la cotisation:* 30$
Membre(s) du bureau directeur:
Serge Pétrin, Président
Publications:
• Le Lien
Type: Newsletter; *Frequency:* Quarterly

General Church of the New Jerusalem in Canada (GCIC)
c/o Olivet Church of the New Jerusalem, 279 Burnhamthorpe Rd., Toronto ON M9B 1Z6
Tel: 416-239-3054; *Fax:* 416-239-4935
assistant@olivetnewchurch.org
www.newchurch.ca
Overview: A small national organization founded in 1971
Mission: An incorporated national organization of individual church members, groups & congregations devoted to the Christian life & teaching expounded in the works of Emanuel Swedenborg.
Chief Officer(s):
James Cooper, Pastor
pastor@olivetnewchurch.org
Brian Smith, Assistant Pastor
brian.smith@olivetnewchurch.org

General Conference of the Canadian Assemblies of God / Conférence générale des assemblées de dieu canadiennes
5845, boul Couture, St-Léonard QC H1P 1A8
Tel: 514-279-1100; *Fax:* 514-279-1131
info@caogonline.org
www.caog.ca
Also Known As: CAOG
Previous Name: Italian Pentecostal Church of Canada
Overview: A small national charitable organization founded in 1912
Mission: To provide distinctive ministry to all Canadians, regardless of language, nationality, or race; To proclaim the gospel of Jesus Christ in the power of the Holy Spirit throughout Canada & the world, based on the biblical standard of ministry in the New Testament
Member of: The Evangelical Fellowship of Canada; Canadian Council of Christian Charities
Finances: *Annual Operating Budget:* $100,000-$250,000
Staff Member(s): 2; 3 volunteer(s)
Membership: 6,000 + 21 affiliated churches
Activities: National Youth Convention (May); Annual General Conference (October); *Internships:* Yes
Chief Officer(s):
Dino Cianflone, General Treasurer
Daniel Ippolito, Overseer Emeritus

David Di Staulo, General Superintendent
Raymond Narula, General Secretary
Giulio Gabeli, Overseer

General Insurance OmbudService (GIO) / Service de conciliation en assurance de dommages (SCAD)
#701, 10 Milner Business Ct., Toronto ON M1B 3C6
Fax: 416-299-4261
Toll-Free: 877-225-0446
www.giocanada.org
Overview: A medium-sized national organization founded in 2002
Mission: To provide dispute resolution services for consumers of home, automobile, & business insurance in Canada; To ensure that services are provided in a cost-free, confidential, impartial, knowledgeable, timely, & courteous manner
Member of: Financial Services OmbudsNetwork (FSON)
Chief Officer(s):
Brian Maltman, Executive Director
Publications:
• General Insurance OmbudService Annual Report
Type: Yearbook; Frequency: Annually

General Practice Psychotherapy Association (GPPA)
312 Oakwood Ct., Newmarket ON L3Y 3C8
Tel: 416-410-6644; Fax: 866-328-7974
info@gppaonline.ca
www.gppaonline.ca
Overview: A small national organization founded in 1984
Mission: To support & encourage quality psychotherapy by physicians in Canada; To promote professional development through ongoing education & collegial interaction
Finances: Funding Sources: Membership fees; educational fees, conference
Membership: Fees: $275 clinical, certificant or mentor member; $175 associate member; $80 inactive; $10 student; Member Profile: Doctors who practice psychotherapy, either full-time or part-time
Activities: Annual conference; workshops & seminars
Chief Officer(s):
Carol Ford, Manager

Générations Unies Ontario See United Generations Ontario

Genesis Research Foundation
92 College St., 3rd Fl., Toronto ON M5G 1L4
Tel: 416-978-2667
www.genesisresearch.org
www.linkedin.com/company/genesis-research-foundation
twitter.com/GenesisOrg
Overview: A small provincial charitable organization founded in 1983
Mission: To fund & promote research & understanding in women's health in the areas of obstetrics & gynaecology
Membership: Member Profile: Women
Activities: Speaker Service: Yes
Chief Officer(s):
Alan Bocking, MD, FRCSC, Chair

Geneva Centre for Autism (GCA)
112 Merton St., Toronto ON M4S 2Z8
Tel: 416-322-7877; Fax: 416-322-5894
Toll-Free: 866-436-3829
info@autism.net
www.autism.net
www.linkedin.com/company/geneva-centre-for-autism
www.facebook.com/genevacentre
twitter.com/geneva_centre
Overview: A medium-sized national charitable organization founded in 1974
Mission: To provide people with autism & other related disorders with opportunities & resources to fully participate in their communities
Member of: Autism Society of Canada; Autism Society of Ontario; Autism Society of America
Finances: Annual Operating Budget: $3 Million-$5 Million
Staff Member(s): 170; 50 volunteer(s)
Membership: 1,200; Fees: Level 1: $40 professionals, $25 parents & students; Level 2: $80 professionals, $50 parents & students; Member Profile: Parents & professionals
Activities: Services to families of children with autism; training events & workshops; international symposium on autism; Awareness Events: The Autists, a fundraising gala in support of children, youth & adults with autism.; Butterfly Classic Charity Golf Tournament; Trailblazers Track & Field Championships, a track & field competition for children & youth with autism;

Internships: Yes; Speaker Service: Yes; Library: Resource Library (for members); by appointment
Chief Officer(s):
Abe Evreniadis, Interim Chief Executive Officer
Susan Walsh, Chief Operations Officer
Wayne Edwards, Director, Human Resources
Ellie Rusonik, Director, Development

Genome Canada
#2100, 150 Metcalfe St., Ottawa ON K2P 1P1
Tel: 613-751-4460; Fax: 613-751-4474
info@genomecanada.ca
www.genomecanada.ca
www.linkedin.com/company/genome-canada
www.facebook.com/GenomeCanada
twitter.com/genomecanada
www.youtube.com/genomecanada
Overview: A medium-sized national organization
Mission: To develop & implement a national strategy in genomics & proteomics research for the benefit of all Canadians; to enable Canada to become a world leader in genomics & proteomics research in key selected areas as agriculture, environment, fisheries, forestry & health
Chief Officer(s):
Marc LePage, President & CEO
Cindy Bell, Executive Vice-President, Corporate Development
cbell@genomecanada.ca

Genome Alberta
#200, 3215 - 33 St. NW, Calgary AB T2L 2A6
Tel: 403-210-5275; Fax: 403-503-5225
info@genomealberta.ca
www.genomealberta.ca
Chief Officer(s):
David Bailey, President/CEO
dbailey@genomealberta.ca
Mike Spear, Director, Corporate Communications
mspear@genomealberta.ca

Genome Atlantic
#123, 1344 Summer St., Halifax NS B3H 0A8
Tel: 902-421-5683; Fax: 902-421-2733
info@genomeatlantic.ca
www.genomeatlantic.ca
www.facebook.com/pages/Genome-Atlantic/113846955323882
twitter.com/GenomeAtlantic
Chief Officer(s):
Steven Armstrong, President/CEO
sarmstrong@genomeatlantic.ca
Sue Coueslan, Director, Communications & Government Relations
sue@genomeatlantic.ca

Genome British Columbia
#400, 575 West 8th Ave., Vancouver BC V5Z 0C4
Tel: 604-738-8072; Fax: 604-738-8597
info@genomebc.ca
www.genomebc.ca
www.linkedin.com/company/genome-british-columbia
www.facebook.com/genomebc
twitter.com/genomebc
www.youtube.com/user/genomicseducation
Chief Officer(s):
Alan E. Winter, President & CEO
Sally Greenwood, Vice-President, Communication & Education

Genome Prairie
Innovation Place, Atrium Bldg., #101, 111 Research Dr., Saskatoon SK S7N 3R2
Tel: 306-668-3570; Fax: 306-668-3580
info@genomeprairie.ca
www.genomeprairie.ca
Chief Officer(s):
David Gauthier, President/CEO
dgauthier@genomeprairie.ca

Génome Québec
#2660, 630, boul René-Lévesque ouest, Montréal QC H3B 1S6
Tél: 514-398-0668; Téléc: 514-398-0883
gqinfo@genomequebec.com
www.genomequebec.com
www.linkedin.com/company/genome-quebec?trk=NUS_CMPY_TWIT
www.facebook.com/GenomeQc
twitter.com/GenomeQuebec
www.youtube.com/channel/UCPN6xorJnmYU_SBUdkwoW6Q?feature=plcp

Chief Officer(s):
Marc LePage, Président-directeur général

Ontario Genomics Institute
MaRS Centre, West Tower, #490, 661 University Ave., Toronto ON M5G 1M1
Tel: 416-977-9582; Fax: 416-977-8342
info@ontariogenomics.ca
www.ontariogenomics.ca
Chief Officer(s):
Mark J. Poznansky, President/CEO
mpoznansky@OntarioGenomics.ca

Georgian Bay Association
ON
www.gbabaptist.org
Overview: A small local organization overseen by Canadian Baptists of Ontario and Quebec
Mission: To support their members in achieving their goals
Member of: Canadian Baptists of Ontario & Quebec
Membership: 15 churches; Member Profile: Baptist churches in Georgian Bay
Chief Officer(s):
Steve Barker, Moderator
office@hopecommunitysite.com

GEOIDE Network
Pavillon Louis-Jacques-Casault, Cité Universitaire, #2306, 1055, av du Séminaire, Québec QC G1V 0A6
Tel: 418-656-7758; Fax: 418-656-2611
info@geoide.ulaval.ca
www.geoide.ulaval.ca
Previous Name: Geomatics for Informed Decisions Network
Overview: A medium-sized national organization
Mission: To consolidate & strengthen the Canadian geomatics industry, while making optimum use of Canada's research & development resources
Member of: Networks of Centres of Excellence
Membership: 395 scholars; 1437 students; 174 affiliates; 95 governmental entities
Activities: Funding; Research; Training activities
Chief Officer(s):
Chantal Arguin, President
Nicholas Chrisman, Scientific Director
Nicholas.Chrisman@geoide.ulaval.ca

Geological Association of Canada (GAC) / Association géologique du Canada (AGC)
c/o Department of Earth Sciences, Memorial University of Newfoundland, #ER4063, Alexander Murray Bldg., St. John's NL A1B 3X5
Tel: 709-864-7660; Fax: 709-864-2532
gac@mun.ca
www.gac.ca
Overview: A large national organization founded in 1947
Mission: To advance the wise use of geoscience in academic, professional, & public circles
Member of: Canadian Federation of Earth Sciences
Affiliation(s): American Geophysical Union; Atlantic Geoscience Society; Canadian Geophysical Union; Canadian Quaternary Association; Canadian Society of Petroleum Geologists; Toronto Geological Discussion Group
Finances: Funding Sources: Membership fees; Publication sales
Membership: 1,000-4,999; Fees: $15 students & teachers; $25 spousal; $55 seniors & unemployed; $110 full members;
Committees: Science Program; Finance; Publications; Communications
Activities: Providing professional development opportunities for members; Disseminating information about geoscience; Offering networking opportunities; Internships: Yes; Speaker Service: Yes
Chief Officer(s):
Victoria Yehl, President, 604-699-4342
victoria.yehl@teck.com
Graham Young, Vice-President
James Conliffe, PhD, Secretary-Treasurer, 709-729-4014
jamesconliffe@gov.nl.ca
Dène Tarkyth, Chair, Finance, 604-684-1454 Ext. 158
dene.tarkyth@angloamerican.com
Chris White, Chair, Publications, 902-424-2519
whitece@novascotia.ca
Awards:
• Logan Medal
To honour an individual for sustained distinguished achievement in Canadian earth science Contact: Stephen Johnston, E-mail: stj@uvic.ca

Canadian Associations / Geomatics Industry Association of Canada (GIAC) / Association canadienne des entreprises de géomatique

- W.W. Hutchison Medal
To recognize a young person for exceptional advances in Canadian earth science research *Contact:* Daniel Lebel, E-mail: Daniel.lebel@ec.gc.ca
- E.R. Ward Neale Medal
To honour an individual for sustained outstanding efforts in sharing earth science with Canadians *Contact:* Tim Corkery, E-mail: timothy.corkery@gov.mb.ca
- J. Willis Ambrose Medal
To recognize a person for dedicated service to the Canadian earth science community *Contact:* Stephen Rowins, E-mail: stephen.rowins@gov.bc.ca
- Yves O. Fortier Earth Science Journalism Award
To honour excellence in journalistic presentation of earth science in the newsprint media *Contact:* Eileen van der Flier-Keller, E-mail: fkeller@uvic.ca
- CJES Best Paper Award
Presented jointly by the Geological Association of Canada & the National Research Council Press for the best paper published in the Canadian Journal of Earth Sciences
- Distinguished Member Award
A service award of the Geological Association of Canada *Contact:* Carolyn Relf, Phone: 867-667-8892; E-mail: carolyn.relf@gov.yk.ca
- Distinguished Service Award
To recognize outstanding contributions to the Geological Association of Canada through volunteer work *Contact:* Tim Corkery, Phone: 204-945-6554; E-mail: timothy.corkery@gov.mb.ca
- Voluntary Service Award
Awarded to members or non-members for significant voluntary contributions to the Geological Association of Canada *Contact:* Tim Corkery, Phone: 204-945-6554; E-mail: timothy.corkery@gov.mb.ca
- Honorary Life Members
To honour individuals for long-term distinguished service to the Geological Association of Canada *Contact:* Tim Corkery, Phone: 204-945-6554; E-mail: timothy.corkery@gov.mb.ca
- Certificate of Appreciation
To recognize both members of the Geological Association of Canada & non-members for voluntary service to the association
- Mary-Claire Ward Geoscience Award
Awarded to a graduate student at a Canadian university whose thesis incorporates geoscience mapping *Contact:* Lisa McDonald, E-mail: lmcdonald@pdac.ca
- Jerome H. Remick Poster Awards
Awards & certificates of merit given to outstanding poster presenters at each Geological Association of Canada Annual Meeting

Meetings/Conferences:
- Geological Association of Canada 2018 Annual Meeting, June, 2018, Vancouver, BC
Scope: National
- Geological Association of Canada 2019 Annual Meeting, 2019, Québec, QC
Scope: National
- Geological Association of Canada 2020 Annual Meeting, 2020, Calgary, AB
Scope: National

Publications:
- Geolog
Type: Magazine; *Frequency:* Quarterly; *Accepts Advertising*; *Price:* Free with membership in the Geological Association of Canada
Profile: News items & short articles of interest to Geological Association of Canada members
- Geological Association of Canada Membership Directory
Type: Directory
- Geoscience Canada
Type: Journal; *Frequency:* Quarterly; *Accepts Advertising*; *Editor:* R.A. Wilson (reg.wilson@gnb.ca); *Price:* Free with membership in the GeologicalAssociation of Canada
Profile: A general interest, earth-science journal featuring review papers, topical articles, conference reports, book reviews, & commentary

Edmonton Section (EGS)
c/o Matt Grobe, Alberta Geological Survey, 4999 - 98 Ave., 4th Fl., Edmonton AB T6B 2X3
Tel: 780-427-2843
www.egs.ab.ca
Mission: To facilitate communication between earth scientists in Edmonton, Alberta & the surrounding area; To promote the science of geology
Chief Officer(s):
Marilyn Huff, President
huff@ualberta.ca
Rob L'Heureux, Treasurer
Matt Grobe, Manager, Publications, 780-427-2843
matt.grobe@ercb.ca
- Edmonton Beneath Our Feet: A Guide to the Geology of the Edmonton Area
Type: Book; *Price:* $12.95
Profile: A guide, containing walking routes
- EGS Notices
Type: Newsletter; *Price:* Free with membership in the Edmonton Geological Society
Profile: Information about field trips & other events of the Edmonton section of the Geological Association of Canada
- Report on the Great Landslide at Frank, Alta., 1903
Type: Book; *Price:* $9.95
- The Valley Beneath Our Feet: An Earth Science Walk Across Edmonton's River
Price: $6.95
Profile: A guide to the North Saskatchewan River Valley

Newfoundland & Labrador Section
c/o Heather Rafuse, Department of Natural Resources, Geological Survey, PO Box 8700, St. John's NL A1B 4J6
gac.esd.mun.ca/nl/nfsection.htm
Chief Officer(s):
Sam Bentley, President
sbentley@mun.ca
Joe McQuaker, Vice-President
jmacquaker@mun.ca
Larry Hicks, Secretary-Treasurer
larryhicks@gov.nl.ca
Andrew Kerr, Chair, Technical Program
andykerr@gov.nl.ca
- Field Trip
Type: Guide
Profile: Guides from the section's annual field trips
- Travellers Guide to the Geology of Newfoundland & Labrador
Type: Guidebook
Profile: Including a list of geological localities & a highway geology map

Québec Section (AQUEST)
QC
gac.esd.mun.ca/AQUEST/index_anglais.htm
Mission: To promote geoscience throughout Québec
Chief Officer(s):
Robert Marquis, Contact, Membership
robert.marquis@mrnf.gouv.qc.ca
- AQUEST Newsletter
Type: Newsletter
Profile: Information about current activities for members of the Québec section of the Geological Association of Canada

Vancouver (Cordilleran) Section
Bentall Centre, PO Box 398, Stn. A, Vancouver BC V6C 2N2
webmaster@gac-cs.ca
www.gac-cs.ca
Chief Officer(s):
Thomas Bissig, President
Peter Friz, Treasurer
- Garibaldi Geology
Type: Guide; *Number of Pages:* 48; *Author:* W.H Matthews; *Price:* $4.95 members; $9 non-members
Profile: The geology of the Garibaldi Lake region
- Geological Association of Canada, Cordilleran Section Newsletter
Type: Newsletter; *Editor:* Stuart Sutherland
Profile: Articles & announcements of interest to members of the section
- Geological Field Trips in Southern British Columbia
Type: Guide
- Geology Tours of Vancouver's Buildings & Monuments
Type: Guide; *Number of Pages:* 143; *Author:* P. Mustard; Z.D. Hora; C. Hansen; *ISBN:* 10: 0-919216-85-4; *Price:* $11.22 members; $20.40 non-members
- Guidebook for Geological Field Trips in Southwestern British Columbia & Northern Washington
Type: Guide
Profile: A guidebook edited by G.J. Woodsworth, L.E. Jackson, J.L. Nelson, & B.C. Ward
- A Transect of the Southern Canadian Cordillera from Calgary to Vancouver
Type: Guide; *Number of Pages:* 165; *Author:* R.A. Price; J.W.H. Monger; *ISBN:* 10: 0-9687005-3-5; *Price:* $24.75 members; $45 non-members
Profile: A field trip

Winnipeg Section (WGS)
#360, 1395 Ellice Ave., Winnipeg MB R3G 3P2
Tel: 204-945-6561; *Fax:* 204-945-1406
wgs-gac@hotmail.com
www.umanitoba.ca/faculties/science/geological_sciences/gacwpg/
Mission: To promote geoscience in Winnipeg, Manitoba & the surrounding area
Chief Officer(s):
Scott Anderson, President
scott.anderson@gov.mb.ca

Geomatics for Informed Decisions Network *See* GEOIDE Network

Geomatics Industry Association of Canada (GIAC) / Association canadienne des entreprises de géomatique
1460 Merivale Rd., Ottawa ON K2E 1B1
Tel: 613-851-1256
Previous Name: Canadian Association of Aerial Surveyors
Overview: A medium-sized national organization founded in 1961
Mission: To strengthen business climate; to maintain cooperative relations with government; to promote expanded role for members in provision of geomatics products & services; to encourage adoption by governments of improved policies & practices for procurement of geomatics products & services; to promote member firms as source of high quality, professional services; to promote Canadian geomatics industry abroad.
Member of: Alliance of Manufacturers & Exporters Canada
Finances: *Funding Sources:* Membership fees

Géomètres professionnels du Canada *See* Professional Surveyors Canada

George Bray Sports Association (GBSA)
9606 Tower Rd., RR#3, St Thomas ON N5P 3S7
Tel: 519-633-9411
www.georgebraysports.ca
www.facebook.com/563729230361725
Overview: A small local organization founded in 1968
Mission: To organize hockey games for children with learning disabilities
Chief Officer(s):
Murray Howard, President
murrayhoward@execulink.com

George Cedric Metcalf Charitable Foundation
38 Madison Ave., Toronto ON M5R 2S1
Tel: 416-926-0366; *Fax:* 416-926-0370
info@metcalffoundation.com
www.metcalffoundation.com
twitter.com/metcalf_ca
Also Known As: Metcalf Foundation
Overview: A small local organization founded in 1967
Staff Member(s): 9
Chief Officer(s):
Sandy Houston, President
shouston@metcalffoundation.com

George Grant Society
1073 Bank St., Ottawa ON K1S 3W9
Tel: 613-600-3405
grantstudies@gmail.com
www.georgegrantsociety.org
Overview: A small national organization founded in 2015
Mission: To promote progressive-conservative & nationalist ideas in Canada; To facilitate commentary & debate about public institutions, foreign policy, Canadian sovereignty, & other values that were defended by philosopher George Grant in his lifetime
Activities: Publishing content in print & online; Organizing cultural events, readings, & symposia
Chief Officer(s):
Daniel Velarde, Founding Editor

George Morris Centre
#107, 100 Stone Rd. West, Guelph ON N1G 5L3
Tel: 519-822-3929; *Fax:* 855-482-3245
info@georgemorris.org
www.georgemorris.org
www.linkedin.com/company/george-morris-centre
www.facebook.com/georgemorriscentre
twitter.com/GMCagrifood
Overview: A small provincial charitable organization founded in 1990

Mission: To provoke quality dialogue on relevant policies & issues & to encourage innovations that enhance insight & excellence in the agriculture & food sector
Finances: *Funding Sources:* Membership fees, sales of goods & services
Staff Member(s): 5
Membership: *Fees:* $250 individual; $1,000 association; $2,500 corporate
Activities: Canadian AgriFood Executive Development Program; Introduction to Commodity Risk Management Using Futures & Options; Designing Hedging Strategies Using Technical Analysis, Futures & Options; Workshop on Strategic Alliances; Canadian Total Excellence in Agricultural Management; *Library:* Not open to public
Chief Officer(s):
Bob Funk, Chair
Bob Funk, Chair
Frank Ingratta, Vice-Chair
Bob Hunsberger, Sec.-Treas.
John F.T. Scott, Managing Director, 519-822-3929 Ext. 205
Publications:
• Agri-food for Thought
Type: Newsletter; *Frequency:* Quarterly

George Street Association
PO Box 7301, Stn. C, #103, 127B Queen's Rd., St. John's NL A1E 3Y5
info@georgestreetlive.ca
www.georgestreetlive.ca
www.facebook.com/GeorgeStLive
twitter.com/GeorgeStLive
www.instagram.com/GeorgeStLive
Overview: A small local organization
Mission: To represent the interests of the pubs, clubs, bars, & shops on George Street in St. John's
Activities: Organizing annual events, including Mardi Gras & the George Street Festival
Chief Officer(s):
Jonathan Galgay, Executive Director

Georgeville Historical Society / Société d'histoire de Georgeville
4600, rue Georgeville, Georgeville QC J0B 1T0
Tel: 819-562-8036
Overview: A small local organization founded in 1992
Mission: Documents the history of the village of Georgeville, Québec.
Chief Officer(s):
Steve Moore, Contact
Publications:
• The Georgevill Enterprise
Type: Newsletter; *Frequency:* Semiannually; *Price:* Free for members

Georgian Bay Country Tourism Association (GBC)
Parry Sound ON
Overview: A small local organization
Mission: To increase tourism in the Georgian Bay area
Affiliation(s): Tourism Industry Association of Ontario; Ontario Accommodation Association; Attractions Ontario

Georgian Bay Folk Society (GBFS)
PO Box 521, Owen Sound ON N4K 5R1
Tel: 519-371-2995; *Fax:* 519-371-2973
gbfs@bmts.com
summerfolk.org
twitter.com/GeorgianBayFolk
ww.flickr.com/photos/gbfs
Overview: A small local charitable organization founded in 1978
Member of: Ontario Council of Folk Festivals; North American Folk Alliance
Finances: *Funding Sources:* Corporate & private donations; fundraising concerts; government grants
Staff Member(s): 2
Membership: *Fees:* $15 folkie; $25 student; $40 individual; $70 family; $500 lifetime
Activities: Winterfolk year round concert series; *Awareness Events:* Summerfolk Music & Craft Festival, August
Chief Officer(s):
James Keelaghan, Artistic Director
artisticdirector@summerfolk.org

Georgian Bay Native Friendship Centre (GBNFC)
175 Yonge St., Midland ON L4R 2A7
Tel: 705-526-5589; *Fax:* 705-526-7662
gbnfc@gbnfc.com
www.gbnfc.com

Overview: A small local charitable organization founded in 1984
Mission: To provide youth activities & programs, to create opportunities for them to have a voice & participate in the community.
Member of: Ontario Federation of Indian Friendship Centres
Staff Member(s): 16
Activities: L'il Beavers; youth social/recreation program; arts & crafts; drug & alcohol intervention programming; child & family services; life long care; native language program; tenant counsellor; employment & training; healing & wellness; desktop publishing services; *Internships:* Yes; *Speaker Service:* Yes
Chief Officer(s):
Compton Khan, Executive Director
edirector@gbnfc.com

Georgian Bay Steam & Antique Association
c/o Eileen Stephens, 1 Peartree Ct., Barrie ON L4N 2N7
Tel: 705-252-3235
info@steamshow.ca
www.steamshow.ca
Also Known As: Georgian Bay Steam Show
Previous Name: Georgian Bay Steam Association
Overview: A small local organization
Finances: *Annual Operating Budget:* Less than $50,000
500 volunteer(s)
Membership: 500
Activities: Heritage & farm-related displays of antiques
Chief Officer(s):
Gary Frampton, President

Georgian Bay Steam Association *See* Georgian Bay Steam & Antique Association

Georgian Bay Symphony (GBS)
PO Box 133, 994 3rd Ave. East, Owen Sound ON N4K 5P1
Tel: 519-372-0212; *Fax:* 519-372-9023
gbs@bmts.com
www.georgianbaysymphony.ca
www.facebook.com/GeorgianBaySymphony
twitter.com/GeorgianBaySymp
Overview: A small local charitable organization founded in 1972 overseen by Orchestras Canada
Mission: To enhance appreciation of music which includes growth & development of regional orchestra
Member of: Orchestras Canada
Affiliation(s): Owen Sound Chamber of Commerce
Finances: *Funding Sources:* Ticket sales; Donations; Private & corporate sponsorship; Fundraising; endowment fund; OAC grant
Membership: *Member Profile:* Subscribers & musicians in the orchestra
Chief Officer(s):
François Koh, Music Director

The Georgian Triangle Tourist Association & Tourist Information Centre
45 St. Paul St., Collingwood ON L9Y 3P1
Tel: 705-445-7722; *Fax:* 705-444-6158
Toll-Free: 888-227-8667
info@georgiantriangle.com
www.georgiantriangle.com
www.facebook.com/114000537662
twitter.com/SGeorgianBay
Overview: A small local organization founded in 1979
Mission: To promote tourism & convention industries in the Georgian Triangle
Member of: Tourism Industry Association of Canada
Staff Member(s): 4
Membership: *Fees:* Schedule available dependant on business type & size; *Member Profile:* Tourism or tourism-related businesses, municipalities, counties
Activities: *Internships:* Yes

Georgina Association for Business *See* South Lake Community Futures Development Corporation

Georgina Association for Community Living
PO Box 68, 26943 Hwy. 48, Sutton West ON L0E 1R0
Tel: 905-722-8947; *Fax:* 905-722-9591
admin@communitylivinggeorgina.com
communitylivinggeorgina.com
Overview: A small local organization
Mission: To provide services & support to people with developmental disabilities
Member of: Community Living Ontario
Staff Member(s): 6

Membership: *Fees:* $10 single; $15 family; $50 group/business; *Committees:* Administration; Finance & Property; Public Relations & Fundraising
Chief Officer(s):
Susan Rome, Executive Director
srome@communitylivinggeorgina.com
Ross Diamond, Officer, Finance
finance@communitylivinggeorgina.com
Robin Hannah, Manager, Program
rhannah@communitylivinggeorgina.com
Publications:
• Communicator [a publication of Georgina Association for Community Living]
Type: Newsletter; *Frequency:* Quarterly; *Accepts Advertising*

Georgina Chamber of Commerce
430 The Queensway South, Keswick ON L4P 2E1
Tel: 905-476-7870; *Fax:* 905-476-6700
Toll-Free: 888-436-7446
admin@georginachamber.com
www.georginachamber.com
Overview: A small local organization founded in 1990
Mission: To focus on the current & future success of its members
Member of: Ontario Chamber of Commerce
Finances: *Funding Sources:* Membership fees; golf tournament; trade show
Membership: *Member Profile:* Entrepreneur, voice of business in Georgina
Activities: *Rents Mailing List:* Yes
Chief Officer(s):
Robin Smith, Chair

Georgina Family Life Centre *See* Family Services York Region (Georgina)

Geotechnical Society of Edmonton (GSE)
c/o Danadeo Innovation Center for Engineering, 9211 - 116 St. NW, 7th Fl., Edmonton AB T6G 1H9
gse@geotechnical.ca
www.geotechnical.ca
Overview: A small local organization founded in 1969
Membership: 190; *Fees:* $15
Activities: Student presentations; lecture series & talks; professional development events; Reinforced Soil Wall Competition
Chief Officer(s):
Kim Askew, President
Awards:
• Morgenstern Student Award

Gerald Hardy Memorial Society
PO Box 131, 22657 Hwy. 7, Sheet Harbour NS B0J 2K0
Tel: 902-885-2300; *Fax:* 902-885-2054
ghms@ns.sympatico.ca
geraldhardymemorialsociety.webs.com
Overview: A small local organization
Mission: To provide intellectually disabled adults with job skills & work experience
Member of: DIRECTIONS Council for Vocational Services Society
Activities: Operates a thrift store & the Rainbow Food Bank

Geraldton & District Chamber of Commerce *See* Geraldton Chamber of Commerce

Geraldton Chamber of Commerce
PO Box 128, Geraldton ON P0T 1M0
Tel: 807-854-0895
chamber@geraldtonchamber.com
www.geraldtonchamber.com
www.facebook.com/320247071347640
Previous Name: Geraldton & District Chamber of Commerce
Overview: A small local organization
Member of: Northwestern Ontario Associated Chambers of Commerce
Membership: 1-99

German Canadian Association of Nova Scotia
c/o Cox & Palmer, PO Box 2380, #1100, 1959 Upper Water St., Halifax NS B3J 3E5
Tel: 902-401-6409
info@germancanadianassociation.ca
www.germancanadianassociation.ca
www.facebook.com/gcanovascotia
twitter.com/gca_ns
Overview: A small provincial organization founded in 1972

Mission: To preserve the cultural heritage of German speaking immigrants & descendants in Nova Scotia; To promote the understanding & appreciation of the German language & culture in Nova Scotia
Finances: *Funding Sources:* Membership fees; Sponsorships
Activities: Providing cultural & educational activities; Supporting the teaching of the German language; Facilitating networking opportunities among German speaking persons; *Awareness Events:* Halifax Oktoberfest; Family Sommerfest
Chief Officer(s):
Jessica Wyss, President
Stefan Eisebraun, Treasurer

German Canadian Business Association
PO Box 91462, West Vancouver BC V7V 3P2
Tel: 604-925-2664
rebecca@germancanadianbusinessassociation.com
www.germancanadianbusinessassociation.com
Previous Name: German-Canadian Business Association of British Columbia
Overview: A small provincial organization founded in 1963
Mission: To actively promote & foster professional & social relationships; to contribute to the enhancement of our European heritage
Finances: *Funding Sources:* Membership fees
7 volunteer(s)
Membership: 70; *Fees:* $385; *Member Profile:* German speaking business in Canada
Activities: Monthly dinner meetings
Chief Officer(s):
Rebecca Lees, Secretary, 604-925-2664
rebecca@germancanadianbusinessassociation.com

German Canadian Cultural Association
German Canadian Cultural Centre, 8310 Roper Rd., Edmonton AB T6E 6E3
Tel: 780-466-4000; *Fax:* 780-440-6963
gcca@shaw.ca
www.gcca.ca
Overview: A small local organization founded in 1983
Member of: German-Canadian Association of Alberta
Finances: *Annual Operating Budget:* $500,000-$1.5 Million
Staff Member(s): 25; 11 volunteer(s)
Membership: 750; *Fees:* $40 individual; $80 family; *Member Profile:* To preserve & promote the heritage & culture of all persons of German language origin
Activities: *Library:* Open to public

German Canadian Cultural Association of Manitoba Inc.
#15, 1110 Henderson Hwy., Winnipeg MB R2G 1L1
Tel: 204-334-8491
Overview: A small provincial organization founded in 1983
Membership: *Member Profile:* Interest in German language & culture
Activities: *Library:* by appointment

German Society of Winnipeg
121 Charles St., Winnipeg MB R2W 4A6
Tel: 204-589-7724; *Fax:* 204-589-2137
gswmb@shaw.ca
gswmb.ca
Overview: A small local organization founded in 1892
Membership: *Fees:* $75 regular; $55 seniors; *Member Profile:* German Canadians living in Manitoba
Activities: *Library:*

German-Canadian Association of Alberta (GCAA)
8310 Roper Rd., Edmonton AB T6E 6E3
Tel: 780-465-7466
mail@gcaa.ca
www.gcaa.ca
Overview: A medium-sized provincial organization founded in 1967
Mission: To promote German culture in Alberta
Finances: *Funding Sources:* Membership fees
15 volunteer(s)
Chief Officer(s):
Annemarie Juravel, President
juravel.fam@shaw.ca

German-Canadian Business & Professional Association of Kitchener-Waterloo
332 Charles St. East, Kitchener ON N2G 2P9
Tel: 519-744-3586; *Fax:* 519-744-3587
info@german-canadian-business.ca
german-canadian-business.com
www.facebook.com/GermanCanadianBPA
twitter.com/GermanCdnBusPro
Overview: A small local organization
Mission: To represent business owners & other professionals of German-Canadian heritage in the K-W area
Membership: *Member Profile:* Business owner/operators, entrepreneurs, professionals, & academics with basic German language knowledge & fluency; prospective members must be sponsored by current members
Activities: Bitzer Award & German-Canadian Education Fund; *Awareness Events:* German Pioneers Day, October; Christkindl Market; Christmas Celebration

German-Canadian Business Association of British Columbia *See* German Canadian Business Association

German-Canadian Congress (Manitoba) Inc.
#58, 81 Garry St., Winnipeg MB R3C 4J9
Tel: 204-989-8300; *Fax:* 204-989-8304
info@gccmb.ca
www.gccmb.ca
www.facebook.com/German.Canadian.Congress
Also Known As: Deutschkanadischer Kongress
Overview: A large provincial organization founded in 1985
Mission: To cultivate & promote language, culture, customs & traditions of German Canadians within the scope of Canadian multiculturalism
Finances: *Annual Operating Budget:* Less than $50,000
Staff Member(s): 2; 10 volunteer(s)
Membership: 170; *Fees:* $35 individual; $50 family; $15 student; $30 senior; $125 corporate; *Committees:* Media; German-Canadian Studies Foundation; Seniors
Activities: Disseminating information about German-Canadian activity & history; Establishing charity fund to benefit multiculturalism & German language education in Canada; *Library:* Office Library; Open to public
Chief Officer(s):
Carola Lange, President
Victoria Prodivus, Secretary
Meetings/Conferences:
• German-Canadian Congress (Manitoba) Inc. Annual General Meeting 2018, 2018, MB
Scope: Provincial
Publications:
• Infoblatt [a publication of the German-Canadian Congress (Manitoba) Inc.]
Type: Newsletter; *Frequency:* Quarterly

German-Canadian Congress (Ontario) (GCC)
41B River Rd. East, Kitchener ON N2B 2G3
Tel: 519-571-8980
Other Communication: Alt. URL: www.dkkont.org
dkkont@gmail.com
www.dkkont.net
Overview: A small provincial organization founded in 1984
Mission: To cultivate & promote the language, culture & customs of German speaking Canadians
Staff Member(s): 1
Membership: 1,400; 44 clubs; *Fees:* $30 single; $40 family; $20 senior; $15 student; $100 companies/clubs
Chief Officer(s):
Gerhard Griebenow, President

German-Canadian Historical Association Inc. (GCHA)
Department of Modern Languages, University of Prince Edward Island, Charlottetown PE C1A 4P3
Fax: 902-566-0359
german-canadian.ca
Overview: A small provincial organization founded in 1973
Mission: To collect, promote & disseminate information regarding the development & contributions of the German-speaking groups in Canada.
Membership: *Fees:* $14 student/pensioners; $28 individual; $42 sustaining; $400 life
Chief Officer(s):
Lothar Zimmermann, Contact
zimmmermann@upei.ca
Publications:
• Canadiana Germanica
Type: Journal; *Frequency:* Quarterly; *Number of Pages:* 45
Profile: Presents original articles, reprints of relevant material & announcements concerning new publications & upcoming meetings

German-Canadian Mardi Gras Association Inc. (BDKK) / Bund Deutscher Karnevalsgesellschaften Kanada
119 Glendonwynne Rd., Toronto ON M6P 3E7
Overview: A small local organization founded in 1963
Membership: 19 institutional; 1,200 individual
Activities: *Rents Mailing List:* Yes
Chief Officer(s):
Herbert H. Wittig, Contact

Gerontological Nursing Association of British Columbia (GNABC)
c/o 328 Nootka St., New Westminster BC V3L 4X4
Tel: 604-484-5698; *Fax:* 604-874-4378
gnabc@shaw.ca
gnabc.com
Overview: A medium-sized provincial organization founded in 1981 overseen by Canadian Gerontological Nursing Association
Mission: To promote a high standard of nursing care & related health services for older adults; To enhance professionalism in the practice of gerontological nursing
Membership: *Fees:* $32.50 student; $45 RPN/LPN (affiliate); $65 RN; *Member Profile:* Registered Nurses, Registered Psychiatric Nurses, & Licensed Practical Nurses within the province of BC; *Committees:* Membership & Local Group Development; Education; Media
Activities: Offering professional networking opportunities; Providing professional development; Advocating for comprehensive services for older adults; Supporting research related to gerontological nursing; Promoting gerontological nursing to the public
Chief Officer(s):
Kim Martin, President
k_martin@shaw.ca
Meetings/Conferences:
• Gerontological Nurses Association of British Columbia 2018 Conference & AGM, April, 2018, Coast Bastion Hotel, Nanaimo, BC
Scope: Provincial
Description: Theme: "What Really Matters"

Gerontological Nursing Association of Ontario (GNAO)
PO Box 368, Stn. K, Toronto ON M4P 2E0
info@gnaontario.org
www.gnaontario.org
www.facebook.com/811284002323318
twitter.com/GNAOntario
Overview: A medium-sized provincial charitable organization founded in 1974 overseen by Canadian Gerontological Nursing Association
Mission: To promote a high standard of nursing care & related health services for older adults; To enhance professionalism in the practice of gerontological nursing
Affiliation(s): Registered Nurses Association of Ontario
Membership: 1,200+; *Fees:* $65 regular; $30 associate; $30 student/retired; *Member Profile:* Registered Nurses; Registered Practical Nurses; Full time students enrolled in a nursing program; Associate members interested in the GNA
Activities: Offering professional networking opportunities; Providing professional development; Advocating for comprehensive services for older adults; Supporting research related to gerontological nursing; Promoting gerontological nursing to the public
Chief Officer(s):
Julie Rubel, President
julie.rubel@gmail.com
Gwen Harris, Treasurer
gcharris@ebtech.net
Awards:
• Education & Research Funding Grant
For educational or research initiatives related to gerontological nursing practice
Meetings/Conferences:
• Gerontological Nursing Association of Ontario Conference & AGM 2018, April, 2018, Embassy Suites, Niagara Falls, ON
Scope: Provincial
Description: Theme: "It Takes a Village"

The Gershon Iskowitz Foundation
19 Whiterock Dr., Toronto ON M1C 3N3
Tel: 416-530-4133
Overview: A small local organization
Mission: To provide grants in order to promote the development of artists in Canada
Chief Officer(s):

Nancy Hushion, Executive Director
nlh@hushion.ca
Awards:
• Gershon Iskowitz Prize
$25,000 to recognize achievements in visual art

Gethsemane Ministries
84008 Wellandport Rd., Wellandport ON L0R 2J0
Tel: 905-368-1111; *Fax:* 647-560-4557
info@gethsemaneministries.com
www.gethsemaneministries.com
www.facebook.com/GethsemaneMinistriesCanada
twitter.com/GethYouthMin
www.instagram.com/gethsemaneministries
Overview: A small local charitable organization founded in 1997
Mission: To preach the Word of God & advance the teachings, religious tenets & observances associated with the Catholic Faith
Finances: *Funding Sources:* Donations
Membership: *Fees:* Free
Activities: Counselling; Providing faith instruction & spiritual guidance; Participating in sacramental life; Offering prayer groups, with Rosary, praise & worship, intercession & fellowship; Assisting the ill, elderly & needy; Helping youth in their Catholic faith formation, including catechism classes for grades 1-8; Providing youth programs, retreats & summer camps; Offering retreats for married couples, mainly conducted by preachers; Supporting other parish & diocesan activities; Offering adult & youth music ministry
Chief Officer(s):
Stan Rodrigo, Contact
stan.rodrigo@gmail.com
Publications:
• The Gethsemane Newsletter
Type: Newsletter; *Editor:* Agnello Desa
Profile: Articles, testimonies, & forthcoming activities

GI (Gastrointestinal) Society
#231, 3665 Kingsway, Vancouver BC V5R 5W2
Tel: 604-873-4876; *Fax:* 604-875-4429
Toll-Free: 866-600-4875
www.badgut.org
www.facebook.com/CISociety
twitter.com/GISociety
www.youtube.com/user/badgutcanada
Overview: A medium-sized national organization
Mission: To improve the lives of people with GI and liver conditions, support research, advocate for appropriate patient access to healthcare & promote gastrointestinal & liver health
Finances: *Funding Sources:* Subscription fees; donations; fundraising events
Staff Member(s): 6
Activities: Support Groups; Lectures; Information on: Constipation, Celiac Disease, Crohn's Disease, Diverticular Disease, GERD, Hemorrhoids, Hiatus Hernia, Inflammatory Bowel Disease, Intestinal Gas, IBS, Functional Dyspepsia, Liver conditions, Pancreatitis, Stress Management, Ulcer Disease, Ulcerative Colitis, Ulcerative Proctitis; *Awareness Events:* IBS Awareness Month, April; Crohn's disease Awareness Month, November; Celiac disease awareness month, May
Chief Officer(s):
Lynda Cranston, Chairperson
Gail Attara, Co-Founder & President/CEO

Gibsons & District Chamber of Commerce
PO Box 1190, #20, 900 Gibsons Way, Gibsons BC V0N 1V0
Tel: 604-886-2325; *Fax:* 604-886-2379
staff@gibsonschamber.com
www.gibsonschamber.com
Overview: A small local organization founded in 1947
Mission: To support & promote local businesses; To address the issues impacting members & businesses in the community
Member of: BC Chamber of Commerce
Staff Member(s): 2
Membership: *Fees:* $99-$250; *Committees:* Communications; Economic Development; Member Recognition; Membership; Professional Development; Visitor Services
Chief Officer(s):
William Baker, President & Treasurer
Chris Nicholls, Executive Director

Gideons International in Canada / Les Gédéons - L'Association Internationale des Gédéons au Canada
PO Box 3619, 501 Imperial Rd. North, Guelph ON N1H 7A2
Tel: 519-823-1140; *Fax:* 519-767-1913
Toll-Free: 888-482-4253
info@gideons.ca
www.gideons.ca
www.linkedin.com/company/the-gideons-international-in-canada
www.facebook.com/gideonscanada
twitter.com/GideonsCanada
www.youtube.com/user/GideonsCanadaMedia
Overview: A medium-sized international charitable organization founded in 1911
Mission: The interdenominational lay association communicates/gives away freecopies of God's Word in Canada & around the world.
Finances: *Annual Operating Budget:* Greater than $5 Million; *Funding Sources:* Membership fees; voluntary donations; funds from other registered charities
Membership: 4,500; *Fees:* $100; *Member Profile:* Christian business & professional people
Activities: Sharing faith; Placing Bibles & New Testaments to the public; Distributing New Testaments to selected groups
Chief Officer(s):
Paul Mercer, Executive Director
Publications:
• The Canadian Gideon: The Official Publication of The Gideons International in Canada
Type: Magazine; *Editor:* Neil Bramble; *Price:* $15
Profile: Information & resources for Gideon & Auxiliary members
• Gideon News
Type: Newsletter

Gillam Chamber of Commerce
c/o Town of Gillam, PO Box 100, 323 Railway Ave., Gillam MB R0B 0L0
Tel: 204-652-3150; *Fax:* 204-652-3199
www.townofgillam.com
Overview: A small local organization
Mission: To support businesses in the community
Member of: The Manitoba Chambers of Commerce
Membership: *Fees:* $25
Chief Officer(s):
Alex Muzyczka, President

Gina Lori Riley Dance Enterprises
Jackman Dramatic Art Centre, #210, 401 Sunset Ave., Windsor ON N9B 3P4
Tel: 519-253-3000
www.ginaloririleydanceenterprises.com
Overview: A small local organization founded in 1979
Mission: To advance art through the development of new work, the presentation of contemporary dance, & the presentation & promotion of community education
Finances: *Funding Sources:* Private & public; box office; fundraising
Chief Officer(s):
Gina Lori Riley, Artistic Director
riley2@uwindsor.ca

Gioventù Studentesca (Student Youth) *See* Communion & Liberation Canada

Girl Guides of Canada (GGC) / Guides du Canada
50 Merton St., Toronto ON M4S 1A3
Tel: 416-487-5281; *Fax:* 416-487-5570
Toll-Free: 800-565-8111
Other Communication: www.flickr.com/photos/girlguidesofcan
www.girlguides.ca
www.facebook.com/GirlGuidesofCanada.GuidesduCanada
twitter.com/girlguidesofcan
www.youtube.com/user/ggcanada
Overview: A large national charitable organization founded in 1910
Mission: To prepare girls to meet the challenges of life, in a safe environment, by teaching them such skills as bandaging wounds & coping with bullies; To encourage girls to foster friendships & develop a sense of leadership
Member of: World Association of Girl Guides & Girl Scouts
Affiliation(s): World Association of Girl Guides & Girl Scouts
Finances: *Annual Operating Budget:* $3 Million-$5 Million
Staff Member(s): 50; 18,0 volunteer(s)
Membership: 70,000+ individual; *Committees:* Finance; Provincial; National Audit; Program Stewardship
Activities: Programs for: Sparks, Brownies; Guides; Pathfinders; Rangers; Women 18+; *Awareness Events:* Annual Cookie Campaign, Oct. to June *Library:* Resource Centre; Open to public by appointment
Chief Officer(s):
Pamela Rice, Chair
Jill Zelmanovits, CEO

Publications:
• Canadian Guider [a publication of Girl Guides of Canada]
Type: Magazine; *Frequency:* 3 pa.; *ISSN:* 0300-435X
• Guiding Matters [a publication of Girl Guides of Canada]
Type: Newsletter

Alberta, Northwest Territories & Yukon Council
11055 - 107 St. NW, Edmonton AB T5H 2Z6
Tel: 780-424-5510; *Fax:* 780-426-1715
info@albertagirlguides.com
www.albertagirlguides.com
twitter.com/GGCAlberta
Chief Officer(s):
Margaret Utgoff, Provincial Commissioner

British Columbia Council
1476 West 8th Ave., Vancouver BC V6H 1E1
Tel: 604-714-6636; *Fax:* 604-714-6645
Toll-Free: 800-565-8111
info@bc-girlguides.org
www.bc-girlguides.org
Chief Officer(s):
Dawnette Humphrey, Provincial Commissioner

Manitoba Council
#213, 530 Century St., Winnipeg MB R3H 0Y4
Tel: 204-774-4475; *Fax:* 204-774-9271
Toll-Free: 800-565-8111
info@girlguides.mb.ca
www.girlguides.mb.ca
Chief Officer(s):
Elaine Cullingham, Executive Director
ecullingham@girlguides.mb.ca

New Brunswick & Prince Edward Island Council
55 Rothesay Ave., Saint John NB E2J 2B2
Tel: 506-634-0808; *Fax:* 506-634-0908
Toll-Free: 800-565-8111
ggcnbc@nb.aibn.com
www.girlguides.nb.ca
www.facebook.com/NBPEI.GirlGuides
Chief Officer(s):
Brenda Malcolm, Provincial Commissioner
pc.ggcnbc@gmail.com

Newfoundland & Labrador Council
63 Roosevelt Ave., St. John's NL A1A 0E8
Tel: 709-726-1116; *Fax:* 709-726-4045
Toll-Free: 800-565-8111
provoffice@ggcnf.org
www.ggcnf.org
twitter.com/GGCNL
Chief Officer(s):
Kay Penney, Provincial Commissioner

Nova Scotia Council
3581 Dutch Village Rd., Halifax NS B3N 2S9
Tel: 902-423-3735; *Fax:* 902-423-5347
Toll-Free: 800-565-8111
ggcns@girlguides.ns.ca
www.girlguides.ns.ca
twitter.com/GGCNovaScotia
Chief Officer(s):
Holly Thompson, Provincial Commissioner
holly.thompson@girlguides.ns.ca

Ontario Council
14 Birch Ave., Toronto ON M4V 1C8
Tel: 416-926-2351; *Fax:* 416-920-1440
Toll-Free: 877-323-4545
executive.coord@guidesontario.org
www.guidesontario.org
Chief Officer(s):
Marcia Powers-Dunlop, Provincial Commissioner
provincial.commissioner@guidesontario.org

Québec Council
#270, 100, boul Alexis-Nihon, Montréal QC H4M 2N7
Tel: 514-933-5839; *Fax:* 514-933-7591
Toll-Free: 800-565-8111
info@guidesquebec.ca
www.guidesquebec.ca
twitter.com/guidesquebec
Chief Officer(s):
Pamela Rice, Provincial Commissioner
pc.cp@guidesquebec.ca

Saskatchewan Council
#200, 1530 Broadway Ave., Regina SK S4P 1E2
Tel: 306-757-4102; *Fax:* 205-347-0995
Toll-Free: 877-694-0383
provincial@girlguides.sk.ca
www.girlguides.sk.ca

Canadian Associations / Girls Action Foundation

Girls Action Foundation
#601, 24, av du Mont Royal ouest, Montréal QC H2T 2S2
Tel: 514-948-1112; *Fax:* 514-948-5926
Toll-Free: 888-948-1112
info@girlsactionfoundation.ca
www.girlsactionfoundation.ca
www.linkedin.com/company/1243793
www.facebook.com/girlsaction.fillesdaction
twitter.com/_GirlsAction
Overview: A medium-sized national organization founded in 1995
Mission: To create a platform that empowers girls & young women in Canada through the sharing of knowledge, resources, & initiatives
Staff Member(s): 6
Membership: 300; *Member Profile:* Organizations that support girls & women in Canada
Activities: Offering resources, training, & networking opportunities; Developing programs & community initiatives for girls
Chief Officer(s):
Rachel Zellars, Executive Director
rachel@girlsactionfoundation.ca
Publications:
• Girls Action Foundation Newsletter
Type: Newsletter

Gitxsan Treaty Office (GTO)
PO Box 229, Hazelton BC V0J 2N0
Fax: 250-842-6709
Toll-Free: 866-842-6780
www.gitxsan.com
www.facebook.com/GitxsanDevelopmentCorporation
Overview: A medium-sized local organization founded in 1975
Mission: To support the Gitxsan people in their treaty & other negotiations, & in their economic & social initiatives
Finances: *Funding Sources:* National & provincial government

Glace Bay Food Bank Society
PO Box 552, 2 Hector St., Glace Bay NS B1A 6G4
Tel: 902-849-0750
glacebayfoodbank@gmail.com
www.facebook.com/GlaceBayFoodBankSociety
Overview: A small local charitable organization
Member of: Nova Scotia Food Bank Association; Atlantic Alliance of Food Banks & C.V.A.'s
Chief Officer(s):
Sandra MacPherson, Coordinator

Glace Bay Literacy Council
c/o Citizen Service League, 150 Commercial St., Glace Bay NS B1A 3C1
Tel: 902-849-2449
Overview: A small local organization
Mission: To promote literacy in the Glace Bay area.
Chief Officer(s):
Leah Skanes, Contact

The Gladys & Merrill Muttart Foundation *See* The Muttart Foundation

Glanbrook Heritage Society
4280 Binbrook Rd., Binbrook ON L0R 1C0
Tel: 905-679-0245
glanbrookheritage@yahoo.ca
www.glanbrookheritage.ca
Previous Name: Glanford Heritage Society
Overview: A small local charitable organization founded in 1995 overseen by Ontario Historical Society
Mission: To collect, maintain & preserve the creation & history of the former Townships of Binbrook & Glanford, now amalgamated into the Township of Glanbrook.
Member of: Hamilton-Wentworth Heritage Association
Finances: *Funding Sources:* Donations; book sales
Membership: *Fees:* $15 family
Activities: *Speaker Service:* Yes; *Library:* Archives; Open to public
Chief Officer(s):
Ron Sinclair, President
Marianne Brown, Secretary

Glanford Heritage Society *See* Glanbrook Heritage Society

Glass & Architectural Metals Association (GAMA)
c/o Calgary Construction Association, 2725 - 12 St. NE, Calgary AB T2E 7J2
www.pgaa.ca/gama
Overview: A small local organization
Mission: To advance the glass & architectural metals industry
Membership: *Member Profile:* Glass contractors, suppliers, & educators from western Canada
Activities: Supporting the glass & architectural metals industry; Providing information about safety; Assisting the apprenticeship training program; Offering networking opportunities
Chief Officer(s):
Al Ryland, President
Becky McLaughlin, Treasurer & Contact, Membership
Meetings/Conferences:
• Glass & Architectural Metals Association 2018 General Meeting, January, 2018
Scope: Provincial
Description: The yearly business meeting of the association
Publications:
• Glass & Architectural Metals Association Member Directory
Type: Directory
Profile: Contact information for association members
• Glass & Architectural Metals Association Newsletter
Type: Newsletter; *Editor:* Jeff Vitale
Profile: Updates from the association of interest to persons interested in or engaged in the glass & architectural metals industry

Glass Art Association of Canada (GAAC) / Association du verre d'art du Canada (AVAC)
gaacanada@gmail.com
www.gaacanada.ca
www.facebook.com/GAACanada
www.instagram.com/GaaCanada
Overview: A large international organization
Mission: To connect a geographically diverse community of artists, craftspeople, educators, curators, collectors, gallerists & students passionate about glass
Membership: 400 worldwide; *Fees:* $35-$145
Activities: Directory of Glass Artists; project grants; workshops; conferences; e-zine; scholarships; exhibitions
Chief Officer(s):
Marcia DeVicque, Treasurer
Publications:
• Contemporary Canadian Glass [a publication of the Glass Art Association of Canada]
Type: Magazine

Glaucoma Research Society of Canada / Société canadienne de recherche sur le glaucome
#215E, 1929 Bayview Ave., Toronto ON M4G 3E8
Tel: 416-483-0200; *Fax:* 416-483-6673
Toll-Free: 877-483-0204
info@glaucomaresearch.ca
www.glaucomaresearch.ca
Overview: A small national charitable organization founded in 1988
Mission: The Glaucoma Research Society of Canada is a national registered charity committed to funding research into the causes, diagnosis, prevention and treatment of glaucoma.
Finances: *Funding Sources:* Donations
Membership: *Committees:* Scientific Advisory
Chief Officer(s):
James M. Park, President
Barbara Ullmann, Administrator

Gleaners Food Bank
PO Box 20029, 25 Wallbridge Cres., Belleville ON K8N 5V1
Tel: 613-962-9043; *Fax:* 613-962-8627
info@gleanersfoodbank.ca
www.gleanersfoodbank.ca
www.facebook.com/gleaners.belleville
twitter.com/GleanersFB
Overview: A small local charitable organization founded in 1986
Mission: To work together to improve the quality of life in Quinte & surrounding area
Member of: Ontario Association of Food Banks; Food Banks Canada; Tri-County Regional Food Network
Affiliation(s): Quinte Coalition for Social Justice; Quinte Region Food Share Shelter
Staff Member(s): 2; 30 volunteer(s)
Activities: Registered site for the Canada Wide Think Food & Phones for Food Recycling Program; School Breakfast & Snack programs; emergency hamper delivery; meal programs; child care; *Awareness Events:* Fall Food Drive, Oct.; Grocery Industry Food Drives, Spring, Fall & Christmas
Chief Officer(s):
Susanne Quinlan, Director, Operations

Glendon & District Business Alliance (GDBA)
c/o Bonnyville & District Chamber of Commerce, PO Box 6054, Hwy. 28 West, Bonnyville AB T9N 2G7
Tel: 780-826-3252
www.bonnyvillechamber.com
Overview: A small local organization overseen by Bonnyville & District Chamber of Commerce
Mission: To drive local economic development; To represent, support & promote businesses in the area
Member of: Bonnyville & District Chamber of Commerce
Chief Officer(s):
Julie Kissel, Chair

Glengarry Association for Community Living *See* Community Living Glengarry

Global Automakers of Canada (GAC) / Constructeurs mondiaux d'automobiles du Canada (CMAC)
PO Box 5, #1804, 2 Bloor St. West, Toronto ON M4W 3E2
Tel: 416-595-8251; *Fax:* 416-595-2864
auto@globalautomakers.ca
www.globalautomakers.ca
Previous Name: Association of International Automobile Manufacturers of Canada; Automobile Importers of Canada
Overview: A medium-sized national organization founded in 1979 overseen by The Canadian Association of Importers & Exporters
Mission: To represent before federal, provincial, & territorial governments the interests of members engaged in the manufacturing, importation, distribution, & servicing of light-duty vehicles
Finances: *Funding Sources:* Membership dues
Staff Member(s): 4; 100 volunteer(s)
Membership: 26; *Committees:* Executive; Consumer Relations; Custom; Finance & Taxation; Financial Services; Government Relations; Legal; Logistics; Parts; Show Exhibitors; Statistical; Technical
Activities: *Library:* Open to public
Chief Officer(s):
David C. Adams, President
Loulia Kouchaji, Analyst, Policy & Commercial Issues
Greg Overwater, Acting Director, Technical & Regulatory Affairs

Global Business Travel Association (Canada) (GBTA)
#301, 1235 Fairview St., Burlington ON L7S 2K9
Tel: 416-840-6128
info@gbta.org
www.gbta.org/canada
www.linkedin.com/groups/697547
www.facebook.com/GBTAonFB
twitter.com/GlobalBTA
www.youtube.com/gbtatv
Previous Name: National Business Travel Association (Canada)
Overview: A large international organization
Mission: To be the leading organization for corporate travel professionals in Canada
Membership: 5,000 worldwide; *Committees:* Leadership Advisory
Activities: Networking & professional development; advocacy; educational programs; *Library:* Resource Library
Chief Officer(s):
Nancy Tudorache, CTE, Director, Operations
ntudorache@gbta.org
Ann Corbitt, Manager, Registration & Pricing, 416-526-5859
acorbitt@gbta.org
Franca Helsdon, Manager, Event & Membership, 647-984-1646
fhelsdon@gbta.org
Meetings/Conferences:
• Global Business Travel Association Canada Conference 2018, April, 2018, Metro Toronto Convention Centre, Toronto, ON
Scope: National
Attendance: 550+
Description: Featuring exhibitors, education sessions & general session featured speakers
Contact Information: canadaconference.gbta.org

Global Commercial Insurers' Association (GCIA)
#1, 189 Queen St. East, Toronto ON M5A 1S2
Tel: 416-968-0183; *Fax:* 416-968-6818
admin@gciassociation.ca
www.gciassociation.ca
Overview: A medium-sized international organization
Mission: To assist foreign-owned commercial insurance companies operating in Canada

Membership: *Member Profile:* Commercial insurance firms with minimum gross premium income of $100 million CDN & 51% of gross written premium income from commercial business, & that are direct insurers & foreign-owned
Chief Officer(s):
Anthony Laycock, General Manager

Global Food Bank Association Inc. *See* The World Job & Food Bank Inc.

Global Network of Director Institutes (GNDI)
c/o Institute of Corporate Directors, #2701, 250 Yonge St., Toronto ON M5B 2L7
Tel: 416-593-7741; *Fax:* 416-593-0636
Toll-Free: 877-593-7741
www.gndi.org
Overview: A large international organization founded in 2012
Mission: To help members stay abreast of leading practices as well as current & emerging governance issues; to foster closer cooperation between members
Affiliation(s): Australian Institute of Company Directors; Brazilian Institute of Corporate Governance; ecoDa; GCC Board Directors Institute; Hong Kong Institute of Directors; Institute of Corporate Directors (Canada); Institute of Directors in New Zealand; Institute of Directors in Southern Africa; Institute of Directors (UK); Malaysian Alliance of Corporate Directors; Mauritius Institute of Directors; National Association of Corporate Directors (US); Singapore Institute of Directors; Swiss Institute of Directors; Thai Institute of Directors; Vereinigung der Aufsichtsräte in Deutschland e.V.
Membership: 19 organizations + 100,000+ members; *Member Profile:* Organizations globally recognized for board & director development activities
Chief Officer(s):
Al-Azhar Khalfan, Contact, Canada, 416-593-7741 Ext. 243
akhalfan@icd.ca

Global Outreach Mission
PO Box 1210, St. Catharines ON L2R 7A7
Tel: 905-684-1401; *Fax:* 905-684-3069
Toll-Free: 866-483-5787
glmiss@on.aibn.com
www.missiongo.org
www.facebook.com/168935979827368
twitter.com/GlobalOutreachM
www.youtube.com/user/missiongo
Previous Name: European Evangelistic Crusade, Inc.
Overview: A small international organization founded in 1943
Mission: To be solely concerned with the propagation of the Gospel of the grace of God as revealed in the Word of God
Affiliation(s): Interdenominational Foreign Mission Association
Activities: International aide ranginf from Christian counselors to hospitals; Radio ministries
Chief Officer(s):
Brian Albrecht, President
balbrecht@missiongo.org
Constable Greg, Vice President, Candidates/Personnel
gconstable@missiongo.org

Global Village Nanaimo (GVN)
204 - 6750 North Island Hwy., Nanaimo BC V9V 1S3
gvnanaimo@gmail.com
www.globalvillagenanaimo.com
www.facebook.com/GlobalVillageNanaimo
Also Known As: The Fair Trade Store
Overview: A small international organization founded in 1975
Mission: To sell fair trade goods in the Central Vancouver Island region
Member of: BC Council for International Cooperation
Finances: *Annual Operating Budget:* Less than $50,000
40 volunteer(s)
Membership: 150; *Fees:* $5; *Member Profile:* General public
Activities: Seasonal store (open Oct.-Dec.)
Chief Officer(s):
Joan Hiemstra, Manager, Operations

Global Youth Network *See* Global Youth Volunteer Network

Global Youth Volunteer Network (GYVN)
PO Box 1450, Blackfalds AB T0M 0J0
Toll-Free: 888-411-0230
info@gyvn.ca
www.gyvn.ca
www.facebook.com/GlobalYouthVolunteerNetwork
twitter.com/gyv_network
www.instagram.com/globalyouthnetwork
Previous Name: Global Youth Network

Overview: A small international organization
Mission: To educate & mobilize young people towards making positive change
Membership: *Fees:* $30; *Committees:* Global Sustainability; Global Education; Global Fundraising; Global Membership
Activities: Global Team program; volunteer engagement programs; summer leadership camps; community action; social justice; child sponsorship; malaria detection clinics
Chief Officer(s):
Dave Skene, Coordinator, Indigenous Program
dave@gyvn.ca
Ruthanne Slofstra, Administrator, Accounts

Global, Environmental & Outdoor Education Council (GEOEC)
c/o Barnett House, Alberta Teachers' Association, 11010 - 142 St. NW, Edmonton AB T5N 2R1
Tel: 780-987-7315; *Fax:* 780-455-6481
Toll-Free: 800-232-7208
Other Communication: membership@geoec.org
info@geoec.org
www.geoec.org
www.facebook.com/geoecalberta
twitter.com/geoec
Previous Name: Environmental & Outdoor Education Council of Alberta
Overview: A small provincial organization founded in 1976
Mission: To encourage professional development for teachers in the area of global, environmental, & outdoor education
Member of: Alberta Teachers' Association
Membership: *Fees:* $25 regular & life memberships; $30 subscription; free for students; *Member Profile:* Active members of the Alberta Teachers' Association; Students members of the Alberta Teachers' Association; Individuals or corporations ineligible for active or associate membership in the Alberta Teachers' Association, such as teaching assistants, parents, & libraries
Activities: Providing workshops
Chief Officer(s):
Don McLaughlin, President
president@geoec.org
Jeffery Siddle, Secretary
Suzanna Wong, Treasurer
Awards:
• Appreciation of Serivce
• Award of Merit
• Distinguished Fellow Award
Meetings/Conferences:
• Global Environmental & Outdoor Education Council 2018 Annual Conference, 2018
Scope: Provincial
Description: Features information sessions, resources, & a keynote speaker

GLOBE Foundation
World Trade Centre, #578, 999 Canada Pl., Vancouver BC V6C 3E1
Tel: 604-695-5001; *Fax:* 604-695-5019
Toll-Free: 800-274-6097
info@globe.ca
www.globe.ca
Overview: A medium-sized national organization founded in 1993
Mission: To strive to find practical business-oriented solutions to environmental problems; To assist companies & individuals realize the value of economically viable environmental business opportunities
Finances: *Funding Sources:* Sponsorships
Activities: Researching & consulting; Managing projects; Providing opportunities for communication; Developing partnerships
Chief Officer(s):
John D. Wiebe, President & Chief Executive Officer
ceo@globe.ca
Freddie Frankling, Vice-President, International Relations
freddie.frankling@globe.ca
Nancy Wright, Vice-President, Marketing
nancy.wright@globe.ca
Cindy Leung, Director, Finance & Administration
cindy.leung@globe.ca
John Gough, Manager, Information Technology
john.gough@globe.ca
Zahida Kanani, Manager, Registration & Database
zahida.kanani@globe.ca
Awards:
• The GLOBE Awards for Environmental Excellence: The Award for Corporate Environmental Excellence
Presented to a Canadian corporation with a record of environmental stewardship & sustainability practices *Contact:* Carine Vindeirinho, GLOBE Awards Coordinator, Phone: 604-695-5002, Fax: 604-695-5019, E-mail: carine@globe.ca
• The GLOBE Awards for Environmental Excellence: The Award for Technology Innovation & Application
Awarded to a Canadian company or group of companies that have developed or applied an innovative technology with a significant environmental application *Contact:* Carine Vindeirinho, GLOBE Awards Coordinator, Phone: 604-695-5002, Fax: 604-695-5019, E-mail: carine@globe.ca
• The GLOBE Awards for Environmental Excellence: The Award for Excellence in Urban Sustainability
To honour a local government, private sector company, or consortium that has developed & applied beneficial urban sustainability principles *Contact:* Carine Vindeirinho, GLOBE Awards Coordinator, Phone: 604-695-5002, Fax: 604-695-5019, E-mail: carine@globe.ca
• The GLOBE Awards for Environmental Excellence: The Award for Best Green Consumer Product
To recognize a Canadian company or group of companies that is pursing new & emerging technologies, or has advanced current environmental technologies *Contact:* Carine Vindeirinho, GLOBE Awards Coordinator, Phone: 604-695-5002, Fax: 604-695-5019, E-mail: carine@globe.ca
• The GLOBE Awards for Environmental Excellence: The Finance Award for Sustainability
To recognize a North American fund manager, a global fund manager, a commercial bank, an investment bank, a private bank, an investment broker, an asset management company, a venture capital firm, or an investment advisor who developed portfolios, investment instruments, analytical tools, or funds for Canadian environmental markets *Contact:* Carine Vindeirinho, GLOBE Awards Coordinator, Phone: 604-695-5002, Fax: 604-695-5019, E-mail: carine@globe.ca
Meetings/Conferences:
• GLOBE Forum 2018, March, 2018, Vancouver, BC
Scope: International
Contact Information: General Information: Phone: 604-695-5000, Toll-Free Phone: 1-800-274-6097, E-mail: info@globeseries.com; URL: www.globeseries.com
Publications:
• GLOBE-Net Environmental Business E-Newsletter
Type: Newsletter; *Frequency:* Weekly

Globe Theatre Society
Globe Theatre, Prince Edward Bldg., 1801 Scarth St., Regina SK S4P 2G9
Tel: 306-525-6400; *Fax:* 306-352-4194
Toll-Free: 866-954-5623
onstage@globetheatrelive.com
www.globetheatrelive.com
www.facebook.com/globetheatrelive
twitter.com/GlobeRegina
www.youtube.com/user/GlobeTheatreRegina
Overview: A small local charitable organization founded in 1966
Mission: To create & produce professional theatre & make it accessible with a view to entertain, educate & challenge
Member of: Professional Association of Canadian Theatres
Affiliation(s): Canadian Actors' Equity
Finances: *Funding Sources:* Canada Council; Saskatchewan Arts Board; City of Regina
Staff Member(s): 18
Activities: *Speaker Service:* Yes
Chief Officer(s):
Ruth Smillie, Artistic Director
ruths@globetheatrelive.com

Gloucester Arts Council *See* Arts Ottawa East-Est

Gloucester Historical Society / Société historique de Gloucester
4550B Bank St., Gloucester ON K1T 3W6
Tel: 613-822-2076
english@gloucesterhistory.com
www.gloucesterhistory.com
Overview: A small local organization
Mission: To research, collect, preserve & promote the history of Gloucester & its environs through its publications & historical documents & photographs.
Finances: *Funding Sources:* Municipal government; donations
Membership: *Fees:* $20 annual; $150 life
Activities: *Library:* Research Room; Open to public

God, Sex, & the Meaning of Life Ministry (GSML Ministry)
889 Finley Ave., Ajax ON L1S 3S5
Tel: 905-427-6137
gsmlministry@gmail.com
www.godsexandthemeaningoflife.com
Also Known As: Theology of the Body Team
Overview: A small national organization founded in 2006
Mission: To provide Catholic Church teaching in areas of sexuality for married, single, & celibate people, based on Pope John Paul II's "Theology of the Body"
Affiliation(s): Archdiocese of Toronto
Membership: *Member Profile:* Lay volunteers help in all areas of the ministry; Trained volunteer facilitators offer workshops
Activities: Offering faith instruction workshops & resources for youth, singles, couples, & seniors
Chief Officer(s):
Susan Kennedy, Primary Contact
Rose Heron, Contact, 905-683-9055
Jan Noonan, Contact, 905-420-8696
Publications:
• God, Sex, & the Meaning of Life Newsletter
Type: Newsletter

Goderich & District Chamber of Commerce *See* Huron Chamber of Commerce - Goderich, Central & North Huron

Goethe-Institut (Montréal)
#100, 1626, boul St-Laurent, Montréal QC H2X 2T1
Tel: 514-499-0159; *Fax:* 514-499-0905
info@montreal.goethe.org
www.goethe.de/montreal
www.facebook.com/GoetheInstitutMontreal
twitter.com/GI_Montreal
Overview: A small local organization
Mission: The Goethe-Institut is the cultural institue of the Federal Republic of Germany with a global reach. They promote knowledge of the German language abroad and foster international cultural cooperation. They convey a comprehensive picture of Germany by providing information on Germany's cultural, social, and political life. They perform the principle talks of cultural and educational policy, they work in partnership with public and private cultural bodies, the German federal states and municipalities, and the corporate sector.

Goethe-Institut (Toronto)
North Tower, PO Box 136, #201, 100 University Ave., Toronto ON M5J 1V6
Tel: 416-593-5257; *Fax:* 416-593-5145
info@toronto.goethe.org
www.goethe.de/toronto
www.facebook.com/GoetheToronto
twitter.com/GoetheToronto
Also Known As: German Cultural Centre
Overview: A medium-sized local organization founded in 1962
Mission: To provide cultural programs, international cultural cooperation, German language teaching, & library & information services
Finances: *Annual Operating Budget:* $500,000-$1.5 Million; *Funding Sources:* Foreign Affairs Dept. of the Federal Republic of Germany
Staff Member(s): 9
Activities: Presenting film series & art exhibitions; Offering language courses; Providing information services on Germany; *Internships:* Yes; *Library:* Open to public
Chief Officer(s):
Uwe Rau, Director, 416-593-5257 Ext. 201
director@toronto.goethe.org

Gogama Chamber of Commerce
PO Box 73, Gogama ON P0M 1W0
Overview: A small local organization

Goh Ballet Society
2345 Main St., Vancouver BC V5T 3C9
Tel: 604-872-4014; *Fax:* 604-872-4011
admin@gohballet.com
www.gohballet.com
www.facebook.com/gohballetcanada
twitter.com/GohBallet
www.youtube.com/user/GohBallet
Overview: A small local organization founded in 1978
Mission: To prepare aspiring dancers for professional careers by providing rigorous training in the vocabulary & artistry of classical ballet
Membership: *Committees:* Volunteer
Chief Officer(s):
Chan Hon Goh, Director

Gold River Chamber of Commerce
PO Box 39, Gold River BC V0P 1G0
Tel: 250-285-2724
www.goldriver.ca
Overview: A small local organization
15 volunteer(s)
Membership: 51; *Fees:* Schedule available

Golden & District Chamber of Commerce *See* Kicking Horse Country Chamber of Commerce

Golden Age Society
4061A - 4th Ave., Whitehorse YT Y1A 1H1
Tel: 867-668-5538; *Fax:* 867-633-6944
goldenagesociety@gmail.com
www.yukon-seniors-and-elders.org/index.php/ga-home
Overview: A small provincial organization founded in 1976
Mission: To promote & give opportunity for social, recreational activities for seniors in the Yukon
Membership: *Fees:* $22
Chief Officer(s):
Deborah Bastien, Office Manager
gas2016@northwestel.net

Golden District Arts Council
PO Box 228, Golden BC V0A 1H0
Tel: 250-344-6186
info@kickinghorseculture.ca
www.kickinghorseculture.ca
twitter.com/goldenculture
www.youtube.com/user/khcgdac
Also Known As: Kicking Horse Culture
Overview: A small local organization founded in 1970
Mission: To stimulate and encourage the development of the arts in the Golden area through interaction with the public
Member of: Assembly of BC Arts Councils; Kootenay Cultural Network of the Rockies
Finances: *Funding Sources:* Private; government
Membership: 800; *Fees:* $10 adults/seniors; $20 family
Activities: Performance Series; Children's Festival; Art Gallery; Student Art Show; X-mas Craft Fair; Summer Music Series; *Internships:* Yes
Chief Officer(s):
Bill Usher, Executive Director
director@kickinghorseculture.ca
Monica Parkinson, Chair

Golden Food Bank
PO Box 1047, #102, 115 - 9th St. South, Golden BC V0A 1H0
Tel: 250-344-2113
info@goldenfoodbank.ca
goldenfoodbank.ca
Overview: A small local charitable organization founded in 1981 overseen by Food Banks British Columbia
Mission: The agency provides food for the needy in the local area
Member of: Food Banks British Columbia
Chief Officer(s):
Barb Davies, Director

Golden Horseshoe Beekeepers' Association
Brantford ON
Tel: 519-752-8766
www.goldenhorseshoebeekeepers.ca
Overview: A small local organization founded in 1980
Mission: To provide educational information to Hamilton & Halton Region's beekeepers
Member of: Ontario Beekeepers' Association
Membership: *Member Profile:* Professional & hobbyist beekeepers in Hamilton & the surrounding region
Activities: Organizing meetings at the Marritt Hall in Jerseyville, Ontario; Providing opportunities to network; Removing swarms of honey bees
Chief Officer(s):
Jim Henderson, President
jimhenderson93@hotmail.com

Golden Horseshoe Co-operative Housing Federation (GHCHF)
#1A, 36 Keefer Crt., Hamilton ON L8E 4V4
Tel: 905-561-2667; *Fax:* 905-561-1153
ghchf@primus.ca
www.ghchf.ca
Overview: A small local organization founded in 1986
Mission: To act as a collective voice for housing co-ops & associated organizations in the Hamilton/Niagara regions
Membership: 52; 44 housing cooperatives; *Member Profile:* Housing co-operatives; Service managers; Property management companies
Activities: Workshops & training for co-op members & staff

Golden Opportunities Vocational Rehabilitation Centre Workshop
PO Box 887, 32 Industrial Park, Springhill NS B0M 1X0
Tel: 902-597-3158
www.nsnet.org/govrc
Also Known As: GOVRC Workshop
Overview: A small local organization
Mission: To offer vocational training for mentally challenged adults
Member of: DIRECTIONS Council for Vocational Services Society
Activities: Woodworking; packaging; ornaments; flyers; fundraising kits; assembling; collating & sorting; wreaths & bow making; gardening
Chief Officer(s):
Paul Williams, Executive Director

Golden Prairie Arts Council (GPAC)
PO Box 2103, 38 Centre Ave. West, Carman MB R0G 0J0
Tel: 204-745-6568
gpaccarman@gmail.com
www.gparts.ca
www.facebook.com/43647958167
Overview: A small local organization founded in 1996
Mission: To support fine arts in Manitoba's south central region
Finances: *Funding Sources:* Manitoba Arts Council; Grants; Fundraising
Activities: Operating a gallery; Hosting art shows; Mentoring artists; Organizing programs, such as "Artists in the School"; Offering an annual members' art sale; Providing music classes; Hosting musical performances; Offering workshops
Chief Officer(s):
Larry Jeffers, Chair
Kathy Wikdahl, Treasurer

Golden Rock & Fossil Club
PO Box 2542, Golden BC V0A 1H0
Tel: 250-344-2108
goldenrockandfossilclub@gmail.com
Overview: A small local organization
Member of: Lapidary, Rock & Mineral Society of British Columbia
Activities: Hunting for rocks & minerals, lapidary
Chief Officer(s):
Stan Walker, Contact

The Golden Triangle Parrot Club
ON
info@gtpc.ca
www.gtpc.ca
Overview: A small local organization
Mission: To provide an informative and entertaining environment for lovers of Psittacines
Member of: Avicultural Advancement Council of Canada

Golden Women's Resource Centre Society (GWRCS)
PO Box 2343, 419C - 9th Ave. North, Golden BC V0H 1H0
Tel: 250-344-5317; *Fax:* 750-344-2565; *Crisis Hot-Line:* 250-344-2101
gwrced@uniserve.com
www.goldenwomencentre.ca
twitter.com/gwrc1
Overview: A small local charitable organization founded in 1978
Mission: GWRCS operates the Golden Women's Resource Centre which provides a safe, non-judgmental, welcoming environment for women to gather, relax, share ideas & get support. It is actively engaged in efforts to end violence against women & their children, & strives to improve the economic, social & legal situation of women in the home, workplace, community & world at large. It is a registered charity, BN: 107438996RR0001.
Affiliation(s): British Columbia/Yukon Society of Transition Houses; British Columbia Coalition of Women's Centres
Finances: *Annual Operating Budget:* $50,000-$100,000; *Funding Sources:* National & provincial government; Status of Women Canada; Ministry of Women's Equality
Membership: 100 individual
Activities: Counselling; educational workshops, internet access; *Awareness Events:* International Women's Day, March 8; Prevention of Violence Against Women Week, April; Take Back the Night, Sept.; Women's History Month, Oct.

Chief Officer(s):
Melanie Myers, Outreach Coordinator & ED
Roni Beauregard, Safehomes Coordinator
safehomes@redshift.bc.ca

Goldstream Food Bank Society
PO Box 28122, Stn. Westshore Town Centre, Victoria BC V9B 6K8
Tel: 250-474-4443
foodbank.islandnet.com
Overview: A small local charitable organization founded in 1983 overseen by Food Banks British Columbia
Mission: To provide food hampers & advocacy to community members in need.
Member of: Food Banks British Columbia
Membership: *Fees:* $5

Golf Association of Ontario (GAO)
PO Box 970, Uxbridge ON L9P 1N3
Tel: 905-852-1101; *Fax:* 905-852-8893
admin@gao.ca
www.gao.ca
www.facebook.com/GolfOntario
twitter.com/TheGolfOntario
www.instagram.com/thegolfontario
Merged from: Ontario Golf Association; Ontario Ladies Golf Association
Overview: A large provincial organization founded in 2001 overseen by Golf Canada
Mission: To develop & promote golf in the province
Finances: *Funding Sources:* Membership dues; Tournament entry fees
Staff Member(s): 19
Membership: 115,000 individuals, 420 member clubs; *Fees:* Schedule available; *Member Profile:* Golfers who are members of private, semi-private or public golf courses; *Committees:* Finance & Risk Management; Governance; Human Resources & Compensation; Nominating
Activities: Offering tournaments, junior camps, & programming; *Internships:* Yes
Chief Officer(s):
Mike Kelly, Executive Director
Judy Crute, Senior Director, Business Operations
Kyle McFarlane, Senior Director, Golf Operations
Craig Loughry, Director, Golf Services
Jason Hraynyk, Manager, Marketing & Business Development
Darren Matte, Coordinator, Marketing & Communications
Awards:
• Marlene Streit Award Fund
• Ken Trowbridge Legacy Fund
• GAO Scholarship Program

Golf Canada / Association royale de golf du Canada
#1, 1333 Dorval Dr., Oakville ON L6M 4X7
Tel: 905-849-9700; *Fax:* 905-845-7040
Toll-Free: 800-263-0009
Other Communication: Member Services e-mail:
members@golfcanada.ca
info@golfcanada.ca
www.golfcanada.ca
www.linkedin.com/company/golf-canada
www.facebook.com/TheGolfCanada
twitter.com/TheGolfCanada
www.youtube.com/user/TheGolfCanada
Previous Name: Royal Canadian Golf Association
Overview: A large national organization founded in 1895
Mission: To work with the provincial golf associations & member clubs to foster the growth & development of golf
Affiliation(s): Canadian Golf Superintendent Association; PGA of Canada; Canadian Society of Club Managers; National Golf Course Owners Association Canada; Canadian Golf Industry Association
Finances: *Funding Sources:* Membership dues; Sponsorships
Membership: 322,000+ at 1,500 clubs; *Fees:* Schedule available; *Member Profile:* Member of a member golf club
Activities: *Awareness Events:* RBC Canadian Open; Canadian Pacific Women's Open; *Speaker Service:* Yes; *Library:* by appointment
Chief Officer(s):
Laurence Applebaum, Chief Executive Officer
Publications:
• Golf Canada Magazine
Type: Magazine; *Frequency:* s-a.; *ISSN:* 1198-2659

Golf Canada Foundation
#1, 1333 Dorval Dr., Oakville ON L6M 4X7
Tel: 905-849-9700; *Fax:* 905-845-7040
Toll-Free: 800-263-0009
www.golfcanadafoundation.com
Also Known As: RCGA Foundation
Previous Name: Canadian Golf Foundation
Overview: A medium-sized national charitable organization founded in 1979
Mission: To raise & grant funds for the betterment of golf in Canada
Finances: *Funding Sources:* Private & corporate donations
Staff Member(s): 2
Activities: *Internships:* Yes
Chief Officer(s):
Spencer Snell, Operations Manager, Golf Canada Foundation
ssnell@golfcanada.ca

Golf Manitoba Inc.
#420, 145 Pacific Ave., Winnipeg MB R3B 2Z6
Tel: 204-925-5730; *Fax:* 204-925-5731
golfmb@golfmanitoba.mb.ca
golfmanitoba.mb.ca
www.facebook.com/217256961725416
twitter.com/golf_manitoba
Previous Name: Manitoba Golf Association Inc.
Overview: A small provincial organization founded in 1915 overseen by Golf Canada
Mission: The Association determines policies & standards relating to the development & promotion of golf in the province.
Chief Officer(s):
Tammy Gibson, President & Representative, Provincial Council
Awards:
• Dr. Dwight Parkinson Award
Eligibility: Young golfers entering or continuing in a post-secondary educational institution in Canada; *Amount:* $3500

Golf Newfoundland & Labrador (GNL)
6 Lester St., St. John's NL A1E 2P6
Tel: 709-364-3534
golf@hnl.ca
www.golfnewfoundland.ca
www.facebook.com/pages/Golf-NL/178044602356289
Previous Name: Newfoundland & Labrador Golf Association
Overview: A medium-sized provincial organization overseen by Golf Canada
Membership: 20 clubs
Activities: Providing information about golf courses in Newfoundland & Labrador; Promoting golf in the province
Chief Officer(s):
Greg Hillier, Executive Director

Good Foundation Inc.
#603, 250 Sydenham St., London ON N6A 5S1
Tel: 519-679-1906
good_foundation@rogers.com
www.goodfoundation.ca
Overview: A small local charitable organization founded in 1974
Mission: To support charitable organizations & strengthen the communities in which members of the foundation are involved
Chief Officer(s):
James Good, President

Good Jobs Coalition *See* Good Jobs for All Coalition

Good Jobs for All Coalition
Toronto ON
Tel: 416-937-9378
communications@goodjobsforall.ca
goodjobsforall.ca
twitter.com/goodjobsforall
Previous Name: Good Jobs Coalition
Overview: A small local organization founded in 2008
Mission: To be an alliance of community, labour, social justice, youth and environmental organizations in the Toronto region
Membership: *Committees:* Green Economy for All; Empowering Workers; Investing in Social Infrastructure
Chief Officer(s):
Preethy Sivakumar, Coordinator
Publications:
• L'ACELF en Action
Type: Newsletter; *Frequency:* Monthly

Good Shepherd Refuge *See* Good Shepherd Refuge Social Ministries

Good Shepherd Refuge Social Ministries
412 Queen St. East, Toronto ON M5A 1T3
Tel: 416-869-3619
www.goodshepherd.ca
www.linkedin.com/company/good-shepherd-ministries
www.facebook.com/goodshepherdTO
twitter.com/goodshepherd_to
www.youtube.com/user/GoodShepherdToronto
Also Known As: Good Shepherd Ministries
Previous Name: Good Shepherd Refuge
Overview: A small local charitable organization founded in 1963
Mission: To provide services to homeless, disadvantaged & marginalized people; To provide the basic necessities of food, shelter & ancillary services, ensuring each client justice, equality, dignity & acceptance; To provide human services that will assist clients in regaining freedom from homelessness
Member of: Ontario Hostels Association
Finances: *Annual Operating Budget:* Greater than $5 Million; *Funding Sources:* Donations; government grants
Staff Member(s): 70; 7000 volunteer(s)
Membership: *Committees:* Fundraising
Activities: Operating Good Shepherd Centre: provides shelter, clothing, daily meals, drop-in, medical & housing services; Barrett House: residence for people living with HIV/AIDS; St. Joseph's Residence: longterm care supportive housing for elderly homeless men with physical &/or mental health problems
Chief Officer(s):
Werner Zapfe, Chair
David Lynch, Executive Director
Aklilu Wendaferew, Assistant Executive Director
Publications:
• Good Shepherd Journal
Type: Newsletter; *Frequency:* Bi-annually; *Editor:* Adrienne Urquhart; *Price:* Free to supporters
Profile: Provides client, service & donor updates.

Goodsoil & District Chamber of Commerce
PO Box 157, Goodsoil SK S0M 1A0
Tel: 306-238-4747; *Fax:* 306-238-4633
Overview: A small local organization

Goodwill Industries
255 Horton St., London ON N6B 1L1
Tel: 519-850-9000
www.goodwillindustries.ca
twitter.com/Goodwill_OGL
www.youtube.com/user/GoodwillOGLakes
Previous Name: London Goodwill Industries Association
Overview: A medium-sized local charitable organization founded in 1943
Mission: To provide programs & services that enhance the employability of people with barriers or diminished opportunities; To provide & recycle goods
Member of: Goodwill Industries International Inc.
Finances: *Funding Sources:* Retail; government
Activities: Collecting donations of clothing & house wares; Operating retail stores; Administering career centres; *Speaker Service:* Yes
Chief Officer(s):
Michelle Quintyn, President & CEO
mquintyn@goodwillindustries.ca
Terry Off, Chief Financial Officer
Scott Louch, Chief Operations Officer

Goodwill Industries Essex Kent Lambton
1121 Wellington St., Sarnia ON N7S 6J7
Tel: 519-332-0440
www.goodwillekl.com
www.facebook.com/GoodwillEKL
twitter.com/goodwillekl
www.youtube.com/user/GoodwillIntl
Overview: A small local charitable organization founded in 1933
Mission: To promote dignity & independence; To provide employment & training programs to assist people with employment barriers; To help people develop life skills
Finances: *Annual Operating Budget:* Greater than $5 Million; *Funding Sources:* Donations
Staff Member(s): 193; 401 volunteer(s)
Activities: Operating stores
Chief Officer(s):
Kevin Smith, Chief Executive Officer
ksmith@goodwillekl.com
Maryam Foroughian, Chief Financial Officer
mforoughian@goodwillekl.com
Michelle Repuski, Director, Workforce Development
mrepuski@goodwillccc.com
Heather Allen, Manager, Marketing & Communication
hallen@goodwillekl.com

Mary Lynn Bouman, Manager, Human Resources
mbouman@goodwillekl.com
Craig Watters, Manager, Operations
cwatters@goodwillekl.com

Goodwill Industries of Alberta
8761 - 51 Ave., Edmonton AB T6E 5H1
Tel: 780-944-1414
Toll-Free: 866-927-1414
media@goodwill.ab.ca
www.goodwill.ab.ca
www.facebook.com/GoodwillAB
twitter.com/goodwillab
instagram.com/goodwill_ab
Overview: A medium-sized provincial charitable organization founded in 1951
Mission: To help persons with disabilities & disadvantages; To build a strong future through rehabilitation & training
Member of: Goodwill Industries International
Affiliation(s): United Way of the Capital Region
Finances: *Funding Sources:* Revenue from retail thrift stores; United Way; Alberta Family & Social Services
Membership: *Committees:* Review; Governance
Activities: *Awareness Events:* Goodwill Week, 1st week of May
Chief Officer(s):
Larry Brownoff, Chair
Dale Monaghan, President & CEO

Goodwill, The Amity Group
225 King William St., Hamilton ON L8R 1B1
Tel: 905-526-8482
www.goodwillonline.ca
www.facebook.com/GoodwillCareerCentre
twitter.com/JobsGoodwill
www.youtube.com/GoodwillIntl
Previous Name: Amity Goodwill Industries
Overview: A medium-sized national organization founded in 1935
Mission: To enrich the community by providing vocational rehabilitation programs & services to assist people challenged by disabilities & special needs to achieve maximum employment, community participation & self-fulfillment
Affiliation(s): Canadian Association of Goodwill Industries; Goodwill Industries International
Finances: *Annual Operating Budget:* Greater than $5 Million; *Funding Sources:* Provincial government; donations
Activities: Accepting donations of household & business goods; Operating Value Centres; Offering contract services; Providing employment opportunities; *Awareness Events:* Tastes of Downtown Walking Restaurant Tour
Chief Officer(s):
Tim Dobbie, Chair
Paul Chapin, President & CEO, 905-526-8482 Ext. 2222
Albert Deveau, Vice-President, Retail & Donated Goods Operations, 905-875-3533
Awards:
• Annual Outstanding Achievement Awards
Publications:
• Goodwill, The Amity Group Newsletter
Type: Newsletter

Gordon Foundation
#400, 11 Church St., Toronto ON M5E 1W1
Tel: 416-601-4776
info@gordonfn.org
www.gordonfoundation.ca
www.linkedin.com/company/1231849
twitter.com/TheGordonFdn
www.instagram.com/thegordonfoundation
Overview: A small provincial charitable organization
Mission: To support the development of public policies focused on freshwater management & the protection of Canada's water; To ensure the full participation of Indigenous people in decisions impacting their communities
Activities: Conducting & disseminating research; Developing programs including Mackenzie DataStream, an open access platform for knowledge sharing, & the IBA Community Toolkit, a resource for First Nations, Inuit, & Métis communities in Canada; *Library:* Resource Library; Open to public
Chief Officer(s):
Sherry Campbell, President & CEO
sherry@gordonfn.org

Gorsebrook Research Institute for Atlantic Canada Studies
Saint Mary's University, 5960 Inglis St., Halifax NS B3H 3C3
Tel: 902-420-5668; *Fax:* 902-496-8135
gorsebrook@smu.ca
www.smu.ca/administration/gorsebrook/
Overview: A small local organization founded in 1982
Mission: The Institute administers an interdisciplinary research centre concerned with social, economic, & cultural issues specific to Canada's Atlantic Region. It encourages research pertaining to the region, its culture, history, etc.
Finances: *Funding Sources:* Federal government; projects; The Austin Willis Moving Images Research Centre
Staff Member(s): 3
Activities: Ongoing Fisheries & Coastal Seminar series; Labrador Project; James Bay Project; conferences, symposia, workshops; Community Seascapes; History of Moving Images in Nova Scotia; Literacy Project
Chief Officer(s):
John Reid, Chair
Peter L. Twohig, Executive Director, 902-420-5447
peter.twohig@smu.ca

Gospel Tract & Bible Society
PO Box 180, Ste Anne MB R5H 1R1
Tel: 204-355-4975
Other Communication: Alt. URL: e-menno.org/tracts.htm
info@gospeltract.ca
wwww.gospeltract.ca
Overview: A small national organization
Mission: Publishes Christian religious tracts; affiliated with Church of God in Christ, Mennonite.

Governance Professionals of Canada (GPC)
#802, 21 St. Clair Ave. East, Toronto ON M4T 1L9
Tel: 416-921-5449; *Fax:* 416-967-6320
Toll-Free: 800-774-2850
www.cscs.org
www.linkedin.com/company/governance-professionals-of-canada-gpc-
twitter.com/GovProCanada
Previous Name: Canadian Society of Corporate Secretaries
Overview: A medium-sized national organization founded in 1994
Mission: To promote & advance governance practices in private, public, & not-for-profit organizations
Finances: *Annual Operating Budget:* $100,000-$250,000; *Funding Sources:* Membership dues; seminars & courses fees
Staff Member(s): 6; 30 volunteer(s)
Membership: 300; *Fees:* $390 professional (non-commercial interests); $515 professional (commercial interests); $85 non-practicing; *Member Profile:* Individuals involved with or retired from corporate governance
Activities: Training in corporate procedures; Advocacy; Offering access to resources
Chief Officer(s):
Lynn Beauregard, President
lynn.beauregard@gpcanada.org
Albert Orellana, Director, Conference & Sponsorship
albert.orellana@gpcanada.org
Megan McLean, Manager, Professional Development & Special Projects
events@gpcanada.org
Caroline Bucksbaum, Coordinator, Membership & Events
caroline.bucksbaum@gpcanada.org

Governing Board of Dental Technicians of Ontario *See* College of Dental Technologists of Ontario

Government Finance Officers Association of British Columbia (GFOABC)
#408, 612 View St., Victoria BC V8W 1J5
Tel: 250-382-6871
office@gfoabc.ca
www.gfoabc.ca
www.linkedin.com/company/gfoabc-government-finance-officers-association-of-bc-
www.facebook.com/GFOABCVictoria
twitter.com/GFOABC
Also Known As: GFOA of BC
Overview: A medium-sized provincial organization founded in 1989 overseen by Government Finance Officers Association
Mission: To represent local government finance officers in BC; To support, educate & develop finance professionals; To promote excellence in local government
Staff Member(s): 3; 10 volunteer(s)
Membership: 1,000
Activities: Offering courses, workshops, webinars & networking opportunities; Organizing events & trade shows; *Speaker Service:* Yes
Chief Officer(s):
Paul Macklem, Executive Director
execdir@gfoabc.ca
Erica Christie, Manager, Operations
Meetings/Conferences:
• Government Finance Officers Association of BC Annual Conference 2018, May, 2018, Kelowna, BC
Scope: Provincial
Publications:
• Dollars & Sense [a publication of the Government Finance Officers Association of British Columbia]
Type: Newsletter

Government Services Union (GSU) / Syndicat des services gouvernementaux
#705, 233 Gilmour St., Ottawa ON K2P 0P2
Tel: 613-560-4395; *Fax:* 613-230-6774
www.gsu-ssg.ca
Merged from: Supply & Services Union; Union of Public Works Employees
Overview: A medium-sized national organization founded in 1999 overseen by Public Service Alliance of Canada
Mission: Their members provide compensation, audit, procurement, disposal telecommunications and informatics, translation, real property and reciever general services to some 100 federal government departments and agencies. They also provide information about government programmes and research the opinions of Canadians.
Staff Member(s): 9
Membership: 7,000 in 32 locals; *Member Profile:* Employees at Public Works & Government Services Canada, Shared Services Canada, the Royal Canadian Mint & Metcalfe Realty
Chief Officer(s):
Donna Lackie, President, 613-560-4395
lackied@psac-afpc.com

Governor General's Performing Arts Awards Foundation (GGPAAF) / Les Prix du Gouverneur Général pour les arts du spectacle
#400, 280 Metcalfe St., Ottawa ON K2P 1R7
Tel: 613-241-5297
awards@ggpaa.ca
ggpaa.ca
www.facebook.com/ggawards.prixgg
twitter.com/govgpaa
Overview: A medium-sized national charitable organization founded in 1992
Mission: To honour & celebrate the lifetime artistic achievement of Canada's outstanding performing artists; To foster cross-cultural awareness of Anglophone artists in French Canada & of Francophone artists in English Canada; To foster awareness of Canada's diverse linguistic & cultural groups; To foster awareness of indigenous performing artists; To raise profile among Canadians of the achievements & contributions of Canadian performing artists at home & abroad; To inspire future performing artists
Finances: *Funding Sources:* Fundraising; Sponsorships
Staff Member(s): 2
Activities: Coordinating the nomination & selection processes; Organizing events related the the awards presentation; Forming partnerhips
Chief Officer(s):
Whitney Taylor, Executive Director, 613-241-5297 Ext. 203
whitneytaylor@ggpaa.ca
Jami Rundle, Assistant, Communications & Administrative, 613-241-4297 Ext. 203
jamirundle@ggpaa.ca
Awards:
• Governor General's Performing Arts Awards
Established in 1992; honours six performing artists for their lifetime achievement & contribution to the cultural enrichment of Canada; each recipient is awarded $15,000 & a commemorative medal
• The National Arts Centre Award
Recognizes work of an extraordinary nature & significance in the performing arts by an individual artist &/or company in the past performance year; recipients receive a $15,000 cash award donated by the NAC Foundation & an original sculpture by Wei Yew
• Ramon John Hnatyshyn Award for Voluntarism in the Performing Arts
Recognizes outstanding service to the performing arts; the recipient is presented with a specially commissioned artwork by Canadian glass artist Naoko Takenouchi

Grace Communion International Canada
#101, 5668 - 192 St., Surrey BC V3S 2V7
Tel: 604-575-2705; Fax: 604-575-2758
info@gcicanada.ca
www.gcicanada.ca
Previous Name: Worldwide Church of God Canada
Overview: A small national organization
Mission: To proclaim the gospel of Jesus Christ around the world & to help members grow spiritually
Chief Officer(s):
Gary Moore, National Director
gmoore@telus.net
Publications:
• Northern Light
Type: Magazine; Frequency: Quarterly

Graham Boeckh Foundation / Fondation Graham Boeckh
#1725, 1002, rue Sherbooke ouest, Montréal QC H3A 3L6
info@grahamboeckhfoundation.org
www.grahamboeckhfoundation.org
www.linkedin.com/company/graham-boeckh-foundation
www.youtube.com/user/GrahamBoeckh
Overview: A medium-sized national charitable organization
Mission: To transform mental health services & enhance the lives of individuals with or at risk of mental illness
Activities: Funding mental health projects & initiatives; Collaborating with policy makers & community service providers to develop integrated youth services, including primary care, mental health care, addictions counselling, social services, & peer/family support
Chief Officer(s):
Ian Boeckh, President & Director
William Powell, Secretary-Treasurer
Publications:
• GBF [Graham Boeckh Foundation] Newsletter
Type: Newsletter

Grahamdale Community Development Corporation
R.M. Of Grahamdale Administration Office, PO Box 160, 23 Government Rd., Moosehorn MB R0C 2E0
Tel: 204-768-2858; Fax: 204-768-3374
info@grahamdale.ca
www.grahamdale.ca
Overview: A small local organization
Mission: To promote economic development in Grahamdale & surrounding areas
Chief Officer(s):
Sandahl Bauch, Officer, Economic Development
edo@grahamdale.ca

Grain Farmers of Ontario
679 Southgate Dr., Guelph ON N1G 4S2
Tel: 519-767-6537; Fax: 519-767-9713
Toll-Free: 800-265-0550
Other Communication: Wheat Trading Price Line: 1-800-943-2809
info@gfo.ca
www.gfo.ca
www.linkedin.com/company/grain-farmers-of-ontario
twitter.com/grainfarmers
www.youtube.com/user/grainfarmersontario
Merged from: Ontario Soybean Growers; Ontario Corn Producers' Association; Ontario Wheat Producers' Marketing Bd.
Overview: A medium-sized provincial organization
Mission: To develop an innovative & successful business environment to benefit farmer members; To promote the Ontario grain industry to become a global leader
Membership: 15,000-49,999; Member Profile: Ontario's growers of soybeans, corn, & wheat
Activities: Researching; Expanding markets; Encouraging new uses for Ontario grains; Engaging in advocacy activities
Chief Officer(s):
Barry Senft, Chief Executive Officer
bsenft@gfo.ca
Crosby Devitt, Vice-President
cdevitt@gfo.ca
Tom Farfaras, Chief Financial Officer
tfarfaras@gfo.ca
Todd Austin, Manager, Marketing
taustin@gfo.ca
Debra Conlon, Manager, Government Relations
dconlon@gfo.ca
Josh Cowan, Manager, Research
joshcowan@gfo.ca
Nicole Mackellar, Manager, Market Development
nmackellar@gfo.ca
Brenda Miller-Sanford, Manager, Administration
bmsanford@gfo.ca
Meetings/Conferences:
• Grain Farmers of Ontario 2018 March Classic, March, 2018, ON
Scope: Provincial
Attendance: 700+
Description: A gathering of representatives from government, industry, & farms throughout Ontario to attend presentations about trade, world markets, & new oppotunities
Contact Information: E-mail: info@gfo.ca

Grain Growers of Canada (GGC)
#912, 350 Sparks St., Ottawa ON K1R 7S8
Tel: 613-230-9954; Fax: 613-236-3590
office@ggc-pgc.ca
www.ggc-pgc.ca
Overview: A small national organization
Mssion: To supprt policies that allow for a competitive global farming industry
Affiliation(s): Alberta Barley Commission; Alberta Oat, Rye & Triticale Association; Alberta Pulse Growers; Alberta Wheat Commission; Atlantic Grains Council; British Columbia Grain Producers Association; Canadian Canola Growers Association; Canadian Young Farmers Forum; Manitoba Corn Growers Association; Prairie Oat Growers Association; Western Barley Growers Association; Western Canadian Wheat Growers Association
Membership: 14; Member Profile: Groups involved in the grain, pulse & oilseed industries
Chief Officer(s):
Stephen Vandervalk, President
Janet Krayden, Manager, Public Affairs

Grain Services Union (CLC) (GSU) / Syndicat des services du grain (CTC)
2334 McIntyre St., Regina SK S4P 2S2
Tel: 306-522-6686; Fax: 306-565-3430
Toll-Free: 866-522-6686
gsu.regina@sasktel.net
www.gsu.ca
Overview: A medium-sized national organization founded in 1936
Mission: They represent Saskatchewan Wheat Pool Workers and represent members working for a variety of companies within Canada.
Affiliation(s): Interntaionl Longshore and Warehouse Union
Membership: 1,500
Chief Officer(s):
Carolyn Illerbrun, President
Hugh J. Wagner, Secretary/Manager

Grain Workers' Union, Local 333 (GWU)
#103- 3989 Henning Dr., Vancouver BC V5C 6P8
Tel: 604-254-8635; Fax: 604-254-6254
local333@telus.net
www.grainworkersunion.com
Overview: A small provincial organization
Mission: A Canadian Union representing members in the Ports of Vancouver and Prince Rupert.
Member of: National Union of Public and General Employees
Affiliation(s): BC Government & Service Employees' Union; Canadian Labour Congress
Staff Member(s): 2
Membership: 800+
Chief Officer(s):
Gerry Gault, President
gerryis@telus.net
Kevin Ling, Sec.-Treas.

Grand Bend & Area Chamber of Commerce
PO Box 248, #1, 81 Crescent St., Grand Bend ON N0M 1T0
Tel: 519-238-2001
Toll-Free: 888-338-2001
info@grandbendchamber.ca
grandbendchamber.ca
Overview: A small local organization founded in 1975
Finances: Funding Sources: Membership dues
Membership: 180
Activities: Library;
Chief Officer(s):
Susan Mills, Manager

Grand Centre Canadian Native Friendship Centre See Cold Lake Native Friendship Centre

Grand Chapitre des Maçons de l'Arche Royale du Québec See Grand Chapter, Royal Arch Masons of Québec

Grand Chapter, R.A.M. of Nova Scotia
NS
www.grandchapterram.org
Overview: A medium-sized provincial organization founded in 1869
Finances: Annual Operating Budget: Less than $50,000
Staff Member(s): 1
Membership: 988
Chief Officer(s):
Fred Richard, Grand Secretary

Grand Chapter, Royal Arch Masons of Québec / Grand Chapitre des Maçons de l'Arche Royale du Québec
#404B, 2295, rue Saint-Marc, Montréal QC H3H 2G9
admin@royalarchmasonsofquebec.ca
www.royalarchmasonsofquebec.ca
Overview: A small provincial organization
Mission: To pursue excellence in masonry
Membership: Member Profile: Master Masons in good standing of a Craft Lodge; Committees: Jurisprudence, Grievances & Appeals; State of the Order; Finance; Ritual, Rites & Ceremonies; Credentials; Grand Convocation Social Affair
Chief Officer(s):
Paul Arturi, M.Ex.Comp.

Grand Conseil des Cris See Grand Council of the Crees

Grand Council of the Crees / Grand Conseil des Cris
2, rue Lakeshore, Nemaska QC J0Y 3B0
Tel: 819-673-2600; Fax: 819-673-2606
cree@cra.qc.ca
www.gcc.ca
www.linkedin.com/companies/grand-council-of-the-crees
www.facebook.com/gcccra
twitter.com/gcccra
Overview: A medium-sized provincial organization founded in 1974
Mission: To representg the Cree people; to foster, promote, protect & assist in preserving the way of life, values & traditions of the Cree people of Quebec.
Chief Officer(s):
Mathew Coon Come, Grand Chief
Bill Namagoose, Executive Director, 613-761-1655, Fax: 613-761-1388

  Bureau de Montréal
  #100, 277, rue Duke, Montréal QC H3C 2M2
  Tel: 514-861-5837; Fax: 514-861-0760
  cra@gcc.ca

  Bureau de Ottawa
  #900, 81 Metcalfe St., Ottawa ON K1P 6K7
  Tel: 613-761-1655; Fax: 613-761-1388
  cree@gcc.ca

  Bureau de Québec
  200, Grande Alleé est, Québec QC G1R 2H9
  Tel: 418-691-1111; Fax: 418-523-8478
  cree.embassy@gcc.ca

Grand Falls, Saint-André & Drummond Chamber of Commerce; Grand Falls & Region Chamber of Commerce See Valley Chamber of Commerce

Grand Falls-Windsor Chamber of Commerce See Exploits Regional Chamber of Commerce

Grand Lodge of Alberta See Grand Orange Lodge of Canada

Grand Lodge of Québec - Ancient, Free & Accepted Masons (GLQ) / Grande Loge du Québec
2295, rue Saint-Marc, Montréal QC H3H 2G9
Tel: 514-933-6739; Fax: 514-933-6730
Other Communication: info@glquebec.org
admin@glquebec.ca
www.glquebec.org
Previous Name: Ancient, Free & Accepted Masons of Canada - Grand Lodge of Québec
Overview: A medium-sized provincial organization founded in 1869
Staff Member(s): 1; 5 volunteer(s)

Grand Manan Chamber of Commerce See Grand Manan Tourism Association & Chamber of Commerce

Grand Manan Fishermen's Association (GMFA)
PO Box 907, Grand Manan NB E5G 3M1

Canadian Associations / Grand Manan Museum Inc.

Tel: 506-662-8481; Fax: 506-662-8336
gmfa@nb.aibn.com
www.gmfa.nb.ca
Overview: A small local organization founded in 1981
Mission: To provide advice to the government on fishery management issues; to operate the Fundy Marine Service Center for fishermen to repair, paint & store boats; To manage the Grand Manon Harbour Authority, responsible for the wharves.
Membership: Fees: $100 captain/associate; $50 crew member; $25 retired; Committees: Lobster; Weir Sector
Chief Officer(s):
Brian Guptill, President

Grand Manan Museum Inc.
1141, Rte. 776, Grand Manan NB E5G 4E9
Tel: 506-662-3524; Fax: 506-662-3009
gmadmin@grandmananmuseum.ca
www.grandmananmuseum.ca
www.facebook.com/GrandMananMuseum
twitter.com/GMMuseum
Overview: A small local organization founded in 1962
Mission: To collect, store, display, & interpret Grand Manan's social & natural history with special emphasis on her marine tradition
Affiliation(s): AMNB, CMA
Finances: Annual Operating Budget: Less than $50,000; Funding Sources: Provincial & national governments; donations, fundraising; gift shop
Membership: Fees: $25 individual; $35 family; $50-$250 patron
Activities: Exhibits, archives, slide shows, nature school, tours, tourism information, fundraising; publications on aspects of Grand Manan; Library: Grand Manan Museum Research Library; Open to public by appointment
Chief Officer(s):
MJ Edwards, Museum Director & Curator

Grand Manan Tourism Association & Chamber of Commerce
PO Box 1310, Grand Manan NB E5G 4E9
Tel: 506-662-3442
Toll-Free: 888-525-1655
info@grandmanannb.com
www.grandmanannb.com
Previous Name: Grand Manan Chamber of Commerce
Overview: A small local organization
Mission: To promote & expand business in the Grand Manan & White Head Islands area
Member of: Atlantic Provinces Chamber of Commerce
Finances: Annual Operating Budget: Less than $50,000
Membership: 84; Fees: $130 business; $10 individual
Chief Officer(s):
Patricia Brown, Secretary & Treasurer

Grand Manan Whale & Seabird Research Station (GMWSRS) / Centre de recherche sur la vie marine de Grand Manan
24 Rte. 776, Grand Manan NB E5G 1A1
Tel: 506-662-3804
info@gmwsrs.org
www.gmwsrs.org
www.facebook.com/122376994520768
twitter.com/GMWSRS
Overview: A small local charitable organization founded in 1981
Mission: To conduct research on the Bay of Fundy ecosystem, concentrating on marine mammals & seabirds; To operate a public display of Bay of Fundy Marine Fauna
Member of: New Brunswick Environmental Network
Finances: Annual Operating Budget: $50,000-$100,000
4 volunteer(s)
Activities: Speaker Service: Yes; Library: Gaskin Memorial Library; by appointment
Chief Officer(s):
Laurie Murison, Managing Director

Grand Masters Curling Association Ontario
c/o Art Lobel, 106 Kirk Dr., Thornhill ON L3T 3L2
Tel: 905-881-0547
grandmasterscurling.com
Overview: A medium-sized provincial organization founded in 2007
Affiliation(s): Ontario Curling Association
Membership: 28 teams; Member Profile: Curlers 70 & older; Committees: Executive
Chief Officer(s):
Art Lobel, President
asobel@sympatico.ca

The Grand Orange Lodge of British America See Grand Orange Lodge of Canada

Grand Orange Lodge of Canada
94 Sheppard Ave. West, Toronto ON M2N 1M5
Tel: 416-223-1690; Fax: 416-223-1324
Toll-Free: 800-565-6248
info@grandorangelodge.ca
www.grandorangelodge.ca
Also Known As: Loyal Orange Association
Previous Name: The Grand Orange Lodge of British America
Overview: A large national organization founded in 1830
Mission: To encourage its members to actively participate in the Protestant church of their choice; To actively support the Canadian system of government; To anticipate legislation & its impact on the civil & religious liberties of all Canadians; To provide social activities that will enrich the lives of its members, community and the overall country of Canada
Member of: Imperial Orange Council of the World
Finances: Annual Operating Budget: Less than $50,000; Funding Sources: Membership dues
Staff Member(s): 8
Membership: 100,000
Activities: Awareness Events: Annual Golf Tournament
Chief Officer(s):
Gerald Budden, Grand Master & Sovereign
Don Wilson, Deputy Grand Master
John Chalmers, Grand Secretary
Jodachal@yahoo.ca
Roy Dawe, Grand Treasurer

Grand Lodge of Newfoundland-Labrador
NL
Chief Officer(s):
Clyde Crane, Grand Secretary
clyde.crane@hotmail.com

Grand Orange Lodge of New Brunswick
553 Hwy. 104, Burtts Corner NB E6L 2B2
Tel: 506-363-2827
Chief Officer(s):
Daniel Grasse, Grand Secretary
danielgrasse@outlook.com

Grand Orange Lodge of Ontario East
PO Box 284, Brockville ON K6V 5V5
Tel: 613-342-7353
www.orangelodge.com
Chief Officer(s):
Art Duncan, Grand Master
arthurduncan@sympatico.ca

Grand Orange Lodge of Ontario West
ON
gm@orangeontario.org
www.orangeontario.org
Chief Officer(s):
Keith Wright, Grand Master

Grand Orange Lodge of Québec
3081, rue Allan, Kinnear's Mills QC G0N 1K0
Tel: 418-424-0912
Chief Officer(s):
James Allan, Grand Master

Grand Orange Lodge of Western Canada
407 Falconridge Gardens NE, Calgary AB T3J 2B9
Tel: 587-968-1519
info@grandorangelodgeofwesterncanada.com
grandorangelodgeofwesterncanada.com
Chief Officer(s):
Adrian Cotter, Grand Secretary

Grand River Beekeepers' Association
Branchton ON
Tel: 519-740-1416
grandriverbee@gmail.com
Overview: A small local organization
Mission: To develop the beekeeping skills of members
Member of: Ontario Beekeepers' Association
Membership: Member Profile: Beekeepers who have between one & fifty hives
Activities: Organizing meetings at the Christian Fellowship Church in Waterloo; Providing opportunities for beekeepers to network
Chief Officer(s):
Vince Nevidon, President

Grand River Conservation Foundation (GRCF)
PO Box 729, 400 Clyde Rd., Cambridge ON N1R 5W6
Tel: 519-621-2761; Fax: 519-621-4844
Toll-Free: 866-900-4722
www.grandriver.ca
www.facebook.com/grandriverconservation
twitter.com/grandriverca
www.youtube.com/user/grandriverca
Previous Name: Grand River Foundation
Overview: A small local charitable organization founded in 1965
Mission: To provide leadership & support within the community of the Valley of the Grand River for the protection, conservation, responsible use & management of its natural resources, in response to the needs & wishes & for the ongoing enjoyment of its residents, as well as of the broader community of our province & country
Finances: Annual Operating Budget: Less than $50,000; Funding Sources: Individuals, groups & corporations
Staff Member(s): 1; 22 volunteer(s)
Membership: 1-99
Activities: Speaker Service: Yes
Chief Officer(s):
Sara Wilbur, Executive Director, 519-621-2763 Ext. 2272
swilbur@grandriver.ca
Awards:
- S.C. Johnson Environmental Scholarship
Annual award for a student enrolled in an environmental sciences program with an emphasis on manufacturing, eocnomics, business, chemistry or related applications at a university in the Grand River watershed area; Amount: $4,000

Grand River Foundation See Grand River Conservation Foundation

GRAND Society
c/o #509, 14 Spadina Rd., Toronto ON M5R 3M4
Tel: 416-513-9404
Also Known As: Grandparents Requesting Access & Dignity
Overview: A medium-sized national organization founded in 1983
Mission: To provide emotional support to grandparents who have been denied access to their grandchildren; to make the public & professionals aware of this problem; to influence provincial family law to recognize the rights of grandparents
Finances: Funding Sources: New Horizons Program; federal government
Membership: Fees: $20 individual; $35 a couple
Chief Officer(s):
Joan Brooks, President/Chair

Hamilton Chapter
#19, 317 Limeridge Rd. West, Hamilton ON L9C 7C8
Tel: 905-385-6561
Chief Officer(s):
Sylvia Chappell, President

Ottawa Chapter
1516 Boutier Dr., Ottawa ON K1E 3J5
Tel: 613-837-8371; Fax: 613-837-8371
Chief Officer(s):
Liliane George, Contact

Grand Valley Trails Association (GVTA)
PO Box 40068, Waterloo ON N2J 4V1
Tel: 519-576-6156
info@gvta.on.ca
www.gvta.on.ca
www.facebook.com/20610893171
twitter.com/GrandVTrails
Overview: A small local charitable organization founded in 1973
Mission: To establish & maintain a public trail along or adjacent to the Grand River watershed & to engage in & promote year-round hiking
Member of: Hike Ontario
Membership: Fees: $30 per household; $300 life
Activities: Trail follows the Grand River north from Dunnville on Lake Erie to Alton; connects to the Bruce by sidetrail (255 km)
Chief Officer(s):
Nicholas Dinka, President
president@gvta.on.ca

Grande Cache Chamber of Commerce
PO Box 1342, 4600 Pine Plaza, Grande Cache AB T0E 0Y0
Tel: 780-501-4461
gcc@grandecachechamber.com
www.grandecachechamber.com
www.facebook.com/gchamberchat
twitter.com/gcchambertweets
Overview: A small local organization

Mission: To promote free enterprise; To provide services for members
Affiliation(s): Alberta Chamber of Commerce; Canadian Chamber of Commerce
Finances: *Annual Operating Budget:* Less than $50,000; *Funding Sources:* Membership fees; grants
50 volunteer(s)
Membership: 41; *Fees:* Schedule available; *Committees:* Tourism; Membership; Trade Fair; Programs
Chief Officer(s):
Rick Bambrick, Acting President

Grande Frères Grandes Soeurs du Grand Moncton *See* Big Brothers Big Sisters of New Brunswick

Grande Loge du Québec *See* Grand Lodge of Québec - Ancient, Free & Accepted Masons

Grande Prairie & Area Association of Realtors (GPAAR)
10106 - 102 St., Grande Prairie AB T8V 2V7
Tel: 780-532-3508; *Fax:* 780-539-3515
eo@gpaar.ca
www.grandeprairie-mls.ca
www.facebook.com/GPAAR
Overview: A small local organization overseen by Alberta Real Estate Association
Member of: Alberta Real Estate Association; The Canadian Real Estate Association
Membership: 260+; *Member Profile:* Real estate industry members & partners
Activities: Operating an MLS system for the region
Chief Officer(s):
Susan Rankin, President

Grande Prairie & District Association for Persons with Developmental Disabilities (GPDAPDD)
8702 - 113 St., Grande Prairie AB T8V 6K5
Tel: 780-532-8436; *Fax:* 780-532-5144
www.gpdapdd.org
Previous Name: Grande Prairie & District Association for the Mentally Handicapped
Overview: A small local organization founded in 1956
Mission: To serve the needs of persons with developmental disabilities, both adults & children, & their families, in the City of Grande Prairie & throughout the northwest region of Alberta
Member of: Alberta Council of Disability Services; Alberta Association for Community Living; Alberta Association for Supported Employment
Activities: Offerinf residential services, day programs, and after-school programs
Chief Officer(s):
Darrin Stubbs, Executive Director
dstubbs@signaturesupport.ca

Grande Prairie & District Association for the Mentally Handicapped *See* Grande Prairie & District Association for Persons with Developmental Disabilities

Grande Prairie & District Chamber of Commerce
Centre 2000, #217, 11330 - 106 St., Grande Prairie AB T8V 7X9
Tel: 780-532-5340; *Fax:* 780-532-2926
info@gpchamber.com
www.grandeprairiechamber.com
www.facebook.com/303922827273
twitter.com/grprchamber
Overview: A small local organization founded in 1915
Mission: To enhance the economic well-being of our members, community & region
Finances: *Funding Sources:* Membership dues; trade shows
Staff Member(s): 5
Membership: *Fees:* Schedule available based on number of employees; *Committees:* Membership; Advocacy; Policy; Health Action
Activities: *Speaker Service:* Yes; *Library:* Open to public
Chief Officer(s):
Dan Pearcy, CEO
dan@gpchamber.com

Grande Prairie & Region United Way
#213, 11330 - 106 St., Grande Prairie AB T8V 7X9
Tel: 780-532-1105; *Fax:* 780-532-3532
info@unitedwayabnw.org
www.gpunitedway.org
www.facebook.com/UnitedWayABNW
twitter.com/UnitedWayABNW
www.youtube.com/user/GrowUnitedBreakfast
Overview: A small local organization overseen by United Way of Canada - Centraide Canada
Mission: To bring people together to strengthen the community; To strengthen the capacity of community & other local agencies to bring about positive change
Chief Officer(s):
Brenda Yamkowy, Executive Director
brenda@gpunitedwayabnw.org

Grande Prairie Food Bank
9615 - 102 St., Grande Prairie AB T8V 2T8
Tel: 780-532-3720; *Fax:* 780-532-1960
services@salvationarmygp.ca
www.salvationarmygp.ca
Overview: A small local organization founded in 1978
Mission: To provide food bank family services; To try to help people help themselves & become self-sufficient
Member of: The Salvation Army
Staff Member(s): 6; 500 volunteer(s)
Chief Officer(s):
Kerry Harris, Contact

Grande Prairie Friendship Centre
10507 - 98 Ave., Grande Prairie AB T8V 4L1
Tel: 780-532-5722; *Fax:* 780-539-5121
gpfriend@telusplanet.net
gpfriendshipcenter.wordpress.com
Overview: A small local organization overseen by Alberta Native Friendship Centres Association
Member of: Alberta Native Friendship Centres Association
Chief Officer(s):
Miranda Laroche, Executive Director

Grande Prairie Museum
10329 - 101 Ave., Grande Prairie AB T8V 6V3
Tel: 780-830-7090
info@grandeprairiemuseum.org
www.facebook.com/G.P.Museum
Overview: A small local charitable organization founded in 1961
Mission: To maintain a high standard of collection activity & preserve the historical objects that represent the community
Member of: Alberta Museum Association; Canadian Museum Association; Chamber of Commerce
Affiliation(s): Society of the Peace Museums Network; Pioneer Museum Society of Grande Prairie & District
Finances: *Funding Sources:* Sales; donations; grants
Activities: Educational programs & tours

Grande Prairie Regional College Academic Staff Association (GPRC) / Association des enseignants du collège régional de Grande Prairie
10726 - 106 Ave., Grande Prairie AB T8V 4C4
Tel: 780-539-2843; *Fax:* 780-539-2214
Toll-Free: 888-539-4772
asa@gprc.ab.ca
www.gprc.ab.ca/departments/asa
Overview: A small local organization
Member of: Alberta Colleges & Institutes Faculty Association
Finances: *Annual Operating Budget:* $50,000-$100,000; *Funding Sources:* Membership dues
Staff Member(s): 150
Membership: 260; *Member Profile:* College instructors; *Committees:* Art Acquisition; College Foundation; Degree Equivalence; Early Retirement; Environment; Evaluations; Food Service; Grievance; Negotiating; Nominating; Professional Growth; Professional Standards; Retirement; Staff Development; Tenure; Tribute; Writing Centre Coordinating
Chief Officer(s):
Som Pillay, President
spillay@gprc.ab.ca
Darcy Moss, Vice-President
dmoss@gprc.ab.ca
Charles Backman, Treasurer
cbackman@gprc.ab.ca

Grande Prairie Soaring Society
PO Box 64, Hythe AB T0H 2C0
www.gpsoaringsociety.ca
Overview: A small local organization
Member of: Soaring Association of Canada
Chief Officer(s):
Dwayne Doll, President
dddoll.canada@gmail.com
Lloyd Sherk, Secretary-Treasurer
lsherk@telusplanet.net

Grande Prairie Society for the Prevention of Cruelty to Animals (GPSPCA)
12220 - 104th Ave., Grande Prairie AB T8V 8A8
Tel: 780-538-4030; *Fax:* 780-532-7275
adopt@gpspca.com
www.gpspca.com
www.facebook.com/gpspca
www.youtube.com/GPSPCA
Also Known As: Grande Prairie & District S.P.C.A.
Overview: A small local charitable organization founded in 1984
Mission: To promote respect, humane treatment & compassion toward animals
Member of: Alberta Society for the Prevention of Cruelty to Animals
Staff Member(s): 6
Membership: *Fees:* $25 individual; $50 family; $100 corporate
Activities: Adoption; humane education programs
Chief Officer(s):
Laureen Harcourt, Executive Director

La Grande Région d'Ottawa *See* Habitat for Humanity Canada

Grandparents Raising Grandchildren - British Columbia
c/o Parent Support Services Society of BC, #204, 5623 Imperial St., Burnaby BC V5J 1G1
Tel: 604-669-1616; *Fax:* 604-669-1636
Toll-Free: 877-345-9777
Other Communication: Support Line: 1-855-474-9777
GRGline@parentsupportbc.ca
www.parentsupportbc.ca/grandparents_raising_grandchildren
Overview: A small local organization
Mission: To provide answers & assistance to grandparents & other relatives who are raising a family member's child.

Les Grands Ballets Canadiens de Montréal (GBCM)
4816, rue Rivard, Montréal QC H2J 2N6
Tél: 514-849-8681
info@grandsballets.com
www.grandsballets.com
www.facebook.com/lesgrandsballets
twitter.com/grandsballets
www.youtube.com/user/LesGrandsBallets
Aperçu: *Dimension:* moyenne; *Envergure:* locale; Organisme sans but lucratif; fondée en 1957
Mission: Maintenir la tradition du ballet classique et élargir le champ d'expression de cette forme artistique par la création; faire connaître et apprécier la danse à tous les publics grâce à la qualité de nos presentations et de nos productions
Membre(s) du personnel: 40
Activités: *Service de conférenciers:* Oui
Membre(s) du bureau directeur:
Alain Dancyger, Directeur général
Gradimir Pankov, Directeur artistique

Grands Frères Grandes Soeurs d'Ottawa *See* Big Brothers Big Sisters of Ontario

Les Grands Frères Grandes Soeurs du Canada *See* Big Brothers Big Sisters of Canada

Grands-Parents Tendresse
374, rue Laviotte, Saint-Jérôme QC J7Y 2S9
Tél: 450-436-6664; *Téléc:* 450-436-9885
info@grandsparentstendresse.org
www.grandsparentstendresse.org
Aperçu: *Dimension:* petite; *Envergure:* locale
Mission: D'offrir des activités aux personnes âgées, afin d'affirmer leurs compétences physiques et mentales.
Membre: *Critères d'admissibilite:* Personnes 45 ans et plus; *Comités:* Bibliothèque; Causerie; Cuisine; Intergénération; Journal; Marrainage; Représentation; Social; Tricot
Membre(s) du bureau directeur:
Marlene Girard, Coordonatrice

Grandview & District Chamber of Commerce
PO Box 28, Grandview MB R0L 0Y0
Tel: 204-546-2626
www.grandviewmanitoba.com
Overview: A small local organization
Mission: To promote the town of Grandview & surrounding area
Finances: *Annual Operating Budget:* Less than $50,000; *Funding Sources:* Municipal government
20 volunteer(s)
Membership: 41 individual; *Fees:* $25 individual; $100 business
Activities: Participating in beautification of town; Promoting tourism & business
Chief Officer(s):

Pierce Cairns, President
Robyn Dingwall, Secretary & Treasurer

Grant MacEwan College Faculty Association (GMCFA) / Association des professeurs du Collège Grant MacEwan
City Centre Campus, #7-102, 10700 - 104 Ave., Edmonton AB T5J 4S2
Tel: 780-497-5068; *Fax:* 780-497-5065
faoffice@macewan.ca
www.macewanfa.ca
www.facebook.com/124596214413541
twitter.com/gmufa
Previous Name: Grant MacEwan Community College Faculty Association
Overview: A small local organization founded in 1972
Mission: To advocate for the interests of members
Member of: Alberta College-Institutes Faculties Association
Finances: *Annual Operating Budget:* $100,000-$250,000
Staff Member(s): 3
Membership: 984 individual; *Fees:* 1% of gross salary
Chief Officer(s):
Jasmine French, Executive Director

Grant MacEwan College Non-Academic Staff Association
See MacEwan Staff Association

Grant MacEwan Community College Faculty Association
See Grant MacEwan College Faculty Association

Grape Growers of Ontario
PO Box 100, Vineland ON L0R 2E0
Tel: 905-688-0990; *Fax:* 905-688-3211
info@grapegrowersofontario.com
www.grapegrowersofontario.com
www.facebook.com/174946032541143
twitter.com/grapegrowersont
www.pinterest.com/grapegrowers
Previous Name: Ontario Grape Growers' Marketing Board
Overview: A medium-sized provincial organization
Mission: To implement innovations in the grape growing industry in order to improve the product
Staff Member(s): 8
Membership: *Member Profile:* Grape growers & viticulturalists; *Committees:* Growers'
Chief Officer(s):
Debbie Zimmerman, Chief Executive Officer
d.zimmerman@grapegrowersofontario.com

Graphic Arts Industries Association; Canadian Printing & Imaging Association *See* Canadian Printing Industries Association

Grasslands Naturalists (GN)
PO Box 2491, Medicine Hat AB T1A 8G8
Tel: 403-529-1003
www.natureline.info/gn
Also Known As: Society of Grasslands Naturalists
Overview: A small local charitable organization founded in 1991
Mission: To promote the study, protection, & preservation of natural habitats & nature in general
Member of: Nature Alberta
Affiliation(s): Canadian Nature Federation
Staff Member(s): 1; 25 volunteer(s)
Membership: 140; *Fees:* $20 individuals; $25 families/organizations; *Committees:* Budget; Communications; Field Trips; Fund Raising; Governance; Indoor Program; Issues; Operations
Activities: Offering educational opportunities, such as field trips & lectures; Assisting in the collection & provision of records of species; *Library:* Police Point Park Nature Centre Resource Centre
Chief Officer(s):
Hugh Armstrong, President

Gravelbourg Chamber of Commerce
PO Box 5, Gravelbourg SK S0H 1X0
Tel: 306-648-7559
gravelbourgchamber@gmail.com
gravelbourg.ca
www.facebook.com/gravelbourgchamber
Overview: A small local organization
Mission: To support the business community of Gravelbourg
Member of: Saskatchewan Chamber of Commerce
Finances: *Annual Operating Budget:* Less than $50,000; *Funding Sources:* Membership fees
Membership: 52; *Fees:* $50; *Member Profile:* Businesses
Chief Officer(s):

Fred Hundersmarck, President

Gravenhurst Board of Trade *See* Gravenhurst Chamber of Commerce/Visitors Bureau

Gravenhurst Chamber of Commerce/Visitors Bureau
275 Muskoka Rd. South, Gravenhurst ON P1P 1J1
Tel: 705-687-4432; *Fax:* 705-687-4382
info@gravenhurstchamber.com
www.gravenhurstchamber.com
www.facebook.com/TheGravenhurstChamberOfCommerce
twitter.com/GhurstChamber
Previous Name: Gravenhurst Board of Trade
Overview: A small local organization founded in 1948
Mission: To work together to advance the commercial, financial, & investment interests of the community
Member of: Ontario Chamber of Commerce
Finances: *Funding Sources:* Membership fees; Special events
Staff Member(s): 7
Membership: *Fees:* Schedule available; *Member Profile:* Individuals; Businesses
Chief Officer(s):
Bob Collins, President
president@gravenhurstchamber.com
Danielle Millar, Executive Director
manager@gravenhurstchamber.com

Great Divide Trails Association (GDTA)
229 - 18A St. NW, Calgary AB T2N 2H1
greatdividetrail@gmail.com
www.greatdividetrail.com
www.facebook.com/144747792203345
twitter.com/GDTAssociation
Overview: A small local organization founded in 2013
Mission: To advocate the completion and long-term preservation of the Great Divide Trail.
Finances: *Funding Sources:* Donations
Membership: *Fees:* $30
Activities: Hiking
Chief Officer(s):
David Hockey, Chair

The Great Herd of Bisons of the Fertile Plains
6 Melness Bay, Winnipeg MB R2K 2T5
Overview: A small local organization founded in 1984
Affiliation(s): The Bootmakers of Toronto
Finances: *Annual Operating Budget:* Less than $50,000
Membership: 32; *Fees:* $10
Chief Officer(s):
Ihor Mayba, Contact

Great Lakes Gliding Club (GLGC)
7272 - 6 Line, RR#3, Tottenham ON L0G 1W0
Tel: 416-466-7016
postmaster@greatlakesgliding.com
www.greatlakesgliding.com
www.facebook.com/flyglgc
Overview: A small local organization founded in 1998
Mission: The club offers license training as well as flying competitions
Membership: 35; *Fees:* $250 associate; $375 students; $550 full; *Member Profile:* Students; Licenced pilots

Great Lakes Institute for Environmental Research (GLIER)
401 Sunset Ave., Windsor ON N9B 3P4
Tel: 519-253-3000; *Fax:* 519-971-3616
glier@uwindsor.ca
www.uwindsor.ca/glier
Overview: A small provincial organization founded in 1981
Mission: Multidisciplinary facility with members from many disciplines, including biology, geology, chemistry, engineering, marine biology, molecular biology, genetics and ecology.
Chief Officer(s):
Brian Fryer, Contact
bfryer@uwindsor.ca

The Great Lakes Marine Heritage Foundation
55 Ontario St., Kingston ON K7L 2Y2
Tel: 613-542-2261; *Fax:* 613-542-0043
marmus@marmuseum.ca
www.marmuseum.ca
Overview: A small local charitable organization founded in 1991
Staff Member(s): 1
Chief Officer(s):
Doug Cowie, Manager
manager@marmuseum.ca

Great Lakes Waterways Development Association *See* Chamber of Marine Commerce

Great Slave Snowmobile Association
4209 - 49A Ave., Yellowknife NT X1A 1B3
Tel: 867-766-4353
Also Known As: GSSA Trail Riders
Overview: A small provincial organization founded in 1988
Mission: The Association is a non-profit organization that is dedicated to promoting safe, responsible snowmobiling in Yellowknife.
Affiliation(s): Canadian Council of Snowmobile Organizations; International Snowmobile Council
Finances: *Annual Operating Budget:* Less than $50,000
6 volunteer(s)
Membership: 300 individual; *Fees:* $35 single; $50 family
Activities: Community fund-raising; clearing trails; adding signage along trail system
Chief Officer(s):
Bill Braden, President

Great White North Franchisee Association (GWNFA) / L'Association des franchisés Great White North
#23, 2133 Royal Windsor Dr., Mississauga ON L5J 1K5
Tel: 905-823-2222
Fax: 905-823-2222
Toll-Free: 877-855-7788
Other Communication: Membership E-mail: membership@gwnfa.ca
info@gwnfa.ca
gwnfa.ca
Overview: A small national organization founded in 2017
Mission: To protect & promote the interests of store owners across Canada, who are committed to preserving the integrity of the Tim Hortons brand
Finances: *Funding Sources:* Donations; member dues
Membership: *Fees:* $1,000 per store; *Member Profile:* Tim Hortons franchisees
Activities: Advocacy; discounted insurance & cell phone plans for members
Chief Officer(s):
David Hughes, President

Greater Arnprior Chamber of Commerce (GACC)
#111, 16 Edward St. South, Arnprior ON K7S 3W4
Tel: 613-623-6817; *Fax:* 613-623-6826
info@gacc.ca
www.gacc.ca
www.facebook.com/greaterarnprior
Overview: A small local organization founded in 1995
Mission: To improve economic prosperity & quality of life in Arnprior & McNab/Braeside
Member of: Ontario Chamber of Commerce
Finances: *Funding Sources:* Membership fees
Staff Member(s): 1
Membership: 150; *Fees:* $100
Activities: Providing networking opportunities; Arranging speaker meetings; Organizing events including Canada Day & golf tournament
Chief Officer(s):
Pamela Cox, President
Cheryl Sparling, Administrative Assistant

Greater Barrie Chamber of Commerce
97 Toronto St., Barrie ON L4N 1V1
Tel: 705-721-5000; *Fax:* 705-726-0973
admin@barriechamber.com
barriechamber.com
www.facebook.com/BarrieChamber
twitter.com/barriechamber
www.youtube.com/barriechamber
Overview: A small local organization
Mission: To assist new & existing businesses with their promotional/advertising needs of their product or products; To provide effective administrative functions to carry out the policies & procedures of the Board for the continual enhancement of the membership
Finances: *Annual Operating Budget:* $250,000-$500,000; *Funding Sources:* Membership dues; events
Staff Member(s): 3; 100 volunteer(s)
Membership: 900; *Fees:* Schedule available; *Committees:* Communications; Events; Finance; Government Relations & Advocacy; Membership; Special Events
Activities: Organizing Gala Awards; Offering networking events & seminars
Chief Officer(s):
Rod Jackson, CEO
rjackson@barriechamber.com

Greater Bathurst Chamber of Commerce / Chambre de commerce du Grand Bathurst
Keystone Bldg., #101, 270 Douglas Ave., Bathurst NB E2A 1M9
Tel: 506-546-8100; Fax: 506-548-2200
info@bathurstchamber.ca
www.bathurstchamber.ca
www.facebook.com/335718759975
twitter.com/bathurstchamber
Overview: A medium-sized local organization founded in 1913
Mission: To facilitate economic growth in the Chaleur area; To advocate for the business community of Greater Bathurst
Affiliation(s): Canadian Chamber of Commerce
Staff Member(s): 4
Membership: 300+; *Fees:* Schedule available based upon number of employees; *Member Profile:* Business & professional individuals of the Chaleur business community, from Allardville to Belledune
Activities: Providing resources; Offering networking opportunities; Providing education for members
Chief Officer(s):
Mitch Poirier, General Manager
mitch.poirier@bathurstchamber.ca
Bernard Cormier, President
Linda Rogers, Treasurer

Greater Charlottetown & Area Chamber of Commerce
PO Box 67, #230, 134 Kent St., Charlottetown PE C1A 7K2
Tel: 902-628-2000; Fax: 902-368-3570
www.charlottetownchamber.com
www.linkedin.com/company/the-greater-charlottetown-area-chamber-of-commerce
www.facebook.com/CharlottetownChamber
twitter.com/GCACCbuzz
Previous Name: Charlottetown Board of Trade
Overview: A medium-sized local organization founded in 1887
Mission: To be the voice of business on economic issues; to provide services & opportunities for members to enhance their ability to do business
Member of: Canadian Chamber of Commerce
Affiliation(s): Atlantic Provinces Chamber of Commerce
Finances: *Annual Operating Budget:* $250,000-$500,000; *Funding Sources:* Membership dues; fundraising
Staff Member(s): 6
Membership: 800; *Fees:* $220-$1,050 based on number of employees; *Committees:* Policy; Business Development; Human Resources; Communications; Business Under Forty; Event; Immigration; Stratford Business Community Forum; Cornwall Business Community Forum; Bonding By
Chief Officer(s):
Pam Williams, President
Penny Walsh McGuire, Executive Director
pwmcguire@charlottetownchamber.com
Angela Smith, Office Manager
asmith@charlottetownchamber.com
Awards:
• Entrepreneurial Award of Excellence
Publications:
• Greater Charlottetown & Area Chamber of Commerce E-Newsletter
Type: Newsletter

Greater Corner Brook Board of Trade (GCBBT)
PO Box 475, 11 Confederation Dr., Corner Brook NL A2H 6E6
Tel: 709-634-5831; Fax: 709-639-9710
www.gcbbt.com
twitter.com/cornerbrookbot
Previous Name: Corner Brook Chamber of Commerce
Overview: A small local organization
Membership: 178; *Fees:* Schedule available
Activities: Seminars; luncheons, workshops
Chief Officer(s):
Chris Noseworthy, President

Greater Dufferin Area Chamber of Commerce; Orangeville & District Chamber of Commerce *See* Dufferin Board of Trade

Greater Edmonton Library Association (GELA)
PO Box 60104, Stn. U of A Postal Outlet, Edmonton AB T6G 2S4
info@gela.ca
www.gela.ca
twitter.com/gela_edmonton
Previous Name: Edmonton Library Association
Overview: A small local organization founded in 1945
Mission: To support library workers in the city of Edmonton & the surrounding region
Membership: *Fees:* $25; *Member Profile:* Librarians, library technicians, library staff, students, & others who are interested in library activities in Edmonton & the surrounding area
Activities: Offering programs addressing library issues in the Greater Edmonton area; Promoting continuing education opportunities; Providing professional development activities; Organizing community outreach initiatives, through the Women's Prison & Reintegration Subcommittee & the Community Bookshelf Subcommittee; Facilitating the exchange of ideas between local library workers; Offering networking opportunities
Chief Officer(s):
Ali Grotkowski, President
Alison Foster, Secretary
Kalin Jensen, Treasurer
Awards:
• GELA Professional Development Grant
Awarded to a GELA member to attend library-related conferences, workshops, seminars, or lectures *Deadline:* March; *Amount:* $300

Greater Fort Erie Chamber of Commerce
#1, 660 Garrison Rd., Fort Erie ON L2A 6E2
Tel: 905-871-3803; Fax: 905-871-1561
info@forteriechamber.com
www.forteriechamber.com
www.facebook.com/FEChamber
Overview: A small local organization founded in 1947
Staff Member(s): 2
Membership: *Fees:* Schedule available; *Member Profile:* Local businesses; organizations; *Committees:* Human Resources; Education; Bursary; Golf; International Women's Day; Business After Five; Business & Government Affairs; Bursary; Technology; Strategic Planning; Auction
Activities: Business networking; social outings; professional workshops & seminars; annual general meetings
Chief Officer(s):
Rick Phibbs, President
Karen Audet, Operations Manager

Greater Halifax Conventions & Meetings Bureau *See* Destination Halifax

Greater Hamilton Technology Enterprise Centre *See* Hamilton Technology Centre

Greater Hamilton Tourism & Convention Services *See* Tourism Hamilton

Greater Innisfil Chamber of Commerce (GICC)
8034 Yonge St., #B, Innisfil ON L9S 1L6
Tel: 705-431-4199; Fax: 705-431-6628
manager@innisfilchamber.com
www.innisfilchamber.com
twitter.com/InnisfilChamber
Previous Name: Innisfil Chamber of Commerce
Overview: A small local organization founded in 1973
Mission: To provide one voice for a prosperous Innisfil
Member of: Canadian Chamber of Commerce; Ontario Chamber of Commerce
Affiliation(s): Alcona Business Association; South Innisfil Business & Community Association; Cookstown Chamber of Commerce; 400 Industrial Group
Finances: *Funding Sources:* Membership fees; Fundraising; Municipal grant
Staff Member(s): 2
Membership: *Fees:* Schedule available; *Member Profile:* Business leaders; *Committees:* Communications; Events; Policies & Procedures/Governance; Education; People/Nominations; Value Proposition/Membership; Finance
Activities: Hosting the Annual Business Awards & an annual golf tournament; Promoting existing business; Attracting & welcoming new business; Communicating between business, community, & government; *Speaker Service:* Yes; *Library*
Chief Officer(s):
Mary-Ellen Madeley, Manager
Shannon MacIntyre, President

Greater Kamloops Chamber of Commerce
615 Victoria St., Kamloops BC V2C 2B3
Tel: 250-372-7722; Fax: 250-828-9500
mail@kamloopschamber.ca
www.kamloopschamber.ca
www.linkedin.com/groups/4087107/profile
www.facebook.com/KamloopsChamberofCommerce
twitter.com/KamloopsChamber
www.youtube.com/watch?v=_55-O-Wp6Ko
Also Known As: Kamloops Chamber of Commerce
Overview: A small local organization founded in 1896
Mission: To create an environment that ensures the greatest opportunity for the success of the membership
Member of: BC Chamber of Commerce; Canadian Chamber of Commerce
Finances: *Annual Operating Budget:* $250,000-$500,000; *Funding Sources:* Membership dues; Fundraising
Staff Member(s): 5; 10 volunteer(s)
Membership: 715; *Fees:* $48.30 non-profit; $69.56 businesses with 1-10 employees; $93.71 businesses with 11-50 employees; $159.34 businesses with 51+ employees
Activities: Holding luncheons, seminars, & socials; *Awareness Events:* Chamber Week; Small Business Week *Library:* Business Information Centre; Open to public
Chief Officer(s):
Deb McClelland, Executive Director
Awards:
• Community Futures Business of the Year Award
• Excel Personnel Business Person of the Year Award
• City of Kamloops Community Service Award
• Coast Kamloops Hotel & Conference Centre Employer of the Year Award
• Kamloops Home Hardware Building Centre Aboriginal Business of the Year Award
• BC Hydro Green Award (1-10 Staff)
• Rocky Mountaineer Green Award (11+ Staff)
• KGHM International - Ajax Project Home Based Business of the Year Award
• BDC Manufacturer Award
• Venture Kamloops Resource Industry Award
• Aberdeen Mall Retailer Award (1-10 Staff)
• Underwriters Insurance Brokers Retailer Award (11+ Staff)
• Berwick on the Park Service Provider Award (1-10 Staff)
• Kamloops Lincoln Service Provider Award (11+ Staff)
• BCLC Technology Innovator Award
• TRU Faculty of Adventure, Culinary Arts & Tourism and Tourism Sun Peaks Tourism Award
• Nutech Safety Young Entrepreneur of the Year Award
• President's Award

Greater Kingston & Frontenac *See* Habitat for Humanity Canada

Greater Kingston Chamber of Commerce (GKCC)
945 Princess St., Kingston ON K7L 3N6
Tel: 613-548-4453; Fax: 613-548-4743
info@kingstonchamber.on.ca
www.kingstonchamber.on.ca
www.linkedin.com/company/greater-kingston-chamber-of-commerce
www.facebook.com/greaterkingstonchamber
twitter.com/kingstonchamber
www.youtube.com/channel/UC1Pmf1i3uKXFF7PM_3_5cAA
Previous Name: Kingston Board of Trade
Overview: A medium-sized local organization founded in 1841
Mission: To advance economic progress, free enterprise, & the quality of life
Member of: Canadian Chamber of Commerce; Ontario Chamber of Commerce
Finances: *Funding Sources:* Membership dues; programs; events
Staff Member(s): 5
Membership: 800; *Committees:* Advocacy; Events; Marketing & Membership; Connect - The Business Expo; Chamber Classic; Gala & Business Achievement Awards; Finance; Nominations
Activities: Offering a group benefits plan & a discount program; Organizing business mixers, breakfast clubs, & a golf tournament; *Awareness Events:* Tourism Awareness Week; Small Business Week; *Rents Mailing List:* Yes
Chief Officer(s):
Martin Sherris, CEO

Greater Kitchener & Waterloo Chamber of Commerce
PO Box 2367, 80 Queen St. North, Kitchener ON N2H 6L4
Tel: 519-576-5000; Fax: 519-742-4760
admin@greaterkwchamber.com
www.greaterkwchamber.com
www.linkedin.com/groups/Greater-KW-Chamber-Commerce-2056325
www.facebook.com/GKWCC
twitter.com/gkwcc
www.youtube.com/user/GreaterKWChamber
Overview: A medium-sized local charitable organization founded in 2001

Mission: To serve business in the Greater Kitchener Waterloo area & be its voice in the betterment of the community
Member of: Canadian Chamber of Commerce; Ontario Chamber of Commerce
Finances: *Funding Sources:* Membership fees; special projects
Staff Member(s): 15; 300+ volunteer(s)
Membership: 1,800; *Committees:* Business After 5; Business Excellence Awards (Nominations); Communications; Chamber Young Professionals; Energy & Environment; Federal/Provincial Affairs; Golf Scramble; Membership; Networking & Breakfast Club; Regional/Municipal Affairs; Women's Leadership
Activities: *Rents Mailing List:* Yes; *Library:* Chamber of Commerce Resource Centre; Open to public
Chief Officer(s):
Ian McLean, President & CEO, 519-749-6038

Greater Langley Chamber of Commerce
#207, 8047 - 199 St., Langley BC V2Y 0E2
Tel: 604-371-3770; *Fax:* 604-371-3731
info@langleychamber.com
www.langleychamber.com
www.facebook.com/langleychamber
twitter.com/LangleyChamber
Overview: A small local organization
Staff Member(s): 5
Membership: 1,000; *Fees:* Schedule available
Chief Officer(s):
Scott Johnstone, President
Lynn Whitehouse, Executive Director
Publications:
• Greater Langley Chamber of Commerce Newsletter
Type: Newsletter; *Frequency:* Monthly

Greater Miramichi Chamber of Commerce *See* Miramichi Chamber of Commerce

Greater Moncton Chamber of Commerce (GMCC) / Chambre de commerce du Grand Moncton
#200, 1273 Main St., Moncton NB E1C 0P4
Tel: 506-857-2883
info@gmcc.nb.ca
www.gmcc.nb.ca
www.linkedin.com/company/greater-moncton-chamber-of-commerce
www.facebook.com/GreaterMonctonChamberOfCommerce
twitter.com/MonctonChamber
www.youtube.com/user/GreaterMonctonCham
Overview: A medium-sized local organization founded in 1891
Mission: To strengthen business & community in the Greater Moncton area through leadership, member services, & advocacy on business issues at the municipal, provincial, & national levels
Member of: Atlantic Provinces Chamber of Commerce (APCC); New Brunswick Chamber of Commerce; Canadian Chamber of Commerce
Finances: *Funding Sources:* Membership dues and events
Staff Member(s): 5
Membership: 820; *Fees:* Schedule available based upon number of employees; *Member Profile:* Businesses in the Greater Moncton area
Activities: Offering training sessions; Providing networking opportunities; advocacy
Chief Officer(s):
Carol O'Reilly, CEO, 506-857-2883
ceo@gmcc.nb.ca
Scott Lewis, Chair
Awards:
• Greater Moncton Excellence Awards
Categories include the following: Excellence in Business, Emerging Business, Marketing, Innovation, Service Excellence, & Community Service

Greater Moncton Chinese Cultural Association (GMCCA)
Moncton NB
www.gmcca.ca
Previous Name: Moncton Chinese Friendship Association (MCFA)
Overview: A small local organization founded in 1981
Mission: To promote the appreciation & understanding of Chinese culture among both members of the Chinese community & general public in the Greater Moncton area
Member of: Chinese Canadian National Council
Chief Officer(s):
Mingkun Gu, President

Greater Moncton Real Estate Board Inc.
541 St. George Blvd., Moncton NB E1E 2B6
Tel: 506-857-8200; *Fax:* 506-857-1760
gmreb@nb.aibn.com
www.monctonrealestateboard.com
Overview: A small local organization overseen by New Brunswick Real Estate Association
Mission: To provide its members with the strcuture & services to enhance REALTOR professionalism, standards of business practice and ethics in meeting the real estate needs of the community.
Member of: Canadian Real Estate Association
Staff Member(s): 3
Membership: 310; *Committees:* Arbitration; Audit & Finance; Governance; Nominating; Rules & Regulations
Chief Officer(s):
Kerry Rakuson, Executive Officer
Roxanne Maillet, President, 506-866-6295

Greater Moncton Society for the Prevention of Cruelty to Animals (GMSPCA) / Société de protection des animaux du Grand Moncton (SPAGM)
116 Greenock St., Moncton NB E1H 2J7
Tel: 506-857-8698; *Fax:* 506-854-1473
info@monctonspca.ca
www.monctonspca.ca
www.facebook.com/gmspca.spagm
twitter.com/GrMonctonSPCA
www.youtube.com/monctonspca
Overview: A small local charitable organization founded in 1956
Mission: To provide a safe haven for unwanted & abused animals until which time they can be adopted into loving homes
Member of: Canadian Federation of Humane Societies
Affiliation(s): New Brunswick Society for the Prevention of Cruelty to Animals
Activities: Education/Awareness Program; Pets & People (Therapy Program); Dog Jog; radio spots with pet tips
Chief Officer(s):
Karen Nelson, Executive Director

Greater Montreal Athletic Association (GMAA) / Association régionale du sport scolaire
#101, 5925, av Monkland, Montréal QC H4A 1G7
Tel: 514-482-8555; *Fax:* 514-487-0121
Other Communication: Sportsline, Phone: 514-482-3055
gmaa@gmaa.ca
www.gmaa.ca
www.facebook.com/RSEQ-Greater-Montreal-GMAA-419767904880749
Overview: A small local charitable organization founded in 1975
Mission: Devoted to the promotion of athletics in the English schools of the greater Montreal region.
Member of: Réseau du sport étudiant du Québec
Finances: *Annual Operating Budget:* $250,000-$500,000
Staff Member(s): 3
Membership: 152; *Fees:* User fees by activity; *Member Profile:* Principals of elementary & secondary schools
Activities: Organize & run sports activities & leagues for English schools on the Island of Montreal
Chief Officer(s):
Amanda Maks, Executive Director
amanda@gmaa.ca

Greater Montréal Convention & Tourism Bureau *Voir* Tourisme Montréal/Office des congrès et du tourisme du Grand Montréal

Greater Montréal Real Estate Board *Voir* Chambre immobilière du Grand Montréal

Greater Nanaimo Chamber of Commerce
2133 Bowen Rd., Nanaimo BC V9S 1H8
Tel: 250-756-1191; *Fax:* 250-756-1584
info@nanaimochamber.bc.ca
www.nanaimochamber.bc.ca
Overview: A medium-sized local organization founded in 1889
Mission: To act as the voice of business in Greater Nanaimo; To ensure a healthy economic base & socio-economic structure to benefit the central Vancouver Island area
Finances: *Annual Operating Budget:* $500,000-$1.5 Million; *Funding Sources:* Membership dues; Fundraising
Staff Member(s): 4
Membership: 700+; *Fees:* Schedule available based upon number of employees; *Member Profile:* Businesses, professionals, & community groups in Greater Nanaimo; *Committees:* Executive; Finance & Budget; Nomination; Government Affairs; Successful Cities; Succession Planing; Transportation
Activities: Promoting business in Nanaimo; Encouraging investment; Researching business issues; Liaising with politicians to benefit the business environment; Providing information about the community to newcomers; Offering educational seminars & training sessions; *Speaker Service:* Yes
Chief Officer(s):
Kim Smythe, CEO
David Littlejohn, Chair
Justin Schley, Treasurer
Awards:
• Sterling Awards
To recognize excellence in business & customer service in Greater Nanaimo

Greater Niagara Chamber of Commerce (GNCC)
#103, 1 St. Paul St., St Catharines ON L2R 7L2
Tel: 905-684-2361; *Fax:* 905-684-2100
info@gncc.ca
www.gncc.ca
www.linkedin.com/groups/4151488
www.facebook.com/NiagaraChamber
twitter.com/The_GNCC
Previous Name: St Catharines-Thorold Chamber of Commerce; St Catharines Chamber of Commerce
Overview: A medium-sized local organization founded in 1867
Mission: To support business growth & prosperity in the Niagara region
Member of: Ontario Chamber of Commerce; Canadian Chamber of Commerce
Finances: *Annual Operating Budget:* $500,000-$1.5 Million; *Funding Sources:* Membership dues; special events; programs
Staff Member(s): 8
Membership: 1,500+; *Fees:* Schedule available; *Committees:* Government Affairs Council; Next Niagara Council; Non-Profit Council; Small Business Niagara Council; Women in Niagara Council
Activities: Organizing events including trade shows & presentations; Providing networking opportunities; *Awareness Events:* Business After 5; Business Achievement Awards; NEXTNiagara, Women in Niagara; *Internships:* Yes; *Speaker Service:* Yes; *Library:* Chamber Education Centre
Chief Officer(s):
Mishka Balsom, President & CEO
mishka@gncc.ca

Greater Oshawa Chamber of Commerce
#100, 44 Richmond St. West, Oshawa ON L1G 1C7
Tel: 905-728-1683; *Fax:* 905-432-1259
info@oshawachamber.com
www.oshawachamber.com
www.facebook.com/oshawachamber
twitter.com/oshawachamber
www.youtube.com/oshawachamber
Previous Name: Oshawa/Clarington Chamber of Commerce
Overview: A small local organization founded in 1928
Mission: To be the voice of business or Greater Oshawa, by providing positive leadership in support of members, business & the private enterprise system
Affiliation(s): Ontario Chamber of Commerce; Canadian Chamber of Commerce
Finances: *Annual Operating Budget:* $250,000-$500,000; *Funding Sources:* Membership dues
Staff Member(s): 4; 70 volunteer(s)
Membership: 890; *Fees:* Schedule available; *Committees:* Ambassador; Awards; Events; Federal Provincial Municipal Affairs; Golf
Activities: Providing seminars, training, & networking opportunities
Chief Officer(s):
Natalie Sims, President
Nancy Shaw, CEO & General Manager
ceo@oshawachamber.com

Greater Peterborough Chamber of Commerce (GPCC)
175 George St. North, Peterborough ON K9J 3G6
Tel: 705-748-9771; *Fax:* 705-743-2331
Toll-Free: 887-640-4037
info@peterboroughchamber.ca
www.peterboroughchamber.ca
www.linkedin.com/groups/Peterborough-Chamber-2934106
www.facebook.com/peterboroughchamber
twitter.com/ptbochamber
www.youtube.com/user/PeterboroughChamber
Previous Name: Peterborough Chamber of Commerce
Overview: A medium-sized local organization founded in 1889

Mission: To create a prosperous community by promoting the free enterprise system, a healthy business environment, & acting as the voice of business
Member of: Ontario Chamber of Commerce; Canadian Chamber of Commerce
Finances: *Funding Sources:* Members fees
Staff Member(s): 7
Membership: *Fees:* $800 five star; $500 four star; $260 three star
Activities: *Speaker Service:* Yes; *Rents Mailing List:* Yes; *Library:* Not open to public
Chief Officer(s):
Stuart Harrison, President & CEO
stuart@peterboroughchamber.ca

Greater Sackville Chamber of Commerce (GSCC)
87 Main St., Sackville NB E4L 4A9
Tel: 506-364-8911
gscc@eastlink.ca
greatersackvillechamber.com
www.facebook.com/GSCC2014
twitter.com/SackvilleCC
Overview: A small local organization founded in 1991
Mission: To enhance economic prosperity & quality of life in Greater Sackville
Finances: *Funding Sources:* Membership fees; fundraising events; administration of Mainstreet Redevelopment Sackville Inc.
Membership: *Fees:* Schedule available
Activities: *Library:* Open to public
Chief Officer(s):
Gwen Zwicker, Executive Administrator
Awards:
• Business Recognition Award
Excellence in innovation & creativity, management skills, growth, job creation & contributions to the community

Greater Saskatoon Chamber of Commerce
#104, 202 - 4th Ave. North, Saskatoon SK S7K 0K1
Tel: 306-244-2151; *Fax:* 306-244-8366
chamber@saskatoonchamber.com
www.saskatoonchamber.com
www.facebook.com/saskatoonchamber
twitter.com/StoonChamber
Previous Name: Saskatoon & District Chamber of Commerce
Overview: A small local organization founded in 1903
Mission: To build the business climate, thereby creating a city of opportunity
Member of: Saskatchewan Chamber of Commerce; Canadian Chamber of Commerce; World Chambers
Affiliation(s): Enterprise Centre; Leadership Saskatoon; Raj Manek Mentorship Program; Saskatchewan Agrivision Corporation; Saskatchewan Economic Development Authority; Saskatchewan Young Professionals & Entrepreneurs; Saskatoon Aboriginal Employment & Business Opportunities Inc., Saskatoon Air Services; Saskatoon Regional Economic Development Authority; Tourism Saskatoon; United Way of Saskatoon; Vision 2000
Staff Member(s): 8
Membership: *Fees:* Schedule available; *Member Profile:* Local businesses; *Committees:* Agribusiness Development; Health Opportunities; Celebrate Success; Future Opportunities; Business Growth; Business of Science; First Nations & Métis; Sustainability Opportunities; Going Global; Government Affairs
Activities: Advocating for business; Hosting business luncheons & community & other chamber events
Chief Officer(s):
Kent Smith-Windsor, Executive Director
Awards:
• SABEX New Product
Awarded to a company that has launched a new Saskatchewan made product or service that is original & currently available to consumers
• SABEX Innovation
Awarded to a business that has demonstrated the application of knowledge or ability to create new forms and/or ways of doing things that provide a competitive advantage; may include involvement of people or new technology to successfully compete in a changing marketplace
• SABEX Marketing
Awarded to a company that has development and implemented a marketing strategy which has contributed to the success of an operation
• SABEX New Business Venture
Awarded to a business that has been in existence for 3 years or less & has shown positive performance in terms of current or expected profitability, job creation or entrance into new markets
• SABEX Customer Service
Awarded to a company providing excellent customer services to customers
• SABEX Export
Awarded to a company exporting Saskatchewan goods or services nationally or internationally
• SABEX Growth & Expansion
Awarded to a business that has made changes resulting in growth or expansion of markets, creation of jobs, increases in physical size, that enhance its ability to increase revenues, investments & profits
• SABEX Hall of Fame
One individual, or business, will be inducted into the Hall of Fame each year; the recipient will abe a long-standing member of the Saskatoon Business community
• SABEX Business of the Year
Awarded to a business which has demonstrated excellence in areas they consider key to their success
• SABEX Community Involvement
Awarded to a business demonstrating exceptional performanc in its support of the arts, culture, amateur sports, education or volunteer groups within the community

Greater Shediac Chamber of Commerce / Chambre de commerce du Grand Shediac
#301, 290 Main St., Shediac NB E4P 2E3
Tel: 506-532-7000; *Fax:* 506-532-6156
www.greatershediacchamber.com
www.facebook.com/1430680673875830
Overview: A small local organization
Mission: To represent the business community of the Shediac area
Membership: 61; *Fees:* $55 individual/non-profit; $125 1-10 employees; $200 11-50 employees; $350 51-100 employees; $450 101+ employees
Chief Officer(s):
Ronald Cormier, President

Greater Sudbury Association for Community Living *See* Community Living Greater Sudbury

Greater Sudbury Chamber of Commerce / Chambre de commerce du Grand Sudbury
#100, 40 Elm St., Sudbury ON P3C 1S8
Tel: 705-673-7133; *Fax:* 705-673-1951
cofc@sudburychamber.ca
www.sudburychamber.ca
www.linkedin.com/company/1025331
www.facebook.com/greatersudburychamber
twitter.com/sudburycofc
Overview: A small local organization founded in 1895
Mission: To act as the voice of business in Ontario's Greater Sudbury area; To advocate for business & community prosperity
Staff Member(s): 9
Membership: 1,000; *Fees:* Schedule available
Chief Officer(s):
Debbi Nicholson, President & Chief Executive Officer, 705-673-7133 Ext. 225
debbi@sudburychamber.ca

Greater Summerside Chamber of Commerce (GSCC)
#10, 263 Heather Moyse Dr., Summerside PE C1N 5P1
Tel: 902-436-9651; *Fax:* 902-436-8320
info@summersidechamber.com
www.summersidechamber.com
www.linkedin.com/groups/8208866/profile
www.facebook.com/120850442004
twitter.com/GSSideCC
www.instagram.com/summersidechamber
Overview: A medium-sized local organization founded in 1900
Mission: To provide a voice on behalf of business in the City of Summerside & area; To work towards the prosperity & betterment of Greater Summerside
Member of: Atlantic Provinces Chamber of Commerce; Canadian Chamber of Commerce
Finances: *Funding Sources:* Membership dues; Sponsorships
Staff Member(s): 2
Membership: *Fees:* Schedule available, based upon number of employees; *Member Profile:* Professional & business people in the Greater Summerside area; *Committees:* Education / Training; Business; Membership / Public Relations; Transportation; Government Relations; Special Projects; Primary Resources; City of Summerside; Business
Activities: Promoting trade & commerce; Providing networking opportunities; Creating business opportunities; Advocating of behalf of members' concerns to municipal, provincial, national, & international governments
Chief Officer(s):
Jan Sharpe, Executive Director, 902-436-9651
jane.sharpe@summersidechamber.com
Awards:
• Wendell J. Gallant Memorial Scholarship
Eligibility: The son or daughter of a Greater Summerside Chamber of Commerce member, or of a member's employee, who has applied for enrollment in an undergraduate program at a post-secondary institution and has maintained a high academic standing at their school within the geographic area; *Amount:* $500
• Excellence In Business Awards
Meetings/Conferences:
• Greater Summerside Chamber of Commerce Annual General Meeting 2018, 2018, PE
Scope: Local

Greater Toronto Al-Anon Information Services (GTAIS)
PO Box 75094, 20 Bloor St. East, Toronto ON M4W 3T3
Tel: 416-410-3809
Toll-Free: 888-425-2666
gtais.updates@gmail.com
al-anon.alateen.on.ca/gtais
Overview: A small local organization
Mission: To provide a forum for the Al-Anon & Alateen groups within the Toronto geographic area to exchange information; To offer a variety of services, such as lists of meeting schedules, post office box, & telephone answering
Affiliation(s): Toronto Al-Anon Family Groups Public Outreach
Activities: Public outreach

Greater Toronto Apartment Association (GTAA)
#103, 20 Upjohn Rd., Toronto ON M3B 2V9
Tel: 416-385-3435
info@gtaaonline.com
www.gtaaonline.com
twitter.com/GTAAONLINE
Previous Name: Metropolitan Toronto Apartment Builders Association
Overview: A medium-sized local organization founded in 1969
Mission: To promote the well-being & interests of the apartment development industry; to regulate relations between employers & employees & to promote new development
Affiliation(s): Joint Construction Council
Membership: 200+ companies; *Fees:* $2 per suite, $325 minimum, owner/property manager membership; $1,500 milennium membership; *Member Profile:* Firms involved in multifamily rental housing industry; *Committees:* Executive; Education & Training; Members' Services & Fundraising; Political & Municipal Liaison; Policy, Finance & Administration; Utilities, Environment & Communications
Chief Officer(s):
Mitch Rasussen, Secretary
Ivan Murgic, Chair

Greater Toronto CivicAction Alliance
#1800, 110 Yonge St., Toronto ON M5C 1T6
Tel: 416-309-4480; *Fax:* 416-309-4481
www.civicaction.ca
www.linkedin.com/companies/civicaction
www.facebook.com/civicactiongta
twitter.com/civicactiongta
www.youtube.com/civicactiongta
Overview: A small local organization
Chief Officer(s):
Mina Mawani, Chief Development Officer
mina.mawani@civicaction.ca

Greater Toronto Electrical Contractors Association
#207, 23 Lesmill Rd., Toronto ON M3B 3P6
Tel: 416-391-3226; *Fax:* 416-391-3926
mail@greatertorontoeca.org
www.greatertorontoeca.org
Overview: A small local organization founded in 1970
Mission: To represent electrical contractors for industrial, commercial, institutional, residential, line/utility, & communications construction & service markets within the Greater Toronto Area; to advocate for its members in labour relations matters, commercial & tendering practices, & government & regulatory issues.
Affiliation(s): International Brotherhood of Electrical Workers (IBEW)
Activities: Supplementary training courses & seminars; funding for the Joint Apprenticeship Council; apprentice recruiting

Canadian Associations / Greater Toronto Hotel Association (GTHA)

Chief Officer(s):
Paul Sheridan, President

Greater Toronto Hotel Association (GTHA)
#404, 207 Queens Quay West, Toronto ON M5J 1A7
Tel: 416-351-1276; Fax: 416-351-7749
info@gtha.com
www.gtha.com
www.facebook.com/GreaterTorontoHotelAssoc
twitter.com/GTHAtweets
Previous Name: Hotel Association of Metropolitan Toronto
Overview: A medium-sized local organization founded in 1925
Mission: To provide the membership with a proactive, informative & cohesive service-oriented organization whose objective is to raise the profile & prosperity of its members
Staff Member(s): 3
Activities: Speaker Service: Yes
Chief Officer(s):
Terry Mundell, President & CEO

Greater Toronto Marketing Alliance (GTMA)
#901, 225 King St. West, Toronto ON M5V 3M2
Tel: 416-360-7320
Toll-Free: 800-411-4482
www.greatertoronto.org
www.linkedin.com/company/greater-toronto-marketing-alliance
www.facebook.com/205700379494353
twitter.com/ThinkCanada2015
www.flickr.com/photos/gtmatoronto
Overview: A small local organization founded in 1998
Mission: To attract international investment & employment to the Greater Toronto Area
Member of: Toronto Board of Trade; EDCO; Canadian Urban Institute; World Teleport Association; EDAC; CoreNet
Finances: Annual Operating Budget: Greater than $5 Million
Staff Member(s): 6
Membership: 80; Member Profile: Municipalities; boards of trade; chambers of commerce; government; private sector; NGO; Committees: Automotive; Information Technology; Energy Environment; Call Centres; Aerospace; Industrial Design
Activities: GTA Luncheon series; Council Investment missions; Corporate call programs; Incoming delegation hosting; Speaker Service: Yes; Library: Not open to public
Chief Officer(s):
George Hanus, President & CEO
ghanus@greatertoronto.org
Gerald Pisarzowski, Vice-President, Business Development
gpisarzowski@greatertoronto.org
Tony Romano, Vice-President, Corporate & Investor Services
tromano@greatertoronto.org
Awards:
• GTA International Awards of Distinction

Greater Toronto Rose & Garden Horticultural Society
9 Tarlton Rd., Toronto ON M5P 2M5
Tel: 416-485-5907
GTRoses@aol.com
www.gardenontario.org/site.php/rosegarden
Also Known As: Toronto Rose
Previous Name: York Rose & Garden Society
Overview: A small local organization founded in 1979 overseen by Ontario Horticultural Association
Mission: Dedicated to cultivation & enjoyment of roses
Member of: Canadian Rose Society, American Rose Society, Ontario Horticultural Association
Membership: 150; Fees: $10 regular; $15 family
Activities: Annual "Roses" garden tour; lectures; public meetings
Chief Officer(s):
Iris Hazen, Contact

Greater Toronto Water Garden & Horticultural Society (GTWGHS)
4691 Hwy. 7A, RR#1, Nestleton Station ON L0B 1L0
Tel: 416-438-4862
info@onwatergarden.com
www.onwatergarden.com
Previous Name: Ontario Water Garden Society
Overview: A small local organization
Member of: Ontario Horticultural Association
Membership: Fees: $20 single; $25 family
Chief Officer(s):
Susan Rightmyer, President
president@onwatergarden.com

Greater Vancouver Apartment Owners Association See British Columbia Apartment Owners & Managers Association

Greater Vancouver Association of the Deaf (GVAD)
2125 West 7th Ave., Vancouver BC V6K 1X9
Fax: 604-738-4645; TTY: 604-738-4644
gvadoffice@gmail.com
www.gvad.com
www.facebook.com/gvad.vancouver
twitter.com/GVAD2
Overview: A small local charitable organization founded in 1926
Mission: To promote all matters of the welfare of the deaf; to foster the social, cultural, educational & recreational activities of the deaf; To affiliate & serve with provincial, regional & national organizations of the deaf & hard of hearing; To ensure that the activities of the society always be intended to contribute positively to the Greater Vancouver area or to any other district within the society's areas of operation
Affiliation(s): BC Deaf Sports Federation
Finances: Funding Sources: Grants, members, donation
Membership: 1-99; Fees: free for youth (up to 25); $10/regular
Activities: Annual Corn Party; Talent Night
Chief Officer(s):
Leanor Vlug, President

The Greater Vancouver Board of Trade
World Trade Centre, #400, 999 Canada Place, Vancouver BC V6C 3E1
Tel: 604-681-2111; Fax: 604-681-0437
contactus@boardoftrade.com
www.boardoftrade.com
www.linkedin.com/company/vancouver-board-of-trade
www.facebook.com/VancouverBoardofTrade
twitter.com/BoardofTrade
Previous Name: The Vancouver Board of Trade; World Trade Centre Vancouver
Overview: A small local organization
Mission: To promote, enhance & facilitate the development of the region as a Pacific centre for trade, commerce & travel
Member of: Canadian Chamber of Commerce; World Trade Centres Association
Staff Member(s): 35
Membership: 5,800; Committees: Advanced Technology; Business & Arts; Communications; Community Affairs; Contract Club; Economic Development & Environment; Government Budget & Finance; Membership & Marketing; Leaders of Tomorrow; Urban Transportation
Activities: Offering Speakers Programs, networking roundtables, seminars, & workshops; Speaker Service: Yes; Library: Not open to public
Chief Officer(s):
Iain Black, President & CEO
ceo@boardoftrade.com
Chris Barry, Director, Membership Services
membership@boardoftrade.com
Greg Hoekstra, Manager, Communications
media@boardoftrade.com
Jennifer Johnson, Manager, Events
events@boardoftrade.com
Awards:
• Rix Award for Engaged Community Citizenship
• Rix Award for Engaged Corporate Citizenship

Greater Vancouver Community Services Society (GVCSS)
#500, 1212 West Broadway, Vancouver BC V6H 3V1
Tel: 604-737-4900; Fax: 604-737-2922
info@gvcss.bc.ca
www.gvcss.bc.ca
Overview: A small provincial organization
Mission: Non-profit provider of in-home health care services to the elderly and individuals with physical and/or developmental disabilities
Activities: Home support; assisted living
Chief Officer(s):
Ron McLeod, CEO

Greater Vancouver Food Bank Society (GVFBS)
1150 Raymur Ave., Vancouver BC V6A 3T2
Tel: 604-876-3601; Fax: 604-876-7323
www.foodbank.bc.ca
www.facebook.com/VanFoodBank
twitter.com/vanfoodbank
www.instagram.com/vanfoodbank
Overview: A small local charitable organization founded in 1982 overseen by Food Banks British Columbia

---

Mission: To provide food & related assistance to those in need in the local area; registered charity, BN: 107449787RR0001
Member of: Food Banks British Columbia; Food Banks Canada; Foodchain; Burnaby Chamber of Commerce; Vancouver Board of Trade; Vancouver Food Policy Organization; Volunteer Vancouver
Finances: Annual Operating Budget: $1.5 Million-$3 Million; Funding Sources: Donations
Staff Member(s): 6; 500 volunteer(s)
Membership: 250; Fees: $10; Committees: Advisory; Audit; Executive; Finance; Fundraising
Activities: 18 direct food distribution centres; Awareness Events: Annual Christmas in July; Christmas Campaign
Chief Officer(s):
Aart Schuurman Hess, Chief Executive Officer
Craig Edwards, Director, Operations
Diane Collis, Director, Food & Education
Iryn Vekay, Director, Finance
Trish Kelly, Director, Community Food Hub

Greater Vancouver Home Builders' Association (GVHBA)
#1003, 7495 - 132 St., Surrey BC V3W 1J8
Tel: 778-565-4288; Fax: 778-565-4289
info@gvhba.org
www.gvhba.org
ca.linkedin.com/groups?gid=5069902
www.facebook.com/gvhba/
twitter.com/GVHBA
www.youtube.com/GreaterVancouverHBA;
www.flickr.com/photos/gvhba/sets
Overview: A small local organization founded in 1974 overseen by Canadian Home Builders' Association
Mission: To promote professionalism in the homebuilding industry; To provide timely new home & renovation information to consumers
Member of: Canadian Home Builders' Association
Staff Member(s): 8
Membership: 740+; Fees: Schedule available; Member Profile: Home builders, renovators, architects, manufacturers, suppliers, sub-contractors, government agencies, utilities, publishers, bankers, lawyers & other professionals
Activities: Offering certification courses & industry workshops; Facilitating consumer seminars; Liaisoning with local governments & housing industry groups to represent membership; Awareness Events: Fall Classic Golf Tournament, September
Chief Officer(s):
Robert de Wit, Chief Executive Officer
bob@gvhba.org
Awards:
• Greater Vancouver Home Builders' Association Ovation Awards Program
• People's Choice Award
Meetings/Conferences:
• Greater Vancouver Home Builders' Association 2018 Annual General Meeting, 2018, BC
Scope: Local
• Greater Vancouver Home Builders' Association Members Expo 2018, May, 2018, Molson Canadian Theatre, Coquitlam, BC
Scope: Provincial
Description: A networking & showcase event at which members can exchange information about products & services, as well as communicate directly with suppliers

Greater Vancouver International Film Festival Society (VIFF)
1181 Seymour St., Vancouver BC V6B 3M7
Tel: 604-685-0260; Fax: 604-688-8221
Other Communication: Submissions: submissions@viff.org
info@viff.org
viff.org
www.facebook.com/VIFFest
twitter.com/VIFForum
youtube.com/user/VIFFest; vimeo.com/viff;
flickr.com/photos/viffest
Also Known As: Vancouver International Film Festival
Overview: A small international charitable organization founded in 1982
Mission: To operate the Annual Vancouver International Film Festival & year-round programming of the Vancity Theatre at the Vancouver International Film Centre
Finances: Annual Operating Budget: $1.5 Million-$3 Million; Funding Sources: Corporate sponsorship; box office; government funding
750 volunteer(s)

Membership: 42,000; *Fees:* $2
Activities: *Awareness Events:* Vancouver International Film Festival; *Internships:* Yes
Chief Officer(s):
Dave Hewitt, Chair
Jacqueline Dupuis, Executive Director
Awards:
• BC Spotlight Awards
Includes the Ignite Award, Best BC Film Award & BC Emerging Filmmaker Award
• Canadian Film Awards
Includes Best Canadian Film, Best Canadian Documentary, Best BC Short Film, Best Canadian Short Film & Most Promising Director of a Canadian Short Film
• Impact Awards
Includes the Radcliffe Foundation Refugee Crisis Awareness Short Film Competition, VIFF Impact Award & VIFF Industry Builder Award
• Audience Awards
Includes Super Channel People's Choice Award, VIFF Most Popular International Feature, VIFF Most Popular International Documentary, VIFF Most Popular Canadian Documentary & #mustseebc

Greater Vancouver Japanese Canadian Citizens' Association (GVJCAA)
#200, 6688 Southoaks Cres., Burnaby BC V5E 4M7
Tel: 604-777-5222; *Fax:* 604-777-5223
gvjcca@gmail.com
jccabulletin-geppo.ca/about-2/jcca-bulletin
twitter.com/bulletin_geppo
instagram.com/bulletin_geppo
Previous Name: Japanese Canadian Citizens Association
Overview: A small local organization founded in 1949
Mission: To represent the Japanese Canadian community in Vancouver & the surrounding area
Member of: National Association of Japanese Canadians
Membership: *Fees:* $40 regular; $30 senior; $50 USA; $75 overseas
Chief Officer(s):
Derek Iwanaka, President
Publications:
• The Bulletin [a publication of the Greater Vancouver Japanese Canadian Citizens' Association]
Type: Journal; *Accepts Advertising*; *Editor:* John Endo Greenaway

Greater Vancouver Professional Theatre Alliance (GVPTA)
1405 Anderson St., 3rd Fl., Vancouver BC V6H 3R5
Tel: 604-608-6799; *Fax:* 604-608-6923
info@gvpta.ca
www.gvpta.ca
www.facebook.com/GVPTA
twitter.com/gvptatheatre
Previous Name: Vancouver Professional Theatre Alliance
Overview: A medium-sized local organization founded in 1987
Mission: To promote live theatre & foster a thriving environment for the continued growth & development of theatre in Greater Vancouver
Member of: Alliance for Arts & Culture; Granville Island Business and Community Association; Tourism Vancouver; Vantage Point
Finances: *Funding Sources:* Self-generated; government grants
Staff Member(s): 3
Membership: *Member Profile:* Theatre companies & venues; *Committees:* Marketing; Membership Development; Conferences & Meetings; Fundraising
Activities: Offering membership programs, workshops & guest speakers; *Internships:* Yes
Chief Officer(s):
Kenji Maeda, President

Greater Vancouver Regional District Employees' Union (GVRDEU)
#102, 3060 Norland Ave., Burnaby BC V5B 3A6
Tel: 604-220-7052
gvrdeu@telus.net
www.gvrdeu.org
Overview: A small local organization founded in 1946
Mission: The Union serves the outside workers of Metro Vancouver & is their sole bargaining agent in collective agreements.
Membership: 500+; *Member Profile:* Workers in water distribution & disinfection, watershed management, watershed security, social housing across the region, regional parks, wastewater collection & treatment, construction, including temporary summer workers
Chief Officer(s):
Bob Beaumont, Secretary

Greater Vancouver Taiwanese Canadian Association
7663 Nanaimo St., Vancouver BC V5P 4M6
Tel: 604-688-3738
www.facebook.com/1893837410828228
Overview: A small local organization
Mission: To help Taiwanese immigrants to the Greater Vancouver area in adapting to Canadian society

Greater Vernon Chamber of Commerce (GVCC)
#102, 2901 - 32nd St., Vernon BC V1T 5M2
Tel: 250-545-0771; *Fax:* 250-545-3114
info@vernonchamber.ca
www.vernonchamber.ca
www.linkedin.com/groups?mostPopular=&gid=2710540
www.facebook.com/VernonChamber
twitter.com/VernonChamber
Also Known As: Vernon Chamber of Commerce
Overview: A small local organization founded in 1897
Mission: To facilitate, enhance & improve the region's unique quality of life; To support positive & sustainable development; To encourage growth in commerce & industry for the prosperity of its members & the Greater Vernon area
Member of: BC Chamber of Commerce
Affiliation(s): Canadian Chamber of Commerce
Finances: *Annual Operating Budget:* $250,000-$500,000; *Funding Sources:* Membership dues; sponsors; banner ads on website
Staff Member(s): 3
Membership: 500+; *Fees:* Schedule available based on number of employees; *Member Profile:* Businesses in Vernon & area
Activities: Annual Business Excellence Awards; luncheons; Business After 5; seminars; *Internships:* Yes; *Speaker Service:* Yes; *Library*
Chief Officer(s):
Dan Rogers, General Manager
manager@vernonchamber.ca
Tracy Cobb-Reeves, President

Greater Victoria Chamber of Commerce (GVCC)
#100, 852 Fort St., Victoria BC V8W 1H8
Tel: 250-383-7191; *Fax:* 250-385-3552
chamber@victoriachamber.ca
www.victoriachamber.ca
www.linkedin.com/groups?mostPopular=&gid=1795424
www.facebook.com/VictoriaChamber
twitter.com/ChamberVictoria
www.youtube.com/user/victoriachamber
Also Known As: Victoria Chamber of Commerce
Overview: A medium-sized local organization founded in 1863
Mission: To act as the voice of business for the Greater Victoria region; To ensure that the area maintains & enhances its prosperous & vibrant business climate
Member of: BC Chamber of Commerce; Canadian Chamber of Commerce
Finances: *Funding Sources:* Membership fees; Sponsorships
Membership: 1,500+; *Fees:* Schedule available based upon number of employees; *Member Profile:* Businesses in the Greater Victoria region; *Committees:* Greater Victoria Development Agency; Prodigy Group; Ambassadors; Policy & Government Affairs; Government; Our Vibrant Community; Capital Region Governance Review; Finance & Audit; Governance
Activities: Influencing public policy to support a healthy enterprise system; Advancing existing business; Attracting new economic opportunities to Greater Victoria; Forming partnerships; Hosting events; Offering networking opportunities; Providing educational programs
Chief Officer(s):
Bruce Carter, CEO, 250-360-3470
ceo@victoriachamber.ca
Frank Bourree, Chair
Sang-Kiet Ly, Treasurer

Greater Victoria Hospitals Foundation *See* Victoria Hospitals Foundation

Greater Victoria Philatelic Society (GVPS)
928 Claremont Ave., Victoria BC V8Y 1K3
gvps@vicstamps.com
www.vicstamps.com/gvps.htm
Overview: A small local organization
Member of: Royal Canadian Philatelic Society; Northwest Federation of Stamp Clubs
Activities: Annual local stamp show, Oct. & May; PIPEX International Show; meetings 3rd Fri. every month

Greater Victoria Youth Orchestra (GVYO)
1611 Quadra St., Victoria BC V8W 2L5
Tel: 250-360-1121; *Fax:* 250-381-3573
gvyo@telus.net
www.gvyo.org
www.facebook.com/GreaterVictoriaYouthOrchestra
Overview: A small local charitable organization founded in 1986 overseen by Orchestras Canada
Mission: To affirm & nourish the love of music in young people; to foster musical development of orchestra members; to serve as musical resource to the community at large
Affiliation(s): Community Arts Council of Greater Victoria
Finances: *Funding Sources:* Provincial & municipal government; Individual & corporate donations; Fundraising; Player fees; Box office revenue
Activities: *Speaker Service:* Yes; *Library:* by appointment
Chief Officer(s):
Sheila Redhead, Manager
Yariv Aloni, Music Director

Greater Westside Board of Trade
2372 Dobbin Rd., West Kelowna BC V4T 2H9
Tel: 250-768-3378; *Fax:* 250-768-3465
admin@gwboardoftrade.com
www.gwboardoftrade.com
www.facebook.com/Greater.Westside.Board.Of.Trade
twitter.com/WSBoardOfTrade
Previous Name: Westbank & District Chamber of Commerce
Overview: A small local organization founded in 1947
Mission: To pursue activities that enhance the social & economic prosperity of our community
Member of: BC Chamber of Commerce
Staff Member(s): 3
Membership: *Fees:* Schedule available; *Committees:* Membership; Policy & Advocacy; Finance; Transportation & Tourism; Communication
Activities: *Rents Mailing List:* Yes
Chief Officer(s):
Norm LeCavalier, Chair
Karen Beaubier, Executive Director
Awards:
• Key Business Awards

Greater Woodstock Chamber of Commerce
#2, 220 King St., Woodstock NB E7M 1Z8
Tel: 506-325-9049; *Fax:* 506-328-4683
info@gwcc.ca
www.gwcc.ca
Overview: A small local organization
Mission: To promote & improve tourism, trade & commerce & the economic, civic & social welfare of the district
Member of: Atlantic Provinces Chamber of Commerce
Membership: *Fees:* $180-$360 business; $84 non-profit
Activities: *Awareness Events:* Small Business Week, Oct.
Chief Officer(s):
Lance Minard, President
minard.lance@brunswicknews.com

Greek Community of Toronto
30 Thorncliffe Park Dr., Toronto ON M4H 1H8
Tel: 416-425-2485; *Fax:* 416-425-2954
info@greekcommunity.org
www.greekcommunity.org
Overview: A medium-sized local charitable organization founded in 1965
Mission: To promote Greek culture & heritage in Toronto
Membership: *Fees:* $100 individual/family; $40 seniors; $20 student; $1000 lifetime
Chief Officer(s):
Andonis Artemakis, President

Greek Orthodox Church (Canada) *See* Greek Orthodox Metropolis of Toronto (Canada)

Greek Orthodox Community of East Vancouver
C/O Saints Nicholas & Dimitrios Greek Orthodox Church, 4641 Boundary Rd., Vancouver BC V5R 2N5
Tel: 604-438-6432; *Fax:* 604-438-6400
greekcommunity@telus.net
www.sts-nicholas-and-dimitrios.org
Overview: A small local organization
Member of: Greek Orthodox Church

Canadian Associations / Greek Orthodox Metropolis of Toronto (Canada)

Membership: 100-499; *Fees:* $60; $30 seniors; $120 family; *Member Profile:* Orthodox Christians living in conformity with the canons of the Church; *Committees:* Educational; Entertainment
Chief Officer(s):
Konstantin Nikolaou, President

Greek Orthodox Metropolis of Toronto (Canada)
86 Overlea Blvd., Toronto ON M4H 1C6
Tel: 416-429-5757; *Fax:* 416-429-4588
metropolis@gometropolis.org
www.gometropolis.org
www.facebook.com/gometropolis
twitter.com/GO_Metropolis
www.youtube.com/user/GOMetropolisToronto
Previous Name: Greek Orthodox Church (Canada)
Overview: A medium-sized national organization
Member of: The Canadian Council of Churches
Staff Member(s): 21
Membership: 76 churches + 350,000 members
Chief Officer(s):
Dimitrios Anas, President
George Seretis, Vice President
Costas Misthios, Secretary
Steve Ramphos, Treasurer

Greek-Canadian Cultural Centre (GCCA)
2349 Portage Rd., Niagara Falls ON L2E 6S4
Tel: 905-374-7044
Also Known As: Greek-Canadian Community Association
Overview: A small local charitable organization founded in 1977
Mission: To promote Greek heritage & culture; to support local community charities.
Affiliation(s): Greek Canadian Community Association of Niagara
Finances: *Funding Sources:* Bingo/Nevada; hall rentals; dances; donations

Green Acres Art Centre
PO Box 545, Teulon MB R0C 3B0
Tel: 204-886-3192
gaac@mymts.net
www.greenacresartcentre.org
Overview: A small local organization founded in 1976
Mission: To provide arts, music & cultural activties for the Town of Teulon & environs.
Member of: Manitoba Association of Community Arts Councils Inc.
Staff Member(s): 1
Activities: Dance, music, oil painting, & yoga classes; astronomy club
Chief Officer(s):
Lana Knor, President
gaacpresident@mymts.net

Green Action Centre (RCM)
303 Portage Ave., 3rd Fl., Winnipeg MB R3B 2B4
Tel: 204-925-3777; *Fax:* 204-942-4207
Toll-Free: 866-394-8880
info@greenactioncentre.ca
greenactioncentre.ca
www.facebook.com/GreenActionCentre
twitter.com/greenactionctr
www.pinterest.com/gacentre/
Previous Name: Recycling Council of Manitoba; Resource Conservation Manitoba Inc.
Overview: A medium-sized provincial organization founded in 1985
Mission: To promote ecological sustainability by developing alternatives to currently unsustainable practices; their principal activity is environmental education; our partners & clients include businesses, schools, non-profit groups, governments, recyclers, home gardeners & general public
Member of: Canadian Environment Network; Manitoba Eco-Network; Manitoba Environmental Industries Association
Finances: *Annual Operating Budget:* $100,000-$250,000; *Funding Sources:* 3 levels of government; corporate; private foundations; membership dues
Staff Member(s): 11; 20 volunteer(s)
Membership: 200; *Committees:* Membership; Policy
Activities: Public Infoline; Environmental Speaker's Bureau; The R-Report; Public Forums; Green Commuting Program; Composting Education Program; *Speaker Service:* Yes; *Library:* Resource Centre
Chief Officer(s):
Tracy Hucul, Executive Director, 204-925-3770
tracy@greenactioncentre.ca

Green Calgary
#100, 301 - 14th St. NW, Calgary AB T2N 2A1
Tel: 403-230-1443
products@greencalgary.org
www.greencalgary.org
www.facebook.com/136497856363082
twitter.com/greencalgary
Previous Name: Clean Calgary Association
Overview: A medium-sized local charitable organization founded in 1978
Mission: To provide educational programs which assist Calgarians to develop an environmentally friendly lifestyle
Member of: City of Calgary Environment Advisory Committee
Finances: *Annual Operating Budget:* $250,000-$500,000; *Funding Sources:* Municipal government; Corporate; Casino; Goods & services
Staff Member(s): 7; 125 volunteer(s)
Membership: 90; *Fees:* $15 low-income/student; $25 individual; $75 non-profit; $200 business; *Member Profile:* Individuals interested in a sustainable lifestyle
Activities: *Speaker Service:* Yes
Chief Officer(s):
Areni Kelleppan, Executive Director
areni@greencalgary.org

Green Communities Association See Green Communities Canada

Green Communities Canada (GCC)
PO Box 928, 416 Chambers St., 2nd Fl., Peterborough ON K9J 7A5
Tel: 705-745-7479; *Fax:* 705-745-7294
info@greencommunitiescanada.org
www.gca.ca
www.facebook.com/125118647578545
twitter.com/GCCCanada
Previous Name: Green Communities Association
Overview: A small national organization founded in 1995
Mission: To support member organizations in achieving environmental sustainability
Member of: Canadian Renewable Energy Alliance
Membership: *Fees:* $500 full membership; $250 associate membership; *Member Profile:* Non-profit community-based organizations that deliver environmental programs
Activities: Sharing information & resources; joint member projects; Water Programs; Energy Programs; Walking Programs/Safe Routes to School; Green IT
Chief Officer(s):
Clifford Maynes, Executive Director, 705-745-7479 Ext. 118
cmaynes@greencommunitiescanada.org
Sé Keohane, Manager, Finance, 705-745-7479 Ext. 112
finance@greencommunitiescanada.org
Jacky Kennedy, Director, Canada Walks, 416-488-7263, Fax: 416-488-2296
info@saferoutestoschool.ca
Sharyn Inward, Director, Water Programs, 705-745-7479 Ext. 113
sharyn@greencommunitiescanada.org
Bruce Roxburgh, Manager, Green Information Technology, 705-745-7479 Ext. 117
broxburgh@greencommunitiescanada.org
Publications:
• Green Community News
Type: Newsletter; *Frequency:* Weekly
Profile: Association activities, resources, & events

Green Kids Inc.
#251, 162-2025 Corydon Ave., Winnipeg MB R3P 0N5
Tel: 204-940-4745; *Fax:* 204-201-0676
Toll-Free: 800-441-6751
www.greenkids.com
www.facebook.com/greenkidsinc
Overview: A small national charitable organization founded in 1991
Mission: To empower children to take positive action & change the world
Membership: *Committees:* Honorary Advisory; Technical Advisory
Activities: Educates children (K-8) about environmental issues in schools using interactive theatre
Chief Officer(s):
Jeff Golfman, Volunteer President

The Green Party of Alberta
PO Box 45066, Stn. Brentwood, #319, 3630 Brentwood Rd. NW, Calgary AB T2L 1Y4
info@greenpartyofalberta.ca
greenpartyofalberta.ca
www.facebook.com/GreenPartyOfAlberta
twitter.com/greenpartyab
Previous Name: Evergreen Party of Alberta; Vision 2012; Alberta Greens
Overview: A small provincial organization founded in 1990 overseen by Green Party of Canada
Mission: To encourage the development of an attitude that everyone is part of the land; to encourage strict control of all forms of pollution; to promote programs teaching consensus & facilitation; to facilitate the process of all interested community members becoming involved in education, both learning & teaching, guided by the long-term sustainability of the Earth community; to create the opportunity for Albertans to become involved in the strategic planning process
Finances: *Funding Sources:* Donations; membership
Membership: *Member Profile:* Environmentally & socially concerned Albertans
Activities: Organizing for provincial elections; education; raising awareness of issues; *Speaker Service:* Yes
Chief Officer(s):
Janet Keeping, Party Leader
leader@greenpartyofalberta.ca
Carl Svoboda, President
president@greenpartyofalberta.ca
Matt Burnett, Chief Financial Officer
cfo@greenpartyofalberta.ca

Green Party of Canada (GPC) / Parti vert du Canada
PO Box 997, Stn. B, Ottawa ON K1P 5R1
Tel: 613-562-4916; *Fax:* 613-706-1424
Toll-Free: 866-868-3447
info@greenparty.ca
www.greenparty.ca
www.facebook.com/GreenPartyofCanada
twitter.com/canadiangreens
www.youtube.com/user/canadiangreenparty
Overview: A medium-sized national organization founded in 1983
Mission: To promote a platform that includes debt reduction, eco-jobs, saving Canada's forests, supporting small business, use of soft energies, sovereignty for First Nations, & a guarantee of full rights for women
Member of: CanAmex; World Greens Coordination
Finances: *Annual Operating Budget:* $50,000-$100,000; *Funding Sources:* Individual contributions
Staff Member(s): 1; 40 volunteer(s)
Membership: 4,000; *Fees:* $10+; *Committees:* Ombuds
Activities: *Speaker Service:* Yes
Chief Officer(s):
Elizabeth May, Party Leader
leader@greenparty.ca
Daniel Green, Deputy Leader
Bruce Hyer, Deputy Leader
Ken Melamed, President
ken.melamed@greenparty.ca

The Green Party of Manitoba
PO Box 26023, Stn. Maryland, 120 Sherbrook St., Winnipeg MB R3G 3R3
Tel: 204-488-2831
Toll-Free: 866-742-4292
www.greenparty.mb.ca
www.facebook.com/GreenPartyofManitoba
twitter.com/Green_Party_MB
www.youtube.com/user/GreenPartyofManitoba
Also Known As: Manitoba Greens
Overview: A medium-sized provincial organization founded in 1996 overseen by Green Party of Canada
Membership: *Fees:* $5
Chief Officer(s):
James R. Beddome, Party Leader
Dirk Hoeppner, President

Green Party of New Brunswick / Parti Vert du Nouveau Brunswick
#102, 403 Regent St., Fredericton NB E3B 3X6
Tel: 506-447-8499; *Fax:* 506-447-8489
Toll-Free: 888-662-8683
www.greenpartynb.ca
www.facebook.com/GPNB.PVNB
twitter.com/greenpartynb
www.youtube.com/user/GPVNB
Overview: A small provincial organization overseen by Green Party of Canada

Chief Officer(s):
David Coon, Party Leader
david.coon@greenpartynb.ca
Carmen Budilean, Executive Director
carmen.budilean@greenpartynb.ca

Green Party of Nova Scotia
PO Box 36044, 5665 Spring Garden Rd., Halifax NS B3J 3S9
Tel: 902-252-3995
Toll-Free: 877-707-5775
gpns@greenpartyns.ca
greenpartyns.ca
www.facebook.com/NSGreens
twitter.com/NSGreens
Overview: A small provincial organization overseen by Green Party of Canada
Chief Officer(s):
Thomas Trappenberg, Party Leader

The Green Party of Ontario (GPO) / Parti Vert d'Ontario
PO Box 1132, Stn. F, #035, 67 Mowat Ave., Toronto ON M4Y 2T8
Tel: 416-977-7476; *Fax:* 416-977-5476
Toll-Free: 888-647-3366
admin@gpo.ca
www.gpo.ca
Previous Name: The Ontario Greens
Overview: A small provincial organization founded in 1983 overseen by Green Party of Canada
Finances: *Funding Sources:* Membership dues
Staff Member(s): 1; 900 volunteer(s)
Membership: 1,000; *Fees:* $10; *Committees:* Policy; Candidate Facilitation
Activities: Annual Fall Meeting
Chief Officer(s):
Mike Schreiner, Party Leader
leader@gpo.ca
Becky Smit, Executive Director, 647-830-6486
beckysmit@gpo.ca

Green Party of Prince Edward Island
81 Prince St., Charlottetown PE C1A 4R3
Tel: 902-940-3598
info@greenparty.pe.ca
www.greenparty.pe.ca
www.facebook.com/GreenPartyPEI
twitter.com/PEIgreens
Overview: A small provincial organization overseen by Green Party of Canada
Chief Officer(s):
Peter Bevan-Baker, Party Leader
leader@greenparty.pe.ca

Green Party of Québec *Voir* Parti Vert du Québec

Green Party Political Association of British Columbia (GPBC)
PO Box 8088, Stn. Central, Victoria BC V8W 3R7
Fax: 250-590-4537
Toll-Free: 888-473-3686
info@bcgreens.ca
www.bcgreens.ca
www.facebook.com/BCGreens
twitter.com/BCGreens
www.instagram.com/GreenPartyBC
Also Known As: Green Party of BC
Overview: A medium-sized provincial charitable organization founded in 1983 overseen by Green Party of Canada
Mission: To form healthy communities with diverse economies by involving the citizens of British Columbia in the political process; To offer voters in British Columbia fiscal responsibility, socially progressive policies, & environmental sustainability
Finances: *Funding Sources:* Donations
Membership: 4,000; *Fees:* $10+; *Member Profile:* Residents of British Columbia, fourteen years of age & older, who are not members of any other provincial political party; *Committees:* Fundraising; Administration; Media; Organizing; Membership
Chief Officer(s):
Andrew Weaver, Party Leader

Green Roofs for Healthy Cities (GRHC)
406 King St. East, Toronto ON M5A 1L4
Tel: 416-971-4494
www.greenroofs.org
www.linkedin.com/company/green-roofs-for-healthy-cities
www.facebook.com/GreenRoofsForHealthyCities

twitter.com/GRHCna
www.instagram.com/grhcna
Overview: A medium-sized international organization founded in 1999
Mission: To promote the green roof industry throughout North America
Membership: *Member Profile:* Corporate suppliers & manufacturers; Individuals who practise the art of living architecture; Supporters (LAM subscribers); *Committees:* Advanced Maintenance; Corporate Members; Green Roof Professional; Green Walls; Policy; Research; Rooftop Urban Food Production
Activities: Increasing awareness of the environmental, economic, & social benefits of green roofs & green walls; Providing education; Offering networking opportunities
Chief Officer(s):
Steven Peck, President
speck@greenroofs.org
Publications:
• Living Architecture Monitor [a publication of Green Roofs for Healthy Cities]
Type: Magazine; *Frequency:* Quarterly; *Accepts Advertising*; *Editor:* Steven Peck
Profile: For Green Roofs for Healthy Cities members only

Green Thumb Theatre for Young People
#210, 49 Dunlevy Ave., Vancouver BC V6A 3A3
Tel: 604-254-4055; *Fax:* 604-251-7002
info@greenthumb.bc.ca
www.greenthumb.bc.ca
www.facebook.com/GreenThumbTheatre
twitter.com/gr_thumbtheatre
Also Known As: Green Thumb Players Society
Overview: A small international organization founded in 1975
Mission: To tour schools, festivals & theatres across Canada & the world with productions which explore contemporary issues for young audiences
Affiliation(s): Professional Association of Canadian Theatres
Finances: *Annual Operating Budget:* $500,000-$1.5 Million; *Funding Sources:* Canada Council for the Arts; City of Vancouver; BC Arts Council
Staff Member(s): 8; 50 volunteer(s)
Chief Officer(s):
Victoria Henderson, President
Patrick McDonald, Artistic Director
pmcdonald@greenthumb.bc.ca
Nadine Carew, General Manager
nadine.carew@greenthumb.bc.ca

Greenest City
220 Cowan Ave., Toronto ON M6K 2N6
Tel: 647-438-0038
info@greenestcity.ca
www.greenestcity.ca
www.facebook.com/GreenestCityToronto
twitter.com/Greenest_City
pinterest.com/greenestcity
Overview: A small local organization
Mission: To reduce pollution; To regenerate urban life; To promote social equity
Activities: Walk to School Day; Active & Safe Routes to School; Walking School Bus; projects & campaigns embrace community diversity & engage people in finding locally appropriate solutions to global environmental problems
Chief Officer(s):
Angela ElzingaCheng, Executive Director
angela@greenestcity.ca

Greenpeace Canada
33 Cecil St., Toronto ON M5T 1N1
Tel: 416-597-8408; *Fax:* 416-597-8422
Toll-Free: 800-320-7183
supporter.ca@greenpeace.org
www.greenpeace.org/canada
www.facebook.com/greenpeace.canada
twitter.com/greenpeaceCA
www.youtube.com/user/GreenpeaceCanada
Overview: A large international organization founded in 1971
Mission: To raise awareness on issues such as biodiversity, pollution of the Earth, nuclear threats, & disarmament; To bring public opinion to bear on decisions makers; To conduct scientific, economic & political research, publicize environmental problems, recommend environmentally sound solutions, & lobby for change
Member of: Greenpeace International; Canadian Renewable Energy Alliance

Finances: *Annual Operating Budget:* $1.5 Million-$3 Million; *Funding Sources:* Donations; shop sales
Staff Member(s): 35
Membership: 100,000+ in Canada + over 2.5 million internationally; *Fees:* $30
Activities: Communications; e-news; reports; *Speaker Service:* Yes
Chief Officer(s):
Joanna Kerr, Executive Director
Publications:
• Greenpeace Canada Annual Report
Type: Yearbook
• Greenpeace Canada E-News
Type: Newsletter
• Greenpeace Magazine
Type: Magazine
Edmonton Office
6328 104 St. W, Unit B, Edmonton AB T6H 2K9
Tel: 780-430-9201; *Fax:* 780-430-9282
Toll-Free: 800-320-7183
Montréal Office
454, Laurier est, 3e étage, Montréal QC H2J 1E7
Tel: 514-933-0021; *Fax:* 514-933-1017
Toll-Free: 800-320-7183
Vancouver Office
1726 Commercial Dr., Vancouver BC 4A3
Tel: 604-253-7701; *Fax:* 604-253-0111
Toll-Free: 800-320-7183

Greenspace Alliance of Canada's Capital
PO Box 55085, 240 Sparks St., Ottawa ON K1P
greenspace@greenspace-alliance.ca
www.greenspace-alliance.ca
Overview: A medium-sized local organization founded in
Mission: To preserve green spaces in the National Capital
Membership: *Fees:* $15 group; $5 student; $30 associate
Chief Officer(s):
Amy Kempster, Chair, 613-722-6039

Greenwood Board of Trade
c/o City of Greenwood, PO Box 129, 202 South Government Ave., Greenwood BC V0H 1J0
Tel: 250-445-6644; *Fax:* 250-445-6441
greenwoodbot@gmail.com
www.greenwoodbot.com
Overview: A small local organization founded in 1899
Mission: To promote & improve trade, commerce & the economic, civic & social welfare of the district
Member of: Canadian Chamber of Commerce; BC Chamber of Commerce; Thompson Okanagan Tourist Association
Finances: *Funding Sources:* Municipal grants
Membership: 86; *Member Profile:* Any related or interested individual
Chief Officer(s):
Dave Evans, President

Greniers de Joseph
#300, 4975, boul Sir Wilfred Laurier, Saint-Hubert QC J3Y 7R6
Tél: 450-445-3511; *Téléc:* 450-445-2812
info@greniersdejoseph.com
greniersdejoseph.com
www.facebook.com/181077338602972
Aperçu: *Dimension:* petite; *Envergure:* locale
Mission: Pour aider les familles défavorisées en leur fournissant de la nourriture, des meubles et des vêtements
Activités: Coin des enfants; Événements de collecte de fonds
Membre(s) du bureau directeur:
Denise Dubuc, Administrateur
Christiane Poisson, Administrateur

Grenville County Historical Society (GCHS)
Grand Trunk / CN Railway Station, PO Box 982, 500 Railway Ave., Prescott ON K0E 1T0
Tel: 613-925-0489
gchs@ripnet.com
www.grenvillecountyarchives.ca
Overview: A small local charitable organization founded in 1891
Mission: To collect, preserve, exhibit, & publish material about Ontario's Grenville County; To provide historical records for research, such as local birth, marriage, & death records, microfilmed newspapers, & census, church, & cemetery records; To promote the preservation of historical buildings & monuments
Finances: *Funding Sources:* Archive & research fees; Fundraising; Sale of publications
Membership: *Fees:* $20 individuals; $200 life memberships

Canadian Associations / Grey Bruce Beekeepers' Association

Activities: Offering research for a fee; *Library:* Grenville County Historical Society Archival Resource Centre; Open to public
Chief Officer(s):
Valerie Schulz, Manager, Collections
Publications:
• The Grenville Sentinel
Type: Newsletter; *Frequency:* 6 pa; *Price:* Free with membership in the Grenville County Historical Society

Grey Bruce Beekeepers' Association
ON
Tel: 519-794-3335
Overview: A small local organization
Mission: To provide education about beekeeping skills
Member of: Ontario Beekeepers' Association
Membership: *Member Profile:* Beekeepers from the Grey Bruce region of Ontario
Activities: Assisting local beekeepers with the challenges of the industry
Chief Officer(s):
Toby Bruce, President
tobyjcbruce@gmail.com

Grey Bruce Real Estate Board *See* REALTORS Association of Grey Bruce Owen Sound

Grey County Kiwanis Festival of Music
PO Box 456, Owen Sound ON N4K 5P7
www.kiwanismusicfestival.net
Overview: A small local organization founded in 1932
Affiliation(s): Federation of Canadian Music Festivals
Finances: *Funding Sources:* Kiwanis Club of Owen Sound; Kiwanis Club of Meaford; Golden "K"; fundraising; private donations
Staff Member(s): 1
Activities: Producing an annual competition music festival
Chief Officer(s):
Becky Azzano, Festival Coordinator
festivalcoordinator@kiwanismusicfestival.net
Kevin Dandeno, Chair

Grey County Kiwanis Music Festival *See* Grey County Kiwanis Festival of Music

Grey County Law Association
611 - 9th Ave. East, Owen Sound ON N4K 6Z4
Tel: 519-371-5495; *Fax:* 519-371-4606
Toll-Free: 866-578-5841
Overview: A small local organization
Member of: Law Society of Upper Canada; Ontario Courthouse Librarians Association
Finances: *Annual Operating Budget:* $50,000-$100,000; *Funding Sources:* Law Foundation of Ontario
Staff Member(s): 1
Membership: 80; *Member Profile:* Practising lawyers; *Committees:* Executive; Library
Activities: *Library:* Courthouse Library
Chief Officer(s):
Ronn Cheney, Librarian

Grey Highlands Chamber of Commerce
774310 Hwy. 10, Flesherton ON N0C 1E0
Tel: 226-910-1393
Toll-Free: 888-986-4612
info@greyhighlandschamber.com
greyhighlandschamber.com
Previous Name: Markdale Chamber of Commerce
Overview: A small local organization
Mission: To support, promote & strengthen business & tourism in the area
Member of: Ontario Chamber of Commerce
Finances: *Annual Operating Budget:* Less than $50,000; *Funding Sources:* Membership dues; donations; grants
Membership: 100; *Fees:* $125
Activities: Sponsoring seminars; Providing information; Supporting community & beautification projects; Organizing events such as the Santa Claus Parade & Classic Cruise Night
Chief Officer(s):
Aakash Desai, President
Ann Detar, Office Administrator

Grey Wooded Forage Association (GWFA)
PO Box 1448, 5039 - 45 St., Rocky Mountain House AB T4T 1B1
Tel: 403-844-2645; *Fax:* 403-844-2642
gwfa1@telus.net
www.greywoodedforageassociation.com
www.facebook.com/3425016126491987
Overview: A small local organization overseen by Agricultural Research & Extension Council of Alberta
Mission: To create awareness about the uses of forages; to help the agricultural community be more environmentally & economically sustainable through knowledge & innovation
Member of: Agricultural Research & Extension Council of Alberta
Staff Member(s): 2
Membership: *Fees:* $20; *Member Profile:* Those interested in forage production & grazing management
Chief Officer(s):
Albert Kuipers, Manager
gwfa2@telus.net
Muriel Finkbeiner, Office Manager
gwfa1@telus.net
Publications:
• The Blade [a publication of the Grey Wooded Forage Association]
Type: Newsletter; *Frequency:* Monthly
• The Newsletter [a publication of the Grey Wooded Forage Association]
Type: Newsletter; *Frequency:* 2 pa

Grey, Bruce, Dufferin, & Simcoe Postal History Study Group (PHSC)
PO Box 163, Stn. C, Kitchener ON N2G 3X9
phscdb@postalhistorycanada.net
www.postalhistorycanada.net/php/StudyGroups/GreyBruce/
Overview: A small local organization founded in 1998
Mission: To study the postal history of the Ontario counties of Grey, Bruce, Dufferin, & Simcoe
Affiliation(s): Postal History Society of Canada
Membership: *Fees:* $12; *Member Profile:* Individuals interested in the postal history of the Grey, Bruce, Dufferin, & Simcoe region of Ontario
Chief Officer(s):
Justus (Gus) Knierim, Contact
Publications:
• Grey, Bruce, Dufferin, & Simcoe Postal History Study Group Newsletter
Type: Newsletter; *Frequency:* Quarterly; *Editor:* Justus (Gus) Knierim
Profile: Local postal history information

Greyhound Pets of Atlantic Canada Society (GPACS)
343 West Petpeswick Rd., Musquodoboit Harbour NS B0J 2L0
Tel: 902-889-2214; *Fax:* 902-443-7731
greyhnd@ns.sympatico.ca
www.gpac.ca
Overview: A small local charitable organization
Mission: To rehoming retired greyhounds across Atlantic Canada.
Finances: *Funding Sources:* Corporate sponsors; private donations
Chief Officer(s):
Jeanette Reynolds, President
Jennifer Melanson, Vice-President & Director, Marketing
jen_wagner77@yahoo.ca

Grieving Children at Seasons Centre *See* Seasons Centre for Grieving Children

Grimsby & District Chamber of Commerce
33 Main St. West, Grimsby ON L3M 3H1
Tel: 905-945-8319; *Fax:* 905-945-1615
www.grimsbychamber.ca
www.facebook.com/grimsbychamberofcommerce
twitter.com/grimsbychamber
www.youtube.com/channel/UCN036EfnmnpKPG2rWqElCqA
Overview: A medium-sized local organization
Mission: To promote commerce in the community
Membership: *Fees:* Schedule available; *Committees:* Annual Events; Budget & Finance; Communications; Golf Tournament; Human Resources; Information Services; Jail 'N Bail; Policy & Government Affairs; Programs & Education; Sponsorship & Partners
Chief Officer(s):
Marion Thorp, President

Grimsby/Lincoln & District Association for Community Living Inc. *See* Community Living Grimsby, Lincoln & West Lincoln

Grimshaw & District Chamber of Commerce
PO Box 919, Grimshaw AB T0H 1W0
Tel: 780-617-4654
info@grimshawchamber.com
www.grimshawchamber.com
www.facebook.com/grimshawcc
Overview: A small local organization
Mission: To strengthen the business community of Grimshaw & district
Member of: Alberta Chamber of Commerce
Finances: *Annual Operating Budget:* Less than $50,000
Staff Member(s): 1; 12 volunteer(s)
Membership: 52; *Fees:* $110-$235
Activities: *Awareness Events:* Trade Show, June; Business Awards Banquet, Oct.
Chief Officer(s):
Daryl Billings, President
Joan Billings, Secretary

GRIS-Mauricie/Centre-du-Québec
#232, 255 rue Brock, Drummondville QC J2C 1M5
Tél: 819-445-0007
Ligne sans frais: 877-745-0007
info@grismcdq.org
www.grismcdq.org
Nom précédent: L'Association des gais, lesbiennes et bisexuel(le)s du Québec
Aperçu: *Dimension:* petite; *Envergure:* locale; fondée en 1998
Mission: De promouvoir la diversité de l'acceptation
Membre(s) du personnel: 3
Membre: *Montant de la cotisation:* 10$
Membre(s) du bureau directeur:
Nathalie Niquette, Directrice générale

Grocery Products Manufacturers of Canada; Food & Consumer Products Manufacturers of Canada *See* Food & Consumer Products of Canada

Groundfish Enterprise Allocation Council (GEAC)
1362 Revell Rd., Manotick ON K4M K84
Tel: 902-526-4582; *Fax:* 613-692-8250
vascotto@vrsi.ca
www.geaconline.com
Overview: A medium-sized national organization founded in 1997
Mission: To generally promote the common interests of its members; To promote the wise use, development & conservation of the Atlantic Canadian groundfish resource; To provide an organization that permits Atlantic groundfish enterprise allocation license holders to speak with a unified voice to the general public & all levels of government on matters of broad concern to the members; To provide an organization that permits groundfish enterprise allocation license holders to interface with similar organizations in Canada; To conduct research that has the potential to produce information & data that will be helpful or useful to the members; to monitor regional, national & international corporate & political activities which have a bearing on the members; To provide a platform for the views of members with regard to these activities
Membership: 19 companies

Group 25 Model Car Builders' Club
Toronto ON
Tel: 416-781-0757
www.group25.org
Overview: A small local organization founded in 1976
Chief Officer(s):
Douglas Mawson, Secretary/Treasurer
KeepemFlyingDM@yahoo.ca

The Group Halifax
Halifax NS
info@thegrouphalifax.com
thegrouphalifax.com
www.linkedin.com/groups/Group-Professional-Networking-Association-2403135?trk=myg_ugrp_ovr
www.facebook.com/TheGroupHalifax
twitter.com/TheGroupHalifax
Overview: A medium-sized local organization founded in 2008
Mission: A Halifax Metro-based business networking association with the aim of bringing together professionals in different sectors and industries to develop new skills, expand business networks, and promote the growth of their businesses.
Membership: *Fees:* $300
Activities: Weekly meetings

Group of 78 / Groupe des 78
#244, 211 Bronson Ave., Ottawa ON K1R 6H5
Tel: 613-230-0860; *Fax:* 613-563-0017
group78@group78.org
group78.org
www.facebook.com/groupof78
Overview: A small international charitable organization founded in 1980
Mission: To advocate for peace, disarmament, sustainable development & strengthening of the United Nations.
Membership: *Fees:* $125 regular; $180 family; $50 limited income; $25 student
Activities: Annual policy conference with guest speakers
Chief Officer(s):
Richard Harmston, Chair

Groupe Brosse Art
8245, rue St-Laurent, Brossard QC J4X 2A6
Tel: 450-656-6610
www.groupebrosseart.com
Overview: A small local organization
Mission: D'unir les artistes de Montérégie en tant que groupe, afin de promouvoir et vendre leur art.
Staff Member(s): 6
Membership: 30; *Member Profile:* Artistes amateurs et semi-professionnels
Activities: Expositions
Chief Officer(s):
Louise Lacasse, Présidente, Conseil d'administration
louloulacasse@hotmail.com

Groupe canadien d'aphérèse See Canadian Apheresis Group

Groupe canadien d'endocrinologie pédiatrique See Canadian Pediatric Endocrine Group

Groupe CDH
#201, 1000, rue Amherst, Montréal QC H2L 3K5
Tél: 514-849-7800; *Téléc:* 514-849-1495
info@groupecdh.com
www.groupecdh.com
Aperçu: *Dimension:* petite; *Envergure:* locale; fondée en 1976
Mission: Pour créer des logements abordables qui est détenue par les locataires

Groupe CTT Group
3000, rue Boullé, Saint-Hyacinthe QC J2S 1H9
Tél: 450-778-1870; *Téléc:* 450-778-3901
Ligne sans frais: 877-288-8378
info@gcttg.com
www.gcttg.com
www.linkedin.com/company/groupe-ctt
www.facebook.com/GroupeCTT
twitter.com/GroupeCTTGroup
Nom précédent: CTT Group Centre for Textile & Geosynthetic Technologies
Aperçu: *Dimension:* grande; *Envergure:* nationale; Organisme sans but lucratif; fondée en 1987
Mission: Favoriser le développement des matériaux textiles et de stimuler l'avancement technologique de l'industrie textile et géosynthétique par des activités telles que la recherche et le développement, l'assistance technique, la formation sur mesure, l'information spécialisé et l'animation du milieu
Affiliation(s): Fédération canadienne du textile; Association canadienne des coloristes et chimistes du textile; Société des textiles du Canada; Association des textiles des Cantons de l'Est; Institut canadien du tapis; Institut canadien des textiles; Institut québécois des revêtements de sol; Société des diplômés en textile
Finances: *Budget de fonctionnement annuel:* $3 Million-$5 Million
Membre(s) du personnel: 40
Membre: 3,000 entreprises; *Montant de la cotisation:* 100$ - 750$; *Critères d'admissibilite:* Industriel
Activités: Expo-Hightex; Forum Geosynthetiques; *Service de conférenciers:* Oui
Membre(s) du bureau directeur:
Jacek Mlynarek, Ph.D., Président-directeur-général
jmlynarek@gcttg.com
Meetings/Conferences:
• Expo Hightex 2018, 2018
Scope: National
Contact Information: URL: www.expohightex.com
Publications:
• Groupe CTT Group Newsletter
Type: Newsletter

Groupe d'action pour la prévention de la transmission du VIH et l'éradication du Sida (GAP-VIES)
3330, rue Jarry est, Montréal QC H1Z 2E8
Tél: 514-722-5655; *Téléc:* 514-722-0063
gapvies@gapvies.ca
www.gapvies.ca
Nom précédent: Groupe haïtien pour la prévention du sida; Groupe d'action pour la prévention du sida
Aperçu: *Dimension:* petite; *Envergure:* provinciale; fondée en 1987 surveillée par Canadian AIDS Society
Mission: Prévenir la transmission du VIH/sida et d'aider les personnes atteintes du virus de l'immunodéficience humaine dans la population en général et dans la communauté haïtienne en particulier; informer et d'éduquer sur les implications de la maladie et les moyens de la prévenir; accompagner les personnes atteintes ainsi que leurs proches
Membre de: Coalition des organismes communautaires québécois de lutte contre le sida
Membre(s) du personnel: 7
Membre: *Critères d'admissibilité:* Professionnels; individus; institutions
Activités: Kiosques; conférences; ateliers; *Bibliothèque*
Membre(s) du bureau directeur:
Joseph Jean-Gilles, Directeur général

Le groupe d'action sida See AIDS Action Now

Groupe d'aide et d'information sur le harcèlement sexuel au travail de la province de Québec (GAIHST)
2231, rue Bélanger, Montréal QC H2G 1C5
Tél: 514-526-0789; *Téléc:* 514-526-8891
info@gaihst.qc.ca
www.gaihst.qc.ca
Aperçu: *Dimension:* petite; *Envergure:* provinciale; Organisme sans but lucratif; fondée en 1980
Mission: Briser le mur du silence entourant les victimes d'harcèlement sexuel; éduquer la population sur le harcèlement sexuel au travail; conseiller les femmes sur les démarches à suivre, pour tenter de régler le problème d'harcèlement sexuel au travail; aider les femmes à surmonter le problème dont elles ont été victimes; rédiger, publier et diffuser des documents, manuels, et périodiques sur la problématique
Finances: *Budget de fonctionnement annuel:* $100,000-$250,000; *Fonds:* Municipal Government
Membre(s) du personnel: 4; 11 bénévole(s)
Membre: 25
Activités: *Stagiaires:* Oui; *Service de conférenciers:* Oui

Groupe d'entraide à l'intention des personnes séropositives, itinérantes et toxicomanes (GEIPSI)
1223, rue Ontario est, Montréal QC H2L 1R5
Tél: 514-523-0979; *Téléc:* 514-523-3075
info@geipsi.ca
www.geipsi.ca
Aperçu: *Dimension:* petite; *Envergure:* locale; fondée en 1992
Mission: Pour apporter soutien et assistance aux personnes qui sont séropositives
Membre: *Critères d'admissibilité:* Les personnes qui sont séropositives
Activités: Dîners communautaires; Sorties; Ateliers éducatifs
Membre(s) du bureau directeur:
Olivier Lourdel, Président
Yvon Coulliard, Directeur général
Publications:
• Le Sans-Mots

Groupe d'entraide G.E.M.E.
#232, 1085, boul Ste-Foy, Longueuil QC J4K 1W7
Tél: 450-332-4463
Ligne sans frais: 866-443-4363
info@geme.qc.ca
geme.qc.ca
www.facebook.com/281207001891651
Aperçu: *Dimension:* moyenne; *Envergure:* locale; fondée en 1996
Mission: Pour fournir un soutien aux personnes souffrant de maladies mentales et les troubles anxieux
Membre: 6,500+; *Montant de la cotisation:* 20$
Activités: Méditation; Conférences

Groupe de droit collaboratif du Québec
445, boul Saint-laurent, 5e étage, Montréal QC H2Y 3T8
Tél: 514-954-3471; *Téléc:* 514-954-3451
info@quebeccollaborativelaw.ca
www.droitcollaboratifquebec.ca

Aperçu: *Dimension:* petite; *Envergure:* provinciale; fondée en 2002
Mission: Pour promouvoir la pratique du droit collaboratif
Membre: *Montant de la cotisation:* 169,31$
Activités: Conférences; Formation
Membre(s) du bureau directeur:
Diane Chartrand, Présidente, Conseil d'administraion, 514-847-8989 Ext. 238

Groupe de recherche appliquée en macroécologie (GRAME)
#202, 735, rue Notre-Dame, Montréal QC H8S 2B5
Tél: 514-634-7205
info@grame.org
www.grame.org
Aperçu: *Dimension:* petite; *Envergure:* locale
Mission: Promotion du développement durable et à la protection de l'environnement
Membre: *Montant de la cotisation:* 5$
Activités: Recherche
Membre(s) du bureau directeur:
Jonathan Théorêt, Directeur
jonathantheoret@grame.org

Groupe de recherche d'intérêt public de l'Ontario See Ontario Public Interest Research Group

Groupe de recherche d'intérêt public du Québec - McGill *Voir* Québec Public Interest Research Group - McGill

Groupe de recherche en animation et planification économique (GRAPE)
#280, 4765 - 1e av, Québec QC G1H 2T3
Tél: 418-522-7356; *Téléc:* 418-522-0845
legrape@videotron.ca
www.legrape.ca
Aperçu: *Dimension:* petite; *Envergure:* locale; Organisme sans but lucratif; fondée en 1979 surveillé par Coalition des associations de consommateurs du Québec
Mission: Intervenir en consultation budgétaire individuelle particulièrement auprès des gens à faibles revenus du Grand Québec
Membre de: Coalition des associations de consommateurs du Québec (CACQ)
Finances: *Budget de fonctionnement annuel:* $100,000-$250,000
Membre: 99; *Critères d'admissibilite:* Habitant du Grand Québec intéressé à ce qui touche la consommation
Activités: Consultations budgétaires individuelles; ateliers budget; défense des droits du consommateur; *Stagiaires:* Oui; *Bibliothèque:* Centre de documentation; Bibliothèque publique rendez-vous
Membre(s) du bureau directeur:
Laurence Marget, Directrice générale

Groupe de recherche en écologie sociale (GRESOC) / Social Ecology Research Group (SERG)
#3, 953 rue Cherrier, Montréal QC H2L 1J2
Aperçu: *Dimension:* petite; *Envergure:* locale; Organisme sans but lucratif; fondée en 1978
Mission: Le GRESOC est constitué de chercheurs universitaires qui s'intéressent à l'écologie sociale, à l'écosociologie et à la sociologie de l'environnement; les recherches en cours portent sur le mouvement vert (écologisme et environnementalisme), le développement durable, les pluies acides, les déchets, et les aspects sociaux des changements environnementaux globaux; plusieurs rapports de recherches, livres, chapitres et articles ont été publiés
Membre de: Réseau des Groupes Écologistes Québécois; Conseil Régional de l'Environnement de Montréal
Finances: *Budget de fonctionnement annuel:* Moins de $50,000; *Fonds:* Hydro-Québec; Agence de l'efficacité énergétique; étalez votre science
2 bénévole(s)
Membre: 25; *Critères d'admissibilite:* Chercheurs universitaires
Activités: *Stagiaires:* Oui; *Bibliothèque* Not open to public
Membre(s) du bureau directeur:
Jean-Guy Vaillancourt, Président

Groupe de recherche et d'intervention sociale (GRIS-Montréal)
CP 476, Succ. C, Montréal QC H2L 4K4
Tél: 514-590-0016; *Téléc:* 514-590-0764
info@gris.ca
www.gris.ca
www.facebook.com/grismontreal
twitter.com/GRISmontreal

Canadian Associations / Groupe export agroalimentaire Québec - Canada (GEAQC) / Agri-Food Export Group Québec - Canada

Aperçu: Dimension: petite; *Envergure:* locale
Mission: Favoriser un meilleur connaissance des réalités homosexuelles et de faciliter l'intégration des gais, lesbiennes et bisexuel(les) dans la société
Membre(s) du personnel: 6
Membre: *Comités:* Appartenance; Formation; Démystification; Communications; Financement; Recherche
Membre(s) du bureau directeur:
David Platts, Président

Groupe de recherches sur les transports au Canada See Canadian Transportation Research Forum

Groupe des 78 See Group of 78

Groupe export agroalimentaire Québec - Canada (GEAQC) / Agri-Food Export Group Québec - Canada
1971, rue Léonard-De Vinci, Sainte-Julie QC J3E 1Y9
Tél: 450-649-6266; *Téléc:* 450-461-6255
Ligne sans frais: 800-563-9767
info@groupexport.ca
www.groupexport.ca
www.linkedin.com/company/1742471
Nom précédent: Club export agro-alimentaire du Québec
Aperçu: Dimension: moyenne; *Envergure:* provinciale; Organisme sans but lucratif; fondée en 1990
Mission: Développer des services adaptés aux besoins réels de nos membres afin d'augmenter leurs ventes sur les marchés internationaux; faciliter l'accès aux programmes gouvernementaux dont nous avons la gestion.
Membre de: SIAL Group; Chambre de commerce de Montréal
Finances: *Budget de fonctionnement annuel:* Plus de $5 Million*Fonds:* Services offerts aux membres; Agriculture Canada; Ministère de l'Agriculture des pêcheries et de l'alimentation du Québec
Membre(s) du personnel: 12
Membre: 400; *Montant de la cotisation:* 675$; *Critères d'admissibilité:* Exportateurs alimentaires
Activités: Conférence annuelle; Encadrement à l'exportation agroalimentaire; salon internationaux; accueil d'acheteur; Programme d'aide financière; *Stagiaires:* Oui; *Service de conférenciers:* Oui
Membre(s) du bureau directeur:
André A. Coutu, Président-directeur général
andrecoutu@groupexport.ca
Francine Lapointe, Directrice, Programme et affaires gouvernemntale
francinelapointe@groupexport.ca
Publications:
• Répertoire des exportateurs agroalientaire du Québec
Type: Newsletter; *Editor:* Dominique Girard
Profile: Liste détaillée des entreprises membre du Groupe Export qui sont actifs sur les différents marchés

Groupe familiaux Al-Anon See Al-Anon Family Groups (Canada), Inc.

Groupe gai de l'Outaouais
#003, 109, rue Wright, Gatineau QC J8X 2G7
Tél: 819-776-2727; *Téléc:* 819-776-2001
Ligne sans frais: 877-376-2727
info@lebras.qc.ca
www.algi.qc.ca/asso/gdhgfo/
Aperçu: Dimension: petite; *Envergure:* locale; fondée en 1991
Mission: Discussions, rencontres, activités sociales; les rencontres ont lieu les mercredis soir à 19h30, au Bureau régional d'action sida, 109, rue Wright, local 003 (Gatineau, secteur Hull).

Groupe gai de l'Université Laval (GGUL)
Pavillon Mauice-Pollack, #2223, 2305, rue de l'Université, Québec QC G1V 0A6
Tél: 418-656-2131
ggul@public.ulaval.ca
www.ggul.org
ca.linkedin.com/pub/ggul-ulaval/28/37a/23
twitter.com/ggul_ulaval
www.youtube.com/user/GGULULAVAL
Aperçu: Dimension: petite; *Envergure:* locale; fondée en 1978

Groupe haïtien pour la prévention du sida; Groupe d'action pour la prévention du sida Voir Groupe d'action pour la prévention de la transmission du VIH et l'éradication du Sida

Groupe intervention vidéo (GIV)
#105, 4001, rue Berri, Montréal QC H2L 4H2
Tél: 514-271-5506; *Téléc:* 514-271-6890
info@givideo.org
www.givideo.org
Aperçu: Dimension: petite; *Envergure:* internationale; Organisme sans but lucratif; fondée en 1975
Mission: Nous privilégions sensibilisation et de discussion sur la condition féminine; le GIV organise des visionnements publics et offre des formations en vidéo légère de montage aux femmes
Membre de: Alliance du film et vidéo indépendant du Canada
Finances: *Budget de fonctionnement annuel:* $100,000-$250,000
Membre(s) du personnel: 4
Membre: 60; *Montant de la cotisation:* 25-35
Activités: Visionnement publiques; ateliers; *Stagiaires:* Oui; *Service de conférenciers:* Oui; *Bibliothèque:* rendez-vous

Le groupe multimédia du Canada / The Multimedia Group of Canada
261, rue Saint-Sacrement, Montréal QC H2Y 3V2
Tél: 514-844-3636; *Téléc:* 514-844-4990
Aperçu: Dimension: petite; *Envergure:* internationale
Membre(s) du personnel: 2

Groupe régional d'intervention social - Québec (GRIS-Québec)
#202, 363, rue de la Couronne, Québec QC G1K 6E9
Tél: 418-523-5572
info@grisquebec.org
www.grisquebec.org
www.facebook.com/GrisQuebec
Aperçu: Dimension: petite; *Envergure:* locale
Finances: *Budget de fonctionnement annuel:* $100,000-$250,000
Membre(s) du personnel: 3
Membre: *Montant de la cotisation:* 10$ individuel bénévole; 15$ individuel régulier
Activités: Activités sportives, sociales et culturelles; groupes de discussion; ateliers d'information
Membre(s) du bureau directeur:
André Tardiff, Directeur général
direction@grisquebec.org

Groupement des assureurs automobiles (GAA)
Tour de la Bourse, CP 336, #2410, 800, Place Victoria, Montréal QC H3A 3C6
Tél: 514-288-4321
Ligne sans frais: 877-288-4321
cinfo@gaa.qc.ca
www.gaa.qc.ca
Aperçu: Dimension: moyenne; *Envergure:* provinciale; fondée en 1978
Mission: Administrer, de façon efficace et selon les décisions du conseil d'administration, tous les mandats certifiés au Groupement des assureurs automobiles par la Loi sur l'assurance automobile du Québec
Membre de: Chambre de commerce du Québec
Finances: *Budget de fonctionnement annuel:* $1.5 Million-$3 Million
Membre(s) du personnel: 46
Membre: 100-499; *Critères d'admissibilite:* Regroupe tous les assureurs privés autorisés à pratiquer l'assurance automobile au Québec; *Comités:* Exécutif; Candidatures; Audit; Actuariat; Normes et pratiques en assurance automobile; Discipline des estimateurs; Arbitrage
Activités: *Service de conférenciers:* Oui; *Bibliothèque:* Centre de documentation; Not open to public
Membre(s) du bureau directeur:
Patricia St-Jean, Présidente
Johanne Lamanque, Directrice générale

Grunthal & District Chamber of Commerce
PO Box 451, Grunthal MB R0A 0R0
Tel: 204-371-1081
grunthal.ca/chamber.php
Overview: A small local organization
Mission: To promote & strengthen trade & commerce in the area
Membership: *Fees:* $50-$80
Chief Officer(s):
Tim Driedger, Interim President

GS1 Canada
#800, 1500 Don Mills Rd., Toronto ON M3B 3L1
Tel: 416-510-8039; *Fax:* 416-510-1916
Toll-Free: 800-567-7084
info@gs1ca.org
www.gs1ca.org
Also Known As: Electronic Data Interchange Council of Canada
Previous Name: Electronic Commerce Council of Canada
Overview: A medium-sized national organization founded in 1985
Mission: To act as a facilitator for the use of electronic information transactions in support of Canadian users.
Finances: *Funding Sources:* Membership dues; conferences; education courses; books
Membership: 20,000; *Fees:* $60 individual; $150 basic; $500 limited; $900 advanced; $1500 corporate; *Member Profile:* Businesses; *Committees:* Standards & Services Governance; Carenet Healthcare Sector; Foodservice Service Sector; Grocery Sector; General Merchandise, Appeal & Hardlines Sector; Healthcare Pharmacy
Activities: Provides a standard for company-to-company exchange of business transactions; *Speaker Service:* Yes; *Rents Mailing List:* Yes; *Library:* Open to public
Chief Officer(s):
N. Arthur Smith, President/CEO

Calgary Office
#110, 720 - 28th St. NE, Calgary AB T2A 6R3
Tel: 403-291-2235
images@gs1ca.org

Montréal Office
9200, boul Golf, Montréal QC H1J 3A1
Tel: 514-355-8929; *Fax:* 514-356-3235
ECCnetlandV@gs1ca.org

Guaranteed Funeral Deposits of Canada (GFD)
#408, 701 Evans Ave., Toronto ON M9C 1A3
Tel: 416-626-7225; *Fax:* 416-626-1766
Toll-Free: 800-268-2466
info@gfd.org
www.gfd.org
Overview: A small national organization founded in 1961
Chief Officer(s):
Heather Kiteley, Manager, 416-407-9343

Guelph & District Labour Council
PO Box 293, Guelph ON N1H 6J9
Tel: 519-823-1030; *Fax:* 519-823-0102
www.guelphdistrictlabourcouncil.ca
Overview: A small local organization
Chief Officer(s):
Janice Folk-Dawson, President

Guelph & District Multicultural Centre See Immigrant Services - Guelph Wellington

Guelph & District Real Estate Board
400 Woolwich St., Guelph ON N1H 3X1
Tel: 519-824-7270
info@gdar.ca
www.gdar.ca
www.linkedin.com/company/guelph-&-district-association-of-realtors-r-
www.facebook.com/AssociationofREALTORS
twitter.com/_gdar_
Overview: A small local organization founded in 1959 overseen by Ontario Real Estate Association
Member of: The Canadian Real Estate Association
Finances: *Funding Sources:* Membership dues

Guelph & Wellington United Way Social Planning Council See United Way of Guelph, Wellington & Dufferin

Guelph Arts Council (GAC)
#404, 147 Wyndham St., Guelph ON N1H 4E9
Tel: 519-836-3280; *Fax:* 519-766-9212
administration@guelpharts.ca
guelpharts.ca/guelphartscouncil
www.facebook.com/GuelphArtsCouncil
twitter.com/guelpharts
Overview: A small local charitable organization founded in 1975
Mission: To foster & coordinate the development of the arts in the region
Affiliation(s): Community Arts Ontario; Canadian Conference of the Arts; Theatre Ontario; Visual Arts Ontario; Canadian Artists Representation; Ontario Crafts Council; Dance Ontario; Ontario Historical Society; Surfacing; Arts Education Council of Ontario
Finances: *Funding Sources:* Ontario Arts Council; City of Guelph; membership fees; donations; fundraising; Ontario Trillium Foundation
Staff Member(s): 3
Membership: 450; *Fees:* $20 youth; $30 family/individual; $45 not-for-profit; $60 business

Activities: Doors Open Guelph; Historical Walking Tours; Artist Workshops; Resource Centre; *Library:* Open to public
Chief Officer(s):
Brad E. Hutton, President
Sonya Poweska, Executive Director

Guelph Chamber of Commerce (GCC)
PO Box 1268, 111 Farquhar St., Guelph ON N1H 3N4
Tel: 519-822-8081; *Fax:* 519-822-8451
chamber@guelphchamber.com
www.guelphchamber.com
www.linkedin.com/groups/2053342
www.facebook.com/guelphchamber
www.youtube.com/user/GuelphChamberComerc1
Overview: A medium-sized local organization founded in 1868
Mission: To serve as the voice of the business community in Guelph; To help strengthen the economy of Guelph & adjacent townships; To provide a forum for the development of discussion & programs that will contribute to the social, economic & physical quality of life in Guelph; To promote Guelph as a good place to live, work & visit
Member of: Canadian Chamber of Commerce; Ontario Chamber of Commerce
Affiliation(s): Guelph Business Enterprise Centre; Guelph Partnership for Innovation
Finances: *Annual Operating Budget:* $500,000-$1.5 Million
Staff Member(s): 7; 200 volunteer(s)
Membership: 775; *Fees:* Schedule available; *Member Profile:* Businesses; *Committees:* Advocacy; Events; Food & Agriculture; Industrial; Membership & Marketing
Chief Officer(s):
Kithio Mwanzia, President & CEO
kithio@guelphchamber.com
Awards:
• Guelph Awards of Excellence

Guelph Coin Club *See* South Wellington Coin Society

Guelph Creative Arts Association (GCAA)
c/o Miriam Bellamy, 79 Wendy Crt., Cambridge ON N1R 8A6
guelphcreativearts.com
Overview: A small local organization founded in 1948
Mission: Guelph Creative Arts Association (GCAA) is a welcoming visual arts organization, open to everyone practicing or interested in the arts in Guelph and surrounding areas.

Guelph Equine Area Rescue Stables
RR#3, Hanover ON N4N 3B9
Tel: 519-369-3330
info@gearstables.com
Overview: A small local organization
Mission: To give equines in hardship the opportunity at life they deserve, whether they are unwanted, retired, abused, neglected, abandoned, heading to auction or slaughter; to assess, vet and retrain these horses to make them fit for reintegration to the general public; to put all proceeds from adoption back into the mission

Guelph Food Bank
#12C, 100 Crimea St., Guelph ON N1H 2Y6
Tel: 519-767-1380; *Fax:* 519-824-1640
gfb@spiritwind.ca
spiritwind-christian-centre.ca/guelphfoodbank.html
Overview: A small local charitable organization founded in 1989
Mission: To supply food to the less fortunate in the community; to help people to become self-sufficient by offering a number of social programs.
Member of: Spiritwind Christian Centre
Affiliation(s): Ontario Association of Food Banks; Canadian Association of Food Banks
Activities: Job & placement programs; skills training; credit counselling; clothing exchange

Guelph Hiking Trail Club (GHTC)
PO Box 1, Guelph ON N1H 6J6
Tel: 519-822-3672
www.guelphhiking.com
Overview: A small local organization founded in 1970
Mission: To generate interest in hiking; To promote environmental conservation
Member of: Hike Ontario
Finances: *Annual Operating Budget:* Less than $50,000
300 volunteer(s)
Membership: 200; *Fees:* $25
Activities: Building & maintaining hiking trails, including Kissing Bridge Trail, Radial Line Trail, Speed River Trail, & Starkey Trail
Chief Officer(s):
Christine Bando, Secretary, Membership

Guelph Historical Society (GHS)
100 Crimea St., #A102, Guelph ON N1H 2Y6
www.guelphhistoricalsociety.ca
twitter.com/GuelphHistSoc
Overview: A small local charitable organization founded in 1961
Mission: To bring together individuals interested in the research, preservation, promotion & advancement of the history of Guelph
Member of: Guelph Arts Council; Guelph Museums
Affiliation(s): Ontario Historical Society; Wellington County Historical Society
Finances: *Annual Operating Budget:* Less than $50,000
16 volunteer(s)
Membership: 275; *Fees:* $30 individual/institutional; $40 family; $15 student; $200 lifetime (individual); $300 lifetime (family)
Activities: Lectures; bus trip; journal; newsletter; essay contest; plaques; *Library:* by appointment
Chief Officer(s):
David Cameletti, President
Awards:
• Vern McIlwraith Essay Contest
Publications:
• Historic Guelph [a publication of Guelph Historical Society]
Type: Journal; *Frequency:* Annual

Guelph Information *See* Volunteer Centre of Guelph/Wellington

Guelph International Resource Centre (GIRC)
75 Norfolk St., Guelph ON N1H 4J2
Tel: 519-822-3110; *Fax:* 519-822-7089
Overview: A small local organization
Mission: To promote awareness, analysis & action on issues of social justice & global sustainability; To help Canadians understand their connection to people in Asia, Africa & the Americas
Member of: Global Education Centres of Ontario
Finances: *Annual Operating Budget:* $100,000-$250,000; *Funding Sources:* Membership fees; donations; fundraising
Staff Member(s): 4
Membership: 1-99; *Fees:* $15
Activities: Sponsors speakers; seminars; workshops; offers educational programs; *Speaker Service:* Yes

Guelph Musicfest
521 Kortright Rd. West, Guelph ON N1G 3R5
Tel: 519-993-7591
musicfest@artset.net
guelphmusicfest.ca
www.facebook.com/guelphmusicfest
twitter.com/guelphmusicfest
Overview: A small local organization founded in 2007
Mission: Annual spring chamber music festival
Member of: Guelph Arts Council; Festivals & Events Ontario
Finances: *Annual Operating Budget:* Less than $50,000; *Funding Sources:* Ticket sales; advertising sponsorship
Membership: *Member Profile:* Members of the community interested in classical music & the status of arts in Guelph
Activities: Annual presentation of four concert series in the Recital Hall of the Guelph Youth Music Centre
Chief Officer(s):
Ken Gee, Artistic Director

Guelph Police Association Inc. / Association de la police de Guelph inc.
PO Box 472, Stn. Main, Guelph ON N1H 6K9
Tel: 519-763-0111
www.guelphpa.ca
twitter.com/gpapres
Overview: A small local organization
Membership: 100-499
Chief Officer(s):
Matthew Jotham, President

Guelph Symphony Orchestra (GSO)
10 Carden St., Guelph ON N1H 3A2
Tel: 519-820-4111
info@guelphsymphony.com
www.guelphsymphony.com
www.facebook.com/GuelphSymphony
twitter.com/GuelphSymphony
Overview: A small local charitable organization founded in 2001 overseen by Orchestras Canada
Mission: To provide symphonic performances to audiences in Guelph and surrounding area
Member of: Orchestras Canada
Finances: *Funding Sources:* Individual & corporate donations; Sponsorships
Staff Member(s): 2
Activities: Performing concerts; Participating in youth engagement programs; *Library:* by appointment
Chief Officer(s):
Catherine Molina, General Manager
gm@guelphsymphony.com
Judith Yan, Artistic Director
jyan@guelphsymphony.com

Guelph-Wellington Counselling Centre *See* Family Counselling & Support Services for Guelph-Wellington

Guelph-Wellington Women in Crisis
PO Box 1451, Guelph ON N1H 6N9
Tel: 519-836-1110; *Fax:* 519-836-1979; *Crisis Hot-Line:* 519-836-5710
feedback@gwwomenincrisis.org
www.gwwomenincrisis.org
www.facebook.com/gwwomenincrisis
twitter.com/gwwic
www.youtube.com/user/gwwic
Previous Name: Sexual Assault Centre of Guelph
Overview: A small local organization founded in 1979
Mission: To end violence against women & children in all its forms
Member of: Ontario Association of Interval & Transition Houses; Ontario Coalition of Rape Crisis Center
Activities: Operating Marianne's Place, a shelter for women & their children who have been physically, emotionally, mentally, financially, or sexually abused (Phone 519-836-5710 or 1-800-265-7233); Providing the Rural Women's Support Program (Phone 519-833-2301 in Erin; 519-843-6834 in Fergus; 519-323-3638 in Mount Forest; or 519-519-5192 or 1-800-661-6041 in Palmerston); *Awareness Events:* Dec. 6 Vigil; Take Back the Night

Guid'amies franco-manitobaines
273, av Taché, Winnipeg MB
Tél: 204-237-6217
guidesfm@mymts.net
www.guidamiesfm.wix.com/guidamies
Nom précédent: Guides franco-manitobaines
Aperçu: *Dimension:* petite; *Envergure:* provinciale; Organisme sans but lucratif; fondée en 1935
Mission: Notre association constitue un organisme visant à l'éducation et à l'épanouissement des filles de 5 à 13 ans et des femmes d'expression francaise du Canada.
Membre de: Guides franco-canadiennes
Finances: *Budget de fonctionnement annuel:* Moins de $50,000; *Fonds:* Centraide; Francofonds
Membre(s) du personnel: 1; 10 bénévole(s)
Membre: 60; *Montant de la cotisation:* 135$; *Comités:* United Way Winnipeg
Activités: Travail en équipe; bonnes actions; service; la vie dans la nature
Membre(s) du bureau directeur:
Paulette Hamilton, Présidente

Guide Outfitters Association of British Columbia (GOABC)
#103, 19140 - 28th Ave., Surrey BC V3S 6M3
Tel: 604-541-6332; *Fax:* 604-541-6339
info@goabc.org
www.goabc.org
www.facebook.com/GOABC1966
twitter.com/GOABC
Overview: A small provincial organization founded in 1966
Mission: To market the Canadian northwest as the premeir hunting destination in Canada while endorsing the responsible, sustainable & ethical use of wildlife as a recreational resource
Affiliation(s): Council of Tourism Associations of British Columbia
Finances: *Annual Operating Budget:* $500,000-$1.5 Million
Staff Member(s): 5
Membership: 200; *Fees:* $320 general; $25 sportsman or family; $200 conservation; *Member Profile:* Licensed guide outfitter; Angling guide
Activities: *Speaker Service:* Yes
Chief Officer(s):
Dale Drown, General Manager
Meetings/Conferences:
• 52nd Annual General Meeting & 25th Annual Convention, March, 2018, Delta Grand Okanagan, Kelowna, BC

Publications:
- Mountain Hunter Magazine
Type: Magazine; Frequency: 3 times pa

Guides du Canada See Girl Guides of Canada

Guides franco-manitobaines Voir Guid'amies franco-manitobaines

Guild of Industrial, Commercial & Institutional Accountants / Guilde des comptables industriels, commerciaux et institutionnels
36 Tandian Ct., Woodbridge ON L4L 8Z9
Tel: 905-264-2713; Fax: 905-264-1043
iciaguild@aol.com
www.guildoficia.ca
Also Known As: Guild of ICIA
Overview: A medium-sized national organization founded in 1961
Mission: To support & promote interest in vocational accountancy; To encourage acceptance of modern accounting methods & procedures
Finances: Funding Sources: Membership fees
Membership: Fees: $150 accredited; $75 associate; Member Profile: Graduates of accounting programs or related fields, who have also finished the requisite practical work & administrative experience; Individuals who possess bookkeeping basic skills & general accounting skills, & who work in the accounting field, may be associate members; Students in accounting or a related field
Activities: Presenting seminars on accounting & other matters of interest to Guild members; Offering an educational program in association with the Granton Institute of Technology
Publications:
- The Journal
Type: Newsletter; Frequency: Quarterly
Profile: Recent & forthcoming activities of the Guild available to members

The Guild Society
27 - 14th Ave., Whitehorse YT Y1A 6K9
Tel: 867-633-3550
guildhall@northwestel.net
www.guildhall.ca
Overview: A small local charitable organization
Mission: To produce community theatre productions in Whitehorse
Activities: Producing three to four shows a season between September & May
Chief Officer(s):
Brandon Wicke, General Manager
Brian Fidler, Artistic Director
Adrian Burrill, Production Manager

La Guilde canadienne des médias See Canadian Media Guild

Guilde canadienne des métiers d'art See Canadian Guild of Crafts

La Guilde canadienne des réalisateurs See Directors Guild of Canada

Guilde canadienne des relieurs et des artisans du livre See Canadian Bookbinders & Book Artists Guild

Guilde de la marine marchande du Canada See Canadian Merchant Service Guild

Guilde des comptables industriels, commerciaux et institutionnels See Guild of Industrial, Commercial & Institutional Accountants

La Guilde des Musiciens/Musiciennes du Québec (GMMQ)
#900, 505, boul René-Lévesque ouest, Montréal QC H2Z 1Y7
Tél: 514-842-2866; Téléc: 514-842-0917
Ligne sans frais: 800-363-6688
info@gmmq.com
www.gmmq.com
www.facebook.com/327272200684984
twitter.com/GMMQ
Aperçu: Dimension: petite; Envergure: provinciale; fondée en 1897
Mission: To promote the economic, social, moral & professional interests of its members & all other musicians in general; To negotiate collective agreements; To establish favourable tariff-of-fees & working conditions
Membre(s) du personnel: 12
Membre: Montant de la cotisation: $195 regular; $50 band; free for students
Activités: Setting minimum working conditions for musicians; Lobbying on behalf of music & musicians to government bodies & communities; Offering services to members & musicians;
Stagiaires: Oui; Service de conférenciers: Oui
Membre(s) du bureau directeur:
Luc Fortin, Président
lfortin@gmmq.com
Mylène Cyr, Directrice générale, 514-842-2866 Ext. 236
mcyr@gmmq.com
Publications:
- Le Cyberbulletin [publication de Guilde des musiciens et musiciennes du Québec]
Type: Infolettre; Frequency: Mensuel
- Entracte [publication de Guilde des musiciens et musiciennes du Québec]
Type: Magazine

Guillain-Barré Support Group of Canada
c/o Muscular Dystrophy Canada, #901, 2345 Yonge St., Toronto ON M4P 2E5
Tel: 416-488-2699; Fax: 416-488-7523
Toll-Free: 800-567-2873
info@muscle.ca
www.muscle.ca
Also Known As: GBS Support Group of Canada
Overview: A small national organization overseen by Muscular Dystrophy Canada
Mission: To offer support to persons who have Guillain-Barré Syndrome.
Chief Officer(s):
Lynn Potvin, Coordinator, Client Services

Guillain-Barré Syndrome Foundation of Canada (GBSFCI)
PO Box 80060, Stn. Rossland Garden, 3100 Garden St., Whitby ON L1R 0H1
Tel: 647-560-6842
Toll-Free: 866-224-3301
www.gbs-cidp.org/canada
www.facebook.com/gbscidp
Overview: A medium-sized national charitable organization founded in 1985
Mission: To provide information about GBS & CIDP; To provide education, research, & support to individuals, families & friends affected by GBS, CIDP & related disorders
Affiliation(s): Guillain-Barré Syndrome Foundation International
Finances: Annual Operating Budget: Less than $50,000
12 volunteer(s)
Membership: 1-99
Chief Officer(s):
Donna Hartlen, Executive Director

Guitar Society of Toronto
Toronto ON
Tel: 416-964-8298
info@GuitarSocietyofToronto.com
www.guitarsocietyoftoronto.com
www.facebook.com/GuitarToronto
twitter.com/GuitarToronto
Overview: A small local organization founded in 1956
Mission: To further the study & appreciation of the classical guitar (predominately but not exclusively)
Finances: Annual Operating Budget: Less than $50,000
Membership: Fees: $80; Committees: Concert; Promotion & Publicity; Development; Finance; Outreach & Education; Communications; 2016 GFA; Eli Kassner's 90th; By-laws
Chief Officer(s):
Jack Silver, President
Timothy Smith, Communications Officer

Gulf of Maine Council on the Marine Environment
c/o New Brunswick Dept. of Environment & Local Government, PO Box 6000, 850 Lincoln Rd., Fredericton NB E3B 5H1
www.gulfofmaine.org
www.linkedin.com/company/gulf-of-maine-council-on-the-marine-environment
www.facebook.com/GulfofMaineCouncil
twitter.com/gomcnews
www.pinterest.com/gomcnews
Mission: This U.S.-Canadian partnership of government & non-government organizations works to maintain & enhance environmental quality in the Gulf of Maine to allow for sustainable resource use. The Council organizes conferences & workshops; offers grants & recognition awards; conducts environmental monitoring; provides science translation to management; raises public awareness about the Gulf. The secretariat rotates annually among the member jurisdictions.
Affiliation(s): ME Coastal Program; NB Department of Environment & Local Government; NH Department of Environmental Services; NS Department of Environment
Activities: Programs include: EcoSystem Indicator Partnership (ESIP), a web-based marine ecosystem monitoring system; Climate Network; State of the Gulf of Maine modular report; Habitat Restoration funding; Gulfwatch Contaminant Monitoring; & Coastal & Marine Spatial Planning (CMSP) for environmentally sound uses of ocean & coastal spaces.
Chief Officer(s):
Joan LeBlanc, Council Coordinator
jleblanc@gulfofmaine.org
Peter McLaughlin, New Brunswick Contact, 506-457-4850
Peter.McLaughlin@gnb.ca
Sophia Foley, Nova Scotia Contact, 902-424-1996
foleysm@gov.ns.ca
Awards:
- Gulf of Maine Visionary Awards
- Gulf of Maine Sustainable Community Award
- Gulf of Maine Industry Award
- Longard Volunteer Award
- Susan Snow-Cotter Leadership Award

Gustav Levinschi Foundation / La fondation Gustav Levinschi
#110, 1820, av Dr Penfield, Montréal QC H3H 1B4
Tel: 514-932-2595
Overview: A small provincial charitable organization founded in 1967
Mission: To improve physical & mental health & alleviate poverty with special focus on children, adolescents & the elderly, by supporting institutions & organization in this area
Activities: Grants are made mainly for seed money, program funding, special projects, equipment funds, research projects & scholarships as agreed by the board of directors

Guyana Cultural Association of Montréal (GCAM)
PO Box 29640, Stn. CSP Prom du Parc, Saint-Hubert QC J3Y 9A9
Tel: 450-445-0747
gcaminfo@yahoo.com
www.gcaom.org
Overview: A small local organization founded in 1967
Mission: To help the Guyanese community in Montreal
Membership: Committees: Benevolent; Information; Entertainment; Youth
Chief Officer(s):
U. Leebert Sancho, President

Guyana Ottawa Cultural Association (GOCA)
Ottawa ON
Tel: 613-808-2482
www.guyanaottawaculturalassociation.org
Overview: A small local organization founded in 1986
Mission: To foster & promote Guyana's cultural heritage among Guyanese individuals residing in the National Capital Region; To promote respect for Canadian values & institutions by working with similar associations in the area
Activities: Working with NGOs in Guyana to provide assistance to disadvantaged groups; Focusing on ways to deal with & adapt to challenges in health & education for the Guyanese Canadian community

Guyanese Canadian Cultural Association of BC (GCCABC)
PO Box 2869, Vancouver BC V6B 3X4
www.guyanabc.ca
www.facebook.com/GCCABC
Overview: A small provincial organization
Mission: To unite Guyanese Canadians living in BC; To contribute to the surrounding community; To foster & maintain an environment in which members can communicate
Membership: Fees: $20; Member Profile: Guyanese Canadians living in BC
Activities: Offering youth leadership programs; Donating to community organizations; Organizing social events for membership
Chief Officer(s):
Basil Statia, President

Guysborough Antigonish Pictou Arts & Culture Council See Antigonish Culture Alive

Guysborough County Inshore Fishermen's Association (GCIFA)
PO Box 98, 990 Union St., Canso NS B0H 1H0
Tel: 902-366-2266; *Fax:* 902-366-2679
gcifa@gcifa.ns.ca
www.gcifa.ns.ca
www.facebook.com/GuysboroughCountyInshoreFishermensAssociation
Overview: A small local organization
Mission: To provide community based management of the fishing resource & to ensure a sustainable resource fishery & habitat, healthy fish stocks & act as an information liaison between inshore fishermen & the Dept. of Fisheries, as well as provide effective representation within the industry & other associations.
Staff Member(s): 2
Membership: 134
Chief Officer(s):
Eugene O'Leary, President
Virginia Boudreau, Manager
Katherine Newell, Lab Technician/Researcher
knewell@gcifa.ns.ca

Guysborough Historical Society (GCHA)
PO Box 232, Guysborough NS B0H 1N0
Tel: 902-533-4008
guysborough.historical@ns.sympatico.ca
www.guysboroughhistoricalsociety.ca
Also Known As: Old Court House Museum
Overview: A small local charitable organization founded in 1972
Mission: To collect, preserve, study & exhibit these objects that serve to illustrate the story of Guysborough county & its people
Finances: *Annual Operating Budget:* Less than $50,000
8 volunteer(s)
Membership: 60; *Fees:* $25/family
Activities: Operating Old Court House Museum
Chief Officer(s):
Mary Armstrong, Curator

Gymnastics B.C. (GBC)
#268, 828 West 8 Ave., Vancouver BC V5Z 1E2
Tel: 604-333-3496; *Fax:* 604-333-3499
Toll-Free: 800-556-2242
info@gymbc.org
www.gymbc.org
www.linkedin.com/groups/3800514
www.facebook.com/GymnasticsBC
twitter.com/GymnasticsBC
www.youtube.com/user/gymnasticsbc1
Also Known As: British Columbia Gymnastics Association
Overview: A large provincial organization founded in 1969
Mission: To provide, promote & guide positive lifelong gymnastics experiences by: directing the development & delivery of quality, comprehensive provincial programs; promoting the benefits of gymnastics as a foundation for human movement, sport, health, wellness & enjoyment; coordinating, suppporting & promoting programs in the pursuit of national & international excellence in consultation with Gymnastics Canada Gymnastique
Member of: Gymnastics Canada Gymnastique
Finances: *Annual Operating Budget:* $1.5 Million-$3 Million; *Funding Sources:* Membership dues; sponsorship; programs
Staff Member(s): 13
Membership: 46,000; *Committees:* Gymnastics For All; Men's Technical; Trampoline Gymnastics Technical; Women's Technical
Activities: Provincial championships, Fall congress, Gymnaestrada; *Library:* Resource Library; Not open to public
Chief Officer(s):
Brian Forrester, CEO
bforrester@gymbc.org
Awards:
• Member of Distinction
• Volunteer of the Year
• Volunteer Team of the Year
• PLAY Gymnastics For All Leader of the Year
• PLAY Gymnastics BC Club of the Year
• PLAY Gymnastics Coaches of the Year
• ProMOTION Plus Emerging Gymnastics Leader of the Year

Gymnastics Canada Gymnastique (GCG)
#120, 1900 Promenade City Park Dr., Ottawa ON K1J 1A3
Tel: 613-748-5637; *Fax:* 613-748-5691
info@gymcan.org
www.gymcan.org
www.facebook.com/CDNgymnastics
twitter.com/CDNGymnastics
www.youtube.com/user/gymnasticscanada
Previous Name: Canadian Gymnastics Federation
Overview: A large national charitable organization founded in 1969
Mission: To lead, promote, facilitate & guide gymnastics in Canada as a sport for the pursuit of excellence & world prominence, & as an activity for lifelong participation; To act as the national umbrella organization for provincial & territorial associations which are members; To publish & enforce a standard set of rules & regulations to serve as guidelines for all members; To represent Canadian gymnastics as a member of national & international agencies & federations; To coordinate application of regulations in Canada; To promote, develop & direct high performance gymnastics programs; To promote, facilitate & guide development of national gymnastics programs; To promote, guide & encourage general gymnastics activities; To promote gymnastics as a healthy & safe sport/activity
Affiliation(s): Fédération internationale de gymnastique
Finances: *Funding Sources:* Sport Canada; Membership; Marketing; Fundraising
Staff Member(s): 20
Membership: 250,000 individuals; *Committees:* Artistic Gymnastics; Communications & Marketing; Executive; Events; Finance; Rhythmic Gymnastics; Sport Development/Education; Trampoline Gymnastics
Activities: National & international programs & competitions; *Awareness Events:* National Gymnastics Week; *Internships:* Yes; *Library*
Chief Officer(s):
Peter Nicol, President/CEO
pnicol@gymcan.org
Ian Moss, Director, High Performance
imoss@gymcan.org
Karl Balisch, Director, Corporate Services & Development
kbalisch@gymcan.org
Awards:
• Life Membership
• Jay Goold Memorial Award
• Malcolm Hogarth Leadership Award
• Ed Brougham Club Awards
• Dr. Gene Sutton Memorial Award

Gymnastics Newfoundland & Labrador Inc. (GNL)
1269A Kenmount Rd., Paradise NL A1L 1N3
Tel: 709-576-0146; *Fax:* 709-576-7493
Other Communication: Alt. Phone: 709-576-0144
gymnastics@sportnl.ca
www.gymnastics.nl.ca
www.facebook.com/gymnasticsnl
twitter.com/gymnastics_nl
Overview: A small provincial organization
Mission: GNL promotes & supports the development of gymnastics throughout the province.
Member of: Canadian Gymnastics Federation
Membership: 8 clubs
Chief Officer(s):
Carol White, Executive Director

Gymnastics Nova Scotia (GNS)
5516 Spring Garden Rd., 4th Fl., Halifax NS B3J 1G6
Tel: 902-425-5450; *Fax:* 902-425-5606
gns@sportnovascotia.ca
www.gymns.ca
www.facebook.com/GymnasticsNovaScotia
twitter.com/gymnasticsns
Previous Name: Nova Scotia Gymnastics Association
Overview: A small provincial organization
Mission: To operate as the governing body of gymnastics in Nova Scotia; To promote gymnastics, from the recreational level to the high performance level; To encourage participation, fitness, & well-being; To promote safe & positive gymnastics environments
Membership: *Fees:* Schedule available; *Member Profile:* Active & associatte gymnastics clubs throughout Nova Scotia; Judges; Recreational & competitive coaches; Pre-school, recreational, & competitive gymnasts & trampolinists; *Committees:* Men's Program; Trampoline Program; Women's Program; Education & Recreation; Fair Play & Equity; Competition
Activities: Training & certifying coaches, officials, & judges; Organizing & sanctioning gymnastics competitions; Providing resources about gymnastics; Offering the introductory Tumblebugs progam for children from 3.5 to 5 years of age
Chief Officer(s):
Nick Lenehan, President
Angela Gallant, Executive Director
David Brown, Technical Director
gnscoach@sportnovascotia.ca
Meetings/Conferences:
• Gymnastics Nova Scotia 2018 Annual General Meeting, 2018, NS
Scope: Provincial
Description: A yearly gathering to establish the general policy & direction of the association, consider committee reports, & elect the new executive committee
Publications:
• Gymnastics Nova Scotia Newsletter
Type: Newsletter; *Price:* Free for Gymnastics Nova Scotia members
Profile: Updates of the association's activities
• Gymnastics Nova Scotia Policy Manual
Type: Manual; *Number of Pages:* 107
Profile: Information about the association's structure, registration, meetings, elections, financials, travel, competitions, fair play, & awards

Gymnastics PEI
Sport PEI, 40 Enman Cres., Charlottetown PE C1E 1E6
Tel: 902-368-6570; *Fax:* 902-368-4548
Toll-Free: 800-247-6712
Other Communication: Toll-Free Fax: 1-800-235-5687
www.gymnasticspei.ca
Overview: A small provincial organization
Chief Officer(s):
Valerie Vuillemot, Executive Director
vvuillemot@sportpei.pe.ca
Awards:
• ADL/Sport PEI Achievement Awards
Honour excellence in various categories

Gymnastics Saskatchewan
1870 Lorne St., Regina SK S4P 2L7
Tel: 306-780-9229; *Fax:* 306-780-9475
info@gymsask.com
www.gymsask.com
www.facebook.com/gymsask
twitter.com/gymsask
Previous Name: Saskatchewan Gymnastics Association
Overview: A medium-sized provincial organization
Member of: Sask Sport Inc.; Canadian Gymnastics Federation
Finances: *Annual Operating Budget:* $250,000-$500,000; *Funding Sources:* Grants; self-generated revenues
Staff Member(s): 5
Membership: 9,000
Activities: *Awareness Events:* Gymnastics Awareness Week
Chief Officer(s):
Klara Miller, Chief Executive Officer
kmiller@gymsask.com
Cheryl Russell, Manager, Operations
crussell@gymsask.com

Gymn-eau Laval inc
2465, rue Honoré-Mercier, Laval QC H7L 2S9
Tél: 450-625-2674; *Téléc:* 450-625-3698
laval@gymno.org
www.gymno.org
Aperçu: *Dimension:* petite; *Envergure:* locale; Organisme sans but lucratif; fondée en 1978
Membre: *Critères d'admissibilite:* Parents utilisateurs
Activités: Loisirs adaptés aux enfants ayant des difficultés d'apprentissage; 8 programmes d'activités sont offerts annuellement dont des camps de jour et de séjour

Habitat Acquisition Trust (HAT)
PO Box 8552, Victoria BC V8W 3S2
Tel: 250-995-2428; *Fax:* 250-920-7975
hatmail@hat.bc.ca
www.hat.bc.ca
www.facebook.com/HabitatAcqTrust
twitter.com/HabitatAcqTrust
Overview: A small local charitable organization founded in 1996
Mission: To promote the preservation of the natural environment on Southern Vancouver Island & the Southern Gulf Island by: conserving habitats by acquisition, conservation coverants or other legal mechanisms; & promoting habitat stewardship, education & research
Member of: Land Trust Alliance of British Columbia
Affiliation(s): Victoria Natural History Society
Finances: *Annual Operating Budget:* $250,000-$500,000; *Funding Sources:* Private; foundations; provincial & municipal government
Staff Member(s): 4; 100 volunteer(s)

Canadian Associations / Habitat for Humanity Canada (HFHC) / Habitat pour l'Humanité Canada

Membership: 100-499; *Fees:* $30 regular; $45 family; $100 corporate; $20 Victoria Natural History Society member
Activities: Land purchase; conservation covenants (easements); environmental education; *Library:* Bob Ogilvie Bioregional Resource Library; Open to public by appointment
Chief Officer(s):
Adam Taylor, Executive Director

Habitat faunique Canada *See* Wildlife Habitat Canada

Habitat for Humanity Canada (HFHC) / Habitat pour l'Humanité Canada
#403, 477 Mount Pleasant Rd., Toronto ON M4S 2L9
Tel: 416-644-0988; *Fax:* 416-646-0574
Toll-Free: 800-667-5137
habitat@habitat.ca
www.habitat.ca
www.facebook.com/HabitatCanada
twitter.com/HabitatCanada
Overview: A large national charitable organization founded in 1985
Mission: To provide affordable & adequate housing for God's people in need by mobilizing local communities, volunteers & material & financial resources in wide-ranging, inclusive partnerships; To support, encourage, facilitate & empower those affiliates to build affordable homes in partnership with needy families
Member of: Habitat for Humanity International
Finances: *Annual Operating Budget:* $3 Million-$5 Million; *Funding Sources:* Corporate & individual donations of cash & building materials
Staff Member(s): 20; 15 volunteer(s)
Membership: 56 local affiliates
Activities: Ed Schreyer Work Project; All Women Build Project; *Speaker Service:* Yes; *Library:* Not open to public
Chief Officer(s):
Mark Rodgers, President & CEO

Alberta - Camrose
#1, 5007 - 46th St., Camrose AB T4V 3G3
Tel: 780-672-4484; *Fax:* 780-672-4453
info@habitatcamrose.com
www.habitatcamrose.com
www.facebook.com/HabitatCamrose
twitter.com/HabitatCamrose
Chief Officer(s):
Tamara Saby, President

Alberta - Edmonton
8210 Yellowhead Trail NW, Edmonton AB T5B 1G5
Tel: 780-479-3566; *Fax:* 780-479-0762
habitat@hfh.org
www.hfh.org
www.facebook.com/Habitatedm
twitter.com/Habitatedm
www.youtube.com/user/HabitatEdmGuy
Chief Officer(s):
Alfred Nikolai, President & Chief Executive Officer
anikolai@hfh.org

Alberta - Lethbridge
20 Rocky Mountain Blvd. West, Lethbridge AB T1K 8E1
Tel: 403-327-6612; *Fax:* 403-331-2195
lethbridgehabitatforhumanity@gmail.com
www.habitatlethbridge.ca
www.facebook.com/habitatforhumanitylethbridge

Alberta - Red Deer
4732 - 78A St. Close, Red Deer AB T4P 2J2
Tel: 403-309-6080; *Fax:* 403-309-0915
info@habitatreddeer.ca
www.habitatreddeer.ca
www.facebook.com/habitatforhumanityreddeer
twitter.com/habitatreddeer

Alberta - Southern Alberta
#210, 805 Manning Rd. NE, Calgary AB T2E 7M8
Tel: 403-253-9331; *Fax:* 403-253-9335
info@habitatsouthernab.ca
www.habitatsouthernab.ca
www.facebook.com/HFHSouthernAB
twitter.com/hfhsouthernab
Chief Officer(s):
Gerrad Oishi, President & Chief Executive Officer

Alberta - Wood Buffalo
The Red Poll Centre at Shell Place, 1 C.A. Knight Way, Fort McMurray AB T9H 5C5
Tel: 780-804-1311
habitatwoodbuffalo@gmail.com
www.habitatwoodbuffalo.ca

www.facebook.com/HabitatWoodBuffalo
twitter.com/HabitatFHWB
Chief Officer(s):
Eric Tokay, Chair

British Columbia - Greater Vancouver
7977 Enterprise St., Burnaby BC V5A 1V5
Tel: 604-681-5618; *Fax:* 604-326-0122
info@vancouverhabitat.bc.ca
www.vancouverhabitat.bc.ca
www.facebook.com/HabitatVan
twitter.com/HabitatVan
Chief Officer(s):
Dennis Coutts, Chief Executive Officer

British Columbia - Kamloops
#28, 1425 Cariboo Pl., Kamloops BC V2C 5Z3
Tel: 250-314-6738; *Fax:* 250-374-9370
info@habitatkamloops.com
www.habitatkamloops.com
Chief Officer(s):
Kim Cassar Torreggiani, Executive Director
executivedirector@habitatkamloops.ca

British Columbia - Okanagan
1793 Ross Rd., Kelowna BC V1Z 3E7
Tel: 778-755-4346
www.habitatforhumanityokanagan.ca
www.facebook.com/HabitatforHumanityKelowna
twitter.com/hfhokanagan

British Columbia - Mid-Vancouver Island
#1, 4128 Mostar Rd., Nanaimo BC V9T 6C9
Tel: 250-758-8078; *Fax:* 250-758-8096
info@habitatmvi.org
www.habitatmvi.org
www.facebook.com/HabitatforHumanityMidVancouverIsland
twitter.com/HFHMVI
Rob Hallam, Executive Director
rhallam@habitatmvi.org

British Columbia - Southeast BC
7281 - 5th St., Grand Forks BC V0H 1H0
Tel: 778-632-0006
hfhboundary@hughes.net
www.hfhsebc.org
www.facebook.com/habitatsoutheastBC
Chief Officer(s):
Bob Huff, Executive Director, 778-632-0006
bob.huff@hfhsebc.org

British Columbia - Sunshine Coast
PO Box 2356, 4494 Hilltop Rd., Sechelt BC V0N 3A0
Tel: 604-885-6773; *Fax:* 604-885-0298
www.habitatsc.ca
www.facebook.com/habitatcoast
twitter.com/@Habitatsc1
Chief Officer(s):
Cori Lynn Germiquet, Executive Director, 604-885-6737
executivedirector@habitatsc.ca

British Columbia - Upper Fraser Valley Society
#2, 34220 South Fraser Way, Abbotsford BC V2T 1T9
Tel: 604-557-1020; *Fax:* 604-557-9991
Toll-Free: 866-856-2434
info@habitatufv.ca
www.habitatufv.ca
www.facebook.com/403131583068845
Chief Officer(s):
James Barlow, Chair
james.barlow@habitatufv.ca

British Columbia - Vancouver Island North
1755 - 13th St., Courtenay BC V9N 7B6
Tel: 250-334-3777; *Fax:* 250-334-2528
info@HabitatNorthIsland.com
www.habitatnorthisland.com
www.facebook.com/HabitatVin
twitter.com/VINHabitat
Chief Officer(s):
John Newman, Chair

British Columbia - Victoria
849 Orono Ave., Victoria BC V8B 2T9
Tel: 250-480-7688; *Fax:* 250-480-7648
info@habitatvictoria.com
www.habitatvictoria.com
www.facebook.com/HabitatVictoria
twitter.com/habitatvictoria
Chief Officer(s):
Yolanda Meijer, Chief Executive Officer, 250-480-7688 Ext. 102
ceo@habitatvictoria.com

Manitoba
60 Archibald St., Winnipeg MB R2J 0V8
Tel: 204-233-5160; *Fax:* 204-233-5271
info@habitat.mb.ca
www.habitat.mb.ca
www.facebook.com/HabitatforHumanityMB
twitter.com/habitat_MB
www.youtube.com/user/HFHWPG
Chief Officer(s):
Sandy Hopkins, Chief Executive Officer
shopkins@habitat.mb.ca

New Brunswick - Fredericton Area Inc.
PO Box 643, 800 St. Mary's St., Fredericton NB E3B 5A6
Tel: 506-474-1520; *Fax:* 506-452-7213
info@habitatfredericton.com
www.habitatfredericton.com
www.facebook.com/HabitatForHumanityFredericton
twitter.com/HabitatFton

New Brunswick - Moncton
950 Mountain Rd., Moncton NB E1C 2S2
Tel: 506-384-4663; *Fax:* 506-384-4661
www.habitatmoncton.com
www.facebook.com/hfhmoncton
twitter.com/habitatmoncton
Chief Officer(s):
Chantal Landry, Executive Director
chantal@habitatmoncton.com

New Brunswick - Saint John
727 Rothesay Ave., Saint John NB E2H 2H6
Tel: 506-635-7867
restore@nb.aibn.com
www.habitatsaintjohn.ca
www.facebook.com/SJHabitat
twitter.com/SJHabitat

Newfoundland & Labrador
6 Robin Hood Bay Rd., St. John's NL A1A 5V3
Tel: 709-753-5743; *Fax:* 709-753-9380
contact@habitatnl.ca
www.habitatnl.ca
www.facebook.com/HabitatNLCA
twitter.com/HabitatNLCA
Chief Officer(s):
Sandra Whiffen, Executive Director

Northwest Territories
YK Centre Mall, Lower Level, PO Box 243, Yellowknife NT X1A 2N2
Tel: 867-920-4010
admin@habitatnwt.ca
www.habitatnwt.ca
www.facebook.com/HabitatNWT
twitter.com/HabitatNWT
Chief Officer(s):
Dave Hurley, President

Nova Scotia
81 Wright Ave., Dartmouth NS B3B 1H4
Tel: 902-464-0274
info@habitatns.ca
habitatns.ca
www.facebook.com/HabitatNovaScotia
twitter.com/habitatns
Chief Officer(s):
Rick Gant, Chief Executive Officer, 782-414-6791
rick@habitat.ca

Nunavut - Iqaluit
PO Box 1989, #103, 8-Storey, Iqaluit NU X0A 0H0
Tel: 867-979-7810
admin@habitaiqaluit.ca
habitatiqaluit.ca
www.facebook.com/HabitatIqaluit
twitter.com/habitatiqaluit

Ontario - Brant-Norfolk
408 Henry St., Brantford ON N3S 7W1
Tel: 519-759-8600; *Fax:* 519-751-2032
habitatbn.org
www.facebook.com/HabitatforHumanityBN
twitter.com/habitatbn
Chief Officer(s):
Dan Brooks, Chief Executive Officer, 519-759-8600 Ext. 22
dbrooks@habitatbn.org

Ontario - Chatham-Kent
566 Riverview Dr., Chatham ON N7M 0N2
Tel: 519-354-0506
info@habitatchatham-kent.ca

www.habitatchatham-kent.ca
www.facebook.com/hfhck
Durham Region, Ontario
#7, 85 Chambers Dr., Ajax ON L1Z 1E2
Tel: 905-428-7434; *Fax:* 905-428-7494
info@habitatdurham.com
www.habitatdurham.com
www.facebook.com/hfhdurhaminc
twitter.com/HFHDurham
Mission: To provide families with affordable home ownership opportunities
Affiliation(s): Habitat for Humanity Durham, Clarington Chapter
Chief Officer(s):
Mary Bone, CEO, 905-428-7434
CEO@habitatdurham.com
Ontario - Kingston Limestone Region
607 Gardiners Rd., Kingston ON K7M 3Y4
Tel: 613-548-8763; *Fax:* 613-547-4119
office@habitatkingston.com
www.habitatkingston.com
www.facebook.com/habitatkingston
twitter.com/HabitatKingston
Chief Officer(s):
Susan Zambonin, Chief Executive Officer
ceo@habitatkingston.com
Ontario - Grey Bruce
223017 Grey Rd. 17, Owen Sound ON N4K 5N7
Tel: 519-371-6776; *Fax:* 519-371-2642
Toll-Free: 866-771-6776
info@habitatgreybruce.ca
habitatgreybruce.ca
www.facebook.com/habitatgreybruce
twitter.com/HFHGB
Chief Officer(s):
Greg Fryer, Executive Director
Ontario - Hamilton
#1, 285 Nash Rd. North, Hamilton ON L8H 7P4
Tel: 905-560-6707; *Fax:* 905-560-6703
info@habitathamilton.ca
www.habitathamilton.ca
www.facebook.com/HabitatHamilton
twitter.com/HabitatHamilton
Chief Officer(s):
Sean Ferris, Executive Director, 905-560-6707 Ext. 108
sean@habitathamilton.ca
Ontario - Huron County
PO Box 453, Goderich ON N7A 4C7
Tel: 519-612-1614
habitatboard@hurontel.on.ca
www.habitathuroncounty.ca
Ontario - Huronia
128 Brock St., Barrie ON L4N 2M2
Tel: 705-727-0802; *Fax:* 705-727-0214
info@habitathuronia.com
www.habitathuronia.com
www.facebook.com/HabitatHuronia
twitter.com/HabitatHuronia
Chief Officer(s):
Ken Kirk, Chief Executive Officer
Ontario - Halton-Mississauga
#10-12, 1705 Argentia Rd., Mississauga ON L5N 3A9
Tel: 905-828-0987
www.habitathm.ca
www.facebook.com/habitathaltonmississauga
twitter.com/HabitatHM
Chief Officer(s):
John Gerrard, Chief Executive Officer
jgerrard@habitathm.ca
Ontario - Ontario Gateway North
1964 Muskoka Beach Rd., RR#1, Gravenhurst ON P1P 1R1
Tel: 705-646-0106; *Fax:* 705-646-2948
habitatgatewaynorth.com
www.facebook.com/HabitatOGN
twitter.com/HFHGatewayNorth
Chief Officer(s):
Tom Phillips, Acting Chief Executive Officer
tphillips@habitatgatewaynorth.com
Ontario - Greater Ottawa
768 Belfast Rd., Ottawa ON K1G 0Z5
Tel: 613-749-9950; *Fax:* 613-749-8991
www.habitatgo.com
www.facebook.com/HabitatGO
twitter.com/HabitatGO

Chief Officer(s):
Alexis Ashworth, Chief Executive Officer
aashworth@habitatgo.com
Ontario - Niagara
150 Bunting Rd., St Catharines ON L2P 3G5
Tel: 905-685-7395; *Fax:* 905-685-7396
info@habitatniagara.ca
www.habitatniagara.ca
www.facebook.com/HFHNiagara
twitter.com/habitatniagara
Chief Officer(s):
Alastair Davis, Chief Executive Officer
alastair@habitatniagara.ca
Ontario - Northumberland
764 Division St., Cobourg ON K9A 5V2
Tel: 289-252-0999; *Fax:* 289-252-2211
info@habitatnorthumberland.ca
www.habitatnorthumberland.ca
www.facebook.com/HabitatNorthumberland
twitter.com/hfhnrestore
Chief Officer(s):
Meaghan Macdonald, Executive Director
mmacdonald@habitatnorthumberland.ca
Ontario - Heartland Ontario
#2, 40 Pacific Crt., London ON N5V 3K4
Tel: 519-455-6623; *Fax:* 519-455-8479
info@habitat4home.ca
habitat4home.ca
www.facebook.com/HabitatHeartlandOntario
twitter.com/Habitat4HOME
Chief Officer(s):
Brian Elliott, Chief Executive Officer
belliot@habitat4home.ca
Ontario - Peterborough & Kawartha Region
550 Braidwood Ave., Peterborough ON K9J 1W1
Tel: 705-750-1546; *Fax:* 705-775-0621
info@habitatpeterborough.ca
www.habitatpeterborough.ca
www.facebook.com/HabitatPtbo
twitter.com/habitatpd
Chief Officer(s):
Sarah Burke, Chief Executive Officer, 705-750-1456 Ext. 222
sarah@habitatpkr.ca
Ontario - Prince Edward-Hastings
365 Bell Blvd., Belleville ON K8P 5N9
Tel: 619-962-7526; *Fax:* 613-969-1415
info@habitatpeh.org
www.habitatpeh.org
www.facebook.com/113997471993077
twitter.com/HFH_PEH
Chief Officer(s):
Bob Clute, Executive Director, 613-962-7526 Ext. 203
bob.clute@habitatpeh.org
Ontario - Sarnia/Lambton
460 Christina St. North, Sarnia ON N7T 5W4
Tel: 519-336-7075
info@habitatsarnia.org
www.habitatsarnia.org
www.facebook.com/HabitatSarnia
twitter.com/habitatsarnia
Chief Officer(s):
Sarah Reaume, Executive Director, 519-339-7957 Ext. 222
sreaume@habitatsarnia.org
Ontario - Sault Ste Marie (HFHSSMA)
32 White Oak Dr. East, Sault Ste Marie ON P6B 4J8
Tel: 705-941-9646; *Fax:* 705-941-9100
www.habitatsault.ca
www.facebook.com/hfhssma
twitter.com/habitatssm
Chief Officer(s):
David Thompson, Chair
Ontario - Seaway Valley
1400 Vincent Massey Dr., Cornwall ON K6J 5N4
Tel: 613-938-0413; *Fax:* 613-938-0446
info@habitatseawayvalley.org
www.habitatseawayvalley.org
Chief Officer(s):
Leigh Taggart, Executive Director, 613-938-0413 Ext. 202
Ontario - South Georgian Bay
155 Sandford Fleming Dr., Collingwood ON L9Y 5A6
Tel: 705-446-9542; *Fax:* 705-446-3210
info@habitatgeorgianbay.ca
www.habitatgeorgianbay.ca

Ontario - Thousand Islands
PO Box 383, Brockville ON K6V 5V6
Tel: 613-342-3521; *Fax:* 613-342-3501
admin@habitat1000islands.org
www.habitat1000islands.com
Ontario - Thunder Bay
660 Squier St., Thunder Bay ON P7B 4A8
Tel: 807-345-5520; *Fax:* 807-346-4401
office@habitattbay.com
www.habitattbay.com
www.facebook.com/hfhtbay
twitter.com/habitat_tbay
Chief Officer(s):
Dan Stezenko, Chief Executive Officer
Ontario - Greater Toronto Area
155 Bermondsey Rd., Toronto ON M4A 1X9
Tel: 416-755-7353; *Fax:* 416-916-2333
info@habitatgta.ca
habitatgta.ca
www.facebook.com/HabitatforHumanityGTA
twitter.com/HabitatGTA
Chief Officer(s):
Ene Underwood, Chief Executive Officer
Ontario - Waterloo Region
120 Northfield Dr. East, Waterloo ON N2J 4G8
Tel: 519-747-0664; *Fax:* 519-747-2153
mail@habitatwr.ca
www.habitatwr.ca
www.facebook.com/HFHWR
twitter.com/habitatwaterloo
www.flickr.com/photos/hfhwr
Chief Officer(s):
Karen Redman, Cheif Executive Officer
KRedman@habitatwr.ca
Ontario - Wellington Dufferin Guelph
#300, 104 Dawson Rd., Guelph ON N1H 1A7
Tel: 519-767-9752; *Fax:* 519-767-9096
info@habitatwdg.ca
habitatwdg.ca
twitter.com/HabitatWDG
Chief Officer(s):
Steve Howard, Chief Executive Officer
steve@habitatwdg.ca
Ontario - Windsor-Essex
3064 Devon Dr., Windsor ON N8X 4L2
Tel: 519-969-3762; *Fax:* 519-969-7832
office@habitatwindsor.org
www.habitatwindsor.org
www.facebook.com/HabitatForHumanityWindsorEssex
twitter.com/HFHWindsorEssex
Prince Edward Island
365 Mount Edward Rd., Charlottetown PE C1A 2A1
Tel: 902-368-7539; *Fax:* 902-368-3951
www.habitatpei.ca
twitter.com/Habitat_PEI
Chief Officer(s):
Aaron Brown, Executive Director
executivedirector@habitatpei.ca
Québec
#108, 4377, rue Notre Dame ouest, Montréal QC H4C 1R9
Tél: 514-937-0643; *Téléc:* 514-937-7437
info@habitatqc.ca
habitatqc.ca
twitter.com/Habitatquebec
Chief Officer(s):
Jean-Maurice Forget, Président
Saskatchewan - Lloydminster
PO Box 143, Lloydminster SK S9V 0Y1
Tel: 306-825-4611
hab4hum@sasktel.net
www.habitatlloydminster.ca
www.facebook.com/habitatlloydminster
twitter.com/HabitatLloyd
Chief Officer(s):
Brad Onofrychuk, Chair
Saskatchewan - Prince Albert
PO Box 644, Prince Albert SK S6V 5S2
Tel: 306-764-4662
habitatpa@sasktel.net
www.habitatpa.ca
Chief Officer(s):
John Van Leeuwen, Executive Director, 306-764-4662
director@habitatpa.ca

Saskatchewan - Regina
1740 Broder St., Regina SK S4N 2H7
Tel: 306-522-9700; *Fax:* 306-522-9703
www.habitatregina.ca
www.facebook.com/Habitatregina
twitter.com/habitatregina
www.youtube.com/user/habitatregina
Chief Officer(s):
Terry Heavisides, Executive Chair

Saskatchewan - Saskatoon
320 - 21st St. West, Saskatoon SK S7M 4E6
Tel: 306-343-7772; *Fax:* 306-343-7801
www.habitatsaskatoon.ca
www.facebook.com/HabitatYXE
twitter.com/H4H_Saskatoon
Chief Officer(s):
Barb Cox-Lloyd, Chief Executive Officer

Yukon
PO Box 31118, Whitehorse YT Y1A 5P7
Tel: 867-456-4349
info@habitatyukon.org
www.habityukon.org
Chief Officer(s):
Arthur Mitchell, President

Habitat pour l'Humanité Canada *See* Habitat for Humanity Canada

Hagersville & District Chamber of Commerce
PO Box 1090, Hagersville ON N0A 1H0
Tel: 905-768-0422; *Fax:* 289-282-0105
Overview: A small local organization
Membership: *Fees:* Schedule available
Chief Officer(s):
Robert C. Phillips, President
rphillips@heaslipford.com

Haida Gwaii Arts Council
PO Box 35, Queen Charlotte BC V0T 1S0
Tel: 250-559-4691
info@hgartscouncil.ca
www.hgartscouncil.ca
Previous Name: Queen Charlotte Islands Arts Council
Overview: A small local organization
Member of: Assembly of BC Arts Councils
Chief Officer(s):
Astrid Egger, President
abegger@haidagwaii.net

Haines Junction Chamber of Commerce *See* St. Elias Chamber of Commerce

Hal Jackman Foundation
165 University AVe., 10th Fl., Toronto ON M5H 3B8
Tel: 416-350-5877; *Fax:* 416-362-7961
www.haljackmanfoundation.org
Overview: A small national charitable organization founded in 1964
Mission: To increase access to & cultivate appreciation of arts & culture; To build the audiences of the future
Chief Officer(s):
Victoria Jackman, Executive Director
victoria@jackman.org

HALCO
#400, 65 Wellesley St. East, Toronto ON M4Y 1G7
Tel: 416-340-7790; *Fax:* 416-340-7248
Toll-Free: 888-705-8889
talklaw@halco.org
www.halco.org
Also Known As: HIV & AIDS Legal Clinic of Ontario
Overview: A small provincial organization founded in 1995
Mission: Community-based legal clinic that provides free legal services to people living with HIV/AIDS in Ontario
Staff Member(s): 10
Membership: 175; *Fees:* Free
Chief Officer(s):
Ryan Peck, Executive Director

Haldimand Association for the Developmentally Challenged *See* Community Living Haldimand

Haldimand Community Support Centre *See* Community Support Centre Haldimand-Norfolk

Haldimand-Norfolk District Beekeepers' Association
Simcoe ON
Tel: 519-428-5386
Overview: A small local organization
Mission: To develop the beekeeping skills of interested persons in Haldimand-Norfolk
Membership: *Member Profile:* Beekeepers in Ontario's Haldimand-Norfolk District
Activities: Providing a forum for networking for district beekeepers
Chief Officer(s):
David Bowen, President
president@halnorbeekeepers.com

Haldimand-Norfolk Information Centre (HNIC)
643 Park Rd. North, Brantford ON N3T 5L8
Tel: 519-758-8228
haldimand.cioc.ca
Overview: A small local charitable organization founded in 1974 overseen by InformOntario
Mission: To provide human service information to community
Member of: On-Line Ontario
Activities: Electronic Data-Bases; Public Access Terminal; Ontario Business Connects Workstation; Provincial government forms & resources; *Speaker Service:* Yes; *Rents Mailing List:* Yes; *Library:* Open to public

Haldimand-Norfolk Literacy Council (HNLC)
200 West St., Simcoe ON N3Y 1S9
Tel: 519-428-0064
Toll-Free: 866-973-7323
info@hnliteracy.com
www.hnliteracy.com
Overview: A small local charitable organization founded in 1986
Mission: To work with adults to upgrade their literacy & math skills.
Affiliation(s): Laubach Literacy of Canada - Ontario
Finances: *Funding Sources:* United Way; provincial government; private donations
Activities: ESL classes, in small groups & 1-to-1, free to adults over 18
Chief Officer(s):
Anita Hillis-Krause, Interim Executive Director
ed@hnliteracy.com
Sherry Black-Schrubb, Coordinator, Norfolk
sherry@hnliteracy.com

Dunnville Office & Adult Learning Centre
227 Queen St., Dunnville ON N1A 2X5
Tel: 905-774-9141
Chief Officer(s):
Gina McIntee, Coordinator
hc@hnliteracy.com

Haley Street Adult Services Centre Society
26 Haley St., North Sydney NS B2A 3L3
Tel: 902-794-3517; *Fax:* 902-794-9650
www.haleystreet.ca
Overview: A small local organization
Mission: To provide vocational training for adults with disabilities
Member of: DIRECTIONS Council for Vocational Services Society
Activities: Nora's New to You thrift store; woodworking; recreation & leisure program
Chief Officer(s):
Judy Gouthro Snow, President

Haliburton County Association for Community Living *See* Community Living Haliburton County

Haliburton Highlands Chamber of Commerce (HHCofC)
PO Box 670, 195 Highland St., #L1, Haliburton ON K0M 1S0
Tel: 705-457-4700; *Fax:* 705-457-4702
admin@haliburtonchamber.com
www.haliburtonchamber.com
www.facebook.com/HaliburtonHighlandsChamberofCommerce
twitter.com/HHCofC
Overview: A small local organization founded in 1964 overseen by Ontario Chamber of Commerce
Mission: To act as the voice of business for Haliburton County
Finances: *Annual Operating Budget:* $50,000-$100,000; *Funding Sources:* Membership dues
Staff Member(s): 2; 25 volunteer(s)
Membership: 250; *Fees:* Schedule available; *Committees:* Advocacy; Member Services; Networking & Special Events; Young Professionals
Activities: Supporting & developing businesses in the Haliburton County; *Internships:* Yes
Chief Officer(s):
Jerry Walker, President
Autumn Smith, Chamber Manager
autumn@haliburtonchamber.com
Awards:
- Business of the Year
- Highlander of the Year

Haliburton Highlands Guild of Fine Arts (HHGFA)
PO Box 912, 23 York St., Haliburton ON K0M 1S0
Tel: 705-457-2330
info@railsendgallery.com
www.railsendgallery.com
www.facebook.com/railsend
twitter.com/RailsEnd
www.pinterest.com/railsend
Also Known As: Rails End Gallery & Arts Centre
Overview: A small local charitable organization founded in 1966
Mission: To maintain a not-for-profit, public art gallery & arts centre which focuses on contemporary art of the region; to offer programs open to the public to foster exploration, appreciation, expression & exchange of creativity.
Finances: *Funding Sources:* Municipal government
Membership: *Fees:* $28.25 adult/artist; $45.20 family/studio; $22.60 senior; $11.30 student

Halifax Amateur Radio Club (HARC)
PO Box 8895, Halifax NS B3K 5M5
Tel: 902-490-6421
www.halifax-arc.org
Overview: A small local organization founded in 1932
Mission: To promote amateur radio and Ham radio and provide a forum for the exchange of ideas and information related to radio communications and technical experimentation in Nova Scotia.
Membership: 125; *Fees:* $30 full; $15 associate; $45 family; *Committees:* Government & Media Relations; Membership; Web page; Basic ham course
Chief Officer(s):
Scott Wood, President
ve1qd@rac.ca

Halifax Area Leisure & Therapeutic Riding Association
196 Moss Close, Lawrencetown NS B2Z 1S5
Tel: 902-435-9344
haltr2@live.ca
www.bengallancers.com/special-needs-haltr
www.facebook.com/HalifaxJrBengalLancers
twitter.com/Bengal_Lancers
instagram.com/hfxjrbengallancers
Previous Name: Lancer Rehab Riders
Overview: A small local charitable organization
Mission: HALTR is a volunteer-run group that provides horse-riding & driving programs for people with special needs. It is a registered charity, BN: 890783947RR0001.
Member of: Equine Canada; Canadian Therapeutic Riding Association
Affiliation(s): Sport Canada
Membership: *Member Profile:* Mostly children & young adults with disabilities
Chief Officer(s):
Sallie Murphy, Program Manager

Halifax Association of Vegetarians (HAV)
PO Box 3087, Tantallon NS B3Z 4G9
halifaxvegetarians@gmail.com
www.halifaxvegetarians.ca
Overview: A medium-sized local organization
Mission: To promote a vegetarian lifestyle, and unite vegetarians and those interested in vegetarianism in the Halifax area and throughout Nova Scotia.
Member of: International Vegetarian Union
Membership: *Fees:* $20 individual; $25 family; $15 senior/student

Halifax Chamber of Commerce
#100, 32 Akerley Blvd., Dartmouth NS B3B 1N1
Tel: 902-468-7111; *Fax:* 902-468-7333
info@halifaxchamber.com
www.halifaxchamber.com
www.linkedin.com/groups/LnkdIn-Group-Halifax-Chamber-Commerce-1865797
www.facebook.com/halifaxchamberofcommerce
twitter.com/halifaxchamber
Previous Name: Metropolitan Halifax Chamber of Commerce
Merged from: Bedford Board of Trade; Halifax Board of

Trade; Dartmouth Chamber of Commerce; Sackville Chamber of
Overview: A large local organization founded in 1995
Mission: To build & strengthen the business culture in Metro Halifax through advocacy, networking & leadership
Member of: Canadian Chamber of Commerce
Finances: *Funding Sources:* Membership dues; event revenue
Staff Member(s): 14; 400 volunteer(s)
Membership: 1,500+; *Fees:* Schedule available, based upon number of employees; *Committees:* Provincial Government Affairs; Municipal Government Affairs; Transportation; Energy Advisory Group; Ambassadors; Chamber Councils; Small Business
Activities: *Awareness Events:* Annual Golf Tournament; Annual Spring & Fall Dinners; Halifax Business Awards; *Speaker Service:* Yes; *Library:* Policy Work Library; Open to public
Chief Officer(s):
Valerie Payn, President & CEO, 902-468-7111
president@halifaxchamber.com
Publications:
• Business Voice [a publication of the Halifax Chamber of Commerce]
Type: Magazine; *Frequency:* 11 pa

Halifax Citadel Regimental Association (HCRA)
PO Box 9080, Stn. A, Halifax NS B3K 5M7
Tel: 902-426-1990; *Fax:* 902-426-7806
info@regimental.com
www.citadel.colourdigital.to
Overview: A small local organization founded in 1993
Mission: To assist Parks Canada in the administration & delivery of the historical interpretive program & associated activities at the Halifax Citadel National Historic Site of Canada and raise funds in support of that program.
Chief Officer(s):
James Bruce, President

Halifax County United Soccer Club
#7, 102 Chain Lake Dr., Halifax NS B3S 1A7
Tel: 902-876-8784; *Fax:* 902-446-3620
info@hcusoccer.ca
www.hcusoccer.ca
Overview: A medium-sized local organization founded in 1998
Mission: To foster a love of soccer & help individuals of all ages achieve their full potential.
Membership: 1,600 players; *Fees:* Schedule available

Halifax Elizabeth Fry Society *See* Canadian Association of Elizabeth Fry Societies

Halifax Employers Association (HEA)
#200, 5121 Sackville St., Halifax NS B3J 1K1
Tel: 902-422-4471; *Fax:* 902-422-7550
hea@hfxemp.ca
www.halifaxemployers.com
Overview: A medium-sized local organization founded in 1996
Mission: To negotiate efficient labour agreements on behalf of its members and to develop and maintain positive employer/employee work relations and oversee the training of employees in the Longshore industry in the port of Halifax.
Membership: 12 corporate
Chief Officer(s):
Fritz Burns King, Chair

Halifax Field Naturalists (HFN)
c/o Nova Scotia Museum of Natural History, 1747 Summer St., Halifax NS B3H 3A6
hfninfo@yahoo.ca
halifaxfieldnaturalists.ca/hfnWP
Overview: A small local charitable organization founded in 1975
Mission: To promote the enjoyment & preservation of Nova Scotia's history & natural areas through education, discussion & fellowship
Member of: Federation of Nova Scotia Naturalists
Affiliation(s): Canadian Nature Federation; Canadian Parks & Wilderness Society; The Nature Conservancy of Canada
Finances: *Annual Operating Budget:* Less than $50,000; *Funding Sources:* Membership dues; sales; donations
Membership: 120; *Fees:* $15 student; $20 individual; $25 family; $30 supporting/institutional; $5 Nature Nova Scotia; *Committees:* Colin Stewart Conservation Award; Conservation; Newsletter; Programme
Activities: Presentations, field trips; *Speaker Service:* Yes
Chief Officer(s):
Burkhard Plache, President

Publications:
• The Halifax Field Naturalist
Type: Newsletter; *Frequency:* Quarterly

Halifax Foundation
PO Box 2635, Stn. CPO, Halifax NS B3J 3A5
halifax_foundation@hotmail.com
www.halifax.ca/foundation
Overview: A small local charitable organization
Chief Officer(s):
Jack Keith, Chair

Halifax Hurricanes Ringette Association
NS
hhringette.ca
Merged from: Halifax Chebucto Ringette Association; Halifax - St. Margaret's Ringette Association
Overview: A small local organization overseen by Ringette Nova Scotia
Member of: Ringette Nova Scotia
Membership: 1-99; *Fees:* Schedule available
Chief Officer(s):
Chad Mombourquette, President
president@hhringette.ca
Mark Whidden, Director, Coaching
dc@hhringette.ca

Halifax Library Association
Nova Scotia Community College, Waterfront Campus Library Tech Services, 80 Mawiomi Pl., Halifax NS B2Y 0A5
halifaxlibraryassociation@gmail.com
halifaxla.wordpress.com
Overview: A medium-sized local organization
Mission: To promote libraries & library services; To promote cooperation among libraries in the Halifax Regional Municipality; To serve the interests of library workers
Membership: *Fees:* $5 student; $10 personal
Chief Officer(s):
Erin Morice, President

Halifax North West Trails Association (HNWTA)
c/o 27 Warwick Lane, Halifax NS B3M 4J3
Tel: 902-443-5051
info@halifaxnorthwesttrails.ca
www.halifaxnorthwesttrails.ca
www.facebook.com/124497311008207
twitter.com/HalifaxNWTrails
Overview: A medium-sized local organization
Mission: To promote the creation, protection and maintenance of trails within the Halifax Mainland North area.
Chief Officer(s):
Todd Beal, Chair

Halifax Professional Fire Fighters Association
PO Box 2330, Dartmouth NS B2W 3Y4
Tel: 902-453-5242; *Fax:* 902-453-1812
secretary@hpff.ca
www.hpff.ca
www.facebook.com/460302050722807
twitter.com/HFXFirefighters
Also Known As: IAFF Local 268
Overview: A medium-sized local organization

Halifax Regional CAP Association (HRC@P)
Halifax NS
Tel: 902-293-8122
admin@halifaxcap.ca
www.halifaxcap.ca
www.facebook.com/HRCAP
twitter.com/hrcap
Overview: A small provincial organization founded in 2000
Mission: To deliver quality service to communities through their locally operated Community Access Program (CAP) sites.
Chief Officer(s):
Paul Hudson, Chair

Halifax Regional Cerebral Palsy Association
PO Box 33075, Stn. Quinpool, Halifax NS B3L 4T6
Tel: 902-423-3025
hfxrcpa@gmail.com
www.facebook.com/HalifaxRegionalCerebralPalsyAssociation
Overview: A small local organization
Mission: To improve the lives of individuals in Nova Scotia who are affected by cerebral palsy
Finances: *Annual Operating Budget:* Less than $50,000
Membership: 100-499; *Fees:* $25 family; $15 individual
Chief Officer(s):
Joy Moulton, President

Halifax Regional Coin Club
c/o Dartmouth Seniors' Service Centre, 45 Ochterloney St., Dartmouth NS B2Y 4M7
Overview: A small local organization
Member of: Royal Canadian Numismatic Association

Halifax Regional Municipality Association *See* Habitat for Humanity Canada

Halifax Regional Police Association (HRPA)
103 Thorne Ave., Dartmouth NS B3B 0A4
Tel: 902-490-5234; *Fax:* 902-490-4188
unifiedstrengthhalifax.ca
Overview: A small local organization founded in 1990
Mission: To protect the rights & interests of the men & women who protect & serve the citizens of the Halifax Regional Municipality
Affiliation(s): Canadian Professional Police Association
Chief Officer(s):
Mark Hartlen, President
hartlema@halifax.ca

Halifax Sexual Health Centre
#201, 6009 Quinpool Rd., Halifax NS B3K 5J7
Tel: 902-455-9656; *Fax:* 902-429-3853
www.hshc.ca
www.facebook.com/HSHCNS
twitter.com/HfxSexualHealth
www.youtube.com/HSHCTV
Previous Name: Planned Parenthood Metro Clinic
Overview: A small local charitable organization founded in 1970
Mission: To promote sexual & reproductive health within an environment that respects & supports individual choice
Member of: Canadian Federation for Sexual Health
Activities: Sexual health clinic; annonymous HIV testing; education; *Awareness Events:* Sexual & Reproductive Health Day; *Speaker Service:* Yes; *Library:* Open to public by appointment
Chief Officer(s):
Kelly Grover, Executive Director

Halifax Sport & Social Club (HSSC)
PO Box 8821, Halifax NS B3K 5M5
Tel: 902-431-8326
info@halifaxsport.ca
www.halifaxsport.ca
www.facebook.com/HalifaxSSC
twitter.com/HalifaxSSC
Overview: A medium-sized local organization
Mission: To offer co-ed recreational sport leagues, tournaments & social events for adults.
Staff Member(s): 5
Chief Officer(s):
Lael Morgan, Executive Director, 902-431-8326 Ext. 113

Halifax Transition House Association - Bryony House
3358 Connaught Ave., Halifax NS B3L 3B5
Tel: 902-429-9002; *Fax:* 902-429-0954; *Crisis Hot-Line:* 902-422-7650
info@bryonyhouse.ca
www.bryonyhouse.ca
www.facebook.com/pages/Bryony-House/159269017458704
twitter.com/BryonyHouse
Overview: A small provincial charitable organization founded in 1978
Mission: To operate a 24-bed shelter for abused women & their children; to advocate for legislative, social & economic change to end violence against women & their children.
Finances: *Funding Sources:* Provincial government
Activities: Counselling service

Halifax Wildlife Association
PO Box 31055, Halifax NS B3K 5T9
Tel: 902-818-7642
admin@halifaxwildlife.ns.ca
www.halifaxwildlife.ns.ca
Overview: A small local charitable organization founded in 1853
Mission: To promote the responsible management of renewable natural resources in Halifax & Nova Scotia
Membership: *Fees:* $30 single; $40 family
Activities: Organizing & supporting educational programs; *Awareness Events:* Members Night
Chief Officer(s):
Richard Lee, President
richard.lee@halifaxwildlife.ns.ca

Halifax-Dartmouth Automobile Dealers' Association (HDADA)
PO Box 142, #502, 5657 Spring Garden Rd., Halifax NS B3J 3R4
Tel: 902-425-2445; Fax: 902-425-2441
info@hdada.ca
www.hdada.ca
Overview: A small local organization
Member of: Nova Scotia Automobile Dealers' Association
Membership: 35; *Committees:* Executive

Halton Children's Aid Society
1445 Norjohn Ct., Burlington ON L7L 0E6
Tel: 905-333-4441; Fax: 905-333-1844
Toll-Free: 866-607-5437
www.haltoncas.ca
Overview: A large local charitable organization founded in 1914
Mission: To protect children & youth while respecting their diverse needs; To strengthen families
Member of: Ontario Association of Children's Aid Societies
Activities: Providing foster care & adoption services; Investigating possible child abuse; *Internships:* Yes; *Library:* Not open to public
Chief Officer(s):
Nancy MacGillivray, Executive Director

Halton District Educational Assistants Association (HDEAA)
#202, 3425 Harvester Rd., Burlington ON L7N 3N1
Tel: 905-639-3680; Fax: 905-639-8517
www.hdeaa.com
Previous Name: Halton Instructional Assistants Association
Overview: A small local organization founded in 1995
Membership: 600; *Member Profile:* 95% Female Educational Assistants; special education support staff

Halton Family Services (HFS)
235 Lakeshore Rd. East, Oakville ON L6J 7R4
Tel: 905-845-3811; Fax: 905-845-3537
info@haltonfamilyservices.org
www.haltonfamilyservices.org
Overview: A small local charitable organization founded in 1954 overseen by Ontario Association of Credit Counselling Services
Mission: To assist individuals, couples, & families in Oakville & the Halton region cope with challenges, by providing a professional counselling service; To operate the Halton-Peel Consumer Credit Counselling Service, to help persons find solutions to their financial problems
Member of: Ontario Association of Credit Counselling Services
Finances: *Funding Sources:* United Ways in Halton; Ministry of Community and Social Services; Donations; Fees, on a sliding scale, for some programs
Activities: Providing individual, couple, family, bereavement, & credit & debt counselling; Offering services for children, men, & abused women; Providing the Employee Assistance Program; Presenting seminars & workshops on topics such as separtation & divorce, healthy relationships, & anger management
Publications:
• Halton Family Services Annual Report
Type: Yearbook; *Frequency:* Annually

Halton Foundation *See* Conservation Halton Foundation

Halton Hills Chamber of Commerce
8 James St., Halton Hills ON L7G 2H3
Tel: 905-877-7119
tourism@haltonhillschamber.on.ca
www.haltonhillschamber.on.ca
www.linkedin.com/company/halton-hills-chamber-of-commerce
www.facebook.com/HHCOC
twitter.com/HHCoC
Overview: A small local organization founded in 1918
Mission: To promote economic prosperity & sustainable development in Halton Hills
Member of: Ontario Chamber of Commerce; Canadian Chamber of Commerce
Finances: *Annual Operating Budget:* $100,000-$250,000; *Funding Sources:* Private sector; memberships
Staff Member(s): 3; 60 volunteer(s)
Membership: 495; *Fees:* Schedule available; *Committees:* Committee Composition, Membership & Procedure; Economic Development; Marketing & Communications; Membership Services
Activities: Providing business & tourist information; Organizing annual golf day, after business networking & business development seminars; Municipal lobbying; *Speaker Service:* Yes; *Rents Mailing List:* Yes

Chief Officer(s):
Kathleen Dills, General Manager
generalmanager@haltonhillschamber.on.ca

Halton Instructional Assistants Association *See* Halton District Educational Assistants Association

Halton Mississauga Youth Orchestra (HMYO)
159 Cavendish Ct., Oakville ON L6J 5S3
Tel: 905-842-5569
info@hmyo.ca
www.hmyo.ca
www.facebook.com/haltonmississaugayouthorchestra
twitter.com/HMYOmusic
Merged from: Halton Youth Symphony; Mississauga Youth Orchestr
Overview: A small local charitable organization founded in 2014 overseen by Orchestras Canada
Mission: To inspire, encourage & challenge young musicians to build their musical skills through the experience of various forms of orchestral music; to create an enjoyable environment that promotes teamwork, leadership & community involvement
Member of: Orchestras Canada
Finances: *Funding Sources:* Provincial & municipal grants; Membership fees
Staff Member(s): 10
Membership: 130; *Member Profile:* Musicians
Chief Officer(s):
Gregory Burton, Music Director
Publications:
• HMYO Newsletter
Type: Newsletter; *Frequency:* Irregular

Halton Multicultural Council (HMC)
1092 Speers Rd., Oakville ON L6L 2X4
Tel: 905-842-2486; Fax: 905-842-8807
info@halton-multicultural.org
www.halton-multicultural.org
www.facebook.com/HaltonMC
Overview: A small local organization founded in 1979 overseen by Ontario Council of Agencies Serving Immigrants
Mission: To offer settlement services, employment & language training, interpretation & translation services, TOEFL testing, social & cultural programs, transitional housing consultation.
Affiliation(s): United Way of Oakville; Ontario Trillium Foundation
Activities: Host Match program; programs for youth, seniors, individuals and families; Transracial Parenting Initiative; *Speaker Service:* Yes
Chief Officer(s):
Trivi Mehendale, President

Halton Peel Hispanic Association
1092 Speers Rd., Oakville ON L6L 2X4
Tel: 905-842-2486
information@hphispanicassociation.org
www.hispaniccanadian.or
ca.linkedin.com/in/hphassociation
www.facebook.com/halton.peel
Overview: A small local organization founded in 2008
Mission: To preserve & promote Hispanic culture & identity in Canada
Membership: *Fees:* $20 Individual; *Member Profile:* Individuals as well as organizations; *Committees:* Events; Web Master; Legal; Translation; Library Advisory
Activities: Cultural festivals
Chief Officer(s):
Alberto Rincon, President, Board of Directors

Halton Regional Police Association (HRPA)
#6, 2333 Wyecroft Rd., Oakville ON L6L 6L4
Tel: 905-825-8789; Fax: 905-825-0826
Toll-Free: 866-843-9993
info@hrpa.com
www.hrpa.com
Overview: A small local organization founded in 1974
Mission: To promote the interests of members & raise the standards of policing; to promote the individual rights of members, including working conditions, wages, benefits & pensions
Staff Member(s): 2
Membership: *Member Profile:* Members of Burlington, Oakville, Milton & Halton Hills police
Chief Officer(s):
Duncan Foot, President
Paul Lacourse, Chief Administrator

Halton Social Planning Council & Volunteer Centre *See* Community Development Halton

Halton Trauma Centre *See* Radius Child & Youth Services

Hamber Foundation
Toronto Dominion Tower, PO Box 10083, Stn. Pacific Centre, 700 West Georgia St., 18th Fl., Vancouver BC V7Y 1B6
Tel: 604-659-7448; Fax: 604-659-7469
www.hamberfoundation.ca
Overview: A small provincial charitable organization
Mission: To award grants to organizations registered as charitable or educational & projects arising & undertaken in the province of British Columbia
Membership: 1-99

Hamilton & District Health Library Network
Hamilton ON
Overview: A small local organization founded in 1970
Mission: To promote resource sharing & cooperation to enhance the quality of library & information services within the healthcare community
Membership: 10; *Member Profile:* Health-related libraries & library resource centres

Hamilton & Region Arts Council *See* Hamilton Arts Council

Hamilton AIDS Network (HAN)
#101, 140 King St. East, Hamilton ON L8N 1B2
Tel: 905-528-0854; Fax: 905-528-6311
Toll-Free: 866-563-0563
www.aidsnetwork.ca
www.facebook.com/TheAIDSNetwork
Previous Name: Hamilton AIDS Network for Dialogue & Support
Overview: A medium-sized local organization founded in 1986 overseen by Canadian AIDS Society
Mission: To help mobilize community-based responses to the needs created & exacerbated by the HIV epidemic in Hamilton & the surrounding community
Member of: Ontario AIDS Network; Canadian AIDS Society
Finances: *Funding Sources:* Ontario Ministry of Health; Health Canada; Region of Hamilton-Wentworth
Staff Member(s): 11
Activities: *Library:* Hamilton AIDS Network Resource Centre
Chief Officer(s):
Tim McClemont, Executive Director
tmcclemont@aidsnetwork.ca
James Finlay, Director, Finance & Administration
jfinlay@aidsnetwork.ca
Leanne Parsons, Director, Support & Volunteer Services
lparsons@aidsnetwork.ca
Karyn Cooper, Director, Community Engagement
dcep@aidsnetwork.ca

Hamilton AIDS Network for Dialogue & Support *See* Hamilton AIDS Network

Hamilton Arts Council
22 Wilson St., Hamilton ON L8R 1C5
Tel: 905-481-3218; Fax: 905-529-9738
info@hamiltonartscouncil.ca
hamiltonartscouncil.ca
www.facebook.com/people/Arts-Hamilton/1266965869
twitter.com/hamartscouncil
Previous Name: Hamilton & Region Arts Council
Overview: A small local charitable organization founded in 1969
Mission: To serve the community & its artists as an advocate for the arts & as a forum for promoting the arts in Hamilton & region
Member of: Community Arts Ontario; Ontario Crafts Council; Canadian Artists' Representation Ontario; Canadian Conference of the Arts; Theatre Ontario
Finances: *Annual Operating Budget:* $100,000-$250,000; *Funding Sources:* City of Hamilton; membership; Ontario Arts Council; donations; Trillium Foundation
Staff Member(s): 4; 55 volunteer(s)
Membership: 400; *Fees:* Schedule available; *Member Profile:* Artists; arts organizations; educators; businesses; individuals; *Committees:* Craft; Fundraising; Literary; Music; Theatre; Visual Arts
Activities: Lit Awards; Designer Crafts; Crafts Award; designer crafts exhibition; Lit Chats; Photophobia; Monologic; Gallery in the Mall; studio walking tour; Class & Trash; *Speaker Service:* Yes; *Library:* Open to public
Chief Officer(s):
Stephanie Vegh, Executive Director
stephanie@hamiltonartscouncil.ca

David Premi, President

Hamilton Association for Community Living See Community Living Hamilton

Hamilton Baseball Umpires' Association (HBUA)
Hamilton ON
Tel: 905-538-6071
hamiltonbaseballumpires@gmail.com
hbua.ca
www.facebook.com/190866890945303
Overview: A small local organization
Chief Officer(s):
Bill Tunney, President & Assignor
b.tunney@cogeco.ca

Hamilton Chamber of Commerce (HCC)
Plaza Level, 120 King St. West, Hamilton ON L8P 4V2
Tel: 905-522-1151; Fax: 905-522-1154
hcc@hamiltonchamber.ca
www.hamiltonchamber.ca
www.linkedin.com/company/hamilton-chamber-of-commerce
www.facebook.com/140038556040986
twitter.com/hamiltonchamber
Overview: A medium-sized local licensing organization founded in 1845
Mission: To make greater Hamilton a great place to live, work, play, visit & invest; To recognize the importance of the individual as the most significant contributor to achieving community objectives
Member of: Ontario Chamber of Commerce; Canadian Chamber of Commerce
Finances: Annual Operating Budget: $1.5 Million-$3 Million; Funding Sources: Membership dues; special events; publications
Staff Member(s): 12; 100 volunteer(s)
Membership: 1,650; Fees: Schedule available; Member Profile: Businesses; Committees: Connections; Human Resources; Ancaster, Dundas, Glanbrook & YEP Divisions
Activities: Offering general business networking opportunities & seminars; Organizing events such as Business After Business & orientation breakfasts; Speaker Service: Yes; Rents Mailing List: Yes; Library: Business Reference Library; Open to public
Chief Officer(s):
Keanin Loomis, President & CEO
k.loomis@hamiltonchamber.ca
Awards:
• Outstanding Business Achievement Awards (OBAA)
• Dundas, Ancaster & Hamilton Citizen of the Year & Youth Volunteer
• Athena Award

Hamilton Community Foundation (HCF)
#700, 120 King St. West, Hamilton ON L8P 4V2
Tel: 905-523-5600; Fax: 905-523-0741
info@hamiltoncommunityfoundation.ca
hamiltoncommunityfoundation.ca
www.facebook.com/HamCommFdn
twitter.com/HamCommFdn
Overview: A small local charitable organization founded in 1954
Mission: To distribute grants in perpetuity to those of Hamilton/Wentworth & Burlington region. Grants in the past have been for adult basic education, theatre arts, residential redevelopment, environment, poverty reduction, youth activities, preschool, sexual assualt centre, community healthcare.
Member of: Canadian Centre for Philanthropy; Council on Foundations; Community Foundations of Canada
Finances: Annual Operating Budget: Greater than $5 Million; Funding Sources: Estate gifts; private sector donations; investment revenue
Staff Member(s): 21
Membership: 191 foundations
Activities: Speaker Service: Yes
Chief Officer(s):
Brent J. Foreman, Chair
Terry Cooke, President & CEO Ext. 224
terry.cooke@hamiltoncommunityfoundation.ca

Hamilton District Society for Disabled Children (HDSDC)
325 Wellington St., Hamilton ON L8L 0A4
Tel: 905-385-5391
Overview: A small local organization founded in 1951
Mission: To assist in addressing the needs of children (under 21 years of age) who have physical disabilities that affect gross or fine motor control & that limit their ability to function in activities of daily living, by providing financial assistance to projects not funded by other agencies or government
Finances: Annual Operating Budget: $50,000-$100,000
Staff Member(s): 1
Membership: 10 individual
Activities: Speaker Service: Yes
Chief Officer(s):
Mark Matson, President

Hamilton Folk Arts Heritage Council
#1, 12 Walnut St. South, Hamilton ON L8N 2K7
Tel: 905-525-2297
www.hamiltonfolkarts.org
Overview: A small local charitable organization founded in 1969
Mission: To promote ethnic awareness among the communities through the avenues of arts, crafts, food & entertainment; to provide activity & fun that are essential to a healthy lifestyle; to promote cultural heritage & public awareness of the diversity of cultures & ethnic lifestyle throughout Canada
Member of: Greater Hamilton Tourism Committee; Ontario Craft Council; Hamilton & Region Art Council
Affiliation(s): Festival & Events Ontario
Membership: Member Profile: Non-commercial & non-political organizations
Activities: Art exhibitions; theatrical presentation; exhibits; cultural events; "It's Your Festival" multi-arts celebration
Chief Officer(s):
Harnald Toomsalu, Acting President

Hamilton Food Share
339 Barton St., Stoney Creek ON L8E 2L2
Tel: 905-664-9065; Fax: 905-664-2108
www.hamiltonfoodshare.org
Overview: A small local charitable organization
Mission: To collect & distribute food to people in need in the Hamilton region; to reduce hunger in the community
Staff Member(s): 3
Chief Officer(s):
Joanne Santucci, Executive Director

Hamilton Industrial Environmental Association (HIEA)
PO Box 35545, Hamilton ON L8H 7S6
Tel: 905-561-4432
info@hiea.org
www.hiea.org
Overview: A medium-sized local organization
Mission: To improve the local environment - air, land and water - through joint and individual activities, and by partnering with the community to enhance future understanding of environmental issues and help establish priorities for action.
Membership: 15 companies
Chief Officer(s):
Jim Stirling, Chair

Hamilton Jewish Federation
#506, 105 Main St. East, Hamilton ON L8N 1G6
Tel: 905-648-0605
www.jewishhamilton.org
twitter.com/JewishHamilton
Also Known As: Jewish Hamilton
Overview: A small local charitable organization founded in 1932
Mission: To govern & represent the Jewish community of Hamilton
Affiliation(s): UIA Federations Canada
Staff Member(s): 5
Activities: Speaker Service: Yes; Library: Holocaust Library; by appointment
Chief Officer(s):
Gustavo Rymberg, Chief Executive Officer, 905-648-0605 Ext. 305
grymberg@jewishhamilton.org

Hamilton Law Association (HLA)
John Sopinka Court House, #500, 45 Main St. East, Hamilton ON L8N 2B7
Tel: 905-522-1563; Fax: 905-572-1188
hla@hamiltonlaw.on.ca
www.hamiltonlaw.on.ca
www.linkedin.com/company/hamilton-law-association
www.facebook.com/hamiltonlawassociation
twitter.com/HLAlibrary
Overview: A small local organization founded in 1879
Mission: To educate & support its members in the practice of law, as well as to advocate their interests as lawyers.
Member of: County & District Law Presidents' Association
Staff Member(s): 10
Membership: 832; Fees: Schedule available; Member Profile: Lawyers; judges; articling students; Committees: Family Law; Real Estate; Continuing Professional Development; Corporate Commercial; New Lawyers
Activities: Maintaining library; legal seminars; lobbying for professional issues; social functions; Speaker Service: Yes; Library: Anthony Pepe Memorial Law Library; Not open to public
Chief Officer(s):
David W. Howell, President, 905-572-5830, Fax: 905-526-0732
dhowell@rossmcbride.com
Rebecca Bentham, Executive Director, 905-522-7992
rbentham@hamiltonlaw.on.ca
Awards:
• Emilius Irving Award
Awarded for outstanding contribution to association
Publications:
• Hamilton Law Association Journal
Type: Journal; Frequency: Bimonthly; Price: $30 pa, non-members

Hamilton Naturalists' Club (HNC)
PO Box 89052, Hamilton ON L8S 4R5
Tel: 905-381-0329
info@hamiltonnature.org
www.hamiltonnature.org
www.facebook.com/386408715600
Overview: A small local charitable organization founded in 1919
Mission: To promote the enjoyment of nature through environmental appreciation & conservation; To foster public interest & education in the appreciation & study of nature; To encourage wise use & conservation of natural resources; to promote environmental protection
Member of: Federation of Ontario Naturalists
Affiliation(s): Canadian Nature Federation
Finances: Annual Operating Budget: Less than $50,000; Funding Sources: Donations; membership dues; grants 80 volunteer(s)
Membership: 500; Fees: $30 senior/student; $35 individual/institution; $40 family; $750 lifetime; Committees: Bird Study Group; Conservation; Hamilton Bird Records; Education; Sanctuary; Newsletter; Plant Study Group
Activities: Monthly public meetings from Sept.-May; public hikes; Speaker Service: Yes
Chief Officer(s):
Michael Fischer, President, 905-526-0325
fischermj@sympatico.ca

Hamilton Niagara Haldimand Brant Community Care Access Centre (HNHB CCAC)
#4, 195 Henry St., Bldg. 4, Brantford ON N3S 5C9
Tel: 519-759-7752
Toll-Free: 800-810-0000
healthcareathome.ca
Overview: A small local organization
Mission: To provide access to community health care services
Finances: Funding Sources: Government of Ontario
Chief Officer(s):
Melody Miles, CEO

Hamilton Philharmonic Orchestra
10 MacNab St. South, Hamilton ON L8P 4Y3
Tel: 905-526-1677
communications@hpo.org
www.hpo.org
www.facebook.com/HamiltonPhilharmonic
twitter.com/h_p_o/
www.youtube.com/user/HamiltonPhilharmonic
Previous Name: New Hamilton Orchestra
Overview: A medium-sized local charitable organization founded in 1996 overseen by Orchestras Canada
Mission: To provide artistically excellent music to patrons; to educate music students of all ages
Member of: Orchestras Canada
Finances: Funding Sources: Ticket revenue; Municipal & regional funding; Federal & provincial arts councils
Staff Member(s): 9
Activities: Performing concert series; facilitating workshops; Library
Chief Officer(s):
Carol Kehoe, Executive Director
ckehoe@hpo.org
Neil Spaulding, Operations and Personnel Manager
personnel@hpo.org
Gemma New, Music Director

Hamilton Philharmonic Youth Orchestra (HPYO)
#129, 2 - 140 King St. East, Hamilton ON L8N 1B2

Tel: 905-869-4796
info@hpyo.com
www.hpyo.com
www.facebook.com/HamiltonPhilharmonicYouthOrchestra
Overview: A small local charitable organization founded in 1965 overseen by Orchestras Canada
Mission: To provide young people with the joy & discipline of orchestral music and perform regular concerts to enrich the cultural landscape of Hamilton & area.
Member of: Orchestras Canada
Finances: *Funding Sources:* Donations; Membership fees; Fundraising
Staff Member(s): 3
Membership: *Member Profile:* Persons from ages 12 to 23
Activities: Offering 10 concerts each year; Facilitating regular rehearsals; *Library:* Not open to public
Chief Officer(s):
Debra French, Executive Director
Colin Clarke, Music Director

Hamilton Police Association (HPA) / Association de la police de Hamilton
555 Upper Wellington St., Hamilton ON L9A 3P8
Tel: 905-574-6044; *Fax:* 905-574-3223
hpa@hpa.on.ca
www.hpa.on.ca
Previous Name: Hamilton-Wentworth Police Association
Overview: A medium-sized local organization founded in 1974
Mission: To promote high quality professional policing through labour relations & political activity
Affiliation(s): Police Association of Ontario; Canadian Police Association
Finances: *Funding Sources:* Membership dues
Staff Member(s): 6
Activities: *Speaker Service:* Yes
Chief Officer(s):
Brad Boyce, Administrator
bboyce@hpa.on.ca
Mike Cruse, Executive Officer
mcruse@hpa.on.ca

Hamilton Program for Schizophrenia (HPS)
#102, 350 King St. East, Hamilton ON L8N 3Y3
Tel: 905-525-2832; *Fax:* 905-546-0055
info@hpfs.on.ca
www.hpfs.on.ca
Overview: A small local organization founded in 1979
Mission: The organization is a comprehensive, community-based treatment & rehabilitation program for adults with schizophrenia. It promotes an understanding of schizophrenia in the community.
Affiliation(s): McMaster University Clinical Teaching Unit
Finances: *Annual Operating Budget:* $1.5 Million-$3 Million; *Funding Sources:* Provincial government
Staff Member(s): 22
Activities: Social gatherings
Chief Officer(s):
Peter E. Cook, Executive Director

Hamilton Regional Indian Centre
34 Ottawa St. North, Hamilton ON L8N 3Y7
Tel: 905-548-9593; *Fax:* 905-545-4077
support@hric.ca
www.hric.ca
www.facebook.com/hric.hamilton
twitter.com/hric2013
Overview: A small local organization founded in 1972
Mission: To serve the needs of the Native People in Hamilton & surrounding areas; to assist those in an urban environment by sponsoring programs that maintain Native traditions & culture.
Member of: Ontario Federation of Indian Friendship Centres
Affiliation(s): National Association of Friendship Centres
Staff Member(s): 25
Membership: *Fees:* $2 elder; $3 individual; $5 family; $10 organization
Activities: *Library:* Resource Library
Chief Officer(s):
Carol Hill, President
Susan Barberstock, Executive Director
sbarberstock@hric.ca

Hamilton Right to Life
209 MacNab St. North, Hamilton ON L8R 2M5
Tel: 905-528-3065; *Fax:* 905-528-5593
info@hamiltonrighttolife.org
hamiltonrighttolife.org
Overview: A small local charitable organization founded in 1972
Mission: To promote public awareness of the sanctity of all life from conception to natural death, of the impact of abortion on women's health, of parent's rights, & of the medical professionals' responsibility to patients & to society
Affiliation(s): Alliance for Life
Finances: *Annual Operating Budget:* $50,000-$100,000; *Funding Sources:* Membership dues; donations
Staff Member(s): 1; 7 volunteer(s)
Membership: 100 student + 15 lifetime + 1,900 individual; *Fees:* Schedule available; *Committees:* Speakers Bureau; Membership; Public Advocacy
Activities: *Speaker Service:* Yes; *Library:* Open to public
Chief Officer(s):
Renato Brun del Re, President
Sandra Dykstra, Office Manager
sandra@hamiltonrighttolife.org

Hamilton Stamp Club (HSC)
Bishop Ryan Catholic Secondary School, 1824 Rymal Rd. East, Hamilton ON L0R 1P0
elsaclare@cogeco.ca
www.hamiltonstampclub.com
Overview: A small local organization founded in 1897
Member of: Grand River Valley Philatelic Association; Royal Philatelic Society of Canada; American Philatelic Society
Affiliation(s): Grand River Valley Philatelic Association
Finances: *Annual Operating Budget:* Less than $50,000
20 volunteer(s)
Membership: 140; *Fees:* $15; *Member Profile:* Family
Activities: *Awareness Events:* Fall Show, 1st weekend in Nov.; Springex, 4th weekend in April; *Speaker Service:* Yes; *Library:* Open to public
Chief Officer(s):
Wuchow Than, President
wthan@cogeco.ca
Brenda Froome, Secretary

Hamilton Technology Centre (HIT)
#200, 7 Innovation Dr., Flamborough ON L9H 7H9
Tel: 905-689-2400; *Fax:* 905-689-2200
www.hitcentre.ca
Previous Name: Greater Hamilton Technology Enterprise Centre
Overview: A small local organization founded in 1977
Mission: To create wealth-generating jobs by helping form & grow technology-focussed business
Member of: City of Hamilton
Finances: *Funding Sources:* City of Hamilton
Activities: Incubating, mentoring & coaching tech business start-ups
Chief Officer(s):
Penny Gardiner, Facilities Director
penny.gardiner@hamilton.ca

Hamilton/Burlington See Bereaved Families of Ontario

Hamilton-Brantford Building & Construction Trades Council
#213, 1104 Fennell Ave. East, Hamilton ON L8T 1R9
Tel: 905-389-1574; *Fax:* 905-389-2207
www.hamiltonbuildingtrades.com
Overview: A small local organization
Mission: To represent the interests of its member trade unions
Membership: *Member Profile:* Trade unions in the Hamilton-Brantford area
Activities: Operating a Joint Labour/Management Safety Committee to bring awareness to the importance of employee safety; Offering training programs for members
Chief Officer(s):
Joseph Beattie, Business Manager

Hamilton-Burlington & District Real Estate Board (HBDREB)
505 York Blvd., Hamilton ON L8R 3K4
Tel: 905-529-8101; *Fax:* 905-529-4349
info@rahb.ca
www.rahb.ca
Also Known As: REALTORS Association of Hamilton-Burlington
Previous Name: Metropolitan Hamilton Real Estate Board
Overview: A medium-sized local organization founded in 1921 overseen by Ontario Real Estate Association
Mission: To pursue excellence & professionalism in real estate through commitment & service
Member of: The Canadian Real Estate Association; Real Estate Council of Ontario
Finances: *Funding Sources:* Membership dues; Fees for service
Membership: 1,000-4,999
Chief Officer(s):
George O'Neill, Chief Executive Officer, 905-529-8101 Ext. 230
George.ONeill@rahb.ca

Hamilton-Wentworth Police Association See Hamilton Police Association

Hamiota Chamber of Commerce
PO Box 403, Hamiota MB R0M 0T0
Tel: 204-764-3050; *Fax:* 204-764-3055
www.hamiota.com/chamber_commerce.html
Overview: A small local organization
Mission: To participate in community fundraisers; To act as liaison between the Manitoba Chamber of Commerce, the Manitoba Government, & local entrepreneurs; To address the issues affecting the business community
Chief Officer(s):
Larry Oakden, President
Bonnie Michaudville, Secretary

Hampton Area Chamber of Commerce (HACC)
#7, 27 Centennial Rd., Hampton NB E5N 6N3
Tel: 506-832-2559; *Fax:* 506-832-2807
hacc@nbnet.nb.ca
www.facebook.com/HamptonACC
Overview: A small local organization founded in 1979
Member of: New Brunswick Chamber of Commerce; Atlantic Provinces Chamber of Commerce

Hampton Food Basket & Clothing Centre Inc.
#2, 39 Tilley St., Hampton NB E5N 5B4
Tel: 506-333-3962
www.facebook.com/HamptonFoodBasket
Overview: A small local charitable organization founded in 1985
Mission: To provide food to families in the Town of Hampton & surrounding areas
Member of: Association of Food Banks & C.V.A.'s for New Brunswick; Atlantic Alliance of Food Banks & C.V.A.'s
Finances: *Annual Operating Budget:* Less than $50,000; *Funding Sources:* Private donations; churches; service clubs; government grants
30 volunteer(s)
Activities: Distribution of food, clothes, small appliances & bedding to the needy; fundraisers; yard sale
Chief Officer(s):
Catherine Peacock, Coordinator
Betty Kennett, Secretary/Founder

Handball Association of Newfoundland & Labrador
St. John's NL
www.nlhandballontherock.com
www.facebook.com/nlhandballontherock
Also Known As: NL Handball Association; Handball on the Rock
Overview: A small provincial organization
Mission: To promote & develop the sport of handball in Newfoundland & Labrador, with emphasis on junior programs
Member of: Canadian Team Handball Federation
Chief Officer(s):
Wayne Amminson, President

Handball Association of Nova Scotia (HANS)
NS
nshandball.com
twitter.com/nshandball
Overview: A small provincial organization
Mission: To promote & develop the sport of handball in Nova Scotia
Activities: Tournaments; junior program
Chief Officer(s):
Daniel Marcil, President & CEO
dan@nshandball.com

Handicap International Canada
#400, 50, rue Sainte-Catherine ouest, Montréal QC H2X 3V4
Tel: 514-908-2813; *Fax:* 514-937-6685
Toll-Free: 877-908-2813
info@handicap-international.ca
www.handicap-international.ca
www.facebook.com/Handicap.International.Canada
twitter.com/HI_Canada
www.youtube.com/user/HandicapInterCan
Overview: A large international charitable organization founded in 1982
Mission: To provide assistance through work in various fields for people in developing countries with disabilities; To prevent disabilities through the clearing of anti-personnel mines & cluster

munitions; To provide support for disabled persons in the aftermath of natural disasters & other humanitarian crises
Finances: *Funding Sources:* Donations; Department of Foreign Affairs, Trade and Development; Canadian Landmine Foundation; Lochmaddy Foundation
Activities: Providing emergency response to national disasters; Supporting teams that engage in landmine clearance; Providing prostheses & physical rehabilitation to the physically disabled; Facilitating & advocating for the inclusion of disabled individuals in the workforce & their communities at large
Chief Officer(s):
Jérôme Bobin, Executive Director
jerome.bobin@handicap-international.ca
Publications:
• Handicap International Canada Newsletter
Type: Newsletter
Profile: Provides important news & international field work updates

Handicapped Organization Promoting Equality
PO Box 562, 84 Main St., Yarmouth NS B5A 4B4
Tel: 902-742-6579; *Fax:* 902-742-1281
hopecentre@ns.sympatico.ca
www.facebook.com/HOPECentreanddialaride
Also Known As: HOPE
Overview: A small local charitable organization founded in 1981
Mission: To provide life skill courses for adults & programs for children with special needs
Affiliation(s): Nova Scotia League for Equal Opportunities
Finances: *Funding Sources:* Federal, provincial governments

Handidactis *See* Disability Awareness Consultants

Hands on Summer Camp Society
1309 Hillside Ave., Victoria BC V8T 2B3
Tel: 250-995-6425; *Fax:* 250-995-6428
info@handsonsummercamp.com
www.handsonsummercamp.com
Also Known As: Elizabeth Buckley School
Overview: A small national charitable organization
Mission: To foster & promote recreational & educational opportuniities for all children; To meet their individual communication needs, with an emphasis on Sign Language
Finances: *Funding Sources:* Fundraising; fees
Activities: Operates the Elizabeth Buckley School & the Hands on Summer Camp
Chief Officer(s):
Choloe Elias, Camp Director

The Hanen Centre
#515, 1075 Bay St., Toronto ON M5S 2B1
Tel: 416-921-1073; *Fax:* 416-921-1225
Toll-Free: 877-426-3655
info@hanen.org
www.hanen.org
www.facebook.com/thehanencentre
twitter.com/TheHanenCentre
Overview: A medium-sized local licensing charitable organization founded in 1975
Mission: To provide specialized services & resources to parents, teachers & caregivers of language delayed children; To provide training to speech-language pathologists
Affiliation(s): Canadian Association of Speech-Language Pathologists & Audiologists; American Speech & Hearing Association
Finances: *Funding Sources:* Provincial government
Membership: *Member Profile:* Hanen certified speech-language pathologists
Activities: *Speaker Service:* Yes
Chief Officer(s):
Elaine Weitzman, Executive Director
elaine.weitzman@hanen.org

Hang Gliding & Paragliding Association of Atlantic Canada (HPAAC)
hpaac.ca
www.facebook.com/HPAAC
Previous Name: Hang Gliding Association of Newfoundland
Overview: A small local organization founded in 1979
Mission: To develop & promote the sports of hang gliding & paragliding in Atlantic Canada
Affiliation(s): Hang Gliding & Paragliding Association of Canada
Membership: 1-99; *Fees:* $140
Activities: Paragliding & hang gliding at coastal cities in Nova Scotia, Prince Edward Island, New Brunswick & Newfoundland & Labrador; *Awareness Events:* Atlantic Annual Paragliding/Hang Gliding Festival, May

Hang Gliding & Paragliding Association of Canada (HPAC) / Association canadienne de vol libre (ACVL)
#404, 1718 Venables St., Vancouver BC V5L 2H4
Fax: 604-731-4407
Toll-Free: 877-370-2078
admin@hpac.ca
www.hpac.ca
www.facebook.com/groups/HPAC.ACVL
Overview: A medium-sized national organization founded in 1977
Mission: To promote unpowered foot-launched flight in hang gliders & paragliders.
Member of: Aero Club of Canada; Fédération aéronautique internationale
Finances: *Annual Operating Budget:* $50,000-$100,000; *Funding Sources:* Membership fees
Staff Member(s): 1
Membership: 890; *Fees:* Schedule available; *Committees:* Safety
Chief Officer(s):
Margit Nance, Executive Director

Hang Gliding Association of British Columbia *See* British Columbia Hang Gliding & Paragliding Association

Hang Gliding Association of Newfoundland *See* Hang Gliding & Paragliding Association of Atlantic Canada

Hanley Agricultural Society
Hanley SK
hanleyagsociety@gmail.com
Overview: A small local organization founded in 1982
Mission: To improve agriculture & the quality of life in the community by providing a forum for discussion of agricultural issues
Member of: Saskatchewan Association of Agricultural Societies & Exhibitions
Activities: Agricultural & domestic displays; beef show; light horse show; co-ed slow pitch; men's fastball; children's activities
Chief Officer(s):
Patti Prosofsky, President, 306-544-2226

Hanna & District Chamber of Commerce
PO Box 2248, Hanna AB T0J 1P0
Tel: 403-854-4004
info@hannachamber.ca
www.hannachamber.ca
Overview: A small local organization
Member of: Alberta Chamber of Commerce; Canadian Chamber of Commerce
Staff Member(s): 1
Membership: 80
Activities: *Library:* The Learning Centre; Open to public
Chief Officer(s):
Will Warwick, President

Hanna Museum & Pioneer Village
502 Pioneer Trail, Hanna AB T0J 1P0
Tel: 403-854-4244
www.facebook.com/hannamuseum
Overview: A small local charitable organization founded in 1965
Mission: To preserve the history of the rural pioneer of this area & of Western Canada; To operate Hanna Pioneer Village & Museum
Finances: *Annual Operating Budget:* Less than $50,000
Staff Member(s): 1; 10 volunteer(s)
Membership: 25; *Fees:* $1; *Committees:* Building; Machinery; Membership; Archives
Activities: Conducting visiting patrons tours; *Library:* Archives; by appointment

Hanover Chamber of Commerce
214 - 10th St., Hanover ON N4N 1N7
Tel: 519-364-5777; *Fax:* 519-364-6949
info@hanoverchamber.ca
www.hanoverchamber.ca
Overview: A small local organization
Member of: Ontario Chamber of Commerce
Finances: *Funding Sources:* Membership fees
Chief Officer(s):
Curtis Schmalz, President

Hantsport & Area Historical Society
PO Box 525, Hantsport NS B0P 1P0
hantsportareahistoricalsociety@gmail.com
nsgna.ednet.ns.ca/hantsport
Overview: A small local charitable organization founded in 1977
Mission: To preserve history of area & make it accessible to the public; To provide index for genealogy
Member of: Federation of Nova Scotia Heritage
Finances: *Annual Operating Budget:* Less than $50,000
Membership: 50; *Fees:* $10
Activities: *Library:* Open to public

Harbourfront Centre
235 Queens Quay West, Toronto ON M5J 2G8
Tel: 416-973-4600; *Fax:* 416-973-6055
info@harbourfrontcentre.com
www.harbourfrontcentre.com
www.facebook.com/HarbourfrontCentre
twitter.com/HarbourfrontTO
Overview: A medium-sized local charitable organization founded in 1974
Mission: To nurture the growth of new cultural expression; to stimulte Canadian & international interchange; to provide a dynamic, accessible environment for the public to experience the marvels of the creative imagination
Finances: *Funding Sources:* Corporate; government; individual donations
2000 volunteer(s)
Chief Officer(s):
Braye Marah, Chief Executive Officer

Harbourfront Community Centre (HCC)
627 Queen's Quay West, Toronto ON M5V 3G3
Tel: 416-392-1509; *Fax:* 416-392-1512
hcc@harbourfrontcc.ca
www.harbourfrontcc.ca
Overview: A medium-sized local charitable organization founded in 1991
Mission: To advocate for provision of necessary services to the community, provide a range of responsive programs and services in an atmosphere of belonging and meet the needs of a diverse and changing multicultural community.
Finances: *Funding Sources:* City of Toronto
Membership: *Fees:* Schedule available
Chief Officer(s):
Leona Rodall, Executive Director
leona@harbourfrontcc.ca

Harmony Foundation of Canada / Fondation Harmonie du Canada
PO Box 50022, #15, 1594 Fairfield Rd., Victoria BC V8S 1G1
Tel: 250-380-3001; *Fax:* 250-380-0887
harmony@islandnet.com
www.harmonyfdn.ca
www.facebook.com/HarmonyFoundationCanada
twitter.com/HarmonyFDN
www.youtube.com/user/harmonyfdn
Previous Name: Society for the Preservation & Encouragement of Barber Shop Quartet Singing in America Inc.
Overview: A medium-sized international charitable organization founded in 1985
Mission: To encourage development which is socially & environmentally sustainable; To strive towards ecological stability, long-term prosperity, & social harmony
Finances: *Funding Sources:* Donations; Sponsorships
Activities: Working with organizations & individuals around the world through the Building Sustainable Societies Program; Improving environmental practices in workplaces; Providing community service opportunities for young people; Publishing action guides for homes, workplaces, & communities; Implementing training programs; Forming partnerships to establish meaningful results around environment & development issues; Educating about sustainable development & global change
Chief Officer(s):
Robert Bateman, Honorary Chair
Jean-Pierre Soublière, President
Michael Bloomfield, Founder & Executive Director

East York Chapter, Barbershoppers
c/o Barbershoppers, 2 Gower St., Toronto ON M1R 3S1
Tel: 416-861-0334
www.east-york-barbershoppers.ca
www.facebook.com/pages/East-York-Barbershoppers/152937108090639
Chief Officer(s):
Pat Hannon, Music Director
pat.hannon21@gmail.com

Greater Toronto Chapter, MegaCity Chorus
c/o MegaCity Chorus, 2 Gower St., Toronto ON M1R 3S1
Tel: 416-361-0025
megacitychorus.com

Harmony, Inc.
Toll-Free: 855-750-3341
info@harmonyinc.org
www.harmonyinc.org
www.facebook.com/HarmonyIncorporated
Also Known As: International Organization of Women Barbershop Singers
Overview: A small international organization founded in 1959
Mission: To perform & promote four-part a cappella harmony in the barbershop style; To promote personal growth & development through education & the practice of democratic principles
45 volunteer(s)
Membership: 2,500 individual
Chief Officer(s):
Jeanne O'Connor, International President
president@harmonyinc.org
Denise Dyer, Executive Secretary
exsecretary@harmonyinc.org
Meetings/Conferences:
• Harmony, Inc. 2018 International Convention & Contests, October, 2018, Lake Buena Vista, FL
Attendance: 1,000

Harold Crabtree Foundation
Varette Building, #603, 130 Albert St., Ottawa ON K1P 5G4
Tel: 613-563-4589
Overview: A small local charitable organization founded in 1951
Mission: To support education, health & social services in Ontario, Quebec, & Atlantic provinces; does not support individual requests or annual compaigns

The Harold Greenberg Fund
Astral Media, Brookfield Place, PO Box 787, #100, 181 Bay St., Toronto ON M5J 2T3
Tel: 416-956-5432; Fax: 416-956-2087
hgfund@astral.com
www.astral.com/en/about-astral/astrals-harold-greenberg-fund
Previous Name: Foundation to Underwrite New Drama for Pay Television (FUND)
Overview: A small national organization founded in 1986
Mission: To foster the development & production of feature-length movies written by Canadians & the production of family television series
Finances: Annual Operating Budget: $3 Million-$5 Million; Funding Sources: The Movie Network; Viewer's Choice Canada; Family Channel
Staff Member(s): 4
Chief Officer(s):
John Galway, President

Harrison Agassiz Chamber of Commerce
PO Box 429, Harrison Hot Springs BC V0M 1K0
info@harrison.ca
www.harrison.ca
twitter.com/HAChamber
Overview: A small local organization founded in 1982
Mission: To actively explain, promote & support the free enterprise system & democratic principle in order to improve trade, commerce & the economic, social & human welfare of the people
Chief Officer(s):
Robert Reyerse, President

Harriston-Minto & District Chamber of Commerce See Minto Chamber of Commerce

Harrow & Colchester Chamber of Commerce
PO Box 888, Harrow ON N0R 1G0
www.harrowchamber.ca
Overview: A small local organization
Membership: Fees: $75-$125 business; $25 individual; $15 retired
Chief Officer(s):
Murdo Mclean, President

Harrow Early Immigrant Research Society (HEIRS)
PO Box 53, Harrow ON N0R 1G0
Tel: 519-738-3700
www.heirs.ca
Overview: A small local charitable organization founded in 1971
Mission: To collect & safeguard local historical information & genealogical data relating to Harrow & Colchester South areas of Essex County, Ontario; to act as a link for other researchers in the field and strives to foster community interest in local history & promotes conservation of historical artifacts
Member of: Southwestern Heritage Association (Essex County)
Affiliation(s): Ontario Historical Society; Ontario Genealogical Society
Finances: Funding Sources: Sale of books; donations; provincial grants; federal student employment grants
Membership: Fees: $20; Member Profile: Interest in local & family history
Activities: Speaker Service: Yes; Library: by appointment
Chief Officer(s):
Richard Herniman, President

Harrowsmith Beekeepers Guild See Limestone Beekeepers Guild

Harry & Martha Cohen Foundation
#550, 1640 - 16th Ave. NW, Calgary AB T2M 0L6
Tel: 403-284-3103
hmcohenfoundation@shaw.ca
www.hmcohenfoundation.com
Overview: A small local charitable organization
Mission: To support Calgary-based charities & projects in the areas of arts & culture, health & welfare, social services, youth development, & animal welfare
Chief Officer(s):
Cheryl Cohen, Executive Director

Harry A. Newman Memorial Foundation
#423, 157 Adelaide St. West, Toronto ON M5H 4E7
Tel: 416-962-2786
Overview: A small local charitable organization
Mission: To supply funds to develop leadership potential in the community
Affiliation(s): Lions Club
Finances: Annual Operating Budget: Less than $50,000
Membership: 8

Harry E. Foster Foundation
204 Shipway Ave., Newcastle ON L1B 1M9
www.harryefosterfoundation.org
Overview: A small provincial charitable organization founded in 1954
Mission: To offer grants to programs focused on assisting individuals with intellectual disabilities & Alzheimers' disease, as well as community organizations for the disadvantaged
Chief Officer(s):
James P. Thomson, President
Carol Davis-Kerr, Administrator
c.davis-kerr@rogers.com

Hart House Orchestra
University of Toronto, 7 Hart House Circle, Toronto ON M5S 3H3
www.harthouseorchestra.ca
www.facebook.com/hhorchestra
twitter.com/hhorchestra
Overview: A small local organization founded in 1976 overseen by Orchestras Canada
Membership: 80-90; Fees: $50 students; $175.60 non students; $134.28 seniors; Member Profile: Students, alumni, senior members
Activities: Three concerts per year
Chief Officer(s):
Zoe Dille, Programme Advisor
zoe.dille@utoronto.ca
Henry Janzen, Director, Music

Hartney & District Chamber of Commerce
PO Box 224, Hartney MB R0M 0X0
Tel: 204-858-2098
Overview: A small local organization

Hashomer Hatzair Canada / Young Guard
#120, 215 Spadina Ave., Toronto ON M5T 2C7
Tel: 416-736-1339; Fax: 647-693-7359
mail@campshomria.ca
www.hashomerhatzair.ca
www.facebook.com/CampShomriaCanada
twitter.com/CampShomria
Also Known As: Camp Shomria Canada
Overview: A small international charitable organization founded in 1923
Mission: To promote Jewish cultural identity & social justice, participation & commitment to Israel & the Jewish community
Member of: Canadian Jewish Congress
Staff Member(s): 5; 50 volunteer(s)
Membership: 400; Fees: $180 individual
Activities: Organizing weekly meetings, special outings, educational activities, residential camps, Purim Ball, Chanukah Party, Passover Seder, Rabin Memorial, & 8-week leadership training; Running youth-led programs; Rents Mailing List: Yes
Chief Officer(s):
Uri Ron Amit, Director, Shaliach & Camp
uri@campshomria.ca

Hastings Centre Rockhounds
c/o Hastings Community Centre, 3096 East Hastings St., Vancouver BC V5K 2A3
Tel: 604-718-6222; Fax: 604-718-6226
Previous Name: Hastings Community Centre Rockhounds
Overview: A small local organization
Member of: Lapidary, Rock & Mineral Society of British Columbia

Hastings Children's Aid Society See Highland Shores Children's Aid

Hastings Community Centre Rockhounds See Hastings Centre Rockhounds

Hastings County Historical Society
154 Cannifton Rd. North, Cannifton ON K0K 1K0
Tel: 613-962-1110
info@hastingshistory.ca
www.hastingshistory.ca
Overview: A small local charitable organization founded in 1957
Mission: To promote & conduct research into the history of Hastings County. It maintains archives on historical documents & encourages community interest in the preservation of local history.
Member of: Ontario Historical Society
Membership: Fees: $25 individual; $30 family; $20 senior/student; $25 non-profit organization; $100 corporate; $150 lifetime
Activities: Monthly meetings with speaker, open to public; Library: Resource Centre; by appointment
Chief Officer(s):
Richard Hughes, President
president@hastingshistory.ca

Hastings County Law Association (HCLA)
Quinte Consolidated Courthouse, #2900, 15 Bridge St. West, Belleville ON K8P 0C7
Tel: 613-962-2280; Fax: 613-962-1611
hcla@on.aibn.com
www.communitylegalcentre.ca/hcla
www.facebook.com/HastingsCountyLawAssociation
twitter.com/HastingsCty_Law
Overview: A small local organization
Mission: To act as a lobbying voice for its members & provides research resources through its library.
Membership: Committees: Library; Social
Activities: Library: Courthouse Library
Chief Officer(s):
Judith Dale, Librarian

Hatzoloh Toronto
#219, 534 Lawrence Ave. West, Toronto ON M6A 1A2
Tel: 416-398-2300
office@hatzolohtoronto.org
www.hatzolohtoronto.ca
Overview: A small local organization
Mission: To offer emergency medical services to Toronto's Jewish community
Chief Officer(s):
Yisroel Dovid Goldstein, Executive Director

Haute Yamaska Real Estate Board Voir Chambre immobilière de la Haute Yamaska Inc.

Hautes études internationales (IQHEI)
Pavillon Charles de Koninck, Université Laval, #5456, 1030 av des Sciences-Humaines, Québec QC G1V 0A6
Tél: 418-656-7771
hei@hei.ulaval.ca
www.hei.ulaval.ca
www.linkedin.com/groups?mostRecent=&gid=4487818
wwww.facebook.com/HEIulaval
twitter.com/hei_ulaval
Nom précédent: Institut québécois des hautes études internationales
Aperçu: Dimension: petite; Envergure: internationale; fondée en 1994

Mission: Assurer à la société des services spécialisés d'information, d'animation et d'expertise sur les problèmes internationaux ainsi que sur les sociétés et cultures étrangères et leur signification dans un context canadien et québécois
Affiliation(s): Université Laval; Défense nationale; Ministère étrangères et du Commerce international; Le Devoir; Canal Savoir
Membre(s) du personnel: 12
Membre: 60; *Comités:* Directeur; Programmes
Activités: Études et de recherches sur l'Asie contemporaine; recherches sur les aspects juridiques internationaux et transitionaux de l'intégration économique; programme de maîtrise en relations internationales; programme pluridisciplinaire incluant un stage pratique de fin d'études au Canada ou à l'étranger; centre d'études interaméricaines; cercle Europe; programme paix et sécurité internationale; chaîne de recherche du Canada en sécurité, en droit de l'environnement, maghrébines Rabah-Bitat; *Stagiaires:* Oui; *Service de conférenciers:* Oui
Membre(s) du bureau directeur:
Louis Bélanger, Directeur

Havelock, Belmont, Methuen & District Chamber of Commerce
PO Box 779, Havelock ON K0L 1Z0
Tel: 705-778-7873; *Fax:* 866-822-2182
havelockchamber@hotmail.com
www.havelockchamber.com
Overview: A small local organization
Mission: To promote business, trade & commerce in the area
Membership: *Fees:* $30-$100
Chief Officer(s):
Phil Higgins, President

Le Havre *See* Our Harbour

Hawkesbury & Region Chamber of Commerce / Chambre de Commerce de Hawkesbury et région
PO Box 36, #35A, 151 Main St. East, Hawkesbury ON K6A 2R4
Tel: 613-632-8066
info@hawkesburychamberofcommerce.ca
www.hawkesburychamberofcommerce.ca
www.facebook.com/190878677617612
Overview: A small local organization founded in 1930
Mission: To promote tourism, commerce & industries
Finances: *Annual Operating Budget:* Less than $50,000; *Funding Sources:* Membership dues
Staff Member(s): 1; 13 volunteer(s)
Membership: 225
Activities: Promoting business
Chief Officer(s):
Bonnie Jean-Louis, Coordinator

Hay River Chamber of Commerce
10K Gagnier St., Hay River NT X0E 1G1
Tel: 867-874-2565; *Fax:* 867-874-3631
www.hayriverchamber.com
Overview: A small local organization
Mission: To build a strong economic environment through business promotion & representation
Membership: 70; *Fees:* $77.75-$735; *Committees:* Public Relations & Tourism; Finance, Admin & Education; Member Services; Special Events; Business & Government Affairs; Taxes & Utilities; Retail Business; Chamber Park; Business, Home & Leisure Show
Chief Officer(s):
Janet-Marie Fizer, President

Head & Hands / A deux mains
5833, rue Sherbrooke ouest, Montréal QC H4A 1X4
Tel: 514-481-0277; *Fax:* 514-481-2336
info@headandhands.ca
www.headandhands.ca
www.facebook.com/headandhands
twitter.com/headandhands
www.youtube.com/user/HeadandHands
Overview: A small local charitable organization founded in 1970
Mission: Medical, social, and legal services with an approach that is harm-reductive, holistic, and non-judgmental.
Membership: *Member Profile:* Anyone who makes a donation within a given year
Activities: Jeunesse 2000 drop-in centre; Community Workshops; Street Work; Young Parents Program; Sense Project
Chief Officer(s):
Jon McPhedran Waitzer, Director
admin@headandhands.ca

Juniper Belshaw, Contact, Fundraising and Development
membres@headandhands.ca

Headache Network Canada (HNC)
210 Georgian Dr., Oakville ON L6H 6T8
Tel: 905-330-9657
headachenetwork.ca
twitter.com/HeadacheNetwork
Overview: A large national charitable organization
Mission: To raise awareness about headache disorders in Canada; To encourage government assistance to the field; To educate the public about headache disorders
Affiliation(s): Neurological Health Charities Canada
Chief Officer(s):
Valerie South, Executive Director
Publications:
• Canadian Headache Society Guideline for Migraine Prophylaxis
Profile: To assist the doctor in recommending the appropriate medication for a migraine sufferer

Headingley Chamber of Commerce
#1, 126 Bridge Rd., Headingley MB R4H 1G9
Tel: 204-837-5766; *Fax:* 204-831-7207
hello@headingleychamber.ca
www.headingleychamber.ca
twitter.com/HeadingleyCham
Overview: A small local organization founded in 1993
Mission: To promote & improve trade & commerce & the economic, civic & social welfare of the district
Member of: Manitoba Chamber of Commerce
Affiliation(s): Central Plains Development Corporation; White Horse Plains Development Corporation; Headingley Heritage Centre
Finances: *Funding Sources:* Membership dues; local government grant; fundraisers
Membership: *Fees:* Schedule available based on number of employees; *Member Profile:* Business owners, associate members, honorary members
Activities: Annual dinner dance; awards night; annual golf tournament; summer tourist booth; family fun day; *Library*
Chief Officer(s):
Graham Hawryluk, President
John Van Massenhoven, Secretary
Dave White, Executive Director
Awards:
• Corporate Citizen Award
• Community Volunteer Award
• Member Appreciation Award

Head-of-the-Lake Historical Society
PO Box 896, Hamilton ON L8N 3P6
Tel: 905-524-0805
contactus@headofthelake.ca
www.headofthelake.ca
Overview: A small local organization founded in 1944
Staff Member(s): 11
Membership: 215; *Fees:* $20 individual; $35 family; $500 life
Chief Officer(s):
Sean Carney, President
Publications:
• The Herald [a publication of the Head-of-the-Lake Historical Society]
Type: Newsletter; *Frequency:* Quarterly; *Price:* Free with membership in the Head-of-the-Lake Historical Society

Healing Our Nations (HON)
31 Gloster Ct., Dartmouth NS B3B 1X9
Tel: 902-492-4255
ea@accesswave.ca
www.hon93.ca
www.facebook.com/Healing.Our.Nations
Also Known As: Atlantic First Nations AIDS Task Force
Overview: A small local organization founded in 1991 overseen by Canadian AIDS Society
Mission: To educate First Nation people about HIV/AIDS; to improve the community by eliminating family violence, substance abuse, mental & spiritual malaise leading to depression & suicide.
Member of: Canadian HIV/AIDS Legal Network
Affiliation(s): Union of NS Indians; Union of NB Indians; Atlantic Policy Congress; Mawiw Council; Confederacy of Mainland Mi'Kmaq
Staff Member(s): 7
Activities: HIV/AIDS education & awareness workshops & training; *Speaker Service:* Yes; *Library:* Resource Centre
Chief Officer(s):

Julie Thomas, Program Manager

Healing Our Spirit BC Aboriginal HIV/AIDS Society
137 East 4 Ave., Vancouver BC V5T 1G4
Tel: 604-879-8884; *Fax:* 604-879-9926
Toll-Free: 866-745-8884
info@healingourspirit.org
www.healingourspirit.org
Overview: A medium-sized local charitable organization founded in 1992
Mission: To prevent & reduce the spread of HIV infection in First Nation communities & to support those affected by HIV/AIDS.
Member of: Canadian Aboriginal AIDS Network
Affiliation(s): Red Road HIV/AIDS Network; BC Aboriginal AIDS Awareness Program; AIDS Vancouver; BC Persons with AIDS
Finances: *Annual Operating Budget:* $500,000-$1.5 Million; *Funding Sources:* Ministry of Health; Health Canada; Healing Foundation; fundraising
Staff Member(s): 19; 57 volunteer(s)
Membership: 150; *Fees:* full membership: $5; association membership:$15; *Member Profile:* Clients, family, friends, societies, organizations; *Committees:* Conference
Activities: Preventive HIV educational workshops; housing subsidy program; community health programs; advocacy; peer support; volunteer & fundraising programs; speakers bureau; research & community development; healing project-residential schools; *Awareness Events:* Aboriginal AIDS Awareness Week, Nov./Dec.; *Speaker Service:* Yes; *Library:* Not open to public
Chief Officer(s):
Winston Thompson, Executive Director
winston@healingourspirit.org
Leonard George, President

Health & Safety Conference Society of Alberta (HSCSA)
PO Box 38009, Calgary AB T3K 5G9
Tel: 403-236-2225; *Fax:* 780-455-1120
Other Communication: Trade Fair Information e-mail: tradefair@hsconference.com
info@hsconference.com
www.hsconference.com
Overview: A small provincial organization
Mission: To promote the importance of health & safety for safer workplaces
Finances: *Funding Sources:* Sponsorships
Membership: 1-99; *Member Profile:* Health & safety associations; Professional societies; Employer associations
Activities: Hosting an annual multi-partner conference; Providing health & safety education
Chief Officer(s):
Guy Clyne, President
Arlene Ledi-Thom, Vice-President
Dianne Paulson, Secretary
Jerald Richelhoff, Treasurer
Meetings/Conferences:
• 17th Annual Health & Safety Conference & Trade Fair, February, 2019, Shaw Conference Center, Edmonton, AB
Scope: Provincial
Description: Theme: "Facing Forward"

Health Action Network Society (HANS)
#214, 5589 Rumble Rd., Burnaby BC V5J 3J1
Tel: 604-435-0512; *Fax:* 604-435-1561
Toll-Free: 855-787-1891
hans@hans.org
www.hans.org
www.facebook.com/HANSHealthAction
twitter.com/JoinHANS
Overview: A medium-sized national charitable organization founded in 1984
Mission: To support complementary & alternative health care; To provide resources about preventive medicine & natural therapeutics; To facilitate delivery of integrated health care; To act as a voice for natural health consumers in Canada
Finances: *Funding Sources:* Donations
Membership: *Member Profile:* Lay & professional individuals with an interest in a natural approach to health care
Activities: Providing educational seminars; Organizing events & workshops; Enabling change at the regulatory level; *Library:* HANS Reference Library
Chief Officer(s):
Lorna Hancock, Director

Health Association Nova Scotia
2 Dartmouth Rd., Halifax NS B4A 2K7

Tel: 902-832-8500; *Fax:* 902-832-8505
www.healthassociation.ns.ca
twitter.com/HealthAssnNS
Previous Name: Nova Scotia Association of Health Organizations
Overview: A medium-sized provincial organization founded in 1960 overseen by Canadian Healthcare Association
Mission: To promote an effective, efficient & integrated quality health system for all Nova Scotians through leadership in influencing the development of public policy, representing & advocating members' interests & providing services to assist its members meet the health care needs of their communities
Member of: Canadian Alliance for Long Term Care
Staff Member(s): 84
Membership: 133; *Member Profile:* Health care & community services providers, including nursing care facilities, adult residential centres, rehabilitation centres, home care organizations, group homes, foundations, regulatory bodies & community-based health care providers; individuals active or interested in the provision of health care services
Activities: *Rents Mailing List:* Yes; *Library:* by appointment
Chief Officer(s):
Gerald Pottier, Chair
Mary Lee, President/CEO, 902-832-8500 Ext. 236
Alex Cross, Communications Assistant, 902-832-8500 Ext. 295
alex.cross@healthassociation.ns.ca

Bedford Office
Clinical Engineering, 2 Dartmouth Rd., Bedford NS B4A 2K7
Tel: 902-832-8500; *Fax:* 902-832-8507
contactus@healthassociation.ns.ca
Chief Officer(s):
Steve Smith, Director, Clinical Engineering
steve.smith@healthassociation.ns.ca

Central Region Office
Clinical Engineering, 150 Exhibition St., Kentville NS B4N 5E3
Tel: 902-678-7090; *Fax:* 902-578-0565
Chief Officer(s):
Ed Ezekiel, Coordinator, Central Region
edward.ezekiel@healthassociation.ns.ca

Northern Region Office
Clinical Engineering, 835 East River Rd., New Glasgow NS B2H 3S6
Tel: 902-752-5487; *Fax:* 902-755-6297
Chief Officer(s):
John Inch, CET, CBET, Coordinator, Northern Region
john.inch@healthassociation.ns.ca

Southern Region Office
Clinical Engineering, 90 Glenn Allen Dr., Bridgewater NS B4V 3S6
Tel: 902-527-5234; *Fax:* 902-543-1662
Chief Officer(s):
Philip Bradfield, CET, CBET, Technical Support & Development Officer
phil.bradfield@healthassociation.ns.ca

Health Association of African Canadians (HAAC)
c/o Black Cultural Centre for Nova Scotia, 10 Cherry Brook Rd., Cherry Brook NS B2Z 1A8
Tel: 902-405-4222
info@haac.ca
www.haac.ca
Overview: A medium-sized provincial organization founded in 2000
Mission: To promote & improve the health of African Canadians in Nova Scotia through community engagement, education, policy recommendations, partnerships, & research participation
Staff Member(s): 4
Chief Officer(s):
Donna Smith-Darrell, Co-Chair
Sharon Davis-Murdoch, Co-Chair

Health Association of PEI (HAPEI)
10 Pownal St., Charlottetown PE C1A 3V6
Tel: 902-368-3901
Previous Name: Hospital Association of PEI
Overview: A small provincial organization founded in 1961 overseen by Canadian Healthcare Association
Mission: To influence the change & development of the health delivery system; to provide services which assist members in managing their human, financial & physical resources.
Finances: *Funding Sources:* Membership dues
Activities: *Library:*

Health Care Public Relations Association (HCPRA) / Association des relations publiques des organismes de la santé (ARPOS)
PO Box 36029, 1106 Wellington St., Ottawa ON K1Y 4V3
Tel: 613-729-2102; *Fax:* 613-729-7708
info@hcpra.org
www.hcpra.org
twitter.com/HCPRA
Overview: A medium-sized national organization founded in 1973
Mission: To address the concerns of the public relations professionals in Canadian health care settings
Affiliation(s): Association for Healthcare Philanthropy
Staff Member(s): 1
Membership: 300; *Member Profile:* Health care communicators from across Canada with responsibilities for the public relations of a health region, institution or organization, or a national, provincial, or community health delivery organization; Students pursuing a full-time course of study in public relations with an interest in health care communications; *Committees:* Professional Development; Recognition; Membership; Communications
Activities: Providing professional development opportunities; Sharing research & best practices; Offering networking opportunities; *Speaker Service:* Yes; *Library*
Chief Officer(s):
Jane Adams, National Coordinator
Awards:
• The Hollobon Awards
Presented to members of the media whose work has contributed significantly to the public's understanding of health care
Eligibility: Media representatives whose work has appeared in print or television with a health care focus
• HYGEIA Awards
Awarded for excellence in health care communications

Health Charities Coalition of Canada (HCCC) / Coalition canadienne des organismes bénévoles en santé
41 Empress Ave., Annex D, Ottawa ON K1R 7E9
Tel: 613-232-7266
www.healthcharities.ca
Overview: A small national organization founded in 2000
Mission: To provide health policy leadership for the health of all people of Canada; To act as a collective authoritative voice of national health charities in public policy & health research issues that affect the lives of the people of Canada
Staff Member(s): 2
Membership: 29; *Fees:* Schedule available based on annual revenue; *Member Profile:* Amyotrophic Lateral Sclerosis Society of Canada; Canadian Breast Cancer Fdn.; Canadian Cancer Society; Canadian Cystic Fibrosis Fdn.; Canadian Diabetes Assn.; Canadian Hospice Palliative Care Assn.; Canadian Lung Assn.; Canadian Mental Health Assn.; The Fdn. Fighting Blindness - Canada; Heart & Stroke Fdn. of Canada; The Kidney Fdn. of Canada; Muscular Dystrophy Canada; Multiple Sclerosis Society of Canada; Osteoporosis Canada; Parkinson Society Canada; Schizophrenia Society of Canada; Sick Kids Fdn.; The Arthritis Society
Chief Officer(s):
Connie Côté, Executive Director
Awards:
• Health Charities Coalition of Canada's Award of Distinction

Health Employers Association of British Columbia (HEABC)
#200, 1333 West Broadway, Vancouver BC V6H 4C6
Tel: 604-736-5909; *Fax:* 604-736-2715
contact@heabc.bc.ca
www.heabc.bc.ca
www.linkedin.com/company/heabc
twitter.com/heabcnews
www.youtube.com/user/BCHealthCareAwards
Overview: A medium-sized provincial organization founded in 1993 overseen by Canadian Healthcare Association
Mission: To serve a diverse group of over 250 publicly funded healthcare employers; To deliver high quality labour relations services; To advance the efficiency & productivity of human resources system-wide
Membership: 250 employers; *Member Profile:* Publicly funded health care employers in British Columbia
Activities: Providing legal services & strategic negotiation; Offering physician consulting services; Recruiting health care professionals through the Health Match BC program
Chief Officer(s):
David Logan, President & CEO
Lyn Kocher, Executive Director

Health Food Dealers Association *See* Canadian Health Food Association

Health Initiatives for Youth Hamilton
151 York Blvd., Lower Level, Hamilton ON L8R 3M2
Tel: 905-528-3009; *Fax:* 905-528-4702
info@hifyhamilton.com
www.hifyhamilton.com
Previous Name: Planned Parenthood Society of Hamilton
Overview: A small local charitable organization founded in 1932
Mission: To advance healthy sexuality & reproductive wellness for all individuals in Hamilton, by acting as a resource for services, education, advocacy & community partnerships
Member of: Canadian Federation for Sexual Health
Finances: *Funding Sources:* City of Hamilton; Hamilton Community Foundation; donations; memberships; special events
Staff Member(s): 4
Activities: Clinical services; community outreach education; *Speaker Service:* Yes; *Library:* Thelma Will Resource Centre; Open to public
Chief Officer(s):
Hannelore Oettgen, Administrative Services Coordinator

Health Law Institute (HLI)
Faculty of Law, University of Alberta, #468, 111 - 89 Ave., Edmonton AB T6G 2H5
Tel: 780-492-6127
hliadmin@ualberta.ca
www.hli.ualberta.ca
Overview: A small international organization founded in 1977
Mission: To research needs & be proactive to emerging health law issues; To disseminate research findings & information through publications; To provide public lectures & educational presentations
Finances: *Funding Sources:* Alberta Law Foundation; Alberta Heritage Foundation for Medical Research; Federal government; grants
Staff Member(s): 8
Activities: *Library:* by appointment
Chief Officer(s):
Robyn Hyde-Lay, Executive Director, 780-492-7577
rhydelay@ualberta.ca
Publications:
• Health Law Journal
Type: Journal; *Frequency:* Annually
Profile: Papers that explore innovative and original issues in the interdisciplinary area of health law. The HLJ is a peer-reviewed publication.

Health Libraries Association of British Columbia (HLABC)
c/o Antje Helmuth, Ministry of Health, Health & Human Services Library, PO Box 9637, Stn. Prov Govt, 1515 Blanshard St., Victoria BC V8W 9P1
Tel: 250-952-1478; *Fax:* 250-952-2180
hlabc.chla-absc.ca
Overview: A small provincial organization founded in 1980 overseen by Canadian Health Libraries Association
Mission: To support the work of health librarians throughout British Columbia
Membership: *Fees:* $30 regular members; $20 students (first year is free for students); *Member Profile:* Librarians working in health services throughout British Columbia
Activities: Delivering continuing education programs for librarians
Chief Officer(s):
Kristina McDavid, President
Chantalle Jack, Secretary
Antje Helmuth, Treasurer & Contact, Membership
antje.helmuth@gov.bc.ca
Awards:
• David Noble Prize
Recognizes excellence in student health information research
• C. William Fraser Prize
Recognizes performance in health librarianship & coursework at the School of Library and Information Studies at UBC
Meetings/Conferences:
• Health Libraries Association of British Columbia (HLABC) Annual General Meeting 2018, 2018, BC
Scope: Provincial
Publications:
• Health Libraries Association of British Columbia Directory
Type: Directory
Profile: Detailed listing of association members

Health Record Association of British Columbia (HRABC)
c/o Faye Jones, 397 Rindle Ct., Kelowna BC V1W 5G5
www.hrabc.net
Overview: A small provincial organization founded in 1949
Mission: To contribute to the promotion of wellness & the provision of quality healthcare through excellence in information management
Member of: National Health Information Management Alliance
Affiliation(s): Canadian Health Information Management Association
Membership: Fees: $80 active; $40 inactive/associate; Member Profile: Health information management professionals; Committees: Membership & Credentials; Program & Arrangements; Communications; Professional Practice
Chief Officer(s):
Dawn Lawrie, President
Faye Jones, Treasurer
Awards:
• Academic Award
• Leadership Award

Health Sciences Association of Alberta (HSAA) / Association des sciences de la santé de l'Alberta (ind.)
10212 - 112 St., Edmonton AB T5K 1M4
Tel: 780-488-0168; Fax: 780-488-0534
Toll-Free: 800-252-7904
www.hsaa.ca
www.facebook.com/349561555109272
twitter.com/HSAAlberta
Overview: A medium-sized provincial organization founded in 1971
Mission: To conduct activities as a labour union to enhance the quality of life for HSAA members & society
Member of: National Union of Public and General Employees
Finances: Funding Sources: Membership dues; Merchandise sales
Staff Member(s): 31
Membership: 17,000; Member Profile: Professional, paramedical technical, general support, & EMS employees in the public & private health care sectors of Alberta; Committees: Bylaws & Resolutions; Community Relations; Elections/Credentials; EMAC; Environmental; Finance; Human Rights & Equality; Labour Relations Appeals; Members' Benefits; OHS&W; Political Action / Education
Activities: Offering educational workshops; Awarding bursaries
Chief Officer(s):
Elisabeth Ballermann, President
elisabethb@hsaa.ca
Lynette McAvoy, Executive Director
lynettem@hsaa.ca
Awards:
• Barb Mikulin Award
To honour an HSAA member who has made extraordinary efforts to improve the world
Publications:
• Challenger [a publication of the Health Sciences Association of Alberta]
Type: Magazine; Frequency: Quarterly; Accepts Advertising Profile: Feature articles, labour relations updates, HSAA activities, affiliate & member news, forthcoming workshops & events

Health Sciences Association of British Columbia (HSABC)
180 East Columbia St., New Westminster BC V3L 0G7
Tel: 604-517-0994; Fax: 604-515-8889
Toll-Free: 800-663-2017
www.hsabc.org
www.facebook.com/HSABC
twitter.com/hsabc
Overview: A large provincial organization founded in 1971
Mission: To negotiate collective agreements for members; To preserve & promote public health care in Canada
Member of: National Union of Public and General Employees
Finances: Annual Operating Budget: Greater than $5 Million; Funding Sources: Union dues
Membership: 16,000+; Member Profile: Health Care & Social services professionals; Committees: Education; Equality & Social Action; Occupational Health & Safety; Political Action; RPN Outreach & Engagement; Women
Chief Officer(s):
Val Avery, President
webpres@hsabc.org
Janice Morrison, Vice-President

Marg Beddis, Secretary-Treasurer
Meetings/Conferences:
• 2018 Health Sciences Association Convention, April, 2018, Hyatt Regency, Vancouver, BC
Scope: Provincial
Description: A gathering of health care & social services professionals

Health Sciences Association of Saskatchewan (HSAS) / Association des sciences de la santé de la Saskatchewan (ind.)
#42, 1736 Quebec Ave., Saskatoon SK S7K 1V9
Tel: 306-955-3399; Fax: 306-955-3396
Toll-Free: 888-565-3399
hsasstoon@hsas.ca
www.hsas.ca
www.facebook.com/124779960928913
www.youtube.com/user/HealthScienceSask
Overview: A medium-sized provincial organization founded in 1972
Mission: To conduct activities as an independent union representing its members who are health sciences professionals in Saskatchewan
Staff Member(s): 9
Membership: 3,600+; Member Profile: Health professionals from all health regions in Saskatchewan
Activities: Conducting public relations campaigns to increase public awareness about the profession; Presenting bursaries & scholarships
Chief Officer(s):
Karen Wasylenko, President
president@hsa-sk.com
Bill Feldbruegge, Vice-President
mt@hsas.ca
Maureen Kraemer, Secretary
sw1@hsas.ca

Health Sciences Centre Foundation (HSCF)
700 William Ave., #PW112, Winnipeg MB R3E 0Z3
Tel: 204-515-5612; Fax: 204-813-0131
Toll-Free: 800-679-8493
info@hscfoundation.mb.ca
www.hscfoundation.mb.ca
www.facebook.com/hscfdn
twitter.com/hscfoundation
Also Known As: HSC Foundation
Previous Name: Health Sciences Centre Research Foundation
Overview: A small national charitable organization founded in 1981
Mission: HSC Foundation supports the men and women who provide health care at Health Sciences Centre Winnipeg by funding research, education, advanced technology and infrastructure enhancements.
Member of: Association of Healthcare Philanthrophy; Association of Fundraising Professionals
Affiliation(s): Health Sciences Centre; Foundations for Health; Breakthrough!
Finances: Annual Operating Budget: Greater than $5 Million; Funding Sources: Donations, Events, Lottery revenue
Staff Member(s): 11; 12 volunteer(s)
Membership: 40; Committees: Executive, Donor Development, Finance & Audit, Grants & Allocations, Marketing & Communications, Nominating & Governance, Honourary Directors, Lottery
Activities: Speaker Service: Yes
Chief Officer(s):
Jonathon Lyon, President & CEO
jlyon@hscfoundation.mb.ca
Susan Robinson, Vice-President, Operations
srobinson@hscfoundation.mb.ca
Awards:
• Grants for Research & Patient Care
Provision of grants for research & patient care locallyLocation: Local

Health Sciences Centre Research Foundation See Health Sciences Centre Foundation

HealthBridge Foundation of Canada
#1004, 1 Nicholas St., Ottawa ON K1N 7B7
Tel: 613-241-3927; Fax: 613-241-7988
admin@healthbridge.ca
www.healthbridge.ca
www.facebook.com/HealthBridgeCan
twitter.com/HealthBridgeCan
Previous Name: PATH Canada
Overview: A small national organization founded in 1982

Mission: Works with partners worldwide to improve health & health equity through research, policy & action
Staff Member(s): 13
Chief Officer(s):
Sian Fitzgerald, Executive Director
sfitzgerald@healthbridge.ca

HealthCareCAN / SoinsSantéCAN
#100, 17 York St., Ottawa ON K1N 5S7
Tel: 613-241-8005; Fax: 613-241-5055
Toll-Free: 855-236-0213
info@healthcarecan.ca
www.healthcarecan.ca
www.linkedin.com/company/1363724?trk=cws-btn-overview-0-0
www.facebook.com/healthcarecan.soinssantecan
twitter.com/healthcarecan
Merged from: Canadian Healthcare Association; Association of Canadian Academic Healthcare Organizations
Overview: A large national charitable organization
Mission: To improve the delivery of health services in Canada through policy development, advocacy & leadership
Affiliation(s): American Hospital Association; Canadian Council on Health Services Accreditation
Finances: Annual Operating Budget: $1.5 Million-$3 Million; Funding Sources: Membership fees; Services
Staff Member(s): 22
Membership: 56; Fees: Schedule available; Member Profile: Federation of 56 provinicial & territorial hospital/health associations & serves as a voice for over 1,200 health care facilities & health service agencies
Activities: Rents Mailing List: Yes
Chief Officer(s):
Bill Tholl, Presiden & Chief Executive Officer, 613-241-8005 Ext. 202
btholl@healthcarecan.ca
Awards:
• Legacy of Leadership Award
To honour achievements in the administration & governance in the healthcare sector
• Patient Safety Champion Award
To recognize outstanding contributions to community care
Meetings/Conferences:
• Canadian Healthcare Association 2018 Annual General Meeting, 2018
Scope: National
Description: The association's business meeting, including the presentation of the Marion Stephenson Award & the CHA Award for Distinguished Service by the Board of Directors
• 2018 National Health Leadership Conference, June, 2018, St. John's, NL
Scope: National

Healthy Indoors Partnership (HIP) / Partenariat pour des environnements intérieurs sains
2699 Priscilla St., Ottawa ON K2B 7E1
Tel: 613-224-3800
mail@cullbridge.com
www.cullbridge.com/Projects/Healthy_Indoors.htm
Overview: A small national organization
Mission: To involve private, public & not-for-profit organizations & individuals in the development, implementation & financing of a broad range of collaborative actions to improve indoor environments in Canada
Membership: Fees: $100
Chief Officer(s):
Jay Kassirer, President
kassirer@healthyindoors.com

Healthy Minds Canada
#300, 1920 Yonge St., Toronto ON M4S 3E2
Tel: 416-351-7757
Toll-Free: 800-915-2773
admin@healthymindscanada.ca
www.healthymindscanada.ca
www.linkedin.com/company/healthy-minds-canada
www.facebook.com/healthymindscanada
twitter.com/Healthy_Minds
www.instagram.com/healthymindscanada
Overview: A medium-sized national charitable organization founded in 1980
Mission: To support & enhance the well-being of individuals with mental health issues & addictions; To emphasize the value of mental health to society

Finances: Annual Operating Budget: $500,000-$1.5 Million; *Funding Sources:* Fundraising; Donations; Corporations; Family foundations
Staff Member(s): 3; 70 volunteer(s)
Membership: 1,000-4,999
Activities: Offering educational conferences, workshops, youth programs, youth & workplace initiatives, online tool development, resources, & research; Exploring wearable health technologies; Funding research projects at universities & teaching hospitals; Advocating for mental health & addiction research investment; *Awareness Events:* Anti-Stigma Youth Summits; Silver Dinner; Open Minds Across Canada; *Speaker Service:* Yes; *Library:* Resource Centre; Open to public
Chief Officer(s):
Katie Robinette, Executive Director
krobinette@healthymindscanada.ca
Chelsea Ricchio, Manager, Communications
chelsea@healthymindscanada.ca
Publications:
• Healthy Minds Canada Annual Report
Type: Yearbook; *Frequency:* Annually
• HMC [Healthy Minds Canada] Newsletter
Type: Newsletter; *Editor:* Chelsea Ricchio
• When Something's Wrong: Ideas for Families
Type: Handbook
Profile: For parents & caregivers to help children
• When Something's Wrong: Strategies for the Workplace
Type: Handbook
Profile: For employers, human resource personnel, managers, disability management providers, occupational health & safety personnel, union representatives, & employees
• When Something's Wrong: Strategies for Teachers
Type: Handbook
Profile: For elementary & secondary school teachers & administrators

Hearing Foundation of Canada / La Fondation canadienne de l'ouïe
#1801, 1 Yonge St., Toronto ON M5J 2N8
Tel: 416-364-4060; *Fax:* 416-369-0515
Toll-Free: 866-432-7968
info@hearingfoundation.ca
www.hearingfoundation.ca
www.linkedin.com/company/the-hearing-foundation-of-canada
www.facebook.com/TheHearingFoundationofCanada
twitter.com/HearFdnCan
Previous Name: Canadian Hearing Society Foundation
Overview: A medium-sized national charitable organization founded in 1979
Mission: To eliminate the devastating effects of hearing loss on the quality of life of Canadians by promoting prevention, early diagnosis, leading edge medical research & successful intervention
Member of: Association of Development Professionals; Canadian Society of Association Executives
Finances: *Funding Sources:* Individual & corporate donations; foundations; service clubs
Staff Member(s): 5
Membership: *Committees:* Finance; Fundraising; Medical Research; Advisory
Activities: Infant Hearing Screening Awareness Program; Medical Research Program; Sound Sense: Save Your Hearing for the Music; *Speaker Service:* Yes
Chief Officer(s):
John Pepperell, Chair Ext. 2
Andrea Swinton, Executive Director Ext. 2

Hearst & Area Association for Community Living / Association de Hearst et de la région pour l'intégration communautaire
PO Box 12000, Hearst ON P0L 1N0
Tel: 705-362-5758
Overview: A small local charitable organization founded in 1970
Mission: To promote & realize the well-being & integration of developmentally challenged persons
Member of: Community Living Ontario
Finances: *Funding Sources:* Fundraising; MCSS
Activities: *Awareness Events:* Access Awareness Week; Community Living Month
Chief Officer(s):
Chantal G. Dillon, Executive Director

Hearst, Mattice - Val Côté & Area Chamber of Commerce
PO Box 987, #60, 9th St., Hearst ON P0L 1N0
Tel: 705-362-5880
info@hearstcommerce.ca
hearstcommerce.ca
Previous Name: Hearst, Mattice Chamber of Commerce
Overview: A small local organization founded in 1994
Mission: To provide leadership to the commercial, industrial & professional community; To bring about economic prosperity to the Hearst, Mattice-Val Côté area
Member of: Chambre économique de l'Ontario; James Bay Frontier Travel Association; Northeastern Ontario Chamber of Commerce
Finances: *Annual Operating Budget:* Less than $50,000; *Funding Sources:* Membership
15 volunteer(s)
Membership: 80; *Fees:* $110-$610; *Committees:* Tourism; Economic Development
Chief Officer(s):
Lise Joanis, President, 705-362-4325

Hearst, Mattice Chamber of Commerce *See* Hearst, Mattice - Val Côté & Area Chamber of Commerce

Heart & Stroke Foundation of Alberta *See* Heart & Stroke Foundation of Alberta, NWT & Nunavut

Heart & Stroke Foundation of Alberta, NWT & Nunavut (HSFA)
#100, 119 - 14 St. NW, Calgary AB T2N 1Z6
Tel: 403-351-7030; *Fax:* 403-237-0803
Toll-Free: 888-473-4636
www.hsf.ab.ca
Previous Name: Heart & Stroke Foundation of Alberta
Overview: A medium-sized provincial charitable organization founded in 1956 overseen by Heart & Stroke Foundation of Canada
Mission: To disseminate information about heart disease & stroke; to promote research into new drugs, therapies, treatments in disorders leading to heart disease & stroke; to conduct several events to campaign for funds.
Finances: *Annual Operating Budget:* $100,000-$250,000
Activities: Advocating in areas such as the promotion of a smoke-free world & eqaual access to quality stroke care; *Awareness Events:* Jump Rope for Heart; Ski for Heart; Heart & Stroke Month
Chief Officer(s):
Michael Hill, Chair
Donna Hastings, CEO
Edmonton Office
10985 - 124 St., Edmonton AB T5M 0H9
Tel: 780-451-4545; *Fax:* 780-454-1593
Grande Prairie Office
#109, 10126 - 120 Ave., Grande Prairie AB T8V 8H9
Tel: 780-513-0439; *Fax:* 780-513-0941
Lethbridge Office
PO Box 2211, Lethbridge AB T1J 4K7
Tel: 403-327-3239; *Fax:* 403-327-9928
Medicine Hat Office
#124, 430 - 6 Ave. SE, Medicine Hat AB T1A 2S8
Tel: 403-527-0028; *Fax:* 403-526-9655
Red Deer Office
#202, 5913 - 50 Ave., Red Deer AB T4N 4C4
Tel: 403-342-4435; *Fax:* 403-342-7088

Heart & Stroke Foundation of British Columbia & Yukon (HSFBCY)
#200, 1212 West Broadway, Vancouver BC V6H 3V2
Tel: 778-372-8000; *Fax:* 604-736-8732
Toll-Free: 888-473-4636
Other Communication: Resuscitation Certification & CPR Courses: 877-473-0333
www.heartandstroke.ca
Previous Name: BC & Yukon Heart Foundation
Overview: A large provincial charitable organization founded in 1955 overseen by Heart & Stroke Foundation of Canada
Mission: To further the study, prevention & relief of cardiovascular disease
Finances: *Annual Operating Budget:* Greater than $5 Million
Activities: *Awareness Events:* Heart Month, Feb.; Stroke Month, June; *Speaker Service:* Yes
Chief Officer(s):
Adrienne Bakker, CEO
Coastal Vancouver Area Office - Vancouver/North Shore
1216 West Broadway, Vancouver BC V6H 1G6
Tel: 778-372-8052; *Fax:* 604-736-4087
Fraser North & East Area Office - Tri-Cities/Fraser Valley/Burnaby/New Westminster
2239C McAllister Ave., Port Coquitlam BC V3C 2A5
Tel: 604-342-8070; *Fax:* 604-472-0055
Toll-Free: 877-472-0045
Kamloops Area Office - Kamloops/Cariboo
729 Victoria St., Kamloops BC V2C 2B5
Tel: 250-372-3938; *Fax:* 250-372-3940
Kelowna Area Office - Okanagan/Kootenays
#4, 1551 Sutherland Ave., Kelowna BC V1Y 9M9
Tel: 778-313-8090; *Fax:* 250-860-8790
Toll-Free: 866-432-7833
Prince George Area Office Northern BC/Yukon
1480 - 7th Ave., Prince George BC V2L 3P2
Tel: 250-562-8611; *Fax:* 250-562-8614
Toll-Free: 866-226-6784
Richmond Office - Richmond/South Delta
#260, 7000 Minoru Blvd., Richmond BC V6Y 3Z5
Tel: 778-234-8080; *Fax:* 604-279-7134
Surrey Area Office - Surrey/Langley/Whiterock/Cloverdale/Aldergrove/North Delta
#101, 13569 - 76th Ave., Surrey BC V3W 2W3
Tel: 778-612-8063; *Fax:* 604-591-2624
Vancouver Island Area Office - Nanaimo
#401, 495 Dunsmuir St., Nanaimo BC V9R 6B9
Tel: 250-754-5274; *Fax:* 250-754-2575
Victoria Office
#106, 1001 Cloverdale Ave., Victoria BC V8X 4C9
Tel: 250-410-8091; *Fax:* 250-382-0231

Heart & Stroke Foundation of Canada (HSFC) / Fondation des maladies du coeur du Canada
#1402, 222 Queen St., Ottawa ON K1P 5V9
Tel: 613-569-4361; *Fax:* 613-569-3278
www.heartandstroke.ca
www.facebook.com/heartandstroke
twitter.com/TheHSF
www.youtube.com/heartandstrokefdn
Overview: A medium-sized national charitable organization founded in 1983
Mission: To further the study, prevention & reduction of disability & death from heart disease & stroke through research, education & the promotion of healthy lifestyles
Member of: Imagine Canada
Affiliation(s): International Society & Federation of Cardiology; Canadian Coalition for High Blood Pressure Prevention & Control
Finances: *Funding Sources:* Personal & corporate donations
Staff Member(s): 620; 1400 volunteer(s)
Activities: Providing more than 60% of non-industry funding for cardiovascular research in Canada; Supporting successful education programs for healthy living; *Awareness Events:* Stroke Month, Feb.; Heart Month, Feb.; CPR Awareness Month, Nov.; *Speaker Service:* Yes; *Library*
Chief Officer(s):
David Sculthorpe, Chief Executive Officer

Heart & Stroke Foundation of Manitoba (HSFM)
The Heart & Stroke Bldg., #200, 6 Donald St., Winnipeg MB R3L 0K6
Tel: 204-949-2000; *Fax:* 204-957-1365
www.heartandstroke.mb.ca
Previous Name: Manitoba Heart Foundation
Overview: A medium-sized provincial charitable organization founded in 1957 overseen by Heart & Stroke Foundation of Canada
Mission: To eliminate heart disease & stroke through education, advocacy, & research
Finances: *Funding Sources:* Donations; Fundraising
Staff Member(s): 46; 6000 volunteer(s)
Chief Officer(s):
Debbie Brown, CEO

Heart & Stroke Foundation of New Brunswick / Fondation des maladies du coeur du Nouveau-Brunswick
133 Prince William St., 5th Fl, Saint John NB E2L 2B5
Tel: 506-634-1620; *Fax:* 506-648-0098
Toll-Free: 800-663-3600
www.heartandstroke.nb.ca
Previous Name: New Brunswick Heart Foundation
Overview: A medium-sized provincial organization founded in 1967 overseen by Heart & Stroke Foundation of Canada

Mission: To improve the health of residents of New Brunswick by preventing & reducing disability & death from heart disease & stroke, through research, health promotion & advocacy
Finances: *Funding Sources:* Donations; Fundraising
Activities: Organizing the Hearts in Motion Walking Club to improve heart health; Establishing the Wellness at Heart Award for New Brunswick businesses; Coordingating the Heart & Stroke Big Bike fundraising event across New Brunswick; Developing the New Brunswick Food Bank Project; Providing health information resources available free of charge; *Awareness Events:* Jump Rope for Heart; World Hypertension Day; Mud Run for Heart *Library:* Video Library
Chief Officer(s):
Kurtis Sisk, CEO

Heart & Stroke Foundation of Newfoundland & Labrador
1037 Topsail Rd., Mount Pearl NL A1N 5E9
Tel: 709-753-8521; *Fax:* 709-753-3117
www.heartandstroke.nf.ca
Overview: A medium-sized provincial organization founded in 1964 overseen by Heart & Stroke Foundation of Canada
Mission: To work in Newfoundland & Labrador to advance research, advocate, & promote healthy lifestyles so that heart disease & stroke will be eliminated & their impact reduced
Activities: Supporting the Active School program in the central Newfoundland area; Offering the Heart to Heart Cardiac Rehabilitation program for patients & their families; Providing pillows to cardiac patients through the Heart Pillow program, in partnership with Aliant Telephone Pioneers; Introducing the product known as CPR Anytime: Family & Friends to assist in teaching resuscitation; Ensuring that the quality of care is high through the Provincial Integrated Stroke Strategy; *Awareness Events:* Jump Rope for Heart
Chief Officer(s):
Mary Ann Butt, CEO

Heart & Stroke Foundation of Nova Scotia (HSFNS)
Park Lane - Mall Level 3, PO Box 245, 5657 Spring Garden Rd., Halifax NS B3J 3R4
Tel: 902-423-7530; *Fax:* 902-492-1464
Toll-Free: 800-423-4432
www.heartandstroke.ns.ca
Previous Name: Nova Scotia Heart Foundation
Overview: A medium-sized provincial charitable organization founded in 1958 overseen by Heart & Stroke Foundation of Canada
Mission: To eliminate heart disease & stroke; To advance research; To promote healthy living; To engage in advocacy activities
Member of: The Heart and Stroke Foundation of Canada
Finances: *Funding Sources:* Donations
4500 volunteer(s)
Activities: Funding research; Helping Nova Scotians to be more active & healthy; Offering CPR programs; Providing healthy living information, including multilingual & multicultural resources; Liaising with Nova Scotia's provincial & municipal governments; Delivering patient programs; *Library:* Resource Centre
Chief Officer(s):
Menna MacIsaac, CEO

Heart & Stroke Foundation of Ontario (HSFO)
PO Box 2414, #1300, 2300 Yonge St., Toronto ON M4P 1E4
Tel: 416-489-7111; *Fax:* 416-489-6885
Previous Name: Ontario Heart Foundation
Overview: A medium-sized provincial charitable organization founded in 1952 overseen by Heart & Stroke Foundation of Canada
Mission: To eliminate heart disease & stroke by advancing research & promoting healthy living; To advocate in areas such as a smoke-free world, equal access to quality stroke care, obesity targeting, elimination of trans-fat, & resuscitation/CPR
Member of: Heart & Stroke Foundation of Canada
Finances: *Funding Sources:* Donations
Activities: Funding research; Providing health information; *Awareness Events:* Polo for Heart
Chief Officer(s):
Darrell Reid, Chief Executive Officer

Barrie Office
#1, 112 Commerce Park Dr., Barrie ON L4N 8W8
Tel: 705-737-1020; *Fax:* 705-737-0902
www.heartandstroke.on.ca

Belleville Office
#106A, 121 Dundas St. East, Belleville ON K8N 1C3
Tel: 613-962-2502; *Fax:* 613-962-6080
www.heartandstroke.on.ca

Brantford Office
442 Grey St., #A, Brantford ON N3S 7N3
Tel: 519-752-1301; *Fax:* 519-752-5554
www.heartandstroke.on.ca

Brockville Office
Brockville General Hospital, 75 Charles St., Brockville ON K6V 1S8
Tel: 613-345-5645; *Fax:* 613-345-8348
www.heartandstroke.on.ca
Chief Officer(s):
Jay Bhatt, Director

Chatham-Kent Office
214 Queen St., Chatham ON N7M 2H1
Tel: 519-354-6232; *Fax:* 519-354-6351
www.heartandstroke.on.ca

Chinese Canadian Council
PO Box 2414, #1300, 2300 Yonge St., Toronto ON M4P 1E4
Tel: 416-489-7111; *Fax:* 416-489-9179
www.heartandstroke.on.ca

Cornwall Office
36 - 2nd St. East, Cornwall ON K6H 1Y3
Tel: 613-938-8933; *Fax:* 613-938-0655
www.heartandstroke.on.ca

Durham Regional Office
#2, 105 Consumers Dr., Whitby ON L1N 1C4
Tel: 905-666-3777; *Fax:* 905-666-9956
www.heartandstroke.on.ca

Guelph Office
#204, 21 Surrey St. West, Guelph ON N1H 3R3
Tel: 519-837-4858; *Fax:* 519-837-9209
www.heartandstroke.on.ca

Halton Region Office
#7, 4391 Harvester Rd., Burlington ON L7L 4X1
Tel: 905-634-7732; *Fax:* 905-634-1353
www.heartandstroke.on.ca

Hamilton Office
#7, 1439 Upper Ottawa St., Hamilton ON L8W 3J6
Tel: 905-574-4105; *Fax:* 905-574-4380
www.heartandstroke.on.ca

Kingston Office
720 Progress Ave., Kingston ON K7M 4W9
Tel: 613-384-2871; *Fax:* 613-384-2899
www.heartandstroke.on.ca

Kitchener Office
#2A, 1373 Victoria St. North, Kitchener ON N2B 3R6
Tel: 519-571-9600; *Fax:* 519-571-9832
www.heartandstroke.on.ca

London Office
#180, 633 Colborne St., London ON N6B 2V3
Tel: 519-679-0641; *Fax:* 519-679-6898
www.heartandstroke.on.ca

Niagara District Office
#3, 300 Bunting Rd., St Catharines ON L2M 7X3
Tel: 905-938-8800; *Fax:* 905-938-8811
www.heartandstroke.on.ca

Ottawa Office
#100, 1101 Prince of Wales Dr., Ottawa ON K2C 3W7
Tel: 613-727-5060; *Fax:* 613-727-1895
www.heartandstroke.on.ca

Owen Sound Office
795 - 1st Ave. East, Owen Sound ON N4K 2C6
Tel: 519-371-0083; *Fax:* 519-371-8164
www.heartandstroke.on.ca

Peel Office
#306, 201 County Court Blvd., Brampton ON L6W 4L2
Tel: 905-451-0021; *Fax:* 905-452-0503
www.heartandstroke.on.ca

Peterborough Office
#3, 824 Clonsilla Ave., Peterborough ON K9J 5Y3
Tel: 705-749-1044; *Fax:* 705-749-1470
www.heartandstroke.on.ca

Sarnia Office
774 London Rd., Sarnia ON N7T 4Y1
Tel: 519-332-1415; *Fax:* 519-332-3139
www.heartandstroke.on.ca

Sault Ste. Marie Office
59 Great Northern Rd., Sault Ste Marie ON P6B 4Y7
Tel: 705-253-3775; *Fax:* 705-946-5760
www.heartandstroke.on.ca

Stratford Office
556 Huron St., Stratford ON N5A 5T9
Tel: 519-273-5212; *Fax:* 519-273-7024
www.heartandstroke.on.ca

Sudbury Office
#130, 43 Elm St., Sudbury ON P3C 1S4
Tel: 705-673-2228; *Fax:* 705-673-7406
www.heartandstroke.on.ca

Thunder Bay Office
#104, 979 Alloy Dr., Thunder Bay ON P7B 5Z8
Tel: 807-623-1118; *Fax:* 807-622-9914
www.heartandstroke.on.ca

Timmins Office
#301, 60 Wilson Ave., Timmins ON P4N 2S7
Tel: 705-267-4645; *Fax:* 705-268-6721
www.heartandstroke.on.ca

Toronto Office
#1300, 2300 Yonge St., Toronto ON M4P 1E4
Tel: 416-489-7111; *Fax:* 416-489-6885
www.heartandstroke.on.ca

Windsor Office
#350, 4570 Rhodes Dr., Windsor ON N8W 5C2
Tel: 519-254-4345; *Fax:* 519-254-4215
www.heartandstroke.on.ca

York Region North Office
#29, 17665 Leslie St., Newmarket ON L3Y 3E3
Tel: 905-853-6355; *Fax:* 905-853-7961
www.heartandstroke.on.ca

York South Office
#204, 9251 Yonge St., Richmond Hill ON L4C 9T3
Tel: 905-709-4899; *Fax:* 905-709-0883
www.heartandstroke.on.ca

Heart & Stroke Foundation of Prince Edward Island Inc.
PO Box 279, 180 Kent St., Charlottetown PE C1A 7K4
Tel: 902-892-7441
Overview: A medium-sized provincial charitable organization overseen by Heart & Stroke Foundation of Canada
Mission: To improve the health of Islanders through the funding of heart disease & stroke research & the provision of heart & stroke education & programs
Finances: *Funding Sources:* Donations
Activities: Delivering programs, such as Live Life Well, to create heart-healthy workplaces on PEI; Providing professional development grants; Initiating community-based strategies, such as the Healthy Living Strategy, to address chronic disease risk factors; *Awareness Events:* Stroke Month, June
Chief Officer(s):
Charlotte Comrie, Chief Executive Officer
charlotte.comrie@heartandstroke.ca
Sarah Crozier, Manager, Health Promotion

Heart & Stroke Foundation of Québec *Voir* Fondation des maladies du coeur du Québec

Heart & Stroke Foundation of Saskatchewan (HSFS) / Fondation des maladies du coeur de la Saskatchewan
#26, 1738 Quebec Ave., Saskatoon SK S7K 1V9
Fax: 306-664-4016
Toll-Free: 888-473-4636
www.linkedin.com/company/heart-and-stroke-foundation-saskatchewan
www.youtube.com/saskheart
Overview: A medium-sized provincial charitable organization founded in 1956 overseen by Heart & Stroke Foundation of Canada
Mission: To eliminate & reduce the impact of heart disease & stroke; To advance research, promote healthy living, & advocates a healthy public policy
Finances: *Funding Sources:* Donations
Activities: Liaising with government; Engaging in fund development activities; *Awareness Events:* Heart Month, Feb.; Stroke Month, June
Chief Officer(s):
Dale Oughton, Director, Development

Hearth Stet Association of Canada *See* Hearth, Patio & Barbecue Association of Canada

Hearth, Patio & Barbecue Association of Canada (HPBAC)
#8, 15 South Mary Lake Rd., Port Sydney ON P0B 1L0
Tel: 705-385-2223; *Fax:* 705-385-1636
Toll-Free: 800-792-5284
admin@hpbacanada.org
www.hpbacanada.org

www.facebook.com/HPBACan
twitter.com/hpbacanada
Previous Name: Hearth Stet Association of Canada
Overview: A small national organization founded in 1994
Mission: To serve as a voice for its members; To promote the interests of those in the industry; To address the needs of the industry
Member of: HPBA
Affiliation(s): Association des Professionels du Chauffage
Finances: *Annual Operating Budget:* $100,000-$250,000
Staff Member(s): 3; 18 volunteer(s)
Membership: 502; *Fees:* Schedule available; *Member Profile:* Hearth, patio & barbecue product manufacturers, distributors & retailers & associated suppliers; *Committees:* Communications; Education; Executive; Finance; Government Affairs; Member Services
Activities: *Awareness Events:* Great Woodstove Changeout; Ener Choice
Chief Officer(s):
Kim Davis, President
Tony Gottschalk, Director, Government
tony@hpbacanada.org
Laura Litchfield, Director, Operations
laura@hpbacanada.org
Michelle Murat, Coordinator, Programs
michelle@hpbacanada.org
Anne Deslauriers, Administrator
anne@hpbacanada.org
Publications:
• HPBAC [Hearth, Patio & Barbecue Association of Canada] Voice
Type: Newsletter; *Frequency:* 3 pa

Heartwood Centre for Community Youth Development
#202, 5516 Spring Garden Rd., Halifax NS B3J 1G6
Tel: 902-444-5885; *Fax:* 902-444-3140
home-place@heartwood.ns.ca
www.heartwood.ns.ca
www.facebook.com/heartwood.centre
twitter.com/HeartWoodNS
www.youtube.com/heartwoodcentre
Previous Name: Heartwood Institute for Leadership in Youth Development
Overview: A small local charitable organization founded in 1989
Mission: To nurture personal leadership qualities through adventure, teamwork, environmental appreciation & service to others.
Staff Member(s): 8
Activities: Youth leadership camp; professional development services for adults & organizations; *Internships:* Yes; *Library:* Not open to public
Chief Officer(s):
Christopher Hayes, Co-Chair
Laura Swaine, Executive Director

Heartwood Institute for Leadership in Youth Development
See Heartwood Centre for Community Youth Development

Heatherton Activity Centre (HAC)
377 Heatherton Village Rd., Antigonish NS B0H 1R0
Tel: 902-386-2808
www.facebook.com/HeathertonActivityCentre
Overview: A small local organization
Member of: DIRECTIONS Council for Vocational Services Society
Chief Officer(s):
Treena Grace, Executive Director/Manager

Heating, Refrigeration & Air Conditioning Institute of Canada (HRAI) / Institut canadien du chauffage, de la climatisation et de la réfrigération (ICCCR)
Bldg. 1, #201, 2800 Skymark Ave., Mississauga ON L4W 5A6
Tel: 905-602-4700; *Fax:* 905-602-1197
Toll-Free: 800-267-2231
hraimail@hrai.ca
www.hrai.ca
www.linkedin.com/company/heating-refrigeration-and-air-conditioning-institute-of-canada
www.facebook.com/322711681086830
twitter.com/HRAI_Canada
www.youtube.com/hraichannel
Overview: A large national organization founded in 1969
Mission: To serve the HRAI membership & HVACR industry in Canada by facilitating industry solutions, coordinating a strong national membership, representing the industry to their publics, conducting accountable association activities, providing quality member/customer services, & educating & training industry members
Finances: *Annual Operating Budget:* $1.5 Million-$3 Million; *Funding Sources:* Membership dues; Education programs
Staff Member(s): 24
Membership: 900 corporate; *Fees:* Schedule available; *Member Profile:* Voting members divided into three divisions based on industry sector - manufacturers, wholesalers & contractors; Associate members include utilities, municipalities, manufacturers' agents & distributors, builders, educational institutions, building maintenance, other associations, & consultants
Activities: Hosting Canadian Mechanicals Exposition (C.M.X.), a national trade show held every two years in Toronto at the end of March; Offering educational programs
Chief Officer(s):
Warren J. Heeley, President, 905-602-4700 Ext. 227
Martin Luymes, Director, Programs & Relations, 905-602-4700 Ext. 235
Frank Diecidue, Director, Operations & Services, 905-602-4700 Ext. 253
Awards:
• HRAI Manufacturer Distinguished Service Awards
Meetings/Conferences:
• Heating, Refrigeration & Air Conditioning Institute of Canada Canadian Mechanical & Plumbing Exposition (CMPX) 2018, March, 2018, Metro Toronto Convention Centre, Toronto, ON
Scope: National
Contact Information: Phone: 416-444-5225, E-mail: cmpx@salshow.com, www.cmpxshow.com
British Columbia - Regional Chapter
Refrigeration & Air Conditioning Contractors Assn. of BC, 26121 Fraser Hwy., Aldergrove BC V4X 2E3
Tel: 604-856-8644; *Fax:* 604-856-7768
raccabc@hrai.ca
Chief Officer(s):
Blair Mastlezav, Chapter President
Manitoba - Regional Chapter
c/o Refrigeration & Air Conditioning Contractors Assn. of Manitoba, 807 McLeod Ave., Winnipeg MB R2G 0Y4
Chief Officer(s):
Ryan Dalgleish, Regional Manager, 204-956-5888
rdalgleish@hrai.ca
Ontario - Brant/Haldimand/Norfolk Chapter
c/o Bowser Technical Ltd., 200 St. George St., Brantford ON N3R 1W4
brant@hrac.ca
www.hracbrant.com
Chief Officer(s):
Dave Murtland, President, 519-428-4000, Fax: 519-428-2591
Dara Bowser, Secretary, 519-756-9116, Fax: 519-756-9227
Ontario - Essex/Kent/Lambton Chapter
c/o Ideal Heating & Cooling Ltd, PO Box 1030, Stn. A, 1900 North Talbot Rd., Windsor ON N9A 6P4
essex_kent_lambton@hrai.ca
Chief Officer(s):
Peter Steffes, Chapter President, 519-737-6797
Ontario - Golden Horseshoe Chapter
c/o Arvin Air Systems, 331 Glover Rd., Stoney Creek ON L8E 5M2
goldenhorseshoe@hrai.ca
Ontario - Greater Toronto Area Chapter
c/o Carrier Canada Ltd., 1515 Drew Rd., Mississauga ON L5S 1Y8
Chief Officer(s):
Marisa Soulis, Chapter Meeting Manager, 905-405-3201
Ontario - Huronia Chapter
c/o LifeBreath Indoor Air Systems, 511 McCormick Blvd., Oro Station ON N5W 4C8
Chief Officer(s):
Wayne Fischer, Chapter President, 705-791-3418
wfischer@airiabrands.com
Ontario - Kawartha Lakes Chapter
c/o Coulter Heating & Air Conditioning, 89 West St., Fenelon Falls ON K0M 1N0
Chief Officer(s):
Laverne Coulter, Chapter President, 705-887-5559
Ontario - Loyalist Chapter
c/o McKeown & Wood Ltd., 373 Centre St. North, Napanee ON K7R 1P7
Ontario - National Capital Region Chapter
c/o E.N. Blue Ltd., PO Box 535, Stittsville ON K2S 1A6
Chief Officer(s):
Darrell McCagg, Chapter President, 613-831-1430, Fax: 613-831-2969
enblue@enblue.com
Ontario - Waterloo/Wellington Chapter
c/o BRC Mechanical Inc., 92 Woolwich St. South, Breslau ON N0B 1M0
Québec - Montréal Chapter
c/o Corporation des maîtres mécaniciens en tuyauterie du Québec, 8175, boul Saint-Laurent, Montréal QC H2P 2M1

Heaven Can Wait Equine Rescue
c/o Claire Malcolm, 95 Cameron Rd., Cameron ON K0M 1G0
Tel: 705-359-3766; *Fax:* 705-359-3769
HCWEquineRescue@sympatico.ca
www.heavencanwaitequinerescue.org
Overview: A small local organization founded in 1997
Mission: To help save horses & ponies from slaughter, & take in any unwanted horse or pony & find them a new, loving home
Chief Officer(s):
Claire Malcolm, Founder

Heavy Civil Association of Newfoundland & Labrador, Inc. (HCANL)
PO Box 23038, 25 Kenmount Rd., St. John's NL A1B 4J9
Tel: 709-364-8811; *Fax:* 709-364-8812
heavycivilnl.ca
Overview: A small provincial organization founded in 1968 overseen by Canadian Construction Association
Mission: To act as the voice of the heavy construction industries in Newfoundland & Labrador; To develop standard tendering & contractual practices & procedures
Membership: *Fees:* $1,243 road builders & water & sewer members; $847.50 associate members; *Member Profile:* Individuals in the highway construction & paving, concrete structure construction, & the marine construction industries; Persons engaged in water & sewer, civil construction, & municipal infrastructure projects; *Committees:* Specification; NLCSA/OH&S; Pits & Quarries; Motor Vehicle; AGM/Seminars/West Coast Meeting; Funding; Dispute Resolution; Charity/Scholarships; Membership; National Education/Training; By-laws; Paving; Staff
Activities: Liaising with provincial government departments & agencies, municipal councils, engineering consultants, & the public; Assisting in the development of occupational health & safety regulations; Developing rental rates for equipment; Awarding scholarships
Chief Officer(s):
Jim Organ, Executive Director, 709-364-8811
jorgan.hcanl@gmail.com
Lorraine Richards, Manager, Operations, 709-364-8811
nlrbhca@nf.aibn.com
Publications:
• Newfoundland & Labrador Road Builders / Heavy Civil Association Membership Directory
Type: Directory
• NLRB/HCA Newsletter
Type: Newsletter
Profile: Association activities & accomplishments, committee reports & updates on the industry
• Road Builders Bulletin
Type: Newsletter; *Frequency:* Weekly; *Accepts Advertising*; *Editor:* Cliff Wight; *Price:* $700
Profile: Bulletin sections include the notebook, open tender report, closed tender report, & advertising

Heavy Equipment & Aggregate Truckers Association of Manitoba (HEAT)
2215 Henderson Hwy., East St. Paul MB R2E 0B8
Tel: 204-654-9426; *Fax:* 204-224-4907
admin@heatmb.ca
heatmb.ca
Overview: A small provincial organization
Mission: To provide education & information to the general public about Winnipeg's growing constuction industry
Membership: 187; *Member Profile:* Members of the heavy equipment operating trade in Manitoba
Activities: Develop standards; Education programs for general public
Chief Officer(s):
Ken McKeen, President

Les Hebdos du Québec inc. *Voir* Hebdos Québec

Hebdos Québec
#345, 2250, boul Daniel-Johnson, Laval QC H7T 2L1
Tél: 514-861-2088
communications@hebdos.com

www.hebdos.com
www.facebook.com/hebdosqc
twitter.com/HebdosQuebec
Nom précédent: Les Hebdos du Québec inc.
Aperçu: *Dimension:* moyenne; *Envergure:* provinciale; fondée en 1932
Mission: Favoriser et stimuler le développement du secteur des hebdomadaires en offrant à ses membres divers services en matière de recherche, de marketing et de formation; projeter une image crédible de la presse hebdomadaire, de la défendre, et de la rendre plus visible et plus accessible
Affiliation(s): Association des professionels de la communication et du marketing
Finances: *Budget de fonctionnement annuel:* $250,000-$500,000
Membre(s) du personnel: 3
Membre: 30 journaux; *Critères d'admissibilite:* Journal hebdomadaire francophone à tirage certifié
Activités: Porte-parole; Recherches; Echanges; Cccasions d'affaires; Économies et rabais; Plaques de presse; Alliances stratégiques; *Stagiaires:* Oui; *Listes de destinataires:* Oui
Membre(s) du bureau directeur:
Gilber Paquette, Directeur général
gpaquette@hebdos.com
Prix, Bourses:
• Les Grands prix des hebdos
18 Prix des Hebdos, des prix d'excellence décernés selon trois catégories d'hebdomadaires, dont le prix de l'hebdo de l'année dans chaque catégorie; et 10 Prix du Jury couronnant les artisans des hebdos

Hébergement la casa Bernard-Hubert
La Casa, 1215, boul Ste-Foy, Longueuil QC J4K 1X4
Tél: 450-442-4777
casa.bernardhubert@videotron.ca
www.la-casa-bernard-hubert.org
Aperçu: *Dimension:* petite; *Envergure:* locale; fondée en 1988
Mission: Pour aider les hommes sans-abri restructurer leur vie et de se réinsérer dans la société
Membre de: L'Association des intervenants en Toxicomanie du Québec; La Fédération des OSBL, d'Habitation Roussillon, Jardins du Québec, Suroît; e Regroupement pour la valorisation de la paternité; Le Réseau d'aide aux personnes seules et itinérantes de Montréal; Le Réseau Solidarité Itinérance du Québec
Affiliation(s): La Fondation Les Amis de La Casa; L'Abri de la Rive-Sud; La Corporation de développement communautaire de Longueuil; La table Itinérance Rive-Sud
Activités: Ateliers et séances de groupe; Encadrement psychosicial; Interventions
Membre(s) du bureau directeur:
Claire Desrosiers, Directrice générale
Lucie Pelletier, Présidente, Conseil d'administration

Hébergements de l'envol
6984, rue Fabre, Montréal QC H2E 2B2
Tél: 514-374-1614; *Téléc:* 514-593-9227
hebergementlenvol@hotmail.com
pages.infinit.net/lenvol2/
Aperçu: *Dimension:* petite; *Envergure:* locale
Mission: Foyer collectif pour personnes en perte d'autonomie
Affiliation(s): Coalition des organismes communautaires québécois de lutte contre le sida

Heiltsuk Tribal Council
PO Box 880, Bella Bella BC V0T 1Z0
Tel: 250-957-2381; *Fax:* 250-957-2544
Toll-Free: 877-957-2381
reception@heiltsuknation.ca
www.heiltsuknation.ca
www.facebook.com/heiltsuk.council
Overview: A small local organization
Chief Officer(s):
Roger Nopper, Executive Director

Helderleigh Foundation
Toronto ON
Tel: 416-200-1492
www.thehelderleighfoundation.org
Overview: A small provincial charitable organization founded in 1992
Mission: To improve nutrition literacy in Canada; To strengthen the physical health & wellness of Canadians
Activities: Funding nutrition literacy projects; Advancing food nutrition in Toronto through a partnership with the Centre for Hospitality & Culinary Arts at George Brown College; Working with the Canadian Food Funder Collaborative to support Canada's Healthy Eating Strategy; Promoting nutrient-dense foods from Canadian grown ingredients
Chief Officer(s):
Teresa Sutton, Administrator

HeliCat Canada
PO Box 968, Revelstoke BC V0E 2S1
Tel: 250-837-5770
info@helicatcanada.com
www.helicatcanada.com
www.youtube.com/channel/UCmMNdyDIRkF3Udowcl5R-2A
Previous Name: BC Helicopter & Snowcat Skiing Operators Association
Overview: A small provincial organization founded in 1975
Member of: Council of Tourism Associations BC; Wilderness Tourism Association
Membership: *Committees:* Environmental; Standards; Communications; Conduct Review; Government Relations
Chief Officer(s):
Rob Rohn, President
Ian Tomm, Executive Director
ed@helicatcanada.com

Helicopter Association of Canada (HAC)
#500, 130 Albert St., Ottawa ON K1P 5G4
Tel: 613-231-1110; *Fax:* 613-369-5097
www.h-a-c.ca
Overview: A small national organization
Mission: To ensure the financial viability of the Canadian civil helicopter industry; To promote flight safety; To expand utilization of helicopter transport
Membership: *Member Profile:* Individuals who operate helicopters in Canada; Non-operator organizations; *Committees:* Air Taxi; Finance; Flight Training Units; Heli Logging; IFR / EMS; Law Enforcement; Maintenance & Manufacturing; Oil & Gas Producers; Safety; Utility Flight Operations
Activities: Educating members, civil servants, & the public about issues important to the industry; Providing opportunities for members to exchange maintenance practices & common issues
Chief Officer(s):
Teri Northcott, Chair
teri_northcott@telus.net
Fred L. Jones, BA LLB, President & Chief Executive Officer, 613-231-1110 Ext. 239, Fax: 613-236-2361
Fred.Jones@h-a-c.ca
Sylvain Seguin, Vice-President & Director, Marketing
sseguin@canadianhelicopters.com
Gary McDermid, Secretary
gary.mcdermid@helifor.com
Maureen Crockett, Treasurer
mcrockett@dt-avn.com
Awards:
• Helicopter Association of Canada Carl Agar / Alf Stringer Award
To honour a leader in the helicopter industry *Deadline:* February
Contact: Barb Priestley, Office Manager, Fax: 613-369-5097; E-mail: barb.priestley@h-a-c.ca
Meetings/Conferences:
• Helicopter Association of Canada 2018 23rd Annual Convention & Trade Show, November, 2018, Vancouver, BC
Scope: National
Attendance: 800+
Description: Professional development programs & information sessions to help Helicopter Association of Canada members achieve in the present economic & regulatory climate
Contact Information: Office Manager & Contact, Member Services: Barb Priestley, Phone: 613-231-1110, ext. 237, Fax: 613-369-5097, E-mail: barb.priestley@h-a-c.ca
Publications:
• Class "D" External Loads Training Guidelines
Type: Guide
Profile: An outline of industry training guidelines to support operations specifications allowing carriage of class D external loads
• HAC [Helicopter Association of Canada] Newsletter
Type: Newsletter
Profile: Association & general information updates
• Helicopter Association of Canada Utility Flight Operations Committee Best Practices Safety Guide for Helicopter Operators
Type: Guide; *Number of Pages:* 90
Profile: Chapters include background information, basic utility infrastructure, helicopter patrol safeguidelines, power line construction & maintenance, safety guide for utilities in evaluating & selecting qualified helicopter contractors, & safety guide for utilities performing utility flight operations
• Helicopter Guidelines for Canadian Onshore Seismic Operations
Type: Guide; *Number of Pages:* 89
Profile: Sections include safety management systems (SMS), program operations, training, competency, & staffing levels, personal protective equipment (PPE), helicopterperformance & role equipment standards, & base camp / staging area / helipad requirements
• Heli-skiing Guidelines
Type: Guide
Profile: Information about performance, weight management, ski baskets, pilot flight & duty time, weather, training, safety briefings, & flagging
• Mountain Flying Training Guidelines
Type: Guide
Profile: Helicopter Association of Canada recommended guidelines for mountain flying training
• Pilot Competencies for Helicopter Wildfire Operations - Best Practices Training & Evaluation
Type: Guide; *Number of Pages:* 26
Profile: Guidance for members of the Helicopter Association of Canada, prepared by the Air Tax Committee, Pilot Qualifications WorkingGroup

Helios Nudist Association (HNA)
Box 8, Site 1, RR#2, Tofield AB T0B 4J0
Tel: 587-986-5522
membership@heliosnudistassociation.ca
heliosnudistassociation.ca
Overview: A small local organization founded in 1964
Mission: To promote the practice of social nudism & recreation in 27 acres of natural setting.
Affiliation(s): Federation of Canadian Naturists; International Naturist Federation; American Association of Nude Recreation
Finances: *Funding Sources:* Membership dues
Membership: 165; *Fees:* Full: $325 single, $500 couple; Associate: $120 single, $180 couple; *Member Profile:* Couples & single adults; board reserves the right to maintain the family-oriented environment
Activities: Dances, dinners, barbecues, swimming, hiking; camping

Hellenic Canadian Board of Trade (HCBT)
PO Box 801, 31 Adelaide St. East, Toronto ON M4C 2K1
Tel: 416-410-4228
membership@hcbt.com
www.hcbt.com
www.facebook.com/helleniccanadianboardoftrade
twitter.com/HCBT_Toronto
www.instagram.com/helleniccanadianboardoftrade
Overview: A medium-sized international organization
Membership: *Fees:* $110 individual; $150 corporate; *Member Profile:* Business executives, lawyers, health professionals & visionaries
Chief Officer(s):
Michael Gekas, President
president@hcbt.com

Hellenic Canadian Congress of BC (HCC(BC))
PO Box 129, 4500 Arbutus St., Vancouver BC V6J 4A2
Tel: 604-780-2460
info@helleniccongressbc.ca
www.helleniccongressbc.ca
www.facebook.com/124766634268645
Overview: A medium-sized national organization
Mission: Fosters education, communication, and cooperation between Hellenic Canadians and other ethnic groups, and promotes the development of just and equitable policies and legislation concerning all citizens.
Chief Officer(s):
Jimmy Sidiropoulos, President

Hellenic Community of Vancouver
St. George Greek Orthodox Cathedral, 4500 Arbutus St., Vancouver BC V6J 4A2
Tel: 604-266-7148; *Fax:* 604-266-7140
hellenic@telus.net
www.hellenic community.org
Overview: A small local organization founded in 1927
Mission: To serve as a spiritual, cultural & social gathering place for all Greeks of Vancouver and the Lower Mainland.
Membership: *Fees:* $150 family; $75 individual; $40 senior/student
Activities: Greek language classes; traditional dance instruction; book club; cooking lessons; arts & crafts; a variety of sports; rental/catering; *Library:* Open to public
Chief Officer(s):

Effie Kerasiotis, President

Help Fill a Dream Foundation of Canada
4085 Quadra St., #D, Victoria BC V8X 1K5
Tel: 250-382-3135; Fax: 250-382-2711
Toll-Free: 866-382-2711
contact@helpfilladream.com
helpfilladream.com
www.facebook.com/helpfilladream
twitter.com/helpfilladream
Overview: A small national charitable organization founded in 1986
Mission: To fill the dreams of children under 19 years of age who have life-threatening illness in BC
Finances: Funding Sources: Telephone campaign; various events
Activities: Speaker Service: Yes
Chief Officer(s):
Craig Smith, Executive Director

Help for Headaches (HFH)
PO Box 1568, Stn. B, 515 Richmond St., London ON N6A 5M3
Tel: 519-434-0008
www.helpforheadaches.org
Also Known As: Headache Support Group
Overview: A small provincial charitable organization founded in 1995
Mission: To provide research, education, advocacy & support for headache sufferers & the public at large
Member of: World Headache Alliance; Canadian Pain Society
Finances: Annual Operating Budget: Less than $50,000
Staff Member(s): 2; 9 volunteer(s)
Membership: 3 student; 20 individual; 5 associate
Activities: Offering presentations, seminars, awareness displays, online programs, newsletters, factsheets, & brochures; Providing a library for members; Speaker Service: Yes; Library: by appointment
Chief Officer(s):
G. Brent Lucas, Director
brent@helpforheadaches.org
Publications:
• Chronic Daily Headache
Type: Book; Price: $25.95
• Non-Drug Treatments for Headache
Type: Book; Price: $25.25
Profile: Educational book discussing various treatment options for headaches & migraines

Help Honduras Foundation See Horizons of Friendship

Help the Aged (Canada) See HelpAge Canada

HelpAge Canada / Aide aux aînés Canada
1300 Carling Ave., Ottawa ON K1Z 7L2
Tel: 613-232-0727; Fax: 613-232-7625
Toll-Free: 800-648-1111
info@helptheaged.ca
www.helptheaged.ca
www.facebook.com/helpagecanada
twitter.com/HelpAgeCanada
www.youtube.com/user/helpage
Previous Name: Help the Aged (Canada)
Overview: A medium-sized international charitable organization founded in 1975
Mission: To meet the needs of poor or destitute elderly people in Canada & the developing world
Affiliation(s): HelpAge International
Finances: Annual Operating Budget: $500,000-$1.5 Million; Funding Sources: Donations; Sponsorships; Foundations; Corporations
Activities: Providing services & programs to relieve the distress, poverty, & sickness of the elderly; Supporting the independence & inclusion of the elderly; Collaborating with other nongovernmental organizations; Obtaining funding; Internships: Yes
Chief Officer(s):
Jacques Bertrand, Executive Director
Jack Panozzo, Chair
Ivan Hale, Vice-Chair
Rosalie Gelderman, Secretary
Donald Hefler, Treasurer

Helping Other Parents Everywhere Inc. (HOPE)
1740 Kingston Rd., Pickering ON L1V 2R2
Tel: 905-239-3577
Toll-Free: 866-492-1299
info@hope4parents.ca
www.hope4parents.ca
Overview: A small local organization
Mission: To provide support, resources, & education to parents of disruptive youth; To offer a confidential & non-judgemental environment for parents who want to deal more effectively with the behaviour of their children; To empower concerned parents to handle situations with their children
Membership: Fees: $50; Member Profile: Parents of acting out youth in Toronto & Durham Region
Activities: Offering a community based support network for parents whose children experience problems, such as drug & alcohol abuse, running away, legal issues, & skipping or dropping out of school; Hosting weekly meetings for parents; Providing telephone support for members at all times; Organizing workshops; Disseminating informational resources; Creating networking opportunities with people who have experience in dealing with similar problems
Chief Officer(s):
Leanne Lewis, President
president@hope4parents.ca

Helping Spirit Lodge Society (HSLS)
3965 Dumfries St., Vancouver BC V5N 5R3
Tel: 604-874-6629; Fax: 604-873-4402
reception@hsls.ca
www.hsls.ca
Overview: A small local organization founded in 1991
Mission: To provide support & a safe place for aboriginal women & children affected by family violence; to provide holistic education programs
Chief Officer(s):
Doris Peters, President

Helping Unite Grandparents & Grandchildren (HUGG)
607 Pine Ridge Ave., Amherstburg ON N9V 3W3
Tel: 519-736-5116; Fax: 519-736-0189
Overview: A small local organization
Chief Officer(s):
Linda Casey, Contact

Henan Fellowship Association of Canada
#130, 8351 Alexandra Rd., Richmond BC V6X 3P3
Tel: 778-869-2033
info@henancanada.ca
www.henancanada.ca
Overview: A small national organization
Mission: To promote Chinese culture; To protect the interests of Henan persons in Canada; To foster the friendship between Henan & Canada

The Henry White Kinnear Foundation
#3910, Toronto Dominion Bank Tower, Toronto ON M5K 1E6
Tel: 416-361-3117; Fax: 416-944-5718
Overview: A small local charitable organization
Chief Officer(s):
Susan Scace, President

Hepatitis Outreach Society of Nova Scotia (HepNS)
PO Box 29120, RPO Halifax Shopping Centre, Dartmouth NS B2Y 1C3
Tel: 902-420-1767; Fax: 902-463-6725
Toll-Free: 800-521-0572
info@hepns.ca
www.hepns.ca
www.facebook.com/114379611934070
twitter.com/HepNSca
www.youtube.com/user/HepNSca
Overview: A medium-sized provincial organization
Mission: To educate Nova Scotians about Hepatitis & its prevention; To reduce social stigmatization & isolation; To prevent the spread of Hepatitis
Chief Officer(s):
Carla Densmore, Executive Director
director@hepns.ca

Heraldry Society of Canada See Royal Heraldry Society of Canada

Heralds of the Gospel / Hérauts de l'Évangile
PO Box 698, Nobleton ON L0G 1T0
Tel: 905-939-0807; Fax: 905-939-9778
www.heralds.ca
www.facebook.com/heralds.herauts
Also Known As: The Heralds
Overview: A small international organization founded in 1999
Mission: To follow a spirituality based on The Eucharist, Mary, & the Pope; to strive for perfection; to live a life of recollection, study, & prayer alternates, with evangelizing activities in dioceses & parishes, with emphasis placed on the formation of youth
Finances: Funding Sources: Donations
Membership: Member Profile: Members practice celibacy & are dedicated to apostolate

Hérauts de l'Évangile See Heralds of the Gospel

Herb Society of Manitoba
PO Box 61004, Stn. Grant Park, Winnipeg MB R3M 3X8
herbs@herbsocietymb.com
www.herbsocietymb.com
Overview: A small provincial organization founded in 1995
Mission: To promote knowledge, use & enjoyment of herbs through education, programs, research & sharing the experience of its members with the community
Membership: 100; Fees: $25 individual; $35 family; $50 business
Activities: Awareness Events: International Herb Day, Oct. 14 Library: The Bev Lloyd Memorial Library; Not open to public
Chief Officer(s):
Dawn Hicks, President
pres@herbsocietymb.com
Publications:
• Prairie Sage Quarterly [a publication of Herb Society of Manitoba]
Type: Newsletter; Frequency: Quarterly
Profile: Available to members

Herbert & District Chamber of Commerce
PO Box 700, Herbert SK S0H 2A0
Tel: 306-784-2588
Overview: A small local organization

Heritage Agricultural Society
5411 - 51 St., Stony Plain AB T7Z 1X7
Tel: 780-963-2777
info@multicentre.org
www.multicentre.org
www.facebook.com/143010392428737
twitter.com/MultiCentre
www.pinterest.com/multicentre
Also Known As: Multicultural Heritage Centre
Overview: A small local charitable organization founded in 1974
Mission: To preserve the region's cultural heritage
Finances: Funding Sources: Alberta Museums Association; Donations
Activities: Tours; School programs for classes K-12; Farm demonstrations; Farmers' market; Canada Day; Library: Wild Rose Library; Open to public
Chief Officer(s):
Locksley McGann, Contact

Heritage Association of Antigonish
20 East Main St., Antigonish NS B2G 2E9
Tel: 902-863-6160
antheritage@parl.ns.ca
www.heritageantigonish.ca
Overview: A small local organization founded in 1982
Member of: Federation of the Nova Scotian Heritage
Membership: Committees: Finance; Membership; Projects; Programs/Events
Chief Officer(s):
Angus MacGillivray, Chair

Heritage Belleville
c/o City Hall, 169 Front St., Belleville ON K8N 2Y8
Tel: 613-967-3319
www.belleville.ca/city-hall/page/heritage-belleville
Also Known As: Municipal Heritage Committee
Overview: A small local organization founded in 1979
Mission: To conduct research & inventory the city's architecture to advise Belleville City Council which buildings should be designated pursuant to the Ontario Heritage Act.
Member of: Ontario Historical Society; Community Heritage Ontario
Finances: Funding Sources: Municipal council; donations
Activities: Library: Open to public by appointment
Chief Officer(s):
Stanley Jones, Chair

Heritage Canada Foundation See National Trust for Canada

L'Héritage canadien du Québec (HCQ) / The Canadian Heritage of Québec (CHQ)
#1201, 1350 rue Sherbrooke ouest, Montréal QC H3G 1J1
Tél: 514-393-1417; Téléc: 514-393-9444
mail@hcq-chq.org
www.hcq-chq.org
www.facebook.com/1723406467941985
Aperçu: *Dimension:* petite; *Envergure:* provinciale; fondée en 1960
Mission: Organisme qui se consacre à la préservation des terrains & des constructions revêtant une valeur historique/architecturale dans la province du Québec
Finances: *Budget de fonctionnement annuel:* $250,000-$500,000; *Fonds:* Annual income; donations
Membre(s) du personnel: 1
Membre: 250; *Montant de la cotisation:* $20-$1,000; *Critères d'admissibilite:* Students; "Friends"; Artisans; Curators; Benefactors; Patrons
Membre(s) du bureau directeur:
Jacques Archambault, General Manager

L'Héritage de L'Ile Rouge
CP 190, RR#1, Lourdes NL A0N 1R0
Courriel: heritagedeilerouge@gmail.com
www.francotnl.ca/HIR
Aperçu: *Dimension:* petite; *Envergure:* locale; fondée en 1982
Mission: Préserver et promouvoir la culture et la langue française
Membre de: Association Regional Côte Ouest
Activités: Festival folklorique; carnaval d'hiver; Chandeleur; March du St. Jean Baptiste; Parade de Noël; *Bibliothèque:* Bibliothèque Ste-Anne; Bibliothèque publique
Membre(s) du bureau directeur:
Eileen Rafuse, Présidente

Heritage Foundation of Newfoundland & Labrador (HFNL)
The Newman Building, PO Box 5171, 1 Springdale St., St. John's NL A1C 5V5
Tel: 709-739-1892; Fax: 709-739-5413
Toll-Free: 888-739-1892
info@heritagefoundation.ca
www.heritagefoundation.ca
Overview: A small provincial charitable organization founded in 1984
Mission: To stimulate an understanding of & appreciation for the architectural heritage of Newfoundland & Labrador; To support & contribute to the preservation, maintenance & restoration of buildings of architectural or historical significance; To designate buildings & structures as Registered Heritage Structures; may make grants for purpose of preservation, maintenance, or restoration (Deadline for submitting grant application is Mar. 1 & Sept. 1 of each year)
Member of: Heritage Canada; Newfoundland & Labrador Homebuilders Association; Heritage Coalition of Newfoundland & Labrador; Newfoundland Historic Trust
Finances: *Annual Operating Budget:* $100,000-$250,000; *Funding Sources:* Provincial government; private
Staff Member(s): 3
Membership: 11; *Member Profile:* Appointed Board by Lt. Governor in council; *Committees:* Buildings; Grants; Finance; Public Relations; Policy
Activities: Education & advisory service in restoration of older structures; *Library:* by appointment
Chief Officer(s):
George Chalker, Executive Director
george@heritagefoundation.ca
Frank Crews, Chairperson

Héritage Kinnear's Mills
122, rue des Églises, Kinnear's Mills QC G0N 1K0
Tel: 418-424-3377; Fax: 418-424-3015
info@kinnearsmills.com
www.kinnearsmills.com
twitter.com/kinnears_Mills
Overview: A small local organization founded in 1991
Mission: To enhance historical site of Kinnear's Mills & its cultural heritage
Affiliation(s): Culture, Communications et Condition féminine Québec; Patrimoine candien; Desjardins Caisse de la Région de Thetford; Camping Soleil
Membership: *Committees:* Library; Beautification; Family; Events & Parties; Heritage Kinnear's Miller; Recreation; Rural Pacte

Héritage Montréal (HM)
#0500, 100, rue Sherbrooke est, Montréal QC H2X 1C3
Tél: 514-286-2662; Téléc: 514-286-1661
www.heritagemontreal.org
www.facebook.com/heritagemontreal
twitter.com/heritagemtl
Également appelé: Fondation Héritage Montréal
Aperçu: *Dimension:* moyenne; *Envergure:* locale; Organisme sans but lucratif; fondée en 1975
Mission: Encourager auprès des décideurs publics et privés la transformation des attitudes et favoriser l'introduction et la mise en oeuvre des méthodes et des stratégies permettant la conservation du patrimoine urbain architectural de Montréal, le patrimoine naturel, les espaces publics ainsi que l'environnement culturel et social
Membre de: Forum québécois du patrimoine; Conseil régional de l'environnement de Montréal
Affiliation(s): International Council on Monuments & Sites
Finances: *Budget de fonctionnement annuel:* $250,000-$500,000
Membre(s) du personnel: 5; 30 bénévole(s)
Membre: 700; *Montant de la cotisation:* 50$ (individuel); 125-500 (corporatif); *Comités:* Patrimoine et aménagement
Activités: Promenades architecturales; cours de rénovation; conférences; recherches; publications; *Bibliothèque:* Bibliothèque publique
Membre(s) du bureau directeur:
Robert Turgeon, Directeur général
rturgeon@heritagemontreal.org

Heritage Ottawa
2 Daly Ave., Ottawa ON K1N 6E2
Tel: 613-230-8841; Fax: 613-564-4428
info@heritageottawa.org
www.heritageottawa.org
www.facebook.com/HeritageOttawa
twitter.com/HeritageOttawa
Overview: A small local charitable organization founded in 1967
Mission: To advocate on behalf of the preservation of heritage buildings & historic landscapes; to educate & inform residents & visitors to Ottawa on the benefits of preserving the city's heritage
Membership: *Fees:* $30 individual; $35 family; $20 student/senior; $120 corporate/institutional
Activities: Lecture Series; Walking Tours
Chief Officer(s):
Leslie Maitland, President

Heritage Park Society
1900 Heritage Dr. SW, Calgary AB T2V 2X3
Tel: 403-268-8500; Fax: 403-268-8501
info@heritagepark.ab.ca
www.heritagepark.ca
www.facebook.com/HeritageParkYYC
twitter.com/HeritageParkYYC
Overview: A small local charitable organization founded in 1964
Mission: To connect people with the settlement of Western Canada 1864-1914
Finances: *Annual Operating Budget:* Greater than $5 Million
Staff Member(s): 76; 2600 volunteer(s)
Activities: Railway Days; Festival of Quilts; Rural Roots; Heritage Day; Fall Fair; Frontier Fun day; Harvest Sale; OctoberWest Weekend; Weekend of Thanks; Twelve Days of Christmas; *Library:* Archives; by appointment

Heritage Society of British Columbia
1459 Barclay St., Victoria BC V6G 1J6
Tel: 604-417-7243
hsbc@islandnet.com
www.heritagebc.ca
www.facebook.com/heritagebcanada
twitter.com/HeritageBCanada
Also Known As: Dogwood Heritage Society of British Columbia
Overview: A medium-sized provincial organization founded in 1981
Mission: To support heritage conservation across British Columbia
Affiliation(s): Heritage Canada
Activities: Presenting awards; Organizing conferences; Preserving historical sites, such as trails; Restoring the built environment; Funding community participation in workshops; *Awareness Events:* Heritage Week, February
Chief Officer(s):
Laura Saretsky, Heritage Program Manager
pgravett@heritagebc.ca
Nathan Macdonald, Coordinator, Operations & Events
nmacdonald@heritagebc.ca

Heritage Toronto
St. Lawrence Hall, 157 King St. East, 3rd Fl., Toronto ON M5C 1G9
Tel: 416-338-0684; Fax: 416-392-1772
email@heritagetoronto.org
www.heritagetoronto.org
www.facebook.com/HeritageToronto
twitter.com/heritagetoronto
www.instagram.com/heritagetoronto
Previous Name: Toronto Historical Board
Overview: A large local charitable organization founded in 1960
Mission: To advise city on heritage matters; To fundraise for heritage activities; To provide heritage programming
Member of: Heritage Canada
Finances: *Annual Operating Budget:* $500,000-$1.5 Million; *Funding Sources:* Donations
Staff Member(s): 9; 160 volunteer(s)
Membership: 1200; *Fees:* Schedule available
Activities: *Awareness Events:* Awards of Merit; Weekend Walking Tours
Chief Officer(s):
Allison Bain, Executive Director
allison.bain@toronto.ca
Kaitlin Wainwright, Director, Programming
kaitlin.wainwright@toronto.ca
LUcy Di Pietro, Manager, Marketing & Outreach
lucy.dipietro@toronto.ca
Publications:
• Heritage Toronto Annual Report
Type: Report; *Frequency:* Annually

Heritage Trust of Nova Scotia (HTNS)
PO Box 36111, Stn. Spring Garden, Halifax NS B3J 3S9
Tel: 902-423-4807; Fax: 902-423-3977
contact@htns.ca
www.htns.ca
Overview: A medium-sized provincial charitable organization founded in 1959
Mission: To promote interest in the preservation of historic structures & sites in Nova Scotia
Member of: Federation of the Nova Scotian Heritage
Affiliation(s): Heritage Canada
Finances: *Funding Sources:* Donations; federal funding; membership dues; sales of goods & services
Membership: *Fees:* $5 student; $15 single; $20 family; $10 senior; $15 senior couple; $25 group/institutions; $500 life membership; *Member Profile:* Individuals & groups who are committed to the protection & rehabilitation of Nova Scotia's heritage; *Committees:* Buildings-at-Risk; Communities; Education; Events/Programs; HRM; Quarterly; Painted Rooms; Publications; Public Relations; Tax Incentives; Places of Worship; Awards
Activities: Providing a public lecture series; Offering input on legislative policy at the municipal & provincial levels; *Speaker Service:* Yes; *Library:* Open to public
Chief Officer(s):
Linda Forbes, President, 902-423-4807
president@htns.ca
Awards:
• Heritage Trust of Nova Scotia Built Heritage Award
Presented for outstanding contribution to building restoration
Contact: Joyce McCulloch, HTNS Awards Chair
Publications:
• The Griffin [a publication of the Heritage Trust of Nova Scotia]
Type: Newsletter; *Frequency:* Quarterly; *Price:* Free with Heritage Trust of Nova Scotia membership

Heritage Winnipeg Corp. (HW)
#509, 63 Albert St., Winnipeg MB R3B 1G4
Tel: 204-942-2663; Fax: 204-942-2094
info@heritagewinnipeg.com
www.heritagewinnipeg.com
Overview: A small local charitable organization founded in 1978
Mission: To promote & encourage preservation of historic sites & structures in Winnipeg; To educate the public on heritage issues & make them aware of the richness of their material culture; To advocate & lobby on behalf of heritage related issues
Member of: Heritage Canada; Manitoba Historical Society; St. Boniface Historical Society; Manitoba Heritage Federation
Affiliation(s): Downtown Biz; Exchange Biz, Destination Winnipeg; Parks Canada; City of Winnipeg; Province of Manitoba
Finances: *Annual Operating Budget:* Less than $50,000; *Funding Sources:* Private donations; provincial government; city of Winnipeg; membership dues; fundraisers
Staff Member(s): 1

Membership: 170; Fees: $20 individual; $15 student/senior; $30 family/organization; corporate $100-$1,000; Committees: Public Service & Information; Legal & Economic Instruments; Advocacy; Preservation Awards; Education
Activities: Museum & Heritage Exposition; heritage auctions; annual preservation awards; school presentations; walking tours; Manitoba Day events; heritage fairs; Doors Open Winnipeg; Awareness Events: Heritage Preservation Awards; Doors Open Winnipeg; 3rd Mon. in Feb.; Speaker Service: Yes; Library: Open to public by appointment
Chief Officer(s):
Cindy Tugwell, Executive Director
Awards:
• Heritage Conservation Award
• Distinguished Service Award
• Youth Awards
Publications:
• Illustrated Guide to Winnipeg's Exchange District
Type: Brochure

Heritage York
Lambton House, 4066 Old Dundas St., Toronto ON M6S 2R6
Tel: 416-767-5472; Fax: 416-767-7191
admin@lambtonhouse.org
www.lambtonhouse.org
Overview: A small local charitable organization founded in 1991
Mission: To preserve & restore the historical heritage of the City of York, starting with the 1847 landmark building, Lambton House.
Affiliation(s): Ontario Historical Society
Finances: Funding Sources: Private; various government sources
Membership: Fees: $25 family; $15 adult; $10 junior (under 14)
Activities: At Lambton House - lecture series; annual carol singing; dinners; pub night; room rental; Speaker Service: Yes
Publications:
• The Heritage York Reporter
Type: newsletter

Herstreet Voir La rue des femmes

High Level & District Chamber of Commerce
10803 - 96 St., High Level AB T0H 1Z0
Tel: 780-926-2470; Fax: 780-926-4017
info@highlevelchamber.com
www.highlevelchamber.com
Overview: A small local charitable organization founded in 1962
Mission: To promote the economic & social well-being of High Level & district as a unified voice of free enterprise
Member of: Alberta Chamber of Commerce; Canadian Chamber of Commerce
Finances: Funding Sources: Membership fees
Membership: 117; Fees: Schedule available; Committees: Executive; Health Services; MacKenzie Crossroads; Merchants; Policy; REDI
Chief Officer(s):
Margaret Carroll, President

High Level Native Friendship Centre
PO Box 1735, 11000 - 95 St., High Level AB T0H 1Z0
Tel: 780-926-3355; Fax: 780-926-2038
hlnfcs.ed@gmail.com
anfca.com/friendship-centres/high-level
Overview: A small local organization overseen by Alberta Native Friendship Centres Association
Member of: Alberta Native Friendship Centres Association
Chief Officer(s):
Barb Adekat, Executive Director

High Prairie & Area Chamber of Commerce
PO Box 3600, #107, 4806 - 53rd Ave., High Prairie AB T0G 1E0
Tel: 780-507-1565
office@hpchamber.net
www.hpchamber.net
Overview: A small local organization
Mission: To enhance the business, economic, & social communities of High Prairie
Affiliation(s): Alberta Chamber of Commerce; Canadian Chamber of Commerce
Membership: 70; Fees: $125-$250; $75 non-profit/individual
Chief Officer(s):
Tracy Sherkawi, President

High Prairie Association for Community Living
PO Box 345, High Prairie AB T0G 1E0
Overview: A small local charitable organization founded in 1971
Mission: To improve & enhance the lives of people with handicaps; To advocate for those who need support, as well as providing support for them & their families.
Member of: Alberta Association for Community Living

High Prairie Native Friendship Centre
PO Box 1448, 4919 - 51 Ave., High Prairie AB T0G 1E0
Tel: 780-523-4511; Fax: 780-523-3055
edhpnfc@gmail.com
www.facebook.com/260735773965759
Overview: A small local organization founded in 1975 overseen by Alberta Native Friendship Centres Association
Mission: To improve the quality of life for Aboriginal people in urban areas by supporting self-determined activities that encourage: the development of human and community resources; the improvement of socio-economic and physical conditions; better understanding and relationships between Aboriginal and non-Aboriginal citizens; and the enhancement of Aboriginal culture among Aboriginal people and the communities they reside in.
Member of: Alberta Native Friendship Centres Association
Activities: friendship centre facilitation; health & wellness; arts & culture; elders; youth

High River & District Chamber of Commerce
PO Box 5244, #6, 28 - 12 Ave. SE, High River AB T1V 1M4
Tel: 403-652-3336; Fax: 403-652-2627
hrdcc@telus.net
www.hrchamber.ca
www.facebook.com/HighRiverChamber
twitter.com/Chamber_HR
Overview: A small local organization founded in 1968
Mission: To enhance the economy in High River & district for the benefit of the community
Member of: High River Agricultural Society; Kinsmen Club of High River
Finances: Funding Sources: Fundraising; membership fees
Membership: Fees: Schedule available based on number of employees
Activities: Operates a year-round tourist information centre; annual trade fair; parades, rodeo; Awareness Events: Santa Parade, Dec. 1; Rodeo Parade, May; Speaker Service: Yes
Chief Officer(s):
Steve Muth, President
Lynette McCracken, Executive Director

Highland Shores Children's Aid
363 Dundas St. West, Belleville ON K8P 1B3
Tel: 613-962-9291; Fax: 613-966-3868
Toll-Free: 800-267-0570; TTY: 613-962-1019
info@highlandshorescas.com
www.highlandshorescas.com
Previous Name: Hastings Children's Aid Society
Overview: A small local charitable organization founded in 1907
Member of: Ontario Association of Children's Aid Societies
Membership: Fees: $5; Member Profile: Individuals, 18 or older; corporations who do business in the area served by the society
Activities: Awareness Events: Purple Ribbon Campaign, Oct.; Adoption Awareness Month, Nov.
Chief Officer(s):
Michael McLeod, President
Awards:
• Outstanding Leadership in Child Welfare Award
Cobourg
1005 Burnham St., Cobourg ON K9A 5J6
Tel: 905-372-1821; Fax: 905-372-5284
Toll-Free: 800-267-0570
North Hastings
PO Box 837, #104, 16 Billa St., Bancroft ON K0L 1C0
Tel: 613-332-2425; Fax: 613-332-5686
Toll-Free: 866-532-2269
Picton
16 MacSteven Dr., Picton ON K0K 2T0
Tel: 613-476-7957; Fax: 613-476-2316
Toll-Free: 800-267-0570; TTY: 613-962-1019
Quinte West
469 Dundas St. West, Trenton ON K8V 3S4
Tel: 613-965-6261; Fax: 613-965-0930
Toll-Free: 800-267-0570

Hiiye'yu Lelum Society House of Friendship
PO Box 1015, Duncan BC V9L 3Y2
Tel: 250-748-2242; Fax: 250-748-2238
hofduncan.org
Previous Name: Valley Native Friendship Centre Society
Overview: A small local organization
Mission: To develop Aboriginal leadership in the community, as well as provide a bridge between cultures in the Cowichan Valley; to promote well-being in the community by offering counselling, information & referral services, in addition to a centre for communal recreation, education & meetings.
Staff Member(s): 38
Chief Officer(s):
Debbie Williams, Executive Director
DebbieWilliams@hofduncan.org

Hike Ontario
262 Lavender Dr., Ancaster ON L9K 1E5
Tel: 905-277-4453
Toll-Free: 800-894-7229
info@hikeontario.com
www.hikeontario.com
www.facebook.com/hikeontario
twitter.com/HikeOntario
www.youtube.com/takeahikeontario;
www.instagram.com/hikeontario
Overview: A medium-sized provincial charitable organization founded in 1974
Mission: To act as the voice for hikers & walkers in Ontario; To encourage hiking, walking & trail development in Ontario; To promote trail maintenance. best practices, & safe hiking; To enhance environmental awareness, conservation & sustainable trails
Affiliation(s): Carolinian Coalition Canada; Conservation Ontario; Friends of the Greenbelt Foundation; Hike Canada En Marche; Older Adult Centres' Association of Ontario; Ontario Nature; Ontario Trails Council
Finances: Funding Sources: Membership dues; Grants; Sponsorships; Donations
Membership: Member Profile: Not-for-profit trail building & hiking organizations; Individuals; Corporations, government agencies, & organizations other than hiking or trail building organizations
Activities: Providing hiking information & services throughout Ontario; Offering the Hike Leader Certification Program & the Young Hikers Program; Supporting trails across the province; Advocating for clubs; Liaising with government; Promoting research & education into the health benefits of walking & hiking; Presenting awards to celebrate dedicated hikers; Awareness Events: Ontario Hiking Week, Oct.
Chief Officer(s):
Tom Friesen, President
Stacey Hodder, Secretary
Roma Juneja, Treasurer
Awards:
• Long Distance Hiker Awards
Includes the Red Pine Award (550km), Trillium Award (950km) & Tamarack Award (1500km)
• Volunteer of the Year Award

Hilal Committee of Metropolitan Toronto & Vicinity
1015 Danforth Ave., Toronto ON M4J 1M1
Tel: 416-230-5229; Fax: 416-467-9787
Other Communication: Alt. Phone: 416-970-5786
info@hilaalcommittee.com
www.hilalcommittee.com
twitter.com/HilalCommittee
Overview: A small local organization
Mission: To coordinate the beginnings of Islamic months & holidays through local sightings of the moon.
Membership: 90; Member Profile: Islamic & masjid centres & organizations
Activities: Publishing an Islamic calendar based on calculations of the moon's visibility
Chief Officer(s):
Khalil Sufi, Chair

Hillel of Greater Toronto
Wolfond Centre, University of Toronto, 36 Harbord St., Toronto ON M5S 1G2
Tel: 416-913-2424
info@hilleltoronto.org
www.hilleltoronto.org
www.facebook.com/hilleluoft
Previous Name: University of Toronto Menorah Society
Overview: A small local organization founded in 1917
Mission: To promote Jewish identity, religious & political diversity, & student leadership
Affiliation(s): UJA Federation of Greater Toronto; Jewish Federations of Canada - UIA
Finances: Funding Sources: Donations
Staff Member(s): 20

Membership: *Member Profile:* Jewish students who attend universities & community colleges throughout the Greater Toronto Area
Activities: Offering programming & events
Chief Officer(s):
Marc Newburgh, Executive Director
Lior Cyngiser, Director, Israel Engagement, Education & Advocacy
Aaron Greenberg, Director, Jewish Learning Initiative

Hillfield-Strathallan College Foundation
299 Fennell Ave. West, Hamilton ON L9C 1G3
Tel: 905-389-1367; *Fax:* 905-389-6366
www.hsc.on.ca
Overview: A small local organization
Chief Officer(s):
Tom Matthews, Contact
headmaster@hillstrath.on.ca

Hincks-Dellcrest Treatment Centre & Foundation
440 Jarvis St., Toronto ON M4Y 2H4
Tel: 416-924-1164; *Fax:* 416-924-8208
Toll-Free: 855-944-4673
info@hincksdellcrest.org
www.hincksdellcrest.org
www.facebook.com/hincksdellcrest
twitter.com/hincksdellcrest
www.youtube.com/thehincksdellcrest
Overview: A small local organization founded in 1998
Mission: To offer a comprehensive range of mental health services to infants, children, youth, & their families; to provide a variety of programs, including prevention & early intervention, outpatient & residential treatment.
Affiliation(s): University of Toronto
Finances: *Annual Operating Budget:* Greater than $5 Million
Chief Officer(s):
Ian Smith, Chair
Donna Duncan, President & CEO

Gail Appel Institute
114 Maitland St., Toronto ON M4Y 1E1
Tel: 416-924-1164; *Fax:* 416-924-9808

Treatment Centre
1645 Sheppard Ave. West, Toronto ON M3M 2X4
Tel: 416-924-1164; *Fax:* 416-633-7141

Hindu Society of Alberta
14225 - 133 Ave., Edmonton AB T5L 4W3
Tel: 780-451-5130
hindu.society@hotmail.com
www.hindusociety.ab.ca
www.facebook.com/hindusociety.ab.ca
twitter.com/Hindu_Society
Overview: A small provincial charitable organization founded in 1967
Mission: The Society is a cultural, social & religious institute catering to the needs of those influenced by Hinduism.
Activities: Classes in yoga & meditation; language classes; lectures & seminars on history & religion; religious celebrations; music & dance performances; hall rentals; *Library:* library
Chief Officer(s):
Hansa Thaleshvar, President, 587-269-3440
hthalesh@gmail.com

Hinton & District Chamber of Commerce
309 Gregg Ave., Hinton AB T7V 2A7
Tel: 780-865-2777; *Fax:* 780-865-1062
info@hintonchamber.com
www.hintonchamber.com
www.facebook.com/hintonchamber
twitter.com/HintonChamber
Overview: A small local organization founded in 1957
Staff Member(s): 2
Membership: 170; *Fees:* Schedule available based on number of employees
Activities: Business Awards Gala, Oct.
Chief Officer(s):
Brian LeBerge, President
Natalie Charlton, Executive Director

Hinton Friendship Centre
PO Box 6720, Stn. Main, 965 Switzer Dr., Hinton AB T7V 1X6
Tel: 780-865-5189; *Fax:* 780-865-1756
main@fchinton.com
www.hintonfriendshipcentre.ca
Overview: A small local organization founded in 1995 overseen by Alberta Native Friendship Centres Association
Member of: Alberta Native Friendship Centres Association

Chief Officer(s):
Yvonne Oshanyk, Executive Director

Hinton-Edson & District Real Estate Board See Alberta West Realtors' Association

Hispanic Canadian Arts & Culture Association (HCACA)
ON
info@hispaniccanadianarts.org
www.hispaniccanadianarts.org
www.facebook.com/HispanicCanadianArts
twitter.com/hcaca_info
Overview: A small local organization founded in 2010
Mission: To promote Hispanic culture in the Greater Toronto Area
Staff Member(s): 3; 5 volunteer(s)
Activities: Exhibitions; Music festivals
Chief Officer(s):
Carlos Bastidas, Executive Director
Roger Marles, President, Board of Directors

Hispanic Canadian Heritage Council (HCHC)
#203, 1280 Finch Ave., Toronto ON M3J 3K6
www.hispaniccanadianheritage.ca
www.facebook.com/HispanicCanadianHeritageCouncil
twitter.com/hispaniccanada
Overview: A small national organization
Mission: To promote Hispanic culture in Canada; To bring together organizations from the Canadian Hispanic community
Activities: Promoting Hispanic Heritage Month
Chief Officer(s):
Claudio Ruiz-Pilarte, President

Hispanic Development Council (HDC)
#203, 1280 Finch Ave. West, Toronto ON M3J 3K6
Tel: 416-516-0851
www.hispaniccouncil.ca
Overview: A small national organization
Mission: To serve the local Hispano/Latin community, forming a network of member organizations & individuals to assist with such services as immigrant settlement & youth counselling, the ultimate goal being a strengthening of community & a chance for all to integrate & participate fully in society
Chief Officer(s):
Duberlis Ramos, Executive Director

Hispanic-Canadian Alliance of Ontario See Alianza Hispano-Canadiense Ontario

Histoire Canada See Canada's History

Historic Restoration Society of Annapolis County (HRS)
PO Box 503, 136 St. George St., Annapolis Royal NS B0S 1A0
Tel: 902-532-7754; *Fax:* 902-532-0700
annapolisheritage@gmail.com
www.annapolisheritagesociety.com
twitter.com/odellmuseum
Also Known As: Annapolis Heritage Society
Overview: A small local charitable organization founded in 1967
Mission: To preserve local heritage; To strive to be a leader in preserving heritage through the rehabilitation of buildings, through direct example or advocacy; To be responsible for the operation of museums &/or resource centres; To support relevant community & provincial aims
Finances: *Funding Sources:* Provincial Government
Activities: Owns & operates O'Dell & Sinclair Inn Museums; operates North Hills Museum; *Library:* Archives; Open to public
Chief Officer(s):
Wayne Smith, Executive Director

Historic Sites Association of Newfoundland & Labrador (HSANL)
Chelsea Building, #204, 10 Forbes St., St. John's NL A1E 3L5
Tel: 709-753-5515; *Fax:* 709-753-0879
Toll-Free: 877-753-9262
marketing@historicsites.ca
www.historicsites.ca
www.facebook.com//131036186980761
twitter.com/historicsitesnl
Overview: A small provincial charitable organization founded in 1984
Mission: To preserve, promote & present the history & heritage of Newfoundland & Labrador
Affiliation(s): Parks Canada; Museum Association of Newfoundland & Labrador; Canadian Museum Association

Finances: *Annual Operating Budget:* $1.5 Million-$3 Million; *Funding Sources:* Operation of Heritage Shops of NL
Staff Member(s): 10; 30 volunteer(s)
Membership: 15; *Member Profile:* Board of Directors & Members Emeritus
Activities: Manning Awards; Joan Woods Exhibition; Book launches; Heritage Fairs; Bartlett Lectures; Operates the Hawthorne Cottage
Chief Officer(s):
Andrea MacDonald, Executive Director, 709-753-2566
director@historicsites.ca
Mandy White, Financial Officer, 709-753-1940
info@historicsites.ca
Awards:
• The Manning Award
To recognize community heritage projects and the work of heritage champions. *Deadline:* February 15th
• History and Heritage Writer's Award
• Paul O'Neill Scholarship
Eligibility: Undergraduate student at Memorial University enrolled in the Bachelor of Arts program.; *Amount:* $1000
• The Craft Award
Recognizing artisans in the province who preserve traditional crafts or use their work to interpret Provincial History

Historic Vehicle Society of Ontario (HVSO)
c/o Canadian Transportation Museum & Heritage Village, 6155 Arner Town Line, RR#2, Kingsville ON N9Y 2E5
Tel: 519-776-6909; *Fax:* 519-776-8321
Toll-Free: 886-776-6909
info@ctmhv.com
www.ctmhv.com
Overview: A medium-sized provincial charitable organization founded in 1959
Mission: To collect, restore & display vehicles, buildings & artifacts that serve to demonstrate the founding settlement of Essex County; to preserve the past to enhance the future.
Finances: *Annual Operating Budget:* $250,000-$500,000
Staff Member(s): 7; 100 volunteer(s)
Membership: 140; *Fees:* $35; *Member Profile:* Lovers of history, antiques, old cars
Chief Officer(s):
Kim Brimner, Contact

Historica Canada
East Mezzanine, 2 Carlton St., Toronto ON M5B 1J3
Tel: 416-506-1867; *Fax:* 416-506-0300
Toll-Free: 866-701-1867
info@historicacanada.ca
www.historicacanada.ca
www.facebook.com/Historica.Canada
twitter.com/HistoricaCanada
www.youtube.com/c/HistoricaCanada;
www.instagram.com/historicacanada
Previous Name: Historica-Dominion Institute
Merged from: The Historica Foundation of Canada; The Dominion Institute
Overview: A medium-sized national charitable organization founded in 2009
Mission: To conduct original research into Canadians' knowledge of the country's past & to build innovative programs that broaden appreciation of the richness & complexity of Canadian history
Activities: Lectures; articles; TV documentaries (Heritage Minutes); interactive websites; teaching tools; publications; operates www.blackhistorycanada.ca & Encounters With Canada (www.ewc-rdc.ca)
Chief Officer(s):
Anthony Wilson-Smith, President & CEO
awilson-smith@historicacanada.ca
Brigitte d'Auzac de Lamartinie, Director, Programs & Development
bdauzac@historicacanada.ca
Publications:
• General News [a publication of Historica Canada]
Type: Newsletter
Profile: Information on contests, events, promitions & more.
• Teacher News [a publication of Historica Canada]
Type: Newsletter
Profile: Information on contests, learning tools, teaching aids, guest speakers & more.

Historica-Dominion Institute See Historica Canada

Historical Association of Annapolis Royal
PO Box 659, Annapolis Royal NS B0S 1A0

Canadian Associations / Historical Automobile Society of Canada, Inc. (HASC)

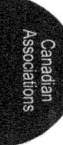

Tel: 902-532-3035; *Fax:* 902-532-2911
tours@tourannapolisroyal.com
www.tourannapolisroyal.com
www.facebook.com/CandlelightGraveyardTours
twitter.com/explorerguide
www.youtube.com/user/TourAnnapolisRoyal
Overview: A small local organization founded in 1919
Mission: The Association is known, not only for its walking tours through historic areas of the city, where history is presented in fun, accessible fashion, but also for its work in designating local sites with heritage plaques.
Affiliation(s): Royal Nova Scotia Historical Society
Membership: *Fees:* $5 regular; $100 lifetime
Activities: Candlelight Graveyard Tours; National Historic District Tours; Acadian Heritage Tours; maintenance of local lighthouse
Chief Officer(s):
Durline Melanson, President
Lorna McLagan, Secretary

Historical Automobile Society of Canada, Inc. (HASC)
c/o Don Mossey, 6 Themer Ct., Tottenham ON L0G 1W0
www.historical-automobile-society.ca
Overview: A small national organization founded in 1963
Mission: To collect, restore & operate an antique, classic & special interest automobiles, motorcycles, trucks, etc. & to preserve related materials
Finances: *Annual Operating Budget:* Less than $50,000; *Funding Sources:* Membership fees
Membership: 1,135; *Fees:* $8 regional; $42 national
Activities: *Awareness Events:* The Family Picnic, July; Normoska, Aug. *Library:* HASC Library; Not open to public
Chief Officer(s):
Don Mossey, Director, National Membership
Publications:
• The Canadian Klaxon [a publication of the Historical Automobile Society of Canada]
Type: Magazine; *Frequency:* 5 pa; *Price:* Free to members of the HASC.

Historical Society of Alberta (HSA)
PO Box 4035, Stn. C, Calgary AB T2T 5M9
Tel: 403-261-3662; *Fax:* 403-269-6029
info@albertahistory.org
www.albertahistory.org
Overview: A medium-sized provincial charitable organization founded in 1907
Mission: To preserve & promote the history of Alberta; to encourage the study & preservation of Canadian & Albertan history; to rescue from oblivion the memories, experiences & knowledge of early inhabitants.
Affiliation(s): Heritage Canada; Alberta Heritage Council
Finances: *Funding Sources:* Membership fees; donations; provincial government grant
Membership: *Fees:* $15 individual; $25 family; $55 affiliate; $120 associate
Activities: Historic Edmonton Week, Historic Calgary Week & Doors Open, Historic Red Deer Week & Doors Open, Historic Lethbridge Week & Doors, summer; monthly meetings held by four chapters, fall & winter
Chief Officer(s):
Belinda Crowson, President
Awards:
• Award of Merit & Lifetime Membership

Central Alberta Historical Society
4525 - 47A Ave., Red Deer AB T4N 6Z6
Tel: 403-347-7873; *Fax:* 403-340-7521
contact@centralalbertahistory.org
centralalbertahistory.org
www.facebook.com/ca.history
Chief Officer(s):
Lianne Kruger, President

Chinook Country Historical Society
#311, 223 - 12 Ave. SW, Calgary AB T2R 0G9
Tel: 403-261-4667
info@chinookcountry.org
www.chinookcountry.org
www.facebook.com/ChinookCountryHistoricalSociety
twitter.com/chinookchs
Chief Officer(s):
David Sztain, Treasurer
david.sztain@replicon.com

Edmonton & District Historical Society
7730 - 106 St., 3rd Fl., Edmonton AB T6E 4W3
Tel: 780-439-2797; *Fax:* 888-692-9019
info@historicedmonton.ca
www.historicedmonton.ca
www.facebook.com/HistoricEdmonton
twitter.com/EdmontonDHS
Chief Officer(s):
Dean Wood, President

Lethbridge Historical Society
PO Box 974, Lethbridge AB T1J 4A2
Tel: 403-320-4994
lhs@albertahistory.org
albertahistory.org/lethbridge
Chief Officer(s):
Belinda Crowson, President, 403-381-4316

Peace Country Historical Society (PCHS)
PO Box 23394, RPO Prairie Mall, Grande Prairie AB T8V 7G7
contactus@pc-hs.ca
www.pc-hs.ca
Chief Officer(s):
Daryl White, President

Historical Society of Fort McMurray See Fort McMurray Historical Society

Historical Society of Ottawa / Société historique d'Ottawa
PO Box 523, Stn. B, Ottawa ON K1P 5P6
hsottawa@storm.ca
hsottawa.ncf.ca
Previous Name: Women's Canadian Historical Society of Ottawa
Overview: A small local charitable organization founded in 1898
Mission: To encourage the study of Canadian history & literature; to collect, preserve, exhibit & publish Canadian historical records & artifacts, especially those that illustrate the origin, growth & development of Ottawa; to foster Canadian loyalty & patriotism
Member of: Canadian Museums Association; Ontario Museum Association; Ontario Historical Society
Membership: *Fees:* $10 student; $35 individual; $50 family; $350 single lifetime; *Committees:* Awards; Library/Archives; Membership; Nominations; Newsletter; Publications; Telephone
Activities: *Internships:* Yes; *Speaker Service:* Yes; *Library:* by appointment
Chief Officer(s):
George Neville, President, 613-729-0579
george.neville@ncf.ca
Margaret Back, Secretary, 613-236-7166
ea590@freenet.carleton.ca

Historical Society of St. Boniface & Maryhill Community
1338 Maryhill Rd., #B, Maryhill ON N0B 2B0
info@maryhillroots.com
www.maryhillroots.com
Also Known As: Maryhill Historical Society
Overview: A small local organization founded in 1977
Mission: To collect, preserve, exhibit & publishe historical material pertaining to the parish, school & Maryhill community.
Member of: Ontario Historical Society
Finances: *Funding Sources:* Membership, donations, publications, research
Membership: *Fees:* $5; $25 life individual; $40 life couple; *Committees:* St. Boniface Church; St. Boniface School; Building Maintenance; Community; Resource Centre; Fundraising; Wayside Shrines; Birthday Club; Geneology; Publications; Program; Membership
Activities: *Awareness Events:* Heritage Day, 3rd Sun. in Sept. *Library:* Resource Centre (summer); by appointment
Chief Officer(s):
Marlene Bruckhardt, President

Historical Society of St. Catharines (HSSC)
Pen Centre, PO Box 25017, 221 Glendale Ave., St Catharines ON L2T 4C4
stcatharineshistory.wordpress.com
Overview: A small local organization founded in 1927
Mission: To increase the knowledge & appreciation of the history of St Catharines & vicinity
Member of: Ontario Historical Society
Finances: *Annual Operating Budget:* Less than $50,000; *Funding Sources:* Membership fees; Donations; Ontario Heritage Development grant
14 volunteer(s)
Membership: 200; *Fees:* $10 single; $15 family; *Committees:* Programme
Activities: Holding public general meetings once a month featuring speakers or presentations on local history topics; Publishing quarterly newsletter & other publications; *Awareness Events:* Observance of the birthday of William Hamilton Merritt, July 3
Chief Officer(s):
Nancy Cameron, President
ncport33@gmail.com
Dave Willer, Vice-President, 289-968-0025
dave.willer@hotmail.com
Elizabeth Finnie, Secretary
finnies@sympatico.ca
Publications:
• Historical Society of St. Catharines Newsletter
Type: Newsletter; *Frequency:* Quarterly; *Editor:* Dave Willer

Historical Society of Sherbrooke *Voir* Société d'histoire de Sherbrooke

HIV Community Link (ACAA)
#110, 1603 - 10th Ave. SW, Calgary AB T3C 0J7
Tel: 403-508-2500; *Fax:* 403-263-7358
Toll-Free: 877-440-2437
www.hivcl.org
www.linkedin.com/company/aids-calgary-awareness-association
www.facebook.com/AIDSCalgary
twitter.com/hivcommlink
Also Known As: AIDS Calgary
Previous Name: AIDS Calgary Awareness Association
Overview: A small local charitable organization founded in 1983 overseen by Canadian AIDS Society
Mission: To reduce the harm associated with HIV & AIDS for all individuals & communities in the Calgary region; to provide HIV education & support; to enhance the quality of life & advocate on behalf of people living with HIV; to promote awareness & understanding of HIV issues; to work together with partners in the community to create a caring & compassionate society in the face of HIV & AIDS
Member of: Canadian AIDS Society; Alberta Community Council on HIV/AIDS; Canadian HIV/AIDS Legal Network; Calgary Coalition on HIV & AIDS
Finances: *Funding Sources:* Alberta Health; Health Canada; United Way of Calgary; City of Calgary
Staff Member(s): 18
Membership: *Fees:* $5 individual; $20 corporate; *Committees:* Operations; Development; Prevention & Engagement; HIV Support; Shift Support
Activities: Offering outreach & education programs to members & to the community; Providing counselling; Advocating on behalf of people living with HIV; *Awareness Events:* AIDS Walk; World AIDS Day; *Speaker Service:* Yes; *Library:* Open to public
Chief Officer(s):
Leslie Hill, Executive Director

HIV Network of Edmonton Society
9702 - 111 Ave. NW, Edmonton AB T5G 0B1
Tel: 780-488-5742; *Fax:* 780-488-3735
Toll-Free: 877-388-5742
www.hivedmonton.com
www.facebook.com/home.php#!/hiv.edmonton?fref=ts
twitter.com/HIVEdmonton
www.youtube.com/user/hivedmontonvideo
Also Known As: HIV Edmonton
Previous Name: AIDS Network of Edmonton Society
Overview: A small local charitable organization founded in 1984
Mission: HIV Edmonton is a community-based, not-for-profit organization that works to reduce HIV/AIDS related stigma & discrimination. It works to educate, support & advocate on behalf of those infected & affected by HIV & related conditions.
Member of: Canadian AIDS Society; Canadian Centre for Philanthropy Canadian HIV/AIDS Legal Network; Canadian Palliative Care Association; Chamber of Commerce
Affiliation(s): Alberta Community Council on HIV
Finances: *Funding Sources:* Government; foundations; fundraising
Staff Member(s): 11
Activities: Support; health promotion; harm reduction; advocacy; *Awareness Events:* AIDS Walk; AIDS Awareness Week; *Internships:* Yes; *Speaker Service:* Yes
Chief Officer(s):
Ken MacDonald, Chair
Shelley Williams, Executive Director
shelley.w@hivedmonton.com

Awards:
• Bob Mills Community Leadership Award

HIV North Society
9607 - 102 St., Grande Prairie AB T8V 2T8
Tel: 780-538-3388; *Fax:* 780-538-3368
www.hivnorth.org
www.facebook.com/106064926090085
Also Known As: HIV North
Previous Name: South Peace AIDS Council of Grande Prairie; Society of the South Peace AIDS Council
Overview: A small local charitable organization founded in 1987 overseen by Canadian AIDS Society
Mission: To provide outreach, education, harm reduction & support programs & services, working collaboratively with other agencies, to fight against HIV/AIDS
Member of: Alberta Community Council on HIV; Canadian AIDS Society; Canadian Society of Association Executives
Finances: *Annual Operating Budget:* $500,000-$1.5 Million; *Funding Sources:* Health Canada; Alberta Health; Fundraising; Individual & corporate donations
Staff Member(s): 17; 25 volunteer(s)
Membership: *Member Profile:* Interest in & knowledge of AIDS/HIV
Activities: Providing client support through education & awareness; Offering drop in centres; Offering mentor programs for LGBTQ youth; Facilitating harm reduction programs; *Internships:* Yes; *Speaker Service:* Yes; *Library:* Open to public
Chief Officer(s):
Susan Belcourt, Executive Director
director@hivnorth.org

HIV West Yellowhead Society
PO Box 5005, 152 Athabasca Ave., Hinton AB T7V 1X3
Tel: 780-740-0066; *Fax:* 780-740-0060
Toll-Free: 877-291-8811
www.hivwestyellowhead.com
Previous Name: AIDS Jasper Society
Overview: A small local organization founded in 1988 overseen by Canadian AIDS Society
Mission: To promote healthy lifestyles & relationships & prevent the spread of HIV
Member of: Alberta Community Council on HIV
Finances: *Annual Operating Budget:* $50,000-$100,000; *Funding Sources:* Health Canada; Alberta Health; community donations
Staff Member(s): 2; 15 volunteer(s)
Membership: 10; *Fees:* $5; *Member Profile:* Community members
Activities: Prevention education & awareness; information & referral; community outreach; *Awareness Events:* AIDS Walk; National AIDS Awareness Week; World AIDS Day
Chief Officer(s):
Lori Phillips, Executive Director
director@hivwestyellowhead.com

HIV/AIDS Regional Services (HARS)
844A Princess St., Kingston ON K7L 1G5
Tel: 613-545-3698; *Fax:* 613-545-9809
Toll-Free: 800-565-2209
hars@kingston.net
www.hars.ca
www.facebook.com/harskingston
Previous Name: Kingston AIDS Project
Overview: A medium-sized local charitable organization founded in 1986
Mission: To prevent spread of Human Immunodeficiency Virus (HIV); To educate people about AIDS & HIV; To support people affected by AIDS & HIV infection
Affiliation(s): Ontario AIDS Network; Canadian AIDS Society; Canadian HIV/AIDS Legal Network
Finances: *Funding Sources:* Federal, provincial & city governments & fundraising
Staff Member(s): 8
Membership: *Fees:* $15 regular; $5 Senior/Student; $0 Person with HIV/AIDS
Activities: *Awareness Events:* AIDS Vigil, May; Red Ribbon Campaign, Dec.; *Library:* Open to public
Chief Officer(s):
John MacTavish, Executive Director
Amanda Girling, Coordinator, Education
amanda@kingston.net

HIV/AIDS Resources and Community Health (ARCH)
#115, 89 Dawson Rd., Guelph ON N1H 1B1
Tel: 519-763-2255; *Fax:* 519-763-8125
Toll-Free: 800-282-4505
education@archguelph.ca
www.archguelph.ca
www.facebook.com/archguelph?fref=ts
twitter.com/archguelph
Previous Name: AIDS Committee of Guelph & Wellington County
Overview: A small local charitable organization founded in 1989
Mission: To provide exemplary services, education & support in the area of HIV & AIDS through innovative health promotion strategies & community partnerships
Member of: Ontario AIDS Network; Canadian AIDS Society
Finances: *Annual Operating Budget:* $500,000-$1.5 Million; *Funding Sources:* Ontario Ministry of Health; Health Canada; United Way
Staff Member(s): 14; 42 volunteer(s)
Membership: 1-99; *Fees:* $24; *Member Profile:* Those infected & affected by HIV & Hepatitis C; *Committees:* Fundraising; Treatment Advisory; Youth Advisory
Activities: Gala Auction; outreach; needle exchange; education; support; *Awareness Events:* Red Ribbon Week, Dec.; AIDS Awareness Campaign, Nov. 24 - Dec. 1; *Speaker Service:* Yes; *Library:* Open to public
Chief Officer(s):
Tom Hammond, Executive Director, 519-763-2255 Ext. 129
director@archguelph.ca
Tashauna Devonshire, Coordinator, Support Services, 519-763-2255 Ext. 126
support@archguelph.ca

HMWN (Holy Mother World Networks) Radio Maria
1247 Lawrence Ave. West, Toronto ON M6L 1A1
Tel: 416-245-7117; *Fax:* 416-245-2668
info@hmwn.net
www.hmwn.net
Also Known As: Radio Maria Canada
Overview: A small local charitable organization
Mission: To promote the Gospel message of joy & hope for the family, the sick, & the lonely, in accordance with the teaching of the Roman Catholic Church; to provide 24-hour Catholic radio broadcasting services as part of an evangelization project
Affiliation(s): Archdiocese of Toronto; World Family of Radio Maria
Finances: *Funding Sources:* Donations
Membership: *Member Profile:* Religious & lay volunteers, devoted to the Holy Mother, to operate HMWN Radio Maria
Activities: Offering programming in faith instruction & prayer

Hockey Alberta / Hockey l'Alberta
PO Box 5005, #2606, 100 College Blvd., Red Deer AB T4N 5H5
Tel: 403-342-6777; *Fax:* 403-346-4277
info@hockeyalberta.ca
www.hockeyalberta.ca
www.facebook.com/HockeyAlberta
twitter.com/HockeyAlberta
Overview: A large provincial organization founded in 1907 overseen by Hockey Canada
Mission: To act as the governing body for organized hockey in Alberta; To create positive opportunities & experiences for players through service & leadership
Member of: Hockey Canada
Staff Member(s): 30; 500+ volunteer(s)
Membership: 450 organizations + 90,000+ individual members
Activities: Hosting regional & provincial tournaments & competitions; Providing access to certified coaching clinics; Holding an appeal board to which any member, team, or player can appeal disciplinary measures; Issuing permits for tournaments & exhibition games to ensure that teams meet eligibility requirements; Providing rule books, training manuals, & bulletins for teams & officials; *Internships:* Yes; *Speaker Service:* Yes; *Rents Mailing List:* Yes
Chief Officer(s):
Rob Litwinski, CEO
rlitwinski@hockeyalberta.ca
Justin Fesyk, Senior Manager, Hockey Development
jfesyk@hockeyalberta.ca
Mike Klass, Senior Manager, Business Operations
mklass@hockeyalberta.ca
Publications:
• Hockey Alberta Annual Report
Type: Yearbook
• Home Ice Magazine [a publication of Hockey Alberta]
Type: Magazine

Hockey Canada
801 King Edward Ave., #N204, Ottawa ON K1N 6N5
Tel: 613-696-0211; *Fax:* 613-696-0787
www.hockeycanada.ca
www.linkedin.com/company/hockey-canada
www.facebook.com/HockeyCanada
twitter.com/hockeycanada
www.youtube.com/hockeycanadavideos;
www.instagram.com/hockeycanada
Also Known As: Canadian Hockey Association
Merged from: Canadian Amateur Hockey Association; Hockey Canada
Overview: A large national organization founded in 1914
Mission: To advance amateur hockey for all individuals through progressive leadership, ensuring meaningful opportunities & enjoyable experiences in a safe, sustainable environment
Affiliation(s): International Ice Hockey Federation
Finances: *Funding Sources:* Government; Sponsorship; Sales; Fundraising
Chief Officer(s):
Tom Renney, President
Lisa Dornan, Director, Communications
ldornan@hockeycanada.ca
Awards:
• Female Hockey Breakthrough Award
• Liz MacKinnon Award
• Hal Lewis Award
• Gordon Juckes Award
• Officiating Award
• Hockey Canada Award of Merit (East)
• Hockey Canada Award of Merit (West)
• Hockey Canada Award of Merit (Central)
• Outstanding Volunteer Award

Calgary Office
#201, 151 Canada Olympic Rd. SW, Calgary AB T3B 6B7
Tel: 403-777-3636; *Fax:* 403-777-3635
www.hockeycanada.ca

Hockey Canada Foundation
151 Canada Olympic Rd. SW, Calgary AB T3B 6B7
Tel: 403-777-3636; *Fax:* 403-777-3635
foundation@hockeycanada.ca
www.hockeycanada.ca
Overview: A large national charitable organization
Mission: To establish & grow endowment & general purpose funds for Hockey Canada
Finances: *Funding Sources:* Donations; fundraising
Activities: Focus areas: Skill Development & Qualified Coaching; Accessibility & Diversity; Health & Wellness; Athlete & Alumni Support; Facilities; *Awareness Events:* Golf Gala
Chief Officer(s):
Donna Iampieri, Executive Director

Hockey Development Centre for Ontario (HDCO)
#215, 19 Waterman Ave., Toronto ON M4B 1Y2
Tel: 416-426-7252; *Fax:* 416-426-7348
Toll-Free: 888-843-4326
hockey@hdco.on.ca
www.hdco.on.ca
twitter.com/theHDCO
Overview: A medium-sized provincial organization founded in 1984
Mission: To provide educational, developmental & financial opportunities for amateur hockey participants in Ontario
Finances: *Annual Operating Budget:* $500,000-$1.5 Million; *Funding Sources:* Provincial government; sponsorships
Staff Member(s): 3
Membership: 10 institutional; 2 associate
Activities: Hockey Trainers Certification Program; *Rents Mailing List:* Yes; *Library:* Hockey Resources; Open to public
Chief Officer(s):
Wayne Dillon, Executive Director
wdillon@hdco.on.ca
Awards:
• Barrie Davis Memorial Award
Awarded to a volunteer who has contributed to the development of amateur hockey in Ontario in an outstanding way for at least 10 years
Publications:
• Ice Times [a publication of the Hockey Development Centre for Ontario]
Type: Magazine
Profile: Profiles & updates on people, programs & events from the ten amateur hockey associations in Ontario

Hockey Eastern Ontario (HEO)
813 Shefford Rd., Ottawa ON K1J 8H9

Canadian Associations / Hockey Manitoba

Tel: 613-224-7686; Fax: 613-224-6079
info@hockeyeasternontario.ca
www.hockeyeasternontario.ca
www.facebook.com/HockeyEasternOntario
twitter.com/HEOhockey
www.youtube.com/channel/UClc6D9wLXpCkGsA2ETjpkhg
Overview: A medium-sized provincial organization founded in 1920 overseen by Hockey Canada
Mission: To act as the governing body of amateur hockey in Eastern Ontario; To foster, improve, & encourage amateur hockey through leadership
Staff Member(s): 4
Chief Officer(s):
Debbie Rambeau, Executive Director, 613-224-7686 Ext. 201
drambeau@hockeyeasternontario.ca

Hockey l'Alberta See Hockey Alberta

Hockey Manitoba
145 Pacific Ave., Winnipeg MB R3B 2Z6
Tel: 204-925-5755; Fax: 204-925-5761
info@hockeymanitoba.ca
www.hockeymanitoba.ca
www.facebook.com/hockeymanitoba
twitter.com/hockeymanitoba
www.youtube.com/hockeymanitoba;
www.instagram.com/hockeymanitoba
Also Known As: Manitoba Amateur Hockey Association
Overview: A medium-sized provincial organization founded in 1914 overseen by Hockey Canada
Mission: To foster, develop, & promote amateur hockey throughout Manitoba; To encourage fair play; To secure the enforcement of rules as adopted by by the assosication; To conduct games between member clubs to determine provincial champions
Staff Member(s): 15
Membership: 30,000; *Committees:* Officials Development; Athlete Development
Activities: Administering clinics & skills camps; Collaborating in development programs for players, coaches & officials
Chief Officer(s):
Peter Woods, Executive Director, 204-925-5757
peter@hockeymanitoba.ca
Bernie Reichardt, Director, Hockey Development, 204-925-5759
bernie@hockeymanitoba.ca
Awards:
• Hockey Manitoba Scholarship Program
Eligibility: Student athletes who are Hockey Manitoba members & attending post-secondary education in Canada *Contact:* Scott Furman, Director, Business Operations, E-mail: scott@hockeymanitoba.ca, Phone: 204-925-5756
• Todd Davison Memorial Scholarship
Eligibility: A Hockey Manitoba member who has risen above personal challenges in life, shows a diligent approach to the game of hockey, displays leadership skills, & is enrolling in post-secondary education on a full- or part-time basis; *Amount:* $1,000 *Contact:* Scott Furman, Director, Business Operations, E-mail: scott@hockeymanitoba.ca, Phone: 204-925-5756
• Trudy Galloway Memorial Bursary
Eligibility: A Hockey Manitoba certified official who is graduating from high school & is registered in an approved post-secondary facility; eligible nominees must maintain an 80% average & be involved with their community; *Amount:* $750 *Contact:* Scott Furman, Director, Business Operations, E-mail: scott@hockeymanitoba.ca, Phone: 204-925-5756
• Jerry Kruk Memorial Hockey Scholarship
Eligibility: A Hockey Manitoba member who is graduating from high school & is proceeding to a post-secondary institution on a full- or part-time basis, who demonstrates a commitment to academic achievement, & displays strong leadership skills in the sport of hockey & in the community at large; *Amount:* $1,000 *Contact:* Scott Furman, Director, Business Operations, E-mail: scott@hockeymanitoba.ca, Phone: 204-925-5756
• Volunteer of the Month Award
Contact: Scott Furman, Director, Business Operations, E-mail: scott@hockeymanitoba.ca, Phone: 204-925-5756
• Volunteer of the Year Award
Contact: Scott Furman, Director, Business Operations, E-mail: scott@hockeymanitoba.ca, Phone: 204-925-5756
• Grassroots Coaching Award
Eligibility: An active coach registered with Hockey Manitoba who is certified to coach at the grassroots level, displays respect for fair play, demonstrates concern for the full development of the player athlete, & shows respect for players, parents, officials & opponents *Contact:* Scott Furman, Director, Business

Operations, E-mail: scott@hockeymanitoba.ca, Phone: 204-925-5756

Hockey New Brunswick (HNB) / Hockey Nouveau-Brunswick
PO Box 456, 861 Woodstock Rd., Fredericton NB E3B 4Z9
Tel: 506-453-0089; Fax: 506-453-0868
www.hnb.ca
www.facebook.com/148777865135246
twitter.com/HockeyNB
Previous Name: New Brunswick Amateur Hockey Association
Overview: A medium-sized provincial organization founded in 1968 overseen by Hockey Canada
Mission: To act as the governing body for hockey in New Brunswick
Staff Member(s): 5; 120 volunteer(s)
Chief Officer(s):
Nic Jansen, Executive Director, 506-453-0866
njansen@hnb.ca

Hockey Newfoundland & Labrador (NLHA) / Association de hockey de Terre-Neuve et Labrador
PO Box 176, 32 Queensway, Grand Falls-Windsor NL A2A 2J4
Tel: 709-489-5512; Fax: 709-489-2273
office@hockeynl.ca
www.hockeynl.ca
twitter.com/Hkynl
Overview: A medium-sized provincial organization founded in 1935 overseen by Hockey Canada
Mission: To act as the governing body for hockey in Newfoundland & Labrador; To foster & encourage positive player experiences through development & leadership
Member of: Hockey Canada
Staff Member(s): 2
Chief Officer(s):
Craig Tulk, Executive Director
ctulk@hockeynl.ca

Hockey North
c/o Kyle Kugler, Executive Director, Hockey North, 237 Borden Dr., Yellowknife NT X1A 3R2
Tel: 867-446-8890
www.hockeynorth.ca
Overview: A small provincial organization overseen by Hockey Canada
Mission: To govern & register all amateur hockey programs in the Northwest Territories & Nunavut Territory
Chief Officer(s):
Kyle Kugler, Executive Director
kylek@hockeynorth.ca

Hockey Northwestern Ontario (HNO)
#301, 214 Red River Rd., Thunder Bay ON P7B 1A6
Tel: 807-623-1542; Fax: 807-623-0037
info@hockeyhno.com
www.hockeyhno.com
www.facebook.com/HNOHockey
twitter.com/HNOHockey
Previous Name: Thunder Bay Amateur Hockey Association
Overview: A small provincial organization overseen by Hockey Canada
Mission: To encourage & improve the sport of amateur hockey throughout Northwestern Ontario
Member of: Hockey Canada
Staff Member(s): 3
Chief Officer(s):
Trevor Hosanna, Executive Director, 807-623-1542 Ext. 2
thosanna@hockeyhno.com

Hockey Nouveau-Brunswick See Hockey New Brunswick

Hockey Nova Scotia
#17, 7 Mellor Ave., Dartmouth NS B3B 0E8
Tel: 902-454-9400; Fax: 902-454-3883
www.hockeynovascotia.ca
www.facebook.com/hockeynovascotia
twitter.com/HockeyNS
www.youtube.com/channel/UC8gbE0o_HAAQ6bj2c8S6kdg
Previous Name: Nova Scotia Hockey Association
Overview: A medium-sized provincial organization founded in 1974 overseen by Hockey Canada
Mission: To act as the governing body for hockey in Nova Scotia; To encourage positive player experiences through development, resources, & leadership
Member of: Hockey Canada
Staff Member(s): 8
Membership: 20,000

Chief Officer(s):
Darren Cossar, Executive Director
dcossar@hockeynovascotia.ca

Hockey PEI
PO Box 302, #209, 40 Enman Cres., Charlottetown PE C1E 1E6
Tel: 902-368-4334; Fax: 902-368-4337
info@hockeypei.com
hockeypei.com
twitter.com/hockeypei
Previous Name: Prince Edward Island Hockey Association
Overview: A medium-sized provincial organization founded in 1974 overseen by Hockey Canada
Mission: To act as the governing body for hockey in Prince Edward Island
Member of: Hockey Canada
Finances: *Annual Operating Budget:* $250,000-$500,000
Staff Member(s): 3; 100 volunteer(s)
Membership: 6,000
Chief Officer(s):
Rob Newson, Executive Director
rob@hockeypei.com

Hockey Québec (FQHG)
#210, 7450, boul les Galeries d'Anjou, Montréal QC H1M 3M3
Tél: 514-252-3079; Téléc: 514-252-3158
communication@hockey.qc.ca
www.hockey.qc.ca
www.facebook.com/HockeyQuebecOfficielle
twitter.com/HockeyQuebec
Nom précédent: Fédération québécoise de hockey sur glace
Aperçu: *Dimension:* grande; *Envergure:* provinciale; fondée en 1976 surveillé par Hockey Canada
Mission: Assurer l'encadrement du hockey sur glace; favoriser la promotion et le développement de la personne qui pratique le hockey
Membre de: Hockey Canada
Membre(s) du personnel: 23
Activités: La Méthode d'apprentissage de hockey sur glace; excellence; développement régional; entraîneurs et officiels; formation des administrateurs bénévoles; hockey féminin; franc jeu; sports-études; *Service de conférenciers:* Oui; *Listes de destinataires:* Oui
Membre(s) du bureau directeur:
Paul Ménard, Directeur général
pmenard@hockey.qc.ca

Hockey sur gazon Canada See Field Hockey Canada

Hockey sur gazon C-B See Field Hockey BC

Hockey Yukon
4061 - 4th Ave., Whitehorse YT Y1A 1H1
Tel: 867-393-4501
yaha@sportyukon.com
hockeyyukon.ca
Previous Name: Yukon Amateur Hockey Association
Overview: A small provincial organization
Mission: The Yukon Amateur Hockey Association is the sports governing body for amateur hockey in the Yukon.
Member of: British Columbia Amateur Hockey Association; Sport Yukon

Hola
c/o 519 Church Street Community Centre, 519 Church St., Toronto ON M4Y 2C9
Tel: 416-925-9872
latinogrouphola@gmail.com
Overview: A small local organization founded in 1991
Mission: Hola offers opportunities to socialize, runs workshops on HIV/AIDS prevention, takes part in immigration panels, holds drug and alcohol abuse seminars, and battles homophobia.
Finances: *Funding Sources:* Grants and fundraisers
Membership: 65

Holland Centre See Jeffery Hale Community Services in English

Holocaust Education Centre
Lipa Green Centre, Sherman Campus, 4600 Bathurst St., 4th Fl., Toronto ON M2R 3V2
Tel: 416-631-5689
neuberger@ujafed.org
www.holocaustcentre.com
twitter.com/Holocaust_Ed
Also Known As: Sarah & Chaim Neuberger Holocaust Education Centre
Overview: A small international organization founded in 1985

Member of: UJA Federation of Greater Toronto
Staff Member(s): 8; 150 volunteer(s)
Membership: 5,000-14,999
Activities: Providing professional aid & support groups for survivors, child survivors, & the second generation; Offering forums for discussion; Organizing conferences; *Awareness Events:* Raoul Wallenberg Day, January 17; International Holocaust Remembrance Day, January 27; Holocaust Education Week, November; *Internships:* Yes; *Speaker Service:* Yes; *Library:* Ekstein Library; Open to public by appointment
Chief Officer(s):
Carson Phillips, Ph.D, Managing Director
Rachel Libman, Manager, Public Programs
Mary Siklos, Manager, Operations
Anna Skorupsky, Librarian

Holstein Canada
PO Box 610, 20 Corporate Pl., Brantford ON N3T 5R4
Tel: 519-756-8300; *Fax:* 519-756-3502
Toll-Free: 855-756-8300
www.holstein.ca
www.facebook.com/HolsteinCanada
twitter.com/HolsteinCanada
www.instagram.com/holstein_canada
Overview: A large national organization founded in 1884
Mission: To improve the Holstein breed by ascertaining the most desirable characteristics of the breed for current & prospective conditions in Canada; To prepare, maintain & make available a genealogical record of the breed; To promote the best interests of breeders & owners of Holstein cattle
Member of: Canadian Agricultural Hall of Fame; Canadian Livestock Genetics Association; Dairy Farmers of Canada
Finances: *Funding Sources:* Service & membership fees
Staff Member(s): 90
Membership: 12,000 regular, affiliate, honorary life, & junior members; *Fees:* Schedule available
Chief Officer(s):
Ann Louise Carson, Chief Executive Officer, 519-756-8300 Ext. 240
annlouise@holstein.ca
Awards:
- Master Breeders Award Program
- Member Awards Program
- Young Leader Awards Program
- Cow of the Year Award
- Animal Awards Program
- Sire Awards
- Cow Awards
- Top LPI Females
- Top LPI Males
- Education Award
Contact: Kelly Velthuis, Coordinator, Programs, E-mail: kvelthuis@holstein.ca; Phone: 855-756-8300, ext. 288
Meetings/Conferences:
- Holstein Canada National Holstein Convention 2018, April, 2018, Québec, QC
Scope: National
Publications:
- Info Holstein [a publication of Holstein Canada]
Type: Magazine; *Frequency:* Bimonthly; *Editor:* Jennifer Kyle
Profile: Contains information & topical news for members
Alberta Branch
Alberta Holstein Association Office, RR#1, Didsbury AB T0M 0W0
Tel: 403-335-5916; *Fax:* 403-335-4751
info@albertaholstein.ca
www.albertaholstein.ca
www.facebook.com/270585993034177
www.youtube.com/user/mountainsab
Chief Officer(s):
Heidi Voegeli-Bleiker, Contact
British Columbia Branch
c/o Secretary, 847 Garnett Rd., Cobble Hill BC V0R 1L0
Tel: 250-743-8690; *Fax:* 250-743-8691
bcbranch@telus.net
www.bcholsteins.com
Chief Officer(s):
Joan Wikkerink, Secretary
Manitoba Branch
PO Box 750, Blumenort MB R0C 0H0
Tel: 204-326-6539
info@manitobaholsteins.ca
www.manitobaholsteins.ca
Chief Officer(s):

Darcy Heapy, President
dheapy@mymts.net
New Brunswick Branch
c/o Secretary, 436 Route 616, Keswick Ridge NB E6L 1S5
Tel: 506-363-2534; *Fax:* 506-363-3701
kitkat@nb.sympatico.ca
www.facebook.com/300481096665386
Chief Officer(s):
Lorraine Allen, Secretary
Nova Scotia & Newfoundland Branch
PO Box 2155, RR#1, Corner Brook NL A2H 2N2
Tel: 709-660-0434
Chief Officer(s):
Dave Simmons, President
simmons_david@hotmail.com
Ontario Branch
285 Fountain St. South, Cambridge ON N3H 1J2
Tel: 519-653-6180; *Fax:* 519-653-2129
branch@ontario.holstein.ca
www.ontario.holstein.ca
Chief Officer(s):
Jason French, General Manager
Prince Edward Island Branch
487 Frenchfort Rd., Frenchfort PE C1C 0G9
Tel: 902-368-2804; *Fax:* 902-566-4264
www.holsteinpei.com
Chief Officer(s):
Tom Robinson, President
bluediamondfarm@live.ca
Saskatchewan Branch
c/o Tricia Flaman, PO Box 40, Vibank SK S0G 4Y0
Tel: 306-762-2241
saskbranch@sasktel.net
Chief Officer(s):
Tymen Vanzessen, President
vanzessendairy@hotmail.com
Section de Québec
3955, boul Laurier ouest, Saint-Hyacinthe QC J2S 3T8
Tél: 450-778-9636; *Téléc:* 450-778-9637
info@holsteinquebec.com
www.holsteinquebec.com
www.facebook.com/holsteinqc
twitter.com/holstein_quebec
Chief Officer(s):
Valérie Tremblay, Directrice générale
tremblay@holsteinquebec.com

Holy Face Association / Association de la Sainte Face
PO Box 310, Stn. B, Montréal QC H3B 3J7
Tel: 514-747-0357; *Fax:* 514-747-9147
holyface@holyface.com
www.holyface.com
Overview: A small national charitable organization founded in 1976
Mission: The goal of this apostolate is reparation to God (Father, Son & Holy Spirit) through contemplative devotion to the Holy Face of Jesus
Finances: *Annual Operating Budget:* $250,000-$500,000; *Funding Sources:* Donations
20 volunteer(s)
Membership: 15,000-49,999
Activities: *Speaker Service:* Yes; *Library:* by appointment
Publications:
- Holy Face Association Newsletter
Type: Newsletter
- The Holy Face of Jesus Christ, Discovery, Journey, Destination [a publication of the Holy Face Association]
Type: Book

Home Business Association of the National Capital Region
See Small Business Association

Home Care Program for Metropolitan Toronto
See Toronto Community Care Access Centre

Home Child Care Association of Ontario (HCCAO)
756 Ossington Ave., Toronto ON M6G 3T9
Tel: 416-233-1506; *Fax:* 416-530-1924
info@hccao.com
www.hccao.com
Previous Name: Private Home Day Care Association of Ontario
Overview: A small provincial organization founded in 1983
Mission: To promote, develop & support home-based child care services for families through licensed agencies

Membership: 70 home child care agencies; *Fees:* Schedule available; *Member Profile:* Child care staff; educators; providers; parents; students
Chief Officer(s):
Marni Flaherty, President
mflaherty@todaysfamily.ca
Janene Parr, Secretary
jparr@ccrconnect.ca
JoAnn Gillan, Treasurer
gjoann@region.waterloo.on.ca
Publications:
- Liaison
Type: Newsletter; *Frequency:* Quarterly

Home Inspectors Association BC (HIABC)
#5, 3304 Appaloosa Rd., Kelowna BC V1V 2W5
Toll-Free: 800-610-5665
info@hiabc.ca
www.hiabc.ca
www.linkedin.com/company/2647618
www.facebook.com/HomeInspectorsAssociationBC
Overview: A small provincial organization
Mission: To protect consumers in British Columbia, through membership requirements, a Standards of Practice & Code of Ethics, & mandatory ongoing training programs for home & property inspectors
Membership: 300+; *Member Profile:* Professional home & property inspectors from all regions of British Columbia; *Committees:* Bylaws & Policies; Complaints & Ethics; Discipline; Education Presentations; Professional Insurance; Report Compliance; Training
Chief Officer(s):
Helene T. Barton, Executive Director
htbarton@hiabc.ca

Home School Legal Defence Association of Canada (HSLDA)
#32B, 980 Adelaide St. South, London ON N6E 1R3
Tel: 519-913-0318; *Fax:* 519-913-0321
info@hslda.ca
www.hslda.ca
www.facebook.com/hsldacanada
twitter.com/hsldacanada
pinterest.com/hsldacanada
Overview: A small national organization
Mission: To promote home education & protect parent educators
Staff Member(s): 8
Membership: *Fees:* $135.60 full time pastor/missionary/single parent; $162.72 regular
Chief Officer(s):
Gerald Huebner, Chair
Paul D. Faris, President & Legal Counsel

H.O.M.E. Society
31581 South Fraser Way, Abbotsford BC V2T 1T8
Tel: 604-852-7888; *Fax:* 604-852-7801
www.homesociety.com
www.facebook.com/TheHomeSociety
Also Known As: Healthy Opportunities for Meaningful Experience Society
Overview: A small local organization
Mission: To provide support for men & women who need a supportive home
Chief Officer(s):
Cam Doré, Executive Director
cam.dore@homesociety.ca
Dave Lappin, Executive Director
dave.lappin@homesociety.ca

Homeopathic College of Canada (HCC)
info@homeopathy.edu
www.homeopathy.edu
Also Known As: International Academy of Homeopathy
Overview: A small national organization founded in 1995
Mission: To maintain the highest professional standards of homeopathy; To provide international leadership in the fields of homeopathy & complementary medicine; To promote homeopathy as an alternative & complement within the health care system; To provide treatment effectively & economically within the health care system
Member of: Ontario Homeopathic Association; Homeopathic Medical Council of Canada
Finances: *Funding Sources:* Tuition
Membership: *Member Profile:* Homeopath professionals; full-time homeopathy students

Activities: *Speaker Service:* Yes; *Library:* The Homeopathic Library
Chief Officer(s):
John Crellin, M.D., Ph.D., Dean
Idoia Ania, Contact, Student Affairs

Homeopathic Medical Association Of Canada (HMAC)
2649 Islington Ave., Toronto ON M9V 2X6
info@hmac.ca
www.hmac.ca
Overview: A small national organization
Mission: To serve homeopathic practitioners across Canada; To uphold the code of ethics
Membership: *Fees:* $200 professionals; $75 students; *Member Profile:* Homeopathic doctors throughout Canada; Homeopathic students
Activities: Maintaining the National Homeopathic Doctor's Resgistry; Offering educational seminars & practice management sessions
Chief Officer(s):
Gangadhar Hanchate, President, 647-668-3567
grao_hanchate@yahoo.com
Publications:
• Homeopathic Medical Council of Canada Journal
Type: Journal
Profile: Featuring a list of homeopathic doctors who are members of the council

Homestead Christian Care
249 Caroline St. South, #A, Hamilton ON L8P 3L6
Tel: 905-529-0454; *Fax:* 905-529-0355
Toll-Free: 866-529-0454
info@hscc.ca
homesteadchristiancare.ca
www.facebook.com/homesteadchristiancare
Overview: A small local charitable organization founded in 1974
Mission: To assist those with mental illness, through affordable housing & rehabilitation services, in order to help them reach personal recovery goals
Finances: *Funding Sources:* Donations; Funding through churches
Chief Officer(s):
Jeffrey Neven, Executive Director

Hominum
2197 261 St., Maple Ridge BC V2W 2A5
www.hominum.ca
Overview: A small local organization founded in 1982
Mission: To serve as support group for gay men presently or previously married
Membership: 50; *Fees:* $15; *Member Profile:* Married men coming out as gay seeking support

Honey Harbour/Port Severn District Chamber of Commerce
See Southeast Georgian Bay Chamber of Commerce

Hong Fook Mental Health Association (HFMHA)
#201, 3320 Midland Ave., Toronto ON M1V 5E6
Tel: 416-493-4242; *Fax:* 416-493-2214
www.hongfook.ca
Overview: A small local charitable organization founded in 1982 overseen by Ontario Council of Agencies Serving Immigrants
Mission: To empower Canadians, including those of Cambodian, Chinese, Korean & Vietnamese, & other Asian communities, who reside within the Greater Toronto Area; to obtain ethno-racial equity in the mental health system & to achieve optimal mental health status through activities of direct services, promotion & prevention & system advocacy.
Affiliation(s): Ontario Federation of Community Mental Health & Addiction Programs; Canadian Mental Health Association
Finances: *Annual Operating Budget:* $3 Million-$5 Million; *Funding Sources:* Ministry of Health & Long-Term Care; United Way; fundraising
432 volunteer(s)
Membership: *Fees:* $5 student; $10 individual; $250 silver life membership; $1,000 gold membership
Activities: Case management & supportive housing services; family initiatives; prevention & promotion; volunteer development; community outreach; collaborative efforts with other mental health providers; ESL classes; *Library:* Resource Centre; by appointment
Chief Officer(s):
Bonnie Wong, Executive Director
   Downton Branch
   130 Dundas St. West, 3rd Fl., Toronto ON M5G 1C3
   Tel: 416-493-4242; *Fax:* 416-595-6332

Hong Kong-Canada Business Association (HKCBA) / L'Association commerciale Hong Kong-Canada
#600, 1285 West Broadway, Vancouver BC V6H 3X8
Tel: 604-684-2410; *Fax:* 604-684-6208
nationaled@hkcba.com
national.hkcba.com
Overview: A medium-sized international organization founded in 1984
Mission: To encourage & promote trade & commercial activities across a broad range of industries between Canada & Hong Kong, & through Hong Kong to China & the Asia Pacific Region.
Member of: Federation of Hong Kong Business Associations Worldwide
Affiliation(s): Hong Kong Trade Development Council; Hong Kong Economic & Trade Office, HKSAR Government; Hong Kong Tourism Board; Invest HK; Canadian Chamber of Commerce in Hong Kong; Federation of Hong Kong Business Associations Worldwide; Canadian Consulate General in Hong Kong; Cathay Pacific Airways
Finances: *Funding Sources:* Membership dues
Staff Member(s): 1
Membership: 1,300 corporate
Activities: *Internships:* Yes; *Speaker Service:* Yes
Chief Officer(s):
Wayne Berg, National Chair
Joyce Chung, Executive Director
vancouver@hkcba.com
   Atlantic Office
   PO Box 29086, 7001 Mumford Rd., Halifax NS B3L 4T8
   www.hkcba.com/halifax
   Mission: To help its members conduct business between Canada and Hong Kong and encourage Canadian companies to utilize Hong Kong as their business "Smart Link"- to China and the rest of the world.
   Chief Officer(s):
   Bill Bu, President
   Calgary Section Office
   PO Box 22308, Stn. Bankers Hall, Calgary AB T2P 4J1
   admin@calgaryhkcba.com
   calgaryhkcba.com
   Mission: To help its members conduct business between Canada and Hong Kong and encourage Canadian companies to utilize Hong Kong as their business "Smart Link"- to China and the rest of the world
   Chief Officer(s):
   Bonita Wong, President
   Edmonton Section Office
   #90, 11215 Jasper Ave., Edmonton AB T5K 0L5
   hkcba.edmonton@gmail.com
   www.edmontonhkcba.com
   www.facebook.com/331342930211327
   twitter.com/HKCBAEdmonton
   Mission: To help its members conduct business between Canada and Hong Kong and encourage Canadian companies to utilize Hong Kong as their business "Smart Link"- to China and the rest of the world.
   Chief Officer(s):
   David Tam, President
   Monica Barclay, Interim Executive Director
   London Section Office
   c/o Q Integrators, 42 Chalfont Cres., London ON N6H 4Y4
   Tel: 519-473-6227; *Fax:* 519-657-4499
   ctse@qint.com
   www.hkcba.com/london
   Mission: To help its members conduct business between Canada and Hong Kong and encourage Canadian companies to utilize Hong Kong as their business "Smart Link"- to China and the rest of the world. It also facilitates business relationships amongst its membership in Canada.
   Montréal Section Office
   #200, 1010, rue Gauchetière ouest, Montréal QC H3B 2N2
   Tel: 514-931-6333; *Fax:* 450-227-9164
   montreal@hkcba.com
   montreal.hkcba.com
   www.linkedin.com/profile/view?id=167781838
   www.facebook.com/239670779452083
   Mission: To help its members conduct business between Canada and Hong Kong and encourage Canadian companies to utilize Hong Kong as their business "Smart Link"- to China and the rest of the world.
   Chief Officer(s):
   Geoffrey Bush, Executive Director
   Ottawa Section Office
   c/o Virginia Lock, 131 Queen St., Ottawa ON K1P 0A1
   Fax: 613-238-3553
   hkcbaottawa@hkcba.com
   national.hkcba.com/ottawa.html
   Mission: To help its members conduct business between Canada and Hong Kong and encourage Canadian companies to utilize Hong Kong as their business "Smart Link"- to China and the rest of the world.
   Chief Officer(s):
   Ruby Williams, President
   Saskatchewan Section Office
   c/o Saskatchewan Trade & Export Partnership, PO Box 1787, Regina SK S4P 3C6
   Tel: 306-787-1550; *Fax:* 306-787-6666
   www.hkcba.com/saskatchewan
   Mission: To help its members conduct business between Canada and Hong Kong and encourage Canadian companies to utilize Hong Kong as their business "Smart Link"- to China and the rest of the world. It also facilitates business relationships amongst its membership in Canada.
   Chief Officer(s):
   John Treleaven, Representative
   jtreleaven@sasktrade.sk.ca
   Toronto Section Office
   9 Temperance St., 2nd Fl., Toronto ON M5H 1Y6
   Tel: 416-366-2642; *Fax:* 416-366-1569
   toronto@hkcba.com
   www.toronto.hkcba.com
   www.facebook.com/HKCBAToronto
   twitter.com/HKCBATO
   Mission: To help its members conduct business between Canada and Hong Kong and encourage Canadian companies to utilize Hong Kong as their business "Smart Link"- to China and the rest of the world. It also facilitates business relationships amongst its membership in Canada.
   Chief Officer(s):
   Robert Brown, Executive Director
   bob@hkcba.com
   Vancouver Section Office
   #600, 1285 West Broadway, Vancouver BC V6H 3X8
   Tel: 604-684-2410; *Fax:* 604-684-6208
   vancouver@hkcba.com
   vancouver.hkcba.com
   www.linkedin.com/groups?gid=2644089
   twitter.com/HKCBA
   www.youtube.com/user/hkcbavancouver
   Mission: To help its members conduct business between Canada and Hong Kong and encourage Canadian companies to utilize Hong Kong as their business "Smart Link"- to China and the rest of the world. It also facilitates business relationships amongst its membership in Canada.
   Chief Officer(s):
   Carmen Lee, Executive Director
   Winnipeg Section Office
   c/o 201 Alexander Ave., Winnipeg MB R3B 3C1
   Tel: 613-789-8388
   hkcba-winnipeg@mts.net
   national.hkcba.com/Winnipeg_Section_Home.html
   Mission: To help its members conduct business between Canada and Hong Kong and encourage Canadian companies to utilize Hong Kong as their business "Smart Link"- to China and the rest of the world.
   Chief Officer(s):
   Dave Speirs, President

Hope & District Chamber of Commerce
PO Box 588, 519 - 6 Ave., #J, Hope BC V0X 1L0
Tel: 604-249-1246
info@hopechamber.net
hopechamber.net
www.facebook.com/HopeChamberofCommerce
Overview: A small local organization founded in 1923
Mission: To improve & promote trade, economic, civic & social welfare of Hope & the scenic Fraser Canyon
Member of: BC Chamber of Commerce; Canadian Chamber of Commerce; Vancouver Coast & Mountains Tourism Association
Finances: *Funding Sources:* Provincial government; District of Hope; fundraising; membership dues; retail sales
Membership: 100+; *Fees:* Schedule available; *Member Profile:* Business, organization or individual wishing to improve or promote trade, economic, civic & social welfare in Hope & the Fraser Canyon
Activities: Hope Business Info. Centre & Visitor Info. Centre; *Awareness Events:* Chamber of Commerce Week, Feb.; *Library:* Not open to public
Chief Officer(s):

Stephen Au-Yeung, President

Hope Air / Vols d'espoir
#207, 124 Merton St., Toronto ON M4S 2Z2
Tel: 416-222-6335; *Fax:* 416-222-6930
Toll-Free: 877-346-4673
mail@hopeair.ca
www.hopeair.ca
www.linkedin.com/company-beta/1222696
www.facebook.com/hopeair
twitter.com/Hope_Air
www.youtube.com/user/HopeAirHealth#p/a
Previous Name: Mission Air Transportation Network
Overview: A small national charitable organization founded in 1986
Mission: To provide free air transportation to Canadians in financial need who must travel between their own communities & recognized facilities for medical care
Finances: *Annual Operating Budget:* $250,000-$500,000; *Funding Sources:* Corporate; private donations; government
Staff Member(s): 6; 30 volunteer(s)
Membership: 1-99; *Committees:* Air Coordination; Funding; Finance; Office Administrations; Planning; Public Relations
Activities: Providings airfare for those in need of medical assitance
Chief Officer(s):
Doug Keller-Hobson, Executive Director, 416-222-6335 Ext. 228
dkeller-hobson@hopeair.ca

Hope Association for Community Living *See* Tillicum Centre - Hope Association for Community Living

Hope Food Bank
PO Box 74, Hope BC V0X 1L0
Tel: 604-869-2466; *Fax:* 604-869-3317
info@hopecommunityservices.com
www.hopecommunityservices.com
Also Known As: Hope Community Services
Overview: A small local organization founded in 1979 overseen by Food Banks British Columbia
Mission: The food bank is run by Hope Community Services which offers a range of social services to seniors, children, youth, & families in the Hope & Fraser Canyon region of BC. The organization also operates a volunteer bureau, thrift store, emergency shelter, emergency social services, drug & alcohol addiction programs.
Member of: Food Banks British Columbia; Food Banks Canada
Finances: *Funding Sources:* Thrift store sales; private donations

Hope for the Nations
#222, 1889 Springfield Rd., Kelowna BC V1Y 5V5
Tel: 250-712-2007; *Fax:* 250-862-2942
community@hopeforthenations.com
www.hopeforthenations.com
www.linkedin.com/company/hope-for-the-nations
www.facebook.com/thisishopeforthenations
twitter.com/nations4hope
Overview: A medium-sized international charitable organization founded in 1994
Mission: An international organization established to help address the needs of exploited children around the world; participates in community development, poverty reduction & gender equity in areas where these issues affect children
Affiliation(s): HFTN Children's Charity (UK), HFTN USA (Western Division, AZ)
Finances: *Funding Sources:* Donations; funds from other charities
Staff Member(s): 5
Chief Officer(s):
Ralph Bromley, President
Patrick Elaschuk, Executive Director
patrick@hopeforthenations.com

Hope for Wildlife Society
5909 Hwy. 207, Seaforth NS B0J 1N0
Tel: 902-452-3339; *Crisis Hot-Line:* 902-407-9453
info@hopeforwildlife.net
www.hopeforwildlife.net
www.facebook.com/hopeforwildlife
twitter.com/hopeforwildlife
Overview: A small provincial organization founded in 1997
Mission: Specializing in the care, treatment and rehabilitation of injured or orphaned native fur bearing mammals, sea birds and songbirds both indigenous to the Nova Scotia area as well as non-indigenous species and pets.
70 volunteer(s)
Chief Officer(s):

Hope Swinimer, Founder & Director

HOPE International Development Agency
214 Sixth St., New Westminster BC V3L 3A2
Tel: 604-525-5481; *Fax:* 604-525-3471
Toll-Free: 866-525-4673
hope@hope-international.com
www.hope-international.com
twitter.com/HOPEInt
Overview: A large international charitable organization founded in 1975
Mission: To help the poverty-stricken section of Third World people to attain the basic necessities of life; To inform Canadians regarding issues related to the developing world & HOPE's activities; To provide alternative technological & educational support to people in developing countries where environmental, economic, &/or social circumstances have interfered with the ability of local communities to sustain themselves by using traditional methods. Other offices in Afghanistan, Australia, Cambodia, Ethiopia, Japan, Myanmar, New Zealand, the U.K., & the U.S.
Member of: Canadian Council of Christian Charities
Finances: *Annual Operating Budget:* Greater than $5 Million; *Funding Sources:* Government; Coalitions; Donations
Staff Member(s): 10; 50 volunteer(s)
Activities: *Internships:* Yes; *Speaker Service:* Yes
Chief Officer(s):
Brian Cannon, Interim Executive Director, 604-525-5481 Ext. 117
brianc@hope-international.com
Publications:
• HOPE International Development Agency Annual Report
Type: Report; *Frequency:* Annual

Hope Studies Central
11032 - 89 Ave., Edmonton AB T6G 0Z6
Tel: 780-492-5897; *Fax:* 780-492-1318
www.ualberta.ca/hope/
www.youtube.com/user/HopeStudiesCentral
Overview: A small provincial charitable organization
Mission: To increase understanding of the role of hope in human life so that people can be intentional in using hope to enhance quality of life
Chief Officer(s):
Denise Larsen, Team Lead
denise.larsen@ualberta.ca

Hôpital général juif fondation *See* Jewish General Hospital Foundation

Horatio Alger Association of Canada / Association Horatio Alger du Canada
#1010, 1410 Stanley St., Montréal QC H3A 1P8
Toll-Free: 855-753-9565
www.horatioalger.ca
www.facebook.com/HoratioAlgerCA
twitter.com/horatioalgerca
www.instagram.com/horatioalgerassociation
Overview: A large national charitable organization founded in 2009
Mission: To honour the achievements of Canadians who have succeeded despite adversity; To encourage youth to pursue their dreams through higher education; To provide scholarship assistance to young Canadians; To promote the values espoused in Canadian author Horatio Alger, Jr.'s books
Finances: *Funding Sources:* Donations; Children's Aid Foundation; The Forum for Young Canadians; The Learning Partnership; Pathways to Education Canada
Membership: *Member Profile:* Recipients of the International Horatio Alger Award
Activities: Awarding scholarships to deserving Canadian youth
Chief Officer(s):
Prem Watsa, President
Awards:
• National Entrepreunerial Scholarships, Horatio Alger Scholarship Program
5 scholarships are available to eligible students *Eligibility:* Students who are enrolled full time in their final year of high school with plans to enter a post-secondary institution immediately following graduation; eligible students demonstrate critical financial need, display integrity & perseverance in overcoming adversity, & maintain a minimum grade percentage of 65 *Deadline:* October 25; *Amount:* $10,000
• Canadian Scholarships, Horatio Alger Scholarship Program
80 scholarships are available to eligible students *Eligibility:* Students who are enrolled full time in their final year of high school with plans to enter a post-secondary institution immediately following graduation; eligible students must demonstrate critical financial need; display integrity & perseverance in overcoming adversity, & maintain a minimum grade percentage of 65 *Deadline:* October 25; *Amount:* $5,000
• The Fairfax Financial Holdings Entrance Awards, Horatio Alger Scholarship Program
45 scholarships are available to eligible students *Eligibility:* Students who plan to enroll full-time at one of 21 eligible post-secondary institutions, demonstrate critical financial need, & maintain a minimum grade percentage of 80
• International Horatio Alger Awards, Horatio Alger Awards
Eligibility: Potential winners must have overcome humble beginnings or adversity to achieve success; they must also have strong philanthropic commitments & a willingness to lead Canadian youth by example while honouring a lifelong membership to the Association

Horizon Achievement Centre
780 Upper Prince St., Sydney NS B1P 5N6
Tel: 902-539-8553; *Fax:* 902-567-0415
www.horizon-ns.ca
www.facebook.com/HorizonAchievement
Overview: A small local charitable organization founded in 1984
Mission: Providing services & employment opportunities to people with disabilities
Member of: DIRECTIONS Council for Vocational Services Society
Activities: Services include: banquets, catering, baking, mail services & printing, assembly & promotions, & job placements

Horizons of Friendship (HOF)
PO Box 402, 50 Covert St., Cobourg ON K9A 4L1
Tel: 905-372-5483; *Fax:* 905-372-7095
Toll-Free: 888-729-9928
info@horizons.ca
www.horizons.ca
www.facebook.com/horizonsoffriendship
twitter.com/HorizonsFriends
www.youtube.com/user/HorizonsofFriendship
Also Known As: Horizons
Previous Name: Help Honduras Foundation
Overview: A medium-sized international charitable organization founded in 1973
Mission: To address the root causes of poverty & injustice through the cooperation of people from the south & north; To support Central American & Mexican partner organizations which undertake local initiatives; To raise awareness in Canada of global issues; To work with Canadian organizations at the local & national levels
Member of: Canadian Council for International Cooperation
Affiliation(s): Americas Policy Group
Finances: *Annual Operating Budget:* $500,000-$1.5 Million; *Funding Sources:* Private donations; government grants
Staff Member(s): 9; 80 volunteer(s)
Membership: *Committees:* Executive; Nominating
Activities: 2 thrift shops; Special Events; Education Sessions; *Awareness Events:* International Development Week, Feb.; Writers & Friends, November; *Speaker Service:* Yes; *Rents Mailing List:* Yes; *Library:* Open to public
Chief Officer(s):
Patricia Rebolledo, Executive Director

Hornby Island Food Bank
3130 Cannon Rd., Hornby Island BC V0R 1Z0
Tel: 250-335-1629
hornby@valleylinks.net
Overview: A small local organization overseen by Food Banks British Columbia
Mission: The agency provides food to the needy in the local area.
Member of: Food Banks British Columbia
Chief Officer(s):
Susan Crowe, Contact
crosusan@yahoo.ca

Hors sentiers
10229, rue Chambord, Montréal QC H2C 2R3
Tél: 450-433-7508
sentiers@hotmail.ca
www.algi.qc.ca/asso/horssentiers/
Également appelé: Groupe de plein air Hors sentiers
Aperçu: *Dimension:* petite; *Envergure:* locale
Mission: Groupe de plein air
Affiliation(s): Équipe Montréal
Membre: *Montant de la cotisation:* 15$

Horse Council British Columbia (HCBC)
27336 Fraser Hwy., Aldergrove BC V4W 3N5
Tel: 604-856-4304; Fax: 604-856-4302
Toll-Free: 800-345-8055
reception@hcbc.ca
www.hcbc.ca
www.linkedin.com/company/horse-council-bc
www.facebook.com/HorseCouncil
twitter.com/horsecounciIbc
www.youtube.com/user/HorseCouncilBC/
Overview: A medium-sized provincial organization founded in 1980
Mission: To represent members & work on behalf of their equine interests in British Columbia; To preserve equestrian use of public lands; To foster & promote participation in equine activities; To ensure the well-being of horses
Member of: Equestrian Canada
Finances: *Funding Sources:* Membership dues; Province of British Columbia
Staff Member(s): 10; 20 volunteer(s)
Membership: 24,000+; *Fees:* $57.75; *Member Profile:* Clubs; Individuals & families; Businesses; Affiliates
Activities: Collaborating with individuals, professionals, industry, businesses, & governments to improve education, safety, & communication; Representing the industry in areas of sport, recreation, agriculture, & industry; Providing education; Granting funds & supporting clubs; Presenting awards; *Awareness Events:* Horse Week, June *Library:* Horse Council BC Library
Chief Officer(s):
Lisa Laycock, Executive Director
administration@hcbc.ca
Liz Saunders, President, 250-359-7293
l.saunders@hcbc.ca
Lisa Mander, Secretary, 604-719-1989
l.mander@hcbc.ca
Carolyn Farris, Treasurer, 250-546-6083
c.farris@hcbc.ca
Awards:
• Horse Council BC Post Secondary Scholarships
Eligibility: Horse Council BC members in good standing, who are a BC graduate from grade 12 and entering into a accredited College or University Study program. *Deadline:* June 30; *Amount:* $1,000.00 (5)
Publications:
• BC's Equine Lifestyles [a publication of Horse Council British Columbia]
Type: Magazine; *Frequency:* Biannually
Profile: Information about HCBC programs, events, & members, as well as industry & horse news
• Horse Council British Columbia Newsletter
Type: Newsletter

Horse Industry Association of Alberta (HIAA)
97 East Lake Ramp NE, Airdrie AB T4A 0C3
Tel: 403-420-5949; Fax: 403-948-2069
www.albertahorseindustry.ca
Overview: A small provincial organization founded in 1982
Mission: To act as a unified voice for the Alberta horse industry to foster a growing & profitable industry
Activities: Advocating for the horse industry in Alberta; Engaging in research; Presenting educational seminars, such as "Getting Started with Horses"
Chief Officer(s):
Peter Fraser, President
Darrell Dalton, Vice-President
Doug Milligan, Secretary
Bruce Roy, Treasurer
Teresa van Bryce, Manager
tvanbryce@albertahorseindustry.ca
Heather Mitchell-Matheson, Program Assistant
heathermm@albertahorseindustry.ca
Awards:
• Alberta Horse Industry Distinguished Service Award
In recognition of an individual who has provided a significant contribution toward the development of the horse industry in Alberta *Contact:* Teresa van Bryce, tvanbryce@albertahorseindustry.ca
Meetings/Conferences:
• Annual Alberta Horse Conference 2019, 2019
Scope: Provincial
Description: Internationally recognized speakers of interest to horse breeders, owners, & professionals
Publications:
• HIAA eNews
Type: Newsletter; *Frequency:* Monthly
Profile: Information about the association & horses, plus upcoming events

Horse Trials New Brunswick
c/o Suzanne Stevenson, 16 Gallaway Dr., Lakeside NB E5N 0K9
Fax: 506-696-4403
info@htnb.org
www.htnb.org
Overview: A small provincial organization
Affiliation(s): Horse Trials Canada
Finances: *Annual Operating Budget:* Less than $50,000; *Funding Sources:* Provincial government; membership fees
Membership: 35; *Fees:* $10
Chief Officer(s):
Lori Leach, President

Horse Trials Nova Scotia (HTNS)
c/o Pam Macintosh, 53 Normandy Ave., Truro NS B2N 3J6
Tel: 902-893-2042
www.htns.org
www.facebook.com/groups/290523457701524
Overview: A small provincial organization
Mission: To foster & encourage safe & fun enjoyment of the sport of Horse Trials (eventing) through regular training & education of riders, coaches, horses & officials
Member of: Canadian Equestrian Federation
Affiliation(s): Horse Trials Canada; Nova Scotia Equestrian Federation
Finances: *Annual Operating Budget:* Less than $50,000
Staff Member(s): 7
Membership: 1-99; *Fees:* $25 senior; $20 junior; $45 family; $10 associate; *Committees:* Athlete Development; Coaching; Competitions; Officials & Technical Delegate; Crosss Country Course Advisors Panel; Eventing Rules
Activities: Clinics (lessons); course design seminars; competitions; booth & brochures; seminars
Chief Officer(s):
Pam Macintosh, President
pmacintosh@bellaliant.net

Horseshoe Canada
NS
Tel: 902-852-3231
www.horseshoecanada.ca
www.facebook.com/Horseshoe-Canada-Association-361777939646
Overview: A medium-sized national organization founded in 1979
Mission: To promote & foster the sport of horseshoe pitching in Canada.
Membership: 10 member associations with 3,500 individual members
Activities: *Awareness Events:* Canadian Horseshoe Pitching Championship
Chief Officer(s):
Jason Rideout, President
jrideout.tp@gmail.com

Horseshoe New Brunswick
c/o Jason Rideout, President, 14 Nicholas Dr., Old Ridge NB E3L 4Y6
Tel: 506-467-9100
Other Communication: Alt. Phone: 506-467-1129
www.horseshoenb.com
www.facebook.com/HorseshoeNB
twitter.com/SSHPC
Overview: A small provincial organization overseen by Horseshoe Canada
Mission: To promote the sport of horseshoe pitching in New Brunswick.
Member of: Horseshoe Canada
Chief Officer(s):
Jason Rideout, President
jrideout.tp@gmail.com

Horseshoe Ontario
c/o Terrie Singbeil, 103 John St. East, Waterloo ON N2J 1G2
www.horseshoeontario.com
Overview: A small provincial organization overseen by Horseshoe Canada
Mission: To promote the sport of horseshoe pitching in Ontario.
Member of: Horseshoe Canada
Membership: 450; *Fees:* $25 regular; $1 junior
Chief Officer(s):
Terrie Slingbeil, Contact
tsingbeil@rogers.com

Horseshoe Saskatchewan Inc.
PO Box 29029, Saskatoon SK S7N 4Y2
horseshoesask@sasktel.net
www.horseshoesask.ca
Overview: A small provincial organization founded in 1973 overseen by Horseshoe Canada
Mission: Clubs in this horseshoe-pitching association represent areas in Saskatchewan, Alberta & Manitoba.
Member of: Horseshoe Canada
Finances: *Annual Operating Budget:* Less than $50,000; *Funding Sources:* Raffles; merchandise sales; Saskatchewan Lotteries
Staff Member(s): 2; 30 volunteer(s)
Membership: 13 clubs
Activities: Annual Western Classics Tournament
Chief Officer(s):
Tammy Christensen, President, 306-565-1409
Denise Squires, Executive Coordinator, 306-374-8233

Horticulture Nova Scotia (HORT NS)
Kentville Agricultural Centre, 32 Main St., Kentville NS B4N 1J5
Tel: 902-678-9335; Fax: 902-678-1280
info@horticulturens.ca
www.horticulturens.ca
Previous Name: Vegetable & Potato Producers' Association of Nova Scotia
Merged from: Vegetables NS and Berries NS
Overview: A small provincial organization founded in 1998
Mission: To enhance collaborative efforts among members which will strengthen & provide leadership to the horticultural industry
Affiliation(s): Nova Scotia Potato Marketing Board
Finances: *Funding Sources:* Membership fees
Staff Member(s): 2
Membership: *Fees:* Schedule available; *Member Profile:* Vegetable & berry growers; agribusiness
Activities: Administers NS Potato Marketing Board
Chief Officer(s):
Marlene Huntley, Executive Director
Marlene@horticulturens.ca
Mark Sawler, President
Meetings/Conferences:
• Scotia Horticultural Congress 2018, 2018, NS
Scope: Provincial

Hospice & Palliative Care Manitoba *See* Palliative Manitoba

Hospice Niagara
#2, 403 Ontario St., St Catharines ON L2N 1L5
Tel: 905-984-8766; Fax: 905-984-8242
info@hospiceniagara.ca
www.hospiceniagara.ca
www.facebook.com/hospiceniagara1
twitter.com/HospiceNiagara
Overview: A small local charitable organization founded in 1993
Mission: To improve the quality of life for individuals with a life-limiting, progressive illness
Member of: Hospice Palliative Care Ontario
Finances: *Annual Operating Budget:* $1.5 Million-$3 Million; *Funding Sources:* Provincial funding; Donations; Fundraising
Staff Member(s): 50; 400 volunteer(s)
Activities: Providing information on palliative care; Maintaining a lending library; Offering a speaker's bureau to educate the community; Offering bereavement support to children, adolescents, & adults; *Internships:* Yes; *Speaker Service:* Yes; *Library*
Chief Officer(s):
Carol Nagy, Executive Director, 905-984-8766 Ext. 225
cnagy@hospiceniagara.ca

Hospice of Waterloo Region
298 Lawrence Ave., Kitchener ON N2M 1Y4
Tel: 519-743-4114; Fax: 519-743-7021
hospice@hospicewaterloo.ca
www.hospicewaterloo.ca
www.facebook.com/hospicewaterloo
twitter.com/hospicewaterloo
www.youtube.com/channel/UCUd8GumvtdxvoGo0WGT2Fog
Overview: A small local charitable organization
Mission: To provide comfort, care & support to people affected by life-threatening illness; To offer services in hospitals, long-term care facilities or in the home
150 volunteer(s)
Chief Officer(s):
Judy Nairn, Executive Director
judy@hospicewaterloo.ca

Hospice Palliative Care Association of Prince Edward Island
c/o Hospice PEI, 5 Brighton Rd., Charlottetown PE C1A 8T6
Tel: 902-368-4498
hpca@hospicepei.ca
www.hospicepei.ca
www.facebook.com/253154211534608
Previous Name: Island Hospice Association
Overview: A medium-sized provincial organization founded in 1985
Mission: To provide care & support to the terminally ill & their families & to those who are bereaved
Member of: Canadian Hospice Palliative Care Association
Activities: *Awareness Events:* Let Their Lights Shine; Hospice Dog Walk
Chief Officer(s):
Linda Callard, Chair

Hospice Palliative Care Ontario (HPCO)
#707, 2 Carlton St., Toronto ON M5B 1J3
Tel: 416-304-1477; *Fax:* 416-304-1479
Toll-Free: 800-349-3111
info@hpco.ca
www.hpco.ca
twitter.com/hpcontario
www.youtube.com/user/hpcotube
Merged from: Hospice Association of Ontario; Ontario Palliative Care Association
Overview: A medium-sized provincial charitable organization founded in 2011
Mission: To act as a voice on issues related to the provision of quality end-of-life care for Ontarians; To advance palliative care standards of practice; To advocate for the development of hospice palliative care services in Ontario
Member of: Canadian Hospice Palliative Care Association (CHPCA)
Finances: *Funding Sources:* Donations; Fundraising
Membership: *Member Profile:* Individuals from the interdisciplinary field of hospice palliative care; Family representatives; Persons with an interest in hospice palliative care
Activities: Providing educational opportunities; Offering information; Increasing public awareness of end-of-life care; Liaising with local, regional, provincial, & national palliative care organizations; Engaging in advocacy activities; Providing networking opportunities with colleagues
Chief Officer(s):
Rick Firth, President & CEO, 416-304-1477 Ext. 24
rfirth@hpco.ca
Paula Neil, Director, Operations
pneil@hpco.ca
Michelle Colero, Manager, Development
mcolero@hpco.ca
Awards:
• Dorothy Ley Award of Excellence in Hospice Palliative Care
• The Dr. S. Lawrence Librach Award for Palliative Medicine in the Community
• Hospice Palliative Care Ontario Outstanding Philanthropist Award
• June Callwood Circle of Outstanding Volunteers
• The Richard R. Walker Visionary Award
• The Joan Lesmond Scholarship
; *Amount:* $2,000
• The Frances Montgomery Personal Support Worker Hospice Palliative Care Award
Meetings/Conferences:
• Hospice Palliative Care Ontario Annual Conference 2018, April, 2018, Sheraton Parkway Toronto North Hotel & Suites, Richmond Hill, ON
Scope: Provincial
Description: Theme: "Striving for Equity in Hospice Palliative Care"
Publications:
• Hospice Palliative Care Ontario Newsletter
Type: Newsletter
Profile: Association reports, conferences, & articles
• Ontario Palliative Care Association Annual Report
Type: Yearbook; *Frequency:* Annually

Hospital Association of PEI *See* Health Association of PEI

Hospital Auxiliaries Association of Ontario (HAAO)
#2800, 200 Front St. West, Toronto ON M5V 3L1
Tel: 416-205-1407; *Fax:* 416-205-1596
www.haao.com
www.facebook.com/193203857388754
Overview: A medium-sized provincial charitable organization founded in 1910
Mission: To advocate for community partnerships to support health care in Ontario; To promote volunteer services
Membership: *Fees:* Schedule available based on number of beds facility houses; *Member Profile:* Auxiliaries & associations in healthcare facilities throughout Ontario
Activities: Fund-raising; Providing education; Offering networking opportunities; Disseminating resource materials; Organizing conventions; *Speaker Service:* Yes
Awards:
• HAAO Student Award

Hospital Employees' Union (HEU) / Syndicat des employés d'hôpitaux
5000 North Fraser Way, Burnaby BC V5J 5M3
Tel: 604-438-5000; *Fax:* 604-739-1510
Toll-Free: 800-663-5813
info@heu.org
www.heu.org
www.facebook.com/hospitalemployeesunion
twitter.com/HospEmpUnion
www.youtube.com/user/MyHEUTube
Overview: A large provincial organization founded in 1944
Mission: To unite & associate together all employees employed in hospital, medical or related work for the purpose of securing concerted action in whatever may be regarded as conducive to their best interests; To embrace the concept of equality of treatment for all in hospital, medical or related employment, with respect to wages & job opportunities, recognizing their obligation to provide high-quality care; To defend & preserve the right of all persons to high standards of medical & hospital treatment
Member of: CUPE; Canadian & BC Health Coalitions; BC Federation of Labour
Affiliation(s): Labour Councils
Membership: 43,000; *Member Profile:* LPNS; care aids; clerical; food service workers & supervisors; technical support; trades people; laundry housekeeping; maintenance; stores; transportation
Activities: *Internships:* Yes; *Library:* Not open to public
Chief Officer(s):
Victor Elkins, President
Jennifer Whiteside, Secretary & Business Manager
Awards:
• HEU Bursaries
Eligibility: HEU members, their children and spouses, including common-law and same-sex partners.; *Amount:* $350-$1,000
Publications:
• The Guardian [a publication of Hospital Employees' Union]
Type: Magazine; *Frequency:* 3-4 pa

Hospital for Sick Children Foundation (HSCF)
525 University Ave., 14th Fl., Toronto ON M5G 2L3
Tel: 416-813-6166; *Fax:* 416-813-5024
Toll-Free: 800-661-1083
www.sickkidsfoundation.com
www.linkedin.com/company/sickkids-foundation
www.facebook.com/sickkidsfoundation
twitter.com/sickkids
www.youtube.com/sickkidsfoundation
Overview: A medium-sized national charitable organization founded in 1972
Mission: To invest contributions in paediatric care, research & education to help children at The Hospital for Sick Children, throughout Canada, & around the world
Staff Member(s): 22
Chief Officer(s):
Kathleen Taylor, Chair
Ted Garrard, President/CEO
L. Robin Cardozo, Chief Operating Officer, 416-813-2937
robin.cardozo@sickkidsfoundation.com
Heather Clark, Vice-President, Direct & Digital Marketing, 416-813-2935
heather.clark@sickkidsfoundation.com
Lori Davison, Vice-President, Brand Strategy & Communications, 416-813-8518
lori.davison@sickkidsfoundation.com
Seanna Millar, Vice-President, Corporate Partnerships, 416-813-2115
seanna.millar@sickkidsfoundation.com
Awards:
• New Investigator Research Grants
Up to three years of support for research in the biomedical, clinical, health systems & services, population & public health sectors. *Eligibility:* Early-career researchers
• Community Conference Grants
Supports events which are organized by or for families with children with health challenges

Hospitality Food Service Employees Association *See* University of Guelph Food Service Employees Association

Hospitality New Brunswick *See* Tourism Industry Association of New Brunswick Inc.

Hospitality Newfoundland & Labrador (HNL)
#102, 71 Goldstone St., St. John's NL A1B 5C3
Tel: 709-722-2000; *Fax:* 709-722-8104
Toll-Free: 800-563-0700
hnl@hnl.ca
hnl.ca
www.facebook.com/HospitalityNL
twitter.com/hospitalitynl
Also Known As: Tourism Industry Association of Newfoundland & Labrador
Overview: A medium-sized provincial organization founded in 1983
Mission: To develop & promote tourism & hospitality industry throughout Newfoundland & Labrador
Member of: Atlantic Canada Tourism Partnership; Canadian Tourism Human Resources Council; Hotel Association of Canada; Tourism Industry Association of Canada
Finances: *Funding Sources:* Membership dues; fees for service; government grants; fundraising
Staff Member(s): 12
Membership: 508; *Fees:* Schedule available; *Member Profile:* Person, business or organization directly or indirectly related to the tourism industry; *Committees:* Policy; Finance; Governance; Professional Development; Membership
Chief Officer(s):
Carol-Ann Gilliard, Chief Executive Officer, 709-722-2000 Ext. 229
cgilliard@hnl.ca

Hostelling International - Canada (HI-C)
#301, 20 James St., Ottawa ON K2P 0T6
Tel: 613-237-7884; *Fax:* 613-237-7868
info@hihostels.ca
www.hihostels.ca
www.facebook.com/hostelling.canada
twitter.com/HIcanadahostels
www.youtube.com/canadahostels
Overview: A medium-sized international charitable organization
Mission: Hostelling International-Canada (HI-Canada or HI-C) is a not-for-profit, member-based organization with a network of 60 hostels.
Member of: International Youth Hostel Federation
Activities: *Internships:* Yes
Chief Officer(s):
Alistair McLean, Acting Executive Director, 613-237-7884 Ext. 30

Atlantic Region (HI-C)
1253 Barrington St., Halifax NS B3J 1Y3
Tel: 902-422-3863; *Fax:* 902-422-0116
atlantic@hihostels.ca
www.hihostels.ca

Pacific Mountain Region (HI-C)
#300, 761 Cardero St., Vancouver BC V6G 2G3
Tel: 604-684-7101; *Fax:* 604-684-7184
westerncanada@hihostels.ca
www.hihostels.ca

Québec & Ontario Region (HI-C)
3514, ave Lacombe, Montréal QC H3T 1M1
Fax: 514-731-1715
Toll-Free: 866-754-1015
quebecontario@hihostels.ca
www.hihostels.ca

Hotel Association of Canada Inc. (HAC) / Association des hôtels du Canada
#1206, 130 Albert St., Ottawa ON K1P 5G4
Tel: 613-237-7149; *Fax:* 613-237-8928
info@hotelassociation.ca
www.hotelassociation.ca
www.linkedin.com/company/hotel-association-of-canada
twitter.com/hotelassoc
Overview: A large national organization founded in 1913
Mission: To represent members both nationally & internationally; To provide cost-effective services which stimulate & encourage a free market accommodation industry; To bring prosperity to the hotel & lodging industry in Canada
Affiliation(s): American Hotel & Lodging Association;

Canadian Associations / Hotel Association of Nova Scotia (HANS)

International Hotel & Restaurant Association; Canadian Tourism Commission; Tourism Industry Association of Canada; Meeting Planners International
Finances: *Annual Operating Budget:* $500,000-$1.5 Million; *Funding Sources:* Membership fees; program sales; contract trade shows
Staff Member(s): 6; 60 volunteer(s)
Membership: 8,400+ hotels; *Fees:* Schedule available; *Member Profile:* Hotel corporations, provincial hotel associations
Activities: Access Canada Training Program; Asia Pacific Program for Canadian Hotels; Certified Rooms Division Executive designation; Certified Hospitality Housekeeping Executive designation; Research & Data; Resource center; Trade show; Government relations; *Speaker Service:* Yes; *Rents Mailing List:* Yes; *Library:* by appointment
Chief Officer(s):
Philippe Gadbois, Chair
Susie Grynol, President, 613-237-7149 Ext. 105
Linda Hartwell, Director, Marketing Communications & Program Management, 613-237-7149 Ext. 103
Awards:
• The Humanitarian Award
• The Human Resources Award
• The Green Key Energy & Environment Award
• The Green Key Meetings Award
Meetings/Conferences:
• Hotel Association of Canada 2018 Annual National Conference, February, 2018, Toronto, ON
Scope: National
Contact Information: Executive Assistant: Linda Crouch, E-mail: crouch@hotelassociation.ca; Phone: 613-237-7149, ext. 101
Publications:
• RooMers [a publication of the Hotel Association of Canada Inc.]
Type: Magazine; *Frequency:* 6 pa.; *Accepts Advertising*; *Editor:* Linda Hartwell
Profile: Includes regulatory updates, industry trends, & Association news

Hotel Association of Metropolitan Toronto *See* Greater Toronto Hotel Association

Hotel Association of Nova Scotia (HANS)
PO Box 473, Stn. M, Halifax NS B3J 2P8
Overview: A medium-sized provincial organization founded in 1993 overseen by Hotel Association of Canada Inc.
Mission: To make Nova Scotia a year-round travel destination; To act as the official voice of the collective member hotels; To provide support for appropriate advisory boards & committees; To develop & encourage a coordinated joint marketing effort
Membership: 36
Activities: Informing members on issues important to the industry

Hotel Association of Prince Edward Island
c/o Murphy Hospitality Group, 96 Kensington Rd., Charlottetown PE C1A 5J4
Tel: 902-566-3137
Overview: A medium-sized provincial organization overseen by Hotel Association of Canada Inc.
Chief Officer(s):
Kevin Murphy, President

Hotel Association of Vancouver (HAV)
30045 - 8602 Granville St., Vancouver BC V6P 6S3
Tel: 778-574-1954
hotelassocvan@shaw.ca
hotelassociationofvancouver.com
Overview: A small local organization founded in 1986
Mission: The Vancouver Hotel Association strives to promote the benefits of the hotel industry to all levels of government, the media and public
Member of: BC & Yukon Hotels Association; Hotel Association of Canada
Staff Member(s): 1
Membership: 60; *Member Profile:* Full-service hotels in Greater Vancouver
Chief Officer(s):
Jonas Melin, Chair

Hotels Association of Saskatchewan *See* Saskatchewan Hotel & Hospitality Association

House of Commons Security Services Employees Association / Association des employés du Service de sécurité de la Chambre des communes
PO Box 903, Confederation Bldg., Ottawa ON K1A 0A6
Tel: 613-992-9802
Overview: A small local organization founded in 1987
Membership: 203
Chief Officer(s):
Roch Lapensée, President

Housing & Urban Development Association of Canada *See* Canadian Home Builders' Association

Houston & District Chamber of Commerce *See* Houston Chamber of Commerce

Houston Chamber of Commerce
PO Box 396, 3289 Hwy. 16, Houston BC V0J 1Z0
Tel: 250-845-7640; *Fax:* 250-845-3682
info@houstonchamber.ca
www.houstonchamber.ca
Previous Name: Houston & District Chamber of Commerce
Overview: A small local organization founded in 1961
Mission: To enable the local businesses to achieve that which they could not do alone
Member of: BC Chamber of Commerce; Canadian Chamber of Commerce
Membership: *Fees:* Schedule available
Activities: Operates the Visitor Info. Centre; provides business & volunteer community awards; *Speaker Service:* Yes
Chief Officer(s):
Jean Marr, President

Houston Friendship Centre Society *See* Dze L K'ant Friendship Centre Society

Houston Link to Learning (HLL)
PO Box 1294, Houston BC V0J 1Z0
Tel: 250-845-2727; *Fax:* 250-845-5629
www.facebook.com/237646302964028
Overview: A small local charitable organization founded in 1990
Mission: To ensure that all adults in Houston area have the opportunity to develop the literacy skills they need to lead satisfying & productive lives in the community
Finances: *Funding Sources:* National government; provincial government

Hoy Ping Benevolent Association of Canada - Vancouver Branch
440 Main St., Vancouver BC V6A 2T4
Tel: 604-669-1042
hoypingvancouver@gmail.com
www.facebook.com/hoypingvancouver
Overview: A small local charitable organization founded in 1925
Mission: To provide support for Vancouver's Hoy Ping community; To promote Hoy Ping family values; To educate youth on their Hoy Ping heritage & family traditions
Activities: Supporting charities, research foundations, hospitals, & Chinese language schools; Donating to relief funds in China; Organizing recreational activities & events

H.R. MacMillan Space Centre Society (HRMSC)
1100 Chestnut St., Vancouver BC V6J 3J9
Tel: 604-738-7827; *Fax:* 604-736-5665
info@spacecentre.ca
www.spacecentre.ca
www.facebook.com/MacMillanSpaceCentre
twitter.com/AskAnAstronomer
www.youtube.com/user/MacMillanSpaceCentre
Also Known As: H.R. MacMillan Planetarium
Previous Name: Pacific Space Centre Society
Overview: A medium-sized local charitable organization founded in 1968
Mission: To promote education concerning astronomy
Member of: Canadian Association of Science Centres
Affiliation(s): Canadian Museums Association
Finances: *Annual Operating Budget:* $1.5 Million-$3 Million; *Funding Sources:* Government; foundations; corporate sponsors; individuals; admissions to facility
Staff Member(s): 50; 30 volunteer(s)
Membership: 700; *Fees:* $20 general membership
Activities: New star show productions; Teacher workshops; Classroom activities; Community astronomy; Starlab; Video-conferences; Planetarium & observatory; Demonstrations, exhibits, games & shows
Chief Officer(s):
Raylene Marchand, Interim Executive Director
Lisa McIntosh, Director, Learning

HRMS Professionals Association (HRMSP) / Association des professionnels en SGRH (PSGRH)
#301, 250 Consumers Rd., Toronto ON M2J 4V6
Tel: 416-221-4559; *Fax:* 416-495-8723
Toll-Free: 866-878-3899
info@hrmsp.org
www.hrmscanada.com
Overview: A medium-sized national organization
Mission: To serve human resource management systems professionals by sharing knowledge, best practices, & industry trends
Membership: *Fees:* $160 Individual; $35 Student; *Member Profile:* Professionals, practitioners, consultants, & product & service vendors from the human resources & payroll fields
Activities: Offering networking opportunities; Providing educational programs; Facilitating communication between users of technology in the business sector, vendors, & consultants
Chief Officer(s):
Richard Rousseau, President
richard.rousseau@hrmsp.org
Martine Castellani, Vice-President & Treasurer
martine.castellani@hrmsp.org
John Allen Doran, Secretary
aldoran@pmihrm.com

Hub for Active School Travel (HASTe)
Haste Worker's Cooperative, 90-425 Carrall St., Vancouver BC V6B 6E3
Tel: 778-883-7962
info@hastebc.org
www.hastebc.org
www.facebook.com/150876098306478
twitter.com/HASTeBC
Overview: A small provincial organization founded in 2007
Mission: To connect children, schools & communities through walking & cycling; To help schools work towards reducing their emissions; To increase safe & active travel in BC communities
Finances: *Funding Sources:* Government
Staff Member(s): 5
Activities: Facilitates communication between schools, parents, students, planners & engineers to encourage active travel to and from school; Supporting School Travel Planning (STP); Offering workshops, consulting & education; *Internships:* Yes
Chief Officer(s):
Omar Bhimji, Project Manager
omar@hastebc.org
Cailey Armstrong, Operations Coordinator
cailey@hastebc.org

HUDAM *See* Manitoba Home Builders' Association

Hudson Bay Chamber of Commerce
PO Box 730, Hudson Bay SK S0E 0Y0
www.townofhudsonbay.com
Overview: A small local organization
Membership: *Fees:* $25 individual; $75 business
Activities: *Awareness Events:* Annual Golf Tournament, May
Chief Officer(s):
Corinne Reine, President
Janice Dyck, Secretary

Hudson's Hope Museum
PO Box 98, 9510 Beattie Dr., Hudson's Hope BC V0C 1V0
Tel: 250-783-5735; *Fax:* 250-783-5770
Other Communication: hhmuseum@gmail.com
hhmuseum@pris.ca
www.hudsonshopemuseum.com
twitter.com/hhmuseum
Also Known As: Hudson's Hope Historical Society
Overview: A small local charitable organization founded in 1967
Mission: To preserve & display the history of Hudson's Hope & area through artifacts collection, oral histories & records
Member of: Canadian Museums Association; BC Museums Association; BC Heritage Society
Finances: *Annual Operating Budget:* Less than $50,000
Staff Member(s): 2; 3 volunteer(s)
Membership: 1-99; *Fees:* $20
Activities: Operating museum; *Library:* Resource Centre; by appointment

Human Concern International (HCI)
PO Box 3984, Stn. C, Ottawa ON K1Y 4P2
Tel: 613-742-5948
Toll-Free: 800-587-6424
info@humanconcern.org
www.humanconcern.org
www.facebook.com/HCICanada
twitter.com/humanconcernint
www.youtube.com/user/HumanConcernInt
Overview: A small national organization founded in 1980

Mission: To help alleviate human suffering by investing in humanity, through long-term development projects for sustainability, & emergency relief assistance during times of dire need
Staff Member(s): 10
Activities: Sustainable development projects; Emergency relief assistance; Child sponsorship program; Education/school support; Higher education; Scholarship; Human resource development; Micro-enterprise; Skill development training
Chief Officer(s):
Kaleem Akhtar, Executive Director
kaleem@humanconcern.org
Garnayl Abdi, Program Officer

Human Factors Association of Canada See Association of Canadian Ergonomists

Human Resource Management Association of Manitoba; Personnel Association of Greater Winnipeg See Chartered Professionals in Human Resources Manitoba

Human Resources Association of New Brunswick (HRANB) / Association des ressources humaines du Nouveau-Brunswick (ARHNB)
PO Box 23128, Moncton NB E1A 6S8
Tel: 506-855-4466; *Fax:* 506-855-4424
Toll-Free: 888-803-4466
solange@hranb.org
www.hranb.org
www.linkedin.com/company/hranb-arhnb
Overview: A medium-sized provincial organization founded in 1996
Mission: Promotes a professional standard of knowledge and proficiency in Human Resources.
Member of: Canadian Council of Human Resources Associations
Membership: *Fees:* $100 + HST: regular & associate; $35 + HST: student & retired.
Chief Officer(s):
Pierre Simoneau, President
simoneap@nbnet.nb.ca

Human Resources Association of Nova Scotia
#103, 84 Chain Lake Dr., Halifax NS B3S 1A2
Tel: 902-446-3660; *Fax:* 902-446-3677
www.cphrns.ca
Also Known As: Chartered Professionals in Human Resources of Nova Scotia
Overview: A small provincial organization founded in 1945
Mission: Dedicated to providing leadership and advocacy in the human resource profession; To enhance the contribution of the human resource profession to humanity by developing our members and through partnerships with business and society.
Member of: Canadian Council of Human Resources Associations
Staff Member(s): 3
Membership: 1,100+; *Fees:* $140 + tax full & association members; $40 + tax students
Chief Officer(s):
Sheila McLean, Chief Executive Officer
Meetings/Conferences:
• Human Resources Association of Nova Scotia 2018 Conference, 2018, NS
Scope: Provincial

Human Resources Institute of Alberta See Chartered Professionals in Human Resources of Alberta

Human Resources Management Association See Chartered Professionals in Human Resources of British Columbia & Yukon

Human Resources Professionals Association (HRPA)
#200, 150 Bloor St. West, Toronto ON M5S 2X9
Tel: 416-923-2324; *Fax:* 416-923-7264
Toll-Free: 800-387-1311; *TTY:* 866-620-3848
info@hrpa.ca
www.hrpa.ca
www.linkedin.com/company/HRPA
www.facebook.com/TheHRPA
twitter.com/HRPA
www.youtube.com/user/HRPATV
Previous Name: Personnel Association of Ontario
Overview: A medium-sized provincial organization founded in 1954
Mission: To empower human resources professionals by providing management & leadership support, through information resources, events, professional development, & networking opportunities.
Member of: Canadian Council of Human Resources Associations
Membership: 20,000+ members in 28 Ontario chapters & internationally; *Fees:* Schedule available; *Member Profile:* Human resources practitioners; Students; Individuals interested in the practice of human resources, such as lawyers, specialists, consultants, retirees, academics, & line managers; *Committees:* Appeals; Audit & Finance; Awards; Academic Standards; Complaints & Investigation; Discipline; Editorial Advisory; Experience Assessment; Board Nominating; Governance & Nominating; Human Resources & Compensation; Professional Development; Annual Conference; Professional Regulation & Standards; Continuing Professional Development; Summit Awards Judges; Registration; SHRP Review; Ethos; Health & Safety
Activities: Granting the Certified Human Resources Professional (CHRP) designation; promoting the profession; engaging in government relations; *Library:* HRPAO Resource Centre; by appointment
Chief Officer(s):
Gary Monk, Interim CEO
Awards:
• Honourary Life Award
• TOSI/HRPAO Scholarship
• Ross A. Hennigar Memorial Award
Presented each year to the outstanding CHRM (Certificate in Human Resources Management) candidate who has completed the program in the current year; it was established to encourage participants of the CHRM program to achieve a high standard in their studies, their human resources careers, & their personal & community endeavours *Eligibility:* Recipients must be at a professional or supervisory level for at least one year & show evidence of growth or the potential for growth & achievement
• HRPAO Outstanding CHRP Achievement Award
• HRPAO Professional Leadership Award
• HRPAO Volunteer Leadership Awards
Meetings/Conferences:
• Human Resources Professionals Association 2018 Annual Conference & Trade Show, January, 2018, Metro Toronto Convention Centre, Toronto, ON
Scope: Provincial
Publications:
• HR Professional
Type: Magazine; *Frequency:* Bimonthly; *Accepts Advertising*; *Price:* Free for members; $29 non-members in Canada; $49 non-members in U.S.A
Profile: A membership magazine for HRPAO, with events & products of interest to HR professionals

Algoma Chapter
Algoma ON
www.hrpa.ca/algoma
Chief Officer(s):
Lorri Kennis, President
lorri.kennis@ssmpuc.com

Barrie & District Chapter
#124, 92 Caplan Ave., Barrie ON L4N 0Z7
Chief Officer(s):
Bonnie Firth, President
president@hrpabarrie.ca

Brockville Chapter
Brockville ON
Tel: 613-340-4427
info@hrpabrockville.ca
Chief Officer(s):
Leah Wales, President, 613-533-6000 Ext. 75435
leah.wales@queensu.ca

Chatham-Kent Chapter
Chatham-Kent ON
Chief Officer(s):
Elise Marentette, President, 519-682-0470 Ext. 1229
emarentette@anchordanly.com

Durham Chapter
105 Consumers Dr., Whitby ON L1N 1C4
Tel: 905-721-9564; *Fax:* 647-689-2264
hrpad@adminedge.com
twitter.com/HRPADurham
Chief Officer(s):
Tracey Starrett, President
Rebecca Lauzon, Administrator

Grand Valley Chapter
PO Box 40043, RPO Waterloo Square, Waterloo ON N2J 4V1
Tel: 519-747-8102; *Fax:* 519-489-2736
office@gvhrpa.on.ca
www.linkedin.com/groups?gid=3689596
www.facebook.com/HRPAGV
twitter.com/HRPA_GV
Chief Officer(s):
Anna Aceto-Guerin, President

Grey Bruce Chapter
Owen Sound ON
Chief Officer(s):
Audrey Bross, President, 519-367-3174
audreyb@wightman.ca

Guelph & District Chapter
Guelph ON
www.gdhrpa.ca
Chief Officer(s):
Stephen Goodwin, President
sgoodwin@gdhrpa.ca

Halton Chapter
ON
communications@hrpahalton.org
www.linkedin.com/Human-Resources-Professionals-Association-Halton
twitter.com/HRPAHalton
Chief Officer(s):
Rebecca Weber, President
president@hrpahalton.org

Hamilton Chapter
PO Box 73010, Hamilton ON L9A 4X0
Tel: 905-667-6622
info@hamiltonhrpa.ca
Chief Officer(s):
Silvia Stankovic, President
president@hamiltonhrpa.ca

Kingston & District
PO Box 1709, Kingston ON K7L 5J7
Tel: 613-547-2962; *Fax:* 613-547-8265
admin@hrpakingston.ca
www.hrpa.ca
Mission: To advance relationships between employees & management & to educate HR professionals
Chief Officer(s):
Emily Koolen, President
president@hrpakingston.ca

Kingston District
PO Box 1709, Kingston ON K7L 5J6
Tel: 613-547-2962
www.hrpa.ca/HRPAChapters/kingston
Mission: To provide support to & connect HR professionals for the exchange of knowledge, expertise, best practices, & resources
Member of: The Human Resources Professional Association of Ontario
Chief Officer(s):
Kayla Fenn, Director, Communications
communication@hrpakingston.ca
Devon Lee Massouh, Director, Membership
membership@hrpakingston.ca

London & District Chapter
#321, 509 Commissioners Rd. West, London ON N6J 1Y5
Tel: 519-645-7741
info@hrpld.ca
Chief Officer(s):
Stephen Sesar, President
president@hrpld.ca

Niagara Chapter
PO Box 30084, RPO Ridley Square, St Catharines ON L2S 4A1
admin@hrpaniagara.ca
www.hrpan.ca
Chief Officer(s):
Marcey Saunders, President
msaunders@hrpaniagara.ca
Jodi Fitzgerald, Communications Director
jfitzgerald@hrpaniagara.ca

North Bay Chapter
North Bay ON
Chief Officer(s):
Marsha Cresswell, President
cresswellm@sympatico.ca

Northumberland Chapter
northumberlandhrpa@gmail.com
Chief Officer(s):

Canadian Associations / Human Resources Professionals of Durham (HRPAD)

Wendy Perry, President
wperry@nhh.ca
Northwestern Ontario Chapter
#421, 1100 Memorial Ave., Thunder Bay ON P7B 4A3
executive@hrpano.org
Chief Officer(s):
Allane Danchuk, President, 807-684-1892
allane@tbaycounselling.com
Ottawa Chapter
PO Box 315, Stn. Main, Stittsville ON K2S 1A4
Tel: 613-224-6477; *Fax:* 613-369-4347
infohr@hrpaottawa.ca
www.hrpaottawa.ca
Chief Officer(s):
Elizabeth Roberts, President
Peel Chapter (HRPAP)
PO Box 538, #6, 2400 Dundas St. West, Mississauga ON L5K 2R8
Tel: 905-337-7141
info@hrpapeel.ca
www.linkedin.com/groups?gid=2219644
twitter.com/HRPA_Peel
Member of: Human Resources Professionals Association of Ontario
Chief Officer(s):
Jeannette Schepp, President
president@hrpapeel.ca
Peterborough Chapter
www.hrpapeterborough.ca
Chief Officer(s):
Pat Cole, President
Quinte Chapter
info@hrpaquinte.ca
Chief Officer(s):
Barb Frederick, President
barbf@pathwaysind.com
Sarnia & District Chapter
Chief Officer(s):
Rebecca Mitchell, President, 519-869-2679
rebeccawmitchell@sympatico.ca
Stormont, Dundas & Glengarry Chapter
Chief Officer(s):
Dora Cameron, President
Sudbury Chapter
Sudbury ON
Chief Officer(s):
Peter Bonish, President
peter@petesrentall.ca
Timmins & District Chapter
Timmins ON
Chief Officer(s):
Jamie Klomp, President, 705-360-7502
jklomp@dumasmining.com
Toronto Chapter
Toronto ON
communications@hrpatoronto.ca
www.hrpa.ca/toronto
www.linkedin.com/groups?home=&gid=4112691
www.facebook.com/HRPATO
twitter.com/HRPATO
Andrea Fraser, President
West Toronto Chapter
Toronto ON
communications@hrpwt.com
hrpwt.com
twitter.com/WestTorontoHRPA
Chief Officer(s):
Heather Wannamaker, President
president@hrpwt.com
Windsor & District Chapter
Windsor ON
info@hrpawindsor.ca
www.hrpawindsor.ca
Chief Officer(s):
Jody Merritt, President
jmerritt@stclaircollege.ca
York Region Chapter
#256, 14845-6 Yonge St., Aurora ON L4G 6H8
Tel: 416-483-2070
Toll-Free: 866-977-9975
public_relations@hrpyr.org
www.hrpyr.org
www.linkedin.com/groups?gid=132598
Chief Officer(s):
Jodi Zigelstein-Yip, President
president@hrpyr.org

Human Resources Professionals of Durham (HRPAD)
105 Consumers Dr., Whitby ON L1N 1C4
Tel: 905-721-9564; *Fax:* 647-689-2264
hrpad@adminedge.com
www.hrpad.org
twitter.com/HRPADurham
Overview: A small local organization
Mission: Advocates excellence in the leadership of Human Resources; provides opportunities for professional development and advancement; and promoting the Human Resources profession and designation.
Member of: Human Resources Professionals Association of Ontario
Membership: *Committees:* Professional Development; Membership; Communications; Education
Activities: *Awareness Events:* Annual Social, Dec.
Chief Officer(s):
Tracey Starrett, President
Morgan Kerby, Vice-President

Human Resources Professionals of Newfoundland & Labrador (HRPNL)
PO Box 21454, St. John's NL A1A 5G6
Tel: 709-351-4134
hrpnl@hrpnl.ca
www.hrpnl.ca
www.linkedin.com/groups/Human-Resources-Professionals-Newfoundland-Labrador-3452445
Overview: A medium-sized provincial organization founded in 1994
Mission: Serves as a community of HR interest with a commitment to promoting the HR profession and advancing HR professionals.
Member of: Canadian Council of Human Resources Associations
Membership: *Fees:* $120 annual; $60 half-year; $25 student
Chief Officer(s):
Neil Coombs, President
president@hrpnl.ca
Leroy Murphy, Vice-President
vicepresident@hrpnl.ca
Kelly Gould, Contact, Administration

Human Rights & Race Relations Centre
#500, 120 Eglinton Ave. East, Toronto ON M4P 1E2
Tel: 416-481-7793
Toll-Free: 888-667-5877
humanrights@sympatico.ca
Previous Name: The South Journalists Club
Overview: A small local organization founded in 1994
Mission: To protect & work for the rights of journalists of South Asian origin
Finances: *Annual Operating Budget:* Less than $50,000
Staff Member(s): 1; 10 volunteer(s)
Membership: 40 individual; 5 associate; *Fees:* $10 student; $20 individual/associate
Activities: *Speaker Service:* Yes
Chief Officer(s):
Hasanat Ahmad Syed, President

Human Rights Internet (HRI) / Internet des droits humains
#1105, 1 Nicholas St., Ottawa ON K1N 7B7
Tel: 613-789-7407
info@hri.ca
www.hri.ca
Overview: A medium-sized international charitable organization founded in 1976
Mission: Consulting & capacity building organization committed to the promotion of human rights in the areas of social justice, good governance & conflict prevention
Affiliation(s): Network on International Human Rights
Finances: *Funding Sources:* International government
Membership: *Member Profile:* Non-governmental, inter-governmental organizations worldwide
Activities: *Internships:* Yes
Chief Officer(s):
Hazel Postma, Chair

Human Rights Research & Education Centre (HRREC) / Centre de recherche et d'enseignement sur les droits de la personne
University of Ottawa, Fauteux Hall, #550, 57 Louis Pasteur, Ottawa ON K1N 6N5
Tel: 613-562-5775; *Fax:* 613-562-5125
hrrec@uottawa.ca
www.cdp-hrc.uottawa.ca
www.facebook.com/265881216771281
Also Known As: Human Rights Centre
Overview: A medium-sized international organization founded in 1981
Mission: To further the discussion of the linkages between human rights, governance, legal reform & development; to support national human rights institutions; to improve social justice institutions/programs
Affiliation(s): University of Ottawa; Canadian Centre for International Justice; Canadian Civil Liberties Association; Canadian Commission for UNESCO; Canadian Red Cross; Interdisciplinary Research Laboratory on the Rights of the Child; Lique des droits et libertés; Office of the Prosecutor of the International Criminal Court
Finances: *Annual Operating Budget:* $1.5 Million-$3 Million; *Funding Sources:* University of Ottawa
Staff Member(s): 4; 3 volunteer(s)
Membership: 33
Activities: *Library:* HRREC Documentation Centre; Open to public
Chief Officer(s):
Penelope Simons, Acting Research Director
penelope.simons@uOttawa.ca

Humane Society International/Canada (HSI Canada)
#320, 4035, rue Saint-Ambroise, Montréal QC H4C 2E1
Tel: 514-395-2914
info@hsicanada.ca
www.hsicanada.ca
www.facebook.com/hsiglobal
twitter.com/hsi_canada
www.instagram.com/hsiglobal
Overview: A large international organization
Mission: To protect all animals, including companion animals, farm animals, & animals in the wild
Finances: *Funding Sources:* Donations
Activities: Engaging in advocacy, education, investigation, litigation, & field work; programs including habitat protection, marine mammal preservation, & farm animal welfare; projects to stop puppy mills, commercial sealing, confinement of farm animals, horse slaughter, trophy hunting, & dog & cat fur; Animal Rescue Fund
Chief Officer(s):
Rebecca Aldworth, Executive Director, Humane Society International/Canada

Humane Society of Ottawa-Carleton *See* Ottawa Humane Society

Humane Society Yukon
126 Tlingit Rd., Whitehorse YT Y1A 6J2
Tel: 867-633-6019; *Fax:* 867-633-2210
info@humanesocietyyukon.ca
www.humanesocietyyukon.ca
www.facebook.com/153522391419947
Also Known As: Mae Bachur Animal Shelter
Overview: A medium-sized provincial organization founded in 1989 overseen by Canadian Federation of Humane Societies
Mission: To foster a caring, compassionate atmosphere; To promote a humane ethic & responsible pet ownership; To prevent cruelty to animals
Finances: *Funding Sources:* Public donations
Membership: *Fees:* $20 individual; $200 corporate
Chief Officer(s):
Brent Slobodin, President

Humanist Canada (HC) / Humaniste Canada (HC)
#1150, 45 O'Connor St., Ottawa ON K1P 1A4
Fax: 613-739-5969
Toll-Free: 877-486-2671
info@humanistcanada.com
www.humanistcanada.com
Also Known As: Humanist Association of Canada
Overview: A medium-sized national charitable organization founded in 1968
Mission: To bring together people who share a non-theistic view of the world; to educate the public about humanism & its ethics & values

Member of: Coalition for Secular Humanism & Free Thought
Affiliation(s): International Humanist & Ethical Union (UK)
Finances: *Annual Operating Budget:* Less than $50,000; *Funding Sources:* Membership fees & donations
12 volunteer(s)
Membership: 800; *Fees:* $500 life; $50 household; $40 individual
Activities: Licensed officiants to perform legal marriages, funeral services; *Awareness Events:* Humanist of the Year *Library:* HAC Library; by appointment Not open to public
Awards:
• Humanist of the Year

Humaniste Canada *See* Humanist Canada

Humanity First Canada
#40, 600 Bowes Rd., Concord ON L4K 4A3
Tel: 416-440-0346
info@humanityfirst.ca
www.humanityfirstcanada.ca
www.facebook.com/humanityfirstcanada
twitter.com/humanityfirst
Overview: A small international charitable organization founded in 2004
Mission: To provide hunmanitarian aid & arrange response to disasters; To help restore communities & help them build a future; To relieve poverty by establishing, operating, & maintaining training centres in developing countries
Finances: *Annual Operating Budget:* $500,000-$1.5 Million; *Funding Sources:* Donations; Grants
Staff Member(s): 2; 100 volunteer(s)
Activities: Operating food banks & the Feed the Hungry/Feed the Homeless programs; Arranging care for orphans; Providing water wells through the Water for Life program; Offering basic health care; *Awareness Events:* Humanity First Awareness Event; *Speaker Service:* Yes
Chief Officer(s):
Aslam Daud, Chair
adaud@humanityfirst.ca
Publications:
• Humanity Matters [a publication of Humanity First Canada]
Type: Newsletter; *Frequency:* Quarterly; *Accepts Advertising Profile:* Articles about disasters & assistance provided, plus information about local events & fundraising efforts

Humboldt & District Chamber of Commerce
PO Box 1440, Humboldt SK S0K 2A0
Tel: 306-682-4990; *Fax:* 306-682-5203
admin@humboldtchamber.ca
www.humboldtchamber.ca
www.facebook.com/humboldtchamber
www.youtube.com/user/humboldtchamber
Overview: A small local organization
Mission: To serve the needs of businesses in Humboldt & District
Member of: Saskatchewan Chamber of Commerce
Finances: *Annual Operating Budget:* $100,000-$250,000; *Funding Sources:* Membership dues
Staff Member(s): 2
Membership: 263; *Fees:* Schedule available, based upon number of employees; *Committees:* Executive; Public Relations & Promotions; Business Retention & Expansion; Campground & Tourist Booth
Activities: Acting as a spokesperson for businesses & other professional communities; Promoting the commercial interests of the community
Chief Officer(s):
Debra Nyczai, Executive Director, 306-682-4990
debra@humboldtchamber.ca
Awards:
• Business of the Year Awards
Two awards: one offered to a business with less than 10 employees, and one offered to a business with 10 or more employees *Deadline:* December
• Young Entrepreneur of the Year Award
Deadline: December
• New Business Venture Award
Deadline: December
• Community Involvement Award
Deadline: December
• Community Merit Award
Deadline: December
• Service Award
Deadline: December
• Marketing Award
Deadline: December

• People's Choice Award
Deadline: December
• Courtesy Service Award
Awarded in four quarters (1st quarter: January-March, 2nd: April-June, 3rd: July-September, 4th: October-December) to an employee that provides exceptional customer service

Humboldt & District Labour Council
200 - 9th St., Humboldt SK S0K 2A0
Tel: 306-682-1528
Overview: A small local organization overseen by Saskatchewan Federation of Labour
Mission: To support union members & workers in Humboldt, Saskatchewan & the surrounding area; To advance the economic & social welfare of workers; To act as the voice of labour
Activities: Promoting the interests of affiliates; Liaising with local elected officials to ensure the issues of workers are heard; Offering educational programs, such as farm safety seminars

Hungarian Canadian Cultural Centre
1170 Sheppard Ave. West, Toronto ON M3K 2A3
Tel: 416-654-4926
office@hccc.org
www.hccc-e.org
Also Known As: Hungarian House
Previous Name: Hungarian Canadian Federation
Overview: A small national charitable organization founded in 1945
Mission: To preserve & showcase Hungarian heritage in the Canadian mosaic.
Activities: Provides space, guidance & funding to several cultural & sports groups; *Library:* Hungarian Library; by appointment

Hungarian Canadian Engineers' Association (HCEA)
57 Drew Kelly Way, Markham ON L3R 5R2
Tel: 905-474-9225
magyar_mernok@kmme.org
kmme.org
Overview: A small national charitable organization founded in 1953
Finances: *Annual Operating Budget:* Less than $50,000
10 volunteer(s)
Membership: 165; *Fees:* $20-$50; *Member Profile:* Engineers; technicians, etc.
Activities: Monthly meetings

Hungarian Canadian Federation *See* Hungarian Canadian Cultural Centre

Hungarian Studies Association of Canada (HSAC) / Association canadienne des études hongroises
c/o Margit Lovrics, #1804, 75 Graydon Hall Dr., Toronto ON M3A 3M5
www.hungarianstudies.org
Also Known As: Kanadai Magyarsagtudományi Tàrsasàg
Overview: A small national organization founded in 1985
Mission: To study Hungarian culture & history at the academic level
Finances: *Funding Sources:* Membership fees
Membership: *Fees:* $45 regular; $30 retired & students; $75 family; *Member Profile:* Interested academics & professionals; *Committees:* Conference Program; Planning & Nominations; Publications
Activities: Annual conference; occasional special events
Chief Officer(s):
Agatha Schwartz, Acting President
agathas@uottawa.ca
Nandor Dreisziger, Vice-President
nandor@kingston.net
Margit Lovrics, Treasurer
margitlovrics@gmail.com
Awards:
• F. Harcsar Award
Meetings/Conferences:
• 2018 Conference of the Hungarian Studies Association of Canada, May, 2018, University of Regina, Regina, SK
Description: Held in conjunction with the Congress of the Humanities & Social Sciences

The Hunger Project Canada / Le Projet Faim
11 O'Connor Dr., Toronto ON M4K 2K3
Tel: 416-429-0023
www.thehungerproject.ca
www.facebook.com/TheHungerProjectCanada
Also Known As: THP-Canada

Overview: A medium-sized international charitable organization founded in 1977
Mission: Committed to the sustainable end of world hunger
Member of: Canadian Council for International Cooperation
Chief Officer(s):
Malgorzata Smelkowska, Director

Hunter Family Foundation
#1700, 521 - 3rd Ave. SW, Calgary AB T2P 3T3
info@hunterfamilyfoundation.ca
www.hunterfamilyfoundation.ca
Overview: A small local charitable organization founded in 1984
Mission: To drive change by assisting Calgary-based organizations & causes that meet significant needs within the community, as well as demonstrate entrepreneurial thinking
Chief Officer(s):
V. Diane Hunter, President

Huntington Society of Canada (HSC) / Société Huntington du Canada
#400, 151 Frederick St., Kitchener ON N2H 2M2
Tel: 519-749-7063; *Fax:* 519-749-8965
Toll-Free: 800-998-7398
info@huntingtonsociety.ca
www.huntingtonsociety.ca
www.linkedin.com/company/huntington-society-of-canada
www.facebook.com/HuntingtonSC
twitter.com/HuntingtonSC
www.youtube.com/user/HuntSocCanada
Also Known As: Huntington Society
Overview: A medium-sized national charitable organization founded in 1973
Mission: To aspire for a world free of Huntington disease; To maximize the quality of life of people living with HD
Member of: Canadian Coalition for Genetic Fairness; Health Charities Coalition of Canada; HealthPartners; Neurological Health Charities Coalition of Canada; International Huntington Association
Finances: *Annual Operating Budget:* $3 Million-$5 Million; *Funding Sources:* Donations; Fundraising; Sponsorships
Staff Member(s): 35; 10,0 volunteer(s)
Membership: 350; *Committees:* Executive/Finance; Board Governance/Nominating; Investment; Audit; Research
Activities: Delivering services; Increasing understanding of the disease; Furthering research; *Awareness Events:* Amaryllis Month, Nov.; Annual Indy Go-Kart Challenge, September; Huntington Disease Awareness Month, May
Chief Officer(s):
Bev Heim-Myers, CEO
bheimmyers@huntingtonsociety.ca
   British Columbia Chapter
   c/o Centre for Huntington Disease, #S179, 2211 Wesbrook Mall, Vancouver BC V6T 2B5
   Tel: 604-682-3269
   britishcolumbiahd@gmail.com
   www.britishcolumbiahd.ca
   Chief Officer(s):
   Manny Abecia, Co-President
   mabecia@gmail.com
   Graham Cook, Co-President
   grahamc@sfu.ca
   East Central Ontario Resource Centre
   PO Box 103, 71 Old Kingston Rd., Ajax ON L1T 3A6
   Tel: 905-426-4333
   Toll-Free: 855-426-4333
   Chief Officer(s):
   Marilyn Mitchell, Director
   mmitchell@huntingtonsociety.ca
   Individual & Family Services
   PO Box 31355, Richmond Hill ON L4C 0V7
   Tel: 905-787-8359
   Toll-Free: 877-573-7011
   Chief Officer(s):
   Rozi Andrejas, Director
   randrejas@huntingtonsociety.ca
   Manitoba Chapters
   c/o Sandra Funk, 200 Woodlawn St., Winnipeg MB R3J 2H7
   Tel: 204-772-4617; *Fax:* 204-940-8414
   www.hdmanitoba.ca
   Chief Officer(s):
   Sandy Funk, Brandon Contact, 204-726-8323
   sandson10@hotmail.com
   Vern Barrett, Winnipeg Contact, 204-694-1779
   vbarrett@mts.net

Manitoba Resource Centre
200 Woodlawn St., Winnipeg MB R3J 2H7
Tel: 204-772-4617; *Fax:* 204-940-8414
www.hdmanitoba.ca
Chief Officer(s):
Sandra Funk, Director
sfunk@huntingtonsociety.ca

Newfoundland/Labrador Resource Centre
NL
Tel: 709-745-1155
Toll-Free: 877-745-1155
Chief Officer(s):
Elaine Smith, Director
esmith@huntingtonsociety.ca

Northern Alberta Chapter - Peace Country
PO Box 6, RR#2, Site 1, Sexsmith AB T0H 3C0
peacecountryhd.ca
Chief Officer(s):
Mack Erno, President, 780-897-8048

Northern Alberta Resource Centre
#102, 11747 Kingsway NW, Edmonton AB T5G 0X5
Tel: 780-434-3229
Chief Officer(s):
Bernadette Modrovsky, Director
bmodrovsky@huntingtonsociety.ca

Northern Ontario Resource Centre
PO Box 1072, Chelmsford ON P0M 1L0
Tel: 705-897-1969; *Fax:* 705-897-3026
Toll-Free: 855-897-1969
Chief Officer(s):
Angèle Bénard, Director
abenard@huntingtonsociety.ca

Nova Scotia & PEI Chapters - Atlantic
Halifax NS
Chief Officer(s):
Jim Russell, President, Nova Scotia, 902-576-5660
jimrussell@eastlink.ca
Danny Drouin, President, PEI, 902-853-3066
ddrouin@pei.sympatico.ca

Nova Scotia & PEI Resource Centre
#101, 3845 Joseph Howe Dr., Halifax NS B3L 4H9
Tel: 902-446-4803
Chief Officer(s):
Barbara Horner, Director
bhorner@huntingtonsociety.ca

Saskatoon & Area
PO Box 26012, Saskatoon SK S7K 8C1
Tel: 306-979-9111
hdsaskatoon@gmail.com
www.facebook.com/HuntingtonSocietyOfCanadaSaskatoon
Chief Officer(s):
June Nichol, President

Southern Alberta Chapter
AB
www.southernalbertahd.ca

Southern Alberta Resource Centre
Westech Bldg., #102, 5636 Burbank Cres. SE, Calgary AB T2H 1Z6
Tel: 403-532-0609; *Fax:* 403-532-3952
Chief Officer(s):
Shannon MacKinnon, Director
smackinnon@huntingtonsociety.ca

Toronto Chapter
c/o HSC National Office, #400, 151 Frederick St., Kitchener ON N2H 2M2
Toll-Free: 800-998-7398
info@hdtoronto.org
www.hdtoronto.org
Chief Officer(s):
Tim Irwin, President

West Central Ontario Resource Centre
#400, 151 Frederick St., Kitchener ON N2H 2M2
Tel: 519-576-6102
Toll-Free: 866-796-8016
Chief Officer(s):
Maike Zinabou, Director
mzinabou@huntingtonsociety.ca

Huntington Society of Québec *Voir* Société Huntington du Québec

Huntley Township Historical Society
PO Box 313, Carp ON K0A 1L0
HuntleyHistory@gmx.net
www.huntleyhistory.ca
Overview: A small local charitable organization founded in 1987
Mission: To gather, preserve & display to the public information pertaining to the history of the former Huntley Township & its people
Affiliation(s): Ontario Historical Society
Finances: *Funding Sources:* Membership dues; grants; book sales; provincial & municipal funding
Membership: *Fees:* $25 regular; US$25 foreign; *Member Profile:* Interest in local history
Activities: *Library:* Resource Centre at Carp Branch, Ottawa Public Library; Open to public

Huntsville & District Association for the Mentally Retarded
See Community Living Huntsville

Huntsville & Lake of Bays Railway Society
Muskoka Heritage Place, 88 Brunel Rd., Huntsville ON P1H 1R1
Tel: 705-789-7576; *Fax:* 705-789-6169
www.portageflyer.org
Also Known As: The Portage Railway
Overview: A small local charitable organization founded in 1984
Mission: Maintains & displays original artifacts of the old Huntsville & Lake of Bays Railway, plus vintage railway equipment from the turn of the century
Affiliation(s): Muskoka Heritage Place
Finances: *Funding Sources:* Fundraising; Rotary Club; local industry; donations
Membership: *Fees:* $35 regular; $45 international
Activities: A fully functional operating railway
Chief Officer(s):
David Topps, President
president@portageflyer.org

Huntsville, Lake of Bays Chamber of Commerce
37 Main St. East, Huntsville ON P1H 1A1
Tel: 705-789-4771; *Fax:* 705-789-6191
chamber@huntsvillelakeofbays.on.ca
huntsvillelakeofbays.on.ca
www.facebook.com/HLOBChamber
twitter.com/HuntsvilleChamb
Overview: A small local organization
Mission: To help with the economic growth of their members
Member of: Canadian Chamber of Commerce
Staff Member(s): 8
Membership: *Fees:* $92 non-profit; $211 1 employee; $273 2-10 employees; $342 11-40 employees; $667 40+ employees
Chief Officer(s):
Kelly Haywood, Executive Director, 705-789-4771 Ext. 22
kelly@huntsvillelakeofbays.on.ca

Huron Chamber of Commerce - Goderich, Central & North Huron
56 East St., Goderich ON N7A 1N3
Tel: 519-440-0176; *Fax:* 519-440-0305
Toll-Free: 855-440-0176
info@huronchamber.ca
www.huronchamber.ca
www.linkedin.com/company/huron-chamber-of-commerce
www.facebook.com/huronchamber
twitter.com/huronchamber
instagram.com/huronchamber
Previous Name: Goderich & District Chamber of Commerce
Overview: A small local organization
Mission: To promote & improve trade & commerce & the economic, civic & social welfare of the Goderich, Central & North Huron regions
Member of: Ontario Chamber of Commerce
Finances: *Funding Sources:* Membership fees
Staff Member(s): 1
Membership: *Fees:* Schedule available
Chief Officer(s):
Gerry Rogers, Chair
Heather Boa, Operations Manager

Huron East Chamber of Commerce
c/o Ralph Laviolette, PO Box 433, Seaforth ON N0K 1W0
Tel: 519-440-6206
www.huroneastcc.ca
Overview: A small local organization
Mission: To act as a voice for its members; To support businesses
Member of: Canadian Chamber of Commerce
Membership: 67
Chief Officer(s):
Ralph Laviolette, Secretary

Huron Perth Association of Realtors
#6, 55 Lorne Ave. East, Stratford ON N5A 6S4
Tel: 519-271-6870; *Fax:* 519-271-3040
www.hpar.ca
Merged from: Huron Real Estate Board; Perth County Real Estate Board
Overview: A small local organization overseen by Ontario Real Estate Association
Mission: To maintain a professional standard among its members in order to better serve the public
Member of: The Canadian Real Estate Association
Membership: 252
Chief Officer(s):
Gwen Kirkpatrick, Executive Officer
gwen@wightman.ca

Huronia & District Beekeepers' Association (HDBA)
c/o Peter Dickey, Dickey Bee Honey Inc., 4031 - 3rd Line., Cookstown ON L0L 1L0
Tel: 705-458-1258
www.huroniabeekeepers.com
www.facebook.com/huroniabeekeepers
Overview: A small local organization
Mission: To inform members of current developments in beekeeping
Member of: Ontario Beekeepers' Association
Membership: *Fees:* $30; *Member Profile:* Persons from the Huronia area who are dedicated to the practice of keeping honey bees
Activities: Organizing lectures, meetings, beekeeping field trips, seminars, & demonstrations; Providing networking opportunities with professional & amateur beekeepers; Recommending literature about beekeeping to members; Offering beekeeping mentors to teach beginners interested in beekeeping
Chief Officer(s):
Peter Dickey, President
Publications:
• Bee Talker
Type: Newsletter

Huronia Symphony Orchestra (HSO)
PO Box 904, Stn. Main, Barrie ON L4M 4Y6
Tel: 705-721-4752
office@huroniasymphony.com
www.huroniasymphony.ca
www.facebook.com/huroniasymphony
twitter.com/huroniasymphony
Overview: A small local charitable organization founded in 1966 overseen by Orchestras Canada
Mission: To operate & support a symphony orchestra in Simcoe County; to provide symphonic music for people of the area as well as an opportunity for children & youth to receive instruction in orchestral music
Member of: Orchestras Canada
Finances: *Funding Sources:* Corporate & individual donations; Ticket revenue; Grants
Membership: 55; *Committees:* Logistics; Marketing; Human Resources; Youth Program; Artistic Advisory
Activities: Performing concert series; participating in Culture Days to build an audience base by performing in casual settings like shopping malls
Chief Officer(s):
John Hemsted, President
Don MacLeod, General Manager
Oliver Balaburski, Artistic Director & Conductor

Huronia Tourism Association *See* Tourism Simcoe County

Huron-Perth Beekeepers' Association
ON
Overview: A small local organization
Mission: To provide education about beekeeping; To promote the beekeeping industry in Huron-Perth
Member of: Ontario Beekeepers' Association
Membership: *Member Profile:* Beekeepers in the Huron-Perth area of Ontario
Activities: Offering networking opportunities for members; Helping local beekeepers deal with problems that arise for beekeepers

Hussar Fish & Game Association
c/o Alberta Fish & Game Association, 6924 - 104th St., Edmonton AB T6H 2L7
Tel: 780-437-2342; *Fax:* 780-438-6872
office@afga.org
www.afga.org/html/content/clubandzones
Overview: A small local organization

Member of: Alberta Fish & Game Association
Chief Officer(s):
Deb Clarke, Director, Zone 2, Alberta Fish & Game Association

Hydro-Québec Foundation for the Environment *Voir* Fondation Hydro-Québec pour l'environnement

Hydro-Québec Professional Engineers Union *Voir* Syndicat professionnel des ingénieurs d'Hydro-Québec

Hypertension Canada
#211, 3780 - 14th Ave., Markham ON L3R 9Y5
Tel: 905-943-9400; *Fax:* 905-943-9401
www.hypertension.ca
twitter.com/HTNCANADA
www.youtube.com/user/hypertensioncanada
Merged from: Blood Pressure Canada; Canadian Hypertension Society; & Canadian Hypertension Education Program
Overview: A medium-sized national organization
Mission: To advance health by preventing & controlling high blood presseure
Finances: *Funding Sources:* Membership fees: Donations; Sponsorships
Membership: *Fees:* $25 associates (fellows, residents, medical student, or graduate students); $100 individuals; *Member Profile:* Professionals who support goals of Hypertension Canada; Individuals in training for practice in the field of hypertension; Pharmaceutical industrries & other companies with an interest in hypertension
Activities: Supporting research; Engaging in advocacy activities; Providing education
Chief Officer(s):
Nadia Khan, President
Angelique Berg, Chief Executive Officer
Glen Doucet, Vice-President
Trevor Hudson, Treasurer
Meetings/Conferences:
• 2018 Canadian Hypertension Congress, 2018
Scope: National
Publications:
• Hypertension Therapeutic Guide
Type: Textbook
Profile: A reference tool to help physicians, nurses, & pharmacistsin the management of hypertension

IAB Internet Advertising Bureau of Canada *See* Interactive Advertising Bureau of Canada

IAESTE Canada (International Association for the Exchange of Students for Technical Experience) (IAESTE)
194 Boteler St., Ottawa ON K1N 5A7
canada@iaeste.org
iaestecanada.org
Overview: A small international organization founded in 1953
Mission: To provide technical students with international work experience related to their studies
Member of: IAESTE International
Finances: *Annual Operating Budget:* $100,000-$250,000
Staff Member(s): 2; 4 volunteer(s)
Membership: 80+ countries
Chief Officer(s):
David Fraser, National Secretary
nationalsecretary@iaestecanada.org

IAMAW District 78
#102, 557 Dixon Rd., Toronto ON M9W 6K1
Tel: 416-225-9003
iamdl78.org
Previous Name: Northern Independent Union
Overview: A small provincial organization
Member of: International Association of Machinists & Aerospace Workers
Chief Officer(s):
Terry Rennette, President

IBD Foundation
#200, 205 Catherine St., Ottawa ON K2P 1C3
Tel: 613-293-7050
info@ibdfoundation.org
www.ibdfoundation.org
Overview: A small national charitable organization
Mission: To improve the quality of life of people affected by IBD (Inflammatory Bowel Disease)
Membership: *Committees:* Medical Advisory
Activities: Organizing fundraising events; Developing nutrition education programs; *Awareness Events:* World IBD Day, May 19; Embassy Chef Challenge
Chief Officer(s):
Michele Hepburn, President

I.C.C. Foundation
#1001, 75 Albert St., Ottawa ON K1P 5E7
Tel: 613-563-2642; *Fax:* 613-565-3089
icc@inuitcircumpolar.com
www.inuitcircumpolar.com
Also Known As: Inuit Circumpolar Council
Overview: A small national charitable organization
Mission: To promote Inuit culture in Canada & the circumpolar region, & the knowledge of its members concerning social, economic & cultural studies of same
Chief Officer(s):
Corinne Gray, Executive Director
cgray@inuitcircumpolar.com

Ice Skating Association of Ontario *See* Ontario Speed Skating Association

Icelandic National League of North America (INLNA)
#103, 94 - 1st Ave., Gimli MB R0C 1B1
Tel: 204-642-5897; *Fax:* 204-642-9382
www.inlofna.org
www.facebook.com/IcelandicNationalLeagueofNorthAmerica
Overview: A medium-sized national organization founded in 1919
Mission: To foster & promote good citizenship among people of Icelandic descent; to foster & strengthen a mutual understanding of kinship, language, literature & cultural bonds among people of Icelandic origin & descent in North America & the people of Iceland; to cooperate with organizations which have similar purposes & objectives; to actively support various cultural & ethnic developments including education, history, publishing & the arts
Affiliation(s): Icelandic National League
Finances: *Annual Operating Budget:* Less than $50,000; *Funding Sources:* Membership fees; donations
Membership: 2,000; *Fees:* $25 individual; $100 associate club & provisional; chapters - formula
Activities: International tours; INL Reads; Donald K. Johnson Film Screenings; Snorri West
Chief Officer(s):
Sunna Furstenau, President
Awards:
• Laurence S. G. Johnson Lifetime Achievement Award
Meetings/Conferences:
• Icelandic National League of North America 2018 Annual Convention, April, 2018, Edmonton, AB
Scope: National

ICOM Musées Canada *See* ICOM Museums Canada

ICOM Museums Canada / ICOM Musées Canada
#400, 280 Metcalfe St., Ottawa ON K2P 1R7
Tel: 613-567-0099
www.linkedin.com/groups/ICOM-Canada-4263110
www.facebook.com/150364635019516
twitter.com/ICOMCanada
Also Known As: International Council of Museums
Overview: A medium-sized national charitable organization founded in 1946
Mission: To advance the cause of museums throughout the world & in Canada; to provide liaison with International Council of Museums in Paris; to hold annual meeting in conjunction with Canadian Museums Association.
Member of: Canadian Museums Association & Société des musées québécois
Finances: *Funding Sources:* Membership dues
Membership: *Member Profile:* Museologists
Activities: *Library:* Open to public
Chief Officer(s):
Audrey Vermette, Director, Programs & Public Affairs
avermette@museums.ca

ICOMOS Canada
PO Box 737, Stn. B, Ottawa ON K1P 5P8
Tel: 613-749-0971; *Fax:* 613-749-0971
secretariat@canada.icomos.org
canada.icomos.org
Also Known As: International Council on Monuments & Sites Canada
Overview: A medium-sized international organization founded in 1975
Mission: To further the conservation, protection, rehabilitation, & enhancement of monuments, groups of buildings & sites; To encourage primary research in many important fields
Affiliation(s): UNESCO; International Centre for the Study of the Preservation & Restoration of Cultural Property (ICCROM)
Finances: *Annual Operating Budget:* Less than $50,000
Staff Member(s): 1
Membership: 500; *Fees:* $175 individual; $50 young professional/student; $100 affiliate; institutional available; *Member Profile:* Conservation professionals & advocates concerned with developing & promoting, through international exchange, the highest professional standards of practice in the conservation of the built environment; *Committees:* 100 national committees & 28 international scientific committees
Activities: Researching; communicating; providing professional services
Chief Officer(s):
Christophe Rivet, President
Robert Buckle, Vice-President, Strategic Planning
Michael McClelland, Vice-President, Memberships & Funding
Meetings/Conferences:
• ICOMOS Canada 2018 Annual Meeting, 2018
Scope: National

The Identification Clinic
#101, 260 Wyse Rd., Dartmouth NS B3A 1N3
Tel: 902-292-4587
theidclinic@gmail.com
www.theidclinic.org
www.facebook.com/theidentificationclinic
twitter.com/theidclinic
Overview: A small local organization founded in 2015
Mission: To assist homeless & disadvantaged individuals in the Halifax area acquire pieces of standard identification
Finances: *Funding Sources:* Individual donations
Staff Member(s): 5
Activities: Transporting individuals to government offices to obtain provincial photo cards, birth certificates, Nova Scotia health cards, &/or social insurance cards
Chief Officer(s):
Darren Greer, Founder/Coordinator

Ikaluktutiak Paddling Association
NU
Overview: A small provincial organization
Member of: Paddle Canada

Ile-a-la-Crosse Friendship Centre Inc.
PO Box 160, Lajeunesse Ave., Ile-a-la-Crosse SK S0M 1C0
Tel: 306-833-2313; *Fax:* 306-833-2216
ilx.friendctr.inc@sasktel.net
ilealacrossefc.weebly.com
www.facebook.com/4925553507971
Overview: A small local organization founded in 1980
Mission: The Centre provides referrals, information, social, cultural, health awareness & sports & recreational programs to help ensure a better quality of life for the community & area.
Member of: Aboriginal Friendship Centres of Saskatchewan; National Association of Friendship Centres
Chief Officer(s):
Myra Malboeuf, Executive Director

Ileostomy & Colostomy Association of Montréal (ICAM) / Association d'iléostomie et colostomie de Montréal (AICM)
5151, boul de l'Assomption, Montréal QC H1T 4A9
Tel: 514-255-3041; *Fax:* 514-645-5464
www.aicm-montreal.org
Overview: A small local charitable organization founded in 1958
Mission: To act for the welfare for ostomates & their families
Affiliation(s): United Ostomy Association of Canada Inc.
Finances: *Funding Sources:* Donations; Sponsorships
Membership: *Fees:* $20 regular members
Activities: Hosting monthly meetings; Providing information to members & the public; Organizing social activities
Chief Officer(s):
Jean-Pierre Lapointe, President & Treasurer, 514-645-4023
Huguette Fortier, Secretary, 514-355-1245

Imagine Canada
#700, 65 St. Clair Ave. East, Toronto ON M4T 2Y3
Tel: 416-597-2293; *Fax:* 416-597-2294
Toll-Free: 800-263-1178
info@imaginecanada.ca
www.imaginecanada.ca
www.linkedin.com/groups/1866345
www.facebook.com/ImagineCanada

Canadian Associations / Immigrant & Multicultural Services Society (IMSS)

twitter.com/ImagineCanada
www.youtube.com/ImagineCanada
Merged from: Canadian Centre for Philanthropy; Coalition of National Voluntary Organizations
Overview: A large national charitable organization founded in 1980
Mission: To support Canada's charities, non-profit organizations, & socially conscious businesses
Finances: *Funding Sources:* Foundations; Corporations; Government; Earned income; Donations
Membership: *Member Profile:* Charities, foundations & businesses
Activities: Conducting research about the charitable sector; Providing information resources; *Library:* John Hodgson Library; by appointment
Chief Officer(s):
Bruce MacDonald, President & CEO
bmacdonald@imaginecanada.ca
Cathy Barr, Vice-President, Mission Effectiveness
cbarr@imaginecanada.ca
Bill Harper, Vice-President, Finance & Operations, 416-597-2293 Ext. 233
bharper@imaginecanada.ca
Marnie Grona, Director, Strategic Communications, 416-597-2293 Ext. 244
mgrona@imaginecanada.ca
 Ottawa
 Ottawa ON
 Tel: 613-238-7555; *Fax:* 613-238-9300
 Toll-Free: 800-263-1178

Immigrant & Multicultural Services Society (IMSS)
1270 - 2nd Ave., Prince George BC V2L 3B3
Tel: 250-562-2900; *Fax:* 250-563-4852
Toll-Free: 877-562-2977
imss.pg@shawcable.com
www.imss.ca
www.facebook.com/274005189316931
Overview: A small provincial charitable organization founded in 1976
Mission: The Society works to promote multiculturalism & to develop cross-cultural understanding in the community. It acts as a central resource & information center for smaller agencies & professionals, & the agency also provides orientation counselling & assistance to immigrants in this northern region of the province. It is a registered charity, BN: 107504045RR0001.
Member of: Affiliation of Multicultural Societies & Service Agencies of BC
Finances: *Annual Operating Budget:* $500,000-$1.5 Million; *Funding Sources:* Provincial and Federal government
Staff Member(s): 25; 30 volunteer(s)
Membership: 80; *Fees:* $10
Activities: English Language Services for Adults; Youth Against Racism; Employment Assistance Program; Settlement Program; Women's Program; information & referral services; computer classes; *Awareness Events:* BC Multicultural Week, November
Chief Officer(s):
Ben Levine, President
Baljit Sethi, Executive Director
baljit.imss@shawcable.com
Ann Saa, Settlement Practitioner/Executive Assistant
ann@imss.ca

Immigrant & Visible Minority Women Against Abuse *See* Immigrant Women Services Ottawa

Immigrant Centre Manitoba Inc.
100 Adelaide St., Winnipeg MB R3A 0W2
Tel: 204-943-9158; *Fax:* 204-949-0734
info@icmanitoba.com
icmanitoba.com
Also Known As: International Centre of Winnipeg
Previous Name: Citizenship Council of Manitoba Inc.
Overview: A medium-sized provincial charitable organization founded in 1965
Mission: To encourage pride in Canada & appreciation of Canadian citizenship; to encourage intercultural understanding in multicultural Canada; to support immigration & provide caring services to newcomers.
Member of: Canadian Citizenship Federation
Affiliation(s): Canadian Council for Refugees; Canadian Citizenship Federation
Finances: *Annual Operating Budget:* $1.5 Million-$3 Million; *Funding Sources:* Federal government; Provincial government; United Way
Staff Member(s): 34; 300 volunteer(s)

Membership: 70 corporate + 130 individual; *Fees:* $10 individual; $25 group
Activities: Immigrant serving agency; multicultural centre; hostels & residences
Chief Officer(s):
Cec Hanec, President

Immigrant Services - Guelph Wellington
#4 & 5, 926 Paisley Rd., Guelph ON N1K 1X5
Tel: 519-836-2222
info@is-gw.ca
www.is-gw.ca
Previous Name: Guelph & District Multicultural Centre
Overview: A small local organization founded in 1976 overseen by Ontario Council of Agencies Serving Immigrants
Mission: To help settle & integrate newcomers into their community; to encourage individuals to participate fully in all aspects of society, social, economic, political & cultural.
Finances: *Annual Operating Budget:* $500,000-$1.5 Million; *Funding Sources:* Citizenship & Immigration Canada; Canadian Heritage; National Crime Prevention Centre; United Way of Guelph & Wellington; City of Guelph
Staff Member(s): 21
Activities: Settlement integration; citizenship program; interpreter & translation services; anti-racism program; employment services; language assessment; *Awareness Events:* Guelph Multicultural Festival; *Library*
Chief Officer(s):
Roger Manning, President
Roya Rabbani, Executive Director

Immigrant Services Association of Nova Scotia (ISANS)
Mumford Professional Centre, #2120, 6960 Mumford Rd., Halifax NS B3L 4P1
Tel: 902-423-3607; *Fax:* 902-423-3154
Toll-Free: 866-431-6472
info@isans.ca
www.isans.ca
www.facebook.com/isans.immigrantservices
twitter.com/isans_ca
vimeo.com/isans
Previous Name: Immigrant Settlement & Integration Services (ISIS)
Merged from: Metropolitan Immigrant Settlement Association (MISA); Halifax Immigrant Learning Centre (HILC)
Overview: A medium-sized provincial organization founded in 1980
Mission: To assist immigrants settling in Nova Scotia
Finances: *Annual Operating Budget:* Greater than $5 Million; *Funding Sources:* Provincial & federal government grants; United Way; Family Learning Initiative Endowment Fund
Staff Member(s): 115
Activities: Refugee resettlement; Professional programs; Family counselling; English in the Workplace
Chief Officer(s):
Catharine Penney, Chair
Basia Dzierzanowska, Vice-Chair
Lilani Kumaranayake, Secretary-Treasurer
Gerry Mills, Executive Director

Immigrant Services Calgary (CIAS)
#1200, 910 - 7th Ave. SW., Calgary AB T2P 3N8
Tel: 403-265-1120; *Fax:* 403-266-2486
info@calgaryimmigrantaid.ca
www.immigrantservicescalgary.ca
www.linkedin.com/company/immigrant-services-calgary
www.facebook.com/ImmigrantServicesCalgary
twitter.com/askISCmmigrantServicesCalgary
Previous Name: Calgary Immigrant Aid Society
Overview: A small local charitable organization founded in 1977
Mission: To offer information to newcomers & helps them to settle in, find employment, access language training, send children to Canadian schools, & become a part of the Calgary community.
Member of: Canadian Citizenship Federation
Finances: *Funding Sources:* Federal/provincial/local government; foundations; IDA & casino
Staff Member(s): 150; 730 volunteer(s)
Membership: *Fees:* $5
Activities: Certified translation; interpretation services; language assessment; career counseling
Chief Officer(s):
Wilson Ho, Chair
Krystyna Biel, CEO

Awards:
• Immigrants of Distinction Awards
Publications:
• ESL Directory
Type: guide
Profile: A general guide to ESL programs & services offered around Calgary

Immigrant Services Society of BC (ISSofBC)
2610 Victoria Dr., Vancouver BC V5N 4L2
Tel: 604-684-2561; *Fax:* 604-684-2266
info@issbc.org
www.issbc.org
www.linkedin.com/company/83044
www.facebook.com/issbc
twitter.com/issbc
Overview: A small provincial charitable organization founded in 1972
Mission: To be a leader in identifying the needs of immigrants & refugees & in developing, demonstrating & delivering effective, quality programs & services which serve those needs; To provide integration services; To deliver educational programs; To advocate for our clients & communities
Member of: Affiliation of Multicultural Societies & Service Agencies of BC; Assn. of Service Providers for Employability & Career Training; Better Business Bureau; Canadian Council for Refugees; Volunteer Vancouver; Vancouver Refugee Council
Finances: *Annual Operating Budget:* Greater than $5 Million
Staff Member(s): 220; 600 volunteer(s)
Membership: 150; *Fees:* $10 individual; $50-$1,000 corporate; $25 non-profit; *Committees:* Bursary; Community Relations; Executive; Finance; Governance; Membership; Nominations; Personnel; Premises
Activities: *Awareness Events:* Refugee Children's Christmas Party
Chief Officer(s):
Patricia Woroch, CEO
Awards:
• Susan Paulson Bursary Award
 Burnaby - Settlement & Career Services
 #207, 7355 Canada Way, Burnaby BC V3N 4Z6
 Tel: 604-395-8000; *Fax:* 604-395-8003
 settlement@issbc.org
 Coquitlam - Settlement Services
 #200, 504 Cottonwood Ave., Coquitlam BC V3J 2R5
 Tel: 778-383-1438; *Fax:* 604-931-8558
 settlement@issbc.org
 Richmond - LINC & Settlement Services
 #150, 8400 Alexandra Rd., Richmond BC V6X 3L4
 Tel: 604-233-7077; *Fax:* 604-233-7040
 linc.richmond@issbc.org
 Port Coquitlam - LINC
 #204, 3242 Westwood St., Port Coquitlam BC V3C 3L8
 Tel: 778-372-6560; *Fax:* 604-945-4534
 linc.tricities@issbc.org
 Coquitlam - Career & Settlement Services
 #240A, 3020 Lincoln Ave., Coquitlam BC V3B 6B4
 Tel: 778-284-7026; *Fax:* 604-942-1730
 skillsconnect@issbc.org
 Maple Ridge - LINC, Settlement & Career Services
 #320, 22470 Dewdney Trunk Rd., Maple Ridge BC V2X 5Z6
 Tel: 778-372-6567; *Fax:* 604-477-1154
 linc.mr@issbc.org
 Langley - Settlement & Career Services
 #204, 20621 Logan Ave., Langley BC V3A 7R3
 Tel: 604-510-5136; *Fax:* 604-530-5519
 settlement@issbc.org
 New Westminster - LINC, Settlement & Career Services
 #280, 610 Sixth St., New Westminster BC V3L 3C2
 Tel: 604-522-5902; *Fax:* 604-522-5908
 linc.nwest@issbc.org
 Squamish - LINC & Assessment Services
 PO Box 2229, 38085 Second Ave., 1st Fl., Squamish BC V8B 0B5
 Tel: 604-567-4490
 Richmond - LINC
 #110, 5751 Cedarbridge Way, Richmond BC V6X 2A8
 Tel: 604-637-1307; *Fax:* 604-303-8711
 linc.richmond@issbc.org
 Coquitlam - LINC
 #136, 3030 Lincoln Ave., Coquitlam BC V3B 6B4
 Tel: 604-942-1777; *Fax:* 604-942-1780
 linc.tricities@issbc.org

Burnaby - LINC & Settlement Services
#105, 4180 Lougheed Hwy., Burnaby BC V5C 6A7
Tel: 604-936-0210; Fax: 604-559-6664
Vancouver - Language & Career College
#601, 333 Terminal Ave., Vancouver BC V6A 4C1
Tel: 604-684-7561; Fax: 604-684-2266
settlement@issbc.org

Immigrant Settlement & Integration Services (ISIS) See Immigrant Services Association of Nova Scotia

Immigrant Welcome Centre (MISA)
#A114, 740 Robron Rd., Campbell River BC V9W 6J7
Tel: 250-830-0171; Fax: 250-830-1010
Toll-Free: 855-805-0171
www.immigrantwelcome.ca
www.facebook.com/157900677578942
twitter.com/immigrantcentre
Also Known As: Immigrant Welcome Centre of Campbell River
Previous Name: Campbell River & Area Multicultural & Immigrant Services Association
Overview: A small local organization founded in 1992
Mission: To develop services & programs that provide an on-going opportunity for immigrants & their families to learn skills to adapt to Canadian society; To sponsor opportunities to celebrate cultural diversity & learn about the issues of cultural acceptance, network & support other agencies as the provide services to the multicultural community
Member of: Affiliation of Multicultural Societies & Service Agencies of BC
Finances: Funding Sources: Government; bingo
Staff Member(s): 4
Membership: 90; Fees: $5 youth; $10 individual; $20 family; $30 organization
Activities: ESL; Intercultural Friendship Program; Multicultural Settlement; Community Kitchen; Multicultural & Anti-Racism workshop; interpreter; referral; drop-in centre; crisis counselling; citizenship classes; Youth 4 Diversity; Family Night; Seniors Group; Women's Group; Diversity Health Fair; Inclusive Leadership Adventure; Meaningful Media Night; Speaker Service: Yes; Library: Video & Resource Library

Immigrant Women of Saskatchewan See Regina Immigrant Women Centre

Immigrant Women of Saskatchewan, Saskatoon Chapter See International Women of Saskatoon

Immigrant Women Services Ottawa (IWSO) / Services pour femmes immigrantes d'Ottawa
#400, 219 Argyle St., Ottawa ON K2P 2H4
Tel: 613-729-3145; Fax: 613-729-9308
infomail@immigrantwomenservices.com
www.immigrantwomenservices.com
www.facebook.com/immigrantwomenservicesottawa
twitter.com/ImmigrantWomen
Previous Name: Immigrant & Visible Minority Women Against Abuse
Overview: A small local organization founded in 1989
Mission: To empower & enable immigrant women in the Ottawa region to participate in the elimination of all forms of abuse against women; to raise awareness among immigrant women who are abused, in order to break down their isolation & enable them to advocate on their own behalf; to develop a crisis service for immigrant women who are abused to give them full access to mainstream resources; to develop cross-cultural training for shelters & mainstream agencies regarding the special needs of immigrant women in order to ensure that existing services are accessible & appropriate to them & their families; to educate immigrant communities to work toward ending violence against women.
Activities: Information & referrals to services; crisis counselling & group support; cultural interpretation to communicate with service agencies

Immigrant Women's Health Centre (IWHC)
#200, 489 College St., Toronto ON M6G 1A5
Tel: 416-323-9986; Fax: 416-323-0447
info@immigranthealth.info
immigranthealth.info
Overview: A small local charitable organization founded in 1975 overseen by Ontario Council of Agencies Serving Immigrants
Mission: To help immigrant & refugee women who have difficulty accessing health services due to cultural, physical, economic, linguistic, political, racial, sexual orientation, age & religious barriers.

Member of: Ontario Sexual Health Network; Metro Network for Social Justice; Toronto Health Coalition
Activities: Free clinical services; workshops at ESL classes, factories, schools, support groups, etc.; mobile clinic
Chief Officer(s):
Ayesha Adhami, Administrative Coordinator
aadhami@immigranthealth.info

Immigrant Women's Job Placement Centre See Toronto Community Employment Services

Immunisation Canada See Immunize Canada

Immunize Canada / Immunisation Canada
c/o Canadian Public Health Association, #404, 1525 Carling Ave., Ottawa ON K1Z 8R9
Tel: 613-725-3769; Fax: 613-725-9826
www.immunize.ca
www.facebook.com/ImmunizeCanada
twitter.com/immunizedotca
www.youtube.com/user/ImmunizeCanada
Previous Name: Canadian Coalition for Immunization Awareness & Promotion
Overview: A small national organization founded in 2004
Mission: To contribute to the control, elimination, & eradication of vaccine preventable diseases in Canada; To increase awareness of the benefits & risks of immunization for all ages
Finances: Funding Sources: NGOs; federal government; private sector
Membership: 27 organizations; 3 government members; 6 sponsor members
Activities: Awareness Events: National Immunization Awareness Week, April; Influenza Awareness Month, Oct.
Chief Officer(s):
Shelly McNeil, Chair
Nicole Le Saux, Vice-Chair

Impact Society
#830, 105 - 12th Ave. SE, Calgary AB T2G 1A1
Tel: 403-280-1856
Toll-Free: 888-224-3762
info@impactsociety.com
www.impactsociety.com
www.facebook.com/heroesimpact
twitter.com/heroesimpact
www.youtube.com/heroesimpact
Overview: A small national charitable organization
Mission: To provide leadership & innovation for character development across Canada; To offer a framework of support for youth & the persons who influence them
Finances: Funding Sources: United Way; Donations; Grants; Sponsorships; Agencies; Fundraising
Activities: Offering experiential-learning programs, such as the HEROES Across Canada program; Awareness Events: Night of Impact gala fund; Speaker Service: Yes
Chief Officer(s):
Jack Toth, Chief Executive Officer
jack@impactsociety.com
Gerald Auger, Director, Indigenous Leadership & Development
gerald.auger@impactsociety.com
Ben Clayton, Director, Innovation
ben.clayton@impactsociety.com
Yvette Starlight, Director, Community Advancement
yvette.starlight@impactsociety.com

Imperial Order Daughters of the Empire See IODE Canada

Import Vintners & Spirits Association
#125A, 1030 Denman St., Vancouver BC V6G 2M6
Tel: 778-840-4872
admin@ivsa.ca
www.ivsa.ca
Overview: A medium-sized provincial organization
Mission: To promote & protect the interests of agents, importers, & organizations in the beverage alcohol industry in British Columbia & Alberta
Affiliation(s): BC Hospitality Foundation
Membership: 169; Fees: Schedule available; Member Profile: Import agencies; Consular & hospitality trade groups; Associate members
Activities: Promoting industry events; Awareness Events: New Product Salon
Chief Officer(s):
Richard Loewen, Executive Director
richard@ivsa.ca

IMS Health Canada See Quintiles IMS Canada

INAS (Canada) See Patronato INAS (Canada)

INCA See Canadian National Institute for the Blind

Incident Prevention Association of Manitoba (IPAM)
#51, 162 - 2025 Corydon Ave., Winnipeg MB R3P 0N5
Tel: 204-275-3727
office@ipam-manitoba.com
ipam-manitoba.com
Overview: A small provincial organization founded in 1961
Membership: Member Profile: Government & individuals in the Province of Manitoba, who are interested in health and safety
Chief Officer(s):
Karen Turner, President, 204-582-3932
protec1@mymts.net
Meetings/Conferences:
• Incident Prevention Association of Manitoba 2018 Safety Saves Conference & Tradeshow, 2018, MB
Scope: Provincial

Inclusion Alberta (AACL)
11724 Kingsway Ave., Edmonton AB T5G 0X5
Tel: 780-451-3055; Fax: 780-453-5779
Toll-Free: 800-252-7556
mail@inclusionalberta.org
inclusionalberta.org
www.linkedin.com/company/3831926
www.facebook.com/InclusionAlberta
twitter.com/inclusionAB
Previous Name: Alberta Association for Community Living; Alberta Association for the Mentally Handicapped
Overview: A medium-sized provincial charitable organization founded in 1956 overseen by Canadian Association for Community Living
Mission: To advocate for fully inclusive community lives for children & adults with developmental disabilities
Member of: Canadian Association for Community Living; Inclusion International
Affiliation(s): Alberta Community Living Foundation
Finances: Funding Sources: Alberta Community Living Foundation; Provincial government grants; Fundraising; Donations
Staff Member(s): 67
Membership: Member Profile: Non-profit community organizations throughout Alberta
Activities: Offering an annual summer institute on inclusive education in partnership with other organizations; Hosting an annual leadership series for families; Developing networks of families, known as Family Voices, throughout the province to advocate regionally; Communicating through social media; Speaker Service: Yes; Library: Reg Peters Library; Open to public
Chief Officer(s):
Bruce Uditsky, Chief Executive Officer
buditsky@inclusionalberta.org
Shawn Ergang, Chief Operating Officer
sergang@inclusionalberta.org
Trish Bowman, Executive Director, Community Devlopment
pbowman@inclusionalberta.org
Meetings/Conferences:
• Inclusion Alberta Annual Family Conference 2018, 2018, AB
Scope: Provincial
Publications:
• Connections [a publication of Inclusion Alberta]
Type: Magazine
Profile: News & updates for members

Inclusion BC
227 - 6th St., New Westminster BC V3L 3A5
Tel: 604-777-9100; Fax: 604-777-9394
Toll-Free: 800-618-1119
info@inclusionbc.org
www.inclusionbc.org
www.facebook.com/InclusionBC
twitter.com/InclusionBC
www.youtube.com/user/BCACL
Previous Name: British Columbia Association for Community Living; British Columbians for Mentally Handicapped People
Overview: A medium-sized provincial charitable organization founded in 1955 overseen by Canadian Association for Community Living
Mission: To enhance the lives of persons with developmental disabilities & their families; To promote the participation of people with developmental disabilities in all aspects of community life; To support activities dedicated to building inclusive communities that value the diverse abilities of all people

Member of: Canadian Association for Community Living; United Way of Lower Mainland
Finances: *Funding Sources:* Donations
Membership: *Member Profile:* Individuals; Families; Volunteers; Associations; *Committees:* Self Advocacy Advisory
Activities: Advocating for children, youth, & adults with developmental disabilities & their families; Ensuring justice, rights & opportunities for people with developmental disabilities; Presenting scholarships for personal & professional development opportunities; Communicating through social media; *Speaker Service:* Yes; *Rents Mailing List:* Yes; *Library:* British Columbia Association for Community Living Library
Chief Officer(s):
Jackie Carpenter, President
Faith Bodnar, Executive Director, 604-777-9100 Ext. 516
fbodnar@inclusionbc.org
Karen De Long, Director, Community Development, 604-777-9100 Ext. 530
kdelong@inclusionbc.org
Jillian Bradley, Director, Employment Initiatives, 604-777-9100 Ext. 533
jbradley@inclusionbc.org
Frank Peng, Director, Finance & Administration, 604-777-9100 Ext. 513
fpeng@inclusionbc.org
Karla Verschoor, Director, Strategic Initiatives, 604-777-9100 Ext. 519
kverschoor@inclusionbc.org
Pam Ratcliff, Office Manager, 604-777-9100 Ext. 518
pratcliff@inclusionbc.org
Meetings/Conferences:
• Inclusion BC 2018 Conference & AGM, 2018
Scope: Provincial
Publications:
• Inclusion BC Annual Report
Type: Yearbook; *Frequency:* Annually
• Inclusion BC Membership Directory
Type: Directory
Profile: Information on programs & services provided by British Columbia Association for Community Living & its member associations

Inclusion Powell River Soceity
#201, 4675 Marine Ave., Powell River BC V8A 2L2
Tel: 604-485-6411
info@pracl.ca
inclusionpr.ca
www.facebook.com/241189675918848
Overview: A small local charitable organization founded in 1954
Mission: Supports people with disabilities, children who are at risk for, or who have a developmental delay, & their families; offers respectful, lifelong supports with the goal that each individual will have a change to have the life they want; advocates with & for individuals & families; strengthens the community by offering education that celebrates differences by valuing contributions of all citizens
Member of: British Columbia Association for Community Living
Affiliation(s): Association for the Severely Handicapped; Council for Exceptional Children; Family Support Institute; Cerebral Palsy Association; Learning Disabilities Association
Finances: *Funding Sources:* Provincial government; fundraising
Membership: *Member Profile:* Attendance at 3 meetings to have voting privilege at annual general meeting
Activities: Powell River Infant Development Program; early childhood community therapy service; employment support service; Cranberry Children's Centre; family support service; Community Living Place (multi purpose facility); Free Spirit Leisure Club; residential service; supported child care; day programs for adults; *Library:* Open to public
Chief Officer(s):
Lilla Tipton, Executive Director

Indefinite Arts Society (IDAS)
8038 Fairmount Dr. SE, Calgary AB T2H 0Y1
Tel: 403-253-3174; *Fax:* 403-255-2234
ida@indefinitearts.com
www.indefinitearts.com
www.facebook.com/IndefiniteArts
twitter.com/IndefiniteArts
Overview: A small local charitable organization founded in 1975
Mission: To provide opportunities for people with developmental disabilities to express themselves & to grow, through their involvement in art; to strive to increase community awareness of the talents & diversity of artists with disabilities. It has been certified by the Alberta Council of Disability Services.
Finances: *Funding Sources:* Provincial government

Staff Member(s): 9
Activities: Programs in fiberarts, ceramics, drawing, painting, sculpture & woodworking; *Speaker Service:* Yes
Chief Officer(s):
John Lee, Chair
Darlene Murphy, Executive Director

Independence Plus Inc.
#115, 66 Waterloo St., Saint John NB E2L 3P4
Tel: 506-643-7004; *Fax:* 506-643-7009
Overview: A small local charitable organization
Mission: To provide residential service for persons who are physically or mentally challenged & operates a Handi-Bus transit service for people with mobility concerns.
Finances: *Funding Sources:* Saint John Transit Commission
Chief Officer(s):
David Black, Executive Director
DavidBlack@nb.aibn.com

Independent Assemblies of God International - Canada (IAOGI)
PO Box 653, Chatham ON N7M 5K8
Tel: 519-352-1743; *Fax:* 519-351-6070
pmcphail@ciaccess.com
www.iaogcan.com
Also Known As: IAOGI Canada
Previous Name: Scandinavian Assemblies of God in the United STates of America, Canada & Foreign Lands
Merged from: The Scandinavian Assemblies of God & the Independent Pentecostal Churches
Overview: A medium-sized national charitable organization founded in 1918
Mission: To provide credientials for pastors and missionaries in all provinces & territories of Canada
Member of: Independent Assemblies of God International
Affiliation(s): Independent Assemblies of God International
Finances: *Annual Operating Budget:* $100,000-$250,000; *Funding Sources:* Membership fees; Offerings
Staff Member(s): 2; 12 volunteer(s)
Membership: 700+ Christian ministers; *Fees:* $155; *Member Profile:* Must be called by God to preach His Word
Activities: *Awareness Events:* National Convention, May; *Speaker Service:* Yes
Chief Officer(s):
Paul McPhail, General Secretary
pmcphail@ciaccess.com
Publications:
• The Canadian Mantle
Type: Newsletter; *Frequency:* 3 pa

Independent Association of Support Staff (IASS) / Association indépendante des employés de soutien
121, av Summerhill, Pointe-Claire QC H9R 2L8
Tel: 514-426-1003; *Fax:* 514-426-5814
office-info@iass.ca
www.iass.ca
Overview: A medium-sized local organization
Mission: To represent the Lester B. Pearson School Board's administrative, technical, & paratechnical staff
Staff Member(s): 3
Membership: 1,600; *Committees:* Professional Development; Labour Relations; Executive
Activities: Secretarial; classroom; librarians; daycare; supervisor; computer techs
Chief Officer(s):
Allison Provost, President

Independent Canadian Extrusion Workers Union (CNFIU)
836 Fuller Ave., Penetanguishene ON L9M 1G8
Tel: 705-549-8728
Overview: A small national organization
Membership: 165 + 1 local
Chief Officer(s):
David Miller, President

Independent Contractors & Businesses Association of British Columbia (ICBA)
#211, 3823 Henning Dr., Burnaby BC V5C 6P3
Tel: 604-298-7795; *Fax:* 604-298-2246
Toll-Free: 800-663-2865
info@icba.bc.ca
www.icba.bc.ca
www.linkedin.com/company/independent-contractors-and-businesses-association-of-b-c-
www.facebook.com/theicba
twitter.com/icbabc

Overview: A medium-sized provincial organization founded in 1975 overseen by Merit Canada
Mission: To market & raise profile of open shop sector; To provide members with construction information & programs which assist them in labour relations efforts; To promote ongoing improvement of skills & knowledge of new entrants to the construction industry (scholarships, apprenticeships, grants)
Member of: Coalition of BC Businesses; Merit Canada
Affiliation(s): Merit Contractors Group
Finances: *Annual Operating Budget:* $500,000-$1.5 Million
Staff Member(s): 16
Membership: 1,200; *Fees:* $400-$1425 based on annual volume; *Member Profile:* Companies active in the construction industry
Chief Officer(s):
Philip Hochstein, President
philip@icba.ca

Independent Federation of Autonomous Unions *Voir*
Fédération indépendante des syndicats autonomes

Independent Film & Video Alliance *See* Independent Media Arts Alliance

Independent Filmmakers' Co-operative of Ottawa (IFCO)
#140, 2 Daly Ave., Ottawa ON K1N 6E2
Tel: 613-569-1789; *Fax:* 613-564-4428
admin@ifco.ca
www.ifco.ca
Overview: A small local organization founded in 1992
Mission: To promote independent filmmaking in the Ottawa region; to foster film production by providing access to training programs, equipment rentals, on-site facilities, & grants.
Member of: Independent Media Arts Alliance
Affiliation(s): Ottawa Arts Court Tenants (City of Ottawa)
Staff Member(s): 3
Membership: *Fees:* $80; $25 student; *Member Profile:* Independent filmmakers
Activities: Training; exhibition of film; news/communications; technical support; equipment rentals; open house; premiere of members' films; *Internships:* Yes; *Library:* Open to public
Chief Officer(s):
Deniz Berkin, President
Patrice James, Executive Director
director@ifco.ca

Independent Financial Brokers of Canada (IFB) / Courtiers indépendants en sécurité financière du Canada (CISF)
#740, 30 Eglinton Ave. West, Mississauga ON L5R 3E7
Tel: 905-279-2727; *Fax:* 905-276-7295
Toll-Free: 888-654-3333
general@ifbc.ca
www.ifbc.ca
www.linkedin.com/company/independent-financial-brokers-of-canada
twitter.com/IFBcanada
Previous Name: Independent Life Insurance Brokers of Canada
Overview: A small national organization founded in 1985
Mission: To enhance & protect businesses of members; to support consumer choice
Finances: *Annual Operating Budget:* $500,000-$1.5 Million; *Funding Sources:* Membership fees; conference registration
Membership: 4,000; *Fees:* Schedule available; *Member Profile:* Independent insurance, mutual fund & other financial service brokers & professionals; *Committees:* Executive; Nominating
Activities: Frequent Educational Summits
Chief Officer(s):
John Dargie, Chair & President
Scott Findlay, Vice-Chair
Marie Jose (MJ) Comtois, Treasurer

Independent First Nations' Alliance (IFNA)
PO Box 5010, 98 King St., Sioux Lookout ON P8T 1K6
Tel: 807-737-1902; *Fax:* 807-737-3501
Toll-Free: 888-253-4362
receptionist@ifna.ca
www.ifna.ca
Overview: A small local organization
Mission: IFNA provides its member communities with technical support & community development programs. The Alliance tries to meet the needs & aspirations of its First Nations on a collective basis, while each member First Nation maintains its autonomy.
Staff Member(s): 7

Membership: *Member Profile:* 4 communities: Lac Seul First Nation, Muskrat Dam First Nation, Pikangikum First Nation, & Kitchenubmaykossib First Nation
Chief Officer(s):
Gerry McKay, CEO
gmckay@ifna.ca

Independent Life Insurance Brokers of Canada *See* Independent Financial Brokers of Canada

Independent Living Canada (ILC) / Vie autonome Canada (VAC)
#1170, 343 Preston St., Ottawa ON K1S 1N4
Tel: 613-563-2581; *Fax:* 613-563-3861
info@ilcanada.ca
www.ilcanada.ca
Previous Name: Canadian Association of Independent Living Centres
Overview: A medium-sized national charitable organization founded in 1986
Mission: To represent & coordinate the network of independent living centres; To guide & support independent living centres in the delivery of programs & services
Finances: *Funding Sources:* Membership fees; Sponsorships; Fundraising
Membership: *Committees:* Centre Development & Accreditation; Communications & Marketing; External Relations; Governance Policy & Structure; Resources & Fund Development
Activities: Developing policies to support programs offered by independent living centres; Providing training & resources; Creating networking opportunities for the exchange of information & ideas; Liaising with government & other organizations; Raising public awareness of independent living centres; Offering information about independent living centres to the public, the media, & governments; *Library:* Independent Living Library
Chief Officer(s):
Diane Kreuger, National Chair
Paula Sanders, Secretary
Awards:
• John Lord Award
• Canada Consumer Award of Excellence
• The Allan Simpson Award for Programming
• Canada Volunteer Award
Publications:
• Independent Living Canada Annual Report
Type: Yearbook; *Frequency:* Annually
• The Perspective: The National Independent Living News Bulletin
Type: Newsletter
Profile: Organizational updates, current events, articles, social policy & research, & fundraising intiatives

Independent Living Nova Scotia (ILNS)
#151L, 7071 Bayers Rd., Halifax NS B3L 2C2
Tel: 902-453-0004
Toll-Free: 877-310-4567
ilnsadmin@ilns.ca
www.ilns.ca
www.facebook.com/146896108683919
twitter.com/ILNS2014
Overview: A medium-sized local organization founded in 1992
Mission: To support persons with disabilities make informed choices about their lives by providing programs and services that support independent living.
Staff Member(s): 5
Activities: *Library:* Open to public
Chief Officer(s):
Sherry Costa, Executive Director

Independent Lumber Dealers Co-operative (ILDC)
#100, 596 Kingston Rd. West, Ajax ON L1T 3A2
Tel: 905-428-0690; *Fax:* 905-428-0690
ildc@ildc.com
www.ildc.com
Overview: A small local organization founded in 1964
Member of: SPANCAN
Finances: *Annual Operating Budget:* $250,000-$500,000
Membership: 20; *Member Profile:* Independent home improvement chains
Chief Officer(s):
A. Battagliotti, General Manager
P. Bonhomme, President

Independent Media Arts Alliance (IMAA) / Alliance des arts médiatiques indépendants (AAMI)
#200-A, 4067, boul Saint-Laurent, Montréal QC H2W 1Y7
Tel: 514-522-8240; *Fax:* 514-987-1862
info@imaa.ca
www.imaa.ca
www.facebook.com/imaa.aami
twitter.com/IMAA_AAMI
www.youtube.com/channel/UC4dulDEsR21dbEg_0hTqNiw?feature=mhee
Previous Name: Independent Film & Video Alliance
Overview: A small national organization founded in 1980
Mission: To promote discussion among media art centres; To coordinate independent film & video centres
Finances: *Annual Operating Budget:* $100,000-$250,000; *Funding Sources:* Canada Council; Canadian Heritage; Telefilm; NFB
Staff Member(s): 2; 11 volunteer(s)
Membership: 80 organizations, 16,000 individuals; *Fees:* $100-300; *Member Profile:* Independent film, video, audio & new media organizations; *Committees:* Advocacy Tasks Forces; 2016 National Media Arts Summit; Exhibition Standards; Preservation; 2016 Media Arts Prize; Distribution Roundtable; Media Arts Delegation Working Group; Review of General Policies
Activities: Annual meetings; newsletter; lobbying; *Internships:* Yes
Chief Officer(s):
Emmanuel Madan, National Director
dir@imaa.ca
Mercedes Pacho, Director, Communications & Development

Independent Meeting Planners Association of Canada, Inc. *See* Canadian Society of Professional Event Planners

The Independent Order of Foresters *See* Foresters

Independent Power Association of BC *See* Clean Energy British Columbia

Independent Power Producers Society of Alberta (IPPSA)
#2600, 144 - 4th Ave. SW, Calgary AB T2P 3N4
Fax: 403-256-8342
www.ippsa.com
Overview: A small provincial organization founded in 1993
Mission: To represent Alberta's major power producers; To encourage dialogue among power producers in Alberta
Membership: 100+; *Fees:* $15,000 power member; $7,500 junior power member; $1,000 corporate member; $250 associate member; *Member Profile:* Operators of Alberta's power supply
Activities: Engaging with Alberta's government & its agencies in policy development; Reviewing legislation, regulations & market rules; Promoting competition in Alberta's electrical market; Providing news about the industry; Sponsoring a bursary for a student at the University of Calgary's Schulich School of Engineering (Electricity Department)
Chief Officer(s):
Evan Bahry, Executive Director, 403-282-8811, Fax: 403-256-8342
Evan.Bahry@ippsa.com
Joe Novecosky, Contact, Membership & Events, 403-256-1587, Fax: 403-256-8342
joeno@telusplanet.net
Meetings/Conferences:
• Independent Power Producers Society of Alberta Annual Conference 2018, 2018, AB
Scope: Provincial
Attendance: 500+
Description: An event featuring guest speakers, panel discussions, debates, a trade show, social events, & networking opportunities
Contact Information: Executive Director: Evan Bahry, Phone: 403-282-8811, E-mail: Evan.Bahry@ippsa.com
Publications:
• IPPSA [Independent Power Producer Society of Alberta] News
Type: Newsletter; *Frequency:* 5 pa
Profile: Industry happenings for IPPSA members

Independent Power Producers Society of Ontario (IPPSO) *See* Association of Power Producers of Ontario

Independent Practice Nurses Interest Group (IPNIG)
Attn: RNAO Membership Services, 158 Pearl St., Toronto ON M5H 1L5
Tel: 416-599-1925; *Fax:* 416-599-1926
Toll-Free: 800-268-7199
admin@ipnig.ca
www.ipnig.ca
Previous Name: Ontario Association of Nurses in Independent Practice
Overview: A small national organization
Mission: To facilitate unity within our diverse profession by supporting our members through educational & networking opportunities; To promote direct access to independent nursing services through political & social action, public awareness & professional liaisons
Member of: Registered Nurses Association of Ontario
Affiliation(s): Canadian Nurses Association
Finances: *Funding Sources:* Membership fees
Membership: *Member Profile:* Must be Registered Nurse & member of RNAO; *Committees:* Professional Nursing Practice/Best Practice Guidelines; Research, Education & Resources; Public Policy & Political Action; Public Relations/Networking; Membership; Communication Newsletter
Activities: *Speaker Service:* Yes; *Rents Mailing List:* Yes; *Library:* by appointment

Independent Production Fund (IPF) / Fonds indépendant de production
#1709, 2 Carlton St., Toronto ON M5B 1J3
Tel: 416-977-8966; *Fax:* 416-977-0694
info@ipf.ca
ipf.ca
Previous Name: Canadian Television Series Development Foundation
Overview: A small national charitable organization founded in 1989
Mission: To support the production of Canadian dramatic television series by independent producers through financial investment.
Finances: *Funding Sources:* Mountain Cablevision Ltd.; Broadcast Distribution Undertaking (BDU) contributions
Staff Member(s): 9
Activities: Funding Canadian dramatic television series & pilots; awarding special project grants for professional development activities, training & promotional programs
Chief Officer(s):
Charles Ohayon, Chair
Andra Sheffer, Executive Director
Carly McGowan, Program Manager
Québec Office
#503, 4200, boul St-Laurent, Montréal QC H2W 2R2
Tel: 514-845-4334; *Fax:* 514-845-5498
fipinfo@ipf.ca
Chief Officer(s):
Claire Dion, Associate Director

Independent School Bus Operators Association
PO Box 514, Arthur ON N0G 1A0
Tel: 416-560-4963
info@isboa.ca
www.isboa.ca
www.facebook.com/isboa
twitter.com/ISBOASchoolBus
Overview: A medium-sized provincial organization founded in 2008
Mission: To represent school bus operators & companies in Ontario
Membership: 120; *Fees:* $150-$5,000; *Member Profile:* School bus operators & suppliers; *Committees:* Media; Organization & Meetings; Research & Education
Activities: Providing training, products & services
Chief Officer(s):
Brian Crow, Executive Director

Independent Telecommunications Providers Association (ITPA)
29 Peevers Cres., Newmarket ON L3Y 7T5
Tel: 519-595-3975; *Fax:* 519-595-3976
www.ota.on.ca
Previous Name: Ontario Telecommunications Association
Overview: A small provincial organization
Mission: To represent the interests of small incumbent local exchange carriers (SILECs) from Ontario & British Columbia & to act as a forum for sharing expertise between member companies
Finances: *Funding Sources:* Membership dues
Staff Member(s): 1
Membership: 20; *Fees:* $395.50 associate; *Member Profile:* Independent Local Exchange Carriers in British Columbia and Ontario.

Canadian Associations / Indexing Society of Canada (ISC) / Société canadienne d'indexation (SCA)

Activities: Liaising with government departments & agencies & industry associates; Setting policies & compliance guidelines; Offering a forum to share expertise
Chief Officer(s):
Jonathan L. Holmes, Executive Director
Meetings/Conferences:
• Independent Telecommunications Providers Association 53rd Annual Convention 2018, 2018
Scope: Provincial
Description: An event featuring guest speakers, informative seminars, the annual general meeting, social events, & opportunities to meet with telecommunications industry representatives

Indexing & Abstracting Society of Canada / Société canadienne pour l'analyse de documents See Indexing Society of Canada

Indexing Society of Canada (ISC) / Société canadienne d'indexation (SCA)
133 Major St., Toronto ON M5S 2K9
www.indexers.ca
www.linkedin.com/groups/8248555/profile
twitter.com/indexerscanada
www.pinterest.com/iscsci
Also Known As: Indexers.ca
Previous Name: Indexing & Abstracting Society of Canada / Société canadienne pour l'analyse de documents
Overview: A medium-sized national organization founded in 1977
Mission: To encourage the production & use of indexes & abstracts; To promote the recognition of indexers & abstractors; To improve indexing & abstracting techniques; To improve communication among individual indexers & abstractors
Affiliation(s): American Society of Indexers; Association of Southern African Indexers and Bibliographers; Australian and New Zealand Society of Indexers; China Society of Indexers; Deutsches Netzwerk der Indexer; International Committee of Representatives of Indexing Societies; Netherlands Indexing Network; Society of Indexers; Publishing Technology Group of SI; Editors' Association of Canada; Society for Editors and Proofreaders; Editorial Freelancers Association; American Library Association; American Society for Information Science and Technology; Canadian Publishers' Council
Finances: *Funding Sources:* Membership fees
Staff Member(s): 4
Membership: *Fees:* $155 institutional; $150 individuals; $115 student; *Member Profile:* Any institution, service, or individual interested in promotion of the society's objectives
Chief Officer(s):
Margaret de Boer, Co-President
margaretdeboer.indexer@gmail.com
Alexandra Pearce, Co-President
alex@alexandrapeace.com
Frances Robinson, Membership Secretary
membership@indexers.ca
Awards:
• Ewart-Daveluy Indexing Award
Awarded to recognize excellence in indexing *Eligibility:* Canadian citizens or citizens of other countries who reside in Canada; nominees are not required to be a member of ISC/SCI
• Tamarack Award
Presented to an ISC member to recognize outstanding volunteer contributions to the organization
Meetings/Conferences:
• Indexing Society of Canada Annual Conference 2018, June, 2018, Winnipeg, MB
Scope: National
Publications:
• The Indexing Society of Canada Bulletin
Type: Newsletter; *Frequency:* 3 pa; *Editor:* Andrea Hatley; *ISSN:* 1914-3192
Profile: Information resource including Society news & important dates
• The Indexing Society of Canada Membership Directory
Type: Yearbook; *Frequency:* Annually
Profile: Resource for members only

India Rainbow Community Services of Peel (IRCS)
#206 & Unit 1, 3038 Hurontario St., Mississauga ON L5B 3B9
Tel: 905-275-2369; *Fax:* 905-275-6799
info@indiarainbow.org
www.indiarainbow.org
Overview: A small local charitable organization founded in 1985
Mission: To provide non-religious & non-political services for integration into Canadian society; To meet the need for social services & training in the Peel immigrant community
Affiliation(s): Multicultural Inter-Agency Group; Volunteer Centre of Peel; Mayors Breakfast Group; Peel Community Against Woman Abuse; Caregivers of Peel Network
Finances: *Annual Operating Budget:* $500,000-$1.5 Million; *Funding Sources:* CIC/OASIS; COSTI/OCASI; Ministry of Health; Ministry of Community & Social Services; United Way of Peel Region
Staff Member(s): 40; 80 volunteer(s)
Membership: 200; *Fees:* $10 individual; $15 family
Activities: Job search workshops in Mississauga 905/275-1976; English language training in Mississauga 905/273-4932; Adult Day Centre for Long Term Care; English Language Training Brampton; Job Search Brampton; LINC Brampton; Mississauga Training Centre; Rainbow Long Term Care Centre
Chief Officer(s):
Samuel Malvea, President

Indian & Metis Friendship Centre of Prince Albert (IMFCPA)
1409 - 1st Ave. East, Prince Albert SK S6V 1G2
Tel: 306-764-3431; *Fax:* 306-763-3205
paimfc.reception@sasktel.net
www.facebook.com/IMFCPA
Previous Name: Prince Albert Indian & Métis Friendship Centre
Overview: A small local organization founded in 1963
Mission: To promote understanding, cooperation, & trust; To recognize the social, cultural, & recreational needs of aboriginal people in Prince Albert & the surrounding area
Affiliation(s): Aboriginal Friendship Centres of Saskatchewan
Activities: Information & referral services; home visits; advocacy; housing; income tax services; transient aid, elder & youth programming; fine option program; native court-workers program
Chief Officer(s):
Connie Farber, Executive Director
Publications:
• Prince Albert Indian & Métis Friendship Centre Newsletter
Type: Newsletter; *Frequency:* Monthly

Indian & Metis Friendship Centre of Winnipeg Inc. (IMFC)
45 Robinson St., Winnipeg MB R2W 5H5
Tel: 204-586-8441; *Fax:* 204-582-8261
imfcentre.net
twitter.com/IMFC_BINGO
Overview: A small local organization founded in 1959
Staff Member(s): 11
Chief Officer(s):
Jim Sinclair, Executive Director

Indian Agricultural Program of Ontario (IAPO)
PO Box 100, 220 North St., Stirling ON K0K 3E0
Tel: 613-395-5505; *Fax:* 613-395-5510
Toll-Free: 800-363-0329
info@indianag.on.ca
www.indianag.on.ca
Overview: A small provincial organization founded in 1984
Mission: IAPO is a non-profit corporation that fosters sustainable economic growth of Ontario First Nations People through agricultural programs involved in all sectors, including dairy, beef, swine, poultry, crops, farm retail, repair, & agri-forestry.
Membership: *Member Profile:* Status Indians registered in Ontario with businesses on or off reserve
Activities: Loans program; agriculture advisory service; seminars; conferences
Chief Officer(s):
Jamie Hall, General Manager
jamie@indianag.on.ca
Bill Bateman, Financial Administrator
bill@indianag.on.ca
Publications:
• Native Agri Update
Type: Newsletter; *Frequency:* Monthly
  Western/Southern Office
  1010 Adelaide St. South, London ON N6E 1R4
  Tel: 519-652-2440; *Fax:* 519-652-0085
  Toll-Free: 800-663-6912
  Chief Officer(s):
  Grant Edwards, Business Advisor
  grant@indianag.on.ca

Indian Friendship Centre in Sault Ste Marie
122 East St., Sault Ste Marie ON P6A 3C7
Tel: 705-256-5634; *Fax:* 705-942-3227
info@ssmifc.ca
www.ssmifc.com
www.facebook.com/ssm.ifc
twitter.com/ssmifc
Overview: A small local organization founded in 1972
Mission: To provide a comprehensive range of social programs to improve the overall well-being of its community; to nurture Indian self-expression & leadership, & it encourages the study of Indian needs, the planning of services from both public & private agencies. 2nd location: 29 Welington St., East, Sault Ste. Marie.
Member of: Ontario Federation of Indian Friendship Centres
Affiliation(s): National Association of Friendship Centres
Finances: *Funding Sources:* Provincial & federal funding; fundraising
Staff Member(s): 39
Membership: *Fees:* $2 single; $5 family; elders - free; *Member Profile:* Urban aboriginal
Activities: A wide variety of services & programs, including employment unit, crisis intervention, life long care, literacy, alternative school, Ojibway language, family support, foster care, healing & wellness, alcohol/drug prevention, homeless initiative, health access centre
Chief Officer(s):
Cathy Syrette, Executive Director
director@ssmifc.ca

Indian Métis Christian Fellowship (IMCF)
3131 Dewdney Ave., Regina SK S4T 0Y5
Tel: 306-359-1096
imcf.info@sasktel.net
www.imcf.ca
Overview: A small local organization founded in 1978
Mission: IMCF is an urban aboriginal ministry supported by the Christian Reformed Church in North America - Canada. Its mission is to develop a worshipping, working community through serving the spiritual & social needs of aboriginal people in Regina.
Affiliation(s): Canadian Ministry Board; Indian Family Center, Winnipeg; Native Healing Centre, Edmonton
Finances: *Annual Operating Budget:* $100,000-$250,000
Membership: 30 individual
Activities: Drop-in ministry; daily prayer circle; soup & bannock lunch; computer club
Chief Officer(s):
Ben Vandezande, Interim Director

Indigenous Bar Association
c/o Anne Chalmers, 70 Pineglen Cres., Ottawa ON K2G 0G8
www.indigenousbar.ca
Overview: A medium-sized national organization
Mission: To recognize & respect the spiritual basis of our Indigenous laws, customs & traditions; To promote the advancement of legal & social justice for Indigenous peoples in Canada; To promote reform of policies & laws affecting Indigenous peoples in Canada; To foster public awareness within the legal community, the Indigenous community & the general public in respect of legal & social issues of concern to Indigenous peoples in Canada; To provide a forum & network amongst Indigenous lawyers
Membership: *Fees:* $200 full; $50 students; *Member Profile:* Full - Indigenous person who is a member of the Bar or law society of any province or territory in Canada; Indigenous person who is a judge or a retired judge of any Court of Record in Canada; Indigenous person in Canada who has graduated from a recognized law school; Student - Indigenous person in Canada who is enrolled in a recognized law school; Honourary - person who has distinguished himself/herself in the field of Indigenous law, or has made a significant contribution to the advancement of justice for Indigenous peoples in Canada; *Committees:* Federal Court Liaison; Missing & Murdered Aboriginal Women; Student
Chief Officer(s):
Koren Lightning-Earle, President, 780-721-2345
klightning-earle@indigenousbar.ca
Anne Chalmers, Administrative Support
achalmers@indigenousbar.ca
Awards:
• Indigenous Peoples' Counsel Award
Contact: Anne Chalmers, Contact, Awards & Scholarships, E-mail: achalmers@indigenousbar.ca
• Indigenous Bar Association Law Student Scholarship
; *Amount:* $2,000 *Contact:* Anne Chalmers, Contact, Awards & Scholarships, E-mail: achalmers@indigenousbar.ca
Meetings/Conferences:
• Indigenous Bar Association 30th Annual Fall Conference 2018,

2018
Scope: National
Contact Information: Assistant, Administration: Anne Chalmers,
E-mail: achalmers@indigenousbar.ca

Indigenous Literary Studies Association (ILSA)
indigenouslsa@gmail.com
www.indigenousliterarystudies.org
www.facebook.com/IndigenousLiteraryStudiesAssociation
Overview: A small national organization founded in 2013
Mission: To promote the continued production & teaching of Indigenous literature
Membership: *Fees:* $40 faculty; $20 students/community members/underwaged
Activities: Offering resources for studying, research, teaching, publishing & conferences
Chief Officer(s):
Jesse Archibald-Barber, President
Awards:
• Unpublished Literary Art by Emerging Writers, Indigenous Voice Awards
Five categories: Best Unpublished Prose Piece in English; Best Unpublished Poetic Piece(s) in English; Best Unpublished Prose Piece in French; Best Unpublished Poetic Piece(s) in French; Best Unpublished Piece in an Indigenous Language; *Amount:* $2,000
• Published or Performed Literary Art by Emerging Writers, Indigenous Voice Awards
Three categories: Most Significant Book of Prose by an Emerging Indigenous Writer; Most Significant Book of Poetry by an Emerging Indigenous Writer; Most Significant Work in an Alternative Format by an Emerging Indigenous Writer; *Amount:* $5,000
Meetings/Conferences:
• Indigenous Literary Studies Association 2018 4th Annual Gathering, 2018
Scope: National

Indigenous Physicians Association of Canada (IPAC)
#305, 323 Portage Ave., Winnipeg MB R3B 2C1
info@ipac-amic.org
www.ipac.amic.org
Overview: A small national organization
Mission: To serve the interests of Indigenous physicians, medical students & the health related interests of Indigenous people in Canada
Chief Officer(s):
Darlene Kitty, President

Indigenous Works
#2, 2510 Jasper Ave., Saskatoon SK S7J 2K2
Tel: 306-956-5360; *Fax:* 306-956-5361
Toll-Free: 866-711-5091
contact.us@indigenousworks.ca
indigenousworks.ca
www.linkedin.com/company/aboriginal-human-resource-council
www.facebook.com/aboriginalhr
twitter.com/inclusionworks
www.youtube.com/user/aboriginalhr
Previous Name: Aboriginal Human Resources Council
Overview: A medium-sized national organization founded in 1988
Mission: To build partnerships between corporations & First Nations, Métis & Inuit communities; to advance workplace inclusion efforts
Chief Officer(s):
Kelly Lendsay, President & CEO, 306-291-0424
klendsay@indigenousworks.ca
Paula Sawyer, Membership Coordinator, Leadership Circle, 306-956-5395
psawyer@indigenousworks.ca

Indo-Canada Chamber of Commerce (ICCC) / Chambre de commerce Indo-Canada
924 The East Mall, Toronto ON M9B 6K1
Tel: 416-224-0090; *Fax:* 416-916-0086
Other Communication: Alt. Phone: 416-224-0482
iccc@iccconline.org
www.iccconline.org
www.linkedin.com/groups/96776/profile
www.facebook.com/ICCCONLINE
twitter.com/Indocanadacc
Overview: A small international organization founded in 1977
Mission: To promote Indo-Canadian professionals & businesses; to facilitate business & trade between Canada & India & the Indian diaspora throughout the world; to highlight Indo-Canadian contributions in the economic, cultural & social fabric of Canada
Member of: Toronto Board of Trade; Ontario Chamber of commerce
Finances: *Funding Sources:* Sponsorships
Staff Member(s): 1
Membership: 850; *Fees:* $100 regular; $60 youth; $1,150 lifetime; *Member Profile:* Business; *Committees:* Business Development; Events; Energy; Finance; Golf; iCATS; IT; New Immigrants; SME; Trade
Activities: Business seminars; IT seminars; social events; *Awareness Events:* Cricket Tournament & Festival; Golf Tournament; Annual Awards & Gala Nite
Chief Officer(s):
Sanjay Makkar, President

Indspire
Six Nations of the Grand River, PO Box 5, #100, 50 Generations Dr., Ohsweken ON N0A 1M0
Tel: 519-445-3021; *Fax:* 866-433-3159
Toll-Free: 855-463-7747
Other Communication: E-mails: donate@indspire.ca; education@indspire.ca
communications@indspire.ca
indspire.ca
www.facebook.com/Indspire
twitter.com/Indspire
Previous Name: National Aboriginal Achievement Foundation
Overview: A small national charitable organization founded in 1985
Mission: To provide scholarships to Indigenous people that help them pay for a post-secondary educations
Finances: *Annual Operating Budget:* Greater than $5 Million
Staff Member(s): 34
Activities: Educational programs & resources; financial assistance to Aboriginal Youth; runs the Indspire Institute;
Internships: Yes; *Speaker Service:* Yes
Chief Officer(s):
Roberta Jamieson, President & CEO
Awards:
• Indspire Awards
Created in 1993 to recognize Indigenous professionals & youth who demonstrate outstanding career achievement.
• Indspire Scholarships
Designed to assist First Nation, Inuit, and Métis students in obtaining post-secondary education
   Toronto Office
   #1002, 555 Richmond St. West, Toronto ON M5V 3B1
   Tel: 416-987-0249; *Fax:* 416-926-7554
   Toll-Free: 855-463-7747
   Winnipeg Office
   #440, 70 Arthur St., Winnipeg MB R3B 1G7

Industrial Accident Victims Group of Ontario (IAVGO)
55 University Ave., 15th Fl., Toronto ON M5J 2H7
Tel: 416-924-6477; *Fax:* 416-924-2472
Toll-Free: 877-230-6311
Other Communication: Migrant Workers Toll-Free: 1-866-521-8535
www.iavgo.org
www.facebook.com/167369409975545
Overview: A medium-sized provincial charitable organization founded in 1975
Mission: To provide free services to injured workers in Ontario including legal advice, legal representation, public legal education, advocacy training & community development
Finances: *Annual Operating Budget:* $100,000-$250,000
Staff Member(s): 8
Membership: *Fees:* $10
Activities: Library: by appointment

Industrial Developers Association of Canada *See* Economic Developers Association of Canada

Industrial Fabrics Association International Canada (IFAI Canada)
1485 Laperriere Ave., Ottawa ON K1Z 7S8
Tel: 613-792-1218; *Fax:* 613-729-6206
Toll-Free: 800-225-4324
Other Communication: membership@ifai.com
ifaicanada@ifai.com
www.ifaicanada.com
Overview: A small national organization overseen by Industrial Fabrics Association International
Mission: To promote the welfare of the Canadian technical textile industry; To work towards solutions to common industry problems; To improve efficiency, quality, & maintenance within the Canadian industrial textile industry; To ensure ethical business practices; To benefit users of Canadian textile products
Membership: *Fees:* $285 affiliate membership; $385 sponsoring membership; $435 - $985 end product manufacturing companies (fee based on sales range); $1,135 supplier; *Member Profile:* Canadian corporations, proprietorships, or partnerships involved in the manufacture or sale of industrial textile products; Suppliers of goods or services to the industrial fabrics industry in Canada; Canadian designers & architects, who are involved in the textile industry
Activities: Directing work towards standardizing materials & production methods; Liaising with related organizations; Representing members before legislative bodies; Informing members of new & better materials & techniques; Creating networking opportunities with industry peers & experts; Offering training & educational opportunities
Chief Officer(s):
Kathy Jones, Executive Director
Frank Braeuer, Chair
Craig Fawcett, Vice-Chair
Meetings/Conferences:
• Industrial Fabrics Association International 2018 Expo, October, 2018, Kay Bailey Hutchison Convention Center, Dallas, TX
Scope: International
Publications:
• Industrial Fabrics Association International Membership Directory
Type: Directory

Industrial First Aid Attendants Association of British Columbia *See* Occupational First Aid Attendants Association of British Columbia

Industrial Gas Users Association (IGUA) / L'association des consommateurs industriels de gaz (ACIG)
#202, 260 Centrum Blvd., Orleans ON K1E 3P4
Tel: 613-236-8021; *Fax:* 613-830-7196
info@igua.ca
www.igua.ca
Overview: A medium-sized national organization founded in 1973
Mission: To provide a coordinated & effective voice for industrial firms depending on natural gas as fuel or feedstock; To represent industrial users of natural gas before regulatory boards & governments
Finances: *Annual Operating Budget:* $500,000-$1.5 Million; *Funding Sources:* Membership dues
Staff Member(s): 3
Membership: 39 corporate; *Fees:* Based on gas consumption, $1,200-$36,099; *Member Profile:* Industrial firms that use natural gas in Ontario & Quebec
Activities: Regulatory intervention; Government advocacy; Creating networking opportunities
Chief Officer(s):
Shahrzad Rahbar, President
srahbar@igua.ca
Yves Seguin, Chairman
Meetings/Conferences:
• 2018 Industrial Gas Users Association Spring Seminar, 2018
Scope: National

Industrial Instrument Manufacturers Association *See* Canadian Process Control Association

l'Industrie forestière de l'Ontario *See* Ontario Forest Industries Association

Industry Training Authority (ITA)
8100 Granville Ave., 8th Fl., Richmond BC V6Y 3T6
Tel: 778-328-8700; *Fax:* 778-328-8701
Toll-Free: 866-660-6011
customerservice@itabc.ca
www.itabc.ca
www.facebook.com/IndustryTrainingAuthority
twitter.com/ita_bc
Overview: A small provincial organization founded in 2004
Mission: A provincial government agency with legislated responsibility to govern and develop the industry training system in B.C.

Infant & Toddler Safety Association (ITSA) / Association pour la sécurité des bébés et des tout petits
#154, 23 - 500 Fairway Rd. South, Kitchener ON N2C 1X3
Tel: 519-570-0181; *Fax:* 519-570-1078
Toll-Free: 888-570-0181
www.infantandtoddlersafety.ca
Overview: A small national charitable organization founded in 1980
Mission: To offer information & resources to promote & increase the safety of young children & prevent paediatric injury & death
Finances: *Annual Operating Budget:* Less than $50,000
25 volunteer(s)
Membership: 1-99
Activities: Offering child car seat clinics, safety workshops, & speaker services; Providing healthcare training; Maintaining listings of child product safety notices; *Speaker Service:* Yes

Infant Feeding Action Coalition
533 Colborne St., London ON N6B 2T5
Tel: 416-595-9819
info@infactcanada.ca
www.infactcanada.ca
Also Known As: INFACT Canada
Previous Name: Infant/Maternal Nutrition Education Association
Overview: A small local organization
Mission: To protect, promote & support breastfeeding in Canada & globally; to promote better infant & maternal health; to foster appropriate mother & infant nutrition
Member of: Canadian Council for International Cooperation
Finances: *Funding Sources:* Membership dues; foundations; government
Activities: *Awareness Events:* World Breastfeeding Week, 1st week of Oct.; *Speaker Service:* Yes; *Library:* Breastfeeding Information Resource Centre; by appointment
Chief Officer(s):
Elisabeth Sterken, National Director
esterken@infactcanada.ca

Infant/Maternal Nutrition Education Association *See* Infant Feeding Action Coalition

Infection & Prevention Control Canada
PO Box 46125, Stn. Westdale, Winnipeg MB R3R 3S3
Tel: 204-897-5990; *Fax:* 204-895-9595
Toll-Free: 866-999-7111
info@ipac-canada.org
www.ipac-canada.org
www.linkedin.com/company/3590721
www.facebook.com/IPACCanada
twitter.com/IPACCanada
plus.google.com/110560934212739734281
Also Known As: IPAC Canada
Previous Name: Community & Hospital Infection Control Association Canada
Overview: A medium-sized national charitable organization founded in 1976
Mission: To promote excellence in the practice of infection prevention & control; to employ evidence based practice & application of epidemiological principles to improve the health of Canadians
Member of: International Federation of Infection Control (IFIC)
Staff Member(s): 2
Membership: *Fees:* $202 individual; $122 student/retired
Activities: Education; Communication; Standards; Research; Consumer awareness; *Library*
Chief Officer(s):
Gerry Hansen, Execurive Director
executivedirector@ipac-canada.org
Meetings/Conferences:
• IPAC Canada 2018 National Education Conference, May, 2018, Banff Centre, Banff, AB
Scope: National
Publications:
• Canadian Journal of Infection Control
Type: Journal; *Frequency:* Quarterly; *Editor:* Pat Piaskowski, RN, HBScN, CIC; *Price:* Free with CHICA-Canada membership
Profile: Information relevant to the practice of infection control in hospitals & communities
• Community & Hospital Infection Control Association Canada Annual Member & Source Guide
Type: Yearbook; *Frequency:* Annually; *Price:* Free with CHICA-Canada membership

Infertility Awareness Association of Canada (IAAC) / Association canadienne de sensibilisation à l'infertilité (ACSI)
#201, 475, av Dumont, Dorval QC H9S 5W2
Tel: 514-633-4494
Toll-Free: 800-263-2929
info@iaac.ca
www.iaac.ca
www.facebook.com/57435550753
twitter.com/iaac_acsi
www.pinterest.com/iaac1
Overview: A medium-sized national charitable organization founded in 1990
Mission: To offer assistance, support & education to individuals with infertility concerns; to increase the awareness & understanding of the causes, treatments & the emotional impact of infertility through the development of educational programs.
Member of: International Federation of Infertility Patient Associations (IFIPA)
Affiliation(s): Canadian Fertility & Andrology Society; Society of Obstetricians & Gynaecologists of Canada
Finances: *Funding Sources:* Government; membership dues; donations
Activities: Chapter Establishment Program (assists individuals who wish to contact existing chapters or who wish to establish an IAAC chapter in their area); information seminars; support groups; resource centres; telephone assistance programs; information package; *Awareness Events:* National Infertility Awareness Week; *Library:* by appointment
Chief Officer(s):
Janet Fraser, President

Infertility Network
160 Pickering St., Toronto ON M4E 3J7
Tel: 416-691-3611; *Fax:* 416-690-8015
info@infertilitynetwork.org
www.infertilitynetwork.org
Overview: A small national charitable organization founded in 1990
Mission: To provide information, support & referral on infertility & related issues; To help people make informed choices for family-building options; To advocate for reform of gamete donation practices
Finances: *Annual Operating Budget:* $50,000-$100,000
Staff Member(s): 2; 10 volunteer(s)
Membership: 7,000; *Fees:* $10
Activities: Offering seminars & support groups
Chief Officer(s):
Patricia Silver, President
Diane Allen, Executive Director

Infirmières de l'Ordre de Victoria du Canada *See* Victorian Order of Nurses for Canada

Infirmières et infirmiers en santé communautaire au Canada *See* Community Health Nurses of Canada

Infirmières unies de l'Alberta *See* United Nurses of Alberta

Info Northumberland
#700, 600 William St., Cobourg ON K9A 5J4
Tel: 905-372-8913; *Fax:* 905-372-4417
Toll-Free: 800-396-6626
Northumberland@fourinfo.com
www.fourinfo.com
twitter.com/fourinfo2
Also Known As: SHARE INFO Community Information Centre Inc.
Previous Name: Cobourg Community Information Centre Inc.
Overview: A small local charitable organization founded in 1979 overseen by InformOntario
Mission: To aid all citizens of Northumberland County giving them, upon request, information &/or referring them to the proper organization or service; To assess trends which meet needs of the community by careful evaluation of demands made by citizens
Member of: Community Information Online Consortium
Finances: *Funding Sources:* United Way; fundraising; Ministry of Community, Family & Children's Services; Trillium Foundation

Information & Communication Technologies Association of Manitoba (ICTAM)
#412, 435 Ellice Ave., Winnipeg MB R3B 1Y6
Tel: 204-944-0533; *Fax:* 204-957-5628
info@ictam.ca
www.ictam.ca
www.linkedin.com/company-beta/2050183
www.facebook.com/ICTAMMB
twitter.com/ICTAM
Overview: A medium-sized provincial organization
Mission: To provide programming, advocacy & collaboration to the information & communication technologies industry in Manitoba, in order to accelerate growth, prosperity & sustainability
Membership: 85; *Fees:* $25 student; $650 affiliate; $150-$3,000 business
Chief Officer(s):
Kathy Knight, CEO, 204-943-7133
kathy.knight@ictam.ca
Tammy Zagari, Chief Financial Officer, 204-953-2796
tzagari@ictam.ca
Publications:
• The HUB [a publication of the Information & Communication Technologies Association of Manitoba]
Type: Newsletter

Information & Communications Technology Council of Canada (ICTC) / Conseil des technologies de l'information et des communications du Canada (CTIC)
#300, 116 Lisgar St., Ottawa ON K2P 0C2
Tel: 613-237-8551; *Fax:* 613-230-3490
info@ictc-ctic.ca
www.ictc-ctic.ca
www.linkedin.com/company/information-and-communications-technology-council
www.facebook.com/196829353752455
twitter.com/@ictc_ctic
www.youtube.com/user/DigitalEconomyPulse
Previous Name: Software Human Resource Council (Canada) Inc.
Overview: A medium-sized national organization
Mission: To serve the software development profession by developing joint ventures in courseware design & delivery, by integrating training & education processes, by helping to ensure sufficient supply & quality of new entrants to the profession & by promoting an attractive image & definition of software workers
Member of: Canadian Advanced Technology Association (CATA); Information Technology Association of Canada (ITAC); Canadian Information Processing Society (CIPS)
Finances: *Annual Operating Budget:* Greater than $5 Million; *Funding Sources:* Private
Staff Member(s): 10
Membership: 1,000-4,999; *Fees:* Schedule available
Activities: *Internships:* Yes; *Speaker Service:* Yes
Chief Officer(s):
Faye West, Chair
Namir Anani, President & CEO
Sandra Saric, Vice-President, Talent Innovation

Information Agincourt; Information Scarborough *See* Agincourt Community Services Association

Information Barrie
Barrie Public Library, 60 Worsley St., Barrie ON L4M 1L6
Tel: 705-728-1010; *Fax:* 705-728-4322
infobarrie@barrie.ca
library.barrie.ca/about/information-barrie
Overview: A small local organization founded in 1977 overseen by InformOntario
Mission: To provide community information & referral; To work with other community agencies
Member of: Inform Canada; InformOntario
Affiliation(s): Information Providers Coalition (Simcoe County); 211 Simcoe County; Community Connection (Collingwood & Dist.); Information Orillia; Contact (Alliston)
Chief Officer(s):
Cathy Bodle, Coordinator

Information Brock
PO Box 131, 30 Allan St., Cannington ON L0E 1E0
Tel: 705-432-2636
Previous Name: Brock Information Centre
Overview: A small local organization founded in 1963 overseen by InformOntario
Mission: Free & confidential information & referral service; on-site thrift shop
Member of: InformOntario

Information Burlington
c/o Burlington Public Library, 2331 New St., 2nd Floor, Burlington ON L7R 1J4

Tel: 905-639-3611; Fax: 905-681-7277
infoburlington@bpl.on.ca
www.bpl.on.ca/resources/community-info
Overview: A small local organization founded in 1971 overseen by InformOntario
Mission: To offer a free, confidential information service to the citizens of Burlington; To connect people with the community & government services they need; To ensure that the public is aware of the programmes & services offered in the community
Member of: InformOntario
Affiliation(s): Halton Information Providers
Finances: *Annual Operating Budget:* $50,000-$100,000; *Funding Sources:* City of Burlington
Activities: Database: www.halinet.on.ca/hcd/sql/start.asp; *Library:* Open to public
Chief Officer(s):
Glynis Maxwell, Coordinator

Information Durham
345 Simcoe St. South, Oshawa ON L1H 4J2
Tel: 905-434-4636
Toll-Free: 866-463-6910
informationdurham@unitedwaydr.com
www.informdurham.com
www.facebook.com/informationdurham
twitter.com/InfoDurham
Also Known As: United Way Information Services
Overview: A small local organization overseen by InformOntario
Member of: InformOntario
Affiliation(s): United Way of Oshawa/Whitby/Clarington/Brock & Scugog; United Way of Ajax/Pickering/Uxbridge
Finances: *Annual Operating Budget:* $50,000-$100,000
Staff Member(s): 1; 5 volunteer(s)
Activities: Providing information on & referral to community, social & government services
Chief Officer(s):
Michele Watson, Manager, Information Services

Information Markham
101 Town Centre Blvd., Markham ON L3R 9W3
Tel: 905-415-7500
imarkham@markham.ca
www.informationmarkham.ca
www.facebook.com/InformationMarkham
Overview: A small local organization founded in 1972 overseen by InformOntario
Mission: To deliver quality information services to our clients; To enhance community life & promote Markham & York Region
Affiliation(s): Community Information & Volunteer Centre - York Region
Chief Officer(s):
Dianne Murray, Executive Director

Information Niagara
#10, 235 Martindale Rd., St Catharines ON L2W 1A5
Tel: 905-682-6611; Fax: 905-682-4314
Toll-Free: 800-263-3695
info@incommunities.ca
www.informationniagara.com
www.facebook.com/InformationNiagara
twitter.com/211CentralSouth
Also Known As: 211 Central South
Overview: A small local charitable organization founded in 1974 overseen by InformOntario
Mission: The organization offers community information & referral services, including an online searchable information database & another database of volunteers. It also maintains an interpretation service for a wide range of languages.
Member of: United Way
Finances: *Funding Sources:* Ontario Trillium Foundation
Staff Member(s): 12
Chief Officer(s):
Terri Bruce, Information Services Manager, 905-682-1900 Ext. 221
terri@informationniagara.com

Information Oakville
c/o Oakville Public Library, Central Branch, 120 Navy St., Oakville ON L6J 2Z4
Tel: 905-815-2046
Other Communication: Editorial e-mail:
informationoakville@oakville.ca
oplreference@oakville.ca
www.informationoakville.org
Also Known As: Community Information Service of the Oakville Public Library
Overview: A small local organization founded in 1980
Mission: To provide accurate information on the community of Oakville; information & referral services. Information Oakville is a founding member of Halton Information Providers, & Community Information Online Consortium (CIOC). Halton Community Services Database URL: halton.cioc.ca
Member of: Inform Canada; Inform Ontario; Oakville Public Library
Finances: *Annual Operating Budget:* $50,000-$100,000; *Funding Sources:* Library
Staff Member(s): 3
Activities: *Library:* Resource Centre; Open to public
Chief Officer(s):
Marcus Logan, Manager, Community Information
marcus.logan@oakville.ca

Information Orillia
c/o Orillia Public Library, 33 Mississauga St. West, Orillia ON L3V 3A6
Tel: 705-326-7743
info@informationorillia.org
www.informationorillia.org
www.facebook.com/Info.Orillia
twitter.com/InfoOrillia
Overview: A small local organization founded in 1969 overseen by InformOntario
Mission: To bring people & services together in Orillia & surrounding townships by information & referral
Member of: InformCanada; InformOntario
Affiliation(s): Coalition of Information Providers of Simcoe County
Finances: *Funding Sources:* City of Orillia; publications; bazaars; public donations
Staff Member(s): 3
Activities: *Library:* Resource Centre
Chief Officer(s):
Shannon O'Donnell, Executive Director

Information Resource Management Association of Canada (IRMAC)
PO Box 5639, Stn. A, Toronto ON M5W 1N8
Tel: 416-887-2837
www.irmac.ca
Also Known As: Database Association of Ontario
Overview: A medium-sized national organization founded in 1971
Mission: To provide a forum for members to exchange information about data administration & information resource management
Affiliation(s): DAMA International; British Columbia Data Management Association
Finances: *Funding Sources:* Membership dues
Membership: 100-150 individuals; *Member Profile:* Information management professionals, such as systems professionals; Industry suppliers
Activities: Sponsoring conferences, seminars, & workshops; Organizing the Data Warehouse Special Interest Group; *Speaker Service:* Yes
Chief Officer(s):
Allie Harris, President
Gordon Irish, Vice-President
J. Eduardo Martinez, Secretary
Afsaneh Afkari, Treasurer

Information Sarnia Lambton (ISL)
PO Box 354, Sarnia ON N7T 7J2
Tel: 519-542-1949
www.informationsarnialambton.org
www.facebook.com/167455956644103
Overview: A small local organization founded in 1960 overseen by InformOntario
Mission: To maintain a database of social & human service organizations in Lambton County

Information Services Vancouver
Vancouver BC
Tel: 604-875-6431; Fax: 604-660-9415; TTY: 604-875-0885; *Crisis Hot-Line:* 800-563-0808
info@bc211.ca
www.bc211.ca
www.facebook.com/bc211
Also Known As: BC211
Overview: A small local charitable organization founded in 1953
Mission: Information & referral to community, social & government agencies
Member of: BC Alliance of Information & Referral Services; InformCanada
Affiliation(s): Alliance of Information & Referral Systems (AIRS)
Finances: *Annual Operating Budget:* $500,000-$1.5 Million; *Funding Sources:* United Way; provincial government; City of Vancouver
Staff Member(s): 31; 2 volunteer(s)
Membership: 39; *Fees:* $25
Activities: Free & confidential assistance; links to more than 4,000 social, community & government agencies & services across the Lower Mainland & British Columbia; *Library:* by appointment
Chief Officer(s):
Nathan Wright, Executive Director, 604-708-3200
nathan.wright@bc211.ca
Rob Conley, Manager, Human Resources & Administration
rob@bc211.ca
Louise Ghoussoub, Manager, Information & Referral Services
louise@bc211.ca
Kanwaljit Sanghera, Manager, Resources & Publicatons/IT
ken@bc211.ca
Shane Dopson, Office Administrator
shane@bc211.ca

Information Technology Association of Canada (ITAC) / Association canadienne de la technologie de l'information
#801, 5090 Explorer Dr., Mississauga ON L4W 4T9
Tel: 905-602-8345; Fax: 905-602-8346
info@itac.ca
www.itac.ca
twitter.com/ITAC_Online
www.youtube.com/user/itacacti
Merged from: Strategic Microelectronics Council; Strategic Microelectronics Consortium
Overview: A medium-sized national organization founded in 1997
Mission: To represent companies in the computing & telecommunications hardware, software, services & electronic content sectors; To identifys & lead resolution on issues that affect the industry; To advocate for initiatives that enable continued growth & development in the industry
Staff Member(s): 17
Membership: 1,300 companies
Chief Officer(s):
Robert Watson, President & CEO
rwatson@itac.ca
Andrew Leduc, Vice President, GR & Policy
aleduc@itac.ca
Carlo Viola, Director, Finance
cviola@itac.ca
Montréal Office
#401, 465, rue St-Jean, Montréal QC H2Y 2R6
Tel: 514-287-0449
Chief Officer(s):
Claude Lemay, Vice-President, Quebec Region
clemay@itac.ca
Ottawa Office
#1120, 220 Laurier Ave. West, Ottawa ON K1P 5Z9
Tel: 613-238-4822; Fax: 613-238-7967
info@itac.ca
www.itac.ca
Chief Officer(s):
Christine Leonard, Director, Communications
cleonard@itac.ca

Information Technology Industry Alliance of Nova Scotia; Software Industry Association of Nova Scotia *See* Digital Nova Scotia

Information Tilbury & Help Centre
PO Box 309, 20 Queen St. North, Tilbury ON N0P 2L0
Tel: 519-682-2268; Fax: 519-682-3771
Overview: A small local charitable organization founded in 1982 overseen by InformOntario
Mission: To act as a "middle person" connecting people with services or volunteers who can help & to become involved with the community when & where needed; to provide the community with mediation information & referrals to community services by accessing individual & community needs by formulating programs services & resources in cooperation with existing organizations
Finances: *Funding Sources:* United Way
Activities: Food bank; community outreach; resume writing; emergency clothing; *Library:* Open to public
Chief Officer(s):
Karen Kirkwood-Whyte, Executive Director
karen@uwock.ca

Information Tillsonburg See Tillsonburg & District Multi-Service Centre

Information Windsor See 211 Southwest Ontario

InformCanada (ICF)
PO Box 41146, 1910 St-Laurent Blvd., Ottawa ON K1G 1A4
Tel: 613-683-5400; Fax: 613-761-9077
info@informcanada.ca
www.informcanada.ca
www.facebook.com/informcanada
Also Known As: Inform Canada Federation
Overview: A medium-sized national organization
Mission: To act as a resource for our members; to develop & promote national standards in our field, strengthen a national I&R network, & represent information & referral at a national level
Membership: Fees: $150 individual; $400-$675 non-profit; $1,475 for-profit; Member Profile: Public, not-for-profit & government information & referral services & practitioners
Activities: Awareness Events: Annual General Meeting
Chief Officer(s):
Kristen Buckley, President
president@informcanada.ca

InformOntario (IO)
c/o 3010 Forest Glade Dr., Windsor ON N8R 1L5
Tel: 519-735-9344
info@informontario.on.ca
www.informontario.on.ca
Also Known As: Association of Community Information Centres in Ontario
Overview: A medium-sized provincial charitable organization founded in 1980
Mission: To provide leadership to the organizations it represents so that they are able to best serve their members
Finances: Funding Sources: Membership fees
Membership: 60 community information centres; Committees: Standards
Chief Officer(s):
Sylvia Mueller, President
Barbara McLachlan, Coordinator

Inforoute Santé du Canada See Canada Health Infoway

Infrastructure Health & Safety Association (IHSA)
Centre for Health & Safety Innovation, #400, 5110 Creekbank Rd., Mississauga ON L4W 0A1
Tel: 905-625-0100; Fax: 905-625-8998
Toll-Free: 800-263-5024
info@ihsa.ca
www.ihsa.ca
ca.linkedin.com/pub/ihsa-news/41/986/aa3
twitter.com/IHSAnews
Merged from: CSAO; E&USA; THSAO
Overview: A medium-sized provincial organization founded in 2010
Mission: To serve the utilities, electrical, natural gas, aggregates, ready-mix, construction & transportation industries in Ontario; To develop prevention solutions for work environments
Membership: Committees: Advisory Councils; CVOR Review Panel; Fleet Safety Council; Labour - Management Committees; Section 21 Committees
Activities: Providing training that meets regulatory requirements & compliance standards
Chief Officer(s):
Michael Frolick, Chief Executive Officer & President
Meetings/Conferences:
• Infrastructure Health & Safety Association 2018 Annual General Meeting, 2018
Scope: Provincial
Description: A business meeting featuring a guest speaker & the presentation of awards
Publications:
• IHSA.ca Magazine
Type: Magazine; Frequency: Quarterly
• Infrastructure Health & Safety Association Annual Report
Type: Yearbook; Frequency: Annually
Profile: Departmental updates & financial statements

Ingénieurs Canada See Engineers Canada

Ingénieurs Canada See Engineers Canada

Ingénieurs sans Frontières See Engineers Without Borders

Ingénieurs Sans Frontières Québec (ISFQ) / Engineers Without Borders Quebec
#204, 8440, boul St-Laurent, Montréal QC H2P 2M5
Tél: 438-320-4737
isfq@isfq.ca
www.isfq.ca
www.linkedin.com/company/ing-nieurs-sans-fronti-res-qu-bec-isfq-
www.facebook.com/ingenieurssansfrontieresquebec
www.instagram.com/isf_qc
Aperçu: Dimension: grande; Envergure: internationale; fondée en 1994
Mission: Améliorer la qualité de vie dans les pays en développement à travers le développement durable; Fournir des services d'ingénierie dans les pays en développement; Informer le public sur l'importance de la coopération internationale
Finances: Fonds: Donations
Membre(s) du personnel: 5
Membre: Montant de la cotisation: 55$ régulier; 15$ étudiant; 1000$ corporation; Critères d'admissibilite: Ingénieurs actifs ou retraités du Québec
Activités: Design et construction des infrastructures; Formation & developpement
Membre(s) du bureau directeur:
Léanne Bonhomme, Directrice générale
direction-generale@isfq.ca
Raffaela Siniscalchi, Coordonnatrice, Projets de coopération

Ingersoll Coin Club
Ingersoll ON
Tel: 519-643-6541
woodydoesit-icc@yahoo.ca
Overview: A small local organization
Chief Officer(s):
Lorne Barnes, Contact

Ingersoll District Chamber of Commerce
132 Thames St. South, Ingersoll ON N5C 2T4
Tel: 519-485-7333; Fax: 519-485-6606
ingersollchamber.com
www.facebook.com/ingersollchamber
twitter.com/ingersollchambe
Overview: A small local organization founded in 1960
Membership: Fees: Schedule available; Committees: Strategic Planning; AGM & Awards of Excellence; Annual Fundraiser; Golf Tournament; Public Relations; Audit; Retail & Industrial; Nominating; Finance; Executive
Chief Officer(s):
Robin Schultz, President
Ann Campbell, General Manager

Ingersoll District Nature Club
c/o Lana Graham, Treasurer, 255 Mutual St., Ingersoll ON N5C 2A9
ingersolldistrictnatureclub@gmail.com
ingersollnatureclub.com
www.facebook.com/230279593830908
twitter.com/IngersollDNC
Overview: A small local charitable organization founded in 1952
Mission: To promote the enjoyment of nature through environmental appreciation & conservation; To encourage wise use & conservation of natural resources; To promote environmental protection
Member of: Federation of Ontario Naturalists
Finances: Annual Operating Budget: Less than $50,000; Funding Sources: Donations
Membership: 45; Fees: $10 youth; $15 single; $25 family
Chief Officer(s):
Sheila Fleming, Contact, 519-485-2645
Wayne Walden, Contact, 519-485-4220

Ininew Friendship Centre
PO Box 1499, 190 - 3rd Ave., Cochrane ON P0L 1C0
Tel: 705-272-4497; Fax: 705-272-3597
reception@ininewfriendshipcentre.ca
www.ininewfriendshipcentre.ca
www.facebook.com/www.ininewfriendshipcentre.ca
Overview: A small local organization
Mission: To improve the quality of life for everyone in the community by offering a wide variety of programs, covering health management, social work, sports & other communal activities.
Activities: Programs & services include life-long care, community development, drug & alcohol counselling, family support, a 10-bed facility for young offenders, employment counselling & continuous training programs
Chief Officer(s):
Desmond O'Connor, President
president@ininewfriendshipcentre.ca
Jack Solomon, Executive Director
executive@ininewfriendshipcentre.ca

Initiative nationale pour le soin des personnes âgées See National Initiative for the Care of the Elderly

Initiatives canadiennes oecuméniques pour la justice See KAIROS: Canadian Ecumenical Justice Initiatives

Injured Workers Association of Manitoba Inc. (IWAM)
Injured & Disabled Centre, 734 Polson Ave., Winnipeg MB R2X 1M2
Tel: 204-586-8183
Overview: A small provincial charitable organization founded in 1971
Mission: To reduce the resulting psychological impact of workplace injuries on workers & families by assisting them to understand the policies & procedures of the Workers Compensation Board or other disability related insurance policies; free services include consultations, information & referrals to appropriate resources
Member of: Canadian Injured Workers Alliance
Finances: Annual Operating Budget: Less than $50,000
Staff Member(s): 2; 12 volunteer(s)
Membership: 20; Fees: $10; Member Profile: Injured workers of Manitoba
Activities: One-to-one promotions; Counselling; Seminars

Inland Refugee Society of BC
#615, 525 Seymour St., Vancouver BC V6B 3K4
Tel: 778-328-8888; Fax: 604-873-6620
inlandrefugeesociety@live.ca
inlandrefugeesociety.ca
Overview: A small provincial organization founded in 1984
Mission: To assist asylum seekers with basic necessities
Member of: Affiliation of Multicultural Societies & Service Agencies of BC; Canadian Council for Refugees
Affiliation(s): Vancouver Refugee Council
Finances: Annual Operating Budget: $100,000-$250,000; Funding Sources: Private donation; provincial & municipal grants; gaming
Staff Member(s): 2; 35 volunteer(s)
Membership: 250; Fees: $5 individual; $20 organization; Member Profile: Friends & supporters; Committees: Nominations; Finances; Program; Personnel
Activities: Food bank, clothing & household items distribution; information & referral; orientation & advocacy; ESL classes
Chief Officer(s):
Mario Ayala, Director

Inland Terminal Association of Canada (ITAC)
PO Box 283, Elbow SK S0H 1J0
Tel: 306-854-4554
www.inlandterminal.ca
Overview: A small national organization founded in 1995
Mission: To supprt & promote the interests of people working with inland terminals
Staff Member(s): 2
Membership: 9; Member Profile: Inland terminal grain handling facilities
Chief Officer(s):
Kevin Hursh, Executive Director, 306-933-0138
kevin@hursh.ca

Inn From the Cold Society
110 - 11 Ave. SE, Calgary AB T2G 0X5
Tel: 403-263-8384; Fax: 403-263-9067
inn@innfromthecold.org
innfromthecold.org
www.linkedin.com/company/inn-from-the-cold
www.facebook.com/innfromthecold
twitter.com/innfromthecold
www.youtube.com/user/innfromthecoldyyc
Overview: A small local charitable organization
Mission: To provide shelter & programs to homeless people in hopes that they can become self-sufficient
Staff Member(s): 60
Chief Officer(s):
Linda McLean, Executive Director

Inner City Angels (ICA)
Distillery Historic District, #203, 15 Case Goods Lane, Toronto ON M5A 3C4
Tel: 416-598-0242; Fax: 416-598-9338
innercityangels@mac.com

www.innercityangels.ca
www.facebook.com/innerangels
twitter.com/innerangels
Overview: A small local organization founded in 1969
Mission: To provide quality arts education opportunities in diverse & innovative ways for children & youth who would otherwise have little opportunity for them; To offer arts experiences to foster the personal growth & creative potential of young people
Finances: *Annual Operating Budget:* $250,000-$500,000; *Funding Sources:* Ontario Arts Council; Toronto Arts Council; Ontario Trillium Foundation; donations
Staff Member(s): 3; 15 volunteer(s)
Membership: 400; *Committees:* Artist & Board Development; Fundraising
Activities: Over 400 visits annually by Angels artists to Toronto priority community schools; *Internships:* Yes
Chief Officer(s):
Jane Howard Baker, Executive Director

Inner City Home of Sudbury (ICHOS)
251 Elm St., Sudbury ON P3C 1V5
Tel: 705-675-7550; *Fax:* 705-675-1652
ichos1986@gmail.com
www.innercityhomesudbury.ca
Overview: A small local charitable organization
Mission: To provide food & counselling to the less fortunate
Staff Member(s): 3
Chief Officer(s):
Mary Ali, Executive Director

Inner Peace Movement of Canada
PO Box 1138, Stn. B, Ottawa ON K1R 5R2
Tel: 613-238-7844
Toll-Free: 877-969-0095
www.innerpeacemovementptyltd.com
Overview: A small national organization founded in 1969
Mission: To promote self-help techniques by following 4 steps, each step providing tools to allow for a deeper self-awareness as a spiritual being

Innisfail & District Chamber of Commerce
5202 50 St., Innisfail AB T4G 1S1
Tel: 403-227-1177; *Fax:* 403-227-6749
Overview: A small local organization founded in 1939
Mission: To support & encourage business & members of the Innisfail community
Member of: Alberta Chamber of Commerce
Finances: *Annual Operating Budget:* Less than $50,000; *Funding Sources:* Membership dues; fundraising
Staff Member(s): 1; 17 volunteer(s)
Membership: 210; *Fees:* $52-$315
Activities: Organizing Junior 4-H Show, Trade Show, Small Business Week, rodeo, parade, car show, & Christmas promotion; *Speaker Service:* Yes
Chief Officer(s):
Carla Gabert, Manager

Innisfil Chamber of Commerce *See* Greater Innisfil Chamber of Commerce

Innkeepers Guild of Nova Scotia (IGNS)
PO Box 66, Tatamagouche NS B0K 1V0
Tel: 902-496-7478
www.innkeeperguild.com
Overview: A small provincial charitable organization founded in 1939
Mission: To work toward improved standards & facilities to better serve the travelling public
Affiliation(s): American Hotel/Motel Association
Finances: *Annual Operating Budget:* Less than $50,000; *Funding Sources:* Membership dues
30 volunteer(s)
Membership: 240 corporate + 25 associate + 5 senior/lifetime; *Fees:* Schedule available; *Member Profile:* Licensed fixed roof accommodation operations & suppliers
Activities: *Speaker Service:* Yes; *Library:* Open to public
Chief Officer(s):
Peter Sheehan, President
ocean.haven@ns.sympatico.ca

Innkeepers of Ontario *See* Ontario's Finest Inns & Spas

Innovate Calgary
Alastair Ross Technology Centre, 3553 - 31 St. NW, Calgary AB T2L 2K7
Tel: 403-284-6400; *Fax:* 403-267-5699
info@innovatecalgary.com
www.innovatecalgary.com
www.linkedin.com/company/innovate-calgary
www.facebook.com/innovatecalgary
twitter.com/innovatecalgary
Overview: A medium-sized local organization founded in 2010
Mission: To aid in acceleration & innovation of business in the technology sector
Chief Officer(s):
Peter Garrett, President, 403-284-6424
pgarrett@innovatecalgary.com
Susan Delesalle, Chief Financial Officer

Innovation & Technology Association of Ontario (ITAP)
646 Davis Dr., Markham ON L3P 2M4
Tel: 905-294-3650
www.itap.ca
Overview: A small provincial organization
Mission: To develop & grow the tech industry in Ontario, with the help of new innovations
Membership: 14+; *Member Profile:* Businesses in the technology sector; Suppliers; Public sector representatives; Students

Innovation Norway
#2120, 2 Bloor St. West, Toronto ON M4W 3E2
Tel: 416-920-0434; *Fax:* 416-920-5982
toronto@innovationnorway.no
www.innovasjonnorge.no/canada
Previous Name: Norwegian Trade Council
Overview: A small international organization
Mission: To promote industrial development beneficial to both Norway & local businesses; to encourage alliances & partnerships between Norwegian & Canadian enterprises.
Staff Member(s): 5
Chief Officer(s):
Rolf H. Sorland, Trade Commissioner & Manager, 416-920-0434 Ext. 123
rolf.h.sorland@innovasjonnorge.no

Innovative Medicines Canada
#1220, 55 Metcalfe St., Ottawa ON K1P 6L5
Tel: 613-236-0455
info@imc-mnc.ca
www.innovativemedicines.ca
www.linkedin.com/company/rx&d
twitter.com/innovativemeds
Previous Name: Canada's Research-Based Pharmaceutical Companies; Pharmaceutical Manufacturers Association of Canada
Overview: A medium-sized national organization founded in 1914
Mission: To discover new medicines that improve the quality of health care available for every Canadian
Member of: Canadian Institute of Biotechnology
Membership: 52 companies
Activities: Administering the Health Research Foundation
Chief Officer(s):
Michael Tremblay, Chair
Elaine Campbell, Interim President
ecampbell@imc-mnc.ca
Awards:
• Post-Doctoral Fellowships in Pharmacy, PMAC Health Research Foundation
Provides highly-qualified individuals the opportunity to undertake post-graduate research & research training in the area of therapeutics or drug evaluation; the four annual awards are tenable only at Canadian faculties of pharmacy for two years
• Research Career Awards in Medicine, PMAC Health Research Foundation
Provides protected time for independent investigators in the fields of clinical pharmacology, therapeutics or drug evaluation; tenable for a five-year period
• Research Studentships in Pharmacology, PMAC Health Research Foundation
Provides the opportunity for students to undertake research in either basic or clinical pharmacology; tenable only at the faculties of medicine at the University of Calgary & McMaster University
• Summer Student Research Scholarships in Pharmacy, PMAC Health Research Foundation
Provides the opportunity for students to undertake research in the fields of medicine & therapeutics during the summer; tenable only at Canadian faculties of pharmacy; two scholarships per faculty are available
• Graduate Research Scholarships in Pharmacy, PMAC Health Research Foundation
Provides the opportunity for graduate students to undertake research training in the fields of medicine & therapeutics; tenable only at Canadian schools of pharmacy for two years
• Summer Student Research Scholarships in Medicine, PMAC Health Research Foundation
Provides promising students the opportunity to undertake research in either basic or clinical pharmacology during the summer; tenable only at Canadian faculties of medicine (the University of Calgary & McMaster University excepted)
• Medal of Honour
Established 1945; awarded periodically when an individual has made an invaluable contribution to the advancement of science

InScribe Christian Writers' Fellowship (ICWF)
PO Box 99509, Edmonton AB T5B 0E1
query@inscribe.org
www.inscribe.org
www.facebook.com/CanadianWriters
twitter.com/InscribeCWF
Overview: A small national organization founded in 1980
Mission: To stimulate, encourage & support Christians across Canada who write; To advance effective Christian writing; To promote the availability & influence of all Christians who write
Finances: *Annual Operating Budget:* Less than $50,000
Membership: 200+; *Fees:* $40
Activities: Fall Conference; Spring workshops; Local Writing Groups; FellowScript (quarterly magazine); Inscribe Press; Writing contests for members; Blogging opportunities; *Speaker Service:* Yes
Chief Officer(s):
Ruth Snyder, President
president@inscribe.org
Tracy Krauss, Vice-President
VP@InScribe.org

Inside Education
11428 - 100 Ave., Edmonton AB T5K 0J4
Tel: 780-421-1497; *Fax:* 780-425-4506
Toll-Free: 888-421-1497
info@insideeducation.ca
www.insideeducation.ca
www.linkedin.com/company/1409777
www.facebook.com/InsideEducation
twitter.com/insideeducation
www.vimeo.com/insideeducation
Previous Name: FEESA - An Environmental Education Society
Overview: A medium-sized provincial charitable organization founded in 1985
Mission: To empower all Albertans to make informed choices about the environment by providing bias-balanced environmental education; To communicate, coordinate, & initiate the development & support of bias-balanced environmental education in Alberta through a variety of programs & services; To ensure that the views of business, industry, government, the environment, & community sector are represented in any programming or communication
Member of: Environmental Outdoor Education Council; Alberta Environmental Network; Canadian Environmental Network
Affiliation(s): North American Association for Environmental Education; EECOM
Finances: *Annual Operating Budget:* $500,000-$1.5 Million; *Funding Sources:* Industry; government; private/users
Staff Member(s): 9; 1000 volunteer(s)
Membership: 300 associates; 18 members (Board); *Fees:* $15 student; $25 individual; $50 institution; $250 corporate
Activities: Promotion of environmental education in formal & public education areas; presentations, conferences & conventions; coordination & development of education resources that focus on a variety of environmental & educational needs; teacher-training institutes focusing on a variety of environmental issues; *Awareness Events:* Environment Week, 1st week of June
Chief Officer(s):
Steve McIsaac, Executive Director
smcisaac@insideeducation.ca
  Calgary
  #205, 1117 - 1st St. SW, Calgary AB T2R 0T9
  Tel: 403-263-7720; *Fax:* 403-263-7709

Inside Out Lesbian & Gay Film & Video Festival *See* Inside Out Toronto LGBT Film & Video Festival

Inside Out Toronto LGBT Film & Video Festival
#219, 401 Richmond St. West, Toronto ON M5V 3A8

Tel: 416-977-6847; Fax: 416-977-8025
inside@insideout.ca
www.insideout.ca
www.facebook.com/InsideOutFilmFestival
twitter.com/InsideOutTO
www.youtube.com/InsideOutToronto
Previous Name: Inside Out Lesbian & Gay Film & Video Festival
Overview: A small international organization founded in 1991
Mission: To promote, produce, & present films & videos created by members of the LGBT community
Staff Member(s): 20; 100 volunteer(s)
Membership: 350+; *Fees:* $35 basic; $100 supporter; $175 associate; $350 benefactor; $600 patron; $2,500 deluxe
Activities: *Awareness Events:* Inside Out Toronto LGBT Film & Video Festival, May
Chief Officer(s):
Andria Wilson, Executive Director
andria@insideout.ca
Deanna Bickford, Director, Development
deanna@insideout.ca
Brad Campbell, Director, Corporate Sales
brad@insideout.ca
Winnie Luk, Director, Operations & Events
winnie@insideout.ca
Andrew Murphy, Director, Programming
andrew@insideout.ca
Awards:
• Mark S. Bonham Scholarship for Queer Studies in Film and Video
Eligibility: Individual who identifies as part of the LGBT community; pursuing undergraduate studies in film; Canadian citizen *Deadline:* May 30

Insitut canadien des économistes en construction - Québec
8615, rue Lafrenaie, Saint-Léonard QC H1P 2B6
Tél: 514-324-0968; *Téléc:* 514-324-2807
info@ocec-quebec.org
www.ciqs.org
Également appelé: ICÉC - Québec
Nom précédent: Association des Estimateurs et Économistes en Construction du Québec
Aperçu: *Dimension:* petite; *Envergure:* provinciale; fondée en 1973
Mission: Promouvoir et avancer le statut professionnel des Économistes en construction; établir et maintenir un haut degré de compétence professionnelle et d'intégrité en limitant l'adhésion à ceux rencontrant les critères de l'Association; assurer la solidarité et servir d'intermédiaire dans les échanges de connaissance en matière de construction afin de promouvoir l'avancement de la profession
Finances: *Budget de fonctionnement annuel:* Moins de $50,000
Membre: 180
Activités: *Service de conférenciers:* Oui
Membre(s) du bureau directeur:
Jean Paradis, Président
André Lavoie, Vice-président
Hervé Couture, Trésorier
Bernard Mercier, Secrétaire
Isabelle Buisson, Coordonnatrice administrative

Inspirit Foundation
Artscape Youngplace, #314, 180 Shaw St., Toronto ON M6J 2W5
Tel: 416-644-3600
info@inspiritfoundation.org
www.inspiritfoundation.ca
www.facebook.com/InspiritFoundation
twitter.com/InspiritFdn
www.youtube.com/user/InspiritFoundation
Overview: A medium-sized national organization
Mission: To support Canadians, particularly young adults, in building a more inclusive & pluralist Canada
Chief Officer(s):
Andrea Nemtin, Founding President & CEO
anemtin@inspiritfoundation.ca
Chris Lee, Manager, Grants & Media Impact Funding
clee@inspiritfoundation.org
Awards:
• Inspirit Bridge Building Grants
Support projects that bring together young Canadians of different religious, spiritual, and secular beliefs for a common goal at the community level. *Eligibility:* Canadian; aged 18-30; *Amount:* $5,000-$25,000

Installation, Maintenance & Repair Sector Council & Trade Association (IMR)
#300, 180 Attwell Dr., Toronto ON M9W 6A9
Tel: 905-602-8877; Fax: 416-679-9234
Toll-Free: 866-602-8877
info@electrofed.com
www.electrofed.com/imr
www.linkedin.com/company/1458895?trk=tyah
twitter.com/EFC_Tweets
Overview: A medium-sized national organization
Mission: To ensure that there is an adequate supply of trained people with the skills required for today's appliances & electronics
Chief Officer(s):
Jeff Miller, Executive Director, 647-258-7478
jmiller@electrofed.com

Instit du Chrysotile *See* Chrysotile Institute

Institut aéronautique et spatial du Canada *See* Canadian Aeronautics & Space Institute

Institut agréé de la logistique et des transports Amérique du Nord *See* The Chartered Institute of Logistics & Transport in North America

Institut agricole du Canada *See* Agricultural Institute of Canada

L'Institut canadien *See* The Canadian Institute

Institut canadien d'administration de la justice *See* Canadian Institute for the Administration of Justice

Institut canadien d'éducation des adultes *Voir* Institut de coopération pour l'éducation des adultes

Institut canadien d'études méditerranéennes *See* Canadian Institute for Mediterranean Studies

Institut canadien d'études ukrainiennes *See* Canadian Institute of Ukrainian Studies

Institut canadien d'information sur la santé *See* Canadian Institute for Health Information

Institut canadien de concessionnaires, manufacturiers et distributeurs de portes *See* Canadian Door Institute of Dealers, Manufacturers & Distributors

Institut canadien de conservation *See* Canadian Conservation Institute

Institut canadien de formation *See* Canadian Training Institute

Institut canadien de formation de l'énergie *See* Canadian Institute for Energy Training

Institut canadien de gemmologie *See* Canadian Institute of Gemmology

Institut canadien de gestion *See* Canadian Institute of Management

Institut canadien de l'immeuble *See* Real Estate Institute of Canada

Institut canadien de la construction en acier *See* Canadian Institute of Steel Construction

Institut canadien de la recherche sur la condition physique et le mode de vie *See* Canadian Fitness & Lifestyle Research Institute

Institut canadien de la retraite et des avantages sociaux *See* Canadian Pension & Benefits Institute

Institut canadien de la santé animale *See* Canadian Animal Health Institute

Institut canadien de la santé infantile *See* Canadian Institute of Child Health

Institut canadien de la tôle d'acier pour le bâtiment *See* Canadian Sheet Steel Building Institute

Institut canadien de plomberie et de chauffage *See* Canadian Institute of Plumbing & Heating

L'Institut canadien de Québec (ICQ)
350, rue Saint-Joseph est, 4e étage, Québec QC G1K 3B2
Tél: 418-641-6788; *Téléc:* 418-641-6787
courrier@institutcanadien.qc.ca
www.institutcanadien.qc.ca
www.linkedin.com/company/l'institut-canadien-de-qu-bec
www.facebook.com/176468254731
twitter.com/ICQ_Quebec
Aperçu: *Dimension:* grande; *Envergure:* nationale; fondée en 1848
Mission: Démocratiser l'accès au savoir et aux oeuvres d'imagination par un service de bibliothèque universellement accessible; Sensibiliser le public aux arts et à la culture; Gestion de bibliothèques publiques de la Ville de Québec
Membre de: Association des Bibliothèques publiques du Québec
Finances: *Budget de fonctionnement annuel:* Plus de $5 Million
Membre(s) du personnel: 150
Membre: Over 50,000
Activités:; *Bibliothèque:* Bibliothèque de Québec
Membre(s) du bureau directeur:
Marie-Claire Lévesque, Présidente
Publications:
• Lettre de la Maison de la littérature [a publication of L'Institut canadien de Québec]
Type: Bulletin

Institut canadien de recherche sur le Judaïsme *See* Canadian Institute for Jewish Research

Institut canadien de recherches avancées *See* Canadian Institute for Advanced Research

Institut canadien de recherches sur les femmes *See* Canadian Research Institute for the Advancement of Women

Institut canadien de relations avec les investisseurs *See* Canadian Investor Relations Institute

Institut canadien de science et technologie alimentaires *See* Canadian Institute of Food Science & Technology

Institut canadien des actuaires *See* Canadian Institute of Actuaries

Institut canadien des affaires culturelles *See* Canadian Institute of Cultural Affairs

Institut canadien des concominiums *See* Canadian Condominium Institute

Institut canadien des évaluateurs *See* Appraisal Institute of Canada

L'Institut canadien des experts en évaluation d'entreprises *See* Canadian Institute of Chartered Business Valuators

L'Institut canadien des ingénieurs *See* The Engineering Institute of Canada

Institut Canadien des ingénieurs en transports *See* Canadian Institute of Transportation Engineers

Institut Canadien des inspecteurs en santé publique *See* Canadian Institute of Public Health Inspectors

Institut canadien des mines, de la métallurgie et du pétrole *See* Canadian Institute of Mining, Metallurgy & Petroleum

L'Institut Canadien des Technologies Scénographiques *See* Canadian Institute for Theatre Technology

Institut canadien des urbanistes *See* Canadian Institute of Planners

L'Institut canadien des valeurs mobilières *See* Canadian Securities Institute

Institut canadien du béton préfabriqué et précontraint *See* Canadian Precast / Prestressed Concrete Institute

Institut canadien du chauffage, de la climatisation et de la réfrigération *See* Heating, Refrigeration & Air Conditioning Institute of Canada

L'Institut canadien du crédit *See* Credit Institute of Canada

L'Institut canadien du droit des ressources *See* Canadian Institute of Resources Law

Institut canadien du film *See* Canadian Film Institute

Institut canadien du marketing *See* Canadian Institute of Marketing

Institut canadien du sucre *See* Canadian Sugar Institute

Institut canadien du tapis *See* Canadian Carpet Institute

Institut canadien du trafic et du transport *See* Canadian Institute of Traffic & Transportation

Institut canadien pour la résolution des conflits See Canadian Institute for Conflict Resolution

Institut canadien pour la sécurité des patients See Canadian Patient Safety Institute

Institut Cardinal Léger contre la lèpre Voir Fondation Jules et Paul-Émile Léger

Institut C.D. Howe See C.D. Howe Institute

Institut circumpolaire canadien See Canadian Circumpolar Institute

L'Institut Cooper See Cooper Institute

Institut culturel et éducatif montagnais; Institut éducatif et culturel Attikamek-Montagnais Voir Institut Tshakapesh

Institut d'administration publique du Canada See Institute of Public Administration of Canada

Institut d'arbitrage et de médiation du Canada See ADR Institute of Canada

L'Institut d'assurance de dommages du Québec (IADQ)
#575, 2055, rue Peel, Montréal QC H3A 1T6
Tél: 514-393-8156; Téléc: 514-393-9222
iadq@institutdassurance.ca
insuranceinstitute.ca/fr/institutes-and-chapters/Quebec.aspx
Nom précédent: L'Institut d'assurance du Québec
Aperçu: *Dimension:* moyenne; *Envergure:* provinciale; Organisme sans but lucratif; fondée en 1927 surveillé par Insurance Institute of Canada
Mission: Organiser des cours, des séminaires et des conférences; promouvoir le rayonnement des titres professionnels PAA et FPAA d'assurance du Canada (AIAC & FIAC). Organisme sans but lucratif, qui a été mis sur pied par l'industrie de l'assurance de dommages pour donner la formation professionnelle à tous ceux qui oeuvrent dans ce secteur au Québec
Membre(s) du personnel: 5
Activités: Formation professionnelles en assurance de dommages; *Evénements de sensibilisation:* Gala; Tournoi de golf; *Service de conférenciers:* Oui
Membre(s) du bureau directeur:
Julie Saucier, Directrice générale
Bureau de Québec
#1300, 2875, boul Laurier, Québec QC G1V 2M2
Tél: 418-623-3688; Téléc: 418-623-6935

Institut d'assurance du Canada See Insurance Institute of Canada

L'Institut d'assurance du Québec Voir L'Institut d'assurance de dommages du Québec

Institut d'éthiques mondiales (Canada) See Institute for Global Ethics (Canada)

L'Institut d'études canadiennes de McGill See McGill Institute for the Study of Canada

Institut d'histoire de l'Amérique française (IHAF)
a/s Département d'histoire, Université de Montréal, CP 6128, Succ. Centre-Ville, #6097c, 3150, rue Jean-Brillant, Montréal QC H3C 3J7
Tél: 514-343-6111; Téléc: 514-343-2483
ihaf@ihaf.qc.ca
www.ihaf.qc.ca
Aperçu: *Dimension:* petite; *Envergure:* nationale; Organisme sans but lucratif; fondée en 1946
Membre: *Critères d'admissibilité:* Professeurs, porfessionnels, et amateurs d'histoire
Membre(s) du bureau directeur:
Alain Beaulieu, Président
beaulieu.alain@uqam.ca
Ollivier Hubert, Vice-président
ollivier.hubert@umontreal.ca
Brigitte Caulier, Secrétaire
Brigitte.Caulier@hst.ulaval.ca
Dominique Marquis, Trésorière
marquis.dominique@uqam.ca
Publications:
• Revue d'histoire de l'Amérique française
Type: Journal; *Editor:* Louise Bienvenue

L'Institut d'Ingénierie Simultanée Voir L'Institut de développement de produits

Institut de cardiologie de Montréal (ICM) / Montréal Heart Institute (MHI)
5000, rue Bélanger, Montréal QC H1T 1C8
Tél: 514-376-3330
Ligne sans frais: 855-922-6387
www.icm-mhi.org
www.facebook.com/institutcardiologiemontreal
twitter.com/ICMtl
www.youtube.com/user/InstitutdeCardioMtl
Aperçu: *Dimension:* petite; *Envergure:* locale; fondée en 1954
Mission: Un centre uniquement consacré au développement des traitements des maladies cardiovasculaires
Membre: *Comités:* Ressources financières, matérielles et informatiques; Gouvernance et éthique; Éthique de la recherche / dév. des nouvelles technologies; Usagers; Vigilance et de la qualité; Gestion des risques; Révision des plaintes; Recherche; Prévention; Éthique clinique; Ressources humaines
Activités: Bibliothèque:
Membre(s) du bureau directeur:
Pierre Anctil, Président
Denis Roy, Directeur général

Institut de chimie du Canada See Chemical Institute of Canada

Institut de coopération pour l'éducation des adultes (ICEA)
4321, av Papineau, Montréal QC H2H 1T3
Tél: 514-948-2044
icea@icea.qc.ca
www.icea.qc.ca
www.linkedin.com/company-beta/1865366
www.facebook.com/icea.reseau
twitter.com/icea_
Nom précédent: Institut canadien d'éducation des adultes
Aperçu: *Dimension:* petite; *Envergure:* nationale; Organisme sans but lucratif; fondée en 1946
Mission: Promouvoir l'exercice du droit des adultes à l'éducation tout au long de la vie
Membre de: Centre de documentation sur l'éducation des adultes et la condition féminine; Communautique; Conseil international de l'éducation des adultes
Finances: *Budget de fonctionnement annuel:* $1.5 Million-$3 Million
Membre(s) du personnel: 15
Membre: 160; *Montant de la cotisation:* Schedule available
Activités: Recherche et analyse stratégiques; intervention publique; concertation; réalisation, production d'outils; *Bibliothèque:* CDEACF
Membre(s) du bureau directeur:
Daniel Baril, Directeur général
dbaril@icea.qc.ca

L'Institut de développement de produits (IDP) / Institute for Product Development (IPD)
4805, rue Molson, Montréal QC H1Y 0A2
Tél: 514-383-3209; Téléc: 514-383-3266
info@idp-ipd.com
www.idp-ipd.com
Nom précédent: L'Institut d'Ingénierie Simultanée
Aperçu: *Dimension:* petite; *Envergure:* provinciale; Organisme sans but lucratif; fondée en 1995
Mission: Accélérer l'adoption des meilleurs pratiques développement de produits au sein des entreprises québécoises afin de les rendre nos performantes
Membre de: Reseau canadien de technologie
Membre(s) du personnel: 11
Membre: *Montant de la cotisation:* Barème; *Critères d'admissibilite:* Manufacturier
Activités: Atelier visite en entreprise; séminaire de sensibilisation aux meilleures pratiques en développement de produits
Membre(s) du bureau directeur:
Bertrand Derome, Directeur général

Institut de développement urbain du Canada See Urban Development Institute of Canada

Institut de l'énergie et de l'environnement de la Francophonie Voir Institut de la Francophonie pour le développement durable

Institut de la fourrure du Canada See Fur Institute of Canada

Institut de la Francophonie pour le développement durable (IFDD)
56, rue St-Pierre, 3e étage, Québec QC G1K 4A1
Tél: 418-692-5727; Téléc: 418-692-5644
ifdd@francophonie.org
www.ifdd.francophonie.org
Nom précédent: Institut de l'énergie et de l'environnement de la Francophonie
Aperçu: *Dimension:* moyenne; *Envergure:* internationale; Organisme sans but lucratif; fondée en 1988
Mission: Contribuer au renforcement des capacités nationales et au développement des partenariats dans les domaines de l'énergie et de l'environnement
Membre de: Agence de la Francophonie
Finances: *Budget de fonctionnement annuel:* $3 Million-$5 Million
Membre(s) du personnel: 17
Activités: *Bibliothèque:* Service information et documentation
Membre(s) du bureau directeur:
Jean-Pierre Ndoutoum, Directeur

Institut de la gestion financière See Financial Management Institute of Canada

Institut de la propriété intellectuelle du Canada See Intellectual Property Institute of Canada

Institut de médiation et d'arbitrage de l'Atlantique See Alternative Dispute Resolution Atlantic Institute

Institut de médiation et d'arbitrage du Québec (IMAQ)
#1501, 1445, rue Stanley, Montréal QC H3A 3T1
Tél: 514-282-3327; Téléc: 514-282-2214
Ligne sans frais: 855-482-3327
info@imaq.org
www.imaq.org
www.linkedin.com/company/institut-de-m-diation-et-d%27arbitrage-du-qu-bec
www.youtube.com/user/IMAQuebec
Aperçu: *Dimension:* petite; *Envergure:* provinciale; fondée en 1977
Mission: Promouvoir les méthodes alternatives de résolution de conflits (médiation, arbitrage); donner accès par internet à la population et aux entreprises à une banque de médiateurs et d'arbitres accrédités selon leur: spécialité (médiateur ou arbitre), région, langue de communication, catégorie de membre, profession, domaine d'expertise
Affiliation(s): ADR Institute of Canada, Inc.
Membre: 300+; *Montant de la cotisation:* 50$; *Comités:* Accréditation; Arbitrage civil et commercial; Communications; Construction; Déjeuners-causeries; Environnement et aménagement du territoire; Propriété intellectuelle; Gestion des plaintes; International; Jeunesse; Médiation dans le domaine de la santé; Regroupement des organismes PRD; Travail
Membre(s) du bureau directeur:
Pierre Grenier, Président
Ginette Gamache, Directrice, Opérations

Institut de prévention des sinistres catastrophiques See Institute for Catastrophic Loss Reduction

Institut de radioprotection du Canada See Radiation Safety Institute of Canada

Institut de réadaptation en déficience physique de Québec (IRDPQ)
525, boul Wilfrid-Hamel, Québec QC G1M 2S8
Tél: 418-529-9141; TTY: 418-649-3733
communications@irdpq.qc.ca
www.irdpq.qc.ca
www.facebook.com/IRDPQ
www.youtube.com/user/VideosIRDPQ
Nom précédent: Institut de réadaptation physique de Québec
Aperçu: *Dimension:* petite; *Envergure:* provinciale; fondée en 1996
Mission: Offrir des services de réadaptation, d'adaptation et de soutien à l'intégration sociale aux enfants, adultes et ainés qui ont des incapacités et vivent des situations de handicap en raison de leur déficience auditive, motrice, neurologique, visuelle, de la parole ou du langage, de même que des services d'accompagnement et de soutien à l'entourage
Membre de: Association des établissements de réadaptation en déficience physique du Québec
Finances: *Budget de fonctionnement annuel:* Plus de $5 Million
Membre(s) du personnel: 1300; 200 bénévole(s)
Membre: *Comités:* Administratif; Évaluation du directeur général; Orientation et de planification stratégique; Éthique clinique; Usagers; Gestion des risques; Vigilance et de la qualité; Gouvernance et d'éthique; Révision; Vérification et d'utilisation des ressources; Éthique de la recherche

Canadian Associations / Institut de recherche en biologie végétale (IRBV) / Plant Biology Research Institute (PBRI)

Activités: *Stagiaires:* Oui; *Bibliothèque:* Centre de documentation
Membre(s) du bureau directeur:
Marc Prenevost, Directeur général

Institut de réadaptation physique de Québec *Voir* Institut de réadaptation en déficience physique de Québec

Institut de recherche - brassage et orge de maltage *See* Brewing & Malting Barley Research Institute

Institut de recherche en biologie végétale (IRBV) / Plant Biology Research Institute (PBRI)
4101, rue Sherbrooke est, Montréal QC H1X 2B2
Tél: 514-343-2121; *Téléc:* 514-343-2288
irbv@irbv.umontreal.ca
www.irbv.umontreal.ca
Aperçu: *Dimension:* petite; *Envergure:* locale; Organisme sans but lucratif; fondée en 1990
Mission: To develop a centre of excellence in plant biology; both in fundamental research and its applicaitons; train students in plant biology at the master, doctoral, and post-doctoral levels; further training and knowledge of its researchers and technical personnel; promote the technological transfer of its scientific research results to users; provide complementary services to the community in fields relevant to plant biology, where expertise in the field is lacking.
Finances: *Budget de fonctionnement annuel:* $1.5 Million-$3 Million
Membre(s) du personnel: 100
Membre: 200
Activités: *Service de conférenciers:* Oui; *Bibliothèque* Not open to public
Membre(s) du bureau directeur:
Anne Bruneau, Directrice, 514-343-2121

Institut de recherche en politiques publiques *See* Institute for Research on Public Policy

Institut de recherche en services de santé *See* Institute for Clinical Evaluative Sciences

Institut de recherche et de développement en agroenvironnement *See* Research & Development Institute for the Agri-Environment

Institut de recherche Robert-Sauvé en santé et en sécurité du travail (IRSST) / Robert Sauvé Occupational Health & Safety Research Institute
505, boul de Maisonneuve ouest, Montréal QC H3A 3C2
Tél: 514-288-1551; *Téléc:* 514-288-7636
communications@irsst.qc.ca
www.irsst.qc.ca
www.linkedin.com/company/irsst
www.facebook.com//207703664186
twitter.com/IRSST
Aperçu: *Dimension:* moyenne; *Envergure:* provinciale; fondée en 1980
Mission: Contribuer par la recherche et le développement à l'amélioration de la santé et de la sécurité des travailleurs et plus spécifiquement, à l'élimination à la source des dangers pour leur santé, leur sécurité et leur intégrité physique ainsi qu'à la réadaptation des travailleurs victimes d'accidents ou de maladies professionnelles; fournir au Réseau public québécois de la prévention en santé et en sécurité du travail - composé de CSST, des Centres locaux de services communautaires, des Régies de la santé et des services sociaux et des associations sectorielles paritaires - les services et l'expertise nécessaires à leur action; diffuser les connaissances issues de ces recherches et de ces expertises auprès des milieux de travail et en favoriser le transfert; accorder des bourses d'études supérieures en santé et en sécurité du travail; agir comme laboratoire de référence au Québec, dans le domaine de l'hygiène industrielle
Affiliation(s): International Occupational Safety & Health Information Centre
Finances: *Budget de fonctionnement annuel:* Plus de $5 Million*Fonds:* Près de 85 % des revenus proviennent d'une subvention de la Commission de la santé et de la sécurité du travail du Québec (CSST)
Membre(s) du personnel: 130
Membre: *Comités:* Executive; Follow-up
Activités: Mène des recherches dans les domaines jugés prioritaires; Fait la promotion du développement de nouvelles connaissances en santé et en sécurité du travail en collaboration avec la communauté scientifique; Contribue à la formation de chercheurs en santé et en sécurité du travail; Contribue au développement de normes et règlements touchant la santé et la sécurité du travail; Diffuse les connaissances issues des recherches auprès du monde du travail et de la communauté scientifique; *Bibliothèque:* Bibliothèque publique
Membre(s) du bureau directeur:
Marie Larue, Présidente-directrice générale
Prix, Bourses:
• Bourse de maîtrise
 Deadline: octobre; *Amount:* 14 100$ *Contact:* Michel Asselin, Téléphone: 514-288-1551 poste 377
• Bourse de doctorat
 Deadline: octobre; *Amount:* 18 000$ *Contact:* Michel Asselin, Téléphone: 514-288-1551 poste 377
• Bourse de doctorat hors du Québec
 Deadline: octobre; *Amount:* 24 000$ *Contact:* Michel Asselin, Téléphone: 514-288-1551 poste 377
• Bourse de formation postdoctorale au Québec
 Deadline: octobre; *Amount:* 30 000$ *Contact:* Michel Asselin, Téléphone: 514-288-1551 poste 377
• Bourse de stagiaire postdoctoral invité à l'IRSST
 Deadline: octobre; *Amount:* 30 000$ *Contact:* Michel Asselin, Téléphone: 514-288-1551 poste 377
• Bourse de formation postdoctorale hors du Québec
 Deadline: octobre; *Amount:* 36 000$ *Contact:* Michel Asselin, Téléphone: 514-288-1551 poste 377
• Programme de subvention de recherche par concours
 Contact: Michel Asselin, Téléphone: 514-288-1551 poste 377
• Programme de subvention de recherche concertée
 Contact: Michel Asselin, Téléphone: 514-288-1551 poste 377
• Programme de subvention d'activité concertée
 Contact: Michel Asselin, Téléphone: 514-288-1551 poste 377
Publications:
• Bulletin d'information du REM
 Type: Bulletin électronique; *Frequency:* semi-annuel
 Profile: Un bulletin qui constitue un moyen d'échanges entre les membres du Réseau d'échange sur la manutention (REM)
• INFO LABO - Des nouvelles de nos laboratoires
 Type: Bulletin électronique
 Profile: Un bulletin qui contient des communiqués, des avis ainsi que des recommandations s'adressant plus spécifiquement aux intervenants du réseau québécois de la santéet de la sécurité du travail
• infoIRSST - Des nouvelles de la recherche
 Type: Bulletin électronique; *Frequency:* 10 fois par an
 Profile: Un bulletin qui présente toute l'actualité de la recherche réalisée ou financée par l'IRSST : les communiqués, les dernières parutions et les nouveaux projets derecherche, les colloques et les conférences et les dernières nouvelles de nos laboratoires
• Prévention au travail
 Type: Magazine; *Frequency:* trimestriel; *Number of Pages:* 31
 Profile: Un magazine qui vise à fournir une information utile pour prévenir les accidents du travail et les maladies professionnelles

Institut de recherche sur le travail et la santé *See* Institute for Work & Health

Institut de recherches cliniques de Montréal (IRCM)
110, av des Pins ouest, Montréal QC H2W 1R7
Tél: 514-987-5500; *Téléc:* 514-987-5532
info@ircm.qc.ca
www.ircm.qc.ca
www.facebook.com/IRCM.Montreal
Aperçu: *Dimension:* petite; *Envergure:* locale; fondée en 1967
Mission: Pour comprendre les causes et les mécanismes des maladies; Pour découvrir des outils diagnostiques et des moyens de prévention et traitement des maladies; Pour faciliter le développement commercial de nouvelles découvertes
Membre(s) du personnel: 425
Membre: *Comités:* Direction; Direction scientifique; Scientifique; Consultatif scientifique
Activités: Former les scientifiques; Favoriser les collaborations nationales et internationales pour faire avancer la science
Membre(s) du bureau directeur:
Tarik Möröy, President & Scientific Director
André Veillette, Executive Director, Academic Affairs
Louis-Gilles Durand, Executive Director, Administration & Research Services
Yves Berthiaume, Executive Director, Clinic & Clinical Research
Stéphane Létourneau, Executive Director, Corporate & Legal Affairs

Institut de tourisme et d'hôtellerie du Québec (ITHQ)
3535, rue Saint-Denis, Montréal QC H2X 3P1
Tél: 514-282-5111
Ligne sans frais: 800-282-5111
info@ithq.qc.ca
www.ithq.qc.ca
www.linkedin.com/company/588922
www.facebook.com/ITHQofficiel
twitter.com/ithqofficiel
Aperçu: *Dimension:* grande; *Envergure:* provinciale; fondée en 1968
Mission: l'ITHQ est la plus importante école de gestion hôtelière au Canada spécialisée en tourisme, hôtellerie, restauration et sommellerie.
Finances: *Budget de fonctionnement annuel:* Plus de $5 Million
Membre(s) du personnel: 280
Activités: *Stagiaires:* Oui; *Bibliothèque:* Bibliothèque; Bibliothèque publique
Membre(s) du bureau directeur:
Liza Frulla, Directrice générale

Institut des administrateurs de sociétés *See* Institute of Corporate Directors

Institut des Affaires Culturelles International *See* Institute of Cultural Affairs International

L'Institut des agronomes du Nouveau-Brunswick *See* New Brunswick Institute of Agrologists

Institut des communications et de la publicité *See* Institute of Communication Agencies

L'Institut des fonds d'investissement du Canada *See* Investment Funds Institute of Canada

Institut des planificateurs professionnels de l'Ontario *See* Ontario Professional Planners Institute

Institut des sciences textiles *See* Institute of Textile Science

Institut des secrétaires et administrateurs agréés au Canada *See* Institute of Chartered Secretaries & Administrators - Canadian Division

Institut des Urbanistes de l'atlantique *See* Atlantic Planners Institute

Institut du cancer de Montréal (ICM) / Montréal Cancer Institute
900, rue Saint-Denis, Montréal QC H2X 0A9
Tél: 514-890-8213
info@icm.qc.ca
www.icm.qc.ca
twitter.com/cancermtl
Aperçu: *Dimension:* petite; *Envergure:* locale; fondée en 1942
Mission: Favoriser la recherche fondamentale et clinique sur le cancer et de préparer la relève dans ce domaine par le biais de l'enseignement et de la formation
Affiliation(s): CHUM, Université de Montréal
Membre(s) du bureau directeur:
André Boulanger, Président
Maral Tersakian, Directrice générale
maral.tersakian@icm.qc.ca

Institut féminin francophone du Nouveau-Brunswick
1746, rte 133, Grand-Barachois NB E4P 8J1
Tél: 506-532-5157
www.institut-feminin-francophone.sitew.ca
www.facebook.com/122062274607399
Aperçu: *Dimension:* petite; *Envergure:* provinciale
Mission: Le mandat est de regrouper les femmes francophones du Nouveau-Brunswick dans le but de promouvoir les intérêts & de défendre les droits des femmes & des francophones
Membre de: Alliance des femmes de la francophonie canadienne
Membre(s) du bureau directeur:
Francine Gallant, Présidente
fgallant@cott.com

Institut forestier du Canada *See* Canadian Institute of Forestry

Institut généalogique des Provinces Maritimes *See* Genealogical Institute of The Maritimes

L'Institut international canadien de la négociation pratique *See* Canadian International Institute of Applied Negotiation

Institut international des sciences humaines intégrales *See* International Institute of Integral Human Sciences

Institut international du développement durable *See* International Institute for Sustainable Development

Institut manitobain des conseillers en administration agréés *See* Institute of Certified Management Consultants of Manitoba

Institut national d'optique (INO) / National Optics Institute
2740, rue Einstein, Québec QC G1P 4S4
Tel: 418-657-7006
Toll-Free: 866-657-7406
info@ino.ca
www.ino.ca
Overview: A large national licensing organization founded in 1985
Mission: To be an international leader in optics & photonics R&D, promoting economic expansion in the country by providing assistance to companies seeking to be more competitive
Member of: Canadian Advanced Technology Alliance
Finances: *Budget de fonctionnement annuel:* Plus de $5 Million*Funding Sources:* 70% self-supporting; 30% government
Staff Member(s): 200
Membership: 11 affiliate + 19 associate + 4 individual; *Fees:* $10,000 affiliate; $1,000 associate; $100 individual; *Member Profile:* Company, individual, organization interested in photonics research & development; *Committees:* Executive; Health & Safety; R&D Advisory; ISO 9001
Activités: Provides a full range of R&D services in optics & photonics; *Stagiaires:* Oui; *Bibliothèque* Not open to public
Membre(s) du bureau directeur:
Jean-Yves Roy, Chair
Prix, Bourses:
• INO Fellowship Program
   Ontario Branch
   #316A, 175 Longwood Rd. South, Hamilton ON L8P 0A1
   Tel: 905-529-7016
   info-ontario@ino.ca

Institut national de la magistrature *See* National Judicial Institute

Institut national de recherche et de gestion de l'incapacité au travail *See* National Institute of Disability Management & Research

Institut Nazareth et Louis-Braille (INLB)
1111, rue St-Charles ouest, Longueuil QC J4K 5G4
Tél: 450-463-1710; Téléc: 450-463-0243
Ligne sans frais: 800-361-7063
info.inlb@ssss.gouv.qc.ca
www.inlb.qc.ca
www.facebook.com/InstitutNazarethEtLouisBraille
Aperçu: *Dimension:* petite; *Envergure:* locale; fondée en 1861
Mission: Pour trouver de nouvelles façons d'aider les personnes ayant une déficience visuelle deviennent autonomes
Membre: *Critères d'admissibilite:* Les personnes ayant une déficience visuelle ou ont de graves dommages à vue
Activités: *Stagiaires:* Oui
Membre(s) du bureau directeur:
Richard Deschamps, Président-directeur général

L'Institut Nord-Sud *See* The North-South Institute

Institut pour tuyaux de tôle ondulée *See* Corrugated Steel Pipe Institute

Institut professionnel de la fonction publique du Canada *See* The Professional Institute of the Public Service of Canada

L'Institut professionnel du personnel municipal *See* Civic Institute of Professional Personnel

Institut québécois de planification financière (IQPF)
#501, 3, Place du Commerce, Montréal QC H3E 1H7
Tél: 514-767-4040; Téléc: 514-767-2845
Ligne sans frais: 800-640-4050
www.iqpf.org
www.facebook.com/IQPF.Planification.Financiere
twitter.com/IQPF
www.youtube.com/user/IQPFplanification
Aperçu: *Dimension:* petite; *Envergure:* provinciale; Organisme sans but lucratif; fondée en 1989
Mission: Contribuer à la protection et au mieux-être économique des consommateurs québécois, en veillant sur la formation et la qualification des professionnels regroupés en un réseau de planificateurs financiers solidaires d'une approche intégrée de la planification financière
Finances: *Budget de fonctionnement annuel:* $1.5 Million-$3 Million
Membre(s) du personnel: 19
Membre: 5 000; *Critères d'admissibilite:* Planificateur financier; *Comités:* Comité développement professionnel; comité d'audit; comité de gouvernance; comité du meilleur formateur; comité bourse de recherche; groupe de travail sur le congrès 2014; groupe des mentors; groupe de rédaction de la cible
Activités: Formation professionnelle des planificateurs financiers du Québec
Membre(s) du bureau directeur:
Jocelyne Houle-LeSarge, Présidente/Directrice Générale

Institut québécois des hautes études internationales *Voir* Hautes études internationales

Institut québécois des revêtements de sol inc. *Voir* Fédération québécoise des revêtements de sol

Institut royal d'architecture du Canada *See* Royal Architectural Institute of Canada

Institut Séculier Pie X (ISPX) / Pius X Secular Institute
CP 87731, Succ. Succ. Charlesbourg, 1645, boul Louis-XIV, Québec QC G1G 5W6
Tél: 418-626-5882; Téléc: 418-624-2277
info@ispx.org
www.ispx.org
Aperçu: *Dimension:* petite; *Envergure:* internationale; Organisme sans but lucratif; fondée en 1939
Mission: Évangéliser les milieux populaires par la présence et par des activités apostoliques
Membre de: Conférence canadienne des instituts séculiers; Conférence mondiale des instituts séculiers
Finances: *Budget de fonctionnement annuel:* $100,000-$250,000
Membre: 17 consacrés + 250 associés
Activités: Apostolat catholique; évangélisation; présence au monde; *Service de conférenciers:* Oui
Membre(s) du bureau directeur:
Christian Beaulieu, Directeur général

Institut sur la gouvernance *See* Institute On Governance

Institut Tshakapesh
1034, av Brochu, Uashat QC G4R 2Z1
Tél: 418-968-4424; Téléc: 418-968-1841
Ligne sans frais: 800-391-4424
reception@tshakapesh.ca
www.tshakapesh.ca
www.facebook.com/institut.tshakapesh
Nom précédent: Institut culturel et éducatif montagnais; Institut éducatif et culturel Attikamek-Montagnais
Aperçu: *Dimension:* moyenne; *Envergure:* locale; fondée en 1978
Mission: Préserver le patrimoine montagnais; sauvegarder la langue montagnaise; promouvoir l'éducation des montagnais
Membre de: Confédération des centres éducatifs et culturels des Premières Nations
Finances: *Budget de fonctionnement annuel:* $500,000-$1.5 Million
Membre(s) du personnel: 12
Membre: 8
Activités:; *Bibliothèque:* rendez-vous
Membre(s) du bureau directeur:
Jean-Pierre Donat, Président

Institut Vanier de la famille *See* Vanier Institute of The Family

Institut Voluntas Dei / Voluntas Dei Institute
7385, boul Parent, Trois-Rivières QC G9A 5E1
Tél: 819-375-7933; Téléc: 819-691-1841
ivd.cent@cgocable.ca
www.voluntasdei.org
www.facebook.com/voluntasdei
twitter.com/voluntasdei
www.youtube.com/voluntasdeis?feature=mhee#p/u/22/
Également appelé: I.V. Dei
Aperçu: *Dimension:* petite; *Envergure:* internationale; Organisme sans but lucratif; fondée en 1958
Mission: To make known & communicate God's love for all to all people; To be present in every milieu; apostolic objective is "to create peace & brotherhood in Jesus Christ"
Membre de: Roman Catholic Church
Finances: *Budget de fonctionnement annuel:* $100,000-$250,000
Membre(s) du personnel: 3
Membre: 974; *Critères d'admissibilite:* Baptised & consecrated people who live the evangelical counsels of obedience, poverty & chastity
Activités: *Stagiaires:* Oui
Membre(s) du bureau directeur:
Henri-Louis Parent, Founder

Institute for Catastrophic Loss Reduction (ICLR) / Institut de prévention des sinistres catastrophiques (IPSC)
#210, 20 Richmond St. East, Toronto ON M5C 2R9
Tel: 416-364-8677; Fax: 416-364-5889
www.iclr.org
www.facebook.com/instituteforcatastrophiclossreduction
twitter.com/ICLRCanada
www.youtube.com/user/ICLRinfo
Overview: A small national licensing organization founded in 1998
Mission: Reduce the loss of life & property caused by severe weather & earthquakes through the identification & support of sustained actions that improve society's capacity to adapt to, anticipate, mitigate, withstand & recover from natural disasters
Affiliation(s): The University of Western Ontario
Membership: *Fees:* $4,000 general; *Member Profile:* Organizations interested in disaster prevention; *Committees:* Advisory; Management
Activities: Protecting Kids from Disaster Program; Safety Upgrades for Child Care Centres; *Speaker Service:* Yes
Chief Officer(s):
Paul Kovacs, Executive Director
pkovacs@iclr.org
   London Office
   Boundary Layer Wind Tunnel Laboratory, Univ. of Western Ontario, 1151 Richmond St., London ON N6A 5B9
   Tel: 519-661-3234; Fax: 519-661-4273

Institute for Change Leaders
Ryerson University, 350 Victoria St., Toronto ON M5B 2K3
changeleaders@ryerson.ca
www.changeleaders.ca
Overview: A medium-sized national organization
Mission: To help community organizers & organizations acquire & develop the skills needed to enact social change
Activities: Teaching organizing skills & strategies
Chief Officer(s):
Olivia Chow, Distinguished Visiting Professor
Ben DW, Coordinator
Kat Horne, Financial Administrator

Institute for Clinical Evaluative Sciences (ICES) / Institut de recherche en services de santé
#G1 06, 2075 Bayview Ave., Toronto ON M4N 3M5
Tel: 416-480-4055
www.ices.on.ca
www.facebook.com/105181509564479
twitter.com/ICESOntario
www.youtube.com/user/ICESOntario
Overview: A small provincial organization founded in 1992
Mission: Conducts research that contributes to the effectiveness, quality, equity & efficiency of health care in Ontario
Finances: *Annual Operating Budget:* Greater than $5 Million
Staff Member(s): 294
Activities: *Library:* Resource Centre; Not open to public
Chief Officer(s):
Michael Baker, Chair
Michael Schull, President & CEO
Publications:
• At A Glance [a publication of the Institute for Clinical Evaluative Sciences]
Type: Bulletin; *Frequency:* Monthly; *Number of Pages:* 2

Institute for Global Ethics (Canada) / Institut d'éthiques mondiales (Canada)
#208 - 431 Pacific St., Vancouver BC V6Z 2P5
Tel: 604-688-6216
Toll-Free: 800-729-2613
canada@globalethics.org
www.globalethics.org/canada.php
Overview: A small national organization founded in 1997
Mission: To promote ethical action in a global context; to explore the global common ground of shared values, elevate awareness of ethics & provide practical tools for making ethical decisions
Membership: *Fees:* $100-$1,000
Chief Officer(s):
Rushworth M. Kidder, President, 800-729-2615 Ext. 133
rush.kidder@globalethics.org

Institute for Optimizing Health Outcomes
#600, 151 Bloor St. West, Toronto ON M5S 1S4
Tel: 416-969-7431
www.optimizinghealth.org

Previous Name: Anemia Institute for Research & Education
Overview: A small national organization
Mission: Promotes patient-centred programs, education, research & advocacy to improve care & support for persons at risk for, or living with, health conditions (including, but not limited to, anemia)
Affiliation(s): Ontario Patient Self-Management Network

Institute for Performance & Learning
#315, 720 Spadina Ave., Toronto ON M5S 2T9
Tel: 416-367-5900
Toll-Free: 866-257-4275
hello@performanceandlearning.ca
www.performanceandlearning.ca
www.linkedin.com/company/the-institute-for-performance-and-learning
www.facebook.com/institutepl
twitter.com/InstitutePL
Previous Name: Canadian Society for Training & Development
Overview: A medium-sized national organization founded in 1946
Mission: To bring together individuals who share a common interest in training, personnel development & organizational development
Member of: Conference Board of Canada
Finances: *Annual Operating Budget:* $500,000-$1.5 Million
Staff Member(s): 7; 100 volunteer(s)
Membership: 2,300; *Fees:* $295 new member; $225 renewal; *Member Profile:* Training & development professionals; *Committees:* Member Services; Professional Certification; Government Relations; Conference
Activities: Annual conference
Chief Officer(s):
Mary Brodhead, Chair
Jane Duffy, Director, Member Experience & Marketing
Elsa Lee, Manager, Finance & Operations
Meetings/Conferences:
• Institute for Performance & Learning 2018 Conference, 2018
Scope: National

Institute for Policy Analysis *See* Rotman Institute for International Business

Institute for Product Development *Voir* L'Institut de développement de produits

Institute for Research on Public Policy / Institut de recherche en politiques publiques
#200, 1470, rue Peel, Montréal QC H3A 1T1
Tel: 514-985-2461; *Fax:* 514-985-2559
irpp@irpp.org
www.irpp.org
Overview: A medium-sized national organization founded in 1972
Mission: To improve public policy in Canada by generating research, providing insight, & sparking debate that will contribute to the public policy decision-making process & strengthen the quality of public policy decisions made by Canadian governments, citizens, institutions, & organizations
Finances: *Funding Sources:* Government; general donations
Staff Member(s): 15
Activities: *Library:*
Chief Officer(s):
Graham Fox, President, 514-787-0741
gfox@irpp.org

Institute for Risk Research (IRR)
University of Waterloo, 200 University Ave. West, Waterloo ON N2L 3G1
Tel: 519-885-4027; *Fax:* 519-725-4834
irr-neram@uwaterloo.ca
www.irr-neram.ca
Overview: A small local organization founded in 1982
Mission: To promote safety for Canadians by improving the understanding of risk & risk policy decisions
Finances: *Funding Sources:* Corporations; government grants & contracts
Membership: 146
Activities: Includes Environmental Risk Management shortcourse; environmental conferences; *Speaker Service:* Yes; *Library:* Open to public by appointment
Chief Officer(s):
John Shortreed, Director
shortree@uwaterloo.ca

Institute for Safe Medication Practices Canada (ISMP Canada)
#501, 4711 Yonge St., Toronto ON M2N 6K8
Tel: 416-733-3131; *Fax:* 416-733-1146
Toll-Free: 866-544-7672
info@ismp-canada.org
www.ismp-canada.org
Overview: A medium-sized national organization
Mission: To promote medication safety in the healthcare industry; To analyze & provide information about safe medication practices; To conduct research on patient safety; To assess medication incidents for future prevention
Activities: Providing information; Offering educational & quality improvement programs
Chief Officer(s):
Sylvia Hyland, Chief Operating Officer
Publications:
• ISMP Canada [Institute for Safe Medication Practices Canada] Safety Bulletin
Frequency: Monthly
Profile: Information on medication safety & medication incidents

Institute for Stuttering Treatment & Research & the Communication Improvement Program (ISTAR, CIP)
College Plaza, #1500, 8215 - 112 St., Edmonton AB T6G 2C8
Tel: 780-492-2619; *Fax:* 780-492-8457
istar@ualberta.ca
www.istar.ualberta.ca
www.facebook.com/UofARehabMedicine
twitter.com/ISTAR_UofA
www.youtube.com/user/RehabMedicineUofA
Overview: A small international charitable organization founded in 1986
Mission: To provide treatment solutions to adults & children who stutter; to conduct research regarding stuttering.
Member of: Institute Faculty of Rehabilitation Medicine, University of Alberta
Affiliation(s): The University of Alberta; Alberta College of Speech-Language Pathologists & Audiologists; Canadian Association of Speech-Language Pathology & Audiology
Finances: *Funding Sources:* Elks of Alberta; Elks & Royal Purple Fund for Children; Clinic fees; Donations
Staff Member(s): 13
Activities: Providing treatment for stuttering; Conducting research into the nature & treatment of stuttering; Providing advanced professional training for speech pathologists; Offering presentations to university students, teachers, parents, speech-language pathologists, & the general public; Publishing
Chief Officer(s):
Deryk Beal, Executive Director
Awards:
• Scholarships
Available to clients depending on need

Institute for Sustainable Energy, Economy & Environment Student's Association *See* Fuse Collective

Institute for the Advancement of Aboriginal Women (IAAW)
#201, 10812 - 178 St., Edmonton AB T5S 1J3
Tel: 780-479-8195
Toll-Free: 877-471-2171
iaaw@iaaw.ca
www.iaaw.ca
www.facebook.com/esquao
Overview: A small provincial organization
Mission: To support the leadership of Aboriginal women in Alberta; To promote the rights of Aboriginal women & their families; To address the economic, cultural, social, & political issues affecting Aboriginal women & communities at the provincial, federal, & international levels; To create a better future for Aboriginal women
Activities: Developing support services & projects for Aboriginal women; Organizing conferences & seminars; Advocating on behalf of Aboriginal women
Chief Officer(s):
Rachelle Venne, Chief Executive Officer

Institute for the Study & Treatment of Pain (ISTOP)
#280, 5655 Cambie St., Vancouver BC V5Z 3A4
Tel: 604-264-7867; *Fax:* 604-264-7860
istop@istop.org
www.istop.org
Overview: A small international charitable organization founded in 1995
Mission: A non-profit organization dedicated to the understanding & treatment of soft tissue pain
Activities: *Internships:* Yes
Chief Officer(s):
Chan Gunn, President
Allan Lam, Clinic Director

Institute for Work & Health (IWH) / Institut de recherche sur le travail et la santé
#800, 481 University Ave., Toronto ON M5G 2E9
Tel: 416-927-2027; *Fax:* 416-927-4167
info@iwh.on.ca
www.iwh.on.ca
www.linkedin.com/company/institute-for-work-and-health
twitter.com/iwhresearch
www.youtube.com/user/iwhresearch
Previous Name: Ontario Workers' Compensation Institute
Overview: A medium-sized provincial organization founded in 1990
Mission: To conduct & share research with workers, labour, employers, clinicians & policy-makers to promote, protect & improve the health of working people
Finances: *Annual Operating Budget:* $3 Million-$5 Million; *Funding Sources:* Public & private sector; research grants
Staff Member(s): 75
Activities: *Awareness Events:* Alf Nachemson Memorial Lecture; *Library:* Not open to public
Chief Officer(s):
Cameron Mustard, President & Senior Scientist
Mary Cicinelli, Director, Human Resources & Corporate Services
Emma Irvin, Director, Research Operations
Awards:
• Mustard Fellowship in Work Environment & Health
Deadline: April

Institute of Air & Space Law (IASL)
3690, rue Peel, Montréal QC H3A 1W9
Tel: 514-398-5095; *Fax:* 514-398-8197
maria.damico@mcgill.ca
www.mcgill.ca/iasl/
www.facebook.com/157123617679546
twitter.com/IASLMcGill
Overview: A small national organization
Mission: To educate air & space lawyers to serve the needs of the air & space community worldwide; To publish interdisciplinary research of value to governments & multinational institutions, the airline & aerospace industries, & the legal profession; To create a global network for faculty, students & subject experts
Membership: 500-999
Activities: *Speaker Service:* Yes
Chief Officer(s):
Paul Stephen Dempsey, Director
paul.dempsey@mcgill.ca
Publications:
• Annals of Air & Space Law / Annales de droit aérien et spatial
Type: Journal; *Frequency:* Annually

Institute of Asian & Slavonic Studies *See* Institute of Asian Research

Institute of Asian Research (IAR)
C.K. Choi Building, University of British Columbia, 1855 West Mall, Vancouver BC V6T 1Z2
Tel: 604-822-4688; *Fax:* 604-822-5207
iar@mail.ubc.ca
www.iar.ubc.ca
Previous Name: Institute of Asian & Slavonic Studies
Overview: A medium-sized international organization founded in 1978
Mission: To promote interdisciplinary research on the Asia Pacific region through its programs of research, training, information & public policy; To collaborate with other Asian researchers in documenting the processes of cultural, economic, political, social & technological change in the region
Member of: CANCAPS; Canadian-Asian Studies Association; American Oriental Society
Finances: *Funding Sources:* Provincial government; grants; contracts; endowments
Staff Member(s): 20
Activities: International Associates Forum; Research Associates & Visiting Scholars Program; Program in inter-cultural studies in Asia; China Program for Integrative Research & Development (CPIRD); Program on Canada-Asia Policy Studies; China Transport & Communication Systems Project; *Library:* Asian Library; Open to public
Chief Officer(s):
Marietta Lao, Manager, Administration
mlao@exchange.ubc.ca

Institute of Association Executives *See* Canadian Society of Association Executives

Institute of Canadian Advertising; Institute of Communications & Advertising *See* Institute of Communication Agencies

Institute of Canadian Bankers *See* Canadian Securities Institute

Institute of Certified Management Consultants of Alberta (CMC-Alberta)
c/o CMC-Canada National Office, PO Box 20, #2004, 410 Bay St., Toronto ON M5H 2Y4
Tel: 416-860-1515; *Fax:* 416-860-1535
Toll-Free: 800-268-1148
consulting@cmc-canada.ca
www.cmc-canada.ca/provincial_institutes.cfm?Portal_ID=1
Overview: A medium-sized provincial organization founded in 1991 overseen by Canadian Association of Management Consultants
Mission: To act under the regulations of the Professional & Occupational Associations Registration Act; To work as the regulatory authority for provisional registrants, certified management consultants, & fellow certified management consultants in Alberta; To ensure that members abide by professional & ethical standards
Membership: *Member Profile:* Certified management consultants; Fellow certified management consultants; *Committees:* Membership
Activities: Offering professional development opportunities
Chief Officer(s):
Greg McIntyre, Vice-President
Jeff Griffiths, Registrar

Institute of Certified Management Consultants of Atlantic Canada
c/o CMC-Canada National Office, PO Box 20, #2004, 401 Bay St., Toronto ON M5H 2Y4
Tel: 416-860-1515; *Fax:* 416-860-1535
Toll-Free: 800-268-1148
consulting@cmc-canada.ca
www.cmc-canada.ca/provincial_institutes.cfm?Portal_ID=2
Also Known As: CMC-Atlantic Canada
Overview: A small provincial organization founded in 1982 overseen by Canadian Association of Management Consultants
Mission: To foster excellence & integrity in the management consulting profession.
Finances: *Funding Sources:* Membership fees
Membership: *Member Profile:* University graduation; 3 years full-time consulting experience; completion of 8 exams or equivalent
Chief Officer(s):
Jerrold White, President
Blaine Atkinson, Registrar

Institute of Certified Management Consultants of British Columbia (CMC-BC)
c/o CMC-Canada National Office, PO Box 20, #2004, 401 Bay St., Toronto ON M5H 2Y4
Tel: 416-860-1515; *Fax:* 416-860-1535
Toll-Free: 800-268-1148
Other Communication: cmc-bc@shaw.ca
consulting@camc.com
www.cmc-canada.ca/provincial_institutes.cfm?Portal_ID=3
Previous Name: Institute of Management Consultants of BC
Overview: A medium-sized provincial organization founded in 1973 overseen by Canadian Association of Management Consultants
Mission: To protect the general public & clients by ensuring that the Institute's Code of Professional Conduct is followed by the certified management consultant profession; To ensure that certified members comply with all applicable legislation & laws
Finances: *Annual Operating Budget:* Less than $50,000
Membership: *Member Profile:* Persons primarily engaged in management consulting in British Columbia
Activities: Presenting awards; Organizing annual general meetings; Ensuring that members are aware of all legislation & laws that affect the profession
Chief Officer(s):
Stephen Spooner, President
Lyn Blanchard, Vice-President
Shayda Kassam, Treasurer

Institute of Certified Management Consultants of Canada
See Canadian Association of Management Consultants

Institute of Certified Management Consultants of Manitoba (CMC-Manitoba) / Institut manitobain des conseillers en administration agréés
c/o CMC-Canada National Office, PO Box 20, #2004, 401 Bay St., Toronto ON M5H 2Y4
Tel: 416-860-1515; *Fax:* 416-860-1535
Toll-Free: 800-268-1148
consulting@cmc-canada.ca
www.cmc-canada.ca/provincial_institutes.cfm?Portal_ID=4
Overview: A small provincial organization founded in 1977 overseen by Canadian Association of Management Consultants
Mission: To foster & promote the development & acceptance of the profession of management consulting; to promote excellence in the practice of the profession for the benefit of members, clients & the community at large.
Finances: *Annual Operating Budget:* Less than $50,000; *Funding Sources:* Membership fees; exams
6 volunteer(s)
Membership: *Member Profile:* Consultants (full-time) with a university degree, three years consulting experience & completing exam process
Activities: *Speaker Service:* Yes
Chief Officer(s):
Timothy Wildman, President
Warren Thompson, Registrar

Institute of Certified Management Consultants of Saskatchewan
c/o CMC-Canada National Office, PO Box 20, #2004, 401 Bay St., Toronto ON M5H 2Y4
Tel: 416-860-1515; *Fax:* 416-860-1535
Toll-Free: 800-662-2972
consulting@cmc-canada.ca
www.cmc-canada.ca/provincial_institutes.cfm?Portal_ID=7
www.facebook.com/CMC.Saskatchewan
Also Known As: CMC-Saskatchewan
Overview: A medium-sized provincial licensing charitable organization founded in 1990 overseen by Canadian Association of Management Consultants
Chief Officer(s):
Richmond Graham, President
Jeremy Hall, Registrar

Institute of Chartered Accountants of the Northwest Territories & Nunavut (ICANTNU)
PO Box 2433, 5016 - 50th Ave., Yellowknife NT X1A 2P8
Tel: 867-873-3680; *Fax:* 867-873-4469
Overview: A small provincial organization founded in 1977 overseen by Chartered Professional Accountants Canada
Mission: To use financial management in order to improve the function of businesses
Membership: *Fees:* Schedule available; *Member Profile:* Chartered Accountants (CAs) in the Northwest Territories & Nunavut
Activities: Providing professional development opportunities (note that ICANTNU will integrate under the CPA banner once legislation is approved)

Institute of Chartered Secretaries & Administrators - Canadian Division (ICSA Canada) / Institut des secrétaires et administrateurs agréés au Canada
#202, 300 March Rd., Ottawa ON K2K 2E2
Tel: 613-595-1151; *Fax:* 613-595-1155
Toll-Free: 800-501-3440
info@icsacanada.org
www.icsacanada.org
www.linkedin.com/groups/4119251
www.facebook.com/ICSA-Canada-297017093984978
twitter.com/ICSACanada
Also Known As: Chartered Secretaries Canada
Previous Name: Chartered Institute of Secretaries
Overview: A medium-sized national organization founded in 1920
Mission: To represent & serve Chartered Secretaries & Administrators, professionals who are hired by organizations to administer key areas such as corporate governance, director/officer/shareholder matters, compliance & regulatory matters & financial matters
Affiliation(s): International Institute of Chartered Secretaries & Administrators
Finances: *Annual Operating Budget:* $250,000-$500,000
Staff Member(s): 3; 20 volunteer(s)
Membership: 1,700+; *Fees:* Schedule available; *Member Profile:* By examination; entry by academic pre-qualification & professional experience; *Committees:* Governance; Education; Admissions; Editorial; Continuing Professional Development
Activities: Training courses in corporate governance & corporate law are available at the head office as well as through its branch offices nationally
Chief Officer(s):
Nancy Barrett, CAE, Executive Director
nancy@icsacanada.org
David Miriguay, CAE, Director, Education
david@icsacanada.org
Publications:
• Corporate Governance Quarterly [a publication of Institute of Chartered Secretaries & Administrators - Canadian Division]
Type: Magazine; *Frequency:* Quarterly
• Corporate Governance Weekly [a publication of Institute of Chartered Secretaries & Administrators - Canadian Division]
Type: E-Newsletter

Institute of Communication Agencies (ICA) / Institut des communications et de la publicité (ICP)
PO Box 2350, #3002, 2300 Yonge St., Toronto ON M4P 1E4
Tel: 416-482-1396; *Fax:* 416-482-1856
Toll-Free: 800-567-7422
ica@icacanada.ca
www.icacanada.ca
www.linkedin.com/company/institute-of-communication-agencies
twitter.com/icacanada
www.youtube.com/user/TheICAcanada
Previous Name: Institute of Canadian Advertising; Institute of Communications & Advertising
Overview: A small national organization founded in 1905
Mission: To anticipate, serve & promote the collective interests of ICA members, with regard to defining, developing & helping to maintain the highest possible standards of professional practice
Membership: *Committees:* ACTRA; CASSIES; CEPO/Advocacy; Client/Agency Relationships; Client of the Year; FFWD Advertising & Marketing Week; Forum of Independent Agencies; FutureFlash; Future of the ICA Task Force; Great Creative & ROI; Innovation and Agency Transformation; Talent Development; Traffic
Activities: Canadian Advertising Agency Practitioners program, a two-year course open to those already in the business; *Library:* by appointment
Chief Officer(s):
Paul Reilly, Chair
Knox Scott, CEO, 416-482-1396 Ext. 225
sknox@icacanada.ca
Awards:
• Cassie Awards
Established 1993; jointly administered with the Association of Canadian Advertisers; Cassies - an acronym for Canadian Advertising Success Stories - are judged on their effectiveness in attaining the advertiser's objectives; awards are presented annually

Institute of Corporate Directors (ICD) / Institut des administrateurs de sociétés
#2701, 250 Yonge St., Toronto ON M5B 2L7
Tel: 416-593-7741; *Fax:* 416-593-0636
Toll-Free: 877-593-7741
info@icd.ca
www.icd.ca
www.linkedin.com/groups?gid=4163769
twitter.com/ICDCanada
Overview: A medium-sized national organization founded in 1980
Mission: To enhance the quality of corporate governance in Canada
Affiliation(s): Institute of Directors
Finances: *Annual Operating Budget:* $500,000-$1.5 Million; *Funding Sources:* Membership fees
Staff Member(s): 20
Membership: 10,000+; *Fees:* Schedule available; *Member Profile:* Full - corporate director; associate - senior executive or professional; *Committees:* Audit; Governance & Human Resources
Activities: Monthly luncheons/breakfast seminars; annual conference; Fellowship Awards Dinner; education programs
Chief Officer(s):
Stan Magidson, President & CEO
Maliha Aqeel, Director, Communications, 416-593-7741 Ext. 229
maqeel@icd.ca
Al-Azhar Khalfan, Director, Marketing & Sales, 416-593-7741 Ext. 243
akhalfan@icd.ca

Institute of Cultural Affairs International (ICAI) / Institut des Affaires Culturelles International
c/o ICA Canada, #405, 401 Richmond St. West, Toronto ON M5V 3A8
Tel: 416-691-2316; *Fax:* 416-691-2491
icai@ica-international.org
ica-international.org
www.facebook.com/icainternational
twitter.com/icai
Also Known As: ICA International
Overview: A medium-sized international charitable organization founded in 1977
Mission: To be engaged in human development activities globally by promoting global ecological perspectives, facilitating organizational change, enabling sustainable development efforts, & advancing lifelong learning & training
Affiliation(s): Has Category II consultative status with The United Nations Economic & Social Council (ECOSOC) & consultative status with the Food & Agricultural Organization (FAO) & a working relationship with the World Health Organization (WHO); consultative status with the United Nations Children's Fund (UNICEF); Service on the Non Governmental Organisation Consultative Group for the International Fund of Agriculture Development (IFAD); membership in CIVICUS, the World Alliance for Citizen Participation
Finances: *Annual Operating Budget:* $500,000-$1.5 Million; *Funding Sources:* Membership dues; Individual/family donations; Institutional/program support (grants)
Staff Member(s): 5; 5 volunteer(s)
Membership: 30 national member organizations, global network of individual and family members; *Fees:* $1,050 statutory; $525 provisional statutory; $330 associate; $150 individual; $250 family; $500 facilitator; $1,000 supporter; *Member Profile:* Global non-profit organizations
Chief Officer(s):
Lisseth Lorenz, President
Archana Deshmukh, Secretary
Seva Gandhi, Treasurer
Publications:
- Winds & Waves [a publication of the Institute of Cultural Affairs International]
Type: Magazine; *Editor:* John Miesen

ICA Canada
#405, 401 Richmond St. West, Toronto ON M5V 3A8
Tel: 416-691-2316
ica@icacan.org
www.icacan.org
Chief Officer(s):
Suzanne Jackson, Chair

Institute of Electrical & Electronics Engineers Inc. - Region 7
685 Woodcrest Blvd., London ON N6K 1P8
Tel: 519-472-7842
www.ieee.ca
Also Known As: IEEE Canada
Overview: A medium-sized national charitable organization founded in 1884
Mission: To advance the theory & practice of electrical, electronics, & computer engineering & computer science
Member of: Institute of Electrical and Electronics Engineers (IEEE)
Affiliation(s): The Engineering Institute of Canada
Finances: *Funding Sources:* Membership dues; Publications; Sponsorship; Sale of products & services
Membership: *Member Profile:* Professional engineers or technologists; *Committees:* Audit; Conference Advisory; Executive; Nominations & Appointments; Steering
Activities: Sponsoring technical conferences, symposia & local meetings worldwide; Providing resources to assist members in increasing their professional skills; Facilitating networking capabilities
Chief Officer(s):
Ashfaq (Kash) Husain, IEEE Canada Administrator
a.husain@ieee.org
Awards:
- A.G.L. McNaughton Gold Medal
- R.A. Fessenden Award
- Power Engineering Award
- Computer Award
- Outstanding Engineer Award
- Outstanding Engineering Educator Award
- W.S. Read Outstanding Service Award
- J.J. Archambault Eastern Canada Merit Award
- M.B. Broughton Central Canada Merit Award
- E.F. Glass Western Canada Merit Award
- RAB Achievement Award
- RAB Innovation Award
- RAB Leadership Award
- RAB Larry K. Wilson Transnational Award
- RAB GOLD Achievement Award
- William W. Middleton Distinguished Service Award
- Friend of IEEE Regional Activities Award
- RAB Section Recognition Awards

Publications:
- Canadian Journal of Electrical & Computer Engineering
Type: Journal; *Frequency:* Quarterly; *Editor:* Shahram Yousefi; *ISSN:* 0840-8688; *Price:* $30 IEEE member; $60 other individual; $90 institution
Profile: Refereed scientific papers in all areas of electrical & computer engineering
- IEEE [Institute of Electrical & Electronics Engineers Inc.] Canada Newsletter / Bulletin de IEEE Canada
Type: Newsletter; *Frequency:* Monthly; *Editor:* Lena Jin
Profile: IEEE activities & industry trends
- IEEE [Institute of Electrical & Electronics Engineers Inc.] Canadian Review / La revue canadienne de l'IEEE
Type: Magazine; *Frequency:* 3 pa; *Accepts Advertising*; *Editor:* Bruce Van-Lane; *ISSN:* 1481-2002; *Price:* Free to members in Canada; $35 non-members; $37.50 corporations & libraries

Institute of Health Economics (IHE)
#1200, 10405 Jasper Ave., Edmonton AB T5J 3N4
Tel: 780-448-4881; *Fax:* 780-448-0018
info@ihe.ca
www.ihe.ca
www.facebook.com/IHECanada
twitter.com/HTAatIHE
vimeo.com/ihe/channels
Previous Name: Institute of Pharmaco-Economics
Overview: A small local organization founded in 1996
Mission: To deliver outstanding health economics, health outcomes, health policy research & related services to governments, health care providers, the health industry & universities
Affiliation(s): Health Technology Assessment International; University of Alberta; University of Calgary; Canadian Association for Health Services & Policy Research; International Health Economics Association; Health Technology Assessment International
Staff Member(s): 37
Membership: *Member Profile:* Government, academia, pharmaceutical industry
Activities: Research; training; knowledge transfer; *Library:* by appointment
Chief Officer(s):
Egon Jonsson, Executive Director & CEO
ejonsson@ihe.ca

Institute of Housing Management (IHM)
#310, 2175 Sheppard Ave. East, Toronto ON M2J 1W8
Tel: 416-493-7382; *Fax:* 416-491-1670
Toll-Free: 866-212-4377
ihm@taylorenterprises.com
ihm-canada.com
Overview: A small provincial organization founded in 1976
Mission: To promote the art & science of property management & the education & training of people engaged in the management & operations of private & public rental housing
Staff Member(s): 1; 11 volunteer(s)
Membership: *Fees:* $69-$307; *Member Profile:* Practising property managers & those with an interest in property management issues
Chief Officer(s):
Kevin O'Hara, President
kohara@regionofwaterloo.ca
Carolyne Vigon, Administrator
carolyne@taylorenterprises.com

Institute of Law Clerks of Ontario (ILCO)
PO Box 44, #502, 20 Adelaide St. East, Toronto ON M5C 2T6
Tel: 416-214-6252; *Fax:* 416-214-6255
Other Communication: Membership E-mail:
members@ilco.on.ca
reception@ilco.on.ca
www.ilco.on.ca
www.linkedin.com/company/institute-of-law-clerks-of-ontario
www.facebook.com/InstituteLCO
twitter.com/InstituteLCO

Overview: A medium-sized provincial organization founded in 1968
Mission: To provide an organized network for promoting unity, cooperation & mutual assistance among law clerks in Ontario; to advance & protect their status & interests; to promote their education for the purpose of increasing their knowledge, efficiency & professional ability
Member of: Canadian Association of Legal Assistants
Finances: *Annual Operating Budget:* $250,000-$500,000; *Funding Sources:* Membership fees
Staff Member(s): 4; 50 volunteer(s)
Membership: 1,700+; *Fees:* Schedule available
Activities: Courses for law clerks available at a number of community colleges throughout Ontario; seminars & workshops; job hotline
Chief Officer(s):
Lisa Matchim, President
Karen Daly, Office Administrator
karen_daly@ilco.on.ca
Meetings/Conferences:
- Institute of Law Clerks of Ontario 28th Annual Conference 2018, May, 2018, Delta Ottawa City Centre, Ottawa, ON
Scope: Provincial
Publications:
- Law Clerks' Review [a publication of the Institute of Law Clerks of Ontario]
Type: E-Newsletter; *Frequency:* Quarterly

Institute of Management Consultants of BC *See* Institute of Certified Management Consultants of British Columbia

Institute of Municipal Assessors (IMA)
#206, 10720 Yonge St., Richmond Hill ON L4C 3C9
Tel: 905-884-1959; *Fax:* 905-884-9263
Toll-Free: 877-877-8703
info@theima.ca
www.assessorsinstitute.ca
Overview: A medium-sized provincial organization founded in 1957
Mission: The IMA is the largest Canadian professional association representing members that practice in the field of Property Assessment & related Property Taxation functions
Finances: *Annual Operating Budget:* $250,000-$500,000
Staff Member(s): 4
Membership: 1,000+; *Fees:* $159 affiliate; $264 associate & accredited; *Committees:* Accreditation; Annual Conference; Bylaw & Resolutions; Communications; Continuing Professional Development; Membership; Nominating
Activities: Administrating the M.I.M.A. & related designations; *Library:* by appointment
Chief Officer(s):
Rose McLean, President
rose.mclean@mpac.ca
Mario Vittiglio, Executive Director, 905-884-1959 Ext. 301
mario@theima.ca
Awards:
- Lifetime Achievement Award
- W.J. Lettner Memorial Award
; *Amount:* $3,000
- The IMA & Legal Group Scholarship
; *Amount:* $5,000
- The IMA & Altus Group Scholarship
; *Amount:* $5,000
- The IMA Achievement Award
; *Amount:* $1,000
- Christian G. Schulze Award for Excellence
; *Amount:* $400
- The IMA Assessors Recognition Award
Meetings/Conferences:
- Institute of Municipal Assessors 62nd Annual Conference 2018, June, 2018, Caesars Windsor Hotel, Windsor, ON
Scope: National

Institute of Pharmaco-Economics *See* Institute of Health Economics

Institute of Power Engineers (IPE)
PO Box 878, Burlington ON L7R 3Y7
Tel: 905-333-3348; *Fax:* 905-333-9328
ipenat@nipe.ca
www.nipe.ca
www.linkedin.com/groups/3973487/profile
Overview: A medium-sized national organization founded in 1940
Mission: To promote business relations, social activities & mutual understanding among power engineers
Finances: *Annual Operating Budget:* $50,000-$100,000

1400 volunteer(s)
Membership: 1,420; *Fees:* $110; *Member Profile:* Individuals holding any class Certificate of Qualification in the Power Engineering field; Individuals enrolled in recognized power engineering courses; Individuals engaged in any pursuit identified or allied with power engineering
Chief Officer(s):
Jude Rankin, National President
Bruce King, 1st National Vice President
Don Purser, National Secretary

Institute of Professional Bookkeepers of Canada (IPBC)
10185 - 164 St., Surrey BC V4N 2K4
Toll-Free: 866-616-4722
info@ipbc.ca
www.ipbc.ca
www.linkedin.com/groups?gid=3759620
www.facebook.com/ipbc.ca
twitter.com/ipbc_canada
Overview: A medium-sized national organization
Mission: To increase excellence in the bookkeeping industry in Canada; To strengthen the credentials & professional standing of bookkeepers
Membership: *Fees:* $415 bookkeeper & accountant; $149.95 student; *Member Profile:* Bookkeepers & accountants throughout Canada
Activities: Providing timely information; Coordinating continuing education events; Offering networking opportunities with other industry professionals; Organizing national phone conferences; Increasing recognition of the bookkeeping profession
Chief Officer(s):
Dianne Mueller, Chair
Peter Lindop, Secretary
Louie Prosperi, Chief Executive Officer
Publications:
• Tips & Topics Newsletter [a publication of the Institute of Professional Bookkeepers of Canada]
Type: Newsletter; *Frequency:* Semiannually; *Price:* Free
Profile: Industry news articles & advice from experts in the industry

Institute of Professional Management (IPM)
#2210, 1081 Ambleside Dr., Ottawa ON K2B 8C8
Tel: 613-721-5957; *Fax:* 613-721-5850
info@workplace.ca
www.workplace.ca
www.facebook.com/InstituteofProfessionalManagement
Overview: A small national organization founded in 1984
Affiliation(s): Association of Professional Recruiters of Canada; Canadian Management Professional Association
Staff Member(s): 8
Activities: Management training & development; workplace.ca gateway to management and workplace resources; publications; *Speaker Service:* Yes
Publications:
• Workplace Today
Type: Journal; *Frequency:* Monthly

Institute of Public Administration of Canada (IPAC) / Institut d'administration publique du Canada (IAPC)
#401, 1075 Bay St., Toronto ON M5S 2B1
Tel: 416-924-8787; *Fax:* 416-924-4992
www.ipac.ca
https://www.linkedin.com/grps?gid=1937184
twitter.com/IPAC_IAPC
Overview: A medium-sized national charitable organization founded in 1947
Mission: To advance public service excellence, by sharing effective practices & policy in public administration; To lead public administration research in Canada; To further professional, non-artisan public service
Staff Member(s): 14
Membership: *Member Profile:* Public servants; Academics; Persons interested in public administration
Activities: Offering learning opportunities; Encouraging research; Providing networking activities; *Speaker Service:* Yes
Chief Officer(s):
Robert P. Taylor, Chief Executive Officer, 416-924-8787 Ext. 230
rtaylor@ipac.ca
Gabriella Ciampini, Director, Special Events, 416-924-8787 Ext. 223
gciampini@ipac.ca
Andrea Migone, Director, Research & Outreach, 416-924-8787 Ext. 228
amigone@ipac.ca
Marta Guzik, Lead, Membership, 416-924-8787 Ext. 221
mguzik@ipac.ca
Suzanne Patterson, Director, Finance & Special Projects, 416-924-8787 Ext. 226
spatterson@ipac.ca
Christy Paddick, Managing Editor & Manager, Public Sector Management Magazine, 905-447-6351
cpaddick@ipac.ca
Awards:
• IPAC / Deloitte Public Sector Leadership Awards
To recognize organizations that have demonstrated outstanding leadership by advancing public policy & management *Contact:* Carole Humphries, IPAC, Phone: 416-924-8787, ext. 234, E-mail: chumphries@ipac.ca
• IPAC Promising New Professional Award
To recognize a promising new public service professional *Deadline:* June 18 *Contact:* Carole Humphries, Dir, Membership & Marketing, Phone: 416-924-8787, ext 234; E-mail: chumphries@ipac.ca
• Innovative Management Award
To recognize exceptional management within the public sector of Canada
• Vanier Medal
Awarded annually to a person who has shown leadership in public administration & public service in Canada, or who, by his or her writings or other endeavours, has made a significant contribution in the field of public administration or public service
• Regional Group Excellence Award
Awarded to a Regional IPAC group that exhibits excellence
• J.E. Hodgetts Award
Awarded annually for the best article in English appearing in the journal Canadian Public Administration
• IPAC Pierre De Celles Award for Excellence in Teaching Public Administration
• Prix Roland Parenteau
Awarded annually for the best article in French appearing in the journal Canadian Public Administration
• National Student & Thought Leadership Awards in Public Administration
To recognize talent in Canadian schools at the regional & national levels
Meetings/Conferences:
• Institute of Public Administration of Canada National Leadership Conference & Awards Gala 2018, February, 2018, Chelsea Hotel, Toronto, ON
Scope: National
Description: Conference for IPAC members featuring leadership seminars & professional development opportunities; theme is "Facing New Frontiers: Leadership Without Borders"
Contact Information: URL: leadership.ipac.ca
• 70th Annual Institute of Public Administration of Canada Conference 2018, August, 2018, Hilton Québec, Québec, QC
Scope: National
Contact Information: URL: 2018.ipac.ca
Publications:
• Canadian Public Administration Journal
Type: Journal; *Frequency:* Quarterly; *Editor:* Christy Paddick
Profile: A refereed scholary publication to examine the structures & processes of public management & public policy at all three level of Canadian government
• Case Studies Program
Editor: Andrew Graham
Profile: Descriptions of situations which public administrators made or influenced
• Collection IPAC en Management Public et Gouvernance
Profile: A French language series, published with the Presses de l'Université Laval, to broaden discussion around policy, governance, & administration
• Institute of Public Administration of Canada Annual Report
Type: Yearbook; *Frequency:* Annually
• IPAC E-newsletter
Type: Newsletter
Profile: Happenings at IPAC, including membership information, research, awards, & forthcoming conferences
• IPAC Series in Public Management & Governance
Editor: Patrice Dutil
Profile: Published in collaboration with the University of Toronto Press to promote excellent scholarship in the field of public sector management
• New Directions Series
Profile: Results of issue-oriented working goups of public servants & academics, such as "Managing Service Transformation Relationships Between Government & Industry: Best Practices"
• Public Sector Management Magazine
Type: Magazine
Profile: Feature articles on topics such as IPAC international programs & country profiles

Institute of Space & Atmospheric Studies (ISAS)
University of Saskatchewan, #260, 116 Science Pl., Saskatoon SK S7N 5E2
Tel: 306-966-6445; *Fax:* 306-966-6400
isas.office@usask.ca
artsandscience.usask.ca/physics/isas
Overview: A small national organization
Mission: Focus is on space & atmospheric studies, solar terrestrial physics, space weather, & atmospheric change
Staff Member(s): 35
Membership: 1-99; *Member Profile:* Professors, research associates, post-doctoral fellow, research engineers
Chief Officer(s):
J.-P. St-Maurice, Chair, 306-966-2906
jp.stmaurice@usask.ca
Alan Manson, Executive Secretary, 306-966-6449
alan.manson@usask.ca

Institute of Textile Science (ITS) / Institut des sciences textiles
c/o CTT Group, 3000, av Boullé, Saint-Hyacinthe ON J2S 1H9
Tel: 450-778-1870
info@textilescience.ca
www.textilescience.ca
Overview: A small national organization founded in 1956
Mission: To promote the dissemination & interchange of knowledge concerning textile science; to encourage research & development related to textile science & technology, including the establishment & granting of awards
Member of: Textile Federation of Canada
Finances: *Annual Operating Budget:* Less than $50,000; *Funding Sources:* Membership fees; scientific sessions
Membership: 180; *Fees:* $30 non-professional; $95 professional
Chief Officer(s):
Patricia Dolez, P. Eng., Ph.D, President, 450-778-1870 Ext. 4255
Dominic Tessier, Ph.D, Membership Secretary, 450-778-1870 Ext. 4240
Meetings/Conferences:
• Institute of Textile Science 117th Scientific Session 2018, 2018
Scope: National

Institute of Urban Studies (IUS)
University of Winnipeg, 599 Portage Ave., 3rd Fl., Winnipeg MB R3C 0G2
Tel: 204-982-1140; *Fax:* 204-943-4695
ius@uwinnipeg.ca
www.uwinnipeg.ca/ius
Overview: A medium-sized national organization founded in 1969
Mission: To undertake policy-oriented research in the field of Urban Studies; To serve as a resource centre for the community; To provide educational services to the University community & the community-at-large
Member of: National Housing Research Committee
Finances: *Funding Sources:* University of Winnipeg; contracts
Staff Member(s): 5
Activities: Areas of expertise include: housing, planning, urban Aboriginal issues, sustainable development, municipal government & finance, & socio-economic & demographic analysis; Research services include: trend analysis, market analysis, cost/benefit analysis, database development, survey & data analysis, community needs assessment, program/policy development & evaluation, community consultation & consensus building, & literature search & review, bibliography development; conference, workshop & publishing services; *Library:* by appointment
Chief Officer(s):
Jino Distasio, Director
j.distasio@uwinnipeg.ca
Publications:
• The Canadian Journal of Urban Research (CJUR)
Type: Journal; *Editor:* Marc Vachon
Profile: A multidisciplinary, scholarly journal dedicated to publishing articles that address a wide range of issues relevant to the field of urbanstudies

Canadian Associations / Institute On Governance (IOG) / Institut sur la gouvernance

Institute On Governance (IOG) / Institut sur la gouvernance
60 George St., Ottawa ON K1N 1J4
Tel: 613-562-0090; *Fax:* 613-562-0087
info@iog.ca
www.iog.ca
www.linkedin.com/groups/Institute-On-Governance-4179557
www.facebook.com/IOGca
twitter.com/IOGca
Overview: A medium-sized national charitable organization founded in 1990
Mission: To advance governance in the public interest
Finances: *Funding Sources:* Public & private sector organizations
Membership: 1-99
Activities: Building policy capacity; Providing advice to public organizations on governance matters in Canada & internationally; Offering professional development activities to promote learning & dialogue on governance issues; *Library:* Information Resource Centre; Not open to public
Chief Officer(s):
Maryantonett Flumian, President
mflumian@iog.ca
Jennifer Smith, Chief Operating Officer
Laura Edgar, Vice President, Board & Organizational Governance
Sylvain Dubois, Vice President, Public Governance
Toby Fyfe, Vice President, Learning Lab
Barry Christoff, Vice President, Indigenous Governance

Institutional Limited Partners Association (ILPA)
#1200, 55 Yonge St., Toronto ON M5J 1R7
Tel: 416-941-9393; *Fax:* 416-941-9307
info@ilpa.org
www.ilpa.org
Overview: A medium-sized national organization
Mission: To serve limited partner investors in the global private equity industry
Staff Member(s): 15
Membership: 300; *Fees:* US$3,000 1-5 member organization; US$3,500 6-10 member organization; US$4,000 11+ member organization; *Committees:* Audit & Finance; Membership; Education; Research, Benchmarking and Standards; Nominating; GP Summit
Chief Officer(s):
Kathy Jeramaz-Larson, Executive Director
Michael Mazzola, Chair
Richard Hall, Vice Chair
Jennifer Kerr, Treasurer

Insurance Agents Association of Manitoba *See* Insurance Brokers Association of Canada

Insurance Brokers Association of Canada (IBAC) / Association des courtiers d'assurances du Canada (ACAC)
#1210, 18 King St. East, Toronto ON M5C 1C4
Tel: 416-367-1831; *Fax:* 416-367-3687
ibac@ibac.ca
www.ibac.ca
Overview: A medium-sized national organization founded in 1922
Mission: The national voice of P&C (Property & Casualty) insurance brokers & an advocate for insurance consumers. IBAC represents their interests to the government of Canada.
Staff Member(s): 7
Membership: 36,000
Chief Officer(s):
Peter Braid, Chief Executive Officer
pbraid@ibac.ca

Insurance Brokers Association of Alberta (IBAA)
3010 Calgary Trail NW, Edmonton AB T6J 6V4
Tel: 780-424-3320; *Fax:* 780-424-7418
Toll-Free: 800-318-0197
ibaa@ibaa.ca
www.ibaa.ca
www.facebook.com/insurancebrokersassociationofalberta
twitter.com/ibaa1
Member of: Insurance Brokers Association of Canada (IBAC)
Chief Officer(s):
George Hodgson, Chief Executive Officer, 780-702-3719 Ext. 194
ghodgson@ibaa.ca
Rikki McBridge, Chief Operating Officer, 780-702-3715 Ext. 101
rmcbride@ibaa.ca

Insurance Brokers Association of British Columbia (IBABC)
#1600, 543 Granville St., Vancouver BC V6C 1X6
Tel: 604-606-8000; *Fax:* 604-683-7831
www.ibabc.org
twitter.com/ibabc
twitter.com/@ibabcEdu
Member of: Insurance Brokers Association of Canada (IBAC)
Chief Officer(s):
Charles (Chuck) Byrne, Executive Director & Chief Operating Officer, 604-606-8001
• BC Broker [a publication of the Insurance Brokers Association of British Columbia]
Type: Magazine; *Editor:* Trudy Lancelyn
Profile: First published in 1978

Insurance Brokers Association of Manitoba (IBAM)
#600, 1445 Portage Ave., Winnipeg MB R3G 3P4
Tel: 204-488-1857; *Fax:* 204-489-0316
Toll-Free: 800-204-5649
info@ibam.mb.ca
www.ibam.mb.ca
www.facebook.com/IBAManitoba
twitter.com/IBAManitoba
Member of: Insurance Brokers Association of Canada (IBAC)
Chief Officer(s):
Olivia Doerksen, Director, Director of Public Relations & Marketing, 204-488-1857 Ext. 1
oliviadoerksen@ibam.mb.ca

Insurance Brokers Association of New Brunswick (IBANB)
PO Box 1523, #202, 334 Queen St., Fredericton NB E3B 5G2
Tel: 506-450-2898; *Fax:* 506-450-1494
ibanb@nbinsurancebrokers.ca
www.nbinsurancebrokers.ca
www.facebook.com/nbbrokers
twitter.com/nbbrokers
www.youtube.com/nbbrokerstv
Member of: Insurance Brokers Association of Canada (IBAC)
Chief Officer(s):
Jay Kimball, Chair, 506-633-2121
jay@gtisj.ca
Andrew McNair, Chief Executive Officer, 506-450-2898
amcnair@ibanb.ca
• Atlantic Insurance Broker Magazine
Type: Magazine; *Frequency:* Quarterly
Profile: Printed on behalf of the Atlantic Canada affiliates of the Insurance Brokers Association of Canada
• Atlantic Insurance Directory
Type: Directory; *Frequency:* Annual
Profile: Printed on behalf of the Atlantic Canada affiliates of the Insurance Brokers Association of Canada

Insurance Brokers Association of Newfoundland (IBAN)
Chimo Bldg., 151 Crosbie Rd., 3rd Floor, St. John's NL A1B 4B4
Tel: 709-726-4450; *Fax:* 709-726-5850
iban@nfld.net
www.iban.ca
www.facebook.com/InsuranceBrokersNewfoundland
twitter.com/IbanSocial
Member of: Insurance Brokers Association of Canada (IBAC)
Chief Officer(s):
Jason Sharpe, President, 709-570-1471, Fax: 709-722-9961
jasons@steersinsurance.com
• Atlantic Insurance Broker Magazine
Type: Magazine; *Frequency:* Quarterly
Profile: Printed on behalf of the Atlantic Canada affiliates of the Insurance Brokers Association of Canada
• Atlantic Insurance Directory
Type: Directory; *Frequency:* Annual
Profile: Printed on behalf of the Atlantic Canada affiliates of the Insurance Brokers Association of Canada

Insurance Brokers Association of Nova Scotia (IBANS)
380 Bedford Hwy, Halifax NS B3M 2L4
Tel: 902-876-0526; *Fax:* 902-876-0527
info@ibans.com
www.ibans.com
www.facebook.com/brokersns
twitter.com/InsuranceNS
Member of: Insurance Brokers Association of Canada (IBAC)
Chief Officer(s):
Cathie Robski, Chair
• Atlantic Insurance Broker Magazine
Type: Magazine; *Frequency:* Quarterly
Profile: Printed on behalf of the Atlantic Canada affiliates of the Insurance Brokers Association of Canada
• Atlantic Insurance Directory
Type: Directory; *Frequency:* Annual
Profile: Printed on behalf of the Atlantic Canada affiliates of the Insurance Brokers Association of Canada

Insurance Brokers Association of Ontario (IBAO)
#700, 1 Eglinton Ave. East, Toronto ON M4P 3A1
Tel: 416-488-7422; *Fax:* 416-488-7526
Toll-Free: 800-268-8845
www.ibao.org
www.facebook.com/IBAO1
twitter.com/IBAOntario
Member of: Insurance Brokers Association of Canada (IBAC)
Colin Simpson, Chief Executive Officer, 416-488-7422 Ext. 120
csimpson@ibao.on.ca
Brett Broadway, Director, Operations, 416-488-7422 Ext. 127
bboadway@ibao.on.ca

Insurance Brokers Association of Prince Edward Island (IBAPEI)
c/o Cooke Insurance Group, PO Box 666, 125 Pownal St., Charlottetown PE C1A 3W4
Tel: 902-566-5666; *Fax:* 855-566-4662
Member of: Insurance Brokers Association of Canada (IBAC)
Chief Officer(s):
Mark Hickey, President, 902-436-9215
mark.hickey@hickeyhyndman.ca
Stephanie Cooke-Landry, Secretary
scooke-landry@cooke.ca
• Atlantic Insurance Broker Magazine
Type: Magazine; *Frequency:* Quarterly
Profile: Printed on behalf of the Atlantic Canada affiliates of the Insurance Brokers Association of Canada
• Atlantic Insurance Directory
Type: Directory; *Frequency:* Annual
Profile: Printed on behalf of the Atlantic Canada affiliates of the Insurance Brokers Association of Canada

Insurance Brokers Association of Saskatchewan (IBAS)
#305, 2631 - 28 Ave., Regina SK S4S 6X3
Tel: 306-525-5900; *Fax:* 306-569-3018
www.ibas.ca
www.facebook.com/270988899613418
twitter.com/SKbrokers
twitter.com/IBASedu
Member of: Insurance Brokers Association of Canada (IBAC)
Chief Officer(s):
Derek Lothian, Chief Executive Officer, 306-545-4075
derek.lothian@ibas.ca
Michael Gaschler, Chief Operating Officer, 306-525-4076
mike.gaschler@ibas.ca
• Saskatchewan Broker [a publication of the Insurance Brokers' Association of Saskatchewan]
Type: Magazine; *Frequency:* Quarterly

Regroupement des cabinets de courtage d'assurance du Québec (RCCAQ)
Complexe Saint-Charles, #550, 1111, rue Saint-Charles ouest, Tour est, Longueuil QC J4K 5G4
Tél: 450-674-6258
Ligne sans frais: 800-516-6258
info@rccaq.com
www.rccaq.com
www.linkedin.com/company/rccaq
www.facebook.com/RCCAQ
twitter.com/rccaq
Membre de: Insurance Brokers Association of Canada (IBAC)
Guy Parent, Directeur général, 450-674-6258 Ext. 282
gparent@rccaq.com

Insurance Brokers Association of Québec - Assembly *Voir* Insurance Brokers Association of Canada

Insurance Bureau of Canada (IBC) / Bureau d'assurance du Canada
Head Office / Ontario Office, PO Box 121, #2400, 777 Bay St., Toronto ON M5G 2C8
Tel: 416-362-2031; *Fax:* 416-361-5952
Toll-Free: 844-227-5422
Other Communication: Membership E-mail: memberservices@ibc.ca
www.ibc.ca
www.linkedin.com/company/15105
www.facebook.com/insurancebureau
twitter.com/InsuranceBureau
www.youtube.com/insurancebureau
Previous Name: Insurance Council of Canada

Overview: A medium-sized national organization founded in 1964
Mission: To foster a healthy property & casualty insurance marketplace & strenghten the ability of our members to serve the needs of Canada's insurance consumers; to advocate public policies that foster a healthy insurance marketplace; to facilitate communication, seek consensus & when in a unique position to do so, undertake industry solutions to common insurance industry concerns
Membership: 80 companies & groups
Activities: *Speaker Service:* Yes; *Library:* Open to public by appointment
Chief Officer(s):
Don Forgeron, President & CEO
Tamara Stoll, Communications Officer, 416-362-2031 Ext. 4303
tstoll@ibc.ca
Meetings/Conferences:
• National Insurance Conference of Canada 2018, September, 2018, Hilton Lac Leamy, Gatineau, QC
Scope: National
Description: Sponsored by the Insurance Bureau of Canada, among other companies & organizations
Contact Information: Web Site: www.niccanada.com; Phone: 416-368-0777; Fax: 416-363-7454

   Alberta & the North
   #2603, 10104 - 103 Ave., Edmonton AB T5J 0H8
   Tel: 780-423-2212; *Fax:* 780-423-4796
   Chief Officer(s):
   William A. Adams, Vice-President, Western & Pacific Region

   Atlantic Canada Office
   Tower II, Purdy's Wharf, #1706, 1969 Upper Water St., Halifax NS B3J 3R7
   Tel: 902-429-2730; *Fax:* 902-420-0157
   Chief Officer(s):
   Amanda Dean, Vice-President, Atlantic

   British Columbia, Saskatchewan & Manitoba Office
   #901, 510 Burrard St., Vancouver BC V6C 3A8
   Tel: 604-684-3635; *Fax:* 604-684-6235
   Chief Officer(s):
   William A. Adams, Vice-President, Western & Pacific Region

   Insurance Information Services & Investigative Services
   #1100, 2235 Sheppard Ave. East, Atria II, Toronto ON M2J 5B5
   Tel: 416-445-5912; *Fax:* 416-449-9357
   Mission: Investigates insurance crime, including fraud & auto theft, & personal injury fraud
   Chief Officer(s):
   Richard Dubin, Vice-President, Investigative Services

   Ottawa Office
   #200, 8 York St., Ottawa ON K1N 5S6
   Tel: 613-236-5043; *Fax:* 613-236-5208

   Québec Office
   Tour de la Bourse, CP 336, #2410, 800, Place-Victoria, Montréal QC H4Z 0A2
   Tél: 514-288-1563; *Téléc:* 514-288-0753
   Ligne sans frais: 877-288-4321
   Chief Officer(s):
   Johanne Lamanque, Vice-President, Québec

Insurance Council of British Columbia
PO Box 7, #300, 1040 West Georgia St., Vancouver BC V6E 4H1
Tel: 604-688-0321; *Fax:* 604-662-7767
Toll-Free: 877-688-0321
info@insurancecouncilofbc.com
www.insurancecouncilofbc.com
Overview: A medium-sized provincial licensing organization founded in 1930
Mission: Has the authority to license insurance agents, salespersons, & adjusters, & to investigate & discipline licensees. The Council is accountable to the provincial government & reports to the Minister of Finance.
Finances: *Annual Operating Budget:* $1.5 Million-$3 Million
Staff Member(s): 30
Membership: *Member Profile:* Insurance agents, salespersons, & adjusters
Chief Officer(s):
Gerald Matier, Executive Director

Insurance Council of Canada *See* Insurance Bureau of Canada

Insurance Council of Manitoba (ICM)
#466, 167 Lombard Ave., Winnipeg MB R3B 0T6
Tel: 204-988-6800; *Fax:* 204-988-6801
contactus@icm.mb.ca
www.icm.mb.ca
Overview: A small provincial licensing organization founded in 1992
Mission: The Council's role is to administer the regulatory legislation governing insurance agents/brokers operating in Manitoba
Staff Member(s): 9
Chief Officer(s):
Erin Pearson, Executive Director
epearson@icm.mb.ca

Insurance Councils of Saskatchewan (ICS)
#310, 2631 - 28th Ave., Regina SK S4S 6X3
Tel: 306-347-0862; *Fax:* 306-569-3018
info@skcouncil.sk.ca
www.insurancecouncils.sk.ca
Overview: A small provincial licensing organization founded in 1986
Mission: Comprising the General Insurance Council, the Life Insurance Council, & the Hail Insurance Council, Insurance Councils of Saskatchewan are committed to promoting a fair, ethical & professional industry, & responsible advice to consumers
Membership: 5,000-14,999
Chief Officer(s):
Ron Fullan, Executive Director

Insurance Institute of British Columbia (IIBC)
#1110, 800 West Pender St., Vancouver BC V6C 2V6
Tel: 604-681-5491; *Fax:* 604-681-5479
Toll-Free: 888-681-5491
IIBCmail@insuranceinstitute.ca
www.insuranceinstitute.ca
Overview: A medium-sized provincial organization overseen by Insurance Institute of Canada
Membership: 4,488; *Committees:* Education; Future Directions; Marketing & Communications; Seminars; Events; Okanagan
Activities: Offering educational opportunities
Chief Officer(s):
Danielle Bolduc, Manager, 604-681-5491 Ext. 22

Insurance Institute of Canada (IIC) / Institut d'assurance du Canada (IAC)
18 King St. East, 6th Fl., Toronto ON M5C 1C4
Tel: 416-362-8586; *Fax:* 416-362-1126
Toll-Free: 866-362-8585
IICmail@insuranceinstitute.ca
www.insuranceinstitute.ca
www.linkedin.com/company/insurance-institute
Overview: A large national licensing organization founded in 1952
Mission: To design, develop, & delivers insurance educational programs & texts; To prepare examinations & awards diplomas; To provide a graduate society; To develop career information on behalf of the property/casualty insurance industry
Member of: Institute for Global Insurance Education
Affiliation(s): Insurance Institute of America; Chartered Insurance Institute; Australian Insurance Institute; Insurance Institute of India; Insurance Institute of Malaysia
Finances: *Annual Operating Budget:* Greater than $5 Million; *Funding Sources:* Fees for services & voluntary corporate subscriptions
Staff Member(s): 28; 100 volunteer(s)
Membership: 36,000 individuals; *Fees:* $50; $95 CIP Society; *Member Profile:* Employed in property/casualty insurance industry; *Committees:* Academic Council; Professionals' Council; Executive
Activities: Offers education programs through local institutes (Chartered Insurance Professionals Program - CIP) & through participating Canadian universities, including the University of Toronto, School of Continuing Studies (Fellowship Program - FCIP), parent organization of the Chartered Insurance Professional Society; *Internships:* Yes; *Speaker Service:* Yes; Library
Chief Officer(s):
Peter G. Hohman, MBA, FCIP, ICD., President & CEO

Insurance Institute of Manitoba (IIM)
#303, 175 Hargrave St., Winnipeg MB R3C 3R8
Tel: 204-956-1702; *Fax:* 204-956-0758
IIMmail@insuranceinstitute.ca
www.insuranceinstitute.ca
Overview: A medium-sized provincial organization founded in 1923 overseen by Insurance Institute of Canada
Mission: To provide educational services in the general insurance industry in both English and French, such as the Chartered Insurance Professional (CIP), & Fellow Chartered Insurance Professional (FCIP) programs
Membership: 1,092; *Member Profile:* Individuals in Manitoba who want to acquire or expand their knowledge of the insurance industry through educational programs provided by the Institute
Activities: Offering continuing educational seminars
Chief Officer(s):
Holly Anderson, Manager

Insurance Institute of New Brunswick (IINB)
#101, 1010 St-George Blvd., Moncton NB E1E 4R5
Tel: 506-386-5896; *Fax:* 506-386-1130
IINBmail@insuranceinstitute.ca
www.insuranceinstitute.ca
Overview: A medium-sized provincial organization founded in 1952 overseen by Insurance Institute of Canada
Activities: Library
Chief Officer(s):
Monique LeBlanc, Manager
mleblanc@insuranceinstitute.ca

Insurance Institute of Newfoundland & Labrador Inc. (IINL)
Chimo Bldg., 151 Crosbie Rd., St. John's NL A1B 4B4
Tel: 709-754-4398; *Fax:* 709-754-4399
IINLmail@insuranceinstitute.ca
www.insuranceinstitute.ca
Overview: A medium-sized provincial organization founded in 1956 overseen by Insurance Institute of Canada
Membership: 469
Activities: *Speaker Service:* Yes; Library
Chief Officer(s):
Leona Rowsell, Manager

Insurance Institute of Northern Alberta (IINA)
#204, 10109 - 106 St., Edmonton AB T5J 3L7
Tel: 780-424-1268; *Fax:* 780-420-1940
IINAmail@insuranceinstitute.ca
www.insuranceinstitute.ca
Overview: A medium-sized local charitable organization overseen by Insurance Institute of Canada
Mission: The Insurance Institute of Northern Alberta provides products and sevices to the general insurance industry, and ensures the maintenance of a uniform standard of education for the general Insurance Business throughout Canada
Affiliation(s): CIP Society of Canada
Finances: *Annual Operating Budget:* $500,000-$1.5 Million
Membership: *Committees:* Education; Seminars; Operations; External Communications
Activities: Seminars; fundraising; social events
Chief Officer(s):
Dawn Horne, Manager

Insurance Institute of Nova Scotia (IINS)
#220, 250 Baker Dr., Dartmouth NS B2W 6L4
Tel: 902-433-0070; *Fax:* 902-433-0072
IINSmail@insuranceinstitute.ca
www.insuranceinstitute.ca
twitter.com/insuranceinsns
Overview: A medium-sized provincial organization founded in 1953 overseen by Insurance Institute of Canada
Mission: To provide educational products & services to the general insurance industry, such as the Chartered Insurance Professional (CIP) & the Fellow Chartered Insurance Professional (FCIP) designation programs
Staff Member(s): 2
Membership: *Member Profile:* Any individual in Nova Scotia who wants to acquire or expand their knowledge of the general insurance industry
Activities: Presenting continuing education seminars; Supervising examinations; Providing networking opportunities
Chief Officer(s):
Jenny Renyo, Manager
jreyno@insuranceinstitute.ca

Insurance Institute of Ontario (IIO)
18 King St. East, 16th Fl., Toronto ON M5C 1C4
Tel: 416-362-8586; *Fax:* 416-362-8081
iiomail@insuranceinstitute.ca
insuranceinstitute.ca/en/institutes-and-chapters/Ontario.aspx
Overview: A medium-sized provincial organization founded in 1899 overseen by Insurance Institute of Canada
Mission: To deliver general insurance educational services in English & French, which are consistent with the standardized curriculum offered throughout Canada, such as the Fellow

Chartered Insurance Professional (FCIP) & the Fellow Chartered Insurance Professional (FCIP) designation programs
Membership: *Member Profile:* Any person in Ontario who would like to acquire or expand their knowledge of the insurance industry
Activities: Arranging instruction; Supervising examinations; Presenting continuing education seminars; Presenting scholarships
Chief Officer(s):
Dawna Matton, BA, FCIP, Senior Director

Cambrian Shield Chapter
18 King St. East, 16th Fl., Toronto ON M5C 1C4
Tel: 416-362-8585; *Fax:* 416-362-8081
cambrianshieldmail@insuranceinstitute.ca
twitter.com/IIOCambrian
Chief Officer(s):
Livia Tersigni, Chapter Manager

Conestoga Chapter
#101, 515 Riverbend Dr., Kitchener ON N2K 3S3
Tel: 519-579-0184; *Fax:* 519-579-1692
conestogamail@insuranceinstitute.ca
twitter.com/IIOConestoga
Chief Officer(s):
Heather Graham, B.Ed, FCIP, CRM, Chapter Manager

Hamilton/Niagara Chapter
#4-5, 1439 Upper Ottawa St., Hamilton ON L8W 3J6
Tel: 905-574-1820; *Fax:* 905-574-8457
hamiltonniagaramail@insuranceinstitute.ca
twitter.com/IIOHam_Nia
Chief Officer(s):
Dawn Cant Elliott, FCIP, CRM, ACS, Chapter Manager

Kawartha/Durham Chapter
18 King St. East, 16th Fl., Toronto ON M5C 1C4
Fax: 416-362-8081
Toll-Free: 866-362-8585
kawarthadurhammail@insuranceinstitute.ca
twitter.com/IIOKaw_Dur
Chief Officer(s):
Livia Tersigni, Chapter Manager

Ottawa Chapter
#300, 1335 Carling Ave., Ottawa ON K1Z 8N8
Tel: 613-722-7870; *Fax:* 613-722-3544
ottawamail@insuranceinstitute.ca
twitter.com/IIOOttawa
Chief Officer(s):
Ellen Legault, BA, FCIP, Chapter Manager

Southwestern Ontario Chapter
#101, 200 Queens Ave., London ON N6A 1J3
Tel: 519-432-3666; *Fax:* 519-432-5919
southwesternmail@insuranceinstitute.ca
twitter.com/IIOSouthWest
Chief Officer(s):
Robert Munford, BA, CIP, Chapter Manager

Insurance Institute of Prince Edward Island (IIPEI)
c/o The Insurance Institute of Canada, 18 King St. East, 6th Fl., Toronto ON M5C 1C4
Tel: 902-892-1692; *Fax:* 902-368-7305
IIPEImail@insuranceinstitute.ca
www.insuranceinstitute.ca
twitter.com/insuranceinspei
Overview: A small provincial organization founded in 1960 overseen by Insurance Institute of Canada
Finances: *Funding Sources:* Membership fees; seminar fees
Activities: Courses; seminars
Chief Officer(s):
Kent Hudson, Marketing Coordinator
khudson@insuranceinstitute.ca

Insurance Institute of Saskatchewan (IIS)
#310, 2631 - 28 Ave., Regina SK S4S 6X3
Tel: 306-525-9799; *Fax:* 306-525-8169
IISmail@insuranceinstitute.ca
www.insuranceinstitute.ca
Overview: A medium-sized provincial organization overseen by Insurance Institute of Canada
Mission: To offer educational products & services to the general insurance industry in both English & French, such as the Fellow Chartered Insurance Professional (FCIP) & the Chartered Insurance Professional (CIP) designation programs
Membership: *Member Profile:* Any person in Saskatchewan who wishes to attain or expand their knowledge of the insurance industry by registering for Insurance Institute courses
Activities: Providing continuing education credits for persons who have completed CIP courses

Chief Officer(s):
Shannon Karok, Manager

Insurance Institute of Southern Alberta (IISA)
#1110, 833 - 4 Ave. SW, Calgary AB T2P 3T5
Tel: 403-266-3427; *Fax:* 403-269-3199
IISAmail@insuranceinstitute.ca
www.insuranceinstitute.ca
Overview: A medium-sized local organization founded in 1954 overseen by Insurance Institute of Canada
Mission: To advance the efficiency, expertise & ability of people employed in the insurance & financial services industry
Finances: *Funding Sources:* Membership dues; industry
100+ volunteer(s)
Membership: 2,530; *Committees:* Education & Membership; Seminar; Career Connections; Marketing
Chief Officer(s):
Seti Mazaheri, Manager

Insurance Professionals of Calgary
c/o Orla McGregor - Intact Insurance, #1200, 321 - 6 Ave. SW, Calgary AB T2P 3H3
Tel: 403-269-7961; *Fax:* 403-263-1839
www.ipcalgary.ca
www.facebook.com/108424839228674
twitter.com/ipcalgary
Previous Name: Calgary Insurance Women
Overview: A small local organization
Mission: Association of individuals employed in the insurance industry or related service providers
Member of: Canadian Association of Insurance Women
Membership: *Fees:* $55
Chief Officer(s):
Orla McGregor, President
president@ipcalgary.org
Evanne Shepherdson, Vice-President
vpresident1@ipcalgary.org
Jane Emslie, Treasurer
treasurer@ipcalgary.org

Insurance Women of Edmonton *See* Edmonton Insurance Association

Insurance Women's Association of Manitoba *See* Manitoba Association of Insurance Professionals

Insurance Women's Association of Western Manitoba
c/o Portage Mutual, 749 Saskatchewan Ave. East, Portage la Prairie MB R1N 2B8
Tel: 204-857-3415; *Fax:* 204-239-6655
www.caiw-acfa.ca/member_associations/iwawm
Overview: A medium-sized local organization founded in 1988
Mission: To encourage & foster education programs for members; to foster & cultivate good fellowship & loyalty among members; to make members more responsive to requirements of the Canadian insurance industry as a whole
Member of: Canadian Association of Insurance Women
Finances: *Annual Operating Budget:* Less than $50,000
30 volunteer(s)
Membership: 30; *Fees:* $45 individual; *Member Profile:* Those employed in the insurance industry
Activities: Monthly meeetings; seminars; golf tournament, Aug.; Wine & Cheese, April; *Awareness Events:* Insurance Information Week
Chief Officer(s):
Andrea Mitchell, President
amitchell@portagemutual.com
Lori Penner, Director
lpenner@portagemutual.com

Integrated Vegetation Management Association of British Columbia (IVMA of BC)
#720, 999 West Broadway, Vancouver BC V5Z 1K5
Tel: 604-732-7117
reception@ivma.com
www.ivma.com
Overview: A small provincial organization
Mission: To advocate for the responsible practice of all aspects of vegetation management
Membership: *Member Profile:* Independent contractors, consultants, manufacturers, suppliers
Chief Officer(s):
Peter Mohammed, Executive Director

Intégration communautaire Chapleau Community Living
PO Box 1377, Chapleau ON P0M 1K0

Tel: 705-864-2932
chapleau.aclhousing@bellnet.ca
Overview: A small local organization
Member of: Community Living Ontario

Intégration communautaire Cochrane Association for Community Living
PO Box 2330, 18 - 2nd Ave., Cochrane ON P0L 1C0
Tel: 705-272-2999; *Fax:* 705-272-4983
Also Known As: Community Living
Overview: A small local charitable organization founded in 1970
Mission: To ensure that all persons live in a state of dignity, share all elements of living, have equal opportunity to maximize inividual potential for personal growth & independence in the community
Member of: Community Living Ontario
Activities: Adult retraining; accommodations services; developmental services
Chief Officer(s):
Chantal Paquette, Executive Director

Intégration communautaire comté de Stormont *See* Community Living Stormont County

Intégration communautaire de Nipissing ouest *See* Community Living West Nipissing

Integration Communautaire Grand Sudbury *See* Community Living Greater Sudbury

Intégration Communautaire Kingston *See* Community Living Kingston

Intégration Communautaire North Bay *See* Community Living North Bay

Intégration communautaire Ontario *See* Community Living Ontario

Integrity Toronto
PO Box 873, Stn. F, Toronto ON M4Y 2N9
Tel: 416-925-9872
toronto@integritycanada.org
www.toronto.integritycanada.org
Overview: A small local organization founded in 1975
Mission: To be an organization of gay & lesbian Anglicans & their friends; To help its members discover & affirm that they can be both Christian & LGBTQ
Affiliation(s): Integrity Inc. - USA
Finances: *Annual Operating Budget:* Less than $50,000; *Funding Sources:* Donations
6 volunteer(s)
Membership: 100 individual; *Fees:* $15 single, $20 couple
Activities: Meetings; Parish education; Newsletters; Retreats; Synod Presence
Chief Officer(s):
Chris Ambidge, Co-Convener

IntegrityLink
#302, 880 Ouellette Ave., Windsor ON N9A 1C7
Tel: 519-258-7222; *Fax:* 519-258-1198
Other Communication: Complaints, E-mail:
complaints@integritylink.ca
info@integritylink.ca
www.integritylink.ca
Previous Name: Better Business Bureau of Windsor & Southwestern Ontario
Overview: A medium-sized local organization
Mission: Their mission is to promote & foster the highest ethical relationship between businesses & the public through voluntary self-regulation, consumer & business education & service education.
Chief Officer(s):
Joe Amort, President & CEO

Intellectual Property Institute of Canada (IPIC) / Institut de la propriété intellectuelle du Canada (IPIC)
Constitution Square, #550, 360 Albert St., Ottawa ON K1R 7X7
Tel: 613-234-0516; *Fax:* 613-234-0671
admin@ipic.ca
www.ipic.ca
Previous Name: Patent & Trademark Institute of Canada
Overview: A medium-sized national organization founded in 1926
Mission: To promote the protection of intellectual property in Canada & abroad in order to enhance Canada's economic prospects as a sovereign nation; To foster cooperation between

Canada & its trading partners around the world
Affiliation(s): Industry Canada
Finances: *Annual Operating Budget:* $250,000-$500,000; *Funding Sources:* Membership dues; meetings
Staff Member(s): 3; 27 volunteer(s)
Membership: 1,700+; *Member Profile:* Professionals who specialize in intellectual property: patents for inventions, trademarks, copyrights, & industrial designs; *Committees:* Alternative Dispute Resolution; Anti-Counterfeiting; Basics of Law Course; Competeton; Copyright Policy; Copyright Technical; Editorial Board of the CIPR; Forums & Seminars; Foundation; Indigenous IP; Industrial Design; Information, Communication & Technogy; Insurance; International Patent Issues; International Trademark Issues; Internet; Invervention; IP Trade Policy; Licensing; Life Science; Litigation; Membership & Information; Patent Agent Examination Standards; Patent Agent Training Course; Patent Legislation; Patent Practice; Professional Regulation; Public Awareness + 7 more
Activities: Professional Development; Promoting the competetiveness of the Canadian IP System; Produce information (publish journals, newsletters, articles, etc); *Rents Mailing List:* Yes
Chief Officer(s):
Adam Kingsley, Executive Director, 613-234-0516 Ext. 25
akingsley@ipic.ca
Kaylee Thambiah, Finance & Administration Officer, 613-234-0516 Ext. 23
klebuis@ipic.ca

Intelligent Sensing for Innovative Structures (ISIS) Canada Research Network *See* Structural Innovation & Monitoring Technologies Resources Centre

Inter Pares / Among Equals
221 Laurier Ave. East, Ottawa ON K1N 6P1
Tel: 613-563-4801; *Fax:* 613-594-4704
Toll-Free: 866-563-4801
info@interpares.ca
www.interpares.ca
www.linkedin.com/company/inter-pares
www.facebook.com/InterParesCanada
twitter.com/Inter_Pares
www.youtube.com/InterParesCanada
Overview: A medium-sized international charitable organization
Mission: To build equality of people, North & South, by collaborating with & supporting justice for people around the world; To advance peace & justice through the provision of programs that address global issues, including food sovereignty, women's equality, democracy, economic justice, health, & migration
Member of: Canadian Council for International Cooperation
Finances: *Annual Operating Budget:* $3 Million-$5 Million
Staff Member(s): 17
Membership: 1-99
Activities: Advocating for equitable policies; Raising funds to support activists & organizations; Carrying out public campaigns to encourage the participation of Canadians; Bringing together activists; *Rents Mailing List:* Yes
Chief Officer(s):
Rita Morbia, Executive Director, 613-563-4801 Ext. 131
rmorbia@interpares.ca
Publications:
• Inter Pares Annual Report
Type: Report; *Frequency:* Annually
Profile: Review of social justice work done by Inter Pares & counterparts in Canada & the South

Inter University Committee on Canadian Slavs (IUCCS) *See* Canadian Ethnic Studies Association

Interac Association / L'Association Interac
Royal Bank Plaza, North Tower, #2400, 200 Bay St., Toronto ON M5J 2J1
Tel: 416-362-8550
Toll-Free: 855-789-2979
info@interac.org
www.interac.org
www.linkedin.com/companies/1328202/Interac+Association
www.facebook.com/interac
twitter.com/interac
youtube.ca/InteracBrand
Overview: A medium-sized national organization founded in 1984
Mission: The Association is a recognized leader in debit card services in Canada
Membership: 80+ organizations; *Member Profile:* Banks; trust companies; credit unions; caisses populaires; technology & payment related companies
Activities: Responsible for the development of a national network of two shared electronic financial services: Shared Cash Dispensing Service at automated banking machines, & Interac Direct Payment Services, a national debit service
Chief Officer(s):
Mark O'Connell, President & CEO

Interactive Advertising Bureau of Canada
#602, 2 St. Clair Ave. West, Toronto ON M4V 1L5
Tel: 416-598-3400; *Fax:* 416-598-3500
Other Communication: quebec@iabcanada.com; west@iabcanada.com
information@iabcanada.com
www.iabcanada.com
www.linkedin.com/groups?home=&gid=4942473&trk=groups_guest_about-h-logo
www.facebook.com/IABCanada
twitter.com/iabcanada
www.youtube.com/iabcanada
Also Known As: IAB Canada
Previous Name: IAB Internet Advertising Bureau of Canada
Overview: A small national organization
Mission: To establish & communicate interactive advertising best practices that optimize advertising investment, leading to increased stakeholder value
Membership: *Member Profile:* Publishers, advertisers, advertising agencies & service associates in the Canadian interactive marketing industry; *Committees:* Ad Operations; Big Data; Content Marketing; Emerging Platforms; Mobile; Research; Programmatic Trading; Search; Social Media; Video
Chief Officer(s):
Chris Williams, President
Julie Ford, Vice President, Operations

Interactive Gaming Council (IGC)
#175, 2906 West Broadway, Vancouver BC V6K 2G8
Tel: 604-732-3833; *Fax:* 604-677-5785
www.igcouncil.org
Overview: A small national organization founded in 1996
Mission: To provide a forum for interested parties to address issues & advance common interests in the global interactive gaming industry; to establish fair & responsible trade guidelines & practices that enhance consumer confidence in interactive gaming products & services; to serve as the industry's public policy advocate & information clearinghouse
Staff Member(s): 3
Chief Officer(s):
Keith Furlong, Cheif Executive
keithf@igcouncil.org
John Anderson, Chair

Interactive Ontario (IO)
#600, 431 King St. West, Toronto ON M5V 1K4
Tel: 416-516-0077
Other Communication: Membership E-mail: membership@interactiveontario.com
info@interactiveontario.com
www.interactiveontario.com
www.linkedin.com/groups?about=&gid=2096721&trk=anet_ug_grppro
www.facebook.com/28971906704
twitter.com/ionews
www.flickr.com/photos/32406922@N04/
Previous Name: New Media Business Alliance
Overview: A medium-sized provincial organization
Mission: To advance the digital media industry in Ontario, including e-Learning, video & online games, mobile, television & social media.
Member of: Canadian Interactive Alliance
Membership: *Fees:* Based on size of company
Chief Officer(s):
Peter Miller, Chair
Lucie Lalumière, Vice-Chair
Spence McDonnell, Treasurer
David Dembroski, Secretary
Christa Dickenson, Executive Director
christa@interactiveontario.com

Inter-American Commercial Arbitration Commission (IACAC)
Canadian Arbitration Centre & Amicable Composition Center, Inc., c/o Faculty of Law, University of Ottawa, Ottawa ON
Tel: 613-232-1476
sice@sice.oas.org
www.sice.oas.org/dispute/comarb/iacac/iacac1e.asp
Overview: A medium-sized international organization founded in 1934
Mission: To promote conciliation, amicable composition & arbitration in the international commercial settling of disputes in the Western hemisphere
Member of: International Federation of Commercial Arbitration Institutions
Finances: *Annual Operating Budget:* $50,000-$100,000; *Funding Sources:* Case fees; grants
Staff Member(s): 2
Membership: 15
Activities: *Internships:* Yes; *Speaker Service:* Yes
Chief Officer(s):
Julio Gonzales Soria, President
Paul J. Davidson, Director, Canada

Canadian National Section
Canadian Arbitration Centre & Amicable Composition Centre, Inc., 57 Louis-Pasteur St., Fauteux Hall, University of Ottawa, Ottawa ON K1N 6N5
Tel: 613-232-1476; *Fax:* 613-564-9800
Chief Officer(s):
Paul J. Davidson, Contact

Intercede International
201 Stanton St., Fort Erie ON L2A 3N8
Tel: 905-871-1773; *Fax:* 905-871-5165
Toll-Free: 800-871-0882
friends@intercedenow.ca
www.intercedenow.ca
Previous Name: Christian Aid Mission
Overview: A medium-sized international charitable organization founded in 1953
Mission: To aid, encourage & strengthen indigenous New Testament Christianity, particularly where Christians are impoverished, few, or persecuted; To encourage Christian witness & ministry to the international community in North America
Member of: Canadian Council of Christian Charities
Affiliation(s): Evangelical Fellowship of Canada
Finances: *Annual Operating Budget:* $500,000-$1.5 Million; *Funding Sources:* Private donations
Staff Member(s): 10; 50 volunteer(s)
Membership: 10; *Committees:* Audit Review
Activities: Sponsorship programs; Relief aid; Equipment & materials provisions; Missions cafe held in major cities; *Speaker Service:* Yes; *Library:* Intercede International Library; by appointment Not open to public
Chief Officer(s):
James S. Eagles, President
Publications:
• Mission Gateway
Type: Magazine; *Frequency:* 3x/yr.; *Editor:* Alan Doerksen
Profile: Publication keeping churches, friends and donors current on indigenous mission work at various global sites.

Inter-Cultural Association of Greater Victoria (ICA)
930 Balmoral Rd., Victoria BC V8T 1A8
Tel: 250-388-4728; *Fax:* 250-386-4395
www.icavictoria.org
www.linkedin.com/company/intercultural-association-of-victoria
www.facebook.com/ICAVictoria
twitter.com/ICAVictoria
www.youtube.com/user/icagreatervictoria
Overview: A small local charitable organization founded in 1971
Mission: To encourage sensitivity, appreciation & respect for individuals of all cultures in our changing community; to assist newcomers to settle in the Greater Victoria area & to facilitate their inclusion & full participation in the community; to advocate for the human rights of people of all cultures; to animate cultural awareness by promoting public multicultural events within Greater Victoria
Member of: Affiliation of Multicultural Societies & Service Agencies of BC
Staff Member(s): 62
Membership: *Member Profile:* Individuals & ethnic member groups
Activities: FolkFest - festival of music, dance & food; ESL; citizenship classes; parenting programs; Women's & Youth Groups; family counselling; interpretation & translation; employment services; Host Family
Chief Officer(s):
Jean McRae, Executive Director

Intercultural Heritage Association
70 Lancaster Rd., Moncton NB E1C 7P6
interculturalheri.association@gmail.com
www.facebook.com/231828396947539
Overview: A small local organization
Mission: To increase the participation & contribution of immigrants & minorities to the social & economic fibres of the New Brunswick community
Chief Officer(s):
JoAnne Gittens, President

Interfaith Food Bank Society of Lethbridge
1103 - 3 Ave. North, Lethbridge AB T1H 0H7
Tel: 403-320-8779; *Fax:* 403-328-0521
info@interfaithfoodbank.ca
www.interfaithfoodbank.ca
www.facebook.com/lethbridgeinterfaith
twitter.com/IFBLethbridge
Overview: A medium-sized local charitable organization founded in 1989 overseen by Food Banks Alberta Association
Mission: To provide food & access to services & resources for those in need
Member of: Food Banks Alberta Association; Food Banks Canada
Chief Officer(s):
Danielle McIntyre, Executive Director
danielle@interfaithfoodbank.ca

Intergovernmental Committee on Urban & Regional Research *See* Muniscope

Interior Designers Association of Saskatchewan (IDAS)
PO Box 32005, Stn. Erindale, Saskatoon SK S7S 1N8
Tel: 306-343-3311
idasadmin@idas.ca
www.idas.ca
Overview: A small provincial organization overseen by Interior Designers of Canada
Mission: To promote an understanding of the profession to the public & to support members in their profession through continuing education & networking
Finances: *Funding Sources:* Auction
Membership: 54; *Fees:* $26.25 student; $156.06 retired; $411.08 registered; $227.23 provisional/out of province; *Member Profile:* 7 years combined education & experience; successful completion of NCIDQ exam; *Committees:* CEU; Events
Activities: Lunch & Learn, monthly
Chief Officer(s):
Kenda Owens, President
kenda.owens@siast.sk.ca

Interior Designers Institute of British Columbia (IDIBC)
#400, 601 West Broadway, Vancouver BC V5Z 4C2
Tel: 604-298-5211; *Fax:* 604-421-5211
info@idibc.org
www.idibc.org
www.linkedin.com/company/idibc---the-interior-designers-institute-of-bc/
www.facebook.com/IDIBC
twitter.com/idibc
Overview: A medium-sized provincial organization founded in 1950 overseen by Interior Designers of Canada
Mission: To act as the single representative voice of the Interior Design profession in British Columbia; to advance the profession through public recognition & provide leadership & services to members through programs, communication & education; to benefit public health, safety & welfare, contribute to the enhancement of the environment & increase the perception, appreciation & value of design in the community.
Affiliation(s): Design Resource Association
Finances: *Annual Operating Budget:* $100,000-$250,000; *Funding Sources:* Corporate; fundraising
Staff Member(s): 1
Membership: 230; *Fees:* $424 professional; $201 associate; $69 pre-professional; $275 affiliate; $32 student; *Member Profile:* Professional; Associate; Pre-Professional; Fellow; Charter; Honorary; Inactive; Student; *Committees:* Newsletter; Fundraising; Design Awards; Special Projects; Education; Membership Services; Programs
Activities: Continuing education; Awards of Excellence Design Competition; professional recognition; seminars; *Rents Mailing List:* Yes
Chief Officer(s):
Erica Wickes, President

Interior Designers of Alberta (IDA)
c/o ManageWise Inc., PO Box 21171, #202, 5405 - 99 St., Edmonton AB T6R 2V4
Tel: 780-413-0013; *Fax:* 780-413-0076
info@idalberta.ca
www.idalberta.ca
Also Known As: Registered Interior Designers of Alberta
Overview: A small provincial organization founded in 1960 overseen by Interior Designers of Canada
Mission: To develop & maintain standards of practice of interior design; to encourage excellence in interior design; to develop standards of & encourage continuing education of practicing designers; & to provide a liaison between the profession & the general public.
Affiliation(s): Interior Designers of Canada; National Council for Interior Design Qualification; Council for Interior Design Accreditation; Interior Design Continuing Education Council Inc.; Interior Designers Institute of British Columbia; Interior Designers Association of Saskatchewan; Professional Interior Designers Institute of Manitoba; Association of Registered Interior Designers of Ontario; Association professionnelle des designers d'intérieur du Quebec; Association of Registered Interior Designers of New Brunswick; Association of Interior Designers of Nova Scotia
Membership: 160; *Fees:* $30 student; $300 provisional; $355 registered-licensed; $405 registered; $390 associate; *Member Profile:* People involved with the interior design profession & students
Chief Officer(s):
Kelly Vander Hooft, President
Adele Bonetti, Registrar

Interior Designers of Canada (IDC) / Designers d'intérieur du Canada
#C536, 43 Hanna Ave., Toronto ON M6K 1X1
Tel: 416-649-4425; *Fax:* 416-921-3660
Toll-Free: 877-443-4425
www.idcanada.org
www.facebook.com/147037918674277?v=info
twitter.com/IDCanadaTweets
Overview: A medium-sized national organization founded in 1972
Mission: To advance the interior design industry in Canada through high standards of education for the profession, professional responsibility, professional development, & communication
Finances: *Funding Sources:* Sponsorships
Activities: Providing educational programs & professional qualifications; Offering national liability insurance; Liaising with federal government committees to represent the interior design profession; Promoting environmental consciousness; Initiating The Interior Designers of Canada Foundation to provide scholarships, bursaries, & fellowships to interior design students & practitioners
Chief Officer(s):
Susan Wiggins, Chief Executive Officer, 416-649-4434
swiggins@idcanada.org

Interior Designers of New Brunswick *See* Association of Registered Interior Designers of New Brunswick

Interior Designers of Newfoundland & Labrador (IDNL)
NL
idnl.ca
Overview: A small provincial organization overseen by Interior Designers of Canada

Interior Designers of Ontario (IDO) *See* Association of Registered Interior Designers of Ontario

Interior Indian Friendship Society
125 Palm St., Kamloops BC V2B 8J7
Tel: 250-376-1296; *Fax:* 250-376-2275
www.iifs.ca
Overview: A small local charitable organization founded in 1972
Mission: To improve the quality of life for Aboriginal People
Finances: *Annual Operating Budget:* $500,000-$1.5 Million
Staff Member(s): 28
Membership: 30-80; *Fees:* $2; *Member Profile:* Urban Aboriginal People; *Committees:* Education; Personnel
Activities: Social programs; Mental Health programs; Alcohol and Drug Counseling; Family Preservation & Roots; Life Skills Housing programs; *Awareness Events:* Aboriginal Day; *Library:* Open to public
Chief Officer(s):
Delphine Terbasket, Executive Director

Interior Running Association
BC
Tel: 250-374-1652
www.interiorrunningassociation.com
www.facebook.com/InteriorRunningAssociation
twitter.com/interiorrunning
Overview: A small national organization
Mission: To promote fitness & running in the Southern Interior of British Columbia.
Activities: Road & trail races
Chief Officer(s):
Cindy Rhodes, Co-President
John Wilson, Co-President

Interior Systems Contractors Association of Ontario (ISCA)
60 Sharer Rd., Woodbridge ON L4L 8P4
Tel: 416-746-4722; *Fax:* 416-746-1522
info@isca.ca
www.isca.ca
Previous Name: Drywall Association of Ontario
Overview: A small provincial organization founded in 1971
Member of: National Trade Contractors Coalition of Canada
Membership: 80 contractors + 30 suppliers/manufacturers; *Fees:* Schedule available; *Member Profile:* Members are engaged in the following areas: Drywall & Acoustical Installation; Thermal Insulation; Exterior Insulated Finishing Systems; Asbestos Removal; Drywall Taping & Plastering; Fireproofing Applications; Residential Steel Framing; & Mold Remediation
Activities: Programs include: Health and Safety Training; Computer Estimating; Foreman Upgrade Training Programs; & a WSIB Safety Group
Chief Officer(s):
Hugh Laird, Executive Director
hlaird@isca.ca

Inter-loge
1503, rue La Fontaine, Montréal QC H2L 1T7
Tél: 514-522-2107; *Téléc:* 514-522-7070
www.linkedin.com/company/inter-loge
www.facebook.com/Interloge
twitter.com/interloge
Aperçu: *Dimension:* petite; *Envergure:* locale; fondée en 1978
Mission: Pour fournir des logements abordables pour les locataires à faible revenu et d'aide à la reconversion de la communauté

International Academy of Energy, Minerals & Materials (IAEMM)
PO Box 62047, Stn. Convent Glen, Orléans ON K1C 7H8
Tel: 613-830-1760
info@iaemm.com
iaemm.com
twitter.com/iaemm1
Overview: A medium-sized international organization
Mission: To advance energy, minerals & materials technologies through education, conferences & scientific publishing
Activities: Provides training & workshops; Organizes conferences; Publishes practical information
Meetings/Conferences:
• International Academy of Energy, Minerals & Materials 2018 International Conference & Exhibition on Advanced and Nano Materials, August, 2018, Québec, QC
Scope: International
Contact Information: icanm2018.iaemm.com
• International Academy of Energy, Minerals & Materials 2018 International Conference & Exhibition on Clean Energy, August, 2018, Québec, QC
Scope: International
Description: Conference topics include the following: Biomass energy, materials & technologies; Hydro energy, materials & technologies; Wind energy resources & technologies; Solar cells energy, materials & technologies; Fuel cells materials & hydrogen energy; Battery materials & technologies; Energy storage techniques; Nanotechnology & energy; Green buildings; Energy process & system simulation, modelling & optimization; & more
Contact Information: icce2018.iaemm.com
• International Academy of Energy, Minerals & Materials 2018 International Conference and Exhibition on Mining, Material and Metallurgical Education, 2018
Scope: International
Publications:
• International Academy of Energy, Minerals, & Materials Conference Proceedings
Type: Report

• International Academy of Energy, Minerals, & Materials Technical Reports
Type: Report

International Academy of Law & Mental Health (IALMH) / Académie internationale de droit et de santé mentale (AIDSM)
c/o Philippe Pinel, Faculty of Medicine, University of Montreal, PO Box 6128, Stn. Centre-Ville, Montréal QC H3C 3J7
Tel: 514-343-5938; *Fax:* 514-343-2452
admin@ialmh.org
www.ialmh.org
Overview: A small international organization founded in 1981
Membership: *Fees:* $100 USD regular; $50 USD student
Chief Officer(s):
George Woods, President
Meetings/Conferences:
• International Academy of Law & Mental Health 2019
International Congress on Law and Mental Health, 2019
Scope: International
Publications:
• International Journal of Law and Psychiatry [a publication of the International Academy of Law & Mental Health]
Type: Journal; *Frequency:* q.; *ISSN:* 0160-2527
Profile: Multidisciplinary forum for the exchange of information and ideas among professionals that relate tothe intersection of law and psychiatry

International Academy of Science, Engineering & Technology
#414, 1376 Bank St., Ottawa ON K1H 7Y3
Tel: 613-695-3040
info@international-aset.com
www.international-aset.com
www.linkedin.com/company/1169039
www.facebook.com/207827708283
twitter.com/ASET_INC
www.youtube.com/user/InternationalASET
Also Known As: International ASET Inc.
Overview: A medium-sized international organization
Mission: The International Academy of Science, Engineering and Technology (International ASET Inc.) is a young, growing and independent institution created to serve in the matters of education involving science and engineering.
Meetings/Conferences:
• 2018 International Conference of Control, Dynamic Systems & Robotics, June, 2018, Niagara Falls, ON
Scope: National
Description: Annual conference in fields related to traditional & modern control and dynamic systems.
Contact Information: cdsr.net
• 7th International Conference on Mechanics & Industrial Engineering 2018, August, 2018, Madrid
Scope: International
Contact Information: icmie.net
• 9th International Conference on Nanotechnology: Fundamentals and Applications 2018, August, 2018, Madrid
Scope: International
Contact Information: icnfa.com
• 8th International Conference on Environmental Pollution & Remediation 2018, August, 2018, Madrid
Scope: International
Contact Information: icepr.org

International Air Transport Association (IATA) / Association du transport aérien international
PO Box 113, 800, Place Victoria, Montréal QC H4Z 1M1
Tel: 514-874-0202; *Fax:* 514-874-9632
www.iata.org
www.linkedin.com/groups/3315879/profile
www.facebook.com/iata.org
twitter.com/iata
www.youtube.com/iatatv
Overview: A small international organization founded in 1945
Mission: To promote safe, regular & economical air transport for the benefit of the peoples of the world; To foster air commerce; To study the problems connected with air transport; To provide a means for collaboration among the air transport enterprises engaged directly or indirectly in international air transport service; To cooperate with the International Civil Aviation Organization & other international organizations; To coordinate international fares & rates; To simplify the travelling process for the general public
Affiliation(s): International Civil Aviation Organization
Membership: 275 member airlines; *Fees:* US$14,450; *Member Profile:* International passenger & cargo airlines; *Committees:* Avionics & Telecommunications; Engineering & Environment; Airports; Flight Operations; Medical; Security; Air Law; Financial; Traffic Coordination; Traffic Services
Activities: Training programs; Policy development; Produce & distribute publications; Webinars; Annual meetings
Chief Officer(s):
Tony Tyler, Director General
Meetings/Conferences:
• International Ait Transport Association 74th Annual General Meeting & World Air Transport Summit, June, 2018, Sydney
Description: Annual meeting of aviation leaders and media representatives; Presentations, debates & panel discussions

International Airborne Geophysics Safety Association (IAGSA)
144 Harry MacKay Rd., Woodland ON K0A 2M0
Tel: 613-832-1646
www.iagsa.ca
Overview: A small international organization founded in 1995
Mission: To promote & enhance safety in airborne geophysics
Finances: *Funding Sources:* Membership fees
Membership: 98; *Fees:* Schedule available based on number of employees; *Member Profile:* Companies involved in airborne geophysics
Activities: *Library:* Not open to public

International Alliance of Breast Cancer Organizations *See* Alliance of Cancer Consultants

International Alliance of Theatrical Stage Employees, Moving Picture Technicians, Artists & Allied Crafts of the U.S. *Voir* Alliance internationale des employé(e)s de scène, de théâtre et de cinéma

International Association for Educational & Vocational Guidance (IAEVG) / Association internationale d'orientation scolaire et professionnelle (AIOSP)
c/o University of Calgary, Division of Applied Psychology, #202, 119 Ross Ave., Ottawa ON K1Y 0N6
Tel: 613-729-6164; *Fax:* 613-729-3515
membership@iaevg.org
www.iaevg.org
Overview: A small international organization founded in 1951
Mission: To promote communication between persons & organizations active in educational & vocational guidance; to encourage the permanent development of ideas, practice & research in this field on national & international levels; to advise governments on the development of guidance & counselling programs
Affiliation(s): Canadian Career Development Foundation; Centre de recherche sur l'éducation au travail (CRET); National Life/Work Centre; Canada WorkInfoNet Partnership
Finances: *Annual Operating Budget:* $100,000-$250,000
Membership: 400 individuals + 50 national associations; *Fees:* US$84
Chief Officer(s):
Lester Oakes, President
Suzanne Bultheel, Secretary General
Suzanne.Bultheel@gmail.com

International Association for Impact Assessment - Western & Northern Canada
2215 - 19th St. SW, Calgary AB T2T 4X1
Tel: 403-245-6404
IAIA-WNC@praxis.ca
www.iaia-wnc.ca
Overview: A small local organization
Chief Officer(s):
Susan P. Wilkins, President

International Association for Literary Journalism Studies (IALJS)
c/o Ryerson University School of Journalism (Attn: Bill Reynolds), 350 Victoria St., Toronto ON M5B 2K3
Tel: 416-979-5000
www.ialjs.org
Overview: A small international organization founded in 2006
Mission: To promote scholarly research & education in literary journalism (narrative journalism, creative non-fiction, or journalism as literature)
Membership: *Fees:* USD$100 sponsoring; USD$50 regular/associate; USD$25 student/retired
Activities: Online newsletter; blog
Chief Officer(s):
Norman Sims, President
normsims@me.com
Bill Reynolds, Editor in Chief & Treasurer
reynolds@ryerson.ca
Publications:
• Literary Journalism Studies
Type: Journal; *Editor:* Bill Reynolds; *ISSN:* 1944-897X

International Association for Medical Assistance to Travellers (IAMAT)
#036, 67 Mowat Ave., Toronto ON M6K 3E3
Tel: 416-652-0137; *Fax:* 416-652-1983
www.iamat.org
www.facebook.com/IAMATHealth
twitter.com/IAMAT_Travel
www.flickr.com/photos/iamat_photo_contest/
Overview: A medium-sized international charitable organization founded in 1960
Mission: To make competent care available to the traveller around the world; to make direct grants to medical institutions
Member of: Foundation for the Support of International Medical Training (Canada)
Finances: *Funding Sources:* Donations
Membership: *Fees:* Free
Activities: World directory of IAMAT physicians; traveller clinical record; world immunization, malaria & schistosomiasis risk & climate charts; scholarship & grant funding in the field of travel medicine; *Speaker Service:* Yes; *Library:* Online Library
Chief Officer(s):
Assunta Uffer-Marcolongo, President
Tullia Marcolongo, Director, Programs & Development
Nadia Sallete, Director, Membership Services
Guelph Office
2162 Gordon St., Guelph ON N1L 1G6

International Association for Public Participation Canada (IAP2)
info@iap2canada.ca
www.iap2canada.ca
www.linkedin.com/groups/3805500
www.facebook.com/iap2canada
twitter.com/IAP2CDN
Overview: A large national organization founded in 1990
Mission: To promote & improve the practice of public participation at the individual, government, & institutional level; To serve the learning needs of members in various ways; To advocate for public participation in Canada & abroad
Finances: *Funding Sources:* Membership fees
Membership: *Fees:* $150 individual; $50 student; schedule for groups; *Committees:* Research
Activities: Providing educational opportunities & technical assistance to member groups to improve public participation; Promoting a results-oriented research agenda; Acting as a connector to build partnerships & foster collaboration between members
Chief Officer(s):
Amelia Shaw, Executive Manager
Awards:
• Project of the Year Award, IAP2 Canada Core Values Awards
• Award for Indigenous Engagement, IAP2 Canada Core Values Awards
• Organization of the Year Award, IAP2 Canada Core Values Awards
• P2 for the Greater Good Award, IAP2 Canada Core Values Awards
• Diversity & Inclusion Award, IAP2 Canada Core Values Awards
Meetings/Conferences:
• International Association for Public Participation Canada 2018 Skills Symposium, March, 2018, Four Points Sheraton, Ottawa, ON

International Association of Art Critics - Canada (IAAC) / Association internationale des Critiques d'art - Canada (AICA)
c/o Ninon Gauthier, President, #301, 150, rue Berlioz, Montréal QC H3E 1K3
Tel: 514-658-2538
aica-canada.org
Overview: A small international organization founded in 1955
Mission: To contribute to the promotion of contemporary art & freedom of expression in the visual arts; To develop national & international cooperation in art criticism
Affiliation(s): International Association of Art Critics
Membership: 70; *Fees:* $80; *Committees:* Archives & Living Memories; Censorship & Freedom of Expression;

Canadian Associations / International Association of Hydrogeologists - Canadian National Chapter (IAH-CNC) / Internationale association des hydrogeologists (AIC)

Communication & Publishing; Financing; Honorary Membership & Awards; Scientific
Chief Officer(s):
Ninon Gauthier, President
Earl Miller, Treasurer & Secretary
earledwinmiller@gmail.com

International Association of Hydrogeologists - Canadian National Chapter (IAH-CNC) / Internationale association des hydrogeologists (AIC)
c/o WESA, 3108 Carp Rd., Carp ON K0A 1L0
Tel: 613-839-3053
www.iah.ca
Overview: A medium-sized national organization founded in 1972
Mission: To advance the science of hydrogeology & exchange hydrogeologic information internationally
Member of: Canadian Geoscience Council
Affiliation(s): International Union of Geological Congresses
Finances: Annual Operating Budget: Less than $50,000
Membership: 378; Fees: $105-$125; $35-$40 student; $680 corporate; Member Profile: Hydrogeologists, scientists, engineers & others with an interest in groundwater resources
Activities: Seminars, talks, conferences & networking opportunities; Speaker Service: Yes
Chief Officer(s):
Diana Allen, President

International Association of Infant Massage Canada
Toll-Free: 877-532-2323
aimbiaim@gmail.com
www.iaim-aimbcanada.org
Overview: A small national organization
Mission: To promote the nuturing touch and communication through training, education and research.
Membership: Fees: $80
Chief Officer(s):
Manon Salois, President

International Association of Outplacement Professionals
See Association of Career Professionals International

International Association of Science & Technology for Development (IASTED)
Bldg B6, #101, 2509 Dieppe Ave. SW, Calgary AB T3E 7J9
Tel: 403-288-1195; Fax: 403-247-6851
calgary@iasted.com
www.iasted.org
www.linkedin.com/in/iastedconferences
www.facebook.com/IASTED
twitter.com/IASTED_Calgary
Overview: A medium-sized international organization founded in 1977
Mission: To further economic development by promoting science & technology
Membership: Fees: $120 individual; $30 developping country; Committees: Technical
Activities: Interchange & circulation of information on science & technology; organizing international conferences, symposia, courses
Publications:
• Alternative Energy
Type: Journal; Frequency: Quarterly; Editor: Dr. M. Hamza
• Biomedical Engineering
Type: Journal; Frequency: Quarterly; Editor: Dr. M. Hamza
• Communications
Type: Journal; Frequency: Quarterly; Editor: Dr. Leone C. Monticone
• Communications & Computer Security
Type: Journal; Frequency: Quarterly; Editor: Dr. M. Hamza
• Control & Intelligent Systems
Type: Journal; Frequency: Quarterly; Editor: Prof. Clarence W. de Silva
• International Journal of Computational Bioscience
Type: Journal; Frequency: Quarterly; Editor: Dr. M. Hamza
• International Journal of Power & Energy Systems
Type: Journal; Frequency: Quarterly; Editor: Dr. A. Domijan
• International Journal of Robotics & Automation
Type: Journal; Frequency: Quarterly; Editor: Prof. Simon X. Yang
• Parallel & Distributed Computing & Networks
Type: Journal; Frequency: Quarterly; Editor: Prof. Amiya Nayak
• Software Engineering
Type: Journal; Frequency: Quarterly; Editor: Dr. Albert M. K. Cheng

• Technology for Education & Learning
Type: Journal; Frequency: Quarterly; Editor: Dr. M. Hamza

International Bible Correspondence School
PO Box 98590, 873 Jane St., Toronto ON M6N 4C0
www.ibcschool.ca
Overview: A small international organization founded in 1968
Mission: To provide students with tools for Bible study
Staff Member(s): 1; 25 volunteer(s)
Membership: Member Profile: Any individual wishing to engage in Bible studies
Chief Officer(s):
Richard Kruse, Director

International Board on Books for Young People - Canadian Section (IBBY - Canada) / Union internationale pour les livres de jeunesse
c/o Canadian Children's Book Centre, #217, 40 Orchard View Blvd., Toronto ON M4R 1B9
Tel: 416-975-0010; Fax: 416-975-8970
info@ibby-canada.org
www.ibby-canada.org
www.facebook.com/ibbycanada
twitter.com/IBBYCanada
flickr.com/photos/50914640@N08
Overview: A small international organization founded in 1980
Mission: To promote the belief that all children everywhere should have the ability to read a wide & rich selection of books at the level of their needs & interests; To build bridges of understanding & tolerance through children's books
Affiliation(s): Canadian Children's Book Centre
Finances: Funding Sources: Private donations & membership fees
Membership: Fees: $15 student; $50 individual; $125 supporter; $250 donor; $750 patron; Member Profile: General interest in children's literature
Chief Officer(s):
Susane Duchesne, President
president@ibby-canada.org
Stephanie Dror, Secretary, Membership
membership@ibby-canada.org
Awards:
• Elizabeth Mrazik-Cleaver Picture Book Award
Awarded for distinguished Canadian picture book illustration; submissions to Children's Literature Service, National Library of Canada, 395 Wellington St., Ottawa, ON K1A 0N4; Amount: $1,000
• Frances E. Russell Award
Awarded to initiate & encourage research in children's literature in Canada; Amount: $1,000
• Claude Aubry Award
Awarded biennially for distinguished contributions to Canadian children's literature by a librarian, teacher, author, illustrator, publisher, bookseller, or editor; Amount: $1,000

International Catholic Deaf Association (ICDA)
mhysell@op.dspt.edu
www.icdacanadasection.wordpress.com
www.facebook.com/ICDACanadianSection
Also Known As: ICDA-Canada
Overview: A small international organization founded in 1949
Mission: To promote religion, religious education, fellowship & leadership among deaf people of all ages; to promote in Canada & the ICDA various programs in foreign countries with a view to enhancing the life of deaf people
Finances: Annual Operating Budget: Less than $50,000
40 volunteer(s)
Membership: 150 + 5,000 non-members; 16 Canadian chapters; Fees: $10 single; $15 couple; Member Profile: Practicing Catholics; deaf diaconates; lay ministries
Activities: National conference/workshop; Canadian Catholic Pastoral Workers for the Deaf meetings; fundraising; retreats; signed Mass; assists the Pastoral Workers, seminarians to learn sign languages; spreads the knowledge of the deaf culture among the hearing parishioners
Chief Officer(s):
Wanda Berrette, President
wberrette@rogers.com
Giuliana Grobelski, Vice-President
julianamusso3@hotmail.com
John Shores, Treasurer
jshores@shaw.ca
Awards:
• The Frank Crough Award
For the outstanding member of the year

• The Sr. Columbiere Award
For the outstanding pastoral worker of the year

International Centre See Queen's University International Centre

International Centre for Comparative Criminology Voir Centre international de criminologie comparée

International Centre for Criminal Law Reform & Criminal Justice Policy (ICCLR)
1822 East Mall, Vancouver BC V6T 1Z1
Tel: 604-822-9875; Fax: 604-822-9317
icclr@allard.ubc.ca
www.icclr.law.ubc.ca
twitter.com/theicclr
Overview: A medium-sized international charitable organization founded in 1991
Mission: To improve the quality of justice through reform of criminal law, policy & practice; To provide advice, information, research & proposals for policy development & legislation
Affiliation(s): UN Crime Prevention & Criminal Justice Programme
Staff Member(s): 10
Membership: 1-99
Activities: Publications; Speaker Service: Yes
Chief Officer(s):
Peter German, President & Executive Director

International Centre for Science in Drug Policy (ICSDP)
c/o Li Ka Shing Knowledge Institute of St. Michael's Hospital, 30 Bond St., Toronto ON M5B 1W8
Tel: 647-694-9199
info@icsdp.org
www.icsdp.org
www.linkedin.com/company/international-centre-for-science-in-drug-policy
www.facebook.com/icsdp
twitter.com/icsdp
Overview: A large international organization
Mission: To improve the health & safety of communities & individuals who are affected by illicit drug use
Staff Member(s): 2
Activities: Conducting research into best policy practices; Working collaboratively with communities, policy makers, & law enforcement to guide effective policy responses; Organizing campaigns to educate communities & individuals about the need for evidence-based drug policies
Chief Officer(s):
Dan Werb, Executive Director
Publications:
• The Effectiveness of Anti-Illicit-Drug Public-Service Announcements [a publication of the ICSDP]
Type: Report; Author: Dan Werb et al.; ISSN: 0143-005X
Profile: Reviews existing studies on the effectiveness of anti-illicit-drug public service announcements
• Effects of Drug Law Enforcement on Drug-Related Violence [a publication of the ICSDP]
Type: Report; Number of Pages: 26; Author: Dan Werb et al.
Profile: Scientific review illustrating the relationship between drug law enforcement & drug-related violence
• State of the Evidence: Cannabis Use & Regulation [a publication of the International Centre for Science in Drug Policy]
Type: Report; Number of Pages: 41; Author: Nazlee Maghsoudi et al.
Profile: Provides an overview of the scientific research on major claims about cannbisuse & regulation
• The Temporal Relationship Between Drug Supply Indicators [a publication of the ICSDP]
Type: Report; Number of Pages: 8; Author: Dan Werb et al.
Profile: Contains information on the relationship between illegal drug prices, purity, & international law enforcement efforts toreduce drug supply
• Tools for Debate: U.S. Federal Government Data on Cannabis Prohibition [a publication of the ICSDP]
Type: Report; Number of Pages: 25; Author: Dan Werb et al.
Profile: Reviews the U.S. government's cannabis prohibition policy
• Using Evidence to Talk about Cannabis [a publication of the International Centre for Science in Drug Policy]
Type: Report; Number of Pages: 16; Author: Nazlee Maghsoudi & Dan Werb
Profile: Provides evidence-based responses to commonly heard claims about cannabis use &regulation

International Centre for Sustainable Cities (ICSC)
#210, 128 West Hastings St., Vancouver BC V6B 1G8
Tel: 778-712-0965
sustainablecities.net
Overview: A small international charitable organization founded in 1993
Mission: To support sustainable city projects around the world through demonstration projects using Canadian experience & expertise
Finances: Funding Sources: Projects
Membership: 40 member cities; Committees: Executive
Activities: Supports sustainable urban development demonstration projects in India, China, Columbia, Thailand, SE Asia (Thailand, Indonesia, Philippines), Turkey, Poland, Slovakia, Hungary; Plus-30 Network; Internships: Yes; Library: by appointment Not open to public
Chief Officer(s):
Jane McRae, CEO
jcmcrae@icsc.ca
Beth Johnson, Chair

International Centre for the Prevention of Crime Voir Centre international pour la prévention de la criminalité

International Cheese Council of Canada (ICCC)
c/o Welch LLP, 100-123 Slater St., Ottawa ON K1P 5H2
Overview: A medium-sized national organization founded in 1976 overseen by The Canadian Association of Importers & Exporters
Mission: To act as the representative voice of Canadian importers of cheese, with respect to the activities of the federal & provincial governments & agencies & all other bodies affecting the commercial interests of cheese importers in Canada; To monitor & analyze all developments relating to the importation of cheese into Canada; To contribute to the formulation, revision & amendment of government policy relating to the commercial regulatory framework within which Canadian cheese importers operate their businesses; To promote the commercial interests of members in a public relations capacity; To liaise with other industry & trade associations working in cheese-related sectors
Finances: Funding Sources: Membership fees
Membership: 100-499
Chief Officer(s):
Amesika Baëta, Director, Member Relations & Development, 613-595-5333 Ext. 41
abaeta@iecanada.com

International Civil Aviation Organization: Legal Affairs & External Relations Bureau
999, boul Robert-Bourassa, Montréal QC H3C 5H7
Tel: 514-954-8219; Fax: 514-954-6077
icaohq@icao.int
www.icao.int
twitter.com/icao
www.youtube.com/icaovideo
Overview: A large international organization
Mission: To promote the safe & orderly development of civil aviation in the world; To set international standards & regulations necessary for the safety, security, efficiency & regularity of air transport & To serve as the medium for cooperation in all fields of civil aviation
Activities: Library: ICAO Library; by appointment
Chief Officer(s):
John V. Augustin, Director

International College of Traditional Chinese Medicine of Vancouver (ICTCMV)
#201, 1508 West Broadway, Vancouver BC V6J 1W8
Tel: 604-731-2926; Fax: 604-731-2964
info@tcmcollege.com
www.tcmcollege.com
www.facebook.com/tcmcollegevan
Overview: A medium-sized provincial organization founded in 1986
Mission: To provide TCM training to foster effective & ethical TCM doctors; To raise awareness of TCM; To promote medical ethics; To support TCM research
Membership: Committees: Program Advisory
Chief Officer(s):
Laina Ho, President

International Commission of Jurists (Canadian Section) (ICJ) / La Commission internationale de juristes (section canadienne) (CIJ)
#500, 865 Carling Ave., Ottawa ON K1S 5S8
Tel: 613-237-2925; Fax: 613-237-0185
patw@cba.org
www.icjcanada.org
Also Known As: ICJ Canada
Overview: A small international organization founded in 1952
Mission: To works internationally with the parent organization to monitor & promote the rule of law & the impartiality & independence of the judiciary in countries where these are threatened or non-existent; to act nationally & locally to promote awareness of these issues & human rights generally
Member of: International Commission of Jurists, Geneva
Finances: Annual Operating Budget: Less than $50,000; Funding Sources: Membership fees
Staff Member(s): 2
Membership: 600; Fees: $75; Member Profile: Judges, lawyers & law professionals
Activities: Library:
Chief Officer(s):
Paul D.K. Fraser, President
Pat Whiting, Executive Director
Awards:
- Walter S. Tarnopolsky Award for Human Rights

International Commission on Irrigation & Drainage - Canadian National Committee See Canadian National Committee for Irrigation & Drainage

International Commission on Radiological Protection (ICRP)
280 Slater St., Ottawa ON K1P 5S9
Tel: 613-947-9750; Fax: 613-944-1920
admin@icrp.org
www.icrp.org
www.facebook.com/ICRP1
twitter.com/ICRP
Overview: A small international charitable organization founded in 1928
Mission: To advance for the public benefit the science of radiological protection, in particular by providing recommendations & guidance on all aspects of protection against ionisary radiation
Finances: Annual Operating Budget: $250,000-$500,000; Funding Sources: Grants from intergovernmental/governmental organizations & national sources
Staff Member(s): 2; 100 volunteer(s)
Membership: 1-99; Committees: Radiation Effects; Doses from Exposures; Protection in Medicine; Application of the Commission's Recommendations; Radiological Protection of the Environment
Chief Officer(s):
Christopher Clement, Scientific Secretary
sci.sec@icrp.org
Meetings/Conferences:
- International Commission on Radiological Protection 5th International Symposium, November, 2019, Adelaide
Scope: International

International Community for Relief of Suffering & Starvation Canada (ICROSS)
PO Box 3, Stn. Main, Saanichton BC V8M 2C3
Tel: 250-652-4137
Overview: A small national charitable organization founded in 1998
Mission: To provide medical supplies to developing countries
Finances: Funding Sources: Donations
Chief Officer(s):
Billy Willbond, CEO & President
billywillbond@shaw.ca

International Cospas-Sarsat Programme / Mission du Programme Cospas-Sarsat
#4215, 1250, boul René-Lévesque ouest, Montréal QC H3B 4W8
Tel: 514-500-7999; Fax: 514-500-7996
mail@cospas-sarsat.int
www.cospas-sarsat.int
www.linkedin.com/company/international-cospas-sarsat-programme
www.facebook.com/InternationalCospasSarsatProgramme
twitter.com/cospas_sarsat
Overview: A large international organization founded in 1979
Mission: To provide accurate, reliable distress alert & location data to assist search & rescue authorities using the satellite-based search & rescue (SAR) system
Affiliation(s): International Maritime Organization (IMO); International Civil Aviation Organization (ICAO); International Telecommunication Union (ITU)
Membership: 4 countries; 29 ground segment providers; 9 user states; 2 organizations
Activities: Operating the SAR system to locate persons in distress; Maintaining constant communication with member organizations to assist search & rescue authorities
Chief Officer(s):
Steven Lett, Chief Executive

International Council for Canadian Studies (ICCS) / Conseil international d'études canadiennes (CIEC)
PO Box 64016, Stn. Holland Cross, #8, 1620 Scott St., Ottawa ON K1R 6K7
Tel: 613-789-7834; Fax: 613-789-7830
www.iccs-ciec.ca
www.facebook.com/ICCS.CIEC.page
twitter.com/ICCS_CIEC
Overview: A medium-sized international organization founded in 1981
Mission: To promote scholarly study, research, teaching & publication about Canada in all disciplines & all countries; to enhance communications among its members to facilitate & develop such scholarly activities; to disseminate research results & to publicize researchers' activities in the area of Canadian Studies; to encourage the development of an international community of Canadianists.
Affiliation(s): Assn. for Cdn. Studies in the US; Assn. for Cdn. Studies; British Assn. of Cdn. Studies; Assn. française d'études canadiennes; Associazione Italiana di Studi Canadesi; Japanese Assn. for Cdn. Studies; Gesellschaft für Kanada-Studien; Assn. for Cdn. Studies in Australia & New Zealand; Assn. of Cdn. Studies in Ireland; Nordic Assn. for Cdn. Studies; Assn. for Cdn. Studies in China; Assn. for Cdn. Studies in The Netherlands; Indian Assn. for Cdn. Studies; Israel Assn. for Cdn. Studies; Asociacion Espanola de Estudios Canadienses; Russian Assn. for Cdn. Studies; Associacao Brasileira de Estudios
Finances: Annual Operating Budget: $500,000-$1.5 Million
Staff Member(s): 7
Membership: 21 Canadian Studies associations, 6 associate members in 39 countries; Member Profile: Full - national or multi-national Canadian Studies association, anywhere in the world; associate - Canadian Studies centres or organizations
Activities: Speaker Service: Yes; Library: Open to public
Chief Officer(s):
Cristina Frias, Executive Director
cristina.frias@iccs-ciec.ca
Nadyne Lacroix, Coordinator, Finance & Programs
nadyne.lacroix@iccs-ciec.ca
Awards:
- ICCS Award of Merit
- Governor General's International Award in Canadian Studies
- Graduate Student Thesis/Dissertation Scholarship
- Graduate Students Scholarship Program
- Pierre Savard Awards
- Best Doctoral Thesis in Canadian Studies Award
- Canadian Studies Postdoctoral Fellowships
Publications:
- International Journal of Canadian Studies [a publication of the International Council for Canadian Studies]
Type: Journal

International Council of AIDS Service Organizations (ICASO) / Le Conseil international des organisations de lutte contre le SIDA
#311, 120 Carlton St., Toronto ON M5A 4K2
Tel: 416-921-0018
www.icaso.org
Overview: A small international organization founded in 1990
Mission: To promote & support the work of community-based organizations around the world in the prevention of AIDS, & care & treatment for people living with HIV/AIDS, with particular emphasis on strengthening the response in communities with fewer resources; To accomplish these objectives through information sharing, advocacy & network building
Chief Officer(s):
Mary Ann Torres, Executive Director
maryannt@icaso.org
Margaret Quish, Manager, Finance
margaretq@icaso.org
Zhanna Kasperskaya, Coordinator, Program
zhannak@icaso.org

International Council of Design / Conseil international des associations de design graphique
#208, 456, rue de la Gauchetière ouest, Montréal QC H2Z 1E3
Tel: 514-875-7545
info@ico-D.org

www.ico-D.org
www.linkedin.com/company/516069
www.facebook.com/intcouncildesign
twitter.com/theicod
www.instagram.com/theicod
Also Known As: ico-D
Previous Name: International Council of Graphic Design Associations
Overview: A medium-sized international organization founded in 1963
Mission: To raise internationally the standards of graphic design & its professional practice, & the professional status of the graphic designer; To improve & expand the contribution of graphic design towards a greater understanding between people everywhere & towards a better solution of social, cultural, economic & environmental problems; To promote cooperation & exchange of information & research between designers & with professionals in related fields; To contribute to the theory & practice of graphic design education & research; To establish international standards
Affiliation(s): Society of Graphic Designers of Canada; Société des graphistes du Québec
Finances: *Funding Sources:* Membership
Staff Member(s): 7
Membership: 140; *Fees:* Schedule available; *Member Profile:* National professional associations; national design promotional organizations
Activities: Gathering young designers to exchange knowledge on issues of interest to them; Promoting standards in liaison with the International Chamber of Commerce & the International Standards Organization; Holding annual International Student Seminars, competitions, exhibitions, archives, international congresses & meetings; *Awareness Events:* World Design Day, April *Library:* Icograda Library at the Design Museum in London; Open to public by appointment
Chief Officer(s):
Ana Masut, Managing Director, 514-875-7545 Ext. 321
Awards:
• Adobe Design Achievements Award
Awarded in conjunction with Adobe to honour talented & promising student graphic designers, illustrators, photographers, filmmakers, animators, computer artists, & game developers
Publications:
• Communication Design: Interdisciplinary & Graphic Design Research [a publication of the International Council of Design]
Type: Journal; *Editor:* Teal Triggs
Profile: A peer-reviewed publication that includes works from various graphic & communicationdesign disciplines
• ico-D [International Council of Design] Newsletter
Type: Newsletter; *Frequency:* Bimonthly
Profile: An information resource featuring member profiles, news, issues, & initiatives by ico-D

International Council of Graphic Design Associations *See* International Council of Design

International Council on Active Aging (ICAA)
3307 Trutch St., Vancouver BC V6L 2T3
Tel: 604-734-4466; *Fax:* 604-708-4464
Toll-Free: 866-335-9777
info@icaa.cc
www.icaa.cc
www.linkedin.com/groups?gid=2294475
www.facebook.com/ICAAhome
Overview: A small international organization founded in 2001
Mission: Dedicated to changing the way we age by uniting professionals in the retirement, assisted living, fitness, recreation, rehabilitation, & wellness fields to help dispel society's myths about aging; to help these professionals to empower aging Baby Boomers & older adults to improve their quality of life & maintain their dignity.
Membership: 9,200 organizations; *Fees:* $209 regular; $619 organizations
Chief Officer(s):
Colin Milner, CEO
colinmilner@icaa.cc
Julie Milner, COO
juliemilner@icaa.cc

International Council on Global Privacy & Security, By Design
admin@gpsbydesign.org
www.gpsbydesign.org
Also Known As: GPS By Design
Overview: A medium-sized international organization founded in 2016
Mission: To promote the development of technologies that embed privacy-protecting measures during design & production; To collaborate with organizations & governments to innovate systems that will protect both privacy & public safety; To provide people around the world with technologies that keep society safe & secure without compromising the privacy of individuals
Finances: *Funding Sources:* Donations
Activities: Conducting research & creating policy templates on the application of privacy to technologies; Educating politicians, businesses, government, media, & the public about privacy by design; Supporting technology innovation in academic institutions; Providing resources; Promoting Privacy by Design Certification (offered by Ryerson University's Privacy by Design Centre of Excellence)
Chief Officer(s):
Ann Cavoukian, Founder & Chair
George Tomko, Director, Research & Technology

International Credential Assessment Service of Canada (ICAS) / Service canadien d'évaluation de documents scolaires internationaux
Ontario AgriCentre, #102, 100 Stone Rd. West, Guelph ON N1G 5L3
Tel: 519-763-7282; *Fax:* 519-763-6964
Toll-Free: 800-321-6021
info@icascanada.ca
www.icascanada.ca
Overview: A medium-sized international organization founded in 1958
Mission: Committed to providing reliable information that will help individuals achieve personal, career and educational goals and help employers, educational institutions, immigration authorities, community agencies and other organizations to understand international credentials.
Member of: Canadian Education Association; Ontario School Counsellors' Association; Association of International Educators; America-Mideast Educational Training Service; European Association of International Educators; Canadian Association of Prior Learning Assessment; Canadian Bureau of International Educatio

International Curling Information Network Group (ICING)
73 Appleford Rd., Hamilton ON L9C 6B5
Tel: 905-389-7781
www.icing.org
Overview: A small international organization founded in 1995
Mission: To provide information about the sport of curling worldwide
Staff Member(s): 2; 4 volunteer(s)
Chief Officer(s):
Peter M. Smith, Contact
psmith@icing.org

International Development & Relief Foundation (IDRF)
908 The East Mall, 1st Fl., Toronto ON M9B 6K2
Tel: 416-497-0818; *Fax:* 416-497-0686
Toll-Free: 866-497-4373
office@idrf.ca
www.idrf.ca
www.linkedin.com/pub/idrf-canada
www.facebook.com/IDRFCANADA
twitter.com/IDRF
www.youtube.com/IDRFCANADA
Overview: A small international organization founded in 1984
Mission: To empower the disadvantaged peoples of the world, through emergency relief & participatory development programs based on the Islamic principles of human dignity, self-reliance, & social justice
Affiliation(s): Canadian Council for International Cooperation
Finances: *Annual Operating Budget:* $500,000-$1.5 Million
Staff Member(s): 9
Membership: *Member Profile:* People who regularly donate $100 or more yearly
Activities: Providing relief, rehabilitation & development aid to communities in need, both overseas & in Canada; *Speaker Service:* Yes
Chief Officer(s):
Zeib Jeeva, Chair
Jessica Ferne, Director, Programs
Maheen A. Rashdi, Manager, Communications, Events, Media & Volunteers

International Development Research Centre (IDRC) / Centre de recherches pour le développement international
PO Box 8500, 150 Kent St., Ottawa ON K1G 3H9
Tel: 613-236-6163; *Fax:* 613-238-7230
Other Communication: www.flickr.com/photos/idrccrdi
info@idrc.ca
www.idrc.ca
www.facebook.com/IDRC.CRDI
twitter.com/idrc_crdi
www.youtube.com/user/IDRCCRDI
Overview: A large international organization founded in 1970
Mission: To help scientists in developing countries identify long-term, practical solutions to pressing development problems; support is given directly to scientists in universities, private enterprise, government & non-profit organizations; priority given to equitable & sustainable development; projects are designed to maximize the use of local materials & to strengthen human & institutional capacity; research is undertaken by Third World recipients independently or in collaboration with Canadian partners
Affiliation(s): Regional offices in Asia & Africa
Finances: *Annual Operating Budget:* Greater than $5 Million
Staff Member(s): 408
Activities: Environment & natural resource management; social & economic equity; information & communication technologies for development; innovation, policy & science; *Internships:* Yes
Library: IDRC Library; Open to public
Chief Officer(s):
Jean Lebel, President
Awards:
• AGROPOLIS-Farming in the City
Awards programme that supports innovative master's & doctoral level research. It aims to add to the body of knowledge of urban & peri-urban agriculture, & thereby to support interventions that address critical areas in the industry *Eligibility:* Award intended primarily for researchers from developing countries, including those studying in a developed country & returning to the South after their studies. However, up to a third of all awards may be granted to citizens or permanent residents of a developed country (currently only Canada). The research must be for a master's or a doctoral thesis. Researchers must be registered at a university-in the South or the North-that; *Amount:* Maximum of $20,000 per year *Contact:* AGROPOLIS International & Graduate Research, 613-236-6163; Fax: 567-7749; Email AGROPOLIS@irdc.ca
• IDRC Doctoral Research Awards (IDRA)
Supports the field research of Canadian graduate students enrolled in a Canadian university for doctoral research on a topic of relevance to sustainable & equitable development *Eligibility:* Applicants must hold Canadian citizenship or permanent residency status; be registered at a Canadian university; research proposal is for a doctoral thesis; provide evidence of affiliation with an institution or organization in the region in which the research will take place; have completed course work & passed comprehensive examinations by the time of award tenure *Deadline:* May; *Amount:* Maximum of $20,000 per year *Contact:* Centre Training & Awards Unit, 613/236-6163 ext 2098; Fax: 613/563-0815; Email: cta@irdc.ca
• John G. Bene Fellowship: Community Forestry, Trees & People
Contributes to the expenses of Canadian graduate students undertaking field research in social forestry in a developing country *Eligibility:* Applicants must be Canadian citizens or hold permanent residency status; be registered in a Canadian university at the master's or doctoral level; have an academic background that combines forestry or agroforestry with social sciences. Applicants from interdisciplinary programs (e.g. environmental studies) may also be eligible, provided their programs contain the specified elements *Deadline:* March; *Amount:* $15,000 per year *Contact:* Centre Training & Awards Unit, 613/236-6163 ext. 2098; Fax: 613/563-0815; Emails cta@irdc.ca
• Canadian Window on International Development Awards
Award offered for doctoral research that explores the relationship between Canadian aid, trade, immigration & diplomatic policy, & international development & the alleviation of global policy *Eligibility:* Applicants must hold Canadian citizenship or permanent residency status; be registered at a Canadian university; be conducting the proposed research for a doctoral dissertation & have completed course work & passed comprehensive examinations by the time of the award tenure *Deadline:* April; *Amount:* $20,000 per year *Contact:* Centre Training & Awards Unit, 613/236-6163 ext 2098; Fax: 613/563-0815; Email: cta@irdc.ca

- Bentley Fellowship: Use of Fertility Enhancing Food, Forage & Cover Crops in Sustainably Managed Agroecosystems Supports applied research of Canadian graduate students on how increased use of forage crops in cropping systems can improve agricultural production by farmers in developing countries *Eligibility:* Applicants must be Canadian citizens or hold permanent residency status; be registered in a Canadian university at the master's or doctoral level; have an academic background in agriculture or biology undertaking research on the role of forage crops in improved sustainable tropical farming. Applicants from interdisciplinary programs (e.g. environmental studies) may be eligible provided their programs contain the specified elements *Deadline:* October; *Amount:* $20,000 *Contact:* Centre Training & Awards Unit, 613/236-6163 ext 2098; Fax: 613/563-0815; Email: cta@idrc.ca
Publications:
- IDRC [International Development Research Centre] Bulletin
Type: Newsletter

International Economuseum Network Society *Voir* Société internationale du réseau ÉCONOMUSÉE et Société ÉCONOMUSÉE du Québec

International Electrotechnical Commission - Canadian National Committee (CNC/IEC) / Commission Électrotechnique Internationale - Comité National du Canada (CEI-CNC)
c/o Standards Council of Canada, #600, 55 Metcalfe St., Ottawa ON K1P 6L5
Tel: 613-238-3222; *Fax:* 613-569-7808
Overview: A medium-sized international organization founded in 1912
Mission: To look at issues related to Canada's participation in the International Electrotechnical Commission (IEC); To advise Council through the Advisory Committee on Standards (ACS); To coordinate the work of the many advisory and technical committees that provide Canadian input to IEC
Member of: Standards Council of Canada
Finances: *Funding Sources:* Parliamentary appropriation; corporate sponsors; individuals
Staff Member(s): 2; 1000 volunteer(s)
Membership: 16; *Committees:* Approx. 100, paralleling the IEC committee structure
Chief Officer(s):
Jacques Régis, President
Lynne M. Gibbens, Secretary

International Federation of Broomball Associations (IFBA)
4, rue du Chambertin, Montréal QC H9H 5E5
secretary@internationalbroomball.org
www.internationalbroomball.org
www.facebook.com/internationalbroomball
Overview: A large international organization founded in 1998
Mission: To serve as the international governing body of broomball; To provide national broomball federations & associations with a means to be certified & recognized at a global level; To offer materials, training, & initiatives to broomball federations; To organize the World Broomball Championships & other sanctioned international membership competitions; To promote the sport of broomball on behalf of members; To encourage fair play & a healthy lifestyle through participation in broomball
7 volunteer(s)
Membership: *Fees:* $500
Activities: Organizing &/or facilitating broomball tournaments; Representing member associations & non-current members at the international level; Working to introduce broomball into new markets to enhance local communities socially & health-wise; Administering the official broomball international rule book; Coaching & officiating programs
Chief Officer(s):
Marc Desparois, President, Operations
president@internationalbroomball.org
Alan Jabs, General Secretary, Administration
secretary@internationalbroomball.org

International Federation of Corporate Football (FIFCO) / Fédération internationale de football corporatif
#2500, 1155 boul René Lévesque ouest, Montréal QC H3B 2K4
Tel: 514-907-7600; *Fax:* 514-409-2570
info@fifco.org
www.fifco.org
www.linkedin.com/company/international-federation-of-corporate-football-fifco-
www.facebook.com/122241874475698
twitter.com/FIFCO
Overview: A small international organization founded in 2008
Mission: To serve as the world governing body of corporate football (soccer); To unite working professionals & promote healthy lifestyles & team-building through football; To establish & implement the World Corporate Champions Cup
Membership: 6 continental members; 10 country members
Activities: Organizing regional, national, continental, & international tournaments
Chief Officer(s):
Albert Zbily, President
Akram Srour, Vice-President, Finance
Daniel Curcio, Vice-President, Officiating

International Federation on Aging (IFA) / Fédération internationale du vieillissement (FIV)
Castleview Wichwood Towers, 351 Christie St., Toronto ON M6G 3C3
Tel: 416-342-1655; *Fax:* 416-392-4157
www.ifa-fiv.org
www.facebook.com/378160352195791
twitter.com/IntFedAgeing
Overview: A medium-sized international organization founded in 1973
Mission: To provide a worldwide forum for ageing issues & concerns; to foster the development of associations & agencies that serve or represent older people; to develop a universal charter of rights & responsibilities for the elderly; to advocate for the rights & respect of older people
Affiliation(s): World Health Organization; International Labour Organization; United Nations Educational, Scientific & Cultural Organization
Finances: *Funding Sources:* Membership fees; service fees; grants; special projects
Staff Member(s): 7
Membership: *Fees:* Schedule available; *Member Profile:* Full - reserved for national voluntary organizations either representing or serving older people; Associate - several categories of international organizations, governmental agencies, professional associations, voluntary organizations whose activities are less than national in scope; Individual; Corporate - any business interested in or providing products & services for older persons; Government associate; Professional associate
Activities: *Internships:* Yes; *Speaker Service:* Yes; *Rents Mailing List:* Yes
Chief Officer(s):
Bjarne Hastrup, President
Jane Barratt, Secretary General
jbarratt@ifa-fiv.org

International Fellowship of Christians & Jews of Canada
Corporate Office, #218, 449 The Queensway South, Keswick ON L4P 2C9
Tel: 416-596-9307; *Fax:* 416-981-7293
Toll-Free: 888-988-4325
info@IFCJ.ca
www.ifcj.ca
www.facebook.com/FellowshipFan
www.youtube.com/channel/UCGubM5If4CS84hmm9VGYujw
Overview: A medium-sized national charitable organization
Mission: To encourage improved understanding between Christian & Jewish people; To promote cooperation between Christian & Jewish communities on issues of shared biblical concern; and support Israel & Jews in crises or need
Member of: International Fellowship of Christians and Jews
Finances: *Funding Sources:* Donations
Activities: Ministry progams; Television programs, Newsletter; *Library:* Pastor's Library
Chief Officer(s):
Yechiel Eckstein, President & Founder

International Finance Club of Montréal *Voir* Cercle de la finance internationale de Montréal

International Financial Centre of Montréal (IFC) / Le Centre Financier International - Montréal (CFI)
c/o Finance Montreal, #1600, 1130, rue Sherbrooke ouest, Montréal QC H3A 2M8
Tel: 514-287-1477; *Fax:* 514-287-1694
www.cfimontreal.com
www.linkedin.com/company/centre-financier-international-montreal
Also Known As: IFC Montréal
Overview: A small local organization founded in 1986
Mission: To facilitate the establishment, development & preservation in the Montréal City region of companies specializing in international financial transactions
Membership: 60 companies
Chief Officer(s):
Mario Albert, CEO

International Fiscal Association Canada
#310, 4 Cataraqui St., Kingston ON K7K 1Z7
Tel: 613-531-8292; *Fax:* 613-531-0626
office@ifacanada.org
www.ifacanada.org
Also Known As: IFA Canada
Overview: A small national organization
Mission: To study & advance international & comparative law in regard to public finance, specifically international & comparative fiscal law & the financial & economic aspects of taxation
Affiliation(s): International Fiscal Association
Membership: *Fees:* $195; $135 fulltime academic; $70 Young IFA Network; *Committees:* Research; Communications; Events; Governance; Finance
Chief Officer(s):
Ron Durand, President

International Fund for Animal Welfare Canada (IFAW) / Fonds international pour la protection des animaux
#2, 301 1/2 Bank St., Ottawa ON K2P 1X7
Tel: 613-241-8996; *Fax:* 613-241-0641
Toll-Free: 888-500-4329
info-ca@ifaw.org
www.ifaw.org
www.facebook.com/ifaw
twitter.com/IFAWCanada
www.youtube.com/ifawvideo
Overview: A small international organization founded in 1969
Mission: Works to improve the welfare of wild & domestic animals throughout the world by reducing the commercial exploitation of animals, protecting wildlife habitats & assisting animals in distress; seeks to motivate the public to prevent cruelty to animals; promotes animal welfare & conservation policies that advance the well-being of animals & people
Finances: *Annual Operating Budget:* $500,000-$1.5 Million
Staff Member(s): 12
Membership: 45,000
Activities: Campaigns against the commercial seal hunt in Canada, supporting anti-cruelty legislations for Canada
Chief Officer(s):
Azzedine Downes, President & Chief Executive Officer
Patricia Zaat, Canadian Director
Publications:
- Gaining Ground: In Pursuit of Ecological Sustainability
Type: Book; *Number of Pages:* 425; *Editor:* Lavigne, D.M.
Profile: 26 chapters written by a variety of conservationists, spanning the fields of conservation biology, fishery science, wildlife biology, ethics, economics, engineering, and the social sciences.
- World of Animals
Type: Magazine; *Frequency:* Bi-Annual

International Geographical Union - Canadian Committee
Dept. of Geography & Environmental Management, University of Waterloo, 200 University Ave. West, Waterloo ON N2L 3G1
Tel: 519-504-7985; *Fax:* 519-746-0658
www.igu-net.org
Overview: A small national organization
Mission: To promote international programs in geography within Canada; to promote activities within IGU programs relevant to Canada & to coordinate Canadian participation; to formulate Canadian position & advise the National Research Council on Canadian participation in IGU activities
Finances: *Funding Sources:* National Research Council; SSHRCC
Chief Officer(s):
Jean Andrey, Contact
jandrey@uwaterloo.ca

The International Grenfell Association (IGA)
PO Box 75, 430 Topsail Rd., St. John's NL A1E 4N1
Tel: 709-745-6162; *Fax:* 709-745-6163
iga@nfld.net
www.grenfellassociation.org
Overview: A small provincial charitable organization founded in 1914
Mission: To provide funds in support of initiatives that benefit the health, education, social & cultural well-being of the people

Canadian Associations / International Institute for Sustainable Development (IISD) / Institut international du développement durable (IIDD)

of Northern Newfoundland & Coastal Labrador, working in partnership with government & other agencies
Finances: Funding Sources: Investments; endowments
Activities: Grant program (75 current grants); scholarships; bursaries
Chief Officer(s):
Paul Canning, Administrator

International Hockey Hall of Fame & Museum; International Ice Hockey Federation Museum Inc. See Original Hockey Hall of Fame & Museum

International Institute for Sustainable Development (IISD) / Institut international du développement durable (IIDD)
#325, 111 Lombard Ave., Winnipeg MB R3B 0T4
Tel: 204-958-7700; *Fax:* 204-958-7710
info@iisd.org
www.iisd.org
www.facebook.com/IISDnews
twitter.com/IISD_news
Overview: A large international organization founded in 1990
Mission: To promote sustainable development in decision-making in Canada & abroad by undertaking sustainable development research, advising government, business & organizations, analyzing & reporting on issues & events, & publishing & disseminating sustainable development information. Offices in Winnipeg, Ottawa, New York, & Geneva.
Finances: Annual Operating Budget: Greater than $5 Million; *Funding Sources:* Federal & provincial government; government of other countries; philanthropic foundations
Staff Member(s): 80
Activities: Trade & sustainable development; community adaptation & sustainable livelihoods; greening national budgets; business & industry accountability; Great Plains Sustainable Development; sustainable development measurement & indicators; *Internships:* Yes; *Speaker Service:* Yes; *Library:* Open to public by appointment
Chief Officer(s):
Scott Vaughan, President/CEO
Grace Mota, Treasurer & Chief Financial Officer
Zahra Sethna, Director, Communications
Awards:
• IISD Scholar
To assist post-secondary students (up to the Ph.D. level) studying issues related to sustainable development

International Institute for Transportation & Ocean Policy Studies; Oceans Institute of Canada See International Oceans Institute of Canada

International Institute of Concern for Public Health (IICPH)
PO Box 40017, 292 Dupont St., Toronto ON M5R 0A2
Tel: 905-906-6128
info@concernforhealth.org
concernforhealth.org
Overview: A medium-sized international charitable organization founded in 1984
Mission: To engage in advocacy on health issues; to assist in promoting & protecting people in their work & living environment in Ontario; to provide expertise on health, scientific & environmental issues
Member of: Ontario Environment Network; Earth Appeal; Nuclear Waste Watch
Finances: Funding Sources: Private donations
Activities: Speaker Service: Yes

International Institute of Integral Human Sciences (IIIHS) / Institut international des sciences humaines intégrales
PO Box 1387, Stn. H, Montréal QC H3G 2N3
Tel: 514-937-8359; *Fax:* 514-937-5380
Toll-Free: 877-937-8359
iiihs@iiihs.org
www.iiihs.org
www.facebook.com/spiritualsciencef
twitter.com/SSF_IIIHS
Overview: A medium-sized international organization founded in 1975
Mission: To explore new sciences of consciousness & healing; To identify paradigms for the convergence of science & spirituality in the global village landscape
Finances: Annual Operating Budget: $100,000-$250,000; *Funding Sources:* Classes; Workshops; International Conferences; Donations
Staff Member(s): 3; 25 volunteer(s)

Membership: 10,000; *Committees:* Local; International
Activities: Offering seminars, lectures, & programs; Conducting international outreach projects; *Internships:* Yes; *Speaker Service:* Yes; *Library*
Chief Officer(s):
Marilyn Rossner, President
mrossner@iiihs.org
Fadel Behman, Vice-President
fadelbehman@sympatico.ca
Meetings/Conferences:
• 43rd Annual International Institute of Integral Human Sciences International Conference 2018, August, 2018, Montréal, QC
Scope: International

International Law Association - Canadian Branch
#1920, 2020, boul Robert-Bourassa, Montréal QC H3A 2A5
Tel: 514-288-2726
www.ila-canada.ca
www.linkedin.com/groups/8498205
www.facebook.com/502073426600173
twitter.com/ILA_Canada
Overview: A medium-sized national organization founded in 1967
Mission: To develop & advance international law in Canada & the world
Finances: Annual Operating Budget: Less than $50,000; *Funding Sources:* Membership
20 volunteer(s)
Membership: 100; *Fees:* $150; *Committees:* International Committees
Activities: Organizing conferences; *Awareness Events:* Biennial Conference; *Speaker Service:* Yes
Chief Officer(s):
Bernard Colas, President
president@ila-canada.ca
Kostantia Koutouki, Director, Communication
communication@ila-canada.ca

International Live Events Association Canada (ILEA)
312 Oakwood Ct., Newmarket ON L3Y 3C8
Tel: 905-898-7434; *Fax:* 905-895-1630
Toll-Free: 866-729-4737
info@ileacanada.com
ileacanada.com
Previous Name: International Special Events Society Canada
Overview: A medium-sized national organization founded in 1979
Mission: To provide a forum for creative events professionals in all disciplines across the country to foster creativity, find inspiration, promote teamwork & communication, & learn & share best practices
Affiliation(s): ILEA International
Finances: Funding Sources: Membership dues
Membership: Fees: $57.52 - $618.58; *Member Profile:* Professionals in the special events industry
Activities: Administers "Certified Special Events Professional" (CSEP) designation through professional accreditation program; Monthly dinner meetings; Annual gala auction
Chief Officer(s):
Dustin Westling, Chair
chair@ileacanada.com
Awards:
• Toronto Chapter Awards
Honours leaders in the industry for the Toronto chapter

International Log Builders' Association
PO Box 1641, Montebello QC J0V 1L0
Tel: 819-983-1494; *Fax:* 819-983-2094
info@logassociation.org
www.logassociation.org
Previous Name: American/Canadian Log Builders' Association
Overview: A medium-sized international organization founded in 1974
Mission: To further the craft of handcrafted log building & the advancement of log builders; To promote the highest standards of the trade
Chief Officer(s):
Symphonie Nadeau, Administrator
symphonie@logassociation.org

International Machine Cancel Research Society of Canada (IMCRSC)
39 Silver Trail, Barrie ON L4N 3K2
www.postalhistorycanada.net/php/StudyGroups/IMCRSC
Overview: A small national organization
Mission: To study the uses of the International Postal Supply Company of New York's rapid cancelling machine models in Canada; To investigate related areas of historical interest, such as the relationship between the Canada Post Office Department & the International Postal Supply Company
Affiliation(s): Postal History Society of Canada
Membership: Member Profile: Individuals interested in the history of the machine cancellations of Canada & Newfoundland, & especially the International machine era
Activities: Undertaking research projects, such as the identification of individual daters in Canadian post offices with an International machine; Publishing the results of research activities involving International machines; Developing a database of International machines; *Library:* International Machine Cancel Research Society of Canada Library
Chief Officer(s):
David Collver, Contact

International Mennonite Health Association Inc. (IMHA)
15 Coleridge Park Dr., Winnipeg MB R3K 0B2
Tel: 204-831-1699; *Fax:* 204-985-3226
info@africancanadianhealth.ca
www.intermenno.net
Overview: A small international charitable organization
Mission: Providing resources and services to Mennonite and Brethren in Christ health programs in developing countries.
Chief Officer(s):
Murray Nickel, President
nickel.murray@gmail.com

International Napoleonic Society (INS) / Société Napoléonienne Internationale
#3315, 81 Navy Wharf Crt., Toronto ON M5V 3S2
Other Communication: www.societenapoleonienne.com
ins@napoleonicsociety.com
www.napoleonicsociety.com
Overview: A small international organization founded in 1995
Mission: To promote the study of the Napoleonic Era in accordance with proper academic standards; to gather the leading minds in this field for the purpose of creating, reviewing, commenting, awarding & financially supporting Napoleonic scholarship; to encourage the publication of works of academic merit; to make available original documents, as well as material available only in languages not commonly read by western scholars; to encourage & support the translation &/or publication of such materials; to encourage the creation & expansion of programs of study in the Napoleonic Era at accredited institutions of learning
Finances: Annual Operating Budget: $100,000-$250,000
Staff Member(s): 6; 6 volunteer(s)
Membership: 650; *Member Profile:* Napoleonic historians; *Committees:* Literary; Awards
Activities: International congress
Chief Officer(s):
Rowayda Guirguis, Executive Secretary & Webmaster
J. David Markham, President
Rafe Blaufarb, Chair, Awards Committee
Awards:
• Literary Award
• Legion of Merit Medal

International Network for Cultural Diversity / Réseau international pour la diversité culturelle
5 Brulé Cres., Toronto ON M6S 4H8
Tel: 416-268-5665
incd@neilcraigassociates.com
www.incd.net
Overview: A small national organization
Mission: INCD is a worldwide network working to counter the adverse affects of globalization on world cultures.
Chief Officer(s):
Garry Neil, Executive Director

International Oceans Institute of Canada (IOIC)
c/o Dalhousie Univ., PO Box 15000, 6414 Coburg Rd., Halifax NS B3H 4R2
Tel: 902-494-1977; *Fax:* 902-494-1334
ioi@dal.ca
internationaloceaninstitute.dal.ca
Previous Name: International Institute for Transportation & Ocean Policy Studies; Oceans Institute of Canada
Overview: A small national organization founded in 1976
Mission: To promote responsible management of the world's oceans & sustainable development of marine resources; to protect the integrity of the ocean environment; to promote sustainable resource development; to improve the quality of ocean-dependent human life, including health & safety of maritime communities; to further these objectives, all aspects of

the ocean environment are pursued - resource management & development, marine environmental quality, ocean law & policy, high seas management, coastal zone management, marine transportation, ocean science & technology, tourism & recreation, ocean industries & maritime boundary delimitation
Affiliation(s): International Oceans Institute; Atlantic Coastal Zone Information Steering Committee
Staff Member(s): 4
Activities: Services of the institute are available nationally & internationally for governments, organizations & private sector concerns, including industry, special interest groups & foundations; services include project development & management, policy development, education & training, conference & workshop coordination, research & information
Chief Officer(s):
Michael J.A. Butler, Director
michael.butler@dal.ca

International Organization of Ukrainian Communities "Fourth Wave"
#2, 15 Canmotor Ave., Toronto ON M8Z 4E4
Tel: 416-251-2244
canadafourthwave@hotmail.com
www.4thwave.org
Overview: A medium-sized international organization founded in 2004
Mission: To contribute to the strengthening & development of the Ukrainian community in Canada; To develop & promote Ukrainian national heritage as an element of the Canadian multicultural environment; To liaise with Ukrainian in Ukraine to promote mutual achievements of Ukrainian Canadians in science, technology, culture, & business; To provide social support to Ukrainian Canadians who are in need
Member of: Ukrainian Canadian Congress
Activities: Organizing community events
Chief Officer(s):
Anna Kisil, President

International Peat Society - Canadian National Committee
c/o Canadian Society for Peat and Peatlands, 196 - 15 St., Shippagan NB E8S 1E8
Tel: 506-336-6600; *Fax:* 506-336-6601
www.peatsociety.org
Overview: A small national organization founded in 1970
Mission: To foster the advancement, exchange and communication of scientific, technical and social knowledge and understanding for the wise use of peatlands and peat.
Affiliation(s): International Peat Society
Finances: *Annual Operating Budget:* Less than $50,000; *Funding Sources:* Membership fees
Activities: *Rents Mailing List:* Yes
Chief Officer(s):
Jean-Yves Daigle, Chair
jydaigle@nb.sympatico.ca
Paul Short, Secretary
cspma@peatmoss.com

International Pension & Employee Benefits Lawyers Association (IPEBLA)
#200, 411 Richmond St. East, Toronto ON M5A 3S5
Tel: 416-693-7775; *Fax:* 416-929-5256
Toll-Free: 866-444-3387
contactipebla@managingmatters.com
www.ipebla.org
www.linkedin.com/groups/4184783
Overview: A medium-sized international organization
Mission: To provide educational resources & networking opportunities for pension & benefits lawyers
Membership: *Fees:* $210 USD; *Committees:* Membership & Regional Meetings; Steering; Teleconference
Activities: Offering surveys, journals & teleconferences
Chief Officer(s):
Caroline Helbronner
Jana Steele

International Personnel Management Association - Canada (IPMA-Canada)
National Office, 20 Edwards Pl., Mount Pearl NL A1N 3V5
Toll-Free: 888-226-5002
national@ipmaigp.ca
ipma-aigp.com
www.linkedin.com/in/ipmaaigpcanada
twitter.com/IPMACanada
Previous Name: Canadian Public Personnel Management Association

Overview: A medium-sized national organization founded in 1906
Mission: To promote excellence in the practice of human resource management; to promote & enhance the HR profession in Canada & globally; to provide professional development & training for the HR community; to maintain a code of ethics & standards of practice; to recognize excellence through national & local awards programs
Affiliation(s): IPMA-HR
Finances: *Annual Operating Budget:* $100,000-$250,000
Membership: 1,000; *Member Profile:* Human resources managers & practitioners across the country
Activities: Provides local courses & speakers programs; national & local newsletters; national & local awards program; Certification Program; National Human Resource Management Certificate Program; *Rents Mailing List:* Yes
Chief Officer(s):
Glenn Saunders, Executive Director
national@ipma-aigp.ca

Alberta & North Chapter
#154, 21 - 10405 Jasper Ave., Edmonton AB T5J 3S2
ipma.abn@shaw.ca
www.linkedin.com/groups?gid=3647281
www.facebook.com/164286233597783

Manitoba Chapter
MB

National Capital Region Chapter
Ottawa ON

New Brunswick Chapter
c/o Peter Trask, Centennial Bldg., PO Box 6000, Fredericton NB E3B 5H1
Chief Officer(s):
Peter Trask, Contact, 506-444-5099, Fax: 506-444-4724
peter.trask@gnb.ca

Newfoundland & Labrador Chapter
Chief Officer(s):
John Peddle, President
john.peddle@nl.rogers.com

Nova Scotia Chapter
NS

Saskatchewan Chapter
PO Box 601, Regina SK S4P 3A3
www.saskatchewanipma.com
www.facebook.com/373753279756
Chief Officer(s):
Alison Biese, President, 306-787-9161
alison.biese@gov.sk.ca

International PhotoTherapy Association
Photo Therapy Centre, 890 The Grove Rd., Gambier Island BC V0N 1V0
Tel: 604-202-3431
www.phototherapy-centre.com
www.facebook.com/groups/PhotoTherapy.and.Therapeutic.Photography
Overview: A small international organization
Mission: To educate about therapeutic uses of still & video photography
Finances: *Annual Operating Budget:* Less than $50,000
Staff Member(s): 3
Membership: 100-499
Activities: *Library:* Open to public by appointment
Chief Officer(s):
Judy Weiser, Contact
jweiser@phototherapy-centre.com

International Police Association - Canada (IPA Canada)
179 Greak Oak Trail, Binbrook ON L0R 1C0
www.ipa.ca
Overview: A medium-sized national organization founded in 1960
Mission: To encourage contact in social & cultural activities among members throughout the world

International Political Science Association (IPSA) / Association internationale de science politique (AISP)
#331, 1590, av Docteur-Penfield, Montréal QC H3G 1C5
Tel: 514-848-8717; *Fax:* 514-848-4095
info@ipsa.org
www.ipsa.org
www.facebook.com/IPSA.AISP
twitter.com/IPSN_AISP

Overview: A medium-sized international charitable organization founded in 1949
Mission: To promote the advancement of political science through the collaboration of scholars in different parts of the world
Member of: International Social Sciences Council
Finances: *Annual Operating Budget:* $250,000-$500,000; *Funding Sources:* Member fees; Royalties
Staff Member(s): 7
Membership: 4,045 individuals; 53 associations
Activities: Congress; Symposiums; Publications; Research; *Rents Mailing List:* Yes
Chief Officer(s):
Guy Lachapelle, Secretary General
guy.lachapelle@concordia.ca
Helen Milner, President
Mathieu St-Laurent, Manager, Membership Services & External Relations

International Relief Agency Inc. (IRA)
#84, 95 Wood St., Toronto ON M4Y 2Z3
Tel: 416-928-0901
ira@ica.net
Overview: A medium-sized international organization founded in 1979
Mission: To promote free enterprise, national freedoms & democracy
Affiliation(s): Best of 7 Continents Inc.; International Hippocrates Foundation; Council of Nations
Activities: Foreign aid & relief; international investment; health care services; overseas adoption services; *Library:* Open to public by appointment

International Ringette Federation - Canada
#201, 5510 Canotek Rd., Ottawa ON K1J 9J4
Tel: 613-748-5655; *Fax:* 613-748-5860
ringette@ringette.ca
www.ringette.ca
www.facebook.com/RingetteCanada
twitter.com/redringette
www.youtube.com/ringettecanada
Overview: A small national organization
Mission: To promote the game of Ringette around the world.
Staff Member(s): 7
Membership: *Committees:* Coach Developement; Officials Development; High Performance; National Ringette League
Activities: *Awareness Events:* Canadian Ringette Championships - Apr.
Chief Officer(s):
Natasha Johnston, Executive Director
natasha@ringette.ca
Jane Casson, President
president@ringette.ca

International Sanitary Supply Association Canada
PO Box 10009, 910 Dundas St. West, Whitby ON L1P 1P7
Tel: 905-665-8001
Toll-Free: 866-684-8273
info@issa-canada.com
www.issa-canada.com
twitter.com/CSSA1957
Also Known As: ISSA Canada
Previous Name: Canadian Sanitation Supply Association; Canadian Sanitation Standards Association
Overview: A large national organization overseen by International Sanitary Supply Association, Inc.
Mission: To provide a high degree of professionalism, technical knowledge & business ethics within the membership; To promote greater public awareness, appreciation & understanding of the sanitation industry
Member of: International Sanitary Supply Association (ISSA)
Affiliation(s): BOMA Toronto; Building Owners and Managers Association (BOMA); Canadian Association of Environmental Management (CAEM); Canadian Commercial Cleaners Association (CCCA); Canadian Consumer Specialty Product Association (CCSPA); Manufacturers Representatives of America (MRA); Ontario Healthcare Housekeepers Association (OHHA)
10 volunteer(s)
Membership: 395 corporate + 10 associate + 15 senior/lifetime; *Fees:* Schedule available; *Member Profile:* Manufacturer or distributor of sanitation products & services; *Committees:* Long Range Planning; Government Liaison
Activities: *Library:* by appointment
Chief Officer(s):

Canadian Associations / International Schizophrenia Foundation (ISF)

Mike Nosko, Executive Director
mike@issa-canada.com
Tracy MacDonald, Manager, Operations
tracy@issa-canada.com
Awards:
• Member of the Year Award
Recognizes a member who contributes significantly to the association in the previous year
• The Builder Award
Given to the member who has donated time and effort to building the association over the years
• Sam Tughan Achievement Award
Recognizes a member individual, group, or organization that represents a high degree of professionalism in business
Publications:
• Clean Canada [a publication of ISSA Canada]
Type: Magazine
• ISSA Canada E-Newsletter
Type: Newsletter; *Price:* Free with membership
Profile: ISSA Canada activities, awards, chapter news, & events

International Schizophrenia Foundation (ISF)
16 Florence Ave., Toronto ON M2N 1E9
Tel: 416-733-2117; *Fax:* 416-733-2352
centre@orthomed.org
www.isfmentalhealth.org
www.facebook.com/178337749007188
twitter.com/ISFMentalHealth
Previous Name: Canadian Schizophrenia Foundation
Overview: A medium-sized international charitable organization founded in 1968
Mission: To raise the levels of diagnosis, treatment & prevention of the schizophrenias & related disorders; to reduce the fear & stigma; to provide the best possible treatment & rehabilitation services.
Member of: International Society for Orthomolecular Medicine
Finances: *Funding Sources:* Donations; literature sales; membership fees
Membership: *Fees:* $35 Canada & US; $40 international
Activities: *Speaker Service:* Yes; *Library:* Open to public by appointment
Chief Officer(s):
Trevor Roberts, Executive Director

International Social Service Canada (ISSC) / Service Social International Canada (SSIC)
#201, 1376 Bank St., Ottawa ON K1H 7Y3
Tel: 613-733-9938; *Fax:* 613-733-4868
www.issc-ssic.ca
Overview: A small international charitable organization founded in 1979
Mission: To provide linkages to social service organizations worldwide; To help resolve individual & family problems resulting from the movement of people across national borders
Member of: Canadian Council for Refugees; Canadian Coalition for the Rights of Children; Family Service Canada; Child Welfare League of Canada; United Nations Association in Canada; Canadian Society of Association Executives
Affiliation(s): International Social Service - Geneva, Switzerland
Finances: *Annual Operating Budget:* $100,000-$250,000; *Funding Sources:* Federal & provincial contracts; fees for service; membership fees; donations
Staff Member(s): 4; 25 volunteer(s)
Membership: 100; *Fees:* Schedule available; *Member Profile:* Residents of Canada
Activities: Provides a professional social work liaison to social service agencies & government departments in Canada when assistance is required in other countries to help resolve a client's individual & family problems (divorce, custody, placement, visiting rights, abandonment, abduction, family reunification, child welfare investigations & service of child welfare documents overseas); also provides assistance in matters relating to health & other relevant social services requiring intercountry linkages; *Speaker Service:* Yes
Chief Officer(s):
Sylvie J. Lapointe, Director, Services
lapointesylvie71@sympatico.ca

International Society for Augmentative & Alternative Communication (ISAAC) / Société internationale de communication non-orale
#216, 312 Dolomite St., Toronto ON M3J 2N2
Tel: 905-850-6848; *Fax:* 905-850-6852
isaac@isaac-online.org
www.isaac-online.org

Overview: A small international charitable organization founded in 1983
Mission: To promote the best possible communication for people with complex communication needs
Membership: 1,000-4,999; *Fees:* Schedule available; *Member Profile:* People who use AAC, families, researchers, providers & manufacturers of communication devices; *Committees:* Committee for People Who Use AAC; Emerging AAC Countries; Research; Nominations
Activities: *Rents Mailing List:* Yes
Chief Officer(s):
Gregor Renner, President
gregor.renner@kh-freiburg.de
Franklin Smith, Executive Director
franklin@isaac-online.org
Teraiz El-Deir, Coordinator, Membership
Awards:
• Lifetime Achievement Award
Honours an individual linked with the field of AAC who has made a sustained & significant lifetime contribution to the field
• Outstanding Consumer Lecture Award
Awarded to provide a platform for person who uses AAC to present a topic in which he/she has special expertise; person will speak at Biennial Conference *Deadline:* Nov. 30, 2017; *Amount:* $5,000
• President's Award
Awarded to acknowledge extraordinary support of ISAAC by an individual *Deadline:* Apr. 28, 2018
• Distinguished Service Award
Recognizes an outstanding contrbution to the field of AAC by an individual or group through clinical work, research, and knowledge distribution *Deadline:* Apr. 28, 2018
• Fellowship Award
Recognizes an ISAAC member who has earned distinction within the ISAAC community; the title "Fellow of the International Society of Augmentative and Alternative Communication" shall be given for life and may be abbreviated/indicated as F.ISAAC *Deadline:* Apr. 28, 2018
• The Bridge School/ISAAC Teacher in Residence Award
Offers an opportunituy to learn and teach AAC methods through a teacher-in-training program at The Bridge School in the U.S. *Contact:* Contact: Vicki Casella, E-mail: vcasella@bridgeschool.org
• AAC Editors' Awards
Awarded by Editorial Board of the Augmentative and Alternative Communication (AAC) journal in two categories: Most Significant Research Article & Most Significant Student Article
Meetings/Conferences:
• International Society for Augmentative & Alternative Communication (ISAAC) Biennial Conference 2018, July, 2018, Gold Coast Convention and Exhibition Centre, Gold Coast *Scope:* International
Publications:
• Augmentative and Alternative Communication [pub. of the International Society for Augmentative & Alternative Communication]
Type: Journal; *Frequency:* Quarterly; *Editor:* Martine Smith & Bronwyn Hemsley; *ISSN:* 0743-4618; *Price:* $98 individual; $293 corporate; $59 people who use AAC/Family; $59 retired/student *Profile:* Contains scientific articles related to thefield of AAC that report on research, treatment, rehabilitation, education

International Society for Cellular Therapy (ISCT)
#400, 570 West 7th Ave., Vancouver BC V5Z 1B3
Tel: 604-874-4366; *Fax:* 604-874-4378
isct@celltherapysociety.org
www.celltherapysociety.org
www.linkedin.com/groups?gid=1943676
twitter.com/ISCTglobal
Previous Name: International Society for Hematotherapy & Graft Engineering
Overview: A medium-sized international organization founded in 1992
Mission: To serve as a voice for investigators, clinicians & technical personnel working in cell therapies & research
Membership: *Fees:* Schedule available; *Committees:* Scientific; Commercialization; Regulatory & Quality/Operations; Communications & Publications
Activities: Cord blood; Ex Vivo Expansion; Gene Therapy; Graft Evaluation; Immunotherapy & Dendritic Cells; Nonhematopoietic Mesenchymal Stem Cells; Transplantation; Tumor Evaluation; Legal & Regulatory Affairs
Chief Officer(s):
Queenie Jang, Executive Director
queenie@celltherapysociety.org

International Society for Emotion Focused Therapy (ISEFT)
8 Brynhurst Ct., Toronto ON M4P 2K1
contact.iseft@gmail.com
www.iseft.org
Overview: A small international organization
Mission: To promote the practice of Emotion Focused Therapy (EFT)
Chief Officer(s):
Jeanne Watson, Contact

International Society for Evolutionary Protistology (ISEP)
c/o Andrew J. Roger, President, Dalhousie University, 5850 College St., #8B1, Halifax NS B3H 1X5
Tel: 902-494-2620; *Fax:* 902-494-1355
www.isepsociety.com
Overview: A small international organization
Membership: *Fees:* $35 per 2-year period
Chief Officer(s):
Andrew Roger, President

International Society for Hematotherapy & Graft Engineering *See* International Society for Cellular Therapy

International Society for Krishna Consciousness (Toronto Branch) *See* Toronto's Hare Krishna Centre

International Society for Labour & Social Security Law - Canadian Chapter (ISLSSL) / Société internationale de droit du travail et de la sécurité sociale
Faculty of Law, University of Montreal, Maximilien-Caron Pavillon, PO Box 6128, Stn. Centre-Ville, Montréal QC H3C 3J7
Tel: 514-343-6124; *Fax:* 514-343-2199
islssl.org
Overview: A small international organization founded in 1958
Mission: To promote the study of labour law & social security law both at national & international levels; to promote the exchange of ideas & information, & collaboration between jurists & other experts in the fields of labour law & social security
Chief Officer(s):
Gilles Trudeau, Contact
gilles.trudeau@umontreal.ca

International Society for Research in Palmistry Inc. / Société internationale de recherches en chirologie inc.
576 rte 315, Chénéville QC J0V 1E0
Tel: 819-428-4298; *Fax:* 819-428-4495
Toll-Free: 866-428-3799
info@birlacenter.com
www.birlacenter.com/palmistry
Also Known As: Birla Center for Hast Jyotish
Overview: A small international organization founded in 1977
Mission: The Society offers individual & group counselling through palmistry & astrology based on Eastern Vedic System.
  Consultation Center
  351, av Victoria, Westmount QC H3Z 2N1
  Tel: 514-488-2292; *Fax:* 514-488-3822

International Society for the History of Medicine - Canadian Section (ISHM) / Société internationale d'histoire de la médecine (SIHM)
c/o Isabelle Perreault, Université d'Ottawa, Pavillon FSS, #14022, 120 Université, Ottawa ON K1N 6N5
Tel: 613-562-5700
iperreault@uottawa.ca
Overview: A small international charitable organization founded in 1921
Mission: To hold biennial conferences; to publish proceedings, abstracts & periodical
Staff Member(s): 2
Membership: 15 Canadian members; 300 internationally; *Fees:* Regular: $60; Corporate: $75; Retired & students: $30; *Member Profile:* Professional historians (medical) & physician historians of medicine; *Committees:* Administrative; Executive
Chief Officer(s):
Isabelle Perreault, PhD, Secretary-Treasurer, Canada
Publications:
• Canadian Bulletin of Medical History
Type: Journal; *Frequency:* Semiannually; *Editor:* Kristin Burnett, Jayne Elliott; *Price:* Free to members

International Special Events Society - Toronto Chapter *See* International Live Events Association

International Special Events Society - Vancouver Chapter; International Special Events Society Pacific Northwest See International Live Events Association

International Special Events Society Canada See International Live Events Association Canada

International Symphony Orchestra of Sarnia, Ontario & Port Huron, Michigan
251 North Vidal St., Sarnia ON N7T 5Y5
Tel: 519-337-7775
Other Communication: Alt. Phone: 519-337-1822
iso@rivernet.net
www.theiso.org
www.facebook.com/153787894700056
Overview: A small local charitable organization founded in 1957 overseen by Orchestras Canada
Mission: To provide cultural enrichment within the community by providing high calibre choral & symphonic performances; To reinforce strong commitment to youth music education and initiatives
Member of: Choirs Ontario; Orchestras Canada
Affiliation(s): American Federation of Symphony Orchestras; Michigan Orchestra Association
Finances: Funding Sources: Individual & corporate sponsors; Ticket revenue
Activities: Speaker Service: Yes; Rents Mailing List: Yes
Chief Officer(s):
Thomas K. Andison, President
Anne Brown, Executive Director
Douglas Bianchi, Music Director & Conductor

International Symphony Orchestra Youth String Ensemble
251 North Vidal St., Sarnia ON N7T 575
Tel: 519-337-7775; Fax: 519-337-1822
www.theiso.org
www.facebook.com/153787894700056
Overview: A small local organization
Mission: To support & work with amateur musicians; To serve as a musical resource for the Sarnia, Ontario & Port Huron, Michigan communities
Member of: Association of Canadian Youth Orchestras
Finances: Annual Operating Budget: Less than $50,000
Membership: 30+; Fees: $120; Member Profile: Musicians 6 to 18
Activities: Offering workshops & string education programs in schools
Chief Officer(s):
Anne Brown, Executive Director

International Union of Food Science & Technology (IUFoST)
IUFoST Secretariat, 112 Bronte Rd., Oakville ON L6L 3C1
Tel: 905-815-1926; Fax: 905-815-1574
secretariat@iufost.org
www.iufost.org
www.linkedin.com/company/2754293
www.facebook.com/437738436247543
twitter.com/iufost
Overview: A large international organization founded in 1970
Mission: To improve the distribution & conservation of the world's food supply; To promote international cooperation among food technologists & scientists
Affiliation(s): Institute of Food Technologists
Membership: 200,000; Fees: $100 USD entrance fee; annual fees calculated from HDI and other factors; Member Profile: Food scientists, technologists, & engineers from around the world; Committees: Food Safety; Food Security Task Force
Activities: Promoting training in food science & technology; Sponsoring international conferences & workshops; Fostering the international exchange of knowledge in the food science & technology community
Chief Officer(s):
Rickey Yada, President
Dietrich Knorr, President-Elect
Judith Meech, Secretary-General & Treasurer
Daryl Lund, Chair, Scientific Council
Publications:
• International Union of Food Science & Technology Scientific Information Bulletins (SIBs)
Type: Bulletin
Profile: Food science issues, presented by scientific experts & reviewed & approved by the IUFoST Scientific Council, for members of IUFoSTadhering bodies, legislators, food scientists & technologists, & consumers

• IUFoST [International Union of Food Science & Technology] Newsline
Type: Newsletter; Frequency: Irregular
Profile: The official newsletter of the International Union of Food Science & Technology, featuring activities of the General Assembly, theBoard, the Governing Council, the International Academy, & adhering bodies, for adhering bodies in more than 100 countries around the world
• Sustainable Development at Risk: Ignoring the Past
Type: Book; Author: Robert D. Reichert; ISBN: 9788175965218
Profile: The challenge of improving third world nations, while conserving critical resources & protecting the environment
• The Textbook of Food Science & Technology
Type: Book; Editor: Geoffrey Campbell-Platt; ISBN: 978-0-632-06421-2
Profile: Chapters from international industry researchers, experts, & teachers, written for students, teachers, & professionals in the food industry
• Trends in Food Science & Technology [a publication of the International Union of Food Science & Technology]
Type: Journal; ISSN: 0924-2244
Profile: A peer-reviewed journal, featuring critical synopses of advances in food research
• Using Food Science & Technology to Improve Nutrition & Promote National Development: Selected Case Studies
Type: Book; Editor: Gordon Robertson & John Lupien; ISBN: 978-0-9810247-0-7
Profile: A handbook about the application of food science & technology toimprove nutrition & promote national development in developing countries
• World of Food Science [a publication of the International Union of Food Science & Technology]
Profile: A joint publication of the IUFoST & the Institute of Food Technologists (IFT)

International Watercolour Society - Canada
34, rue du Plateau du Réservoir, Gatineau QC J8V 1G2
www.iwscanada.com
www.facebook.com/CanadaIWS
Overview: A small international organization
Mission: To promote watercolour painting; To unite watercolour artists
Membership: Committees: Biennale Organizing
Activities: Offering seminars, workshops & discussions designed to help artists display their work & improve watercolour technique
Chief Officer(s):
Alfonso Tejada, Head

International Women of Saskatoon
#412, 230 Ave. R South, Saskatoon SK S7M 2Z1
Tel: 306-978-6611; Fax: 306-978-6614
iwssaskatoon@sasktel.net
www.internationalwomenofsaskatoon.org
Previous Name: Immigrant Women of Saskatchewan, Saskatoon Chapter
Overview: A small local organization
Member of: Regina Immigrant Women Centre
Chief Officer(s):
April Sora, President
Ijeoma Udemgba, Executive Director

Internationale association des hydrogeologists See International Association of Hydrogeologists - Canadian National Chapter

Internet des droits humains See Human Rights Internet

Interpretation Canada - A Professional Association for Heritage Interpretation (IC)
c/o Kerry Wood Nature Centre, 6300 - 45 Ave., Red Deer AB T4N 3M4
Tel: 604-947-0483
membership@interpscan.ca
www.interpcan.ca
Previous Name: Canadian Association for Interpretation
Overview: A small national organization founded in 1974
Mission: To foster greater public appreciation, understanding & enjoyment of Canadian heritage & its resources through interpretation; to reveal meanings & relationships of our cultural & natural heritage to the public through first-hand experience with an object, artifact, landscape or site
Finances: Funding Sources: Membership dues
Membership: Fees: $50 student/volunteer; $65 individual; $75 subscription; $95 small institution/consultant; $190 company; Member Profile: Heritage interpreters & heritage interpretation institutions

Activities: Professional development; networking; workshops & conferences; service & product suppliers; employment opportunities & recruitment; awards; on-line discussion; training; advertising; fun activities; Library
Chief Officer(s):
Chris Mathieson, Chair
chris.mathieson@interpscan.ca
Sue Ellen Fast, Executive Director
editor@interpcan.ca
Stephanie Yuill, Secretary
stephanie.yuill@interpscan.ca
Awards:
• Annual Awards of Excellence

Interpreting Services of Newfoundland & Labrador Inc. (ISNL)
The Viking Building, #100A, 136 Crosbie Rd., St. John's NL A1B 3K3
Tel: 709-753-5621; Fax: 709-753-5682; TTY: 709-753-5620
info@isnl.ca
www.isnl.ca
Previous Name: Newfoundland & Labrador Interpreting Service
Overview: A small provincial charitable organization founded in 2001
Mission: To provide interpretive services for Newfoundland & Labrador residents
Affiliation(s): Canadian Hard of Hearing Association
Finances: Annual Operating Budget: $50,000-$100,000; Funding Sources: Provincial government
Staff Member(s): 10
Membership: 200; Fees: $10; Member Profile: Deaf, deafened & hard of hearing people
Activities: Awareness Events: Deaf Culture Month, Sept.; Library: Open to public

Inter-Provincial Association on Native Employment (IANE)
#316, 35-2855 Pembina Hwy., Winnipeg MB R3T 2H5
Tel: 204-257-2754; Fax: 204-255-1182
www.ianeinc.ca
Overview: A small national organization
Mission: To reflect the needs of Native peoples regarding employment; to provide advice & assistance; to assist companies & other groups employing or assisting Native persons; to provide information about pertinent government policies & programs to industry & labour groups; to encourage development of education & training programs
Chief Officer(s):
Lynda Highway, Event Coordinator
lhighway@shaw.ca

Interprovincial Brotherhood of Electrical Workers (CLC) Voir Fraternité interprovinciale des ouvriers en électricité (CTC)

Interprovincial Denturist Societies See Denturist Association of Canada

Interprovincial School Development Association (ISDA)
5940 South St., Halifax NS B3H 1S6
Tel: 902-424-8500; Fax: 902-424-0543
apsea@apsea.ca
www.apsea.ca
Overview: A small provincial organization
Mission: To provide & extend opportunities, activities & experiences for children who are deaf or hard of hearing in Atlantic Canada up to the age of 21 years; To achieve these goals by administering funds for post-secondary scholarships, graduation awards & prizes, research grants & grants to support recreational, social & cultural activities
Chief Officer(s):
Heather Conrad, Director, Finance & Administration
Heather_Conrad@apsea.ca

Interval House
#200, 131 Bloor St., Toronto ON M5S 1R8
Tel: 416-924-1411; Fax: 416-928-9020; TTY: 416-924-0899; Crisis Hot-Line: 416-924-1491
info@intervalhouse.ca
www.intervalhouse.ca
www.facebook.com/IntervalHouseTO
twitter.com/interval_house
Overview: A small local charitable organization
Mission: To provide a continuum of services that enable abused women & children to have access to safe shelter & responsive services that help them establish lives free from violence; To provide integrated & specialized services related to counselling,

advocacy, outreach, legal & housing support, as well as programs to help build economic self-sufficiency

Inter-Varsity Christian Fellowship (IVCF)
1 International Blvd., Toronto ON M9W 6H3
Tel: 416-443-1170; *Fax:* 416-443-1499
Toll-Free: 800-668-9766
info@ivcf.ca
www.ivcf.ca
Overview: A medium-sized national charitable organization founded in 1929
Mission: To help the transformation of youth, students & graduates into fully committed followers of Jesus Christ, regardless of background or ethnicity
Finances: *Funding Sources:* Donations
Activities: Offering Pioneer Camps across Canada; Providing ministry at university & college campuses; Offering travel opportunities through Inter-Varsity's World Services' Global Partnerships; Participating in the Urbana Student Mission Convention
Chief Officer(s):
Geri Rodman, President

Intervention régionale et information sur le sida en Estrie
505, rue Wellington sud, Sherbrooke QC J1H 5E2
Tél: 819-823-6704
www.iris-estrie.com
Également appelé: IRIS/Estrie
Aperçu: *Dimension:* petite; *Envergure:* locale; Organisme sans but lucratif; fondée en 1988
Mission: Stimuler et développer une action communautaire pour faire face à la problématique du Sida dans la région de l'Estrie; pour remplir sa mission, l'organisme a regroupé ses actions dans trois programmes spécifiques: Soutien, Prévention, Intervention
Affiliation(s): Coalition québécoise des organismes communautaires de lutte contre le sida
Membre(s) du personnel: 9
Membre: *Comités:* Ressources Humaines; Levée de Fonds; Gestion Interne; Activités de l'Organisme; Action Bénévole; Communication, Développement et Marketing social régional et provincial; Santé Sexuelle régional et provincial; Femmes Vulnérables régional et provincial; HARSAH régional et provincial; Ethnoculturelle régional et provincial; UDI régional et provincial; Droit pronvincial
Activités: *Stagiaires:* Oui; *Service de conférenciers:* Oui; *Listes de destinataires:* Oui; *Bibliothèque:* Centre de documentation; Bibliothèque publique
Membre(s) du bureau directeur:
Yannick Dallaire, Directeur général
ydallaire.irisestrie@hotmail.com

Intrepid Theatre Co. Society
#2, 1609 Blanshard St., Victoria BC V8W 2J5
Tel: 250-383-2663
www.intrepidtheatre.com
www.facebook.com/IntrepidTheatre
twitter.com/IntrepidTheatre
www.instagram.com/intrepidtheatre
Also Known As: Victoria Fringe Festival; UNO Festival of Solo Performance
Overview: A small local charitable organization founded in 1986
Mission: To educate & enhance the public's awareness & aesthetic appreciation of contemporary & progressive styles of modern theatre by encouraging, developing & producing new or experimental works for public performance; by coordinating & producing the annual Fringe Theatre Festival in Victoria
Member of: Canadian Association of Fringe Festivals
Affiliation(s): Pro Art Alliance of Greater Victoria
Finances: *Annual Operating Budget:* $500,000-$1.5 Million; *Funding Sources:* Government; Sponsors; Bingo/casino; Box office
Staff Member(s): 5; 250+ volunteer(s)
Membership: 75+
Activities: Organizing festivals & presentation series; *Internships:* Yes; *Rents Mailing List:* Yes
Chief Officer(s):
Janet Munsil, Artistic Director/Producer
janet@intrepidtheatre.com
Heather Lindsay, Executive Director
gm@intrepidtheatre.com

Inuit Art Foundation (IAF) / Fondation d'art Inuit
c/o Centre of Social Innovation, #400, 215 Spadina Ave., Toronto ON M5T 2C7
Tel: 647-498-7717
Toll-Free: 855-274-0109
info@inuitartfoundation.org
www.inuitartfoundation.org
Overview: A medium-sized national charitable organization founded in 1985
Mission: To facilitate the creative expression of Inuit artists; To foster an increased understanding of this expression in a local & global context; To assist in the marketing of Inuit art; To promote Inuit art through exhibits, publications & public events
Finances: *Funding Sources:* Donations
Membership: *Member Profile:* Inuit artists
Activities: Managing the Inuit Artists' Shop; Assisting organizations to obtain copyright permission; Providing marketing brochures for dealers & artists
Chief Officer(s):
Jimmy Manning, President
William Huffman, Director, Development & Stakeholder Relations
Publications:
• Inuit Art Quarterly
Type: Magazine; *Frequency:* Quarterly; *Editor:* Nancy Campbell
Profile: A magazine comprising scholarly and popular content that connects readers to Inuit art.

Inuit Community Centre
604 Laurier Ave. West, Ottawa ON K1R 6L1
Tel: 613-565-5885; *Fax:* 613-563-4136
info@tungasuvvingatinuit.ca
www.tungasuvvingatinuit.ca
Also Known As: Tungasuvvingat Inuit
Overview: A small local organization founded in 1987
Mission: A social, cultural & counselling organization serving the Inuit
Finances: *Annual Operating Budget:* $3 Million-$5 Million
Activities: Programs: Addiction treatment; lunch; homeless support; employment support; head start; youth; diabetes prevention & awareness; community support
Chief Officer(s):
Kevin Kablutsiak, President

Inuit Tapiriit Kanatami (ITK)
#1101, 75 Albert St., Ottawa ON K1P 5E7
Tel: 613-238-8181; *Fax:* 613-234-1991
Toll-Free: 866-262-8181
info@itk.ca
www.itk.ca
www.facebook.com/inuittapiriitkanatami
twitter.com/ITK_CanadaInuit
www.youtube.com/inuitofcanada
Previous Name: Inuit Tapirisat of Canada
Overview: A large local organization founded in 1971
Mission: To ensure the survival of Inuit culture in Canada
Staff Member(s): 38
Membership: Represents 55,000 Inuit; *Member Profile:* Members come from 4 geographic regions: Nunatsiavut (Labrador), Nunavik (Québec), Nunavut, and the Inuvialuit Settlement Region (NWT)
Activities: *Library:*
Chief Officer(s):
Natan Obed, President
Elizabeth Ford, Acting Executive Director, 613-238-8181 Ext. 224
Publications:
• Inuit Tapiriit Kanatami Annual Report
Type: Report; *Frequency:* Annually

Inuit Tapirisat of Canada *See* Inuit Tapiriit Kanatami

Inuvik Chamber of Commerce
PO Box 3039, Inuvik NT X0E 0T0
inuvikchamber.com
Overview: A small local organization founded in 1971
Mission: To improve & promote commerce in Inuvik
Member of: Canadian Chamber of Commerce
Membership: 49; *Fees:* $100
Chief Officer(s):
Lee Smallwood, President
president@inuvikchamber.com

Inventors Association of Ottawa
PO Box 4028, Stn. E, Ottawa ON K1S 5B1
Tel: 613-788-0688
Overview: A small local organization
Chief Officer(s):
Gene Shershen, President

Inverness Cottage Workshop (ICW)
PO Box 485, 46 Lower Railway St., Inverness NS B0E 1N0
Tel: 902-258-3316; *Fax:* 902-258-3351
www.invernesscottageworkshop.ca
www.facebook.com/ICottageWorkshop
twitter.com/InvernessCW
Overview: A small local organization founded in 1981
Member of: DIRECTIONS Council for Vocational Services Society
Staff Member(s): 7
Activities: Daily programs include: Bakery, Used Clothing Store, Shredding, Recylcing, Bags-n-Tags, & Village Market
Chief Officer(s):
Donna MacLean, President
Cindy O'Neill, Executive Director/Manager

Inverness County Centre for the Arts (ICCA)
PO Box 709, 16080 Hwy. 19, Inverness NS B0E 1N0
Tel: 902-258-2533; *Fax:* 902-258-2277
manager@invernessarts.ca
www.invernessarts.ca
Overview: A small local organization founded in 1984
Mission: The Inverness County Council of the Arts is a charitable organization, dedicated to promoting exhibitions and cultural events that showcase artists in the community and creating awareness of the opportunities and benefits associated with the arts
Membership: *Fees:* $10-$50
Activities: Annual visual art shows
Chief Officer(s):
Kathy Hannigan, Executive Director

Invest Ottawa / Investir Ottawa
7 Bayview Rd., Ottawa ON K1Y 2C5
Tel: 613-828-6274
worldclass@investottawa.ca
www.investottawa.ca
www.linkedin.com/company/invest-ottawa
www.facebook.com/InvestOttawa
twitter.com/Invest_Ottawa
Previous Name: Ottawa Centre for Research & Innovation; Ottawa Carleton Research Institute
Overview: A small local organization founded in 1983
Mission: To foster the advancement of Ottawa & area's globally competitive knowledge-based industries & institutions
Finances: *Funding Sources:* Membership fees; Professional development programs; Municipal, provincial & federal governments; Private sector contributions
Staff Member(s): 35
Membership: 500-999
Activities: Connecting business, research, education, government, & talent; Marketing Ottawa to business; Offering access to market research; *Internships:* Yes
Chief Officer(s):
Jon Milne, Managing Director, Innovation
jmilne@investottawa.ca
Blair Patacairk, Managing Director, Investment & Trade
bpatacairk@investottawa.ca
Karen Letain, Director, Marketing & Communications
kletain@investottawa.ca
Publications:
• Invest Ottawa Spotlight [a publication of Invest Ottawa]
Type: Newsletter; *Frequency:* bi-weekly
Profile: A resource for members featuring Invest Ottawa's upcoming events, recent news, & job listings
• Ottawa Spotlight Guides [a publication of Invest Ottawa]
Type: Report
Profile: Guides that provide an overview of innovation & companies in various fields: Film, Television & Interactive Digital Media; Aerospace, Defence & Security; WirelessTelecom; & Optics & Photonics

Investir Ottawa *See* Invest Ottawa

Investment Counsel Association of Canada *See* Portfolio Management Association of Canada

Investment Funds Institute of Canada (IFIC) / L'Institut des fonds d'investissement du Canada
11 King St. West, 4th Fl., Toronto ON M5H 4C7
Tel: 416-363-2150
Toll-Free: 866-347-1961
member-services@ific.ca
www.ific.ca
www.linkedin.com/company/266541
twitter.com/ific
Previous Name: Canadian Mutual Fund Association

Overview: A medium-sized national organization founded in 1962
Mission: To act as the voice of the investment funds industry in Canada; To enhance the integrity & growth of the Canadian mutual fund industry
Affiliation(s): The Canadian Institute of Financial Planning
Membership: 150; *Member Profile:* Fund managers; Distributors; Industry service organizations; *Committees:* Governance; Regulatory Watch; Compliance; Operations; Communications
Activities: Advocating on industry issues; Providing an investor resource centre; Improving members' knowledge & proficiency; Communicating with members; Providing a job board & networking opportunities; *Library:* Advisor Resource Centre
Chief Officer(s):
John Adams, Chair
Ross Kappele, 1st Vice-Chair
Paul C. Bourque, Q.C., President & CEO
Parker John, CFO & Vice-President, Finance
Meetings/Conferences:
• Investment Funds Institute of Canada (IFIC) Annual Leadership Conference 2018, September, 2018, The Carlu, Toronto, ON
Scope: National
> Bureau du Québec - Le Conseil des fonds d'investissement du Québec
> #1800, 1010, rue Sherbrooke ouest, Montréal QC H3A 2R7
> *Tel:* 514-985-7025
> cfiqinfo@ific.ca

Investment Industry Association of Canada (IIAC) / Association canadienne du commerce des valeurs mobilières (AACVM)
PO Box 173, #1910, 100 Wellington St. West, Toronto ON M5K 1H6
Tel: 416-364-2754; *Fax:* 416-364-4861
PublicAffairs_AffairesPubliques@iiac.ca
www.iiac.ca
www.linkedin.com/company/investment-industry-association-of-canada
www.facebook.com/1605407876404528
twitter.com/IIACACCVM
www.youtube.com/channel/UC_UOj1wFC6YmpghyCRWigUw
Overview: A small national organization founded in 2006
Mission: Advances the growth and development of the Canadian investment industry; acts as a proactive voice for the industry; endeavours to create efficient and competitive capital markets, stimulate the savings and investment process, and provide support and services that contribute to member success. Montreal Office: Place Montreal Trust, 1800, av McGill College, bureau 2112, Montreal QC H3A 3J6, Ph. 514-843-8380. Vancouver Office: 888 Dunsmuir St., Suite 1230, Vancouver BC V6C 3K4, Ph. 604-482-1790.
Membership: *Member Profile:* Bank-owned securities firms; independent integrated firms; institutional boutiques; *Committees:* Communications; Compliance; Debt Markets; Derivatives; Equity Markets; Insurance; Investment Banking; Private Client; Regional; Small Dealers; Tax Reporting; U.S. Tax
Activities: Continuing education; publications; job search resources
Chief Officer(s):
Ian Russell, President

Investment Industry Regulatory Organization of Canada (IIROC) / Organisme canadien de réglementation du commerce des valeurs mobilières (OCRCVM)
#2000, 121 King St. West, Toronto ON M5H 3T9
Tel: 416-364-6133; *Fax:* 416-364-0753
Toll-Free: 877-442-4322
Other Communication: Enforcement Matters, Fax: 416-364-2998
publicaffairs@iiroc.ca
www.iiroc.ca
Merged from: Investment Dealers Association of Canada; Canada & Market Regulation Services Inc.
Overview: A large national licensing organization founded in 2008
Mission: To oversee investment dealers & trading activity on debt & equity marketplaces in Canada; To focus on regulatory & investment industry standards, protecting investors & strengthening market integrity
Membership: 100-499; *Member Profile:* Investment dealer firms & their employees; *Committees:* Corporate Governance; Finance & Audit; Human Resources & Pension
Activities: Providing continuing education & member events
Chief Officer(s):
Andrew J. Kriegler, President & CEO

Ian Campbell, Chief Information Officer
Lucy Becker, Vice-President, Public Affairs & Member Education Services
Bureau de Montréal
#1550, 5, Place Ville-Marie, Montréal QC H3B 2G2
Tél: 514-878-2854; *Téléc:* 514-878-3860
Chief Officer(s):
Claudyne Bienvenu, Vice-président, Québec
Calgary Office
Bow Valley Square 3, #800, 255 - 5 Ave. SW, Calgary AB T2P 3G6
Tel: 403-262-6393; *Fax:* 403-234-0861
Chief Officer(s):
Warren Funt, Vice-President, Western Canada
Vancouver Office
Royal Centre, PO Box 11164, #2800, 1055 West Georgia St., Vancouver BC V6E 3R5
Tel: 604-683-6222; *Fax:* 604-683-3491
Chief Officer(s):
Warren Funt, Vice-President, Western Canada

Investment Property Owners Association of Cape Breton (IPOACB)
105 Bentinck St., Sydney NS B1P 1G3
Tel: 902-562-1813
ipoacb@syd.eastlink.ca
www.ipoacb.ca
www.facebook.com/IPOACB
twitter.com/IPOACB
Overview: A medium-sized local organization founded in 1978
Mission: To represent owners of residential properties in the Cape Breton area while providing members with services.
Affiliation(s): Investment Property Owners Association of Nova Scotia
Membership: 300+
Chief Officer(s):
Priscilla Lotherington, President

Investment Property Owners Association of Nova Scotia Ltd. (IPOANS)
Vantage Business Centre, #208-209, 102 Chain Lake Dr., Halifax NS B3S 1A7
Tel: 902-425-3572; *Fax:* 902-422-0700
association@ipoans.ca
www.ipoans.ca
www.linkedin.com/groups/Investment-Property-Owners-Association-Nova-6623377
www.facebook.com/ipoansca
twitter.com/ipoans
Overview: A medium-sized provincial organization founded in 1979
Mission: To protect, enhance & contribute to the ability of rental housing owners & operators to profit from their investments; to provide educational programs for members; to serve as an information centre
Member of: Canadian Society of Association Executives; Canadian Federation of Apartment Associations
Affiliation(s): National Apartment Association
Finances: *Annual Operating Budget:* $50,000-$100,000; *Funding Sources:* Membership fees; education
Staff Member(s): 2
Membership: 100-499; *Member Profile:* Must own or operate rental/commercial property; *Committees:* Education; Legislative; Membership; Public Relations
Activities: Lobbying; legislative task forces; Certified Management Program discounts; property management advice; *Speaker Service:* Yes; *Rents Mailing List:* Yes
Chief Officer(s):
Rose Marie Howell, Executive Director

Investor Learning Centre of Canada *See* Canadian Securities Institute Research Foundation

IODE Canada (IODE)
#219, 40 Orchard View Blvd., Toronto ON M4R 1B9
Tel: 416-487-4416
Toll-Free: 866-827-7428
iodecanada@bellnet.ca
www.iode.ca
www.facebook.com/IODECanada
twitter.com/IODECanada
Previous Name: Imperial Order Daughters of the Empire
Overview: A medium-sized national charitable organization founded in 1900

Mission: To operate as a women's charitable organization; to provide education support, community service & citizenship programs
Finances: *Funding Sources:* Membership fees; Donations; Foundations
4,00 volunteer(s)
Activities: *Library:* The National Chapter of Canada IODE Resource Centre; by appointment
Chief Officer(s):
Bonnie G. Rees, National President
Awards:
• Labrador Bursary
; *Amount:* $1,000
• IODE 100th Anniversary Grant to Child Protection Workers
; *Amount:* $20,000
• The National Chapter of Canada IODE Violet Downey Book Award
Awarded annually for the best English-language book, containing at least 500 words of text, preferably with Canadian content, in any category suitable for children aged 13 & under; *Amount:* $3,000
• IODE War Memorial Doctoral Scholarships
• National IODE (RCMP) Police Community Relations Award
Publications:
• Echoes [a publication of IODE Canada]
Type: Newsletter
Profile: Published since 1902; features information on IODE members & supported programs
• IODE Canada Express News
Type: Newsletter

Iqaluit Chamber of Commerce
PO Box 1107, Iqaluit NU X0A 0H0
Tel: 867-979-4095; *Fax:* 867-979-2929
Overview: A small local organization

Iranian Community Association of Ontario
#205, 5330 Yonge St., Toronto ON M2N 5P9
Tel: 416-441-2656; *Fax:* 416-691-8466
info@iranianassociation.ca
www.iranianassociation.ca
Overview: A small local organization founded in 1986
Mission: To provide basic orientation for Iranian newcomers in Ontario; To refer clients to appropriate governmental organizations; To help newcomers find a place to live & a job
Finances: *Annual Operating Budget:* $50,000-$100,000
Staff Member(s): 5
Membership: 800
Activities: *Library:* Open to public
Chief Officer(s):
Mohammad Asari, Chief of the Board

Iraqi Canadian Society of Ontario
1057 McNicoll Ave., Toronto ON M1W 3W6
Tel: 416-494-1438; *Fax:* 416-494-1438
Overview: A small provincial organization founded in 1991
Mission: To create a healthy & friendly environment so that Iraqis regardless of their race, religion, age & background, can come together, cooperate & unite

Iraqi Jewish Association of Ontario
7026 Bathurst, Thornhill ON L4J 8K3
Tel: 416-488-6262
info@ijao.ca
ijao.ca
Overview: A small provincial organization
Chief Officer(s):
Reuven Ahron, President

The Ireland Funds, Canada
#1620, 44 Victoria St., Toronto ON M5C 1Y2
Tel: 416-367-8311
irelandfunds.org/chapters/worldwide/canada
www.linkedin.com/company/11200963
twitter.com/IrelandFundCda
Overview: A medium-sized international charitable organization
Mission: To raise funds to support programs of peace, reconciliation, arts, culture, education, & community development in Ireland & Canada
Chief Officer(s):
Jane Noonan, Executive Director
jnoonan@irelandfunds.org

Ireland-Canada Chamber of Commerce (ICCC)
121 Decarie Circle, Toronto ON M9B 3J6

www.icccto.com
www.facebook.com/1417845151804118
twitter.com/icccto
Overview: A small international organization founded in 1991
Mission: To bring together individuals & corporations interested in the development & enhancement of commercial relations between Ireland & Canada; To provide a forum for its members to network within the business community in Canada & Ireland
Finances: *Funding Sources:* Membership dues
Membership: *Fees:* $25 under 25/new member; $50 under 30/over 65; $100 standard; $500 gold
Activities: Supporting community organizations; Providing speakers & networking opportunities
Chief Officer(s):
Matthew Cotter, President

Irish Canadian Cultural Association of New Brunswick (ICCA NB)
c/o Patricia O'Leary-Coughlan, 189 Carlisle Rd., Douglas NB E3A 7M8
info@newirelandnb.ca
www.newirelandnb.ca
Overview: A small provincial organization founded in 1983
Mission: To recognize & honour the contributions made by our ancestors to Canada by holding an annual Irish Festival, promoting an Irish Studies program at universities & sponsoring Irish cultural & social programs & events
Finances: *Funding Sources:* Membership dues
Membership: *Fees:* $20 individuals; $25 families
Chief Officer(s):
Patricia O'Leary-Coughlan, Contact

Irish Dance Teacher's Association of Eastern Canada
c/o Ryan Carroll, Goggin-Carroll School of Irish Dance, 1040 South Service Rd. East, Oakville ON L6J 2X7
www.irishdancecanada.com
Overview: A small local organization
Mission: To promote Irish dance throughout eastern Canada
Membership: *Member Profile:* Registered teachers (TCRG) & adjudicators (ADCRG) in eastern Canada
Activities: Regulating Feiseanna in the eastern Canadian region; Maintaining a standardized syllabus of competitions & rules
Chief Officer(s):
Ryan Carroll, Regional Director
ryan@goggin-carroll.com
Bernadette Short, Vice Regional Director
Fiona Cunningham, Treasurer

Irish Loop Chamber of Commerce
PO Box 114, Trepassey NL A0A 4B0
Tel: 709-438-1189; *Fax:* 709-438-2405
info@IrishLoopChamber.com
irishloopchamber.com
twitter.com/IrishLoopCofC
Overview: A small local organization
Mission: To strengthen business & stimulate economic development in the Irish Loop area
Chief Officer(s):
Derrick Thompson, Interim President

Irma & District Chamber of Commerce
PO Box 284, Irma AB T0B 2H0
Tel: 780-754-3996
Overview: A small local organization

Irma Fish & Game Association
General Delivery, Irma AB T0B 2H0
Tel: 780-754-3937
Overview: A small local organization
Member of: Alberta Fish & Game Association; National Firearms Association
Finances: *Annual Operating Budget:* Less than $50,000
Membership: 75
Activities: Hide collection program
Chief Officer(s):
Brad Hill, Contact
Ken Veer, Contact, 780-754-3969

Iroquois Falls & District Chamber of Commerce
723 Synagogue Ave., Iroquois Falls ON P0K 1G0
Tel: 705-232-4656; *Fax:* 705-232-4656
office@iroquoisfallschamber.com
www.iroquoisfallschamber.com
Overview: A small local organization founded in 1924

Mission: To promote & improve economic & social development of the community
Member of: Canadian & Ontario Chambers of Commerce; James Bay Frontier
Finances: *Annual Operating Budget:* Less than $50,000; *Funding Sources:* Membership fees
Staff Member(s): 2; 16 volunteer(s)
Membership: 71; *Fees:* Schedule available; *Member Profile:* Businesses; *Committees:* Business & Commerce; Community Programs; Economic Development; Tourism
Activities: *Speaker Service:* Yes; *Library:* Tourism & Info Centre; Open to public
Chief Officer(s):
Linda Anderson, Business Director

Iroquois Falls Association for Community Living
PO Box 310, 9 Veterans Dr., Iroquois Falls ON P0K 1E0
Tel: 705-258-3971; *Fax:* 705-258-3119
ifacl@onlink.net
Overview: A small local organization
Member of: Community Living Ontario
Chief Officer(s):
Carol Gauthier, Chief Executive Officer

Iroquois Falls Historical Society
245 Devonshire Ave., Iroquois Falls ON P0K 1E0
Tel: 705-258-3730; *Fax:* 705-258-3730
ifpioneermuseum@outlook.com
iroquoisfallschamber.com/web-content/Pages/historicalsociety.html
Overview: A small local charitable organization
Mission: To preserve the local history of the area
Member of: Ontario Historical Society; Ontario Museum Association
Affiliation(s): Cochrane Temiskaming Museum & Galleries Assoc.
Finances: *Funding Sources:* Grants; admissions; gift shop; membership fees
Membership: *Fees:* $5 single; $10 family; $25 corporate
Activities: Operates a Pioneer Museum; *Library:* Open to public
Chief Officer(s):
Denis Charette, President

Irritable Bowel Syndrome Self Help & Support Group
PO Box 94074, Toronto ON M4N 3R1
Tel: 416-932-3311; *Fax:* 416-932-8909
www.ibsgroup.org
www.facebook.com/ibsgroup
twitter.com/ibsgroup
Also Known As: IBS Self Help Group
Overview: A medium-sized international organization founded in 1987
Mission: To educate & provide support for people who have IBS; To use membership to encourage both medical & pharmaceutical research to make the lives of those with IBS easier
Member of: Self Help Resource Centre; American Self-Help Clearinghouse
Affiliation(s): IBS Association
Finances: *Funding Sources:* Membership dues; industry sponsors
Activities: *Rents Mailing List:* Yes
Chief Officer(s):
Jeffrey Roberts, Founder

Is Five Foundation
#302, 161 Eglinton Ave. East, Toronto ON M4P 1J5
Tel: 416-480-2408; *Fax:* 416-480-2546
Overview: A small local organization

Islamic Association of Nova Scotia (IANS)
PO Box 103-136, 287 Lacewood Dr., Dartmouth NS B3M 3Y7
Tel: 902-469-9490
info@islamnovascotia.ca
www.islamnovascotia.ca
Previous Name: Islamic Association of the Maritimes
Overview: A small local organization founded in 1966
Membership: *Fees:* $50 single; $100 family; $25 student
Chief Officer(s):
Iftikhar Baig, President, 902-471-8998
Sami Mirza, Vice President

Islamic Association of Saskatchewan
222 Copland Cres., Saskatoon SK S7H 2Z5
Tel: 306-665-6424
info@islamiccenter.sk.ca
www.islamiccenter.sk.ca

Overview: A small provincial organization founded in 1968
Affiliation(s): Multi-Faith Group; Saskatchewan Organization for Heritage Language; Saskatchewan Intercultural Association; Saskatchewan Forum for "Racialized" Canadians; Saskatchewan Council for International Cooperation
Membership: *Fees:* $40 family; $25 single; *Committees:* The Muslim Communications and Outreach Committee (MCOC); The Takaful Fund Committee (TFC)
Activities: Operates Islamic Centre; Represents Muslims; Provides activities; Responsible for Muslim Cemetery
Chief Officer(s):
Khalil-ur-Rehman, President
president@islamiccenter.sk.ca
Naeem Sader, Vice President
vp@islamiccenter.sk.ca
Hanan Elbardouh, Vice President, Sisters
vps@islamiccenter.sk.ca
Faiyaz Ahmed, Secretary
info@islamiccenter.sk.ca
Taimur Samad, Treasurer
treasurer@islamiccenter.sk.ca

Islamic Association of the Maritimes *See* Islamic Association of Nova Scotia

Islamic Care Centre (ICC)
312 Lisgar St., Ottawa ON K2P 0E2
Tel: 613-232-0210; *Fax:* 613-232-0210
info@islamcare.ca
www.islamcare.ca
Also Known As: Daw'ah Centre
Overview: A small national charitable organization founded in 1999
Mission: Islam Care Centre provides the Canadian (Ottawa) Muslim community with resources to meet religious and social needs with the objective of establishing a better relationship with the larger Canadian society.
Member of: Muslim Community Council of Ottawa
Affiliation(s): Islam Care Centre
Finances: *Annual Operating Budget:* $50,000-$100,000
Staff Member(s): 2; 10 volunteer(s)
Membership: 35; *Fees:* $50
Activities: *Speaker Service:* Yes; *Library:* Islamic Information; Open to public
Chief Officer(s):
Omar Mahfoudhi, Executive Director

Islamic Foundation of Toronto (IFT)
441 Nugget Ave., Toronto ON M1S 5E1
Tel: 416-321-0909; *Fax:* 416-321-1995
info@islamicfoundation.ca
www.islamicfoundation.ca
www.facebook.com/iftlive
twitter.com/iftlive
www.youtube.com/user/islamicfoundationca
Also Known As: Nugget Mosque
Overview: A small local charitable organization founded in 1969
Finances: *Annual Operating Budget:* $3 Million-$5 Million
Staff Member(s): 72
Membership: 1,000-4,999; *Committees:* Dawah; Library; School Board; Social Services
Activities: Full time Islamic school, JK to Grade 10; part-time evening Islamic school; Arabic language centre for adults; Friday & Sunday schools
Chief Officer(s):
Shakil Akhter, Administrator, 416-321-0909 Ext. 233
Shabbir Gangat, Coordinator, Funerals, 416-876-3000

Islamic Information Foundation (IIF)
8 Laurel Lane, Halifax NS B3M 2P6
Tel: 902-445-2494; *Fax:* 902-445-2494
iif@geocities.com
www.institutealislam.com/dr-jamal-badawi
Overview: A small national charitable organization founded in 1981
Mission: To promote better understanding of Islam among Muslims & Christians through information provided in print, audio & video forms & through lecture, seminars & interfaith dialogues
Finances: *Annual Operating Budget:* $100,000-$250,000; *Funding Sources:* Sale of religious material; donations
4 volunteer(s)
Membership: 40 individuals
Activities: *Speaker Service:* Yes
Chief Officer(s):
Jamal Badawi, Founder & Chair
Jamal.Badawi@StMarys.ca

Islamic Propagation Centre International (Canada) See
Islamic Propagation Centre of Ontario

Islamic Propagation Centre of Ontario (IPC)
Jame Masjid Mississauga, 5761 Coopers Ave., Mississauga ON L4Z 1R9
Tel: 905-507-3323
Secretary@jamemasjid.org
www.jamemasjid.org
Also Known As: Jama Masjid Mississauga
Previous Name: Islamic Propagation Centre International (Canada)
Overview: A small local charitable organization founded in 1984
Mission: The Centre offers a selection of resource material for those interested in learning about Islam. Topics covered include comparative religion, history, culture, lifestyle, politics, law & women in Islam. It is a registered charity, BN: 886810191RR0001.
Finances: Annual Operating Budget: $50,000-$100,000
Staff Member(s): 2; 100 volunteer(s)
Membership: 100 student; 1,000 individual; Fees: $200 individual; Committees: Fundraising; Eid & Ramadhan; Executive
Activities: Congregation; marriages; family counselling; summer & evening school for kids; Speaker Service: Yes; Library: IPC Office Library; Open to public by appointment
Chief Officer(s):
Nafis Bhayat, Director, Religious Services, 416-844-9373
Imamjamemasjid.org

Islamic Relief Canada
3506 Mainway, Burlington ON L7M 1A8
Tel: 905-332-4673
Toll-Free: 855-377-4673
info@islamicreliefcanada.org
islamicreliefcanada.org
www.facebook.com/islamicrelief.canada
twitter.com/IRCanada
www.youtube.com/user/IslamicReliefC
Overview: A small international charitable organization founded in 1984
Mission: To provide food & supplies to people in developing countries in order to help them establish better living situations for themselves
Affiliation(s): Islamic Relief Worldwide; People in Aid
Finances: Annual Operating Budget: Greater than $5 Million
Staff Member(s): 3

Island Deaf & Hard of Hearing Centre (IDHHC)
#201-754 Broughton St., Victoria BC V8W 1E1
Tel: 250-592-8144; Fax: 250-592-8199
Toll-Free: 800-667-5448; TTY: 250-592-8147
victoria@idhhc.ca
www.idhhc.ca
www.facebook.com/145668377075
twitter.com/IDHHC
Overview: A small local charitable organization founded in 1991
Mission: To enable individuals who are deaf, hard of hearing or deafened, their supporters & the communities they represent, to have full & active access, recognition & involvement in society
Finances: Annual Operating Budget: $500,000-$1.5 Million; Funding Sources: Government; contract; donations; United Way
Staff Member(s): 14; 50 volunteer(s)
Membership: 200; Fees: $15-40
Activities: Counselling; interpreting; employment services; technical aids; family services; Spring Family Celebration; aural rehabilitation; support groups; Awareness Events: Sound & Silence Run/Walk, Aug.; Internships: Yes; Speaker Service: Yes; Rents Mailing List: Yes; Library
Chief Officer(s):
Denise Robertson, Executive Director
Nanaimo Branch Office
#101, 75 Front St., Nanaimo BC V9R 5G9
Tel: 250-753-0999; Fax: 250-753-9601
Toll-Free: 877-424-3323; TTY: 250-753-0977
nanaimo@idhhc.ca
www.idhhc.ca
Chief Officer(s):
Alexandra Walker, Office Manager
alex@idhhc.ca

Island Fishermen Cooperative Association Ltd. Voir
Association coopérative des pêcheurs de l'île Itée

Island Fitness Council
Sport PEI, PO Box 302, Charlottetown PE C1A 7K7
Tel: 902-368-4110; Fax: 902-368-4548
Toll-Free: 800-247-6712
sports@sportpei.pe.ca
Overview: A small provincial organization
Mission: A volunteer driven organization that is committed to developing a competent and enthusiastic core of active living leaders through leadership programs and standards which have been designed to establish professional competency and credibility, and ultimately enhance the health of all Islanders.
Affiliation(s): National Fitness Leadership Alliance
Finances: Funding Sources: Provincial government
Activities: Fitness Leader Certification

Island Horse Council (IHC)
c/o Sport PEI, 40 Enman Cres., Charlottetown PE C1E 1E6
www.islandhorsecouncil.ca
www.facebook.com/islandhorsecouncil
twitter.com/pei_IHC
Overview: A small provincial organization overseen by Sport PEI Inc.
Mission: The objectives of Island Horse Council are: to promote, conduct and manage a Council for the benefit of Prince Edward Island equestrians; to provide a unified voice for the horse industry on Prince Edward Island; to establish a liaison with any authorities, including federal, provincial, and municipal governments, and provincial or national Horse Councils or Equestrian Federations; and to encourage the development of all aspects of horsemanship, health, education, training, competition, breeding, facilities and humane practices.
Member of: Equine Canada; Sport PEI
Finances: Funding Sources: Sponsorships; PEI Provincial Government, Community & Cultural Affairs
Membership: 600+ individuals & 12 clubs; Fees: $35; Committees: Insurance/Membership; Provincial Coaching; Strathgartney; Trails & Recreation
Activities: Offering seminars, on topics such as first aid; Liaising with governments & other authorities; Encouraging the certification of coaches
Chief Officer(s):
Gary Evans, Chair
gevans@upei.ca
Frank Szentmiklossy, Treasurer
frank.szentmiklossy@systronix.net
Awards:
• Annual Volunteer of the Year
Publications:
• Business Directory
Type: Directory
• Island Horse Council Newsletter
Type: Newsletter; Accepts Advertising
Profile: Council activities & upcoming shows & event

Island Hospice Association See Hospice Palliative Care Association of Prince Edward Island

Island Lake Tribal Council
338 Broadway Ave., 4th Fl., Winnipeg MB R3C 0T2
Tel: 204-982-3300
wpgsuboffice@iltc.ca
www.iltc.ca
Overview: A small local organization
Mission: To generally unify, maintain and expand the interests, lives and identity of the Membership in every manner and respect whatsoever by facilitating leadership of all Island Lake Tribal Council communities; strengthening first nations communities; and working with first nations staff to bring in resources to strengthen skills and knowledge.
Affiliation(s): Assembly of Manitoba Chiefs; Manitoba Keewatinowi Okimakanak; Assembly of First Nations
Staff Member(s): 17
Membership: Member Profile: Represents four member reserves: Garden Hill; Red Sucker Lake; St. Theresa Point; Wasagamack
Activities: Education Advisory Services; Financial Advisory Services; First Nation Child Care Program; Social Development Advisory Services; Technical Services
Chief Officer(s):
Jonathan Flett, Executive Director
jflett@iltc.ca

Island Media Arts Co-op (IMAC)
PO Box 2726, Charlottetown PE C1A 8C3
Tel: 902-892-3131
director@imac.coop
www.islandmedia.pe.ca
Overview: A small provincial organization founded in 1982
Mission: To provide support & equipment for independent films produced on Prince Edward Island
Member of: Independent Film & Video Alliance
Staff Member(s): 1
Membership: Fees: $25 general; $40 producer
Activities: Film & video training workshops; Awareness Events: Reel Island Film Festival
Chief Officer(s):
Renee Laprise, Executive Director

Island Mountain Arts
PO Box 65, Wells BC V0K 2R0
Tel: 250-994-3466; Fax: 250-994-3433
Toll-Free: 800-442-2787
info@imarts.com
www.imarts.com
www.facebook.com/islandmountainarts
twitter.com/@ima_arts
Overview: A small local organization founded in 1977
Staff Member(s): 4
Chief Officer(s):
Julie Fowler, Executive Director
media@imarts.com

Island Nature Trust (INT)
PO Box 265, Charlottetown PE C1A 7K4
Tel: 902-566-9150; Fax: 902-628-6331
admin@islandnaturetrust.ca
www.islandnaturetrust.ca
www.facebook.com/islandnaturetrust
Also Known As: Prince Edward Island Nature Trust
Overview: A small provincial charitable organization founded in 1979
Mission: To acquire & manage natural areas on PEI
Member of: Tourism Industry Association of PEI
Affiliation(s): Canadian Nature Federation; Tree Canada Foundation
Finances: Funding Sources: Donations; fundraising; contract work
Membership: Fees: $20 single; $25 family; $10 student; $50 sustaining; $100 active; $250 supporting; $500 membership
Activities: Educational programs; acquisition, protection & management of natural areas; Speaker Service: Yes

The Island Party of Prince Edward Island
PE
theislandparty@yahoo.com
theislandpartypei.ca
Also Known As: The Island Party of P.E.I.
Overview: A small provincial organization
Chief Officer(s):
Billy Cann, Party Leader

Island Technology Professionals (ITP)
PO Box 1436, 92 Queen St., Charlottetown PE C1A 7N1
Tel: 902-892-8324
registrar@techpei.ca
www.techpei.ca
www.facebook.com/IslandTechnologyProfessionals
twitter.com/Tech_PEI
Previous Name: Association of Certified Engineering Technicians & Technologists of PEI; Prince Edward Island Society of Certified Engineering Technologists
Overview: A small provincial licensing organization founded in 1972 overseen by Canadian Council of Technicians & Technologists
Mission: To benefit society by advancing the professions of applied science & engineering technology in Prince Edward Island
Affiliation(s): The Association of Engineering Technicians and Technologists of Newfoundland and Labrador; TechNova; New Brunswick Society of Certified Engineering Technicians and Technologists; l'Ordre des technologues professionnels du Québec; The Certified Technicians and Technologists Association of Manitoba
Activities: Certifying engineering / applied science technicians & technologists; Conferring the designations C.Tech., C.E.T., & A.Sc.T.; Awareness Events: Career Options Day, November; National Skilled Trades Day, November; National Technology Week, November
Chief Officer(s):
Bryan Burt, CET, President
Marea O'Halloran, CET, Vice-President
Laurie Eveleigh, CET, Treasurer
Troy Livingstone, CET, Registrar
Publications:
• AtlanTECH News

Type: Newsletter
Profile: Information for technology professionals in New Brunswick, Prince Edward Island, & Newfoundland & Labrador

Island Writers' Association (P.E.I.)
c/o Debbie Gamble, 1320 Pownal Rd., RR#1, Alexandra, Charlottetown PE C1A 7J6
Tel: 902-569-3913
Overview: A small provincial organization founded in 1979
Mission: To facilitate information for P.E.I. freelance writers
Membership: *Member Profile:* Writer or aspiring writer
Activities: Writers & photographers workshops; conferences
Chief Officer(s):
Debbie Gamble, Contact
debbiegamble@pei.sympatico.ca

Islands Historical Society
PO Box 67, Freeport NS B0V 1B0
Tel: 902-839-2034; *Fax:* 902-839-2018
islandshistorical@cwswireless.ca
www.islandshistoricalsociety.com
Overview: A small local organization founded in 1984
Mission: To preserve, protect and promote the social history of Long and Brier Islands.
Member of: Association of Nova Scotia Museums; Council of Nova Scotia Archives; Canadian Heritage Information Network; Nova Scotia Lighthouse Preservation Society; Federation of the Nova Scotian Heritage

Islands Organic Producers Association (IOPA)
3490 Glenora Rd., Duncan BC V9L 6S2
Tel: 250-748-2791; *Fax:* 250-748-2741
admin@iopa.ca
www.iopa.ca
Overview: A small local organization founded in 1990
Affiliation(s): Certified Organic Associations of BC
Finances: *Funding Sources:* Membership fees
30 volunteer(s)
Membership: 60; *Member Profile:* Organic farmers

Israel Aliyah Center
#210, 4600 Bathurst St., Toronto ON M2R 3V3
Tel: 416-633-4766; *Fax:* 416-633-2758
aliyahto@jafi.org
www.aliyah.org
Overview: A small local organization
Mission: Committed towards maintaining Israel as a prominent focus of Jews everywhere and of stimulating interest in Israel as a viable living option.
Member of: Jewish Agency for Israel

Israel Cancer Research Fund (ICRF)
PO Box 29, #616, 1881 Yonge St., Toronto ON M4S 3C4
Tel: 416-487-5246; *Fax:* 416-487-8932
Toll-Free: 866-207-4949
research@icrf.ca
www.icrf.ca
www.facebook.com/ICRFToronto
twitter.com/icrftoronto
www.youtube.com/user/ICRFOnline
Overview: A small international charitable organization founded in 1975
Mission: To support scientists who are conducting cancer research in Israel
Staff Member(s): 3
Membership: *Member Profile:* Those committed to finding the cures for cancer; *Committees:* Scientific Advisory
Activities: Postdoctoral fellowships; project grants; Research Career Development Awards (RCDAs) & professorships; Women of Action Luncheon; The ICRF Gala; *Speaker Service:* Yes
Chief Officer(s):
Bryna Goldberg, President
Joy Wagner Arbus, Executive Director
joy.wagner@icrf.ca

The Israel Economic Mission to Canada
#700, 180 Bloor St. West, Toronto ON M5S 2V6
Tel: 416-847-0227
itrade.gov.il/canada
ca.linkedin.com/pub/israel-economic-mission-to-canada/35/530/410
facebook.com/112558825499912
twitter.com/IsraelFTA
Overview: A small international organization
Mission: To forge trade & investment relations between Israel & Canada

Activities: *Library:*
Chief Officer(s):
Michael Khoury, Head
Montréal
#650, 1, carré Westmount, Montréal QC H3Z 2P9
Tel: 514-940-8518

Israel Medical Association-Canadian Chapter (IMA)
#309, 788 Marlee Ave., Toronto ON M6B 3K1
Tel: 416-781-9562; *Fax:* 416-781-3166
Overview: A small international charitable organization founded in 1958
Mission: Devoted to promotion of professional & cultural ties between physicians in Israel & their colleagues abroad
Affiliation(s): Israel Medical Association World Fellowship
Activities: *Speaker Service:* Yes
Chief Officer(s):
Rose Geist, President
rgeist@thc.on.ca

Italian Canadian Benevolent Corporation (Toronto District)
See Villa Charities Inc. (Toronto District)

Italian Canadian Cultural Association of Nova Scotia (ICCA NS)
PO Box 9044, Stn. A, 2629 Agricola St., Halifax NS B3K 5M7
Tel: 902-453-5327; *Fax:* 902-453-1852
icca@eastlink.ca
www.iccans.org
Overview: A small provincial organization
Mission: To enrich & share Italian Canadian culture throughout Nova Scotia; To honour Italian heritage
Membership: *Fees:* $25 students (full time, from age 18 to 25) & seniors (over 65 years of age); $35 single members; $70 fammilies; *Member Profile:* Persons of Italian heritage; Individuals of non-Italian heritage, who have an interest in Italian history & culture
Activities: Providing educational services, such as instruction in the Italian language; Organizing social, cultural, & recreational events which build family & community ties; Offering a forum for members to share their experiences; *Library:* Italian Canadian Cultural Association of Nova Scotia Library
Publications:
• La Voce
Type: Newsletter; *Accepts Advertising; Editor:* Giovanni Da Ros
Profile: Announcements of upcoming events in the Italian community

Italian Chamber of Commerce in Canada (ICCC)
#1150, 550, rue Sherbrooke ouest, Montréal QC H3A 1B9
Tel: 514-844-4249; *Fax:* 514-844-4875
info.montreal@italchamber.qc.ca
www.italchamber.qc.ca
twitter.com/CCICmontreal
Overview: A small international organization
Mission: ICCC is a private, non-profit organization that nurtures economic ties between Italy & Canada, with a special focus on Quebec. It encourages the development of business relations between major public & private economic players, & provides a range of services that contribute to clients' internationalization projects. It has experience in advanced technology sectors, such as aeronautics, biotechnology, telecommunications, genomics, nanotechnology & chemical industries.
Staff Member(s): 7
Membership: *Fees:* $450 corporate; $1200 sustaining
Activities: Trade shows in Canada & Italy
Chief Officer(s):
Emanuele Triassi, President
Danielle Virone, Executive Director
virone.montreal@italchamber.qc.ca

Italian Chamber of Commerce in Canada - West
#405, 889 West Pender St., Vancouver BC V6C 3B2
Tel: 604-682-1410; *Fax:* 604-682-2997
iccbc@iccbc.com
www.iccbc.com
www.facebook.com/Italian.Chamber.Commerce.Canada
twitter.com/Italian_Chamber
Overview: A small international organization founded in 1992
Mission: The Chamber is private, non-profit, membership organization with the mandate of promoting & enhancing business, trade & investment exchanges between Italy & Western Canada
Staff Member(s): 7
Membership: *Fees:* $100 friend; $200 associate; $350 business; $550 corporate; *Member Profile:* Open to all

individuals & companies with an interest in business links between BC, Alberta & Italy
Activities: Trade shows; seminars
Chief Officer(s):
Celso Boscariol, President
Giorgio Puppin, Executive Director
Publications:
• Conexus
Type: Magazine; *Frequency:* Quarterly
Profile: www.conexusmagazine.ca
Calgary Office
#9, 3927 Edmonton Trail NE, Calgary AB T2E 6T1
Tel: 403-283-0453; *Fax:* 403-283-0484
calgary@iccbc.com
Chief Officer(s):
Petra Saccani, Contact

Italian Chamber of Commerce of Ontario (ICCO)
#201F, 622 College St., Toronto ON M6G 1B6
Tel: 416-789-7169; *Fax:* 416-789-7160
businessinfo@italchambers.ca
www.italchambers.ca
www.linkedin.com/company/icco-italian-chamber-of-commerce-of-ontario
www.facebook.com/IccoItalianChamberOfCommerceOfOntario
twitter.com/Italchambers
www.instagram.com/italchambers
Previous Name: Italian Chamber of Commerce of Toronto
Overview: A medium-sized international organization founded in 1961
Mission: To enhance & promote business, trade & cultural relations between Canada & Italy
Member of: European Union Chambers of Commerce; Greater Toronto Business Alliance
Membership: *Fees:* Schedule available
Activities: *Library:*
Chief Officer(s):
George Visintin, President
Corrado Paina, Executive Director
paina@italchambers.ca

Italian Chamber of Commerce of Toronto *See* Italian Chamber of Commerce of Ontario

Italian Cultural Centre Society
3075 Slocan St., Vancouver BC V5M 3E4
Tel: 604-430-3337; *Fax:* 604-430-3331
info@iccvancouver.ca
italianculturalcentre.ca
www.facebook.com/ilcentrovan
twitter.com/IlCentroVan
Overview: A small local organization founded in 1978
Mission: To promote Italian culture and bring together Italians in Vancouver
Member of: BC Chamber of Commerce; Business in Vancouver; Commercial Drive BIA; Tourism Vancouver; Vancouver Board of Trade
Activities: Italian Language Classses; Italian Sports; Bingo
Chief Officer(s):
Mauro Vescera, Executive Director, 604-430-3337 Ext. 226
executivedirector@iccvancouver.ca

Italian Cultural Institute (Istituto Italiano di Cultura)
496 Huron St., Toronto ON M5R 2R3
Tel: 416-921-3802; *Fax:* 416-962-2503
Other Communication: Courses, E-mail: corsi.iictoronto@esteri.it
iicToronto@esteri.it
www.iictoronto.esteri.it
www.facebook.com/iictoronto
twitter.com/IICToronto
www.youtube.com/user/IICCulturalToronto
Overview: A medium-sized international organization founded in 1976
Mission: To promote Italian culture & language in its many expressions in a spirit of vital interaction with the host country; To provide information on Italy's cultural heritage & contemporary cultural production
Finances: *Funding Sources:* Italian Ministry of Foreign Affairs; Private sponsors
Membership: 5,000-14,999; *Fees:* $50
Activities: *Speaker Service:* Yes; *Rents Mailing List:* Yes; *Library:* Open to public by appointment
Chief Officer(s):
Alessandro Ruggera, Acting Director, 416-921-3802 Ext. 221
alessandro.ruggera@esteri.it

Carlo Settembrini, Technical Manager, 416-921-3802 Ext. 222
carlo.settembrini@esteri.it
Tiziana Miano, Assistant to the Director
tiziana.miano@esteri.it

Italian Cultural Society of Edmonton
14230 - 133 Ave. NW, Edmonton AB T5L 4W4
Tel: 780-453-6182; *Fax:* 780-451-0669
Overview: A small local organization
Mission: To foster retention of Italian cultural heritage; to operate a Cultural Centre in order to provide its members and other community organizations with facilities for carrying out their activities; To initiate and undertake activities which bring closer ties between the Italian community and the Canadian community at large.
Activities: Annual Senior's dinner; monthly dinner dances; annual banquets
Chief Officer(s):
Alfredo Pitrini, Contact

Italian Pentecostal Church of Canada See General Conference of the Canadian Assemblies of God

IWK Health Centre Foundation (IWKF)
#B220, 5855 Spring Garden Rd., Halifax NS B3H 4S2
Tel: 902-470-8085
Toll-Free: 800-595-2266
foundationmail@iwk.nshealth.ca
iwkfoundation.org
www.facebook.com/iwkfoundation
twitter.com/IWKFoundation
www.instagram.com/iwkfoundation
Overview: A small local charitable organization
Mission: To raise money on behalf of the IWK Health Centre that helps fund research & improve patient care
Finances: *Annual Operating Budget:* Greater than $5 Million
Staff Member(s): 31
Chief Officer(s):
Jennifer Gillivan, ICD.D, President & CEO
jennifer.gillivan@iwk.nshealth.ca

Iyengar Yoga Association of Canada
c/o Theresa McDiarmid, 22 Langley Ave., Toronto ON M4K 1B5
info@iyengaryogacanada.com
www.iyengaryogacanada.com
www.facebook.com/IYAC.ACYI
twitter.com/CanadaIyengar
Overview: A small national organization
Membership: *Fees:* $42-$173.25
Chief Officer(s):
Theresa McDiarmid, Membership

J. Armand Bombardier Foundation / Fondation J. Armand Bombardier
#2100, 115 rue Metcalfe, Montréal QC H3B 2V6
Tel: 514-876-4555
fondation@fjab.qc.ca
www.fondationbombardier.ca
www.linkedin.com/company/3200024
www.facebook.com/FondationBombardier
twitter.com/FondationJAB
Overview: A small national charitable organization founded in 1965
Mission: To support organizations focused on the social & economic development of their communities
Activities: Providing resources on issues relevant to community & philanthropic organizations; Offering training sessions, conferences, workshops, & networking activities through Philagora, a capacity building program for non-profits
Chief Officer(s):
Maeva Dourthe, Coordinator, Administration

J. Douglas Ferguson Historical Research Foundation
PO Box 5079, Shediac NB E4P 8T8
Tel: 506-532-6025
www.nunet.ca/jdfhrf/main.php
Overview: A small national charitable organization founded in 1971
Mission: To give financial support to a broad range of activities aimed at preserving the heritage of early historical currency, banks & other issuers of money, coins, tokens & paper money issued throughout Canada since the 18th century.
Finances: *Funding Sources:* Bequests; donation
Activities: Undergraduate/Graduate Essay Contests
Chief Officer(s):
Geoffrey G. Bell, Deputy Chair
gbel@nb.sympatico.ca
Chris Faulkner, Chairman
Len Buth, Treasurer
Awards:
• Rev. Dr. Bernard O'Connor Scholarship
Eligibility: Applicants must be numismatic students, advanced collectors, university students & educators wishing to pursue post-graduate studies in Canadian numismatics, banking history, economics, currency development & related studies; *Amount:* Up to $10,000 *Contact:* Graham Esler, 56 Glass Ave., London, ON

Jack Miner Migratory Bird Foundation, Inc.
360 RR#3 West, Kingsville ON N9Y 2E5
Tel: 519-733-4034; *Fax:* 519-733-0932
info@jackminer.com
www.jackminer.ca
www.facebook.com/JackMinerMigratoryBirdSanctuary
twitter.com/JM_Sanctuary
instagram.com/Jackminer1865
Overview: A small local charitable organization founded in 1904
Mission: The sanctuary provides food, shelter & protection to migratory water fowl, tags birds & tracks migration patterns
Finances: *Funding Sources:* Private
Staff Member(s): 3; 12 volunteer(s)
Activities: *Awareness Events:* National Wildlife Week, April
Chief Officer(s):
Mary E. Baruth, Executive Director

Jack.org
#505, 192 Spadina Ave., Toronto ON M5T 2C2
Tel: 416-425-2494
www.jack.org
www.facebook.com/jackdotorg
twitter.com/jackdotorg
www.instagram.com/jackdotorg
Overview: A medium-sized national charitable organization
Mission: To eliminate the stigmatization of mental illness; To enhance the lives of young people through programs, initiatives & outreach
Activities: Providing workshops & presentations on mental health; *Speaker Service:* Yes
Chief Officer(s):
Eric Windeler, Executive Director
Meetings/Conferences:
• Jack Summit 2018 6th Annual Conference, March, 2018, Toronto, ON
Scope: National

Jacob's Ladder - The Canadian Foundation for Control of Neurodegenerative Disease
#400, 505 Consumers Rd., Toronto ON M2J 4V8
Tel: 416-485-0078; *Fax:* 800-611-2449
info@jacobsladder.ca
www.jacobsladder.ca
www.facebook.com/1544472979109094
twitter.com/JacobsLadder_
Overview: A medium-sized national charitable organization founded in 1998
Mission: To raise awareness of neurodegenerative disease; To lower occurrences of neurodegenerative disease in the future
Chief Officer(s):
Jeff Schwartz, Co-Founder
Ellen Schwartz, Co-Founder

Jake Thomas Learning Centre
7575 Townline Rd., Site 1, RR#1, Wilsonville ON N0E 1Z0
Tel: 519-445-0779; *Fax:* 519-445-0802
www.jakethomaslearningcentre.ca
www.facebook.com/jake.centre?fref=ts
Also Known As: The Friends of the Jake Thomas Learning Centre
Overview: A small local charitable organization founded in 1993
Mission: To raise funds both on & off Six Nations Reserve to enhance & support the Jake Thomas Learning Centre which is dedicated to preserve & promote Iroquoian Heritage & the traditional way of life; fundraising for the Jake Thomas Learning Centre building & the Friends of the Jake Thomas Learning Centre organization to be able to operate all events to the aims stated above
Finances: *Annual Operating Budget:* $50,000-$100,000
Staff Member(s): 2; 8 volunteer(s)
Membership: *Committees:* Archive; Building
Activities: Workshops: Wampum-bead making, Cornhusk weaving; Tutoring languages: Mohawk, Cayuga, Onondaga; *Library:* Open to public by appointment

Chief Officer(s):
Phyllis Hill, Treasurer
Dan Longboat, Director
Ken Maracle, Director
Yvonne Thomas, Executive Director

Jaku Konbit
211 Bronson Ave., Ottawa ON K1R 6H5
Tel: 613-567-0600
www.jakukonbit.com
Overview: A small local organization founded in 2000
Mission: To enhance the quality of life for underpriviledged youth & minority groups, particularly those of African & Caribbean descent.
Chief Officer(s):
Kenneth Campbell, President

Jamaica Association of Montréal Inc.
4065, rue Jean-Talon ouest, Montréal QC H4P 1W6
Tel: 514-737-8229
www.jam-montreal.com
www.facebook.com/JamaicaAssociationOfMontrealInc
Overview: A small local organization
Mission: Educational, cultural & social activities for the Jamaican community; after-school & evening classes & programs for youth & adults; Saturday morning program for children; restaurant on site

Jamaican Canadian Association (JCA)
995 Arrow Rd., Toronto ON M9M 2Z5
Tel: 416-746-5772; *Fax:* 416-746-7035
info@jcaontario.org
jcaontario.org
Overview: A small international charitable organization founded in 1962
Mission: To provide social interaction among members & to facilitate desirable relations with Canadian society; to represent the Caribbean community on public matters; to respond to the diverse social service needs of members; to facilitate economic, social & cultural integration of Caribbean people within Canadian society
Membership: *Member Profile:* People of Jamaican & Caribbean descent
Activities: Immigrant Settlement & Adaption Program (ISAP); Caribbean Canadian Seniors' Club; Program for Abused & Assaulted Black Women; Pal Program (provides supportive, one-on-one relationship between Caribbean/Black children ages 7-16 & caring adults); Caribbean Youth & Family Services; Youth Development Programs; Multicultural Community Outreach; Parenting/Healthy Babies; Meals on Wheels; Job Assistance; Computer Training; Teen Drop-In; Spring & Summer Camp; Under 12 Program on Delinquency; *Library:* Marcus Garvey Resource Library; Open to public
Chief Officer(s):
Audrey Campbell, President
Awards:
• "I Have a Dream" Scholarship
• Marcus Mosiah Garvey Scholarship
• Dr. Ezra Nesbeth Scholarship

Jamaican Ottawa Community Association (JOCA)
211 Bronson Ave., Ottawa ON K1R 6H5
Tel: 613-523-9085
jamaicanottawaassn@yahoo.com
www.jakukonbit.com
www.facebook.com/136531216361229
Overview: A small local organization
Mission: To enhance the quality of life for the Jamaican communtiy in Ottawa
Membership: *Fees:* $20 student/associate; $25 senior; $30 general; $50 family; *Committees:* Jamday; Youth; Brunch; Education; Heroes Gala; Building Fund; Variety Concert; Christmas Party; Seniors; Fundraising
Chief Officer(s):
Joanne Robinson, President

Jamaican Self-Help Organization (JSH)
PO Box 1992, Peterborough ON K9J 7X7
Tel: 705-743-1671
info@jshcanada.org
jshcanada.org
Overview: A small international charitable organization founded in 1981 overseen by Ontario Council for International Cooperation
Mission: To foster the development of healthy Jamaican communities through partnership based on mutual respect, understanding & a shared vision of self determination; To foster

an understanding of global forces North & South & their interconnectedness
Member of: Canadian Council for International Cooperation
Finances: *Annual Operating Budget:* $250,000-$500,000; *Funding Sources:* Donations; foundations; religious groups 100 volunteer(s)
Membership: 25; *Committees:* Finance; Fundraising; Personnel; Strategic Planning; Global Education; Jamaican Program
Activities: Supporting education & youth programs in Jamaica; *Speaker Service:* Yes
Chief Officer(s):
Cathie Morrissey, President

James Bay Association for Community Living
PO Box 460, #18, 4 St., Moosonee ON P0L 1Y0
Tel: 705-336-2378; *Fax:* 705-336-2694
www.jbacl.org
Previous Name: Moosonee-Moose Factory Association for Community Living
Overview: A small local charitable organization
Mission: To address the residential requirements of individuals with developmental disabilities; To integrate developmentally disabled people into their home communities; To work towards supported employment & independent living (area covers west coast of James Bay) so that all persons live in a state of dignity, share in all elements of living in the community & have the opportunity to participate effectively
Member of: Community Living Ontario
Finances: *Annual Operating Budget:* $250,000-$500,000; *Funding Sources:* Ministry of Community & Social Services; Ministry of Municipal Affairs & Housing
Staff Member(s): 13
Membership: 1-99
Activities: *Awareness Events:* Community Living Month, May
Chief Officer(s):
Weena Saunders, President
Mark Storey, Executive Director
mark.storey@jbacl.org

James Bay Tourism *Voir* Tourisme Baie-James

Jane Austen Society of North America (JASNA)
#105, 195 Wynford Dr., Toronto ON M3C 3P3
Toll-Free: 800-836-3911
info@jasna.org
www.jasna.org
www.facebook.com/285332054855712
Overview: A medium-sized international organization founded in 1979
Mission: To promote an appreciation of Jane Austen & her writings
Finances: *Funding Sources:* Membership dues; contributions
Membership: 4,500; *Fees:* $18 student; $30 individual; $45 family; $60 sustaining; $500 life; $700 family life
Activities: Tours of Austen sites in England; scholarly publishing; student essay contest; lectures; teas; Jane Austen's birthday Dec. 16; *Speaker Service:* Yes
Chief Officer(s):
Nancy Stokes, Canadian Membership Secretary
naristo@rogers.com
Publications:
• Persuasions: The Jane Austen Journal
Type: Journal; *Frequency:* Annually; *ISSN:* 0821-0314

Alberta - Calgary Chapter
Calgary AB
jasnacalgary@jasnacalgary.ca
www.jasnacalgary.ca
twitter.com/JasnaCalgary

Alberta - Edmonton Chapter
Edmonton AB
Tel: 780-451-9243
Chief Officer(s):
Bridget Toms, Contact
twolegsgood@telus.net

British Columbia - Vancouver Chapter
698 Wellington Place, North Vancouver BC V7K 3A1
Tel: 604-988-6806
www.jasnavancouver.ca
Chief Officer(s):
Michelle Siu, Coordinator
jasnavancouverRC@gmail.com

British Columbia - Victoria Chapter
Victoria BC
Tel: 250-384-0193
Chief Officer(s):
Joan Millar, Contact
sophycroft-at-sea@shaw.ca

Manitoba Region
Winnipeg MB
Tel: 204-475-3200
Chief Officer(s):
Celine Kear, Contact
Lorna Pyrih, Contact

Nova Scotia Region
NS
janeausteninnovascotia.wordpress.com
Chief Officer(s):
Anne Thompson, Regional Coordinator, 902-477-2341
anne_thompson@ns.sympatico.ca

Ontario - London Chapter
12569 Boston Dr., RR#41, London ON N6H 5L2
Tel: 519-657-3994
jasnalondonchapter@hotmail.com
Chief Officer(s):
Nancy Johnson, Contact

Ontario - Ottawa Chapter
Ottawa ON
Tel: 613-523-1485
Chief Officer(s):
Emily Arrowsmith, Coordinator
emily_arrowsmith@caf-fca.org

Ontario - Toronto Chapter
Toronto ON
Chief Officer(s):
Louise Yearwood, Coordinator
lyearwood@havergal.on.ca

Québec - Montréal & Québec Chapters
Montréal QC
Tel: 514-481-4555
jasna.montrealqc@gmail.com
jasna-mtl.weebly.com
Chief Officer(s):
Elaine Bander, Coordinator

Saskatchewan - Moose Jaw Chapter
Moose Jaw SK
Chief Officer(s):
Brenda Babich, Contact, 306-692-3224
babich.brenda@sasktel.net

Jane Finch Community & Family Centre
#108, 440 Jane St., Toronto ON M3N 2K4
Tel: 416-663-2733; *Fax:* 416-663-3816
admin@janefinchcentre.org
www.janefinchcentre.org
www.facebook.com/people/Jane-Finch-Centre/1518951464
Overview: A medium-sized local charitable organization
Mission: To operate with a strong commitment to social justice, community engagement, & collaboration
Membership: *Fees:* $3 individual; $5 non-resident; $10 group
Chief Officer(s):
Michelle Dagnino, Executive Director

The Jane Goodall Institute of Canada
c/o University of Toronto Mailroom, 563 Spadina Cres., Toronto ON M5S 2J7
Tel: 416-978-3711; *Fax:* 416-978-3713
Toll-Free: 888-882-4467
info@janegoodall.ca
www.janegoodall.ca
www.facebook.com/JaneGoodallCAN
twitter.com/JaneGoodallCAN
www.youtube.com/user/JaneGoodallCAN
Overview: A small national charitable organization founded in 1994
Mission: To support wildlife research, education & conservation; To promote informed & compassionate action to improve the environment shared by all Earth's living creatures
Affiliation(s): The Jane Goodall Institute - USA; The Jane Goodall Institute - UK
Finances: *Annual Operating Budget:* $250,000-$500,000; *Funding Sources:* Private donations; lecture honorariums
Staff Member(s): 8; 32 volunteer(s)
Membership: 100-499
Activities: Chimp Guardian Program - sponsor orphan chimpanzees; Roots & Shoots - Jane Goodall Institute's global environmental & humanitarian program; Providing training in environmental & humanitarian education; Raising awareness of endangered animals; Promoting activities to aid the well-being of wild & captive chimpanzees; *Awareness Events:* Earth Day, April 22; Peace Day, Sept. 21; *Internships:* Yes
Chief Officer(s):
Andria Teather, CEO
andria.teather@janegoodall.ca
Publications:
• Jane Goodall Institute of Canada eNewsletter
Type: Newsletter; *Frequency:* 2 pa; *Price:* Free online
• Roots & Shoots Canada eNewsletter [a publication of the Jane Goodall Institute of Canada]
Type: Newsletter; *Price:* Free online

Janeway Children's Hospital Foundation
300 Prince Philip Dr., St. John's NL A1B 3V6
Tel: 709-777-4640; *Fax:* 709-777-4489
janewayfoundation@easternhealth.ca
www.janewayfoundation.nf.ca
www.facebook.com/JanewayNL
twitter.com/JanewayNL
www.youtube.com/user/janewayfoundation
Overview: A small local charitable organization
Mission: To raise money on behalf of the Janeway Childnren's Hospital that helps fund research & improve patient care
Chief Officer(s):
Lynn Sparkes, Executive Director

Japan Automobile Manufacturers Association of Canada
#460, 151 Bloor St. West, Toronto ON M5S 1S4
Tel: 416-968-0150; *Fax:* 416-968-7095
jama@jama.ca
www.jama.ca
Also Known As: JAMA Canada
Overview: A medium-sized international organization founded in 1984
Mission: To promote increased understanding of economic & trade matters pertaining to the motor vehicle industry; To encourage closer cooperation between Canada & Japan; To represent the interests of members
Activities: Providing information about the Japanese-affiliated auto industry in Canada; Producing statistics on Japanese-affiliated motor vehicle production, imports & expors & sales in Canada
Chief Officer(s):
Takashi Sekiguchi, Chairman

Japan External Trade Organization (Toronto) (JETRO)
#1600, 181 University Ave., Toronto ON M5H 3M7
Tel: 416-861-0000; *Fax:* 416-861-9666
inquiry@jetro.go.jp
www.jetro.go.jp/canada
Also Known As: JETRO Toronto
Overview: A medium-sized international organization founded in 1958
Mission: A non-profit organization that promotes trade and investment between Japan and the rest of the world. Canadian branches in Toronto and Vancouver.
Activities: Trade & investment promotion; Research

The Japan Foundation, Toronto / Kokosai Koryu Kikin Toronto Nihon Bunka Centre
#213, 131 Bloor St. West, Toronto ON M5S 1R1
Tel: 416-966-1600; *Fax:* 416-966-9773
info@jftor.org
www.japanfoundationcanada.org
www.facebook.com/JFToronto
twitter.com/JFToronto
Overview: A medium-sized international organization founded in 1972
Mission: To promote Japanese culture abroad; to offer a broad range of programs designed to further cultural exchange with Japan, with an emphasis on Japanese studies at the post-secondary level & Japanese language study
Finances: *Funding Sources:* Japanese Ministry of Foreign Affairs
Staff Member(s): 14
Activities: *Library:* Open to public
Chief Officer(s):
Ishida Takashi, Executive Director
Chieko Kono, Director
Awards:
• The Japan Foundation Fellowships
Scholars, researchers, artists & other professionals are provided an opportunity to conduct research or pursue projects in Japan. Term of award is from two to 14 months, depending on category; annual application deadline is Dec. 1 for funding year beginning the following April 1

• The Japan Foundation Scholarships & Programs
The Foundation offers a wide range of programs in more than 180 countries, including the following: exchange of persons (fellowships); support for Japanese-language instruction; support for Japanese studies; support for arts-related exchange; support for media exchange

The Japan Society Canada
#604, 157 Adelaide St. West, Toronto ON M5H 4E7
Tel: 416-366-4196; *Fax:* 416-366-4176
www.japansocietycanada.com
Overview: A small international organization founded in 1989
Mission: To enable Canadian & Japanese executives & academic leaders to meet on a continuing basis to discuss matters of mutual interest; To further economic relationships between Canada & Japan; To acquire greater cultural understanding; To support business, educational, & cultural exchanges
Member of: Canadian Society of Association Executives
Affiliation(s): National Association of Japan-America Societies
Finances: *Funding Sources:* Membership fees
Membership: 100-499
Chief Officer(s):
John Craig, Chair, 416-865-7128
Ben Ciprietti, President
ben@japansocietycanada.com

Japanese Canadian Association of Yukon (JCAY)
jcayukon@gmail.com
info.jcayukon.org/intro-e.html
Overview: A medium-sized provincial organization

Japanese Canadian Citizens Association *See* Greater Vancouver Japanese Canadian Citizens' Association

Japanese Canadian Cultural Centre (JCCC)
6 Garamond Ct., Toronto ON M3C 1Z5
Tel: 416-441-2345; *Fax:* 416-441-2347
jccc@jccc.on.ca
www.jccc.on.ca
twitter.com/jccc_toronto
www.youtube.com/jccctoronto
Overview: A small national charitable organization founded in 1964
Mission: To serve as a gathering place for Japanese-Canadians & those interested in Japanese culture.
Finances: *Funding Sources:* Membership fees; donations; space rental; class fees; special events
Staff Member(s): 9
Membership: 4,300; *Fees:* Schedule available
Activities: Cultural & martial arts classes & performances; festivals; *Awareness Events:* Spring Festival, March; Natsu Matsuri, July; Issei Day, Oct.; *Speaker Service:* Yes
Chief Officer(s):
James Heron, Executive Director
Gary Kawaguchi, President
Sharon Marubashi, Secretary

Japanese Cultural Association of Manitoba (JCAM)
180 McPhillips Ave., Winnipeg MB R3E 2J9
Tel: 204-774-5909; *Fax:* 204-775-6029
m.jccc@shaw.ca
www.mjccc.org
Merged from: Manitoba Japanese Canadian Citizens' Association; Manitoba Japanese Canadian Cultural Centre
Overview: A small local organization
Mission: To promote a strong Japanese Canadian identity in Manitoba; To advocate for equal rights for all persons
Member of: National Association of Japanese Canadians (NAJC)
Membership: *Fees:* Family $30; Individual $20
Activities: Raising funds for the Canadian Museum of Human Rights; Presenting events to celebrate Japanese Canadian arts & culture; Sponsoring workshops related to Japanese culture, heritage, & history; *Library:* MJCCC Library
Chief Officer(s):
Art Miki, President
Awards:
• Harold Hirose Education Fund
Eligibility: Student; *Amount:* $1,500
Publications:
• The History of Japanese Canadians in Manitoba
Type: Book

Les jardins botaniques royaux *See* Royal Botanical Gardens

Jasper Environmental Association (JEA)
PO Box 2198, Jasper AB T0E 1E0
Tel: 780-852-4152
jea2@telus.net
www.jasperenvironmental.org
Overview: A medium-sized local organization
Mission: To support Parks Canada in administering Jasper National Park in accordance with Canadian legislation, Parks Canada principles and policies and the wishes of the Canadian public.
Finances: *Funding Sources:* Membership fees
Membership: *Fees:* $5

Jasper Park Chamber of Commerce
Robson House, PO Box 98, 409 Patricia St., Jasper AB T0E 1E0
Tel: 780-852-4621
admin@jpcc.ca
www.jasperparkchamber.ca
www.linkedin.com/company/jasper-park-chamber-of-commerce
www.facebook.com/JasperParkChamber
twitter.com/JasperParkChamb
Overview: A small local organization founded in 1952
Mission: To advocate on behalf of its members
Staff Member(s): 3
Membership: 180; *Member Profile:* Local businesses
Chief Officer(s):
Rusty Noble, President
Pattie Pavlov, General Manager

Jazz Yukon
PO Box 31307, Whitehorse YT Y1A 5P7
Tel: 867-334-2789
info@jazzyukon.ca
www.jazzyukon.ca
Overview: A medium-sized provincial charitable organization
Mission: To promote & present jazz in the Yukon through an annual integrated program of live jazz presentations & jazz education outreach
Membership: *Member Profile:* Jazz musicians & fans
Activities: Offering the Jazz on the Wing concert series

Jean Tweed Treatment Centre (JTC)
215 Evans Ave., Toronto ON M8Z 1J5
Tel: 416-255-7359; *Fax:* 416-255-9021
info@jeantweed.com
www.jeantweed.com
www.facebook.com/JeanTweedCentre
twitter.com/jeantweedcentre
Overview: A small provincial charitable organization founded in 1983
Mission: To provide services for women with substance abuse or gambling problems & their families with a focus on children 0-6
Member of: Federation of Community Mental Health & Addictions Programs; Toronto Area Addictions Services Committee; Residential Addiction Services of Ontario
Finances: *Annual Operating Budget:* $3 Million-$5 Million
Staff Member(s): 98; 30 volunteer(s)
Activities: Child care; parenting services; *Awareness Events:* Staying on Course Charity Golf Classic, Sept.; *Internships:* Yes
Chief Officer(s):
Nancy Bradley, Executive Director
Katherine Devlin, Chair
Erin MacRae, Vice Chair/ Treas.

Jeffery Hale Community Services in English
1250, ch Sainte-Foy, Québec QC G1S 2M6
Tel: 418-684-5333
Toll-Free: 888-984-5333
www.jhsb.ca
Previous Name: Holland Centre
Overview: A small local organization
Staff Member(s): 35

The Jerrahi Sufi Order of Canada
Canadian Sufi Cultural Centre, 270 Birmingham St., Toronto ON M8V 2E4
jerrahi@jerrahi.ca
www.jerrahi.ca
Overview: A medium-sized national organization
Mission: To disseminate knowledge about Islam and the Halveti-Jerrahi Order of Dervishes to which the Jerrahi Sufi Order members belong
Activities: Weekly gatherings; Discussions and discourse on Sufi music, art & poetry; Prayer & Zikrullah (Sufi remembrance ceremony)

Jersey Canada (JC)
#9, 350 Speedvale Ave. West, Guelph ON N1H 7M7
Tel: 519-821-1020; *Fax:* 519-821-2723
info@jerseycanada.com
www.jerseycanada.com
www.linkedin.com/company-beta/8435935
www.facebook.com/jerseycanada
twitter.com/@jerseycanada
www.instagram.com/jerseycanada
Previous Name: Jersey Cattle Association of Canada
Overview: A medium-sized national organization founded in 1901
Mission: To represent & promote the Jersey breed & encourage market development domestically & internationally; To provide & maintain a registration system, catalogues & pedigree information; To update classification & milk production records
Member of: Canadian Livestock Genetics Association
Finances: *Funding Sources:* Membership fees; The Jersey Store; Federal government
Membership: *Committees:* Executive; Finance; Youth; Genetic Improvement; Marketing; Milk Marketing; Strategic Planning; Publications; Joint Classification Representatives; Show; Disciplinary; Awards Review
Activities: Communicating with members & liaising with industry; Providing classification & herdbook services; Presenting awards & scholarships
Chief Officer(s):
Tim Sargent, President, 905-263-8823
David Morey, First Vice-President, 780-698-2267
Patrick MacDougall, Second Vice-President, 450-921-0520
Kathryn Roxburgh, General Manager, 519-821-1020 Ext. 102
kathryn@jerseycanada.com
Atlantic
10032 Hwy. 224, Middle Musquodoboit NS B0N 1X0
Tel: 902-568-2211
Chief Officer(s):
David Cole, Secretary
dhcole2010@gmail.com
British Columbia
27336 River Rd., Langley BC V1M 3L7
Tel: 604-857-5445
Chief Officer(s):
Caryl Fair, Secretary
caryl.fair@ledalite.com
Manitoba
PO Box 7, St Alphonse MB R0K 1Z0
Tel: 204-836-2072; *Fax:* 204-836-2371
Chief Officer(s):
Henry Delichte, Secretary
clubmilk@xplornet.com
Ontario
#9, 350 Speedvale West, Guelph ON N1H 7M7
Tel: 519-766-9980; *Fax:* 519-766-9981
ontario@jerseycanada.com
www.jerseyontario.ca
Chief Officer(s):
Kristie Rivington, Secretary
Québec
4685, boul Laurier ouest, Saint-Hyacinthe QC J2S 3T8
Tel: 450-771-2227; *Fax:* 450-778-9637
quebec@jerseycanada.com
Chief Officer(s):
Sandra Berthiaume, Provincial Secretary
West
RR#2, Didsbury AB T0M 0W0
Tel: 403-335-3028
Chief Officer(s):
Adrian Haeni, Co-Secretary
lonepinej@xplornet.com

Jersey Cattle Association of Canada *See* Jersey Canada

Jersey West
c/o Adrian Haeni, Didsbury AB
Tel: 403-335-3028
www.jerseycanada.com/jerseywest
www.facebook.com/gowestjerseywest
Overview: A small provincial organization overseen by Jersey Canada
Activities: Promoting Jersey cattle; Organizing showcase sales
Chief Officer(s):
Adrian Haeni, Contact
lonepinej@cciwireless.ca

Jerusalem Foundation of Canada Inc / La Fondation de Jerusalem du Canada Inc
#1040, 2, Place Alexis Nihon, Montréal QC H3Z 3C1

Canadian Associations / Jessie's - The June Callwood Centre for Young Women

Tel: 514-484-1289; Fax: 514-482-9640
Toll-Free: 877-484-1289
www.jerusalemfoundation.ca
Overview: A small national organization founded in 1970
Mission: To enhance & enrich the quality of life for all residents of the city of Jerusalem
Membership: Committees: Gala Tribute
Activities: Funds are raised in Canada to support a host of programs which span the arts, social services, health care, historical preservation & beautification
Chief Officer(s):
Monica E. Berger, National Executive Director

Jessie's - The June Callwood Centre for Young Women
205 Parliament St., Toronto ON M6A 2Z4
Tel: 416-365-1888; Fax: 416-365-1944
mail@jessiescentre.org
jessiescentre.org
www.facebook.com/jessiescentre
Overview: A small local charitable organization
Mission: To provide help & social services to pregnant teenagers, young parents & their children
Finances: Annual Operating Budget: $500,000-$1.5 Million
Staff Member(s): 21
Chief Officer(s):
Maritza Sanchez, Executive Director

Jessie's Hope Society
#400, 601 West Broadway St., Vancouver BC V5Z 4C2
Tel: 604-466-4877; Fax: 604-466-4897
Toll-Free: 877-288-0877
www.jessieshope.org
Previous Name: Association for Awareness & Networking around Disordered Eating
Overview: A small national organization founded in 1985
Staff Member(s): 2
Chief Officer(s):
Heather Quick Rajala

Jesuit Development Office (JDO)
c/o Jesuit in English Canada, Provincial Office, 43 Queen's Park Cres. East, Toronto ON M5S 2C3
Tel: 416-962-4500; Fax: 416-962-4501
jdo@jesuits.ca
www.jesuits.ca
Overview: A medium-sized international charitable organization founded in 1940
Mission: To raise & provide the funds necessary for the support of Jesuit brothers & priests in formation, in ministry & in their senior years
Member of: Jesuit Fathers & Brothers of Upper Canada
Staff Member(s): 6
Membership: under 200
Chief Officer(s):
Erica Zlomislic, Communications Officer
communications@jesuits.ca

Jesus Youth Canada
canada@jesusyouth.org
canada.jesusyouth.org
www.facebook.com/280977068632989
twitter.com/jycanada
Overview: A small international organization
Mission: To reach out to other young people as witnesses of the joy of life in Christ & in service of the Catholic Church; To offer ministries of youth, intercession, prayer, & Angel's Army; To provide a focus on a Jesus-centred life; To take guidance from the international Jesus Youth International Team which coordinates worldwide activities
Affiliation(s): Toronto Archdiocese
Membership: Member Profile: Open to young people
Activities: Offering prayer programs, the sacraments, & worship programs; Working with youth in local parishes in faith & leadership development; Providing monthly youth meetings, fellowship, eFellowship, youth camps, & retreats
Chief Officer(s):
Soby Joseph, East Area Coordinator, 647-459-9360
Xavier Mathew, Central Area Coordinator, 647-988-2659
Thomas Varghese, West Area Coordinator, 416-456-7050
Publications:
• Jesus Youth International Newsletter
Type: Newsletter; **Frequency:** Quarterly
Profile: Global JY initiatives & activities

Jeune Barreau de Québec
#300, boul Jean-Lesage, #RC-21, Québec QC G1K 8K6
Tél: 418-802-5816; Téléc: 418-522-4560
jbq@jeunebarreaudequebec.ca
jeunebarreaudequebec.ca
www.facebook.com/379908232065460
twitter.com/JBQ_Quebec
Aperçu: Dimension: petite; Envergure: provinciale; fondée en 1914
Mission: Pour représenter les intérêts de ses membres au niveau national et international
Affiliation(s): Barreau de Québec; Desjardins; Juris Concept; SOQUIJ; Médicassurance
Membre: 1000+; Critères d'admissibilite: Les avocats qui exercent au Québec qui ont moins de 10 ans d'expérience; Comités: La formation; les services aux membres; Service de consultations à la Cour du Québec, Division des petites créances; Tournoi de hockey bottines; Concours oratoire; Tournoi de soccer; Tournoi de balle-molle; Cocktail de Noël; Journée Noël des enfants; Relations extérieures
Activités: Formations; Consultations pro bono; Tournoi de balle-molle; Concours oratoire; Tournoi de soccer; Tournoi de Hockey
Membre(s) du bureau directeur:
Jad-Patrick Barsoum, Président, Conseil d'administration

Jeune chambre de commerce de Montréal (JCCM)
#700, 1435, rue Saint-Alexandre, Montréal QC H3A 2G4
Courriel: info@jccm.org
www.jccm.org
www.facebook.com/jeunechambremtl
twitter.com/jccm_mtl
Aperçu: Dimension: petite; Envergure: locale; fondée en 1931
Mission: De favoriser le développement professionnel & personnel des jeunes gens d'affaires de Montréal, de promouvoir leurs intérêts & de contribuer à l'essor du milieu dans lequel ils évoluent
Membre de: Chambre de commerce du Québec
Membre: Montant de la cotisation: 70$ étudiant; 150$ individuel; 120$ 3 à 10 membres corporatif; 95$ 11 à 20 membres; 85$ 21 membres et plus; Critères d'admissibilite: Être âgé entre 18 et 40 ans; Comités: Gestion
Membre(s) du bureau directeur:
Sandrine Archambault, Directrice générale, 514-845-4951 Ext. 23
sarchambault@jccm.org

Jeune chambre de commerce de Québec
#249, 4600, boul Henri-Bourassa, Québec QC G1H 3A5
Tél: 418-622-6937
jccq@jccq.qc.ca
www.jccq.qc.ca
www.facebook.com/JeunechambredecommercedeQuebec
twitter.com/jccdequebec
www.youtube.com/user/JeunechambredeQuebec
Aperçu: Dimension: petite; Envergure: locale
Mission: Créer des opportunités de développement personnel et professionnel pour des gens d'affaires
Membre(s) du personnel: 3
Membre: 600; Montant de la cotisation: 66$ étudiant; 66-120 corporatif; Comités: Activités sociales; Intégration; International; Affaires publiques
Membre(s) du bureau directeur:
Justine Audy, Présidente
Virginie Gourdeau, Directrice générale par intérim
vgourdeau@jccq.qc.ca

Jeune chambre internationale du Canada See Junior Chamber International Canada

Jeunes canadiens pour une civilisation chrétienne
880, av Louis Fréchette, Québec QC G1S 3N3
Tél: 418-683-5222
Aperçu: Dimension: petite; Envergure: locale; fondée en 1977
Mission: Travailler avec la jeunesse pour préserver les principes catholiques et éducatifs
Finances: Budget de fonctionnement annuel: Moins de $50,000
Membre(s) du bureau directeur:
Frank R. Murphy, President

Jeunes en forme Canada See Active Healthy Kids Canada

Jeunes en partage
CP 441, Chibougamau QC G8P 2X8
Tél: 418-748-2935
Aperçu: Dimension: petite; Envergure: locale
Membre(s) du bureau directeur:
Dany Larouche, Responsable

Jeunes Entreprises du Canada See Junior Achievement Canada

Jeunesse Acadienne et Francophone de l'Île-du-prince-Édouard (JAFLIPE)
Centre Belle-Alliance, 5, av Maris Stella, Summerside PE C1N 6M9
Tél: 902-888-3346; Téléc: 902-436-6936
coord1@ssta.org
www.jeunesseacadienne.ca
www.facebook.com/JeunesseAcadienne
twitter.com/JeunesseAcadie
Aperçu: Dimension: petite; Envergure: provinciale; Organisme sans but lucratif
Mission: Permettre aux jeunes acadiens et francophones de la province à vivre et s'épanouir en français
Membre de: Fédération de la jeunesse canadienne-française inc; Société Nationale de l'Acadie
Finances: Budget de fonctionnement annuel: $50,000-$100,000
Membre(s) du personnel: 1; 20 bénévole(s)
Membre: 150+; Montant de la cotisation: 10$
Activités: Regroupements de jeunes pour promouvoir des activités en sports, éducation, économie, politique et communications; promouvoir la langue française et la culture acadienne auprès des jeunes
Membre(s) du bureau directeur:
Myranda Kelly, Présidente
myranda_4@hotmail.com
Katelyn Gill, Vice-Président
Kelly McGrath, Secrétaire-trésorière

Jeunesse Canada Monde See Canada World Youth

Jeunesse du Monde
920, rue Richelieu, Québec QC G1R 1L2
Tél: 418-694-1222; Téléc: 418-694-1227
Aperçu: Dimension: petite; Envergure: internationale; Organisme sans but lucratif; fondée en 1959
Mission: Former des jeunes à devenir des citoyens responsables et à s'engager dans la lutte contre toutes les formes de racisme, l'éducation à la paix, le respect des droits humains, la création de rapports de justice entre les peuples, le développement durable; proposer des programmes d'éducation planétaire dans les institutions scolaires et dans les groupes communautaires; appuyer des projects de développement durable menés par des partenaires en Amérique latine, en Afrique, en Asie; offrir aux jeunes la possibilité de vivre des stages au sud et au nord
Finances: Budget de fonctionnement annuel: $500,000-$1.5 Million
Membre(s) du personnel: 9; 200 bénévole(s)
Membre(s) du bureau directeur:
Nicole Riberdy, Directrice

Jeunesse j'écoute See Kids Help Phone

Jeunesse Lambda
CP 321125, Succ. Saint-André, Montréal QC H2L 4Y5
Tél: 514-528-7535
info@jeunesselambda.org
www.algi.qc.ca/asso/jlambda/
www.facebook.com/JLAMBDA.MTL
Aperçu: Dimension: petite; Envergure: locale
Mission: Groupe d'accueil francophone de discussion et d'activités par et pour les jeunes gais, lesbiennes, bisexuel(les).
Membre: 60

La Jeunesse Youth Orchestra (LJYO)
PO Box 134, Port Hope ON L1A 3W3
Toll-Free: 866-460-5596
info@ljyo.ca
www.ljyo.ca
www.facebook.com/lajeunesseyouthorchestra
Previous Name: North York Symphony Youth Orchestra
Overview: A small local charitable organization overseen by Orchestras Canada
Mission: To provide young musicians from the Port Hope area with the enriching experience of performing a wide range of symphonic music.
Member of: Orchestras Canada
Staff Member(s): 10
Membership: Member Profile: Musicians aged 10-22 in woodwinds, brass, strings or percussion
Activities: Performing three public concerts per year; Holding regular rehearsals
Chief Officer(s):
Michael Lyons, Music Director

Laurie Mitchell, Music Director

Jeunesses Musicales du Canada (JMC) / Jeunesses Musicales of Canada (JMC)
305, av du Mont-Royal est, Montréal QC H2T 1P8
Tél: 514-845-4108; *Téléc:* 514-845-8241
Ligne sans frais: 877-377-7951
www.jmcanada.ca
www.facebook.com/330606301320
twitter.com/JMC_1949
www.youtube.com/user/jeunessesmusicalesca
Aperçu: *Dimension:* moyenne; *Envergure:* nationale; Organisme sans but lucratif; fondée en 1949
Mission: To promote Canadian musical artists & develop audiences
Membre de: Jeunesses Musicales International; Conseil québécois de la musique
Finances: *Budget de fonctionnement annuel:* $500,000-$1.5 Million
Membre(s) du personnel: 15; 400 bénévole(s)
Membre: 40 member centres in Ontario, Québec & New Brunswick; *Montant de la cotisation:* Schedule available
Activités: Family concerts; school concerts; touring artists (Ovation Series); Jeunesses Musicales World Orchestra (Orchestre mondial des jeunesses musicales) held each summer in a different member country of the JMI; *Stagiaires:* Oui; *Bibliothèque:* Bibliothèque publique rendez-vous
Membre(s) du bureau directeur:
Danièle LeBlanc, Directeur général et artistique, 514-845-4108 Ext. 226
dleblanc@jmcanada.ca
Claudia Morissette, Directrice, Artistic Operations, 514-845-4108 Ext. 250
cmorissette@jmcanada.ca
Nathalie Allen, Directrice, Services financiers, 514-845-4108 Ext. 248
nallen@jmcanada.ca
Marie Lamoureux, Directrice, Communications, 514-845-4108 Ext. 222
mlamoureux@jmcanada.ca

Jeunesses Musicales of Canada *Voir* Jeunesses Musicales du Canada

Jeux du Commonwealth Canada *See* Commonwealth Games Canada

Jeux Olympiques Spéciaux du Québec Inc. (OSQ) / Québec Special Olympics
#200, 1274, rue Jean-Talon est, Montréal QC H2R 1W3
Tél: 514-843-8778; *Téléc:* 514-843-8223
Ligne sans frais: 877-743-8778
www.olympiquesspeciaux.qc.ca
www.facebook.com/olympiquesspeciauxquebec
twitter.com/athletesOSQ
Aperçu: *Dimension:* petite; *Envergure:* provinciale; fondée en 1981 surveillé par Special Olympics Canada
Mission: Les Olympiques spéciaux, actifs dans plus de 170 pays, ont pour mission d'enrichir, par le sport, la vie des personnes présentant une déficience intellectuelle. Plus de 3.7 millions d'athlètes spéciaux, de tous âges, sont inscrits dans le monde dont plus de 31,000 au Canada et 4,850 aux programmes récréatifs scolaire ou compétitifs offerts dans toutes les régions du Québec. Les 14 sports officiels sont pratiqués à l'intérieur d'un réseau de compétitions annuelles, comptant plus de 80 événements conçus pour tous les niveaux d'habiletés.
Membre de: Special Olympics Canada
Membre: *Comités:* Comité provincial des programmes
Membre(s) du bureau directeur:
Daniel Granger, Président

Les Jeux Olympiques Spéciaux du Yukon *See* Special Olympics Yukon

Jewellers Vigilance Canada Inc. (JVC)
#600, 27 Queen St. East, Toronto ON M5C 2M6
Tel: 416-368-4840; *Fax:* 416-368-5552
Toll-Free: 800-636-9536
info@jewellersvigilance.ca
www.jewellersvigilance.ca
Overview: A small national organization founded in 1987
Mission: To advance ethical practices, establish a level playing field for the Canadian jewellery industry & provide crime prevention education for the trade.

Jewish Chamber of Commerce / Chambre de commerce juive
1, carré Cummings, Montréal QC H3W 1M6
Tel: 514-345-2645
info@jccmontreal.com
www.jccmontreal.com
www.linkedin.com/groups/3063
www.facebook.com/jccmontreal
twitter.com/jccmontreal
Overview: A small local organization founded in 1995
Mission: To provide a network for Jewish business people in Montréal
Member of: A division of Federation CJA
Chief Officer(s):
Elana Minz, Director
elana.minz@federationcja.org

Jewish Child & Family Services (JCFS)
123 Doncaster St., #C200, Winnipeg MB R3N 2B2
Tel: 204-477-7430; *Fax:* 204-477-7450
Other Communication: After Hours Emergency Phone: 204-946-9510
info@jcfswinnipeg.org
www.jcfswinnipeg.org
www.linkedin.com/company/jewish-child-and-family-service
Overview: A small local charitable organization founded in 1952
Mission: To provide social services that focus on 3 areas: care of children, family problems, & concern for the needs of recent immigrants
Finances: *Funding Sources:* Jewish Federation of Winnipeg/Combined Jewish Appeal; United Way; Provincial government; Jewish Foundation of Manitoba
Staff Member(s): 40
Activities: Providing counselling & child welfare services; Offering newcomer support services; Facilitating workshops on contemporary family issues; *Library*
Chief Officer(s):
Al Benarroch, Executive Director

Jewish Community Centre of Greater Vancouver
950 West 41 Ave., Vancouver BC V5Z 2N7
Tel: 604-257-5111; *Fax:* 604-257-5119
reception@jccgv.bc.ca
www.jccgv.com
www.facebook.com/256610085406
Overview: A small local organization founded in 1928
Mission: To bring together the Jewish community in Vancouver & provide activities & programs to the population
Member of: Vancouver Cultural Alliance
Membership: *Fees:* Schedule available
Activities: *Library:* Isaac Waldman Jewish Public Library; Open to public
Chief Officer(s):
Eldad Goldfarb, Executive Director
eldad@jccgv.bc.ca

Jewish Community Centre of Winnipeg *See* Rose & Max Rady Jewish Community Centre

Jewish Community Council of Montreal
6825, boul Decarie, Montréal QC H3W 3E4
Tel: 514-739-6363; *Fax:* 514-739-7024
Toll-Free: 866-739-6363
info@mk.ca
www.mk.ca
Also Known As: Montréal Kosher
Overview: A small local licensing organization founded in 1922
Affiliation(s): Synagogues, Jewish organisations
Activities: Kosher supervision, counselling, divorces, disputes, community work

Jewish Community Foundation of Montréal / Fondation communautaire juive de Montréal
#510, carré Cummings, Montréal QC H3W 1M6
Tel: 514-345-6414; *Fax:* 514-345-6410
info@jcfmontreal.org
www.jcfmontreal.org
www.facebook.com/jcfmontreal
Overview: A small local charitable organization founded in 1971
Finances: *Funding Sources:* Donations
Chief Officer(s):
Robert A. Kleinman, FCA, Executive Director
robert.kleinman@jcfmontreal.org
Joel Segal, President
president@jcfmontreal.org
Brenda Gewurz, Vice-President
seniorvp@jcfmontreal.org
Marlene Gerson, Director, Marketing
marlene.gerson@jcfmontreal.org
Joelle Mamane, Director, Finance
joelle.mamane@jcfmontreal.org
Awards:
• Jewish Community Foundation of Montreal Undergraduate Scholarships Program
• Jewish Community Foundation of Montreal Specialized & Postgraduate Study Scholarships Program
• Jewish Community Foundation of Montreal Scholarships for Study in Israel

Jewish Family & Child (JFCS)
4600 Bathurst St., 1st Fl., Toronto ON M2R 3V3
Tel: 416-638-7800; *Fax:* 416-638-7943
info@jfandcs.com
www.jfandcs.com
www.linkedin.com/company/jewish-family-&-child
www.facebook.com/JFandCS
www.youtube.com/user/jewishfamilyandchild
Overview: A small local charitable organization founded in 1868
Mission: To support the healthy development of individuals, families & communities in the Greater Toronto Area through prevention, protection, counselling, education & advocacy services, within the context of Jewish values
Affiliation(s): Family Service Ontario; Association of Jewish Family & Children's Agencies; Canadian Family Services Accreditation Program; Children's Mental Health Ontario; Council on Accreditation; Ontario Association of Children's Aid Societies; Ontario Association of Social Workers; Ontario College of Social Workers and Social Service Workers
Staff Member(s): 120
Activities: *Internships:* Yes; *Speaker Service:* Yes
Chief Officer(s):
Brian Prousky, Executive Director
Publications:
• Family Matters [a publication of Jewish Family & Child]
Type: Newsletter; *Frequency:* Monthly
Profile: Contains agency updates & important news
• Jewish Family & Child Annual Report
Type: Report; *Frequency:* a.

Downtown Branch
35 Madison Ave., Toronto ON M5R 2S2
Tel: 416-961-9344; *Fax:* 416-961-9351

Thornhill Branch - Family Resource Centre & Clothing Cupboard
Promenade Mall, #313, 1 Promenade Circle, Thornhill ON L4J 1Z8
Tel: 905-882-8509; *Fax:* 905-695-0157

Toronto Branch - Jerome D. Diamond Adolescent Centre
196 Keewatin Ave., Toronto ON M4P 1Z8
Tel: 416-482-3023; *Fax:* 416-482-3014

York Region Branch
Joseph & Wolf Lebovic JCC, #242, 9600 Bathurst St., Vaughan ON L6A 3Z8
Tel: 905-303-5838; *Fax:* 905-303-5892

Jewish Family Services - Calgary (JESC)
#420, 5920 - 1A St. SW, Calgary AB T2H 0G3
Tel: 403-287-3510; *Fax:* 403-287-3735
info@jfsc.org
www.jfsc.org
Overview: A medium-sized local charitable organization founded in 1961
Mission: To strengthen the community by helping people in the spirit of Jewish tradition & values
Member of: Association of Jewish Family & Children's Agencies; Family Service Canada
Finances: *Annual Operating Budget:* $500,000-$1.5 Million; *Funding Sources:* United Way; Calgary Foundation; Jewish Community Council; City of Calgary; B'Nai B'Rith Lodge; Mazon Canada
Staff Member(s): 21; 70 volunteer(s)
Activities: *Library:* by appointment
Chief Officer(s):
Marty Hornstein, Executive Director

Jewish Family Services Edmonton
#100, 8702 Meadowlark Rd. NW, Edmonton AB T5R 5W5
Tel: 780-454-1194; *Fax:* 780-482-4784
info@jfse.org
www.jfse.org
www.facebook.com/jfs.edmonton
twitter.com/JFS_Edmonton
Overview: A small local charitable organization founded in 1955

Canadian Associations / Jewish Family Services of Ottawa-Carleton (JFSOC)

Mission: To provide strength & support to individuals & families in need, in a manner sensitive to Jewish values; To promote economic & social justice
Member of: Edmonton Camber of Voluntary Organizations
Finances: *Annual Operating Budget:* $1.5 Million-$3 Million; *Funding Sources:* Claims Conference; United Way; FCSS; Foundations; Donations; Service fees
Staff Member(s): 50; 100 volunteer(s)
Membership: 120
Activities: Offering bereavement support, counselling, & seniors & immigrant support services; *Internships:* Yes; *Speaker Service:* Yes; *Library:* Edmonton Bereavement Support Library
Chief Officer(s):
Larry Derkach, Executive Director

Jewish Family Services of Ottawa-Carleton (JFSOC)
#300, 2255 Carling Ave., Ottawa ON K2B 7Z5
Tel: 613-722-2225; *Fax:* 613-722-7570
info@jfsottawa.com
www.jfsottawa.com
Also Known As: Jewish Social Service Agency of Ottawa-Carleton
Overview: A small local charitable organization founded in 1979
Mission: Through Jewish traditions, values & culture, to build a community where people can learn to care for themselves & each other with dignity, respect & compassion
Affiliation(s): Family Service Ontario Agencies; Family Service Canada Agencies
Activities: Social services; seniors services; settlement services; employment services; *Internships:* Yes *Library:* Resource Centre; Not open to public
Chief Officer(s):
Mark Zarecki, Executive Director
mzarecki@jfsottawa.com

The Jewish Federation of Greater Toronto *See* UJA Federation of Greater Toronto

Jewish Federation of Greater Vancouver (JFGV)
#200, 950 West 41 Ave., Vancouver BC V5Z 2N7
Tel: 604-257-5100; *Fax:* 604-257-5110
reception@jewishvancouver.com
www.jewishvancouver.com
www.facebook.com/jewishvancouver
twitter.com/JewishVancouver
Overview: A medium-sized local charitable organization founded in 1932
Mission: Committed to building a strong, vibrant & enduring Jewish community in the Lower Mainland, in Israel & throughout the world by nurturing those values, practices & traditions which sustain & enrich Judaism & the Jewish people; to serve the Greater Vancouver Jewish community by working in partnership with community members & other agencies to: identify & plan for community needs; enhance mutual cooperation; raise & allocate funds for programs & services locally, nationally, in Israel & worldwide; develop & sustain leadership; encourage involvement in Jewish communal life
Affiliation(s): United Israel Appeal Federations Canada; United Jewish Communities
Finances: *Annual Operating Budget:* Greater than $5 Million
Staff Member(s): 21
Membership: *Committees:* Executive; Finance; Allocations Planning; Israel & Overseas Affairs; Yom Hazikaron; High School Debate; Axis Steering
Chief Officer(s):
Ezra S. Shanken, Chief Executive Officer
eshanken@jewishvancouver.com

Jewish Federations of Canada - UIA (JFC-UIA)
#315, 4600 Bathurst St., Toronto ON M2R 3V3
Tel: 416-636-7655; *Fax:* 416-636-9897
info@jfcuia.org
www.jewishcanada.org
www.facebook.com/JewishFederationsofCanadaUIA
twitter.com/jfcuia
www.youtube.com/user/JewishFedofCanada
Also Known As: United Israel Appeal of Canada
Overview: A small international organization founded in 1967
Mission: To raise money for Canadian Jewish organizations & to promote their efforts
Chief Officer(s):
Linda Kislowicz, President & CEO
Awards:
• Aviva Barth Scholarship Fund
Awarded to assist Jewish youth attend & participate in Israel programs & Jewish summer camps *Eligibility:* Post-Bar/Bat Mitzvah teens living in small Jewish communities in Ontario

Jewish Foundation of Manitoba (JFM)
123 Doncaster St., #C400, Winnipeg MB R3N 2B2
Tel: 204-477-7520; *Fax:* 204-477-7527
Toll-Free: 855-284-1918
info@jewishfoundation.org
www.jewishfoundation.org
twitter.com/jfm_mb
Overview: A small provincial charitable organization
Mission: To encourage & facilitate the creation & growth of endowment funds to enable the community to reach its potential
Staff Member(s): 10
Membership: *Committees:* Board of Directors; Governors; Jewish Foundation of Manitoba USA, Inc.; Audit & Finance; Distributions; Endownment Book of Life; Governance & Nominating; Grants; Investment; Scholarship; Special Awards; Special Grants; Women's Endowment Fund Grants
Activities: Provide scholarships & grants
Chief Officer(s):
Marsha Cowan, Chief Executive Officer, 204-477-7520
mcowan@jewishfoundation.org

Jewish Free Loan Toronto (JFLT)
Lipa Green Centre for Jewish Community Services, Sherman Campus, #340, 4600 Bathurst St., Toronto ON M2R 3V3
Tel: 416-635-1217; *Fax:* 416-635-8926
info@jewishfreeloan.ca
www.jewishfreeloan.ca
www.facebook.com/JewishFreeLoanToronto
Previous Name: Toronto Jewish Free Loan Cassa
Overview: A small local charitable organization founded in 1924
Mission: Offering interest-free loans to needy individuals of the Jewish community in the Greater Toronto Area
Affiliation(s): UJA Federation of Greater Toronto; United Way Toronto
Staff Member(s): 3
Chief Officer(s):
Marra Messinger, Executive Director
Publications:
• Free Loan Matters [a publication of Jewish Free Loan Toronto]
Type: Newsletter; *Frequency:* s-a.
Profile: Features profiles on borrowers

Jewish Genealogical Institute of British Columbia
c/o 950 West 41 Ave., Vancouver BC V5Z 2N7
Tel: 604-321-9870
jgibc@yahoo.com
jgibc.shutterfly.com
Overview: A small provincial organization founded in 1992
Mission: To research genealogy & encourage the exploration of the community's Jewish heritage.
Membership: *Fees:* $30 individual; $45 family

Jewish Genealogical Society of Canada *See* Jewish Genealogical Society of Toronto

Jewish Genealogical Society of Toronto (JGST)
2901 Bayview Ave., Toronto ON M2K 2S3
Tel: 647-247-6414
info@jgstoronto.ca
www.jgstoronto.ca
www.facebook.com/jgstoronto
twitter.com/jgsoftoronto
www.jgstoronto.blogspot.com
Also Known As: JGS of Toronto
Previous Name: Jewish Genealogical Society of Canada
Overview: A medium-sized local charitable organization founded in 1985
Mission: To foster interest in Jewish genealogical research; To facilitate the pursuit of Jewish genealogical research domestically & internationally; To provide a forum for the exchange of knowledge & information among people interested in Jewish genealogy
Member of: International Association of Jewish Genealogical Societies (IAJGS)
Finances: *Annual Operating Budget:* Less than $50,000; *Funding Sources:* Membership fees; Donations; Product sales 25 volunteer(s)
Membership: 165; *Fees:* $40 individual; $18 student; *Committees:* Cemetery Records; Memorial Plaques; Newsletter; Programming; Social Media; Speaker's Bureau; Toronto Jewish Families Research Project; Website
Activities: Monthly programming from Septembr to June, with speakers & workshops of interest to people researching their Jewish roots; Publishing newsletter; Conducting the Cemetery Digital Photography Project; *Internships:* Yes; *Speaker Service:* Yes; *Library:* JGS of Toronto Collection, Toronto Reference Library

Chief Officer(s):
Marla Waltman, President
president@jgstoronto.ca
Les Kelman, Past President
lkelman@jgstoronto.ca
Neil Richler, Coordinator, Membership
membership@jgstoronto.ca
Publications:
• Shem Tov [a publication of the Jewish Genealogical Society of Toronto]
Type: Newsletter; *Editor:* Judy Kasman
Profile: Includes practical research techniques, book reviews, personal research accounts, society news, & information onJewish genealogy & history

Jewish General Hospital Foundation (JGHF) / Hôpital général juif fondation (HGJF)
3755, ch de la Côte-Sainte-Catherine, #A107, Montréal QC H3T 1E2
Tel: 514-340-8251; *Fax:* 514-340-8220
info@jghfoundation.org
www.jghfoundation.org
www.facebook.com/FHGJ.JGHF
Overview: A small local charitable organization founded in 1969
Mission: To raise money on behalf of the Jewish General Hospital in order to fund research & improve patient care
Finances: *Annual Operating Budget:* Greater than $5 Million
Staff Member(s): 31
Membership: *Committees:* Executive; Invesment & Finance; Audit; Governance; Strategic Planning; Human Resources; Nominating; Grants
Chief Officer(s):
Myer Bick, President & CEO
mbick@fon.jgh.mcgill.ca

Jewish Heritage Centre of Western Canada Inc. (JHC)
123 Doncaster St., #C140, Winnipeg MB R3N 2B2
Tel: 204-477-7460; *Fax:* 204-477-7465
jewishheritage@jhcwc.org
www.jhcwc.org
Also Known As: Jewish Heritage Centre
Previous Name: Jewish Historical Society of Western Canada
Overview: A small local charitable organization founded in 1999
Mission: The Jewish Heritage Centre is composed of The Jewish Historical Society of Western Canada, Marion & Ed Vickar Jewish Museum of Western Canada, Freeman Foundation Holocaust Education Centre & Genealogical Institute
Membership: 300+; *Fees:* $50
Activities: Research; Holocaust education; preservation of documents, photos, sound; *Speaker Service:* Yes; *Library:* Archives
Chief Officer(s):
Ilana Abrams, General Manager

Jewish Historical Society of BC (JHS)
c/o Jewish Museum & Archives of BC, 6184 Ash St., Vancouver BC V5Z 3G9
Tel: 604-257-5199
info@jewishmuseum.ca
www.jewishmuseum.ca
Overview: A small provincial charitable organization founded in 1971
Mission: To document & preserve the history of the Jewish community in BC & its contribution to the development of BC
Member of: Vancouver Historical Society; Canadian Jewish Historical Society; British Columbia Museum Association; Association for Canadian Jewish Studies; BC Historical Federation
Finances: *Funding Sources:* Membership dues; donations; sale of books, videos, cards; government & foundation grants
Membership: *Fees:* $54 basic; $75 institutions; *Member Profile:* Members of the British Columbia Jewish Community
Activities: Lecture series; exhibits & displays; archival reference service; *Library:* Nemetz Jewish Community Archives; by appointment
Chief Officer(s):
Perry Seidelman, President

Jewish Historical Society of Southern Alberta (JHSSA)
1607 - 90 Ave. SW, Calgary AB T2V 4V7
Tel: 403-444-3171; *Fax:* 403-253-7915
jhssa@shaw.ca
www.jhssa.org
twitter.com/JHSSA1
Overview: A small local charitable organization founded in 1990

Mission: To preserve the history of Jewish individuals, businesses, organizations & activities of southern Alberta
Finances: *Funding Sources:* Fundraising; private donations; membership fees
Staff Member(s): 1
Membership: *Fees:* $18 individual; $36 family; $50 patrons; $100 benefactors
Activities: Oral history interviews; gathering of museum & archival material; *Library:* Harry & Martha Cohen Library; Open to public by appointment
Chief Officer(s):
Betty Sherwood, President

Jewish Historical Society of Western Canada *See* Jewish Heritage Centre of Western Canada Inc.

Jewish Immigrant Aid Services of Canada (JIAS) / Services canadiens d'assistance aux immigrants juifs
#300, 2255 Carling Ave., Ottawa ON K2B 7Z5
Tel: 613-722-2225; *Fax:* 613-722-5750
national@jias.org
www.jias.org
Overview: A medium-sized international charitable organization founded in 1922
Mission: To serve the needs of Jewish immigrants & refugees; To facilitate the legal entry of Jewish immigrants to Canada; to provide services for immigration, naturalization, resettlement & integration
Finances: *Funding Sources:* Jewish community; Government grants
Activities: *Speaker Service:* Yes
Chief Officer(s):
Mark Zarecki, Executive Director, 613-722-2225, Fax: 613-722-5750
mzarecki@jfsottawa.com
Awards:
• Jewish Immigrant Aid Services of Canada General Scholarships Program
Eligibility: Jewish immigrant students who have been in Canada for nine years or less
• John Hirsch Awards For The Arts And The Performing Arts
Eligibility: Jewish immigrant students who have been in Canada for nine years or less
• The Michael And Marta Herling Award
Eligibility: Jewish immigrant students who have been in Canada for nine years or less
• Stephan and Sophie Lewar JIAS Canada Endowment Fund
Agence Ometz
1 carré Cummings, 515s, ch de la Côte-Sainte-Catherine, Montréal QC H3W 1M6
Tel: 514-342-0000; *Fax:* 514-342-2371
info@ometz.ca
www.ometz.ca
www.linkedin.com/company/agence-ometz
www.facebook.com/AgenceOmetz
twitter.com/ometz
www.youtube.com/agenceometz
Mission: To provide employment, family, and immigration services to the Montreal Jewish Community.
Chief Officer(s):
Howard Berger, Co-Executive Director
Gail Small, Co-Executive Director

Jewish Immigrant Aid Services of Canada - Montreal *See* Jewish Immigrant Aid Services of Canada

Jewish Information Referral Service Montréal (JIRS) / Le Service juif d'information et de référence
1, carré Cummings, Montréal QC H3W 1M6
Tel: 514-735-3541; *Fax:* 514-735-8972
fcja@federationcja.org
www.federationcja.org
www.facebook.com/federationcja
twitter.com/federationcja
www.youtube.com/federationcja
Previous Name: Jewish Information Service Montreal
Overview: A small local organization
Mission: To bring together the Jewish community in Montréal
Affiliation(s): Alliance of Information & Referral Systems Inc.
Finances: *Annual Operating Budget:* Greater than $5 Million
Membership: *Committees:* Allocations & Community Relations; Audit; Budget & Finance; Compensation; Development; Governance & Ethics
Activities: *Rents Mailing List:* Yes; *Library:* Not open to public
Chief Officer(s):
Deborah Corber, CEO

Jewish Information Service Montreal *See* Jewish Information Referral Service Montréal

Jewish Information Service of Greater Toronto (JIST)
4600 Bathurst St., Toronto ON M2R 3V3
Tel: 416-635-5600; *Fax:* 416-849-1005
jinfo@ujafed.org
www.jewishtoronto.com
Overview: A small local organization founded in 1973
Mission: To offer information & referral to walk-ins, by phone, & by e-mail; To support & maintain "Doing Jewish in Toronto"
Member of: UJA Federation of Greater Toronto
Affiliation(s): Latner Centre for Jewish Knowledge & Heritage of UJA Federation

Jews for Jesus
10 Huntingdale Blvd., Toronto ON M1W 2S5
Tel: 416-444-7020; *Fax:* 805-267-4141
toronto@jewsforjesus.ca
www.jewsforjesus.ca
www.facebook.com/jewsforjesuscanada
twitter.com/jewsforjesuscan
Overview: A small local charitable organization founded in 1981
Mission: Jews for Jesus Canada is a Jewish evangelistic agency dedicated to bringing the Gospel into places where a significantly Jewish testimony is needed.
Member of: Canadian Council of Christian Charities; Evangelical Fellowship of Canada; Interdenominational Foreign Mission Association
Staff Member(s): 6; 10 volunteer(s)
Chief Officer(s):
Andrew Barron, Canadian Director/Missionary
andrew.barron@jewsforjesus.ca

Jews for Judaism
PO Box 41032, 2795 Bathurst St., Toronto ON M6B 4J6
Tel: 416-789-0020; *Fax:* 416-789-0030
Toll-Free: 866-307-4362
toronto@jewsforjudaism.ca
www.jewsforjudaism.ca
www.facebook.com/jewsforjudaismcanada
twitter.com/JewsforJudaism1
www.youtube.com/user/JewsforJudaismCanada
Overview: A small international organization
Mission: To counteract the efforts of numerous cults & Christian missionary groups that target Jews in Canada for conversion
Finances: *Funding Sources:* Corporate sponsorship, donations
Activities: Free preventative educational programs, innovative educational materials & specialized counselling services
Chief Officer(s):
Julius Ciss, Executive Director
juliusciss@bellnet.ca

JMJ Children's Fund of Canada Inc
PO Box 20051, 390 Rideau St. East, Ottawa ON K1N 9N5
amdg3@rogers.com
www.jmjchildren.ca
Overview: A small national organization founded in 1972
Mission: To assist children in need of food, medication & schooling; to provide physiotherapy for the physically disabled
Activities: sponsoring students in schools in Malawi, Zaire, Haiti, and the Dominican Republic; supporting medical clinics that treat children for malnutrition, tuberculosis, tropical diseases and AIDS; Providing support to children so that the family unit stays together in difficult times; Emergency relief to children in crisis situations; providing food, clothing and medical assistance when required

Jobs Unlimited
1079 York St., Fredericton NB E3B 3S4
Tel: 506-458-9380
www.jobsunlimited.nb.ca
Overview: A small local charitable organization
Mission: To facilitate work placement for individuals who face barriers to employment
Affiliation(s): United Way
Staff Member(s): 45
Activities: *Awareness Events:* Employers Appreciation Night, Oct.; *Internships:* Yes; *Speaker Service:* Yes
Chief Officer(s):
Maynard Shore, Chair
Abdel Belhadjsalah, Executive Director

Jockey Club du Canada *See* Jockey Club of Canada

Jockey Club of Canada / Jockey Club du Canada
PO Box 66, Stn. B, Toronto ON M9W 5K9
Tel: 416-675-7756; *Fax:* 416-675-6378
jockeyclub@bellnet.ca
www.jockeyclubcanada.com
twitter.com/jockeyclubofCAN
Overview: A small national licensing organization founded in 1973
Mission: Promote good quality racing throughout Canada
Member of: Thoroughbred Racing Industry participants in Canada
Affiliation(s): The Jockey Club (New York)
Membership: *Member Profile:* Liaises with foreign Jockey Clubs; promotes Thoroughbred ownership; and represents Canada at international racing conferences.
Activities: *Library:* Open to public by appointment
Chief Officer(s):
James Lawson, Chief Steward
Stacie Roberts, Executive Director

Jockeys Benefit Association of Canada (JBAC)
c/o Thoroughbred Race Office, 555 Rexdale Blvd., Toronto ON M9W 5L2
Overview: A small national organization
Mission: The Jockey's Benefit Association of Canada (JBAC) has been in operation for over 40 years as a non profit corporation which operates to assist & represent jockeys as a group across Canada. Operated under a number of directors across the country, the JBAC is the official spokesperson of jockeys in Canada.
Membership: 150

Jodo Shinshu Buddhist Temples of Canada
11786 Fentiman Pl., Richmond BC V7E 6M6
Tel: 604-272-3330; *Fax:* 604-272-6865
jsbtcheadquarters@gmail.com
www.bcc.ca
www.facebook.com/654327614577625
www.youtube.com/user/livingdharmacentre
Previous Name: Buddhist Churches of Canada
Overview: A medium-sized national charitable organization founded in 1933
Mission: Propagation of Buddhism
Affiliation(s): Jodo Shinshu Hongwanji, Kyoto
Finances: *Annual Operating Budget:* $100,000-$250,000
Staff Member(s): 9
Membership: 2,500; *Fees:* $45
Activities: *Speaker Service:* Yes; *Library:* by appointment
Chief Officer(s):
Tatsuya Aoki, Bishop
Leslie Kawamura, Director, Living Dharma Centre

The Joe Brain Foundation
#1700, 360 Main St., Winnipeg MB R3C 3Z3
Overview: A small provincial charitable organization founded in 1977
Mission: To advance education, with particular emphasis on mining research & education, medical research & relief of poverty
Finances: *Annual Operating Budget:* $50,000-$100,000; *Funding Sources:* Investment income
4 volunteer(s)
Membership: 1-99

John Gordon Home
596 Pall Mall St., London ON N5Y 2Z9
Tel: 519-433-3951; *Fax:* 519-433-1314
johngordonhome@lrah.ca
www.johngordonhome.ca
Also Known As: London Regional AIDS Hospice
Overview: A small local organization founded in 1991 overseen by Canadian AIDS Society
Mission: To provide compassionate care to people with AIDS & HIV in a comforting, non-discriminatory, homelike environment; to provide medical, psychosocial, spiritual & personal support
Member of: Ontario AIDS Network; Canadian AIDS Society; Ontario Non-Profit Housing Association
Finances: *Annual Operating Budget:* $250,000-$500,000; *Funding Sources:* Donations; Ministry of Health - Long-Term Care Division
Membership: 200; *Fees:* $10
Activities: Personal care; palliative care; psychological support; supportive housing; *Internships:* Yes; *Speaker Service:* Yes
Chief Officer(s):
Bruce Rankin, Executive Director
brucerankin@lrah.ca

John Howard Society of Alberta
10523 - 100 Ave., 2nd Fl., Edmonton AB T5J 0A8
Tel: 780-423-4878
info@johnhoward.ab.ca
www.johnhoward.ab.ca
www.linkedin.com/company/john-howard-society-of-alberta
www.facebook.com/JohnHowardSocietyOfAlberta
twitter.com/johnhowardab
Overview: A medium-sized provincial organization overseen by The John Howard Society of Canada
Mission: To advance the work of the John Howard Societies across Alberta through education, research, & promotion on issues of crime prevention & public safety
Activities: Preparing research papers on criminal justice issues; Responding to & communicating with government regarding legislation & policy; Administering pension, health, & insurance benefits for the local Societies

Calgary
917 - 9 Ave. SE, Calgary AB T2G 0S5
Tel: 403-266-4566; Fax: 403-265-2458
info@calgaryjohnhoward.org
www.calgaryjohnhoward.org
www.facebook.com/315661361870559
www.youtube.com/channel/UC8K2Vtof0HHMJU46BN3sC2Q
Chief Officer(s):
Gordon Sand, Executive Director
gord.sand@cjhs.ca

Edmonton
#401, 10010 - 105 St., Edmonton AB T5J 1C4
Tel: 780-426-7590; Fax: 780-425-1549
www.johnhoward.ab.ca/services/edmonton
www.facebook.com/YEGJohnHoward
twitter.com/YEGJohnHoward
Chief Officer(s):
Maureen Collins, Executive Director
mcollins@johnhoward.org

Grande Prairie
#200, 10135 - 101 Ave., Grande Prairie AB T8V 0Y4
Tel: 780-532-0373; Fax: 780-538-4931
info@johnhowardgp.ca
www.johnhoward.ab.ca/services/grande-prairie
www.facebook.com/268350653203939
twitter.com/gpjohnhoward
Chief Officer(s):
Penny Mickanuck, Executive Director

Lethbridge
903 - 3rd Ave. North, Lethbridge AB T1H 0H5
Tel: 403-327-8202; Fax: 403-320-6613
lethjhs@telus.net
www.johnhoward.ab.ca/services/lethbridge
Chief Officer(s):
Lynne Harrold, Executive Director

Medicine Hat
#208, 535 - 3 St. SE, Medicine Hat AB T1A 0H2
Tel: 403-526-5916; Fax: 403-526-4636
mhjhs@telusplanet.net
www.johnhoward.ab.ca/services/medicine-hat
Chief Officer(s):
Gary Straub, Executive Director

Red Deer
4916 - 50 St., Red Deer AB T4N 1X7
Tel: 403-343-1770; Fax: 403-346-8740
admin@jhsrd.ca
www.jhsrd.ca
Chief Officer(s):
Marion Carlson, Executive Director
marionc@jhsrd.ca

The John Howard Society of British Columbia
763 Kingsway, Vancouver BC V5V 3C2
Tel: 604-872-5651; Fax: 604-872-8737
info@johnhowardbc.ca
www.johnhowardbc.ca
Overview: A medium-sized provincial charitable organization founded in 1931 overseen by The John Howard Society of Canada
Mission: To prevent crime & reform the justice system through alternative programming
Finances: *Funding Sources:* Government; Foundations; Non-profit Organizations; Donations
Chief Officer(s):
Tim Veresh, Executive Director
Awards:
- The Ed Griffin Educational Bursary

The John Howard Society of Canada / Société John Howard du Canada
809 Blackburn Mews, Kingston ON K7P 2N6
Tel: 613-384-6272; Fax: 613-384-1847
national@johnhoward.ca
www.johnhoward.ca
twitter.com/JohnHoward_Can
Overview: A medium-sized national charitable organization founded in 1978
Mission: To promote effective, just, & humane responses to the causes & consequences of crime; To assist individuals who have come into conflict with the law; To advocate for change in the criminal justice process; To educate the community on matters involving prison conditions, criminal law, & its applications today
Finances: *Annual Operating Budget:* $250,000-$500,000; *Funding Sources:* Federal Grant; Donations; Project Contracts
Staff Member(s): 2; 15 volunteer(s)
Membership: *Fees:* Schedule available; *Member Profile:* Provincial/territorial societies
Activities: Providing education, advocacy, & outreach activities; Working with individuals in federal & provincial correctional facilities; Disseminating information to encourage change; *Speaker Service:* Yes
Chief Officer(s):
Catherine Latimer, Executive Director
Publications:
- John Howard Society of Canada Annual Report
Type: Report; *Frequency:* Annually

The John Howard Society of Manitoba (JHSMB)
583 Ellice Ave., Winnipeg MB R3B 1Z7
Tel: 204-775-1514; Fax: 204-775-1670
office@johnhoward.mb.ca
www.johnhoward.mb.ca
www.facebook.com/137026123009646
twitter.com/JHSofMB
Previous Name: Manitoba Prisoner's Aid Group
Overview: A medium-sized provincial organization founded in 1957 overseen by The John Howard Society of Canada
Mission: To achieve restorative justice through measures that resolve conflicts, repair them, & restore peaceful relations in society
Member of: John Howard Society of Canada
Finances: *Funding Sources:* Solicitor General of Canada; United Way; Manitoba Department of Justice
Staff Member(s): 13
Activities: *Library:* Justice Resource Centre; Open to public
Chief Officer(s):
John Hutton, Executive Director
jhutton@johnhoward.mb.ca
Publications:
- The Inside Scoop [a publication of The John Howard Society of Manitoba, Inc.]
Type: Newsletter
Profile: Prison literacy & art, created by inmates for inmates
- The John Howard Society of Manitoba, Inc. Annual Report
Type: Yearbook; *Frequency:* Annually
Profile: Reports on the society's key areas, such as reintegration, literacy, volunteers, & finances

The John Howard Society of New Brunswick, Inc.
68 Carleton St., Saint John NB E2L 2Z4
Tel: 506-657-5547; Fax: 506-649-2006
info@johnhowardsj.ca
www.johnhowardnb.ca
www.facebook.com/JohnHowardSocietyOfSaintJohn
twitter.com/JHS_SaintJohn
Overview: A small provincial organization overseen by The John Howard Society of Canada
Mission: To promote peace through understanding & reaction of problems with the criminal disciplinary system
Staff Member(s): 5
Activities: Providing education, advocacy, & outreach services
Chief Officer(s):
William Bastarache, Executive Director

Southeastern New Brunswick
15 Flanders Ct., Moncton NB E1C 0K6
Tel: 506-854-3499; Fax: 506-854-2057
info@johnhowardsenb.com
www.johnhowardsenb.com
www.facebook.com/JHSSENB
twitter.com/jhssenb
Chief Officer(s):
Joanne Murray, Executive Director

The John Howard Society of Newfoundland & Labrador (JHSNL)
342 Pennywell Rd., St. John's NL A1E 1V9
Tel: 709-726-5500; Fax: 709-726-5509
info@jhsnl.ca
www.johnhowardnl.ca
www.facebook.com/631568636899443
twitter.com/JohnHowardNL
Overview: A medium-sized provincial charitable organization founded in 1951 overseen by The John Howard Society of Canada
Mission: To reduce crime primarily by providing program opportunities for the rehabilitation of offenders
Member of: John Howard Society of Canada
Finances: *Annual Operating Budget:* $500,000-$1.5 Million
Membership: *Committees:* Executive; Personnel; Scholarship; Nomination
Activities: Providing public education & reform activities; Offering group home services; *Awareness Events:* John Howard Society Week, Feb.
Chief Officer(s):
Bryan Purcell, President

Corner Brook
278 Curling St., Corner Brook NL A2H 6G1
Tel: 709-785-7656; Fax: 709-785-2927
johnhowardnl.ca/service/loretta-bartlett-home-youth
Chief Officer(s):
Rosemary Mullins, Coordinator

Stephenville
92 West St., Stephenville NL A2N 1E4
Tel: 709-643-2903; Fax: 709-643-3084
johnhowardnl.ca/local-offices/stephenville-office
Chief Officer(s):
Audrey Gracie, Director
audreygracie@nf.aibn.com

The John Howard Society of Northwest Territories
4901 - 48th St., Yellowknife NT X1A 3S3
Tel: 867-920-4276; Fax: 867-669-9715
reception_jhsnwt@theedge.ca
Overview: A small local charitable organization founded in 1992 overseen by The John Howard Society of Canada
Member of: John Howard Society of Canada
Finances: *Funding Sources:* Dept. of Justice; Revenue
Activities: Organizing diversion programs; Providing community education services

The John Howard Society of Nova Scotia
#1, 541 Sackville Dr., Lower Sackville NS B4C 2S1
Tel: 902-429-6429
contact@ns.johnhoward.ca
ns.johnhoward.ca
Overview: A small provincial organization overseen by The John Howard Society of Canada
Chief Officer(s):
Flora MacLeod, President

The John Howard Society of Ontario
#603, 111 Peter St., Toronto ON M5V 2H1
Tel: 416-408-4282; Fax: 416-408-2991
info@johnhoward.on.ca
www.johnhoward.on.ca
twitter.com/reducingcrime
www.youtube.com/user/JohnHowardSocietyON
Overview: A medium-sized provincial charitable organization founded in 1929 overseen by The John Howard Society of Canada
Mission: To promote effective, just, & humane responses to crime & its causes
Member of: John Howard Society of Canada; Criminal Justice Association
Finances: *Annual Operating Budget:* $500,000-$1.5 Million
Staff Member(s): 8
Activities: *Rents Mailing List:* Yes; *Library:* Open to public
Chief Officer(s):
Paula Osmok, Executive Director
Publications:
- John Howard Society of Ontario Annual Report
Type: Report; *Frequency:* Annually

Belleville
#19, 21 Wallbridge Cres., Belleville ON K8P 2Z3
Tel: 613-968-6628; Fax: 613-968-6696
reception@johnhowardbelleville.ca
johnhoward.on.ca/belleville
Chief Officer(s):

Debbie Woods, Executive Director
dwoods@johnhowardbelleville.ca
Durham Region
75 Richmond St. West, Oshawa ON L1G 1E3
Tel: 905-579-8482; *Fax:* 905-435-0352
johnhoward.on.ca/durham
www.linkedin.com/company/john-howard-society-of-durham-region
www.facebook.com/539273192757476
twitter.com/JHSDurhamRegion
Chief Officer(s):
Dianna Eastwood, Executive Director
Hamilton, Burlington & Area
645 Barton St. East, Hamilton ON L8L 3A2
Tel: 905-522-4446; *Fax:* 905-524-2223
johnhoward.on.ca/hamilton
twitter.com/jhshamilton
Kawartha Lakes & Haliburton
31 Peel St., Lindsay ON K9V 3L9
Tel: 705-328-0472; *Fax:* 705-328-2549
Toll-Free: 888-665-6615
info@jhscklh.on.ca
johnhoward.on.ca/kawartha
Mission: To prevent crime by offering services such as community education, reform, & advocacy
Kingston & District
771 Montreal St., Kingston ON K7K 3J4
Tel: 613-542-7373; *Fax:* 613-542-2733
ed@johnhowardkingston.ca
johnhoward.on.ca/kingston
Chief Officer(s):
Tyler Fainstat, Executive Director
London & District
601 Queens Ave., London ON N6B 1Y9
Tel: 519-438-4168; *Fax:* 519-438-7670
jhslondon@execulink.com
johnhoward.on.ca/london
Chief Officer(s):
Taghrid Hussain, Executive Director
Niagara
210 King St., St Catharines ON L2R 3J9
Tel: 905-682-2657; *Fax:* 905-984-6918
jobgym@jhs-niagara.ca
www.jhs-niagara.com
Chief Officer(s):
Jay Gemmell, Executive Director
Ottawa
550 Old St. Patrick St., Ottawa ON K1N 5L5
Tel: 613-789-7418; *Fax:* 613-789-7431
jhsottawa@ottawa.johnhoward.ca
johnhoward.on.ca/ottawa
Chief Officer(s):
Don Wadel, Executive Director
Peel, Halton & Dufferin
134 Main St. North, Brampton ON L6V 1N8
Tel: 905-459-0111; *Fax:* 905-459-5954
johnhoward.on.ca/peel-halton-dufferin
Chief Officer(s):
Patricia E. Anderson, President
Peterborough
305 Stewart St., Peterborough ON K9J 3N2
Tel: 705-743-8331; *Fax:* 705-743-8340
jhsptbo@jhsptbo.com
johnhoward.on.ca/peterborough
Chief Officer(s):
Kathy Neill, Executive Director
Sarnia & Lambton
300 Christina St. North, Sarnia ON N7T 5V5
Tel: 519-336-1020; *Fax:* 519-336-1046
johnhoward.on.ca/sarnia-lambton
Chief Officer(s):
Anne Doan, President
Sault Ste Marie & District
27 King St., Sault Ste Marie ON P6A 6K3
Tel: 705-759-1703
johnhoward.on.ca/sault-ste-marie
Chief Officer(s):
Suzanne Lajambe, Executive Director
Simcoe & Muskoka
#336, 80 Bradford St., Barrie ON L4N 6S7
Tel: 705-759-1703
contact@jhssm.ca
johnhoward.on.ca/muskoka
Chief Officer(s):

Keith Kacsuta, Executive Director
Sudbury
204 Pine St., Sudbury ON P3C 1X5
Tel: 705-673-9576; *Fax:* 705-673-1543
office@johnhowardsudbury.com
johnhoward.on.ca/sudbury
The John Howard Society of Toronto
1669 Eglinton Ave. West, Toronto ON M6E 2H4
Tel: 416-925-4386; *Fax:* 416-925-9112
Toll-Free: 866-265-4434
contact@johnhowardtor.on.ca
www.johnhowardon.ca/toronto
www.facebook.com/108442035933591
twitter.com/jhstoronto
Chief Officer(s):
Sonya Spencer, Executive Director, 416-925-4386 Ext. 225
sspencer@johnhowardtor.on.ca
Thunder Bay & District
315 Syndicate Ave. South, Thunder Bay ON P7E 1E2
Tel: 807-623-5355; *Fax:* 807-623-4191
info@johnhowardtbay.on.ca
johnhoward.on.ca/thunderbay
www.facebook.com/johnhowardtbay
twitter.com/jhstbay
Chief Officer(s):
Sandy Lychowyd, Executive Director
Waterloo - Wellington
310 Charles St. East, Kitchener ON N2G 2P9
Tel: 519-743-6071; *Fax:* 519-743-9632
inquiries@waterloo.johnhoward.on.ca
johnhoward.on.ca/waterloo
Chief Officer(s):
Ted Sehl, President
Windsor - Essex County
275 Oak St., Windsor ON N9A 5E5
Tel: 519-252-3461; *Fax:* 519-252-0439
info@jhswindsor.org
johnhoward.on.ca/windsor-essex
York Region
#202, 16600 Bayview Ave., Newmarket ON L3X 1Z9
Tel: 905-895-9943; *Fax:* 905-895-0861
johnhoward.on.ca/yorkregion
Chief Officer(s):
Christin Cullen, Executive Director

The John Howard Society of Prince Edward Island
PO Box 1211, 163 Queen St., Charlottetown PE C1A 7M8
Tel: 902-566-5425; *Fax:* 902-628-6842
johnhowardsociety@pei.aibn.com
pei.johnhoward.ca
Overview: A small provincial charitable organization founded in 1960 overseen by The John Howard Society of Canada
Mission: To assist at-risk individuals, or individuals who are involved in the criminal justice process
Finances: *Annual Operating Budget:* $100,000-$250,000
Staff Member(s): 5; 9 volunteer(s)
Activities: Providing prevention, transitional & support services
Chief Officer(s):
Donna Hartley, Executive Director

The John Howard Society of Saskatchewan
#7, 2010 - 11th Ave., Regina SK S4P 0J3
Tel: 306-757-6657
www.sk.johnhoward.ca
www.facebook.com/218360001561654
twitter.com/JHSocietySask
Overview: A small provincial charitable organization overseen by The John Howard Society of Canada
Mission: To provide effective, just, & humane responses to the causes & consequences of crime
Activities: Providing youth, victims, offenders, & families with education & outreach programs
Chief Officer(s):
Greg Fleet, Executive Director
g.fleet@sk.johnhoward.ca
Moose Jaw
15 Hochelaga St. West, Moose Jaw SK S6H 2E9
Tel: 306-693-0777; *Fax:* 306-692-7655
Toll-Free: 866-485-0777
www.sk.johnhoward.ca
Chief Officer(s):
Jamie Boldt, Executive Director
jboldt@sk.johnhoward.ca
Saskatoon
#202, 220 - 3rd Ave. South, Saskatoon SK S7K 1M1

Tel: 306-244-8347; *Fax:* 306-244-9923
Toll-Free: 877-244-8347
www.sk.johnhoward.ca
Chief Officer(s):
Shaun Dyer, Executive Director
sdyer@sk.johnhoward.ca

John Milton Society for the Blind in Canada
#202, 40 St. Clair Ave. East, Toronto ON M4T 1M9
Tel: 416-960-3953; *Fax:* 416-960-3570
Overview: A small national charitable organization
Mission: To provide Christian materials in alternative formats to blind, deafblind, & visually impaired Canadians
Chief Officer(s):
Barry Brown, Executive Director
bbrown@jmsblind.ca

Joint Centre for Bioethics
University of Toronto, #754, 155 College St., Toronto ON M5T 1P8
Tel: 416-978-2709; *Fax:* 416-978-1911
jcb.info@utoronto.ca
www.jcb.utoronto.ca
www.facebook.com/uoftjcb
twitter.com/utjcb
Overview: A small national organization founded in 1995
Mission: To improve health care through leadership in bioethics research, education, practice, & public engagement
Finances: *Funding Sources:* Government (56%), academic institutions (37%), individuals and foundations (4%), and private sector (3%)
Membership: 215
Chief Officer(s):
Jennifer L. Gibson, Director
Rhonda Martin, Executive Assistant

Joint Forum of Financial Market Regulators / Forum conjoint des autorités de réglementation du marché financier
c/o Joint Forum Secretariat, PO Box 85, 5160 Yonge St., 17th Fl., Toronto ON M2N 6L9
Tel: 416-590-7526; *Fax:* 416-590-7070
jointforum@fsco.gov.on.ca
www.jointforum.ca
Overview: A small national organization founded in 1999
Mission: Established as a mechanism through which pension, securities and insurance regulators could co-ordinate, harmonize and streamline the regulation of financial products and services in Canada.
Affiliation(s): Canadian Council of Insurance Regulators (CCIR); the Canadian Securities Administrators (CSA); Canadian Association of Pension Supervisory Authorities (CAPSA)
Activities: Strategic planning; publications; meetings
Chief Officer(s):
Sabitha Kanagasabai, Acting Policy Manager, 416-226-7781
sabitha.kanagasabai@fsco.gov.on.ca

Joint Regional Library Boards Association of Nova Scotia
See Library Boards Association of Nova Scotia

Jour de la terre Canada *See* Earth Day Canada

Journalistes canadiens pour la liberté d'expression *See* Canadian Journalists for Free Expression

Journaux Canadiens *See* Newspapers Canada

Judo Alberta
Percy Page Centre, 11759 Groat Rd., Edmonton AB T5M 3K6
Tel: 780-427-8379; *Fax:* 780-447-1915
Toll-Free: 866-919-5836
judo@judoalberta.com
www.judoalberta.com
www.facebook.com/judoalberta
twitter.com/JudoAlberta
www.flickr.com/photos/judoalberta
Also Known As: Alberta Kodokan Black Belt Association - AKBBA
Overview: A small provincial organization founded in 1960 overseen by Judo Canada
Mission: To promote the principles & teachings of the sport of kodokan judo to all levels in all parts of Alberta; To have qualified facilities & equipment in places throughout Alberta; To promote judo as a lifelong interest; to develop competitive opportunities throughout Alberta; To promote greater public awareness of the sport; To increase the number of participants in the sport; To develop & maintain qualified judo officials & coaches throughout

Canadian Associations / Judo BC

Alberta; To develop high performance athletes; To develop recreational opportunities throughout Alberta
Member of: Judo Canada
Affiliation(s): International Judo Federation
Finances: *Annual Operating Budget:* $100,000-$250,000
Staff Member(s): 2; 200 volunteer(s)
Membership: 1,200; *Fees:* Schedule available; *Committees:* Grading; Technical; Referee; Coaching; Women's Ctee
Activities: *Library:* Video Library; Open to public
Chief Officer(s):
Kelly Thornton, President
kellyt4d@telus.net
Nate MacLellan, Executive Director

Judo BC
#523, 4438 West 10th Ave., Vancouver BC V6R 4R8
Tel: 604-333-3513; *Fax:* 604-333-3514
www.judobc.ca
www.facebook.com/JudoBritishColumbia
twitter.com/OfficialJudoBC
Overview: A medium-sized provincial organization founded in 1952 overseen by Judo Canada
Mission: To promote & support the development of all aspects of Judo in the province; To inform & report on all aspects of Judo & planned activities in BC & elsewhere; To promote Judo & public awareness of the sport; To increase the number of participants in the sport; To keep close liaison with Judo clubs in BC in order to share all things of common interest to members
Member of: Judo Canada; Sport BC; Pan-American Confederation of Judo; International Judo Federation; Kodokan Judo Institute
Finances: *Annual Operating Budget:* $100,000-$250,000; *Funding Sources:* Provincial government; self-generated revenue; gaming
Staff Member(s): 1
Membership: 2,200; *Fees:* Schedule available; *Committees:* Technical; Grading & Kata Board; Referee; NCCP; Membership
Activities: Offering coaching clinics; Organizing tournaments; Providing athlete & referee training; *Awareness Events:* Judo Awareness Week, 3rd week of Sept.; *Library:* by appointment
Chief Officer(s):
Sandy Kent, President
Katie Thomson, Executive Director
executivedirector@judobc.ca

Judo Canada
c/o Judo Canada, #201, 1155 Lola St., Ottawa ON K1K 4C1
Toll-Free: 877-738-5836
info@judocanada.org
www.judocanada.org
www.facebook.com/judocanada
twitter.com/judocanada
Also Known As: Canadian Kodokan Black Belt Association
Overview: A large national charitable organization founded in 1956
Mission: To promote the principles & teachings of the sport of Kodokan Judo; To work towards the advancement of Judo throughout Canada
Member of: Pan American Judo Union
Affiliation(s): International Judo Federation
Finances: *Funding Sources:* Sport Canada; Membership dues; Sponsorships
Staff Member(s): 9
Membership: *Member Profile:* Black belt & provincial members; *Committees:* High Performance; NCCP/LTAD; Women's Programs; Grading; Kata; Referee; Aboriginal & Territorial Affairs; Tournament; Legal; Awards; Finance & Audit
Activities: Providing Rendez-Vous Canada & the Canadian Championships; *Library:* by appointment
Chief Officer(s):
Andrien Landry, Executive Director
a.landry@judocanada.org
Andrzej Sadej, Director, Sports
a.sadej@judocanada.org
Stewart Tanaka, Coordinator, Events
s.tanaka@judocanada.org
Francine Latreille, Office Manager
f.latreille@judocanada.org

National Training Centre
Parc olympique de Montréal, 4141, av Pierre-de-Coubertin, Montréal QC H1V 3N7
Toll-Free: 877-738-5836
hp@judocanada.org
www.judocanada.org/national-training-centre
Chief Officer(s):
Nicolas Gill, Director/National Head Coach
n.gill@judocanada.org
Isabelle Pearson, Chief Therapist

Judo Manitoba
c/o Sport Manitoba, #311, 145 Pacific Ave., Winnipeg MB R3B 2Z6
Tel: 204-925-5691; *Fax:* 204-925-5703
judo@sportmanitoba.ca
www.judomanitoba.mb.ca
Also Known As: Manitoba Judo Black Belt Association Inc.
Overview: A small provincial organization founded in 1963 overseen by Judo Canada
Mission: To propagate & perpetuate the sport of Judo; To improve the calibre of athletes, referees & coaches
Member of: Judo Canada; Sport Manitoba; International Judo Federation; Canadian Olympic Committee
Finances: *Annual Operating Budget:* $100,000-$250,000
Staff Member(s): 2
Membership: 86 Black Belts + 594 others; *Fees:* Schedule available; *Committees:* Fundraising; Officials; Grading; Bingo; NCCP; Grassroots; Awards
Activities: *Library:*
Chief Officer(s):
Oscar Li, Executive Director
David Minuk, President

Judo New Brunswick / Judo Nouveau Brunswick
#13, 900 Hanwell St., Fredericton NB E3B 6A3
Tel: 506-451-1322; *Fax:* 506-451-1325
judonb@nb.aibn.com
www.judonb.org
www.facebook.com/judonewbrunswick
twitter.com/judo_nb
Also Known As: Judo NB
Overview: A small local organization overseen by Judo Canada
Mission: To promote judo in New Brunswick
Member of: Judo Canada
Membership: 500; *Committees:* Grading
Chief Officer(s):
Curtis Lauzon, Executive Director, 506-261-0867

Judo Nouveau Brunswick *See* Judo New Brunswick

Judo Nova Scotia
NS
Tel: 902-425-5450
admin@judons.ca
www.judons.ca
www.facebook.com/judons
twitter.com/judonovascotia
Overview: A small provincial organization overseen by Judo Canada
Mission: To promote the principles of judo &, in collaboration with members & interested parties, to work towards the advancement of judo, at all levels & areas of Nova Scotia
Member of: Judo Canada
Chief Officer(s):
Chris Hattie, President
chattie@judons.ca
Scott Tanner, Provincial Coach
stanner@judons.ca

Judo Nunavut
PO Box 2135, Iqaluit NU X0A 0H0
Tel: 867-979-4540
judo.nunavut@gmail.com
www.facebook.com/NunavutJudo
Overview: A small provincial organization overseen by Judo Canada
Member of: Judo Canada

Judo Ontario
#2040, 875 Morningside Ave., Toronto ON M1C 0C7
Tel: 416-447-5836; *Fax:* 416-449-5836
Toll-Free: 866-553-5836
info@judoontario.ca
www.judoontario.ca
www.facebook.com/JudoOntario
Overview: A small provincial organization founded in 1959 overseen by Judo Canada
Mission: To govern the sport of Judo in Ontario
Member of: Judo Canada; International Judo Federation
Finances: *Annual Operating Budget:* $250,000-$500,000
Staff Member(s): 2; 100 volunteer(s)
Membership: 1,000-4,999; *Fees:* Schedule available; *Committees:* HPC; Grading Board; Referee; LTAD; NCCP; Aboriginal; Differently Abled; Quest for Gold; Website; Membership
Chief Officer(s):
Aartje Sheffield, President, 905-251-0202
aartjes@judoontario.ca
Pedro Guedes, Technical Coach & Director
pedrog@judoontario.ca
Steve Sheffield, Administrator
Awards:
• Judo Ontario Recognition Awards

Judo Prince Edward Island
PO Box 302, 40 Enman Cres., Charlottetown PE C1A 7K7
Tel: 902-368-4262
www.judopei.ca
www.facebook.com/JUDOPEI
twitter.com/judopei
Overview: A small provincial organization overseen by Judo Canada
Mission: To promote and govern the sport of Judo in Prince Edward Island
Member of: Sport PEI Inc.; Judo Canada
Chief Officer(s):
Michael Sheppard, President
president@judopei.ca
Trish Shaw, Secretary
secretary@judopei.ca

Judo Saskatchewan
c/o Sandy Taylor, Treasurer, PO Box 1464, Warman SK S0K 4S0
Tel: 306-668-6879
www.judosask.ca
Also Known As: Saskatchewan Kodokan Black Belt Association
Overview: A small provincial licensing organization founded in 1950 overseen by Judo Canada
Mission: To govern the sport of Judo in Saskatchewan
Member of: Judo Canada; Pan-American Judo Federation
Affiliation(s): International Judo Federation
Finances: *Annual Operating Budget:* $100,000-$250,000
Staff Member(s): 1; 10 volunteer(s)
Membership: 300+; *Fees:* Schedule available
Chief Officer(s):
T.V. Taylor, President, 306-668-6879
tvtaylor@sasktel.net
Sandy Taylor, Treasurer
taylor.s@sasktel.net

Judo Yukon
4061 - 4th Ave., Whitehorse YT Y1A 1H1
Tel: 867-668-4236; *Fax:* 867-667-4237
judoyukon@gmail.com
www.judoyukon.ca
Overview: A small provincial charitable organization founded in 1995 overseen by Judo Canada
Mission: To govern the sport of Judo in the Yukon
Member of: Judo Canada; Sport Yukon; True Sport; Sport Officials Canada
Finances: *Annual Operating Budget:* Less than $50,000
Membership: 100+; *Member Profile:* Juniors & seniors; ages 8 & up; *Committees:* NCCP; Officials
Activities: Organizing competitions & demonstrations; *Awareness Events:* Judo Yukon Open Tournament, April *Library:* Resource Library; Not open to public
Chief Officer(s):
Richard Zebruck, President
Bianca Ockedahl, Head Coach
judoyukon.hc@gmail.com

Judo-Québec inc
4545, av Pierre-de Coubertin, Montréal QC H1V 0B2
Tél: 514-252-3040; *Téléc:* 514-254-5184
info@judo-quebec.qc.ca
www.judo-quebec.qc.ca
www.facebook.com/JudoQuebec
www.youtube.com/user/judoquebec
Également appelé: Association québécoise de judo-kodokan
Aperçu: *Dimension:* moyenne; *Envergure:* provinciale; Organisme sans but lucratif; fondée en 1966 surveillé par Judo Canada
Mission: Assurer la promotion et le développement du judo au Québec; éduquer, développer et servir nos membres
Membre de: Judo Canada; Sport Québec
Affiliation(s): Fédération internationale de Judo; Union panaméricaine du Judo

Finances: *Budget de fonctionnement annuel:* $500,000-$1.5 Million; *Fonds:* Secrétariat au loisirs et aux sports
Membre(s) du personnel: 6; 200 bénévole(s)
Membre: 10 000; *Montant de la cotisation:* Barème; *Critères d'admissibilite:* Personne de 7 à 77 ans; *Comités:* Arbitrage; excellence; développement; grade; éthique; ju-jutsu
Activités: Competition; stage; colloque; gala; formation; *Stagiaires:* Oui; *Service de conférenciers:* Oui; *Bibliothèque*
Membre(s) du bureau directeur:
Daniel De Angelis, Président
Jean-François Marceau, Directeur général, 514-252-3040 Ext. 27
jfmarceau@judo-quebec.qc.ca
Patrick Vesin, Coordonnateur technique, 514-252-3040 Ext. 24
pvesin@judo-quebec.qc.ca

Jump Alberta
#132, 250 Shawville Blvd. SE, Calgary AB T2Y 2Y7
jumpalberta@gmail.com
www.jumpalberta.com
Overview: A small provincial organization
Affiliation(s): Alberta Equestrian Federation
Chief Officer(s):
Kristi Beunder, President

Junior Achievement Canada (JACAN) / Jeunes Entreprises du Canada
161 Bay St., 27th Fl., Toronto ON M5J 2S1
Tel: 416-622-4602; *Fax:* 416-622-6861
Toll-Free: 800-265-0699
www.jacan.org
www.facebook.com/JAchievement
twitter.com/ja_canada
www.youtube.com/user/junioriachievementcan
Overview: A large national charitable organization founded in 1967
Mission: To provide practical business & economic education programs & experience for young people, through partnerships with business & education communities
Member of: Junior Achievement Worldwide
Affiliation(s): Temple de la renommée de l'entreprise canadienne
Finances: *Annual Operating Budget:* $500,000-$1.5 Million; *Funding Sources:* Corporate contributions
Staff Member(s): 10; 150 volunteer(s)
Membership: 250,000 students; *Member Profile:* Senior business representatives; *Committees:* Finance; Canadian Business Hall of Fame; Strategic Planning; Marketing; Programs
Activities: Operates in 114 countries around the world; Programs delivered by experienced business people through a network of 40 chartered organizations across Canada; *Awareness Events:* Junior Achievement Month, Feb.; *Speaker Service:* Yes
Chief Officer(s):
Scott Hillier, President & Chief Executive Officer, 647-427-9548
shillier@jacanada.org
Karen Gallant, Vice President, Programs & Charter Services, 647-435-1113
kgallant@jacanada.org
Kristina Fixter, Director, Marketing & Events, 647-428-9097
kfixter@jacanada.org
Andre Gallant, Director, Program Development, Services & Volunteer Inquiries, 647-428-6532
agallant@jacanada.org
Vanessa Underwood, Director, Finance, 647-428-7544
vunderwood@jacanada.org

Junior Achievement of Nova Scotia
#300, 1550 Bedford Hwy., Bedford NS B4A 1E6
Tel: 902-425-4564; *Fax:* 902-454-4514
info@janovascotia.org
www.janovascotia.ca
www.facebook.com/janovascotia
twitter.com/janovascotia
www.youtube.com/user/janovascotia
Chief Officer(s):
Kristin Williams, President & Chief Executive Officer, 902-454-4564 Ext. 107
kwilliams@janovascotia.org

Junior Achievement of British Columbia
#360, 475 West Georgia St., Vancouver BC V6B 4M9
Tel: 604-688-3887; *Fax:* 604-689-5299
info@jabc.org
jabc.ca
www.linkedin.com/company/ja-british-columbia
www.facebook.com/JABritishColumbia
twitter.com/JA_of_BC
www.youtube.com/user/JuniorAchievementBC
Chief Officer(s):
Kristi Miller, Chair

Junior Achievement of Central Ontario
#405, 133 Richmond St. West, Toronto ON M5H 2L3
Tel: 416-360-5252; *Fax:* 416-366-5252
companyprogram@jacentralontario.org
www.jacocompanyprogram.ca
www.facebook.com/JACOCompanyProgram
twitter.com/JACO_CP
Chief Officer(s):
Lynn Gonsalves, Senior Manager, Company Program, 416-360-5252 Ext. 238
lgonsalves@jacentralontario.org

Junior Achievement of Ottawa
#205, 900 Morrison Dr., Ottawa ON K2H 8K7
Tel: 613-366-3085; *Fax:* 613-726-3443
www.onfe-rope.ca
www.facebook.com/onfe.rope
twitter.com/ONFE_ROPE
Chief Officer(s):
Albert Wong, Director, 913-366-3085 Ext. 251
awong@onfe-rope.ca

Junior Achievement of London & District
15 Wharncliffe Rd. North, London ON N6H 2A1
Tel: 519-439-4201; *Fax:* 519-438-2331
Toll-Free: 877-229-9925
info@jalondon.org
jacanada.org/london-district
www.facebook.com/JALondonAndDistrict
twitter.com/JA_London
www.youtube.com/user/JALondonTV
Chief Officer(s):
Bev Robinson, President & Chief Executive, 519-439-4201 Ext. 224
brobinson@jalondon.org

Junior Achievement of Manitoba
1149 St. Matthews Ave., Winnipeg MB R3G 0J8
Tel: 204-956-6088; *Fax:* 204-831-5284
jacanada.org/manitoba
www.facebook.com/191061872629
twitter.com/JAManitoba
Chief Officer(s):
Greg Leipsic, President & Chief Executive Officer, 204-956-6082
gleipsic@jamanitoba.org

Junior Achievement of Newfoundland and Labrador
Delgado Bldg., PO Box 7468, 171 Water St., 3rd Fl., St. John's NL A1E 4V8
Tel: 709-753-9533; *Fax:* 709-753-2612
info@janl.org
janl.org
www.facebook.com/juniorachievementofnl
Chief Officer(s):
Sandra Patterson, President & Chief Executive Officer
spatterson@janl.org

Junior Achievement of Northern Alberta & Northwest Territories
#200, 10150 - 100 St., Edmonton AB T5J 0P6
Tel: 780-428-1421; *Fax:* 780-428-1031
Toll-Free: 877-626-7666
www.janorthalberta.org
www.facebook.com/JANorthernAlberta
twitter.com/JA_northalberta
www.youtube.com/user/JANorthernAlberta
Chief Officer(s):
Jen Panteluk, President & Chief Executive Officer
jpanteluk@janorthalberta.org

Junior Achievement of P.E.I.
Holland College, Montgomery Hall, #406-408 & 410, 305 Kent St., Charlottetown PE C1A 1P5
Tel: 902-892-6066; *Fax:* 902-892-1993
jacanada.org/pei
www.facebook.com/JuniorAchievementPEI
Chief Officer(s):
Betty Ferguson, President & Chief Executive Officer
bferguson@japei.org

Junior Achievement of Québec
#505, 300, rue du Saint-Sacrement, Montréal QC H2Y 1X4
Tel: 514-285-8944
info@jaquebec.org
jaquebec.org
www.facebook.com/JAQuebec

Junior Achievement of Peterborough, Lakeland & Muskoka
PO Box 1, 270 George St. North, Peterborough ON K9J 3H1
Tel: 705-748-0024; *Fax:* 844-275-5123
info@ja-plm.ca
jacanada.org/plm
www.facebook.com/JuniorAchievementPeterboroughLakelandMuskoka
Chief Officer(s):
John McNutt, President & Chief Executive Officer
jmcnutt@ja-plm.ca

Junior Achievement of Saskatchewan
#1110, 410 - 22nd St. East, Saskatoon SK S7K 5T6
Tel: 306-955-5267; *Fax:* 306-653-1507
info@jasask.org
www.jasask.org
www.facebook.com/JASask
twitter.com/JASask
Chief Officer(s):
Brenda Garneau, Chair

Junior Achievement of Southern Alberta
#870, 105 - 12 Ave. SE, Calgary AB T2G 1A1
Tel: 403-237-5252; *Fax:* 403-261-6988
info@jasouthalberta.org
jasab.ca
www.facebook.com/JASouthAlberta
twitter.com/jasouthalberta
www.youtube.com/user/JASouthAlberta
Chief Officer(s):
Rick Gallant, Board Chair

Junior Achievement of New Brunswick
PO Box 631, Stn. A, Fredericton NB E3B 5A6
Tel: 506-634-8409; *Fax:* 506-454-5752
jafrednb@nb.aibn.com
www.janewbrunswick.ca
www.facebook.com/janewbrunswick
twitter.com/JA_NB
Chief Officer(s):
Connie Woodside, President & Chief Executive Officer, 506-455-6552

Junior Achievement of Southwestern Ontario
60 William St. South, Chatham ON N7M 4S3
Tel: 519-352-0151; *Fax:* 519-352-6180
jacanada.org/sw-ontario
twitter.com/JA_SWO
www.youtube.com/user/JASWONT
Chief Officer(s):
Barb Smith, President & Chief Executive Officer, 519-352-0151

Junior Achievement of Waterloo Region
40 Shirley Ave., Kitchener ON N2B 2E1
Tel: 519-576-6610; *Fax:* 519-576-3210
info@jawaterlooregion.org
jacanada.org/waterloo
www.facebook.com/JAWaterlooRegion
twitter.com/JAWatRegion
www.youtube.com/user/JAWaterlooRegion
Chief Officer(s):
Brian Breckles, President & Chief Executive Officer, 519-576-6610 Ext. 1
bbreckles@jawaterlooregion.org

Junior Achievement Mainland Nova Scotia *See* Junior Achievement of Canada

Junior Achievement of Chatham-Kent *See* Junior Achievement of Canada

Junior Achievement of Eastern Newfoundland *See* Junior Achievement of Canada

Junior Chamber International Canada / Jeune chambre internationale du Canada
14 Bruce Farm Dr., Toronto ON M2H 1G3
Tel: 416-226-9756; *Fax:* 416-221-9389
Toll-Free: 800-265-0484
administration@jcicanada.com
www.jcicanada.com
Also Known As: JAYCEES
Previous Name: Canadian Junior Chamber
Overview: A medium-sized national organization
Mission: To contribute to the advancement of the global community by providing the opportunity for young people to develop the leadership skills, social responsibility & fellowship necessary to create positive change. Chapters across Canada.
Affiliation(s): Junior Chamber International

Canadian Associations / Junior Farmers' Association of Ontario (JFAO)

Finances: Funding Sources: Membership fees; fundraising; sponsorship
Membership: Member Profile: Ages 18-40
Chief Officer(s):
Francois Begin, Chairman of the Board
fbegin@jci.cc
Jason Ranchoux, National President
president@jcicanada.com

Junior Farmers' Association of Ontario (JFAO)
Ontario AgriCentre, #206, 100 Stone Rd. West, Guelph ON N1G 5L3
Tel: 519-780-5326; *Fax:* 519-821-8810
info@jfao.on.ca
www.jfao.on.ca
www.facebook.com/547606885270544
Overview: A medium-sized provincial organization founded in 1944
Mission: To build future rural leaders through self-help & community betterment
Membership: Member Profile: People ages 15-29
Chief Officer(s):
Sarah McLaren, President
president@jfao.on.ca

Junior League of Calgary (JLC)
511 - 22 Ave. SW, Calgary AB T2S 0H5
Tel: 403-244-5355; *Fax:* 403-244-2217
jlc@juniorleaguecalgary.com
www.juniorleaguecalgary.com
www.facebook.com/JuniorLeagueofCalgary
twitter.com/juniorleagueyyc
www.youtube.com/juniorleaguecalgary
Overview: A small local charitable organization founded in 1950 overseen by Canadian Federation of Junior Leagues
Mission: To promote voluntarism; To foster the potential of women; To enhance communities through the leadership of trained volunteers
Member of: Canadian Federation of Junior Leagues; Association of Junior Leagues International
Finances: Annual Operating Budget: $50,000-$100,000; *Funding Sources:* Membership fees; Fund-raising events
Staff Member(s): 2; 98 volunteer(s)
Membership: 300; *Fees:* $155; *Member Profile:* Women 18 & over; *Committees:* Junior Chefs; Distribution Centre; Training
Activities: Assisting Young Mothers; Moms U Matter (MUM); Teen Totes; Youth In The Kitchen
Chief Officer(s):
Kate Hanna, President

Junior League of Edmonton (JLE)
10447 - 86 Ave. NW, Edmonton AB T6E 2M4
Tel: 780-433-9739; *Fax:* 780-431-0138
info@jledmonton.org
www.jledmonton.org
www.facebook.com/JuniorLeagueEdmonton
twitter.com/jledmonton
Overview: A small local charitable organization founded in 1928 overseen by Canadian Federation of Junior Leagues
Mission: To promote voluntarism; To foster the potential of women; To enhance the community through the leadership of trained volunteers
Member of: Canadian Federation of Junior Leagues; Association of Junior Leagues International
Finances: Annual Operating Budget: $50,000-$100,000; *Funding Sources:* Fundraising; grants; donations; casinos
Staff Member(s): 1; 163 volunteer(s)
Membership: 120+ active & sustaining members; *Fees:* $135 provisional; $110 active; $70 sustaining
Activities: Girls in the Know; Kids in the Kitchen; Diaper Drive; C&E Railway Station Museum; *Awareness Events:* Indulgence: A Canadian Epic of Food & Wine, June; Homes for the Holidays, Nov.
Chief Officer(s):
Hannah Barrington, President
Amanda Mouait, President-Elect
Awards:
• Community Assistance Fund Grant

Junior League of Halifax
PO Box 8011, Stn. A, Halifax NS B3K 5L8
Tel: 902-429-9437
info@juniorleagueofhalifax.org
www.juniorleagueofhalifax.org
www.facebook.com/JuniorLeagueofHalifaxNS
twitter.com/jl_halifax

Overview: A small local charitable organization founded in 1934 overseen by Canadian Federation of Junior Leagues
Mission: To promote voluntarism; To foster the potential of women; To enhance communities through the leadership of trained volunteers
Member of: Canadian Federation of Junior Leagues; Association of Junior Leagues International
Affiliation(s): Supportive Housing for Young Mothers
Finances: Annual Operating Budget: Less than $50,000
150 volunteer(s)
Membership: 150; *Member Profile:* Female over 19 years of age
Activities: Backpacks for Kids; Laing House; Kids in the Kitchen; Healthy Families; Youth Run Club; Amanda's Gift; *Awareness Events:* Homes for the Holidays, Nov.
Chief Officer(s):
Carole Thompson, President
Kate Murphy, President-Elect

Junior League of Hamilton-Burlington, Inc. (JLHB)
1424 Plains Rd. West, Burlington ON L7T 1H6
Tel: 289-337-9526; *Fax:* 289-337-0369
info@juniorleague.ca
www.juniorleague.ca
www.facebook.com/JuniorLeagueHamiltonBurlington
twitter.com/JuniorLeagueHB
www.instagram.com/juniorleaguehb
Overview: A small local charitable organization founded in 1934 overseen by Canadian Federation of Junior Leagues
Mission: To promote voluntarism, to develop the potential of women & to improve the community through the effective action & leadership of trained volunteers
Member of: Canadian Federation of Junior Leagues; Association of Junior Leagues International
Finances: Annual Operating Budget: $100,000-$250,000
Staff Member(s): 1; 166 volunteer(s)
Membership: 166; *Fees:* $125; *Committees:* Kids on the Block; House Tour; PR; New Member; Community Research Link; Nominating; Member Placement & Development
Activities: Empowerment Hour; Discretionary Fund; Kids in the Kitchen; *Awareness Events:* Holiday House Tour of Distinctive Homes, Nov.
Chief Officer(s):
Marion Goard, President, 289-337-9526
president@juniorleague.ca
Linda Daniels-Smith, Office Manager, 289-337-9526
info@juniorleague.ca

Junior League of Toronto
539A Mount Pleasant Rd., Toronto ON M4S 2M5
Tel: 416-485-4218; *Fax:* 416-485-5949
info@jlt.org
www.jlt.org
www.facebook.com/JuniorLeagueOfToronto
twitter.com/jrleaguetoronto
Also Known As: JLT
Overview: A small local charitable organization founded in 1926 overseen by Canadian Federation of Junior Leagues
Mission: To promote voluntarism; To foster the potential of women; To enhance communities through the leadership of trained volunteers
Member of: Canadian Federation of Junior Leagues; Associaton of Junior Leagues International Inc.
Finances: Annual Operating Budget: $250,000-$500,000
Staff Member(s): 1; 450 volunteer(s)
Membership: 100-499; *Fees:* Schedule available
Activities: Gifts of Light Partnership; Tea to Help Teens; Done in a Day
Chief Officer(s):
Emily Beckett Sward, President
Melissa Ostrosser, President-Elect

Junior Symphony Society *See* Vancouver Youth Symphony Orchestra Society

Justice Centre for Constitutional Freedoms (JCCF)
#253, 7620 Elbow Dr. SW, Calgary AB T2V 1K2
Tel: 403-475-3622
www.facebook.com/165911043462459
twitter.com/JCCFCanada
www.youtube.com/user/JCCFdotCA
Overview: A small national organization founded in 2010
Mission: To defend constitutional freedoms through litigation & education
Chief Officer(s):
John Carpay, President

Justice for Children & Youth (JFCY)
55 University Ave., 15th Fl., Toronto ON M5J 2H7
Tel: 416-920-1633; *Fax:* 416-920-5855
Toll-Free: 866-999-5329
info@jfcy.org
www.jfcy.org
Also Known As: Canadian Foundation for Children, Youth & the Law
Overview: A medium-sized provincial charitable organization founded in 1978
Mission: To assist & empower children & youth in obtaining fair & equal access to legal, educational, medical & social resources; To provide direct legal assistance in all areas of children's law to eligible children & youth of Metro Toronto & vicinity; To provide summary legal advice, information & assistance to young people, parents, professionals & community groups on a province-wide basis; To advocate for law & policy reform; To monitor & respond to developments & changes to the laws which affect children
Finances: Annual Operating Budget: $250,000-$500,000
Staff Member(s): 6; 20 volunteer(s)
Membership: 40 institutional + 150 individual; *Fees:* $20 individual; $50 organization; $100 sustaining member; *Committees:* Legal Services; Policy; Community Development; Personnel; Youth Advisory
Activities: Internships: Yes; *Speaker Service:* Yes; *Library:* Resource Centre; Open to public
Chief Officer(s):
Emily Chan, Acting Executive Director
Karien Gibson, Office Manager

Justice for Girls
Tel: 604-689-7887; *Fax:* 604-689-5600
justiceforgirls@justiceforgirls.org
www.justiceforgirls.org
Overview: A small national organization
Mission: To promote support, justice & equality for homeless, low income & street-involved teenage girls who have experienced violence
Activities: Court monitoring; public education; advocacy & legal education; internship for young women
Chief Officer(s):
Annabel Webb, Director
annabel@justiceforgirls.org

Justice Institute of British Columbia (JIBC)
715 McBride Blvd., New Westminster BC V3L 5T4
Tel: 604-525-5422; *Fax:* 604-528-5518
Toll-Free: 888-865-7764
infodesk@jibc.ca
www.jibc.ca
www.linkedin.com/company/justice-institute-of-british-columbia
www.facebook.com/justiceinstitute
twitter.com/JIBCnews
www.youtube.com/user/JusticeInstitute
Overview: A small provincial organization
Activities: Library: Open to public
Chief Officer(s):
Michel Tarko, President

Juvenile Diabetes Research Foundation Canada (JDRF)
#800, 2550 Victoria Park Ave., Toronto ON M2J 5A9
Tel: 647-789-2000; *Fax:* 416-491-2111
Toll-Free: 877-287-3533
general@jdrf.ca
www.jdrf.ca
www.facebook.com/JDRFCanada
twitter.com/JDRF_Canada
www.youtube.com/JDRFCanada
Previous Name: Diabetes Research Foundation
Overview: A medium-sized national charitable organization founded in 1974
Mission: To support research to find a cure for diabetes & its complications; To increase awareness of diabetes, particularly Juvenile (Type 1) diabetes
Finances: Funding Sources: Donations
Activities: Liaising with government; Advocating for diabetes research
Chief Officer(s):
Matt Varey, Chair
Dave Prowten, President/CEO
David Kozloff, Secretary
Alex Davidson, Treasurer
Calgary
#204, 1608 - 17th Ave. SW, Calgary AB T2T 0E3

Tel: 403-255-7100; Fax: 403-253-6683
Toll-Free: 877-287-3533
calgary@jdrf.ca
Edmonton
17321 - 107 Ave., Edmonton AB T5S 1E9
Tel: 780-428-0343; Fax: 780-428-0348
Toll-Free: 855-428-0343
edmonton@jdrf.ca
Chief Officer(s):
Cheryl Vickers, Coordinator, Fundraising & Development
cvickers@jdrf.ca
Halifax Region
Bedford Place Mall, #2055, 1658 Bedford Hwy., Bedford NS B4A 2X9
Tel: 902-453-1009; Fax: 902-453-2528
Toll-Free: 888-439-5373
Chief Officer(s):
Marilyn Holm, Atlantic Regional Manager
mholm@jdrf.ca
Hamilton
#12, 442 Millen Rd., Stoney Creek ON L8E 6H2
Tel: 905-664-1432; Fax: 905-664-2408
Toll-Free: 866-602-6662
London
309 Commissioners Rd. West, #A, London ON N6J 1Y4
Tel: 519-641-7006; Fax: 519-641-7837
london@jdrf.ca
Québec
#330, 615, boul Rene-Levesque ouest, Montréal QC H3B 1P5
Tel: 514-744-5537; Fax: 514-744-0516
Toll-Free: 877-634-2238
montreal@jdrf.ca
www.facebook.com/FRDJQuebec
Chief Officer(s):
Francine Bourdeau, Regional Director, 514-744-0516 Ext. 243
fbourdeau@jdrf.ca
Saskatoon
959 Patrick Way, Saskatoon SK S7M 0G1
Tel: 306-380-1588
saskatoon@jdrf.ca
South Saskatchewan
PO Box 3924, Regina SK S4P 3S9
Tel: 306-789-8474
regina@jdrf.ca
www.facebook.com/JdrfRegina
Toronto-York
#800, 2550 Victoria Park Ave., Toronto ON M2J 5A9
Tel: 647-789-2000; Fax: 416-491-2111
Toll-Free: 877-287-3533
www.facebook.com/jdrftoronto
twitter.com/jdrftoronto
Chief Officer(s):
Shannon Carkner, Regional Director
scarkner@jdrf.ca
Vancouver
Sperling Plaza II, #150, 6450 Roberts St., Burnaby BC V5G 4E1
Tel: 604-320-1937; Fax: 604-320-1938
vancouver@jdrf.ca
twitter.com/jdrf_bc
Chief Officer(s):
Chris Lowe, Regional Manager
clowe@jdrf.ca
Waterloo
#103, 684 Belmont Ave. West, Kitchener ON N2M 1N6
Tel: 519-745-2426; Fax: 519-745-2626
waterloo@jdrf.ca
Winnipeg
#1101, 191 Lombard Ave., Winnipeg MB R3B 0X1
Tel: 204-953-4477; Fax: 204-953-4470
winnipeg@jdrf.ca

JVS of Greater Toronto
74 Tycos Dr., Toronto ON M6B 1V9
Tel: 416-787-1151
services@jvstoronto.org
www.jvstoronto.org
www.linkedin.com/company/jvs-toronto
www.facebook.com/JVSToronto
twitter.com/JVSToronto
www.youtube.com/JVSTorontoOnline
Also Known As: Jewish Vocational Service
Overview: A small local charitable organization founded in 1947
Mission: To provide leadership in the development & delivery of educational & vocational services of the highest quality in order to assist clients to identify educational & vocational goals & to develop the skills & knowledge to achieve those goals; To deal effectively with educational or vocational barriers
Member of: International Association of Counselling Services; International Association of JVS
Affiliation(s): United Way; Agency of UJA
Staff Member(s): 220
Activities: Library: Open to public
Chief Officer(s):
Jeff Goldfarb, Chair
Bathurst Finch
540 Finch Ave. West, Toronto ON M2R 1N9
Tel: 416-633-1240
Jane-Finch
Jane Finch Mall, #3, 1911 Finch Ave. West, Toronto ON M3N 2V2
Tel: 416-636-2481
www.jvstoronto.org
Toronto North
#607, 1280 Finch Ave. West, Toronto ON M3J 3K6
Tel: 416-661-3010
www.jvstoronto.org
Al Green Resource Centre
74 Tycos Dr., Toronto ON M6B 1V9
Tel: 416-782-3976
www.jvstoronto.org

The J.W. McConnell Family Foundation / La fondation de la famille J.W. McConnell
#1800, 1002, rue Sherbrooke ouest, Montréal QC H3A 3L6
Tel: 514-288-2133; Fax: 514-288-1479
information@mcconnellfoundation.ca
www.mcconnellfoundation.ca
Overview: A small national charitable organization founded in 1937
Mission: To fund initiatives of national significance, which address challenges for Canadian society, by engaging people & by developing a strong knowledge base for the work supported
Member of: Private Foundations Canada; Council on Foundations; Canadian Centre for Philanthropy
Membership: 1-99
Chief Officer(s):
Stephen Huddart, President & Chief Executive Officer
John Cawley, Director, Programs & Operations
jcawley@mcconnellfoundation.ca
Brianna Hunter, Officer, Communications
bhunter@mcconnellfoundation.ca

K3C Community Counselling Centres / Centre de Conseil Communautaire
Unison Place, 417 Bagot St., Kingston ON K7K 3C1
Tel: 613-549-7850; Fax: 613-544-8138
Toll-Free: 800-379-5556
info@k3c.org
www.k3c.org
www.facebook.com/1394815584088014
Previous Name: Kingston Community Counselling Centre
Overview: A medium-sized local charitable organization founded in 1968 overseen by Ontario Association of Credit Counselling Services
Mission: To assist persons in Kingston & the surrounding area to solve their debt & money management troubles for free, or a small fee; To provide a variety of educational presentations about financial matters
Member of: Canadian Association of Credit Counselling Services; Ontario Association of Credit Counselling Services; United Way
Finances: Annual Operating Budget: $3 Million-$5 Million
Activities: Counselling persons in a confidential & unbiased manner about credit concerns; Offering debt management programs; Liaising with creditors; Teaching budgeting & money management skills; Offering alternatives to declaring bankruptcy; Speaker Service: Yes
Chief Officer(s):
Danielle Brown, Administrator
Publications:
• K3C Newsletter [a publication of K3C Community Counselling Centres]
Type: Newsletter; Frequency: bi-monthly
Profile: Information about agency & topical articles.

K3C Credit Counselling Belleville
235 Bridge St. East, Belleville ON K8N 1P2
Tel: 613-966-3556
Toll-Free: 800-379-5556
belleville@k3c.org
Mission: To provide confidential, unbiased professional counselling & support to persons in Quinte Region
Member of: Canadian Association of Credit Counselling Services; Ontario Association of Credit Counselling Services
K3C Credit Counselling Brockville
7B Perth St., Brockville ON K6V 6C5
Tel: 613-341-8788
Toll-Free: 800-379-5556
brockville@k3c.org
Mission: To assist individuals & families in Brockville & the surrounding area who are experiencing financial problems
Member of: Canadian Association of Credit Counselling Services; Ontario Association of Credit Counselling Services; United Way
K3C Credit Counselling Cornwall
26 Montreal Rd., Cornwall ON K6H 1B1
Toll-Free: 866-202-0425
cornwall@k3c.org
Mission: To offer free, qualified, & confidential financial advice to persons in the Cornwall area
Member of: Canadian Association of Credit Counselling Services; Ontario Association of Credit Counselling Services; United Way
K3C Credit Counselling Oshawa
Oshawa Executive Centre, 203A, 419 King St. West, Oshawa ON L1J 2K5
Tel: 905-665-6204
Toll-Free: 800-379-5556
oshawa@k3c.org
Mission: To provide confidential credit counselling services to individuals & families, in Whitby & Oshawa, who are experiencing financial concerns; To offer education about financial well-being
Member of: Canadian Association of Credit Counselling Services; Ontario Association of Credit Counselling Services; United Way
K3C Credit Counselling Ottawa - Carling Ave.
#209, 1300 Carling Ave., Ottawa ON K1Z 7L2
Tel: 613-728-2041
Toll-Free: 866-202-0425
ottawa@k3c.org
Mission: To help persons in Ottawa & area find solutions to their debt difficulties
Member of: Canadian Association of Credit Counselling Services; Ontario Association of Credit Counselling Services; United Way
K3C Credit Counselling Ottawa - McArthur Ave.
311 McArthur St., Ottawa ON K1L 8M3
Tel: 613-728-2041
Toll-Free: 866-202-0425
ottawa@k3c.org
Mission: To offer free, qualified, & confidential financial advice to persons in the Ottawa area
Member of: Canadian Association of Credit Counselling Services; Ontario Association of Credit Counselling Services; United Way

Kababayan Community Centre See Kababayan Multicultural Centre

Kababayan Multicultural Centre
#133, 1313 Queen St. West, Toronto ON M6K 1L8
Tel: 416-532-3888; Fax: 416-532-0037
office@kababayan.org
www.kababayan.org
www.facebook.com/KababayanCommunity
Previous Name: Kababayan Community Centre
Overview: A small local charitable organization founded in 1977 overseen by Ontario Council of Agencies Serving Immigrants
Mission: To develop a strong immigrant community in Canada
Staff Member(s): 7
Chief Officer(s):
Flordeliz M. Dandal, Executive Director

Kabuki Syndrome Network Inc. (KSN)
8060 Struthers Cres., Regina SK S4Y 1J3
Tel: 306-543-8715
margot@kabukisyndrome.com
kabukisyndrome.com
Overview: A small national charitable organization founded in 1997

Mission: To provide information on Kabuki syndrome
Finances: *Annual Operating Budget:* Less than $50,000
Membership: 200; *Fees:* $20
Chief Officer(s):
Dean Schmiedge, Contact
Margot Schmiedge, Contact

Kainai Chamber of Commerce
PO Box 350, Stand Off AB T0L 1Y0
Tel: 403-737-8124; *Fax:* 403-737-2116
Overview: A small local organization founded in 1999

KAIROS: Canadian Ecumenical Justice Initiatives / Initiatives canadiennes oecuméniques pour la justice
#200, 310 Dupont St., Toronto ON M5R 1V9
Tel: 416-463-5312; *Fax:* 416-463-5569
Toll-Free: 877-403-8933
info@kairoscanada.org
www.kairoscanada.org
www.facebook.com/19277141685
twitter.com/kairoscanada
www.youtube.com/user/KAIROSCanada
Previous Name: Ecumenical Coalition for Economic Justice; GATT-Fly
Overview: A small national organization founded in 2001
Mission: To undertake a program of research & action with churches & popular groups emphasizing coalition-building & social transformation; five churches have participated in the Coalition since its inception: the Anglican Church of Canada, the Canadian Conference of Catholic Bishops, the Evangelical Lutheran Church in Canada, the Presbyterian Church in Canada, the United Church of Canada
Member of: Canadian Network on Corporate Accountability
Affiliation(s): Canadian Council of Churches
Finances: *Annual Operating Budget:* $1.5 Million-$3 Million; *Funding Sources:* Member denominations; Religious communities; Individual & group donations; Grants
Staff Member(s): 18; 300 volunteer(s)
Membership: 11; *Member Profile:* Canadian Churches; Religious organizations
Activities: *Speaker Service:* Yes
Chief Officer(s):
Jennifer Henry, Executive Director, 416-463-5312 Ext. 236
jhenry@kairoscanada.org
Ed Bianchi, Manager, Programs, 613-235-9956 Ext. 221
ebianchi@kairoscanada.org

Kaleidoscope Theatre Productions Society (KTPS)
3130 Jutland Rd., Victoria BC V8T 2T3
Tel: 250-383-8124; *Fax:* 250-383-8911
Toll-Free: 800-811-5777
info@kaleidoscope.bc.ca
www.kaleidoscope.bc.ca
facebook.com/kaleidoscopetheatre
twitter.com/kaleidoscope_ca
youtube.com/kaleidoscopetps
Also Known As: Kaleidoscope Theatre
Overview: A medium-sized national charitable organization founded in 1974
Mission: To create & present original, innovative & relevant theatre that stimulates & inspires the minds & imaginations of families & young people, using a style of presentation that emphasizes timeless & universal themes, is centered on the lives of young people & is enhanced by the integration of visuals, music & movement
Member of: ProArt; Greater Victoria Community Arts Council; Artstarts in Schools; BC Touring Council
Affiliation(s): Canadian Actors' Equity Association
Finances: *Annual Operating Budget:* $250,000-$500,000; *Funding Sources:* Federal, provincial & regional governments; performance fees; fundraising
Staff Member(s): 3
Membership: 40
Activities: Annual theatre productions; local, national & international touring; Annual Family Concert Series; Annual Young Playwright's Competition & Festival
Chief Officer(s):
Roderick Glanville, Artistic Director
David Ferguson, General Manager

Kali-Shiva AIDS Services
646 Logan Ave., Winnipeg MB R3A 0S7
Tel: 204-783-8565; *Fax:* 204-772-7237
kalishiv@mts.net
www.kalishiva.wix.com/shiva
Overview: A small local charitable organization founded in 1987 overseen by Canadian AIDS Society
Mission: To provide community-based support services for persons with HIV/AIDS
Activities: *Speaker Service:* Yes

Kamloops & District Labour Council (KDLC)
PO Box 369, Stn. Main, 929 Laval Cres., Kamloops BC V2C 5K9
www.kdlc.ca
Overview: A medium-sized local organization overseen by British Columbia Federation of Labour
Mission: To promote the interests of affiliates in Kamloops & the surrounding area; To advance the economic & social welfare of workers
Membership: 10,000; *Member Profile:* Unionized workers in British Columbia's Kamloops area, including Clearwater, Merritt, Ashcroft, & Chase
Activities: Raising awareness of issues, such as the Northern Gateway Pipeline Project & offshore oil exploration; Promoting social justice & human rights; Organizing Day of Mourning ceremonies, to remember persons who were injured or died on the job; Contributing to the community by participating in the Day of Caring
Chief Officer(s):
Barb Nederpel, President, 250-320-1635
Brad Gerow, First Vice-President
John Hall, Secretary-Treasurer
Awards:
• Kamloops & District Labour Council Bursaries
; *Amount:* $1,000

Kamloops & District Real Estate Association (KADREA)
#101, 418 St. Paul St., Kamloops BC V2C 2J6
Tel: 250-372-9411
kadrea.realtyserver.com
Overview: A small local organization founded in 1973 overseen by British Columbia Real Estate Association
Member of: Canadian Real Estate Association

Kamloops Exploration Group
#1100, 235 First Ave., Kamloops BC V2C 3J4
Tel: 250-828-2585
info@keg.bc.ca
www.keg.bc.ca
www.facebook.com/107234792716213
twitter.com/KamloopsExplora
Overview: A small local organization
Mission: To generally promote the interests of mining & prospecting for minerals, metals, & petroleum to the general public; to further the member's knowledge of mineral exploration & mining by offering informational lectures to members & the general public; to hold prospecting classes & promote other educational projects in connection with mining & prospecting; to further the general public's knowledge on the subject of Geoscience
Chief Officer(s):
Colin Russell, President, 250-578-2068
russellgeoscience@gmail.com

Kamloops Foodbank & Outreach Society
PO Box 1513, Stn. Main, 171 Wilson St., Kamloops BC V2C 6L8
Tel: 250-376-2252
Other Communication:
www.flickr.com/photos/kamloopsfoodbank
kamloopsfoodbank.org
www.facebook.com/kamloopsfoodbank
twitter.com/kamfoodbank
www.youtube.com/user/kamloopsfoodbank
Overview: A small local organization founded in 1985
Mission: To provide & support programs & services that feed the hungry, promote long-term food security & improve the social well-being of people in our community
Affiliation(s): Canadian Association of Food Banks
Finances: *Annual Operating Budget:* $500,000-$1.5 Million
Staff Member(s): 6; 70 volunteer(s)
Membership: 17; *Fees:* $1; *Committees:* Health Promotion; Fundraising; Maintenance; Personnel; Public Relations; Food Bank
Activities: Confidential services; hamper distribution on a monthly basis; hampers to last 3-58 days; nutritionally designed hampers; bread & bread products on a daily basis; birthday packages for children; pre-natal hampers; hampers for special needs diets; school snacks for students & children; free clothing *when available;* referrals to alternate agencies when needed; *Awareness Events:* Food Bank Month, Dec.

Kamloops Immigrant Services (KIS)
448 Tranquille Rd., Kamloops BC V2B 3H2
Tel: 778-470-6101; *Fax:* 778-470-6102
Toll-Free: 866-672-0855
kis@immigrantservices.ca
www.immigrantservices.ca
Overview: A small local organization founded in 1982
Mission: To assist immigrants, visible minorities & new Canadians to be full & equal participants in Canadian society; to promote positive race relations & organizational change in diversity
Member of: Affiliation of Multicultural Societies & Service Agencies of BC
Finances: *Annual Operating Budget:* $500,000-$1.5 Million; *Funding Sources:* Federal & provincial government; United Way; fundraising
Staff Member(s): 16; 60 volunteer(s)
Membership: *Committees:* Race Relations
Activities: Direct settlement; integration services; employment programs; ESL programs; counselling; interpretation/translation; diversity training & organizational change training; Safe Harbour Program; *Speaker Service:* Yes; *Rents Mailing List:* Yes; *Library:* ESL Library; Not open to public
Chief Officer(s):
David Cruz, Chair
Paul Lagace, Executive Director, 778-470-6101 Ext. 101
kcris@shaw.ca

Kamloops Multicultural Society (KMS)
PO Box 1515, Stn. Main, Kamloops BC V2C 6L8
Tel: 250-682-0289
info@kmsociety.ca
www.kmsociety.ca
Overview: A small local organization
Mission: To increase public awareness about issues surrounding multiculturalism
Member of: Affiliation of Multicultural Societies & Service Agencies of BC
Membership: 30 member groups; *Fees:* $50 group; $10 individual; *Member Profile:* Cultural organizations & interested individuals from Kamloops & area
Activities: Educational programmes in schools, festivals; *Speaker Service:* Yes
Chief Officer(s):
Ray Dhaliwal, President

Kamloops Naturalist Club (KNC)
PO Box 625, Kamloops BC V2C 5L7
Tel: 250-554-1285
marggraham@shaw.ca
www.kamloopsnaturalistclub.ca
Overview: A small local charitable organization founded in 1981 overseen by Federation of BC Naturalists
Mission: To promote the enjoyment of nature through environmental appreciation & conservation; to encourage wise use & conservation of natural resources & environmental protection
Member of: Canadian Nature Federation
Affiliation(s): Nature Canada
Finances: *Annual Operating Budget:* Less than $50,000; *Funding Sources:* Membership fees; grants; raffles
Membership: 1-99; *Fees:* $25 single; $35 family; *Member Profile:* All ages, but predominately retired
Activities: Field trips; workshops; monthly meetings; speakers

Kamloops Society for Community Living (KSCL)
521 Seymour St., Kamloops BC V2C 2G8
Tel: 250-374-3245; *Fax:* 250-374-2133
Overview: A small local charitable organization founded in 1956
Mission: To provide opportunities for persons with a developmental disability to experience a full life in as many aspects as they so choose by providing supports and services
Member of: British Columbia Association for Community Living
Finances: *Funding Sources:* Public support
Staff Member(s): 3

Kamloops Symphony (KSO)
PO Box 57, Kamloops BC V2C 5K3
Tel: 250-372-5000; *Fax:* 250-372-5089
info@kamloopssymphony.com
www.kamloopssymphony.com
www.facebook.com/kamloopssymphony
Also Known As: Kamloops Symphony Society
Overview: A small local charitable organization founded in 1976 overseen by Orchestras Canada
Mission: To operate & promote a symphony orchestra for the Kamloops region

Finances: *Funding Sources:* Provincial, federal & municipal government; Ticket sales; Donations; Fundraising
Staff Member(s): 7
Chief Officer(s):
Kathy Humphreys, General Manager
kathy@kamloopssymphony.com
Bruce Dunn, Music Director
bruce@kamloopssymphony.com

Kamloops Wildlife Park Society
9077 Dallas Dr., Kamloops BC V2C 6V1
Tel: 250-573-3242; *Fax:* 250-573-2406
info@bczoo.org
www.bczoo.org
www.facebook.com/BCzoo
Also Known As: BC Wildlife Park
Overview: A small local charitable organization founded in 1965
Mission: To encourage the appreciation of & respect for BC's wildlife; to assist in preserving biodiversity through education, research, captive breeding & rehabilitation service
Affiliation(s): Canadian Association of Zoos & Aquariums
Finances: *Annual Operating Budget:* $500,000-$1.5 Million; *Funding Sources:* Regional government; self-generated revenue
Staff Member(s): 15; 200 volunteer(s)
Membership: 2,000; *Fees:* $32 adults; $24 seniors; $20 children (age 3-17); $99 family (up to 5 members); *Member Profile:* Families from Kamloops region
Activities: Captive breeding for release endangered Burrowing Owls; *Awareness Events:* BC Hydro Wildlights, Dec.-Jan.; Family Farm, May-Sept.; BC Wildlife Day, 1st Mon. in Aug.; *Internships:* Yes; *Speaker Service:* Yes; *Library:* by appointment
Chief Officer(s):
Glenn Grant, General Manager, 250-573-3242 Ext. 231
glenn@bczoo.org
Jeff Stone, President
Jack Madryga, 1st Vice-President
Rod Simmons, 2nd Vice-President
Don Bogie, Treasurer

Kamloops, Revelstoke, Okanagan & District Building & Construction Trades Council
785 Tranquille Rd., Kamloops BC V2B 3J3
Tel: 250-554-2278; *Fax:* 250-554-1766
Overview: A small local organization
Member of: AFL-CIO
Chief Officer(s):
Leroy Vollans, Secretary-Treasurer
Andy Semenoff, Vice-President
Gary Kinnear, President

Kamsack & District Arts Council
PO Box 1496, Kamsack SK S0A 1S0
Tel: 306-590-0196
clachambre@aol.com
kamsackarts.weebly.com
www.facebook.com/KamsackArt
Overview: A small local charitable organization founded in 1981
Mission: To promote enjoyment & education in visual & performing arts
Member of: Organization of Saskatchewan Arts Councils
Finances: *Annual Operating Budget:* Less than $50,000; *Funding Sources:* Trust Initiatives Program; Saskatchewan Lotteries
7 volunteer(s)
Membership: 7; *Committees:* Visual Arts; Performing Arts

Kamsack & District Chamber of Commerce
PO Box 817, Kamsack SK S0A 1S0
Tel: 306-542-3553; *Fax:* 306-542-3553
Overview: A small local organization

Kanada Türk Dernekleri Federasyonu *See* Federation of Canadian Turkish Associations

Kanadsko Hrvatski Kongres *See* Canadian Croatian Congress

Kanata Chamber of Commerce *See* West Ottawa Board of Trade

Kanien'kehaka Onkwawen'na Raotitiohkwa *See* Kanien'kehaka Onkwawen'na Raotitiohkwa Language & Cultural Centre

Kanien'kehaka Onkwawen'na Raotitiohkwa Language & Cultural Centre (KORLCC)
PO Box 969, Kahnawake QC J0L 1B0
Tel: 450-638-0880; *Fax:* 450-638-0920
kor@korkahnawake.org
www.korkahnawake.org
Previous Name: Kanien'kehaka Onkwawen'na Raotitiohkwa
Overview: A small local charitable organization founded in 1978
Mission: To lead & support all Kanien'kehaka; to practice, maintain, respect, renew & enhance Kanien'kehaka language, beliefs, values, customs & traditions through the development, delivery & sharing with all peoples; to provide cultural & educational activities which will ensure the continued existence of present & future generations of Kanien'kehaka
Member of: First Nations Confederacy of Cultural Education Centres
Staff Member(s): 12
Activities: Kanien'keha language courses; cultural workshops; translation services; *Library:* Open to public
Chief Officer(s):
Reaghan Tarbell, Executive Director
Joe Deom, Chair

Kapuskasing & District Chamber of Commerce
25 Millview Rd., Kapuskasing ON P5N 2X6
Tel: 705-335-2332; *Fax:* 705-335-2359
info@kapchamber.ca
www.kapchamber.ca
www.facebook.com/KDCofC
twitter.com/KDCC2
Overview: A medium-sized local organization
Mission: To help businesses & the community thrive & grow
Activities: *Awareness Events:* Business Drive Golf Tournament, June
Chief Officer(s):
Martin Proulx, President

Kapuskasing Friendship Centre (KFC)
41 Murdock St., Kapuskasing ON P5N 1H9
Tel: 705-337-1935; *Fax:* 705-335-6789
kifc@ntl.sympatico.ca
www.ofifc.org/centre/kapuskasing-friendship-centre
Previous Name: Kapuskasing Indian Friendship Centre
Overview: A small local organization founded in 1985
Mission: To help improve the lives of the Aboriginal community in the Kapuskasing area through participation in Canadian society which values Native culture
Member of: Ontario Federation of Indian Friendship Centres

Kapuskasing Indian Friendship Centre *See* Kapuskasing Friendship Centre

Kapuskasing, Cochrane & District Association for Community Living
12 Kimberly Dr., Kapuskasing ON P5N 1L5
Tel: 705-337-1417; *Fax:* 705-337-6538
Overview: A small local organization
Member of: Community Living Ontario
Chief Officer(s):
Carole Theriault, Executive Director
ctheriault@neacl.ca

Karate Alberta Association (KAA)
c/o Stewart Price, 56 Auburn Crest Park, Calgary AB T3M 0Z3
Tel: 403-601-1610
www.karateab.org
www.facebook.com/karateAlberta
Overview: A small provincial organization overseen by Karate Canada
Mission: To be the provincial governing body for the sport of karate in Alberta
Member of: Karate Canada
Finances: *Funding Sources:* Government of Alberta
Membership: *Committees:* Bylaws; Casino; Coaching; Communications; Officials; Tournament; Technical
Chief Officer(s):
Marc Ward, President, 403-991-1821
Dean Tucker, Membership Officer, 403-691-5323

Karate BC (KBC)
Fortius Athlete Development Centre, Sydney Landing, #2002A, 3713 Kensington Ave., Burnaby BC V5B 0A7
Tel: 604-333-3610; *Fax:* 604-333-3612
Toll-Free: 855-806-8126
www.karatebc.org
www.facebook.com/OfficalKarateBC
twitter.com/KarateBC
Overview: A small provincial charitable organization founded in 1974 overseen by Karate Canada
Mission: To promote the traditions & integrity of karate-do; to improve opportunities to excel in a competitive environment; to be the governing body of the sport of karate in British Columbia.
Member of: Karate Canada; BC Recreation & Parks Association; BC Coaches Association; Sport BC
Finances: *Annual Operating Budget:* $250,000-$500,000; *Funding Sources:* Provincial government; gaming; fundraising
Staff Member(s): 2
Membership: 4,000; *Fees:* Schedule available; *Member Profile:* Instructor must hold bona-fide Dan certificate, be certified at level I NCCP & pass a criminal records check; *Committees:* Executive; Officials; Technical; Tournament; Marketing; Newsletter; High Performance
Activities: Tournaments; coaching clinics; officials seminars; athlete assistance program; coaching grants; first aid clinics; BC Winter Games; mall demos; annual recognition banquet for outstanding athletes & volunteers; *Internships:* Yes; *Speaker Service:* Yes; *Library:* by appointment
Chief Officer(s):
Norma Foster, President
guseikai@hotmail.com
Jonathan Wornell, Executive Director
jwornell@karatebc.org
Conan Cooper, Coordinator, Coaching Development
coachdev@karatebc.org
Meetings/Conferences:
• Karate BC Annual General Meeting 2018, 2018, BC
Scope: Provincial
Publications:
• Karate BC Newsletter
Type: Newsletter

Karate Canada
c/o Canadian Olympic Committee, 500, boul René-Lévesque ouest, Montréal QC H2Z 1W7
Tel: 514-252-3209; *Fax:* 514-252-3211
info@karatecanada.org
www.karatecanada.org
www.facebook.com/459465044133223
Previous Name: National Karate Association of Canada
Overview: A medium-sized national organization founded in 1963
Mission: To be the national governing body for the sport of karate in Canada
Member of: Sport Canada; Canadian Olympic Committee; World Karate Federation
Membership: 10 provincial & territorial associations; 13,000 individuals; *Committees:* Finance; Communications & Marketing; Governance & Policy; Domestic Development; Events; High Performance; Officials; NCCP/LTAD; Technical; Para-Karate
Chief Officer(s):
Olivier Pineau, Executive Director
olivier@karatecanada.org
Alexandra Roy, Program Manager
alexandra.roy@karatecanada.org

Karate Manitoba
145 Pacific Ave., Winnipeg MB R3B 2Z6
Tel: 204-925-5605; *Fax:* 204-925-5916
info@karatemanitoba.ca
www.karatemanitoba.ca
www.facebook.com/KarateManitobaWKF
twitter.com/KarateManitoba
www.youtube.com/user/KarateManitoba
Also Known As: Manitoba Karate Association
Overview: A small provincial organization founded in 1974 overseen by Karate Canada
Mission: To promote & develop karate in the province of Manitoba at all levels (grassroots to elite athlete) & as recreation.
Member of: Karate Canada; World Karate Federation; Sport Manitoba
Membership: 600; *Committees:* NCCP; Officials; Athlete Development; Finance; Grassroots
Chief Officer(s):
Debra Kofsky, President
president@karatemanitoba.ca
Sharon Andrews, Secretary
km.officials@live.ca

Karate New Brunswick
NB
karatenb.com
Previous Name: New Brunswick Karate Association
Overview: A small provincial organization overseen by Karate Canada

Member of: Karate Canada
Finances: Funding Sources: Provincial government
Staff Member(s): 1; 15 volunteer(s)
Membership: 600 individual
Activities: Rents Mailing List: Yes
Chief Officer(s):
Don Mazerolle, President
djmaz@bellaliant.net

Karate Newfoundland & Labrador (KNL)
c/o 3 Albert Pl., Torbay NL A1K 0J4
karatenl@gmail.com
www.karatenl.ca
Overview: A small provincial organization overseen by Karate Canada
Mission: To be the provincial governing body for the sport of karate in Newfoundland & Labrador
Member of: Karate Canada
Chief Officer(s):
Derek J. Ryan, President

Karate Nova Scotia (KNS)
5516 Spring Garden Rd., 4th Fl., Halifax NS B3J 3G6
info@karatens.org
karatens.org
Overview: A small provincial organization overseen by Karate Canada
Mission: To be the provincial governing body for the sport of karate in Nova Scotia
Member of: Karate Canada
Activities: Tournaments; Athlete Development; Awards
Chief Officer(s):
Gary Walsh, President
garywalsh.ns@hotmail.com
Greg Da Ros, Vice President
info@karatens.org

Karate Ontario (KAO)
#160, 2 County Court Blvd., Brampton ON L6W 4V1
Tel: 647-706-4835
info@karate-ontario.com
karate-ontario.com
www.facebook.com/309961174058
www.youtube.com/channel/UCnjL8YhmflRwiK1FZQBAIUA
Overview: A medium-sized provincial organization overseen by Karate Canada
Mission: To promote & perpetuate karate as a martial art & lifetime activity; to promote karate for physical fitness, mental fitness, & as a way of life; to develop provincial standards & programs; to encourage all participants in safely achieving their maximum at the recreational or competitive level; to provide safe competitive opportunities for karate-ka wishing to participate in the sport aspect of karate; to govern the amateur sport of karate & the conduct of all karate-ka under its jurisdiction
Member of: Karate Canada
Affiliation(s): World Karate Federation; Sport Alliance of Ontario; Coaches Assocation of Ontario
Membership: Committees: Technical; Referee; Coaching; Constitution; Dispute Resolution; Medical; Women's Affairs; Communications; Awards
Activities: Awareness Events: Sport Science Karate Symposium, June
Chief Officer(s):
Pravilal Pravibhavan, President
ppravibhavan@karate-ontario.com

Karaté Québec
CP 1000, Succ. M, 4545, av Pierre-de Coubertin, Montréal QC H1V 3R2
Tél: 514-252-3161; Téléc: 514-252-3036
Ligne sans frais: 877-527-2835
info@karatequebec.com
www.karatequebec.com
www.facebook.com/karatequebec
Aperçu: Dimension: moyenne; Envergure: provinciale; fondée en 1995 surveillé par Karate Canada
Mission: Karaté Québec est une organisation structurée et démocratique qui vise à promouvoir, à organiser et à administrer la pratique du karaté au Québec de manière à ce que cet art martial ne perde jamais son sens premier : favoriser une progression saine et équilibrée des karatékas dans une société en mouvance perpétuelle
Membre de: Karate Canada

Kashmiri Canadian Council (KCC)
#44516, 2376 Eglinton Ave. East, Toronto ON M1K 5K3
Tel: 416-282-6933; Fax: 416-282-7488
kcc@kashmiri-cc.ca
www.kashmiri-cc.ca
Overview: A small international organization
Finances: Annual Operating Budget: $100,000-$250,000
Staff Member(s): 3

Kashruth Council of Canada
#308, 3200 Dufferin St., Toronto ON M6A 3B2
Tel: 416-635-9550; Fax: 416-635-8760
questions@cor.ca
www.cor.ca
www.facebook.com/CORKosher
twitter.com/CORKosher
Also Known As: COR
Previous Name: Kashruth Council of Toronto
Overview: A small local organization founded in 1956
Mission: To promote awareness among consumers and manufacturers about kosher products.
Affiliation(s): Vaad Harabonim of Toronto
Staff Member(s): 20
Activities: Kosher cooking demos; holiday recipes & updates; kosher food supervision
Chief Officer(s):
Tuvia Basser, Chief Executive Officer

Kashruth Council of Toronto See Kashruth Council of Canada

Kaslo & Area Chamber of Commerce
PO Box 329, Kaslo BC V0G 1M0
Toll-Free: 866-276-3212
thekaslochamber@gmail.com
www.kaslochamber.com
www.facebook.com/kaslochamber
Previous Name: Kaslo Chamber of Commerce
Overview: A small local organization founded in 1897
Mission: To promote & improve trade & commerce & the economic, civic & social welfare of the district.
Finances: Funding Sources: Membership dues
Membership: 70+; Fees: $80 business; $55 associate
Chief Officer(s):
John Addison, President
Awards:
• Kaslo Citizen of the Year Award
• Business Excellence Awards
Publications:
• Kaslo & Area Chamber of Commerce Newsletter
Type: Newsletter

Kaslo Arts Counci See Langham Cultural Society

Kaslo Chamber of Commerce See Kaslo & Area Chamber of Commerce

Katimavik
429, av Viger est, Montréal QC H2L 2N9
Tel: 514-868-0898; Fax: 514-868-0901
Toll-Free: 888-525-1503
info@katimavik.org
www.katimavik.org
www.facebook.com/KatimavikFans?ref=stream&fref=nf
Overview: A small national organization founded in 1977
Mission: To engage youth in volunteer service and foster sustainable communities through challenging national youth service programs.
Chief Officer(s):
Robert Landry, Executive Director
Andréanne Sylvestre, Coordinator, Communications

Kawartha Baseball Umpires Association (KBUA)
ON
Overview: A small local organization

Kawartha Chamber of Commerce & Tourism
PO Box 537, 12 Queen St., Lakefield ON K0L 2H0
Tel: 705-652-6963; Fax: 705-652-9140
Toll-Free: 888-565-8888
www.kawarthachamber.ca
www.linkedin.com/company/kawarthachamberofcommerce&tourism
www.facebook.com/KawarthaChamber
twitter.com/KawarthaChamber
www.instagram.com/kawarthachamber
Previous Name: Kawartha Lakes Chamber of Commerce
Overview: A small local organization founded in 1947
Mission: To promote the commercial, industrial, agricultural & civic welfare of the community; To maintain just & equitable principles in business & the professions
Member of: Canadian Chamber of Commerce; Ontario Chamber of Commerce; Canadian Society of Association Executives
Finances: Annual Operating Budget: $50,000-$100,000
Staff Member(s): 4; 14 volunteer(s)
Membership: 350; Fees: $170-$620; Committees: Marketing; Membership; Programs & Events; Public Policy; Human Resources; Finance; Governance; Nominating
Activities: Library:
Chief Officer(s):
Kris Keller, President
Sherry Boyce-Found, General Manager
generalmanager@kawarthachamber.ca

Kawartha Lakes Chamber of Commerce See Kawartha Chamber of Commerce & Tourism

Kawartha Lakes Real Estate Association
31 Kent St. East, Lindsay ON K9V 2C3
Tel: 705-324-4515
www.kawarthalakes-mls.ca
www.facebook.com/184458454969478
Previous Name: Lindsay & District Real Estate Board
Overview: A small local organization founded in 1958 overseen by Ontario Real Estate Association
Mission: To provide its members with resources that allow them to grow within the profession
Member of: The Canadian Real Estate Association
Chief Officer(s):
Susan Schell, Executive Officer
sschell@kawarthalakes-mls.ca

Kawartha Sexual Assault Centre
#102, 411 Water St., Peterborough ON K9H 3L9
Tel: 705-748-5901; Fax: 705-741-0405
Toll-Free: 866-298-7778; Crisis Hot-Line: 705-741-0260
ksac@nexicom.net
www.kawarthasexualassaultcentre.com
www.facebook.com/125032707554367
twitter.com/KSACstaff
Previous Name: Sexual Violence Support & Information Centre of the Kawarthas
Overview: A small local charitable organization founded in 1977
Mission: To provide sexual assault services & public education for the community
Finances: Funding Sources: Ministry of the Attorney General; City of Peterborough; Trent University Student Levy
Activities: 24-hour crisis line; outreach counselling; in-house counselling; public education; Speaker Service: Yes

Kawartha World Issues Centre (KWIC)
PO Box 895, Peterborough ON K9J 7A2
Tel: 705-748-1680; Fax: 705-748-1681
info@kwic.info
www.kwic.info
www.facebook.com/KWICPeterborough
twitter.com/KWICnews
www.youtube.com/user/KWICpeterborough
Overview: A small international charitable organization founded in 1988
Mission: To further an understanding of global issues; to create links between global & local community development; to promote analysis & action for positive social change
Member of: Eastern Ontario Coalition of Internationally-Minded NGOs; Ontario Council for International Cooperation
Finances: Funding Sources: Public donations; Trent student donations; CIDA; special grants
Staff Member(s): 2
Membership: Fees: Donations
Activities: Public Programming on global issues; skills training; networking; special projects: Person's Day Breakfast, International Development Week; One World (Vegetarian) Dinner; Global Youth Day, Volunteer Recruitment & Training, Annual Secondary School Symposium; Speaker Service: Yes; Library: Open to public
Chief Officer(s):
Julie Cosgrove, Coordinator

Kawartha-Haliburton Children's Aid Society
1100 Chemong Rd., Peterborough ON K9H 7S2
Tel: 705-743-9751; Fax: 757-437-858
Toll-Free: 800-661-2843
www.khcas.on.ca
Overview: A small local organization
Mission: To protect children, youth, & young adults by engaging & cooperating with families & the wider community
Member of: Ontario Association of Children's Aid Societies

Finances: *Annual Operating Budget:* Greater than $5 Million
Staff Member(s): 100; 50 volunteer(s)
Activities: Providing adoption & foster care services; Investigating possible instances of child abuse & neglect; *Speaker Service:* Yes
Chief Officer(s):
Deirdre Thomas, President
  Haliburton
  HALCO Plaza, PO Box 958, 83 Maple Ave., Haliburton ON K0M 1S0
  Tel: 705-457-1661
  Toll-Free: 800-661-1979
  Lindsay
  42 Victoria Ave. North, Lindsay ON K9V 4G2
  Tel: 705-324-3594
  Toll-Free: 800-567-9136

Kaye Nickerson Adult Service Centre
PO Box 3, 87 Parade St., Yarmouth NS B0H 1R0
Tel: 902-742-2238; *Fax:* 902-386-2808
kayenick@ns.aliantzinc.ca
Overview: A small local organization
Mission: To provide mentally challenged adults in Yarmouth with vocational training & work experience
Membership: *Member Profile:* Adults with special needs, aged 18+
Activities: Provides services involving pallets, lawn furniture, survey stakes, rough boxes, garbage bins, kindling wood & buttons, as well as special orders
Chief Officer(s):
Darrell Foster, Executive Director/Manager

Keewatin Chamber of Commerce *See* Kivalliq Chamber of Commerce

Keewatin Tribal Council (KTC)
23 Nickel Rd., Thompson MB R8N 0Y4
Tel: 204-677-2341; *Fax:* 204-677-0256
www.ktc.ca
Previous Name: Winnipeg Tribal Council
Overview: A small provincial organization
Chief Officer(s):
Irvin Sinclair, Grand Chief
Walter Spence, Chair
Gilbert G. Andrews, Vice-Chair
Peter Thorassie, Sec.-Treas.

Kelowna *See* Habitat for Humanity Canada

Kelowna & District Arts Council *See* Arts Council of the Central Okanagan

Kelowna & District Stamp Club
4740 Parkridge Dr., Kelowna BC V1W 3A5
Overview: A small local organization
Mission: To provide an opportunity for stamp collectors to exhibit, buy & sell stamps & to share their knowledge of philately
Activities: Monthly meetings, every 1st Wed. at Odd Fellows Hall

Kelowna Chamber of Commerce
544 Harvey Ave., Kelowna BC V1Y 6C9
Tel: 250-861-3627; *Fax:* 250-861-3624
info@kelownachamber.org
www.kelownachamber.org
www.linkedin.com/groups/Kelowna-Chamber-Commerce-3972388
www.facebook.com/KelownaChamberofCommerce
twitter.com/KelownaChamber
Overview: A medium-sized local organization
Mission: To improve trade & commerce & the economic, civic & social welfare of the city of Kelowna
Affiliation(s): BC Chamber of Commerce
Staff Member(s): 8
Membership: *Fees:* Schedule available; *Committees:* Advocacy; Ambassadors; Local Issues; Member Care; Provincial & Federal Policy; Taxation Advisory; Women's Leadership; Young People in Business
Activities: *Rents Mailing List:* Yes; *Library:* Open to public
Chief Officer(s):
Tom Dyas, President
Caroline Grover, Chief Executive Officer
caroline@kelownachamber.org

Kelowna Visitor & Convention Bureau *See* Tourism Kelowna

Kemptville & District Chamber of Commerce *See* North Grenville Chamber of Commerce

Kenaston & District Chamber of Commerce
PO Box 70, Kenaston SK S0G 2N0
www.kenaston.ca/pages/chamber.htm
Overview: A small local organization
Chief Officer(s):
Susan Anbolt, Sec.-Treas.
Mary Lou Whittles, President
r.m.whittles@sasktel.net

Kennebecasis Naturalists' Society
c/o Ms. H. Folkins, 827 Main St., Sussex NB E4E 2N1
www.macbe.com/kns/
Overview: A small local organization
5 volunteer(s)
Membership: 80
Activities: Field trips
Chief Officer(s):
Gart Bishop, Chair

Kenneth M Molson Foundation
PO Box 50, 1 First Canadian Pl., Toronto ON M5X 1B8
kennethmolsonfoundation@gmail.com
www.kennethmolsonfoundation.ca
Overview: A small national charitable organization
Mission: To support charitable & educational organizations in Canada that focus on aeronautical engineering education & research, aviation history & libraries, wildlife research, conservation, & habitat
Activities: Providing grants

Kenora & District Chamber of Commerce (KDCC)
PO Box 471, Kenora ON P9N 3X5
Tel: 807-467-4646; *Fax:* 807-468-3056
kenorachamber@kmts.ca
www.kenorachamber.com
www.facebook.com/KenoraChamber
twitter.com/KenoraChamber
Overview: A small local organization founded in 1888
Mission: To promote a favourable business climate; To enhance quality of life; To stimulate the growth & prosperity of members
Member of: Northwestern Ontario Associated Chambers of Commerce; Canadian Chamber of Commerce
Membership: 230+; *Fees:* Schedule available; *Committees:* Education; Government Affairs & Tendering Home & Leisure Show; Membership Services/Membership Recruitment; Policy & Procedures/By-law & Constitution; Special Events/After Hour Mixers
Chief Officer(s):
Carlee Hakenson, Manager

Kenora Association for Community Living (KACL)
501 - 8th Ave. South, Kenora ON P9N 3Z9
Tel: 807-467-5225; *Fax:* 807-467-5247
www.kacl.ca
www.facebook.com/kenora.acl
twitter.com/KenoraACL
www.youtube.com/user/KenoraACL
Overview: A medium-sized local charitable organization founded in 1961
Mission: To ensure that all people with special needs have the chance to enjoy a meaningful lifestyle & full participation in their community through the provision of education, training, support, advocacy, & other personal growth opportunities
Member of: Community Living Ontario
Finances: *Annual Operating Budget:* $3 Million-$5 Million
Staff Member(s): 160; 20 volunteer(s)
Membership: 50; *Fees:* $10
Activities: *Speaker Service:* Yes; *Library:* Open to public
Chief Officer(s):
Deborah Everley, Executive Director, 807-467-5251
debbie.everley@kacl.ca
Diane Pelletier, Senior Director, 807-467-5236
Kelly Williams, Senior Director, 807-467-5232

Kenora District Labour Council
Kenora ON
Previous Name: Kenora-Keewatin & District Labour Council
Overview: A small local organization overseen by Ontario Federation of Labour
Membership: 2,700

Kenora Fellowship Centre
PO Box 447, Kenora ON P9N 3X4
Tel: 807-467-8205; *Fax:* 807-468-9063
kenorafellowship@kmts.ca
www.kenorafellowshipcentre.ca
Overview: A small local charitable organization
Mission: To offer emergency shelter to the less fortunate
Staff Member(s): 20
Chief Officer(s):
Henry Hildebtrandt, Executive Director

Kenora-Keewatin & District Labour Council *See* Kenora District Labour Council

Kensington & Area Chamber of Commerce
PO Box 234, Kensington PE C0B 1M0
Tel: 902-836-3209; *Fax:* 902-836-3206
info@kensingtonchamber.ca
kensingtonchamber.ca
www.linkedin.com/groups/Kensington-Area-Chamber-Commerce-3837839
www.facebook.com/KensingtonAreaChamberofCommerce
twitter.com/KTownChamber
www.youtube.com/user/KtownChamber
Overview: A small local organization founded in 1961
Mission: To protect the interests of the business community; To promote & strengthen trade & commerce
Member of: PEI Chamber of Commerce; Atlantic Provinces Chambers of Commerce
Finances: *Annual Operating Budget:* Less than $50,000; *Funding Sources:* Membership fees
Membership: 129; *Fees:* $85
Chief Officer(s):
Patricia Bennett, President
Jessica Caseley, Coordinator, Membership & Events

Kensington & Area Tourist Association
PO Box 600, Kensington PE C0B 1M0
Tel: 902-836-3031; *Fax:* 902-836-3674
mail@kata.pe.ca
www.kata.pe.ca
Overview: A small local organization
Staff Member(s): 3; 6 volunteer(s)
Membership: *Fees:* $26+

Kensington Cooperative Association Ltd
48 Victoria St. East, Kensington PE C0B 1M0
Tel: 902-836-3116; *Fax:* 902-836-3770
Overview: A small local organization

Kensington Foundation
25 Brunswick Ave., Toronto ON M5S 2L9
Tel: 416-964-3636; *Fax:* 416-963-9811
www.kensingtonhealth.org/Kensington-Foundation
Overview: A small local charitable organization
Mission: To raise money of behalf of Kensington Health, a long term care organization
Finances: *Annual Operating Budget:* Greater than $5 Million
Membership: *Committees:* Audit; Investment; Kensington Golf; Grants/Donations; Strategic Planning
Chief Officer(s):
Brian McFarlane, Executive Director

Kent Centre Chamber of Commerce
#1, 9235 rue Main, Richibucto NB E4W 4B4
Tel: 506-523-7870; *Fax:* 506-523-7850
www.kentcentre.com
Previous Name: Richibouctou chambre de commerce
Overview: A small local organization
Mission: To serve the needs & interests of local entrepreneurs; To address issues affecting local business & community
Member of: Atlantic Chamber of Commerce
Finances: *Annual Operating Budget:* Less than $50,000
10 volunteer(s)
Membership: 45+; *Fees:* $25
Activities: *Speaker Service:* Yes; *Library*
Chief Officer(s):
Jody Pratt, President & Treasurer

Kent Coin Club
27 Peter St., Chatham ON N7M 5B2
Tel: 519-352-5477
Overview: A small local organization founded in 1963
Mission: To encourage & promote the collection and study of coins, tokens, paper money, medals, badges, trade money, and other currency related collectibles; to cultivate fraternal relations among collectors.
Finances: *Funding Sources:* Membership fees
Membership: *Fees:* $2 child; $5 adult; $7 family
Activities: Annual Coin Show
Chief Officer(s):
Lucien Wagenaer, President

Kent County Cattlemen's Association
7189 - 9th Line, RR#6, Chatham ON N7M 5J6
Tel: 519-436-0701
Overview: A small local organization
Affiliation(s): Ontario Cattlemen's Association
Chief Officer(s):
Mike Buis, President

Kent County Community Volunteer Action Organization
PO Box 2706, #4, 9358 Main St., Richibucto NB E4W 4C8
Tel: 506-523-7580; *Fax:* 506-523-4086
Also Known As: Kent County C.V.A. Organization
Overview: A small local organization
Member of: Association of Food Banks & C.V.A.'s for New Brunswick

Kent County Stamp Club
43 Sudbury Dr., Chatham ON N7L 2K1
Tel: 519-354-1845
Overview: A small local organization founded in 1960
Mission: Provides an opportunity for members & guests to trade, deal & learn about stamps in a friendly, informal setting
Member of: Royal Philatelic Society of Canada
Membership: *Fees:* $10
Activities: *Awareness Events:* KENTPEX, annual Stamp Exhibition & Bourse
Chief Officer(s):
Allan Burk, Contact

Kentville & Area Board of Trade; Eastern Kings Chamber of Commerce *See* Annapolis Valley Chamber of Commerce

Kerby Centre for the 55 Plus
1133 - 7th Ave. SW, Calgary AB T2P 1B2
Tel: 403-265-0661; *Fax:* 403-705-3211
information@kerbycentre.com
kerbycentre.com
www.facebook.com/pages/Kerby-Centre-for-the-55/514905501859242
twitter.com/KerbyCentre
www.youtube.com/user/hheerema29
Overview: A medium-sized local charitable organization founded in 1976
Mission: To assist older people to live as well as possible for as long as possible as residents in the community. Services include Adult Day Support, grocery delivery, food services, housing registry, wellness centre
Finances: *Annual Operating Budget:* $3 Million-$5 Million; *Funding Sources:* Provincial & regional government (38%); remaining funds are self-generated
Membership: 2,997 individual; *Member Profile:* Anyone age 55 and over
Activities: Sr. Multi Service Centre; *Library:* Resource Centre for the Aging Family; Open to public
Chief Officer(s):
Luanne Whitmarsh, CEO
Hank Heerema, President

Kermode Friendship Centre *See* Kermode Friendship Society

Kermode Friendship Society
#201, 3240 Kalum St., Terrace BC V8G 2N4
Tel: 250-635-1476; *Fax:* 250-635-7696
Toll-Free: 877-635-1476
info@kermode-fs.ca
kermodefriendship.ca
www.facebook.com/KermodeFS
Previous Name: Kermode Friendship Centre
Overview: A small local charitable organization founded in 1976
Mission: To provide cultural services & programs to the Aboriginal community in the Terrace area
Staff Member(s): 38
Activities: Health; education; parenting; youth
Chief Officer(s):
Calvin Albright, Executive Director
execdir@kermode-fs.ca

Keroul, Tourism & culture for people with restricted physical ability *Voir* Kéroul, Tourisme pour personnes à capacité physique restreinte

Kéroul, Tourisme pour personnes à capacité physique restreinte / Keroul, Tourism & culture for people with restricted physical ability
4545, av Pierre-de Coubertin, Montréal QC H1V 0B2
Tél: 514-252-3104; *Téléc:* 514-254-0766
infos@keroul.qc.ca
www.keroul.qc.ca
www.facebook.com/keroul1979
Aperçu: *Dimension:* moyenne; *Envergure:* provinciale; fondée en 1979
Mission: Rendre le tourisme et la culture accessibles aux personnes à capacité physique restreinte
Affiliation(s): Regroupement loisir Québec
Finances: *Budget de fonctionnement annuel:* $250,000-$500,000
Membre(s) du personnel: 7; 9 bénévole(s)
Membre: 400 individus; 40 institutionnel; *Montant de la cotisation:* 25$ individus; 60$ organismes
Activités: Représentation; information et promotion; recherche; formation; organisation d'événements; *Stagiaires:* Oui; *Service de conférenciers:* Oui
Membre(s) du bureau directeur:
André Leclerc, Président-directeur général et fondateur
aleclerc@keroul.qc.ca
Lyne Ménard, Directrice adjointe
lmenard@keroul.qc.ca

Kerrobert Chamber of Commerce
433 Manitoba Ave., Kerrobert SK S0L 1R0
Tel: 306-834-5423
kerrobertchamber@sasktel.net
www.kerrobertsk.com
Overview: A small local organization
Member of: Saskatchewan Chamber of Commerce
Chief Officer(s):
Darryl Morris, President

Kerry's Place Autism Services
34 Berczy St., Aurora ON L4G 1W9
Tel: 905-841-6611; *Fax:* 905-841-1461
info@kerrysplace.org
www.kerrysplace.org
www.facebook.com/kerrysplaceautismservices
twitter.com/kerrysplace
Overview: A medium-sized local charitable organization founded in 1974
Mission: To enhance the quality of life of individuals with Autism Spectrum Disorder through support, expertise, collaboration & advocacy
Finances: *Annual Operating Budget:* Greater than $5 Million; *Funding Sources:* Donations, Fundraising events
Staff Member(s): 1000
Membership: *Fees:* $20 individual/associate; $15 people with autism/seniors/students; $60 corporate; *Member Profile:* Parents; professionals
Activities: *Library:* Resource Centre; by appointment
Chief Officer(s):
Isabel Meharry, Interim President & CEO
imeharry@kerrysplace.org

Central Region
38B Berczy St., Aurora ON L4G 1W9
Tel: 905-713-6808
Chief Officer(s):
Tracy Mansell, Regional Executive Director, 905-713-6808 Ext. 318
tracy.mansell@kerrysplace.org

Eastern Office
189 Victoria Ave., Belleville ON K8N 2B9
Tel: 613-968-5554; *Fax:* 613-967-4555
Chief Officer(s):
Lisa Binns, Regional Executive Director
lisa.binns@kerrysplace.org

Kerry's Place Toronto
#12A, 219 Dufferin St., Toronto ON M6K 3J1
Tel: 416-537-2000; *Fax:* 416-537-7715
Chief Officer(s):
Kelly West, Regional Executive Director
kelly.west@kerrysplace.org

Kerry's Place Hastings *See* Kerry's Place Autism Services

Kerry's Place South East *See* Kerry's Place Autism Services

Keyano College Faculty Association (KCFA) / Association des professeurs du Collège Keyano
8115 Franklin Ave., Fort McMurray AB T9H 2H7
Tel: 780-791-4800
Overview: A small local organization
Chief Officer(s):
C. Vincella Thompson, Contact
vincella.thompson@keyano.ca

Keystone Agricultural Producers (KAP)
#203, 1700 Ellice Ave., Winnipeg MB R3H 0B1
Tel: 204-697-1140; *Fax:* 204-697-1109
kap@kap.mb.ca
www.kap.mb.ca
twitter.com/KAP_Manitoba
Previous Name: Manitoba Farm Bureau
Overview: A medium-sized provincial organization founded in 1985 overseen by Canadian Federation of Agriculture
Mission: To be a democratic & effective policy organization, promoting the social, economic & physical well-being of all Manitoban agricultural producers
Staff Member(s): 6
Membership: *Fees:* $200 farm; $210 associate; $1,050 group
Chief Officer(s):
James Battershill, General Manager
james.battershill@kap.mb.ca
Dan Mazier, President
Meetings/Conferences:
• Keystone Agricultural Producers 2018 Annual Meeting, January, 2018, Delta Hotel, Winnipeg, MB
Scope: National
Publications:
• Manitoba Farmers' Voice [a publication of Keystone Agricultural Producers]
Type: Journal; *Frequency:* Quarterly

Khalsa Diwan Society
8000 Ross St., Vancouver BC V5X 4C5
Tel: 604-322-5610; *Fax:* 604-322-0504
kdsross@live.com
kdsross.com
www.facebook.com/kdsross
twitter.com/kdsross
Also Known As: Gurdwara Sahib Ross Street
Overview: A large local organization founded in 1906
Mission: To act as a Sikh society in BC; To build a strong community based on Sikhi values & principles
Finances: *Annual Operating Budget:* $500,000-$1.5 Million
Activities: Raising awareness of Sikhi issues in the community; Offering Punjabi classes at the temple and in various schools in Vancouver; Establishing a computer training centre for new immigrants, youth, & seniors; Organizing sports activities & tournaments
Chief Officer(s):
Gurdwara Sahib, Director, 604-322-5610
Joginder Singh Sunner, Secretary, 604-317-5454

Kicking Horse Country Chamber of Commerce (KHCCC)
PO Box 1320, #500, 10 North Ave., Golden BC V0A 1H0
Tel: 250-344-7125; *Fax:* 250-344-6688
Toll-Free: 800-622-4653
www.goldenchamber.bc.ca
www.facebook.com/KHCCC
twitter.com/KHCchamber
Previous Name: Golden & District Chamber of Commerce
Overview: A small local organization
Mission: To actively encourage, develop & represent the business community of Golden & District
Member of: BC Chamber of Commerce; Tourism Rockies
Finances: *Funding Sources:* Membership dues
Staff Member(s): 1
Membership: 240; *Committees:* Policy & Advocacy; Events; Education & Training; Finance
Chief Officer(s):
Ruth Hamilton, Manager
Michele La Point, President

KickStart Disability Arts & Culture
PO Box 2749, Stn. Terminal, Vancouver BC V6B 3X2
Tel: 604-559-6626
info@kickstart-arts.ca
www.kickstart-arts.ca
www.facebook.com/318968627521
Previous Name: Society for Disability Arts & Culture
Overview: A small national organization founded in 1998
Mission: Kickstart's mission is to produce and present works by artists with disabilities and to promote artistic excellence among artists with disabilities working in a variety of disciplines.
Chief Officer(s):
Nisse Gustafson, Operations Director
Emma Kivisild, Artistic Director

Kidney Cancer Canada Association
#226, 4936 Yonge St., Toronto ON M2N 6S3

Tel: 416-603-0277; *Fax:* 416-603-0277
Toll-Free: 866-598-7166
info@kidneycancercanada.ca
www.kidneycancercanada.ca
www.linkedin.com/company/kidney-cancer-canada
www.facebook.com/KidneyCancerCanada
twitter.com/KidneyCancer_Ca
www.youtube.com/KidneyCancerCanada
Also Known As: Kidney Cancer Canada
Overview: A medium-sized national charitable organization founded in 2007
Mission: To support & improve the lives of patients & families living with kidney cancer; To raise awareness of kidney cancer treatment options; To promote quality care across Canada; To increase funding for kidney cancer research
Finances: *Annual Operating Budget:* $500,000-$1.5 Million; *Funding Sources:* Sponsorships; Donations
Staff Member(s): 4; 10 volunteer(s)
Membership: 2,000+; *Committees:* Executive; Finance
Activities: Providing peer support, information, & education; Researching; Engaging in advocacy
Chief Officer(s):
Andrew Weller, Chair
aweller@kidneycancercanada.ca
Heather Chappell, Executive Director
hchappell@kidneycancercanada.ca
Jan Coleman, Coordinator, Administration & Program Development
Meetings/Conferences:
• Kidney Cancer Canada 2018 Patient & Caregiver Forum, 2018
Scope: National
Publications:
• KCC [Kidney Cancer Canada] Newsletter
Type: Newsletter
• Kidney Cancer Canada Brochure
Type: Brochure

Kidney Foundation of Canada (KFOC) / Fondation canadienne du rein
#310, 5160, boul Decarie, Montréal QC H3X 2H9
Tel: 514-369-4806; *Fax:* 514-369-2472
Toll-Free: 800-361-7494
Other Communication: Website Management: webmaster@kidney.ca
info@kidney.ca
www.kidney.ca
www.facebook.com/kidneyfoundation
twitter.com/kidneycanada
www.youtube.com/kidneycanada
Overview: A large national charitable organization founded in 1964
Mission: To improve the health & quality of life of people living with kidney disease; To fund research & related clinical education; To provide services for the special needs of individuals living with kidney disease; To advocate for access to high quality health care; To actively promote awareness of & commitment to organ donation
Member of: Healthpartners; Imagine Canada; Health Charities Coalition; Canadian Coalition for Genetic Fairness
Finances: *Annual Operating Budget:* Greater than $5 Million; *Funding Sources:* Fundraising programs
Staff Member(s): 145
Membership: 5,000; *Fees:* $10; *Committees:* Allied Health Scientific; Biomedical Scientific; Governance Implementation Task Force; National Executive; National Finance & Audit; National Fund Development Task Force; National Governance; National Nominations; National Public Benefit
Activities: Offering monthly support group meetings in Ontario, in Kitchener, Brantford, Thunder Bay, Mississauga & Oshawa; *Awareness Events:* Kidney Month, March; Organ Donor Awareness Week, 3rd week in April; *Speaker Service:* Yes
Chief Officer(s):
Paul Kidston, National President
Elizabeth Myles, National Executive Director
Elisabeth Fowler, National Director, Research
Teresa Havill, National Director, Human Resources
Carole Larouche, National Director, Finance
Wendy Kudeba, National Director, Communications & Marketing
Awards:
• Bresinger Award of Excellence
• Medal for Research Excellence
• The Gavin Turley Scholarship for Civic Engagement
Meetings/Conferences:
• Kidney Foundation of Canada 2018 Kidney Care Conference, 2018
Scope: National
Publications:
• Living with Kidney Disease
Type: Manual
Profile: Published in English, French, Italian, Chinese, & Punjabi

Atlantic Canada Branch
#204, 56 Avonlea Ct., Fredericton NB E3C 1N8
Tel: 506-453-0533; *Fax:* 506-454-3639
Toll-Free: 877-453-0533
kidneyatlantic@kidney.ca
www.kidney.ca/atlantic
Chief Officer(s):
Trina Ralph, Executive Director
trina.ralph@kidney.ca

British Columbia & Yukon Branch
#200, 4940 Canada Way, Burnaby BC V5G 4K6
Tel: 604-736-9775; *Fax:* 604-736-9703
Toll-Free: 800-567-8112
info@kidney.bc.ca
www.kidney.ca/BC
Chief Officer(s):
Pia Schindler, Executive Director, 604-558-6875
pias@kidney.bc.ca

Division du Québec
2300, boul René-Lévesque ouest, Montréal QC H3H 2R5
Tél: 514-938-4515; *Téléc:* 514-938-4757
Ligne sans frais: 800-565-4515
infoquebec@kidney.ca
www.kidney.ca/quebec
Chief Officer(s):
Martin Munger, Directeur général
martin.munger@kidney.ca

Eastern Ontario Chapter
#401, 1376 Bank St., Ottawa ON K1H 7Y3
Tel: 613-724-9953; *Fax:* 613-722-5907
Toll-Free: 800-724-9953
Chief Officer(s):
Sarah Hart, Program Coordinator
shart@kidney.on.ca

Hamilton & District Chapter
#201, 1599 Hurontario St., Mississauga ON L5G 4S1
Fax: 905-271-4990
Toll-Free: 800-387-4474
Chief Officer(s):
Tony Tirone, Contact
ttirone@kidney.on.ca

Kingston Chapter
PO Box 24003, Stn. Barriefield, Kingston ON K7L 0B4
Tel: 613-542-2121
Toll-Free: 800-387-4474
Chief Officer(s):
Kerry McCloy, Fund Development Officer
kmccloy@kidney.on.ca

Manitoba Branch
#1, 452 Dovercourt Dr., Winnipeg MB R3Y 1G4
Tel: 204-989-0800
Toll-Free: 800-729-7176
info@kidney.mb.ca
www.kidney.ca/manitoba
twitter.com/KidneyFdnMB
Chief Officer(s):
Valerie Dunphy, Executive Director
vdunphy@kidney.mb.ca

Niagara & District Chapter
#201, 1599 Hurontario St., Mississauga ON L5G 4S1
Fax: 905-271-4990
Toll-Free: 800-387-4474
Chief Officer(s):
Jennifer Fraser, Chapter Manager
jfraser@kidney.on.ca

Northern Alberta & The Territories Branch
#202, 11227 Jasper Ave. NW, Edmonton AB T5K 0L5
Tel: 780-451-6900; *Fax:* 780-451-7592
Toll-Free: 800-461-9063
info@kidney.ab.ca
www.kidney.ca/Page.aspx?pid=266
Chief Officer(s):
Flavia Robles, Executive Director

Northern Superior Chapter - Thunder Bay
PO Box 22043, Stn. Northwood, Thunder Bay ON P7E 6P2
Tel: 807-624-2680
Chief Officer(s):
Marion Harms, Fundraising Coordinator
mharms@tbaytel.net

Ontario Branch
#201, 1599 Hurontario St., Mississauga ON L5G 4S1
Tel: 905-278-3003; *Fax:* 905-271-4990
Toll-Free: 800-387-4474
kidney@kidney.on.ca
www.kidney.ca/ontario
twitter.com/kidneyontario
Chief Officer(s):
Jim O'Brien, Executive Director, 905-278-3003 Ext. 4950
jobrien@kidney.on.ca

Outaouais-Québécois Chapter
CP 89027, Succ. Cité des jeunes, 207, boul Mont-Bleu, Gatineau QC J8Z 3G3
Tél: 819-661-5079
Chief Officer(s):
Bruno Tousignant, Responsable
bruno.tousignant@kidney.ca

Prince Edward Island Chapter
565 North River Rd., Charlottetown PE C1E 1J7
Tel: 902-892-9009
Toll-Free: 877-892-9009
kidneypei@kidney.ca
Chief Officer(s):
Harry McLellan, Fundraising Coordinator
harry.mclellan@kidney.ca

Québec Chapter
#101, 1675, ch Ste-Foy, Québec QC G1S 2P7
Tél: 418-683-1449; *Téléc:* 418-683-7079
Chief Officer(s):
Maryse Neron, Coordonnatrice
maryse.neron@kidney.ca

Regina & District Chapter
1545C McAra St., Regina SK S4N 6H4
Tel: 306-347-0711; *Fax:* 306-586-8287
regina@kidney.sk.ca
Chief Officer(s):
Iris Lord, Fund Development Manager
ilord@kidney.sk.ca

Saguenay/Lac Saint-Jean Chapter
#301, 23, rue Racine est, Chicoutimi QC G7H 1P4
Tél: 418-543-9644
Chief Officer(s):
Nathalie Sauliner, Coordinatrice
nathalie.saulnier@kidney.ca

Sarnia-Lambton Chapter
#405B, 546 Christina St. North, Sarnia ON N7T 5W6
Tel: 519-344-3462; *Fax:* 519-344-4038
Chief Officer(s):
Elaine Hayter, Senior Development Manager
ehayter@kidney.on.ca

Saskatchewan Branch
#1, 2217 Hanselman Ct., Saskatoon SK S7L 6A8
Tel: 306-664-8588; *Fax:* 306-653-4883
Toll-Free: 888-664-8588
info@kidney.sk.ca
www.kidney.ca/sk
Chief Officer(s):
Joyce VanDeurzen, Executive Director
executivedirector@kidney.sk.ca

Sault Ste Marie Chapter
PO Box 20057, RPO Churchill Place, Sault Ste Marie ON P6A 6W3
Tel: 705-949-0400
Chief Officer(s):
Tannis McMillan, Fund Development Officer
tmcmillan@kidney.on.ca

Southern Alberta Branch
6007 - 1A St. SW, Calgary AB T2H 0G5
Tel: 403-255-6108; *Fax:* 403-255-9590
Toll-Free: 800-268-1177
info@kidneyfoundation.ab.ca
www.kidney.ca/sab
Chief Officer(s):
Joyce Van Deurzen, Executive Director
joyce.vandeurzen@kidneyfoundation.ab.ca
Karen Thomas, Director, Community Relations
karen.thomas@kidneyfoundation.ab.ca

Southwestern Ontario Chapter
#203, 785 Wonderland Rd. South, London ON N6K 1M6
Fax: 519-850-5360
Toll-Free: 800-667-3597
Chief Officer(s):

Canadian Associations / Kids Cancer Care Foundation of Alberta

Rizwana Ramzanali, Fund Development Officer
rramzanali@kidney.on.ca
Timmins-Porcupine Chapter
11357 Hwy. 101 East, Connaught ON P0N 1A0
Tel: 705-235-3233; *Fax:* 705-235-3237
Marlene Smith, President
Western Ontario Chapter
#201, 1599 Hurontario St., Mississauga ON L5G 4S1
Fax: 905-271-4990
Toll-Free: 800-387-4474
Chief Officer(s):
Evelina Turney, Fund Development Officer
eturney@kidney.on.ca
Windsor & District Chapter
PO Box 22033, 11500 Tecumseh Rd. East, Windsor ON N8N 5G6
Tel: 519-977-9211
Toll-Free: 800-387-4474
Chief Officer(s):
Anne Brinkman, Ontario Program Manager
peersupport@kidney.ca

Kids Cancer Care Foundation of Alberta
#302, 609 - 14 St. NW, Calgary AB T2N 2A1
Tel: 403-216-9210; *Fax:* 403-216-9215
Toll-Free: 888-554-2267
staff@kidscancercare.ab.ca
www.kidscancercare.ab.ca
www.facebook.com/KCCFA
twitter.com/KidsCancerCare
instagram.com/kidscancercare
Overview: A small provincial charitable organization
Mission: To help improve the lives of children who are suffering from cancer
Finances: *Annual Operating Budget:* Greater than $5 Million
Staff Member(s): 31
Chief Officer(s):
Christine McIver, Founder & CEO

Kids First Parent Association of Canada
8337 Shaske Cres., Edmonton AB T6R 0B4
Tel: 604-291-0088
info@kidsfirstcanada.org
www.kidsfirstcanada.org
Overview: A medium-sized national charitable organization founded in 1987
Mission: To lobby to protect their right & choice to raise children in a family setting; to provide support to anyone wanting to further this cause in other communities
Finances: *Funding Sources:* Donations; membership fees
Activities: Political lobbying; public information meetings; parenting workshops; *Speaker Service:* Yes; *Library:* Open to public by appointment
Chief Officer(s):
Helen Ward, President

Kids Help Phone (KHP) / Jeunesse j'écoute
#300, 439 University Ave., Toronto ON M5G 1Y8
Tel: 416-586-5437
Toll-Free: 800-668-6868
info@kidshelpphone.ca
kidshelpphone.ca
www.linkedin.com/company/kids-help-phone
www.facebook.com/KidsHelpPhone
twitter.com/kidshelpphone
www.youtube.com/user/KidsHelpPhone
Overview: A medium-sized national charitable organization founded in 1989
Mission: To provide a national, bilingual, 24-hours a day, 365 days of the year, toll-free, professionally staffed, confidential counselling service to young people; To help young people deal with concerns large or small; To contribute to awareness of children's issues & the development of policies & practices to help Canadian children
Member of: Child Helpline International; Alliance of Information & Referral Systems
Finances: *Funding Sources:* Donations; Sponsorships
Activities: *Awareness Events:* Walk for Kids Help Phone; Boolathon, October; *Internships:* Yes; *Library:* by appointment
Not open to public
Chief Officer(s):
Sharon Wood, President & CEO
Alberta/Northwest Territories
4331 Manhattan Rd. SE, Calgary AB T2G 4B1
Tel: 403-476-0385
Toll-Free: 866-297-4101
alberta@kidshelpphone.ca
Atlantic Region
#301, 1600 Bedford Hwy., Bedford NS B4A 1E8
Tel: 902-457-4779
Toll-Free: 888-470-8880
atlantic@kidshelpphone.ca
British Columbia/Yukon
#1100, 1200 West 73 Ave., Vancouver BC V6P 6G5
Tel: 604-267-7057
Toll-Free: 877-267-7057
bc@kidshelpphone.ca
Manitoba
#320, 145 Pacific Ave., Winnipeg MB R3B 2Z6
Tel: 204-770-8053
manitoba@kidshelpphone.ca
Ontario
#300, 439 University Ave., Toronto ON M5G 1Y8
Tel: 416-586-5437
Toll-Free: 800-268-3062
ontario@kidshelpphone.ca
Québec
#303, 5605, av de Gaspé, Montréal QC H2T 2A4
Tel: 514-273-7007
Toll-Free: 866-814-1010
quebec@kidshelpphone.ca
Saskatchewan
#120, 2150 Scarth St., Regina SK S4P 2H7
Tel: 306-780-9492
Toll-Free: 866-321-4125
saskatchewan@kidshelpphone.ca

Kids Kottage Foundation
10107 - 134 Ave., Edmonton AB T5E 1J2
Tel: 780-448-1752; *Crisis Hot-Line:* 780-944-2888
info@kidskottage.org
www.kidskottage.org
www.facebook.com/kidskottageYEG
twitter.com/KidsKottageEDM
Previous Name: Canadian Foundation for the Love of Children
Overview: A medium-sized local charitable organization founded in 1987
Mission: To promote the health & well-being of children & their families; To prevent child abuse & neglect by supporting families in crisis
Activities: *Awareness Events:* Premier's Breakfast; Radiothon
Chief Officer(s):
Lori Reiter, Executive Director
Dianne Petersen, Program Manager

Kids Now
PO Box 1314, 1500 Avenue Rd., Toronto ON M5M 0A1
Tel: 416-488-4848; *Fax:* 647-436-3126
Toll-Free: 877-407-4848
info@kidsnowcanada.org
www.kidsnowcanada.org
www.linkedin.com/company/kids.now
www.facebook.com/kidsnow
twitter.com/kids_now
www.youtube.com/mentorkidsnow
Overview: A small local charitable organization founded in 1999
Mission: To provide guidance & counselling to students in grades 7 & 8 in order to give them more skills & confidence to help their future
Staff Member(s): 8
Membership: *Committees:* Advisory
Chief Officer(s):
Janet King, President & Founder

Kids Up Front
Corus Quay, 25 Dockside Dr., Toronto ON M5A 0B5
www.kidsupfronttoronto.com
www.facebook.com/kidsupfrontto
twitter.com/kidsupfrontto
Overview: A medium-sized national charitable organization
Mission: Provides access to arts, culture, sport and recreation for children who otherwise do not have the opportunity.
Finances: *Funding Sources:* Donations
Activities: Ticket donations; CIBC Theatre of ALL; Kids Count; Kids' City Park Project
Chief Officer(s):
Lindsay Oughtred, Executive Director, 416-479-6926
lindsay@kidsupfronttoronto.com

Kidsfest *See* Start2Finish

kidsLINK; Mosaic Counselling & Family Services; Catholic Family Counselling Centre; Catholic Social Services; Catholic Welfare Bureau *See* Carizon Family & Community Services

KidSport Alberta
Percy Page Centre, 11759 Groat Rd., Edmonton AB T5M 3K6
www.kidsport.ab.ca
www.facebook.com/KidSportAlberta
twitter.com/KidSportAlberta
Overview: A small provincial organization overseen by KidSport Canada
Mission: To provide financial assistance to children in Alberta, aged 18 & under, who are interested in playing sports; help with registration fees & equipment
Member of: KidSport Canada
Membership: *Member Profile:* Local chapters
Activities: Providing grants from $100-$500
Chief Officer(s):
Erin Bilawchuk, Executive Director, 780-644-1815
ebilawchuk@kidsport.ab.ca

KidSport British Columbia
#230, 3820 Cessna Dr., Richmond BC V7B 0A2
Tel: 604-333-3434; *Fax:* 604-333-3401
www.kidsportcanada.ca
twitter.com/kidsport
Overview: A small provincial organization overseen by KidSport Canada
Mission: To provide financial assistance to children in British Columbia, aged 18 & under, who are interested in playing sports; help with registration fees & equipment
Member of: KidSport Canada; Sport BC
Membership: *Member Profile:* Local chapters
Activities: Providing grants from $100-$500
Chief Officer(s):
Thea Culley, Manager
thea.culley@sportbc.com

KidSport Canada
Sport for Life Centre, #423, 145 Pacific Ave., Winnipeg MB R3B 2Z6
Tel: 204-925-5914; *Fax:* 204-925-5916
www.kidsportcanada.ca
www.facebook.com/kidsportcanada
twitter.com/KidSportCA
Overview: A medium-sized national organization founded in 2005
Mission: To provide financial assistance to children aged 18 & under who are interested in playing sports; help with registration fees & equipment
3600 volunteer(s)
Membership: 11 provincial/territorial chapters + 177 community chapters
Activities: Providing grants from $100-$500
Chief Officer(s):
Bryan Ezako, Manager
bezako@kidsportcanada.ca

KidSport Manitoba
145 Pacific Ave., Winnipeg MB R3B 2Z6
Tel: 204-925-5600; *Fax:* 204-925-5916
Toll-Free: 866-774-2220
kidsport@sportmanitoba.ca
www.kidsportcanada.ca
www.facebook.com/sportmb
twitter.com/SportManitoba
Overview: A small provincial organization overseen by KidSport Canada
Mission: To provide financial assistance to children in Manitoba, aged 18 & under, who are interested in playing sports; help with registration fees & equipment
Member of: KidSport Canada; Sport Manitoba
Membership: *Member Profile:* Local chapters
Activities: Providing grants from $100-$500

KidSport New Brunswick
#13, 900 Hanwell Rd., Fredericton NB E3B 6A2
Tel: 506-451-1320; *Fax:* 506-451-1325
www.kidsportcanada.ca
twitter.com/KidSportNB
Overview: A small provincial organization overseen by KidSport Canada
Mission: To provide financial assistance to children in New Brunswick, aged 18 & under, who are interested in playing sports; help with registration fees & equipment
Member of: KidSport Canada; Sport New Brunswick

Membership: *Member Profile:* Local chapters
Activities: Providing grants from $100-$500

KidSport Newfoundland & Labrador
1296A Kenmount Rd., Paradise NL A1L 1N3
Tel: 709-579-5977; Fax: 709-576-7493
www.kidsport.nl.ca
Overview: A small provincial organization overseen by KidSport Canada
Mission: To provide financial assistance to children in Newfoundland & Labrador, aged 18 & under, who are interested in playing sports; help with registration fees & equipment
Member of: KidSport Canada; Sport Newfoundland & Labrador
Membership: *Member Profile:* Local chapters
Activities: Providing grants from $100-$500
Chief Officer(s):
Alicia Curran, Coordinator, Events & Marketing, Sport NL
acurran@sportnl.ca

KidSport Northwest Territories
Don Cooper Bldg., 4908 - 49th St., 3rd Fl., Yellowknife NT X1A 3X7
Tel: 867-669-8332; Fax: 867-669-8327
www.kidsportcanada.ca
Overview: A small provincial organization overseen by KidSport Canada
Mission: To provide financial assistance to children in the Northwest Territories, aged 18 & under, who are interested in playing sports; help with registration fees & equipment
Member of: KidSport Canada; Sport North Federation
Membership: *Member Profile:* Local chapters
Activities: Providing grants from $100-$500

KidSport Nova Scotia
5516 Spring Garden Rd., 4th Fl., Halifax NS B3J 1G6
Tel: 902-425-5450; Fax: 902-425-5606
kidsport@sportnovascotia.ca
www.sportnovascotia.ca/KidSport
Overview: A small provincial organization overseen by KidSport Canada
Mission: To provide financial assistance to children in Nova Scotia, aged 18 & under, who are interested in playing sports; help with registration fees & equipment
Member of: KidSport Canada; Sport Nova Scotia
Membership: *Member Profile:* Local chapters
Activities: Providing grants from $100-$500
Chief Officer(s):
Colin Gillis, Coordinator

KidSport Ontario
#2041, 875 Morningside Ave., Toronto ON M1C 0C7
Tel: 416-283-0940
www.kidsportcanada.ca/ontario
www.facebook.com/KidSportOntario
twitter.com/KidSportOntario
Overview: A small provincial organization overseen by KidSport Canada
Mission: To provide financial assistance to children in Ontario, aged 18 & under, who are interested in playing sports; help with registration fees & equipment
Member of: KidSport Canada
Membership: *Member Profile:* Local chapters
Activities: Providing grants from $100-$500

KidSport PEI
40 Enman Cres., Charlottetown PE C1E 1E6
Tel: 902-368-4110; Fax: 902-368-4548
www.kidsportcanada.ca/prince-edward-island
www.facebook.com/176050449103403
Overview: A small provincial organization overseen by KidSport Canada
Mission: To provide financial assistance to children in Prince Edward Island, aged 18 & under, who are interested in playing sports; help with registration fees & equipment
Member of: KidSport Canada; Sport PEI Inc.
Membership: *Member Profile:* Local chapters
Activities: Providing grants from $100-$500
Chief Officer(s):
Terry Bernard, Contact
tbernard@sportpei.pe.ca

KidSport Québec *Voir* Sport Jeunesse

KidSport Saskatchewan
1870 Lorne St., Regina SK S4P 2L7
Tel: 306-780-9345; Fax: 306-781-6021
Toll-Free: 800-319-4263
kidsport@sasksport.sk.ca
www.kidsportcanada.ca/saskatchewan
Overview: A small provincial organization overseen by KidSport Canada
Mission: To provide financial assistance to children in Saskatchewan, aged 18 & under, who are interested in playing sports; help with registration fees & equipment
Member of: KidSport Canada; Sask Sport Inc.
Membership: *Member Profile:* Local chapters
Activities: Providing grants from $100-$500
Chief Officer(s):
Nathan Cole, Provincial Coordinator

Kikinahk Friendship Centre
PO Box 254, 320 Boardman St., La Ronge SK S0J 1L0
Tel: 306-425-2051
www.facebook.com/141174299305567
Previous Name: Neginuk Friendship Centre
Overview: A small local organization founded in 1977
Mission: To provide a cultural centre for Indian, Métis & non-status Indian persons
Activities: Social welfare services; recreational activities; job training; leadership skills programs
Chief Officer(s):
Ron Woytowich, Executive Director

Killam & District Chamber of Commerce
PO Box 189, Killam AB T0B 2L0
Tel: 780-385-7050
Overview: A small local organization
Mission: To serve as the voice for the area's businesses
Member of: Canadian Chamber of Commerce; Alberta Chamber of Commerce
Finances: *Annual Operating Budget:* Less than $50,000; *Funding Sources:* Fundraising; membership fees
5 volunteer(s)
Membership: 31; *Fees:* $30-$70

Killarney & District Chamber of Commerce
433 Broadway Ave., Killarney MB R0K 1G0
Tel: 204-523-4202
Overview: A small local organization

Les Kilomaîtres de LaSalle
CP 3022, Succ. Succursale Lapierre, LaSalle QC H8N 3H2
Tél: 514-582-5494
www.kilomaitreslasalle.com
Aperçu: *Dimension:* petite; *Envergure:* locale
Mission: Pour offrir un moyen à faible coût pour l'exercice et le rester en bonne santé
Membre: *Montant de la cotisation:* $115 Adultes; 40$ Jeunes
Membre(s) du bureau directeur:
Richard Proulx, Président, Conseil d'administration

Ki-Low-Na Friendship Society (KFS)
442 Leon Ave., Kelowna BC V1Y 6J3
Tel: 250-763-4905; Fax: 250-861-5514
reception@kfs.bc.ca
www.kfs.bc.ca
Previous Name: Central Okanagan Indian Friendship Society
Overview: A small national charitable organization founded in 1974
Mission: To promote total well-being for Native people in all human dimensions: physical, spiritual, mental & emotional
Member of: United Way
Finances: *Annual Operating Budget:* $500,000-$1.5 Million
Staff Member(s): 15
Membership: 236; *Fees:* $5
Activities: Recreational activities; advocacy; employment & educational services; counselling in alcohol & drugs, family violence & other topics
Chief Officer(s):
Edna Terbasket, Executive Director

Kimberley & District Chamber of Commerce (KBSCC)
253 Wallinger Ave., Kimberley BC V1A 1Z2
Tel: 250-427-3666
info@kimberleychamber.com
www.kimberleychamber.com
www.linkedin.com/groups/Kimberley-District-Chamber-Commerce-3678646
www.facebook.com/KimberleyChamber
twitter.com/KimberleyCofC
www.youtube.com/channel/UCzQjb9dgpA0GYNjlB2s3K4g
Overview: A small local organization founded in 1925

Mission: To play a leadership role in the promotion, development, growth & prosperity of businesses in the community
Member of: British Columbia Chamber of Commerce; Canadian Chamber of Commerce
Finances: *Annual Operating Budget:* $100,000-$250,000; *Funding Sources:* City of Kimberly; Tourism BC
Staff Member(s): 3; 40 volunteer(s)
Membership: 185; *Fees:* Schedule available
Activities: Supporting community events such as Julyfest; *Speaker Service:* Yes; *Rents Mailing List:* Yes; *Library:* Open to public
Chief Officer(s):
Mike Guarnery, Manager

Kimberley Arts Council *See* Kimberley Arts Council - Centre 64 Society

Kimberley Arts Council - Centre 64 Society
64 Deer Park Ave., Kimberley BC V1A 2J2
Tel: 250-427-4919; Fax: 250-427-4920
kimberleyarts@telus.net
www.kimberleyarts.com
Also Known As: Centre 64
Previous Name: Kimberley Arts Council
Overview: A small local organization founded in 1977
Mission: To increase & broaden the opportunities of Kimberley citizens to enjoy & participate in cultural activities & arts & crafts
Member of: Assembly of BC Arts Councils
Finances: *Annual Operating Budget:* $50,000-$100,000; *Funding Sources:* City of Kimberley; cultural services; lotteries
Staff Member(s): 1; 50 volunteer(s)
Membership: 150; *Fees:* $20
Activities: Art gallery; theatre; fibrearts studio; concerts; workshops

Kimberley Helping Hands Food Bank
All Saint's Anglican Church, 340 Leadenhall St., Kimberley BC V1A 2X6
Tel: 250-427-5522
allaboutkimberley.com/foodbankhours.html
Overview: A small local organization founded in 1985
Mission: To supply food to individuals & families in need
Activities: *Awareness Events:* Canada Day Duck Race, July

Kin Canada
PO Box 3460, 1920 Rogers Dr., Cambridge ON N3H 5C6
Tel: 519-653-1920; Fax: 519-650-1091
Toll-Free: 800-742-5546
kinhq@kincanada.ca
www.kincanada.ca
www.facebook.com/kincanada
twitter.com/kincanada
Also Known As: Association of Kinsmen, Kinette & Kin Clubs
Previous Name: Kinsmen & Kinette Clubs of Canada; The Association of Kin Clubs
Overview: A large national organization founded in 1920
Mission: To enrich communities through service, while embracing national pride, positive values, personal development, & lasting friendships; To support Cystic Fibrosis research & care in Canada
Affiliation(s): Cystic Fibrosis Canada
Finances: *Annual Operating Budget:* $500,000-$1.5 Million; *Funding Sources:* Membership dues; sponsorship; sales of items to members
Staff Member(s): 8
Membership: 6,505 individuals in 462 clubs; *Fees:* Schedule available; *Member Profile:* Men & women over ages of 19; *Committees:* Awards & Recognition; Club Support; Education & Training; Marketing & Membership Development; Service
Activities: *Awareness Events:* Great Strides Walk; *Speaker Service:* Yes
Chief Officer(s):
Grant Ferron, Executive Director
gferron@kincanada.ca
Awards:
• National Awards
• Hal Rogers Endowment Fund
; *Amount:* $1,000
• Recognition Awards
• Personal Awards
Meetings/Conferences:
• Kin Canada 2018 National Convention, 2018, Sarnia, ON
Scope: National

Kin Canada Foundation
PO Box 3460, 1920 Rogers Dr., Cambridge ON N3H 5C6

Tel: 519-653-1920; Fax: 519-650-1091
Toll-Free: 800-742-5546
kinhq@kincanada.ca
www.kincanada.ca/kin-canada-foundation
www.facebook.com/kincanada
twitter.com/kincanada
Overview: A large national charitable organization founded in 2005
Mission: To support Kin, Kinsmen & Kinette clubs across Canada; To function as the official charitable organization of Kin Canada
Activities: Providing funding for clubs' local service projects
Chief Officer(s):
Carmen Preston, Contact, 800-742-5546 Ext. 205
Awards:
• Hal Rogers Fellow Award

Kinark Child & Family Services
#200, 500 Hood Rd., Markham ON L3R 9Z3
Tel: 905-944-7086; Fax: 905-474-1448
Toll-Free: 800-230-8533
info@kinarkfoundation.org
www.kinarkfoundation.org
www.facebook.com/kinark
twitter.com/mykinark
Overview: A small provincial organization founded in 1972
Mission: To strengthen the well-being of children & their families, thereby contributing to safe & healthy communities; seek to achieve this goal by being a provider of choice in the delivery of the highest quality services to our clients in partnership with community resources
Affiliation(s): Children's Mental Health Ontario
Finances: *Funding Sources:* Provincial government; donations
Chief Officer(s):
Cheri Smith, Director, Development
cheri.smith@kinarkfoundation.org

Kincardine & District Chamber of Commerce
777B Queen St., Kincardine ON N2Z 2Y2
Tel: 519-396-9333; Fax: 519-396-5529
kincardine.cofc@bmts.com
www.kincardinechamber.com
Overview: A small local organization
Mission: To promote business & tourism in the Kincardine area
Member of: Ontario Chamber of Commerce
Finances: *Funding Sources:* Membership dues
Staff Member(s): 1
Membership: 140; *Fees:* $110
Chief Officer(s):
Matt Smith, President
Jackie Pawlikowski, Office Manager

Kind Space
#404, 222 Somerset St. West, Ottawa ON K2P 0J4
Tel: 613-563-4818
welcome@kindspace.ca
www.kindspace.ca
Previous Name: Pink Triangle Services; Association of Lesbians, Gays & Bisexuals of Ottawa
Overview: A small local charitable organization founded in 1984
Mission: To foster the wellness of all lesbian, gay & bisexual persons in the National Capital Region; To provide leadership to identify & address the needs of diverse groups, through communtiy development, delivery of & advocacy for, respectful & inclusive services & programs, provided in a safe environment; To build partnerships with other groups that share cultural & sociopolitical history, in order to work on common goals, issues, needs, & services
Finances: *Annual Operating Budget:* $100,000-$250,000; *Funding Sources:* Donations; Grants
Staff Member(s): 2; 82 volunteer(s)
Membership: *Fees:* $2-$10
Activities: Discussion groups; peer support; Gayline/Télégai; library; *Library:* Dr. Kelly McGinnis Library
Chief Officer(s):
Carling Miller, Executive Director
carling@kindspace.ca

Kindersley Chamber of Commerce
PO Box 1537, 605 Main St., Kindersley SK S0L 1S0
Tel: 306-463-2320; Fax: 306-463-2312
kindersleychamber@sasktel.net
www.kindersleychamber.com
www.facebook.com/404457099601540
twitter.com/kindersleycoc
Overview: A small local organization founded in 1989
Mission: To promote town of Kindersley & local business
Member of: Saskatchewan Chamber of Commerce; Sask Tourism
Finances: *Annual Operating Budget:* Less than $50,000; *Funding Sources:* Membership fees; Trade show
Staff Member(s): 1; 10+ volunteer(s)
Membership: 105; *Fees:* $175-$275; *Committees:* Tourism; Business Development; Membership; Promotion
Activities: *Awareness Events:* Kindersley Chamber of Commerce Annual Trade Show, June; Goose Festival, Sept.; Winter Wonderland, Dec.
Chief Officer(s):
Heather Wall, Office Manager

The Kindness Club / Le Cercle Saint-François
#142, 527 Dundonald St., Fredericton NB E3B 1X5
Tel: 506-459-3379
info@kindnessclub.ca
www.kindnessclub.nb.ca
Overview: A small international charitable organization founded in 1959
Mission: To educate children to be kind to animals & people & to respect the environment
Member of: Canadian Federation of Humane Societies; World Society for the Protection of Animals; Nature Canada; Zoocheck Canada
Affiliation(s): New Brunswick Naturalists
Finances: *Funding Sources:* Donations; interest from small capital
Membership: *Fees:* $5 child; $10 adult
Activities: Essay contest for students, grades 4-8; pet shows; displays; weekly column in 6 New Brunswick newspapers; liaison teacher program; *Library*

Kinesis Dance Society
Scotia Bank Dance Centre, 677 Davie St., Level 7, Vancouver BC V6B 2G6
Tel: 604-684-7844; Fax: 604-684-7834
admin@kinesisdance.org
www.kinesisdance.org
Overview: A small local charitable organization founded in 1986
Mission: To contribute new & provocative works of contemporary dance to the local, national & international dance scene; To educate through workshops & cultural exchanges & to collaborate with other media, such as film, video & theatre
Finances: *Funding Sources:* Canada Council; BC Arts Council; BC Gaming
Staff Member(s): 2
Membership: *Member Profile:* Women & men; urban; ages 26-45; university degree/certificate
Activities: *Library:* Open to public
Chief Officer(s):
Paras Terezakis, Artistic Director

King Chamber of Commerce
PO Box 381, Schomberg ON L0G 1T0
Tel: 905-717-7199; Fax: 416-981-7174
info@kingchamber.ca
kingchamber.ca
Overview: A small local organization founded in 2008
Mission: To act as a voice for its members; To help promote business
Member of: Canadian Chamber of Commerce; Ontario Chamber of Commerce
Staff Member(s): 1
Membership: 200; *Fees:* $110 non-profit; $100 1 employee; $135 2-10 employees; $225 11-25 employees; $300 26-50 employees; $400 51+ employees; *Committees:* Events; Communications; Tourism; Educational Outreach
Chief Officer(s):
Tom Allen, President
Helen Neville, Administrator

King's County Historical Society
27 Centennial Rd., Hampton NB E5N 6N3
Tel: 506-832-6009
kingscm@nbnet.nb.ca
www.kingscountymuseum.com
www.facebook.com/434926949879214
Also Known As: King's County Museum
Overview: A small local charitable organization founded in 1968
Mission: To preserve the history of archives; to make history alive; to collect artifacts that reflect the County lifestyle
Member of: Museums New Brunswick; New Brunswick Historical Society; Canadian Heritage Information Network; New Burnswick Genealogical Society; Queen's County Historical Society
Finances: *Funding Sources:* Municipal government
Membership: *Fees:* $20 single; $25 couple

Kings County Wildlife Association (KCWA)
Kings County NS
kingscountywildlife@outlook.com
www.facebook.com/kingscountywildlife
Overview: A small local organization founded in 1926
Mission: To implement conservation projects & programs in order to enhance wildlife populations & habitats

Kings Historical Society
Kings County Museum, 37 Cornwallis St., Kentville NS B4N 2E2
Tel: 902-678-6237; Fax: 902-678-2764
museum@okcm.ca
www.okcm.ca
www.facebook.com/kingscountymuseum
twitter.com/Kings_Co_Museum
www.youtube.com/embed/JBOKCFM_Do8
Overview: A small local charitable organization founded in 1979
Mission: To preserve the cultural & natural history of Kings County, Nova Scotia
Member of: Federation of the Nova Scotian Heritage; Council of Nova Scotia Archives; Heritage Canada; Genealogical Association of Nova Scotia
Affiliation(s): Kings Historical Scoeity
Finances: *Annual Operating Budget:* $50,000-$100,000; *Funding Sources:* Government; private
Staff Member(s): 3; 25 volunteer(s)
Membership: 400; *Fees:* $20 adult; $25 family/organizations; *Committees:* Family History
Activities: Administrative & financial support to Kings County Museum; Christmas Homes Tour & Tea; Heritage Homes Tours; Heritage Fashion Shows; *Awareness Events:* Heritage Day; *Internships:* Yes; *Speaker Service:* Yes; *Library:* Kings County Museum; Open to public
Chief Officer(s):
Bria Stokesbury, Curator

Kingston & Area Real Estate Association
720 Arlington Park Pl., Kingston ON K7M 8H9
Tel: 613-384-0880; Fax: 613-384-0863
info@karea.ca
www.karea.ca
Overview: A small local organization overseen by Ontario Real Estate Association
Member of: The Canadian Real Estate Association
Membership: 550+
Chief Officer(s):
Adam Rayner, President

Kingston & District Association for Community Living *See* Community Living Kingston

Kingston & District Labour Council
105 Sutherland Dr., Kingston ON K7K 5V6
Tel: 613-548-4952; Fax: 613-545-1659
kingstonlabourcouncil@gmail.com
kingstonlabourcouncil.wordpress.com
Overview: A small local organization
Chief Officer(s):
Lisa Marion, President
unionlisa@gmail.com

Kingston AIDS Project *See* HIV/AIDS Regional Services

Kingston Area Economic Development Commission *See* Kingston Economic Development Corporation

Kingston Arts Council (KAC)
PO Box 1005, Kingston ON K7L 4X8
Tel: 613-546-2787
info@artskingston.com
www.artskingston.com
www.facebook.com/kingstonartscouncil
twitter.com/artsking
www.youtube.com/kingstonartscouncil
Overview: A small local charitable organization founded in 1961
Mission: To serve as an advocate for the arts & arts education; To sponsor, encourage, & foster the visual, performing & literary arts; To encourage excellence in artistic expression; To coordinate & facilitate the exchange of information about the arts; To educate & encourage public interest in the arts & to actively seek partnership opportunities with governments, business, the community & the media
Member of: Ontario Arts Council; Communty Arts Ontario
Finances: *Annual Operating Budget:* $50,000-$100,000
Staff Member(s): 2; 20 volunteer(s)

Membership: 300 individual + 75 groups; *Fees:* Schedule available; *Member Profile:* Individual or group interested in supporting the arts & arts-related activities in the Kingston region; *Committees:* Executive; Advancement & Development; Nominating; Human Resources; Advocacy; Arts Salon; Arts Events; Membership; Marketing
Activities: Art workshops, community conferences on arts; juried arts salon; Town & Country Studio Tour; student art contest; Beat Bethoven foundraising run (annual); Timepieces Dance Festival (annual); *Library:* by appointment
Chief Officer(s):
Karen Dolan, Executive Director
karen@artskingston.ca
Awards:
• Kingston Prize for Contemporary Canadian Portraiture ; *Amount:* $3,000
• Kingston Art Awards
• Student Art Contest

Kingston Association of Museums, Art Galleries & Historic Sites (KAM)
PO Box 1921, Stn. Main, Kingston ON K7L 5J7
Tel: 613-538-4014
www.kingstonmuseums.ca
Overview: A medium-sized local organization founded in 1978
Mission: To work for the promotion & growth of museums & museum-based tourism in the Kingston area
Staff Member(s): 2
Membership: 26 institutional; *Member Profile:* Museums, art galleries & historic sites in Kingston, ON; *Committees:* Education; Governance; Marketing; Professional Development
Activities: Monthly meetings; group advertising & promotional projects; coordinate/partner on many diverse projects
Chief Officer(s):
Ann Blake, Managing Director
managing.director@kingstonmuseums.ca

Kingston Board of Trade *See* Greater Kingston Chamber of Commerce

Kingston Community Counselling Centre *See* K3C Community Counselling Centres

Kingston Construction Association (KCA)
1575 John Counter Blvd., Kingston ON K7M 3L5
Tel: 613-542-9431; *Fax:* 613-542-2417
staff@kca.on.ca
www.kca.on.ca
Overview: A small local organization founded in 1950 overseen by Canadian Construction Association
Mission: To foster and advance the interests of those engaged in, or who are directly or indirectly connected with, or affected by the construction industry (ICI sector), in the Province of Ontario
Affiliation(s): Council of Ontario Construction Associations; Canadian Construction Association
Staff Member(s): 2
Membership: 400+; *Member Profile:* Firms working in the industrial, commercial & institutional construction industry
Activities: *Library:* Not open to public
Chief Officer(s):
Brian McMullen, President

Kingston Economic Development Corporation (KEDCO)
945 Princess St., Kingston ON K7L 3N6
Tel: 613-544-2725; *Fax:* 613-546-2882
Toll-Free: 866-665-3326
business@kingstoncanada.com
business.kingstoncanada.com
www.linkedin.com/company/kingston-economic-development-corporation
www.facebook.com/KingstonEconomicDevelopmentCorporation
twitter.com/kingstoncanada
Previous Name: Kingston Area Economic Development Commission
Overview: A small local organization founded in 1997
Mission: To work with the community to develop world-class products & services that are competitive in global markets; to enhance economic development partnerships including private/public initiatives related to economic development policy; to position Kingston as an innovative jurisdiction, a place for new models of wealth creation; to expand the private sector in the tourism, culture, advance materials, biotechnology, information technology & environmental cluster; to stimulate entrepreneurship
Member of: Economic Development Council of Ontario
Affiliation(s): Canadian Manufacturing & Exporters
Finances: *Annual Operating Budget:* $1.5 Million-$3 Million; *Funding Sources:* Municipal government; private sector; provincial & federal government on a per project basis
Staff Member(s): 20
Activities: Small Business Self-Help Office; KANnet; provides on-line searchable Business directory, the Jobs & Prosperity Guide, on-line searchable Available Property Guide, on-line media releases, & downloadable Community Profile; *Library:* Entrepreneurship Centre/Self-Help Resource Centre; Open to public
Chief Officer(s):
Jeff Garrah, Chief Executive Officer, 613-544-2725 Ext. 7230
garrah@kingstoncanada.com
Rob Carnegie, Director, Tourism & Marketing Development, 613-544-2725 Ext. 7245
carnegie@kingstoncanada.com
Cyril Cooper, Director, Business Development, 613-544-2725 Ext. 7242
cooper@kingstoncanada.com

Kingston Field Naturalists (KFN)
PO Box 831, Kingston ON K7L 4X6
info@kingstonfieldnaturalists.org
kingstonfieldnaturalists.org
Overview: A small local charitable organization founded in 1949
Mission: To acquire, record & disseminate knowledge of natural history; To stimulate public interest in nature & in the protection & preservation of wildlife
Member of: Ontario Nature
Affiliation(s): Canadian Nature Federation; Thousand Islands-Frontenac Arch Biosphere Reserve Network
Finances: *Annual Operating Budget:* Less than $50,000; *Funding Sources:* Membership fees
Membership: 500; *Fees:* $30 individual; $32 family; $20 young adult/junior; $800 life; *Committees:* Conservation; Education; Bird Records; Field Trips; Nature Reserves
Activities: Junior naturalists club (6-12); bird counts; Helen Quillam Sanctuary; Amherst Island Reserve; teen naturalists (13-17); habitat protection projects; *Awareness Events:* Spring/Fall Leisure Shows - Kingston
Chief Officer(s):
Gaye Beckwith, President, 613-376-3716
Awards:
• Scholarship
For junior members to attend camp

Kingston Historical Society (KHS)
PO Box 54, Kingston ON K7L 4V6
Tel: 613-544-9925
kingstonhs@gmail.com
www.kingstonhistoricalsociety.ca
Overview: A small local organization founded in 1893
Mission: To preserve, promote & publicize local history & heritage through the presentation/publication of learned papers & the commemoration & celebration of people, events, institutions and the military related to local heritage; to operate Murney Tower Museum
Member of: Ontario Historical Society
Finances: *Annual Operating Budget:* Less than $50,000; *Funding Sources:* Membership dues; grants
20 volunteer(s)
Membership: 250+; *Fees:* $40 individual; $50 family; $25 student
Activities: Operates museum at Murney Tower National Historic Site May-Sept.; Military Day; *Speaker Service:* Yes; *Library:* Resource Centre - Queen's University Archives
Chief Officer(s):
Gordon Sinclair, President

Kingston Independent Nylon Workers Union (KINWU)
662D Progress Ave., Kingston ON K7M 4W9
Tel: 613-389-5255; *Fax:* 613-389-8265
www.kinwu.com
Overview: A small local organization founded in 1968
Mission: To represent workers in the nylon industry.
Chief Officer(s):
Larry Garrah, President
Sean Foley, Treasurer

Kingston Kiwanis Music Festival
PO Box 883, Kingston ON K7L 4X8
Tel: 613-876-3577
info@kiwaniskingston.ca
www.kiwaniskingston.ca
Overview: A small local charitable organization founded in 1972
Mission: To nurture a friendly, mainly non-competitive atmosphere where amateur musicians of all ages can enjoy performing & hearing others perform, while at the same time gaining new artistic insights from experienced adjudicators
Affiliation(s): Ontario Music Festivals Association
Finances: *Funding Sources:* Entry fees; donations; grants
Membership: *Member Profile:* Parents, teachers, students, general public interested in performing arts
Activities: Planning & organizing a 10-day performing arts festival annually
Chief Officer(s):
Philip Wilson, President

Kingston Lapidary & Mineral Club
623 King St. West, Kingston ON K7M 2E7
www.mineralclub.ca
Overview: A small local organization founded in 1962
Mission: To encourage the growth of silversmithing work, & mineral, fossil, & crystal collecting
Member of: The Central Canadian Federation of Mineralogical Societies (CCFMS)
Membership: *Fees:* $10 junior; $15 adult; $20 family; *Member Profile:* Rockhounds; Lapidary enthusiasts; Silversmiths
Activities: Hosting meetings & workshops; Organizing field trips; *Library:* Kingston Lapidary & Mineral Club Library
Chief Officer(s):
Paul Blaney, President, 613-544-5138
paulrichardblaney@hotmail.com
Eileen Moss, Vice-President, Social & Publicity, 613-384-4439
emoss@cogeco.net
Wendy Dawes, Secretary, 613-876-2505
wdawes1@cogeco.ca
Publications:
• The Streak Plate: The Kingston Lapidary & Mineral Club Newsletter
Type: Newsletter; *Frequency:* 5 pa; *Editor:* John Casnig
Profile: Upcoming events & articles about the hobby

Kingston Orchid Society (KOS)
c/o Gian Frontini, 66 Earl St., Kingston ON K7L 2G6
kingstonorchidsociety@yahoo.ca
www.kingstonorchidsociety.ca
www.facebook.com/456078307817916
Overview: A small local organization founded in 1988
Member of: Canadian Orchid Congress; American Orchid Society
Membership: 60; *Fees:* $20 single; $25 family
Chief Officer(s):
Gian Frontini, President
gianfrontini@bell.net

Kingston Police Association / Association de la police de Kingston
705 Division St., Kingston ON K7K 4C2
Tel: 613-549-4660; *Fax:* 613-549-7111
kpf.ca
Overview: A small local organization
Mission: To represent all members of the Kingston Police Force.
Chief Officer(s):
Sean Bambrick, President
sbambrick@kpf.ca

Kingston Stamp Club
c/o Ongwanada Resource Centre, 191 Portsmouth Ave., Kingaston ON K0H 1G0
Tel: 613-389-6536
www.kingstonstampclub.ca
Overview: A small local organization founded in 1975
Member of: Royal Philatelic Society of Canada
Finances: *Annual Operating Budget:* Less than $50,000
10 volunteer(s)
Membership: 80; *Fees:* $8
Activities: Kingston Stamp Festival, Oct.; bi-monthly meetings; auctions
Chief Officer(s):
Richard Weigand, President, 613-352-8775
rweigand@kos.net

Kingston Symphony Association (KSA)
PO Box 1616, #206, 11 Princess St., Kingston ON K7L 5C8
Tel: 613-546-9729; *Fax:* 613-546-8580
info@kingstonsymphony.on.ca
www.kingstonsymphony.on.ca
www.facebook.com/KingstonSymphonyAssociation
twitter.com/KingstonSymph
www.youtube.com/user/Kingstonsymphony

Overview: A small local charitable organization founded in 1956 overseen by Orchestras Canada
Mission: To maintain & produce professional orchestral & symphonic music in the Kingston area
Finances: *Funding Sources:* Corporate & individual donations; Ticket revenue; Grants
Staff Member(s): 6
Membership: 55; *Committees:* KSA Volunteer Committee
Activities: Performing concerts; Facilitating youth training; *Internships:* Yes
Chief Officer(s):
Andrea Haughton, General Manager
ahaughton@kingstonsymphony.on.ca
Evan Mitchell, Music Director
emitchell@kingstonsymphony.on.ca

Kingston Youth Orchestra
c/o Kingston Symphony Association, PO Box 1616, Kingston ON K7L 5C8
Tel: 613-546-9729; *Fax:* 613-546-8580
info@kingstonsymphony.on.ca
www.kingstonsymphony.on.ca/youth.cfm
Overview: A small local organization founded in 1968 overseen by Orchestras Canada
Affiliation(s): Kingston Symphony Association
Membership: *Member Profile:* High school aged musicians who want to develop their ensemble skills and are considering a career in music
Activities: Performing concerts; Providing students with professional leadership
Chief Officer(s):
Linda Craig, Manager

Kinistino & District Chamber of Commerce
PO Box 803, Kinistino SK S0J 1H0
Tel: 306-864-2244; *Fax:* 306-864-2244
Overview: A small local organization

Kinsight
#300, 218 Blue Mountain St., Coquitlam BC V3K 4H2
Tel: 604-525-9494; *Fax:* 604-936-3013
info@sfscl.org
www.sfscl.org
Previous Name: Simon Fraser Society for Community Living; Simon Fraser Society for Mentally Handicapped People
Overview: A large local charitable organization founded in 1954
Mission: To provide choices & opportunities for children who require extra support, adults with intellectual abilities & their families
Member of: British Columbia Association for Community Living
Finances: *Annual Operating Budget:* Greater than $5 Million; *Funding Sources:* Donations; membership fees
55 volunteer(s)
Membership: *Member Profile:* Open except for employees of society; can include individuals & corporations
Activities: Community fund-raisers; services for children/youth, families & adults; individual, family & community support; *Awareness Events:* Community Inclusion Month, Oct.; *Internships:* Yes; *Speaker Service:* Yes; *Library:* Open to public
Chief Officer(s):
Christine Scott, Executive Director
cscott@sfscl.org

Kinsmen & Kinette Clubs of Canada; The Association of Kin Clubs See Kin Canada

Kinsmen Foundation of British Columbia & Yukon (KRF)
c/o David Owen, #3, 33361 Wren Cres., Abbotsford BC V2S 5V9
Tel: 604-852-4501; *Fax:* 604-852-4501
kinsmenfoundationofbc@shaw.ca
www.kinsmenfoundationofbc.ca
Overview: A medium-sized provincial charitable organization founded in 1952 overseen by Easter Seals Canada
Mission: Committed to providing funding for services & technologies empowering British Columbians with physical disabilities to live more independently
Finances: *Funding Sources:* Annual Kinsmen Tag Day; Direct mail appeals; Special events
Membership: *Member Profile:* Kinsmen & kinette clubs of BC & Yukon
Activities: Supports Technology for Independent Living division that assists persons with severe physical disabilities by providing assistive technology; supports disability awareness to elementary school children through the "Kids on the Block"

educational puppetry program; *Awareness Events:* Disability Tag Day, Apr. 2; *Speaker Service:* Yes
Chief Officer(s):
David Owen, Volunteer Chief Administrative Officer

Kipling Chamber of Commerce
PO Box 700, Kipling SK S0G 2S0
Tel: 306-736-9065; *Fax:* 306-736-2962
www.townofkipling.ca/business/chamber-of-commerce
Overview: A small local organization
Chief Officer(s):
Buck Bright, Secretary
Tammy Frater, Chair

Kirkland & District Association for the Developmentally Handicapped See Kirkland Lake Association for Community Living

Kirkland Lake Association for Community Living
PO Box 274, 51 Government Rd. West, Kirkland Lake ON P2N 3H7
Tel: 705-567-9331; *Fax:* 705-567-5005
www.communitylivingkl.com
Previous Name: Kirkland & District Association for the Developmentally Handicapped
Overview: A small local organization
Mission: To provide support & services for people with intellectual disabilities
Member of: Community Living Ontario
Chief Officer(s):
Annice Tilley, President
Heather Topliss, Executive Director
heather.topliss@communitylivingkl.com

Kirkland Lake District Chamber of Commerce (KLCC)
PO Box 966, 23 Government Rd. East, Kirkland Lake ON P2N 3L1
Tel: 705-567-5444; *Fax:* 705-567-1666
kirklandchamber@ntl.sympatico.ca
www.kirklandlakechamberofcommerce.com
www.facebook.com/KLChamberofCommerce
Overview: A small local organization founded in 1920
Mission: To promote & strengthen trade & commerce in the Kirkland Lake area
Member of: Canadian Chamber of Commerce
Affiliation(s): Ontario Chamber of Commerce
Finances: *Annual Operating Budget:* Less than $50,000; *Funding Sources:* Membership dues
Staff Member(s): 2; 20 volunteer(s)
Membership: 120; *Committees:* Retail; Annual Meeting; Exposition; Membership; Municipal & Government Affairs
Activities: Offering business programs & services; *Awareness Events:* Annual Golf Tournament; Small Business Week
Chief Officer(s):
Chantal Ayotte, President

The Kitchener & Waterloo Community Foundation (KWCF)
29 King St. East, #B, Kitchener ON N2G 2K4
Tel: 519-725-1806; *Fax:* 519-725-3851
info@kwcf.ca
www.kwcf.ca
www.facebook.com/TheKWCF
twitter.com/thekwcf
Overview: A small local charitable organization founded in 1984
Mission: To improve the quality of life in Kitchener-Waterloo & area, now & for generations to come, by building community endowment, addressing needs through grant-making & providing leadership on key community issues
Member of: Community Foundations of Canada; Canadian Association of Gift Planners
Finances: *Funding Sources:* Donations
Staff Member(s): 9
Membership: *Committees:* Grants; Investment; Audit; Leadership Identification; Nominating; Ontario Endowment for Children and Youth in Recreation Fund; Random Act of Kindness Day
Activities: Town Hall Meeting; *Library:* by appointment
Chief Officer(s):
Bethan Llewellyn, Director, Foundation Services
bllewellyn@kwcf.ca

Kitchener Sports Association (KSA)
50 Ottawa St. South, Kitchener ON N2G 3S7
Tel: 519-208-9302
www.kitchenersports.ca

www.facebook.com/492371234132957
twitter.com/KitchenerSA
Overview: A small local organization founded in 1944
Mission: To govern sports & sporting facilities in Kitchener
Membership: *Committees:* Operating
Chief Officer(s):
Bill Pegg, President
ksapresident@kitchenersports.ca

Kitchener-Waterloo See Bereaved Families of Ontario

Kitchener-Waterloo Building & Construction Trades Council See Waterloo, Wellington, Dufferin & Grey Building & Construction Trades Council

Kitchener-Waterloo Chamber Music Society (KWCMS)
57 Young St. West, Waterloo ON N2L 2Z4
Tel: 519-886-1673
kwcms@yahoo.ca
www.k-wcms.com
www.facebook.com/203443633010012
Overview: A small local charitable organization founded in 1974
Mission: To organize & present chamber music concerts in the Waterloo area
Affiliation(s): Faculty of Music, Wilfrid Laurier University
Finances: *Annual Operating Budget:* $100,000-$250,000; *Funding Sources:* Donations; Subscriptions; Ticket sales
10 volunteer(s)
Membership: 65; *Fees:* Full: $390 regular; $225 student; $360 senior
Activities: Presenting 70 concerts per year; Radio program "The World of Chamber Music"
Chief Officer(s):
Jan Narveson, President
jnarveso@uwaterloo.ca
Jean Narveson, Board Member
midnightediting@gmail.com
Meetings/Conferences:
• Kitchener-Waterloo Chamber Music Society 2018 Annual General Meeting, 2018, The Music Room, Waterloo, ON
Publications:
• Kitchener-Waterloo Chamber Music Society E-mail Letter
Type: Newsletter; *Frequency:* Weekly
• Kitchener-Waterloo Chamber Music Society Brochure
Type: Brochure
Profile: Provides list of concerts

Kitchener-Waterloo Chamber Orchestra (KWCO)
F-168 Lexington Ct., Waterloo ON N2J 4R9
info@kwchamberorchestra.ca
www.kwchamberorchestra.ca
www.facebook.com/75294799995
twitter.com/KW_Chamber
Overview: A small local charitable organization founded in 1985 overseen by Orchestras Canada
Mission: To present lesser-known orchestral music from the 18th and 19th century to the residents of the Kitchener-Waterloo area
Member of: Orchestras Canada
Finances: *Funding Sources:* Ticket sales; Individual & corporate sponsors
Membership: *Member Profile:* Professional and semi-professional musicians; Highly skilled music students
Activities: *Library:* Not open to public
Chief Officer(s):
Matthew Jones, Music Director

Kitchener-Waterloo Field Naturalists
317 Highland Rd. East, Kitchener ON N2M 3W6
www.kwfn.ca
Overview: A small local charitable organization founded in 1934
Mission: To promote the enjoyment of nature through environmental appreciation & conservation; To encourage wise use & conservation of natural resources
Member of: Federation of Ontario Naturalists
Finances: *Annual Operating Budget:* Less than $50,000
Membership: 250; *Fees:* $20
Activities: Walks; speakers; social; photography; plant study; *Library:* Not open to public
Chief Officer(s):
Janet Ozaruk, President, 519-893-0490
janeto@golden.net

Kitchener-Waterloo Kiwanis Music Festival
#193, 55 Northfield Dr. East, Waterloo ON N2K 3T6

Tel: 519-496-7085
admin@kwkiwanismusicfestival.org
www.kwkiwanismusicfestival.org
www.facebook.com/kwmusicfestival
twitter.com/KWKMF
Overview: A small local organization
Chief Officer(s):
Heidi Wall, Coordinator

Kitchener-Waterloo Multicultural Centre
102 King St. West, Kitchener ON N2G 1A6
Tel: 519-745-2531; *Fax:* 519-745-5857
kwmc@kwmc-on.com
www.kwmc.on.ca
www.facebook.com/128710583884871
twitter.com/kwmcED
Overview: A small local organization founded in 1970 overseen by Ontario Council of Agencies Serving Immigrants
Mission: To foster diversity & encourage participation in community life
Finances: *Funding Sources:* Federal, provincial & municipal government
Staff Member(s): 19
Membership: 40 groups; *Member Profile:* Multicultural groups & social service providers
Activities: *Speaker Service:* Yes
Chief Officer(s):
Lucia Harrison, Executive Director
lucia@kwmc-on.com

Kitchener-Waterloo Parents of Multiple Births Association
PO Box 48001, Stn. Williamsburg, Kitchener ON N2E 4K6
kitchenerwaterloo@multiplebirthscanada.org
www.multiplebirthscanada.org/~kwpomba
Also Known As: K-W POMBA
Overview: A small local organization overseen by Multiple Births Canada
Mission: Providing support services for parents of multiple birth children in Durham Region.
Membership: *Fees:* $25-$30
Activities: *Library:*
Chief Officer(s):
Jenna Aylott, President

Kitchener-Waterloo Philatelic Society (KWPS)
c/o C. Pinchen, PO Box 904, Stn. C, Kitchener ON N2G 4C5
kwps-president@kwstampclub.org
www.kwstampclub.org
Also Known As: K-W Philatelic Society
Overview: A small local organization founded in 1935
Member of: Royal Philatelic Society of Canada; Grand River Valley Philatelic Association
Membership: *Fees:* $15 adult; $20 family; $8 associate
Activities: Monthly meetings; annual exhibition; *Awareness Events:* Stampfest, March; *Speaker Service:* Yes
Chief Officer(s):
George Pepall, Treasurer
treasurer@kwstampclub.org

Kitchener-Waterloo Symphony Orchestra Association Inc. (KWSOA)
36 King St. West, Kitchener ON N2G 1A3
Tel: 519-745-4711; *Fax:* 519-745-4474
Toll-Free: 888-745-4717
info@kwsymphony.on.ca
kwsymphony.on.ca
www.facebook.com/kwsymphony
twitter.com/kw_symphony
www.youtube.com/user/kwsymphony
Overview: A small local charitable organization founded in 1945 overseen by Orchestras Canada
Mission: To cultivate the tradition of live performance through the presentation of classical orchestral & popular music for the edification, enrichment, education & excitement of our community & beyond
Member of: Orchestras Canada
Finances: *Funding Sources:* Government; Corporate & individual donations; Ticket revenue
Staff Member(s): 29
Membership: *Fees:* Schedule available; *Member Profile:* Arts patrons; *Committees:* Finance; Development; Audience Engagement; Operations, Education & Community
Activities: Performing concerts; Facilitating education & outreach programs; *Library:* KWS Music Library; Not open to public
Chief Officer(s):
Andrew Bennett, Executive Director
Edwin Outwater, Music Director, Artistic

Kitchener-Waterloo Symphony Youth Orchestra (KWSYO)
36 King St. West, Kitchener ON N2G 1A3
Tel: 519-745-4711; *Fax:* 519-745-4474
Toll-Free: 888-745-4717
info@kwsymphony.on.ca
www.kwsymphony.on.ca
Overview: A small local charitable organization founded in 1975 overseen by Orchestras Canada
Member of: Orchestras Canada
Membership: *Fees:* $470
Activities: Offers the following ensembles: Youth Orchestra; Youth Strings; Senior Youth Sinfonia; Valhalla Brass; Chamber Music
Chief Officer(s):
Barbara Kaplanek, Education & Community Programs Manager, Youth Orchestra & Schools
bkaplanek@kwsymphony.on.ca
Evan Mitchell, Youth Orchestra Conductor

Kitikmeot Regional Board of Trade (KRBT)
Kugaaruk NU
www.krbt.ca
twitter.com/kitikmeotgrowth
Overview: A small local organization
Mission: To represent businesses in the Kitikmeot region
Membership: *Committees:* Governance; Urban/rural Planning; Resource Development; Workforce Development; Funding Models; Marketing & Branding; Membership Development; Governance
Chief Officer(s):
Greg Holitzki, Director

Kitimat Chamber of Commerce
PO Box 214, 2109 Forest Ave., Kitimat BC V8C 2G7
Tel: 250-632-6294; *Fax:* 250-632-4685
Toll-Free: 800-664-6554
info@kitimatchamber.ca
www.kitimatchamber.ca
www.facebook.com/tourismkitimat
twitter.com/KitimatChamber
Overview: A small local organization founded in 1955
Mission: To protect the business interests of members; To build a strong business community in Kitimat
Member of: BC Chamber of Commerce; Canadian Chamber of Commerce
Finances: *Annual Operating Budget:* $100,000-$250,000
Staff Member(s): 3; 16 volunteer(s)
Membership: 200+; *Fees:* $130+
Activities: *Rents Mailing List:* Yes; *Library:* Resource Centre; Open to public
Chief Officer(s):
Wendy Kraft, Chair
Trish Parsons, Executive Director
tparsons@kitimatchamber.ca

Kitimat Child Development Centre
1515 Kingfisher Ave., Kitimat BC V8C 1S5
Tel: 250-632-3144; *Fax:* 250-632-3120
info@kitimatcdc.ca
www.kitimatcdc.ca
Overview: A small local organization founded in 1974
Mission: To ensure that special needs children have equal opportunities to be the best that they can be
Member of: BC Association for Community Living; Canadian Council for Exceptional Children; Spina Bifida Association of BC; Child Development & Rehabilitation Network; Association for the Care of Children's Health
Finances: *Annual Operating Budget:* $500,000-$1.5 Million; *Funding Sources:* Fundraising; donations; government funding
Staff Member(s): 32; 75 volunteer(s)
Membership: 60
Activities: Children's & Family Resource Centre; prenatal program; car seat program; Building Healthier Babies; family resources programs; physiotherapy; occupational therapy; speech-language therapy; preschool; school-aged programs; parenting classes; *Awareness Events:* Walk-for-Kids, June; *Library:* Open to public
Chief Officer(s):
Margaret Warcup, Executive Director
mwarcup@kitimatcdc.ca

Kitimat Community Services Society
#102, 170 City Centre, Kitimat BC V8C 1T6
Tel: 250-632-9107; *Fax:* 250-632-6599
Toll-Free: 877-632-9101
kcss@telus.net
www.kitimatcommunityservices.ca
Overview: A small local charitable organization founded in 1989
Affiliation(s): Literacy BC
Finances: *Annual Operating Budget:* Less than $50,000; *Funding Sources:* Regional government; donations; BC gaming
Staff Member(s): 1; 15 volunteer(s)
Membership: 27; *Fees:* $5; *Member Profile:* Residents of Kitimat area
Activities: Conversation groups; one-to-one tutoring; upgrading; *Awareness Events:* National Literacy Day
Chief Officer(s):
Janette Camazzola, Contact
Denise O'Neil, Executive Director

Kitimat Food Bank
14 Morgan St., Kitimat BC V8C 1J3
Tel: 250-632-6611
Overview: A small local organization
Chief Officer(s):
Marjorie Phelps, Contact
marjon@citywest.ca

Kitimat Valley Naturalists
c/o Walter Thorne, 12 Farrow St., Kitimat BC V8C 1E2
Tel: 250-632-7632
Overview: A small local organization
Mission: To engage with & explore birding, wildflowers, ecology, & environmental issues in the region
Membership: 10; *Fees:* $16.10
Chief Officer(s):
Walter Thorne, Contact
swthorne@telus.net

Kitimat, Terrace & District Labour Council
3312 Sparks St., Terrace BC V8G 2T7
Tel: 250-635-5080; *Fax:* 250-635-5083
Overview: A small local organization overseen by British Columbia Federation of Labour
Mission: To advance the economic & social welfare of workers in Kitimat, Terrace & the surrounding area in British Columbia
Affiliation(s): Canadian Labour Congress (CLC)
Activities: Promoting the interests of affiliates; Providing training, in areas such as campaign organizing, women & leadership, & problem solving; Raising awareness of local issues, such as the Northen Gateway project to transport oil; Hosting a ceremony for the annual Day of Mourning for Workers Killed or Injured On the Job
Chief Officer(s):
Larry Huntus, President

Kitsilano Showboat Society
PO Box 74526, 2300 Cornwall Ave., Vancouver BC V6K 4P9
Tel: 604-734-7332
kitsilanoshowboat@hotmail.com
www.kitsilanoshowboat.com
Overview: A small local organization
Mission: To showcase talent during the summer season
Chief Officer(s):
Bea Leinbach, President

Kivalliq Chamber of Commerce
PO Box 819, Rankin Inlet NU X0C 0G0
Tel: 867-645-2823; *Fax:* 867-645-2082
Previous Name: Keewatin Chamber of Commerce
Overview: A small local organization
Chief Officer(s):
Paul Delany, Contact

Kivalliq Inuit Association
PO Box 340, #164, 1 Mivvik Ave., Rankin Inlet NU X0C 0G0
Tel: 867-645-5725; *Fax:* 867-645-2348
reception@kivalliqinuit.ca
www.kivalliqinuit.ca
www.facebook.com/169387666467868
Overview: A small local organization
Mission: To promote the interests of Inuit living in the Kivalliq Region
Staff Member(s): 19
Chief Officer(s):
Steve Hartman, Executive Director, 867-645-5733
shartman@kivalliqinuit.ca

Kiwanis International (Eastern Canada & the Caribbean District)
PO Box 26040, Stn. Terrace Hill, Brantford ON N3R 7X4

Tel: 519-304-0745; Fax: 519-304-5362
Toll-Free: 888-921-9054
district@kwanisecc.org
www.kiwanisecc.org
Overview: A medium-sized local organization
Chief Officer(s):
Hope Markes, Governor

Kiwanis International (Western Canada District)
#303, 6010 - 48 Ave., Camrose AB T4V 0K3
Tel: 780-608-1417; Fax: 780-672-8369
WeCanDST@gmail.com
www.ikiwanis.ca
Overview: A medium-sized local organization founded in 1919
Activities: Youth programs; community services
Chief Officer(s):
Dirk Bannister, Secretary-Treasurer
Richard Le Sueur, Governor
Cheryl Storrs, Governor-Elect

Kiwanis Music Festival See Sault Ste. Marie Music Festival

Kiwanis Music Festival Association of Greater Toronto
1422 Bayview Ave., #A, Toronto ON M4G 3A7
Tel: 416-487-5885; Fax: 416-639-5340
office@kiwanismusictoronto.org
kiwanismusictoronto.org
Overview: A small local charitable organization
Mission: To bring together various choirs in music competitions
Member of: Ontario Music Festivals Association; The Federation of Canadian Music Festivals
Staff Member(s): 3
Chief Officer(s):
Pam Allen, General Manager

Kiwanis Music Festival of Windsor/Essex County
PO Box 941, Windsor ON N9A 6P2
Tel: 226-783-9686
info@wkmf.ca
www.wkmf.ca
www.facebook.com/131126860274386
twitter.com/WKMFestival
Overview: A small local organization founded in 1947
150+ volunteer(s)
Chief Officer(s):
Kim Beneteau, Contact

Kiwassa Neighbourhood Services Association
2425 Oxford St., Vancouver BC V5K 1M7
Tel: 604-254-5401; Fax: 604-254-7673
info@kiwassa.ca
www.kiwassa.ca
Overview: A small local charitable organization
Mission: To bring the community together
Member of: Affiliation of Multicultural Societies & Service Agencies of BC
Staff Member(s): 21
Activities: Social, recreational & educational services for youth, families, seniors & the unemployed
Chief Officer(s):
Mark Gifford, Executive Director
markg@kiwassa.ca

Klondike Placer Miners' Association
3151B Third Ave., Whitehorse YT Y1A 1G1
Tel: 867-667-2267; Fax: 867-668-7127
kpma@kpma.ca
www.kpma.ca
Overview: A small provincial organization founded in 1974
Membership: Fees: $159-$3210
Chief Officer(s):
Mike McDougall, President

Klondike Snowmobile Association (KSA)
4061 - 4th Ave., Whitehorse YT Y1A 1H1
Tel: 867-667-7680
klonsnow@yknet.ca
www.ksa.yk.ca
www.facebook.com/253094448062816
Overview: A small local organization
Member of: Canadian Council of Snowmobile Organizations
Affiliation(s): Trans Canada Trail - Yukon
Membership: 500; Fees: $20 single; $30 family; $100 corporate
Chief Officer(s):
Mark Daniels, President
mnd@northwestel.net

Klondike Visitors Association (KVA)
PO Box 389, Dawson City YT Y0B 1G0
Tel: 867-993-5575; Fax: 867-993-6415
Toll-Free: 877-465-3006
kva@dawson.net
www.dawsoncity.ca
www.facebook.com/dawsoncity
Overview: A small local organization founded in 1952 overseen by Tourism Industry Association of the Yukon
Mission: To respond to visitor information requests & liaises with municipal & territorial governments to encourage Tourism-related initiatives; to promote Dawson City, Yukon & the Klondike Region as a year-round tourist destination.
Finances: Funding Sources: Casino gaming; entertainment venue
Membership: Fees: $210 corporate
Activities: Diamond Tooth Gerties Gambling Hall; Thaw-di-Gras Spring Carnival; Klondike Outhouse Races; Yukon Goldpanning; Gaslight Follies; Jack London Interpretive Centre
Chief Officer(s):
Gary Parker, Executive Director

Kneehill Historical Society
PO Box 653, 1301 2nd St. North, Three Hills AB T0M 2A0
Tel: 403-443-2092; Fax: 403-443-7941
www.threehills.ca
Overview: A small local charitable organization founded in 1975
Mission: To collect, preserve & display artifacts pertaining to local history
Affiliation(s): Big Country Tourist Association
Finances: Funding Sources: Alberta Museum Association; Alberta Lotteries; local support
Staff Member(s): 2; 10 volunteer(s)
Membership: 30; Fees: $15
Activities: Operates Three Hills Museum
Chief Officer(s):
Gordon Park, President
Alice Park, Secretary
George Boles, Vice-President

Knights Hospitallers, Sovereign Order of St. John of Jerusalem, Knights of Malta, Grand Priory of Canada (OSJ)
#301, 2800 Hwy. 7 West, Concord ON L4K 1W8
Also Known As: Knights Hospitallers of Cyprus, Rhodes, Malta & Russia
Overview: A medium-sized international charitable organization founded in 1048
Mission: To propagate the principles of chivalry; care for the sick, aged, invalid, poor & children in need; protect & defend Christianity throughout the world; combat errors; champion the truth; promote & encourage the spirit of Brotherhood & charity within the order; members are expected to be united in brotherhood & charity
Member of: International Chivalric Congress
Affiliation(s): United Nations - Canada, participant
Finances: Funding Sources: Members' donations
Membership: Member Profile: Exemplary Christians of any official denomination, active in community charitable works
Activities: Supreme Council; Priory Councils; Hospitaller Service; Awareness Events: Feast of St. John, June 24; Great Siege Day, Sept. 8; Internships: Yes; Speaker Service: Yes; Library: Gr. Priory OSJ Library; by appointment Not open to public
Chief Officer(s):
Mario Cortellucci, Contact
Awards:
• Cross of Merit
; Amount: Pro merito medal for volunteer work

Knights of Columbus of Québec Voir Les Chevaliers de Colomb du Québec

Knights of Pythias - Domain of British Columbia
BC
knightsofpythiasbritishcolumbia.ca
Overview: A small provincial organization founded in 1880
Affiliation(s): Supreme Lodge Knights of Pythias
Activities: Rents Mailing List: Yes
Chief Officer(s):
Roger Murray, Chancellor

Knights of St. John International - Canada
26 Royce Ave., Brampton ON K61 1J5
Also Known As: Knights of St. John International Commandery 710
Overview: A large international organization founded in 2010
Mission: To advance the interests of the Roman Catholic Church; to foster fraternity & fellowship among members; to promote undiscriminating charity
Affiliation(s): Archdiocese of Toronto
Membership: Member Profile: Catholic males aged 16 & above
Chief Officer(s):
Peter Ozemoyah, Contact

Kokosai Koryu Kikin Toronto Nihon Bunka Centre See The Japan Foundation, Toronto

Kolbe Eucharistic Apostolate
c/o St. Brigid's Church, 300 Wolverleigh Blvd., Toronto ON M4C 1S6
www.kolbeapostolate.com
Overview: A small local organization founded in 1996
Mission: To make the Eucharistic Christ the heart of lives, through Eucharistic Adoration
Affiliation(s): Archdiocese of Toronto
Membership: Member Profile: Any Catholic individual who lives in accordance with the teaching of the Catholic Church, & who wishes to deepen his or her knowledge of God
Activities: Developing faith formation; Providing mini-retreats, prayer groups, Bible study, & catechesis
Chief Officer(s):
Maria De Manche, Event Co-Coordinator & Animator
Therese De Manche, Event Co-Coordinator & Animator
Charles Anang, Spiritual Advisor

Kootenay Lake Chamber of Commerce
PO Box 120, Crawford Bay BC V0B 1E0
Tel: 250-227-9655
info@kootenaylake.bc.ca
www.kootenaylake.bc.ca
Overview: A small local organization
Mission: To promote & advance area businesses
Membership: 46; Fees: $65-$110
Activities: Providing networking opportunities; Fundraising; Supporting community efforts & events
Chief Officer(s):
Gina Medhurst, Chair

Kootenay Real Estate Board (KREB)
#208, 402 Baker St., Nelson BC V1L 4H8
Tel: 250-352-5477; Fax: 250-352-7184
Toll-Free: 877-295-9375
kreb@telus.net
www.kreb.ca
www.facebook.com/217611504946687
Overview: A small local organization founded in 1965 overseen by British Columbia Real Estate Association
Mission: To promote interest in real estate markets in all aspects through service to members & the public.
Member of: The Canadian Real Estate Association
Finances: Funding Sources: Membership dues
Chief Officer(s):
Cathy Graham, President
Marianne Bond, Executive Officer
kreb_eo@telus.net

Kootenay Rockies Tourism
1905 Warren Ave., Kimberley BC V1A 1S2
Tel: 250-427-4838; Fax: 250-427-3344
Toll-Free: 800-661-6603
info@kootenayrockies.com
www.krtourism.ca
www.linkedin.com/company/kootenay-rockies-tourism
www.facebook.com/KootRock
twitter.com/kootrock
www.youtube.com/kootrock
Previous Name: Tourism Rockies
Overview: A medium-sized local organization founded in 1978
Mission: To coordinate & execute tourism marketing initiatives of private sector partners.
Staff Member(s): 7
Membership: 600; Member Profile: Tourism business in the Kootenay Rockies Region
Chief Officer(s):
Kathy Cooper, CEO & Travel Trade Manager
Kathy@KootenayRockies.com

Kootenay Society for Community Living (KSCL)
2224 - 6th Ave., Castlegar BC V1N 2V9
Tel: 250-365-2624; Fax: 250-365-5679
info@kscl.ca
ksclcastlegar.net
www.facebook.com/670132373006601

Overview: A small local organization founded in 1950
Mission: TO support people with mental disabilities so that they may have fulfilling & productive lives, independent, but integrated in the community
Member of: British Columbia Society for Community Living
Membership: Fees: Schedule availables
Activities: Day program; residences
Chief Officer(s):
Kathleen Elias, Executive Director, 250-365-2624 Ext. 3
keliaskscl@telus.net

Korea Veterans Association of Canada Inc., Heritage Unit (KVA) / Association canadienne des vétérans de la Corée (ACVC)
#12, 280 Thaler Ave., Kitchener ON N2A 1R6
Tel: 519-896-6466
www.kvacanada.com
Overview: A medium-sized national charitable organization founded in 1974
Mission: To promote awareness of Canada's role in the Korean War; To represent veterans & their families
Finances: Funding Sources: Membership dues; Fundraising
Membership: Member Profile: Persons who served in the Canadian Armed Forces (Navy, Army, Air Force) in Korea during the 1950-1953 war & on peacekeeping duties in Korea from 1953 to 1955; Korea veterans who served with United Nations Forces from other countries; Members of ancillary units that served UN Forces, such as the Red Cross, Salvation Army, & Merchant Navy
Activities: Presenting awards & bursaries; Operating a kit shop
Chief Officer(s):
Dave Davidson, Chair, Membership
 Atlantic Region
 www.kvacanada.com
 Ontario Region
 ON
 www.kvacanada.com
 Chief Officer(s):
 Terry Wickens, President
 Pacific Region
 BC
 Tel: 250-743-3383
 www.kvacanada.com
 Chief Officer(s):
 John R. Bishop, President
 Prairie Region
 AB
 www.kvacanada.com
 Québec Region
 QC
 www.kvacanada.com

Korean Association of Newfoundland & Labrador
42 McNeilly St., St. John's NL A1B 1Y8
Overview: A small provincial organization founded in 1978
Mission: To preserve Korean heritage & culture across Newfoundland
Membership: Member Profile: Korean Canadians who live in Newfoundland
Activities: Arranging networking opportunities & cultural activities for Korean Canadians in Newfoundland
Chief Officer(s):
Chung Won Cho, Contact
cho@physics-mun.ca

Korean Business Association
499 Main St. East, Hamilton ON L8N 1K8
Tel: 905-549-2210
Overview: A small local organization

Korean Businessmen's Cooperative Association of British Columbia (KBCABC)
6373 Arbroath St., Burnaby BC V5E 1C3
Tel: 604-431-7373; Fax: 604-431-7374
www.kbcabc.com
Overview: A small international organization

Korean Canadian Association of Ottawa (KCAO)
645 Somerset St. West, Ottawa ON K1R 5K3
Tel: 613-236-4720; Fax: 613-236-4720
ottawakorean@gmail.com
www.ottawakorean.com
Overview: A small local organization founded in 1960
Mission: To retain Korean heritage & traditions; To promote appreciation of Korean heritage & culture; To support Korean Canadians in the Ottawa area through the provision of social services, such as interpretation & counselling
Finances: Funding Sources: Membership fees
Membership: 2,000; Member Profile: Korean Canadians from Ottawa & the surrounding area; Person interested in furthering the objects of the association
Activities: Offering Korean cultural activities; Presenting exhibitions; Contributing to ethnocultural events in the Ottawa area; Providing information about Korean heritage & culture; Organizing educational events, such as lectures & discussions; Assisting members by providing social & legal services; Helping victims financially or through moral support; Providing recreational activities for the welfare of members

Korean Canadian Association of Waterloo & Wellington
PO Box 176, St Mitchell ON N0K 1N0
Tel: 519-348-8126
Overview: A small local organization founded in 1970
Mission: To retain Korean culture & heritage
Membership: Member Profile: Korean Canadians from the Waterloo & Wellington regions of Ontario
Activities: Promoting appreciation for Korean heritage & culture in Ontario's Waterloo & Wellington regions

Korean Canadian Cultural Association of the Greater Toronto Area (KCCA)
1133 Leslie St., Toronto ON M3C 2J6
Tel: 416-383-0777; Fax: 416-383-1116
kcca1133@gmail.com
www.koreancentre.on.ca
www.facebook.com/koreancanadianculturalassociation
twitter.com/kccagta
www.youtube.com/user/koreancentre
Overview: A large local organization founded in 1965
Mission: To promote Korean heritage & culture in Toronto & the surrounding area; To develop cooperation in the local Korean community
Finances: Funding Sources: Membership fees; Ontario Trillium Foundation
Membership: 100,000; Fees: $30 regular individual; $50 family; $20 senior; $30 senior couple; Member Profile: Korean Canadians in Toronto & the surrounding region
Activities: Organizing cultural & recreational activities, such as traditional Korean dance classes, & Taekwondo & Kuk Sool classes; Offering English as a Second Language classes; Assisting new Korean immigrants to the Greater Toronto Area; Internships: Yes
Chief Officer(s):
Daniel Lee, President

Korean Canadian Society of London
#718, 595 Proudfoot Lane, London ON N6H 4S1
Tel: 519-670-2883
Overview: A small local organization founded in 1970
Mission: To assist Korean Canadians in the London, Ontario region, in areas such as language
Finances: Funding Sources: Membership fees
Membership: Member Profile: Korean Canadians in London, Ontario & the surrounding area
Activities: Arranging social & recreational activities for Korean Canadians in the London area; Hosting a Korean seniors' group; Providing a Korean language school
Chief Officer(s):
David Sangwoo Kim, President
davidkim88@yahoo.ca

Korean Canadian Students Federation See Korean Students' Association of Canada

Korean Canadian Women's Association (KCWA)
27 Madison Ave., Toronto ON M5R 2S2
Tel: 416-340-1234; Fax: 416-340-7755
kcwa@kcwa.net
www.kcwa.net
www.facebook.com/kcwaservice
Also Known As: KCWA Family and Social Services
Overview: A medium-sized national organization founded in 1985
Mission: To empower Korean Canadian families and other vulnerable members of the community-at-large to live free from violence, poverty and inequity through the provision of culturally sensitive and linguistically appropriate services for the purpose of enhancing the well-being of immigrant families and promoting their successful integration into Canadian society
Chief Officer(s):
Shine Chung, Executive Director, 416-340-7198
shine.chung@kcwa.net
Eunyoung Baek, Operations Manager, 416-340-1831

Korean Community of Greater Montréal / La communauté coréenne du grand Montréal
3480, boul Décarie, 2e étage, Montréal QC H4A 3J5
Tel: 541-481-6661; Fax: 514-481-0062
Overview: A medium-sized local organization founded in 1965
Mission: To support Korean Canadians in the Greater Montréal Area
Membership: Member Profile: Korean Canadians in the Montréal area
Activities: Offering classes in English, French, & Korean at the Korean Community Center of Montréal; Providing social & cultural activities

Korean Senior Citizens Society of Toronto (KSCST)
KSCST Centre, 476 Grace St., Toronto ON M6G 3A9
Tel: 416-532-8077; Fax: 416-532-9964
kscst@hotmail.com
www.kscst.com
Overview: A medium-sized local charitable organization founded in 1973
Mission: To provide social services & programs to Korean senior citizens in the Greater Toronto Area; To promote welfare among members; To promote traditional Korean arts, culture, & values to younger Korean generations
Finances: Funding Sources: Membership fees; Donations
Membership: 2,000+; Fees: $30; Member Profile: Korean Canadian seniors, over sixty years of age, who live in Toronto & the surrounding area
Activities: Offering educational, recreational, & cultural programming; Assisting Korean seniors who have recently moved to Canada & the Greater Toronto Area; Providing social services, such as counselling, & assistance in applying for government support programs; Awareness Events: Annual Korean Harvest Thanksgiving Festival & Walk-a-Thon; Hyo-Do Arts Festival
Chief Officer(s):
Bae Kim Jeong, President
Yong Hoo Chung, Chief Director
Kil Yeo Whang, Vice-Chief Director
Kum Suk Hwang, General Manager
Sang-Im Kim, Executive Manager
Hyun-Ju Shin, Coordintor, Programs
Publications:
• Korean Senior Citizens Society of Toronto Newsletter
Type: Newsletter; Frequency: Quarterly; Price: Free with membership in the Korean Senior Citizens Society of Toronto
Profile: Information & upcoming events for society members

Korean Society of British Columbia for Fraternity & Culture
1320 East Hastings St., Vancouver BC V5L 1S3
Tel: 604-255-3739; Fax: 604-255-3443
Overview: A medium-sized provincial organization founded in 1966
Mission: To retain Korean heritage & culture
Membership: Over 50,000; Member Profile: Korean Canadians residing in British Columbia
Activities: Offering cultural, recreational, & social activities for Korean Canadians in British Columbia; Facilitating networking opportunities; Promoting appreciation for Korean heritage & culture

Korean Society of Manitoba
#800, 150 River Ave., Winnipeg MB R3L 0A9
Tel: 204-668-7326
www.ksmanitoba.com
Overview: A small provincial organization founded in 1967
Mission: To promote & preserve the Korean culture
Member of: Asian Heritage Society of Manitoba
Membership: 350; Member Profile: Korean Canadians who reside in Manitoba
Activities: Organizing social & cultural activities for Korean Canadians in Manitoba; Sponsoring the Korean Pavilion at Winnipeg's Folklorama

Korean Students' Association of Canada (KSAC)
www.ksacanada.com
Previous Name: Korean Canadian Students Federation
Overview: A medium-sized national organization founded in 1998
Mission: To act as a voice for Korean Canadian students; To assist Korean youth in the exploration of their future; To organize

projects to engage the Korean Canadian student community; To cultivate healthy Korean Canadian identities
Membership: *Member Profile:* Korean Canadian students
Activities: Hosting academic, cultural, & social events, such as career conferences, identity conferences, & the KSAC Games; Creating networking opportunities for all Korean Canadian students across Canada; Acting as a bridge between students & professionals in order to assist students; Providing technical knowledge about developing careers for Korean Canadian students; Raising awareness of matters in the Korean Canadian community; *Awareness Events:* KSAC Festival, November
Chief Officer(s):
Dyland Chang, President
ksacpresident@gmail.com
Jennie Yeo, Vice-President, External
tdiad.jyeo@gmail.com
Steve Kwon, Vice-President, Internal
sts6373@gmail.com
Publications:
• Sponge & Open
Type: Magazine; *Frequency:* Semiannually
Profile: A place for Korean students to express their views

Korean-Canadian Symphony Orchestra (KGSO)
#203, 28 Finch Ave. West, Toronto ON M2N 2G7
Tel: 647-532-2578
info@kcso.ca
www.kcso.ca
www.facebook.com/KoreanCanadianSymphonyOrchestra
Overview: A small local charitable organization overseen by Orchestras Canada
Mission: To provide concerts to people in the GTA & to promote Korean-Canadian musicians
Finances: *Funding Sources:* Provincial government; Corporate & indivdual donations
Staff Member(s): 13
Membership: 34
Activities: Performing concerts; Operating a youth orchestra; Operating summer music camps; *Library:* by appointment
Chief Officer(s):
June Choi, President
Richard Lee, Music Director

Kosher Check
#401, 1037 West Broadway, Vancouver BC V6H 1E3
Tel: 604-731-1803; *Fax:* 604-731-1804
info@koshercheck.org
www.koshercheck.org
www.linkedin.com/company/3110427
www.facebook.com/Koshercheck
twitter.com/koshercheck
www.youtube.com/watch?v=ujujK_r3xAc
Previous Name: BC Kosher; Orthodox Rabbinical Council of British Columbia
Overview: A medium-sized international charitable organization founded in 1983
Finances: *Annual Operating Budget:* $100,000-$250,000
Staff Member(s): 5; 6 volunteer(s)
Membership: 100-499
Activities: Providing information about Kashruth (kosher food - kashruth symbol BCK); *Speaker Service:* Yes
Chief Officer(s):
Avraham Feigelstock, Av Beis Din, 604-731-1803 Ext. 101
Richard Wood, Director, Business & Marketing, 604-731-1803 Ext. 103

Kugluktuk Chamber of Commerce
11 Coronation Dr., Kugluktuk NU X0B 0E0
Tel: 867-982-3232; *Fax:* 867-982-3229
Overview: A small local organization
Member of: Nunavut Tourism; NWT Chamber of Commerce; Canadian Chamber of Commerce
Activities: *Rents Mailing List:* Yes; *Library:* Open to public
Chief Officer(s):
Ken Brandly, Executive Director

Kurdish Community & Information Centre of Toronto (TKCC)
#7, 1290 Finch Ave. West, Toronto ON M3J 3K3
Tel: 416-654-2049; *Fax:* 647-748-2051
contact@kurdishcommunity.com
www.kurdishcc.com
www.facebook.com/KurdishCommunity
twitter.com/TorontoKurdCC
Overview: A small international organization founded in 1992
Mission: To help the Kurdish community in Toronto

K-W Hang Gliding Club; Hang-On-Tario *See* Southwestern Ontario Gliding Association

Kwakiutl District Council
PO Box 489, 695 Headstart Cres., Campbell River BC V9W 5C1
Tel: 250-286-3263; *Fax:* 250-286-3268
Toll-Free: 866-999-3262
www.kdchealth.com
Overview: A small local organization
Chief Officer(s):
Bev Hills, Administrator
admikdc@uniserve.com

Kwantlen College Faculty Association *See* Kwantlen Faculty Association

Kwantlen Faculty Association (KFA) / Association des professeurs de Kwantlen
Birch Bldg., #201, 12666 - 72nd Ave., Surrey BC V3W 2M8
Tel: 604-599-2200; *Fax:* 604-599-0797
kfa@kfa.bc.ca
www.kfa.bc.ca
www.facebook.com/YourKFA
Previous Name: Kwantlen College Faculty Association
Overview: A small local organization
Mission: To represent their memebers' interests during collective bargaining agreements
Member of: College Institute Educators Association
Affiliation(s): BC Federation of Labour; Canadian Association of University Teachers; National Union of Canadian Association of University Teachers; Canadian Labour Congress; Federation of Post Secondary Educators of BC; New Westminster & District Labour Council; Vancouver & District Labour Council
Membership: 750; *Committees:* Disability Management Rehabilitation; Labour Management Relations; Occupational Health and Safety; Performance Review; Negotiations; Union Counselling; Working Conditions
Chief Officer(s):
Terri Van Steinburg, President, 604-599-2259
Suzanne Pearce, Secretary-Treasurer, 604-599-2197
suzanne.pearce@kpu.ca

Laboratoires des assureurs du Canada *See* Underwriters' Laboratories of Canada

Labour Council of Metropolitan Toronto & York Region *See* Toronto & York Region Labour Council

Labrador Friendship Centre
PO Box 767, Stn. B, 49 Grenfell St., Happy Valley-Goose Bay NL A0P 1E0
Tel: 709-896-8302; *Fax:* 709-896-8731
www.lfchvgb.ca
Overview: A small local organization
Mission: To meet the needs of Aboriginal people in Labrador through the provision of programs & services
Chief Officer(s):
Jennifer Hefler-Elson, Executive Director
jhefler-elson@lfchvgb.ca

Labrador Literacy Information & Action Network
PO Box 2516, Stn. B, Happy Valley-Goose Bay NL A0P 1E0
Tel: 709-896-9088; *Fax:* 709-896-2970
Overview: A small provincial organization

Labrador Native Women's Association
PO Box 542, Stn. B, Happy Valley-Goose Bay NL A0P 1S0
Tel: 709-896-5071; *Fax:* 709-896-5071
www.exec.gov.nl.ca/exec/wpo/aboriginalwomen
Overview: A small provincial organization

Labrador North Chamber of Commerce (LNCC)
PO Box 460, Stn. B, 6 Hillcrest Rd., Happy Valley-Goose Bay NL A0P 1E0
Tel: 709-896-8787; *Fax:* 709-896-8039
Toll-Free: 877-920-8787
www.chamberlabrador.com
www.linkedin.com/company/1209666
www.facebook.com/chamberlabrador
twitter.com/LabradorChamber
Overview: A small local organization
Mission: To provide & improve trade & commerce & the economic, civic & social welfare of the community
Member of: Canadian Chamber of Commerce; Nfld & Labrador Chamber of Commerce; Atlantic Provinces Chamber of Commerce
Finances: *Annual Operating Budget:* $50,000-$100,000
Staff Member(s): 4; 9 volunteer(s)

Membership: 123; *Fees:* Based on number of employees
Chief Officer(s):
Sterling Peyton, President
Brian Fowlow, Chief Executive Officer

Labrador Straits Chamber of Commerce
PO Box 179, Forteau NL A0K 2P0
Tel: 709-931-2073; *Fax:* 709-931-2073
Overview: A small local organization

Labrador West Association for Community Living *See* Newfoundland & Labrador Association for Community Living

Labrador West Chamber of Commerce
PO Box 273, 118 Humphrey Rd., Labrador City NL A2V 2K5
Tel: 709-944-3723; *Fax:* 709-944-4699
lwc@crrstv.net
www.labradorwestchamber.ca
Overview: A small local organization
Mission: To improve the economic environment of the area
Chief Officer(s):
Alice Regular, President

Lac du Bonnet & District Chamber of Commerce
PO Box 598, Lac du Bonnet MB R0E 1A0
Tel: 204-340-0497
ldbchamberofcommerce@gmail.com
www.lacdubonnetchamber.com
www.facebook.com/LdBChamberOfCommerce
Overview: A small local organization
Mission: To promote economic development & tourism marketing in & around Lac du Bonnet, Manitoba
Affiliation(s): Manitoba Chambers of Commerce
Finances: *Funding Sources:* Town; Rural Municipality; Membership dues
Membership: 137; *Fees:* $80 1-2 employees; $105 3-10 employees; $155 11 or more employees; $80 non-profit; *Member Profile:* Businesses; Services; Non-profit organizations; Individuals
Chief Officer(s):
Jennifer Hudson Stewart, Administrator

Lac La Biche & District Chamber of Commerce
PO Box 804, 10307 100 St., Lac La Biche AB T0A 2C0
Tel: 780-623-2818; *Fax:* 780-623-7217
info@llbchamber.ca
www.llbchamber.ca
www.facebook.com/127175950658710
twitter.com/LLBCHAMBER
Overview: A small local organization founded in 1922
Mission: To help promote business & tourism in the area
Affiliation(s): Alberta Chamber of Commerce
Finances: *Funding Sources:* Membership fees; events
Membership: *Member Profile:* Local businesses
Chief Officer(s):
Rik Nikoniuk, President

Lac La Biche Canadian Native Friendship Centre
PO Box 2338, 10105 Churchill Dr., Lac La Biche AB T0A 2C0
Tel: 780-623-3249; *Fax:* 780-623-1846
www.llb-cnfc.com
www.facebook.com/llbcnfc
twitter.com/LLBCNFC
Overview: A small local organization overseen by Alberta Native Friendship Centres Association
Mission: Dedicated to providing culturally-based programs and services that respond to the distinct needs of urban Aboriginal people in their communities and bridging the gaps that occur between Aboriginal and non-Aboriginal peoples in urban areas.
Member of: Alberta Native Friendship Centres Association
Staff Member(s): 9
Chief Officer(s):
Donna Webster, Executive Director
donna@llb-cnfc.com

Lac La Biche Disability Services
PO Box 2078, 10018 - 103 Ave., Lac La Biche AB T0A 2C0
Tel: 780-623-2800; *Fax:* 780-623-3874
llbds@telus.net
www.llbds.com
Previous Name: Community Living Association for the Little Divide; Lac La Biche & District Association for the Handicapped
Overview: A small local charitable organization founded in 1979 overseen by Alberta Association for Community Living
Mission: To support & serve individuals with disabilities; To encourage community inclusion & participation
Member of: Alberta Association for Community Living; Alberta Association of Rehabilitation Centres

Finances: *Funding Sources:* Government funds
Staff Member(s): 3
Activities: Promoting public education & awareness; Providing individualized community support for individuals with disabilities; *Internships:* Yes; *Speaker Service:* Yes; *Library:* Open to public
Chief Officer(s):
Shauna Quintal, Executive Director
shauna@llbds.com

Lace Up Your Cleats (LUYC)
Toronto ON
info@laceupyourcleats.com
www.laceupyourcleats.com
Overview: A small local organization
Mission: To provide marginalized people & communities with opportunities to play recreational soccer
Activities: Organizing sporting & social events; *Rents Mailing List:* Yes
Chief Officer(s):
Cristina Murano, Founder

Lachine Black Community Association
PO Box 34042, Lachine QC H8S 4H4
Tel: 514-634-1862
Overview: A small local organization
Chief Officer(s):
Marcia Babb, Contact
msmbabb@sympatico.ca

LaCloche Foothills Chamber of Commerce
PO Box 4311, 91 Barber St., Espanola ON P5E 1S4
Tel: 705-869-7671
www.laclochefoothillschamber.com
Previous Name: Espanola & District Chamber of Commerce
Overview: A small local organization
Mission: To represent Espanola, Sable-Spanish, Baldwin, & Nairn & Hyman
Membership: *Fees:* Schedule available
Chief Officer(s):
Cheryl Kay, President
cheryl@laclochefoothillschamber.com

Lacombe & District Chamber of Commerce
6005 - 50 Ave., Lacombe AB T4L 1K7
Tel: 403-782-4300; *Fax:* 403-782-4302
info@lacombechamber.ca
www.lacombechamber.ca
www.facebook.com/lacombeanddistrictchamberofcommerce
twitter.com/LacombeChamber
Overview: A small local organization founded in 1924
Mission: To promote & enhance the economic well-being of Lacombe & district businesses, industries & residents
Member of: Alberta Chamber of Commerce; Canadian Chamber of Commerce
Finances: *Annual Operating Budget:* $100,000-$250,000; *Funding Sources:* Trade show; membership fees; events; grants
Staff Member(s): 1
Membership: 254; *Fees:* Schedule available
Chief Officer(s):
Monica Bartman, Executive Director

Lacombe Handicraft & Lapidary Guild
c/o Bea Ganter, 5539 - 53 Ave., Lacombe AB T4L 1L3
Tel: 403-782-6221
Previous Name: Lacombe Lapidary Club
Overview: A small local organization
Member of: Alberta Federation of Rock Clubs
Chief Officer(s):
Bea Ganter, Contact

Lacombe Lapidary Club *See* Lacombe Handicraft & Lapidary Guild

Lacrosse New Brunswick
211 rte 616, Keswick Ridge NB E6L 1R9
Tel: 506-440-1227
www.laxnb.ca
www.facebook.com/128267803907009
Also Known As: Lacrosse NB
Overview: A small provincial organization overseen by Canadian Lacrosse Association
Mission: To be the provincial governing body for the sport of lacrosse in New Brunswick
Member of: Canadian Lacrosse Association
Chief Officer(s):
Chris Gallop, President, 506-440-1227
chris.gallop@nbed.bd.ca

Tim Jackson, Treasurer, 506-674-1597
tjackson@nb.sympatico.ca
Jennifer Gendron, Secretary, 506-651-4848
jqgendron@gmail.com

Lacrosse Nova Scotia
5516 Spring Garden Rd., 4th Fl., Halifax NS B3J 1G6
Tel: 902-425-5450; *Fax:* 902-425-5606
lacrosse@sportnovascotia.ca
lacrossens.ca
www.facebook.com/421011914655642
Overview: A small provincial organization founded in 1971 overseen by Canadian Lacrosse Association
Member of: Canadian Lacrosse Association; Sport Nova Scotia
Finances: *Funding Sources:* Provincial government
Chief Officer(s):
Greg Knight, Executive Director
Chet Koneczny, Technical Director
lacrossetechdirector@sportnovascotia.ca

The Ladies of the Lake
ON
Tel: 905-476-4045
Other Communication: sponsorship@lakeladies.ca
ladies@lakeladies.ca
www.lakeladies.ca
Overview: A small local organization founded in 2005
Mission: To promote a greater sense of connection with Lake Simcoe; to get people involved in what the future brings - both in terms of the lake itself & for those who share it; to offer a set of possible actions to restore the Lake to health for the communities around the Lake & watershed
Membership: 100+; *Member Profile:* Women of all ages who are working to rescue Lake Simcoe and its watershed.
Activities: Calendar; "Naked Truth" series of events
Chief Officer(s):
Annabel Slaight, President

Ladies' Morning Musical Club (LMMC) / Les Matinées de musique de chambre
#12, 1410, rue Guy, Montréal QC H3H 2L7
Tel: 514-932-6796; *Fax:* 514-932-0510
lmmc@qc.aibn.com
www.lmmc.ca
Also Known As: LMMC Concerts
Overview: A small local charitable organization founded in 1892
Member of: Conseil québécois de la musique
Finances: *Annual Operating Budget:* $100,000-$250,000
Staff Member(s): 1; 10 volunteer(s)
Membership: 480; *Fees:* $80 student subscription; $250 adult subscription; *Member Profile:* Men & women
Activities: Presenting chamber music concerts
Chief Officer(s):
Constance V. Pathy, President
Rosemary Neville, Secretary-Treasurer

Ladies' Orange Benevolent Association of Canada (LOBA)
c/o Grand Orange Lodge of Canada, 94 Sheppard Ave. West, Toronto ON M2N 1M5
Tel: 416-223-1690; *Fax:* 416-223-1324
Toll-Free: 800-565-6248
Overview: A medium-sized national organization founded in 1894 overseen by Grand Orange Lodge of Canada
Mission: To provide women with an opportunity to practice Orange beliefs & participate in benevolent activities
Chief Officer(s):
John Chalmers, Grand Secretary, Grand Lodge of Canada

Ladysmith Chamber of Commerce
PO Box 598, 33 Roberts St., Ladysmith BC V9G 1A4
Tel: 250-245-2112; *Fax:* 250-245-2124
www.ladysmithcofc.com
Overview: A small local organization founded in 1930
Mission: To promote & improve the commercial, industrial, civic & social welfare of the Town of Ladysmith & surrounding area; To develop programs for the business community; To represent the business community municipally, provincially & federally
Member of: BC Chamber of Commerce
Affiliation(s): Cowichan Regional Valley
Finances: *Annual Operating Budget:* $100,000-$250,000; *Funding Sources:* Membership fees; Town of Ladysmith; fundraising
Staff Member(s): 2; 200 volunteer(s)
Membership: 220; *Fees:* Schedule available; *Member Profile:* Local businesses & services
Chief Officer(s):

Alana Newton, President

Ladysmith Food Bank
PO Box 1653, 630 2nd Ave., Ladysmith BC V9G 1B2
Tel: 250-245-3079; *Fax:* 250-245-3798
www.lrca.ca/programs/food-bank
Overview: A small local organization founded in 1998 overseen by Food Banks British Columbia
Mission: To provide food & service to those in need in the Ladysmith area
Member of: Food Banks British Columbia

LaHave Islands Marine Museum Society (LIMM)
PO Box 69, 100 LaHave Islands Rd., LaHave NS B0R 1C0
Tel: 902-688-2973
www.lahaveislandsmarinemuseum.ca
www.facebook.com/179807478711382
Overview: A small local charitable organization founded in 1979
Mission: To maintain & preserve the history & culture of the LaHave Islands & the Inshore Fisheries
Member of: Federation of the Nova Scotian Heritage; South Shore Tourism Association; LaHave River Valley Association
Finances: *Annual Operating Budget:* Less than $50,000; *Funding Sources:* Membership fees; donations
40 volunteer(s)
Membership: 70; *Fees:* $5
Activities: Manage LaHave Islands Marine Museum; Municipal Heritage Church; *Awareness Events:* Fishermen's Memorial Service, Aug.
Chief Officer(s):
Douglas Berrigan, President
Mary Fulleman, Treasurer

Laidlaw Foundation
#2000, 365 Bloor St. East, Toronto ON M4W 3L4
Tel: 416-964-3614; *Fax:* 416-975-1428
www.laidlawfdn.org
www.facebook.com/LaidlawFoundation
twitter.com/laidlawfdn
www.youtube.com/user/LaidlawFdn
Overview: A medium-sized national charitable organization founded in 1949
Mission: Committed to a Canada where communities are inclusive, creative & answerable, where all children & families are valued for their capacities & potential; to fund ideas, convince shareholders & advocate for change
Affiliation(s): Canadian Environmental Grantmakers Network; FUNDERS Alliance for Children & Youth; Grantmakers for Children Youth & Families; Grantmakers in the Arts; Philanthropic Foundation Canada
Finances: *Annual Operating Budget:* $3 Million-$5 Million; *Funding Sources:* Private endowment
Staff Member(s): 8; 100 volunteer(s)
Membership: 1-99; *Committees:* Youth Engagement; Youth Arts; Contaminants & Child Health; Inclusive Communication for Children, Youth & Family
Activities: *Internships:* Yes; *Speaker Service:* Yes; *Library:* Laidlaw Foundation Library; by appointment
Chief Officer(s):
Jehad Aliweiwi, Executive Director, 416-964-3614 Ext. 304

Lake Abitibi Model Forest
PO Box 129, Cochrane ON P0L 1C0
Tel: 705-272-7800; *Fax:* 705-272-2744
Overview: A small local organization
Member of: Canadian Model Forest Network
Chief Officer(s):
Sue Parton, General Manager, 705-272-8449
parton.sue@gmail.com

Lake Country Chamber of Commerce
Winfield Professional Building, #106, 3121 Hill Rd., Lake Country BC V4V 1G1
Tel: 250-766-5670
manager@lakecountrychamber.com
www.lakecountrychamber.com
Overview: A small local organization
Mission: To promote & serve members, businesses & the community
Chief Officer(s):
Kirbey Lockhart, President
Kimberley Kristiansen, Manager

Lake Country Food Assistance Society
3130C Berry Rd., Winfield BC V4V 1Z7
Tel: 250-766-0125

Canadian Associations / Lake of the Woods Adult Learning Line

Overview: A small local organization overseen by Food Banks British Columbia
Member of: Food Banks British Columbia
Chief Officer(s):
Phyllis MacPherson, Contact
pmacpher@shaw.ca

Lake of the Woods Adult Learning Line
#203, 115 Chipman St., Kenora ON P9N 1V7
Tel: 807-468-8202; *Fax:* 807-468-3921
Overview: A small local organization founded in 1980
Member of: Ontario Council of Agencies Serving Immigrants
Chief Officer(s):
Bonnie Boucha, Program Coordinator
bonnie.boucha@shaw.ca

Lake of the Woods Ojibway Cultural Centre
237 Airport Rd., Kenora ON P9N 0A2
Tel: 807-548-5744; *Fax:* 807-548-1591
Other Communication: lowocc@gmail.com
ojibwaycrafts@shaw.ca
www.ojibwayculturalcentre.com
www.facebook.com/467406369968488
Overview: A small local organization founded in 1977
Activities: Craft display; job search assistance; *Library:* Open to public

Lake Simcoe Region Conservation Foundation
PO Box 282, 120 Bayview Pkwy., Newmarket ON L3Y 4X1
Tel: 905-895-1281
Toll-Free: 800-465-0437
lakesimcoefoundation.ca
Overview: A small local organization
Mission: The Lake Simcoe Conservation Foundation (LSCF) invests in projects designed to protect and restore Lake Simcoe. Working in partnership with the Lake Simcoe Region Conservation Authority (LSRCA), watershed municipalities and other partners, they enable vital work to be done that maintains the natural environment, and in many places return the land and the rivers and the streams to a natural state.
Activities: Undertaken a million dollar fundraising campaign to help restore the lake
Chief Officer(s):
Cheryl Taylor, Executive Director

Lake Superior Coin Club
PO Box 10245, Thunder Bay ON P7B 6T7
Tel: 807-577-5416
Overview: A small local organization founded in 1980
Member of: Royal Canadian Numismatic Association
Chief Officer(s):
Germain Tremblay, Treasurer

LakeCity Employment Services Association
386 Windmill Rd., Dartmouth NS B3A 1J5
Tel: 902-465-5000; *Fax:* 902-465-5009
lesa@lakecityemployment.com
www.lakecityemployment.com
Also Known As: LakeCity Woodworkers
Overview: A small local organization founded in 1972
Mission: To assist mental health consumers in improving their quality of life by helping them to assume responsibility & independence through work
Member of: DIRECTIONS Council for Vocational Services Society
Affiliation(s): Workshop Council of Nova Scotia; Teamwork Co-Operative Ltd.
Finances: *Funding Sources:* Provincial government
Staff Member(s): 31
Chief Officer(s):
Andre McConnell, Chair
Chris Fyles, Executive Director

Lakehead Association for Community Living *See* Community Living Thunder Bay

Lakehead Japanese Cultural Association (LJCA)
West Thunder Community Centre, 915 Edward St. South, Thunder Bay ON P7E 6R2
Tel: 807-475-9396; *Fax:* 807-473-9055
westthunder@tbaytel.net
my.tbaytel.net/westthunder/Lakehead_Japanese_Cultural_Association
Overview: A small local organization
Chief Officer(s):
Steve Sellar, President

Lakehead Social Planning Council (LSPC)
Victoria Mall, #28, 125 Syndicate Ave. South, Thunder Bay ON P7E 6H8
Tel: 807-624-1720; *Fax:* 807-625-9427
Toll-Free: 866-624-1729; *TTY:* 888-622-4651
info@lspc.ca
lspc-circ.on.ca
Overview: A small local charitable organization founded in 1963
Mission: To strengthen Thunder Bay by providing collaborative community responses to social issues, research & access to human service information; to bring people together, promote social & economic justice, develop programs & services, link people to services; to research social, economic, environmental & health issues
Member of: Inform Ontario; Ontario Social Development Council; Canadian Council on Social Development
Finances: *Funding Sources:* All levels of government; sale of goods & services; fundraising
Staff Member(s): 10
Membership: *Fees:* $20 individual; $40 organizations
Activities: *Speaker Service:* Yes; *Library:* Open to public
Chief Officer(s):
Marie Klassen, Director, Services

Lakehead Stamp Club
c/o Daryl Lein, 232 Dease St., Thunder Bay ON P7C 2H8
Tel: 807-623-2179
Overview: A small local organization founded in 1947
Member of: Royal Philatelic Society of Canada
Finances: *Funding Sources:* Membership fees
Activities: Selling stamps at meetings; Maintaining a library of stamp catalogues; Sponsoring annual spring show
Chief Officer(s):
Daryl Lein, Secretary

Lakehead University Faculty Association (LUFA) / Association des professeurs de l'Université Lakehead
#CB-4108, Lakehead University, 855 Oliver Rd., Thunder Bay ON P7B 5E1
Tel: 807-343-8789; *Fax:* 807-766-7142
LUFA@lakeheadu.ca
www.lufa.org
www.linkedin.com/company/lakehead-university-faculty-association
www.facebook.com/136377669839280
Overview: A small local organization founded in 1960
Finances: *Annual Operating Budget:* $100,000-$250,000
Membership: 290
Chief Officer(s):
Glenna Knutson, President
glenna.knutson@lakeheadu.ca

Lakeland Agricultural Research Association (LARA)
PO Box 7068, Bonnyville AB T9N 2H4
Tel: 780-826-7260; *Fax:* 780-826-7099
livestock.lara@mcsnet.ca
www.laraonline.ca
Overview: A small local organization overseen by Agricultural Research & Extension Council of Alberta
Mission: To achieve a profitable & sustainable future for agricultural producers by conducting agricultural research programs
Member of: Agricultural Research & Extension Council of Alberta
Chief Officer(s):
Alyssa Krone, Manager, Forage & Livestock Program
Kellie Nichiporik, Manager, Environmental Program
Charlene Rachynski, Office Administrator
Publications:
• LARA [Lakeland Agricultural Research Association] Newsletter
Type: Newsletter

Lakeland College Faculty Association (LCFA) / Association des professeurs du Collège de Lakeland
c/o Lakeland College, 5707 College Dr., Vermilion AB T9X 1K5
Overview: A small local organization
Membership: 100-499
Chief Officer(s):
Neil Maclean, President, 780-853-8561
neil.maclean@lakelandcollege.ca

Lakeland District Soccer Association (LDSA)
PO Box 4801, Bonnyville AB T9N 0H2
Tel: 780-201-4346
lakelandsoccer.ca
Overview: A small local organization overseen by Alberta Soccer Association
Member of: Alberta Soccer Association
Membership: 1-99
Chief Officer(s):
Kristy L'Hirondelle, Executive Director
execdir@lakelandsoccer.ca

Lakeland Industry & Community Association (LICA)
PO Box 8237, 5107W - 50 St., Bonnyville AB T9N 2J5
Tel: 780-812-2182; *Fax:* 780-812-2186
Toll-Free: 877-737-2182
lica2@lica.ca
www.lica.ca
Overview: A small local organization
Mission: To protect the environment by collecting ecological information about the Lakeland area and using it to further their cause
Membership: *Fees:* $0 - $1,000; *Member Profile:* People who are of legal age & who live or work in the LICA area; Corporations; Non-profit organizations; *Committees:* Education & Info; Governance; Resolution; Airshed Zone; Beaver River Watershed Alliance
Activities: Commitee meetings
Chief Officer(s):
Delano Tolley, Chairman, Board of Directors

Lakeland United Way
Marina Mall, PO Box 8125, #3, 901 - 10 St., Cold Lake AB T9M 1N1
Tel: 780-826-0045; *Fax:* 780-639-2699
www.lakelandunitedway.com
Overview: A small local charitable organization founded in 1987 overseen by United Way of Canada - Centraide Canada
Finances: *Annual Operating Budget:* Less than $50,000
Staff Member(s): 1; 8 volunteer(s)
Chief Officer(s):
Ajaz Quraishi, President
president@lakelandunitedway.com

Lakelands Association of Realtors (MHAR)
34 Cairns Cres., Huntsville ON P1H 1Y3
Tel: 705-788-1504; *Fax:* 705-788-2040
comms@thelakelands.ca
www.thelakelands.ca
www.facebook.com/179085482158066
twitter.com/TheLakelands
Overview: A small local organization overseen by Ontario Real Estate Association
Mission: To provide realtors within the Muskoka, Haliburton & Orillia with information & services that allow them to better serve their customers
Membership: 700
Chief Officer(s):
Crystal Henderson, Executive Officer
chenderson@thelakelands.ca

Lakes District Festival Association
c/o Jana Epkens-Shaffer, PO Box 202, Francois Lake BC V0J 1R0
Tel: 250-695-6400
www.ldfestival.com
Overview: A small local organization founded in 1957
Mission: To celebrate each spring with competitions in piano, band, speech arts, instrumental, strings, highland dance, modern dance, ballet, jazz, ethnic dance & musical theatre
Membership: *Member Profile:* Interest in music, drama or dance & willingness to work as on festival & planning committee & during festival; *Committees:* Awards; Advertising; Publicity; Hospitality
Activities: Annual Festival competitions in the performing arts; *Awareness Events:* Lake District Festival of the Performing Arts
Chief Officer(s):
Lois Koop, President, 250-695-6699

Lakeshore Area Multi-Service Project (LAMP)
185 - 5th St., Toronto ON M8V 2Z5
Tel: 416-252-6471; *Fax:* 416-252-4474
www.lampchc.org
www.facebook.com/LAMPCHEALTHC
Overview: A medium-sized local charitable organization
Mission: To offer community health centre services in South Etobicoke, Toronto West
Finances: *Annual Operating Budget:* Greater than $5 Million; *Funding Sources:* Government; Donations; United Way
Staff Member(s): 6
Membership: *Fees:* $3

Activities: Offering a variety of integrated programs & services to meet the health needs of the community
Chief Officer(s):
Russ Ford, Executive Director

Lakeshore Coin Club
PO Box 46004, Pointe-Claire QC H9R 5R4
Tel: 514-289-9761
medievalcoins@gmail.com
Overview: A small local organization founded in 1962
Member of: Canadian Numismatic Association; Ontario Numismatic Association
Activities: *Library:* Lakeshore Coin Club Library at City of Pointe Claire, Stewart Hal
Chief Officer(s):
Michael Joffre, President

Lakeshore Community Services (LCS)
PO Box 885, 499 Notre Dame St., Belle River ON N0R 1A0
Tel: 519-728-1435; *Fax:* 519-728-4713
Toll-Free: 855-728-1433
www.lakeshorecommunity.net
www.facebook.com/542559895805728
twitter.com/CscEssexCounty
Previous Name: Community Information Centre Belle River
Overview: A small local organization overseen by InformOntario
Mission: The Mission of LCS is to service the Community of Lakeshore responsibly by providing information about and access to health, government, and community and support services and through this research social needs.
Activities: Meals on Wheels; vistor services; transit bus; Coats for Kids; job bank; Keep the Heat; income tax clinic
Chief Officer(s):
Tracey Bailey, Executive Director

Lakeshore Stamp Club Inc.
PO Box 1, Stn. Pointe-Claire, Dorval QC H9R 4N5
www.lakeshorestampclub.ca
Overview: A small local organization founded in 1961
Mission: To promote stamp collecting
Affiliation(s): American Philatelic Society; Fédération québécoise de philatélie; Royal Philatelic Society of Canada; The American Association of Philatelic Exhibitors; The American Topical Association
Finances: *Funding Sources:* Membership dues
Membership: 180; *Fees:* $30 adults; $1 juniors; *Committees:* Philatelic Study Group; Bourse; Exhibitions; House; Library; Publicity; Shoebox; Social Events
Activities: Exchange & exhibition of philatelic items; annual exhibition
Chief Officer(s):
Chuck Colomb, President
president@lakeshorestampclub.ca
Robert Carswell, Secretary
secretary@lakeshorestampclub.ca

Lambton County Association for the Mentally Handicapped
See Lambton County Developmental Services

Lambton County Developmental Services (LCDS)
PO Box 1210, 339 Centre St., Petrolia ON N0N 1R0
Tel: 519-882-0933; *Fax:* 519-882-3386
administration@lcds.on.ca
lcdspetrolia.ca
www.facebook.com/lambtoncountydevelopmentalservices
twitter.com/lcds_ontario
Previous Name: Lambton County Association for the Mentally Handicapped
Overview: A large local organization founded in 1955
Mission: To provide support services for children & adults with developmental disabilities in Lambton County
Affiliation(s): Ontario Agencies Supporting Individuals with Special Needs
Finances: *Funding Sources:* Ministry of Community & Social Services; fundraising; donations
Membership: *Fees:* $25
Activities: Supported employment services; community skills development program; adult residential services; supported *independent living services; respite care*; drop-in centre; recreation & leisure resources
Chief Officer(s):
Tom McCallum, Executive Director
Publications:
• LCDS [Lambton County Developmental Services] Focus Newsletter
Type: Newsletter; *Frequency:* 3 pa

Lambton County Historical Society (LCHS)
3775 Shiloh Line, #RR4, Petrolia ON N0N 1R0
Tel: 519-882-0881
Overview: A small local charitable organization founded in 1960
Mission: To encourage the preservation of the history of the county by publication, exhibition & collection of books, manuscripts, artifacts
Affiliation(s): Ontario Historical Society
Finances: *Annual Operating Budget:* Less than $50,000; *Funding Sources:* Membership fees; book sales
Staff Member(s): 5; 65 volunteer(s)
Membership: 60; *Fees:* $10 corporate; $5 individual; *Committees:* Publication; Special Events
Activities: *Library:* Lambton County Library; Open to public
Chief Officer(s):
Betty Lou Snetselaar, Secretary

Lambton Industrial Society: An Environmental Co-operative
See Sarnia-Lambton Environmental Association

Lambton Wildlife Inc. (LWI)
PO Box 681, Sarnia ON N7T 7J7
Tel: 519-542-7914
info@lambtonwildlife.com
www.lambtonwildlife.com
Overview: A small local charitable organization founded in 1966
Mission: To preserve our natural heritage for present & future generations; Particularly concerned with the natural history of Lambton County & the establishment & care of conservation areas & wildlife sanctuaries therein
Member of: Federation of Ontario Naturalists
Affiliation(s): Canadian Nature Federation
Finances: *Annual Operating Budget:* Less than $50,000; *Funding Sources:* Membership fees; donations
75 volunteer(s)
Membership: 210; *Fees:* $20 individual; $25 family; *Committees:* Adopt-a-Highway; Arbor Week; Ausable Trail; Binational Public Advisory; Bluebird Nesting; Conservation; Education; Environment; Indoor; Mandaumin Woods; Outdoor; Rural Lambton Stewardship; Wawanosh Wetlands Management; Wildlife Inventory; Woodlot Protection; Howard Watson Nature Trail; Port Franks Property Management
Activities: Education programs in environmental studies & natural history; lectures in natural history at Lambton County schools & other organizations; special public lectures; regular field trips; sponsors the annual Audubon Christmas Bird census in Lambton area; purchase & management of Mandaumin Woods Nature Reserve; establishment of Ausable Trail; sponsorship of the World Wildlife studies of the Port Franks Karner Blue Butterfly & the Walpole Island Life Science Inventory
Chief Officer(s):
Janet Bremner, President

LAMP Community Health Centre
185 - 5th St., Toronto ON M8V 2Z5
Tel: 416-252-6471; *Fax:* 416-252-4474
volunteering@lampchc.org
www.lampchc.org
www.facebook.com/LAMPCHEALTHC
twitter.com/LAMPCHC_info
www.pinterest.com/lampchc
Also Known As: Lakeshore Area Multi-Services Project Inc.
Overview: A large local charitable organization founded in 1976
Mission: To meet the community's health needs through integrated programs & services
Finances: *Annual Operating Budget:* Greater than $5 Million
Staff Member(s): 6
Membership: *Fees:* $3
Activities: Occupational health & safety program; primary health care; speech & language program; "Equally Healthy Kids" program; chiropody; adult literacy; community development; mental health program; child psychiatry; community information centre; *Library:* Toy Lending Library & Parenting Library; Open to public
Chief Officer(s):
Anne Brennan, Director, HR & Operations
Awards:
• Awards of Merit
Publications:
• LAMP Community Health Centre Newsletter
Type: Newsletter

Lanark County Beekeepers' Association (LCBA)
c/o Paul Lacelle, 126 Bruce St., Carleton Place ON K7C 3P1
Tel: 613-253-0566
lanarkcountybeekeepers@gmail.com
sites.google.com/site/lanarkcountybeekeepers
Overview: A small local organization founded in 1998
Mission: To promote the beekeeping & honey industry in Lanark County; To provide information about beekeeping to members
Member of: Ontario Beekeepers' Association
Membership: *Fees:* $15; *Member Profile:* Individuals interested in beekeeping from Ontario's Lanark County; *Committees:* Membership; Library
Activities: Organizing four meetings each year at the McMartin House in Perth; Assisting new beekeepers through a mentoring program; Showing honey & honey bee products, such as displays at the Perth Fair; Capturing swarms of honey bees
Chief Officer(s):
Paul Lacelle, President

Lanark County Food Bank
5 Allan St., Carleton Place ON K7C 1T1
Tel: 613-257-8546
Overview: A small local charitable organization
Member of: Ontario Association of Food Banks
30 volunteer(s)
Chief Officer(s):
Nadine Kennedy, Executive Director

The Lanark County Museums Network (LCMN)
c/o Carleton Place & Beckwith Heritage Museum, 267 Edmund St., Carleton Place ON K7C 3E8
Tel: 613-253-7013
www.lanarkcountymuseums.ca
Overview: A small local organization founded in 1991
Mission: To offer self-help in every phase of museum activity; to promote all twelve museums & the Lanark County Archives in Lanark County
Member of: Ontario Museums Association
Affiliation(s): Lanark County Tourism Association
Finances: *Funding Sources:* Donations; membership dues
Membership: 12; *Member Profile:* Community museums in Lanark County: Lanark & District Museum; Mill of Kintail Conservation Area; Mississippi Valley Textile Museum; Middleville & District Museum; North Lanark Historical Society; Naismith Museum & Hall of Fame; Matheson House; Heritage House Museum; Inge-Va

Lanark County Therapeutic Riding Program (LCTRP)
30 Bennett St., Carleton Place ON K7C 4J9
Tel: 613-257-7121; *Fax:* 613-257-2675
info@therapeuticriding.ca
www.therapeuticriding.ca
Overview: A small local charitable organization founded in 1986
Mission: To provide individuals a holistic approach to therapy, rehabilitation & recreation; the opportunity to experience freedom & movement astride a horse
Member of: Canadian Therapeutic Riding Association; Ontario Therapeutic Riding Association; Lanark Health & Community Services
Finances: *Annual Operating Budget:* $50,000-$100,000; *Funding Sources:* Local fundraising events; fees for service
Staff Member(s): 1; 45 volunteer(s)
Membership: 105 riders; *Committees:* Advisory; Fundraising
Activities: Provides individuals a holistic approach to therapy, rehabilitation & recreation & the opportunity to experience freedom when riding a horse; *Internships:* Yes
Chief Officer(s):
Maria Hofbauer, Head Instructor

Lancer Rehab Riders *See* Halifax Area Leisure & Therapeutic Riding Association

Land Improvement Contractors of Ontario
231 Dimson Ave., Guelph ON N1G 3C7
Tel: 519-836-1386; *Fax:* 519-836-4059
www.drainage.org
Overview: A small provincial organization founded in 1995
Mission: To represent the interests of professional contractors, suppliers of drainage pipe & equipment, engineers, & municipal drainage superintendents involved in Ontario's agriculture & land drainage industries
Finances: *Annual Operating Budget:* Less than $50,000
Membership: *Fees:* $146.90 general membership
Chief Officer(s):
John Johnston, Secretary-Treasurer
john.johnston@gto.net

Landis & District Chamber of Commerce
PO Box 400, Landis SK S0K 2K0

Canadian Associations / Landlord's Self-Help Centre

Tel: 306-658-2100; *Fax:* 306-658-4455
Overview: A small local organization

Landlord's Self-Help Centre
425 Adelaide St. West, 4th Fl., Toronto ON M5V 3C1
Tel: 416-504-5190; *Fax:* 416-504-1932
Toll-Free: 800-730-3218
info@landlordselfhelp.com
www.landlordselfhelp.com
www.facebook.com/landlordselfhelp
twitter.com/LSHC1
Overview: A small local organization founded in 1975
Mission: To provide information, assistance & educational programs to Ontario's small scale landlords free of charge
Chief Officer(s):
Jonathan Lau, President

LandlordBC
830B Pembroke St., Victoria BC V8T 1J9
Tel: 250-382-6324; *Fax:* 877-382-6006
Toll-Free: 888-330-6707
info@landlordbc.ca
www.landlordbc.ca
www.linkedin.com/company/landlordbc
www.facebook.com/landlordBC
twitter.com/LandlordBC
Previous Name: Rental Owners & Managers Society of British Columbia; Apartment Owners & Property Managers Association of Vancouver Island
Overview: A small provincial organization founded in 1971
Mission: To serve & represent our members & enhance the residential rental industry in B.C.
Member of: Canadian Federation of Apartment Associations
Staff Member(s): 7
Membership: 3,200+; *Member Profile:* Owners & managers of residential rental properties in B.C.
Activities: Lobbying, service
Chief Officer(s):
David Hutniak, CEO

Landmark & Community Chamber of Commerce
PO Box 469, Landmark MB R0A 0X0
Tel: 204-355-5323
Overview: A small local organization
Chief Officer(s):
Evan Rodgers, President

Landscape Alberta Nursery Trades Association
#200, 10331 - 178 St. NW, Edmonton AB T5S 1R5
Tel: 780-489-1991; *Fax:* 780-444-2152
Toll-Free: 800-378-3198
Other Communication: Member Services:
member.services@landscape-alberta.com
admin@landscape-alberta.com
www.landscape-alberta.com
www.linkedin.com/company/landscape-alberta-nursery-trade-association
twitter.com/LandscapeAB
Also Known As: Landscape Alberta
Overview: A medium-sized provincial organization founded in 1957 overseen by Canadian Nursery Landscape Association
Mission: To advance the Alberta ornamental horticulture industry through unity, education & professionalism
Affiliation(s): Saskatchewan Nursery Landscape Association
Finances: *Funding Sources:* Membership fees; Fundraising programs
Staff Member(s): 6
Membership: 250 +; *Fees:* Schedule available; *Member Profile:* Must be engaged in the horticultural industry or a supplier
Activities: Providing professional development tools; Advocating for the industry's interests & concerns at various levels of government
Chief Officer(s):
Joel Beatson, Executive Director
joel.beatson@landscape-alberta.com
Awards:
• Lifetime Member Award
• Green Thumb Award
• Executive Choice Award
Meetings/Conferences:
• Green Industry Show & Conference 2018, November, 2018, Edmonton Expo Centre at Northlands, Edmonton, AB
Scope: National
Description: An opportunity for members of the landscape, greenhouse, nursery, garden centre, tree care, & turf industries to network

Publications:
• Green for Life
Type: Magazine; *Frequency:* 6 pa; *Accepts Advertising; Editor:* Joel Beatson; *ISSN:* 1929-7114
Profile: Addresses green industry issues across Alberta that affect the landscape horticulture trade
• LANDX [a publication of the Landscape Alberta Nursery Trades Association]
Type: Report; *Frequency:* Annually; *Accepts Advertising*
Profile: Contains an annual membership directory

Landscape New Brunswick Horticultural Trades Association (LNBHTA)
PO Box 742, Saint John NB E2L 4B3
Fax: 866-595-5467
Toll-Free: 866-752-6862
lnb@nbnet.nb.ca
www.landscapenbmember.com
www.facebook.com/Landscapenewbrunswick
Overview: A small provincial organization
Mission: To further the development of the ornamental horticulture industry by focusing on the environment, education, promotion & professionalism; to represent members & to help them achieve their goals
Membership: *Fees:* $375 active; $425 commercial; $225 out-of-province; $25 affiliate; *Committees:* Environment; Education; Landscape Horticulture Training Institute; Awards; Membership; All Commodity Education Sessions; Certification; Garden Centre Canada; HortEast; Summer Tour
Chief Officer(s):
Joe Wynberg, President

Landscape Newfoundland & Labrador (LNL)
PO Box 8062, St. John's NL A1B 3M9
Fax: 866-833-8603
Toll-Free: 855-872-8722
lnl@landscapenl.com
members.landscapenl.com
facebook.com/landscapenlevents
twitter.com/@landscapeNL
pinterest.com/landscapenl/
Overview: A small provincial organization founded in 1992 overseen by Canadian Nursery Landscape Association
Mission: To promote professionalism at all levels of the Industry, and achieve the highest standards of excellence in delivery of services and products across all sectors of our industry.
Membership: 75; *Fees:* $50 individual; $125 affiliated; $310 associate/active
Chief Officer(s):
David Kiell, Executive Director
Meetings/Conferences:
• Landscape NL Annual General Meeting 2018, 2018
Scope: Provincial

Landscape Nova Scotia
Executive Plus Business Centre, Burnside Industrial Park, #44, 201 Brownlow Ave., Dartmouth NS B3B 1W2
Tel: 902-463-0519; *Fax:* 902-446-8104
Toll-Free: 877-567-4769
info@landscapenovascotia.ca
www.landscapenovascotia.ca
www.facebook.com/199135136822813
Overview: A medium-sized provincial organization overseen by Canadian Nursery Landscape Association
Mission: To promote high standards in product quality, professional service and conduct in the landscape and horticulture industry
Staff Member(s): 1
Membership: 3,700 companies; *Fees:* $452 active; $78 affiliate; $130 out of province
Chief Officer(s):
Pam Woodman, Executive Director
pam@landscapenovascotia.ca

Landscape Ontario Horticultural Trades Association (LOHTA)
7856 - 5th Line South, RR#4, Milton ON L9T 2X8
Tel: 416-848-7575; *Fax:* 905-875-3942
Toll-Free: 800-265-5656
www.horttrades.com
Overview: A medium-sized provincial organization founded in 1973 overseen by Canadian Nursery Landscape Association
Mission: To be a leader in representing, promoting & fostering a favourable environment for the advancement of the horticulture industry in Ontario
Affiliation(s): American Nursery Landscape Association;

Canadian Nursery Landsape Association; Canadian Ornamental Plant Foundation; Communities in Bloom; International Association of Horticultural Producers; International Garden Centre Association; Irrigation Association; North American Plant Protection Organization; Ontario Parks Association; Professional Landcare Network; Trees for Life; Vineland Research and Innovation Centre
Finances: *Funding Sources:* Membership dues; congress
Staff Member(s): 28
Membership: 2,000+; *Member Profile:* Active - firms with at least 3 years experience in the field; Interim/Active - firms with at least 1 year but less than 3 years experience in the field; Associate - suppliers to the industry & the association
Activities: *Speaker Service:* Yes
Chief Officer(s):
Tony DiGiovanni, Executive Director
tonydigiovanni@landscapeontario.com
Awards:
• The Landscape Awards Program
Publications:
• Landscape Ontario
Type: Magazine; *Frequency:* Monthly; *Editor:* Lee Ann Knudsen
Profile: Industry news, association news, industry issue features, profiles, event announcements, extension bulletins and more.

Langara Faculty Association / Association des professeurs de Langara
100 - West 49th Ave., Vancouver BC V5Y 2Z6
Tel: 604-323-5343
langarafacultyassociation@lfaweb.ca
www.lfaweb.ca
Overview: A small local organization
Mission: To facilitate collective bargaining agreements for the faculty of Langara College in Vancouver, BC.

Langdon & District Chamber of Commerce
PO Box 18, Langdon AB T0J 1X0
Tel: 403-936-5524
www.langdonchamber.ca
Overview: A small local organization
Mission: To support local businesses
Affiliation(s): Alberta Chamber of Commerce; Canadian Chamber of Commerce
Membership: 184; *Fees:* $75
Chief Officer(s):
Al Schule, President

Langenburg & District Chamber of Commerce
PO Box 610, Langenburg SK S0A 2A0
Tel: 306-743-2231; *Fax:* 306-743-2873
Overview: A small local organization
Mission: To promote the Town of Langenburg & District
Finances: *Funding Sources:* Membership fees

Langham Cultural Society
PO Box 1000, 447A Ave., Kaslo BC V0G 1M0
Tel: 250-353-2661; *Fax:* 250-353-2671
langham@netidea.com
www.thelangham.ca
Previous Name: Kaslo Arts Counci
Overview: A small local charitable organization founded in 1974
Mission: To preserve Langham Building, Kaslo; To stimulate educational & cultural awareness of the community & surrounding area through the introduction of works in performing & visual arts; To foster interest & pride in cultural heritage of community of Kaslo & the West Kootenay region
Member of: North Kootenay Lake Arts & Heritage Council
Finances: *Annual Operating Budget:* $50,000-$100,000;
Funding Sources: Provincial & federal government; private foundation grants; memberships; donations
Membership: 200; *Fees:* $12 single; $20 family; $450 lifetime;
Committees: Building; Windows; Contracts
Activities: Operates Langham Gallery & gallery programs, The Langham Theatre & the Japanese Canadian Museum; *Library:* Langham Arts Instruction Library; Open to public
Chief Officer(s):
Alice Windsor, Administrator
Brent Bukowski, Curator

Langley & Aldergrove Food Bank
5768 - 203 St., Langley BC V3A 1W3
Tel: 604-533-0671; *Fax:* 604-533-0891
info@langleyfoodbank.com
www.langleyfoodbank.com
Overview: A small local organization
Mission: To help bring food & services to the needy in the Langley area

Finances: Funding Sources: Donations from local churches, organizations and individuals

Langley Arts Council (LAC)
#206, 20641 Logan Ave., Langley BC V3R 7R3
Tel: 604-534-0781; *Fax:* 604-534-0781
administrator@langleyartscouncil.com
www.langleyartscouncil.com
Overview: A small local organization founded in 1968
Mission: To promote & support the Arts by participating in cultural & multicultural events; To solicit funds from private & government sources; to support heritage conservation; To continue to campaign for community cultural affairs; to act as a resource centre for information on the Arts; To help to initiate new arts groups & activities; To act as a liaison between government & arts organizations
Member of: Assembly of BC Arts Councils; Langley Chamber of Commerce
Membership: Member Profile: Interest in supporting & promoting the arts
Activities: Speaker Service: Yes; *Library:* Open to public
Chief Officer(s):
Don Shilton, Interim General Manager

Langley Association for Community Living (LACL)
23535 - 44th Ave., Langley BC V2Z 2V2
Tel: 604-534-8611; *Fax:* 604-534-4763
main@langleyacl.com
www.langleyacl.com
www.facebook.com/392209904180351
twitter.com/LangleyACL
Overview: A small local organization founded in 1959
Mission: To support the participation & inclusion of people with developmental disabilities in the community; To provide quality services
Member of: British Columbia Association for Community Living
Affiliation(s): Canadian Association for Community Living
Finances: Funding Sources: Government; fundraising
Membership: Fees: $5
Activities: Speaker Service: Yes
Chief Officer(s):
Dan Collins, Executive Director
dcollins@langleyacl.com

Langley District Help Network
5768 - 203 St., Langley BC V3A 1W3
Tel: 604-533-0671; *Fax:* 604-533-0891
info@langleyfoodbank.com
www.langleyfoodbank.com
Also Known As: Langley Food Bank
Overview: A small local organization
Mission: To help individuals & communities in need in Langley

Langley Field Naturalists Society (LFN)
PO Box 56052, Stn. Valley Centre, Langley BC V3A 8B3
Langleyfieldnaturalists@shaw.ca
www.langleyfieldnaturalists.org
Overview: A small local organization founded in 1973
Mission: To promote the enjoyment of nature; to learn about natural history; to promote preservation of the environment through active participation in conservation projects
Member of: The Federation of BC Naturalists; Canadian Nature Federation
Finances: Annual Operating Budget: Less than $50,000; *Funding Sources:* Langley Arts Council Grant; membership fees
Membership: 60-70; *Fees:* $25 single; $30 family; *Committees:* Conservation education; Watson nature reserve
Activities: Monthly field trips from Sept.-June, weekly walks July-Aug.; Maintenance of Brydan Lagoon & Irene Pearce Trail; *Awareness Events:* Rivers Day; Earth Day; Campbell Valley Country Celebration

Langley Heritage Society (LHS)
PO Box 982, Fort Langley BC V1M 2S3
Tel: 604-513-8787
info@langleyheritage.ca
www.langleyheritage.ca
www.facebook.com/LangleyHeritageSociety
Overview: A small local charitable organization founded in 1979
Mission: To plan for restoration & ongoing use for Langley's heritage buildings & sites
Member of: BC Heritage Society; Langley Arts Council
Membership: Fees: $8 individual; $15 family; $50 contributing; $100 sustaining
Chief Officer(s):
Fred Pepin, President

Language Industry Association (AILIA) / Association de l'industrie de la langue
25 Rockcastle Dr., Toronto ON M9R 2V2
Toll-Free: 888-510-1148
communication@ailia.ca
www.ailia.ca
www.linkedin.com/groups?gid=3026714
www.facebook.com/ailia.langindustryassoc
twitter.com/AILIA_LANG
www.youtube.com/user/AILIALang
Overview: A small national organization founded in 2003
Mission: To promote & increase the competitiveness of the Canadian language industry nationally & internationally throug advocacy, accreditation & information sharing
Finances: Annual Operating Budget: $100,000-$250,000; *Funding Sources:* Grants
Staff Member(s): 1; 10 volunteer(s)
Membership: 150; *Fees:* $400; *Member Profile:* Enterprises; Individuals in translation, language training, language technologies; *Committees:* Canadian & ISO Standards; Interpreting; Terminology; Translation
Activities: Canadian Annual Tour in seven cities, Jan. - Mar.; *Speaker Service:* Yes
Chief Officer(s):
Lola Bendana, Chair
Publications:
• Info-AILIA [a publication of the Language Industry Association] *Type:* Newsletter
Profile: News about the Canadian language industry

Languages Canada / Langues Canada
c/o Member Services, 27282 - 12B Ave., Aldergrove BC V4W 2P6
Tel: 604-574-1532; *Fax:* 888-277-0522
Other Communication: French Phone: 581-888-3568
info@languagescanada.ca
www.languagescanada.ca
www.linkedin.com/company/languages-canada
www.facebook.com/languagescanada
twitter.com/LangCanada
www.instagram.com/langcanada
Merged from: Canadian Association of Private Language Schools; Canada Language Council
Overview: A large national organization founded in 2008
Mission: To promote quality, accredited English & French language training in Canada, & to represent Canada as a destination for excellent English & French language training
Staff Member(s): 6; 16 volunteer(s)
Membership: 204 programs; *Member Profile:* Language schools which meet the rigorous standards of the association
Chief Officer(s):
Gonzalo Peralta, Executive Director
Meetings/Conferences:
• Languages Canada 2018 Conference, February, 2018, Toronto Marriott Downtown Eaton Centre Hotel, Toronto, ON
Scope: National
Attendance: 200+
Contact Information: conference@languagescanada.ca

Langues Canada *See* Languages Canada

Lansdowne Outdoor Recreational Development Association (LORDA)
#1480, Hwy. 289, Lansdowne NS B0K 2A0
Tel: 902-396-4470; *Fax:* 902-396-1399
www.facebook.com/614534051970994
Overview: A small local organization founded in 1986
Mission: To operate a recreational park for seniors, disabled individuals, & those who have limited access to facilities for the elderly & infirmed
Finances: Annual Operating Budget: $50,000-$100,000; *Funding Sources:* Federal & provincial grants; Private donations
12 volunteer(s)
Activities: Offering wheelchair accessible park facilities including an indoor recreational center, a fishing pond, a camping area for trailers & tents, outdoor barbecue & picnic tables; Organizing annual maple syrup production & fundraisers
Chief Officer(s):
Dave Leese, Park Curator
dave@lorda.org

Lao Association of Ontario
956 Wilson Ave., Toronto ON M3K 1E7
Tel: 416-398-3057
info@laoweb.org
www.laoweb.org
www.facebook.com/249069225233477
Overview: A small provincial charitable organization founded in 1979
Mission: To assist Lao people settle into Canadian society; to promote Lao culture
Member of: Canadian Multiculturalism Council; Ontario Council of Agencies Serving Immigrants; Laotian Federation of Canada
Activities: Information exchange; interpretation & translation services; supportive counselling

Lao Community of Québec *Voir* Communauté Laotienne du Québec

Lapidary Club of West Vancouver
PO Box 91233, West Vancouver BC V7V 2N6
Tel: 604-922-0072
Overview: A small local organization
Member of: Lapidary, Rock & Mineral Society of British Columbia

Last Post Fund (LPF) / Fonds du Souvenir
#401, 505, boul René-Lévesque ouest, Montréal QC H2Z 1Y7
Tel: 514-866-2727; *Fax:* 514-866-1471
Toll-Free: 800-465-7113
info@lastpost.ca
www.lastpostfund.ca
Overview: A medium-sized national charitable organization founded in 1909
Mission: To ensure that no war veterans, or certain other persons who meet the wartime service eligibility criteria, are denied a funeral & burial due to lack of funds
Finances: Funding Sources: Donations
Activities: Conveying Last Post Fund resolutions to Veterans Affairs Canada; *Awareness Events:* Annual Commemorative Ceremonies, Last Post Fund National Field of Honour, Pointe-Claire, Québec, first Sunday each June
Chief Officer(s):
Barry Keeler, President
Raymond Mikkola, Vice-President, West
Derek Sullivan, Vice-President, East
Jean-Pierre Goyer, Executive Director
Alberta Branch
Canada Place, #1130, 9700 Jasper Ave., Edmonton AB T5J 4C3
Tel: 780-495-3766; *Fax:* 780-495-6960
Toll-Free: 888-495-3766
British Columbia Branch
#307, 7337 - 137th St., Surrey BC V3W 1A4
Tel: 604-572-3242; *Fax:* 604-572-3306
Toll-Free: 800-268-0248
Newfoundland-Labrador Branch
Prudential Bldg., 49 Elizabeth Ave., St. John's NL A1A 1W9
Tel: 709-579-4288; *Fax:* 709-579-0966
Toll-Free: 888-579-4288
Nova Scotia Branch
Chebucto Place, #200A, 7105 Chebucto Rd., Halifax NS B3L 4W8
Tel: 902-455-5283; *Fax:* 902-455-4058
Toll-Free: 800-565-4777
Ontario Branch
#905, 55 St. Clair Ave. East, Toronto ON M4T 1M2
Tel: 416-923-1608; *Fax:* 416-923-3695
Toll-Free: 800-563-2508
Saskatchewan Branch
Princeton Towers, #400, 123 - 2e Ave. South, Saskatoon SK S7K 736
Tel: 306-975-6045; *Fax:* 306-975-4306
Toll-Free: 800-667-3668
lastpost@sasktel.net
United Kingdom Representative
High Commission of Canada, Canada House, Trafalgar Sq., London SW1Y 5BJ United Kingdom
Tel: 44 (0) 207 004 6075
Chief Officer(s):
Suzanne Happe, Veterans Affairs Officer
suzanne.happe@international.gc.ca

Latin American Mission Program (LAMP)
81 Prince St., Charlottetown PE C1A 4R3
Tel: 902-368-7337; *Fax:* 902-368-7180
lamp@pei.sympatico.ca
www.dioceseofcharlottetown.com
Overview: A small international organization founded in 1967
Mission: To send out & receive back missionaries; To learn from the dispossessed & oppressed & to stand with them in building a society of justice; To develop & encourage a Faith response based on the life & struggle of dispossessed peoples;

To participate in "return mission" by working with groups committed to social justice in Canada & developing education programs in PEI that analyze the causes of exploitation of the poor & expose the reality of their lives
Affiliation(s): Diocese of Charlottetown; Les missionnaires du Sacre-Coeur; Scarboro Foreign Mission Society
Finances: *Annual Operating Budget:* $50,000-$100,000; *Funding Sources:* Share Lent collections taken up annually in all parishes
Membership: 20
Activities: Educational events; Orientation & support for missionaries

Latino Canadian Cultural Association (LCCA) / Association Culturelle Latino Canadienne (ACLC)
#254, 601 Christie St., Toronto ON M6G 4C7
info@lccatoronto.com
www.lccatoronto.com
Also Known As: Asociacion Cultural Latino Canadiense
Overview: A small local organization
Mission: To support Latino artists & help them connect to the Canadian community
Activities: Exhibitions; Cultural events
Chief Officer(s):
Dinoi Toledo, President, Board of Directors
Alejandro Freeland, Executive Director

Latvian Canadian Cultural Centre (LCCC)
4 Credit Union Dr., Toronto ON M4A 2N8
Tel: 416-759-4900; *Fax:* 416-759-9311
office@latviancentre.org
www.latviancentre.org
www.facebook.com/143970339032047
Overview: A small national charitable organization founded in 1977
Mission: To acquire, maintain & operate a Centre; to foster & sustain the Latvian heritage & cultural tradition; to provide social & cultural exchange with the various cultural communities in Canada; to provide facilities for meetings, concerts, dances, seminars, theatre & film shows & similar social/recreational activities for the general public & members
Finances: *Annual Operating Budget:* $250,000-$500,000
Staff Member(s): 10; 60 volunteer(s)
Membership: 800; *Fees:* $1,000; *Member Profile:* Latvian or Latvian background
Activities: *Library:* Latvian Centre Library; Open to public
Chief Officer(s):
Sylvia Shedden, President & CEO

Latvian National Federation in Canada (LNAK) / Fédération nationale lettone au Canada
4 Credit Union Dr., Toronto ON M4A 2N8
Tel: 416-755-2353
Other Communication: Alt. E-mail: lnak@lnak.net
lnak@lnak.org
www.lnak.net/eng
www.facebook.com/latviannationalfederationincanada
Overview: A small national organization overseen by Baltic Federation in Canada
Mission: To represent the interests of Latvian Canadians at the city, provincial & federal levels; To maintain contact with other Canadian non-governmental organizations & expedite projects both in Canada & in Latvia
Member of: Canadian Ethnocultural Council; Baltic Federation of Canada
Chief Officer(s):
Andris Kesteris, Chair
Vilnis Petersons, Administrator

The Latvian Relief Society of Canada
4 Credit Union Dr., Toronto ON M4A 2N8
Tel: 647-727-4310
dvkvbirojs@gmail.com
www.daugavasvanagi.ca
Also Known As: Daugavas Vanagi
Overview: A small national charitable organization founded in 1953
Mission: To provide financial assistance to Latvian-Canadians who demonstrate financial need; To encourage Latvian-Canadian youth to pursue post-secondary education
Finances: *Funding Sources:* Donations
Activities: Providing financial assistance & scholarships
Chief Officer(s):
Gunta Reynolds, President
vanadze@hotmail.com
Astride Sile, Secretary
astride.silis@sympatico.ca

Latviesu Dailamatnieku Savieniba *See* Association of Latvian Craftsmen in Canada

Laubach Literacy New Brunswick
347 Mountain Rd., Moncton NB E1C 2M7
Tel: 506-384-6371; *Fax:* 506-388-9314
laubachliteracynb@nb.aibn.com
www.llnb.ca
Overview: A medium-sized provincial organization
Staff Member(s): 2
Chief Officer(s):
Deanna Allen, Executive Director

Laubach Literacy Ontario
#8A, 65 Noecker St., Waterloo ON N2J 2R6
Tel: 519-743-3309; *Fax:* 519-743-7520
Toll-Free: 866-608-2574
literacy@laubach-on.ca
www.laubach-on.ca
www.facebook.com/LaubachLiteracyOntario
twitter.com/LLOntario
Overview: A medium-sized provincial organization
Mission: To provide their students with skills in order to combat illiteracy in Ontario
Affiliation(s): Laubach Literacy of Canada is the Canadian affiliate of ProLiteracy Worldwide (formerly Laubach Literacy International)
Staff Member(s): 3
Membership: 80; *Fees:* $50 organizational; $75 associate; *Committees:* Social Enterprise; Student
Chief Officer(s):
Gary Porter, President
Lana Faessler, Executive Director

LAUDEM, L'Association des musiciens liturgiques du Canada
1085, rue de la Cathédrale, Montréal QC H3B 2V3
Courriel: info@laudem.org
www.laudem.org
www.facebook.com/laudemcanada
Nom précédent: L'Association des organistes liturgiques du Canada
Aperçu: *Dimension:* petite; *Envergure:* nationale; fondée en 1992
Mission: De réunir les organistes liturgiques pour la promotion et le développement de leur ministère dans l'Église catholique romaine
Membre de: Fédération francophone des amis de l'orgue
Membre: 45
Membre(s) du bureau directeur:
Paul Cadrin, Président et directeur, Revue
paulcadrin@hotmail.com
Jean-Pierre Couturier, Vice-Président
Alexandra Fol, Secrétaire-trésorière
Publications:
• Éditions LAUDEM
Editor: Paul Cadrin
• Revue LAUDEM
Type: Magazine; *Frequency:* semi-annuel; *Editor:* Paul Cadrin

Laurentian University Faculty Association (LUFA) / Association des professeurs de l'Université Laurentienne
#C105, Laurentian University, 935 Ramsey Lake Rd., Sudbury ON P3E 2C6
Tel: 705-675-1151; *Fax:* 705-673-6536
admind@lufappul.org
www.news.lufapul.ca
Overview: A small local organization
Affiliation(s): Canadian Association of University Teachers; Ontario Confederation of University Faculty Associations; Sudbury and District Labour Council; Ontario Federation of Labor; Canadian Labor Congress
Finances: *Annual Operating Budget:* $100,000-$250,000
Staff Member(s): 1
Membership: 391 individual; *Fees:* Based on salary; *Member Profile:* Professors; librarians
Chief Officer(s):
Anis Farah, President
afarah@laurentian.ca

Laurentian University Staff Union (LUSU) / Syndicat des employé(es) de l'Université Laurentienne (SEUL)
Laurentian University, 935 Ramsey Lake Rd., Sudbury ON P3E 2C6
Tel: 705-675-1151
www.lusu-seul.ca
Overview: A small local organization founded in 1973
Member of: Confederation of Canadian Unions
Affiliation(s): Confederation of Ontario University Staff Associations
Membership: 270
Chief Officer(s):
Tom Fenske, President
tc_fenske@laurentian.ca
Awards:
• Lynn McGlade Memorial Bursary
• Dan MacLean Memorial Bursary
• Evelyn Ham/LUSU Bursary

The Laurier Institution
UBC Robson Square, #1600, 800 Robson St., Vancouver BC V6Z 2C5
Tel: 604-822-2054
info@thelaurier.ca
www.thelaurier.ca
www.facebook.com/thelaurier
www.youtube.com/user/thelaurierca
Overview: A small national charitable organization founded in 1989
Mission: To provide research & educational projects on Canada's cultural diversity
Finances: *Funding Sources:* Membership fees; Donations
Membership: 100-499; *Member Profile:* Individuals & students
Activities: Conducting research studies; Providing education; Offering support services; *Library:* by appointment
Chief Officer(s):
Farid Rohani, Board Member

Laurier Teachers Union (LTU) / Syndicat des enseignantes et enseignants Laurier
#210, 2292, boul Industriel, Laval QC H7S 1P9
Tel: 450-667-7037; *Fax:* 450-667-9506
Toll-Free: 800-301-1351
laurierteachersunion@ltu.ca
www.ltu.ca
Previous Name: North Island Laurentian Teachers' Union
Overview: A small local organization founded in 1998
Mission: To promote & defend the interests of teachers & public education
Member of: Québec Provincial Association of Teachers
Finances: *Annual Operating Budget:* $250,000-$500,000
Staff Member(s): 4; 50 volunteer(s)
Membership: 1,200; *Fees:* $650 individual
Chief Officer(s):
Stephanie McLellan, President
smclellan@ltu.ca
Stephan Ethier, Director, Membership Welfare
sethier@ltu.ca
Serge Landry, Director, Pedagogical Affairs
slandry@ltu.ca

Laval University Faculty Union *Voir* Syndicat des professeurs de l'Université Laval

Law Foundation of British Columbia
#1340, 605 Robson St., Vancouver BC V6B 5J3
Tel: 604-688-2337; *Fax:* 604-688-4586
info@lawfoundationbc.org
www.lawfoundationbc.org
Overview: A medium-sized provincial charitable organization founded in 1969
Mission: To allocate funds to programs that will benefit the general public of British Columbia; To act in accordance with The Legal Profession Act & distribute income in areas such as legal aid, law libraries, legal education, legal research & law reform; To conduct operations with recognition of the diverse population of British Columbia
Finances: *Funding Sources:* Income is the result of interest on client's funds that are held in lawyers' pooled trust accounts maintained in financial institutions
Activities: Accepting grant applications from non-profit organizations; Funding projects
Chief Officer(s):
Wayne Robertson, Executive Director
Jo-Anne Kaulius, Director, Finance

Law Foundation of Newfoundland & Labrador
PO Box 5907, #49, 55 Elizabeth Ave., St. John's NL A1C 5X4
Tel: 709-754-4424; *Fax:* 709-754-4320
lfnl@lawfoundationl.com
www.lawfoundationnl.com

Overview: A medium-sized provincial organization founded in 1980
Mission: To provide grants that advance public understanding of the law & access to legal services, in the areas of: law libraries; legal research; legal education; scholarships for studies relevant to law; law reform; legal aid; & legal referral services
Activities: Providing grants
Chief Officer(s):
Lawrence E. Collins, Executive Director
Janet Kielly, Office Secretary

Law Foundation of Nova Scotia
Cogswell Tower, #1305, 2000 Barrington St., Halifax NS B3J 3K1
Tel: 902-422-8335; *Fax:* 902-492-0424
nslawfd@nslawfd.ca
www.nslawfd.ca
Overview: A small provincial organization founded in 1976
Mission: To establish & maintain a fund to be used for the examination, research, revision & reform of & public access to the law, legal education, the administration of justice in the province & any other purposes incidental or conducive to or consequential upon the attainment of any such objects
Finances: *Funding Sources:* Interest acquired from lawyers' general trust accounts
Staff Member(s): 1
Chief Officer(s):
Kerry L. Oliver, Executive Director

Law Foundation of Ontario (LFO) / La fondation du droit de l'Ontario
PO Box 19, #3002, 20 Queen St. West, Toronto ON M5H 3R3
Tel: 416-598-1550; *Fax:* 416-598-1526
Other Communication: grants@lawfoundation.on.ca
general@lawfoundation.on.ca
www.lawfoundation.on.ca
www.facebook.com/LawFoundationOn
twitter.com/LawFoundationOn
Overview: A small provincial charitable organization founded in 1974
Mission: An organization that provides funding to a wide range of organizations to foster excellence in the work of lawyers, paralegals and other legal professionals.
Chief Officer(s):
Mark J. Sandler, Chair
Elizabeth Goldberg, Chief Executive Officer
egoldberg@lawfoundation.on.ca
Awards:
• Guthrie Award
The Guthrie Award recognizes outstanding individuals and organizations for their contributions to access to justice and excellence in the legal profession.
• Roy and Ria McMurtry Endowment
The Guthrie Award recognizes outstanding individuals and organizations for their contributions to access to justice and excellence in the legal profession. *Eligibility:* Students who are enrolled in courses related to law.

Law Foundation of Prince Edward Island
49 Water St., Charlottetown PE C1A 7K2
Tel: 902-620-1763
info@lawfoundationpei.ca
www.lawfoundationpei.ca
Overview: A small provincial organization founded in 1973
Mission: To establish & maintain a fund & use the proceeds for the purposes of: legal education & research on law reform; the editing & printing of decisions of the Supreme Court & the Provincial Court of PEI; the promotion of legal aid; aid in the establishment, operation & maintenance of law libraries in PEI
Affiliation(s): Association of Canadian Law Foundations
5 volunteer(s)
Membership: 5
Chief Officer(s):
Sheila Lund MacDonald, Executive Director

Law Foundation of Saskatchewan
#200, 2208 Scarth St., Regina SK S4P 2J6
Tel: 306-352-1121; *Fax:* 306-522-6222
www.lawfoundation.sk.ca
Overview: A medium-sized provincial organization founded in 1971
Mission: To maintain a fund to support legal aid, law reform, law libraries, legal education & legal research in Saskatchewan
Finances: *Funding Sources:* Interest on the sums in lawyers' mixed trust accounts
Activities: Consider grant applications
Chief Officer(s):
Bob Watt, Executive Director
Eileen Libby, Chair

Law Society of Alberta (LSA)
#500, 919 - 11th Ave. SW, Calgary AB T2R 1P3
Tel: 403-229-4700; *Fax:* 403-228-1728
Toll-Free: 800-661-9003
www.lawsocietyalberta.com
www.linkedin.com/company/the-law-society-of-alberta
twitter.com/LawSocietyofAB
Overview: A large provincial licensing organization founded in 1907
Mission: To serve the public by promoting a high standard of legal services & professional conduct through the governance & regulation of an independent legal profession; To govern all lawyers who practise law in Alberta; To admit lawyers to the Bar; To supervise professional conduct & disciplinary actions as required
Affiliation(s): Federation of Law Societies of Canada
Finances: *Funding Sources:* Membership fees
Staff Member(s): 85
Membership: 5,000-14,999; *Fees:* Schedule available; *Committees:* Access to Justice; Appeal; Audit; Civil Practice Advisory; Conduct; Continuing Competence; Corporate & Commercial Advisory; Credentials & Education; Criminal Practice ADvisory; Executive; Family Law Advisory; Finance; Governance; Insurance & Claims; Joint Library; Practice Review; Professional Responsibility; Re-Engagment & Retention; Third Party Funding Policy; Trust Safety
Chief Officer(s):
Don Thompson, Executive Director
James Eamon, President, 403-298-1851, Fax: 403-263-9193
Drew Thomson, Director, Corporate Services, 403-229-4763
Ally Taylor, Manager, Communications, 403-229-4744
Awards:
• Distinguished Service Awards
• The Viscount Bennett Scholarship
; *Amount:* Up to $20,000
• Peter Freeman, QC, Bursary for Indigenous Students in Law
• W.B. Kelly, QC, Memorial Prize
; *Amount:* Two at $1,000
   Edmonton Office
   Bell Tower, #800, 10104 - 103 Ave., Edmonton AB T5J OH8
   Tel: 780-429-3343

Law Society of British Columbia
845 Cambie St., 8th Fl., Vancouver BC V6B 4Z9
Tel: 604-669-2533; *Fax:* 604-669-5232
Toll-Free: 800-902-5300; *TTY:* 604-443-5700
communications@lsbc.org
www.lawsociety.bc.ca
www.linkedin.com/company/law-society-of-british-columbia
twitter.com/LawSocietyofBC
www.youtube.com/user/lawsocietyofbc
Overview: A large provincial licensing organization founded in 1884
Mission: To ensure that the public is well served by a competent, honourable & independent legal profession
Affiliation(s): Federation of Law Societies of Canada
Finances: *Annual Operating Budget:* Greater than $5 Million; *Funding Sources:* Membership dues
50 volunteer(s)
Membership: 10,210 practising; 1,298 non-practising; *Fees:* $855 practising; $180 non-practising; *Member Profile:* Completed requirement for call to B.C. Bar; *Committees:* Benchers; Executive; Treasurer's; Audit; Competency; Credentials; Discipline; Audit; Ethics; Special Compensation Fund; Finance
Activities: *Speaker Service:* Yes; *Library*
Chief Officer(s):
E. David Crossin, President
Timothy E. McGee, CEO & Executive Director
Awards:
• The Law Society Award
• Law Society Gold Medals
• Law Society Scholarship for Graduate Legal Studies
• Jack Webster Award for Excellence in Legal Journalism
Publications:
• Benchers' Bulletins
Type: Bulletin

Law Society of Manitoba (LSM) / La Société du Barreau du Manitoba
219 Kennedy St., Winnipeg MB R3C 1S8
Tel: 204-942-5571; *Fax:* 204-956-0624
Other Communication: Membership E-mail:
membership@lawsociety.mb.ca
admin@lawsociety.mb.ca
www.lawsociety.mb.ca
twitter.com/lawsocietymb
Overview: A medium-sized provincial licensing organization founded in 1877
Mission: To ensure the public in Manitoba is well served by the legal profession
Member of: Canadian Lawyers Insurance Association (CLIA)
Membership: *Committees:* Executive & Administration; Admissions & Education; Complaints Investigation, Competence, & Discipline; Spot Audit Program; Professional Liability Insurance Program; Practice Issues; Equity Initiatives
Activities: Admitting persons to the Bar; Providing continuing professional education; Conducting investigations of complaints, & disciplinary procedures; Auditing of law firms; Offering professional liability insurance; Publishing legal studies
Chief Officer(s):
Kristin Dangerfield, CEO
kdangerfield@lawsociety.mb.ca
Richard Porcher, Director, Admissions & Membership
rporcher@lawsociety.mb.ca

Law Society of New Brunswick / Barreau du Nouveau-Brunswick
68 Avonlea Court, Fredericton NB E3C 1N8
Tel: 506-458-8540; *Fax:* 506-451-1421
general@lawsociety-barreau.nb.ca
www.lawsociety-barreau.nb.ca
Overview: A medium-sized provincial licensing organization founded in 1846
Mission: The Law Society was officially created in 1846. The Provincial Legislative Assembly adopted Chapter 48 of the Provincial Statutes which in effect incorporated what was then called the "Barristers' Society" for the "purpose of securing in the Province a learned and honourable legal profession, for establishing order and good conduct among its members and for promoting knowledgeable development and reform of the law".
Affiliation(s): Federation of Law Societies of Canada
Membership: 1,000-4,999; *Member Profile:* Open to individuals in accordance with the criteria & procedures established in the Law Society Act & the regulations under that Act; *Committees:* Admissions; Articling; Audit & Risk Management; Bar Admission Course; Compensation; Competence; Complaints; Continuing Professional Development; Discipline; Ethics; Examining; File Retention & Destruction Guidelines; Human Resources; Insurance Management; Law Libraries; Mandatory Continuing Professional Development; New Brunswick Law Foundation; Practice Review; Property Law Advisory; Provincial Libraries; Strategic Development; TRC Calls to Action
Activities: *Library:*
Chief Officer(s):
Hélène L. Beaulieu, President, 506-856-9800
hbeaulieu@coxandpalmer.com
Marc L. Richard, Executive Director
mrichard@lawsociety-barreau.nb.ca

Law Society of Newfoundland & Labrador
PO Box 1028, 196-198 Water St., St. John's NL A1C 5M3
Tel: 709-722-4740; *Fax:* 709-722-8902
thelawsociety@lawsociety.nf.ca
www.lawsociety.nf.ca
Overview: A medium-sized provincial licensing organization founded in 1826
Mission: To ensure that law students are appropriately educated and trained through articling and Bar Admission programs and exams, and provides continuing legal education to practititoners.
Affiliation(s): Federation of Law Societies of Canada
Staff Member(s): 16
Membership: 719; *Committees:* Executive; Accounts and Finance; Archives; Bar Admission; Claims Review; Complaints Authorization; Custodianship; Discipline; Education; Honours & Awards; Insurance; Law Society Act & Rules; Law Society of Newfoundland & Labrador Medical Legal Liason; Legislation; Library; Life Membership; Practice Rules Compliance; Professional Law Corporations; Professionals' Assistance; Real Estate; The SS Daisy Legal History; Student Awards; Unauthorized Practice
Activities: *Library:* Open to public by appointment
Chief Officer(s):
Brenda B. Grimes, Executive Director
brenda.grimes@lawsociety.nf.ca

Law Society of Nunavut (LSNU)
PO Box 149, Iqaluit NU X0A 0H0

Tel: 867-979-2330; Fax: 867-979-2333
administrator@lawsociety.nu.ca
lawsociety.nu.ca
Overview: A medium-sized provincial licensing organization founded in 1999
Mission: To govern its membership & protect the public
Member of: Federation of Law Societies of Canada
Staff Member(s): 5
Membership: 262; *Committees:* Executive; Membership & Admissions; Discipline; Ethics & Unauthorized Practice; Finance
Chief Officer(s):
Nalini Vaddapalli, CEO

Law Society of Prince Edward Island
PO Box 128, 49 Water St., Charlottetown PE C1A 7K2
Tel: 902-566-1666; Fax: 902-368-7557
lawsociety@lspei.pe.ca
www.lspei.pe.ca
Overview: A small provincial licensing organization founded in 1876
Mission: To uphold & protect the public interest in the administration of justice; to establish standards for the education, professional responsibility & competence of members & applicants for membership; to ensure the independence, integrity & honour of the society & its members; to regulate the practice of law; to uphold & protect the interests of members.
Affiliation(s): Federation of Law Societies of Canada
Finances: *Funding Sources:* Membership fees
Staff Member(s): 5
Membership: Law firm members: 152; government members: 59; corporate members: 19; *Committees:* Annual and Mid-Winter Meeting; Articling & Admissions/ Board of Examiners; Continuing Legal Education; Credentials; Discipline; Discipline Policies and Procedure; Ethics; Insurance; Law Foundation; Legislation; Library, Court House; Nominating; Practice Standards/Competence; Real Property; Scholarship; Unauthorized Practice
Activities: *Internships:* Yes *Library:* Law Library; Open to public
Chief Officer(s):
Susan M. Robinson, Executive Director & Sec.-Treas.

Law Society of Saskatchewan
#1100, 2002 Victoria Ave., Regina SK S4P 0R7
Tel: 306-569-8242; Fax: 306-352-2989
reception@lawsociety.sk.ca
www.lawsociety.sk.ca
Overview: A small provincial licensing organization founded in 1907
Mission: To govern the legal profession by upholding high standards of competence & integrity; ensuring the independence of the profession; advancing the administration of justice, the profession & the rule of law, all in the public interest
Affiliation(s): Federation of Law Societies of Canada
Staff Member(s): 29
Membership: *Committees:* Admission & Education; Discipline; Insurance; Ethics; Professional Standards
Chief Officer(s):
Donna Sigmeth, Deputy Director
Tim Huber, Counsel
tim@lawsociety.sk.ca
Ruth Armstrong, Office Administrator
ruth@lawsociety.sk.ca

Law Society of the Northwest Territories / Le Barreau des Territoires du Nord-Ouest
Diamond Plaza, PO Box 1298, Stn. Main, 5204 - 50th Ave., 4th Fl., Yellowknife NT X1A 2N9
Tel: 867-873-3828; Fax: 867-873-6344
info@lawsociety.nt.ca
www.lawsociety.nt.ca
twitter.com/LawSocietyNWT
Overview: A small provincial licensing organization founded in 1978
Mission: To serve the public by an independent, responsible & responsive legal profession.
Affiliation(s): Federation of Law Societies of Canada
Finances: *Funding Sources:* Membership fees
Staff Member(s): 3
Membership: 547 individuals; *Fees:* $1,470 practising member; $236.25 non practising member; *Member Profile:* Graduate of common law faculty of Canadian law school or equivalent; *Committees:* Access to Justice; Admissions; Continuing Professional Development; Discipline; Finance; Insurance; Legal Ethics & Practice; Rules; Social; Civil Bench & Bar; Criminal Bench & Bar; Judicial Appointments Advisory; Federal Judicial Appointments; Legal Aid Commission; M.M. de Weerdt Law Library; Judicial Council for Territorial Court Judges; Northwest Territories Law Foundation; Territorial Bench & Bar (Civil & Criminal); Territorial Court Rules; Professionalism
Activities: Referral service; *Internships:* Yes
Chief Officer(s):
Pamela Naylor, Executive Director
pamela.naylor@lawsociety.nt.ca

Law Society of Upper Canada / Barreau du Haut-Canada
Osgoode Hall, 130 Queen St. West, Toronto ON M5H 2N6
Tel: 416-947-3300; Fax: 416-947-3924
Toll-Free: 800-668-7380; TTY: 416-644-4886
lawsociety@lsuc.on.ca
www.lsuc.on.ca
www.linkedin.com/company/the-law-society-of-upper-canada
www.facebook.com/lawsocietylsuc
twitter.com/LawsocietyLSUC
www.youtube.com/lawsocietylsuc
Overview: A large provincial licensing organization founded in 1797
Mission: To govern the legal profession in the public interest by ensuring that the people of Ontario are served by lawyers who meet high standards of learning, competence & professional conduct
Affiliation(s): Federation of Law Societies of Canada
Finances: *Annual Operating Budget:* $3 Million-$5 Million; *Funding Sources:* Membership fees; Law Foundation of Ontario
Membership: 27,500; *Committees:* Access to Justice; Audit & Finance; Compensation; Compensation Fund; Equity and Indigenous Affairs; Government & Public Affairs; Inter-Jurisdictional Mobility; Law Society Awards; Litigation; Paralegal Awards; Paralegal Standing; Priority Planning; Proceedings Authorization; Professional Development & Competence Regulation; Summary Disposition; Tribunal
Activities: Lawyer/Paralegaldirectory; Helping individuals choose the right legal professional; Providing access to legal services; Member Assistance Program (MAP); *Library:* Great Library; Not open to public
Chief Officer(s):
Robert G. W. Lapper, CEO
Diana Miles, Director, Professional Development & Competence
Awards:
• The Law Society Medal
• Distinguished Paralegal Award
• The Lincoln Alexander Award
To recognize an Ontario lawyer who has demonstrated a commitment to the public through community service.
• The Laura Legge Award
Recognizes woman lawyers from Ontario who have exemplified leadership within the profession.
Meetings/Conferences:
• The Annual General Meeting of the Law Society of Upper Canada, 2018
Scope: Provincial

Law Society of Yukon (LSY)
#202, 302 Steele St., Whitehorse YT Y1A 2C5
Tel: 867-668-4231; Fax: 867-667-7556
info@lawsocietyyukon.com
www.lawsocietyyukon.com
Also Known As: Yukon Law Society
Overview: A small provincial licensing organization founded in 1985
Mission: To govern legal profession in the Yukon.
Affiliation(s): Federation of Law Societies of Canada
Staff Member(s): 1
Membership: 329; *Fees:* Schedule available
Activities: *Library:* Law Library; Open to public
Chief Officer(s):
Lynn Daffe, Executive Director

Law Union of Ontario
31 Prince Arthur Ave., Toronto ON M5R 1B2
Tel: 416-927-9662; Fax: 416-960-5456
law.union.of.ontario@gmail.com
www.lawunion.ca
Overview: A small provincial organization founded in 1974
Mission: Coalition of progressive & socialist lawyers, law students & legal workers providing an alternative bar in Ontario which seeks to counter the traditional protections afforded by the legal system to social, political & economic privilege
Membership: 200
Meetings/Conferences:
• Law Union of Ontario 2018 Annual Conference, 2018, ON
Scope: Provincial

Lawn Bowls Association of Alberta
11759 Groat Rd., Edmonton AB T5M 3K6
Tel: 780-427-8119
office@bowls.ab.ca
www.bowls.ab.ca
Overview: A small provincial organization founded in 1989 overseen by Bowls Canada Boulingrin
Affiliation(s): Commonwealth; Highlands; Royal Lawn Bowling Club; Edmonton Indoor Lawn Bowling Club; Bow Valley; Calgary Lawn; Rotary Park; Stanley Park; Ted Petrunia Lawn Bowling Green; Medicine Hat Lawn Bowling Green
Staff Member(s): 1
Chief Officer(s):
Anthony Peter Spencer, President
Dave Cox, Vice-President
Laura Lochanski, Vice-President

Lawn Bowls Canada Boulingrin *See* Bowls Canada Boulingrin

Lawson Foundation
c/o Foundation House, #300, 2 St. Clair Ave. East, Toronto ON M4T 2T5
www.lawson.ca
www.linkedin.com/company/583873
www.facebook.com/lawsonfoundation
twitter.com/Lawson_Fdn
Overview: A small provincial charitable organization founded in 1956
Mission: To advance the well-being of children & youth; To enhance early child development for the benefit of children & families; To provide opportunities for children & youth to be active & healthy; To promote the value of youth & the environment
Activities: Providing grants for community action, knowledge development & mobilization, & other activities; Facilitating conversations & knowledge sharing; Impact investing; Advocating for investment in Early Childhood Education; Supporting charitable & non-profit organizations
Chief Officer(s):
Marcel Lauzière, President & CEO, 416-775-9458 Ext. 203
mlauziere@lawson.ca
Amanda Mayer, Director, Governance & Communications
amayer@lawson.ca
Awards:
• Miggsie Fund
Eligibility: Charities in the London, Ontario area

Lawyers Without Borders Canada *Voir* Avocats sans frontières Canada

Lay Missionaries of Charity - Canada (LMC)
www.laymc.com
Also Known As: Lay Missionaries of Charity of Mother Teresa
Overview: A large international organization
Mission: To advance the interests of the Roman Catholic Church; to foster fraternity & fellowship among members; to promote undiscriminating charity
Affiliation(s): Archdiocese of Toronto
Membership: *Member Profile:* Catholic males aged 16 & above

LC Line Contractors' Association of BC
#222, 7455 - 132 St., Surrey BC V3W 1J8
Tel: 604-599-9228; Fax: 604-599-4433
Toll-Free: 877-439-9827
info@lca.ca
www.lca.ca
Also Known As: LCA of BC
Overview: A small provincial organization founded in 1999
Member of: Mining, Suppliers, Contractors & Consultants Association of British Columbia
Affiliation(s): Electrical Industry Training Institute; IBEW Local 258
Activities: Safety Program; Skills Upgrading; Safety Database; *Internships:* Yes
Chief Officer(s):
Jeff Skosnik, CEO
jeff@lca.ca
Awards:
• Annual Safety Awards

LEAD Canada Inc.
PO Box 250, 3202, rang de Tullochgorum, Ormstown QC J0S 1K0
Toll-Free: 866-532-3539
office@leadcanada.net
www.leadcanada.net

Also Known As: Leadership for Environment & Development Canada
Overview: A small national organization
Membership: Fees: $15
Chief Officer(s):
John Lewis, President
john@intelligentfutures.ca

Leader Board of Trade
PO Box 104, Leader SK S0N 1H0
Tel: 306-628-3687; Fax: 306-628-3674
Overview: A small local organization
Membership: 23; Fees: $50
Chief Officer(s):
K. Wagman, Secretary
Gordon Stueck, President
gstueck@sasktel.net

Leaf Rapids Chamber of Commerce
PO Box 26, Leaf Rapids MB R0B 1W0
Tel: 204-473-2491; Fax: 204-473-2284
Overview: A small local organization founded in 1974
Mission: To promote tourism & business in Leaf Rapids; To attract new members of the community
Member of: Manitoba Chamber of Commerce
Finances: Annual Operating Budget: Less than $50,000; Funding Sources: Membership dues
6 volunteer(s)
Membership: 1-99; Member Profile: Businesses; Non-governmental offices; educators; artists; Committees: Tourism
Activities: Promoting economic & social development; Library: by appointment

League for Human Rights of B'nai Brith Canada / Ligue des droits de la personne de B'nai Brith Canada
15 Hove St., Toronto ON M3H 4Y8
Tel: 416-633-6224; Fax: 416-630-2159
Toll-Free: 800-892-2624; Crisis Hot-Line: 800-892-2624
league@bnaibrith.ca
www.bnaibrith.ca/league
Previous Name: Anti-Defamation League of B'nai Brith
Overview: A medium-sized national charitable organization founded in 1965
Mission: To strive for human rights for all Canadians; to improve inter-community relations; to combat racism & racial discrimination; to prevent bigotry & anti-Semitism.
Member of: B'nai Brith Canada
Affiliation(s): Anti-Defamation League
Finances: Funding Sources: Private donations; B'nai Brith Foundation; grants
Membership: Committees: Legal/Legislative; Community Action; Intercultural Dialogue; Education; Holocaust & Hope; Human Rights Youth League; Young Leadership Network
Activities: Multicultural anti-racist workshops for students, teachers & administrators, police services, businesses, government, health services, community organizations; intercultural & interfaith dialogue programs; monitoring hate group activity & etc.; Internships: Yes; Speaker Service: Yes; Library: Education & Training Centre; by appointment
Chief Officer(s):
Frank Dimant, CEO
Awards:
• Student Human Rights Achievement Award
• Special Human Rights Award
• Friend of the League
• Media Human Rights Awards
Eligibility: Awards for "alerting, informing, sensitizing the public with regard to the nature & value of human rights"; one major award & one honourable mention is presented to organizations in each of press, television, advertising
  Winnipeg Office
  123 Doncaster St., #C403, Winnipeg MB R3N 2B2
  Tel: 204-487-9623; Fax: 204-487-9648
  winnipeg@bnaibrith.ca
  Vancouver Office
  Vancouver BC
  Tel: 604-282-3952
  vancouver@bnaibrith.ca
  Ontario Region Office
  15 Hove St., Toronto ON M3H 4Y8
  Tel: 416-633-6224; Fax: 416-630-2159
  toronto@bnaibrith.ca
  Montréal Office
  #202, 7155, rue Cote-St-Luc, Montréal QC H4V 1J2

Tel: 514-733-5377
montreal@bnaibrith.ca
  Western Region - Calgary Office
  Calgary AB
  Tel: 403-262-9255
  calgary@bnaibrith.ca
  Western Region - Edmonton Office
  Edmonton AB
  Tel: 780-483-6939
  edmonton@bnaibrith.ca

The League of Canadian Poets (LCP)
#312, 192 Spadina Ave., Toronto ON M5T 2C2
Tel: 416-504-1657; Fax: 416-504-0096
info@poets.ca
www.poets.ca
www.facebook.com/canadianpoets
twitter.com/CanadianPoets
Overview: A medium-sized national organization founded in 1966
Mission: To develop the art of poetry; to enhance the status of poets & nurture a professional poetic community; to facilitate the teaching of Canadian poetry at all levels of education; to enlarge the audience for poetry by encouraging publication, performance & recognition of poetry nationally & internationally; to uphold freedom of expression
Member of: Canadian Conference of the Arts
Affiliation(s): Book & Periodical Council
Finances: Annual Operating Budget: $250,000-$500,000; Funding Sources: Canada Council; Ontario Arts Council; Toronto Arts Council; Metro Cultural Affairs
Staff Member(s): 3; 50 volunteer(s)
Membership: 700; Fees: $185 full membership; $70 associate; $30 student; Member Profile: Full - poets who have published at least one book of poetry or two chapbooks & have substantial publication credits in periodicals; associate - poets who have begun publishing in print or online but are not ready for full membership; students; Committees: Membership; Feminist Caucus
Activities: Lectures; feminist caucus; funding programs; Poetry City; Awareness Events: National Poetry Month, April; Poem in Your Pocket Day, April Library: Poetry Library; Open to public
Chief Officer(s):
Lesley Fletcher, Executive Director
lesley@poets.ca
Nicole Brewer, Coordinator, Administration & Communications
nicole@poets.ca
Awards:
• Gerald Lampert Memorial Award
Established 1979; awarded annually for excellence in a first book of poetry, written by a Canadian citizen or landed immigrant, & published in the preceding year; Amount: $1,000
• Pat Lowther Memorial Award
Awarded annually for excellence in a book of poetry, written by a Canadian female citizen or landed immigrant, & published in the preceding year; Amount: $1,000
• Raymond Souster Award
Honours a book of poetry written by a member of the League; Amount: $1,000
• Sheri-D Wilson Golden Beret Award
For lifetime achievement in spoken word; Amount: $1,000
• Jessamy Stursberg Poetry Prize for Canadian Youth
$2,000 in prizes for poems written by young poets, grades 7-12
Meetings/Conferences:
• The League of Canadian Poets 2018 Annual Conference & AGM, June, 2018, Toronto, ON
Scope: National
Publications:
• Between the Lines [a publication of The League of Canadian Poets]
Type: Newsletter

The League of Canadian Theatres See Professional Association of Canadian Theatres

League of Ukrainian Canadian Women (LUCW)
#204, 2282 Bloor St. West, Toronto ON M6S 1N9
Tel: 416-763-8907
info@lucw.ca
www.lucw.ca
Overview: A large national organization founded in 1951
Mission: To support the development & sustainment of a strong Ukrainian community in Canada; To promote Ukraine's right to protect its national independence & security in the European family of nations

Member of: Ukrainian Canadian Congress
Affiliation(s): League of Ukrainian Canadians (LUC)
Activities: Organizing humanitarian initiatives, like the Guardian Angels Ukraine Project; Sponsoring events that align with association goals; Communicating with government representatives
Chief Officer(s):
Oksana Kuzyshyn, President

League of Ukrainian Canadians
9 Plastics Ave., Toronto ON M8Z 4B6
Tel: 416-516-8223; Fax: 416-516-4033
luc@lucorg.com
www.lucorg.com
www.facebook.com/LeagueofUkrainianCanadians
Overview: A medium-sized national organization
Mission: To aid Ukrainian people living in Canada & in Ukraine; To contribute to the growth & development of a prosperous Ukrainian community in Canada
Member of: Ukrainian Canadian Congress
Affiliation(s): Ukrainian World Congress; League of Ukrainian Canadian Women
Activities: Education projects; cultural events; research; publications; networking
Chief Officer(s):
Orest Steciw, President

Leamington District Chamber of Commerce
PO Box 321, Leamington ON N8H 3W3
Tel: 519-326-2721; Fax: 519-326-3204
www.leamingtonchamber.com
twitter.com/Leam_Chamber
Overview: A small local organization founded in 1936
Staff Member(s): 2
Membership: 300; Fees: Schedule available
Chief Officer(s):
Wendy Parsons, General Manager

Learning Assistance Teachers' Association (LATA)
c/o BC Teachers' Federation, #100, 550 West 6th Ave., Vancouver BC V5Z 4P2
Fax: 250-377-0860
www.latabc.com
www.facebook.com/LATABC
twitter.com/latabc
Overview: A small provincial organization
Mission: To provide equal access to the educational system, a position that supports the opportunity for students to pursue their goals in all aspects of education; To work together with parents and the community, and give all students the best opportunities for success
Member of: BC Teachers' Federation
Membership: Fees: $35 BCTF member; $54.50 non-BCTF member; Member Profile: Classroom teachers; learning assistance specialists; administrators; parents
Chief Officer(s):
Janice Neden, President
jneden@sd73.bc.ca
Gail Bailey, Vice-President
gailbailey@shaw.ca

Learning Centre for Georgina (LCG)
23324 Woodbine Ave., Keswick ON L4P 3E9
Tel: 905-476-9900; Fax: 905-476-3085
info@lcgeorgina.org
www.lcgeorgina.org
www.facebook.com/learningcentregeorgina
Overview: A small local charitable organization founded in 1985
Mission: To help people (must be 16 years of age or older to access cost free services & not in full-time attendance in school) improve their basic reading, writing, spelling, & math skills
Member of: Georgina Board of Trade; United Way
Affiliation(s): Metro Toronto Movement for Literacy; Ontario Literacy Coalition; Community Literacy Ontario
Finances: Funding Sources: Provincial government; United Way; fundraising events; Trillium Foundation
Staff Member(s): 5
Chief Officer(s):
Yvonne Parker, President
Grant Peckford, Executive Director
grantp@lcgeorgina.org

Learning Disabilities Association of Alberta (LDAA) / Troubles d'apprentissage - Association de l'Alberta
PO Box 29011, Stn. Pleasantview, Edmonton AB T6H 5Z6

Canadian Associations / Learning Disabilities Association of British Columbia (LDAV) / Troubles d'apprentissage - Association de la Colombie-Britannique

Tel: 780-448-0360
www.ldalberta.ca
www.facebook.com/185386404841119
Overview: A medium-sized provincial charitable organization founded in 1968 overseen by Learning Disabilities Association of Canada
Mission: To foster public understanding & build support networks to maximize the potential of individuals with learning disabilities; To support children, families, & adults affected by learning disabilities & ADHD
Finances: *Annual Operating Budget:* $100,000-$250,000; *Funding Sources:* Government; Donations
Staff Member(s): 1; 15 volunteer(s)
Membership: 300 + 3 provincial chapters; *Fees:* $40 individual/family; $20 student/senior; $75 school/non-profit; $125 corporation
Activities: Representing the learning disabilities community at the provincial level; Providing support programs & resources to children, adults, & families, including the Right to Read program; Offering support; *Awareness Events:* Learning Disabilities Month, March; *Speaker Service:* Yes
Chief Officer(s):
Ellie Shuster, Executive Director
execdir@ldalberta.ca
Awards:
• Siobhan Isabella Reid Memorial Scholarship
Eligibility: A student enrolled full time at a post-secondary institution in Alberta who has already completed two full academic years in the program; the program must lead to that individual being able to assist children & adults with learning disabilities *Deadline:* May 15; *Amount:* $1,000
• Mandin Award
Awarded to assist a child or youth participate in a summer camp, social skill development courses, or tutoring & assessments; Funds will be disbursed directly to the program or service provider *Eligibility:* An individual between 4 & 21 years of age with a learning disability or ADHD *Deadline:* May 15; *Amount:* up to $400

Edmonton Chapter
L.Y. Cairns School, 10510 - 45 Ave., Edmonton AB T6H 0A1
Tel: 780-466-1011; Fax: 780-466-1095
info@ldedmonton.com
www.ldedmonton.ca
www.facebook.com/LDEdmonton
twitter.com/LDEdmonton
Chief Officer(s):
Karen Popal, Programs Coordinator

Red Deer Chapter
3757 - 43 Ave., Lower Level, Red Deer AB T4N 3B7
Tel: 403-340-3885; Fax: 403-340-3884
ldreddeer.ca
Chief Officer(s):
Marg Dunlop, Administrative Coordinator

Learning Disabilities Association of British Columbia (LDAV) / Troubles d'apprentissage - Association de la Colombie-Britannique
#5, 774 Bay St., Victoria BC V8T 5E4
Tel: 250-370-9513
info@ldabc.ca
www.ldabc.ca
www.facebook.com/LDABC
twitter.com/LDABC
Overview: A medium-sized provincial organization founded in 1974 overseen by Learning Disabilities Association of Canada
Mission: To advance the education, employment, social development, legal rights & general well-being of people with learning disabilities; To operate as a coordinating body, information centre & provincial representative for chapters within BC
Member of: Learning Disabilities Association of B.C.
Finances: *Annual Operating Budget:* $100,000-$250,000
Staff Member(s): 5; 50 volunteer(s)
Membership: 1,000+; *Fees:* $35
Activities: *Internships:* Yes *Library:* Learning Centre; Open to public
Chief Officer(s):
Lynne Kent, Chair
lynne.k@ldabc.ca

Learning Disabilities Association of Canada (LDAC) / L'association Canadienne des troubles d'apprentissage (ACTA)
#20, 2420 Bank St., Ottawa ON K1V 8S1
Tel: 613-238-5721
info@ldac-acta.ca
www.ldac-acta.ca
www.facebook.com/ldacacta
twitter.com/ldacacta
www.youtube.com/ldacacta
Overview: A large national charitable organization founded in 1971
Mission: To advance the education, employment, social development, legal rights & general well-being of people with learning disabilities; To create a greater public awareness & understanding of learning disabilities; To promote & develop early recognition, diagnosis, treatment & appropriate educational, social, recreational & career-oriented programs for people with learning disabilities; To promote legislation, research & training of personnel in the field of learning disabilities
Finances: *Funding Sources:* Direct mail; publications; sales; government
Staff Member(s): 2
Membership: *Fees:* $20-$50; *Member Profile:* Parents; teachers; individuals with learning disabilities; buyers; physicians
Activities: Representing people with learning disabilities at national meetings, & through briefs & position papers to the federal government & agencies; Acting as a clearinghouse for information, communication & joint action; *Awareness Events:* Learning Disabilities Awareness Month, Oct.; *Library:* by appointment
Chief Officer(s):
Thealzel Lee, Chair
Claudette Larocque, Executive Director
claudette@ldac-acta.ca
Publications:
• National [a publication of the Learning Disabilities Association of Canada]
Type: Newsletter; *Frequency:* Quarterly

Learning Disabilities Association of Manitoba (LDAM) / Troubles d'apprentissage - Association de Manitoba
617 Erin St., Winnipeg MB R3G 2W1
Tel: 204-774-1821; Fax: 204-788-4090
ldamb@mts.net
www.ldamanitoba.org
Also Known As: LDA Manitoba
Overview: A medium-sized provincial charitable organization founded in 1966 overseen by Learning Disabilities Association of Canada
Mission: To provide support to all those who are concerned with learning disabilities; To represent individuals & families with learning disabilities
Affiliation(s): Learning Disabilities Association of Canada
Finances: *Funding Sources:* The City of Winnipeg; United Way of Winnipeg; Manitoba Lotteries; Sponsorships; Fundraising
Staff Member(s): 7
Membership: *Member Profile:* Parents; Professionals; Persons with learning disabilities &/or attention deficit disorders; Individuals interested in learning disabilities
Activities: Providing educational workshops, courses, & seminars, such as parenting courses; Offering programs, such as Destination Employment & a literacy tutoring program; Providing information about learning disabilities & attention deficit disorders; Giving referrals to community, government, & private services; *Awareness Events:* Date With a Star Dinner; Annual Mercer Learning Disabilities Golf Classic *Library:* LDAM Resource Library; by appointment
Chief Officer(s):
Marilyn MacKinnon, Executive Director
ldamanitoba4@mymts.net

Learning Disabilities Association of New Brunswick (LDANB) / Troubles d'apprentissage - Association du Nouveau-Brunswick (TA-ANB)
#203, 403 Regent St., Fredericton NB E3B 3X6
Tel: 506-459-7852; Fax: 506-455-9300
Toll-Free: 877-544-7852
admin@ldanb-taanb.ca
www.ldanb-taanb.ca
www.facebook.com/LDANBTAANB
twitter.com/LDANB
vimeo.com/user19549796
Also Known As: LDA New Brunswick
Overview: A medium-sized provincial charitable organization founded in 1980 overseen by Learning Disabilities Association of Canada
Mission: Promotes the understanding & acceptance of the ability of persons with learning disabilities to lead meaningful & successful lives. Satellite office in Saint John.
Finances: *Funding Sources:* Membership fees; Human Resources Development Canada
Staff Member(s): 2
Membership: *Fees:* $25
Activities: *Speaker Service:* Yes; *Library:* LDANB Resource Library & ADHD Resource Centre; Open to public by appointment
Chief Officer(s):
Deschênes André, Executive Director
Awards:
• Tia Klarissa Rickard Memorial Award
Publications:
• Reflexions [a publication of the Learning Disabilities Association of New Brunswick]
Type: Newsletter

Moncton Chapter
63 Peter St., Moncton NB E1A 3W3
Tel: 506-383-5077; Fax: 506-383-5077
lmlebinc@nbnet.nb.ca

Saint John Chapter (LDASJ)
c/o St. John The Baptist/King Edward School, 223 St. James St., Saint John NB E2L 1W3
Tel: 506-642-4956
ldasj@nb.aibn.com
www.ldasj.ca

Learning Disabilities Association of Newfoundland & Labrador Inc. (LDANL)
The Board of Trade Bldg., #301, 66 Kenmount Rd., St. John's NL A1B 3V7
Tel: 709-753-1445; Fax: 709-753-4747
info@ldanl.ca
www.ldanl.ca
www.facebook.com/LearningDisabilitiesNL
twitter.com/LDANL
Also Known As: LDA Newfoundland & Labrador
Overview: A medium-sized provincial charitable organization founded in 2001 overseen by Learning Disabilities Association of Canada
Mission: To work towards the advancement of legal rights, social development, education, employment, & the general well-being of people with learning disabilities
Member of: Learning Disabilities Association of Canada (LDAC)
Finances: *Funding Sources:* Donations; Fundraising; Sponsorships
Membership: *Fees:* $30 individual & family; $100 schools & associated organizations; *Member Profile:* Individuals & organizations wishing support services & resources
Activities: Increasing public awareness & understanding of learning disabilities; Liaising with all levels of government & the community; Providing information & support services; Offering assistive technology demonstrations; Advocating on behalf of people with learning disabilities & parents; Organizing conferences; *Library:* Resource Library; Not open to public
Chief Officer(s):
David Banfield, Executive Director
david@ldanl.ca
Karen Nelson, Office Manager

Learning Disabilities Association of Ontario (LDAO) / Troubles d'apprentissage - Association de l'Ontario
#202, 365 Evans Ave., Toronto ON M8Z 1K2
Tel: 416-929-4311; Fax: 416-929-3905
resource@ldao.ca
www.ldao.ca
www.facebook.com/LDAOntario
twitter.com/ldatschool
Overview: A medium-sized provincial charitable organization founded in 1964 overseen by Learning Disabilities Association of Canada
Mission: To provide leadership in learning disabilities advocacy, research, education & services; To advance the full participation of children, youth & adults with learning disabilities in today's society
Finances: *Annual Operating Budget:* $1.5 Million-$3 Million; *Funding Sources:* Public & private donations
Staff Member(s): 6; 30 volunteer(s)
Membership: 1,000 in 18 chapters; *Fees:* $50 individual/family; $20 student; $75 professional; $125 institutional; *Member Profile:* Open to all who are interested in the needs & interests of people with learning disabilities; *Committees:* Legislation & Policy; Fundraising/Finance
Activities: Providing information & services to individuals & families; *Awareness Events:* Learning Disabilities Month, Oct. *Library:* LDAO Resource Library; by appointment

Chief Officer(s):
Lawrence Barns, President & CEO
lawrence@ldao.ca
Karen Quinn, Director, Operations
karenq@ldao.ca
Diane Wagner, Senior Manager, Public Policy & Education
dianew@ldao.ca
Awards:
• Gloria Landis Memorial Bursary
For adult student with a learning disability returning to school for further education
• Roy Cooper Scholarship

Learning Disabilities Association of Prince Edward Island (LADPEI)
#149, 40 Enman Cres., Charlottetown PE C1E 1E6
Tel: 902-894-5032
ldapei@eastlink.ca
www.ldapei.ca
www.facebook.com/ldapei
twitter.com/LDAPEI
Overview: A medium-sized provincial charitable organization founded in 1975 overseen by Learning Disabilities Association of Canada
Mission: To advance the interests of people with learning disabilities; To act as a voice for learning disabled people of Prince Edward Island
Member of: Prince Edward Island Literacy Alliance Inc.
Affiliation(s): Learning Disabilities Association of Canada (LDAC)
Finances: Funding Sources: Donations
Staff Member(s): 8
Membership: Member Profile: Individuals & organizations who wish support services & resources
Activities: Advocating for improved education, health & employment opportunities; Offering programs, such a job-readiness program for adults with learning disabilities & strategies for caregivers; Organizing educational workshops; Offering monthly support groups; Increasing public awareness; Presenting awards; Library: LDAPEI Resource Library
Chief Officer(s):
Martin Dutton, Executive Director
martin@ldapei.ca

Learning Disabilities Association of Québec Voir Association québécoise des troubles d'apprentissage

Learning Disabilities Association of Saskatchewan (LDAS) / Troubles d'apprentissage - Association de la Saskatchewan
221 Hanselman Ct., Saskatoon SK S7L 6A8
Tel: 306-652-4114; Fax: 306-652-3220
reception@ldas.org
www.ldas.org
Overview: A medium-sized provincial charitable organization founded in 1973 overseen by Learning Disabilities Association of Canada
Mission: To advance the education, employment, social development, legal rights & general well-being of people with learning disabilities. Branches in Regina & Prince Albert.
Member of: The United Way of Saskatoon
Finances: Annual Operating Budget: $500,000-$1.5 Million
Staff Member(s): 20; 30 volunteer(s)
Membership: 300; Fees: $35
Activities: Awareness Events: Learning Disabilities Month, October; Speaker Service: Yes; Library: Kinsmen Resource Centre; Open to public
Chief Officer(s):
Dale Rempel, Provincial Executive Director
dale.rempel@ldas.org
Laurie Garcea, Director, Psychological Services
Eldeen Kabatoff, Director, Program
Colette Gauthier, Director, Operations
Awards:
• Memorial Scholarship
; Amount: $250
• High Voltage Scholarship
; Amount: $200
   Prince Albert Branch
   1106 Central Ave., Prince Albert SK S6V 4V6
   Tel: 306-922-1071; Fax: 306-922-1073
   pabranch1@sasktel.net
   Chief Officer(s):
   Prema Arsiradam, Director
   Regina Branch
   438 Victoria Ave. East, Regina SK S4N 0N7
   Tel: 306-352-5327; Fax: 306-352-2260
   ldas.reginabranch@sasktel.net
   Chief Officer(s):
   Shelley Kemp, Branch Director

Learning Disabilities Association of The Northwest Territories (LDA-NWT)
PO Box 242, Yellowknife NT X1A 2N2
Tel: 867-873-6378; Fax: 867-873-6378
lda-nwt@arcticdata.ca
Previous Name: The Northwest Territories Association for Children (& Adults) with Learning Disabilities
Overview: A medium-sized provincial organization founded in 1981 overseen by Learning Disabilities Association of Canada
Mission: To help people with learning disabilities achieve their potential in school, the workplace, & in society
Activities: Offering information & workshop; Advocating for children & adults with learning disabilities; Library: Resource Centre

Learning Disabilities Association of Yukon Territory (LDAY)
128A Copper Rd., Whitehorse YT Y1A 2Z6
Tel: 867-668-5167; Fax: 867-668-6504
office@ldayukon.com
www.ldayukon.com
Also Known As: LDA Yukon
Previous Name: Yukon Association for Children & Adults with Learning Disabilities
Overview: A medium-sized provincial charitable organization founded in 1973 overseen by Learning Disabilities Association of Canada
Mission: To provide services & programs for Yukoners with learning disabilities so that they reach their potential & become productive members of society
Finances: Funding Sources: City of Whitehorse, Yukon, & Federal Government; Corporate sponsorships; Service clubs & organizations; Individual donations
Staff Member(s): 7
Membership: Fees: $20 family/individual; $40 organization; Member Profile: Parents; Adults; Professionals; Persons with Learning Disabilities
Activities: Presenting tutorials & demonstrations for assistive technologies; Offering a computer lab to assist the public; Mentoring & tutoring; Offering learning disability assessments; Organizing summer & winter camps; Providing workshops; Library: The LDAY Library
Chief Officer(s):
Stephanie Hammond, Executive Director
ed@ldayukon.com
Barb Macrae, President
Awards:
• Roland Sanders Boone Scholarship
For students attending the Learning for Success Course at Yukon College
• Tutoring Bursary
For children, youth, or adults in need of tutoring

Learning Enrichment Foundation (LEF)
116 Industry St., Toronto ON M6M 4L8
Tel: 416-769-0830; Fax: 416-769-9912
info@lefca.org
www.lefca.org
Overview: A medium-sized local charitable organization founded in 1978
Mission: To provide programs & services to help individuals become contributors to their community's social & economic development
Activities: Offering workshops, training programs; Providing employment services; Presenting language instruction for newcomers to Canada & literacy & numeracy classes; Operating LEF's licensed Child Care Centres, child care consulting, & after care programs
Chief Officer(s):
James McLeod, President
Fotios Saratsiotis, Vice-President
Alex Kroon, Vice-President
Arthur Kennedy, Secretary-Treasurer

Learning for a Sustainable Future (LSF)
York University, 343 York Lanes, Toronto ON M3J 1P3
Toll-Free: 877-250-8202
info@lsf-lst.ca
www.lsf-lst.ca
www.facebook.com/lsf.lst.ca
twitter.com/LSF_LST
Overview: A medium-sized national charitable organization founded in 1991
Mission: LSF is a non-profit Canadian organization that was created to integrate sustainability education into Canada's education system.
Chief Officer(s):
Lisa Roy, Chair
liseroy@health.nb.ca

Learning for Living South Muskoka
690 - 2 Muskoka Rd. South, Gravenhurst ON P1P 1K2
Tel: 705-687-9323; Fax: 705-687-2020
Toll-Free: 800-293-9020
lssm@bellnet.ca
Previous Name: Literacy Society of South Muskoka Inc.
Overview: A small local organization founded in 1982
Mission: To provide one-to-one literacy training & small group tutoring; To promote awareness of literacy
Member of: Simcoe/Muskoka Literacy Network; Community Literacy of Ontario
Affiliation(s): Laubach Literacy of Ontario; Laubach Literacy Canada
Finances: Annual Operating Budget: $50,000-$100,000; Funding Sources: Provincial government
Staff Member(s): 2; 35 volunteer(s)
Membership: 50; Fees: $10 individual
Activities: Family literacy; ESL tutoring; one-to-one tutoring; small groups tutoring; Awareness Events: Tee-off for Literacy, Labour Day Weekend; Library: Not open to public
Chief Officer(s):
Brent Cooper, President

Leave Out Violence Everywhere (LOVE)
#202, 3130 Bathurst St., Toronto ON M6A 2A1
Tel: 416-785-8411
toronto@leaveoutviolence.org
www.leaveoutviolence.com
www.facebook.com/leaveoutviolence
twitter.com/love_ontario
Overview: A small local organization founded in 1993
Mission: Leave Out Violence (LOVE) is a not-for-profit, grass roots youth organization that is an effective means of social change, providing hope, motivation and opportunity to thousands of young people.
Membership: Committees: In-School Violence Prevention
Activities: Media Arts Program; Leadership Training; School and Community Violence Prevention Outreach Program
   British Columbia
   #103, 2780 East Broadway, Vancouver BC V5M 1Y8
   Tel: 604-709-5728
   vancouver@leaveoutviolence.org
   Nova Scotia
   #106, 1657 Barrington St., Halifax NS B3J 2A1
   Tel: 902-429-6616; Fax: 902-429-0097
   love@eastlink.ca
   Québec
   #300, 400, rue Saint Jacques, Montréal QC H2Y 1S1
   Tel: 514-938-0006; Fax: 514-938-2377
   info@vivresansviolence.org

Lebanese Canadian Heritage Association
1555, ch Rockland, Mont-Royal QC H3P 2Y4
Overview: A small local organization founded in 1919
Mission: To support the Lebanese community of Montreal
Finances: Funding Sources: Fundraising
Activities: Organizing social, cultural & sporting events
Chief Officer(s):
Selma Nawar, Contact

Lebanese Syrian Canadian Ladies Aid Society
1406 - 1400, rue Sauvé ouest, Montréal QC H4N 1C5
Tel: 514-274-3583
Overview: A small local charitable organization
Mission: To support needy members of Montréal's Lebanese Syrian community

La Leche League Canada (LLLC) / Ligue La Leche Canada
PO Box 307, Silton SK S0G 4L0
Tel: 306-992-2125
Other Communication: Alt. E-mails: media@lllc.ca; events@lllc.ca
adc@lllc.ca
www.lllc.ca
Overview: A medium-sized national charitable organization founded in 1961

Canadian Associations / Leduc & District Food Bank Association

Mission: To act as a support network for breastfeeding mothers; To promote the importance of breastfeeding in Canada; To disseminate information on how to help mothers succeed in breastfeeding
Affiliation(s): La Leche League International; LLL Great Britain; LLL New Zealand
Finances: *Funding Sources:* Membership fees; Donations
Activities: Providing educational seminars for the public & health professionals
Chief Officer(s):
Kirsten Goa, Chair
chair@lllc.ca

Leduc & District Chamber of Commerce *See* Leduc Regional Chamber of Commerce

Leduc & District Food Bank Association
PO Box 5008, Leduc AB T9E 6L5
Tel: 780-986-5333; *Fax:* 780-986-4803
leducfb@shaw.ca
www.leducfoodbank.ca
www.facebook.com/LeducFoodBank
twitter.com/leducfoodbank
Overview: A small local charitable organization overseen by Food Banks Alberta Association
Mission: To provide for Leduc & the surrounding areas of Beaumont, Calmar, Devon, New Sarepta, Thorsby, Warburg & Leduc County
Affiliation(s): Canadian Association of Food Banks; Alberta Food Bank Network Association
Staff Member(s): 4
Activities: Fall Food Round Up
Chief Officer(s):
Gert Reynar, Executive Director
gert@ldfb.ca

Leduc Regional Chamber of Commerce
6420 - 50 St., Leduc AB T9E 7K9
Tel: 780-986-5454; *Fax:* 780-986-8108
info@leduc-chamber.com
www.leduc-chamber.com
www.linkedin.com/groups/4904841
www.facebook.com/LeducChamberofCommerce
twitter.com/LeducChamber
www.instagram.com/leducchamber
Previous Name: Leduc & District Chamber of Commerce
Overview: A small local organization founded in 1906
Mission: To be the premier business organization in the region; To be a business advocate for members; To strengthen the economic climate; To promote the free enterprise system
Member of: Alberta Chambers of Commerce; Edmonton Tourism; Greater Edmonton Regional Chambers of Commerce; Canadian Chamber of Commerce
Finances: *Funding Sources:* Membership dues; Special events; Mixers
Staff Member(s): 6
Membership: 713; *Fees:* Schedule available
Activities: Organizing trade shows, seminars, promotional & tourism services, & parades; Providing a business directory; Engaging in advocacy
Chief Officer(s):
Jennifer Garries, Executive Director
jgarries@leduc-chamber.com
Jessica Roth, Coordinator, Communications & Marketing
jroth@leduc-chamber.com

Lee's Benevolent Association of Canada
313 East Pender St., Vancouver BC V6A 1V1
Tel: 604-681-9070; *Fax:* 604-685-7804
info@leesofcanada.org
www.leesofcanada.org
Overview: A medium-sized national organization
Mission: To serve as a clan association for persons with the surname Lee
Membership: *Committees:* Steering

Legal & District Chamber of Commerce
PO Box 338, Legal AB T0G 1L0
Tel: 780-961-7634
www.legalchamberofcommerce.ca
Overview: A small local organization
Mission: To promote local business & community
Affiliation(s): Greater Edmonton Regional Chambers of Commerce
Staff Member(s): 1
Membership: 100; *Fees:* $30-$60; *Committees:* Membership; "Legal-Lerie"; Tourism; Trade & Craft Fair; Nominations

Chief Officer(s):
Ken Evans, President
Carol Tremblay, Secretary & Treasurer

Legal Aid New Brunswick
PO Box 20026, Saint John NB E2L 5B2
Tel: 506-633-6030; *Fax:* 506-633-8994
Overview: A small provincial organization
Mission: Provides Duty Counsel lawyers at Provincial Court in Sussex, Hampton, Saint John & St. Stephen in adult & youth courts; provides lawyers for trials to successful applicants for serious criminal charges & for parents when the Dept. of Health & Community Services is applying for permanent custody of the child/children

Legal Aid Ontario (LAO) / Aide juridique Ontario
#200, 40 Dundas St. West, Toronto ON M5G 2H1
Tel: 416-979-1446; *Fax:* 416-979-8669
Toll-Free: 800-668-8258
info@lao.on.ca
www.legalaid.on.ca
twitter.com/legalaidontario
www.youtube.com/user/LegalAidOntario
Overview: A small provincial organization founded in 1998
Mission: To promote access to justice throughout Ontario for low income individuals by means of providing consistently high quality legal aid services in a cost-effective & efficient manner
Chief Officer(s):
John McCamus, Chair
Bob Ward, President/CEO

Legal Aid Society of Alberta (LAA)
Revillion Building, #400, 10320 - 102 Ave., Edmonton AB T5J 4A1
Tel: 780-644-4971; *Fax:* 780-415-2618
Toll-Free: 888-845-3342
Other Communication: Tollfree fax: 1-866-382-7253
lsc@legalaid.ab.ca
www.legalaid.ab.ca
Also Known As: Legal Aid Alberta
Overview: A small provincial organization founded in 1970
Mission: To provide a continuum of innovative & cost-effective legal services for people in need throughout Alberta
Finances: *Annual Operating Budget:* $50,000-$100,000; *Funding Sources:* Government of Alberta; Federal Government; Alberta Law Foundation; Client contributions; Interest
Activities: Five offices in Alberta; *Speaker Service:* Yes
Chief Officer(s):
Suzanne Polkosnik, President/CEO

Legal Archives Society of Alberta (LASA)
#400, 1015 - 4th St. SW, Calgary AB T2R 1J4
Tel: 403-244-5510; *Fax:* 403-454-4419
lasa@legalarchives.ca
legalarchives.ca
Overview: A small provincial charitable organization founded in 1990
Mission: To preserve complete & accurate documentation & provide resources for research on the evaluation of law & society in Alberta
Affiliation(s): Archives Society of Alberta; Association of Canadian Archivists
Finances: *Annual Operating Budget:* $250,000-$500,000; *Funding Sources:* Donations; Grant from the Law Society of Alberta
Membership: 450 individual; *Member Profile:* Members of Alberta's legal profession
Activities: Direct mail campaigns; Historical dinners; Auctions; Book launches; Display openings; *Library:* Legal History Library; Open to public by appointment
Chief Officer(s):
Shaun MacIsaac, Chair

Legal Education Society of Alberta (LESA)
#2610, 10104 - 103 Ave., Edmonton AB T5J 0H8
Tel: 780-420-1987; *Fax:* 780-425-0885
Toll-Free: 800-282-3900
lesa@lesa.org
www.lesaonline.org
www.linkedin.com/company/legal-education-society-of-alberta
www.facebook.com/lesaonline
twitter.com/lesaonline
Overview: A medium-sized provincial organization founded in 1975
Mission: To educate providers of legal services in Alberta; To increase awareness of issues affecting the legal profession; To maintain & increase professional responsibility & competence; To develop & provide education in law, skills, & ethics
Activities: Providing continuing legal education seminars for lawyers & support staff; Publishing seminar materials, practice manuals, & Canadian Centre for Professional Legal Education (CPLED) materials
Chief Officer(s):
Tamara Buckwold, Chair
Aaron D. Martens, Secretary-Treasurer
Jennifer Flynn, Executive Director & Director, Canadian Centre for Professional Legal Education (CPLED) Alberta, 780-420-1988

Legal Information Society of Nova Scotia (LISNS)
5523B Young St., Halifax NS B3K 1Z7
Tel: 902-454-2198; *Fax:* 902-455-3105
Toll-Free: 800-665-9779
lisns@legalinfo.org
www.legalinfo.org
www.facebook.com/LegalSeagull
twitter.com/LegalInfoNS
Previous Name: Public Legal Education Society of Nova Scotia
Overview: A medium-sized provincial charitable organization founded in 1982
Mission: To provide Nova Scotians easy access to information & resources about the law
Finances: *Funding Sources:* Law Foundation of Nova Scotia; Department of Justice Canada; Nova Scotia Department of Justice; Donations
Activities: Providing legal information through online resources, publications on various topics, dial-a-law, a legal information line, the lawyer referral service, workshops, & training sessions; Fundraising; *Awareness Events:* Annual Law Day Lunch, April; *Speaker Service:* Yes
Chief Officer(s):
Kevin A. MacDonald, President

A Legal Resource Centre for Persons with Disabilities *See* ARCH Disability Law Centre

Legal Services Society (LSS)
#400, 510 Burrard St., Vancouver BC V6C 3A8
Tel: 604-601-6000; *Fax:* 604-682-7967
Other Communication: Blog: factum.mylawbc.com
www.lss.bc.ca
www.facebook.com/legalaidbc
twitter.com/legalaidbc
Also Known As: Legal Aid
Overview: A large provincial organization founded in 1979
Mission: To assist low income individuals to resolve their legal problems by providing a spectrum of services that promote their effective participation in the justice system
Finances: *Annual Operating Budget:* Greater than $5 Million; *Funding Sources:* Provincial government; Law Foundation of BC; Notary Foundation
Membership: *Committees:* Executive; Finance; Stakeholder Engagement
Chief Officer(s):
Mark Benton, CEO
Publications:
• Legal Aid BC Update
Type: Newsletter

Légion de Marie - Senatus de Montréal / Legion of Mary - Senatus of Montréal
1071, rue de la Cathédrale, Montréal QC H3B 2V4
Tél: 514-866-1661
info@smlm.org
www.smlm.org
Aperçu: *Dimension:* petite; *Envergure:* internationale
Membre(s) du bureau directeur:
Farida Moubayed, Présidente
Publications:
• Alfie Lambe Newsletter
Type: Newsletter
• Manuel officiel de la légion de Marie
Type: Handbook

Legion of Mary - Senatus of Montréal *Voir* Légion de Marie - Senatus de Montréal

La Légion royale canadienne *See* The Royal Canadian Legion

Legislative Recording & Broadcast Association
c/o Broadcasting & Recording Service, Queen's Park, Toronto ON M7A 1A2
Tel: 416-325-7900; *Fax:* 416-325-7916
Overview: A small provincial organization

Member of: Legislative Assemblies
Finances: *Annual Operating Budget:* Less than $50,000
2 volunteer(s)
Membership: 16; *Member Profile:* Employees of Canadian legislative assemblies

Lennox & Addington Association for Community Living
99 Richmond Blvd., Napanee ON K7R 3S3
Tel: 613-354-2185; *Fax:* 613-354-0815
Previous Name: Lennox & Addington Association for the Mentally Retarded
Overview: A small local organization
Mission: To offer day support & services to people with disabilities as well as family support
Member of: Community Living Ontario
Chief Officer(s):
Barb Fabius, Executive Director

Lennox & Addington Association for the Mentally Retarded
See Lennox & Addington Association for Community Living

Lennox & Addington County Law Association
97 Thomas St. East, Napanee ON K7R 4B9
Tel: 613-654-5469
Toll-Free: 866-603-6383
lalaw@kingston.net
Overview: A small local organization founded in 1953
Membership: 30 individual
Activities: *Library:*

Lennox & Addington Historical Society
PO Box 392, Napanee ON K7R 3P5
Tel: 613-354-3027; *Fax:* 613-354-1005
Membership@LennoxandAddingtonHistoricalSociety.ca
www.lennoxandaddingtonhistoricalsociety.ca
Also Known As: Macpherson House & Park
Overview: A small local organization founded in 1907
Mission: To promote the study, practice, knowledge & preservation of the history of the county of Lennox & Addington
Member of: Ontario Historical Society; Ontario Museums Association
Membership: *Fees:* $25 single; $30 corporate; $35 family; $525 lifetime
Activities: Operates Lennox & Addington County Museum & Archives & MacPherson House; *Library:* Archives; Open to public
Chief Officer(s):
Jane Foster, Manager, Museum
jfoster@lennox-addington.on.ca

Lennoxville-Ascot Historical & Museum Society (LAHMS) / Société d'histoire et de musée de Lennoxville-Ascot
9, rue Speid, Sherbrooke QC J1M 1R9
Tel: 819-564-0409; *Fax:* 819-564-8951
uplands@uplands.ca
www.uplands.ca
www.facebook.com/uplandslahms
Overview: A small local organization founded in 1970
Mission: To collect, preserve, & exhibit material from the Lennoxville-Ascot region of Québec; To provide genealogical & historical information
Finances: *Funding Sources:* Donations; Fundraising
Activités: Displaying local antiques at the Uplands Cultural & Heritage Centre; Promoting local history; *Service de conférenciers:* Oui; *Bibliothèque:* Lennoxville-Ascot Historical & Museum Society Reference Library

The Leon & Thea Koerner Foundation
PO Box 39209, Stn. Point Grey, 3695 West 10th Ave., Vancouver BC V6R 4P1
Tel: 604-224-2611
www.koernerfoundation.ca
Overview: A small provincial charitable organization founded in 1955
Mission: To assist & support development projects by registered charitable organizations in cultural & creative arts & social services areas in BC

Leprosy Relief (Canada) Inc. *Voir* Secours aux lépreux (Canada) inc.

Lesbian & Gay Community Appeal Foundation *See* Community One Foundation

Lesbian & Gay Immigration Task Force
1170 Bute St., Vancouver BC V6E 1Z6
legitvancouver@gmail.com
www.legit.ca
Overview: A small local organization
Mission: To provide immigration information & support to queer, lesbian, gay, bisexual, & transgendered people; To end discrimination in Canada's immigration regulations

LEGIT - Toronto
PO Box 111, Stn. F, Toronto ON M4Y 2L4
Tel: 416-392-6874
toronto@legit.ca

Lésions Médullaires Canada *See* Spinal Cord Injury Canada

Lesser Slave Lake Indian Regional Council (LSLIRC)
PO Box 269, Slave Lake AB T0G 2A0
Tel: 780-849-4943; *Fax:* 780-849-4975
www.lslirc.com
Overview: A small local organization founded in 1971
Mission: To help improve the ecnomimic, social & educational well being of its member First Nations
Finances: *Funding Sources:* Federal & provincial government
Membership: 5; *Member Profile:* First Nations band governments

Let's Talk Science
1584 North Routledge Park, London ON N6H 5L6
Tel: 519-474-4081; *Fax:* 519-474-4085
Toll-Free: 877-474-4081
www.letstalkscience.ca
www.facebook.com/LetsTalkScience
twitter.com/LetsTalkScience
Overview: A medium-sized national organization
Mission: Strives to improve Science literacy through leadership, innovative educational programs, research and advocacy. It motivates and empowers youth to use science, technology and engineering to develop critical skills, knowledge and attitudes needed to thrive in our world.
Finances: *Funding Sources:* Public & private sponsorship
Chief Officer(s):
Bonnie Schmidt, President

Lethbridge & District Association of Realtors
522 - 6 St. South, Lethbridge AB T1J 2E2
Tel: 403-328-8838; *Fax:* 403-328-8906
eo@ldar.ca
www.ldar.ca
twitter.com/LDAR2013
Previous Name: Lethbridge Real Estate Board
Overview: A small local organization overseen by Alberta Real Estate Association
Mission: To provide real estate information on the Lethbridge area; to serve as a forum to network & build connections within the real estate community.
Member of: Alberta Real Estate Association; Canadian Real Estate Association
Membership: 291; *Member Profile:* Brokers; associate brokers
Activities: Training & educational courses & seminars; advocacy at all levels of government, regulatory bodies, CREA & AREA

Lethbridge & District Humane Society
PO Box 783, 2920 - 16th Ave. North, Lethbridge AB T1J 3Z6
Tel: 403-320-8991
pets4you2@hotmail.com
www.humanehaven.ab.ca
Overview: A small local charitable organization founded in 1970
Mission: To spay/neuter all adult animals prior to adoption; To shelter, protect & provide for stray, abandoned, orphaned & unwanted cats & dogs & to place them in the best possible homes; To provide information, advice & counsel to help people understand the fundamentals of responsible pet ownership
Member of: Canadian Federation of Humane Societies; Alberta Society for the Prevention of Cruelty to Animals
Finances: *Annual Operating Budget:* Less than $50,000; *Funding Sources:* Adoption fees; donations; fundraising; sale of promotional items
Staff Member(s): 1; 80 volunteer(s)
Membership: 275; *Fees:* $15 single; $20 family; $10 senior/child; *Committees:* Shelter; Adoption; Office & Cleaning; Fundraising; Public Relations; Building Maintenance & Office Supply; Dogwalking; Youth Group; Statistician; Building
Activities: *Awareness Events:* Annual Dog Jog
Chief Officer(s):
Sherry VanderGriendt, Contact

Lethbridge & District Japanese Garden Society
PO Box 751, Lethbridge AB T1J 3Z6
Tel: 403-328-3511; *Fax:* 403-328-0511
info@nikkayuko.com
www.nikkayuko.com
www.facebook.com/123765594310823
twitter.com/NikkaYuko
Also Known As: Nikka Yuko Japanese Garden
Overview: A small local organization founded in 1965
Mission: To acquaint visitors with cultural & historical background; to create support for garden philosophy of authenticity & meditative/contemplative setting; to create a unique attraction drawing large numbers to foster economic betterment of the community; to contribute to education fields such as arts, botany & general gardening
Member of: Lethbridge Chamber of Commerce
Affiliation(s): Chinook Tourist Association; Community Volunteer Centre
Membership: *Fees:* $30 single; $40 family
Chief Officer(s):
John Harding, President

Lethbridge & District Pro-Life Association
#1805 - 9 Ave. North, Lethbridge AB T1H 1H8
Tel: 403-320-5433; *Fax:* 403-380-2827
lprolife@shaw.ca
www.lifelethbridge.org
www.facebook.com/lprolife
Overview: A small local charitable organization founded in 1977 overseen by Alliance for Life
Mission: To increase public awareness concerning life issues; To recognize the right to life; To maintain the principle of the intrinsic value of human life
Finances: *Funding Sources:* Membership dues; churches; Knights of Columbus; individual donors; Hike for Life
Membership: *Fees:* $10 students; $20 regular
Activities: Speaker's Forum; *Speaker Service:* Yes; *Library:* Open to public
Awards:
• Elsie Alexander Pro-Life Scholarship
; *Amount:* $1,000

Lethbridge AIDS Connection Society *See* Lethbridge HIV Connection

Lethbridge Association for Community Living (LACL)
527 - 6 St. South, Lethbridge AB T1J 2E1
Tel: 403-327-2911; *Fax:* 403-320-7054
mail@lacl.ca
www.lacl.ca
Overview: A small local charitable organization founded in 1957
Mission: To advocate for & to provide support to individuals with developmental disabilities & their families/guardians; to assist in gaining full inclusion in the community
Finances: *Annual Operating Budget:* $100,000-$250,000
Staff Member(s): 3; 40 volunteer(s)
Membership: 75; *Fees:* $10 individual; $20 family; *Member Profile:* Individuals; families/guardians
Activities: *Speaker Service:* Yes
Chief Officer(s):
Dave Lawson, Executive Director
dave.lawson@lacl.ca

Lethbridge Chamber of Commerce
#200, 529 - 6 St. South, Lethbridge AB T1J 2E1
Tel: 403-327-1586; *Fax:* 403-327-1001
office@lethbridgechamber.com
www.lethbridgechamber.com
www.facebook.com/LethbridgeChamber
twitter.com/lethchamber
www.youtube.com/lethchamber
Overview: A medium-sized local organization founded in 1889
Mission: To serve and represent the interests of its members by promoting and enhancing free enterprise, for the benefit of the social and economic environment of the City of Lethbridge
Member of: Alberta Chamber of Commerce; Canadian Chamber of Commerce
Finances: *Annual Operating Budget:* $50,000-$100,000; *Funding Sources:* Membership
Staff Member(s): 3; 150 volunteer(s)
Membership: 750 businesses; *Fees:* Schedule available, based upon number of employees; *Member Profile:* Representatives from all business sectors; *Committees:* Business Affairs; Special Events; Business & Education; Finance; Government Relations; Member Services; Tourism Connection
Activities: Holding workshops, seminars, & speaker sessions; Offering business education opportunities; *Speaker Service:* Yes
Chief Officer(s):

Karla Pyrch, Executive Director
karla@lethbridgchamber.com

Lethbridge Community College Faculty Association (LCCFA)
3000 College Dr. South, Lethbridge AB T1K 1L6
Tel: 403-320-3217
Overview: A small local organization
Member of: Alberta Colleges Institute Faculty Association
Staff Member(s): 1
Chief Officer(s):
Rika Snip, Acting President
Rika.Snip@LethbridgeCollege.ca

Lethbridge Fish & Game Association (LFGA)
PO Box 495, Lethbridge AB T1J 3Z1
Tel: 403-308-3541
lfga.info@gmail.com
www.lfga.org
Overview: A small local organization founded in 1923
Mission: To promote, through education, lobbying and programs, the conservation & utilization of fish & wildlife & to protect & enhance the habitat upon which they depend
Member of: Alberta Fish & Game Association
Finances: Annual Operating Budget: Less than $50,000
900 volunteer(s)
Membership: 1,300; Fees: $15 youth; $35 regular; $60 family; Committees: Big Game; Bird Game; Casino; Outdoor Education; Political Action; Publicity
Chief Officer(s):
Ken Peterson, President
lfga.president@gmail.com

Lethbridge Handicraft Guild
Bowman Art Centre, 811 - 5 Ave. South, Lethbridge AB T1J 0V2
Tel: 403-328-7488
Overview: A small local organization
Affiliation(s): Handweavers, Spinners & Dyers of Alberta
Finances: Annual Operating Budget: $250,000-$500,000
Staff Member(s): 40

Lethbridge HIV Connection (LHC)
1206 - 6th Ave. South, Lethbridge AB T1J 1A4
Tel: 403-328-8186; Fax: 403-328-8564
info@lethbridgehiv.com
www.lethbridgehiv.com
Previous Name: Lethbridge AIDS Connection Society
Overview: A medium-sized local charitable organization founded in 1986 overseen by Canadian AIDS Society
Mission: To support, educate, advocate & facilitate compassionate & effective community responses to HIV
Member of: Alberta Community Council on HIV; United Way of Southwestern Alberta
Finances: Funding Sources: Alberta Community HIV Fund; Alberta Community Council on HIV; Health Canada; Alberta Health & Wellness; Public Health Agency of Canada; Donations
Activities: Information line; educational presentations; support groups; counselling; advocacy; volunteer program; Awareness Events: World AIDS Day Candlelight Vigil, Dec; Speaker Service: Yes; Library: Open to public

Lethbridge Lacrosse Association
PO Box 874, Lethbridge AB T1J 3Z8
Tel: 403-715-3291
www.lethbridgelacrosse.com
www.facebook.com/lethbridge.lacrosse
twitter.com/lethlax
Overview: A small local organization
Mission: To promote lacrosse in southern Alberta
Chief Officer(s):
Mark Stewart, Program Director
progdirector@lethbridgelacrosse.com

Lethbridge Naturalists' Society
PO Box 1691, Stn. Main, Lethbridge AB T1J 4K4
Overview: A small local organization founded in 1966
Mission: To encourage knowledge & appreciation of natural history & understanding of ecological processes; To organize lectures, visual presentations & field trips; to conduct research on natural history; To become involved in environmental issues relating to conservation of the natural environment
Member of: Federation of Alberta Naturalists
Finances: Funding Sources: Membership fees
Activities: Winter programs; summer field trips
Chief Officer(s):
Becky Little, Contact
becky.little@lethbridge.ca

Lethbridge Oldtimers Sports Association (LOSA)
PO Box 84, Lethbridge AB T1J 3Y3
www.losa.ca
Overview: A small local organization
Mission: To organize recreational hockey games for adults
Membership: Fees: $50
Chief Officer(s):
Brian Wright, President

Lethbridge Real Estate Board See Lethbridge & District Association of Realtors

Lethbridge Soccer Association
2501 - 28 St. South, Lethbridge AB T1K 7L6
Tel: 403-320-5425; Fax: 403-327-5847
lethbridgesoccer.com
www.facebook.com/LethbridgeSoccerAssociation
twitter.com/LethSoccer
Overview: A small local organization overseen by Alberta Soccer Association
Member of: Alberta Soccer Association
Chief Officer(s):
Steven Dudas, General Manager
steve@lethbridgesoccer.com

Lethbridge Soup Kitchen Association
802 - 2A Ave. North, Lethbridge AB T1H 0C9
Tel: 403-320-8688
www.soupbridge.org
Overview: A small local charitable organization founded in 1984
Mission: To feed the hungry of Lethbridge & area
Staff Member(s): 1
Activities: Provision of hot lunch meals; referrals to other agencies
Chief Officer(s):
Joyce Crittenden, Executive Director

Lethbridge Symphony Orchestra (LSO)
PO Box 1101, Lethbridge AB T1J 4A2
Tel: 403-328-6808; Fax: 403-380-4418
Toll-Free: 855-328-6808
info@lethbridgesymphony.org
www.lethbridgesymphony.org
ca.linkedin.com/company/lethbridge-symphony-orchestra
www.facebook.com/lethbridgesymphony
twitter.com/LethSymphony
Also Known As: Lethbridge Symphony Association
Overview: A small local charitable organization founded in 1960 overseen by Orchestras Canada
Mission: To promote the orchestra & provide memorable musical experiences for their audiences
Member of: Allied Arts Council of Lethbridge; Orchestras Canada
Finances: Annual Operating Budget: $250,000-$500,000; Funding Sources: Box office; Donations; Government grants; Advertising
Staff Member(s): 8; 100 volunteer(s)
Membership: 500; Fees: Schedule available; Committees: Fund Development; Marketing; Policy & By-Law; Love Notes; Golf Tournament
Activities: Performing concert series; Introducing children to live, classical music through education & outreach programs; Collaborating with community music ensembles; Internships: Yes
Chief Officer(s):
Melanie Gattiker, Executive Director
melanie@lethbridgesymphony.org
Glenn Klassen, Director, Music
Mary Opyr, Manager, Finance
mary@lethbridgesymphony.org
Meetings/Conferences:
• Lethbridge Symphony Orchestra 2018 Annual General Meeting, 2018
Scope: Local

Lethbridge Therapeutic Riding Association (LTRA)
RR#8-24-6, Lethbridge AB T1J 4P4
Tel: 403-328-2165; Fax: 403-317-0235
info@ltra.ca
www.ltra.ca
Also Known As: Rainbow Riding Centre
Overview: A small local charitable organization founded in 1977
Mission: To provide the opportunity for improved physical & emotional well-being for people of all ages & abilities who participate in therapeutic, recreational, educational & competitive riding programs at Rainbow Riding Centre
Member of: Canadian Therapeutic Riding Association

Finances: Annual Operating Budget: $100,000-$250,000
Staff Member(s): 2; 200 volunteer(s)
Membership: 260; Fees: Schedule available; Committees: Facility; Program; Fundraising; Public relations; Foundation
Activities: 5-6 riding sessions per year; summer Ride On camp; Easter clinic
Chief Officer(s):
Rick Austin, Executive Director
raustin@ltra.ca

Leucan - Association for Children with Cancer Voir Leucan - Association pour les enfants atteints de cancer

Leucan - Association pour les enfants atteints de cancer / Leucan - Association for Children with Cancer
#300, 550, av Beaumont, Montréal QC H3N 1V1
Tél: 514-731-3696; Téléc: 514-731-2667
Ligne sans frais: 800-361-9643
www.leucan.qc.ca
www.linkedin.com/company/1115189
www.facebook.com/leucanpageprovinciale
twitter.com/leucan
instagram.com/leucan
Aperçu: Dimension: moyenne; Envergure: provinciale; fondée en 1978
Mission: Accroître la confiance en l'avenir des enfants atteints de cancer et de leurs familles
Membre de: Imagine Canada; Association des camps certifiés du Québec; Children's Oncology Camp Association International; Association canadienne des camps pédiatriques en oncologie
Finances: Budget de fonctionnement annuel: Plus de $5 Million; Fonds: Campagnes; dons
Membre(s) du personnel: 70; 2000 bénévole(s)
Membre: 3600 familles; Montant de la cotisation: Barème
Activités: Camp Vol d'été Leucan-CSN; Fête de Noël; Karting; Défi têtes rasées; Marche et course à la fête des Mères; Camp d'Halloween Leucan-Simple Plan; Fins de semaine de répit; Cueillette de pommes; Cabane à sucre; Événements de sensibilisation: Omnium Michel Blouin; Campagne de tirelires; Défi ski 12 h Leucan; L'Expérience Leucan; Défi Loïc 12 h vélo; Stagiaires: Oui; Bibliothèque: Centre d'information Leucan; Bibliothèque publique rendez-vous
Membre(s) du bureau directeur:
Pascale Bouchard, Directeur général
pascale.bouchard@leucan.qc.ca
Prix, Bourses:
• Prix Jocelyn-Demers
; Amount: 1,000$
• Prix Coup de Coeur
Meetings/Conferences:
• Leucan - Association pour les enfants atteints de cancer Assemblée générale annuelle 2018, 2018
Scope: Provincial
Publications:
• L'espoir [publication de Leucan - Association pour les enfants atteints de cancer]
Type: Newsletter; Frequency: s-a.

The Leukemia & Lymphoma Society of Canada (LLSC) / Société de leucémie et lymphome du Canada
#804, 2 Lansing Square, Toronto ON M2J 4P8
Tel: 416-661-9541; Fax: 416-661-7799
Toll-Free: 877-668-8326
AdminCanada@lls.org
www.llscanada.org
www.linkedin.com/company/5127044
www.facebook.com/LeukemiaandLymphomaSocietyofCanada
twitter.com/llscanada
www.youtube.com/llscanada
Previous Name: Leukemia Research Fund of Canada
Overview: A medium-sized national charitable organization founded in 1955
Mission: To cure leukemia, lymphoma, Hodgkin's disease & myeloma, & to improve the quality of life of patients & their families
Affiliation(s): Canadian Centre for Philanthropy
Finances: Funding Sources: Fundraising
Membership: Committees: Medical & Scientific Advisory
Activities: Awareness Events: Leukemia Awareness Month, June; Internships: Yes
Chief Officer(s):
Shelagh Tippet-Fagyas, President
Ted Moroz, Chair

Atlantic Canada Branch
#H2, 1660 Hollis St., Halifax NS B3J 1V7
Tel: 902-422-5999
Toll-Free: 855-515-5572
www.llscanada.org/atlantic-region
www.facebook.com/llsatlantic
Chief Officer(s):
Joe DiPenta, Regional Director, 905-422-5999 Ext. 7520, Fax: 902-422-5968
joe.dipenta@lls.org
British Columbia/Yukon Branch
#303, 1401 West Broadway, Vancouver BC V6H 1H6
Tel: 604-733-2873
Toll-Free: 866-547-5433
Chief Officer(s):
Donna McLennan, Regional Director
donna.mclennan@lls.org
Sharon Paulse, Manager, Patient Services
sharon.paulse@lls.org
Scott Kehoe, Manager, Fund Development
scott.kehoe@lls.org
Ontario Branch
#804, 2 Lansing Sq., Toronto ON M2J 4P8
Tel: 647-253-5530
Chief Officer(s):
Sandra Harris, Regional Director
Ontario Branch - Ottawa
#701, 116 Albert St., Ottawa ON K1P 5G3
Tel: 613-234-1274
Prairies/Territories Branch - Calgary
#316, 1212 31 Avenue NE, Calgary AB T2E 7S8
Tel: 403-263-5300
www.llscanada.org/prairies-region
Chief Officer(s):
Lauren Atkinson, Regional Director, Fax: 403-263-5303
lauren.atkinson@lls.org
Prairies/Territories Branch - Edmonton
#208, 10240 - 124th St., Edmonton AB T5N 3W6
Tel: 780-758-4261
Prairies/Territories Branch - Saskatoon
#202, 402 - 21st St. East, Saskatoon SK S7K 0C3
Tel: 306-242-6611
Québec Branch
#602, 740, rue St-Maurice, Montréal QC H3C 1L5
Tel: 514-875-1000
Chief Officer(s):
Andy Fratino, Acting Regional Director
andy.fratino@lls.org

Leukemia Research Fund of Canada See The Leukemia & Lymphoma Society of Canada

Lewisporte & Area Chamber of Commerce
395B Main St., Lewisporte NL A0G 3A0
Tel: 709-535-2500; *Fax:* 709-535-2482
Overview: A small local organization

LGBT Family Coalition *Voir* Coalition des familles LGBT

Liaison of Independent Filmmakers of Toronto (LIFT)
1137 Dupont St., Toronto ON M6K 3P6
Tel: 416-588-6444; *Fax:* 416-588-7017
lift.ca
www.facebook.com/LIFT.ca
twitter.com/LIFTfilm
Overview: A small local charitable organization founded in 1979
Mission: To support & encourage independent filmmaking through the exchange of information, access to film production equipment & post-production facilities, regular series of workshops & regular public film exhibitions
Member of: Independent Media Arts Alliance; Artist-run Centres & Collectives of Ontario
Affiliation(s): Independent Film & Video Alliance; Association of National Non-Profit Artist-Run Centres; Artist Run Centres Toronto
Finances: *Annual Operating Budget:* $500,000-$1.5 Million
Staff Member(s): 5
Membership: 600+ individual; *Fees:* $60 individual; $70 associate; $130 full; *Member Profile:* Three levels of membership: affiliate, associate, full; all new members join at affiliate level & upgrade (via volunteer hours & an additional fee) to associate or full status, if desired; *Committees:* Workshops; Equipment; Lobbying; Programming; Magazine
Activities: *Library:*
Chief Officer(s):

Kathryn MacKay, Chair
Ben Donoghue, Executive Director

The Liberal Party of Canada (LPC) / Le Parti Libéral du Canada (PLC)
#920, 350 Albert St., Ottawa ON K1P 6M8
Fax: 613-235-7208
Toll-Free: 888-542-3725
assistance@liberal.ca
www.liberal.ca
www.linkedin.com/company/liberal-party-of-canada
www.facebook.com/LiberalCA
twitter.com/Liberal_party
www.youtube.com/user/liberalvideo
Previous Name: The National Liberal Federation
Overview: A large national organization founded in 1867
Mission: To seek a common ground of understanding among the people of the provinces & territories of Canada; To advocate liberal philosophies, principles & policies; To promote the election of candidates of the Liberal Party to the Parliament of Canada
Affiliation(s): Liberal International
Finances: *Annual Operating Budget:* Greater than $5 Million; *Funding Sources:* Donations
Staff Member(s): 30
Membership: Over 50,000; *Committees:* Policy Development; Organization; Constitutional & Legal; Communications & Publicity; Multiculturalism; Platform; National Campaign; Permanent Appeal; Management; Financial Management; Young Liberals of Canada; National Women's Liberal Commission; Aboriginal Peoples' Commission; Seniors' Commission
Activities: *Speaker Service:* Yes
Chief Officer(s):
Justin Trudeau, Prime Minister & Party Leader
Anna Gainey, National President
Azam Ishmael, National Director
Suzanne Cowan, National Vice-President, English
Sébastien Fassier, National Vice-President, French

The Liberal Party of Canada (British Columbia) (LPCBC) / Parti libéral du Canada (Colombie-Britannique)
#460, 580 Hornby St., Vancouver BC V6C 3B6
Tel: 604-664-3777; *Fax:* 877-411-6511
Toll-Free: 888-542-3725
bcinfo@liberal.ca
bc.liberal.ca
www.facebook.com/LPCBC
twitter.com/lpcbc
www.youtube.com/user/liberalvideo
Overview: A medium-sized provincial organization overseen by The Liberal Party of Canada
Staff Member(s): 6; 10 volunteer(s)
Membership: 15,000
Activities: *Internships:* Yes; *Speaker Service:* Yes
Chief Officer(s):
Manjot Hallen, Party Chair
mhallen@liberal.ca

The Liberal Party of Canada (Manitoba)
Molgat Place, 635 Broadway, Winnipeg MB R3C 0X1
Fax: 204-284-1492
Toll-Free: 888-542-3725
manitoba.liberal.ca
www.facebook.com/LPCMB.PLCMB
twitter.com/liberalpartymb
Overview: A medium-sized provincial organization overseen by The Liberal Party of Canada
Chief Officer(s):
David Johnson, Executive Director
djohnson@liberal.ca

Liberal Party of Canada (Ontario) (LPC(O)) / Parti libéral du Canada (Ontario)
#420, 10 St. Mary St., Toronto ON M4Y 1P9
Tel: 416-921-2844; *Fax:* 416-921-3880
Toll-Free: 800-361-3881
ontario@liberal.ca
ontario.liberal.ca
www.facebook.com/LPCO.PLCO
twitter.com/lpc_o
Overview: A medium-sized provincial organization overseen by The Liberal Party of Canada
Staff Member(s): 14
Chief Officer(s):

Tyler Banham, President
president@lpco.ca
Mike Rosati, Director, Operations
mrosati@lpco.ca

Liberal Party of Canada in Alberta (LPC(A))
#308, 10240 - 124 St. NW, Edmonton AB T5N 3W6
Tel: 780-328-3889; *Fax:* 613-235-7208
alberta@liberal.ca
alberta.liberal.ca
www.facebook.com/lpcalberta
twitter.com/lpca
Overview: A medium-sized provincial organization overseen by The Liberal Party of Canada
Chief Officer(s):
Robbie Schuett, Chair
robert.m.schuett@schuettlaw.com

Liberal Party of Newfoundland & Labrador / Parti libéral de Terre-Neuve et du Labrador
#102, 1 Crosbie Place, St. John's NL A1B 3Y8
Tel: 709-754-1813
Toll-Free: 888-971-6991
info@nlliberals.ca
nlliberals.ca
www.facebook.com/nlliberals
twitter.com/nlliberals
www.youtube.com/nlliberals
Overview: A medium-sized provincial organization overseen by The Liberal Party of Canada
Chief Officer(s):
Dwight Ball, Leader

Liberal Party of Nova Scotia
PO Box 723, #1400, 5151 George St., Halifax NS B3J 2T3
Tel: 902-429-1993; *Fax:* 902-423-1624
office@liberal.ns.ca
www.liberal.ns.ca
www.facebook.com/NSLiberalParty
twitter.com/NSLiberal
www.youtube.com/nsliberalparty
Also Known As: Nova Scotia Liberal Party
Overview: A small provincial organization overseen by The Liberal Party of Canada
Staff Member(s): 4
Chief Officer(s):
Stephen McNeil, Leader
mcneilsr@gov.ns.ca
John Gillis, President

Liberal Party of Prince Edward Island / Parti libéral de l'Ile du Prince Édouard
PO Box 2559, 6 Pownal St., Charlottetown PE C1A 8C2
Tel: 902-368-3449; *Fax:* 902-368-3687
Toll-Free: 877-740-3449
officialagent@liberalpei.ca
www.liberalpei.ca
www.facebook.com/PEILiberals
twitter.com/peiliberalparty
Overview: A medium-sized provincial organization overseen by The Liberal Party of Canada
Chief Officer(s):
Wade MacLauchlan, Leader
Isaac MacDonald, Executive Director
Carol Doyle, Office Manager
carol@liberalpei.ca

The Libertarian Party of Canada
#126, 372 Rideau St., Ottawa ON K1N 1G7
Tel: 613-288-9089
www.libertarian.ca
www.linkedin.com/company/libertarian-party-of-canada
www.facebook.com/libertarianCDN
twitter.com/libertarianCDN
Overview: A small national organization
Chief Officer(s):
Timothy Moen, Party Leader

Libertel de la Capitale Nationale See National Capital FreeNet

Libra House Inc.
PO Box 449, Stn. B, Happy Valley-Goose Bay NL A0P 1E0
Tel: 709-896-8022; *Fax:* 709-896-8223
Toll-Free: 877-896-3014; *Crisis Hot-Line:* 709-896-3014
librahouse@nf.aibn.com
www.librahouse.ca
Overview: A small local organization founded in 1983

Mission: To provide crisis shelter services for abused women & their children; To offer support & education to women
Member of: Provincial Association Against Family Violence
Staff Member(s): 7
Activities: Providing a 24-hour crisis support line
Chief Officer(s):
Janet O'Donnell, Executive Director

Librarians Without Borders (LWB)
info@lwb-online.org
www.lwb-online.org
www.facebook.com/librarianswithoutborders
twitter.com/LWB_Online
www.flickr.com/photos/librarians-without-borders
Overview: A small international organization founded in 2005
Mission: To address the information resource inequity in different regions of the world; To improve access to information, regardless of geography, language, or religion; To build sustainable libraries & support their librarians
Finances: *Funding Sources:* Donations; Fundraising
Membership: *Fees:* Free; *Committees:* Dalhousie University; McGill University; University of British Columbia; University of Toronto; University of Western Ontario; University of Ottawa
Activities: Partnering with community organizations in developing regions
Chief Officer(s):
Melanie Sellar, Co-Executive Director
melanie.sellar@lwb-online.org
Mark Gelsomino, Co-Executive Director
mark.gelsomino@lwb-online.org
Erika Heesen, Director, Membership & Communications
erika.heesen@lwb-online.org
Gavin Woltjer, Director, Operations
gavin.woltjer@lwb-online.org

Library Association of Alberta (LAA)
80 Baker Cres. NW, Calgary AB T2L 1R4
Tel: 403-284-5818
Toll-Free: 877-522-5550
info@laa.ca
www.laa.ca
www.linkedin.com/groups/Library-Association-Alberta-4735949
www.facebook.com/LibraryAssociationOfAlberta
twitter.com/Lib_Assn_AB
plus.google.com/114726559596090866928
Previous Name: Alberta Library Association
Overview: A medium-sized provincial organization founded in 1931
Mission: To facilitate the improvement of library services in Alberta; To promote library service throughout Alberta; To encourage cooperation among libraries & information centres across the province; To promote intellectual freedom in Alberta
Finances: *Funding Sources:* Sponsorships
Membership: *Fees:* Schedule available; *Member Profile:* Individuals, institutions, & organizations involved in library service; *Committees:* Advocacy; Association Governance; Continuing Education; Personnel; Finance; Intellectual Freedom; Member Services; Nominations & Elections
Activities: Liaising with other library organizations; Engaging in advocacy activities; Influencing government policy & legislation regarding library services; Providing continuing education opportunities; Facilitating communication among persons concerned with library & information services in Alberta
Chief Officer(s):
Christine Sheppard, Executive Director
Awards:
• Punch Jackson Award of Excellence in Library Service
Awarded to honour excellence in service, program or public relations/advocacy achievement in library service *Deadline:* March 1
• President's Award
Awarded to recognize the efforts of an individual who has made a notable impact, on a province-wide basis, in the library field in Alberta
• Student Awards
Four awards are available: two for graduating students from the School of Library & Information Studies at the University of Alberta; one graduating student from the Library & Information Technology Program at the Southern Alberta Institute of Technology; & one graduating student from the Library Technician program at Grant MacEwan University *Eligibility:* Students graduating from library programs in Alberta; *Amount:* $200
• Library Association of Alberta Scholarship
Awarded to provide Alberta residents with the opportunity to acquire education/training to enter into the profession of librarianship in the province *Eligibility:* LAA members entering the first or second year of a full-time library program *Deadline:* May 31; *Amount:* $1,500
Meetings/Conferences:
• Library Association of Alberta Annual Conference 2018, April, 2018, AB
Scope: Provincial
Description: A conference held each spring for members of the Alberta library community, featuring association annual general meetings, session presentations, networking opportunities, & a trade show. Beginning this year, the conference is no longer held jointly with the Alberta Library Trustees Association (ALTA).
Contact Information: Library Association of Alberta, Phone: 403-284-5818, Toll-Free Phone: 1-877-522-5550, Fax: 403-282-6646, E-mail: info@laa.ca, info@albertalibraryconference.com
• Library Association of Alberta Annual Conference 2019, April, 2019, AB
Scope: Provincial
Description: A conference held each spring for members of the Alberta library community, featuring association annual general meetings, session presentations, networking opportunities, & a trade show. Beginning this year, the conference is no longer held jointly with the Alberta Library Trustees Association (ALTA).
Contact Information: Library Association of Alberta, Phone: 403-284-5818, Toll-Free Phone: 1-877-522-5550, Fax: 403-282-6646, E-mail: info@laa.ca, info@albertalibraryconference.com
• Library Association of Alberta Annual Conference 2020, April, 2020, AB
Scope: Provincial
Description: A conference held each spring for members of the Alberta library community, featuring association annual general meetings, session presentations, networking opportunities, & a trade show. Beginning this year, the conference is no longer held jointly with the Alberta Library Trustees Association (ALTA).
Contact Information: Library Association of Alberta, Phone: 403-284-5818, Toll-Free Phone: 1-877-522-5550, Fax: 403-282-6646, E-mail: info@laa.ca, info@albertalibraryconference.com
Publications:
• Library Association of Alberta Membership Directory
Type: Directory; *Price:* Free with membership in the Library Association of Alberta
Profile: Contact information, place of work, & position for association members

Library Boards Association of Nova Scotia (LBANS)
135 North Park St., Bridgewater NS B4V 9B3
Tel: 902-543-2548
www.standupforlibraries.ca
Previous Name: Joint Regional Library Boards Association of Nova Scotia
Overview: A small provincial organization founded in 1976
Mission: To preserve & support quality public library service throughout Nova Scotia
Membership: *Member Profile:* Appointed persons from the nine regional library boards in Nova Scotia, such as elected councillors or volunteers with an interest in public libraries & their services
Activities: Promoting public library services across Nova Scotia; Offering a forum for the exchange of ideas; Encouraging cooperation between regional library boards; Advocating on behalf of public libraries; Liaising with government & other stakeholders
Chief Officer(s):
Christina Pottie, Executive Assistant
cpottie@southshorepubliclibraries.ca
Meetings/Conferences:
• Library Boards Association of Nova Scotia Annual Conference 2018, 2018
Scope: Provincial

Licensed Paralegals Association (Ontario) (LPA)
#100, 400 Applewood Cres., Vaughan ON L4K 0C3
Tel: 416-944-1020; *Fax:* 416-482-4922
licensedparalegalsassociation.com
Overview: A medium-sized provincial organization
Mission: To act as the self-regulating body for all paralegals who provide legal services to the public in Ontario
Membership: *Member Profile:* Paralegals licensed and regulated as of May 2008 by the Law Society of Upper Canada.
Chief Officer(s):
Robert Burd, President, 905-456-0038
burd@licensedparalegalsassociation.com
Brian Eminovski, Treasurer
eminovski@tcslegalservices.com

Licensed Practical Nurses Association & Regulatory Board of PEI *See* College of Licensed Practical Nurses of PEI

Licensed Practical Nurses Association of British Columbia (LPNABC)
#211, 3030 Lincoln Ave., Coquitlam BC V3B 6B4
Tel: 604-434-1972
info@lpnabc.ca
www.lpnabc.ca
www.facebook.com/LPNABC
twitter.com/LPNABC
www.youtube.com/user/LPNABC
Overview: A small provincial organization founded in 1951 overseen by Practical Nurses Canada
Mission: To promote professional excellence among the licensed practical nurses of British Columbia; To offer a unified voice for the province's licensed practical nurses
Member of: Practical Nurses Canada
Membership: *Fees:* $25 students & retired persons; $60 active members; *Member Profile:* Licensed practical nurses in British Columbia; Retired persons; Students; *Committees:* Communications; Conference; Finance; Legislation and Bylaw; Nominations; Promotions
Activities: Supporting licensed practical nurses in British Columbia; Lobbying for the profession; Liaising with the government & employers; Promoting the profession to the public; Organizing educational & mentoring opportunities; Facilitating provincial & national networking opportunities; Awarding education bursaries
Chief Officer(s):
Teresa McFadyen, President
Meetings/Conferences:
• Licensed Practical Nurses Association of BC AGM 2018, 2018, BC
Scope: Provincial
Publications:
• In Touch
Type: Newsletter; *Frequency:* 3 pa; *Price:* Free with membership in Licensed Practical Nurses Association of British Columbia
Profile: Association activities

Licensed Practical Nurses Association of Nova Scotia; Nova Scotia Certified Nursing Assistants Association *See* College of Licensed Practical Nurses of Nova Scotia

Lieutenant Governor's Circle on Mental Health & Addiction
#208, 14925 - 111th Ave., Edmonton AB T5M 2P6
Tel: 780-453-2201
execdir@lgcirclealberta.org
www.lgcircle.ca
www.facebook.com/LGCircle
Overview: A small provincial organization
Chief Officer(s):
Sol Rolingher, Chair
Awards:
• True Grit, True Awards
An individual who has made use of mental health &/or addictions services & inspired others to get help in the management of mental illness; or who has helped to further mental health & addictions programmes
• True Compassion, True Awards
An individual who has provided guidance in effecting the improvement of mental health & addictions programmes
• True Leadership, True Awards
An individual who has provided exceptional leadership in improving mental health & addictions programmes
• True Service, True Awards
A public body that has provided service in the improvement of mental health & addictions reduction
• True Imagination, True Awards
An individual, group or organization that has used treatment or programmes in the imaginative improvement of mental health or reduction of addictions

Life Insurance Institute of Canada *See* LOMA Canada

Life Science Association of Manitoba (LSAM)
1000 Waverley St., Winnipeg MB R3T 0P3
Tel: 204-272-5095; *Fax:* 204-272-2961
info@lsam.ca
www.lsam.ca
www.linkedin.com/groups?about=&gid=3753791&trk=anet_ug_grppro

www.facebook.com/123001494423036
twitter.com/LifeScienceMB
www.youtube.com/user/LifeScienceMB
Overview: A medium-sized provincial organization founded in 1990
Mission: To represent the life science industry in Manitoba; to provide services for companies in the industry; to promote economic development
Affiliation(s): BIOTECanada; BioTalent Canada; Life Sciences British Columbia; BioAlberta; Ag-West Biotech Inc.; Ontario Agri-Food Technologies; MaRS; Ottawa Life Sciences Council; Toronto Biotechnology Initiative; TechAlliance; The Golden Horseshoe Biosciences Network; York Biotech; BioQuebec; BioAtlantech; BioNova; PEI BioAlliance; Newfoundland & Labrador Assn of Technology Industries
Finances: Funding Sources: Membership dues
Staff Member(s): 4
Membership: 107 member organizations; Fees: Schedule available; Member Profile: Corporations involved in the manufacturing & research health care industries
Chief Officer(s):
Tracey Maconachie, President, 204-272-5096
tmaconachie@lsam.ca

Life Sciences Ontario (LSO)
#109, 1 Concorde Gate, Toronto ON M3C 3N5
Tel: 416-426-7293; Fax: 416-426-7280
admin@lifesciencesontario.ca
www.lifesciencesontario.ca
www.linkedin.com/groups?gid=91161
www.facebook.com/LifeSciencesOntario
twitter.com/LifeSciencesON
www.youtube.com/user/LifeSciencesON
Previous Name: Toronto Biotechnology Initiative
Overview: A small local organization founded in 1989
Mission: LSO collaborates with governments, academia, industry and other life science organizations in Ontario and across Canada to promote and encourage commercial success throughout this diverse sector.
Affiliation(s): Biotechnology Industry Organization; Council of Biotechnology Centres; BIOTECanada
Finances: Annual Operating Budget: $50,000-$100,000; Funding Sources: Membership fees
Membership: 400; Fees: $200 regular; $76 student;
Committees: Biofinance; Breakfast Meetings; Education; Membership; Public Interest Forum; Regulatory; Technology Transfer
Activities: Biofinance (events, awards dinner); Bioscan newsletter; community service award; education; entrepreunership program; international program; monthly meetings; public interest forum; regulatory affairs
Chief Officer(s):
Paul Lucas, Chair

Life Underwriters Association of Canada See Advocis

Life's Vision
388 Portage Ave., #A, Winnipeg MB R3C 0C8
Tel: 204-233-8047; Fax: 204-233-0523
Toll-Free: 877-233-8048
lifesvision@shaw.ca
lifesvision.ca
www.facebook.com/pages/Lifes-Vision/244844832240237
twitter.com/LifesVision1
Also Known As: League for Life in Manitoba, Inc.
Overview: A medium-sized provincial charitable organization founded in 1974
Mission: To engage in non-sectarian educational activities in order to encourage & promote among the general public an understanding & awareness of the dignity & worth of each individual human life, whatever its state & circumstances; to foster respect for all human life. Life's Vision provides information & referral services dealing with pregnancy & end of life issues, such as abortion, euthanasia & assisted suicide, & provides a voice for those opposed to abortion.
Finances: Funding Sources: Membership dues; private donations; fundraising
Activities: Field calls from people in crisis pregnancies 1-800-665-0570; Create awareness in community with truth booth display; Presentations for schools, youth groups on pre-natal development, abortion & post-abortion healing resources; Awareness Events: Life Hike; Respect for Life Week, Feb.; Annual Banquet; Speaker Service: Yes; Library: Open to public

LifeCanada / VieCanada
PO Box 138, Carleton Place ON K7C 3P3
Tel: 613-722-1552; Fax: 613-482-4937
Toll-Free: 866-780-5433
Other Communication: Local BC: 778-805-2171
info@lifecanada.org
www.lifecanada.org
www.facebook.com/LifeCanada1
twitter.com/LifeCanadaOrg
Overview: A medium-sized national organization
Mission: To represent educational pro-life groups in Canada; To promote the respect & dignity of all human life
Membership: Fees: $25 individual; $50 supporting; $5 per member, affliate/associate
Meetings/Conferences:
• The National Pro-Life Conference 2018, 2018
Scope: National
Description: A 3-day national gathering of experts and pro-life professionals from across the country and abroad.
Publications:
• LifeCanada Journal
Type: Journal; Frequency: Bi-Monthly; Price: $20 for 6 issues
Profile: Sent to every Member of Parliament and Senator as well as to pro-life organizations, supporters and benefactors.
• Reflections [a publication of LifeCanada]
Type: Magazine; Frequency: Bi-Annually; Price: $20

Lifeforce Foundation
PO Box 3117, Vancouver BC V6B 3X6
Tel: 604-649-5258
lifeforcesociety@hotmail.com
www.lifeforcefoundation.org
www.facebook.com/196062246185
Also Known As: Lifeforce
Overview: A small international charitable organization founded in 1981
Mission: To raise public awareness of the interrelationship of human, animal & environmental problems; to urge society to address & solve problems by taking into consideration the long-term effects on all parts of the ecosystem
Finances: Funding Sources: Donations; membership fees; bequests
Activities: Whale & dolphin hotline; Orca research; Lifewatch program distributes whale watching regulations & stops boaters who harass marine mammals; Marine Wildlife Rescue; educational materials & displays; all animal rights & issues

Lifesaving Society / Société de sauvetage
400 Consumers Rd., Toronto ON M2J 1P8
Tel: 416-490-8844; Fax: 416-490-8766
www.lifesavingsociety.com
www.facebook.com/lifesavingsocietyON
twitter.com/LifesavingON
Previous Name: Royal Life Saving Society Canada
Overview: A large national charitable organization founded in 1908
Mission: To prevent drowning & water-related incidents by providing lifesaving, lifeguarding & leadership education
Affiliation(s): Canadian Armed Forces; Canadian Parks & Recreation Association; Canadian Red Cross Society; L'Institut Maritime du Québec; Professional Association of Diving Instructors Canada; Royal Canadian Mounted Police; St. John Ambulance; Swimming Canada; YMCA Canada
Finances: Annual Operating Budget: $500,000-$1.5 Million
Staff Member(s): 8; 100 volunteer(s)
Membership: 87 organizations in Canada; Committees: Strategic Units - Communications & Marketing; Behavioural Change/Injury Prevention; Education; Lifeguarding; Research & Development; International Affairs
Activities: Awareness Events: National Drowning Prevention Day, July Library: Resource Centre; by appointment
Chief Officer(s):
Yvan Chalifour, Executive Director

Alberta & North West Territories Branch
13123 - 156th St., Edmonton AB T5V 1V2
Tel: 780-415-1755; Fax: 780-427-9334
experts@lifesaving.org
www.lifesaving.org
www.facebook.com/LifesavingABNWT
twitter.com/lifesavingabnwt
Chief Officer(s):
Kelly Carter, Executive Director
kelly@lifesaving.org

British Columbia & Yukon Branch
#112, 3989 Henning Dr., Burnaby BC V5C 6N5
Tel: 604-299-5450; Fax: 604-299-5795
www.lifesaving.bc.ca
www.facebook.com/LifesavingBCYK

Chief Officer(s):
Dale Miller, Executive Director

Manitoba Branch
#100, 383 Provencher Blvd., Winnipeg MB R2H 0G9
Tel: 204-956-2124; Fax: 204-944-8546
aquatics@lifesaving.mb.ca
www.lifesaving.mb.ca
www.facebook.com/lifesavingsociety.mb
twitter.com/LifesavingMB
Carl Shier, Chief Executive Officer
cshier@lifesaving.mb.ca

New Brunswick Branch
70 Melissa St., Fredericton NB E3A 6W1
Tel: 506-455-5762; Fax: 506-450-7946
www.lifesavingnb.ca
Doug Ferguson, Chief Executive Officer

Newfoundland & Labrador Branch
PO Box 8065, Stn. A, 11 Austin St., St. John's NL A1B 3M9
Tel: 709-576-1953; Fax: 709-738-1475
lifeguard@bellaliant.com
www.lifesavingnl.ca
www.facebook.com/LifesavingSocietyNL
twitter.com/LifesavingNL
Chief Officer(s):
Christopher Mercer, Executive Director

Nova Scotia Branch
5516 Spring Garden Rd., 4th Fl., Halifax NS B3J 1G6
Tel: 902-425-5450; Fax: 902-425-5606
experts@lifesavingsociety.ns.ca
www.lifesavingsociety.ns.ca
www.facebook.com/NovaScotiaLifesavingSociety
twitter.com/NSLifesaving
Chief Officer(s):
Mike Maguire, Executive Director
mike.maguire@nsls.ns.ca

Ontario & Nunavut Branch
400 Consumers Rd., Toronto ON M2J 1P8
Tel: 416-490-8844; Fax: 416-490-8766
www.lifesavingsociety.com
www.facebook.com/lifesavingsocietyON
twitter.com/LifesavingON
Chief Officer(s):
Doug Ferguson, Executive Director

Prince Edward Island Branch
40 Enman Cres., Charlottetown PE C1E 4E6
Tel: 902-368-7757; Fax: 902-368-1593
info@lifesavingsocietypei.ca
lifesavingsocietypei.ca
www.facebook.com/152048238151395
twitter.com/lifesavingpei
www.youtube.com/user/OntarioLifesaving
Chief Officer(s):
Adam Ross, President

Québec Branch
4545, av Pierre-de Coubertin, Montréal QC H1V 0B2
Tél: 514-252-3100; Téléc: 514-254-6232
Ligne sans frais: 800-265-3093
alerte@sauvetage.qc.ca
www.sauvetage.qc.ca
www.facebook.com/sauvetage1
twitter.com/sauvetage
Chief Officer(s):
Raynald Hawkins, Directeur général
rhawkins@sauvetage.qc.ca

Saskatchewan Branch
2224 Smith St., Regina SK S4P 2P4
Tel: 306-780-9255
lifesaving@sasktel.net
www.lifesavingsociety.sk.ca
www.facebook.com/SKLifesaving
twitter.com/sklifesaving
Chief Officer(s):
Shelby Rushton, Chief Executive Officer
lifesavingceo@sasktel.net

LifeSciences British Columbia
#580, 1285 West Broadway, Vancouver BC V6H 3X8
Tel: 604-669-9909; Fax: 604-669-9912
info@lifesciencesbc.ca
www.lifesciencesbc.ca
www.facebook.com/lifesciencesbc
twitter.com/lifesciences_bc
Previous Name: BC Biotech

Canadian Associations / Lifewater Canada

Overview: A medium-sized provincial organization founded in 1991
Mission: To improve the climate in which the business of biotechnology is conducted in BC; To be an advocate for the industry; To improve the level of awareness & understanding of biotechnology
Finances: *Funding Sources:* Membership fees
Membership: *Member Profile:* Producers & users of biotechnology, including companies, colleges & universities, government agencies & students; *Committees:* Finance; Med-tech; Membership; Policy
Chief Officer(s):
Gordon McCauley, Chair
Paul V. Drohan, President & CEO
Awards:
• Annual BC Biotechnology Awards

Lifewater Canada
457 Heather Cres., Thunder Bay ON P7E 5L1
Tel: 807-622-4848; *Fax:* 807-577-9798
Toll-Free: 888-543-3426
info@lifewater.ca
www.lifewater.ca
www.facebook.com/lifewater.ca
Overview: A small international organization founded in 1995
Mission: To be dedicated to ensuring that people everywhere have access to adequate supplies of safe water; To train & equip nationals with drill rigs & hand pumps so they can solve their own water problems
Membership: *Member Profile:* Hydrogeologists, well drillers, educators, engineers, environmental scientists, businessmen & many other people with diverse skills & training
Chief Officer(s):
Alanna Drost, Contact

Lighthouse Food Bank Society
PO Box 179, Chester NS B0J 1J0
Tel: 902-275-5304
Overview: A small local charitable organization founded in 1986
Member of: Nova Scotia Food Bank Association
Finances: *Annual Operating Budget:* Less than $50,000
10 volunteer(s)
Membership: *Fees:* $25
Chief Officer(s):
Madge Cook, Chair

Lighthouse Mission
669 Main St., Winnipeg MB R3B 1E3
Tel: 204-943-9669; *Fax:* 204-949-9479
info@lighthousemission.ca
www.lighthousemission.ca
www.facebook.com/lighthousemission.ca
Overview: A small local organization founded in 1911
Mission: To provide food and services to the needy in Winnipeg
Staff Member(s): 3
Activities: Operates a soup kitchen; Distributes clothing
Chief Officer(s):
Joel Cormie, Operations Manager
J'Lynn Johnson, Manager, Donor Relations
Joan Vezeau, Administrative Assistant
Richard Kunzelman, Door-to-Door Embassador

Lights, Camera, Access!
#447, 155 Dalhousie St., Toronto ON M5B 2P7
Tel: 416-363-9948; *Fax:* 416-551-9977
www.lightscameraaccess.ca
www.facebook.com/217700321585546
twitter.com/lca_canada
Overview: A medium-sized national charitable organization
Mission: To expand the presence of disabled individuals in Canadian media
Activities: Connecting disabled artists with employment opportunities in Canada's entertainment & media industries
Chief Officer(s):
Leesa Levinson, Founder

La Ligue canadienne de compositeurs *See* Canadian League of Composers

Ligue canadienne de football *See* Canadian Football League

Ligue de dards Ungava
331, 2e rue, Chibougamau QC G8P 1M4
Tél: 418-748-8060
Aperçu: *Dimension:* petite; *Envergure:* locale
Membre(s) du bureau directeur:
Claude Patoine, Président

Ligue de sécurité de l'Ontario *See* Ontario Safety League

Ligue des cadets de l'air du Canada *See* Air Cadet League of Canada

Ligue des cadets de l'armée du Canada *See* Army Cadet League of Canada

Ligue des droits de la personne de B'nai Brith Canada *See* League for Human Rights of B'nai Brith Canada

La Ligue des Noirs du Québec *See* Black Coalition of Québec

Ligue des propriétaires de Montréal / Property Owners League of Montréal
8565, rue Saint-Denis, Montréal QC H2P 2H4
Tél: 514-381-1182; *Téléc:* 514-381-2214
Ligne sans frais: 888-381-1182
ligue@liguedespropriaires.ca
www.liguedespropriaires.ca
Aperçu: *Dimension:* petite; *Envergure:* locale; Organisme sans but lucratif; fondée en 1921
Mission: Promouvoir les droits des propriétaires d'immeuble de logements locatifs
Membre: *Montant de la cotisation:* Barème; *Critères d'admissibilité:* Être propriétaire d'un immeuble à logements locatifs
Activités:; *Bibliothèque:* Bibliothèque publique
Membre(s) du bureau directeur:
Pierre Aubry, Président, 514-381-1182
Jeanne-Mance Calvé, Secretariat

Ligue La Leche Canada *See* La Leche League Canada

Ligue Monarchiste du Canada *See* Monarchist League of Canada

Ligue navale du Canada *See* Navy League of Canada

Ligue pour le bien-être de l'enfance du Canada *See* Child Welfare League of Canada

Ligue trotskyste du Canada *See* Trotskyist League of Canada

Likely & District Chamber of Commerce
PO Box 29, Likely BC V0L 1N0
Tel: 250-790-2127
www.likely-bc.ca
Overview: A small local organization founded in 1965
Mission: To support area businesses
Member of: BC Chamber of Commerce
Finances: *Annual Operating Budget:* Less than $50,000; *Funding Sources:* Fundraising
Membership: 50; *Fees:* $10-$25; $100 corporate; *Member Profile:* Business & community members; *Committees:* Community Forest; Community School; Likely Cemetary; Seniors; Likely Community Hall
Chief Officer(s):
Lisa Kraus, President

Lillooet & District Chamber of Commerce
PO Box 650, Lillooet BC V0K 1V0
Tel: 250-256-3578; *Fax:* 250-256-4882
info@lillooetchamberofcommerce.ca
www.lillooetchamberofcommerce.com
Overview: A small local organization
Mission: To promote local businesses & build a strong, sustainable business community in Lillooet; To support initiatives for tourism & economic development
Staff Member(s): 2
Membership: 87
Chief Officer(s):
Bob Sheridan, Co-President
Bain Gair, Co-President & Secretary-Treasurer

Lillooet Food Bank
PO Box 2170, 357 Main St., Lillooet BC V0K 1V0
Tel: 250-256-4400; *Fax:* 250-256-7928
Overview: A small local organization overseen by Food Banks British Columbia
Mission: To provide food to the needy in the Lillooet area
Member of: Food Banks British Columbia

Lillooet Tribal Council
PO Box 1420, 80 Seton Lake Rd., Lillooet BC V0K 1V0
Tel: 250-256-7523; *Fax:* 250-256-7119
lillooet_tribal_council@yahoo.ca
Overview: A small local organization
Membership: *Member Profile:* Bridge River Indian Band; Cayoose Creek Band; Mount Currie Band Council; Seton Lake Band; T'it'q'et Administration; Ts'kw'aylaxw First Nation
Chief Officer(s):
Susan James, Data Provider

Limestone Beekeepers Guild
c/o Bill Lake, 2712 Round Lake Rd., Battersea ON K0H 1H0
Tel: 613-353-6768
betsybhoney@hotmail.com
www3.sympatico.ca/lovegrove1//bees
Previous Name: Harrowsmith Beekeepers Guild
Overview: A small local organization founded in 1987
Mission: To promote apiculture in the Kingston, Ontario region; To provide education about beekeeping
Member of: Ontario Beekeepers' Association
Membership: *Fees:* $15 individuals; $20 families; *Member Profile:* Beekeepers from Kingston & area, with one to several hundred hives
Activities: Organizing meetings with guest speakers; Hosting an annual honey contest; Supporting the Ontario Bee Research Fund; *Speaker Service:* Yes
Chief Officer(s):
Bill Lake, President, 613-353-6768
Publications:
• Bee Space: The Limestone Beekeepers Guild Newsletter
Type: Newsletter
Profile: Guild information, including upcoming meetings & honey contests

Lincoln Chamber of Commerce
PO Box 493, 4961 King St., #T2, Beamsville ON L0R 1B0
Tel: 905-563-5044; *Fax:* 905-563-7098
info@lincolnchamber.ca
www.lincolnchamber.ca
twitter.com/LCOCbusiness
Overview: A small local organization
Mission: To serve local businesses; To promote economic prosperity in the community
Chief Officer(s):
Cathy McNiven, Executive Director

Lincoln County Humane Society
160 - 4th Ave., St Catharines ON L2S 0B6
Tel: 905-682-0767; *Fax:* 905-682-8133
myconnect@lchs.ca
www.lchs.ca
Overview: A small local charitable organization founded in 1927
Mission: Cruelty investigation & prosecution; animal rescue & protection; to promote humane treatment of animals; to provide shelter to animals & pet therapy
Affiliation(s): Ontario Humane Society
Finances: *Funding Sources:* Regional government
Chief Officer(s):
Kevin Strooband, Executive Director

Lincoln County Law Association
59 Church St., St Catharines ON L2R 3C3
Tel: 905-685-9094; *Fax:* 905-685-0981
Toll-Free: 866-637-6829
library@thelcla.ca
www.thelcla.ca
Overview: A small local organization
Mission: To provide information for lawyers practicing in the Niagara North area
Membership: 220 individual
Activities: *Library:*
Chief Officer(s):
Keith Newell, Librarian

Lindsay & District Chamber of Commerce
180 Kent St. West, Lindsay ON K9V 2Y6
Tel: 705-324-2393; *Fax:* 705-324-2473
info@lindsaychamber.com
www.lindsaychamber.com
www.linkedin.com/company/lindsay-&-district-chamber-of-commerce
twitter.com/LDChamber
Overview: A medium-sized local organization
Mission: To protect the interests of the business community of Lindsay & district
Membership: 400+; *Fees:* Schedule available; *Committees:* Advocacy; Executive; Membership; Programs & Events
Chief Officer(s):
Marlene Morrison Nicholls, President
Colleen Collins, Administrative Officer

Lindsay & District Real Estate Board See Kawartha Lakes Real Estate Association

Lions Eye Bank of Manitoba & Northwest Ontario, Incorporated
320 Sherbrook St., Winnipeg MB R3B 2W6
Tel: 204-772-1899; *Fax:* 204-943-6823
Toll-Free: 800-552-6820
lfmnoi@mts.net
www.eyebankmanitoba.com
Overview: A small provincial charitable organization founded in 1984
Mission: To maintain professional staff to procure, process, & distribute human donor eye tissue for surgical transplantation in recipients of Manitoba & Norhwest Ontario
Member of: Eye Bank Association of America
Affiliation(s): Lions Eye Bank
Membership: *Member Profile:* Lions clubs of Manitoba & northwestern Ontario
Activities: Increasing public awareness; Arranging funding assistance
Chief Officer(s):
Chris Barnard, Chair
cbarnard@mts.net
Awards:
• Stew Peever Memorial Award

Lions Foundation of Canada
152 Wilson St., Oakville ON L6J 5E8
Tel: 905-842-2891; *Fax:* 905-842-3373
Toll-Free: 800-768-3030; *TTY:* 905-842-1585
info@dogguides.com
www.dogguides.com
www.facebook.com/LFCDogGuides
twitter.com/LFCDogGuides
Overview: A small national charitable organization founded in 1983
Mission: To provide service to physically challenged Canadians in the areas of mobility, safety & independence
Affiliation(s): Lions Clubs of Canada
Finances: *Annual Operating Budget:* $3 Million-$5 Million; *Funding Sources:* Donations; fundraising; gift shop
Staff Member(s): 40
Activities: Canine Vision Canada; Hearing Ear Dogs of Canada; Special Skills Dogs of Canada; *Awareness Events:* Walk for Dog Guides; *Speaker Service:* Yes
Chief Officer(s):
Sandy Turney, Executive Director, 905-842-2891 Ext. 224
sandyturney@dogguides.com
Julie Jelinek, Director of Development, 905-842-2891 Ext. 223
jjelinek@dogguides.com

Lions Gate Hospice Society See North Shore Hospice Society

Lions Gate Hospital Foundation
231 East 15th St., North Vancouver BC V7L 2L7
Tel: 604-984-5785; *Fax:* 604-984-5786
info@lghfoundation.com
www.lghfoundation.com
www.facebook.com/lghfoundation
twitter.com/LGHFoundation
instagram.com/lghfoundation
Overview: A small local charitable organization
Mission: To help raise money on behalf of 10 health care centres to fund research & improve patient care
Finances: *Annual Operating Budget:* Greater than $5 Million
Staff Member(s): 11
Chief Officer(s):
Judy Savage, President
judy.savage@vch.ca

Lions Legacy International
Tel: 778-868-0776
Overview: A small international organization
Mission: To democratize education across the globe; To develop schools with 1:1 gender parity & open source education technology
Activities: Building schools in Ethiopia & other countries
Chief Officer(s):
Jered Love, Executive Director, Marketing
jered@lionslegacy.ca

Lions Quest Canada - The Centre for Positive Youth Development
#1, 427 Elgin St. North, Cambridge ON N1R 8G4
Tel: 519-624-1170; *Fax:* 519-624-3354
Toll-Free: 800-265-2680
qbear@lionsquest.ca
www.lionsquest.ca
Overview: A medium-sized national organization founded in 1988
Mission: To provide leadership, knowledge and resources to develop capable young Canadians of positive character.
Finances: *Funding Sources:* Private sponsorship
Staff Member(s): 3
Chief Officer(s):
Joanne McQuiggan, Executive Director

Listowel Chamber of Commerce See North Perth Chamber of Commerce

Literacy Alberta
3060 - 17 Ave. SW, Calgary AB T3E 7G8
Tel: 403-410-6990; *Fax:* 403-410-9024
Toll-Free: 800-410-6584
office@literacyalberta.ca
www.literacyalberta.ca
www.linkedin.com/company/1511757
www.facebook.com/literacyalberta
twitter.com/literacyalberta
Previous Name: Literacy Co-ordinators of Alberta
Overview: A small provincial charitable organization founded in 2003
Mission: To support people involved in literacy activities; to influence public policy on literacy issues
Member of: Movement for Canadian Literacy
Staff Member(s): 10
Membership: 300+; *Fees:* $5 student; $50 individual; $150 small organization; $250 large organization; *Member Profile:* Literacy program coordinators, tutors, students, professionals & general public
Activities: To conceive & administrate projects that provide funding, resources & professional development opportunities for literacy programs in Alberta; *Speaker Service:* Yes; *Library:* Literacy Alberta Library; Open to public by appointment
Chief Officer(s):
Phillip Hoffmann, Executive Director
Awards:
• Literacy Awards of Excellence

Literacy Alliance of West Nipissing
210 Holditch St., Sturgeon Falls ON P2B 1S6
Tel: 705-753-0537; *Fax:* 705-753-7942
yes2literacy.ca
www.facebook.com/1406891759532704
Previous Name: Sturgeon Falls Literacy Alliance
Overview: A small local organization
Mission: To provide free service to adults in the West Nipissing area who wish assistance in upgrading their English literacy skills
Finances: *Funding Sources:* National government
Staff Member(s): 1; 15 volunteer(s)
Membership: 9 institutional; 10 student; 15 individual
Activities: Workshops; literary events
Chief Officer(s):
Isabel Mosseler, Contact

Literacy Central Vancouver Island
19 Commercial St., Nanaimo BC V9R 5G3
Tel: 250-754-8988; *Fax:* 250-754-8114
info@literacycentralvi.org
www.literacynanaimo.org
www.facebook.com/literacycentralvi
Also Known As: Literacy Central VI
Previous Name: Nanaimo Literacy Association
Overview: A small local charitable organization founded in 1990
Mission: To promote literacy for all individuals
Member of: Literacy BC
Affiliation(s): National Adult Literacy Database
Staff Member(s): 8; 200 volunteer(s)
Activities: Volunteer Tutor Program; Computer Recycling Program; Computer learning centre; Used book store; Book fair; Community access internet site; Adult learning centre; *Library:* Tutor Resource Centre; Open to public by appointment
Chief Officer(s):
Rebecca Kirk, Cheif Executive Officer

Literacy Coalition of New Brunswick (LCNB) / Coalition pour l'alphabétisme du Nouveau-Brunswick
#303, 212 Queen St., Fredericton NB E3B 1A8
Tel: 506-457-1227; *Fax:* 506-458-1352
Toll-Free: 800-563-2211
lcnb@nbliteracy.ca
www.nbliteracy.ca
www.facebook.com/LiteracyNB
twitter.com/LiteracyNB
Previous Name: New Brunswick Coalition for Literacy
Overview: A small provincial charitable organization founded in 1988
Mission: To increase literacy in partnership with others; To maintain &/or extend network of NB Literacy groups & stakeholders; To increase public understanding of the literacy issue & its impact on every facet of society; To facilitate & mobilize activities which will result in opportunites for higher levels of literacy among the people of New Brunswick
Affiliation(s): Frontier College; ABC Canada; Laubach Literacy New Brunswick; Literacy New Brunswick Inc.; La Fédération d'alphabétisation du Nouveau-Brunswick; Provincial Partners for Literacy; Learning Disabilities Association of New Brunswick
Finances: *Funding Sources:* National Literacy Secretariat; corporate donations
Staff Member(s): 2
Membership: *Member Profile:* Persons with a high interest in promoting, supporting & delivering literacy services; family, adult & workplace; *Committees:* Adult/Workplace Literacy & Essential Skills; Communications & Government Relations; Executive; Family Literacy & Lifelong Learning
Activities: Referring learners to programs; Collecting & distributing new & used reading materials for adults & children; Promoting literacy through television & radio campaigns; Forming partnerships with groups that have an interest in literacy; Continuing to build a literacy community; Participating in policy discussions provincially & nationally; *Awareness Events:* Peter Gzowski Invitational Golf Tournament, May
Chief Officer(s):
Christy McLean, Executive Director
Matthew Garneau, Officer, Communications
matthew@nbliteracy.ca

Literacy Co-ordinators of Alberta See Literacy Alberta

Literacy Council of Brantford & District See Brant Skills Centre

The Literacy Council of Burlington
Upper Canada Place, #21, 460 Brant St., Burlington ON L7R 4B6
Tel: 905-631-1770; *Fax:* 905-631-5533
info@literacycouncil.ca
www.literacycouncil.ca
Overview: A small local charitable organization founded in 1980
Mission: To assist adults in Burlington, Ontario to improve their quality of life, by offering individual tutoring & small classes in reading, writing, mathematics, & computer literacy
Member of: Employment Ontario; Laubach Literacy of Ontario; Peel-Halton-Dufferin Adult Learning Network
Finances: *Annual Operating Budget:* $50,000-$100,000; *Funding Sources:* Ministry of Training, Colleges & Universities; Donations
Staff Member(s): 4; 40 volunteer(s)
Membership: 60; *Fees:* $20
Activities: Providing classes & workshops
Chief Officer(s):
Elaine Austin, Executive Director
elaine@literarycouncil.ca

Literacy Council of Durham Region (LCDR)
115 Simcoe St. South, 2nd Fl., Oshawa ON L1H 4G7
Tel: 905-434-5441; *Fax:* 905-725-6015
lcdr@bellnet.ca
www.literacydurham.ca
Overview: A small local charitable organization
Mission: To tutor adults to read & write in the Durham region; to recruit & train adult volunteers to become literacy tutors
Member of: Laubach Literacy of Canada - Ontario
Finances: *Annual Operating Budget:* $50,000-$100,000; *Funding Sources:* Ministry of Training, Colleges & Universities
Staff Member(s): 1; 100 volunteer(s)
Membership: 1-99
Activities: *Speaker Service:* Yes
Chief Officer(s):
Brad Cook, Executive Director

Literacy Council of Lincoln See Niagara West Employment & Learning Resource Centres

Literacy Council York-Simcoe (LCYS)
#15, 1100 Gorham St., Newmarket ON L3Y 8Y8
Tel: 905-853-6279; *Fax:* 905-836-7323
info@lcys.ca

www.lcys.ca
www.facebook.com/LCYorkS
twitter.com/LCYorkS
Overview: A small local charitable organization founded in 1987
Mission: To promote adult literacy in York Region & South Simcoe & provide a free tutoring service; to recruit & train volunteer tutors to help non-literate adults become fully functioning members of our community
Affiliation(s): Laubach Literacy International; Laubach Literacy of Canada; Laubach Literacy Ontario; Newmarket Chamber of Commerce; Community Literacy of Ontario; Ontario Literacy Coalition
Finances: *Funding Sources:* Provincial government; fundraising
Staff Member(s): 6
Membership: *Fees:* $15
Activities: *Speaker Service:* Yes; *Library:* by appointment
Chief Officer(s):
Trisha Patrick, Executive Director
trishap@lcys.ca
Natalie Cholewa, Coordinator, Learning
nataliec@lcys.ca

The Literacy Group of Waterloo Region
40 Ainslie St. South, 2nd Fl., Cambridge ON N1R 3K1
Tel: 519-621-7993; *Fax:* 519-743-6203
info@tlgwr.ca
www.theliteracygroup.com
www.facebook.com/323565181054788
Previous Name: Cambridge Literacy Council; Literacy Council of Kitchener-Waterloo
Overview: A small local charitable organization founded in 1980
Mission: To improve the basic literacy skills of adults in the community by providing accessible literacy programs
Member of: Laubach Literacy Ontario; Ontario Literacy Coalition; Community Literacy Ontario; Project Read Literacy Network
Finances: *Annual Operating Budget:* $250,000-$500,000
Staff Member(s): 7; 150 volunteer(s)
Membership: 150; *Fees:* $20; *Committees:* Program Development; Community Relations; Executive; Programming
Activities: *Awareness Events:* International Literacy Day, Sept.; *Speaker Service:* Yes; *Library*
Chief Officer(s):
Chris Prosser, Executive Director
Kitchener Branch
#200, 151 Frederick St., Kitchener ON N2H 2M2
Tel: 519-743-6090; *Fax:* 519-743-6203
info@tlgwr.ca

Literacy Link South Central (LLSC)
255 Horton St., 3rd Fl., London ON N6B 1L1
Tel: 519-681-7307; *Fax:* 519-681-7310
Toll-Free: 800-561-6896
literacylink@bellnet.ca
www.llsc.on.ca
Previous Name: Southwestern Ontario Adult Literacy Network
Overview: A small local charitable organization founded in 1991
Mission: To support all literacy programs equally & inclusively, respecting diversities in service delivery based on their individual community needs in counties of Brant, Haldimand/Norfolk, Elgin, Middlesex & Oxford
Member of: Ontario Literacy Coalition; Community Literacy of Ontario; London Council for Adult Education
Finances: *Annual Operating Budget:* $100,000-$250,000
Staff Member(s): 4
Membership: 15; *Fees:* $20 individual voting & non-voting; $40 organizational; *Member Profile:* Literacy programs; adult educators; employment service organizations; youth service organizations
Activities: Provide ongoing support for literacy agencies to deliver quality programming; support lifelong learning through a variety of community planning activities; enchance communication among literacy deliverers & funders; participate in the regional plan for information & referral services; support literacy initiatives through regional coordination of training; coordinate & manage literacy development projects; educate the public about literacy; network/link with other regional, provincial & national organizations; *Awareness Events:* Literacy Awareness Workshops; Clear Writing Workshops; *Library:* Not open to public
Chief Officer(s):
Tamara Kaattari, Executive Director

Literacy Nova Scotia (LNS)
NSCC Truro Campus, Forrester Hall, PO Box 1516, #125, 36 Arthur St., Truro NS B2N 5V2
Tel: 902-897-2444; *Fax:* 902-897-4020
Toll-Free: 800-255-5203
literacyns@nscc.ca
www.literacyns.ca
www.facebook.com/LiteracyNovaScotia
twitter.com/literacyns1
www.youtube.com/LiteracyNS
Previous Name: Nova Scotia Provincial Literacy Coalition
Overview: A small provincial organization founded in 1992
Mission: To provide Nova Scotians with access to literacy, skills, & learning opportunities
Membership: *Fees:* $5 individual; $50 organizational; *Committees:* Executive; NS PGI; PGI Grant Selection; Scholarship/Bursary
Activities: *Awareness Events:* International Literacy Day, Sept.; The Word On The Street Halifax, Sept.; Literacy Action Week, Nov.
Chief Officer(s):
Jayne Hunter, Executive Director
Awards:
• Learner Recognition Awards
Publications:
• Literacy Nova Scotia News
Type: Newsletter

Literacy Ontario Central South (LOCS)
#203, 113 Park St. South, Peterborough ON K9J 3R8
Tel: 705-749-0675; *Fax:* 705-749-1883
www.locs.on.ca
www.facebook.com/179735928825157
twitter.com/LOCSLiteracy
Overview: A small local organization founded in 1990
Mission: To serve literacy programs in the counties of Haliburton, Northumberland, Peterborough, Renfrew & the City of Kawartha Lakes
Affiliation(s): Ontario Literacy Coalition
Finances: *Funding Sources:* National & provincial government
Staff Member(s): 3; 6 volunteer(s)
Activities: Literacy programs; information & referral; resources & reference material
Chief Officer(s):
Joan Connolly, Executive Director
joan@locs.on.ca

Literacy Society of South Muskoka Inc. *See* Learning for Living South Muskoka

Literacy Volunteers of Quebec (LVQ)
#230A, 1001, rue Lenoir, Montréal QC H4C 2Z6
Tel: 514-508-6805; *Fax:* 514-508-4985
Toll-Free: 855-890-1587
info@literacyvolunteersquebec.org
www.literacyquebec.org
www.facebook.com/literacyquebec.org
Overview: A medium-sized provincial organization founded in 1980
Mission: A coalition of volunteer groups offering literacy services to the Anglophone population of Quebec.
Staff Member(s): 3
Membership: 13; *Fees:* $50; *Member Profile:* Literacy organizations
Chief Officer(s):
Margo Legault, Executive Director
margolegault@literacyvolunteersquebec.org

Literary & Historical Society of Québec (LHSQ) / Société littéraire et historique de Québec
44, Chaussée des Écossais, Québec QC G1R 4H3
Tel: 418-694-9147; *Fax:* 418-694-0754
info@morrin.org
www.morrin.org
Overview: A small provincial charitable organization founded in 1824
Mission: To preserve, develop & share the diverse cultural life of the Québec City region's English-speaking community through innovative, responsive & effective services
Member of: Heritage Canada Foundation; Champlain Society; Québec Anglophone Heritage Network
Staff Member(s): 7
Membership: *Fees:* $20 student; $45 individual; $60 family; $100 friend of LHSQ; $250 corporate
Activities: Lectures; courses (poetry, social history); readings; bake sale; raffle; *Library:* Open to public
Chief Officer(s):
Barry McCullough, Executive Director
barrymccullough@morrin.org

The Literary Press Group of Canada (LPG)
#700, 425 Adelaide St. West, Toronto ON M5V 3C1
Tel: 416-483-1321; *Fax:* 416-483-2510
www.lpg.ca
www.facebook.com/lpgcanada
twitter.com/LPGCanada
Overview: A medium-sized national organization founded in 1976
Mission: To advocate on behalf of members; To foster the survival, growth & maintenance of strong Canadian-owned & controlled literary book publishing houses; To help members with the selling & distribution of their books
Member of: Book & Periodical Council
Affiliation(s): Association of Canadian Publishers
Finances: *Annual Operating Budget:* $250,000-$500,000; *Funding Sources:* Membership fees & commissions
Staff Member(s): 5; 7 volunteer(s)
Membership: 60 companies; *Fees:* $450; *Member Profile:* Publishing houses that are 80% Canadian owned, in operation for at least two years & primarily based in Canada, & that publish original Canadian books with 50% in literary categories such as poetry, fiction, drama, literary criticism & creative non-fiction
Activities: Providing cooperative sales & marketing projects
Chief Officer(s):
Christen Thomas, Executive Director Ext. 1
Tanya Snyder, Manager, Marketing

Literary Translators' Association of Canada (LTAC) / Association des traducteurs et traductrices littéraires du Canada (ATTLC)
Concordia University LB 601, 1455, boul Maisonneuve ouest, Montréal QC H3G 1M8
Tel: 514-848-2424
info@attlc-ltac.org
www.attlc-ltac.org
www.facebook.com/ATTLC.LTAC
Overview: A small national organization founded in 1975
Mission: To promote literary translation & interests of literary translators.
Member of: Fédération internationale des Traducteurs
Finances: *Funding Sources:* Membership dues; Canada Council
Membership: *Fees:* $140 full; $70 associate; $25 student; *Member Profile:* Canadian citizen or landed immigrant; published one book-length work of literary translation or equivalent
Activities: Brings together Canadian translators of literature (fiction, non-fiction, film, theatre, poetry, juvenile); provides members with sample contracts; lobbies & liaises with cultural & government agencies & literary associations
Chief Officer(s):
Beatriz Hausner, President
Awards:
• John Glassco Prize
Awarded annually for a translator's first work in book-length literary translation into French or English, published in Canada during the previous calendar year *Deadline:* July; *Amount:* $1,000 & one year's membership in the association

The Lithuanian Canadian Community (LCC) / La Communauté lithuanienne du Canada
1 Resurrection Rd., Toronto ON M9A 5G1
Tel: 416-533-3292; *Fax:* 416-533-2282
klb@on.aibn.com
www.klb.org
Overview: A medium-sized national organization founded in 1952 overseen by Baltic Federation in Canada
Mission: To promote, maintain, & encourage the survival of the Lithuanian culture & language in Canada & abroad
Member of: Canadian Ethnocultural Council; Baltic Federation of Canada
Membership: *Member Profile:* Some Lithuanian heritage
Chief Officer(s):
Joana Kuraite-Lasiene, President

Lithuanian Community Association of Toronto
1573 Bloor St. West, Toronto ON M6P 1A6
Tel: 416-955-4810; *Fax:* 416-532-4745
Other Communication: Alternate Phone: 416-532-3311
litn@rogers.com
www.lithuanianbanquethalls.ca
www.facebook.com/LithuanianBanquetHalls
Also Known As: Lithuanian House
Overview: A small local organization founded in 1952
Mission: To promote, support & fund Lithuanian organizations
Affiliation(s): Labdara Foundation
Membership: 1,000-4,999

The Lithuanian Society of Edmonton
11629 - 83 St., Edmonton AB T5B 2Y7
Tel: 780-474-0350
Overview: A small local organization founded in 1953
Affiliation(s): Lithuanian Canadian Community
Finances: *Annual Operating Budget:* Less than $50,000;
Funding Sources: Membership fees; shares; donations
Membership: 100

Lithuanian-Canadian Foundation (LCF)
1 Resurrection Rd., Toronto ON M9A 5G1
Tel: 416-889-5531
Overview: A small national charitable organization

Little Bits Therapeutic Riding Association
PO Box 29016, Stn. Pleasantview, Edmonton AB T6H 5Z6
Tel: 780-476-1233; *Fax:* 780-476-7252
Other Communication: Volunteering Inquiries, E-mail:
volunteers@littlebits.ca
info@littlebits.ca
www.littlebits.ca
www.facebook.com/LittleBitsVolunteers
Overview: A small local charitable organization founded in 1978
Mission: To provide recreational riding programs that have therapeutic benefits for disabled children & adults in Edmonton & surrounding area. Physical address: Whitemud Equine Learning Centre Asociation, 12504 Fox Dr. NW, Edmonton, AB T6G 2L6
Member of: Central Canadian Therapeutic Riding Association; North American Riding for the Handicapped Association
200 volunteer(s)
Membership: 200; *Committees:* Finance; Fundraising; Public Relations; Riding Program; Camp Horseshoe
Chief Officer(s):
Linda Rault, Riding Administrator
Publications:
• Little Bits Therapeutic Riding Association e-Newsletter
Type: Newsletter

Little Brothers of the Good Shepherd *See* The Brothers of the Good Shepherd

Little Burgundy Sports Centre *Voir* Centre Sportif de la Petite Bourgogne

Little Faces of Panama Association
#1202, 2177 Sherobee Rd., Mississauga ON L5A 3G9
Tel: 647-262-2353
www.littlefacesofpanama-association.com
www.facebook.com/littlefacesofpanama
Overview: A small local organization
Mission: To promote the culture of Panama and raise funds for impoverished children in the country
Activities: Carnival; Dance recitals
Chief Officer(s):
Waldy Marcucci, President, Board of Directors

Little League Canada / Petite ligue Canada
#500, 2210 Prince of Wales Dr., Ottawa ON K2E 6Z9
Tel: 613-731-3301; *Fax:* 613-731-2829
Other Communication: media@littleleague.ca
canada@littleleague.org
www.littleleague.ca
www.facebook.com/LittleLeagueCanada
twitter.com/LittleLgeCanada
www.youtube.com/DugoutTheMascot
Overview: A large national charitable organization founded in 1951
Mission: To provide baseball & softball programs to every boy or girl wishing to participate
Member of: Little League Baseball International
Finances: *Funding Sources:* Membership dues; corporate
Staff Member(s): 2
Membership: 35,000
Chief Officer(s):
Roy Bergerman, President & Chair
rbergerman@littleleague.ca
Joe Shea, Regional Director
jshea@littleleague.ca

Little People of Manitoba (LPM)
4 Lakepoint Rd., Winnipeg MB R3T 4R4
Tel: 204-226-0110
www.lpmanitoba.ca
Overview: A small provincial charitable organization founded in 1981
Mission: Dedicated to helping people of small stature become useful members of society through education, employment and social adjustment, and to focus public attention to the fact that the magnitude of any physical limitation is a function of attitude of both the small and the average-sized person and desire to assist in these matters.
Finances: *Annual Operating Budget:* Less than $50,000
25 volunteer(s)
Membership: 60; *Fees:* $25 family; $15 single
Activities: Monthly meetings; socials; fundraising
Chief Officer(s):
Connie Magalhaes, President

Little People of Ontario (LPO)
108 Rosedale Heights Dr., Toronto ON M4T 1C6
Tel: 647-874-8766; *Fax:* 647-977-1211
info@lpo.on.ca
www.littlepeopleofontario.com
Overview: A small provincial charitable organization founded in 1965
Mission: To provide support & information to little people, as well as their families & friends; To raise awareness about dwarfism
Finances: *Annual Operating Budget:* Less than $50,000
6 volunteer(s)
Membership: 100; *Fees:* $25 individual; $35 family; $55 corporate
Activities: Social events; newsletter; education; *Library*
Chief Officer(s):
Allan Redford, President

Living Bible Explorers (LBE)
600 Burnell St., Winnipeg MB R3G 2B7
Tel: 204-786-8667; *Fax:* 204-775-7525
Toll-Free: 866-786-8667
lbe@mymts.net
livingbibleexplorers.com
www.facebook.com/livingbibleexplorers
Overview: A small provincial charitable organization founded in 1969
Mission: To help children, youth & their families become productive, responsible & spiritually mature individuals
Member of: Canadian Council of Christian Charities
Finances: *Annual Operating Budget:* $250,000-$500,000;
Funding Sources: Individual and cooperate donations; Provincial government; individual churches; foundations
Staff Member(s): 10; 200 volunteer(s)
Membership: 700 individual; *Committees:* New Bible Camp; Board of Directors
Activities: Boys & Girls Clubs; Summer & weekend camps; Ministry for kids & teens; Food distribution; Weekly home visitation; Annual banquet; *Awareness Events:* Mission Fest - Feb; Annual Fundraising Banquet - Mar; Garage Sale - May; *Internships:* Yes; *Speaker Service:* Yes; *Library:* Living Bible Explorers' Resource Library; Not open to public
Chief Officer(s):
Curtis Klassen, General Manager
Cheryl Peters, Assistant Manager
Mary Ann Funk, Children's Program Coordinator
Nicola Plett, Children's Program Coordinator

Living Positive
#50, 9912 - 106 St., Edmonton AB T5K 1C5
Tel: 780-424-2214
living-positive@telus.net
www.facebook.com/LivingPoz
Previous Name: Edmonton Persons Living with HIV Society
Overview: A small local charitable organization founded in 1990 overseen by Canadian AIDS Society
Mission: To provide persons living with HIV infection nurturing, supportive environments in which to develop positive attitudes & self image
Member of: Alberta Community Council on HIV
Finances: *Funding Sources:* Provincial AIDS Program; Alberta Health
Membership: *Member Profile:* HIV positive persons & their supporters
Activities: *Awareness Events:* AIDS Walk; *Internships:* Yes; *Speaker Service:* Yes; *Library:* Open to public

Living Positive Resource Centre, Okanagan (LPRC)
168 Asher Rd., Kelowna BC V1X 3H6
Tel: 778-753-5830; *Fax:* 778-753-5832
info@lprc.ca
www.livingpositive.ca
www.facebook.com/lprcokanagen
Previous Name: ARC, AIDS Resource Centre, Okanagan & Region
Overview: A small local charitable organization founded in 1992
Mission: To educate & inform the public about HIV/AIDS & hepatitis, its transmission, prevention, treatment & care, providing the most accurate & up-to-date information available; to develop & promote community based partnerships for the delivery of education & support; to dispel the myths & misunderstandings & to promote awareness of the discrimination & marginalization of persons infected & affected by HIV/AIDS & hepatitis & to advocate for change; to advocate & lobby for programs & services, necessary to promote wellness & quality of life of persons infected & affected by HIV/AIDS & hepatitis; to facilitate access to emotional, spiritual, social & practical support for persons infected & affected by HIV/AIDS & hepatitis, respectful of their right to determine the direction of their lives; to provide accessible services in non-judgmental, safe, confidential environments; to identify & seek solutions to existing gaps in services
Member of: Canadian AIDS Society; Pacific AIDS Network
Affiliation(s): Central Okanagan Hospice Society; Vernon Hospice; Salmon Arm Hospice; North Okanagan Youth & Family Services; Columbia-Shuswap HIV/AIDS Project; Outreach Health Services
Finances: *Funding Sources:* Provincial government; Ministry of Health; fundraising; HRDC
Staff Member(s): 5
Activities: Information & referral telephone service; counselling & education; support groups & wellness workshops; *Awareness Events:* MDS Walk; World AIDS Day; AIDS Walk; Annual Candlelight Vigil; *Speaker Service:* Yes; *Library:* LPRC; Open to public
Chief Officer(s):
Clare Overton, Executive Director

Livres Canada Books
#504, 1 Nicholas St., Ottawa ON K1N 7B7
Tel: 613-562-2324; *Fax:* 613-562-2329
info@livrescanadabooks.com
www.livrescanadabooks.com
www.linkedin.com/company/livres-canada-books
www.facebook.com/LivresCanadaBooks
twitter.com/livresCAbooks
Previous Name: Association for the Export of Canadian Books
Overview: A medium-sized international organization founded in 1972
Mission: To defend the interests of Canadian book publishers by providing market intelligence products & services, information & resources on digital publishing, as well as financial, promotion & logisitical support; To administer the Foreign Rights Marketing Assistance Program, a component of the Canada Book Fund, as well as mentoring programs & other funding initiatives
Affiliation(s): Association of Canadian Publishers; Canadian Publishers Council; Association of Canadian University Presses; Association nationale des éditeurs de livres
Finances: *Annual Operating Budget:* $3 Million-$5 Million
Staff Member(s): 6
Membership: *Committees:* Executive & Finance; Export Expertise; Nominating & Governance
Activities: Providing financial assistance to Canadian book publishers through the Export Marketing Assistance Program & the Foreign Rights Marketing Assistance Program; Coordinating Canada's collective presence at international book fairs; Conducting workshops on foreign markets; Providing information on foreign markets & on opportunities for export sales
Chief Officer(s):
Robert Dees, Chair
François Charette, Executive Director
fcharette@livrescanadabooks.com

Lloydminster & District Fish & Game Association (LDFGA)
PO Box 116, Lloydminster AB T9V 0X9
Tel: 780-875-5100
lloyddfga@gmail.com
www.lloydfishandgame.org
Overview: A medium-sized local organization founded in 1927
Mission: To advocate for & assist in the conservation & management of fish, wildlife & habitat for the continuing benefit of association members & the general public
Affiliation(s): Saskatchewan Wildlife Federation; Alberta Fish & Game Association; Canadian Wildlife Federation; Ducks Unlimited Canada
Membership: 650; *Fees:* $15 youth; $35 regular; $65 family
Activities: Recreational hunting & fishing; trout ponds; outdoor rifle range & Pistol Club; archery; gun show
Chief Officer(s):
Dwayne Davison, President, 780-808-6420
dwayne.teagan@sasktel.net

Lloydminster & District United Way
4419 - 52nd Ave., Lloydminster AB T9V 0Y8
Tel: 780-875-3743; Fax: 780-875-3793
Other Communication: office@lloydminster.unitedway.ca
luw@telusplanet.net
www.lloydminster.unitedway.ca
Overview: A small local organization overseen by United Way of Canada - Centraide Canada
Mission: To strengthen the community by supporting local agencies

Lloydminster Agricultural Exhibition Association (LAEA)
PO Box 690, 5521 - 49 Ave., Lloydminster SK S9V 0Y7
Tel: 306-825-5571; Fax: 306-825-7017
lloydexh@lloydexh.com
www.lloydexh.com
www.facebook.com/LloydExh
Overview: A small local charitable organization founded in 1904
Mission: Dedicated in continuing to foster and develop the tourism industry of Lloydminster, and providing support to the business, social and cultural sectors of the reason.
Member of: Saskatchewan Association of Agricultural Societies & Exhibitions
Affiliation(s): Alberta Association of Agricultural Associations; Canadian Association of Fairs & Exhibitions; International Association of Fairs & Exhibitions
Finances: Annual Operating Budget: $1.5 Million-$3 Million
Staff Member(s): 15; 300 volunteer(s)
Membership: 100-499; Fees: $10 with $40 on demand
Activities: Agricultural activities; rentals; seminars; livestock sales & shows; social receptions
Chief Officer(s):
Michael Sidoryk, Manager
Owen Noble, President

Lloydminster Chamber of Commerce
4419 - 52 Ave., Lloydminster AB T9V 0Y8
Tel: 780-875-9013; Fax: 780-875-0755
info@lloydminsterchamber.com
www.lloydminsterchamber.com
www.facebook.com/LloydChamber
twitter.com/LloydChamber
www.youtube.com/user/LloydminsterChamber
Overview: A medium-sized local organization founded in 1934
Mission: To enhance private enterprise in Lloydminster & surrounding area
Member of: Canadian Chamber of Commerce; Alberta Chamber of Commerce; Saskatchewan Chamber of Commerce
Finances: Funding Sources: Membership fees; fundraising
Staff Member(s): 7
Membership: 584; Fees: Schedule available
Activities: Organizing Christmas Preview Trade Show, Business Week, Service with a Smile Program, & other events & services; Library: Chamber Reference Library; Open to public
Chief Officer(s):
Serena Sjodin, Executive Director
Awards:
• J.A. McLean Agricultural Scholarship
 Deadline: May; Amount: $600
• Dunstan Scholarship
 Deadline: May; Amount: $600

Lloydminster Early Childhood Intervention Program See Early Childhood Intervention Program (ECIP) Sask. Inc.

Lloydminster German Heritage Society Inc.
4708 - 49 St., Lloydminster SK S9V 0L8
Tel: 306-825-3177
Overview: A small local organization
Member of: German-Canadian Association of Alberta; Saskatchewan German Council

Lloydminster Interval Home Society
PO Box 1523, Lloydminster SK S9V 1K5
Tel: 780-808-5282; Fax: 780-875-0609
lihsi@telusplanet.net
www.intervalhome.ab.ca
Overview: A small local organization founded in 1980
Mission: To provide safe short-term accommodation & supportive counselling for women & their children who are in a family violence or crisis situation
Finances: Funding Sources: Community donations; fundraising; government; Sask Lotteries; United Way
Staff Member(s): 38
Membership: Fees: $5
Chief Officer(s):
Angela Rooks-Trotzuk, Executive Director

Lloydminster Native Friendship Centre (LNFC)
PO Box 1364, 4602 - 49 Ave., Lloydminster SK S9V 1K4
Tel: 306-825-6558; Fax: 306-825-6565
reception@LNFC.org
www.lnfc.org
Overview: A small local charitable organization founded in 1982 overseen by Alberta Native Friendship Centres Association
Mission: To provide services to residents from SK & AB, within an approximate 11 km radius; to promote better understanding & relations between the different cultures within our community; to develop wellness, education, cultural & social programs & activities for children & their families; to promote the well-being & enhancement of quality of life for all people within the community through partnership with community & government agencies; to seek avenues of financial security to ensure viable & sustainable operation
Member of: Alberta Native Friendship Centres Association
Staff Member(s): 8; 50 volunteer(s)
Membership: 200; Fees: $2; Member Profile: Aboriginal & non-Aboriginal of all ages
Activities: Teen & young parent program; extrajudicial sanctions program; day program for youth; planting the seeds of tolerance program; soup & bannock weekly program; skill enhancement & pre-employment preparedness; help n' hand youth centre; Cree conversational classes; young ladies self-esteem program; family craft classes; elder socials; summer day camp for children; healing circles; tutor services; educational opportunities workshops; Métis culture awareness campaign; family dances, drumming & drama; Awareness Events: National Indigenous Peoples Day, June 21
Chief Officer(s):
Audrey Parke, President & Secretary
Bonnie Start, Executive Director

Lloydminster Real Estate Board See Realtors Association of Lloydminster & District

Lloydminster Region Health Foundation (LRHF)
#116, 4910 - 50 St., Lloydminster SK S9V 0Y5
Tel: 306-820-6161; Fax: 306-825-3680
lrhf.ca
www.facebook.com/LloydRHF
Overview: A small local charitable organization founded in 1983
Mission: To help raise money on behalf of 4 health care centres to fund research & improve patient care
Staff Member(s): 7
Chief Officer(s):
Wendy Plandowski, CEO
wendy.plandowski@lrhf.ca

Lloydminster Society for the Prevention of Cruelty to Animals
PO Box 566, Lloydminster SK S9V 0Y6
Tel: 780-875-2809; Fax: 780-875-2819
www.lloydminsterspca.org
www.facebook.com/280509945522
twitter.com/LloydSPCA
Also Known As: Lloydminster & District SPCA
Overview: A small local charitable organization founded in 1972
Mission: To provide shelter & care to unwanted & neglected companion animals; To investigate & enact laws in the prevention of cruelty to animals; To educate the community about the proper care & maintenance of animals towards the goal of reducing the number of unwanted & neglected animals in Lloydminster & area
Member of: Alberta SPCA; Saskatchewan SPCA
Finances: Annual Operating Budget: $100,000-$250,000; Funding Sources: Donations; fundraising
Staff Member(s): 6; 100 volunteer(s)
Membership: 10
Activities: Awareness Events: Dog Jog; Dinner Theatre; Garage Sale
Chief Officer(s):
Shelly Zimmerman, Executive Director
execetivedirector@lloydminsterspca.org

L.M. Montgomery Institute (LMMI)
University of Prince Edward Island, 550 University Ave., Charlottetown PE C1A 4P3
Tel: 902-628-4346; Fax: 902-628-4305
lmmi@upei.ca
www.lmmontgomery.ca
www.facebook.com/LMMInstitute
twitter.com/LMMI_PEI
Overview: A small international organization founded in 1993
Mission: To focus on scholarship & teaching, while providing resources & educational opportunities to students & scholars researching the life, works & influence of L.M. Montgomery
Activities: Biennial international conferences; Lectures; Involvement in campus & community activities related to L.M. Montgomery; Library: KindredSpaces: L.M. Montgomery Research Collections Online
Chief Officer(s):
Mark Leggott, Chair
Meetings/Conferences:
• The L.M. Montgomery Institute's 13th Biennial Conference, June, 2018, University of Prince Edward Island, Charlottetown, PE

Loaves & Fishes Community Food Bank
1009 Farquhar St., Nanaimo BC V9R 2G2
Tel: 250-754-8347; Fax: 250-754-8349
info@nanaimoloavesandfishes.org
www.nanaimoloavesandfishes.org
www.facebook.com/NanLoavesFishes
twitter.com/nanaimofoodbank
Overview: A small local organization founded in 1996 overseen by Food Banks British Columbia
Member of: Food Banks British Columbia
Chief Officer(s):
Peter Sinclair, Executive Director

Local Government Administrators of the Northwest Territories (LGANT)
PO Box 2083, 5018 - 52nd St., 2nd Fl., Yellowknife NT X1A 2P6
Tel: 867-765-5630; Fax: 867-765-5635
information@lgant.com
www.lgant.com
Overview: A medium-sized provincial organization founded in 1981
Mission: To ensure effectiveness & professionalism in the Northwest Territories' local government administration field
Membership: Member Profile: Individuals employed in community governments or municipal corporations in the Northwest Territories
Activities: Offering education & career development programs
Chief Officer(s):
Grant Hood, President
Awards:
• LGANT Award of Excellence
Eligibility: Current NWT community government employees who have held an LGA position for at least two years
Meetings/Conferences:
• Local Government Administrators of the Northwest Territories Conference & Annual General Meeting, 2018
Scope: Provincial

Local Government Management Association of British Columbia (LGMA BC)
710 - 880 Douglas St., Victoria BC V8W 1B7
Tel: 250-383-7032; Fax: 250-384-4879
office@lgma.ca
www.lgma.ca
Previous Name: Municipal Officers' Association of British Columbia
Overview: A medium-sized provincial organization founded in 1919
Mission: To promote professional management & leadership excellence in local government; To create awareness of local government officers' roles in the community; To support professional networking & connections development; To encourage idea exchanges among members
Member of: Canadian Society of Association Executives
Finances: Annual Operating Budget: $1.5 Million-$3 Million; Funding Sources: Membership dues; Conference fees; Workshop fees; Sponsorships
Staff Member(s): 6; 200 volunteer(s)
Membership: 900; Fees: $130 retired; $285 regular; $335 affiliate; fee for corporate membership based on number of members; Member Profile: Municipal & regional district managers, administrators, clerks, treasurers, & other local government officials in the province of British Columbia; Persons with an interest in local government administration may be affiliate members; Committees: Audit & Financial Management; Governance; Professional Development & Education
Activities: Providing educational programs for local government professionals to encourage fellowship & networking; Offering career transition counselling services & training; Providing personal pension & retirement planning counselling services for members; Internships: Yes; Speaker Service: Yes
Chief Officer(s):

Nancy Taylor, Executive Director, 250-383-7032 Ext. 223
Ana Fuller, Manager, Programs, 250-383-7032 Ext. 227
afuller@lgma.ca
Randee Platz, Officer, Finance, 250-383-7032 Ext. 224
rplatz@lgma.ca
Awards:
• LGMA Member Recognition Awards
Awarded to recognize members for their service; distinctions include Life Membership, Distinguished Membership, Professional Service (Leadership, Innovation, Community & Volunteer), Distinguished Partners, Long Service *Deadline:* May
Meetings/Conferences:
• Local Government Management Association of British Columbia 2018 Annual Conference & AGM, May, 2018, Victoria Conference Centre, Victoria, BC
Scope: Provincial
Contact Information: Program Manager: Ana Fuller, Phone: 250-383-7032, ext. 227, E-mail: afuller@lgma.ca
• Local Government Management Association of British Columbia 2019 Annual Conference & AGM, June, 2019, Westin Bayshore, Vancouver, BC
Scope: Provincial
Contact Information: Program Manager: Ana Fuller, Phone: 250-383-7032, ext. 227, E-mail: afuller@lgma.ca
Publications:
• Election Manual [a publication of the Local Government Management Association of BC]
Type: Book; *Price:* $250 with LGMA membership; $295 without LGMA membership
Profile: Provides practical advice & best practices on local government elections
• Exchange [a publication of the Local Government Management Association of British Columbia]
Type: Magazine; *Frequency:* Quarterly; *Accepts Advertising*
Profile: A magazine, featuring best practices, ideas, & professional development, distributed to more than 1,000 localgovernment managers, mayors, & regional district chairs throughout British Columbia, as well as business affiliates
• Freedom of Information & Protection of Privacy Act [a publication of the Local Government Management Association of BC]
Type: Book; *Price:* $250 with LGMA membership; $295 without LGMA membership
Profile: A toolkit including information on privacy breaches, privacy management,& social media & electroniccommunications
• Guide for Approving Officers for Local Governments [a publication of the Local Government Management Association of BC]
Type: Book; *Price:* $250 with LGMA membership; $295 without LGMA membership
Profile: Includes information on approving officers, commentary on procedural fairness, civil liabilityinformation, & services agreements
• Human Resource Toolkit [a publication of the Local Government Management Association of BC]
Type: Book; *Price:* $250 with LGMA membership; $295 without LGMA membership
Profile: A sourcebook for best practices in Human Resources management
• Local Government Management Association of British Columbia Annual Report
Type: Yearbook; *Frequency:* Annually
Profile: A review of the year's activities, including chapter reports & financial statements
• Records Management Manual [a publication of the Local Government Management Association of BC]
Type: Book; *Price:* $250with LGMA membership; $295 without LGMA membership
Profile: Includes information on records management, including limitation periods, government aufits, elections, & anti-spam laws
  Lower Mainland Chapter
  BC
  Chief Officer(s):
  Susan Rauh, President, 604-927-5413, Fax: 604-927-5360
  rauhs@portcoquitlam.ca
  North Central Chapter
  BC
  Chief Officer(s):
  Ron Bowles, President, 250-638-4725, Fax: 250-638-4777
  rbowles@terrace.ca
  Eliana Clements, Secretary, 250-569-2229, Fax: 250-569-3276
  eliana@mcbride.ca

Karla Jensen, Treasurer, 250-960-4444, Fax: 250-563-7520
kjensen@rdffg.bc.ca
  Rocky Mountain Chapter (RMLGMA)
  c/o Raeleen Manjak, District of Sparwood, PO Box 520, 136 Spruce Ave., Sparwood BC V0B 2G0
  Chief Officer(s):
  Curtis Helgesen, President & Treasurer, 250-865-4000, Fax: 250-865-4001
  chelgesen@elkford.ca
  Jon Wilsgard, Vice-President, 250-344-2271 Ext. 237, Fax: 250-344-6577
  jon.wilsgard@golden.ca
  Thompson Okanagan Chapter
  BC
  Chief Officer(s):
  Stephen Fleming, President, 250-469-8660, Fax: 250-862-3399
  sfleming@kelowna.ca
  Ian Wilson, Vice-President, 250-469-8500, Fax: 250-862-3399
  iwilson@kelowna.ca
  Stephen Banmen, Treasurer, 250-766-5650, Fax: 250-766-0116
  sbanmen@lakecountry.bc.ca
  Vancouver Island Chapter (VILGMA)
  BC
  Chief Officer(s):
  Don Schaffer, President, 250-361-0549, Fax: 250-361-0348
  dschaffer@victoria.ca
  Andrew Hicik, Vice-President, 250-665-5410, Fax: 250-665-4508
  ahicik@sidney.ca
  Anja Nurvo, Secretary, 250-414-7135, Fax: 250-414-7111
  anja.nurvo@esquimalt.ca
  Michael Dillabaugh, Treasurer, 250-642-1634, Fax: 250-642-0541
  mdillabaugh@sooke.ca
  West Kootenay Boundary Chapter
  BC
  Chief Officer(s):
  Theresa Lenardon, President, 250-368-0225, Fax: 250-368-3990
  tlenardon@rdkb.com
  Bryan Teasdale, Vice-President, 250-368-9148, Fax: 250-368-3990
  bteasdale@rdkb.com
  Amy Gurnett, Secretary-Treasurer, 250-367-7234, Fax: 250-367-7288
  montvill@telus.net

LOFT Community Services (LOFT)
15 Toronto St., 9th Fl., Toronto ON M5C 2E3
Tel: 416-979-1994; *Fax:* 416-979-3028
info@loftcs.org
www.loftcs.org
www.facebook.com/loftcs
Previous Name: Anglican Houses
Overview: A large local organization founded in 1953
Mission: To promote recovery & independence for people marginalized by mental illness, addiction & homelessness; To offer housing & support services that are respectful, voluntary & responsive to individual needs
Member of: CARF Canada
Finances: *Annual Operating Budget:* Greater than $5 Million; *Funding Sources:* Donations
Staff Member(s): 350; 50 volunteer(s)
Activities: Community outreach & supportive housing services to over 4,000 vulnerable & homeless people at 50 sites in Toronto, York Region & South Simcoe Region; *Awareness Events:* Annual Holiday Benefit Concert, December; *Speaker Service:* Yes
Chief Officer(s):
Heather McDonald, CEO, 416-259-5995
hmcdonald@loftcs.org
Jim Nason, Director, Operations, 416-979-1994 Ext. 234
jnason@loftcs.org
Rosa Galluzzo, Director, Finance, 416-979-1994 Ext. 229
rgalluzzo@loftcs.org
Jane Corbett, Director, Development, 416-979-1994 Ext. 227
jcorbett@loftcs.org

Logan Lake Arts Council (LLAC)
PO Box 299, Logan Lake BC V0K 1W0

Tel: 250-523-2390
llac@ocis.net
llac.d3ross.info
Overview: A small local organization founded in 1983
Mission: To promote arts & culture in community
Member of: Assembly of BC Arts Councils
Membership: 1-99
Activities: *Library:* Not open to public
Chief Officer(s):
Joan Wankel, President

The Logistics Institute
#405, 501 Alliance St., Toronto ON M6N 2J1
Tel: 416-363-3005; *Fax:* 416-363-5598
loginfo@loginstitute.ca
www.loginstitute.ca
www.linkedin.com/groups?home=&gid=1581887
www.facebook.com/129220600590938
twitter.com/LogInstitute
Overview: A medium-sized national organization founded in 1990
Mission: To provide certification for the P.Log. designation
Finances: *Funding Sources:* Human Resources Services Development of Canada
Activities: Provides comprehensive training, development and support programs; Workshops; Certifications; Continuous learning
Chief Officer(s):
Victor S. Deyglio, Founding President, 416-363-3005 Ext. 1200
vdeyglio@loginstitute.ca
Ben Avery, Manager, Marketing, 416-363-3005 Ext. 1500
bavery@loginstitute.ca
Jasmine Gill, Coordinator, Program & Membership, 416-363-3005 Ext. 1700
jgill@loginstitute.ca
Stephanie Char, Program Assistant, 416-363-3005 Ext. 1400
schar@loginstitute.ca
Priscilla Ng, Fianance, 416-363-3005 Ext. 1000
priscilla@loginstitute.ca

Loisir littéraire du Québec *Voir* Fédération québécoise du loisir littéraire

LOMA Canada
East Tower, 675 Cochrane Dr., 6th Floor, Markham ON L3R 0B8
Tel: 905-530-2309; *Fax:* 905-530-2001
lomacanada@loma.org
www.loma.org/canada
Previous Name: Life Insurance Institute of Canada
Overview: A medium-sized national organization founded in 2002
Mission: To serve its member companies by encouraging & assisting individuals to acquire knowledge & understanding of business of life & health insurance & related financial services.
Member of: Life Office Management Association
Membership: *Member Profile:* Chartered life & health insurance companies, with their head or a branch office operating in Canada; organizations that provide services to life & health insurance companies; academic institutions that provide education in & outside the life & health insurance industry
Meetings/Conferences:
• LOMA 2018 Annual Conference, September, 2018
Scope: National
Contact Information: E-mail: meetings@loma.org

London & District Labour Council
#1, 380 Adelaide St. North, London ON N6B 3P6
Tel: 519-432-3188; *Fax:* 519-642-7834
www.ldlc.on.ca
www.facebook.com/londonlabour
twitter.com/ldnlabour
Overview: A small local organization overseen by Ontario Federation of Labour
Chief Officer(s):
Patti Dalton, President

London & Middlesex Historical Society (LMHS)
PO Box 303, Stn. B, London ON N6A 4W1
www.londonheritage.ca/LondonMiddlesexHistoricalSociety
Overview: A small local charitable organization founded in 1901
Mission: To promote awareness of local heritage through public meetings, historical tours & demonstrations; to encourage the preservation of records, documents, pictures, buildings & sites relating to history of London & Middlesex
Member of: Ontario Historical Society
Finances: *Funding Sources:* Membership fees; donations; grants

Membership: *Fees:* $20 single; $15 senior/student
Activities: Meetings; bus tours; displays
Chief Officer(s):
Sandy McRae, President
smcrae@gtn.on.ca

London & St. Thomas Association of Realtors
342 Commissioners Rd. West, London ON N6J 1Y3
Tel: 519-641-1400; *Fax:* 519-641-4613
info@lstar.ca
www.lstar.ca
www.facebook.com/LSTAR.REALTORS
twitter.com/LSTARtweets
www.youtube.com/user/LSTARMembers
Overview: A small local organization overseen by Ontario Real Estate Association
Mission: To provide its members with the necessary tools that enable them to deliver excellent service to the community
Member of: The Canadian Real Estate Association
Membership: 1,500
Activities: *Library:*
Chief Officer(s):
Betty Doré, Executive Vice President
Joanne Shannon, Director, Administration

London Building & Construction Trades Council
56 Firestone Blvd., London ON N5W 5L4
Tel: 519-455-8083; *Fax:* 519-455-0712
Overview: A small local organization founded in 1946
Member of: AFL-CIO
Finances: *Annual Operating Budget:* $50,000-$100,000
Membership: 6,000+; *Member Profile:* Skilled construction trades
Activities: Trade shows; career days; volunteer labour for community projects; *Speaker Service:* Yes
Chief Officer(s):
Jim MacKinnon, Contact
jmackinnon@liuna1059.ca

London Chamber of Commerce
#101, 244 Pall Mall St., London ON N6A 5P6
Tel: 519-432-7551; *Fax:* 519-432-8063
info@londonchamber.com
www.londonchamber.com
www.facebook.com/303537065706
twitter.com/LondonCofC
Overview: A small local organization founded in 1857
Mission: To serve as the voice of business committed to the enhancement of economic prosperity & quality of life in London
Member of: Ontario Chamber of Commerce; Canadian Chamber of Commerce
Finances: *Funding Sources:* Membership dues; fundraising
Staff Member(s): 7; 1500 volunteer(s)
Membership: 980; *Fees:* Schedule available; *Committees:* Agri-Business; Executive; Global Business Opportunities; Government Affairs; Marketing & Communications; Membership Services
Activities: Organizing events such as Business After Five, Business Before Business, Breakfast with the Mayor, Comedy Auction, Corporate Challenge, Past Presidents' Golf Classic, Volunteer Appreciation Night & Speed Networking; *Speaker Service:* Yes; *Rents Mailing List:* Yes; *Library:* Open to public
Chief Officer(s):
Jeff Macoun, President
Gerry MacCartney, CEO
gerry@londonchamber.com
Awards:
- Innovation & Agribusiness Award
- Environmental Leadership Award
- Business of the Year
- Corporate Social Responsibility Award
- Excellence in Human Resources Award

London Community Foundation (LCF)
Covent Garden Market, 130 King St., London ON N6A 1C5
Tel: 519-667-1600; *Fax:* 519-667-1615
info@lcf.on.ca
www.lcf.on.ca
www.facebook.com/LdnCommFdn
twitter.com/LdnCommFdn
www.youtube.com/user/Ldncommfdn
Overview: A small local charitable organization founded in 1954
Mission: To create a vibrant & caring community; To strengthen the community by making strategic & effective grants; To build & manage a permanent endowment; To serve the community as a resource & partner so that each member has the opportunity for an enriched quality of life

Staff Member(s): 5; 50 volunteer(s)
Chief Officer(s):
Martha Powell, President & CEO, 519-667-1600 Ext. 101
mpowell@lcf.on.ca
Stephanie Winterton, Executive Administrator, 519-667-1600 Ext. 108
stephanie@lcf.on.ca
Vanessa Dolishny, Manager, Communications, 519-667-1600 Ext. 107
vanessa@lcf.on.ca

London Community Orchestra (LCO)
838 Wellington St., London ON N6A 3S7
info@lco-on.ca
lco-on.ca
www.facebook.com/LondonCommunityOrchestra
twitter.com/LCO_ON
Previous Name: Fanshawe Community Orchestra
Overview: A small local charitable organization founded in 1974 overseen by Orchestras Canada
Mission: To give concerts & to sponsor local young artists as soloists
Member of: Orchestras Canada
Finances: *Funding Sources:* Membership fees; Donations; Ticket sales
Activities: 4 symphony concerts per season
Chief Officer(s):
Sally Vernon, President
Leonard Ingrao, Music Director

London District Chief's Council *See* Southern First Nations Secretariat

London Food Bank
926 Leathorne St., London ON N5Z 3M5
Tel: 519-659-4045; *Fax:* 519-680-1627
londonfb@web.net
www.londonfoodbank.net
www.facebook.com/LondonFoodBank
twitter.com/LondonFoodBank1
Overview: A small local charitable organization founded in 1987
Mission: To help a caring community share its food resources
Member of: Ontario Association of Food Banks; Canadian Association of Food Banks
Finances: *Annual Operating Budget:* $100,000-$250,000
Staff Member(s): 3; 200 volunteer(s)
Membership: 100-499
Activities: *Internships:* Yes; *Speaker Service:* Yes
Chief Officer(s):
Brian Ratcliffe, General Manager
Glen Peason, Director
Jane Roy, Director

London Goodwill Industries Association *See* Goodwill Industries

London Health Sciences Foundation (LHSF)
747 Base Line Rd. East, London ON N6C 2R6
Tel: 519-685-8409; *Fax:* 519-685-8265
foundation@lhsc.on.ca
www.lhsf.ca
www.facebook.com/lhsf.ca
twitter.com/LHSFCanada
www.youtube.com/LHSFCanada
Overview: A small local charitable organization
Mission: To help raise money on behalf of the London Health Sciences Centre to fund research & improve patient care
Staff Member(s): 44
Chief Officer(s):
John H. MacFarlane, President, 519-685-8409 Ext. 58482

London Insurance Professionals Association
London ON
www.caiw-acfa.com
Overview: A small local organization
Member of: Canadian Association of Insurance Women
Chief Officer(s):
Mary Hooper, Director, 519-661-0200, Fax: 519-661-0972
mhooper@preferred-ins.com

London Jewish Community Council; London Jewish Community Foundation *See* London Jewish Federation

London Jewish Federation
536 Huron St., London ON N5Y 4J5
Tel: 519-673-3310; *Fax:* 519-673-1161
ljf@ljf.on.ca
www.jewishlondon.ca

www.facebook.com/jcclondonontario
twitter.com/jcclondonon
Previous Name: London Jewish Community Council; London Jewish Community Foundation
Overview: A medium-sized local charitable organization founded in 1974 overseen by Ontario Council of Agencies Serving Immigrants
Mission: To support & enrich the quality of Jewish life in London; to assist in enhancing Jewish values in Israel & throughout the world
Member of: Council of Jewish Federations; Jewish Community Centre Association
Affiliation(s): United Israel Appeal of Canada
Finances: *Funding Sources:* United Jewish Appeal; United Way
Staff Member(s): 11
Activities: Annual Holocaust program; Israel Day; Special Event programs at Chanukah, Purim, etc.; Speaker series; *Internships:* Yes; *Speaker Service:* Yes
Chief Officer(s):
Esther Marcus, Executive Director
jccexec@ljf.on.ca

London Multiple Births Association (LMBA)
PO Box 52031, RPO Commissioners Road East, London ON N6C 0A1
london@multiplebirthscanada.org
www.londonmultiples.com
Overview: A small local organization founded in 1977 overseen by Multiple Births Canada
Membership: *Committees:* Sales; Social; Parent Outreach
Chief Officer(s):
Tammy Langendyk, Co-President
lmba.president@rogers.com
Erika Kafka, Co-President
lmba.president@rogers.com

London Musicians' Association
#9, 30 Forward Ave., London ON N6H 1B7
Tel: 519-685-2540
Other Communication: londonmusicians279@gmail.com
admin@londonmusicians.com
www.londonmusicians.com
Also Known As: American Federation of Musicians, Local 279
Overview: A small local organization founded in 1903
Mission: To represent professional musicians in the London area
Affiliation(s): American Federation of Musicians
Membership: 300+; *Fees:* $100 initiation; $180 annual; *Committees:* By-Laws; Finance; Membership/Diversity
Activities: Booking referral service; legal assistance; immigration/travel assistance; *Library*

London Numismatic Society
543 Kininvie Dr., London ON N6G 1P1
Tel: 519-472-9679
Overview: A small local organization founded in 1951
Mission: To study coins, discuss purchases, present educational material, & auction items
12 volunteer(s)
Activities: *Awareness Events:* Numismatic Society Annual Coin Show, September
Chief Officer(s):
Ted Leitch, Contact

London Orchid Society
#162, 509 Commissioners Rd. West, London ON N6J 1Y5
los.lon.imag.net
Overview: A small local organization founded in 1976
Mission: To promote the cultivation of orchids
Member of: Canadian Orchid Congress; American Orchid Society
Membership: *Fees:* $20 single; $25 family
Chief Officer(s):
Sean Moore, President
spmoore@rogers.com

London Philatelic Society
London ON
Overview: A small local organization founded in 1892
Mission: To promote the study & collecting of stamps in the London area
Finances: *Annual Operating Budget:* Less than $50,000; *Funding Sources:* Membership dues
Staff Member(s): 6
Membership: 100; *Fees:* $10; *Member Profile:* Stamp collecting
Activities: *Library:* Not open to public

London Police Association (LPA) / Association de la police de London
330 William St., London ON N6B 3C7
Tel: 519-661-5360; *Fax:* 519-660-6018
carolyn@lpa.on.ca
www.lpa.on.ca
Overview: A small local organization founded in 1947 overseen by Police Association of Ontario
Mission: To represent all police & civilian members of the London Police Service; To promote the mutual interests of members
Member of: Police Association of Ontario
Finances: *Funding Sources:* LPA facility rental fees
Membership: 801; *Member Profile:* Police & civilian members of London Ontario's police service
Activities: Supporting charities
Chief Officer(s):
Rick Terrio, Vice-President
rterrio@lpa.on.ca
Brian Urquhart, President
Dan Axford, Administrator
lpa@lpa.on.ca

London Regional Art & Historical Museums *See* Museum London

London Regional Resource Centre for Heritage & the Environment
1017 Western Rd., London ON N6G 1G5
Tel: 519-645-2845; *Fax:* 519-645-0981
info@grosvenorlodge.com
www.heritagelondonfoundation.org/Grosvenor/indexgrosvenor.html
www.facebook.com/events/1431960477024890
Also Known As: Grosvenor Lodge
Overview: A small local organization founded in 1992
Mission: To promote heritage & environmental activities & organizations in the London area
Member of: Heritage London Foundation
Staff Member(s): 3

London Soaring Club
315816 - 31st Line, Embro ON N0J 1J0
Tel: 519-661-7844
info@londonsoaringclub.ca
www.londonsoaringclub.ca
www.facebook.com/124146337603689
twitter.com/Londonsoaring
Overview: A small local organization
Member of: Soaring Association of Canada

London Youth Symphony (LYS)
PO Box 553, Stn. B, London ON N6A 4W8
Tel: 519-868-6983
lysymphony@hotmail.com
www.windmillwebworks.ddns.net/londonyouthsymphony/
www.facebook.com/169142799797422
Overview: A small local organization overseen by Orchestras Canada
Mission: To provide the region's most talented young musicians with the opportunity to build self-discipline, confidence & team spirit within an outstanding symphonic environment that offers professional directorship & coaching
Member of: Orchestras Canada
Finances: *Funding Sources:* Tuition; Corporate and individual sponsors; Municipal donations
Staff Member(s): 3
Membership: *Fees:* $700; *Member Profile:* Orchestral musicians ages 13 to 23
Chief Officer(s):
Len Ingrao, Artistic Director

London-Middlesex Children's Aid Society
PO Box 7010, 1680 Oxford St. East, London ON N5Y 5R8
Tel: 519-455-9000; *Fax:* 519-455-4355
Toll-Free: 888-661-6167; *TTY:* 519-455-6498
info@caslondon.on.ca
www.caslondon.on.ca
www.linkedin.com/company/children's-aid-society-of-london-&-middlesex
Overview: A small local organization
Mission: To protect & care for at-risk children & families
Member of: Ontario Association of Childrens' Aid Societies
196 volunteer(s)
Activities: Providing protection & counselling services to children, youth, & families; Offering foster care placement services; *Speaker Service:* Yes

Chief Officer(s):
Regina Bell, Interim Executive Director

Long Point Bird Observatory *See* Bird Studies Canada

Long Term & Continuing Care Association of Manitoba (LTCAM)
#103, 1483 Pembina Hwy., Winnipeg MB R3T 2C6
Tel: 204-477-9888; *Fax:* 204-477-9889
Toll-Free: 855-477-9888
info@ltcam.mb.ca
www.ltcam.mb.ca
www.facebook.com/ltccam
twitter.com/LTCAManitoba
www.youtube.com/LTCAManitoba
Overview: A small provincial organization founded in 1959 overseen by Canadian Alliance for Long Term Care
Mission: To advance long term & continuing care by promoting awareness to government, regional health authorities, health agencies & the community
Membership: 4,500+; *Member Profile:* Long term & continuing care organizations in Manitoba
Chief Officer(s):
Linda Sundevic, President

Longlac Chamber of Commerce
PO Box 877, Longlac ON P0T 2A0
info@longlacchamber.com
www.longlacchamber.com
www.facebook.com/longlacchamber
Overview: A small local organization
Mission: To promote local businesses & help them grow
Chief Officer(s):
Vaughn Arsenault, President

Lookout Emergency Aid Society
429 Alexander St., Vancouver BC V6A 1C6
Tel: 604-255-0340; *Fax:* 604-255-0790
info@lookoutsociety.bc.ca
www.lookoutsociety.bc.ca
www.facebook.com/LookoutSociety
twitter.com/LookoutSociety
www.youtube.com/user/LookoutSociety
Also Known As: Lookout Society
Overview: A medium-sized local charitable organization founded in 1971
Mission: To provides housing and a range of support services to adults with low or no income who have few, if any, housing or support optionss. Operating in 4 municipalities within Metro Vancouver, Lookout serves the homeless popoulation by providing 4 permanent emergency shelters, 3 temporary extreme weather shelters, 6 tranitional and 14 permanent supported residences as well as a drop in activity centre for people living with mental illness within Vancouver's Downtown Eastside.
Member of: Shelter Net BC; Home & Homeless Network; Health Employers Association of BC; Greater Vancouver Shelter Strategy; Burnaby Homeless Task Force; Vancouver Urban Core Community Workers Assocation; Surrey Board of Trade
Affiliation(s): Vancouver Urban Care Community Workers Association; Adult Mental Health Service Providers Committee
Finances: *Annual Operating Budget:* Greater than $5 Million; *Funding Sources:* Provincial government; federal grants; donations; health authorities
Staff Member(s): 360; 5231 volunteer(s)
Membership: 11; *Fees:* $11; *Committees:* Board of Directors; H'Arts Annual Gala Committee
Activities: Housing & support services; Blanket drive in December; *Awareness Events:* Coins for Change; *Internships:* Yes; *Speaker Service:* Yes
Chief Officer(s):
Shayne Williams, Executive Director, 604-255-0340
shaynew@lookoutsociety.ca
Leonard Levy, Director of Operations
leonardl@lookoutsociety.ca

Lord Reading Law Society / Association de droit Lord Reading
5161, boul Décarie, Montréal QC H2X 2H9
info@lordreading.org
lordreading.org
Overview: A small local organization founded in 1948
Mission: Pour faire avancer les droits de l'homme et des libertés des juristes juifs
Membership: *Member Profile:* Jewish jurists; *Committees:* Communications; Careers; Membership; Sponsorship; Program; Young Bar

Chief Officer(s):
Morris Chaikelson, Executive Director
Heather Michelin, President, Board of Directors
president@lordreading.org

The Lord Selkirk Association of Rupert's Land (TLSARL)
Winnipeg MB
www.lordselkirk.ca
Overview: A small local organization founded in 1908
Mission: To serve as a link to bind together the descendants of the hardy men & women who first settled on the bank of the Red River in the early 1800s; to perpetuate the memory & preserve the spirit, traditions & history of those first agricultural settlers
Finances: *Funding Sources:* Membership fees
Membership: *Member Profile:* Descendants of settlers resident at Red River prior to 1835

The Lord's Flock Charismatic Community
Our Lady of Fatima Shrine, 3170 St. Clair Ave. East, Toronto ON M1L 1V6
Tel: 416-317-9599
lordsflock.intl@gmail.com
www.lordsflock.org
Overview: A medium-sized international organization
Mission: To promote the Christian faith while preserving culture & heritage for future generations
Affiliation(s): Archdiocese of Toronto
Finances: *Annual Operating Budget:* Less than $50,000
Activities: Pilgrimages; Christian holiday celebrations; seminars
Chief Officer(s):
Jun Silva, Contact
Cynthia Silva, Contact
Georgia Gaceta, Contact
Pilar Acosta, Contact

Lorne Agricultural & Industrial Society *See* Prince Albert Exhibition Association

Lorraine Kimsa Theatre for Young People *See* Young People's Theatre

Lost Villages Historical Society
PO Box 306, Ingleside ON K0C 1M0
Tel: 613-534-2197
lostvillages.ca
Overview: A small local charitable organization founded in 1977
Mission: To collect, preserve & display the heritage of the Lost Villages, the communities which were inundated in the Hydro & Seaway flooding of July 1, 1958; to operate the Lost Villages Museum, open mid-June to late Sept.
Membership: *Fees:* $10 individual; $15 family; $50 life
Activities: Historical tours of St. Lawrence Seaway & Lost Villages area; *Library:* by appointment

Lo-Se-Ca Foundation
#215, 1 Carnegie Dr., St Albert AB T8N 5B1
Tel: 780-460-1400
www.loseca.ca
www.facebook.com/115663645142959
twitter.com/losecafdn
Overview: A small local charitable organization founded in 1988
Mission: To promote the quality of life of families & individuals by providing services within a Christian environment; to enhance human well-being, worth & dignity of life for all persons with disabilities
Member of: Alberta Association of Rehabilitation Centres; Persons with Developmental Disabilities
Activities: Day service; thrift shop; in-services; seminars; respite care
Chief Officer(s):
Marie Renaud, Executive Director
mrenaud@loseca.ca

Lotus Car Club of Canada
460 Barclay Cres., Oakville ON L6J 6H9
www.lotusclubcanada.ca
Overview: A small national charitable organization founded in 1977
Member of: British Car Council
Affiliation(s): Specialty Vehicle Association of Ontario
Membership: 141; *Fees:* $15; *Member Profile:* Lotus car owners & enthusiasts

Louise Bédard Danse
#300, 2022, rue Sherbrooke est, Montréal QC H2K 1B9
Tél: 514-982-4580
infos@lbdanse.org

www.lbdanse.org
www.facebook.com/lbdanse
twitter.com/lbdanse
www.youtube.com/lbdanse
Aperçu: Dimension: petite; *Envergure:* locale; fondée en 1990
Mission: De poursuivre les activités modernes création de danse, de sensibilisation et d'éducation, et en offrant des créations chorégraphiques originales pour le grand public
Membre de: Circuit-Est centre chorégraphique; Regroupement québécois de la danse; La danse sur les routes du Québec
Membre(s) du personnel: 4
Membre(s) du bureau directeur:
Louise Bédard, Directrice artistique

Lower Mainland Independent Secondary School Athletic Association (LMISSAA)
BC
athletics@yorkhouse.ca
www.lmissaa.com
Overview: A small local organization
Member of: BC School Sports
Chief Officer(s):
Carm Renzullo, President

Lower Mainland Local Government Association (LMLGA)
#60, 10551 Shellbridge Way, Richmond BC V6X 2W9
Tel: 250-356-5122; *Fax:* 604-270-9116
www.lmlga.ca
Overview: A small local organization
Mission: To enhance & improve the level of services provided by local governments; To promote the welfare of residents of member governments; To advance proposed changes to legislation, regulations, or government policies
Membership: 31 local governments + 3 regional districts; *Member Profile:* Local governments from Lillooet to Hope, British Columbia; Regional districts
Activities: Offering information & educational activities; Providing networking opportunities
Chief Officer(s):
Iris Hesketh-Boles, Executive Coordinator
Iris@lmlga.bc.ca
James Atebe, President
Sav Dhaliwal, 1st Vice President
Barbara Steele, 2nd Vice President
Meetings/Conferences:
• Lower Mainland Local Government Association 2018 Annual General Meeting & Conference, May, 2018, Whistler, BC
Scope: Local
Description: Tradeshow, workshops, & seminars for persons involved in local government

Lower Mainland Spina Bifida Association *See* Spina Bifida & Hydrocephalus Association of British Columbia

Lower Mainland Wildlife Rescue Association *See* Wildlife Rescue Association of British Columbia

Loyola Arrupe Centre for Seniors *See* LA Centre for Active Living

Lu'ma Native Housing Society (LNHS)
25 West 6th Ave., Vancouver BC V5Y 1K2
Tel: 604-876-0811; *Fax:* 604-876-0999
www.lnhs.ca
Also Known As: New Beginnings Native Housing Society
Overview: A small provincial organization founded in 1981
Mission: To provide affordable, adequate & accessible housing to meet the needs of Aboriginal people; To assist tenants with the transition to urban living
Member of: National Aboriginal Housing Association
Affiliation(s): First Funds Society
Finances: *Annual Operating Budget:* $3 Million-$5 Million; *Funding Sources:* Canada Mortgage & Housing Society; BC Housing Management Commission
Staff Member(s): 29; 10 volunteer(s)
Membership: 100; *Fees:* $1; *Committees:* Membership; Finance; Development; AGM
Activities: Advocates for low-cost affordable housing to Aboriginal peoples & finding best practice methods in providing housing services & homelessness initiatives
Chief Officer(s):
Marcel Swain, Consultant

Lucie & André Chagnon Foundation *Voir* Fondation Lucie et André Chagnon

Lucie Grégoire Danse
#302, 4416 boul St-Laurent, Montréal QC HW2 1Z5
Tél: 514-278-1620
infos@luciegregoiredanse.ca
www.luciegregoiredanse.ca
www.facebook.com/luciegregoiredanse
Aperçu: Dimension: petite; *Envergure:* locale, fondée en 1981
Membre de: Regroupement québécois de la danse
Finances: *Fonds:* Conseil des Arts du Canada; Conseil des arts et des lettres du Québec
Membre(s) du bureau directeur:
Lucie Grégoire, Directrice artistique

Lucknow & District Chamber of Commerce
PO Box 313, Lucknow ON N0G 2H0
Tel: 519-357-8454
info@lucknowchamber.ca
www.lucknowchamber.ca
www.facebook.com/422493221143383
twitter.com/LucknowChamber
Overview: A small local organization founded in 1993
Mission: To enhance the economic prosperity & quality of life in Lucknow & the surrounding district
Member of: Ontario Chamber of Commerce
Finances: *Funding Sources:* Membership dues
Membership: *Fees:* $80; *Member Profile:* Local businesses
Activities: Promoting the business community
Chief Officer(s):
Morten Jakobsen, President
Awards:
• Citizen of the Year

LUE-42 Enterprises
PO Box 11021, Stn. Main, Edmonton AB T5J 3K3
Tel: 780-466-9938; *Fax:* 780-468-4449
lue42@shaw.ca
www.LUE42.com
Overview: A small provincial organization founded in 1999
Member of: Canadian Society of Association Executives (CSAE), Institute of Chartered Secretaries & Administrators (ICSA), Institute of Corporate Directors (ICD)
Finances: *Annual Operating Budget:* $100,000-$250,000
Staff Member(s): 1
Activities: Consulting businesses; Providing crisis management; Writing & speaking for events
Chief Officer(s):
Linda Wood Edwards, President
Publications:
• Exceptional Board Members [a publication of LUE-42 Enterprises]
Type: Book; *Author:* Linda Wood Edwards; *ISBN:* 978-0-9866030-1-3; *Price:* $40
Profile: A guide for board members; assists in developing their skills
• LUE-42 E-zine
Type: Newsletter; *Frequency:* Monthly; *Accepts Advertising*; *Author:* Linda Wood Edwards
Profile: News & updates for members
• Understanding Bylaws: A Guide for Directors of Not-For-Profit Organizations [a publication of LUE-42 Enterprises]
Type: Book; *Author:* Linda Wood Edwards; *ISBN:* 978-0-9866030-0-6; *Price:* $75
Profile: A guide for directors of not-for-profit organizations; assistsin the development of bylaws & improving governance

Luggage, Leathergoods, Handbags & Accessories Association of Canada (LLHA)
PO Box 144, Stn. A, Toronto ON M9C 4V2
Fax: 519-624-6408
Toll-Free: 866-872-2420
info@llha.ca
www.llha.ca
www.facebook.com/LLHAShow
twitter.com/llhatradeshow
Overview: A medium-sized national organization
Mission: To promote the growth of the industry in Canada; To foster the interchange of ideas
Membership: *Member Profile:* Manufacturers; Distributors; Importers; Wholesalers; Agents; Retailers
Activities: Presenting educational speakers & seminars; organizing the annual LLHA Show; *Awareness Events:* Trade Show, April
Chief Officer(s):
Catherine Genge, Executive Administrator
Meetings/Conferences:
• 38th Annual Luggage, Leathergoods, Handbags & Accessories Show 2018, April, 2018, International Centre, Toronto, ON
Scope: National

Lumber & Building Materials Association of Ontario (LBMAO)
391 Matheson Blvd. East, #A, Mississauga ON L4Z 2H2
Tel: 905-625-1084; *Fax:* 905-625-3006
Toll-Free: 888-365-2626
www.lbmao.on.ca
Previous Name: Ontario Retail Lumber Dealers Association
Overview: A medium-sized provincial organization founded in 1917
Mission: To promote the welfare of members so that they are able to build a competitive advantage & remain at the leading edge of the lumber & building materials industry
Membership: *Member Profile:* Manufacturers; Distributors; Purchasing organizations; Wholesalers; Service firm
Activities: Providing educational opportunities; Offering support services; Engaging in advocacy activities
Chief Officer(s):
Ken Forbes, Chair

Lumby Chamber of Commerce
PO Box 534, 1882 Vernon St., Lumby BC V0E 2G0
Tel: 250-547-2300; *Fax:* 250-547-2300
www.monasheetourism.com
Overview: A small local organization founded in 1979
Mission: To facilitate, enhance & improve Lumby's quality of life; To support positive & sustainable development; To encourage growth in commerce & industry for the prosperity of members & the Lumby area
Member of: BC Chamber of Commerce
Finances: *Annual Operating Budget:* Less than $50,000; *Funding Sources:* Memberships; fee for service
Staff Member(s): 3; 10 volunteer(s)
Membership: 100; *Fees:* $95-$255; *Member Profile:* Business; tourism; service groups; *Committees:* Arts & Parks; Business Development; Tourism
Activities: Engaging in revitalization efforts & other projects; Maintaining Lumby Visitor Infocentre; *Speaker Service:* Yes
Chief Officer(s):
Stephanie Sexsmith, Executive Director

Lumsden & District Chamber of Commerce
PO Box 114, Lumsden SK S0G 3C0
Tel: 306-731-2862
Overview: A small local organization founded in 1985
Membership: *Fees:* $100

Lundy's Lane Historical Society (LLHS)
5810 Ferry St., Niagara Falls ON L2G 1S9
Tel: 905-358-5082
Overview: A small local organization founded in 1887
Mission: To arouse & stimulate interest in the history of Niagara Falls, the Battle of Lundy's Lane, the Niagara Peninsula & Ontario by means of public lectures, field trips & publications
Member of: Ontario Historical Society
Finances: *Annual Operating Budget:* Less than $50,000; *Funding Sources:* Membership fees; sale of books; donations
Membership: 140; *Fees:* $8 individual; $10 family; *Committees:* Executive; Publications; Museum
Activities: Monthly meetings; two walking tours; annual commemorative service
Chief Officer(s):
Bill Houston, President
Marg Lamb, Contact, 905-227-1632

Lunenburg Board of Trade
Visitor's Information Centre, PO Box 1300, 11 Blockhouse Hill Rd., Lunenburg NS B0J 2C0
Tel: 902-634-3170; *Fax:* 902-634-3194
Toll-Free: 888-615-8305
ed@lunenburgns.com
www.lunenburgns.com/lunenburg-board-of-trade
Overview: A small local organization founded in 1927
Mission: To advance commercial, industrial & civic interests of Lunenburg and its area
Affiliation(s): Canadian Chamber of Commerce; Atlantic Chamber of Commerce; NS Economic Development & Tourism; Tourism Industry Association of NS; Destination Bluenose Coast
Membership: *Member Profile:* Sole Proprietors; Partnerships; Corporations; Associations; Societies; Business-minded individuals
Chief Officer(s):
Mike Smith, President

Lunenburg County Historical Society (LCHS)
PO Box 99, LaHave NS B0R 1C0
Tel: 902-688-1632; *Fax:* 902-688-1632
Other Communication: fortpointmuseum.wordpress.com
lchsftpt@gmail.com
www.fortpointmuseum.com
www.facebook.com/fort.point.5
twitter.com/fortpointmuseum
Also Known As: Fort Point Museum
Overview: A small local organization founded in 1969
Mission: To preserve the LeHave River Estuary cultural & historical heritage while educating & learning
Member of: Federation of the Nova Scotian Heritage
Finances: *Annual Operating Budget:* Less than $50,000; *Funding Sources:* Membership fees; donations
Staff Member(s): 1; 50 volunteer(s)
Membership: 105; *Fees:* $10
Activities: Fort Point Museum; concerts; art events; workshop

Lunenburg County Wildlife Association
PO Box 1934, Lunenburg NS B0J 2C0
Overview: A small local organization
Mission: To promote outdoor activities, including fishing & hunting

Lunenburg Heritage Society
PO Box 674, 125 Pelham St., Lunenburg NS B0J 2C0
Tel: 902-634-3498; *Fax:* 902-634-3194
lunenburgheritagesociety@hotmail.com
www.lunenburgheritagesociety.ca
www.facebook.com/lunenburg.heritage.9
twitter.com/lunenburghs
Overview: A small local charitable organization founded in 1972
Mission: To promote & preserve the architectural & cultural heritage of the Town of Lunenburg
Member of: Heritage Trust of Nova Scotia; National Historic Site(Knaut-Rhuland House Museum)
Affiliation(s): Heritage Advisory - Town of Lunenburg; South Shore Tourism Association; Lunenburg Board of Trade
Finances: *Annual Operating Budget:* Less than $50,000; *Funding Sources:* Fundraising
Staff Member(s): 1; 10 volunteer(s)
Membership: 100-200; *Fees:* $10 individual; $15 family; *Committees:* Marketing; Cabaret; Bandstand; House Tour; Knaut-Rhuland House Museum; NS Folk Art Festival
Activities: Heritage House Tour; Knaut-Rhuland House Museum; NS Folk Art Festival; Bandstand Summer Concerts; Christmas Cabaret
Chief Officer(s):
Don Wilson, President

Lunenburg Marine Museum Society
PO Box 1363, 68 Bluenose Dr., Lunenburg NS B0J 2C0
Tel: 902-634-4794; *Fax:* 902-634-8990
Toll-Free: 866-579-4909
fma@gov.ns.ca
www.fisheries.museum.gov.ns.ca
Also Known As: Fisheries Museum of the Atlantic
Overview: A small local organization founded in 1965
Mission: To protect, enhance & celebrate the heritage of the Atlantic Canada Fishery; to collect, interpret & share this valuable heritage with special emphasis on the traditional Nova Scotia fisheries for all Atlantic Canadians & our visitors
Member of: Canadian Museums Association
Finances: *Annual Operating Budget:* $500,000-$1.5 Million; *Funding Sources:* Nova Scotia Museum; admissions; gift shop
Staff Member(s): 9; 21 volunteer(s)
Membership: 184; *Fees:* $10
Activities: Programs & demonstrations during open season, first weekend in May - last weekend in October; *Library:* Open to public
Chief Officer(s):
Angela Saunders, General Manager

Lunenfeld-Tanenbaum Research Institute
Sinai Health System, 600 University Ave., Toronto ON M5G 1X5
Tel: 416-596-4200
www.lunenfeld.ca
www.youtube.com/SamuelLunenfeld
Overview: A large international organization founded in 1985
Mission: To advance scientific knowledge; To ensure the application of such knowledge to the promotion of human health; To assist Mount Sinai Hospital in meeting its mission as a leading health care facility
Affiliation(s): Mount Sinai Hospital; University of Toronto Faculty of Medicine; Ontario Health Study
Finances: *Funding Sources:* Sinai Health Foundation; medical research granting agencies; pharmaceutical companies
Staff Member(s): 264
Membership: *Committees:* Research
Activities: Conducting medical & scientific research; Publishing papers in scientific journals; *Speaker Service:* Yes
Chief Officer(s):
Jim Woodgett, Director, Research, 416-586-4800 Ext. 8811
Paul Kranjac, Director, Finance & Information Technology, 416-586-4800 Ext. 5398
Mark Toone, Director, Operations, 416-586-4800 Ext. 8252

The Lung Association of Nova Scotia (LANS)
#200, 6331 Lady Hammond Rd., Halifax NS B3K 2S2
Tel: 902-443-8141; *Fax:* 902-445-2573
Toll-Free: 888-566-5864
info@ns.lung.ca
www.ns.lung.ca
www.facebook.com/LungNS
twitter.com/NSLung
www.instagram.com/ns_lung
Overview: A small provincial charitable organization founded in 1909 overseen by Canadian Lung Association
Mission: To control & prevent lung disease in Nova Scotia; To help people who live with lung disease
Finances: *Funding Sources:* Donations; Fundraising; Sponsorships
Staff Member(s): 10
Activities: Offering lung health education to Nova Scotians; Supporting research; Engaging in advocacy activities; Providing information & peer support to help people with COPD & lung disease; Offering a camp for children with asthma; *Library:* Nova Scotia Lung Association Resource Library; Open to public
Chief Officer(s):
Robert MacDonald, President & CEO, 902-443-8141 Ext. 22
robertmacdonald@ns.lung.ca
Mohammed Al-Hamdani, Director, Health Initiatives
mohammedalhamdani@ns.lung.ca
Maria Caines, Senior Manager, Finance
mariacaines@ns.lung.ca
Michelle Donaldson, Manager, Communications & Special Projects
michelledonaldson@ns.lung.ca
Lynette Hollett, Manager, Donor Relations
lynettehollett@ns.lung.ca

Lupus Canada
#306, 615 Davis Dr., Newmarket ON L3Y 2R2
Tel: 905-235-1714
Toll-Free: 800-661-1468
info@lupuscanada.org
www.lupuscanada.org
www.facebook.com/LupusCanada
twitter.com/lupuscanada
Overview: A medium-sized national charitable organization founded in 1987
Mission: To improve the lives of people living with lupus; To encourage cooperation among the lupus organizations in Canada
Finances: *Funding Sources:* Individual & corporate donations; Fundraising; Bequests; Memorials; Grants; Contributions from member organization
Staff Member(s): 2
Membership: *Member Profile:* Provincial & regional organizations
Activities: Promoting public awareness; Providing general education about lupus; Engaging in advocacy activities; Encouraging research; Offering support to people living with lupus; Organizing annual patient symposia; *Awareness Events:* Lupus Awareness Month, Oct.; World Lupus Day, May 10
Chief Officer(s):
Tanya Carlton, President
Malcolm Gilroy, Vice-President
Patricia Morzenti, Treasurer
Leanne Mielczarek, Executive Director
leanne.mielczarek@lupuscanada.org

Lupus Foundation of Ontario (LFO)
PO Box 687, 294 Ridge Rd. North, Ridgeway ON L0S 1N0
Tel: 905-894-4611; *Fax:* 905-894-4616
Toll-Free: 800-368-8377
lupusont@vaxxine.com
www.vaxxine.com/lupus
Overview: A medium-sized provincial charitable organization founded in 1977 overseen by Lupus Canada
Mission: To serve the lupus patient community as a charitable organization
Finances: *Funding Sources:* Donations; Member support; Fundraising
Staff Member(s): 1; 94 volunteer(s)
Membership: *Fees:* $25 yearly
Activities: Raising public awareness & understanding of lupus; Providing support services; Encouraging research; Engaging in advocacy activities; Offering educational opportunities to learn about lupus & develop coping strategies; Providing literature about lupus; Donating funds to research projects & treatment facilities; *Awareness Events:* Walk for Lupus, May; World Lupus Day, May 10; Lupus Awareness Month, October; *Speaker Service:* Yes; *Library:* The Lupus Foundation of Ontario Library
Chief Officer(s):
Laurie Kroeker, President

Lupus New Brunswick
#17, 55 Grant St., Moncton NB E1A 3R3
Tel: 506-384-6227
Toll-Free: 877-303-8080
lupins@rogers.com
www.lupusnb.ca
Overview: A small provincial organization founded in 1986 overseen by Lupus Canada
Mission: To promote eduction & public awareness of lupus; To bring together lupus patients, friends, family, & other interested persons for a network of support
Member of: Lupus Canada
Membership: *Fees:* $25
Activities: *Awareness Events:* Walk for Lupus, May
Chief Officer(s):
Nancy Votour, President

Lupus Newfoundland & Labrador
PO Box 8121, Stn. A, St. John's NL A1B 3M9
Tel: 709-368-8130
lupus.nl.ca@gmail.com
www.envision.ca/webs/lupusnfldlab
Previous Name: Lupus Society of Newfoundland
Overview: A small provincial charitable organization overseen by Lupus Canada
Mission: To support individuals with lupus; to promote education & awareness of lupus; to support research & treatment of the disease
Membership: *Fees:* $10
Activities: *Awareness Events:* Walk for Lupus, June; Diane Bartlett Memorial Ride, Sept.

Lupus Ontario
#10, 25 Valleywood Dr., Toronto ON L3R 5L9
Tel: 905-415-1099; *Fax:* 905-415-9874
Toll-Free: 877-240-1099
info@lupusontario.org
www.lupusontario.org
twitter.com/LupusON
Merged from: Ontario Lupus Association; Lupus Society of Hamilton
Overview: A medium-sized provincial charitable organization founded in 2004 overseen by Lupus Canada
Mission: To serve the needs of Lupus sufferers in Ontario
Member of: Lupus Canada
Finances: *Funding Sources:* Donations; Memberships; Memorials; Item Sales; Special Events
Staff Member(s): 3
Membership: *Fees:* $25
Activities: Providing information about lupus; Offering support groups; Increasing public awareness; Encouraging research; Organizing annual general meetings & clinical updates; *Awareness Events:* Lupus Awareness Month, Oct.; Annual Walk a Block for Lupus in Ontario, May (Part of Walk the World for Lupus event); World Lupus Day, May
Chief Officer(s):
Linda Keill, President
Karen Furlotte, Office Manager & Coordinator
kfurlotte@lupusontario.org

Kingston Branch
Kingston ON
Chief Officer(s):
Sherrill Ritchie, Contact

Kitchener Branch
Zehrs Laurentian, 750 Ottawa St. South, Kitchener ON N2E 1B6
Toll-Free: 877-240-1099

London Branch
London ON

Canadian Associations / Lupus PEI

lupuslondonontario@gmail.com

Mississauga/Oakville/Brampton/West Toronto Branch
Toronto ON
Toll-Free: 877-240-1099
Chief Officer(s):
Juanita Butler, Contact, Support Group
jbutler@lupusontario.org

Ottawa Branch
Ottawa ON
Toll-Free: 877-240-1099
Chief Officer(s):
David Boal, Contact
david.boal@sympatico.ca

Sudbury Branch
Sudbury ON
Tel: 705-280-0900
Chief Officer(s):
Ruth Tarvudd, Contact
rtarvudd@gmail.com

Thunder Bay Branch
Thunder Bay ON
info@lupusontario.org

Timmins Branch
Timmins ON
Tel: 705-268-5299; *Fax:* 877-240-1099
Chief Officer(s):
Juanita Butler, Contact, Support Group
jbutler@lupusontario.org

Windsor Branch
1395 Albert Rd., Windsor ON N8Y 3R1
Tel: 519-919-6717
Chief Officer(s):
Kevin Stannard, President
kevin.stannard@sympatico.ca

Lupus PEI
PO Box 23002, Charlottetown PE C1E 1Z6
Tel: 902-892-3875; *Fax:* 902-626-3585
Toll-Free: 800-661-1468
info@lupuscanada.org
www.lupuscanada.org/pei
Overview: A small provincial organization founded in 1993 overseen by Lupus Canada
Mission: To promote public awareness of lupus on PEI, while offering support & educational materials to lupus patients, their families & friends.
Finances: *Funding Sources:* Donations
Activities: *Speaker Service:* Yes

Lupus SK Society
c/o Royal University Hospital, PO Box 88, 103 Hospital Dr., Saskatoon SK S7N 0W8
Toll-Free: 877-566-6123
lupus@lupussk.com
www.lupussk.com
www.facebook.com/Lupus-SK-254959414545218
twitter.com/Lupus_SK
www.youtube.com/user/sasklupus?
Overview: A small provincial charitable organization founded in 1981 overseen by Lupus Canada
Mission: To assist individuals affected by lupus by providing education, raising awareness, & supporting research
Finances: *Funding Sources:* Donations
Membership: *Fees:* $20
Activities: *Library:* Not open to public
Chief Officer(s):
Tammy Hinds, First Vice-President
Katie Thompson, Secretary

Lupus Society of Alberta (LESA)
#202, 1055 - 20 Ave. NW, Calgary AB T2M 1E7
Tel: 403-228-7956; *Fax:* 403-228-7853
Toll-Free: 888-242-9182
lupuslsa@shaw.ca
www.lupus.ab.ca
www.youtube.com/channel/UCAvO7nEVN3TdOzMo_pJif4Q
Overview: A small provincial charitable organization founded in 1973 overseen by Lupus Canada
Mission: To provide education & support on lupus issues & enable research to find a cure
Member of: Imagine Canada; Leave a Legacy Calgary; Volunteer Calgary
Finances: *Funding Sources:* Membership dues; corporate; individual; casino

Membership: *Fees:* $25; *Committees:* Communications & Public Awareness; Fund Development; Education & Support; Nominating
Activities: *Awareness Events:* Lupus Awareness Month, Oct.; *Speaker Service:* Yes
Chief Officer(s):
Mike Sewell, President
Rosemary E. Church, Executive Director

Lupus Society of Manitoba
#105, 386 Broadway Ave., Winnipeg MB R3X 1G2
Tel: 204-942-6825; *Fax:* 204-942-4894
lupus@mymts.net
www.lupusmanitoba.com
www.facebook.com/lupus.manitoba
Overview: A small provincial charitable organization founded in 1988 overseen by Lupus Canada
Mission: To provide support, encouragement & education to lupus patients & their families
Finances: *Funding Sources:* Fundraising; donations
Activities: *Awareness Events:* Lupus Awareness Month, Oct.; Golf Tournament, June; Walk For Lupus, May; *Library:* Open to public
Chief Officer(s):
Debbie Dohan, President

Lupus Society of Newfoundland *See* Lupus Newfoundland & Labrador

Lutheran Association of Missionaries & Pilots (LAMP)
4966 - 92 Ave. NW, Edmonton AB T6B 2V4
Tel: 780-466-8507; *Fax:* 780-466-6733
Toll-Free: 800-307-4036
Other Communication: www.mistyriverministries.blogspot.ca
office@lampministry.org
www.lampministry.org
www.facebook.com/lampministry
twitter.com/lampministry
www.youtube.com/user/LAMPMinistry/videos
Overview: A small international organization founded in 1970
Mission: To share Jesus Christ with the people of remote areas of Canada
Affiliation(s): Lutheran Church Canada; Evangelical Lutheran Church in Canada
Finances: *Annual Operating Budget:* $500,000-$1.5 Million
300 volunteer(s)
Activities: *Speaker Service:* Yes
Chief Officer(s):
Ron Ludke, Executive Director

Lutheran Bible Translators of Canada Inc. (LBTC)
137 Queen St. South, Kitchener ON N2G 1W2
Tel: 519-742-3361
Toll-Free: 866-518-7071
info@lbtc.ca
www.lbtc.ca
Overview: A small international charitable organization founded in 1974
Mission: To bring people to faith in Jesus Christ through Bible translations & literacy work
Affiliation(s): Canadian Council of Christian Charities
Finances: *Annual Operating Budget:* $250,000-$500,000
Staff Member(s): 5
Membership: 1-99
Activities: *Speaker Service:* Yes
Chief Officer(s):
James Keller, Executive Director
JKeller@lbtc.ca

Lutheran Church - Canada (LCC) / Église Luthérienne du Canada
3074 Portage Ave., Winnipeg MB R3K 0Y2
Tel: 204-895-3433; *Fax:* 204-832-3018
Toll-Free: 800-588-4226
Other Communication: communications@lutheranchurch.ca
info@lutheranchurch.ca
www.lutheranchurch.ca
www.facebook.com/lutheranchurch.canada
twitter.com/CanLutheran
Overview: A medium-sized national organization founded in 1988
Mission: To share the Gospel of Jesus Christ; To proclaim the Lutheran belief & faith in word & deed
Affiliation(s): Canadian Lutheran World Relief; Lutheran Women's Missionary League - Canada; Lutheran Laymen's League; Concordia Lutheran Mission Society

Finances: *Funding Sources:* Donations
Membership: 75,000+ members in 319 congregations
Activities: Supporting LCC missionaries in other countries; Working with Canadian Lutheran World Relief; Responding to social needs in local communities, such as establishing food banks & offering English as a Second Language classes; Educating children through Sunday schools, Vacation Bible Schools & confirmation classes; Offering various resources, such as congregation resources, statistical data & theological documents; Organizing Synod conventions; *Awareness Events:* National Lutheran Open House; National Youth Gathering
Chief Officer(s):
Robert Bugbee, President, 204-895-3433 Ext. 212
president@lutheranchurch.ca
Dwayne Cleave, Treasurer, 204-895-3433 Ext. 219
treasurer@lutheranchurch.ca
Leonardo Neitzel, Mission & Social Ministry, 204-895-3433 Ext. 215
missions@lutheranchurch.ca
Matthew Block, Communications
communications@lutheranchurch.ca
Publications:
• The Canadian Lutheran
Type: Magazine; *Frequency:* Bimonthly; *Editor:* Mathew Block; *ISSN:* 0383-4247; *Price:* $20/yr.

Alberta-British Columbia District
7040 Ada Blvd., Edmonton AB T5B 4E3
Tel: 780-474-0063; *Fax:* 780-479-3067
Toll-Free: 888-474-0063
info@lccabc.ca
www.lccabc.ca
Chief Officer(s):
Glenn Schaeffer, Dr., District President
president@lccabc.ca

Central District
3074 Portage Ave., Winnipeg MB R3K 0Y2
Tel: 204-832-7242; *Fax:* 204-897-4319
Toll-Free: 800-663-5673
lcccentral@lutheranchurch.ca
www.lcccentral.ca
Chief Officer(s):
Thomas Prachar, District President
tprachar@lutheranchurch.ca

East District
275 Lawrence Ave., Kitchener ON N2M 1Y3
Tel: 519-578-6500
Toll-Free: 800-465-8179
info@lcceastdistrict.ca
www.lcceastdistrict.ca
www.facebook.com/508588585897092
Chief Officer(s):
Paul Zabel, District President, 519-578-6500 Ext. 1
pzabel@lcceast.ca

Lutheran Laymen's League of Canada (LLL-C)
270 Lawrence Ave., Kitchener ON N2M 1Y4
Tel: 519-578-7420; *Fax:* 519-742-8091
Toll-Free: 800-555-6236
helpful@lll.ca
www.lll.ca
www.facebook.com/162406453805301
Also Known As: Lutheran Hour Ministries
Overview: A small national charitable organization founded in 1967
Mission: To proclaim gospel of Jesus Christ through the use of media; To bring Christ to the nations & the nation to the Christ
Affiliation(s): International Lutheran Layman's League
Finances: *Annual Operating Budget:* $500,000-$1.5 Million; *Funding Sources:* Donations
Staff Member(s): 2; 200 volunteer(s)
Membership: 1,000-4,999
Activities: Christian radio & TV programs; print & Internet resources; communication workshops
Chief Officer(s):
Klinck Stephen, Managing Director
director@lll.ca
Publications:
• Media Matters [a publication of the Lutheran Layman's League of Canada]
Type: Newsletter

Lutsel K'E Development Corporation *See* Denesoline Corporation Ltd.

Lutte NB Wrestling (LNBW)
NB

www.luttenbwrestling.com
Overview: A small provincial organization overseen by Wrestling Lutte Canada
Mission: Lutte New Brunswick Wrestling (LNBW) is a non-profit, equal opportunity organization, dedicated to the development, administration and promotion of amateur wrestling throughout the Province.
Staff Member(s): 2
Chief Officer(s):
Mary Singh, Executive Director
exec@luttenbwrestling.com
Chris Falconer, President

Lymphedema Association of Québec *Voir* Association Québécoise du Lymphoedème

Lymphoma Canada
#202, 6860 Century Ave., Mississauga ON L5N 2W5
Tel: 905-858-5967; *Fax:* 905-858-5967
Toll-Free: 866-659-5556
info@lymphoma.ca
www.lymphoma.ca
www.linkedin.com/company/lymphoma-foundation-canada
www.facebook.com/LymphomaCanada
twitter.com/lymphomacanada
www.youtube.com/user/LymphomaTV
Previous Name: Lymphoma Foundation Canada
Merged from: Lymphoma Research Foundation of Canada (LRFC); Canadian Lymphoma Foundation (CLF)
Overview: A medium-sized national charitable organization founded in 2000
Mission: To provide education & support for individuals with lymphoma & their support network; To fund medical research to find a cure for lymphatic cancer; To advocate for the best treatment & care for lymphoma patients; To promote further research & new treatments in lymphoma & to promote rapid access to new developments
Finances: *Annual Operating Budget:* $500,000-$1.5 Million; *Funding Sources:* Donations; Fundraising
Activities: *Awareness Events:* World Lymphoma Awareness Day, Sept.
Chief Officer(s):
Robin Markowitz, Chief Executive Officer
robin@lymphoma.ca
Publications:
• Lymphoma & You: A Guide for Patients Living with Hodgkin's & Non-Hodgkin's Lymphoma
Type: Guide; *Editor:* C. Tom Kouroukis
Profile: Contents include an overview of lymphoma, Non-Hodgkin's & Hodgkin's Lymphoma, new developments in treatment, living withcancer, & a glossary
• Lymphoma Patient Resource
Type: Manual; *Number of Pages:* 146
Profile: A useful resource for patients recently diagnosed with lymphoma

> **Bureau du Québec**
> QC
> www.lymphoma.ca
> **Chief Officer(s):**
> Patricia Gimore, Directrice, Québec
> patricia@lymphoma.ca

Lymphoma Foundation Canada *See* Lymphoma Canada

Lymphovenous Association of Ontario (LAO)
#203, 4800 Dundas Street West, Toronto ON M9A 1B1
Tel: 416-410-2250; *Fax:* 416-546-8991
Toll-Free: 877-723-0033
lymphontario@yahoo.com
www.lymphontario.org
Overview: A small provincial charitable organization founded in 1996
Mission: To educate the public; To promote improved treatments for lymphovenous disorders; To support research for a cure
Affiliation(s): Canadian Disability Organization; Canadian Organization for Rare Disorders
Finances: *Annual Operating Budget:* Less than $50,000; *Funding Sources:* fundraising
15 volunteer(s)
Membership: 200; *Fees:* $50 individual; $150 professional; $200 business; *Member Profile:* Family or individual suffering lymphodema or lymphovenous disorder; *Committees:* Education; Newsletter; Conference; Fundraising; Research
Activities: Providing public education; Supporting research; Offering workshops

Chief Officer(s):
Denise Lang, President
Anne Blair, Vice-Chair

Lyndhurst Seeleys Bay & District Chamber of Commerce
PO Box 89, Lyndhurst ON K0E 1N0
Tel: 613-331-2063
lsbchamber@hotmail.com
www.lyndhurstseeleysbaychamber.com
Overview: A small local organization founded in 1993
Mission: To promote local businesses & help them grow
Member of: Ontario Chamber of Commerce
Finances: *Funding Sources:* Membership dues
Membership: 83; *Fees:* $75; *Member Profile:* Local businesses
Chief Officer(s):
Mel Magalas, President

Lynn Canyon Ecology Centre
3663 Park Rd., North Vancouver BC V7J 3G3
Tel: 604-990-3755
ecocentre@dnv.org
www.lynncanyonecologycentre.ca
Overview: A small local organization founded in 1971
Mission: To educate people about ecology
Finances: *Funding Sources:* District of North Vancouver
Staff Member(s): 3; 12 volunteer(s)
Membership: 1,000-4,999; *Committees:* Stream Keepers - Maplewood Conservation Area
Activities: School & public education program; displays; leaflets

Lynn Lake Friendship Centre
625 Gordon Ave., Lynn Lake MB R0B 0W0
Tel: 204-356-2407
Overview: A small local organization
Mission: Provides programs and services to meet the needs of the Aboriginal and Non Aboriginal people in Lynn Lake and surrounding area.
Activities: Family First Project; Partners for Careers; Eagle Feather Youth Council

Lytton & District Chamber of Commerce
PO Box 460, 400 Fraser St., Lytton BC V0K 1Z0
Tel: 250-455-2523
Other Communication: Visitor Centre e-mail:
visitorcentre@lyttonchamber.com
info@lyttonchamber.com
lyttonchamber.com
Also Known As: Lytton Infocentre
Overview: A small local organization founded in 1949
Mission: To encourage social & economic development in the area; To promote growth & sustainability among businesses
Member of: BC Chamber of Commerce
Affiliation(s): Vancouver Coast & Mountains Tourism Region
Finances: *Annual Operating Budget:* Less than $50,000; *Funding Sources:* Membership fees
Staff Member(s): 4; 4 volunteer(s)
Membership: 69; *Fees:* $50-$150
Activities: Supporting community initiatives & projects
Chief Officer(s):
Bernie Fandrich, President
Sheila Maguire, Secretary
secretary@lyttonchamber.com

Lytton Community Food Bank
PO Box 87, Lytton BC V0K 1Z0
Tel: 250-455-2316; *Fax:* 250-455-6669
Overview: A small local organization overseen by Food Banks British Columbia
Member of: Food Banks British Columbia

M2/W2 Association - Restorative Christian Ministries (M2/W2)
#208, 2825 Clearbrook Rd., Abbotsford BC V2T 6S3
Tel: 604-859-3215; *Fax:* 604-859-1216
Toll-Free: 800-298-1777
info@m2w2.com
www.m2w2.com
www.linkedin.com/groups/5100601
www.facebook.com/M2W2Association?ref=hl
twitter.com/M2W2Association
Also Known As: Man-to-Man/Woman-to-Woman
Overview: A small provincial charitable organization founded in 1966
Mission: To mutually transform lives - one relationship at a time; To see individuals & communities in British Columbia safer, transformed, reconciled, & restored through justice, accountability, partnerships, mutual support, mediation, education & prevention; To provide one-to-one volunteers for men & women in British Columbia prisons, combined with pre- & post-release support & resources; To counsel prisoners, ex-prisoners, & their families; To prevent crime through one-to-one support for parents of young children at risk
Member of: Canadian Council of Christian Charities
Finances: *Annual Operating Budget:* $250,000-$500,000; *Funding Sources:* 65% community fundraising; 35% federal & provincial government contracts
Staff Member(s): 11; 400 volunteer(s)
Membership: 190; *Fees:* $10; *Member Profile:* Wide range of people whose common interest is the focus of M2/W2; *Committees:* Finance/Promotion; Program/New Initiatives; Personnel
Activities: Organizing annual promotion dinners; *Speaker Service:* Yes
Chief Officer(s):
Raymond Robyn, Executive Director

Maccabi Canada
PO Box 20090, Stn. Carrville, 9200 Dufferin St., Concord ON L4K 0C8
Tel: 416-398-0515
info@maccabicanada.com
www.maccabicanada.com
www.facebook.com/213044145375553
twitter.com/MaccabiCanada
www.youtube.com/channel/UCD4r-hlafAAlXXvi9HGXIUg
Overview: A small national organization
Mission: To promote Jewish identity & traditions through athletic, cultural, social & educational activities.
Deliveries/shipping address: #1, 8150 Keele St., Concord, ON L4K 2A5
Member of: Maccabi World Union
Membership: *Fees:* Schedule available; *Committees:* National Athletic
Activities: *Awareness Events:* Maccabiah Games: every 4 years, in Israel; Pan-American Maccabiah Games: every 4 years in South America
Chief Officer(s):
Tali Dubrovsky, Executive Director
tali@maccabicanada.com
Michele Bass, Director, Operations
michele@maccabicanada.com

Macedonian Human Rights Movement International (MHRMI) / Mouvement canadien de défense des droits de la personne dans la communauté macédonienne
#434, 157 Adelaide St., Toronto ON M5H 4E7
Tel: 416-850-7125; *Fax:* 416-850-7127
info@mhrmi.org
www.mhrmi.org
www.facebook.com/MHRMI
twitter.com/mhrmi
Previous Name: Macedonian Human Rights Movement of Canada
Overview: A small national organization founded in 1986
Mission: To secure & maintain the human rights of all Macedonians wherever they live through advocacy & education
Member of: Macedonian World Congress; Canadian Macedonian Federation
Finances: *Annual Operating Budget:* $50,000-$100,000; *Funding Sources:* Donations; Publications sales; Membership fees
Staff Member(s): 2; 25 volunteer(s)
Membership: 600; *Fees:* $10; *Committees:* Data Collection; Executive; Fundraising; Membership; Publication; Public Relations
Activities: *Library:* by appointment Not open to public
Chief Officer(s):
Bill Nicholov, President
Luby Vidinovski, Vice-President
Mark Opashinov, Secretary
Andy Plukov, Treasurer
Publications:
• Ancient Macedonians - Differences Between The Ancient Macedonians and The Ancient Greeks [a publication of MHRMI]
Type: Book; *Number of Pages:* 318; *Author:* J.S.G. Gandeto; *ISBN:* 0-595-76032-5; *Price:* $35
Profile: An overview of the basic differences between the ancient Macedonians & theancient Greeks
• The Descendants of Alexander the Great of Macedon [a publication of the MHRMI]
Type: Book; *Number of Pages:* 247; *Author:* Aleksandar Donski;

ISBN: 0-9581162-5-3; *Price:* $35
Profile: An analysis of the elements of Macedonian folklore
• Diary of an Uncivil War: The Violent Aftermath of the Kosovo Conflict [a publication of MHRMI]
Type: Book; *Number of Pages:* 201; *Author:* Scott Taylor; *ISBN:* 1-895890-20-7; *Price:* $30
Profile: An collection of first-hand observations & interviews relating to the Kosovo War
• History of the Macedonian People from Ancient Times to the Present [a publication of the MHRMI]
Type: Book; *Number of Pages:* 424; *Author:* Chris Stefou; *ISBN:* 0-9737256-0-5; *Price:* $30
Profile: An overview of Macedonian history
• Minorities in the Balkans [a publication of MHRMI]
Type: Book; *Number of Pages:* 350; *Author:* Vladimir Ortakovski; *ISBN:* 1-57105-129-5; *Price:* $35
Profile: An overview of minorities in the Balkan states before the First World War & the interwar period
• Oshchima - The Story of a Small Village in Western Macedonia [a publication of the MHRMI]
Type: Book; *Number of Pages:* 384; *Author:* Chris Stefou; *Price:* $35
Profile: An overview of the life experience of the Oschimian community, who lived through social & political unrest

Macedonian Human Rights Movement of Canada *See* Macedonian Human Rights Movement International

MacEwan Staff Association (MSA)
MacEwan University, City Centre Campus, #7-102D, 10700 - 104 Ave., Edmonton AB T5J 2P2
Tel: 780-497-5697; *Fax:* 780-497-5696
msa@macewan.ca
www.macewanstaff.ca
www.facebook.com/macewanstaffassociation
twitter.com/MacEwanMSA
Previous Name: Grant MacEwan College Non-Academic Staff Association
Overview: A small local organization founded in 1982
Mission: To enhance the work environment; to advocate the interests of its members while contributing to the success of the college
Affiliation(s): Non-Academic Staff Association, Univ. of Alberta
Finances: *Funding Sources:* Membership fees
Staff Member(s): 4
Membership: *Member Profile:* Support or supervisory employees of Grant MacEwan College; *Committees:* Academic Governance Council; Admissions & Selections; Bylaw; Job Evaluation & Classification Review; Negotiations; Performance Management; Professional Development; Sick Leave & Disability Management; Social; MSA Financial; Health & Wellness; Employee Benefits; MSA Human Resources
Chief Officer(s):
Donna-Mae Winquist, President
WinquistD@MacEwan.ca

MacGregor Chamber of Commerce
PO Box 685, MacGregor MB R0H 0R0
Tel: 204-685-2390
Overview: A small local organization
Mission: To facilitate the creation of an economic & social base in MacGregor & District that will encourage development & promotion in all sectors of the community
Member of: Manitoba Chamber of Commerce; Canadian Chamber of Commerce
Finances: *Annual Operating Budget:* Less than $50,000; *Funding Sources:* Membership dues
Staff Member(s): 1
Membership: 165; *Fees:* $50; *Committees:* Promotion; Lobby
Activities: Organizing & promoting events including BLPOM & Pancake Breakfast, townwide garage sale & MacGregor & District Rodeo; *Library*
Chief Officer(s):
Jason McKelvy, President
mckelv@mts.net
Awards:
• Citizen of the Year

Mackenzie & District Museum Society
PO Box 934, 86 Centennial Dr., Mackenzie BC V0J 2C0
Tel: 250-997-3021
museum@mackbc.com
www.mackenziemuseum.ca
www.facebook.com/mackenziemuseum
Overview: A small local charitable organization founded in 1991
Mission: To ensure the public has the opportunity to learn history & have fun while doing it
Member of: British Columbia Museums Association
Affiliation(s): Fraser-Fort George Regional Museum
Finances: *Annual Operating Budget:* Less than $50,000
Staff Member(s): 1; 7 volunteer(s)
Membership: 19; *Fees:* $10 individual; $15 family; *Member Profile:* Residents of Mackenzie
Activities: Displays are borrowed from residents & other museums; communication with schools & public advertising display; participates in Mackenzie Children's Festival; leisure fair; school tours; *Library:* Archives; Open to public by appointment
Chief Officer(s):
Christopher Johansen, President

Mackenzie Applied Research Assciation (MARA)
PO Box 646, 1 River Road Experimental Farm, Fort Vermilion AB T0H 1N0
Tel: 780-927-3776; *Fax:* 780-927-4747
mara3@telus.net
www.areca.ab.ca/marahome.html
Overview: A small local organization overseen by Agricultural Research & Extension Council of Alberta
Mission: To conduct agricultural research, trials & rural extension in Northern Alberta's Mackenzie county
Chief Officer(s):
Jim Ludwig, Coordinator/Manager, 780-285-0843
ludwig41@telus.net

Mackenzie Chamber of Commerce
PO Box 880, 88 Centennial Dr., Mackenzie BC V0J 2C0
Tel: 250-997-5459; *Fax:* 250-997-6117
office@mackenziechamber.bc.ca
www.mackenziechamber.bc.ca
Overview: A small local charitable organization founded in 1984
Mission: To promote & support business; To improve trade & commerce; To enhance civic & social welfare in Mackenzie & area
Member of: BC Chamber of Commerce; Canadian Chamber of Commerce
Affiliation(s): Retail Merchants Association of BC
Finances: *Annual Operating Budget:* $100,000-$250,000; *Funding Sources:* District of Mackenzie; membership fees; fundraising; advertising; workshops
Staff Member(s): 4; 23 volunteer(s)
Membership: 77; *Fees:* $94.76-$355.35 business; $39.65 individual; $71.07 non-profit
Activities: Providing information, resources, networking events, & benefit programs; Lobbying; Organizing & supporting events; *Library:* Open to public by appointment
Chief Officer(s):
Debbie Wallace, President

Mackenzie Community Arts Council
Ernie Bodine Centre, PO Box 301, 86 Centennial Dr., Mackenzie BC V0J 2C0
Tel: 250-997-5818
Overview: A small local charitable organization founded in 1974
Mission: To support, encourage & promote arts & culture in the community through education, coordination of programs & raising public awareness
Member of: Assembly of BC Arts Councils; Central Interior Regional Arts Council; Canadian Artists Representation-CARFAC
Affiliation(s): Mackenzie Potters Guild
Finances: *Annual Operating Budget:* Less than $50,000
Staff Member(s): 1; 20 volunteer(s)
Membership: 111; *Fees:* $15 individual; $25 family; *Member Profile:* Potters, painters; artists; crafters & supporters; *Committees:* Advocacy; Finance; Programs; Festival of Bells; Mountain Gifts 'n Gallery; Children's Festival
Activities: Children's & adult programming; craft fair; children's festival; gift store; art gallery; monthly meetings; *Library:* Resource Centre; Open to public by appointment
Chief Officer(s):
Michele Gillespie, President
Awards:
• Mackenzie Secondary School Scholarship
• Mackenzie Secondary School Bursary

The Mackenzie Institute
PO Box 338, Stn. Adelaide, Toronto ON M5C 2J4
Tel: 416-686-4063
institute@mackenzieinstitute.com
www.mackenzieinstitute.com
Overview: A small international charitable organization founded in 1986
Mission: To provide comment on terrorism, organized crime, political extremism, propaganda, conflict & other such matters
Finances: *Annual Operating Budget:* $100,000-$250,000
Staff Member(s): 3; 2 volunteer(s)
Membership: 500-999; *Fees:* $60 minimum annual donation
Activities: *Speaker Service:* Yes

Macklin Chamber of Commerce
PO Box 642, Macklin SK S0L 2C0
Tel: 306-753-9394; *Fax:* 306-753-2849
www.macklinchamber.com
www.facebook.com/macklinchamber
Overview: A small local organization
Mission: To promote free enterprise; To protect the interests of members
Finances: *Annual Operating Budget:* Less than $50,000
Membership: *Fees:* $50
Chief Officer(s):
Christy Veller, President

Macleod Institute
#223, 20 Coachway Rd. SW, Calgary AB T3H 1E6
Tel: 403-240-2573; *Fax:* 403-246-1852
Toll-Free: 866-204-6123
macleod@macleodinstitute.com
www.macleodinstitute.com
Previous Name: Macleod Institute for Environmental Analysis
Overview: A small national organization founded in 1995
Mission: To provide impartial advice on regulatory & environmental issues
Affiliation(s): University of Calgary
Finances: *Annual Operating Budget:* $100,000-$250,000; *Funding Sources:* Contract
Staff Member(s): 5
Membership: 1-99
Chief Officer(s):
Elaine McCoy, President

Macleod Institute for Environmental Analysis *See* Macleod Institute

Mactaquac Country Chamber of Commerce
PO Box 1163, Nackawic NB E6G 2N1
Tel: 506-575-9622; *Fax:* 506-575-2035
mccc@mactaquaccountry.com
www.mactaquaccountry.com
www.facebook.com/97733447857
twitter.com/mccc_nb
Overview: A small local organization founded in 1997
Mission: To promote & represent members as well as business in Mactaquac Country
Finances: *Annual Operating Budget:* Less than $50,000
Membership: 75; *Fees:* $75; *Committees:* Awards Banquet; Artisans Sale; Charity Casino
Chief Officer(s):
Melanie Sloat, President
Marc Jesmer, Secretary

Madawaska Forest Products Marketing Board / Office de vente des produits forestiers du Madawaska
PO Box 5, 870 Canada St., Edmundston NB E3V 3X3
Tel: 506-739-9585; *Fax:* 506-739-0859
odvdm@nbnet.nb.ca
Overview: A small local charitable organization founded in 1962
Mission: Mise en marché des produits forestiers bruts; encourager les bonnes pratiques d'aménagement forestier
Member of: La Fédération des Propriétaires de Lots Boissés du Nouveau Brunswick
Finances: *Annual Operating Budget:* $100,000-$250,000
Staff Member(s): 7
Membership: 2 200 individu; 400 associé
Chief Officer(s):
Claude A. Pelletier, Manager

Madawaska Valley Association for Community Living *See* Madawaska Valley Association for Community Living

Madawaska Valley Association for Community Living
19491 Opeongo Line, Barry's Bay ON K0J 1B0
Tel: 613-756-3817; *Fax:* 613-756-0616
info@mvacl.ca
www.mvacl.ca
Previous Name: Madawaska Valley Association for Community Living
Overview: A small local charitable organization overseen by Community Living Ontario

Mission: To advocates for individuals with intellectual disabilities, so they may participate fully in their communities
Member of: Community Living Ontario
Membership: Fees: $15
Activities: Library: Resource Library; Open to public
Chief Officer(s):
Darcy Lacombe, Executive Director

MADD Canada / Les mères contre l'alcool auvolant
#500, 2010 Winston Park Dr., Oakville ON L6H 5R7
Tel: 905-829-8805; Fax: 905-829-8860
Toll-Free: 800-665-6233
info@madd.ca
www.madd.ca
www.facebook.com/maddcanada.ca
twitter.com/maddcanada
Also Known As: Mothers Against Drunk Driving
Previous Name: PRIDE - People to Reduce Impaired Driving Everywhere (Ontario)
Overview: A medium-sized national charitable organization founded in 1982
Mission: To stop impaired driving & to support victims of this crime
Finances: Funding Sources: Donations; Sponsorships
7 volunteer(s)
Activities: Increasing public awareness about the dangers of drinking & driving; Offering programs such as youth/school outreach; Engaging in legislative & public policy advocacy; Providing education; Offering support services to victims; Publishing & distributing brochures, statistics & research papers; Awareness Events: Annual MADD Canada National Victims' Weekend & Candlelight Vigil of Hope and Remembrance; Rents Mailing List: Yes; Library: MADD Canada Research Library
Chief Officer(s):
Andrew Murie, CEO
amurie@madd.ca

Madoc & District Chamber of Commerce
PO Box 669, 20 Davidson St., Madoc ON K0K 2K0
Tel: 613-473-1616
madocchamber@gmail.com
www.centrehastings.com/business/chamber-of-commerce/
www.facebook.com/MadocDistrictChamberofCommerce
twitter.com/MadocChamber
Overview: A small local organization
Mission: To act as a voice for its members
Member of: Canadian Chamber of Commerce
Staff Member(s): 1
Membership: Fees: $50
Chief Officer(s):
Leigh Anne Lavender, Coordinator

Madonna House Apostolate
2888 Dafoe Rd., RR#2, Combermere ON K0J 1L0
Tel: 613-756-3713; Fax: 613-756-0211
Other Communication: publications@madonnahouse.org
combermere@madonnahouse.org
www.madonnahouse.org
www.facebook.com/MadonnaHouse
twitter.com/madonnahouse
www.youtube.com/MadonnaHouseCanada
Overview: A small national charitable organization founded in 1947
Affiliation(s): Roman Catholic Church; Diocese of Pembroke
Finances: Funding Sources: Donations
Membership: 200+; Member Profile: Christian lay men, women, & priests, who are dedicated to promises of poverty, chastity, & obedience
Activities: Offering the Cana Colony summer program for families; Distributing gooods to the poor; Operating a gift shop, flea market, & used book shop to raise funds
Chief Officer(s):
David Linder, Director General
Elizabeth Bassarear, Director General
Publications:
• Friends of Madonna House
Type: Newsletter; Frequency: Monthly; Price: Free
• Restoration: The Madonna House Catholic Newspaper
Type: Newspaper; Frequency: Monthly; ISSN: 0708-2177

Edmonton
Marian Centre, 10528 - 98th St. NW, Edmonton AB T5H 2N4
Tel: 780-424-3544; Fax: 780-424-4806
MCEEdmonton@shaw.ca
Mission: To offer friendship & hospitality to all who visit
Affiliation(s): Archdiocese of Edmonton

Ottawa
440 Kensington Ave., Ottawa ON K1Z 6G8
Tel: 613-729-0956
Mission: To pray for salvation, the world, & for the people of the Archdiocese of Ottawa
Affiliation(s): Archdiocese of Ottawa

Regina
Marian Centre, 1835 Halifax St., Regina SK S4P 1T4
Mission: To care for the poor; To pray for those who serve, benefactors, all those who enter the doors of Madonna House Apostolate, & for the people of the Regina area
Affiliation(s): Archdiocese of Regina

Toronto (MHA)
501 Parkside Dr., Toronto ON M6R 2Z9
Tel: 416-761-9965
madonnahousetoronto@rogers.com
www.madonnahouse.org/locations/madonna-house-toronto
Mission: To form a community of love; to be a house of hospitality, with a focus on evangelization; To provide availability to persons of every walk of life
Affiliation(s): Archdiocese of Toronto

Vancouver
5450 Trafalgar St., Vancouver BC V6N 1B9
Tel: 604-267-1757
madonna02@shaw.ca
Mission: To be a place of welcome and friendship; To proclaim the Gospel of Jesus Christ; To provide an evangelizing presence in the Archdiocese of Vancouver
Affiliation(s): Archdiocese of Vancouver

Whitehorse
Maryhouse, 504 Cook St., Whitehorse YT Y1A 2R4
Tel: 867-667-7146
maryhouse@klondiker.com
Mission: To provide for the needs of the poor; To aim to preach the Gospel

Windsor
1307 Pelissier St., Windsor ON N8X 1M4
Tel: 519-252-9236
mhwindsor@dol.ca
Mission: To offer a prayer-listening house to serve the Diocese of London; To pray & fast in support of priestly vocations
Affiliation(s): Diocese of London

Magazines Canada
#700, 425 Adelaide St. West, Toronto ON M5V 3C1
Tel: 416-504-0274; Fax: 416-504-0437
info@magazinescanada.ca
www.magazinescanada.ca
www.linkedin.com/company/magazines-canada
twitter.com/magscanada
www.youtube.com/user/magazinescanada
Previous Name: Canadian Periodical Publishers' Association; Canadian Magazine Publishers Association (CMPA)
Overview: A medium-sized national organization founded in 1973
Mission: To represent Canadian-owned magazines with Canadian content
Finances: Funding Sources: Dept. of Canadian Heritage; ON Media Development Corp.; ON Arts Council; ON Ministry of Culture; Canada Council for the Arts; Private sponsorships
Staff Member(s): 13
Membership: 350+; Member Profile: Magazine companies that have published at least one issue available to the general public, at least 51% Canadian owned, at least 80% Canadian-authored content, & have distinction between advertising & editorial content; Committees: Advertising Services; Circulation Services; Executive; Government Relations; Market Intelligence; Membership
Activities: Offering member services such as direct-to-retail distribution, marketing, & advertising services; Providing professional development opportunities; Liaising with all levels of government; Internships: Yes
Chief Officer(s):
Matthew Holmes, President & CEO, 416-504-0274 Ext. 223
mholmes@magazinescanada.ca
Barbara Zatyko, Vice-President, Operations & Development, 416-504-0274 Ext. 222
bzatyko@magazinescanada.ca
Barbara Bates, Executive Director, Circulation Marketing, 416-504-0274 Ext. 229
bbates@magazinescanada.ca
Mascod Abid, Senior Director, Finance & Administration
mabid@magazinescanada.ca
Melanie Rutledge, Director, Government & Industry Engagement
mrutledge@magazinescanada.ca

Magen David Adom canadien pour Israël See Canadian Magen David Adom for Israel

Maggie's: The Toronto Prostitutes' Community Service Project; Prostitute's Safe Sex Project See Maggie's: The Toronto Sex Workers Action Project

Maggie's: The Toronto Sex Workers Action Project
298A Gerrard St. East, 2nd Fl., Toronto ON M5A 2G7
Tel: 416-964-0150
maggiescoord@gmail.com
www.maggiestoronto.ca
www.facebook.com/Maggiestoronto
Also Known As: Maggie's
Previous Name: Maggie's: The Toronto Prostitutes' Community Service Project; Prostitute's Safe Sex Project
Overview: A small local charitable organization founded in 1991
Mission: To provide education & support to assist sex workers in our efforts to live & work with safety & dignity
Member of: Ontario AIDS Network
Finances: Funding Sources: Ontario Ministry of Health; AIDS Bureau; Donations
Membership: Member Profile: Sex trade workers
Activities: Speaker Service: Yes

The Magic of Christmas
PO Box 76097, Stn. Millrise, 9136 - 52 St., Calgary AB T2Y 2Z9
Tel: 403-803-1619; Fax: 403-256-8443
info@themagicofchristmas.org
www.themagicofchristmas.org
Also Known As: The Spirit of Christmas
Overview: A small local charitable organization founded in 1980
Mission: To spread the love, caring & sharing associated with the most joyous time of year
Finances: Annual Operating Budget: Less than $50,000
200 volunteer(s)
Membership: 200; Member Profile: People of all ages bringing love, care & sharing at Christmas; Committees: Transportation; Beneficiaries; Pickups; Sewing & Repairs; Media & Newsletter; Fundraising; Santa Shows; Phone; Office & Sorting; Decorating
Activities: Visiting private homes, hospitals, shelters, nursing homes on Christmas Eve; Awareness Events: Santa Clause Parade, Dec.; Christmas Eve Run, Dec. 24

Magnificat Charismatic Prayer Community
19309 Warden Ave., Queensville ON L0G 1R0
Tel: 905-478-4264
sanctuary-magnificat@rogers.com
reginamundimagnificat.com
Also Known As: Regina Mundi Retreat Centre
Overview: A small local organization founded in 1990
Mission: To provide spiritual care to all community members
Affiliation(s): Regina Mundi Retreat Centre
Chief Officer(s):
Lita Malixi, Treasurer

Magog Historical Society Voir Société d'histoire de Magog

Magrath & District Chamber of Commerce
PO Box 1165, Magrath AB T0K 1J0
www.magrathchamber.com
www.facebook.com/magrathchamber
twitter.com/magrathchamber
Overview: A small local organization
Mission: To improve business & the community
Affiliation(s): Alberta Chamber of Commerce; Canadian Chamber of Commerce
Membership: 46; Fees: $50 1-4 employees; $60 5-10 employees; $70 11-15 employees; $75 16+ employees; Committees: Membership/Budget; Business Development/Planning/Beautification; Public Relations/Communication/Education; Programs/Events
Chief Officer(s):
Jay Mackenzie, President

Mahatma Gandhi Canadian Foundation for World Peace
PO Box 60002, RPO University of Alberta, Edmonton AB T6G 2S4
Tel: 780-492-5504; Fax: 780-492-0113
gandhifoundationcanada@gmail.com
www.gandhi.ca
Overview: A small local charitable organization founded in 1986

Mission: To conduct programs & activities that promote the teachings & philosophy of Mahatma Gandhi in order to advance peace & understanding amongst peoples of the world
Finances: *Annual Operating Budget:* Less than $50,000; *Funding Sources:* Banquet; casino funds
28 volunteer(s)
Membership: 40; *Fees:* $10
Activities: Speakers; public lectures; banquet; annual debate in school; summer institute; *Awareness Events:* Gandhi Memorial Day, Jan. 30; *Speaker Service:* Yes; *Library:* by appointment
Chief Officer(s):
Jaime Beck, Educational Coordinator
Awards:
• Mahatma Gandhi Scholarship
; *Amount:* $1,000

Mahone Bay & Area Chamber of Commerce
PO Box 59, Mahone Bay NS B0J 2E0
Tel: 902-624-6151; *Fax:* 902-624-6152
Toll-Free: 888-624-6151
info@mahonebay.com
www.mahonebay.com
Overview: A small local organization
Mission: To promote local business & the community
Chief Officer(s):
Sue Bourinot, Chair

Maidstone & District Chamber of Commerce
PO Box 208, Maidstone SK S0M 1M0
Tel: 306-893-2373; *Fax:* 306-893-4378
maidstonechamberofcommerce@gmail.com
www.facebook.com/733573566749480
Overview: A small local organization
Membership: *Fees:* $50

Mainland Nova Scotia Building & Construction Trades Council
#205, 14 McQuade Lake Cres., Halifax NS B3S 1B6
Tel: 902-450-1012; *Fax:* 902-450-1013
info@mainlandbuildingtrades.ca
www.mainlandbuildingtrades.ca
Overview: A small local organization
Mission: Committed to providing easy access to highly trained, safe working industrial tradesmen; to forge partnerships with owners & developers to become synonymous with sound investment & industrial growth in mainland Nova Scotia
Member of: AFL-CIO
Finances: *Annual Operating Budget:* $100,000-$250,000
Staff Member(s): 1; 5 volunteer(s)
Membership: 12,000; *Member Profile:* Construction, maintenance & service
Chief Officer(s):
Brad Smith, Executive Director

Mainland South Heritage Society (MSHS)
16 Sussex St., Halifax NS B3R 1N9
Tel: 902-868-2553
www.rootsweb.ancestry.com/~nsmshs
Overview: A small local charitable organization
Mission: To preserve the heritage of Mainland South
Membership: *Fees:* $10; $15 senior couples
Chief Officer(s):
Leslie Harnish, President, 902-686-2553
harnish@hfx.eastlink.ca

Mainstream Association for Proactive Community Living
See posAbilities Association of BC

Maintenance, Engineering & Reliability (MER) Society (MER)
c/o Secretary, Marcel M. Djivre, 2058 Latimer Cres., Sudbury ON P3E 5L6
Tel: 705-621-1945
www.cim.org
Previous Name: Mechanical-Electrical Division of The Canadian Institute of Mining, Metallurgy & Petroleum
Overview: A medium-sized national organization overseen by Canadian Institute of Mining, Metallurgy & Petroleum
Mission: To advance the theory & practice of electrical & mechanical arts & sciences in the mining industry; To improve mechanical-electrical standards
Activities: Facilitating the exchange of information & data on electrical & mechanical subjects; Publishing technical papers; Providing educational assistance; Promoting methods & devices to increase safety
Chief Officer(s):

Jo-Anne Boucher, Chair, 705-675-7720 Ext. 214
jo-anne_boucher@bestech.com
R.A. (Dick) McIvor, Treasurer
dmcivor@sympatico.ca
Awards:
• The McParland Memorial Medal
• JD (Pat) Patterson Memorial Scholarship
• The CIM Fellow-ship Award
• Centennial Scholarship
• Distinguished Lecturer

Maison Amaryllis
1462, rue Panet, Montréal QC H2L 2Z3
Tél: 514-526-3635; *Téléc:* 514-521-9209
maison.amaryllis@sympatico.ca
Aperçu: *Dimension:* petite; *Envergure:* locale; Organisme sans but lucratif; fondée en 1990 surveillé par Canadian AIDS Society
Affiliation(s): Coalition des organismes communautaires québécois de lutte contre le sida
Finances: *Budget de fonctionnement annuel:* $250,000-$500,000
Membre(s) du personnel: 10; 7 bénévole(s)
Membre: 1-99
Activités: Maison d'hébergement pour personnes vivant avec le VIH/Sida, sans-abri et polytoxicomanes; *Evénements de sensibilisation:* Souper bénéfice

La Maison Benoit Labre / The Benoit Labre House
308, rue Young, Montréal QC H3C 2G2
Tél: 514-937-5973
www.benedictlabre.org
www.facebook.com/106194182796549
twitter.com/LabreHouse
Aperçu: *Dimension:* petite; *Envergure:* locale; Organisme sans but lucratif; fondée en 1952
Mission: Offre aux personnes itinérantes et vulnérables des services de premières ligne
Finances: *Fonds:* Donations
Activités: Espace de centre de jour; distribue des items d'hygiène personnelle et des vêtements

Maison D'Haiti (MH)
8883, boul Saint-Michel, Montréal QC H1Z 3G3
Tél: 514-326-3022; *Téléc:* 514-326-3024
mhaiti@mhaiti.org
www.mhaiti.org
www.facebook.com/maison.haiti.1
Aperçu: *Dimension:* petite; *Envergure:* locale; fondée en 1972
Mission: L'organisme a pour missions, la promotion, l'intégration, l'amélioration des conditions de vie et la défense des droits des québécois d'origine haïtienne et des personnes immigrantes ainsi que la promotion de leur participation au développement de la société d'accueil.
Membre de: Issu de la communauté, issu des organisations, membres sympathisants et amis de la Maison d'Haïti
Finances: *Budget de fonctionnement annuel:* $1.5 Million-$3 Million; *Fonds:* MELS, MIDI, MSP, MSSS, Santé Canada, DRHC, Lutte à la pauvreté, Centraide, Québec jeunes, Dufresne Gauthier
Membre(s) du personnel: 19; 65 bénévole(s)
Membre: 125; *Montant de la cotisation:* 5$
Activités: Volet Éducation:alphabétisation, francisation, persévérance scolaire, camps éducatifs; Volet Femmes:sécurité alimentaire des familles, Réseau de jeunes parents, insertion des mères adolescentes; Volet Jeunesse: Animations culturelles et sportives, prévention contre la violence les gangs de rue et l'exploitation sexuelle; Volet Intégration et insertion sociale: Accueil des nouveaux immigrants, orientation, recherche d'emploi
Membre(s) du bureau directeur:
Marjorie Villefranche, Directrice générale
dg@mhaiti.org

Maison de Campagne & d'Entraide Communautaire du Lac
Succ. 184, 2915, rte du Lac ouest, Alma QC G8B 5V6
Tél: 418-662-2102; *Téléc:* 418-662-6471
Nom précédent: Association des citoyennes averties Alma
Aperçu: *Dimension:* petite; *Envergure:* locale; fondée en 1976
Mission: Vise à informer, sensibiliser, et conscientiser les personnes à faible revenu de leurs droits; offrir une maison communautaire sans but lucratif, et permettre des vacances aux familles à faible revenu, un lieu privilégié pour des rencontres familiales, sessions de formation et d'éducation populaire, session de cuisine collective

Finances: *Budget de fonctionnement annuel:* $100,000-$250,000; *Fonds:* Gouvernements régional et provincial
Membre(s) du personnel: 7; 20 bénévole(s)
Membre: 77; *Montant de la cotisation:* 5$
Activités: *Listes de destinataires:* Oui
Membre(s) du bureau directeur:
Germaine Gauthier, Coordonnatrice
maicam@cgocable.ca

La Maison de la culture inc. (MC)
#123, 218, boul J.D. Gauthier, Shippagan NB E8S 1P6
Tél: 506-336-3423; *Téléc:* 506-336-3434
mculture@umcs.ca
www.maisonculture.ca
Aperçu: *Dimension:* petite; *Envergure:* locale; Organisme sans but lucratif; fondée en 1983
Mission: Viser le développement et le rayonnement culturel communautaire, en français, dans toute la région, de Pokemouche à Miscou
Membre de: Conseil de promotion de diffusion de la culture
Affiliation(s): Conseil provincial des sociétés culturelles; Réseau atlantique de diffusion des arts de la scène
Finances: *Budget de fonctionnement annuel:* Moins de $50,000; *Fonds:* Patrimoine canadien
Membre(s) du personnel: 2; 9 bénévole(s)
Membre: 84 individuels; 9 familles; 2 entreprise; *Montant de la cotisation:* 3$ étudiant(e)/aîné(e); $5 individuel; $15 famille; 30$ organisme; *Comités:* Bureau de direction; Conseillières-Conseillers
Activités: Spectacle, pièces de théâtre; expositions, ventes; ateliers; camp musical et artistique; revendications; lancement de disques et de livres
Membre(s) du bureau directeur:
Carole Savoie, Présidente
Denise Haché, Secrétaire

Maison de la famille de la Vallée du Richelieu
91, boul Cartier, Beloeil QC J3G 6R4
Tél: 450-446-0852
famillevr@videotron.ca
mfvr.ca
Aperçu: *Dimension:* petite; *Envergure:* locale
Mission: Pour aider les parents à apprendre plus de compétences parentales pour aider à améliorer leur vie et celle de leurs enfants
Membre: *Montant de la cotisation:* 15$
Activités: Ateliers; Conférences; Halte-garderie; Services de soutien; *Stagiaires:* Oui

Maison de Ribatejo *Voir* Casa do Ribatejo

La Maison des Açores du Québec *Voir* La Maison des Açores du Québec

La Maison des Açores du Québec / La Maison des Açores du Québec
229, rue Fleury ouest, Montréal QC H3L 1T8
Tél: 514-388-4129; *Téléc:* 514-388-2813
casadosacoresdoquebeque@hotmail.com
casasdosacores.org
Également appelé: Quebec Acores House
Aperçu: *Dimension:* petite; *Envergure:* internationale; fondée en 1978
Mission: Maintenir la communauté açores et la culture açores et préserver leur indentité
Membre(s) du bureau directeur:
Damiao Sousa, Président, Consil d'administration
José Machado, Vice-Président, Consil d'administration
Maria Alice Macedo, Trésorière, Consil d'administration

Maison des femmes de Québec inc.
CP 48023, Québec QC G1R 5R5
Tél: 418-522-0042; *Téléc:* 418-522-8034
maisondesfemmes.qc@videotron.ca
www.lamaisondesfemmesdequebec.com
Aperçu: *Dimension:* petite; *Envergure:* locale; Organisme sans but lucratif; fondée en 1980
Mission: Pourvoir hébergement gratuit & protection pour femmes et enfants victimes de violence conjugale; assurer un lieu sécuritaire d'intervention
Membre de: Regroupement provincial des maisons d'hébergement
Finances: *Budget de fonctionnement annuel:* $250,000-$500,000; *Fonds:* Gouvernement provincial
Membre(s) du personnel: 7; 25 bénévole(s)
Membre: 25; *Montant de la cotisation:* 2$

Activités: Représentation extérieure (écoles, universités, etc.); écoute téléphonique consultation à l'externe; support et accompagnement dans les démarches; intervention individuelle et de groupe; *Stagiaires:* Oui; *Service de conférenciers:* Oui

Maison des marins de Montréal *See* Mariners' House of Montréal

Maison du Parc
1287, rue Rachel est, Montréal QC H2J 2J9
Tél: 514-523-6467; *Téléc:* 514-523-6800
info@maisonduparc.org
www.maisonduparc.org
Aperçu: Dimension: petite; *Envergure:* locale; fondée en 1991 surveillé par Canadian AIDS Society
Membre de: Coalition des Organismes Communautaires Québécois-Sida
Activités: Centre d'hébergement pour personnes vivant avec le VIH-Sida (12 places); repas préparés sont distribués

Maison du Tourisme
892, rte 111 est, Amos QC J9T 2K4
Tél: 819-727-1242; *Téléc:* 819-727-3437
www.ville.amos.qc.ca/tourisme
Également appelé: Tourism Harricana
Nom précédent: Tourisme Harricana
Aperçu: Dimension: petite; *Envergure:* locale; Organisme sans but lucratif; fondée en 1995
Mission: Accueil; promotion; développement
Finances: *Budget de fonctionnement annuel:* $100,000-$250,000
Membre(s) du personnel: 2

Maison Elizabeth *See* Elizabeth House

Maison internationale de la Rive-Sud (MIRS)
#220, 2152, boul Lapinière, Brossard QC J4W 1L9
Tél: 450-445-8777; *Téléc:* 450-445-1222
info@mirs.qc.ca
www.mirs.qc.ca
Aperçu: Dimension: petite; *Envergure:* locale; fondée en 1975
Membre(s) du personnel: 10
Membre(s) du bureau directeur:
Gérard Deschênes, Président
Nicole Diessenes, Vice-présidente
Miguel Del Rio, Trésorier
Pierre Faubert, Secrétaire
Noureddine Belhocine, Directeur général

Maison Kekpart
1000, boul Roland-Therrien, Longueuil QC J4J 5H3
Tél: 450-677-3821; *Téléc:* 450-677-1907
maisonkekpart@videotron.ca
www.maisonkekpart.com
www.linkedin.com/company/maison-kekpart
www.facebook.com/rkekpart
Également appelé: Action jeunesse St-Pie X de Longueuil, inc.
Aperçu: Dimension: petite; *Envergure:* locale; Organisme sans but lucratif; fondée en 1981
Mission: Favoriser, chez les 12 à 18 ans, l'accessibilité à un statut de citoyen critique, actif et responsable; offre un lieu de rencontre animé où les jeunes peuvent choisir, organiser et participer à des activités de groupe
Membre de: Boys & Girls Clubs of Canada (Québec Region)
Activités: Bowling; spectacle extérieur; cueuillette de pommes; marche en montagne; équitation; ateliers; soupers communautaires; conférences
Membre(s) du bureau directeur:
Richard Desjardins, Directeur général
richardkekpart@videotron.ca

Maison Plein Coeur
1611, rue Dorion, Montréal QC H2K 4A5
Tél: 514-597-0554; *Téléc:* 514-597-2788
infompc@maisonpleincoeur.org
www.maisonpleincoeur.org
twitter.com/mpleincoeur
Aperçu: Dimension: petite; *Envergure:* locale; fondée en 1991
Mission: Contribuer à prévenir le VIH-SIDA, et à promouvoir la santé chez les personnes vivant avec la maladie; offrir des services sans aucune discrimination; favoriser des services communautaires visant à stabiliser la situation des personnes présentant des troubles de santé et d'organisation; améliorer la qualité de vie de la personne en offrant un lieu de partage et d'informations
Membre de: Société canadienne du sida; Coalition des organismes communautaires québécois de lutte contre le sida; Table des Organismes Montréalais de VIH-sida; Centre d'action bénévole de Montréal; Chambre de commerce LGBT du Québec; Conseil canadien de surveillance sur l'accès aux traitements
Finances: *Budget de fonctionnement annuel:* $500,000-$1.5 Million; *Fonds:* Gouvernementaux; privés
Membre(s) du personnel: 8; 100 bénévole(s)
Membre: 50
Activités: Accompagnement en voiture; intervention à domicile; massages; résidence supervisée transitoire; Entraide Positive; centre de jour; Souper Agora; VIH des Arts; Zone+; intervention individuelle; *Stagiaires:* Oui
Membre(s) du bureau directeur:
Elaine Mayrand, Présidente
Chris Lau, Directeur général, 514-597-0554 Ext. 222
chris@maisonpleincoeur.org

Maisons Adrianna
2500, rue Sainte-Catherine est, Montréal QC H2K 2K2
Tél: 514-527-9233
info@maisons-adrianna.org
maisons-adrianna.org
Aperçu: Dimension: petite; *Envergure:* locale; fondée en 1988
Mission: Pour aider à améliorer la qualité de vie des personnes défavorisées vivant dans la région centre-sud et de leur offrir une éducation sur la malnutrition
Activités: Bazar; Friperie; Librairie; Bingo
Membre(s) du bureau directeur:
Reynald Leboeuf, Directeur général

The Maitland Trail Association (MTA)
PO Box 443, Goderich ON N7A 4C7
mta.goderich@gmail.com
www.maitlandtrail.cjb.net
Overview: A small local organization founded in 1975
Mission: To develop & maintain low impact recreational trails in the natural areas of the Maitland River Valley
Member of: Hike Ontario
Finances: *Funding Sources:* Membership dues; donations; grants; Nevada outlet funding
Membership: *Fees:* $20 individual; $25 family
Activities: Trail follows the north side of the Maitland River from Lake Huron at Goderich to the Village of Auburn; developed & maintains the Goderich to Auburn Rail Trail (GART) in cooperation with the Colborne Snowmobile Club, a 2.5 km trail in the Maitland Woods (owned by Town of Goderich); work on new trail on the south bank of the Maitland River, called the Millennium Trail
Chief Officer(s):
Susanna Reid, President

Make-A-Wish Canada / Fais-Un-Voeu Canada
#520, 4211 Yonge St., Toronto ON M2P 2A9
Tel: 416-224-9474; *Fax:* 416-224-8795
Toll-Free: 888-822-9474
nationaloffice@makeawish.ca
makeawish.ca
www.linkedin.com/company/422218
www.facebook.com/makeawish.ca
twitter.com/MakeAWishCA
www.youtube.com/user/makeawishcanada
Overview: A large national charitable organization founded in 1980
Mission: The Foundation grants wishes to children suffering from a high risk, life-threatening illnesses
Finances: *Annual Operating Budget:* Greater than $5 Million; *Funding Sources:* Donations
Staff Member(s): 18
Chief Officer(s):
Jennifer Klotz-Ritter, President & Chief Executive Officer Ext. 6112
jennifer.ritter@makeawish.ca

Maker Kids
2241 Dundas St. West, Toronto ON M6R 1X6
Tel: 416-534-4560
info@makerkids.ca
www.makerkids.ca
www.facebook.com/MakerKids
twitter.com/Maker_Kids
Overview: A small local charitable organization
Mission: To help children & adults become more creative using physical tools & materials in areas including electronics, cooking, crafts & woodworking
Staff Member(s): 7; 4 volunteer(s)
Activities: *Internships:* Yes
Chief Officer(s):
Andy Forest, Co-Founder & Chief Investigator
Marianne Mader, Co-Founder

Makivik Corporation / Société Makivik
PO Box 179, Kuujjuaq QC J0M 1C0
Tel: 819-964-2925
Toll-Free: 877-625-4825
www.makivik.org
Previous Name: Northern Quebec Inuit Association
Overview: A large local charitable organization founded in 1978
Mission: A non-profit organization owned by the Inuit of Nunavik, the Corporation promotes the social & economic interests of the Inuit people; receives, administers & invests Inuit compensation funds received under the James Bay & Northern Québec Agreement, & promotes the political, social & economic development of the Nunavik region. Offices in Kuujjuaq, Montreal, Ottawa, Quebec City
Member of: Inuit Tapirisat Kanatami; Inuit Circumpolar Conference
Finances: *Annual Operating Budget:* Greater than $5 Million; *Funding Sources:* JBNQA compensation; investments; subsidiary corporations
Staff Member(s): 83
Membership: 9,838; *Member Profile:* Inuit as defined in James Bay Agreement
Activities: *Awareness Events:* Signing of James Bay & Northern Québec Agreement, Nov. 11, 1975; *Speaker Service:* Yes
Chief Officer(s):
Jobie Tukkiapik, President
jtukkiapik@makivik.org
Andy Pirti, Treasurer
apirti@makivik.org
Andy Moorhouse, Corporate Secretary
amoorhouse@makivik.org
Publications:
• Makivik Magazine [a publication of the Makivik Corporation]
Type: Magazine; *Frequency:* Quarterly
• Nunavik Newsletter [a publication of the Makivik Corporation]
Type: Newsletter
  Inukjuak Office
  Inukjuak QC J0M 1M0
  Tél: 819-254-1173; *Téléc:* 819-254-1040
  Kuujjuaraapik Office
  Kuujjuaraapik QC J0M 1G0
  Tél: 819-929-3925; *Téléc:* 819-929-3982
  Montréal Office
  1111, boul Dr.-Frederic-Philips, 3e étage, Montréal QC H4M 2X6
  Tél: 514-745-8880
  Ligne sans frais: 800-361-7052
  Québec City Office
  555, Grande-Allée est, Québec QC G1R 2J5
  Tél: 418-522-2224

Malaspina Printmakers Society (MPS)
1555 Duranleau St., Vancouver BC V6H 3S3
Tel: 604-688-1724
www.malaspinaprintmakers.com
www.facebook.com/malaspinaprintmakers
twitter.com/malaspinaprint
www.youtube.com/malaspinaprintmakers
Overview: A small international charitable organization founded in 1975
Mission: To support the development of printmaking as a contemporary art form and promotes and preserves traditional print practice; to advance knowledge of printmaking in the community; to facilitate the critical and technical exploration of printmaking in contemporary visual art practice.
Member of: Vancouver Cultural Alliance
Finances: *Funding Sources:* All levels of government; membership fees; fundraising; sales; studio rent
Membership: *Fees:* $35 individual; $50 friend; $150 patron; $300-$599 supporter; $600+ benefactor
Activities: *Internships:* Yes *Library:* Resource Centre; Open to public
Chief Officer(s):
Justin Muir, Executive Director

Malcolm Scottish Society
PO Box 8102, Canmore AB T1W 2T8
Tel: 403-678-9454; *Fax:* 403-678-3385
info@canmorehighlandgames.ca
www.canmorehighlandgames.ca
www.facebook.com/canmore.highlandgames
twitter.com/Canmorehighland
Overview: A small local organization founded in 2017

Mission: To establish the Canmore Highland Games as an entertainment/cultural destination event
Activities: *Awareness Events:* Canmore Highland Games, September

Mallaig Chamber of Commerce
PO Box 144, Mallaig AB T0A 2K0
Tel: 780-635-3952
Overview: A small local organization
Member of: Alberta Chambers of Commerce

Malta Band Club, Inc.
5745 Coopers Ave., Mississauga ON L4Z 1R9
Tel: 905-890-8507; *Fax:* 905-890-1306
maltabandclub@bellnet.ca
www.maltabandclub.net
Overview: A medium-sized local organization founded in 1971
Mission: To promote Maltese culture
Affiliation(s): Maltese Canadian Federation
Activities: Musical instruction; *Library:* Open to public
Chief Officer(s):
Anthony Vella, President

Maltese Veterans Association of Canada
3 Baby Point Cres., Toronto ON M6S 2B7
Tel: 416-767-8185
Overview: A small national organization founded in 1975
Member of: Maltese-Canadian Federation
Membership: *Member Profile:* Maltese-Canadians

Maltese-Canadian Federation Inc.
c/o St. Paul the Apostle Church, 3223 Dundas St. West, Toronto ON M6P 2A4
Overview: A small national organization
Affiliation(s): Maltese Veterans Association of Canada
Membership: *Member Profile:* Maltese-Canadians
Chief Officer(s):
Joe Sherri, President
joesherri21@gmail.com

Maltese-Canadian Society of Toronto, Inc. (MCST)
3132 Dundas St. West, Toronto ON M6P 2A1
Tel: 416-767-3645
Also Known As: The Maltese Society
Overview: A small local organization founded in 1922
Mission: The organization strives for the betterment of the Maltese community in Toronto. It also preserves & promotes the Maltese language & culture in Canada.
Affiliation(s): Maltese-Canadian Federation Inc.
Finances: *Annual Operating Budget:* Less than $50,000
9 volunteer(s)
Membership: *Member Profile:* Persons of Maltese-Canadian background
Activities: Outings; social events; Miss Malta of Canada Pageant

Malton Neighbourhood Services
3540 Morning Star Dr., Mississauga ON L4T 1Y2
Tel: 905-677-6270; *Fax:* 905-677-6281
www.mnsinfo.org
www.facebook.com/181976788507092
Overview: A small local charitable organization founded in 1978 overseen by Ontario Council of Agencies Serving Immigrants
Mission: To identify community needs; to promote community participation in planning; to ensure services are accessible & available to Malton residents; to promote community pride
Affiliation(s): City of Mississauga Recreation Department
Membership: *Member Profile:* Resident/worker in ward 5, Mississauga
Activities: Malton Community Information Service; *Speaker Service:* Yes; *Library:* Open to public
Chief Officer(s):
Joyce Temple-Smith, Executive Director
Tony Patey, Chair
Awards:
• Citizenship & Immigration Citation for Citizenship

Mamawehetowin Crisis Centre
PO Box 133, Pukatawagan MB R0B 1G0
Tel: 204-553-2198; *Fax:* 204-553-2302; *Crisis Hot-Line:* 866-432-1041
Previous Name: Mamawehetowin Crisis Centre for Abused Women & Children
Overview: A small local organization
Mission: To provide shelter & servies to battered aboriginal women & their children
Member of: National Aboriginal Circle Against Family Violence
Activities: Emergency shelter; Support groups; Crisis counselling & intervention; Referrals to medical, legal & social service agencies; Follow-up services

Mamawehetowin Crisis Centre for Abused Women & Children *See* Mamawehetowin Crisis Centre

Mamingwey Burn Survivor Society
#303, 83 Garry St., Winnipeg MB R3C 4J9
Tel: 204-272-0945
info@mamingwey.ca
www.mamingwey.ca
Overview: A small local organization
Mission: To offer support to persons with burn injuries
Membership: *Member Profile:* Burn survivors; Family members & friends of burn survivors; Persons who work with burn victims
Activities: Providing networking opportunities
Chief Officer(s):
Barbara-Anne Hodge, Chair

Ma-Mow-We-Tak Friendship Centre Inc. / The Gathering Place
4 Nelson Rd., Thompson MB R8N 0B4
Tel: 204-677-0950
www.mamowwetak.com
Overview: A small local organization founded in 1976
Mission: To support Aboriginal people making the transition from life on the reserve or isolated communities to urban life in Thompson, Manitoba; To operate as a non-sectarian, non-political, non-profit, charitable organization, geared to meeting the needs of Aboriginal people in Thompson and the surrounding area
Activities: Northern Council of Youth; Youth Employment Assistant Services; Parent/Child Centre Initiative; New Beginnings
Chief Officer(s):
Anita Campbell, Executive Director

Managers Association of Financial Advisors of Canada *See* GAMA International Canada

Manitoba & Northwestern Ontario CGIT Association
131 Woodside Cres., Winnipeg MB R3W 1B5
Tel: 204-254-2378
cgit@cgitmanitoba.ca
www.cgitmanitoba.ca
www.facebook.com/groups/5409037069
twitter.com/CGITManitoba
www.instagram.com/cgit_manitoba
Also Known As: Canadian Girls in Training - Manitoba
Previous Name: National CGIT Association - Manitoba & Northwestern Ontario
Overview: A small provincial organization

Manitoba 5 Pin Bowlers' Association (M5PBA)
#432, 145 Pacific Ave., Winnipeg MB R3B 2Z6
Tel: 204-925-5766; *Fax:* 204-925-5792
Toll-Free: 800-282-8069
www.m5pba.com
Overview: A small provincial organization overseen by Manitoba Five Pin Bowling Federation, Inc.
Member of: Manitoba Five Pin Bowling Federation, Inc.
Chief Officer(s):
Marilyn McMullan, President
mgmc.hdqtrs@shaw.ca

Manitoba Aboriginal Education Counselling Association Inc.
#305, 352 Donald St., Winnipeg MB R3B 2H8
Tel: 204-947-0421
Overview: A small provincial organization founded in 1989
Awards:
• Abraham McPherson Scholarship Award
Eligibility: High school graduate with an overall average of 70% upon graduation; *Amount:* $250

Manitoba Amateur Bodybuilding Association (MABBA)
23 Forestgate Ave., Winnipeg MB R3P 2L2
mabba@shaw.ca
www.bodybuilding.ca
www.facebook.com/groups/231959203612085
Overview: A small provincial organization overseen by Canadian Bodybuilding Federation
Mission: To be the provincial governing body for the sport of amateur bodybuilding in Manitoba
Member of: Canadian Bodybuilding Federation; International Federation of Bodybuilding; Sport Manitoba
Membership: *Fees:* $50; *Committees:* Fitness; Figure; Bikini; Bodybuilding; Physique
Chief Officer(s):
Chris McKee, Executive Director
mabba@shaw.ca

Manitoba Amateur Boxing Association *See* Boxing Manitoba

Manitoba Amateur Broomball Association (MABA)
145 Pacific Ave., Winnipeg MB R3B 2Z6
Tel: 204-925-5668; *Fax:* 204-925-9792
Toll-Free: 866-792-7666
broomballmb@shaw.ca
www.manitobabroomball.com
Overview: A medium-sized provincial organization founded in 1982 overseen by Ballon sur glace Broomball Canada
Mission: To promote the sport of broomball in Manitoba; to offer opportunities to members in competing in provincial & national championships
Member of: Ballon sur glace Broomball Canada; Sport Manitoba
Staff Member(s): 1
Membership: 500
Activities: School clinics; competitions; tournaments; provincials
Chief Officer(s):
Cathy Derewianchuk, Executive Director

Manitoba Amateur Wrestling Association (MAWA)
c/o Sport Manitoba, 145 Pacific Ave., Winnipeg MB R3B 2Z6
mawawrestling@mts.net
www.mawawrestling.ca
Overview: A small provincial organization founded in 2007 overseen by Canadian Amateur Wrestling Association
Mission: The Manitoba Amateur Wrestling Association (MAWA) is the recognised provincial sport organization (PSO) for the sport of wrestling in Manitoba. MAWA is dedicated to the continuing development of wrestling across the province and to maintain a safe, fun environment for all its members. MAWA is an organization that promotes teamwork, leadership and healthy lifestyles through wrestling in Manitoba for all ages.
Membership: *Fees:* Schedule available; *Member Profile:* Individual wrestlers & clubs; *Committees:* Tournament; Athlete Development; Marketing
Chief Officer(s):
Sally McNabb, President

Manitoba Animal Health Technologists Association (MAHTA)
1590 Inkster Blvd., Winnipeg MB R2X 2W4
Tel: 204-832-1394; *Fax:* 204-896-6756
office@mahta.ca
www.mahta.ca
Overview: A small provincial organization
Member of: Canadian Association of Animal Health Technologists & Technicians
Membership: *Fees:* Schedule available

Manitoba Antique Association (MAA)
PO Box 2881, Winnipeg MB R3C 4B4
mbantiqueassociation@gmail.com
mbantiqueassociation.com
www.facebook.com/MBAntiqueAssociation
Overview: A medium-sized provincial organization founded in 1967
Mission: To preserve & restore antiques; to promote the admiration of all antiques
Finances: *Annual Operating Budget:* Less than $50,000
Membership: 300; *Fees:* $25 individual; $35 family
Activities: Organizing educational programs; presenting shows & sales; monthly meetings; *Speaker Service:* Yes; *Library*
Chief Officer(s):
Laurie Paradis, President, 204-663-4311
lparadis@shaw.ca
Audrey German, Contact, Membership, 204-224-5282
agerman@shaw.ca
Publications:
• Manitoba Antique Association Newsletter
Type: Newsletter; *Frequency:* Monthly; *Accepts Advertising*; *Editor:* Audrey German
Profile: Printed between September & June; contains news, activities & upcoming events

Manitoba Arm Wrestling Association (MAWA)
MB
Tel: 204-285-9873
info@manitobaarmwrestling.com
www.manitobaarmwrestling.com
www.facebook.com/groups/375248869203923/

Overview: A small provincial organization overseen by Canadian Arm Wrestling Federation
Mission: To be the provincial governing body for the sport of arm wrestling in Manitoba
Member of: Canadian Arm Wrestling Federation
Chief Officer(s):
Darrell Steffenson, Contact

Manitoba Arts Council (MAC) / Conseil des arts du Manitoba (CAM)
#525, 93 Lombard Ave., Winnipeg MB R3B 3B1
Tel: 204-945-2237; *Fax:* 204-945-5925
Toll-Free: 866-994-2787
info@artscouncil.mb.ca
artscouncil.mb.ca
www.facebook.com/mbartscouncil
Overview: A medium-sized provincial organization founded in 1969
Mission: An arms-length agency of the provincial government dedicated to artistic excellence; offers a broad based grant program for professional artists & arts organizations; promotes, preserves, supports & advocates for the arts as essential to the quality of life of all people of Manitoba.
Finances: *Annual Operating Budget:* Greater than $5 Million; *Funding Sources:* Dept. of Culture, Heritage & Tourism
Staff Member(s): 18
Activities: *Speaker Service:* Yes
Chief Officer(s):
Akoulina Connell, Chief Executive Officer
aconnell@artscouncil.mb.ca
Charlene Brown, Executive Coordinator
cbrown@artscouncil.mb.ca
Elly Wittens, Office Manager
ewittens@artscouncil.mb.ca
Awards:
• Performing Arts
• Arts Development
• Writing & Publishing
• Aboriginal Arts
• Visual Arts
• Multidisciplinary

Manitoba Arts Network
#203, 100 Arthur St., Winnipeg MB R3B 1H3
Tel: 204-943-0036; *Fax:* 204-943-1126
Toll-Free: 866-919-2787
info@communityarts.mb.ca
www.manitobaartsnetwork.ca
www.facebook.com/mbartsnet
twitter.com/search/manitoba%20arts
www.flickr.com/search/?q=manitoba+arts
Also Known As: Manitoba Association of Community Arts Councils Inc.
Overview: A small provincial charitable organization founded in 1984
Mission: To represent community arts councils & community arts programming organizations throughout Manitoba; to enhance community life by providing opportunities for individuals in rural & remote communities to participate in & gain knowlege from arts & cultural activities that enrich their lives; to provide support for the growth & development of community arts councils throughout Manitoba; to provide programs & services designed to foster the development of arts & cultural activity in rural & remote communities
Staff Member(s): 5; 50 volunteer(s)
Membership: 150; *Member Profile:* Arts organizations & individual artists; *Committees:* Visual Arts; Northern Touring; Southern Touring
Activities: Tour Visual arts exhibitions; arrange block booking for performance tours; *Library*
Chief Officer(s):
Rose-Ann Harder, Director
director@mbartsnet.ca

Manitoba Association for Art Education (MAAE)
Winnipeg MB
maae.weebly.com
Overview: A small provincial organization
Mission: To promote & improve visual art education in Manitoba
Affiliation(s): Manitoba Teachers' Society; Canadian Society for Education through Art
Membership: *Fees:* $20; $10 (student); *Member Profile:* Teachers; artists; students; *Committees:* Grants; SAGE Conference
Chief Officer(s):
Dawn Knight, President
dknight@pembinatrails.ca

Manitoba Association for Behaviour Analysis (MABA)
PO Box 53017, Stn. South St. Vital, Winnipeg MB R2N 3X2
president@maba.ca
www.maba.ca
Overview: A small provincial organization
Membership: *Committees:* Executive Public Relations; Newsletter; Membership; Conference
Chief Officer(s):
Genevieve Roy-Wsiaki, President
president@maba.ca
Meetings/Conferences:
• 13th Annual Manitoba Association for Behaviour Analysis Conference 2018, 2018, MB
Scope: Provincial

Manitoba Association for Business Economics (MABE)
MB
www.cabe.ca/mabe
Overview: A small provincial organization overseen by Canadian Association for Business Economics
Mission: To bring together individuals in Manitoba interested in the field of economics; To provide regular meetings for discussion & the exchange of ideas on current economic problems, issues & achievements; To foster further education in the field of economics
Member of: Canadian Association for Business Economics
Chief Officer(s):
John Harper, President, 204-292-5827
john.harper@canada.ca

Manitoba Association for Medical Laboratory Science (MAMLS)
585 London St., Winnipeg MB R2K 2Z6
Tel: 204-669-9050; *Fax:* 204-667-1747
mamlsprez1@gmail.com
www.mamls.ca
www.facebook.com/manitobaamls
twitter.com/MAMLS1
Previous Name: Manitoba Society of Medical Laboratory Science; Manitoba Society of Medical Laboratory Technologists
Overview: A medium-sized provincial organization overseen by Canadian Society for Medical Laboratory Science
Mission: To protect public safety by maintaining & improving standards of medical laboratory technology practice in Manitoba, & promoting closer cooperation between its members & other health care professionals to more effectively aid in the diagnosis of disease
Affiliation(s): Canadian Society for Medical Laboratory Science
Finances: *Funding Sources:* Member fees
Membership: *Member Profile:* Certified technologists & trainees
Chief Officer(s):
Melanie Couture, President

Manitoba Association for Volunteer Administration (MAVA)
PO Box 3099, Winnipeg MB R3C 4B3
MAVAmanitoba@gmail.com
www.mavamanitoba.ca
www.facebook.com/840199486025116
twitter.com/MAVA_MB
Overview: A small provincial organization
Mission: To unite individuals involved in the administration of volunteer services & programs in a professional association; promotes volunteer administration as a profession; provides opportunities for the exchange of knowledge & experience in the administration of volunteer services & programs; promotes professional standards, education, growth & development
Member of: Canadian Administrators of Volunteer Resources
Membership: *Fees:* $35 student; $65 adult
Chief Officer(s):
Lesley Camaso-Catalan, President

Manitoba Association of Architects (MAA)
137 Bannatyne Ave., 2nd Fl., Winnipeg MB R3B 0R3
Tel: 204-925-4620; *Fax:* 204-925-4624
info@mbarchitects.org
www.mbarchitects.org
Overview: A medium-sized provincial licensing organization founded in 1914
Mission: To protect the public interest and advance the profession of architecture.
Finances: *Funding Sources:* Membership dues

Staff Member(s): 2
Membership: *Fees:* Schedule available; *Committees:* Registration; Executive; Practice; Education; Public Affairs; Investigation; Inquiry; Internship in Architecture
Activities: *Internships:* Yes; *Rents Mailing List:* Yes
Chief Officer(s):
Judy Pestrak, Executive Director

Manitoba Association of Asian Physicians (MAAP)
c/o Dr. Rajat Kumar, President, 675 McDermot Ave., Winnipeg MB R3E 0V9
www.maap.ca
Overview: A small provincial organization founded in 1985
Membership: *Fees:* $200 life; $50 annual; $0 resident/medical student; *Member Profile:* Practicing physicians, residents and students of Asian decent.

Manitoba Association of Cheerleading (MAC)
MB
Tel: 204-888-0317
info@cheermanitoba.ca
www.cheermanitoba.ca
www.facebook.com/ManitobaAssociationofCheerleading
twitter.com/MAC_Cheer_MB
instagram.com/mac_cheer_mb
Overview: A small provincial organization founded in 1986 overseen by Cheer Canada
Mission: To be the official regulating body for cheerleading in Manitoba.
Member of: Cheer Canada
Chief Officer(s):
Patricia McNeill, President

Manitoba Association of Christian Home Schools (MACHS)
PO Box 13 RPO SO St Vital, Winnipeg MB R2N 3X9
info@machs.ca
www.machs.mb.ca
Overview: A small provincial organization founded in 1983
Mission: MACHS is a non-profit, volunteer provincial organization that seeks to connect, support and equip all those who are involved in Christian Home Education in the Province of Manitoba.
Activities: *Library:* MACHS Library
Chief Officer(s):
Edgar Donelle, Président

Manitoba Association of Fire Chiefs (MAFC)
PO Box 1208, Portage la Prairie MB R1N 3J9
Tel: 204-857-6249
mb.firechiefs@mymts.net
mafc.ca
Overview: A small provincial organization founded in 1950
Membership: *Fees:* $150 regular; *Committees:* Annual Conference; Finance & Audit; Nominating; Resolutions
Chief Officer(s):
Martin Haller, President
Meetings/Conferences:
• 2018 Manitoba Association of Fire Chiefs Annual Conference & Trade Show, May, 2018, Selkirk, MB
Scope: Provincial

Manitoba Association of Friendship Centres (MAC)
#102, 150 Henry Ave., Winnipeg MB R3B 0J7
Tel: 204-942-6299
www.friendshipcentres.ca
www.facebook.com/FriendshipCentres
Overview: A medium-sized provincial charitable organization founded in 1971 overseen by National Association of Friendship Centres
Mission: To assist friendship centres in communication, funding & training
Finances: *Funding Sources:* Provincial & federal government
Membership: 11 centres; *Committees:* Personnel & Finance; Constitution & Policy; National Issues
Chief Officer(s):
Adam Blanchard, Executive Director

Manitoba Association of Health Care Professionals (MAHCP) / Association des professionnels de la santé du Manitoba
#101, 1500 Notre Dame Ave., Winnipeg MB R3E 0P9
Tel: 204-772-0425; *Fax:* 204-775-6829
Toll-Free: 800-315-3331
info@mahcp.ca
mahcp.com

www.facebook.com/manitobaahcp
twitter.com/MAHCP_MB
Overview: A medium-sized provincial organization
Mission: To protect, advocate for & advance the rights of its members through labour relations activities
Staff Member(s): 12
Membership: *Committees:* Communication; Governance; Management; Oversight; Social Action & Strategic Partnership; Strike Readiness
Activities: *Library:* Not open to public
Chief Officer(s):
Bob Moroz, President
bobm@mahcp.ca
Lee Manning, Executive Director
lee@mahcp.ca

Manitoba Association of Health Information Providers (MAHIP)
c/o Neil John Maclean Health Sciences Library, University of Manitoba, 727 McDermott Ave., Winnipeg MB R3E 3P5
Fax: 204-789-3922
contact.mahip@gmail.com
mahip.chla-absc.ca
Previous Name: Manitoba Health Libraries Association
Overview: A small provincial organization founded in 1979 overseen by Canadian Health Libraries Association
Mission: To promote the provision of quality library service to the health community in Manitoba by communication & mutual assistance.
Membership: *Fees:* $50 institutional; $30 professional librarian; $20 library technician/assistant; $10 student
Chief Officer(s):
Grace Romund, President
grace.romund@umanitoba.ca
Andrea Szwajcer, Secretary
andrea.szwajcer@umanitoba.ca
Meetings/Conferences:
• Manitoba Association of Health Information Providers Annual General Meeting 2018, 2018, MB
Scope: Provincial

Manitoba Association of Home Economists (MAHE)
PO Box 582, Stn. Main, Winnipeg MB R3C 2J3
Tel: 204-885-0718
Toll-Free: 866-261-0707
Other Communication: Home & Family URL:
www.homefamily.net
mahe@mahe.ca
www.mahe.ca
www.facebook.com/HomeAndFamily.net
twitter.com/HomeFamily_PHEc
Overview: A small provincial organization
Mission: To enable families, both as individual units & generally as a social institution, to build & maintain systems of action which lead to maturing in individual self-formation & enlightened, co-operative participation in the critique & formulation of social goals & means for accomplishing them.
Chief Officer(s):
Debra Durnin-Richards, President

Manitoba Association of Insolvency & Restructuring Professionals (MAIRP)
c/o Deloitte, #2300, 360 Main St., Winnipeg MB R3C 3Z3
Tel: 204-944-3611; *Fax:* 204-947-2689
www.mairp.ca
Previous Name: Manitoba Insolvency Association
Overview: A small provincial organization overseen by Canadian Association of Insolvency & Restructuring Professionals
Member of: Canadian Association of Insolvency & Restructuring Professionals
Chief Officer(s):
Brent Warga, President
bwarga@deloitte.ca

Manitoba Association of Insurance Professionals (MAIP)
MB
Tel: 204-269-7032
www.caiw-acfa.ca
Previous Name: Insurance Women's Association of Manitoba
Overview: A small provincial organization founded in 1966
Mission: To preserve and enhance the value of its members through education and networking, and to foster personal growth
Member of: Canadian Association of Insurance Women

Activities: Monthly dinner meetings & speakers; continuing education, awards; *Awareness Events:* Annual Golf Tournament; Annual Wine & Cheese; Annual Public Speaking Contest
Chief Officer(s):
Katherine Morgan Clark, President
katherine.morganclark@intact.net

Manitoba Association of Landscape Architects (MALA)
131 Callum Cres., Winnipeg MB R2G 2C7
Tel: 204-663-4863; *Fax:* 204-668-5662
www.mala.net
Overview: A medium-sized provincial organization founded in 1973 overseen by Canadian Society of Landscape Architects
Mission: To promote, improve & advance the profession; to maintain standards of professional practice & conduct consistent with the need to serve & protect public interest; to support improvement &/or conservation of the natural, cultural, social & built environment
Member of: Canadian Society of Landscape Architects
Finances: *Annual Operating Budget:* Less than $50,000
Staff Member(s): 1
Membership: 49 individual + 5 honorary + 28 associate + 40 student affiliates + 4 friend; *Committees:* CSLA Awards/Annual Symposium; Communications; Examining Board; Ethics; University Liaison
Activities: *Internships:* Yes; *Rents Mailing List:* Yes
Chief Officer(s):
Monica Giesbrecht, President

Manitoba Association of Library Technicians (MALT)
PO Box 1872, Winnipeg MB R3C 3R1
malt.mb.ca@gmail.com
www.malt.mb.ca
www.facebook.com/malt.mb.ca
Overview: A medium-sized provincial organization founded in 1971
Mission: To promote & advance the role of library technicians throughout Manitoba; To respond to issues that relate to the library & information services community
Membership: *Fees:* $12.50 students/unemployed members; $25 regular; $40 institutional (1-5 people); $100 institutional (6+ people); *Member Profile:* Library technician students throughout Manitoba; Individuals from all types of libraries in Manitoba; Institutions
Activities: Offering workshops; Sponsoring programs; Maintaining a job bank to advertise library positions; Promoting libraries in Manitoba
Chief Officer(s):
Cassie Page, President
Ebony Novakowski, Vice-President
Alice Klumper, Treasurer
Brad Rogowsky, Secretary
Justin Fuhr, Editor, Newsletter
Leslie McDonald, Coordinator, Membership
Dana Van Aert Pattrosson, Coordinator, Communications
Awards:
• Library Technician of the Year Award
Eligibility: A graduate of a recognized Library Technician program
• Library Support Worker of the Year Award
Eligibility: An individual working in a library without holding a Library Technician Diploma or Master of Library Science
• Rising Star Award
Eligibility: A Library Technician who has graduated from a recognized program within the last six years
• Red River College Library & Information Technology Student Award
Eligibility: A student with the highest marks in library-related courses in the first year of the Red River College Library Information Technician program
Meetings/Conferences:
• Manitoba Association of Library Technicians 2018 Annual General Meeting, 2018, MB
Scope: Provincial
Publications:
• Manitoba Association of Library Technicians Newsletter
Type: Newsletter; *Frequency:* q.; *Editor:* Justin Fuhr; *ISSN:* 1188-3804
Profile: Continuing education information, meeting highlights, association business, & awards

Manitoba Association of Medical Radiation Technologists (MAMRT)
Sargent Professional Centre, #202, 819 Sargent Ave., Winnipeg MB R3E 0B9

Tel: 204-774-5346
admin@mamrt.ca
www.mamrt.ca
Overview: A small provincial organization founded in 1929 overseen by Canadian Association of Medical Radiation Technologists
Mission: To support the Medical Radiation Technology profession, consisting of the four disciplines of Radiological Technology, Radiation Therapy, Magnetic Resonance Technology & Nuclear Medicine Technology, within Manitoba
Finances: *Funding Sources:* Membership dues & fees; Sponsorships
Staff Member(s): 2; 12+ volunteer(s)
Membership: *Fees:* Schedule available; *Member Profile:* Medical radiation technologists in Manitoba; *Committees:* Standing; Special
Activities: Promotion and education for both the general public and members; *Library:* MAMRT Lending Library; Not open to public
Chief Officer(s):
Jenna Bruderer, President
Salín Guttormsson, Executive Director
Jordan Veale, Director, Communications
Jason Lewis, Director, Finance & Administration
Corey Baschuk, Office Administrator
Awards:
• Colin Maxwell Memorial Award
• Bill Doern Service Award
• Claude Bodle Memorial Lecture Award
Meetings/Conferences:
• Manitoba Association of Medical Radiation Technologists 2018 Annual General Conference, 2018
Scope: Provincial
Description: A conference providing educational sessions, held each spring
Publications:
• MAMRT News: A Newsletter of the Manitoba Association of Medical Radiation Technologists
Type: Newsletter; *Frequency:* 3 pa; *Accepts Advertising*
Profile: Information from the association for members

Manitoba Association of Non-Teaching Employees (MANTE) / Association des employés non enseignants du Manitoba
#210, 2281 Portage Ave., Winnipeg MB R3J 0M1
Tel: 204-931-2397
mante@mante.ca
mante.ca
Overview: A small provincial organization founded in 1978
Chief Officer(s):
Joan McEachern, President

Manitoba Association of Optometrists (MAO)
#217, 530 Century St., Winnipeg MB R3H 0Y4
Tel: 204-943-9811; *Fax:* 204-943-1208
mao@optometrists.mb.ca
www.optometrists.mb.ca
Previous Name: Manitoba Optometric Society
Overview: A medium-sized provincial organization founded in 1909 overseen by Canadian Association of Optometrists
Mission: To regulate the practice of optometry in Manitoba, in accordance with The Optometry Act & Regulation; To represent optometrists in Manitoba; To protect & promote the vision care needs & eye health of Manitobans
Member of: Canadian Association of Optometrists (CAO)
Membership: *Member Profile:* Doctors of optometry in Manitoba
Activities: Registering practitioners; Establishing & ensuring standards of practice; Communicating the role of optometrists' in the health care system; Answering inquiries & concerns from patients & the public; Encouraging regular, preventitive eye examinations
Chief Officer(s):
Neil Campbell, President
Laureen Goodridge, Executive Director
Lorne Ryall, Registrar

Manitoba Association of Parent Councils (MAPC)
#1005, 401 York Ave., Winnipeg MB R3C 0P8
Tel: 204-956-1770; *Fax:* 204-948-2855
Toll-Free: 877-290-4702
info@mapc.mb.ca
www.mapc.mb.ca
www.facebook.com/mapcmb
twitter.com/mapcmb
www.youtube.com/MBParentCouncils

Overview: A small provincial charitable organization overseen by Canadian Home & School Federation
Mission: An organization of school-based parent groups throughout Manitoba.
Finances: *Annual Operating Budget:* Less than $50,000; *Funding Sources:* Grants; membership dues; donations
Staff Member(s): 1; 14 volunteer(s)
Membership: 295; *Fees:* $50; *Member Profile:* Parent groups involved in their child's school
Activities: *Speaker Service:* Yes; *Library:* Open to public
Chief Officer(s):
Naomi Kruse, Executive Director
Meetings/Conferences:
• 2018 Manitoba Association of Parent Councils AGM & Conference, May, 2018, Victoria Inn Hotel & Convention Centre, Winnipeg, MB
Scope: Provincial

Manitoba Association of Personal Care Home Social Workers (MAPCHSW)
PO Box 2591, Stn. Main, Winnipeg MB R3C 4B3
www.mapchsw.com
Overview: A small provincial organization founded in 1972
Mission: To provide a forum for discussion of topics pertinent to social workers in long-term care settings
Finances: *Funding Sources:* Membership dues
Membership: *Fees:* $30
Chief Officer(s):
Lori Orford, Contact

Manitoba Association of Playwrights (MAP)
#503, 100 Arthur St., Winnipeg MB R3B 1H3
Tel: 204-942-8941
mbplay@mts.net
www.mbplays.ca
www.facebook.com/mbplaywrights
Overview: A small provincial charitable organization founded in 1979
Mission: To provide support for playwrights in Manitoba through the operation of programs for emerging & established playwrights
Membership: *Fees:* $60; $25 student; *Member Profile:* Directors, actors & anyone interested in the continuing health of playwriting & the production of new plays in Manitoba theatres
Activities: Offering play development workshops, seminars, programs, mentorships, resources, & services to playwrights; *Speaker Service:* Yes; *Library:* Open to public
Chief Officer(s):
James Durham, President

Manitoba Association of Prosthetists & Orthotists
c/o Orthotics Prosthetics Canada, #202, 300 March Rd., Ottawa ON K2K 2E2
Overview: A small provincial organization overseen by Orthotics Prosthetics Canada
Mission: To promote quality care for prosthetic & orthotic patients in Manitoba; To encourage professionalism in Manitoba's prosthetic & orthotic field
Membership: *Member Profile:* Certified prosthetic & orthotic practitioners, registered technicians, allied health professionals, students, & retired persons in Manitoba
Activities: Promoting continuing education; Liaising with related organizations in Manitoba
Chief Officer(s):
Daniel Mazur, Contact

Manitoba Association of Registered Nurses See College of Registered Nurses of Manitoba

Manitoba Association of Registered Respiratory Therapists, Inc. (MARRT) / L'Association des thérapeutes respiratoires du Manitoba, inc.
#206, 629 McDermot Ave., Winnipeg MB R3A 1P6
Tel: 204-944-8081
www.marrt.ca
Overview: A medium-sized provincial licensing organization founded in 1981
Affiliation(s): Canadian Society of Respiratory Therapists
Staff Member(s): 2
Membership: *Member Profile:* Respiratory therapists; student respiratory therapists; *Committees:* Complaints; Discipline; Education; Finance; License & Audit; Nominating; Public Relations; Standards of Practice
Activities: *Speaker Service:* Yes
Chief Officer(s):
Cory Campbell, President
Shane McDonald, Registrar

Manitoba Association of School Business Officials (MASBO)
PO Box 547, Morris MB R0G 1K0
Tel: 204-254-7570; *Fax:* 204-254-3606
www.masbo.ca
Overview: A small provincial organization founded in 1965
Mission: To provide leadership in the areas of finance, maintenance & transportation
Membership: 160; *Fees:* $318
Chief Officer(s):
Roy Seidler, Executive Director

Manitoba Association of School Psychologists Inc.
#562, 162 - 2025 Corydon Ave., Winnipeg MB R3P 0N5
www.masp.mb.ca
Overview: A small provincial organization founded in 1981
Mission: To promote & support school psychology in Manitoba; to develop a network of communication among practitioners of school psychology in Manitoba; to encourage & provide information to educators & the public regarding the practice of school psychology & other related educational issues
Membership: *Fees:* $100 full; $50 affiliate; $50 retired; $18 student; *Committees:* Issues; Membership; Professional Development; Publications/Communications; Website
Chief Officer(s):
Barry Mallin, President

Manitoba Association of School Superintendents (MASS)
375 Jefferson Ave., Winnipeg MB R2V 0N3
Tel: 204-487-7972; *Fax:* 204-487-7974
www.mass.mb.ca
Overview: A small provincial organization founded in 1956
Mission: To provide leadership for public education by advocating in the best interest of learners, & supports its members through professional services.
Affiliation(s): Canadian Association of School Administrators
Finances: *Funding Sources:* Membership fees
Staff Member(s): 2
Membership: 110; *Member Profile:* Senior professional administrator in education; *Committees:* Curriculum; Education Finance; ICT; Legislation/Policy; Professional Learning; Public Relations/Membership Services; Research; Aboriginal Education Advisory
Activities: *Library:* by appointment Not open to public
Chief Officer(s):
Ken Klassen, Executive Director
ken.klassen@7oaks.org

Manitoba Association of School Trustees See Manitoba School Boards Association

Manitoba Association of Sheet Metal & Air Handling Contractors Inc. (MASMAHC)
24 Trottier Bay, Winnipeg MB R3T 3Y5
Tel: 204-284-2882
info@masmahc.org
www.masmahc.org
Overview: A medium-sized provincial organization
Mission: To improve the industry & image of the sheet metal contractor; To upgrade procedures & workmanship; To address mutual problems of trade contractors & construction; To educate members on government regulations
Affiliation(s): Sheet Metal & Air Conditioning Contractors' National Association, Inc.
Finances: *Annual Operating Budget:* Less than $50,000; *Funding Sources:* Membership dues
Membership: 30
Activities: *Library:*

Manitoba Association of the Appraisal Institute of Canada See The Appraisal Institute of Canada - Manitoba

Manitoba Association of Visual Language Interpreters (MAVLI)
PO Box 68056, Stn. Osborne Village, Winnipeg MB R3L 2V9
www.mavli.com
Overview: A small provincial organization founded in 1976 overseen by Association of Visual Language Interpreters of Canada
Mission: To promote the profession of visual language interpretation through advocacy & education
Member of: Association of Visual Language Interpreters of Canada (AVLIC)
Affiliation(s): Winnipeg Community Centre of the Deaf

Membership: *Member Profile:* Those involved in the provision of sign language interpretation or who support the aims of the organization; *Committees:* Education
Chief Officer(s):
Mandy MacDonald, President
president@mavli.com

Manitoba Association of Women's Shelters (MAWS)
c/o Genesis House, PO Box 389, Winkler MB R6W 4A6
Tel: 204-325-9957; *Crisis Hot-Line:* 877-977-0007
maws@maws.mb.ca
www.maws.mb.ca
Overview: A medium-sized provincial organization founded in 1991
Mission: To eliminate violence against women; To provide support to member shelters for abused women & their children; To share information & resources with its member shelters, increase training of staff & increase services for clients.
Finances: *Funding Sources:* Provincial government; private donations
Membership: 9 provincially funded shelters & several affiliate members; *Member Profile:* Shelters for abused women & children
Activities: *Speaker Service:* Yes
Chief Officer(s):
Karen Peto, Co-Chair
Sharon Morgan, Co-Chair

Manitoba Athletic Therapists Association Inc. (MATA)
145 Pacific Ave., Winnipeg MB R3B 2Z6
Tel: 204-925-5930; *Fax:* 204-925-5624
mata@sportmanitoba.ca
www.mata.mb.ca
www.facebook.com/162809277115285
twitter.com/MATATherapist
Overview: A small provincial organization founded in 1983
Mission: Committed to the prevention and care of activity-related injuries, at all levels of sport and recreation, ranging from the grass roots level to the elite athlete, throughout Manitoba.
Member of: Canadian Athletic Therapists Association; Sports Medicine Council of Manitoba; Sport Manitoba
Finances: *Annual Operating Budget:* $50,000-$100,000
Staff Member(s): 2
Membership: 200; *Fees:* Schedule available
Activities: Athletic First Aid Programs; medical coverage for sport & recreation; *Library:* Open to public
Chief Officer(s):
Mike Hutton, President
mhutton@mbteach.org
Publications:
• Manitoba Athletic Therapists Association Inc. Newsletter
Type: Newsletter
Profile: News & updates for members

Manitoba Audio Recording Industry Association See Manitoba Music

Manitoba Badminton Association (MBA)
#323, 145 Pacific Ave., Winnipeg MB R3B 2Z6
Fax: 204-925-5703
www.badminton.mb.ca
twitter.com/badmintonmb
Overview: A small local organization overseen by Badminton Canada
Mission: To provide the leadership that promotes the growth of badminton throughout Manitoba as a lifelong sport
Staff Member(s): 3
Membership: *Member Profile:* Athletes, coaches, officials & badminton clubs
Chief Officer(s):
Ryan Giesbrecht, Executive Director, 204-925-5621
ryan@badminton.mb.ca

Manitoba Ball Hockey Association (MBHA)
#306, 145 Pacific Ave., Winnipeg MB R3B 2Z6
Tel: 204-808-8770
mbha1@hotmail.com
www.winnipegballhockey.com
Overview: A small provincial organization founded in 1978
Mission: To promote & encourage the development of competitive & recreational ball hockey in Manitoba
Member of: Sport Manitoba
Membership: 2,500+

Canadian Associations / Manitoba Band Association

Manitoba Band Association
131 Rouge Road, Winnipeg MB R3K 1J5
Tel: 204-663-1226
mbband@shaw.ca
www.mbband.org
Previous Name: Manitoba Instrumental Music Association
Overview: A small provincial charitable organization founded in 1977 overseen by Canadian Band Association
Mission: To promote growth & development of bands in Manitoba
Affiliation(s): Canadian Band Association; Manitoba Music Educators' Association; Coalition for Music Education in Canada
Finances: Annual Operating Budget: $50,000-$100,000; *Funding Sources:* Corporate & government sponsors
Membership: 350; *Fees:* $50 general; $20 student; $25 senior; $85 corporate; *Member Profile:* Music teachers; music students; music dealers; others who share the goals of the association
Chief Officer(s):
John Balsillie, Executive Director

Manitoba Bar Association (MBA) / Association du barreau du Manitoba
#1020, 444 St. Mary Ave., Winnipeg MB R3C 3T1
Tel: 204-927-1210; *Fax:* 204-927-1212
admin@cba-mb.ca
cba-mb.ca
Overview: A medium-sized provincial organization founded in 1896
Mission: To serve as the voice of lawyers, judges, notaries, law teachers, & law students in Manitoba
Member of: Canadian Bar Association
Finances: Funding Sources: Membership fees; member services
Staff Member(s): 2; 17 volunteer(s)
Membership: 1,400; *Fees:* Schedule available; *Member Profile:* Lawyer; Law Student; Law Professor; Judiciary; *Committees:* Law Day Organizing; Legislation & Law Reform; MBA-CBA Wellness; Mid-Winter Organizing; Provincial Court Informal Concerns; Queen's Bench Informal Concerns
Activities: Awareness Events: Law Day, April 17; *Speaker Service:* Yes
Chief Officer(s):
Stacy A. Nagle, Executive Director
snagle@cba-mb.ca
Meetings/Conferences:
• Manitoba Bar Association 2018 Mid-Winter Conference, January, 2018, Fairmont Hotel, Winnipeg, MB
Scope: Provincial

Manitoba Baseball Association
145 Pacific Ave., Winnipeg MB R3B 2Z6
Tel: 204-925-5763; *Fax:* 204-925-5928
baseball.info@sportmanitoba.ca
www.baseballmanitoba.ca
www.facebook.com/171229052909245
twitter.com/BaseballMB
Also Known As: Baseball Manitoba
Overview: A small provincial organization founded in 1968 overseen by Baseball Canada
Mission: To foster the participation, development & competition of amateur baseball in Manitoba
Membership: 15,000; *Committees:* Management
Chief Officer(s):
Morgan de Peña, Executive Director
baseball.morgan@sportmanitoba.ca

Manitoba Baton Twirling Sportive Association (MBTSA)
MB
www.manitobabaton.com
twitter.com/mbtsa
www.youtube.com/channel/UCBovtBVe1clqI7XIkWzj7hw
Overview: A small provincial organization overseen by Canadian Baton Twirling Federation
Mission: To be the provincial governing body for the sport of baton twirling in Manitoba
Member of: Canadian Baton Twirling Federation
Chief Officer(s):
Edie Parisian, Chairperson
Patti Sabeski, Vice Chairperson

Manitoba Beef Cattle Performance Association (MBCPA)
PO Box 1190, Carberry MB R0K 0H0
Tel: 204-763-4696; *Fax:* 204-763-4102
bulltest@mts.net
www.manitobabulltest.com
Also Known As: Douglas Bull Test Station
Overview: A small provincial organization founded in 1964
Staff Member(s): 2
Membership: 215; *Fees:* $10
Chief Officer(s):
Ivan Ahntholz, Manager
Tod Wallace, President

Manitoba Beef Producers (MBP)
#220, 530 Century St., Winnipeg MB R3H 0Y4
Tel: 204-772-4542; *Fax:* 204-774-3264
Toll-Free: 800-772-0458
www.mbbeef.ca
www.facebook.com/manitobabeef.producers.7
twitter.com/ManitobaBeef
www.youtube.com/user/mcpacom
Previous Name: Manitoba Cattle Producers Association
Overview: A medium-sized provincial organization
Mission: To protect the interests of beef producers in Manitoba; To bring prosperity & sustainability to Manitoba's beef industry
Member of: Canadian Cattlemen's Association
Staff Member(s): 6
Membership: 7,000; *Member Profile:* Cattle producers in Manitoba; *Committees:* AGM/Nominations/Resolutions; Animal Health; Beef-Forage Research Farm; Communications; Crown Lands; Environment; Executive; Finance; Governance; Production Management; Research
Activities: Lobbying; Researching; Providing education; *Awareness Events:* Manitoba Beef Week
Chief Officer(s):
Brian Lemon, General Manager
blemon@mbbeef.ca
Chad Saxon, Coordinator, Communications
csaxon@mbbeef.ca
Awards:
• Environmental Stewardship Award
Meetings/Conferences:
• Manitoba Beef Producers 2018 39th Annual General Meeting, 2018, MB
Scope: Provincial
Publications:
• Cattle Country: The Voice of Manitoba's Cattle Industry
Type: Magazine; *Frequency:* 8 pa; *Accepts Advertising*
Profile: Information for cattle producers & industry supporters in Manitoba & eastern Saskatchewan

Manitoba Beekeepers' Association (MBA)
c/o Hilary Stewart, PO Box 192, Baldur MB R0K 0B0
Tel: 204-535-2167
manitobabeekeepers@mts.net
www.manitobabee.org
Overview: A small provincial organization founded in 1903
Mission: To represent the interests of Manitoba honey producers
Affiliation(s): Canadian Honey Council
Finances: Funding Sources: Membership fees; Donations
Membership: Fees: $60 associate members; $200 + $.40 colony levy (maximum 1,000 colonies) or $.13 (1,001 colonies or more); *Member Profile:* Manitoba honey producers, who are sole proprietors, with 50 or more colonies; Honey producers in Manitoba who represent a Hutterite colony, partnership, or corporation; Associate members include out-of-province beekeepers, industry supporters, or volunteers; *Committees:* Convention & Annual General Meeting; Fee/Levy; Finance; Foreign Worker; KAP; Newsletter; Nomination; Pests & Pest Management; Pollination; Promotion/Education; Resolution; Research; Safety Nets; Stock Replacement
Activities: Supporting bee research projects in Manitoba; Facilitating networking opportunities to discuss industry issues
Chief Officer(s):
Allan Campbell, President, 204-638-6515
allan.campbell@durstonhoneyfarms.com
Jake Maendel, Vice-Chair, 204-513-0529, Fax: 204-886-2215
jake@destinyroad.ca
Jim Campbell, Secretary, 204-467-5246
mbasecretary@mts.net
Hilary Stewart, Treasurer, 204-535-2167
Publications:
• Manitoba Beekeeper
Type: Newsletter; *Frequency:* Quarterly; *Accepts Advertising;*
Editor: Dan Lecocq; *Price:* Free with membership in the Manitoba Beekeepers' Association
Profile: Reports from the Manitoba Beekeepers' Association, CHC, & the provincial apiarist, plus honey prices, honey shows, & beekeeping issues

Manitoba Bison Association (MBA)
PO Box 64, Inwood MB R0C 1P0
Tel: 204-278-3302; *Fax:* 204-278-3737
vwdyck@mts.net
www.manitobabison.ca
Overview: A small provincial organization
Member of: Canadian Bison Association
Chief Officer(s):
Len Epp, President
sepp@mts.net

Manitoba Blind Sports Association (MBSA)
145 Pacific Ave., Winnipeg MB R3B 2Z6
Tel: 204-925-5694; *Fax:* 204-925-5792
blindsport@shawbiz.ca
www.blindsport.mb.ca
Previous Name: Manitoba Sport & Recreation Association for the Blind
Overview: A medium-sized provincial organization founded in 1976 overseen by Canadian Blind Sports Association Inc.
Mission: To provide blind & visually impaired Manitobans with the opportunity to participate in sport at all levels of skill & ability
Finances: Annual Operating Budget: Less than $50,000
20 volunteer(s)
Membership: 45; *Fees:* $100 ($10 for membership, $40 program fee, $50 refundable fundraising fee)
Activities: Awareness Events: Run for Light; *Speaker Service:* Yes; *Library:* by appointment

Manitoba Block Parent Program *See* Block Parent Program of Canada

Manitoba Blues Society Inc. (MBS)
PO Box 56036, Stn. Portage Place, Winnipeg MB R3B 0G9
Tel: 204-667-3491
Overview: A small provincial organization founded in 1995
Mission: To foster an understanding of & appreciation for the music form known as The Blues
Finances: Funding Sources: Membership dues; fundraising events
Membership: 1-99; *Committees:* Advertising; Communications; Education; Events; Marketing; Volunteers/Membership; Jams
Activities: Blues jams; blues events
Publications:
• Blues News [a publication of the Manitoba Blues Society Inc.]
Type: Journal

Manitoba Boxing Commission *See* Manitoba Combative Sports Commission

Manitoba Brain Injury Association Inc.
#204, 825 Sherbrook St., Winnipeg MB R3A 1M5
Tel: 204-975-3280; *Fax:* 204-975-3027
Toll-Free: 866-327-1998
info@mbia.ca
www.mbia.ca
www.facebook.com/449153225157899
Also Known As: MBIA
Overview: A small provincial charitable organization founded in 1987 overseen by Brain Injury Association of Canada
Mission: To improve the quality of life & give hope to those affected by acquired brain injury; To support persons affected by acquired brain injury in Manitoba
Finances: Funding Sources: Membership fees; Donations; Fundraising; Sponsorships
Membership: 400+; *Fees:* $15 individuals; $20 families; $30 non-profit organizations; $50 corporate members; *Member Profile:* Survivors of brain injuries & their families throughout Manitoba
Activities: Preparing prevention programs; Raising awareness of acquired brain injury in Manitoba; Engaging in advocacy activities on behalf of those with acquired brain injury; Offering peer support programs & support groups in Dauphin & Parkland region, Winnipeg, Steinbach & area, & Brandon; Providing education, such as a lecture series called the Empowerment Series & discussion groups; Planning social & recreational activities for members & other acquired brain injury survivors; *Library:* Manitoba Brain Injury Association Inc. Library
Chief Officer(s):
Kristyn Cain, President
David Sullivan, Executive Director
david@mbia.ca
Satoshi Yamashita, Office Administrator
Publications:
• MBIA [Manitoba Brain Injury Association] News
Type: Newsletter; *Frequency:* Quarterly

Profile: Association activities, provincial news, meetings, events, & programs, plus member information

Manitoba Brown Swiss Association
PO Box 428, Austin MB R0H 0C0
Tel: 204-637-2589
Overview: A small provincial organization
Member of: Canadian Brown Swiss Association
Chief Officer(s):
Linda Doerksen, Provincial Secretary

Manitoba Building & Construction Trades Council (MBCTC)
Marshall-Wells Warehouse, #510, 136 Market Ave., Winnipeg MB R3B 0P4
Tel: 204-956-7425; *Fax:* 204-956-7427
info@mbtrades.ca
www.mbtrades.ca
twitter.com/mbtcouncil
Also Known As: MBT
Previous Name: Winnipeg Building & Construction Trades Council
Overview: A small provincial organization founded in 1908
Mission: To represent the common goals of construction & trades professionals in Manitoba
Member of: AFL-CIO
Staff Member(s): 3
Membership: 6,000 professionals in 12 member unions
Chief Officer(s):
Sudhir Sandhu, Chief Executive Officer

Manitoba Building Envelope Council (MBEC)
PO Box 2052, Winnipeg MB R3C 3R3
www.mb-bec.ca
Overview: A small provincial organization founded in 1983
Mission: To promote excellence in the building envelope through technology transfer.
Member of: National Building Envelope Council
Membership: *Fees:* $150 corporate; $35 individual
Chief Officer(s):
Ryan Dalgleish, President
rdalgleish@buildingprofessionals.com

Manitoba Building Officials Association
PO Box 2063, Winnipeg MB R3C 3R4
Tel: 204-832-1512; *Fax:* 204-897-8094
info@mboa.mb.ca
www.mboa.mb.ca
Overview: A small provincial organization
Mission: To promote building safety through training & awareness in order to help their members
Membership: 200; *Fees:* $60 government; $500 government group; $70 associate; $600 associate group; $25 student
Chief Officer(s):
Rick Grimshaw, President
rgrimshaw@gov.mb.ca

Manitoba Call Centre Association *See* Manitoba Customer Contact Association, Inc.

Manitoba Camping Association (MCA)
Manitoba Camping Association Sunshine Fund, 545 Telfer St. South, Winnipeg MB R3G 2Y4
Tel: 204-784-1134
sunshinefund@mbcamping.ca
www.mbcamping.ca
www.facebook.com/sunshinefundmb
twitter.com/SunshineFundMB
Overview: A medium-sized provincial organization founded in 1937 overseen by Canadian Camping Association
Mission: To act as a coordinating body for organized camping in Manitoba; To promote organized camping as an educational and recreational experience
Member of: Canadian Camping Association
Finances: *Funding Sources:* Donations; Membership dues
Membership: *Member Profile:* Organizations & individuals who support organized childrens & family camps & the mission of the MCA
Activities: Developing standards for organized camping in Manitoba; Communicating information about regulations & developments that affect organized camping; Representing member camps to government agencies & to the public; Administering the Winnipeg Free Press Sunshine Fund which allows financially disadvantaged children to attend camps; Offering workshops; Providing networking opportunities; *Awareness Events:* Manitoba Parade of Camps
Chief Officer(s):
Liz Kovach, Executive Director
lkovach@manitobacamping.ca
Kelly Giddings, Coordinator, Outdoor Learning & Member Services
kgiddings@manitobacamping.ca
Sydney Kazina, Coordinator, Sunshine Fund

Manitoba Cardiac Institute (Reh-Fit) Inc.
1390 Taylor Ave., Winnipeg MB R3M 3V8
Tel: 204-488-8023; *Fax:* 204-488-4819
reh-fit@reh-fit.com
www.reh-fit.com
Also Known As: Kinsmen Reh-Fit Centre
Overview: A small provincial organization
Mission: To enhance the health and well-being of its members and the community by providing innovative health and fitness services through assessment, education, and exercise in a suportive environment.
Chief Officer(s):
Rosanna Buonpensiere, Director

Manitoba Cattle Producers Association *See* Manitoba Beef Producers

Manitoba Cerebral Palsy Sports Association (MCPSA)
MB
Overview: A small provincial organization overseen by Canadian Cerebral Palsy Sports Association
Mission: To assist in the development of sport for the disabled in Manitoba by providing an opportunity for a wider participation for persons with cerebral palsy & other neuromuscular disorders
Member of: Canadian Cerebral Palsy Sports Association
Membership: 60
Activities: Track; Field; Swimming; Boccia

Manitoba Chamber Orchestra (MCO)
Portage Place, #y300, 393 Portage Ave., Winnipeg MB R3B 3H6
Tel: 204-783-7377; *Fax:* 204-783-7383
info@themco.ca
www.manitobachamberorchestra.org
www.facebook.com/mcocanada
Overview: A small provincial charitable organization founded in 1972 overseen by Orchestras Canada
Mission: To perform chamber orchestra repertoire with emphasis on premiering new Canadian works & Canadian soloists
Member of: Orchestras Canada
Finances: *Annual Operating Budget:* $500,000-$1.5 Million; *Funding Sources:* Government grants; Individual & corporate donations; Ticket revenue
Staff Member(s): 15; 60 volunteer(s)
Membership: 728
Activities: Performing 8 concert subscription series, Facilitating educational programs; *Speaker Service:* Yes; *Library*
Chief Officer(s):
Anne Manson, Music Director
Vicki Young, General Manager

The Manitoba Chambers of Commerce
227 Portage Ave., Winnipeg MB R3B 2A6
Tel: 204-948-0100; *Fax:* 204-948-0110
Toll-Free: 877-444-5222
www.mbchamber.mb.ca
www.linkedin.com/company/manitoba-chambers-of-commerce
www.facebook.com/118694504008
twitter.com/mbchambersofcom
Overview: A medium-sized provincial organization founded in 1931
Member of: Canadian Chamber of Commerce
Finances: *Funding Sources:* Membership dues; advertising; special events
Staff Member(s): 7
Membership: 10,000+ businesses; *Member Profile:* Registered business or organization
Activities: Small Business Week; Youth Business Institute; Rural Forum; Invest in Manitoba; Forum for International Trade; *Internships:* Yes; *Speaker Service:* Yes; *Rents Mailing List:* Yes; *Library:* by appointment
Chief Officer(s):
Chuck Davidson, President, 204-948-0107
cdavidson@mbchamber.mb.ca

Manitoba Cheer Federation Inc. (MCF)
PO Box 42010, 1881 Portage Ave., Winnipeg MB R3J 0J0
info@mbcheer.ca
www.mbcheer.ca
www.facebook.com/145664425448394
twitter.com/MCF_Cheer
Overview: A small provincial organization founded in 2010 overseen by Cheer Canada
Mission: To regulate, promote & develop cheerleading in Manitoba.
Member of: Cheer Canada
Chief Officer(s):
Marian Henry, President
Kait Allen, Director, Judging
Amanda Barnes, Director, Communications
Mallory Mitchell, Director, Event

Manitoba Chicken Producer Board *See* Manitoba Chicken Producers

Manitoba Chicken Producers (MCP)
1357 Kenaston Blvd., Winnipeg MB R3P 2P2
Tel: 204-489-4603; *Fax:* 204-488-1163
chicken@chicken.mb.ca
www.chicken.mb.ca
Previous Name: Manitoba Chicken Producer Board
Overview: A medium-sized provincial organization founded in 1968 overseen by Chicken Farmers of Canada
Mission: To represent the needs of hatching egg & chicken producers of Manitoba by providing leadership in maintaining a viable & stable hatching egg & chicken production industry
Member of: Canadian Hatching Egg Producers; Chicken Farmers of Canada
Staff Member(s): 6
Chief Officer(s):
Wayne Hiltz, Executive Director
whiltz@chicken.mb.ca

Manitoba Child Care Association (MCCA)
2350 McPhillips St., 2nd Fl., Winnipeg MB R2V 4J6
Tel: 204-586-8587; *Fax:* 204-589-5613
Toll-Free: 888-323-4676
info@mccahouse.org
www.mccahouse.org
twitter.com/MCCAHOUSE
Overview: A medium-sized provincial charitable organization founded in 1974
Mission: To act as the voice of child care in Manitoba; To advocate for a quality system of child care; To advance early childhood education as a profession
Affiliation(s): Canadian Child Care Federation
Finances: *Annual Operating Budget:* $500,000-$1.5 Million; *Funding Sources:* Membership dues
Staff Member(s): 5; 120 volunteer(s)
Membership: 4,000; *Fees:* Schedule available; *Member Profile:* Early childhood educators; Child care assistants; Centre administrators; Academics; Licensed family child care providers; Parents who volunteer on boards of their children's programs; Students; *Committees:* Board Operations & Development; Finance; Child Care Benefits; Conference; Editorial; Ethics; Family Child Care; Regional Branch; Public Policy & Professionalism; School Age
Activities: Informing members about issues; Providing professional development opportunities; Offering networking occasions; Presenting awards; Building broad coalitions; Encouraging research; Participating in the development of standards & guidelines to maintain quality child care services; Organizing conferences; *Awareness Events:* Week of the ECE
Library: Manitoba Child Care Association Resource Library
Chief Officer(s):
Pat Wege, Executive Director, 204-336-5060
patwege@mccahouse.org
Meetings/Conferences:
• Manitoba Child Care Association 2018 Annual Conference, May, 2018, Victoria Inn, Winnipeg, MB
Scope: Provincial
Description: Keynote speakers, a trade show, & an awards banquet
Publications:
• Child Care Bridges [a publication of the Manitoba Child Care Association]
Type: Journal; *Frequency:* q.; *Accepts Advertising; Editor:* Karen Houdayer; *Price:* Free with membership in the Manitoba Child Care Association
Profile: An information resource including updates & current issues affecting child care & Early ChildhoodEducators

Manitoba Chiropractors' Association (MCA)
#610, 1445 Portage Ave., Winnipeg MB R3G 3P4
Tel: 204-942-3000; *Fax:* 204-942-3010
www.mbchiro.org

Canadian Associations / Manitoba Choral Association (MCA)

Overview: A medium-sized provincial licensing organization founded in 1945 overseen by Canadian Chiropractic Association
Mission: To act as both a regulatory body & a professional association to serve the public & the chiropractors of Manitoba; To foster high standards of chiropractic health care for Manitobans; To ensure that safe, ethical, & competent services are provided by Manitoba chiropractors
Finances: *Annual Operating Budget:* $500,000-$1.5 Million; *Funding Sources:* Membership dues
Membership: *Committees:* Standards; Licensing; Complaints
Activities: Licensing Manitoba chiropractors; Enforcing a Code of Ethics & Standards of Practice; Investigating & resolving complaints; Advocating for accessible & affordable health care
Chief Officer(s):
Taras Luchak, Executive Director
Ernie Miron, Registrar

Manitoba Choral Association (MCA)
#5, 276 Marion St., Winnipeg MB R2H 0T7
Tel: 204-942-6037; *Fax:* 204-947-3105
mca@manitobasings.org
www.manitobasings.org
Overview: A small provincial charitable organization founded in 1976
Mission: To advance knowledge & appreciation of, & to stimulate interest in the choral arts
Affiliation(s): Manitoba Music Educators Association; American Choral Directors Association; International Federation for Choral Music; Manitoba Opera; Association of Canadian Choral Conductors; Chorus America; Arts & Cultural Industries Association of Manitoba
Finances: *Annual Operating Budget:* $100,000-$250,000
Staff Member(s): 1; 300 volunteer(s)
Membership: 63 individuals; 168 choirs; *Fees:* $40 individual; $80 choirs; *Member Profile:* Choirs choral directors; *Committees:* Choral Fest; Provincial Honour Choir; Manitoba Youth Choir; Professional Development; Volunteer Coordination; 30th Anniversary
Activities: Diversity Sings Project; *Library:* MCA Choral Library; Not open to public
Chief Officer(s):
Robert Neufeld, Executive Director

Manitoba Christmas Tree Growers Association (MCTGA)
900 Corydon Ave., Winnipeg MB R3M 0Y4
Tel: 204-453-3128
mctga@realchristmastrees.mb.ca
www.realchristmastrees.mb.ca
Overview: A small provincial organization
Mission: To assist membership in promoting benefits of Christmas trees
Chief Officer(s):
Cliff Freund, President
Dorothy Freund, Treasurer

Manitoba Clearinghouse Concerning Disabilities Inc. *See* Society for Manitobans with Disabilities Inc.

Manitoba Coin Club
PO Box 321, Stn. Main, Winnipeg MB R3C 2H6
Tel: 204-260-9717
manitobacoinclub@hotmail.com
www.manitobacoinclub.org
Overview: A small provincial organization founded in 1954
Mission: To promote numismatics in the province of Manitoba
Membership: *Fees:* $2 youth; $10 adult; $15 family
Activities: Shows; Auctions; Guest speakers; Videos; Show-and-tell nights; Grading challenges
Chief Officer(s):
Landon Taraschuk, President

Manitoba College of Registered Social Workers (MIRSW)
#101, 2033 Portage Ave., Winnipeg MB R3J 0K6
Tel: 204-888-9477; *Fax:* 204-831-6359
admin@mcsw.ca
www.mcsw.ca
Previous Name: Manitoba Institute of Registered Social Workers
Overview: A medium-sized provincial organization founded in 1963
Mission: To certify members; To act as the regulatory arm of the social work profession; To encourage ethical standards of practice to protect the public
Membership: *Fees:* $360 practicing; $180 non-practicing; *Member Profile:* Individuals with a Bachelor of Social Work degree or a Master of Social Work degree from a school accredited by the Canadian Association of Schools of Social Work or the Council of Social Work Education
Activities: Investigating public complaints in its role as a disciplinary body; Ensuring registrants maintain current knowledge
Chief Officer(s):
Liz McLeod, President

Manitoba Combative Sports Commission (MCSC)
#628, 213 Notre Dame Ave., Winnipeg MB R3B 1N3
Tel: 204-945-1788; *Fax:* 204-948-3649
www.mbcombativesports.com
twitter.com/MBCombatSports
Previous Name: Manitoba Boxing Commission
Overview: A small provincial licensing organization founded in 1993 overseen by Canadian Professional Boxing Council
Mission: To regulate professional boxing, kickboxing and mixed martial arts throughout the province
Member of: Canadian Professional Boxing Federation
Activities: Licensing participants, promoters, & athletes; Supervising events
Chief Officer(s):
Joel Fingard, Executive Director

Manitoba Community Newspapers Association (MCNA)
943 McPhillips St., Winnipeg MB R2X 2J9
Tel: 204-947-1691; *Fax:* 204-947-1919
Toll-Free: 800-782-0051
www.mcna.com
Overview: A medium-sized provincial organization founded in 1919 overseen by Canadian Community Newspapers Association
Mission: To serve community newspaper publishers in Manitoba; To act as the industry voice for the issues of community newspaper publishers; To encourage high standards in publishing
Affiliation(s): Canadian Community Newspapers Association (CCNA); Atlantic Community Newspapers Association
Membership: 50+ newspapers; *Member Profile:* Community newspaper publishers throughout Manitoba which meet MCNA publishing standards
Activities: Liaising with the federal, provincial, & municipal levels of government; Providing education & training opportunities for the betterment of the industry; Communicating recent publishing trends & technological advancements to members; Representing the industry to advertisers
Chief Officer(s):
Vanessa Gensiorek, Manager, Member Services & Administration
vanessa@mcna.com
Tanis Hutchinson, Manager, Display Ad Sales
tanis@mcna.com
Awards:
• Better Newspapers Competition Awards

Manitoba Conservation Districts Association (MCDA)
#4, 940 Princess Ave., Brandon MB R7A 0P6
Tel: 204-570-0164
info@mcda.ca
www.mcda.ca
www.facebook.com/176771465790644
twitter.com/MBConsDistAssoc
Overview: A small provincial organization
Mission: Manitoba Conservation Districts Association (MCDA) is a non-profit organization which represents the 18 Conservation Districts (CD's) within Manitoba.
Chief Officer(s):
Shane Robins, Executive Director, 204-570-0164
Meetings/Conferences:
• 43rd Manitoba Conservation Districts Association Conference, 2018, MB
Scope: Provincial

Manitoba Cooperative Association (MCA) Inc.
#400, 317 Donald St., Winnipeg MB R3B 2H6
Tel: 204-989-5930
info@manitoba.coop
www.manitoba.coop
www.facebook.com/290929227626052
twitter.com/MBIYC
Overview: A medium-sized provincial organization
Mission: To promote a united, growing & influential co-operative movement through focussed, collective energies & resources
Membership: 11 representing 150 co-ops
Chief Officer(s):
Dale Ward, President
Awards:
• Cooperative Awards

Manitoba Cooperative Honey Producers Ltd.
625 Roseberry St., Winnipeg MB R3H 0T1
Tel: 204-786-8977; *Fax:* 204-783-8468
Toll-Free: 866-788-8030
www.beemaid.com
www.facebook.com/BeeMaidHoney
Overview: A small provincial organization
Chief Officer(s):
Ida MacLeod, Contact

Manitoba Council for Exceptional Children (MCEC)
PO Box 43035, Winnipeg MB R2C 4J2
manitobacec@gmail.com
www.manitobacec.ca
www.facebook.com/home.php#!/manitobacec
Overview: A medium-sized provincial organization overseen by Council for Exceptional Children
Membership: *Committees:* Public Policy; Council for Children with Behavioural Disorders; Historian; Provincial Conference; Membership; SAGE Liaison; Scholarships/Yes I Can); Communication Action Team
Chief Officer(s):
Todd Long, President

Manitoba Council for International Cooperation (MCIC) / Conseil du Manitoba pour la coopération internationale
#302, 280 Smith St., Winnipeg MB R3C 1K2
Tel: 204-987-6420; *Fax:* 204-956-0031
Other Communication: mcic@web.ca
info@mcic.ca
www.mcic.ca
www.facebook.com/mcic.ca
twitter.com/MCIC_CA
Overview: A medium-sized international charitable organization founded in 1974
Mission: To promote international development that protects the environment; To coordinate the development work of member agencies
Member of: Canadian Council for International Cooperation (CCIC)
Finances: *Funding Sources:* Federal & provincial Government; Members; Winnipeg Foundation; Assiniboine Credit Union
Staff Member(s): 8
Membership: 40+ non-governmental organizations; *Member Profile:* Non-governmental organizations working in Manitoba which support international development cooperation
Activities: Administering funds for international development through the Manitoba Government Matching Grant Program (MGMGP); Supporting overseas projects that deal with development, community solidarity or relief & rehabilitation of countries in Africa, Asia & Latin America; Providing development education in Manitoba; Increasing awareness of international issues through youth conferences & public engagement groups; Fostering member interaction; Building solidarity with the developing world through the Fair Trade Manitoba Program; *Awareness Events:* International Development Week
Chief Officer(s):
Janice Hamilton, Executive Director
janice@mcic.ca
Awards:
• Paul LeJeune Volunteer Service Award
• Global Citizenship Award for Graduating Grade 12 Students
Eligibility: Grade 12 students in Manitoba who have engaged in meaningful global citizenship activities aimed at making a more just and sustainable world*Location:* Manitoba *Deadline:* February; *Amount:* $250
• Global Citizenship Award for Educators
Eligibility: Manitoba teachers and administrators who have been leaders in promoting global citizenship*Location:* Manitoba *Deadline:* February

Manitoba Council of Archives *See* Association for Manitoba Archives

Manitoba Crafts Council (MCC)
#553, 70 Arthur St., Winnipeg MB R3B 1G7
Tel: 204-946-0803
media@manitobacraft.ca
manitobacraft.ca
www.facebook.com/ManitobaCraftCouncil

twitter.com/mbcraftcouncil
pinterest.com/manitobacraft/
Also Known As: Council of Manitoba Artisans Inc.
Overview: A medium-sized provincial charitable organization founded in 1978
Mission: To promote the development & appreciation of fine craft; to facilitate a supportive environment in which fine, contemporary craft may flourish.
Member of: Canadian Crafts Federation
Finances: *Funding Sources:* Manitoba Arts Council; Winnipeg Arts Council; Canada Council for the Arts; WH & SE Loewen Foundation; Art Gallery of Southwestern Manitoba
Membership: *Fees:* $45 individual; $25 student/low income/friend; *Member Profile:* Craft artists & those with an interest in contemporary craft
Activities: *Internships:* Yes; *Speaker Service:* Yes; *Library:* Open to public
Chief Officer(s):
Alison Norberg, President
Awards:
• Judith Ryan Award for Best in Show
• Marilyn Levett Award for Excellence in Clay
• Jurors Awards for Excellence & Innovation

Manitoba Cricket Association (MCA)
145 Pacific Ave., Winnipeg MB R3B 2Z6
Tel: 204-925-5672; *Fax:* 204-925-5703
www.cricket.mb.ca
Overview: A small provincial organization founded in 1937 overseen by Cricket Canada
Mission: To make cricket available to all Manitobans.
Member of: Cricket Canada
Finances: *Annual Operating Budget:* $50,000-$100,000; *Funding Sources:* Manitoba government; Lotteries Foundation
Staff Member(s): 1; 10 volunteer(s)
Membership: 362; *Fees:* $900 per team
Activities: *Library*
Chief Officer(s):
Garvin Budhoo, President
garvin.budhoo@shaw.ca
Rawle Manoosingh, Executive Secretary

Manitoba Criminal Justice Association (MCJA)
#510, 405 Broadway, Winnipeg MB R3C 3L6
Tel: 204-945-8547; *Fax:* 204-945-1260
info@mcja.ca
www.mcja.ca
Previous Name: Manitoba Society of Criminology Inc.
Overview: A small provincial organization founded in 1969
Mission: The MCJA reflects the views of people from all areas of the criminal justice system, and to addresses problems arising within this system.
Affiliation(s): Canadian Criminal Justice Association; Alberta Criminal Justice Association; British Columbia Criminal Justice Association; Criminal Justice Association of Ontario; New Brunswick/Prince Edward Island Criminal Justice Association; Newfoundland & Labrador Criminology & Corrections Association; Nova Scotia Criminal Justice Association; Société de Criminologie du Québec; Saskatchewan Justice Institute
Membership: *Fees:* Student $25; Individual $60-$145; Patron $200; Corporate $500
Chief Officer(s):
Mike Cook, President

Manitoba Cultural Society of the Deaf (MCSD)
101-285 Pembina Hwy., Winnipeg MB R3L 2E1
Tel: 204-284-0802; *Fax:* 204-284-0802; *TTY:* 204-284-0802
www.deafmanitoba.org
Overview: A small provincial organization
Affiliation(s): Winnipeg Community Centre of the Deaf; Canadian Cultural Society of the Deaf
Finances: *Annual Operating Budget:* Less than $50,000
Membership: 60+; *Fees:* $10
Activities: Deaf entertainment; Forrest C. Nickerson Day; *Speaker Service:* Yes
Chief Officer(s):
Sheila Montney, Executive Director

Manitoba Customer Contact Association, Inc. (MCCA)
1000 Waverley St., Winnipeg MB R3T 0P3
Tel: 204-975-6464; *Fax:* 204-975-6460
deb@mcca.mb.ca
www.mcca.mb.ca
www.linkedin.com/company/418143
www.facebook.com/MBCustContact
twitter.com/MBCustContact
Previous Name: Manitoba Call Centre Association
Overview: A small provincial organization founded in 1997
Mission: To promote the development & sustainability of a growing, healthy & dynamic contact centre industry
Member of: Manitoba & Winnipeg Chambers of Commerce, CSAE; Alliance of MB Sector Councils; Contact Centre Canada
Finances: *Annual Operating Budget:* $250,000-$500,000; *Funding Sources:* Government; Membership fees; Events
Staff Member(s): 4; 20 volunteer(s)
Membership: *Fees:* $250 - $1,500 various levels; *Committees:* Human Resources; Events; Advisory; Training & Development; Conference Planning; Awards; Membership Survey; Website Review; MECCA Promotion; Decorations/Mementoes; Sponsorship; Judging; Representative Workforce Strategy
Activities: MECCA Awards; *Awareness Events:* March Forum; AGM, May; MECCA Awards, Nov.
Chief Officer(s):
Bruce Rose, Executive Director
bruce@mcca.mb.ca
Carmen Ferris, Manager, Education & Development
carmen@mcca.mb.ca

Manitoba Cycling Association (MCA)
Sport for Life Centre, 145 Pacific Ave., Winnipeg MB R3B 2Z6
Tel: 204-925-5686
cycling.ed@sportmanitoba.ca
mbcycling.ca
www.facebook.com/ManitobaCycling
twitter.com/ManitobaCycling
vimeo.com/mbcycling
Overview: A small provincial organization overseen by Cycling Canada Cyclisme
Mission: To be the provincial governing body for the sport of cycling in Manitoba
Member of: Cycling Canada Cyclisme
Membership: *Fees:* $50-$125 individual; $75 affiliate
Chief Officer(s):
Andy Romanovych, President
tpeabody@shaw.ca
Twila Pitcher, Executive Director, 204-925-5686
cycling.ed@sportmanitoba.ca

Manitoba Darts Association Inc. (MDAI)
c/o MDAI Membership Director, 720 Consol Ave., Winnipeg MB R2K 1T2
info@manitobadarts.com
www.manitobadarts.com
www.facebook.com/ManitobaDartsAssociationInc
Overview: A small provincial organization overseen by National Darts Federation of Canada
Member of: National Darts Federation of Canada
Membership: *Fees:* $30
Chief Officer(s):
Ron Looker, President, 204-997-7579
ronlooker@hotmail.com
Kim Clawson, Provincial Director
kimmyclawson@live.com

Manitoba Deaf Sports Association Inc. (MDSA)
c/o Sport Manitoba, 145 Pacific Ave., Winnipeg MB R3B 2Z6
www.mdsaassoc.com
Overview: A small provincial organization overseen by Canadian Deaf Sports Association
Mission: To provide sporting opportunities for deaf people in Manitoba
Member of: Canadian Deaf Sports Association
Membership: 6 organizations
Chief Officer(s):
Brenda Comte, President
mdsapresident72@gmail.com
Shawna Joynt, Vice-President
Kenneth Anderson, Treasurer
Joseph Comte, Technical Director

Manitoba Dental Assistants Association
#142, 99 Scurfield Blvd., Winnipeg MB R3Y 1Y1
Tel: 204-586-7378; *Fax:* 204-489-8033
Toll-Free: 877-475-6322
mdaa@mdaa.ca
www.mdaa.ca
www.facebook.com/manitobaRDA
twitter.com/MDAA_RDA
Overview: A small provincial organization overseen by Canadian Dental Assistants Association
Mission: To promote & advance the profession of dental assisting
Chief Officer(s):
Kathleen Cook, Executive Director
Meetings/Conferences:
• Manitoba Dental Assistants Association 2018 Annual General Meeting, 2018, MB
Scope: Provincial
Publications:
• Manitoba Dental Assistants Association Newsletter
Type: Newsletter; *Accepts Advertising*; *Price:* Free with membership in the Manitoba Dental Assistants Association
Profile: Association updates, including notice of professional development courses & Dental Assisting Week events, plus information from the Manitoba DentalAssociation regulatory body

Manitoba Dental Association (MDA)
#202, 1735 Corydon Ave., Winnipeg MB R3N 0K4
Tel: 204-988-5300; *Fax:* 204-988-5310
office@manitobadentist.ca
www.manitobadentist.ca
Overview: A medium-sized provincial licensing organization founded in 1883 overseen by Canadian Dental Association
Mission: To act as the governing body for dentists & dental assistants in Manitoba; To ensure that the oral health of Manitobans is met
Activities: Carrying out the requirements of The Dental Association Act; Developing clinical standards; Ensuring professional & ethical standards; Encouraging continuing dental education
Chief Officer(s):
Carla Cohn, President
Catherine Dale, Vice-President
Rafi Mohammed, Executive Director & Secretary-Treasurer
Meetings/Conferences:
• Manitoba Dental Association's 2018 Annual Convention, January, 2018, RBC Convention Centre, Winnipeg, MB
Scope: Provincial
Description: A conference & trade show, with business meetings, educational presentations, & networking opportunities, for dentists, dental hygienists, the oral health team, lab personnel, practice consultants, & dental students

Manitoba Dental Hygienists Association (MDHA)
#200E, 1215 Henderson Hwy., Winnipeg MB R2G 1L8
Tel: 204-981-7327
info@mdha.ca
www.mdha.ca
www.facebook.com/208495962663337
twitter.com/MDHA_MB
Overview: A small provincial organization founded in 1966
Mission: To cultivate, promote & sustain the art & science of dental hygiene; To represent, maintain & safeguard the honour & common interests of members; To promote closer communication, unity & social intercourse among members; To contribute toward the education & the improvement of public health
Affiliation(s): Canadian Dental Hygienists Association
Membership: *Committees:* Mentorship; U of M Endowment Fund Advisory; Membership; Sponsorship
Chief Officer(s):
Kim Wozniak, Executive Director

Manitoba Diving Association
#430, 145 Pacific Ave., Winnipeg MB R3B 2Z6
Tel: 204-925-5654; *Fax:* 204-925-5792
www.manitobadiving.ca
www.facebook.com/mbdiving
twitter.com/manitobadiving
Overview: A small provincial organization
Mission: Provides strong ethical and values driven foundation for diving throughout Manitoba and Canada, and supports athletic development, personal growth and community awareness through excellence in leadership
Member of: Diving Plongeon Canada
Chief Officer(s):
Ken Stevens, Executive Director
diving@sportmanitoba.ca

Manitoba Down Syndrome Society (MDSS)
#204, 825 Sherbrook St., Winnipeg MB R3A 1M5
Tel: 204-992-2731; *Fax:* 204-975-3027
www.manitobadownsyndromesociety.com
www.facebook.com/ManitobaDownSyndromeSociety
twitter.com/manitobadss
Overview: A small provincial charitable organization founded in 1991
Mission: To provide support, information & opportunities for individuals with Down Syndrome, parents, professionals and other interested persons; To seek resolutions to issues of

concern
Affiliation(s): Canadian Down Syndrome Society
Finances: *Funding Sources:* Donations; Fundraising
Membership: *Fees:* $30 family/individual; $55 organization
Activities: Visiting Parents Program; Parent Networking Evenings; Family Fun Days; *Awareness Events:* World Down Syndrome Day, March
Chief Officer(s):
Lorraine Baydack, President
Val Surbey, Vice-President

Manitoba Eco-Network Inc. (MEN) / Réseau écologique du Manitoba inc.
#3, 303 Portage Ave., Winnipeg MB R3B 2B4
Tel: 204-947-6511; *Fax:* 866-237-3130
info@mbeconetwork.org
www.mbeconetwork.org
www.facebook.com/Manitoba.Eco.Network
twitter.com/MB_EcoNetwork
www.youtube.com/user/ManitobaEcoNetwork
Also Known As: Manitoba Environmental Network
Overview: A small provincial charitable organization founded in 1988 overseen by Canadian Environmental Network
Mission: To educate the public on environmental issues; to conduct research on environmental issues; to facilitate communications between environmental groups & the general public
Member of: Canadian Environmental Network
Finances: *Funding Sources:* Project work; donations; membership dues; grants
Staff Member(s): 11
Membership: 80; *Fees:* $100 associate; $50 group; $30 individual; *Member Profile:* Open to any non-profit non-governmental group which has as one of its objectives the enhancing or furthering of environmental quality, protecting the environment or environmental education
Activities: Sponsors public forums, speakers, workshops on a broad variety of issues; operates projects regarding climate change, water issues & organic lawn care; offers GIS & mapping services to environmental projects; meets regularly with officials of the provincial government; *Speaker Service:* Yes; *Library:* Alice Chambers Memorial Library; Open to public
Chief Officer(s):
Peters Karen, Executive Director
executivedirector@mbeconetwork.org
Awards:
• Annual Environmental Awards

Manitoba Egg Farmers
Waverley Square, #18, 5 Scurfield Blvd., Winnipeg MB R3Y 1G3
Tel: 204-488-4888; *Fax:* 204-488-3544
www.eggs.mb.ca
www.facebook.com/eggsmanitoba
twitter.com/eggsmanitoba
www.instagram.com/eggsmanitoba
Previous Name: Manitoba Egg Producers
Overview: A small provincial organization
Mission: To provide an adequate supply of eggs to the marketplace at a fair price to the consumer & equitable return to the producer
Membership: 170; *Member Profile:* Egg & pullet farmers
Chief Officer(s):
Cory Rybuck, General Manager
Brenda Bazylewski, Director, Communication & Public Relations
Heather Ward, Coordinator, Administration & Logistics

Manitoba Egg Producers *See* Manitoba Egg Farmers

Manitoba Electrical League Inc. *See* Electrical Association of Manitoba Inc.

Manitoba Environment Officers Association Inc. (MEOA)
147 Norcross Cres., Winnipeg MB R3X 1J2
meoa@mts.net
www.meoa.ca
Overview: A medium-sized provincial organization
Mission: To enhance the public health and safety of Manitobans and to protect, maintain and rehabilitate Manitoba's environment ecosystems through the diligent duties of educated Environment Officers and to obtain for Environment Officers continued education and recognition of their efforts.
Membership: *Fees:* $25
Chief Officer(s):
Bill Barr, President

Manitoba Environmental Industries Association Inc. (MEIA)
#100, 62 Albert St., Winnipeg MB R3B 1E9
Tel: 204-783-7090; *Fax:* 204-783-6501
admin@meia.mb.ca
www.meia.mb.ca
Overview: A medium-sized provincial organization founded in 1991
Mission: To assist members in the business of the environment; To connect business, government, & stakeholders with environmental issues
Finances: *Funding Sources:* Membership fees; Sponsorships
Membership: *Fees:* Schedule available, based upon number of employees & number of representatives; *Member Profile:* Professionals, companies, & organizations in Manitoba who practise in the area of environment & sustainable development; *Committees:* Executive; Member Services; Legislation & Regulation; Programs Development
Activities: Providing professional development training, including courses, MEIA learning sessions, & environment industry workshops; Collaborating with other organizations; Providing networking opportunities
Chief Officer(s):
John Fjeldsted, Executive Director
Vaughn Bullough, President
Rosemary Deans, Coordinator, Education & Training
Deb Tardiff, Coordinator, Education & Training
Sheldon McLeod, Secretary
John Pikel, Treasurer
Meetings/Conferences:
• Manitoba Environmental Industries Association 2018 Annual General Meeting, 2018, MB
Scope: Provincial
Description: A gathering of members to address the business of the association & to provide networking opportunities
Publications:
• Manitoba Environmental Industries Association Inc. Members' Directory
Type: Directory
Profile: Contact information for association members
• MEIA [Manitoba Environmental Industries Association Inc.] Information Bulletin
Type: Newsletter; *Frequency:* Biweekly
Profile: Information for Manitoba Environmental Industries Association Inc. members about events, technology updates, & emerging regulatory & policyissues

Manitoba Farm Bureau *See* Keystone Agricultural Producers

Manitoba Farm Vacations Association; Manitoba Country Vacations Association Inc *See* Manitoba Rural Tourism Association Inc.

Manitoba Federation of Independent Schools Inc. (MFIS)
630 Westminster Ave., Winnipeg MB R3C 3S1
Tel: 204-783-4481
director@mfis.ca
www.mfis.ca
Overview: A medium-sized provincial organization founded in 1974 overseen by Canadian Accredited Independent Schools
Mission: To support & encourage high educational standards & values unique to members' various school communities; Tto represent interests & concerns of member independent schools in Manitoba
Finances: *Annual Operating Budget:* $100,000-$250,000; *Funding Sources:* Membership fees
Membership: 51; *Committees:* Education; Government Liaison; Public Relations; Membership
Chief Officer(s):
Bruce Neal, Executive Director

Manitoba Federation of Labour / Fédération du travail du Manitoba
#303, 275 Broadway, Winnipeg MB R3C 4M6
Tel: 204-947-1400; *Fax:* 204-943-4276
admin@mfl.mb.ca
www.mfl.mb.ca
www.facebook.com/ManitobaLabour
twitter.com/MFLabour
www.youtube.com/user/MFLabour/featured
Overview: A medium-sized provincial organization founded in 1956 overseen by Canadian Labour Congress
Mission: To advance economic & social welfare of working people in Manitoba; To encourage workers to vote & exercise full rights & responsibilities
Finances: *Annual Operating Budget:* $500,000-$1.5 Million; *Funding Sources:* Membership dues
Staff Member(s): 7
Membership: 90,000; *Member Profile:* Members of affiliated unions; Sectors include manufacturing, government, business, retail, health care, schools, tourism industry, agriculture, transportation; *Committees:* Occupational Health & Safety; Workers Compensation; Environment; Women; Human Rights; Political Education; Education
Activities: *Internships:* Yes; *Speaker Service:* Yes; *Library:* Occupational Health Centre
Chief Officer(s):
Kevin Rebeck, President
krebeck@mfl.mb.ca
Sylvia Farley, Executive Director
sfarley@mfl.mb.ca
Meetings/Conferences:
• Manitoba Federation of Labour 2018 Convention, May, 2018, Winnipeg, MB
Scope: Provincial
Contact Information: Coordinator, Communications: Andrew Tod, E-mail: atod@mfl.mb.ca

Manitoba Fencing Association (MFA)
#308, 145 Pacific Ave., Winnipeg MB R3B 2Z6
Tel: 204-925-5696; *Fax:* 204-925-5703
fencing@sportmanitoba.ca
www.fencing.mb.ca
www.facebook.com/199898656787720
Overview: A small provincial organization founded in 1978 overseen by Canadian Fencing Federation
Mission: To promote & develop the sport of fencing in Manitoba
Finances: *Funding Sources:* Fundraising
Staff Member(s): 2
Membership: *Member Profile:* Fencing clubs in Manitoba
Activities: Organizing training programs for high level athletes; Offering coaching training opportunities & clinics; Providing certification opportunities for officials; Conducting school & community outreach programs
Chief Officer(s):
David Cohen, Executive Director

Manitoba Five Pin Bowling Federation, Inc. (MFPBF)
145 Pacific Ave., Winnipeg MB R3B 2Z6
Tel: 204-925-5766; *Fax:* 204-925-5767
www.mfpbf.com
Overview: A small provincial organization overseen by Sport Manitoba
Mission: To provide services & resources to its members which enable them to increase membership & promote bowling as a lifetime sport through effective programs at all levels of participation
Member of: Canadian 5 Pin Bowlers' Association; Sport Manitoba
Affiliation(s): Manitoba 5 Pin Bowlers' Association; Master Bowlers Association of Manitoba; Youth Bowling Canada - Manitoba Division
Staff Member(s): 2
Chief Officer(s):
Deanne Zilinsky, Executive Director

Manitoba Food Processors Association (MFPA)
#12, 59 Scurfield Blvd., Winnipeg MB R3Y 1V2
Tel: 204-982-6372
mfpa@mfpa.mb.ca
www.mfpa.mb.ca
www.linkedin.com/company/manitoba-food-processors-association
Overview: A small provincial organization founded in 1993
Mission: To act as the voice of the food processing industry in Maniboba; To promote food products made in Manitoba to both local & international markets; To increase awareness of locally grown & processed food products
Staff Member(s): 5
Membership: 260+ companies; *Fees:* Schedule available, based upon number of employees; *Member Profile:* Food processing companies in Manitoba, ranging from start-up operations to multi-national companies; Food growers; Suppliers; Retailers; Marketing boards; Government agencies
Activities: Providing continuing education & networking opportunities; Liaising with government
Chief Officer(s):
Dave Shambrock, Executive Director, 204-982-6372 Ext. 102
Dave_Shambrock@mfpa.mb.ca
Caroline Wiley, Executive Assistant, 204-982-6372 Ext. 101
Caroline_Wiley@mfpa.mb.ca

Awards:
• Industry Excellence Awards
To recognize Manitoba food industry leaders

Manitoba Forage & Grassland Association (MFGA)
145 Edstan Pl., Selkirk MB R1A 2E8
Tel: 204-770-3548
info@mfga.net
www.mfga.net
Overview: A small provincial organization overseen by Canadian Forage & Grassland Association
Mission: To achieve healthy grasslands & prosperous forage crops on agricultural lands in Manitoba; To promote the economic prosperity of grasslands, forages, cover crops, & healthy soils
Member of: Canadian Forage & Grassland Association
Activities: Conducting research related to the forage industry; Promoting Manitoba products; Lobbying; Offering information about forage issues in Manitoba
Chief Officer(s):
Duncan Morrison, Executive Director
duncan@mfga.net

Manitoba Forestry Association Inc.
900 Corydon Ave., Winnipeg MB R3M 0Y4
Tel: 204-453-3182; *Fax:* 204-477-5765
www.thinktrees.org
Previous Name: Prairie Provinces Forestry Association
Overview: A medium-sized provincial charitable organization founded in 1972 overseen by Canadian Forestry Association
Mission: To promote the wise use & management of all natural renewable resources, with emphasis on forests; to promote the planting of trees; to promote private land forestry (woodlots); to act as liaison among government, industry & the general public.
Finances: *Funding Sources:* Government: industry; individuals
Staff Member(s): 8
Membership: *Fees:* $25 individual; $250 corporate
Activities: School programs; forest centres; Private Land Forests Program; operates Forest Museum; conservation kits for use by teachers; wildfire prevention campaigns; *Speaker Service:* Yes; *Library:* Not open to public
Chief Officer(s):
Patricia Pohrebnuk, Executive Director
Christina McDonald, President
Awards:
• Alan B. Beaven Forestry Scholarship
Manitoba resident; must be a recent graduate of high school, entering a Canadian university or technical school in forestry or an allied field *Deadline:* July; *Amount:* $500

Manitoba Freestyle Ski Association
145 Pacific Ave., Winnipeg MB R3B 2Z6
Tel: 204-795-9754
info@mbfreestyle.com
www.mbfreestyle.com
Overview: A small provincial organization overseen by Canadian Freestyle Ski Association
Mission: To promote the sport of freestyle skiing in Manitoba.
Member of: Canadian Freestyle Ski Association
Chief Officer(s):
Steve Carpenter, President
president@mbfreestyle.com
Meetings/Conferences:
• Manitoba Freestyle Ski Association Annual General Meeting 2018, 2018
Scope: Provincial

Manitoba Funeral Service Association (MFSA)
#610, 55 Garry St., Winnipeg MB R3C 4H4
Tel: 204-947-0927
info@mfsa.mb.ca
www.mfsa.mb.ca
Overview: A small provincial organization founded in 1964
Mission: To serve funeral directors & funeral homes throughout Manitoba; To advance funeral service; To uphold a code of ethics
Affiliation(s): Western Canada Cemetery Association
Membership: 38; *Member Profile:* Funeral homes in Manitoba; Organizations which serve funeral homes; *Committees:* Government Affairs; FSAC; Member & Public Affairs; Continuing Education; Finance
Activities: Providing educational opportunities
Chief Officer(s):
Owen McKenzie, President, 204-857-4021
mckpfc@gmail.com
Thorunn Petursdottir, Executive Director, 204-947-0927
mfsa63@gmail.com

Matt Nichol, Secretary-Treasurer, 204-523-7791
matt@wheatlandfs.com

Manitoba Genealogical Society Inc. (MGS)
1045 St. James St., #E, Winnipeg MB R3H 1B1
Tel: 204-783-9139; *Fax:* 204-783-0190
contact@mbgenealogy.com
www.mbgenealogy.com
www.facebook.com/pages/Manitoba-Genealogical-Society-Inc/7054423205
twitter.com/MbGenealogy
Overview: A small provincial charitable organization founded in 1976
Mission: To collect & preserve local genealogical & historical records & materials; To foster education in genealogical research through society workshops & seminars; To encourage production of genealogical publications relating especially to Manitoba
Member of: Manitoba Heritage Federation Inc.
Finances: *Funding Sources:* Membership fees; Government grants; Fundraising; Donations
Membership: 18 institutional + 25 associate + 61 lifetime + 441 individual; *Fees:* $20 associate; $40 individual & institutional; $115 corporate; *Committees:* Education; Membership; Library; Research; Special Projects
Activities: Seminars & workshops; Genealogical research; *Library:* Resource Centre; Open to public
Chief Officer(s):
Kathy Stokes, President
Mary Bole, Library Chair
library@mbgenealogy.com

  Beautiful Plains
  PO Box 2620, Neepawa MB R0J 1H0
  Chief Officer(s):
  Maxine Woodcock, President

  Dauphin Branch
  c/o Tammy Zurba, 37 - 6th Ave. SE, Dauphin MB R7N 2C3
  dauphinbranch@yahoo.ca
  Chief Officer(s):
  Tammy Zurba, Secretary

  South West Branch
  327 Kirkaldy Dr., Brandon MB R7A 0C3
  info@swmanitobagenealogy.ca
  www.swmanitobagenealogy.ca
  Chief Officer(s):
  Laura Crookshanks, President
  crooks@wcgwave.ca

  Southeast & Winnipeg Branch
  1045 St. James St., #E, Winnipeg MB R3H 1B1
  Tel: 204-453-1431
  Virginia Braid, President
  vbraid@mts.net

  Swan Valley Branch
  PO Box 6, Swan River MB R0L 1Z0
  Tel: 204-734-2170
  Chief Officer(s):
  Eric Neufeld, Contact
  eneufeld@mts.net

Manitoba Gerontological Nurses' Association (MGNA)
c/o Leslie Dryburgh, 300 Booth Dr., Winnipeg MB R3J 3M7
Tel: 204-831-2547
info@mbgna.com
mbgna.ca
Overview: A medium-sized provincial organization overseen by Canadian Gerontological Nursing Association
Mission: To promote a high standard of nursing care & related health services for older adults; To enhance professionalism in the practice of gerontological nursing
Membership: *Fees:* $27.50 associate; $70 regular; *Member Profile:* Nurses interested in gerontology; *Committees:* Membership; Education; Media
Activities: Offering professional networking opportunities; Providing professional development; Advocating for comprehensive services for older adults; Supporting research related to gerontological nursing; Promoting gerontological nursing to the public
Chief Officer(s):
Poh Lin Lim, President
plim@vgh.mb.ca
Awards:
• MGNA Nursing Distinction Award - Clinical Category
• MGNA Nursing Distinction Award - Education/Research/Administration

Manitoba Golf Association Inc. *See* Golf Manitoba Inc.

Manitoba Government & General Employees' Union (MGEU)
#601, 275 Broadway, Winnipeg MB R3C 4M6
Tel: 204-982-6438; *Fax:* 204-942-2146
Toll-Free: 866-982-6438; *TTY:* 204-982-6599
resourcecentre@mgeu.ca
www.mgeu.ca
www.facebook.com/174238299256105
twitter.com/MGEUnion
www.youtube.com/user/mgeulogin
Overview: A medium-sized provincial organization
Member of: National Union of Public and General Employees
Membership: 40,000
Activities: *Library:*
Chief Officer(s):
Michelle Gawronsky, President
Debbie O'Hare, Executive Assistant

Manitoba Gymnastics Association (MGA)
145 Pacific Ave., Winnipeg MB R3B 2Z6
Tel: 204-925-5781; *Fax:* 204-925-5932
mga@sportmanitoba.ca
www.gymnastics.mb.ca
www.facebook.com/427931587283744
twitter.com/GymnasticsMB
Overview: A small provincial organization founded in 1968
Mission: To develop, promote & guide gymnastics as a lifetime activity in Manitoba
Member of: Canadian Gymnastics Federation
Staff Member(s): 2
Membership: *Committees:* Women's Technical; Men's Technical; Development; Trampoline & Tumbling Technical
Chief Officer(s):
Karly Miller, Executive Director
mga.kmiller@sportmanitoba.ca

Manitoba Hairstylists' Association
PO Box 12, Stn. L, Winnipeg MB R3H 0Z4
Tel: 204-775-8633
www.manitobahairstylists.com
Overview: A small provincial organization
Membership: *Member Profile:* Hairstylists in Manitoba
Activities: Educational seminars, workshops, guest speakers, and platform artists; *Library:* Video Library
Chief Officer(s):
Mary Elliott, President
Publications:
• Clippings
Type: Newsletter

Manitoba Handball Association Inc. *See* Manitoba Team Handball Federation

Manitoba Hang Gliding Association (MHGA)
c/o Sport Manitoba, 145 Pacific Ave., Winnipeg MB R3B 2Z6
mhga.ca
Overview: A small provincial organization founded in 1980 overseen by Hang Gliding & Paragliding Association of Canada
Mission: To be the provincial governing body for the sport of hang gliding in Manitoba
Member of: Hang Gliding & Paragliding Association of Canada

Manitoba Health Libraries Association *See* Manitoba Association of Health Information Providers

Manitoba Health Organizations *See* The Regional Health Authorities of Manitoba

Manitoba Heart Foundation *See* Heart & Stroke Foundation of Manitoba

Manitoba Heavy Construction Association (MHCA)
#3, 1680 Ellice Ave., Winnipeg MB R3G 0Z2
Tel: 204-947-1379; *Fax:* 204-943-2279
info@mhca.mb.ca
www.mhca.mb.ca
twitter.com/ManitobaHeavy
Overview: A small provincial organization founded in 1943 overseen by Canadian Construction Association
Mission: To promote a safe workplace for employees in Manitoba's heavy construction industry; To represent the heavy construction industry in Manitoba
Membership: 340+ organizations & businesses; *Member Profile:* Heavy construction (heavy civil) & related industries in Manitoba; *Committees:* Safety Program; Winnipeg; Aggregate Producers; Highways; Events; Equipment Rental Rates;

Education, Training, Education, Training, & Gold Seal; Membership
Activities: Providing government approved career & vocational training; Liaising with government; Facilitating networking opportunities
Chief Officer(s):
Christopher Lorenc, President
clorenc@mhca.mb.ca
Wendy Greund Summerfield, Manager, Finance & Human Resources
wendy@mhca.mb.ca
Don Hurst, Director, WORKSAFELY, Education & Training
don@mhca.mb.ca
Christine Miller, Manager, Operations
christine@mhca.mb.ca
Catherine Mitchell, Manager, Policy & Communications
catherine@mhca.mb.ca
Meetings/Conferences:
• Manitoba Heavy Construction Association 2018 Expo, 2018, MB
Scope: Provincial
Description: An educational event to help train & educate workers in the heavy construction industry
Contact Information: Manager, Operations: Christine Miller, Phone: 204-947-1379
Publications:
• Heavy News Weekly
Type: Newsletter; *Frequency:* Weekly
Profile: Articles about the heavy construction industry & association activities
• Manitoba Heavy Construction Association Annual Report
Type: Yearbook; *Frequency:* Annually
• Manitoba Heavy Construction Association Directory
Type: Directory; *Frequency:* Annually
Profile: Listings of Manitoba Heavy Construction Association member & a guide to equipment rental rates in Manitoba
• Perspectives [a publication of the Manitoba Heavy Construction Association]
Type: Magazine; *Frequency:* Annually; *Accepts Advertising*
Profile: Information about public policy, industry positions, & safety & environment related issues

Manitoba Hereford Association
PO Box 7, Stn. Site 520, Brandon MB R7A 5Y5
Tel: 204-769-4459
www.mbhereford.ca
www.facebook.com/255808637782090
www.youtube.com/mbhereford
Overview: A small provincial organization founded in 1990
Mission: To promote the hereford breed of cattle in Manitoba.
Member of: Canadian Hereford Association
Membership: 75
Chief Officer(s):
Brent Blaine, President
bblaine2002@yahoo.ca
Kailey Penner, Contact
kjpenner@hotmail.ca

Manitoba High Schools Athletic Association (MHSAA)
145 Pacific Ave., Winnipeg MB R3B 2Z6
Tel: 204-925-5640; *Fax:* 204-925-5624
info@mhsaa.ca
www.mhsaa.ca
www.facebook.com/MBHighSchoolsAthleticsAssociation
twitter.com/MHSAA_
Overview: A medium-sized provincial charitable organization founded in 1962 overseen by School Sport Canada
Mission: To promote the value of sports in Manitoba secondary schools; To provide athletic & educational opportunities so that students reach their full potential
Member of: School Sport Canada
Finances: *Funding Sources:* Sport Manitoba grants; Membership fees; Corporate support; Revenues from admissions to provincial championships; Fundraising
Staff Member(s): 3
Membership: 192 schools + 37,000 athletes; *Fees:* Schedule available, based upon school size; *Member Profile:* Secondary schools in Manitoba
Activities: Encouraging participation in high school sports; Assisting in running equitable & fair sporting events for high schools; Presenting awards & scholarships for athletes, coaches, & volunteeers; Promoting volunteer involvement; Seeking support for the association; Providing educational materials for coaches & teachers
Chief Officer(s):
Chad Falk, Executive Director, 204-925-5641
chad@mhsaa.ca

Manitoba Historical Society (MHS)
#710A, 1 Lombard Place, Winnipeg MB R3B 0X3
Tel: 204-947-0559
info@mhs.mb.ca
www.mhs.mb.ca
Overview: A medium-sized provincial organization founded in 1879
Mission: To promote public interest in, & preservation of Manitoba's historical resources; To encourage research relating to the history of Manitoba
Finances: *Funding Sources:* Donations
Membership: *Fees:* $45 regular; $25 youth/student; $50 family; $55 nonprofit; $275 corporate; *Member Profile:* Individuals, families, students, organizations, & businesses interested in the history of Manitoba & Western Canada; *Committees:* Centennial Business; Centennial Farm; Centennial Organization; McWilliams Award; Young Historians; Publications; Program; Macdonald Dinner; Historic Preservation; Manitoba History
Activities: Assisting in the work of local historical societies; Organizing field trips; Preserving heritage buildings & historical landmarks; Operating Ross House Museum; Hosting programs with historical themes; Organizing annual general meetings & conferences; *Library:* The Edwin Nix Memorial Library
Chief Officer(s):
Gary McEwen, President
president@mhs.mb.ca
Gordon Clarke, Chief Administrative Officer
cao@mhs.mb.ca
Victor Sawelo, Manager, Ross House
rosshouse@mhs.mb.ca
Awards:
• Centennial Farm Award
• Centennial Business Award
• Margaret McWilliams Award
• Young Historians Award
• Centennial Organization Award
• Charles N. Bell Award
• George Bryce Award
• Dr. Edward C. Shaw Award
• Douglas Kemp Award
Publications:
• Manitoba History [a publication of the Manitoba Historical Society]
Type: Journal; *Editor:* Greg Thomas & Sheila Grover
• MHS [Manitoba Historical Society] Gazette
Type: Newsletter; *Editor:* Greg Thomas & Sheila Grover

Manitoba Holiday Festival of the Arts Inc.
PO Box 147, Neepawa MB R0J 1H0
Tel: 204-476-3232
mhfa@mts.net
www.mts.net/~mhfa
Overview: A small provincial charitable organization founded in 1967
Mission: To provide art opportunities to all members of a family, regardless of age or experience
Finances: *Funding Sources:* Regional Government; Manitoba Culture, Heritage and Tourism
Staff Member(s): 1; 7 volunteer(s)
Chief Officer(s):
Greg Heschuk, Administrator
Moira Woods, President

Manitoba Home Builders' Association (MHBA)
#1, 1420 Clarence Ave., Winnipeg MB R3T 1T6
Tel: 204-925-2560; *Fax:* 204-925-2567
info@homebuilders.mb.ca
www.homebuilders.mb.ca
www.linkedin.com/company/manitoba-home-builders'-association
www.facebook.com/220906100079
Previous Name: HUDAM
Overview: A small provincial organization founded in 1937 overseen by Canadian Home Builders' Association
Mission: To act as the voice of Manitoba's residential construction industry; To promote affordability & choice in housing in Manitoba; To uphold the MHBA Code of Ethics & the Code of Discipline
Affiliation(s): Canadian Home Builders' Association
Membership: *Member Profile:* Builders, conducting business in Manitoba, who have been members of a new home warranty program for two years, & who have completed COR registration, or have a Simplified Safety certificate; Renovators, conducting business in Manitoba, for at least two years, who are members of a new home warranty program, if they build complete new homes; Developers in Manitoba; Professionals registered to provide services to the housing industry; Sub-contractors; Suppliers to the housing industry; Manufacturers; Government; Persons employed by or enrolled in any educational institution, in study related to the housing industry; *Committees:* Government Liaison; Technical Research; Show Management; Education & Training; Workplace Safety & Health; Parade of Homes; Renovators; Nominating; Marketing; Membership Services; Past Chairman's Advisory
Activities: Offering information about the housing industry in Manitoba; Providing educational opportunities; Supporting Habitat for Humanity
Chief Officer(s):
Mike Moore, President, 204-925-2565
mmoore@homebuilders.mb.ca
Janet Constable, Coordinator, Special Events & Membership, 204-925-2578
jconstable@homebuilders.mb.ca
Publications:
• Builders' Voice
Type: Newsletter
Profile: Association activities & forthcoming events

Manitoba Horse Council Inc.
145 Pacific Ave., Winnipeg MB R3B 2Z6
Tel: 204-925-5719; *Fax:* 204-925-5703
mhc.admin@sportmanitoba.ca
www.manitobahorsecouncil.ca
www.facebook.com/ManitobaHorseCouncil
Overview: A medium-sized provincial organization founded in 1974
Mission: To represent clubs & individuals involved with equestrian
Member of: Equine Canada; Canadian Equestrian Federation
Finances: *Funding Sources:* Manitoba Lotteries Foundation; membership dues
Staff Member(s): 3
Membership: *Fees:* $60.50 senior; $49.50 junior; $121 family; friends of Horses $27.50; *Committees:* Athlete Development; Bingo; Breeds & Industry; Coaching; Competitions; Equestrian Centre; Officials; Recreation; Special Events; Marketing
Activities: *Rents Mailing List:* Yes; *Library:* Open to public
Chief Officer(s):
Geri Sweet, President
Bruce Rose, Executive Director
mhc.exec@sportmanitoba.ca

Manitoba Hotel Association (MHA)
#200, 1534 Gamble Pl., Winnipeg MB
Tel: 204-942-0671; *Fax:* 204-942-6719
Toll-Free: 888-859-9976
www.manitobahotelassociation.ca
Overview: A small provincial organization founded in 1927
Mission: To serve the needs of the hotel & accommodation industry in Manitoba; To promote the interests of the industry; To encourage growth & excellence in Manitoba's hospitality industry
Membership: *Member Profile:* Members of the hotel & accommodation industry from Manitoba, including hotels & suppliers
Activities: Promoting professionalism, accountability, & ethical principles in Manitoba's hotel & accommodation industry; Organizing regional meetings throughout Manitoba; Liaising with government organizations, regarding changes to legislation & regulations that affect the hotel industry; Arranging networking opportunities; Awarding bursaries to students in Red River College's Hotel Restaurant Administration program
Chief Officer(s):
Reid Kelner, Chair
Jim Baker, President & Chief Executive Officer
jbaker@manitobahotelassociation.ca
Jerry Weir, Executive Director
jweir@manitobahotelassociation.ca
Ryan Kirkness, Manager, Membership & Corporate Relations
rkirkness@manitobahotelassociation.ca
Jeremy Leroux, Manager, Communications
jleroux@manitobahotelassociation.ca
Awards:
• Alexander Campbell Scholarship Fund
To assist Manitoba students who are enrolled in a four year degree course in hotel management
Meetings/Conferences:
• Manitoba Hotel Association Convention & Tradeshow 2018, 2018, MB
Scope: Provincial

Canadian Associations / Manitoba Library Association (MLA)

Description: Presentations from government ministers, educational speakers, & others from the hospitality industry
Publications:
• Manitoba Hotel Association Newsletter
Type: Newsletter; *Frequency:* Monthly; *Accepts Advertising*; *Editor:* Ryan Kirkness
Profile: Hotel & accommodation industry issues, programs, & information for association members

Manitoba Independent Insurance Adjusters' Association
c/o Craig Shanks, Network Adjusters Ltd., 64 Regent Cres., Brandon MB R7B 2W9
Tel: 204-725-7436; *Fax:* 204-725-7437
www.ciaa-adjusters.ca
Overview: A small provincial organization overseen by Canadian Independent Adjusters' Association
Member of: Canadian Independent Adjusters' Association
Chief Officer(s):
Craig Shanks, President
craig.shanks@mymts.net

Manitoba Indian Cultural Education Centre (MICEC)
119 Sutherland Ave., Winnipeg MB R2W 3C9
Tel: 204-942-0228; *Fax:* 204-947-6564
info@micec.com
www.micec.com
www.facebook.com/micec.mb
Overview: A medium-sized provincial charitable organization founded in 1975
Mission: To stimulate, reidentify, maintain, expand & promote the cultural interests, lives & identity of Manitoba First Nations in every manner & respect whatsoever, & to promote an awareness of the traditional history of the First Nation Peoples of Manitoba; to advance the interests of First Nation Peoples who are registered members of the reserves within Manitoba, whether residing on or outside them; to cooperate with other organizations concerned with the interests of First Nation Peoples; to establish & promote research services; to assist in the development of accurate curriculum for use in schools within Manitoba; to produce audio, visual, & written materials relevant to cultural education development
Member of: First Nations Confederacy of Cultural Education Centres
Finances: *Funding Sources:* Federal government
Activities: Library; video & television production & editing services & equipment; community school liaison programme; *Speaker Service:* Yes; *Library:* People's Library; Open to public

Manitoba Indian Education Association Inc. (MIW)
PO Box 1250, Lake Manitoba First Nation MB R0C 3K0
Tel: 204-947-0421; *Fax:* 204-942-3067
www.miea.ca
Overview: A small provincial organization founded in 1981
Activities: Providing a student services office (#200, 70 Albert St., Winnipeg, MB, R3C 1E7); Offering support programs in academic, social, & financial counselling, tutorial services, orientation, & recreation; Providing a computer lab with internet access; Engaging in community relations; Offering referrals

Manitoba Insolvency Association *See* Manitoba Association of Insolvency & Restructuring Professionals

Manitoba Institute of Agrologists (MIA)
#201, 38 Dafoe Ave., Winnipeg MB R3T 2N2
Tel: 204-275-3721; *Fax:* 888-315-6661
agrologist@mia.mb.ca
www.mia.mb.ca
www.linkedin.com/company/manitoba-institute-of-agrologists
Overview: A small provincial organization founded in 1950 overseen by Agricultural Institute of Canada
Mission: To act in accordance with the Agrologists Act of Manitoba; To regulate the practice of agrology in Manitoba; To ensure the knowledge, competence, & integrity of institute members, in order to protect the public interest; To act as the voice of the agrology profession
Membership: *Member Profile:* Agricultural professionals in Manitoba; *Committees:* Admission & Registration; Professional Standards & Compliance; Complaint Review; Judiciary; Audit; Ownership Linkage; Governance
Activities: Licensing agrologists; Promoting high standards in research; Advancing the professional status of members; Providing educational & networking opportunities
Chief Officer(s):
Jim Weir, Executive Director & Registrar
miaweir@mia.mb.ca

Awards:
• Distinguished Agrologist Award
• H.D. McRorie Recognition Award
• Journalism Award
Meetings/Conferences:
• Manitoba Institute of Agrologists 2018 68th Annual General Meeting & Professional Development Event, 2018, MB
Scope: Provincial
Description: The business meeting of the institute, plus presentations & networking opportunities

Manitoba Institute of Registered Social Workers *See* Manitoba College of Registered Social Workers

Manitoba Institute of the Purchasing Management Association of Canada *See* Supply Chain Management Association - Manitoba

Manitoba Instrumental Music Association *See* Manitoba Band Association

Manitoba Interfaith Welcome Place
521 Bannatyne Ave., Winnipeg MB R3A 0E4
Tel: 204-977-1000; *Fax:* 204-956-7548
www.miic.ca
Overview: A small provincial organization
Mission: To welcome & extend hospitality to all refugees/immigrants & to serve them as brothers & sisters
Finances: *Annual Operating Budget:* $1.5 Million-$3 Million
Membership: *Committees:* Finance; Funding Diversification; Governance; Property; Human Resources
Chief Officer(s):
Rita Chahal, Executive Director
Ruth Magnuson, Chair

Manitoba Islamic Association (MIA)
2445 Waverley St., Winnipeg MB R3Y 1S3
Tel: 204-256-1347
www.miaonline.org
www.facebook.com/ManitobaIslamicAssociation
Overview: A small provincial organization founded in 1969
Mission: Large collection of English and Arabic books on major Islamic sciences & theology
Membership: *Fees:* $30; *Member Profile:* Muslim persons in Manitoba who abide by the association's rules & regulations; *Committees:* Takaful Fund
Activities: Owns & operates the Manitoba Grand Mosque; Providing funeral services to the Muslim community, through partnership with Cropo Funeral Services; Offering services for marriage; Conducting Sunday Qur'an classes for children & the MIA Al Nur Weekend Islamic School; Sponsoring the Al-Hamd Learning Center, which offers an Arabic & Islamic educational program for preschoolers; *Library:* Al-Hikmah (Wisdom) Library; by appointment
Chief Officer(s):
Osaed Khan, President
Salman Qureshi, Vice President 1
Reda Elgazzar, Vice President 2
Ferdose Skeikheldin, Secretary
Salman Idris, Treasurer
Awards:
• MIA / MSA University Scholarships
Publications:
• Manitoba Muslim
Type: Newsletter; *Accepts Advertising*
Profile: Editorials, reports, articles, announcements, community news, & local events

Manitoba Lacrosse Association
145 Pacific Ave., Winnipeg MB R3B 2Z6
Tel: 204-925-5684; *Fax:* 204-925-5792
lacrosse@sportmanitoba.ca
manitobalacrosse.com
www.facebook.com/ManitobaLacrosse
twitter.com/MBLacrosse
www.instagram.com/manitobalacrosse
Overview: A small provincial organization overseen by Canadian Lacrosse Association
Mission: To be the provincial governing body for the sport of lacrosse in Manitoba
Member of: Canadian Lacrosse Association
Chief Officer(s):
Paul Magnan, President
pmagnan@sunrisesd.ca
Dallas Smith, Executive Director, 204-925-5684, Fax: 204-925-5792
lacrosse@sportmanitoba.ca

The Manitoba Law Foundation / La Fondation manitobaine du droit
#300, 207 Donald St., Winnipeg MB R3C 1M5
Tel: 204-947-3142; *Fax:* 204-942-3221
mblawfoundation@gatewest.net
manitobalawfoundation.org
Overview: A medium-sized provincial organization founded in 1986
Mission: To provide funds for legal education, legal research, legal aid, law reform & the establishment, operation & maintenance of law libraries
Chief Officer(s):
Barbara Palace Churchill, Executive Director

Manitoba Lawn Bowling Association *See* Bowls Manitoba

Manitoba League of Persons with Disabilities (MLPD)
#909, 294 Portage Ave., Winnipeg MB R3C 0B9
Tel: 204-943-6099; *Fax:* 204-943-6654
Toll-Free: 888-330-1932; *TTY:* 204-943-6099
contact@mlpd.mb.ca
www.mlpd.mb.ca
Overview: A medium-sized provincial charitable organization founded in 1974
Mission: To remove systemic barriers to community participation for people with disabilities
Member of: Council of Canadians with Disabilities
Affiliation(s): Disabled Peoples' International
Finances: *Annual Operating Budget:* $100,000-$250,000
Staff Member(s): 5
Membership: *Fees:* $5 individuals; *Member Profile:* People with disabilities; *Committees:* Ethics; Fundraising; Housing; Transportation
Activities: Advocacy; Great Obstacle Race; *Library:* Open to public
Chief Officer(s):
Jennifer Sande, Provincial Coordinator
Awards:
• Access Awareness Achievement Award

Manitoba Liberal Party (MLP)
635 Broadway, Winnipeg MB R3C 0X1
Tel: 204-988-9380; *Fax:* 204-284-1492
Toll-Free: 800-567-5746
executive.director@manitobaliberals.ca
www.manitobaliberals.ca
www.facebook.com/manitobaliberals
www.youtube.com/user/manitobaliberals
Overview: A medium-sized provincial organization overseen by The Liberal Party of Canada
Membership: 14,000; *Fees:* $10
Chief Officer(s):
Dougald Lamont, Leader
Paul Brault, President

Manitoba Library Association (MLA)
#606, 100 Arthur St., Winnipeg MB R3B 1H3
Tel: 204-943-4567; *Fax:* 866-202-4567
www.mla.mb.ca
www.linkedin.com/in/manitoba-library-association-2a24325b
www.facebook.com/MBLibAssn
twitter.com/MB_Lib_Assn
Overview: A medium-sized provincial charitable organization founded in 1936
Mission: To develop, support, & promote library & information services in Manitoba for the benefit of the library community & Manitoba residents
Membership: *Fees:* Schedule available, based on the annual salary for individuals & the operating budget for institutions; *Member Profile:* Persons in Manitoba, representing all types of libraries & information services; *Committees:* Advocacy; Communications; Finance; Prison Library; Scholarships & Awards
Activities: Advocating for the development of accessible & comprehensive library & information services; Increasing public awareness of library services in Manitoba; Providing professional development activities; Offering up-to-date information about professional issues; Fostering cooperation between the library community & the information resource management sector; Facilitating interaction with members of Manitoba's library & information services field
Chief Officer(s):
Alix-Rae Stefanko, President
president@mla.mb.ca
Megan O'Brien, Director, Membership
membership@mla.mb.ca

Ellen Tisdale, Director, Communications
communications@mla.mb.ca
Dee Wallace, Director, Advocacy
advocacy@mla.mb.ca
Christine Janzen, Secretary
secretary@mla.mb.ca
Awards:
- John Edwin Bissett Scholarship
  Deadline: June
- Jean Thorunn Law Scholarship
  Deadline: June
- Library Innovation of the Year Award
  Deadline: June
- Manitoba Library Service Award
  Deadline: June
- Manitoba Library Association Award: Library and Information Technology Program
  Eligibility: A full-time graduating student in the Library and Information Technology program at Red River College who has demonstrated academic excellence

Manitoba Library Consortium Inc. (MLCI) / Consortium de bibliothèques du Manitoba
c/o Library Administration, University of Winnipeg, 515 Portage Ave., Winnipeg MB R3B 2E9
Fax: 204-783-8910
manitobalibraryconsortium@gmail.com
www.mlcinc.mb.ca
Overview: A medium-sized provincial organization
Mission: To facilitate resource sharing among the libraries in Manitoba; To build a public information network to contribute to a community's economic goals; To strengthen library services for the residents of Manitoba; To promote the exchange of information related to preservation
Membership: *Fees:* Schedule available, based upon library's annual budget; *Member Profile:* Library systems or libraries in Manitoba which support the purposes of the Manitoba Library Consortium
Activities: Planning & managing cooperative projects to enable efficient & equitable access to library resources for Manitobans; Initiating the Manitobia.ca project to gather & provide access to historically significant documents & publications; Offering "Library Express" to provide timely delivery of materials to clients; Arranging consortial licensing; Creating a Manitoba Union List of Serials
Chief Officer(s):
Betty Braaksma, Chair, 204-727-9688
Colleen Slight, Secretary, 204-775-9741
Carlos G. Wong-Martinez, Treasurer, 204-632-3761

Manitoba Library Trustees Association (MLTA)
MB
Tel: 204-984-5132
manitobalibrarytrusteesassn@gmail.com
www.mlta.ca
Overview: A small provincial organization
Mission: To foster & promote the effectiveness of public library boards through leadership & advocacy; To promote a better understanding of the role of the library trustee; To maintain channels of communication between other trustee associations to exchange information & ideas
Finances: *Funding Sources:* Membership dues
Membership: *Fees:* Schedule available, based upon library size
Activities: Representing members at the government level to discuss key issues; Providing resources to assist members' advocacy efforts; Producing a newsletter; Organizing a trustee handbook & resource lists for members
Chief Officer(s):
Andrew Robert, Chair
Awards:
- Trustee of Distinction Award
  Deadline: September 30
Publications:
- Manitoba Library Trustees Association Newsletter
Type: Newsletter

Manitoba Lung Association
#301, 1 Wesley Ave., Winnipeg MB R3C 4C6
Tel: 204-774-5501
info@mb.lung.ca
www.mb.lung.ca
www.facebook.com/manitobalungassociation
twitter.com/ManitobaLung
www.youtube.com/channel/UC3OyzjhurY-5KBPZvsG1G4Q
Overview: A small provincial charitable organization founded in 1904 overseen by Canadian Lung Association
Mission: To improve lung health
Member of: Sanatorium Board of Manitoba
Finances: *Funding Sources:* Donations; Fundraising; Sponsorships
Staff Member(s): 17
Activities: Providing information about lung health; Supporting & promoting research; Offering education programs in areas such as asthma, chronic obstructive pulmonary disease (COPD), & air quality
Chief Officer(s):
Deborah Harri, Chair
Bill Pratt, President & CEO
Kathi Neal, Director, Fund Development
Malcolm Harwood, Coordinator, Finance
Tracy Fehr, Coordinator, Tobacco Reduction
Publications:
- Manitoba Lung Association Annual Report
Type: Yearbook; *Frequency:* Annually

Manitoba Magazine Publishers Association (MMPA)
#606 - 100 Arthur St., Winnipeg MB R3B 1H3
Tel: 204-942-0189; *Fax:* 204-257-2467
exedir@manitobamagazines.ca
manitobamagazines.ca
www.linkedin.com/pub/manitoba-magazine-publishers-associatio n-inc/80/5a1/81
www.facebook.com/553448658032785?fref=ts
plus.google.com/111826288530235237421
Overview: A small provincial organization founded in 1988
Mission: The Manitoba Magazine Publishers' Association (MMPA) aims to represent and promote Manitoba magazines.
Chief Officer(s):
Brenda Johnstone, President
bjj@convenienceandcarwash.com
Meetings/Conferences:
- Manitoba Magazine Publishers Association 2018 Annual General Meeting, 2018
Scope: Provincial

Manitoba Medical Association *See* Doctors Manitoba

Manitoba Medical Service Foundation Inc. (MMSF)
PO Box 1046, Stn. Main, Winnipeg MB R3G 3P3
Tel: 204-788-6801; *Fax:* 204-774-1761
info@mmsf.ca
www.mmsf.ca
Overview: A medium-sized provincial organization founded in 1971
Mission: To consider the provision of funds for the advancement of scientific, educational, & other activities to maintain & improve the health & welfare of the citizens of Manitoba
Affiliation(s): Manitoba Blue Cross
Activities: Supporting medical research in Manitoba by awarding grants to researchers in the health care field
Chief Officer(s):
Greg Hammond, Executive Director
Lindsay Du Val, Chair
Awards:
- The Norman and Margaret Corne Memorial Scholarship
To recognize research excellence
- The Morris Neaman Memorial Award
To recognize research excellence
- The Richard Hoeschen Memorial Award
To permit students in clinical chemistry to travel to national & international meetings
- Basic Science Career Development Research Award

Manitoba Medical Students' Association (MMSA)
c/o Faculty of Medicine, University of Manitoba, #260, 727 McDermot Ave., Winnipeg MB R3E 3P5
Tel: 204-789-3424; *Fax:* 204-789-3929
mmsa.online
twitter.com/UofMMSA
Overview: A small provincial organization
Mission: To represent & promote the interests of students at the Max Rady College of Medicine at the University of Manitoba
Membership: *Committees:* Curriculum; Clerkship; Pre-Clerkship; Pre-Clerkship Organizing; Clinical; Evaluation; Admissions; Bachelor of Science (Medicine); Academic Standing; Faculty Executive Council; Manitoba Medical College Foundation; Student Affairs Awards; Introduction to Clerkship; Manitoba Medical College Foundation; Association of Canadian Medical Colleges; Internal Medicine Undergraduate; Curriculum Evaluation Seminar
Chief Officer(s):
Matthew Kochan, Contact, Communications
kochanm3@myumanitoba.ca

Manitoba Mennonite Historical Society (MMHS)
c/o Mennonite Heritage Centre, 600 Shaftesbury Blvd., Winnipeg MB R3P 0M4
Tel: 204-888-6781; *Fax:* 204-831-5675
Toll-Free: 866-888-6785
mmhs@mmhs.org
www.mmhs.org
Overview: A small provincial organization founded in 1958
Mission: To foster interest in Manitoba's Mennonite heritage & culture; To preserve Mennonite stories
Membership: 150; *Fees:* $15 students; $40 regular; $65 couples
Activities: Conducting workshops & seminars in Mennonite studies
Chief Officer(s):
Conrad Stoesz, President
Publications:
- Heritage Postings
Type: Newsletter; *Frequency:* Quarterly
Profile: Reports about members' historical interests

Manitoba Métis Federation / Fédération des Métis du Manitoba
Head Office, #300, 150 Henry Ave., Winnipeg MB R3B 0J7
Tel: 204-586-8474; *Fax:* 204-947-1816
mmf@mmf.mb.ca
www.mmf.mb.ca
www.facebook.com/ManitobaMetisFederationOfficial
twitter.com/MBMetis_MMF
www.youtube.com/ManitobaMetisMMF
Overview: A medium-sized provincial organization
Mission: To promote & instill pride in the history & culture of the Métis people; to educate members with respect to their legal, political, social & other rights; to promote the participation & representation of the Métis people in key political & economic bodies & organizations; to promote the political, legal, social and economic interests & rights of its members.
Affiliation(s): Infinity Women; Louis Riel Capital Corporation; Louis Riel Institute; Metis Child and Family Services; Metis Economic Development Organization; Metis Economic Development Fund; Metis Generation Fund; Pemmican Publications
Membership: *Member Profile:* People who have Métis ancestors
Chief Officer(s):
David Chartrand, President

Manitoba Milk Prices Review Commission
Norquay Building, #812, 401 York Ave., Winnipeg MB R3C 0P8
Tel: 204-945-3854; *Fax:* 204-948-2844
Overview: A small provincial organization founded in 1980
Mission: To set a price for producers of fluid milk; to monitor & control wholesale & retail milk prices
Finances: *Funding Sources:* Provincial government
Chief Officer(s):
Randy Ozunko, Chair
randy.ozunko@gov.mb.ca

Manitoba Milk Producers *See* Dairy Farmers of Manitoba

Manitoba Model Forest
PO Box 6500, 3 Walnut St., Pine Falls MB R0E 1M0
Tel: 204-367-4541; *Fax:* 204-367-4768
admin@manitobamodelforest.net
www.manitobamodelforest.net
Overview: A small provincial organization founded in 1992
Member of: Canadian Model Forest Network
Chief Officer(s):
Brian Kotak, General Manager
gm@manitobamodelforest.net

Manitoba Motion Picture Industries Association *See* On Screen Manitoba

Manitoba Motor Dealers Association (MMDA)
#112, 1790 Wellington Ave., Winnipeg MB R3H 1B2
Tel: 204-985-4200; *Fax:* 204-775-9125
Toll-Free: 800-949-6632
info@mmda.mb.ca
www.mmda.mb.ca
www.facebook.com/MBMotorDealers
twitter.com/MBMotorDealers
Overview: A medium-sized provincial organization founded in 1944

Mission: To represent franchised automobile & truck dealers in Manitoba by dealing with provincial issues that affect this membership; To advance the automotive industry in Manitoba; To uphold the code of ethics
Membership: *Member Profile:* Regular members consist of franchised automobile dealerships in Manitoba that sell new cars & trucks; Associate members consist of companies that supply products & services to dealers; *Committees:* Driver's Ed Revitalization
Activities: Offering a Sales Certification Program; Providing professional development programs; Liaising wtih other companies & organizations
Chief Officer(s):
Geoff Sine, Executive Director
Publications:
• Advertising & Marketing Guidelines
Type: Guide
Profile: Distributed to Manitoba Motor Dealers Association members, in order to improve relations between dealers & customers
• Manitoba Motor Dealers Association Newsletter
Type: Newsletter; *Frequency:* Bimonthly

Manitoba Municipal Administrators' Association Inc.
533 Buckingham Rd., Winnipeg MB R3R 1B9
Tel: 204-255-4883; *Crisis Hot-Line:* 800-668-9920
mmaa@mts.net
www.mmaa.mb.ca
Overview: A medium-sized provincial organization
Mission: To promote the needs of membership & their professional development.
Membership: *Committees:* Certificate Advisory; Conference; Executive; Finance; Professional Development
Chief Officer(s):
Mel Nott, Executive Director
mnott@qworks.biz

Manitoba Music
#1, 376 Donald St., Winnipeg MB R3B 2J2
Tel: 204-942-8650; *Fax:* 204-942-6083
info@manitobamusic.com
www.manitobamusic.com
www.facebook.com/manitobamusic
twitter.com/manitobamusic
www.youtube.com/musicmanitoba
Previous Name: Manitoba Audio Recording Industry Association
Overview: A medium-sized provincial organization founded in 1987
Mission: To develop and sustain the Manitoba music community and industry to their fullest potential
Affiliation(s): Foundation to Assist Canadian Talent on Records; Manitoba Film & Music; Aboriginal Music Program
Finances: *Funding Sources:* Member fees; government funding
Staff Member(s): 9
Membership: 700+; *Fees:* $50 individual; $200 corporate; $35 youth; $75 band; *Member Profile:* Members of the music industry, including artists; bands; studios; managers; agents; songwriters; venues; promoters; producers
Activities: Promotion, education & lobbying for Manitoba's recording industry
Chief Officer(s):
Sean McManus, Executive Director, 204-975-5191
sean@manitobamusic.com

Manitoba Naturopathic Association (MNA)
PO Box 434, 971 Corydon Ave., Winnipeg MB R3M 0Y0
Tel: 204-947-0381
info@mbnd.ca
www.mbnd.ca
Overview: A small provincial licensing organization founded in 1946 overseen by The Canadian Association of Naturopathic Doctors
Mission: To act as a regulatory body for the profession of naturopathy, in accordance with The Naturopathic Act of Manitoba
Staff Member(s): 1
Membership: 28; *Fees:* $2,000; *Member Profile:* Licensed naturopathic physicians in Manitoba, who employ natural methods of healing in their treatment
Activities: Licensing naturopathic doctors in Manitoba
Chief Officer(s):
Lesley Phimister, Executive Director & Registrar

Manitoba Non-Profit Housing Association (MNPHA)
#200A, 1215 Henderson Hwy., Winnipeg MB R2G 1L8
Tel: 204-797-6746; *Fax:* 204-336-3809
info@mnpha.com
mnpha.com
www.facebook.com/380849451979226?ref=ts&fref=ts
twitter.com/mnpha_
Overview: A small provincial organization
Mission: To build, support and strengthen its members who are diverse non-profit housing providers in Manitoba through services, educational opportunities and advocacy.
Membership: *Committees:* Aboriginal Housing; Conference; Membership; Government; Sponsorship; Policy
Activities: Training and workshops
Chief Officer(s):
Menno Peters, President, 204-949-2886
mpeters@whrc.ca
Meetings/Conferences:
• Manitoba Non-Profit Housing Association 2018 Building Partnerships Conference, October, 2018, MB
Scope: Provincial
Attendance: 150+

Manitoba Nurses' Union (MNU) / Syndicat des infirmières du Manitoba
#301, 275 Broadway, Winnipeg MB R3C 4M6
Tel: 204-942-1320; *Fax:* 204-942-0958
Toll-Free: 800-665-0043
manitobanurses.ca
www.facebook.com/ManitobaNurses
twitter.com/ManitobaNurses
www.youtube.com/user/mbnursesunion
Previous Name: Manitoba Organization of Nurses' Associations (MONA); Manitoba Staff Nurses' Council
Overview: A medium-sized provincial organization founded in 1975
Mission: To represent & support all categories of licensed nurses in Manitoba; To safeguard the role of nurses in the health care system of Manitoba
Member of: Canadian Federation of Nurses' Unions; Manitoba Council of Health Care Unions; Canadian Labour Congress
Staff Member(s): 32
Membership: 11,000; *Member Profile:* Unionized nurses in Manitoba, including Registered Nurses, Registered Psychiatric Nurses, Licensed Practical Nurses, & Operating Room Technicians; *Committees:* Discipline; Executive; Finance; Nominations; Provincial Collective Bargaining; Resolutions & Constitution
Activities: Liaising with registering & licensing bodies; Organizing an annual general meeting; Preparing briefs & reports about issues relevant to members
Chief Officer(s):
Sandi Mowat, President
Monica Girouard, Director, Operations
mgirouard@manitobanurses.ca
Eric Jorgensen, Director, Labour Relations
ejorgensen@manitobanurses.ca
Wes Payne, Director, Communications & Government Relations
wpayne@manitobanurses.ca

Manitoba Opera Association Inc.
#1060, 555 Main St., Winnipeg MB R3B 1C3
Tel: 204-942-7479; *Fax:* 204-949-0377
mbopera@manitobaopera.mb.ca
www.manitobaopera.mb.ca
www.facebook.com/ManitobaOpera
twitter.com/ManitobaOpera
www.youtube.com/user/ManitobaOpera
Overview: A small provincial charitable organization founded in 1969
Mission: To present & develop appreciation for art of opera in Manitoba; To assist in development of Canadian talent, with emphasis on Manitobans
Affiliation(s): Opera America; Canadian Actor's Equity; Opera.ca
Finances: *Funding Sources:* Ticket Sales; Government; Donations
Staff Member(s): 10
Activities: Presenting two full opera productions & one concert per season
Chief Officer(s):
Larry Desrochers, General Director & CEO

Manitoba Operating Room Nurses Association (MORNA)
MB
www.ornac.ca/en/morna
Overview: A medium-sized provincial organization overseen by Operating Room Nurses Association of Canada
Mission: To promote professional standards for perioperative nursing practice
Membership: *Member Profile:* Registered Nurses in Manitoba who are engaged in operating room nursing or involved in the Perioperative setting; *Committees:* Communications & Newsletter; Constitution & By-Laws; Education; Nominations
Activities: *Awareness Events:* Perioperative Nurses Week, November
Chief Officer(s):
Kim Goodman, President
Meetings/Conferences:
• Manitoba Operating Room Nurses Association Annual Meeting 2018, 2018
Scope: Provincial

Manitoba Optometric Society *See* Manitoba Association of Optometrists

Manitoba Orchid Society (MOS)
c/o Harvey Keselman, 8 Vassar Rd., Winnipeg MB R3T 3M9
www.manitobaorchidsociety.ca
www.facebook.com/126535720751112
Overview: A small provincial organization founded in 1970
Member of: Canadian Orchid Congress
Membership: *Fees:* $25 single; $35 family
Activities: *Library:* Not open to public
Chief Officer(s):
Harvey Keselman, President
president@manitobaorchidsociety.ca

Manitoba Organization of Disc Sports (MODS)
#402, 145 Pacific Ave., Winnipeg MB R3B 2Z6
Tel: 204-925-5665; *Fax:* 204-925-5916
bsddirector@mods.mb.ca
mods.mb.ca
www.facebook.com/MBDiscSports
twitter.com/modsmbca
Overview: A small provincial organization founded in 1988
Mission: To be the provincial governing body for disc sports in Manitoba
Member of: Sport Manitoba
Chief Officer(s):
Billy Donaldson, President
president@mods.mb.ca

Manitoba Organization of Nurses' Associations (MONA); Manitoba Staff Nurses' Council *See* Manitoba Nurses' Union

Manitoba Orienteering Association Inc. (MOA)
145 Pacific Ave., Winnipeg MB R3B 2Z6
Tel: 204-925-5706; *Fax:* 204-925-5792
info@orienteering.mb.ca
www.orienteering.mb.ca
Overview: A medium-sized provincial organization
Mission: Promotes and supports orienteering in Manitoba.
Member of: Canadian Orienteering Federation
Affiliation(s): Sports Manitoba
Membership: *Fees:* $5 adult; $3 junior

Manitoba Ozone Protection Industry Association (MOPIA)
1980B Main St., Winnipeg MB R2V 2B6
Tel: 204-338-0804; *Fax:* 204-338-0810
Toll-Free: 888-667-4203
mopia@mts.net
www.mopia.ca
Overview: A medium-sized provincial organization
Mission: To work towards protection of the stratospheric ozone layer; To control, reduce, & eventually eliminate emissions of ozone depleting substances
Activities: Liaising with industry, interest groups, & Manitoba Environment; Raising public awareness of the impact of ozone depleting substances
Chief Officer(s):
Mark E. Miller, Executive Director
George Kurowski, Chair
John Kub, Secretary
Laverne Dalgleish, Treasurer
Publications:
• Environmental Awareness Training for Ozone Depleting Substances (ODS) & Other Halocarbons
Type: Manual; *Price:* $45
Profile: A training manual for persons working on refrigeration or air conditioning equipment that contains a regulated substance

- Manitoba Ozone Protection Industry Association Annual Report
Type: Yearbook; *Frequency:* Annually
Profile: Featuring messages from the Chair of the Board of Directors & the Executive Director, reports from the treasurer & auditor, as well as highlights of the year
- MOPIA [Manitoba Ozone Protection Industry Association] E-Bulletin
Type: Newsletter; *Frequency:* Monthly; *Editor:* Mark Miller; Vanessa Krahn
Profile: Information for Manitoba Ozone Protection Industry Association members & select stakeholders

Manitoba Paddling Association Inc. (MPA)
145 Pacific Ave., Winnipeg MB R3B 2Z6
Tel: 204-925-5681; *Fax:* 204-925-5792
mpa@sportmanitoba.ca
www.mpa.mb.ca
www.facebook.com/ManitobaPaddlingAssociation
twitter.com/MBPaddling
Overview: A medium-sized provincial organization founded in 1982 overseen by CanoeKayak Canada
Mission: To act as the governing body for all competitive paddling sports in Manitoba, including kayak, canoe, & dragon boat; To develop high performance athletes to compete for Manitoba nationally & to qualify for the national team; To develop coaches to coach from the grassroots to the high performance levels; To service paddlers from beginners to elite athletes; To ensure the existence of paddling clubs in Manitoba
Member of: CanoeKayak Canada; Sport Manitoba
Finances: *Funding Sources:* Sport Manitoba
Membership: *Member Profile:* Paddling clubs & athletes from Manitoba
Activities: Hosting paddling events; Promoting paddling

Manitoba Paraplegia Foundation Inc.
825 Sherbrook St., Winnipeg MB R3A 1M5
Tel: 204-786-4753; *Fax:* 204-786-1140
winnipeg@canparaplegic.org
www.cpamanitoba.ca/mpf
Overview: A small provincial organization founded in 1980
Mission: To provide support for research & prevention activities; To provide direct aid to paraplegics & quadriplegics for home modifications, vocational aid & other items to assist spinal cord injured Manitobans to lead independent lives within the community; To provide support for special projects undertaken on behalf of spinal cord injured persons in Manitoba
Finances: *Annual Operating Budget:* $50,000-$100,000
Staff Member(s): 2; 12 volunteer(s)
Membership: *Member Profile:* Interest in spinal cord research
Activities: *Library:* by appointment
Chief Officer(s):
Doug Finkbeiner, President

Manitoba Percheron & Belgian Club
c/o Brenda Hunter, PO Box 159, Kenton MB R0M 0Z0
Tel: 204-764-3789
bhunterphoto@gmail.com
www.manpercheronbelgianclub.com
Overview: A small provincial organization
Mission: To promote the Percheron & Belgian horse breeds throughout Manitoba & eastern Saskatchewan
Finances: *Funding Sources:* Membership fees; Sponsorships; Fundraising
Membership: 80; *Fees:* $35 individuals; $50 families; *Member Profile:* Heavy horse enthusiasts from Manitoba & eastern Saskatchewan; *Committees:* Executive; Futurity
Activities: Hosting shows; Sponsoring various events; Offering youth clinics; Presenting awards
Chief Officer(s):
Robert Berry, President
Rod Delaquis, Vice-President
Brenda Hunter, Secretary
Jodi Denbrok, Treasurer
Janice Rutherford, Coordinator, Youth Program
Meetings/Conferences:
- Manitoba Percheron & Belgian Club 2018 Annual Meeting, 2018, MB
Scope: Provincial
Publications:
- Manitoba Percheron & Belgian Club Breeder Directory
Type: Directory

Manitoba Pest Management Association (MPMA)
MB
www.mpma.ca
Overview: A small provincial organization
Mission: To encourage best practices & proper licensing within the pest management industry in Manitoba
Membership: 17 companies; *Fees:* $305-$430; *Member Profile:* Pest management companies in Manitoba
Activities: Education & training resources
Chief Officer(s):
Shaun Jeffrey, President, 204-292-2260
sjeffrey@abellgroup.com
Debbie Lapointe, Treasurer
lowcost@mymts.net
Amanda Richardson, Secretary
arichardson@orkincanada.com

Manitoba Pharmaceutical Association *See* College of Pharmacists of Manitoba

Manitoba Physical Education Teachers Association *See* Physical & Health Educators of Manitoba

Manitoba Physiotheraphy Association (MPA)
145 Pacific Ave., Winnipeg MB R3B 2Z6
Tel: 204-925-5701; *Fax:* 204-925-5624
Toll-Free: 877-925-5701
ptassociation@mbphysio.org
www.mbphysio.org
www.facebook.com/MBPhysiotherapy
twitter.com/MBPhysiotherapy
Overview: A medium-sized provincial organization overseen by Canadian Physiotherapy Association
Mission: To provide leadership & direction to the physiotherapy profession; To foster excellence in practice, education & research
Member of: Canadian Physiotherapy Association
Finances: *Funding Sources:* Membership dues; Educational activities
Membership: 500; *Committees:* Professional Development; Business Affairs Private Practice; Awards; Communications
Chief Officer(s):
Allison Guerico, President

Manitoba Poison Control Centre
Children's Hospital Health Sciences Centre, 840 Sherbrook St., Winnipeg MB R3A 1S1
Tel: 204-787-2444; *Crisis Hot-Line:* 204-787-2591
Overview: A small provincial organization
Mission: To provide poison information, by physicians, for the public & health care advisers
Member of: Canadian Association of Poison Control Centres
Activities: Providing poison control phones, answered by physicians; Offering treatment advice, toxicology information, & veterinary toxicology information

Manitoba Pork Council
28 Terracon Place, Winnipeg MB R2J 4G7
Tel: 204-237-7447; *Fax:* 204-237-9831
Toll-Free: 888-893-7447
info@manitobapork.com
www.manitobapork.com
www.facebook.com/mbpork
twitter.com/MBPork
www.youtube.com/user/MBPorkfan
Overview: A small provincial organization founded in 1964
Mission: To represent Manitoba hog producers in related associations; To conduct promotion & market development campaigns for Manitoba Pork Marketing Agency
Staff Member(s): 13
Membership: *Committees:* Public Relations; Sustainable Development & Research; Industry Performance & Services
Chief Officer(s):
Andrew Dickson, General Manager
adickson@manitobapork.com

Manitoba Powerlifting Association (MPA)
MB
manitobapowerlifting.ca
Overview: A small provincial organization founded in 1967 overseen by Canadian Powerlifting Union
Member of: Manitoba Sports Federation; Manitoba Sports Directorate; Canadian Powerlifting Union; International Powerlifting Federation

Manitoba Printmakers Association
11 Martha St., Winnipeg MB R3B 1A2
Tel: 204-779-6253; *Fax:* 204-944-1804
printmakers@mymts.net
www.printmakers.mb.ca
www.facebook.com/marthastreet
Also Known As: Martha Street Studio
Overview: A small provincial organization founded in 1984
Mission: To promote printmaking & digital & photographic art in Manitoba
Finances: *Funding Sources:* Membership dues; Donations
Membership: *Fees:* $35 regular; $20 student
Chief Officer(s):
Larry Glawson, Executive Director
director.printmakers@mymts.net

Manitoba Prisoner's Aid Group *See* The John Howard Society of Manitoba

Manitoba Professional Painting Contractors Association (MPPCA)
1447 Waverley St., Winnipeg MB R3T 0P7
Tel: 204-479-8279; *Fax:* 204-958-5740
Overview: A small provincial organization
Mission: To elevate & promote professionalism & quality in the industry of painting contracting, paint & wall covering suppliers, & the related paint industry business

Manitoba Professional Planners Institute (MPPI)
137 Bannatyne Ave., 2nd Fl., Winnipeg MB R3B 0R3
Tel: 204-943-3637; *Fax:* 204-925-4624
mppiadmin@shaw.ca
www.mppi.mb.ca
Overview: A medium-sized provincial organization overseen by Canadian Institute of Planners
Mission: To handle membership applications & services & to enforce the Code of Professional Conduct.
Member of: Canadian Institute of Planners (CIP)
Membership: 147; *Fees:* Schedule available; *Member Profile:* University graduates working in planning & student planners; *Committees:* Continuous Professional Learning; Events; Membership; Communications & Events
Chief Officer(s):
Valdene Buckley, President
Kari MacKinnon, Administrator
Meetings/Conferences:
- Manitoba Planning Conference 2018, 2018
Scope: Provincial

Manitoba Provincial Handgun Association (MPHA)
PO Box 314, Stn. Corydon Ave., Winnipeg MB R3M 3S7
www.handgunmb.ca
Overview: A small provincial organization
Mission: To provide opportunities & programming for handgun athletes, coaches & officials; to help participants learn, practice & develop skills in the sport of handgun shooting.
Member of: Sport Manitoba
Membership: *Fees:* $10 individual; $25 club
Chief Officer(s):
Randy Myrdal, President
Meetings/Conferences:
- Manitoba Provincial Handgun Association Annual General Meeting 2018, 2018
Scope: Provincial

Manitoba Provincial Rifle Association Inc. (MPRA)
795 Valour Rd., Winnipeg MB R3G 3B3
Tel: 204-783-0768
www.manitobarifle.ca
Overview: A medium-sized provincial organization founded in 1872
Mission: To promote & encourage safe firearm handling & competitive target shooting in Manitoba
Member of: Shooting Federation of Canada; Dominion of Canada Rifle Association
Affiliation(s): Sports Manitoba
Membership: *Fees:* $40 full member; $25 associate member/under 25; $65 family; $350 lifetime; *Member Profile:* Individuals & clubs interested in rifle target shooting
Activities: Shooting practices & competitions

Manitoba Public Health Association (MPHA)
c/o Klinic Community Health Centre, 870 Portage Ave., Winnipeg MB R3G 0P1
manitobapha@mts.net
www.manitobapha.ca
Overview: A small provincial organization founded in 1940 overseen by Canadian Public Health Association
Mission: To influence health, social, environmental, & economic policy decisions, in order to improve the well-being of people in Manitoba; To ensure that health promotion, health protection, & disease protection are part of services
Member of: Canadian Public Health Association (CPHA)
Membership: *Fees:* Schedule available

Activities: Advocating for healthy public policies; Liaising with community & professional associations & the government
Chief Officer(s):
Barb Wasilewski, President

Manitoba Pulse & Soybean Growers Inc.
PO Box 1760, 38 - 4th Ave. NE, Carman MB R0G 0J0
Tel: 204-745-6488; *Fax:* 204-745-6213
Toll-Free: 866-226-9442
www.manitobapulse.ca
Overview: A medium-sized provincial organization founded in 1984
Mission: To provide production knowledge to members of the Manitoba pulse growers industry
Membership: 3,000; *Member Profile:* Farmers in Manitoba who grow edible beans, peas, lentils, chickpeas, faba beans & soybeans; *Committees:* Executive; Edible Bean; Finance; Market Development; MASC; Peas, Faba beans, Lentils & Chickpeas; Soybean; Variety Trial Results
Chief Officer(s):
Francois Labelle, Executive Director, 204-745-6488 Ext. 2
francois@manitobapulse.ca
Toban Dyck, Director, Communications
toban@manitobapulse.ca
Daryl Domitruk, Director, Research & Production
daryl@manitobapulse.ca
Melissa Denys-Roulette, Officer, Finance
melissa@manitobapulse.ca
Sandy Robinson, Manager, Business
sandy@manitobapulse.ca
Awards:
• Manitoba Pulse & Soybean Growers Degree Scholarship
; *Amount:* $1,000
• Manitoba Pulse & Soybean Growers Diploma Scholarship
; *Amount:* $1,000
• Manitoba Pulse & Soybean Growers Agribusiness Bridging Award
; *Amount:* $1,000

Manitoba Quality Network
#660, 175 Hargrave St., Winnipeg MB R3C 3R8
Tel: 204-949-4999; *Fax:* 204-949-4990
www.qnet.ca
Also Known As: QNET
Overview: A medium-sized provincial organization
Mission: To help organizations pursue continuous excellence & improvement
Membership: 400 individuals + 200 businesses; *Fees:* $135-$2,000; *Member Profile:* Members of various sectors, including: manufacturing, service, health care, government, education, consultant & non-profit
Chief Officer(s):
Trish Wainikka, Executive Director

Manitoba Reading Association
c/o Child Guidance Clinic, Winnipeg School Division, 700 Elgin Ave., Winnipeg MB R2E 1B2
Tel: 204-786-7841
www.readingmanitoba.org
Also Known As: Council No: CG150
Overview: A medium-sized provincial organization overseen by International Reading Association
Chief Officer(s):
Carol Hryniuk-Adamov, Coordinator
cadamov@shaw.ca
Meetings/Conferences:
• Manitoba Reading Association 5th Adolescent Literacy Summit, April, 2019, Winnipeg, MB
Scope: Provincial
Contact Information: mrasummit.weebly.com

Brandon Reading Council
Brandon MB
www2.brandonsd.mb.ca/brc/
Chief Officer(s):
Carole McCurry, President
mccurry.carole@bsd.ca

Manitoba Council of Reading Clinicians (MCRC)
MB
www.mcrc-online.ca

Pembina Escarpment Reading Council
MB
pereadingcouncil.pbworks.com/w/page/30555408/FrontPage

Manitoba Ready Mixed Concrete Association *See* Concrete Manitoba

Manitoba Real Estate Association (MREA)
1873 Inkster Blvd., Winnipeg MB R2R 2A6
Tel: 204-772-0405; *Fax:* 204-775-3781
Toll-Free: 800-267-6019
www.realestatemanitoba.com
Overview: A medium-sized provincial organization founded in 1949
Mission: To represent the interest of Manitoba's licensed realtors
Membership: 1,700 real estate professionals + 4 real estate boards; *Member Profile:* Real estate professionals & real estate boards in Manitoba
Activities: Training real estate agents; Advocating for improvements to government policies & programs in Manitoba
Chief Officer(s):
David Salvatore, Chief Executive Officer
dsalvatore@mrea.mb.ca
Jill Johnston, Director, Operations
jjohnston@mrea.mb.ca
Caroline Duheme, Reception
cduheme@mrea.mb.ca

Manitoba Recreational Canoeing Association *See* Paddle Manitoba

Manitoba Regional Lily Society
PO Box 846, Neepawa MB R0J 1H0
nigel@lilynook.mb.ca
www.manitobalilies.ca
Overview: A small provincial organization
Mission: To promote the growing and care of lillies in Manitoba.
Membership: *Fees:* $10
Chief Officer(s):
Deborah Petrie, President
petrie@mymts.net

Manitoba Restaurant & Food Services Association (MRFA)
103-D Scurfield Blvd., Winnipeg MB R3Y 1M6
Tel: 204-783-9955; *Fax:* 204-783-9909
Toll-Free: 877-296-2909
info@mrfa.mb.ca
www.mrfa.mb.ca
www.facebook.com/105407752852372
twitter.com/ManRFA
Overview: A medium-sized provincial organization founded in 1947
Mission: To lobby government and other regulatory bodies on issues affecting you and your business; to present educational seminars and social programs; to provide member services such as insurance programs and credit card savings; to represent the restaurant and foodservice industry effectively through a large membership.
Finances: *Funding Sources:* Membership; seminars; special events
Staff Member(s): 2
Membership: 500; *Fees:* $225 restaurant/food service; $275 associate; *Member Profile:* Organizations in the restaurant/food service industry & suppliers; *Committees:* Membership; Finance; Government Affairs; Events
Chief Officer(s):
Scott Jocelyn, Executive Director
Meetings/Conferences:
• Manitoba Hotel Association & Manitoba Restaurant & Foodservices Association 2018 Tradeshow, 2018, MB
Scope: Provincial

Manitoba Rhythmic Sportive Gymnastics Association *See* Rhythmic Gymnastics Manitoba Inc.

Manitoba Riding for the Disabled Association Inc. (MRDA)
145 Pacific Ave., Winnipeg MB R3B 2Z6
Tel: 204-925-5905; *Fax:* 204-925-5792
exedir@mrda.cc
www.mrda.cc
www.facebook.com/105010909544565
Overview: A small provincial charitable organization founded in 1977
Mission: To provide a therapeutic horseback riding program for children with disabilities.
Member of: Canadian Therapeutic Riding Association
Finances: *Funding Sources:* corporate sponsors
100 volunteer(s)
Chief Officer(s):
Peter Manastyrsky, Executive Director

Manitoba Ringette Association (MRA) / Association de ringuette du Manitoba
145 Pacific Ave., Winnipeg MB R3B 2Z6
Tel: 204-925-5710; *Fax:* 204-925-5925
ringette.admin@sportmanitoba.ca
www.manitobaringette.ca
twitter.com/MBRingette
Overview: A medium-sized provincial organization founded in 1970 overseen by Ringette Canada
Mission: To develop, encourage and promote Ringette for the enjoyment of all Manitobans through the provision of programs, services and resources that inform, educate and teach skills.
Member of: International Ringette Federation
Affiliation(s): Sport Manitoba
Finances: *Funding Sources:* Sponsorship; grants & registration fees
Staff Member(s): 4
Activities: Tournaments; provincial competitions; national competitions; world competitions; *Library:* Open to public
Chief Officer(s):
Laralie Higginson, Executive Director
edringette@sportmanitoba.ca
Melanie Reimer, Coordinator, Program
ringette@sportmanitoba.ca

Manitoba Rowing Association
Sport for Life Centre, 145 Pacific Ave., Winnipeg MB R3B 2Z6
Tel: 204-925-5653
rowing@sportmanitoba.ca
rowingmanitoba.ca
twitter.com/manitobarowing
Overview: A medium-sized provincial organization founded in 1981 overseen by Rowing Canada Aviron
Mission: To govern the sport of rowing in Manitoba
Member of: Rowing Canada Aviron
Chief Officer(s):
Kelly Malcolmson, President
Andrea Katz, Executive Director

Manitoba Runners' Association (MRA)
PO Box 34148, Winnipeg MB R3T 5T5
Tel: 204-477-5185
office@mraweb.ca
www.mraweb.ca
www.facebook.com/188241213063
Overview: A small provincial organization
Mission: To encourage road running in Manitoba.
Membership: *Fees:* Schedule available
Activities: Fun runs; races
Chief Officer(s):
Kathy Wiens, Executive Director

Manitoba Rural Tourism Association Inc. (MRTA)
PO Box 11, Lake Audy MB R0J 0Z0
Tel: 204-848-7354
info@countryvacations.mb.ca
www.countryvacations.mb.ca
Previous Name: Manitoba Farm Vacations Association; Manitoba Country Vacations Association Inc
Overview: A small provincial organization founded in 1972
Mission: To provide a quality, rural alternative to tourism
Membership: 15; *Fees:* $125
Chief Officer(s):
Jim Irwin, Contact

Manitoba Safety Council *See* Safety Services Manitoba

Manitoba Sailing Association Inc. *See* Sail Manitoba

Manitoba Schizophrenia Society, Inc. (MSS)
#100, 4 Fort St., Winnipeg MB R3C 1C4
Tel: 204-786-1616; *Fax:* 204-783-4898
info@mss.mb.ca
www.mss.mb.ca
www.facebook.com/ManitobaSchizophreniaSociety
twitter.com/mbschizophrenia
www.youtube.com/user/recoverytree?
Overview: A medium-sized provincial charitable organization founded in 1979
Mission: To improve the quality of life for individuals affected by schizophrenia / psychosis & co-occurring disorders
Finances: *Funding Sources:* Donations; Fundraising; Sponsorships
Staff Member(s): 6; 40 volunteer(s)
Membership: *Fees:* $15 single members; $25 families; $50 corporate members; *Committees:* Gala; Golf; Walk

Activities: Engaging in advocacy activities; Raising public awareness; Providing public educational opportunities; Offering the "Name That Feeling" program, for children who have a family member with a mental illness; Providing peer support programs; *Awareness Events:* Journey of Hope Walk for People with Schizophrenia; Iris Gala; Golf for Schizophrenia Tournament *Library:* Mental Health Education Resource Centre (MHERC); Open to public
Chief Officer(s):
Chris Summerville, Executive Director
chris@mss.mb.ca
Jane Burpee, Coordinator, Public Education
jane@mss.mb.ca
Katrina Tinman, Administrator, Special Events
katrina@mss.mb.ca
Publications:
• Reasons for Hope [a publication of the Manitoba Schizophrenia Society]
Type: Newsletter; *Frequency:* Quarterly; *Editor:* Chris Summerville; Kim Heidinger
• The Sharing Tree [a publication of the Manitoba Schizophrenia Society]
Type: Newsletter; *Editor:* Jo-Ann Paley

Manitoba School Boards Association
191 Provencher Blvd., Winnipeg MB R2H 0G4
Tel: 204-233-1595; *Fax:* 204-231-1356
Toll-Free: 800-262-8836
webmaster@mbschoolboards.ca
www.mbschoolboards.ca
twitter.com/mbschoolboards
Previous Name: Manitoba Association of School Trustees
Overview: A medium-sized provincial organization overseen by Canadian School Boards Association
Mission: To provide services to school boards in Manitoba; To advocate for public education
Member of: Manitoba Chamber of Commerce; Manitoba Council for Leadership in Education; Physical Activity Coalition of Manitoba; Social Planning Council of Winnipeg; Winnipeg Chamber of Commerce
Staff Member(s): 16
Membership: 38 public school boards; *Member Profile:* Public school boards in Manitoba; *Committees:* Aboriginal Education; Convention Planning; MB Public School Employees Dental & Extended Health Care Plan Trust; Finance/Audit; General Insurance Management; Group Life Insurance; MSBA Universal Standards Trust Fund; Nominating; Pension; Resolutions & Policy
Activities: Providing labour relations & personnel services to member school boards; Administering benefit programs; Offering guidance in risk management areas; Assisting school boards to obtain insurance through the Manitoba Schools Insurance (MSI) program; Providing professional development opportunities for trustees & senior administrators
Chief Officer(s):
Josh Watt, Executive Director
jwatt@mbschoolboards.ca
Heather Demetrioff, Director, Education & Communication Services
hdemetrioff@mbschoolboards.ca
George Coupland, Director, Labour Relations & Human Resource Services
gcoupland@mbschoolboards.ca
Awards:
• Student Citizenship Awards
Deadline: January
• Presidents' Council Award
Deadline: January
• Premier Award for School Board Innovation
Deadline: January
Meetings/Conferences:
• Manitoba School Boards Association Convention 2018, March, 2018, Delta Winnipeg, Winnipeg, MB
Scope: Provincial
Description: Theme: "Leadership, Service & Advocacy"
Publications:
• Manitoba School Boards Association School Board Member Handbook
Type: Booklet; *Number of Pages:* 48
Profile: A reference guide for Manitoba school trustees

Manitoba School Counsellors' Association (MSCA) / Association manitobaine des conseillers d'Orientation
c/o Manitoba Teachers' Society, 77 John Forsyth Rd., Winnipeg MB R2N 1R3
Tel: 204-254-0120; *Fax:* 204-253-7981
www.msca.mb.ca
Previous Name: School Counsellors' Association of Manitoba
Overview: A small provincial organization founded in 1965
Mission: To promote & develop guidance & counselling services for children & youth; To provide a forum & a voice for those interested in promoting the personal, social, educational & career development of young Manitobans
Member of: Manitoba Teachers' Society
Finances: *Annual Operating Budget:* $50,000-$100,000
22 volunteer(s)
Membership: 340; *Fees:* $25 regular; $15 student; *Member Profile:* Individual involved in, or interested in counselling; *Committees:* Awards; Career Symposium; Ethics; Membership; Professional Development; Public Relations; Social
Chief Officer(s):
Carla Bennett, President
Charu Gupta, President-Elect

Manitoba School Library Association (MSLA)
307 Shaftesbury Blvd., Winnipeg MB R3P 0L9
www.manitobaschoollibraries.ca
twitter.com/_MSLA_
Previous Name: Manitoba School Library Audio-Visual Association
Overview: A small provincial organization
Mission: To advocate for school library programs in Manitoba; To provide professional development opportunities for members
Membership: *Fees:* $10 student; $30 regular; *Member Profile:* Library personnel in Manitoba
Activities: Liaising with the Department of Education, as well as provincial, national, & international associations
Chief Officer(s):
Jo-Anne Gibson, President
mslapresident@gmail.com
Dorothy McGinnis, Secretary
dmcginnis@mcbi.mb.ca
Joyce Riddell, Treasurer
mslatreasurer@gmail.com
Awards:
• Outstanding Teacher-Librarian of the Year Award
Eligibility: Practicing teacher-librarians in Manitoba who are MSLU members
• School Administrator Award for Distinguished Service
Eligibility: A Principal or Vice-Principal who is responsible for a Manitoba elementary or secondary school
• Distinguished Service Award
Eligibility: A Principal or Vice-Principal who is responsible for a Manitoba elementary or secondary school
Meetings/Conferences:
• Manitoba School Library Association 2018 Annual General Meeting, 2018, MB
Scope: Provincial
Publications:
• Manitoba School Library Association Journal
Frequency: 3 pa; *Price:* Free for all members of the Manitoba School Library Association Journal
Profile: Current research & topics about school libraries in Manitoba, Canada, & around the world

Manitoba School Library Audio-Visual Association *See* Manitoba School Library Association

Manitoba Schools' Orchestra *See* Winnipeg Youth Orchestras

Manitoba Securities Commission (MSC)
#500, 400 St. Mary Ave., Winnipeg MB R3C 4K5
Tel: 204-945-2548; *Fax:* 204-945-0330
Toll-Free: 800-655-5244
Other Communication: Real Estate Division, Phone: 204-945-2562; Fax: 204-948-4627
securities@gov.mb.ca
www.mbsecurities.ca
Overview: A medium-sized provincial organization founded in 1968 overseen by Canadian Securities Administrators
Mission: To regulate securities trading in Manitoba, through the administration of the Securities Act; To report to the Legislature, through the minister responsible for the administration of the Securities Act; To foster a fair & competitive securities market; To protect investors & market integrity
Member of: Canadian Securities Administrators
Finances: *Funding Sources:* Fees collected from market participants under the legislation
Chief Officer(s):
Donald Murray, Chair & Chief Executive Officer
Publications:
• Manitoba Securities Commission Annual Report
Type: Report; *Frequency:* Annually

Manitoba Sign Association
850 Main St., Steinbach MB R5G 2H4
Tel: 204-326-4282; *Fax:* 204-326-5572
Toll-Free: 877-938-7446
mansa.ca
Overview: A small provincial organization
Mission: To promote the welfare of the sign industry in Manitoba; to benefit the users of signs
Member of: Sign Association of Canada / Association canadienne de l'enseigne
Membership: *Committees:* Events; Regulatory
Chief Officer(s):
Andrew Wrolstad, President
Matt Voth, Vice-President
Rona Jackson, Secretary/Treasurer

Manitoba Simmental Association (MSA)
PO Box 142, Cartwright MB R0K 0L0
Tel: 204-529-2444
mbsimmental.com
Overview: A small provincial organization founded in 1971
Mission: To assist in and promote the breeding of the Simmental breed of cattle in Manitoba.
Member of: Canadian Simmental Association
Membership: *Fees:* $50; *Member Profile:* Purebred simmental cattle breeders; *Committees:* Test Station; Show/Sale; Advertising; 4H/YCS
Chief Officer(s):
Everett Olson, President
everettolson@hotmail.com
Donalee Jones, Secretary-Treasurer
donalee@midcan.com

Manitoba Snowboard Association
15 Winterhaven Dr., Winnipeg MB R2N 4L2
Tel: 204-930-2724
info@manitobasnowboard.com
manitobasnowboard.com
twitter.com/MBSnowboard
Overview: A small provincial organization overseen by Canadian Snowboard Federation
Mission: To be the provincial governing body of competitive snowboarding in Manitoba
Member of: Canadian Snowboard Federation
Chief Officer(s):
Glenn Luff, Contact
gkluff@mymts.net

Manitoba Soaring Council
200 Main St., Winnipeg MB R3C 4M2
www.wgc.mb.ca/msc/Manitoba_Soaring_Council_Home_Page.htm
Overview: A small provincial organization founded in 1970 overseen by Soaring Association of Canada
Mission: To foster the art of soaring as an environmentally friendly safe & competitive life sport accessible to all Manitobans
Membership: 1,000-4,999

Manitoba Society of Artists (MSA)
c/o Luba Olesky, 2018 Henderson Hwy., Winnipeg MB R2G 1P2
www.mbsa.ca
Overview: A small provincial charitable organization founded in 1902
Mission: To foster & promote professional visual arts in Manitoba
Membership: 90+; *Fees:* $50
Activities: Hosting workshops, lectures, & slide presentations; Sponsoring juried exhibitions; Organizing rotating exhibits for members; Arranging social activities
Chief Officer(s):
Bonnie Taylor, President
president@mbsa.ca
Heather Robbins, Vice-President
John Mills, Secretary
Jack Watts, Treasurer
Luba Olesky, Chair, Membership
rlo@mts.net
Lori Zebiere, Chair, Publicity
lori@zebiereart.com
Awards:
• Brian J. Hyslop Memorial Award
Presented at the Manitoba Society of Artists Provincial Annual Open Juried Exhibition

- Lynn Sisson Watercolour Award
Awarded at the Manitoba Society of Artists Provincial Annual Open Juried Exhibition
- W. Cliff Packer Memorial Award
An award presented at the Annual Open Juried Exhibition of the Manitoba Society of Artists
Meetings/Conferences:
- Manitoba Society of Artists 2018 86th Annual Open Juried Art Exhibition, March, 2018, Warehouse Artworks Gallery, Winnipeg, MB
Scope: Provincial
Description: A major exhibition & the presentation of awards for both professional & amateur artists
Publications:
- Manitoba Society of Artists Newsletter
Type: Newsletter; *Editor:* Rachel Ines; Tom Andrich

Manitoba Society of Certified Engineering Technicians & Technologists Inc. See Certified Technicians & Technologists Association of Manitoba

Manitoba Society of Criminology Inc. See Manitoba Criminal Justice Association

Manitoba Society of Medical Laboratory Science; Manitoba Society of Medical Laboratory Technologists See Manitoba Association for Medical Laboratory Science

Manitoba Society of Occupational Therapists (MSOT)
#7, 120 Maryland St., Winnipeg MB R3G 1L1
Tel: 204-957-1214; *Fax:* 204-775-2340
msot@msot.mb.ca
www.msot.mb.ca
www.facebook.com/TheMSOT
Overview: A medium-sized provincial organization founded in 1963
Mission: To build & strengthen occupational therapy in Manitoba
Membership: *Fees:* $100 active; $37.50 associate & affiliate; $45 out of province; Free, first year students; $50 new grad; *Member Profile:* Occupational therapists, students & people working in occupational therapy in a support role; *Committees:* Executive; Communications; Newsletter; Website; Nominating & Awards; Public Relations; Professional Development; Special Events; Archives
Activities: Providing professional representation to government & professional groups; Promoting occupational therapy in Manitoba; Offering networking opportunities; Providing continuing education courses; *Library:* MSOT Resource Library
Chief Officer(s):
Pearl Soltys, Executive Officer
Katie Kitchen, President
Esther Hawn, Secretary
Kathy Kelly, Treasurer
Awards:
- MSOT Book Prize
Awarded to the student with the second highest standing in the final year of the Master of Occupational Therapy program at the University of Manitoba
- Outstanding Occupational Therapists Award
To honour an MSOT member who has made an outstanding contribution to the profession
- 25 Year Membership Acknowledgement
- MSOT Award for Professional Excellence in Fieldwork
For the graduating student of the Masters of Occupational Therapy program at the University of Manitoba who has demonstrated excellence in fieldwork
- MSOT Student Research Award
To honour the University of Manitoba Occupational Therapy student with the highest marks in Statistics & Research Methods
- OT Memorial Bursary
Eligibility: All students in the Masters of Occupational Therapy program at the University of Manitoba
Publications:
- MSOT Update
Type: Newsletter; *Frequency:* Bimonthly; *Accepts Advertising*
Profile: MSOT executive functions, current projects, & forthcoming events

Manitoba Society of Pharmacists Inc. (MSP)
#202, 90 Garry St., Winnipeg MB R3C 4H1
Tel: 204-956-6680; *Fax:* 204-956-6686
Toll-Free: 800-677-7170
www.pharmacistsmb.ca
Also Known As: Pharmacists Manitoba
Previous Name: Manitoba Society of Professional Pharmacists Inc.
Overview: A small provincial organization founded in 1973
Mission: To act as the voice of pharmacists in Manitoba on economic & professional issuess
Finances: *Funding Sources:* Membership fees; Sponsorships
Membership: *Fees:* Schedule available; *Member Profile:* Licensed, practising pharmacists in Manitoba, who are in good standing under the Pharmaceutical Act; Licensed, practising new graduates in Manitoba, who are in good standing under the Pharmaceutical Act; Canadian Society of Hospital Pharmacists members, whose practice is hospital-based; Non-practising & retired members are associate members of the society; *Committees:* Government Relations; Membership Services; Public Relations; Finance & Compensation; Professional Relations; Good Governance
Activities: Engaging in advocacy activities; Promoting pharmacists & their services
Chief Officer(s):
Brenna Shearer, Executive Director
bshearer@msp.mb.ca
Awards:
- Bonnie Schultz Memorial Award For Pharmacy Practice Excellence
- Centennial Award
- Magnum Opus Award
- Award of Merit
- Canadian Foundation for Pharmacy Past President Award
- Pfizer Consumer Health Bowl of Hygeia
- Patient Safety Award
- Pharmacist of the Year
- Young Leaders Award
Meetings/Conferences:
- 2018 Pharmacists Manitoba Conference, April, 2018, RBC Convention Centre, Winnipeg, MB
Scope: Provincial
Publications:
- Communication [a publication of the Manitoba Society of Pharmacists]
Type: Journal; *Frequency:* Bimonthly; *Accepts Advertising*;
Price: Free with membership in the Manitoba Society of Pharmacists; $72 non-members
Profile: Includes accredited & non-accredited continuing education units
- Communication Plus [a publication of the Manitoba Society of Pharmacists]
Type: Newsletter; *Price:* Free with membership in the Manitoba Society of Pharmacists
Profile: Updated information for society members

Manitoba Society of Professional Pharmacists Inc. See Manitoba Society of Pharmacists Inc.

Manitoba Special Olympics See Special Olympics Manitoba

Manitoba Speech & Hearing Association See College of Audiologists and Speech-Language Pathologists of Manitoba

Manitoba Speed Skating Association
145 Pacific Ave., Winnipeg MB R3B 2Z6
Tel: 204-925-5657; *Fax:* 204-925-5792
Toll-Free: 888-628-9921
office@mbspeedskating.ca
www.mbspeedskating.org
twitter.com/mbspeedskating
instagram.com/mbspeedskating
Overview: A small provincial organization overseen by Speed Skating Canada
Mission: The MSSA is dedicated to the development, growth & effective administration of the sport of speed skating in Manitoba through the provision of leadership, support & promotion of its members & clubs.
Member of: Speed Skating Canada
Membership: *Committees:* Finance; High Performance; Coaching; Officials; Competitions
Activities: Short-track, long-track speed skating
Chief Officer(s):
Brad Chambers, President

Manitoba Sport & Recreation Association for the Blind See Manitoba Blind Sports Association

Manitoba Sport Parachute Association (MSPA)
145 Pacific Ave., Winnipeg MB R3B 2Z6
Other Communication: Events E-mail: events@mspa.mb.ca;
Marketing: marketing@mspa.mb.ca
membership@mspa.mb.ca
www.mspa.mb.ca
Overview: A small provincial organization founded in 1978 overseen by Canadian Sport Parachuting Association
Mission: To promote awareness & participation in skydiving in Manitoba
Member of: Canadian Sport Parachuting Association
Finances: *Funding Sources:* Manitoba Sports Federation; Manitoba Lotteries; Sport Directorate
Membership: *Fees:* $25
Chief Officer(s):
Kaneena Vanstone, President
president@mspa.mb.ca

Manitoba Sports Federation Inc. See Sport Manitoba

Manitoba Sports Hall of Fame & Museum (MSHF&M)
145 Pacific Ave., Winnipeg MB R3B 2Z6
Tel: 204-925-5735; *Fax:* 204-925-5916
halloffame@sportmanitoba.ca
www.halloffame.mb.ca
www.facebook.com/sportmb
twitter.com/SportManitoba
www.youtube.com/user/sportmanitoba
Overview: A small provincial charitable organization founded in 1980
Mission: The mandate of the Manitoba Sports Hall of Fame is to recognize and honour those people who have made their mark in Manitoba's rich sports history through their activities and achievements. The core business of the Hall of Fame is to honour people by telling their story through articles and exhibits, or right here on this website.
Member of: Association of Manitoba Museums (AMM), the Association of Manitoba Archives (AMA), the Canadian Association for Sport Heritage (CASH) and the Canadian Heritage Information Network (CHIN).
Affiliation(s): Association of Manitoba Museums; Association of Manitoba Archives; Canadian Association for Sport Heritage; Canadian Heritage Information Network
Finances: *Funding Sources:* Fundraising; lotteries; provincial government
Activities: Casino Fun Nite; Stanley Cup Nite; Induction Dinner
Chief Officer(s):
Rick Brownlee, Sport Heritage Manager

Manitoba Square & Round Dance Federation
c/o President, PO Box 44, Hamiota MB R0M 0T0
Tel: 204-764-2108
www.squaredancemb.com
Overview: A medium-sized provincial organization overseen by Canadian Square & Round Dance Society
Mission: To promote & govern square, round, clog, & line dancing in Manitoba
Finances: *Funding Sources:* Member fees
Membership: *Member Profile:* Organizations & individuals participating in square, round, line, contra, clog, country/western, or related dancing
Chief Officer(s):
Edward Beamish, Co-President
Rosalie Beamish, Co-President

Manitoba Table Tennis Association (MTTA)
145 Pacific Ave., Winnipeg MB R3B 2Z6
Tel: 204-925-5690; *Fax:* 204-925-5916
table.tennis@sportmanitoba.ca
www.mtta.ca
Overview: A small provincial organization founded in 1959 overseen by Table Tennis Canada
Mission: To develop & promote the sport of table tennis at all levels within Manitoba
Member of: Table Tennis Canada; Sport Manitoba
Affiliation(s): International Table Tennis Federation
Finances: *Annual Operating Budget:* $100,000-$250,000;
Funding Sources: Sport Manitoba; Manitoba Lotteries; program revenue
Staff Member(s): 2; 25 volunteer(s)
Membership: 504; *Fees:* $25 active (adult); $15 active (junior); $10 associate (adult); $5 associate (junior); $35 associate (club); *Committees:* Tournaments; Leagues; Athlete Development; Grass Roots & Regional Developments; Coaching Development; Officials Development; Facilities & Equipment; Special Events; Finance & Administration; Bylaws & Policy Review; Privacy Officer; Fundraising & Bingos; Publicity & Promotion; Membership, Stats & Ranking; Banquets & Awards; Disciplinary; Nominations
Activities: *Library:* MTTA Resource Library; Open to public
Chief Officer(s):

Canadian Associations / Manitoba Teachers' Society (MTS)

Ron Edwards, Executive Director

Manitoba Tae Kwon-Do Association See Taekwondo Manitoba

Manitoba Teachers' Society (MTS)
McMaster House, 191 Harcourt St., Winnipeg MB R3J 3H2
Tel: 204-888-7961; *Fax:* 204-831-0877
Toll-Free: 800-262-2803
www.mbteach.org
www.facebook.com/manitobateachers
twitter.com/mbteachers
Overview: A large provincial organization founded in 1919 overseen by Canadian Teachers' Federation
Mission: Envisions a public education system that provides equal accessibility & equal opportunity for all children, that optimizes the potential of all students as individuals & citizens, that fosters lifelong learning & that ensures a safe learning environment respectful of diversity & human dignity
Finances: *Annual Operating Budget:* Greater than $5 Million; *Funding Sources:* Membership fees
Staff Member(s): 70; 500 volunteer(s)
Membership: 15,000; *Fees:* Schedule available; *Member Profile:* Manitoba public school teachers
Chief Officer(s):
Bobbi Taillefer, General Secretary, 204-888-7961 Ext. 232
btaillefer@mbteach.org
Dave Tate, Chief Financial Officer, 204-888-7961 Ext. 202
dtate@mbteach.org
Meetings/Conferences:
• Manitoba Teachers' Society 2018 Annual General Meeting, 2018, MB
Scope: Provincial

Manitoba Team Handball Federation
MB
www.manitobahandball.wixsite.com/mthf
www.facebook.com/teamhandballmb
twitter.com/TeamHandballMB
www.instagram.com/teamhandballmb
Previous Name: Manitoba Handball Association Inc.
Overview: A small provincial organization
Mission: To promote & develop the sport of handball in Manitoba
Member of: Canadian Team Handball Federation
Chief Officer(s):
Rhoni McKenzie, Coordinator, Operations

Manitoba Tenpin Federation
#407, 145 Pacific Ave., Winnipeg MB R3B 2Z6
Tel: 204-925-5705
www.mbtenpinfed.com
Overview: A small provincial organization overseen by Canadian Tenpin Federation, Inc.
Mission: To oversee the sport of tenpin bowling in Manitoba.
Member of: Canadian Tenpin Federation, Inc.

Manitoba Tobacco Reduction Alliance
192 Goulet St., Winnipeg MB R2H 0R8
Tel: 204-784-7030; *Fax:* 204-784-7039
info@mantrainc.ca
www.mantrainc.ca
Also Known As: ManTRA
Previous Name: Council for a Tobacco-Free Manitoba
Overview: A small provincial organization founded in 1977
Mission: To strive for a tobacco-free society for Manitobans; to encourage & support legislation to restrict smoking in public places & workplaces; to maintain awareness of the hazards of tobacco consumption to identified high-risk target groups
Member of: Canadian Council on Smoking & Health
Finances: *Annual Operating Budget:* $250,000-$500,000
Membership: *Member Profile:* Open to organizations which are interested in achieving a tobacco-free society for Manitobans; associate - available for those who wish to receive minutes only at a reduced fee
Chief Officer(s):
Rick Lambert, Chair
Murray Gibson, Executive Director

The Manitoba Tourism Education Council (MTEC)
#3, 75 Scurfield Blvd., Winnipeg MB R3Y 1P6
Tel: 204-957-7437; *Fax:* 204-956-1700
Toll-Free: 800-820-6832
www.mtec.mb.ca
Overview: A medium-sized provincial organization founded in 1989
Mission: To build the quality and performance of Manitoba's tourism and hospitality industry through excellence in training, education and recognition.
Staff Member(s): 11
Chief Officer(s):
Shannon Fontaine, Chief Executive Officer

Manitoba Trail Riding Club Inc. (MTRC)
838 Alfred Ave., Winnipeg MB R2X 0T6
www.mbtrailridingclub.ca
Overview: A small provincial organization founded in 1979
Mission: To meet the needs of a growing number of horse people who wanted a type of riding other than in the show ring which could demonstrate good horsemanship and promote sound, sensible trail horses
Member of: Manitoba Horse Council
Affiliation(s): Canadian Long Distance Riding Association
Membership: *Fees:* $25 individual; $40 family
Chief Officer(s):
Iris Oleksuk, President
irisolek@yahoo.com
Mary Anne Kirk, Treasurer, 204-955-7388
yaknow3@hotmail.com

Manitoba Trucking Association (MTA)
25 Bunting St., Winnipeg MB R2X 2P5
Tel: 204-632-6600; *Fax:* 204-694-7134
info@trucking.mb.ca
www.trucking.mb.ca
www.linkedin.com/manitobatruckingassociation
www.facebook.com/manitobatruckingassociation
twitter.com/truckingmb
Overview: A medium-sized provincial organization founded in 1932 overseen by Canadian Trucking Alliance
Mission: To develop & maintain a safe and healthy business environment for its members
Affiliation(s): Canadian Trucking Alliance; Canadian Council of Motor Transport Administrators; Canadian Trucking Human Resource Council; Winnipeg Chamber of Commerce; Manitoba Chamber of Commerce; Infrastructure Council of Manitoba; Employers' Task Force on Workers' Compensation; Manitoba Employers' Council
Finances: *Funding Sources:* Membership dues & fundraising through services
Staff Member(s): 6
Membership: 250 organizations; *Member Profile:* PSV Carriers; City Transportation; Private Fleet; Household Goods Carriers; Associated Trades; Vehicle Maintenance; *Committees:* Safety; Professional Truck Driving Championships; Scholarship Fund; Human Resources; Workers Compensation
Activities: *Speaker Service:* Yes
Chief Officer(s):
Terry Shaw, Executive Director
Awards:
• RBC Service to Industry Award
• Payne Transportation Associate of the Year Award
• Shaw Tracking Distinguished Member Award
• Volvo Truck North America MB Driver of the Year Award
Meetings/Conferences:
• Manitoba Trucking Association Annual General Meeting 2018, April, 2018, RBC Convention Center, Winnipeg, MB
Scope: Provincial
Contact Information: E-mail: info@trucking.mb.ca
Publications:
• [Manitoba Trucking Association] Manitoba Trucking Guide for Shippers
Type: Guide; *Frequency:* a.; *Accepts Advertising*; *Number of Pages:* 95; *Price:* Free download
Profile: A general guide to trucking information in Manitoba

Manitoba Underwater Council (MUC)
PO Box 711, Winnipeg MB R3C 2K3
Tel: 204-632-8508
info@manunderwater.com
www.manunderwater.com
Overview: A medium-sized provincial charitable organization founded in 1962
Mission: To coordinate, preserve, support & promote sport diving clubs & associations; to promote safety in diving; to exchange & disseminate information concerning the sport of skin & scuba diving & to foster conservation
Member of: Sport Manitoba
Finances: *Annual Operating Budget:* Less than $50,000; *Funding Sources:* Provincial Government & membership fees
Staff Member(s): 10; 10 volunteer(s)
Membership: 27 institutional + 150 individual; *Fees:* $20; *Member Profile:* Certified scuba divers, divers in training
Activities: Spear fishing competition, pumpkin dive, super dive, underwater football competition
Chief Officer(s):
Ronals Hempel, President
president@manunderwater.com

Manitoba UNIX User Group (MUUG)
PO Box 130, Stn. St-Boniface, Winnipeg MB R2H 3B4
Tel: 204-474-8161; *Fax:* 204-474-7609
Other Communication: membership@muug.mb.ca
info@muug.mb.ca
www.muug.mb.ca
Overview: A small provincial organization founded in 1986
Mission: To provide a forum for sharing ideas & information about open systems & their applications
Member of: Computer User Groups of Manitoba Inc.
Finances: *Annual Operating Budget:* Less than $50,000; *Funding Sources:* Membership fees; corporate sponsorships & donations
Membership: 65; *Fees:* $20
Chief Officer(s):
Gilbert Detillieux, Contact

Manitoba Used Car Dealers Association (MUCDA)
PO Box 53023, RPO South St. Vital, Winnipeg MB R2N 3X2
Tel: 204-254-1891
Toll-Free: 877-386-8232
info@mucda.mb.ca
www.mucda.mb.ca
Overview: A small provincial organization founded in 1991
Mission: To enhance & improve the automobile industry in Manitoba for the benefit of the Province's consumers through identifying public agenda issues affecting the industry and contributing to the decision-making process.
Membership: *Fees:* $255; *Member Profile:* Independent used car dealers
Activities: Scholarship Program

Manitoba Uske
c/o Gord Bluesky, Brokenhead Ojibway First Nation, PO Box 180, Scanterbury MB R0E 1W0
Tel: 204-766-2494
Overview: A small provincial organization founded in 1998 overseen by National Aboriginal Lands Managers Association
Staff Member(s): 1
Chief Officer(s):
Gord Bluesky, Chair
gordbluesky@gmail.com

Manitoba Veterinary Medical Association (MVMA)
1590 Inkster Blvd., Winnipeg MB R2X 2W4
Tel: 204-832-1276; *Fax:* 204-832-1382
Toll-Free: 866-338-6862
www.mvma.ca
Overview: A small provincial organization overseen by Canadian Veterinary Medical Association
Mission: To enhance professional excellence for the health & welfare of animals & Manitobans.
Finances: *Funding Sources:* Membership fees
Staff Member(s): 4
Membership: 300; *Fees:* Schedule available; *Committees:* Council Advisory
Activities: *Internships:* Yes; *Rents Mailing List:* Yes
Chief Officer(s):
Andrea Lear, Executive Director
alear@mvma.ca

Manitoba Volleyball Association (MVA)
#412, 145 Pacific Ave., Winnipeg MB R3B 2Z6
Tel: 204-925-5783; *Fax:* 204-925-5786
www.volleyballmanitoba.ca
twitter.com/VBManitoba
Overview: A small provincial organization founded in 1977 overseen by Volleyball Canada
Mission: To govern the sport of volleyball in Manitoba; To promote the development & growth of volleyball in the province
Finances: *Funding Sources:* Fundraising
Staff Member(s): 4
Membership: *Member Profile:* Elite & recreational athletes, coaches, officials; *Committees:* Grassroots Development; Competitions; Finance & Audit; Marketing; Awards & Recognition; Conduct & Ethics; Nominations; Governance; High Performance Development; Hall of Fame
Activities: Offering coaching clinics; Training & certifying officials; Providing competitive programs; Conducting Youth

Talent Identification Camps; *Library:* Manitoba Volleyball Association Resource Library
Chief Officer(s):
John Blacher, Executive Director
volleyball.ed@sportmanitoba.ca
Awards:
• Nikki Redekop Memorial Scholarship
Eligibility: Graduating high school students pursuing academics & volleyball excellence at the post-secondary level; *Amount:* 2 at $500 *Contact:* Anthony Roberts, Director, Programs, E-mail: volleyball.pd@sportmanitoba.ca; Phone: 204-925-5912
• Dale Iwanoczko Scholarship
Eligibility: Manitoba residents, 2 female and 2 male students currently attending highschool and pursuing post-secondary studies after graduation; eligible nominees must demonstrate volleyball ability, leadership, & participate in extra-curricular activities; *Amount:* 4 at $750 *Contact:* Anthony Roberts, Director, Programs, E-mail: volleyball.pd@sportmanitoba.ca; Phone: 204-925-5912
• Stefan Savoie Scholarship
Eligibility: A grade 12 student who is a Manitoba resident; *Amount:* $1,000 *Contact:* Anthony Roberts, Director, Programs, E-mail: volleyball.pd@sportmanitoba.ca; Phone: 204-925-5912
• Volleyball Manitoba Age Class Awards

Manitoba Wall & Ceiling Association (MWCA)
1447 Waverley St., Winnipeg MB R3T 0P7
Tel: 204-772-1700
info@mwca.ca
mwca.ca
www.facebook.com/568487016545116
Overview: A small provincial organization
Membership: 25; *Member Profile:* Contractors, manufacturers & dealers
Chief Officer(s):
Tom Robson, President

Manitoba Water & Wastewater Association (MWWA)
PO Box 1600, #215, 9 Saskatchewan Ave. West, Portage la Prairie MB R1N 3P1
Tel: 204-239-6868; *Fax:* 204-239-6872
Toll-Free: 866-396-2549
mwwaoffice@shaw.ca
www.mwwa.net
www.facebook.com/Manitobawaterandwastewater
Overview: A small provincial organization founded in 1975
Mission: To provide operator members with educational opportunities for operating & maintaining water & wastewater treatment facilities & water distribution & wastewater collection systems; To promote operator certification & facility classification
Member of: Western Canada Water & Wastewater Association
Membership: *Fees:* $52.50
Activities: Exchanging information & experiences; Seminars & workshops; Awards
Chief Officer(s):
Alan Howe, Executive Director
Awards:
• Lorne Sayer Award
• Jim Warrener Rookie of the Year Award
• George Balacko Operator of the Year Award
• Supplier of the Year Award
Meetings/Conferences:
• Manitoba Water & Wastewater Association Annual Conference & Trade Show 2018, February, 2018, Keystone Centre, Brandon, MB
Scope: Provincial
Description: The presentation of technical papers plus the opportunity to view industry products & services
Contact Information: Executive Director: Iva Last, Phone: 204-239-6868, Toll-Free Phone: 1-866-396-2549, Fax: 204-239-6872, E-mail: mwwaoffice@shaw.ca
• Manitoba Water & Wastewater Association Annual Conference & Trade Show 2019, February, 2019, Victoria Inn Airport, Winnipeg, MB
Scope: Provincial
Description: The presentation of technical papers plus the opportunity to view industry products & services
Contact Information: Executive Director: Iva Last, Phone: 204-239-6868, Toll-Free Phone: 1-866-396-2549, Fax: 204-239-6872, E-mail: mwwaoffice@shaw.ca

Manitoba Water Polo Association Inc.
#307, 145 Pacific Ave., Winnipeg MB R3B 2Z6
Tel: 204-925-5777; *Fax:* 204-925-5730
mwpa@shaw.ca
www.mbwaterpolo.com
Overview: A small provincial organization overseen by Water Polo Canada
Mission: To promote & govern the sport of water polo in Manitoba
Member of: Water Polo Canada
Affiliation(s): Sport Manitoba
Chief Officer(s):
Bruce Rose, Executive Director
Cindra Leclerc, President

Manitoba Water Well Association (MWWA)
PO Box 1648, Winnipeg MB R3C 2Z6
Tel: 204-479-3777
info@mwwa.ca
www.mwwa.ca
Overview: A medium-sized provincial organization founded in 1958
Mission: To promote & support the water well industry in Manitoba
Membership: *Member Profile:* Manufacturers; Technicians; Suppliers; Contractors
Activities: Offering workshops & seminars; Providing networking opportunities; Fostering & promoting scientific education, research, & standards
Chief Officer(s):
Jeff Bell, President
Ray Ford, Vice-President
Lynn Giersch, Business Manager
Marilyn Schneider, Secretary-Treasurer
Publications:
• Manitoba Water Well Association Newsletter
Type: Newsletter; *Frequency:* Quarterly
Profile: Featuring the president's report, membership information

Manitoba Welsh Pony & Cob Association
c/o Donna Hunter, PO Box 135, Kenton MB R0M 0Z0
Tel: 204-848-2411
mwpca.webs.com
Overview: A small provincial organization founded in 1975 overseen by Welsh Pony & Cob Society of Canada
Mission: To promote & develop the Welsh pony breed in Manitoba
Membership: *Member Profile:* Welsh pony breeders & other interested persons in Manitoba
Activities: Increasing public awareness of the Welsh pony breed; Hosting annual shows
Chief Officer(s):
Marg Allen, President, 204-352-4324
Donna Hunter, Secretary, 204-838-2411
kenview@inethome.ca

Keystone Region
c/o Norman Kalinski, PO Box 45, Carroll MB R0K 0K0
Tel: 204-483-2222; *Fax:* 204-483-3687
kalinski@mts.net
Mission: To promote the Welsh ponies & Cobs in Manitoba's Keystone area
Chief Officer(s):
Norman Kalinski, Contact, 204-483-2222

Manitoba Wheelchair Sports Association
145 Pacific Ave., Winnipeg MB R3B 2Z6
Tel: 204-925-5790; *Fax:* 204-925-5792
mwsa@sportmanitoba.ca
www.mwsa.ca
www.facebook.com/manitobawheelchairsports
Overview: A small provincial organization founded in 1962
Mission: Committed to leadership in the promotion of well being and a healthy lifestyle through the development of sport and fitness related opportunities for physically disabled Manitobans.
Member of: Canadian Wheelchair Sports Association
Staff Member(s): 2
Membership: *Fees:* $5
Chief Officer(s):
Samuel Unrau, Interim Executive Director

Manitoba Wildlife Federation (MWF)
70 Stevenson Rd., Winnipeg MB R3H 0W7
Tel: 204-633-5967
Toll-Free: 877-633-4868
info@mwf.mb.ca
www.mwf.mb.ca
Overview: A medium-sized provincial charitable organization founded in 1944 overseen by Canadian Wildlife Federation
Mission: To devote members to the causes of conservation & the participation in the wise use of natural resources; To encourage the propagation of game & fish; To promote the enforcement of game laws; To cooperate with government departments
Finances: *Funding Sources:* Membership fees; Donations; Sponsorships
Staff Member(s): 5
Membership: 14,000+; *Fees:* $9 youth (12 to 17 years of age); $30 individuals; $40 families; *Member Profile:* Anglers; Hunters; Outdoor enthusiasts
Activities: Offering hunting skills & firearms training programs; Developing the Hunters Sharing the Harvest program; Supporting the MWF Habitat Foundation
Chief Officer(s):
Rob Olson, Managing Director
Publications:
• Outdoor Edge [a publication of the Manitoba Wildlife Federation]
Type: Magazine; *Frequency:* Bimonthly; *Price:* Free with Manitoba Wildlife Federation membership
Profile: Information for Manitoba's hunters & anglers

Manitoba Wildlife Rehabilitation Organization *See* Wildlife Haven Rehabilitation Centre

Manitoba Women's Enterprise Centre *See* Women's Enterprise Centre of Manitoba

Manitoba Women's Institutes (MWI)
1129 Queens Ave., Brandon MB R7A 1L9
Tel: 204-726-7135; *Fax:* 204-726-6260
mbwi.ca
www.facebook.com/557282304320877
Overview: A medium-sized provincial charitable organization founded in 1910 overseen by Federated Women's Institutes of Canada
Mission: Focuses on personal development, the family, agriculture, rural development & community action, locally & globally
Member of: Federated Women's Institutes of Canada; Associated Country Women of the World
Finances: *Funding Sources:* Government; membership fees
Membership: *Member Profile:* Any woman 18 years of age & older
Chief Officer(s):
Joni Swidnicki, Executive Administrator

Manitoba Writers' Guild Inc. (MWG)
#218, 100 Arthur St., Winnipeg MB R3B 1H3
Tel: 204-944-8013
Other Communication: Events E-mail: events@mbwriter.mb.ca
info@mbwriter.mb.ca
www.mbwriter.mb.ca
www.facebook.com/mbwriters
twitter.com/mbwriters
Overview: A medium-sized provincial charitable organization founded in 1981
Mission: To provide services & support writers in Manitoba
Membership: 100-499; *Fees:* $60 regular; $30 student/low income; *Member Profile:* Manitoba writers at all stages of their writing careers
Activities: Offering a wide range of programs, such as the Blue Pencil Sessions & Master Classes; Providing manuscript evaluation services; Offering writing contests; *Awareness Events:* Winnipeg International Writers Festival; Manitoba Book Awards *Library:* Writers Resource Library
Chief Officer(s):
Melanie Matheson, Executive Director
Awards:
• McNally Robinson Book of the Year Award
To the Manitoba author judged to have written the best book in the calendar year
• John Hirsch Award for Most Promising Manitoba Writer
Awarded annually to the most promising Manitoba writer working in poetry, fiction, creative non-fiction or drama
• Alexander Kennedy Isbister Award for Non-Fiction
Presented to the Manitoba writer whose book is judged the best book of adult non-fiction written in English
• Margaret Laurence Award for Fiction
Presented to the Manitoba writer whose book is judged the best book of adult fiction written in English
• McNally Robinson Book for Young People Awards
Awarded annually to the writer whose young person's book is judged the best written by a Manitoba author; two categories: children's & young adult
• Le Prix littéraire Rue Deschambault
Biennial award presented to the author whose published book or play is judged to be the best French language work by a Manitoba author

- Carol Shields Winnipeg Book Award
To honour books that evoke the special character of & contribute to the appreciation & understanding of the City of Winnipeg
- Eileen McTavish Sykes Award for Best First Book
Awarded annually to a Manitoba author whose first professionally published book is deemed the best written
Eligibility: Must have been written in the previous year
- Mary Scorer Award for Best Book by a Manitoba Publisher
Awarded to the best book published by a Manitoba publisher & written for the trade, bookstore, educational, academic or scholarly market
- Lansdowne Prize for Poetry
Awarded to the best-written full-length adult book of poetry in either English or French.
- Beatrice Mosionier Aboriginal Writer of the Year Award
Awarded to an Aboriginal writer who demonstrates excellence in writing & engagement in work that encourages & supports Aboriginal writing in the province.
- The Manuela Dias Book Design & Illustration Award(s)
This award consists of four categories: Book Design; Children's Illustrated; General Illustration; & Graphic Novel.
- Lifetime Achievement Award
Awarded to individuals whose work in the writing & publishing community is both exemplary & spans at least a 25-year period.
- Chris Johnson Award for Best Play by a Manitoba Playwright
Awarded to the best play published or produced in Manitoba by a Manitoba-based playwright.
- Michael Van Rooy Award for Genre Fiction
Awarded to the best book of genre fiction written in English by a Manitoba writer, & published within a two-year period.

Manitoba/Saskatchewan Gelbvieh Association *See* Saskatchewan/Manitoba Gelbvieh Association

Manitoba-Saskatchewan Prospectors & Developers Association (MSPDA)
PO Box 306, 12 Mitchell Rd., Flin Flon MB R8N 1N1
Tel: 204-687-3500; *Fax:* 204-687-4762
more@mts.net
Overview: A medium-sized provincial organization founded in 1950
Mission: To act on behalf of individuals & firms engaged in mineral exploration in Manitoba & Saskatchewan in their dealings with government with respect to acts & regulations; to promote interest in mineral exploration in these provinces; to provide members with access to technical improvement
Membership: *Member Profile:* Geoscientists; prospectors; suppliers
Activities: Participation in provincial committees (Manitoba, Saskatchewan) dealing with land access, aboriginal concerns, mining, exploration & development; arrange technical speakers
Chief Officer(s):
Steve Masson, President

Manitoulin District Association for Community Living *See* Community Living Manitoulin

Manitouwadge Chamber of Commerce *See* Manitouwadge Economic Development Corporation

Manitouwadge Economic Development Corporation
c/o Township of Manitouwadge, 1 Mississauga Dr., Manitouwadge ON P0T 2C0
Tel: 807-826-3227; *Fax:* 807-826-4592
Toll-Free: 877-826-7529
www.manitouwadge.ca
Previous Name: Manitouwadge Chamber of Commerce
Overview: A small local organization
Activities: Education seminars; community & special events; supports local organizations; information booth; represents the community to the provincial government
Chief Officer(s):
Karen Robinson, Economic Development Assistant, 807-826-3255
karen@manitouwadge.com

Mannawanis Native Friendship Centre
PO Box 1358, 4901 - 50 St., St Paul AB T0A 3A0
Tel: 780-645-4630; *Fax:* 780-645-1980
Other Communication: Alt. E-mail: mannawanis@hotmail.com
mannatfc@mcsnet.ca
Overview: A small local charitable organization overseen by Alberta Native Friendship Centres Association
Mission: To co-exist in a safe & unified environment that supports the development of healthy aboriginal families, providers & members of the community
Member of: Alberta Native Friendship Centres Association

Affiliation(s): Alberta Food Bank Association; Canadian Food Bank Association
Membership: 100-499
Activities: Annual talent show; Family day celebration; National Addictions Awareness Powerwalk; Monthly soup & bannock day for general public; *Library:* Open to public

Manning & District Chamber of Commerce
PO Box 130, Manning AB T0H 2M0
Tel: 780-836-4045; *Fax:* 780-836-4048
manningchamber@gmail.com
www.facebook.com/Manningchamber
Overview: A small local organization
Member of: Alberta Chamber of Commerce
Finances: *Funding Sources:* Membership fees
Membership: *Member Profile:* To promote & enhance the business community through creation, participation & support of innovative programs
Chief Officer(s):
Kevin Albright, Chair

Mannville & District Chamber of Commerce
PO Box 54, Mannville AB T0B 2W0
Tel: 780-763-6455; *Fax:* 780-763-6451
Overview: A small local organization
Mission: To serve local businesses in the surrounding districts & community
Finances: *Annual Operating Budget:* Less than $50,000
Membership: 20; *Fees:* $20 business; $10 single
Activities: Organizing events such as Parade, Hollydaze, & Agricultural Fair
Chief Officer(s):
Hinton Erin, Secretary

Manufacturiers et Exportateurs Canada *See* Canadian Manufacturers & Exporters

Many Rivers Counselling & Support Services
4071 - 4th Ave., Whitehorse YT Y1A 1H3
Tel: 867-667-2970; *Fax:* 867-633-3557
www.manyrivers.yk.ca
Previous Name: Yukon Family Services Association
Overview: A small provincial charitable organization founded in 1969
Mission: To support & strengthen families & individuals throughout the Yukon while striving for supportive & responsive communities
Member of: Family Service Canada
Finances: *Annual Operating Budget:* $1.5 Million-$3 Million; *Funding Sources:* Yukon government; Membership fees; Contracts; Donations
Staff Member(s): 19
Membership: *Fees:* $10
Activities: Counselling; Psycho-educational groups; Workshops; Parenting programs; Youth outreach; Intervention workers; *Awareness Events:* National Family Week, Oct.; *Library:* Open to public
Chief Officer(s):
Brent Ramsay, Executive Director
bramsay@manyrivers.yk.ca
  Dawson City
  PO Box 595, 853 - 3rd Ave., 2nd Fl., Dawson City YT Y0B 1G0
  Tel: 867-993-6455; *Fax:* 867-993-6456
  Haines Junction
  PO Box 2109, 108 Auriol St., Haines Junction YT Y0B 1L0
  Tel: 867-634-2111; *Fax:* 867-634-2333
  Watson Lake
  PO Box 537, 714 Adela Trail, Watson Lake YT Y0A 1C0
  Tel: 867-536-2330; *Fax:* 867-536-7854
  www.manyrivers.yk.ca

Maple Creek Chamber of Commerce
PO Box 1766, Maple Creek SK S0N 1N0
Tel: 306-662-8119; *Fax:* 306-662-4005
info@maplecreekchamber.ca
www.maplecreekchamber.ca
Overview: A small local organization
Mission: To build an economic environment that will allow for thriving & sustainable businesses
Member of: Saskatchewan Chamber of Commerce; Canadian Chamber of Commerce
Finances: *Annual Operating Budget:* Less than $50,000; *Funding Sources:* Membership fees
6 volunteer(s)

Membership: 50; *Committees:* Business Retention & Expansion; Finance; Membership; Public Relations & Promotions
Chief Officer(s):
Blaine Filthaut, President

Maple Ridge Lapidary Club
23750 Fern Cres., Maple Ridge BC V4R 2S9
Tel: 604-466-4938
m.ridge_lapiclub@yahoo.ca
www.mrlclub.com
Overview: A small local organization founded in 1958
Mission: To provide a venue to develop appreciation of & skill in the lapidary & mineral arts
Member of: Lapidary, Rock & Mineral Society of British Columbia; Gem & Mineral Association of Canada
Finances: *Funding Sources:* Membership fees; workshop fees; annual gem show
Membership: *Fees:* $25 single; $45 family
Activities: Silversmithing; gem cutting; stone carving; enamelling; classroom discussions; workshops; displays; *Speaker Service:* Yes; *Library:* Not open to public
Chief Officer(s):
Carol Kostachuk, President

Maple Ridge Museum & Community Archives
22520 - 116 Ave., Maple Ridge BC V2X 0S4
Tel: 604-463-5311; *Fax:* 604-463-5317
mapleridgemuseum.org
Also Known As: Maple Ridge Historical Society
Overview: A small local organization founded in 1957
Mission: To provide current, former & potential residents of Maple Ridge with the means to understand the community's history through the collection, preservation & sharing of historical images, documents & artifacts; The Museum is home to the Maple Ridge Heritage Society & the Dewdney-Alouette Railway Society, which preside over the Haney House Museum & St. Andrew's Heritage Church Hall
Affiliation(s): National Model Railway Association; Pacific Northwest Region 7th Division Society; BC Heritage Society; Maple Ridge Historical Society; Maple Ridge Museum
Finances: *Funding Sources:* Membership fees, donations, admissions
Membership: *Fees:* $20 individual; $25 family; $120 corporate; $120 sustaining member; *Member Profile:* Individuals interested in Maple Ridge and its history
Chief Officer(s):
Val Patenaude, Executive Director
Allison White, Museums Curator

Maple Ridge Pitt Meadows Arts Council
11944 Haney Pl., Maple Ridge BC V2X 6G1
Tel: 604-476-2787; *Fax:* 604-476-2187
info@mract.org
www.theactmapleridge.org
www.facebook.com/mapleridgeact
twitter.com/mapleridgeact
Previous Name: Community Arts Council of T'Lagunna
Overview: A small local charitable organization founded in 1971
Mission: To serve the artistic & cultural needs of the Maple Ridge & Pitt Meadows area; To act as a voice for arts & culture in Maple Ridge & Pitt Meadows; To encourage appreciation for the arts
Affiliation(s): Assembly of British Columbia Arts Councils
Finances: *Annual Operating Budget:* $500,000-$1.5 Million; *Funding Sources:* Membership; Fundraising; Grants
118 volunteer(s)
Membership: *Member Profile:* Individuals; Families; Corporations; Groups
Activities: Operating & managing The Arts Centre & Theatre (The Act); Promoting all disciplines of the arts; Organizing arts programs, such as arts & crafts classes; *Awareness Events:* Annual Family Arts Fair
Chief Officer(s):
Lindy Sisson, Executive Director, 604-476-2780
lindys@mract.org
Karen Pighin, Communications Manager, 604-476-2784
karenp@mract.org

Maple Ridge Pitt Meadows Chamber of Commerce
12492 Harris Rd., Pitt Meadows BC V3Y 2J4
Tel: 604-457-4599; *Fax:* 604-457-4598
info@ridgemeadowschamber.com
www.ridgemeadowschamber.com
www.facebook.com/RidgeMeadowsChamber
twitter.com/PMMRChamber
instagram.com/pmmrchamber

Overview: A medium-sized local organization founded in 1910
Affiliation(s): BC Chamber Executive; Canadian Chamber of Commerce; Southwestern BC Tourism
Finances: *Funding Sources:* Membership fees
Staff Member(s): 3
Membership: *Fees:* Schedule available
Activities: *Library:* Open to public
Chief Officer(s):
Andrea Madden, Executive Director

Marathon & District Chamber of Commerce
PO Box 988, Marathon ON P0T 2E0
Tel: 807-229-1340
marathonchamber@live.ca
www.marathon.ca
Overview: A small local organization founded in 1962
Mission: To preserve & promote entrepreneurial spirit & the free enterprise system; To provide a framework to help members expand their business, practice or service
Member of: Ontario Chamber of Commerce
Affiliation(s): Northwestern Ontario Associated Chambers of Commerce
Finances: *Annual Operating Budget:* Less than $50,000
Staff Member(s): 1; 20 volunteer(s)
Membership: 35; *Fees:* $75
Activities: Providing professional & social networking opportunities; *Internships:* Yes
Chief Officer(s):
Greg Vallance, President

Marathon canadien de ski *See* Canadian Ski Marathon

March of Dimes Canada (MODC) / Mars de dix sous du Canada
10 Overlea Blvd., Toronto ON M4H 1A4
Tel: 416-425-3463; *Fax:* 416-425-1920
Toll-Free: 800-263-3463
www.marchofdimes.ca
www.facebook.com/marchofdimescanada
twitter.com/modcanada
www.youtube.com/user/marchofdimescda
Also Known As: Rehabilitation Foundation for Disabled Persons, Canada
Overview: A large national charitable organization founded in 2001
Mission: To provide support services to people with disabilities, their families & caregivers across Canada
Affiliation(s): OMOD Independence Non-Profit Corporation; Rehabilitation Foundation for Disabled Persons Inc., U.S.; Polio Canada; Stroke Recovery Canada
Finances: *Annual Operating Budget:* Greater than $5 Million; *Funding Sources:* Fundraising
Staff Member(s): 4; 10 volunteer(s)
Membership: *Member Profile:* Consumers, donors, sustaining & volunteers
Activities: Advocacy; Research; Offering information & peer support services; Accessible modifications programs; Alternative communication services; Assistive services; Attendant care services; Development disability programs; Employment services; *Awareness Events:* Polio Awareness Month, March; Stroke Awareness Month, May
Chief Officer(s):
Jenelle Ross, Chair
Andria Spindel, President & CEO
Zulfikar Chaggan, Chief Financial Officer
Chris Harrison, Chief Administrative Officer
Jerry Lucas, Chief Operating Officer
Awards:
• Vocational Rehabilitation Award
Contact: Awards Selection Committee, *Phone:* 416-425-3463; *E-mail:* awardscommittee@Marchofdimes.ca
• Jeannette Shannon Post-Polio Program Volunteer Award
Contact: Awards Selection Committee, *Phone:* 416-425-3463; *E-mail:* awardscommittee@Marchofdimes.ca
• Award of Merit for Barrier-Free Design
Contact: Awards Selection Committee, *Phone:* 416-425-3463; *E-mail:* awardscommittee@Marchofdimes.ca
• Judge George Ferguson Award
Contact: Awards Selection Committee, *Phone:* 416-425-3463; *E-mail:* awardscommittee@Marchofdimes.ca
• Rick Hansen Award of Excellence
Contact: Awards Selection Committee, *Phone:* 416-425-3463; *E-mail:* awardscommittee@Marchofdimes.ca
• Breaking the Barrier Award
Contact: Awards Selection Committee, *Phone:* 416-425-3463; *E-mail:* awardscommittee@Marchofdimes.ca

• Jonas Salk Award
Presented annually to a Canadian scientist, physician or researcher who has made a new and outstanding contribution in science or medicine to prevent, alleviate or eliminate a physical disability. *Contact:* Awards Selection Committee, *Phone:* 416-425-3463; *E-mail:* awardscommittee@Marchofdimes.ca

March of Dimes Non-Profit Housing Corporation (NPHC)
March of Dimes Canada Head Office, 10 Overlea Blvd., Toronto ON M4H 1A4
Tel: 416-425-3463; *Fax:* 416-425-1920
Toll-Free: 800-263-3463
nphc@marchofdimes.ca
www.marchofdimes.ca/nphc
Overview: A small national charitable organization founded in 1992
Mission: To develop & promote affordable supportive housing for people with physical disabilities
Affiliation(s): March of Dimes Canada
Finances: *Annual Operating Budget:* $500,000-$1.5 Million
Membership: *Member Profile:* Consumers; donors; sustaining & volunteers
Activities: Operates supportive housing projects.
Chief Officer(s):
Cameron Whale, Chair
Publications:
• Ontario March of Dimes Non-Profit Housing Corporation Annual Report
Type: Yearbook; *Frequency:* Annually

Margaree Salmon Association
PO Box 108, Margaree Centre NS B0E 1Z0
Tel: 902-248-2578; *Fax:* 902-248-2578
margareesalmon@gmail.com
www.margareesalmon.ca
Overview: A small local organization founded in 1982
Mission: Dedicated to the conservation, protection & enhancement of Atlantic salmon, trout & their habitat
Affiliation(s): Atlantic Salmon Federation; Nova Scotia Salmon Association
Membership: *Fees:* $30 regular; $50 family; $10 junior; $300 lifetime
Chief Officer(s):
Lester Wood, President

Margaret Laurence Home, Inc.
PO Box 2099, 312 First Ave., Neepawa MB R0J 1H0
Tel: 204-476-3612
mlhome@mts.net
www.mts.net/~mlhome
Overview: A small local charitable organization founded in 1986
Mission: To operate as a Provincial Heritage Site & museum; To preserve & display the possessions of Margaret Laurence
Finances: *Funding Sources:* Admission fees; Grants; Donations
Activities: Providing books, magazines, letters & tapes for research; Hosting writers' workshops, book launchings, & Elder Hostel education programs; Offering meeting space; *Awareness Events:* Annual Margaret Laurence Home Antiques & Collectibles Sale

Margaret M. Allemang Centre for the History of Nursing
c/o Judith Young, Treasurer, 355 Millwood Rd., Toronto ON M4S 1J9
Tel: 416-488-0597
secretary@allemang.on.ca
www.allemang.on.ca
Previous Name: Ontario Society for the History of Nursing
Overview: A small provincial organization founded in 1994
Mission: To promote the study of the history of nursing; to establish & maintain a collection of archival resources relating to the history of nursing
Finances: *Annual Operating Budget:* Less than $50,000; *Funding Sources:* Membership dues
Membership: 86 nurses; *Fees:* $50; $15 retired, student or associate; *Committees:* Archives; Acquisition
Activities: Public lectures; collection of nursing archival material (Ontario focus); oral history; *Speaker Service:* Yes
Chief Officer(s):
Judith Young, Treasurer

Margaret Morris Method (Canada) (MMM)
Tel: 613-938-7066
www.mmmcanada.ca
Also Known As: MMM (Canada)
Overview: A small national organization founded in 1951
Mission: To promote Margaret Morris exercise & dance methods & techniques
Affiliation(s): International Association of M.M.M. Ltd.
Finances: *Annual Operating Budget:* Less than $50,000
50 volunteer(s)
Membership: 200; *Fees:* $20 individual; $10 junior; $50 registered teacher
Activities: *Library:*
Chief Officer(s):
Marie Paquette-Rivard, Contact
mariepr.mmm@gmail.com
Awards:
• Special Junior Achievement Award
• Outstanding Contribution to MMM
Bronze trophy awarded annually

Margie Gillis Dance Foundation / Fondation de danse Margie Gillis
#304, 1908, rue Panet, Montréal QC H2L 3A2
Tel: 514-845-3115; *Fax:* 514-845-4526
info@margiegillis.org
www.margiegillis.org
www.facebook.com/fdmargiegillis
twitter.com/fdmargiegillis
Overview: A small local charitable organization founded in 1981
Mission: To reach as large a public as possible with a dance program of physical & emotional integrity; To make the audience aware of the potential of their own lives
Staff Member(s): 7
Activities: *Awareness Events:* Dancing from the Inside Out Workshop
Chief Officer(s):
Margie Gillis, Artistic Director

Marguerite Bourgeoys Family Centre Fertility Care Programme (MBFC)
Coxwell Medical Bldg., #100, 688 Coxwell Ave., Toronto ON M4C 3B7
Tel: 416-465-2868; *Fax:* 416-465-3538
www.fertilitycare.ca
www.facebook.com/FertilityCareToronto
twitter.com/FertilityCareTO
Overview: A small national charitable organization
Mission: To help families manage & care for their reproductive health, by providing health care & resources; To educate women, couples, & youth about sexuality, fertility, & family relationships, in the framework of Catholic values; To respect the dignity & differences of people
Member of: ShareLife Catholic Charities
Affiliation(s): Archdiocese of Toronto
Finances: *Funding Sources:* Donations
Staff Member(s): 12
Activities: Offering marriage preparation & family planning services
Chief Officer(s):
Krystyna Zasowski, President
Hemingway Karen, CFCS, Executive Director

Marigold Enterprises Rehabilitation Services Society
PO Box 2207, 4724 - 53 Ave., High Prairie AB T0G 1E0
Tel: 780-523-4588; *Fax:* 780-523-5350
dhpmari@telus.net
Overview: A small local organization
Mission: To serve & support both adults & children with developmental disabilities in High Prairie
Member of: Alberta Council of Disability Services
Affiliation(s): Alberta Association for Community Living
Activities: Offering vocational training; Encouraging supported & independent living
Chief Officer(s):
Donna Geertsma, Chief Administrative Officer

Marijuana Party / Parti Marijuana
5535, av Bourbonnière, Montréal QC H1X 2N3
Tel: 514-725-8103
info@marijuanaparty.ca
www.marijuanaparty.ca
Overview: A small national organization founded in 2000
Chief Officer(s):
Blair T. Longley, Leader

Marine Insurance Association of British Columbia (MIABC)
c/o Tina Antonio, Aon Risk Solutions, PO Box 3228, #1200, 401 West Georgia St., Vancouver BC V6B 3X8

Tel: 604-844-7654; Fax: 604-682-4026
marineinsuranceassociationbc.ca
Previous Name: Association of Marine Underwriters of British Columbia
Overview: A medium-sized provincial organization
Mission: To represent the goals & interests of the marine insurance industry in British Columbia
Finances: Funding Sources: Membership fees
Membership: Fees: $200 associate; $350 full; Member Profile: Marine underwriters, brokers, surveyors & lawyers; Committees: Education; Legislative; Underwriting; Social; Claims; Communications
Activities: Educational courses; drafting of clauses for industry use
Chief Officer(s):
Tina Antonio, President
Kristina.antonio@aon.ca

Marine Renewables Canada
PO Box 34066, 1690 Hollis St., 10th Fl., Halifax NS B3J 3S1
www.marinerenewables.ca
www.linkedin.com/groups/Marine-Renewables-Canada-2689413
www.facebook.com/marinerenewablescanada
twitter.com/Canadian_MRE
Previous Name: Ocean Renewable Energy Group
Overview: A medium-sized national charitable organization founded in 2004
Mission: To align industry, academia & government to ensure that Canada is a leader in providing marine renewable energy solutions to a world market
Membership: Fees: $50 student; $300 individual; $750 organization; $1,000 government dept.; $3,000-$10,000 Marine Energy Leader/Champion; Member Profile: Leaders in Canada's marine renewable energy industry
Activities: Conferences
Chief Officer(s):
Elisa Obermann, Executive Director, 902-817-4317
elisa@marinerenewables.ca
Amanda White, Director, Operations, 902-717-0716
amanda@marinerenewables.ca
Meetings/Conferences:
• Marine Renewables Canada 2018 Annual Conference, 2018
Scope: National
Description: Multiple networking opportunities to meet leaders and experts from business, government, and academia that will help build connections and support emerging industry needs.
• 8th International Conference on Ocean Energy 2018, June, 2018, Normandy
Scope: International
Description: Global marine renewable energy event focused on the industrial development of marine renewable energy.
Contact Information: www.icoe-conference.com
  Atlantic Office
  PO Box 34066, #400, 1533 Barrington St., Halifax NS B3J 3S1
  Chief Officer(s):
  Elisa Obermann, Atlantic Director, 902-817-4317
  elisa@marinerenewables.ca

Mariners' House of Montréal / Maison des marins de Montréal
PO Box 128, Stn. Place d'Armes, Montréal QC H2Y 3E9
Tel: 514-849-3234; Fax: 514-849-2874
manager@marinershouse.ca
www.marinershouse.ca
Also Known As: Montréal Seafarers Centre
Previous Name: Montreal Sailors' Institute & Catholic Sailors' Club
Overview: A small local charitable organization founded in 1862
Mission: To aid & assist seafarers temporarily in the City of Montréal & surrounding vicinity; to provide a place of repose for such seafarers & to provide for their spiritual, moral & social welfare
Finances: Annual Operating Budget: $100,000-$250,000
Staff Member(s): 5; 8 volunteer(s)
Membership: 1-99
Activities: A home away from home for some 15,000 seafarers annually; services include local & overseas calls, currency exchange, postal services, recreation, library & snack bar
Chief Officer(s):
Carolyn Osborne, Manager

Mario Racine Foundation Voir Fondation Mario-Racine

Mariposa Folk Foundation
PO Box 383, Orillia ON L3V 6J8
Tel: 705-326-3655; Fax: 705-326-5963
officemanager@mariposafolk.com
www.mariposafolk.com
www.facebook.com/MariposaFolkFestivalOfficial
twitter.com/mariposafolk
www.youtube.com/mariposafolk
Overview: A medium-sized national organization founded in 1961
Mission: To promote & preserve folk arts in Canada through song, story, dance, & craft
Member of: North America Folk Alliance; Ontario Council of Folk Festivals; Archives Association of Ontario; Orillia & District Arts Council
Staff Member(s): 6
Membership: Fees: $20 regular; $5 student/unwaged/accredited volunteer voting; Committees: Festival
Activities: Presenting festivals & concerts; Library: by appointment
Chief Officer(s):
Pam Carter, President

Maritime Aberdeen Angus Association (MAA)
c/o Betty Lou Scott, 840 Mount Thom Rd., Upper Mount Thom NS B0K 1P0
Tel: 902-925-2057; Fax: 902-925-2265
maritimeangus.blogspot.ca
Overview: A small local organization founded in 1905
Mission: To provide services that enhance the growth & position of the Angus breed in the Maritime provinces; To promote Aberdeen Angus cattle; To monitor the record keeping & integrity of the Aberdeen Angus cattle breed
Member of: Canadian Aberdeen Angus Association
Finances: Annual Operating Budget: Less than $50,000; Funding Sources: Grants from parent organization; Fundraising
8 volunteer(s)
Membership: 70+; Fees: $25
Activities: Organizing annual Junior Member show & Field Day
Chief Officer(s):
Betty Lou Scott, Secretary-Treasurer
windcrest.farm@ns.sympatico.ca
Awards:
• Maritime Angus Association Scholarship
Eligibility: Member of the Maritime Junior or Canadian Junior Angus Associations in first year post-secondary studies
Deadline: March 31; Amount: $500
Meetings/Conferences:
• Maritime Angus Field Day and Junior Show 2018, 2018
Scope: Provincial

Maritime Aboriginal Peoples Council (MAPC)
172 Truro Heights Rd., Truro NS B6L 1X1
Tel: 902-895-2982; Fax: 902-895-3844
mapcorg.ca
Overview: A medium-sized provincial organization
Mission: Represents the Traditional Ancestral Homeland Mi'Kmaq, Maliseet, and Passamaquoddy Aboriginal Peoples of Canada.

Maritime Appaloosa Horse Club See Appaloosa Horse Club of Canada

Maritime Association of Professional Sign Language Interpreters (MAPSLI)
PO Box 2625, Halifax NS B3J 1P7
www.mapsli.ca
www.facebook.com/367468123385697
twitter.com/MAPSLI_Canada
Overview: A small local organization founded in 1992 overseen by Association of Visual Language Interpreters of Canada
Member of: Association of Visual Language Interpreters of Canada (AVLIC)
Membership: Committees: Newsletter; Membership; Professional Development
Chief Officer(s):
Brenna D'Arcy, Acting President
president@mapsli.ca
Jessica Bezanson, Secretary
secretary@mapsli.ca

Maritime Auto Wreckers Association See Automotive Recyclers Association of Atlantic Canada

Maritime Breeders Association (MBA)
c/o PEI Harness Racing Industry Association, #204A, 420 University Ave., Charlottetown PE C1A 7Z5
Tel: 902-569-1682; Fax: 902-569-1827
peracing@eastlink.ca
Overview: A small local organization founded in 1982
Member of: Prince Edward Island Harness Racing Industry Association
Membership: Member Profile: Maritime stallion owners
Activities: Sponsoring the Maritime Breeders Association championship series; Registering stallions
Chief Officer(s):
Wayne Pike, Executive Director, PEI Harness Racing Industry Association

Maritime Broomball Association
NB
Merged from: New Brunswick Broomball Association; Nova Scotia Broomball Association
Overview: A small provincial organization overseen by Ballon sur glace Broomball Canada
Member of: Ballon sur glace Broomball Canada

Maritime Fire Chiefs' Association (MFCA)
PO Box 6, Dartmouth NS B2Y 3Y2
www.mfca.ca
Overview: A medium-sized local organization founded in 1914
Mission: To advance the science of the fire service in the Atlantic provinces
Membership: Member Profile: Persons in the position of fire chief, deputy fire chief, assistant fire chief, platoon fire chief, division fire chief, district fire chief, fire marshal, deputy fire marshal, fire commissioner, deputy fire commissioner, & individuals with an equivalent rank; Committees: Constitution & Bylaws; Resolutions; Training & Education; Conference; Finance; Nominating; Honours
Activities: Advocating & supporting educational programs for fire chiefs in fire protection & prevention, firefighting, administration, & training; Liaising with government; Rendering financial assistance to families of deceased members
Chief Officer(s):
Neville Wheaton, President
nwheaton@cornerbrook.com
Al Duchesne, First Vice-President
duchesea@halifax.ca
Vince Mackenzie, Second Vice-President
firechief@grandfallswindsor.ca
Charles Kavanaugh, Sergeant at Arms
charles.kavanaugh@inspection.gc.ca
Meetings/Conferences:
• 104th Maritime Fire Chiefs Association Annual Conference, July, 2018, Moncton, NB
Scope: Provincial
Description: Information about the latest trends & innovations within the fire service

Maritime Fishermen's Union (CLC) (MFU) / Union des pêcheurs des Maritimes (CTC) (UPM)
408 Main St., Shediac NB E4P 2G1
Tel: 506-532-2485; Fax: 506-532-2487
shediac@mfu-upm.com
www.mfu-upm.com
Overview: A medium-sized local organization founded in 1977
Mission: To maintain a sustainable inshore fishery & defend the principal of the fishermen/owner-operator.
Membership: 1,300+
Chief Officer(s):
Christian Brun, Executive Secretary
christian@mfu-upm.com

Maritime Hereford Association
RR#1, New Ross NS B0J 2M0
Tel: 902-425-7427; Fax: 902-425-7427
Overview: A small local organization
Mission: To increase the demand for Hereford & Hereford-influence cattle in the Maritime provinces
Member of: Canadian Hereford Association
Activities: Encouraging the breeding of purebred Hereford cattle in the Maritimes
Chief Officer(s):
Bobby Jo Hickey, Secretary-Manager, 506-523-7543
bobjhickey@hotmail.com
Philip Thorne, President
philshel@yahoo.ca
Gordie Raymond, Vice-President
garay@nb.sympatico.ca

Maritime Library Association See Atlantic Provinces Library Association

Maritime Limousin Association
c/o Sandra Othberg, Summerfield NB
Tel: 506-433-5245
www.maritimelimousin.com
Overview: A small provincial organization
Mission: To promote the limousin breed in the Maritime provinces
Member of: Canadian Limousin Association
Membership: *Member Profile:* Breeders of limousine cattle in the Maritimes
Activities: Providing member services
Chief Officer(s):
Michael Byrne, President, 902-485-6731
Sandra Othberg, Secretary-Treasurer

Maritime Lumber Bureau (MLB) / Bureau de bois de sciage des Maritimes
PO Box 459, Amherst NS B4H 4A1
Tel: 902-667-3889; *Fax:* 902-667-0401
Toll-Free: 800-667-9192
info@mlb.ca
www.mlb.ca
Overview: A medium-sized local organization founded in 1938
Mission: An accredited quality control agency for the lumber industry in the region.
Member of: Canadian Lumber Standards Accreditation Board; Canadian Wood Council
Staff Member(s): 12
Activities: *Speaker Service:* Yes
Chief Officer(s):
Diana L. Blenkhorn, President & CEO

Maritime Lumber Dealers Association *See* Atlantic Building Supply Dealers Association

Maritime Model Horse Collectors & Showers Association (MMHC&SA)
c/o Debbie Gamble-Arsenault, Alexandra RR#1, Charlottetown PE C1A 7J6
Overview: A small local organization
Mission: To bring together people who collect model horses & to foster growth in the hobby
Affiliation(s): Canadian Model Club & Registry
Membership: *Fees:* $1; *Member Profile:* Residents of the Maritimes who collect model horses
Chief Officer(s):
Debbie Gamble-Arsenault, Contact
dgamble@isn.net

Maritime Professional Photographers Association (MPPA)
See Professional Photographers of Canada

Maritime Regional CGIT Committee
130 Wellington St., Pictou NS B0K 1H0
Tel: 902-485-4011
g.cmacdonald@eastlink.ca
Also Known As: Canadian Girls in Training - Maritimes
Previous Name: National CGIT Association - Maritime Regional Committee
Overview: A small provincial organization
Chief Officer(s):
Chris MacDonald, Contact

Maritime Shorthorn Association
NS
Tel: 902-384-2964
Overview: A small local organization
Mission: To promote the use & breeding of Canadian Shorthorn cattle
Member of: Canadian Shorthorn Association
Chief Officer(s):
Jim Poole, Contact
Lynn Poole, Contact

Maritime Sikh Society (MSS)
10 Parkhill Rd., Halifax NS B3P 1R3
Tel: 902-477-0008
info@maritimesikhsociety.com
www.maritimesikhsociety.com
www.facebook.com/msssikhsociety
Overview: A small provincial organization founded in 1968
Member of: Multicultural Association of Nova Scotia
Finances: *Annual Operating Budget:* Less than $50,000
Membership: 46; *Fees:* $12
Activities: Weekly Sunday service; Panjabi classes for teaching religion, language & other activities
Chief Officer(s):
Kulvinder Singh Dhillon, President, 902-477-1949

Surinder Singh Kang, Vice President, 902-434-8368
Kanwal K Sidhu, Secretary, 902-462-2051
Jeginger Singh Bajwa, Treasurer, 902-443-5699

The Maritimes Energy Association
Cambridge Tower 1, #420, 202 Brownlow Ave., Dartmouth NS B3B 1T5
Tel: 902-425-4774; *Fax:* 902-422-2332
communications@maritimesenergy.com
www.maritimesenergy.com
twitter.com/MEnergyAssoc
Previous Name: Offshore / Onshore Technologies Association of Nova Scotia (OTANS)
Overview: A medium-sized provincial organization founded in 1982
Mission: To support the maximization of Atlantic Canadian participation in the supply of both goods & services to meet the needs of the energy industry; To identify, promote & support the development of opporunitities for member companies
Membership: 300+; *Fees:* $30 student membership; $498 companies with 1-10 employees; $760 businesses with 11-50 employees; $998 for companies with 51+ employees; *Member Profile:* Businesses in the Maritimes that supply goods & services to the energy industry in Eastern Canada, including the offshore & onshore, renewable & non-renewable, domestic & export markets; *Committees:* Audit; Executive; Events; Energy Industry
Activities: Networking & information activities; Industry advocacy & policy research; Conferences & trade missions
Chief Officer(s):
Ray Ritcey, Chief Executive Officer, 902-496-3182
ray@maritimesenergy.com
Lori Peddle, Manager, Business & Operations
lori@maritimesenergy.com
Louise Hawkins, Coordinator, Member Relations, 902-425-4285
membership@MaritimesEnergy.com
Torrie George, Coordinator, Communications & Events, 902-496-3180
communications@MaritimesEnergy.com
Meetings/Conferences:
• The Maritimes Energy Association Annual General Meeting & Dinner 2018, January, 2018, Westin Nova Scotian, Halifax, NS
Scope: Provincial
Description: A gathering of interest to decision makers in the offshore & onshore & renewable & non-renewable energy sectors to participate in roundtable discussions & networking events
Publications:
• The Maritimes Energy Association Annual Report with Financials
Type: Yearbook; *Frequency:* Annually
Profile: Contents include messages from the chair, executive committee, & board of directors, as well as industry activity in the maritime region, events, &committees
• The Maritimes Energy Association Daily Energy Bulletin
Type: Newsletter; *Frequency:* Daily
Profile: Current events of interest to members of the energy industry in Eastern Canada, such as notices of trade shows, association events, news releases from membercompanies, & procurement opportunities
• The Maritimes Energy Association Directory
Type: Directory
Profile: A listing of association members with company profiles & contact information

Maritimes Health Libraries Association (MHLA) / Association des bibliothèques de la santé des Maritimes (ABSM)
c/o Robin Parker, W.K. Kellogg Health Sciences Library, Dalhousie Uni., PO Box 1500, 5850 College St., Halifax NS B3H 4R2
mhla.absm@gmail.com
library.nshealth.ca/friendly.php?s=MHLA
Overview: A medium-sized provincial organization overseen by Canadian Health Libraries Association
Mission: To support members in the provision of quality information services for the health care community in the Maritime provinces
Member of: Canadian Health Libraries Association / Association des bibliothèques de la santé du Canada
Membership: *Fees:* $25 regular; free for students; *Member Profile:* Health library specialists in the Maritime provinces
Activities: Advocating for the value of health library specialists & health libraries; Providing educational opportunities; Communicating with members
Chief Officer(s):

Jackie Phinney, President
j.phinney@dal.ca
Awards:
• Ann Manning Professional Development Grant
Awarded to enhance access to professional development opportunities for an individual MHLA member *Deadline:* March 1; *Amount:* up to $500

Markdale Chamber of Commerce *See* Grey Highlands Chamber of Commerce

Marketing Research & Intelligence Association (MRIA) / L'Association de la recherche et de l'intelligence marketing (ARIM)
#1102, 21 St. Clair Ave. East, Toronto ON M4T 1L9
Tel: 416-942-9793; *Fax:* 416-644-9793
Toll-Free: 888-602-6742
info@mria-arim.ca
mria-arim.ca
www.linkedin.com/groups/MRIA-113690
www.facebook.com/MRIAARIM
twitter.com/MRIAARIM
Merged from: Canadian Association of Marketing Research Organizations; Canadian Survey Research Council
Overview: A medium-sized national licensing organization founded in 2004
Mission: To benefit the public & its members by developing & delivering ethical, professional practice standards, promoting the industry, & advocating for public policy that balances the need for research with privacy & consumer rights
Finances: *Funding Sources:* Member fees
Staff Member(s): 6
Membership: 2,000+; *Fees:* Schedule available; *Member Profile:* Members represent all aspects of the market intelligence & survey research industry, including practitioners, research houses, & buyers of research services, such as financial institutions, retailers, insurance companies, & manufacturers.; *Committees:* Certification Advisory; Communications; Conference; Fellowship Review; Litigation & Regulatory Resources; Membership; Research & Development; Field Management Group
Activities: Advancing the industry through education & accreditation; Offering industry surveys & reports; *Library:* Not open to public
Chief Officer(s):
Kara Mithcelmore, Chief Executive Officer
kmitchelmore@mria-arim.ca
Erica Klie, Manager, Member Support Services
eklie@mria-arim.ca
Lee Robinson, Officer, Compliance
lrobinson@mria-arim.ca
Awards:
• Excellence in Research Awards
• Blankenship Award
• John F. Graydon Award
• Joseph Doyle Award
• Commins Award
For best paper in the Canadian Journal of Marketing Research
Publications:
• Canadian Journal of Marketing Research
Type: Journal; *Price:* $50
Profile: Articles by Canadian researchers
• The Research Buyers Guide
Type: Directory; *Frequency:* Annually; *Accepts Advertising*; *Editor:* Barbara Justason; *Price:* Free to members
Profile: Listing of companies & organizations that provide marketing research services & products in Canada
• Vue Magazine
Type: Magazine; *Frequency:* Monthly; *Accepts Advertising*
Profile: Articles relating to research methods & practices, book reviews, industry conference reviews, upcoming events, & member news

Markham Board of Trade (MBT)
Markham Convergence Centre, 7271 Warden Ave., Markham ON L3R 5X5
Tel: 905-474-0730; *Fax:* 905-474-0685
info@markhamboard.com
www.markhamboard.com
Also Known As: Markham Chamber of Commerce
Overview: A medium-sized local organization founded in 1982
Mission: To enhance the success of members & the Markham business community
Member of: Ontario Chamber of Commerce; Canadian Chamber of Commerce

Affiliation(s): Scarborough York Region Chinese Business Association
Finances: *Annual Operating Budget:* $500,000-$1.5 Million; *Funding Sources:* Membership dues; programs & services
Staff Member(s): 6; 100 volunteer(s)
Membership: 800; *Fees:* Schedule available; *Committees:* Leaders/Nominating; Strategic Planning; Breakfast Committee; Government Affairs; Annual Awards Selection; Membership; Youth; International Business
Activities: Luncheons; golf tournaments
Chief Officer(s):
Richard Cunningham, President/CEO
Mary Ann Quagliara, Director, Member Services
Awards:
• Business Excellence Awards

Markham District Historical Society
c/o Markham District Historical Museum, 9350 Hwy. 48, Markham ON L3P 3J3
Tel: 905-294-4576; *Fax:* 905-294-4590
Overview: A small local charitable organization founded in 1969
Mission: To research, record & preserve Markham's history & to present a series of programs for its members
Affiliation(s): Ontario Historical Society
Finances: *Funding Sources:* Membership dues; Provincial government; Dinners; Festival days
Activities: Museum activities; Meetings; Bus tours; *Speaker Service:* Yes
Chief Officer(s):
Lorne R. Smith, Historian
lorne.smith@sympatico.ca

Markham Federation of Filipino Canadians
#10 & 11, 1151 Denison St., Markham ON L3R 3Y4
Tel: 905-305-1320; *Fax:* 905-284-6191
www.mffc.ca
Overview: A small local organization founded in 1989
Mission: To promote & preserve the Filipino culture & heritage through dialogue & activites
Affiliation(s): National Council of Canadian Filipino Associations
Finances: *Funding Sources:* Membership dues; Fundraising
Membership: *Fees:* $10 individual; $20 family; $50 organizations
Chief Officer(s):
Ester Toribio, Secretary
Yoly Ladines, President

Markham Stouffville Hospital Foundation
PO Box 1800, 381 Church St., Markham ON L3P 7P3
Tel: 905-472-7059; *Fax:* 905-472-7018
mshfoundation@msh.on.ca
www.mshf.on.ca
www.facebook.com/markhamstouffvillehospital
twitter.com/mshospital
www.youtube.com/mshospital
Also Known As: MSH Foundation
Overview: A small local charitable organization
Mission: To raise money on behalf of the Markham Stouffville Hospital in order to fund research & improve patient care
Finances: *Funding Sources:* Donations
Staff Member(s): 19
Chief Officer(s):
Suzette Strong, Chief Executive Officer, 905-472-7396
suzette@msh.on.ca

Markland Homes Association (MHA)
PO Box 11, Toronto ON M9C 4V2
mhapresident@marklandwood.org
www.marklandwood.org
Overview: A small local organization
Mission: To create, foster & maintain a community spirit
Membership: *Fees:* $20; *Member Profile:* Residents of the Markland Wood neighbourwood in Toronto's west end.; *Committees:* Environmental; Government Relations; Positively Promoting Markland; Safety; Social; Youth Awards
Chief Officer(s):
Anna Schaefer, President

Marmot Recovery Foundation
PO Box 2332, Stn. A, Nanaimo BC V9R 6X6
Tel: 250-390-0006
Toll-Free: 877-462-7668
marmots@telus.net
www.marmots.org
Overview: A small local organization founded in 1998
Mission: To manage the recovery effort for one of North America's most endangered mammals: the Vancouver Island marmot (Marmota vancouverensis)
Affiliation(s): Vancouver Island Marmot Recovery Team
Chief Officer(s):
Viki Jackson, Executive Director

The Marquis Project, Inc.
PO Box 50045, Brandon MB R7A 7E4
Tel: 204-727-5675; *Fax:* 204-727-5683
marquis@marquisproject.com
www.marquisproject.com
Overview: A small international charitable organization founded in 1979
Mission: To inform rural Manitobans of global issues; to link concerns to those of Third World peoples; to encourage concrete positive action in response to global concerns
Affiliation(s): Canadian Council for International Cooperation; Manitoba Council for International Cooperation; Partnership Africa-Canada; Canadian Peace Alliance; Manitoba Eco-Network
Finances: *Annual Operating Budget:* $100,000-$250,000; *Funding Sources:* Government; membership dues; donations; foundations
Staff Member(s): 3; 100 volunteer(s)
Membership: 30 institutional + 25 student + 50 senior/lifetime + 450 individual; *Fees:* $30; *Committees:* Overseas Projects; Education; Program; Finance
Activities: Operates a 3rd world craft store "Worldly Goods"; *Internships:* Yes; *Speaker Service:* Yes; *Library:* Laura Delamater Resource Centre; Open to public
Chief Officer(s):
Al Friesen, President

Mars de dix sous du Canada *See* March of Dimes Canada

Marsh Collection Society
235A Dalhousie St., Amherstburg ON N9V 1W6
Tel: 519-736-9191
research@marshcollection.org
www.marshcollection.org
Overview: A small local charitable organization founded in 1983
Mission: To collect, preserve & encourage research into the heritage of Amherstburg & the lower Detroit River
Member of: Ontario Museum Association; Ontario Historical Society; Ontario Genealogical Society; Archives Association of Ontario; Amherstburg Museums & Galleries; Association for Great Lakes Maritime History; Essex County Historical Society
Activities: *Library:* Open to public

The Martello Tower Society *See* Community Foundation for Kingston & Area

Martin Prosperity Institute
Rotman School of Management, University of Toronto, #9000, 105 St. George St., Toronto ON M5S 3E6
Tel: 416-946-7300; *Fax:* 416-946-7606
assistant@martinprosperity.org
www.martinprosperity.org
www.linkedin.com/company/629089
twitter.com/MartinProsperiT
Overview: A small local organization founded in 2007
Mission: To promote, provide information about, & broaden understandings of sustainable prosperity as part of democratic capitalism
Chief Officer(s):
Roger Martin, Institute Director
Jamison Steeve, Executive Director
jamison.steeve@martinprosperity.org
Jennifer Riel, Managing Director, Strategy & Innovation
jennifer.riel@martinprosperity.org
Stefanie Schram, Director, Intervention Design
stefanie.schram@martinprosperity.org
Sarah Soteroff, Community Manager
sarah.soteroff@martinprosperity.org

Marwayne & District Chamber of Commerce
PO Box 183, Marwayne AB T0B 2X0
Tel: 780-847-2538
Overview: A small local organization
Member of: Alberta Chamber of Commerce
Finances: *Annual Operating Budget:* Less than $50,000
Staff Member(s): 6; 20 volunteer(s)
Membership: 1-99
Chief Officer(s):
Sharon Kneen, President

Mary Undoer of Knots
#1, 271 Richvale Dr. South, Brampton ON L6Z 4W6
Tel: 905-495-4614
novena@maryundoerofknots.com
www.maryundoerofknots.com
Overview: A small local organization
Mission: To be devoted to Mary Undoer of Knots; To pray, as described in the Novena booklet, which is translated in 19 languages & Braille
Affiliation(s): Archdiocese of Toronto
Activities: Providing faith instruction; Offering prayer groups for youth, singles, & seniors

Masaryk Memorial Institute Inc. / The New Homeland
450 Scarborough Golf Club Rd., Toronto ON M1G 1H1
Tel: 416-439-4354
office@masaryktown.org
masaryktown.ca
Also Known As: Masarykuv Ustav
Overview: A small national charitable organization founded in 1945 overseen by Czech & Slovak Association of Canada
Mission: To keep tradition alive; to maintain heritage
Membership: *Fees:* $20; *Member Profile:* Canadians of Czech or Slovak origins & people with an interest in Czech culture
Activities: Newspaper, library, school, courses, cultural events; *Library:* MMI Library; Open to public
Chief Officer(s):
Frantisek Jecmen, President

Mascall Dance
1130 Jervis St., Vancouver BC V6E 2C7
Tel: 604-669-9337
admin@mascalldance.ca
www.mascalldance.ca
twitter.com/MascallDance
Overview: A small local organization founded in 1989
Mission: To provide a forum for research, creation, performance, education, documentation & dissemination of contemporary dance & related disciplines
Member of: Dance Centre; Alliance for Arts & Culture; Shape; CADA
Finances: *Funding Sources:* The Canadian Council; BC Arts Council; City of Vancouver; fundraising
Staff Member(s): 4
Activities: Offering workshops, summer school, programs & educational tours
Chief Officer(s):
Jennifer Mascall, Artistic Director

Masonic Foundation of Manitoba Inc.
420 Corydon Ave., Winnipeg MB R3L 0N8
Tel: 204-453-7410
Overview: A small provincial charitable organization founded in 1976
Chief Officer(s):
C.R. Haldane-Wilsone, Secretary-Treasurer

Masonic Foundation of Ontario
361 King St. West, Hamilton ON L8P 1B4
Tel: 905-527-9105; *Fax:* 905-527-8859
www.masonicfoundation.on.ca
Overview: A small provincial charitable organization founded in 1964
Mission: To provide bursaries for needy students attending universities & colleges in Ontario
Finances: *Annual Operating Budget:* Greater than $5 Million
Chief Officer(s):
Mel Duke, Secretary
mel_duke@masonicfoundation.on.ca

Masonry Industry Employers Council of Ontario (MIECO)
360 Superior Blvd., Mississauga ON L5T 2N7
Tel: 905-564-6622; *Fax:* 905-564-5744
www.canadamasonrycentre.com/mieco
Overview: A small provincial organization
Mission: To maintain a fair working relationship with local & provincial unions across Ontario
Member of: Ontario Masonry Contractors Association
Staff Member(s): 7
Membership: 500-999
Activities: *Library:* Canada Masonry Centre; Open to public
Chief Officer(s):
D. Webb, Contact
dwebb@canadamasonrycentre.com

MasonryWorx
#10, 150 Jardin Dr., Concord ON L4K 3P9

Tel: 905-760-9679; Fax: 866-700-4974
info@masonryworx.com
www.masonryworx.com
www.facebook.com/MasonryWorx
twitter.com/masonryworx
www.youtube.com/user/MasonryWorx1
Overview: A small local organization
Mission: To create beautiful communities across the Greater Toronto Area, that will increase in value & stand the test of time; To promote the use, understanding & benefits of masonry professionals, masonry products & masonry systems in the design & construction of our communities throughout the GTA

Massage Therapist Association of Alberta (MTAA)
#2, 7429 - 49 St., Red Deer AB T4P 1N2
Tel: 403-340-1913; Fax: 403-346-2269
info@mtaalberta.com
www.mtaalberta.com
www.facebook.com/MTAAlberta
Overview: A small provincial organization founded in 1953
Mission: To promote massage therapy through member services, education, professional standards & advocacy
Member of: Canadian Massage Therapist Alliance
Membership: Fees: $575 active

Massage Therapist Association of Saskatchewan (MTAS)
#16, 1724 Quebec Ave., Saskatoon SK S7K 1V9
Tel: 306-384-7077; Fax: 306-384-7175
mtas@sasktel.net
www.saskmassagetherapy.com
www.linkedin.com/company/massage-therapist-association-of-saskatchewan
www.facebook.com/145260445598968
twitter.com/SaskMassage
Overview: A small provincial licensing organization founded in 1997
Mission: To encourage the science & practice of massage therapy
Member of: Canadian Massage Therapist Alliance; Saskatchewan Chamber of Commerce
Finances: Annual Operating Budget: $250,000-$500,000; Funding Sources: Membership dues
Staff Member(s): 2; 11 volunteer(s)
Membership: 860; Fees: Schedule available; Member Profile: Registered massage therapists; Committees: Education; Competency; Complaints & Discipline; Intergovernmental; Public Relations & Membership; Finance; Executive; Insurance
Activities: Providing information & resources on continuing education; Licensing members; Awareness Events: Massage Therapy Awareness Week, October; Speaker Service: Yes
Chief Officer(s):
Lori Green, Executive Director
lorigreen@saskmassagetherapy.com
Jayne Little, Manager, Member Services
Meetings/Conferences:
• Massage Therapist Association of Saskatchewan 5th Annual Research Symposium 2018, 2018, SK
Scope: Provincial
Description: Includes information & research on massage therapy from keynote presenters

Massage Therapists' Association of Nova Scotia (MTANS)
PO Box 9410, Stn. A, Halifax NS B3K 5S3
Tel: 902-429-2190; Fax: 902-425-2441
info@mtans.ca
www.mtans.ca
Overview: A small provincial organization founded in 1990
Mission: To promote the science, art & philosophy of Massage Therapy for the betterment of public health & in the public interest; to represent membership before governmental & regulating bodies concerned with Massage Therapy; to foster & encourage professional & ethical standards among its members; to encourage high standards of education for students of Massage Therapy; to increase the awareness & knowledge of the general public concerning the benefits of Massage Therapy; to liaise with & recommend potential students to recognized schools of Massage Therapy which meet the standards of the Association; to offer post-graduate education & to set post-graduate standards
Member of: Canadian Massage Therapist Alliance
Affiliation(s): Alliance of Complemeniary Health Professions
Finances: Funding Sources: Membership dues
Membership: Fees: $400 regular; $100 associate/inactive; $0 student; Member Profile: Massage therapists; Committees:
Public Relations; Complaints; Continuing Education; Examination & Education Standards; Conference & Tradeshow; Legislation
Activities: Annual booth at Labatt's 24-Hour Relay, a fundraiser for Abilities Foundation of Nova Scotia
Chief Officer(s):
Kelly Carrington, President
Donna Noddin, Executive Director

Massage Therapy Association of Manitoba Inc. (MTAM)
#304, 428 Portage Ave., Winnipeg MB R3C 0E2
Tel: 204-927-7979; Fax: 204-927-7978
Toll-Free: 866-605-1433
info@mtam.mb.ca
www.mtam.mb.ca
www.linkedin.com/company/2511272
www.facebook.com/MTAManitoba
twitter.com/MTAManitoba
Overview: A small provincial organization founded in 1973
Mission: To promote & enhance massage therapy in Manitoba; To ensure safe & ethical massage therapy practice; To represent members & support their professional growth
Membership: Fees: Schedule available; Member Profile: Massage Therapists who have successfully completed two years of study from a recognized school/college of massage therapy & who have attained a minimum grade point average of 75%
Chief Officer(s):
Sheila Molloy, Executive Director

Massey Centre for Women
1102 Broadview Ave., Toronto ON M4K 2S5
Tel: 416-425-6348; Fax: 416-425-4056
giving@massey.ca
www.massey.ca
www.facebook.com/MasseyCentre
twitter.com/MasseyCentre
Overview: A small local charitable organization founded in 1901
Mission: To improve the lives of disadvantaged young women & their children
Affiliation(s): The United Church of Canada
Finances: Annual Operating Budget: $3 Million-$5 Million; Funding Sources: Donations; Municipal, provincial & federal government grants; Fundraising
Staff Member(s): 81; 57 volunteer(s)
Activities: Speaker Service: Yes
Chief Officer(s):
Ekua Asabea Blair, CEO

Master Bowlers' Association of Alberta
1 Oxbow St., Red Deer AB T4N 5C3
Tel: 403-309-6916
mbaofalberta@gmail.com
mbaofa.ca
Also Known As: MBA of A
Overview: A small provincial organization overseen by Master Bowlers' Association of Canada
Member of: Master Bowlers' Association of Canada
Chief Officer(s):
Brian Rossetti, President

Master Bowlers' Association of British Columbia
11048 83A Ave., Surrey BC V3C 2J5
www.mbaofbc.com
Overview: A small provincial organization overseen by Master Bowlers' Association of Canada
Member of: Master Bowlers' Association of Canada
Chief Officer(s):
Laddie MacKinnon, President
ladmac99@telus.net
Lee-Anne Wilson, Technical Director

Master Bowlers' Association of Canada
c/o Master Bowlers' Association of Alberta, 1 Oxbow St., Red Deer AB T4N 5C3
www.mastersbowling.ca
www.facebook.com/MBAofCanada
Overview: A medium-sized national organization founded in 1970
Mission: To connect master bowlers across Canada
Membership: Member Profile: NCCP certified coaches & athletes competing as Teaching Masters, Tournament Masters & Senior Masters
Activities: Annual National Championships

Master Bowlers' Association of Manitoba (MBAM)
MB
Overview: A small provincial organization overseen by Master Bowlers' Association of Canada
Member of: Manitoba Five Pin Bowling Federation, Inc.; Master Bowlers' Association of Canada

Master Bowlers' Association of Ontario (MBAO)
PO Box 22, 41 Temperance St., Bowmanville ON L1C 3A0
mbao.ca
www.facebook.com/185964874757498
Overview: A small provincial organization overseen by Master Bowlers' Association of Canada
Member of: Master Bowlers' Association of Canada
Chief Officer(s):
Brenda Walters, President

Master Insulators' Association of Ontario Inc.
Building 1, #101, 2600 Skymark Ave., Mississauga ON L4W 5B2
Tel: 905-279-6426; Fax: 905-279-6422
miapublic1@miaontario.org
www.miaontario.org
Overview: A small provincial organization founded in 1942
Mission: To promote & advance the insulation industry
Membership: 102; Member Profile: Companies who install thermal insulation; suppliers, distributors & manufacturers of thermal insulation; Committees: Joint Apprentice; Labour Advisory; Charity Golf; Health & Safety
Chief Officer(s):
Caroline O'Keeffe, Office Manager

Master Mariners of Canada
c/o Captain Patrick Gates, 5591 Leeds St., Halifax NS B3K 2T3
www.mastermariners.ca
www.facebook.com/mastermarinersofcanada
twitter.com/MMofCanada
Overview: A medium-sized national organization founded in 1967
Mission: To encourage and maintain a high and honourable standard of ability & profesional conduct of the officers of the Canadian Merchant Service; Provide a central body of command representing senior officers; Encourage and further develop education, training & qualifications of young seafarers; Promote & maintain efficient & friendly cooperation between the commerical, government & military fleets of Canada
Member of: Canadian Maritimes Law Association (CMLA); International Federation of Shipmasters' Associations (IFSMA); International Maritimes Organization (IMO)
Affiliation(s): Master Mariner organizations in the UK, USA, South Africa, Australia & NZ
Finances: Funding Sources: Membership dues
Membership: Fees: $80 senior/associate/companion; $50 full; Member Profile: Master Mariners
Activities: Organizes conventions and seminars; Participates, and provides input into, National and International groups; Speaker Service: Yes
Chief Officer(s):
Patrick Gates, National President
patrickgates@bellaliant.net
Chris Hearn, National Vice President
christopher.hearn@mi.mun.ca
Chris Hall, National Assistant Vice President
chall@sjport.com
Awards:
• Captain G.O. Baugh Memorial Fund
Eligibility: A second - fourth year student enrolled in a Deck Officer/Nautical Science Cadet program or a Navigation Officer planning to upgrade their nautical certification Deadline: September 30; Amount: $2000 Contact: Captain David Whitaker, whitknit@telus.net
Publications:
• From The Bridge
Type: Newsletter; Frequency: Quarterly; Editor: David Whitaker
   Capital Division
   PO Box 56104, 407 Laurier Ave. West, Ottawa ON K1R 7Z1
   Chief Officer(s):
   Michael Hubbard, Divison Master
   Fundy Division
   c/o 33 Cove Cres., Rothesay NB E2E 5C6
   Chief Officer(s):
   John McCann, Division Master
   Great Lakes Division
   8 Unwin Ave., Toronto ON M5A 1A1
   Chief Officer(s):
   Frank Hough, Division Master
   Maritimes Division
   PO Box 315, Stn. Main, Dartmouth NS B2Y 3Y5
   Chief Officer(s):

Rick Gates, Division Master
patrickgates@bellaliant.net
Montréal Division
#326, 300, rue St-Sacrement, Montréal QC H2Y 1X4
Chief Officer(s):
Don Coelho, Division Master
Newfoundland & Labrador Division
PO Box 4920, St. John's NL A1C 5R3
Chief Officer(s):
Christopher Hearn, Division Master
christopher.hearn@mi.mun.ca
Vancouver Division
c/o D. Rose, 6050 Cartier St., Vancouver BC V6M 3A9
Chief Officer(s):
Don Rose, Division Master
Vancouver Island Division
#6, 912 Brulette Pl., Mill Bay BC V0R 2P2
Chief Officer(s):
Geoffrey Vale, Division Master, 250-743-9656
gvale33@hotmail.com

Master Painters & Decorators Association (MPDA)
2800 Ingleton Ave., Burnaby BC V5C 6G7
Tel: 604-298-7578; *Fax:* 604-298-7571
Toll-Free: 888-674-8708
Other Communication: Toll-Free Fax: 1-888-211-8708
info@paintinfo.com
www.paintinfo.com/assoc/mpda
Previous Name: Master Painters & Decorators Association of British Columbia
Overview: A medium-sized provincial organization founded in 1911
Mission: To set & raise standards of industrial organizations
Affiliation(s): Master Painters Institute
Finances: *Annual Operating Budget:* $250,000-$500,000
Staff Member(s): 4
Membership: 1-99; *Committees:* Technical; Program
Activities: *Speaker Service:* Yes; *Library*
Chief Officer(s):
Greg Boshard, President
Joe Racanelli, Vice-President
Doreen Tan, Secretary-Treasurer

Master Painters & Decorators Association of British Columbia *See* Master Painters & Decorators Association

Matane Historical & Genealogical Society *Voir* Société d'histoire et de généalogie de Matane

MATCH International Women's Fund
1404 Scott St., Ottawa ON K1Y 4M8
Fax: 613-798-0990
Toll-Free: 855-640-1872
info@matchinternational.org
www.matchinternational.org
www.facebook.com/matchinternational
twitter.com/MATCHIntFund
www.youtube.com/user/MATCHIntCentre;
www.instagram.com/thematchfund
Also Known As: MATCH International
Overview: A small international charitable organization founded in 1977
Mission: To encourage sustained development in the global South, through a focus on women's rights & empowerment; To support women in the global South in executing their ideas regarding women's rights & equality; To advance women's rights through international cooperation
Member of: Canadian Council for International Cooperation; South Asia Partnership
Finances: *Annual Operating Budget:* $500,000-$1.5 Million; *Funding Sources:* Government; Donations; Foundations
Staff Member(s): 7; 40 volunteer(s)
Membership: 5,000 supporters; *Fees:* Donation
Activities: Providing grants to women working for change in their communities; Financially supporting progressive projects & initiatives; *Awareness Events:* International Women's Day, March 8; *Speaker Service:* Yes; *Library:* Resource Clearing Centre; Open to public by appointment
Chief Officer(s):
Jessica Tomlin, Executive Director, 613-761-3695

Mathematics of Information Technology & Complex Systems (MITACS)
Technology Enterprise Facility, University of British Columbia, #301, 6190 Agronomy Rd., Vancouver BC V6T 1Z3
Tel: 604-822-9189; *Fax:* 604-822-3689
mitacs@mitacs.ca
www.mitacs.math.ca
www.linkedin.com/company/mitacs
www.facebook.com/MITACS
twitter.com/DiscoverMITACS
Also Known As: MITACS Inc.
Overview: A medium-sized national organization
Mission: MITACS leads Canada's effort in the generation, application and commercialization of new mathematical tools and methodologies within a world-class research program. The network initiates and fosters linkages with industrial, governmental, and not-for-profit organizations that require mathematical technologies to deal with problems of strategic importance to Canada. MITACS is driving the recruiting, training, and placement of a new generation of highly mathematically skilled personnel that is vital to Canada's future social and economic wellbeing. Offices in Vancouver, Toronto, Montréal, St. John's & Fredericton.
Member of: Networks of Centres of Excellence
Chief Officer(s):
Arvind Gupta, CEO & Scientific Director

Les Matinées de musique de chambre *See* Ladies' Morning Musical Club

Matsqui Sumas Abbotsford Museum Society
2313 Ware St., Abbotsford BC V2S 3C6
Tel: 604-853-0313; *Fax:* 866-373-2771
info@msamuseum.ca
www.msamuseum.ca
Also Known As: MSA Museum
Overview: A small local charitable organization founded in 1969
Mission: To be the memory of the community by preserving & interpreting its history
Member of: Abbotsford Chamber of Commerce; BC Museums Association; Canadian Museum Association
Affiliation(s): Abbotsford Public Art
Staff Member(s): 4
Membership: *Fees:* $5 student; $10 senior; $20 individual; $30 family; $30+ club; $50 corporate
Activities: Halloween House; Easter Egg Hunt; school programs; tours; av production & presentations; *Awareness Events:* International Museums Day, May; *Speaker Service:* Yes
Chief Officer(s):
Dororthy van der Ree, Executive Director

Matsqui-Abbotsford Food Bank *See* Abbotsford Food Bank & Christmas Bureau

Max Bell Foundation
#380, 1201 - 5th St. SW, Calgary AB T2R 0Y6
Tel: 403-215-7310
www.maxbell.org
Overview: A small national charitable organization
Mission: To support Canadian charities whose projects & programs inform policies & practices in the areas of health & wellness, education, & the environment
Activities: Providing financial support to partner organizations; Offering professional development through a Public Policy Training Institute
Chief Officer(s):
Allan Northcott, President
Alida White, Administrator
white@maxbell.org
Publications:
• Max Bell Foundation Annual Report
Type: Yearbook; *Frequency:* Annually

Maxville & District Chamber of Commerce
PO Box 279, Maxville ON K0C 1T0
www.maxvillechamber.ca
www.facebook.com/1375339476044961
Overview: A small local organization founded in 1991
Mission: To promote its members
Member of: Canadian Chamber of Commerce
Membership: 25; *Fees:* $25 individual; $50 business
Chief Officer(s):
Deirdre Hill, President
deirdre@maxvillechamber.ca

Mayne Island Community Chamber of Commerce (MICCC)
PO Box 2, Mayne Island BC V0N 2J0
executiveofficer@mayneislandchamber.ca
www.mayneislandchamber.ca
www.facebook.com/mayneislandcommunitychamberofcommerce
Overview: A small local organization
Mission: To promote & support local businesses
Membership: 60; *Fees:* $5 community; $60 business
Chief Officer(s):
Toby Snelgrove, Chair
Lauren Underhill, Executive Officer

Maytree Foundation
#1600, 77 Bloor St. West, Toronto ON M5S 1M2
Tel: 416-944-2627
info@maytree.com
www.maytree.com
www.linkedin.com/company/maytree-foundation
www.facebook.com/Maytree.Canada
twitter.com/maytree_canada
www.youtube.com/user/MaytreeToronto
Overview: A medium-sized national charitable organization founded in 1982
Mission: To address the systemic problems that drive poverty; To develop & advance solutions to poverty; To protect the economic & social rights of all persons in Canada
Activities: Developing programs & initiatives aimed at enhancing knowledge & strengthening leadership, including CivicsXchange, Five Good Ideas, & Maytree Policy School
Chief Officer(s):
Elizabeth McIsaac, President

Mazda Sportscar Owners Club (MSOC)
3327 Charmaine Heights, Mississauga ON L5A 3C2
Tel: 416-625-1532
thelimit@rogers.com
www.wiredmotorsports.com/pitl
Previous Name: RX-7 Club of Toronto
Overview: A small provincial organization
Mission: To provide a car club for all Mazda sportscar owners; officially recognized by Mazda Canada Inc.
Affiliation(s): Canadian Automobile Sportscar Club
Finances: *Annual Operating Budget:* Less than $50,000; *Funding Sources:* Advertising; membership fees
8 volunteer(s)
Membership: 50; *Fees:* $40
Activities: Caravans; autoslalom racing; "Push it to the Limit" performance driving competitions
Chief Officer(s):
Darryl Dimitroff, President

MB Mission (MBMSI) / Mennonite Brethren Mission & Service International
International & Western Canada (BC), #300, 32040 Downes Rd., Abbotsford BC V4X 1X5
Tel: 604-859-6267; *Fax:* 604-859-6422
Toll-Free: 866-964-7627
mbmission@mbmission.org
www.mbmission.org
www.facebook.com/mbmission
twitter.com/MBMission
www.youtube.com/MBMissionVideos
Also Known As: Board of Missions & Services of the Mennonite Brethren Churches of North America
Previous Name: MBMS International
Overview: A medium-sized local charitable organization founded in 1900 overseen by Canadian Conference of Mennonite Brethren Churches
Mission: To make disciples & plant churches globally through church planting & envangelism, discipleship & leadership training & social ministry
Member of: Evangelical Fellowship of Mission Agencies
Finances: *Funding Sources:* Voluntary contributions; grants
Activities: Cross-cultural mission agency of Mennonite Brethren churches in Canada & the US; *Internships:* Yes; *Speaker Service:* Yes
Chief Officer(s):
Randy Friesen, General Director
randyf@mbmission.org
Central Canada
1310 Taylor Ave., Winnipeg MB R3M 3Z6
Tel: 204-415-0670; *Fax:* 204-654-1865
Toll-Free: 888-866-6267
winnipeg@mbmission.org
Eastern Canada
#208, 50 Kent Ave., Kitchener ON N2G 3R1
Tel: 519-886-4378
Toll-Free: 888-866-6267
waterloo@mbmission.org

MBMS International *See* MB Mission

MBTelehealth Network
John Buhler Research Centre, #772, 715 McDermot Ave., Winnipeg MB R3E 3P4
Tel: 204-272-3063; *Fax:* 204-975-7787
Toll-Free: 866-667-9891
www.mbtelehealth.ca
Overview: A small provincial organization
Mission: To promote the use of information technology to link people to health care expertise at a distance
Finances: *Funding Sources:* Provincial Government
Staff Member(s): 28
Chief Officer(s):
Liz Loewen, Director, Coordination of Care

McBride & District Chamber of Commerce
PO Box 2, McBride BC V0J 2E0
Tel: 250-569-3366; *Fax:* 250-569-3276
Toll-Free: 866-569-3366
www.mcbridechamber.ca
www.facebook.com/867154639975109
twitter.com/McBrideChamber
Overview: A small local organization
Mission: To protect the interests of local businesses; To promote industry & tourism in the area
Member of: BC Chamber of Commerce
Finances: *Annual Operating Budget:* Less than $50,000
Membership: 50+
Chief Officer(s):
Brenda Molendyk, Chair

McCord Museum of Canadian History / Musée McCord d'histoire canadienne
690, rue Sherbrooke ouest, Montréal QC H3A 1E9
Tel: 514-398-7100
info@mccord.mcgill.ca
www.mccord-museum.qc.ca
www.facebook.com/museemccord
twitter.com/MuseeMcCord
www.youtube.com/user/MuseeMcCordMuseum
Also Known As: The McCord
Overview: A small local charitable organization founded in 1921
Mission: To preserve, study, diffuse & appreciate Canadian history; to make available to the general public & specialized researchers collections of artifacts & documents which record all facets of Canadian history, with special focus on the history of Montréal & Québec.
Member of: Canadian Museums Association; Société des directeurs des musées montréalais
Affiliation(s): Société des musées québécois
Finances: *Annual Operating Budget:* Greater than $5 Million; *Funding Sources:* National government
Staff Member(s): 57
Membership: *Committees:* Ball; Wine & Food; Development; Marketing & Communications; Sugar Ball
Activities: Permanent & temporary exhibitions; educational, cultural & native programs; WEB exhibitions; research databases & pedagogical resources; hall rental service; bookstore & giftshop café; annual conference; *Internships:* Yes *Library:* Archive & Documentation Centre; by appointment
Chief Officer(s):
Suzanne Sauvage, President & CEO
Cynthia Cooper, Head, Collections & Research
Pascale Grignon, Director, Marketing & Communications

McCreary Centre Society (MCS)
3552 Hastings St. East, Vancouver BC V5K 2A7
Tel: 604-291-1996; *Fax:* 604-291-7308
mccreary@mcs.bc.ca
www.mcs.bc.ca
Previous Name: Friends of the McCreary Centre Society
Overview: A small local charitable organization founded in 1977
Mission: To raise awareness & understanding of youth health & related issues; To address the health needs of young people through the development of projects & initiatives
Member of: Canadian Health Network
Finances: *Annual Operating Budget:* $250,000-$500,000; *Funding Sources:* Membership fees; donations; grants; contracts
Staff Member(s): 6; 25 volunteer(s)
Membership: 48; *Fees:* $20; *Member Profile:* Open
Activities: Community-based research; Education; Youth participation projects; *Library:* ERC; by appointment
Chief Officer(s):
Annie Smith, Executive Director

McGill Centre for Medicine, Ethics & Law
McGill University, 3690, rue Peel, Montréal QC H3A 1W9
Tel: 514-398-7400; *Fax:* 514-398-4668
Overview: A small national organization founded in 1986
Mission: To undertake & promote research across the fields of health law & bioethics
Chief Officer(s):
Margaret Somerville, Founding Director
margaret.somerville@mcgill.ca

McGill Chamber Orchestra / Orchestre de chambre McGill
5459, av Earnscliffe, Montréal QC H3X 2P8
Tel: 514-487-5190; *Fax:* 514-487-7390
info@ocm-mco.org
www.ocm-mco.org
www.facebook.com/ocm.mco.montreal
twitter.com/ocm_mco
Overview: A small local charitable organization founded in 1939
Member of: Association of Canadian Orchestras
Staff Member(s): 7
Chief Officer(s):
Boris Brott, Artistic Director
Marc-Antione d'Aragon, Executive Director
directeurgeneral@ocm-mco.org

McGill Institute for the Study of Canada (MISC) / L'Institut d'études canadiennes de McGill
3463, rue Peel, Montréal QC H3A 1W7
Tel: 514-398-8346; *Fax:* 514-398-7336
misc.iecm@mcgill.ca
www.mcgill.ca/misc
www.facebook.com/150347341735712
twitter.com/MISCCAN
Overview: A small national charitable organization founded in 1994
Mission: To promote a better understanding of Canada through the study & appreciation of our heritage; to provide new understanding about our social, political & economic future; to identify & explore the benefits that a pluralistic society offers; to breathe new life into the field of Canadian studies
Member of: Association for Canadian Studies
Finances: *Funding Sources:* Charles & Andrea Bronfman Foundation; McGill University; Seagram Co. Ltd.
Staff Member(s): 19
Activities: Seminars, conferences & publications on a wide range of issues; Interdisciplinary courses in Canadian studies at McGill University; Graduate fellowships; *Library:* MISC Reading Room; Open to public by appointment
Chief Officer(s):
Will Straw, Director

McGill University Health Centre Foundation
#900, 2155, rue Guy, Montréal QC H3H 2R9
Tel: 514-931-5656; *Fax:* 514-931-5696
www.muhcfoundation.com
Also Known As: MUHC Foundation
Overview: A small local charitable organization
Mission: To raise money on behalf of the McGill University Health Centre in order to fund research & improve patient care
Finances: *Funding Sources:* Donations
Staff Member(s): 7
Chief Officer(s):
Julie Quenneville, President
julie.quenneville@muhc.mcgill.ca
Lorraine Balleine, Director, Finance & Administration
lorraine.balleine@muhc.mcgill.ca

McGill University Non Academic Certified Association (MUNACA) / Association accréditée du personnel non enseignant de l'université McGill
3483, rue Peel, Montréal QC H3A 1W7
Tel: 514-398-6565; *Fax:* 514-398-6892
reception@munaca.com
www.munaca.com
www.facebook.com/McGillStrike
Overview: A small local organization founded in 1994
Membership: *Member Profile:* Technical, clerical & library assistants; *Committees:* Communications; Health & Safety; Social Justice
Chief Officer(s):
Kevin Whittaker, President
president@munaca.com

McGill University Sexual Identity Centre *Voir* Centre d'orientation sexuelle de l'université McGill

McGregor Model Forest
PO Box 2640, Prince George BC V2N 4T5
Tel: 250-612-5840; *Fax:* 250-612-5848
Overview: A small local organization
Member of: Canadian Model Forest Network
Chief Officer(s):
Al Gorley, President
Dan Adamson, General Manager
dan.adamson@mcgregor.bc.ca

McIlwraith Field Naturalists
PO Box 24008, London ON N6H 5C4
Tel: 519-457-4593
info@mcilwraith.ca
www.mcilwraith.ca
Overview: A small local organization founded in 1890
Mission: To promote the enjoyment of nature through environmental appreciation & conservation; to encourage wise use & conservation of natural resources; to promote environmental protection
Affiliation(s): Canadian Nature Federation; Federation of Ontario Naturalists
Finances: *Annual Operating Budget:* $50,000-$100,000
Membership: 5 institutional + 400 individual; *Fees:* $30 individual; $10 student; $50 contributing; $100 sustaining; *Member Profile:* Interest in natural world; *Committees:* Conservation; Education; Birding; Junior Naturalists
Activities: Field trips; tree & wild flower plantings; nature reserve; life science inventories; *Speaker Service:* Yes

The McLean Foundation
#1008, 2 St. Clair Ave. West, Toronto ON M4V 1L5
Tel: 416-964-6802; *Fax:* 416-964-2804
info@mcleanfoundation.ca
mcleanfoundation.ca
Overview: A small national charitable organization founded in 1945
Mission: To provide grants to registered charitable organizations in Canada
Finances: *Annual Operating Budget:* $500,000-$1.5 Million
Staff Member(s): 2
Chief Officer(s):
Paul McLean, President
Ev McTaggart, Secretary

McLennan Chamber of Commerce
PO Box 90, McLennan AB T0H 2L0
Tel: 780-324-3300
mclennanchamber@serbernet.com
mclennan.ca/town-a-government/businesses/chamber-of-commerce
Overview: A small local organization
Mission: To serve as the voice of the community's businesses
Chief Officer(s):
Louis Gagne, President

McMan Youth, Family & Community Services Association
11016 - 127 St., Edmonton AB T5M 0T2
Tel: 780-482-4461; *Fax:* 780-409-9419
mcman@mcman.ca
www.mcman.ca
Also Known As: McMan Community Services
Overview: A medium-sized local charitable organization founded in 1975
Mission: To help individuals & families across Alberta develop the skills & supports to function effectively as members of their communities; to exercise advocacy & leadership in the community
Affiliation(s): Alberta Association of Services for Children & Families; Alberta Association of Rehabilitation Centres
Finances: *Annual Operating Budget:* Greater than $5 Million; *Funding Sources:* Provincial Government
Staff Member(s): 800; 100 volunteer(s)
Membership: 1-99; *Fees:* $10 individual; *Committees:* Fund Development; Edmonton & North
Activities: *Library:* McMan Library Services
Chief Officer(s):
Mikk Peek, President

Calgary
#1, 4004 - 19 St. NW, Calgary AB T2L 2B6
Tel: 403-508-6259; *Fax:* 403-508-7757
Calgary@mcman.ca
www.mcmancalgary.ca
www.facebook.com/McManofCalgary
twitter.com/McManCalgary

Canadian Associations / McMaster University Faculty Association (MUFA) / Association des professeurs de l'Université McMaster

Chief Officer(s):
Carolyn Koltutsky, President
Soraya Saliba, Executive Director
Laura Foster, Office Administrator
laura.foster@mcman.ca
Central Alberta
#121, 4804 - 50 St., Innisfail AB T4G 1C2
Tel: 403-227-5580; *Fax:* 403-227-5541
central@mcman.ca
www.mcmancentral.ca
www.facebook.com/mcmancentral
www.twitter.com/mcmancentral
Chief Officer(s):
Pat Johnson, President
Sherri McAllister, Executive Director
sherri.mcallister@mcman.ca
Southern Alberta
#4, 941 South Railway St. SE, Medicine Hat AB T1A 2W3
Tel: 403-527-1588; *Fax:* 403-526-8249
www.mcmansouth.ca
www.facebook.com/McManMedicineHat
Chief Officer(s):
Tom Coulter, President
Chris Christie, Executive Director
chris.christie@mcman.ca

McMaster Symphony Orchestra; Greater Hamilton Symphony Association *See* Symphony on the Bay

McMaster University Faculty Association (MUFA) / Association des professeurs de l'Université McMaster
McMaster University, Hamilton Hall, #103A, 1280 Main St. West., Hamilton ON L8S 4K1
Tel: 905-525-9140; *Fax:* 905-522-8320
mufa@mcmaster.ca
www.mcmaster.ca/mufa
Overview: A small local organization founded in 1951
Mission: To protect the interests & negotiate terms & conditions of employment for the faculty members & librarians of McMaster University
Member of: Ontario Confederation of University Faculty Associations; Canadian Association of University Teachers
Finances: *Annual Operating Budget:* $250,000-$500,000; *Funding Sources:* Membership fees
Staff Member(s): 2; 13 volunteer(s)
Membership: 900; *Committees:* Academic Affairs; Grievance; Human Rights; Library; Membership; Pension; Public Relations; Renumerations; Tenure
Chief Officer(s):
Phyllis DeRosa Koetting, Executive Director
Martin Dooley, President
dooley@mcmaster.ca
Awards:
• MUFA Service Award

McMaster University Retirees Association (MURA)
c/o McMaster University, Gilmour Hall, #B108, 1280 Main St. West, Hamilton ON L8S 4L8
Tel: 905-525-9140
mura@mcmaster.ca
www.mcmaster-retirees.ca
Overview: A medium-sized local organization founded in 1984
Mission: To contribute in as many ways as possible to the welfare, prestige & excellence of the University; To encourage & promote a spirit of fraternity & unity among the members of the Association; To provide means for continuing the associations which retirees enjoyed as employees of the University
Membership: 1685; *Member Profile:* Retired McMaster University faculty & staff

McMaster University Staff Association (MUSA)
Gilmour Hall, #B111, 1280 Main St. West, Hamilton ON L8S 4L8
Tel: 905-525-9140; *Fax:* 905-524-3111
caw555@cawlocal555.ca
www.cawlocal555.ca
Also Known As: CAW Local 555
Overview: A small local organization
Membership: 2,220+; *Member Profile:* Support staff, regional medical associates, parking & transit services staff & special constables working at McMaster University; *Committees:* Bylaws; Community Services; Elections; Education; Environment; Health & Safety; Human Rights; Recreation; Social Justice; Union in Politics; Women's; WSIB
Chief Officer(s):
Maggie Wilson, Administrative Assistant

Meadow Lake & District Chamber of Commerce
PO Box 847, Meadow Lake SK S9X 1Y6
Tel: 306-236-4061; *Fax:* 306-236-4031
Overview: A small local organization
Member of: Saskatchewan Chamber of Commerce
Affiliation(s): Northwest Regional Economic Development Authority
Finances: *Annual Operating Budget:* Less than $50,000; *Funding Sources:* Membership dues; local government
Staff Member(s): 1; 30 volunteer(s)
Membership: 100; *Fees:* $25-$160

Meadow Lake Tribal Council (MLTC)
8003 Flying Dust Reserve, Meadow Lake SK S9X 1T8
Tel: 306-236-5654; *Fax:* 306-236-6301
receptionist@mltc.net
www.mltc.ca
Overview: A small local organization founded in 1981
Mission: To create & improve programs & services that meet the needs of the member First Nations
Membership: 9 First Nations; *Member Profile:* Birch Narrows Dene Nation; Buffalo River Dene Nation; Canoe Lake Cree Nation; Clearwater River Dene Nation; English River First Nation; Flying Dust First Nation; Makwa Sahgaiehcan First Nation; Ministikwan Lake Cree Nation; Waterhen Lake First Nation
Activities: Economic development programs
Chief Officer(s):
Eric Sylvestre, Tribal Chief
Larry Iron, Vice-Chief

Meaford Chamber of Commerce (MDCC)
16 Trowbridge St. West, Meaford ON N4L 1N2
Tel: 519-538-1640; *Fax:* 519-538-5493
Toll-Free: 888-632-3673
info@meafordchamber.ca
www.meafordchamber.ca
Previous Name: Meaford Community Partners
Overview: A small local organization founded in 1857
Mission: To be the voice of businesses in Meaford & the body through which all the members work in order to achieve their goals
Member of: Ontario Chamber of Commerce; Canadian Chamber of Commerce
Finances: *Funding Sources:* Municipal; Membership dues; Grants
Staff Member(s): 2
Membership: 200+; *Fees:* Schedule available
Activities: Organizing events such as information nights, After 5's, business seminars, Community Awards & community Christmas party
Chief Officer(s):
Dan White, President

Meaford Community Partners *See* Meaford Chamber of Commerce

Meals on Wheels Ontario Inc. *See* Ontario Community Support Association

Meanskinisht Village Historical Association
PO Box 155, Kitwanga BC V0J 2A0
Tel: 250-849-5732
Overview: A small local organization founded in 1979
6 volunteer(s)
Membership: *Member Profile:* Descendents of original inhabitants
Activities: Operates Cedarvale Museum; looks after graveyard of original inhabitants & descendants
Chief Officer(s):
Mary Dalen, Contact

Meat Packers Council of Canada *See* Canadian Meat Council

Mechanical Contractors Association of Alberta (MCA AB)
#204, 2725 - 12 St. NE, Calgary AB T2E 7J2
Tel: 403-250-7237; *Fax:* 403-291-0551
Toll-Free: 800-251-0620
info@mca-ab.com
www.mca-ab.com
Overview: A small provincial organization founded in 1900 overseen by Mechanical Contractors Association of Canada
Mission: To promote plumbing & mechanical contractors; To provide educational programs to foster improved management & productivity in mechanical contracting; To represent mechanical contractors with their various publics - governments, design authorities, labour; To foster professional advancement & profitability of the plumbing, heating & mechanical contracting industry through its member services; To advocate on behalf of members
Member of: Mechanical Contractors Association of Canada; Alberta Construction Association
Finances: *Annual Operating Budget:* $500,000-$1.5 Million; *Funding Sources:* Membership dues; Non-dues revenue
Staff Member(s): 3; 16 volunteer(s)
Membership: 300; *Fees:* $750-$3,750; *Member Profile:* Contractors & suppliers of the mechanical, heating, & plumbing industry
Activities: Offering education, seminars, & certification; Organizing issue-based member meetings; Providing social networking opportunities
Chief Officer(s):
Russ Evans, Executive Director
russ@mca-ab.com
Vicky Derkson, Member Services
vicky@mca-ab.com
Publications:
• MCA [Mechanical Contractors Association] Connections
Type: Newsletter; *Editor:* Russ Evans

Mechanical Contractors Association of British Columbia (MCABC)
#223, 3989 Henning Dr., Burnaby BC V5C 6N5
Tel: 604-205-5058; *Fax:* 604-205-5075
Toll-Free: 800-663-8473
www.mcabc.org
www.linkedin.com/company/mechanical-contractors-association-of-bc
twitter.com/mcabc
www.flickr.com/photos/mcabc
Previous Name: Canadian Plumbing & Mechanical Contractors Association, BC Branch
Overview: A medium-sized provincial organization founded in 1905 overseen by Mechanical Contractors Association of Canada
Mission: To encourage, support & promote the advancement of the mechanical contracting industry; to provide leadership, assistance & training to members.
Staff Member(s): 6
Membership: 192; *Member Profile:* Licensed contractors in the mechanical trades; suppliers; manufacturers; distributors; servce providers
Activities: *Speaker Service:* Yes; *Library*
Chief Officer(s):
Dana Taylor, Executive Vice President
danat@mcabc.org

Mechanical Contractors Association of Canada (MCAC) / Association des entrepreneurs en mécanique du Canada
#701, 280 Albert St., Ottawa ON K1P 5G8
Tel: 613-232-0492
mcac@mcac.ca
www.mcac.ca
www.linkedin.com/groups/4893930
www.facebook.com/MechanicalContractorsAssociationofCanada
twitter.com/MecConCA
Overview: A medium-sized national organization founded in 1895
Mission: To promote plumbing & mechanical contractors; to provide educational programs to foster improved management & productivity in mechanical contracting; to represent mechanical contractors to their various publics - governments, design authorities, labour.
Member of: National Trade Contractors Coalition of Canada
Affiliation(s): Council of Construction Trade Associations
Membership: 1,000 companies
Chief Officer(s):
Richard McKeagan, President
rick@mcac.ca
Awards:
• Life Member Award
• Lloyd MacLean Memorial Award
• Gary Greig Memorial Award
• 100th Anniversary Award
• Doug Crawford Memorial Award
Meetings/Conferences:
• Mechanical Contractors Association of Canada 77th Annual National Conference, September, 2018, Whistler, BC
Scope: National
Publications:
• Information Guide [a publication of the Mechanical Contractors Association of Canada]

Type: Guide
Profile: Lists hundreds of manuals, books, videos & more
• Just the Fax [a publication of the Mechanical Contractors Association of Canada]
Type: E-Newsletter; *Frequency:* weekly
• National Bulletin [a publication of the Mechanical Contractors Association of Canada]
Type: Newsletter; *Frequency:* bi-annual

Mechanical Contractors Association of Manitoba (MCAM)
#320, 830 King Edward St., Winnipeg MB R3H 0P4
Tel: 204-774-2404; *Fax:* 204-772-0233
mcam@mts.net
www.mca-mb.com
Overview: A medium-sized provincial organization founded in 1970 overseen by Mechanical Contractors Association of Canada
Mission: To continually improve mechanical industry standards while providing a high level of value performance & customer service for our members
Staff Member(s): 2
Membership: 77; *Member Profile:* Plumbing & heating contractors; *Committees:* Associate Members; Education; Finance; Government Liaison; Long Range Planning; MCAM Golf Tournament; Mechanical Service Contractors; Pipe Trades Pre-Employment Advisory; Social; Membership
Chief Officer(s):
Betty McInerney, Executive Director
bmcinerney@mts.net

Mechanical Contractors Association of New Brunswick (MNECA)
c/o Moncton Northeast Construction Association, 297 Collishaw St., Moncton NB E1C 9R2
Tel: 506-857-4038; *Fax:* 506-857-8861
info@@mneca.ca
www.mneca.ca
Also Known As: MCA New Brunswick Inc.
Previous Name: Mechanical Contractors Association of New Brunswick; Plumbing & Mechanical Contractors Association of New Brunswick
Overview: A small provincial organization founded in 1976 overseen by Mechanical Contractors Association of Canada
Mission: To provide leadership & service to members; To act on behalf of members in labour relations matters, including collective bargaining; To advance & develop the industry, primarily in New Brunswick; To endeavour to improve legislation affecting the industry; To promote sound labour relations
Affiliation(s): Canadian Construction Association
Finances: *Annual Operating Budget:* $100,000-$250,000; *Funding Sources:* Membership fees
Staff Member(s): 1
Membership: 28; *Fees:* $1,058 contractor/sub-contractor/supplier; $575 associate; *Member Profile:* Open to individual firms engaged in contracting trades
Chief Officer(s):
Nadine Fullarton, President, 506-857-4128
nfullarton@mneca.ca

Mechanical Contractors Association of New Brunswick; Plumbing & Mechanical Contractors Association of New Brunswick *See* Mechanical Contractors Association of New Brunswick

Mechanical Contractors Association of Newfoundland & Labrador
PO Box 1674, 240 Waterford Bridge Rd., St. John's NL A1C 5P5
Tel: 709-745-0225; *Fax:* 709-368-3502
ddawe@cahill.ca
Also Known As: MCA Newfoundland & Labrador
Overview: A small provincial organization overseen by Mechanical Contractors Association of Canada
Chief Officer(s):
David Dawe, Executive Director

Mechanical Contractors Association of Nova Scotia (CANS)
#103, 134 Eileen Shabbs Ave., Dartmouth NS B3B 0A9
Tel: 902-468-2267; *Fax:* 902-468-2470
dwilliams@cans.ns.ca
www.cans.ns.ca
Also Known As: Mechanical Contractors Section of The Construction Association of Nova Scotia
Overview: A small provincial organization overseen by Mechanical Contractors Association of Canada
Mission: To be the leading voice of the construction industry in Nova Scotia
Membership: *Fees:* $1,620 full; $735 associate
Chief Officer(s):
Duncan Williams, President, 902-468-2267 Ext. 700
dwilliams@cans.ns.ca

Mechanical Contractors Association of Ontario (MCAO)
#103, 10 Director Ct., Woodbridge ON L4L 7E8
Tel: 905-856-0342; *Fax:* 905-856-0385
mcao@mcao.org
www.mcao.org
Also Known As: MCA Ontario
Overview: A medium-sized provincial organization overseen by Mechanical Contractors Association of Canada
Mission: To provide leadership & assistance to members of the mechanical contracting industry in Ontario
Chief Officer(s):
Steve Coleman, Executive Vice-President
steve@mcao.org

Mechanical Contractors Association of Ottawa / Association des entrepreneurs en mécanique d'Ottawa
#401, 2039 Robertson Rd., Ottawa ON K2H 8R2
Tel: 613-237-1491; *Fax:* 613-567-3177
info@mcaottawa.com
www.mcaottawa.ca
Overview: A small local organization founded in 1966
Mission: To advance the unionized trades in the mechanical contracting industry; To improve working conditions & safety laws for the mechanical trades; To promote improved relations between employer & employee
Membership: *Member Profile:* Trade contractors (sheet metal, pipefitting & plumbing); Manufacturers, suppliers, & dealers
Activities: Providing information & education programs to members; Conducting trade promotion activities; Upholding a code of ethics
Chief Officer(s):
Mary Gauthier, General Manager
Publications:
• Safety Matters
Type: Newsletter

Mechanical Contractors Association of Saskatchewan Inc. (MCAS)
Heritage Business Park, #105, 2750 Faithfull Ave., Saskatoon SK S7K 6M6
Tel: 306-664-2154; *Fax:* 306-653-7233
admin@mca-sask.com
www.mca-sask.com
Overview: A small provincial organization founded in 1919 overseen by Mechanical Contractors Association of Canada
Mission: To represent plumbing & heating contractors in relation to the construction industry, legislative departments of municipal & provincial government & other industry-related bodies.
Affiliation(s): Mechanical Contractors Association of Canada
Finances: *Funding Sources:* Membership fees
Staff Member(s): 3
Membership: 251; *Fees:* $450; *Member Profile:* Mechanical contractors
Chief Officer(s):
Ryan Tynning, President, 306-778-2830, Fax: 306-778-2833
Carolyn Bagnell, Executive Director
carolyn@mca-sask.com

Mechanical Service Contractors of Canada (MSCC)
#701, 280 Albert St., Ottawa ON K1P 5G8
Tel: 613-232-0017; *Fax:* 613-235-2793
Toll-Free: 877-622-2668
daryl@mcac.ca
www.servicecontractor.ca
Overview: A medium-sized national organization overseen by Mechanical Contractors Association of Canada
Mission: To be dedicated to mechanical service, repair & retrofit contractors
Chief Officer(s):
Daryl Sharkey, Chief Operating Officer

Mechanical-Electrical Division of The Canadian Institute of Mining, Metallurgy & Petroleum *See* Maintenance, Engineering & Reliability (MER) Society

Médecins francophones du Canada
8355, boul Saint-Laurent, Montréal QC H2P 2Z6
Tél: 514-388-2228; *Téléc:* 514-388-5335
Ligne sans frais: 800-387-2228
www.medecinsfrancophones.ca
Nom précédent: Association des médecins de langue française du Canada
Aperçu: *Dimension:* moyenne; *Envergure:* nationale; fondée en 1902
Membre(s) du bureau directeur:
Marie-Françoise Mégie, Présidente
Céline Monette, Directrice générale

Médecins pour la survie mondiale (Canada) *See* Physicians for Global Survival (Canada)

Médecins pour un Canada sans fumée *See* Physicians for a Smoke-Free Canada

Médecins sans frontières Canada *See* Doctors without Borders Canada

Media Access Canada (MAC)
2 Bellwoods Park, Toronto ON M6J 1S4
Tel: 239-529-8785
mac@mediac.ca
www.mediac.ca
Overview: A medium-sized national organization
Mission: To improve accessibility in broadcasting & telecommunications; To drive the growth of an independent accessible content production industry; To commission & produce research on accessibility in broadcasting & telecommunications
Activities: Advocating for better accessibility in the broadcasting industry
Chief Officer(s):
Beverley Milligan, CEO

Media Awareness Network *See* Media Smarts

Media Smarts
#120, 950 Gladstone Ave., Ottawa ON K1Y 3E6
Tel: 613-224-7721; *Fax:* 613-761-9024
Toll-Free: 800-896-3342
info@mediasmarts.ca
mediasmarts.ca
www.facebook.com/MediaSmarts
twitter.com/MediaSmarts
Previous Name: Media Awareness Network
Overview: A small national organization
Mission: To ensure children and youth possess the necessary critical thinking skills and tools to understand and safely and actively engage with media, and to be the leading Canadian provider of media education resources and awareness programs for educators, parents, children and youth.
Chief Officer(s):
Cathy Wing, Co-Executive Director
Jane Tallim, Co-Executive Director

Mediate BC Society
#177, 800 Hornby St., Vancouver BC V6Z 2C5
Tel: 604-684-1300; *Fax:* 604-684-1306
Toll-Free: 877-656-1300
info@mediatebc.com
www.mediatebc.com
Merged from: D.R. Innovation Society; B.C. Mediator Roster Society
Overview: A small provincial organization founded in 2010
Mission: To provide practical, accessible & affordable mediation & dispute resolution choices
Affiliation(s): Family Mediation Canada
Finances: *Funding Sources:* Ministry of Attorney General; Law Foundation of British Columbia; Ministry of Children & Family Development; Training fees; Membership fees
Activities: Training; Mediator roster
Chief Officer(s):
Monique Steensma, CEO, 604-684-1300 Ext. 200
monique.steensma@mediatebc.com
Melanie Carfantan-Mclachlan, Executive Director, 604-684-1300 Ext. 105
melanie.mclachlan@mediatebc.com

Médiation Familiale Canada *See* Family Mediation Canada

Mediation Saskatchewan *See* Conflict Resolution Saskatchewan

Mediation Yukon Society
PO Box 31102, Whitehorse YT Y1A 5P7
mediationyukon@gmail.com
mediationyukon.com

Overview: A small provincial organization
Mission: To encourage alternate methods for dispute resolution
Affiliation(s): Family Mediation Canada
Chief Officer(s):
Christiane Boisjoly, Mediator, 867-668-6794; Fax: 867-668-6795
boisjoly@northwestel.net

Medical Council of Canada (MCC) / Le Conseil médical du Canada (CMC)
1021 Thomas Spratt Pl., Ottawa ON K1G 5L5
Tel: 613-521-6012; Fax: 613-248-5234
service@mcc.ca
www.mcc.ca
www.linkedin.com/company/medical-council-of-canada
www.facebook.com/MedicalCouncilOfCanada
twitter.com/MedCouncilCan
www.youtube.com/user/medicalcouncilcanada
Overview: A large national licensing organization founded in 1912
Mission: To establish & promote a qualification in medicine, known as the Licentiate of the Medical Council of Canada, such that the holders thereof are acceptable to medical licensing authorities for the issuance of a licence to practise medicine
Finances: *Funding Sources:* Examination & related service fees
Membership: *Committees:* Appeals; Finance; Legislation; Nominating; Research & Development; Selection
Chief Officer(s):
Ian Bowmer, Executive Director
Awards:
- Outstanding Achievement Award
- Louis Levasseur Award
- Medical Council of Canada Grants
Eligibility: To interested faculty members, staff members or graduate students of Canadian medical faculties; *Amount:* Up to $37,500
Meetings/Conferences:
- Medical Council of Canada 2018 Annual Meeting, 2018
Scope: National
Publications:
- ECHO [a publication of the Medical Council of Canada]
Type: Newsletter; *Frequency:* Biannually

Medical Council of Prince Edward Island *See* College of Physicians & Surgeons of Prince Edward Island

Medical Device Reprocessing Association of Ontario (MDRAO)
PO Box 225, Timmins ON P4N 7C9
Tel: 705-268-4763; Fax: 705-268-4421
mdrao@ntl.sympatico.ca
www.mdrao.ca
www.linkedin.com/groups/5036123
www.facebook.com/CSAO-237386583016742
twitter.com/CSAOCanada
Previous Name: Central Service Association of Ontario
Overview: A medium-sized provincial organization founded in 1963
Mission: To promote standards of practice & education in the medical device reprocessing industry; To provide opportunities for all members
Finances: *Funding Sources:* Membership dues & services
Membership: *Fees:* $30 technician & associate; $40 management; *Member Profile:* Those involved in instrument/device reprocessing in a health care setting; *Committees:* Executive
Chief Officer(s):
Louis Konstant, President
Rohan Jagasar, Vice-President
Stephenie Naugler, Director, Communications

Medical Group Management Association of Canada
102 Allen Cove, Hinton AB T7V 2A6
Tel: 780-865-7956
info@mgmac.org
www.mgmac.org
Overview: A small national organization
Mission: To provide support for clinic managers across Canada
Chief Officer(s):
Tom Malone, President
Karen Chezick, Secretary

Medical Laboratory Science Association of Yukon (MLSAY)
c/o Laboratory, Whitehorse General Hospital, 5 Hospital Rd., Whitehorse YT Y1A 3H7
Overview: A medium-sized provincial organization overseen by Canadian Society for Medical Laboratory Science

Medical Marijuana Association
#2500, 120 Adelaide St. West, Toronto ON M5H 1T1
Toll-Free: 855-420-8222
www.medicinalmarijuanaassociation.com
www.facebook.com/512945362172098
twitter.com/MedMarijuanaA
plus.google.com/+Medicinalmarijuanaassociation
Overview: A large national organization
Mission: To promote & support medical marijuana producers, patients, & doctors by providing information about the benefits of medicinal marijuana
Membership: *Fees:* $9.99/month

Medical Services Association; CU&C Health Services Society *See* Canadian Association of Blue Cross Plans

Medical Society of Nova Scotia *See* Doctors Nova Scotia

Medical Society of Prince Edward Island (MSPEI)
2 Myrtle St., Stratford PE C1B 2W2
Tel: 902-368-7303; Fax: 902-566-3934
www.mspei.org
twitter.com/MSPEI_Docs
Overview: A medium-sized provincial organization founded in 1855 overseen by Canadian Medical Association
Mission: To promote health & improvement of medical services; To prevent disease; To represent members at national bodies & government; To consider all matters concerning the professional welfare of members
Finances: *Funding Sources:* Membership dues
Staff Member(s): 4
Membership: 400 physicians; *Member Profile:* Individuals licensed to practise medicine in PEI; *Committees:* Executive; Medical Society; Finance; Nominating; Human Resources; Continuing Medical Education; Physician Support; Health Care & Promotion; Economics
Activities: *Internships:* Yes; *Library:* by appointment
Chief Officer(s):
Lea Bryden, Chief Executive Officer
lea@mspei.org
Erica Jenkins, Office Coordinator
erica@mspei.org

Medical Women's International Association (MWIA)
7555 Morley Dr., Burnaby BC V5E 3Y2
Tel: 604-522-1960; Fax: 604-522-1960
www.mwia.net
twitter.com/MedWIA
Overview: A small international organization founded in 1919
Mission: To offer medical women the opportunity to meet so as to confer upon questions concerning the health & well-being of humanity; to overcome gender-related differences in health & healthcare between women & men, girls & boys throughout the world; to overcome gender-related inequalities in the medical profession; to promote health for all throughout the world with particular interest in women, health & development
Affiliation(s): Federation of Medical Women of Canada
Finances: *Funding Sources:* Membership dues & donations
Membership: *Member Profile:* Fully-qualified women doctors; *Committees:* Finance; Ethics & Resolution; Scientific & Research; Centennial
Chief Officer(s):
Shelley Ross, Secretary General

Medicine Hat & District Chamber of Commerce
413 - 6th Ave. SE, Medicine Hat AB T1A 2S7
Tel: 403-527-5214; Fax: 403-527-5182
info@medicinehatchamber.com
www.medicinehatchamber.com
www.linkedin.com/company/medicine-hat-and-district-chamber-of-commerce
www.facebook.com/MHChamber
twitter.com/mhdchamber
Overview: A medium-sized local organization founded in 1900
Mission: To promote a healthy business environment
Member of: Canadian Society of Association Executives; National Association of Member Development
Affiliation(s): Alberta Chamber of Commerce; Canadian Chamber of Commerce
Finances: *Annual Operating Budget:* $500,000-$1.5 Million; *Funding Sources:* Trade shows; events
Staff Member(s): 7
Membership: 700+; *Fees:* Schedule available based on number of employees
Activities: Trade shows; tourism; President's Ball; membership networking; speaking series; *Speaker Service:* Yes
Chief Officer(s):
Khrista Vogt, President
Lisa Kowalchuk, Executive Director
Awards:
- Hospitality/Tourism Award
- Business of the Year Award
- Industry of the Year Award
- Citizen of the Year Award
- Keeper of the Gates Award
- Silver Spade Award
- Athlete of the Year Award

Medicine Hat & District Food Bank
532 South Railway St. SE, Medicine Hat AB T1A 2V6
Tel: 403-528-4313; Fax: 403-528-4381
mhfbank@telus.net
www.mhfoodbank.com
www.facebook.com/mhfoodbank
twitter.com/MedHatFoodBank
Overview: A medium-sized local charitable organization overseen by Food Banks Alberta Association
Member of: Food Banks Alberta Association; Food Banks Canada
Chief Officer(s):
Celina Symmonds, Executive Director

Medicine Hat Coin & Stamp Club
c/o Ron Schmidt, #324, 2800 - 13 Ave. SE, Medicine Hat AB T1A 3P9
Tel: 403-526-5158
medhatcsc@live.com
www.mhcasc.ca
Overview: A small local organization
Chief Officer(s):
Ron Schmidt, Secretary

Medicine Hat Fibre Arts Society
c/o Cultural Centre, Medicine Hat College, 299 College Dr. SE, Medicine Hat AB T1A 3Y6
Tel: 403-529-1174
Overview: A small local organization
Affiliation(s): Handweavers, Spinners & Dyers of Alberta
Chief Officer(s):
Sharon Regehr, Vice-President

Medicine Hat Fish & Game Association
PO Box 883, Medicine Hat AB T1A 7G8
Tel: 403-526-9261
mhfga1@gmail.com
www.mhfishandgame.com
Overview: A small local organization founded in 1973
Member of: Alberta Fish & Game Association
Finances: *Annual Operating Budget:* Less than $50,000; *Funding Sources:* Donations; fundraising
14 volunteer(s)
Membership: 250+; *Fees:* $25; *Committees:* Fish; Big Game; Membership; Habitat; Bird; Fundraising; Environment
Activities: Stocking fish; releasing pheasants; planting shelterbelt trees & securing habitat; *Awareness Events:* Sportsmen's Trade Show, Jan.
Chief Officer(s):
Glen Heather, President

Medicine Hat Police Association / Association des policiers de Medicine Hat
884 - 2 St. SE, Medicine Hat AB T1A 8H2
Tel: 403-529-8400
www.mhpoliceassociation.com
twitter.com/medhatpa
Overview: A small local organization
Chief Officer(s):
Brent Secondiak, President

Medicine Hat Real Estate Board Co-operative Ltd.
403 - 4 St. SE, Medicine Hat AB T1A 0K5
Tel: 403-526-2879; Fax: 403-526-0307
www.mhreb.ca
Overview: A small local organization overseen by Alberta Real Estate Association
Member of: Alberta Real Estate Association; The Canadian Real Estate Association
Membership: 140
Chief Officer(s):
Murray Schlenker, President
Randeen Bray, Executive Officer

Medicine Hat Rock & Lapidary Club
826 - 11th St. SE, Medicine Hat AB T1A 1T7

Tel: 403-526-8113
www.afrc.ca/medicinehat.htm
Overview: A small local charitable organization founded in 1989
Member of: Alberta Federation of Rock Clubs; Gem & Mineral Federation of Canada
Finances: *Funding Sources:* Membership fees; Casino revenues
Membership: *Fees:* $20 individual; $25 family or couple
Activities: Workshops & training seminars
Chief Officer(s):
Marilyn Jetyter, President

Medicine Hat Soccer Association
#101, 533 - 2nd St. East, Medicine Hat AB T1A 0C5
Tel: 403-529-6931; *Fax:* 403-526-6590
mhsa@telusplanet.net
www.medicinehatsoccer.com
www.facebook.com/medicinehatsoccer
twitter.com/mhsasoccer
Overview: A small local organization founded in 1971 overseen by Alberta Soccer Association
Member of: Alberta Soccer Association
Membership: 2,700
Chief Officer(s):
Jeff Vangen, President
Heather Bach, Director, Communications

Medicine Hat Society for the Prevention of Cruelty to Animals (MHSPCA)
55 Southwest Dr. SW, Medicine Hat AB T1A 8E8
Tel: 403-526-7722; *Fax:* 403-504-5740
contact@medhatspca.ca
www.medhatspca.com
Also Known As: Medicine Hat SPCA
Overview: A small local charitable organization founded in 1979
Mission: To provide protective care for sick, injured, homeless & unwanted animals; to promote humane attitudes & responsible pet ownership; to promote wildlife conservation
Member of: Canadian Federation of Humane Societies
Affiliation(s): Alberta SPCA
Finances: *Funding Sources:* Bingos; raffles; membership dues; coin banks; dog jog; bequests; donations
Activities: Open house; mall displays; garage sale; dog jogs; Christmas Party for the Animals

Medico-Legal Society of Toronto
#1700, 438 University Ave., Toronto ON M5G 2L9
Tel: 416-523-4469; *Fax:* 416-585-7860
mlst@mlst.ca
www.mlst.ca
www.facebook.com/220520598037210
twitter.com/MLSTExDir
Overview: A small local organization founded in 1950
Mission: To promote the medical & legal professions as well as information involving those subjects.
Membership: *Fees:* $45 student/senior; $260 full; *Committees:* Submissions; Outreach; Membership; Program
Chief Officer(s):
Clare Samworth, Executive Director
Phillipa Samworth, President

Meetings & Conventions Prince Edward Island (MCPEI)
9 Queen St., Charlottetown PE C1A 4A2
Tel: 902-629-1655
Toll-Free: 855-368-3688
info@peimc.com
www.meetingsandconventionspei.com
www.facebook.com/meetinpei
twitter.com/MeetInPEI
www.youtube.com/user/MeetOnPEI;
www.flickr.com/photos/64609093@N05
Previous Name: Prince Edward Island Convention Partnership; Meetings Prince Edward Island; Prince Edward Island Convention Bureau
Overview: A medium-sized provincial organization founded in 1987
Mission: To promote & confirm PEI as the destination for meetings, conferences & special events
Affiliation(s): Canadian Society of Professional Event Planners; Canadian Society of Association Executives; Prince Edward Island Business Women's Association; Tourism Industry Association of Prince Edward Island; Meeting Professionals International; Religious Conference Management Association; Destination Management Association of Canada
Finances: *Funding Sources:* Government funding
Staff Member(s): 10
Membership: *Fees:* Schedule available; *Member Profile:* Meetings & conventions industry
Chief Officer(s):
Michael Matthews, Executive Director
mmatthews@peimc.com
Jo-Ann Thomsen, Director, Business Development, 902-368-2191
jthomsen@peimc.com

Meewasin Valley Authority (MVA)
402 - 3rd Ave. South, Saskatoon SK S7K 3G5
Tel: 306-665-6887; *Fax:* 306-665-6117
meewasin@meewasin.com
www.meewasin.com
www.facebook.com/Meewasin
twitter.com/meewasin
Overview: A small local organization founded in 1979
Mission: To ensure a healthy & vibrant river valley with a balance between human use & conservation by: providing leadership in the management of its resources; promoting understanding, conservation & beneficial use of the valley; undertaking programs & projects in river valley development & conservation for the benefit of present & future generations
Finances: *Funding Sources:* Donations; Government of Saskatchewan; City of Saskatoon; University of Saskatchewan
Staff Member(s): 6
Membership: *Committees:* Development Review; Resource Conservation Advisory; Design Advisory; Education Advisory; Fund Development
Activities: Clean-up Campaign; Stewardship Program; Dragon Boat Races
Chief Officer(s):
Lloyd Isaak, CEO

MEFM Myalgic Encephalomyelitis & Fibromyalgia Society of British Columbia
PO Box 462, 916 West Broadway Ave., Vancouver BC V5Z 1K7
Tel: 604-878-7707
Toll-Free: 888-353-6322
info@mefm.bc.ca
www.mefm.bc.ca
Merged from: British Columbia Fibromyalgia Society; Myalgic Encephalomyelitis Society of British Columbia
Overview: A medium-sized provincial organization
Mission: To provide support to people with (ME) Myalgic Encephalomyelitis, (Chronic Fatique Syndrome) & (FM) Fibromyalgia & their families; to help educate physicians, paramedical professionals, family members & the community at large regarding ME & FM; to promote research aimed at improving treatment & ultimately finding a cure; to help to encourage early diagnosis & effective treatment

Megantic County Historical Society
#701, 6550, rue Sherbrooke ouest, Montréal QC H4R 1N6
Tel: 514-489-8354
Other Communication: Alt Phone: 418-424-3258
Overview: A small local organization founded in 1971
Chief Officer(s):
Sheila Allan, President

Melfort & District Chamber of Commerce
PO Box 2002, 102 Spruce Haven Rd., Melfort SK S0E 1A0
Tel: 306-752-4636; *Fax:* 306-752-9505
melfortchamber@sasktel.net
www.melfortchamber.com
Overview: A small local organization founded in 1907
Mission: To identify & fulfill development needs through communication, implementation of strategies, & promotion, for the growth of the business community
Member of: Saskatchewan Chamber of Commerce; CANAM International Highway Association
Finances: *Annual Operating Budget:* $50,000-$100,000
Staff Member(s): 3; 50 volunteer(s)
Membership: 173; *Fees:* $75-$310
Activities: *Awareness Events:* Light Up Melfort, Nov.; *Rents Mailing List:* Yes
Chief Officer(s):
Warren Salen, President

Melfort Agricultural Society
PO Box 816, Melfort SK S0E 1A0
Tel: 306-752-2240; *Fax:* 306-752-2240
info@melfortex.com
www.melfortex.com
Overview: A small local charitable organization founded in 1906
Mission: To improve agriculture & the quality of life in the community by educating members & the community; to provide a community forum for discussing agricultural issues; to foster community development & community spirit; to help provide markets for Saskatchewan products; to encourage conservation of natural resources, including soil conservation, reforestation, rural & urban beautification
Member of: Saskatchewan Association of Agricultural Societies & Exhibitions; Canadian Association of Fairs & Exhibitions
Finances: *Annual Operating Budget:* $100,000-$250,000; *Funding Sources:* Bingo; flea markets; exhibition; grants
Staff Member(s): 1; 101 volunteer(s)
Membership: 101; *Fees:* $5
Chief Officer(s):
Christy Vodicka, President

Melfort Real Estate Board
PO Box 3157, Melfort SK S0E 1A0
Tel: 306-752-5751; *Fax:* 306-752-5754
Overview: A small local organization overseen by Saskatchewan Real Estate Association
Member of: The Canadian Real Estate Association
Chief Officer(s):
Derwood Dodds, President
derwooddodds@royallepage.ca

Melita & District Chamber of Commerce
PO Box 666, Melita MB R0M 1L0
Tel: 204-522-3278
www.melitamb.ca
Overview: A small local organization founded in 1902
Mission: To promote tourism & trade in the town of Melita
Chief Officer(s):
Darren Stewart, President

Melville & District Agri-Park Association Inc.
PO Box 2678, Melville SK S0A 2P0
Tel: 306-728-5277; *Fax:* 306-728-4544
agripark@sasktel.net
www.melvilleagripark.com
Also Known As: Melville Agri-Park
Overview: A small local organization founded in 1981
Mission: To promote agriculture events in Melville & surrounding district
Member of: Saskatchewan Association of Agricultural Societies & Exhibitions; Canadian Association of Exhibitions; Saskatchewan Horse Federation
Finances: *Annual Operating Budget:* $50,000-$100,000
Staff Member(s): 1; 100 volunteer(s)
Membership: 200 senior/lifetime; *Fees:* $100; *Committees:* 4-H Organization; Horse Show; Showstoppers ATV; Archery Club; Homecrafts; Horse Racing; Rodeo; Cattle; Team Roping; Barrel Racing
Activities: *Internships:* Yes; *Rents Mailing List:* Yes
Chief Officer(s):
Jamie D. McDonald, Manager

Melville & District Chamber of Commerce
PO Box 429, 76 Halifax Ave., Melville SK S0A 2P0
Tel: 306-728-4177
melvillechamber@sasktel.net
www.melvillechamber.com
www.facebook.com/melvillechamberofcommerce
twitter.com/ChamberMelville
Overview: A small local charitable organization founded in 1988
Mission: To promote business for Melville & district
Finances: *Annual Operating Budget:* Less than $50,000; *Funding Sources:* City grants; memberships; proceeds from Bingo
Staff Member(s): 1; 20 volunteer(s)
Membership: 80; *Committees:* Economic Development; Marketing & Membership; Minor Events; Railway Dayz; Trade Show
Chief Officer(s):
Joe Kirwan, President

Melville Arts Council
PO Box 309, 800 Prince Edward St., Melville SK S0A 2P0
Tel: 306-728-4494
mcworks@accesscomm.ca
www.melvillecommunityworks.ca
www.facebook.com/MelvilleCommunityWorks
Also Known As: Melville Community Works
Overview: A small local charitable organization founded in 2001
Mission: To foster & promote opportunities for Melville & district citizens to enjoy & participate in cultural & artistic activities; to stimulate & encourage development of cultural projects & activities; to make a available high standard of performing & visual arts events; to encourage municipal government, private

corporations & individuals to participate & assist in growth, development & appreciation of the arts
Member of: Organization of Saskatchewan Arts Councils
Finances: Annual Operating Budget: $50,000-$100,000
Staff Member(s): 4; 12 volunteer(s)
Membership: 12 senior + 100 subscribers; Fees: $20; Member Profile: Interest in performing &/or visual arts; willing volunteer &/or leader; Committees: Membership; Volunteer; Reception
Activities: Internships: Yes
Chief Officer(s):
Lorie Dietz-Rathgeber, Administrator

Melville Dance Association
PO Box 1101, Melville SK S0A 2P0
www.melvilledance.citymax.com
www.facebook.com/MelvilleDance
Overview: A small local organization founded in 1985
Mission: To encourage friendships & self confidence in our youth by promoting the art of dance through various styles & music
Member of: Multicultural Council of Saskatchewan; Dance Saskatchewan Inc.
Membership: Member Profile: Students 4-18
Activities: Annual dance recital; ballet examinations through Royal Academy of Dance; Rents Mailing List: Yes
Chief Officer(s):
Shannon Bell, President
4bells@sasktel.net

Memorial Society of British Columbia (MSBC)
#205, 640 West Broadway, Vancouver BC V5Z 1G4
Tel: 604-733-7705; Fax: 604-733-7730
Toll-Free: 888-816-5902
mail@memorialsocietybr.org
www.memorialsocietybc.org
www.facebook.com/MemorialSocietyBC
Overview: A large provincial organization founded in 1956
Mission: To promote simple, dignified funeral rites through education; To assist members in pre-recording the kind of funeral arrangements preferred through a written record; To ensure availability of suitable low-cost funeral arrangements through written contracts with selected funeral homes
Member of: Better Business Bureau
Finances: Annual Operating Budget: $250,000-$500,000; Funding Sources: Membership fees; Service fees; Donations
Staff Member(s): 3; 30 volunteer(s)
Membership: 200,000; Fees: $40 individual lifetime; $50 individual sustaining
Activities: Speaker Service: Yes
Chief Officer(s):
Barrie Webster, President
Nicole Renwick, Executive Director

Memorial Society of Calgary See Calgary Co-operative Memorial Society

Memorial Society of Edmonton & District (MSED)
#1108, 10235 - 124 St. NW, Edmonton AB T5N 1P9
Tel: 780-944-0196; Fax: 780-944-0791
info@memorialsocietyedmonton.ca
www.msedmonton.com
Overview: A small local charitable organization founded in 1958
Mission: To assist members in final needs preparation
Finances: Annual Operating Budget: Less than $50,000
Staff Member(s): 1; 10 volunteer(s)
Membership: 5,000-14,999; Fees: $40; Member Profile: General public
Activities: Pre-planning simple, low-cost funeral arrangements; public consumer education

Memorial Society of Kitchener-Waterloo & Area
299 Sydney St. South, Kitchener ON N2G 3V8
Tel: 519-603-2550
kwmemsoc@gmail.com
www.kwmemsoc.org
Also Known As: KW Memorial Society; Kitchener-Waterloo Memorial Society
Overview: A small local organization founded in 1971
Mission: To promote & ensure affordable funerals; To monitor practices & performances of funeral providers; To promote environmentally sound disposal of human remains
Member of: Federation of Ontario Memorial Societies - Funeral Consumers Alliance
Membership: Fees: $30
Chief Officer(s):
Ellen Papenburg, President

Publications:
• Perspective [a publication of the Memorial Society of Kitchener-Waterloo & Area]
Type: Newsletter; Frequency: Annual

Memorial Society of London; London Memorial Society; Memorial & Funeral Advisory Society of London See Funeral Consumers Advocacy of London & Windsor

Memorial Society of Northern Ontario (MSNO)
PO Box 1355, Stn. B, Sudbury ON P3E 5K4
Tel: 705-671-3753
Toll-Free: 866-203-5139
msnont@gmail.com
www.memorialsociety.ca
Overview: A small local organization founded in 1979
Mission: To promote simple, dignified funerals at moderate cost; To educate the public with respect to funeral arrangements; To advise members concerning funeral arrangements & funeral planning
Member of: Federation of Ontario Memorial Societies - Funeral Consumers Alliance
Finances: Annual Operating Budget: Less than $50,000
25 volunteer(s)
Membership: 2,300; Fees: $50; Committees: Executive; Promotion; Membership; Nominations
Activities: Board & committee meeting; public presentations; media promotions; Speaker Service: Yes
Publications:
• Memorial Society of Northern Ontario Newsletter
Type: Newsletter

Memorial Society of Red Deer & District
3030 - 55 St., Red Deer AB T4P 3S6
Tel: 403-340-3898
info@memorialsocietyrd.ca
www.memorialsocietyrd.ca
Overview: A small local charitable organization founded in 1978
Mission: To provide pre-planned, dignified, reasonably priced funerals to our members & to offer personal assistance to their families
Affiliation(s): Continental Association of Funeral & Memorial Societies, Inc.
Finances: Funding Sources: Membership fees; donations; record fees
Membership: 2,500; Fees: $25

Memorial Society of Saskatchewan See Funeral Advisory & Memorial Society of Saskatchewan

Men for Change (M4C)
PO Box 33005, Halifax NS B3L 4T6
Tel: 902-492-4104
www.chebucto.ns.ca/CommunitySupport/Men4Change
Overview: A small local organization
Mission: To promote positive masculinity; To end sexism & violence

Meningitis BC
20 Hallman St., Kitimat BC V8C 2R1
Tel: 250-632-5946
www.meningitisbc.org
www.facebook.com/meningitisbc.org
Overview: A small provincial organization
Mission: To educate the public about meningitis & prevention by vaccination; To promote meningitis awareness initiatives; To advocate for the use of MCV4 & 4CMenB vaccines in the public immunization program

Meningitis Relief Canada
266 Thorndale Rd., Brampton ON L6P 3H2
Tel: 647-702-7447; Fax: 905-915-7434
info@meningitisrelief.com
www.meningitisrelief.com
www.facebook.com/MeningitisReliefCanada
Overview: A small national charitable organization
Mission: To raise awareness of meningitis in Canada; To prevent deaths caused by meningitis; To provide support & services for individuals & families affected by meningitis
Chief Officer(s):
Furakh Mir, President

Meningitis Research Foundation of Canada
PO Box 28015, Stn. Parkdale, Waterloo ON N2L 6J8
Tel: 519-664-0244
Toll-Free: 800-643-1303
fund@meningitis.ca
www.meningitis.ca

www.facebook.com/meningitisca
twitter.com/meningitisCA
Overview: A small national charitable organization
Mission: To raise funds to promote education & research in order to prevent death & disability from meningitis & other infections of the central nervous system; To provide support & education to patients & their families affected by meningitis; To increase public awareness of meningitis; To promote better understanding of the disease among healthcare professionals; To provide funds for research into improved diagnosis, treatment, & prevention of meningitis
Chief Officer(s):
Kathryn Blain, Chair

Mennonite Brethren Church of Manitoba (MBCM)
1310 Taylor Ave., Winnipeg MB R3M 3Z6
Tel: 204-654-5771; Fax: 204-654-1865
Toll-Free: 888-669-6575
info@mbcm.ca
mbcm.ca
www.facebook.com/mbManitoba
twitter.com/mbcmonline
Overview: A small provincial organization overseen by Canadian Conference of Mennonite Brethren Churches
Mission: To foster & encourage an inclusive community of Jesus
Staff Member(s): 4
Chief Officer(s):
Elton DaSilva, Executive Director, 204-654-5779
elton@mbcm.ca

Mennonite Brethren Mission & Service International See MB Mission

Mennonite Central Committee Canada (MCCC)
134 Plaza Dr., Winnipeg MB
Tel: 204-261-6381; Fax: 204-269-9875
Toll-Free: 888-622-6337
canada@mennonitecc.ca
mcccanada.ca
www.facebook.com/MennoniteCentralCommittee
twitter.com/mccan
www.instagram.com/mccpeace
Overview: A large national charitable organization founded in 1920
Mission: To share God's love and compassion for all by responding to basic human needs & working for peace & justice
Member of: Mennonite Central Committee
Chief Officer(s):
Don Peters, Executive Director
donpeters@mcccanada.ca
Publications:
• A Common Place
Type: Magazine; Frequency: Quarterly

MCC Alberta
#210, 2946 - 32 St. NE, Calgary AB T1Y 6J7
Tel: 403-275-6935; Fax: 403-275-3711
Toll-Free: 888-622-6337
officeab@mccab.ca
mccalberta.ca
www.facebook.com/mccalberta
twitter.com/mccalberta
Member of: Mennonite Central Committee
Chief Officer(s):
Abe Janzen, Executive Director, 403-275-6935
abejanzen@mccab.org

MCC British Columbia
#201, 33933 Gladys Ave., Abbotsford BC V2S 2E8
Tel: 604-850-6639; Fax: 604-850-8734
Toll-Free: 888-622-6337
admin@mccbc.com
bc.mcc.org
www.facebook.com/mccbritishcolumbia
twitter.com/mccbctalk
Member of: Mennonite Central Committee
Chief Officer(s):
Len Block, Chair

MCC Ontario
#203, 50 Kent Ave., Kitchener ON N2G 3R1
Tel: 519-745-8458
Toll-Free: 800-313-6226
info@mcco.ca
mcco.ca
www.facebook.com/MCCOntario
twitter.com/MCCOntario
Member of: Mennonite Central Committee

Chief Officer(s):
Karen Cornies, Chair

MCC Québec
#200, 4824, ch de la Côte-des-Neiges, Montréal QC H3V 1G4
Tél: 514-278-3008; *Téléc:* 514-278-3008
quebec@mcccanada.ca
mccquebec.ca
twitter.com/MCCQuebec
Membre de: Mennonite Central Committee
Chief Officer(s):
Muriel Queval, Directrice régionaux
MurielQueval@mennonitecc.ca
Claude Queval, Directeur régionaux
MurielQueval@mennonitecc.ca

MCC Saskatchewan
600 - 45th St. West, Saskatoon SK S7L 5W9
Tel: 306-665-2555; *Fax:* 306-665-5564
Toll-Free: 888-622-6337
saskoffice@mccsk.org
mccsk.org
www.facebook.com/mccsask
twitter.com/MCCSask
Member of: Mennonite Central Committee
Chief Officer(s):
Claire Ewert Fisher, Executive Director
claireewertfisher@mccs.org

Mennonite Central Committee Supportive Care Services Society *See* Communitas Supportive Care Society

Mennonite Church Canada (MC Canada)
600 Shaftesbury Blvd., Winnipeg MB R3P 0M4
Tel: 204-888-6781; *Fax:* 204-831-5675
Toll-Free: 866-888-6785
office@mennonitechurch.ca
www.mennonitechurch.ca
Also Known As: Conference of Mennonites in Canada
Overview: A medium-sized national charitable organization founded in 1903
Mission: To form a people of God; To become a global church; To grow leaders
Finances: *Funding Sources:* Donations
Staff Member(s): 40
Membership: 31,000 baptized believers in 225 congregations & 5 area churches
Activities: *Library:* Mennonite Church Canada Resource Centre
Chief Officer(s):
Willard Metzger, Executive Director, 204-888-6781 Ext. 116
wmetzger@mennonitechurch.ca
Coreena Stewart, Chief Administrative Officer, 204-888-6781 Ext. 122
cstewart@mennonitechurch.ca

Mennonite Church Alberta
Box 1839, Pincher Creek AB T0K 1W0
info@mennonitechurch.ab.ca
www.mennonitechurch.ab.ca
Chief Officer(s):
Dan Lowell Graber, Area Church Minister, 403-909-5105
dan@mennonitechurch.ab.ca

Mennonite Church Eastern Canada
#201, 50 Kent Ave., Kitchener ON N2G 3R1
Tel: 226-476-2500
Toll-Free: 855-476-2500
mcec@mcec.ca
www.mcec.ca
www.facebook.com/MennoniteChurchEasternCanada
www.youtube.com/user/MennoEasternCanada
Chief Officer(s):
David Martin, Executive Minister
dmartin@mcec.ca

Mennonite Church Manitoba
#200, 600 Shaftesbury Blvd., Winnipeg MB R3P 2J1
Tel: 204-896-1616; *Fax:* 204-832-7804
office@mennochurch.mb.ca
www.mennochurch.mb.ca
Mission: Their vision is to be a community of congregrations unified in Jesus Christ, living a biblical Anabaptist faith, together presenting Jesus Christ to the world. Their mission is to resource and empower each other, and to facilitate spiritual growth, service, and evangelism.
Member of: Mennonite Church Canada
Chief Officer(s):
Ken Warkentin, Executive Director
kwarkentin@mennochurch.mb.ca

Mennonite Church Saskatchewan
#101A, 301 Pawka Place, Saskatoon SK S7L 6A3
Tel: 306-249-4844; *Fax:* 306-249-4441
mcsask@mcsask.ca
www.mcsask.ca
Chief Officer(s):
Ryan Siemens, Area Church Minister, Congregational & Pastoral Relations, 306-249-4844 Ext. 1
minister@mcsask.ca

Mennonite Economic Development Associates Canada
155 Frobisher Dr., #I-106, Waterloo ON N2V 2E1
Tel: 519-725-1633; *Fax:* 519-725-9083
Toll-Free: 800-665-7026
meda@meda.org
www.meda.org
www.linkedin.com/company-beta/1314159
www.facebook.com/MEDAdotorg
twitter.com/medadotorg
Also Known As: MEDA Canada
Overview: A medium-sized international charitable organization founded in 1953 overseen by Manitoba Council for International Cooperation
Mission: To be committed to the nurture & expression of Christian faith in a business setting; To enable members to integrate biblical values & business principles in their daily lives; To address the needs of the disadvantaged through programs of economic development
Finances: *Annual Operating Budget:* $1.5 Million-$3 Million
Membership: 3,000 Canada & US
Activities: Publish magazines & reports; Videos & weblinks; Learning Centre; *Library:* Mennonite Economic Development Associates Canada Library; by appointment
Chief Officer(s):
Allan Sauder, President
Kim Pityn, CEO
Gerald Morrison, Chief Financial Officer
Michael White, Chief Strategic Engagement Officer
Publications:
• The Marketplace [a publication of the Mennonite Economic Development Associates Canada]
Type: Magazine; *Frequency:* Bimonthly; *Editor:* Wally Kroeker; *ISSN:* 0199-7130

Mennonite Foundation of Canada *See* Abundance Canada

Mennonite Historical Society of Canada (MHSC)
c/o Mennonite Historical Society of British Columbia, 36199 Sandringham Dr., Abbotsford BC V3G 2M4
info@mhsc.ca
www.mhsc.ca
Overview: A small local organization
Mission: To produce publications about Mennonite history & to coordinate provincial historical & archival societies
Chief Officer(s):
Richard Thiessen, President

Mensa Canada Society / La Société Mensa Canada
#503, 386 Broadway, Winnipeg MB R3C 3R6
Toll-Free: 844-202-6761
info@mensacanada.org
www.mensacanada.org
www.linkedin.com/groups/40194
www.facebook.com/MensaCanada
twitter.com/MensaCanada
google.com/+mensacanada
Also Known As: The High IQ Society
Overview: A medium-sized national organization founded in 1967
Mission: To identify & foster human intelligence for the benefit of humanity; To encourage research; To provide an intellectual & social environment for members
Member of: Mensa International Inc.
Finances: *Funding Sources:* Membership dues
Membership: *Fees:* $70 individual; $45 student; $90 family; *Member Profile:* Individuals who have shown that they have an IQ higher than 98% of the world's population
Activities: Offering networking opportunities & international contacts; Presenting annual scholarships; Providing assistance for gifted children; Administering the Mensa Supervised Entrance Examination
Chief Officer(s):
Vicki Herd, President
president@mensacanada.org
Mary Susan MacDonald, Vice-President, Communications
vpcomm@mensacanada.org

Awards:
• Distinguished Educator Award
To recognize a teacher, professor, instructor, teaching assistant or other educator at any educational level who has had a positive influence on the education or life of a Mensa member.
• Mensa Canada Scholarship Program
To recognize a teacher, professor, instructor, teaching assistant or other educator at any educational level who has had a positive influence on the education or life of a Mensa member.; *Amount:* $2,000-$3,000

Mental Illness Foundation *Voir* Fondation des maladies mentales

Mercaz-Canada
#201, 55 Yeomans Rd., Toronto ON M3H 3J7
Tel: 416-667-1717
Toll-Free: 866-357-3384
info@masorti-mercaz.ca
www.mercaz.ca
www.facebook.com/MercazCanada
Also Known As: Movement to Reaffirm Conservative Zionism
Overview: A medium-sized international organization founded in 1994
Mission: To support the State of Israel as a democratic & pluralistic national home for all Jews, secure & at peace with its Arab neighbours, committed to protecting the rights of all its citizens & supporting all streams of Jewish practices; in Canada, to promote Aliyah, trips to Israel & local Zionist programming
Member of: Canadian Zionist Federation; World Zionist Organization; Mercaz-Olami
Affiliation(s): United Synagogues of Conservative Judaism
Staff Member(s): 3
Membership: *Fees:* $18 individual; $36 couple; $9 student ages 18-25
Chief Officer(s):
Jennifer Gorman, Executive Director

Mercy for Animals Canada
#22033, 131 Bloor St. West, Toronto ON M5S 1R1
Toll-Free: 866-632-6446
www.mercyforanimals.org
www.facebook.com/mercyforanimals
twitter.com/mercyforanimals
www.instagram.com/mercyforanimals
Overview: A medium-sized national organization
Mission: To protect farmed animals & prevent animal suffering; To promote compassionate consumer choices & policies
Activities: Conducting undercover investigations of factory farms & slaughterhouses; Working with law enforcement to ensure the prosecution of individuals who violate animal cruelty statutes; Helping businesses adopt animal welfare reforms; Promoting vegan diets through education
Chief Officer(s):
Nathan Runkle, President
Nick Cooney, Executive Vice-President
Matt Rice, Executive Vice-President
Jake Morton, Vice-President, Operations
Ari Solomon, Vice-President, Communications
Geetika Sripathi, Vice-President, Education
Vandhana Bala, General Counsel

Mères avec pouvoir (MAP)
2015A, rue Fullum, Montréal QC H2K 3N5
Tél: 514-282-1882
info@mapmontreal.org
www.mapmontreal.org
www.facebook.com/meresavecpouvoir
www.youtube.com/user/mapmontreal
Aperçu: *Dimension:* petite; *Envergure:* locale; fondée en 2001
Mission: Pour aider les mères célibataires à trouver un travail ou poursuivre leurs études grâce à des logements abordables et de garderie
Affiliation(s): Inter-lodge; CPE du Carrefour
Membre: *Critères d'admissibilite:* Femmes qui habitent à Montréal, qui sont monoparentale avec un enfant de la naissance à cinq ans et avoir un manumim de deux enfants, qui ont la garde pour plus de 50% du temps, qui terminent leurs études ou qui travaillent ou cherchent du travail

Les mères contre l'alcool auvolant *See* MADD Canada

Merit Canada
Toll-Free: 877-416-3748
info@meritcanada.ca
meritcanada.ca
Overview: A small national organization founded in 2008

Canadian Associations / Merit Contractors Association of Alberta

Mission: A united national voice for eight different provincial Open Shop construction associations.
Finances: *Annual Operating Budget:* Less than $50,000
Staff Member(s): 1
Membership: *Member Profile:* Construction contractors
Activities: Training and education programs

Merit Contractors Association of Alberta
#103, 13025 St. Albert Trail, Edmonton AB T5L 4H5
Tel: 780-455-5999; *Fax:* 780-455-2109
Toll-Free: 888-816-9991
meritedm@meritalberta.com
www.meritalberta.com
www.facebook.com/meritalberta
twitter.com/merit_ab
www.youtube.com/user/meritalberta
Overview: A small provincial organization overseen by Merit Canada
Mission: Merit Contractors Association provides the construction industry with benefits and benefit programs, industry specific training programs, employee education support, human resource tools and advocacy specifically related to open shop contractors.
Membership: *Member Profile:* Construction contractors
Chief Officer(s):
Stephen Kushner, President

Merit Contractors Association of Manitoba
#112, 131 Provencher Blvd., Winnipeg MB R2H 0G2
Tel: 204-888-6202; *Fax:* 204-888-6204
info@meritmb.com
www.meritmb.com
Overview: A small provincial organization founded in 1994 overseen by Merit Canada
Finances: *Annual Operating Budget:* Less than $50,000
Staff Member(s): 1
Membership: 83; *Member Profile:* Construction contractors
Chief Officer(s):
Harvey Millier, Executive Director
hmiller@meritmb.com

Merit Contractors Association of Newfoundland & Labrador
#213, 446 Newfoundland Dr., St. John's NL A1A 4G7
Tel: 709-576-3748; *Fax:* 709-576-3749
Toll-Free: 877-544-3748
merit@merit-nl.ca
www.merit-nl.ca
Overview: A small provincial organization overseen by Merit Canada
Mission: Merit Contractors Association is the voice of the open shop construction industry in Newfoundland and Labrador.
Membership: *Member Profile:* Construction contractors
Chief Officer(s):
Paul Dubé, Executive Director
paul@merit-nl.ca

Merit Contractors Association of Nova Scotia
#216, 30 Damascus Rd., Bedford NL B4A 0C1
Tel: 902-453-6248; *Fax:* 902-453-0689
Toll-Free: 877-525-9205
info@meritns.com
meritns.com
www.facebook.com/MeritNovaScotia?ref=hl
twitter.com/MeritNS
Also Known As: Merit Nova Scotia
Overview: A small provincial organization overseen by Merit Canada
Mission: To support open shop contractors seeking fair opportunities to compete and do business in Nova Scotia.
Membership: 135 companies (2,000 employees); *Member Profile:* Construction contractors
Chief Officer(s):
Bill McLellan, Executive Director, 902-453-6248

Merit Contractors Association of Saskatchewan
#102, 70 - 17th St. West, Prince Albert SK S6V 3X3
Tel: 306-764-4380; *Fax:* 306-764-4390
info@meritsask.com
www.meritcontractors.sk.ca
twitter.com/meritsask
Overview: A small provincial organization founded in 1988 overseen by Merit Canada
Mission: An open shop association in Saskatchewan
Membership: 200; *Member Profile:* Construction contractors
Chief Officer(s):
Karen Low, Executive Director

Merit OpenShop Contractors Association of Ontario
11 Kodiak Cres., Toronto ON M3J 3E5
Toll-Free: 888-303-9878
www.meritontario.com
twitter.com/meritontario
Also Known As: Merit Ontario
Previous Name: United Independent Contractors' Group of Ontario
Overview: A small provincial organization founded in 1990 overseen by Merit Canada
Mission: To represent and support the growth of open shop construction by encouraging sound business practices and ensuring a fair and competitive marketplace for construction in Ontario.
Membership: 3,500; *Member Profile:* Construction contractors
Chief Officer(s):
Gordon Sproule, Chair

Merritt & District Chamber of Commerce
City Hall, 2185 Voght St., Merritt BC V1K 1B8
Tel: 250-378-5634; *Fax:* 250-378-6561
www.merrittchamber.com
www.facebook.com/merrittchamber
twitter.com/Merritt_Chamber
Overview: A small local organization founded in 1914
Mission: To support members & the community by strengthening the business environment
Staff Member(s): 4
Membership: 198; *Fees:* $100 individual; $175 business
Activities: Organizing & supporting events including the Merritt Mountain Music Festival, trade shows, business awards shows, parades, & shopping events
Chief Officer(s):
Etelka Gillespie, Manager

Merry Go Round Children's Foundation
#410, 463 King St. West, Toronto ON M5V 1K4
Tel: 647-426-1252; *Fax:* 416-849-2514
www.kidscopscomputers.org
www.facebook.com/KidsCopsComputers
twitter.com/KidCopComputer
www.youtube.com/user/kidscopscomputers
Overview: A small local organization founded in 1997
Mission: To help children who do not have access to computers or internet, by providing them with laptops, internet connections & police mentorship
Affiliation(s): Toronto District School Board; Toronto Catholic District School Board; Toronto Police Service
Staff Member(s): 3
Membership: *Member Profile:* Underpriviledged children in grades 7 - 12
Chief Officer(s):
Clayton Shold, Executive Director, 647-426-1280
clayton@merrygoround.ca

Messagères de Notre-Dame de l'Assomption (MNDA)
#4, 45, rue de la Sapiniere-dorion, Québec QC G1L 1A3
Tél: 418-626-7492
Aperçu: *Dimension:* petite; *Envergure:* locale; Organisme sans but lucratif; fondée en 1964
Finances: *Budget de fonctionnement annuel:* $50,000-$100,000
Membre: 100-499

Méta d'âme
2250, rue Florian, Montréal QC H2X 2P5
Tél: 514-528-9000; *Téléc:* 514-527-6999
administration@metadame.org
www.metadame.org
Aperçu: *Dimension:* petite; *Envergure:* locale
Mission: Pour prodiguer des soins médicaux aux personnes souffrant de dépendance aux médicaments d'ordonnance et à faciliter leur réinsertion dans la société
Membre: *Critères d'admissibilite:* Les personnes qui sont accro aux médicaments d'ordonnance

The Metal Arts Guild of Canada (MAGC)
151 Marion St., Toronto ON M6R 1E6
communications@metalartsguild.ca
www.metalartsguild.ca
twitter.com/MAGcanada
Overview: A medium-sized national charitable organization founded in 1946
Mission: To be committed to the exchange of information & ideas encouraging appreciation for the metal arts; To promote & develop the metal arts; To further education in the metal arts; To encourage members to experiment with all the forms that metal takes
Affiliation(s): Ontario Crafts Council
Finances: *Funding Sources:* Membership; Ontario Arts Council; private funding; corporate sponsorship
Membership: *Fees:* Schedule available
Activities: Workshops; lectures & seminars; *Internships:* Yes; *Speaker Service:* Yes; *Library:* Archives & Resource Centre; Open to public by appointment
Chief Officer(s):
Delane Cooper, President
president@metalartsguild.ca

Metal Industries Association *See* Western Employers Labour Relations Association

The Metal Working Association of New Brunswick (MWANB) / Association des entreprises métallurgiques du Nouveau-Brunswick
PO Box 7129, #12, 567 Coverdale Rd., Riverview NB E1B 4T8
Tel: 506-861-9071; *Fax:* 506-857-3059
nb@cme-mec.ca
www.mwanb.com
Also Known As: SPARK
Overview: A small provincial organization founded in 1976
Mission: To be a voice for the metal working sector in New Brunswick & to provide a forum for members to network & discuss opportunities
Affiliation(s): Canadian Manufacturers & Exporters
Membership: 30; *Fees:* $300
Chief Officer(s):
Corey MacDonald, President
Scott Black, Vice President
Publications:
• Metal Working Matters [a publication of The Metal Working Association of New Brunswick]
Type: Newsletter

Metallurgy & Materials Society of the Canadian Institute of Mining, Metallurgy & Petroleum (MetSoc)
#1250, 3500, boul de Maisonneuve ouest, Montréal QC H3Z 3C1
Tel: 514-939-2710; *Fax:* 514-939-2714
metsoc@cim.org
www.metsoc.org
www.twitter.com/AnnualCOM
Overview: A medium-sized national organization founded in 1967 overseen by Canadian Institute of Mining, Metallurgy & Petroleum
Mission: To expand the professional horizons of society members in order to serve the metals & materials industry
Membership: *Member Profile:* Persons involved in the development & application of technologies for the extraction, fabrication, & utilization of metals & materials in Canada; *Committees:* CIM Journal; Student Activities; Historical Metallurgy; Membership Services; Publications; Trustees
Activities: Providing information to the government & the public; Offering continuing education; Recognizing excellence; Providing networking opportunities
Chief Officer(s):
Zhenghe Xu, President
Brigitte Farah, Manager, Administration & Conferences, 514-939-2710 Ext. 1329
bfarah@cim.org
Meetings/Conferences:
• Metallurgy & Materials Society 2018 57th Annual Conference of Metallurgists, October, 2018, Hyatt Regency Columbus, Columbus, OH
Scope: International
Description: A technical program, with short courses & industrial tours, plus a metals trade show, the poster session, plenary sessions, & student activities
Publications:
• Canadian Metallurgical Quarterly: The Canadian Journal of Metallurgy & Materials Science
Type: Journal; *Frequency:* Quarterly; *Accepts Advertising*; *Editor:* J.R. McDermid; *ISSN:* 0008-4433
Profile: Research in the areas of mineral processing, extraction, synthesis, processing, characterization properties,& performance of metals & materials
• mLink: The The Electronic Newsletter of the METSOC of CIM
Type: Newsletter
Profile: News for members & students about MetSoc meetings & publications

Métis Child & Family Services Society (Edmonton) (MCFS)
10437 - 123rd St., Edmonton AB T5N 1N8

Tel: 780-452-6100; *Fax:* 780-452-8944
reception@metischild.com
www.metischild.com
Overview: A small local organization founded in 1984
Mission: To promote the health & well-being of Aboriginal children & families by building the capacity of the Métis community through the provision of culturally sensitive & appropriate services & programs
Staff Member(s): 42
Chief Officer(s):
Don Langford, Executive Director
ed1@metischild.com

Métis Nation - Saskatchewan
231 Robin Cres., Saskatoon SK S7L 6M8
Tel: 306-343-8285; *Fax:* 306-343-0171
Toll-Free: 888-343-6667
reception@mn-s.ca
www.mn-s.ca
www.facebook.com/metisnationsaskatchewan
twitter.com/metisnationsask
www.youtube.com/user/MetisSK2012
Overview: A medium-sized provincial organization
Mission: To represent Saskatechwan Métis & act as its legislative assembly
Affiliation(s): Métis National Council; Métis Women of Saskatchewan; Métis Nation of Saskatchewan Youth Council
Membership: *Committees:* CDC; Woodland Caribou Recovery Strategy; Sturgeon River Plains Bison Management; North Saskatchewan River Basin Council
Activities: *Awareness Events:* Louis Riel Day, Nov.; Back to Batoche Days

Métis Nation of Alberta
Delia Gray Bldg., #100, 41738 Kingsway Ave., Edmonton AB T5G 0X5
Tel: 780-455-2200; *Fax:* 780-452-8948
Toll-Free: 800-252-7553
www.albertametis.com
twitter.com/AlbertaMetis
Overview: A medium-sized provincial organization founded in 1932
Mission: To represent the interests of the Métis people of Alberta & ensure the advancement of their culture & well-being
Affiliation(s): Métis Urban Housing; Métis Child & Family Services; Métis Development Inc.
Finances: *Funding Sources:* Donations
Membership: *Fees:* $40 replacement card fee
Activities: *Awareness Events:* Louis Riel Week *Library:* Culture & Resource Centre; Open to public by appointment
Chief Officer(s):
Audrey Poitras, President

  Regional Office - Zone 1
  PO Box 1350, Lac La Biche AB T0A 2C0
  Tel: 780-623-3039; *Fax:* 780-623-2733
  Chief Officer(s):
  William Landstrom, President

  Regional Office - Zone 2
  PO Box 6497, Bonnyville AB T9N 2H1
  Tel: 780-826-7483; *Fax:* 780-826-7603
  Chief Officer(s):
  Karen (KC) Collins, President

  Regional Office - Zone 3
  1415 - 28th St. NE, Calgary AB T2A 2P6
  Tel: 403-569-8800; *Fax:* 403-569-8959
  Toll-Free: 800-267-5844
  Chief Officer(s):
  Marlene Lanz, President

  Regional Office - Zone 4
  11724 - 95 St., Edmonton AB T5G 1L9
  Tel: 780-944-9288; *Fax:* 780-455-5546
  Toll-Free: 888-588-4088
  Chief Officer(s):
  Cecil Bellrose, President

  Regional Office - Zone 5
  353 Main St. North, Slave Lake AB T0G 2A3
  Tel: 780-849-4654; *Fax:* 780-849-2890
  Toll-Free: 866-849-4660
  Chief Officer(s):
  Bev New, President

  Regional Office - Zone 6
  9621 - 90 Ave., Peace River AB T8S 1G8
  Tel: 780-624-4219; *Fax:* 780-624-3477
  Toll-Free: 800-668-5319
  Chief Officer(s):

Sylvia Johnson, President

Métis Nation of Ontario
#3, 500 Old St. Patrick St., Ottawa ON K1N 9G4
Tel: 613-798-1488; *Fax:* 613-722-4225
Toll-Free: 800-263-4889
www.metisnation.org
www.facebook.com/147602041992683
Overview: A medium-sized provincial organization
Mission: To bring Métis people together to celebrate and share their rich culture and heritage and to forward the aspirations of the Métis people in Ontario as a collective.
Affiliation(s): Métis National Council
Staff Member(s): 150
Membership: 15,000
Chief Officer(s):
Gary Lipinski, President
garyl@metisnation.org

Métis National Council (MNC) / Ralliement national des Métis
#4, 340 MacLaren St., Ottawa ON K2P 0M6
Tel: 613-232-3216; *Fax:* 613-232-4262
Toll-Free: 800-928-6330
info@metisnation.ca
www.metisnation.ca
www.facebook.com/186735084697421
twitter.com/MNC_tweets
www.youtube.com/user/MetisNationalCouncil
Overview: A medium-sized provincial organization founded in 1983
Mission: To represent the Métis both nationally & internationally; To secure a healthy space for the Métis Nation's existence within Canada
Finances: *Funding Sources:* Government of Canada
Chief Officer(s):
Clément Chartier, President

Métis National Council of Women (MNCW) / Conseil national des femmes métisses, inc. (CNFM)
PO Box 293, Woodlawn ON K0A 3M0
Tel: 613-567-4287; *Fax:* 613-567-9644
Toll-Free: 888-867-2635
info@metiswomen.ca
www.metiswomen.ca
Overview: A medium-sized national organization founded in 1992
Mission: To unite & organize Métis women in Canada and to maintain & promote respect for the individual rights, freedoms & gender equality of Métis women.
Finances: *Annual Operating Budget:* $100,000-$250,000
Activities: Youth programs; research & publishing; *Speaker Service:* Yes
Chief Officer(s):
Sheila D. Genaille, President

Métis Provincial Council of British Columbia
30691 Simpson Rd., Abbotsford BC V2T 2C7
Tel: 604-557-5851; *Fax:* 604-557-2024
Toll-Free: 800-940-1150
reception@mnbc.ca
www.mnbc.ca
www.facebook.com/metisnationbc
Also Known As: Métis Nation BC
Overview: A medium-sized provincial organization founded in 1996
Mission: To support the Métis population in British Columbia.
Affiliation(s): Métis National Council
Staff Member(s): 18
Membership: 35 Métis communities; *Committees:* Operations & Finance; Priorities & Planning; Governance; Human Resource
Chief Officer(s):
Bruce Dumont, President
bdumont@mnbc.ca
Dale Drown, Chief Executive Officer

Métis Settlements General Council
#101, 10335 - 172 St., Edmonton AB T5S 1K9
Tel: 780-822-4096; *Fax:* 780-489-9558
Toll-Free: 888-213-4400
reception@msgc.ca
www.msgc.ca
www.facebook.com/alberta.settlements
www.youtube.com/user/MSGCHistoryOnline
Also Known As: Alberta Federation of Métis Settlement Associations
Overview: A medium-sized provincial organization

Mission: To represent settlements & address socio-economic issues on their behalf; to promote good governance & community involvement
Chief Officer(s):
Randy Hardy, President

Métis Women's Council of Edmonton *See* Edmonton Aboriginal Senior Centre

Metro (Toronto) Association of Family Resource Programs (MAFRP)
1117 Gerrard St. East, Toronto ON M4M 1Z9
Tel: 416-463-7974; *Fax:* 416-463-0316
mafrp@web.net
Overview: A small local organization founded in 1993
Mission: To encourage the healthy growth & development of young children, their families & care givers; to collaborate with family resource programes to develop the networks & resources necessary to enhance & maintain a high level of program quality
Finances: *Annual Operating Budget:* Less than $50,000
Staff Member(s): 1
Membership: 1-99
Activities: *Rents Mailing List:* Yes
Chief Officer(s):
Cheryl Lajoie, Contact

Metro Action Committee on Public Violence Against Women & Children *See* Metropolitan Action Committee on Violence Against Women & Children

Metro Food Bank Society *See* Feed Nova Scotia

Metro Toronto Chinese & Southeast Asian Legal Clinic (MCSA)
#1701, 180 Dundas St. West, Toronto ON M5G 1Z8
Tel: 416-971-9674; *Fax:* 416-971-6780
mtcsalc.org
www.facebook.com/mcsalegal
twitter.com/mcsalegalclinic
plus.google.com/116850532419152142411
Overview: A small local organization founded in 1987
Mission: To provide free legal services to low income Torontonians who do not speak English & are originally from China, Vietnam, Loas or Cambodia.
Staff Member(s): 5
Membership: *Fees:* Free

Metro Toronto Movement for Literacy (MTML) / Rassemblement pour l'alphabétisation de la communauté urbaine de Toronto
#405, 344 Bloor St. West, Toronto ON M5S 3A7
Tel: 416-961-4013; *Fax:* 416-961-8138
literacyinfo@mtml.ca
www.mtml.ca
www.facebook.com/240716686100834
twitter.com/MTMLTorontoYork
Overview: A small local charitable organization founded in 1978
Mission: To provide leadership & work actively to develop & promote adult literacy in Toronto & York Region
Member of: Ontario Literacy Coalition
Finances: *Annual Operating Budget:* $100,000-$250,000; *Funding Sources:* Ontario Ministry of Training, Colleges & Universities; National Literacy Secretariat; Ontario Trillium Foundation; City of Toronto; Canada Post
Staff Member(s): 3
Membership: 100-499; *Fees:* $15-$50 individual (pay what you can); $60-$240 organization; $30 subscriber; *Member Profile:* Community groups; school boards; libraries; workplaces; community colleges; individual members: literacy workers, volunteer tutors & learners
Activities: Public education; information & referral services to learners & volunteers through the Literacy Access Network hotline; community planning coordination; professional development for literacy workers & volunteers; *Awareness Events:* The Word On The Street; International Literacy Day; CBC Book Sale
Chief Officer(s):
Alicia Homer, Executive Director
aliciah@mtml.ca

Metro United Way (Halifax-Dartmouth) *See* United Way of Halifax Region

Metronome Canada
118 Sherbourne St., Toronto ON M5A 2R2
Tel: 416-367-0162; *Fax:* 416-367-1569
Toll-Free: 877-411-7456
info@metronomecanada.com

Canadian Associations / Metropolitan Action Committee on Violence Against Women & Children (METRAC)

www.metronomecanada.com
www.facebook.com/MetronomeCanada?ref=search&sid=6
Overview: A small local charitable organization
Mission: To transform the historic Canada Malting Silo Complex on Toronto's waterfront into a facility to integrate, educate, celebrate & promote all facets of the Canadian music industry
Activities: *Internships:* Yes; *Speaker Service:* Yes
Chief Officer(s):
John Harris, Contact
johnharris@metronomecanada.com

Metropolitan Action Committee on Violence Against Women & Children (METRAC)
158 Spadina Rd., Toronto ON M5R 2T8
Tel: 416-392-3135; *Fax:* 416-392-3136
Toll-Free: 877-558-5570; *TTY:* 416-392-3031
info@metrac.org
www.metrac.org
www.facebook.com/metracorg
twitter.com/metracorg
www.youtube.com/user/metracorg
Previous Name: Metro Action Committee on Public Violence Against Women & Children
Overview: A small local charitable organization founded in 1984
Mission: To promote the rights of women & children to live free of violence; to decrease & finally eliminate all forms of violence against women & children; to work with agents of change at the municipal, provincial & federal levels; to work with other community-based organizations & with educators, urban planners, police, health & legal professionals; to seek to identify the need for action & to determine appropriate solutions to violence against women & children; to promote education of the public, of professionals & of public officials on the causes of, & appropriate solutions to, violence against women & children
Member of: National Association of Women & the Law
Affiliation(s): Ontario Women's Justice Network (OWJN)
Finances: *Annual Operating Budget:* $250,000-$500,000
Staff Member(s): 9; 20 volunteer(s)
Membership: 200; *Fees:* Sliding scale; *Member Profile:* Violence against women organizations; community activists; researchers; students; *Committees:* Fundraising; Finance; HR & Nominations; Communications; Planning & Evaluation; Social Action; Executive
Activities: Consultations; research; public education; workshops; annual meeting; training; violence prevention; "Night out with a Difference" event; handbooks; pamphlets; kits & links; *Awareness Events:* Women's Safety Audit Night; *Speaker Service:* Yes; *Library:* by appointment
Chief Officer(s):
Wendy Komiotis, Executive Director
executivedirector@metrac.org

Metropolitan Community Church of Toronto
115 Simpson Ave., Toronto ON M4K 1A1
Tel: 416-406-6228; *Fax:* 416-466-5207
Overview: A small local charitable organization founded in 1984
Mission: Ministry by and for the LGBT community of Toronto
Member of: Universal Fellowship of Metropolitan Community Churches
Finances: *Annual Operating Budget:* Less than $50,000
Staff Member(s): 1; 8 volunteer(s)
Membership: 30
Activities: Weekly worship services; Baptism, weddings & funerals; Volunteer ministries & programs; Leading social programs conccerning same-sex marriage, trans education, black education awareness & refugee support & sponsorship
Chief Officer(s):
Brent Hawkes, Senior Pastor

Metropolitan Halifax Chamber of Commerce *See* Halifax Chamber of Commerce

Metropolitan Hamilton Real Estate Board *See* Hamilton-Burlington & District Real Estate Board

The Metropolitan Toronto & Region Conservation Foundation; The Conservation Foundation of Greater Toronto *See* Conservation Foundation of Greater Toronto

Metropolitan Toronto Apartment Builders Association *See* Greater Toronto Apartment Association

Metropolitan Toronto Convention & Visitors Association *See* Tourism Toronto

Metropolitan Toronto Lawyers Association; County of York Law Association *See* Toronto Lawyers Association

Metropolitan Toronto Police Association *See* Toronto Police Association

Mi'kmaq Association for Cultural Studies (MACS)
PO Box 243, Sydney NS B1P 6H1
Tel: 902-567-1752; *Fax:* 902-567-0776
macs@mikmaq-assoc.ca
www.mikmaqculture.com
Overview: A medium-sized local organization founded in 1974
Mission: To promote, maintain & protect the customs, language, history, tradition & culture of the Mi'kmaq people; to facilitate & promote understanding & awareness of our culture among the public; to teach the culture, language & history of the Mi'kmaq people to others
Membership: *Member Profile:* All registered Mi'kmaq in 12 First Nations communities
Chief Officer(s):
Deborah Ginnish, Executive Director

Mi'kmaq Native Friendship Centre
2158 Gottingen St., Halifax NS B3K 3B4
Tel: 902-420-1576; *Fax:* 902-423-6130
www.mymnfc.com
www.facebook.com/121366117945828
Overview: A small local charitable organization founded in 1973 overseen by National Association of Friendship Centres
Mission: To promote the educational & cultural advancement of native people in & about the Halifax/Dartmouth area; to assist people of native descent who have newly arrived in the area to settle in; to strive to create & improve mutual understanding between people of native descent & others.
Staff Member(s): 17
Activities: Alcohol & Drug Counselling; Community & Cultural Development Program; Crisis Intervention Program; DayCare Program; Employment & Education Program; Justice Program; Micmac Native Learning Centre; Mainline Needle Exchange Program
Chief Officer(s):
Tony Thomas, Chair

Micah House
205 Holton Ave. South, Hamilton ON L8M 2L8
Tel: 905-296-4387
info@micahhouse.ca
www.micahhouse.ca
www.facebook.com/MicahHouseHamilton
twitter.com/micah_house
Overview: A small local organization founded in 2006
Mission: To demonstrate God's love to newly arrived refugees in Hamilton, Ontario
Finances: *Funding Sources:* Donations
Staff Member(s): 6
Membership: *Member Profile:* Christians from a variety of churches & organizations in Hamilton, Ontario
Activities: *Awareness Events:* Walkathon
Chief Officer(s):
Scott Jones, Executive Director
scott@micahhouse.ca

Michael Smith Foundation for Health Research (MSFHR)
#200, 1285 West Broadway, Vancouver BC V6H 3X8
Tel: 604-730-8322
Toll-Free: 866-673-4722
info@msfhr.org
www.msfhr.org
www.linkedin.com/MichaelSmithFoundationforHealthResearch
twitter.com/msfhr
www.youtube.com/themsfhr
Overview: A medium-sized provincial organization founded in 2001
Mission: To build British Columbia's capacity for excellence in clinical, biomedical, health services & population health research
Staff Member(s): 33
Chief Officer(s):
Diane Finegood, President & CEO
Bev Holmes, Vice-President Research & Impact
Gordon Schwark, Vice-President, Finance & Corporate Services

Michaëlle Jean Foundation / Fondation Michaëlle Jean
143 Séraphin-Marion Pvt., Ottawa ON K1N 6N5
Tel: 613-562-5751
Toll-Free: 855-626-8296
info@fmjf.ca
www.fmjf.ca
www.facebook.com/FondationMichaelleJeanFoundation
twitter.com/FMJF143
www.youtube.com/user/FMJF2011
Overview: A small local charitable organization
Mission: To use the arts to empower underserved youth to create solutions to issues affecting them & to change their communities
Activities: Supporting youth-driven organizations through the Youth Community Action initiative; Enabling emerging artists from disadvantaged backgrounds to create exhibitions through the 4th Wall: Make the Invisible Visible initiative; Funding research into the arts
Chief Officer(s):
Jean-Daniel Lafond, Executive Director
Peter Flegel, Director, Programs & Communications

The Michener Institute for Applied Health Sciences
222 St. Patrick St., Toronto ON M5T 1V4
Tel: 416-596-3101
Toll-Free: 800-387-9066
info@michener.ca
www.michener.ca
www.facebook.com/TheMichenerInstitute
twitter.com/michenerinst
www.youtube.com/user/TheMichenerInstitute
Previous Name: Toronto Institute of Medical Technology
Overview: A medium-sized national organization founded in 1967
Mission: To design, develop & deliver the best educational programs, products & services in applied health sciences
Affiliation(s): 170 hospitals, labs, & clinics across Canada
Finances: *Funding Sources:* Ontario Ministry of Health
Activities: *Library:* by appointment
Chief Officer(s):
Cliff Nordal, Chair
President Adamson, President & CEO

Microscopical Society of Canada (MSC) / Société de Microscopie du Canada (SMC)
c/o Line Mongeon, McGill University, Strathcona Bldg., #1-48, Montréal QC H3A 2B2
Tel: 514-398-2878; *Fax:* 514-398-5047
www.msc-smc.org
Overview: A medium-sized national organization founded in 1973
Membership: *Fees:* $40 individual; $28 retired; $15 student; $195 corporate
Chief Officer(s):
Michael Robertson, President
michael.robertson@acadiau.ca
Pierre M. Charest, Treasurer
pierre-mathieu.charest.1@ulaval.ca
Line Mongeon, Executive Secretary
line.mongeon@mcgill.ca
Meetings/Conferences:
• Microscopical Society of Canada 45th Annual Meeting, 2018
Scope: National
Publications:
• Bulletin [a publication of the Microscopical Society of Canada]
Type: Newsletter; *Editor:* Nadi Braidy

Middle River & Area Historical Society
Cape Breton NS
middleriverhistoricalsociety.wordpress.com
Overview: A small local organization founded in 1984
Member of: Federation of the Nova Scotian Heritage
Finances: *Annual Operating Budget:* Less than $50,000; *Funding Sources:* Donations; sale of books; fundraising
15 volunteer(s)
Membership: 13; *Fees:* $2; *Committees:* Auditing
Chief Officer(s):
Shirley Hart, Contact, 902-295-2686
mrhs844@gmail.com
Peggy MacLeod, Contact, 902-295-2669
pegnsandy@ns.sympatico.ca
Publications:
• Middle River Cemetery Book [a publication of the Middle River & Area Historical Society]
Type: Book
Profile: A full name index, stone inscriptions, history & photographs relating to the Middle River Cemetery
• Middle River Past & Present [a publication of the Middle River & Area Historical Society]
Type: Book; *Number of Pages:* 310; *Author:* John A. Nicholson; *ISBN:* 0-9696854-0-8
Profile: A history of Middle River from 1806-1985

- Name Index for Middle River [a publication of the Middle River & Area Historical Society]
Type: Book; Number of Pages: 69

Middlesex Community Living
82 Front St. West, Strathroy ON N7G 1X7
Tel: 519-245-1301; Fax: 519-245-5654
www.middlesexcl.on.ca
Overview: A small local charitable organization
Mission: To support developmentally disabled individuals in the Strathroy-Caradoc community
Member of: Community Living Ontario
Chief Officer(s):
Sherri Kroll, Executive Director
skroll@middlesexcl.on.ca

Middlesex Federation of Agriculture (MFA)
PO Box 820, 633 Lions Park Dr., Mount Brydges ON N0L 1W0
Tel: 519-457-8444; Fax: 519-264-9173
mfa4h@bellnet.ca
www.ofa.on.ca/about/county-federation-sites/middlesex.aspx
Overview: A small local organization founded in 1939 overseen by Ontario Federation of Agriculture
Mission: To advance agriculture & the rural community through partnerships, education & advocacy
Finances: Annual Operating Budget: $50,000-$100,000
Staff Member(s): 1; 50 volunteer(s)
Membership: 2500; Committees: Education; Communication; Special Events; Political Awareness
Chief Officer(s):
Lucia Lilbourne, Coordinator

Middlesex Law Association (MLA)
80 Dundas St., #N, Gr. Fl., London ON N6A 6A1
Tel: 519-679-7046; Fax: 519-672-5917
Toll-Free: 866-556-5570
library@middlaw.on.ca
www.middlaw.on.ca
Overview: A small local organization founded in 1879
Finances: Funding Sources: Law Society of Upper Canada; membership dues
Staff Member(s): 3
Membership: 850; Fees: $125 regular member; $60 first-year member & retired member; Member Profile: Hold a L.L.B.
Activities: Library: Not open to public
Chief Officer(s):
Bill Woodward, President, 519-673-1100, Fax: 519-679-6108
wwoodward@dyerbrownlaw.com

Middlesex, Oxford, Elgin Beekeepers' Association
c/o Bob Crowhurst, 21977 Wonderland Rd. North, RR#1, Arva ON N0M 1C0
Tel: 519-666-1670
www.moebeea.com
Overview: A small local organization
Mission: To educate & assist local beekeepers
Member of: Ontario Beekeepers' Association
Membership: Member Profile: Persons interested in beekeeping in Middlesex, Oxford, & Elgin, Ontario
Activities: Organizing meetings for members to provide timely information about beekeeping techniques & issues
Chief Officer(s):
Bob Crowhurst, President
robert.crowhurst@sympatico.ca

Middlesex-Lambton-Huron Association of Baptist Churches
ON
www.mlha.ca
Overview: A small local organization overseen by Canadian Baptists of Ontario and Quebec
Member of: Canadian Baptists of Ontario & Quebec
Membership: 19 churches; Member Profile: Baptist churches in Southwestern Ontario
Activities: Camp site; Golf tournament; Annual Picnic
Chief Officer(s):
Dave Stephens, Moderator

Mid-Island Coin Club
c/o West Coast Stamp & Coin, 4061 Norwell Dr., Nanaimo BC V9T 1Y8
Tel: 250-758-5896
relmcoin@shaw.ca
Overview: A small local organization

Mid-Pro Rock & Gem Society
c/o Prince Albert Arts Centre, 1010 Central Ave., Prince Albert SK S6V 4V5
Tel: 306-763-6581
Overview: A small local organization
Affiliation(s): Gem & Mineral Federation of Canada
Membership: Fees: $20 individual; $30 family

Mid-Toronto Community Services (MTCS)
192 Carlton St., 2nd Fl., Toronto ON M5A 2K8
Tel: 416-962-9449; Fax: 416-962-5541
admin@midtoronto.com
www.midtoronto.com
Overview: A small local charitable organization founded in 1965
Mission: Provides programs & services to support the independence of seniors & adults with disabilities to continue living in their own homes
Member of: Ontario Community Support Association
Finances: Funding Sources: Provincial government, municipal Government; United Way
Membership: Fees: Free
Activities: Alzheimer Day Program; Adult Day Program; Adult Enrichment & Wellness Program; Meals on Wheels; critical housing support; community transportation; volunteer opportunities; social work services; Korean social work; Internships: Yes; Speaker Service: Yes; Rents Mailing List: Yes
Chief Officer(s):
Kaarina Luoma, Executive Director
kluoma@midtoronto.com
Susan Burns, Chair

Midwives Association of British Columbia
#2, 175 - 15th Ave. East, Vancouver BC V5T 2P6
Tel: 604-736-5976; Fax: 604-736-5957
mabc@telus.net
www.bcmidwives.com
www.facebook.com/196300877987
twitter.com/bcmidwives
Overview: A small provincial organization founded in 1980
Mission: Supports the profession of midwifery in British Columbia
Member of: International Confederation of Midwives; Canadian Association of Midwives
Finances: Funding Sources: Membership dues
Chief Officer(s):
Ganga Jolicoeur, Executive Director

Midwives Association of Saskatchewan (MAS)
c/o Birdene Keefe, 439 Assiniboia St., Weyburn SK S4H 0R5
glk@sasktel.net
www.saskatchewanmidwives.com
Overview: A small provincial organization founded in 1987
Mission: To support midwives working in Saskatchewan; To promote midwifery in the province
Finances: Funding Sources: Membership fees
Membership: Fees: $50 non-voting members, such as students & others interested in midwifery; $100 voting members; Member Profile: Practicing & non-practicing persons in Saskatchewan with midwifery training & experience
Activities: Providing education about midwifery
Chief Officer(s):
Birdene Keefe, Treasurer

Midwives Collective of Toronto
1203 Bloor St. West, Toronto ON M6H 1N3
Tel: 416-963-8842; Fax: 416-963-4398
midwivescollective@bellnet.ca
www.midwivescollective.ca
Overview: A small local organization founded in 1983
Finances: Funding Sources: Provincial government
Staff Member(s): 3; 1 volunteer(s)
Activities: Prenatal care; birth care; postnatal care
Chief Officer(s):
Heather Douglas, Administrator

Military Collectors Club of Canada (MCC of Canada)
1442 - 26A St. SW, Calgary MB T3C 1K8
Tel: 204-669-0871
militarycollectorsclubofcanada@yahoo.ca
www.mccofc.ca
Overview: A medium-sized international organization founded in 1963
Mission: To serve as the focal point for collectors of all types of military artifacts, including medals, badges, artwork, military arms, vehicles or any other militaria-related item
Membership: 500+; Fees: $25 Canada; US$25 US; $30 International; Member Profile: Individuals in Canada, the US or internationally who are interested in militaria, military history & research
Activities: Preserving military artifacts; Researching military history; Organizing conventions
Chief Officer(s):
Doug Styles, President, 780-483-7985
dstyles@shaw.ca
Garry Milne, Vice President, 403-242-7704
gemilne@telus.net
Martin Urquhart, Secretary-Treasurer
mccofc@shaw.ca

Militia of the Immaculata Canada (M.I.)
PO Box 21003, 314 Harwood Ave. South, Ajax ON L1S 2J0
Tel: 905-686-1256
immaculatacanada@yahoo.com
consecration.ca
Overview: A small national organization founded in 1922
Mission: To recognize the consecration to God through the Immaculata the primacy of vocation to sanctity; to bring together spiritual life & action; To live out its ecclesial dimension, by taking on pastoral programs of the bishops' conferences; To listen to the needs of the New Evangelization
Affiliation(s): Archdiocese of Toronto
Membership: Member Profile: Members of the Militia of the Immaculata Canada live consecration in the Church, love the Church, & recognize & profess their Catholic faith; Individuals are called to work with creativity & unity, while combining Church teaching, Kolbean inspiration, & environmental concerns
Activities: Contributing in all areas in the form of catechesis, social work, humanitarian initiatives, & cultural proposals; Participating in the apostolate of the Church, in the spirit of our Marian consecration

Mill Woods Society for Community Living (MSCL)
1911 - 42 St., Edmonton AB T6L 5P8
Tel: 780-450-9884; Fax: 780-465-3897
mscl@shaw.ca
Previous Name: Millwoods Society for Community Living
Overview: A small local charitable organization founded in 1986
Mission: To support & advocate for individuals with multiple disabilities in their home & their community; To enhance awareness & understanding for all individuals with disabilities
Member of: Alberta Association of Rehabilitation Centres; Alberta Council of Disability Services
Finances: Annual Operating Budget: $250,000-$500,000; Funding Sources: Provincial government
Staff Member(s): 18
Membership: 60
Chief Officer(s):
Henriette Groeneveld, Executive Director

Millarville Racing & Agricultural Society (MRAS)
PO Box 68, Millarville AB T0L 1K0
Tel: 403-931-3411; Fax: 403-931-3485
www.millarvilleracetrack.com
www.facebook.com/131119606994283
twitter.com/MillarvilleFM
Overview: A small local organization founded in 1907
Mission: To build a strong community
Member of: Alberta Association of Agricultural Societies
Finances: Annual Operating Budget: $250,000-$500,000
Staff Member(s): 3; 300 volunteer(s)
Membership: 500; Fees: $38.50 individual; $44 family; $26.25 student/senior
Activities: Organizing rodeos, races, farmers' markets, & fairs
Chief Officer(s):
Barb Castell, Staff
Don Stewart, President

Millbrook & Cavan Historical Society
PO Box 334, Millbrook ON L0A 1G0
Tel: 705-932-2713
millbrookcavanhs@gmail.com
www.millbrookcavanhs.com
Overview: A small local organization
Mission: To preserve & promote local history
Member of: Ontario Historical Society
Membership: Fees: $15 single; $25 family; $5 student

Millbrook & District Chamber of Commerce
PO Box 271, 46 King St. East, Millbrook ON L0A 1G0
Tel: 705-932-7007
www.millbrook.ca
twitter.com/millbrookon
Overview: A small local organization founded in 1953
Mission: To promote the Millbrook community
Membership: Fees: $100
Chief Officer(s):

Karen Irvine, Office Manager

Millet & District Chamber of Commerce
PO Box 389, Millet AB T0C 1Z0
Tel: 780-387-4554; *Fax:* 780-387-4459
Overview: A small local organization
Mission: To promote business & tourism in the Millet area

Millet & District Historical Society (MDHS)
PO Box 178, Millet AB T0C 1Z0
Tel: 780-387-5558
info@milletmuseum.ca
www.milletmuseum.ca
Overview: A small local charitable organization founded in 1977
Mission: To maintain, preserve, further develop & expand Millet's cultural resources; & ensure them for future generations; to operate Millet & District Museum & Archives
Member of: Museums Alberta; Archives Society of Alberta; Central Alberta Regional Museums Network
Finances: *Funding Sources:* Bingos; Grants; Donations
Membership: *Member Profile:* Interested in preserving Millet history
Activities: School curriculum tours; Interpretation guided tours; Trade show; Parade; Conservation; *Library:* Museum Archives; by appointment
Chief Officer(s):
Tracey Leavitt, Executive Director

Millwoods Society for Community Living *See* Mill Woods Society for Community Living

Milton Chamber of Commerce
#104, 251 Main St. East, Milton ON L9T 1P1
Tel: 905-878-0581; *Fax:* 905-878-4972
info@miltonchamber.ca
www.miltonchamber.ca
www.linkedin.com/groups/Milton-Chamber-Commerce-44704?trk=myg_ugrp_ovr
www.facebook.com/miltonchamber
twitter.com/miltonchamber
www.youtube.com/miltonchamber
Overview: A small local organization founded in 1888
Mission: To strengthen the business climate of the community
Membership: 700; *Fees:* Schedule available; *Committees:* Business After Hours; Escarpment Country Tourism; Milton Farmers' Market; Golf Tournament; Government Relations; Marketing & Communications; Meetings & Seminars; Membership Services; Milton Young Professionals; Scholarship Fund Selection; Special Events; Sports Celebrity Dinner & Auction
Activities: Organizing networking events & business seminars; Providing programs & advertising; Advocating on behalf of members
Chief Officer(s):
Scott McCammon, President & CEO
scott@miltonchamber.ca

Milton Historical Society (MHS)
16 James St., Milton ON L9T 2P4
Tel: 905-875-4156
miltonhistoricalsociety@bellnet.ca
www.miltonhistoricalsociety.ca
www.facebook.com/184811598254298
twitter.com/miltonsoldiers
Overview: A small local charitable organization founded in 1977
Mission: To provide a friendly forum for those interested in the Milton community; to search out Milton's heritage & make it known to the community; to recognize those who have helped preserve our heritage; to cooperate with other heritage organizations & Town Council on heritage projects & concerns; to stimulate public interest in Milton's historic people & places; to encourage & assist educational heritage programs
Member of: Ontario Historical Society
Finances: *Funding Sources:* Membership dues; government grants; plaquing; books
15 volunteer(s)
Membership: 50; *Fees:* $20
Activities: Awards; 10 monthly meetings; outreach; research; publishing; community displays; Mayor's Levee; *Library:* Milton Historical Society Collection; by appointment
Chief Officer(s):
Jan Mowbray, President
Awards:
• Heritage Awards for Visual Arts, Education, & Writing
• President's Award
Given to a home owner who has preserved & maintained an older home

Minalliance
#2200, 1250, boul René-Lévesque ouest, Montréal QC H3B 4W8
Tel: 514-983-1382; *Fax:* 514-989-3136
minalliance.ca
www.linkedin.com/company/minalliance
Overview: A medium-sized provincial organization founded in 2010
Mission: Minalliance is the Quebec mining industry's communications fund that brings together Quebec and Canadian mining exploration and production companies, suppliers of goods and services, industry associations and other partners.
Chief Officer(s):
Isabelle Poirier, Executive Director

MindFuel
#260, 3512 - 33 St. NW, Calgary AB T2L 2A6
Tel: 403-220-0077; *Fax:* 403-284-4132
info@mindfuel.ca
mindfuel.ca
Previous Name: Science Alberta Foundation
Overview: A medium-sized provincial organization founded in 1990
Mission: To increase science literacy by creating innovative programs for all Albertans
Finances: *Funding Sources:* Provincial government; private donations
Activities: Science-in-a-Crate; science festivals
Chief Officer(s):
Cassy Weber, CEO
Alma Abugov, Director, Development & Community Engagement

La Mine d'Or, entreprise d'insertion sociale
542, 3e rue, Chibougamau QC G8P 1N9
Tél: 418-748-4183
dglaminedor@outlook.com
Aperçu: *Dimension:* petite; *Envergure:* provinciale
Mission: Organisme sans but lucratif, qui a pour mission l'insertion sociale & professionnelle des personnes en situation d'exclusion; offre une passerelle aux participants vers le marché du travail, la formation ou d'autres alternatives
Membre de: Collectif des entreprises d'insertion du Québec
Membre(s) du bureau directeur:
France Bureau, Présidente

The Mineral & Gem Society of Nova Scotia *See* The Nova Scotia Mineral & Gem Society

Mineral Society of Manitoba (MSM)
c/o The Manitoba Museum, 190 Rupert Ave., Winnipeg MB R3B 0N2
mineralsocietyofmanitoba.weebly.com
Overview: A small provincial organization founded in 1971
Mission: To promote the study of minerals, rocks, & fossils for both scientific & recreational purposes
Membership: *Fees:* $15 individuals; $20 families
Activities: Hosting monthly meetings at the Manitoba Museum; organizing field trips; planning educational exhibits; guest speakers
Chief Officer(s):
Jacques Bourgeois, President
Publications:
• The Mineral Vein: The Mineral Society of Manitoba Newsletter
Type: Newsletter; *Frequency:* 9 pa
Profile: Upcoming events, presentation summaries, & articles about rockhounding & mineralogy

Mineralogical Association of Canada (MAC) / Association minéralogique du Canada
490, rue de la Couronne, Québec QC G1K 9A9
Tel: 418-653-0333; *Fax:* 418-653-0777
office@mineralogicalassociation.ca
www.mineralogicalassociation.ca
Overview: A medium-sized national charitable organization founded in 1955
Mission: To promote & advance knowledge of mineralogy & the allied disciplines of petrology, crystallography, mineral deposits, & geochemistry
Membership: *Member Profile:* Individuals or organizations engaged or interested in mineralogy, crystallography, petrology, geochemistry, & economic geology; *Committees:* Finance
Activities: Organizing annual meetings & symposia; Providing short courses; Disseminating information about mineralogy; Providing reference books & textbooks in the mineral sciences; Presenting awards & scholarships; Increasing public awareness of science
Chief Officer(s):
Lee A. Groat, President
lgroat@eos.ubc.ca
Johanne Coran, Manager, Business
jcaron@mineralogicalassociation.ca
Publications:
• The Canadian Mineralogist: The Journal of the Mineralogical Association of Canada
Type: Journal; *Frequency:* Bimonthly; *Editor:* Robert F. Martin
Profile: Subjects include mineralogy, mineral deposits, petrology, crystallography, & geochemistry
• Elements: An International Magazine of Mineralogy, Geochemistry, & Petrology
Type: Magazine; *Frequency:* Bimonthly; *Accepts Advertising;* *Editor:* Pierrette Tremblay; *ISSN:* 1811-5209; *Price:* Free with membership in the Mineralogical Association of Canada
Profile: An international magazine published by organizations such as the Mineralogical Association of Canada, theMineralogical Society of America, the Mineralogical Society of Great Britain & Ireland, the European Association of Geochemistry, the Clay Minerals Society, & the Geochemical Society

Mines Alerte Canada *See* MiningWatch Canada

Miniature Horse Association of Canada
c/o David Trus, #316, 1305 Baseline Rd., Tower 5, Ottawa ON K1A 0C5
Tel: 613-773-0229; *Fax:* 613-759-6316
Overview: A small national organization founded in 1992
Mission: To establish standards of breeding for miniature horses; To encourage the breeding, exhibiting, & uses of miniature horses
Affiliation(s): Canadian Livestock Records Corporation
Membership: *Fees:* $45 initiation fee for persons other than juniors; $25 / year Canadian & foreign members; $5 junior members; *Member Profile:* Owners, associations, clubs, & enthusiasts of miniature horses
Activities: Publicizing miniature horses to increase public awareness; Providing educational programs for miniature horse owners & enthusiasts; Liaising with similar organizations
Chief Officer(s):
Mavis MacDonald, Registrar, 613-731-7110 Ext. 311, Fax: 613-731-0704
David Trus, Officer, Animal Registration, 613-773-0229, Fax: 613-759-6316

Miniature Horse Association of Nova Scotia (MHANS)
c/o Brenda Green, 260 Dagger Woods Rd., Heatherton NS B0H 1R0
www.mhans.ca
Also Known As: Nova Scotia Mini Club
Overview: A small provincial organization founded in 2003
Mission: To promote the miniature horse breed in Nova Scotia; To support activities that will benefit miniature horses in Nova Scotia; To encourage communication among Nova Scotia's miniature horse community
Finances: *Annual Operating Budget:* Less than $50,000; *Funding Sources:* Fundraising
20 volunteer(s)
Membership: 50; *Fees:* $10 individual; $20 family; *Member Profile:* Persons involved in the miniature horse industry in Nova Scotia; *Committees:* Audit; Show
Activities: Presenting educational clinics about showing miniature horses; Sanctioning & participating in shows; Increasing public awareness of miniature horses in Nova Scotia; Organizing regular meetings; Providing information about the breed for members; Offering networking opportunities; Liaising with similar organizations
Chief Officer(s):
Dorothy Best, President
Brenda Green, Vice-President
Dorrie Mosel, Secretary
Kim Horton, Treasurer, 902-364-2258
horton.rk@ns.sympatico.ca

Miniature Horse Club of Ontario (MHCO)
c/o Carolyn Aarup, PO Box 2, RR#1, Meaford ON N4L 1W5
Tel: 519-538-3114
mhco@mhco.ca
www.mhco.ca
www.facebook.com/120325871333053
Overview: A small provincial organization
Mission: To provide information & opportunity for those in Ontario who are interested in the miniature horse breed; To encourage improvement of miniature horse stock through proper breeding programs

Member of: Ontario Equestrian Federation
Affiliation(s): American Miniature Horse Registry
Membership: *Fees:* $20 youth members, age 17 & under; $35 single members; $45 families; $55 farms; *Member Profile:* Miniature horse enthusiasts of any age in Ontario; *Committees:* Advertising, Promotion & Public Relation; MHCO Club Point Shows; AMHR Sanction Show; Social; Fundraising; MHCO Awards; Administration, Rules, & By-Laws; Youth Club Plus; Electronic Media
Activities: Promoting the miniature horse breed in Ontario at various public events, such as equine events; Providing educational clinics on topics such as show preparation, conformation, & driving principles; Participating in competitions for miniature horses; Hosting shows, such as the annual American Miniature Horse Registry sanctioned show; Presenting awards; Offering recreational activities; Hosting two general meetings each year to plan club activities; Planning fun days for members & their horses, such as pleasure drives
Chief Officer(s):
Doug Savage, President, 905-936-6873
savagemoor@hotmail.com
John McCallum, Vice-President, 519-285-5683
ajmccallum@rogers.com
Angie Trumpler, Secretary
trumpler56@gmail.com
Carolyn Aarup, Treasurer & Coordinator, Promotions
kacahana@sympatico.ca

Mining Association of British Columbia (MABC)
#900, 808 West Hastings St., Vancouver BC V6C 2X4
Tel: 604-681-4321; *Fax:* 604-681-5305
mabcinfo@mining.bc.ca
www.mining.bc.ca
www.facebook.com/MABCMining
twitter.com/ma_bc
Overview: A medium-sized provincial organization founded in 1901 overseen by Mining Association of Canada
Mission: To speak on behalf of mineral producers; To represent the interests of British Columbia's mining industry; To communicate with senior government decision-makers, communities, NGOs, First Nations, & the media; To act as the industry's voice regarding issues such as environmental regulations, taxation, infrastructure demands, labour issues, health & safety, & international trade
Staff Member(s): 4
Membership: 48; *Member Profile:* Corporations with producing operations within BC, service & supply organizations, institutions, & non-profit organizations
Activities: Liaising with government legislators; Lobbying for regulatory advancement; Promoting the economic & social value of mining; Updating members on regulatory change; Facilitating exchange of information among members
Chief Officer(s):
Karina Briño, President & CEO
kbrino@mining.bc.ca
Bryan Cox, Vice-President, Corporate Affairs
bcox@mining.bc.ca
Awards:
• Mining Person of the Year
• Mining & Sustainability Award

Mining Association of Canada (MAC) / Association minière du Canada
#1100, 275 Slater St., Ottawa ON K1P 5H9
Tel: 613-233-9392; *Fax:* 613-233-8897
communications@mining.ca
www.mining.ca
twitter.com/theminingstory
Overview: A large national organization founded in 1935
Mission: To represent the interests of member companies engaged in mineral exploration, extraction & refining; To work with governments on public policy pertaining to minerals
Finances: *Annual Operating Budget:* $1.5 Million-$3 Million; *Funding Sources:* Membership dues
Staff Member(s): 12
Membership: 55
Activities: *Awareness Events:* National Mining Week, May; Mining Weeks in Canada, April - June
Chief Officer(s):
Pierre Gratton, President & CEO
Justyna Laurie-Lean, Vice-President, Environment & Regulatory Affairs
Jessica Draker, Director, Communications
Awards:
• Paul Stothart Memorial Scholarship in Mineral Economics
Eligibility: Candidates must be enrolled full-time in their second, third or fourth year of a Bachelors of Economics degree or in their first or second year of a Master of Economics or MBA program; must demonstrate an interest, supported by current or intended course work, in mineral economics or mining commerce *Deadline:* May; *Amount:* $3,500 *Contact:* Marilyn Fortin, Director, Corporate Services, E-mail: mfortin@mining.ca
Publications:
• Crisis Management Planning Reference Guide [a publication of the Mining Association of Canada]
Type: Report
• Energy & GHG Emissions Management Reference Guide [a publication of the Mining Association of Canada]
Type: Report
• Tailings Facility Management Guides [a publication of the Mining Association of Canada]
Type: Report
Profile: A series of guides on site-specific issues

Mining Association of Manitoba Inc. (MAMI)
#700, 305 Broadway Ave., Winnipeg MB R3C 3J7
Tel: 204-989-1890
www.mines.ca
www.linkedin.com/company/the-mining-association-of-manitoba-inc-
Overview: A medium-sized provincial organization founded in 1940 overseen by Mining Association of Canada
Mission: To represent mining & exploration companies in Manitoba
Finances: *Funding Sources:* Membership dues
Membership: 27; *Member Profile:* Mining companies with more than 50 employees; *Committees:* Exploration; Environment; Tax; Aboriginal Relations; Safety; Mine Rescue
Activities: *Speaker Service:* Yes; *Library:* by appointment
Chief Officer(s):
Lovro Paulic, Chair
Awards:
• John T. Ryan Award
Awarded to Canadian mines who have recorded the lowest reportable injury frequency per 200,000 hours worked from the previous year
Publications:
• Guidelines for Mineral Exploration in Manitoba [a publication of the Mining Association of Manitoba Inc.]
Type: Report
• Mining Association of Manitoba Inc. Annual Report
Type: Report; *Frequency:* Annually

Mining Association of Nova Scotia (MANS)
7744 St. Margaret's Bay Rd., Ingramport NS B3Z 3Z8
Tel: 902-820-2115
info@tmans.ca
tmans.ca
www.facebook.com/MiningNS
twitter.com/MiningNS
Overview: A medium-sized provincial organization founded in 1981
Mission: To ensure Nova Scotia is recognized internationally as having mineral resources worthy of investment; to develop mineral deposits; to work for government policies that provide a framework for a competitive mining industry within the global marketplace; to promote mining as a corporate industry creating wealth & long-term stable employment, with responsible environmental & social attitudes
Affiliation(s): Mining Association of Canada
Staff Member(s): 2
Membership: 90; *Fees:* Schedule available
Activities: *Library:* by appointment
Chief Officer(s):
Sean Kirby, Executive Director
sean@tmans.ca

Mining Industry Human Resources Council (MIHR) / Conseil des ressources humaines de l'industrie minière (RHIM)
#401, 260 Hearst Way, Kanata ON K2L 3H1
Tel: 613-270-9696; *Fax:* 613-270-9399
info@mihr.ca
www.mihr.ca
Overview: A medium-sized national organization
Mission: Contributes to the strength, competitiveness & sustainability of the Canadian mining industry by collaborating with all communities of interest in the development & implementation of solutions to the industry's national human resource challenges
Finances: *Annual Operating Budget:* $3 Million-$5 Million; *Funding Sources:* Government; Industry
Chief Officer(s):
Patricia Dillon, Chair
Ryan Montpellier, Executive Director

Mining Industry NL
Prince Charles Bldg., PO Box 21463, #W280, 120 Torbay Rd., St. John's NL A1A 2G8
Tel: 709-722-9542; *Fax:* 709-722-8588
info@miningnl.com
www.miningnl.com
Overview: A medium-sized provincial organization
Mission: To represent all sectors of the mineral industry in the province; to be a central contact for government, media & the public
Membership: 60 corporate; *Fees:* Schedule available; *Member Profile:* Exploration companies, mine operators, service & supply companies
Chief Officer(s):
Ed Moriarity, Executive Director
edmoriarity@miningnl.com
Jennifer Kelly, Communications Advisor
jkelly@miningnl.com

Mining Society of Nova Scotia
88 Leeside Dr., Sydney NS B1R 1S6
Tel: 902-567-2147; *Fax:* 902-567-2147
www.miningsocietyns.ca
Overview: A small provincial organization founded in 1887 overseen by Mining Association of Canada
Mission: To provide services in order to help & improve the mining industry
Affiliation(s): Canadian Institute of Mining, Metallurgy & Petroleum
Staff Member(s): 2
Chief Officer(s):
Bob MacDonald, President
Meetings/Conferences:
• Mining Society of Nova Scotia 131st Annual Meeting 2018, 2018, NS
Scope: Provincial

Mining Suppliers Trade Association Canada (MSTA)
#130, 7111 Syntex Dr., Mississauga ON L5N 8C3
Tel: 905-513-0046; *Fax:* 905-513-1834
minesupply@mstacanada.ca
www.mstacanada.ca
www.linkedin.com/company/mstacanada
www.facebook.com/mstacanada/
twitter.com/miningsuppliers
Previous Name: Canadian Association of Mining Equipment & Services for Export
Overview: A medium-sized international organization founded in 1981
Mission: To assist members with marketing to the mining world
Member of: Canadian Institute of Mining, Metallurgy & Petroleum; Prospectors & Developers Association of Canada; Canadian Manufacturers & Exporters
Finances: *Annual Operating Budget:* $500,000-$1.5 Million; *Funding Sources:* Membership dues; Special projects; Government support
Staff Member(s): 5; 8 volunteer(s)
Membership: 250; *Fees:* Schedule available; *Member Profile:* Organizations, with an office or employee in Canada, that seek to export goods & services to the global mining industry; Organizations that assist others to export goods & services; *Committees:* Audit; Personnel
Activities: Providing selling advice to members; Participating in international mining trade exhibitions; Networking with other firms in the mining sector; Researching target makets for member firms; Advocating; Offering information through the website & publications
Chief Officer(s):
Ryan McEachern, Managing Director,
mceachern@mstacanada.ca
Spencer Ramshaw, Director, Information & Communication
Dolores Wharton, Manager, Exhibition
Linda Collins, Manager, Office

Mining Suppliers, Contractors & Consultants Association of BC (MSCCA)
#900, 808 West Hastings St., Vancouver BC V6C 2X4
Tel: 604-681-4321; *Fax:* 604-681-5305
miningsuppliersbc.ca
Overview: A medium-sized provincial licensing organization founded in 1986

Mission: To promote the development of a sustainable mining industry in BC
Affiliation(s): Mining Association of British Columbia
Finances: *Annual Operating Budget:* $100,000-$250,000; *Funding Sources:* Membership dues; special events
Staff Member(s): 1; 3 volunteer(s)
Membership: 225 companies; *Fees:* Based on sales to BC mining
Activities: Networking functions with the mining industry
Chief Officer(s):
Terry B. Mulligan, President & CEO, 604-681-4321 Ext. 111
tmulligan@mining.bc.ca

MiningWatch Canada / Mines Alerte Canada
City Centre Building, #508, 250 City Centre Ave., Ottawa ON K1R 6K7
Tel: 613-569-3439; *Fax:* 613-569-5138
info@miningwatch.ca
www.miningwatch.ca
www.facebook.com/MiningWatch
twitter.com/MiningWatch
www.youtube.com/miningwatch
Overview: A small national organization founded in 1999
Mission: To address the urgent need for a coordinated public interest response to the threats to public health, water & air quality, fish & wildlife habitat & community interests posed by irresponsible mineral policies & practices in Canada & around the world
Member of: Canadian Environmental Network; Canadian Council for International Cooperation; Halifax Initiative
Staff Member(s): 5
Membership: 1-99; *Fees:* Sliding scale; *Member Profile:* Aboriginal, labour, environmental, international groups
Chief Officer(s):
Catherine Coumans, Research Coordinator

Minnedosa Chamber of Commerce
PO Box 857, Minnedosa MB R0J 1E0
Tel: 204-867-2951; *Fax:* 204-867-3641
minnedosachamber@gmail.com
www.discoverminnedosa.ca
Overview: A small local organization
Mission: To be the voice of the business community & enhance trade & commerce in the Minnedosa area
Member of: Manitoba Chamber of Commerce
Finances: *Annual Operating Budget:* Less than $50,000; *Funding Sources:* Membership fees & fundraising
4 volunteer(s)
Membership: 140; *Fees:* $30-160; *Committees:* Retail; Business Improvement; Membership; Executive
Activities: Organizing community events, parade, & town clean-up; Promoting tourism & economic development; Offering educational features
Chief Officer(s):
Brad Ross, President
Awards:
• Business of the Year
• Lifetime Achievement Award

Minor Hockey Alliance of Ontario
71 Albert St., Stratford ON N5A 3K2
Tel: 519-273-7209; *Fax:* 519-273-2114
www.alliancehockey.com
www.facebook.com/114981545258512
twitter.com/ALLIANCE_Hockey
Also Known As: Alliance Hockey
Overview: A small provincial organization founded in 1993
Mission: To organize, coordinate & develop hockey programs for all ages
Member of: Canadian Hockey Association; Ontario Hockey Federation
Staff Member(s): 5
Membership: 29,734; *Committees:* Development; Constitution; House League & Select; Minor Development; Group Structure; Insurance & Risk Management; Discipline & Suspension; Championship; Overseas; AGM
Chief Officer(s):
Tony Martindale, Executive Director

Minto Chamber of Commerce
PO Box 864, Harriston ON N0G 1Z0
Tel: 519-510-7400
info@mintochamber.on.ca
www.mintochamber.on.ca
Previous Name: Harriston-Minto & District Chamber of Commerce
Overview: A small local organization

Mission: To promote & support local businesses
Membership: 56; *Fees:* $65
Chief Officer(s):
John Burgess, President

Mirabel Morgan Special Riding Centre
1201 - 2nd Line South, Bailieboro ON K0L 1B0
Tel: 705-939-6485
mirabelmf@gmail.com
Overview: A small local organization
Mission: Year round program for anyone who wishes to ride who has medical, physical, or emotional needs; for those who enjoy the outdoors & animals, want to improve flexibility, balance, joint, muscle & nerve stimulation; designed to meet unique needs, limitations & abilities of the rider
Member of: Canadian Therapeutic Riding Association

Miramichi Board of Trade
6506 Rte. 8, Boiestown NB E6A 1Z7
Tel: 506-369-8889; *Fax:* 506-369-2468
Overview: A small local organization founded in 1953

Miramichi Chamber of Commerce (MCC)
PO Box 342, #2, 120 Newcastle Blvd., Miramichi NB E1N 3A7
Tel: 506-622-5522; *Fax:* 506-622-5959
mirchamber@nb.aibn.com
www.miramichichamber.com
www.facebook.com/miramichichamberofcommerce
twitter.com/MiramichiCofC
instagram.com/miramichichamber
Previous Name: Greater Miramichi Chamber of Commerce
Overview: A small local organization founded in 1981
Affiliation(s): New Brunswick Chamber of Commerce; Atlantic Provinces Chamber of Commerce; Canadian Chamber of Commerce
Membership: 231; *Fees:* Schedule available
Activities: Golf Tournament; Lunch and Learns
Chief Officer(s):
Jason Harris, President
Joyce Buckley, Executive Director

Miramichi Historical Society, Inc.
2224 King George Hwy., Miramichi NB E1V 6N3
Tel: 506-733-3448
Overview: A small local organization founded in 1959
Mission: To acquire & preserve papers, articles & artifacts of historical or architectural interest; to maintain archives of genealogical & historical information
Finances: *Funding Sources:* Provincial government; public donations
Activities: Operates Rankin House Museum

Miramichi Salmon Association
485 Rte. 420, South Esk NB E1V 4L9
Tel: 506-622-4000
nola@miramichisalmon.ca
www.miramichisalmon.ca
www.facebook.com/MiramichiSalmonAssociation
Overview: A small local organization founded in 1953
Mission: To preserve, protect & propagate the Atlantic salmon
Member of: Atlantic Salmon Federation
Finances: *Annual Operating Budget:* $500,000-$1.5 Million; *Funding Sources:* Fundraising; Membership dues; Donations; Government grants
Staff Member(s): 6
Membership: *Fees:* $10 junior/guide/camp staff; $50 regular; $100 sustaining; $250-$500 Corporations; $1000 lifetime
Chief Officer(s):
Mark Hambrook, President
mark@miramichisalmon.ca
Kenneth Kyle, Secretary-Treasurer

Miriam Foundation / Fondation Miriam
#620, 8000, boul Décarie, Montréal QC H4P 2S4
Tel: 514-345-1300; *Fax:* 514-345-6904
Toll-Free: 855-365-1300
info@miriamfoundation.ca
www.miriamfoundation.ca
www.linkedin.com/company/miriam-foundation
www.facebook.com/FondationMiriamFoundation
twitter.com/FondationMiriam
Overview: A small provincial organization founded in 1970
Mission: To provide services & support for individuals with autism spectrum disorder & intellectual disabilities; To enhance the quality of life for people with autism spectrum disorders & intellectual disabilities; To promote inclusion

Activities: Offering educational resources & training; Promoting research on diagnosis & treatment
Chief Officer(s):
Warren Greenstone, Chief Executive Officer

Mirror & District Museum Association
PO Box 246, Mirror AB T0B 3C0
Tel: 403-788-3828; *Fax:* 403-788-3828
mmuseum@telus.net
Overview: A small local charitable organization founded in 1977
Mission: To collect & display artifacts & specimens that depict the district's past in terms of natural resources, native peoples, exploration, transportation, settlement, education, cultural achievements, agriculture, petroleum, mining, manufacturing & with special emphasis of the contribution made by the railroad as an important factor in its economic base
Member of: Museum's Alberta
Chief Officer(s):
Ernie Schafer, President

Miss G Project
PO Box 557, Stn. A, Toronto ON K1N 9H1
missg@themissgproject.org
themissgproject.wix.com
www.facebook.com/missgproject
twitter.com/missgproject
Overview: A small provincial organization
Mission: The Miss G Project for Equity in Education is a grassroots feminist organization working to combat all forms of oppression in and through education.
Chief Officer(s):
Sarah Ghabrial, Political Action & Communications
sarah@themissgproject.org
Dilani Mohan, Finances & Events Coordinator
dilani@themissgproject.org
Sheetal Rawal, Research & High School Coordinator
sheetal@themissgproject.org
Lara Shkordoff, Education & University Coordinator
lara@themissgproject.org

Missing Children Quebec *Voir* Enfant-Retour Québec

Missing Children Society of Canada (MCSC)
#219, 3501 - 23 St. NE, Calgary AB T2E 6V8
Tel: 403-291-0705; *Fax:* 403-291-9728
Toll-Free: 800-661-6160
info@mcsc.ca
www.mcsc.ca
www.facebook.com/MissingChildrenSocietyofCanada
twitter.com/MCSCanada
www.youtube.com/user/MissingChildCanada
Overview: A medium-sized national charitable organization founded in 1986
Mission: To return missing children to a safe haven through professional investigations, emergency response, public awareness, & family support programs; To eliminate child abduction in Canada
Finances: *Funding Sources:* Donations
Staff Member(s): 8
Activities: Facilitating searches nationally & internationally through professional investigations & public awareness; Offering family support programs; Organizing fundraising activities; *Awareness Events:* "Light the Way Home"; National Missing Children's Day, May 25
Chief Officer(s):
Amanda Pick, Executive Director
apick@mcsc.ca
Craig Peterson, Contact
cpeterson@mcsc.ca
Brenda Mantle, Contact
bmantle@mcsc.ca
  Toronto Office
  #201, 446 Spadina Ave., Toronto ON M5T 2T7
  Toll-Free: 800-661-6160

Mission à l'intérieur de l'Afrique (Canada) *See* Africa Inland Mission International (Canada)

Mission Air Transportation Network *See* Hope Air

Mission Association for Community Living (MACL)
33345 - 2nd Ave., Mission BC V2V 1K4
Tel: 604-826-9080; *Fax:* 604-826-9611
macl@macl.bc.ca
www.macl.bc.ca
Overview: A small local charitable organization founded in 1958
Mission: To advocate for & build an inclusive & caring community where the empowerment & rights of all individuals

are realized
Member of: British Columbian Association for Community Living
Finances: *Annual Operating Budget:* $3 Million-$5 Million; *Funding Sources:* Provincial government; bingo & gaming revenue
Staff Member(s): 120; 15 volunteer(s)
Membership: 75; *Fees:* Schedule available; *Member Profile:* People with developmental disabilities; their families; staff; *Committees:* Advocacy; Public Relations; Executive
Activities: *Awareness Events:* Illuminaria, 3rd Sat. of Sept. *Library:* MACL Library; Not open to public
Chief Officer(s):
Kerridan Dougan, President

Mission Aviation Fellowship of Canada (MAFC)
264 Woodlawn Rd. West, Guelph ON N1H 1B6
Tel: 519-821-3914; *Fax:* 519-823-1650
Toll-Free: 877-351-9243
info@mafc.org
www.mafc.org
www.facebook.com/mafcanada
twitter.com/mafcanada
www.youtube.com/MAFCanada
Overview: A small international charitable organization founded in 1973
Mission: To provide aviation & communications help to overseas missions; To operate approximately 145 aircraft in over 30 developing countries
Member of: Canadian Council of Christian Charities
Affiliation(s): Mission Aviation US; Mission Aviation Australia; Mission Aviation Europe; Mission Aviation South Africa; Asas de Socorro, Brazil
Finances: *Annual Operating Budget:* $1.5 Million-$3 Million; *Funding Sources:* Donations
Staff Member(s): 60; 20 volunteer(s)
Membership: 1-99
Activities: *Awareness Events:* Charity Air Fair, last weekend in May
Chief Officer(s):
Robert Roebuck, Chair

Mission Bon Accueil / Welcome Hall Mission
606, rue de Courcell, Montréal QC M4C 3C1
Tel: 514-523-5288; *Fax:* 514-523-6456
info@missionba.com
www.missionbonaccueil.com
www.linkedin.com/company/welcome-hall-mission-mission-bon-accueil
www.facebook.com/MissionBonAccueil
twitter.com/whmba
www.youtube.com/user/whmba
Overview: A small local charitable organization founded in 1982
Mission: Pour fournir les moins fortunés à Montréal avec des services essentiels tels que le logement, le traitement de la toxicomanie, de la nourriture, des conseils et éducation
Finances: *Annual Operating Budget:* Less than $50,000
Staff Member(s): 110
Chief Officer(s):
Cyril Morgan, Directeur exécutif

Mission Community Services Food Bank *See* Mission Community Services Food Centre

Mission Community Services Food Centre (MCSS)
32646 Logan Ave., Mission BC V2V 6C7
Tel: 604-814-3333
missionfoodcentre@hotmail.ca
www.missionfoodcentre.ca
Previous Name: Mission Community Services Food Bank
Overview: A small local charitable organization founded in 1972
Mission: To identify & respond to the needs of individuals, families, & the community
Member of: Mission Community Services Society
Finances: *Annual Operating Budget:* Less than $50,000 10 volunteer(s)
Membership: *Committees:* Mission Food Coalition
Activities: *Awareness Events:* Christmas in July

Mission du Programme Cospas-Sarsat *See* International Cospas-Sarsat Programme

Mission Heritage Association (MHA)
PO Box 3341, Mission BC V2V 4J5
Tel: 604-826-0277; *Fax:* 604-826-0333
mhadmin@telus.net
www.heritagepark-mission.ca
www.facebook.com/FraserRiverHeritagePark

Overview: A small local organization founded in 1979

Mission Indian Friendship Centre (MIFC)
33150A - 1st Ave., Mission BC V2V 1G4
Tel: 604-826-1281; *Fax:* 604-826-4956
www.mifcs.ca/programs.html
www.facebook.com/missionfriendshipcentresociety
Overview: A small local charitable organization founded in 1973
Mission: To provide acceptable assistance & services to the community, without prejudice from an aboriginal perspective
Affiliation(s): all First Nations organizations
Finances: *Funding Sources:* Federal & provincial government
Staff Member(s): 14
Activities: *Awareness Events:* National Indigenous Peoples Day, June *Library:* Resource Centre; Open to public

Mission Old Brewery / Old Brewery Mission
902, boul Saint-Laurent, Montréal QC H2Z 1J2
Tél: 514-866-6591
info@missionoldbrewery.ca
www.oldbrewerymission.ca
www.facebook.com/168973503131279
twitter.com/missionOBM
www.instagram.com/mission_old_brewery
Aperçu: *Dimension:* petite; *Envergure:* locale; Organisme sans but lucratif
Mission: Offrir des services répondant aux besoins des personnes sans abri à Montréal
Finances: *Fonds:* Donations
Activités: Services d'urgence et de soutien; ressources
Membre(s) du bureau directeur:
Matthew Pearce, Président et chef de la direction
Alain Laurendeau, Vice-président, Finances et systèmes administratifs

Mission Regional Chamber of Commerce
34033 Lougheed Hwy., Mission BC V2V 5X8
Tel: 604-826-6914; *Fax:* 604-826-5916
info@missionchamber.bc.ca
www.missionchamber.bc.ca
www.facebook.com/Mission.Business.Network
twitter.com/MissionCommerce
www.youtube.com/TheMissionChamber
Overview: A medium-sized local organization founded in 1893
Mission: To foster a network for entrepreneurial leaders to partner in education, communication & representation
Member of: aC Chamber of Commerce; Vancouver Coast Mountains Tourism Association
Membership: 444; *Fees:* Schedule available; *Committees:* Membership; Events; Government Affairs; Tourism
Activities: *Awareness Events:* Annual Business Excellence Awards
Chief Officer(s):
Kristin Parsons, Executive Director
execdir@missionchamber.bc.ca

The Mission to Lepers *See* effect:hope

Missionaires de la Royauté du Christ *See* The Secular Institute of Missionaries of the Kingship of Christ

Missionary Sisters of Our Lady of the Angels *Voir* Soeurs missionnaires de Notre-Dame des Anges

Missionary Sisters of The Precious Blood of North America
St Bernard's Convent, 685 Finch Ave. West, Toronto ON M2R 1P2
Tel: 416-630-3298
www.preciousbloodsisters.com
www.facebook.com/PreciousBloodSisters
Overview: A small international organization founded in 1885
Mission: To be devoted to missionary service regardless of language, people or nation
Finances: *Funding Sources:* donations
Staff Member(s): 60

Missions catholiques au Canada *See* Catholic Missions in Canada

Les Missions des Soeurs Missionnaires du Christ-Roi
4730, boul Lévesque ouest, Chomedey QC H7W 2R4
Tél: 450-687-2100
missionsmcr@hotmail.com
www.missa.org/dc_m_smcr.php
Également appelé: Missions MCR

Aperçu: *Dimension:* moyenne; *Envergure:* internationale; Organisme sans but lucratif; fondée en 1979
Mission: Organiser, administrer, maintenir une oeuvre dont les fins sont la religion, la charité; promouvoir l'éducation et le bien-être, particulièrement en ce qui a trait aux différents buts qu'il s'est fixé; aide internationale
Finances: *Budget de fonctionnement annuel:* $100,000-$250,000; *Fonds:* Fondations; Subventions
Membre(s) du personnel: 1
Membre: 213 institutionnel
Activités: *Bibliothèque:* Not open to public

Missisquoi Historical Society / Société d'histoire de Missisquoi
2, rue River, Stanbridge East QC J0J 2H0
Tel: 450-248-3153; *Fax:* 450-248-0420
info@missisquoimuseum.ca
www.missisquoimuseum.ca
Overview: A small local charitable organization founded in 1899
Mission: To administer the Missisquoi Museum, including the Cornell Mill, Hodge's Store & Bill's Barn; UEL archives & to collect, preserve, research, exhibit & publish items of historical interest
Finances: *Annual Operating Budget:* $100,000-$250,000
Staff Member(s): 3; 75 volunteer(s)
Membership: 600; *Fees:* $10 single; $15 family; $125 life
Activities: Apple Pie Festival; *Library:* Archives; by appointment
Chief Officer(s):
Pamela Realffe, Executive Secretary

Mississauga *See* Habitat for Humanity Canada

Mississauga Arts Council (MAC)
#1055, 300 City Centre Dr., Mississauga ON L5B 3C9
Tel: 905-615-4278; *Fax:* 905-615-4171
mac@mississaugaartscouncil.com
www.mississaugaartscouncil.com
www.facebook.com/missartscouncil
twitter.com/missartscouncil
www.youtube.com/user/MACLimelight
Overview: A small local charitable organization founded in 1981
Mission: To foster & develop, support & champion a vibrant, dynamic arts community in the city of Mississauga through services; To enrich the lives of Mississauga citizens
Affiliation(s): Ontario Arts Council; City of Mississauga; Boards of Education in Peel; Mississauga Board of Trade
Finances: *Annual Operating Budget:* $500,000-$1.5 Million; *Funding Sources:* City of Mississauga; Sponsors; Donors; Membership fees; Ontario Trillium Foundation; Foundations
Staff Member(s): 6; 60 volunteer(s)
Membership: 250 groups + 250 corporate + 700 individuals; *Fees:* $19 student/senior; $29 individual; $35 family; $50 charity/non-profit/artist collective; $65 corporate; *Member Profile:* Individuals; organizations; corporations
Activities: Facilitating breakfasts, workshops, & other networking events; Advocating for the arts community; *Library:* by appointment
Chief Officer(s):
Anu Vittal, Executive Director
execdir@mississaugaartscouncil.com
Awards:
• MARTY Awards Program

The Mississauga Astronomical Society *See* Royal Astronomical Society of Canada

Mississauga Board of Trade (MBOT)
#701, 77 City Centre Dr., Mississauga ON L5B 1M5
Tel: 905-273-6151; *Fax:* 905-273-4937
info@mbot.com
www.mbot.com
www.linkedin.com/groups/Mississauga-Board-Trade-1851210
www.facebook.com/MississaugaBoardofTrade
twitter.com/MBOTOntario
www.youtube.com/user/MBOTMississauga
Overview: A small local organization founded in 1976
Mission: To provide a forum for business; To work together to influence public policy; To promote a better understanding of the marketplace among policy makers, educators, & the general public
Member of: Ontario Chamber of Commerce; Canadian Chamber of Commerce
Finances: *Funding Sources:* Membership fees
Staff Member(s): 9
Membership: 1,500; *Committees:* Ambassadors; Environment; Health & Safety; Human Resources; Independent Business;

Technology; International Trade; Education & Training; Transportation, Supply, Chain
Activities: *Speaker Service:* Yes; *Rents Mailing List:* Yes
Chief Officer(s):
Sheldon Leiba, President & CEO
sleiba@mbot.com

Mississauga Choral Society (MCS)
PO Box 59505, Mississauga ON L5H 1G9
Tel: 905-278-7059
info@mcschorus.ca
www.mcschorus.ca
www.facebook.com/pages/Mississauga-Choral-Society/273190841879
Overview: A small local organization founded in 1975
Mission: To present to its audiences the major works of the choral repertoire from the 16th to 21st century; to provide choristers an opportunity to improve vocal skills while learning & performing works
Member of: Mississauga Arts Council
Affiliation(s): Oakville Arts Council; Choirs Ontario
Finances: *Annual Operating Budget:* $100,000-$250,000; *Funding Sources:* Government
Staff Member(s): 3; 8 volunteer(s)
Membership: 90 individual + 12 associate; *Fees:* $10; *Member Profile:* Volunteer choir with paid section leads; *Committees:* Marketing; Programming; Finance; Fundraising
Activities: Resident choir of the Living Arts Centre, Mississauga; concert series
Chief Officer(s):
Mervin William Fick, Artistic Director & Conductor
Rosanne Caruso, Administrator
George Hrubecky, President

Mississauga Food Bank
3121 Universal Dr., Mississauga ON L4X 2E2
Tel: 905-270-5589; *Fax:* 905-270-4076
info@themississaugafoodbank.org
www.themississaugafoodbank.org
www.facebook.com/themississaugafoodbank
twitter.com/food_bank
Overview: A small local charitable organization
Mission: To distribute to food to the less fortunate in Mississauga
Staff Member(s): 8
Membership: *Fees:* $50
Chief Officer(s):
Christopher Hatch, Executive Director
chris@themississaugafoodbank.org

Mississauga Heritage Foundation Inc. (MHF)
1921 Dundas St. West, Mississauga ON L5K 1R2
Tel: 905-828-8411; *Fax:* 905-828-8176
Toll-Free: 877-223-3605
info@heritagemississauga.org
www.heritagemississauga.com
www.facebook.com/HeritageMississauga
Also Known As: Heritage Mississauga
Overview: A small local charitable organization founded in 1960
Mission: To identify, research, interpret, promote & encourage awareness of the heritage resources relating to the city of Mississauga
Member of: Heritage Canada
Affiliation(s): City of Mississauga
Finances: *Funding Sources:* City of Mississauga grant; service fees; fundraising
Staff Member(s): 5
Membership: *Fees:* $30 individual; $50 family/small business; $10 senior/students; $35 school/non-profit; *Committees:* Marketing
Activities: Organizing & promoting tours, lectures, exhibits, outreach efforts, events, awards dinner, & Heritage Mississauga Showcase; *Internships:* Yes; *Speaker Service:* Yes; *Library:* Resource Centre; by appointment
Chief Officer(s):
Jayme Gaspar, Executive Director
jgaspar@heritagemississauga.org
Awards:
• Modern Heritage Award
• Lifetime Achievement Award
• Special Recognition Certificate
Publications:
• Heritage News [a publication of the Mississauga Heritage Foundation]
Type: Newsletter

Mississauga Real Estate Board
#1, 3450 Ridgeway Dr., Mississauga ON L5L 0A2
Tel: 905-608-6732; *Fax:* 905-608-9988
membership@mreb.ca
www.mreb.ca
twitter.com/MREBca
Overview: A small local organization founded in 1954 overseen by Ontario Real Estate Association
Mission: To represent its members & keep them informed about events involving real estate so that they are able to provide knowledgable service to the public
Member of: The Canadian Real Estate Association
Staff Member(s): 5
Membership: 1,000-4,999; *Fees:* $160; *Committees:* CMC; Communications; Education; Finance; Golf; Governance; Government Relations; Membership; Nominations; Related Services
Chief Officer(s):
Donna Metcalfe, Executive Officer, 905-608-6732 Ext. 26
executiveofficer@mreb.ca

Mississauga-Etobicoke Coin Stamp & Collectibles Club (MECSCC)
5261 Naskapi Ct., Mississauga ON L5R 2P4
Tel: 905-677-3765
info@gta-collects.ca
www.gta-collects.ca
Previous Name: Thistletown Coin & Stamp Club
Overview: A small local organization
Mission: To promote collectors in various numismatic & related groups
Member of: Ontario Numismatic Association; Royal Canadian Numismatic Association
Membership: 25+
Activities: Monthly meetings
Chief Officer(s):
Bob Wilson, Chair

Mississippi Mills Chamber of Commerce
PO Box 1244, Almonte ON K0A 1A0
Tel: 613-216-5177
admin@mississippimills.com
www.mississippimills.com
www.facebook.com/MMChamber
Overview: A small local organization founded in 1996
Mission: To host networking events for its members
Member of: Canadian Chamber of Commerce
Membership: 109; *Fees:* $100 1-3 employees; $150 4-5 employees

Mittimatalik Hunters' & Trappers' Organization
PO Box 189, Pond Inlet NU X0A 0S0
Tel: 867-899-8856; *Fax:* 867-899-8095
Overview: A small local organization founded in 1974

Mizrachi Organization of Canada
296 Wilson Ave., Toronto ON M3H 1S8
Tel: 416-630-9266; *Fax:* 416-630-2305
mizrachi@rogers.com
www.mizrachi.ca
www.facebook.com/186778775014
twitter.com/MizrachiCanada
Also Known As: Mizrachi-Hapoel Hamizrachi Men's Organization
Overview: A medium-sized international charitable organization
Mission: To coordinate Zionist-oriented programming for the Orthodox Jewish communities in Canada; to raise funds for educational & social welfare institutions in Israel
Member of: Canadian Zionist Federation; World Religious Zionist Movement; World Mizrachi Organization
Finances: *Funding Sources:* Private donations
Staff Member(s): 4
Activities: Adult educational programs; *Speaker Service:* Yes; *Library:* Open to public by appointment
Chief Officer(s):
Meir Rosenberh, Executive Director
mizrachi@rogers.com

Mobilité Électrique Canada *See* Electric Mobility Canada

Model "A" Owners of Canada Inc. (MAOC)
PO Box 31, Stn. A, Toronto ON M1K 5B9
maocinc@rogers.com
www.modelaowners.com
www.youtube.com/user/ModelAOwners
Overview: A small national organization founded in 1959
Mission: To grow & maintain enthusiasm about the Ford Model A car
Finances: *Funding Sources:* Membership fees
Membership: 350+
Activities: Meetings held the first Tues. of every month
Chief Officer(s):
Ross Walter, President
rosswalter@cogeco.ca

Model Aeronautics Association of Canada Inc. (MAAC) / Modélistes Aéronautiques Associés du Canada
#9, 5100 South Service Rd., Burlington ON L7L 6A5
Tel: 905-632-9808; *Fax:* 905-632-3304
Toll-Free: 855-359-6222
www.maac.ca
Overview: A medium-sized national organization founded in 1949
Mission: To foster, enhance, assist, aid & engage in scientific development; To provide central organization to record & disseminate information relating to model aeronautics; To guide & direct national model aviation activities; To direct technical organization of national & international model aircraft contests
Affiliation(s): Aero Club of Canada; Fédération aeronautique internationale
Finances: *Funding Sources:* Membership fees
Membership: 13,000+; *Fees:* Schedule available; *Member Profile:* Aircraft modelling enthusiasts; *Committees:* Over 30 committees including all disciplines of model aviation
Activities: *Library:* Archives; by appointment Not open to public
Chief Officer(s):
Craig Ekstrand, President
Awards:
• MAAC [Model Aeronautics Association of Canada] Hall of Fame Award
To recognize a significant contribution to model aviation in Canada
Meetings/Conferences:
• Model Aeronautics Association of Canada 2018 Annual Meeting, 2018
Scope: National

Alberta Zone
4209 - 36 Ave., Leduc AB T9E 6A3
Tel: 780-986-9230
zone-a@maac.ca
Chief Officer(s):
Roger Ganley, Zone Director

Atlantic Zone
Kingston NB
Chief Officer(s):
Cato Hansen, Zone Director

British Columbia & Yukon Zone
#27, 2080 Pacific Way, Kamloops BC V1S 1V3
Tel: 250-374-4405
Chief Officer(s):
Roly Worsfold, Zone Director

British Columbia Coastal Zone
PO Box 1376, 129 Butler Ave., Parksville BC V9P 2H3
Tel: 250-951-4947
Chief Officer(s):
William (Bill) Rollins, Zone Director

Manitoba/Northwestern Ontario Zone
1256 Heenan Pl., Kenora ON P9N 2Y8
Tel: 807-468-7507
Chief Officer(s):
Peter Schaffer, Zone Director

Middle Ontario Zone
1546 - 8th Ave., St Catharines ON L2R 6P7
Tel: 905-685-1170; *Fax:* 905-641-1082
Chief Officer(s):
Roy R.R. Rymer, Zone Director

Northern Ontario Zone
40 Parkshore Ct., Sault Ste Marie ON P6A 5Z3
Tel: 705-759-1670
Chief Officer(s):
Kevin McGrath, Zone Director

Ottawa Valley Zone
Oxford Station ON
Chief Officer(s):
Geoff Strotmann, Zone Director

Quebec Zone
19, Martel de Brouage, Baie Comeau QC G4Z 2B2
Tel: 418-296-8791
Chief Officer(s):

Jean Paul Le Guilcher, Zone Director
St. Lawrence Zone
5763, av McAlear, Côte Saint-Luc QC H4W 2H2
Tel: 514-944-8241
Chief Officer(s):
Steve Woloz, Zone Director
Saskatchewan Zone
Swift Current SK
Chief Officer(s):
Jamie Skerten, Zone Director
Southeast Ontario Zone
Thornhill ON
Chief Officer(s):
Athol Cohen, Zone Director
Southwest Ontario Zone
450 Broadway St., Tillsonburg ON N4G 3S7
Tel: 519-550-7955
Chief Officer(s):
Frank Klenk, Zone Director

Model Forest of Newfoundland & Labrador (MFNL)
Humber Trust Building, PO Box 68, #11, 19 - 21 West St., Corner Brook NL A2H 6C3
Tel: 709-637-7300
Previous Name: Western Newfoundland Model Forest
Overview: A small local organization
Mission: The Model Forest is a not-for-profit corporation formed as a partnership of organizations & individuals working on the implementation of activities that advance their abilities to practice sustainable forest management & community-based economic development utilizing forest resources
Member of: Canadian Model Forest Network
Chief Officer(s):
Sean Dolter, General Manager
Glenda Garnier, Contact
glendagarnier@mfnl.ca

Modélistes Aéronautiques Associés du Canada *See* Model Aeronautics Association of Canada Inc.

Modern Baroque Opera Society
1895 Venables St., Vancouver BC V5L 2H6
Tel: 604-216-1114
Overview: A small local organization

Modular Housing Association Prairie Provinces (MMHA)
PO Box 3538, Stn. Main, Sherwood Park AB T8H 2T4
Tel: 780-429-1798; *Fax:* 780-429-1871
Toll-Free: 866-866-8106
www.mhaprairies.ca
www.linkedin.com/company/modular-housing-association-prairie-provinces
www.facebook.com/ModularHousingAssociationPrairieProvinces
Also Known As: Modular Housing Association
Previous Name: Modular Manufactured Housing Association - Alberta & Saskatchewan
Overview: A small provincial organization founded in 1975
Mission: To promote the interests of the manufactured housing industry in Alberta, Manitoba, & Saskatchewan
Finances: *Annual Operating Budget:* $100,000-$250,000; *Funding Sources:* Industry-funded
Staff Member(s): 1
Membership: 150; *Committees:* Advertising; Finance; Membership
Activities: Building green & sustainable housing; *Speaker Service:* Yes; *Library:* Not open to public
Chief Officer(s):
Sandra Nigro, Executive Director
snigro@mhaprairies.ca
Meetings/Conferences:
• 42nd Anniversary Modular Housing Association Prairie Provinces Annual General Meeting, 2018
Scope: Provincial

Modular Manufactured Housing Association - Alberta & Saskatchewan *See* Modular Housing Association Prairie Provinces

Moelle Épinière et Motricité Québec / Quebec Paraplegics Association
#400, 6020, rue Jean-Talon est, Montréal QC H1S 3B1
Tél: 514-341-7272; *Téléc:* 514-341-8884
Ligne sans frais: 877-341-7272
info@moelleepiniere.com
www.moelleepiniere.com
www.facebook.com/MEMOQuebec
twitter.com/MEMOQuebec
Aperçu: *Dimension:* moyenne; *Envergure:* provinciale; fondée en 1946 surveillé par Spinal Cord Injury Canada
Mission: Pour aider les personnes souffrant de lésions de la moelle épinière se réinsérer dans la société
Finances: *Fonds:* Emploi-Québec
Membre: 2,000
Activités: Intégration sociale; employabilité; défense des droits; sensibilisation et prévention; recherche scientifique
Membre(s) du bureau directeur:
Walter Zelaya, Directeur général
wzelaya@moelleepiniere.com

Mohawk Council of Akwesasne
PO Box 579, Cornwall ON K6H 5T3
Tel: 613-575-2250; *Fax:* 613-575-2181
info@akwesasne.ca
www.akwesasne.ca
Overview: A small local organization
Chief Officer(s):
Russell Roundpoint, CAO

Moisson Laurentides
25, rue Rolland-Brière, Blainville QC J7C 5R8
Tél: 450-434-0790; *Téléc:* 450-434-9235
reception@moissonlaurentides.org
www.moissonlaurentides.org
Aperçu: *Dimension:* petite; *Envergure:* locale; Organisme sans but lucratif; fondée en 1987
Mission: Une banque alimentaire dont le rôle est la récupération gratuite des surplus de l'industrie alimentaire et la distribution gratuite d'aliments aux plus démunis par l'intermédiaire d'organismes communautaires
Membre de: Reseau banques alimentaires du Québec; Banques alimentaires Canada
Finances: *Budget de fonctionnement annuel:* $250,000-$500,000
Membre(s) du personnel: 3; 500 bénévole(s)
Activités: Tournoi du golf
Membre(s) du bureau directeur:
Anne Bélanger, Directrice générale
direction@moissonlaurentides.org

Moisson Mauricie/Centre-du-Québec
1579, rue Laviolette, Trois-Rivières QC G9A 1W5
Tél: 819-371-7778
info@moisson-mcdq.org
www.moisson-mcdq.org
www.facebook.com/1499037073744555
Aperçu: *Dimension:* petite; *Envergure:* locale; Organisme sans but lucratif; fondée en 1988
Mission: Récupération et distribution d'aliments aux personnes économiquement défavorisées; lutte contre la pauvreté avec les organismes partenaires; utilisation de divers moyens pour favoriser la prise en mains des personnes démunies et développer leur autonomie
Membre de: Association québécoise des banques alimentaires et des moissons; Banques alimentaires Canada
Finances: *Budget de fonctionnement annuel:* $250,000-$500,000; *Fonds:* Centraide; Régie Régionale de la Santé et des Services Sociaux
Membre(s) du personnel: 6; 250 bénévole(s)
Membre: 60; *Critères d'admissibilite:* Organismes d'aide alimentaire; *Comités:* De soutien; d'accréditation des organismes; de bénévolat
Activités: Deux grandes collectes annuelles; Fête des bénévoles; Rencontres annuelle des organismes; *Evénements de sensibilisation:* Grande collecte de denrées; *Stagiaires:* Oui; *Service de conférenciers:* Oui
Membre(s) du bureau directeur:
Monique Trépanier, Directrice générale

Moisson Québec / Québec Harvest
2125, rue Hertz, Québec QC G1N 4E1
Tél: 418-682-5061; *Téléc:* 418-682-3549
info@moissonquebec.com
www.moissonquebec.com
www.facebook.com/moissonquebec
www.youtube.com/user/Moissonqc
Aperçu: *Dimension:* moyenne; *Envergure:* locale; Organisme sans but lucratif; fondée en 1987
Mission: Enrayer la faim et la pauvreté; récupérer et redistribuer gratuitement aux organismes communautaires les surplus agro-alimentaires; sensibiliser la population et les instances concernées à la faim et à la pauvreté; implanter des solutions favorisant l'autonomie des personnes en difficulté
Membre de: Fédération québécoise des banques alimentaires; Association canadienne des banques alimentaires
Affiliation(s): Centraide Québec & Chaudière-Appalaches
Finances: *Budget de fonctionnement annuel:* $500,000-$1.5 Million
Membre(s) du personnel: 8; 100 bénévole(s)
Membre: 80
Activités: *Evénements de sensibilisation:* Grande Collecte, avril; Soupe populaire, sept.; Guignolée des Médias, dec.; *Stagiaires:* Oui; *Service de conférenciers:* Oui; *Bibliothèque:* Centre de ressources éducatives; rendez-vous
Membre(s) du bureau directeur:
Elaine Côté, Directrice générale

The Molson Family Foundation / Fondation Famille Molson
1555, rue Notre-Dame est, Montréal QC H2L 2R5
Tel: 514-521-1786; *Fax:* 514-599-5396
Previous Name: The Molson Foundation
Overview: A small national charitable organization
Mission: To support innovative projects in fields of health & welfare, education, social development, national development & the humanities; registered Canadian charitable organizations only

The Molson Foundation *See* The Molson Family Foundation

Mon Réseau Plus, Association professionnelle des massothérapeutes spécialisés du Québec inc.
2285, rue St-Pierre, Drummondville QC J2C 5A7
Téléc: 819-472-2900
Ligne sans frais: 800-461-1312
info@monreseauplus.com
www.monreseauplus.com
www.linkedin.com/company/mon-r-seau-plus
www.facebook.com/MonReseauPlus.Massotherapie
twitter.com/MonReseauPlus
Également appelé: Mon Réseau +
Merged from: AMOC; CMA; CMAPPAC
Aperçu: *Dimension:* petite; *Envergure:* provinciale; fondée en 2008
Mission: Représenter les activités professionnelles de ses membres
Membre: *Montant de la cotisation:* 200$
Membre(s) du bureau directeur:
Martin Vallée, Président-directeur général
mvallee@monreseauplus.com

Mon Sheong Foundation
11211 Yonge St., Richmond Hill ON L4S 0E9
Tel: 905-883-9288; *Fax:* 905-883-9855
Toll-Free: 866-708-0002
msf@monsheong.org
www.monsheong.org
twitter.com/MonSheong
instagram.com/monsheong
Overview: A medium-sized local organization founded in 1964
Mission: To recognize the Chinese language & philosophy through caring for the elderly & edifying the young; To provide programs & services which respond to the needs of communities
Member of: Ontario Association of Nonprofit Homes & Services for Seniors
Affiliation(s): Ontario Hospital Association
Finances: *Funding Sources:* Ministry of Health; Donations; Membership fees
Membership: *Committees:* Chinese School; Finance; Development & Communications; Governane; Home; Human Resources; Senior Home; Volunteer Services & Youth Group
Activities: Operating the Mon Sheong Home for the Aged, the Mon Sheong Foundation Chinese Schools, & the Mon Sheong Youth Group
Chief Officer(s):
Stephanie Wong, CEO

Monarchist League of Canada (MLC) / Ligue Monarchiste du Canada
PO Box 1057, Stn. Lakeshore West, Oakville ON L6K 0B2
Tel: 905-912-0916
Other Communication: youth@monarchist.ca (Young Monarchists)
domsec@monarchist.ca
www.monarchist.ca
www.facebook.com/canadamonarchist
twitter.com/monarchist
www.youtube.com/LigueMonarchLeague?hl=en-GB
Overview: A large national organization founded in 1970

Canadian Associations / Moncton Area Lawyers' Association (MALA) / Association des avocats et avocates de la région de Moncton (AAARM)

Mission: To promote loyalty to the Sovereign & a broader understanding of constitutional monarchy as part of Canada's parliament, history, social fabric, culture & traditions
Affiliation(s): Canadian Royal Heritage Trust
Finances: *Annual Operating Budget:* $250,000-$500,000; *Funding Sources:* Membership fees; Donations
Staff Member(s): 2; 15 volunteer(s)
Membership: 25 institutional + 500 student + 13,500 individual + 3,000 other; *Fees:* $24; *Member Profile:* Loyalty to Crown
Activities: Promotion of education & support for the Canadian Crown; "Red Boxes" for schools & youth groups; *Awareness Events:* Royal Week, 3rd week of May *Library:* King George III Library; by appointment
Chief Officer(s):
Robert Finch, Dominion Chairman
chairman@monarchist.ca
Publications:
- Canadian Monarchist News [a publication of the Monarchist League of Canada]
Type: Newsletter

Moncton Archers & Bowhunters Association *See* Tir-à-l'arc Moncton Archers Inc.

Moncton Area Lawyers' Association (MALA) / Association des avocats et avocates de la région de Moncton (AAARM)
145 Assomption blvd., Moncton NB E1C 0R2
Tel: 506-389-1649; *Fax:* 506-856-6031
mala@nbnet.nb.ca
Previous Name: Moncton Barristers' Society
Overview: A small provincial organization founded in 1937
Mission: To procure & maintain a law library; to advance the science of jurisprudence; to promote the administration of justice; to uphold the honour of the profession of the law; to foster relations & cooperation among members; to encourage a high standard of legal education, training & ethics; to foster goodwill & better understanding of the legal system in the community
Finances: *Annual Operating Budget:* $50,000-$100,000; *Funding Sources:* Law Society of N.B.
Staff Member(s): 1
Membership: 204; *Fees:* $160
Activities: *Library:* Law Library; Open to public
Chief Officer(s):
Jacqueline A. Cormier, Librarian

Moncton Barristers' Society *See* Moncton Area Lawyers' Association

Moncton Chinese Friendship Association (MCFA) *See* Greater Moncton Chinese Cultural Association

Moncton Coin Club
PO Box 54, Moncton NB E1C 8R9
coincbnt@nbnet.nb.ca
Overview: A small local organization founded in 1961
Member of: Canadian Numismatic Association

Moncton Retriever Club
434 Charles Lutes Rd., Lutes Mountain NB E1G 2T4
Tel: 506-852-7107; *Fax:* 506-852-7107
yeloros@nb.sympatico.ca
Overview: A small local organization
Member of: New Brunswick Wildlife Federation
5 volunteer(s)
Membership: 20 individual
Chief Officer(s):
Brian Dempsey, President
Evelyn Hoyt, Secretary

Moncton University Employees Association *Voir* Association des employés de l'Université de Moncton

Monde des mots *See* People, Words & Change

Money Mentors
Airstate Bldg., #150, 1200 - 59 Ave. SE, Calgary AB T2H 2M4
Fax: 403-265-2240
Toll-Free: 888-294-0076
info@moneymentors.ca
www.moneymentors.ca
www.facebook.com/MoneyMentors
twitter.com/MoneyMentors
www.youtube.com/user/moneymentors
Previous Name: Credit Counselling Services of Alberta
Overview: A small provincial organization founded in 1997
Mission: Not-for-profit credit counselling agency helping consumers resolve debt & money problems & gain control over their finances
Member of: Credit Counselling Canada
Staff Member(s): 38
Activities: Offices in Red Deer, Lethbridge, Medicine Hat, Edmonton and Grande Prairie.
Chief Officer(s):
Jim Thorne, Executive Director

Montreal Advocates' Mutual Assistance Assocation *Voir* Association d'entraide des avocats de Montréal

Montréal Association for the Blind (MAB) / Association montréalaise pour les aveugles
Head Office, 7000, rue Sherbrooke ouest, Montréal QC H4B 1R3
Tel: 514-488-5552; *Fax:* 514-489-3477
info@mabmackay.ca
www.mabmackay.ca
Overview: A medium-sized local organization founded in 1908
Mission: To offer rehabilitation services (low vision, social work, occupational therapy, activites of daily living, orientation & mobility, computer adaptation, early intervention etc.) to blind & visually impaired persons; to offer residential services to blind & visually impaired seniors. The MAB-Mackay Rehabilitation Centre, located at 3500, boul Decarie in Montréal, provides family-centred adaptation, rehabilitation & social integration services to persons with a visual disability, and/or deaf or hard of hearing.
Finances: *Funding Sources:* Provincial government
Membership: *Member Profile:* Blind & visually impaired persons; *Committees:* Users'
Activities: *Internships:* Yes; *Speaker Service:* Yes

Montreal Association for the Intellectually Handicapped *Voir* Association de Montréal pour la déficience intellectuelle

Montréal Association of Insurance Women *Voir* Association des femmes d'assurance de Montréal

Montréal Association of Law Libraries *Voir* Association des bibliothèques de droit de Montréal

Montréal Cancer Institute *Voir* Institut du cancer de Montréal

Montreal CFA Society *Voir* Association CFA Montréal

Montréal Chamber Orchestra *Voir* Orchestre de chambre de Montréal

Montréal Children's Hospital Foundation *See* Fondation de l'Hôpital de Montréal pour enfants

Montréal Council of Women (MCW) / Le Conseil des femmes de Montréal (CFM)
1195 rue Sherbrooke ouest, Montréal QC H3A 1H9
Tel: 514-932-1154; *Fax:* 514-271-8914
mcwcfm@gmail.com
www.mcw-cfm.org
www.facebook.com/175809462469517
Overview: A small local organization founded in 1893
Mission: To improve the quality of life for women & their families in Québec
Affiliation(s): Canadian National Council of Women; Quebec Provincial Council of Women
Membership: 30,000; *Member Profile:* 70 federated societies
Activities: Monthly meetings; *Awareness Events:* Intl. Woman's Day (UN Day for Women's Rights & Intl. Peace), March 8
Awards:
- Woman of the Year Award

Montréal Danse
#109, 372, rue Sainte-Catherine ouest, Montréal QC H3B 1A2
Tél: 514-871-4005
questions@montrealdanse.com
www.montrealdanse.com
www.facebook.com/montrealdanse
Aperçu: *Dimension:* petite; *Envergure:* locale; Organisme sans but lucratif; fondée en 1986
Mission: Se voue à la création de vibrantes oeuvres chorégraphiques avec le concours de plusieurs chorégraphes nationaux et internationaux
Membre de: Regroupement québécois de la danse
Finances: *Fonds:* Conseil des Arts du Canada; Conseil des Arts et des Lettres du Québec; Conseil des Arts de Montréal
Membre(s) du personnel: 7
Membre(s) du bureau directeur:
Kathy Casey, Directrice artistique

Montréal Federation of Housing Cooperatives *Voir* Fédération des coopératives d'habitation intermunicipale du Montréal métropolitain

Montréal Field Naturalists Club
42, av Ballantyne nord, Montréal QC H4X 2B8
Tel: 514-769-1542
montrealfieldnaturalists.wordpress.com
Overview: A small local organization founded in 1971
Mission: To increase knowledge of nature through outdoor & indoor activities; to act when nature seems to be threatened, by expressing protests, participating in meetings
10 volunteer(s)
Membership: 150 individual; *Fees:* $15 individual
Chief Officer(s):
Pat Borlace, President
p.borlace@yahoo.ca

Montréal Firefighters' Association Inc. *Voir* Association des Pompiers de Montréal inc.

Montréal Gem & Mineral Club (MGMC) / Le Club de gemmologie et de minérlogie de Montréal
PO Box 32522, Stn. Lucerne, Ville Mont-Royal QC H3R 3L7
Tel: 514-878-9110
geminews@gmail.com
www.montrealgemmineralclub.com
Overview: A small local organization founded in 1957
Mission: To provide information about gems & minerals
Membership: *Fees:* $25 individuals; $35 families; *Member Profile:* Rockhounds, collectors lapidaries, jewelers, & persons interested in learning about gems & minerals in the Montréal area
Activités: Organizing programs & field trips; Planning workshops; *Evénements de sensibilisation:* Annual Gem & Mineral Show; *Bibliothèque:* Montréal Gem & Mineral Club Library
Publications:
- Geminews
Type: Newsletter; *Frequency:* Monthly; *Price:* Free for Montréal Gem & Mineral Club members
Profile: Club activities & forthcoming events

Montréal General Hospital Foundation *See* Fondation de l'Hôpital Général de Montréal

Montréal Heart Institute *Voir* Institut de cardiologie de Montréal

Montréal Heart Institute Foundation *See* Fondation Institut de Cardiologie de Montréal

The Montréal Holocaust Memorial Centre (MHMC) / Le Centre commémoratif de l'Holocauste à Montréal
Cummings House, 5151, ch de la Côte-Sainte-Catherine, Montréal QC H3W 1M6
Tel: 514-345-2605; *Fax:* 514-344-2651
info@mhmc.ca
www.mhmc.ca
www.facebook.com/78382729139
Overview: A medium-sized local organization founded in 1979
Mission: To provide services & programs for survivors of the Holocaust, their children & the general public (Jewish & non-Jewish, English & French speaking); to collect, document & preserve the record of Jewish life in Europe before, during & after the Holocaust
Member of: Canadian Museum Association; Société des musées québécois; International Council of Museums; American Association of Museums; American Association of State & Local History; Association of Holocaust Organizations; Canadian Jewish Historical Society
Staff Member(s): 10; 180 volunteer(s)
Membership: *Committees:* Education; Finance; Remembrance; Holocause Education Series; Human Rights; Kristallnacht; Museum; 35th Anniversary Event; Public Position; Rememberance; Yom Hashoah
Activities: Museum open throughout the year; provides guided tours, three major travelling exhibits; exhibits & museum, education & outreach are based on art, culture, historical reference & testimony & artifacts collected in Montréal; provides docent training, archives; Community Outreach - commemoration, testimonies, lectures/films, interfaith programs; Educational Resources - seminars/workshops, roundtable discussions, teachers' training, instructional material, speakers' bureau; CEGEP Holocaust Symposium; *Internships:* Yes; *Speaker Service:* Yes; *Library:* MHMC Library; Open to public
Chief Officer(s):
Alice Herscovitch, Executive Director
Helen Malkin, President

Montreal Numismatic Society
c/o Michael Joffre, #900, 1117, rue Sainte-Catherine ouest, Montréal QC H3B 1H9
Tel: 514-289-9761
medievalcoins@gmail.com
Overview: A small local organization
Chief Officer(s):
Michael Joffre, President

Montréal Opera Voir L'Opéra de Montréal

Montréal Print Collectors' Society Voir Société des collectionneurs d'estampes de Montréal

Montreal Sailors' Institute & Catholic Sailors' Club See Mariners' House of Montréal

Montréal Science Fiction & Fantasy Association / Association montréalaise de science-fiction et de fantastique
4456, boul Ste-Rose, Laval QC H7R 1Y6
president@monsffa.ca
www.monsffa.ca
Also Known As: MonSFFA
Overview: A small local organization founded in 1987
Membership: Fees: $25 standard; $35 platinum; $40 family;
Member Profile: Fans of the science fiction & fantasy genres in literature, movies, television, comics, gaming, art, animation, scale-model building, costuming, memorabilia collecting, & film & video production
Activities: Hosting meetings, lectures, & hands-on demonstrations

Montréal Soaring Council (MSC) / Club de Vol à Voile MSC
PO Box 147, Montréal QC H4L 4V4
Tel: 613-632-5438
info@montrealsoaring.ca
montrealsoaring.com
www.facebook.com/montrealsoaring
twitter.com/MontrealSoaring
Overview: A small local organization founded in 1946
Mission: To promote the sport of soaring & gliding, including the provision of gliding training
Member of: Soaring Association of Canada
Finances: Annual Operating Budget: $100,000-$250,000
Staff Member(s): 11; 30 volunteer(s)
Membership: 100; Fees: Schedule available; Member Profile: Open to individuals interested in soaring
Chief Officer(s):
Kurt Sermeus, Vice-President, 514-919-7374

Montréal SPCA
5215, rue Jean-Talon ouest, Montréal QC H4P 1X4
Tél: 514-735-2711; Téléc: 514-735-7448
admin@spcamontreal.com
www.spcamontreal.com
www.facebook.com/SPCAMontreal
twitter.com/SPCAMontreal
Également appelé: Société pour la prévention de la cruauté envers les animaux
Aperçu: Dimension: petite; Envergure: locale; fondée en 1869 surveillée par Canadian Federation of Humane Societies
Mission: Recueillir, héberger et soigner les animaux errants ou abandonnés; Rendre les animaux perdus à leurs propriétaires; mettre en adoption les animaux en santé; Inspecter et enquêter sur les plaintes de cruauté
Membre(s) du bureau directeur:
Nicholas Gilman, Directeur général

Monument canadien pour les droits de la personne See Canadian Tribute to Human Rights

Mood Disorders Association of British Columbia (MDA)
#1450, 605 Robson St., Vancouver BC V6B 5J3
Tel: 604-873-0103; Fax: 604-873-3095
info@mdabc.net
www.mdabc.net
www.facebook.com/mdasupport
twitter.com/MDA_BC
Overview: A small provincial charitable organization founded in 1982
Mission: To provide support & education for people with a mood disorder, & those around them, in order to help them live a healthy & active life
Staff Member(s): 7
Membership: Fees: $30

Activities: Awareness Events: National Mental Health Week; May; Speaker Service: Yes
Chief Officer(s):
Martin Addison, Executive Director

Mood Disorders Association of Manitoba (MDAM)
#100, 4 Fort St., Winnipeg MB R3C 1C4
Tel: 204-786-0987; Fax: 201-786-1906
Toll-Free: 800-263-1460
info@mooddisordersmanitoba.ca
www.mooddisordersmanitoba.ca
www.facebook.com/MoodDisordersMB
twitter.com/MoodDisordersMB
Overview: A small provincial charitable organization
Mission: To help others through peer support, education & advocacy; to increase public awareness about mood disorders & empower people to develop & manage mental wellness
Membership: Fees: $15
Chief Officer(s):
Tara Brousseau, Executive Director
TaraS@mooddisordersmanitoba.ca

Mood Disorders Association of Ontario (MDAO)
#602, 36 Eglinton Ave. West, Toronto ON M4R 1A1
Tel: 416-486-8046; Fax: 416-486-8127
Toll-Free: 888-486-8236
www.mooddisorders.ca
www.facebook.com/MoodDisordersAssociationON
twitter.com/mooddisorderson
instagram.com/mooddisordersassociation
Overview: A small provincial charitable organization founded in 1985
Mission: To provide information, education & support to those affected by depression & manic depression, their families & friends; to develop & maintain a network of supportive self-help groups; to improve the quality of life of people who experience mood disorders, their families & friends; to advocate for a flexible & responsive system of care
Member of: Federation of Community Mental Health & Addictions; Consumer Survivor Development Initiative
Finances: Annual Operating Budget: $250,000-$500,000
Staff Member(s): 6; 150 volunteer(s)
Membership: 1,500; Fees: Schedule available; Member Profile: Consumers/families with mood disorders; community mental health professionals; Committees: Conference; Nominating
Activities: Support groups; telephone information; information meetings; resource centre; public outreach; conferences; workshops; resource materials for group development; Distinguished Speakers Series; Speaker Service: Yes; Library: Paul Horner Resource Centre; Open to public
Chief Officer(s):
Ann Marie MacDonald, Executive Director, 416-486-8046 Ext. 226
annmariem@mooddisorders.ca
Publications:
• Mood Disorders Association of Ontario Fact Sheets
Type: Reports
Profile: A series of fact sheets about various mood disorders

Mood Disorders Society of Canada (MDSC) / La Société pour les troubles de l'humeur du Canada
#325, 110 North Front St., Unit A3, Belleville ON K8P 0A6
Tel: 613-921-5565
info@mdsc.ca
www.mdsc.ca
www.linkedin.com/company/mood-disorders-society-of-canada
www.facebook.com/MoodDisordersSocietyCanada
twitter.com/MoodDisordersCa
www.youtube.com/user/MDSofC?
Overview: A large national organization founded in 2001
Mission: To ensure that issues related to mood disorders are understood & considered in the setting of research priorities, the development of treatment strategies, & the creation of government programs & policies
Chief Officer(s):
Dave Gallson, National Executive Director
John Starzynski, President
Awards:
• Jordan James Pickell Mental Health Achievement Recognition Award
Awarded to organizations that have had an impact on the mental health community through contributions to mental health & anti-stigma education & activities
• Marg Starzynski Mental Health Leadership Award
Awarded to individuals who have demonstrated leadership in raising awareness of mental illness

Mooredale Youth Concert Orchestra
c/o Mooredale House, 146 Crescent Rd., Toronto ON M4W 1V2
Tel: 416-922-3714
orchestras@mooredaleconcerts.com
www.mooredaleconcerts.com/youth-orchestras
www.facebook.com/MooredaleConcerts
twitter.com/mooredaleconcrt
Overview: A small local organization founded in 1989 overseen by Orchestras Canada
Mission: To give serious young musicians an opportunity to prepare and perform orchestral selections at a high standard
Affiliation(s): Mooredale Concerts
8 volunteer(s)
Membership: 120; Fees: $400 senior; $375 intermediate; $325 junior; Member Profile: Junior, intermediate & senior string orchestras
Activities: Three performances per season
Chief Officer(s):
Christina A. Cavanagh, Managing Director
marketing@mooredaleconcerts.com

Moorelands Community Services
#501, 250 Merton St., Toronto ON M4S 1B1
Tel: 416-466-9987; Fax: 416-466-0727
info@moorelands.ca
www.moorelands.ca
www.facebook.com/moorelandscommunityservices
twitter.com/MoorelandsCS
www.instagram.com/moorelandscs
Previous Name: The Downtown Churchworkers' Association
Overview: A small local charitable organization founded in 1912
Mission: To provide positive experiences for children & youth in Toronto affected by poverty
Finances: Funding Sources: Donations; Foundations; Corporations; Churches; Individuals
Staff Member(s): 9
Membership: 1-99; Committees: Fundraising; Finance & Programs
Activities: Offering a summer camp; Providing year-round city programs for youth from ages six to eighteen; Arranging assistance for new mothers; Organizing a Christmas relief program; Raising public awareness; Speaker Service: Yes
Chief Officer(s):
Lynda Tilley, Executive Director, 416-466-9987 Ext. 308
Maureen Lewis, Director, Development & Communications, 416-466-9987 Ext. 307

Moose Jaw & District Chamber of Commerce
88 Saskatchewan St. East, Moose Jaw SK S6H 0V4
Tel: 306-692-6414; Fax: 306-694-6463
chamber@mjchamber.com
www.mjchamber.com
www.facebook.com/MooseJawChamber
Overview: A small local licensing organization founded in 1888
Mission: To act as the voice of business in Moose Jaw on matters affecting its membership & concerning the economic climate & directly related to social well-being of Moose Jaw & trading area
Member of: Canadian Chamber of Commerce; Saskatchewan Chamber of Commerce
Finances: Annual Operating Budget: $100,000-$250,000; Funding Sources: Membership dues; special events
Staff Member(s): 2; 20 volunteer(s)
Membership: 485; Fees: $105-$787.50; Member Profile: Businesses & individuals; Committees: Focus on Trade; Business Excellence Awards; Golf Tour
Activities: Providing business information & promotion; Library: Business Resource Centre; Open to public
Chief Officer(s):
Rob Clark, CEO
Heather Bergdahl, Office Administrator

Moose Jaw & District Food Bank
350 Fairford St. West, Moose Jaw SK S6H 1V8
Tel: 306-692-2911
Overview: A small local organization
Member of: Food Banks of Saskatchewan Inc.

Moose Jaw & District Labour Council
1402 Caribou St. West, Moose Jaw SK S6H 7S9
Tel: 306-693-6507
www.facebook.com/moosejawdistrictlabourcouncil
Overview: A small local organization overseen by Saskatchewan Federation of Labour
Mission: To support union members & workers in Moose Jaw, Saskatchewan & the surrounding region; To advance the the economic & social welfare of workers

Activities: Presenting educational seminars; Liaising with local elected officials to present workers' issues; Promoting the interests of affiliates; Increasing awareness of the plight of workers, by organizing events such as a ceremony on the Day of Mourning to remember workers who were killed & injured on the job; Supporting local community organizations, such as the Moose Jaw Health Foundation & the Transition House
Chief Officer(s):
Stacey Landin, President
staceylandin@sasktel.net

Moose Jaw Exhibition Company Ltd.
250 Thatcher Dr. East, Moose Jaw SK S6J 1L7
Tel: 306-692-2723; *Fax:* 306-692-2762
moosejawexh@sasktel.net
www.moosejawex.com
Overview: A small local organization founded in 1884
Mission: To provide quality entertainment, recreation & education for rural & urban communities
Member of: Saskatchewan Association of Agricultural Societies & Exhibitions
Affiliation(s): Canadian Association of Exhibitions; Western Canada Fair Association
Finances: *Annual Operating Budget:* $1.5 Million-$3 Million
Staff Member(s): 20; 200 volunteer(s)
Membership: 100; *Fees:* $5; *Member Profile:* Rural & urban
Activities: Spring & fall rodeo; Hometown Fair; *Awareness Events:* Moose Jaw Hometown Fair, June

Moose Jaw Humane Society Inc.
PO Box 1658, Stn. Main, 1755 Stadacona St. West, Moose Jaw SK S6H 7K7
Tel: 306-692-1517; *Fax:* 306-694-0720
contact@mjhs.ca
www.mjhs.ca
Overview: A small local organization founded in 1966
Mission: To promote the belief that all animals have intrinsic value, deserving humane & compassionate treatment
Member of: Canadian Federation of Humane Societies
Staff Member(s): 13
Membership: *Fees:* $20 senior; $25 regular; $500 lifetime/corporate
Activities: Provide shelter & care for lost & abandoned animals
Chief Officer(s):
Kristyn McEwen, Executive Director
kmcewen@mjhs.ca

Moose Jaw Multicultural Council (MJMC)
60 Athabasca St. East, Moose Jaw SK S6H 0L2
Tel: 306-693-4677; *Fax:* 306-694-0477
reception@mjmcinc.ca
www.mjmcinc.ca
Overview: A small local organization founded in 1974
Mission: Welcomes & integrates newcomers to Canada & develops harmonious relations among Canadians, through programs & activities that recognize, respect & promote the positive aspects of cultural diversity & that seek seek to discover, encourage & develop commmonalities among peoples
Member of: Multicultural Council of Saskatchewan
Affiliation(s): Saskatchewan Organization of Heritage Languages; Moose Jaw Chamber of Commerce; Saskatchewan Cultural Exchange Society; Saskatchewan Literacy Network
Membership: 15 organizations
Activities: Immigrant settlement & adaptation; *Awareness Events:* Motif, Moose Jaw Multicultural Festival, July *Library:* Moose Jaw Multicultural Council Library; Open to public

Moose Jaw Music Festival
1437 Duffield St. West, Moose Jaw SK S6H 5K5
Tel: 306-694-0953
moosejawmusicfestival@hotmail.com
www.smfa.ca/festivals/MooseJaw.php
Overview: A small local organization
Member of: Saskatchewan Music Festival Association
Chief Officer(s):
Marcie Carswell, Corresponding & Recording Secretary

Moose Jaw Real Estate Board
88 Saskatechewan St. East, Moose Jaw SK S6H 0V4
Tel: 306-693-9544; *Fax:* 306-692-4463
eo.mjreb@sasktel.net
www.moosejawrealestateboard.com
Overview: A small local organization overseen by Saskatchewan Real Estate Association
Mission: To promote the real estate sector in the area & provides a forum for local realtors to exchange information.
Member of: The Canadian Real Estate Association

Membership: *Committees:* Finance; Advertising & Public Relations; Membership & Education; Professional Standards; MLS Legislation & Standard Forms; Social
Activities: Fundraising for local charities
Chief Officer(s):
Jami Thorn, President
jamithorn@royallepage.ca
Jim Millar, Executive Officer

Moose Mountain Friendship Centre
PO Box 207, 112 Main St., Carlyle SK S0M OJO
Tel: 306-453-2425; *Fax:* 306-453-6777
Overview: A small local organization

Moosomin Chamber of Commerce
PO Box 819, Moosomin SK S0G 3N0
Tel: 306-435-2445
www.moosomin.com/chamber
Overview: A small local organization
Mission: To support & strengthen local businesses
Member of: Saskatchewan Chamber of Commerce
Finances: *Annual Operating Budget:* Less than $50,000; *Funding Sources:* Membership fees; projects
15 volunteer(s)
Membership: 93; *Fees:* $26.50-$254.40
Chief Officer(s):
Kevin Weedmark, Secretary
Janelle Davidson, Treasurer

Moosonee Native Friendship Centre
PO Box 478, Moosonee ON P0L 1Y0
Tel: 705-336-2808; *Fax:* 705-336-2929
www.onlink.net/~mcap
Overview: A small local organization founded in 1982
Mission: To assist the Aboriginal population of Moosonee with establishing a better quality of life, spiritually, culturally, socially & economically
Member of: Ontario Federation of Indian Friendship Centres

Moosonee-Moose Factory Association for Community Living *See* James Bay Association for Community Living

Morden & District Chamber of Commerce
#100, 379 Stephen St., Morden MB R6M 1V1
Tel: 204-822-5630
execdirector@mordenchamber.com
www.mordenchamber.com
www.facebook.com/mordenchamberofcommerce
twitter.com/MordenChamber
Previous Name: Morden Chamber of Commerce
Overview: A small local organization founded in 1890
Mission: To make Morden a better place to live & work
Member of: Manitoba Chamber of Commerce; Canadian Chamber of Commerce, Canadian Taxpayers Association
Finances: *Annual Operating Budget:* $50,000-$100,000; *Funding Sources:* Membership dues; grants; fundraising
Staff Member(s): 1; 8 volunteer(s)
Membership: 235; *Fees:* Schedule available; *Member Profile:* Small businesses; Home-based businesses; Individuals; *Committees:* Executive; Advocacy; Farmer's Market; Marketing & Communications; Programming; Information & Technology; Tourism; Board Development; Human Resource; Fundraising; Membership; Governance
Activities: Organizing annual meetings, spring golf tournament, seminars, farmer's market & events; *Library:* Canada/Manitoba Business Service Centre; Open to public
Chief Officer(s):
Candace Olafson, Executive Director

Morden Chamber of Commerce *See* Morden & District Chamber of Commerce

Morgan Sports Car Club of Canada (MSCCC)
21 Penn Dr., Burlington ON L7N 2B6
www.morgansportscarclubofcanada.com
Overview: A small national organization founded in 1965
Finances: *Annual Operating Budget:* Less than $50,000; *Funding Sources:* Membership dues; membership
Membership: 100; *Fees:* $25; *Member Profile:* Owners of Morgan sports cars or otherw with an interest in Morgans
Activities: Participation in British car events
Chief Officer(s):
Martin Beer, President

Morinville & District Chamber of Commerce
10113 - 100 Ave., Morinville AB T8R 1P8

Tel: 780-939-9462
www.morinvillechamber.com
twitter.com/MoriChamber
Overview: A small local organization
Mission: To promote the Morinville District as a leading business centre; To support, expand, & diversify business opportunities
Membership: 89; *Fees:* $75-$200
Chief Officer(s):
Simon Boersma, President

Morning Light Ministry
c/o St. Mary Star of the Sea Church, 11 Peter St. South, Mississauga ON L5H 2G1
Tel: 647-781-9300
morninglightministry@yahoo.ca
www.morninglightministry.org
www.facebook.com/139540882897810
Overview: A small local organization founded in 1996
Mission: To provide Catholic ministry for bereaved parents who have experienced the death of a baby through ectopic pregnancy, miscarriage, stillbirth, or infant death up to two years of age; To help families who have received an adverse prenatal diagnosis; To offer suuport to couples who are experiencing infertility
Affiliation(s): Archdiocese of Toronto
Membership: *Member Profile:* Bereaved Catholic parents, as well as bereaved parents of other Christian denominations, other faiths, & those with no religious affiliation who struggle with the notion of faith
Activities: Providing information at no cost; Counselling; Offering faith instruction; Providing support by e-mail, telephone, & individual & group meetings; Conducting an annual memorial Mass

Moroccan Association of Toronto (AMDT) / Association Marocaine de Toronto
Toronto ON
Tel: 416-834-3420
info@amdt.ca
www.amdt.ca
www.facebook.com/amdtoronto
Overview: A small local organization
Mission: To promote & defend the cultural interests of Moroccans in Toronto
Membership: *Member Profile:* Persons of Moroccan origin who reside in the Greater Toronto Area
Activities: Establishing traditional events & services to link the Moroccan community of Toronto: Providing information to newcomers to Toronto from Morocco; *Awareness Events:* Annual Cultural Party
Chief Officer(s):
Faouzi Metouilli, President
Salaheddine Tahori, General Director
Publications:
• Moroccan Association of Toronto Report of Activities
Type: Yearbook; *Frequency:* Annually

Morris & District Chamber of Commerce
141 Main St. South, Morris MB R0G 1K0
Tel: 204-712-6162
info@morrischamberofcommerce.com
www.morrischamberofcommerce.com
www.facebook.com/143472332424547
Overview: A small local organization founded in 1974 overseen by The Manitoba Chambers of Commerce
Mission: To promote & enhance business in the community; To promote tourism & recreational activities
Member of: Manitoba Chambers of Commerce
Finances: *Annual Operating Budget:* Less than $50,000; *Funding Sources:* Membership fees; Municipal levy
6 volunteer(s)
Membership: 75+; *Fees:* $75; *Member Profile:* Business & services in Morris & District
Activities: *Awareness Events:* Moonlight Madness, Dec.; Stampede Kickoff, July
Chief Officer(s):
Bruce Third, President
Andy Anderson, Secretary
Awards:
• Business of the Year Award
• Entrepreneur of the Year Award
• Community Contribution Award

Morrisburg & District Chamber of Commerce *See* South Dundas Chamber of Commerce

Mortgage Investment Association of British Columbia (MIABC)
The Marine Bldg., #1000, 355 Burrard St., Vancouver BC V6C 2G8
Tel: 604-380-1107
contactus@miabc.com
www.miabc.com
Overview: A small provincial organization founded in 1917
Membership: 200+; Fees: $346.50 corporate; Member Profile: Commercial & residential lenders; banks; trust companies; life insurance companies; mortgage companies & credit unions; mortgage insurers; appraisers; law firms; accountants; environmental consultants; mortgage brokers; technology suppliers
Activities: Dealing with the government & public regarding matters of concern; networking opportunities; Awareness Events: Annual Golf Tournament, Summer; Summer Social
Chief Officer(s):
Jeff Puhl, President, 604-406-6004
jeff.puhl@centract.com
Michelle Holst, Executive Coordinator, 778-245-9559
michelle_holst@miabc.com

Mortgage Professionals Canada
Atria II, #1401, 2235 Sheppard Ave. East, Toronto ON M2J 5B5
Tel: 416-385-2333; Fax: 416-385-1177
Toll-Free: 888-442-4625
info@MortgageProsCan.ca
www.mortgageproscan.ca
Previous Name: Canadian Association of Accredited Mortgage Professionals; Canadian Institute of Mortgage Brokers & Lenders
Overview: A medium-sized national organization founded in 1994
Mission: To act as the voice of the mortgage industry with legislators, government, & the media; To increase the level of professionalism in the mortgage industry through the creation of the Accredited Mortgage Professional (AMP) designation
Membership: Member Profile: Mortgage professionals, including mortgage brokers, lenders, insurers, & other stakeholders in the industry; Committees: Communications; Education; Government Relations; Membership; National Ethics; Professional Standards
Activities: Promoting professional development
Chief Officer(s):
Paul Taylor, President/CEO
Publications:
• CAAMP [Mortgage Professionals Canada] Update
Type: Newsletter; Frequency: Monthly
Profile: Review of CAAMP activities & issues that affect the mortgage industry
• Mortgage Journal hypothécaire [a publication of Mortgage Professionals Canada]
Type: Magazine
Profile: CAAMP / ACCHA news, member information, conference reports, upcoming events, & articles related to the industry
• Mortgage Professionals Canada Annual Report
Type: Yearbook; Frequency: Annually

Mosaic Institute
#1730, 2 Bloor St. West, Toronto ON M4W 3E2
Tel: 416-644-6000; Fax: 416-644-6001
www.mosaicinstitute.ca
www.linkedin.com/company/the-mosaic-institute
www.facebook.com/themosaicinstitute
twitter.com/MosaicInstitute
Overview: A medium-sized national charitable organization founded in 2007
Mission: To facilitate dialogue & interaction among the diverse communities of Canada for the advancement of peace & justice
Activities: Offering programs that encourage dialogue; Conducting research & developing resources; Awareness Events: Mosaic in Conversation; Next Generation; New Beginnings
Chief Officer(s):
Bernie Farber, Executive Director
bmf@mosaicinstitute.ca

Mosaïque centre d'action bénévole et communautaire
1650, av de l'Église, Le Moyne QC J4P 2C8
Tél: 450-465-1803; Téléc: 450-465-5440
info@lamosaique.qc.ca
lamosaique.org
Aperçu: Dimension: petite; Envergure: locale; fondée en 1985
Mission: De renforcer la communauté et aider à l'autonomie et l'intégration des personnes défavorisées dans la communauté
Activités: Evénements de sensibilisation: Donner pour changer leur vie collecte de fonds (novembre)
Membre(s) du bureau directeur:
Danielle Lavigne, Directrice générale
Lyse Summerside, Présidente, Conseil d'administration

Mossley Post Heritage & Citizenship Society (MPH&CS)
4006 Elgin Rd., Mossley ON N0L 1V0
mossleypost@hotmail.com
www.mossleyheritagesociety.com
Overview: A small local charitable organization founded in 1987
Mission: Provides educational scholarships, bursaries & prizes for Canadian citizens under the age of 19; Nurtures an appreciation of aesthetic matters; Provides a social & cultural facility for the benefit of the Mossley area community
Member of: Ontario Historical Society
Finances: Funding Sources: Fundraising; Donations; Government
Membership: Member Profile: People interested in Mossley's heritage
Activities: Monthly meetings; Social events; Addressing & assisting in producing heritage events when needed

Mother of Red Nations Women's Council of Manitoba (MORN)
#300, 141 Bannatyne Ave., Winnipeg MB R3B 0R3
Tel: 204-942-6676
morn.cimnet.ca/cim/92C270_397T18346.dhtm
Previous Name: Aboriginal Women of Manitoba
Overview: A small provincial organization overseen by Native Women's Association of Canada
Mission: To represent Aboriginal women in Manitoba & serve as their primary political & advocacy organization; To promote, protect & support the spiritual, emotional, physical & mental well-being of all Aboriginal women & children in the province
Affiliation(s): Native Woman's Association of Canada
Staff Member(s): 5
Membership: 1,200; Member Profile: Girl or woman 14 years of age or older; of the Aboriginal Peoples of Canada, as defined in the Constitution Act of 1982; and a resident of Manitoba.

Motion Picture Association - Canada / Association Cinématographique - Canada
#210, 55 St. Clair Ave. West, Toronto ON M4V 2Y7
Tel: 416-961-1888; Fax: 416-968-1016
info@mpa-canada.org
mpa-canada.org
twitter.com/mpacanada
Previous Name: Canadian Motion Picture Distributors Association
Overview: A small national organization founded in 1920
Mission: To act as the voice of U.S.A. studios who market feature films, prime time entertainment programming for television & pay TV, & pre-recorded videos & DVDs in Canada; To coordinate recommendations on matters affecting national distributors of feature films, pre-recorded videocassettes, & television programs; To protect the rights of copyright owners
Affiliation(s): Motion Picture Association of America; Motion Picture Association
Membership: Member Profile: Associations in the motion picture, video, & television programming industry
Activities: Promoting the interests of the industry; Liaising with federal & provincial government departments & ministries; Directgn an anti-piracy program to protect films, videos, & television programs
Chief Officer(s):
Katherine Ward, Director, Public Affairs, 416-355-7459
katherine_ward@mpa-canada.org

Motion Picture Theatre Association of Alberta
#400, 2555 - 32nd St. NE, Calgary AB T1Y 7J6
Tel: 403-381-1251
Overview: A small provincial organization
Mission: To help sustain the general welfare & prosperity of motion picture exhibitors
Member of: The Motion Picture Theatre Associations of Canada
Membership: Member Profile: Theatre exhibitors, owners, executives & managers

Motion Picture Theatre Association of British Columbia
20090 - 91A Ave., Langley BC V1M 3Y9
Overview: A small provincial organization
Member of: The Motion Picture Theatre Associations of Canada

Motion Picture Theatre Association of Central Canada
www.mptaccentral.ca
Also Known As: MPTAC Central
Overview: A small provincial organization
Member of: The Motion Picture Theatre Associations of Canada
Chief Officer(s):
Kellen Jasper, President
Meetings/Conferences:
• Motion Picture Theatre Association of Central Canada 2018 Annual General Meeting, 2018
Scope: Provincial

Motor Carrier Passenger Council of Canada (MCPCC) / Conseil canadien du transport de passages
#306, 9555 Yonge St., Richmond Hill ON L4C 9M5
Tel: 905-884-7782; Fax: 905-884-8335
Toll-Free: 866-271-1107
info@buscouncil.ca
www.buscouncil.ca
Overview: A small national organization
Mission: To develop, promote & enhance human capability by sharing resources, talents & best practices resulting in business & personal growth within the motor carrier passenger industry
Finances: Funding Sources: Government of Canada's Sector Council Program
Chief Officer(s):
Joan Crawford, Executive Director & CEO

Motor Coach Canada (MCC) / L'Association des autocaristes Canadiens (AAC)
#505, 555 Burnhamthorpe Rd., Toronto ON M9C 2Y3
Tel: 416-229-9305; Fax: 416-229-6281
info@motorcoachcanada.com
www.motorcoachcanada.com
Overview: A medium-sized international organization
Mission: To provide a united voice at the national level for motor coach tour operators & bus operators & to create an environment that supports members investments & growth
Finances: Funding Sources: Membership dues; services
Staff Member(s): 7
Membership: Fees: Schedule available; Member Profile: Bus operators; tour operators; product & service members
Chief Officer(s):
Réal Boissonneault, Chair
Doug Switzer, President & CEO, 416-229-9305 Ext. 222
doug@motorcoachcanada.com

Motor Dealers' Association of Alberta (MDA)
9249 - 48 St., Edmonton AB T6B 2R9
Tel: 780-468-9552; Fax: 780-465-6201
info@mdaalberta.com
www.mdaalberta.com
www.facebook.com/MDAofAlberta
Overview: A medium-sized provincial charitable organization founded in 1950
Mission: To serve the collective interest of all its members and promote positive relationships with government, industry, suppliers, consumers and media, by offering needed and effective programs and services.
Member of: Canadian Automobile Dealers' Association
Finances: Funding Sources: Membership dues; training program; endorsements
Staff Member(s): 2
Membership: Member Profile: New vehicle franchise dealers
Activities: Annual celebrity golf classic in support of special olympics; staff training programs; Library: Not open to public
Chief Officer(s):
Denis Ducharme, President
dducharme@mdaalberta.com
Awards:
• Alberta Dealer of Excellence

Motor Dealers' Association of BC; BC Automobile Dealers' Association See BCADA - The New Car Dealers of BC

Motorcycle & Moped Industry Council (MMIC) / Le Conseil de l'industrie de la motocyclette et du cyclomoteur (CIMC)
#201, 3000 Steeles Ave. East, Markham ON L3R 4T9
Tel: 416-491-4449; Fax: 416-493-1985
Toll-Free: 877-470-6642
info@mmic.ca
www.mmic.ca
www.facebook.com/MotorcycleMopedIndustryCouncil
Overview: A small national organization founded in 1971

Mission: To serve as a forum to identify and act on issues of importance to the motorcycle & scooter communities; To monitor & respond to changes in legislation and regulations affecting the use of motorcycles & scooters; To serve as a statistical gathering base for the industry
Staff Member(s): 10
Membership: 12; *Fees:* Schedule available; *Member Profile:* Companies involved in the manufacturing or distribution of motorcycles, mopeds or scooters in Canada
Activities: Data collection and organization; Motorcycle & OHV shows; Training programs; Ride! events
Chief Officer(s):
Jo-Anne Farquhar, Director, Communications & Public Affairs
jfarquhar@mmic.ca
Luc Fournier, Director, Policy & Government Relations
lfournier@mmic.ca
Tim Stover, Contact, Motorcycle Shows
tstover@mmic.ca

Motorsport Club of Ottawa (MCO) / Club des sports moteur d'Ottawa
PO Box 65006, Stn. Merivale, Ottawa ON K2G 5Y3
www.mco.org
www.facebook.com/mcofb
twitter.com/TheOfficialMCO
www.youtube.com/c/McoOrgRacersGatherHere
Previous Name: Ottawa Light Car Club
Overview: A small local organization founded in 1949
Mission: To foster a spirit of unity & comradership among car owners; to encourage courtesy both to other drivers & to pedestrians; To provide information which may be of aid & interest to car owners; to organize & to encourage the organization of legitimate sporting events
Affiliation(s): ASN Canada FIA; CASC-OR; Rallysport Ontario
Finances: *Annual Operating Budget:* $50,000-$100,000
10 volunteer(s)
Membership: 380; *Fees:* $60 single; $75 family; *Member Profile:* Road racing participants; enthusiasts; all involved at grassroots level; *Committees:* Race; Rally; Solo; Social
Activities: Winter & Summer Solo II; winter driving school; go-karting; rallying; road racing; summer high-performance driving school; Canaska Cup; group tours
Chief Officer(s):
John Hodge, President
vicepresident@mco.org

Mount Allison Faculty Association (MAFA) / Association des professeurs de Mount Allison
PO Box 6314, Sackville NB E4L 1G6
Tel: 506-364-2289; *Fax:* 506-364-2288
mafa@mta.ca
www.mafa.ca
Overview: A small local organization founded in 1839
Member of: Canadian Association of University Teachers
Membership: 117
Chief Officer(s):
Stephen Law, President
slaw@mta.ca

Mount Forest District Chamber of Commerce
514 Main St. North, Mount Forest ON N0G 2L0
Tel: 519-323-4480; *Fax:* 519-323-1557
chamber@mountforest.ca
www.mountforest.ca
www.facebook.com/mountforest
Overview: A small local organization
Mission: To promote the civic, commercial & industrial progress of the district served by this organization
Member of: Ontario Chamber of Commerce
Finances: *Funding Sources:* Membership dues; advertising sales
Staff Member(s): 1
Membership: *Fees:* $200; *Committees:* Annual Community, Visitor & Business Guide; Excellence Awards; Seasonal Chamber Events; Retail Promotions; Mount Forest Fireworks Festival; Website Development; Networking Events
Activities: Community awareness; festivals
Chief Officer(s):
David Ford, President

Mount Pearl-Paradise Chamber of Commerce
365 Old Placentia Rd., Mount Pearl NL A1N 0G7
Tel: 709-364-8513; *Fax:* 709-364-8500
info@mppcc.ca
www.mtpearlparadisechamber.com
www.facebook.com/MPPChamber
twitter.com/MPPChamber

Overview: A small local organization
Mission: To promote economic development & provide an information base for all employees & employers in the area; To represent the membership to local & provincial governments
Member of: Canadian Chamber of Commerce; Atlantic Provinces Chamber of Commerce; Newfoundland & Labrador Chamber of Commerce
Finances: *Annual Operating Budget:* $50,000-$100,000; *Funding Sources:* Membership dues; special projects; annual auction; fundraising
Staff Member(s): 1; 25 volunteer(s)
Membership: 200; *Fees:* $192-$368; *Committees:* Advocacy & Policy; Events; Finance & Local Office; Marketing, Promotion & Branding
Activities: *Speaker Service:* Yes; *Library:* Open to public
Chief Officer(s):
David Mercer, President

Mount Pleasant Group
info@mountpleasantgroup.com
www.mountpleasantgroup.com
Previous Name: Mt. Pleasant Group of Cemeteries; Commemorative Services of Ontario
Overview: A small local organization founded in 1826
Activities: Operates Mount Pleasant Memorial Services, Mount Pleasant Group of Cemeteries, & Canadian Memorial Services.
Chief Officer(s):
Diane Chabot, President & CEO
Angie Aquino, President, Funeral
Glenn McClary, President, Cemetery

Mount Royal Staff Association (MRSA)
#W301, 4825 Mount Royal Gate SW, Calgary AB T3E 6K6
Tel: 403-440-5993; *Fax:* 403-440-6763
mrsa@mtroyal.ca
www.mrssa.ca
Previous Name: Mount Royal Support Staff Association
Overview: A small local organization founded in 1976
Mission: To ensure Mount Royal University staff work in a fair environment
Finances: *Annual Operating Budget:* $50,000-$100,000
Staff Member(s): 1
Membership: 650; *Committees:* Education, Development & Training; Develop, Train & Learn; Professional Development Days; Policies & Procedures; Negotiating; Audit & Finance; Labour Relations; Social Engagement & Communications
Chief Officer(s):
Baset Zarrugr, President
bzarrug@mtroyal.ca

Mount Royal Support Staff Association *See* Mount Royal Staff Association

Mount Saint Vincent University Faculty Association (MSVUFA) / Association des professeurs de l'Université Mount Saint Vincent
166 Bedford Hwy., Halifax NS B3M 2J5
Tel: 902-457-6265; *Fax:* 902-457-2118
msvufa@msvu.ca
www.msvufa.ca
Overview: A small local organization founded in 1987
Membership: 150; *Fees:* 1.15% of gross annual salary
Chief Officer(s):
Linda Mann, President

Mount Sinai Hospital Foundation
#1001, 522 University Ave., Toronto ON M5G 1W7
Tel: 416-586-8203; *Fax:* 416-586-8639
Toll-Free: 877-565-8555
foundation@mtsinai.on.ca
www.mshfoundation.ca
www.youtube.com/user/MountSinaiFoundation
Overview: A small local charitable organization founded in 1923
Mission: The Foundation raises & stewards funds to support the Mount Sinai Hospital's patient care, research & education. In 2008, more than $344 million has been raised to fund The Best Medicine Campaign, to support research, innovative programs, improved facilities & technology. Mount Sinai Hospital's Centres of Excellence include: the Samuel Lunenfeld Research Institute, Women's & Infants' Health, Oncology, Acute & Chronic Medicine, & Laboratory Medicine & Infection Control
Activities: *Awareness Events:* Mount Sinai Annual Golf Classic; Unicorn Gala; Mother Daughter Tea
Chief Officer(s):
Brent S. Belzberg, Chair
Kevin Goldthorp, President

Publications:
• The Best Medicine Matters [a publication of the Mount Sinai Hospital Foundation]
Type: Newsletter; *Frequency:* q.

Mount View Special Riding Association (MVSRA)
PO Box 1637, Didsbury AB T0M 0W0
Tel: 403-335-9146; *Fax:* 403-556-6480
www.mountviewriding.com
Previous Name: Mountview Handicapped Riding Association
Overview: A small local charitable organization founded in 1983
Mission: To provide recreational & therapeutic riding to specially abled adults & children with mental &/or physical disabilities
Member of: Canadian Therapeutic Riding Association
Finances: *Annual Operating Budget:* Less than $50,000
40 volunteer(s)
Membership: 75; *Fees:* $5
Chief Officer(s):
Karla Brautigam, President
Karla@asc-mva.ab.ca

Mounted Police Professional Association of Canada (MPPAC) / Association canadienne de la police montée professionnelle
PO Box 76004, Langley BC
Fax: 855-530-4720
Toll-Free: 855-530-4720
national@mppac.ca
www.mppac.ca
www.facebook.com/MPPAC
Overview: A medium-sized national organization
Mission: To lead & represent members of the Royal Canadian Mounted Police; To address justice issues, as well as professional & employment concerns
Membership: *Fees:* $300

Mountview Handicapped Riding Association *See* Mount View Special Riding Association

Mourir dans la dignité *See* Dying with Dignity

Mouvement action chômage de Longueuil
1194, rue Marquette, Longueuil QC J4K 4H8
Tél: 450-670-7615; *Téléc:* 450-670-1347
info@macl.org
www.macl.org
www.facebook.com/486550318183440
Aperçu: *Dimension:* petite; *Envergure:* locale

Mouvement ATD Quart Monde Canada / ATD Fourth World Movement Canada
6747, rue Drolet, Montréal QC H2S 2T1
Tél: 514-279-0468; *Téléc:* 514-279-7759
www.atdquartmonde.ca
www.facebook.com/AtdQMCanada
Nom précédent: Association des Amis d'ATD Quart-Monde
Aperçu: *Dimension:* moyenne; *Envergure:* nationale; fondée en 1982
Mission: Développer un courant de refus de la misère en donnant la priorité aux plus pauvres, dans le respect des droits et de la dignité de la personne; contribuer à l'action du Mouvement dans le monde
Affiliation(s): Mouvement international ATD Quart-Monde (France)
Membre: 1,000-4,999; *Montant de la cotisation:* 3$
Activités: Soirées Quart Monde thématiques, groupes de travail avec différents intervenants sociaux (groupes communautaires, travailleurs sociaux, syndicats, écoles) participation à différents collectifs de lutte contre la pauvreté, recrutement et formation de volontaires-permanents (pour le Canada et des équipes du Mouvement dans le monde); *Evénements de sensibilisation:* Journée mondiale pour l'élimination de la pauvreté, 17 oct.; *Stagiaires:* Oui; *Service de conférenciers:* Oui
Publications:
• Actualités Quart Monde
Type: Newsletter

Mouvement canadien de défense des droits de la personne dans la communauté macédonienne *See* Macedonian Human Rights Movement International

Mouvement contre le viol et l'inceste (MCVI)
CP 50009, Succ. Jarry, Montréal QC H2P 0A1
Tél: 514-278-9383; *Téléc:* 514-278-9385
mcvi@contreleviol.org
www.mcvicontreleviol.org
www.facebook.com/mcvicontreleviol

Aperçu: *Dimension:* petite; *Envergure:* locale; Organisme sans but lucratif; fondée en 1976
Mission: Contrer la violence sexuelle dont sont victimes les femmes et les enfants
Affiliation(s): Regroupement québécois des Centre d'aide et de lutte contre les agressions à caractère sexuel
Activités: Counselling individuel; Groupes de soutien; informations et références médico-légales; ateliers de sensibilisation et de prévention; *Bibliothèque:* Centre de documentation

Mouvement d'éducation et de défense des actionnaires (MÉDAC)
82, rue Sherbrooke ouest, Montréal QC H2X 1X3
Tél: 514-286-1155; *Téléc:* 514-286-1154
Ligne sans frais: 866-332-7347
admin@medac.qc.ca
www.medac.qc.ca
twitter.com/MEDACtionnaires
Nom précédent: Association de protection des épargnants et investisseurs du Québec
Aperçu: *Dimension:* moyenne; *Envergure:* provinciale; Organisme sans but lucratif; fondée en 1994
Mission: Le MÉDAC a pour mission: faire valoir auprès des gouvernements le point de vue des membres sur le fonctionnement des marchés financiers; promouvoir une meilleure représentation des actionnaires aux conseils d'administration des entreprises; favoriser une plus grande transparence dans la gestion des sociétés par actions; constituer un espace de débats et d'échanges; et assurer la formation des membres
Membre de: International Corporate Governance Network
Membre(s) du personnel: 1; 9 bénévole(s)
Membre: 1,000-4,999; *Montant de la cotisation:* 35$ individuel; 250$ institutionnel
Membre(s) du bureau directeur:
Daniel Thouin, Président

Mouvement d'éducation populaire et d'action communautaire du Québec (MÉPACQ)
#392, 1600, av De Lorimier, Montréal QC H2K 3W5
Tél: 514-843-3236
info@mepacq.qc.ca
www.mepacq.qc.ca
Aperçu: *Dimension:* moyenne; *Envergure:* provinciale
Mission: Mouvement national et multisectoriel qui travaille à la transformation sociale dans une perspective de justice sociale. Il regroupe 11 Tables régionales en éducation populaire autonome (ÉPA) qui regroupent 333 groupes populaires et communautaires autonomes
Membre: 11
Activités: Publications

Mouvement d'étudiant(e)s chrétien(ne)s *See* Student Christian Movement of Canada

Mouvement d'information et d'entraide dans la lutte contre le sida à Québec
625, av Chouinard, Québec QC G1S 3E3
Tél: 418-649-1720; *Téléc:* 418-649-1256
miels@miels.org
www.miels.org
www.facebook.com/mielsQC
Également appelé: MIELS-Québec
Aperçu: *Dimension:* petite; *Envergure:* provinciale; fondée en 1986 surveillé par Canadian AIDS Society
Mission: Soutenir les personnes vivant avec le VIH/sida et leurs proches; prévenir la transmission du VIH; accueillir et héberger personnes vivant avec le sida
Affiliation(s): Société canadienne du sida
Membre(s) du personnel: 27
Membre: *Critères d'admissibilite:* Personnes qui vivent avec le VIH-sida et qui s'inscrivent au organisme; *Comités:* Personnes vivant avec le VIH-sida
Activités: *Evénements de sensibilisation:* Soirée Tangô; Party de Noël; *Bibliothèque:* Bibliothèque publique
Membre(s) du bureau directeur:
Martin Masson, Président
Thérèse Richer, Directrice générale
dgmiels@miels.org

Mouvement d'information, d'éducation et d'entraide dans la lutte contre le sida (MIENS)
CP 723, Chicoutimi QC G7H 5E1
Tél: 418-693-8983; *Téléc:* 418-693-0409
Ligne sans frais: 800-463-3764
lemiens@lemiens.com
www.lemiens.com
Aperçu: *Dimension:* petite; *Envergure:* provinciale; Organisme sans but lucratif; fondée en 1988
Mission: Pour fournir des informations sur la prévention du VIH ainsi que de soutenir et d'aider les personnes infectées par le VIH et à leurs proches
Affiliation(s): Coalition des organismes québécois de lutte contre le sida
Membre: *Critères d'admissibilite:* Avoir un intérêt particulier pour la problématique de l'infection au VIH et le sida
Activités: Information; éducation; entraide

Mouvement de sainteté biblique *See* The Bible Holiness Movement

Mouvement des femmes Chrétiennes (MFC)
Secrétariat nationale du MFC, 625 - 1300, chemin Sainte-Foy, Québec QC G1S 0A6
Tél: 581-742-7176
Nom précédent: Fédération nationale du MFC - Mouvement des Femmes Chrétiennes
Aperçu: *Dimension:* grande; *Envergure:* nationale; Organisme sans but lucratif; fondée en 1962
Mission: Un mouvement d'action catholique générale, il forme des femmes efficaces et dynamiques sur le plan familial, paroissial, social, et chrétien afin de transformer le milieu de vie par des projects concrets et en utilisant la méthode de l'action catholique
Membre de: Regroupement des Organismes Volontaires d'Éducation Populaire
Finances: *Budget de fonctionnement annuel:* Moins de $50,000
Membre(s) du personnel: 1; 700 bénévole(s)
Membre: 3 000; *Montant de la cotisation:* 15$; *Critères d'admissibilite:* Femmes de tout âge, condition et culture
Activités: Rencontre mensuelle sur le programme d'action; formation
Membre(s) du bureau directeur:
Pierrette Vachon, Présidente
Publications:
• La Famille Chrétienne [a publication of the Fédération nationale du MFC - Mouvement des Femmes Chrétiennes]
Type: Revue; *Frequency:* Quarterly

Mouvement des Focolari *See* Focolare Movement - Canada

Mouvement du Renouveau charismatique
#102, 161, rue du Parc, Chibougamau QC G8P 2H3
Tél: 418-748-4951
Aperçu: *Dimension:* petite; *Envergure:* locale
Membre(s) du bureau directeur:
Réjeanne Lalancette, Responsable

Mouvement national des québécoises et québécois (MNQ)
2207, rue Fullum, Montréal QC H2K 3P1
Tél: 514-527-9891; *Téléc:* 514-527-9460
mnq@mnq.quebec
www.mnq.qc.ca
www.facebook.com/MouvementnationaldesQuebecois
twitter.com/mouvnatqc
Aperçu: *Dimension:* moyenne; *Envergure:* nationale; fondée en 1947
Mission: Regroupe dix-neuf sociétés nationales et Saint-Jean-Baptiste réparties dans les régions du Québec; défendre, promouvoir la langue française, la souveraineté du Québec et la fierté nationale; est coordonnateur de la Fête à échelle du Québec
Membre(s) du personnel: 9
Membre: 19 institutionnel; *Critères d'admissibilite:* Société nationale ou Société Saint-Jean-Baptiste
Activités: Fête nationale du Québec
Membre(s) du bureau directeur:
Martine Desjardins, Présidente

SN de l'Est du Québec
75, boul Arthur-Buies ouest, Rimouski QC G5L 5C2
Tél: 418-723-9259; *Téléc:* 418-724-7201
sneq@globetrotter.net
www.sneq.qc.ca
Membre(s) du bureau directeur:
Alain Martineau, Président

SN Gaspésie/Iles-de-la-Madeleine
#2, 14, rue Comeau, Carleton-sur-Mer QC G0C 1J0
Tél: 418-364-6313; *Téléc:* 418-364-2005
snatgim@hotmail.com
Membre(s) du bureau directeur:
Marcel Landry, Président

SNQ d'Abitibi-Témiscamingue et du Nord-du-Québec inc.
CP 308, 127, 8e rue, Rouyn-Noranda QC J9X 5C3
Tél: 819-764-4556
info@snqat-nq.com
www.snqat-nq.com
Membre(s) du bureau directeur:
Chantal Tremblay, Directrice générale
ctremblay@snqat-nq.com

SNQ de Chaudière-Appalaches
2217, ch du Fleuve, Saint-Romuald QC G6W 5P7
Tél: 418-834-1160
snqca@bellnet.ca
Membre(s) du bureau directeur:
Pierre-Paul Sénéchal, Président

SNQ de l'Outaouais
30A, rue Bourque, Gatineau QC J8Y 1X1
Tél: 819-773-2221
snqoutaouais@gmail.com
Membre(s) du bureau directeur:
Mathieu-Henri Jetté, Président par intérim

SNQ de la Capitale
#222, 157, rue Des Chênes ouest, Québec QC G1L 1K6
Tél: 418-640-0799; *Téléc:* 418-640-0880
snqc@snqc.qc.ca
www.snqc.qc.ca
www.facebook.com/SNQCapitale
twitter.com/SNQCapitale
Membre(s) du bureau directeur:
Anne Beaulieu, Présidente

SNQ de la Côte-Nord
126, av Laval, Baie-Comeau QC G4Z 1R2
Tél: 418-296-4158
Membre(s) du bureau directeur:
Viviane Richard, Présidente
v-richard@globetrotter.net

SNQ de la région de Thetford
479, rue des Rosiers, Thetford Mines QC G6G 1B3
Tél: 418-755-1251
Membre(s) du bureau directeur:
Gaston St-Jacques, Président
gastonstjac@hotmail.com

SNQ de Lanaudière
414, rue Beaudry nord, Joliette QC J6E 6A8
Tél: 450-759-0100; *Téléc:* 450-759-9238
info@snql.com
www.snql.com
Membre(s) du bureau directeur:
Yvon Blanchet, Président

SNQ des Hautes-Rivières
#201, 332, rue de la Madone, Mont-Laurier QC J9L 1R9
Tél: 819-623-3617; *Téléc:* 819-623-6464
snqhr@tlb.sympatico.ca
www.snqhr.com
Membre(s) du bureau directeur:
Richard Gagnon, Président

SNQ des Laurentides
487, rue Laviolette, Saint-Jérôme QC J7Y 2T8
Tél: 450-438-4129; *Téléc:* 450-438-8895
info@snql.qc.ca
www.snql.qc.ca
Membre(s) du bureau directeur:
Gilles Broué, Président

SNQ du Saguenay/Lac-Saint-Jean
CP 308, 512, boul Auger est, Alma QC G8B 5V8
Tél: 418-668-2357; *Téléc:* 418-668-2313
snqalma@cgocable.ca
Membre(s) du bureau directeur:
Claire Bouchard, Présidente

SNQ du Suroît
2898, rue Honoré-Mercier, Vaudreuil-Dorion QC J7V 8P5
Tél: 450-455-3636; *Téléc:* 450-455-3636
Membre(s) du bureau directeur:
Lise Dandurand, Présidente

SNQ Richelieu/Saint-Laurent
219, rue Jacques-Cartier nord, Saint-Jean-sur-Richelieu QC J3B 6T3
Tél: 450-346-1141; *Téléc:* 450-346-2953
information@snqrsl.qc.ca
www.snqrsl.qc.ca
Membre(s) du bureau directeur:
Christian Haché, Président

SSJB de la Mauricie
CP 1059, 3239, rue Papineau, Trois-Rivières QC G9A 5K5

Canadian Associations / Mouvement québécois de la qualité (MQQ)

Tél: 819-375-4881; *Téléc:* 819-375-5854
ssjbm@ssjbmauricie.qc.ca
www.ssjbmauricie.qc.ca
Membre(s) du bureau directeur:
Sandra Dessureault, Présidente
SSJB de Montréal
82, rue Sherbrooke ouest, Montréal QC H2X 1X3
Tél: 514-843-8851; *Téléc:* 514-844-6369
reception@ssjb.com
www.ssjb.com
Membre(s) du bureau directeur:
Mario Beaulieu, Président
SSJB de Richelieu/Yamaska
515, av Robert, Saint-Hyacinthe QC J2S 4L7
Tél: 450-773-8535; *Téléc:* 450-773-8262
ssjb@maskatel.net
www.ssjbry.org
Membre(s) du bureau directeur:
Lise Lavoir, Présidente
SSJB du Centre-du-Québec
449, rue Notre-Dame, Drummondville QC J2B 2K9
Tél: 819-478-2519; *Téléc:* 819-472-7460
info@ssjbcq.qc.ca
www.ssjbcq.qc.ca
www.facebook.com/ssjbcq
Membre(s) du bureau directeur:
Gisèle Denoncourt, Directeur général

Mouvement québécois de la qualité (MQQ)
#1710, 360, rue Saint-Jacques ouest, Montréal QC H2Y 1P5
Tél: 514-874-9933; *Téléc:* 514-866-4600
Ligne sans frais: 888-874-9933
mqq@qualite.qc.ca
www.qualite.qc.ca
www.facebook.com/MouvementQuebecoisQualite
Aperçu: *Dimension:* moyenne; *Envergure:* provinciale
Mission: Promouvoir et rendre accessibles aux organisations les meilleures pratiques d'affaire pour accroître leur performance et leur compétitivité
Finances: *Budget de fonctionnement annuel:* $250,000-$500,000
Membre(s) du personnel: 10
Membre: 1 600
Activités:; *Bibliothèque:* Centre de documentation; Bibliothèque publique rendez-vous
Membre(s) du bureau directeur:
Roch Dubé, Président

Mouvement québécois des camps familiaux inc. *Voir*
Mouvement québécois des vacances familiales inc.

Mouvement québécois des chantiers jeunesse *Voir*
Chantiers jeunesse

Mouvement québécois des vacances familiales inc. (MQVF)
4545, av Pierre-de Coubertin, Montréal QC H1V 3R2
Tél: 514-252-3118; *Téléc:* 514-252-4302
mqvf@vacancesfamiliales.qc.ca
www.vacancesfamiliales.qc.ca
www.facebook.com/Vacancesfamiliales
Nom précédent: Mouvement québécois des camps familiaux inc.
Aperçu: *Dimension:* moyenne; *Envergure:* provinciale; Organisme sans but lucratif; fondée en 1982
Mission: Le Mouvement vise à favoriser l'accessibilité aux loisirs et aux vacances pour les familles à faible revenu en particulier et soutenir les organismes oeuvrant dans ce domaine
Finances: *Fonds:* Gouvernement provincial
Membre(s) du personnel: 3
Membre(s) du bureau directeur:
Colette Casavant, Présidente
Robert Rodrigue, Directeur général

Mouvement Retrouvailles
#201, 150, rue Grant, Longueuil QC J4H 3H6
Tél: 450-646-1060; *Téléc:* 450-646-7401
Ligne sans frais: 888-646-1060
mouvement-retrouvailles.qc.ca
Aperçu: *Dimension:* petite; *Envergure:* locale; fondée en 1983
Mission: Pour réunir les parents biologiques avec les enfants qu'ils avaient donnés en adoption
Membre: 13,000+; *Montant de la cotisation:* 35$; *Critères d'admissibilité:* Les enfants adoptés; Les parents de naissance; Les parents adoptifs
Membre(s) du bureau directeur:

Caroline Fortin, Présidente, Conseil d'administration
cfortin@mouvement-retrouvailles.qc.ca

Movement for Marriage Enrichment (MME)
57 Spiers Cres., Ajax ON L1S 6Z1
Tel: 905-428-6137
mmeenrich.tripod.com
Overview: A small local organization founded in 1992
Mission: To enrich the lives of married couples within the Filipino community in Toronto by caring for the spiritual, moral & temporal needs of members
Affiliation(s): Archdiocese of Toronto
Activities: Weekend activites; mass; pilgrimages
Chief Officer(s):
Jorge Isidro, Coordinator
Elsa Isidro, Coordinator

Moving Images Distribution
#103, 511 - 14th Ave., Vancouver BC V5Z 1P5
Tel: 604-684-3014; *Fax:* 604-684-7165
Toll-Free: 800-684-3014
mailbox@movingimages.ca
www.movingimages.ca
Overview: A small local organization
Mission: To promote Canadian culture & the recognition of film as an art form through the distribution of film & video created by its membership of Canadian independent producers
Chief Officer(s):
Sylvia Jonescu Lisitza, Executive Director

Mr. & Mrs. P.A. Woodward's Foundation
#300, 1055 West Hastings St., Vancouver BC V6E 2E9
Tel: 604-682-8116; *Fax:* 604-682-8153
pawoodwardfoundation@gmail.com
www.woodwardfoundation.ca
Overview: A medium-sized provincial charitable organization founded in 1951
Mission: To assist in projects that will contribute to better health care for British Columbians
Staff Member(s): 2
Membership: 8
Chief Officer(s):
Christopher Woodward, President
Jill Leversage, Treasurer

MSA Society for Community Living
2391 Crescent Way, Abbotsford BC V2S 3M1
Tel: 604-852-6800
info@msasociety.com
www.msasociety.com
Also Known As: MSA Society
Overview: A medium-sized local charitable organization founded in 1957
Mission: To promotes active participation of people with disabilities in the community; To support those people & their families to maximize their potential for growth & community participation
Member of: British Columbia Association for Community Living
Finances: *Funding Sources:* Government; Donations; Fundraising
Membership: *Member Profile:* Open (full, associate, & organizational)
Activities: Offering residential & day services
Chief Officer(s):
Richard Ashton, Executive Director, 604-852-6800 Ext. 102
ashton@msasociety.com

The M.S.I. Foundation
12230 - 106 Ave. NW, Edmonton AB T5N 3Z1
Tel: 780-421-7532; *Fax:* 780-425-4467
info@msifoundation.ca
www.msifoundation.ca
Also Known As: Medical Services Incorporated
Overview: A small provincial charitable organization founded in 1971
Mission: To foster & support research into any aspect of the provision of medical & allied health services to the people of Alberta
Finances: *Funding Sources:* Interest from invested capital
Activities: Supports medical research through universities & hospitals in Alberta
Chief Officer(s):
Doug Wilson, Chairperson

Mt. Pleasant Group of Cemeteries; Commemorative Services of Ontario *See* Mount Pleasant Group

MuchFACT
299 Queen St. West, Toronto ON M5V 2Z5
Tel: 416-384-5000; *Fax:* 416-384-2791
info@muchfact.ca
muchfact.ca
www.facebook.com/muchfact
twitter.com/muchfact
Previous Name: VideoFACT, A Foundation to Assist Canadian Talent
Overview: A small national charitable organization founded in 1984
Mission: To stimulate production of Canadian music videos, websites & electronic press kits
Finances: *Funding Sources:* Sponsored by MuchMusic/MuchMoreMusic/MusiquePlus Network
Activities: *Library:* Resource Centre; Open to public by appointment
Chief Officer(s):
Tiffany Ferguson, Program Manager, 416-384-2616
tiffany.ferguson@bellmedia.ca
David Kines, Chairperson

Mulgrave Road Theatre Foundation (MRT)
PO Box 219, Guysborough NS B0H 1N0
Tel: 902-533-2092; *Fax:* 902-533-3320
admin@mulgraveroad.ca
www.mulgraveroad.ca
www.facebook.com/mulgraveroad
Overview: A small local charitable organization founded in 1977
Mission: To create theatre that is inspired by the Atlantic Canadian experience
Member of: Theatre Nova Scotia; Playwrights Atlantic Resource Centre; Professional Association of Canadian Theatres; Guysborough Antigonish Pictou Arts & Culture Council
Finances: *Funding Sources:* Canada Council for the Arts; Nova Scotia Department of Communities, Culture & Heritage
Staff Member(s): 2
Activities: Touring Theatre; Script Development
Chief Officer(s):
Emmy Alcorn, Artistic Director
emmy@mulgraveroad.ca
Awards:
• Fogarty's Cove Scholarship

Multicultural Association of Carleton County Inc.
#4, 330 Centreville Rd., Florenceville NB E7L 3K6
Tel: 506-392-6011; *Fax:* 506-392-6411
admin@maccnb.ca
www.maccnb.ca
www.facebook.com/108327792575549
Overview: A small local organization
Mission: To help newcomers adapt to our rural area as well as to promote intercultural respect & awareness
Activities: English as a Second Language Training (E.S.L.); job counseling; social activities; neighborhood liaison; Canadian lifestyle guidance

Multicultural Association of Fredericton (MCAF) / Association multiculturelle de Fredericton Inc.
28 Saunders St., Fredericton NB E3B 1N1
Tel: 506-454-8292; *Fax:* 506-450-9033
www.mcaf.nb.ca
Overview: A small local organization founded in 1974
Mission: To establish communication & to foster understanding between the community, settled immigrants & newcomers
Membership: *Fees:* $5 student; $10 individual; $15 family; $25 organization
Chief Officer(s):
Arthur Jaucian, President
Lisa Bamford De Gante, Executive Director
bamford@mcaf.nb.ca

Multicultural Association of Kenora & District
136 Main St. South, Kenora ON P9N 1S9
Tel: 807-468-7140; *Fax:* 807-468-3895
makd@kmts.ca
www.kenoramulticultural.com
Overview: A small local organization
Mission: To promote the concept of multiculturalism; to encourage cultural awareness, appreciation & cooperation; to preserve cultural freedom, heritage & cultural identity; to work toward anti-racism & cultural diversity within the community
Member of: Multicultural Association of Northwestern Ontario
Activities: Settlement & interpreter service
Chief Officer(s):
Darlene Smeaton, Contact

Multicultural Association of Northwestern Ontario (MANWO)
511 East Victoria Ave., Thunder Bay ON P7C 1A8
Tel: 807-622-4666; *Fax:* 807-622-7271
Toll-Free: 800-692-7692
manwoyc@tbaytel.net
Overview: A small local organization founded in 1981
Mission: To promote the concept of multiculturalism; to provide information, training & resources on citizenship, multiculturalism & race relations.
Affiliation(s): Other multicultural associations; Native Friendship Centres; Race Relations Committees; Association des Francophones du Nord-Ouest de L'Ontario
Activities: *Internships:* Yes; *Speaker Service:* Yes; *Rents Mailing List:* Yes; *Library:* Open to public

Multicultural Association of Nova Scotia (MANS) / Association multiculturelle de la Nouvelle-Écosse
1113 Marginal Rd., Halifax NS B3H 4P7
Tel: 902-423-6534; *Fax:* 902-422-0881
Overview: A medium-sized provincial organization founded in 1975
Mission: To develop & influence multicultural policy & to promote equality; To create a sense of belonging & respect for all cultures
Membership: *Committees:* Education & Programming; Festival Management; Finance; Fundraising; Membership; Nomination; Personnel; Advisory; By-Laws; Immigration
Activities: Partnering with community agencies & stakeholders; Providing resources & education to members & the public; Presenting awards for exemplary services to multiculturalism; Advocating for multicultural issues; Initiating the development of legislation that reflects multiculturalism; Delivering multicultural programs; *Awareness Events:* Multicultural Festival; *Internships:* Yes *Library:* MANS Library
Chief Officer(s):
Sylvia Parris, Vice-President

Multicultural Association of Saint John Inc.
5 Bartlett Rd., Rothesay NB E2H 2W8
Tel: 506-849-8778
masjinc@gmail.com
Overview: A small local organization founded in 1984
Member of: Canadian Citizenship Federation; New Brunswick Multicultural Council
Finances: *Funding Sources:* Fundraising; provincial government
Membership: *Fees:* $5 Senior/student; $20 individual; $25 family; $35 not for profit; $175 corporation; *Member Profile:* People of all races & diverse ethnic backgrounds
Activities: *Speaker Service:* Yes; *Library:* Open to public
Chief Officer(s):
Melana Iverson, Executive Director
daba@rogers.com

Multicultural Association of the Greater Moncton Area (MAGMA) / Association multiculturelle, Grand Moncton (AMGM)
#C170, 22 Church St., Moncton NB E1C 0P7
Tel: 506-858-9659; *Fax:* 506-857-9430
info@magma-amgm.org
www.magma-amgm.org
www.facebook.com/people/Magma-Amgmorg-Moncton/746910498
Overview: A small local organization founded in 1980
Mission: To promote & protect human rights; to assist various groups to develop & preserve their cultural identities; to foster harmonious relations among people of all cultures; to create cultural awareness & encourage sharing for the benefit of all Canadians; to be the medium of contact & communications between the members & the various ethnic, cultural & affiliated groups
Member of: New Brunswick Multicultural Council
Finances: *Funding Sources:* Municipal, provincial & federal government; United Nations Association in Canada
Staff Member(s): 23
Activities: Multicultural dinner
Chief Officer(s):
Tradina Meadows Forgeron, Executive Director
Paul Vautour, President

Multicultural Council of Windsor & Essex County (MCC)
245 Janette Ave., Windsor ON N9A 4Z2
Tel: 519-255-1127; *Fax:* 519-255-1435
contact@themcc.com
www.themcc.com
www.facebook.com/MultiCulturalCI
twitter.com/MultiCulturalCI
www.youtube.com/user/MCCWEC
Overview: A small local organization founded in 1973 overseen by Ontario Council of Agencies Serving Immigrants
Mission: To create a harmonious multicultural society
Finances: *Annual Operating Budget:* $100,000-$250,000
Staff Member(s): 60; 200 volunteer(s)
Membership: 50; *Fees:* $20 individual; $60 organization; *Committees:* Human Rights; Race Relations; Education; Carousel of the Nations; Folk Arts
Activities: *Awareness Events:* Carrousel of the Nations; Herb Gray Harmony Award Gala; Harmony Ribbon Campaign; *Internships:* Yes; *Library:* Open to public by appointment
Chief Officer(s):
Pat Reid Crichton, President
Awards:
- Herb Gray Harmony & Champion Award
Eligibility: Individuals, businesses & organizations that act as champions & role models and aid in creating and sustaining a community that is multicultural and works toward social equality of cultures*Location:* Windsor-Essex *Deadline:* December

Multicultural History Society of Ontario (MHSO)
c/o Oral History Museum, #307, 901 Lawrence Ave. West, Toronto ON M5S 1C3
Tel: 416-979-2973; *Fax:* 416-979-7947
mhso.mail@utoronto.ca
www.mhso.ca
www.facebook.com/multiculturalhistorysociety
www.youtube.com/user/MulticulturalHistory
Overview: A medium-sized provincial organization founded in 1976
Mission: Working with communities, schools, cultural agencies and institutions to preserve, record and make accessible archival and other material which demonstrate the role of immigration and ethnicity in shaping the culture and economic growth of Ontario and Canada. Library is located at St. Michael's College, University of Toronto.
Finances: *Annual Operating Budget:* $250,000-$500,000; *Funding Sources:* Government; corporate; private
Staff Member(s): 3; 25 volunteer(s)
Membership: 250; *Fees:* Schedule available; *Member Profile:* Interest in multiculturalism
Activities: *Speaker Service:* Yes; *Rents Mailing List:* Yes; *Library:* Resource Centre; by appointment
Chief Officer(s):
Cathy Leekam, Program Manager
cathy.leekam@mhso.ca

Multicultural Marketing Society of Canada
Toronto ON
Overview: A small national organization
Chief Officer(s):
Gautam Nath, Founder

Multi-Ethnic Association for the Integration of Persons with Disabilities *Voir* Association multi-ethnique pour l'intégration des personnes handicapées

Multifaith Action Society (MAS)
949 West 49 Ave., Vancouver BC V5Z 2T1
Tel: 604-321-1302
admin@multifaithaction.org
www.multifaithaction.org
www.facebook.com/113668295376729
twitter.com/mfcalendar
Previous Name: Canadian Ecumenical Action
Overview: A small national charitable organization founded in 1972
Mission: To promote interfaith & multifaith dialogue & understanding; To provides information & resources on world religions to the community & develops community service programs
Staff Member(s): 1
Membership: *Fees:* Schedule available
Activities: Lectures & conferences promoting interreligious dialogue; forums on faith; environmental awareness programs within religious communities; faith centre visits; *Speaker Service:* Yes
Chief Officer(s):
Acharya Shrinath Dwivedi, President
Marcus Hynes, Operations Coordinator

Multilingual Association of Regina, Inc. (MLAR)
2144 Cornwall St., Regina SK S4P 2K7
Tel: 306-757-3171; *Fax:* 306-757-3172
mlar@accesscomm.ca
www.mlar.ca
Overview: A small local organization founded in 1978
Mission: To advance education in heritage languages, other than the official languages of Canada, in Regina & the surrounding areas; To promote cultural diversity
Finances: *Funding Sources:* Saskatchewan Organization for Heritage Languages; SaskCulture; Saskatchewan Ministry of Education; Saskatchewan Lotteries
Membership: 35 language schools; *Member Profile:* Non-profit heritage language schools in the Regina region
Activities: Developing heritage language curriculum & resource materials; Organizing training workshops for heritage language teachers; Providing materials, such as teaching aids, course materials, & technology; Conducting heritage language school visitations; Negotiating with the City of Regina, the Public School Board, & individual collegiates, for access to public school facilities; Assisting members to secure funding for schools; Promoting literature written in heritage languages
Chief Officer(s):
Jim Leskun, President
Emile Carignan, Coordinator, Office
Publications:
- The Multilingual Association of Regina Newsletter
Type: Newsletter; *Frequency:* Quarterly; *ISSN:* 1483-9660
Profile: Executive reports, meeting summaries, & reports from schools

Multilingual Orientation Service Association for Immigrant Communities (MOSAIC)
1720 Grant St., 2nd Fl., Vancouver BC V5L 2Y7
Tel: 604-254-9626; *Fax:* 604-254-3932
mosaic@mosaicbc.com
www.mosaicbc.com
www.linkedin.com/in/mosaicbc
www.facebook.com/mosaicbc
twitter.com/mosaicbc
www.youtube.com/mosaicbc
Overview: A small local charitable organization founded in 1976
Mission: To empower immigrants & refugees with settlement & immigration needs; to promote respect for people of different cultures, beliefs & abilities; to advocate for social justice & equality for all
Affiliation(s): Canadian Council for Refugees
Finances: *Funding Sources:* Federal, provincial & municipal governments; donations; translation fees; foundation grants 46 volunteer(s)
Membership: *Member Profile:* Staff, volunteers, organizations, business, individuals
Activities: Interpretation; translation; settlement support; employment services; family support services; English training for adults
Chief Officer(s):
Gabrielle Smith, President
Eyob Naizghi, Executive Director
Awards:
- MOSAIC Human Rights Award
- Dr. Kes Chetty Education Award
- Employer Recognition Award
- Britannia Scholarship Award

The Multimedia Group of Canada *Voir* Le groupe multimédia du Canada

Multiple Birth Families Association (MBFA)
PO Box 5532, Stn. F, Ottawa ON K2C 3M1
Tel: 613-860-6565
www.mbfa.ca
Previous Name: Ottawa Twins' Parents Association
Overview: A small local charitable organization founded in 1961
Mission: Giving parents an opportunity to get together & share ideas on raising multiples - the joys & the pitfalls
Finances: *Funding Sources:* Membership dues; Advertising in newsletter
Membership: 350; *Fees:* $45; *Member Profile:* Parents & expectant parents of twins, triplets, quadruplets & higher order multiples
Chief Officer(s):
Olga Kutikov, President
president@mbfa.ca

Multiple Births Canada (MBC) / Naissances multiples Canada
PO Box 432, Wasaga Beach ON L0L 2P0
Tel: 613-834-8946
Toll-Free: 866-228-8824

office@multiplebirthscanada.org
www.multiplebirthscanada.org
www.facebook.com/MultipleBirthsCanada
twitter.com/Multiple_Births
Previous Name: Parents of Multiple Births Association of Canada Inc.
Overview: A small national organization founded in 1978
Mission: To improve the quality of life for multiple birth individuals & their families through research, education, service & advocacy
Member of: International Society for Twin Studies
Finances: *Annual Operating Budget:* Less than $50,000
10 volunteer(s)
Membership: 60 corporate + 10 institutional + 50 individual; *Fees:* $20-$30; *Member Profile:* Individual & multiple birth families; caregivers; professionals; healthcare; *Committees:* Single Parents of Multiple Births; Parents of Multiples With Special Needs; Parents of Triplets; Quads & Quints; Loss of Multiples Registry
Activities: Speakers seminars; workshops; publications; referrals; *Awareness Events:* National Multiple Births Awareness Day, May 28; *Library:* Not open to public

Multiple Births Guelph-Wellington
PO Box 21012, 35 Harvard Rd., Guelph ON N1G 4T3
Tel: 519-829-5337
Other Communication: guelphmultiples@live.ca
guelph@multiplebirthscanada.org
www.multiplebirthscanada.org/~guelphwellington
twitter.com/guelphmultiples
Overview: A small local organization founded in 1977 overseen by Multiple Births Canada
Mission: To offer support and encouragement to families in our area who are experiencing the joys and challenges of raising multiple-birth children.
Membership: *Fees:* $20-$30
Chief Officer(s):
Ruth Morton, President

Multiple Organ Retrieval & Exchange Program of Ontario
See Trillium Gift of Life Network

Multiple Sclerosis Society of Canada (MS) / Société canadienne de la sclérose en plaques
North Tower, #500, 250 Dundas St. West, Toronto ON M5T 2Z5
Tel: 416-922-6065; *Fax:* 416-922-7538
Toll-Free: 800-268-7582
info@mssociety.ca
www.mssociety.ca
www.linkedin.com/company/ms-society-of-canada
www.facebook.com/MSSocietyCanada
twitter.com/mssocietycanada
www.youtube.com/MSSocietyCanada
Also Known As: MS Society
Overview: A medium-sized national charitable organization founded in 1948
Mission: To be a leader in finding a cure for multiple sclerosis & enabling people affected by MS to enhance their quality of life
Member of: Multiple Sclerosis International Federation
Affiliation(s): Canadian Medical Association
Finances: *Funding Sources:* Fundraising; Donations; Membership fees
1350 volunteer(s)
Membership: 28,000; *Member Profile:* People with MS & their families
Activities: Funding of MS medical research; Providing services for persons with MS; Offering education; *Awareness Events:* MS Carnation Campaign, May; RONA MS Bike Tours, July-Sept.; *Internships:* Yes; *Speaker Service:* Yes; *Library:* Information Resource Centre; by appointment
Chief Officer(s):
Yves Savoie, President & CEO
Karen Lee, Vice-President, Research
Lori Radke, Vice-President, Marketing & Development
Publications:
• MS Canada [a publication of the Multiple Sclerosis Society of Canada]
Type: Magazine; *Frequency:* Semiannually; *Editor:* Tiffany Regaudie; Meaghan Kelly; *ISSN:* 0315-1131; *Price:* Free with membership inthe Multiple Sclerosis Society of Canada
Profile: MS Society programs & services, plus the latest advance in MS research & treatments

Alberta & Northwest Territories Division
#150, 9405 - 50 St., Edmonton AB T6B 2T4
Tel: 403-463-1190; *Fax:* 403-479-1001
Toll-Free: 800-268-7582
info.alberta@mssociety.ca
mssociety.ca/division/alberta-and-northwest-territories-division
Chief Officer(s):
Garry Wheeler, President
garry.wheeler@mssociety.ca

Atlantic Division
#1, 109 Ilsley Ave., Dartmouth NS B3B 1S8
Tel: 902-468-8230; *Fax:* 902-468-5328
Toll-Free: 800-268-7582
info.atlantic@mssociety.ca
mssociety.ca/division/atlantic-division
www.facebook.com/170182879748684
twitter.com/MSAtlantic
Chief Officer(s):
Benjamin Davis, President, 800-268-7582 Ext. 1003
Mary Long, Coordinator, Communications & Community Engagement, 902-468-8230 Ext. 1004
mary.long@mssociety.ca

British Columbia & Yukon Division
Metrotower II, #1103, 4720 Kingsway, Burnaby BC V5H 4N2
Tel: 604-689-3144; *Fax:* 604-689-0377
info.bc@mssociety.ca
www.mssociety.ca/division/bc-and-yukon-division
www.facebook.com/mssocietybcy
twitter.com/mssocietybc
www.flickr.com/photos/mssociety_bcyukon
Chief Officer(s):
Chelsea Seaby, Chair
Tania Vrionis, President, 604-602-3217 Ext. 7241
tania.vrionis@mssociety.ca

Calgary & Area Chapter
Emerson Bldg., #150, 110 Quarry Park Blvd. SE, Calgary AB T2C 3G3
Tel: 403-250-7090; *Fax:* 403-250-8937
info.calgary@mssociety.ca
www.mssociety.ca/calgary
www.facebook.com/MSSocietyCalgary
twitter.com/MS_Calgary
www.youtube.com/user/calgaryms
Chief Officer(s):
Darrel Gregory, Southern Regional Director
darrel.gregory@mssociety.ca

Division du Québec
Tour Est, #1010, 550, rue Sherbrooke ouest, Montréal QC H3A 1B9
Tél: 514-849-7591; *Téléc:* 514-849-8914
Ligne sans frais: 800-268-7582
info.qc@mssociety.ca
www.mssociety.ca/division/quebec-division
www.linkedin.com/company/soci-t-canadienne-de-la-scl-rose-en-plaques-division-du-qu-bec
www.facebook.com/SocieteSPCanada
twitter.com/SocCanDeLaSP
www.flickr.com/photos/societesp-quebec
Louis Adam, Executive Director
louis.adam@mssociety.ca

Manitoba Division
#100, 1465 Buffalo Pl., Winnipeg MB R3T 1L8
Tel: 204-943-9595; *Fax:* 204-988-0915
Toll-Free: 800-268-7582
info.manitoba@mssociety.ca
mssociety.ca/division/manitoba-division
www.facebook.com/mssocietymanitoba
twitter.com/mssocietyMB
www.instagram.com/mssocietymb
Chief Officer(s):
Erin Kuan, President
erin.kuan@mssociety.ca
Ilona Niemczyk, Director, Development
ilona.niemczyk@mssociety.ca
Darell Hominuk, Director, Programs & Services
darell.hominuk@mssociety.ca

Ontario & Nunavut Division
#500, 250 Dundas St. West, Toronto ON M5T 2Z5
Tel: 416-922-6065; *Fax:* 416-922-7538
Toll-Free: 800-268-7582
info.ontario@mssociety.ca
www.mssociety.ca/ontario
twitter.com/MSSocietyON
Chief Officer(s):
Marie Vaillant, Chair

Saskatchewan Division
150 Albert St., Regina SK S4R 2N2
Tel: 306-522-5600; *Fax:* 306-565-0477
Toll-Free: 800-268-7582
info.sask@mssociety.ca
mssociety.ca/division/saskatchewan-division
twitter.com/MSSocietySK
www.flickr.com/photos/mssocietysask/
Chief Officer(s):
Lisa Smith, Director, Development
lisa.smith@mssociety.ca
Laurie Murphy, Director, Client Services
laurie.murphy@mssociety.ca

Multiple Sclerosis Society of Canada (Québec Division) *Voir* Société canadienne de la sclérose en plaques (Division du Québec)

MultiPrévention
#301, 2271, boul Fernand-Lafontaine, Longueuil QC J4G 2R7
Tél: 450-442-7763; *Téléc:* 450-442-2332
info@multiprevention.org
multiprevention.org
Nom précédent: ASPHME
Aperçu: *Dimension:* grande; *Envergure:* provinciale; Organisme sans but lucratif; fondée en 1986
Mission: L'union rejoindre de sécurité pour les secteurs de la santé et sécurité:métallique, électricité, vêtements, & gravures
Finances: *Budget de fonctionnement annuel:* $500,000-$1.5 Million
Membre(s) du personnel: 7
Activités: *Stagiaires:* Oui; *Service de conférenciers:* Oui
Membre(s) du bureau directeur:
Nathalie Laurenzi, Directrice générale

Québec
#570, 979, av de Bourgogne, Québec QC G1W 2L4
Tel: 418-652-7682; *Fax:* 418-652-9348

MultiPrévention ASP: Association paritaire pour la santé et la sécurité au travail des secteurs: métal, électrique, habillement et imprimerie
#150, 2405 boul Fernand-Lafontaine, Longueuil QC J4N 1N7
Tél: 450-442-7763; *Téléc:* 450-442-2332
multiprevention.org
www.facebook.com/MultiPrévention-214272358763722/
Merged from: Association paritaire pour la santé et la sécurité du travail Produits en métal et électriques; ASP
Aperçu: *Dimension:* moyenne; *Envergure:* provinciale; fondée en 2016
Membre(s) du personnel: 25
Membre(s) du bureau directeur:
Marie-Josée Ross, Conseillère en gestion
mjross@multiprevention.org
Caroline Godin, Conseiller technique
cgodin@multiprevention.org

The Municipal Chapter of Toronto IODE
#219, 40 Orchard View Blvd., Toronto ON M4R 1B9
Tel: 416-925-5078
iodetoronto@bellnet.ca
Overview: A small local charitable organization founded in 1912
Mission: To improve the quality of life for children, youth & those in need through educational, social service & citizenship programs
Member of: The National Chapter of Canada IODE; The Provincial Chapter of Ontario IODE
Finances: *Funding Sources:* Donations; special programs; trusts
Chief Officer(s):
Mary K. Anderson, President
Awards:
• IODE Book Award
Established in 1975; an inscribed scroll & not less than $1,000 awarded annually to the author or illustrator of the best children's book written or illustrated by a Canadian resident in Toronto or surrounding area & published by a Canadian publisher within the preceding 12 months
• Music Awards
• Education Bursaries

Municipal Electric Association *See* Electricity Distributors Association

Municipal Engineers Association (MEA)
#22, 1525 Cornwall Rd., Oakville ON L6J 0B2
Tel: 289-291-6472; *Fax:* 289-291-6477
www.municipalengineers.on.ca
Overview: A medium-sized provincial organization founded in 1974

Mission: To provide focus & unity for licensed engineers employed by municipalities in Ontario; To address issues of common concern to members; To facilitate the dissemination of information
Membership: *Fees:* Schedule available; *Member Profile:* Public sector professional engineers in full time municipal employment who perform functions in the field of municipal engineering; *Committees:* 36 Committees
Activities: Organizing training events; Advocating for sound municipal engineering; Championing positions on municipal engineering issues; Recognizing achievements of municipal engineers
Chief Officer(s):
Reg Russwurm, President
rrusswurm@thebluemountains.ca
Alan Korell, Executive Director
alan.korell@municipalengineers.on.ca
Awards:
• MEA Bursary
Eligibility: Children or dependents of Ontario municipal employees & Councillors entering a university engineering program *Deadline:* April; *Amount:* 10 at $1500
Meetings/Conferences:
• Municipal Engineers Association 2018 Annual General Meeting, November, 2018
Scope: Provincial
Publications:
• Municipal Engineers Association Members Directory
Type: Directory

Municipal Equipment & Operations Association (Ontario) Inc.
38 Summit Ave., Kitchener ON N2M 4W2
Tel: 519-741-2600; *Fax:* 519-741-2750
Other Communication: stcc@meoa.org (safety matters)
admin@meoa.org
www.meoa.org
Also Known As: MEOA
Overview: A small provincial organization founded in 1965
Mission: To promote high standards & cost effectiveness in public services across Ontario
Finances: *Funding Sources:* Annual membership dues
Staff Member(s): 7
Membership: 250; *Fees:* $75; *Member Profile:* Supervisory employees & management support staff from any government body; Suppliers of equipment & services used by municipal corporate organizations; Individuals who have been beneficial to the association or have an interest in the association
Activities: Offering education & training; Organizing field trips; Facilitating the exchange of information; Providing networking opportunities
Chief Officer(s):
Mike Beattie, President
Meetings/Conferences:
• Municipal Equipment & Operations Association (Ontario) Inc. 2018 Annual Spring Meeting, 2018
Scope: Provincial
Description: An event to elect the new executive, to address the business of the association, to participate in a plant tour, to hear guest speakers, & to attend educational presentations
• Municipal Equipment & Operations Association (Ontario) Inc. 2018 Annual Professional Development Day, 2018
Scope: Provincial
Description: A learning opportunity for members of the association
• Municipal Equipment & Operations Association (Ontario) 2018 Annual Municipal & Contractor Fall Equipment Show, 2018
Scope: Provincial
Description: An opportunity for suppliers to promote & demonstrate their products & services

Municipal finance & development agency for emergency 9-1-1 call centres in Quebec *Voir* Agence municipale de financement et de développement des centres d'urgence 9-1-1 du Québec

Municipal Finance Officers' Association of Ontario (MFOA)
2169 Queen St. East, 2nd Fl., Toronto ON M4L 1J1
Tel: 416-362-9001; *Fax:* 416-362-9226
office@mfoa.on.ca
www.mfoa.on.ca
Overview: A medium-sized provincial organization founded in 1989
Mission: To represent the interests of municipal finance officers throughout Ontario; To promote the interests of members
Affiliation(s): Association of Municipalities of Ontario (AMO)
Finances: *Funding Sources:* Sponsorships
Staff Member(s): 8
Membership: 2,300+ individuals; *Member Profile:* Municipalities; Provincial Employees; Corporate individuals; *Committees:* Accounting & Financial Reporting; Professional Development
Activities: Organizing annual meetings; Presenting awards; Sponsoring seminars; Initiating studies; Developing positions on policy & financial management issues
Chief Officer(s):
Dan Cowin, Executive Director, 416-362-9001 Ext. 223
dan@mfoa.on.ca
Shelley Stedall, President
sstedall@northdumfries.ca
Nancy Taylor, Vice-President
ntaylor@clarington.net
Meetings/Conferences:
• Municipal Finance Officers' Association of Ontario 2018 Annual Conference, September, 2018, Niagara Falls, ON
Scope: Provincial

Municipal Information Systems Association of Canada (MISA)
#2201, 250 Yonge St., Toronto ON M5B 2L7
Tel: 905-789-1356
info@misa.on.ca
www.misa-asim.ca
Overview: A small provincial organization
Mission: To promote the efficient & effective use of municipal information systems & technology; to provide a medium of communication for interchange of information between members & interested persons or groups leading to a more efficient use of information systems.
Finances: *Annual Operating Budget:* Less than $50,000; *Funding Sources:* Chapter membership dues; National vendor partners
Staff Member(s): 1
Membership: 5 associations; *Fees:* Schedule available
Activities: *Speaker Service:* Yes
Chief Officer(s):
Kathryn Bulko, President, 416-397-9921
president@misa.ca
Roy Wiseman, Executive Director
roy.wiseman@misa.ca
Awards:
• Peter Bennett Award
Presented annually to an individual who has made an outstanding contribution to the Canadian municipal IT community & who aligns with the MISA objectives *Deadline:* May 3
• Dennis Steen Award
Presented to an individual who is not a municipal employee and has made exceptional contributions to the Canadian municipal IT community

Municipal Law Departments Association of Ontario (MLDAO)
c/o The City of Greater Sudbury, PO Box 5000, Stn. A, Sudbury ON P3A 5P3
Tel: 705-671-2489
www.mldao.ca
Previous Name: Regional Solicitors' Association of Ontario
Overview: A small provincial organization founded in 2002
Mission: To exchange information & advice on municipal issues; to hold meetings & seminars as a forum for sharing information & education of members; to advocate reform of legislation to the benefit of municipalities; to participate in consultation with governments & other associations interested in matters affecting municipalities
Member of: Association of Municipalities of Ontario
Membership: 45 departments; *Member Profile:* Municipal law departments of all those municipalities in Ontario that maintain in-house legal services
Activities: Five plenary meetings/seminars annually; Annual conference
Chief Officer(s):
Jamie M. Canapini, Chair
jamie.canapini@greatersudbury.ca
Alan Barber, Vice-Chair
abarber@peterborough.ca
Jennifer A. Smout, Vice-Chair
jsmout@london.ca
Elizabeth Waight, Vice-Chair
elizabeth.waight@mississauga.ca

Municipal Law Enforcement Officers' Association (MLEOA)
1 Carden St., Guelph ON N1H 3A1
Tel: 519-822-1260
mleo@mleoa.ca
www.mleoa.ca
www.facebook.com/mleoaOntario
Overview: A medium-sized provincial organization founded in 1979
Mission: To help bring members into association with each other to maintain professional standards; To encourage & assist in the education & training programs for Municipal Law Enforcement Officers
Finances: *Annual Operating Budget:* $50,000-$100,000; *Funding Sources:* Membership fees
9 volunteer(s)
Membership: 1,500; *Fees:* $17 retired; $83 associate & student; $110 individual; *Committees:* Newsletter; Website Management; Communications & Public Relations; Government Liaison; Strategic Planning; Procedures & Elections; Certification & Awards; Professional Valyes & Awards; Associations Joint Working; National Association
Activities: Annual training seminars; Training courses; *Speaker Service:* Yes
Chief Officer(s):
Doug Godfrey, President
doug.godfrey@guelph.ca
Yves Roy, Vice President
yroy@nationamun.ca

Municipal Officers' Association of British Columbia *See* Local Government Management Association of British Columbia

Municipal Pension Retirees Association (MPRA)
Unit 22, #525, 2475 Dobbin Rd., West Kelowna BC V4T 2E9
Tel: 250-768-1519
mpra@shawbiz.ca
www.mpra.ca
Overview: A small national organization
Membership: 32 districts + 1 out of province; *Fees:* $20 individual; $35 couples; *Member Profile:* Individuals who recieve a Municipal Pension
Activities: Networking; newsletters; access to travel & home insurance; discounts at select retailers
Chief Officer(s):
Steven Polak, President

Municipal Police Authorities *See* Ontario Association of Police Services Boards

Municipal Waste Association (MWA)
PO Box 1894, Guelph ON N1H 7A1
Tel: 519-823-1990; *Fax:* 519-823-0084
www.municipalwaste.ca
Previous Name: Association of Municipal Recycling Coordinators
Overview: A medium-sized provincial organization founded in 1987
Mission: To expedite the flow of information regarding 3R programs to municipalities & other community & government groups; To act as an information forum for municipal recycling coordinators; To allow member municipalities to act as a unified voice in promoting progressive waste reduction & recycling alternatives
Member of: Recycling Council of Ontario
Finances: *Funding Sources:* Membership fees; Project sponsorship
Membership: 100-499; *Fees:* Schedule available, based upon population; *Committees:* Household Hazardous Waste; Markets Operation & Contracts; Organic Waste Diversion; Policy & Program
Activities: *Speaker Service:* Yes
Chief Officer(s):
Ben Bennett, Executive Director
ben@municipalwaste.ca
Melissa Campbell, Coordinator, Membership
melissa@municipalwaste.ca
Meetings/Conferences:
• Municipal Waste Association 2018 Annual General Meeting, 2018, ON
Scope: Provincial
Description: A yearly event featuring a business meeting, trade show, & networking opportunities
Publications:
• For R Information [a publication of the Municipal Waste Association]
Type: Newsletter

Municipalities Newfoundland & Labrador (MNL)
460 Torbay Rd., St. John's NL A1A 5J3
Tel: 709-753-6820; Fax: 709-738-0071
Toll-Free: 800-440-6536
info@municipalnl.ca
www.municipalitiesnl.com
www.linkedin.com/groups/4094976
www.facebook.com/MunicipalitiesNL
twitter.com/MunicipalNL
www.instagram.com/municipal_nl
Previous Name: Newfoundland & Labrador Federation of Municipalities
Overview: A medium-sized provincial charitable organization founded in 1951
Mission: To assist communities in their endeavour to achieve & sustain strong & effective local government thereby improving the quality of life for all the people of this province.
Member of: Federation of Canadian Municipalities
Membership: 276 municipalities; Fees: Sliding scale based on population; Member Profile: Incorporated municipal governments in Newfoundland; Committees: Executive; Advocacy; Finance; UMC; Small Towns Advisory; Convention
Activities: Internships: Yes; Rents Mailing List: Yes
Chief Officer(s):
Tony Keats, President
tkeats@municipalnl.ca
Craig Pollett, Chief Executive Officer
cpollett@municipalnl.ca
Gail Woodfine, Contact, Communications & Public Relations
gwoodfine@municipalnl.ca
Awards:
• James Hiscock Scholarship
Eligibility: Must be a child or ward of any municipal council member or any municipal employee, from a member municipality upon high school graduation.
Meetings/Conferences:
• Municipalities Newfoundland & Labrador Municipal Symposium, 2018, Gander, NL
Scope: Provincial
Description: Held each spring in Gander, NL.
Contact Information: Contact, Christine Carter, E-mail: ccarter@municipalnl.ca.

Municipality of Port Hope Historical Society (EDHS)
PO Box 116, Port Hope ON L1A 3V9
Tel: 905-885-2981
info@porthopehistorical.ca
www.porthopehistorical.ca
Previous Name: East Durham Historical Society
Overview: A small local organization founded in 1964
Mission: Responsible for Dorothy's House Museum & preserving local history
Membership: 100; Fees: $15 single; $25 family; $40 business; $75 lifetime
Chief Officer(s):
Joan Parrott, President

Muniscope (ICURR)
#210, 40 Wynford Dr., Toronto ON M3C 1J5
Fax: 647-345-7004
www.muniscope.ca
twitter.com/muniscope
Previous Name: Intergovernmental Committee on Urban & Regional Research
Overview: A medium-sized national organization founded in 1967
Mission: To support local and regional governments, as well as private & non-profit companies through subsidized information & networking services; to act as a national resource on municipal issues, with subscription-based research & library services available on economic development, finance and taxation, housing and infrastructure, transportation, planning, & sustainability
Finances: Funding Sources: Canadian Mortgage & Housing Corporation
Staff Member(s): 4
Activities: Providing information exchange & research resources; Rents Mailing List: Yes; Library
Chief Officer(s):
Mathieu Rivard, Director, 418-455-4485
mrivard@muniscope.ca
Mark Rose, Manager, Information Services, 647-345-7004
mrose@muniscope.ca

Murray Grey International, Incorporated (MGI)
c/o Canadian Livestock Records Coroporation, 2417 Holly Lane, Ottawa ON K1V 0M7
Tel: 613-731-7110; Fax: 613-731-0704
clrc@clrc.ca
www.murraygrey.org
Also Known As: Murray Grey International Association
Overview: A small international organization
Mission: To promote the Murray Grey breed; To provide a registry of Murray Grey breeding
Affiliation(s): Canadian Livestock Records Corporation
Membership: Fees: Schedule available based on number of bulls; Member Profile: Murray Grey breeders in North America & South America, & other areas of the world
Chief Officer(s):
Terry Anderson, Contact, 819-632-7352
Publications:
• Breeder Directory
Type: Directory; Frequency: Annually
• Murray Grey International, Incorporated Newsletter
Type: Newsletter

Musagetes Foundation
6 Dublin St. South, Guelph ON N1H 4L5
Tel: 519-836-7300; Fax: 519-836-7320
info@musagetes.ca
www.musagetes.ca
www.facebook.com/musagetesfoundation
twitter.com/musagetesf
Overview: A small international organization
Mission: To function as a catalyst to generate ideas & actions that bring artistic creativity into daily life. It sponsors Cafés, multi-year projects which occur at comfortable, social places where people with common interests can explore & apply creative ideas for community change & development.
Staff Member(s): 4
Activities: Café meetings in Barcelona (Spain), Lecce (Italy), London (UK), Rijeka (Croatia), Sudbury (Canada)
Chief Officer(s):
Joy Roberts, President
Shawn Van Sluys, Executive Director

Muscular Dystrophy Canada (MDC) / Dystrophie musculaire Canada (DMC)
#900, 2345 Yonge St., Toronto ON M4P 2E5
Fax: 416-488-7523
Toll-Free: 866-687-2538
info@muscle.ca
www.muscle.ca
www.linkedin.com/company/466761
www.facebook.com/muscle.ca
twitter.com/md_canada
www.youtube.com/user/musculardystrophycan
Overview: A large national charitable organization founded in 1954
Mission: To improve the quality of life of persons who have muscular dystrophy through a broad range of programs, education, support of research & the delivery of needed services to people with muscular dystrophy & their families
Member of: Canadian Coalition for Genetic Fairness
Finances: Annual Operating Budget: Greater than $5 Million
Staff Member(s): 53
Membership: Committees: Executive; Marketing & Communications; Services & Advocacy; Human Resources; Chapter Relations; Medical & Scientific Advisory; National Fire Fighter Relations; Governance & Mandate
Activities: Awareness Events: Walk for Muscular Dystrophy; Muscular Dystrophy Month, Sept.
Chief Officer(s):
Buzz Green, Chair
Barbara Stead-Coyle, Chief Executive Officer
Eitan Dehtiar, Interim Chief Financial Officer
Eitan.Dehtiar@muscle.ca
Awards:
• Courage to Inspire Award
• Dr. George Karpati Award
• Fire Department of the Year Award
• Fire Fighter of the Year Award
• Mary Ann Wickham Award for Volunteer of the Year
• Michel Louvain Award for Client of the Year

Atlantic Regional Office
100 Ilsley Ave., #N, Dartmouth NS B3B 1L3
Tel: 902-429-6322; Fax: 902-425-4226
Toll-Free: 800-884-6322
infoatlantic@muscle.ca

Ontario & Nunavut Regional Office
#901, 2345 Yonge St., Toronto ON M4P 2E5
Tel: 416-488-2699; Fax: 416-488-0107
Toll-Free: 800-567-2873
infoontario@muscle.ca

Québec Regional Office
#506, 1425, boul René-Lévesque ouest, Montréal QC H3G 1T7
Tel: 514-393-3522; Fax: 514-393-8113
Toll-Free: 800-567-2236
infoquebec@muscle.ca

Western Canada Regional Office
#302, 601 West Broadway, Vancouver BC V5Z 4C2
Tel: 604-732-8799; Fax: 604-731-6127
Toll-Free: 800-336-8166
infowest@muscle.ca
www.facebook.com/MDCBCYUKON

Musée Colby-Curtis See Stanstead Historical Society

Le Musée de chemin de fer de Sydney à Louisburg See Sydney & Louisburg Railway Historical Society

Le Musée et la fondation du patrimoine de l'Ile-du-Prince-Édouard See Prince Edward Island Museum & Heritage Foundation

Musée et Temple canadien de la renommée du golf See Canadian Golf Hall of Fame & Museum

Musée McCord d'histoire canadienne See McCord Museum of Canadian History

Musée minéralogique et minier de Thetford Mines
711, boul Frontenac ouest, Thetford Mines QC G6G 7Y8
Tél: 418-335-2123; Téléc: 418-335-5605
Ligne sans frais: 855-335-2123
Autres numéros: communication@museemineralogique.com
secretariat@museemineralogique.com
www.museemineralogique.com
www.facebook.com/333048121773
Aperçu: Dimension: petite; Envergure: nationale; Organisme sans but lucratif; fondée en 1976
Mission: Le Musée vise à faire connaître la région de L'Amiante, son patrimoine minier, géologique et minéralogique; collectionner et présenter des minéraux et roches du monde entier; conserver, présenter et interpréter les témoins du patrimoine minier régional; initier jeunes et moins jeunes aux sciences de la terre; et, favoriser les échanges avec d'autres musées du Québec, du Canada et de l'étranger
Membre de: Société des musées québécois; Association des musées canadiens
Finances: Budget de fonctionnement annuel: $250,000-$500,000; Fonds: Ministère de la culture et des communications du québec
Membre(s) du personnel: 10; 35 bénévole(s)
Membre: 13 institutionnel; 181 individu; Montant de la cotisation: 50$ institutionnel; 75$ commerce; 9,20$ étudiant; 20$ individuel; 30$ familial; Critères d'admissibilite: 18 ans et plus
Activités: Expositions; excursions géologiques; forfait mine-musée en été; boutique souvenirs; 8 livres ont été publiés par le Musée; collections de roches et de minéraux produites par les musée pour la vente; Jounrées de la Culture; Expo-Cadeaux
Membre(s) du bureau directeur:
Yvan Faucher, Président
François Cinq-Mars, Directeur
f.cinq-mars@museemineralogique.com
Monique Laberge, Secrétaire

Museum Association of Newfoundland & Labrador (MANL)
PO Box 5785, St. John's NL A1C 5X3
Tel: 709-722-9034; Fax: 709-722-9035
www.manl.nf.ca
www.facebook.com/museumassociationofnl
twitter.com/manltweets
www.flickr.com/photos/manl
Overview: A medium-sized provincial charitable organization founded in 1980
Mission: To protect & preserve the cultural & natural heritage of Newfoundland & Labrador; To unite, support & promote members; To improve & promote museums
Member of: Canadian Museums Association
Finances: Funding Sources: Donations
Staff Member(s): 4
Membership: 115 individuals; 150 museums & heritage societies; Member Profile: Individuals, museums, & heritage

groups of Newfoundland & Labrador interested in the preservation & promotion of the province's material & cultural heritage
Activities: Providing training; Advocating for members; Encouraging standards of excellence; Connecting with other provincial & national associations & organizations to provide members with up-to-date information; Disseminating information to museums & concerned individuals; Presenting awards; Organizing conferences; *Awareness Events:* Museum Week, June *Library:* Resource Centre
Chief Officer(s):
Ken Flynn, Executive Director
kflynn@nf.aibn.com
Awards:
• Award of Merit
• Honorary Life Membership
Publications:
• Beginner's Guide to Living History
Type: Report; *Price:* $40
Profile: A guide that presents the basic principles of living history interpretation; Assists readers through the process of developing their own living history programs
• Museum Association of Newfoundland & Labrador Technical Bulletins
Type: Report
Profile: A series of technical bulletins on topics relating to conservation & article care

Museum London
421 Ridout St. North, London ON N6A 5H4
Tel: 519-661-0333
www.museumlondon.ca
Previous Name: London Regional Art & Historical Museums
Overview: A medium-sized local charitable organization founded in 1989
Mission: To enrich public knowledge & enjoyment of the art & history of the London region & Canada
Member of: Ontario Museums Association; Ontario Association of Art Galleries; Canadian Museums Association
Finances: *Annual Operating Budget:* $3 Million-$5 Million; *Funding Sources:* All levels of government; Fees; Fundraising; Sponsorship; Revenues
Staff Member(s): 20
Membership: *Committees:* Property & Finance; Art Collection; Material Culture; Policy; Marketing & Development; Museum Underground
Activities: Exhibitions of art & artifacts with related programs & special events
Chief Officer(s):
Brian Meehan, Executive Director
bmeehan@museumlondon.ca

Museum of Contemporary Canadian Art (MOCCA)
MOCCA Temporary Offices, #99, 80 Ward St., Toronto ON M6H 4A6
Tel: 416-395-0067
info@mocca.ca
www.mocca.ca
www.facebook.com/MOCCA.Toronto
twitter.com/MOCCA_TO
www.youtube.com/user/MOCCAToronto
Previous Name: Art Gallery of North York
Overview: A small local charitable organization founded in 1999
Mission: To exhibit, research, & promote contemporary art by Canadian & international artists; To provide a forum for emerging artists; To champion work that is ground-breaking, innovative, timely, & influential
Finances: *Funding Sources:* Membership dues; Individual & corporate sponsors; Local & provincial government
Staff Member(s): 5
Membership: *Fees:* Schedule available; *Member Profile:* Artists, arts patrons, educators, philanthropists, gallerists, other professionals in the arts field
Activities: Organizing exhibitions throughout the year in two exhibition spaces; Hosting artist events; Facilitating workshops for children
Chief Officer(s):
Chantal Pontbriand, Chief Executive Officer
David Liss, Artistic Director & Curator
Awards:
• The MOCCA Award
Awarded to honour a Canadian in the field for innovation, accomplishment, extended contribution, or for a project that has garnered national or international recognition & significance; *Amount:* $25,000

Publications:
• Museum of Contemporary Canadian Art e-Newsletter
Type: Newsletter
Profile: An information resource for members; includes association news & important event dates

Museums Association of Saskatchewan (MAS)
424 McDonald St., Regina SK S4N 6E1
Tel: 306-780-9279; *Fax:* 306-780-9463
Toll-Free: 866-568-7386
mas@saskmuseums.org
www.saskmuseums.org
www.facebook.com/saskmuseums
twitter.com/saskmuseums
Previous Name: Saskatchewan Museums Association
Overview: A medium-sized provincial charitable organization founded in 1967
Mission: To work for the advancement of strong & vibrant museums in Saskatchewan; To encourage the preservation & understanding of the province's cultural & natural heritage; To serve Saskatchewan museums
Finances: *Funding Sources:* Department of Canadian Heritage Museums Assistance Program; Saskatchewan Lotteries Trust for Sport, Culture & Recreation
Staff Member(s): 6
Membership: 400+; *Fees:* Schedule available; *Member Profile:* Individuals; Museums; Associate organizations
Activities: Offering training opportunities; Providing support to First Nations & Métis communities; Advising museums through an information & referral service & on-site visits; Administering grants; *Library:* MAS Resources Library
Chief Officer(s):
Wendy Fitch, Executive Director, 306-780-9280
wendy.fitch@saskmuseums.org
Robert Hubick, President

Museums of Niagara Association (MONA)
c/o Helen Booth, Jordan Historical Museum of the Twenty, 3800 Main St., Jordan ON L0R 1S0
Tel: 905-562-5242; *Fax:* 905-562-7786
Overview: A small local organization founded in 1979
Mission: To advocate, educate & cooperate with Niagara's cultural facilities
Membership: *Member Profile:* Museums & art galleries of Niagara
Activities: Production of area brochure of member institutions; meetings featuring workshops & speakers on current & relevant issues; *Speaker Service:* Yes

Musgamagw Tsawataineuk Tribal Council
#1-2, 2005 Eagle Dr., Campbell River BC V9H 1V8
Tel: 250-914-3402; *Fax:* 250-914-3406
Overview: A small local organization

Mushrooms Canada (CMGA)
7660 Mill Rd., RR#4, Guelph ON N1H 6J1
Tel: 519-829-4125; *Fax:* 519-837-0729
info@canadianmushroom.com
www.mushrooms.ca
www.facebook.com/mushroomscanada
twitter.com/mushroomscanada
www.youtube.com/cdnmushroom
Previous Name: Canadian Mushroom Growers' Association
Overview: A medium-sized national organization founded in 1955
Mission: To encourage cooperation & communication within the Canadian industry, with various levels of government, & with related organizations internationally; To promote mushroom consumption
Affiliation(s): International Society for Mushroom Science (ISMS)
Finances: *Funding Sources:* Membership dues
Membership: *Fees:* Schedule available; *Member Profile:* Mushroom growers; Consultants; Suppliers to the industry; Research scientists
Activities: Researching in mushroom cultivation; Marketing

Music BC Industry Association (PMIA)
#100, 938 Howe St., Vancouver BC V6Z 1N9
Tel: 604-873-1914; *Fax:* 604-873-9686
Toll-Free: 888-866-8570
info@musicbc.org
www.musicbc.org
twitter.com/musicbc
www.youtube.com/user/MusicBCofficial
Also Known As: Music BC
Previous Name: Pacific Music Industry Association

Overview: A medium-sized provincial organization founded in 1990
Mission: To address key issues; To implement positive change by presenting a strong voice to government, business & community; To enhance the profile of the BC music industry in the international marketplace; To promote communication; To stimulate activity & employment
Member of: Western Canadian Music Alliance
Affiliation(s): FACTOR; MROC
Finances: *Funding Sources:* Provincial government; membership dues; events; Socan Foundation
Staff Member(s): 3
Membership: *Fees:* Schedule available
Activities: Professional development sessions throughout the province; *Library:* by appointment
Chief Officer(s):
Alex Grigg, Executive Director
alex@musicbc.org
Lindsay MacPherson, Program Manager
lindsay@musicbc.org
Becky Wosk, Coordinator, Membership & Communications
becky@musicbc.org
Awards:
• West Coast Music Awards

Music Canada
85 Mowat Ave., Toronto ON M6K 3E3
Tel: 416-967-7272; *Fax:* 416-967-9415
info@musiccanada.com
www.musiccanada.com
www.facebook.com/MusicCanada
twitter.com/music_canada
instagram.com/music_canada
Previous Name: Canadian Recording Industry Association
Overview: A medium-sized national organization
Mission: To develop & promote high ethical standards in the creation, manufacture and marketing of sound recordings.
Membership: 20
Chief Officer(s):
Graham Henderson, President

Music for Young Children (MYC) / Musique pour jeunes enfants
39 Leacock Way, Kanata ON K2K 1T1
Tel: 613-592-7565; *Fax:* 613-592-8632
Toll-Free: 800-561-1692
myc@myc.com
www.myc.com
www.facebook.com/Music.for.Young.Children.MYC
www.youtube.com/user/MYCKanata
Overview: A medium-sized local licensing organization founded in 1980
Mission: To develop, deliver & support comprehensive entry level music education programs of the finest quality
Member of: Registered Music Teachers Association
Finances: *Funding Sources:* Private
Membership: 900 individual; *Fees:* Schedule available; *Member Profile:* Teachers must have completed a training seminar
Activities: *Library:* by appointment
Chief Officer(s):
Janice Reade, Manager, Public Relations
janice@myc.com
Awards:
• Helena Evans Memorial Scholarship
Awarded annually to an MYC graduate pursuing music at the post-secondary level; *Amount:* $500

Alberta
326 Superior Ave. SW, Calgary AB T3C 2J2
Tel: 403-244-9080
Toll-Free: 866-244-9008
Chief Officer(s):
Judy Causgrove, Coordinator
j.causgrove@myc.com

British Columbia & Western United States
4350 - 13th St. South, Cranbrook BC V1C 7A6
Tel: 250-489-1746
Chief Officer(s):
Wendy Guimont, Coordinator
w.guimont@myc.com

Manitoba
2735 Hallama Dr., Grande Pointe MB R5A 1H5
Tel: 204-257-1071; *Fax:* 204-257-1071
www.facebook.com/MYC.MB.NWON
Chief Officer(s):

Canadian Associations / Music Managers Forum Canada

Marilyn Unrau, Coordinator
m.unrau@myc.com
New Brunswick & Prince Edward Island
34 Llangollen Rd., Moncton NB E1E 3W5
Tel: 506-382-0280; *Fax:* 506-382-0280
Toll-Free: 888-371-5577
Chief Officer(s):
Doris Sabean, Coordinator
d.sabean@myc.com
Newfoundland & Labrador
21 Connemara Pl., St. John's NL A1A 3E3
Tel: 709-753-0218
Chief Officer(s):
Heather Meaney, Coordinator
h.meaney@myc.com
Nova Scotia
49 Charles St., Timberlea NS B3T 1J7
Tel: 902-434-3929
Chief Officer(s):
Megan Henley, Coordinator
m.henley@myc.com
Ontario - Central
c/o Muskoka Music Centre, 36 Lorne St. South, Huntsville ON P1H 1V7
Tel: 705-224-0070
Toll-Free: 866-999-1091
play@muskokamusiccentre.com
Chief Officer(s):
Frank Berg, Coordinator
f.berg@myc.com
Ontario - Eastern
1599 Winterport Way, Ottawa ON K4A 4C2
Tel: 613-841-5811
Chief Officer(s):
Eileen Leversedge, Coordinator
e.leversedge@myc.com
Ontario - Southern
Elmira ON
Tel: 519-669-8941
Toll-Free: 866-884-3080
Chief Officer(s):
Sandra Poolton, Coordinator
s.poolton@myc.com
Prince Edward Island Sunrise Program
Wildon St., Summerside PE C1N 4H6
Tel: 902-436-2674
Chief Officer(s):
Nancy Rogerson, Coordinator
n.rogerson@myc.com
Québec
Montréal QC
Tel: 514-696-0008
www.facebook.com/MYC.Quebec.MJE
Chief Officer(s):
Cathy Morabito, Coordinator
c.morabito@myc.com
Saskatchewan
493 Willow Bay, Estevan SK S4A 2G3
Tel: 306-636-2692
Chief Officer(s):
Anita Kuntz, Coordinator
a.kuntz@myc.com

Music Industry Association of Newfoundland & Labrador
See MusicNL

Music Managers Forum Canada
1731 Lawrence Ave. East, Toronto ON M1R 2X7
Tel: 416-462-9160
info@musicmanagersforum.ca
musicmanagersforum.ca
twitter.com/MMFCanada
Also Known As: MMF Canada
Overview: A small national organization
Mission: To be a source of information for Canadian musicians, artists & managers
Affiliation(s): International Music Managers Forum
Membership: 150+ members serving 300+ Canadian & international acts
Chief Officer(s):
Meg Symsyk, President
Jordan Safer, Manager, Operations, Events & Sponsorship
jordan@musicmanagersforum.ca

Music Nova Scotia
2169 Gottingen St., Halifax NS B3K 3B5
Tel: 902-423-6271; *Fax:* 902-423-8841
Toll-Free: 888-343-6426
info@musicnovascotia.ca
www.musicnovascotia.ca
www.facebook.com/MusicNovaScotia
twitter.com/musicnovascotia
www.youtube.com/user/MusicNS
Overview: A large provincial organization founded in 1989
Mission: To encourage the creation, development, growth & promotion of Nova Scotia's music industry
Staff Member(s): 9
Membership: *Fees:* $20 student; $50 individual; $60 band; $70 small business/non-profit/venue; $135 corporate
Chief Officer(s):
Scott Long, Executive Director
scott@musicnovascotia.ca

Music NWT
PO Box 127, Yellowknife NT X1A 2N1
info@musicnwt.ca
www.musicnwt.ca
twitter.com/musicnwt
Overview: A medium-sized provincial organization
Mission: To bring together musicians, offers workshops & other resources, & provides networking opportunities
Staff Member(s): 2
Membership: *Fees:* $10 supporter; $15 senior/youth; $30 individual; $250 venue; $500 corporate; *Member Profile:* Musicians, including bands; music-related associations & corporations
Chief Officer(s):
Mike Filipowitsch, Executive Director
mike@musicnwt.ca

Music PEI
PO Box 2371, Charlottetown PE C1A 8C1
Tel: 902-894-6734; *Fax:* 902-894-4404
music@musicpei.com
www.musicpei.com
www.facebook.com/MusicPEI
twitter.com/MusicPEI
Overview: A large provincial organization founded in 2001
Mission: To promote, foster, & develop artists & the music industry in PEI
Staff Member(s): 2
Membership: 200+; *Fees:* $30 artist; $60 band; $75 corporate; $15 student; $20 music lover
Activities: Exposing emerging artists through showcases & awards; *Awareness Events:* Music PEI Week, February; Music PEI Awards
Chief Officer(s):
Rob Oakie, Executive Director
roboakie@musicpei.com
Awards:
• Music PEI Awards
Eligibility: PEI musicians

Music Yukon
#416, 108 Elliott St., Whitehorse YT Y1A 6C4
Tel: 867-456-8742
office@musicyukon.com
www.musicyukon.com
www.facebook.com/musicyukon
twitter.com/musicyukon
Overview: A medium-sized provincial organization
Mission: To promote the Yukon music industry
Affiliation(s): Canadian Academy of Recording Arts & Sciences; Yukon Film & Sound Commission; Canadian Independent Record Production Association; Folk Alliance Canada; Foundation to Assist Canadian Talent on Records; Songwriters Association of Canada; Society of Composers, Authors & Music Publishers of Canada
Finances: *Funding Sources:* Member fees; Government grants
Membership: *Fees:* $200 corporate; $40 full service; $20 associate; No fee for affiliates or supporting cast members; *Member Profile:* Individuals, groups, organizations, companies & entities involved in the Yukon's music industry
Chief Officer(s):
Kelly Proudfoot, President
Kim Winnicky, Executive Director

Music/Musique NB
PO Box 1638, #30, 140 Botsford St., Moncton NB E1C 4X5
Tel: 506-383-4662; *Fax:* 506-383-6171
contact@musicnb.org
musicnb.org
www.facebook.com/MusicMusiqueNB
twitter.com/MusicMusiqueNB
instagram.com/musicmusiquenb
Also Known As: Music New Brunswick
Overview: A medium-sized provincial organization
Mission: To support musicians, managers & businesses involved in the music industry in New Brunswick
Affiliation(s): The Foundation Assisting Canadian Talent on Recordings
Membership: *Fees:* Schedule available
Chief Officer(s):
Richard Hornsby, President
Jean Surette, Executive Director
jean@musicnb.org
Awards:
• Prix MNB Awards
Awarded annually to recognize excellence in music in New Brunswick. Categories include: Album of the Year, Solo Recording of the Year, Emerging Artist of the Year & Music Industry Professional of the Year.

Musicaction
#2, 4385, rue Saint-Hubert, Montréal QC H2J 2X1
Tél: 514-861-8444; *Téléc:* 514-861-4423
Ligne sans frais: 800-861-5561
info@musicaction.ca
www.musicaction.ca
www.facebook.com/musicaction.ca
Aperçu: *Dimension:* petite; *Envergure:* nationale; Organisme sans but lucratif; fondée en 1985
Mission: Développement de la musique vocale francophone au Canada
Finances: *Budget de fonctionnement annuel:* Plus de $5 Million
Membre(s) du personnel: 15
Activités: *Service de conférenciers:* Oui
Membre(s) du bureau directeur:
Louise Chenail, Directrice générale
lchenail@musicaction.ca

Musicians' Association of Victoria & the Islands, Local 247, AFM
#201, 732 Princess Ave., Victoria BC V8T 1K6
Tel: 250-385-3954; *Fax:* 250-480-1518
afm247.com
Previous Name: Victoria Musicians' Association
Overview: A small local organization founded in 1902
Mission: To organize professional musicians within our jurisdiction in order to provide services & work towards the betterment of their working conditions & benefits
Member of: American Federation of Musicians of the United States & Canada
Affiliation(s): Canadian Labour Congress
Finances: *Annual Operating Budget:* $50,000-$100,000; *Funding Sources:* Membership dues
Staff Member(s): 2
Membership: 120; *Fees:* $110
Activities: *Speaker Service:* Yes
Chief Officer(s):
Paul Wainwright, President

Musiciens amateurs du Canada *See* Canadian Amateur Musicians

MusicNL
186 Duckworth St., St. John's NL A1C 1G5
Tel: 709-754-2574; *Fax:* 709-754-5758
info@musicnl.ca
www.musicnl.ca
www.facebook.com/MusicNL
twitter.com/_MusicNL_
www.youtube.com/channel/UCEQj7GHNh3HvjGh5EG0su7Q
Previous Name: Music Industry Association of Newfoundland & Labrador
Overview: A small provincial organization founded in 1992
Mission: To promote, encourage & develop the music from Newfoundland & Labrador, in all its forms, whether written, recorded or in live performances
Affiliation(s): Foundation to Assist Canadian Talent on Records (FACTOR)
Finances: *Funding Sources:* Provincial government
Staff Member(s): 1
Membership: 700; *Fees:* Schedule available
Chief Officer(s):
Glenda Tulk, Interim Executive Director
Rebekah Robbins, Officer, Communications & Programs

Musique pour jeunes enfants *See* Music for Young Children

Muskoka *See* Habitat for Humanity Canada

Muskoka Arts & Crafts Inc. (MAC)
PO Box 376, Bracebridge ON P1L 1T7
Tel: 705-645-5501; *Fax:* 705-645-0385
info@muskokaartsandcrafts.com
www.muskokaartsandcrafts.com
www.facebook.com/MuskokaArtsandCraftsInc
Overview: A small local organization founded in 1963
Mission: To assure the strength & vitality of the arts & crafts community in Muskoka
Member of: Ontario Crafts Council
Finances: *Funding Sources:* Fundraising; Membership fees
Staff Member(s): 1
Membership: *Fees:* $39.55 individual; $32.77 senior; $20.34 student; $53.11 family
Activities: Craft shows, workshops, lectures, special events, public art gallery
Chief Officer(s):
Elene J. Freer, Executive Director

Muskoka Community Futures Development Corporation
111 Manitoba St., Bracebridge ON P1L 2B6
Tel: 705-646-9511; *Fax:* 705-646-9522
Toll-Free: 800-414-6570
www.muskokafutures.ca
www.facebook.com/652906441425560
twitter.com/MuskokaFutures
www.youtube.com/channel/UCY-VoZwDpkVPTVKeKTwys2w
Also Known As: Muskoka Futures
Overview: A small local organization
Mission: To enable long-term employment & economic growth by providing professionally guided access to business information, counselling, mentoring & business financing for start-up, maintenance & expansion; facilitation services for community economic development projects & activities taking place throughout the region
Finances: *Annual Operating Budget:* $250,000-$500,000
Staff Member(s): 4
Activities: *Internships:* Yes; *Speaker Service:* Yes; *Library:* Open to public
Chief Officer(s):
David Brushey, Executive Director, 705-646-9511 Ext. 220

Muskoka Lakes Association
PO Box 289, 65 Joseph St., 2nd Fl., Port Carling ON P0B 1J0
Tel: 705-765-5723; *Fax:* 705-765-3203
info@mla.on.ca
www.mla.on.ca
www.facebook.com/muskokalakesassociation
twitter.com/MuskokaLakes
Overview: A medium-sized local organization founded in 1894
Mission: To represent the interests of lakeshore residents in preserving the unique beauty of Muskoka
Staff Member(s): 2; 104 volunteer(s)
Membership: 2,458 members; *Fees:* $95 family; *Member Profile:* Permanent & seasonal residents of the Muskoka Lakes & area; anyone interested in the preservation & safety of the lakes
Chief Officer(s):
Lisa Noonan, Senior Manager
lisa@mla.on.ca

Muskoka Lakes Chamber of Commerce
PO Box 536, 3181 Muskoka Rd. 169, Bala ON P0C 1A0
Tel: 705-762-5663; *Fax:* 705-762-5664
info@muskokalakeschamber.com
www.muskokalakeschamber.com
www.linkedin.com/company/muskoka-lakes-chamber-of-commerce
www.facebook.com/533787036692064
twitter.com/muskokalkscc
www.youtube.com/user/MuskokaLksCC;
www.instagram.com/MuskokaLksCC
Previous Name: West Muskoka Chamber of Commerce
Overview: A small local organization
Member of: Ontario Chamber of Commerce
Finances: *Annual Operating Budget:* Less than $50,000
Staff Member(s): 1; 10 volunteer(s)
Membership: 325; *Fees:* $198.26 general business; $123.05 private members/associations/affiliates; $150.40 young professional (owner under 30); $56.50 not-for-profit
Activities: *Internships:* Yes; *Speaker Service:* Yes
Chief Officer(s):
Jane Templeton, Manager

Muskoka Pioneer Power Association
PO Box 2256, Bracebridge ON P1L 1W2
Tel: 705-645-6546
www.bracebridgechamber.com/mppa/
Overview: A small local organization founded in 1984
Mission: To preserve the farming & logging artifacts of Muskoka & to provide a demonstration show each year
Activities: Annual show second weekend of July; participate at local fall fair in Sept.
Chief Officer(s):
Ray Leng, President

Muskoka Ratepayers' Association (MRA)
PO Box 336, Port Carling ON P0B 1J0
Tel: 705-765-0022; *Fax:* 705-765-0023
muskokaratepayers@vianet.ca
www.tmlra.on.ca
Overview: A small local organization founded in 1976
Mission: Preservation, fairness & enhancement for & with property owners in the Township of Muskoka Lakes & beyond
Chief Officer(s):
J. Douglas Bryden, President

Muskoka Steamship & Historical Society
c/o Muskoka Boat & Heritage Centre, 275 Steamship Bay Rd., Gravenhurst ON P1P 1Z9
Tel: 705-687-2115; *Fax:* 705-687-7820
info@realmuskoka.com
www.realmuskoka.com
www.facebook.com/MuskokaSteamships
twitter.com/rmssegwun
www.youtube.com/user/muskokasteamships
Overview: A small local charitable organization founded in 1973
Mission: To preserve & promote the traditions of boat building & steamships in the Muskoka region of Ontario
Finances: *Funding Sources:* Ship ticket sales; Muskoka Boat & Heritage Centre admissions & room rentals; Membership fees; Government grants; Donations; Fundraising
Staff Member(s): 71; 100 volunteer(s)
Membership: 600; *Fees:* $10 juniors; $52 individual; $63 family; $150 corporate; *Committees:* Fundraising; Communciations/Newsletter; Membership; Marketing; Muskoka Boat & Heritage Centre Management; Archives & Curatorial; Education; Collections; Program; Heritage Boatworks; Volunteer; Muskoka Steamships Management; Safety & Technical Standards
Activities: Providing education about boat building & steamships; Operating the Muskoka Boat & Heritage Centre as well as the Royal Mail Ship Segwun, Wenonah II, & Wanda III
Chief Officer(s):
John Miller, General Manager
Ann Curley, Manager, MDC Operations
Inguna Ramina, Manager, Sales
Prisca Campbell, Manager, Marketing & Fundraising
Jordan Waines, Manager, Operations
Publications:
• The Real Muskoka Story
Type: Newsletter; *Frequency:* Quarterly; *Price:* Free with membership
Profile: News & events from the Muskoka Steamship & Historical Society

Muskoka Tourism
1342 Hwy. 11 North, RR#2, Kilworthy ON P0E 1G0
Tel: 705-689-0660; *Fax:* 705-689-9118
Toll-Free: 800-267-9700
info@muskokatourism.ca
www.discovermuskoka.ca
www.facebook.com/discovermuskoka
twitter.com/DiscoverMuskoka
www.youtube.com/user/MuskokaTourism
Also Known As: Muskoka Tourism Marketing Agency
Overview: A medium-sized local organization founded in 1984
Mission: To market the region's tourism resources to the public, media & group tour travel markets
Member of: Ontario Motor Coach Association; Tourism Industry Association of Canada; Meeting Professionals International
Finances: *Funding Sources:* Municipal
Membership: *Fees:* Schedule available
Activities: Travel counselling; event planning; *Speaker Service:* Yes; *Rents Mailing List:* Yes; *Library:* by appointment
Chief Officer(s):
Michael Lawley, Executive Director
mlawley@muskokatourism.ca

Muskoka-Parry Sound Beekeepers' Association
c/o Robert Key, 92 West Rd., Huntsville ON P1H 1M1
Tel: 705-783-3320
robertjkey@hotmail.com
Overview: A small local organization
Mission: To provide education & information about beekeeping in the Muskoka - Parry Sound region; To assist local beekeepers with problems encountered
Member of: Ontario Beekeepers' Association
Membership: *Member Profile:* Persons working in apiculture in the Muskoka - Parry Sound area of Ontario
Activities: Hosting meetings for members; Offering networking opportunities to exchange information about beekeeping
Chief Officer(s):
Robert Key, President
robertjkey@hotmail.com

Muslim Association of Canada (MAC)
2270 Speakman Dr., Mississauga ON L5K 1B4
Tel: 905-822-2626; *Fax:* 905-822-2727
mac@macnet.ca
www.macnet.ca
Overview: A medium-sized national organization
Mission: Seeks to promote a balanced, constructive & integrated Islamic presence in Canada; operates in 13 Canadian cities
Activities: Schools & community centres; educational & other projects; youth projects; outreach
Chief Officer(s):
Abu Nazir, CPA, CMA, Chair

Muslim Association of New Brunswick (MANB)
1100 Rothesay Rd., Saint John NB E2H 2H8
Tel: 506-633-1675
info@manb.ca
www.manb.ca
Overview: A medium-sized provincial organization founded in 1985
Mission: To strengthen access to Islamic education, facilitate community outreach & interaction with other religious organizations & community groups; consolidate the social fabric of the community; & sustain Islamic work by encouraging & building endowments
Membership: *Fees:* $25; *Committees:* Maintenance; Cemetery; Constitutional Amendments; Religion Affairs; Imam Selection; Financial Affairs; Syrian Refugees Liaison; Dawa'; Ladies Liasion; Social Activities; Islamic School
Activities: *Library:*
Chief Officer(s):
Husni Abou El Niaj, President
Abdul Sattar Rahimi, Vice President
Kamran Gill, Treasurer
Nasir Mahmood, General Secretary

Muslim Community of Québec (MCQ) / Communauté musulmane du Québec (CMQ)
7445, av Chester, Montréal QC H4V 1M4
Tel: 514-484-2967; *Fax:* 514-484-3802
mrdeen25@hotmail.com
www.muslimcommunityofquebec.com
Also Known As: Mosque of Montréal
Overview: A small local organization founded in 1979
Mission: To facilitate Muslim religious life
Finances: *Annual Operating Budget:* $500,000-$1.5 Million
Membership: 500
Activities: *Speaker Service:* Yes
Chief Officer(s):
Muhammed Romizuddin, Contact

Muslim Council of Montréal (MCM)
PO Box 180, Stn. St-Laurent, Montréal QC H4L 4Z8
Tel: 514-748-8427
info@muslimcouncil.org
www.muslimcouncil.org
Overview: A small local organization
Mission: Seeks effective cooperation among Islamic organizations & Muslims of all nationalities or schools of thought; seeks better understanding of Islam; assists media by open discussion; takes part in multicultural activities
Finances: *Annual Operating Budget:* Less than $50,000
5 volunteer(s)
Membership: 40 Muslim institutions

Muslim World League - Canada
2550 Argentia Rd., Mississauga ON L5N 5R1

Tel: 905-542-1050; Fax: 905-542-1054
mwl@mwlcanada.org
themwl.org/GLOBAL/node/1205
Overview: A small national organization founded in 1985
Mission: The League is a non-profit, non-governmental organization that serves the religious needs of Muslims in Canada. It promotes Islam & Islamic teachings among Canadian Muslims & helps non-Muslims grasp an accurate understanding of the religion. It also serves as a resource centre, publishing booklets & flyers on current issues.
Affiliation(s): Muslim World League, Makkah, Saudia Arabia
Staff Member(s): 4
Membership: *Member Profile*: Muslims
Activities: *Rents Mailing List*: Yes; *Library*: Open to public
Chief Officer(s):
Mohamad Zuhair El-Khateeb, Director

Musquodoboit Trailways Association
PO Box 336, Musquodoboit Harbour NS B0J 2L0
Tel: 902-889-3447
www.mta-ns.ca
Overview: A small local organization founded in 1997
Mission: To provide world-class hiking & cycling trails while preserving the ecosystem & wildlife habitats of the area
Member of: Nova Scotia Regional Trails Federation; Trans Canada Trail
Membership: *Fees*: $10 individual; $15 family; $25 corporate
Activities: Manages & maintains 40 kms of non-motorized trails
Chief Officer(s):
Stanley Van Dyke, Chair
stanley.vandyke@gmail.com

Mustard Seed Food Bank
625 Queens Ave., Victoria BC V8T 1L9
Tel: 250-953-1575; Fax: 250-385-0430
contact@mustardseed.ca
www.mustardseed.ca
www.facebook.com/MustardSeedVictoria
twitter.com/mustardseedvic
www.instagram.com/mustardseedvic
Overview: A small local charitable organization overseen by Food Banks British Columbia
Mission: To provide good nutritional food to people in need
Member of: Food Banks British Columbia; Food Banks Canada
Staff Member(s): 4; 50 volunteer(s)
Chief Officer(s):
Bruce Curtiss, Executive Director
Jackie Cox-Ziegler, Director, Administration
Janine Boice, Director, Development
Publications:
• Street Beat
Frequency: Monthly
Profile: Newsletter

The Muttart Foundation
Scotia Place, #1150, 10060 Jasper Ave., Edmonton AB T5J 3R8
Tel: 780-425-9616; Fax: 780-425-0282
Toll-Free: 877-788-5437
www.muttart.org
Previous Name: The Gladys & Merrill Muttart Foundation
Overview: A small local charitable organization founded in 1953
Mission: To support projects that improve the effectiveness of the charitable sector; funding limited to Alberta, Saskatchewan, NWT & the Yukon
Affiliation(s): Canadian Centre for Philanthropy; Council on Foundations; Association of Canadian Foundations
Finances: *Annual Operating Budget*: $500,000-$1.5 Million; *Funding Sources*: Private endowment
Staff Member(s): 8; 12 volunteer(s)
Activities: *Speaker Service*: Yes
Chief Officer(s):
Bob Wyatt, Executive Director
bwyatt@muttart.org
Marion Gracey, President

Mutual Fund Dealers Association of Canada (MFDA) / Association canadienne des courtiers de fonds mutuels
#1000, 121 King St. West, Toronto ON M5H 3T9
Tel: 416-361-6332
Toll-Free: 888-466-6332
Other Communication: Member Fax: 416-943-1218; HR Fax: 416-361-6381
mfda@mfda.ca
www.mfda.ca
www.linkedin.com/company/mfda
twitter.com/MFDA_News
Overview: A large national organization founded in 1998
Mission: To be the national self-regulatory organization (SRO) for the distribution side of the Canadian mutual fund industry
Membership: *Fees*: Schedule available; *Committees*: Audit & Finance; Governance; Regulatory Issues
Chief Officer(s):
Christopher Nicholls, BA, LL.B., LL.M, Chair
Mark T. Gordon, LLB, President & CEO
Shaun Devlin, Senior Vice-President, Member Regulation - Enforcement
Karen L. McGuinness, Senior Vice-President, Member Regulation - Compliance
Paige L. Ward, General Counsel, Corporate Secretary & VP, Policy
Publications:
• MFDA [Mutual Fund Dealers Association of Canada] Bulletins
Type: Bulletin

 Pacific Regional Office
 PO Box 11603, #1220, 650 West Georgia St., Vancouver BC V6B 4N9
 Tel: 604-694-8840; Fax: 604-683-6577
 PacificOffice@mfda.ca
 Chief Officer(s):
 Jeff Mount, Vice-President, Pacific Region

 Prairie Regional Office
 #850, 800 - 6th Ave. SW, Calgary AB T2P 3G3
 Tel: 403-266-8826; Fax: 403-266-8858
 PrairieOffice@mfda.ca
 Chief Officer(s):
 Mark Stott, Vice-President, Prairie Region

Myalgic Encephalomyelitis Association of Halton/Hamilton-Wentworth
#5, 2230 Mountainside Dr., Burlington ON L7P 1B5
Tel: 905-319-7966
Overview: A small local charitable organization
Finances: *Funding Sources*: Membership fees; private donations
Activities: Public awareness; fundraising; support group; *Library*: Resource Centre; Open to public
Chief Officer(s):
Sally Hansen, President

Myalgic Encephalomyelitis Association of Ontario (MEAO)
#370, 170 Donway West, Toronto ON M3C 2G3
Tel: 416-222-8820
Toll-Free: 877-632-6682
info@meao.ca
www.meao.ca
Overview: A small provincial charitable organization founded in 1992
Mission: To support individuals who have Myalgic Encephalomyelitis/Chronic Fatigue Syndrome & their families; to provide medical professionals, government & the general public with information on the illness & its effects & consequences
Finances: *Funding Sources*: Membership dues; Donations; City of Toronto; Trillium Foundation
Membership: *Fees*: $25

Myasthenia Gravis Association of British Columbia (MGABC)
2805 Kingsway, Vancouver BC V5R 5H9
Tel: 604-451-5511; Fax: 604-451-5651
mgabc@centreforability.bc.ca
www.mystheniagravis.ca
Overview: A small provincial charitable organization founded in 1955
Mission: To provide information & support to British Columbians who suffer from Myasthenia Gravis (Grave Muscular Disease) & to their caregivers; to increase public awareness of the disease; to gather & disseminate specific information on Myasthenia Gravis to healthcare providers in British Columbia; to foster & support research into the causes & treatment of Myasthenia Gravis
Finances: *Funding Sources*: Donations; Membership; Charity gaming funds
Membership: *Member Profile*: People with Myasthenia Gravis; friends; family; health professionals
Activities: *Speaker Service*: Yes; *Library*: Open to public by appointment
Chief Officer(s):
Brenda Kelsey, President

 North Island MG Association
 BC
 Chief Officer(s):
 John Skalos, Contact
 lisaandjohn@shaw.ca
 Victoria
 Victoria BC

Mycological Society of Toronto (MST)
c/o 42 Eastwood Cres., Markham ON L3P 5Z7
info@myctor.org
www.myctor.org
Overview: A small local organization
Mission: To provide opportunities for members to develop their interest in mycology through discussions, exhibits, lectures, forays, field trips & contacts with professional mycologists; to stimulate public interest & awareness in the broad area of mycology; and to foster a responsible & caring attitude towards the natural environment
Affiliation(s): North American Mycological Association
Membership: *Fees*: $30
Activities: *Speaker Service*: Yes; *Library*: Not open to public
Chief Officer(s):
Margaret Faye, Membership Director
Kevin McAuslan, President

Myeloma Canada / Myélome Canada
#138, 1800, boul Le Corbusier, Laval QC H7S 2K1
Tel: 579-934-3885; Fax: 514-505-1055
Toll-Free: 888-798-5771
contact@myeloma.ca
www.myelomacanada.ca
Overview: A small national organization founded in 2004
Mission: To support persons living with multiple myeloma; To promote clinical research & improved access to drug trials in Canada
Member of: Canadian Cancer Action Network
Affiliation(s): International Myeloma Foundation
Finances: *Funding Sources*: Fundraising; Donations
Activities: Increasing awareness of myeloma; Providing educational information about myeloma; Facilitating access to new treatment options; Offering emotional support; Liaising with support groups across Canada
Chief Officer(s):
Aldo Del Col, Chair
adelcol@myeloma.ca
Olivier Jerome, Director, Operations
ojerome@myeloma.ca
Martine Elias, Director, Access, Advocacy & Community Relations
melias@myeloma.ca
Josee Rainville, Senior Manager, Communication & Events
jrainville@myeloma.ca
Michelle Oana, Manager, Community Events & Fundraising
moana@myeloma.ca
Publications:
• Multiple Myeloma Patient Handbook
Type: Handbook; *Price*: Free
Profile: Education for myeloma patients & their loved ones, so that they can be an active partner in their care
• Myeloma Canada Newsletter
Type: Newsletter; *Frequency*: Quarterly
Profile: News & developments related to the disease, plus upcoming meetings & fundraisers

Myélome Canada *See* Myeloma Canada

N'Amerind (London) Friendship Centre
260 Colbourne St., London ON N6B 2S6
Tel: 519-672-0131; Fax: 519-672-0717
www.namerind.on.ca
www.facebook.com/namerindfc
Overview: A small local organization founded in 1967
Mission: To promote the intellectual, spiritual & physical well being of Native people, with a focus on Urban Natives
Member of: Ontario Federation of Indian Friendship Centres
Staff Member(s): 30
Chief Officer(s):
Donna Phillips, President
Al Day, Executive Director
aday@namerind.on.ca

N'swakamok Native Friendship Centre
110 Elm St., Sudbury ON P3C 1T5
Tel: 705-674-2128; Fax: 705-671-3539
nnfcadmin@on.aibn.com
www.nfcsudbury.org
Overview: A small local organization founded in 1967
Mission: To provide social programs & services to the Native population

Chief Officer(s):
Marie Meawasige, Executive Director

Na'amat Canada Inc.
#212, 5555 av Westminster, Montréal QC H4W 2J2
Tel: 514-488-0792; *Fax:* 514-487-6727
Toll-Free: 888-278-0792
naamat@naamatcanada.org
www.naamat.com
www.facebook.com/NaamatCanada
twitter.com/NaamatCanada
www.youtube.com/user/NaamatCanada
Previous Name: Pioneer Women Organization of Canada Inc.
Overview: A medium-sized national charitable organization founded in 1925
Mission: To support social programs in Canada & Israel; to help protect women, children & families in both nations; to support the state of Israel
Member of: Canadian Zionist Federation; National Council of Women of Canada
Affiliation(s): National Action Committee on the Status of Women
Staff Member(s): 6; 3,00 volunteer(s)
Membership: 2,000; *Fees:* Schedule available; *Committees:* Israel Information; Leadership Development; Social Action; Status of Women
Activities: Social program for seniors; daycare; events for children; legal aid; women's rights support
Chief Officer(s):
Doris Wexler-Charow, President

Edmonton Council
Edmonton AB
edmonton.info@naamat.com
Chief Officer(s):
Darlene Bushewsky, President

Montréal Council
#212, 5555 Westminster Dr., Montréal QC H4W 2J2
Tel: 514-484-0252; *Fax:* 514-487-6727
montreal.info@naamat.com
Chief Officer(s):
Anita Blanshay, Contact
Brenda Fayerman Noodelman, Contact
Heather Gordon, Contact

Ottawa Council
#633, 1500 Bank St., Ottawa ON K1H 1B8
Tel: 613-788-2913; *Fax:* 613-822-8194
ottawa.info@naamat.com
Chief Officer(s):
Toby Herscovitch, Co-President
Marilyn Schwartz, Co-President

Toronto Council
272 Codsell Ave., Toronto ON M3H 3X2
Tel: 416-636-5425; *Fax:* 416-636-5248
Toll-Free: 888-622-6280
toronto.info@naamat.com
Chief Officer(s):
Roni Maderer, President

Vancouver Council
#303, 950 - 41st Ave. West, Vancouver BC V5Z 2N7
Tel: 604-257-5177; *Fax:* 604-266-2561
vancouver.info@naamat.com
Chief Officer(s):
Tamar Glaser, Co-President
Ruth Stewart, Co-President

Calgary Council
Calgary AB
calgary.info@naamat.com
Chief Officer(s):
Susan Inhaber, President

Winnipeg Council
1010 Sinclair St., Winnipeg MB R2V 3H7
Tel: 204-334-3637; *Fax:* 204-338-4500
naamatw@mts.net

NABET 700 CEP
#203, 100 Lombard St., Toronto ON M5C 1M3
Tel: 416-536-4827; *Fax:* 416-536-0859
info@nabet700.com
www.nabet700.com
Overview: A medium-sized local organization founded in 1970
Mission: To be a union serving television & film technicians in Toronto; in 1994 NABET 700 merged with the Communications, Energy & Paperworkers Union of Canada (CEP).
Membership: 1,000; *Member Profile:* Television & film technicians

Chief Officer(s):
Jonathan Ahee, President
Craig Steele, Senior Vice-President
Frank Iacobucci, Secretary-Treasurer

NAID Canada
95 King St. East, 4th Fl., Toronto ON M5C 1G4
Toll-Free: 800-825-0864
info@naidcanada.org
www.naidcanada.org
Also Known As: National Association for Information Destruction Canada
Overview: A small national organization
Mission: To raise awareness & understanding of the importance of secure information & document destruction; to ensure that private personal & business information is not used for purposes other than originally intended; to develop & implement industry standards & certification; to provide a range of member services which include advocacy, communication, education & professional development
Member of: National Association for Information Destruction in United States
Membership: *Member Profile:* Companies that specialize in secure information & document destruction
Chief Officer(s):
Kevin Perry, Chair

NAIMA Canada
#500, 150 Laurier Ave. West, Ottawa ON K1P 5J4
Tel: 613-232-8093; *Fax:* 613-232-9149
contact@naimacanada.ca
www.naimacanada.ca
twitter.com/NAIMACanada
www.youtube.com/user/NAIMAVideo
Overview: A small national organization founded in 2004
Mission: To promote energy efficiency & sustainable building while promoting safe use of members products; to support standardization in insulation systems & installation
Affiliation(s): North American Insulation Manufacturers Association, USA
Finances: *Funding Sources:* Membership
Membership: 7 companies; *Committees:* Steering; Government Affairs; Technical/Product
Activities: *Speaker Service:* Yes
Chief Officer(s):
Michelle Bunch, Director, Finance & Administration
Angus Crane, Secretary
Jay Nordenstrom, Executive Director

NAIOP Greater Toronto
#300, 1100 Burloak Dr., Burlington ON L7L 6B2
Tel: 905-332-2322; *Fax:* 905-331-1768
Toll-Free: 877-331-9668
info@torontonaiop.org
www.torontonaiop.org
www.linkedin.com/company/naiop-greater-toronto-chapter
www.facebook.com/146718738715302?v=wall
twitter.com/torontonaiop
Also Known As: National Association of Industrial & Office Properties
Overview: A small local organization founded in 1977
Mission: To serve owners & developers of industrial & office properties in the Greater Toronto
Membership: 1,000; *Committees:* Programs; Real Estate Excellence (REX) Awards; Membership; Developing Leaders; Government Affairs; Education; Sustainability; Sponsorship; Annual Ski Day; Annual Golf Tournament
Chief Officer(s):
Constance Wrigley-Thomas, Executive Director
constance@torontonaiop.org

Naissances multiples Canada *See* Multiple Births Canada

Naissances multiples Temiskaming *See* Temiskaming Multiple Births

Nakiska Alpine Ski Association (NASA)
Stn. PO Box 68080, RPO Crowfoot, Calgary AB T3G 3N8
Tel: 403-613-5935
info@skinasa.org
www.skinasa.org
Overview: A small local organization founded in 2009 overseen by Alberta Alpine Ski Association
Mission: To introduce as many athletes as possible to the sport of alpine ski racing; To create the best alpine development system in Canada
Membership: 6 clubs + 300 individual

Chief Officer(s):
Scott Zahn, Director, Program & Technical
szahn@skinasa.org

Nakusp & District Chamber of Commerce
PO Box 387, 92 - 6th Ave. NW, Nakusp BC V0G 1R0
Tel: 250-265-4234; *Fax:* 250-265-3808
Toll-Free: 800-909-8819
nakusp@telus.net
www.nakusparrowlakes.com
www.facebook.com/nakusp.bc
Overview: A small local organization
Mission: To promote & improve trade & commerce & the economic welfare of the area
Member of: British Columbia Chamber of Commerce; Kootenay Rockies Tourism
Affiliation(s): Tourism British Columbia
Finances: *Annual Operating Budget:* Less than $50,000; *Funding Sources:* Fee for service
Staff Member(s): 1; 2 volunteer(s)
Membership: 140; *Fees:* Schedule available
Activities: *Awareness Events:* Nakusp Celebration of Light, July
Chief Officer(s):
Cedra Eichenauer, Office Manager

Nanaimo Association for Community Living (NACL)
#201, 96 Cavan St., Nanaimo BC V9L 2V1
Tel: 250-741-0224; *Fax:* 250-741-0227
info@nanaimoacl.com
www.nanaimoacl.com
www.facebook.com/nanaimoacl
Overview: A medium-sized local organization founded in 1986
Mission: To support all people with disabilities to achieve the highest quality of life through participation, independence, inclusion & education
Member of: British Columbia Association for Community Living
Finances: *Funding Sources:* Donations; provincial & municipal funding
Membership: *Fees:* By donation
Activities: Actions Day Program; 7 residential programs: Hammond Bay Home, Jingle Pot Home, Kennedy Home, Morningside Home, Portsmouth Road Home, Turner Connection Home, McCauley Drive Home; annual general meeting; Community Living event; *Library:* NACL Resource Library
Chief Officer(s):
Marlena Stewart, Executive Assistant
marlena.stewart@nanaimoacl.com

Nanaimo Community Foundation
#106, 619 Comox Rd., Nanaimo BC V9R 5V8
Tel: 250-714-0047
administrator@nanaimocommunityfoundation.com
www.nanaimocommunityfoundation.com
Overview: A small local charitable organization founded in 1982
Finances: *Funding Sources:* Bequests; Public & private donations
Membership: 1-99

Nanaimo District Museum (NDM)
100 Museum Way, Nanaimo BC V9R 5J8
Tel: 250-753-1821
info@nanaimomuseum.ca
www.nanaimomuseum.ca
www.facebook.com/NanaimoMuseum
Also Known As: Nanaimo & District Museum Society
Overview: A small local charitable organization founded in 1967
Mission: To promote & engage the community & visitor in meaningful experiences to the cultural heritage of the City of Nanaimo & its surrounding district
Member of: BC Museums Association
Finances: *Annual Operating Budget:* $250,000-$500,000; *Funding Sources:* Municipal & provincial government; earned revenue
Staff Member(s): 7; 50 volunteer(s)
Membership: 350; *Fees:* $8-$30; *Member Profile:* Community based; *Committees:* Finance; Personal Collection; Marketing; Volunteer
Activities: Coal mine bus tours; photo contest; exhibits; special events; educational programs; daily summer cannon firing; outreach; *Awareness Events:* Chinese New Year, Jan./Feb.; Heritage Week, Feb.; *Library:* Not open to public
Chief Officer(s):
Debbie Trueman, General Manager
debbie@nanaimomuseum.ca
Aimee Greenaway, Curator
aimee@nanaimomuseum.ca

Canadian Associations / Nanaimo Family Life Association (NFLA)

Awards:
- Don Sale Annual Scholarship for Excellence in History

Nanaimo Family Life Association (NFLA)
1070 Townsite Rd., Nanaimo BC V9S 1M6
Tel: 250-754-3331; *Fax:* 250-753-0268
reception@nflabc.org
www.nflabc.org
www.facebook.com/447668528623973
twitter.com/NanaimoFamLife
Overview: A medium-sized local charitable organization founded in 1967
Mission: To provide counselling & support services to individuals & families in Nanaimo
Finances: *Funding Sources:* Provincial government; foundations
Staff Member(s): 6
Membership: *Fees:* $10
Chief Officer(s):
Deborah Hollins, Executive Director

Nanaimo Historical Society (NHS)
PO Box 933, Nanaimo BC V9R 5N2
Overview: A small local organization founded in 1953
Mission: To collect, preserve & disseminate local & BC history
Member of: British Columbia Historical Federation
Activities: Monthly meetings; field trips; historic gatherings; book publications; *Library:* Historical Society Archives; by appointment
Awards:
- Annual Award to Student in the History Course at Malaspina University College

Nanaimo Literacy Association *See* Literacy Central Vancouver Island

Nanaimo Volunteer and Information Centre Society (NVICS)
3148 Barons Rd., #E, Nanaimo BC V9T 4B5
Tel: 250-758-7121; *Fax:* 250-758-7106
vn@volunteernanaimo.ca
www.volunteernanaimo.ca
www.facebook.com/volunteernanaimo
Also Known As: Volunteer Nanaimo
Overview: A small local charitable organization founded in 1979
Mission: To build the community's quality of life through volunteer development; To raise awareness of the power of volunteer service & the value of volunteering; To connect people with volunteering opportunities through recruitment & referral
Finances: *Funding Sources:* Donations; Sponsorship
Membership: *Fees:* $60 organizational; $10 individual; *Member Profile:* Volunteer organizations in Nanaimo; Individuals interested in volunteering in their community
Activities: Building capacity & staff of non-profit & community-based organizations; Connecting people with volunteer opportunities through recruitment services; Delivering current resources & news to volunteers & volunteer organizations

Nanaimo, Duncan & District Labour Council (NDDLC)
PO Box 822, Nanaimo BC V9R 5N2
Tel: 250-760-0547; *Fax:* 250-760-0548
labour@telus.net
www.nddlc.ca
Overview: A small local organization founded in 1958 overseen by British Columbia Federation Of Labour
Mission: To represent 65 affiliated local unions from British Columbia's Nanaimo, Duncan, & district; To build a strong labour movement & community; To promote quality social programs & public services
Affiliation(s): Canadian Labour Congress (CLC)
Membership: 14,000; *Member Profile:* Male & female trade unionists from the central area of Vancouver Island & the Gulf Islands north of Saltspring; *Committees:* Mid Island Health Coalition; Budget; Education; Political Action; Social; Social Justice; Strike / Labour Support; Union Label
Activities: Organizing workers; Providing education to members, such as labour & social justice education courses; Promoting workers' issues, such as pay equity & employment equity; Lobbying government; Raising awareness of social issues, such as the Ban Log Rally in Nanaimo; Supporting striking or locked out workers; Campaigning for economic & social justice; Supporting the community, by working with local organizations, such as the United Way; Offering networking opportunities; Providing labour news; Hosting monthly meetings
Chief Officer(s):
Ellen Oxman, President
eoxman@shaw.ca

Nanton & District Chamber of Commerce
PO Box 711, Nanton AB T0L 1R0
Tel: 403-646-2111
info@nantonchamber.com
www.nantonchamber.com
Overview: A small local organization
Finances: *Annual Operating Budget:* Less than $50,000
Membership: 65
Chief Officer(s):
Pam Woodall, President
Simon Hunt, Vice-President

Napanee & District Chamber of Commerce
Napanee Business Centre, 47 Dundas St. East, Napanee ON K7R 1H7
Tel: 613-354-6601
Toll-Free: 877-354-6601
inquiry@napaneechamber.ca
www.napaneechamber.ca
www.facebook.com/137245796288349
twitter.com/NapaneeChamber
Overview: A small local organization founded in 1995 overseen by Ontario Chamber of Commerce
Mission: To advocate on behalf of local businesses & promote their members
Membership: *Fees:* Schedule available
Chief Officer(s):
Brad Way, President

Napanee Sports Association
16 McPherson Dr., Napanee ON K7R 3L1
Tel: 613-354-4423; *Fax:* 613-354-2212
info@napaneesportsassociation.com
www.losa.ca
Overview: A small local organization founded in 2006
Mission: To provide funding to local sports teams
Chief Officer(s):
Chuck Airhart, Chair

Napi Friendship Association
PO Box 657, 622 Charlotte St., Pincher Creek AB T0K 1K0
Tel: 403-627-4224; *Fax:* 403-627-2564
napiyouthcoordinator@gmail.com
www.okinapi.com
www.facebook.com/napiyouthprograms
Overview: A small provincial charitable organization overseen by Alberta Native Friendship Centres Association
Mission: To create better communication & understanding between the residents of Pincher Creek & the Peigan Nation
Member of: Alberta Native Friendship Centres Association

Nar-Anon Family Groups of Ontario
PO Box 20046, 2900 Warden Ave., Toronto ON M1W 3Y9
Tel: 416-239-0096
Toll-Free: 877-239-0096
info@naranonontario.com
www.naranonontario.com
Overview: A medium-sized provincial organization
Mission: To support & provide weekly meetings for those who know or have known a feeling of desperation due to the addiction problem of someone close to them

Narcotics Anonymous *See* Canadian Assembly of Narcotics Anonymous

Narcotiques Anonymes
Chibougamau QC
Ligne sans frais: 800-463-0162
www.naquebec.org
Aperçu: *Dimension:* petite; *Envergure:* provinciale

Natation Canada *See* Swimming Canada

Natation Nouveau-Brunswick *See* Swimming New Brunswick

National & Provincial Parks Association (NPPAC) *See* Canadian Parks & Wilderness Society

National Aboriginal Achievement Foundation *See* Indspire

National Aboriginal Capital Corporations Association (NACCA)
#908, 75 Albert St., Ottawa ON K1P 5E7
Tel: 613-688-0894; *Fax:* 613-688-0895
Toll-Free: 844-827-0327
info@nacca.ca
www.nacca.ca
www.facebook.com/NACCAinfo
twitter.com/NACCAinfo
Overview: A small national organization founded in 1996
Mission: To promote the growth of aboriginal business by providing products & services to Aboriginal financial institutions & Aboriginal focused organizations including institutional capacity, building, training, access to capital, advocacy, partnerships & member services with quality & accountability
Finances: *Annual Operating Budget:* $1.5 Million-$3 Million
Staff Member(s): 6; 13 volunteer(s)
Membership: 56 corporate; *Member Profile:* Aboriginal financial institutions; Aboriginal Capital Corporations; Community Future Development Centres; Development Corporations
Activities: Business loans; financial consulting services; aftercare; start-up support; Youth Entrepreneur Symposium
Chief Officer(s):
Shannin Metatawabin, CEO, 613-688-0894 Ext. 517
smetatawabin@nacca.ca

National Aboriginal Circle Against Family Violence
Kahnawake Business Complex, PO Box 2169, Kahnawake QC J0L 1B0
Tel: 450-638-2968; *Fax:* 450-638-9415
www.nacafv.ca
Overview: A medium-sized national organization
Mission: To reduce & eliminate family violence in our Aboriginal communities; programs are culturally appropriate, & support shelters & family violence prevention centres
Activities: Advocacy; research; promotion of public awareness
Chief Officer(s):
Brenda Combs, Chair, 705-941-9054, Fax: 705-941-9055
bcombs@nimkii@shaw.ca

National Aboriginal Diabetes Association Inc. (NADA)
#B1, 90 Garry St, Winnipeg MB R3C 4H1
Tel: 204-927-1220; *Fax:* 204-927-1222
Toll-Free: 877-232-6232
diabetes@nada.ca
www.nada.ca
www.facebook.com/nadasugarfree
twitter.com/nadasugarfree
Overview: A small national organization founded in 1995
Mission: To be the driving force in addressing diabetes & Aboriginal people as a priority health issue by working together with people, Aboriginal communities & organizations in the culturally respectful manner in promoting healthy lifestyles among Aboriginal people today & for future generations
Staff Member(s): 3
Membership: *Fees:* $0 community membership; $40 health professional; $75 corporate
Chief Officer(s):
Anita Ducharme, Executive Director
Alisher Kabildjanov, Program Assistant

National Aboriginal Forestry Association (NAFA)
#302, 359 Kent St., Ottawa ON K2P 0R6
Tel: 613-233-5563; *Fax:* 613-233-4329
www.nafaforestry.org
Overview: A medium-sized national organization founded in 1989
Mission: To promote & support increased Aboriginal involvement in forest management & related commercial opportunities; to assist Aboriginal communities in their quest to achieve a standard of land care which is balanced, sustainable & reflective of the traditional knowledge & forest values of Aboriginal peoples; to facilitate capacity-building in forest management through the development of human resource strategies & models for increased participation in natural resource decision making; to address the need for Aboriginal forest land rehabilitation & increased Aboriginal control over forest resources through the development of appropriate policy & programming
Member of: Encouraging responsible forest management & land care
Staff Member(s): 4
Membership: *Fees:* $150 regional, organization, individual, associate; $20 student; *Member Profile:* Organizations controlled by more than one First Nation or by one or more Tribal Councils; Aboriginal individuals; Non-Aboriginal organizations interested in furthering the goals of the association; Students
Activities: Cooperating with various levels of government, the forest industry, & other institutions to achieve its goals; Developing human resources strategies & models to increase participation in natural resource decision-making
Chief Officer(s):

Bradley Young, Executive Director
byoung@nafaforestry.org
Janet Pronovost, Office Manager
janet@nafaforestry.org

National Aboriginal Lands Managers Association (NALMA) / Association nationale des gestionnaires des terres autochones
1024 Mississauga St., Curve Lake ON K0L 1R0
Tel: 705-657-7660; Fax: 705-657-7177
Toll-Free: 877-234-9813
info@nalma.ca
www.nalma.ca
www.facebook.com/134580736635130
Overview: A small national organization
Mission: To enhance professional development & technical expertise in the functions of land management; To incorporate First Nations values & beliefs, keeping in mind the grass-root practices
Membership: Member Profile: First Nation Lands managers
Chief Officer(s):
Leona Irons, Executive Director
lirons@nalma.ca

National Aboriginal Trust Officers Association (NATOA)
468 New Credit Rd., RR#6, Hagersville ON N0A 1H0
natoa.ca
ca.linkedin.com/in/natoa
www.facebook.com/natoa.canada
twitter.com/NATOA_ca
Overview: A small national charitable organization
Mission: To build knowledge about trusts & investments within aboriginal communities; to foster & encourage professionalism & accountability
Staff Member(s): 1
Membership: Fees: $350 aboriginal individual; $450 individual corporate; $800 aboriginal org.; $1,075 industry org.; $1,500 gold; $10,000 platinum; $25,000 diamond; Committees: Membership
Activities: Annual conferences; accreditation program; Library: Research Library; Not open to public
Chief Officer(s):
Mark Sevestre, President, 289-260-4088
mark_sevestre@natoa.ca
Michele Young-Crook, Management Coordinator, 416-302-7399

National Academy Orchestra (NAO)
301 Bay St. South, Hamilton ON L8P 3J7
Tel: 905-525-7664; Fax: 905-526-9934
Toll-Free: 888-475-9377
www.nationalacademyorchestra.com
Overview: A small local organization founded in 1989 overseen by Orchestras Canada
Mission: To professionally train emerging young Canadian musicians through education, rehearsal, and public performance
Finances: Funding Sources: Government grants
Membership: 43; Member Profile: Emerging young Canadian professional musicians from 18-30; preferably with a post-secondary degree
Activities: Performing concerts; Holding regular rehearsal; Facilitating mock auditions; Holding seminars, lectures, and master classes
Chief Officer(s):
Boris Brott, Musical Director

National Action Committee on the Status of Women (NAC) / Comité canadien d'action sur le statut de la femme (CCA)
#417, 215 Spadina Ave., Toronto ON M5T 2C7
Tel: 416-932-1718; Fax: 416-979-3936
Overview: A large national organization founded in 1971
Mission: To shape public opinion, influence decision makers & mobilize membership & the Canadian public to work for equality & justice for all women
Finances: Annual Operating Budget: $500,000-$1.5 Million; Funding Sources: Member groups; individual contributions; Women's program
Staff Member(s): 5; 100 volunteer(s)
Membership: 604 organizations; Member Profile: Commitment to working to improve the status of women in Canada; member groups include national women's organizations, women's centres, service delivery groups, native women's groups, women's committees of church groups, unions & major political parties
Activities: Internships: Yes; Speaker Service: Yes; Rents Mailing List: Yes; Library: by appointment

National Adult Literacy Database See Copian

National Advertising Benevolent Society (NABS) / Société nationale de bienfaisance en publicité
#403, 55 St. Clair Ave. West, Toronto ON M4V 2Y7
Tel: 416-962-0446; Fax: 416-962-9149
Toll-Free: 800-661-6227
www.nabs.org
www.linkedin.com/company/nabs-canada
www.facebook.com/nabsCanada
twitter.com/NABS_Canada
www.youtube.com/user/NABSCan
Overview: A medium-sized national charitable organization founded in 1983
Mission: To relieve the suffering of individuals & their families who have derived the majority of their income from advertising
Member of: Canadian Centre of Philanthropy
Affiliation(s): Canadian Society of Association Executives
Finances: Funding Sources: Donations; fundraising events
Staff Member(s): 4
Activities: Advice Directory - resource information & assistance; Stress Line 1-888-355-5548; Speaker Service: Yes; Rents Mailing List: Yes; Library: NABS Resource Room
Chief Officer(s):
Manuela Yarhi, Executive Director
myarhi@nabs.org
Publications:
- NABS [National Advertising Benevolent Society] Newsletter
Type: Newsletter

NABS West
PO Box 35096, #409, 15940 Fraser Way, Surrey BC V4N 9E9
Tel: 604-580-8036; Fax: 877-397-3163
nabswest@nabswest.org
www.nabswest.org
www.linkedin.com/groups/3350104/profile
www.facebook.com/nabswest
twitter.com/NABSWest
Chief Officer(s):
Loraine Brown, Regional Manager

National African Integration & Families of Ontario (NAIFA)
60 Wellesley St. West, Toronto ON M5S 3L2
Tel: 416-975-0877; Fax: 416-925-9112
www.naifatoronto.ca
Overview: A medium-sized provincial organization founded in 1993
Mission: To support new beginnings for those involved in the justice and immigration systems, especially youth, by providing them with support services and programs that both empower and offer them genuine alternatives.

National Alliance for Autism Research See Autism Speaks Canada

National Alliance for Children & Youth (NACY) / Alliance nationale pour l'enfance et la jeunesse (ANEJ)
#707, 331 Cooper St., Ottawa ON K2P 0G5
Tel: 613-292-0569
info@nacy.ca
www.nacy.ca
www.facebook.com/189588222849
twitter.com/NACY_ANEJ
Overview: A medium-sized national organization founded in 1996
Mission: To promote the health & well being of children in Canada.
Membership: 50
Chief Officer(s):
Gordon Floyd, Chair

National Angel Capital Organization (NACO)
MaRS Centre, PO Box 23, 101 College St., HL 30B, Toronto ON M5G 1L7
Tel: 416-581-0009; Fax: 647-317-1649
Other Communication: Alt. E-mails: membership@nacocanada.com; events@nacocanada.com
contact@nacocanada.com
nacocanada.com
www.linkedin.com/groups/National-Angel-Capital-Organization-687677
www.facebook.com/NACOCanada
twitter.com/angelcapcanada
Overview: A medium-sized national organization founded in 2002
Mission: To create & promote a thriving community of Angel investors in Canada
Membership: 2,000+; Fees: $250 individual; $750 Angel group; Member Profile: Individual investors, Angel groups & industry partners
Activities: Networking opportunities; intelligence, tools & resources; industry events
Chief Officer(s):
Michelle Scarborough, Chair
Yuri Navarro, Executive Director, 416-581-0009 Ext. 3
ynavarro@nacocanada.com

National Anti-Poverty Organization See Canada Without Poverty

National Arts Centre Foundation
PO Box 1534, Stn. B, Ottawa ON K1P 5W1
Tel: 613-947-7000
donorscircle@nac-cna.ca
nacfoundation.ca
Overview: A small national charitable organization founded in 2000
Mission: To raise money on behalf on behalf of the National Arts Centre which funds performing arts projects across Canada
Staff Member(s): 6
Chief Officer(s):
Jayne Watson, CEO

National Arts Centre Orchestra of Canada (NACO) / Orchestre du Centre national des Arts (OCNA)
PO Box 1534, Stn. B, Ottawa ON K1P 5W1
Tel: 613-947-7000
Toll-Free: 866-850-2787
info@nac-cna.ca
nac-cna.ca
www.linkedin.com/company/national-arts-centre
www.facebook.com/NACOrchCNA
twitter.com/NACOrchCNA
Overview: A small national charitable organization founded in 1969 overseen by Orchestras Canada
Member of: League of American Orchestras; Orchestras Canada
Finances: Funding Sources: Federal government; Individual & corporate donations
Activities: Performing a regular concert season; Touring nationally & internationally; Facilitating master classes & open rehearsals; Internships: Yes; Library
Chief Officer(s):
Peter Herrndorf, President & Chief Executive Officer
peter.herrndorf@nac-cna.ca
Alexander Shelley, Music Director
alexander.shelley@nac-cna.ca
Awards:
- Vic Pomer Award
; Amount: $2,000
- The NAC Orchestra Bursary
; Amount: $7,000
- The Crabtree Foundation Award
Eligibility: Promising young musicians interested in pursuing an orchestral career.; Amount: $5,000
- Friends of the NAC Orchestra Award
; Amount: $3,000
- Piccolo Prix
; Amount: $1,000
- The NAC Orchestra Special Prize for Excerpts
; Amount: $1,000

National Association of Canadian Film & Video Distributors See Canadian Association of Film Distributors & Exporters

National Association of Canadian Optician Regulators (NACOR)
#2708, 83 Garry St., Winnipeg MB R3C 4J9
Tel: 204-949-1950; Fax: 204-949-9153
Toll-Free: 866-949-1950
general@nacor.ca
www.nacor.ca
Overview: A medium-sized national organization
Mission: To offer a platform that enables Canadian optician regulators to network & exchange information; To establish opticianry accreditation standards & processes; To assess & examine opticianry issues
Affiliation(s): College of Opticians of British Columbia; Alberta Opticians Association; Saskatchewan Ophthalmic Dispensers Association; The Opticians of Manitoba; The College of Opticians of Ontario; Ordre des Opticiens d'ordonnances du Qubec; Board of Dispensing Opticians of Newfoundland and

Labrador; Opticians Association of New Brunswick; Nova Scotia Board of Dispensing Opticians; P.E.I. Board of Dispensing Opticians

National Association of Canadians of Origins in India (NACOI) / Association nationale des Canadiens d'origine indienne (ANCOI)
PO Box 2308, Stn. D, Ottawa ON K1P 5W5
dbdavis@web.net
www.nacoi.ca
Overview: A medium-sized national organization founded in 1976
Mission: To encourage Canadians of origins in India to fully participate in Canadian society and to provide them with a national voice; To provide a forum for exchanges of ideas, issues & common concerns; To facilitate communication within & with other organizations; To assure & protect rights of Canadians of origins in India
Member of: Canadian Ethnocultural Council
Finances: *Annual Operating Budget:* $50,000-$100,000
4 volunteer(s)
Membership: 40 chapters + 60 organizations; *Fees:* $10 individual/family; $100 corporation; *Member Profile:* Canadian of origins in India
Chief Officer(s):
Dharam Pal Verma, President

National Association of Career Colleges (NACC) / Association nationale des collèges de carrières (ANCC)
#270, 44 Byward Market Sq., Ottawa ON K1N 7A2
Tel: 613-800-0340; *Fax:* 613-789-9669
www.nacc.ca
www.facebook.com/155709131139991
twitter.com/NACCCanada
Overview: A medium-sized national organization founded in 1896
Mission: To encourage excellence in the private training sector and to promote the interests of its members and their students at the national level.
Staff Member(s): 3
Chief Officer(s):
James Loder, Chair
Serge Buy, CEO
Meetings/Conferences:
• 2018 National Association of Career Colleges Conference, October, 2018, Ottawa, ON
Scope: National
Publications:
• Career Connections
Type: Magazine; *Frequency:* Quarterly; *Editor:* Shannon Lutter

National Association of Computer Consulting Business (Canada)
2233 Argentia Rd., Mississauga ON L5N 2X7
Tel: 905-826-6665; *Fax:* 905-826-4873
naccb@naccb.ca
www.naccb.ca
Also Known As: NACCB Canada
Overview: A small national organization founded in 1999
Mission: To provide education & awareness on public policy issues that impact the IT services industry in Canada; to represent interests of our members to policy makers to ensure that legislation does not inhibit the growth of IT services industry
Finances: *Annual Operating Budget:* $50,000-$100,000
20 volunteer(s)
Membership: 71; *Fees:* $500-$1,500; *Member Profile:* IT placement agencies
Chief Officer(s):
Terry Power, President
Terry_Power@eagleonline.com
Amanada Curtis, Executive Director
acurtis@naccb.ca
Ian MacMillan, Chair

National Association of Federal Retirees (FSNA) / Association nationale des retraités fédéraux (ANRF)
865 Shefford Rd., Ottawa ON K1J 1H9
Tel: 613-745-2559; *Fax:* 613-745-5457
Toll-Free: 855-304-4700
service@federalretirees.ca
www.federalretirees.ca
www.linkedin.com/company/1278904
www.facebook.com/FederalRetirees
twitter.com/fedretirees
Previous Name: Federal Superannuates National Association
Overview: A large national organization founded in 1963
Mission: To protect & enhance the rights & benefits of retired federal employees, & seniors in general, & to cooperate with other seniors'/pensionsers' organizations on objectives of mutual interest
Finances: *Annual Operating Budget:* $1.5 Million-$3 Million; *Funding Sources:* Membership fees
Staff Member(s): 28; 1000 volunteer(s)
Membership: 180,000+; *Fees:* $47.76 individual; $62.04 couple; *Member Profile:* Retired federal public service employees, retired Canadian Forces employees, & retired RCMP employees & their spouses
Chief Officer(s):
Jean-Guy Soulière, President
Simon Coakeley, Chief Executive Officer
Publications:
• Sage [a publication of the National Association of Federal Retirees]
Type: Magazine; *Frequency:* Quarterly; *Price:* Free to members
Profile: Includes analysis, news and other features of interest to members; available in both English & French

National Association of Friendship Centres (NAFC) / Association nationale des centres d'amitié
275 MacLaren St., Ottawa ON K2P 0L9
Tel: 613-563-4844; *Fax:* 613-594-3428
Toll-Free: 877-563-4844
nafcgen@nafc.ca
nafc.ca
www.linkedin.com/company/national-association-of-friendship-centres
www.facebook.com/TheNAFC
twitter.com/NAFC_ANCA
Overview: A medium-sized national organization founded in 1971
Mission: To assist friendship centres in communication, funding & training
Finances: *Funding Sources:* Secretary of State; project funding; membership fees
Staff Member(s): 14
Membership: 119 Friendship Centres
Activities: *Library:* by appointment
Chief Officer(s):
Erin Corston, Executive Director
ecorston@nafc.ca

National Association of Japanese Canadians (NAJC)
207 Donald St., 3rd Fl., Winnipeg MB R3C 1M5
Tel: 204-943-2910; *Fax:* 888-515-3192
national@najc.ca
www.najc.ca
Previous Name: National Japanese Canadian Citizens Association
Overview: A medium-sized national organization founded in 1947
Mission: To promote & develop a strong Japanese Canadian identity, thereby strengthening local communities & the national organization; to strive for equal rights & liberties for all persons & racial & ethnic minorities in particular.
Affiliation(s): Canadian Ethnocultural Council; Canadian Council for Refugees; National Capital Alliance on Race Relations
Finances: *Funding Sources:* Membership; government
Membership: *Fees:* $600 organizations; $100 associate organizations; $50 individuals; $25 senior/youth; *Committees:* Human Rights; Community Development; Heritage
Activities: NAJC Funds established to assist individuals & groups within the Japanese Canadian Community - Sports Education Arts Development (SEAD) Fund; Cultural Development Fund; Special Projects Fund; *Speaker Service:* Yes
Chief Officer(s):
Ken Noma, President

National Association of Major Mail Users, Inc. (NAMMU) / Association nationale des grands usagers postaux inc. (ANGUP)
#302, 517 Wellington St. West, Toronto ON M5V 1G1
Tel: 416-977-3703; *Fax:* 416-977-4513
Toll-Free: 800-453-1308
Other Communication: Membership E-mail: membership@nammu.ca
admin@nammu.ca
nammu.ca
www.linkedin.com/company/national-association-of-major-mail-users
Overview: A large national organization founded in 1983
Mission: To work in cooperation with Canada Post to improve cost & service
17 volunteer(s)
Membership: 200; *Member Profile:* Mail users of $200,000+ in lettermail or other Canada Post products, annually
Activities: *Awareness Events:* Golf Event, Aug.

National Association of Occupational Health Nurses *See* Canadian Occupational Health Nurses Association

National Association of Painters - Local 99 *Voir* Association nationale des peintres - locale 99

National Association of PeriAnesthesia Nurses of Canada
8753 Rte. 11, New Brandon NB E2A 5R3
Tel: 506-546-2890; *Fax:* 506-546-2890
info@napanc.org
www.napanc.org
Overview: A small national organization
Mission: To promote high standards of PeriAnesthesia Nursing practices in Canada
Finances: *Funding Sources:* Fundraising; Membership dues
Membership: *Committees:* Standards; Conference; Website; Newsletter; Nominations; Fundraising; Certification
Chief Officer(s):
Laura McNulty, President

National Association of Pharmacy Regulatory Authorities (NAPRA) / Association nationale des organismes de réglementation de la pharmacie
#750, 220 Laurier Ave. West, Ottawa ON K1P 5Z9
Tel: 613-569-9658; *Fax:* 613-569-9659
info@napra.ca
www.napra.ca
Overview: A medium-sized national organization founded in 1995
Mission: To facilitate the activities of provincial pharmacy regulatory authorities in their service of public interest
Finances: *Annual Operating Budget:* $1.5 Million-$3 Million
Staff Member(s): 6
Membership: 11; *Member Profile:* Provincial/territorial pharmacy licensing body; *Committees:* Executive; Advisory
Chief Officer(s):
Carole Bouchard, Executive Director

National Association of Physical Activity & Health (NAPAH)
info@napah.ca
www.napah.ca
Overview: A medium-sized national organization
Mission: Committed to empowering Canadians in acheiving optimum wellness through physical activity & healthy lifestyles; To networking & affiliating with a diversity of groups, organizations & volunteers who are strong advocates for public policies that support long-term physical activity programs as prevention to combat increasing rates of obesity, cancer, diabetes & cardiovascular disease

National Association of Women & the Law (NAWL) / Association nationale de la femme et du droit (ANFD)
PO Box 46008, 2339 Ogilvie Rd., Gloucester ON K1J 9M7
Tel: 613-241-7570
www.nawl.ca
Overview: A medium-sized national charitable organization founded in 1974
Mission: To promote the equality rights of women through legal education, research & law reform advocacy; to improve the legal status of women in Canada through law reform; to dismantle barriers to all women's equality
Member of: National Action Committee on the Status of Women; Women's Future Fund
Finances: *Annual Operating Budget:* $250,000-$500,000; *Funding Sources:* Women's Program; Status of Women Canada; donations; projects
Staff Member(s): 3; 100 volunteer(s)
Membership: 1,000; *Fees:* $10 student; $50 new graduates; $100 professional; *Member Profile:* Supports goals of the association
Activities: Education; research & advocacy; membership support; *Library:* by appointment
Chief Officer(s):
Julie Shugarman, Executive Director
Awards:
• Alison Dewar Scholarship in Women's Equality, Labour & Human Rights Law

National Automobile, Aerospace, Transportation & General Workers Union of Canada See UNIFOR

National Automotive Trades Association of Canada
#1, 8980 Fraserwood Ct., Burnaby BC V5J 5H7
Tel: 604-432-7987; Fax: 604-432-1756
www.natacanada.ca
Overview: A small national organization
Mission: To act as the unified voice for the Canadian Automotive Trades industry
Chief Officer(s):
Rene Young, Executive Vice-President
Rob Lang, President

National Ballet of Canada
Walter Carsen Centre, 470 Queens Quay West, Toronto ON M5V 3K4
Tel: 416-345-9686; Fax: 416-345-8323
info@national.ballet.ca
national.ballet.ca
www.facebook.com/nationalballet
twitter.com/nationalballet
www.youtube.com/user/nationalballetcanada
Overview: A medium-sized national organization
Chief Officer(s):
Karen Kain, Artistic Director
Barry Hughson, Executive Director
David Briskin, Music Director/Principal Conductor

National Brotherhood of Foresters & Industrial Workers (CLC) Voir Fraternité nationale des forestiers et travailleurs d'usine (CTC)

National Building Envelope Council (NBEC) / Conseil National de l'Enveloppe du Bâtiment (CNEB)
c/o 5041 Regent St., Burnaby BC V5C 4H4
Tel: 604-473-9587
nbec@cebq.org
www.nbec.net
Overview: A small national organization
Mission: To pursue excellence in the design, construction & performance of the building envelope
Chief Officer(s):
Dominique Derome, President Elect
Meetings/Conferences:
• Canadian Conference on Building Science and Technology 2018, 2018
Scope: National
Description: Provides a forum for the presentation, discussion and sharing of practical building science research, knowledge and field experience

National Business Travel Association (Canada) See Global Business Travel Association (Canada)

National Campus & Community Radio Association (NCRA) / Association nationale des radio étudiantes et communautaires (ANREC)
#608, 180 Metcalfe St., Ottawa ON K2P 1P5
Tel: 613-321-1440
Toll-Free: 866-859-8086
www.ncra.ca
www.facebook.com/groups/2295724894
twitter.com/NCRACanada
Overview: A medium-sized national organization founded in 1986
Mission: To encourage development of community & student radio in Canada by providing core services to community-oriented radios & representing them to government, industry, agencies & the public; To promote community radio in Canada
Affiliation(s): World Association of Community Radio Broadcasters (AMARC); Canadian Radio-Television & Telecommunications Commission (CRTC); Canadian Society of Independent Radio Producers
Finances: Annual Operating Budget: $250,000-$500,000; Funding Sources: Membership fees; Grants; Fundraising
Staff Member(s): 3; 20 volunteer(s)
Membership: 98; Fees: $100-$2,000; Member Profile: Community &/or student-oriented broadcasting enterprise; Committees: Conference; Equity; External Policy; Finance & Fundraising; Hiring; Human Resources; Indigenous; Policy & Governance; Technical Advisory
Activities: Supporting campus & community radio; Lobbying; Providing training & education; Awareness Events: Dig Your Roots; Internships: Yes; Speaker Service: Yes
Chief Officer(s):
Barry Rooke, Executive Director
barry@ncra.ca
Luke Smith, Coordinator, Membership
luke@ncra.ca
Meetings/Conferences:
• National Campus & Community Radio Association 2018 Conference, June, 2018, Fredericton, NB
Scope: National
Publications:
• NCRA [National Campus & Community Radio Association] Newsletter
Type: Newsletter; Frequency: Monthly

National Cancer Institute of Canada See Canadian Cancer Society Research Institute

National Capital FreeNet (NCF) / Libertel de la Capitale Nationale
Richmond Square, #206, 1305 Richmond Rd., Ottawa ON K2B 7Y4
Tel: 613-721-1773
ncf@ncf.ca
www.ncf.ca
Overview: A medium-sized local organization founded in 1992
Member of: Telecommunities Canada
Finances: Funding Sources: Member donations
500 volunteer(s)
Membership: 7,500; Fees: Free; Committees: Complaints; Finance; Francophone
Activities: Free, computer-based information sharing network; links the people & organization of the National Capital region; provides useful information & enablesan open exchange of ideas with the world; prepares people for full participation in a rapidly changing communications environment

National Capital Music Academy See Ottawa Youth Orchestra Academy

National CGIT Association - BC Provincial Board See Provincial CGIT Board of BC

National CGIT Association - Manitoba & Northwestern Ontario See Manitoba & Northwestern Ontario CGIT Association

National CGIT Association - Maritime Regional Committee See Maritime Regional CGIT Committee

National CGIT Association - Ontario See Ontario CGIT Association

National CGIT Association - Saskatchewan Committee See Saskatchewan CGIT Committee

National Chinchilla Breeders of Canada (NCBC)
9575 Winston Churchill Blvd., Brampton ON L6X 0A4
Tel: 905-451-8736; Fax: 905-457-5326
ncbc@idirect.com
Overview: A small national organization founded in 1946
Affiliation(s): Agriculture Canada; Canadian National Livestock Records
Membership: Fees: $30 resident; $12.50 non-resident
Chief Officer(s):
Marie Riedstra, Secretary-Manager

The National Citizens Coalition / Coalition nationale des citoyens inc.
#501, 27 Queen St. East, Toronto ON M5C 2M6
Tel: 416-869-3838; Fax: 416-869-1891
ncc@nationalcitizens.ca
www.nationalcitizens.ca
www.facebook.com/nationalcitizens
twitter.com/NatCitizens
Overview: A small national organization founded in 1967
Mission: To promote free markets, individual freedom & responsibility under limited government & a strong defence
Finances: Annual Operating Budget: $1.5 Million-$3 Million
Staff Member(s): 5
Membership: 40,000
Activities: Engaging in political advocacy; Speaker Service: Yes
Chief Officer(s):
Colin T. Brown, Chair
Peter Coleman, President & CEO
pcoleman@ncc-on.org

National Colorectal Cancer Campaign See Colon Cancer Canada

National Committee of Schools of Social Work; Canadian Association of Schools of Social Work (CASSW) See Canadian Association for Social Work Education

National Congress of Italian-Canadians (NCIC) / Congrès national des italo-canadiens
#202, 340 Falstaff Ave., Toronto ON M6L 3E8
Tel: 416-531-9964
info@canadese.org
www.facebook.com/pg/ncictoronto
Also Known As: NCIC Toronto District
Overview: A medium-sized international organization founded in 1974
Mission: To promote Italian language & culture among Italian-Canadians
Member of: Canadian Ethnocultural Council
Membership: Over 50,000
Activities: Speaker Service: Yes; Library: by appointment Not open to public
   National Capital Region
   PO Box 8144, Stn. Terminal, Ottawa ON K1G 3H6
   ottawancic@gmail.com
   www.cnicottawa.ca
   twitter.com/OttawaNCIC
   Chief Officer(s):
   Trina Costantini-Powell, President
   Congrès national des Italo-Canadiens du Québec (CNIC)
   #302, 8370, boul Lacordaire, Saint-Léonard QC H1R 3Y6
   Tél: 514-279-6357; Téléc: 514-955-8527
   info@italcongresso.qc.ca
   www.italcongresso.qc.ca
   Chief Officer(s):
   Pino Asaro, Président
   Josie Verrillo, Directrice générale

National Contingency Fund See Canadian Investor Protection Fund

National Convenience Stores Distributors Association See Association nationale des distributeurs aux petites surfaces alimentaires

National Council of Barbadian Associations in Canada (NCBAC) / Conseil national des associations barbadiennes au Canada
#300, 211 Consumers Rd., Toronto ON M2J 4G8
www.ncbac.ca
Overview: A small national organization founded in 1984
Mission: To incorporate Barbadians into Canadian society
Member of: Canadian Ethnocultural Council
Chief Officer(s):
Malcolm Flatts, President
presidentncbacmflatts@hotmail.com

National Council of Canadian Filipino Associations / Conseil national des associations canadiennes des Philippines
180 Larkin Dr., Ottawa ON K2J 1H9
Tel: 613-815-6314
Overview: A small national organization

National Council of Canadian Muslims (NCCM)
PO Box 13219, Ottawa ON K2K 1X4
Tel: 613-254-9704; Fax: 613-254-9810
Toll-Free: 866-524-0004
info@nccm.ca
www.nccm.ca
www.facebook.com/NCCMuslims
twitter.com/NCCM
www.youtube.com/NCCMtv
Previous Name: Council on American-Islamic Relations Canada
Overview: A large international organization founded in 2000
Mission: To promote the civic engagement of Canadian Muslims, the protection of their human rights & the education of non-Muslims so they may hold an accurate understanding of Islam
Activities: Seminars & workshops; Publication of guides, handbooks & media resource kits
Chief Officer(s):
Ihsaan Gardee, Executive Director, 613-853-4111

National Council of Jamaicans & Supportive Organizations in Canada
4065, rue Jean Talon ouest, Montréal QC H4P 1W6
Tel: 514-737-8299; Fax: 514-737-4861
Overview: A small national organization founded in 1987
Activities: Speaker Service: Yes

National Council of Jewish Women of Canada (NCJWC)
#118, 1588 Main St., Winnipeg MB R2V 1Y3
Tel: 416-633-5100; *Fax:* 416-633-1956
Toll-Free: 866-625-9274
www.ncjwc.org
Overview: A medium-sized national charitable organization founded in 1897
Mission: To further human welfare in the Jewish & general communities; To help fulfill unmet needs & to serve the individual & the community
Affiliation(s): International Council of Jewish Women; UNESCO Sub commission on the Status of Women; Coalition of Jewish Women against Domestic Violence & the Coalition for Agunot Rights
Finances: *Funding Sources:* Donations
Membership: *Fees:* $36

Edmonton Section
#200, 10235 - 124 St., Edmonton AB T5N 1P9
Tel: 780-454-1194; *Fax:* 780-482-4784
ncjwc.edmonton@gmail.com
www.jfse.org
Chief Officer(s):
Larry Derkach, Executive Director
tikunolam@jfse.org

Toronto Section
4700 Bathurst St., Toronto ON M2R 1W8
Tel: 416-633-5100; *Fax:* 416-633-1956
info@ncjwc-ts.org
www.ncjwc-ts.org
Chief Officer(s):
Ena Cord, Co-President
Dahlia Rusinek, Co-President

Vancouver Section
#302, 950 - West 41st Ave., Vancouver BC V5Z 2N7
Tel: 604-339-5180; *Fax:* 604-339-5158
info@ncjwvancouver.org
www.ncjwvancouver.org
www.facebook.com/NCJWvancouver

Winnipeg Section
1588 Main St., Winnipeg MB R2V 1Y3
Tel: 204-339-7291; *Fax:* 204-334-3779
ncjwws@mts.net

National Council of Trinidad & Tobago Organizations in Canada (NCTTOC)
66 Oakmeadow Blvd., Toronto ON M1E 4G5
Tel: 416-283-9672; *Fax:* 416-283-9672
Overview: A small national organization founded in 1983
Mission: To provide a national focus for representing the concerns of Trinidad & Tobago Nationals; to advocate on behalf of Trinidad & Tobago Nationals & their families in Canada; to develop & maintain a system of communication, information sharing & networking among Trinidad & Tobago organizations; to provide information, referrals, advocacy & support to new arrivals from Trinidad & Tobago
Member of: Canadian Ethnocultural Council
Affiliation(s): National Visible Minority Council on Labour Force Development
Finances: *Funding Sources:* Government projects; contributions
Membership: *Member Profile:* Trinidad & Tobago provincial organizations
Activities: *Speaker Service:* Yes
Chief Officer(s):
Emmanuel Dick, Contact

National Council of Veteran Associations (NCVA) / Conseil national des associations d'anciens combattants au Canada (CNAAC)
2827 Riverside Dr., Ottawa ON K1V 0C4
Tel: 613-731-3821; *Fax:* 613-731-3234
Toll-Free: 800-465-2677
ncva@waramps.ca
www.ncva-cnaac.ca
twitter.com/NCVACanada
Overview: A medium-sized national organization
Mission: To provide a voice on issues which are of significant interest to the Veterans' community
Membership: 55
Chief Officer(s):
Brian N. Forbes, Chair

The National Council of Women of Canada (NCWC) / Le Conseil national des femmes du Canada
PO Box 67099, Ottawa ON K2A 4E4
Tel: 902-422-8485
ncwc@magma.ca
www.ncwcanada.ca
www.facebook.com/thencwc
Overview: A large national organization founded in 1893
Mission: To empower all women to work together towards improving the quality of life for women, families & society through a forum of member organizations & individuals
Member of: International Council of Women
Finances: *Annual Operating Budget:* $100,000-$250,000
Staff Member(s): 3; 100 volunteer(s)
Membership: 20 local + 5 provincial councils; *Committees:* Citizenship & Immigration; Culture & Heritage; Environment; Global Affairs; Health; Social & Seniors Issues; Economics & Employments; Status of Women; Youth
Chief Officer(s):
Karen Monnon Dempsey, President

National Council on Canada-Arab Relations (NCCAR) / Conseil National des Relations Canado-Arabes
116, promenade du Portage, Gatineau QC J8X 2K1
Tel: 613-238-3795; *Fax:* 613-235-9185
nccar@nccar.ca
www.nccar.ca
www.facebook.com/Connecting.Canadians.Arabs
Overview: A small national organization
Mission: The National Council on Canada-Arab Relations (NCCAR) is a charitable organization whose mission is to build ties between Canadians and people of the Arab World in order to develop stronger relations and cooperation between them, as well as raise an appreciation of their common values.
Membership: *Fees:* $35 youth; $100 regular; $500 sustaining; $1000 corporate
Chief Officer(s):
Bahija Reghai, President

National Council on Ethics in Human Research / Conseil national d'éthique en recherche chez l'humain
#208, 240 Catherine St., Ottawa ON K2P 2G8
Tel: 613-233-5445; *Fax:* 613-233-0658
www.ncehr-cnerh.org
Overview: A small national organization
Mission: To advance the protection & promotion of the well-being of human participants in research; to foster high ethical standards for the conduct of research involving humans
Staff Member(s): 4
Chief Officer(s):
Richard Carpentier, Executive Director

National Crowdfunding Association of Canada (NCFA)
#1801, 1 Yonge St., Toronto ON M5E 1W7
Tel: 416-618-0254
info@ncfacanada.org
www.ncfacanada.org
www.linkedin.com/company/national-crowdfunding-association-of-canada
www.facebook.com/NCFACanada.org
twitter.com/NCFACanada
Overview: A medium-sized national organization
Mission: To work with industry groups, government, academia, & other businesses to create a vibrant crowdfunding industry and voice across Canada
Member of: World Crowdfund Federation
Membership: *Fees:* Donation
Activities: Researching & consulting to find solutions to issues affecting the crowdfunding industry; Educating businesses, entrepreneurs, the public, & the media on crowdfunding trends & best practices; Assisting both members & the public in ways to identify & report fraud in the crowdfunding industry
Chief Officer(s):
Craig Asano, Executive Director
casano@ncfacanada.org
Publications:
• Canadian Crowdfunding Directory
Type: Directory

National Darts Federation of Canada (NDFC) / Fédération nationale de dards du Canada
Tel: 902-401-9650
secretary@ndfc.ca
www.ndfc.ca
Overview: A medium-sized national organization founded in 1977
Mission: To promote & organize darts events & promote the betterment of the game
Affiliation(s): World Darts Federation
Finances: *Annual Operating Budget:* $50,000-$100,000
Staff Member(s): 7
Membership: 5,000-14,999
Activities: Provincial/national championships; international events
Chief Officer(s):
Bill Hatter, President
president@ndfc.ca

National Dental Assisting Examining Board (NDAEB) / Bureau national d'examen d'assistance dentaire (BNEAD)
#205, 2255 St. Laurent Blvd., Ottawa ON K1G 4K3
Tel: 613-526-3424; *Fax:* 613-526-5560
office@ndaeb.ca
www.ndaeb.ca
Overview: A medium-sized national organization founded in 1997
Mission: To ensure that individuals entering the practice of dental assisting have met a national baseline standard in the knowledge, skills & attitudes necessary to practice as a dental assistant
Chief Officer(s):
Leslie Riva, President

National Dental Examining Board of Canada / Le bureau national d'examen dentaire du Canada
80 Elgin St., 2nd Fl., Ottawa ON K1P 6R2
Tel: 613-236-5912; *Fax:* 613-236-8386
info@ndeb-bned.ca
www.ndeb-bned.ca
Overview: A small national organization
Mission: To establish qualifying conditions for a national standard of dental competence for general practitioners; To establish & maintain an examination facility to test for this national standard of dental competence; To issue certificates to dentists who successfully meet this national standard
Chief Officer(s):
Jack D. Gerrow, DDS, MS, MEd, C, Executive Director & Registrar

National Dental Hygiene Certification Board
#322, 1929 Russell Rd., Ottawa ON K1G 4G3
Tel: 613-260-8156; *Fax:* 613-260-8511
exam@ndhcb.ca
www.ndhcb.ca
Overview: A small national licensing organization founded in 1994
Mission: To issue the National Dental Hygiene Certification Examination (NDHCE)
Chief Officer(s):
Doris Lavoie, Executive Director
dlavoie@ndhcb.ca

National Eating Disorder Information Centre (NEDIC)
200 Elizabeth St., #ES7-421, Toronto ON M5G 2C4
Tel: 416-340-4156; *Fax:* 416-340-4736
Toll-Free: 866-633-4220
nedic@uhn.ca
www.nedic.ca
www.facebook.com/thenedic
Overview: A small national charitable organization founded in 1985
Mission: To provide information & resources on eating disorders, food & weight preoccupation; To raise public awareness about eating disorders & related issues
Member of: Toronto General Hospital
Finances: *Annual Operating Budget:* $100,000-$250,000; *Funding Sources:* Community Mental Health Branch, Ontario Ministry of Health; donations; sales of materials
Staff Member(s): 3; 7 volunteer(s)
Membership: 1-99; *Committees:* Advisory
Activities: Lectures & workshops for schools, community groups & individuals; support groups; information & consultation for public health professionals & interested individuals to enable them to start support groups; national referral to treatment; *Awareness Events:* Eating Disorder Awareness Week, 1st full week in Feb.; International No Diet Day, May 6; *Speaker Service:* Yes; *Library*
Chief Officer(s):
Elizabeth Pottinger, Officer, Development
elizabeth.pottinger@uhn.ca
Suzanne Phillips, Manager, Program
suzanne.phillips@uhn.ca

Marbella Carlos, Coordinator, Education & Outreach
marbella.carlos@uhn.ca

National Educational Association of Disabled Students (NEADS) / Association nationale des étudiant(e)s handicapé(e)s au niveau postsecondaire
Carleton University, Unicentre, #514, 1125 Colonel By Dr.,
Ottawa ON K1S 5B6
Tel: 613-380-8065; *Fax:* 613-369-4391
Toll-Free: 877-670-1256
info@neads.ca
www.neads.ca
www.facebook.com/myNEADS
Overview: A small national organization founded in 1986
Mission: To encourage the self-empowerment of post-secondary students with disabilities; To advocate for increased accessibility at all levels so that disabled students may gain equal access to a college or university education; To provide an information resource base on services for disabled students nationwide according to a file of material from post-secondary institutions
Affiliation(s): Association québécoise des étudiant(e)s handicapé(e)s au post-secondaire; Council of Canadians with Disabilites
Membership: 400; *Fees:* $10 regular & associate; $20 institutional; *Member Profile:* Disabled persons; regular - student; associate - professional; institutional - business
Activities: *Library:* Open to public by appointment
Chief Officer(s):
Frank Smith, National Coordinator, 613-380-8065 Ext. 201
frank.smith@neads.ca

National Electricity Roundtable (NER) / La Table ronde nationale de l'électricité (TRNE)
c/o Bryan Simonson, 148 Park Estates Pl. SE, Calgary AB T2J 3W5
Tel: 403-619-8967
nationaler@shaw.ca
www.nationalelectricityroundtable.com
Overview: A medium-sized national organization founded in 1994
Mission: To act as a forum for companies operating in the Canadian electric power industry; To work with government to develop a sustainable industry
Membership: 24 companies; 5 federal departments
Chief Officer(s):
Pierre Marquis, Chair, 450-449-3999
pmarquis@hmiconstruction.ca
Bryan Simonson, President

National Elevator & Escalator Association (NEEA)
#708, 6299 Airport Rd., Mississauga ON L4V 1N3
Tel: 905-678-9940
Overview: A medium-sized national organization founded in 1977
Chief Officer(s):
Andrew Reistetter, Executive Director

National Emergency Nurses Association (NENA) / Association des infirmières et infirmiers d'urgence
144 - 8485 Young Rd., Chilliwack BC V2P 7Y7
www.nena.ca
www.facebook.com/NationalEmergencyNursesAssociation
Overview: A medium-sized national organization
Mission: To represent the Canadian emergency nursing profession
Affiliation(s): Canadian Nurses Association
Membership: 800; *Fees:* $20; *Committees:* Nominations/Awards; Certification; Nursing Practice; Professional Practice Documents
Chief Officer(s):
Sherry Uribe, President
Meetings/Conferences:
• National Emergency Nurses Association 2018 Conference, April, 2018, Kelowna, BC
Scope: National

National Farmers Foundation
2717 Wentz Ave., Saskatoon SK S7K 4B6
Tel: 306-652-9465; *Fax:* 306-664-6226
nfu@nfu.ca
www.nfu.ca/about/national-farmers-foundation
twitter.com/NFUcanada
Overview: A large national charitable organization founded in 1987

Mission: To stimulate rural/urban cooperation; To fund education & research that will further the progressive farm movement in Canada
Affiliation(s): National Farmers Union
Finances: *Funding Sources:* Fundraising; donations
Chief Officer(s):
Patty Englund, General Manager
Joan Lange, Director, Finance & Administration
Cathy Holtslander, Director, Research & Policy

National Farmers Union (NFU) / Syndicat national des cultivateurs
2717 Wentz Ave., Saskatoon SK S7K 4B6
Tel: 306-652-9465; *Fax:* 306-664-6226
nfu@nfu.ca
www.nfu.ca
www.facebook.com/nfuCanada
twitter.com/NFUcanada
Overview: A large national organization founded in 1969
Mission: To improve economic & social well-being of rural people & rural communities
Member of: Rural Dignity of Canada
Affiliation(s): Action Canada Network
Finances: *Annual Operating Budget:* $500,000-$1.5 Million; *Funding Sources:* Membership dues; fundraising; donations
Staff Member(s): 7; 300 volunteer(s)
Membership: *Fees:* $195 family; $98 youth; $65 associate; *Committees:* Women's Advisory; Youth Advisory; International Program
Activities: *Speaker Service:* Yes; *Library*
Chief Officer(s):
Patty Englund, General Manager
Joan Lange, Director, Finance & Administration
Cathy Holtslander, Director, Research & Policy
Awards:
• The Paul Beingessner Award for Excellence in Writing
; *Amount:* $500
Publications:
• Union Farmer Monthly [a publication of the National Farmers Union]
Type: Newsletter; *Frequency:* Monthly
• Union Farmer Quarterly [a publication of the National Farmers Union]
Type: Magazine; *Frequency:* Quarterly
New Brunswick Office
Tel: 506-260-0087
nfu.nb.office@gmail.com
www.nfunb.org
Maritimes - NFU Financial Services
120 Bishop Dr., Summerside PE C1N 5Z8
Tel: 902-436-1872
Chief Officer(s):
Gayle Read, Contact
Maritimes - Taxation Office
559 Rte. 390, Rowena NB E7H 4N2
Tel: 506-273-4328; *Fax:* 506-273-4328
Chief Officer(s):
Judy Barr, Contact
Ontario Office
5420 Hwy. 6 North, RR#5, Guelph ON N1H 6J2
Tel: 705-738-3993
Toll-Free: 888-832-9638
office@nfuontario.ca
www.nfuontario.ca
Chief Officer(s):
Emery Huszka, President
president@nfuontario.ca
Sarah Bakker, General Manager
office@nfuontario.ca

National Federation for the Sports of Triathlon, Duathlon & Aquathlon in Canada *See* Triathlon Canada

National Federation of Communication Workers (CNTU) *Voir* Fédération nationale des communications (CSN)

National Federation of Nurses' Unions *See* Canadian Federation of Nurses Unions

National Federation of Québec Teachers *Voir* Fédération nationale des enseignants et des enseignantes du Québec

National Federation of the Blind: Advocates for Equality *See* Alliance for Equality of Blind Canadians

National Firearms Association *See* Canada's National Firearms Association

National Floor Covering Association (NFCA) / Association nationale des revêtements de sol
987 Clarkson Rd. South, Mississauga ON L5J 2V8
Tel: 905-822-2280; *Fax:* 905-822-2494
www.nfcaonline.ca
Overview: A small national organization founded in 1987
Mission: To unite the Canadian regional & provincial associations in a spirit of cooperation; to improve & enhance the floorcovering industry; to share information & ideas; to undertake & support programs which will improve communications at all levels of the industry
Finances: *Annual Operating Budget:* $50,000-$100,000; *Funding Sources:* Membership fees
Staff Member(s): 1; 10 volunteer(s)
Membership: 4 provincial/regional floor covering associations

National Golf Course Owners Association Canada (NGCOA) / L'Association nationale des propriétaires de terrains de golf du Canada (ANPTG)
#810, 515 Legget Dr., Ottawa ON K2K 3G4
Tel: 613-226-3616; *Fax:* 613-226-4148
Toll-Free: 866-626-4262
ngcoa@ngcoa.ca
www.ngcoa.ca
www.facebook.com/nationalgolfcourseownersassociationcanada
twitter.com/ngcoacanada
Overview: A large national organization founded in 1993
Mission: To provide business support to Canadian golf course operators & related stakeholders, networking opportunities, purchasing programs, & education
Staff Member(s): 20
Membership: *Fees:* Schedule available; *Member Profile:* Golf course owner/operators
Activities: Golfmax Purchasing Program; GOLFEXPOs; Take A Kid To The Course; Golf Business Canada magazine; *Awareness Events:* Take a Kid to the Course Week, July; GolfBusiness Canada Conference & Trade Show; NGCOA Canada Golf Invitationals
Chief Officer(s):
Jeff Calderwood, Chief Executive Officer, 613-226-3616 Ext. 20
jcalderwood@ngcoa.ca
Nathalie Lavallée, Chief Operating Officer, 613-226-3616 Ext. 15
nlavallee@ngcoa.ca
Meetings/Conferences:
• 2018 Golf Business Canada Conference & Trade Show, 2018
Scope: National
Publications:
• Golf Business Canada
Type: Magazine
Alberta Chapter
AB
Tel: 403-335-2834
Chief Officer(s):
Brent Hutcheon, Regional Director
bhutcheon@ngcoa.ca
Atlantic Chapter
NB
Toll-Free: 866-626-4262
Chief Officer(s):
Jim Thompson, Interim Regional Director
jthompson@ngcoa.ca
British Columbia Chapter
BC
Tel: 778-808-6711
Toll-Free: 866-262-4262
Chief Officer(s):
Erica Beck, Regional Director
ebeck@ngcoa.ca
Central Ontario Chapter
ON
Tel: 705-812-1254
Toll-Free: 866-626-4262
Chief Officer(s):
Mike Bell, Regional Director
mbell@ngcoa.ca
Eastern Ontario / Outaouais Chapter
ON
Tel: 613-528-1994
Toll-Free: 866-626-4262
Chief Officer(s):
Carol Ann Campbell, Regional Director
cacampbell@ngcoa.ca
Prairie Chapter
MB

Tel: 204-282-6422
Toll-Free: 866-626-4262
Chief Officer(s):
Kevin O'Donovan, Regional Director
kodonovan@ngcoa.ca
Québec Chapter
QC
Toll-Free: 866-626-4262
Chief Officer(s):
Mark Fraser, Regional Director
mfraser@ngcoa.ca
Southwestern Ontario Chapter
ON
Tel: 519-637-3361
Chief Officer(s):
Shawn Hunter, Regional Director
shunter@ngcoa.ca

National Health Union (NHU) / Syndicat national de la santé (SNS)
#1202, 233 Gilmour St., Ottawa ON K2P 0P2
Tel: 613-237-2732; Fax: 613-237-6954
Toll-Free: 888-545-6305
www.nhu-sns.ca
Overview: A medium-sized national organization overseen by Public Service Alliance of Canada
Mission: To protect members by ensuring safe working conditions & fair wage rights & benefits
Membership: 5,000 + 24 Locals; *Member Profile:* Employees at Health Canada & Public Health Agency of Canada; *Committees:* Finance; Health & Safety; Honours & Awards; Organization & Structure
Chief Officer(s):
Tony Tilley, President

National Hockey League Alumni Association (NHLA)
400 Kipling Ave., Toronto ON M8V 3L1
Tel: 416-798-2586; Fax: 416-798-2582
info@nhlalumni.net
nhlalumni.net
la.linkedin.com/groups?gid=1039337
www.facebook.com/nhlalumni
twitter.com/NHLAlumni
Also Known As: NHL Alumni Association
Overview: A medium-sized national charitable organization founded in 1999
Mission: Provides programs and assistance for all retired NHL players, including career transition with the BreakAway Program.
Affiliation(s): National Hockey League (NHL); National Hockey League Players' Association
Staff Member(s): 7
Membership: 28 chapters + 2,500 members
Activities: *Speaker Service:* Yes; *Rents Mailing List:* Yes
Chief Officer(s):
Mark Napier, Executive Director
mark@nhlalumni.net
Mike Pelyk, Chair
Awards:
• NHL Alumni 'Man of the Year'
• Keith McCreary '7th Man Award'
• Ace Bailey 'Award of Courage'
• Scholarships for Members
Contact: Wendy McCreary, wendymccreary@nhlalumni.net
• Scholarships for Members Descendants
Contact: Wendy McCreary, wendymccreary@nhlalumni.net

National Hockey League Players' Association (NHLPA)
#1700, 20 Bay St., Toronto ON M5J 2N8
www.nhlpa.com
www.facebook.com/nhlpa
twitter.com/nhlpa
www.youtube.com/user/NHLPA
Overview: A medium-sized national organization founded in 1967
Mission: The union for professional hockey players in the National Hockey League (NHL).
Affiliation(s): National Hockey League (NHL); National Hockey League Players' Association
Membership: *Committees:* Competition
Chief Officer(s):
Don Fehr, Executive Director

National Indian Brotherhood *See* Assembly of First Nations

National Information Program on Antibiotics (NIPA)
#700, 160 Bloor St. East, Toronto ON M4W 3P7
www.antibiotics-info.org
Overview: A small national organization
Mission: NIPA's objectives are to help Canadians understand the difference between viral and bacterial infections, and the importance of using antibiotics only for the treatment of bacterial infections. NIPA wants to raise awareness and understanding of the issue of antibiotic resistance and motivate behavioural changes in the prescribing and use of antibiotics.
Activities: Provides information for consumers & healthcare professionals on the issue of antibiotic resistance in Canada; *Awareness Events:* National Antibiotics Awareness Week, Feb.

National Initiative for the Care of the Elderly (NICE) / Initiative nationale pour le soin des personnes âgées
#234, 246 Bloor St. West, Toronto ON M5S 1V4
Tel: 416-978-7037
nicenetadmin@utoronto.ca
www.nicenet.ca
www.facebook.com/NICEIderly
twitter.com/NICEIderly
Overview: A small national organization
Mission: To represent researchers, practitioners, students, & seniors involved in or dedicated to caring for the elderly; To improve the care of elderly individuals in Canada & the world
Member of: Network of Centres of Excellence
Chief Officer(s):
Lynn McDonald, Scientific Director
Raza M. Mirza, Network Manager
raza.mirza@nicenet.ca
Meetings/Conferences:
• 13th Annual National Initiative for the Care of the Elderly Knowledge Exchange 2018, 2018
Scope: National

National Institute for Cannabis Health & Education (NICHE)
#170, 422 Richards St., Vancouver BC V6B 2Z4
Tel: 604-805-3272
info@nichecanada.com
www.nichecanada.com
www.linkedin.com/company/18016221
www.facebook.com/Canada.NICHE
twitter.com/nichecanada
www.instagram.com/niche_canada
Overview: A large national organization
Mission: To provide a forum for public dialogue about cannabis across Canada; To strengthen knowledge about cannabis in the areas of public health & safety, education, legislation & regulatory reforms, research, & industry standards & accreditation; To protect public health & safety after the legalization of cannabis in Canada
Activities: Providing resources, information, & education; Promoting & organizing events
Chief Officer(s):
Barinder Rasode, CEO

National Institute of Broadcasting
1498 Yonge St., Toronto ON M4T 1Z6
Tel: 416-922-2556; Fax: 416-922-5470
Overview: A small national organization founded in 1962

National Institute of Disability Management & Research (NIDMAR) / Institut national de recherche et de gestion de l'incapacité au travail
c/o Pacific Coast University for Workplace Health Sciences, 4755 Cherry Creek Rd., Port Alberni BC V9Y 0A7
Tel: 778-421-0821; Fax: 778-421-0823
nidmar@nidmar.ca
www.nidmar.ca
Overview: A medium-sized national charitable organization
Mission: Committed to reducing the human, social, & economic cost of disability to workers, employers, & society by providing education, research, policy development, & implementation resources to promote workplace-based integration programs
Finances: *Funding Sources:* Disabled Workers Foundation of Canada; Endowment fund
Staff Member(s): 8
Activities: Training; Education; Research; Disability management resources; Collection of databases
Chief Officer(s):
Wolfgang Zimmermann, Executive Director
wolfgang@nidmar.ca
Meetings/Conferences:
• International Forum on Disability Management, October, 2018, Vancouver, BC
Scope: International

National Inuit Youth Council (NIYC)
#1101, 75 Albert St., Ottawa ON K1P 5E7
Tel: 613-238-8181; Fax: 613-234-4482
Toll-Free: 866-262-8181
www.niyc.ca
www.facebook.com/332933250073292
twitter.com/inuityouth
Overview: A small national organization founded in 1994
Mission: To provide information on political & environmental issues, Inuit rights & opportunities, legal assistance; to improve communications & assist Inuit youth achieve full participation in Canadian society; to fulfill wishes & needs of all Inuit Canadians
Affiliation(s): Inuit Tapiriit Kanatami
Finances: *Annual Operating Budget:* $50,000-$100,000
Staff Member(s): 2; 13 volunteer(s)
Membership: 7; *Member Profile:* Inuit youth 13-30 years; *Committees:* Canadian Inuit HIV/AIDS Network; Inuit Action Plan; National Inuit Committee on Health; Urban Inuit Committee
Activities: Culture & Language; Education & Suicide; Urban Multi-Purpose Aboriginal Youth Centres
Chief Officer(s):
David Joanasie, Contact
Jesse Mike, Contact

National Investor Relations Institute Canada (NIRI Canada) *See* Canadian Investor Relations Institute

National Japanese Canadian Citizens Association *See* National Association of Japanese Canadians

National Judicial Institute (NJI) / Institut national de la magistrature (INM)
#400, 250 Albert St., Ottawa ON K1P 6M1
Tel: 613-237-1118; Fax: 613-237-6155
nji@nji-inm.ca
www.nji.ca
Overview: A small national charitable organization founded in 1988
Mission: Based in Ottawa, the National Judicial Institute (NJI) is an independent, not-for-profit institution committed to building better justice through leadership in the education of judges in Canada and internationally. Since its inception in 1988, the NJI has continued to develop and deliver stimulating programs and a variety of electronic resources that foster judicial excellence. Alone or in partnership with courts and other organizations, the NJI is involved in the delivery of the majority of education taken by judges in Canada.
Finances: *Annual Operating Budget:* Greater than $5 Million; *Funding Sources:* Federal & provincial governments
Staff Member(s): 50
Membership: 1-99
Activities: *Library:* Not open to public
Chief Officer(s):
C. Adèle Kent, Executive Director
Lynn O'Shaughnessy, Library/Information Technician, Operations

National Karate Association of Canada *See* Karate Canada

The National Liberal Federation *See* The Liberal Party of Canada

National Literacy & Health Program (NLHP)
c/o Canadian Public Health Association, #404, 1525 Carling Ave., Ottawa ON K1Z 8R9
Tel: 613-725-3769; Fax: 613-725-3769
www.cpha.ca/en/portals/h-l/h-l5.aspx
Overview: A small national organization
Mission: To promote awareness among health professionals of the links between literacy and health.
Member of: Canadian Public Health Association
Chief Officer(s):
Greg Penney, Director, National Programs, Canadian Public Health Association

National Magazine Awards Foundation (NMAF) / Fondation nationale des prix du magazine canadien
#3500, 2 Bloor St. East, Toronto ON M4W 1A8
Tel: 416-422-1358
staff@magazine-awards.com
www.magazine-awards.com
www.linkedin.com/groups/National-Magazine-Awards-Foundation-4002310?trk=myg_ugrp_ovr
www.facebook.com/190062084384867?
twitter.com/magawards
youtube.com/magazineawards
Also Known As: NMAs
Overview: A small national organization founded in 1977

Mission: To recognize & promote excellence in the content & creation of Canadian print & digital publications through an annual program of awards & national publicity efforts
Finances: *Annual Operating Budget:* $500,000-$1.5 Million; *Funding Sources:* Government, corporate, individual
Staff Member(s): 4; 250 volunteer(s)
Membership: *Committees:* Judging; fundraising
Activities: *Library:* Archive
Chief Officer(s):
Barbara Gould, Managing Director
Awards:
• National Magazine Awards
Awards are presented annually in 48 categories including new categories Blogs, Online Video & Tablet Magazine of the Year; all awards go to individual magazine writers, photographers, illustrators, or art directors; Magazine of the Year recognizes continual overall excellence *Deadline:* January; *Amount:* $500 to $1000 cash prizes

National Marine Manufacturers Association Canada (NMMA)
#8, 14 McEwan Dr., Bolton ON L7E 1H1
Tel: 905-951-0009; *Fax:* 905-951-0018
sanghel@nmma.org
www.cmma.ca
Also Known As: NMMA Canada
Previous Name: Canadian Marine Manufacturers Association
Overview: A medium-sized national organization
Mission: The CMMA is committed to being a leader; in promoting boating, advocacy with government and providing value added services to foster the financial success of the marine industry.
Membership: *Member Profile:* Marine industry
Chief Officer(s):
Sara Anghel, Executive Director
sanghel@nmma.org

National ME/FM Action Network / Réseau national d'action EM/FM encéphalomyélite myalgique/fibromyalgie
#512, 33 Banner Rd., Nepean ON K2H 8V7
Tel: 613-829-6667; *Fax:* 613-829-8518
mefminfo@mefmaction.com
www.mefmaction.net
www.facebook.com/MEFMActionNetwork
twitter.com/mefmaction
Also Known As: Myalgic Encephalomyelitis/Chronic Fatigue Syndrome & Fibromyalgia Action Network
Overview: A small provincial charitable organization founded in 1993
Mission: To offer support, advocacy, education & research into the many, varied, anomalies connected with Myalgic Encephalomyelitis/Chronic Fatigue Syndrome & Fibromyalgia (ME/FM)
Member of: National Voluntary Health Organization; Health Charities Council of Canada
Affiliation(s): Volunteer Ottawa; Volunteer Canada
Finances: *Annual Operating Budget:* Less than $50,000; *Funding Sources:* Membership; donations
Staff Member(s): 1; 27 volunteer(s)
Membership: 1,400; *Fees:* $30
Chief Officer(s):
Lydia E. Neilson, M.S.M., Founder & CEO

National Native Addictions Partnership Foundation (NNAPF) / Fondation autochtone nationale de partenariat pour la lutte contre les dépendances
PO Box 183, Muskoday SK S0J 3H0
Tel: 306-763-4714; *Fax:* 306-763-5993
Toll-Free: 866-763-4714
info@nnapf.org
www.nnapf.org
www.facebook.com/423836911040446
twitter.com/NNAPF
Overview: A small national organization founded in 1998
Mission: To advocate, develop, facilitate, & monitor strategies designed to continuously upgrade & enhance the quality of ideas, information, program methodologies, financial allociations & skills of service providers comprising the program
Chief Officer(s):
Austin Bear, President
Janice Nicotine, Vice-President

National Network for Mental Health (NNMH) / Réseau national pour la santé mentale
#604, 55 King St., St Catharines ON L2R 3H5
Tel: 905-682-2423; *Fax:* 905-682-7469
Toll-Free: 888-406-4663
info@nnmh.ca
www.nnmh.ca
www.facebook.com/pages/National-Network-for-Mental-Health/52563059509
twitter.com/NNMH_RNSM
Overview: A small national organization founded in 1992
Mission: To advocate, educate & provide expertise & resources for the increased health & well-being of the Canadian mental health consumer/survivor community
Staff Member(s): 4
Membership: *Fees:* $10 individual; $50 organization
Chief Officer(s):
Julie L. Flatt, Executive Director
Jean Beckett, President

National NewsMedia Council (NNC)
#200, 37 Front St. East, Toronto ON M5E 1B3
Tel: 416-340-1981
info@mediacouncil.ca
www.mediacouncil.ca
Merged from: B.C. Press Council; Ontario Press Council; Atlantic Press Council
Overview: A large national organization founded in 2015
Mission: To promote ethical practice in the news media industry; To serve as a forum for complains against its member news organizations; To represent the rights of the public in regards to free speech & freedom of the media
Staff Member(s): 3
Membership: 50; *Member Profile:* Representatives from the public & from news organizations that support the Council
Activities: Providing a forum for the public to voice complaints; Representing the public through hearings; Providing information & resources for news organizations & the general readership
Chief Officer(s):
John Fraser, President & Chief Executive Officer, 416-340-1981 Ext. 3
jfraser@mediacouncil.ca
Patricia Perkel, Executive Director, 416-340-1981 Ext. 2
pperkel@mediacouncil.ca
Brent Jolly, Director, Communications, 416-340-1981 Ext. 3
bjolly@mediacouncil.ca

National Optics Institute *See* Institut national d'optique

National Organization for the Reform of Marijuana Laws Canada
Tel: 613-546-6266
info@norml.ca
www.norml.ca
twitter.com/NORMLCanada
Also Known As: NORML Canada
Overview: A large international organization founded in 1978
Mission: To move public opinion sufficiently to legalize the responsible use of marijuana by adults, & to serve as an advocate for consumers
Chief Officer(s):
Craig Jones, Executive Director
 NORML Saskatchewan
 2923 Dewdney Ave., Regina SK S4T 0Y1

National Organization of Immigrant & Visible Minority Women of Canada (NOIVMWC) / Organisation nationale des femmes immigrantes et des femmes appartenant à une minorité visible du Canada (ONFIFAMVC)
#225, 219 Argyle St., Ottawa ON K2P 2H4
www.noivmwc.org
Overview: A medium-sized national organization founded in 1986
Mission: To ensure equality for immigrant & visible minority women within bilingual Canada by putting into place strategies that will combat sexism, racism, poverty, isolation & violence & by acting as an advocate on issues dealing with immigrant & visible minority women.
Finances: *Annual Operating Budget:* $500,000-$1.5 Million; *Funding Sources:* Federal & provincial government; membership dues; foundations
Membership: 500; *Fees:* Schedule available; *Committees:* Advocacy; Membership; Constitution & Policy; Newsletter; Personnel; Financial
Activities: *Library:* by appointment

National Ovarian Cancer Association *See* Ovarian Cancer Canada

National Pensioners & Senior Citizens Federation *See* National Pensioners Federation

National Pensioners Federation (NPF) / Fédération nationale des retraités
c/o Mary Forbes, Treasurer, 2186 Stanfield Rd, Mississauga ON L4Y 1R5
Tel: 519-359-3221
www.nationalpensionersfederation.ca
www.facebook.com/NPFederation
twitter.com/npfederation
www.youtube.com/user/npfederation
Previous Name: National Pensioners & Senior Citizens Federation
Overview: A large national organization founded in 1945
Mission: To act as an advisory body providing central contacts, facilities for research, surveys, uniform objectives & a national expansion of the pensioners movement; To stimulate public interest in the welfare of senior citizens by means of adequate pensions & social security that will provide comfortable housing & decent living; To protect the rights & interests of pensioners & prospective pensioners; To prevent discrimination & undue delay in granting pensions; To project a social friendly fellowship among the pensioners of Canada
Affiliation(s): International Senior Citizens Association
Finances: *Annual Operating Budget:* Less than $50,000; *Funding Sources:* Membership dues; donations
Membership: 1 million in 350 seniors groups; *Fees:* $25 individual; $35 family; $35-$350 groups
Activities: *Library:* Open to public by appointment
Chief Officer(s):
Herb John, President, 519-350-3221
herb.john@npfmail.com
Patrick Brady, Secretary, 604-856-2430
patbrady@uniserve.com
Mary Forbes, Treasurer, 905-306-1830
mary.forbes@npfmail.com

National People First *See* People First of Canada

National Press Club of Canada Foundation / Cercle national des joualistes du Canada
Sheraton Ottawa Hotel, 150 Albert St., 2nd Fl., Ottawa ON K1P 5G2
info@pressclubcanada.ca
pressclubcanada.ca
Overview: A small national organization founded in 1928
Mission: To provide a medium for the exchange of ideas; to foster friendly relationships among members of the news media & allied professions; to promote the prestige & standards of the news media & safeguard its freedoms; to improve the status & advance the profession of journalism
Finances: *Annual Operating Budget:* $500,000-$1.5 Million
Staff Member(s): 30; 14 volunteer(s)
Membership: 120 active + 50 associate + 12 affiliate; *Fees:* $199 + GST
Activities: Social events, newsmaker breakfasts, speaker luncheons, snooker tournaments, golf tournaments, business luncheons; *Speaker Service:* Yes; *Library:* McClung Library
Chief Officer(s):
James Baxter, President
Awards:
• Charles Lynch Award
• World Press Freedom Award

National Processing Human Resources Council *See* National Seafood Sector Council

National Quality Institute *See* Excellence Canada

National Reading Campaign, Inc.
#300, 2 Toronto St., Toronto ON M5C 2B6
Tel: 416-847-0309
Other Communication:
plus.google.com/116043634923630958858
info@nationalreadingcampaign.ca
www.nationalreadingcampaign.ca
www.facebook.com/NationalReadingCampaign
twitter.com/readingcampaign
www.youtube.com/user/NationalReadCampaign
Overview: A small national charitable organization founded in 2012
Mission: To help make Canada a nation of readers
Finances: *Funding Sources:* Donations & sponsorship
Staff Member(s): 3
Activities: National Reading Plan; Canlit for new Canadians; Aboriginal Policy Initiative

Canadian Associations / National Retriever Club of Canada

Chief Officer(s):
Sandy Crawley, Executive Director

National Retriever Club of Canada
c/o Mark Laberge, 1970 Paris St., Sudbury ON P3E 3C8
Tel: 613-797-4330
secretary@nrcc-canada.com
www.nrcc-canada.com
www.facebook.com/679064212138775
Overview: A small national organization
Chief Officer(s):
Jim Ling, President, 613-849-4801
jim_ling101@sympatico.ca
Mark Laberge, Treasurer, 705-523-0272
Mark.Laberge@mnp.ca

National Screen Institute - Canada (NSI)
#400, 141 Bannatyne Ave., Winnipeg MB R3B 0R3
Tel: 204-956-7800; *Fax:* 204-956-5811
Toll-Free: 800-952-9307
info@nsi-canada.ca
www.nsi-canada.ca
www.facebook.com/nsicanada
twitter.com/nsicanada
Previous Name: Canadian Screen Institute
Overview: A medium-sized national charitable organization founded in 1984
Mission: To supply innovative, focused, applied professional training to lead participants in successful careers as writers, directors & producers in Canada's film & television industry
Finances: *Annual Operating Budget:* $1.5 Million-$3 Million; *Funding Sources:* Telefilm Canada through Canadian Heritage; Manitoba Culture, Heritage & Tourism; *Patrons:* CTV; CBC TV
Staff Member(s): 10
Activities: Offers courses; *Awareness Events:* Annual Film Festival; *Speaker Service:* Yes
Chief Officer(s):
John Gill, Chief Executive Officer, 416-505-1036
john.gill@nsi-canada.ca

National Seafood Sector Council (NSSC) / Le conseil national du secteur des produits de la mer (CNSPM)
38B John St., Yarmouth NS B5A 3H2
Tel: 902-742-6167; *Fax:* 902-742-8391
info@nssc.ca
www.nationalseafood.ca
Previous Name: National Processing Human Resources Council
Overview: A small national organization founded in 1995
Mission: To work toward one common goal: a strong & prosperous seafood prcessing industry created by a well trained & productive workforce
Member of: Canadian Society of Association Executives; Sector Councils' Steering Committee
Affiliation(s): British Columbia Seafood Sector Council
Membership: 1-99; *Member Profile:* Managment & labour representatives on the Board; Seafood processing industry members
Activities: Works on behalf of of the entire seafood processing industry to provide up-to-date training courses & products; *Internships:* Yes
Chief Officer(s):
Carey Bonnell, Head

National Shevchenko Musical Ensemble Guild of Canada
626 Bathurst St., Toronto ON M5S 2R1
Tel: 416-533-2725; *Fax:* 416-533-6348
info-sme@bellnet.ca
www.shevchenkomusic.com
Also Known As: Shevchenko Musical Ensemble
Overview: A medium-sized national charitable organization founded in 1972
Mission: To provide instruction in vocal, instrumental & dance for youth & adults by maintaining the Shevchenko Musical Ensemble & Shevchenko School of Dance & Music; To perpetuate Ukrainian cultural traditions
Member of: Ontario Choral Federation; Balalaika & Domra Association of America; Metropolitan Toronto Community Folk Arts Council; Classical Mandolin Society of America
Finances: *Funding Sources:* Individual & corporate donations; fundraising events & projects; concert receipts; grants
Staff Member(s): 2
Activities: *Library:* Eugene Dolny Library of Ukrainian & Slavic Music; Open to public by appointment
Chief Officer(s):
Ginger Kautto, Administrator

National Society of Critical Care Nurses *See* Canadian Association of Critical Care Nurses

National Spa & Pool Institute of Canada *See* Pool & Hot Tub Council of Canada

National Sunflower Association of Canada (NSAC)
PO Box 1269, 38 - 4th Ave. NE, Carman MB R0G 0J0
Tel: 204-745-6776; *Fax:* 204-745-6122
www.canadasunflower.com
www.facebook.com/142997522440563
Overview: A small national organization founded in 1996
Mission: To ensure the profitability and long term growth of the sunflower crop through industry wide leadership
Membership: 950; *Fees:* $50 producers; $500 corporate
Chief Officer(s):
Kelly Dobson, President
Darcelle Graham, Executive Director

National Taekwon-Do Federation (NTF)
c/o Whitecroft Hall, #314, 52313 Range Rd. 232, Sherwood Park AB T8B 1B5
Tel: 780-468-3418
www.ntf.ca
www.facebook.com/CanadaNTF
Overview: A medium-sized national organization
Mission: To develop the art of Tae-Kwon-Do; To encourage overall fitness, stress reduction, well-being, & self-defense
Membership: *Fees:* $70/month adults & children; $140/month family
Chief Officer(s):
Wilfred Ho, President & Founder
wilfho@ntf.ca

National Trade Contractors Coalition of Canada (NTCCC)
#601, 280 Albert St., Ottawa ON K1P 5G8
Tel: 613-232-0492
ntccc@ntccc.ca
www.ntccc.ca
Overview: A small national organization
Mission: To identify issues of common interest among like-minded national trade associations
Affiliation(s): Mechanical Contractors Association of Canada; Canadian Electrical Contractors Association; Canadian Masonry Contractors Association; Canadian Automatic Sprinkler Association; Canadian Roofing Contractors Association; Contractors Division of the Heating, Refrigeration and Air Conditioning Contractors of Canada; Ontario Sheet Metal Contractors Association; Thermal Insulation Association of Canada; Interior Systems Contractors Association of Ontario; Canadian Institute of Steel Construction; Terrazzo, Tile, Marble Stone Guild of Ontario
Membership: 10 organizations; *Fees:* $5,000 annually
Activities: Current issues of concern are: Promotion of Unaltered Forms of Contracts; Prompt Payment Legislation; & Change Orders
Chief Officer(s):
Richard McKeagan, Contact
rick@mcac.ca
Publications:
• A Guide to CCA's Stipulated Price Subcontract
Type: Guide
Profile: Developed by the National Trade Contractors Coalition of Canada with permission from the Canadian Construction Association.

National Transportation Brokers Association (NTBA)
PO Box 31047, RPO Westney Heights, Ajax ON L1T 3V2
www.ntba-brokers.com
Overview: A medium-sized national organization
Mission: To promotes & continually improve business relationships among shippers, carriers, government & freight brokers
Finances: *Funding Sources:* Member fees
Membership: *Fees:* $300; *Member Profile:* Freight brokerage services providers
Chief Officer(s):
Mark Linton, Chairman, 905-842-0422
service@kml-logistics.com

National Trust for Canada (HCF) / Fiducie Nationale du Canada
190 Bronson Ave., Ottawa ON K1R 6H4
Tel: 613-237-4262; *Fax:* 613-237-5987
Toll-Free: 866-964-1066
Other Communication: Blog: blog.nationaltrustcanada.ca
nationaltrust@nationaltrustcanada.ca
www.nationaltrustcanada.ca
www.facebook.com/NationalTrustCanada
twitter.com/nationaltrustca
www.instagram.com/nationaltrustca
Previous Name: Heritage Canada Foundation
Overview: A large national charitable organization founded in 1973
Mission: To foster & ensure the understanding, protection & sustainable evolution of Canada's heritage buildings & historic places
Finances: *Annual Operating Budget:* $500,000-$1.5 Million; *Funding Sources:* Membership; Donations; Government endowment
Staff Member(s): 12
Membership: 2,400 voting members; 100,000 network members; *Fees:* Schedule available
Activities: Offering projects & programs that strengthen local identity; *Internships:* Yes *Library:* Building Stories; by appointment
Chief Officer(s):
Natalie Bull, Executive Director, 613-237-1066 Ext. 222
nbull@nationaltrustcanada.ca
Jim Mountain, Director, Regeneration Projects, 613-237-1066 Ext. 226
jmountain@nationaltrustcanada.ca
Alison Faulknor, Director, New Initiatives, 613-237-1066 Ext. 225
afaulknor@nationaltrustcanada.ca
Awards:
• Prince of Wales Prize
Awarded to the government of a municipality which has demonstrated a strong & sustained commitment to the conservation of its historic places
• Gabrielle Léger Medal for Lifetime Achievement
Recognizes individuals for their outstanding service to Canada in the cause of heritage conservation
• Lieutenant Governor's Award for Heritage Conservation
Awarded to honour outstanding achievement in heritage conservation at the provincial & territorial level
• Ecclesiastical Insurance Cornerstone Awards for Building Heritage
Awarded to recognize excellence in the regeneration of heritage sites & buildings
• Prix du XXe siècle
Awarded to celebrate the excellence of nationally significant architecture that is in Canada or a building anywhere designed by a Canadian architect *Eligibility:* Existing buildings completed after 1950 & before 1988
• Herb Stovel Scholarship Fund
Eligibility: Canadian students or professionals between 20-35 years of age & either studying or working in built heritage conservation; *Amount:* $2,500
Meetings/Conferences:
• National Trust for Canada National Heritage Conference 2018, October, 2018, Fredericton, NB
Scope: National
Publications:
• Heritage [a publication of the National Trust for Canada]
Type: Magazine; *Frequency:* q.; *Editor:* Sara Lynne Levine; *Price:* $40
Profile: Articles, information & profiles on the conservation & rehabilitation of Canada's historic places

National Union of Public & General Employees (NUPGE)
15 Auriga Dr., Nepean ON K2E 1B7
Tel: 613-228-9800; *Fax:* 613-228-9801
nupge.ca
Overview: A medium-sized national organization
Mission: A family of 11 component unions that works to deliver public services of every kind to the citizens of their home provinces.
Membership: 340,000
Chief Officer(s):
James Clancy, National President

National United Professional Association of Trained Homeopaths (NUPATH)
#102, 2680 Matheson Blvd., Mississauga ON L4W 0A5
Tel: 905-267-8539; *Fax:* 905-267-3401
info@nupath.org
www.nupath.org
Overview: A medium-sized national organization founded in 1993
Mission: To represent homeopathic practitioners in Canada

Membership: *Fees:* $200 active; $30 associate; $25 supporting; no fee for students; *Member Profile:* Practitioners of homeopathy
Chief Officer(s):
Sushila Lalsingh, President
Meetings/Conferences:
• National United Professional Association of Trained Homeopaths Conference, 2018
Scope: National

National Winter Sports Association (NWSA)
c/o Cross Country Canada, Bill Warren Training Centre, #100, 1995 Olympic Way, Canmore AB T1W 2T6
Tel: 403-678-6791; *Fax:* 403-678-3885
Toll-Free: 877-609-3215
info@cccski.com
www.cccski.com
www.facebook.com/CrossCountryCanada
twitter.com/cccski
www.youtube.com/user/xccanada
Overview: A small national organization founded in 2007 overseen by Cross Country Canada
Mission: To provide financial assistance to cross country ski coaches, athletes & racing programs across Canada; grants administered through Cross Country Canada
Member of: Cross Country Canada
Chief Officer(s):
Pierre Lafontaine, Executive Director, Cross Country Canada, 403-678-4791 Ext. 38
plafontaine@cccski.com

National Youth Bowling Council *See* Youth Bowling Canada

National Youth in Care Network *See* Youth in Care Canada

National Youth Orchestra Canada (NYOC) / Orchestre national des jeunes Canada (ONJC)
#500, 59 Adelaide St. East, Toronto ON M5C 1K6
Tel: 416-532-4470; *Fax:* 416-532-6879
Toll-Free: 888-532-4470
info@nyoc.org
www.nyoc.org
www.facebook.com/nyoconjc
twitter.com/nyoc_onjc
www.youtube.com/nyoconjc
Overview: A medium-sized national charitable organization founded in 1961 overseen by Orchestras Canada
Mission: To provide comprehensive training for Canada's best young classical musicians
Member of: Orchestras Canada
Finances: *Funding Sources:* Ontario Arts Council; Grants; Corporate & individual donations
Staff Member(s): 8
Activities: Facilitating in-depth training programs for youth ages 16-28; Touring nationally and internationally; *Library:* Not open to public
Chief Officer(s):
Barbara Smith, Executive Director, 416-532-4470 Ext. 222

Native Addictions Council of Manitoba (NACM)
160 Salter St., Winnipeg MB R2W 4K1
Tel: 204-586-8395; *Fax:* 204-589-3921
info@nacm.ca
www.mts.net/~nacm/
Also Known As: Pritchard House
Overview: A small provincial charitable organization founded in 1972
Mission: To provide traditional holistic healing services to First Peoples through treatment of addictions; each member of First Peoples has the right to wellness.
Activities: Woman's program, youth program, gambling program, and an outreach program.; *Library*

Native Alliance of Québec *Voir* Alliance autochtone du Québec

Native Brotherhood of British Columbia (NBBC) / Fraternité des Indiens de la Colombie-Britannique
#110, 100 Park Royal South, West Vancouver BC V7T 1A2
Tel: 604-913-2997; *Fax:* 604-913-2995
nativebrotherhood.ca
Overview: A medium-sized provincial organization founded in 1931
Mission: To improve the social, spiritual, economic & physical conditions of its members, including education, health & living; To cooperate with other organizations which are involved with the advancement of Indian welfare; To focus on capacity building, particularly resources with economic potential
Membership: 450 current individual members; 6,000 charter community members; *Fees:* Schedule available

Native Canadian Centre of Toronto (NCCT)
16 Spadina Rd., Toronto ON M5R 2S7
Tel: 416-964-9087; *Fax:* 416-964-2111
reception@ncct.on.ca
www.ncct.on.ca
www.facebook.com/nativecentre
twitter.com/NativeCentre
Overview: A medium-sized local charitable organization
Mission: To provides a gathering place to deliver programs & services for Native people while striving to reflect the traditional
Member of: National Association of Friendship Centres
Staff Member(s): 30
Membership: *Fees:* Schedule available
Activities: Traditional Awareness Gathering; *Speaker Service:* Yes; *Library:* Community History Project; by appointment
Chief Officer(s):
Larry Frost, Executive Director
larry.frost@ncct.on.ca
Gene Jamieson, President
J'net Cavanagh, Officer, Communications & Referrals
Jnet.Cavanagh@ncct.on.ca

Native Child & Family Services of Toronto (NCFST)
30 College St., Toronto ON M5G 1K2
Tel: 416-969-8510; *Fax:* 416-928-0706
Other Communication: After Hours Emergency Service: 416-924-4646
info@nativechild.org
www.nativechild.org
twitter.com/ncfst
Overview: A medium-sized local charitable organization founded in 1986
Mission: To provide caring, well-being, quality of life, & healing to children in need in Toronto's Native community
Finances: *Annual Operating Budget:* Greater than $5 Million; *Funding Sources:* Government; Organizations
Staff Member(s): 180
Activities: Operating an Aboriginal Head Start program; Offering summer camps, youth programs, & developmental services; Facilitating transitional housing services for youth; *Internships:* Yes
Chief Officer(s):
Kenn Richard, Executive Director

Native Clan Organization Inc. (NCO)
94 McGregor St., Winnipeg MB R2W 4V5
Tel: 204-943-7357
ednco@nativeclan.org
www.nativeclan.org
Overview: A small local organization founded in 1972
Mission: To supply social services to male & female inmates of Native origin incarcerated in southern Manitoba
Affiliation(s): Canadian Criminal Justice Association
Finances: *Funding Sources:* Services fees
Chief Officer(s):
Ken Fleury, Executive Director

Native Communications Society of the Northwest Territories (NCS)
PO Box 2193, Yellowknife NT X1A 2P6
Tel: 320-295-7700
Toll-Free: 888-627-6208
www.ncsnwt.com
Overview: A small provincial organization
Mission: To promote & develop improved communications between aboriginal & non-aboriginal people & communities in the NWT, as well as between northerners & southern Canadians; to help educate aboriginal people through the communications media in order for them to readily understand the implications of the European way of living & the developments taking place in the NWT
Chief Officer(s):
Les L. Carpenter, CEO
lcarpenter@ncsnwt.com

Native Coordinating Council
2010 - 1st Ave. East, Prince Albert SK S6V 2B7
Tel: 306-764-6690; *Fax:* 306-764-8072
sundance.staff@sasktel.net
Also Known As: Sundance Haven
Overview: A medium-sized local organization founded in 1978
Mission: To develop programs that support Native culture; to provide needed services to Prince Albert community; to provide employment opportunities to Native People
Affiliation(s): Indian Metis Friendship Center; Local 269; Local 109
Finances: *Funding Sources:* Provincial government

Membership: *Member Profile:* Aboriginal - Métis descent
Activities: Family counselling; crisis centre; parent aid program

Native Council of Canada *See* Congress of Aboriginal Peoples

Native Council of Nova Scotia (NCNS)
PO Box 1320, 129 Truro Heights Rd., Truro NS B2N 5N2
Tel: 902-895-1523; *Fax:* 902-895-0024
Toll-Free: 800-565-4372
www.ncns.ca
twitter.com/NativeCouncilNS
Overview: A medium-sized provincial organization founded in 1975 overseen by Congress of Aboriginal Peoples
Mission: To aid & assist people of Aboriginal ancestry in Nova Scotia; To work with all levels of government, public & private agencies & industries to improve social, educational & employment opportunities for Aboriginal people; To foster & strengthen cultural identity & pride; To inform the public of the special needs of Native People; To cooperate with other Native organizations
Membership: 1,000-4,999; *Member Profile:* Full - 16 years of age & over, resident of Nova Scotia, of Aboriginal ancestry & non-resident band member; Honorary - at discretion of Executive Committee, Board of Directors & General Assembly
Activities: APTEC & SARSET Programs - employment & training assistance for off-reserve Mi'kmaq/Aboriginal people in NS; Education Program - educational assistance through awards, scholarships & loans for off-reserve Mi'kmaq/Aboriginal people in NS; CHIP Program - community action program for Mi'kmaq/Aboriginal parents with young children ages 0-6 yrs.; Prenatal Program - support program for first-time Mi'kmaq/Aboriginal expectant mothers & babies; RNH Program: assists off-reserve Mi'kmaq/Aboriginal homeowners with CMHC, RRAP & ERP; *Library:* Open to public
Chief Officer(s):
Grace Conrad, Chief & President
chiefconrad@ncns.ca
Theresa Hare, Financial Comptroller, 902-899-1431
theresa.veniott@eastlink.ca

Native Council of Prince Edward Island (NCPEI)
6 F.J. McAuley Ct., Charlottetown PE C1A 9M7
Tel: 902-892-5314; *Fax:* 902-368-7464
Toll-Free: 877-591-3003
admin@ncpei.com
www.ncpei.com
Overview: A small provincial organization overseen by Congress of Aboriginal Peoples
Mission: To be the self governing authority for all off-reserve Aboriginal people living on Epekwitk (PEI)
Member of: Prince Edward Island Literacy Alliance Inc.
Staff Member(s): 13
Chief Officer(s):
Lisa Cooper, President & Chief, 902-892-5314, Fax: 902-368-7464
chief@ncpei.com

Native Counselling Services of Alberta (NCSA)
10975 - 124 St., Edmonton AB T5M 0H9
Tel: 780-451-4002; *Fax:* 780-428-0187
www.ncsa.ca
Overview: A medium-sized provincial organization founded in 1970
Mission: To promote wellness for Aboriginal individuals, families and communities.
Finances: *Funding Sources:* Federal & provincial governments; private foundations
Staff Member(s): 9
Activities: *Library:*
Chief Officer(s):
Allen Benson, CEO
allen-benson@ncsa.ca

Native Courtworker & Counselling Association of BC (NCCABC)
#207, 1999 Marine Dr., North Vancouver BC V7P 3J3
Tel: 604-985-5355; *Fax:* 604-985-8933
Toll-Free: 877-811-1190
nccabc@nccabc.net
www.nccabc.ca
Also Known As: NCCA of BC
Overview: A small provincial charitable organization founded in 1973
Mission: To provide culturally appropriate services to aboriginal people & communities consistent with their needs; To provide access to counselling & referral services to clients with substance abuse & detox support issues; To provide advocacy

Canadian Associations / Native Earth Performing Arts Inc. (NEPA)

service for aboriginal family & youth; To facilitate & enhance access to justice by assisting clients involved in the criminal justice system
Finances: *Annual Operating Budget:* $1.5 Million-$3 Million
Staff Member(s): 50
Membership: *Committees:* Executive; Finance; Planning

Native Earth Performing Arts Inc. (NEPA)
#250, 585 Dundas St. East, Toronto ON M5A 2B7
Tel: 416-531-1402; *Fax:* 416-531-6377
Toll-Free: 877-854-9708
office@nativeearth.ca
www.nativeearth.ca
www.facebook.com/NativeEarthPerformingArts
twitter.com/NativeEarth
Overview: A medium-sized local charitable organization founded in 1983
Mission: To enable Native actors, writers, designers, directors & technicians to work together to produce quality theatre that is vital to their development as artists & their identity as Native people; To encourage the use of theatre as form of communication within the Native community, including the use of the Native languages
Member of: Theatre Ontario
Affiliation(s): Professional Association of Canadian Theatres; Toronto Theatre Alliance
Finances: *Funding Sources:* Government; corporate; private donations; special events; membership dues; merchandise sales
Staff Member(s): 11
Activities: *Internships:* Yes; *Speaker Service:* Yes
Chief Officer(s):
Ryan Cunningham, Artistic Director
ryan@nativeearth.ca
Isaac Thomas, Managing Director
isaac@nativeearth.ca

Native Fishing Association (NFA)
#110, 100 Park Royal South, West Vancouver BC V7T 1A2
Tel: 604-913-2997; *Fax:* 604-913-2995
reception@shoal.ca
www.shoal.ca
www.facebook.com/native.fishing
twitter.com/nativefishing
Overview: A small local organization founded in 1985
Mission: To enhance, stabilize, & support Native participation in British Columbia's commercial fishing industry
Chief Officer(s):
Violet Hill, Executive Director
vhill@shoal.ca

Native Friendship Centre of Montréal Inc. (NFCM) / Centre d'amitié autochtone de Montréal Inc.
2001, boul St-Laurent, Montréal QC H2X 2T3
Tel: 514-499-1854; *Fax:* 514-499-9436
Toll-Free: 855-499-1854
info@nfcm.org
www.nfcm.org
Overview: A medium-sized local charitable organization founded in 1974
Mission: To promote, develop & enhance the quality of life of the urban Aboriginal community of Montréal
Member of: National Association of Friendship Centres
Finances: *Funding Sources:* Heritage Canada
Membership: *Fees:* $5; *Member Profile:* Status & non-status First Nations, Inuit, Métis, & non-native
Activities: Cultural activities; Training & Employment; AIDS/HIV Workshops; Substance Abuse Therapy
Chief Officer(s):
Brett W. Pineau, Executive Director

Native Investment & Trade Association (NITA)
6520 Salish Dr., Vancouver BC V6N 2C7
Tel: 604-275-6670; *Fax:* 604-275-0307
Toll-Free: 800-337-7743
Overview: A small national licensing organization founded in 1989
Mission: To promote, establish & maintain trade/investment opportunities in Native communities; encourages free enterprise solutions to economic & social problems confronting Native communities, but remains sensitive to their special cultural heritage, needs, requirements; views non-governmental business involvement with First Nations as a vital step towards greater self-reliance; fosters business ventures with high employment potential; promotes projects with potential for sustainable economic growth; conducts research into innovative approaches to economic development of Native communities
Finances: *Funding Sources:* Registration fees
Activities: Online business directory; conferences; scholarships; business products and services; *Library:* NITA Resource Library

Native North American Traveling College
1 Ronathahon:ni Lane, Ahkwesahsne ON K6H 5R7
Tel: 613-932-9452; *Fax:* 613-932-0092
info@nnatc.org
www.nnatc.org
Overview: A small national organization founded in 1974
Mission: The cultural centre has been and continues today to be instrumental in preserving and maintaining the Mohawk cultural, history and language.
Finances: *Annual Operating Budget:* $100,000-$250,000
Staff Member(s): 10
Activities: *Awareness Events:* Friendship Days, July; *Speaker Service:* Yes; *Library*
Chief Officer(s):
Russell Roundpoint, Executive Director

Native Orchid Conservation Inc.
45 Skowron Cres., Winnipeg MB R3W 1N6
Tel: 204-223-8209
www.nativeorchid.org
Overview: A small local organization
Mission: To protect unique mini-ecosystems & their plant communities
Membership: *Fees:* $10 individual; $25 group
Chief Officer(s):
Doris Ames, President
adames@mts.net

Native Women's Association of Canada (NWAC) / L'Association des femmes autochtones du Canada (AFAC)
#4, 155 International Rd., Akwesasne ON K6H 5R7
Tel: 613-722-3033
Toll-Free: 800-461-4043
reception@nwac.ca
www.nwac.ca
www.facebook.com/NWAC.AFAC
twitter.com/NWAC_CA
Overview: A medium-sized national organization founded in 1974
Mission: To enhance, promote & foster the social, economic, cultural & political well-being of First Nations & Métis women with First Nations & Canadian societies; To help empower women by being involved in developing & changing legislation which affects them, & by involving them in the development & delivery of programs promoting equal opportunity for Aboriginal women. Satellite office located at 1 Nicholas St., 9th Fl., Ottawa.
Member of: Indigenous Survival International
Finances: *Funding Sources:* Canadian Heritage; Corrections Service Canada
Staff Member(s): 8
Activities: The Indian Act; The Constitution; Family Violence; AIDS; Justice; Health Issues; Child Welfare; Aboriginal Rights; *Library:* Resource Centre; Open to public
Chief Officer(s):
Francyne Joe, Interim President

Native Women's Association of the Northwest Territories
Post Office Building, 2nd Fl., PO Box 2321, Yellowknife NT X1A 2P7
Tel: 867-873-5509; *Fax:* 867-873-3152
Toll-Free: 866-459-1114
nativewomensnwt.com
www.facebook.com/NativeWomensAssociationOfTheNwt
Overview: A medium-sized provincial organization founded in 1978
Mission: Provides training & education programs for native women in the Western Arctic
Member of: Native Women's Association of Canada
Affiliation(s): Yellowknife Victim Services
Activities: Adult education; pre-employment programme; workshops
Chief Officer(s):
Marilyn Napier, Executive Director
marilyn_napier@hotmail.com

Native Women's Resource Centre of Toronto (NWRCT)
191 Gerrard St. East, Toronto ON M5A 2E5
Tel: 416-963-9963; *Fax:* 416-963-5062
info@nwrct.ca
www.nwrct.ca
www.facebook.com/292090724136835
twitter.com/NWRCT
Overview: A small local charitable organization founded in 1985
Mission: To provide ongoing support for native women in the GTA through a variety of programs; To incorporate spiritual, physical, social, economic & intellectual components into all programs
Affiliation(s): Toronto Aboriginal Social Services Association
Finances: *Funding Sources:* Government & fundraising
Membership: *Fees:* Free
Activities: Client information & referral; food bank; clothing give-away; youth activities; circles; craft classes; Pimaatisiwin developmental programs for children 0-6; Student Advancement program; Adult Literacy; Adult Education; workshops; native language class; summer day camps; Annual Winter Solstice Celebration; Women's Full Moon Ceremonies; *Library:* Open to public

Native Women's Transition Centre Inc.
105 Aikins St., Winnipeg MB R2W 4E6
Tel: 204-989-8240; *Fax:* 204-586-1101
rswnwt1@nwtc.cc
www.nativewomens.mb.ca
Overview: A small local organization founded in 1979
Mission: To provide shelter to Native women & children; to provide social services to woman in need
Activities: Programs: Crisis/Addiction; Learning; Parenting; Compulsive coping behavior; Women's healing/Play circle; Breaking the Silence; Practical skillsFamily violence prevention
Chief Officer(s):
Phil Lancaster, Acting-Chair

Natural Family Planning Association
c/o #205, 3050 Yonge St., Toronto ON M4N 2K4
Tel: 416-481-5465
www.naturalfamilyplanning.ca
Also Known As: The Billings Group
Overview: A small national charitable organization
Mission: To promote the Billings Ovulation Method of natural family planning which is based on an awareness of a woman's physical systems to gauge optimum fertility state.
Member of: WOOMB International
Finances: *Funding Sources:* Government
Activities: *Internships:* Yes; *Speaker Service:* Yes; *Library:* by appointment
Chief Officer(s):
Christian Elia, Executive Director

Natural Gas Employees' Association (NGEA)
#316, 9426 - 51 Ave., Edmonton AB T6E 5A6
Tel: 780-483-9330; *Fax:* 780-469-2504
Toll-Free: 877-912-9330
ngea@telus.net
www.ngea.ca
Overview: A small national organization
Mission: To provide equal & effective representation to ensure growth, development & the well-being of its members
Membership: *Member Profile:* Employees of ATCO Gas & Pipelines Limited-Gas Division & Pipelines Division
Chief Officer(s):
Jordan Smeland, President, 780-999-7779
Danny Burrell, Business Agent, 780-783-9330
danny.ngea@telus.net

Natural Health Practitioners of Canada (NHP)
10339 - 124 St., 6th Fl, Edmonton AB T5N 3W1
Tel: 780-484-2010; *Fax:* 780-484-3605
Toll-Free: 888-711-7701
growingtogether@nhpcanada.org
www.nhpcanada.org
www.linkedin.com/companies/nhpcanada
www.facebook.com/nhpcanada
twitter.com/NHPCANADA
www.youtube.com/nhpcanada
Previous Name: Association of Massage Therapists & Wholistic Practitioners
Overview: A medium-sized national organization founded in 1988
Mission: To maintain professional standards of practitioners practising in massage therapy & wholistic practice in order to benefit services to clients
Staff Member(s): 21
Membership: *Member Profile:* Canadian massage therapists & wholistic practitioners
Activities: Providing information to members; Promoting wellness
Chief Officer(s):

Kelly Sloan, Executive Director

Natural Health Practitioners of Canada Association (NHPCA) / Association des Praticiens de la santé naturelle du Canada (PSNC)
10339 - 124 St. NW, 6th Fl, Edmonton AB T5N 3W1
Tel: 780-484-2010; Fax: 780-484-3605
Toll-Free: 888-711-7701
growingtogether@nhpcanada.org
www.nhpcanada.org
www.linkedin.com/companies/nhpcanada
www.facebook.com/nhpcanada
twitter.com/NHPCANADA
www.youtube.com/nhpcanada
Overview: A medium-sized national organization founded in 1988
Mission: To provide programs, services and products for members in the service of public wellness and to serve the public by promoting and advocating the wellness professions.
Staff Member(s): 21
Membership: Committees: Leadership
Chief Officer(s):
Kelly Sloan, Executive Director
Publications:
• Connections [a publication of the Natural Health Practitioners of Canada]
Type: Magazine; Frequency: Quarterly

Natural History Society of Manitoba; Manitoba Naturalists Society See **Nature Manitoba**

Natural History Society of Newfoundland & Labrador
PO Box 1013, St. John's NL A1C 5M3
naturenl@naturenl.ca
naturenl.ca
www.facebook.com/128262310581874
Overview: A small provincial charitable organization founded in 1963
Mission: To promote the enjoyment & protection of all wildlife and natural history resources in the Province of Newfoundland & Labrador & surrounding waters.
Member of: Canadian Nature Federation
Finances: Annual Operating Budget: Less than $50,000; Funding Sources: Membership fees; donations
Membership: Fees: $25
Activities: Field trips; monthly meetings
Chief Officer(s):
Dave Innes, Secretary
Awards:
• Wild Things Scholarship

Natural Products Marketing Council
PO Box 890, Truro NS B2N 5G6
Tel: 902-893-6511; Fax: 902-893-6573
www.novascotia.ca
Overview: A small provincial organization founded in 1946
Mission: To assure the orderly marketing of natural products
Staff Member(s): 3; 6 volunteer(s)
Chief Officer(s):
Elizabeth Crouse, General Manager
crouseea@gov.ns.ca
Ken Peacock, Chair

Natural Resources Union (NRU) / Syndicat des ressources naturelles (SRN)
#600, 233 Gilmour St., Ottawa ON K2P 0P2
Tel: 613-560-4378; Fax: 613-233-7012
info@nru-srn.com
www.nru-srn.com
twitter.com/NRUSRN
Also Known As: PSCA
Previous Name: Union of Energy, Mines & Resources Employees
Overview: A medium-sized national organization founded in 1978 overseen by Public Service Alliance of Canada
Finances: Annual Operating Budget: $250,000-$500,000
Staff Member(s): 2
Membership: 1,600 + 20 locals; Member Profile: Government employees, Natural Resources Canada, Canadian Space Agency & various other agencies & boards; Committees: Occupational Safety & Health; Equal Opportunities; Labour Management Consultation
Activities: Library:
Chief Officer(s):
Mike Sargent, National President
sargentm@nru-srn.com

Natural Sciences & Engineering Research Council of Canada (NSERC) / Conseil de recherches en sciences naturelles et en génie du Canada (CRSNG)
350 Albert St., 16th Fl., Ottawa ON K1A 1H5
Tel: 613-995-4273; Fax: 613-992-5337
Toll-Free: 855-275-2861
Other Communication: President's Office e-mail:
exec@nserc-crsng.gc.ca
comm@nserc-crsng.gc.ca
www.nserc-crsng.gc.ca
www.linkedin.com/company/natural-sciences-and-engineering-research-council-of-canada
www.facebook.com/EurekaCanadaEnglish
twitter.com/nserc_crsng
www.youtube.com/user/NSERCTube
Overview: A large national organization
Mission: To support university students in advanced studies; to promote discovery research; to foster innovation through Canadian investment in postsecondary research projects
Finances: Annual Operating Budget: Greater than $5 Million
Membership: Committees: Standing & Advisory; Selection; Prizes; Membership
Chief Officer(s):
B. Mario Pinto, President, 613-995-5840
Pres@nserc-crsng.gc.ca
Daniel Muzyka, Vice-President & Chair

The Natural Step Canada
#208, 251 Bank St., Ottawa ON K2P 1X3
Tel: 613-748-3001; Fax: 613-748-1649
info@naturalstep.ca
www.naturalstep.ca
www.linkedin.com/groups?mostPopular=&gid=1169257
www.facebook.com/TheNaturalStepCanada
twitter.com/TNS_Canada
www.youtube.com/user/TNSCanada
Overview: A large national charitable organization
Mission: To help organizations & individuals make meaningful progress toward sustainability
Staff Member(s): 12
Chief Officer(s):
David Hughes, President & Chief Executive Officer

Nature Alberta
Percy Page Centre, 11759 Groat Rd., 3rd Fl., Edmonton AB T5M 3K6
Tel: 780-427-8124; Fax: 780-422-2663
info@naturealberta.ca
naturealberta.ca
www.facebook.com/NatureAB
twitter.com/naturealberta
www.youtube.com/user/naturealberta
Overview: A medium-sized provincial charitable organization founded in 1970
Mission: To encourage Albertans to increase knowledge & understanding of natural history & ecological processes; to provide a unified voice for naturalists on conservation issues; to organize field meetings, conferences, nature camps, research symposia, & other activities.
Member of: Canadian Nature Federation
Finances: Funding Sources: Donations; grants; projects
Staff Member(s): 6
Membership: 5,000 individual + 40 clubs; Fees: Schedule available
Chief Officer(s):
Petra Rowell, Executive Director
petrar@naturealberta.ca
Awards:
• Loran L. Goulden Memorial Award

Nature Canada / Canada Nature
#300, 75 Albert St., Ottawa ON K1P 5E7
Tel: 613-562-3447
Toll-Free: 800-267-4088
info@naturecanada.ca
www.naturecanada.ca
www.linkedin.com/company/nature-canada
www.facebook.com/NatureCanada
twitter.com/NatureCanada
www.youtube.com/user/NatureCanada1;
www.pinterest.com/NatureCanada
Previous Name: Canadian Nature Federation
Overview: A large national charitable organization founded in 1971
Mission: To protect & conserve wildlife & habitats throughout Canada

Finances: Funding Sources: Donations
Staff Member(s): 10
Membership: 350+ organizations + 40,000 supporters; Member Profile: Naturalist organizations across Canada; Individual supporters
Activities: Offering outreach & educational programs; Organizing action campaigns for nature
Chief Officer(s):
Graham Saul, Executive Director, 613-562-3447 Ext. 247
gsaul@naturecanada.ca
Stephen Hazell, Director, Conservation & General Counsel, 613-562-3447 Ext. 240
shazell@naturecanada.ca
Jodi Joy, Director, Development, 613-562-3447 Ext. 239
jjoy@naturecanada.ca
Awards:
• Charles Labatiuk Volunteer Award
To recognize individuals who have made outstanding contributions to Canadian conservation Eligibility: A resident of Canada under the age of 18
• Conservation Partner Award
To recognize the conservation efforts of a partner organization or volunteer who has supported a Nature Canada conservation project
• Douglas H. Pimlott Award
Eligibility: An individual with outstanding contributions to Canadian conservation
• Charles Labatiuk Scholarship
Eligibility: Any student enrolled in an entrance level course or program at an accredited college or university in Canada, in the interdisciplinary study of natural environmental systems;
Amount: $2,000
Meetings/Conferences:
• Nature Canada 2018 Annual General Meeting, 2018
Scope: National
Description: The annual meeting usually features the election of the Board of Directors, the presentation of Nature Canada awards, & the adoption of resolutions
Contact Information: Executive Assistant & Manager, Office Operations: Marie du Plessis, Phone: 800-267-4088, ext. 298, E-mail: mduplessis@naturecanada.ca

The Nature Conservancy of Canada (NCC) / Société canadienne pour la conservation de la nature
#400, 36 Eglinton Ave. West, Toronto ON M4R 1A1
Tel: 416-932-3202
Toll-Free: 800-465-0029
nature@natureconservancy.ca
www.natureconservancy.ca
www.linkedin.com/company/the-nature-conservancy-of-canada
www.facebook.com/natureconservancy.ca
twitter.com/NCC_CNC
www.instagram.ca/ncc_cnc
Overview: A large national charitable organization founded in 1962
Mission: To protect Canada's biodiversity through long-term stewardship & property securement
Finances: Funding Sources: Donations
Membership: Committees: Executive; Governance & Nominating; Audit; Investment; Conservation
Activities: Partnering with landowners & corporations to protect Canada's natural areas
Chief Officer(s):
John Lounds, President & Chief Executive Officer
Michael Bradstreet, Vice-President, Conservation
Publications:
• The Ark [a publication of The Nature Conservancy of Canada]
Type: Newsletter; Frequency: 3 pa; Price: A donation of $20+
Profile: A national newsletter, with updates on featured projects & properties, stewardship work, & threatened or vulnerable species
• The Nature Conservancy of Canada Annual Report to our Donors
Type: Yearbook; Frequency: Annually
Profile: The year in review for each region of Canada
Alberta
#830, 105 - 12 Ave. SE, Calgary AB T2G 1A1
Tel: 403-262-1253; Fax: 403-515-6987
Toll-Free: 877-262-1253
alberta@natureconservancy.ca
Chief Officer(s):
Bob Demulder, Regional Vice President, 866-262-1253 Ext. 6988
bob.demulder@natureconservancy.ca

Canadian Associations / Nature Manitoba

British Columbia
#200, 825 Broughton St., Victoria BC V8W 1E5
Tel: 250-479-3191
Toll-Free: 888-404-8428
bcoffice@natureconservancy.ca
Chief Officer(s):
Linda Hannah, Regional Vice President

Manitoba
#200, 611 Corydon Ave., Winnipeg MB R3L 0P3
Tel: 204-942-6156; *Fax:* 204-942-1016
Toll-Free: 866-683-6934
manitoba@natureconservancy.ca
Chief Officer(s):
Jeff Polakoff, Regional Vice President

New Brunswick
#180, 924 Prospect St., Fredericton NB E3B 2T9
Tel: 506-450-6010; *Fax:* 506-450-6013
Toll-Free: 877-231-4400
atlantic@natureconservancy.ca
Chief Officer(s):
Linda M. Stephenson, Regional Vice President

Newfoundland & Labrador
#103, 136 Crosbie Rd., St. John's NL A1B 3K3
Tel: 709-753-5540
atlantic@natureconservancy.ca
Chief Officer(s):
Linda Stephenson, Regional Vice-President

Nova Scotia
#337, 7071 Bayer's Rd., Halifax NS B3L 2C2
Tel: 902-405-4334
atlantic@natureconservancy.ca
Chief Officer(s):
Linda Stephenson, Regional Vice-President

Ontario
PO Box 443, London ON N6A 4W1
Toll-Free: 866-281-5331
ontario@natureconservancy.ca
Chief Officer(s):
James Duncan, Regional Vice President

Prince Edward Island
PO Box 2859, Charlottetown PE C1A 8C4
Toll-Free: 877-231-4400
atlantic@natureconservancy.ca
Chief Officer(s):
Linda Stephenson, Regional Vice-President

Québec
#1000, 55, av Mont-Royal ouest, Montréal QC H2T 2S6
Tél: 514-876-1606; *Téléc:* 514-876-7901
Ligne sans frais: 877-876-5444
quebec@natureconservancy.ca
Chief Officer(s):
Nathalie Zinger, Regional Vice President

Saskatchewan
1777 Victoria Ave., Regina SK S4P 4K5
Tel: 306-347-0447; *Fax:* 306-347-2345
Toll-Free: 866-622-7275
saskatchewan@natureconservancy.ca
Chief Officer(s):
Mark Wartman, Regional Vice President

Nature Council of British Columbia See British Columbia Nature (Federation of British Columbia Naturalists)

Nature Manitoba
Hammond Building, #401, 63 Albert St., Winnipeg MB R3B 1G4
Tel: 204-943-9029; *Fax:* 204-943-9029
Other Communication: editor@naturemanitoba.ca (Newsletter)
info@naturemanitoba.ca
www.naturemanitoba.ca
www.facebook.com/naturemanitoba
Previous Name: Natural History Society of Manitoba; Manitoba Naturalists Society
Overview: A medium-sized provincial charitable organization founded in 1920
Mission: To foster the popular & scientific study of nature; To preserve the natural environment; To act as a voice for people interested in the outdoors & natural history
Finances: *Funding Sources:* Donations; Nature Manitoba Store
Membership: *Fees:* $20 students; $35 seniors; $40 individuals; $55 families; *Member Profile:* Manitobans who share a passion for nature
Activities: Conducting research; Engaging in advocacy activities; Offering educational & recreational programs & field trips to observe botany, butterflies, & birds; *Library:* Nature Manitoba Library
Chief Officer(s):
Roger Turenne, President
Donald Himbeault, Executive Vice-President
Alain Louer, Secretary
Sean Worden, Treasurer
Susan McLarty, Office Administrator
Meetings/Conferences:
• Nature Manitoba 2018 Annual General Meeting, 2018
Scope: Provincial
Description: An opportunity for Nature Manitoba members to discuss & advance policy positions about nature in Manitoba
Publications:
• The Birds of Manitoba
Type: Book; *Price:* $63.95
Profile: Information about & illustrations & photographs of the 382 species of birds known in Manitoba
• Checklist of the Birds of Manitoba
Price: $1
Profile: A checklist of 391 confirmed species in Manitoba
• Finding Birds in Southern Manitoba
Type: Guide; *Price:* $20
Profile: A birding guide for southern Manitoba, featuring photographs & maps
• Nature Manitoba News
Type: Newsletter; *Frequency:* Bimonthly; *Accepts Advertising*; *Editor:* Tommy Allen; *Price:* Free with membership in Nature Manitoba
Profile: Information about Nature Manitoba's meetings & workshops, activities, members, & nature in the news
• Naturescape Manitoba
Type: Book; *Number of Pages:* 200; *Price:* $24.95
Profile: A source book about native planting & water conservation for the Prairies Ecozone of Manitoba

Nature NB
#110, 924 Prospect St., Fredericton NB E3B 2T9
Tel: 506-459-4209; *Fax:* 506-459-4209
nbfn@nb.aibn.com
www.naturenb.ca
www.facebook.com/naturenb
twitter.com/NatureNB
Previous Name: New Brunswick Federation of Naturalists
Overview: A medium-sized provincial charitable organization founded in 1979
Mission: To preserve wildlife & protect its natural habitat; to promote a public interest in & a knowledge of natural history; to promote, encourage & cooperate with organizations & individuals who have similar interests & objectives; to consider matters of environmental concern.
Member of: Nature Canada
Staff Member(s): 4
Membership: *Fees:* $25 individual; $30 family membership; *Member Profile:* Nature clubs
Chief Officer(s):
Danielle Smith, Executive Director

Nature Nova Scotia (Federation of Nova Scotia Naturalists)
c/o Nova Scotia Museum of Natural History, 1747 Summer St., Halifax NS B3H 3A6
Tel: 902-582-7176
doug@fundymud.com
www.naturens.ca
Previous Name: Federation of Nova Scotia Naturalists
Overview: A medium-sized provincial charitable organization founded in 1990
Mission: To support the interests of naturalists clubs; To represent naturalists clubs throughout Nova Scotia
Member of: Nature Conservancy of Canada (NCC); Canadian Parks & Wilderness Society (CPAWS)
Affiliation(s): Nature Canada
Finances: *Funding Sources:* Donations
Membership: *Fees:* $5 students & seniors; $20 single adults & families; *Member Profile:* Naturalists clubs & organizations within Nova Scotia; Members-at-large
Activities: Providing educational opportunities; Hosting field trips; Conducting research; Serving on committees & advisory boards involving issues that affect the health of the natural environment
Chief Officer(s):
Bob Bancroft, President, 902-386-2501
Sue Abbot, Vice-President, 902-453-0435
Doug Linzey, Secretary, 902-582-7176
Jean Gibson, Treasurer, 902-678-4725
Meetings/Conferences:
• Nature Nova Scotia 2018 Annual General Meeting & Conference, 2018, NS
Scope: Provincial
Description: A weekend event, with an annual meeting featuring reports on the past year's activities to the membership, plus educational talks & field trips
Publications:
• Nature Nova Scotia Annual Report
Type: Yearbook; *Frequency:* Annually
Profile: A summary of Nature Nova Scotia's yearly activities

Nature Québec
#207, 870, av de Salaberry, Québec QC G1R 2T9
Tél: 418-648-2104; *Téléc:* 418-648-0991
conservons@naturequebec.org
www.naturequebec.org
www.linkedin.com/company-beta/2794658
www.facebook.com/naturequebec
twitter.com/NatureQuebec
Nom précédent: Union québécoise pour la conservation de la nature
Aperçu: *Dimension:* moyenne; *Envergure:* provinciale; Organisme sans but lucratif; fondée en 1981
Mission: Regrouper les individus et les sociétés oeuvrant en sciences naturelles et en environnement; Maintenir des processus écologiques essentiels; Préserver la diversité génétique; Utiliser soutenablement des espèces et des écosystèmes
Membre de: Union internationale pour la conservation de la nature
Finances: *Budget de fonctionnement annuel:* $500,000-$1.5 Million
Membre(s) du personnel: 8
Membre: 120 institutionnel; 5 000 individuel; *Montant de la cotisation:* 25$
Activités: *Stagiaires:* Oui; *Service de conférenciers:* Oui
Membre(s) du bureau directeur:
Christian Simard, Directeur général, 418-648-2104 Ext. 2071
christian.simard@naturequebec.org

Nature Saskatchewan
#206, 1860 Lorne St., Regina SK S4P 2L7
Tel: 306-780-9273; *Fax:* 306-780-9263
Toll-Free: 800-667-4668
info@naturesask.ca
www.naturesask.ca
www.facebook.com/NatureSask
twitter.com/naturesask
www.instagram.com/naturesaskatchewan
Also Known As: Saskatchewan Natural History Society
Overview: A medium-sized provincial charitable organization founded in 1949
Mission: To foster appreciation & understanding for the natural environment; To document & protect the biological diversity of Saskatchewan; To preserve the natural eco-systems of the province
Finances: *Annual Operating Budget:* $500,000-$1.5 Million; *Funding Sources:* Membership fees; Donations; Sponsorships
Staff Member(s): 7; 900 volunteer(s)
Membership: 1,000; *Fees:* $15 students; $20 seniors; $25 individuals; $30 families, institutions, & foreign members; $600 lifetime members; *Member Profile:* Naturalists in Saskatchewan
Activities: Conducting research; Providing education; Producing special publications, such as: Ferns & Fern Allies; Lilies, Irises & Orchids; Dragonflies & Damselflies in the Hand; Getting to know Saskatchewan Lichens; *Speaker Service:* Yes; *Library:* Nature Saskatchewan Resource Centre
Chief Officer(s):
Jordan Ignatiuk, Executive Director
jignatiuk@naturesask.ca
Lacey Weekes, Manager, Conservation & Education
lweekes@naturesask.ca
Melissa Ranalli, Manager, Species at Risk
mranalli@naturesask.ca
Becky Quist, Office Coordinator
Awards:
• Volunteer of the Year Award
• Cliff Shaw Award
• Fellows Award
• Larry Morgotch Memorial Award
• Conservation Award
Publications:
• Blue Jay
Type: Journal; *Accepts Advertising*; *Editor:* Chris Somers; Vicky Kjoss; *Price:* $25 / year
Profile: Conservation, nature, & scientific research news, plus artwork & poetry

- Nature Views
Type: Newsletter; *Frequency:* Quarterly; *Accepts Advertising*; *Editor:* Robert Warnock; Angela Dohms; *Price:* Free with Nature Saskatchewan membership
Profile: Discussions of environmental issues, contributions from well known naturalists, & forthcoming events

Fort Qu'Appelle Branch
PO Box 294, Balcarres SK S0G 0C0
Tel: 306-334-2862
Chief Officer(s):
Keith Stephens, President

Indian Head Natural History Society
PO Box 995, Indian Head SK S0G 2K0
Chief Officer(s):
Irv Escott, President, 306-695-3987

Kelsey Ecological Society
PO Box 549, Preeceville SK S0A 3B0
Tel: 306-547-2008
Chief Officer(s):
Kathleen Pitt, President
kathleentpitt@icloud.com

Nature Moose Jaw
Moose Jaw SK
Chief Officer(s):
Lorna Arnold, Coordinator

Nature Prince Albert
PO Box 235, Prince Albert SK S6V 5R5

Nature Regina
PO Box 291, Regina SK S4P 3A1
natureregina@gmail.com
Chief Officer(s):
Gary Seib, President

Saskatoon Nature Society
PO Box 448, RPO University, Saskatoon SK S7N 4J8
Tel: 306-665-1915
www.saskatoonnaturesociety.sk.ca
www.facebook.com/SaskatoonNatureSociety
Chief Officer(s):
Joan Feather, President, 306-653-3160
jfeather@sasktel.net

Southwest Naturalists
370 - 4th Ave. SE, Swift Current SK S9H 3L8
Tel: 306-778-2775
info@swnaturalists.org
www.swnaturalists.org
Chief Officer(s):
Gerald Handley, President

Weyburn Nature Society
PO Box 131, McTaggart SK S0G 3G0
Chief Officer(s):
Val Thomas, Secretary, 306-842-5005
van_doyle_thomas@hotmail.com

Yellowhead Flyway Birding Trail Association
PO Box 460, Saltcoats SK S0A 4R0
yfbta.com
Chief Officer(s):
Rob Wilson, Secretary

Yorkton Natural History Society
45 Darlinton St. East, Yorkton SK S3N 0C3
Chief Officer(s):
Geoffrey Rushowick, President, 306-783-5898
rushg@sasktel.net

Nature Trust of New Brunswick (NTNB) / Fondation pour la protection des sites naturels du Nouveau-Brunswick
PO Box 603, Stn. A, 404 Queen St., 3rd Fl., Fredericton NB E3B 5A6
Tel: 506-457-2398; *Fax:* 506-450-2137
naturetrust@ntnb.org
www.naturetrust.nb.ca
www.linkedin.com/company/the-nature-trust-of-new-brunswick
www.facebook.com/NatureTrustNB
twitter.com/naturetrustNB
www.youtube.com/user/NatureTrustNB
Overview: A small provincial charitable organization founded in 1987
Mission: To identify, classify & preserve natural areas which are outstanding for their biological, geological or aesthetic value; to foster in the people of New Brunswick an awareness of their natural heritage & to educate persons in connection therewith
Finances: *Annual Operating Budget:* $500,000-$1.5 Million; *Funding Sources:* Donations; Government grants; Membership dues

Staff Member(s): 7
Membership: *Fees:* $25 individual; $35 family/group; $75 supporting; $150 sponsoring; $250 donor; $500 benefactor; $10 student; $1000+ corporate; $5000 lifetime; *Committees:* Partnership; Membership; Communications; Nomination
Chief Officer(s):
Renata Woodward, Executive Director
Lynn MacKinnon, President
Mike Bonga, Vice-President
Andy Hardie, Treasurer

Nature Vancouver
PO Box 3021, Vancouver BC V6B 3X5
Tel: 604-737-3074
info@naturevancouver.ca
www.naturevancouver.ca
www.facebook.com/naturevancouver
Previous Name: Vancouver Natural History Society
Overview: A small local charitable organization founded in 1918
Mission: To promote the enjoyment of nature; to foster public interest & education in appreciation & study of nature; To encourage wise use & conservation of natural resources; To work for complete protection of endangered species & ecosystems; To promote access to & maintenance of natural areas in vicinity of Vancouver
Member of: The Federation of BC Naturalists
Affiliation(s): Nature Canada
Finances: *Annual Operating Budget:* $50,000-$100,000; *Funding Sources:* Membership fees
100 volunteer(s)
Membership: 700; *Fees:* $40 individual; $50 family; $20 student; *Committees:* Conservation; Birding; Botany; Marine Biology
Activities: Marsh & bog restoration; bird & plant survey; conservation - briefs, forums & public information meetings; monthly speakers; annual summer camp to allow participants to learn about a special wilderness area in the province
Awards:
- Nature Vancouver Annual Scholarship
Eligibility: Members or members' families

Naut'sa mawt Resource Group (NRG)
1921 Tsawwassen Dr., Tsawwassen BC V4M 4G2
Tel: 604-943-6712; *Fax:* 604-943-5367
Toll-Free: 888-382-7711
info@nautsamawt.com
www.nautsamawt.com
Previous Name: Naut'sa mawt Tribal Council, The Alliance Tribal Council
Overview: A medium-sized local organization founded in 1975
Mission: To advance the Aboriginal rights, & the concept of Indian self-government; To provide services in the fields of oil & gas, construction, manufacturing, & project management

Naut'sa mawt Tribal Council, The Alliance Tribal Council
See Naut'sa mawt Resource Group

Naval Club of Toronto
1910 Gerrard St. East, Toronto ON M4L 2C1
Tel: 416-924-2811
info@navalcluboftoronto.com
www.navalcluboftoronto.com
Previous Name: Naval Veterans Association
Overview: A small local organization
Staff Member(s): 4; 3 volunteer(s)
Membership: *Committees:* Budget & Finance
Chief Officer(s):
Joeann Coulson, Chief Steward
Michael A. Roger, President
Publications:
- Telegraph
Type: Newsletter; *Frequency:* Monthly

Naval Museum of Alberta Society (NMAS)
4520 Crowchild Trail SW, Calgary AB T2T 5J4
Tel: 403-974-2807
Previous Name: Tecumseh Historical Society
Overview: A small local charitable organization founded in 1984
Mission: To promote an awareness & understanding of the role played by the Royal Canadian Navy to our country, province & community, with emphasis on naval establishments in Alberta & those HMC ships that were named for cities, towns & communities in the province of Alberta
Member of: Alberta Museums Association; Calgary Convention & Visitors Bureau
Affiliation(s): Museum Association of Canada

Finances: *Annual Operating Budget:* $50,000-$100,000; *Funding Sources:* Donations
Staff Member(s): 1; 75 volunteer(s)
Membership: 300; *Fees:* $20; *Member Profile:* Retired military; students & scholars of military history
Activities: Naval Museum of Alberta; *Awareness Events:* Battle of Atlantic Day, May 2; Remembrance Day Service, Nov. 11
Library: John Burgess Library; by appointment
Chief Officer(s):
Glenn Hardie, President
Terry Thompson, Vice-President
Murray Bialek, General Manager, Naval Museum of Alberta

The Naval Officers' Association of Canada (NOAC) / L'Association des officiers de la marine du Canada
c/o Ottawa Branch, PO Box 505, Stn. B, Ottawa ON K1P 5P6
Tel: 613-841-4358
noacexdir@msn.com
www.navalassoc.ca
Overview: A medium-sized national organization founded in 1946
Mission: To maintain active interest in the Maritime affairs of Canada; To oversee 15 member branches in major cities from coast to coast & a member branch in Brussels, Belgium
Finances: *Funding Sources:* Membership dues; Grants; Donations
Membership: *Member Profile:* Former career officers & reserve officers who have served in the several components of the Royal Canadian Navy or the Maritime Command of the Canadian Forces
Activities: *Library:* by appointment
Chief Officer(s):
Jim Carruthers, President
jimc@rruthers.com
Ken Lait, Executive Director

Naval Veterans Association *See* Naval Club of Toronto

Navy League of Canada / Ligue navale du Canada
#201, 1505 Laperriere Ave., Ottawa ON K1Z 7T1
Toll-Free: 800-375-6289
info@navyleague.ca
www.navyleague.ca
www.facebook.com/navyleaguecanada
twitter.com/NavyLeagueCA
Overview: A large national organization founded in 1895
Mission: To promote an interest in maritime affairs generally throughout Canada; To prepare, publish & disseminate information & encourage debate relating to the role & importance of maritime matters in the interests of Canada; To promote, organize, sponsor, support & encourage the education & training of the youth of the country through Cadet movements & other youth groups with a maritime orientation; To hold conferences, symposia & meetings for the discussion & exchange of views in matters relating to the objects of The League; To raise funds as may be deemed necessary, for the welfare & benefit of seamen, for their dependents & for Seamen's Homes, Hostels & other institutions in Canada, including the establishment, operation & maintenance thereof; To co-operate with any kindred society having either in whole or in part comparable objects to The League
Member of: National Cadet Council
Affiliation(s): Conference of Defence Associates; Department of National Defence; The Army Cadet League of Canada; The Air Cadet League of Canada
Finances: *Funding Sources:* Donations; government grant
Staff Member(s): 3
Activities: *Library:* by appointment Not open to public
Chief Officer(s):
Earle Corn, National President
Awards:
- Rear-Admiral Fred Mifflin Memorial Scholarship
Awarded to an active Sea Cadet entering an accredited post-secondary maritime program; *Amount:* $3,000
- Lockheed Martin Centennial Award
Awarded to serving & former Royal Canadian Sea Cadets entering their first year in university or college
- Robert I. Hendy Award
- J.J. Kinley Award
Meetings/Conferences:
- The Navy League of Canada 2018 Annual General Meeting, 2018
Scope: National

Cape Breton
821 Donkin Hwy., Donkin NS B1A 6N9
Tel: 902-737-2257

Chief Officer(s):
Jack Griffin, President
jgriffin@navyleague.ca

Manitoba
c/o HMCS Chippawa, 1 Navy Way, Winnipeg MB R3C 4J7
www.mb.navyleague.ca
Chief Officer(s):
Debra Barrett, President
dbarrett@navyleague.ca

Newfoundland & Labrador
5 Davis Pl., Mount Pearl NL A1N 3W8
Tel: 709-368-5620; *Fax:* 709-758-9709
Chief Officer(s):
Clayton Bailey, President
cbailey@navyleague.ca

Nova Scotia Mainland
c/o Earle Corn, 65 Grennan Dr., Lower Sackville NS B4C 2C4
Tel: 902-864-8156
www.nsmainlanddivision.ca
Chief Officer(s):
Earle Corn, President
ecorn@navyleague.ca

Ontario
#600, 4900 Yonge St., Toronto ON M2N 6B7
Tel: 416-635-2791; *Fax:* 416-635-2794
Toll-Free: 877-635-2791
navyleag@bellnet.ca
www.navyleagueont.ca
www.facebook.com/NLOntDiv
Chief Officer(s):
Gordon King, President
gking@navyleague.ca

Prince Edward Island
c/o Lise Munger, 2474 Fort Augustus, RR#21, Glenfinnan PE C1B 0Z9
Tel: 902-892-4642
Chief Officer(s):
Reg Shields, President
rshields@navyleague.ca
Lise Munger-Perry, Sec.-Treasurer
lmunger@ymail.com

Québec
a/s Jean-Claude Poirier, Unité régionale de soutien aux cadets (est), CP 1000, Succ. Forces, Courcelette QC G0A 4Z0
Tél: 800-681-8180
division@liguenavaleducanada.qc.ca
www.liguenavaleducanada.qc.ca
Chief Officer(s):
Germain Poitras, Président
president@liguenavaleducanada.qc.ca
Jacques Aubrey, Secrétaire
secretaire@liguenavaleducanada.qc.ca

Saskatchewan
1860 Lorne St., Regina SK S4P 2L7
Tel: 306-780-9294
Toll-Free: 877-335-7245
nlcsd@sasktel.net
www.nlcsd.ca
Chief Officer(s):
Marty Mollison, President

Vancouver Island
PO Box 28143, Stn. Canwest, Victoria BC V9B 6K8
www.vidcadets.ca
Chief Officer(s):
Peter Betcher, President
vid.pres@vidcadets.ca
Mike Dietrich, Treasurer
vid.tres@vidcadets.ca

Nawican Friendship Centre
1320 - 102 Ave., Dawson Creek BC V1G 2C6
Tel: 250-782-5202; *Fax:* 250-782-8411
community@nawican.ca
Overview: A small local organization founded in 1971

Ne'Chee Friendship Centre
PO Box 241, 1301 Railway St., Kenora ON P9N 3X3
Tel: 807-468-5440; *Fax:* 807-468-5340
reception@nechee.org
www.nechee.org
Overview: A small local charitable organization founded in 1976
Member of: Ontario Federation of Indian Friendship Centres; National Association of Friendship Centres
Staff Member(s): 24

Membership: *Member Profile:* All persons of aboriginal descent
Chief Officer(s):
Patti Fairfield, Executive Director
aces@nechee.org

NEC Native Education College Society
285 East 5th Ave., Vancouver BC V5T 1H2
Tel: 604-873-3772; *Fax:* 604-873-9152
info@necvancouver.org
www.necvancouver.org
Previous Name: Urban Native Indian Education Society
Overview: A small local organization founded in 1967
Mission: To provide adult Aboriginal students with developmental, vocational, & applied academic programs
Affiliation(s): Vancouver Community College
Finances: *Annual Operating Budget:* $3 Million-$5 Million
Staff Member(s): 40
Membership: 1-99; *Fees:* $2
Activities: *Library:* NEC Library
Chief Officer(s):
Dan Guinan, President
Awards:
• First Nations Health Careers Bursary Program
; *Amount:* A limited number of bursaries up to $2,500

Nechi Training, Research & Health Promotions Institute
PO Box 2039, Stn. Main, St. Albert AB T8N 2G3
Tel: 780-459-1884; *Fax:* 780-458-1883
Toll-Free: 800-459-1884
www.nechi.com
Also Known As: Nechi Institute
Overview: A small international charitable organization founded in 1974
Mission: To promote holistic healing & healthy, addictions-free lifestyles
Member of: Canadian Society of Association Executives
Affiliation(s): First Nations Adult & Higher Education Consortium
Staff Member(s): 7
Activities: Training; Aboriginal population health research; health promotions; *Internships:* Yes *Library:* Aboriginal Resource Centre; Open to public
Chief Officer(s):
Geraldine Potts, Director, Operations

Neepawa & District Chamber of Commerce
PO Box 726, 282 Hamilton St., Neepawa MB R0J 1H0
Tel: 204-476-5292; *Fax:* 204-476-5231
info@neepawachamber.com
www.neepawachamber.com
Overview: A small local organization founded in 1900
Mission: To promote Neepawa Manitoba & the surrounding area
Member of: Yellowhead Highway Association; Manitoba Chamber of Commerce; Canadian Chamber of Commerce
Finances: *Funding Sources:* Membership dues; Projects; Grants
Membership: *Member Profile:* Business owners

Neepawa & District United Way
PO Box 1545, Neepawa MB R0J 1H0
Tel: 204-476-3410
unitedwayneepawa@mymts.net
www.neepawaunitedway.org
Overview: A small local organization overseen by United Way of Canada - Centraide Canada
Mission: Local United Way Chapter raising funds to help community organization.

Neginuk Friendship Centre *See* Kikinahk Friendship Centre

Neighbourhood Information Post (NIP)
269 Gerrard St. East, 2nd Fl., Toronto ON M5A 2G3
Tel: 416-924-2543; *Fax:* 416-924-4748
nipost@nipost.org
www.nipost.org
twitter.com/nip_toronto
Overview: A small local organization founded in 1970
Mission: Non-profit community help centre established to provide information, assistance & support to all persons in order to improve the quality of individual & community life; serves the eastern area of the City of Toronto
Member of: Association of Community Information Centres in Ontario
Affiliation(s): Advocacy Centre for Tenants Ontario; African Women

Finances: *Funding Sources:* Municipal, provincial & federal government; United Way
Activities: Toronto Rent Bank program; Energy Assistance programs; Community outreach & education; Crisis intervention; Housing Trusteeship program; Immigrant women's support group; Income tax clinic; Self-help drop in; Senior activities

Neighbourhood Pharmacy Association of Canada
#301, 45 Sheppard Ave. East, Toronto ON M2N 5W9
Tel: 416-226-9100; *Fax:* 416-226-9185
info@neighbourhoodpharmacies.ca
www.cacds.com
Overview: A small national organization founded in 1995
Mission: Neighbourhood Pharmacy Association of Canada strives to ensure a strong chain drug store sector access to high quality products & health care services to Canadians.
Finances: *Funding Sources:* Membership dues; programs
Membership: *Member Profile:* Retail members include chain drug stores, grocery chains, & mass merchandisers with pharmacies. Associate members include suppliers & service providers to the retail pharmacy industry.
Activities: Promoting the role & value of chain pharmacies & their pharmacists; Communicating issues to governments & regulators; Working with suppliers to increase consumer satisfaction; Providing information to members about industry issues; *Library:* Neighbourhood Pharmacy Association of Canada Documentation Centre
Chief Officer(s):
Denise Carpenter, President/CEO
Vivek Sood, Chair
Publications:
• CACDS [Canadian Association of Chain Drug Stores] News Bulletin
Type: Newsletter; *Frequency:* Weekly
Profile: CACDS achievements, member news, & national industry issues
• State of the Industry Report [a publication of the Canadian Association of Chain Drug Stores]
Type: Yearbook; *Frequency:* Annually; *Price:* $80.25 members; $215 non-members
Profile: Report on community pharmacy trends in Canada

The Neighbouring Rights Collective of Canada *See* Re:Sound Music Licensing Company

The Neil Squire Foundation (NSF)
#220, 2250 Boundary Rd., Burnaby BC V5M 3Z3
Tel: 604-473-9363; *Fax:* 604-473-9364
Toll-Free: 877-673-4636
info@neilsquire.ca
www.neilsquire.ca
www.linkedin.com/company/neil-squire-society
www.facebook.com/neilsquiresoc
twitter.com/NeilSquireSoc
www.youtube.com/user/NeilSquireSociety
Overview: A medium-sized national organization founded in 1984
Mission: To respond to the needs of individuals who have significant physical disabilities; to research & develop appropriate innovative technology & services; to create opportunities for greater independence in all aspects of life
Finances: *Annual Operating Budget:* Greater than $5 Million; *Funding Sources:* National government; provincial government
Membership: *Committees:* Client Services; Audit & Financial Management; Technology & Partnership; Marketing; Fundraising; Nominations
Chief Officer(s):
Greg Pyc, National Operations Manager
Gary Birch, Executive Director

Atlantic Regional Office
#104, 440 Wilsey Rd., Fredericton NB E3B 7G5
Tel: 506-450-7999; *Fax:* 506-453-9681
Toll-Free: 866-446-7999
nb.info@neilsquire.ca
Chief Officer(s):
Diana Hall, Regional Manager
dianah@neilsquire.ca

Central Regional Office
#150, 34 Colonnade Rd., Ottawa ON K2E 7J6
Tel: 613-723-3575; *Fax:* 613-723-3579
on.info@neilsquire.ca
Chief Officer(s):
Cheryl Comer, Regional Manager
cherylc@neilsquire.ca

Prairie Regional Office
#100, 2445 - 13th Ave., Regina SK S4P 0W1

Tel: 306-781-6023; *Fax:* 306-522-9474
sk.info@neilsquire.ca
Chief Officer(s):
Nikki Langdon, Regional Manager
nikkil@neilsquire.ca

Nellie's Shelter
PO Box 98118, 970 Queen St. East, Toronto ON M4M 1J8
Tel: 416-461-8903; *Fax:* 416-461-0970; *Crisis Hot-Line:* 416-461-1084
community@nellies.org
www.nellies.org
www.facebook.com/nelliesshelter
twitter.com/nelliesshelter
www.youtube.com/user/nelliesshelter
Overview: A small local charitable organization founded in 1974
Mission: To advocate for social justice for all women & children
Finances: *Annual Operating Budget:* $500,000-$1.5 Million; *Funding Sources:* Ministry of Community and Social Services; City of Toronto; Canada Mortgage & Housing Corporation; United Way; Donations
Membership: *Member Profile:* Women over age 16 & community organizations
Chief Officer(s):
Margarita Mendez, Executive Director, 416-461-9849, Fax: 416-461-0970

Outreach Office
754 Queen St. East, Toronto ON M4M 1H4
Tel: 416-461-3404
Chief Officer(s):
Margarita Mendez, Executive Director

Nelson & District Arts Council (NDAC)
PO Box 422, Nelson BC V1L 5R2
Tel: 250-352-2402; *Fax:* 250-352-2405
ndac@direct.ca
ndac.ca
www.facebook.com/NelsonDistrictArtsCouncil
Overview: A small local organization founded in 1969
Mission: To stimulate & encourage the development of cultural pride & activities; to render service to all participatory groups; to foster interest & pride in the cultural heritage of the district; to bring to the attention of governments the cultural needs of the district
Member of: Assembly of BC Arts Councils; BC Arts Council
Affiliation(s): West Kootenay Regional Arts Council; Columbia Kootenay Cultural Alliance
Finances: *Annual Operating Budget:* Less than $50,000
Staff Member(s): 1; 20 volunteer(s)
Membership: 20 groups + 3 individual + 3 associate; *Fees:* $25 group; $10 individual; *Member Profile:* Community art, cultural, heritage groups; *Committees:* Artwalk; Nelson Public Art Gallery Committee; Museum
Activities: Artwalk & Community Arts of all Disciplines Event
Chief Officer(s):
Pat Henman, Executive Director
Ron Robinson, President

Nelson & District Chamber of Commerce
91 Baker St., Nelson BC V1L 4G8
Tel: 250-352-3433; *Fax:* 250-352-6355
Toll-Free: 877-663-5706
info@discovernelson.com
www.discovernelson.com
Overview: A small local organization founded in 1893
Mission: To promote & improve trade & commerce & the economic, civic & social welfare of the City of Nelson & the surrounding districts; To support & advance the interests of its members in local, provincial & national issues
Affiliation(s): British Columbia Chamber of Commerce; Canadian Chamber of Commerce
Finances: *Annual Operating Budget:* $100,000-$250,000
Staff Member(s): 3
Membership: 460; *Fees:* $150 regular; $100 associate/non-profit; $75 private citizen; *Committees:* Tourism; Resource; Economic Development; Education; Health
Activities: Organizing Canada Day event at Lakeside Park; *Library:* Open to public
Chief Officer(s):
Ed Olthof, President

Nelson & District Hospice Society
PO Box 194, Nelson BC V1L 5P9
Tel: 250-352-2337; *Fax:* 250-227-9017
nelsonhospice@netidea.com
www.nelsonhospice.org
Overview: A small local charitable organization
Mission: To offer hospice & palliative care in the Nelson & District region
Chief Officer(s):
Jane DiGiacomo, Executive Director

Nelson & District Museum, Archives, Art Gallery & Historical Society; Kootenay Museum Association & Historical Society *See* Touchstones Nelson Museum of Art & History

The Neocatechumenal Way
Tel: 905-951-2155
neocatechumenalcanada@gmail.com
www.camminoneocatecumenale.it
Overview: A small international charitable organization founded in 1964
Mission: To assist the church to renew herself in response to Vatican II, The Neocatechumenal Way started during the Second Vatican Council; To send missionaries from all parts of the world to evanglize & to be a Christian presence; To gift the Church with Redemptoris Mater Seminaries
Finances: *Funding Sources:* Donations
Membership: *Member Profile:* Members are Christian baptized adults; The charism of the Neocatechumenal Way is the rediscovery of the gift of Christian baptism through an itinerary of Christian formation; Everyone may freely participate in the catecheses, especially the following groups: Those who have drifted away from the Church; Persons who have not been sufficiently evangelized; Individuals who wish to deepen & mature their faith; & Those who come from Christian denominations not in full communion with the Catholic Church; The Neocatechumenal Way is represented in more than 100 countries around the world
Activities: Implementing The Neocatechumenal Way in Dioceses at request of the local Ordinary; Operating under the direction of the local Ordinary with the help & guidance of an international team, a national team, the parish priest, & the community Responsibles; Counselling; Offering programs for couples, seniors, singles, & youth; Providing faith instruction; Offering prayer groups; Presenting catecheses in parishes at the request of pastors; Giving a series of catecheses in parishes during Advent & Lent
Chief Officer(s):
Mario De Marchi, Contact

Nepali Children's Education Project (NCEP)
55 Sunnybrae Cres., Toronto ON M6M 4W6
Tel: 416-899-9904
info@nceponline.org
www.nceponline.org
Overview: A medium-sized international charitable organization
Mission: To help poor & orphaned Nepali children complete primary & secondary education
Finances: *Funding Sources:* Donations
Activities: Organizing fundraising initiatives in Canada; Developing sponsorship programs; *Awareness Events:* Light the Lamp, March
Chief Officer(s):
Sandeep Kembhavi, Chair

Nepisiguit Salmon Association (NSA) / L'Association du saumon Nepisiguit
789 Riverside Dr., Bathurst NB E2A 2M8
Tel: 506-546-5279
nsa@nbnet.nb.ca
Overview: A small local organization founded in 1976
Mission: To enhance & preserve Atlantic Salmon in general & in the Nepisiguit river in particular; to educate the public as to the value of this unique, renewable, natural resource
Member of: Atlantic Salmon Federation
Affiliation(s): New Brunswick Salmon Council; Nepisiguit Watershed Management Committee
Finances: *Funding Sources:* Donations; Grants; Programs; Fundraising
Membership: *Member Profile:* Anglers & those interested in salmon conservation
Activities: Salmon enchancement program
Chief Officer(s):
Bob Baker, President

Neptune Theatre Foundation
1593 Argyle St., Halifax NS B3J 2B2
Tel: 902-429-7300; *Fax:* 902-429-1211
Toll-Free: 800-565-7345
info@neptunetheatre.com
www.neptunetheatre.com
www.facebook.com/neptunetheatre
twitter.com/NeptuneTheatre
www.youtube.com/user/NeptuneHFX
Overview: A small local charitable organization founded in 1962
Mission: To pursue theatrical excellence with artistic vision; To develop local & Canadian artistic talent; To encourage the youth of our community to develop a life-long interest in live theatre
Finances: *Funding Sources:* Box office revenue; fundraising; government
Staff Member(s): 19
Chief Officer(s):
George Pothitos, Artistic Director

Netball Alberta
PO Box 270, 7620 Elbow Dr. SW, Calgary AB T2V 1K2
Tel: 403-238-8041; *Fax:* 888-213-9218
Other Communication: Registration Inquiries, E-mail: registration@netballalberta.com
contact@netballalberta.com
www.netballalberta.com
www.facebook.com/groups/2223869141
Previous Name: Alberta Netball Association
Overview: A small provincial charitable organization founded in 1992 overseen by Netball Canada
Mission: To promote & encourage the sport of netball in Alberta; to facilitate exchange of information & ideas; to promote education & development; to sponsor clinics & classes; to collect & distribute information; to raise funds for the Association; to organize & conduct competitions
Member of: Netball Canada
Affiliation(s): International Federation of Netball Associations
Finances: *Annual Operating Budget:* Less than $50,000; *Funding Sources:* Fundraising
10 volunteer(s)
Membership: 350
Chief Officer(s):
Julie Arnold, President
president@netballalberta.com

Netball Canada
AB
netballcanada@gmail.com
netballcanada.ca
www.facebook.com/netballcanada
twitter.com/NetballCanada
Overview: A small national organization founded in 1976
Mission: To be the national governing body for netball throughout Canada
Affiliation(s): International Federation of Netball Associations
Membership: 4 provincial associations

Netball Ontario
ON
info@netballontario.com
www.netballontario.com
www.facebook.com/NetballOntario
Previous Name: Ontario Amateur Netball Association
Overview: A small provincial organization founded in 1974 overseen by Netball Canada
Mission: To promote & develop the sport of netball in Ontario.
Member of: Netball Canada
Affiliation(s): International Federation of Netball Associations

Netherlands Business & Professional Association *See* Canadian Netherlands Business & Professional Association Inc.

Network of French Speaking Women of South Ontario *Voir* Réseau des femmes du sud de l'Ontario

Neurofibromatosis Association of Saskatchewan
450 Kirkpatrick Ct., Saskatoon SK S7L 6Z3
Tel: 306-384-3540
Also Known As: NF Association of Saskatchewan
Overview: A small provincial charitable organization founded in 1985
Affiliation(s): National NF Foundation
Finances: *Funding Sources:* Membership fees; Donations

Neurofibromatosis Society of Ontario (NFSO)
2004 Underhill Ct., Pickering ON L1X 2M6
Tel: 905-683-0811
Toll-Free: 866-843-6376
info@nfon.ca
www.nfon.ca
www.facebook.com/NFOntario
Also Known As: NF Society of Ontario
Overview: A small provincial charitable organization founded in 1985

Mission: To be a source of information; develop a participating membership; increase public awareness
Affiliation(s): National NF Foundation
Membership: Fees: $25
Activities: Support of NF research; educate members, professionals & public; support affected people
Chief Officer(s):
Angela Bobbett, President
a.bobbett@nfon.ca

Neurolodical Centre & Children's Centre for Ability; Vancouver Neurological Association See British Columbia Centre for Ability

Neurological Health Charities Canada (NHCC)
c/o Parkinson Canada, #316, 4211 Yonge St., Toronto ON M2P 2A9
Tel: 416-227-9700; Fax: 416-227-9600
Toll-Free: 800-565-3000
info@mybrainmatters.ca
www.mybrainmatters.ca
www.facebook.com/MyBrainMatters
twitter.com/MyBrainMatters
www.youtube.com/MyBrainMatters
Overview: A large national charitable organization
Mission: To improve quality of life for persons with chronic brain conditions & their caregivers; To increase awareness in the government about neurological issues; To support research
Membership: Member Profile: Organizations that relate to neurological conditions
Chief Officer(s):
Joyce Gordon, Chair
Publications:
• Brain Matters [a publication of Neurological Health Charities Canada]
Type: Newsletter; Frequency: s-a.

New Apostolic Church Canada
319 Bridgeport Rd. East, Waterloo ON N2J 2K9
Tel: 519-884-2862
Toll-Free: 866-622-7828
info@naccanada.org
www.naccanada.org
Overview: A medium-sized international organization
Mission: The New Apostolic Church takes a balanced approach to bible-based faith, recognizing three sacraments: Holy Baptism, Holy Sealing & Holy Communion.
Member of: New Apostolic Church (International)
Membership: 10 million internationally
Chief Officer(s):
E. Wagner, President
T. Witt, Treasurer

New Beginnings Association of Southern Alberta
2006 - 37 St. South, Lethbridge AB T1K 3T9
Tel: 403-328-6530; Fax: 403-394-0788
newbeginleth@shaw.ca
Overview: A small local organization founded in 1987
Mission: To provide day supports for adults with developmental disabilities
Finances: Funding Sources: Provincial government

New Beginnings for Youth (NBFY)
93 O'Connor St., Ottawa ON K1P 5M8
Tel: 613-236-1656
mail@nbfy.com
www.nbfy.com
Overview: A small local organization founded in 1986
Finances: Funding Sources: Donations
Activities: Variety of programs that encourage life-long learning outside of the traditional classroom, including: The Roasted Cherry, Java Journey, The Can, & Passport

New Boundaries
PO Box 1075, Windsor NS B0N 2T0
Tel: 902-798-5160; Fax: 902-798-5036
new.boundaries@live.ca
newboundaries.org
www.facebook.com/pages/NEW-BOUNDARIES/1398477490404943
Overview: A small local organization
Mission: To provide programs & work experience for mentally challenged adults
Activities: General contracts; cleaning; sorting; woodworking; community employment; Amigos second-hand clothing store
Chief Officer(s):
Marilyn Thomas, Executive Director

Publications:
• New Boundaries E-newsletter
Type: Newsletter

New Brunswick & Prince Edward Island Independent Adjusters' Association
c/o Greg Potten, AMG Claims Inc., #308, 212 Queen St., Fredericton NB E3B 1A8
Tel: 506-458-9000; Fax: 506-458-9595
www.ciaa-adjusters.ca
Overview: A small provincial organization overseen by Canadian Independent Adjusters' Association
Member of: Canadian Independent Adjusters' Association
Chief Officer(s):
Greg Potten, President
greg.potten@amgclaims.ca

New Brunswick Aboriginal Peoples Council (NBAPC)
320 St. Mary's St., Fredericton NB E3A 2S4
Tel: 506-458-8422; Fax: 506-451-6130
Toll-Free: 800-442-9789
www.nbapc.org
Overview: A medium-sized provincial organization founded in 1972 overseen by Congress of Aboriginal Peoples
Mission: To represent Status & Non-status First Nations who reside in New Brunswick
Finances: Funding Sources: Secretary of State; federal & provincial government
Staff Member(s): 15
Membership: Member Profile: Aboriginal ancestry
Activities: Aboriginal & Treat Rights; Aboriginal Human Resources Development Strategy; Aboriginal Fishery Strategy; Aboriginal Seafood Network; Community Diabetes Education & Prevention; Skigin-Elnoog Housing Corp.; Educational Assistance Program; Environmental & Health programs; youth; Wabanaki; employment; Aboriginal Sport Authority
Chief Officer(s):
Wendy Wetteland, Chief & President
chief@nbapc.org
Carol LaBillios-Slocum, Executive Director
executivedirector@nbapc.org

New Brunswick Aboriginal Women's Council
29 Big Cove Rd., Elsipogtog NB E4W 2S5
Tel: 506-523-9518; Fax: 506-523-8350
nbawca@nb.aibn.com
Previous Name: New Brunswick Native Indian Women's Council
Overview: A medium-sized provincial organization overseen by Native Women's Association of Canada
Chief Officer(s):
Sarah Rose, President

New Brunswick Aerospace & Defence Association (NBADA)
1630 Rte. 940, Centre Village NB E4L 1Y6
Tel: 506-878-3348
www.nbada.ca
Overview: A small provincial organization
Mission: To raise customer awareness of the services, products, & expertise provided by the New Brunswick aerospace, defence, & security sector; To develop the aerospace, defence, & security industry
Membership: Fees: Schedule available based on number of employees; Member Profile: Organizations in New Brunswick which supply technology & components to the aerospace, defence, & security sectors
Chief Officer(s):
Terry Malley, Chair & President
Kelly Ashfield, Treasurer
Peter Hess, Managing Director
peter.hess@nbada.ca

New Brunswick African Association Inc.
NB
nbaa.ca
Overview: A small provincial organization
Mission: To support the African community in New Brunswick
Chief Officer(s):
Andrew Gbongbor, President
sagyfly@yahoo.ca

New Brunswick Amateur Hockey Association See Hockey New Brunswick

New Brunswick Arts Board
649 Queen Street, 2nd Fl., Fredericton NB E3B 1C3
Tel: 506-444-4444; Fax: 506-444-5543
Toll-Free: 866-460-2787
artsnb.ca
www.facebook.com/artsnb
twitter.com/artsnb
Also Known As: artsnb
Previous Name: New Brunswick Arts Council Inc.
Overview: A medium-sized provincial charitable organization founded in 1979
Mission: To achieve the vision of New Brunswick as a place where all residents attend a diversity of quality, live performances in their own community; all students attend performances in their own school by performing artists; artists residing in New Brunswick find a supportive arts community & the resources necessary to establish a career in the performing arts in New Brunswick & beyond; maintain a resource centre; assume an advocacy for the performing arts in the community
Member of: Canadian Conference of the Arts
Finances: Annual Operating Budget: Less than $50,000; Funding Sources: Government grants; membership dues; blockbooking fees
Staff Member(s): 1; 20 volunteer(s)
Membership: 50 organizations; Fees: Schedule available; Member Profile: NB presenters, performers, musicians' unions, NB schools, arts councils, arts organizations, towns & municipalites, marketing & promotions firms; Committees: Executive; Membership; Nominations; Booking Services; Sponsorship & Fundraising
Activities: Coordination of provincial performing arts tours; coordination of NB school performances, young audience community performing arts series, promotion of the performing arts in NB; speakers series; booking services; Library: Not open to public
Chief Officer(s):
Akoulina Connell, Executive Director
Pierre McGraw, Chair

New Brunswick Arts Council Inc. See New Brunswick Arts Board

New Brunswick Association for Community Living (NBACL) / Association du Nouveau-Brunswick pour l'intégration communautaire
800 Hanwell Rd., Fredericton NB E3B 2R7
Tel: 506-453-4400; Fax: 506-453-4422
Toll-Free: 866-622-2548
nbacl@nbnet.nb.ca
www.nbacl.nb.ca
www.facebook.com/nbacl
twitter.com/nbacl
www.youtube.com/communitylivingnb
Overview: A medium-sized provincial charitable organization founded in 1957 overseen by Canadian Association for Community Living
Mission: To promote the welfare of people with handicaps & their families; To lobby for developmentally disabled people in New Brunswick; To ensure that every person in New Brunswick has access to supports to live with dignity & participate in the community of his/her choice
Member of: Canadian Association for Community Living
Finances: Funding Sources: Fundraising; Donations
Staff Member(s): 59
Membership: 26 branches
Activities: Speaker Service: Yes
Chief Officer(s):
Krista Carr, Executive Director
ea@nbacl.nb.ca
Tammy Gallant, Director, Finance & Office Administration
tammy@nbacl.nb.ca

New Brunswick Association of Community Business Development Corporations / L'Association des CBDC du Nouveau-Brunswick
Place Harbourview, PO Box 5, #212-R, 275 Main St., Bathurst NB E2A 1A9
Tel: 506-548-2406; Fax: 506-546-2661
Toll-Free: 888-303-2232
www.cbdc.ca/nb
www.facebook.com/AACBDC
twitter.com/CBDCatlantic
www.youtube.com/user/AtlanticCBDCs
Also Known As: New Brunswick Association of CBDCs
Overview: A medium-sized provincial organization
Mission: To assist entrepreneurs in New Brunswick's rural communities to access capital & other business resources

Membership: *Member Profile:* Not-for-profit organizations from local business communities which strive to improve the economic viability of their areas
Activities: Reviewing business plans; Working with entrepreneurs who experience difficulty securing capital from traditional sources; Providing term loans to businesses; Monitoring progress of clients; Counselling clients; Offering training opportunities
Chief Officer(s):
Line Doiron, Executive Director
line.doiron@cbdc.ca
Publications:
• New Brunswick Association of Community Business Development Corporations Annual Report
Type: Yearbook; *Frequency:* Annually

New Brunswick Association of Dietitians (NBAD) / Association des diététistes du Nouveau-Brunswick (ADNB)
PO Box 7022, Riverview NB E1B 4T8
Tel: 506-386-5903; *Fax:* 506-450-9375
registrar@adnb-nbad.com
www.adnb-nbad.com
Overview: A medium-sized provincial licensing organization overseen by Dietitians of Canada
Mission: To regulate & maintain excellence in dietetic practice in New Brunswick
Finances: *Annual Operating Budget:* Less than $50,000
Membership: 100-499; *Fees:* $345; *Committees:* Discipline; Legislation; Quality Assurance; Registration
Activities: *Awareness Events:* Nutrition Month, March
Chief Officer(s):
Nicole Arsenault Bishop, Executive Director & Registrar
registrar@adnb-nbad.com
Véronique Ferguson, President
president@adnb-nbad.com

New Brunswick Association of Family Resource Centres (NBAFRC)
c/o Fredericton Regional Family Resource Centre, 60 Veteran's Dr., Fredericton NB E3A 4C3
Tel: 506-474-0252
nbafrc@frc-crf.com
www.frc-crf.com
Overview: A medium-sized provincial organization
Mission: To promote child development & parent-child communication & bonding in New Brunswick's families; To increase awareness of issues encountered by New Brunswick families with children in the range of 0 to 6 years of age; To support family resource centres throughout New Brunswick; To sustain high standards for family resource centre employees
Finances: *Funding Sources:* Community Action Program for Children (CAPC)
Membership: 13; *Member Profile:* Family resource centres operating in New Brunswick
Activities: Developing & coordinating policies for family resource centres in New Brunswick; Engaging in advocacy activities at the municipal, provincial, & federal levels of government; Offering programs & activities for parents & children, such as support groups & parent education; Promoting family literacy; Increasing public awareness of child development & safety; Partnering with other education & health organizations in New Brunswick, such as Healthy Baby & Me; Enabling networking opportunities for family resource centres; *Library:* Toy & Resource Lending Libraries; Open to public

New Brunswick Association of Food Banks (NBAFB) / Association des banques alimentaires du Nouveau-Brunswick (ABANB)
4270, Rte. 102, Lower Kingsclear NB E3E 1L3
Tel: 506-363-4217; *Fax:* 506-473-6883
www.foodbanksnb.com
Previous Name: Association of Food Banks & CVAs for New Brunswick
Overview: A medium-sized provincial charitable organization founded in 1989
Mission: To support member agencies in their efforts to alleviate hunger; to serve as a provincial voice for same
Member of: Canadian Association of Food Banks
Finances: *Annual Operating Budget:* Less than $50,000
15 volunteer(s)
Membership: 47; *Fees:* $35
Activities: *Speaker Service:* Yes
Chief Officer(s):
George Piers, President
Stéphane Bourgoin, Vice-President

New Brunswick Association of Insolvency & Restructuring Professionals (NBAIRP)
c/o Grant Thornton Poirier Limited, #401, 133 Prince William St., Saint John NB E2L 2B5
Tel: 506-643-1727
Overview: A small provincial organization overseen by Canadian Association of Insolvency & Restructuring Professionals
Member of: Canadian Association of Insolvency & Restructuring Professionals
Chief Officer(s):
Matthew Munro, President
matthew.munro@ca.gt.com

New Brunswick Association of Medical Radiation Technologists (NBAMRT)
Memramcook Institute, #129, 488, rue Centrale, Memramcook NB E4K 3S6
Tel: 506-758-9673
www.nbamrt.ca
Previous Name: New Brunswick Association of Radiation Technologists; Canadian Association of Medical Radiation Technologists - New Brunswick
Overview: A small provincial organization founded in 1957 overseen by Canadian Association of Medical Radiation Technologists
Mission: To register medical radiation techologists in New Brunswick
Membership: *Member Profile:* Technologists from New Brunswick who operate radiographic & radiation therapy equipment to administer radiation treatment & to produce images of the body for diagnosis & treatment of injury & disease
Activities: Offering educational opportunities
Chief Officer(s):
Melanie Roybedy, Registrar

New Brunswick Association of Naturopathic Doctors (NBAND)
c/o Crystal Charest, 2278 King George Hwy., Miramichi NB E1V 6N6
Tel: 506-773-3700; *Fax:* 506-773-3704
www.nband.ca
twitter.com/NewBrunswickNDs
Overview: A small provincial organization overseen by The Canadian Association of Naturopathic Doctors
Mission: To educate the public on the philosophies and values of Naturopathic Medicine and to promote the profession within the province.
Membership: 15; *Fees:* $100 Associated Practitioner; $250 First Year Member; $500 Active Full Member; *Member Profile:* Naturopathic doctors
Chief Officer(s):
Crystal Charest, Contact

New Brunswick Association of Nursing Homes, Inc. (NBANH) / Association des foyers de soins du Nouveau-Brunswick, inc. (AFSNB)
#206, 1113 Regent St., Fredericton NB E3B 3Z2
Tel: 506-460-6262; *Fax:* 506-460-6253
communication@nbanh.com
www.nbanh.com
www.facebook.com/afsnb.nbanh
twitter.com/NBANH_AFSNB
Overview: A medium-sized provincial organization founded in 1972 overseen by Canadian Alliance for Long Term Care
Mission: To assist members in the provision of quality & efficient care to their residents
Member of: Canadian Alliance for Long Term Care
Finances: *Funding Sources:* Membership dues
Staff Member(s): 8
Membership: *Member Profile:* Licensed nursing homes in New Brunswick
Activities: *Awareness Events:* Nursing Home Week, June
Library: Resource Centre; Not open to public
Chief Officer(s):
Jean-Eudes Savoie, President
Michael Keating, Executive Director
mkeating@nbanh.com
Robert Stewart, Treasurer

New Brunswick Association of Occupational Therapists (NBAOT) / Association des ergothérapeutes du Nouveau-Brunswick
PO Box 184, Stn. A, Fredericton NB E3B 4Y9
Tel: 506-458-1001; *Fax:* 506-364-8464
info@nbaot.org
nbaot.org
Overview: A small provincial licensing organization founded in 1967
Mission: To license & to provide professional support to occupational therapists in New Brunswick
Member of: Canadian Association of Occupational Therapists
Finances: *Funding Sources:* Membership fees
Staff Member(s): 3
Membership: 367; *Fees:* $350; *Committees:* Awards; Archives; Public Relations; Clinical Practice; ErgOTour; Professioal Development; Registration; Complaints; Discipline/Appeals
Activities: *Awareness Events:* OT Week, Oct.; *Internships:* Yes; *Rents Mailing List:* Yes
Chief Officer(s):
Catherine Pente, Registrar, 506-536-4394, *Fax:* 888-896-2299
registrar@nbaot.org
Ellen Snider, Executive Director
executivedirector@nbaot.org
Awards:
• Evelyn Fleiger Award

New Brunswick Association of Optometrists (NBAO) / Association des optométristes du Nouveau-Brunswick
#1, 490 Gibson St., Fredericton NB E3A 4E9
Tel: 506-458-8759; *Fax:* 506-450-1271
nbao@nbao.ca
www.nbao.ca
Overview: A medium-sized provincial organization overseen by Canadian Association of Optometrists
Mission: To represent Doctors of Optometry in New Brunswick
Membership: *Member Profile:* Passed provincial board exams; graduate of recognized school of optometry
Activities: *Speaker Service:* Yes
Chief Officer(s):
Krista McDevitt, President

New Brunswick Association of Radiation Technologists; Canadian Association of Medical Radiation Technologists - New Brunswick See New Brunswick Association of Medical Radiation Technologists

New Brunswick Association of Real Estate Appraisers (NBAREA) / Association des évaluateurs immobiliers du Nouveau-Brunswick (AEIN-B)
#204, 403 Regent St., Fredericton NB E3B 3X6
Tel: 506-450-2016; *Fax:* 506-450-3010
nbarea@nb.aibn.com
www.nbarea.org
Overview: A medium-sized provincial licensing organization founded in 1995 overseen by Appraisal Institute of Canada
Mission: To enhance the profession & to protect the public
Finances: *Funding Sources:* Membership dues
Membership: 185; *Committees:* Examiners; Discipline; Complaints; Nominations, Elections & Public Relations; Standards; Membership & Public Relations
Activities: Education; government lobbying; *Internships:* Yes; *Speaker Service:* Yes; *Library:* NBAREA Library; Not open to public
Chief Officer(s):
Andrew Leech, President

The New Brunswick Association of Respiratory Therapists Inc. (NBART) / L'Association des thérapeutes respiratoires du Nouveau-Brunswick inc. (ATRNB)
500 St. George St., Moncton NB E1C 1Y3
Tel: 506-389-7813; *Fax:* 506-389-7814
Toll-Free: 877-334-1851
info@nbart.ca
www.nbart.ca
www.facebook.com/nbartinfo
twitter.com/nbart_info
Overview: A medium-sized provincial organization founded in 1984 overseen by Canadian Society of Respiratory Therapists
Mission: To protect the public by ensuring that the respiratory therapists practicing in the province of New Brunswick deliver safe & ethical care
Finances: *Annual Operating Budget:* Less than $50,000; *Funding Sources:* Membership dues
Staff Member(s): 1; 7 volunteer(s)
Membership: 400; *Fees:* $450; *Committees:* Complaints; Fitness to Practice & Discipline
Chief Officer(s):
Pam Taylor, President
president@nbart.ca
Troy Denton, Registrar
registrar@nbart.ca

Canadian Associations / New Brunswick Association of Social Workers (NBASW) / Association des travailleurs sociaux du Nouveau-Brunswick

Publications:
• New Brunswick Association of Respiratory Therapists Membership Registry
Type: Directory
Profile: A listing of active, associate, & student members

New Brunswick Association of Social Workers (NBASW) / Association des travailleurs sociaux du Nouveau-Brunswick
PO Box 1533, Stn. A, Fredericton NB E3B 5G2
Tel: 506-459-5595; *Fax:* 506-457-1421
Toll-Free: 877-495-5595
nbasw@nbasw-atsnb.ca
www.nbaslw-atsnb.ca
Overview: A medium-sized provincial licensing organization founded in 1965
Mission: To regulate the profession of social work; to protect the public; To set standards; To promote the profession
Member of: Canadian Association of Social Workers; Association of Social Work Boards
Finances: *Funding Sources:* Membership dues
Staff Member(s): 4
Membership: 1,600; *Fees:* $60 regular; $30 student; *Committees:* Examiners; Complaints; Discipline; Educaton; Social Action; By-Laws; Practice Issues, Ethics & Professional Standards; Scope of Practice
Chief Officer(s):
Miguel LeBlanc, Executive Director, 506-472-6148
mleblanc@nbasw-atsnb.ca

New Brunswick Association of Speech-Language Pathologists & Audiologists (NBASLPA) / Association des orthophonistes et des audiologistes du Nouveau-Brunswick
147 Ellerdale Ave., Moncton NB E1A 3M8
Tel: 506-858-1788; *Fax:* 506-854-0343
Toll-Free: 877-751-5511
nbaslpa@nb.aibn.com
www.nbaslpa.ca
Previous Name: New Brunswick Speech & Hearing Association
Overview: A small provincial licensing organization founded in 1976
Mission: To represent the professions of speech language pathology & audiology including registration of members which outlines requirements for working in New Brunswick
Member of: Canadian Association of Speech-Language Pathologists & Audiologists
Finances: *Annual Operating Budget:* Less than $50,000
6 volunteer(s)
Membership: 100-499; *Fees:* Schedule available; *Member Profile:* Individuals qualified for practice of speech-language pathology &/or audiology according specific standards; *Committees:* Legislation; Quality Assurance; Public Relations; Schools; Discipline; Translation; Audiology; Membership; Budget
Activities: *Awareness Events:* Speech & Hearing Month, May; *Rents Mailing List:* Yes
Chief Officer(s):
Darin Quinn, President
president.nbaslpa@gmail.com

New Brunswick Ball Hockey Association
NB
site2865.goalline.ca/index.php?league_id=53684
Overview: A small provincial organization
Member of: Canadian Ball Hockey Association
Membership: *Member Profile:* Ball hockey leagues throughout New Brunswick; *Committees:* Disciplinary
Activities: Establishing rules for ball hockey in New Brunswick; Maintaining high standards of officiating; Offering the Rookie Officiating Program

New Brunswick Beekeepers Association
488 Cape Breton Rd., Sainte Phillippe NB E1H 1W2
Tel: 506-388-5127
www.nbba.ca
Overview: A small provincial organization
Finances: *Funding Sources:* Membership dues
Membership: 250; *Fees:* Schedule available based on number of colonies
Chief Officer(s):
Calvin Hicks, President
cfhicks18@gmail.com
Brian M. Pond, Secretary-Treasurer
beehivePond@gmail.com

New Brunswick Branch of the Royal Caledonian Curling Club of Scotland *See* New Brunswick Curling Association

New Brunswick Building Officials Association (NBBOA) / L'Association des officiels de la construction du Nouveau-Brunswick
PO Box 3193, Stn. B, Fredericton NB E3A 5G9
Tel: 506-470-3375; *Fax:* 506-450-4924
admin@nbboa.ca
www.nbboa.ca
www.facebook.com/NBBOA
twitter.com/THENBBOA
Overview: A small provincial organization founded in 1976
Mission: To achieve & maintain the highest levels of professionalism in membership, education & qualifications; legislative interpretation; building inspection service; building & construction safety.
Staff Member(s): 3
Membership: 125; *Fees:* $250 regular; $500 corporate; *Member Profile:* Professionals; technicians; technologists; carpenters; tradesmen; *Committees:* Education; Publicity; Membership; Website; Certification
Activities: Certification courses; annual meetings; training; *Speaker Service:* Yes; *Rents Mailing List:* Yes
Chief Officer(s):
Sherry Sparks, President
sherry.sparks@moncton.ca
Robert Pero, Secretary
rob.pero@vonm.ca
Lucas Roze, Executive Director
lucas.roze@nbboa.ca

New Brunswick Camping Association (NBCA)
NB
nbcamping.ca
Overview: A small provincial organization overseen by Canadian Camping Association
Mission: To advance outdoor recreation in residential camps & day-camps in New Brunswick
Member of: Canadian Camping Association
Finances: *Funding Sources:* Sponsorships
Membership: *Member Profile:* Camps in New Brunswick that have met the association's standard for accreditation
Activities: Advocating the benefits of outdoor recreation; Developing an accreditation program; Providing educational opportunities, such as the annual directors' workshop & the annual counsellor conference; Distributing information; Creating networking opportunities
Chief Officer(s):
Rheal Williams, Director, Communications
Rheal.Williams@diabetes.ca

New Brunswick Candlepin Bowlers Association
7 Lilac Cres., Fredericton NB E3A 2G7
Tel: 516-472-7592
Overview: A medium-sized provincial organization
Mission: To promote candlepin bowling, a sport unique to the Maritimes & New England
Member of: Sport NB
Finances: *Funding Sources:* Provincial government
Chief Officer(s):
Don Leger, President

New Brunswick Cattle Marketing Agency *See* New Brunswick Cattle Producers

New Brunswick Cattle Producers (NBCP)
PO Box 1567, #302, 259 Brunswick St., Fredericton NB E3B 5G2
Tel: 506-458-8534; *Fax:* 506-453-1985
nbcattle@nb.aibn.com
www.bovinsnbcattle.ca
Previous Name: New Brunswick Cattle Marketing Agency
Overview: A small provincial organization founded in 1982
Mission: To promote, control, & regulate the production & marketing of cattle in New Brunswick; To advocate on behalf of cattle producers in New Brunswick; To develop competitive & efficient practices in the cattle producing industry
Affiliation(s): Canadian Cattlemen's Association (CCA); Maritime Beef Council (MBC)
Finances: *Funding Sources:* The collection of a mandatory $3.00 levy per head of cattle sold each year.
Membership: *Member Profile:* Beef cattle producers in New Brunswick
Activities: Undertaking research activities; Providing educational opportunities; Promoting the consumption & use of beef; Liaising with government, other sectors of the beef cattle industry, consumers, & the public
Chief Officer(s):

Cedric MacLeod, Chair, 506-472-8033
cedric@localvalleybeef.ca

New Brunswick Chamber of Commerce (NBCC)
1, ch Canada, Edmundston NB E3V 1T6
Tel: 506-737-1868; *Fax:* 506-737-1862
Overview: A medium-sized provincial organization founded in 1985
Staff Member(s): 2

New Brunswick Chiropractors' Association (NBCA) / Association des chiropraticiens du Nouveau-Brunswick
#206, 944 Prospect St., Fredericton NB E3B 9M6
Tel: 506-455-6800; *Fax:* 506-455-4430
comments@nbchiropractic.ca
www.nbchiropractic.ca
Overview: A medium-sized provincial licensing organization founded in 1958 overseen by Canadian Chiropractic Association
Mission: To regulate the practice of chiropractic medicine & govern its members in accordance with the Act & the by-laws, in order to serve & protect the public interests; To establish, maintain, develop & enforce standards of qualification for the practice of chiropractic, including the required knowledge, skill & efficiency; To establish, maintain, develop & enforce standards of professional ethics; To promote public awareness of the role of the Association & the work of chiropractic, & to communicate & cooperate with other professional organizations for the advancement of the best interests of the Association, including the publication of books, papers & journals; To encourage studies in chiropractic & provide assistance & facilities for special studies & research
Finances: *Funding Sources:* Membership fees
Membership: 65 active; *Member Profile:* Graduate of accredited chiropractic college & successful completion of Canadian Chiropractic Board Examinations & Jurisprudence exam; *Committees:* Admission; Complaint & Discipline; Finance; Government Relations; Marketing & Communications; Third Party Relations
Chief Officer(s):
Mohamed El-Bayoumi, Chief Executive Officer

New Brunswick Choral Federation (NBCF) / Fédération des chorales du Nouveau-Brunswick (FCNB)
Charlotte Street Arts Centre, #203, 732 Charlotte St., Fredericton NB E3B 1M5
Tel: 506-453-3731
nbcf@nbnet.nb.ca
nbchoral.blogspot.ca
Overview: A small provincial charitable organization founded in 1979
Mission: To promote & encourage the art of choral singing in New Brunswick at all levels
Staff Member(s): 1
Membership: 1,000; *Fees:* Schedule available; *Member Profile:* Individual singers & choirs/organizations
Activities: *Awareness Events:* Spring Choral Fest, April; New Brunswick Youth Choir, Oct. *Library:* Music Library
Chief Officer(s):
Dianne Roxborough Brown, Executive Director

New Brunswick Christmas Tree Growers Co-op Ltd. (NBCTGC) / Coop des Producteurs d'arbres de Noël du N.-B. (CPANNB)
226 Montgomery St., Fredericton NB E3B 2X1
Tel: 506-454-8252
Also Known As: The Christmas Tree Growers Association
Overview: A small provincial organization founded in 1976
Mission: To represent producers of natural christmas trees & related products in all matters pertaining to the viability of the industry
Member of: Canadian Christmas Tree Growers Association; National Christmas Tree Association (USA)
Affiliation(s): New Brunswick Agri-Environmental Council; The Tree House
Finances: *Funding Sources:* Membership fees; Ad revenue from newsletter
Membership: *Member Profile:* New Brunswick producer of two or more acres of Christmas trees
Activities: Field Day on the first Saturday in August
Awards:
• Annual Provincial Tree Competition

New Brunswick Coalition for Literacy *See* Literacy Coalition of New Brunswick

New Brunswick Coalition of Transition Houses/Centres for Abused Women
c/o Lynne Matheson, Secretary, PO Box 73, St Stephen NB E3L 2W9
Tel: 506-466-4590; *Fax:* 506-466-4487
frth@nb.aibn.com
Overview: A medium-sized provincial organization
Mission: To act as a provincial voice in advocating for abused women & their children
Membership: *Member Profile:* Made up of approximately 35 representatives from 12 shelters throughout the province
Chief Officer(s):
Lynn Matheson, Secretary

New Brunswick Competitive Festival of Music Inc.
PO Box 2022, Saint John NB E2L 3T5
Tel: 506-635-4128
www.nbfestivalofmusic.ca
Overview: A small provincial charitable organization founded in 1936
Mission: To hold a competitive & non-competitive music festival where students of all ages & music disciplines, including piano, vocal, strings, & band may meet, compete on a friendly basis & learn from expert adjudication
Affiliation(s): New Brunswick Federation of Music Festivals; Canadian Federation of Music Festivals
Staff Member(s): 1
Membership: *Member Profile:* Willingness to work as volunteer for music festival; *Committees:* Adjudicators; Awards; Syllabus; Advertising/Sponsors; Concerts; Program/Scheduling; Volunteers
Chief Officer(s):
Nadine Lane, Festival Administrator
Chris Titus, President

New Brunswick Construction Safety Association (NBCSA)
PO Box 731, 289 Dalton Ave., Miramichi ON E1V 3V4
Tel: 506-627-1477; *Fax:* 506-624-9581
Other Communication: Awards E-mail: awards@nbcsa.ca
info@nbcsa.ca
www.nbcsa.ca
Overview: A small provincial organization
Mission: To support the reduction of human, social & economic loss resulting from work-related accidents, injuries & death
Membership: *Fees:* Schedule available
Activities: E-Learning; JobLine employment service; information sessions; presentations; *Library:* Video Library; Not open to public
Chief Officer(s):
Roy Silliker, General Manager
rsilliker@nbcsa.ca
Awards:
• Safety Professional of the Year
• Leadership Award
• Best Practice
• Safety Star

New Brunswick Continuing Legal Education / Formation juridique permanente du Nouveau-Brunswick
c/o CBA - New Brunswick, 422 York St., Fredericton NB E3B 3P7
Tel: 506-452-7818; *Fax:* 506-459-7959
Toll-Free: 866-452-7818
cle@cbanb.com
www.nb-cba.org
Overview: A small provincial organization
Member of: Canadian Bar Association, New Brunswick
Activities: *Library:* by appointment
Chief Officer(s):
Ginette Little, CLE Program Coordinator

New Brunswick Council for Fitness & Active Living (NBCFAL); New Brunswick Fitness Council See Fitness New Brunswick

New Brunswick Crafts Council / Conseil d'artisanat du Nouveau-Brunswick
PO Box 1231, Stn. A, Fredericton NB E3B 5C8
Tel: 506-450-8989; *Fax:* 506-457-6010
Toll-Free: 866-622-7238
info@nbcraftscouncil.ca
www.nbcraftscouncil.ca
www.facebook.com/2411474486
Overview: A small provincial organization
Mission: To provide opportunities & support to members by developing, promoting & fostering an appreciation of excellence in craft.
Finances: *Annual Operating Budget:* $100,000-$250,000; *Funding Sources:* Provincial government
Staff Member(s): 4
Membership: *Fees:* $25 student; $55 individual; $65 associate; $85 juried craft individual; $125 friend
Chief Officer(s):
Natalie Landry, Executive Director
ed@nbcraftscouncil.ca
Kim Bent, President
kim.bent@unb.ca
Awards:
• Alfred J. Pringle Award for Ingenuity in Crafts
Awarded for devices, techniques &/or processes invented by the craftperson which will improve the quality of the item, lower the cost of production or extend the creative range of the craft; not awarded to the product but to the process *Eligibility:* All craftspeople who have resided in New Brunswick for the last three years *Deadline:* June 30; *Amount:* Two prizes of $250 each
• Strathbutler Award
Awarded in recognition of excellence in the crafts &/or visual arts in New Brunswick as wll as a substantail contribution to their respective fields ove a significant peiod of time (at least 10 years) *Eligibility:* Must be born in New Brunswick or have resided in New Brunswick for at least 10 full years & be actively pursuing a career in the fields of visual arts or fine crafts in New Brunswick *Deadline:* March; *Amount:* $10,000 *Contact:* Administered by Sheila Hugh Mackay
• Susan Vida Judah Travel Award
Created to help defray transportation expenses to help attend craft related conferences, seminars, workshops, courses ect., trade shows & exhibitions excluded unless applicant visiting with the plan to survey them for the purpose of participating at a later date *Eligibility:* Open to all craftspeople who have resided in New Brunswick for three years *Deadline:* March; *Amount:* Amount of regular return airfare to the event, to a maximum of $1,000
• Duffie-Crowell Award for Ecclesiastical Craft
Create to encourage craftspeople to work in the field of ecclesiastical craft & to ecourage religious insitituions to consider the talent withing the provinces when commissioning properties *Eligibility:* Open to anyone who has resided in New Brunswick for the last three years *Deadline:* April; *Amount:* $1,000

New Brunswick Cricket Association See Cricket New Brunswick

New Brunswick Curling Association (NBCA) / Association de Curling du Nouveau-Brunswick (ACNB)
c/o Marg Maranda, 65 Newcastle Centre Rd., Newcastle Centre NB E4B 2L2
Tel: 506-327-3445; *Fax:* 506-388-5708
Toll-Free: 800-592-2875
nbca@nb.sympatico.ca
www.nbcurling.com
Also Known As: Curling NB
Previous Name: New Brunswick Branch of the Royal Caledonian Curling Club of Scotland
Overview: A medium-sized provincial organization founded in 1971 overseen by Canadian Curling Association
Mission: To promote curling in New Brunswick; To establish & govern rules for curling competitions in New Brunswick
Member of: Canadian Curling Association / Association canadienne de curling
Affiliation(s): Curl Atlantic
Finances: *Funding Sources:* Canadian Curling Association; Curling Development Fund; Sponsorships
Membership: *Member Profile:* Members of affiliated curling clubs in New Brunswick
Activities: Organizing curling competitions; Offering learn-to-curl clinics, courses for coaching & instruction, & ice making; Supporting "Business of Curling Clinics"; Lending training equipment & resources
Chief Officer(s):
Marg Maranda, Executive Director
Damien Lahiton, President
damilahi@gmail.com

New Brunswick Dart Association (NBDA)
526 Rte. 845, Kingston NB E3N 1P5
Tel: 506-832-7293
www.nbdarts.com
Overview: A small provincial organization overseen by National Darts Federation of Canada
Mission: To provide recreational & competitive opportunities for darts players of all levels in New Brunswick
Member of: National Darts Federation of Canada
Chief Officer(s):
Rick Kirkpatrick, National Director, 506-609-2860
kirkpatrick@rogers.com
Debbie Mullin, National Youth Director, 506-696-0230
ikemullin@rogers.com
Bill White, President, 506-832-7293

New Brunswick Dental Assistants Association (NBDAA) / Association des Assistantes Dentaires du Nouveau-Brunswick (AADNB)
PO Box 8997, Shediac NB E4P 8W5
Tel: 506-532-9189; *Fax:* 506-532-3635
Toll-Free: 866-530-9189
nbdaa.ca
www.facebook.com/pages/NBDAA/309506835839025
Overview: A small provincial organization founded in 1975 overseen by Canadian Dental Assistants Association
Mission: To provide opportunities Dental Assistants in New Brunswick.
Member of: Canadian Dental Assitants' Association
Membership: 550+; *Fees:* $45 inactive/student; $100 regular
Chief Officer(s):
Amber Caissie, President
Bernice Léger, Office Coordinator
bernioff@nb.sympatico.ca

New Brunswick Dental Society / Société dentaire du Nouveau-Brunswick
HSBC Place, PO Box 488, Stn. A, #820, 520 King St., Fredericton NB E3B 4Z9
Tel: 506-452-8575; *Fax:* 506-452-1872
nbds@nb.aibn.com
www.nbdental.com
www.facebook.com/NBDentalSociety
twitter.com/NBDentalNB
Overview: A small provincial licensing organization founded in 1890 overseen by Canadian Dental Association
Mission: To regulate & promote the dentistry profession in New Brunswick; To support professional growth & ensure the provision of high standards & quality care
Membership: *Member Profile:* Licensed dentists
Activities: *Rents Mailing List:* Yes; *Library:* Open to public by appointment
Chief Officer(s):
Lia A. Daborn, Executive Director

New Brunswick Denturists Society / Société des denturologistes du Nouveau-Brunswick
PO Box 5566, 288 West Blvd. St. Pierre, Caraquet NB E1W 1B7
Tel: 506-727-7411; *Fax:* 506-727-6728
www.nbdenturistsociety.ca
Overview: A small provincial licensing organization founded in 1973 overseen by Denturist Association of Canada
Mission: To promote & support denturists in New Brunswick
Member of: Denturist Association of Canada
Chief Officer(s):
Daniel J. Robichaud, President
dentureguy@nb.aibn.com
Claudette Boudreau, Administrative Assistnat
claudetteboudreau@nb.aibn.com

New Brunswick Egg Marketing Board (NBEMB) / L'Office de commercialisation des oeufs de Nouveau Brunswick
#101, 275 Main St., Fredericton NB E3A 1E1
www.nbegg.ca
Overview: A small provincial organization founded in 1970
Affiliation(s): Canadian Egg Marketing Agency
Membership: 17

New Brunswick Environmental Network (NBEN) / Réseau environnemental du Nouveau-Brunswick (RENB)
167 Creek Rd., Waterford NB E4E 4L7
Tel: 506-433-6101; *Fax:* 506-433-6111
nben@nben.ca
www.nben.ca
www.facebook.com/renb.nben
Overview: A medium-sized provincial organization founded in 1991 overseen by Canadian Environmental Network
Mission: To strengthen the environmental movement throughout New Brunswick; To promote ecologically sound ways

Canadian Associations / New Brunswick Equestrian Association (NBEA)

of life
Affiliation(s): Canadian Environmental Network
Finances: *Funding Sources:* Environment Canada; Health Canada; NB Dept. of Environment; NB Dept. of Health; NB Dept. of Intergovernmental Affairs; NB Dept. of Natural Resources
Membership: *Member Profile:* Non-profit environmental organizations
Activities: Providing educational opportunities
Chief Officer(s):
Mary Ann Coleman, Executive Director
Joanna Brown, Coordinator, Youth Outreach & Events
Raissa Marks, Coordinator, Education & Outreach Programs
Meetings/Conferences:
• New Brunswick Environmental Network 2018 Annual General Meeting, 2018, NB
Scope: Provincial
Description: Featuring the election of a Steering Committee by member groups
Publications:
• Greenprint: Towards a Sustainable New Brunswick
Type: Report; *Number of Pages:* 16
Profile: Lead organizations include the New Brunswick Environmental Network, Canadian Parks & Wilderness Society - New Brunswick Chapter, Conservation Council of New Brunswick,Falls Brook Centre, Meduxnekeag River Association Inc., & Petitcodiac Riverkeeper
• Legal Information for Environmental Groups
Type: Guide; *Number of Pages:* 20
Profile: Topics include civil disobedience, property law, endangered species, & international law

New Brunswick Equestrian Association (NBEA)
#13, 900 Hanwell Rd., Fredericton NB E3B 6A3
Tel: 506-454-2353; *Fax:* 506-454-2363
horses@nbnet.nb.ca
www.nbea.ca
www.facebook.com/equinenb
twitter.com/equinenb
Overview: A small provincial organization
Mission: To promote equestrian & provide education in New Brunswick.
Member of: Equine Canada
Affiliation(s): New Brunswick SPCA; Maritime Saddle & Tack Ltd.; Government of New Brunswick; P'tit Trot; Greenhawk; Sport New Brunswick
Membership: *Fees:* $43 junior; $50 senior; $85 family
Activities: Recreation; Sport; Dressage; Hunter/jumper; Distance riding; Eventing; Racing; Driving; Coaching
Chief Officer(s):
Deanna Phelan, President
deannaphelan@gmail.com
Bonnie Robertson, Secretary
equinenb@gmail.com

New Brunswick Federation of Agriculture *See* Agricultural Alliance of New Brunswick

New Brunswick Federation of Dance Clubs *See* Federation of Dance Clubs of New Brunswick

New Brunswick Federation of Home & School Associations, Inc. (NBFHSA)
#202A, 212 Queen St., Fredericton NB E3B 1A8
Tel: 506-451-6247
www.nbfhsa.org
Overview: A medium-sized provincial organization founded in 1937 overseen by Canadian Home & School Federation
Mission: To ensure a quality education, enhanced by parental involvement, & a safe environment for all children
Finances: *Annual Operating Budget:* Less than $50,000; *Funding Sources:* Membership fees; government grant
Membership: 5,000 members + 152 provincial affiliates; *Fees:* $3; *Committees:* Health Issues; Literacy; Media Violence; Membership; Resolutions
Activities: Workshops for parents & teachers; *Speaker Service:* Yes
Chief Officer(s):
Leola Langille, President
leola.langille@gmail.com

New Brunswick Federation of Labour (NBFL) / Fédération des travailleurs et travailleuses du Nouveau-Brunswick
#314, 96 Norwood Ave., Moncton NB E1C 6L9
Tel: 506-857-2125; *Fax:* 506-383-1597
info@fednb.ca
www.nbfl-fttnb.ca
www.facebook.com/NewBrunswickFederationOfLabour
twitter.com/NBFL_FTTNB
Overview: A medium-sized provincial organization founded in 1914 overseen by Canadian Labour Congress
Mission: To act as the central voice of labour in New Brunswick; To build solidarity & support between unions; To advance the economic & social welfare of New Brunswick's workers
Finances: *Funding Sources:* Membership dues
Membership: 46,000 individuals in 375 local union affiliates + 8 labour councils; *Committees:* Political Education; Occupational Health, Safety, & Environment; Youth; Women's; Education
Activities: Assisting in organizing the unorganized into affiliated unions; Educating members, by hosting seminars & conferences; Liaising with government to discuss concerns of members; Influencing provincial legislation which will promote free collective bargaining & the rights of workers
Chief Officer(s):
Patrick Colford, President
John Gagnon, First Vice-President
Awards:
• James A. Whitebone Memorial Scholarships
• Tim McCarthy Environment Prize
• NBFL Solidarity Bursaries
• J. Harold Stafford Humanitarian Award
• Dermot Kingston Life Long Learning Award
Meetings/Conferences:
• New Brunswick Federation of Labour 54th Biennial Convention 2019, 2019, NB
Scope: Provincial
Description: A biennial gathering where approximately sixty resolutions are normally submitted & handled

New Brunswick Federation of Music Festivals Inc. (NBFMF) / La Fédération des festivals de musique du Nouveau-Brunswick inc. (FFMNB)
NB
info@nbfmf.org
nbfmf.org
Overview: A medium-sized provincial organization founded in 1973 overseen by Federation of Canadian Music Festivals
Finances: *Annual Operating Budget:* Less than $50,000
Chief Officer(s):
Barbara Long, Executive Director/President

New Brunswick Federation of Naturalists *See* Nature NB

New Brunswick Federation of Woodlot Owners Inc. / Fédération des propriétaires de lots boisés du Nouveau-Brunswick inc.
819 Royal Rd., Fredericton NB E3G 6M1
Tel: 506-459-2990; *Fax:* 506-459-3515
www.nbwoodlotowners.ca
Overview: A small provincial organization founded in 1965
Mission: To advocate for woodlot owners; To direct government policy as it affects private woodlots
Staff Member(s): 4
Chief Officer(s):
Andrew Clark, President
Ken Hardie, Manager

New Brunswick Fencing Association *See* Fencing - Escrime New Brunswick

New Brunswick Filmmakers' Co-op
PO Box 1537, 732 Charlotte St., Fredericton NB E3B 4Y1
Tel: 506-455-1632; *Fax:* 506-457-2006
info@nbfilmcoop.com
www.nbfilmcoop.com
Overview: A small provincial charitable organization founded in 1979
Mission: To operate a 16mm/digital video training centre for individuals interested in filmmaking
Affiliation(s): Independent Media Arts Alliance
Finances: *Annual Operating Budget:* Less than $50,000; *Funding Sources:* Federal, provincial & municipal government; corporate sponsors; memberships; equipment rental
Staff Member(s): 2
Membership: 150 individual; *Fees:* $30; *Member Profile:* Interest in film production; *Committees:* Production; Public Relations; Equipment & Materials; Workshops; Training
Activities: Screenings; workshops; committees; film productions; Tidal Wave Film Festival, Nov.; *Library:* Film Co-op Resource Centre; Open to public
Chief Officer(s):
Tony Merzetti, Executive Director

New Brunswick Food & Beverage Processors Association
See Atlantic Food & Beverage Processors Association

New Brunswick Forest Products Association Inc. (NBFPA) / L'Association des produits forestiers du Nouveau-Brunswick (APFNB)
Hugh John Flemming Forestry Centre, 1350 Regent St., Fredericton NB E3C 2G6
Tel: 506-452-6930; *Fax:* 506-450-3128
info@nbforestry.com
www.nbforestry.com
Overview: A small provincial organization founded in 1959
Mission: To represent forest industry members by serving as a common voice in relations with the government and the public, promoting a healthy New Brunswick forest, raise public awareness of sustainable forest management practices & provide a forum for the exchange of information, ideas & concerns.
Staff Member(s): 1
Membership: 31 organizations
Chief Officer(s):
Jacques Cormier, Chair

New Brunswick Fruit Growers Association Inc.
c/o NBFGA Scholarship Committee, #206, 1115 Regent St., Fredericton NB E3B 3Z2
nbapple@nbnet.nb.ca
Overview: A small provincial organization founded in 1904
Staff Member(s): 1
Membership: *Committees:* Scholarship
Chief Officer(s):
Euclide Bourgeois, President

New Brunswick Funeral Directors & Embalmers Association (NBFDEA)
515 Everard H. Daigle Blvd., Grand Falls NB E3Z 2R5
Tel: 506-473-3063; *Fax:* 506-473-3494
nbfdandea@nb.aibn.com
www.nbfuneraldirectors.ca
Overview: A small provincial organization
Mission: To promote quality Funeral Homes in the province of New Brunswick.

New Brunswick Genealogical Society Inc. (NBGS, Inc.) / Société Généalogique du Nouveau-Brunswick Inc.
PO Box 3235, Stn. B, Fredericton NB E3A 5G9
webmanager@nbgs.ca
www.nbgs.ca
Overview: A medium-sized provincial charitable organization founded in 1978
Mission: To promote & facilitate family historical research in New Brunswick
Finances: *Funding Sources:* Donations
Membership: *Fees:* $35; *Member Profile:* Individuals, families, & institutions interested in family historical research in New Brunswick
Chief Officer(s):
Stephanie Heenan-Orr, President
Ron Green, Treasurer
Shirley Graves, Secretary
Publications:
• Generations
Type: Journal; *Frequency:* Quarterly; *Number of Pages:* 68; *Editor:* George Hayward; *Price:* Free withNew Brunswick Genealogical Society Inc. membership
Profile: Genealogical related material associated with New Brunswick, such as rare documents, census information, passenger lists, cemeteries, book reviews, & upcoming genealogical seminars
• New Brunswick Genealogical Society Inc. Membership Directory
Type: Directory
• New Brunswick Genealogical Society Inc. Members' Surname Interests
Editor: Frank Morehouse & Stan Balch
Profile: Listing of family surnames being researched by NBGS members
• The New Brunswick Militia Commissioned Officers' List 1787-1867
Charlotte Branch
c/o Marguerite Garnett, 3701 Rte. 127 Bayside, St Andrews NB E5B 2T1
Chief Officer(s):
Marguerite Garnett, President

• 1861 Census of Charlotte County
Type: Book; *Price:* $35

Miramichi Branch
PO Box 403, Miramichi NB E1N 3A8
info@nbgsmiramichi.org
www.nbgsmiramichi.org
Mission: To promote the collection, preservation, & accessibility of genealogical materials in the Miramichi area
• Anglican Church Records of Northumberland County
Type: Book
Profile: Anglican Church marriage & baptism registers
• Cemetery Records of Northumberland County
Type: Book
Profile: Transcriptions of headstones from cemeteries in New Brunswick's Northumberland County
• Census Books of Northumberland County
Type: Book
Profile: Transcriptions of indexed census returns for Northumberland county in New Brunswick
• First Families of Northumberland County
Type: Book
Profile: Two volumes about the New Brunswick county's early families
• Marriage Stats from Northumberland County Newspapers
Type: Book
Profile: Three volumes of wedding announcements from the county's local newspapers
• NBGS Miramichi Newsletter
Type: Newsletter; *Frequency:* Quarterly; *Price:* Free with New Brunswick Genealogical Society Inc., Miramichi Branch, membership
Profile: Branch updates, current events, & genealogical information
• Obituary Books
Type: Book
Profile: Seven volumes of obituaries & funeral notices for New Brunswick's Northumberland County

Restigouche Branch
PO Box 5453, Dalhousie NB E8C 3C2
Chief Officer(s):
Suzanne Blaquière, President

Saint John Branch
PO Box 2423, 125 Rothesay Ave., Saint John NB E2L 3V9
info@nbgssj.ca
www.nbgssj.ca
Mission: To encourage the study of genealogy & family history in the Saint John area; To develop the preservation & research of family history; To promote the accessibility of heritage records
Chief Officer(s):
Carol Lee Elliot, President
Beverlee Gregg, Secretary
David Laskey, Treasurer
• Burial Records for Church of England Cemetery, Thorne Avenue
Editor: Lennox Bagnell; *Price:* $20
Profile: 6,766 recorded burials from 1837 to 1923
• New Brunswick Genealogical Society Inc. Saint John Branch Newsletter
Type: Newsletter; *Price:* Free with New Brunswick Genealogical Society Inc. Saint John Branch membership
Profile: Information for members, including upcoming meetings
• Records of Rev. James Gray
Price: $15

Southeastern Branch
PO Box 7102, Riverview NB E1B 4T8
Mission: To promote genealogy & genealogical research in New Brunswick's Westmorland, Albert, & Kent counties
• Cemeteries of Westmorland County: Dorchester Parish
Number of Pages: 335; *ISBN:* 978-0-9782223-2-1; *Price:* $42
Profile: An indexed list from twenty-three cemeteries situated in Dorchester Parish
• Cemeteries of Westmorland County: Moncton Parish
Number of Pages: 371; *ISBN:* 978-0-9782223-1-4; *Price:* $42
Profile: Listings of thiry-five cemeteries across Moncton Parish
• Cemeteries of Westmorland County: Sackville Parish
Number of Pages: 421; *ISBN:* 978-0-9782223-3-8; *Price:* $42
Profile: Listings of thirteen cemeteries located in Sackville Parish
• Cemeteries of Westmorland County: Salisbury Parish
Number of Pages: 197; *ISBN:* 0-9782223-0-X; *Price:* $22
Profile: Listings of twenty-six cemeteries located in Salisbury Parish
• Cemeteries of Westmorland County: Westmorland Parish
Number of Pages: 132; *ISBN:* 978-0-9782223-4-5; *Price:* $18

Profile: Listings of eleven cemeteries situated in Westmorland Parish
• News & Notes [a publication of the New Brunswick Genealogical Society Inc.]
Type: Newsletter

New Brunswick Golf Association (NBGA) / Association de golf du nouveau brunswick
PO Box 1555, Stn. A, Fredericton NB E3B 5G2
Tel: 506-451-1324; *Fax:* 888-307-2963
Toll-Free: 877-833-4662
info@golfnb.ca
www.golfnb.ca
Overview: A medium-sized provincial organization founded in 1934 overseen by Golf Canada
Mission: To determine policies & standards relating to the development & promotion of amateur golf in New Brunswick
Staff Member(s): 3
Membership: *Member Profile:* Amateur golfers at member clubs; *Committees:* Executive
Activities: Provincial amateur tournaments; programs & services for members clubs
Chief Officer(s):
Tyson Flinn, Executive Director
tflinn@golfnb.ca

New Brunswick Ground Search & Rescue Association (NBGSARA)
#247, 527 Beaverbrook Ct., Fredericton NB E3E 1X6
media@nbgsara.nb.ca
www.nbgsara.nb.ca
Overview: A small provincial organization
Mission: To represent the Province of New Brunswick's 11 regional ground search and rescue teams.
Membership: *Member Profile:* Ground search and rescue teams
Chief Officer(s):
Matt Cameron, President

New Brunswick Ground Water Association
1278 Route 260, St-Martin de Restigouche NB E8A 2M8
Tel: 506-235-5002
nbgwa@nb.sympatico.ca
www.nbgwa.ca
Overview: A small provincial organization
Mission: To preserve & protect New Brunswick's water; To promote education of members & the public; To encourage the development of ground water guidelines & strategies
Finances: *Annual Operating Budget:* Less than $50,000; *Funding Sources:* Membership dues
Membership: 42; *Fees:* $300
Chief Officer(s):
Danny Constantine, President
Terry Burpee, Sec.-Treas.

New Brunswick Guild of Dispensing Opticians *See* Opticians Association of New Brunswick

New Brunswick Gymnastics Association (NBGA) / Association gymnastique du Nouveau-Brunswick (AGNB)
1991 Route 112, Upper Cloverdale NB E1J 1Z1
Tel: 506-215-0085
nbga@gym.nb.ca
gym.nb.ca
www.facebook.com/NBGym
twitter.com/gymnasticsnb
www.youtube.com/user/GymnasticsNB
Overview: A small provincial organization founded in 1967
Mission: To promote gymnastics in New Brunswick
Member of: Gymnastics Canada Gymnastique
Staff Member(s): 1
Membership: 2500; *Committees:* Executive; Technical
Chief Officer(s):
Nathalie Colpitts-Waddell, Executive Director
director@gym.nb.ca
Diane Kirk, President
president@gym.nb.ca

New Brunswick Heart Foundation *See* Heart & Stroke Foundation of New Brunswick

New Brunswick Historical Society
Loyalist House, 120 Union St., Saint John NB E2L 1A3
Tel: 506-652-3590
info@LoyalistHouse.com
www.loyalisthouse.com
Overview: A medium-sized provincial charitable organization founded in 1874

Mission: To promote the study, research & discussion of New Brunswick history; to collect & preserve New Brunswick history; to publish & educate. The Society owns & operates Loyalist House.
Membership: *Fees:* $20 individual; $100 life
Activities: *Speaker Service:* Yes; *Library:* The Loyalist Library; Open to public by appointment

New Brunswick Hog Marketing Board *See* Porc NB Pork

New Brunswick Hospice Palliative Care Association
Fredericton Medical Clinic, #302, 1015 Regent St., Fredericton NB E3B 6H5
info@nbhpca-aspnb.ca
www.nbhpca-aspnb.ca
www.facebook.com/763652390348798
Previous Name: New Brunswick Palliative Care Association
Overview: A small provincial organization
Mission: To promote principles & standards for hospice palliative care in New Brunswick
Member of: Canadian Palliative Care Association
Finances: *Funding Sources:* Membership dues; Donations
Membership: *Fees:* $35 individual; $20 nurses group; $70 organization; *Member Profile:* Health care professionals, volunteers, & other individuals dedicated to ensuring access to quality end-of-life care for patients in New Brunswick
Chief Officer(s):
Renée Turcotte, President
president@nbhpca-aspnb.ca

New Brunswick Innovation Foundation
King Tower, #602, 440 King St., Fredericton NB E3B 5H8
Tel: 506-452-2884; *Fax:* 506-452-2886
Toll-Free: 877-554-6668
info@nbif.ca
www.nbif.ca
www.facebook.com/NBinnovation
twitter.com/nb_innovation
Overview: A medium-sized provincial organization
Mission: To help create business by investing in startup companies
Chief Officer(s):
Calvin Milbury, President & CEO

New Brunswick Institute of Agrologists (NBIA) / L'Institut des agronomes du Nouveau-Brunswick (IANB)
PO Box 3479, Stn. B, Fredericton NB E3B 5H2
Tel: 506-459-5536; *Fax:* 506-454-7837
www.ianbia.com
Overview: A small provincial organization founded in 1960 overseen by Agricultural Institute of Canada
Mission: To maintain high competency & professional standards for those practicing agrology in New Brunswick; To uphold the NBIA Code of Ethics; to offer advice to the public about agriculture & related areas; To formulate policies & improve the agriculture & food industry
Membership: 200; *Fees:* $25; *Member Profile:* Professional agrologists in New Brunswick, with a degree in agriculture from a recognized university, plus three or more years of training or experience in the field; Individuals with a degree accepted by the Council; Articling agrologists; *Committees:* Admissions; Act / Bylaws; Scholarship; Professional Development; NBIA Strategy; Communication; Discipline; Complaints; Nominating; Executive
Activities: Participating in programs to benefit the agriculture & food industry; Analyzing issues & making recommendations to organizations; Improving standards of research; Providing professional development & networking opportunities; Offering information for members, the farming industry, & the public; Promoting the profession of agrology to famers
Chief Officer(s):
Pat Toner, President
pat.toner@gnb.ca
Duncan Fraser, Secretary
duncan.fraser@gnb.ca
Rita Rattray, Office Administrator
nbia@nbagrologists.nb.ca
Meetings/Conferences:
• New Brunswick Institute of Agrologists 2018 Annual Meeting, 2018, NB
Scope: Provincial

New Brunswick Interscholastic Athletic Association (NBIAA)
PO Box 6000, 125 Hilton Rd., Fredericton NB E3B 5H1

Canadian Associations / New Brunswick Latino Association

Tel: 506-457-4843; Fax: 506-453-5311
nbiaa@gnb.ca
www.nbiaa-asinb.org
Overview: A medium-sized provincial organization overseen by School Sport Canada
Member of: School Sport Canada
Staff Member(s): 2
Membership: 75 schools; Fees: $300 per school; Committees: Executive
Chief Officer(s):
Yvan Arseneault, President, 506-684-7610
Allyson Ouellette, Executive Director
Awards:
• Sportsmanship Awards
• NBIAA Appreciation Award
• Emery Johnson Memorial Award

New Brunswick Karate Association See Karate New Brunswick

New Brunswick Latino Association
c/o Fredericton Multicultural Assn., 28 Saunders St., Fredericton NB E3B 1N1
Tel: 506-454-8292; Fax: 506-450-9033
www.nblatino.ca
Also Known As: NB Latino Association
Overview: A small provincial organization
Mission: To welcome Spanish and Portuguese-speaking newcomers to NB, to offer relevant information that will help them settle in the province, to celebrate and share our unique cultures and to provide the sense of belonging and encouragement for those aspiring to become established in the province of New Brunswick

New Brunswick Law Foundation / La Fondation pour l'avancement du droit au Nouveau-Brunswick
68 Avonlea Court, Fredericton NB E3C 1N8
Tel: 506-458-8540; Fax: 506-451-1421
general@lawsociety-barreau.nb.ca
lawsociety-barreau.nb.ca/en/public/new-brunswick-law-found
Overview: A small provincial organization founded in 1975
Mission: To fund law-related activities related to the areas of legal reform, legal aid & legal education
Affiliation(s): Law Society of New Brunswick
Staff Member(s): 1
Chief Officer(s):
Marc L. Richard, Executive Director
mrichard@lawsociety-barreau.nb.ca
R. Bruce Eddy, Chair

New Brunswick Liberal Association
715 Brunswick St., Fredericton NB E3B 1H8
Tel: 506-453-3950; Fax: 506-453-2476
Toll-Free: 800-442-4902
www.nbliberal.ca
www.facebook.com/nbla.alnb
twitter.com/NBLA_ALNB
www.youtube.com/user/NBLiberalTV
Overview: A medium-sized provincial organization overseen by The Liberal Party of Canada
Chief Officer(s):
Brian Gallant, Leader
Joel Reed, President
joel.b.reed@gmail.com

New Brunswick Library Trustees' Association (NBLTA) / Association des commissaires de bibliothèque du Nouveau-Brunswick, inc.
PO Box 34, St Antoine NB E0A 2X0
Overview: A small provincial organization founded in 1979
Mission: To train effective library trustees in New Brunswick
Finances: Funding Sources: New Brunswick Public Library System
Membership: Member Profile: Any member of a public library board in New Brunswick
Activities: Promoting public library services

New Brunswick Lung Association / Association pulmonaire du Nouveau-Brunswick
65 Brunswick St., Fredericton NB E3B 1G5
Tel: 506-455-8961; Fax: 506-462-0939
Toll-Free: 888-566-5864
info@nb.lung.ca
www.nb.lung.ca
www.facebook.com/nblung
twitter.com/NBlung
Overview: A small provincial charitable organization overseen by Canadian Lung Association
Mission: To promote wellness throughout New Brunswick & prevent lung disease
Finances: Funding Sources: Donations; Sponsorships; Fundraising
Staff Member(s): 10
Activities: Engaging in advocacy activities; Offering education about respiratory health; Providing resources such as fact sheets, booklets, & audio-visual & program resources; Supporting respiratory research; Organizing fundraising events to support children & adults with lung disease; Library: NB Lung Associations' Environment & Health Public Resource Svs.; Open to public
Chief Officer(s):
Barbara MacKinnon, President & CEO
Ted Allingham, Director, Finance & Administration
Monica Brewer, Director, Fundraising & Donor Relations
Barbara Walls, Director, Health Initiatives
Liz Smith, Director, Public Education
Roshini Kassie, Director, Community Outreach Programs
Maggie Estey, Manager, Marketing & Development

New Brunswick Maple Syrup Association (NBMSA)
250 Sheriff St., Grand Falls NB E3Z 3A2
Tel: 506-473-2271
maple.infor.ca
Overview: A medium-sized provincial organization
Mission: To represent the interests of its members, & facilitate the industry through advertisement & the constant improvement of quality & standards of the maple industry
Membership: 154
Chief Officer(s):
Louise Poitras, Executive Director

New Brunswick Massotherapy Association (NBMA) / Association des massothérapeutes du Nouveau-Brunswick (AMNB)
10, rue des Oiseaux, Pointe-Verte NB E8J 2V6
Toll-Free: 855-642-2662
info@nbma-amnb.ca
www.nbma-amnb.ca
Overview: A small provincial organization

New Brunswick Medical Society (NBMS) / Société médicale du Nouveau-Brunswick
21 Alison Blvd., Fredericton NB E3C 2N5
Tel: 506-458-8860; Fax: 506-458-9853
nbms@nb.aibn.com
www.nbms.nb.ca
www.facebook.com/CareFirstLasanteenpremier
twitter.com/nb_docs
Overview: A medium-sized provincial organization founded in 1867 overseen by Canadian Medical Association
Mission: To advance medical science in all its branches; to promote improvement of medical services; to prevent disease in cooperation with health officers & all others engaged in such work; to maintain high scientific & professional status for its members; to promote medical science & related arts & sciences
Staff Member(s): 15
Membership: Fees: Schedule available; Member Profile: Licensed physician by College of Physicians & Surgeons of NB
Activities: Internships: Yes; Speaker Service: Yes; Rents Mailing List: Yes
Chief Officer(s):
Camille Haddad, President

New Brunswick Merit Contractors Association
NB
Tel: 506-333-8845
Toll-Free: 800-521-9731
info@meritnb.ca
www.meritnb.ca
Overview: A small provincial organization overseen by Merit Canada
Mission: To represent and support the growth of open shop construction in New Brunswick
Membership: Member Profile: Construction contractors
Chief Officer(s):
Graeme Scaplen, Executive Director

New Brunswick Multicultural Council (NBMC) / Conseil multiculturel du Nouveau-Brunswick (CMNB)
#200, 494 Queen St., Fredericton NB E3B 1B6
Tel: 506-453-1091
www.nb-mc.ca
www.facebook.com/cmnb.nbmc
twitter.com/nbmc_cmnb
Overview: A medium-sized provincial charitable organization founded in 1983
Mission: To represent multicultural & multi-racial interests of all member associations; to encourage development & formation of new associations; to encourage member associations in their multicultural, inter-cultural & inter-racial programs & activities
Affiliation(s): Canadian Federation of Multicultural Councils
Finances: Annual Operating Budget: Less than $50,000; Funding Sources: Dept. of Canadian Heritage; NB Dept. of Advanced Education & Labour
Staff Member(s): 7; 46 volunteer(s)
Membership: 16 associations; Fees: $100; Member Profile: Multicultural associations; Committees: Public Policy; Race Relations; Education; Newsletter; Constitution; Finance
Activities: Providing training & events; Raising awareness of multicultural issues; Advocating for a more diverse & inclusive New Brunswick; Speaker Service: Yes
Chief Officer(s):
Alex LeBlanc, Executive Director, 506-453-1091 Ext. 226
alex.leblanc@nb-mc.ca
Publications:
• NBMC [New Brunswick Multicultural Council] Newsletter
Type: Newsletter; Frequency: Monthly
Profile: Information on upcoming events; articles on citizenship, refugee & immigration issues & updates in Canada

New Brunswick Musicians' Association, Local 815 of the American Federation of Musicians
82 Germain St., Saint John NB E2L 2E7
Tel: 506-652-6620; Fax: 506-652-6624
local815@afm.org
www.sjfn.nb.ca/local815
Overview: A small provincial organization founded in 1964
Mission: To represent professional musicians in New Brunswick
Member of: American Federation of Musicians of the United States & Canada
Membership: Fees: $30 local intiation fee; $65 federation initiation fee; $152 annual dues; Member Profile: Professional musicians in New Brunswick; Youth members are 20 years or younger
Activities: Administering the Music Performance Funds throughout New Brunswick
Chief Officer(s):
Norman G. Weyman, President
Bernadette Hedar, Vice-President
Brandon Weyman, Secretary-Treasurer

New Brunswick Native Indian Women's Council See New Brunswick Aboriginal Women's Council

New Brunswick Nurses Union (NBNU) / Syndicat des infirmières et infirmiers du Nouveau-Brunswick (SIINB)
103 Woodside Lane, Fredericton NB E3C 2R9
Tel: 506-453-0829; Fax: 506-453-0828
Toll-Free: 800-442-4914
nbnu1@nbnu.ca
www.nbnu.ca
www.facebook.com/212365802133370
twitter.com/NBNU_SIINB
Previous Name: Provincial Collective Bargaining Council
Overview: A medium-sized provincial organization
Mission: To enhance the social, economic, & general work life of nurses; To advocate for nurses & quality health care
Member of: National Federation of Nurses' Unions
Staff Member(s): 16
Membership: 6,200
Activities: Speaker Service: Yes
Chief Officer(s):
Paula Doucet, President
paulad@nbnu.ca
Matt Hiltz, Executive Director
mhiltz@nbnu.ca

New Brunswick Operating Room Nurses (NBORN)
NB
Overview: A medium-sized provincial organization founded in 1974 overseen by Operating Room Nurses Association of Canada
Mission: To represent operating room nurses in New Brunswick
Membership: Member Profile: Registered Nurses in New Brunswick who are engaged in operating room nursing or involved in the Perioperative setting
Activities: Awareness Events: Perioperative Nurses Week, November

Chief Officer(s):
Laura Astle, President

New Brunswick Outfitters Association Inc. (NBOA Inc.)
c/o Mike Roy, PO Box 451, Bathurst NB E2A 3Z4
Tel: 506-548-5157
www.nboa.nb.ca
Overview: A small provincial organization
Mission: To act as the voice of the outfitting industry in New Brunswick; to maintain high standards in New Brunswick's outfitting industry; To uphold the association's Code of Ethics; To ensure safety & satisfaction of guests
Membership: *Member Profile:* Hunting & fishing outfitters or guides in New Brunswick who contract with private parties to host outdoor excursions
Activities: Establishing rating standards & licensing roofed accommodations
Chief Officer(s):
Mike Roy, President
mikeroy@nb.aibn.com

New Brunswick Palliative Care Association *See* New Brunswick Hospice Palliative Care Association

New Brunswick Pharmaceutical Society (NBPhS) / Ordre des pharmaciens du N.-B.
#8, 1224 Mountain Rd., Moncton NB E1C 2T6
Tel: 506-857-8957; *Fax:* 506-857-8838
Toll-Free: 800-463-4434
info@nbpharmacists.ca
www.nbpharmacists.ca
Overview: A small provincial licensing organization overseen by National Association of Pharmacy Regulatory Authorities
Mission: To protect the public by regulating the profession of pharmacy in New Brunswick.
Member of: Canadian Council on Continuing Education in Pharmacy
Staff Member(s): 7
Membership: *Member Profile:* Pharmacists - certified dispensers; pharmacies; hospitals
Activities: *Internships:* Yes; *Library*
Chief Officer(s):
Sam Lanctin, Registrar
sam.lanctin@nbpharmacists.ca
Karen DeGrace, Communications Manager
karen.degrace@nbpharmacists.ca

New Brunswick Pharmacists' Association (NBPA) / Association des pharmaciens du Nouveau-Brunswick (APNB)
#410, 212 Queen St., Fredericton NB E3B 1A8
Tel: 506-459-6008; *Fax:* 506-453-0736
Toll-Free: 888-358-2345
nbpa@nbnet.nb.ca
www.nbpharma.ca
twitter.com/PharmacistsNB
Overview: A small provincial organization founded in 1981
Mission: To advance the profession of pharmacy in New Brunswick; To represent the interests of members & the profession of pharmacy
Staff Member(s): 3
Membership: *Member Profile:* New Brunswick pharmacists or certified dispensers; Corporate members; Hospital members; Persons who have a business association with pharmacists in New Brunswick; Students
Activities: Implementing programs to help members provide quality pharmacy services; Disseminating information to members
Chief Officer(s):
Paul Blanchard, Executive Director

New Brunswick Physiotherapy Association (NBPA)
PO Box 28117, St. John's NL A1B 4J8
Tel: 709-765-1096
atlanticbranches@physiotherapy.ca
Overview: A medium-sized provincial organization overseen by Canadian Physiotherapy Association
Mission: To provide leadership & direction to the physiotherapy profession; To foster excellence in practice, education & research
Member of: Canadian Physiotherapy Association
Finances: *Funding Sources:* Membership dues; Educational activities
Chief Officer(s):
Lisa Pike, Executive Director
Colin Hood, President

New Brunswick Physique & Figure Association (NBPFA)
NB
Tel: 506-850-1515
nbpfa.exec@gmail.com
www.nbpfa.com
www.facebook.com/191517260859626
Overview: A small provincial organization overseen by Canadian Bodybuilding Federation
Mission: To be the provincial governing body for the sport of bodybuilding in New Brunswick
Member of: Canadian Bodybuilding Federation; International Federation of Bodybuilding
Chief Officer(s):
Heather LeBlanc, President, 506-850-1515
figure@heatherleblanc.ca
Adam Walker, Vice President, 506-333-3556
adam@canadianmademuscle.com
Jean LeBlanc, Secretary-Treasurer, 506-536-7084
nbpfa.exec@gmail.com

New Brunswick Potato Agency *See* Potatoes New Brunswick

New Brunswick Purchasing Management Institute *See* Supply Chain Management Association - New Brunswick

New Brunswick Racquetball Association (NBRA)
NB
nbracquetball@gmail.com
www.nbracquetball.ca
twitter.com/nbrball
Overview: A small provincial organization founded in 1977 overseen by Racquetball Canada
Mission: To promote the sport of racquetball throughout New Brunswick
Member of: Racquetball Canada
Activities: Providing racquetball classes; Offering racquetball coaching
Chief Officer(s):
Michael McCabe, Vice-President, Membership

New Brunswick Real Estate Association (NBREA) / L'Association des agents des immobiliers du Nouveau-Brunswick
#1, 22 Durelle St., Fredericton NB E3C 1N8
Tel: 506-459-8055; *Fax:* 506-459-8057
Toll-Free: 800-762-1677
info@nbrea.ca
nbrea.ca
www.facebook.com/NBREALTORS
twitter.com/NBREALTORS
Overview: A medium-sized provincial organization founded in 1958
Mission: To strengthen & promote standards of professionalism in the real estate industry
Member of: The Canadian Real Estate Association
Finances: *Funding Sources:* Membership dues
Staff Member(s): 5
Membership: *Member Profile:* Realtors
Chief Officer(s):
Jamie Ryan, Chief Executive Officer
jryan@nbrea.ca
Jane Girard, Financial Officer
jgirard@nbrea.ca
Caroyln Cameron, Registrar
registrar@nbrea.ca
Meetings/Conferences:
• New Brunswick Real Estate Association 2018 Annual General Meeting, April, 2018

New Brunswick Road Builders & Heavy Construction Association
#5, 59 Avonlea Ct., Fredericton NB E3C 1N8
Tel: 506-454-5079; *Fax:* 506-452-7646
rbanb@nb.aibn.com
www.rbanb.com
Overview: A medium-sized provincial organization founded in 1958 overseen by Canadian Construction Association
Mission: To foster & enhance relations between members, & between the members of other associations in construction; To acquire & disseminate information of value to the industry & to its membership; To improve & extend standards, conditions, methods & practices within the industry
Member of: Transportation Association of Canada
Affiliation(s): Construction Association of New Brunswick
Finances: *Funding Sources:* Membership fees
Staff Member(s): 2
Membership: *Fees:* Schedule available; *Member Profile:* Contractors, Support Service Firms, Suppliers & Engineers; *Committees:* Annual Meetings, Membership & Advertising
Chief Officer(s):
Jamie Weatherbee, President
Tom McGinn, Executive Director
tom@rbanb.com
Awards:
• Two Civil Engineering Scholarships
; *Amount:* $3,000 each
Publications:
• New Brunswick Road Builder
Type: Magazine; *Frequency:* Annually
• Road Builders Association of New Brunswick Newsletter
Type: Newsletter; *Frequency:* Monthly
• Road Builders Association of New Brunswick Membership Directory
Type: Directory; *Frequency:* Annually

New Brunswick Roofing Contractors Association, Inc. (NBRCA) / Association des entrepreneurs en couverture du Nouveau-Brunswick
1010 Fairville Blvd., Saint John NB E2M 5T5
Tel: 506-652-7003; *Fax:* 506-696-0380
Toll-Free: 888-652-7003
info@nbrca.ca
www.nbrca.ca
Overview: A small provincial licensing organization founded in 1969 overseen by Canadian Roofing Contractors' Association
Mission: To protect the public's interest in relation to roofing; To act as the voice of New Brunswick's roofing industry; To facilitate a competent & profitable roofing & sealed membrane system industry in the province; To foster excellence in roofing related activities; to ensure that members uphold the code of ethics
Member of: Canadian Roofing Contractors' Association
Membership: 40; *Member Profile:* Professional roofing contractors, sheet metal contractors, manufacturers, suppliers, roof inspectors, & building consultants in New Brunswick
Activities: Promoting the roofing industry in New Brunswick; Providing safety training; Offering information about the industry, such as materials, practices, & advances; Ensuring that members meet workmanship standards
Chief Officer(s):
Andrew Lunn, President
Ron Hutton, Executive Director
rhutton@nbrca.ca

New Brunswick Rugby Union (NBRU)
#13, 900 Hanwell Rd., Fredericton NB E3B 6A2
Tel: 506-261-2176
www.nbru.ca
Overview: A medium-sized provincial organization overseen by Rugby Canada
Mission: To govern rugby in New Brunswick & organize games between teams
Member of: Rugby Canada
Finances: *Funding Sources:* Membership fees; donations; fund raising
Membership: *Committees:* Selection; Discipline; Executive
Chief Officer(s):
Sherry Doiron, President
sherrydoiron@gmail.com

New Brunswick Safety Council Inc. *See* Safety Services New Brunswick

New Brunswick Sailing Association (NBSA)
c/o Sharon Mills, Executive Director, 105 Bird Ave., Fredericton NB E2A 2H8
Tel: 506-472-2117
www.nbsailing.nb.ca
Overview: A small provincial organization overseen by Sail Canada
Mission: The New Brunswick Sailing Association is the provincial governing body for boating & the sport of sailing. It is the Canadian Yachting Association's representative in New Brunswick.
Member of: Sail Canada
Chief Officer(s):
Sharon Mills, Executive Director
smills@nbsailing.nb.ca

New Brunswick Salmon Council (NBSC)
PO Box 533, Stn. A, Fredericton NB E3B 5A6
Tel: 506-452-1875; *Fax:* 506-454-0336
thenbsc@nbnet.nb.ca
www.nbsalmoncouncil.com

Overview: A small provincial organization overseen by Atlantic Salmon Federation
Affiliation(s): Atlantic Salmon Federation

New Brunswick Salmon Growers Association See Atlantic Canada Fish Farmers Association

New Brunswick Scottish Cultural Association Inc. (NBSCA)
PO Box 781, Fredericton NB E3B 5B4
Fax: 506-454-9936
Toll-Free: 877-627-2234
info@nbscots.com
www.nbscots.com
www.facebook.com/nbscots
twitter.com/nbsca
Overview: A medium-sized provincial organization founded in 1980
Mission: To promote & protect the Scottish culture in New Brunswick; to bring together people of Scottish descent & people interested in the culture; to educate children of the importance of the Scottish people & their contribution to New Brunswick & Canada. Chapters in Bathurst, & Moncton.
Finances: *Funding Sources:* Fundraising; sponsorships; membership dues; donations; government
Membership: *Fees:* $22 individual; $35 group/club; $38 family; $250 life; $500 sustaining; *Committees:* Fundraising; Membership; Nominating; Communications
Activities: *Speaker Service:* Yes; *Library:* NBSCA Kubrart
Chief Officer(s):
Llewellyn Smith, President

New Brunswick Securities Commission See Financial & Consumer Services Commission

New Brunswick Senior Citizens Federation Inc. (NBSCF) / Fédération des citoyens aînés du Nouveau-Brunswick inc. (FCANB)
#214, 23 - 451 Paul St., Dieppe NB E1A 6W8
Tel: 506-857-8242; *Fax:* 506-857-0315
Toll-Free: 800-453-4333
horizons@nbnet.nb.ca
www.nbscf.ca
www.facebook.com/238798849533942
Overview: A medium-sized provincial organization founded in 1968
Mission: To promote the general welfare & leadership of NB's senior citizens regardless of language, race, colour, sex, or creed; to elevate the social, moral, & intellectual standing of NB's senior citizens; to provide information, coordination, communication, & advocating services to members
Finances: *Funding Sources:* Special projects; membership dues
Staff Member(s): 2
Membership: 18,000; *Fees:* $20 individual; $30 couple; *Member Profile:* NB resident 50 years+
Activities: *Awareness Events:* Seniors Products & Services Expo
Chief Officer(s):
Isabelle Arseneault, Director, Operations

New Brunswick Shorthorn Breeders Association
138 Salem Rd., Havelock NB E4Z 5R5
Tel: 506-534-2492
Overview: A small provincial organization founded in 1931
Member of: Canadian Shorthorn Association
Finances: *Funding Sources:* Membership dues; harvest auctions
Membership: *Member Profile:* Owners of shorthorn cattle
Chief Officer(s):
Arthur Carson, President

New Brunswick Signallers Association (NB Sigs)
c/o 3 ASG Signal Squadron, CFB Gagetown, PO Box 17000, Stn. Forces, Oromocto NB E2V 4J5
Tel: 506-357-7314
admin@nbsigs.net
www.nbsigs.net
Overview: A small provincial organization founded in 2003
Membership: *Fees:* $25
Chief Officer(s):
Al Lustig, President

New Brunswick Society for the Prevention of Cruelty to Animals / Société protectrice des animaux du Nouveau-Brunswick
PO Box 1412, Stn. A, Fredericton NB E3B 5E3
Tel: 506-458-8208; *Fax:* 506-458-8209
www.spca-nb.ca
Also Known As: New Brunswick SPCA
Overview: A medium-sized provincial charitable organization founded in 1881 overseen by Canadian Federation of Humane Societies
Mission: To prevent cruelty to & encourage consideration for all animals; To pursue program of humane education
Membership: *Fees:* $10
Chief Officer(s):
Hilary Howes, Executive Director

New Brunswick Society of Cardiology Techologists (NBSCT)
NB
www.nbsct.ca
Overview: A small provincial organization founded in 1968
Mission: To operate in accordance with An Act Respecting the New Brunswick Society of Cardiology Technologists; To maintain high standards for the practice of cardiology technology in New Brunswick
Member of: Canadian Society of Cardiology Technologists
Affiliation(s): Canadian Medical Association
Membership: *Fees:* $125 active members; $75 other memberships; *Member Profile:* Cardiology technologists in New Brunswick educated to test, monitor, & evaluate the human heart & its functions; Students enrolled in a a cardiology program approved by the society; *Committees:* Complaints; Discipline; Legislation / Bylaw; Membership; Public Relations; Translation; CEU
Activities: Upholding the Canon of Ethics of the Canadian Society of Cardiology Technologists as the rules of conduct of society members
Chief Officer(s):
Kathy Walker, Registrar
nbsct.registrar@hotmail.com
Kelsey McEachern, Secretary
nbsct.secretary@hotmail.com
Nadine Hebert, Treasurer
treasurer_nbsct@hotmail.com
Kristine McLaughlin, Coordinator, Provincial Education
nbsct.education@hotmail.com

New Brunswick Society of Certified Engineering Technicians & Technologists (NBSCETT) / Société des techniciens et des technologues agréés du génie du Nouveau-Brunswick (STTAGN-B)
#12B 102 Main St., Fredericton NB E3A 9N6
Tel: 506-454-6124; *Fax:* 506-452-7076
Toll-Free: 800-665-8324
nbscett@nbscett.nb.ca
www.nbscett.nb.ca
Overview: A medium-sized provincial organization founded in 1968 overseen by Canadian Council of Technicians & Technologists
Mission: To grant certification to applied science & engineering technology technicians & technologists; to protect titles & powers of discipline for its members
Finances: *Annual Operating Budget:* $100,000-$250,000; *Funding Sources:* Membership dues
Staff Member(s): 3
Membership: 1,600; *Fees:* Schedule available; *Member Profile:* Certified - in field of engineering, applied science, technology & meets requirements for certification; Technology graduate in training - meet all of academic requirements for certification; Associate - employed in engineering technology field; *Committees:* Accreditation; Certification & Review; Finance; Human Resources
Activities: Awards; Scholarships; *Awareness Events:* Annual Awards; *Internships:* Yes; *Speaker Service:* Yes; *Library:* Open to public
Chief Officer(s):
Jean-Luc Michaud, PTech, President
Edward F. Leslie, Executive Director & CEO

New Brunswick Society of Laboratory Technology See New Brunswick Society of Medical Laboratory Technologists

New Brunswick Society of Medical Laboratory Technologists (NBSMLT) / Association des technologistes de laboratoire médical du Nouveau-Brunswick (ATMLNB)
488 Centrale St., Memramcook NB E4K 3S6
Tel: 506-758-9956; *Fax:* 506-758-9963
office@nbsmlt.nb.ca
www.nbsmlt.nb.ca
Previous Name: New Brunswick Society of Laboratory Technology

Overview: A medium-sized provincial licensing organization founded in 1948 overseen by Canadian Society for Medical Laboratory Science
Mission: To regulate the practice of medical laboratory technology in New Brunswick; To protect the public in matters related to medical laboratory technology; To establish & maintain high standards of practice & regulation in the profession
Staff Member(s): 3
Membership: 650+; *Fees:* $145 active; $100 temporary; $50 assicate/inactive; *Member Profile:* Medical laboratory technologists (MLTs) in the province of New Brunswick; *Committees:* Continuing Education; Publications; Public Relations; PP & R
Activities: Licensing medical laboratory technologists practising in New Brunswick; Supporting partnerships; Promoting continuing education (ce@nbsmlt.nb.ca); *Awareness Events:* National Medical Laboratory Week, April
Chief Officer(s):
Chrystal Allen, President
president@nbsmlt.nb.ca
Paula Steeves, Executive Director
paula.steeves@nbsmlt.nb.ca
William Allen, Registrar
registrar@nbsmlt.nb.ca
Awards:
• NBSMLT Anita Lindsay Award
To recognize the technologist who exemplifies exceptional professional service
Publications:
• MLT Analyzer: Bulletin of the New Brunswick Society of Medicatl Laboratory Technologists
Type: Newsletter; *Editor:* Janelle B. Whitlock
Profile: Society reports, conferences, & professional development activities
• New Brunswick Society of Medical Laboratory Technologist Annual Report
Type: Yearbook; *Frequency:* Annually

New Brunswick Soil & Crop Improvement Association (NBSCIA) / Association pour l'amélioration du sol et des cultures du Nouveau-Brunswick
#302, 259 Brunswick St., Fredericton NB E3B 1G8
Tel: 506-454-1736; *Fax:* 506-453-1985
nbscia@nbnet.nb.ca
www.nbscia.ca
Overview: A small provincial organization founded in 1978
Mission: To improve soil & crop sustainability in New Brunswick; To encourage research & innovation to advance the agricultural industry throughout the province
Affiliation(s): Agricultural Alliance of New Brunswick; Eastern Soil & Water Conservation Centre; Soil Conservation Council of Canada
Membership: *Fees:* $20 provincial membership
Activities: Promoting environmental & economical agricultural practices in New Brunswick; Organizing field days & tours; Distributing educational information to New Brunswick farmers; Conducting research projects; Sponsoring research projects & new farming techniques; Liaising with government
Chief Officer(s):
Susannah Banks, General Manager
John Robinson, President, 506-432-6473
Publications:
• New Brunswick Soil & Crop Improvement Association Newsletter
Type: Newsletter; *Frequency:* Quarterly; *Price:* Free with New Brunswick Soil & Crop Improvement Association membership

New Brunswick Solid Waste Association (NBSWA) / l'Association des déchets solides du Nouveau-Brunswick (ADSNB)
32 Wedgewood Dr., Rothesay NB E2E 3P7
Tel: 506-849-4218; *Fax:* 506-847-1369
Toll-Free: 877-777-4218
nbswa@nbnet.nb.ca
Overview: A small provincial organization
Mission: To promote environmentally friendly solid waste management practices in New Brunswick.

New Brunswick Special Care Home Association Inc.
c/o Seely Lodge Inc., 2081 Route 845, Bayswater NB E5S 1J7
Tel: 506-738-8514; *Fax:* 506-738-0892
www.nbscha.com
Overview: A medium-sized provincial organization
Mission: To assist licensed members of the New Brunswick Special Care Home Association Inc. in providing quality, cost

effective long term care for seniors and special needs adults in cooperation with the Department of Social Development.
Membership: 42 homes; *Member Profile:* Long-term care and special care homes in New Brunswick
Chief Officer(s):
Jan Seely, President

New Brunswick Special Olympics *See* Special Olympics New Brunswick

New Brunswick Speech & Hearing Association *See* New Brunswick Association of Speech-Language Pathologists & Audiologists

New Brunswick Speed Skating Association *See* Speed Skate New Brunswick

New Brunswick Sportfishing Association (NBSFA)
c/o Bert Beek, 758 Rte. 670, Ripples NB E4B 1E9
Tel: 506-385-2335
www.nbsportfishing.ca
www.facebook.com/550441211657133
Overview: A small provincial organization
Mission: To elevate the sport of bass fishing in New Brunswick
Finances: *Funding Sources:* Membership fees; Sponsorships
Membership: *Fees:* $50; *Member Profile:* Persons, 19 years of age or older, who are eligible to purchase a fishing license in New Brunswick; Persons, under age 19, who are recommended by a member; Organizations which provide finanial support to the association
Activities: Hosting tournaments; Promoting catch & release programs; Liaising with the government for new regulations for tournament bass fishing; Improving fish handling methods; Helping to fund studies on smallmouth bass in New Brunswick

New Brunswick Sports Hall of Fame (NBSHF) / Temple de la renommée sportive du N.-B.
503 Queen St., Fredericton NB E3B 5H1
Tel: 506-453-3747
nbsportshalloffame@gnb.ca
www.nbsportshalloffame.com
www.facebook.com/150319378347024
twitter.com/NBSHF
Overview: A small provincial charitable organization founded in 1970
Mission: N.B. Sports Hall of Fame recognizes & honours achievement in competitive sport & its development; with honour comes distinction & a rich sport legacy for the youth of the future; such achievement & legacy are kept alive for inductees, the sport community & generations of New Brunswickers through celebration, public exhibition & preservation of our sport heritage
Member of: Canadian Association for Sport Heritage; Canadian Museums Association
Affiliation(s): International Sports Heritage Association
Finances: *Funding Sources:* Provincial government; fundraising; sponsorships; donations
Activities: Annual dinner & Induction Ceremony; exhibits; receptions; lectures; tours; *Library:* Sports Heritage Resource Centre; Open to public by appointment
Chief Officer(s):
Jamie Wolverton, Executive Director, 506-453-8930
jamie.wolverton@gnb.ca

New Brunswick Teachers' Association (NBTA) / Fédération des enseignants du Nouveau-Brunswick (FENB)
PO Box 752, 650 Montgomery St., Fredericton NB E3B 5G2
Tel: 506-452-8921; *Fax:* 506-453-9795
www.nbta.ca
www.facebook.com/219814221400600
Previous Name: New Brunswick Teachers' Federation (Ind.)
Overview: A medium-sized provincial organization founded in 1970 overseen by Canadian Teachers' Federation
Finances: *Funding Sources:* Membership dues
Staff Member(s): 17
Membership: 8,170 + 47 branches
Activities: *Library:* NBTF Resource Centre; Not open to public
Chief Officer(s):
Guy Arseneault, President
guy.arseneault@nbta.ca
Larry Jamieson, Executive Director, 506-452-1721
larry.jamieson@nbta.ca

New Brunswick Teachers' Federation (Ind.) *See* New Brunswick Teachers' Association

New Brunswick Team Handball Federation
NB
Courriel: info.handballnb@gmail.com
www.handballnb.org
www.facebook.com/handballnb
Également appelé: Handball NB
Aperçu: *Dimension:* petite; *Envergure:* locale; Organisme sans but lucratif
Membre de: Canadian Team Handball Federation
Membre(s) du bureau directeur:
Jason A. Ferguson, President

New Brunswick Turkey Marketing Board *See* Turkey Farmers of New Brunswick

New Brunswick Union (NBU) / Syndicat du Nouveau-Brunswick (SNB)
217 Brunswick St., Fredericton NB E3B 1G8
Tel: 506-458-8440; *Fax:* 506-450-8481
Toll-Free: 800-442-4420
local333@telus.net
www.nbu.ca
twitter.com/NBUSNB
Also Known As: New Brunswick Union of Public and Private Employees
Overview: A small provincial organization
Member of: National Union of Public and General Employees
Membership: *Committees:* Code of Solidarity; Constitution and By-Laws; Executive; Finance; Harassment; Nominations/Elections Credentials; Occupational Health & Safety; Para Medical Educational Assistance; Pension Working Group; Resolutions; Scholarship Bursary; Staff Relations; Union Education Selection; Unison for Retired Members; Women's
Chief Officer(s):
Susie Proulx-Daigle, President
susie@nbu.ca

New Brunswick Veterinary Medical Association (NBVMA) / Association des médecins vétérinaires du Nouveau-Brunswick (AMVNB)
c/o Dr. George Whittle, 1700 Manawagonish Rd., Saint John NB E2M 3Y5
Tel: 506-635-8100
registrar@nbvma-amvnb.ca
www.nbvma-amvnb.ca
Overview: A small provincial licensing organization founded in 1919 overseen by Canadian Veterinary Medical Association
Mission: To act as the regulatory body for the practice of veterinary medicine in New Brunswick; To establish standards of practice in the profession; To promote animal health & welfare; To prevent public health problems related to animal disease
Member of: Canadian Veterinary Medical Association
Membership: *Member Profile:* Veterinarians in New Brunswick
Activities: Offering continuing education programs
Chief Officer(s):
George Whittle, Registrar

New Brunswick Wildlife Federation (NBWF) / Fédération de la faune du Nouveau-Brunswick
PO Box 549, Moncton NB E1C 8L9
nbwildlifefederation.org
Overview: A medium-sized provincial organization founded in 1924 overseen by Canadian Wildlife Federation
Mission: To foster sound management & wise use of the renewable & non-renewable natural resources of New Brunswick; To assist & encourage the enforcement of those game laws which are in keeping with the objectives of the Federation & to strive for better management & game laws where & when necessary; To educate membership & the public, with particular emphasis upon conservation & safety; To represent the interests & concerns of New Brunswick sportsmen; to cooperate with government departments & all related groups, where interests are mutual
Member of: New Brunswick Salmon Council; Fur Institute of Canada
Membership: 30 clubs + 4,000 individual; *Fees:* $40 individual; $400 max. per club; *Committees:* Adopt-a-Stream; Constitution & By-Laws; Environment; Fisheries; Forestry; Master Angler; Membership; Memorial Cards, Merchandise & Prints; Resolutions; Wildlife & Hunter Education; Fundraising; Becoming an Outdoors-Woman
Activities: *Speaker Service:* Yes
Chief Officer(s):
Charlie Leblanc, President, 506-866-4345
cleblan618@rogers.com

New Brunswick Women's Institute (NBWI)
681 Union St., Fredericton NB E3A 3N8
Tel: 506-454-0798; *Fax:* 506-451-8949
nbwi@nb.aibn.com
www.nbwi.ca
www.facebook.com/284295801781170
Overview: A medium-sized provincial charitable organization founded in 1911 overseen by Federated Women's Institutes of Canada
Mission: To help discover, stimulate & develop leadership among women; to assist, encourage & support women to become knowledgeable & responsible citizens; to ensure basic human rights for women & work towards their equality; to network with other organizations sharing similar objectives; to promote the improvement of agricultural & other rural communities & to safeguard the environment
Member of: Federated Women's Institutes of Canada
Affiliation(s): Associated Country Women of the World
Finances: *Funding Sources:* Grants; membership dues
Membership: 1,000 members in 100 branches; *Member Profile:* New Brunswick Women 18 or older
Awards:
• Alma J. Porter Memorial Scholarship
; *Amount:* $500
• Alma J. Porter Educational Scholarship
; *Amount:* $250
• NBWI Educational Scholarship
; *Amount:* 5 at $300
• Music Scholarship
; *Amount:* $300
• NBWI Scholarship for Women's Institute Member
; *Amount:* $300

New Brunswick Youth in Care Network
535 Beaverbrook Ct., #B-10, Fredericton NB E3B 1X6
Tel: 506-462-0323; *Fax:* 506-462-0328
www.partnersforyouth.ca
www.facebook.com/NBYICN
twitter.com/VoicesMYICN
Also Known As: Partners for Youth
Overview: A medium-sized provincial organization founded in 2010 overseen by Youth in Care Canada
Mission: To advocate for & support youth in or from government care in New Brunswick
Affiliation(s): Partners for Youth
Staff Member(s): 1
Membership: *Member Profile:* Youth in or from government care in New Brunswick
Activities: Raising awareness of the challenges youth-in-care face through public education; Operating a leadership group & peer mentor program; Organizing events
Chief Officer(s):
Zoe Bourgeois, Project Coordinator
rlippett@partnersforyouth.ca
Awards:
• The Rosemary McCain McMillin Scholarship
Eligibility: An individual in or from government care in New Brunswick who is successfully enrolled in a graduate-level educational program *Deadline:* June; *Amount:* $5,000

New Canadian Centre Immigrant Service *See* New Canadians Centre Peterborough Immigrant Services

New Canadians Centre Peterborough Immigrant Services (NCC)
221 Romaine St., Peterborough ON K9J 2C3
Tel: 705-743-0882; *Fax:* 705-743-6219
info@nccpeterborough.ca
www.nccpeterborough.ca
www.facebook.com/newcanadianscentre
twitter.com/ncc_ptbo
www.youtube.com/user/newcanadianscentre
Previous Name: New Canadian Centre Immigrant Service
Overview: A small local organization founded in 1979 overseen by Ontario Council of Agencies Serving Immigrants
Mission: To provide direct assistance to New Canadians through resettlement services in Peterborough; to promote cultural bridging through public awareness & community activities
Member of: United Way; Council of Immigrant Services of Eastern Ontario
Finances: *Funding Sources:* Federal; provincial; municipal; United Way; fundraising
Membership: *Fees:* $20 single; $30 organization
Activities: *Speaker Service:* Yes; *Library:* Open to public
Chief Officer(s):

Hajni Hos, Executive Director
hajni@nccpeterborough.ca

New Circles Community Services
161 Bartley Dr., Toronto ON M4A 1E6
Tel: 416-422-2591; *Fax:* 416-422-5946
info@newcircles.ca
newcircles.ca
www.facebook.com/130999970339869
twitter.com/newcircles
Overview: A small local charitable organization
Mission: To provide clothing & social services to families in need living in the Thorncliffe Park, Flemingdon Park & Victoria Village areas of Toronto
Staff Member(s): 7; 200 volunteer(s)
Chief Officer(s):
Alykhan Suleman, Executive Director
alykhan@newcircles.ca

New Clarence-Rockland Chamber of Commerce
#201, 8710 County Rd. 17, Rockland ON K4K 1T2
Tel: 613-761-1954; *Fax:* 866-648-2769
info@ccclarencerockland.com
ccclarencerockland.com
www.facebook.com/formationsncccr
Overview: A small local organization
Mission: To be the voice for its members; To promote commerce in Clarence-Rockland
Member of: Canadian Chamber of Commerce
Membership: *Fees:* $150 self employed; $200 non-profit; $250 1-14 employees; $450 15-39 employees; $850 40+ employees
Chief Officer(s):
Melinda Raymond, President

New College Alumni Association (NCAA)
#118, 300 Huron St., Toronto ON M5S 3J6
Tel: 416-978-8273; *Fax:* 416-978-0554
alumni.newcollege@utoronto.ca
www.utoronto.ca/ncaa
Overview: A medium-sized local organization
Mission: To develop a visible & mutually supportive communication network that connects New College Alumni with the other stake holders of New College & the University of Toronto
Chief Officer(s):
Lesley Reidstra, President

New Democratic Party (NDP) / Nouveau Parti Démocratique
Federal Office, #300, 279 Laurier West, Ottawa ON K1P 5J9
Tel: 613-236-3613; *Fax:* 613-230-9850
Toll-Free: 866-525-2555; *TTY:* 866-776-7742
www.ndp.ca
www.facebook.com/NDP.NPD
twitter.com/NDP
www.youtube.com/user/NDPCanada
Also Known As: Canada's NDP
Overview: A medium-sized national organization founded in 1961
Mission: To offer Canadians an alternative political vision based on the principles of democratic socialism; To protect & expand programs such as Medicare & the Old Age Pension through prudent & effective government, & through a truly fair tax system
Membership: 200,000+
Activities: Library: by appointment
Chief Officer(s):
Jagmeet Singh, Party Leader
Marit Stiles, President
president@ndp.ca

Alberta NDP
#201, 10544 - 114 St. NW, Edmonton AB T5H 3J7
Tel: 780-474-2415; *Fax:* 780-669-9617
Toll-Free: 800-465-6587
info@albertandp.ca
www.albertandp.ca
www.facebook.com/albertandp
twitter.com/AlbertaNDP
www.youtube.com/user/AlbertaNDP
Chief Officer(s):
Rachel Notley, Party Leader
British Columbia NDP (BC NDP)
#301, 4180 Lougheed Hwy., Burnaby BC V5C 6A7
Tel: 604-430-8600; *Fax:* 778-379-4842
Toll-Free: 888-868-3637
info@bcndp.ca
www.bcndp.ca

www.facebook.com/bcndp
twitter.com/bcndp
Chief Officer(s):
John Horgan, Party Leader
Manitoba NDP
#803, 294 Portage Ave., Winnipeg MB R3C 0B9
Tel: 204-987-4857; *Fax:* 204-786-2443
Toll-Free: 877-863-2976
info@todaysndp.ca
todaysndp.ca
www.facebook.com/mbndp
twitter.com/mbndp
www.youtube.com/ndpmanitoba
Chief Officer(s):
Wab Kinew, Party Leader
David Woodbury, President
New Brunswick NDP
#2, 924 Prospect St., Fredericton NB E3B 2T9
Tel: 506-458-5828
Toll-Free: 844-637-6731
www.nbndp.ca
www.facebook.com/nbndp.npdnb
twitter.com/NB_NDP
Chief Officer(s):
Jennifer McKenzie, Leader
Newfoundland & Labrador NDP
PO Box 5275, St. John's NL A1C 5W1
Tel: 709-739-6387; *Fax:* 709-579-6371
info@nl.ndp.ca
nl.ndp.ca
www.facebook.com/NLNDP
twitter.com/nlndp
Chief Officer(s):
Lorraine Michael, Interim Leader
Nova Scotia NDP
#603, 5151 George St., Halifax NS B3J 1M5
Tel: 902-423-9217; *Fax:* 902-423-9618
Toll-Free: 800-753-7696
feedback@nsndp.ca
www.nsndp.ca
www.facebook.com/nsndp
twitter.com/NSNDP
www.youtube.com/nsndp
Chief Officer(s):
Gary Burrill, Party Leader
Ontario NDP
#201, 2069 Lakeshore Blvd. West, Toronto ON M8V 3Z4
Tel: 416-591-8637; *Fax:* 416-599-4820
Toll-Free: 866-390-6637
info@ontariondp.ca
www.ontariondp.ca
www.facebook.com/OntarioNDP
twitter.com/ontariondp
www.youtube.com/user/OntarioNewDemocrat
Chief Officer(s):
Andrea Horwath, Party Leader
Karla Webber-Gallagher, Provincial Secretary
kwebberg@on.ndp.ca
PEI NDP
81 Prince St., Charlottetown PE C1A 4R3
Tel: 902-892-1930
ndppei@ndppei.com
www.ndppei.ca
www.facebook.com/NewDemocraticPartyOfPrinceEdwardIsland
twitter.com/NDPPEI
Chief Officer(s):
Mike Redmond, Party Leader
Québec NDP
#202, 4689, av Papineau, Montréal QC H2H 1V4
Tel: 514-590-0036; *Fax:* 514-590-0555
Toll-Free: 866-525-2555
qc.npd.ca
twitter.com/NPDQuebec
www.flickr.com/photos/npdndpqc
Chief Officer(s):
Jérémy Boulanger-Bonnelly, Co-président
Catherine Hamé, Co-présidente
Saskatchewan NDP
Tommy Douglas House, 1122 Saskatchewan Dr., Regina SK S4P 0C4
Tel: 306-525-1322; *Fax:* 306-569-1363
info@saskndp.ca
www.saskndp.ca

www.facebook.com/SaskNDP
twitter.com/Sask_NDP
www.youtube.com/SaskNDP
David McGrane, Party President
president@saskndp.ca
Yukon NDP
PO Box 31516, Whitehorse YT Y1A 6K8
Tel: 867-668-2203
yukon@ndp.ca
www.yukonndp.ca
www.facebook.com/YukonNDP
twitter.com/yukonndp
Chief Officer(s):
Liz Hanson, Party Leader

New Denmark Historical Society
c/o New Denmark Memorial Museum, 444 Hwy. 380, New Denmark NB E7G 2Y9
Tel: 506-553-6464
Overview: A small local organization founded in 1972
Mission: To operate a museum; To preserve cultural heritage
Member of: Federation of Danish Association in Canada; NB Museum
Finances: *Annual Operating Budget:* Less than $50,000
12 volunteer(s)
Membership: 30 corporate; *Fees:* Schedule available
Chief Officer(s):
Sarah Ouellette, President

New Experiences for Refugee Women *See* Newcomer Women's Services Toronto

New Hamburg Board of Trade
121 Huron St., New Hamburg ON N3A 1K1
Tel: 519-662-6628
www.nhbot.ca
twitter.com/NewHamburgBoT
Overview: A small local organization
Mission: The New Hamburg Board of Trade represents and serves local business interests in this Wilmot-based township.
Membership: 90; *Fees:* $145 basic; $205 full + GST
Chief Officer(s):
Tim Bender, President, 519-662-1221
timbender@nhbot.ca
Steve Wagler, Vice-President, 519-662-1644

New Hamilton Orchestra *See* Hamilton Philharmonic Orchestra

The New Homeland *See* Masaryk Memorial Institute Inc.

New Leaf Enterprises
3670 Kempt Rd., Halifax NS B3K 4X8
Tel: 902-453-6000
www.easterseals.ns.ca
Overview: A small local organization founded in 1960 overseen by Easter Seals Nova Scotia
Mission: To create a collaborative social setting in order to help adults with physical disabilities develop job skills
Member of: Easter Seals Nova Scotia; DIRECTIONS Council for Vocational Services Society
Activities: Catering services; café; business services; job skills training
Chief Officer(s):
Veronica Dale, Executive Director
v.dale@easterseals.ns.ca

New Life League *See* Adventive Cross Cultural Initiatives

New Media Business Alliance *See* Interactive Ontario

New West Theatre Society
#111, 210A - 12A St. North, Lethbridge AB T1H 2J1
Tel: 403-381-9378
info@newwesttheatre.com
www.newwesttheatre.com
www.facebook.com/NewWestTheatreLethbridge
twitter.com/newwesttheatre
Overview: A small local charitable organization
Mission: To provide Lethbridge & surrounding region with a broad-based & diverse program of professional quality theatrical, musical & dramatic performances
Finances: *Funding Sources:* Alberta Foundation for the Arts
Staff Member(s): 2
Activities: Hiring 180 contract actors, directors, designers, technicians per year
Chief Officer(s):
Sharon Peat, Artistic Director
Derek Stevenson, General Manager

New Westminster & District Labour Council (NWDLC)
#105, 3920 Norland Ave., Burnaby BC V5G 4K7
Tel: 604-291-9306; Fax: 604-291-0996
nwdlc@shawcable.com
www.nwdlc.ca
Overview: A large local organization founded in 1966 overseen by British Columbia Federation of Labour
Mission: To represent 123 affiliated unions in New Westminster, British Columbia & the surrounding area; To support community activism for workers & their families; To speak out on issues affecting workplaces & communities; To build a community that supports the needs of working families
Affiliation(s): Canadian Labour Congress (CLC)
Membership: 55,000+; *Member Profile:* Trade union members from New Westminster, British Columbia, & the surrounding area, including Burnaby, Delta, Surrey, Port Moody, White Rock, Pitt Meadows, Port Coquitlam, Langley City, & Langley Township
Activities: Advocating for issues, such as an increase to British Columbia's minimum wage & changes to Workers Compensation regulations to protect employees who work alone; Lobbying all levels of government about social & economic issues; Offering educational seminars & conferences; Providing networking opportunities among local union members; Supporting local community organizations, such as the Protein for People Project & the United Way Days of Caring project
Chief Officer(s):
Lori Mayhew, President
Carolyn Rice, Secretary-Treasurer
Awards:
- Gerry Stoney CLC Harrison Winter School Scholarship
- Bob Fortin CLC Harrison Winter School Scholarship
- Joy Langan CLC Harrison Winter School Scholarship

The New Westminster Board of Trade *See* New Westminster Chamber of Commerce

New Westminster Chamber of Commerce
#201, 309 6th St., New Westminster BC V3L 3A7
Tel: 604-521-7781; Fax: 604-521-0057
nwcc@newwestchamber.com
www.newwestchamber.com
Also Known As: New Westminster Visitor Info Centre
Previous Name: The New Westminster Board of Trade
Overview: A small local organization founded in 1883
Mission: To encourage a business climate which enables members & the community to prosper
Member of: BC Chamber of Commerce
Finances: *Annual Operating Budget:* $250,000-$500,000
Staff Member(s): 2; 2 volunteer(s)
Membership: 327; *Fees:* Schedule available; *Committees:* Community Policing; Heritage Advisory
Activities: Organizing & promoting networking events; Offering benefit programs
Chief Officer(s):
Lizz Kelly, CEO

New Westminster Historical Society (NWHS)
#309, 2559 Parkview Lane, Port Coquitlam BC V3C 6M1
Tel: 604-526-6113
www.nwheritage.org/heritagesite/orgs/nwhs/nwhs.htm
Overview: A small local organization founded in 1976
Mission: To provide monthly programs, free & open to everyone, about the history of New Westminster & other related history topics; to organize speakers
Finances: *Funding Sources:* Membership fees
Membership: *Fees:* $10
Activities: Monthly meetings

New Westminster Hyack Festival Association
204 - 6th St., New Westminster BC V3L 3A1
Tel: 604-522-6894; Fax: 604-522-6094
events@hyack.bc.ca
www.hyack.bc.ca
www.facebook.com/HyackFestivalAssn
twitter.com/HyackFestival
Overview: A small local organization founded in 1971
Mission: To organize & facilitate events in the City of New Westminster while preserving history and tradition, in order to promote the City, stimulate the local economy & entertain and involve people in a fun-filled atmosphere.
Membership: *Fees:* $25 youth/senior; $35 single; $55 couple/family
Chief Officer(s):
Cathie Gibson, Interim Executive Director
execdirector@hyack.bc.ca

Newcastle & District Chamber of Commerce
PO Box 11, 20 King Ave. West, Newcastle ON L1B 1H7
info@newcastle.on.ca
www.newcastle.on.ca
www.facebook.com/NewcastleAndDistrictChamber
twitter.com/NewcastleCofC
Overview: A small local organization
Mission: To support business; To contribute to business growth
Member of: Canadian Chamber of Commerce
Membership: 72; *Fees:* $120
Activities: Providing referrals; Offering networking & advertising opportunities
Chief Officer(s):
Marilia Hjorngaard, President

Newcastle Village & District Historical Society
#3, 20 King Ave. West, Newcastle ON L1B 1H7
Tel: 905-987-5180
newcastle.historic@gmail.com
Overview: A small local organization
Mission: To collect local historical documents & photographs
Member of: Ontario Historical Society
Finances: *Funding Sources:* Membership dues
Activities: *Library:* Massey Memorial Library
Chief Officer(s):
Beverly Jeeves, Director

Newcomer Women's Services Toronto (NEW)
#401, 745 Danforth Ave., Toronto ON M4J 1L4
Tel: 416-469-0196; Fax: 416-469-3307
pa@newcomerwomen.org
www.newcomerwomen.org
twitter.com/NEW_Employment
www.youtube.com/user/NewcomerWomenService
Also Known As: New Experiences for Newcomer Women
Previous Name: New Experiences for Refugee Women
Overview: A small local charitable organization founded in 1983
Mission: To promote the social, cultural & economic integration of newcomer women into Canada's multicultural society
Member of: Advocates for Community Based Training & Education for Women; Ontario Council of Agencies Serving Immigrants; Women's Centres Association Ontario
Finances: *Funding Sources:* Federal, provincial, municipal & city governments; United Way; Trillium Foundation
Staff Member(s): 22
Membership: *Member Profile:* Clients & community supporters
Activities: *Internships:* Yes
Chief Officer(s):
Maya Roy, Executive Director
maya@newcomerwomen.org

 Newcomer Employment Services Toronto (NEST)
 #402, 745 Danforth Ave., Toronto ON M4J 1L4
 Tel: 416-751-8886; Fax: 416-639-1360
 twitter.com/NEW_Employment
 Chief Officer(s):
 Grace Son, Director, Employment Programs
 grace@newcomerwomen.org

Newfoundland & Labrador AIDS Committee *See* AIDS Committee of Newfoundland & Labrador

Newfoundland & Labrador Amateur Bodybuilding Association (NLABBA)
12 Walsh's Rd., Logy Bay NL A1K 3G8
www.nlabba.ca
www.facebook.com/groups/13081045661
Overview: A small provincial organization overseen by Canadian Bodybuilding Federation
Mission: To be the provincial governing body for the sport of amateur bodybuilding in Newfoundland & Labrador
Member of: Canadian Bodybuilding Federation; International Federation of Bodybuilding
Membership: *Fees:* $25
Chief Officer(s):
Candace Critch, President
nlabba.ccritch@gmail.com
Andrew Dove, Vice President
adovenlabba.exec@gmail.com

Newfoundland & Labrador Amateur Sports Federation *See* Sport Newfoundland & Labrador

Newfoundland & Labrador Amateur Wrestling Association (NLAWA)
NL
nlawa.wordpress.com
Overview: A small provincial organization overseen by Canadian Amateur Wrestling Association
Mission: The NLAWA is a small organization comprised of coaches, officials, parents and athletes who are dedicated to advancing the sport of wrestling in Newfoundland and Labrador
Chief Officer(s):
Randy Ralph, President
randolphralph@esdnl.ca

Newfoundland & Labrador Arts Council (NLAC)
The Newman Building, PO Box 98, 1 Springdale St., St. John's NL A1C 5H5
Tel: 709-726-2212; Fax: 709-726-0619
Toll-Free: 866-726-2212
nlacmail@nlac.ca
www.nlac.ca
www.facebook.com/NLArtsCouncil
twitter.com/NLArtsCouncil
Also Known As: ArtsNL
Overview: A medium-sized provincial charitable organization founded in 1980
Mission: To foster & promote the creation & enjoyment of the arts for the people of the province
Member of: Canadian Conference of the Arts
Finances: *Annual Operating Budget:* $500,000-$1.5 Million; *Funding Sources:* Provincial government
Staff Member(s): 4; 12 volunteer(s)
Activities: Provide grant & awards programs; *Library:* Open to public
Chief Officer(s):
Reg Winsor, Executive Director
rwinsor@nlac.ca

Newfoundland & Labrador Association for Community Living (NLACL)
PO Box 8414, 74 O'Leary Ave., St. John's NL A1B 3N7
Tel: 709-722-0790; Fax: 709-722-1325
Toll-Free: 800-701-8511
nlacl@nlacl.ca
www.nlacl.ca
www.facebook.com/nlacl
twitter.com/nlacl1
Previous Name: Labrador West Association for Community Living
Overview: A small provincial charitable organization founded in 1956 overseen by Canadian Association for Community Living
Mission: To develop communities in Newfoundland & Labrador that welcome individuals with developmental disabilities
Member of: Canadian Association for Community Living
Finances: *Funding Sources:* Donations; Sponsorships; Fundraising; Special events; Bequeaths
Membership: *Fees:* $10 individual; $25 family; *Committees:* Executive; Grassroots & Membership; Inclusion & Well-Being Initiative
Activities: Engaging in advocacy activities; Liaising with government & service agencies; Supporting individuals, families, & local associations; Facilitating research; Providing educational opportunities about issues encountered by persons with developmental disabilities; Sponsoring a community inclusion project; *Library:* NL Association for Community Living Resource Centre
Chief Officer(s):
Dennis Gill, President
dennis.gill@nlacl.ca
Gail St. Croix, Vice-President
frisky@nl.rogers.com
Una Tucker, Secretary
harvey.tucker@eastlink.ca
Helen O'Rourke, Treasurer
helenorourke_497@hotmail.com
Sherry Gambin-Walsh, Executive Director
sherrygw@nlacl.ca
Publications:
- Gateway
Type: Magazine; *Frequency:* Quarterly

Newfoundland & Labrador Association of Insolvency & Restructuring Professionals
c/o Janes & Noseworthy Ltd., #201, 516 Topsail Rd., St. John's NL A1E 2C5
Tel: 709-364-8148; Fax: 709-368-2146
Previous Name: Newfoundland & Labrador Insolvency Association
Overview: A small provincial organization overseen by Canadian Association of Insolvency & Restructuring Professionals

Member of: Canadian Association of Insolvency & Restructuring Professionals
Membership: *Member Profile:* Persons in Newfoundland & Labrador who act as trustees in bankruptcy, agents, receivers, monitors, & consultants in insolvency matters
Chief Officer(s):
Derrick Hutchens, President
derrickhutchens@janesnoseworthy.ca

Newfoundland & Labrador Association of Medical Radiation Technologists (NLAMRT)
PO Box 29141, Stn. Torbay Rd. Post Office, St. John's NL A1A 5B5
Tel: 709-777-6036
www.nlamrt.ca
Overview: A small provincial organization founded in 1951 overseen by Canadian Association of Medical Radiation Technologists
Mission: To represent all working medical radiation technologists in Newfoundland & Labrador
Membership: *Member Profile:* Full practice membership is available to those in Newfoundland & Labrador who have passed the Canadian Association of Medical Radiation Technologists; Medical radiation technology students
Activities: Advocating for the profession of medical radiation technology; Upholding the ethical standards of the profession; Providing continuing education
Chief Officer(s):
Nicole Jenkins, President
njenkins668@hotmail.com
Awards:
• NLAMRT Mentoring Award
• Best Price Memorial Award
• Roy Crowley Memorial Award for Clinical Excellence
Meetings/Conferences:
• 67th Newfoundland & Labrador Association of Medical Radiation Technologists Annual General Meeting 2018, 2018, NL
Scope: Provincial

Newfoundland & Labrador Association of Occupational Therapists (NLAOT)
PO Box 5423, St. John's NL A1C 5W2
Tel: 709-738-2434
info@nlaot.ca
www.nlaot.ca
Overview: A small provincial organization
Mission: To advocate for the profession of occupational therapy in Newfoundland & Labrador
Finances: *Funding Sources:* Membership fees; Subscriptions; Bequests; Donations; Grants
Membership: 100-499; *Member Profile:* Occupational therapists who practise or reside in Newfoundland & Labrador
Activities: Developing public awareness & understanding of occupational therapy; Supporting continuing professional education; Encouraging research in occupational therapy; Facilitating communication among occupational therapists
Chief Officer(s):
Sandy Delaney, President
president@nlaot.ca

Newfoundland & Labrador Association of Optometrists (NLAO)
PO Box 8042, St. John's NL A1B 3M7
Tel: 709-765-1096; *Fax:* 709-739-8378
nlao@bellaliant.net
www.nlao.org
Previous Name: Newfoundland Association of Optometrists
Overview: A medium-sized provincial organization overseen by Canadian Association of Optometrists
Mission: To provide an online resource for Doctors of Optometry & other health care providers in Newfoundland & Labrador
Finances: *Funding Sources:* Membership dues
Chief Officer(s):
Ed Breen, Executive Director

Newfoundland & Labrador Association of Public & Private Employees (NAPE)
PO Box 8100, 330 Portugal Cove Pl., St. John's NL A1B 3M9
Tel: 709-754-0700; *Fax:* 709-754-0726
Toll-Free: 800-563-4442
www.nape.ca
Overview: A medium-sized provincial organization founded in 1936
Mission: The largest union in Newfoundland & Labrador
Member of: Canadian Labour Congress; National Union of Public and General Employees
Affiliation(s): Newfoundland & Labrador Federation of Labour; National Union of Public and General Employees; Canadain Labour Congress
Finances: *Funding Sources:* Membership dues
Staff Member(s): 35
Membership: 25,000; *Member Profile:* Public & private workers in government, health care, education, corrections, food processing, hospitality & financial sectors
Activities: *Library:* Open to public by appointment
Chief Officer(s):
Jerry Earle, President
jearle@nape.ca
Bert Blundon, Secretary-Treasurer
bblundon@nape.ca
Arlene Sedlickas, General Vice-President
  Central Office
  PO Box 160, 15 Hardy Ave., Grand Falls-Windsor NL A2A 2J4
  Tel: 709-489-6619; *Fax:* 709-489-6657
  Toll-Free: 800-563-1050
  Chief Officer(s):
  Bernadine Power, Employee Relations Officer
  bpower@nape.ca
  Elaine Price, Employee Relations Officer
  eprice@nape.ca
  Western Office
  PO Box 864, 10 Main St., Corner Brook NL A2H 6H6
  Tel: 709-639-8483; *Fax:* 709-639-1079
  Toll-Free: 800-563-9343
  Chief Officer(s):
  Randy Avery, Employee Relations Officer
  ravery@nape.ca
  Andy Parsons, Employee Relations Officer
  aparsons@nape.ca

Newfoundland & Labrador Association of Realtors (NLAR)
28 Logy Bay Rd., St. John's NL A1A 1J4
Tel: 709-726-5110; *Fax:* 709-726-4221
Toll-Free: 855-726-5110
reception@nlar.ca
www.nlar.ca
www.linkedin.com/company/newfoundland-and-labrador-association-of-realtors-
www.facebook.com/NLAREALTORS
twitter.com/_NLAR
Previous Name: Newfoundland Real Estate Association
Overview: A medium-sized provincial organization
Member of: The Canadian Real Estate Association
Finances: *Funding Sources:* Membership fees
Membership: 700 individual
Chief Officer(s):
Bill Stirling, Chief Executive Officer
bstirling@nlar.ca

Newfoundland & Labrador Association of Respiratory Therapists (NLART)
#133, Bldg. 50, Hamlyn Rd. Plaza, St. John's NL A1A 5X7
nlarrt@gmail.com
www.nlart.ca
Overview: A medium-sized provincial organization overseen by Canadian Society of Respiratory Therapists
Mission: To improve & maintain the standards of respiratory care in Newfoundland & Labrador
Affiliation(s): Canadian Society of Respiratory Therapists (CSRT)
Membership: *Member Profile:* Registered respiratory therapists in Newfoundland & Labrador, who evaluate, treat, & care for persons with heart & breathing disorders

Newfoundland & Labrador Association of Social Workers (NLASW) / Association des travailleurs sociaux de Terre-Neuve et Labrador
PO Box 39039, 177 Hamlyn Rd., St. John's NL A1E 5Y7
Tel: 709-753-0200; *Fax:* 709-753-0120
info@nlasw.ca
www.nlasw.ca
Overview: A medium-sized provincial organization founded in 1993
Mission: To ensure excellence in social work in Newfoundland & Labrador; To speak out & take appropriate action on issues of social concern; To disseminate information & provide opportunities for continuing education; To provide consultation to agencies involved in training for or delivering human services; To promote the development & the enhancement of social service delivery system suited to the needs of Newfoundlanders
Member of: Canadian Association of Social Workers
Finances: *Funding Sources:* Membership fees
Staff Member(s): 5
Membership: 1,507; *Fees:* $400; *Member Profile:* Social workers employed in a wide variety of settings including child welfare, youth & adult corrections, health care, senior citizens homes, hospitals & community health centres, psychiatric institutions, addictions services & social work education; also self-employed in private practice & consulting businesses; *Committees:* Registration; Dosciplinary; Editorial; Professional Issues; Promotion of the Profession; Communitt development network
Activities: *Awareness Events:* National Social Work Week, 1st week of March; *Internships:* Yes; *Speaker Service:* Yes
Chief Officer(s):
Lisa Crockwell, Executive Director
lcrockwell.nlasw.ca

Newfoundland & Labrador Association of Speech-Language Pathologists & Audiologists (NLASLPA)
PO Box 21212, St. John's NL A1A 5B2
info@nlaslpa.ca
www.nlaslpa.ca
www.facebook.com/nlaslpa
twitter.com/nlaslpa
Previous Name: Newfoundland Speech & Hearing Association
Overview: A medium-sized provincial organization founded in 1979
Mission: To foster highest quality of service to the communicatively handicapped; to advance knowledge of speech-language pathology & audiology in the region
Member of: Canadian Association of Speech-Language Pathologists & Audiologists
Finances: *Funding Sources:* Membership dues
Membership: 100+; *Fees:* Schedule available; *Member Profile:* Speech-Language Pathologists & Audiologists
Activities: *Awareness Events:* Speech Hearing Awareness Month, May *Library:* NLASLPA Library; by appointment Not open to public
Chief Officer(s):
Ashley Rossiter, President

Newfoundland & Labrador Association of Technology Industries (NATI)
#5, 391 Empire Ave., St. John's NL A1E 1W6
Tel: 709-772-8324; *Fax:* 709-757-6284
info@nati.net
www.nati.net
www.linkedin.com/company/nati
twitter.com/NATI_NL
Previous Name: Newfoundland Alliance of Technical Industries
Overview: A medium-sized provincial organization founded in 1988
Mission: To act collectively for technical organizations in Newfoundland industry in cooperation with educational & public sectors to promote the growth of innovative technical industries in Newfoundland & Labrador & the rest of Canada
Affiliation(s): Canadian Advanced Technology Association; Information Technology Association of Canada
Finances: *Annual Operating Budget:* $1.5 Million-$3 Million; *Funding Sources:* Membership dues; government
Staff Member(s): 10; 30 volunteer(s)
Membership: 120; *Fees:* $300-$700
Activities: Offering mentorship, corporate & market development programs, networking & communications, export, & program funding; *Internships:* Yes
Chief Officer(s):
Ron Taylor, Chief Executive Officer

Newfoundland & Labrador Association of the Appraisal Institute of Canada *See* The Appraisal Institute of Canada - Newfoundland & Labrador

Newfoundland & Labrador Association of the Deaf (NLAD)
21 Merrymeeting Rd., 3rd Fl., St. John's NL A1C 2V6
Tel: 709-726-6672; *Fax:* 709-726-6650; *TTY:* 709-726-6672
nlad@nlad.org
www.nlad.org
Overview: A small provincial organization founded in 1947
Mission: To protect & promote the rights, needs & concerns of people who have severe hearing disabilities & are profoundly deaf within the Province of Newfoundland & Labrador
Affiliation(s): Canadian Association of the Deaf
Chief Officer(s):

Jodie Burke, Chair
jodie.burke@bellaliant.net

Newfoundland & Labrador Athletics Association (NLAA)
PO Box 3202, Paradise NL A1L 3W4
Tel: 709-576-1303; *Fax:* 709-576-7493
athletics@nlaa.ca
www.nlaa.ca
www.facebook.com/NLAthletics
twitter.com/nlathletics
Previous Name: Newfoundland & Labrador Track & Field Association
Overview: A small provincial organization overseen by Athletics Canada
Member of: Athletics Canada
Affiliation(s): Athletics North-East; Mariners Athletics Club; Nautilus Running Club; New World Running Club; Pearlgate T&F Club; Trappers Running Club; Trinity-Conception Athletics Club; Westerland Track Club
Membership: *Fees:* Schedule available; *Member Profile:* Competitive membership (road running, cross country running, & track & field); Non-competitive membership (coaches & officials); *Committees:* Road Race; Coaches; Officials
Activities: Offering courses & clinics for athletes, officials, & coaches; Supervising events; Ensuring that rules are followed & criteria maintained throughout Newfoundland & Labrador
Chief Officer(s):
Bob Walsh, President
bob@atlantichome.net
Alison Walsh, Treasurer
alisonwalsh3@hotmail.com
George Stanoev, Technical Director

Newfoundland & Labrador Ball Hockey Association (NLBHA)
NL
www.nlbha.com
www.facebook.com/NewfoundlandAndLabradorBallHockeyAssociation
twitter.com/NLBallHockey
Overview: A small provincial organization
Mission: To promote the sport of ball hockey in Newfoundland & Labrador; To maintain rules & regulations of the sport
Member of: Canadian Ball Hockey Association; Sport Newfoundland & Labrador
Activities: Organizing championships

Newfoundland & Labrador Basketball Association
1296A Kenmount Rd., Paradise NL A1L 1N3
Tel: 709-576-0247; *Fax:* 709-576-8787
nlba@sportnf.com
www.nlba.nf.ca
www.facebook.com/nlbasketball
twitter.com/nlbasketball
Previous Name: Basketball Newfoundland
Overview: A medium-sized provincial charitable organization founded in 1988 overseen by Canada Basketball
Mission: To develop & promote the sport of basketball across Newfoundland; to assest in the establishment of basketball clubs throughout Newfoundland & Labrador.
Finances: *Annual Operating Budget:* $250,000-$500,000
Staff Member(s): 3
Membership: *Fees:* Schedule available; *Member Profile:* Clubs, coaches, volunteers, teams, players; *Committees:* Executive; Minor; Coaching; Awards; Hallf of Fame; Policy; Hall of Fame Cup; Nominating
Activities: *Internships:* Yes; *Rents Mailing List:* Yes
Chief Officer(s):
Bill Murphy, Executive Director
nlba@sportnf.com
David Constantine, President

Newfoundland & Labrador Brain Injury Association (NLBIA)
PO Box 21063, St. John's NL A1A 5B8
Tel: 709-579-3070
nlbia2011@gmail.com
www.nlbia.ca
www.facebook.com/119669344782709
Overview: A small provincial organization founded in 1987 overseen by Brain Injury Association of Canada
Mission: To meet the needs of acquired brain injury survivors & their families in Newfoundland & Labrador; To improve access to care & services
Finances: *Funding Sources:* Donations; Fundraising
Staff Member(s): 2

Membership: *Fees:* Free; *Member Profile:* Anyone in Newfoundland & Labrador who has been affected by or is interested in acquired brain injury
Activities: Offering support groups & social activities across Newfoundland & Labrador; Raising public awareness of acquired brain injury throughout the province; Providing education about acquired brain injury; Engaging in advocacy activities
Chief Officer(s):
Chava Finkler, Coordinator, Programs & Services
Michelle Ploughman, President
Marina White, Vice-President
Glen Russell, Treasurer

Newfoundland & Labrador Camping Association
c/o Malcolm Turner, President, 27 Earle Dr., Pasadena NL A0L 1K0
Tel: 709-686-2363
Overview: A medium-sized provincial organization overseen by Canadian Camping Association
Mission: To facilitate the development of organized camping in order to provide educational, character-building & constructive recreational experiences for all people; to develop awareness & appreciation of the natural environment
Member of: Canadian Camping Association
Chief Officer(s):
Malcolm Turner, President
killdevil.camp@gmail.com

Newfoundland & Labrador Cheerleading Athletics (NLCA)
PO Box 39059, Stn. Topsail Road, St. John's NL A1E 5Y7
nlcheerleading.ca
www.facebook.com/groups/10418436853
twitter.com/NLCAnews
Overview: A small provincial organization overseen by Cheer Canada
Mission: To be the governing body of cheerleading in Newfoundland & Labrador.
Member of: Cheer Canada
Membership: 600
Chief Officer(s):
Ashley Wright, President

Newfoundland & Labrador Chiropractic Association
#285W, 120 Torbay Rd., St. John's NL A1A 2G8
Tel: 709-739-7762; *Fax:* 709-739-7703
www.nlchiropractic.ca
Overview: A medium-sized provincial organization overseen by Canadian Chiropractic Association

Newfoundland & Labrador College of Dietitians (NLCD)
PO Box 1756, Stn. C, St. John's NL A1C 5P5
Tel: 709-753-4040; *Fax:* 709-781-1044
Toll-Free: 877-753-4040
registrar@nlcd.ca
www.nlcd.ca
Overview: A medium-sized provincial licensing organization overseen by Dietitians of Canada
Mission: To regulate Registered Dietitians & to ensure competency in the dietetic profession, in the interest of the people in Newfoundland
Member of: Alliance of Canadian Regulatory Boards
Finances: *Annual Operating Budget:* Less than $50,000; *Funding Sources:* Membership fees
6 volunteer(s)
Membership: 150; *Fees:* $450 registration fee; *Member Profile:* Registered dietitians; *Committees:* Continuing Competence; Disciplinary; Registration
Activities: *Internships:* Yes
Chief Officer(s):
Cynthia Whalen, Registrar
Awards:
• Dr. Patricia Giovannetti Memorial Bursary

Newfoundland & Labrador College of Physiotherapists (NLCP)
PO Box 21351, St. John's NL A1A 5G6
Tel: 709-753-6527; *Fax:* 709-753-6526
collegept@nf.aibn.com
nlcpt.com
Overview: A small provincial licensing organization founded in 1972 overseen by Canadian Alliance of Physiotherapy Regulators
Mission: To regulate the profession of physiotherapy in Newfoundland & Labrador

Member of: Canadian Alliance of Physiotherapy Regulators
Affiliation(s): Canadian Physiotherapy Association
Membership: *Member Profile:* Individuals who have completed the following requirements: an undergraduate or master's degree in physiotherapy at a university recognized by College; the national Physiotherapy Competency Examination; & a course of clinical practice; Registrants with the College must also carry current malpractice insurance; *Committees:* Policy Review; CNA Advisory; Membership; Continuing Competency; PTA Advisory; Complaints Authorization; Legislative
Activities: Licensing physiotherapists in Newfoundland & Labrador; Liaising with the provincial Ministry of Health to ensure all physiotherapists are registered and meet standards
Chief Officer(s):
Ryan Johnston, Chair
Josephine Crossan, Executive Director/Registrar
Publications:
• Newfoundland & Labrador College of Physiotherapists Newsletter
Type: Newsletter

Newfoundland & Labrador Construction Association (NLCA)
#202, 397 Stavanger Dr., St. John's NL A1A 0A1
Tel: 709-753-8920; *Fax:* 709-754-3968
info@nfld.com
www.nlca.ca
www.facebook.com/NLCA1
twitter.com/NLCA1
Overview: A small provincial organization founded in 1968 overseen by Canadian Construction Association
Mission: To act as the voice of the construction industry in Newfoundland & Labrador; To enhance the professionalism & productivity of members through the development of policies
Member of: Canadian Construction Association
Staff Member(s): 4
Membership: *Fees:* Schedule available, based upon volume of construction related business; *Member Profile:* Contractors, builders & suppliers in Newfoundland & Labrador's construction industry; *Committees:* Standard Practices; Safety; Membership; Education & Training; Conference Planning; Golf
Activities: Promoting safety practices in the workplace; Facilitating networking opportunities; Offering the Electronic Plans Room for members; Providing the Gold Seal Certification program; Selling CCA / CCDC construction documents & guides; Providing educational programs & seminars; Developing standard tendering & contractual practices & procedures; Awarding scholarships & bursaries; *Speaker Service:* Yes
Chief Officer(s):
Rhonda Collings, Chair, 709-256-2222, Fax: 709-256-8222
Rhonda Neary, President & Chief Operating Officer, 709-753-8920, Fax: 709-754-3968
rneary@nlca.ca
Meetings/Conferences:
• Newfoundland & Labrador Construction Association 2018 Annual Conference & General Meeting, 2018, NL
Scope: Provincial
Description: Sessions & keynote addresses of interest to persons such as general, electrical, & mechanical contractors, manufacturers, suppliers, safety professionals, engineers, training providers, LEED accredited professionals, & municipalities
• Newfoundland & Labrador Construction Association 2018 Annual Awards Gala, 2018, NL
Scope: Provincial
Description: An awards presentation to honour industry professionals, featuring a keynote address to delegates
Publications:
• Newfoundland & Labrador Construction Association Weekly Bulletin
Type: Newsletter; *Frequency:* Weekly
Profile: Updates for NLCA members
• Newfoundland & Labrador Construction Association Membership Directory
Type: Directory
Profile: Featuring a Trade Classification Section

Newfoundland & Labrador Construction Safety Association (NLCSA)
Donovan's Industrial Park, 80 Glencoe Dr., Mount Pearl NL A1N 4S9
Tel: 709-739-7000; *Fax:* 709-739-7001
Toll-Free: 888-681-7233
info@nlcsa.com
www.nlcsa.com
Overview: A small provincial organization founded in 1996

Mission: To be the industry leaders in the creation & maintenance of a positive cultural shift within the construction industry that assists members in achieving reductions in human, social & economic loss as a result of work related accidents, injuries & death
Staff Member(s): 23
Membership: Fees: Schedule available; Member Profile: Construction companies
Activities: Health & safety training; auditing & other services; employer certification
Chief Officer(s):
Jackie Manuel, CEO
jmanuel@nlcsa.com

Newfoundland & Labrador Crafts Development Association
See Craft Council of Newfoundland & Labrador

Newfoundland & Labrador Credit Union
Corporate Office, 240 Water St., St. John's NL A1C 1B7
Tel: 709-754-2630; Fax: 709-576-8771
Toll-Free: 800-563-3300
www.nlcu.com
www.facebook.com/NLCUHOME
twitter.com/NLCU
Previous Name: Credit Union Central of Newfoundland & Labrador
Overview: A medium-sized provincial organization founded in 1977
Mission: To assist each owner to achieve personal financial success
Activities: Offering access to financial & related services; Providing personalized financial solutions
Chief Officer(s):
Michael W. Boland, President
Allison Chaytor-Loveys, CEO & Treasurer
Glenn Bolger, Chief Operating Officer & Secretary
Elizabeth Duff, Chief Financial Officer

Newfoundland & Labrador Cricket Association
NL
cricketnewfoundland@gmail.com
www.canadacricket.com/nlcricket
www.facebook.com/185095814896295
Also Known As: Cricket NL
Overview: A small provincial organization founded in 2010 overseen by Cricket Canada
Mission: To be the provincial governing body of cricket in Newfoundland & Labrador.
Member of: Cricket Canada
Chief Officer(s):
Senthill Selvamani, President
presidentnlca@gmail.com
David Liverman, Secretary
liverman@mun.ca

Newfoundland & Labrador Criminology & Corrections Association
c/o West Coast Correctional Centre, PO Box 660, Stephenville NL A2N 3B5
Overview: A small provincial organization

Newfoundland & Labrador Curling Association
c/o Harold Walters, 114 Ennis Ave., St. John's NL A1A 1Z2
Tel: 709-728-1301
www.curlingnl.ca
Overview: A small provincial organization overseen by Canadian Curling Association
Member of: Canadian Curling Association
Finances: Funding Sources: Membership fees; Sponsorships
Activities: Organizing clinics; Coordinating tournaments
Chief Officer(s):
Harold Walters, President
president@curlingnl.ca
Mark Noseworthy, Vice-President
vicepresident@curlingnl.ca
Steve Routledge, Coordinator, Tournament
tournaments@curlingnl.ca

Newfoundland & Labrador Darts Association
NL
nldarts.webs.com
www.facebook.com/NewfoundlandAndLabradorDartsAssociation
Overview: A medium-sized provincial organization founded in 1977 overseen by National Darts Federation of Canada
Member of: National Darts Federation of Canada
Chief Officer(s):
Cavelle Taylor, President, 709-582-2952
cavtaylor@yahoo.ca

Newfoundland & Labrador Deaf Sports Association (NLDSA)
58 First St., Mount Pearl NL A1N 1Y3
Overview: A small provincial organization overseen by Canadian Deaf Sports Association
Mission: To govern fitness, amateur sports & recreation for deaf people in Newfoundland & Labrador
Member of: Canadian Deaf Sports Association
Chief Officer(s):
Bryan Johnson, Acting President
bryan.johnson@nf.sympatico.ca

Newfoundland & Labrador Dental Association
#102, 1 Centennial St., Mount Pearl NL A1N 0C9
Tel: 709-579-2362; Fax: 709-579-1250
nfdental@nfld.net
www.nlda.net
Overview: A medium-sized provincial licensing organization overseen by Canadian Dental Association
Mission: To promote & advance dentistry or dental surgery & related arts & sciences in all their branches; To increase the knowledge, skill, standard & proficiency of its members in the practice of dentistry or dental surgery; To maintain the honour & integrity of the dental profession; To aid in the furtherance of measures designed to improve dental health & prevent disease & disability; To cooperate with & to assist public & private dental associations, agencies & commissions in the task of providing or financing dental care; To promote measures designed to improve standards of dental care & the practice of dentistry or dental surgery; To improve the welfare & social standards of its members & encourage the cooperation of its members in the protection of their rights
Staff Member(s): 3
Membership: Committees: By-Laws; Continuing Education; Dental Health Awareness; Finance; Hospital Services; Salaried Dentists; Tariff
Activities: Continuing Education; job opportunities listing; Speaker Service: Yes
Chief Officer(s):
Anthony Patey, Executive Director
anthony.patey.nlda@nfld.net

Newfoundland & Labrador Dental Board
#204, 49-55 Elizabeth Ave., St. John's NL A1A 1W9
Tel: 709-579-2391; Fax: 709-579-2392
nldb@nf.aibn.com
www.nldb.ca
Overview: A small provincial licensing organization
Mission: To establish standards of qualification, practice, knowledge, & ethics for the dentistry, dental assisting, & dental technician professions
Member of: Canadian Dental Regulatory Authorities
Affiliation(s): National Dental Hygiene Exam Board; National Dental Assistant Exam Board
Membership: Member Profile: Dentists; hygienists; associations; technicians
Activities: Licensing & discipline
Chief Officer(s):
Paul O'Brien, Secretary-Registrar

Newfoundland & Labrador Drama Society (NLDS)
39 Airport Blvd., Gander NL A1V 2P8
Tel: 709-256-3796
info@nldrama.ca
nldrama.ca
Overview: A small provincial charitable organization founded in 1950
Finances: Funding Sources: Donations; Grants
Activities: Providing theatre workshops; Presenting a competitive festival for drama groups from across the province; Presenting awards; Awareness Events: Newfoundland & Labrador Provincial Drama Festival
Chief Officer(s):
Brian Dove, Chair
chair@nldrama.ca

Newfoundland & Labrador Environment Network (NLEN)
Environmental Gathering Place, PO Box 5125, Stn. C, 172 Military Rd., St. John's NL A1C 5V5
Tel: 709-753-7898; Fax: 709-726-2764
nlen.ed@gmail.com
www.nlenvironmentnetwork.org
www.facebook.com/NLEnvironmentNetwork
twitter.com/nl_environet
www.youtube.com/user/NLenvironet
Overview: A small provincial organization founded in 1990 overseen by Canadian Environmental Network
Mission: To take an active role in protecting, restoring, & enhancing the environment; To educate the public on environmental issues
Finances: Funding Sources: Membership dues
Membership: Fees: $30-$90; Member Profile: Organizations interested in environmental issues
Chief Officer(s):
Chris Hogan, Executive Director

Newfoundland & Labrador Environmental Industry Association (NEIA)
#207, 90 O'Leary Ave., St. John's NL A1B 2C7
Tel: 709-237-8090
info@neia.org
neia.org
www.linkedin.com/company/3194901
www.facebook.com/NEIAssoc
twitter.com/NEIAssoc
Overview: A medium-sized provincial organization founded in 1992
Mission: To promote the growth & development of the environmental industry of Newfoundland & Labrador; to promote ethical behavior & high standards for environmental products & services; to provide a strong, unified voice toward all private sector, government & non-profit entities involved in the Newfoundland environmental industry.
Finances: Annual Operating Budget: $250,000-$500,000; Funding Sources: Government; luncheons; seminars
Staff Member(s): 4
Membership: 124; Member Profile: Full - commercial enterprises that provide environmental products & services in Newfoundland & Labrador; associate - individuals & organizations supportive of the aims & objectives of NEIA
Chief Officer(s):
Ted Lomond, Executive Director
ted@neia.org
Frank Ricketts, Chair

Newfoundland & Labrador Federation of Agriculture
PO Box 1045, 308 Brookfield Rd., Bldg. 4, Mount Pearl NL A1N 3C9
Tel: 709-747-4874; Fax: 709-747-8827
info@nlfa.ca
www.nlfa.ca
www.facebook.com/nlfarms
twitter.com/NLFarms
Overview: A medium-sized provincial organization overseen by Canadian Federation of Agriculture
Mission: To act as the united voice of farmers in Newfoundland & Labrador; To improve the agricultural industry in Newfoundland & Labrador; To advance the economic & social conditions of those in the agricultural industry
Finances: Funding Sources: Membership fees; Federal or provincial government programs
Membership: Fees: Schedule available, based upon farm gate revenue; Member Profile: Farmers & farmer groups in Newfoundland & Labrador
Activities: Assisting in the formulation of agricultural policies; Providing information about the state of the industry
Chief Officer(s):
Melvin Rideout, President, 709-635-7151, Fax: 709-635-7318
melvinrideout@gmail.com
Paul Connors, Executive Director, 709-747-1759
paul@nlfa.ca
Nicole Parrell, Financial Officer
nicole@nlfa.ca
Publications:
• AgriView [a publication of Newfoundland & Labrador Federation of Agriculture]
Type: Newsletter; Frequency: 3 pa.; Accepts Advertising; Editor: Kerry Hann; ISSN: 1911-2297; Price: Free with Newfoundland & Labrador Federation ofAgriculture membership
Profile: Feature articles, news, forthcoming events, & safety information

Newfoundland & Labrador Federation of Labour (NLFL) / Fédération du travail de Terre-Neuve et du Labrador
NAPE Bldg., PO Box 8597, Stn. A, 330 Portugal Cove Pl., 2nd Fl., St. John's NL A1B 3P2
Tel: 709-754-1660; Fax: 709-754-1220
fed@nlfl.nf.ca

www.nlfl.nf.ca
www.facebook.com/189773034381902
twitter.com/NLFL_labour
www.youtube.com/user/NLLABOUR
Overview: A medium-sized provincial organization founded in 1936 overseen by Canadian Labour Congress
Mission: To represent the interests of its members
Staff Member(s): 8
Membership: 65,000; *Committees:* Education; Occupational Health & Safety; Political Action & Legislative Review; Trustee; Women's; Workers' Compensation; Youth
Chief Officer(s):
Mary Shortall, President
president@nlfl.nf.ca
Linda Rideout, Executive Secretary
lrideout@nlfl.nf.ca
Meetings/Conferences:
• Newfoundland & Labrador Federation of Labour Annual Conference 2018, 2018, NL
Scope: Provincial
Contact Information: Executive Secretary: Jennifer Rideout, E-mail: jrideout@nlfl.nf.ca

Newfoundland & Labrador Federation of Municipalities See Municipalities Newfoundland & Labrador

Newfoundland & Labrador Federation of School Councils (NLFSC)
PO Box 23140, St. John's NL A1B 4J9
Tel: 709-834-7300; *Fax:* 709-834-7301
Toll-Free: 877-739-4830
nlfsci@gmail.com
www.nlta.nl.ca/files/nlfsc
Overview: A medium-sized provincial organization founded in 1979
Mission: Advocacy for school-age children
Affiliation(s): Canadian Home & School Federation
Finances: *Funding Sources:* Provincial government
Membership: 231 institutional; *Fees:* Schedule available based on student membership; *Member Profile:* School councils; parent groups
Activities: Providing a forum for school councils, parent associations & other groups; advocating parental participation in education; fostering cooperation; fostering the development of policies, practices & activities that enhance the quality of school programs
Chief Officer(s):
Denise Pike, Executive Director
Peter Whittle, President

Newfoundland & Labrador Fencing Association (N&LFA)
#168, Unit 50 Hamlyn Road Plaza, St. John's NL A1E 5X7
Tel: 709-368-8830
nlfencing@gmail.com
sites.google.com/site/nlfencing
Overview: A small provincial organization overseen by Canadian Fencing Federation
Mission: To promote & develop the sport of fencing in Newfoundland
Membership: 70
Chief Officer(s):
Justin So, President

Newfoundland & Labrador Folk Arts Society (NLFAS)
#206, 223 Duckworth St., St. John's NL A1C 6N1
Tel: 709-576-8508; *Fax:* 709-757-8500
Toll-Free: 866-576-8508
office@nlfolk.com
www.nlfolk.com
www.facebook.com/nlfolk
twitter.com/nlfolkfestival
Overview: A small local organization founded in 1966
Mission: To promote & preserve the folk arts of Newfoundland & Labrador
Finances: *Funding Sources:* Corporate sponsors; Canadian Heritage; CEDA; City of St. John's
Staff Member(s): 4
Membership: *Fees:* $10
Activities: Annual Newfoundland & Labrador Folk Festival; weekly folk music club; educational workshops; *Speaker Service:* Yes
Chief Officer(s):
Erin Whitney, Office Manager

Newfoundland & Labrador Funeral Services Association (NLFSA)
PO Box 138, Winterton NL A0G 3M0
Tel: 709-586-2721; *Fax:* 709-586-2888
Overview: A small provincial organization
Mission: To offer funeral service support for the province.
Affiliation(s): Funeral Service Association of Canada

Newfoundland & Labrador Fur Breeders Association (NLFBA)
info@furfarming.ca
www.furfarming.ca
Overview: A small provincial organization
Mission: To protect the interests of the fur farming industry of Newfoundland & Labrador
Chief Officer(s):
Catherine Moores, President

Newfoundland & Labrador Genealogical Society Inc. See Family History Society of Newfoundland & Labrador

Newfoundland & Labrador Golf Association See Golf Newfoundland & Labrador

Newfoundland & Labrador Ground Water Association
PO Box 160, Doyles NL A0N 1J0
Tel: 709-955-2561; *Fax:* 709-955-3402
gwater@nf.sympatico.ca
Previous Name: Newfoundland & Labrador Water Well Corporation
Overview: A small provincial organization
Mission: To promote the protection & management of ground water in Newfoundland & Labrador
Activities: Increasing public awareness about ground water protection
Chief Officer(s):
Francis Gale, Contact

Newfoundland & Labrador Health Libraries Association (NLHLA)
c/o Health Sciences Library, Memorial University of Newfoundland, St. John's NL A1B 3V6
nlhla@chla-absc.ca
nlhla.chla-absc.ca
Overview: A medium-sized provincial organization founded in 1979 overseen by Canadian Health Libraries Association
Mission: To promote the provision of a high quality library service to the health community in Newfoundland & Labrador through mutual assistance & communication; To provide professional support to the membership by offering continuing education opportunities
Affiliation(s): Canadian Health Libraries Association
Staff Member(s): 3
Membership: *Fees:* $20; *Member Profile:* People who work in hospital & other health-related libraries & resource centres throughout Newfoundland & Labrador
Activities: Initiating & coordinating projects to improve library services & information access in the health care field in Newfoundland
Chief Officer(s):
Shannon McAlorum, President
smcalorum@mun.ca
Alison Farrell, Secretary & Treasurer
alisonr@mun.ca
Meetings/Conferences:
• Newfoundland & Labrador Health Libraries Association (NLHLA) Annual Conference & Annual General Meeting 2018, 2018, NL
Scope: Provincial

Newfoundland & Labrador High School Athletic Federation See School Sports Newfoundland & Labrador

Newfoundland & Labrador Independent Adjusters' Association
c/o Crawford & Company (Canada) Inc., #100, 96 Clyde Ave., Mount Pearl NL A1N 4S2
Tel: 709-753-6351; *Fax:* 709-753-6129
www.ciaa-adjusters.ca
Overview: A small local organization overseen by Canadian Independent Adjusters' Association
Member of: Canadian Independent Adjusters' Association
Chief Officer(s):
Marcel Pitcher, Regional President
Marcel.Pitcher@crawco.ca

Newfoundland & Labrador Insolvency Association See Newfoundland & Labrador Association of Insolvency & Restructuring Professionals

Newfoundland & Labrador Institute of Agrologists (NLIA)
PO Box 978, Mount Pearl NL A1N 3C9
Tel: 709-772-4170
www.aic.ca/agrology/nlia.cfm
Overview: A small provincial licensing organization founded in 1988 overseen by Agricultural Institute of Canada
Mission: Dedicated to the professional aspects of Canadian agriculture.
Finances: *Annual Operating Budget:* Less than $50,000
Membership: 40; *Fees:* $110
Chief Officer(s):
Gary Bishop, President/Treasurer
gary.bishop@agr.gc.ca
Samir Debnath, Registrar

Newfoundland & Labrador Interpreting Service See Interpreting Services of Newfoundland & Labrador Inc.

Newfoundland & Labrador Judo Association
#112, Hamlyn Rd. Plaza, Unit 50, St. John's NL A1E 5X7
nljawebmaster1@gmail.com
www.judonl.ca
Also Known As: Judo Newfoundland & Labrador
Overview: A small provincial organization overseen by Judo Canada
Mission: To govern & promote the sport of Judo in Newfoundland & Labrador
Member of: Judo Canada
15 volunteer(s)
Membership: *Committees:* Provincial Grading Board; Medical; NCCP; Refereeing; Hall of Fame
Chief Officer(s):
Chris Wellon, President, 709-424-4084
cwellon@nf.sympatico.ca

Newfoundland & Labrador Lacrosse Association (NLLA)
PO Box 26037, 250 Lemarchant Rd., St. John's NL A1E 0A5
nllacrossegeneral@gmail.com
nllacrosse.ca
www.facebook.com/nllacrosse
twitter.com/_NLLacrosse
Overview: A small provincial organization founded in 2009 overseen by Canadian Lacrosse Association
Mission: To be the provincial governing body for the sport of lacrosse in Newfoundland & Labrador
Member of: Canadian Lacrosse Association
Chief Officer(s):
Mark Stanford, President
president@nllacrosse.ca
Stan Cook, Vice President
Andy Schmidt, Director, Operations

Newfoundland & Labrador Laubach Literacy Council (NLLLC)
c/o Margie Lewis, PO Box 822, 141 O'Connell Dr., Corner Brook NL A2H 6H6
Tel: 709-634-5081; *Fax:* 709-634-2126
Toll-Free: 800-863-0373
laubach@nf.aibn.com
www.nlllc.ca
www.facebook.com/102784339799297
Overview: A medium-sized provincial charitable organization
Chief Officer(s):
Lewis Margie, Executive Director

Newfoundland & Labrador Library Association (NLLA)
PO Box 23192, Stn. Churchill Square, St. John's NL A1B 4J9
www.nlla.ca
www.facebook.com/newfoundlandandlabradorlibraryassociation
twitter.com/NLLA_NL
Previous Name: Newfoundland Library Association
Overview: A medium-sized provincial organization founded in 1969
Mission: To ensure the excellence of Newfoundland & Labrador's public, special, academic, & school libraries; To foster interest in libraries
Membership: *Fees:* $10 students/retired librarians/library supporters; $15 library technicians/assistants/clerks; $20 librarians/teacher librarians; *Member Profile:* Librarians & library support staff in Newfoundland & Labrador

Activities: Recommending policies; Facilitating networking opportunities; Providing workshops; Offering professional advice & assistance; *Awareness Events:* Canadian Library Month, Oct.; Newfoundland & Labrador Library Week
Chief Officer(s):
Krista Godfrey, President
kgodfrey@mun.ca
Meetings/Conferences:
• Newfoundland & Labrador Library Association Annual Conference & Annual General Meeting 2018, 2018, NL
Scope: Provincial
Description: An annual spring meeting, presenting opportunities to learn about new services, current issues, & research in Newfoundland & Labrador libraries

Newfoundland & Labrador Lung Association (NLLA)
PO Box 13457, Stn. A, St. John's NL A1B 4B8
Tel: 709-726-4664; *Fax:* 709-726-2550
Toll-Free: 888-566-5864
info@nf.lung.ca
www.nf.lung.ca
www.facebook.com/NLLung
twitter.com/nllung
Overview: A small provincial charitable organization founded in 1944 overseen by Canadian Lung Association
Mission: To achieve healthy breathing for the people of Newfoundland & Labrador
Finances: *Funding Sources:* Donations; Fundraising; Sponsorships
Activities: Organizing fundraisers; Supporting research; Providing education; Offering support groups in areas such asthma, COPD, & smoking cessation; Engaging in advocacy activities
Chief Officer(s):
Greg Noel, President & CEO
greg.noel@nf.lung.ca
Publications:
• Newfoundland & Labrador Lung Association Newsletter
Type: Newsletter

Newfoundland & Labrador Massage Therapists' Association (NLMTA)
PO Box 23212, Stn. Churchill Sq., St. John's NL A1B 4J9
Tel: 709-726-4006; *Fax:* 709-895-7767
Toll-Free: 877-744-2468
nlmta@nlmta.ca
www.nlmta.ca
Overview: A small provincial organization founded in 1990
Member of: Canadian Massage Therapy Alliance
Activities: *Library:* Not open to public

Newfoundland & Labrador Medical Association (NLMA)
164 MacDonald Dr., St. John's NL A1A 4B3
Tel: 709-726-7424; *Fax:* 709-726-7525
Toll-Free: 800-563-2003
nlma@nlma.nl.ca
www.nlma.nl.ca
www.facebook.com/nlma.nl.ca
twitter.com/_nlma
www.youtube.com/user/nlmavideo
Overview: A medium-sized provincial organization founded in 1924 overseen by Canadian Medical Association
Mission: To represent & support physicians in Newfoundland & Labrador; provide leadership in the promotion of good health & the provision of quality health care to the people of the province
Finances: *Funding Sources:* Membership dues
Staff Member(s): 11
Membership: 1,200; *Fees:* $2,195 full; $695 non-resident; $333 retired; $150 resident; $20 student; *Member Profile:* Physicians; medical students; residents; retired physicians; *Committees:* Nominating; Governance; Negotiations; Finance & Administration; External Relations
Chief Officer(s):
Wendy Graham, President
president@nlma.nl.ca
Robert Thompson, Executive Director, 709-726-7424 Ext. 302
rthompson@nlma.nl.ca

Newfoundland & Labrador Multicultural and Folk Arts Council See Newfoundland & Labrador Multicultural Council Inc.

Newfoundland & Labrador Multicultural Council Inc. (NLMC)
PO Box 2544, Stn. C, St. John's NL A1C 6K1
Tel: 709-753-2917; *Fax:* 709-726-8201
secretary@nlmfac.ca
www.nlmfac.ca
Previous Name: Newfoundland & Labrador Multicultural and Folk Arts Council
Overview: A small provincial organization founded in 1979
Mission: To advance multiculturalism in Newfoundland & Labrador
Membership: 9; *Fees:* $5 individuals; $50 organizations
Activities: Promoting multiculturalism & folk-arts; Presenting scholarships

Newfoundland & Labrador Nurse Practitioner Association (NLNPA)
NL
www.nlnpa.ca
Overview: A small provincial organization
Mission: Represents the professional interests of Nurse Practitioners (NPs) in NL.
Member of: Association of Registered Nurses of Newfoundland & Labrador
Membership: *Member Profile:* Nurse practitioners from Newfoundland & Labrador
Activities: Providing professional support to nurse practitioners in Newfoundland & Labrador; Offering educational opportunities; Advocating for accessible, high quality health care throughout the province; Creating networking opportunities
Chief Officer(s):
Penney Ralph, Communications Director
pennyjralph@gmail.com
Valda Duke, Treasurer
vjaw1@hotmail.com

Newfoundland & Labrador Nurses' Union (NLNU) / Syndicat des infirmières de Terre-Neuve et du Labrador
PO Box 416, 229 Major's Path, St. John's NL A1C 5J9
Tel: 709-753-9961; *Fax:* 709-753-1210
Toll-Free: 800-563-5100
info@nlnu.ca
www.nlnu.ca
www.facebook.com/rnunl
www.youtube.com/user/RNUNL
Overview: A medium-sized provincial organization founded in 1974
Member of: Canadian Federation of Nurses Unions; Canadian Labour Congress
Staff Member(s): 21
Membership: 5,700; *Member Profile:* Unionized nurses
Chief Officer(s):
John Vivian, Executive Director
jvivian@nlnu.ca
Karyn Whelan, Communications Specialist
kwhelan@rnunl.ca

Newfoundland & Labrador Occupational Therapy Board (NLOTB)
RPO Churchill Square, PO Box 23076, St. John's NL A1B 4J9
Tel: 709-697-4920; *Fax:* 709-383-0135
registrar@nlotb.ca
www.nlaot.ca/board/index.asp
Overview: A small provincial licensing organization founded in 1988
Mission: Protection of the public through implementation of legislation on occupational therapy practice
Affiliation: Canadian Association of Occupational Therapists; Newfoundland & Labrador Association of Occupational Therapists; Association of Canadian Occupational Therapists Registering Organizations
Finances: *Annual Operating Budget:* Less than $50,000; *Funding Sources:* Membership dues
Staff Member(s): 5; 5 volunteer(s)
Membership: 125; *Fees:* $100 full-time; $75 part-time; *Member Profile:* Graduation from WFOT-approved school; CAOT exam completion; *Committees:* Practice Support
Chief Officer(s):
Kim Doyle, Registrar
registrar@nlotb.ca

Newfoundland & Labrador Operating Room Nurses Association (N&LORNA)
NL
Overview: A medium-sized provincial organization overseen by Operating Room Nurses Association of Canada
Mission: To enhance patient care by providing members with professional growth opportunities; To promote perioperative nursing practice standards
Membership: *Member Profile:* Registered Nurses in Newfoundland & Labrador who are engaged in operating room nursing or involved in the Perioperative setting
Activities: *Awareness Events:* Perioperative Nurses Week, November
Chief Officer(s):
Joanne Peddle, President

Newfoundland & Labrador Organization of Women Entrepreneurs (NLOWE)
Regatta Plaza II, 84-86 Elizabeth Ave., 2nd Fl., St. John's NL A1A 1W7
Tel: 709-754-5555; *Fax:* 709-754-0079
Toll-Free: 888-656-9311
www.nlowe.org
www.linkedin.com/company/newfoundland-and-labrador-organization-of-women-entrepreneurs-nlowe-
www.facebook.com/nlowe.org
twitter.com/nlowe_org
www.youtube.com/user/NLOWEVideo
Overview: A medium-sized provincial organization founded in 1997
Mission: To support women's contribution to growth in business & community economic development
Affiliation(s): Atlantic Canada Opportunities Agency; Human Resources Development Canada
Finances: *Funding Sources:* Membership dues; government funding
Staff Member(s): 15
Membership: *Fees:* $100 individual; $175 non-profit; $350 corporate; *Member Profile:* Women business owners in Newfoundland & Labrador
Activities: Annual conference for women entrepreneurs; programs; online training sessions; business advice
Chief Officer(s):
Paula Sheppard, Chief Executive Officer
psheppard@nlowe.org
Alison Stoodley, President, 709-740-4910

Newfoundland & Labrador Outfitters Association (NLOA)
Goodhouse Building, 93 West St., 2nd Fl., Corner Brook NL A2H 2Y5
Tel: 709-639-5926
Toll-Free: 866-420-6562
info@nloa.ca
www.nloa.ca
Overview: A small provincial organization
Mission: To assist hunting & fishing outfitters throughout Newfoundland & Labrador; To work with government departments & other organizations that impact the outfitting industry
Membership: *Member Profile:* Licensed hunting & fishing outfitter operations in Newfoundland & Labrador that uphold the ethics & goals of the association
Activities: Providing information to hunting & fishing outfitters
Chief Officer(s):
Keith Payne, Executive Director, 709-634-9962
keithpayne@nloa.ca
Melissa Byrne, Coordinator, Project Support
melissa@nloa.ca

Newfoundland & Labrador Palliative Care Association (NLPCA)
PO Box 39023, 390 Topsail Rd., St. John's NL A1E 5Y7
www.nlpalliativecareassociation.com
Overview: A medium-sized provincial charitable organization founded in 1993
Mission: To strive for excellence in the care of persons near death; To lessen the suffering & loneliness of people approaching the end of life
Member of: Canadian Hospice Palliative Care Association (CHPCA)
Finances: *Funding Sources:* Fundraising
Membership: *Fees:* $30; *Member Profile:* Individuals & organizations in Newfoundland & Labrador engaged in palliative care education, counselling, & services
Activities: Engaging in advocacy activities; Educating professionals & the public about palliative care; Promoting principles & standards of end of life care; Encouraging research
Chief Officer(s):
Debbie Squires, President
Daphne Crane-Burt, Secretary

Newfoundland & Labrador Parks & Recreation Association
See Recreation Newfoundland & Labrador

Newfoundland & Labrador Pharmacy Board (NLPB)
Apothecary Hall, 488 Water St., St. John's NL A1E 1B3
Tel: 709-753-5877; Fax: 709-753-8615
Toll-Free: 877-453-5877
inforx@nlpb.ca
www.nlpb.ca
www.facebook.com/139887479372029
twitter.com/nlpharmacyboard
Previous Name: Newfoundland Pharmacy Association
Overview: A small provincial organization
Mission: To set, govern & advance the standards & scope of pharmacy practice & pharmacy service for the people of Newfoundland & Labrador
Member of: Canadian Council on Continuing Education in Pharmacy
Chief Officer(s):
Margot Priddle, Registrar
mpriddle@nlpb.ca
Publications:
- The Apothecary [a publication of the Newfoundland & Labrador Pharmacy Board]
Type: Newsletter; *Frequency:* 3 pa

Newfoundland & Labrador Physiotherapy Association (NLPA)
St. John's NL
www.physiotherapy.ca/Atlantic-Branches/Newfoundland
www.facebook.com/NLPhysioAssoc
twitter.com/nlphysioassoc
Overview: A medium-sized provincial organization overseen by Canadian Physiotherapy Association
Mission: To provide leadership & direction to the physiotherapy profession; To foster excellence in practice, education & research
Member of: Canadian Physiotherapy Association
Finances: *Funding Sources:* Membership dues; Educational activities
Chief Officer(s):
Lisa Pike, Executive Director
Sherry Lythgoe, President

Newfoundland & Labrador Powerlifting Association
NL
www.nlpowerlifting.ca
www.facebook.com/NLPowerlifting
Overview: A small provincial organization overseen by Canadian Powerlifting Union
Member of: Canadian Powerlifting Union
Membership: *Fees:* $50 regular; $30 special Olympian
Chief Officer(s):
Jeff Butt, President

Newfoundland & Labrador Prospectors Association (NLPA)
17 Nelder Dr., Mount Pearl NL A1N 4M2
Tel: 709-740-6000
www.nlprospectors.org
Overview: A small provincial organization founded in 2012
Mission: To act as a voice for all member prospectors in the province; to raise awareness about prospecting in Newfoundland & Labrador
Chief Officer(s):
Norm Mercer, President
nmercer@nlprospectors.org

Newfoundland & Labrador Provincial Association of Family Resource Centres
c/o Kilbride to Ferryland Family Resource Centre, PO Box 1039, Goulds NL A1S 1H2
Tel: 709-747-8530; Fax: 709-745-2727
kffrc@avinet.net
Overview: A medium-sized provincial organization
Mission: To promote the well-being of families
Affiliation(s): Canadian Association of Family Resource Programs (FRP Canada)
Activities: Providing resources to those who support families & care for children
Chief Officer(s):
Rhonda Thomas, Contact

Newfoundland & Labrador Public Health Association (NLPHA)
PO Box 8172, St. John's NL A1B 3M9
Tel: 709-364-1589
info@nlpha.ca
www.nlpha.ca
Overview: A small provincial organization founded in 1978 overseen by Canadian Public Health Association
Mission: To advocate for the physical, emotional, social, & environmental well-being of Newfoundland & Labrador's people & communities
Member of: Canadian Public Health Association (CPHA)
Finances: *Funding Sources:* Donations
Membership: *Fees:* $30 individual/affiliate; *Member Profile:* Individuals in Newfoundland & Labrador who are interested in public health & community activities, such as health & community service workers, researchers, & educators
Activities: Raising awareness of public health issues; Addressing public health issues, such as school nutrition, food security, mental health services, family life education, fetal alcohol syndrome, primary health care, & low level flying; Providing education; Offering prevention programming; Liaising with partners & community organizations to strengthen community health; Offering monthly business & educational teleconferences
Chief Officer(s):
Lynn Vivian-Book, President
Elizabeth Wright, Secretary
Pat Murray, Treasurer
Publications:
- Newfoundland & Labrador Public Health Association Newsletter
Type: Newsletter; *Editor:* Douglas Howse

Newfoundland & Labrador Right to Life Association
PO Box 5427, 195 Freshwater Rd., St. John's NL A1C 5W2
Tel: 709-579-1500; Fax: 709-579-1600
centreforlife@centreforlife.ca
www.centreforlife.ca
Also Known As: Centre for Life
Previous Name: Right to Life Association of Newfoundland & Labrador
Overview: A small provincial organization founded in 1977
Mission: To provide support, resources, & referrals to women experiencing unplanned pregnancies
Member of: Alliance for Life
Chief Officer(s):
Linda Holden, President

Newfoundland & Labrador Rugby Union
PO Box 9, Mount Pearl NL A1N 2C1
www.rockrugby.ca
Also Known As: The Rock Rugby
Overview: A small provincial organization overseen by Rugby Canada
Member of: Rugby Canada
Chief Officer(s):
John Cowan, President
jcowan@mun.ca

Newfoundland & Labrador Safety Council See Safety Services Newfoundland & Labrador

Newfoundland & Labrador School Boards Association (NLSBA)
40 Strawberry Marsh Rd., St. John's NL A1B 2V5
Tel: 709-722-7171; Fax: 709-722-8214
www.schoolboardsnl.ca
Overview: A medium-sized provincial organization founded in 1969 overseen by Canadian School Boards Association
Mission: To promote the interests of education in Newfoundland & Labrador
Finances: *Annual Operating Budget:* $250,000-$500,000; *Funding Sources:* Member board fees; Government grants
Staff Member(s): 5; 150 volunteer(s)
Membership: 11 school boards + 180 trustees; *Fees:* Schedule available, based on school population; *Member Profile:* Elected school board members; *Committees:* Finance; Resolution; Legislative; Certification; Communication; Nominating
Activities: *Speaker Service:* Yes
Chief Officer(s):
Brian Shortall, Executive Director
brianshortall@schoolboardsnl.ca

Newfoundland & Labrador School Milk Foundation See School Milk Foundation of Newfoundland & Labrador

Newfoundland & Labrador Sexual Assault Crisis & Prevention Centre Inc. (NLSACPC)
#101, 360 Topsoil Rd., St. John's NL A1E 2B6
Tel: 709-747-7757; Fax: 709-747-7758
coordinator@sexualassaultcentre.nf.net
www.nlsacpc.com
www.facebook.com/EndSV
Previous Name: St. John's Rape Crisis & Information Centre
Overview: A small local organization overseen by Canadian Association of Sexual Assault Centres
Mission: To provide services & support to persons affected by sexual violence; To work towards prevention of sexual violence through education
Finances: *Annual Operating Budget:* $100,000-$250,000; *Funding Sources:* Donations; Fundraising; Government of Newfoundland
10-2 volunteer(s)
Membership: *Member Profile:* Persons who work towards the prevention of sexual assault
Activities: Offering educational presentations for schools, community centres, & workplaces; Providing written information; Raising awareness about matters of sexual violence by participating in community events; Providing support groups & phone support; Offering referrals; Accompanying victims, when requested, to medical & legal procedures
Chief Officer(s):
Barbara Wadman, Centre Coordinator

Newfoundland & Labrador Snowboard Association
PO Box 259, Steady Brook NL A2H 2N2
Tel: 709-634-4664
nlsnowboard@gmail.com
nlsnowboard.com
Also Known As: NL Snowboard
Overview: A small provincial organization overseen by Canadian Snowboard Federation
Mission: To be the provincial governing body of competitive snowboarding in Newfoundland & Labrador
Member of: Canadian Snowboard Federation
Chief Officer(s):
Emily Pittman, Contact

Newfoundland & Labrador Soccer Association
39 Churchill Ave., St. John's NL A1A 0H7
Tel: 709-576-0601; Fax: 709-576-0588
info@nlsa.ca
www.nlsa.ca
Previous Name: Newfoundland Soccer Association
Overview: A large provincial organization overseen by Canadian Soccer Association
Mission: To provide opportunities for the general public to engage in the game of soccer while having fun & competition
Member of: Canadian Soccer Association
Chief Officer(s):
Dragan Mirkovic, Director, Technical, 709-576-2262
dragan@nlsa.ca
Mike Power, Director, Player Development, 709-576-7310
mike@nlsa.ca
Rob Comerford, Manager, Business, 709-576-0601
rob@nlsa.ca

Newfoundland & Labrador Society for Medical Laboratory Science (NLSMLS)
c/o Canadian Blood Services, 7 Wicklow St., St. John's NL A1B 3Z9
Tel: 709-758-8068
www.nlsmls.ca
Previous Name: Newfoundland & Labrador Society of Laboratory Technologists
Overview: A medium-sized provincial organization overseen by Canadian Society for Medical Laboratory Science
Mission: To serve & protect the public
Membership: *Member Profile:* Laboratory technicians in Newfoundland & Labrador
Chief Officer(s):
Colin Power, President
colin.power@blood.ca

Newfoundland & Labrador Society for the Prevention of Cruelty to Animals
PO Box 29053, St. John's NL A1A 5B5
Tel: 709-726-0301; Fax: 709-579-8089
shelter@spcastjohns.com
www.spcastjohns.org
www.facebook.com/SPCAStJohns
twitter.com/spcastjohns
www.instagram.com/spcastjohns;
www.youtube.com/user/SPCAVideos
Also Known As: Newfoundland & Labrador SPCA
Overview: A medium-sized provincial charitable organization founded in 1954 overseen by Canadian Federation of Humane Societies

Canadian Associations / Newfoundland & Labrador Speed Skating Association (NLSSA)

Mission: To act as the voice for animal welfare in Newfoundland & Labrador; To promote humane treatment toward all animals
Member of: Canadian Federation of Humane Societies
Finances: *Funding Sources:* Provincial government; Donations
Activities: Offering animal protection, shelter, & care; Increasing understanding of animal welfare
Chief Officer(s):
Carolyn Hickey, Secretary

Newfoundland & Labrador Society of Laboratory Technologists *See* Newfoundland & Labrador Society for Medical Laboratory Science

Newfoundland & Labrador Speed Skating Association (NLSSA)
NL
Overview: A small provincial organization overseen by Speed Skating Canada
Member of: Speed Skating Canada

Newfoundland & Labrador Table Tennis Association (NLTTA)
NL
Tel: 709-834-8402
nltabletennis.com
Overview: A small provincial organization overseen by Table Tennis Canada
Mission: To promote the sport of Table Tennis in Newfoundland & Labrador
Member of: Sprot NL; Table Tennis Canada
Affiliation(s): International Table Tennis Federation
Membership: *Fees:* $25 full member sr.; $20 full member jr.; $50 club; free for school clubs
Activities: Competetions; Training courses; *Awareness Events:* Memorial University of Newfoundland & Labrador Open
Chief Officer(s):
Barry Hicks, President
president@nltta.com
Merv Greenham, Vice President, Technical
vp-technical@nltta.com
Kenny Curlew, Vice President, Administrative
vp-admin@nltta.com
Harrison Lamswood, Secretary
secretary@nltta.com
Rick Fisher, Treasurer, 709-834-0015
finance@nltta.com

Newfoundland & Labrador Teachers' Association (NLTA) / Association des enseignants de Terre-Neuve
3 Kenmount Rd., St. John's NL A1B 1W1
Tel: 709-726-3223; *Fax:* 709-726-4302
Toll-Free: 800-563-3599
mail@nlta.nl.ca
www.nlta.nl.ca
www.facebook.com/nlta.nl.ca
twitter.com/NLTeachersAssoc
Overview: A medium-sized provincial organization founded in 1890 overseen by Canadian Teachers' Federation
Mission: To strive towards the professional excellence & personal well-being of teachers
Membership: 6,400; *Member Profile:* Teachers in Newfoundland & Labrador; *Committees:* Communications / Political Action; Curriculum; Equity Issues in Education; Electoral; Finance & Property; Group Insurance; Internal Review (Ad Hoc); Membership Benefits & Services; Professional Issues; Teacher Health & Wellness
Activities: Publishing numerous guides & brochures for teachers; Engaging in advocacy activities; Delivering supportive programs & services, such as the employee assistance program & the health & wellness promotion program; Offering professional development opportunities
Chief Officer(s):
Don Ash, Executive Director, 709-726-3223 Ext. 224
dash@nlta.nl.ca
Awards:
• Alan Bishop Award
To recognize outstanding service at the provincial level of the NLTA
• Bancroft Award
To recognize outstanding service at the branch level of the NLTA
• Barnes Award
To recognize outstanding service to the NLTA in the field of professional development by teachers

• Patricia Cowan Award
To recognize individuals or groups outside the school system for outstanding support & promotion of education
• President's Award
To recognize a strong supporter of the NLTA
• Special Recognition Award
To recognize a major contribution by an NLTA member to the cultural, social, or community life of the province
• Roy C. Hill Award
Formerly Hilroy Fellowship

Newfoundland & Labrador Tennis Association *See* Tennis Newfoundland & Labrador

Newfoundland & Labrador Track & Field Association *See* Newfoundland & Labrador Athletics Association

Newfoundland & Labrador Veterinary Medical Association (NALVMA)
PO Box 818, Mount Pearl NL A1N 3C8
nalvmacouncil@gmail.com
www.nalvma.ca
Overview: A small provincial organization founded in 1971 overseen by Canadian Veterinary Medical Association
Mission: To promote better animal health care; to educate the general public & strive towards continued excellence in veterinary medicine.
Activities: *Speaker Service:* Yes; *Rents Mailing List:* Yes
Chief Officer(s):
Heather Hillier, President

Newfoundland & Labrador Volleyball Association (NLVA)
1296A Kenmount Rd., Paradise NL A1L 1N3
Tel: 709-576-0817; *Fax:* 709-576-7493
www.nlva.net
Overview: A small provincial organization founded in 1986 overseen by Volleyball Canada
Mission: To promote volleyball in Newfoundland & Labrador; To provide competitive opportunities for its members
Chief Officer(s):
Russell Jackson, Executive Director
nlvaruss@sportnl.ca
Luke Harris, Director, Technical
nlvaluke@sportnl.ca

Newfoundland & Labrador Water Well Corporation *See* Newfoundland & Labrador Ground Water Association

Newfoundland & Labrador Wildlife Federation (NWLF)
15 Conran St., St. John's NL A1E 5L8
Tel: 709-364-8415
www.nlwf.ca
Overview: A medium-sized provincial organization founded in 1962 overseen by Canadian Wildlife Federation
Mission: To foster awareness & enjoyment of the natural world; To promote the sustainable use of natural resources; To protect wildlife & its habitat through conservation & effective wildlife management
Affiliation(s): Over 15 affiliated conservation groups, including the Canadian Wildlife Federation (CWF), Rod & Gun Clubs from St. John's, Bay Of Islands, Green Bay, Baie d'Espoir, Marystown, South East Placentia & Grand Falls
Activities: Liaising with government agencies & organizations with similar goals; Conducting educational programs in conservation
Chief Officer(s):
Rick Bouzan, President

Newfoundland & Labrador Women's Institutes
c/o Arts & Culture Centre, PO Box 1854, St. John's NL A1C 5P9
Tel: 709-753-8780; *Fax:* 709-753-8708
nlwi@nfld.com
www.nlwi.ca
Overview: A small provincial organization overseen by Federated Women's Institutes of Canada
Mission: To encourage women to work together to expand their skills, broaden their interests, plan meetings, workshops & conferences, & strengthen the quality of life for themselves, their families & their communities
Membership: *Fees:* $20
Chief Officer(s):
Barbara Taylor, Executive Officer
Awards:
• Newfoundland Women's Institutes Scholarship
Students must submit grades, a short essay & letters of reference in the application package *Eligibility:* Male & female students who have completed grade 12 *Deadline:* Oct 31

Newfoundland & Labradour Institute of the Purchasing Management Association of Canada *See* Supply Chain Management Association - Newfoundland & Labrador

Newfoundland Alliance of Technical Industries *See* Newfoundland & Labrador Association of Technology Industries

Newfoundland Amateur Baseball Association *See* Newfoundland Baseball

Newfoundland Aquaculture Industry Association (NAIA)
#209, 11 Austin St., St. John's NL A1B 4C1
Tel: 709-754-2854; *Fax:* 709-754-2981
www.naia.ca
www.facebook.com/207556199255955
twitter.com/naia_nl
Overview: A small provincial organization
Mission: To facilitate the commercial development of aquaculture in Newfoundland; To strive towards excellence in quality, safety, environmental sustainability, & profitability; To act as the voice of the industry in the province
Member of: Canadian Aquaculture Industry Alliance (CAIA); National Seafood Sector Council (NSSC)
Membership: *Fees:* $400 regular members; $200 associate members; *Member Profile:* Finfish & shellfish farmers in Newfoundland; Primary & secondary processors; Hatcheries producers; Supply & service companies; Academic institutions
Activities: Liaising with government; Offering training & advice; Providing business intelligence; *Awareness Events:* Aquaculture Week, June
Chief Officer(s):
Miranda Pryor, Executive Director, 709-754-2854 Ext. 2
miranda@naia.ca
Cyr Couturier, President
Robert Barry, Secretary, 709-576-7292
Jennifer Caines, Treasurer, 709-665-3168
Publications:
• Cold Harvester [a publication of the Newfoundland Aquaculture Industry Association]
Type: Magazine; *Frequency:* Quarterly
Profile: Information about the successes & challenges of the aquaculture industry for Newfoundland Aquaculture Industry Association members
• Newfoundland Aquaculture Industry Association Member Directory
Type: Directory
  St. Alban's Office
  PO Box 27, 88 Main St., St Alban's NL A0H 2E0

Newfoundland Association of Architects
PO Box 5204, 7 Downing St., St. John's NL A1C 5V5
Tel: 709-726-8550; *Fax:* 709-726-1549
nlaa@newfoundlandarchitects.com
www.newfoundlandarchitects.com
Overview: A small provincial organization
Mission: To support architecture & architects in Newfoundland and Labrador.
Membership: *Fees:* Schedule available

Newfoundland Association of Optometrists *See* Newfoundland & Labrador Association of Optometrists

Newfoundland Association of Visual Language Interpreters (NAVLI)
36 Ursula Cres., St. Philips NL A1M 1G6
skinterpreter@nf.sympatico.ca
Overview: A small provincial organization overseen by Association of Visual Language Interpreters of Canada
Member of: Association of Visual Language Interpreters of Canada (AVLIC)
Membership: *Member Profile:* Professional sign language interpreters

Newfoundland Baseball
1296A Kenmount Rd., Paradise NL
Tel: 709-576-3401
www.leaguelineup.com/welcome.asp?url=nlbaseball
twitter.com/BaseballNL
Also Known As: Baseball NL
Previous Name: Newfoundland Amateur Baseball Association
Overview: A small provincial organization founded in 1947 overseen by Baseball Canada
Mission: Supports amatuer baseball in Newfoundland.
Member of: Baseball Canada

Finances: *Annual Operating Budget:* $50,000-$100,000; *Funding Sources:* Membership dues; fundraising; corporate; government
10 volunteer(s)
Membership: 20; *Fees:* Schedule available; *Committees:* Hall of Fame
Activities: Amateur baseball development; *Rents Mailing List:* Yes
Chief Officer(s):
Kevin Legge, President
Ryan Garland, Executive Director

Newfoundland Cancer Treatment & Research Foundation (NCTRF)
300 Prince Philip Dr., St. John's NL A1B 3V6
Tel: 709-777-6484; *Fax:* 709-753-0927
Overview: A medium-sized provincial charitable organization founded in 1971
Mission: To provide excellence in cancer care, including research, cancer prevention, treatment, & support, in Newfoundland & Labrador
Affiliation(s): Canadian Council on Health Services Accreditation
Activities: Conducting & fostering research; Participating in the education of health care professionals & providers; Operating cancer registries; *Library:* Elaine Deluney Patient & Family Resource Library

Newfoundland Cerebral Palsy Association Inc. *See* Cerebral Palsy Association of Newfoundland & Labrador

Newfoundland Chicken Marketing Board *See* Chicken Farmers of Newfoundland & Labrador

Newfoundland Co-operative Union; Newfoundland Co-operative Services *See* Newfoundland-Labrador Federation of Cooperatives

Newfoundland Council for Nursing Assistants *See* College of Licensed Practical Nurses of Newfoundland & Labrador

Newfoundland Dental Assistants Association (NLDAA)
#274, 38 Pearson St., St. John's NL A1A 3R1
Tel: 709-579-2391
nldaa@yahoo.ca
www.nldaa.ca
Overview: A small provincial organization overseen by Canadian Dental Assistants Association
Mission: To advance the career of dental assisting in Newfoundland
Membership: *Fees:* $75 regular; $40 NLDAA membership only; $17 student; *Member Profile:* Individuals employed in the dentistry field in Newfoundland; Persons who have graduated from a dental assisting program; Students enrolled in a school of dental assisting
Activities: Providing educational opportunities
Chief Officer(s):
Vera Walsh, President
Publications:
• Newfoundland Dental Assistants Association Newsletter
Type: Newsletter; *Frequency:* Semiannually
Profile: Updates for members

Newfoundland Equestrian Association (NEA)
PO Box 372, Stn. C, St. John's NL A1C 5J9
equestriannl.ca
www.facebook.com/groups/1529209380693900
Overview: A small provincial organization
Member of: Equine Canada
Membership: *Fees:* $35 individual junior (18 years & under); $35 individual senior (19 years & over); $60 family ($10 for additional juniors); $65 club/corporate; *Member Profile:* Equestrians in Newfoundland; Equestrian associations or clubs
Activities: Offering the Learn to Ride program; Providing coaching programs; *Library:* NEA Library
Chief Officer(s):
Jessica Anstey, President
president@equestriannl.ca
Dominique Lavers, Secretary
secretary@equestriannl.ca
Awards:
• Horsemanship Award
• Sportsmanship Award
• Volunteer of the Year Award
• Most Improved Junior Rider Award
• Most Improved Senior Rider Award
• Horse of the Year Award
• Pony of the Year Award
• Industry Leader Award
• Coach of the Year Award
• Junior Athlete of the Year Award
• Senior Athlete of the Year Award
• Recreational Rider of the Year Award
• Recreational Driver of the Year Award
Meetings/Conferences:
• Newfoundland Equestrian Association Annual General Meeting 2018, 2018
Scope: Provincial

Newfoundland Federation of Music Festivals
1 Marigold Place, St. John's NL A1A 3T1
Tel: 709-722-9376
Overview: A medium-sized provincial organization founded in 1969 overseen by Federation of Canadian Music Festivals
Mission: To coordinate activities of local music festivals & conduct a provincial music festival annually; to participate in the CIBC National Music Festival.
Chief Officer(s):
Joan Woodrow, Provincial Administrator
jwoodrow@bellaliant.net

Newfoundland Historical Society (NHS)
PO Box 23154, Stn. Churchill Square, St. John's NL A1B 4J9
Tel: 709-722-3191; *Fax:* 709-722-9035
nhs@nf.aibn.com
www.nlhistory.ca
Overview: A small provincial charitable organization founded in 1905
Mission: To promote study, research & public discussion of Newfoundland & Labrador's history; to record the history of the province; to promote preservation of historic sites
Finances: *Funding Sources:* Membership fees; government grants; private
Membership: 526; *Fees:* $40 individual/institutional; $400 life; *Committees:* Office; Finance; Membership; Programme; *Publications:* Newfoundland Quarterly; AHI; Nominating
Activities: Fall/winter public lecture series; compilation of database of historical/heritage societies in the province; compilation of database of pre-1949 churches; pamphlets & monographs on Newfoundland history; symposia; *Rents Mailing List:* Yes; *Library:* Open to public
Chief Officer(s):
Fred Smith, President

Newfoundland Horticultural Society
PO Box 28086, Stn. Avalon Mall, St. John's NL A1B 4J8
NHSweb@nl.rogers.com
nfldhort.dhs.org/page2.htm
Overview: A small provincial organization founded in 1963
Mission: To encourage an interest in all aspects of gardening as related to Newfoundland conditions
Affiliation(s): Royal Horticultural Society
Finances: *Annual Operating Budget:* Less than $50,000; *Funding Sources:* Membership fees
Membership: 104; *Fees:* $20
Activities: Monthly meetings; garden visits in summer; *Awareness Events:* Garden Show, August
Chief Officer(s):
Shirley Rooney, President

Newfoundland Library Association *See* Newfoundland & Labrador Library Association

Newfoundland Medical Board *See* College of Physicians & Surgeons of Newfoundland & Labrador

Newfoundland Native Women's Association
PO Box 22, Benoits Cove NL A0L 1A0
Tel: 709-789-3430; *Fax:* 709-789-2207
nf.nativewomen@nf.aibn.com
Overview: A small provincial organization overseen by Native Women's Association of Canada
Mission: To enhance, promote & foster the social, economic, cultural and political well-being of First Nations and Métis women within First Nation, Métis and Canadian societies.
Membership: *Member Profile:* Aboriginal women residing off-reserve living in the region may particiapte if they are unemployed, under-employed or employed and seeking assistance with employment maintenance.

Newfoundland Paddling Club *See* Paddle Newfoundland & Labrador

Newfoundland Pharmacy Association *See* Newfoundland & Labrador Pharmacy Board

Newfoundland Racquetball Association
NL
Overview: A small provincial organization overseen by Racquetball Canada
Member of: Racquetball Canada; Sport Newfoundland & Labrador

Newfoundland Real Estate Association *See* Newfoundland & Labrador Association of Realtors

Newfoundland Rock Garden Society
St. John's NL
Overview: A small provincial organization founded in 1986
Member of: North American Rock Garden Society
Activities: Monthly meetings; Garden visits; Annual guest speaker
Chief Officer(s):
Todd Boland, Chair

Newfoundland Rowing Association *See* Rowing Newfoundland

Newfoundland Soccer Association *See* Newfoundland & Labrador Soccer Association

Newfoundland Society for the Physically Disabled Inc. *See* Easter Seals Newfoundland & Labrador

Newfoundland Speech & Hearing Association *See* Newfoundland & Labrador Association of Speech-Language Pathologists & Audiologists

Newfoundland Symphony Orchestra Association (NSO)
Arts & Culture Centre, PO Box 23125, Stn. Churchill Square, St. John's NL A1B 4J9
Tel: 709-722-4441; *Fax:* 709-753-0561
nso@nsomusic.ca
www.nsomusic.ca
www.linkedin.com/company/newfoundland-symphony-orchestra
www.facebook.com/NSOonline
twitter.com/NSOonline
Overview: A small provincial charitable organization founded in 1979 overseen by Orchestras Canada
Mission: To foster & promote in all age groups of the general public of the province an interest in & an appreciation of music; To provide the province with a symphony orchestra of the highest possible standard; To provide professional musicians, highly skilled amateur players & talented students with the opportunity of performing
Member of: Orchestras Canada
Finances: *Annual Operating Budget:* $500,000-$1.5 Million; *Funding Sources:* Canada Council; Arts Council; Municipal government
Staff Member(s): 4; 30 volunteer(s)
Membership: 50
Activities: Performing more than 25 times annually; Providing music education programs for schools, community groups, and private studios; *Library:* Not open to public
Chief Officer(s):
Hugh Donnan, CEO
hd@nsomusic.ca
Marc David, Music Director

Newfoundland Symphony Youth Orchestra (NSYO)
18 Hazelwood Cres., St. John's NL A1E 6B3
Tel: 709-690-2259
info@nsyo.ca
www.nsyo.ca
www.facebook.com/NSYOmusic
twitter.com/NSYOmusic
www.youtube.com/user/NSYOstjohnsnl
Overview: A small local charitable organization overseen by Orchestras Canada
Mission: To encourage and develop the musical abilities of young musicians; To play high quality orchestral music
Finances: *Funding Sources:* Individual & corporate donations; Government grants
Staff Member(s): 10
Membership: *Member Profile:* Musicians aged 8-23
Activities: Performing public concerts; Holding regular rehearsals
Chief Officer(s):
Laura Ivany, Executive Director
Grant Etchegary, Artistic Director

Newfoundland-Labrador Federation of Cooperatives (NLFC)
Cooperators Bldg., PO Box 13369, Stn. A, #203, 19 Crosbie Pl., St. John's NL A1B 4B7
Fax: 709-726-9433
Toll-Free: 877-726-9431
www.nlfc.coop
Previous Name: Newfoundland Co-operative Union; Newfoundland Co-operative Services
Overview: A medium-sized provincial organization founded in 1981
Mission: To represent the interests of co-operative businesses in Newfoundland & Labrador; To promote the development & growth of the co-operative business sector in the province
Member of: Canadian Co-operative Association
Membership: 40+ local co-ops; *Fees:* $100 - $2000; *Member Profile:* Co-operatives & credit unions in Newfoundland & Labrador
Activities: Liaising with the provincial government, industry associations, & community development agencies; Providing information & advice about the formation of co-operatives; Assisting existing co-operatives; Researching; Training; Offering co-op programs for young people; *Awareness Events:* Co-op Week, Oct.; Credit Union Day, Oct.
Chief Officer(s):
Glen Fitzpatrick, Managing Director
gfitz@nlfc.nf.ca

Newfoundland-Labrador Special Olympics *See* Special Olympics Newfoundland & Labrador

Newman Centre Catholic Chaplaincy and Parish
89 St. George St., Toronto ON M5S 2E8
Tel: 416-979-2468; *Fax:* 416-596-6920
secretary@newmantoronto.com
www.newmantoronto.com
www.facebook.com/newmanchaplaincy
twitter.com/newmanuoft
Also Known As: The Newman Centre
Previous Name: Newman Foundation of Toronto
Overview: A small local charitable organization
Mission: To maintain & support Roman Catholic chaplaincy on University of Toronto campus
Chief Officer(s):
James Milway, President
Peter Turrone, Executive Director
frpeterturrone@newmantoronto.com

Newman Foundation of Toronto *See* Newman Centre Catholic Chaplaincy and Parish

Newmarket & District Association for Community Living *See* Community Living Newmarket/Aurora District

Newmarket Chamber of Commerce
470 Davis Dr., Newmarket ON L3Y 2P3
Tel: 905-898-5900; *Fax:* 905-853-7271
info@newmarketchamber.ca
www.newmarketchamber.ca
www.linkedin.com/company/672395
www.facebook.com/NewmarketChamberofCommerce
twitter.com/NMKTChamber
Overview: A small local organization founded in 1983
Mission: To represent the interests of members through member programs, government representation, & development of public policy
Member of: Ontario Chamber of Commerce; Canadian Chamber of Commerce
Finances: *Annual Operating Budget:* $100,000-$250,000; *Funding Sources:* Membership dues; advertising fees; events
Staff Member(s): 3; 50 volunteer(s)
Membership: 600; *Fees:* $216-$624
Activities: *Library:* Not open to public
Chief Officer(s):
Dave Peters, Chair
Debra Scott, President & CEO
debra@newmarketchamber.ca

Newmarket Parents of Multiple Births Association
Newmarket ON
Other Communication: newmarketpomba@gmail.com
newmarket@multiplebirthscanada.org
yorkregionmultiples.ca
www.facebook.com/NPOMBA?v=wall&ref=ts
twitter.com/NewmarketPOMBA
Also Known As: Newmarket POMBA

Overview: A small local organization founded in 1983 overseen by Multiple Births Canada
Mission: A support network for parents of twins, triplets or more. Serving York region.
Membership: *Fees:* $30-$35

News Photographers Association of Canada (NPAC) / Association des photographes de presse du Canada (APPC)
www.npac.ca
www.facebook.com/NPAC.APPC
twitter.com/npac_appc
www.instagram.com/npac_appc
Overview: A medium-sized national organization
Mission: To improve the standards of the photojournalism industry
Membership: 300; *Fees:* $75 professional; $35 retired professional/student
Activities: Offering photography workshops & competitions, as well as portfolio assessments
Chief Officer(s):
Amber Bracken, President
president@npac.ca

Newspapers Atlantic
#216, 7075 Bayers Rd., Halifax NS B3L 2C2
Tel: 902-832-4480; *Fax:* 902-832-4484
Toll-Free: 877-842-4480
info@newspapersatlantic.ca
newspapersatlantic.ca
Previous Name: Atlantic Community Newspapers Association
Overview: A small local organization founded in 1972 overseen by Canadian Community Newspapers Association
Mission: To promote excellence, credibility, & the economic well-being of member community newspapers throughout Atlantic Canada
Affiliation(s): Canadian Community Newspapers Association; Quebec Community Newspapers Association; Hebdos Québec; Ontario Community Newspapers Association; Manitoba Community Newspapers Association; Saskatchewan Weekly Newspapers Association; Alberta Weekly Newspapers Association; British Columbia & Yukon Community Newspapers Association
Membership: 70 newspapers; *Member Profile:* Community newspapers from Nova Scotia, New Brunswick, Prince Edward Island, & Newfoundland & Labrador which meet certain criteria; Non-publishing members, such as suppliers to the newspaper industry
Activities: Fostering freedom of the press; Offering professional training, through the online training center; Marketing newspapers to corporations & agencies; Providing access to online marketing programs
Chief Officer(s):
Inez Forbes, President
Mike Kierstead, Executive Director
mike@newspapersatlantic.ca
Meetings/Conferences:
• 46th Annual Newspapers Atlantic Conference 2018, 2018
Scope: Provincial
Description: A Maritime meeting with speakers, educational seminars, an awards banquet, networking opportunities with colleagues, & social events
Publications:
• Atlantic Community Newspapers Association Newsletter
Type: Newsletter
Profile: Information about the association & the industry

Newspapers Canada (CNA) / Journaux Canadiens (ACJ)
#200, 37 Front St. East, Toronto ON M5E 1B3
Tel: 416-923-3567; *Fax:* 416-923-7206
Toll-Free: 877-305-2262
info@newspaperscanada.ca
www.newspaperscanada.ca
www.linkedin.com/company/newspapers-canada
www.facebook.com/newspaperscanada
twitter.com/newspapercanada
Previous Name: Canadian Daily Newspaper Association
Merged from: Newspaper Marketing Bureau
Overview: A medium-sized national organization founded in 1996
Mission: To ensure the continuance of a free press to serve readers effectively, by combining the experience, expertise, & dedication of members; To increase the profile & effectiveness of Canada's newspaper industry
Affiliation(s): Canadian Community Newspapers Association

Finances: *Funding Sources:* Membership fees
Staff Member(s): 10
Membership: *Member Profile:* English & French daily newspapers, with circulations which range from 3,500 to over 500,000 each day; Suppliers, vendors, & consultants to the newspaper industry
Activities: Monitoring & analyzing legislation which affects newspapers & the freedom of the press; Representing needs of members & the public in areas of public policy, marketing, & member services; Increasing awareness of the benefits of newspapers; Developing research projects; Providing educational activities; Offering business services, such as the Canadian Media Circulation Audit; Preparing marketing materials; *Library:* Canadian Newspaper Association Library; by appointment
Chief Officer(s):
John Hinds, President & Chief Executive Officer, 416-923-3567 Ext. 3244
jhinds@newspaperscanada.ca
Awards:
• Extra Awards
To recognize outstanding newspaper advertising in Canada
• Goff Penny Awards
A competition for young journalists from daily newspapers
• Great Ideas Awards
To honour the best ad campaigns, promotions, & special sections from community & daily newspapers
• Quill Awards
To recognize longstanding service in the newspaper industry
• Canadian Community Newspaper Awards
To recognize excellence in community newspapers
• National Newspaper Awards
To recognize excellence in daily newspapers
Publications:
• Industry Reports [a publication of the Canadian Newspaper Association]
Type: Yearbook; *Frequency:* Annually
Profile: A series of reports that relay information & statistics on revenue & circulation rates

Niagara Action for Animals (NAfA)
94 Welland Ave., St Catharines ON L2R 2N1
www.niagaraactionforanimals.org
Overview: A small local charitable organization founded in 1989
Mission: To help protect animals through education, community outreach, & fundraising efforts
Membership: *Fees:* $15 individual; $5 junior; $250 lifetime

Niagara Association of REALTORS (NAR)
116 Niagara St., St Catharines ON L2R 4L4
Tel: 905-684-9459; *Fax:* 905-684-4778
www.niagararealtor.ca
www.linkedin.com/company/niagara-association-of-realtors
www.facebook.com/NiagaraRealtors
twitter.com/NiagaraREALTORS
www.pinterest.com/niagararealtors
Merged from: St. Catharines District Real Estate Board; Welland District Real Estate Board
Overview: A medium-sized local organization founded in 2002 overseen by Ontario Real Estate Association
Mission: To provide members with the structure & services to facilitate the marketing of real estate; To ensure a high standard of business practices & ethics; To effectively serve the real estate needs of the members
Member of: Canadian Real Estate Association
Finances: *Annual Operating Budget:* $500,000-$1.5 Million; *Funding Sources:* Membership dues
Staff Member(s): 8; 80 volunteer(s)
Membership: 975; *Member Profile:* Licenced real estate agents/brokers; *Committees:* Professional Standards; Public Relations; Professional Development; Finance
Chief Officer(s):
Stephen Oliver, President

Niagara Cattlemen's Association
4593 Brookfield Rd., Welland ON L3B 5N7
Tel: 289-214-7321
niagaracattlemen@hotmail.com
Previous Name: Niagara County Cattlemen's Association
Overview: A small local organization
Chief Officer(s):
Donna Rauscher, Secretary

Niagara County Cattlemen's Association *See* Niagara Cattlemen's Association

Niagara Economic Development (NED)
PO Box 1042, 2201 St. David's Rd., 3rd Fl., Thorold ON L2V 4T7
Tel: 905-685-4225; Fax: 905-688-5907
info@niagaracanada.com
www.niagaracanada.com
www.linkedin.com/company/952834
www.facebook.com/NEDCanada
twitter.com/NEDCanada
www.youtube.com/nedcanada
Previous Name: Niagara Economic Development Corporation
Overview: A medium-sized local organization founded in 1971
Mission: To attract investment & visitation to the Niagara region; to deliver economic & tourism information to customers; to facilitate decision making among partners
Affiliation(s): Club 2000; Grimsby Chamber of Commerce; Niagara Falls Small Business Enterprise Centre; Niagara Immigrant Employment Council; Niagara Workforce Planning Board; Niagara-on-the-Lake Chamber of Commerce; Southern Ontario Gateway Council; St. Catharines Enterprise Centre; Venture Niagara; World Trade Centre Buffalo Niagara
Finances: *Funding Sources:* Regional government; private & public sectors
Staff Member(s): 6
Activities: Business relocation & expansion information support; information for potential investors; economic development research; business registration, financial programs, & marketing; *Rents Mailing List:* Yes; *Library:* by appointment Not open to public
Chief Officer(s):
Bob Seguin, Director
bob.seguin@niagararegion.ca

Niagara Economic Development Corporation See Niagara Economic Development

Niagara Falls Chamber of Commerce See Chamber of Commerce Niagara Falls, Canada

Niagara Falls Coin Club
c/o Todd Hume, 41 Radfird Ave., Fort Erie ON L2A 5H6
Overview: A small local organization
Member of: Royal Canadian Numismatic Association
Affiliation(s): Ontario Numismatic Association
Membership: *Member Profile:* Coin collectors in the Niagara Falls area
Activities: Conducting monthly meetings at Stamford Lions Hall; Hosting coin shows
Chief Officer(s):
Todd Hume, Contact, 905-871-2451
humebl@aol.com

Niagara Falls Nature Club (NFNC)
PO Box 901, Niagara Falls ON L2E 6V8
winkal@sympatico.ca
niagaranatureclub.tripod.com
Overview: A small local charitable organization founded in 1967
Mission: To promote awareness, understanding, preservation, & protection of the natural habitat of the Niagara area
Membership: *Fees:* $15 students; $25 single members; $35 families
Activities: Arranging programs & field trips; Conducting regular meetings at the Niagara Falls Public Library
Chief Officer(s):
Win Laar, President, 905-262-5057
Awards:
• R.W. Sheppard Award
To honour an individual or organization for their contribution, through education, conservation or research, in the field of nature
Publications:
• Nature Niagara News
Type: Newsletter; *Editor:* Margaret Pickles; *ISSN:* 0829-1241
Profile: Articles about local nature

Niagara Falls Tourism (NFT)
5400 Robinson St, Niagara Falls ON L2G 2A6
Tel: 905-356-6061; Fax: 905-356-5567
Toll-Free: 800-563-2557
www.niagarafallstourism.com
www.facebook.com/niagarafallstourismcanada
twitter.com/nfallstourism
www.youtube.com/user/niagarafallstourism
Previous Name: Niagara Falls, Canada Visitor & Convention Bureau
Overview: A medium-sized local organization
Mission: Niagara Falls Tourism (Visitor and Convention Bureau) is the official tourism marketing organization of the Community, responsible for developing public and private sector programs that produce incremental visitor business and resulting economic development returns for the City, its residents and the business community
Member of: Tourism Industry Association of Canada
Affiliation(s): 180 Marketing; AVW-TELAV Audio Visual Solutions; Bain Printing; Beatties Stationary; Brock University; Crawford Smith & Swallow Chartered Accountants; CTM Media Group; Downtown Niagara Falls; Fallsview BIA; Flexo Products; Meridian Reservation Systems; Niagara College; Niagara Falls Review; Niagara Peninsula Engery Inc.; Olsen-Sottile Insurance; Peninsula Press; Residence & Conference Centres; Robinson Show Services Inc; RVW Printing; Sightseeing & Receptive; St. Joseph's Printing; Stagevision; Stronco Group of Companies; Sullivan Mahoney; Victoria Centre BIA; Waters Meredith & Tchang, LLP
Finances: *Funding Sources:* City funding; membership fees
Staff Member(s): 15
Membership: 400; *Fees:* Schedule available
Chief Officer(s):
Toni Williams, Director, Operations
twilliams@niagarafallstourism.com

Niagara Falls, Canada Visitor & Convention Bureau See Niagara Falls Tourism

Niagara Peninsula Conservation Authority (NPCA)
250 Thorold Rd. West, 3rd Fl., Welland ON L3C 3W2
Tel: 905-788-3135; Fax: 905-788-1121
info@npca.ca
www.npca.ca
www.facebook.com/NPCAOntario
twitter.com/NPCA_Ontario
Also Known As: Conservation Niagara Foundation
Overview: A small local charitable organization founded in 1969
Mission: To raise funds in support of the Niagara Peninsula Conservation Authority in order to undertake programs designed to further the conservation, restoration, development and management of natural resources within the Niagara Watershe.
Member of: Canadian Centre for Philanthropy
Finances: *Annual Operating Budget:* $100,000-$250,000; *Funding Sources:* Donations; bequests; grants
10 volunteer(s)
Membership: 15; *Member Profile:* Member must be approved by conservation authority
Activities: Grants; Donations; Bequests and Special Events; *Awareness Events:* Golf Tournament, June; Elimination Draw & Dinner, Nov.
Chief Officer(s):
Carmen D'Angelo, Chief Administrative Officer, 905-788-3135 Ext. 251
cdangelo@npca.ca

Niagara Peninsula Electrical Contractors Association (NPECA)
34 Scott St. West, St Catharines ON L2R 1C9
Tel: 905-688-0376; Fax: 905-688-5723
ecaniagara@bellnet.ca
www.ecaniagara.ca
Overview: A small local organization founded in 1974
Mission: A not-for-profit organization that represents local electrical contractors working in the Niagara Region.
Member of: Electrical Contractors Association of Ontario
Membership: *Fees:* $30; *Member Profile:* Professional contractors
Chief Officer(s):
Sue Phillips, Executive Director

Niagara Peninsula Geological Society (NPGS)
120 South Dr., St Catharines ON L2R 4V9
www.ccfms.ca/clubs/NPGS
Overview: A small local organization founded in 1962
Mission: To share knowledge in geology, mineralogy, petrology, palaeontology, & lapidary
Member of: Central Canadian Federation of Mineralogical Societies (CCFMS)
Membership: *Fees:* $15 individuals; $20 families; *Member Profile:* Individuals interested in collecting rocks, minerals, & fossils & in jewellery making
Activities: Hosting monthly meetings from September to June; Arranging collecting field trips; Teaching lapidary techniques; Lending equipment, such as a rock splitter, & microscope; *Awareness Events:* Gem, Mineral, & Fossil Show & Sale, June *Library:* Niagara Peninsula Geological Society Lending Library
Chief Officer(s):
Dave Baker, Secretary
bbaker160@cogeco.ca
Publications:
• The Pink Dolomite Saddle Bulletin
Type: Newsletter; *Frequency:* 10 pa; *Editor:* John Tordiff; *Price:* Free with NPGS membership; $10 non-members
Profile: Upcoming regional events, club activities, & general interest articles

Niagara Region Orchid Society
c/o Lydia Stewart, 5831 Murray St., Niagara Falls ON L2G 2J9
nrossociety@gmail.com
www.facebook.com/135801719803197
Overview: A small local organization
Finances: *Funding Sources:* Membership
Membership: *Fees:* $20
Activities: *Library:* Not open to public
Chief Officer(s):
Rick Rempel, President

Niagara Region Police Association (NRPA) / Association de la police de la région de Niagara
1706 Merrittville Hwy., RR#2, Welland ON L3B 5N5
Tel: 905-384-9800; Fax: 905-384-4082
Toll-Free: 866-443-8066
nrpa@nrpa.on.ca
www.nrpa.on.ca
Overview: A small local organization founded in 1971
Mission: To uphold honour of police profession; to elevate standards of police services; To encourage cooperative intercourse among police officers; to provide financial assistance in accordance with by-laws of Association
Affiliation(s): Association Nationale de la Police Professionnelle/National Association of Professional Police
Finances: *Annual Operating Budget:* $500,000-$1.5 Million
Staff Member(s): 4
Membership: 849 individual + 20 temporary members + 240 lifetime; *Fees:* 1.25% of base salary; *Member Profile:* Civilian & uniform members of the Niagara Region Regional Police Service; *Committees:* Member Assistance; Business Plan; Compressed Work Week; Constitution & By-Laws; Equipment & OH&S; Job Evaluation; Legal Assistance Plan; Management Association; Member Athletics; Polical Activity; Shared Services; Special Finance; Special Functions; Strategic Planning; Technology; Uniform Job Posting; Civilian Job Reclassification; Community Policing
Activities: Negotiates two separate collective agreements; handles Police Act Discipline matters; WSIB appeals; grievanace disputes; Human Rights disputes; administers member owned long term disability plan; administers charitable organization & general membership assistance; *Library*

Niagara Region Sexual Assault Centre
#503, 43 Church St., St Catharines ON L2R 7E1
Tel: 905-682-7258; Fax: 905-682-2114; *Crisis Hot-Line:* 905-682-4584
carsa@sexualassaultniagara.org
www.sexualassaultniagara.org
www.facebook.com/CARSAniagara
www.youtube.com/user/SexualAssaultNiagara
Also Known As: CARSA - Committee Against Rape & Sexual Assault
Overview: A small local charitable organization founded in 1976 overseen by Canadian Association of Sexual Assault Centres
Mission: To provide counselling & support programs to survivors of sexual assault, incest & sexual child abuse; emergency services; public education & advocacy
Member of: Ontario Coalition of Rape Crisis Centres; Canadian Association of Sexual Assault Centres
Finances: *Funding Sources:* Ministry of Attorney General; fundraising
Membership: *Fees:* Yearly donations of $1000+
Activities: *Awareness Events:* Take Back the Night, Sept; *Speaker Service:* Yes
Chief Officer(s):
Sharon Pazzaglia, Coordinator, Project Development, 905-682-7258
sharon@nrsac.org

Niagara Regional Labour Council
#2, 1 Ormond St. South, Thorold ON L2V 1Y2
Tel: 289-362-2233; Fax: 905-397-1113
www.niagaralabour.ca
www.facebook.com/niagaralabour
twitter.com/niagaralabour
Previous Name: Welland & District Labour Council

Overview: A small local organization overseen by Ontario Federation of Labour
Chief Officer(s):
Lou Ann Binning, President

Niagara Regional Native Centre (NRNC)
382 Airport Rd., RR#4, Niagara-on-the-Lake ON L0S 1J0
Tel: 905-688-6484; *Fax:* 905-688-4033
www.nrnc.ca
www.facebook.com/NiagaraRegionalNativeCentre
Previous Name: St. Catharines Indian Centre
Overview: A medium-sized local charitable organization founded in 1972
Mission: To promote the development of the Native community: working in unity, to identify & address the needs of the community; To develop competent leadership; To act as an advocate within the larger community; To maintain a positive image of the Native community; To promote a better understanding between Natives & Non-Natives
Affiliation(s): Ontario Federation of Indian Friendship Centres
Staff Member(s): 20
Activities: Programs include healing & wellness, health outreach, prenatal nutrition, programs for children & youth, employment counselling, programs for seniors, literacy & basic skills; emphasis on culturally sensitive approaches
Chief Officer(s):
Mitch Baird, Executive Director
executivedirector@nrnc.ca

Niagara Support Services (NSS)
PO Box 190, 120 Canby St., Port Robinson ON L0S 1K0
Tel: 905-384-1172; *Fax:* 905-384-2691
nssinfo@ntec-nss.com
www.ntec-nss.com
Overview: A medium-sized local charitable organization founded in 1953
Mission: To provide support & services for persons with developmental disabilities
Member of: Ontario Agencies Supporting Individuals with Special Needs (OASIS)
Finances: *Annual Operating Budget:* $3 Million-$5 Million; *Funding Sources:* Provincial government; fundraising; donations
Staff Member(s): 150; 20 volunteer(s)
Membership: 375; *Fees:* $8 single; $10 family; $5 associate; $15 corporate; $50 patron; *Committees:* Health & Safety; Admissions
Activities: Offering community programs & residential, adult consultant, & children's services
Chief Officer(s):
Brent Rolfe, President
Meetings/Conferences:
• Niagara Support Services 2018 65th Annual General Meeting, 2018, ON
Scope: Local
Publications:
• News & Notes [a publication of Niagara Support Services]
Type: Newsletter

Niagara West Employment & Learning Resource Centres (NWELRC)
PO Box 460, 4271 Queen St., Beamsville ON L0R 1B0
Tel: 905-563-1515; *Fax:* 905-563-5612
info@nwelrc.ca
www.nwelrc.ca
www.facebook.com/556944574324383
twitter.com/LCNiagaraWest
Also Known As: Literacy Council of Niagara West
Previous Name: Literacy Council of Lincoln
Overview: A small local charitable organization founded in 1985
Mission: To provide lifelong literacy & basic skills training for sustained employability
Member of: Ont. Alliance of Career Develop Practitioners; Ont. Soc. for Training & Develop.; ONESTEP; Community Based Trainers of Niagara; Lincoln C of C; Ont Literacy Coalition; Movement for Cdn Literacy; Community Literacy Ont; Literacy Link Niagara; Laubach Literacy Ont/Canada
Finances: *Funding Sources:* Provincial government; municipal government; public & private donations
Activities: Upgrading of basic, essential & literacy skills; support services for un/underemployed; specialists in employment services for the 40+ worker; transitional programs towards employability or higher education; one-to-one tutoring & small groups in reading, writing, math, computers; GED prep.; open learning computer lab; professional academic & vocational assessments; Job Finding Clubs; career counseling; résumés & cover letters; internet job search; outreach; customized workshops; research; *Speaker Service:* Yes; *Library:* Lending Library; Open to public

Niagara Youth Orchestra Association
#148, 12 - 111 Fourth Ave., St Catharines ON L2S 3P5
Tel: 905-323-5892
music@niagarayouthorchestra.ca
www.niagarayouthorchestra.ca
www.facebook.com/12038278189
Previous Name: St. Catharines Youth Orchestra
Overview: A small local charitable organization founded in 1965 overseen by Orchestras Canada
Mission: To foster an interest & understanding of orchestral music in the youth of the Niagara Region
Member of: Orchestras Canada
Finances: *Funding Sources:* Membership fees; Fundraising; Donations
Membership: *Fees:* $685 junior member; $775 senior member; *Member Profile:* Young musicians who play an instrument, are interested in orchestral music, and want to develop their skills
Activities: Performing 5-7 concerts yearly; Providing education and instruction for young musicians through regular rehearsal; *Library:* Not open to public
Chief Officer(s):
Laura Thomas, Music Director
Awards:
• Dan Fuzzen Memorial Award
Eligibility: A Niagara Youth Orchestra musician who is going to university or college to major in a subject other than music, and who has shown dedication to the orchestra during his or her membership
• Dr. Charles and Winifred Sankey Scholarship
Eligibility: A graduating member of the Niagara Youth Orchestra who will be continuing music studies in university.
• NYOA Graduation Awards
Eligibility: Graduates who are continuing their post-secondary education at a post-secondary institution and do not qualify for another NYOA scholarship; Recipients must demonstrate a positive attitude, leadership skills, and a dedicated contribution to NYO *Deadline:* April 15

Niagara/Hamilton Association of Baptist Churches
ON
nhachurches@gmail.com
baptist.ca
www.facebook.com/niagarahamiltionassoc
Overview: A small local organization overseen by Canadian Baptists of Ontario and Quebec
Member of: Canadian Baptists of Ontario & Quebec
Membership: *Member Profile:* Baptist churches in the Niagara Falls & Hamilton area
Chief Officer(s):
Peter Dempsey, Moderator
podempsey@yahoo.ca

Niagara-on-the-Lake Bed & Breakfast Association Inc.
PO Box 1228, Niagara-on-the-Lake ON L0S 1J0
Tel: 905-468-0123
Toll-Free: 866-855-0123
info@bbaboard.com
www.niagarabedandbreakfasts.com
www.facebook.com/niagarabedandbreakfasts
twitter.com/OntarioBnBs
www.youtube.com/user/niagarabnb
Overview: A small local organization
Mission: To maintain a standard of bed & breakfasts in Niagara-on-the-Lake; to allow for collaboration amongst bed & breakfast owners
Membership: *Fees:* $170 with Guestbook system; $95 without Guestbook system; *Member Profile:* Licencees of bed & breakfasts or inns

Niagara-on-the-Lake Chamber of Commerce
PO Box 1043, 26 Queen St., Niagara-on-the-Lake ON L0S 1J0
Tel: 905-468-1950; *Fax:* 905-468-4930
tourism@niagaraonthelake.com
www.niagaraonthelake.com
twitter.com/niagaraonlake
Overview: A small local organization founded in 1949
Mission: To nurture the growth & prosperity of the agricultural, cultural, hospitality, retail, heritage, historical, & other sectors of Niagara-on-the-Lake
Member of: Ontario Chamber of Commerce
Finances: *Annual Operating Budget:* $100,000-$250,000; *Funding Sources:* Membership fees; grants; service fees
Staff Member(s): 5
Membership: 360; *Fees:* Schedule available; *Committees:* Economic Development; Industrial; Retail; Tourism
Activities: Organizing & promoting events such as Artistry by the Lake, Polo NOTL, Candlelight Stroll, & Days of Wine & Roses; *Rents Mailing List:* Yes
Chief Officer(s):
Janice Thomson, Executive Director
manager@niagaraonthelake.com

Nickel Belt Coin Club (NBCC)
c/o Larry Seguin, 4349 Chateau Cres., Hanmer ON P3P 1Y6
Tel: 705-969-5023
www.nickelbeltcoinclub.com
www.facebook.com/nickelbeltcoinclub
Overview: A small local organization founded in 1956
Mission: To provide a meeting place, as well as a discussion forum for those interested in coin collection
Membership: 60+
Chief Officer(s):
Larry Seguin, Secretary
Slarryd@hotmail.com

Nickel Development Institute *See* Nickel Institute

Nickel Institute
Brookfield Place, #2700, 161 Bay St., Toronto ON M5J 2S1
Tel: 416-591-7999; *Fax:* 416-572-2201
www.nickelinstitute.org
www.linkedin.com/company/nickel-institute-brussels
twitter.com/NickelInstitute
Previous Name: Nickel Development Institute
Overview: A large national organization founded in 1984
Mission: To provide information for nickel users, designers, specifiers, educators & others interested in nickel-containing materials & their applications
Finances: *Annual Operating Budget:* Greater than $5 Million
Staff Member(s): 9
Membership: 24 corporate; *Member Profile:* Nickel miner, smelter, refiner; *Committees:* Technical Program; Advisory
Activities: *Library:*
Chief Officer(s):
David Butler, President
Hudson Bates, Executive Director
Publications:
• Nickel Magazine [a publication of the Nickel Institute]
Type: Magazine; *Editor:* Clare Richardson; *ISSN:* 0829-8351

Nicola Valley & District Food Bank
PO Box 2719, 2026 Quilchena Ave., Merritt BC V1K 1B8
Tel: 250-378-2282; *Fax:* 250-378-2982
foodbank@mail.ocis.net
Overview: A small local organization overseen by Food Banks British Columbia
Member of: Food Banks British Columbia
Chief Officer(s):
Linda Monkman, Contact

Nicola Valley Community Arts Council
PO Box 2762, Merritt BC V0K 2B0
Tel: 250-378-6515
nicolavalleyartscouncil@gmail.com
www.nvartscouncil.com
Overview: A small local charitable organization founded in 1982
Mission: To increase & broaden the opportunities for residents of Nicola Valley to participate in cultural activities
Affiliation(s): Okanagan Mainline Regional Arts Council; BC Touring Council
Finances: *Annual Operating Budget:* Less than $50,000; *Funding Sources:* Municipal & provincial government
6 volunteer(s)
Membership: 38 individual & family + 7 group + 2 lifetime; *Fees:* $10 individual; $20 family; $25 groups
Chief Officer(s):
Deanna Gage, President

Nicola Valley Museum Archives Association
PO Box 1262, 1675 Tutill Ct., Merritt BC V1K 1B8
Tel: 250-378-4145
nvma@uniserve.com
www.nicolavalleymuseum.org
www.facebook.com/NVMuseum
Overview: A small local charitable organization founded in 1976
Mission: To collect & preserve archival & museum artifacts pertinent to the Nicola Valley area & its history; To display museum articles
Member of: BC Museums Association; Archives Association of

BC; BC Historical Federation
Affiliation(s): Canadian Museums Association
Finances: *Funding Sources:* Provincial government; Municipal government; Regional government
Staff Member(s): 2
Activities: *Library:* Open to public

Nigerian Students Association *See* Association of Nigerians in Nova Scotia

Niijkiwenhwag - Friends of Lake Superior Park
c/o Lake Superior Provincial Park, PO Box 267, Wawa ON P0S 1K0
Tel: 705-856-2284
info@lakesuperiorpark.ca
www.lakesuperiorpark.ca
Overview: A small local organization founded in 1993
Mission: To achieve public awareness, knowledge & appreciation of the park's natural & cultural heritage; To coordinate special events & projects related to the park's theme; To support the development of park interpretive programs; To provide supplementary funds to complement park educational & scientific research projects
Membership: *Fees:* $10 individual; $15 family
Chief Officer(s):
Christina Speer, Chair

The Nile Association of Ontario (NAO)
81 Primrose Crescent, Brampton ON L6Z 1E1
Tel: 905-840-5375
info@nileclub.org
www.nileclub.org
Overview: A small provincial organization founded in 1988
Mission: To promote the social coherence of the Egyptian community & to provide assistance, help, & guidance to new immigrants
Membership: *Fees:* $20 student/senior; $25 adult; $50 family; *Committees:* Social; Culture; Sports; Membership; Business; Youth
Activities: Promotes & teaches Egyptian culture; promotes our heritage; organizes sports activities; promotes business within the Egyptian community; social functions
Chief Officer(s):
Mohamed Elhalwagy, President

Nipawin & District Chamber of Commerce
PO Box 177, Nipawin SK S0E 1E0
Tel: 306-862-5252; *Fax:* 306-862-5350
nipawin.chamber@sasktel.net
www.nipawinchamber.ca
twitter.com/NipawinChamber
Overview: A small local organization founded in 1923
Mission: To promote the commercial, industrial, agricultural, & civic interests of the community & district
Finances: *Annual Operating Budget:* Less than $50,000
Staff Member(s): 2
Membership: 180; *Fees:* Schedule available
Chief Officer(s):
Mark Knox, President

Nipawin Exhibition Association Inc.
PO Box 105, Nipawin SK S0E 1E0
Tel: 306-862-3411; *Fax:* 306-862-9669
nipawinex@sasktel.net
www.nipawinex.com
www.facebook.com/nipawinex
Also Known As: Nipawin AG Society
Overview: A small local licensing organization founded in 1928
Mission: To help promote light horse, heavy horse & beef cattle through exhibitions
Member of: Saskatchewan Association of Agricultural Societies & Exhibitions
Finances: *Annual Operating Budget:* $50,000-$100,000
150 volunteer(s)
Membership: 44; *Fees:* $10; *Committees:* Indoor; Light Horse; Heavy Horse; Beef
Activities: *Awareness Events:* Nipawin Exhibition, July

Nipigon, Red Rock & District Association for Community Living *See* Superior Greenstone Association for Community Living

Nipissing Children's Aid Society for the District of Nipissing & Parry Sound *See* Children's Aid Society of the District of Nipissing & Parry Sound

Nipissing Coin Club
North Bay ON
Tel: 705-474-2141
Overview: A small local organization
Chief Officer(s):
Jeff Fournier, Contact

Nipissing Environmental Watch (NEW)
PO Box 1543, North Bay ON P1B 8K6
Tel: 705-494-8935
new@bell.net
www.nipissingenvironmentalwatch.org
Overview: A small local organization
Mission: To help make positive steps towards environment conservation in Nipissing District

Nipissing Law Association
360 Plouffe St., North Bay ON P1B 9L5
Tel: 705-495-3271; *Fax:* 705-495-3487
Toll-Free: 866-899-6439
nipilaws@onlink.net
nipissinglawassociation.wordpress.com
Overview: A small local organization founded in 1981
Membership: 98
Activities: *Library:* George C. Wallace Q.C. Law Library; Not open to public
Chief Officer(s):
Amanda Adams, Law Librarian

Nisga'a Lisims Government
PO Box 231, 2000 Lisims Dr., Gitlaxt'aamiks BC V0J 1A0
Tel: 250-633-3000; *Fax:* 250-633-2367
Toll-Free: 866-633-0888
comm@nisgaa.net
www.nisgaanation.ca
www.facebook.com/NLGNisgaaNation
twitter.com/NLGNisgaaNation
Also Known As: Nisga'a Tribal Council
Previous Name: Nishga Tribal Council
Overview: A medium-sized local organization founded in 1956
Finances: *Annual Operating Budget:* $3 Million-$5 Million
Staff Member(s): 30
Membership: 6,000; *Member Profile:* People of Nisga'a origin; *Committees:* Planning & Priorities; Ayuukhl Nisga'a; Economic Finance; Personnel Finance; Education; Joint Venture; Working groups - Fisheries; Forest, Lands, Environment; Nisga'a government; Nisga'a highways
Activities: Wilp Wilx'osk Nisga'a (Nisga'a House of Learning); Justice Department (Family Law Program, Access to Justice Program, Victim Assistance Program); Educational training programs; *Library:* Resource Centre; Open to public

Nishga Tribal Council *See* Nisga'a Lisims Government

Nishnawbe - Gamik Friendship Centre
52 King St., Sioux Lookout ON P8T 1B8
Tel: 807-737-1909; *Fax:* 807-737-1805
Toll-Free: 800-619-9519
ches@ngfc.net
www.ngfc.net
Overview: A small local organization founded in 1971
Mission: To provide a meeting place for people of Aboriginal ancestry & others in the Sioux Lookout, Ontario region to exchange ideas & to develop mutual understanding & appreciation; To advance native language & culture
Member of: Ontario Federation of Indian Friendship Centres
Staff Member(s): 16
Activities: Hosting weekly cultural nights; Offering educational & recreational activities; Providing programs such as the Akwe:go High-Risk Urban Aboriginal Children's Program; Wasa-Nabin Urban Aboriginal Youth Program; the Addictions Program, Anokeewin Wiichiiwaawin Employment Program, & the Life Long Care Program
Chief Officer(s):
Che September, Exeuctive Director
Kelly Anderson, President

Nistawoyou Association Friendship Centre
8310 Manning Ave., Fort McMurray AB T9H 1W1
Tel: 780-743-8555; *Fax:* 780-750-0527
nistawoyou@gmail.com
Overview: A small local organization founded in 1964 overseen by Alberta Native Friendship Centres Association
Mission: To develop social & recreational activities in the Aboriginal communities in & around Fort McMurray
Member of: Alberta Native Friendship Centres Association
Affiliation(s): Fort McMurray United Way
Finances: *Funding Sources:* Federal government; provincial government
Staff Member(s): 3
Membership: 100
Activities: Feed the hungry program; Life enhancement & empowerment; Community Assistance; Youth summer camp; Homelessness initiatives; Employment programs
Chief Officer(s):
Theresa Nahwegahbow, Executive Director

Niverville Chamber of Commerce
PO Box 157, Niverville MB R0A 1E0
Tel: 204-388-5340
chamber@niverville.com
www.niverville.com
Overview: A small local organization
Mission: To promote business in the area
Chief Officer(s):
Dawn Harris, Coordinator

NL West SPCA
PO Box 7, 10 Connors Rd., Corner Brook NL A2H 6C3
Tel: 709-785-2747
nlwestspca@gmail.com
www.nlwestspca.com
Previous Name: Bay of Islands SPCA; Bay of Islands Society for the Prevention of Cruelty to Animals
Overview: A small local organization founded in 1979
Mission: To assist animals in need, keep them healthy, & aid in their adoption
Member of: Canadian Federation of Humane Societies
Finances: *Funding Sources:* Donations
Chief Officer(s):
Frances Drover, President

Noia
Atlantic Pl., PO Box 44, #602, 215 Water St., St. John's NL A1C 6C9
Tel: 709-758-6610; *Fax:* 709-758-6611
noia@noia.ca
www.noia.ca
www.linkedin.com/company-beta/2954799
www.facebook.com/noiaNL
twitter.com/NoiaNL
Also Known As: Newfoundland & Labrador Oil & Gas Industries Association
Overview: A medium-sized provincial organization founded in 1977
Mission: To assist, promote & facilitate the participation of members in ocean industries, with particular emphasis on oil & gas, to enhance their growth & development; To promote the growth of ocean industry; To act as a focal point for representations to government bodies & agencies; To act as a source of information & education for members
Finances: *Annual Operating Budget:* $500,000-$1.5 Million; *Funding Sources:* Membership fees; conferences, seminars & special events
Staff Member(s): 10; 100 volunteer(s)
Membership: 600; *Fees:* Schedule available; *Member Profile:* Those who develop, manufacture & market products & services in the oil & gas industry, both offshore & onshore; *Committees:* Board of Directors; Conference; Governance; Industry Achievement Awards; Membership Engagement; Noia-Hibernia Scholarship; Redefining Oil; Research & Development; Supplier Development; Petroleum Industry Human Resources Committee (PIHRC)
Activities: Promotes development of Canada's eastern coast's hydrocarbon resources & facilitates its membership's participation in oil & gas industries; *Library:* Noia Library; by appointment
Chief Officer(s):
Robert Cadigan, President & CEO
Awards:
• Outstanding Contribution Award
• Rising Star Award
Eligibility: Noia members 40 years old or younger
• Noia - Hibernia Scholarship Fund
Eligibility: Graduating high school students in Newfoundland and Labrador who are entering post-secondary studies with the intention of pursuing a petroleum-related career *Deadline:* August; *Amount:* $1,000 *Contact:* Noia - Hibernia Scholarship Committee, #602, PO Box 44, 215 Water St., St. John's, NL A1C 6C9
Meetings/Conferences:
• Noia Conference 2018, June, 2018, St. John's Convention Centre, St. John's, NL
Scope: National
Description: The Annual Noia Conference is a key service that

provides members and the general public with information on trends and business opportunities in the East Coast Canada oil & gas industry.
Contact Information: noiaconference.com
Publications:
• Noia News
Type: Magazine; *Frequency:* Quarterly
Profile: News & information for members

Non-Academic Staff Association for the University of Alberta
1200 College Plaza, 8215 - 112 St., Edmonton AB T6G 2E1
Tel: 780-439-3181; *Fax:* 780-433-5056
Toll-Free: 877-439-3111
nasa@ualberta.ca
www.nasa.ualberta.ca
www.facebook.com/supportstaffunion
twitter.com/UnionNASA
Previous Name: University of Alberta Non-Academic Staff Association
Overview: A medium-sized local organization
100 volunteer(s)
Membership: 6,000+; *Fees:* Schedule available; *Member Profile:* Support staff of the University of Alberta
Chief Officer(s):
Nancy Furlong, Director, Operations
nancy.furlong@ualberta.ca

Nonprescription Drug Manufacturers Association of Canada; NDMAC, Advancing Canadian Self-Care *See* Consumer Health Products Canada

Non-Smokers' Rights Association (NSRA) / Association pour les droits des non-fumeurs
#221, 720 Spadina Ave., Toronto ON M5S 2T9
Tel: 416-928-2900; *Fax:* 416-928-1860
toronto@nsra-adnf.ca
www.nsra-adnf.ca
twitter.com/nsra_adnf
Overview: A medium-sized national organization founded in 1974
Mission: To promote public health by stopping illness & death due to tobacco, including second-hand smoke
Affiliation(s): Smoking & Health Action Foundation (SHAF)
Finances: *Funding Sources:* Membership fees
Membership: *Fees:* $29 individual; $36 family; $18 student or person over age 65; $47 institution
Activities: Advocating for tobacco-control efforts in Canada & throughout the world; Liaising with national, provincial, & local health organizatons & community groups
Chief Officer(s):
Lorraine Fry, Executive Director

Montréal
833, rue Roy est, Montréal QC H2L 1E4
Tel: 514-843-3250
montreal@nsra-adnf.ca
Chief Officer(s):
François Damphousse, Director

Ottawa
#1903, 130 Albert St., Ottawa ON K1P 5G4
Tel: 613-230-4211; *Fax:* 613-230-9454
ottawa@nsra-adnf.ca
Chief Officer(s):
Melodie Tilson, Director, Policy

Nordic Combined Ski Canada (NCSC)
#388, 305 - 4625 Varsity Dr. NW, Calgary AB T3A 0Z9
Tel: 403-863-7951
skijumpingcanada.com
Overview: A small national organization
Mission: To be the national governing body for the sport of ski jumping in Canada, alongside Ski Jumping Canada.
Affiliation(s): Ski Jumping Canada
Chief Officer(s):
Andy Mah, Chair
Savill Wes, Director
wsavill@gmail.com

Nordic Ski Nova Scotia *See* Cross Country Nova Scotia

Nordic Walking Nova Scotia
5545 Stanley Pl., Halifax NS B3K 2E8
Tel: 902-454-2267; *Fax:* 902-482-3380
info@nordicwalkingnovascotia.ca
www.nordicwalkingnovascotia.ca
www.facebook.com/NordicPoleWalkingNS
Also Known As: Nordic Pole Walking Nova Scotia

Overview: A small local organization founded in 2010
Mission: To teach & promote Nordic pole walking in the Atlantic Canada region
Member of: CARP; Serving Seniors Alliance Cooperative
Finances: *Annual Operating Budget:* $100,000-$250,000; *Funding Sources:* Government grants; Poles sales; Not-for-profit partnerships
Staff Member(s): 4; 80 volunteer(s)
Membership: 950; *Committees:* Finance; Instructor Training; Program; Public Relations & Marketing
Activities: Offering free beginner clinics; Marketing & public relations; Certifying instructors; *Internships:* Yes; *Speaker Service:* Yes

Norfolk Association for Community Living (NACL)
644 Ireland Rd., Simcoe ON N3Y 4K2
Tel: 519-426-5000; *Fax:* 519-426-5744
naclinfo@nacl.ca
www.nacl.ca
Overview: A medium-sized local charitable organization founded in 1953
Mission: To promote & support the inclusion of people with disabilities in all aspects of community life
Member of: Ontario Association Supporting Individuals with Special Needs (OASIS); Community Living Ontario
Finances: *Funding Sources:* M.C.S.S.; United Way; donations
Membership: *Fees:* $10 supported person; $20 basic; $30 family
Activities: *Internships:* Yes *Library:* NACL Resource Library; Open to public
Chief Officer(s):
Stella Barker, Executive Director
Ann Engell, President

Norfolk Community Chest *See* United Way of Haldimand-Norfolk

Norfolk County Agricultural Society
172 South Dr., Simcoe ON N3Y 1G6
Tel: 519-426-7280; *Fax:* 519-426-7286
www.norfolkcountyfair.com
Overview: A small local organization
Chief Officer(s):
George Araujo, General Manager

Norfolk Field Naturalists (NFN)
PO Box 995, Simcoe ON N3Y 5B3
Tel: 519-586-2603
info@norfolkfieldnaturalists.org
www.norfolkfieldnaturalists.org
Overview: A small local organization founded in 1962
Mission: Dedicated to the acquisition & extension of knowledge of natural history & appreciation, enjoyment & stewardship of natural environment, especially within the region of Haldimand-Norfolk
Member of: Federation of Ontario Naturalists; Long Point Bird Observatory; Carolinian Canada
Finances: *Annual Operating Budget:* Less than $50,000; *Funding Sources:* Membership dues; donations; LPBO Birdathon
10 volunteer(s)
Membership: 150; *Fees:* $20 single; $30 family; *Committees:* Local Environmental Protection; Waste Management
Activities: Field trips for birding; free identification; nature appreciation; local natural heritage sites; *Speaker Service:* Yes
Chief Officer(s):
Bernie Solymar, President
solymar@nornet.on.ca

Norfolk Historical Society (NHC)
109 Norfolk St. South, Simcoe ON N3Y 2W3
Tel: 519-426-1583; *Fax:* 519-426-1584
office@norfolklore.com
www.norfolklore.com
www.facebook.com/evabrookdonly
twitter.com/museumnorfolk
Also Known As: Eva Brook Donly Museum & Archives
Overview: A small local charitable organization founded in 1900
Mission: Collects, preserves & provides evidence of the history of old Norfolk county in the operation of the Eva Brook Donly Museum, holding its collections in trust for the public & their descendants; Extensive material culture collection, thousands of photographs, archival documents and printed material, reference books; Loyalist Library and Genealogical Resources
Affiliation(s): Ontario Genealogical Society; Ontario Museum Association; Ontario Historical Society; Simcoe Chamber of Commerce

Finances: *Funding Sources:* Membership dues; fundraising; donations; grants
Membership: *Fees:* $5 youth; $40 regular; $50 non-profit; $60 family; $200 commercial
Activities: Operates Eva Brook Donly Museum & Archives; *Speaker Service:* Yes; *Library:* Open to public
Chief Officer(s):
Keitha Davis, President

Norman Wells & District Chamber of Commerce
PO Box 400, Norman Wells NT X0E 0V0
Tel: 867-587-6609
www.normanwellschamber.com
Overview: A small local organization
Mission: To support businesses in the Norman Wells community & surrounding area
Membership: 43
Chief Officer(s):
Peter Spilchak, President
president@normanwellschamber.com

Norman Wells Historical Society (NWHS)
PO Box 145, 23 Mackenzie Dr., Norman Wells NT X0E 0V0
Tel: 867-587-2415
www.facebook.com/NormanWellsHistoricalSociety
Overview: A small local organization founded in 1977
Member of: Canadian Museums Association
Affiliation(s): Canadian Booksellers Association; Prince of Wales Northern Heritage Centre
Staff Member(s): 2; 10 volunteer(s)
Activities: Museum, art gallery, gift shop; annual art show; travelling exhibits

Les normes canadiennes de la publicité *See* Advertising Standards Canada

Les normes canadiennes de la publicité (NCP) / Advertising Standards Canada (ASC)
Tour Sud, #1801, 175, rue Bloor est, Toronto ON M4W 3R8
Tél: 416-961-6311; *Téléc:* 416-961-7904
info@normespub.ca
www.normespub.com
Nom précédent: Conseil des normes de la publicité
Aperçu: *Dimension:* petite; *Envergure:* nationale; Organisme sans but lucratif; fondée en 1957
Mission: Assurer l'autoréglementation de l'industrie canadienne de la publicité à l'aide de codes d'éthique publicitaire
Finances: *Budget de fonctionnement annuel:* $1.5 Million-$3 Million
Membre(s) du personnel: 2; 36 bénévole(s)
Membre: 200; *Comités:* Conseil des normes
Activités: *Service de conférenciers:* Oui; *Bibliothèque:* Centre de documentation de NCP
Membre(s) du bureau directeur:
Jani Yates, Présidente et chef de la direction

Nornet-Yukon *See* Yukon Territory Environmental Network

Norquay & District Chamber of Commerce
PO Box 327, Norquay SK S0A 2V0
Tel: 306-594-2101; *Fax:* 306-594-2347
www.norquay.ca
Previous Name: Norquay Chamber of Commerce
Overview: A small local organization
Mission: To strengthen businesses & the community
Membership: *Fees:* $25 individual; $75 business
Activities: *Awareness Events:* Annual Trade Show
Chief Officer(s):
Kevin Ebert, President

Norquay Chamber of Commerce *See* Norquay & District Chamber of Commerce

North Algoma Literacy Coalition (NALC)
50B Broadway Ave., Wawa ON P0S 1K0
Tel: 705-856-4394; *Fax:* 705-856-4394
wawa-adultlearningcentre.com
Also Known As: Adult Learning Centre for Wawa and Surrounding Area
Overview: A small local charitable organization
Mission: Works with the community to promote & improve life-long learning for adults & families
Staff Member(s): 5
Activities: Deliver literacy & basic skills program; support family literacy activities; *Speaker Service:* Yes
Chief Officer(s):
Lisa Houston, Program Director
director@wawa-nalc.com

North America Railway Hall of Fame (NARHF)
750 Tabot St., St Thomas ON N5P 1E2
Tel: 519-633-2535; *Fax:* 519-633-3087
info@casostation.com
casostation.ca
www.facebook.com/CASOstation
twitter.com/casostation
Overview: A small national charitable organization founded in 1996
Mission: To honour individuals & organizations who have made significant contributions relating to the railway industry in North America; To preserve & display a collection of library materials & railway heritage artifacts related to the Hall of Fame inductees; To educate the public about the impact of railway transportation on history & the development of communities, nations & international relations
Chief Officer(s):
Matt Janes, President

North American Association of Asian Professionals Vancouver (NAAAP)
PO Box 18518, 710 Granville St., Vancouver BC V6Z 0B3
Other Communication: communications@naaap.bc.ca
naaap@naaap.bc.ca
www.naaap.bc.ca
twitter.com/naaap
Overview: A small local organization founded in 1982
Mission: To promote the career advancement of Asian professionals in Vancouver; To support multiculturalism
Finances: *Funding Sources:* Membership fees
Membership: *Fees:* $50; *Member Profile:* Asian Canadian professionals in the Vancouver area
Activities: Encouraging the leadership development of Asian professionals in all areas; Facilitating professional networking opportunities; Presenting professional development workshops & seminars; Providing resources to Asian professionals & university students; Sponsoring community activities to increase cultural awareness of Asians
Chief Officer(s):
Rudy Chung, President
Walt Woo, Vice-President
Linton Chokie, Secretary
Holman Lai, Treasurer
Tammy Tsang, Director, Communications
Publications:
• NAAAP Insight
Type: Newsletter; *Frequency:* Quarterly; *Price:* Free with membership in North American Association of Asian Professionals Vancouver
Profile: Association activities & upcoming events

North American Bird Conservation Initiative Canada (NABCI)
c/o Canadian Wildlife Service-Environment & Climate Change Canada, 351, boul St-Joseph, 3e étage, Gatineau QC K1A 0H3
Tel: 819-994-0512; *Fax:* 819-994-4445
nabci@ec.gc.ca
www.nabci.net
Mission: The NABCI is a coordinated effort among Canada, the United States & Mexico to maintain the diversity & abundance of all North American birds. National coordination of this effort in Canada occurs through the NABCI Canada Council, chaired by the Asst. Deputy Minister of Environment Canada's Environmental Conservation Service. Council members include representatives from provincial governments, non-government organizations, four bird plans (waterfowl, landbirds, shorebirds, waterbirds), & habitat joint ventures. In Canada, the joint venture conservation projects have four habitat joint ventures (Pacific Birds Habitat, Canadian Intermountain, Prairie Habitat, Eastern Habitat) & three species (Arctic Goose, Black Duck, Sea Duck).

North American Broadcasters Association (NABA)
PO Box 500, Stn. A, #6C300, 25 John St., Toronto ON M5V 3G7
Tel: 416-598-9877
contact@nabanet.com
www.nabanet.com
Previous Name: North American National Broadcasters Association
Overview: A large international organization founded in 1972
Mission: To advance the interests of broadcasters in Canada, the United States, & Mexico; To identify & respond to technical, operational, & regulatory issues affecting the broadcasting industry in North America
Member of: World Broadcasting Union
Finances: *Funding Sources:* Membership fees
Staff Member(s): 5

Membership: 10 full; 9 associate; 14 affiliate; *Fees:* US$40,000 full; US$20,000 associate; *Member Profile:* Broadcasters; *Committees:* Legal; Radio; Resilience & Risk; Technical
Activities: Organizing industry events; Developing projects
Chief Officer(s):
Michael McEwen, Director General
Anh Ngo, Director, Administration
Meetings/Conferences:
• North American Broadcasters Association 2018 Annual General Meeting & Conference, 2018
Scope: International

North American Chronic Pain Association of Canada *See* Chronic Pain Association of Canada

North American National Broadcasters Association *See* North American Broadcasters Association

North American Native Plant Society (NANPS)
PO Box 69070, Stn. St. Clair, Toronto ON M4T 3A1
Tel: 416-631-4438
nanps@nanps.org
www.nanps.org
www.facebook.com/nativeplant
twitter.com/tnanps
Previous Name: Canadian Wildflower Society
Overview: A medium-sized provincial charitable organization founded in 1985
Mission: Dedicated to the study, conservation & cultivation of North America's wild flora.
Member of: Ontario Nature; Toronto Botanical Gardens
Staff Member(s): 1; 20+ volunteer(s)
Membership: *Fees:* $25/year (digital subscription to Blazing Star magazine); $30 for print copy); *Committees:* Awards & Nominations; Board of Directors; Communications; Excursions; Fundraising; Land Management; Plant Rescue & Restoration; Plant Sale; Seed Exchange
Activities: Members-only seed exchange; Native Garden Award; Native Plant Sales; Speakers Series; Stewardship of & excursions to 2 conservation properties, Zincan Island Cove & Shining Tree Woods in Ontario; Publication of members-only magazine, The Blazing Star
Publications:
• Blazing Star [a publication of the North American Native Plant Society]
Type: Journal; *Frequency:* Quarterly

North American Recycled Rubber Association (NARRA)
#24, 1621 McEwen Dr., Whitby ON L1N 9A5
Tel: 905-433-7769; *Fax:* 905-433-0905
narra@oix.com
www.recycle.net/recycle/assn/narra
Overview: A small national organization founded in 1994
Mission: The Association provides a unified voice, as well as a communication network & research facility, for issues of concern to those involved in rubber recycling across North America.
Finances: *Funding Sources:* Membership dues; research
Activities: Provides specialized training & feasibility studies; annual convention (March) & newsletter
Chief Officer(s):
Diane Sarracini, Office Manager

North American Waterfowl Management Plan (NAWMP) / Le plan nord-américain de gestion de la sauvagine
Wetlands Office, Place Vincent Massey, 351, boul St-Joseph, 7e étage, Gatineau QC K1A 0H3
Tel: 819-934-6036; *Fax:* 819-934-6017
nawmp@ec.gc.ca
nawmp.wetlandnetwork.ca
Mission: The North American Waterfowl Management Plan is an international action plan to conserve migratory birds throughout the continent. The Plan's goal is to return waterfowl populations to their 1970's levels by conserving wetland & upland habitat. Canada & the United States signed the Plan in 1986 in reaction to critically low numbers of waterfowl. Mexico joined in 1994 making it a truly continental effort. The Plan is a partnership of federal, provincial/state & municipal governments, non-governmental organizations, private companies & many individuals, all working towards achieving better wetland habitat for the benefit of migratory birds, other wetland-associated species & people. The Plan's combination of biology, landscape conservation & partnerships comprise its conservation legacy. Plan projects are international in scope, but implemented at regional levels. These projects contribute to the protection of habitat & wildlife species across North America.

Awards:
• Great Blue Heron Award
Recognizes primary participants in the Plan who have made major, long-term national contributions that result in benefits to waterfowl & other bird populations of North America; for US nominations - Executive Director, N. American Waterfowl & Wetlands Office, US Fish & Wildlife Service, Rm.110, 4401 N. Fairfax Dr., Arlington VA 22203, ph. 703/358-1784; for Mexican nominations - Humberto Berlanga, Instituto Nacional de Ecolgís, Avenida Revoluclon 1425-19, Colonia Tlacopoc San Angel, Mexico D.F.01040, ph.(52-56)24-33-09-09; for Canadian nomination contact above address *Eligibility:* Nominees must demonstrate protection, maintenance, restoration or improvement of habitat for waterfowl & migratory bird populations; or initiation of legislation or major corporate or public policy that helped attain goals of the plan, & benefit waterfowl & migratory bird populations; or donation of a gift valued at $10,000 or more to any plan partner; or fostering of cooperation & coordination that contributes to plan goals
Deadline: February; *Amount:* A carving of a Great Blue Heron & a certificate
• International Canvasback Award
For individuals, corporations, & organizations who have made substantial, long-term international contributions to the implementation & continuation of the plan throughout North America *Deadline:* February; *Amount:* An original decoy carving of a Canvasback & a certificate

Arctic Goose Joint Venture (AGJV)
c/o Prairie & Northern Region, Canadian Wildlife Service, 9250 - 49 St. NW, Edmonton AB T6B 1K5
Tel: 780-951-8652; *Fax:* 780-495-2615
agvj@ec.gc.ca
www.agjv.ca
Chief Officer(s):
Deanna Dixon, Coordinator
deanna.dixon@canada.ca

Black Duck Joint Venture (BDJV)
c/o Canadian Wildlife Service, 17 Waterfowl Lane, Sackville NB E4L 1G6
Tel: 506-354-5085
blackduck.cmi.vt.edu
Chief Officer(s):
Patricia Devers, Coordinator
patricia.edwards@canada.ca

Canadian Intermountain Joint Venture (CIJV)
c/o Environment & Climate Change Canada, Pacific & Yukon Region, 5421 Robertson Rd., Delta BC V4K 3N2
jointventure@ec.gc.ca
www.cijv.ca
Chief Officer(s):
Tasha Sargent, Coordinator
tasha.sargent@canada.ca

Eastern Habitat Joint Venture (EHJV)
c/o Canadian Wildlife Service, 17 Waterfowl Lane, Sackville NB E4L 1G6
Tel: 506-364-5085
www.ehjv.ca
www.facebook.com/EasternHabitatJointVenture
twitter.com/ehjvnews
Chief Officer(s):
Patricia Edwards, Coordinator
patricia.edwards@canada.ca

Pacific Birds Habitat Joint Venture
c/o Environment & Climate Change Canada, 5421 Robertson Rd., Delta BC V4K 3N2
Tel: 604-350-1903
info@pacificbirds.org
www.pacificbirds.org
Mission: Formerly known as the Pacific Coast Joint Venture
Chief Officer(s):
Tasha Sargent, Coordinator
tasha.sargent@canada.ca

Prairie Habitat Joint Venture (PHJV)
c/o Prairie & Northern Region, Canadian Wildlife Service, 9250 - 49 St. NW, Edmonton AB T6B 1K5
phjv@ec.gc.ca
www.phjv.ca
Chief Officer(s):
Deanna Dixon, Coordinator
deanna.dixon@canada.ca

Sea Duck Joint Venture (SDJV)
c/o Québec Region, Canadian Wildlife Service, #801, 1550, av d'Estimauville, Québec QC G1J 0C3
www.seaduckjv.org

Chief Officer(s):
Richard Cotter, Coordinator
richard.cotter@canada.ca

North American Wild Fur Shippers Council
567 Henry Ave., Winnipeg MB R3A 0T8
Tel: 204-774-1705
Toll-Free: 800-745-0693
www.nawfsc.com
Overview: A medium-sized international organization founded in 1996
Mission: To represent & protect the interests of wild fur producers in North America
Activities: Organizing auctions
Chief Officer(s):
Dave Bewick, Executive Director

North Battleford & District Labour Council
PO Box 1719, North Battleford SK S9A 3W2
Tel: 306-445-0660
Overview: A small local organization overseen by Saskatchewan Federation of Labour
Mission: To support union members & workers in North Battleford, Saskatchewan & the surrounding region; To advance the economic & social welfare of workers
Affiliation(s): Canadian Labour Congress (CLC)
Activities: Promoting the interests of affiliates; Liasing with local elected officials to ensure labour's message is heard; Presenting educational opportunities; Raising awareness of occupational health & safety; Organizing ceremonies surrounding the International Day of Mourning for Workers Killed & Injured on the Job
Chief Officer(s):
Colin Lemauviel, President
coconb@sasktel.net

North Battleford Chamber of Commerce *See* Battlefords Chamber of Commerce

North Bay & District Chamber of Commerce
205 Main St. East, North Bay ON P1B 1B2
Tel: 705-472-8480; *Fax:* 705-472-8027
Toll-Free: 888-249-8998
www.nbdcc.ca
www.linkedin.com/company/north-bay-&-district-chamber-of-commerce
www.facebook.com/NBDCC
twitter.com/nbdcc
Overview: A small local organization founded in 1894
Mission: To improve the economic environment & quality of life in North Bay
Member of: Ontario Chamber of Commerce; Canadian Chamber of Commerce
Staff Member(s): 5; 85 volunteer(s)
Membership: 900+; *Fees:* Schedule available
Chief Officer(s):
Patti Carr, Executive Director
patricia@nbdcc.ca

North Bay & District Humane Society
PO Box 1383, 2060 Main St. West, North Bay ON P1B 8K5
Tel: 705-474-1251; *Fax:* 705-474-1259
info@northbayhumanesociety.ca
www.northbayhumanesociety.ca
www.facebook.com/nbHumaneSociety
twitter.com/nbhumanesociety
www.instagram.com/northbayhumanesociety
Overview: A small local charitable organization founded in 1954
Member of: Canadian Federation of Humane Societies
Affiliation(s): Ontario Society for the Prevention of Cruelty to Animals
Finances: *Annual Operating Budget:* $250,000-$500,000
Staff Member(s): 7; 50 volunteer(s)
Activities: Animal control & cruelty prevention; *Awareness Events:* Pawsathon, June; *Speaker Service:* Yes
Chief Officer(s):
Daryl Vaillancourt, Executive Director

North Bay & District Stamp Club
North Bay ON
Overview: A small local organization
Mission: To encourage & promote stamp collecting in & around North Bay; To provide a social medium for the exchange of stamps & philatelic information
Member of: Royal Philatelic Society of Canada
Finances: *Annual Operating Budget:* $100,000-$250,000; *Funding Sources:* Membership fees

Membership: 25; *Fees:* $12

North Bay Food Bank
1016 Fisher St., North Bay ON P1B 2G4
Tel: 705-495-3290; *Fax:* 705-495-0413
nbayfoodbank@gmail.com
www.northbayfoodbank.com
www.facebook.com/NorthBayFoodBank
Also Known As: North Bay Soup Kitchen Inc.
Overview: A small local charitable organization founded in 1986
Mission: To ensure that no child or persons go hungry in the community
Member of: Ontario Association of Food Banks
Finances: *Annual Operating Budget:* $100,000-$250,000; *Funding Sources:* Food & financial donations
Staff Member(s): 2; 12 volunteer(s)
Membership: *Fees:* $100
Chief Officer(s):
Amber Livingstone, Manager

North Bay Indian Friendship Centre (NBIFC)
980 Cassells St., North Bay ON P1B 4A6
Tel: 705-472-2811
info@nbifc.org
www.nbifc.org
www.facebook.com/197057837005772
Overview: A small local organization founded in 1974
Mission: To improve the quality of life for First Nation, Metis, & Inuit people in North Bay, Ontario
Member of: Ontario Federation of Indian Friendship Centres
Activities: Offering services & programs to support Aboriginal people of all ages, such as the the Aboriginal Prenatal Nutrition Program, the Best Start Program, the Aboriginal Healthy Babies Healthy Children Program, Cultural Connections for Aboriginal Youth, the Apatisiwin Employment Unit, the Native Inmate Liaison Program, the Aboriginal Drug & Alcohol Program, the Aboriginal Family Support Program, & the Aboriginal Healing & Wellness Program

North Bay Police Association (NBPA)
135 Princess St. West, North Bay ON P1B 8J8
Tel: 705-197-5555
nbpa@northbaypoliceassociation.ca
www.northbaypoliceassociation.ca
Overview: A small local organization founded in 1882
Mission: To advance the interests of members
Affiliation(s): Police Association of Ontario; Canadian Police Association
Membership: 152; *Member Profile:* Sworn & civilian members of the North Bay Police
Activities: Sponsoring & supporting local organizations, such as One Kids Place
Chief Officer(s):
Mike Tarini, President
Ken Rice, 1st Vice-President
Denis Levasseur, 2nd Vice-President
Karen Pendergast, Secretary
Sally O'Halloran, Treasurer

North Bay Real Estate Board
926 Cassells St., North Bay ON P1B 4A8
Tel: 705-472-6812; *Fax:* 705-472-0529
admin@nbreb.com
www.nbreb.com
Overview: A small local organization founded in 1957 overseen by Ontario Real Estate Association
Mission: To represent real estate agents and member offices in North Bay
Member of: The Canadian Real Estate Association
Membership: 167 real estate agents & 17 member offices
Chief Officer(s):
Susan Nosko, President, 705-474-4500

North Central Labour Council of British Columbia
PO Box 1449, Prince George BC V2L 4V4
Tel: 604-430-6766
nclcboard@gmail.com
www.facebook.com/116669825022245
Overview: A small local organization founded in 1956 overseen by British Columbia Federation of Labour
Mission: To act as the voice of workers from the northern interior of British Columbia
Affiliation(s): Canadian Labour Congress (CLC)
Membership: *Member Profile:* Unions from north central British Columbia, such as Prince George, Fort St. James, Vanderhoof, Valemount, & McBride

Activities: Liaising with locally elected officials; Advocating for political change to benefit workers; Providing local labour news; Participating in ceremonies to mark the annual Day of Mourning to remember workers injured or killed on the job
Chief Officer(s):
Troy Zohner, President
Don Iwaskow, Vice-President
Terry Archibald, Secretary-Treasurer

North Central Library Federation (NCLF)
PO Box 44113, RPO Gorge, Victoria BC V9A 7K1
Tel: 778-817-1108
nclf.ca
Overview: A small local organization
Mission: To unite North Central area public libraries; To advance the profession through service
Member of: BC Libraries Cooperative
Staff Member(s): 1
Membership: 25 member libraries
Chief Officer(s):
Katherine Anderson, Manager
kanderson@northcentral.bclibrary.ca

North Central Local Government Association (NCLGA)
c/o Maxine Koppe, #206, 155 George St., Prince George BC V2L 1P8
Tel: 250-564-6585; *Fax:* 250-564-6514
www.nclga.ca
twitter.com/NCLGA
Overview: A small local organization
Mission: To address the issues of local governments; To mobilize initiatives to benefit member governments
Membership: 40 municipalities; *Member Profile:* Elected officials from member regional municipalities, districts, cities, towns, & villages in the north area of British Columbia
Chief Officer(s):
Mitch Campsall, President
president@nclga.ca
Bruce D. Christensen, First Vice-President
Brian Frenkel, Second Vice-President
Maxine Koppe, Executive Director
mkoppe@nclga.ca
Meetings/Conferences:
• North Central Local Government Association 2018 Convention, 2018
Scope: Local
Publications:
• Issues in Focus [a publication of the North Central Local Government Association]
Type: Newsletter; *Frequency:* 8 pa

North Coast Library Federation *See* North West Library Federation

The North Cumberland Historical Society (NCHS)
PO Box 353, Pugwash NS B0K 1L0
Tel: 902-243-3348
nchs_2@yahoo.ca
nchsociety.wikifoundry.com
www.facebook.com/228243580590378
Overview: A small local charitable organization
Mission: To collect, preserve & make available historical data, including genealogy, pertaining to North Cumberland County
Member of: Council of Nova Scotia Archives
Activities: *Library:* Small Archives; Open to public
Chief Officer(s):
Betty Brown, Co-President, 902-243-2263
Carol Hyslop, Co-President, 902-548-2381

North Durham Social Development Council
ON
Overview: A small local organization founded in 1991
Mission: To identify social needs in the townships of Brock, Scugog & Uxbridge; To initiate & encourage the provision of services to meet the needs identified
Finances: *Annual Operating Budget:* Less than $50,000
12 volunteer(s)
Membership: 100; *Fees:* $10; *Committees:* Transportation; Interagency
Chief Officer(s):
Vanessa Slater, Vice-President

North Eastern Ontario Family & Children's Services / Services à la famille et à l'enfance du Nord Est de l'Ontario
707 Ross Ave. East, Timmins ON P4N 8R1

Tel: 705-360-7100; Fax: 705-360-7200
www.neofacs.org
Previous Name: Child & Family Services of Timmins & District
Overview: A medium-sized local organization
Mission: To ensure the well-being of children & families
Staff Member(s): 160
Chief Officer(s):
Don Anderson, President

North Grenville Chamber of Commerce
PO Box 1047, 509 Kernahan St., Kemptville ON K0G 1J0
Tel: 613-258-4838
www.northgrenvillechamber.com
Previous Name: Kemptville & District Chamber of Commerce
Overview: A medium-sized local organization
Mission: To promote business community & quality of life
Member of: Ontario Chamber of Commerce
Finances: Funding Sources: Fundraising; membership dues
Membership: 193
Chief Officer(s):
Mark Thornton, Chair

North Grenville Historical Society (NGHS)
PO Box 1239, Kemptville ON K0G 1J0
Tel: 613-258-4401
nghsociety@gmail.com
www.northgrenvillehistoricalsociety.ca
www.facebook.com/653609458043693
Overview: A small local organization founded in 2001
Finances: Annual Operating Budget: Less than $50,000
Membership: Fees: $25 adult; $20 youth; $30 household; $100 single patron; $150 household patron
Activities: Creating publications & archives; Hosting guest speakers
Chief Officer(s):
Bill Adams, President

North Hastings Community Integration Association (NHCIA)
PO Box 1508, 2 Alice St., Bancroft ON K0L 1C0
Tel: 613-332-2090; Fax: 613-332-4762
communityliving@nhcia.ca
www.nhcia.ca
Overview: A small local charitable organization founded in 1965
Mission: To support people with an intellectual disability & their families; To facilitate opportunities for all people to live, work & learn together
Member of: Community Living Ontario
Finances: Funding Sources: Ministry of Community & Social Services; fundraising; foundations; corporations; donations
Activities: Library: Open to public
Chief Officer(s):
Aaron Hill, Executive Director, 613-334-7929
Lloyd Churchill, President
Awards:
• John & Evelyn Lock Bursary Award

North Island College Faculty Association (NICFA)
2300 Ryan Rd., Courtenay BC V9N 8N6
Tel: 250-949-2867
www.nicfa.ca
Overview: A small local organization
Member of: College Institute Educators Association of BC
Chief Officer(s):
Shirley Ackland, President
sackland@nic.bc.ca

North Island Laurentian Teachers' Union See Laurier Teachers Union

North Island Wildlife Recovery Association
PO Box 364, 1240 Leffler Rd., Errington BC V0R 1V0
Tel: 250-248-8534; Fax: 250-248-1274
wildlife@niwra.org
www.niwra.org
Overview: A small local charitable organization founded in 1985
Mission: To work with the people of Vancouver Island to care for ill, injured, & orphaned wildlife; To educate the public on issues affecting wildlife & the environment
Finances: Funding Sources: Donations
Membership: Fees: $35 adult; $32 parent; $12 child; $100 corporate
Activities: Offering educational programs & presentations, as well as animal rehabilitation & adoption programs; Operating gift shop; Organizing fundraising events; Providing information on wildlife; Awareness Events: Magical Nights of Light
Chief Officer(s):
Del L. Kristalovich, President

North Lanark Historical Society
PO Box 218, 647 River Rd., Appleton ON K0A 1A0
Tel: 613-256-2866
appletonmuseum@hotmail.com
www.northlanarkregionalmuseum.com
Also Known As: North Lanark Regional Museum
Overview: A small local charitable organization founded in 1965
Mission: To preserve & record area history
Member of: Ontario District Society
Affiliation(s): Ontario Historical Society
Finances: Annual Operating Budget: Less than $50,000
6 volunteer(s)
Membership: 45; Fees: $10
Activities: Operating the North Lanark Regional Museum; Library: Open to public
Chief Officer(s):
Doreen Wilson, Manager, Museum

North of Superior Film Association (NOSFA)
#352, 1100 Memorial Ave., Thunder Bay ON P7B 4A3
Tel: 807-625-5450
info@nosfa.ca
www.nosfa.ca
Overview: A medium-sized provincial organization
Mission: To promote film and appreciation of film in the Thunder Bay area.
Membership: Fees: $10
Activities: Film screenings; Awareness Events: Film Festival
Chief Officer(s):
Marty Mascarin, President
Catherine Powell, Festival Coordinator

North of Superior Tourism Association (NOSTA)
#2, 605 Victoria Ave. East, Thunder Bay ON P7C 1B1
Tel: 807-346-1130; Fax: 807-346-1135
Toll-Free: 800-265-3951
info@northofsuperior.org
www.northofsuperior.org
www.facebook.com/northofsuperior
twitter.com/northosuperior
Also Known As: North of Superior Travel Association Inc.
Overview: A small local organization founded in 1974
Mission: To market the tourism opportunities for vacationing in Northwestern Ontario.
Member of: Ontario Tourism; Canadian Tourism Commission; Tourism Industry Association of Canada
Finances: Funding Sources: Membership fees; government
Activities: Speaker Service: Yes; Rents Mailing List: Yes
Chief Officer(s):
Tim Lukinuk, President
tim@amethystmine.com

North Okanagan Labour Council
1091 Gordon Dr., Kelowna BC V1Y 3E3
nolc@shaw.ca
members.shaw.ca/nolc
Overview: A medium-sized local organization overseen by British Columbia federation of Labour
Mission: To represent labour unions in British Columbia's North & Central Okanagan
Affiliation(s): Canadian Labour Congress (CLC)
Membership: 8,500; Member Profile: Union members in the North & Central Okanagan of British Columbia
Activities: Offering training courses, on topics such as health & safety; Marking the annual Day of Mourning, for workers injured or killed on the job; Providing labour news; Hosting monthly general meetings
Chief Officer(s):
Andrew Pritchard, President
Nikki Inouye, Vice-President
Ronn Dunn, Vice-President
Karen Abramsen, Vice-President
Cheryl Stone, Secretary
nolc.cstone@gmail.com
Ron Bobowski, Secretary-Treaser

North Okanagan Naturalists Club (NONC)
PO Box 473, Vernon BC V1T 6M4
Tel: 250-545-0490
www.nonc.ca
Overview: A small local charitable organization founded in 1951
Mission: To foster an interest in nature; to record data & sightings of flora & fauna; to educate young people; to hold land
Member of: The Federation of BC Naturalists; Canadian Nature Federation
Finances: Annual Operating Budget: Less than $50,000; Funding Sources: Dues; social activities; club sales
3 volunteer(s)
Membership: 180; Fees: $35 adults; $50 family; Committees: Conservation; Education; Land Stewardship; Socials; Trips; Ways & Means
Activities: Awareness Events: Annual Field & Dinner Day, May
Chief Officer(s):
Rod Drennan, President, 250-545-4999
Awards:
• James Grant Memorial Award

North Okanagan Neurological Association (NONA)
2802 - 34th St., Vernon BC V1T 5X1
Tel: 250-549-1281; Fax: 250-549-3771
administration@nona-cdc.com
www.nona-cdc.com
www.facebook.com/NONAChildDevelopmentCentre
Overview: A small local organization founded in 1975
Mission: To provide services for the treatment, education & support of special needs children & their families
Member of: B.C. Association of Child Development & Rehabilitation
Affiliation(s): Cerebral Palsy Association of British Columbia
Finances: Funding Sources: Provincial Government
Chief Officer(s):
Janice Foster, Executive Director

North Okanagan Organic Association (NOOA)
C76 Cedar Hill Rd., RR#1, Vernon BC V0E 1W0
Tel: 250-540-2557
northorganics@gmail.com
Overview: A small local licensing organization
Mission: To encourage the practice of soil regeneration & sustainable food production, through the use of organic methods as per the Canadian definition; To certify members' food products that are organically grown in accordance with the association's guidelines
Affiliation(s): Certified Organic Associations of BC
Finances: Annual Operating Budget: Less than $50,000
Membership: 101; Fees: $325; Committees: Certification; Standards
Activities: Certification of members' food products; monthly meeting for information on organic practices; Library: by appointment
Chief Officer(s):
Molly Thurston, President
Cara Nunn, Administrator

North Okanagan Social Planning Council See Social Planning Council for the North Okanagan

North Okanagan United Way See United Way of North Okanagan Columbia Shuswap

North Pacific Anadromous Fish Commission (NPAFC)
#502, 889 West Pender St., Vancouver BC V6C 3B2
Tel: 604-775-5550; Fax: 604-775-5577
secretariat@npafc.org
www.npafc.org
www.facebook.com/profile.php?id=100014339771216
Overview: A medium-sized international organization founded in 1992
Mission: To promote the conservation of anadromous stocks in the North Pacific Ocean
Member of: Regional Fishery Body Secretariat's Network
Finances: Annual Operating Budget: $500,000-$1.5 Million; Funding Sources: Member state contributions
Staff Member(s): 5
Membership: Committees: Enforcement; Finance & Administration; Scientific Research & Statistics
Activities: Holding meetings & communications in the areas of fisheries enforcement & scientific research; Internships: Yes
Chief Officer(s):
Vladimir Radchenko, Executive Director
vlrad@npafc.org
Nancy Davis, Deputy Director
ndavis@npafc.org
Awards:
• NPAFC Award
   Deadline: January
Meetings/Conferences:
• North Pacific Anadromous Fish Commission Annual Meeting 2018, May, 2018, Khabarovsk
Publications:
• NPAFC [North Pacific Anadromous Fish Commission]

Newsletter
Type: Newsletter; *Editor:* Nancy Davis
Profile: Outlines activities of the Commission & its members

North Pacific Cannery - National Historic Site
1889 Skeena Dr., Port Edward BC V0V 1G0
Tel: 250-628-3538; *Fax:* 250-628-3540
info@northpacificcannery.ca
www.northpacificcannery.ca
www.facebook.com/NorthPacificCannery
Overview: A small local organization
Finances: *Annual Operating Budget:* $100,000-$250,000
Staff Member(s): 10
Chief Officer(s):
Laurie Davie, General Manager
manager@northpacificcannery.ca

North Pacific Marine Science Organization (PICES)
c/o Institute of Ocean Sciences, PO Box 6000, Sidney BC V8L 4B2
Tel: 250-363-6366; *Fax:* 250-363-6827
secretariat@pices.int
www.pices.int
Overview: A medium-sized international organization
Mission: To promote & coordinate marine research in the northern North Pacific & adjacent seas especially northward of 30 degrees North; to advance scientific knowledge about the ocean environment, global weather & climate change, living resources & their ecosystems & the impacts of human activities; to promote the collection & rapid exchange of scientific information on these issues
Staff Member(s): 4
Membership: 334; *Member Profile:* Member scientists come from Canada, Japan, China, Korea, Russia & the U.S.;
Committees: Biological Oceanography; Fishery Science; Marine Environmental Quality; Physical Oceanography & Climate; Data Exchange; Monitoring; Executive; Finance & Administration
Chief Officer(s):
Alexander Bychkov, Executive Secretary
bychkov@pices.int

North Peace Applied Research Association (NPARA)
PO Box 750, 116 - 4th Ave., Manning AB T0H 2M0
Tel: 780-836-3354
npara.ca
Overview: A small local organization founded in 1988 overseen by Agricultural Research & Extension Council of Alberta
Mission: To conduct agricultural research, trials, extension & research plots
Member of: Agricultural Research & Extension Council of Alberta
Membership: *Fees:* $20
Chief Officer(s):
Nora Paulovich, Manager
nora@npara.ca
Tom Fromme, Coordinator, Research
tom@npara.ca
Publications:
• NPARA [North Peace Applied Research Association] Newsletter
Type: Newsletter

North Peace Cultural Society (NPCC)
10015 - 100 Ave., Fort St John BC V1J 1Y7
Tel: 250-785-1992; *Fax:* 250-785-1510
Toll-Free: 877-785-1992
reception@npcc.bc.ca
www.npcc.bc.ca
www.facebook.com/north.peace.cultural.centre
twitter.com/FSJNPCC
Also Known As: North Peace Cultural Centre
Overview: A small local charitable organization founded in 1976
Mission: To stimulate & develop cultural activities in the North Peace; to encourage individuals & groups to promote arts activities & support community events
Member of: BC Touring Council
Finances: *Annual Operating Budget:* $500,000-$1.5 Million
Staff Member(s): 14; 35 volunteer(s)
Membership: 100; *Fees:* $15
Chief Officer(s):
Bettyanne Hampton, Executive Director
ed@npcc.bc.ca

North Peace Historical Society
9323 - 100th St., Fort St John BC V1J 4N4
Tel: 250-787-0430; *Fax:* 250-787-0405
www.fsjmuseum.com

Overview: A small local charitable organization founded in 1965
Mission: To collect, preserve & house articles pertaining to the history of Fort St. John & the North Peace River area, for the education & enjoyment of local residents & tourists
Member of: BC Museum Association; Canadian Museums Association; Archives Association of BC; Northern BC Tourism Association; Fort St. John & District Chamber of Commerce
Finances: *Annual Operating Budget:* $50,000-$100,000;
Funding Sources: Provincial, local & regional government; fundraising
Staff Member(s): 1; 50 volunteer
Membership: 150; *Fees:* $8 adult; $6 senior; $3 student
Activities: *Library:* Fort St. John North Peace Museum Archives; Open to public
Chief Officer(s):
Evelyn Sim, President

North Perth Chamber of Commerce
580 Main St. West, Listowel ON N4W 1A8
Tel: 519-291-1551; *Fax:* 519-291-4151
npchamber.com
Previous Name: Listowel Chamber of Commerce
Overview: A small local organization
Mission: To foster civic, commercial, industrial & agricultural growth in the community
Membership: 185; *Fees:* $125-$390
Chief Officer(s):
Virginia Dunbar, President
Sharon D'Arcey, General Manager

North Queens Board of Trade
North Queens Community School, 40 Caledonia Rd. West, Caledonia NS B0T 1B0
Tel: 902-682-3116
Overview: A small local organization
Mission: To support & promote commerce and trade in the North Queens area
Member of: Nova Scotia Chamber of Commerce
Chief Officer(s):
Peter van Dyk, President
petervandyke@eastlink.ca

North Renfrew Family Services Inc. (NRFS)
PO Box 1334, 109 Banting Dr., Deep River ON K0J 1P0
Tel: 613-584-3358; *Fax:* 613-584-5520
nrfs@drdh.org
bright-ideas-software.com/NRFS
Overview: A small local charitable organization founded in 1968 overseen by Family Service Ontario
Mission: To provide referral & counselling services for individuals & families in North Renfrew
Member of: Renfrew County United Way
Affiliation(s): Family Service Ontario
Finances: *Funding Sources:* United Way; Ministry of Community & Social Services; Private donations; Town of Deep River; Town of Laurentian Hills
Staff Member(s): 3; 50 volunteer(s)
Chief Officer(s):
Kelly Hawley, Executive Director

North Saskatchewan Watershed Alliance
9504 - 49 St., Edmonton AB T6B 2M9
Tel: 780-442-6363; *Fax:* 780-495-0610
water@nswa.ab.ca
www.nswa.ab.ca
www.facebook.com/NorthSaskRiver?fref=ts
twitter.com/NorthSaskRiver
www.youtube.com/user/NSaskRiverWatershed
Overview: A small local organization founded in 2000
Mission: To protect & improve water quality & ecosystem functioning in the North Saskatchewan Watershed within Alberta
Finances: *Annual Operating Budget:* $50,000-$100,000;
Funding Sources: Industry; government; grants
Staff Member(s): 6
Membership: 140
Activities: State of watershed reporting; watershed planning; education & awareness; stewardship; *Library:* by appointment
Chief Officer(s):
David Trew, Executive Director, 780-496-3474
Tom Cottrell, IWMP Coordinator, 780-496-6962
tom.cottrell@edmonton.ca

North Shore Association for the Physically Handicapped
See North Shore Disability Resource Centre Association

North Shore ConneXions Society
1070 Roosevelt Cres., North Vancouver BC V7P 1M3

Tel: 604-984-9321; *Fax:* 604-984-9882
info@nsconnexions.org
www.nsconnexions.org
www.facebook.com/nsconnexions
twitter.com/NSConneXions
Also Known As: ConneXions
Overview: A small local organization founded in 1956
Mission: To advocate for better social & educational services for children with special needs
Finances: *Funding Sources:* Municipal, provincial & federal government; donations; membership fees
Membership: *Fees:* $2 self advocate; $10 associate; $12 individual; $15 family
Chief Officer(s):
Shirley Clarke, President
Publications:
• Community ConneXions [a publication of the North Shore ConneXions Society]
Type: Newsletter; *Frequency:* 6 pa

North Shore Construction Inc. (Ind.) *Voir* Syndicat québécois de la construction

North Shore Disability Resource Centre Association (NSDRC)
3158 Mountain Hwy., North Vancouver BC V7K 2H5
Tel: 604-985-5371; *Fax:* 604-985-7594; *TTY:* 604-985-5371
nsdrc@nsdrc.org
www.nsdrc.org
www.facebook.com/227106267339398
twitter.com/NSDRCcbsProg
Previous Name: North Shore Association for the Physically Handicapped
Overview: A medium-sized local charitable organization founded in 1976
Mission: To provide programs & services based on the belief that all people are important to their community; To work to ensure that people with disabilities can participate actively as members of the community; To work toward a community which is free from physical, financial, & attitudinal barriers
Member of: BC Association for Community Living; United Way of the Lower Mainland
Affiliation(s): BC Federation of Private Child Care Agencies; United Way of the Lower Mainland; BC Coalition of People with Disabilities
Finances: *Funding Sources:* Government; Fundraising; Membership fees
Activities: Information Services Program; Infant Development Program; Special Services to Children; Summer Program; Equipment Technicians; community-based day programs; individual life skills contracts; residential services; Pre-teen & Teen Program; Day Service Program; *Speaker Service:* Yes; *Rents Mailing List:* Yes; *Library:* Open to public
Chief Officer(s):
Liz Barnett, Executive Director
lizb@nsdrc.org

North Shore Forest Products Marketing Board
PO Box 386, Bathurst NB E2A 3Z3
Tel: 506-548-8958
nsfpmb@nb.aibn.com
www.forestrysyndicate.com
Overview: A small local organization founded in 1973
Mission: To negotiate with industry & government on behalf of the private wood producers of the regulated area for fair prices for the products of the woodlots & to promote improved forest management
Affiliation(s): NB Forest Products Commission
Finances: *Annual Operating Budget:* Greater than $5 Million;
Funding Sources: Regional Government
Staff Member(s): 10; 10 volunteer(s)
Membership: 2,000 individual
Activities: *Rents Mailing List:* Yes
Chief Officer(s):
Alain Landry, General Manager
Patrick Doucet, Sylviculture Manager
patrick.doucet@forestrysyndicate.com

North Shore Hospice Society
231 East 15th St., North Vancouver BC V7L 2L7
Tel: 604-984-5785
www.northshorehospicepalliative.com
Previous Name: Lions Gate Hospice Society
Overview: A small local charitable organization founded in 1982
Mission: To support hospice/palliative care for people at the end of their lives & to support their family & friends in the North Vancouver area

Membership: Fees: $25; $15 seniors; $125 life
Chief Officer(s):
Jo-Ann Wood, Chair

North Shore Multicultural Society (NSMS)
#207, 123 - 15th St. East, North Vancouver BC V7L 2P7
Tel: 604-988-2931; Fax: 604-988-2960
office@nsms.ca
www.nsms.ca
Overview: A small local organization founded in 1991
Mission: To assist immigrant families to settle & integrate into Canadian society; To work with community agencies & schools in making services more accessible to North Shore newcomers
Member of: Affiliation of Multicultural Societies & Service Agencies of BC
Finances: Annual Operating Budget: $500,000-$1.5 Million; Funding Sources: Federal & provincial governments; Donations
Staff Member(s): 20; 125 volunteer(s)
Membership: 110; Fees: $15 individual; $25 family; $35 non-profit; $10 student/senior
Activities: Immigrant settlement orientation & orientation in formation; Referral; Lay counselling; Workshops; Short-term ESL classes; Computer classes; Support groups; Employment programs for newcomers; Youth programs; Diversity & anti-racism; Rents Mailing List: Yes
Chief Officer(s):
Vera Radyo, President
Elizabeth Jones, Executive Director
elizabethj@nsms.ca
Stacie Letham, Director, Operations
staciel@nsms.ca

North Shore Numismatic Society (NSNS)
BC
info@northshorenumismaticsociety.org
www.northshorenumismaticsociety.org
Overview: A small local organization founded in 1974 overseen by Royal Canadian Numismatic Association
Mission: To advance numismatica
Membership: Fees: $15 singles; $16 couples; $7.50 juniors
Activities: Conducting monthly meetings
Chief Officer(s):
Mike Souza, President
Publications:
• The Shoreline [a publication of North Shore Numismatic Society]
Type: Newsletter; Accepts Advertising; ISSN: 0380-8866
Profile: Information about collecting & upcoming events

North Shore Stamp Club
135 West 15th St. North, North Vancouver BC
Tel: 604-984-3360
Overview: A small local organization
Member of: Royal Philatelic Society of Canada

North Shuswap Chamber of Commerce
3871 Squilax-Anglemont Rd., #B, Scotch Creek BC V0E 1M5
Tel: 250-955-2113
info@northshuswapbc.com
www.northshuswapbc.com
www.facebook.com/130215783729882
Overview: A small local organization
Mission: To lead the economic development of the community
Membership: 100+; Fees: $100 primary; $50 secondary; $20 individual

North Sydney Historical Society
PO Box 163, North Sydney NS B2A 3M3
Tel: 902-794-2524
nsydmuseum@ns.sympatico.ca
northsydneymuseum.ca
Overview: A small local organization founded in 1980
Member of: Federation of the Nova Scotian Heritage
Finances: Annual Operating Budget: Less than $50,000; Funding Sources: Local & provincial government
20 volunteer(s)
Membership: 20; Fees: $10
Activities: Research, exhibit of artifacts reflecting past of area, histories of Western Union poiticians; Library: Open to public

North Vancouver Chamber of Commerce (NVCC)
1250 Lonsdale Ave., Vancouver BC V7M 2H6
Tel: 604-987-4488; Fax: 604-987-8272
www.nvchamber.ca
www.linkedin.com/company/north-vancouver-chamber-of-commerce
www.facebook.com/nvchamber
www.instagram.com/nvchamber
Overview: A medium-sized local organization founded in 1906
Mission: To ensure a healthy socio-economic base for the benefit of the North Shore region by supporting business prosperity, economic growth, & diversification
Membership: Fees: Schedule available, based upon number of employees; Member Profile: Businesses; Professionals; Residents; Community groups; Committees: Governance; Membership Value; Policy/Advocacy; Emerging Leaders
Activities: Advocating on business issues; Providing networking opportunities; Encouraging partnerships; Liaising with municipal, provincial, & federal committees in order to encourage business; Promoting the North Vancouver city & district economy; Providing business information; Offering seminars & expert speakers; Presenting business excellence awards; Library: Business Resource Centre
Chief Officer(s):
Louise Ranger, Chief Executive Officer
Misha Wilson, Manager, Membership

North Vancouver Community Arts Council (NVCAC)
335 Lonsdale Ave., North Vancouver BC V7M 2G3
Tel: 604-988-6844; Fax: 604-988-2787
info@nvartscouncil.ca
www.nvartscouncil.ca
www.facebook.com/nvartscouncil
twitter.com/NVArtsCouncil
www.youtube.com/northvanartscouncil
Overview: A small local organization founded in 1969
Mission: To promote arts as a way to bridge cultures & build community
Member of: Assembly of BC Arts Councils; Vancouver Cultural Alliance; South West Regional Arts Council; Presentation House Cultural Society; Chamber of Commerce
Finances: Annual Operating Budget: $250,000-$500,000; Funding Sources: Municipal & provincial government; membership dues; programmes; corporations
Staff Member(s): 5; 100 volunteer(s)
Membership: 400; Fees: $35 individual; $30 senior/student; $60 group; $40 family; Committees: Art in Public Places; Picture Rental; Newsletter; Adjudications; Craft Fair; After School Art; Art in Garden; CityScape Community Art Space; Wild Lights Festival; Mountain Mardi Gras
Chief Officer(s):
Linda Feil, Executive Director

North West Commercial Travellers' Association (NWCTA)
39 River St., Toronto ON M5A 3P1
Fax: 877-284-8909
Toll-Free: 800-665-6928
nwcta@nwcta.com
www.nwcta.com
www.linkedin.com/NorthWestCommercialAssociation
twitter.com/NWCTAl
Also Known As: NWCTA, the Business & Travellers' Association
Overview: A medium-sized national organization founded in 1882
Mission: To protect & introduce benefits for individual business travellers
Finances: Annual Operating Budget: $250,000-$500,000
Staff Member(s): 3; 7 volunteer(s)
Membership: 900 senior/lifetime; Fees: $92; Member Profile: Business traveller representing an organization or company involved in marketing goods or providing services to business community
Activities: Speaker Service: Yes
Chief Officer(s):
Peter McClure, President
pmcuct@nb.sympatico.ca
Wendy Sue Lyttle, Executive Director
wlyttle@nwcta.com
Charles Ng, Membership Coordinator
membership@nwcta.com

North West Library Federation (NWLF)
432 - 3rd St., New Westminster BC V3L 2S2
Tel: 604-802-7996
Toll-Free: 800-276-1804
nwlf.ca
Previous Name: North Coast Library Federation
Overview: A small local charitable organization
Mission: To create equitable access to public library services in the region
Membership: 7 libraries; Fees: Schedule available; Member Profile: Public libraries in the communities of Hazelton, Houston, Kitimat, Prince Rupert, Smithers, Stewart, & Terrace
Chief Officer(s):
Lauren Wolf, Director

North York Coin Club (NYCC)
3888 Duke of York Blvd., #PH34, Mississauga ON L5B 4P5
Tel: 416-897-6684
info@northyorkcoinclub.com
www.northyorkcoinclub.com
Overview: A small local organization founded in 1960
Mission: To promote numismatics
Member of: Canadian Numismatic Association; Ontario Numismatic Association
Finances: Annual Operating Budget: Less than $50,000
10 volunteer(s)
Membership: 60; Fees: $10 individual; $15 family; $5 junior
Activities: Educational/collectible social exchange in all areas of numismatics; Speaker Service: Yes; Library: Not open to public
Chief Officer(s):
Bill O'Brien, President
Publications:
• NYCC [North York Coin Club] Bulletin
Type: Newsletter; Frequency: Monthly; Editor: Paul Petch

North York Community House
Lawrence Square Mall, #226, 700 Lawrence Ave., Toronto ON M6A 3B4
Tel: 416-784-0920
www.nych.ca
www.facebook.com/nychonline
twitter.com/nychonline
www.youtube.com/user/nychonline
Overview: A medium-sized local charitable organization founded in 1990
Mission: To assist newcomers settle, integrate and become vibrant members of our community; to help residents improve their economic conditions; and to help build strong neighbourhoods.
Finances: Annual Operating Budget: Greater than $5 Million; Funding Sources: Government, United Way
Staff Member(s): 100; 347 volunteer(s)
Membership: Fees: $5
Chief Officer(s):
Shelley Zuckerman, Executive Director

North York General Foundation
4001 Leslie St., Toronto ON M2K 1E1
Tel: 416-756-6944; Fax: 416-756-9047
foundation@nygh.on.ca
www.nyghfoundation.ca
www.linkedin.com/company/north-york-general-foundation
www.facebook.com/NYGHFoundation
twitter.com/NYGHFoundation
www.youtube.com/NYGHFoundation
Overview: A small local charitable organization
Mission: To raise money on behalf of North York General Hospital in order to fund research & improve patient care
Finances: Annual Operating Budget: Less than $50,000
Chief Officer(s):
Terry Pursell, President & CEO

North York Harvest Food Bank
116 Industry St., Toronto ON M6M 4L8
Tel: 416-635-7771; Fax: 416-635-5599
info@northyorkharvest.com
www.northyorkharvest.com
www.linkedin.com/company/2220838
www.facebook.com/northyorkharvest
twitter.com/nyhfb
instagram.com/nyhfb
Overview: A small local charitable organization
Mission: To feed those in need & work to reduce hunger
Member of: Ontario Association of Food Banks
Staff Member(s): 21
Activities: Collects, sorts & distributes free of charge, 180,000 hampers of fresh & non-perishable items per year, through 47 community agencies; provides direct emergency hamper service; also actively involved in anti-hunger & anti-poverty initiatives
Chief Officer(s):
Ryan Noble, Executive Director
ryan@northyorkharvest.com

North York Symphony Youth Orchestra See La Jeunesse Youth Orchestra

Northeast Avalon ACAP, Inc.
PO Box 8732, St. John's NL A1B 3T1
Tel: 709-726-9673; *Fax:* 709-726-2764
info@naacap.ca
www.naacap.ca
www.facebook.com/NAACAP.NL
twitter.com/naacap
Also Known As: Atlantic Coastal Action Program
Previous Name: St. John's Harbour ACAP
Overview: A small local organization
Member of: NL Environmental Industries Association; NL Environment Network
Finances: *Annual Operating Budget:* $100,000-$250,000
Staff Member(s): 2; 25 volunteer(s)
Membership: 1-99
Activities: *Library:* Open to public by appointment
Chief Officer(s):
Myron King, Office and Outreach Coordinator

Northeast Highlands Chamber of Commerce
PO Box 125, Ingonish NS B0C 1L0
Tel: 902-285-2289; *Fax:* 902-285-2295
Overview: A small local organization founded in 1996
Chief Officer(s):
Ian Green, President

Northeastern Alberta Aboriginal Business Association (NAABA)
PO Box 5993, Stn. Main, 1005 Memorial Dr., Hwy 63, Fort McMurray AB T9H 4V9
Tel: 780-791-0478; *Fax:* 780-714-6485
admin@naaba.ca
www.naaba.ca
www.facebook.com/NAABA93
twitter.com/NAABA_RMWB
Overview: A small provincial organization
Mission: To create partnerships between Aboriginal businesses & industry; To support economic development of Aboriginal people in the Wood Buffalo region
Membership: 236; *Fees:* Schedule available
Chief Officer(s):
Leanne Hawco, Executive Director
leanne@naaba.ca
Tammie Tuccaro, Office Manager
tammie@naaba.ca

Northeastern Ontario Building & Construction Trades Council
2413 Lasalle Blvd., Sudbury ON P3A 2A9
Tel: 705-560-0128; *Fax:* 705-560-4701
Overview: A small local organization
Mission: To act as a trade union in accordance with Ontario's Labour Relations Act

Northeastern Ontario Tourism
#401, 2009 Long Lake Rd., Sudbury ON P3E 6C3
Tel: 705-522-0104
Toll-Free: 800-465-6655
www.northeasternontario.com
www.facebook.com/northeasternontario
twitter.com/NeOntario
Overview: A small local organization founded in 1974
Member of: Tourism Federation of Ontario

The Northern AIDS Connection Society (NACS)
33 Pleasant St., Truro NS B2N 3R5
Tel: 902-895-0931; *Fax:* 902-895-3353
Toll-Free: 866-940-2437
admin@nhcsociety.ca
www.nhcsociety.ca
www.facebook.com/nhcsns
Previous Name: Truro & Area Outreach Project; Pictou County AIDS Coalition
Overview: A small local organization founded in 1996 overseen by Canadian AIDS Society
Mission: To support & promote the health & well-being of individuals living with HIV & those affected by HIV; To provide prevention education within northern region of Nova Scotia
Affiliation(s): Nova Scotia AIDS Coalition
25 volunteer(s)
Activities: Presentations in schools; support work for people living with HIV; displays; art auction; AIDS Walk; *Awareness Events:* International Day Against Homophobia, May; World Hep Day, July; World AIDS Day, Dec. *Library:* Resource Library
Chief Officer(s):
Albert McNutt, Director
super@nhcsociety.ca

Dwight Griffiths, Program Coordinator
programs@nhcsociety.ca
Publications:
• Extreme Reality [a publication of the Northern AIDS Connection Society]
Type: Newsletter; *Frequency:* Quarterly

Northern Air Transport Association (NATA)
c/o Colin Dempsey, PO Box 20102, Yellowknife NT X1A 3X8
Tel: 867-446-6282; *Fax:* 866-977-6282
admin@nata-yzf.ca
www.nata-yzf.ca
Overview: A small local organization founded in 1977
Mission: To promote safe & effective Northern air transportation; To advocate for Northern air transport positions; To establish & maintain partnerships within the industry, governments & other interested parties
Membership: *Fees:* $195-$2,895 operator; $625 associate; $100 sustaining membership; *Member Profile:* Operators, associates & affiliates of the industry; Members can also be Sustaining Members or Honorary Life Members; *Committees:* Training
Activities: Advocating for Northern air transport; Establishing partnerships with governments & within the transportation industry; *Speaker Service:* Yes
Chief Officer(s):
Glenn Priestley, Executive Director, 613-866-2374
exec@nata-yzf.ca
Colin Dempsey, General Manager, 867-466-6282, Fax: 866-977-6282
admin@nata-yzf.ca
Awards:
• Kenn Borek Memorial Scholarship
To assist Western and Northern Canadian students pursuing careers in aviation *Eligibility:* Canadian students in pursuit of pilot or aircraft maintenance training residing in the Yukon, Northwest Territories, Nunavut, British Columbia or Alberta *Deadline:* March 31; *Amount:* $4,000 *Contact:* Christina Hadzoglou, bcmcdonald@parlee.com
• Aviation Career Development Program
To assist students from the Northwest Territories pursuing careers in aviation *Eligibility:* Northwest Territories residents pursuing full-time training in an aviation-related field and planning to work in the North upon completion *Deadline:* July 30; *Amount:* $5,000 x8
Meetings/Conferences:
• Northern Air Transport Association 42nd Annual Conference & Tradeshow, April, 2018, Whitehorse, YT
Description: Conference presentations & exhibitors
Contact Information: admin@nata-yzf.ca

Northern Alberta Brain Injury Society See Brain Care Centre

Northern Alberta Curling Association (NACA)
#110, 9440 - 49 St., Edmonton AB T6B 2M9
Tel: 780-440-4270; *Fax:* 780-463-4519
northernalbertacurling@shaw.ca
northernalbertacurling.com
www.facebook.com/108398119223374
Overview: A small local organization founded in 1918 overseen by Canadian Curling Association
Mission: To develop and promote the sport of curling.
Staff Member(s): 2
Chief Officer(s):
Matt Yeo, President
Vicki Baird, Execurive Director

Northern Alberta Health Libraries Association
c/o J.W. Scott Health Sciences Library, University of Alberta, 2K3.28 Walter MacKenzie Ctr., Edmonton AB T6G 2R7
contact.nahla@gmail.com
nahla.chla-absc.ca
Overview: A small local organization founded in 1984 overseen by Canadian Health Libraries Association
Mission: To provide a forum for networking among librarians, library technicians, & others interested in health libraries & health information; To encourage health information specialists to support health care services & research
Member of: Canadian Health Libraries Association
Membership: *Fees:* $30 regular; $15 student; *Member Profile:* Librarians, library technicians, & others interested in health libraries & health information.
Chief Officer(s):
Sandy Campbell, President
Morgan Truax, Secretary
Awards:
• Continuing Education Award

; *Amount:* $200 + free registration to annual TRENDS mini-conference
Meetings/Conferences:
• Northern Alberta Health Libraries Association TRENDS Mini Conference 2018, 2018, AB
Scope: Provincial
Description: An annual, half-day conference that features keynote speakers
• Northern Alberta Health Libraries Association Annual General Meeting 2018, 2018, AB
Scope: Provincial
• Northern Alberta Health Libraries Association Research Exposition, 2018, AB
Scope: Provincial
Description: An annual event that showcases recent & in-progress research by members through a series of brief presentations on a wide range of topics

Northern Alberta Institute of Technology Academic Staff Association (NASA)
#T110, 11762 - 106 St., Edmonton AB T5G 2R1
Tel: 780-471-8702; *Fax:* 780-474-6736
nasa@nait.ca
Also Known As: NAIT Academic Staff Association
Overview: A small local organization founded in 1982
Mission: To provide a positive work environment & to facilitate members in their delivery of high-quality instruction & their pursuit of personal & professional growth
Member of: Alberta Colleges-Institutes Faculties Association
Finances: *Annual Operating Budget:* $250,000-$500,000; *Funding Sources:* Membership dues
Staff Member(s): 3; 60 volunteer(s)
Membership: 1,000+; *Committees:* Membership Services; Bargaining; Finance
Chief Officer(s):
Doug Short, President, 780-471-8916
dougs@nait.ca

Northern British Columbia Construction Association See British Columbia Construction Association

Northern British Columbia Tourism Association (NBCTA)
1274 - 5th Ave., Prince George BC V2L 3L2
Tel: 250-561-0432
www.travelnbc.com
Overview: A small local organization founded in 1972 overseen by Council of Tourism Associations of British Columbia
Mission: To promote & develop the tourism industry of northern British Columbia
Member of: Tourism Industry Association of Canada
Finances: *Funding Sources:* Private tourism sector contracts; membership fees
Activities: Co-op marketing; *Library:* Not open to public
Chief Officer(s):
Anthony Everett, CEO
anthony@nbctourism.com

Northern Canada Study Group
#570, 188 Douglas St., Victoria BC V8V 2P1
Overview: A small local organization founded in 1994
Mission: To study the postal history of the northern regions of British Columbia, Ontario, & Quebec, early Manitoba, the provincial districts of Alberta, Assiniboia, Athabasca, Saskatchewan & Keewatin, plus Labrador, the Northwest Territories, & Yukon
Affiliation(s): Postal History Society of Canada
Chief Officer(s):
Gray Scrimgeour, Contact
gray@scrimgeour.ca
Publications:
• The Northerner: Newsletter of the Northern Canada Study Group
Type: Newsletter; *Frequency:* 5-6 pa; *Number of Pages:* 32; *Editor:* Gray Scrimgeour; *Price:* $15
Profile: Includes illustrations of covers or post cards, plus information about mail handling, postmarks, & life in northern Canada

Northern Film & Video Industry Association (NFVIA)
PO Box 31340, Whitehorse YT Y1A 5P7
Tel: 867-456-2978
info@nfvia.com
www.nfvia.com
Also Known As: Yukon Film Industry Association
Overview: A medium-sized provincial organization founded in 1999

Mission: To support the film & video sector in the Yukon by focussing on areas such as human resource development in the industry, development of infrastructure & production support, marketing, strategic alliances & partnerships, & membership services

Northern Finance Association (NFA)
c/o Rotman School of Management, 105 St. George St., Toronto ON M5S 3E6
www.northernfinance.org
Overview: A small local organization founded in 1989
Mission: To hear & present the latest research in all areas of finance, including asset pricing, arbitrage, behavioral finance, corporate finance, corporate governance, derivatives, emerging markets, financial development, financial institutions, finance theory, financial regulation, international finance, market efficiency, market microstructure, mathematical finance, real estate finance & others
Membership: Fees: $50
Activities: Annual conference
Chief Officer(s):
Stéphane Chrétien, President
Meetings/Conferences:
• Northern Finance Association 2018 Conference, September, 2018, Charlevoix, QC
Scope: Local

Northern Frontier Visitors Association (NFVA)
#4, 4807 - 49 St., Yellowknife NT X1A 3T5
Tel: 867-873-4262; Fax: 867-873-3654
Toll-Free: 877-881-4262
info@northernfrontier.com
www.northernfrontier.com
www.facebook.com/163871037005160
Overview: A small local organization founded in 1983
Mission: To promote the Northern Frontier Region as an attractive area for tourism; to foster, encourage & assist in any way the growth of tourism into & within the Northern Frontier Region; to increase awareness within the Northern Frontier Region of the potential tourism holds as a viable, clean, labour intensive industry.
Member of: Northwest Territories Arctic Tourism; Yellowknife Chamber of Commerce
Finances: Funding Sources: Government of NWT; City of Yellowknife; membership fees; gift shop retail sales; rental of office
Membership: 180; Fees: $150 voting; $75 artist
Activities: Visitors Centre is open seven days per week, 360 days per year, to serve both residents & visitors; staff assist visitors in locating accommodation, booking tours & recommending other services provided by our members

Northern Independent Union See IAMAW District 78

Northern Interior Wood Workers Association See United Steelworkers Local 1-424

Northern Native Fishing Corporation (NNFC)
#160, 110 First Ave. West, Prince Rupert BC V8J 1A8
Tel: 250-627-8486; Fax: 250-624-6627
Overview: A small local organization founded in 1982
Mission: To preserve & enhance for individual native fishermen the economic opportunity to harvest & market marine resources by creating & ensuring access to the resources
Activities: Fishing licenses

Northern Ontario Aquaculture Association
PO Box 124, 9050 Hwy. 6, #C, Little Current ON P0P 1K0
Tel: 705-368-1345; Fax: 705-368-0685
ontarioaquaculture@manitoulin.net
www.ontarioaquaculture.com
Overview: A small local organization
Mission: The voice of Ontario's sustainable fish farming industry
Membership: 30; Fees: Non-voting members: $100 associate. Voting members: $500 supporting; $1,000 corporate; $4,000 patron; $2,000 sustaining
Chief Officer(s):
Mike Meeker, President
Karen Tracey, Executive Director
noaa@manitoulin.net

Northern Ontario Curling Association
PO Box 940, #4, 214 Main St. West, Atikokan ON P0T 1C0
Tel: 807-597-8730; Fax: 888-622-8884
Toll-Free: 888-597-8730
info@curlnoca.ca
www.curlnoca.ca
www.facebook.com/curlnoca
twitter.com/curlnoca
Merged from: Temiskaming & Northern Ontario Curling Association; Northern Ontario Ladies Curling Association
Overview: A small local organization overseen by Canadian Curling Association
Mission: To promote curling throughout northern Ontario.
Staff Member(s): 8
Membership: Committees: Executive; Finance; Communications; Development; Competitions; Sponsorship
Chief Officer(s):
Leslie Kerr, Executive Director
lesliekerr@curlnoca.ca

Northern Ontario Darts Association (NODA)
c/o Chris Arsenault, #159, 163 Louis St., Sudbury ON P3B 2H4
Tel: 807-625-9373; Fax: 807-625-9391
nodarts.ca
twitter.com/dartsno
Overview: A small provincial organization overseen by National Darts Federation of Canada
Mission: To provide recreational & competitive opportunities for darts players of all levels in Northern Ontario
Member of: National Darts Federation of Canada
Chief Officer(s):
Christine Stark, President
czachary@tbaytel.net
Chris Arsenault, Secretary, 705-626-1030
180king@personainternet.com

Northern Ontario Hockey Association (NOHA)
110 Lakeshore Dr., North Bay ON P1A 2A8
Tel: 705-474-8851; Fax: 705-474-6019
noha@noha.on.ca
www.noha.on.ca
www.facebook.com/NorthernOntarioHockeyAssociation
twitter.com/nohahockey
Overview: A small local organization founded in 1919 overseen by Hockey Canada
Mission: To foster the sport of amateur hockey in northern Ontario
Affiliation(s): Ontario Hockey Federation
Finances: Funding Sources: Sponsorships; Membership fees
Staff Member(s): 13
Membership: Member Profile: Amateur hockey clubs in northern Ontario
Activities: Hosting tournaments; Presenting awards; Organizing specialty clinics
Chief Officer(s):
Jason Marchand, Executive Director
jmarchand@noha.on.ca
Awards:
• Northern Ontario Hockey Association Life Membership
• Angus Campbell Merit Award
• Ken Neeb Memorial Award
• Rick F. Albert Memorial Award
• Tom Pashby Trainer of the Year Award
• Jim Conners Memorial Award
• Hockey Canada/Northern Ontario Hockey Association Officiating Awards
Meetings/Conferences:
• Northern Ontario Hockey Association Annual General Meeting 2018, 2018, ON
Scope: Local
Contact Information: Executive Director: Jason Marchand, E-mail: jmarchand@noha.on.ca
Publications:
• NOHA Managers Manual
Type: Manual
Profile: A reference guide to NOHA bylaws, regulations, & policies

Northern Ontario Native Tourism Association (NONTA)
#200, 710 Victoria Ave. East, Thunder Bay ON P7C 5P7
Tel: 807-623-0497
Overview: A small provincial organization founded in 1987
Finances: Annual Operating Budget: $500,000-$1.5 Million
Activities: Internships: Yes
Chief Officer(s):
Tara Ingram, Contact

Northern Prospectors Association (NPA)
PO Box 535, Kirkland Lake ON P2N 3J5
Tel: 705-679-5500
Overview: A small local organization founded in 1971
Mission: To act as a strong voice for the prospecting & mining industry
Affiliation(s): Ontario Prospectors Association
Membership: Member Profile: Members of the mining exploration community in the Kirkland Lake area, including prospectors & geologists
Activities: Offering courses on topics such as geology & geophysics; Hosting NPA gold panning events for tourists
Chief Officer(s):
Gino Chitaroni, President

Northern Quebec Inuit Association See Makivik Corporation

Northern Ramblers Car Club Inc. (NRCC)
c/o Roman Bratasiuk, 12 Tremont Rd., Toronto ON M9B 3X5
www.northernramblerscarclub.com
Overview: A small national organization founded in 1979
Mission: To honour the American Motors Corporation & its predecessor companies
Member of: Specialty Vehicle Association of Ontario
Finances: Annual Operating Budget: Less than $50,000; Funding Sources: Membership fees; club events
Membership: 250 individual; Fees: $35-$100
Chief Officer(s):
Steve Johnston, President

Northern Rockies Alaska Highway Tourism Association (NRAHTA)
PO Box 6850, #300, 9523 - 100 St., Fort St. John BC V1J 4J3
Tel: 250-785-2544; Fax: 250-785-4424
Toll-Free: 888-785-2544
info@hellonorth.com
www.hellonorth.com
Also Known As: Hello North Ventures
Previous Name: Peace River Alaska Highway Tourism Association
Overview: A medium-sized provincial licensing organization founded in 1977 overseen by Council of Tourism Associations of British Columbia
Mission: To coordinate opportunites for sustainable tourism growth & development by fostering memorable year round visitor experiences; promoting social & economic benefits to members & wider community.
Member of: Tourism Industry Association of Canada
Affiliation(s): Tourism BC
Finances: Funding Sources: Regional district
Membership: Member Profile: Tourism operators, accommodations, restaurants, stores, communities, chambers of commerce

Northern Territories Federation of Labour / Fédération du travail des Territoires du Nord
PO Box 2787, Yellowknife NT X1A 2R1
Tel: 867-873-3695; Fax: 867-873-6979
Toll-Free: 888-873-1956
ntfl@yk.com
www.ntfl.ca
www.facebook.com/NTFed
Previous Name: Northwest Territories Federation of Labour
Overview: A medium-sized local organization founded in 1980 overseen by Canadian Labour Congress
Mission: To promote the interests of its members
Membership: 9,000
Activities: Library: by appointment
Chief Officer(s):
Gayla Thunstrom, Acting President

Northern Youth Abroad Program (NYAP)
#308, 311 Richmond Rd., Ottawa ON K1Z 6X3
Tel: 613-232-9989; Fax: 613-232-2121
Toll-Free: 866-212-2307
www.nya.ca
Also Known As: Nunavut Youth Abroad Program
Overview: A small provincial charitable organization founded in 1996
Mission: To send Nunavut youth to Southern Canada & Africa in a supported program where they live & volunteer in a new setting
Finances: Annual Operating Budget: $250,000-$500,000
Staff Member(s): 2; 100 volunteer(s)
Membership: 100-499
Chief Officer(s):
Lois Philipp, Chair
Rebecca Bisson, Program Director
rebecca@nya.ca

The North-South Institute (NSI) / L'Institut Nord-Sud
River Building, 1124 Colonel By Dr., 5th Floor, Ottawa ON K1S 5B6
Tel: 613-520-6655; *Fax:* 613-520-2889
nsi@nsi-ins.ca
www.nsi-ins.ca
www.facebook.com/NSIINS
twitter.com/NSI_INS
Overview: A small international charitable organization founded in 1976
Mission: To analyze, for Canadians & others, the economic, social & political implications of global change & to propose policy alternatives to promote global development & justice
Finances: *Annual Operating Budget:* $1.5 Million-$3 Million; *Funding Sources:* CIDA; research project income; donations; book sales
Staff Member(s): 20; 6 volunteer(s)
Activities: Areas of research include: international finance; development cooperation; gender equality; civil society & good governance; corporate social responsibility & workers' rights; human security & conflict prevention; & international trade; *Speaker Service:* Yes; *Library:* by appointment

Northumberland Central Chamber of Commerce
The Chamber Bldg., 278 George St., Cobourg ON K9A 3L8
Tel: 905-372-5831
nccofc.ca
www.facebook.com/160134906739
Previous Name: Cobourg & District Chamber of Commerce
Overview: A small local organization
Mission: To provide a voice for businesses in the Town of Cobourg, Hamilton Township, & Alnwick / Haldimand Township; to improve the commercial climate & economic growth of the area; to protect the interests of the business community
Staff Member(s): 2
Membership: 400+; *Fees:* Schedule available; *Member Profile:* Businesses in the Town of Cobourg, & the Townships of Hamilton & Alnwick/Haldimand; *Committees:* Marketing; Business Achievement Awards; Professional Development
Activities: Providing information about local products & services to consumers; Operating the Cobourg Driver & Vehicle Licensing Office; Offering networking opportunities; Providing professional development events; Presenting business awards
Chief Officer(s):
Peter Dounoukos, Chair
Kevin Ward, President & CEO
Publications:
• Business Directory
Type: Directory
Profile: Listings of chamber members
• Chamber Spotlight
Type: Newsletter; *Frequency:* 11 pa; *Accepts Advertising*
Profile: Business updates, events, & articles, circulated to more than 400 owners, managers, & professionals

Northumberland Hills Association of Realtors
#14, 975 Elgin St. West, Cobourg ON K9A 5J3
Tel: 905-372-8630; *Fax:* 905-372-1443
districtrealestate@bellnet.ca
boards.mls.ca/northumberland
Previous Name: Cobourg-Port Hope District Real Estate Board
Overview: A small local organization founded in 1968 overseen by Ontario Real Estate Association
Member of: The Canadian Real Estate Association

Northumberland Orchestra Society (NOC)
PO Box 1012, Cobourg ON K9A 4W4
Tel: 905-376-3021
www.northumberlandmusic.ca
www.facebook.com/186929644677624
twitter.com/nocfriends
Also Known As: Northumberland Orchestra & Choir
Previous Name: Northumberland Philharmonic Choir
Overview: A small local charitable organization founded in 1978 overseen by Orchestras Canada
Mission: To perform orchestral and choral music to the Northumberland area; To encourage young local musicians through inclusion and education
Member of: Orchestras Canada; Arts Council of Northumberland
Finances: *Funding Sources:* Fundraising; Donations; Sponsorships
Membership: *Member Profile:* Orchestra & choir members of all ages from the Northumberland County, Ontario; Orchestra members that have attained the equivalent of a grade 6 RCM music level; Choir members that have experience reading music
Activities: Hosting Northumberland orchestra & choir events; Offering professional training
Chief Officer(s):
John Kraus, Music Director & Conductor

Northumberland Philharmonic Choir *See* Northumberland Orchestra Society

Northumberland Salmon Protection Association (NSPA)
485, rte 420, South Esk NB E1V 4L9
Tel: 506-622-4000
Overview: A small local organization
Member of: Atlantic Salmon Federation
Affiliation(s): New Brunswick Salmon Council
100 volunteer(s)
Membership: 200
Chief Officer(s):
Debbie Norton, President

Northumberland United Way
#700, 600 William St., Cobourg ON K9A 3A5
Tel: 905-372-6955; *Fax:* 905-372-4417
Toll-Free: 800-833-0002
office@nuw.unitedway.ca
www.mynuw.org
www.facebook.com/northumberlandunitedway
twitter.com/nlanduw
www.youtube.com/user/NlandUnitedWay
Overview: A small local organization founded in 1969 overseen by United Way of Canada - Centraide Canada
Mission: To raise & allocate funds in an efficient manner & to promote the effective delivery of services in response to current & emerging social needs in Northumberland County
Finances: *Annual Operating Budget:* $500,000-$1.5 Million; *Funding Sources:* Donations
Staff Member(s): 6; 100 volunteer(s)
Membership: 1-99
Activities: *Speaker Service:* Yes
Chief Officer(s):
Lynda Kay, CEO
lkay@nuw.unitedway.ca

Northwatch (NW)
PO Box 282, North Bay ON P1B 8H2
Tel: 705-497-0373; *Fax:* 705-476-7060
northwatch@northwatch.org
www.northwatch.org
www.facebook.com/pages/Northwatch/191694054468
Overview: A small local organization founded in 1988
Mission: To act as a representative body & to provide support to local citizens groups addressing environmental issues such as energy use, generation & conservation, forest conservation & wild areas protection, waste management & water quality issues, mining & militarization as well as other environmental concerns; to improve forest management, promote community involvement in mine monitoring & management & to prevent northeastern Ontario from becoming the receiving ground for foreign wastes, including Toronto's garbage, Ontario's biomedical waste, Canada's nuclear reactor fuel waste & PCBs from around the world
Member of: Great Lakes United; MiningWatch Canada; Nuclear Waste Watch; Ontario Environment Network
Finances: *Annual Operating Budget:* Less than $50,000
Staff Member(s): 2; 100 volunteer(s)
Membership: 20 organizations; *Fees:* $10 individual; $25 group/supporting; *Committees:* Forest; Mining; Energy; Waste; Water
Activities: Advocacy; public education; regional meetings; workshops; tours; *Internships:* Yes; *Speaker Service:* Yes; *Library:* by appointment
Chief Officer(s):
B. Lloyd, Coordinator

Northwest Atlantic Fisheries Organization (NAFO)
PO Box 638, #100, 2 Morris Dr., Dartmouth NS B2Y 3Y9
Tel: 902-468-5590; *Fax:* 902-468-5538
info@nafo.int
www.nafo.int
www.facebook.com/NAFO.Info
twitter.com/NAFO1979
Overview: A large international organization founded in 1979
Mission: To contribute through consultation & cooperation to the optimum utilization, rational management & conservation of the fishery resources of the Northwest Atlantic
Finances: *Annual Operating Budget:* $500,000-$1.5 Million; *Funding Sources:* Contracting parties
Staff Member(s): 11
Activities: Managing fisheries; *Internships:* Yes *Library:* NAFO Library
Chief Officer(s):
Fred Kingston, Executive Secretary, 902-468-5590 Ext. 202
fkingston@nafo.int
• Journal of Northwest Atlantic Fishery Science
Type: Journal; *Editor:* Dr. Neil Campbell
Profile: The journal features articles about ecosystems in the Atlantic Northwest, as well as articles that focus on living marine resources

Northwest Mennonite Conference
West Zion Mennonite Church, PO Box 1316, 2025 - 20 Ave., Didsbury AB T0M 0W0
Tel: 403-337-3283; *Fax:* 403-337-3258
www.nwmc.ca
Overview: A small provincial organization
Mission: To enable & empower congregations to become communities of Christ's healing & hope
Member of: Mennonite Church North America
Membership: 14 congregations; *Member Profile:* Churches in Alberta; *Committees:* Congregational Ministries; Congregational Leadership; Missions & Service; Stewardship
Chief Officer(s):
Mark Loewen, Conference Moderator, 403-337-3283
David Peters, Conference Minister, 587-225-1072

Northwest Ontario Sunset Country Travel Association
PO Box 647W, Kenora ON P9N 3X6
Tel: 807-468-5853
Toll-Free: 800-665-7567
info@ontariossunsetcountry.ca
www.ontariossunsetcountry.ca
www.facebook.com/SunsetCountry
twitter.com/Sunset_Country
sunsetcountry.tumblr.com
Overview: A medium-sized provincial organization founded in 1974
Mission: To develop, promote & advertise through cooperation, coordination & communication with clients & organizations for the betterment of tourism in Sunset Country & the province.
Member of: Tourism Industry Association of Canada
Finances: *Funding Sources:* Membership dues; provincial & federal government
Membership: *Member Profile:* Tourism-related businesses
Activities: *Rents Mailing List:* Yes
Chief Officer(s):
Gerry Cariou, Executive Director
gcariou@sunsetcountry.net

Northwest Peace Soccer Association (NWPSA)
11727 - 88A St., Grande Prairie AB T8X 1L8
Tel: 780-832-1627
nwpsoccer@gmail.com
www.northwestpeacesoccer.ca
Overview: A small local organization overseen by Alberta Soccer Association
Member of: Alberta Soccer Association

Northwest Territories & Nunavut Association of Professional Engineers & Geoscientists (NAPEG)
#201, 4817 - 49th St., Yellowknife NT X1A 3S7
Tel: 867-920-4055; *Fax:* 867-873-4058
www.napeg.nt.ca
www.facebook.com/208781715979685
twitter.com/napeg_north
Overview: A medium-sized provincial licensing organization founded in 1978 overseen by Engineers Canada
Mission: To license professional engineers & professional geoscientists in the Northwest Territories & Nunavut; To regulate the practices of professional engineering & professional geoscience; To establish & maintain standards of knowledge, skill, care, & professional ethics among registrants
Member of: Engineers Canada
Finances: *Funding Sources:* Membership fees; Dues
100 volunteer(s)
Membership: 397 + 781 Licensees; *Fees:* $300 registration; $220 annual dues; *Committees:* Discipline; Environment; Honours & Awards; Member-in-Training & New Professionals; Membership & Enforcement; Nominating; Professional Development; Professional Practice; Outreach
Activities: *Awareness Events:* National Engineering Week, March; National Science & Technology Week, October
Chief Officer(s):
Sudhir Jha, P.Eng., President

Linda Golding, FEC (Hon), FGC, Executive Director & Registrar

Northwest Territories & Nunavut Chamber of Mines
PO Box 2818, #103, 5102 - 50 Ave., Yellowknife NT X1A 3S8
Tel: 867-873-5281; Fax: 780-669-5681
info@miningnorth.com
www.miningnorth.com
twitter.com/MiningNorth
Also Known As: NWT & Nunavut Chamber of Mines
Previous Name: Northwest Territories Chamber of Mines
Overview: A medium-sized provincial organization founded in 1967
Mission: To promote & assist the development & growth of responsible & sustainable mining & mineral exploration in the Northwest Territories & Nunavut
Affiliation(s): Mining Association of Canada; Canadian Institute of Mining, Metallurgy & Petroleum
Finances: Annual Operating Budget: $100,000-$250,000; Funding Sources: Membership fees
Staff Member(s): 2; 25 volunteer(s)
Membership: 200 corporate + 600 individual + 9 senior/lifetime; Fees: $75 full & government employees; $10 seniors & students; schedule based on earnings for corporate; Member Profile: Persons & corporations interested in, or associated with, the mining industry in the Northwest Territories & Nunavut
Activities: Awareness Events: Mining Week, June; GeoScience Forum, Nov.; Library: by appointment Not open to public
Chief Officer(s):
Tom Hoefer, Executive Director
executivedirector@miningnorth.com

Northwest Territories & Nunavut Construction Association (NNCA)
PO Box 2277, 4921 - 49th St., 3rd Fl., Yellowknife NT X1A 2P7
Tel: 867-873-3949; Fax: 867-873-8366
bulletin@nnca.ca
nnca.ca
Previous Name: Northwest Territories Construction Association
Overview: A medium-sized provincial organization founded in 1976 overseen by Canadian Construction Association
Mission: To act as a voice for construction-related business in the Northwest Territories & Nunavut
Membership: 150+; Fees: Schedule available; Member Profile: Construction-related businesses in the Northwest Territories & Nunavut
Activities: Lobbying governments on behalf of the construction industry
Chief Officer(s):
Louise Elder, Executive Director

Northwest Territories & Nunavut Council of the Canadian Physiotherapy Association (NWTNC)
Yellowknife NT
Tel: 867-669-4117; Fax: 867-669-4137
Overview: A medium-sized provincial organization overseen by Canadian Physiotherapy Association
Member of: Canadian Physiotherapy Association
Finances: Funding Sources: Membership dues; educational activities
Activities: Awareness Events: National Physiotherapy Month, April 20 - May 20

Northwest Territories & Nunavut Dental Association
PO Box 46817, Vancouver BC V6J 5M4
Tel: 867-988-0151; Fax: 877-389-6876
www.nwtnudentalassociation.ca
Overview: A small provincial organization overseen by Canadian Dental Association
Mission: To act as the voice of dentists in the Northwest Territories & Nunavut
Affiliation(s): Canadian Dental Association
Activities: Providing information on dentists in the Northwest Territories & Nunavut
Chief Officer(s):
Elisabeth Specht, President

Northwest Territories 5 Pin Bowlers' Association (NWT5PBA)
PO Box 2643, Yellowknife NT X1A 2P9
www.bowlnwt.ca
Overview: A small provincial organization
Mission: To promote 5 pin bowling in the Northwest Territories

Northwest Territories Amateur Speed Skating Association (NWTASSA)
c/o Sport North, 4908 - 49 St., Yellowknife NT X1A 2P9
Tel: 867-669-8326; Fax: 867-669-8327
Toll-Free: 800-661-0797
nwtspeedskating@gmail.com
sportnorth.com/tso/speed-skating/about-us
Overview: A small provincial organization overseen by Speed Skating Canada
Mission: To promote the sport of speed skating in the NWT
Member of: Sport North Federation; Speed Skating Canada
Finances: Annual Operating Budget: Less than $50,000
40 volunteer(s)
Membership: 140
Chief Officer(s):
Julie Jeffery, Director

Northwest Territories Archives Council (NWTAC)
c/o NWT Archives Council, PO Box 1320, Yellowknife NT X1A 2L9
nwtarchivescouncil@gmail.com
www.nwtarchivescouncil.ca
Overview: A small provincial organization founded in 1985 overseen by Canadian Council of Archives
Mission: To facilitate development of the archival system in the Northwest Territories; To make recommendations about the system's operation & financing; To develop & facilitate implementation & management of programs to assist the archival community; To communicate archival needs & concerns to decision-makers, researchers, & the general public.
Chief Officer(s):
Giselle Marion, President

Northwest Territories Arts Council / Conseil des arts des TNO
c/o GNWT Education, Culture & Employment, PO Box 1320, Yellowknife NT X1A 2L9
Tel: 867-920-6370; Fax: 867-873-0205
Toll-Free: 877-445-2787
www.nwtartscouncil.ca
Also Known As: NWT Arts Council
Overview: A small provincial organization founded in 1985
Mission: To promote and encourage the arts in the Northwest Territories.
Chief Officer(s):
Boris Atamanenko, Manager, Community Programs, 867-920-6370
boris_atamanenki@gov.nt.ca

The Northwest Territories Association for Children (& Adults) with Learning Disabilities See Learning Disabilities Association of The Northwest Territories

Northwest Territories Association of Architects (NWTAA)
Administrative Office, Northern Frontier Visitors Centre, PO Box 1394, Yellowknife NT X1A 2P1
Tel: 867-766-4216; Fax: 867-973-3654
nwtaa@yk.com
www.nwtaa.ca
Overview: A small provincial licensing organization founded in 2002
Mission: To maintain the Register of Architects, in accordance with the NWT Architects Act
Member of: Committee of Canadian Architectural Councils (CCAC)
Membership: Fees: $1000; Member Profile: Persons engaged in the practice of architecture in the Northwest Territories; Committees: Registration & Licence Review; Complaint Review; Practice Review; Continuing Education
Activities: Offering continuing education
Chief Officer(s):
Ben Russo, Executive Director
nwtaa@yk.com
Rod Kirkwood, President

Northwest Territories Association of Communities (NWTAC)
Finn Hansen Bldg., #200, 5105 - 50th St., Yellowknife NT X1A 1S1
Tel: 867-873-8359; Fax: 867-873-3042
Toll-Free: 866-973-8359
communications@nwtac.com
www.nwtac.com
twitter.com/nwtac
www.flickr.com/photos/nwtac
Overview: A medium-sized provincial organization founded in 1967
Mission: To promote the exchange of information amongst the community governments of the Northwest Territories and to provide a united front for the realization of goals.
Member of: Federation of Canadian Municipalities
Staff Member(s): 6
Membership: 32 incorporated communities; Member Profile: Municipal corporations & community governments
Chief Officer(s):
Sara Brown, CEO
sara@nwtac.com

Northwest Territories Association of Landscape Architects (NWTALA)
PO Box 1394, Yellowknife NT X1A 2P1
Tel: 867-920-2986; Fax: 867-920-2986
atborow@internorth.com
www.csla-aapc.ca/society/nwtala
Overview: A medium-sized provincial organization founded in 1991 overseen by Canadian Society of Landscape Architects
Mission: To represent landscape architects in the Northwest Territories
Affiliation(s): Canadian Society of Landscape Architects (CSLA)

Northwest Territories Association of Provincial Court Judges
c/o Judge Garth Malakoe, Territorial Court of Northwest Territories, PO Box 550, 4093 - 49th St., Yellowknife NT X1A 2N4
Tel: 867-873-7602; Fax: 867-873-0291
Toll-Free: 866-822-5864
Overview: A small provincial organization
Affiliation(s): Canadian Association of Provincial Court Judges
Membership: Member Profile: Court judges in the Northwest Territories
Chief Officer(s):
Garth Malakoe, Northwest Territories Director, Canadian Association of Provincial Court Judges

Northwest Territories Badminton Association
PO Box 11089, Yellowknife NT X1A 3X7
Tel: 867-669-8378; Fax: 867-669-8327
Toll-Free: 800-661-0797
www.nwtbadminton.ca
Overview: A small provincial organization overseen by Badminton Canada
Mission: To promote badminton throughout the Northwest Territories
Membership: Member Profile: Athletes, clubs, coaches, & officials

Northwest Territories Biathlon Association
NT
Tel: 867-874-2681
www.nwtbiathlon.com
www.facebook.com/172304639531053
Also Known As: NWT Biathlon Association
Overview: A small provincial organization overseen by Biathlon Canada
Mission: To be the provincial governing body for the sport of biathlon in Northwest Territories
Member of: Biathlon Canada
Chief Officer(s):
Pat Bobinski, President, 867-874-2681
pat@nwtbiathlon.com
Ted Kimmins, Vice President
ted@nwtbiathlon.com
Belinda Whitford, Secretary-Treasurer
belinda@nwtbiathlon.com

Northwest Territories Broomball Association
529 Range Lake Rd., Yellowknife NT X1A 3Y1
www.nwtbroomball.com
Overview: A small provincial organization overseen by Ballon sur glace Broomball Canada
Member of: Ballon sur glace Broomball Canada
Membership: 250; Fees: Schedule available
Chief Officer(s):
Val Pond, President
netmindr@theedge.ca

Northwest Territories Chamber of Commerce
NWT Commerce Place, #13, 4802 - 50th Ave., Yellowknife NT X1A 1C4
Tel: 867-920-9505; Fax: 867-873-4174
admin@nwtchamber.com
www.nwtchamber.com
Overview: A medium-sized provincial charitable organization founded in 1973

Canadian Associations / Northwest Territories Community Futures Association (NWTCFA)

Mission: To act as the voice for northern business; To create a business climate of profitability & competitiveness in the Northwest Territories; To foster business development; To promote business in the Northwest Territories; To involve & assist First Nations organizations; To conduct operations in an environmentally responsible manner
Membership: 865
Activities: Liaising with territorial, national & international governments; Providing input in the development of legislation & policy
Chief Officer(s):
Richard Morland, President
Mike Bradshaw, Executive Director

Northwest Territories Chamber of Mines *See* Northwest Territories & Nunavut Chamber of Mines

Northwest Territories Community Futures Association (NWTCFA)
NT
www.nwtcfa.ca
Overview: A small provincial organization founded in 1999
Mission: To improve communication between community futures organizations in the Northwest Territories; to advocate for members; to establish partnerships on behalf of members
Membership: 7 regional organizations

Northwest Territories Construction Association *See* Northwest Territories & Nunavut Construction Association

Northwest Territories Council for the Disabled; NWT Council for Disabled Persons *See* NWT Disabilities Council

Northwest Territories Curling Association
PO Box 11089, Yellowknife NT X1A 3X7
Tel: 867-669-8339; *Fax:* 867-669-8327
Toll-Free: 800-661-0797
www.nwtcurling.com
www.facebook.com/nwtcurling
twitter.com/nwt_curling
Overview: A small provincial organization founded in 1990 overseen by Canadian Curling Association
Mission: To promote curling in the Northwest Territories.

Northwest Territories Federal Liberal Association
PO Box 965, Stn. Main, Yellowknife NT XIA 2N7
nwtfla.membership@gmail.com
nwt.liberal.ca
www.facebook.com/NWTFLA
Overview: A medium-sized provincial organization
Chief Officer(s):
Charles Blyth, Director

Northwest Territories Federation of Labour *See* Northern Territories Federation of Labour

Northwest Territories Institute of the Purchasing Management Association of Canada *See* Supply Chain Management Association - Northwest Territories

Northwest Territories Law Foundation
PO Box 1298, Yellowknife NT X1A 2P9
Tel: 867-873-3828; *Fax:* 867-873-6344
www.nwtlawfoundation.ca
Overview: A small provincial charitable organization
Mission: To direct funding towards the following areas: research into law reform & the administration of justice, establishing & maintaining law libraries, offering assistance to legal aid programs, contributing to the Assurance Fund, & providing programs & facilities to enhance the legal education available to persons in the Northwest Territories
Activities: Offering grants & scholarships
Chief Officer(s):
Malinda Kellett, Chair
Awards:
• NWT Law Foundation/Graeme Garson Scholarship Fund
Eligibility: Students from the Northwest Territories who are attending law school
Publications:
• Northwest Territories Law Foundation Annual Report
Type: Yearbook; *Frequency:* Annually

Northwest Territories Library Association (NWTLA)
PO Box 2276, Yellowknife NT X1A 2P7
nwtlibraryassociation@gmail.com
nwtlibraryassociation.wordpress.com
www.facebook.com/NWTLA
Overview: A medium-sized provincial organization
Mission: To facilitate the exchange of ideas among persons involved in library services in the Northwest Territories; To recommend policies for the provision of library services; To promote intellectual freedom
Membership: *Fees:* $20 individual; $35 institutional
Chief Officer(s):
John Mutford, President

Northwest Territories Medical Association (NWTMA)
PO Box 1732, Yellowknife NT X1A 2P3
Tel: 867-920-4575; *Fax:* 867-920-4575
nwtmedassoc@ssimicro.com
www.nwtma.ca
Overview: A medium-sized provincial organization overseen by Canadian Medical Association
Mission: To advocate on behalf of its members & citizens for access to quality health care; To provide leadership & guidance to its members
Member of: Canadian Medical Association
Membership: *Fees:* Schedule available
Chief Officer(s):
Steve Kraus, President

Northwest Territories Public Service Association *See* Union of Northern Workers

Northwest Territories Recreation & Parks Association (NWTRPA)
PO Box 841, Yellowknife NT X1A 2N6
Tel: 867-873-5340; *Fax:* 867-669-6791
admin@nwtrpa.org
www.nwtrpa.org
www.facebook.com/260257614047483
Overview: A small provincial organization founded in 1989 overseen by Canadian Parks & Recreation Association
Mission: To increase public awareness of recreation & parks; to enhance the quality of life of residents of the NWT through fostering the development of recreation & parks services
Affiliation(s): Sport North
Finances: *Annual Operating Budget:* $50,000-$100,000; *Funding Sources:* Federal, territorial government
Staff Member(s): 6
Membership: 100; *Fees:* $35 individual; $75 municipal or recreation committee; *Committees:* Executive; Corporate; Sponsorship
Activities: Recreation Code of Ethics; Recreation & Parks Resource Binder; Awards Program; Corporate Sponsorship; Active Living
Chief Officer(s):
Geoff Ray, Executive Director, 867-669-8380
gray@nwtrpa.org

Northwest Territories Registered Nurses Association *See* The Registered Nurses Association of the Northwest Territories & Nunavut

Northwest Territories Ski Division
PO Box 1916, Yellowknife NT X1A 2P4
Tel: 867-445-5855
nwtski@gmail.com
www.nwtski.com
Previous Name: Cross Country Northwest Territories
Overview: A small provincial organization overseen by Cross Country Canada
Member of: Cross Country Canada

Northwest Territories Soccer Association (NWTSA)
PO Box 11089, Yellowknife NT X1A 3X7
Tel: 867-669-8396; *Fax:* 867-669-8327
Toll-Free: 800-661-0797
www.nwtkicks.ca
www.facebook.com/NWTSoccerAssociation
twitter.com/NwtSoccer
Overview: A medium-sized provincial organization overseen by Canadian Soccer Association
Mission: The NWT Soccer Association is a volunteer-run organization & the governing body for all soccer activities in the NWT; focus is on the grassroots development of the game, as well as the promotion of high performance. Physical delivery address: c/o Sport North Federation, 4908 - 49th St., 1st Fl., Yellowknife, NT X1A 2N4
Member of: Canadian Soccer Association
Affiliation(s): Sport North Federation
Finances: *Funding Sources:* Operates on Sport Lottery funding
Activities: Summer camps; leagues & tournaments; developmental clinics
Chief Officer(s):
Ollie Williams, President
Lyric Sandhals, Executive Director
Awards:
• Coach of the Year Award
• Official of the Year Award
• Overlander Sportsmanship of the Year
• First Air Male Player of the Year
• First Air Female Player of the Year
• Northwestel Volunteer of the Year Award
• Paul Stipdonk Memorial Life Member Award

Northwest Territories Society for the Prevention of Cruelty to Animals (NWTSPCA)
PO Box 2278, Yellowknife NT X1A 2P7
Tel: 867-920-7722; *Fax:* 867-920-7723
nwtspcayk@gmail.com
www.nwtspca.com
www.facebook.com/nwtspca
Overview: A medium-sized provincial charitable organization
Mission: To provide animal rescue services in the north; to educate the public about the proper ways to protect & take care of animals
Finances: *Annual Operating Budget:* $250,000-$500,000
Membership: *Fees:* $20 individual; $40 family
Chief Officer(s):
Nicole Spencer, President

Northwest Territories Softball
PO Box 11089, Yellowknife NT X1A 3X7
Tel: 867-669-8339; *Fax:* 867-669-8327
Toll-Free: 800-661-0797
sportnorth.com/tso/softball
Also Known As: NWT Softball
Overview: A small provincial organization overseen by Canadian Amateur Softball Association
Mission: To be the territorial governing body for fastpitch, minor ball & slo-pitch softball in the Northwest Territories
Member of: Canadian Amateur Softball Association
Affiliation(s): Sport North Federation
Chief Officer(s):
Paul Gard, President
paul_gard@gov.nt.ca
Melanie Thompson, Executive Director
mel@movethenorth.ca

Northwest Territories Special Olympics *See* Special Olympics Northwest Territories

Northwest Territories Sport Federation *See* Sport North Federation

Northwest Territories Teachers' Association (NWTTA)
PO Box 2340, 5018 - 48 St., Yellowknife NT X1A 2P7
Tel: 867-873-8501; *Fax:* 867-873-2366
nwtta@nwtta.nt.ca
www.nwtta.nt.ca
Overview: A medium-sized provincial organization overseen by Canadian Teachers' Federation
Mission: The Northwest Territories Teachers' Association is the professional voice of educators as they provide quality education to Northwest Territories students. With commitment to growth, respect & security for its membership, the Association represents all regions equally, advocates for public education & promotes the teaching profession
Finances: *Annual Operating Budget:* $500,000-$1.5 Million
Staff Member(s): 3
Membership: 800; *Fees:* Schedule available; *Member Profile:* Teachers; consultants; administrators; *Committees:* Aboriginal Educators & Leadership Council; Professional Relations; School Administrators; Small Communities; Teacher Welfare; Public Relations; Curriculum; Discipline; Finance; Legislation; Status of Women; other special & ad hoc committees
Chief Officer(s):
Fraser Oliver, President, 867-873-8501
fraser.oliver@nwtta.nt.ca
David Roebuck, Executive Director, 867-873-8501
dave.roebuck@nwtta.nt.ca

Northwest Territories Tennis Association
PO Box 671, Yellowknife NT X1A 2N5
Tel: 867-444-8330
www.tennisnwt.com
Also Known As: Tennis NWT
Previous Name: Tennis Northwest Territories
Overview: A small provincial organization overseen by Tennis Canada

Mission: To grow & promote the sport of tennis in the Northwest Territories
Member of: Tennis Canada
Chief Officer(s):
Jon Brennan, President
Julie Bennett, General Manager

Northwest Territories Tourism (NWTT)
PO Box 610, Yellowknife NT X1A 2N5
Tel: 867-873-5007; *Fax:* 867-873-4059
Toll-Free: 800-661-0788
info@spectacularnwt.com
www.spectacularnwt.com
www.facebook.com/spectacularnwt
twitter.com/spectacularnwt
www.instagram.com/spectacularnwt
Previous Name: Tourism Industry Association of the NWT
Overview: A medium-sized local organization founded in 1996
Mission: To support the development of a strong tourism sector in the Northwest Territories for the benefit of tourists, residents & communities; To promote pan-territorial tourism; To act as a voice for the tourism industry; To preserve the integrity of the cultural & natural heritage of the Northwest Territories
Affiliation(s): Canadian Tourism Commission (CTC); Yukon Travel; Nunavut Tourism; Travel Alberta; Tourism BC
Membership: 200+; *Fees:* $150; *Member Profile:* Tourism industry participants in the Northwest Territories; Aboriginal Land Claims Groups
Activities: Providing industry education; Marketing all sectors of tourism in the Northwest Territories; *Library:* NWTT Visual Library
Chief Officer(s):
Brian Desjardins, Executive Director
Ron Ostrom, Director, Marketing
Julie Warnock, Coordinator, Communications
Margo Thorne, Officer, Finance

Northwest Territories Volleyball Association (NWTVA)
4909 - 49 St., 3rd Fl., Yellowknife NT X1A 3X7
Tel: 867-669-8396; *Fax:* 867-669-8327
www.nwtvolleyball.ca
www.facebook.com/NWTVolleyballAssociation
twitter.com/NWTVA
Overview: A medium-sized provincial organization overseen by Volleyball Canada
Mission: To promote volleyball in the Northwest Territories; To provide competitive opportunities for members
Staff Member(s): 1
Chief Officer(s):
Lyric Sandhals, Executive Director
lsandhals@sportnorth.com

Northwest Territories/Nunavut Council of Friendship Centres
PO Box 2285, #209, 4817 - 49th St., Yellowknife NT X1A 2P6
Tel: 867-669-7063; *Fax:* 867-669-7064
ntnucfc.wildapricot.org
Overview: A small provincial organization overseen by National Association of Friendship Centres
Mission: To assist friendship centres in the Northwest Territories & Nunavut
Membership: 60

Northwest Wildlife Preservation Society (NWPS)
#720, 1190 Melville St., Vancouver BC V6E 3W1
Tel: 604-568-9160; *Fax:* 604-568-6152
info@northwestwildlife.com
www.northwestwildlife.com
www.facebook.com/NorthwestWildlifePreservationSociety
twitter.com/nwpsHQ
www.facebook.com/mwpsVancouverIsland
Overview: A small local organization founded in 1987
Mission: To ensure that healthy wildlife populations are preserved for their own intrinsic value & for the appreciation of all; To develop & provide educational, research & advisory services which can advance the public's awareness & knowledge about wildlife & wildlife systems in northwest North America
Member of: BC Endangered Species Coalition; Vancouver Urban Wildlife Committee; BC Environmental Network
Finances: *Annual Operating Budget:* $100,000-$250,000; *Funding Sources:* Donations; grants; honoria
Staff Member(s): 3; 180 volunteer(s)
Membership: 100+; *Fees:* $35 family/NGO/Classroom; $25 individual; $15 senior/student; $100 corporate

Activities: *Awareness Events:* Green Ribbon Campaign, April; *Speaker Service:* Yes; *Library:* Species Reports; Open to public
Chief Officer(s):
Ann Peters, Executive Director, 604-568-9160, Fax: 604-568-6152
execdirector@northwestwildlife.com
Jim Pigott, President
Michele Kvarnstrom, Vice-President
James McBeath, Sec.-Treas.
Darren Colello, Education Coordinator
edcomm@northwestwildlife.com

Northwestern Ontario Air Search & Rescue Association (NOASARA)
411 John Paterson Dr., Thunder Bay ON P7E 6M8
Tel: 807-577-4329
Other Communication: Cell Phone: 807-627-4433
noasara@tbaytel.net
www.noasara.com
www.facebook.com/22493505586
Overview: A small local charitable organization founded in 1986

Northwestern Ontario Associated Chambers of Commerce (NOACC)
#102, 200 Syndicate Ave. South, Thunder Bay ON P7E 1C9
Tel: 807-624-2626; *Fax:* 807-622-7752
www.noacc.ca
Overview: A medium-sized local licensing organization founded in 1931
Mission: To provide leadership to ensure quality of life & a healthy economy for member chambers, the regional business community & the citizens of Northwestern Ontario; to make representations to government; to provide a network for interaction between local chambers
Affiliation(s): Ontario Chamber of Commerce
Finances: *Annual Operating Budget:* Less than $50,000; *Funding Sources:* Membership dues
Staff Member(s): 1; 60 volunteer(s)
Membership: 2,000; *Fees:* $240.62-$2,838.68, based on business size; *Committees:* Policy Development; Advocacy
Chief Officer(s):
Nathan Lawrence, President
Meetings/Conferences:
• Northwestern Ontario Associated Chambers of Commerce 83rd AGM, 2018
Scope: Local

Northwestern Ontario Building & Construction Trades Council
Thunder Bay ON
Overview: A small local organization
Mission: To respresent the following unions in northwestern Ontario: Construction & Allied Workers, Local 607; Greater Ontario Regional Council of Carpenters, Drywall & Allied Workers, Local 1669; International Union of Painters & Allied Trades, Local 1671; International Association of Heat & Frost Insulators & Asbestos Workers, Local 95; International Association of Bridge, Structural, Ornamental, & Reinforcing Ironworkers, Local 759; International Union of Bricklayers & Allied Craftworkers, Local 25; International Union of Operating Engineers, Local 793; International Brotherhood of Boilermakers, Iron Ship Builders, Blacksmiths, Forgers & Helpers, Local 555 & 128; International Brotherhood of Electrical Workers, Local 402; Millwrights & Machine Erectors, Local 1151; Sheetmetal Workers International Association, Local 397; Teamsters International Union, Local 938; & United Association of Plumbers & Pipefitters, Local 628
Chief Officer(s):
Terry Webb, Contact

Northwestern Ontario Insurance Professionals
c/o Linda Lacroix, The Standard Insurance Brokers Ltd., PO Box 2890, 319 - 2nd St. South, Kenora ON P9N 3X8
Tel: 807-468-6678
Overview: A small local organization
Mission: To be responsive to the requirements of the Canadian insurance industry
Member of: Canadian Association of Insurance Women
Activities: Engaging in educational programs; Providing networking opportunities
Chief Officer(s):
Linda Lacroix, President, 807-468-6678 Ext. 7006
lindal@kmts.ca

Northwestern Ontario Municipal Association (NOMA)
PO Box 10308, Thunder Bay ON P7B 6T8

Tel: 807-683-6662
admin@noma.on.ca
www.noma.on.ca
Overview: A medium-sized local organization founded in 1946
Mission: To consider matters of interest to municipalities in northwestern Ontario; To procure enactment of legislation which may be advantageous to northwestern Ontario's municipalities
Member of: Association of Municipalities of Ontario
Finances: *Funding Sources:* Operating subsidy from the Ministry of Northern Development & Mines; Membership fees
Membership: 100-499; *Fees:* $250 not-for-profit organizations; $500 businesses; *Member Profile:* Membership is attained from the Corporation of the City of Thunder Bay, the Kenora District Municipal Association, the Rainy River District Municipal Association, & the Thunder Bay District Municipal League; Associate membership is comprised of not-for-profit organizations & businesses
Activities: Advocating for northwestern Ontario's regional interests; Acting on matters where municipal rights may be affected; Promoting municipal interests; Offering opportunities for education & discussion to advance the standards of municipal government
Chief Officer(s):
Charla Robinson, Executive Director
Dennis Brown, President
Iain Angus, Vice-President
Meetings/Conferences:
• Northwestern Ontario Municipal Association 2018 Annual Conference & AGM, 2018, ON
Scope: Local
Contact Information: Phone: 807-683-6662, E-mail: admin@noma.on.ca

Northwestern Ontario Prospectors Association (NWOPA)
PO Box 10124, Thunder Bay ON P7B 6T6
nwopa@tbaytel.net
www.nwopa.net
Overview: A small local organization
Mission: To represent & advance the interests of northwestern Ontario's prospectors
Member of: Ontario Prospectors Association
Finances: *Funding Sources:* Sponsorships; Membership fees
Membership: *Fees:* $60 individuals; $200 corporations; *Member Profile:* Prospectors in northwestern Ontario; *Committees:* Communications; Elections; Education & Events; First Nations Issues; General Meetings; Land Use; Minister Mining Act Advisory; MNR N.W. Reg. Advisory; Ontario Prospectors Association; Policies & Procedures; Website
Activities: Engaging in lobbying activities; Planning displays about the mining industry at local events, such as the Children's Festival in Thunder Bay
Chief Officer(s):
Bob Chataway, President
chataway@tbaytel.net
Steven Flank, Vice-President
steve.flank@gmail.com
Cyndee Komar, Secretary
Paul Nielsen, Treasurer
treasurer@nwopa.net
Awards:
• The Lifetime Achievement Award
• The Bernie Schnieders Discovery of the Year Award
• The Developer of the Year Award
Publications:
• The Claim Post
Type: Newsletter; *Frequency:* Semiannually
Profile: Current events in the mining industry

Northwestern Ontario Sports Hall of Fame & Museum
219 May St. South, Thunder Bay ON P7E 1B5
Tel: 807-622-2852; *Fax:* 807-622-2736
nwosport@tbaytel.net
www.nwosportshalloffame.com
www.youtube.com/user/nwosport
Also Known As: NWO Sports Hall of Fame
Overview: A small local charitable organization founded in 1978
Mission: To preserve & honour the sports heritage of northwestern Ontario
Member of: Canadian Association for Sport Heritage; International Association of Sports Museums & Halls of Fame; Ontario Museum Association; Archives Association of Ontario; Canadian Museums Association; Thunder Bay Chamber of Commerce
Finances: *Annual Operating Budget:* $100,000-$250,000

Canadian Associations / Northwestern Ontario Technology Association (NOTA)

Staff Member(s): 3; 25 volunteer(s)
Membership: 400; *Fees:* $25 individual; $40 family; $60 business/organization
Activities: A variety of structured programs are available for different grade levels; Annual Induction Dinner & Ceremony, last Sat. in Sept.; *Library*
Chief Officer(s):
Kathryn Dwyer, Curator
Diane Imrie, Executive Director

Northwestern Ontario Technology Association (NOTA)
#213, 1294 Balmoral St., Thunder Bay ON P7B 5Z5
Tel: 807-768-6687; *Fax:* 807-768-6683
www.linkedin.com/groups/Northwestern-Ontario-Technology-Association-1227697
Overview: A small local organization founded in 2001
Finances: *Annual Operating Budget:* Less than $50,000
5 volunteer(s)
Membership: 40; *Fees:* $100, depends on the size of the firm; *Member Profile:* Technology industry professional, company or stakeholder in N.W.C.
Activities: Networking; marketing; seminars; training

Northwood Neighbourhood Services
#400, 1860 Wilson Ave., Toronto ON M9M 3A7
Tel: 416-748-0788; *Fax:* 416-748-0525
info@northw.ca
www.northw.ca
Overview: A small local charitable organization founded in 1982 overseen by Ontario Council of Agencies Serving Immigrants
Mission: To provide programs & services within the community that will empower individuals, families & groups to achieve, maintain & enhance a state of physical, mental & social well being
Finances: *Annual Operating Budget:* $500,000-$1.5 Million; *Funding Sources:* Federal, provincial & municipal governments; United Way member & charitable donations
Staff Member(s): 35; 70 volunteer(s)
Membership: 210; *Fees:* $5; *Committees:* Program & Development; Policy; Fundraising; Social Enterprise; Health & Safety; Settlement, Sponsorship Holder & English Conversation Circle; Seniors Programs; Child Parent Programs; Women's Program; Training & Professional Development
Activities: Providing settlement services & language training; Facilitating workshops; *Internships:* Yes
Chief Officer(s):
François Yabit, Executive Director
fyabit@northw.ca
Azaria Wolday, Manager, Settlement & Sponsorship
awolday@northw.ca

Norwegian Trade Council *See* Innovation Norway

Nose Creek Valley Museum Society
1701 Main St. SW, Airdrie AB T4B 1C5
Tel: 403-948-6685
ncvm@telus.net
www.nosecreekvalleymuseum.com
Overview: A small local organization founded in 1985
Mission: To operate the Nose Creek Valley Museum & Tourist Information Centre
Finances: *Funding Sources:* Donations; Museum admission fees; Fundraising; Sponsorships
Membership: *Fees:* $10
Activities: Providing geological, natural history, topographical, farm machinery, military, & First Nation's displays; Maintaining a settler's cabin, a blacksmith shop, & a historical general store & barbershop
Chief Officer(s):
Laurie Harvey, Curator

Not Far From The Tree
#365, 401 Richmond St. West, Toronto ON M5V 3A8
Tel: 647-774-7425
info@notfarfromthetree.org
www.notfarfromthetree.org
Overview: A small local organization
Mission: To harvest fruit from trees that the owners would otherwise let go to waste
Membership: *Committees:* Steering
Chief Officer(s):
Danielle Goldfiner, Interim Project Director

Notre-Dame-de-Grâce Community Council *Voir* Conseil communautaire Notre-Dame-de-Grâce

Nouveau Parti Démocratique *See* New Democratic Party

Nova Central Ringette Association
NS
novacentralringette.ca
www.facebook.com/NovaCentralRingetteAssociation
Overview: A small local organization overseen by Ringette Nova Scotia
Member of: Ringette Nova Scotia
Affiliation(s): Bedord Ringette Association; Berwick Ringette Association; Sackville Ringette Association
Membership: 15 teams
Chief Officer(s):
Greg Giffin, President

Nova Forest Alliance
PO Box 208, 285 George St., Stewiacke NS B0N 2J0
Tel: 902-639-2921; *Fax:* 902-639-2981
info@novaforestalliance.com
www.novaforestalliance.com
Overview: A small provincial organization

Nova Scotia Advisory Council on the Status of Women / Conseil consultatif sur la condition féminine de la Nouvelle-Écosse
PO Box 745, Halifax NS B3J 2T3
Tel: 902-424-8662; *Fax:* 902-424-0573
Toll-Free: 800-565-8662
women@novascotia.ca
women.gov.ns.ca
www.facebook.com/StatusofWomenNS
twitter.com/StatusofWomenNS
Overview: A medium-sized provincial organization founded in 1977
Mission: To advise the government on matters relating to the status of women; To propose legislation & policies to promote equality of opportunity & status; To publish reports, studies & recommendations
Finances: *Annual Operating Budget:* $500,000-$1.5 Million; *Funding Sources:* Provincial government
Staff Member(s): 11
Activities: *Library:* NSACSW Resource Centre; Open to public
Chief Officer(s):
Stephanie MacInnis-Langley, Executive Director

Nova Scotia Allergy & Environmental Health Association *See* Environmental Health Association of Nova Scotia

Nova Scotia Amateur Bodybuilding Association (NSABBA)
#612, 137 Solutions Dr., Halifax NS B3S 0G5
nsabba@nsabba.com
www.nsabba.com
www.facebook.com/groups/nsabbagroup
Overview: A small provincial organization founded in 1980 overseen by Canadian Bodybuilding Federation
Mission: To be the provincial governing body for the sport of amateur bodybuilding in Nova Scotia.
Member of: Canadian Bodybuilding Federation; International Federation of Bodybuilding
Chief Officer(s):
Shira Rubin, President
Leah Johnson, Vice President
Chris Johnson, Treasurer
Karen MacLean, Secretary

Nova Scotia Archaeology Society (NSAS)
PO Box 36090, Halifax NS B3J 3S9
nsarchaeology@gmail.com
www.nsarchaeology.com
www.facebook.com/nsarchaeology
twitter.com/NSArchSociety
Overview: A small provincial charitable organization founded in 1987 overseen by Canadian Archaeological Association
Mission: To promote the preservation of Nova Scotia's archaeological sites & resources
Membership: *Fees:* $15 students/seniors; $20 individuals; $25 families; $45 classes & institutions; *Member Profile:* Individuals interested in the study of archaeology & Nova Scotia's heritage resources
Activities: Increasing awareness of archaeology in Nova Scotia; Disseminating knowledge; Facilitating the exchange of information among both professionals & amateurs; Conducting workshops; Organizing field trips to archaeological sites
Chief Officer(s):
Sara Beanlands, President
Allison Fraser, Vice-President
Courtney Glen, Secretary
Rob Ferguson, Treasurer

Publications:
• Nova Scotia Archaeology Society Newsletter
Type: Newsletter
Profile: Current information for society members

Nova Scotia Arm Wrestling Association (NSAWA)
c/o Rick Pinkney, President, 192 Beaver Bank Rd., Lower Sackville NS B4E 1J7
Tel: 902-489-9008
info@novascotiaarmwrestling.com
novascotiaarmwrestling.com
Overview: A small provincial organization overseen by Canadian Arm Wrestling Federation
Mission: To be the provincial governing body for the sport of arm wrestling in Nova Scotia
Member of: Canadian Arm Wrestling Federation
Chief Officer(s):
Rick Pinkney, President, 902-489-9008
info@novascotiaarmwrestling.com
Shawn Ross, Vice-President, 902-765-4656
shawnross1111@gmail.com
Paula O'Connell, Treasurer, 902-222-3169
paula.oconnell@hotmail.com
Mark MacPhail, Director, 902-822-1180
markmacphail3@hotmail.com

Nova Scotia Association for Community Living (NSACL)
#101, 3845 Joseph Howe Dr., Halifax NS B3L 4H9
Tel: 902-469-1174
Toll-Free: 844-469-1174
nsacl.wordpress.com
www.facebook.com/nsacl
twitter.com/NSACL
Overview: A medium-sized provincial organization overseen by Canadian Association for Community Living
Mission: To work for the benefit of persons of all ages who have an intellectual disability in Nova Scotia; To ensure those with an intellectual disability have the same rights & access as all other persons
Member of: Canadian Association for Community Living
Activities: Advocating for the interests of individuals with intellectual disabilities; Promoting research
Chief Officer(s):
Jean Coleman, Executive Director
nsacl@eastlink.ca

Nova Scotia Association of Architects (NSAA)
1361 Barrington St., Halifax NS B3J 1Y9
Tel: 902-423-7607; *Fax:* 902-425-7024
info@nsaa.ns.ca
www.nsaa.ns.ca
Overview: A medium-sized provincial organization founded in 1932
Mission: To administer the practice of architecture in Nova Scotia
Staff Member(s): 2
Membership: *Fees:* Schedule available; *Member Profile:* Individuals who practice architecture in Nova Scotia; Intern architects; Associate members; Architecture students; Retired architects
Activities: Maintaining a registry of architects licensed to practice; Administering NCARB examinations; Hosting technical meetings; Disciplining members; Liaising with governments
Chief Officer(s):
Margo Dauphinee, Executive Director
mdauphinee@nsaa.ns.ca
Jeremy Martell, Coordinator, Membership
jmartell@nsaa.ns.ca
Publications:
• Nova Scotia Association of Architects eBulletin
Type: Newsletter; *Frequency:* Monthly
Profile: Outlines association updates, news & industry events

Nova Scotia Association of Black Social Workers (ABSW)
1018 Main St., Dartmouth NS B2W 4X9
Tel: 902-407-8809; *Fax:* 902-434-6544
www.nsabsw.ca
Overview: A small provincial organization
Mission: To promote the advancement & professional development of Black Social Workers & Human Service Workers in Nova Scotia; To provide educational programs & financial assistance to individuals of African descent studying social work or working in the social services field
Membership: *Fees:* $75 regular; $65 associate; $50 student; *Member Profile:* Regular members consist of registered social

workers; Associate members consist of individuals who work in social services but do not have a social work degree; Student/unemployed/retired members consist of social work students, unemployed social workers & social service workers, & individuals who have retired from the social services field; *Committees:* Bursary; Child Welfare; International; Membership; Social
Activities: Providing educational & professional development programs; Raising awareness on social issues; Offering counselling services; Lobbying
Chief Officer(s):
Veronica Marsman-Murphy, President
vmarsman@me.com
Crystal John, Vice-President
Germaine Howe-Bundy, Treasurer
Chanae Parsons, Secretary

Nova Scotia Association of Health Organizations *See* Health Association Nova Scotia

Nova Scotia Association of Insolvency & Restructuring Professionals (NSAIRP)
c/o PricewaterhouseCoopers Inc., Summit Place, #400, 1601 Lower Water St., Halifax NS B3J 3P6
Tel: 902-491-7431; *Fax:* 902-422-1166
Previous Name: Nova Scotia Insolvency Association
Overview: A small provincial organization overseen by Canadian Association of Insolvency & Restructuring Professionals
Mission: To foster the provision of objective & competent insolvency & restructuring services in Nova Scotia, in order to instill public trust
Affiliation(s): Canadian Association of Insolvency & Restructuring Professionals
Activities: Facilitating communication among members; Providing workshops for association members
Chief Officer(s):
Derek George Cramm, President
derek.cramm@ca.pwc.com

Nova Scotia Association of Medical Radiation Technologists (NSAMRT)
Park Lane Terraces, PO Box 142, #502, 5657 Spring Garden Rd., Halifax NS B3J 3R4
Tel: 902-434-6525; *Fax:* 902-832-8676
Toll-Free: 866-788-6525
info@nsamrt.ca
www.nsamrt.ca
Overview: A small provincial organization overseen by Canadian Association of Medical Radiation Technologists
Mission: To uphold standards of practice in the field of medical radiation technology in Nova Scotia, in order to ensure the public is given optimal care
Membership: 500+; *Member Profile:* Nova Scotia medical radiation technologists from the disciplines of nuclear medicine technology, radiological technology, magnetic resonance imaging technology, & radiation therapy; *Committees:* Continuing Education; Refresher; Historian; Public Relations; Publications; Awards; Conference
Activities: Engaging in advocacy activities; Providing professional development opportunities; Increasing public awareness of the profession of medical radiation technologists (MRTs) in Nova Scotia
Chief Officer(s):
Julie Avery, Executive Director
julieavery@nsamrt.ca
Awards:
• President's Bursary
Awarded to provide financial assistance to members attending the CAMRT Annual Conference; *Amount:* 4 at $500 *Contact:* Julie Avery, E-mail: julieavery@nsamrt.ca
Meetings/Conferences:
• Nova Scotia Association of Medical Radiation Technologists 2018 Annual Fall Education Seminar, 2018, NS
Scope: Provincial
Description: Held the weekend before Medical Radiation Technologists Week, the annual continuing education meeting consists of talks related to the disciplines of radiation therapy, nuclear medicine, & radiological technology, as well as a keynote address related to all medical radiation technology disciplines
• Nova Scotia Association of Medical Radiation Technologists 78th Annual General Conference 2018, 2018
Scope: Provincial

Nova Scotia Association of Naturopathic Doctors (NSAND)
PO Box 245, Lower Sackville NS B4C 2S9
Tel: 902-431-8001
info@nsand.ca
www.nsand.ca
www.facebook.com/novascotiaassociationofNDs
twitter.com/NSAND_
Overview: A small provincial organization founded in 1995 overseen by The Canadian Association of Naturopathic Doctors
Mission: To be a resource for its members & to inform the public about naturopathic medicine.
Membership: *Fees:* $400 full member; $50 associate; $25 student
Chief Officer(s):
Bryan Rade, President
Florence Woolaver, Administrator

Nova Scotia Association of Optometrists (NSAO)
PO Box 9410, Stn. A, #700, 6009 Quinpool Rd., Halifax NS B3K 5S3
Tel: 902-435-2845; *Fax:* 902-425-2441
info@ns.doctorsofoptometry.ca
ns.doctorsofoptometry.ca
Previous Name: Nova Scotia Optometrical Society
Overview: A medium-sized provincial licensing organization founded in 1905 overseen by Canadian Association of Optometrists
Mission: To foster excellence in the delivery of vision & eye health services in Nova Scotia; To act as the voice of optometry in Nova Scotia
Membership: *Member Profile:* Doctors of optometry in Nova Scotia
Activities: Promoting preventative eye health care; Providing educational resources; *Library:* Patient Education Library

Nova Scotia Association of REALTORS (NSAR)
#100, 7 Scarfe Ct., Dartmouth NS B3B 1W4
Tel: 902-468-2515; *Fax:* 902-468-2533
Toll-Free: 800-344-2001
nsrealtors.ca
www.linkedin.com/company/nova-scotia-association-of-realtors-
www.facebook.com/nsarREALTORS
twitter.com/nsarREALTORS
Previous Name: Nova Scotia Real Estate Association
Overview: A medium-sized provincial organization founded in 2000
Mission: To provide Realtors with services & representation to enable them to best serve the public in real estate transactions
Member of: The Canadian Real Estate Association
Finances: *Annual Operating Budget:* $1.5 Million-$3 Million; *Funding Sources:* Membership dues
Staff Member(s): 13
Membership: 1,300; *Fees:* $168; *Member Profile:* Brokers & sales people; *Committees:* Arbitration; By-law; Professional Standards & Conduct Review; Education; Executive; Finance; MLS; Government Relations; Public Relations; Standard Forms & Practices
Chief Officer(s):
Roger Boutilier, Chief Executive Officer, 902-468-3447
rboutilier@nsar.ns.ca
Bonnie Wigg, Director, MLSr & Member Services, 902-468-5870
bwigg@nsar.ns.ca
Nicole Kreiger, Director, Education, 902-468-5765
nkreiger@nsar.ns.ca

Nova Scotia Association of Social Workers (NSASW) / Association des travailleurs sociaux de la Nouvelle-Écosse
#700, 1888 Brunswick St., Halifax NS B3J 3J8
Tel: 902-429-7799; *Fax:* 902-429-7650
nsasw@nsasw.org
www.nsasw.org
www.facebook.com/NSASW
twitter.com/NSASWNEWS
Overview: A medium-sized provincial licensing organization founded in 1963
Mission: To promote & regulate the practice of social work so the members can provide a high standard of service that respects diversity, promotes social justice & enhances the worth, self-determination & potential of individuals, families & communities
Member of: Canadian Association of Social Workers
Finances: *Funding Sources:* Membership fees
Staff Member(s): 6
Membership: 1,600; *Committees:* Social Action/Social Justice; Program; Professional Development; Public Relations; Membership; Standards & Ethics; Nominating; Private Practice
Activities: Social Work Register; publishing; *Internships:* Yes; *Library:* by appointment
Chief Officer(s):
Robert R. Shepherd, Executive Director
robert.shepherd@nsasw.org

Nova Scotia Association of the Appraisal Institute of Canada *See* Nova Scotia Real Estate Appraisers Association

Nova Scotia Automobile Dealers' Association (NSADA)
#700, 6009 Quinpool Rd., Halifax NS B3K 5S3
Tel: 902-425-2445; *Fax:* 902-425-2441
info@nsada.ca
www.nsada.ca
Overview: A medium-sized provincial organization founded in 1966
Mission: To assist & protect association members; To act as the voice of new vehicle franchised dealers in Nova Scotia
Member of: Canadian Automobile Dealer's Association (CADA)
Membership: 100+; *Member Profile:* New vehicle franchised dealers in Nova Scotia
Activities: Liaising with government, automotive manufacturers, & related industries
Chief Officer(s):
John K. Sutherland, Executive Vice-President
Meetings/Conferences:
• Nova Scotia Automobile Dealers' Association AGM 2018, 2018, NS
Scope: Provincial
Description: An event for association members from across Nova Scotia

Nova Scotia Badminton Association
5516 Spring Garden Rd., Halifax NS B3J 1G6
Tel: 902-425-5450; *Fax:* 902-425-5606
badmintonns.ca
www.facebook.com/BadmintonNovaScotia
twitter.com/bdmintonNS
Also Known As: Badminton Nova Scotia
Overview: A small provincial organization overseen by Badminton Canada
Mission: To promote the development of badminton for all Nova Scotians, at all levels; To provide leadership, organization, and fair governance for the sport
Membership: *Fees:* $20 recreational/coach & umpire; $40 competitive; $150 club
Chief Officer(s):
Jennifer Petrie, Executive Director
executive_director@badmintonns.ca
Awards:
• Lifetime Achievement Award
• Volunteer of the Year Award
• Service Award
• Jeff Hebert Memorial Award
• Male Athlete of the Year Award
• Female Athlete of the Year Award

Nova Scotia Ball Hockey Association (NSBHA)
Tel: 902-463-2833
nsbha@hotmail.com
nsbha.weebly.com
Overview: A small provincial organization
Mission: To promote ball hockey in Nova Scotia & to host provincial tournaments
Affiliation(s): Canadian Ball Hockey Association; Sport Nova Scotia
Finances: *Annual Operating Budget:* Less than $50,000
20 volunteer(s)
Membership: 650 individual

Nova Scotia Band Association
108 Grindstone Dr., Halifax NS B3R 0A6
www.novascotiabandassociation.com
www.facebook.com/novascotiabandassociation
twitter.com/nsbandassoc
Overview: A small provincial organization overseen by Canadian Band Association
Mission: To support and promote the development of bands throughout the province of Nova Scotia through communication, coordination, program development, advocacy and lobbying at the provincial level.
Member of: Canadian Band Association

Canadian Associations / Nova Scotia Barristers' Society (NSBS)

Membership: *Fees:* $30 student/retired; $50 teacher; $100 institution; *Member Profile:* Band directors & supporters; Musicians; Music industry workers
Chief Officer(s):
Mark Hopkins, President
Awards:
• James H. Hargreaves Memorial Scholarship
Eligibility: A graduating high school student who has been accepted for post-secondary musical study at a recognized institution & whose band director or music instructor is a member of the Nova Scotia band association *Deadline:* May 30 *Contact:* Hope Gendron, Email: nsband@accesswave.ca
• NSBA Student Recognition Award
Eligibility: A student from the middle school level (grades 6-9) & a student from the high school level (grades 9-12) who demonstrate musical ability, responsibility, loyalty, cooperation, & dependability *Contact:* Katelyn Montgomery, E-mail: kmontgomery2@staff.ednet.ns.ca
• Ron MacKay "Music for Life" Award
Deadline: March 31 *Contact:* Jim Forde, Phone: 902-479-0286; E-mail: jimforde@eastlink.ca
• Ron MacKay's Musical Chair Award
Eligibility: Any participant who has paid tuition

Nova Scotia Barristers' Society (NSBS)
800 - 2000 Barrington St., Halifax NS B3J 3K1
Tel: 902-422-1491; *Fax:* 902-429-4869
www.nsbs.org
https://www.linkedin.com/company/ns-barristers'-society
www.facebook.com/NSBarristers
twitter.com/nsbs
Overview: A medium-sized provincial licensing organization founded in 1825
Mission: To set & enforce standards of professional responsibility & ethics for lawyers; To license & discipline members of the profession, in accordance with the Legal Profession Act
Affiliation(s): Canadian Lawyers' Insurance Association; Federation of Law Societies; Law Foundation of Nova Scotia; Law Reform Commission of Nova Scotia; Lawyers' Insurance Association of Nova Scotia; Nova Scotia Legal Aid Commission; Canadian Bar Association
Membership: 2,500; *Member Profile:* Practising & non-practising lawyers in Nova Scotia; *Committees:* Administration of Justice; Complaints Investigation; Credentials; Distinguished Service Award; Ethics & Professional Responsibility; Executive; Finance; Gender Equity; Hearing; Lawyers Fund for Client Compensation; Nominating; Professional Responsibility Policies & Procedures; Professional Standards; Race Relations; Trust Accounts; Department of Justice Liaison; Service Nova Scotia & Municipal Relations Liaison; Land Registration Act Management
Activities: Providing education & guidance to members; *Library:* Nova Scotia Barristers' Society Library & Information Services; Not open to public
Chief Officer(s):
Darrel Pink, Executive Director
dpink@nsbs.org
Publications:
• InForum [a publication of the Nova Scotia Barristers' society]
Type: Newsletter; *Frequency:* bi-weekly
Profile: Provides regular updates on news & events of importance to Nova Scotia's legal profession
• Nova Scotia Barristers' Society Annual Report
Type: Yearbook; *Frequency:* Annually; *Number of Pages:* Y
• Society Record [a publication of the Nova Scotia Barristers' Society]
Type: Magazine; *Frequency:* 2 pa; *Number of Pages:* Y; *ISSN:* 1186-284X; *Price:* Free with NSBS membership, $30 + HST without membership

Nova Scotia Beekeepers' Association (NSBA)
c/o Barb McLaughlin, 283 McKay Siding Rd., McKay Siding NS B0N 2J0
Tel: 902-639-3064
nsbeekeepers@gmail.com
www.nsbeekeepers.ca
Overview: A small provincial organization
Mission: To help beekeepers in Nova Scotia maintain their bee farms & supply them with educational services
Membership: *Fees:* $46 0-10 hives; $115 11-99 hives; $230 100-500 hives; $402.50 500-1499 hives; $1150 1500+ hives; *Member Profile:* Beekeepers from Nova Scotia
Activities: Informing members about regulations regarding beekeeping; Providing updates on honey bee research; Sharing information on the code of practice for beekeepers in Nova Scotia
Chief Officer(s):
Joe Goetz, President, 902-292-8708
michelleandjoe1@me.com
Perry Brandt, Vice-President, 902-300-4171
brandt@bellaliant.net
Barb McLaughlin, Treasurer, 902-639-2064
bauld.mclau@ns.sympatico.ca

Nova Scotia Boxing Authority (NSBA)
NS
Overview: A small provincial organization founded in 1975
Mission: The Nova Scotia Boxing Authority regulates professional boxing & other combat sports in the province, as well as establishes & enforces rules for the conduct of boxing, & the training of officials in accordance with national standards. The NSBA answers to the minister of health promotion & protection.
Member of: Canadian Boxing Federation

Nova Scotia Cattle Producers (NSCP)
60 Research Dr., Bible Hill NS B6L 2R2
Tel: 902-893-7455; *Fax:* 902-893-7063
office@nscattle.ca
www.nscattle.ca
Previous Name: Nova Scotia Cattlemen's Association
Overview: A medium-sized provincial organization founded in 2004
Mission: To assist in the sustainable development of the beef production industry in Nova Scotia
Member of: Canadian Cattlemen's Association
Affiliation(s): National Check-off Agency; The Beef Cattle Research Agency; Beef Information Centre; Nappan Beef Research Committee; Maritime Beef Council; The Nova Scotia Federation of Agriculture Council of Leaders
Membership: *Fees:* Schedule available; *Member Profile:* Persons involved in Nova Scotia's beef & dairy production industry
Activities: Providing information about beef production & marketing; Promoting the beef industry in Nova Scotia; Monitoring & responding to issues in the industry; Advocating on behalf of producers
Chief Officer(s):
Terry Prescott, Chair
Jim Fraser, Vice-Chair
Publications:
• N.S.C.Action [a publication of Nova Scotia Cattle Producers]
Type: Newsletter

Nova Scotia Cattlemen's Association *See* Nova Scotia Cattle Producers

Nova Scotia Child Care Association / Association des services de garde à l'enfance de la Nouvelle-Écosse
#161, 1083 Queen St., Halifax NS B3H 0B2
Tel: 902-423-8199; *Fax:* 902-492-8106
Toll-Free: 800-565-8199
info@nschildcareassociation.org
nschildcareassociation.org
Overview: A medium-sized provincial organization
Mission: To promote high standards in service in the child care industry; to be a voice for its members
Member of: Canadian Child Care Federation
Membership: *Fees:* $30; $55; *Committees:* Ethics; Membership & Standards; Advocacy
Chief Officer(s):
Kathleen Couture, Chair

Nova Scotia Choral Federation (NSCF) / Fédération des chorales de la Nouvelle-Écosse (FCNE)
1113 Marginal Rd., Halifax NS B3H 4P7
Tel: 902-423-4688; *Fax:* 902-422-0881
Toll-Free: 888-672-3969
office@nscf.ns.ca
www.nscf.ns.ca
twitter.com/nschoralfed
Overview: A small provincial organization founded in 1976
Mission: To promote the art of choral music by encouraging high standards of artistic achievement by providing technical expertise & training; To foster an appreciation of choral music throughout Nova Scotia
Member of: Cultural Federations of Nova Scotia
Affiliation(s): Association of Canadian Choral Conductors; Nova Scotia Music Educators Association; Canadian Music Educators Association; American Choral Directors Association; International Federation for Choral Music; Music Industry Association of Nova Scotia
Finances: *Annual Operating Budget:* $100,000-$250,000; *Funding Sources:* Programs; provincial Dept. of Education; fundraising; membership
Staff Member(s): 2; 35 volunteer(s)
Membership: 230 individual + 140 group + 4 life; *Fees:* $35 individual; $40 student choir; $60 adult choir; *Member Profile:* Individuals engaged in choral singing; students; groups - adult & student choirs; organizations which support objectives of federation; *Committees:* Library; Workshop; Finance & Development; Policy Review; Special Projects
Activities: *Library:* Open to public
Chief Officer(s):
Frances Farrell, President
Tim Callahan-Cross, Executive Director
tim@nscf.ns.ca

Nova Scotia College Conference *See* Atlantic Collegiate Athletic Association

Nova Scotia College of Chiropractors (NSCC)
Park Lane Terraces, PO Box 142, #502, 5657 Spring Garden Rd., Halifax NS B3J 3R4
Tel: 902-407-4255; *Fax:* 902-425-2441
inquiries@chiropractors.ns.ca
www.chiropractors.ns.ca
Overview: A small provincial organization founded in 1953 overseen by Canadian Chiropractic Association
Mission: To promote & improve the proficiency of chiropractors in all matters relating to the practice of chiropractic; To protect the public from untrained & unqualified persons acting as chiropractors; To advance the chiropractic profession
Finances: *Funding Sources:* Membership dues
Membership: *Committees:* Hearing; Peer Assessment; Continuing Education; Advertising Approval; Credentials; Nominating; Regulations & Policy Development; Registration Review
Chief Officer(s):
John K. Sutherland, Executive Director

Nova Scotia College of Medical Laboratory Technologists (NSCMLT)
#202, 380 Bedford Hwy., Dartmouth NS B3M 2L4
Tel: 902-453-9605; *Fax:* 902-454-3535
Toll-Free: 888-897-4095
info@nscmlt.org
www.nscmlt.org
www.facebook.com/683739585020891
Overview: A medium-sized provincial licensing organization overseen by Canadian Society for Medical Laboratory Science
Mission: To provide leadership, establish partnerships & support the professional development of members so as to maintain the highest standards of practice
Membership: *Member Profile:* Laboratory technologists in the province of Nova Scotia; *Committees:* Advocacy & Technology; Professional Practice
Chief Officer(s):
Wanda Thomas, Contact

Nova Scotia College of Pharmacists (NSCP)
#200, 1559 Brunswick St., Halifax NS B3J 2G1
Tel: 902-422-8528; *Fax:* 902-422-0885
info@nspharmacists.ca
www.nspharmacists.ca
Previous Name: Nova Scotia Pharmaceutical Society
Overview: A medium-sized provincial licensing organization founded in 1876 overseen by National Association of Pharmacy Regulatory Authorities
Mission: To govern the practice of pharmacy in Nova Scotia to benefit the health & well being of the public
Member of: Canadian Council on Continuing Education in Pharmacy
Staff Member(s): 11
Membership: 1,152; *Committees:* Executive; Audit; Registrations; Investigations; Standards of Practice; Governance; Nominating; Hearing Panel
Chief Officer(s):
Shelagh Campbell-Palmer, Manager, Professional Practice, 902-422-8528 Ext. 2
Susan Wedlake, Registrar, 902-422-8528 Ext. 7

Nova Scotia College of Physiotherapists (NSCP)
PO Box 309, Stn. Main, Dartmouth NS B2Y 3Y5
Tel: 902-454-0158; *Fax:* 902-484-6381
Toll-Free: 866-225-1060

office@nsphysio.com
www.nsphysio.com
Overview: A small provincial licensing organization founded in 1958 overseen by Canadian Alliance of Physiotherapy Regulators
Mission: To assure that the interests of the public are upheld through the regulation & promotion of safe & effective physiotherapy services; To communicate effectively with the membership & thereby affect change on issues of concern to the public
Member of: Canadian Alliance of Physiotherapy Regulators
Finances: *Funding Sources:* Registration fees
Membership: *Member Profile:* Registered physiotherapists; *Committees:* Peer Assessment; Investigation; Practice Standards
Chief Officer(s):
Joan Ross, Registrar, 902-454-0158 Ext. 1, Fax: 902-245-3134
registrar@nsphysio.com
Patrick King, Executive Director, 902-454-0158 Ext. 2, Fax: 902-484-6381

Nova Scotia College of Respiratory Therapists (NSCRT)
#1301, 1959 Upper Water St., Halifax NS B3J 3N2
Tel: 902-423-3229; *Fax:* 902-422-2388
registrar@nscrt.com
www.nscrt.com
Overview: A small provincial organization founded in 2007
Mission: To serve as the regulatory body of respiratory therapy in Nova Scotia; To establish professional & ethical standards for respiratory therapy practice; To promote excellence & leadership in cardio-respiratory care practice
Finances: *Annual Operating Budget:* $250,000-$500,000; *Funding Sources:* Membership; licence fees
Staff Member(s): 2; 35 volunteer(s)
Membership: 300; *Fees:* $450; *Committees:* Complaints; Credentials; Nominations; Professional Conduct; Professional Practice; Registrations Appeal
Activities: Professional self-regulation
Chief Officer(s):
Shannon McDonald, Registrar
registrar@nscrt.com
Tara Planetta, Deputy Registrar
deputyregistrar@nscrt.com

Nova Scotia Construction Labour Relations Association Limited (NSCLRA)
#1, 260 Brownlow Ave., Dartmouth NS B3B 1V9
Tel: 902-468-2283; *Fax:* 902-468-3705
admin@nsclra.ca
www.nsclra.ca
www.facebook.com/reseaufadoq
www.youtube.com/user/ReseauFADOQ
Previous Name: Construction Management Bureau Limited
Overview: A medium-sized provincial organization founded in 1972
Mission: To represent construction industry employers in collective bargaining with trade unions in the industrial & commercial sectors
Member of: Nova Scotia Construction Sector Council - Industrial-Commercial-Institutional
Membership: *Fees:* $500; *Committees:* Executive; Central Coordinating
Chief Officer(s):
Allan Stapleton, President, 902-222-2036
astapleton@nsclra.ca
Nancy Canales, Administrator
ncanales@nsclra.ca

Nova Scotia Construction Safety Association (NSCSA)
Burnside Industrial Park, 35 MacDonald Ave., Dartmouth NS B3B 1C6
Tel: 902-468-6696; *Fax:* 902-468-8843
Toll-Free: 800-971-3888
nscsa@nscsa.org
www.nscsa.org
www.linkedin.com/company/nova-scotia-construction-safety-association
www.facebook.com/NSCSA
www.youtube.com/user/nscsaassociation
Overview: A small provincial organization founded in 1994
Mission: To develop a positive occupational health & safety culture within the Nova Scotia construction industry through the provision of quality accessible & affordable services
Staff Member(s): 24
Activities: Safety training; audits; member services; Certificate of Recognition; resource room; *Speaker Service:* Yes
Chief Officer(s):
A. Bruce Collins, General Manager
abcollins@nscsa.org

Nova Scotia Construction Sector Council - Industrial-Commercial-Institutional (NSCSC-ICI)
#1, 10 Ragged Lake Blvd., Halifax NS B3S 1C2
Tel: 902-832-4761; *Fax:* 902-832-4763
www.nscsc.ca
Overview: A small provincial organization
Mission: To identify areas of concern related to human resource planning & skills development within Nova Scotia's construction sector
Affiliation(s): Cape Breton Island Building & Construction Trades Council; Nova Scotia Construction Labour Relations Association
Activities: Better SuperVision & Leaders Being Leaders training programs; skills enhancement initiatives; *Library*
Chief Officer(s):
Mike Marsh, Chair
Trent Soholt, Executive Director/Project Manager
tsoholt@nscsc.ca

Nova Scotia Consulting Engineers Association *See* Consulting Engineers of Nova Scotia

Nova Scotia Co-operative Council
347C Willow St., Truro NS B2N 6C7
Tel: 902-893-8966; *Fax:* 902-895-0109
info@novascotia.coop
www.novascotia.coop
www.linkedin.com/company/2332853
www.facebook.com/nscoopcouncil
twitter.com/NovaScotiaCo_op
www.youtube.com/user/NSCoopCouncil
Overview: A small provincial organization
Mission: To encourage co-operatives of all types to work together to form a strong co-operative movement in Nova Scotia; to stimulate, promote & support the creation of new co-operatives across all sectors & industries in Nova Scotia; to advocate for the co-operative movement's interests to all levels of government; to enhance the profile of a "co-operative identity" among the public in Nova Scotia; to ensure innovation within the co-operative sector; to develop new ways of financing which support development opportunities. Branch offices in Sydney, & Yarmouth.
Member of: Canadian Renewable Energy Alliance
Staff Member(s): 8
Membership: *Fees:* Schedule available; *Member Profile:* Co-operatives in all sectors including housing co-ops, retail, agricultural, fisheries and forestry co-ops, credit unions, health co-ops, worker co-ops
Activities: Innovation Council; Renewable Energy Initiative; HealthConnex (Health Care Initiative); Youth Alliance Initiative; small business loan program; immigrant loan program; short-term equity fund; co-operative training; business planning and mentoring; conflict resolution; research; advocacy
Chief Officer(s):
Dianne Kelderman, CEO
diannefk@eastlink.ca
Linda Johnson, Office Manager
linda@novascotia.coop

Nova Scotia Council for the Family (NSCF)
#302, 1888 Brunswick St., Halifax NS B3J 3J8
Tel: 902-422-1316; *Fax:* 902-422-4012
info@nscouncilfamily.org
www.nscouncilfamily.org
Overview: A medium-sized provincial charitable organization founded in 1967
Mission: To be devoted to the well-being of all children & families in Nova Scotia
Affiliation(s): Family Service Canada; Child Welfare League of America/Canada
100 volunteer(s)
Membership: 27; *Committees:* Amanda's Gift Bursary Program Fund Raising; Amanda's Gift Bursary Program Selections; Executive; Nominations; Professional Development; Youth in Care Program
Activities: Presenting education programs for families & children & the public; Providing professional development; Engaging in advocacy activities; Reviewing research; *Speaker Service:* Yes; *Library:* Open to public by appointment
Chief Officer(s):
Jane Boyd Landry, Executive Director
jane@nscouncilfamily.org
Awards:
• Youth Achievement Award
• Award of Merit
• Judge Tramble Award
• Achievement of Excellence Award
• Support Staff Award
• Chuck Lake Distinguished Service Award
; *Amount:* $500
• Honourary Life Membership
• Community Partners Award

Nova Scotia Council on Smoking & Health *See* Coalition for a Smoke-Free Nova Scotia

Nova Scotia Cricket Association (NSCA)
PO Box 31, Lunenburg NS B0J 2C0
Tel: 902-640-2448
info@novascotiacricket.com
www.novascotiacricket.com
www.facebook.com/296868372047
twitter.com/nscricket
Overview: A small provincial organization founded in 1965 overseen by Cricket Canada
Mission: To be the provincial governing body of cricket in Nova Scotia.
Member of: Cricket Canada; Sport Nova Scotia
Chief Officer(s):
Tushar Sehgal, President
Yash Gugle, Secretary
Amit Joshi, Provincial Director

Nova Scotia Criminal Justice Association (NSCJA)
PO Box 31191, Halifax NS B3K 5Y1
Tel: 902-490-5300; *Fax:* 902-490-6596
info@nscja.ca
www.nscja.ca
Previous Name: Nova Scotia Criminology & Corrections Association
Overview: A small provincial organization
Membership: *Fees:* $60; $35 student
Chief Officer(s):
Sebastien Decaens, President

Nova Scotia Criminology & Corrections Association *See* Nova Scotia Criminal Justice Association

Nova Scotia Curling Association (NSCA)
5516 Spring Garden Rd., 4th Fl., Halifax NS B3J 1G6
Tel: 902-421-2875; *Fax:* 902-425-5606
nsca@sportnovascotia.ca
www.nscurl.com
Previous Name: Nova Scotia Ladies Curling Association
Overview: A medium-sized provincial organization overseen by Canadian Curling Association
Affiliation(s): Canadian Curling Association
Staff Member(s): 5
Membership: 6,000; *Member Profile:* Men's, women's & juniors curlers; *Committees:* Operations; Finance; Competitions; Junior Curling; Athlete Development; Ombudsman; Disciplinary; Nominations; Awards; Curl Atlantic Reps
Chief Officer(s):
Kevin Patterson, Technical Director

Nova Scotia Daylily Society
c/o Carol Harvey, Newport RR#3 999 McKay Rd., Hants County NS B0N 2A0
Tel: 902-757-2057
www.nsdaylilysociety.com
www.facebook.com/129889100496214
Overview: A small provincial organization founded in 2003
Mission: To promote the growing of Daylilies
Membership: *Fees:* $10
Chief Officer(s):
Carol Harvey, Chair, Membership
cgharvey@eastlink.ca

Nova Scotia Deaf Sports Association (NSDSA)
5516 Spring Garden Rd., 4th Fl., Halifax NS B3J 1G6
Overview: A small provincial organization overseen by Canadian Deaf Sports Association
Mission: To govern fitness, amateur sports & recreation for deaf people in Nova Scotia.
Member of: Canadian Deaf Sports Association
Chief Officer(s):
Matt Ayyash, President

Nova Scotia Dental Assistants' Association (NSDAA)
PO Box 9142, Stn. A, Halifax NS B3K 5M8
Tel: 902-405-1122; Fax: 902-405-1133
nsdaa@eastlink.ca
www.nsdaa.ca
Overview: A small provincial organization founded in 1950 overseen by Canadian Dental Assistants Association
Mission: To affiliate at local, provincial & national levels for the betterment of the dental assistant profession & patient care
Finances: Annual Operating Budget: Less than $50,000; Funding Sources: Membership dues
Membership: 600-650; Fees: $85
Chief Officer(s):
Michelle Fowler, President
rdamdf@yahoo.ca
Lynda Foran, Executive Director

Nova Scotia Dental Association (NSDA)
#101, 1559 Brunswick St., Halifax NS B3J 2G1
Tel: 902-420-0088; Fax: 902-423-6537
Toll-Free: 888-238-1726
nsda@eastlink.ca
www.nsdental.org
Overview: A medium-sized provincial organization founded in 1891 overseen by Canadian Dental Association
Mission: To help dentists in Nova Scotia better serve their patients
Member of: Canadian Dental Association
Finances: Funding Sources: Membership dues
Membership: 600+ active members; Fees: Schedule available; Member Profile: Licensed to practise dentistry
Activities: Rents Mailing List: Yes
Chief Officer(s):
Steve Jennex, Executive Director
jennexnsda@eastlink.ca
Patricia Pellerine, Manager, Operations
p.pellerinensda@eastlink.ca
Lesley Squarey, Manager, Communications
lsquarey.nsda@eastlink.ca
Kyla Romard, Manager, Clinical Affairs
kromard.nsda@eastlink.ca

Nova Scotia Designer Crafts Council (NSDCC)
1113 Marginal Rd., Halifax NS B3H 4P7
Tel: 902-423-3837; Fax: 902-422-0881
office@nsdcc.ns.ca
www.nsdcc.ns.ca
www.facebook.com/NSDCC
twitter.com/NSDCC
www.youtube.com/user/nsdcc
Overview: A small provincial charitable organization founded in 1973
Mission: To encourage & promote the craft movement in Nova Scotia; to increase public awareness & appreciation of craft products & activities
Member of: Cultural Federations of Nova Scotia; Canadian Crafts Federation; Craft Alliance
Finances: Funding Sources: Core funding from NS Dept. of Education & Culture; Membership fees; Fundraising
Staff Member(s): 4
Membership: Fees: $23 student; $28.75 associate; $34.50 senior; $69 group/general; $115 market; Committees: Communications; Development; Exhibitions; Standards; Jackie Mackay Library Collection; Market Advisory
Activities: Leading workshops, conferences, & educational programs; Facilitating exhibitions & craft shows; Awareness Events: Summer Show, July; Christmas Show, Nov.; Annual Festival of Craft, June Library: Jackie MacKay Library; Open to public
Chief Officer(s):
Susan Hanrahan, Executive Director
susan@nsdcc.ns.ca
Publications:
• Newsflash! [a publication of the Nova Scotia Designer Crafts Council]
Type: Newsletter; Frequency: weekly
Profile: Contains council news & exhibition dates

Nova Scotia Dietetic Association (NSDA)
#301, 380 Bedford Hwy., Halifax NS B3M 2L4
Tel: 902-493-3034
info@nsdassoc.ca
www.nsdassoc.ca
Overview: A medium-sized provincial licensing organization founded in 1953 overseen by Dietitians of Canada
Mission: To regulate dietitians & nutritionists in the province, & register & discipline (when necessary) practitioners to ensure safe, ethical & competent dietetic practice
Finances: Annual Operating Budget: Less than $50,000; Funding Sources: Membership dues
Membership: 450 individuals; Fees: $310 ($155 first time renewal); Member Profile: Must meet standards of Professional Dietitians Act of Nova Scotia; Committees: Continuing Competency; Registration; Registration Appeal; Professional Practice
Activities: Internships: Yes; Speaker Service: Yes; Rents Mailing List: Yes
Chief Officer(s):
Melissa Campbell, President
Jennifer Garus, Executive Manager (ex-officio)

Nova Scotia Drama League See Theatre Nova Scotia

Nova Scotia Egg & Pullet Producers Marketing Board See Nova Scotia Egg Producers

Nova Scotia Egg Producers (NSEP)
PO Box 1096, 55 Queen St., #A, Truro NS B2N 2B2
Tel: 902-895-6341; Fax: 902-895-6343
www.nsegg.ca
www.facebook.com/EggFarmersOfNovaScotia
twitter.com/EggFarmersofNS
Previous Name: Nova Scotia Egg & Pullet Producers Marketing Board
Overview: A small provincial licensing organization founded in 1972
Mission: To promote, control, & regulate the marketing of eggs & pullets in Nova Scotia
Affiliation(s): Canadian Egg Marketing Agency
Finances: Annual Operating Budget: $250,000-$500,000
Staff Member(s): 4; 7 volunteer(s)
Membership: 26
Chief Officer(s):
Patricia Wyllie, General Manager

Nova Scotia Equestrian Federation (NSEF)
5516 Spring Garden Rd., 4th Fl., Halifax NS B3J 1G6
Tel: 902-425-5450; Fax: 902-425-5606
nsefmembership@sportnovascotia.ca
www.horsenovascotia.ca
twitter.com/NSEquestrian
Overview: A small provincial organization
Member of: Equine Canada
Membership: 2,100; Fees: $40
Chief Officer(s):
Heather Myrer, Executive Director
nsef@sportnovascotia.ca
Gidget Oxner, Technical Director
nseftd@sportnovascotia.ca
Awards:
• Volunteer of the Year Award
• Sponsor of the Year Award
• Nova Trophy Service Award
• President's Award
• Scotia Series Youth Sportsmanship Award
• Female Athlete of the Year Award
• Male Athlete of the Year Award
• Long Term Equestrian Development Bursary

Nova Scotia Federation of Agriculture (NSFA)
Perennia Innovation Park, 60 Research Dr., Bible Hill NS B6L 2R2
Tel: 902-893-2293; Fax: 902-893-7063
info@nsfa-fane.ca
www.nsfa-fane.ca
Overview: A medium-sized provincial organization founded in 1895 overseen by Canadian Federation of Agriculture
Mission: To act as the voice for the agricultural community in Nova Scotia; To ensure a competitive & sustainable future for agriculture in Nova Scotia; To build financially viable, ecologically sound, & socially responsible farm businesses in the province
Member of: Canadian Federation of Agriculture
Membership: 1,800+; Member Profile: Individual farm businesses in Nova Scotia which represent all aspects of primary agriculture; Corporations
Activities: Reviewing legislative & regulatory issues & lobbying for change; Developing & delivering programs to meet the needs of the farm community, such a environmental farm planning services
Chief Officer(s):
Chris van den Heuvel, President

Henry Vissers, Executive Director
hvissers@nsfa-fane.ca

Nova Scotia Federation of Anglers & Hunters (NSFAH)
PO Box 654, Halifax NS B3J 2T3
Tel: 902-477-8898; Fax: 902-444-3883
www.nsfah.ca
Overview: A medium-sized provincial organization founded in 1930
Mission: To be dedicated to the conservation & propagation of wildlife in the province for those who hunt, fish, trap or otherwise enjoy the wildlife resources of Nova Scotia, through education, cooperation & exchange of information
Membership: Fees: $20 individual; $30 family; $50 sustaining; $75 corporate; $150 life

Nova Scotia Federation of Home & School Associations (NSFHSA)
PO Box 28123, Stn. Tacoma Dr., Dartmouth NS B2W 6E2
Tel: 902-266-9507
Toll-Free: 800-214-9507
nsfhsapresident@gmail.com
www.nsfhsa.org
Overview: A small provincial organization founded in 1936 overseen by Canadian Home & School Federation
Mission: To provide a forum for discussion between the home & school beyond the parent-teacher interview; To promote & secure legislation for the care & protection of & equality of educational opportunities for children; To give parents an understanding of the school & its work, assisting in interpreting the school to the public; To confer & cooperate with organizations other than the schools which concern themselves with the training & development of children & youth
Member of: Canadian Home & School Federation
Finances: Annual Operating Budget: Less than $50,000; Funding Sources: Government
Staff Member(s): 5; 5 volunteer(s)
Membership: 5,000+ families & 400 group affiliates; Fees: $10/year; Member Profile: Parents; teaching staff
Activities: Internships: Yes; Speaker Service: Yes
Chief Officer(s):
Charla Dorrington, President
Meetings/Conferences:
• Nova Scotia Federation of Home & School Associations 2018 Annual General Meeting, 2018
Scope: Provincial
Publications:
• NSFHSA [Nova Scotia Federation of Home & School Associations] Newsletter
Type: Newsletter

Nova Scotia Federation of Labour / Fédération du travail de la Nouvelle-Écosse
#225, 3700 Kempt Rd., Halifax NS B3K 4X8
Tel: 902-454-6735; Fax: 902-454-7671
nsfl@ns.aliantzinc.ca
www.nsfl.ns.ca
Overview: A medium-sized provincial organization founded in 1956 overseen by Canadian Labour Congress
Mission: To speak on behalf of & represent the interests of organized & unorganized workers; to promote decent wages & working conditions, improved health & safety laws & lobbies for fair taxes & strong social programs; to work for social equality & to end racism & discrimination.
Membership: 70,000 members of affiliated unions in 350+ locals; Committees: Anti-Racism/Human Rights; Political Action; Education; Health Care; Occupational Health & Safety/Workers' Compensation; Women's Committee; Pensions; Young Workers
Activities: Lobbying; strike support; Lighting the Way program (workplace literacy/numeracy skills)
Chief Officer(s):
Rick Clarke, President
Kyle Buott, Secretary-Treasurer

Nova Scotia Federation of Senior Citizens & Pensioners See Federation of Senior Citizens & Pensioners of Nova Scotia

Nova Scotia Fish Packers Association (NSFPA)
38B John St., Yarmouth NS B5A 3H2
Tel: 902-774-0006; Fax: 902-742-8391
fishpackers@ns.aliantzinc.ca
www.fishpackers.ca
Previous Name: Southwestern Nova Scotia Fish Packers Association
Overview: A small provincial organization founded in 1972

Mission: To ensure the survival of a competitive seafood processing industry in Nova Scotia; To provide leadership on industry issues, effective representation with government, R&D, project management, & volume discount purchases
Finances: *Annual Operating Budget:* $50,000-$100,000
Staff Member(s): 1
Membership: 60 seafood companies; *Fees:* $460-$2645 plus HST; *Member Profile:* Fish processing companies dealing with a wide variety of seafood for Canadian & export sales
Chief Officer(s):
Marilyn Clark, Executive Director

Nova Scotia Fishermen Draggers Association *See* Scotia Fundy Mobile Gear Fishermen's Association

Nova Scotia Forest Technicians Association (NSFTA)
164 Forest Hills Dr., Truro NS B2N 2B7
nsfta@nsfta.com
www.nsfta.ca
Overview: A small provincial organization
Finances: *Annual Operating Budget:* Less than $50,000
12 volunteer(s)
Membership: 200 individual; *Fees:* $35 regular; $70 certified; *Member Profile:* Forest technicians; technologists
Activities: *Library:* Open to public
Chief Officer(s):
Cheryl Rudderham, President
rudderca@gov.ns.ca

Nova Scotia Forestry Association (NSFA)
PO Box 696, Truro NS B2N 5E5
Tel: 902-895-1179; *Fax:* 902-893-1197
kari@nsfa.ca
www.nsfa.ca
www.facebook.com/NSENVIROTHON
twitter.com/envirothonns
Overview: A medium-sized provincial charitable organization founded in 1940 overseen by Canadian Forestry Association
Mission: To conserve Nova Scotia's forests; To promote the wise use & management of forest resources
Finances: *Funding Sources:* Sponsorships
Activities: Conducting programs in schools, such as Envirothon; Advocating for the full development, utilization, & protection of forests in Nova Scotia; Promoting reforestation; *Awareness Events:* Arbor Day, September
Chief Officer(s):
Debbie Waycott, Executive Director

Nova Scotia Friends of Schizophrenics *See* Schizophrenia Society of Nova Scotia

Nova Scotia Fruit Growers' Association (NSFGA)
Kentville Agricultural Centre, 32 Main St., Kentville NS B4N 1J5
Tel: 902-678-1093; *Fax:* 902-678-1567
contact@nsapples.com
www.nsfga.ca
www.facebook.com/nsfga
twitter.com/nsfga1863
Overview: A small provincial organization founded in 1863
Mission: To serve the interests of tree fruit growers in Nova Scotia
Member of: Canadian Horticulture Council
Affiliation(s): Nova Scotia Federation of Agriculture
Finances: *Annual Operating Budget:* $100,000-$250,000
16 volunteer(s)
Membership: 220; *Fees:* Schedule available
Chief Officer(s):
C. Andrew Parker, President
Meetings/Conferences:
• Nova Scotia Fruit Growers' Association Annual Convention 2018, January, 2018, Old Orchard Inn, Greenwich, NS
Scope: Provincial

The Nova Scotia Genealogy Network Association (NSGNA)
indexgans@gmail.com
nsgna.ednet.ns.ca
Overview: A small local organization founded in 1996
Finances: *Annual Operating Budget:* Less than $50,000
10 volunteer(s)
Membership: 15; *Fees:* $25

Nova Scotia Gerontological Nurses Association (NSGNA)
PO Box 33101, Stn. Quinpool, Halifax NS B3L 4T6
ssavage@ssdha.nshealth.ca
www.nsgna.com

Overview: A medium-sized provincial organization founded in 1984 overseen by Canadian Gerontological Nursing Association
Mission: To promote a high standard of nursing care & related health services for older adults; To enhance professionalism in the practice of gerontological nursing
Membership: *Member Profile:* Nurses interested in gerontology
Activities: Offering professional networking opportunities; Providing professional development; Advocating for comprehensive services for older adults; Supporting research related to gerontological nursing; Promoting gerontological nursing to the public
Chief Officer(s):
Sohani Welcher, President, 902-473-8413
Sohani.welcher@cdha.nshealth.ca
Awards:
• NSGNA Scholarship
• NSGNA Certification Bursary
• Conference Bursary
Publications:
• NSGNA [Nova Scotia Gerontological Nurses Association] Newsletter
Type: Newsletter

Nova Scotia Golf Association (NSGA)
#216, 30 Damascus Rd., Bedford NS B4A 0C1
Tel: 902-468-8844; *Fax:* 902-484-5327
www.nsga.ns.ca
www.facebook.com/novascotiagolf
twitter.com/novascotiagolf
Overview: A medium-sized provincial organization founded in 1931 overseen by Golf Canada
Mission: To promote, foster & develop golf at all levels in Nova Scotia; to provide a liaison between member clubs & the Royal Canadian Golf Association; to consult & assist with member clubs on turf maintenance, handicap procedures, slope ratings, rule interpretations & junior development; to organize tournaments, in cooperation with member clubs, that determine provincial champions.
Member of: Canadian Golf Foundation; International Association of Golf Administrators; Sport Nova Scotia
Finances: *Funding Sources:* Membership dues; sponsors
Membership: *Member Profile:* Must be a member club
Chief Officer(s):
David Campbell, Executive Director
david@nsga.ns.ca
Jan Gaudette, Executive Assistant
jan@nsga.ns.ca

Nova Scotia Government & General Employees Union (NSGEU) / Syndicat de la fonction publique de la Nouvelle-Écosse
255 John Savage Ave., Dartmouth NS B3B 0J3
Tel: 902-424-4063; *Fax:* 902-424-2111
Toll-Free: 877-556-7438
www.nsgeu.ns.ca
Overview: A medium-sized local organization founded in 1958
Affiliation(s): Canadian Labour Congress; Nova Scotia Federation of Labour; National Union of Public & General Employees
Finances: *Funding Sources:* Membership dues
Staff Member(s): 54
Membership: 30,000 public & private sector employees; *Committees:* Constitution & By-Laws; Finance; Health, Safety & Environment; Human Rights; Political Action; Education; Women's Issues; Social/Recreation
Chief Officer(s):
Joan Jessome, President
Keiren Tompkins, Executive Director

Nova Scotia Government Libraries Council (NSGLC)
NS
Tel: 902-424-7214
www.nsglc.ednet.ns.ca
Overview: A small provincial organization
Mission: To provide a forum for government libraries to discuss common problems & share information
Chief Officer(s):
Ruth Hart, Chair
hartre@gov.ns.ca
Natalie MacPherson, Secretary, 902-424-8474
Anne Van Iderstine, Treasurer, 902-424-2078
vanideal@gov.ns.ca

Nova Scotia Ground Water Association (NSGWA)
#417, 3 - 644 Portland St., Dartmouth NS B2W 2M3
Fax: 902-435-0089
Toll-Free: 888-242-4440

nsgwa@ns.aliantzinc.ca
www.nsgwa.ca
Previous Name: Nova Scotia Well Drillers Association
Overview: A medium-sized provincial organization
Mission: To act as the voice of the industry to all levels of government; To encourage the management & protection of ground water
Membership: *Fees:* $100 associate, non-voting, non-certifed membership; $200 drillers, diggers, pump installers, suppliers, & technical personnel; *Member Profile:* Well drillers; Well diggers; Pump installers; Manufacturers; Suppliers; Technicians
Activities: Increasing public awareness; Encouraging partnerships; Providing continuing education; Presenting awards
Chief Officer(s):
Arthur Jefferson, President
Noreene McGuire, Secretary-Treasurer
Meetings/Conferences:
• Nova Scotia Ground Water Association 2018 Annual General Meeting, 2018, NS
Scope: Provincial
Description: A yearly gathering featuring divisional meetings, presentations, & association business
Publications:
• Water Talk [a publication of the Nova Scotia Ground Water Association]
Type: Newsletter; *Frequency:* Semiannually; *Accepts Advertising Profile:* A publication for Nova Scotia's well drillers & diggers, pump installers, technical personnel, manufacturerer, & suppliers to the ground waterindustry, featuring association happenings & industry news

Nova Scotia Guides Association
PO Box 641, Liverpool NS B0T 1K0
Tel: 902-682-2782
info@nsguides.ca
www.nsguides.ca
Overview: A small provincial organization
Mission: To recruit & train wilderness guides
Member of: Nova Scotia Federation of Anglers & Hunters
Membership: 17; *Member Profile:* Licensed guides in Nova Scotia
Activities: Maintaining a campground for seasonal camping

Nova Scotia Gymnastics Association *See* Gymnastics Nova Scotia

Nova Scotia Head Injury Association *See* Brain Injury Association of Nova Scotia

Nova Scotia Hearing & Speech Foundation
PO Box 120, #401, 5657 Spring Garden Rd., Halifax NS B3S 3R4
Tel: 902-492-8201
contact@hearingandspeech.ca
www.hearingandspeech.ca
twitter.com/NSHSF
Overview: A medium-sized provincial organization founded in 1999
Mission: To provide hearing services to all Nova Scotians & speech-language services to preschool children & adults; To work with community volunteer leaders, the families & friends of those who are hearing or speech impaired, our partners in government, & the medical & academic communities; To raise funds to support critical Centres' needs
Chief Officer(s):
Gordon Moore, Chair

Nova Scotia Heart Foundation *See* Heart & Stroke Foundation of Nova Scotia

Nova Scotia Hereford Club
Overview: A medium-sized provincial organization founded in 1940
Mission: To promote the Hereford breed of beef cattle
Affiliation(s): Maritime Hereford Association
Finances: *Annual Operating Budget:* Less than $50,000
64 volunteer(s)
Membership: 115 institutional + 30 student
Chief Officer(s):
Pat Ward, Director, 902-384-2878

Nova Scotia Hockey Association *See* Hockey Nova Scotia

Nova Scotia Home Builders' Association (NSHBA)
Bayers Lake Business Park, 124 Chain Lake Drive, #B, Halifax NS B3S 1A2
Tel: 902-450-5554; *Fax:* 902-450-5448
Toll-Free: 800-668-2001

nshba@nshba.ns.ca
nshomebuilders.ca
www.facebook.com/nshomebuilders
twitter.com/nshomebuilders
Overview: A small provincial organization founded in 1959 overseen by Canadian Home Builders' Association
Mission: To act as the voice of the residential construction industry in Nova Scotia; To promote quality, choice, & affordable housing for Nova Scotians
Finances: *Annual Operating Budget:* $500,000-$1.5 Million; *Funding Sources:* Membership dues; Program management; Home Show
Staff Member(s): 4; 18 volunteer(s)
Membership: 300 firms; *Fees:* Schedule available; *Member Profile:* Builders, renovators, developers; other stakeholders in the residential construction industry; *Committees:* Technical Research; Training & Education; Marketing; Renovators' Council; Economic Research; Women's Council; R-2000 Advisory Committee
Activities: Holding monthly member meetings; Organizing a Home Show; Offering workshops, courses, & networking opportunities; *Awareness Events:* Renovation Month, October; *Speaker Service:* Yes; *Rents Mailing List:* Yes; *Library:* by appointment
Chief Officer(s):
Sherry Donovan, Chief Executive Officer
sherry@nshba.ns.ca
Awards:
- Peter Kohler Peak Awards

Annapolis Valley
c/o Crowell Construction, 55 Highbury School Rd., RR #2, Kentville NS B4N 4K1
Tel: 902-678-8752; *Fax:* 902-678-8752
Chief Officer(s):
Steven Crowell, Executive Officer
crowlcon@eastlink.ca

Central Nova
Bayers Lake Business Park, 124 Chain Lake Dr., #B, Halifax NS B3S 1A2
Tel: 902-450-5554; *Fax:* 902-450-5448
Chief Officer(s):
Sherry Grant, Interim Chief Executive Officer

South Shore
NS
Chief Officer(s):
Andrew Joudrey, Secretary
andrew@projecthq.ca

Nova Scotia Horseshoe Players Association
NS
Tel: 902-852-3231; *Fax:* 902-852-2311
Overview: A small provincial organization overseen by Horseshoe Canada
Mission: To promote the sport of horseshoes in Canada
Member of: Horseshoe Canada
Chief Officer(s):
Cecil Mitchell, Contact
cmitchell@rainbownetrigging.com

Nova Scotia Horseshoe Players Association (NSHPA)
NS
Overview: A small provincial licensing organization founded in 1973 overseen by Horseshoe Canada
Mission: To promote the enjoyment & health benefits of the sport of horseshoe pitching throughout Nova Scotia
Member of: Sport Nova Scotia; Horseshoe Canada
Affiliation(s): Maritime Horseshoe Players Association
Finances: *Annual Operating Budget:* Less than $50,000; *Funding Sources:* Membership dues; fundraising; government grants
40 volunteer(s)
Membership: 35; *Committees:* Club Forming; Membership; Palladian Construction; Promotion
Activities: 8 sanctioned tournaments; TV Series; conducts Special Olympics for horseshoes; *Rents Mailing List:* Yes

Nova Scotia Hospice Palliative Care Association (NSHPCA)
PO Box 103, Lakeside NS B3T 1M6
Tel: 902-818-9139
info@nshpca.ca
www.nshpca.ca
Overview: A medium-sized provincial charitable organization founded in 1995
Mission: To strive towards achieving comfort & peace for persons living & dying with a life-threatening illness throughout Nova Scotia; to promote the philosophy & principles of palliative care through networking, public & professional education, advocacy & research; to educate & improve public awareness of the needs of those with a life-threatening illness; thus enabling & empowering communities to recognize the values, needs & wishes of all persons across all stages of life
Member of: Canadian Palliative Care Association
Membership: *Fees:* $50 individual; *Member Profile:* Interdisciplinary health professionals & volunteers
Activities: *Awareness Events:* Palliative Care Week, May
Chief Officer(s):
Carolyn Marshall, President

Nova Scotia Independent Adjusters' Association
c/o Michael Connolly, ClaimsPro, #220, 30 Damascus Rd., Halifax NS B4A 0C1
Tel: 902-835-5065; *Fax:* 902-835-0848
www.ciaa-adjusters.ca
Overview: A small local organization overseen by Canadian Independent Adjusters' Association
Member of: Canadian Independent Adjusters' Association
Chief Officer(s):
Michael Connolly, President
michael.connolly@scm.ca

Nova Scotia Insolvency Association *See* Nova Scotia Association of Insolvency & Restructuring Professionals

Nova Scotia Institute of Agrologists (NSIA)
Annapolis Building, 60 Research Dr., Bible Hill NS B6L 2R2
Tel: 902-897-6742
info@nsagrologists.ca
www.nsagrologists.ca
Overview: A medium-sized provincial licensing organization founded in 1953 overseen by Agricultural Institute of Canada
Finances: *Annual Operating Budget:* Less than $50,000; *Funding Sources:* Membership dues
15 volunteer(s)
Membership: 300; *Fees:* $20-$150
Activities: *Internships:* Yes; *Speaker Service:* Yes; *Library:* Not open to public
Chief Officer(s):
Carolyn Van Den Heuvel, President
Awards:
- Outstanding Farmer
- Outstanding Young Agrologist
- Distinguished Life Member
- Distinguished Agrologist
- NSIA Scholarship
; *Amount:* $1,000
- Honourary Member
- C.A. Douglas Award
- NSIA 50th Anniversary Scholarship
; *Amount:* $1,000

Nova Scotia Institute of the Purchasing Management Association of Canada *See* Supply Chain Management Association - Nova Scotia

Nova Scotia Insurance Women's Association (NSIWA)
c/o Lynne Gerhardt, Travelers Canada, #300, 100 Venture Run, Dartmouth NS B3B 0H9
Tel: 902-877-2129; *Fax:* 902-423-6812
www.nsiwa.com
Overview: A small local organization
Member of: Canadian Association of Insurance Women
Chief Officer(s):
Lynne Gerhardt, President
lgerhard@travelers.com

Nova Scotia Ladies Curling Association *See* Nova Scotia Curling Association

Nova Scotia League for Equal Opportunities (NSLEO)
#1211, 5251 Duke St., Halifax NS B3J 1P3
Tel: 902-455-6942; *Fax:* 902-454-4781
Toll-Free: 866-696-7536
nsleo@eastlink.ca
www.novascotialeo.org
www.facebook.com/451050828262446
www.twitter.com/wix
Also Known As: LEO
Overview: A medium-sized provincial charitable organization founded in 1979
Mission: To promote a barrier-free environment; To strive for equality; To achieve recognition of the abilities of people with disabilities so that they may function as equals in society
Member of: Council of Canadians with Disabilities (CCD)
Affiliation(s): Clare Organization Representing Disabilities; Community Involvement of the Disabled; Central Highlands Association of the Disabled; Disabled Consumer Society of Colchester; Richmond County Disabled
Staff Member(s): 2
Membership: 20; *Fees:* $50; *Member Profile:* Nova Scotians with disabilities; *Committees:* Transportation; Health Care; Nominating Constitution; Education
Activities: Challenge legislature; host regular information sessions; conduct research on accessible transportation, universal technical aids, health care/home care, attendant care provisions, building code regulations, regular contact with government officials; *Speaker Service:* Yes; *Library:* Resource Centre; by appointment
Chief Officer(s):
Emily Duffett, Chair
emily.duffett48@gmail.com
Kim Cicchino, Office Manager
Awards:
- Recognition & Lifestyles Awards
- Certificates for Volunteers

Nova Scotia Library Association (NSLA)
c/o Nova Scotia Provincial Library, 6016 University Ave., 5th Fl., Halifax NS B3H 1W4
www.nsla.ns.ca
Overview: A small provincial charitable organization founded in 1973
Mission: To promote the value of libraries; To facilitate the exchange of ideas & information among library workers in Nova Scotia
Membership: *Fees:* $25 individual; $50 institutions; *Member Profile:* Library workers in Nova Scotia
Activities: Enhancing the skills of library workers throughout Nova Scotia; Monitoring local issues at libraries in the province
Chief Officer(s):
Cindy Lelliott, President
president@nsla.ns.ca
Yvette Frost, Secretary
secretary@nsla.ns.ca
Tim Jackson, Treasurer
treasurer@nsla.ns.ca
Awards:
- Norman Horrocks Award for Library Leadership
To recognize contributions to the promotion & development of library service in Nova Scotia *Contact:* Yvette Frost, Secretary, E-mail: secretary@nsla.ns.ca
- Award for Library & Information Technology Student
To recognize the achievement of a graduating student *Contact:* Yvette Frost, Secretary, E-mail: secretary@nsla.ns.ca
- Award for School of Information Management Graduate
To recognize a graduating student with high academic achievement & a demonstrated commitment to public libraries *Contact:* Yvette Frost, Secretary, E-mail: secretary@nsla.ns.ca
- Emile Theriault Library & Information Technology Award
To recognize the efforts of a library support staff member who contributed to their library community *Contact:* Yvette Frost, Secretary, E-mail: secretary@nsla.ns.ca
- NSLA Conference Bursary
To provide financial assistance to a library staff person who is in need of assistance to attend the NSLA annual conference *Contact:* Yvette Frost, Secretary, E-mail: secretary@nsla.ns.ca
- NSLA Professional Support & Development Fund
Provides grants for projects or activities that will further the aims and objectives of NSLA *Contact:* Yvette Frost, Secretary, E-mail: secretary@nsla.ns.ca
Meetings/Conferences:
- Nova Scotia Library Association 2018 Annual Conference, 2018
Scope: Provincial
Description: Hosted by Cumberland Regional Library in the autumn
Contact Information: E-mail: conference@nsla.ns.ca
Publications:
- NSLA [Nova Scotia Library Association] Newsletter
Type: Newsletter; *Frequency:* Quarterly; *Editor:* Rosalind Morrison; *ISSN:* 1182-0209; *Price:* Free with Nova Scotia Library Association membership
Profile: Association business, regional news, & announcements

Nova Scotia Lighthouse Preservation Society (NSLPS)
c/o Maritime Museum of the Atlantic, 1675 Lower Water St., Halifax NS B3J 1S3
info@nslps.com
www.nslps.com
www.facebook.com/NSLPS1993
twitter.com/nslps
Overview: A medium-sized provincial charitable organization founded in 1994
Mission: To promote awareness & preservation of Nova Scotian lighthouses; To assist community groups in leasing or taking ownership of lighthouse sites; To provide access to written research & photographic documentation; To initiate oral history research, & to monitor the status of historic lighthouse sites
Member of: Federation of NS Heritage; World Lighthouse Society
Finances: *Annual Operating Budget:* Less than $50,000
12 volunteer(s)
Membership: 1,500; *Fees:* $20 single; $25 family; $15 single; $30 group affiliates; $50 sustaining; $100 patron; US$20 foreign
Activities: *Speaker Service:* Yes
Chief Officer(s):
Joanne McCormick, President

Nova Scotia Mackerel Fishermen's Association
RR#2, Hubbards NS B0J 1T0
Tel: 902-857-3619; *Fax:* 902-857-2057
Overview: A small provincial organization founded in 1992

The Nova Scotia Mineral & Gem Society (NSMGS)
N.S. Museum of Natural History, 1747 Summer St., Halifax NS B3H 3A6
info@novascotiamineralandgemsociety.com
www.novascotiamineralandgemsociety.com
Previous Name: The Mineral & Gem Society of Nova Scotia
Overview: A small provincial organization founded in 1957
Mission: To encourage & promote mineral collecting, gem cutting & allied activities among the members & the public; to encourage & assist in the exchange of information, technical knowledge, etc., among persons interested in these activities
Member of: Gem & Mineral Federation of Canada
Membership: *Fees:* $20
Activities: Meetings; auctions; lectures; slide shows; field trips
Chief Officer(s):
William Blinn, President

Nova Scotia Mink Breeders' Association
c/o Dan Mullen, 2124 Black Rock Rd., Waterville NS B0P 1V0
Tel: 902-680-5360; *Fax:* 902-538-7799
Overview: A small provincial organization founded in 1938
Mission: To foster better mink breeding among the members; to help secure market advantage.
Finances: *Funding Sources:* Membership fees
Membership: *Member Profile:* Licensed mink farmers; associate members
Activities: Sponsors live mink shows; field days; information meetings; short courses
Chief Officer(s):
Dan Mullen, President

Nova Scotia Minor Hockey Council
c/o Hockey Nova Scotia, #17, 7 Mellor Ave., Dartmouth NS B3B 0E8
Tel: 902-454-9400; *Fax:* 902-454-3883
Overview: A medium-sized provincial organization founded in 1974
Mission: To provide a standard set of playing rules for minor hockey in Nova Scotia
Affiliation(s): Nova Scotia Hockey Association
Chief Officer(s):
Arnie Farrell, Chair, 902-863-0221
arniefarrell@ns.sympatico.ca

Nova Scotia Music Educators' Association (NSMEA)
c/o NSMEA Membership Secretary, 1046 Church St., RR#1, Port Williams NS B0P 1T0
local.nstu.ca/web/nsmea
Overview: A small provincial organization founded in 1959
Mission: To promote & advance music education in Nova Scotia; To hold meetings, exhibitions & conferences for the discussion of problems & the exchange of views on matters relating to music education; To facilitate communication between music educators & the Department of Education through the Nova Scotia Teachers' Union
Member of: Nova Scotia Teachers Union
Finances: *Annual Operating Budget:* Less than $50,000
Staff Member(s): 10; 32 volunteer(s)
Membership: 31 student; 178 individual; *Fees:* $40 active; $19.50 student; $27.75 retired; *Member Profile:* Teachers of music or have an interest in music
Chief Officer(s):
Donalda Westcott, President
djwestcott@nstu.ca
Marg Kristie, Membership Secretary
mekristie@nstu.ca

Nova Scotia Native Women's Society (NSNWA)
PO Box 805, Truro NS B2N 5E8
Tel: 902-893-7402; *Fax:* 902-897-7162
www.facebook.com/nsnwa
Overview: A medium-sized provincial organization founded in 1972 overseen by Native Women's Association of Canada
Member of: Native Women's Association of Canada (NWAC)
Membership: 8,000

Nova Scotia Nature Trust (NSNT)
PO Box 2202, 2085 Maitland St., Halifax NS B3J 3C4
Tel: 902-425-5263; *Fax:* 902-429-5263
Toll-Free: 877-434-5263
nature@nsnt.ca
www.nsnt.ca
www.facebook.com/novascotianaturetrust
twitter.com/nsnaturetrust
www.youtube.com/user/naturetrust/videos
Overview: A medium-sized provincial organization founded in 1994
Mission: To protect Nova Scotia's outstanding natural legacy through land conservation.
Staff Member(s): 9
Chief Officer(s):
Corey Miller, President
Bonnie Sutherland, Executive Director
bonnie@nsnt.ca

Nova Scotia Nurses' Union (NSNU)
150 Garland Ave., Dartmouth NS B3B 0A7
Tel: 902-469-1474; *Fax:* 902-466-6935
Toll-Free: 800-469-1474
www.nsnu.ca
www.youtube.com/user/NSNursesUnion
Overview: A medium-sized provincial organization founded in 1976
Mission: To represent Registered Nurses & Licensed Practical Nurses working in acute & long term care, with the VON & Canadian Blood Services
Affiliation(s): Canadian Nurses Association; Canadian Labour Congress; Canadian Federation of Nurses Unions
Staff Member(s): 17
Membership: 6,500; *Committees:* Executive; Personnel; AGM Operations & Nominations; Constitution/Resolutions; Finance; Education
Chief Officer(s):
Janet Hazelton, President
janet.hazelton@nsnu.ca
Jean Candy, Executive Director
jean.candy@nsnu.ca
Cindy Herbert, Director, Finance & Operations
cindy.herbert@nsnu.ca

Nova Scotia Optometrical Society *See* Nova Scotia Association of Optometrists

Nova Scotia Pharmaceutical Society *See* Nova Scotia College of Pharmacists

Nova Scotia Physiotherapy Association (NSPA)
PO Box 33013, Halifax NS B3L 4T6
Tel: 902-223-0141
info@physiotherapyns.ca
www.physiotherapyns.ca
Overview: A medium-sized provincial organization overseen by Canadian Physiotherapy Association
Mission: To provide leadership & direction to the physiotherapy profession; To foster excellence in practice, education & research
Member of: Canadian Physiotherapy Association
Finances: *Funding Sources:* Membership dues; Educational activities
Membership: *Committees:* Awards; Professional Development; Public Relations
Activities: *Awareness Events:* National Physiotherapy Month, April 20 - May 20
Chief Officer(s):
Morah MacEachern, Executive Director
ed@physiotherapyns.ca
Alison McDonald, President
president@physiotherapyns.ca

Nova Scotia Powerlifting Association
240 Cusack Dr., Sydney NS B1P 6A1
Tel: 902-567-0893
Overview: A small provincial licensing organization overseen by Canadian Powerlifting Association
Mission: To provide opportunities for lifters to learn the sport of powerlifting through seminars, gyms & clubs; to participate in meets locally, nationally & internationally
Member of: International Powerlifting Union
Membership: *Member Profile:* Novice; Junior; Master; Open; Special Olympian divisions; provincial, national & world calibre lifters
Activities: Lifters attend competitions on provincial, national & international levels & receive medallions or trophies according to placement; seminars given upon request
Chief Officer(s):
John Fraser, President
johnfraser56@hotmail.com

Nova Scotia Progressive Conservative Association
#1003, 1660 Hollis St., Halifax NS B3J 1V7
Tel: 902-429-9470; *Fax:* 902-423-2465
Toll-Free: 800-595-8679
www.pcparty.ns.ca
www.facebook.com/nspcparty
twitter.com/nspc
www.youtube.com/user/pcnovascotia
Also Known As: PC Party of Nova Scotia
Overview: A medium-sized provincial organization
Mission: To form a fiscally responsible, socially progressive government
Finances: *Annual Operating Budget:* $250,000-$500,000; *Funding Sources:* Donations
Staff Member(s): 4; 25 volunteer(s)
Membership: 30,000+; *Fees:* $10
Activities: *Speaker Service:* Yes; *Rents Mailing List:* Yes
Chief Officer(s):
Jamie Baillie, Party Leader
JamieBaillie@gov.ns.ca
Jim David, Provincial Director
jim.david@pcparty.ns.ca

Nova Scotia Prospectors Association (NSPA)
65 Amaranth Cres., Dartmouth NS B2W 4L1
www.prospectors.ns.ca
Overview: A medium-sized provincial organization founded in 1993
Mission: The Nova Scotia Prospectors Association was formed to foster prospecting at the professional and recreational level.
Membership: *Fees:* $30 individual; $35 family; $10 student
Chief Officer(s):
Matt Abel, President
president@prospectors.ns.ca
John Wightman, Executive Director
Ken Mallett, Secretary
secretary@prospectors.ns.ca

Nova Scotia Provincial Literacy Coalition *See* Literacy Nova Scotia

Nova Scotia Public Interest Research Group (NSPIRG)
Student Union Building, Dalhousie University, #24, 6136 University Ave., Halifax NS B3H 4J2
Tel: 902-494-6662
Other Communication: board@nspirg.org
info@nspirg.ca
www.nspirg.ca
www.facebook.com/NSPIRG
twitter.com/NSPIRG
Overview: A medium-sized provincial organization
Mission: To link research with social justice & environmental action
Finances: *Annual Operating Budget:* Less than $50,000
Membership: 5,000-14,999; *Fees:* $4; *Member Profile:* Dalhousie University students
Activities: *Speaker Service:* Yes; *Library:* Resource Library
Chief Officer(s):
Clark MacIntosh, Coordinator, Resources & Administration
resource@nspirg.ca
Mahbubur Rahman, Coordinator, Outreach & Administration
outreach@nspirg.ca

Nova Scotia PWA Coalition *See* AIDS Coalition of Nova Scotia

Nova Scotia Real Estate Appraisers Association (NSREAA)
#602, 5670 Spring Garden Rd., Halifax NS B3J 1H6
Tel: 902-422-4077; *Fax:* 902-422-3717
nsreaa@nsappraisal.ns.ca
nsreaa.ca
Also Known As: The Appraisal Institute of Canada - Nova Scotia (AIC-NS)
Previous Name: Nova Scotia Association of the Appraisal Institute of Canada
Overview: A medium-sized provincial licensing organization overseen by Appraisal Institute of Canada
Mission: The Association regulates the practice of real estate appraisal in Nova Scotia, establishes & promotes the interests of appraisers, develops & maintains high standards of knowledge & best practices in the field, develops & enforces professional ethics, promotes public awareness of the profession, & encourages studies in real estate appraisal.
Finances: *Annual Operating Budget:* $50,000-$100,000
Staff Member(s): 1; 12 volunteer(s)
Membership: 250; *Member Profile:* Appraisers; assessors; candidate members; *Committees:* Executive; Examiners; Complaints; Discipline; Education; Membership & Public Relations; Political Action
Chief Officer(s):
Carla Dempsey, President
Davida Mackay, Executive Director & Registrar
Awards:
• Butler Education Award
• NSREAA Certificate of Appreciation

Nova Scotia Real Estate Association *See* Nova Scotia Association of REALTORS

Nova Scotia Real Estate Commission (NSREC)
7 Scarfe Ct., Dartmouth NS B3B 1W4
Tel: 902-468-3511; *Fax:* 902-468-1016
Toll-Free: 800-390-1015
info@nsrec.ns.ca
www.nsrec.ns.ca
Overview: A small provincial organization
Mission: To protect consumers by establishing standards for applicants and licensees in the real estate industry, which will promote higher standards of professionalism, competance and integrity.
Chief Officer(s):
Brad Chisholm, Registrar
bchisholm@nsrec.ns.ca

Nova Scotia Recreation Professionals in Health (NSRPH)
c/o MacGillivray Guest Home, 25 Xavier Dr., Sydney NS B1S 2R9
Tel: 902-539-6110; *Fax:* 902-567-0437
www.nsrph.com
www.facebook.com/NSRPH
Overview: A small provincial organization founded in 1994
Mission: To allow for recreation professionals to communicate, network, & share concerns & ideas; To advocate for the necessity & benefits of recreation in the health care system
Finances: *Funding Sources:* Membership dues
Membership: *Fees:* $50
Chief Officer(s):
Shelly Luddington, President
shelly.luddington@theadmiralltc.com
Dawn MacDonald, Vice-President, Communications
Dawn.MacDonald@nscc.ca

Nova Scotia Rifle Association (NSRA)
PO Box 482, Dartmouth NS B2Y 3Y8
Tel: 902-456-7468
nsrifle@ns.sympatico.ca
www.nsrifle.org
Overview: A small provincial organization founded in 1861
Mission: To promote & organize recreational shooting
Member of: Dominion of Canada Rifle Association
Affiliation(s): Shooting Federation of Canada
Finances: *Annual Operating Budget:* Less than $50,000
12 volunteer(s)
Membership: 300; *Fees:* $295 senior; $20 junior (under 19); *Member Profile:* Residents of the province with a valid firearm license
Chief Officer(s):
Andy S. Webber, President
asw@tangenttheta.com

Dave G. Beaulieu, Secretary

Nova Scotia Road Builders Association
#217, 11 Thornhill Dr., Dartmouth NS B3B 1R9
www.nsrba.ca
Overview: A medium-sized provincial organization founded in 1947 overseen by Canadian Construction Association
Mission: To speak for the heavy construction industry in Nova Scotia; To liaise with provincial Department of Transportation
Finances: *Annual Operating Budget:* $100,000-$250,000
Staff Member(s): 2
Membership: 140 member companies; *Fees:* $2,000-$10,000; *Committees:* Contracts & Specifications; Environment; Municipal Affairs; CCA/TRIP; Communications; TANS/Labour Relations; Rental Rates; Safety; Convention/Membership; Newsletter/Media & Website
Chief Officer(s):
Grant Feltmate, Executive Director, 902-499-7278, Fax: 902-876-1294
grant@nsrba.ca
Carol Ingraham, Office Manager
carol@nsrba.ca

Nova Scotia Rugby Football Union
5516 Spring Garden Rd., 4th Fl., Halifax NS B3J 1G6
Tel: 902-425-5450; *Fax:* 902-425-5606
rugby@sportnovascotia.ca
www.rugbyns.ns.ca
Also Known As: Rugby Nova Scotia
Overview: A small provincial organization founded in 1965 overseen by Rugby Canada
Mission: To promote, control, encourage & develop the game of rugby union football throughout Nova Scotia
Member of: Rugby Canada
Affiliation(s): International Rugby Board
Chief Officer(s):
Geno Carew, President

Nova Scotia Safety Council; The Nova Scotia Highway Safety Council *See* Safety Services Nova Scotia

Nova Scotia Salmon Association (NSSA)
PO Box 396, Chester NS B0J 1J0
nssasalmon@gmail.com
www.nssalmon.ca
Overview: A medium-sized provincial charitable organization founded in 1963 overseen by Atlantic Salmon Federation
Mission: To further the conservation & wise management of wild Atlantic salmon & trout
Member of: Atlantic Salmon Federation
Finances: *Funding Sources:* Donations
Membership: *Fees:* $20 full; $5 junior; *Member Profile:* Individuals with an interest in the welfare of salmon & trout; Affiliate associations
Activities: Increasing public awareness; Offering educational activities; Conducting & supporting research; Administering programs, such as Adopt-A-Stream
Chief Officer(s):
Rene Aucoin, President

Nova Scotia School Athletic Federation (NSSAF)
5516 Spring Garden Rd., Halifax NS B3J 1G6
Tel: 902-425-8662; *Fax:* 902-425-5606
nssaf.ednet.ns.ca
Overview: A small provincial organization overseen by School Sport Canada
Mission: Motto: "Education Through Sport" which thus emphasises the value of sport in relation to the multitude of benefits that participation gives to their students.
Member of: School Sport Canada
Staff Member(s): 3
Membership: 40,000 student athletes; *Member Profile:* Student atheletes and their affiliates including coaches, administrators, and officiates.
Chief Officer(s):
Darrell LeBlanc, Chair, Board of Governors
Darrell Dempster, Executive Director
Dianne Weston, Secretary

Nova Scotia School Boards Association (NSSBA) / Association des conseils scolaires de la Nouvelle-Écosse
#395, 3 Spectacle Lake Dr., Dartmouth NS B3B 1W8
Tel: 902-491-2888
info@nssba.ca
www.nssba.ca
www.linkedin.com/company/nova-scotia-school-boards-associati on
www.facebook.com/NovaScotiaSchoolBoardsAssociation
twitter.com/NSSchoolBoards
www.youtube.com/user/NSSBA2012?feature=mhee
Overview: A medium-sized provincial organization founded in 1954 overseen by Canadian School Boards Association
Mission: To act as the voice for school boards in Nova Scotia; To strive towards excellence in public education for students in the province
Staff Member(s): 3
Membership: *Committees:* Audit; Central Purchasing; Communications; Education; Finance; Leaders Advisory; Members' Employees Benefits; MOU; Nominations; Pension Trustees; Resolutions
Activities: Providing services to school boards such as bulk purchasing; Offering training opportunities; Advocating for school boards; Presenting awards; Providing information for school boards, parents, students, educators, journalists, & others
Chief Officer(s):
Nancy Pynch-Worthylake, Executive Director, 902-491-2855
npynch-worthylake@nssba.ca
Awards:
• The School Board Member Long Service Award
Awarded to recognize long-term members who have dedicated their time to the improvement of public education; awarded in levels of service length (ten years, fifteen years, twenty years, & twenty-five years)
• The Montgomery Award
• The Education Week Partner Award
Awarded to recognize teachers & school board members who have contributed significantly to student achievement

Nova Scotia School Counsellor Association (NSSCA)
c/o Amherst Regional High School, 190 Willow St., Amherst NS B4H 3W5
Tel: 902-661-2540; *Fax:* 902-661-2535
local.nstu.ca/web/nssca
Overview: A small provincial organization founded in 1965
Affiliation(s): Nova Scotia Teachers Union
Finances: *Annual Operating Budget:* Less than $50,000
Membership: 200; *Fees:* $20
Chief Officer(s):
Teri Cochrane, President
trcochrane@nstu.ca

Nova Scotia Securities Commission (NSSC)
Duke Tower, PO Box 458, #400, 5251 Duke St., Halifax NS B3J 2P8
Tel: 902-424-7768; *Fax:* 902-424-4625
nsscinquiries@novascotia.ca
nssc.novascotia.ca
twitter.com/NSSCommission
Overview: A medium-sized provincial organization overseen by Canadian Securities Administrators
Mission: To regulate securities trading in Nova Scotia, through the administration of the Securities Act; To report to the Legislature, through the minister responsible for the administration of the Securities Act; To foster a fair & competitive securities market; To protect investors & market integrity
Member of: Canadian Securities Administrators
Finances: *Funding Sources:* Fees collected from market participants under the legislation
Chief Officer(s):
Paul E. Radford, Chair
Publications:
• Annual Accountability Report [a publication of the Nova Scotia Securities Commission]
Type: Report; *Frequency:* Annually
• Nova Scotia Securities Commission Annual Report
Type: Report; *Frequency:* Annually
• Statement of Mandate [a publication of the Nova Scotia Securities Commission]
Type: Report; *Frequency:* Annually

Nova Scotia Shorthorn Association
1538 Millbrook Rd., RR#2, West River Station NS B0K 1Z0
Tel: 902-396-1937
www.facebook.com/375661389206631
Overview: A small provincial organization
Member of: Canadian Shorthorn Association
Chief Officer(s):
Adam Fraser, President
Kristy Fraser, Secretary

Nova Scotia Snowboard Association *See* Snowboard Nova Scotia

Nova Scotia Society for the Prevention of Cruelty to Animals (NS SPCA)
PO Box 38073, Stn. Burnside, 11 Akerley Blvd., Dartmouth NS B3B 1X2
Tel: 902-835-4798; *Fax:* 902-835-7885
Toll-Free: 844-835-4798
info@spcans.ca
www.spcans.ca
www.facebook.com/nsspca
twitter.com/nsspca
www.instagram.com/nsspca
Also Known As: Nova Scotia SPCA
Overview: A medium-sized provincial charitable organization founded in 1877 overseen by Canadian Federation of Humane Societies
Mission: To prevent abuse & neglect of all animals in Nova Scotia; To provide leadership in humane education through outreach activities & adoption services; To enforce laws on animal cruelty by issuing orders, warrants & laying charges
Member of: Canadian Federation of Humane Societies
Finances: *Annual Operating Budget:* $500,000-$1.5 Million; *Funding Sources:* Donations & bequests
Staff Member(s): 4; 3 volunteer(s)
Membership: 11 branches; *Fees:* $15 single; $30 family; *Committees:* Education; Finance; Fundraising; Investigations
Chief Officer(s):
Elizabeth Murphy, Chief Executive Officer
emurphy@spcans.ca

Antigonish Branch
PO Box 1421, Antigonish NS B2G 2L2
Tel: 902-863-2111; *Fax:* 902-863-1229
antigonish@spcans.ca
spcans.ca/branch-antigonish
www.facebook.com/nsspca.antigonish
Chief Officer(s):
Raylene Dewan, Acting President

Cape Breton Branch
401 East Broadway, Sydney NS B1N 3K1
Tel: 902-539-7722; *Fax:* 902-539-7391
capebreton@spcans.ca
spcans.ca/capebreton_branch
www.facebook.com/nsspca.capebreton
Chief Officer(s):
Barbara Tryon, Vice-President

Colchester Branch
PO Box 914, 408 Industrial Ave., Truro NS B2N 5G7
Tel: 902-893-7968; *Fax:* 902-895-6550
colchester@spcans.ca
spcans.ca/colchester_branch
www.facebook.com/nsspca.colchester
Chief Officer(s):
Leah McDonald, President

Hants Branch
PO Box 2274, Windsor NS B0N 2T0
Tel: 902-757-2000
hants@spcans.ca
spcans.ca/hants_branch
www.facebook.com/nsspca.hants
Chief Officer(s):
Sylvia Hunter, Treasurer

Kings Branch
1285 County Home Rd., Waterville NS B0P 1V0
Tel: 902-538-9075
kings@spcans.ca
spcans.ca/kingscounty
www.facebook.com/nsspca.kings
Chief Officer(s):
Paula Hasler, Secretary

La Baie Branch
PO Box 159, Saulnierville NS B0W 2Z0
Tel: 902-770-0099
labaie@spcans.ca
spcans.ca/labaiebranch
www.facebook.com/nsspca.labaie
Chief Officer(s):
Gail Melanson, Co-Chair

Lunenburg Branch
RR#1, Riverport NS B0J 2W0
Tel: 902-766-4787
lunenburg@spcans.ca
spcans.ca/lunenburg_branch
www.facebook.com/nsspca.lunenburg
Chief Officer(s):
Doreen Gillespie, President

Pictou Branch
PO Box 786, 3504 Granton Rd., New Glasgow NS B2H 5G2
Tel: 902-396-3595
pictou@spcans.ca
spcans.ca/pictoucounty
www.facebook.com/nsspca.pictou
Chief Officer(s):
Lori Sutherland, President

Dartmouth Branch
5 Scarfe Ct., Dartmouth NS B3B 1W4
Tel: 902-468-7877; *Fax:* 902-468-9761
dartmouth@spcans.ca
spcans.ca/dartmouthshelter
www.facebook.com/nsspca.pas

Queens Branch
PO Box 2012, Liverpool NS B0T 1K0
Tel: 902-350-2444
queens@spcans.ca
spcans.ca/queensbranch
www.facebook.com/QueensSpca
Chief Officer(s):
Jill Grafton, Secretary

Yarmouth Branch
RR#4, 298 Hardscratch Rd., Yarmouth NS B5A 4A8
Tel: 902-742-9767
yarmouth@spcans.ca
spcans.ca/yarmouth_branch
www.facebook.com/nsspca.yarmouth
Chief Officer(s):
Elizabeth Murphy, Contact, 902-835-4798 Ext. 228

Nova Scotia Society of Occupational Therapists (NSSOT)
Halifax Shopping Centre, Box 11, #2132B, 6960 Mumford Rd., Halifax NS B3L 4P1
Toll-Free: 866-936-7768
nssot@bellaliant.com
www.nssot.ca
Overview: A small provincial organization
Mission: An organization that strives for occupational therapy to be accessible & effective in order to maximize the independent living potential of all Nova Scotians despite disability or disadvantage; to promote development of occupational therapy practice through continuing education, support & advocacy of members & their clients
Affiliation(s): Canadian Association of Occupation Therapy
Finances: *Annual Operating Budget:* Less than $50,000
Staff Member(s): 2; 10 volunteer(s)
Membership: 330; *Fees:* $75 practicing, $40 non-practicing; $10 student
Activities: *Awareness Events:* National Occupational Therapy Month, Oct.; *Speaker Service:* Yes
Chief Officer(s):
Anne Carswell, Executive Director
Jen Davis, President

Nova Scotia Special Olympics *See* Special Olympics Nova Scotia

Nova Scotia Speed Skating Association *See* Speed Skate Nova Scotia

Nova Scotia Sport Heritage Centre *See* Novia Scotia Sports Hall of Fame

Nova Scotia Stamp Club (NSSC)
102 Birch Bear Run, Lewis Lake NS B3Z 4B8
www.nsstampclub.ca
Overview: A small provincial organization founded in 1922
Mission: To promote awareness & enjoyment of the hobby of philately & provide a forum for discussion of topics related to philately for the advancement of members knowledge
Member of: American Philatelic Society
Affiliation(s): Royal Philatelic Society of Canada
Finances: *Annual Operating Budget:* Less than $50,000
14 volunteer(s)
Membership: 120; *Fees:* $15 individual; $22.50 couple; $20 US; $25 international; *Member Profile:* Individuals 16 years of age & older; *Committees:* Executive; Membership
Activities: *Awareness Events:* NOVAPEX, Sept. *Library:* NSSC Library; Not open to public
Chief Officer(s):
Marilyn Melanson, Treasurer
Publications:
• The Nova Scotia Post [a publication of the Nova Scotia Stamp Club]
Type: Newsletter; *Frequency:* 10 pa

Nova Scotia Swordfish Association
#9, 155 Chainlake Dr., Halifax NS B3S 1B3
Tel: 902-737-4327; *Fax:* 902-457-4990
highliner@ns.sympatico.ca
Overview: A small provincial organization
Chief Officer(s):
George Rennehan, Vice-President

Nova Scotia Table Tennis Association (NSTTA)
5526 Spring Garden Rd., Halifax NS B3J 3G6
Tel: 902-425-5450
info@nstta.ca
nstta.ca
Overview: A small provincial organization overseen by Table Tennis Canada
Member of: Table Tennis Canada
Affiliation(s): International Table Tennis Federation
Chief Officer(s):
Dave Greenough, President
dwg@eastlink.ca

Nova Scotia Teachers Association of Literacy & Learning (NSTALL)
NS
nstall.nstu.ca
Overview: A small provincial organization
Publications:
• NSTALL [Nova Scotia Teachers Association of Literacy & Learning] Newsletter
• Salt Breezes & Fireflies [a publication of the Nova Scotia Teachers Association of Literacy & Learning]
Profile: An online publication collecting writings by Nova Scotia students.

Nova Scotia Teachers Union (NSTU) / Syndicat des enseignants de la Nouvelle-Écosse
Dr. Tom Parker Bldg., 3106 Joseph Howe Dr., Halifax NS B3L 4L7
Tel: 902-477-5621; *Fax:* 902-477-3517
Toll-Free: 800-565-6788
centraloffice@nstu.ca
www.nstu.ca
www.facebook.com/nsteachersunion
twitter.com/NSTeachersUnion
www.youtube.com/nstuwebcast
Overview: A medium-sized provincial organization founded in 1895 overseen by Canadian Teachers' Federation
Mission: To unify the teaching profession in Nova Scotia; To improve the quality of education
Affiliation(s): Canadian Teachers' Federation
Finances: *Funding Sources:* Membership dues
Membership: 10,600; *Member Profile:* K-12 public school teachers; Atlantic Provinces Special Education Authority teachers; Nova Scotia Community College teachers; Professional support staff
Activities: Advocating on behalf of members; Promoting the teaching profession; Offering professional development opportunities; Conducting research; *Library:* Bruce Hunter Memorial Library
Chief Officer(s):
Joan Ling, Executive Director
jling@staff.nstu.ca
Awards:
• Honourary Membership Award
• Life Membership Award
• Special Award
• Local Service Award
• Public Education Advocacy Award
• Retired Member Recognition Award
• Lieutenant Governor's Teaching Award

Nova Scotia Tennis Association
5516 Spring Garden Rd., 4th Fl., Halifax NS B3J 1G6
Tel: 902-425-5454
tennisns@sportnovascotia.ca
www.tennisnovascotia.ca
www.facebook.com/109415259125199
twitter.com/TennisNovaScoti
Overview: A medium-sized provincial organization overseen by Tennis Canada
Mission: To promote & create opportunities for people to play tennis in Nova Scotia
Member of: Tennis Canada
Staff Member(s): 2
Membership: *Member Profile:* Individuals & clubs
Chief Officer(s):
Craig Bethune, President

Roger Keating, Executive Director
Marijke Nel, Technical Director
mnel@sportnovascotia.ca

Nova Scotia Trails Federation (NSTF)
5516 Spring Garden Rd., 4th Fl., Halifax NS B3Z 1E8
Tel: 902-425-5450; Fax: 902-425-5606
www.novascotiatrails.com
www.facebook.com/nstrails
twitter.com/NSTrails
Also Known As: Nova Scotia Trails
Overview: A large provincial organization
Mission: To promote the development & responsible use of recreational trails for the benefit & enjoyment of all Nova Scotians & visitors to the province
Membership: 6000+; Fees: $200 associate/user group/community group; $20 individual
Chief Officer(s):
Holly Woodill, President
president@novascotiatrails.com
Vanda Jackson, Executive Director
vanda@novascotiatrails.com

Nova Scotia Union of Public & Private Employees (CCU) (NSUPE) / Syndicat des employés du secteur public de la Nouvelle-Écosse (CCU)
#402A, 7020 Mumford Rd., Halifax NS B3L 4S9
Tel: 902-422-9495; Fax: 902-429-7655
www.nsupe.ca
Previous Name: Nova Scotia Union of Public Employees (CCU)
Overview: A medium-sized provincial organization founded in 1974
Mission: To better & protect the livelihood and the social and economic well-being of its members, their families and fellow citizens.
Affiliation(s): Confederation of Canadian Unions; Atlantic Council of the Confederation of Canadian Unions
Finances: Funding Sources: Membership dues
Staff Member(s): 3
Membership: 2,000 + 10 locals; Member Profile: Professional; trade & technical; administrative; clerical
Chief Officer(s):
Joe Kaiser, President
Claudia MacFarlane, Vice-President

Nova Scotia Union of Public Employees (CCU) See Nova Scotia Union of Public & Private Employees (CCU)

Nova Scotia Veterinary Medical Association
15 Cobequid Rd., Lower Sackville NS B4C 2M9
Tel: 902-865-1876; Fax: 902-865-2001
info@nsvma.ca
www.nsvma.ca
Overview: A small provincial licensing organization overseen by Canadian Veterinary Medical Association
Mission: To license Nova Scotia veterinarians in small animal, large animal & mixed practice as well as those employed in government, industry or other institutions
Finances: Funding Sources: Membership dues
Staff Member(s): 3
Membership: 317; Fees: Schedule available; Member Profile: Licensed to practice in Nova Scotia
Chief Officer(s):
Frank Richardson, Registrar
Rob Doucette, President

Nova Scotia Water Ski Association See Water Ski Wakeboard Nova Scotia

Nova Scotia Well Drillers Association See Nova Scotia Ground Water Association

Nova Scotia Wild Flora Society
c/o Nova Scotia Museum of Natural History, 1747 Summer St., Halifax NS B3H 3A6
Tel: 902-423-7032
nswildflora@yahoo.ca
www.nswildflora.ca
Overview: A small provincial organization founded in 1990
Member of: Federation of Nova Scotia Naturalists
Affiliation(s): Canadian Wildflower Society
Finances: Annual Operating Budget: Less than $50,000; Funding Sources: Membership dues
2 volunteer(s)
Membership: 50; Fees: $15 individual; $20 family
Chief Officer(s):
Charles Cron, President
ccron72@hotmail.com

Heather Drope, Secretary-Treasurer

Nova Scotia Wool Marketing Board
c/o Natural Products Marketing Council, NS Dept. of Agriculture, PO Box 190, Halifax NS B3J 2M4
Overview: A small provincial organization founded in 1943
Mission: To foster the production of high-quality wool in Nova Scotia, & the effective marketing of this product
3 volunteer(s)
Membership: 250 individual

Nova Scotia Yachting Association See Sail Nova Scotia

Nova Scotia Youth Orchestra
6199 Chebucto Rd., Halifax NS B3L 1K7
Tel: 902-423-5984
info@novascotiayouthorchestra.com
www.novascotiayouthorchestra.com
www.facebook.com/novascotiayouthorchestra
twitter.com/nsyorchestra
Overview: A small provincial charitable organization founded in 1977 overseen by Orchestras Canada
Mission: To provide young musicians with the finest orchestral training; to provide live orchestral music to audiences in Nova Scotia
Finances: Funding Sources: Government; Individual & corporate donations
Membership: 93; Member Profile: Musicians ages 12-22 who are full-time students
Activities: Performing regular concerts; Providing comprehensive musical education for its members through regular rehearsal; Library: Not open to public
Chief Officer(s):
Dinuk Wijeratne, Music Director
dinuk@novascotiayouthorchestra.com
Linda Bull, General Manager
linda@novascotiayouthorchestra.com

Nova Scotian Institute of Science (NSIS)
Science Services, Killam Library, Dalhousie Univ., 6225 University Ave., Halifax NS B3H 4H8
Tel: 902-494-3621; Fax: 902-494-2062
nsis.chebucto.org
Overview: A medium-sized provincial organization founded in 1862
Mission: To provide a forum for scientists & those interested in science
Membership: Fees: $20 regular; $10 student; $300 life members; Member Profile: Individual with an amateur or professional interest in science
Activities: Conducting the NSIS Student Essay Competition; Providing a public lecture series; Library: Killam Library, Dalhousie University, Halifax, NS
Chief Officer(s):
Tom Rand, President
Patrick Ryall, Vice-President
Linda Marks, Secretary
Angelica Silva, Treasurer

Novia Scotia Sports Hall of Fame (NSSHF)
#446, 1800 Argyle St., Halifax NS B3J 3N8
Tel: 902-421-1266; Fax: 902-425-1148
sporthalloffame@eastlink.ca
www.novascotiasporthalloffame.com
www.linkedin.com/company/nova-scotia-sport-hall-of-fame
www.facebook.com/116064731766960
twitter.com/NSSHF
Previous Name: Nova Scotia Sport Heritage Centre
Overview: A small provincial organization founded in 1964
Staff Member(s): 5
Activities: Awareness Events: Golf Tournament, June; Bingo @ the Halifax Forum
Chief Officer(s):
Don Mills, Chair
Bill Robinson, CEO
bill@nsshf.com

NSERC Chair for Women in Science & Engineering
350 Albert St., Ottawa ON K1A 1H5
Tel: 613-944-6240; Fax: 613-996-2589
cwse-cfsg@nserc-crsng.gc.ca
www.nserc-crsng.gc.ca
Overview: A medium-sized national organization founded in 1996
Mission: To encourage women in Canada to enter careers in science, engineering, mathematics & computer sciences; to encourage women in Canada to attain high levels of professional achievement in these fields; to serve as an information centre for & about women in these fields; to make people aware of Canadian women scientists & engineers & of career opportunities available to them; to provide a forum for discussion of subjects of interest to members
Finances: Annual Operating Budget: Less than $50,000
Membership: 360; Fees: $250 corporate; $40 full; $25 associate; $10 student; $20 information (receives newsletter)
Activities: Speaker Service: Yes
Chief Officer(s):
Carolyn J. Emerson, Chair, Atlantic Region
  British Columbia/Yukon
  c/o Westcoast Women in Engineering, Science & Technology, #2054, 6250 Applied Science Ln., Vancouver BC V6T 1Z4
  Tel: 604-822-6584; Fax: 604-822-2403
  wwest@mech.ubc.ca
  wwest.mech.ubc.ca
  Chief Officer(s):
  Jennifer Pelletier, Manager
  Ontario
  c/o Department of Mechanical Engineering, University of Ottawa, 161 Louis Pasteur, Ottawa ON K1N 6H5
  info@scieng-women-ontario.ca
  scieng-women-ontario.ca
  www.facebook.com/CWSE.ON
  twitter.com/CWSE_ON
  pinterest.com/cwseon
  Chief Officer(s):
  Cahterine Mavriplis, Chair
  Prairie Region
  c/o Fort Garry Campus of the University of Manitoba, Winnipeg MB R3T 2N2
  cwse-prairies.ca
  www.facebook.com/cwseprairies
  Chief Officer(s):
  Jackie Onagi, Chair, Prairie Region, 204-474-9556, Fax: 204-474-7644
  Jacqueline.onagi@umanitoba.ca
  WISE (Women in Science & Engineering) Newfoundland & Labrador
  #293, 38 Pearson St., St. John's NL A1A 3R1
  Tel: 709-864-2484
  info@wisenl.ca
  www.wisenl.ca
  www.facebook.com/245047002313019
  Mission: To increase female involvement in the science, technology, engineering & math fields
  Chief Officer(s):
  Gloria Montano, President

Nuclear Insurance Association of Canada (NIAC) / Association canadienne d'assurance nucléaire
#1600, 401 Bay St., Toronto ON M5H 2Y4
Tel: 416-646-6232
www.niac.biz
www.linkedin.com/company/5279485
www.facebook.com/648772525244971
twitter.com/NIACanada
www.youtube.com/channel/UCpwR0r-ONaYt6TDZXwf64hA
Overview: A small national organization founded in 1958
Mission: NIAC is a voluntary, non-profit association of insurers. Members may provide insurance protection by participation in property and liability pools; the association underwrites and accepts nuclear risks located within Canadian territorial limits for Nuclear Liability and Physical Damage (liability &/or property insurance)
Member of: Canadian Nuclear Association
Staff Member(s): 2
Chief Officer(s):
Colleen P. DeMerchant, Manager
colleen@niac.biz

Numeris
1500 Don Mills Rd., 3rd Fl., Toronto ON M3B 3L7
Tel: 416-445-9800; Fax: 416-445-8644
en.numeris.ca
Previous Name: BBM Bureau of Measurement; Bureau of Broadcast Measurement; BBM Canada
Overview: A large national organization founded in 1944
Mission: To provide broadcast measurement & consumer behaviour data to broadcasters, advertisers, & agencies
Finances: Funding Sources: Membership fees
Membership: 1,600 organizations; Member Profile: Licensed radio/TV broadcasters; Advertisers; Agencies

Activities: Surveys, reports & guides
Chief Officer(s):
Neil McEneaney, President & CEO
Lisa Eaton, Senior Vice-President, Member Engagement
Jacques Gaboury, Vice-President, Legal
Anna Giagkou, Vice-President, Finance
Ricardo Gomez-Insausti, Vice-President, Research
Jane Hill, Vice-President, Operations
Dorena Quinn, Vice-President, People & Culture
Shawn Sheridan, Vice-President, Information Technology
- **Moncton Office**
  #600, 1234 Main St., Moncton NB E1C 1H7
  Tel: 506-859-7700; *Fax:* 506-852-4445
- **Montréal Office**
  #840, 800, boul René-Lévesque ouest, Montréal QC H3B 1X9
  Tél: 514-878-9711; *Téléc:* 514-878-4210
- **Western Office**
  #300, 13700 International Place, Richmond BC V6V 2X8
  Tel: 604-248-0770; *Fax:* 604-214-9648

Nunasi Corporation
PO Box 1559, Iqaluit NU X0A 0H0
Tel: 867-979-8920; *Fax:* 867-979-8921
www.nunasi.com
Overview: A small local organization founded in 1976
Mission: To support shareholders & maximize profits; To provide training, employment, & economic opportunities for Inuit of Nunavut
Chief Officer(s):
Greg Cayen, President & CEO
greg@nunasi.com

Nunavummi Disabilities Makinnasuaqtiit Society (NDMS) / Société Nunavummi Disabilities Makinnasuaqtiit
PO Box 4212, #105, 8 Storey Bldg., Iqaluit NU X0A 1H0
Tel: 867-979-2228
Toll-Free: 877-354-0916
connect@nuability.ca
www.nuability.ca
Also Known As: Nunavut Disability Society
Overview: A small provincial organization overseen by Canadian Association for Community Living
Mission: To improve the quality of life for people with disabilities in Nunavut through encouragement, advocacy & promotion of opportunities
Member of: Canadian Association for Community Living

Nunavut Arts & Crafts Association (NACA)
PO Box 1539, Iqaluit NU X0A 0H0
Tel: 867-979-7808; *Fax:* 867-979-6880
Toll-Free: 866-979-7808
communications@nacaarts.org
www.nacaarts.org
Overview: A medium-sized provincial organization
Mission: To promote the growth & appreciation of Nunavut artists & the production of arts & crafts
Membership: *Fees:* Free for artists; $50 organization
Chief Officer(s):
Kathleen Nicholls, Manager, Communications & Membership

Nunavut Association of Landscape Architects (NuALA)
PO Box 58, Iqaluit NU X0A 0H0
nualainfo@gmail.com
Overview: A medium-sized provincial organization overseen by Canadian Society of Landscapre Architects
Membership: 1-99; *Member Profile:* Landscape architects & firms
Chief Officer(s):
Jim Floyd, President
jfloyd@nnet.net

Nunavut Curling Association (NCA)
PO Box 413, Rankin Inlet NU X0C 0G0
Tel: 867-645-2534
Overview: A small provincial organization overseen by Canadian Curling Association

Nunavut Economic Developers Association (NEDA)
PO Box 1990, 1104B Inuksugait Plaza, Phase II, Iqaluit NU X0A 0H0
Tel: 867-979-4620; *Fax:* 867-979-4622
www.nunavuteda.com
www.facebook.com/NEDA-170058311362
Overview: A small provincial organization founded in 2000
Mission: To build & improve communities in Nunavut through the provision of programs & services for economic development professionals
Finances: *Annual Operating Budget:* $250,000-$500,000; *Funding Sources:* Territorial core funding; Government
Staff Member(s): 1; 8 volunteer(s)
Membership: 35; *Fees:* $50 individual associate; $100 institutional associate; *Committees:* Executive
Activities: *Speaker Service:* Yes
Chief Officer(s):
Hal Timar, Executive Director
exdir@nunavuteda.com
Meetings/Conferences:
- Nunavut Economic Developers Association 2018 Annual Conference, 2018
Scope: Provincial

Nunavut Employees Union (NEU)
PO Box 869, Iqaluit NU X0A 0H0
Tel: 867-979-4209; *Fax:* 867-979-4522
Toll-Free: 877-243-4424
reception@neu.ca
www.neu.ca
Overview: A small provincial organization founded in 1999 overseen by Public Service Alliance of Canada
Mission: The Nunavut Employees Union represents the interests of the employees of the Government of Nunavut, the Northwest Territories Power Corporation who live in Nunavut, Workers Compensation Board in Nunavut, Nunavut Housing Corporation, and the unionized employees of Nunavut municipalities and Housing Associations. Most of our members work for the Government of Nunavut and live all across the territory. Others belong to Canada Labour Code bargaining units representing Housing Associations and Authorities, Hamlet and town employees, and support staff in schools. NEU members are social workers and nurses, health care professionals, power plant workers, security guards, hamlet bylaw officers, renewable resource officers, engineers, and many more.
Staff Member(s): 5
Membership: *Member Profile:* Territorial employees
Chief Officer(s):
Bill Fennell, President
bill@neu.ca
Brian Boutilier, Executive Director
brian@neu.ca

Nunavut Harvesters Association (NHA)
c/o Brian Zawadski, PO Box 249, Rankin Inlet NU X0C 0G0
Tel: 867-645-3170; *Fax:* 867-645-3755
www.harvesters.nu.ca
Overview: A small provincial organization
Mission: To develop & promote the sustainable harvesting of natural resources & wildlife in Nunavut
Activities: Promoting conservation of wildlife & natural resources in Nunavut; Administering & delivering the Agriculture & Agri-Food Canada program, entitled Advancing Canadian Agriculture & Agri-Food
Chief Officer(s):
Brian Zawadski, Executive Director, 867-645-3170
brian@ndcorp.nu.ca

Nunavut Library Association (NLA)
c/o Nunavut Legislative Library, PO Box 1200, Iqaluit NU X0A 0H0
nunavutlibraryassociation@gmail.com
www.nunavutlibraryassociation.ca
Overview: A small provincial organization
Mission: To support persons who work in Nunavut libraries; To advocate for excellent library services for Nunavut; To promote library services & literacy; To provide professional development for members.
Membership: *Member Profile:* Professional librarians; library technicians; library support staff; literacy workers; archivists; members of the public who are interested in library issues & NLA's work

Nunavut Securities Office
Brown Bldg., 1st Fl., PO Box 1000, Stn. 570, Iqaluit NU X0A 0H0
Tel: 867-975-6590; *Fax:* 867-975-6594
securities@gov.nu.ca
nunavutlegalregistries.ca/sr_index_en.shtml
Overview: A medium-sized provincial organization overseen by Canadian Securities Administrators
Mission: To govern the sale & trading of securities in Nunavut
Member of: Canadian Securities Administrators
Chief Officer(s):
Jeff Manson, Superintendent, Securities

Nunavut Speed Skating Association
c/o John Maurice, President, PO Box 761, 563 Suputi St., Iqaluit NU X0A 0H0
Tel: 867-979-1226; *Fax:* 867-975-3384
www.nunavutspeedskating.ca
Overview: A small provincial organization overseen by Speed Skating Canada
Member of: Speed Skating Canada
Chief Officer(s):
John Maurice, President
jtmaurice@northwestel.net
Don Galloway, Secretary & Director, Coaching
don.galloway@aandc-aadnc.gc.ca

Nunavut Teachers' Association (NTA)
PO Box 2458, Iqaluit NU X0A 0H0
Tel: 867-979-0750; *Fax:* 867-979-0780
www.ntanu.ca
Previous Name: Federation of Nunavut Teachers
Overview: A small provincial organization founded in 1997 overseen by Canadian Teachers' Federation
Mission: To represent & negotiate for teachers, vice-principals, & principals, as well as RSO & TLC coordinators in Nunavut; To ensure that members' rights & benefits are advocated & protected
Membership: *Member Profile:* Teachers, vice-principals, & principals, as well as RSO & TLC coordinators in Nunavut
Chief Officer(s):
John Fanjoy, President
JFanjoy@ntanu.ca
Emile Hatch, Executive Director, 867-222-1275
emile@ntanu.ca
Jeff Avery, Coordinator, Professional Improvement
Jeff@ntanu.ca

Nunavut Tourism
PO Box 1450, Iqaluit NU X0A 0H0
Toll-Free: 866-686-2888
info@nunavuttourism.com
www.nunavuttourism.com
www.facebook.com/nunavuttourism
twitter.com/NunavutTourism
www.youtube.com/nunavuttourism
Overview: A small provincial organization founded in 1995
Mission: To represent the tourism industry for the private sector in Nunavut; to promote & market Nunavut tourism products
Member of: Tourism Industry Association of Canada
Affiliation(s): Team Canada
Finances: *Funding Sources:* Territorial government; industry partners
Membership: *Member Profile:* Outfitters; accommodation providers; tour operators
Activities: To encourage tourism development by providing knowledge & expertise in: marketing, research, industry development, training, & visitor services
Awards:
- Tourism Operator of the Year

Nuns' Island Tenants Association *Voir* Association des locataires de l'Ile-des-Soeurs

Nurse Practitioner Association of Canada (NPAC) / Association des infirmières et infirmiers practiciens du Canada (AIIPC)
1855 Scarth St., Regina SK S4P 2G9
www.npac-aiipc.org
twitter.com/NPsinCanada
Previous Name: Canadian Association of Advanced Practice Nurses
Overview: A medium-sized national organization
Mission: To represent advanced practice nurses from across Canada
Member of: Canadian Nurses Association (CNA)
Membership: 500+; *Fees:* $60 associate non-voting members; $80 regular members, with full voting privileges; *Member Profile:* Advanced practice nurses (also known as clinical nurse specialists, acute care nurse practitioners, & primary health care nurse practitioners) throughout Canada, with a wide range of specialties; Students of advanced practice programs; *Committees:* Communications; Drug Legislation & Regulation; Finance; Research
Activities: Liaising with other professional nursing organizations; Facilitating local, provincial, national, & international discussions of advanced practice nursing issues; Offering networking opportunities

Canadian Associations / Nurse Practitioners Association of Alberta (NPAA)

Chief Officer(s):
Jennifer Fournier, Director, Communications

Nurse Practitioners Association of Alberta (NPAA)
PO Box 9015, Stn. Aspen Glen, 2 Aspen Glen Dr., Spruce Grove AB T7X 4H5
www.albertanps.com
www.facebook.com/131524033527571
twitter.com/NPalberta
Overview: A small provincial organization
Mission: To develop an evidence based, flexible, & integrated practice for nurse practitioners in Alberta; To support the full scope of the nurse practitioner practice in Alberta, to ensure accessible, efficient, & effective health care system
Membership: Fees: $45 students & associate & out of province members; $100 / year, regular members; Member Profile: Nurse practitioners who are registered with the CARNA; Registered nurses who are committed to the advancement of the nurse practitioner role; Students who are registered full time in nurse practitioner programs; Committees: Communication; Education; Advocacy
Activities: Engaging in advocacy activities to support nurse practitioners; Offering networking opportunities; Facilitating educational & research opportunities; Providing education to the public, other health care professionals, & the government about the role of nurse practitioners
Chief Officer(s):
Daris Klemmer, Interim President
president@albertanps.com
Jolene Medynski, Interim Treasurer
treasurer@albertanps.com

Nurse Practitioners of Saskatchewan (NPOS)
1301 Central Ave., Prince Albert SK S6V 4W1
Tel: 306-765-3876
info@npos.ca
www.npos.ca
Overview: A small provincial organization
Mission: To raise awareness of the roles of the nurse practitioners in Saskatchewan; To develop the role & scope of practice of nurse practitioners; To promote established standards of nursing practice for nurse practitioners
Affiliation(s): Saskatchewan Registered Nurses' Association; Canadian Association of Advanced Practice Nurses (CAAPN)
Finances: Funding Sources: Membership fees; Sponsorships
Membership: Member Profile: Nurse practitioners who are part of the Saskatchewan health care system; Registered nurses who are interested in advanced nursing practice, or who work with nurse practitioners; Students in nurse practitioner programs
Activities: Exchanging information related to the role of the nurse practitioners; Supporting research to improve nursing practice
Chief Officer(s):
Deanna Barlow, President
Meetings/Conferences:
• 14th Annual Saskatchewan Nurse Practitioner Conference & AGM, April, 2018, Regina, SK
Scope: Provincial
Publications:
• Nurse Practitioners of Saskatchewan Newsletter
Type: Newsletter; Frequency: Quarterly

Nurse Practitioners' Association of Nova Scotia (NPANS)
c/o School of Nursing, Dalhousie University, PO Box 15000, Halifax NS B3H 3J5
www.npans.ca
Overview: A small provincial organization
Mission: To promote the practice of nurse practitioners throughout Nova Scotia; To support nurse practitioners in various settings; To advocate for nurse practitioner integration & healthcare access
Affiliation(s): College of Registered Nurses of Nova Scotia
Membership: Fees: $30 students; $60 regular members; Member Profile: Nurse practitioners throughout Nova Scotia; Students enrolled in a nurse practitioner program
Activities: Facilitating exchange of practice experiences among nurse practitioners; Offering continuing education opportunities for nurse practitioners throughout Nova Scotia; Educating the public regarding the work of nurse practitioners
Chief Officer(s):
Barbara Currie, Co-Chair
Kimberly Newton, Co-Chair
Nancy Edgecombe, Treasurer

Nurse Practitioners' Association of Ontario (NPAO)
#1801, 1 Yonge St., Toronto ON M5E 1W7
Tel: 416-593-9779; Fax: 416-369-0515
admin@npao.org
www.npao.org
www.facebook.com/NursePractitionersAssociationofOntario
twitter.com/NPAO2
Overview: A small provincial organization founded in 1973
Mission: To represent nurse practitioners in Ontario
Membership: 1500+; Fees: Schedule available
Chief Officer(s):
Theresa Agnew, Executive Director
tagnew@npao.org
Tannice Fletcher-Stackhouse, President
tfletcher-stackhouse@npao.org
Wendy McKay, President-Elect
rmckay12@cogeco.ca
Awards:
• Jerry Gerow Nurse Practitioner Leadership Award; Amount: $1500.00
• AstraZeneca Award for Innovation in Chronic Disease Management; Amount: $5000.00
• NPAO Member Bursary; Amount: $1000.00
• NPAO President's Award; Amount: $1500.00
• Pfizer Consumer Healthcare Bursary; Amount: $1500.00
• Pfizer Award for Clinical Excellence; Amount: $2500.00
• Huronia Nurse Practitioner Network Bursary; Amount: $1500.00
Meetings/Conferences:
• Nurse Practitioners' Association of Ontario Annual Conference 2018, 2018, ON
Scope: Provincial

Nursery School Teachers Association See Association of Early Childhood Educators of Quebec

Nursery Sod Growers' Association of Ontario
PO Box 25045, Guelph ON N1G 4T4
Tel: 519-265-6742; Fax: 519-265-8873
nsga@rogers.com
www.nsgao.com
Overview: A small provincial organization founded in 1960
Mission: The main objectives of the association are to develop and maintain high standards of turfgrass sod quality, to stimulate consumer knowledge of quality turfgrass sod, to work in close co-operation with allied professions to the benefit of consumer and trade alike, and to gather, analyse and disseminate information of general interest to the public, governmental agencies and other organizations.
Chief Officer(s):
Greg Skotnicki, President

Nurses Association of New Brunswick (NANB) / Association des infirmières et infirmiers du Nouveau-Brunswick (AIINB)
165 Regent St., Fredericton NB E3B 7B4
Tel: 506-458-8731; Fax: 506-459-2838
Toll-Free: 800-442-4417
www.nanb.nb.ca
www.facebook.com/1704804403067899
twitter.com/nanb_aiinb
Overview: A medium-sized provincial licensing organization founded in 1916
Mission: To act as the professional voice & regulatory body of nursing in New Brunswick; To protect the public by maintaining standards for nursing education & practice
Member of: Canadian Nurses Association (CNA)
Finances: Funding Sources: Membership fees
Membership: 8,700
Activities: Registering nurses in New Brunswick in accordance with the 1984 Nurses Act; Advocating for public policy; Offering professional liability protection; Providing continuing education; Preventing undesirable practice; Intervening with unacceptable practice; Presenting awards
Chief Officer(s):
Brenda Kinney, President
president@nanb.nb.ca

NWT Disabilities Council (NWTCPD)
#116, 5102 50th Ave., Yellowknife NT X1A 3S8
Tel: 867-873-8230; Fax: 867-873-4124
Toll-Free: 800-491-8885
admin@nwtdc.net
www.nwtdc.net
www.facebook.com/436138019806132
Previous Name: Northwest Territories Council for the Disabled; NWT Council for Disabled Persons
Overview: A medium-sized provincial charitable organization founded in 1978
Mission: To encourage & support the self-determination of people with disabilities
Affiliation(s): Council of Canadians with Disabilities
Staff Member(s): 8
Membership: Member Profile: Persons with disabilities or committed to disability issues
Activities: Celebrity Auction & Ability Cup; Speaker Service: Yes; Library: Open to public
Chief Officer(s):
Denise McKee, Executive Director
ed@nwtdc.net
Jennifer Winsor, Office Manager
finance@nwtdc.net

NWT School Athletic Federation (NWTSAF)
PO Box 266, Fort Smith NT X0E 0P0
Overview: A medium-sized provincial organization overseen by School Sport Canada
Member of: School Sport Canada
Affiliation(s): Canadian School Sport Federation; Sport North
Activities: Regional tournaments
Chief Officer(s):
Richard Daitch, Executive Director
rwdaitch@yahoo.com

NWT Seniors' Society (NWTSS)
#102, 4916 - 46th Ave., Yellowknife NT X1A 1L2
Tel: 867-920-7444; Fax: 867-920-7601
Toll-Free: 800-661-0878
seniors@yk.com
www.nwtseniorssociety.ca
www.facebook.com/nwtseniorssociety
twitter.com/NWTSeniors
Overview: A small provincial organization
Mission: To promote the independence & well-being of older citizens through the provision of programs & services in partnership with responsible government & other organizations; to serve as a consulting body & advocate for the elderly
Member of: Yukon Council on Aging; Alberta Council on Aging; Saskatchewan Council on Aging
Finances: Funding Sources: Territorial government; Federal funding; Raffle; Bingo
Membership: Member Profile: 50+ age group
Activities: 1-800 Seniors Information Line; Resource library; Advisory council; Workshops; Awareness Events: Intergenerational Day, June 1; World Elder Sbuse Awareness Day, June 15; Senior Citizens' Month, June; Library: Open to public
Chief Officer(s):
Barbara Hood, Executive Director
Leon Peterson, President

NWT Squash
NT
www.nwtsquash.com
twitter.com/NWTSquash
Overview: A small provincial organization overseen by Squash Canada
Mission: To develop & provide squash programs to athletes of all ages in the Northwest Territories.
Member of: Squash Canada
Chief Officer(s):
Bruce Jones, President
Garrett Hinchey, Secretary

O Vertigo Danse
175, rue Sainte-Catherine ouest, Montréal QC H2X 1Z8
Tél: 514-251-9177; Téléc: 514-251-7358
info@overtigo.com
www.overtigo.com
www.facebook.com/108428645874501
www.youtube.com/user/overtigodanse
Aperçu: Dimension: petite; Envergure: locale; Organisme sans but lucratif; fondée en 1984
Mission: Se consacre à la création en nouvelle danse et la diffusion des oeuvres de la fondatrice et directrice artistique de la compagnie
Finances: Budget de fonctionnement annuel: $500,000-$1.5 Million; Fonds: Conseil des Arts du Canada; Donateurs
Membre(s) du personnel: 17
Activités: Stagiaires: Oui; Listes de destinataires: Oui

Membre(s) du bureau directeur:
Ginette Laurin, Directrice générale
Vecerina Jacques, Directeur administratif

O'Keefe Ranch & Interior Heritage Society
PO Box 955, Vernon BC V1T 6M8
Tel: 250-542-7868
info@okeeferanch.ca
www.okeeferanch.ca
www.facebook.com/HistoricOkeefeRanch
twitter.com/okeeferanchca
Also Known As: Historic O'Keefe Ranch
Overview: A small local charitable organization founded in 1977
Mission: Preservation & presentation of the rural history of the North Okanagan
Affiliation(s): BC Museums Association
Finances: *Funding Sources:* Municipal government; provincial Arts Board
Activities: *Rents Mailing List:* Yes; *Library:* O'Keefe Ranch Archives; Open to public by appointment

Oak Ridges Moraine Foundation (ORMF)
120 Bayview Pkwy., Newmarket ON L3Y 4X1
Tel: 289-279-5733
support@ormf.com
www.ormf.com
twitter.com/ormoraine
Overview: A medium-sized local organization
Mission: To provide support and encouragement for activities that preserve, protect, and restore the environmental integrity of the Oak Ridges Moraine and support a trail along it.
Staff Member(s): 1
Chief Officer(s):
Michele Donnelly, Senior Administrative Assistant

Oak Ridges Trail Association (ORTA)
PO Box 28544, Aurora ON L4G 6S6
Tel: 905-833-6600; *Fax:* 905-833-8379
Toll-Free: 877-319-0285
info@oakridgestrail.org
www.oakridgestrail.org
Previous Name: Citizens for an Oak Ridges Trail
Overview: A medium-sized local organization founded in 1992
Mission: To develop a trail across the Oak Ridges moraine linking the Bruce Trail in the west to the Northumberland Forest in the east
Member of: Hike Ontario
Finances: *Annual Operating Budget:* Less than $50,000
20 volunteer(s)
Membership: 800+; *Fees:* $30 individual/family; $20 student; $450 lifetime
Activities: *Awareness Events:* Hike Ontario Day, 1st Sunday Oct.; The Annual Moraine For Life Adventure Relay, June
Chief Officer(s):
Michele Donnelly, Office Manager

Oakville & District Chamber of Commerce
PO Box 263, Oakville MB R0H 0Y0
Tel: 204-267-2730; *Fax:* 888-552-9910
oakvillechamberoffice@gmail.com
Overview: A small local organization
Chief Officer(s):
Sian Taris, President

Oakville & District Humane Society *See* Oakville & Milton Humane Society

Oakville & Milton Humane Society
445 Cornwall Rd., Oakville ON L6J 7S8
Tel: 905-845-1551; *Fax:* 905-845-1973
shelter@omhs.ca
www.omhs.ca
www.facebook.com/OakvilleMiltonHumaneSociety
twitter.com/OakvilleHumane
www.youtube.com/user/oakvillehumane
Previous Name: Oakville & District Humane Society
Overview: A small local charitable organization founded in 1936
Mission: To promote the human/animal bond & relationship; To assist animals which are sick, have been injured, abused, sick, or abandoned, or are in need of rescue; To legally investigate & prosecute on the animals' behalf; To assist in finding suitable homes for unclaimed stray animals & to assist owners in finding their animals which have strayed or become lost; To construct, equip & maintain places for the reception & care of sick, injured or straying animals & for the humane destruction of unwanted animals.
Member of: Canadian Federation of Humane Societies
Affiliation(s): Ontario Society for the Prevention of Cruelty to Animals
Finances: *Annual Operating Budget:* $500,000-$1.5 Million
Staff Member(s): 40; 140 volunteer(s)
Membership: 2,000; *Fees:* $25 single; $40 family; $150 life
Activities: *Awareness Events:* Be Kind to Animals Month, May; *Library:* Open to public
Chief Officer(s):
Kim Millan, Executive Director
kimm@omhs.ca

Oakville Art Society
560 Bronte Rd., Oakville ON L6L 6S1
Tel: 905-827-5711
info@oakvilleartsociety.com
www.oakvilleartsociety.com
www.facebook.com/OakvilleArtSociety
twitter.com/OASInfo
instagram.com/oas_oakville.art.society;
youtu.be/8B5ZEzhPWQQ
Overview: A small local charitable organization founded in 1965
Mission: To create a forum where individuals interested in art may meet to share ideas & appreciate art; To provide the environment & facilities through which artistic skills may be more fully developed; To promote art appreciation within the community; To offer bursaries & other assistance when possible & desirable to the encouragement of suitable students
Finances: *Funding Sources:* Self-supporting; Town Cultural Grants for specific events or initiatives
Staff Member(s): 3
Membership: 170; *Fees:* $80 adult; $140 family
Activities: Classes offered in fall, winter, & spring for adults & youth, including painting, drawing, photography, & jewellery; Adult workshops offered throughout the year generally on weekends; *Awareness Events:* Art in the Park, August
Chief Officer(s):
Carolyn Crosby, President

Oakville Arts Council (OAC)
2302 Bridge Rd., Oakville ON L6L 2G6
Tel: 905-815-5977; *Fax:* 905-815-2024
artscouncil@oakville.ca
www.oakvillearts.com
www.linkedin.com/groups/3955059/profile
www.facebook.com/152380326624
twitter.com/oakvillearts
instagram.com/oakvilleartscouncil
Overview: A medium-sized local charitable organization founded in 1978
Mission: To promote & encourage the development of arts organizations & activities in the town of Oakville
Member of: Community Arts Ontario
Finances: *Annual Operating Budget:* $250,000-$500,000; *Funding Sources:* 40% fundraising; 35% government grants; 25% revenue
Staff Member(s): 4; 60 volunteer(s)
Membership: 500; *Fees:* $50 individual; $150 organization; *Committees:* Cultural Grants; Finance; Mayor's Awards; Artworks; Membership; Fundraising
Activities: Art Works; members' centre; skills training workshops; administrative support; Cultural Grants Advisory; municipal arts advisory; Mayor's Awards for Business & the Arts; Film Festival; Festival for Fibre Arts; *Internships:* Yes; *Speaker Service:* Yes; *Library:* Resource Centre; Open to public
Chief Officer(s):
Bernadette Ward, Executive Director, 905-815-5977 Ext. 3
bward@oakville.ca

Oakville Chamber Ensemble *See* Oakville Chamber Orchestra

Oakville Chamber of Commerce
#200, 700 Kerr St., Oakville ON L6K 3W5
Tel: 905-845-6613; *Fax:* 905-845-6475
info@oakvillechamber.com
www.oakvillechamber.com
www.linkedin.com/company/3527781
www.facebook.com/oakvillechamber
twitter.com/OakvilleChamber
instagram.com/oakvillechamber
Overview: A small local organization founded in 1953
Mission: To provide leadership for the business community in general & its members in particular by: communicating its views regarding economic development in a timely, informed & effective way; acting as a strong business advocate supporting sound government policies which promote economic development & business opportunities in the Oakville area; providing networking opportunities for its primary stakeholders to sustain & develop business; & promoting partnership among its stakeholders & fostering community involvement
Member of: Canadian Chamber of Commerce
Affiliation(s): Ontario Chamber of Commerce; Burlington Chamber of Commerce; Milton Chamber of Commerce; Halton Hills Chamber of Commerce; AmCham; Bronte Village Business Improvement Area; Downtown Oakville Business Improvement Area; Kerr Village Business Improvement Area
Staff Member(s): 8
Membership: 1,100; *Fees:* Schedule available; *Committees:* Executive; Nominating; Government Relations & Advocacy; Golf; Small Business Week; Good Morning Oakville
Chief Officer(s):
Caroline Hughes, Chair

Oakville Chamber Orchestra
PO Box 76036, 1500 Upper Middle Rd. West, Oakville ON L6M 3H5
Tel: 905-483-6787
mail@oakvillechamber.org
www.oakvillechamber.org
www.linkedin.com/company/oakville-chamber-orchestra
www.facebook.com/oakvillemusic
twitter.com/oakvillemusic
www.youtube.com/user/oakvillemusic
Previous Name: Oakville Chamber Ensemble
Overview: A small local charitable organization founded in 1984 overseen by Orchestras Canada
Mission: To enrich the cultural landscape of Oakville by performing chamber music concerts, developing local amateur musicians, and promoting Canadian soloists
Member of: Oakville Chamber of Commerce; Oakville Arts Council; Mississauga Arts Council; Halton Nonprofit Network
Finances: *Funding Sources:* Provincial & municipal government grants; Individual & corporate donations
Chief Officer(s):
Kevin Fernandez, President
Charles Demuynck, Music Director

Oakville Community Centre for Peace, Ecology & Human Rights
PO Box 52007, Oakville ON L6J 7N5
Tel: 905-849-5501
info@oakvillepeacecentre.org
www.oakvillepeacecentre.org
Overview: A small local organization
Chief Officer(s):
Stephen Dankowich, Executive Director

Oakville Distress Centre
PO Box 776, Oakville ON L6K 0A9
Tel: 905-849-4559; *Crisis Hot-Line:* 905-849-4541
info@dchalton.ca
www.dchalton.ca
www.linkedin.com/company/distress-centre-oakville
twitter.com/DCOakville
Overview: A small local charitable organization founded in 1974 overseen by Distress Centres Ontario
Mission: To provide telephone, crisis intervention, & support services for the community of Oakville, Milton, & surrounding areas; To develop & provide outreach & suicide prevention programs to meet the needs of the community
Finances: *Funding Sources:* United Way; Donations

Oakville Historical Society
PO Box 69501, 109 Thomas St., Oakville ON L6J 7R4
Tel: 905-844-2695; *Fax:* 905-844-7380
info@oakvillehistory.org
www.oakvillehistory.org
Overview: A small local organization founded in 1953
Mission: To preserve & promote the historical heritage of the area now making up the Town of Oakville
Membership: *Fees:* $25 individual; $15 student; $20 senior; $35 family/institution; $100 corporate
Chief Officer(s):
George Chisholm, President
pres@oakvillehistory.org

Oakville Symphony Orchestra (OSO)
#310, 200 North Service Rd. West, Oakville ON L6M 2Y1
Tel: 905-338-1462; *Fax:* 905-338-7954
oakville.symphony@cogeco.ca
www.oakvillesymphony.com
www.facebook.com/oakvillesymphony
twitter.com/oaksymphony
Overview: A small local charitable organization founded in 1967 overseen by Orchestras Canada

Mission: To bring audiences a variety of music for all ages & to contribute to the cultural growth of the community
Affiliation(s): Oakville Arts Council
Finances: *Funding Sources:* Town of Oakville; Donations; Sponsors; Fund-raising
Membership: 83; *Member Profile:* Musicians; non-playing members "Friends of OSO"
Activities: Concerts; *Library:* OSO Music Library; by appointment Not open to public
Chief Officer(s):
Peggy Steele, General Manager
Awards:
• Young Artists Awards
• Kenneth Hollier Award

The Oakville, Milton & District Real Estate Board
125 Navy St., Oakville ON L6J 2Z5
Tel: 905-844-6491; *Fax:* 905-844-6699
info@omdreb.on.ca
www.omdreb.on.ca
www.linkedin.com/company/the-oakville-milton-and-district-real-estate-board-omdreb
www.facebook.com/OMDREB
twitter.com/OMDREB_Official
www.youtube.com/user/omdreb
Overview: A small local organization overseen by Ontario Real Estate Association
Mission: To represent its members & provide them with services to help further their career
Member of: The Canadian Real Estate Association
Staff Member(s): 12
Membership: 1,500
Chief Officer(s):
Marta Sponder, Executive Officer
msponder@omdreb.on.ca

Oasis Centre des femmes
CP 73022, Succ. wood Street, 465 Yonge Street, Toronto ON M4Y 2W5
Tél: 416-591-6565; *Téléc:* 416-591-7525
services@oasisfemmes.org
www.oasisfemmes.org
www.facebook.com/oasisfemmes?ref=ts&fref=ts
twitter.com/OasisFemmes
Aperçu: *Dimension:* petite; *Envergure:* locale; Organisme sans but lucratif; fondée en 1995
Mission: OASIS a pour mission d'éliminer la violence et d'améliorer la situation des femmes francophones de la grande région de Toronto
Membre: 1-99
Activités: Nous offrons nos services aux femmes francophones qui sont victimes de violence, qui sont immigrantes, réfugiées ou nouvelles arrivantes, ou qui sont à la recherche d'un emploi
Membre(s) du bureau directeur:
Odette Doumbe, Gestionnaire des programmes
Brampton
CP 74089, 150 Main St., Brampton ON L6V 1M0
Tél: 905-454-3332; *Téléc:* 905-454-9437
josettes@oasisfemmes.org

Oblate Missionaries of Mary Immaculate *Voir* Les Oblates Missionnaires de Marie Immaculée

Les Oblates Missionnaires de Marie Immaculée (OMMI) / Oblate Missionaries of Mary Immaculate
7625, boul Parent, Trois-Rivières QC G9A 5E1
Tél: 819-375-7317
ommi@ommi-is.org
www.ommi-is.org
Aperçu: *Dimension:* petite; *Envergure:* internationale; fondée en 1952

Occupational & Environmental Medical Association of Canada (OEMAC) / Association canadienne de la médecine du travail et de l'environnement (ACMTE)
#503, 386 Broadway, Winnipeg MB R3C 3R6
Toll-Free: 888-223-3808
info@oemac.org
oemac.org
Overview: A medium-sized national organization founded in 1983
Mission: To act as the voice of the Canadian occupational & environmental medicine sector
Affiliation(s): Canadian Medical Association; Canadian Board of Occupational Medicine; Royal College of Physicians & Surgeons of Canada
Finances: *Funding Sources:* Membership fees

Membership: 264; *Fees:* $334.75 active; $200 non-resident; *Member Profile:* Licensed physicians with an interest in occupational medicine
Activities: Exchanging scientific & professional information
Chief Officer(s):
Daniel Gouws, President
president@oemac.org
Jonathan Strauss, Executive Director
Melanie Tsouras, Coordinator, Programs & Services
mtsouras@oemac.org
Chantal Champagne, Event Manager
cchampagne@oemac.org
Publications:
• Liaison [a publication of the Occupational & Environmental Medical Association of Canada]
Type: Newsletter; *Frequency:* Quarterly

Occupational First Aid Attendants Association of British Columbia (OFAAA)
#108, 2323 Boundary Rd., Vancouver BC V5M 4V8
Tel: 604-294-0244; *Fax:* 604-294-0289
Toll-Free: 800-667-4566
ofaaa@ofaaa.bc.ca
www.ofaaa.bc.ca
www.facebook.com/119440864766772
twitter.com/OFAAABC
Previous Name: Industrial First Aid Attendants Association of British Columbia
Overview: A small provincial charitable organization founded in 1935
Mission: To enhance the professional status of first aid attendants & to promote accessibility to high standards of first aid for the workers of the province of British Columbia
Finances: *Annual Operating Budget:* $250,000-$500,000
Staff Member(s): 1; 12 volunteer(s)
Membership: *Fees:* $70 professional; $30 associate; *Member Profile:* First aid attendants
Chief Officer(s):
Allan Zdunic, President
azdunich@ofaaa.bc.ca

Occupational Health Clinics for Ontario Workers (OHCOW)
#606, 1090 Don Mills Rd., Toronto ON M3C 3R6
Tel: 416-510-8713; *Fax:* 416-443-9132
Toll-Free: 877-817-0336
ask@ohcow.on.ca
www.ohcow.on.ca
Overview: A medium-sized provincial organization
Mission: To prevent work-related illnesses & injuries; To improve workers' physical, mental, & social well-being
Chief Officer(s):
David Chezzi, President

Occupational Hygiene Association of Ontario (OHAO)
#100, 6700 Century Ave., Mississauga ON L5N 6A4
Tel: 905-567-7196; *Fax:* 905-567-7191
office@ohao.org
www.ohao.org
Overview: A medium-sized provincial organization founded in 1984
Mission: To protect people's health from hazards arising in or from the workplace; To develop & promote the profession of occupational hygiene; To sponsor professional development, training & research; To provide public education
Finances: *Annual Operating Budget:* $50,000-$100,000; *Funding Sources:* Membership dues; seminars
10 volunteer(s)
Membership: 300; *Fees:* $80 individual; $25 student; *Committees:* Education; Program; Membership; Public Affairs
Activities: Regional meetings; *Awareness Events:* Technical Symposia; *Speaker Service:* Yes; *Rents Mailing List:* Yes
Chief Officer(s):
Letty Wong, President
Awards:
• Hugh Nelson Award
Presented to an individual who has made a significant long-term contribution to the advancement of occupational hygiene in Ontario

Occupational Nurses' Specialty Association of British Columbia (ONSA BC)
Previous Name: British Columbia Occupational Health Nurses Professional Practice Group
Overview: A small provincial organization founded in 2010

Membership: *Member Profile:* Occupational health nurses in British Columbia
Activities: Providing information about occupational issues encountered by British Columbia's occupational health nurses

Ocean Renewable Energy Group *See* Marine Renewables Canada

Oceana Canada
#505, 18 King St. East, Toronto ON M5C 1C4
Tel: 416-583-2350
www.oceana.ca
www.facebook.com/OceanaCanada
twitter.com/OceanaCAN
Overview: A medium-sized national charitable organization founded in 2001
Mission: To conserve, protect, & restore Canada's oceans; To educate the public about ocean conservation & related issues
Activities: Providing ocean conservation resources; Campaigning for policies that benefit fisheries & promote marine sustainability
Chief Officer(s):
Josh Laughren, Executive Director
Alex Ivankine, Director, Finance & Administration
Robert Rangeley, Director, Science
Lesley Wilmot, Director, Communications
Publications:
• Oceana Canada Annual Report
Type: Yearbook; *Frequency:* Annually

Oceanside Community Arts Council (OCAC)
c/o McMillan Arts Centre, PO Box 1662, 133 McMillan St., Parksville BC V9P 2H5
Tel: 250-248-8185; *Fax:* 250-248-8185
mcmillanartscentre.com
www.youtube.com/channel/UCnMExnRHIsZjWiINNnOXi2Q
Previous Name: District 69 Community Arts Council
Overview: A small local charitable organization
Mission: To promote & facilitate the production & appreciation of all creative cultural activities
Member of: Assembly of BC Arts Councils
Finances: *Funding Sources:* Municipal, provincial grants
Membership: *Fees:* $26
Chief Officer(s):
Chris Raines, President

Odawa Native Friendship Centre
250 City Centre Ave., Ottawa ON K1R 6K7
Tel: 613-722-3811; *Fax:* 613-722-4667
info@odawa.on.ca
www.odawa.on.ca
www.facebook.com/Odawa.Friendship
Overview: A small local charitable organization
Affiliation(s): Ontario Federation of Indian Friendship Centres
Staff Member(s): 29
Activities: Administers the following programs: Community Justice; Family Support; Healthy Babies, Healthy Children; Akwe:go; Healing & Wellness; Life Long Care; Healthy Living; Homeless Partnering Strategy; Wasa-Nabin; Recreation; Cultural Awareness; Support/Information Referral. The Centre also runs a drop-in centre, child care agency, & alternative high school
Chief Officer(s):
Neal Freeland, President
president@odawa.on.ca
Morgan Hare, Executive Director, 613-722-3811 Ext. 246
executive.director@odawa.on.ca

Odre des enseignantes et des enseignants de l'Ontario *See* Ontario College of Teachers

Oeuvres pour enfants Ronald McDonald du Canada *See* Ronald McDonald House Charities of Canada

Office canadien de vérification de la diffusion *See* Canadian Circulations Audit Board Inc.

L'Office de Certification Commerciale du Québec Inc. (OCCQ) / Québec Commercial Certification Office Inc. (QCCO)
#206, 1565, boul de l'Avenir, Laval QC H7S 2N5
Tél: 514-905-3893; *Téléc:* 450-663-6316
info@occq-qcco.com
www.occq-qcco.com
Aperçu: *Dimension:* moyenne; *Envergure:* provinciale

L'Office de commercialisation des oeufs de Nouveau Brunswick *See* New Brunswick Egg Marketing Board

Office de Tourisme de Percé *Voir* Office de Tourisme du Rocher-Percé

Office de Tourisme du Rocher-Percé (OTRP)
CP 243, 9, rue du Quai, Percé QC G0C 2L0
Tél: 418-782-2258; *Téléc:* 418-782-2285
services@rocherperce.qc.ca
www.rocherperce.qc.ca
Nom précédent: Office de Tourisme de Percé
Aperçu: Dimension: petite; *Envergure:* locale; Organisme sans but lucratif; fondée en 1998
Mission: Améliorer l'offre touristique de la MRC du Rocher-Percé, sa commercialisation et l'éthique professionnelle, soutenir les événements
Membre de: Association touristique de la Gaspésie
Affiliation(s): Québec Maritime
Finances: *Budget de fonctionnement annuel:* $100,000-$250,000; *Fonds:* Emploi-Québec; Association des centres locaux de développement; Société d'assurance-dépôts du Canada
Membre(s) du personnel: 8; 5 bénévole(s)
Membre: 142; *Montant de la cotisation:* 100$; *Critères d'admissibilité:* Commerçants; villes; organismes de développement; *Comités:* Éthique; Formation
Activités: Billetterie, animation publique

Office de vente des produits forestiers du Madawaska *See* Madawaska Forest Products Marketing Board

Office des normes générales du Canada *See* Canadian General Standards Board

Office du tourisme et des congrès de la communauté urbaine de Québec *Voir* Office du tourisme et des congrès de Québec

Office du tourisme et des congrès de Québec (OTCQ) / Québec City & Area Tourism & Convention Board
399, rue Saint-Joseph est, Québec QC G1K 8E2
Tél: 418-641-6654; *Téléc:* 418-641-6578
Ligne sans frais: 877-783-1608
www.quebecregion.com
www.facebook.com/QuebecRegion
twitter.com/quebecregion
www.instagram.com/quebecregion
Nom précédent: Office du tourisme et des congrès de la communauté urbaine de Québec
Aperçu: Dimension: moyenne; *Envergure:* locale; fondée en 1985 surveillé par Associations touristiques régionales associées du Québec
Mission: Organisme responsable de la mise en marché de la région touristique de Québec
Membre de: Tourism Industry Association of Canada
Finances: *Budget de fonctionnement annuel:* Plus de $5 Million
Membre(s) du personnel: 44
Membre: 800; *Montant de la cotisation:* Barème
Activités: Stagiaires: Oui; *Listes de destinataires:* Oui
Membre(s) du bureau directeur:
Gabriel Savard, Directeur général
Daniel Gagnon, Directeur, Communication et publicité

Office municipal d'habitation de Longueuil (OMHL)
445, rue Labonté, Longueuil QC J4H 2P8
Tél: 450-670-2733; *Téléc:* 450-670-7757
omhl@omhl.org
www.omhl.org
Aperçu: Dimension: petite; *Envergure:* locale
Mission: Pour fournir la qualité, le logement à faible revenu pour les personnes défavorisées
Membre(s) du bureau directeur:
Sylvain Boily, Directeur général
Monique Brisson, Présidente, Conseil d'administration

Office of the Superintendent of Securities of Newfoundland & Labrador
Confederation Bldg., West Block, PO Box 8700, St. John's NL A1B 4J6
Tel: 709-729-4189; *Fax:* 709-729-6187
www.servicenl.gov.nl.ca/securities
Overview: A medium-sized provincial organization overseen by Canadian Securities Administrators
Member of: Canadian Securities Administrators
Activities: Administering the securities laws of Newfoundland & Labrador
Chief Officer(s):
John O'Brien, Superintendent, Securities

Office of the Superintendent of Securities of the Northwest Territories
Stuart M. Hodgson Bldg., PO Box 1320, 5009 - 49th St., 1st Fl., Yellowknife NT X1A 2L9
Tel: 867-767-9305; *Fax:* 867-873-0243
securitiesregistry@gov.nt.ca
www.justice.gov.nt.ca/en/divisions/legal-registries-division
Also Known As: Securities Office
Overview: A medium-sized provincial organization overseen by Canadian Securities Administrators
Mission: To govern the sale & trading of securities in the Northwest Territories; to administer the Securities Act
Member of: Canadian Securities Administrators
Chief Officer(s):
Tom Hall, Superintendent, Securities

Office of the Yukon Superintendent of Securities
PO Box 2703, Stn. C-6, 307 Black St., Whitehorse YT Y1A 2C6
Tel: 867-667-5466; *Fax:* 867-393-6251
Toll-Free: 800-661-0408
securities@gov.yk.ca
www.community.gov.yk.ca/corp/securities_about.html
Overview: A medium-sized provincial organization overseen by Canadian Securities Administrators
Mission: To foster fair & efficient capital markets; to protect investors
Member of: Canadian Securities Administrators
Activities: Administering Yukon's securities laws
Chief Officer(s):
Fred Pretorius, Director, Corporate Affairs, 867-667-5225
Fred.Pretorius@gov.yk.ca

Offshore / Onshore Technologies Association of Nova Scotia (OTANS) *See* The Maritimes Energy Association

Offshore Energy Research Association of Nova Scotia (OERA)
Joseph Howe Building, #1001, 1690 Hollis St., Halifax NS B3J 1V7
Tel: 902-406-7012; *Fax:* 902-406-7019
Toll-Free: 888-257-8688
www.oera.ca
www.linkedin.com/company-beta/3108008
Merged from: Offshore Energy Environmental Research (OEER); Offshore Energy Technical Research (OETR)
Overview: A medium-sized provincial organization founded in 2012
Mission: To foster offshore energy & environmental research & development; To develop offshore petroleum exploration & development for Nova Scotia
Activities: *Library:* Offshore Energy Research - Document Library
Chief Officer(s):
Stephen Dempsey, Executive Director, 902-406-7011, Fax: 902-406-7019
sdempsey@oera.ca
Carey Ryan, Director, Research & Business Development, 902-499-4375, Fax: 902-406-7019
Jennifer Pinks, Manager, Research, 902-406-7013, Fax: 902-406-7019
Nalani Perry, Manager, Operations, 902-406-7012, Fax: 902-406-7019
nperry@oera.ca

Ogemawahj Tribal Council (OTC)
5984 Rama Rd., Rama ON L3V 6H6
Tel: 705-329-2511; *Fax:* 705-329-2509
www.ogemawahj.on.ca
twitter.com/OgemawahjTribal
Overview: A small local organization founded in 1990
Mission: To provide professional & technical services to its members; to promote self-sufficiency for First Nations
Membership: 6 First Nations
Activities: Economic development; education; employment & training; financial management; technical services; policy, planning & intergovernmental relations
Chief Officer(s):
Elizabeth Bigwin, Executive Director
ebigwin@ogemawahj.on.ca

Oil & Gas Services Association of Québec *Voir* L'association québécoise des fournisseurs de services pétroliers et gaziers du Québec

Ojibway & Cree Cultural Centre
150 Brousseau Ave., #B, Timmins ON P4N 5Y4
Tel: 705-267-7911; *Fax:* 705-267-4988
www.occc.ca
Overview: A medium-sized local charitable organization founded in 1975
Mission: To uphold the strength, integrity & growth of the Native culture within the Nishnawbe-Aski Nation; To support the Nisnawbe-Aski Nation in nurturing a sense of pride, independence & self-determination through the development & provision of culturally oriented materials & resources; To assist in the recognition & acceptance of Native culture within mainstream society
Member of: Ontario Library Association
Affiliation(s): First Nations Confederacy of Cultural & Education Centres
Staff Member(s): 5
Activities: Provides curriculum & resource materials for use in Nishnawbe-Aski schools; preserves Cree & Ojibway through the creation of such materials as well as developing vocabularies & archives of Elders' stories; translation services; *Library:* Resource Centre
Chief Officer(s):
Dianne Riopel, Executive Director

Ojibway Power Toboggan Association (OPTA)
PO Box 1466, Sioux Lookout ON P8T 1B9
Tel: 807-737-1976; *Fax:* 807-737-1722
www.opta.ca
Overview: A medium-sized provincial organization
Mission: To keep snowmobile trails in the Sioux Lookout area in good condition and promote safe snowmobiling
Member of: North West Ontario Snowmobile Trails Association; Ontario Federation of Snowmobile Clubs; Sunset Country; Patricia Region Tourist Bureau
Membership: *Committees:* Trails; Membership; Grooming; Safety; Building; Equipment; Signage; Risk Management; STOP
Activities: Training courses; *Awareness Events:* Poker Derby; Snowmobile Raffle; Snowarama
Chief Officer(s):
Gail Sayers, President
president@opta.ca

Okanagan Historical Society (OHS)
PO Box 313, Vernon BC V1T 6M3
okheritagehistory@gmail.com
www.okanaganhistoricalsociety.org
Overview: A small local charitable organization founded in 1925
Mission: To promote the history & geography of the Okanagan & Shuswap areas of British Columbia
Affiliation(s): BC Historical Federation
Finances: *Funding Sources:* Report sales
Chief Officer(s):
Tracy Satin, President, 250-718-5928
Robert Cowan, Treasurer, 250-838-9641
robertscowan@gmail.com

Okanagan Mainline Municipal Association; Okanagan Valley Municipal Association; Okanagan Valley Mayors & Reeves Association *See* Southern Interior Local Government Association

Okanagan Mainline Real Estate Board (OMREB)
#112, 140 Commercial Dr., Kelowna BC V1X 7X6
Tel: 250-491-4560; *Fax:* 250-491-4580
admin@omreb.com
www.omreb.com
www.facebook.com/okanaganmainlineREB
twitter.com/OMREB1
Overview: A small local organization founded in 1959 overseen by British Columbia Real Estate Association
Mission: To provide a forum for the exchange of property-related information between members so that they may provide the public with outstanding service; to establish & maintain optimum standards of business practices; to provide continuing education for the betterment of the members' knowledge; to monitor proposed & legislated laws which inhibit or restrict the right of Canadians or British Columbians to own or use real property
Member of: The Canadian Real Estate Association
Finances: *Funding Sources:* Membership fees
Membership: 90; *Member Profile:* Real estate licensees in Kelowna, Vernon & Salmon Arm areas
Activities: *Library:* Not open to public

Okanagan Miniature Horse Club (OMHC)
c/o Judy Aschenmeier, 4240 Noble Rd., Armstrong BC V0E 1B4

Canadian Associations / Okanagan Orchid Society

Tel: 250-546-9345
aschjudy@hotmail.com
www.miniaturehorsesbc.com/okclubinfo.htm
Overview: A small local organization founded in 2004
Mission: To provide education & information about the miniature horse breed in the Okanagan region of British Columbia
Finances: *Funding Sources:* Membership fees; Fundraising; Sponsorships
Membership: *Fees:* $10 youth members; $15 single members; $25 families; *Member Profile:* Miniature horse owners, breeders, & enthusiasts who are involved in the industry in the central interior of British Columbia & Alberta
Activities: Hosting annual American Miniature Horse Association & American Miniature Horse Registry sanctioned shows in Armstrong, British Columbia; Participating in shows for miniature horses in the Okanagan region; Offering demonstrations of miniature horses at various events; Organizing educational clinics about the miniature horse breed; Providing networking opportunities for members to exchange information
Chief Officer(s):
Barb Aschemeier, President, 250-379-2513
bentfir@telus.net
Joan Cunningham, Vice-President & Member, Show Committee, 250-545-9566
vistavalleyminis@shaw.ca
Anna DeWolff, Secretary, 250-832-9832
adewolff@telus.net
Ann Iceton, Treasurer, 250-832-9832
ann@paragonbc.com
Publications:
• Okanagan Miniature Horse Club Newsletter
Type: Newsletter; *Accepts Advertising*
Profile: Club information, member profiles, informative articles about miniature horses, events, & fun activities for members of the Okanagan Miniature Horse Club

Okanagan Orchid Society
Okanagan BC
www.members.shaw.ca/oos
Overview: A small local organization founded in 1993
Membership: 30; *Fees:* $25

Okanagan Similkameen Parks Society (OSPS)
PO Box 787, Summerland BC V0H 1Z0
Tel: 250-494-8996
okanagansimilkameenparkssociety.ca
Overview: A small local charitable organization founded in 1965
Member of: West Coast Environmental Law; Sierra Club
Affiliation(s): Friends of Stikine; Friends of Strathcona Park; Creston Wildlife; Okanagan Naturalists
Finances: *Annual Operating Budget:* Less than $50,000; *Funding Sources:* Donations; membership fees; bequests; Penticton Foundation
Membership: 273; *Fees:* $10 single; $15 couple/family; $20 organization; *Member Profile:* Interest in parks; land & wildlife stewardship/conservation; historic trails; forestry practices; watershed protection; urban green spaces
Activities: Monthly meetings; special events; seminars; workshops; film; brochures & booklets; *Awareness Events:* Meadowlark Festival, Penticton - May
Chief Officer(s):
Jeremy McCall, Executive Director

Okanagan Similkameen Tourism Association *See* Thompson Okanagan Tourism Association

Okanagan Symphony Society
865 Bernard Ave., Kelowna BC V1Y 6P6
Tel: 250-763-7544
admin@okanagansymphony.com
okanagansymphony.com
www.facebook.com/OkanaganSymphonyOrchestra
twitter.com/oksymphonyorch
Overview: A small provincial charitable organization founded in 1967 overseen by Orchestras Canada
Mission: To provide the communities of the Okanagan Valley with an orchestra that is committed to excellence in the performance of classical music
Finances: *Funding Sources:* Corporate & individual sponsors; Government grants; Ticket revenue
Staff Member(s): 7
Membership: 54
Activities: Performing concert series; Performing at schools; Facilitating master classes and workshops; *Internships:* Yes; *Speaker Service:* Yes; *Library:* by appointment
Chief Officer(s):
Robert Barr, Executive Director
rbarr@okanagansymphony.com
Rosemary Thomson, Music Director
md@okanagansymphony.com

Okotoks & District Chamber of Commerce
PO Box 1053, 4-87 Elizabeth St., Okotoks AB T1S 1B1
Tel: 403-938-2848; *Fax:* 403-995-3338
ceo@okotokschamber.ca
www.okotokschamber.ca
Overview: A small local organization
Mission: To strengthen & support businesses in the Okotoks & District community
Finances: *Funding Sources:* Membership dues
Membership: 265; *Fees:* $175 business; $150 individual/home-based; $50 non-profit
Activities: Organizing events such as Lite-up Okotoks, Okotoks Rocks - Sports Day, Okotoks Pro-Rodeo, Tailgate Sale, & Parade
Chief Officer(s):
Cheryl Actemichuk, Executive Director

Okotoks Arts Council
PO Box 149, Okotoks AB T1S 2A2
Tel: 403-938-3204; *Fax:* 403-938-8963
okotoksartscouncil.ca
www.facebook.com/OkotoksCulture
twitter.com/okotoksarts
Overview: A small local organization founded in 1979
Mission: Developing and promoting cultural activities in the community.
Activities: *Awareness Events:* Alberta Culture Days, September
Chief Officer(s):
Linda Macallum, President

Old Brewery Mission *Voir* Mission Old Brewery

Old Chrysler Corporation Auto Club
57 Pinehurst Cres., Kitchener ON N2N 1E3
Tel: 519-342-1284; *Fax:* 519-342-1285
moparfest@rogers.com
www.moparfest.com
Also Known As: OCC Auto Club
Overview: A small local organization founded in 1979
Mission: To promote the maintenance & restoration of Chrysler/AMC vehicles
Finances: *Annual Operating Budget:* $50,000-$100,000
Staff Member(s): 10; 100 volunteer(s)
Membership: 125; *Fees:* $30; *Member Profile:* Interest in old Chrysler automobiles
Activities: Organizing Moparfest & other automotive events; *Awareness Events:* Mopar Fest, Aug.

Old Strathcona Foundation (OSF)
Queen Alexandra School, 7730 - 106 St., 3rd Fl., Edmonton AB T6E 4W3
Tel: 780-433-5866; *Fax:* 780-431-1938
info@oldstrathconafoundation.ca
www.oldstrathconafoundation.ca
Overview: A small national charitable organization founded in 1974
Staff Member(s): 1; 100 volunteer(s)
Membership: 170; *Fees:* $20; *Committees:* Murals; Planning; Historical
Activities: *Awareness Events:* Silly Summer Parade, July 1; Art Walk, end of July
Chief Officer(s):
Karen Tabor, Executive Director
Wayne Moen, President/Treasurer

Old Sydney Society
225 George St., Sydney NS B1P 1J5
Tel: 902-539-1572; *Fax:* 902-539-1572
oldsydneysociety@ns.aliantzinc.ca
www.oldsydney.com
www.facebook.com/OldSydneySociety
twitter.com/OldSydney
Overview: A small local charitable organization founded in 1966
Mission: To preserve & promote interest in local heritage; To mark historic sites in Sydney & area; To operate museums under its jurisdiction
Member of: Federation of the Nova Scotian Heritage
Finances: *Funding Sources:* NS Museum Assistance; municipal; membership fees; shop; special events
Membership: *Fees:* $10 individual; $15 family; $100 sustaining
Activities: Operates St. Patrick's Church Museum, Cossit House & Jost House, heritage houses (seasonal), & C.B. Centre for Heritage & Science (year-round); works with local school boards to provide educational experiences for students; hosts travelling exhibits & walking tours; *Speaker Service:* Yes; *Library:* Open to public

The Olde Forge Community Resource Centre (OFCRC) / Centre de ressources communautaires Olde Forge
2730 Carling Ave., Ottawa ON K2B 7J1
Tel: 613-829-9777
oldeforge.ca
Overview: A small local charitable organization founded in 1970
Mission: To provide an information & referral service; To operate a support service to enable senior citizens to remain in their own homes as long as possible
Member of: Ontario Community Support Association
Finances: *Annual Operating Budget:* $100,000-$250,000; *Funding Sources:* Municipal & provincial government; Community donations; Fundraising
Staff Member(s): 6; 107 volunteer(s)
Membership: 50
Chief Officer(s):
Anita Bloom, Executive Director, 613-829-9777 Ext. 224

Older Adult Centres' Association of Ontario (OACAO) / Association des centres pour aînés de l'Ontario
PO Box 65, Caledon East ON L7C 3L8
Tel: 905-584-8125; *Fax:* 905-584-8126
Toll-Free: 866-835-7693
admin@oacao.org
www.oacao.org
www.facebook.com/oacao
twitter.com/theoacao
Overview: A large provincial charitable organization founded in 1973
Mission: To ensure that seniors in Ontario have opportunities & choices that lead to healthy, active lifestyles
Member of: Ontario Community Support Association; Ontario Coalition of Senior Citizens Organizations; United Generations Ontario
Finances: *Funding Sources:* Membership fees; Business; Grants; Events
Membership: 145 centres representing over 300 staff & 150,000 seniors; *Fees:* Schedule available; *Member Profile:* Older adult centres in Ontario
Activities: *Library:* Resource Centre; by appointment
Chief Officer(s):
Sue Hesjedahl, Executive Director
sue@oacao.org
Awards:
• Award of Merit
• Person of Distinction Award
• Past President's Award
• Life Membership Award
• Print Media Award of Merit
• Electronic Media Award of Merit
• Community Spirit Award
Meetings/Conferences:
• Older Adult Centres' Association of Ontario Annual Conference 2018, 2018, ON
Scope: Provincial

The Older Women's Network (OWN) / Réseau des femmes aînées
115 The Esplanade, Toronto ON M5E 1Y7
Tel: 416-214-1518
info@olderwomensnetwork.org
olderwomensnetwork.org
Overview: A small provincial charitable organization founded in 1988
Mission: To initiate & support discussion on issues relevant to the well-being of older women; To develop & support legislation to expand opportunities for housing, economic security, & optimum health; To monitor the media in order to encourage a more realistic & positive portrayal of older women; To support the efforts of young women to achieve equal opportunity, freedom from discrimination, abuse & exploitation, & the right to reproductive choice; To support the needs of children; To liaise with movements for social justice in Canada & abroad
Member of: National Action Committee on the Status of Women; Ontario Coalition of Senior Citizens Associations
Affiliation(s): One Voice; National Association of Women & the Law; Women's Legal Education & Action Fund
Finances: *Funding Sources:* Membership fees; individual donors

Membership: *Fees:* $35 individuals; *Member Profile:* Older women who support OWN's objectives; *Committees:* Finance; Anam Cara; Special Interest Groups & Outreach; Housing; Alfreda Mordas Reading Room; Nominating & Bylaws; Membership; Communications
Activities: Engaging in advocacy activities; Providing presentations to all levels of government; *Speaker Service:* Yes

Oldman River Antique Equipment & Threshing Club
PO Box 2496, Pincher Creek AB T0K 1W0
Overview: A small local charitable organization founded in 1987
Mission: To collect, preserve, & demonstrate antique farm equipment from southern Alberta
Finances: *Funding Sources:* Donations; Fundraising
Activities: Operating a museum

Olds & District Chamber of Commerce
PO Box 4210, Olds AB T4H 1P8
Tel: 403-556-7070; *Fax:* 403-556-1515
chamber@oldsalberta.com
www.oldsalberta.com
www.facebook.com/OldsChamberOfCommerce
twitter.com/oldschamber
Overview: A small local organization
Mission: To serve & improve the business, economic, & social communities of the town & area
Membership: *Fees:* Schedule available
Activities: Advocating; Providing services to members
Chief Officer(s):
Barb Babiak, Executive Director

Olds Agricultural Society *See* Olds Regional Exhibition

Olds College Faculty Association (OCFA) / Association des professeurs du Collège Olds
Olds College, 4500 - 50 St., Olds AB T4H 1R6
Tel: 403-556-4636; *Fax:* 403-556-4637
ocfaea@oldscollege.ca
www.oldscollege.ca/staff/faculty-association
Overview: A small local organization founded in 1968
Member of: Alberta Colleges & Institutes Faculties Association (ACIFA)
Finances: *Annual Operating Budget:* Less than $50,000
Staff Member(s): 1
Membership: 93; *Committees:* Academic Council; ACIFA Negotiation Advisory; CLC Governance; Ethics; Faculty Centre; Faculty PD Event(s); Faculty Professional Development; Graduation; Grievance; Legislative; Negotiations; Nominations; OH & S; Professional Practices; Social
Chief Officer(s):
Keith Smyth, President, 403-507-7938
ksmyth@oldscollege.ca
Sandra Hallett, Executive Assistant
Awards:
- OCFA Outstanding Student Award

Olds Regional Exhibition (ORE)
PO Box 3751, Olds AB T4H 1P5
Tel: 403-556-3770; *Fax:* 403-556-3333
office@oldsregionalexhibition.com
www.oldsregionalexhibition.com
www.facebook.com/oldsagsociety
Previous Name: Olds Agricultural Society
Overview: A small local organization founded in 1899
Mission: To organize events that promote awareness of agriculture's role in the community
Member of: Canadian Beef Breeds Council
Membership: *Fees:* $10; *Member Profile:* Individuals over 18 who reside in Alberta; *Committees:* Finance
Activities: Festivals; agricultural shows & events; conferences
Chief Officer(s):
Tami Gardner, Executive Director
tami@oldsregionalexhibition.com
Tracy Gardner, Manager, Events
tracy@oldsregionalexhibition.com
Buck Thompson, Manager, Operations
facilities@oldsregionalexhibition.com

Oliver & District Chamber of Commerce *See* South Okanagan Chamber Of Commerce

Oliver Community Arts Council (OCAC)
PO Box 1711, Oliver BC V0H 1T0
Tel: 250-498-0183; *Fax:* 250-498-0183
olivercac@gmail.com
www.oliverartscouncil.org
Overview: A small local charitable organization founded in 1976
Mission: To increase & broaden the opportunities of Oliver residents to enjoy & participate in cultural activities
Member of: Assembly of BC Arts Councils
Finances: *Annual Operating Budget:* Less than $50,000 60 volunteer(s)
Membership: 12 member groups; 60 individual/family; *Fees:* $10 individual; $15 family; $25 group; $35 business; *Committees:* Executive; Board of Directors; Development & Design; Fall Art Show; Summer Studio; Public Relations; Building Operations; Finance; Entertainment
Activities: Summer Studio; Music in the Park; Fall Arts Show; Showcase of Talent; Arts & Culture Week
Chief Officer(s):
Jo Ann Turner
Terry Irvine
Penelope Johnson

Oliver Food Bank
PO Box 405, Oliver BC V0H 1T0
Tel: 250-498-4555
Overview: A small local organization overseen by Food Banks British Columbia
Member of: Food Banks British Columbia
Chief Officer(s):
Jim Ouellette, Contact
jimo@persona.ca

Oliver-Osoyoos Naturalists
PO Box 1181, Osoyoos BC V0H 1V0
Tel: 250-485-0263
Overview: A small local organization founded in 1973
Mission: To cooperate and communicate with other naturalists. To foster an awareness, appreciation and understanding of our natural environment so that it may be wisely used and maintained for future generations.
Member of: The Federation of BC Naturalists
Finances: *Annual Operating Budget:* Less than $50,000
Membership: 60; *Fees:* $25 individual; $30 family; *Member Profile:* People interested in nature & the environment
Activities: Walks; hiking; bird watching; outdoor education; caretaking of two ecological reserves; environmental restoration; "clean-up" projects.
Chief Officer(s):
Jackie Castellarin, Contact
ivocastellarin@gmail.com

Olivet New Church
279 Burnhamthorpe Rd., Toronto ON M9B 1Z6
Tel: 416-239-3054
contact@olivetnewchurch.org
www.olivetnewchurch.org
www.facebook.com/olivet.newchurch
Also Known As: Olivet
Overview: A small local organization founded in 1893
Mission: To inspire belief in New Church teachings; To encourage spiritual growth practices; To provide & promote service to others; To offer leadership & volunteerism opportunities
Membership: *Committees:* GCIC; Men's Group; Women's Group
Activities: Offering Sunday worship & school services; *Speaker Service:* Yes; Library

Olympic Aid *See* Right to Play

Olympiques spéciaux Canada *See* Special Olympics Canada

OmbudService for Life & Health Insurance (OLHI) / Ombudsman des assurances de personnes (OAP)
PO Box 7, 401 Bay St., Toronto ON M5H 2Y4
Tel: 416-777-9002
Toll-Free: 888-295-8112
Other Communication: Bell Relay Service: 1-800-855-0511
www.olhi.ca
Previous Name: Canadian Life & Health Insurance OmbudService
Overview: A medium-sized national organization
Mission: An independent service that assists consumers with concerns & complaints about life & health insurance products & services.
Member of: Financial Services OmbudsNetwork (FSON)
Chief Officer(s):
Janice MacKinnon, Chair
    Montréal Office
    2001, rue University, 17e étage, Montréal QC H3A 2A6
    Tel: 514-282-2088
    Toll-Free: 866-582-2088
    www.olhi.ca

Ombudsman des assurances de personnes *See* OmbudService for Life & Health Insurance

Ombudsman des services bancaires et d'investissement *See* Ombudsman for Banking Services & Investments

Ombudsman for Banking Services & Investments (OBSI) / Ombudsman des services bancaires et d'investissement (OSBI)
PO Box 5, #1505, 401 Bay St., Toronto ON M5H 2Y4
Tel: 416-287-2877; *Fax:* 416-225-4722
Toll-Free: 888-451-4519; *TTY:* 855-889-6274
Other Communication: Toll-Free Fax: 1-888-422-2865
ombudsman@obsi.ca
www.obsi.ca
Previous Name: Canadian Banking Ombudsman
Overview: A medium-sized national organization founded in 1996
Mission: To investigate complaints from individuals & small businesses about banking services; To provide impartial & prompt resolution of complaints, based on fairness & good business & banking practices
Member of: Financial Services OmbudsNetwork (FSON)
Membership: 500-999; *Member Profile:* Retail & commercial banks; Investment dealers; Mutual fund dealers; Fund companies; *Committees:* Finance & Audit; Governance, Human Resources & Compensation; Policy & Standards
Activities: *Speaker Service:* Yes
Chief Officer(s):
Fernand Bélisle, Chair
Douglas Melville, Ombudsman & CEO

OMF International - Canada (OMF)
#21, 5155 Spectrum Way., Mississauga ON L4W 5A1
Tel: 905-568-9971; *Fax:* 905-568-9974
Toll-Free: 888-657-8010
omfcanada@omf.ca
www.omf.ca
www.facebook.com/omfcanada
twitter.com/OMFcanada
Also Known As: Overseas Missionary Fellowship
Previous Name: China Inland Mission
Overview: A medium-sized international organization founded in 1865
Mission: To share the good news of Jesus Christ with East Asia's peoples
Member of: Interdenominational Foreign Mission Association
Affiliation(s): Evangelical Fellowship of Canada
Staff Member(s): 120
Membership: 1,300 missionaries worldwide; *Member Profile:* Four years post-secondary education
Chief Officer(s):
Ron Adams, Director, Administration & Finance
Jon Fuller, National Director
    Alberta Region
    Tel: 780-483-8025
    george.jakeway@gmail.com
    Chief Officer(s):
    George Jakeway, Regional Ministry Coordinator
    Atlantic Region
    152 Douglas Crescent, Halifax NS E9B 1R8
    Tel: 902-454-9665
    ca.atl.rmc@omfmail.com
    Chief Officer(s):
    Hasell Kerr, Regional Ministry Coordinator
    Manitoba Region
    MB
    Ontario Region
    ON
    Tel: 905-568-9971
    ca.ont.rd@omfmail.com
    Chief Officer(s):
    CY Yan, Region Director
    Pacific Region
    BC
    Tel: 604-278-1208; *Fax:* 604-278-1208
    CA.BC.RD@omfmail.com
    Chief Officer(s):
    Gary Roosma, Regional Director
    Québec Region
    QC
    Tel: 514-488-9383

Canadian Associations / OMID Foundation Canada

Chief Officer(s):
Brian Ludgate, Regional Ministry Coordinator
Saskatchewan Region
SK
Tel: 306-975-1298
Chief Officer(s):
David Ginther, Regional Ministry Coordinator

OMID Foundation Canada
29 Metheun Ave., Toronto ON M6S 1Z7
Tel: 647-708-3633
toronto@omidfoundation.com
www.omidfoundation.com
Overview: A large international organization founded in 2014
Mission: To raise money for the Omid e Mehr program, which strengthens the social, emotional, & economic skills & competencies of disadvantaged young women in Iran
Finances: *Funding Sources:* Donations
Activities: Fundraising; *Internships:* Yes
Chief Officer(s):
Yassi Dadashi, Contact

On Screen Manitoba
#003, 100 Albert St., Winnipeg MB R3B 1H3
Tel: 204-927-5898; *Fax:* 204-272-8792
info@onscreenmanitoba.com
www.onscreenmanitoba.com
www.facebook.com/onscreenmanitoba
twitter.com/OnScreenMB
www.youtube.com/user/OnScreenManitoba
Previous Name: Manitoba Motion Picture Industries Association
Overview: A medium-sized provincial organization founded in 1987
Mission: To build & represent the motion picture industry in Manitoba; To foster excellence & innovation in the industry
Finances: *Funding Sources:* Sponsorships; Department of Culture, Heritage & Tourism; Western Economic Diversification; Telefilm Canada; MB Film & Sound Recording Development Corp
Membership: *Fees:* $25 students & corporate & production company employees; $50 voting individuals; $100 production company producers; $200 procduction companies
Activities: Engaging in advocacy activities; Offering networking opportunities; Providing information about industry statistics, training programs, funding, & festivals; Raising public awareness of the benefits of the industry in the province
Chief Officer(s):
Nicole Matiation, Executive Director, 204-927-5893
nicole@onscreenmanitoba.com
Trevor Suffield, Coordinator, Communications, 204-927-5896
trevor@onscreenmanitoba.com
Awards:
• Blizzard Awards
To recognize excellence in Manitoba film & video production
Publications:
• The Manitoba Film & Television Production Guide
Type: Directory; *Frequency:* Annually
Profile: Published by On Screen Manitoba, in partnership with Manitoba Film & Sound
• On Screen Manitoba Newsletter
Type: Newsletter

On the Border, Lloydminster *See* Habitat for Humanity Canada

On to Ottawa Historical Society
c/o Joey Hartman, Vancouver BC
Tel: 604-254-0703
webmaster@ontoottawa.ca
www.ontoottawa.ca
Overview: A small local organization founded in 1988
Mission: To preserve labour's heritage, specifically the history of the On to Ottawa trek
Chief Officer(s):
Joey Harman, Contact

One Full Circle (OFC)
882, boul Décarie, Montréal QC H4L 3L9
Tel: 514-651-4545
onefullcircleofc@gmail.com
theofc.org
www.facebook.com/theofc
twitter.com/1fullcircle
www.youtube.com/channel/UCHz2HhkluaA112A3g_RNd_Q
Overview: A small local organization founded in 2011
Mission: To provide social & community services to members of the black community in Montréal

Membership: *Fees:* $54 supporting; $108 core; $162 business
Chief Officer(s):
Shiata Lewis, Co-Founder
Pharaoh Freeman, Co-Founder & Head Coordinator

100 Mile & District Arts Council
PO Box 2262, 100 Mile House BC V0K 2E0
Tel: 250-395-2697; *Fax:* 250-791-6420
administration@100milearts.com
www.100milearts.com
Overview: A small local organization founded in 1975
Mission: To develop opportunities for area residents to experience &/or participate in creative & cultural endeavours
Member of: Assembly of BC Arts Councils; Central Interior Regional Arts Council
Finances: *Annual Operating Budget:* Less than $50,000
10 volunteer(s)
Membership: 40; *Fees:* $30 group; $15 individual
Activities: *Awareness Events:* Winter Arts & Crafts Fair, November; Festival of the Arts Recitals & Presentations

100 Mile House Food Bank Society
199 - 7 St., 100 Mile House BC V0K 2E3
Tel: 250-395-3923; *Fax:* 250-397-2579
Overview: A small local organization overseen by Food Banks British Columbia
Member of: Food Banks British Columbia

One Parent Families Association of Canada / Association des familles uniparentales du Canada
PO Box 628, Pickering ON L1V 3T3
Tel: 905-831-7098
Toll-Free: 877-773-7714
oneparentfamilies@gmx.com
oneparentfamilies.net
Overview: A small national charitable organization founded in 1973
Mission: To develop & provide a broad comprehensive program for the enlightenment & guidance of single parents & their children on the special problems they encounter & for assistance on the various readjustments involved.
Membership: *Member Profile:* Separated, divorced, widowed or never married parents; custodial & non-custodial parents
Chief Officer(s):
Greg Mercer, President

One Sky
PO Box 3352, 3768 - 2 Ave., Smithers BC V0J 1N0
Tel: 250-877-6030
www.onesky.ca
Overview: A medium-sized national organization founded in 2000
Mission: To promote sustainable living globally; To inspire and promote solutions, provide practical solutions, and network across sectors with like-minded organizations.
Finances: *Funding Sources:* Donations
Membership: *Fees:* $10
Activities: *Internships:* Yes
Chief Officer(s):
Michael Simpson, Executive Director

1000 Islands Gananoque Chamber of Commerce
215 Stone St. South, Gananoque ON K7G 2V4
Tel: 613-382-7744
info@1000islandsganchamber.com
www.1000islandsganchamber.com
www.linkedin.com/company/1000-islands-gananoque-chamber-of-commerce
www.facebook.com/1000IslandsGananoqueChamber
twitter.com/gananoquechamb
Overview: A small local organization
Mission: To improve commerce in Gananoque
Member of: Eastern Ontario Travel Association; 1,000 Islands International Council; Québec Bus Association; Canadian Chamber of Commerce; Ontario Chamber of Commerce
Affiliation(s): Travel Media Association of Canada
Finances: *Funding Sources:* Membership dues; fundraisers; fee for services from town & township
Membership: 200; *Fees:* $60 non-profit/service club; $120 1-5 employees; $170 6-10 employees; $220 11-15 employees; $270 16+ employees
Activities: *Library:* Resource Centre
Chief Officer(s):
Michael Smith, President

One World Arts (OWA)
323 Chapel St., 3rd Fl., Ottawa ON K1N 7Z2

Tel: 613-238-4659; *Fax:* 613-238-1888
inquiries@oneworldarts.ca
oneworldarts.ca
www.facebook.com/214778781880093
twitter.com/OneWorldArts
Previous Name: World Inter-Action Mondiale; Ottawa-Hull Learner Centre
Overview: A medium-sized local charitable organization founded in 1972
Mission: To raise awareness about global issues, using different types of media & performing arts projects
Member of: Global Education Centres of Ontario; Ontario Council for International Cooperation; Canadian Council for International Cooperation
Staff Member(s): 3
Activities: *Awareness Events:* One World Film Festival, September
Chief Officer(s):
Pixie Cam, Manager, Film Festival Program
pixie.cram@oneworldarts.ca
Micheline Shoebridge, Manager, Arts Program & Festival
micheline.shoebridge@oneworldarts.ca

Onoway & District Chamber of Commerce
PO Box 723, Onoway AB T0E 1V0
Tel: 780-967-2550
info@onowaychamber.ca
www.onowaychamber.ca
Overview: A small local organization
Mission: To support the business community of Onoway & the surrounding area
Chief Officer(s):
Ed Gallagher, President

Ontaria Esperanto-Asocio *See* Esperanto Rondo de Otavo

Ontario 5 Pin Bowlers' Association (O5PBA)
#302, 3 Concorde Gate, Toronto ON M3C 3N7
Tel: 416-426-7167; *Fax:* 416-426-7364
o5pba@o5pba.ca
www.o5pba.ca
Overview: A medium-sized provincial organization founded in 1963
Mission: To act as the governing body for 5 pin bowling in Ontario
Member of: Canadian 5 Pin Bowlers' Association
Staff Member(s): 3
Membership: 10,000
Chief Officer(s):
John Cresswell, President
Rhonda Gifford, Coordinator, Program
Jackie Henriques, Coordinator, Finances
Al Hong, Coordinator, Events
Publications:
• Pinboard
Type: Newsletter; *Frequency:* Monthly
Profile: Event highlights

Ontario Aboriginal Lands Association (OALA)
c/o Wanda McGonigle, Hiawatha First Nation, 123 Paudash St., RR #2, Keene ON K0L 2G0
Tel: 705-295-4421
Overview: A small provincial organization founded in 1995 overseen by National Aboriginal Lands Managers Association
Mission: To network towards the enhancement of professional development & expertise in Lands Management issues; To achieve a recognized role within the federal & provincial governments, & provincial & territorial organizations
Staff Member(s): 1
Membership: 22; *Fees:* $250; *Member Profile:* First Nations in Ontario
Chief Officer(s):
Wanda McGonigle, Chair
wmcgonig@hiawathafn.ca

Ontario Aerospace Council (OAC)
1701 Aberfoyle Ct., Pickering ON L1V 4W4
Tel: 905-492-2296
www.theoac.ca
www.linkedin.com/company/ontario-aerospace-council
Overview: A medium-sized provincial organization
Mission: To enhance Ontario's aerospace industry in the global market; to ensure growth & prosperity
Finances: *Funding Sources:* Membership dues
Staff Member(s): 4
Membership: 250+; *Fees:* $450 associate; $700+ industry; *Member Profile:* Companies in the Ontario aerospace industry

Activities: Fostering relationships between industry stakeholders to promote knowledge & growth; Implementing member programs, events, & initiatives
Chief Officer(s):
Moira Harvey, Executive Director
moira.harvey@theOAC.ca

Ontario Agencies Supporting Individuals with Special Needs (OASIS)
c/o Community Living South Muskoka, 15 Depot Dr., Bracebridge ON P1L 0A1
Tel: 705-645-5494
administrativesupport@oasisonline.ca
www.oasisonline.ca
www.facebook.com/oasis.ontario
twitter.com/oasisontario
Overview: A medium-sized provincial organization
Mission: To facilitate the sharing of ideas, resources, systems & information; to liaise with government on behalf of member organizations with the goal of improving the development of cost effective quality supports for individuals with developmental disabilities
Membership: 181; *Fees:* $1500
Chief Officer(s):
David Barber, President
Amanda Brown, Administrative Contact

Ontario Agri Business Association (OABA)
#104, 160 Research Lane, Guelph ON N1G 5B2
Tel: 519-822-3004; *Fax:* 519-822-8862
info@oaba.on.ca
www.oaba.on.ca
Merged from: Ontario Grain & Feed Association; Fertilizer Institute of Ontario
Overview: A medium-sized provincial organization founded in 1965
Mission: To serve & represent firms engaged in the crop inputs, country grain elevator, & feed & farm supply industy, plus related agricultural businesses operating within Ontario
Member of: Canadian Fertilizer Institute; Animal Nutrition Association of Canada
Finances: *Funding Sources:* Annual membership dues from regular, branch, &c associate members
Staff Member(s): 5
Membership: *Member Profile:* Country grain elevators in Ontario; Ontario crop input supply businesses; Feed manufacturing facilities in the province; Associated businesses that provide products & services to the crop input, grain, & feed industry
Activities: Delivering products, programs, & services to members; Promoting the crop input, grain, & feed industry; Coordinating services of member sectors in areas such as food safety & environmental stewardship; Providing educational opportunities; Liaising with stakeholders, consumers, & government; Studying legislation affecting members; Disseminating information to members; Engaging in & sponsoring research
Chief Officer(s):
Dave Buttenham, Chief Executive Officer
dave@oaba.on.ca
Darcy Oliphant, President
Dave Bender, Vice-President
Cassandra Loomans, Treasurer

Ontario Agri-Food Education Inc. (OAFE)
PO Box 460, 8560 Tremaine Rd., Milton ON L9T 4Z1
Tel: 905-878-1510; *Fax:* 905-878-0342
info@oafe.org
www.oafe.org
www.linkedin.com/company/ontario-agri-food-education-inc-?trk=fc_badge
www.facebook.com/OAFEInc
twitter.com/OntAgriFoodEd
Overview: A small provincial organization founded in 1991
Mission: To build awareness & understanding of the importance of an agriculture & food system; To provide high quality, objective & relevant agriculture & food related learning materials & services for Ontario educators to enhance the learning experiences of students in Ontario classrooms
Membership: *Fees:* $50 individual
Chief Officer(s):
Colleen Smith, Executive Director, 905-878-151 Ext. 22
director@oafe.org

Ontario Agri-Food Technologies (OAFT)
Agri-Technology Commercialization Centre, #200, 120 Research Lane, Guelph ON N1G 0B4
Tel: 519-826-4195; *Fax:* 519-821-7361
info@oaft.org
www.oaft.org
Overview: A medium-sized provincial organization founded in 1997
Mission: To generate wealth & sustainability for the Ontario agriculture & food industries by utilizing current technologies
Affiliation(s): Agriculture and Agri-Food Canada; Ontario Ministry of Agriculture and Food/Ministry of Rural Affairs; Ontario Ministry of Economic Development, Trade and Employment
Membership: *Member Profile:* Grower organizations; Industry; Universities; Government; Affiliates
Chief Officer(s):
Tyler Whale, President
Andrea Murray, Program Administrator
amurray@oaft.org

Ontario Allergy Society *See* Allergy, Asthma & Immunology Society of Ontario

Ontario Alliance of Christian Schools (OACS)
790 Shaver Rd., Ancaster ON L9G 3K9
Tel: 905-648-2100; *Fax:* 905-648-2110
oacs@oacs.org
www.oacs.org
twitter.com/oacsnews
Overview: A medium-sized provincial organization founded in 1952 overseen by Federation of Independent Schools in Canada
Mission: To promote independent schools in Ontario; to promote Christian education in Canada; to provide educational services for member schools; to lobby government for educational choice. Canada's largest & oldest independent school organization, representing 79 schools with approximately 14,000 students.
Affiliation(s): Christian Schools International; Christian Schools Canada
Finances: *Annual Operating Budget:* $500,000-$1.5 Million; *Funding Sources:* Membership dues
Staff Member(s): 12; 200 volunteer(s)
Membership: 1-99; *Fees:* Schedule available; *Committees:* Finance; Education; PR; Planning; Government Relations; Personnel
Activities: *Speaker Service:* Yes; *Rents Mailing List:* Yes
Chief Officer(s):
Julius de Jager, MAT, Executive Director, 905-648-2100 Ext. 15
julesdj@oacs.org

Ontario Amateur Netball Association *See* Netball Ontario

Ontario Amateur Softball Association (OASA)
c/o Registrar, 44 Hilltop Blvd., RR#1, Gormley ON L0H 1G0
Tel: 905-727-5139
www.oasa.ca
www.facebook.com/OntarioAmateurSoftballAssocation
twitter.com/OASASoftball
Overview: A medium-sized provincial organization founded in 1923 overseen by Softball Ontario
Mission: To be the provincial governing body for the sport of amateur softball in Ontario
Member of: Canadian Amateur Softball Association; Softball Ontario
Finances: *Funding Sources:* Sponsors; Partners; Government grants; Player/team fees
Chief Officer(s):
Garry Waugh, President, 519-537-5835
gwaugh@execulink.com
Brad Thomson, Executive Vice President, 519-954-1269
oasabradthomson@gmail.com
Awards:
• Ontatio Amateur Softball Association Scholarship
Rewards the scholarship & academic excellence of OASA players enrolled in either a community college or university
Eligibility: Players who have played at either the Midget or Junior OASA level in the year that the scholarship is to awarded
Contact: Karen Mills, millsy@live.ca

Ontario Amateur Wrestling Association (OAWA)
#213, 3 Concorde Gate, Toronto ON M3C 3N7
Tel: 416-426-7274
admin@oawa.ca
www.oawa.ca
twitter.com/OAWA_Wrestling
Also Known As: Ontario Wrestling
Overview: A medium-sized provincial organization founded in 1980 overseen by Canadian Amateur Wrestling Association
Mission: To provide essential services & programs dedicated to developing amateur wrestling at all age levels within Ontario
Affiliation(s): International Amateur Wrestling Association; Canadian Amateur Wrestling Association
Finances: *Annual Operating Budget:* $100,000-$250,000; *Funding Sources:* Government; private donors; sponsors; fundraising; user fees
Membership: 1,800; *Fees:* $85 coach; $65 official/athlete (older than 9 years); $55 athletes (7-8 years); $45 supporter
Activities: Competitons; demonstrations
Chief Officer(s):
Tim MaGarrey, Provincial Director

Ontario Amputee & Les Autres Sports Association (OALASA)
c/o Rodney Reimer, 15 Tanner Dr., London ON N5W 6B4
oalasa.webs.com
Previous Name: Ontario Amputee Sports Association
Overview: A small provincial organization founded in 1976
Member of: Sport for Disabled Ontario; Canadian Amputee Sports Association
Finances: *Annual Operating Budget:* Less than $50,000; *Funding Sources:* Bingos
15 volunteer(s)
Membership: 100 individual; *Fees:* $20 regular; $15 associate; *Member Profile:* Anyone interested in amputee & les autres sports
Activities: Golf clinics & tournaments; speakers; lawn bowls tournament; boccia tournament; *Speaker Service:* Yes
Chief Officer(s):
Rodney Reimer, President, 519-659-7452
rodreimer@rogers.com

Ontario Amputee Sports Association *See* Ontario Amputee & Les Autres Sports Association

Ontario Angus Association (OAA)
PO Box 331, Fergus ON N1M 3E2
Tel: 519-787-2397; *Fax:* 519-928-9972
secretary@ontarioangus.com
www.ontarioangus.com
Overview: A small provincial organization
Mission: To encourage the breeding of quality livestock
Member of: Canadian Angus Association
Membership: 100-499
Chief Officer(s):
Julie Smith, Secretary-Treasurer

The Ontario Archaeological Society
PO Box 62066, Stn. Victoria Terrace, #102, 1444 Queen St. E, Toronto ON M4A 2W1
Tel: 416-406-5959; *Fax:* 416-406-5959
info@ontarioarchaeology.org
www.ontarioarchaeology.org
twitter.com/ontarchsoc
www.youtube.com/user/OntarioArchaeology
Overview: A medium-sized provincial charitable organization founded in 1950 overseen by Canadian Archaeological Association
Mission: To preserve, promote, investigate, record & publish an archaeological record of the province of Ontario
Finances: *Funding Sources:* Membership dues; Government; Programs; Donations
Staff Member(s): 7
Membership: 600 individual + 25 senior/lifetime + 75 family; *Fees:* Schedule available
Activities: Offering public archaeology programs, trips, & lecture series; *Speaker Service:* Yes; *Library:* by appointment
Chief Officer(s):
Lorie Harris, Executive Director
execdirector@ontarioarchaeology.org
Chris Dalton, Director, Chapter Services
chapters@ontarioarchaeology.org
Dana Millson, Director, Membership
membership@ontarioarchaeology.org
Awards:
• Ian Kenyon Memorial Award
• J. Norman Emerson Silver Medal
• Heritage Conservation Award
• J.V. Wright Lifetime Achievement Award
• Tim Kenyon Memorial Award
• Peggi Armstrong Public Archaeology Award
• Killarney Award for Outstanding Service
• Award for Excellence in Cultural Resource Management
• Award for Excellence in Publishing
• OAS Student Paper-Poster Award
• Valerie Sonstenes Student Research Fund
Publications:
• Arch Notes [a publication of the Ontario Archaeology Society]

Type: Newsletter; *Frequency:* bi-m.; *Editor:* Sheryl A. Smith; *ISSN:* 0048-1742
• Monographs in Ontario Archaeology [a publication of the Ontario Archaeology Society]
Type: Monograph; *ISSN:* 0714-4881
• Ontario Archaeology [a publication of the Ontario Archaeology Society]
Type: Journal; *Editor:* Chris Ellis; *ISSN:* 0078-4672; *Price:* $9 for student members; $12 for all other members

Hamilton Chapter
c/o Dr. Gary Warrick, Laurier Brantford, 73 George St., Brantford ON N3T 2Y3
Tel: 866-243-7028
oashamilton@gmail.com
hamilton.ontarioarchaeology.on.ca
Chief Officer(s):
Emily Anson, President

Huronia Chapter
c/o Huronia Museum, PO Box 638, 549 Little Lake Park, Midland ON L4R 4P4
huronia.ontarioarchaeology.on.ca
Chief Officer(s):
Kristin Thor, Treasurer

London Chapter
Museum of Ontario Archaeology, 1600 Attawandaron Rd., London ON N6G 3M6
www.ssc.uwo.ca/assoc/oas
Chief Officer(s):
Chris Ellis, Treasurer
cjellis@uwo.ca

Ottawa Chapter
PO Box 4939, Stn. E, Ottawa ON K1S 5J1
contact@ottawaoas.ca
www.ottawaoas.ca
www.facebook.com/582145708470231
twitter.com/OttawaOAS
Chief Officer(s):
André Miller, President

Peterborough Chapter
51 Adelaide St. South, Lindsay ON K9V 3J6
Tel: 705-320-9979
www.ontarioarchaeology.org/~peterborough
Chief Officer(s):
Tom Mohr, President
mohr.utsc.utoronto.ca

Thunder Bay Chapter
c/o Lakehead University, 955 Oliver Rd., Thunder Bay ON P7B 5E1
Chief Officer(s):
Clarence Surette, President
clsurett@lakeheadu.ca

Toronto Chapter
Toronto's First Post Office, PO Box 48, 260 Adelaide St. East, Toronto ON M5A 1N1
torontoarchaeology@gmail.com
toronto.ontarioarchaeology.on.ca
Chief Officer(s):
Carole Stimmell, President

Windsor Chapter
218 McKay Ave., Windsor ON N9B 1Z4
oaswindsor@gmail.com
sites.google.com/site/windsoroas
www.facebook.com/WindsorOAS
Chief Officer(s):
Amanda Black, President

Ontario Archery Association *See* Ontario Association of Archers Inc.

Ontario Arenas Association Inc. *See* Ontario Recreation Facilities Association

Ontario Arms Collectors' Association (OACA)
PO Box 477, Richmond Hill ON L4C 4Y8
Overview: A small provincial organization
Mission: To promote interest in the collection, possession, & lawful use of all types of arms by holding matches, competitions, meetings & exhibitions

Ontario Art Education Association (OAEA)
membership@OAEA.ca
www.oaea.ca
www.facebook.com/291406104216483
Overview: A small provincial organization founded in 1942
Mission: Promotes and advocates for learning through visual and media arts.

Member of: Donations; member fees
Affiliation(s): Ontario Teachers' Federation
Staff Member(s): 1
Membership: 100-499; *Committees:* Web; outreach; regional representation; advocacy resources; membership
Chief Officer(s):
Patricia Rocco, President
president@oaea.ca
Meetings/Conferences:
• Ontario Art Education Association Conference 2018, April, 2018, Hamilton, ON
Scope: Provincial
Description: Theme: "Moving Forward with Visual & Media Arts Education"

Ontario Art Therapy Association (OATA)
#103, 611 Wonderland Rd. N, London ON N6H 5N7
president@oata.ca
www.oata.ca
Overview: A small provincial licensing organization founded in 1978
Mission: To provide for the development, the promotion & the maintenance of the field of art therapy in Ontario; to grant registration to its professional members upon successful completion of a rigorous process & documentation of training & experience
Finances: *Annual Operating Budget:* Less than $50,000
Membership: 150-175; *Fees:* $40-$125; *Committees:* Registration; Membership; Newsletter; Education
Activities: *Speaker Service:* Yes
Chief Officer(s):
Susan Richardson, President
president@oata.ca

Ontario Artist Blacksmith Association (OABA)
c/o Les Fairhurst, 851 Zion Rd R.R. #1, Frankford ON K0K 2C0
www.ontarioblacksmiths.ca
Overview: A small provincial organization
Mission: The Ontario Artist Blacksmith Association seeks to promote the work and trade of blacksmithing, both traditional and modern.
Membership: *Fees:* $40

Ontario Arts Council (OAC) / Conseil des arts de l'Ontario
121 Bloor St. East, 7th Fl., Toronto ON M4W 3M5
Tel: 416-961-1660; *Fax:* 416-961-7796
Toll-Free: 800-387-0058
info@arts.on.ca
www.arts.on.ca
www.facebook.com/118143304897633
twitter.com/ONArtsCouncil
Overview: A large provincial organization founded in 1963
Mission: Ontario's primary funding body for professional arts activity; promotes & assists the development of the arts & artists; offers 50+ funding programs
Finances: *Annual Operating Budget:* Greater than $5 Million
Staff Member(s): 55
Membership: *Committees:* Governance; Finance & Audit; Compensation/Management/Resources; Public Affairs
Activities: *Library:* Open to public
Chief Officer(s):
Peter Caldwell, Director & CEO, 416-969-7457
pcaldwell@arts.on.ca
Kirsten Gunter, Director, Communications, 416-969-7403
kgunter@arts.on.ca
Carolyn Vesely, Director, Granting, 416-969-7458
cvesely@arts.on.ca
Awards:
• John Hirsch Director's Award
Established by a bequest to the Ontario Arts Council from the late John Hirsch; presented every three years to a promising theatre director in Ontario
• Pauline McGibbon Award
Annual award alternates between designers, directors & production craftspersons; *Amount:* $7,000
• The Venture Fund
Assists in artistic projects that embody a sense of challenge, experimentation or risk
• The Vida Peene Fund
Provides assistance to projects which benefit the orchestra community as a whole
• John Adaskin Memorial Fund
Established in memorial of the Canadian Music Centre's first executive secretary; supports a project that encourages the promotion & development of Canadian music in the school system
• Tim Sims Encouragement Fund Award
Established in 1995; to be awarded annually to a promising young comedic performer or troupe; *Amount:* $1,000
• K.M. Hunter Artists Awards
Designed to support & encourage artists who have completed their professional training & have begun to establish themselves & make an impact in their chosen field; 1 award in each field of dance, literature, music, theatre & visual arts; *Amount:* $8,000
• Lieutenant-Governor's Awards for the Arts
Approximately $300,000 to be awarded annually for the visual & performing arts that recognize institutional achievements rather than celebrating particular productions or artists; established in 1995 & co-sponsored by the J.P. Bickell Foundation
• Heinz Unger Award for Conducting
Awarded every two years; Established 1968 & awarded biennially to honour the memory of the York Concert Society music director; administered by the Music Office of the Ontario Arts Council in cooperation with the Association of Canadian Orchestras
• Leslie Bell Scholarship for Choral Conducting
Established 1973; awarded biennially in competition; the purpose of the award is to help young emerging choral conductors in Ontario further their studies in the choral music field either in Canada or abroad; competition organized by the Ontario Choral Federation; *Amount:* Up to $2,000
• Ruth Schwartz Children's Book Award
Two awards presented annually; $3,000 for best picture book & $2,000 for best young adult/middle reader book; in conjunction with the Canadian Booksellers Association
• William & Mary Corcoran Craft Award
Established to encourage excellence in crafts in the disciplines of glass, textiles, wood & ceramics; for college students
• Paul de Hueck & Norman Walford Career Achievement Award in the Performing Arts and in Visual Arts
Recognizes the acheivement of outstanding Canadian artists in keyboard artistry, art photography & singing
• Diana Crawford Prize
Established in 1998 in honor of Diana Crawford; awarded annually; recognizes exceptional young professionals employed by Tarragon Theatre for outstanding work in theatrical production
• Fabian Lemieux Award
Established in memory of educator Fabian Lemieux; Recognizes arts educators who have encouraged arts education in schools, colleges and universities in Ontario
• Linda Zwicker Fund
Established in memory of writer/playwright & former Arts Education Officer at the Ontario Arts Council, is designed to encourage women writers
• Hugh D. McKellar Fund
Established by Hugh McKellar to support the Lambton Country Music Festival & St. Michael's Cathedral Choir School.
• Louis Applebaum Composers Award
Established in 1998 by Canadian composer & champion of the arts, Louis Applebaum, the income generated funds an annual award recognizing excellence in composition
• Orford String Quartet Scholarship
Established by the members of the renowned Orford String Quartet; awarded every 2 years; Assists a Canadian string musician with studies, commissions or performances related to work in chamber music; *Amount:* $2,000

Ontario Asbestos Removal Contractors Association *See* Environmental Abatement Council of Ontario

Ontario Asparagus Growers' Marketing Board *See* Asparagus Farmers of Ontario

Ontario Asphalt Pavement Council (OAPC)
#4, 365 Brunel Rd., Mississauga ON L4Z 1Z5
Tel: 905-507-3707; *Fax:* 905-507-3709
info@onasphalt.org
www.onasphalt.org
www.facebook.com/OntarioHotMix
twitter.com/OAPC_ON_Asphalt
Overview: A medium-sized provincial organization
Mission: To provide a voice for hot mix asphalt producers & asphalt cement suppliers in Ontario
Membership: *Member Profile:* Major producers across Ontario; supportive manufacturer/supplier members; *Committees:* Executive; Environment; Marketing; Plant & Paving; Technical
Activities: *Speaker Service:* Yes
Chief Officer(s):

Vince Aurilio, Executive Director
vince@onasphalt.org
Mala Singh, Manager, Marketing & Communications
mala@orba.org

Ontario Association for Behaviour Analysis (ONTABA)
#413, 283 Danforth Ave., Toronto ON M4K 1N2
contact@ontaba.org
www.ontaba.org
twitter.com/ONTABA1
Overview: A small provincial organization
Affiliation(s): Association for Behaviour Analysis International
Membership: *Committees:* Conference; Elections; Membership; Recruitment; Professional Regulation; Newsletter; Webpage; Public and Community Relations; Awards; Satellite Conference
Chief Officer(s):
Albert Malkin, President
Meetings/Conferences:
• Ontario Association for Behaviour Analysis Annual Conference 2018, 2018, ON
Scope: Provincial

Ontario Association for Family Mediation (OAFM)
#204, 2167 Victoria Park Ave., Toronto ON M1R 1V5
Tel: 416-740-6236
Toll-Free: 844-989-3026
www.oafm.on.ca
twitter.com/OAFMEDIATION
Overview: A small provincial organization founded in 1982
Mission: To promote family mediation as a dispute resolution process for separating couples & for families in conflict
Member of: Family Mediation Canada
Affiliation(s): Family Mediation Canada
Membership: *Fees:* $35 student; $95 supporting; $150 associate; $250 accredited; *Member Profile:* Individuals working in the field of mediation in Ontario
Chief Officer(s):
Mary-Ane Popescu, Executive Director
Meetings/Conferences:
• Ontario Association for Family Mediation Conference & AGM 2018, September, 2018, Novotel Toronto Centre, Toronto, ON
Scope: Provincial

Ontario Association for Geographic & Environmental Education (OAGEE) / Association pour l'enseignement de la géographie et de l'environnement en Ontario (AEGEO)
#202, 10 Morrow Ave., Toronto ON M6R 2J1
Tel: 416-538-1650; *Fax:* 416-489-1713
www.oagee.org
www.facebook.com/geoteachersontario
Overview: A small provincial organization founded in 1949
Membership: *Fees:* $25 university students & faculty; $30 retired members; $50 individuals; *Member Profile:* Teachers of geography from across Ontario
Activities: Providing information & resources to elementary & secondary school teachers of geography & environmental education
Chief Officer(s):
Shawn Hughes, President
Ewan Geddes, Vice-President, Membership Services
Jonathan Fletcher, Vice-President, Communications
Ivan Ius, Vice-President, Curriculum
Brenda Scarlett, Secretary
Lew French, Treasurer
Meetings/Conferences:
• Ontario Association of Geographic & Environmental Educators 2018 Spring Conference, 2018
Scope: Provincial
• Ontario Association of Geographic & Environmental Educators 2018 Fall Conference, 2018
Scope: Provincial
Publications:
• The Monograph Editor
Type: Journal; *Frequency:* Quarterly; *Editor:* Gary Birchall; *Price:* Free with Ontario Association of Geographic & Environmental Education membership
Profile: Lesson plans & activities, for geography courses, designed by teachers

Ontario Association for Impact Assessment (OAIA)
144 Marita Pl., Concord ON L4K 3J9
oaiaontario@rogers.com
www.oaia.on.ca
twitter.com/OA_ImpactAssess
Overview: A medium-sized provincial organization

Membership: *Fees:* $50 regular; $10 student; *Committees:* Executive; Conference Planning; Education & Research Liaison; Event Planning; Membership & Liaison
Chief Officer(s):
Jillian Bieser, Director, Communications

Ontario Association for Marriage & Family Therapy (OAMFT)
PO Box 693, Tottenham ON L0G 1W0
Tel: 905-936-3338; *Fax:* 905-936-9192
Toll-Free: 800-267-2638
admin@oamft.com
rmft.oamft.com
Overview: A small provincial organization founded in 1974
Mission: To serve members of the association, the profession of marriage & family therapy, & the public; To uphold the Code of Ethics of the American Association for Marriage & Family Therapy & high professional standards; To advocate for members & communities
Member of: Division of American Association for Marriage & Family Therapy
Affiliation(s): Canadian Registry of Marriage & Family Therapy; American Association for Marriage & Family Therapy (AAMFT)
Finances: *Annual Operating Budget:* $100,000-$250,000; *Funding Sources:* Membership dues; Conference
Staff Member(s): 1; 14 volunteer(s)
Membership: 750; *Fees:* Schedule available; *Member Profile:* Registered marriage & family therapists; Approved supervisors; Associate members who have completed graduate training; Students; Affiliate members who are professionals in other disciplines such as medicine & religious leadership; *Committees:* Commission on Education; Ethics; Finance; Membership; Third Party Payment
Activities: Engaging in advocacy activities; Collaborating with other agencies to provide seminars & workshops; Organizing networking opportunities; Providing public education, awareness programs, & referrals; *Speaker Service:* Yes
Chief Officer(s):
Ron Mellish, President, 905-483-4354
president@oamft.com
Donna Chamberlain, Administrator
Meetings/Conferences:
• Ontario Association for Marriage & Family Therapy 2018 Annual General Meeting, 2018
Scope: Provincial

Ontario Association For Students At Risk (OASAR) / Association Ontario eleves a risque (AOER)
10676 Hedley Dr., RR #2, Ilderton ON N0M 2A0
oasar1@gmail.com
www.oasar.org
Overview: A small provincial organization founded in 1987
Mission: The Ontario Association of Students at Risk (OASAR) is a non-profit association that supports the education for at risk youth in Ontario.
Membership: *Fees:* $35 regular; $15 student/retired

Ontario Association for University Lifelong Learning *See* Ontario Council for University Lifelong Learning

Ontario Association of Acupuncture & Traditional Chinese Medicine (OAATCM)
370B Dupont St., Toronto ON M5R 3G3
Tel: 416-944-2265
Overview: A small provincial organization
Mission: To encourage the standardization of educational requirements for all practitioners of traditional Chinese medicine (TCM); To support high standards of professional training, competency & qualifications of TCM practitioners

Ontario Association of Agricultural Societies (OAAS)
PO Box 189, Glencoe ON N0L 1M0
Tel: 519-287-3553; *Fax:* 519-287-2000
oaas@bellnet.ca
www.ontarioagsocieties.com
Overview: A medium-sized provincial organization founded in 1900
Mission: To provide education, information & leadership to members & to act as a single voice when dealing with members, media, public & government
Member of: Canadian Association of Fairs & Exhibitions; International Association of Fairs & Expositions
Finances: *Annual Operating Budget:* $50,000-$100,000
Staff Member(s): 3
Membership: 234; *Fees:* Depends on size of fair; *Member Profile:* Open to agricultural fair or service manager

Chief Officer(s):
Vince Brennan, Office Manager
oaasofficemanager@gmail.com

Ontario Association of Alternative & Independent Schools *See* Ontario Federation of Independent Schools

Ontario Association of Archers Inc. (OAA)
PO Box 45, Caledon ON L7K 3L3
www.oaa-archery.on.ca
Previous Name: Ontario Archery Association
Overview: A medium-sized provincial organization founded in 1927 overseen by Archery Canada Tir à l'Arc
Member of: Archery Canada Tir à l'Arc
Membership: 800; *Fees:* $70 adult; $55 youth; $140 family; schedule for corporate & club memberships
Chief Officer(s):
Michael Martin, President
president@oaa-archery.on.ca
Kelly Chambers, Secretary-Treasurer
secretary@oaa-archery.on.ca
Lynda Savage, Office Administrator
administration@oaa-archery.on.ca
Awards:
• Reg Edie Merit Award
• Andrea Dopson Volunteer of the Year Award

Ontario Association of Architects (OAA)
111 Moatfield Dr., Toronto ON M3B 3L6
Tel: 416-449-6898; *Fax:* 416-449-5756
Toll-Free: 800-565-2724
Other Communication: practiceadvisor@oaa.on.ca
oaamail@oaa.on.ca
www.oaa.on.ca
Overview: A medium-sized provincial licensing organization founded in 1889
Mission: To operate in accordance with the Government of Ontario's Architects Act; To serve & protect the public interest by promoting & increasing the knowledge, skill, & proficiency of members
Finances: *Funding Sources:* Membership dues; Rental of meeting facilities; Document sales; Sponsorships
Membership: 2,500 licensed architects + 1,200 intern architects + 750 associates (honorary, life, retired, & student associates); *Committees:* Practice; Complaints; Discipline; Experience Requirements; Public Interest Review; Registration; Audit; Perspectives Editorial
Activities: Regulating the profession in the interest of all Ontarians; Presenting the OAA Continuing Education Program; *Internships:* Yes; *Speaker Service:* Yes
Chief Officer(s):
I. Hillel Roebuck, Registrar
hillelr@oaa.on.ca
Gordon Masters, Director, Operations
gordonm@oaa.on.ca
Kristi Doyle, Director, Policy
kristid@oaa.on.ca
Andrew Fuller, Administrator, Accounting & Information Technology
andrewf@oaa.on.ca
Gail Hanselman, Administrator, Certificate of Practice
gailh@oaa.on.ca
Tamara La Pierre King, Administrator, Web site & Communications
tamarak@oaa.on.ca
Jessica O'Rafferty, Administrator, Admission
jessicao@oaa.on.ca
Ellen Savitsky, Administrator, Continuing Education
ellens@oaa.on.ca
Kim Sumi, Administrator, Licence
kims@oaa.on.ca
Awards:
• G. Randy Roberts Service Award
To honour an OAA member for extraordinary service to the membership
• Honour Roll
For prominent members of the architectural profession who are now deceased (a record of achievement is given to a relative)
• Lifetime Design Achievement Award
To honour an individual for career-long achievement in architectural design excellence
• Order of Da Vinci
To reconize architects who have demonstrated exceptional leadership in education, the profession, or in the community
Meetings/Conferences:
• 2018 Ontario Association of Architects Conference, May, 2018,

Metro Toronto Convention Centre & Delta Toronto, Toronto, ON
Scope: Provincial
• 2019 Ontario Association of Architects Conference, May, 2019, Quebec City Convention Centre & Fairmont Le Chateau Frontenac, Québec, QC
Scope: Provincial
Publications:
• Ontario Association of Architects Annual Report
Type: Yearbook; *Frequency:* Annually
Profile: A review of the year, with Ontario Association of Architects programs & services
• Perspectives [a publication of the Ontario Association of Architects]
Type: Journal; *Frequency:* Quarterly

Ontario Association of Art Galleries (OAAG)
#125, 111 Peter St., Toronto ON M5V 2H1
Tel: 416-598-0714; *Fax:* 416-598-4128
oaag@oaag.org
oaag.org
Overview: A medium-sized provincial organization founded in 1968
Mission: To encourage the highest standards for the exhibition, interpretation, & conservation of the visual arts; to develop tools to assist gallery professionals in achieving institutional goals; to advance positive, responsive relations with government, its agencies & the citizens of Ontario
Finances: *Funding Sources:* Ontario Ministry of Citizenship, Culture, Tourism & Recreation; Ontario Arts Council; memberships
Staff Member(s): 2; 9 volunteer(s)
Membership: 200+ art organizations + individuals involved in the visual arts; *Fees:* $30 student; $75 individual; $200-$900 organization; *Member Profile:* Non-profit organization which shares aims of OAAG; individuals are encouraged to join as 'Friends/Colleagues of OAAG'; *Committees:* Awards; Membership; Policy; New Technology; Cultural Equity
Activities: Seminars, workshops, annual meetings; awards; publications; job file; member directory; advisory service; *Speaker Service:* Yes; *Library*
Chief Officer(s):
Demetra Christakos, Executive Director
Veronica Quach, Assistant Director

Ontario Association of Bovine Practitioners
Elora ON
Tel: 519-846-2290; *Fax:* 519-846-8165
admin@oabp.ca
www.oabp.ca
Overview: A medium-sized provincial organization
Mission: To represent the interests of veterinarians working in the dairy, beef, & cattle industries in Ontario
Chief Officer(s):
Ruth Cudmore, Executive Assistant

Ontario Association of Broadcasters (OAB)
PO Box 54040, 5762 Hwy. 7 East, Markham ON L3P 7Y4
Tel: 905-554-2730; *Fax:* 905-554-2731
www.oab.ca
Previous Name: Central Canada Broadcasters Association
Overview: A small provincial organization founded in 1950 overseen by Canadian Association of Broadcasters
Membership: 100-499
Chief Officer(s):
Doug Kirk, President
president@oab.ca
Dave Hughes, Vice-President
dave.hughes@star933.com
Ross Davies, Treasurer
rdavies@bbm.ca
Meetings/Conferences:
• Ontario Association of Broadcasters' 2018 Conference & AGM, 2018, ON
Scope: Provincial
Attendance: 300+

Ontario Association of Cemeteries *See* Ontario Association of Cemetery & Funeral Professionals

Ontario Association of Cemetery & Funeral Professionals (OACFP)
PO Box 10173, 27 Legend Ct., Ancaster ON L9K 1P3
Tel: 905-383-6528; *Fax:* 905-383-2771
Toll-Free: 888-558-3335
info@oacfp.com
www.oacfp.com
www.facebook.com/OACFP
twitter.com/theOACFP
Previous Name: Ontario Association of Cemeteries
Overview: A medium-sized provincial organization founded in 1913
Mission: To promote high standards of service & the professional operation of cemeteries, funeral homes, crematoria & related bereavement services
Membership: *Fees:* $150 regular; $630 supplier; $185 affiliate; free for students; *Member Profile:* All professional sectors of the death care industry including cemeteries, funeral homes, crematoria, monument retailers, casket retailers, funeral transfer services & industry supplers & consultants
Activities: Offering educational seminars & conferences; Emcouraging legislation for the betterment of the death care industry; Advising & cooperating with government in the implementation of legislation
Chief Officer(s):
Patty Harris, President
Ian Merritt, First Vice-President
Ron Hendrix, Second Vice-President
Tim Vreman, Treasurer
Jo-Anne Rogerson, Executive Director

Ontario Association of Certified Engineering Technicians & Technologists (OACETT)
#404, 10 Four Seasons Pl., Toronto ON M9B 6H7
Tel: 416-621-9621; *Fax:* 416-621-8694
info@oacett.org
www.oacett.org
www.linkedin.com/groups/official-oacett-group-149199
www.facebook.com/OACETT
twitter.com/OACETT
Overview: A small provincial organization founded in 1962
Mission: To advance the profession of applied science & engineering technology through standards for society's benefit.
Member of: Canadian Council of Technicians & Technologists
Staff Member(s): 28
Membership: 24,000+; *Fees:* Schedule available; *Member Profile:* Applied science technicians & technologists
Activities: *Internships:* Yes; *Speaker Service:* Yes
Chief Officer(s):
David J. Thomson, CEO
dthomson@oacett.org
Stephen Morley, President
Publications:
• Ontario Technologist
Frequency: Bi-Monthly; *Price:* $24 (Canada), $48 (U.S.A.), $96(International)
Profile: Includes technical features written by experts, cover stories on interesting topics and consistent coverage of major disciplines by knowledgeable columnists.

Ontario Association of Chiefs of Police (OACP)
#605, 40 College St., Toronto ON M5G 2J3
Tel: 416-926-0424; *Fax:* 416-926-0436
Toll-Free: 800-816-1767
oacpadmin@oacp.ca
www.oacp.on.ca
www.facebook.com/OACPOfficial
twitter.com/OACPOfficial
www.youtube.com/OACPOfficial
Overview: A medium-sized provincial organization founded in 1952
Mission: The Association coordinates police training & education. It advocates on behalf of its membership, expressing concerns & priorities to the government, public & to any other bodies.
Finances: *Funding Sources:* Membership dues & programs
Staff Member(s): 4
Membership: 1,500+; *Member Profile:* Police leaders in Ontario
Activities: Conferences; seminars & workshops; zone meetings; communications & networking; advocacy
Chief Officer(s):
Ron Bain, Executive Director Ext. 25
rbain@oacp.ca
Joe Couto, Director, Government Relations & Communications Ext. 22
jcouto@oacp.ca
Sharon Seepersad, Manager, Administration/Member Services Ext. 22
sharons@oacp.ca
Jennifer Evans, President
Meetings/Conferences:
• Ontario Association of Chiefs of Police 2018 Annual Meeting, June, 2018, Deerhurst Resort, Huntsville, ON
Scope: Provincial
Contact Information: www.oacpconference.on.ca

Ontario Association of Child & Youth Care (OACYC) / Association Ontarienne des Techniques (AOTES)
c/o The School of Child & Youth Care, Ryerson University, 350 Victoria St., Toronto ON M5B 2K3
Tel: 416-621-4340; *Fax:* 866-403-5961
office@oacyc.org
www.oacyc.org
Previous Name: Ontario Association of Child & Youth Counsellors
Overview: A medium-sized provincial organization founded in 1969
Member of: Council of Canadian Child & Youth Care Associations
Finances: *Funding Sources:* Membership fees; Donations; Revenue from conferences & workshops; Sale of advertising & print materials
25 volunteer(s)
Membership: *Fees:* $40-$200
Activities: Offering professional liability insurance for members
Chief Officer(s):
Michelle Shelswell, President
Meetings/Conferences:
• 2018 Ontario Association of Child & Youth Care Conference, 2018, ON
Scope: Provincial

Ontario Association of Child & Youth Counsellors *See* Ontario Association of Child & Youth Care

Ontario Association of Children's Aid Societies (OACAS) / Association ontarienne des sociétés de l'aide à l'enfance
#308, 75 Front St. East, Toronto ON M5E 1V9
Tel: 416-987-7725; *Fax:* 416-366-8317
Toll-Free: 800-718-7725
public_editor@oacas.org
www.oacas.org
www.linkedin.com/company/ontario-association-of-children-s-aid-societies
twitter.com/our_children
Overview: A medium-sized provincial organization founded in 1912
Mission: To provide leadership for the achievement of excellence in the protection of children & in the promotion of their well-being within their families & communities
Finances: *Funding Sources:* Membership fees; Government grants; Other revenue producing activities
Activities: Promoting knowledge regarding best practices in child welfare; Providing management leadership training; Ensuring optimal operational practices in child welfare networks; Disseminating key information; Identifying & uniting stakeholders to inform child welfare policy that focuses on Aboriginal children & families
Chief Officer(s):
Nancy MacGillivray, Executive Director
Publications:
• Ontario Association of Children's Aid Societies Child Welfare Report
Type: Report; *Frequency:* Annually
Profile: Outlines recommendations & areas of priority for the child welfare sector
• Ontario Association of Children's Aid Societies Journal
Type: Journal; *Frequency:* s-a.; *Number of Pages:* Y; *Editor:* Bernadette Gallagher; *ISSN:* 0381-985X; *Price:* $16
Profile: Features articles & news on child welfare practice & research in Ontario
• Ontario Association of Children's Aid Societies Annual Report
Type: Report; *Frequency:* Annually
• The Voice [a publication of the Ontario Association of Children's Aid Societies]
Type: Newsletter; *Frequency:* Monthly
Profile: Contains association initiatives & advocacy effort, public engagement opprtunities, & other child welfare sector news

Ontario Association of Children's Rehabilitation Services (OACRS) / Association ontarienne des services de réhabilitation pour enfants (AOSRE)
150 Kilgour Rd., Toronto ON M4G 1R8
Tel: 416-424-3864
info@oacrs.com
www.oacrs.com
www.facebook.com/OACRS
twitter.com/OACRS
www.youtube.com/OACRS

Previous Name: Association of Treatment Centres of Ontario
Overview: A medium-sized provincial charitable organization founded in 1973
Mission: To promote a province-wide, coordinated, community-based service system for children & youth with multiple disabilities & their families; To support members centres to achieve responsive, family-centred care
Affiliation(s): Kid's Coalition
Finances: *Funding Sources:* Membership fees; Donations
Membership: 21 centres; *Member Profile:* Treatment centres for children & youth with physical disabilities &/or communication disorders
Chief Officer(s):
Jennifer Churchill, Chief Executive Officer
jchurchill@oacrs.com

Ontario Association of Committees of Adjustment & Consent Authorities (OACA)
PO Box 568, Cayuga ON N0A 1E0
oaca@primus.ca
www.oaca.info
Overview: A small provincial organization founded in 1973
Mission: To promote laws that benefit its members & set a standard for their practices
Membership: 500-999; *Fees:* $110 active; $120 associate; *Committees:* Finance; Site Selection; Accreditation; Publicity & Website; Conference; Seminar; Education Monitoring; Legislation; Resolutions; Nominations
Activities: March seminar; annual meeting; *Rents Mailing List:* Yes
Chief Officer(s):
Linda Gavey, Secretary-Treasurer
Andreas Peterson, President

Ontario Association of Community Care Access Centres (OACCAC)
#200, 130 Bloor St. West, Toronto ON M5S 1N5
Tel: 416-750-1720
oaccac.com
www.linkedin.com/company/oaccac-the-ontario-association-of-community-care-access-centres-
twitter.com/oaccac
www.youtube.com/user/OACCAC
Overview: A medium-sized provincial organization founded in 1998
Mission: To serve as a collective voice for the contributions made by CCACs to & an integrated health care system, & to provide leadership, inspiration & evidence-based outcomes in support of innovative & cost-effective community health care services
Affiliation(s): Ontario Hospital Association
Membership: 14 community care access centres in Ontario; *Fees:* varies based on CCAC budget
Chief Officer(s):
Catherine Brown, CEO

Ontario Association of Community Futures Development Corporations (OACFDC) / Association des Sociétés d'aide au développement des collectivités de l'Ontario (ASADCO)
300 South Edgeware Rd., St Thomas ON N5P 4L1
Tel: 519-633-2326; *Fax:* 519-633-3563
Toll-Free: 888-633-2326
info@oacfdc.com
www.ontcfdc.com
twitter.com/OACFDC
Overview: A medium-sized provincial organization founded in 1994
Mission: To support members as leaders for rural community economic development in Ontario; To support members to deliver quality services in their communities and to provide the voice for the Community Futures Program in Ontario
Affiliation(s): Community Futures Network of Canada
Finances: *Annual Operating Budget:* $250,000-$500,000
Staff Member(s): 3
Membership: 61 Community Futures Development Corporations (CFDCs)
Chief Officer(s):
Diana Jedig, Executive Director

Ontario Association of Consultants, Counsellors, Psychometrists & Psychotherapists (OACCPP) / Association des consultants et conseillers en santé mentale, psychométriciens, et psychothérapeutes de l'Ontario
#410, 586 Eglinton Ave. East, Toronto ON M4P 1P2
Tel: 416-298-7333; *Fax:* 416-298-9593
Toll-Free: 888-622-2779
oaccpp@oaccpp.ca
www.oaccpp.ca
www.linkedin.com/company/2202979?trk=tyah
twitter.com/OACCPP
Overview: A small provincial organization founded in 1978
Mission: The OACCPP is a provincial body of mental health service providers that provides for the professional needs of its members, and meets the needs of the community in identifying and certifying practitioners.
Membership: *Fees:* $115-$200
Chief Officer(s):
James Whetstone, President
Carol Cox, Administrative Director
admin-director@oaccpp.ca
Meetings/Conferences:
• Ontario Association of Consultants, Counsellors, Psychometrists & Psychotherapists 40th Annual Conference & AGM, 2018
Scope: Provincial
Publications:
• Psychologica Magazine
Type: Magazine; *Frequency:* 2 pa

Ontario Association of Credit Counselling Services (OACCS)
ON
info@oaccs.ca
www.indebt.org
Overview: A medium-sized provincial charitable organization founded in 1968
Mission: To represent member agencies & provide them with a forum for the pursuit of common interests in order to support, strengthen & enhance not-for-profit credit counselling services; to enhance the quality & availability of not-for-profit credit counselling
Finances: *Annual Operating Budget:* $100,000-$250,000; *Funding Sources:* Member agency fees
Membership: 1-99; *Fees:* % of operating budget
Activities: *Speaker Service:* Yes
Chief Officer(s):
Henrietta Ross, Executive Director
hross@indebt.org

Ontario Association of Deans of Education (OADE)
c/o Council of Ontario Universities, #1100, 180 Dundas St. West, Toronto ON M5G 1Z8
Tel: 416-979-2165; *Fax:* 416-979-8635
cou.on.ca
Overview: A small provincial organization
Affiliation(s): Council of Ontario Universities
Finances: *Funding Sources:* 13 participating faculties
Membership: 21 (15 Deans, 6 associate)
Chief Officer(s):
Peter Gooch, Contact

Ontario Association of Dental Specialists (OADS)
4261 Hwy. 7, Unionville ON L3R 9W6
Tel: 905-513-7722; *Fax:* 905-513-7833
Overview: A medium-sized provincial organization founded in 1992
Mission: Organization representing all dental specialties in Ontario
Membership: *Member Profile:* Dental specialist societies
Chief Officer(s):
Neil Applebaum, President
neilapplebaum@rogers.com

Ontario Association of Distress Centres *See* Distress Centres Ontario

Ontario Association of Emergency Managers (OAEM)
c/o McCauley Nichols, 14 Caledonia Terrace, Goderich ON N7A 2M8
Tel: 519-524-5992; *Fax:* 519-612-1992
secretary@oaem.ca
www.oaem.ca
Overview: A small provincial organization
Mission: To unite emergency management professionals in Ontario; To promote, support, & improve the profession of emergency management in Ontario
Finances: *Funding Sources:* Membership dues
Membership: *Fees:* $525 corporate; $125 individual; $65 student; $0 first year student; *Member Profile:* First responders; Health professionals; Risk management professionals; Private consultants; Business community coordinators; IT professionals
Activities: Organizing annual conference; Offering members a network of emergency management contacts; Facilitating professional development workshops & resources
Chief Officer(s):
Amber Rushton, Coordinator, Membership
membership@oaem.ca
Meetings/Conferences:
• Ontario Association of Emergency Managers 2018 Ontario Disaster & Emergency Management Conference, October, 2018, Toronto, ON
Scope: Provincial

Ontario Association of Equine Practitioners (OAEP)
PO Box 27037, 7 Clair Rd. West, Guelph ON N1L 0A0
equinepractitioners@gmail.com
www.ontarioequinevets.ca
Overview: A small provincial organization founded in 1980
Mission: To facilitate communication & collegiality among equine practitioners in Ontario; To support continuing education, & provide a link between equine clinical practice, academia, industry, media, government & the community
Membership: *Fees:* $80; $20 student; *Member Profile:* Equine veterinarians; *Committees:* Animal Welfare; Continuing Education; Racing
Chief Officer(s):
Julie Ballinger, President
Alice Draper, Executive Assistant

Ontario Association of Fire Chiefs (OAFC)
#22, 520 Westney Rd. South, Ajax ON L1S 6W6
Tel: 905-426-9865; *Fax:* 905-426-3032
Toll-Free: 800-774-6651
info@oafc.on.ca
www.oafc.on.ca
www.linkedin.com/company/ontario-association-of-fire-chiefs
www.facebook.com/570718659627505
twitter.com/ONFireChiefs
www.flickr.com/photos/96578349@N02
Overview: A medium-sized provincial organization founded in 1973
Mission: To provide a voice for matters relating to the management & delivery of fire & emergency services in Ontario; To represent fire chief officers in Ontario
Finances: *Funding Sources:* Membership dues
Membership: *Fees:* $285 industry; $245 active & associate; $20 retired; *Member Profile:* Assistant Chiefs; Deputy Chiefs; Platoon Chiefs; Battalion Chiefs; District Chiefs; Division Chiefs; Directors of fire departments in Ontario; *Committees:* Executive; Education; Fire Services; Membership; Legislative
Activities: Organizing annual conventions; Reviewing government regulations & legislation; Providing networking opportunities
Chief Officer(s):
Richard Boyes, Executive Director
Awards:
• The Alf Stone Award
Awarded to honour a member that displays professionalism, takes initiative in improving public fire safety, leads by example, & influences others *Contact:* Mercedes Sturges, Manager, Events, mercedes.sturges@oafc.on.ca
• The Bill Williams Humanitarian Award
Awarded to recognize community contributions, professionalism, &/or leadership from a member of the fire service or fire service industry *Contact:* Mercedes Sturges, Manager, Events, mercedes.sturges@oafc.on.ca
• The VFIS Volunteer Firefighter Recruitment and Retention Award
Awarded in conjunction with VFIS (Volunteer Firemen's Insurance Services, Inc.) to an organization that is successful in its recruitment & retention initiative *Contact:* Mercedes Sturges, Manager, Events, mercedes.sturges@oafc.on.ca
• The Mark Diotte Leadership Award
Awarded to a member of the OAFC that demonstrates exceptional leadership, is committed to honesty & integrity, & exhibits pride as a firefighter *Contact:* Mercedes Sturges, Manager, Events, mercedes.sturges@oafc.on.ca
Meetings/Conferences:
• Ontario Association of Fire Chiefs 2018 Conference & Trade Show, May, 2018, The International Centre, Mississauga, ON
Scope: Provincial
Attendance: 600+
Publications:
• OAFC [Ontario Association of Fire Chiefs] Fire Department

Ontario Association of Food Banks (OAFB)
PO Box 1108, #501, 555 Richmond St. West, Toronto ON M5V 3B1
Tel: 416-656-4100; *Fax:* 416-656-4104
info@oafb.ca
www.oafb.ca
www.facebook.com/Ontario-Association-of-Food-Banks-898232 7261
twitter.com/OAFB
Overview: A small provincial charitable organization
Mission: To support the work of individual member food banks in Ontario which aim to achieve an immediate response to hunger while supporting & initiating long-term solutions to the problems which bring about hunger
Affiliation(s): Canadian Association of Food Banks
Finances: *Annual Operating Budget:* $100,000-$250,000; *Funding Sources:* Government; individual and corporate sponsors
Staff Member(s): 7
Membership: 105; *Fees:* $50; *Member Profile:* Small, medium & large food banks across Ontario that are registered charities.
Activities: *Internships:* Yes
Chief Officer(s):
Sharon Lee, Executive Director, 416-656-4100 Ext. 2931
sharon@oafb.ca

Ontario Association of Former Parliamentarians / Association ontarienne des ex-parlementaires
Whitney Block, #1612, 99 Wellesley St. West, Toronto ON M7A 1A2
Tel: 416-325-4647; *Fax:* 416-326-4650
oafp@ontla.org
www.oafp.ca
Overview: A small provincial organization
Mission: To protect former parliamentarians & to put their skills to use in other sectors of Ontario
Membership: *Fees:* $50; *Member Profile:* Former sitting members of the Legislative Assembly
Chief Officer(s):
Canon Derwyn Shea, Rev., Chair, 416-787-7911
dshea@sthildastowers.com

Ontario Association of Gastroenterology (OAG)
#210, 2800 - 14 Ave., Markham ON L3R 0E4
Tel: 416-494-7233; *Fax:* 416-491-1670
Toll-Free: 866-560-7585
info@gastro.on.ca
www.gastro.on.ca
twitter.com/ontario_gastros
Overview: A small provincial organization
Mission: Serves the practice of gastroenterology in Ontario, promoting, maintaining & improving its knowledge & standards; Represents Ontario gastroenterologists in discussions, meetings & communications with other organizations
Finances: *Funding Sources:* Membership fees
Staff Member(s): 3
Membership: *Fees:* $250 active; $0 residents
Chief Officer(s):
Melonie Hart, Director, Operations

Ontario Association of Insolvency & Restructuring Professionals (OAIRP)
c/o Collins Barrow Toronto Ltd., PO Box 27, #700, 11 King St. West, Toronto ON M5H 4C7
Tel: 416-646-8778; *Fax:* 416-496-9651
www.oairp.com
Previous Name: Ontario Insolvency Practitioners Association
Overview: A small provincial organization overseen by Canadian Association of Insolvency & Restructuring Professionals
Member of: Canadian Association of Insolvency & Restructuring Professionals
Activities: *Rents Mailing List:* Yes
Chief Officer(s):
Daniel Weisz, President
dweisz@collinsbarrow.com

Ontario Association of Interval & Transition Houses (OAITH)
PO Box 27585, Stn. Yorkdale Mall, Toronto ON M6A 3B8
Tel: 416-977-6619
info@oaith.ca
www.oaith.ca
www.facebook.com/OAITH
www.youtube.com/user/OAITH
Overview: A small provincial organization founded in 1977
Mission: To work towards social change by ensuring that the voices of abused women are heard; To remove barriers to equality for women & children
Finances: *Annual Operating Budget:* $250,000-$500,000; *Funding Sources:* Donations
Staff Member(s): 2; 15 volunteer(s)
Membership: 67; *Member Profile:* First stage emergency shelters for abused women & their children; Second stages housing programs; Community-based women's service organizations; *Committees:* Membership; Social Justice & Action/Anti-Racism Anti-Oppression; Member Education & Training; Personnel; Finance
Activities: Engaging in advocacy activities; Raising public awareness; Offering public education; *Internships:* Yes; *Speaker Service:* Yes; *Library*
Chief Officer(s):
Charlene Catchpole, Chair, Board of Directors
Marlene Ham, Provincial Coordinator
marlene@oaith.ca

Ontario Association of Jewish Dayschools; Ontario Jewish Association for Equity in Education See Centre for Jewish Education

Ontario Association of Landscape Architects (OALA)
#506, 3 Church St., Toronto ON M5E 1M2
Tel: 416-231-4181; *Fax:* 416-231-2679
oala@oala.ca
www.oala.ca
www.facebook.com/109687249113317
twitter.com/OALA_ON
Overview: A medium-sized provincial licensing organization founded in 1968 overseen by Canadian Society of Landscapre Architects
Mission: To promote, improve & advance the landscape architecture profession; To maintain standards of professional practice & conduct consistent with the need to serve & to protect the public interest; To support improvement &/or conservation of the natural, cultural, social & built environment
Member of: Canadian Society of Landscape Architects; Council of Landscape Architectural Registration Boards
Affiliation(s): American Society of Landscape Architects
Finances: *Annual Operating Budget:* $3 Million-$5 Million; *Funding Sources:* Membership dues
Staff Member(s): 2; 100 volunteer(s)
Membership: 690 full + 250 associate + 20 affiliate; *Fees:* $776.31 full; $160.46 associate; $186.45 affiliate; *Member Profile:* Professional landscape architects; *Committees:* Ethics; Honours, Awards & Protocol; Discipline; Continuing Education; Marketing
Activities: *Internships:* Yes; *Library:* Not open to public
Chief Officer(s):
Doris Chee, President
Aina Budrevics, Executive Director
Ingrid Little, Registrar
Sarah Manteuffel, Coordinator
Awards:
• Emeritus & Honorary Award
Honorary members being non-landscape architects appointed by Council, nominated by another member
• Public Practice Award
Recognizes the outstanding leadership of a member of the profession in public practice who promotes & enhances landscape architecture by working for improved understanding & appreciation of the work of landscape architects in both public & private practice
• Carl Borgstrom Award for Service to the Environment
Given to an individual landscape architect or landscape architectural group, organization or agency to recognize & encourage a special or unusual contribution to the sensitive, sustainable design for human use of the environment
• OALA Award for Service to the Environment
Given to a non-landscape architectural individual, group, organization or agency to recognize & encourage a special or unusual contribution to the sensitive, sustainable design for human use of the environment
• Pinnacle Award for Landscape Architectural Excellence
Recognizes an OALA member and their professional work
• David Erb Memorial Award
Recognizes an OALA member who has made an exemplary vountary contribution to the work of the association

Publications:
• Ground: Landscape Architect Quarterly [a publication of the Ontario Association of Landscape Architects]
Type: Magazine; *Frequency:* Quarterly
Profile: Articles on the landscape architecture industry

Ontario Association of Library Technicians (OALT) / Association des bibliotechniciens de l'Ontario (ABO)
Abbey Market, PO Box 76010, 1500 Upper Middle Rd. West, Oakville ON L6M 3H5
info@oaltabo.on.ca
oaltabo.on.ca
www.linkedin.com/company/oalt-abo
twitter.com/OALTABO
Overview: A medium-sized provincial organization founded in 1973
Mission: To promote the interests of library & information technician graduates & students throughout Ontario; To advance library & information technician graduates & students
Membership: *Fees:* $40 full; $12 student/unemployed/retired; $34 associate; schedule for groups, based on number of members in group; *Member Profile:* Library & information technician graduates in Ontario; Retired or unemployed individuals; Library & information technician students; Associate members; Institutional members
Activities: Instituting recognized standards; Promoting the value of library information technicians; Liaising with related professions & institutions; Disseminating information; Offering educational & professional development opportunities; Advocating for library information technicians; Providing networking events
Chief Officer(s):
Jessica Reeve, President
Lori O'Connor, Treasurer
Jillann Rothwell, Coordinator, Membership
Awards:
• Presidential Award
• Award for Innovation
• Outstanding Student Award
Meetings/Conferences:
• Ontario Association of Library Technicians / Association des bibliotechniciens de l'Ontario 2018 45th Annual Conference, 2018
Scope: Provincial
Description: Featuring educational sessions, speeches, the annual business meeting, & award presentations
Publications:
• Ontario Association of Library Technicians Newsletter
Type: Newsletter
• Ontario Association of Library Technicians Membership Directory
Type: Directory

Ontario Association of Medical Laboratories (OAML)
#1802, 5000 Yonge St., Toronto ON M2N 7E9
Tel: 416-250-8555; *Fax:* 416-250-8464
oaml@oaml.com
www.oaml.com
Overview: A medium-sized provincial organization founded in 1978
Mission: To act as the voice of Ontario's community laboratory sector; To promote professionalism, technical excellence, & accountability in the delivery of laboratory services throughout Ontario
Membership: 7; *Member Profile:* Independently owned laboratories in Ontario that perform diagnostic testing for patients outside hospitals
Activities: Speaking to government on behalf of the industry; Liaising with other health service professional associations & colleges to bring about positive changes in health care services in Ontario; Administering the OAML quality assurance program
Awards:
• OAML Scholarships
Eligibility: Ontario students enrolled in programs in medical laboratory sciences; *Amount:* $1,000
• OAML Research Trust Small Grants
To recognize innovation & excellence in the clinical laboratory sciences & the delivery of laboratory services in Ontario

Ontario Association of Medical Radiation Sciences (OAMRS)
#415A, 175 Longwood Rd. South, Hamilton ON L8P 0A1
Tel: 289-674-0034; *Fax:* 289-674-0037
Toll-Free: 800-387-4674
www.oamrs.org

www.linkedin.com/company/oamrs—ontario-association-of-medical-radiation-sciences
www.facebook.com/OAMRS1
twitter.com/OAMRS1
Merged from: Ont. Assn. of Medical Radiation Technologists; Ont. Society of Diagnostic Medical Sonographers
Overview: A medium-sized provincial organization founded in 2012 overseen by Canadian Association of Medical Radiation Technologists
Mission: To advocate on behalf of the profession of medical radiation science practitioners to government bodies
Finances: Funding Sources: Membership fees; Sponsorships
Staff Member(s): 8
Membership: Member Profile: Medical radiation technologists, therapists, & students from across Ontario; Committees: Executive & By-Laws; Nominating; Strategic Planning & Advisory Council (SPAC); Marketing & Communications; Professional Recognition; M.E. (Beth) Wastle Research Bursary; Practice Evolution & Extended Learning
Activities: Presenting education programs; Conducing research; Promoting the profession of medical radiation technology
Chief Officer(s):
Greg Toffner, President & CEO
toffnerg@oamrs.org
Meetings/Conferences:
• Ontario Association of Medical Radiation Sciences 2018 Annual General Conference, 2018, ON
Scope: Provincial
Publications:
• Filter: The Journal of The Ontario Association of Medical Radiation Sciences
Type: E-Newsletter; Frequency: Bimonthly; Accepts Advertising
Profile: Information for technologists who specialize in radiography, C.T., P.E.T., M.R.I, radiation therapy, ultrasound, & nuclear medicine

Ontario Association of Midwives See Association of Ontario Midwives

Ontario Association of Naturopathic Doctors (OAND)
#603, 789 Don Mills Rd., Toronto ON M3C 1T5
Tel: 416-233-2001; Fax: 416-233-2924
Toll-Free: 877-628-7284
info@oand.org
www.oand.org
www.facebook.com/ndontario
twitter.com/OANDorg
Previous Name: Ontario Naturopathic Association
Overview: A medium-sized provincial organization founded in 1950 overseen by The Canadian Association of Naturopathic Doctors
Mission: To act as a voice for naturopathic doctors in Ontario
Affiliation(s): Canadian Association of Naturopathic Doctors
Staff Member(s): 6
Membership: Member Profile: Registered / licensed naturopathic doctors in Ontario; Students of accredited colleges of naturopathic medicine; Corporate members
Activities: Advocating for naturopathic doctors; Conducting public awareness campaigns; Providing resources for the profession & the public; Setting standards of practice for clinical excellence; Promoting research in naturopathic medicine; Awareness Events: Naturopathic Medicine Week, May
Chief Officer(s):
Chrystine Langille, CEO
clangille@oand.org
Alfred Hauk, Chair
Angeli Chitale, Secretary
Meetings/Conferences:
• Ontario Association of Naturopathic Doctors 2018 Convention & Tradeshow, 2018
Scope: Provincial

Ontario Association of Non-Profit Homes & Services for Seniors; Ontario Association of Homes for the Aged See AdvantAge Ontario

Ontario Association of Nurses in Independent Practice See Independent Practice Nurses Interest Group

Ontario Association of Optometrists (OAO)
PO Box 16, #801, 20 Adelaide St. East, Toronto ON M5C 2T6
Tel: 905-826-3522; Fax: 905-826-0625
Toll-Free: 800-540-3837
info@optom.on.ca
www.optom.on.ca
www.facebook.com/OntarioOptometrists
twitter.com/ONOptometrists
www.youtube.com/user/OntarioOptometrists
Overview: A medium-sized provincial organization founded in 1909 overseen by Canadian Association of Optometrists
Mission: To advance the profession of optometry at the government, regulatory, & public levels
Staff Member(s): 12
Membership: Fees: Schedule available; Member Profile: Licensed optometrists in Ontario
Activities: Monitoring provincial legislation; Providing education credits; Organizing an annual symposium; Disseminating public information material; Providing the Ethical Guide for OAO Members
Chief Officer(s):
Beth Witney, Chief Executive Officer, 905-826-3522 Ext. 221
Bethany Carey, Director, Member Services, 905-826-3522 Ext. 227
Melissa Secord, Director, Professional Affairs, 905-826-3522 Ext. 243
Sandra Ng, Manager, Policy & Government Relations, 905-826-3522 Ext. 225

Ontario Association of Orthodontists (OAO)
ON
str8smiles@sympatico.ca
www.oao.on.ca
Overview: A small provincial organization
Mission: Official voice of orthodontists to organized dental associations, recognized educational institutions, licensing bodies, the public & government
Finances: Funding Sources: Membership dues
Membership: Member Profile: Orthodontists
Chief Officer(s):
Drew Smith, President
Gayle Fielding, Executive Secretary

Ontario Association of Pathologists (OAP)
#310, 4 Cataraqui St., Kingston ON K7K 1Z7
Tel: 613-507-7663
oap@eventsmgt.com
www.ontariopathologists.org
www.linkedin.com/company/ontario-association-of-pathologists
www.facebook.com/OntarioPathologists
Overview: A small provincial organization founded in 1937
Mission: To advance pathology & its allied sciences; To maintain a high standard of proficiency & ethics among its members; To promote research in pathology; To promote the interests of members
Finances: Annual Operating Budget: Less than $50,000
8 volunteer(s)
Membership: 250 individual; Fees: $100 regular; $50 associate/assistant; Free, resident
Chief Officer(s):
Russell Price, President
Satish Chawla, Secretary-Treasurer
Meetings/Conferences:
• Ontario Association of Pathologists 2018 Annual Meeting, September, 2018, Mont-Tremblant, QC
Scope: Provincial

Ontario Association of Physics Teachers (OAPT)
oaopt.wildapricot.org
Overview: A small provincial organization founded in 1979
Mission: To improve physics teaching in Ontario through the interaction & cooperation of high school teachers & university & college faculty
Affiliation(s): American Association of Physics Teachers
20 volunteer(s)
Membership: 300; Fees: $20 individual; Committees: Executive & Steering
Activities: Annual conference; province-wide high school physics contest
Chief Officer(s):
James Ball, Secretary, Membership

Ontario Association of Police Services Boards (OAPSB)
Suite A, 10 Peel Centre Dr., Brampton ON L6T 4B9
Tel: 905-458-1488; Fax: 905-458-2260
Toll-Free: 800-831-7727
admin@oapsb.ca
www.oapsb.ca
Previous Name: Municipal Police Authorities
Overview: A medium-sized provincial organization founded in 1962
Mission: To act as the voice of police services boards to government; To provide services to assist police services boards in Ontario
Finances: Funding Sources: Membership dues
Activities: Providing educational opportunities; Offering networking opportunities; Advocating on issues & concerns of police services boards
Chief Officer(s):
Fred Kaustinen, Executive Director
Meetings/Conferences:
• Ontario Association of Police Services Boards 2018 Spring Conference & AGM, May, 2018, Blue Mountain Resort, The Blue Mountains, ON
Scope: Provincial

Ontario Association of Property Standards Officers Inc.
PO Box 43209, 3980 Grand Park Dr., Mississauga ON L5B 4A7
www.oapso.ca
www.facebook.com/OAPSO.ca
Overview: A small provincial organization founded in 1974
Mission: To provide training for professionals involved in the governing of property & the environment
Membership: Fees: $74 individual; $29 associate/venerable; $74/$138+ municipality; Member Profile: Municipal government employees
Activities: Speaker Service: Yes
Chief Officer(s):
Italo Joe Luzi, President, 905-832-2281 Ext. 8361
italojoe.luzi@vaughan.ca

Ontario Association of Prosthetists & Orthotists (OAPO)
15 Britannia Ave., Toronto ON M6N 3T6
Other Communication: E-mails: mediarelations@oapo.org; committee@oapo.org
info@oapo.org
oapo.org
Overview: A small provincial organization overseen by Orthotics Prosthetics Canada
Mission: To promote professionalism & high standards of care in the prosthetic & orthotic field in Ontario
Membership: Member Profile: Persons involved in the prosthetic & orthotic field in Ontario
Activities: Reviewing patients' questions about fees; Promoting continuing education
Chief Officer(s):
Eric Bapty, Director

Ontario Association of Quick Printers (OAQP)
PO Box 182, 44 Fox Lane, Foxboro ON K0K 2B0
Tel: 613-966-3081
rutandrut@aol.com
Overview: A small provincial organization founded in 1985
Affiliation(s): Association of Graphic Solutions Providers
Finances: Annual Operating Budget: Less than $50,000
Staff Member(s): 1; 11 volunteer(s)
Membership: 100-499; Fees: $210 printers; $380 suppliers; Member Profile: Copy shops; off set & in-plant printers; trade shops; manufacturers; Committees: Nominating; Programs; Conference; Golf Tournament
Activities: Educational events; networking; support; communications; public relations; public affairs; Print Ontario Trade Show; Graphics Canada Trade Show
Chief Officer(s):
Dean Baxendale, President, 416-921-2111

Ontario Association of Radiology Managers (OARM)
26 Gateway Crt., Whitby ON L1R 3M9
Tel: 905-655-5645
headoffice@oarm.org
www.oarm.org
Overview: A medium-sized provincial organization founded in 1983
Mission: To serve as an education & communication platform for radiology managers in Ontario
Membership: 160
Chief Officer(s):
Mike Mukesh Sharma, President
Meetings/Conferences:
• Ontario Association of Radiology Managers 2018 Annual Fall Conference, September, 2018, ON
Scope: Provincial

Ontario Association of Residences Treating Youth (OARTY)
#210, 550 Alden Rd., Markham ON L3R 6A8

Tel: 905-475-5437; *Fax:* 905-475-5430
info@oarty.net
www.oarty.net
Overview: A medium-sized provincial charitable organization founded in 1990
Mission: To promote the provision of high quality care for vulnerable children, youth, adults, & their families
Membership: 1-99; *Committees:* Conference; Finance & Audit; Government & Stakeholder Affairs; HR & Compensation; Insurance & Risk; IT; Member Services; Nominations & Governance; Research
Chief Officer(s):
Rebecca Harris, Executive Director
rharris@oarty.net

Ontario Association of Residents' Councils (OARC)
#201, 80 Fulton Way, Richmond Hill ON L4B 1J5
Tel: 905-731-3710; *Fax:* 905-731-1755
Toll-Free: 800-532-0201
info@ontarc.com
www.residentscouncils.ca
twitter.com/OARCnews
www.youtube.com/channel/UC9zqu513DgytE8UBLjWo05w
Overview: A small provincial organization founded in 1981
Mission: To represent the views of residents on issues that affect the quality of their lives in long term care facilities & to promote & support the role & development of Residents' Councils
Finances: *Annual Operating Budget:* $100,000-$250,000
Staff Member(s): 5
Membership: 250; *Fees:* $50-$150; *Member Profile:* Residents' councils in long term care facilities
Activities: *Speaker Service:* Yes
Chief Officer(s):
Dee Lender, Executive Director, 905-731-3710 Ext. 24
dlender@ontarc.com
Julie Garvey, Manager, Administration & Finance, 905-731-3710 Ext. 23
jgarvey@ontarc.com

Ontario Association of School Business Officials (OASBO)
#207, 144 Main St., Markham ON L3P 5T3
Tel: 905-209-9704; *Fax:* 905-209-9705
office@oasbo.org
www.oasbo.org
Overview: A medium-sized provincial organization founded in 1945
Mission: Dedicated to the pursuit & support of quality education for all students. OASBO is the professional organization for school business officials in Ontario. The purpose is to improve the quality of school business management and the status, competency, leadership qualities and ethical standards of school business officials at all levels; focus is on information sharing, the promotion of learning at all opportunities, the optimization of operational processes, & the development of partnerships to promote & recognize business practices excellence.
Finances: *Annual Operating Budget:* $250,000-$500,000; *Funding Sources:* PD events; membership fees
Staff Member(s): 2
Membership: 700; *Fees:* $210 active member; $420 business; *Member Profile:* School business officials employed by Ontario school boards; *Committees:* Finance; Health & Safety; Human Resources; Operations, Maintenance & Construction; Payroll & Benefits; Planning; Purchasing; Senior Business Officials; Transportation; Information Technology; Disability Management; Information Management/Privacy & Access; Admissions/Enrolment
Chief Officer(s):
Bill Blackie, Executive Director
Awards:
• McCordic Award
Awarded in recognition of the contribution made to the field of school business by an OASBO member
Meetings/Conferences:
• Ontario Association of School Business Officials 75th Annual Conference & Education Industry Show, May, 2018, Ottawa, ON
Scope: Provincial

Ontario Association of Sign Language Interpreters (OASLI)
233 - 6 St., Toronto ON M8V 3A8
contactus@oasli.on.ca
www.oasli.on.ca

Overview: A small provincial organization founded in 1985 overseen by Association of Visual Language Interpreters of Canada
Mission: To provide support & professional development, & to promote ethical & professional behaviour among our membership; To advocate for professional recognition & to provide public education about the role of sign language interpreters
Member of: Association of Visual Language Interpreters of Canada (AVLIC)
Membership: *Member Profile:* ASL - English Interpreters; LSQ - French Interpreters; Deaf Interpreters; students of interpretation
Activities: Advocacy; Professional development; Public education; Interpreter certification
Chief Officer(s):
Jennifer Best, President
pres_ident@oasli.on.ca

Ontario Association of Social Workers (OASW) / Association des travailleuses et travailleurs sociaux de l'Ontario (ATTSO)
410 Jarvis St., Toronto ON M4Y 2G6
Tel: 416-923-4848; *Fax:* 416-923-5279
info@oasw.org
www.oasw.org
www.linkedin.com/company/ontario-association-of-social-workers
www.facebook.com/ontarioassociationofsocialworkers
twitter.com/oasw_info
Overview: A medium-sized provincial organization founded in 1964
Mission: To act as the voice of social workers in Ontario
Member of: Canadian Association of Social Workers
Finances: *Funding Sources:* Membership fees
Membership: 4,400; *Member Profile:* Individuals with a university degree in social work at the bachelor's, master's or doctoral level; Students in an accredited university-based program in social work
Activities: Offering a wide variety of publications & educational materials; Developing professional practice guidelines; Advocating for improvement of social policies & programs; Increasing public awareness on the role of the profession; Workshops; Webinars; *Awareness Events:* Social Work Week, March
Chief Officer(s):
Joan MacKenzie Davies, Executive Director
jmd@oasw.org
Meetings/Conferences:
• Ontario Association of Social Workers 2018 Provincial Conference, November, 2018, ON
Scope: Provincial
Description: Theme: "Mental Health Across the Lifespan: Social Workers on the Front Line of Real Issues"

Ontario Association of Speech-Language Pathologists & Audiologists (OSLA)
410 Jarvis St., Toronto ON M4Y 2G6
Tel: 416-920-3676; *Fax:* 416-920-6214
Toll-Free: 800-718-6752
mail@osla.on.ca
www.osla.on.ca
www.linkedin.com/groups?home=&gid=4453106
www.facebook.com/162240417157549
twitter.com/osla_ontario
Overview: A medium-sized provincial organization founded in 1958
Mission: Represents & promotes the professional interests of its members; provides a comprehensive range of services that support its professional members in their work on behalf of people with communication disorders
Finances: *Funding Sources:* Membership dues
Staff Member(s): 3
Membership: *Member Profile:* Speech language pathologists; audiologists; students of both
Activities: Private practice referrals; career information; advocacy on behalf of profession, membership benefits; *Awareness Events:* Speech & Hearing Month (May)
Chief Officer(s):
Mary Cook, Executive Director
mcook@osla.on.ca

Ontario Association of Student Financial Aid Administrators (OASFAA)
c/o Student Awards & Financial Aid, University of Waterloo, 200 University Ave. West, 2nd Fl., Waterloo ON N2L 3G1
www.uwindsor.ca/oasfaa

Overview: A medium-sized provincial organization
Mission: To concern itself with the scholastic & need-based assistance programs available to the students of its member institutions, & their effect upon the financial well being of students; To conduct studies & workshops for the exchange of information & professional development; to cooperate & maintain effective liaison with other agencies, councils & committees, as appropriate; To act as a lobby group on issues related to scholastic or need-based assistance programs for students
Affiliation(s): Canadian Association of Student Financial Aid Administrators
Finances: *Annual Operating Budget:* Less than $50,000
10 volunteer(s)
Membership: 60 institutional; 1 associate; *Fees:* $30
Chief Officer(s):
Maureen Jones, Treasurer, 519-888-4567 Ext. 36039
maureen@uwaterloo.ca

Ontario Association of the Appraisal Institute of Canada
See The Appraisal Institute of Canada - Ontario

Ontario Association of Trading Houses (OATH)
PO Box 43086, Toronto ON M2N 6N1
Tel: 416-223-2028; *Fax:* 416-223-5707
info@oath.on.ca
www.oath.on.ca
www.linkedin.com/company/ontario-association-of-trading-houses
Overview: A small provincial organization founded in 1996
Mission: To develop & expand international trade; To help Canadian companies to increase their international trade & investment
Member of: Federation of International Trade Associations
Membership: *Fees:* $500 international; $250 associate; $100 Ontario Trade & Investment Professionals

Ontario Association of Triathletes (OAT)
#2, 2015 Pan Am Blvd., Milton ON L9T 8Y9
Tel: 416-426-7025
info@triathlonontario.com
www.triathlonontario.com
www.facebook.com/TriathlonOntario
twitter.com/TriOntario
Also Known As: Triathlon Ontario
Overview: A small provincial organization overseen by Triathlon Canada
Mission: To encourage participation in multi-sport events & to ensure safety & fair competition; to assist, support & promote Ontario athletes
Member of: Triathlon Canada
Finances: *Funding Sources:* Fees; sponsorship; government
Membership: 1,000-4,999; *Fees:* Schedule available
Chief Officer(s):
Phil Dale, Executive Director
ed@triathlonontario.com
Emma Leeder, Manager, Program
technical@triathlonontario.com
Greg Kealey, Coach, Provincial Development
coach@triathlonontario.com
Publications:
• What's Happenin' @ TriOntario [a publication of the Ontario Association of Triathletes]
Type: Newsletter; *Frequency:* Monthly
Profile: News & updates for members

Ontario Association of Veterinary Technicians (OAVT)
#104, 100 Stone Rd. West, Guelph ON N1G 5L3
Tel: 519-836-4910; *Fax:* 519-836-3638
Toll-Free: 800-675-1859
oavt@oavt.org
www.oavt.org
www.facebook.com/OntarioAssociationOfVeterinaryTechnicians
twitter.com/The_OAVT
Overview: A small provincial licensing organization founded in 1972
Mission: To promote registered veterinary technicians & advocate on behalf of its members
Member of: Canadian Association of Animal Health Technologists & Technicians
Staff Member(s): 9
Membership: *Fees:* $257.64
Chief Officer(s):
Rory Demetrioff, Executive Director & Registrar
rory@oavt.org
Meetings/Conferences:
• Ontario Association of Veterinary Technicians 2018

Conference, March, 2018, Scotiabank Convention Centre, Niagara Falls, ON
Scope: Provincial

Ontario Association on Developmental Disabilities (OADD)
2 Surrey Pl., Toronto ON M5S 2C2
Tel: 416-429-3720; *Fax:* 647-260-2016
oadd@oadd.org
www.oadd.org
Overview: A medium-sized provincial organization
Mission: To support professionals & students in the field of developmental disabilities through the promotion of the highest standards of research, education, & practice
Affiliation(s): Great Lakes Society for Developmental Services of Ontario (GLS); Research Special Interest Group (RSIG)
Finances: *Funding Sources:* Membership dues
Membership: 100-499; *Fees:* $0 general; $25 sustaining student; $50 sustaining; $200 organizational; $250-$500 patron (bronze, silver, gold); *Member Profile:* Professionals & students working in the field of developmental disabilities; Organizations dealing with developmental disabilities
Chief Officer(s):
Tony Vipond, Chair
Meetings/Conferences:
• Ontario Association on Developmental Disabilities Annual Conference 2018, April, 2018, Ambassador Hotel & Conference Centre, Kingston, ON
Scope: Provincial
Description: Theme: "Working Together: Innovative Ideas for Complex Care"
Publications:
• BrOADDcast [a publication of the Ontario Association on Developmental Disabilities]
Type: Newsletter
Profile: Brief articles submitted by families, service providers, students, & researchers
• Journal on Developmental Disabilities
Editor: Maire Percy et. al.
Profile: A peer-reviewed journal, featuring research on issues relevant to developmental disabilities for both a Canadian & international audience

Ontario Athletic Therapists Association (OATA)
#302, 140 Allstate Pkwy., Markham ON L3R 5Y8
Tel: 905-946-8080; *Fax:* 905-946-1517
oatamembers@cggroup.com
www.ontarioathletictherapists.org
www.linkedin.com/groups?gid=4044330&trk=myg_ugrp_ovr
www.facebook.com/187942491304864
twitter.com/ontherapists
www.youtube.com/watch?v=FnbJdWyZD6Y&feature=plcp
Overview: A small provincial organization
Member of: Canadian Athletic Therapists Association
6 volunteer(s)
Membership: 400; *Fees:* $50-$200; *Member Profile:* Must be enrolled or graduate of an accredited institution - Sheridan College, Oakville Athletic Therapy Program or York University, Sport Therapy Program
Chief Officer(s):
Andrew Laskoski, President
drew.laskoski@bellnet.ca

Ontario Automotive Recyclers Association (OARA)
#1, 1447 Upper Ottawa St., Hamilton ON L8W 3J6
Tel: 905-383-9788; *Fax:* 905-383-1904
Toll-Free: 800-390-8743
admin@oara.com
www.oara.com
Overview: A small provincial organization founded in 1992
Mission: The association is the voice of the automotive recycling industry in Ontario. OARA works to improve recycling industry practices, and to promote the benefits of responsbile auto recycling to the general public, to stakeholders, and to local and provincial governments.
Member of: Automotive Recyclers of Canada
Finances: *Funding Sources:* Membership fees
Staff Member(s): 3
Membership: *Fees:* $150 Private vehical recycling businesses; $750 associate member; $500 direct membership; *Member Profile:* Automotvve recyclers; Direct Members must demonstrate compliance with the Ontario Certified Auto Recylcers Program; *Committees:* Certification; Data Collection; Government Affairs; Health & Safety; Meetings; Membership; Member Benefits; Parts Procurement; Transportation; Budget & Audit; Nominations

Activities: *Rents Mailing List:* Yes
Chief Officer(s):
Steve Fletcher, Executive Director
steve@oara.com
Meetings/Conferences:
• Ontario Automotive Recyclers Association 2018 Convention & Trade Show, March, 2018, Hilton Toronto/Markham Suites Conference Centre, Markham, ON
Scope: Provincial
Contact Information: Program & Exhibitors/Sponsors: Steve, Phone: 519-858-8761; Registration/Invoicing: Sherry, Phone: 1-800-390-8743

Ontario Badminton Association *See* Badminton Ontario

Ontario Bailiff Association (OBA)
139 Sutton Pl., Sault Ste Marie ON P6A 6A8
Tel: 705-759-0326
ontariobailiff.org
Overview: A small provincial organization
Mission: Association of recovery and liquidation experts located throughout Ontario

Ontario Ball Hockey Association (OBHA)
#5, 56 Pennsylvania Ave., Concord ON L4K 3V9
Tel: 905-738-3320; *Fax:* 905-738-3321
www.ontarioballhockey.ca
www.facebook.com/643077945729508
twitter.com/OntarioBallHock
Overview: A medium-sized provincial organization founded in 1974
Mission: To promote & increase participation in the sport of ball hockey in Ontario; to improve opportunities for competition at all levels of participation; to create & implement leadership opportunities for officials, coaches & administrators; to establish standards of play & for quality of equipment to ensure good sport & safety for all participants
Affiliation(s): Canadian Ball Hockey Association; International Street & Ball Hockey Association; Sport Canada; Canadian Hockey Association
Finances: *Funding Sources:* Self-generated revenue
Staff Member(s): 2; 12 volunteer(s)
Membership: 18,000; *Fees:* Schedule available
Activities: *Awareness Events:* Provincial Championships; Regional & National Champions
Chief Officer(s):
Jamie Robillard, Coaching & Technical Director
Awards:
• Five Year Silver Certificates
• Ten Year Gold Certificates
• Walter Moncrief Memorial Award
• Stephen Nichols Memorial Award
• Referee of the Year Award
• Girard Award Memorial Gaetanne
• Joey Panetta Memorial Award
• Minor Volunteer of the Year Award
• Steve Rumsey Volunteer of the Year Award
• Minor Male/Female Provincial Athlete of the Year Award
• Male/Female/Minor Athlete of the Year Award
• Mens/Womens/Minor Coach of the Year Award
• Recognition of Team Canada Award
• The Team Canada Award
• League Executive of the Year Award
• President's Award of Excellence
• Penny Meitz Memorial Award
• Hall of Fame Award

Ontario Ballet Theatre
1133 St. Clair Ave. West, Toronto ON M6E 1B1
Tel: 416-656-9568; *Fax:* 416-651-4803
Overview: A small provincial charitable organization
Mission: To nurture & develop an appreciation of contemporary & classical ballet by reaching new audiences through artistic excellence
Member of: Dance Ontario

Ontario Band Association
c/o Membership Co-ordinator, 198 Fincham Ave., Markham ON L3P 4B5
membership@onband.ca
www.onband.ca
www.facebook.com/CanadianBandAssociationOntario
Previous Name: Canadian Band Directors Association (Ontario) Inc.
Overview: A small provincial charitable organization founded in 1934 overseen by Canadian Band Association

Mission: To promote & develop musical, educational & cultural values of bands in Ontario by sponsoring annual band & solo instrument competition, composition competition, original works
Member of: Canadian Band Association
Finances: *Funding Sources:* Membership fees; Donations
Membership: *Fees:* $50; $35 student
Activities: *Rents Mailing List:* Yes
Chief Officer(s):
Andria Kilbride, President
president@onband.ca
Publications:
• In Harmony [a publication of the Ontario Band Association]
Type: Newsletter; *Frequency:* Monthly; *Price:* Free with membership to the OBA
Profile: An information resource for members containing workshop, symposium & conference listings, member profiles & events, upcoming auditions & concerts & festivalresults

Ontario Basketball
Abilities Centre, #2A, 55 Gordon St., Whitby ON L1N 0J2
Tel: 416-477-8075; *Fax:* 416-477-8120
basketball.on.ca
twitter.com/OBANews
www.youtube.com/user/OntarioBasketballOBA
Overview: A medium-sized provincial organization founded in 1977 overseen by Canada Basketball
Mission: To promote & develop basketball on an amateur basis in the province of Ontario.
Affiliation(s): Provincial Sports Organizations Council; Canada Basketball; Toronto Raptors Basketball Club; NBA Canada; Coaches Association of Ontario; Canadian Sports Centre; and other provincial basketball organizations
Finances: *Annual Operating Budget:* $1.5 Million-$3 Million; *Funding Sources:* Sponsorship; fundraising; grants
Staff Member(s): 6
Membership: 9,000; *Fees:* Schedule available; *Member Profile:* Players & coaches
Activities: *Internships:* Yes; *Speaker Service:* Yes; *Library:* Open to public by appointment
Chief Officer(s):
Jason Jansson, Executive Director, 416-477-8075 Ext. 202
jjanson@basketball.on.ca
Lindsay Walsh, Director, Basketball Development, 416-477-8075 Ext. 203
lwalsh@basketball.on.ca

Ontario Baton Twirling Association (OBTA)
#263, 55 Collinsgrove Rd., Toronto ON M1E 4Z2
info@obta.ca
www.obta.ca
www.facebook.com/OntarioBatonTwirlingAssociation
twitter.com/OBTA_ca
Overview: A small provincial organization overseen by Canadian Baton Twirling Federation
Mission: To be the provincial governing body for the sport of baton twirling in Ontario
Member of: Canadian Baton Twirling Federation
Chief Officer(s):
Kim Genton, President
president@obta.ca
Connie Worsnop, Membership Registrar
membership@obta.ca

Ontario Bean Growers Association (OBG)
#D, 59 Lorne Ave. East, Stratford ON N5A 6S4
Tel: 519-271-8641
info@ontariobeans.on.ca
ontariobeans.on.ca
Merged from: Ontario Bean Producers' Marketing Board; Ontario Coloured Bean Growers Association
Overview: A small provincial licensing organization founded in 2013
Member of: Ontario Agricultural Commodity Council; Canadian Special Crops Association; Pulse Canada; National Edible Bean Committee
Membership: *Member Profile:* Farmers of dry beans

Ontario Beef Improvement Association; Ontario Cattlemen's Association *See* Beef Farmers of Ontario

Ontario Beekeepers' Association (OBA)
#476, 8560 Tremaine Rd., Milton ON L9T 4Z1
Tel: 905-636-0661; *Fax:* 905-636-0662
info@ontariobee.com
www.ontariobee.com
Overview: A small provincial organization founded in 1881

Mission: To coordinate & advance the beekeeping industry in Ontario
Member of: Canadian Honey Council; Ontario Federation of Agriculture; Eastern Apicultural Society; Ontario Agricultural Commodity Council; Canadian Agricultural Hall of Fame; AGCare; Agricultural Adaptation Council; Ont. Agricultural Research Coalition
Finances: Annual Operating Budget: $50,000-$100,000
Staff Member(s): 1
Membership: 450; Fees: $85 associate; $100 voting plus $0.50 per hive up to $700; Member Profile: Voting - reside in Ontario; associate (non-voting) - interested in beekeeping; 49 hives or less
Activities: Resources; courses; workshops; information meetings; Speaker Service: Yes; Rents Mailing List: Yes
Chief Officer(s):
Maureen Vandermarel, Business Administrator
Dan Davidson, President
sddavidson@brktel.ca

Ontario Berry Growers' Association (OBGA)
30 Harmony Way, Kemptville ON K0G 1J0
Tel: 613-258-4587; Fax: 613-258-9129
info@ontarioberries.com
ontarioberries.com
www.facebook.com/ontarioberries
twitter.com/OntarioBerries
www.youtube.com/user/ontarioberries
Overview: A small provincial organization founded in 1973
Staff Member(s): 2; 17 volunteer(s)
Membership: 200; Fees: $150 + GST; Member Profile: Berry growers & agribusiness; Committees: Research; Annual Conference; Finance; Promotion; Education & Membership
Chief Officer(s):
Kevin Schooley, Contact

Ontario Bison Association
c/o Secretary, RR#6, Line 45679, St Marys ON N4X 1C8
Tel: 519-229-6316
www.canadianbison.ca/producer/The_CBA/OntarioBisonAssociation.htm
www.facebook.com/OntarioBisonAssociation
Overview: A small provincial organization
Member of: Canadian Bison Association
Membership: Fees: $175
Chief Officer(s):
Shirley Mills, Secretary

Ontario Black History Society (OBHS) / Société historique des Noirs de l'Ontario
#402, 10 Adelaide St. East, Toronto ON M5C 1J3
Tel: 416-867-9420; Fax: 416-867-8691
admin@blackhistorysociety.ca
www.blackhistorysociety.ca
www.facebook.com/109773629168
twitter.com/tweetOBHS
www.youtube.com/user/OntarioBlackHistory
Overview: A medium-sized provincial charitable organization founded in 1978
Mission: To study Black history in Canada; to recognize, preserve & promote the contribution of Black peoples & their collective histories through education, research & cooperation; to promote the inclusion of material on Black history in school curricula; to sponsor & support educational conferences & exhibits in this field.
Affiliation(s): Ontario Historical Society
Finances: Funding Sources: Membership fees; provincial government
Membership: Fees: $15 senior/student; $35 individual; $50 family; $100 organization
Activities: Discover Black History Bus Tour; Black History presentations; travelling exhibits; Awareness Events: Black History Month, Feb.; Speaker Service: Yes; Library: Open to public by appointment

Ontario Blind Sports Association (OBSA)
#104, 3 Concorde Gate, Toronto ON M3C 3N6
Tel: 416-426-7191; Fax: 416-426-7361
blindsports.on.ca
www.facebook.com/OntarioBlindSports
Overview: A small provincial charitable organization founded in 1984 overseen by Canadian Blind Sports Association Inc.
Mission: To organize sporting events & activities for blind & visually impaired athletes in Ontario
Finances: Annual Operating Budget: $100,000-$250,000; Funding Sources: Membership fees; government
Staff Member(s): 2; 20 volunteer(s)
Membership: 200; Fees: $25; Member Profile: Sport association
Activities: Speaker Service: Yes
Chief Officer(s):
Kyle Pelly, Executive Director, 416-426-7244
Greg Theriault, Manager, Programs
greg@blindsports.on.ca
Publications:
• Ontario Blind Sports Association Newsletter
Type: Newsletter
Profile: News & updates for members

Ontario Blonde d'Aquitaine Association
Acres Farms, 2166 McGee Side Rd., Carp ON K0A 1L0
Tel: 613-836-4190
www.ontarioblondecattle.com
Overview: A small provincial organization
Member of: Canadian Blonde d'Aquitaine Association
Activities: Fairs; exhibitions
Chief Officer(s):
Steven J. Acres, President

Ontario Bobsleigh Skeleton Association (OBSA)
22 Lynwood Ave., Ottawa ON K1Y 2B3
Tel: 613-864-0702
www.ontariobobsleighskeleton.ca
www.facebook.com/OntarioBobsleighSkeleton
Overview: A medium-sized provincial organization founded in 1960
Mission: To promote bobsleigh & skeleton in Ontario
Affiliation(s): Bobsleigh Canada Skeleton; International Bobsleigh & Skeleton Federation
Chief Officer(s):
Esther Dalle, Director, High Performance
edalle@hotmail.com

Ontario Book Publishers Organization (OBPO)
#101, 1 Ruttan St., Toronto ON M6P 0A1
Tel: 416-536-7584
www.obpo.ca
Previous Name: Organization of Book Publishers of Ontario
Overview: A medium-sized provincial organization founded in 1990
Mission: To act as a centralized representative of Ontario book publishers in lobbying the provincial government & arts organizations about issues directly of concern to members; To share information & education opportunities that relate to the provincial, national & international book publishing industries; To provide the opportunities for group marketing projects
Member of: ACP
Affiliation(s): Open Book Foundation
Staff Member(s): 2
Membership: 43; Member Profile: Book Publishers based in Ontario
Chief Officer(s):
David Caron, President
Michael Mirolla, Vice-President
Holly Kent, Executive Director

Ontario Brain Injury Association (OBIA)
3550 Schmon Parkway, 2nd Fl., Thorold ON L2V 4Y6
Tel: 905-641-8877; Fax: 905-641-0323
Toll-Free: 800-263-5404
obia@obia.ca
www.obia.ca
www.linkedin.com/company/ontario-brain-injury-association
www.facebook.com/OntarioBIA
twitter.com/OntarioBIA
Overview: A medium-sized provincial organization founded in 1987 overseen by Brain Injury Association of Canada
Mission: To provide on-going support to persons in Ontario whose lives have been affected by acquired brain injury
Finances: Funding Sources: Donations; Directory revenues
Membership: Fees: $5 subsidized membership in OBIA & one other local association; $30 individual membership in OBIA & one other local association; $50 families
Activities: Providing education & information about acquired brain injury; Offering a Peer Support Mentoring Program for people living with acquired brain injury; Increasing public awareness; Liaising with community associations; Library: Ontario Brain Injury Association Library
Chief Officer(s):
Barbara Claiman, President
Brad Borkwood, Treasurer
Ruth Wilcock, Executive Director
rwilcock@obia.on.ca
Publications:
• Directory of ABI Services [a publication of the Ontario Brain Injury Association]
Type: Directory
Profile: Company listings with program descriptions
• OBIA [Ontario Brain Injury Association] Review
Type: Newsletter; Frequency: Quarterly; Accepts Advertising;
Editor: Jennifer Norquay
Profile: Feature articles, survivor stories, upcoming events, & training information

Belleville (BIAQD)
Core Centre, 223 Pinnacle St., Belleville ON K8N 3A7
Tel: 613-967-2756
Toll-Free: 866-894-8884
biaqd@bellnet.ca
www.biaqd.ca
www.facebook.com/154337841305196
Mission: To support persons affected by acquired brain injury in Quinte Distric
Member of: United Way of Quinte
Affiliation(s): Ontario Brain Injury Association
Chief Officer(s):
Mary-Ellen Thompson, President
Kris Bonn, Vice-President
Monique Chartrand, Office Administrator
• On the Sunnier Side
Type: Newsletter; Frequency: Monthly; Accepts Advertising
Profile: Notices of upcoming events, information about programs & services, plus prevention updates

Chatham (BIACK)
9 Maple Leaf Dr., Chatham ON N7M 6H2
Tel: 519-351-0297; Fax: 519-351-7600
lgall@newbeginnings-cksl.com
newbeginnings-cksl.com
www.facebook.com/370648369630107
Mission: To reduce the occurrence of acquired brain injury; To enhance the quality of life for survivors of acquired brain injury & their family members in Chatham-Kent
Chief Officer(s):
Lori Gall, Executive Director
Sean St.Amand, Community Integration Director
sean@newbeginnings-cksl.com
Greg Davenport, Vice-President
Cathy Weir, Vice-President
Kevin Deacon, Treasurer

Fort Erie
649 Niagara Blvd., Fort Erie ON L2A 3H7
Tel: 905-871-7789; Fax: 905-871-7832
hiafeadmin@bellnet.ca
Mission: To support persons with acquired brain injury & their families in Fort Erie & area
Chief Officer(s):
Donna Summerville, Coordinator, Programs
Julie Anthony, President
hiafepresident@bellnet.ca
Shirley Athoe, Treasurer
hiafetreasure@bellnet.ca

Hamilton-Wentworth (HBIA)
822 Main St. East, Hamilton ON L8M 1L6
Tel: 905-521-2100; Fax: 905-521-7927
info@hbia.ca
www.hbia.ca
Mission: To support persons with acquired brain injury in Hamilton; To improve treatment opportunites in Hamilton for persons affected by acquired brain injury; To advocate on behalf of survivors of acquired brain injury
Chief Officer(s):
Jane Grech, President
Ted Newbigging, Vice-President
Diana Velikonja, Secretary
Shannon Moffat, Treasurer
• Headstrong
Type: Newsletter; Frequency: Quarterly; Accepts Advertising;
Editor: Sandra Best; Celeste Gallant
Profile: Updates on association events & groups, plus new developments related to acquired brain injuries

Kingston (BIASEO)
c/o Epilepsy Kingston, 100 Stuart St., Kingston ON K7L 2V6
Tel: 613-547-6969; Fax: 613-548-4162
BIASEO@epilepsykingston.org
braininjuryhelp.ca
www.facebook.com/407323819294054
twitter.com/abi_help

Mission: To enhance the quality of life for people affected by acquired brain injury in southeastern Ontario
Chief Officer(s):
Kim Smith, Contact, 613-536-1555
London
201 King St., London ON N6A 1C9
Tel: 519-642-4539; *Fax:* 519-642-4124
info@braininjurylondon.on.ca
www.braininjurylondon.on.ca
ca.linkedin.com/company/brain-injury-association-of-london-&-region
www.facebook.com/braininjuryassociationoflondonandregion
twitter.com/braininjuryon
www.youtube.com/user/braininjurylondonon
Mission: To maximize the quality of life of persons with acquired brain injury in London & area; To advocate on behalf of those affected by acquired brain injury
Chief Officer(s):
Donna Thomson, Executive Director
Alysia Chrisiaen, President
Colin Fitchett, Vice-President
Julie Willsie, Vice-President
Carla Robertson, Treasurer
Stephanie McGill, Coordinator, Communications & Services
• The Monarch [a publication of the Brain Injury Association of London & Region]
Type: Newsletter; *Frequency:* Quarterly; *Accepts Advertising*
Mississauga (1986)
#204, 2155 Leanne Blvd., Mississauga ON L5K 2K8
Tel: 905-823-2221; *Fax:* 905-823-9960
Toll-Free: 800-565-8594
biaph@biaph.com
www.biaph.com
facebook.com/biaph
twitter.com/BrainAwareBIAPH
Mission: To meet the needs of survivors of acquired brain injury & their families in the Peel & Halton region; To improve the quality of care for persons with acquired brain injury
Chief Officer(s):
Alexis Moskal, Contact
North Bay (BIANBA)
280 Oakwood Ave., North Bay ON P1B 9G2
Tel: 705-840-8882
contact@bianba.ca
www.bianba.ca
Mission: To support & assist persons living with acquired brain injury in North Bay & the surrounding area
Chief Officer(s):
Katy Snoddon, Chair
Robert McKay, Secretary
Michael Cairns, Treasurer
Oshawa (HIAD)
#24, 850 King St. West, Oshawa ON L1J 8N5
Tel: 905-723-2732; *Fax:* 905-723-4936
Toll-Free: 866-354-4464
headinjassoc@rogers.com
Mission: To enrich the lives of people in Durham Region who are affected by acquired brain injury
Chief Officer(s):
Frank Murphy, Executive Director
fmurphy@biad.ca
Frank Welling, President
• The Front Page
Type: Newsletter; *Frequency:* Monthly
Profile: Association activities & forthcoming events
Ottawa (BIAOV)
#300A, 211 Bronson Ave., Ottawa ON K1R 6H5
Tel: 613-233-8303; *Fax:* 613-233-8422
braininjuryottawavalley@bellnet.ca
www.biaov.org
Mission: To support persons with acquired brain injury, their families, caregivers, & friends in the Ottawa Valley
Chief Officer(s):
Wendy Charbonneau, President
Lise Marcoux, Vice-President
Robert Allen, Secretary-Treasurer
Peterborough (FCBIA)
#100, 160 Charlotte St., Peterborough ON K9J 2T8
Tel: 705-741-1172; *Fax:* 705-741-5129
Toll-Free: 800-854-9738
biapr@nexicom.net
biapr.ca
twitter.com/biapeterboro

Mission: To provide services to persons living with the effects of acquired brain injury in the four counties of Haliburton, Northumberland, Peterborough, & the City of Kawartha Lakes
Chief Officer(s):
Cheryl-Ann Hassan, Executive Director
Jeff Lanctot, President
• Heads & Tales
Type: Newsletter; *Frequency:* Monthly; *Accepts Advertising*
Profile: Information about the association & acquired brain injuries for members
Richmond Hill
11181 Yonge St., 3rd Fl., Richmond Hill ON L4S 1L2
Tel: 905-780-1236; *Fax:* 905-780-1524
Toll-Free: 800-263-5404
daveblakemore@rogers.com
Mission: To support acquired brain injury survivors & their families in York Region
Chief Officer(s):
Dave Blakemore, President
• The Headway
Type: Newsletter
Profile: Current information related to acquired brain injury in York Region
St. Catharines (BIAN)
c/o Stokes Community Village, PO Box 2338, 4-36 Page Street, St Catharines ON L2R 4A7
Tel: 905-984-5058; *Fax:* 905-984-5354
Mission: To maximize the quality of life for persons with acquired brain injury & their families in the Niagara region
Chief Officer(s):
Pat Dracup, Program Director
• Brain Injury Association of Niagara Newsletter
Type: Newsletter; *Frequency:* Quarterly
Profile: Association activities for members
Sarnia-Lambton (BIASL)
#1032, 1705 London Line, Sarnia ON N7S 1B2
Tel: 519-337-5657; *Fax:* 519-337-1024
info@sarniabiasl.ca
www.sarniabiasl.ca
Mission: To support individuals with acquired brain injury & their families in the Sarnia & Lambton region
Chief Officer(s):
Roy Marshall, Contact, 519-542-2151
Sault Ste Marie
#127, 31 Old Garden River Rd., Sault Ste Marie ON P6B 5Y7
Tel: 705-946-0172; *Fax:* 705-946-0594
biassmd@shaw.ca
www.braininjuryssm.ca/bia.htm
Mission: To assist persons living with acquired brain injury in Sault Ste Marie & area; To reduce the incidents of brain injury
Chief Officer(s):
Frank Halford, President
Jennifer Trepasso, Secretary
Karen McKinley, Treasurer
Dawn Kuhlenbaumer, Coordinator, Peer Support
• Brain Injury Association of Sault Ste Marie & District Newsletter
Type: Newsletter
Sudbury & District (BIASD)
2750 Bancroft Dr., Sudbury ON P3B 1T9
Tel: 705-670-0200; *Fax:* 705-670-1462
info@biasd.com
www.biasd.com
Mission: To support survivors of acquired brain injury in Sudbury & the surrounding district
Chief Officer(s):
Sean Parsons, President, Chair-Executive
Thunder Bay (BISNO)
#217, 1100 Memorial Ave., Thunder Bay ON P7B 4A3
Tel: 807-621-4164
info@biatba.org
www.biatba.org
Mission: To support individuals of all ages who are affected by acquired brain injury in the Thunder Bay area
Timmins
733 Ross Ave. E., Timmins ON P4N 8S8
Tel: 705-264-2933; *Fax:* 705-264-0350
www.seizurebraininjurycentre.com
www.facebook.com/seizurebraininjurycentre
twitter.com/letstalkbrain
Mission: To ensure that brain injuries or epilepsy are not deciding factors in an individual's opportunities
Affiliation(s): Canadian Epilepsy Alliance; Epilepsy Canada; Epilepsy Ontario

Chief Officer(s):
Rhonda Latendresse, Executive Director
rhondal@seizurebraininjurycentre.com
Stacey DeLaurier, Communications Officer
staceyd@seizurebraininjurycentre.com
Samantha Saley, Client Services Coodinator
sams@seizurebraininjurycentre.com
Toronto (BIST)
#205, 40 St. Clair Ave. East, Toronto ON M4T 1M9
Tel: 416-830-1485
info@bist.ca
www.bist.ca
Mission: To support survivors of acquired brain injury & their family members in the City of Toronto
Chief Officer(s):
Judy Moir, Chair
Paul McCormack, Vice-Chair & Treasurer
Gary Gerber, Secretary
Todd Gotlieb, Treasurer
• BIST Beacon
Type: Newsletter; *Frequency:* Irregular
Profile: Information about the Brain Injury Society of Toronto, available to members & donors to the society
Waterloo-Wellington (BIAWW)
#1, 871 Victoria St. North, Kitchener ON N2B 3S4
Tel: 519-579-5300; *Fax:* 519-579-0118
biaww@bellnet.ca
www.biaww.com
www.linkedin.com/groups/Brain-Injury-Association-WaterlooWellington-3812945
www.facebook.com/biaww
Mission: To support persons suffering from acquired brain injury & their families in the Waterloo-Wellington region
Chief Officer(s):
Patti Lehman, Executive Director
Windsor-Essex (BIAWE)
#201, 200 West Grand Blvd., Windsor ON N9E 3W7
Tel: 519-981-1329
info@biawe.com
www.biawe.com
www.facebook.com/BIAWE
www.youtube.com/channel/UC-VWaZbdUVoC4zw-_9jrKFA
Mission: To enhance the lives of residents of Windsor & Essex County who are affected by acquired brain injury
Chief Officer(s):
Melanie Gardin, President
Lois Caldwell, Vice-President
Cheryl Henshaw, Secretary
Nancy Nicholson, Treasurer
• Step Ahead!
Type: Newsletter; *Accepts Advertising*
Profile: Review of association activites & announcements of future events

Ontario Broiler Hatching Egg & Chick Commission (OBHECC)
#213, 251 Woodlawn Rd. West, Guelph ON N1H 8J1
Tel: 519-837-0005; *Fax:* 519-837-0464
info@obhecc.com
www.obhecc.com
Overview: A medium-sized provincial organization
Mission: To administer the supply management system for broiler hatching eggs & chicks in Ontario
Chief Officer(s):
Bob Guy, General Manager

Ontario Brown Swiss Association (OBSA)
RR#1, Bognor ON N0H 1E0
Tel: 519-372-1803
Overview: A small provincial organization
Mission: To promote Brown Swiss cow as dairy animal in Canada
Member of: Canadian Brown Swiss Association
Membership: *Member Profile:* Ownership of or interest in Brown Swiss breed of cattle
Activities: *Rents Mailing List:* Yes
Chief Officer(s):
Tracy Reid, Sec.-Treas.

Ontario Building Envelope Council (OBEC)
#310, 2175 Sheppard Ave. East, Toronto ON M2J 1W8
Tel: 647-317-5754; *Fax:* 416-491-1670
info@obec.on.ca
www.obec.on.ca
www.facebook.com/147901538606379

Overview: A medium-sized provincial organization founded in 1987
Mission: To promote the pursuit of excellence in the design, construction & performance of the building envelope
Member of: National Building Envelope Council
Finances: *Funding Sources:* Membership fees; seminars
Staff Member(s): 2
Membership: *Fees:* $660 corporate; $165 individual; $240 professional; $25 student
Chief Officer(s):
Paul J. Pushman, President
paul.pushman@exp.com
Sherry Denesha, Operations Manager
sherryd@taylorenterprises.com

Ontario Building Officials Association Inc. (OBOA) / Association de l'Ontario des officers en bâtiment inc.
#8, 200 Marycroft Ave., Woodbridge ON L4L 5X4
Tel: 905-264-1662; *Fax:* 905-264-8696
admin@oboa.on.ca
www.oboa.on.ca
www.linkedin.com/groups/4469807
www.facebook.com/oboa.ontariocanada
www.youtube.com/user/OBOA1956
Overview: A medium-sized provincial organization founded in 1956
Mission: To foster & cooperate in the establishment of uniform regulations relating to the fire protection & structural adequacy of buildings & the safety & health of the occupants; To promote the understanding & uniform interpretation & enforcement of these regulations & their companion documents; To provide assistance in the development & improvement of these regulations & their companion documents; To promote a close liaison & interchange of ideas on these regulations with related associations, the building industry, government & the consumer public
Finances: *Annual Operating Budget:* $500,000-$1.5 Million
Staff Member(s): 2; 24 volunteer(s)
Membership: 2,184 individual; 200 institutions; *Fees:* $100; *Member Profile:* Open to individuals, firms, corporations, associations, governments & government agencies interested or engaged in the administration & enforcement of regulations related to buildings & structures & their planning, construction, demolition, alteration, renovation, maintenance, operation & renewal insofar as such matters relate to fire prevention & protection, structural adequacy, safety, health, durability & the environment; *Committees:* Certification; Education; HRDC; Journal; Nominations; Objective Base Codes; Public Relations; Rural Affairs; Training; Website
Activities: Single-day symposiums & information sessions; seven courses, covering individual & specialized parts of the Building Code; Code & Administrative training seminars; a one-year post diploma community college course; certification program; *Awareness Events:* International Building Safety Week; *Speaker Service:* Yes
Chief Officer(s):
Aubrey LeBlanc, CAO
cao@oboa.on.ca
Michael T. Leonard, Coordinator, Membership, Training, Administration & Registrations

Ontario Business Education Partnership (OBEP)
info@obep.on.ca
www.obep.on.ca
twitter.com/ontbep
Previous Name: Ontario Learning Partnership Group
Overview: A medium-sized provincial organization
Mission: To promote & facilitate mutually beneficial alliances between education, business, community organizations & government that enhance education & employment opportunities for the students of Ontario
Finances: *Annual Operating Budget:* $50,000-$100,000
Staff Member(s): 5
Membership: 25 organizations

Ontario Camelids Association (OCA)
RR#3, Harrowsmith ON K0H 1V0
Tel: 613-372-0290
info@ontariocamelids.org
www.ontariocamelids.org
Overview: A small provincial organization founded in 1991
Mission: To promote llamas & alpacas in Ontario; to enhance the visibility & versatility of camelids
Finances: *Funding Sources:* Membership fees
Membership: 50; *Fees:* $50; *Member Profile:* Llama & alpaca enthusiasts
Activities: Educational displays at fairs; information pamphlets; library containing books & videos; *Speaker Service:* Yes; *Library*
Publications:
• Update [a publication of the Ontario Camelids Association]
Type: Newsletter

The Ontario Campaign for Action on Tobacco
c/o Ontario Medical Association, #900, 150 Bloor St. West, Toronto ON M5S 3C1
Tel: 416-340-2992; *Fax:* 416-340-2995
ocat@oma.org
www.ocat.org
Overview: A small provincial organization founded in 1992
Mission: To secure the passage of Ontario's Tobacco Control Act (TCA)
Chief Officer(s):
Michael Perley, Director

Ontario Camping Association *See* Ontario Camps Association

Ontario Camps Association (OCA)
70 Martin Ross Ave., Toronto ON M3J 2L4
Tel: 416-485-0425; *Fax:* 416-485-0422
info@ontariocamps.ca
www.ontariocamps.ca
www.facebook.com/OntarioCampsAssociation
twitter.com/OCACamps
Previous Name: Ontario Camping Association
Overview: A medium-sized provincial organization founded in 1937 overseen by Canadian Camping Association
Mission: To promote youth camping throughout Ontario; To maintain high standards for organized camping; To advocate on issues which impact members
Staff Member(s): 4
Membership: 600; *Fees:* $300 provisional camp; $100 regular; $60 senior/student; $350 commercial; $250 affiliate; *Member Profile:* Ontario camps which meet the association's standards; Individuals; Like-minded organizations & agencies; *Committees:* Archives; Awards; Educational Events; Finance; Health Care; Human Resources; Legislative; Membership; Nominations; Special Needs; Standards; Standards Review
Activities: Enforcing camp standards, through inspections, in order to ensure sound camp operation & administration & safe camping experiences; Sharing information & ideas; Supporting training seminars & workshops; Informing the public about the benefits of camping & the role of the association; Conducting research, through the OCA Educational Research Task Force
Chief Officer(s):
Adam Kronick, President
Heather Heagle, Executive Director
Jen Gilbert, Coordinator, Membership & Volunteer
Meetings/Conferences:
• Ontario Camps Association 2018 Annual Conference, 2018, ON
Scope: Provincial
Publications:
• OCA [Ontario Camps Association] Camps Guide
Type: Directory; *Frequency:* Annually; *Accepts Advertising*
Profile: Listings & descriptions of accredited camps in Ontario
• Ontario Camps Association's Guidelines for Accreditation
Profile: Addressing aspects of a day or residential camp's operations, such as health & safety, facilities, & leadership

Ontario Campus Radio Organization
c/o CFRU-FM, Radio Gryphon, University of Guelph, Level 2 UC, Guelph ON N1G 2W1
Tel: 519-824-4120
Overview: A small provincial organization founded in 1980
Member of: National Campus Community Radio Association
Staff Member(s): 4; 200 volunteer(s)
Activities: "Raise Your Voice" fundraising campaign

Ontario Canoe Kayak Sprint Racing Affiliation (OCSRA)
c/o Joanne Bryant, 118 Batson Dr., Aurora ON L4G 3T2
Tel: 905-841-5489
www.ocsra.ca
Overview: A small provincial organization founded in 1985 overseen by CanoeKayak Canada
Mission: To represent the sport of Olympic Sprint Canoe Kayak racing in Ontario.
Member of: CanoeKayak Canada
Chief Officer(s):
Joanne Bryant, Chair
joanne.i.bryant@gmail.com

Ontario Catholic School Trustees' Association (OCSTA)
PO Box 2064, #1804, 20 Eglinton Ave. West, Toronto ON M4R 1K8
Tel: 416-932-9460; *Fax:* 416-932-9459
ocsta@ocsta.on.ca
www.ocsta.on.ca
www.facebook.com/CatholicEducationInOntario
twitter.com/catholicedu
www.youtube.com/user/OCSTAVideo1
Overview: A medium-sized provincial organization founded in 1930
Mission: To protect & support the interests of Catholic education in Ontario
Member of: Canadian Catholic School Trustees Association
Staff Member(s): 9
Membership: 29 Catholic School Boards
Chief Officer(s):
Patrick J. Daly, President
Nick Milanetti, Executive Director

Ontario Catholic Supervisory Officers' Association (OCSOA)
730 Courtneypark Dr. West, Mississauga ON L5W 1L9
Tel: 905-564-8206; *Fax:* 905-564-8210
ocsoa@ocsoa.ca
www.ocsoa.ca
www.facebook.com/CatholicEducationInOntario
twitter.com/catholicedu
www.youtube.com/watch?v=T3PYrlpouqU
Overview: A medium-sized provincial organization founded in 1967
Mission: To represent supervisory officers employed in Catholic school boards
Membership: 150 individual; 18 associate
Activities: Offer Catholic Community Delivery Organization (CCDO) Supervisory Officers' Qualifications Program (SOQP)
Chief Officer(s):
John B. Kostoff, Executive Director
Laura Tonkovic, Executive Assistant
lauratonkovic@ocsoa.ca

Ontario Cavy Club (OCC)
c/o Bonnie Dart, 1978 Hilliard St., Selwyn ON K9J 6X2
www.ontariocavyclub.net
Overview: A small provincial organization founded in 1973
Mission: To unite all persons interested in the study, breeding & showing of guinea pigs (cavies); To promote interest in the study & breeding of cavies; To establish & recognize breeds & varieties of cavies & standards with respect thereto; To encourage, hold & sponsor showings & exhibitions, conferences, meetings & discussions; To cooperate, collaborate & affiliate with & to assist other clubs & organizations having objectives in whole or in part similar to those of the club
Finances: *Annual Operating Budget:* Less than $50,000; *Funding Sources:* Membership dues; shows; donations; ads
Membership: 1-99; *Fees:* $15 adult; $20 family; $10 youth
Chief Officer(s):
Bonnie Dart, Secretary-Treasurer

Ontario Centres of Excellence (OCE)
#200, 156 Front St. West, Toronto ON M5J 2L6
Tel: 416-861-1092; *Fax:* 416-971-7164
Toll-Free: 866-759-6014
www.oce-ontario.org
www.linkedin.com/groups/1811772/profile
www.facebook.com/OCEInnovation
twitter.com/oceinnovation
www.youtube.com/ocediscovery;
www.instagram.com/oceinnovation
Previous Name: Ontario Centres of Excellence - Centre for Earth & Environmental Technologies
Overview: A large provincial organization founded in 1987
Mission: To create new jobs, products, services, technologies & businesses by creating partnerships between industry & academia
Affiliation(s): Accelerator Centre for Commercialization Excellence (ACE)
Membership: *Committees:* Social Innovation Steering; Centre for Commercialization of Research Advisory Board; Advanced Health Technologies Sector Advisory Board; Advanced Manufacturing Sector Advisory Board; Energy & Environment Sector Advisory Board; Information, Communications & Digital Media Sector Advisory Board
Activities: Co-investing to commercialize innovation that originates in Ontario's publicly funded colleges, universities, &

research hospitals; Supporting & investing in early-stage projects that show promise for commercial success
Chief Officer(s):
Tom Corr, President & CEO
Tanya Dunn, Executive Assistant, 416-861-1092 Ext. 1003
tanya.dunn@oce-ontario.org
Bob Civak, Senior Vice-President, Business Development & Commercialization, 416-861-1092 Ext. 3229
bob.civak@oce-ontario.org
Sharon Jobity, Vice-President, Human Resources & Talent Acquisition, 416-861-1092 Ext. 1050
sharon.jobity@oce-ontario.org
Awards:
• Martin Walmsley Fellowship for Technological Entrepreneurship

Ontario Centres of Excellence - Centre for Earth & Environmental Technologies See Ontario Centres of Excellence

Ontario Cerebral Palsy Sports Association (OCPSA)
PO Box 60082, Ottawa ON K1T 0K9
Tel: 613-723-1806; *Fax:* 613-723-6742
Toll-Free: 866-286-2772
ocpsa.com
Overview: A small provincial organization overseen by Canadian Cerebral Palsy Sports Association
Mission: To provide, promote & coordinate competitive opportunities for persons with with cerebral palsy & other neuromuscular disorders in Ontario.
Member of: Canadian Cerebral Palsy Sports Association
Affiliation(s): Canadian Sport Institute - Ontario; Coaches Association of Ontario; ParaSport Ontario
Membership: *Fees:* $20
Activities: Athletics; Boccia; other sports
Chief Officer(s):
Don Sinclair, President

Ontario CGIT Association
PO Box 371, Norwich ON N0J 1P0
Tel: 519-863-6760
ontariocgit@dolson.ca
www.cgit.ca
Also Known As: Canadian Girls in Training - Ontario
Previous Name: National CGIT Association - Ontario
Overview: A small provincial organization founded in 1915
Finances: *Annual Operating Budget:* Less than $50,000
Staff Member(s): 1; 150 volunteer(s)

Ontario Chamber of Commerce (OCC)
#1500, 180 Dundas St. West, Toronto ON M5G 1Z8
Tel: 416-482-5222; *Fax:* 416-482-5879
info@occ.on.ca
www.occ.ca
www.linkedin.com/company/876425
twitter.com/OntarioCofC
www.youtube.com/user/OntarioChamber
Previous Name: Associated Boards of Trade of Ontario
Overview: A large provincial organization founded in 1911
Mission: As "Ontario's Business Advocate", the Ontario Chamber of Commerce is a ISO certified organization providing leadership to the province's business community. The focus is on the development of soundly research policy positions, representing the business community to government, & providing consultation, information & programs to the membership
Finances: *Annual Operating Budget:* $500,000-$1.5 Million; *Funding Sources:* Membership dues
Staff Member(s): 29; 600 volunteer(s)
Membership: 140 local chambers of commerce & boards; *Member Profile:* Business organizations of all sizes, from all economic sectors & from all parts of Ontario
Activities: Knowledge is Power Program; Public Awareness; Support to women living with ovarian cancer; Online knowledge centre at www.ovarianknowledge.ca; *Awareness Events:* Ovarian Cancer Walk of Hope
Chief Officer(s):
Rocco Rossi, President & CEO
Ali Mirza, Vice-President, Finance, 647-243-3536
Awards:
• Chair's Awards
• International Trade Contest
For senior high school students
• Membership Marketing Award
• Outstanding Business Achievement Award

Ontario Charterboat Association See Ontario Sportfishing Guides' Association

Ontario Cheerleading Federation (OCF)
21 Oceanpearl Cres., Whitby ON L1N 0C5
registrar@ocfcheer.com
www.ofcheer.com
twitter.com/OntarioCheer
Overview: A small provincial organization overseen by Cheer Canada
Mission: To provide training & certification courses for coaches across Ontario.
Member of: Cheer Canada

Ontario Chiropractic Association (OCA) / Association chiropratique de l'Ontario
#200, 20 Victoria St., Toronto ON M5C 2N8
Tel: 416-860-0070; *Fax:* 416-860-0857
Toll-Free: 877-327-2273
oca@chiropractic.on.ca
www.chiropractic.on.ca
www.facebook.com/ontariochiropracticassociation
twitter.com/ON_Chiropractic
Overview: A medium-sized provincial organization founded in 1929 overseen by Canadian Chiropractic Association
Mission: To serve its members by promoting the philosophy, art, & science of chiropractic & thereby enhance the health & well-being of the citizens of Ontario
Membership: *Member Profile:* Licensed Doctor of Chiropractic
Activities: Providing public education & professional development; *Speaker Service:* Yes
Chief Officer(s):
Kristina Peterson, President
Awards:
• Chiropractor of the Year

Ontario Christian Music Assembly
90 Topcliff Ave., Downsview ON M3N 1L8
Tel: 416-636-9779; *Fax:* 905-775-2230
landmkooy@rogers.com
Overview: A small provincial organization founded in 1961
10 volunteer(s)
Membership: 130 individual
Activities: Spring & Christmas concerts series; Annual Christian festival concert

Ontario Clean Air Alliance (OCAA)
#300, 160 John St., Toronto ON M5V 2E5
Tel: 416-260-2080; *Fax:* 416-598-9520
contact@cleanairalliance.org
www.cleanairalliance.org
twitter.com/NoNukeBailouts
Overview: A medium-sized provincial organization founded in 1997
Mission: To ensure that Ontario's electricity needs are met by ecologically sustainable renewable sources
Finances: *Funding Sources:* Donations
Membership: *Member Profile:* Organizations & individuals who work for cleaner air through a coal phase-out & a move to a renewable electricity future
Chief Officer(s):
Jack Gibbons, Chair, 416-260-2080 Ext. 2
jack@cleanairalliance.org
Angela Bischoff, Director, Outreach, 416-260-2080 Ext. 1
Angela@cleanairalliance.org
Publications:
• Finishing the Coal Phase Out: An Historic Opportunity for Climate Leadership
Type: Report
Profile: A review of the Government of Ontario's coal phase-out to reduce greenhouse gas emission
• Increasing Productivity & Moving Towards a Renewable Future: A New Electricity Strategy for Ontario
Type: Report; *Number of Pages:* 60; *Author:* Jack Gibbons
• Ontario Clean Air Alliance E-Bulletin
Type: Newsletter; *Frequency:* Semimonthly
Profile: The most recent news & reports about energy issues & air quality
• The Ontario Power Authority's Coal Phase-Out Strategy: A Critical Review
Type: Report; *Number of Pages:* 13
• Ontario's Coal Phase-Out: A Major Climate Accomplishment Within Our Grasp
Type: Report; *Number of Pages:* 10
Profile: A review of the coal phase-out's progress
• Ontario's Green Future: How We Can Build a 100% Renewable Electricity Grid by 2027

Type: Report; *Number of Pages:* 32; *Author:* Jack Gibbons
Profile: An Ontario Clean Air Alliance report with recommendations
• Powerful Options: A Review of Ontario's Options for Replacing Aging Nuclear Plants
Type: Report; *Number of Pages:* 18
Profile: A presentation of options for replacing nuclear plants that are less expensive than building new nuclear reactors

Ontario Coalition Against Poverty (OCAP)
#206, 157 Carlton St., Toronto ON M5A 2K3
Tel: 416-925-6939; *Fax:* 416-925-6995
ocap@tao.ca
www.ocap.ca
twitter.com/OCAPtoronto
Overview: A small provincial organization
Mission: To organize campaigns against regressive policies that affect poor & working people
Finances: *Funding Sources:* Donations
Activities: Engaging in advocacy activities; *Rents Mailing List:* Yes

Ontario Coalition for Abortion Clinics (OCAC)
PO Box 3, 427 Bloor St. West, Toronto ON M5S 1X7
Tel: 416-969-8463
ocac88@gmail.com
ocac-choice.com
www.facebook.com/OCAC88
twitter.com/OCAC25
Overview: A medium-sized provincial organization founded in 1982
Mission: To work for reproductive rights & access to abortions
Activities: Presenting workshops & speakers; Lobbying; Organizing demonstration & community action

Ontario Coalition for Better Child Care (OCBCC) / Coalition Ontarienne pour de meilleurs services éducatifs à l'enfance
#206, 489 College St., Toronto ON M6G 1A5
Tel: 416-538-0628; *Fax:* 416-538-6737
Toll-Free: 800-594-7514
info@childcareontario.org
www.childcareontario.org
www.facebook.com/OCBCC
twitter.com/ChildCareON
Also Known As: Better Child Care Ontario, Inc.
Overview: A medium-sized provincial organization founded in 1981
Mission: To advocate on behalf of Ontario's non-profit, licensed child care programs
Affiliation(s): Canadian Child Care Advocacy Association
Finances: *Annual Operating Budget:* $250,000-$500,000; *Funding Sources:* Government research grants; foundations; membership
Staff Member(s): 3; 39 volunteer(s)
Membership: 456; *Fees:* $40 individuals; $30 students; $26.50 unwaged & retired; $37.50 child care workers; $90-$1,000 organizations; $190-$1,000 organizations; *Member Profile:* Child care programs, individuals, trade unions, students, rural, native & francophone groups
Activities: *Library:* Open to public by appointment
Chief Officer(s):
Sheila Olan-MacLean, President
Christine Sbardella, Vice President
Lynn Poole-Cotnam, Treasurer

Ontario Coalition of Aboriginal Peoples (OCAP)
PO Box 189, Wabigoon ON P0V 2W0
Tel: 807-938-1321
www.o-cap.ca
Overview: A large provincial organization founded in 2007 overseen by Congress of Aboriginal Peoples
Mission: To represent the rights & interests of Métis, Status & Non-Status Aboriginal peoples living off-reserve in urban, rural or remote areas
Affiliation(s): 23 organizations
Finances: *Annual Operating Budget:* $1.5 Million-$3 Million
Membership: 15,000-49,999; *Fees:* $5-$25; *Member Profile:* Métis, Status, Non-Status, Inuit people living off-reserve in Ontario
Activities: Providing training & education programs & services
Chief Officer(s):
Brad Maggrah, President
kmaggrah1@gmail.com

Ontario Coalition of Rape Crisis Centres (OCRCC) / Coalition des centres anti-viol de l'Ontario
Toronto ON M5S 1A8
Tel: 416-597-1171; *Crisis Hot-Line:* 416-597-8808
www.sexualassaultsupport.ca
Overview: A medium-sized provincial charitable organization founded in 1977
Mission: To work for prevention & eradication of sexual assault; To help implement legal, social & attitudinal changes regarding sexual assault; To provide mechanism for communication, education & mobilization to alleviate political & geographical isolation of rape crisis centres in Ontario; To encourage, direct & generate research into sexual violence; To work with the Canadian Association of Sexual Assault Centres to develop national policies & to liaise with other provincial organizations addressing similar issues
Member of: Canadian Association of Sexual Assault Centres; National Action Committee on the Status of Women; National Coalition of Sexual Assault (US)
Finances: *Annual Operating Budget:* Less than $50,000; *Funding Sources:* Provincial government
Staff Member(s): 1
Membership: 24; *Fees:* $2; *Member Profile:* Member centres that work for social change & prevention of sexual assault through education & crisis intervention; *Committees:* Executive; Finance; Personnel; Lobby; Policy
Activities: Information Exchange Centre Referrals; *Awareness Events:* Take Back the Night; *Library*
Chief Officer(s):
Jacqueline Benn-John, President

Ontario College & University Library Association (OCULA)
c/o Ontario Library Association, 2 Toronto St., 3rd Fl., Toronto ON M5C 2B6
Tel: 416-363-3388; *Fax:* 416-941-9581
Toll-Free: 866-873-9867
info@accessola.com
www.accessola.org
Overview: A medium-sized provincial charitable organization founded in 1969
Mission: To support librarians & to improve Library Science in Ontario's college & university libraries
Affiliation(s): Ontario Library Association
Membership: *Committees:* Fundraising; Super Conference Planning
Activities: *Rents Mailing List:* Yes
Chief Officer(s):
Sarah Shujah, President
sshujah@centennialcollege.ca
Awards:
• Award for Special Achievement
Honours exceptional achievements in service or research & publication
• Lifetime Achievement Award
Awarded to an indvidiual working in an Ontario library who has made an outstanding contribution to academic or research library development
• Lightning Strikes Student Award
Provides an opportunity for a Library Information Science student to participate in the OLA Super Conference
• New Librarian Residency Award
Awarded to enhance recruitment of new librarians to academic librarianship & to provide entry-level professional work experience in a research library setting
Meetings/Conferences:
• Ontario College & University Library Association Annual General Meeting 2018, 2018, ON
Scope: Provincial
Publications:
• InsideOCULA [a publication of the Ontario College & University Library Association]
Type: Magazine; *Frequency:* 5 pa; *Editor:* Graeme Campbell et al.
Profile: Showcases programs, activities & research happening in university & college libraries inOntario

Ontario College Administrative Staff Associations (OCASA)
PO Box 263, #201-202, 120 Centre St. North, Napanee ON K7R 3M4
Fax: 866-742-5430
Toll-Free: 866-742-5429
info@ocasa.on.ca
www.ocpinfo.com
www.linkedin.com/groups?mostPopular=&gid=3274946
twitter.com/OCASA_APACO
www.flickr.com/photos/ocasa
Overview: A medium-sized provincial licensing organization
Mission: OCASA is a voluntary, professional association which supports and advocates for Ontario's community college administrators, while building and promoting administrative excellence for the betterment of the college system.
Chief Officer(s):
Diane Posterski, Executive Director, 866-742-5429 Ext. 102
diane.posterski@ocasa.on.ca
Meetings/Conferences:
• 2018 Leaders & Innovators Conference, 2018
Scope: Provincial

Ontario College of Certified Social Workers *See* Ontario College of Social Workers & Social Service Workers

Ontario College of Pharmacists (OCP)
483 Huron St., Toronto ON M5R 2R4
Tel: 416-962-4861; *Fax:* 416-847-8200
Toll-Free: 800-220-1921
communications@ocpinfo.com
www.ocpinfo.com
www.linkedin.com/company/ontario-college-of-pharmacists
www.facebook.com/ocpinfo
twitter.com/ocpinfo
Overview: A medium-sized provincial licensing organization founded in 1871 overseen by National Association of Pharmacy Regulatory Authorities
Mission: To administer the Regulated Health Professions Act; To regulate the practice of pharmacy, in accordance with standards of practice; To ensure that members provide quality pharmaceutical service & care to the public
Member of: Canadian Council on Continuing Education in Pharmacy
Activities: Developing & maintaining qualification standards for individuals to be issued certificates of accreditation; Regulating drugs & pharmacies, under the Drug & Pharmacies Regulation Act; Ensuring adherence to professional & operational standards by pharmacists & pharmacies; Collaborating with other health profession colleges; Establishing & maintaining programs to assist members with their response to changes in practice environments, advances in technology, & other emerging issues; Educating the public
Chief Officer(s):
Regis Vaillancourt, President
Publications:
• Pharmacy Connection [a publication of Ontario College of Pharmacists]
Type: Journal; *Frequency:* Bimonthly
Profile: College activities & policies for Ontario's 12,000 pharmacists

Ontario College of Reflexology (OCR)
PO Box 220, New Liskeard ON P0J 1P0
Tel: 705-647-5354; *Fax:* 705-995-3415
Toll-Free: 888-627-3338
Other Communication: info@ocr.edu; membership@ocr.edu; referral@ocr.edu
ocr@ocr.edu
www.ocr.edu
www.facebook.com/ontarioreflexology
twitter.com/profbisson
plus.google.com/+OcrEdu
Overview: A small provincial organization
Mission: To provide accreditation for reflexologists in the province of Ontario, where required & as permitted by applicable statues of Ontario; To improve & maintain the qualifications & standards of the reflexology profession; To promote reflexology in the province
Finances: *Funding Sources:* Membership dues
Membership: *Fees:* $50; *Member Profile:* Certified practitioners; Persons interested in reflexology
Activities: Offering a referral system
Chief Officer(s):
Donald A. Bisson, Chair
Publications:
• OCR [Ontario College of Reflexology] Foot Notes
Type: Newsletter; *Frequency:* Quarterly

Ontario College of Social Workers & Social Service Workers (OCSWSSW) / Ordre des travailleurs sociaux et des techniciens en travail social de l'Ontario
#1000, 250 Bloor St. East, Toronto ON M4W 1E6
Tel: 416-972-9882; *Fax:* 416-972-1512
Toll-Free: 877-828-9380
info@ocswssw.org
www.ocswssw.org
Previous Name: Ontario College of Certified Social Workers
Overview: A medium-sized provincial organization founded in 2000
Mission: To establish & maintain qualification for College membership; To regulate the practice of social work & the practice of social service work in order to protect the public; To investigate complaints agaains members of the College
Staff Member(s): 26
Membership: *Fees:* $280; $180 for new graduates; *Member Profile:* Persons in Ontario who wish to use the titles social worker, social service worker, registered social worker, or registered social service worker; *Committees:* Executive; Complaints; Registration Appeals; Discipline Decisions; Fitness to Practise; Elections; Corporations; Standards of Practice; Finance; Nominating; Governance
Activities: Issuing certificates of registration to members; Approving continuing education programs for members of the College; Dealing wtih issues of discipline or incompetence; Communicating with the public on behalf of members
Chief Officer(s):
Lisa Betteridge, Registrar, 416-972-9882 Ext. 225
lbetteridge@ocswssw.org
Christina Van Sickle, Director, Professional Practice, 416-972-9882 Ext. 226
cvansickle@ocswssw.org
Paul Cucci, Manager, Membership, 416-972-9882 Ext. 202
pcucci@ocswssw.org
Publications:
• Ontario College of Social Workers & Social Service Workers Annual Report
Type: Yearbook; *Frequency:* Annually; *Editor:* Yvonne Armstrong
• Perspective
Type: Newsletter; *Frequency:* Semiannually; *Editor:* Yvonne Armstrong
Profile: College activites, practice notes, council highlights, discipline decision summaries, information sessions, questions & answers, & a bulletin board

Ontario College of Teachers (OCT) / Odre des enseignantes et des enseignants de l'Ontario
101 Bloor St. West, Toronto ON M5S 0A1
Tel: 416-961-8800; *Fax:* 416-961-8822
Toll-Free: 888-534-2222; *TTY:* 416-961-6331
info@oct.ca
www.oct.ca
www.linkedin.com/company/ontario-college-of-teachers
www.facebook.com/OntarioTeachers
twitter.com/OCT_OEEO
www.instagram.com/oct_oeeo
Overview: A large provincial licensing organization founded in 1997
Mission: To ensure Ontario students are taught by skilled teachers who adhere to clear standards of practice & conduct; To establish standards of practice & conduct; To issue teaching certificates & may also suspend or revoke them; To accredit teacher education programs; To provide for ongoing professional learning opportunities for members
Finances: *Annual Operating Budget:* Greater than $5 Million; *Funding Sources:* Membership fees
Staff Member(s): 170
Membership: 213,000+; *Fees:* Schedule available; *Member Profile:* Accredited teachers in Ontario; Vice-principals; Principals; Supervisory officers; Directors of education; *Committees:* Executive; Accreditation; Accreditation Appeal; Discipline; Editorial Board; Finance; Fitness to Practise; Governance; Human Resources; Investigation; Quality Assurance; Registration Appeals; Standards of Practice & Education; Steering
Activities: *Library:* Margaret Wilson Library; Not open to public
Chief Officer(s):
Michael Salvatori, Registrar & CEO
Linda Zaks-Walker, Director, Membership Services
Richard Lewko, Director, Corporate & Council Services
Awards:
• Joseph W. Atkinson Scholarship For Excellence In Teacher Education
Eligibility: Studying in the faculty of education in Ontario; must be in a consecutive program or going into their final year in a concurrent program; outstanding academic achievement while demonstrating a high level of preparedness for teacher education.; *Amount:* $2,000

Meetings/Conferences:
• Ontario College of Teachers 2018 Annual Meeting of Members, 2018
Scope: Provincial
Description: Presentations of interest to teachers
• Ontario College of Teachers Conference 2018, May, 2018, Toronto Marriott Downtown Eaton Centre Hotel, Toronto, ON
Scope: Provincial
Description: Presentations of interest to teachers
Publications:
• Professionally Speaking: The Magazine of The Ontario College of Teachers
Type: Magazine; *Frequency:* Quarterly; *Accepts Advertising*; *Price:* $10 in Canada; $20 outside Canada
Profile: Features, resources & reviews, teacher profiles, & governance reports

Ontario Colleges Athletic Association (OCAA)
#911, 305 Milner Ave., Toronto ON M1B 3V4
Tel: 416-426-7043; *Fax:* 416-426-7308
www.ocaa.com
www.facebook.com/TheOCAA
twitter.com/TheOCAA
www.instagram.com/theocaa
Overview: A small provincial charitable organization founded in 1967
Mission: To govern intercollegiate sports in Ontario; To promote student athlete & sport development as well as academic success; To ensure a safe environment; To provide a forum for personal development; To enhance student life
Member of: Canadian Collegiate Athletic Association
Affiliation(s): Pacific Western Athletic Association; Alberta Colleges Athletic Conference; Fédération Québécoise du Sport Étudiant; Atlantic Colleges Athletic Association; Ontario Federation of School Athletic Associations; Ontario University Athletics; Athletics Ontario; Ontario Badminton Association; Basketball Ontario; Ontario Curling Council; Golf Association of Ontario; Rugby Ontario; Ontario Soccer Association; Softball Ontario; Ontario Volleyball Association
Membership: *Committees:* Awards/Athletic Scholarships; Constitution, By-Laws & Membership; Finance; Eligibility; Marketing & Sport Development; Policies & Procedures; Risk Management/Athletic Therapy; Ways & Means
Chief Officer(s):
Ray Chateau, President
Kyle Pelly, Executive Director
Josh Bell-Webster, Coordinator, Marketing & Communications, 416-426-7041
bell-webster@ocaa.com

Ontario Commercial Fisheries' Association (OCFA)
PO Box 2129, 45 James St., Blenheim ON N0P 1A0
Tel: 519-676-0488; *Fax:* 519-676-0944
Toll-Free: 800-461-7890
info@ocfa.on.ca
www.ocfa.ca
Overview: A medium-sized provincial organization founded in 1945
Mission: To be dedicated to the growth & continued strength of a responsible, competitive, & sustainable licensed commercial fishery in Ontario; To represent the industry's interests & its view to government, the media, & consumers
Finances: *Annual Operating Budget:* $500,000-$1.5 Million; *Funding Sources:* Membership dues; Contractual programs
Staff Member(s): 12; 19 volunteer(s)
Membership: 267; *Fees:* $150; *Member Profile:* Licensed Ontario commercial fishing license holders; Federal registered processing plants
Activities: Maintaining a code of conduct for responsible fishing practices; Hosting an annual convention
Chief Officer(s):
Jane Graham, Executive Director
jane.graham@ocfa.on.ca

Ontario Commercial Rabbit Growers' Association
PO Box 634, Brussels ON N0G 1H0
info@ontariorabbit.ca
www.ontariorabbit.ca
Also Known As: Ontario Rabbit
Overview: A small provincial organization founded in 1964
Mission: To enhance the profitability of meat rabbit production through activities such as lobbying, education, research & market development
Chief Officer(s):
Michelle Sanders, President

Ontario Community Justice Association (OCJA)
Tel: 416-304-1974
www.facebook.com/OntarioCommunityJusticeAssociation
twitter.com/OCJA1979
Overview: A small provincial charitable organization founded in 1979
Mission: To promote community justice through support to service providers; to endorse service provision that embraces inclusivity and human rights; to advocate for the presence & accessibility of community justice programs
Finances: *Annual Operating Budget:* Less than $50,000; *Funding Sources:* Membership dues
11 volunteer(s)
Membership: 20+; *Fees:* $250 agency; $75 individual; *Member Profile:* Any staff person employed by a community based organization in Ontario & affiliated with the justice system
Activities: Providing members with open & ongoing communication networks; Advocating on behalf of community service providers; Enhancing services through collaboration;
Speaker Service: Yes
Chief Officer(s):
Gemma Napoli, President
gnapoli@efrytoronto.org
Amy Roy, Representative, Public Relations
amy_roy@can.salvationarmy.org
Awards:
• Marjorie Blakeney Memorial Award
Awarded to recognize an OCJA member who shows outstanding community involvement through service & volunteering
Meetings/Conferences:
• Ontario Community Justice Association 38th Annual Conference 2018, 2018
Scope: Provincial
Publications:
• Ontario Community Justice Association Newsletter
Type: Newsletter; *Frequency:* Irregular
Profile: An information source for OCJA members including association news & events

Ontario Community Newspapers Association (OCNA)
#200, 37 Front St. East, Toronto ON M5E 1B3
Tel: 416-923-7724
www.ocna.org
www.facebook.com/171125688577
twitter.com/OCNAAdReach
Overview: A large provincial organization founded in 1950 overseen by Canadian Community Newspapers Association
Mission: To support members with information about the Ontario community newspaper industry & market; To improve the competitive position of the industry
Affiliation(s): Newspapers Canada; Atlantic Community Newspapers Association; Québec Community Newspapers Association; Hebdos Québec; Manitoba Community Newspapers Association; Saskatchewan Weekly Newspapers Association; Alberta Weekly Newspapers Association; British Columbia & Yukon Community Newspapers Association
Finances: *Funding Sources:* Membership fees; Grants; Sponsorships
Staff Member(s): 8
Membership: 800+ newspapers; *Fees:* Schedule available, based upon circulation for active members; $250 associate members; *Member Profile:* Newspapers throughout Ontario which serve a specific geographical or ethnic community, publish less frequently than a daily newspaper, but at least once a month, & meet other criteria; Other organizations that support community newspapers
Activities: Engaging in advocacy activities for favourable government policies; Promoting the Ontario community newspaper industry; Working with advertisers, agencies, & government to place advertising in member newspapers, through Ad*Reach; Posting industry-related positions; Providing educational opportunities through the online training center
Chief Officer(s):
Dave Adsett, President
John Willems, Secretary-Treasurer
Caroline Medwell, Executive Director, 416-923-7724 Ext. 4428
c.medwell@ocna.org
Karen Shardlow, Coordinator, Member Services, 416-923-7724 Ext. 4432
k.shardlow@ocna.org
Kelly Gorven, Coordinator, Member Services, 416-923-7724 Ext. 4439
k.gorven@ocna.org
Lucia Shepherd, Coordinator, Accounting/Newsprint, 416-923-7724 Ext. 4423
l.shepherd@ocna.org
Awards:
• General Excellence Awards, Better Newspapers Competition
To honour achievement by circulation class in editorial, layout, & advertising
• Insurance Bureau of Canada Community Award in Memory of Mary Knowles
Awarded to recognize dedicated newspaper employees who constantly serve their communities
• Ontario Junior Citizen Awards
Awarded to recognize a youth who is involved in worthwhile community service, shows excellence in personal achievements, or has performed a brave & heroic act in the past year *Eligibility:* Any resident of Ontario aged 6-17 years
• Quill Awards
Awarded to community newspaper owners & employees for long time service to the industry
Publications:
• NewsClips [a publication of the Ontario Community Newspapers Association]
Type: Newsletter; *Frequency:* Monthly; *Price:* Free with membership in the Ontario Community NewspapersAssociation
Profile: Industry information & details about upcoming association services & events

Ontario Community Support Association (OCSA) / Association ontarienne de soutien communautaire
#104, 970 Lawrence Ave. West, Toronto ON M6A 3B6
Tel: 416-256-3010; *Fax:* 416-256-3021
Toll-Free: 800-267-6272
reception@ocsa.on.ca
www.ocsa.on.ca
twitter.com/OCSAtweets
Previous Name: Meals on Wheels Ontario Inc.
Overview: A medium-sized provincial charitable organization founded in 1992
Mission: To support & represent the common goals of community-based, not-for-profit health & social service organizations which assist individuals to live at home in their own community
Member of: Canadian Centre for Philanthropy
Finances: *Funding Sources:* Membership fees; donations
Staff Member(s): 13
Membership: *Fees:* Schedule available based on budget for full members; $100 associate; $300 corporate; *Member Profile:* A not-for-profit community based agency delivering home support & or Meals on Wheels & or homemaking services
Activities: *Awareness Events:* Community Support Month, Oct.; *Rents Mailing List:* Yes; *Library:* OCSA Resource Collection; Open to public by appointment
Chief Officer(s):
Deborah Simon, Chief Executive Officer
deborah.simon@ocsa.on.ca
Meetings/Conferences:
• Ontario Community Support Association 2018 Annual Conference, 2018, ON
Scope: Provincial

Ontario Community Transit Association *See* Ontario Public Transit Association

Ontario Competitive Trail Riding Association Inc. (OCTRA)
c/o Doug Price, 457102 Conc. 3A, RR#4, Chatsworth ON N0H 1G0
Tel: 519-377-0652
www.octra.on.ca
Overview: A small provincial organization founded in 1967 overseen by Canadian Long Distance Riding Association
Mission: To encourage the growth & popularity of competitive trail, endurance riding & Ride'n'Tie; to establish a set of rules & quality for managing & judging same; to encourage & maintain a high standard of horsemanship & sportsmanship amongst competitors; to encourage the selection, care, training & conditioning of horses for long distance riding; to provide guidance & help to clubs & groups in establishing & running competitive rides; to ensure that all rides are run humanely so as to avoid cruelty & suffering to competing animals; to formulate promotional & educational programs; to foster goodwill & understanding between horse owners, land owners & conservation authorities with a view to opening up more land for riding trails
Member of: Canadian Long Distance Riding Association
Affiliation(s): Horse Ontario; Ontario Equestrian Federation

Canadian Associations / Ontario Concrete Pipe Association (OCPA)

Membership: *Fees:* $60 family; $45 individual; $35 associate non-voting; $25 junior; *Committees:* Awards; Competitive; Education; Endurance; Fundraising; Mileage Programs; Newsletter; Publicity & Promotions; Ride 'n' Tie; Ride Management/Sanctioning; Set Speed; Veterinary; Website; Worker Credit; Youth
Activities: *Speaker Service:* Yes; *Rents Mailing List:* Yes; *Library:* Archives; by appointment
Chief Officer(s):
Doug Price, President
khofire@gmail.com
Nancy Beacon, Vice-President
rabbitrun1@me.com
Jackie Redmond, Secretary
jackieredmond@sympatico.ca
Michelle Bignell, Treasurer
arabians@cayusecreekranch.com

Ontario Concrete Block Association *See* Canadian Concrete Masonry Producers Association

Ontario Concrete Pipe Association (OCPA)
447 Frederick St., 2nd Fl, Kitchener ON N2H 2P4
Tel: 519-489-4488; *Fax:* 519-578-6060
admin@ocpa.com
www.ocpa.com
www.linkedin.com/company-beta/2126103
www.facebook.com/ocpa.fb
Overview: A medium-sized provincial organization founded in 1957
Mission: To represent the concrete pipe & maintenance hole industry throughout Ontario; To promote engineered concrete products of permanence
Member of: Canadian Standards Association
Affiliation(s): Municipal Engineers Association; Canadian Concrete Pipe Association; Tubecon; American Concrete Pipe Association; Canadian Portland Cement Association; Water Environment Association of Ontario; Canadian Public Works Association; Ontario Sewer & Watermain Construction Association; Consulting Engineers of Ontario
Finances: *Annual Operating Budget:* $250,000-$500,000; *Funding Sources:* Membership dues
Staff Member(s): 2; 30 volunteer(s)
Membership: 40; *Member Profile:* Manufacturers of precast concrete pipe & associated products; *Committees:* Prequalification; Public Relations & Communications; Technical
Activities: *Awareness Events:* Construct Canada; Ontario Good Roads; *Speaker Service:* Yes; *Library:* by appointment
Chief Officer(s):
Gerrard F. Mulhern, Executive Director, 519-489-4488 Ext. 3
gerry.mulhern@opca.com

Ontario Confederation of University Faculty Associations (OCUFA) / Union des associations des professeurs des universités de l'Ontario
17 Isabella St., Toronto ON M4Y 1M7
Tel: 416-979-2117; *Fax:* 416-593-5607
ocufa@ocufa.on.ca
www.ocufa.on.ca
www.facebook.com/OCUFA
twitter.com/ocufa
Overview: A small provincial organization founded in 1964 overseen by Canadian Association of University Teachers
Mission: To act as the voice of Ontario's approximately 15,000 university faculty & academic librarians; To advance the professional & economic interests of university faculty & academic librarians; To enhance the quality of Ontario's higher education system
Staff Member(s): 11
Membership: 27 associations; *Member Profile:* Member faculty associations throughout Ontario
Activities: Providing on-campus support to faculty associations; Engaging in advocacy activities; Liaising with government, the media, & higher education stakeholders; Providing research to support collective bargaining & grievance management
Chief Officer(s):
Kate Lawson, President, 519-888-4567 Ext. 33965
klawson@uwaterloo.ca
Judy Bates, Vice-President, 519-884-1970 Ext. 2387
Mark Rosenfeld, Executive Director, 416-979-2117 Ext. 229
mrosenfeld@ocufa.on.ca
Mark Rosenfeld, Associate Executive Director, Research & Communications, 416-979-2117 Ext. 233
Glen Copplestone, Treasurer, 519-433-3491 Ext. 4432
Awards:
• Teaching & Academic Librarianship Awards
• Lorimer Award (Bargaining Award)
• Status of Women Award of Distinction
• The Henry Mandelbaum Graduate Fellowship
Eligibility: A full-time graduate student at a publicly-assisted Ontario University who has demonstrated academic excellence, shows exceptional academic promise, and has provided significant community service in his/her university career.
Publications:
• The Academic Matters
Profile: Highlights of current trends in postsecondary education, of interest to faculty in Ontario
• Ontario University Report
Type: Newsletter; *Frequency:* Semimonthly
Profile: News about postsecondary education & the association's activities
• Trends in Higher Education
Profile: A research series, featuring in-depth analysis

Ontario Conference of Mennonite Brethren Churches (OCMBC)
3970 Glendale Ave., Vineland ON L0R 2C0
Tel: 905-562-7391
info@onmb.org
www.onmb.org
Overview: A small provincial organization overseen by Canadian Conference of Mennonite Brethren Churches
Mission: To glorify God by facilitating collaboration among its member churches
Staff Member(s): 1
Chief Officer(s):
Ed Willms, Executive Director
ewillms@onmb.org
Meetings/Conferences:
• Ontario Conference of Mennonite Brethren Churches 87th Annual Convention 2018, February, 2018, Behta Darya Community Church, Mississauga, ON
Scope: Provincial

Ontario Conference, Church of the United Brethren in Christ *See* The United Brethren Church in Canada

Ontario Construction Secretariat (OCS)
#360, 180 Attwell Dr., Toronto ON M9W 6A9
Tel: 416-620-5210; *Fax:* 416-620-5310
Toll-Free: 888-878-8868
info@iciconstruction.com
www.iciconstruction.com
www.linkedin.com/company/ontario-construction-secretariat
www.facebook.com/OCS.KnowledgeToBuildOn
twitter.com/OntConstSec
Overview: A large provincial organization
Mission: To represent 25 Employee & the 25 Employer Bargaining Agencies of the unionized industrial, commercial, & institutional (ICI) sector of Ontario's construction industry
Staff Member(s): 7
Activities: *Speaker Service:* Yes
Chief Officer(s):
Sean Strickland, CEO
seans@iciconstruction.com
Katherine Jacobs, Director, Research
kjacobs@iciconstruction.com
Christine Allenby, Director, Operations
christine2@iciconstruction.com
Meetings/Conferences:
• Ontario Construction Secretariat State of the Industry & Outlook Conference 2018, March, 2018, Metro Toronto Convention Centre, Toronto, ON
Scope: Provincial
Contact Information: Administrator: Gianluca Cipriani, E-mail: gcipriani@iciconstruction.com
• Ontario Construction Secretariat Future Building 2018, April, 2018, International Centre, Toronto, ON
Scope: Provincial
Attendance: 7,000+
Description: An interactive three-day exhibition that provides young career seekers with the opportunity to experience hands-on activities in all areas of the construction sector; event is targeted towards youth 14-26, Aboriginal youth, youth at risk, & individuals in career transition
Contact Information: Administrator: Gianluca Cipriani, E-mail: gcipriani@iciconstruction.com
Publications:
• Eye on ICI [a publication of the Ontario Construction Secretariat]
Type: Newsletter; *Frequency:* q.

Ontario Consultants on Religious Tolerance (OCRT)
#128, 829 Norwest Rd., Kingston ON K7P 2N3
Toll-Free: 888-806-6115
ocrtfeedback@gmail.com
www.religioustolerance.org
www.facebook.com/groups/115060631838983
Overview: A small provincial organization founded in 1995
Mission: To promote religious tolerance & expose religious hatred & misinformation
Finances: *Annual Operating Budget:* Less than $50,000; *Funding Sources:* Lecture fees; donations; banner ads
Staff Member(s): 1; 5 volunteer(s)
Membership: 1-99
Activities: *Speaker Service:* Yes
Chief Officer(s):
B.A. Robinson, Coordinator

Ontario Convenience Store Association (OCSA)
#217, 466 Speers Rd., Oakville ON L6K 3W9
Tel: 905-845-9152; *Fax:* 905-849-9947
www.conveniencestores.ca
twitter.com/ontariocstores
Overview: A medium-sized provincial organization overseen by Canadian Convenience Store Association
Mission: To represent convenience store retailers in Ontario
Affiliation(s): Canadian Convenience Stores Association; Western Convenience Stores Association; Association Québécoise des dépanneurs en alimentation; Atlantic Convenience Stores Association
Finances: *Funding Sources:* Membership fees
Membership: *Member Profile:* Major convenience store companies; independent owners; food retailers; suppliers & wholesalers; oil companies; gasoline & automotive product vendors
Chief Officer(s):
Dave Bryans, Chief Executive Officer
bryans@conveniencestores.ca

Ontario Co-operative Association
#101, 450 Speedvale Ave. West, Guelph ON N1H 7Y6
Tel: 519-763-8271; *Fax:* 519-763-7239
Toll-Free: 888-745-5521
info@ontario.coop
www.ontario.coop
www.facebook.com/oncoop/
twitter.com/ontariocoops/
www.youtube.com/user/OntarioCoopAssoc/
Also Known As: On Co-op
Overview: A small provincial organization founded in 1979
Mission: The Ontario Co-operative Association (On Co-op) develops, unites and promotes co-operatives throughout the province of Ontario
Member of: The Ontario Rural Council; Foundation for Rural Living; Agricultural Adaptation Council; Association of Co-operative Education
Staff Member(s): 5
Membership: *Fees:* Schedule available; *Member Profile:* Agriculture, finance, insurance, consumer, supply & services cooperatives; *Committees:* Governance & Membership; Regulatory Affairs; Government Relations; Co-operative Development; Nominations; Finance & Human Resources
Chief Officer(s):
Mark Ventry, Executive Director, 519-763-8271 Ext. 30
mventry@ontario.coop

Ontario Cooperative Education Association (OCEA) / Association de l'éducation coopérative de l'Ontario
35 Reynar Dr., Quispamsis NB E2G 1J9
Fax: 506-849-8375
ocea@rogers.com
www.ocea.on.ca
Overview: A medium-sized provincial organization founded in 1976
Mission: To support excellence in the education of Ontario students by providing leadership for the professional development of its members
Affiliation(s): Career, Cooperative Work Education Association of Canada
Finances: *Funding Sources:* Membership fees; conference fees; donations
Membership: *Fees:* $80.75 statutory & non-statutory; $21.55 associate; $37.70 retired; *Member Profile:* Ontario cooperative education & experiential learning professionals; *Committees:* Communications; Finance; Membership; Teacher Professional Learning

Activities: Facilitating access to information, resources, & supports for its members; Providing a forum for the exchange of ideas & experiences among educators, employers, students, & others; Responding to issues; Researching future directions
Chief Officer(s):
Susanna Scocchia, Executive Secretary, 416-395-3330 Ext. 20140, Fax: 416-395-4453
susanna.scocchia@tdsb.on.ca
Donna Flasza, President
donna_flasza@Lakeheadschools.ca
Mona Safarian, Treasurer
safarmo@ecolecatholique.ca
Awards:
- The George King Award of Excellence
- The S.J. "Jack" Ulan Professional Contribution Award
- The Honorary Member Award
- The Career / LifeSkills Resources Award of Excellence in Cooperative Education

Meetings/Conferences:
- 2018 Annual Ontario Cooperative Education Association Spring Conference, April, 2018, The Westin Prince, Toronto, ON
Scope: Provincial
Publications:
- OCEA [Ontario Cooperative Education Association] News
Type: Newsletter; *Frequency:* Semiannually
Profile: Distributed to members

Ontario Council for Exceptional Children (OCEC)
1106 Berkshire Crt., Oakville ON L6J 6K9
manitobacec@gmail.com
www.cecontario.ca
www.linkedin.com/company/2756373
www.facebook.com/cechqanitobacec
twitter.com/cecmembership
www.youtube.com/user/CECHeadquarters
Overview: A medium-sized provincial organization overseen by Council for Exceptional Children
Chief Officer(s):
Dianne Parr, President
dparr@hwdsb.on.ca

Ontario Council for International Cooperation (OCIC) / Conseil de l'Ontario pour la coopération internationale
#209, 344 Bloor St. West, Toronto ON M5S 3A7
Tel: 416-972-6303; *Fax:* 416-972-6996
info@ocic.on.ca
www.ocic.on.ca
www.linkedin.com/groups?gid=4146814&trk=hb_side_g
twitter.com/ocictweets
Overview: A medium-sized international organization founded in 1988
Mission: Community of Ontario-based international development and global education organizations and individual associate members working globally for social justice
Member of: Canadian Council for International Cooperation
Finances: *Annual Operating Budget:* $100,000-$250,000
Staff Member(s): 2; 10 volunteer(s)
Membership: 70 organizations; *Fees:* Depends on the budget; *Committees:* Anti-Racism & Equity; Personnel; Policy; Global Citizenship
Activities: Weekly radio show; international development; public engagement; *Library:* Resource Centre; Open to public by appointment
Chief Officer(s):
Kimberly Gibbons, Executive Director

Ontario Council for University Lifelong Learning
c/o Lakehead University, Thunder Bay ON P7B 5E1
Tel: 807-343-8210; *Fax:* 807-343-8008
www.ocull.ca
Previous Name: Ontario Association for University Lifelong Learning
Overview: A small provincial organization
Mission: To advocate for adult learners at Ontario universities, a collegial network, and a vehicle for professional development for its members.
Affiliation(s): Council of Ontario Universities
Membership: 20; *Fees:* $250 institution; $60 subscriber
Chief Officer(s):
Lisa Fanjoy, President
lfanjoy@wlu.ca

Ontario Council of Agencies Serving Immigrants (OCASI)
#200, 110 Eglinton Ave. West, Toronto ON M4R 1A3
Tel: 416-322-4950; *Fax:* 416-322-8084; *TTY:* 416-322-1498
generalmail@ocasi.org
www.ocasi.org
twitter.com/OCASI_Policy
Overview: A medium-sized provincial charitable organization founded in 1978
Mission: To act as a collective voice for immigrant services; to provide access for immigrants & refugees to settlement services; to provide social organizational development with community groups, policy analysis & government relations, professional development of member agency staff & research into issues facing immigrant service agencies
Member of: Canadian Council for Refugees; United Way; Canadian Council on Social Development; Toronto Refugee Affairs Council
Finances: *Annual Operating Budget:* $1.5 Million-$3 Million; *Funding Sources:* Government; United Way; Foundations
Staff Member(s): 19; 4 volunteer(s)
Membership: 200 agencies; *Fees:* $80-$1,000; *Member Profile:* Non-profit community-based agencies in Ontario whose primary objectives include the provision of social & community services to immigrants; *Committees:* Board Development; Executive; Finance; Management; Personnel; Policy & Research; Membership
Activities: Regional training workshop; technical liaison training; refugee rights week events; *Speaker Service:* Yes; *Rents Mailing List:* Yes; *Library:* Resource Centre; by appointment Not open to public
Chief Officer(s):
Carl Nicholson, President
carl@cic.ca
Debbie Douglas, Executive Director, 416-322-4950 Ext. 229
ddouglas@ocasi.org

Ontario Council of Alternative Businesses (OCAB)
#203, 1499 Queen St. West, Toronto ON M6R 1A3
Tel: 416-504-1693; *Fax:* 416-504-8063
Toll-Free: 866-504-1693
ocab@on.aibn.com
www.ocab.ca
Overview: A small provincial organization founded in 1994
Mission: To increase economic opportunities for psychiatric survivors by developing community businesses; To reduce discrimination & ignorance of general public in regards to psychiatric survivors
Activities: Operating a variety of community businesses, including the Raging Spoon, OTWCafe, & Parkdale Green Thumb; *Rents Mailing List:* Yes
Chief Officer(s):
Joyce Brown, Co-Director
jmbrown@on.aibn.com
Becky McFarlane, Co-Director
becky@on.aibn.com

Ontario Council of University Libraries (OCUL)
Robarts Library, 130 St. George St., 7th Fl., Toronto ON M5S 1A5
ocul@ocul.on.ca
www.ocul.on.ca
Overview: A small provincial organization
Mission: To collaborate in the delivery & development of effective information resources for Ontario's universities
Member of: Council of Ontario Universities
Affiliation(s): Council of Ontario Universities
Staff Member(s): 6
Membership: 21; *Member Profile:* Ontario university libraries; *Committees:* Planning & Assessment; Information Resources; Scholars Portal
Chief Officer(s):
John Barnett, Executive Director, 416-946-0578
john.barnett@ocul.on.ca
Nur Artok, Business Officer, 416-978-0894
nur.artok@ocul.on.ca
Jacqueline Cato, Coordinator, Information Resources, 416-978-0672
jacqueline.cato@ocul.on.ca
Anika Ervin-Ward, Coordinator, Administration & Communications, 416-978-5338
anika.ervin.ward@ocul.on.ca
Awards:
- OCUL Award
Awarded to recognize outstanding contributions from an individual or group within the OCUL consortium *Eligibility:* Individuals or teams employed by OCUL member institutions

Ontario Council on Articulation and Transfer (ONCAT)
#1902, 180 Dundas St. West, Toronto ON M5G 1Z8
Tel: 416-640-6951; *Fax:* 416-640-6959
info@oncat.ca
www.oncat.ca
twitter.com/ONTransfer
Overview: A medium-sized provincial organization founded in 2011
Mission: To enhance transfer opportunities & pathways for students within Ontario's postsecondary system; To support & develop credit transfer policies & practices
Membership: 45; *Member Profile:* Public colleges & universities in Ontario
Activities: Promoting projects designed to develop credit transfer pathways; Supporting research on credit transfer & student transfer experiences; Developing systems for managing & collecting data on credit transfers; Providing students with credit transfer information & opportunities
Chief Officer(s):
Lia Quickert, Director, Strategic Communications & Public Affairs
lquickert@oncat.ca
Shauna Love, Director, Operations
slove@oncat.ca
Alana Wiens, Director, Policy & Programs
awiens@oncat.ca
Meetings/Conferences:
- Ontario Council on Articulation & Transfer 2018 Student Pathways in Higher Education Conference, April, 2018, Toronto Marriott Downtown Eaton Centre, Toronto, ON
Scope: Provincial

Ontario Council on Graduate Studies (OCGS) / Conseil ontarien des études supérieures
#1100, 180 Dundas St. West, Toronto ON M5G 1Z8
Tel: 416-979-2165; *Fax:* 416-979-8635
cou.on.ca/ocgs-1
Overview: A small provincial organization founded in 1965
Mission: To ensure quality graduate education & research across Ontario
Member of: Council of Ontario Universities
Staff Member(s): 1
Membership: 20; *Member Profile:* Deans of Graduate Studies (or equivalent officer) of each provincially assisted universities in Ontario; *Committees:* Executive; Nominating
Activities: Conducts quality reviews of graduate (Master's & Ph.D.) programs that have been proposed for implementation in Ontario's universities, as well as quality reviews of existing programs on a seven-year cycle; *Library*
Chief Officer(s):
Peter Gooch, Secretariat, COU
pgooch@cou.on.ca
Clarke Anthony, Chair
aclarke@registrar.uoguelph.ca
Awards:
- Women's Health Scholar Award
- Autism Scholars Award
- John Charles Polanyi Prizes
In honour of the achievement of John Charles Polanyi, co-recipient of the 1986 Nobel Prize in Chemistry, the Government of Ontario has established a fund to provide annually up to five prizes to persons continuing to post-doctoral studies at an Ontario university; prizes available in the areas of Physics, Chemistry, Physiology or Medicine, Literature & Economic Science; *Amount:* $15,000

Ontario Craft Brewers (OCB)
#1, 75 Horner Ave., Toronto ON M8Z 4X5
Tel: 416-494-2766
Other Communication: pr@ontariocraftbrewers.com
info@ontariocraftbrewers.com
www.ontariocraftbrewers.com
www.facebook.com/OntarioCraftBrewers
twitter.com/OntCraftBrewers
www.youtube.com/OntarioCraftBrewers
Overview: A small provincial organization
Mission: To promote craft brewers in the province on Ontario.
Membership: 35+

Ontario Crafts Council (OCC)
990 Queen St. West, Toronto ON M6J 1H1
Tel: 416-925-4222; *Fax:* 416-925-4223
info@craft.on.ca
www.craft.on.ca
www.facebook.com/OntarioCraftsCouncil
twitter.com/OntarioCrafts

Previous Name: Canadian Guild of Crafts (Ontario); Ontario Craft Foundation
Overview: A medium-sized provincial charitable organization founded in 1976
Mission: To have craft recognized as a valuable part of life and the excellence of Ontario craft and craftspeople acknowledged across Canada and around the world.
Finances: *Funding Sources:* Membership dues; donations; corporate; foundations; government
Staff Member(s): 7
Membership: 1,500; *Fees:* $150 business; $125 affiliate; $130 craft professional; $45 student; $70 standard
Activities: Operates the Craft Gallery & the Guild Shop, Yorkville; *Rents Mailing List:* Yes; *Library:* Open to public
Chief Officer(s):
Emma Quin, Executive Director
equin@craft.on.ca
Awards:
• James H. McPherson Scholarship in Wood
Provides assistance for an individual to pursue further education in woodworking, especially in lathe or inlay work; *Amount:* $225
• Hey Frey Memorial Award
Awarded to an established or emerging artist working in any craft medium whose work demonstrates excellence & a commitment to expand the horizons in their field; *Amount:* $100
• Tommia Vaughan-Jones Award for Excellence in Metal Arts
Award in metal arts; *Amount:* $400
• Don McKinley Award for Excellence in Wood
Awarded to a woodworking student studying at one of the Crafts Councils affiliated educational institutions to recognize excelolene in woodworking design; *Amount:* $150
• Diana Crawford Craft Careet Development Grant
For the development of emerging craftspeople in their first five years of professional practice, to be applied towards the development of business skills; *Amount:* $250
• Hildreth G. Holden Wood Scholarship
For a person intending to pursue further education in wood, including joinery, carving, musical instruments & inlay; *Amount:* $250
• Volunteer Committee Emerging Professional Grant
Intended to enable crafts people who are in their first five years of professional practice to establish or expand their studio or facilities; *Amount:* $1,000 maximum
• RBC-Lakatos Craft Career Award
To enable emerging craftspeople in their first five years of professional practice to participate in an exhibition, craft or trade show in Ontario; *Amount:* Maximum of $450
• Critical Craft Writing Award
Celebrates & recognizes the importance of documenting the work of craftspeople; offered to raise the profile of critical writing about contemporary Canadian craft; *Amount:* $400 & article published in Ontario Crafts magazine
• Helen Frances Gregor Scholarship
Awarded to provide funds for a fibre artist to pursue further study; *Amount:* $550
• Ontario Crafts Council Scholarships
Awarded to craftspeople to further their study; *Amount:* 3 awards of $1,000
• Volunteer Committee Scholarship
For further study in volunteer work; *Amount:* $1,500
• Kingcrafts/Lady Flavelle Award
Granted to a person intending to pursue further education; *Amount:* $1,000
• Mary Diamond Butts Award in Embroidery
Eligibility: Provides assistance to pursue self-directed study or participate in an established couse of study; *Amount:* $250
• Mary Robertson Textile Award
Eligibility: To assist a person intending to pursue further education in textiles, including textile printing, surface embellishments, weaving, basketry & embroidery; *Amount:* $500

Ontario Creamerymen's Association
26 Dominion St., Alliston ON L9R 1L5
Tel: 705-435-6751; *Fax:* 705-435-6797
Overview: A small provincial organization founded in 1935
Finances: *Funding Sources:* Membership dues
Chief Officer(s):
Lloyd Kennedy, President

Ontario Cricket Association Inc. *See* Cricket Council of Ontario

Ontario Criminal Justice Association (CJAO)
PO Box 949, Stn. K, Toronto ON M4P 2V3
cjao.info
Overview: A small local organization
Mission: To encourage co-operation among individuals, groups & governmental organizations interested & active in the field of criminal justice; to further the study of criminal justice issues.
Affiliation(s): Canadian Criminal Justice Association
Membership: 200; *Committees:* Policy Review; Social Issues; Public Awareness & Visibility

Ontario Crown Attorneys Association (OCAA) / Association des procureurs de la couronne de l'Ontario (APCO)
PO Box 30, #1905, 180 Dundas St. West, Toronto ON M5G 1Z8
Tel: 416-977-4517; *Fax:* 416-977-1460
reception@ocaa.ca
www.ocaa.ca
Overview: A medium-sized provincial organization founded in 1946
Mission: To promote & protect the professional interests of crown counsels, assistant crown attorneys, & articling students
Membership: 850; *Member Profile:* Crown counsel, assistant crown attorneys, & articling students employed by the criminal law division of the Ontario Ministry of the Attorney General
Activities: Engaging in collective bargaining on behalf of the association's members; Ensuring the continuing legal education of members
Chief Officer(s):
Scott Childs, President
scott.rogers@ocaa.ca

Ontario Curling Association (OCA)
#10, 1400 Bayly St., Pickering ON L1W 3R2
Tel: 905-831-1757
Toll-Free: 877-668-2875
www.ontcurl.com
www.facebook.com/CurlOntario
twitter.com/CurlON_
Also Known As: CurlON
Overview: A large provincial organization founded in 1875 overseen by Canadian Curling Association
Mission: To promote & facilitate the growth & development of curling
Member of: Canadian Curling Association
Affiliation(s): Ontario Curling Council; Northern Ontario Curling Association; Ontario Special Olympics
Finances: *Funding Sources:* Membership dues; competition fees; sponsorships
Staff Member(s): 7
Membership: 55,000 people in 200 clubs; *Committees:* Communication; Executive; Finance; Governance; Nomination; Rules
Activities: Competitions; seminars; workshops; Marketing & Development Programme
Chief Officer(s):
Stephen Chenier, Executive Director
steve@ontcurl.com
Awards:
• OCA Achievement Award
Deadline: March 31
• OCA Honorary Life Membership
Deadline: May 31
• OCA Past President Scholarship Award
Deadline: May 31
• Sportsmanship Awards
• Coaching Awards
• OCA Media Awards
• Honorary Life Members
Publications:
• OCA [Ontario Curling Association] Annual Report
Type: Yearbook; *Frequency:* Annually

Ontario Cycling Association (OCA) / Association cycliste ontarienne
#2, 2015 Pan Am Blvd., Milton ON L9T 8Y9
Tel: 416-855-1717
Other Communication: Toll-Free Fax: 1-855-488-0812
www.ontariocycling.org
www.linkedin.com/company/ontario-cycling-association
www.facebook.com/129640691224
twitter.com/ontariocycling
Overview: A medium-sized provincial licensing organization founded in 1882 overseen by Cycling Canada Cyclisme
Mission: To act as the provincial governing body for road, track & cyclocross, mountain biking, & BMX racing in Ontario; To develop & deliver quality programs & services for the sport of cycling in Ontario
Member of: Cycling Canada Cyclisme
Finances: *Funding Sources:* Membership fees; Sponsorships
Membership: *Fees:* Schedule available; *Member Profile:* OCA affiliated club members; Riders who wish to compete only in Ontario; Riders who wish to compete out of the province or at national & international events held within Ontario; Non-racers; Certified Can-Bike & OMBI instructors
Activities: Promoting the benefits of cycling, as well as cycling programs & services in Ontario; Advocating for cyclists in Ontario; Sharing resources & expertise; Promoting safe cycling, through the CanBike safe cycling program; Coordinating mountain bike, road, & track race competitions
Chief Officer(s):
Jim Crosscombe, Chief Executive Officer, 416-855-1717 Ext. 1008
Michael Suraci, Manager, High Performance, 416-855-1717 Ext. 1002
Jen Eaton, Coordinator, Sport, 416-855-1717 Ext. 1009
Meetings/Conferences:
• Ontario Cycling Association Annual General Meeting 2018, 2018
Scope: Provincial
Publications:
• Ontario Cycling Association Handbook
Type: Guide

Ontario Dairy Council (ODC)
6533D Mississauga Rd., Mississauga ON L5N 1A6
Tel: 905-542-3620; *Fax:* 905-542-3624
Toll-Free: 866-542-3620
info@ontariodairies.ca
www.ontariodairies.ca
Overview: A medium-sized provincial organization founded in 1971
Mission: To represent interests of dairy product processors, marketers & distributors in Ontario
Affiliation(s): International Dairy Federation
Finances: *Annual Operating Budget:* $500,000-$1.5 Million; *Funding Sources:* Membership fees
Staff Member(s): 3
Membership: 40 corporate + 50 associate; *Fees:* Schedule available; *Member Profile:* Licensed processor, marketer or distributor; *Committees:* Technical; Advisory; Environment; Policy & Technical
Activities: *Library:* by appointment
Chief Officer(s):
Christina Lewis, President
clewis@ontariodairies.ca

Ontario DanceSport (ODS)
ON
Tel: 905-831-2426
publicity@ontariodancesport.com
www.ontariodancesport.com
Overview: A small provincial organization overseen by Canada DanceSport
Chief Officer(s):
Gord Brittain, President
odspresident@rogers.com
Kam Young, Vice President
vicepresident@ontariodancesport.com

Ontario Daylily Society (ODS)
6798 9th Line, R R#2, Beeton ON L0G 1A0
Tel: 905-729-2718
www.ontariodaylily.on.ca
Overview: A small provincial organization founded in 1997
Membership: *Fees:* $8 youth; $20 individual; $25 family
Chief Officer(s):
Faye Collins, President
president@ontariodaylily.on.ca

Ontario Deaf Sports Association (ODSA)
ON
Overview: A small provincial organization founded in 1964 overseen by Canadian Deaf Sports Association
Member of: Canadian Deaf Sports Association

Ontario Delphinium Club
c/o Christine Gill, 4691 Hwy. 7A, RR#1, Nestleton Station ON L0B 1L0
Tel: 905-986-0310
www.ondelphiniums.com
Overview: A small provincial organization
Membership: *Fees:* $10 family
Chief Officer(s):
Don Wick, President

Ontario Dental Assistants Association (ODAA)
869 Dundas St., London ON N5W 2Z8
Tel: 519-679-2566; *Fax:* 519-679-8494
info@odaa.org
www.odaa.org
www.facebook.com/yourODAA
Previous Name: Ontario Dental Nurses & Assistants Association
Overview: A medium-sized provincial licensing organization founded in 1927 overseen by Canadian Dental Assistants Association
Mission: To act as the certifying body for dental assistants in Ontario
Staff Member(s): 6
Membership: *Fees:* $45.20 students; $135.60 regular members; *Member Profile:* Dental assistants in Ontario; Students training to become dental assistants
Activities: Working with the Ontario government to have dental assisting become a regulated profession; Producing brochures for students & brochures about certification; Organizing networking opportunities
Chief Officer(s):
Susan Henderson, President
Goldi Gill, Vice-President
Carolyn Hibbs, Executive Director
cahibbs@odaa.org
Publications:
• The Journal [a publication of the Ontario Dental Assistants Association]
Type: Journal; *Frequency:* 3 pa
Profile: Educational articles, profiles of ODAA members, regulation efforts, & meetings

Ontario Dental Association (ODA)
4 New St., Toronto ON M5R 1P6
Tel: 416-922-3900; *Fax:* 416-922-9005
Toll-Free: 800-387-1393
info@oda.ca
www.oda.ca
www.facebook.com/OntarioDentalAssociation
www.youtube.com/user/OntarioDentalAssoc
Overview: A medium-sized provincial organization overseen by Canadian Dental Association
Mission: To represent the dentists of Ontario; To provide exemplary oral health care & promote the attainment of optimal health for the people of Ontario
Membership: 6,500
Chief Officer(s):
Jack McLister, President
Frank Bevilacqua, Executive Director
Ian Farmer, Director, Finance & Administration
David Gentili, Director, Professional & Government Affairs
Alex Glazduri, Director, Membership Services & Marketing
Marcus Staviss, Director, Communications, Public Affairs & Events
Meetings/Conferences:
• Ontario Dental Association Annual Spring Meeting 2018, April, 2018, Metro Toronto Convention Centre, Toronto, ON
Scope: Provincial
Attendance: 12,000

Ontario Dental Hygienists' Association (ODHA)
#108, 3425 Harvester Rd., Burlington ON L7N 3N1
Tel: 905-681-8883; *Fax:* 905-681-3922
Toll-Free: 800-315-6342
info@odha.on.ca
www.odha.on.ca
www.linkedin.com/company/2777651
www.facebook.com/252476104875579
twitter.com/OntarioODHA
Overview: A medium-sized provincial organization founded in 1963
Mission: To provide a program of services & benefits to members
Affiliation(s): Canadian Dental Hygienists' Association
Membership: *Fees:* $84.75 first year entering practice; $109.35 associate; $129.95 support; $224.87 regular; *Member Profile:* Registered Dental Hygienists

Ontario Dental Nurses & Assistants Association *See* Ontario Dental Assistants Association

Ontario Disc Sports Association (ODSA)
#3, 160 Aberdeen Ave., Hamilton ON L8P 2P6
Tel: 905-808-5993
chris@ontariodiscsports.ca
www.ontariodiscsports.ca
www.facebook.com/OntarioDiscSports.ca
twitter.com/OntarioDisc
www.youtube.com/channel/UCxzSzfCZXwEs3ylfmfngvMg
Overview: A small provincial organization
Mission: To be the provincial governing body for disc sports in Ontario
Membership: *Fees:* $10 individual; $30 club
Activities: Beach ultimate; discathon; disc golf; double disc court; field events; freestyle; Goaltimate; guts; Catch & Fetch; ultimate
Chief Officer(s):
John MacLeod, President
president@ondisc.org
Chris Ozolins, Executive Director
chris@ontariodiscsports.ca
Jacynthe Goulard, Vice President
vicepresident@ondisc.ca

Ontario DX Association (OXDA)
#23, 3211 Centennial Dr., Vernon BC V1T 2T8
odxa@rogers.com
www.odxa.on.ca
Overview: A medium-sized provincial organization founded in 1974
Finances: *Annual Operating Budget:* $50,000-$100,000; *Funding Sources:* Membership fees
20 volunteer(s)
Membership: 500; *Fees:* $40
Activities: Radiofest Convention, Sept.

Ontario East Tourism Association (OETA)
PO Box 730, #200, 104 St. Lawrence St., Merrickville ON K0G 1N0
Tel: 613-269-4113; *Fax:* 613-659-4306
Toll-Free: 800-567-3278
support@realontario.ca
www.realontario.ca
Also Known As: Real Ontario
Previous Name: Eastern Ontario Travel Association
Overview: A small local organization founded in 1974
Mission: To encourage visitation to Eastern Ontario by means of cooperative tourism marketing
Finances: *Annual Operating Budget:* $500,000-$1.5 Million
Staff Member(s): 3
Membership: 110 tourist associations & operators; *Fees:* Schedule available; *Member Profile:* Tourist associations, businesses & municipalities; *Committees:* Marketing; Membership; Motorcoach; Finance; Government Relations; Constitution; Tourism Liaison; Special Projects
Activities: *Speaker Service:* Yes
Chief Officer(s):
Rose Bertoia, Executive Director
John Bonser, President

Ontario Electric Railway Historical Association
PO Box 578, Milton ON L9T 5A2
Tel: 519-856-9802; *Fax:* 519-856-1399
streetcar@hcry.org
www.hcry.org
twitter.com/streetcarmuseum
Also Known As: Halton County Radial Railway
Overview: A small provincial charitable organization founded in 1953
Mission: To collect & return to operating capacity, electric railway equipment representing North American city & interurban systems
Affiliation(s): Association of Railway Museums; Ontario Museum Association; Canadian Museums Association
Finances: *Funding Sources:* Operations; membership fees; donations
Membership: *Member Profile:* Persons interested in restoration/operation of Canadian streetcars
Activities: Operates a museum for the pleasure & education of the public; *Speaker Service:* Yes; *Library:* Archives; by appointment

Ontario Electrical League (OEL)
#109, 93 Skyway Ave., Toronto ON M9W 6N6
Tel: 905-238-1382; *Fax:* 905-238-1420
league@oel.org
www.oel.org
www.linkedin.com/oeleague
www.facebook.com/OntarioElectricalLeague
twitter.com/OEL3
Overview: A medium-sized provincial organization founded in 1922
Mission: To represent & strengthen the electrical industry in Ontario
Staff Member(s): 3
Membership: 20 chapters, with 12,000+ members; *Member Profile:* Educators; Electricians; Electrical contractors; Electrical inspectors; Manufacturers; Consulting engineers; Distributors; *Committees:* Contractor; Contractor Government Relations; Safety Communications
Activities: Promoting Ontario's electrical industry; Providing educational opportunities
Chief Officer(s):
Stephen Sell, President
stephen.sell@oel.org
Wendy Dobinson, Manager, Operations
wendy.dobinson@oel.org
Huong Nguyen, Editor, Dialogue
huong.nguyen@oel.org
Awards:
• EFC / OEL Scholarship
A post-secondary school scholarship, for enrollment in an electrical or related program, for members of the Ontario Electrical League & their families
Publications:
• Contractor News [a publication of the Ontario Electrical League]
Type: Newsletter; *Frequency:* Monthly
Profile: Update on industry news, plus issues that affect contractors & their businesses
• Contractor Newsbrief [a publication of the Ontario Electrical League]
Type: Newsletter
Profile: Contractor Committee activities, for Ontario Electrical League contractor members
• Dialogue [a publication of the Ontario Electrical League]
Type: Magazine; *Frequency:* Quarterly; *Accepts Advertising*; *Price:* Free with membership in the Ontario Electrical League
Profile: League activities, member news, plus updates about industry & government issues
• Ontario Electrical League Chapter Newsletter
Type: Newsletter
Profile: Chapter committee update

Ontario Energy Association (OEA)
#202, 121 Richmond St. West, Toronto ON M5H 2K1
Tel: 416-961-2339; *Fax:* 416-961-1173
Other Communication: committees@energyontario.ca
oea@energyontario.ca
www.energyontario.ca
www.linkedin.com/company/ontario-energy-association
twitter.com/ontarioenergy
Overview: A medium-sized provincial organization
Mission: To represent the energy industry of Ontario
Finances: *Funding Sources:* Sponsorships
Membership: 150+ corporate members; *Member Profile:* Members of Ontario's energy industry, such as power producers, manufacturers, contractors, service providers, energy retailers, marketers, energy distributors & energy consultants; *Committees:* DSM/CDM; Demand Response Working Group; Environment; Energy; Government Relations/Public Affairs; IT; Markets; Regulatory
Activities: Providing education & resources about the energy sector; Engaging in advocacy activities for members; Conducting research into energy matters; *Speaker Service:* Yes
Chief Officer(s):
Vince Brescia, President & Chief Executive Officer, 416-961-8874
vince@energyontario.ca
Roy Hrab, Director, Policy, 647-493-2351
roy@energyontario.ca
Meetings/Conferences:
• Ontario Energy Association Energy Conference 2018, September, 2018, Toronto, ON
Scope: Provincial
Description: Examples of programming includes panel sessions, the presentation of awards, information sharing opportunities, & social events

Ontario English Catholic Teachers' Association (CLC) (OECTA)
#400, 65 St. Clair Ave. East, Toronto ON M4T 2Y8
Tel: 416-925-2493; *Fax:* 416-925-7764
Toll-Free: 800-268-7230
Other Communication: AQ Courses e-mail:
registrar@oecta.on.ca
contact@oecta.on.ca
www.oecta.on.ca

www.facebook.com/OECTA
twitter.com/OECTAProv
Overview: A large provincial organization founded in 1944
Mission: To advance Catholic education; To provide professional services, support, protection, & leadership
Member of: Canadian Teachers' Federation; Canadian Labour Congress; Ontario Federation of Labour
Affiliation(s): Ontario Teachers' Federation
Staff Member(s): 61
Membership: 45,000; *Fees:* $950; *Committees:* Audit; Awards; Beginning Teachers; Catholic Education; Collective Bargaining; Communications & Public Relations; Educational Aid; Elementary Schools; Finance; Health & Safety; Human Rights; Legislation; Occasional Teachers; Personnel; Political Advisory; Program & Structures; Professional Development Steering; Secondary Schools; Status of Women; Teacher Education Network
Activities: *Library:* Resource Library
Chief Officer(s):
Ann Hawkins, President
Marshall Jarvis, General Secretary
m.jarvis@oecta.on.ca
David Church, Deputy General Secretary
d.church@oecta.on.ca
Awards:
• Annual General Meeting Awards
• 25-Year Annual General Meeting Recognition Service Award
• Excellence in Communication Awards
• Fintan Kilbride Memorial Social Justice Recognition Award
• Young Authors Awards/Prix Jeunes Écrivains
Meetings/Conferences:
• Ontario English Catholic Teachers' Association 2018 Annual General Meeting, 2018, ON
Scope: Provincial
Description: Delegates attend to the business of the association, elect Provincial Executive members, & listen to presentations by guest speakers
Publications:
• Agenda [a publication of the Ontario English Catholic Teachers' Association (CLC)]
Type: Newsletter
• e-agenda [a publication of the Ontario English Catholic Teachers' Association (CLC)]
Type: Newsletter

Ontario Environment Industry Association (ONEIA)
#410, 215 Spadina Ave., Toronto ON M5T 2C7
Tel: 416-531-7884; *Fax:* 416-644-0116
info@oneia.ca
www.oneia.ca
www.linkedin.com/groups/3999411
twitter.com/ONEIAnetwork
Previous Name: Canadian Environment Industry Association - Ontario Chapter
Overview: A large provincial organization founded in 1991
Mission: To promote the growth of environment business in Ontario
Member of: Auditing Association of Canada; CRESTech; Retail Council of Canada
Affiliation(s): Canadian Standards Association; Cements Association of Canada; Ontario Concrete Pipe Association; Ontario Sewer & Watermain Construction Association; Ontario Environmental Training Consortium; Ontario Centre for Environmental Technology Advancement
Finances: *Annual Operating Budget:* $100,000-$250,000; *Funding Sources:* Membership dues; projects
Staff Member(s): 4; 12 volunteer(s)
Membership: 130; *Fees:* Schedule available; *Member Profile:* Ontario-based companies, business associations & organizations which actively provide environmental technologies & services that help protect or improve the environment & that help achieve sustainable development; *Committees:* Advocacy; Board Nominations; Communications; Environment Industry Day; Environment & Cleantech Business & Policy Forum; Membership
Activities: Participating in environmental initiatives; Organizing Environmental Business Opportunity Breakfasts & other networking events; Hosting Environment Industry Day & the Environment & Cleantech Business & Policy Forum; Advocacy; Promoting environment companies in Ontario; Managing EnviroChannel, a permission-based email network; *Library:* by appointment
Chief Officer(s):
Alex Gill, Executive Director
Sonia Zorzos, Manager, Operations

Ontario Environmental Network (OEN)
PO Box 192, Georgetown ON L7G 4T1
oen@oen.ca
www.oen.ca
www.facebook.com/OntarioEnvironmentNetwork
www.youtube.com/ontarioenvironment
Overview: A large provincial organization founded in 1981 overseen by Canadian Environmental Network
Mission: To encourage discussions of ways to protect the environment; To increase environmental awareness throughout Ontario; To serve the environmental non-profit, non-governmental community in Ontario
Affiliation(s): Canadian Environmental Network
6 volunteer(s)
Membership: 500+ environmental groups; *Fees:* $15 individuals; $30 government agencies & businesses; $40 organizations; *Member Profile:* Non-government, not-for-profit organizations in Ontario concerned with the preservation of the environment; Government agencies; Businesses; Individuals
Activities: Facilitating communication among environmental organizations; Maintaing a database of Ontario's environmental groups; Increasing awareness of environmental organizations; Operating the First Ontario TimeBank (firstontario.timebanks.org)
Chief Officer(s):
Phillip Penna, Coordinator, 705-840-2888
Meetings/Conferences:
• Ontario Environment Network AGM 2018, 2018
Scope: Provincial
Publications:
• OEN [Ontario Environmental Network] News
Type: Newsletter; *Frequency:* Semimonthly; *Accepts Advertising*; *Price:* Free with Ontario Environmental Network membership
Profile: Ontario Environment Network updates, events, & action alerts sent to member groups & subscribers
• Ontario Environmental Directory [a publication of the Ontario Environmental Directory]
Type: Directory; *Editor:* Peter Blanchard; *Price:* Free with Ontario EnvironmentalNetwork membership
Profile: Comprehensive information about Ontario environmental organizations & agencies

Ontario Equestrian Federation (OEF)
#201, 1 West Pearce St., Richmond Hill ON L4B 3K3
Tel: 905-709-6545; *Fax:* 905-709-1867
Toll-Free: 877-441-7112
horse@horse.on.ca
www.horse.on.ca
www.facebook.com/OEF.Horse
instagram.com/oef_horse
Overview: A medium-sized provincial organization founded in 1977
Mission: Committed to equine welfare & to providing leadership & support to the individuals, associations & industries in Ontario's horse community
Member of: Equine Canada
Affiliation(s): Equine Guelph; Ontario Trails Council; Ontario Federation of Agriculture; Ontario Minitry of Tourism, Culture & Sport
Finances: *Annual Operating Budget:* $250,000-$500,000; *Funding Sources:* Membership dues; government grant; merchandise sales
Staff Member(s): 14; 100 volunteer(s)
Membership: 22,000 individuals; *Fees:* Schedule available; *Member Profile:* Individuals, associations & corporations with interests in equine sport & industry; *Committees:* Associations; Competitions; Horse Facilities; Industry; Recreation
Activities: Education; equine welfare; member services; competitions administration; coaching certification; industry promotion; *Awareness Events:* Horse Day, June; Royal Agricultural Winter Fair, Nov.; Can-Am Equine Emporium, March; *Rents Mailing List:* Yes; *Library:* Open to public
Chief Officer(s):
Mark Nelson, President, 613-227-9784
mark@oakhurstfarm.com
Iryna Konstantynova, Director, Finance, 905-709-6545 Ext. 16
i.konstantynova@horse.on.ca
Pam Coburn, Manager, Coaching & Stables Program, 905-709-6545 Ext. 26
p.coburn@horse.on.ca
Lesley McCoy, Coordinator, Operations, 905-709-6545 Ext. 13
l.mccoy@horse.on.ca
Awards:
• OEF Model Member Award
• Yvonne Collard Award
• Cassie Bonnar Award
• Sponsor of the Year Award
• Sandra Sillcox Award
• Media of the Year Award
• Coach of the Year Award
• "Just Add Horses" Environmental Award
• People Make a Difference Award
Meetings/Conferences:
• Ontario Equestrian Federation Annual General Meeting 2018, 2018
Scope: Provincial
Publications:
• WHOA! [a publication of the Ontario Equestrian Federation]
Type: Newsletter; *Frequency:* Quarterly

Ontario Farm & Country Accommodations Association (OFCA)
8724 Wellington Rd. 18, RR#5, Belwood ON N0J 1J0
www.countryhosts.com
Overview: A small provincial organization founded in 1967
Mission: To be a self-supporting, accredited association whose members provide warm hospitality, country accommodations & farm tours, for guests seeking a unique getaway with the opportunity to experience rural culture, farming & the environment
Activities: *Speaker Service:* Yes; *Rents Mailing List:* Yes
Chief Officer(s):
Paul Faires, Secretary
paul.faires@sympatico.ca

Ontario Farm Fresh Marketing Association (OFFMA)
2002 Vandorf Sideroad, Aurora ON L4G 7B9
Tel: 905-841-9278; *Fax:* 905-726-3369
info@ontariofarmfresh.com
ontariofarmfresh.com
www.facebook.com/OntarioFarmFresh
twitter.com/OFFMA
www.instagram.com/ontariofarmfresh
Overview: A medium-sized provincial organization founded in 1973
Mission: To assist members in marketing skills & to provide knowledge & leadership to grow the farm fresh experience
Affiliation(s): Ontario Fruit & Vegetable Growers Association
Finances: *Annual Operating Budget:* Less than $50,000
Staff Member(s): 1; 9 volunteer(s)
Membership: 193 individual; 27 associate; *Fees:* $129
Chief Officer(s):
Leslie Forsythe, President, 905-887-1086
forsythefamilyfarms@gmail.com
Nicole Judge, Vice President, 905-838-2530
contactus@spirttreecider.com

Ontario Farmland Trust (OFT)
c/o University of Guelph, Johnston Hall, #017, Guelph ON N1G 2W1
Tel: 519-824-4120; *Fax:* 519-767-1686
info@ontariofarmlandtrust.ca
www.ontariofarmlandtrust.ca
Overview: A medium-sized provincial organization founded in 2004
Mission: To protect & preserve farmland in Ontario
Staff Member(s): 3
Chief Officer(s):
Matt Setzkorn, Acting Executive Director

Ontario Fashion Exhibitors (OFE)
PO Box 218, #2219, 160 Tycos Dr., Toronto ON M6B 1W8
Tel: 416-596-2401; *Fax:* 416-596-1808
Toll-Free: 800-765-7508
info@profileshow.ca
www.profileshow.ca
Overview: A medium-sized provincial organization founded in 1955
Mission: To produce fashion marketplace events
Affiliation(s): Canadian Association of Wholesale Sales Representatives (CAWS)
Membership: *Member Profile:* Wholesale sales representatives in the apparel industry who are not part of ownership or management of design, manufacturing, or importing businesses
Activities: Organizing shows & seminars for the ladies wear industry
Chief Officer(s):
Serge Micheli, Executive Director
sm@profileshow.ca
Michael Dargavel, Show Manager
md@profileshow.ca

Canadian Associations / Ontario Federation of School Athletic Associations (OFSAA) / Fédération des associations du sport scolaire de l'Ontario

Meetings/Conferences:
• The Profile Show Spring 2018, March, 2018, ON
Scope: Provincial
• The Profile Show Fall 2018, September, 2018, ON
Scope: Provincial
• The Profile Show Spring 2019, February, 2019, ON
Scope: Provincial
• The Profile Show Fall 2019, September, 2019, ON
Scope: Provincial

Ontario Federation for Cerebral Palsy (OFCP)
#104, 1630 Lawrence Ave. West, Toronto ON M6L 1C5
Tel: 416-244-9686; *Fax:* 416-244-6543
Toll-Free: 877-244-9686
info@ofcp.ca
www.ofcp.ca
www.facebook.com/OntarioFederationforCerebralPalsy
twitter.com/OntarioFCP
Overview: A medium-sized provincial charitable organization founded in 1947
Mission: To address the changing needs of people in Ontario with cerebral palsy; To improve the quality of life of persons with cerebral palsy through a broad range of programs, education, support of research & the delivery of needed services to people with cerebral palsy & other physical disabilities & their families
Affiliation(s): United Way Toronto; Neurological Health Charities Canada; Canada Helps; Ontario Association of Non-Profit Homes & Services for Seniors; The Community Ethics Network (CEN); Ontario Association of Independent Living Service Providers; Federated Health Charities; Neurological Health Charities Canada; Ontario Association of Non-Profit Homes & Services for Seniors
Activities: Programs: Planning Services; Long Term Planning and Support; Assistive Devices Funding; Vacation Funding Assistance; Day Activities Funding Assistance; Membership Services; Educational and Recreational Services; Children and Families Program; Ontario Services Information Database; Household Pickup Service (used clothing and household goods); *Awareness Events:* OFCP Annual Conference, Nov.; Annual Conference for people who provide support for people with disabilities, May
Chief Officer(s):
Gordana Skrba, Interim Executive Director, 416-244-9626 Ext. 241
gordana@ofcp.ca
Publications:
• InformAction
Type: Newsletter; *Frequency:* 3 pa

Ontario Federation of Agriculture (OFA)
Ontario AgriCentre, #206, 100 Stone Rd. West, Guelph ON N1G 5L3
Tel: 519-821-8883; *Fax:* 519-821-8810
Toll-Free: 800-668-3276
www.ofa.on.ca
www.facebook.com/ontariofarms
twitter.com/ontariofarms
www.youtube.com/user/ontariofarms
Overview: A large provincial organization founded in 1936 overseen by Canadian Federation of Agriculture
Mission: To represent farm families throughout Ontario; To champion the interests of Ontario farmers; To work towards a sustainable future for farmers
Member of: Agricultural Credit Corporation; AgEnergy Co-operative Ltd.; Agricultural Adaptation Council; Biosolids Utilization Committee; Canadian Federation of Agriculture; Cooperators Insurance; Drains Action Working Group; Farm & Food Care Ontario; Guelph Chamber of Commerce; and more...
Affiliation(s): SHARE Agriculture Foundation
Finances: *Funding Sources:* Membership fees; Sponsorships
Staff Member(s): 21
Membership: 38,000 individual + 31 organizations; *Fees:* Schedule available
Activities: Engaging in advocacy activities; Providing networking opportunities
Chief Officer(s):
Don McCabe, President
Meetings/Conferences:
• Ontario Federation of Agriculture 2018 Annual General Meeting, 2018
Scope: Provincial
Publications:
• OFA [Ontario Federation of Agriculture] Today
Type: Magazine
Profile: A business magazine about Ontario agriculture

Ontario Federation of Anglers & Hunters (OFAH)
PO Box 2800, 4601 Guthrie Dr., Peterborough ON K9J 8L5
Tel: 705-748-6324; *Fax:* 705-748-9577
ofah@ofah.org
www.ofah.org
www.facebook.com/theOFAH
twitter.com/ofah
www.youtube.com/ofahcommunications
Overview: A medium-sized provincial charitable organization founded in 1928 overseen by Canadian Wildlife Federation
Mission: To save & defend from waste the natural resources of Ontario, its soils, minerals, air, water, forests & wildlife
Finances: *Funding Sources:* Membership fees; Donations
Membership: 83,000 individuals + 655 affiliated clubs; *Fees:* $45.50 adult; $57.50 family; $33.00 youth; $1,000 life; *Member Profile:* Interest in fish & wildlife conservation; *Committees:* Land Access; Forestry; Fisheries; Hunter Education
Activities: *Awareness Events:* Ontario Family Fishing Weekend, July; Project Purple Week, Aug.
Chief Officer(s):
Angelo Lombardo, Executive Director
Meetings/Conferences:
• 90th Ontario Federation of Anglers & Hunters AGM and Fish & Wildlife Conference, 2018, ON
Scope: Provincial

Ontario Federation of Home & School Associations Inc. (OFHSA)
51 Stuart St., Hamilton ON L8L 1B5
Tel: 905-308-9563
info@ofhsa.on.ca
www.ofhsa.on.ca
www.facebook.com/159974104078740
Overview: A medium-sized provincial charitable organization founded in 1916 overseen by Canadian Home & School Federation
Mission: To provide facilities for the bringing together of members of Home & School Associations for discussion of matters of general interest & to stimulate cooperative effort; to assist in forming public opinion favorable to reform & advancement of the education of the child; to develop between educators & the general public such united effort as shall secure for every child the highest advantage in physical, mental, moral & spiritual education; to raise the standard of home & national life; to maintain a non-partisan, non-commercial, non-racial & non-sectarian organization
Membership: *Fees:* $15; *Member Profile:* Parents & others interested in advocating for children in public education
Activities: Annual conference; leadership camps; regional education workshops; *Speaker Service:* Yes
Chief Officer(s):
Teresa Blum, President
Sandra Binns, 1st Executive Vice-President
Michelle Ercolini, 2nd Executive Vice-President

Ontario Federation of Independent Schools (OFIS)
PO Box 27011, 101 Holiday Inn Dr., Cambridge ON N3C 0E6
Tel: 519-249-1665
info@ofis.ca
www.ofis.ca
www.facebook.com/OFISOntario
twitter.com/OFIS_Ontario
www.youtube.com/user/subtlevox
Previous Name: Ontario Association of Alternative & Independent Schools
Overview: A medium-sized provincial charitable organization founded in 1974 overseen by Canadian Accredited Independent Schools
Mission: To secure guarantees from Ontario government for independent schools' right to exist, curricular freedom, self-governance & acceptance by government of its responsibility to let education grants follow a child to any bona fide school that meets acceptable social & educational criteria
Finances: *Funding Sources:* Membership fees
Staff Member(s): 2
Membership: 140 schools; *Fees:* Schedule available; *Committees:* Finance; Professional Developmen; Governance
Activities: *Speaker Service:* Yes
Chief Officer(s):
Barbara Bierman, Executive Director
barbara.bierman@ofis.ca
Barbara Brown, President
barbarakec@bellnet.ca

Ontario Federation of Indian Friendship Centres (OFIFC)
219 Front St. East, Toronto ON M5A 1E8
Tel: 416-956-7575; *Fax:* 416-956-7577
Toll-Free: 800-772-9291
ofifc@ofifc.org
www.ofifc.org
www.facebook.com/TheOFIFC
twitter.com/theofifc
Also Known As: Ontario Federation of Friendship Centres
Overview: A medium-sized provincial organization founded in 1971 overseen by National Association of Friendship Centres
Mission: To represent the collective interests of Ontario's friendship centres; To administer programs delivered by friendship centres, such as justice, health, employment, & family support; To improve the quality of life for Aboriginal people for equal access & participation in Canadian society
Membership: 27 friendship centres; *Member Profile:* Friendship centres located across Ontario
Activities: Managing provincial programs, such as Aboriginal Healing & Wellness Strategy, Ontario Aboriginal Health Advocacy Initiative, & O-GI Employment Services
Chief Officer(s):
Sheila McMahon, President

Ontario Federation of Labour (OFL) / Fédération du travail de l'Ontario
#202, 15 Gervais Dr., Toronto ON M3C 1Y8
Tel: 416-441-2731; *Fax:* 416-441-0722
Toll-Free: 800-668-9138; *TTY:* 416-443-6305
info@ofl.ca
www.ofl.ca
www.linkedin.com/company/ontario-federation-of-labour
www.facebook.com/OFLabour
twitter.com/OFLabour
Overview: A large provincial organization founded in 1957 overseen by Canadian Labour Congress
Mission: To represent the interests of organized workers in Ontario; To provide support services to its affiliated local unions & labour councils
Finances: *Annual Operating Budget:* $3 Million-$5 Million; *Funding Sources:* Per capita revenue; Literature & video sales
Staff Member(s): 35
Membership: 700,000; *Member Profile:* Trade unions; *Committees:* Education; Energy & Environment; Health & Safety; Women's; Human Rights; Social Services; Health Care; Labour Relations; Peace & Disarmament; Political Education; Youth; Visible Minority; Gay, Lesbian & Bisexual; Aboriginal Persons; Persons with Disabilities
Activities: *Speaker Service:* Yes; *Library:* by appointment
Chief Officer(s):
Chris Buckley, President
CBuckley@ofl.ca
Patty Coates, Sec.-Treas.
PCoates@ofl.ca
Meetings/Conferences:
• Ontario Federation of Labour 15th Biennial Convention 2019, 2019, ON
Scope: Provincial

Ontario Federation of School Athletic Associations (OFSAA) / Fédération des associations du sport scolaire de l'Ontario
#204, 3 Concorde Gate, Toronto ON M3C 3N7
Tel: 416-426-7391; *Fax:* 416-426-7317
www.ofsaa.on.ca
www.facebook.com/OFSAA
twitter.com/OFSAA
www.instagram.com/OFSAAGRAM
Overview: A medium-sized provincial charitable organization founded in 1948 overseen by School Sport Canada
Mission: To enhance school sport in Ontario; To handle issues that affect students, coaches, schools, & communities; To work with volunteer teacher-coaches to offer provincial championships & festivals for student-athletes across Ontario
Member of: School Sport Canada
Finances: *Funding Sources:* Sponsorships
Staff Member(s): 9
Membership: 18 associations; *Member Profile:* Regional school athletic associations throughout Ontario, such as the Central Ontario Secondary Schools Association, Northern Ontario Secondary Schools Association, Southern Ontario Secondary Schools Association, & the Toronto District College Athletic Association; *Committees:* Alpine Skiing; Badminton; Baseball; Basketball; Cross Country; Curling; Field Hockey; Field Lacrosse; Football; Golf; Gymnastics; Hockey; Nordic Skiing;

Canadian Associations / Ontario Federation of Snowmobile Clubs (OFSC)

Rugby; Snowboard Racing; Soccer; Swimming; Tennis; Track & Field; Volleyball; Wrestling; Championship Review Ad Hoc; Classifications Ad Hoc; Coaching Ad Hoc; Constitutional Review Ad Hoc; Future Directions Ad Hoc; Gender Equity Ad Hoc; Sanctions Ad Hoc; Transfers Ad Hoc
Activities: Organizing programs, such as student leadership & coach development programs; Sanctioning tournaments; Preparing & distributing resources; Providing professional development opportunities; *Awareness Events:* Canadian School Sport Week
Chief Officer(s):
Donna Howard, Executive Director, 416-426-7438
donna@ofsaa.on.ca
Devin Gray, Coordinator, Communications, 416-426-7437
devin@ofsaa.on.ca
Awards:
- Pete Beach Award
- OFSAA Leadership in School Sport Award
- Colin Hood OFSAA School Sport Award
- Roger Neilson / Toronto Maple Leafs Alumni Scholarship Award
- Ministry Long Service Award
- Syl Apps Special Achievement Award
- Brian Maxwell Memorial Scholarship
- OFSAA Alumni Scholarship

Publications:
- Baseball Coaching Manual
Type: Manual; *Price:* $15
- Curling Coaching Manual
Type: Manual; *Price:* $20
- Rugby Coaching Manual
Type: Manual; *Price:* $16
- Volleyball Coaching Manual
Type: Manual; *Price:* $30

Ontario Federation of Snowmobile Clubs (OFSC)
ON
www.ofsc.on.ca
www.facebook.com/gosnowmobilingontario
twitter.com/GoSnowmobiling
Overview: A medium-sized provincial organization founded in 1966
Mission: To support member snowmobile clubs & volunteers; To establish & maintain quality snowmobile trails; To further the enjoyment of organized snowmobiling
Member of: Canadian Council of Snowmobile Organizations
Finances: *Funding Sources:* Sale of trail permits; Donations; Sponsorships
6 volunteer(s)
Membership: 231 clubs in 17 districts, consisting of 200,000 families; *Member Profile:* Ontario local snowmobile clubs
Activities: Setting policies & procedures; Providing advice to member clubs; Handling trail plans & issues; Promoting concern for the environment & safety; Campaigning to attract new participants

Ontario Federation of Teaching Parents (OFTP)
PO Box 66551, Stn. McCowan, Toronto ON M1J 3N8
Tel: 416-410-5218
Toll-Free: 800-704-0448
enquiries@ontariohomeschool.org
www.ontariohomeschool.org
www.facebook.com/182154071937198
Overview: A small provincial organization founded in 1987
Mission: To support parental choice in education as stated in the UN Declaration of Human Rights; to act as link between home educators & institutions such as the provincial government & school boards
Member of: Ontario Federation of Independent Schools
Affiliation(s): Association of Canadian Home-based Educators
Membership: *Fees:* $30/year; $75/3 years; *Member Profile:* Home educators
Activities: Provides information & support on home education
Chief Officer(s):
Glenda Willemsma, Administrator

Ontario Fencing Association (OFA) / Association d'escrime de l'Ontario
c/o Laurence Bishop, Executive Director, 177 Old River Rd., RR #2, Mallorytown ON K0E 1R0
Tel: 519-496-0613
fencingontario.ca
Overview: A medium-sized provincial organization overseen by Canadian Fencing Federation
Mission: To promote & develop the sport of fencing in Ontario
Staff Member(s): 5
Membership: *Fees:* $5 associate; $20 recreation; $80 competitive; $35 coaches & officials
Chief Officer(s):
Laurence Bishop, Executive Director
lbishop@fencingontario.ca

Ontario Field Ornithologists (OFO)
PO Box 116, Stn. F, Toronto ON M4Y 2L4
membership@ofo.ca
www.ofo.ca
Overview: A medium-sized international charitable organization founded in 1982
Mission: To study bird life in Ontario
Finances: *Funding Sources:* Membership fees; Donations
Membership: *Fees:* $40 Canada; $45 USA; $50 international; $700 Canadian life membership; $800 USA life membership; $900 international life membership; *Member Profile:* Field ornithologists from Ontario & abroad; *Committees:* Convention; Certificates; Field Trips; Website; Membership; Birdathon; Advertising; Ontario Bird Records; ONTBIRDS Listserv; Nomination
Activities: Offering field trips to birding spots in Ontario; Publishing site guides to birding areas of Ontario; Facilitating the exchange of information
Chief Officer(s):
Lynne Freeman, President, 416-671-0325
lynnef.to@gmail.com
Bob Cermak, Vice-President, 613-720-5859
vp@ofo.ca
Brian Gibbon, Treasurer, 705-726-8969
treasurer@ofo.ca
Kevin Seymour, Secretary
secretary@ofo.ca
David Milsom, Director, Field Trips, 705-874-8531
fieldtrips@ofo.ca
Doug Woods, Director, Website, 416-466-4660
admin@ofo.ca
Awards:
- Distinguished Ornithologist Award; Certificates of Appreciation

Meetings/Conferences:
- Ontario Field Ornithologists 2018 Annual Convention, 2018, ON
Scope: Provincial
Description: Activities include guest speakers, birding displays, field trips, & a social event

Publications:
- Field Checklist of Ontario Birds
Type: Booklet; *Price:* $2
- OFO [Ontario Field Ornithologists] News
Type: Newsletter; *Frequency:* 3 pa; *Editor:* Seabrooke Leckie; *Price:* Free with Ontario Field Ornithologists membership
Profile: Announcements, field trip reports, site guides, & Ontario Bird Records Committe reports
- Ontario Birds
Type: Journal; *Frequency:* 3 pa; *Editor:* R. James; G. Coady; D.V. Weseloh; *Price:* Free with Ontario Field Ornithologists membership
Profile: New information about the status, distribution, identification, & behaviour of birds in Ontario
- Ornithology in Ontario
Type: Book; *Number of Pages:* 400; *Editor:* Martin McNicholl; John Cranmer-Byng
Profile: Historical overview, archaeology, early naturalists, biographies, zoology, museums, bird banding, species accounts, & studies

Ontario Fire Buff Associates (OFBA)
PO Box 56, Stn. Don Mills Station, Toronto ON M3C 2R6
ontariofirebuffs@yahoo.ca
www.ofba.ca
Overview: A small provincial organization founded in 1971
Mission: To bring together people who share a common interest - the fire service of Ontario
Member of: International Fire Buff Associates
Finances: *Annual Operating Budget:* Less than $50,000
170 volunteer(s)
Membership: 100-499; *Fees:* $15-$28; *Member Profile:* Open to any eligible individual or organization upon required recommendation, payment of fees & approval of the Board of Directors
Chief Officer(s):
Bob Rupert, President

Ontario Floorball Association
#2, 30 Vogell Rd., Richmond Hill ON L4B 3K6
info@ontariofloorball.com
www.ontariofloorball.com
Overview: A small provincial organization overseen by Floorball Canada
Mission: To be the provincial governing body for the sport of floorball in Ontario
Member of: Floorball Canada; International Floorball Federation
Chief Officer(s):
Kultar Singh, President
David Thomas, Director, Corporate Relations

Ontario Flue-Cured Tobacco Growers' Marketing Board (OFCTGMB)
4B Elm St., Tillsonburg ON N4G 0C4
Tel: 519-842-3661; *Fax:* 519-842-7813
otb@ontarioflue-cured.com
www.ontarioflue-cured.com
Also Known As: Ontario Tobacco Board
Overview: A medium-sized provincial organization founded in 1957
Mission: To administer & enforce the provisions of Regulation 207/09 (Tobacco - Plan) & Regulation 208/09 (Tobacco - Powers of Local Board), made under the Farm Products Marketing Act; To control & regulate the production & marketing of tobacco, within the limits imposed by the Farm Products Marketing Act
Activities: Engaging in a continuing monitoring process, during which Board inspectors, accompanied by Excise Duty Officers from the Canada Revenue Agency, visit tobacco farms

Ontario Fly & Bait Casting Association
c/o Toronto Sportsmen's Association, #66, 2700 Dufferin St., Toronto ON M6B 4J3
Tel: 416-487-4477; *Fax:* 416-487-4478
info@torontosportsmens.ca
www.torontosportsmens.ca/Casting.html
Overview: A small provincial organization
Mission: To teach casting skills, covering fly, bait & spinning
Affiliation(s): Toronto Sportsmen's Association; Canadian Casting Federation

Ontario Folk Dance Association (OFDA)
Toronto ON
ontariofolkdancers@gmail.com
www.ofda.ca
www.facebook.com/ontariofolkdanceassociation
Overview: A small provincial organization founded in 1969
Mission: To promote the practice of international folk arts & dance; To prepare, collect & disseminate information & material relating to folk arts & dance
Finances: *Funding Sources:* Membership fees; events
Membership: *Fees:* $24 single; $30 family; *Committees:* Steering
Activities: Recreational folk dancing
Chief Officer(s):
Janis Smith, Treasurer
Marylyn Peringer, Secretary

Ontario Food Protection Association (OFPA)
PO Box 51575, 2140A Queen St. East, Toronto ON M4E 1C0
Tel: 519-265-4119; *Fax:* 416-981-3368
info@ofpa.on.ca
www.ofpa.on.ca
Overview: A small provincial organization
Mission: Provides a common forum for those associated with food safety in the food industry and enables those interested in food safety to exchange ideas, experiences and information.
Membership: *Fees:* Professional - $59; Sustaining Corporate Member - $188; Student - $16; Retired - $26; *Member Profile:* Food safety professionals
Chief Officer(s):
Jeff Hall, President
Meetings/Conferences:
- Ontario Food Protection Association Spring Technical Meeting, April, 2018, ON
Scope: Provincial
- Ontario Food Protection Association 60th Meeting & Fall Symposium, November, 2018, ON
Scope: Provincial

Ontario Football Alliance
7384 Wellington Rd. 30, #B, Guelph ON N1H 6J2
Tel: 519-780-0200; *Fax:* 519-780-0705
Toll-Free: 888-313-9419
www.ontariofootball.ca
www.facebook.com/ontariofootball

twitter.com/Ontariofootball
www.youtube.com/channel/UCNtsuz7nHyHJOCJfciYPZ3A
Previous Name: Football Ontario
Overview: A medium-sized provincial organization founded in 1971
Mission: To develop football in Ontario by providing programs to improve the game through participation & mandates developed by its membership
Member of: Football Canada
Staff Member(s): 4
Membership: *Fees:* $25 tackle; $10 coach; $100 association; $500 league
Activities: *Rents Mailing List:* Yes; *Library:* by appointment Not open to public
Chief Officer(s):
Tina Turner, Executive Director
director@ontariofootball.ca
Don Edwards, President
president@ontariofootball.ca

Ontario Forest Industries Association (OFIA) / l'Industrie forestière de l'Ontario
#1704, 8 King St. East, Toronto ON M5C 1B5
Tel: 416-368-6188; *Fax:* 416-368-5445
info@ofia.com
www.ofia.com
Overview: A medium-sized provincial organization founded in 1943
Mission: To act as a unified voice on behalf of member companies to ensure industry positions are considered; To respond to industry issues, such as economic, environmental, & technological developments
Membership: 10 member companies + 10 affiliate members + 4 associate members; *Member Profile:* Companies, ranging from large multinational corporations to small businesses, that produce materials such as pulp, paper, paperboard, plywood, panelboard, veneer & lumber
Activities: Liaising with government & other business sectors; Developing partnerships, such as the Ontario Forestry Coalition; Raising awareness of the forest industry in Ontario; Providing opportunities for members to discuss industry issues
Publications:
• Canadian Forests: A Primer
Number of Pages: 50; *Author:* Dr. Ken Armson; *ISBN:* 1-895540-17-8
Profile: Part of the Environmental Literacy Series, the contents address the ownership & governance of forests, forest management, the economy

Ontario Formwork Association (OFA)
#25, 111 Zenway Blvd., Woodbridge ON L4H 3H9
Tel: 905-856-4747; *Fax:* 905-856-4474
ontarioformwork@bellaliant.ca
www.ontarioformworkassociation.com
Overview: A medium-sized provincial organization founded in 1968
Mission: To discuss issues related to the formwork sector of the construction industry in Ontario
Member of: Council of Ontario Construction Associations
Finances: *Annual Operating Budget:* $250,000-$500,000
Membership: 50 member companies; 4,500+ foamworkers; *Fees:* Schedule available

Ontario Foundation for Visually Impaired Children Inc. (OFVIC)
PO Box 1116, Stn. D, Toronto ON M6P 3K2
Tel: 416-767-5977; *Fax:* 416-767-5530
ofvic@look.ca
Overview: A small provincial organization
Chief Officer(s):
April Cornell, Executive Director

Ontario Friends of Schizophrenics *See* Schizophrenia Society of Ontario

Ontario Fruit & Vegetable Growers' Association (OFVGA) / L'Association des fruiticulteurs et des maraîchers de l'Ontario
#105, 355 Elmira Rd. North, Guelph ON N1K 1S5
Tel: 519-763-6160; *Fax:* 519-763-6604
info@ofvga.org
www.ofvga.org
www.facebook.com/ofvga
twitter.com/OntFruitVeg
Overview: A medium-sized provincial organization founded in 1859
Mission: Dedicated to the advancement of horticulture, working proactively through effective lobbying for the betterment of the industry & producers as a whole through advocacy, research, education, communication & marketing
Member of: Canadian Horticultural Council
Finances: *Annual Operating Budget:* $500,000-$1.5 Million; *Funding Sources:* Membership fees; advertising revenue
Staff Member(s): 9
Membership: 8,700
Activities: *Speaker Service:* Yes
Chief Officer(s):
Jason Verkaik, Chair
John Kelly, Executive Vice President, 519-763-6160 Ext. 115
johnkelly@ofvga.org
Meetings/Conferences:
• Ontario Fruit & Vegetable Convention 2018, February, 2018
Scope: Provincial
Description: An annual gathering of horticultural crop enthusiasts involved in producing fruits and vegetables.
Contact Information: www.ofvc.ca

Ontario Funeral Service Association (OFSA)
#103, 3228 South Service Rd., Burlington ON L7N 3N1
Tel: 905-637-3371; *Fax:* 905-637-3583
Toll-Free: 800-268-2727
info@ofsa.org
www.ofsa.org
www.facebook.com/ofsa.socialmedia
twitter.com/OFSAsocialmedia
Previous Name: Embalmers' Association
Overview: A medium-sized provincial organization founded in 1883
Mission: To maintain high standards of services & ethical business practices among Ontario's funeral homes for the welfare of the public; To represent & support Ontario's independently owned funeral establishments
Finances: *Annual Operating Budget:* $250,000-$500,000; *Funding Sources:* Membership dues
Staff Member(s): 2; 8 volunteer(s)
Membership: 575; *Fees:* Schedule available; *Member Profile:* Independent & family owned funeral homes in Ontario; *Committees:* Legislation; Membership; Social Services; Finance; Insurance; Special Events
Activities: Advocating on behalf of funeral homes in Ontario; Liaising with various levels of government; Offering professional development activities & resources; Creating networking opportunities; Raising public awareness of the funeral profession
Chief Officer(s):
Scott Davidson, President, 705-652-3355
Kerri Douglas, Executive Director
kerri@ofsa.org
Awards:
• Cornerstone Award
To recognize members who have made an outstanding contribution to the betterment of the funeral profession
• Humanitarian Award
To recognize excellence in community service
• Association Activist Award
To recognize outstanding contributions to the Ontario Funeral Service Association by volunteers
Meetings/Conferences:
• Ontario Funeral Service Association Annual Convention 2018, September, 2018, Blue Mountain Resort, The Blue Mountains, ON
Scope: Provincial

Ontario Gang Investigators Association (ONGIA)
PO Box 57085, Stn. Jackson Square, Hamilton ON L8P 4W9
ongia.org
Overview: A medium-sized provincial organization
Mission: ONGIA is a non-profit organization that is committed to addressing the street gang phenomenon.
Membership: *Member Profile:* Law enforcement professionals and members of the criminal justice community throughout Ontario.
Chief Officer(s):
Jim Aspiotis, President
president@ongia.org
Meetings/Conferences:
• 17th Annual Gang & Organized Crime Professional Development Conference, 2018, ON
Scope: Provincial

Ontario Gay & Lesbian Chamber of Commerce
#1600, 401 Bay St., Toronto ON M5H 2Y4
Tel: 416-646-1600
info@oglcc.com
www.oglcc.com
www.facebook.com/OGLCC
twitter.com/OGLCC
Overview: A medium-sized provincial organization
Mission: To create an environment in which the Ontario gay & lesbian business & professional communities can thrive through the sharing of knowledge, resources, & communications
Membership: *Fees:* Schedule available
Chief Officer(s):
Chris Matthews, President

Ontario Genealogical Society (OGS)
#202, 2100 Steeles Ave. West, Concord ON L4K 2V1
Tel: 416-489-0734; *Fax:* 855-695-8080
Toll-Free: 855-697-6687
info@ogs.on.ca
www.ogs.on.ca
www.linkedin.com/company/the-ontario-genealogical-society
www.facebook.com/OntarioGenealogicalSociety
twitter.com/OntGenSociety
Overview: A medium-sized provincial charitable organization founded in 1961
Mission: To support, unite & help all those interested in pursuing family history; To promote the study of genealogy & genealogical research in Ontario
Member of: Genealogical Societies Across Canada; Federation of Genealogical Societies
Finances: *Annual Operating Budget:* $1.5 Million-$3 Million; *Funding Sources:* Membership fees; Annual conference; Workshops & seminars; Sale of materials; Grants
Staff Member(s): 3; 300 volunteer(s)
Membership: 3,800; *Fees:* $63 plus individual Branch & Special Interest Group fees; *Committees:* Cemeteries; Finance; Library; Membership; Publications
Activities: Educating Ontario genealogists & promoting the use of ethical research standards; Encouraging the creation & publication of family histories & transcriptions; Collecting, preserving & disseminating genealogical resources; Publishing books & periodicals on genealogy; Fostering communication & networking among the society, members, & the public; *Library:* OGS Library, Hum. & Soc. Serv. Dept., Toronto Reference Library; Open to public
Chief Officer(s):
Peter D. Taylor, Executive Director
ed@ogs.on.ca
Coral Harkies, Administrative Coordinator
officeadmin@ogs.on.ca
Awards:
• Keffer Essay Writing Competition
Eligibility: Membership in the Ontario Genealogical Society
Deadline: November; *Amount:* $100
Meetings/Conferences:
• Ontario Genealogical Society 2018 Annual Conference, June, 2018, University of Guelph, Guelph, ON
Scope: International
Description: Theme: "Upper Canada to Ontario - The Birth of a Nation"
Publications:
• Families [a publication of the Ontario Genealogical Society]
Type: Journal; *Frequency:* Quarterly
Profile: Articles, book reviews, advertisements & a queries column; features submissions from members & others with an interest in genealogy
  Brant County Branch
  #114, 118 Powerline Rd., Brantford ON N3T 5L8
  Tel: 519-753-4140; *Fax:* 519-753-9866
  brant@ogs.on.ca
  www.brant.ogs.on.ca
  Bruce & Grey Branch
  PO Box 66, Owen Sound ON N4K 5P1
  Tel: 416-489-0734
  Toll-Free: 855-697-6687
  brucegreyogs@gmail.com
  brucegrey.ogs.on.ca
  Durham Region Branch
  PO Box 174, Whitby ON L1N 5S1
  Tel: 905-720-0985
  durham@ogs.on.ca
  durham.ogs.on.ca
• Kindred Spirits [a publication of the Ontario Genealogical Society, Durham Region Branch]
Type: Newsletter; *Frequency:* Quarterly

Canadian Associations / Ontario General Contractors Association (OGCA)

Elgin County Branch
c/o Ontario Genealogical Society, #202, 2100 Steeles Ave. West, Concord ON L4K 2V1
elgin@ogs.on.ca
elgin.ogs.on.ca
www.facebook.com/ElginOGS
elgincountyogs.blogspot.ca

Essex County Branch
c/o Ontario Genealogical Society, PO Box 2, Stn. A, Windsor ON N9A 6J5
Tel: 519-255-6770
essex@ogs.on.ca
essex.ogs.on.ca
www.linkedin.com/groups/4483476
twitter.com/EssexOGS
• Trails [a publication of the Ontario Genealogical Society, Essex County Branch]
Type: Newsletter; Frequency: Quarterly

Haldimand & Norfolk Branch
ON
haldimandnorfolk@ogs.on.ca
haldimandnorfolk.ogs.on.ca
Mission: To preserve family history & genealogy in Haldimand & Norfolk Counties

Halton-Peel Branch
PO Box 24, Streetsville ON L5M 2B7
haltonpeel@ogs.on.ca
haltonpeel.ogs.on.ca
twitter.com/HaltonPeelOGS
Chief Officer(s):
Lori Kay, Chair
haltonpeelchair@ogs.on.ca
• Halton-Peel KINnections [a publication of the Ontario Genealogical Society, Halton-Peel Branch]
Type: Newsletter; Frequency: Quarterly

Hamilton Branch
169 West 24th St., Hamilton ON L9C 4W5
Tel: 855-697-6687
hamilton.ogs.on.ca
twitter.com/OGSHamilton
www.youtube.com/c/hamiltonbranch

Huron County Branch
PO Box 469, Goderich ON N7A 4C7
www.hurontel.on.ca/~ogshuron

Kawartha Branch
PO Box 861, Peterborough ON K9J 7A2
kawartha@ogs.on.ca
kawartha.ogs.on.ca
Chief Officer(s):
June James, Treasurer
kawarthapublicationsales@ogs.on.ca

Kent County Branch
PO Box 964, 120 Queen St., Chatham ON N7M 5L3
Tel: 855-697-6687
kent@ogs.on.ca
kent.ogs.on.ca
• Roots, Branches & Twigs [a publication of the Ontario Genealogical Society, Kent County Branch]
Type: Newsletter; Frequency: 3 pa

Kingston Branch
PO Box 1394, Kingston ON K7L 5C6
www.ogs.on.ca/kingston
• Kingston Relations [a publication of the Ontario Genealogical Society, Kingston Branch]
Type: Newsletter; Frequency: 5 pa

Lambton County Branch
PO Box 2857, Sarnia ON N7T 7W1
lambton@ogs.on.ca
www.ogs.on.ca/lambton
• Lambton Lifeline [a publication of the Ontario Genealogical Society, Lambton County Branch]
Type: Newsletter; Frequency: Quarterly

Leeds & Grenville Branch
PO Box 536, 5 Henry St., Brockville ON K6V 5V7
Tel: 613-342-7773
leedsgrenville@ogs.on.ca
leedsandgrenville.ogs.on.ca

London-Middlesex County Branch
611 Wonderland Rd. North, #PMB 235, London ON N6H 5N7
Tel: 855-697-6687
londonmiddlesex@ogs.on.ca
londonmiddlesex.ogs.on.ca
Chief Officer(s):

David Elliott, Acting Chair
dr.david.r.elliott@sympatico.ca

Niagara Peninsula Branch
50 Chapel St. South, Thorold ON L2V 2C6
Tel: 416-489-0734
Toll-Free: 855-697-6687
niagara@ogs.on.ca
niagara.ogs.on.ca
Chief Officer(s):
Steve Fulton, Chair
niagarachair@ogs.on.ca

Nipissing Branch
271 Worthington St. East, North Bay ON P1B 1H1
nipissing@ogs.on.ca
www.nipissing.ogs.on.ca

Ottawa Branch
PO Box 8346, Stn. T, Ottawa ON K1G 3H8
Tel: 613-454-1406
www.ogsottawa.on.ca
Chief Officer(s):
Doug Gray, Chair

Oxford County Branch
PO Box 20091, Woodstock ON N4S 8X8
Tel: 519-421-1700
oxford@ogs.on.ca
www.oxford.ogs.on.ca
• The Tracer [a publication of the Ontario Genealogical Society, Oxford Country Branch]
Type: Newsletter; Frequency: Quarterly

Perth County Branch
c/o Stratford-Perth Archives, 4273 Line 34, RR #5, Stratford ON N5A 6S6
Tel: 519-271-0531
perthcountyogs@gmail.com
perthcountyogs.org

Quinte Branch
PO Box 1371, Trenton ON K8V 5R9
Tel: 613-394-3381
quintebranch@ogs.on.ca
www.rootsweb.ancestry.com/~canqbogs
Chief Officer(s):
Terry Buttler, Chair
• The Quinte Searchlight [a publication of the Ontario Genealogical Society, Quinte Branch]
Type: Newsletter; Frequency: Quarterly

Sault & District Branch
#202, 2100 Steeles Ave. West, Concord ON L4K 2V1
Tel: 416-489-0734; Fax: 855-695-8080
Toll-Free: 855-697-6687
saultanddistrict.ogs.on.ca
• Sault Channels [a publication of the Ontario Genealogical Society, Sault & District Branch]
Type: Newsletter; Frequency: Quarterly

Simcoe County Branch
PO Box 892, Barrie ON L4M 4Y6
simcoe.ogs.ca
Chief Officer(s):
Nancy Leveque, Chair
simcoechair@ogs.on.ca
• Simcoe County Ancestor News (SCAN) [a publication of the Ontario Genealogical Society, Simcoe County Branch]
Type: Newsletter; Frequency: Quarterly

Sudbury District Branch
c/o Greater Sudbury Public Library, 74 Mackenzie St., Sudbury ON P3C 4X8
sudburybranchogs@gmail.com
www.sudburyogs.com
Chief Officer(s):
Lynn Gainer, Chair

Thunder Bay District Branch
PO Box 10373, Thunder Bay ON P7C 6T8
Tel: 807-632-1533
thunderbay@ogs.on.ca
thunderbay.ogs.on.ca
Chief Officer(s):
Janet Bazdarick, Chair
thunderbaychair@ogs.on.ca
• Past Tents [a publication of the Ontario Genealogical Society, Thunder Bay District Branch]
Type: Newsletter; Frequency: Quarterly
• Pick & Shovel [a publication of the Ontario Genealogical Society, Thunder Bay District Branch]
Type: Book
Profile: Northwestern Ontario genealogical resources.

Waterloo Region Branch
525 Highland Rd. West, Kitchener ON N2M 5P4
waterloo.ogs.on.ca
• Our Waterloo Kin [a publication of the Ontario Genealogical Society, Waterloo Region Branch]
Type: Newsletter; Frequency: Quarterly

Wellington County Branch
PO Box 1211, Guelph ON N1H 6N6
wellington@ogs.on.ca
wellington.ogs.on.ca
Chief Officer(s):
Jan Salsberg, Chair
wellingtonchair@ogs.on.ca
• Traces & Tracks [a publication of the Ontario Genealogical Society, Wellington County Branch]
Type: Newsletter; Frequency: Quarterly

York Region Branch
PO Box 95045, Stouffville ON L4A 1J1
york.ogs.on.ca
• York Region Ancestors [a publication of the Ontario Genealogical Society, York Region Branch]
Type: Journal; Frequency: Quarterly

Ontario General Contractors Association (OGCA)
#703, 6299 Airport Rd., Mississauga ON L4V 1N3
Tel: 905-671-3969; Fax: 905-671-8212
www.ogca.ca
Overview: A medium-sized provincial organization founded in 1939 overseen by Canadian Construction Association
Mission: To offer experience & expertise dealing with contractors, architects, engineers & owners
Affiliation(s): Ontario Association of Architects; Consulting Engineers of Ontario; Ontario Realty Corporation; Canadian Construction Association
Finances: Funding Sources: Membership dues
Staff Member(s): 5
Membership: 217 corporate; Fees: Schedule available; Member Profile: General Contractors, industrial, commercial & institutional; Committees: Education; Executive; Marketing; Safety; Best Practices
Chief Officer(s):
Clive Thurston, President
clive@ogca.ca

Ontario Geothermal Association (OGA)
ON
Tel: 905-602-4700
Toll-Free: 800-267-2231
www.ontariogeothermal.ca
Overview: A large provincial organization founded in 2009
Affiliation(s): Heating, Refrigeration & Air Conditioning Institute of Canada
Chief Officer(s):
Jim Bolger, President
Meetings/Conferences:
• Ontario Geothermal Association 2018 Conference, February, 2018, Westin Toronto Airport, Toronto, ON
Scope: Provincial
Description: Theme: "From the Ground Up"

Ontario Gerontology Association (OGA) / Association ontarienne de gérontologie
#601, 90 Eglinton Ave. East, Toronto ON M4P 2Y3
Tel: 416-535-6034; Fax: 416-535-6907
Overview: A small provincial organization founded in 1981
Affiliation(s): Canadian Association on Gerontology
Membership: Fees: $350 business; $100 non profit; $55 individual; $25 senior/student
Activities: Publishing newsletters; Organizing regional events

Ontario Ginseng Growers Association
PO Box 587, 1283 Blueline Rd., Simcoe ON N3Y 4N5
Tel: 519-426-7046; Fax: 519-426-9087
info@ginsengontario.com
www.ginsengontario.com
Overview: A medium-sized provincial organization
Mission: To conduct research on how to improve ginseng growing, as well as new varieties of ginseng; to help market North American ginseng
Staff Member(s): 2
Membership: 140; Committees: Research; Marketing/Buyer Relations; Government/Liason; Social/Public Relations
Chief Officer(s):
Rebecca Coates, Executive Director
rebecca.coates@ginsengontario.com

Ontario Goat Breeders Association (OGBA)
#12, 449 Laird Rd., Guelph ON N1G 4W1
Tel: 519-824-2942; *Fax:* 519-824-2534
info@livestockalliance.ca
www.ontariogoat.ca
twitter.com/ontariogoat
Also Known As: Ontario Goat
Overview: A medium-sized provincial organization founded in 1951
Mission: To provide & circulate sound information about goats in Ontario; To improve & develop the goat breeds in Ontario; To encourage & promote the expansion of the goat industry in Ontario; To assist the development of chevon, fibre & dairy industries
Finances: *Annual Operating Budget:* Less than $50,000; *Funding Sources:* Membership dues; sales; advertising; fundraising; sponsorship donations
8 volunteer(s)
Membership: 300; *Fees:* $60; *Member Profile:* Goat owners, breeders; industry partners; *Committees:* Milk; Chevon; Fibre
Activities: *Library:*

Ontario Golf Superintendents' Association (OGSA)
328 Victoria Rd. South, Guelph ON N1L 0H2
Tel: 519-767-3341; *Fax:* 519-766-1704
Toll-Free: 877-824-6472
admin@ogsa.ca
www.ogsa.ca
Overview: A small provincial organization
Membership: *Committees:* Member Services; Research; Education; Communications; Governance; Gov't Industry Relations; Golf & Events
Chief Officer(s):
Sally E. Ross, Executive Manager, 519-767-3341 Ext. 202
manager@ogsa.ca
Meetings/Conferences:
• Ontario Golf Superintendents' Association 2018 Conference, January, 2018, Fallsview Casino Resort Conference Centre, Niagara Falls, ON
Scope: National
• 2018 Canadian Golf Course Management Conference, February, 2018, Québec, QC
Scope: National

Ontario Good Roads Association (OGRA)
#22, 1525 Cornwall Rd., Oakville ON L6J 0B2
Tel: 289-291-6472; *Fax:* 289-291-6477
info@ogra.org
www.ogra.org
ca.linkedin.com/pub/ontario-good-roads-association/43/b08/829
twitter.com/Ont_Good_Roads
Overview: A medium-sized provincial organization founded in 1894
Mission: To represent the transportation & public works-related interests of Ontario's municipalities & First Nation communities; To deliver programs & services that meet the needs of members; To support municipalities in the provision of effective & efficient transportation systems throughout Ontario
Finances: *Funding Sources:* Membership fees; Sponsorships
Membership: 400+ municipalities; *Member Profile:* Ontario municipalities; First Nations communities; Corporations; Life & honourary members; *Committees:* Municipal Hot Mix Asphalt Liaison; Quality of Asphalt Pavement; Aggregate Recycling Ontario Council; Municipal Concrete Liaison; Smart About Salt; Ontario Roads Coalition (ORC); Ontario Provincial Standards (OPS); The Ontario Road Salt Management Group (ORSMG); Municipal Alliance for Connected and Autonomous Vehicles in Ontario (MACAVO)
Activities: Advocating for the collective interests of municipal transportation & works departments; Analyzing policies; Reviewing legislation; Consulting with stakeholders & partners; Offering education & training opportunities; *Library:* Ontario Good Roads Association Documents Library; Open to public
Chief Officer(s):
Joseph W. Tiernay, Executive Director
joe@ogra.org
James Smith, Manager, Member & Technical Services
james@ogra.org
Scott Butler, Manager, Policy & Research
Heather Crewe, Manager, Education & Training
Rayna Gillis, Manager, Finance & Administration
rayna@ogra.org
Colette Caruso, Coordinator, Communications & Marketing
Janelle Warren, Coordinator, Curriculum
janelle@ogra.org
Cherry-Lyn Sales, Coordinator, Training Services
cherry@ogra.org
Fahad Shuja, Coordinator, Member Services & OPS
fahad@ogra.org
Hilda Esedebe, Coordinator, Infrastructure Service
hilda@ogra.org
Meetings/Conferences:
• Ontario Good Roads Association 2018 Conference, February, 2018, Fairmont Royal York, Toronto, ON
Scope: Provincial
Attendance: 2,200
Description: Workshops, information about current municipal issues, a trade show, & social events
Contact Information: www.ograconference.ca
Publications:
• Milestones [a publication of the Ontario Good Roads Association]
Type: Magazine; *Frequency:* 4 pa; *Accepts Advertising; Editor:* Colette Caruso; Scott Butler
Profile: Articles of interest to the municipal services sector, including a conference issue & a wintermaintenance issue

Ontario Grape Growers' Marketing Board *See* Grape Growers of Ontario

The Ontario Greenhouse Alliance (TOGA)
PO Box 175, #6, 76 Main St., Grimsby ON L3M 1S5
Tel: 905-945-9773; *Fax:* 905-945-5767
Toll-Free: 888-480-0659
info@theontariogreenhousealliance.com
www.theontariogreenhousealliance.com
Overview: A small provincial organization founded in 2003
Mission: To provide an infrastructure & approach that will integrate all the current resources & future potential of the Ontario greenhouse stakeholders into a community & international marketplace presence, with the synergy & standards to be a world leader in greenhouse operations
Membership: *Member Profile:* Ontario's greenhouse vegetable, pepper & flower growers
Chief Officer(s):
Rejean Picard, Chair

Ontario Greenhouse Vegetable Growers (OGVG)
32 Seneca Rd., Leamington ON N8H 5H7
Tel: 519-326-2604; *Fax:* 519-326-7824
Toll-Free: 800-265-6926
admin@ogvg.com
www.ontariogreenhouse.com
www.facebook.com/ONgreenhouseVeg
twitter.com/ONgreenhouseVeg
www.youtube.com/channel/UCk9o96iBk6TUUgHnkfHjGQA
Overview: A large provincial organization founded in 1967
Mission: To represent growers' interests & ensure that they have the necessary resources to continue to prosper
Affiliation(s): Ontario Greenhouse Marketers' Association; Ontario Greenhouse Alliance
Staff Member(s): 8
Membership: 220; *Committees:* Energy & Environment; Finance; Food Safety; Human Resources; Marketing; Research; Trade
Chief Officer(s):
Rick Seguin, General Manager, 519-326-2604 Ext. 201
rseguin@ogvg.com

The Ontario Greens *See* The Green Party of Ontario

Ontario Ground Water Association (OGWA)
48 Front St. East, Strathroy ON N7G 1Y6
Tel: 519-245-7194; *Fax:* 519-245-7196
www.ogwa.ca
Previous Name: Ontario Water Well Association
Overview: A medium-sized provincial organization founded in 1952
Mission: To protect & promote Ontario's ground water; To provide guidance to members, government representatives, & the public
Finances: *Funding Sources:* Membership dues
Membership: *Member Profile:* Ground water professionals
Activities: Disseminating information & providing education about ground water; Promoting technical skills of ground water professional
Chief Officer(s):
Greg Bullock, President
Rob MacKinnon, Secretary-Treasurer
Anne Gammage, Office Manager, 519-245-7194, Fax: 519-245-7196
Meetings/Conferences:
• Ontario Ground Water Association 2018 66th Convention & Annual General Meeting, March, 2018, Brookstreet Hotel, Ottawa, ON
Scope: National
Publications:
• The Source [a publication of the Ontario Ground Water Association]
Type: Newsletter; *Accepts Advertising; Editor:* Shannon Savory
Profile: Ontario Ground Water Association information, plus feature articles & industry news

Ontario Gymnastic Federation (OGF)
#214, 3 Concorde Gate, Toronto ON M3C 3N7
Tel: 416-426-7100; *Fax:* 416-426-7377
Toll-Free: 866-565-0650
info@ogf.com
www.ogf.com
Also Known As: Gymnastics Ontario
Overview: A small provincial organization founded in 1968
Mission: To lead the sport of gymnastics throughout Ontario; To provide services & programs which encourage lifelong involvement in gymnastics
Affiliation(s): Gymnastics Canada
Finances: *Funding Sources:* Fundraising
Activities: Providing professional development & training activities; Offering resources such as technical manuals, workbooks, & videos; Providing a development award program; *Awareness Events:* I Love Gymnastic Week *Library:* Gymnastics Ontario Resource Centre
Chief Officer(s):
Dave Sandford, Chief Executive Officer, 416-426-7095
ceo@gymnasticsontario.ca
Linda Clifford, President
Angel Crossman, Director, Policies & Procedures
Michelle Pothier, Coordinator, Recreation
recreation@gymnasticsontario.ca
Yuliana Korolyova, Coordinator, Education, 416-426-7096
education@gymnasticsontario.ca
Kristina Galloway, Coordinator, Membership Services, 416-426-7096
membership@gymnasticsontario.ca
Siobhan Covington, Manager, Finance, 416-426-7094
scovington@gymnasticsontario.ca
Meetings/Conferences:
• Gymnastics Ontario AGM & Conference, 2018, ON
Scope: Provincial

Ontario Halfway House Association (OHHA)
224 Cornwallis Ct., Oshawa ON L1H 8E8
Tel: 905-571-1999; *Fax:* 877-772-9695
Toll-Free: 800-698-7689
ohha@rogers.com
halfwayhouses.ca/en/region/ohha
Overview: A small provincial organization overseen by Regional Halfway House Assocation
Mission: To help offenders reintegrate themselves into society
Member of: Regional Halfway House Association
Chief Officer(s):
Darrell Rowe, President, Executive Commitee

Ontario Handball Association (OHA)
ON
www.ontariohandball.ca
Overview: A small provincial organization
Mission: To promote & develop the sport of handball in Ontario
Activities: Tournaments; junior programs
Chief Officer(s):
Jenine Wilson, President
president@ontariohandball.ca

Ontario Harness Horse Association *See* Central Ontario Standardbred Association

Ontario Hatcheries Association
39 William St., Elmira ON N3B 1P3
Tel: 519-669-3350
info@ontariohatcheries.ca
www.ontariohatcheries.ca
Overview: A small provincial organization
Mission: To serve as the voice of hatcheries & associated service & supply companies in Ontario
Membership: 58 corporate
Chief Officer(s):
Susan Fitzgerald, Executive Director

Canadian Associations / Ontario Health Libraries Association (OHLA)

Ontario Health Care Housekeepers Association Inc. See Ontario Healthcare Housekeepers' Association Inc.

Ontario Health Libraries Association (OHLA)
c/o Ontario Library Association, 2 Toronto St., 3rd Fl., Toronto ON M5C 2B6
Tel: 416-363-3388; *Fax:* 416-941-9581
Toll-Free: 866-873-9867
www.ohla.on.ca
www.linkedin.com/groups/2670522/profile
www.facebook.com/303797462978073
twitter.com/ohlacommunity
Overview: A medium-sized provincial organization founded in 1985
Mission: To represent views of members; To advocate for the value of health libraries & specialists; To provide a forum for leadership, education, & communications; To build & strengthen relationships with members & other organizations
Chief Officer(s):
Sandra Kendall, President
Meetings/Conferences:
• Ontario Health Libraries Association Annual General Meeting 2018, 2018, ON
Scope: Provincial
Description: Held during OLA's annual Super Conference

Ontario Healthcare Housekeepers' Association Inc. (OHHA)
2053 County Road 22, Bath ON K0H 1G0
Tel: 613-352-5696; *Fax:* 613-352-5840
www.ohha.org
www.facebook.com/ontariohealthcarehousekeepersassociationinc
twitter.com/healthcarehskpr
Previous Name: Ontario Health Care Housekeepers Association Inc.
Overview: A small provincial organization founded in 1957
Affiliation(s): Ontario Hospital Association, CSSA, OLTCA, ISSA
Membership: *Fees:* $85 group; $95 regular; $250 affiliate; *Member Profile:* Supervisors, managers, directors of housekeeping/environmental services in health care facilities
Activities: *Awareness Events:* Pack Your Backpack Conference & Trade Show, May; *Speaker Service:* Yes
Chief Officer(s):
Wendy Boone-Watt, Executive Director
executivedirector@ohha.org

Ontario Healthy Communities Coalition (OHCC) / Coalition des communautés en santé de l'Ontario
#1810, 2 Carlton St., Toronto ON M5B 1J3
Tel: 416-408-4841; *Fax:* 416-408-4843
Toll-Free: 800-766-3418
www.ohcc-ccso.ca
www.facebook.com/OntarioHealthyCommunitiesCoalition
twitter.com/OntarioHCC
www.youtube.com/user/ohcccso
Overview: A medium-sized provincial charitable organization founded in 1992
Mission: To achieve social, environmental, economic & physical well-being for individuals, communities & local governments throughout Ontario
Finances: *Funding Sources:* Trillium Foundation; Ministry of Health & Long Term Care; Ministry of Environment
Staff Member(s): 8
Membership: *Fees:* $25; *Member Profile:* Provincial associations; community; individuals
Activities: *Speaker Service:* Yes; *Library:* Open to public by appointment
Chief Officer(s):
Lorna McCue, Executive Director

Ontario Heart Foundation See Heart & Stroke Foundation of Ontario

Ontario Herbalists Association (OHA)
PO Box 123, Stn. D, Toronto ON M9A 4X2
Tel: 416-236-0090
Toll-Free: 877-642-4372
info@herbalists.on.ca
www.herbalists.on.ca
www.facebook.com/herbalists.on.ca
twitter.com/Ontarioherbs
Overview: A medium-sized provincial organization founded in 1979
Mission: To bring together people with interest in & knowledge about herbs; To facilitate a sharing of information & research; To promote advancement of understanding of medicinal plants; To serve as liaison between herbalists & other healing professionals & to work actively for recognition & promotion of herbal therapy
Member of: British Herbal Medicine Association
Finances: *Funding Sources:* Membership fees; events
Membership: *Fees:* $30 general; $225 professional; $45 student; *Member Profile:* Professional herbalists, gardeners, herbal product manufacturers & retailers, organic herb growers, wildcrafters, etc.; *Committees:* Professional Members; Association Membership
Activities: Herb fair; professional conference; herb walks; seminars; lectures
Chief Officer(s):
Diane Kent, President

Ontario Hereford Association
2253 Concession 14 Greenock Twp., RR#2, Cargill ON N0G 1J0
Tel: 519-366-1260; *Fax:* 519-366-1261
ont.herefords@sympatico.ca
www.ontarioherefords.ca
Overview: A small provincial organization
Mission: To promote & regulate Hereford cattle breeding in Ontario
Member of: Canadian Hereford Association
Staff Member(s): 1
Activities: *Speaker Service:* Yes
Chief Officer(s):
Robert Thurston, President
bob@thurstonlivestock.com
Ron Wells, Secretary-Manager

Ontario Heritage Trust (OHT) / Fiducie du patrimoine ontarien
10 Adelaide St. East, Toronto ON M5C 1J3
Tel: 416-325-5000; *Fax:* 416-325-5071
marketing@heritagefdn.on.ca
www.heritagetrust.on.ca
www.facebook.com/OntarioHeritageTrust
twitter.com/@ONheritage
Overview: A medium-sized provincial charitable organization founded in 1967
Mission: To be dedicated to the preservation, protection & promotion of Ontario's built, natural & cultural heritage for public enjoyment
Affiliation(s): The Elgin & Winter Garden Theatre Centre
Activities: Establishes conservation agreements with owners of heritage properties to ensure that the significant heritage features of these properties are protected; Holds provincially significant heritage properties & collections "in trust" on behalf of the people of Ontario; Provides technical assistance to individuals & groups involved in heritage preservation; Protects significant natural areas & geological land formations through Natural Heritage & Niagara Escarpment Programs; *Awareness Events:* Heritage Week
Chief Officer(s):
Nimet Manji, Executive Assistant, 416-314-4903
nimet.manji@heritagetrust.on.ca

Ontario High School Chess Association
c/o Stephen Leacock Collegiate Institute, 2450 Birchmount Rd., Toronto ON M1T 2M5
Tel: 416-396-8000; *Fax:* 416-396-8042
high.school.chess@gmail.com
www.ohscc.on.ca
Overview: A small provincial organization founded in 1970
Affiliation(s): Chess Federation of Canada; Ontario Chess Association; Chess 'n Math
3 volunteer(s)
Activities: Supprting the Ontario High School Chess Championships
Chief Officer(s):
Chris Field, President

Ontario Historical Society (OHS) / La Société historique de l'Ontario
34 Parkview Ave., Willowdale ON M2N 3Y2
Tel: 416-226-9011; *Fax:* 416-226-2740
Toll-Free: 866-955-2755
ohs@ontariohistoricalsociety.ca
www.ontariohistoricalsociety.ca
www.facebook.com/OntarioHistoricalSociety
twitter.com/OntarioHistory
Previous Name: The Pioneer Association of Ontario
Overview: A medium-sized provincial charitable organization founded in 1888
Mission: To bring people who are interested in preserving some aspect of Ontario's history together; To encourage & assist museums, historical societies & other heritage groups to research, preserve & interpret artifacts, architecture, archaeological sites & archival resources of local communities; To provide a forum to exchange ideas, research & experiences related to the history of Ontario; To sponsor programs & projects with a wide general appeal that help illustrate Ontario's history
Member of: Heritage Canada
Finances: *Annual Operating Budget:* $500,000-$1.5 Million; *Funding Sources:* Membership fees; Donations; Program fees; Book sales; Grants
Staff Member(s): 4; 30 volunteer(s)
Membership: 2,000 individuals + 900 organizations; *Fees:* Schedule available; *Committees:* Museums; Fundraising
Activities: Workshops; Young Ontario Program; Participation program; *Speaker Service:* Yes; *Library:* by appointment
Chief Officer(s):
Robert Leverty, Executive Director
rleverty@ontariohistoricalsociety.ca
Awards:
• Alison Prentice Award
• Scadding Award for Excellence
• Museum Award of Excellence
• Dorothy Duncan Award
• B. Napier Simpson Jr. Award of Merit
• Riddell Award
• Joseph Brant Award
• Fred Landon Award
• J.J. Talman Award
• President's Award
• Cruikshank Gold Medal
• Carnochan Award

Ontario HIV Treatment Network (OHTN)
#600, 1300 Yonge St., Toronto ON M4T 1X3
Tel: 416-642-6486; *Fax:* 416-640-4245
Toll-Free: 877-743-6486
info@ohtn.on.ca
www.ohtn.on.ca
www.facebook.com/theOHTN
twitter.com/theOHTN
www.youtube.com/user/OntarioHIVTreatment
Overview: A small provincial organization
Mission: To optimize the quality of life of people living with HIV in Ontario & to promote excellence & innovation in treatment, research, education & prevention through a collaborative network of excellence representing consumers, providers, researchers & other stakeholders
Staff Member(s): 55
Chief Officer(s):
Jean Bacon, Interim Executive Director
jbacon@ohtn.on.ca
Barry Adam, Scientist & Director, Prevention Research
badam@ohtn.on.ca

Ontario Hockey Federation (OHF)
#9, 400 Sheldon Dr., Cambridge ON N1T 2H9
Tel: 226-533-9070; *Fax:* 519-620-7476
info@ohf.on.ca
www.ohf.on.ca
www.facebook.com/OHFHockey
twitter.com/ohfhockey
Overview: A medium-sized provincial organization founded in 1989 overseen by Hockey Canada
Mission: To foster & promote the sport of amateur hockey in Ontario; To provide opportunities for all players to participate in the sport; To coordinate & conduct competitions & tournaments for branch, regional, & national championships
Member of: Hockey Development Centre for Ontario (HDCO)
Affiliation(s): Minor Hockey Alliance of Ontario; Greater Toronto Hockey League; Northern Ontario Hockey Association; Ontario Minor Hockey Association; Ontario Hockey Association; Ontario Hockey League; Ontario Women's Hockey Association
Staff Member(s): 6
Membership: 228,251 registered players; 33,500 coaches; 7,300 officials; *Committees:* Constitution; Finance; Rules; Risk Management; Registration; Minor Council; Junior Council; Hockey Development Council; Senior / Adult Recreational Council; Female Hockey (operates under the auspices of the Ontario Women's Hockey Association)
Activities: *Internships:* Yes
Chief Officer(s):
Phillip McKee, Executive Director, 226-533-9075
pmckee@ohf.on.ca
Awards:
• Bill Richmond Memorial Award

To recognize outstanding achievement in the area of hockey development within the Ontario Hockey Federation
• Past Referee-in-Chief Recognition
• Past President's Recognition
• Dr. Allan Morris Honour Award
To recognize an individual who has exemplified dedication to amateur hockey
• President's Award
To recognize an individual who has provided service & leadership to amateur hockey
• Ontario Hockey Federation Volunteer of the Year Award
To recognize significant contribution to the game & the hockey community
• Ontario Hockey Federation Order of Merit
To honour individuals who have served amateur hockey for many years
• Ontario Hockey Federation Minor Hockey Award
To recognize an individual who has made a significant contribution to minor hockey in an administrative role
• Ontario Hockey Federation Junior Hockey Award
To recognize an individual who has made a significant contribution to junior hockey in an administrative role
• Ontario Hockey Federation Senior Hockey Award
To recognize an individual who has made a significant contribution to senior hockey in an administrative role
• Ontario Hockey Federation Officiating Program Award
To recognize individuals involved in the officiating program
• Ontario Hockey Federation Staff Award
To honour a staff person who exemplifies commitment to the values & objectives of the Ontario Hockey Federation
• Ontario Hockey Federation Life Membership
To recognize distinctive services & contributions to the Ontario Hockey Federation
• Ontario Hockey Federation Bursary Program
Awarded to recognize & reward dedication in education & hockey *Eligibility:* A player who has been registered with the OHF for three years in any capacity & is enrolling in post-secondary, full-time studies in Canada for the first time
Publications:
• OHF Handbook
Type: Handbook; *Frequency:* Annually
Profile: Featuring the Ontario Hockey Federation constitution, by-laws, regulations, policies, & directory

Ontario Home Builders' Association (OHBA)
#101, 20 Upjohn Rd., Toronto ON M3B 2V9
Tel: 416-443-1545; *Fax:* 416-443-9982
Toll-Free: 800-387-0109
www.ohba.ca
www.linkedin.com/company/2233011?trk=tyah
www.facebook.com/203305789711914
twitter.com/OntarioHBA
Overview: A medium-sized provincial organization overseen by Canadian Home Builders' Association
Mission: To represent the interests of members involved in Ontario's residential construction industry in legislation, regulation & policy issues; To promote association activities to the public, other groups & non-members
Staff Member(s): 9
Membership: 30 local associations + 4,000 member companies; *Member Profile:* Builders, developers, professional renovators, manufacturers, contractors, consultants, marketing companies, suppliers; *Committees:* Builders' Council; Health & Safety; Land Development; Executive Officers'; Ontario Renovators'; Sales & Marketing; Technical; Training & Education; OHBA/Tarion Liaison
Chief Officer(s):
Joe Vaccaro, Chief Executive Officer
jvaccaro@ohba.ca
Awards:
• Awards of Distinction
Meetings/Conferences:
• Ontario Home Builders' Association Annual Conference 2018, 2018, ON
Scope: Provincial
Contact Information: Manager, Business: Sajida Jiwani, E-mail: sjiwani@ohba.ca
Publications:
• Ontario Home Builder [a publication of the Ontario Home Builders' Association]
Type: Magazine; *Frequency:* 6 pa; *Accepts Advertising*; *Editor:* Ted McIntyre; *ISSN:* 1182-1345; *Price:* $12.95 Canada; $29.95USA
Profile: Features resources & information for new home construction industry professionals

• Ontario Home Builders' Association Membership Directory & Buyer's Guide
Type: Report; *Frequency:* a.
Bluewater
34031 Saltford Rd., RR #4, Goderich ON N7A 3Y1
admin@bluewaterbuildersassociation.ca
www.bluewaterbuildersassociation.ca
Chief Officer(s):
Hugh Burgsma, Executive Officer
hughcomplete@hurontel.on.ca
Brantford
PO Box 1322, Brantford ON N3T 5T6
Tel: 519-755-9690
bhba.on.ca
www.linkedin.com/in/brantford-home-builders-association-aa948352
www.facebook.com/418938554933480
twitter.com/bhbabrantford
Chief Officer(s):
Fred DeCator, Executive Officer
Chatham Kent
PO Box 20023, 416 St. Clair St., Chatham ON N7L 5K6
ckhba.ca
www.facebook.com/CKHomeBuildersAssociation
Chief Officer(s):
Kevin Owen, Acting Executive Officer
ckhba.eo@gmail.com
Durham Region
206 King St. East, Oshawa ON L1H 1C0
Tel: 905-579-8080; *Fax:* 905-579-0141
info@drhba.com
drhba.com
www.facebook.com/durhamregionhomebuildersassociation
Chief Officer(s):
Anita DeVries, Executive Officer
Greater Dufferin
PO Box 369, Orangeville ON L9W 2Z7
Tel: 519-938-6086
info@gdhba.ca
gdhba.ca
Chief Officer(s):
Margaret Janssen, Executive Officer
Greater Ottawa
#108, 30 Concourse Gate, Ottawa ON K2E 7V7
Tel: 613-273-2926; *Fax:* 613-723-2982
info@gohba.ca
www.gohba.ca
twitter.com/gohba_ottawa
Chief Officer(s):
John Herbert, Executive Director, 613-723-2926 Ext. 224
jherbert@gohba.ca
Grey - Bruce
PO Box 266, Owen Sound ON N4K 5P3
greybrucehomebuilders.net
Chief Officer(s):
Tara Hall, Executive Officer
thall@gbtel.ca
Guelph & District
7 Clair Rd. West, Guelph ON N1L 0A6
Tel: 519-836-8560; *Fax:* 519-489-1405
guelph.homebuilders@gmail.com
www.gdhba.com
www.facebook.com/GuelphHomeBuilders
Chief Officer(s):
Stacy Cooper, Executive Officer
Haldimand Norfolk
PO Box 191, Simcoe ON N3Y 4L1
www.hnhba.com
Haliburton County
PO Box 299, Haliburton ON K0M 1S0
Tel: 705-457-6901; *Fax:* 705-457-3436
info@hchba.ca
www.hnhba.com
Chief Officer(s):
Aggie Tose, Executive Officer
Hamilton - Halton
1112 Rymal Rd. East, Hamilton ON L8W 3N7
Tel: 905-575-3344; *Fax:* 905-574-3411
info@hhhba.ca
www.hhhba.ca
www.linkedin.com/company/hamilton-halton-home-builders'-association-hhhba-
www.facebook.com/HHHBA

twitter.com/HHHBAOfficial
www.youtube.com/user/hamiltonhaltonhba
Chief Officer(s):
Suzanne Mammel, Executive Officer
Kingston
1575 John Counter Blvd., Kingston ON K7M 3L5
Tel: 613-547-0986; *Fax:* 613-547-5117
khba@khba.ca
khba.ca
www.facebook.com/191358867636681
Chief Officer(s):
Nicholas Harrington, Executive Officer
Lanark - Leeds
PO Box 544, Perth ON K7H 3K4
Tel: 613-523-5656
llhba.on.ca
Chief Officer(s):
Darlene Fendley, Executive Officer
darlenefendley@gmail.com
London
#5, 571 Wharncliffe Rd. South, London ON N6J 2N6
Tel: 519-686-0343; *Fax:* 519-649-2781
newhomes@lhba.on.ca
www.lhba.on.ca
www.facebook.com/LondonHomeBuildersAssociation
twitter.com/LHBA_
www.youtube.com/user/LHBA2011
Chief Officer(s):
Lois Langdon, Executive Officer
Niagara
34 Scott St. West, St Catharines ON L2R 1C9
Tel: 905-646-6281; *Fax:* 905-646-6274
info@niagarahomebuilders.ca
niagarahomebuilders.ca
Chief Officer(s):
Lynda Busch, Executive Officer
North Bay & District
265 Lakeside Dr., North Bay ON P1A 3E2
Tel: 705-495-8976; *Fax:* 705-495-0726
www.northbayhomebuilders.com
Chief Officer(s):
Judy Ochoski, Executive Officer
judy.ochoski@sympatico.ca
Oxford County
PO Box 771, Norwich ON N0J 1P0
Tel: 519-863-2230
oxfordcountyhomebuilders@execulink.com
Chief Officer(s):
Cornelius Van Vliet, Executive Officer
Peterborough & The Kawarthas
#2, 494 The Parkway, Peterborough ON K9J 7L9
Tel: 705-876-7604; *Fax:* 705-876-6630
info@pkhba.com
www.pkhba.com
www.facebook.com/165617243569628
twitter.com/PKHBA
Chief Officer(s):
Holly Richards-Conley, Executive Officer
Quinte
PO Box 22018, Belleville ON K8N 5V7
Tel: 613-970-2216
info@quintehomebuilders.com
www.quintehomebuilders.com
Chief Officer(s):
Ruth Estwick, Executive Officer
Renfrew County
65 Mudd Lake Rd., Laurentian Valley ON K8A 6W4
Tel: 613-735-6291
Chief Officer(s):
Claus Trost, Executive Officer
claus@laurvall.on.ca
St. Thomas & Elgin
PO Box 20126, St Thomas ON N5P 4H4
Tel: 519-476-5811; *Fax:* 519-637-6952
www.twentyfivepercentmorelife.com
www.facebook.com/stehbassociation
Chief Officer(s):
John Gundry, Executive Officer
Sarnia Lambton
PO Box 281, Sarnia ON N7T 7H9
Tel: 519-344-7422; *Fax:* 516-344-3868
office@sarnialambtonhomebuilders.com
www.sarnialambtonhomebuilders.com
Chief Officer(s):

Canadian Associations / Ontario Home Care Association (OHCA)

Kelly McCoy, Executive Officer
Saugeen
9 Robin Cres., Brockton ON N0G 2V0
Chief Officer(s):
Wally Halliday, President
cwhalliday@eastlink.ca
Simcoe County
PO Box 305, Barrie ON L4M 4T5
Tel: 705-728-5030; *Fax:* 705-728-3690
office@simcoehomebuilders.com
simcoehomebuilders.com
Chief Officer(s):
Jennifer Lynch, Executive Officer
Stratford & Area
PO Box 23024, Stratford ON N5A 7V8
Tel: 519-271-4795
admin@stratfordbuilders.ca
stratfordbuilders.ca
www.facebook.com/stratfordbuilders
twitter.com/sabastratford
Chief Officer(s):
Ross Dale, Executive Officer
Sudbury & District
1942 Regent St., #C, Sudbury ON P3E 5V5
Tel: 705-671-6099; *Fax:* 705-671-9590
sudburyhomebuilders@vianet.ca
sudburyhomebuilders.com
Chief Officer(s):
Laura Higgs, Executive Officer
laura@sudburyhomebuilders.com
Thunder Bay
857 May St. North, Thunder Bay ON P7C 3S2
Tel: 807-622-9645; *Fax:* 807-623-2296
Chief Officer(s):
Harold Lindstrom, Executive Officer
harold.lindstrom@catb.on.ca
Waterloo Region
#1C, 625 King St. East, Kitchener ON N2G 4V4
Tel: 519-884-7590; *Fax:* 519-884-7361
www.wrhba.com
www.linkedin.com/company/10127584
www.facebook.com/WaterlooRegionHomeBuildersAssociation
twitter.com/RenoMarkWRHBA
Mission: To represent the residential development, construction, & renovation industry in Waterloo; To drive the success of members; To promote value & choice in housing & renovation
Chief Officer(s):
Marie Schroeder, Executive Officer
marie-schroeder@wrhba.com
Windsor Essex
2880 Temple Dr., Windsor ON N8W 5J5
Tel: 519-948-3247
WEHBA@primus.ca
www.windsoressexhomebuilders.ca
Chief Officer(s):
Dennis Gerrard, Executive Officer

Ontario Home Care Association (OHCA)
PO Box 68018, RPO Blakely, Hamilton ON L8M 3M7
Tel: 905-543-9474
info@homecareontario.ca
www.homecareontario.ca
twitter.com/HomeCareOntario
Previous Name: Ontario Home Health Care Providers' Association
Overview: A medium-sized provincial organization founded in 1987
Mission: To service excellence & client satisfaction in the provision of home health & support services in Ontario
Member of: Canadian Home Care Association; Ontario Health Providers' Alliance; Ontario Home & Community Care Council
Finances: *Funding Sources:* Membership fees
Membership: 80; *Member Profile:* Home care agencies
Chief Officer(s):
Susan D. VanderBent, Chief Executive Officer

Ontario Home Economics Association (OHEA)
c/o Registrar/Office Administrator, 1225 Meadowview Rd., RR#2, Omemee ON K0L 2W0
Tel: 705-799-2081; *Fax:* 705-799-0605
info@ohea.on.ca
www.ohea.on.ca
www.facebook.com/OntarioHomeEconomicsAssociation
twitter.com/OntarioHEA
Overview: A small provincial organization founded in 1979
Mission: To further the field of home economics; Establish standards of professional conduct, ethics & standards of practice
Affiliation(s): Ontario Family Studies/Home Economics Educators' Association; Ontario Family Studies Leadership Council; Ontario Home Economists in Business; International Federation for Home Economics
Membership: 300+; *Fees:* $209.05 registered/provisional/assoc.; $30.79 student; $104.54 new grad; $96.05 ret.; $129.95 active ret.; $45.20 corresp.; $45.20 affiliate; *Member Profile:* Home economists
Chief Officer(s):
Nancy Greiter, Registrar & Office Administrator
nancyohea@rogers.com
Awards:
- Engberg-Fewster International Development Grant
- Edith Rowles Simpson Family Finance Award
- OHEA President's Distinguished Service Award
- OHEA Founder's Honour Award
- Volunteer Recognition Awards
- OHEA Incentive Award
- Federated Women's Institutes of Ontario International Scholarship

Meetings/Conferences:
- Ontario Home Economics Association 2018 Conference & AGM, 2018, ON
Scope: Provincial
Publications:
- The Vegetarian's Complete Quinoa Cookbook [a publication of the Ontario Home Economics Association]
Type: Book
Profile: Cookbook featuring over 125 recipes for quinoa-based meals.

Ontario Home Health Care Providers' Association *See* Ontario Home Care Association

Ontario Home Respiratory Services Association (OHRSA)
#600, 55 University Ave., Toronto ON M5J 2H7
Tel: 416-961-8001
www.ohrsa.ca
twitter.com/OHRSAOntario
Overview: A small provincial organization founded in 1985
Mission: To foster & promote an innovative & viable home respiratory services industry; To provide opportunities for future growth; To offer quality products & services through members
Member of: Ontario Health Providers Alliance
Finances: *Annual Operating Budget:* $100,000-$250,000
Staff Member(s): 1; 8 volunteer(s)
Membership: 30 corporate; *Member Profile:* Home oxygen suppliers
Activities: Promoting Ontario home respiratory services; Addressing industry issues
Chief Officer(s):
Shane Walsh, Chair
Al Benton, Secretary-Treasurer

Ontario Homeopathic Association (OHA)
#801, 60 Pleasant Blvd., Toronto ON M4T 1K1
Tel: 416-516-6109; *Fax:* 416-516-7725
info@ontariohomeopath.com
www.ontariohomeopath.com
www.linkedin.com/pub/ontario-homeopathic-association/5a/614/581
www.facebook.com/OntarioHomeopathicAssociation
twitter.com/OntHomeopath
Overview: A medium-sized provincial organization founded in 1992
Mission: To promote homeopathy; to educate physicians in the areas of homeopathy
Membership: *Fees:* $275 professional; $150 recent grad; $120 associate; $75 professional out of province; $50 student

Ontario Horse Racing Industry Association (OHRIA)
PO Box 456, Stn. B, Toronto ON M9W 5L4
Tel: 416-679-0741; *Fax:* 416-679-9114
ohria@ohria.com
www.ohria.com
twitter.com/value4money_ca
Overview: A small provincial organization founded in 1994
Mission: Promote the horse racing industry as a vital part of Ontario's lifestyle, heritage & agricultural economy
Membership: 21 associations; *Member Profile:* Industry organization/associations
Chief Officer(s):
Sue Leslies, President and Chair

Ontario Horse Trials Association (OHTA)
#201, 1 West Pearce St., Richmond Hill ON L4B 3K3
Tel: 905-709-6545
Toll-Free: 877-441-7112
Other Communication: Membership, E-mail:
membership@horse.on.ca
ohtainfo@gmail.com
www.horsetrials.on.ca
www.facebook.com/Ontariohorsetrials
Previous Name: Ontario Horse Trials Canada
Overview: A small provincial charitable organization founded in 1965
Mission: OHTA is a volunteer, not-for-profit organization whose main functions are to support, develop & promote events in Ontario.
Member of: Canadian Equestrian Federation
Finances: *Annual Operating Budget:* Less than $50,000
Staff Member(s): 1
Membership: 1,257; *Fees:* $35 senior; $25 junior; $126 family; $30 associate; $100 corporate; *Committees:* Championship Selection; Competitions; Young Riders; Event Evaluations; Event Schedule; Funding Programs; Officials; Omnibus; Omnibus Ad Sales; Organizer Meeting; Volunteer Incentive Program; Communications; Memberships; Points/Leaderboard; AGM/Banquet/Royal Winter Fair; Strategic Planning; Coach Outreach Program; Rules; Safety; Budget/Financial Statements
Activities: Overall program development, implementation & monitoring programs regarding the sport
Chief Officer(s):
Katie Holman, President
katieh22@live.com
Lisa Thompson, Secretary
lisat26@sympatico.ca

Ontario Horse Trials Canada *See* Ontario Horse Trials Association

Ontario Horticultural Association (OHA)
448 Paterson Ave., London ON N5W 5C7
secretary@gardenontario.org
www.gardenontario.org
twitter.com/gardenontario
Overview: A medium-sized provincial charitable organization founded in 1906
Mission: To promote civic beautification, preservation of the environment, youth work & education of many aspects of horticulture
Finances: *Annual Operating Budget:* Less than $50,000; *Funding Sources:* Membership dues; Grants; Fundraising
Staff Member(s): 1
Membership: 278 societies; 40,000 members; *Member Profile:* Gardener; *Committees:* Annual Report; Community Initiatives; Competitions; Conservation & Environment; Constitution, By-Laws & Resolutions; Convention; Director's Manual; Fundraising & Merchandising; Historian; Judges Registrar; Judging Schools; In Memoriam; Nominations/Elections; Partners & Associate Members; Promotion & Publicity; Seedy Saturdays; Speakers List; Supplies; Trillium Newsletter; Volunteer Hours; Web; Youth
Chief Officer(s):
Suzanne Hanna, President
president@gardenontario.org
Rose Odell, Vice President
vp@gardenontario.org
Kelly Taylor, Secretary
secretary@gardenontario.org
Mary Donnelly, Treasurer
treasurer@gardenontario.org
Meetings/Conferences:
- Ontario Horticultural Association 112th Convention, July, 2018, Ambassador Hotel & Conference Centre, Kingston, ON
Scope: Provincial

Ontario Hospital Association (OHA)
#2800, 200 Front St. West, Toronto ON M5V 3L1
Tel: 416-205-1300; *Fax:* 416-205-1301
Toll-Free: 800-598-8002
info@oha.com
www.oha.com
www.linkedin.com/company/ontario-hospital-association
www.facebook.com/onthospitalassn
twitter.com/OntHospitalAssn
www.youtube.com/onthospitalassn

Overview: A medium-sized provincial organization founded in 1924 overseen by Canadian Healthcare Association
Mission: To build a strong, innovative, & sustainable health care system that meets patient care needs throughout Ontario; To promote an efficent & effective health care system
Membership: 150 public hospitals; *Member Profile:* Public hospitals throughout Ontario; Affiliated associations & organizations; *Committees:* Audit; Executive; Finance; Governance; Nominating
Activities: Engaging in advocacy activities to help shape health care policy in Ontario; Building partnerships; Providing opportunities for professional development
Chief Officer(s):
Jamie McCracken, Chair
Anthony Dale, President & CEO
Warren DiClemente, Chief Operating Officer & VP, Educational Services
Elizabeth Carlton, Vice-President, Policy & Public Affairs
Hazim Hassan, Vice-President, Business Planning & Strategy
Publications:
• Healthcare Governance Update
Type: Newsletter
Profile: Information from the Governance Centre of Excellence to maintain & increase trustees' knowledge of health care governance issues
• Healthscape [a publication of Ontario Hospital Association]
Type: Newsletter
• Hospital Perspectives
Type: Newsletter; *ISSN:* 1198-0192
Profile: Articles about innovations in health care
• Labour Relations Bulletin [a publication of Ontario Hospital Association]
Type: Newsletter
• OHA [Ontario Hospital Association] Executive Report
Type: Newsletter; *Frequency:* Weekly; *Price:* Free with membership in the Ontario Hospital Association
Profile: Current health care news
• Ontario Hospital Association Annual Report
Type: Yearbook; *Frequency:* Annually

Ontario Hotel & Motel Association *See* Ontario Restaurant, Hotel & Motel Association

The Ontario Imported Wine-Spirit-Beer Association (OIWSBA) *See* Drinks Ontario

Ontario Independent Insurance Adjusters' Association
c/o Maria Joshua, Sedgwick CMS Canada Inc., #100, 21 Four Seasons Pl., Toronto ON M9B 6J8
Tel: 416-695-5100; *Fax:* 416-695-5120
www.ciaa-adjusters.ca
Overview: A small provincial organization overseen by Canadian Independent Adjusters' Association
Member of: Canadian Independent Adjusters' Association
Chief Officer(s):
Maria Joshua, President
maria.joshua@sedgwickcms.ca

Ontario Independent Meat Packers & Processors Society *See* Ontario Independent Meat Processors

Ontario Independent Meat Processors (OIMP)
52 Royal Rd., #B-1, Guelph ON N1H 1G3
Tel: 519-763-4558; *Fax:* 519-763-4164
info@oimp.ca
www.oimp.ca
www.linkedin.com/company-beta/1368588
www.facebook.com/ONTARIOINDEPENDENTMEATPROCESSORS
twitter.com/OIMPa
www.instagram.com/ontariomeatpoultry
Previous Name: Ontario Independent Meat Packers & Processors Society
Overview: A medium-sized provincial organization founded in 1979
Mission: To provide leadership for Ontario's meat & poultry industry by fostering innovation, promoting food safety & recognizing excellence
Staff Member(s): 6; 11 volunteer(s)
Membership: *Member Profile:* Individuals associated with the meat & poultry industry
Activities: Food handler certification; Nutrition analysis; Consumer outreach
Chief Officer(s):
Laurie Nicol, Executive Director, 519-763-4558 Ext. 224

Meetings/Conferences:
• Ontario Independent Meat Processors Meat Industry Expo 2018, 2018, ON
Scope: Provincial
Contact Information: www.meatindustryexpo.ca

Ontario Industrial Development Council Inc. *See* Economic Developers Council of Ontario Inc.

Ontario Industrial Fire Protection Association (OIFPA)
193 James St. South, Hamilton ON L8P 3A8
Tel: 905-527-0700; *Fax:* 905-527-6254
oifpa@interlynx.net
www.oifpa.org
Overview: A medium-sized provincial organization founded in 1981
Mission: To unite individuals with a concern for fire protection within Ontario's industrial community
Finances: *Funding Sources:* Membership fees
Membership: *Member Profile:* Individuals from the chemical industry & the oil & gas industry; Consulting engineers; Emergency response personnel; Municipal fire departments & fire protection consultants; Government agencies; Industrial underwriters
Activities: Creating networking opportunities with members from organizations such as municipal fire departments & government agencies; Providing educational seminars, on topics such as Ontario Fire Code updates, explosion protection, & fire pump installation
Publications:
• Firewatch
Type: Newsletter
Profile: Information updates from the association

Ontario Industrial Roofing Contractors' Association (OIRCA)
#301, 940 The East Mall, Toronto ON M9B 6J7
Tel: 416-695-4114; *Fax:* 416-695-9920
Toll-Free: 888-336-4722
oirca@ontarioroofing.com
www.ontarioroofing.com
www.linkedin.com/company-beta/3499282
Overview: A medium-sized provincial organization founded in 1964 overseen by Canadian Roofing Contractors' Association
Mission: To act as the voice of the industrial-commercial roofing industry in Ontario; To promote excellence in roofing construction
Member of: Canadian Roofing Contractors' Association
Affiliation(s): Construction Safety Association of Ontario
Membership: *Member Profile:* Roofing & sheet metal contractors from Ontario; Engineers; Manufacturers; Product suppliers; Industry members who are interested in roofing activities; *Committees:* Rooftop Rescue Foundation; Labour Relations; Membership; Risk Management; Strategic Planning; Technical; IHSA Roofer Safety
Activities: Promoting good business ethics; Encouraging compliance with standards of occupational health & safety; Providing continuing education & training; Issuing bulletins (Technical, Safety & Member)
Chief Officer(s):
Wesley Lamb, President
Peter Serino, Treasurer
Awards:
• Ontario Industrial Roofing Contractors' Association Annual Zero Frequency Category Awards
To recognize companies in Ontario that worked without a lost time injury during the year
Publications:
• Low-Slope Roofing - Health & Safety Manual
Price: Free
Profile: Released in conjunction with the Infrastructure Health & Safety Association
• Ontario Roofing News
Type: Newsletter
Profile: Articles about current trends in roofing, plus association news, & upcoming events

Ontario Insolvency Practitioners Association *See* Ontario Association of Insolvency & Restructuring Professionals

Ontario Institute of Agrologists (OIA)
Ontario AgriCentre, #108, 100 Stone Rd. West, Guelph ON N1G 5L3
Tel: 519-826-4226; *Fax:* 519-826-4228
Toll-Free: 866-339-7619
www.oia.on.ca

ca.linkedin.com/company/ontario-institute-of-agrologists
www.facebook.com/ontarioinstituteofagrologists
www.youtube.com/playlist?list=PLEF3F4C0E83C69744
Overview: A medium-sized provincial organization founded in 1960 overseen by Agricultural Institute of Canada
Mission: To regulate Ontario's Professional Agrologists & ensure that competencies meet a Standard of Practice within a specific scope of agrology
Affiliation(s): Certified Crop Advisor Program; Ontario Agricultural Hall of Fame Association; Ontario Agricultural Training Institute; Ontario Farm Animal Council; Western Fair Association
Staff Member(s): 2
Membership: *Fees:* Schedule available; *Member Profile:* B.Sc (Agriculture) from Canadian university or equivalent
Activities: *Internships:* Yes
Chief Officer(s):
Drew Orosz, President
Terry Kingsmill, Registrar, 519-826-4226 Ext. 230
Awards:
• Public Relations Award
Presented to a member who has made an outstanding contribution to promoting OIA
• Branch Newsletter Award
Presented to the branch newsletter editor deemed by the Membership Committee to produce the most effective branch newsletter for their members
• Cheryl Somerville Memorial Distinguished Young Agrologist Award
Presented annually to an individual under 40 years of age who has made significant contributions to the agriculture & food industry in this province, the profession of agrology &/or the OIA
• Distinguished Agrologist
Member individuals who have rendered signal service to the agricultural industry of Ontario &/or the affairs of the OIA
• Honourary Life Member
Individuals who have rendered signal service to the agricultural industry of Ontario
• President's Honour Roll
Member individuals who have contributed greatly to branch effectiveness during the year
Meetings/Conferences:
• Canadian Greenhouse Conference 2018, October, 2018, Scotiabank Convention Centre, Niagara Falls, ON
Scope: National
Description: Held annually since 1979 the CGC is committed to providing a high quality conference experience for the extension of information through speakers, workshops, demonstration and exhibits.
  Central Branch
  Toronto ON
  Chief Officer(s):
  Dwight Greer, Contact
  Guelph Branch
  Guelph ON
  Chief Officer(s):
  Dean Anderson, Contact
  Hamilton Branch
  Hamilton ON
  Chief Officer(s):
  Doug Yungblut, Contact
  Huronia Branch
  Midland ON
  Chief Officer(s):
  Mary Ruth McDonald, Contact
  Long Point Branch
  RR#4, Hagersville ON N0E 1W0
  Niagara Branch
  St Catharines ON
  Chief Officer(s):
  George Mitges, Contact
  Northern Branch
  PO Box 555, Emo ON P0W 1E0
  Tel: 807-482-2420
  puritysl@jam21.net
  Ottawa-St. Lawrence Branch
  Ottawa ON
  Chief Officer(s):
  Christopher P. Dufault, Contact
  Quinte Branch
  RR#1, 4727 County Rd. 2, Port Hope ON L1A 3V5
  Tel: 905-475-4908; *Fax:* 905-475-3835
  pcoughler@cogeco.ca

Canadian Associations / Ontario Insurance Adjusters Association (OIAA)

Southwestern Branch
ON
Western Branch
London ON
oaa.westernbranch@gmail.com
Chief Officer(s):
Robin Blythe, Contact

Ontario Institute of the Purchasing Management Association of Canada See Supply Chain Management Association - Ontario

Ontario Insurance Adjusters Association (OIAA)
29 De Jong Dr., Mississauga ON L5M 1B9
Tel: 905-542-0576; Fax: 905-542-1301
Toll-Free: 888-259-1555
manager@oiaa.com
www.oiaa.com
www.facebook.com/OntarioInsuranceAdjustersAssociation
twitter.com/PresidentOIAA
Overview: A medium-sized provincial organization founded in 1930
Mission: To promote & maintain a high standard of ethics in the business of insurance claims adjusting
Membership: Fees: $45.20; Member Profile: Insurance adjusters actively adjusting claims; Committees: Communications; Education; Benevolent & Community; Conferences; Industry; Association Operations; Entertainment
Chief Officer(s):
Tammie Norn, President
tnorn@proadjusting.ca
Meetings/Conferences:
• Ontario Insurance Adjusters Association 2018 Claims Conference, January, 2018
Scope: Provincial

Ontario Jaguar Owners Association (OJOA)
12 Alexander Hunter Pl., Markham ON L6E 1A8
www.ojoa.org
Overview: A small provincial organization founded in 1959
Mission: To promote the preservation, ownership, & operation of Jaguar automobiles
Affiliation(s): Jaguar Clubs of North America (JCNA)
Membership: 260; Fees: $80 individual; $90 family
Chief Officer(s):
John Myers, President
johnamyers@rogers.com
Karen Carlson, Secretary
k.carlson@sympatico.ca

Ontario Jiu-Jitsu Association (OJA)
#7, 40 Bell Farm Rd., Barrie ON L4M 5L3
Tel: 705-725-9186; Fax: 705-725-8562
Toll-Free: 800-352-1338
www.ontariojiujitsu.com
www.facebook.com/jiujitsuontario
Overview: A medium-sized provincial organization founded in 1963
Mission: To promote Jiu Jitsu among amateurs in Ontario
Membership: Fees: $150 club; $20 club; $35 black belt; $25 adult; $190 private training centre; Committees: Finance; Membership & Promotion; Safety & Insurance; Technical; Tournament; Volunteer; Canadian Jiu Jitsu Grading Board
Chief Officer(s):
Doug Knispel, President
dknispel@rci.rogers.com

Ontario Katahdin Sheep Association Inc. (OKSA)
c/o Kim Henzie, Sweetwater Farms, RR#2, Norwood ON K0L 2V0
Tel: 705-696-3193
www.katahdin.ca
Overview: A small provincial organization overseen by Canadian Katahdin Sheep Association Inc.
Mission: To develop & expand the Katahdin sheep industry in Ontario
Membership: 20; Member Profile: Katahdin sheep breeders in Ontario
Activities: Promoting Katahdin sheep; Educating association members & the public about the breeding, raising, uses, & heritage of Katahdin sheep; Hosting inspection clinics for members; Collecting & preserving data; Increasing efficiency in animal husbandry
Chief Officer(s):
Donna Aziz, President, 905-852-9252
rolypolyfarms@yahoo.com

Brian Harris, Vice-President, 705-526-7509
brianrobertharris@gmail.com
Kim Henzie, Secretary-Treasurer
kim@sweetwaterfarms.com

Ontario Kinesiology Association (OKA)
#100, 6700 Century Ave., Mississauga ON L5N 6A4
Tel: 905-567-7194; Fax: 905-567-7191
info@oka.on.ca
www.oka.on.ca
www.linkedin.com/groups?home=&gid=1264707
www.facebook.com/ontariokinesiologyassociation
twitter.com/ONKinesiology
Overview: A medium-sized provincial organization founded in 1982
Mission: To promote the application of the science of human movement to other professionals & to the community; to uphold the standards of the profession of kinesiology; to assist kinesiologists in the performance of their duties & responsibilities
Member of: Canadian Kinesiology Alliance
Finances: Funding Sources: Membership fees; sponsorship; advertising
Membership: 2,000; Fees: $282.50; $141.25 affiliate; $56.50 student
Activities: Awareness Events: Kin Week; Speaker Service: Yes; Rents Mailing List: Yes
Chief Officer(s):
Jennifer Chapman, President
Meetings/Conferences:
• 2018 Ontario Kinesiology Association Conference & AGM, 2018, ON
Scope: Provincial

Ontario Labour-Management Arbitrators Association (OLMAA)
#701, 100 Adelaide St. West, Toronto ON M5H 1S3
Tel: 416-366-3091; Fax: 416-366-0879
info@labourarbitrators.org
www.labourarbitrators.org
Overview: A small provincial organization
Mission: To promote practices that mediate labour relations
Membership: 123; Member Profile: Labour arbitrators

Ontario Lacrosse Association
#306, 3 Concorde Gate, Toronto ON M3C 3N7
Tel: 416-426-7066; Fax: 416-426-7382
www.ontariolacrosse.com
twitter.com/OntarioLacrosse
Overview: A small provincial organization founded in 1897 overseen by Canadian Lacrosse Association
Member of: Canadian Lacrosse Association
Chief Officer(s):
Stan Cockerton, Executive Director
stan@ontariolacrosse.com
Meetings/Conferences:
• Ontario Lacrosse Association 2018 Annual General Meeting, 2018, ON
Scope: Provincial

Ontario Lawn Bowls Association
c/o Edith Pedden, 471 Silvery Lane, Marberly ON K0H 2B0
olba@olba.ca
www.olba.ca
www.facebook.com/groups/138144062931120
Overview: A medium-sized provincial organization overseen by Bowls Canada Boulingrin
Finances: Funding Sources: Membership fees; Sponsorships
Membership: Fees: Schedule available; Member Profile: Ontario lawn bowls clubs; Committees: Annual General Meetings; Achievement Awards; Annual; Bowls Canada Delegates; By-Laws; Championships, Indoors/Short-Mat & Championship Awards; Coaching; Database; Distribution, Sales, New Bowler Kits; E-Banter; Finance; Funding/Grants; Greens; Juniors; Marketing/Go Lawn Bowl; Memorial Fund; Nominating; Officiating; Planning & Development; Player Development; Promotion & Sponsorship; Safety & Risk Management; Visually Impaired/Physically Disabled Bowlers; Website
Activities: Providing programs, information & resources to member clubs; Campaigning for member recruitment; Assisting clubs that want to host provincial or national championships; Presenting awards, plaques, & certificates
Chief Officer(s):
Mike Landry, President
olba@olba.ca
Elaine Stevenson, Contact, Membership
membership@olba.ca

Awards:
• Membership Increase Award
Contact: Deb Hare, Director, Awards Committee, E-mail: hare@olba.ca
• Volunteer of the Year Award
Contact: Deb Hare, Director, Awards Committee, E-mail: hare@olba.ca
Meetings/Conferences:
• Ontario Lawn Bowls Association Spring General Meeting 2018, April, 2018, Holiday Inn Oakville, Oakville, ON
Scope: Provincial
Publications:
• Ontario Lawn Bowls Association e-Bulletin
Type: Newsletter; Editor: Jan Bauer
Profile: Reports on championships & forthcoming events

Ontario Lawn Tennis Association See Ontario Tennis Association

Ontario Learning Partnership Group See Ontario Business Education Partnership

Ontario Liberal Party (OLP)
#210, 10 St. Mary St., Toronto ON M4Y 1P9
Fax: 416-323-9425
Toll-Free: 800-268-7250
info@ontarioliberal.ca
www.ontarioliberal.ca
www.linkedin.com/groups/3410725
www.facebook.com/OntarioLiberalParty
twitter.com/OntLiberal
www.youtube.com/OntarioLiberalTV
Overview: A medium-sized provincial organization overseen by The Liberal Party of Canada
Finances: Funding Sources: Donations
Membership: Fees: $10 regular; $5 youth and seniors
Chief Officer(s):
Kathleen Wynne, Leader
Brian Johns, President

Ontario Library & Information Technology Association (OLITA)
c/o Ontario Library Association, 2 Toronto St., 3rd Fl., Toronto ON M5C 2B6
Tel: 416-363-3388; Fax: 416-941-9581
Toll-Free: 866-873-9867
www.accessola.com/olita
Overview: A medium-sized provincial organization founded in 1992
Mission: To engage in the planning, development, design, application, & integration of technology in the library & information environment with the impact of emerging technologies on library service, & with the effect of automated technologies on people
Activities: Rents Mailing List: Yes
Chief Officer(s):
Mita Williams, President
mita@uwindsor.ca
Awards:
• OLITA Project Award
Honours a project that demonstrates leadership in the application of technology to benefit library users
Meetings/Conferences:
• Ontario Library & Information Technology Association Annual General Meeting 2018, 2018
Scope: Provincial
Publications:
• InsideOLITA [a publication of the Ontario Library & Information Technology Association]
Type: Newsletter; Editor: Elizabeth Mens
Profile: Explains OLITA programming & provides technological news from Ontario's libraries

Ontario Library Association (OLA)
2 Toronto St., 3rd Fl., Toronto ON M5C 2B6
Tel: 416-363-3388; Fax: 416-941-9581
Toll-Free: 866-873-9867
Other Communication: olaprograms@accessola.com
info@accessola.com
www.accessola.org
www.linkedin.com/groups/2747909
www.facebook.com/accessola
twitter.com/onlibraryassoc
www.youtube.com/user/ONLibraryAssoc
Overview: A medium-sized provincial charitable organization founded in 1900

Mission: To provide opportunities for people in the library & information field to share experience & expertise, & to create innovative solutions
Affiliation(s): Ontario College & University Library Association; Ontario Library & Information Technology Association; Ontario Library Boards' Association; Ontario Public Library Association; Ontario School Library Association; L'Association des bibliothécaires francophones de l'Ontario
Finances: *Annual Operating Budget:* $3 Million-$5 Million; *Funding Sources:* Sponsorships; Education programs; Publication sales; Membership fees; Donations
Staff Member(s): 11; 500 volunteer(s)
Membership: 5,000+; *Fees:* Schedule available; *Member Profile:* Librarians, library technicians, library suppliers, library staff, systems specialists, publishers, authors, producers, school administrators, teacher librarians, financial officers, directors, trustees, & friends of libraries; *Committees:* Advocacy; Annual Institute of Library as Place; Audit; Cultural Diversity & Inclusion; Copyright User Group; Forest of Reading; Indigenous Libraries Task Group; Finance; Governance Review; Marketing Libraries Think Tank; Mentoring; Nomination; OLA Awards; OLA Best Bests; OLA Revenue Development Task Force; OPLA Child & Youth Services; OPLA Community Led Libraries; OPLA Reader's Advisory; Special Libraries; Super Conference
Activities: Providing education & information, through seminars & virtual programs; Lobbying & political action; Coordinating mutual interests & needs; Offering services & products; Researching & developing programs & services; Defending free & equitable access to information; Providing networking opportunities through listservs & chat groups; *Awareness Events:* "A Forest of Reading": The Ontario Library Association's Literacy Initiative, April (voting day) & May (ceremony); *Internships:* Yes
Chief Officer(s):
Shelagh Paterson, Executive Director, 416-363-3388 Ext. 224
spaterson@accessola.com
Stephanie Pimentel, Manager, Operations, 416-363-3388 Ext. 225
spimentel@accessola.com
Michelle Arbuckle, Director, Member Engagement & Education, 416-363-3388 Ext. 230
marbuckle@accessola.com
Meredith Tutching, Director, Forest of Reading, 416-363-3388 Ext. 222
mtutching@accessola.com
Lauren Hummel, Coordinator, Event & Marketing, 416-363-3388 Ext. 227
lhummel@accessola.com
Mary-Rose O'Connor, Coordinator, Education, 416-363-3388 Ext. 223
moconnor@accessola.com
Rachelle DesRochers, Coordinator, Administration, 416-363-3388 Ext. 244
rdesrochers@accessola.com
Awards:
• OLA's Larry Moore Distinguished Service Award
Awarded to an OLA member who has made an oustanding contribution to Ontario libraries through service
• OLA President's Award for Exceptional Achievement
Acknowledges an outstanding action or contribution that has furthered librarianship in Ontario in a unique way
• OLA Les Fowlie Intellectual Freedom Award
• OLA Media & Communications Award
• OLA Library Building Award
• OLA Technical Services Award
Awarded to an Ontario librarian, teacher-librarian, technician, library worker or department who has made a substantial achievement in technical library services
• OLA Archival & Preservation Achievement Award
Awarded to Ontario-based individuals or institutions who have made significant achievements in the field of preservation & conservation for libraries or archives
• OLA Champion Award
Awarded to recognize partnerships within the OLA that demonstrate significant contributions & commitment to the association
Meetings/Conferences:
• Ontario Library Association 2018 Super Conference, January, 2018, Metro Toronto Convention Centre, Toronto, ON
Scope: Provincial
Attendance: 4,500+
Description: An annual gathering of delegates, speakers, & exhibitors for a continuing education event in librarianship
Contact Information: superconference@accessola.com

Publications:
• Open Shelf [a publication of the Ontario Library Association]
Type: Magazine; *Accepts Advertising; Editor:* Mike Ridley; *ISSN:* 2368-1837
Profile: Association activities plus trends & issues affecting libraries

Ontario Library Boards' Association (OLBA)
c/o Ontario Library Association, 2 Toronto St., 3rd Fl., Toronto ON M5C 2B6
Tel: 416-363-3388; *Fax:* 416-941-9581
Toll-Free: 866-873-9867
info@accessola.com
www.accessola.org
Previous Name: Ontario Library Trustees Association
Overview: A medium-sized provincial charitable organization
Mission: To represent Ontario public library board members on issues that affect library board leadership; To advance public library board development & improve the management & services of libraries throughout Ontario; To enhance the visibility of library boards
Affiliation(s): Ontario Library Association
Membership: *Member Profile:* Ontario public library board members (trustees)
Activities: Building a professional development program & ensuring continuing education of Ontario public library trustees; Providing information materials about public library governance, board roles, & the legislation on public libraries; Promoting Ontario Public Library Guidelines; Collaborating with related agencies; Promoting government support; Providing the listserv to connect members across the province
Chief Officer(s):
Kerry Badgley, President
Awards:
• W.J. Robertson Medallion
Awarded to a public librarian in Ontario who has demonstrated outstanding leadership in the advancement of public library service
• Joyce Cunningham Award
Awarded to a public library board that demonstrates a high level of collaboration & innovation to produce outstanding results
Meetings/Conferences:
• Ontario Library Boards' Association 2018 Annual General Meeting, 2018, ON
Scope: Provincial
Description: AGM reports from executive members, the business of the association, statement of expenses, & the introduction of the new council
Publications:
• Inside OLBA [Ontario Library Boards' Association]
Type: Newsletter; *Frequency:* Quarterly
Profile: Articles about current library issues, OLBA activities, & profiles of trustees
• Ontario Library Boards' Association Annual Report
Type: Yearbook; *Frequency:* Annually

Ontario Library Trustees Association *See* Ontario Library Boards' Association

Ontario Limousine Owners Association (OLOA)
10 Sunbeam Ave., Toronto ON M3H 1W7
Tel: 416-233-3029; *Fax:* 416-638-1699
Toll-Free: 866-700-6562
info@oloa.ca
www.oloa.ca
Overview: A small provincial organization founded in 1996
Mission: To represent limousine operators in Ontario; To provide members with a unified voice to approach regulatory agencies, politicians, & lawmakers with information regarding issues affecting the limousine industry
Membership: 175
Chief Officer(s):
John Dahdaly, President

Ontario Literacy Coalition *See* Essential Skills Ontario

Ontario Long Term Care Association (OLTCA)
#500, 425 University Ave., Toronto ON M5G 1T6
Tel: 647-856-3490; *Fax:* 416-642-0635
info@oltca.com
www.oltca.com
twitter.com/oltcanews
www.youtube.com/user/OLTCA345
Previous Name: Ontario Nursing Home Association
Overview: A medium-sized provincial licensing organization founded in 1959 overseen by Canadian Alliance for Long Term Care

Mission: Provides professional leadership to the long-term care sector; to empower long-term care facilities to provide high quality & cost-effective health care & accommodation services
Member of: Canadian Alliance for Long Term Care
Finances: *Funding Sources:* Membership dues
Membership: 440 long term care homes
Activities: *Awareness Events:* Long Term Care Facility Month, June; Occupational Health & Safety Week, Oct.; *Rents Mailing List:* Yes
Chief Officer(s):
Candace Chartier, CEO, 905-470-8995 Ext. 22
cchartier@oltca.com
Judy Irwin, Senior Manager, Communications, 904-470-8995 Ext. 33
jirwin@oltca.com

Ontario Luge Association (OLA)
3073 Victoria Heights Cres., Ottawa ON K1T 3M7
Tel: 613-262-5513
ontarioluge@gmail.com
ontarioluge.ca
www.facebook.com/OntarioLugeAssociation
twitter.com/OntarioLuge
Overview: A medium-sized provincial organization
Mission: To promote luge in Ontario
Affiliation(s): Canadian Luge Association
Membership: *Fees:* $5 indiviual; $10 under 16

Ontario Lumber Manufacturers' Association (OLMA) / Association des manufacturiers de bois de sciage de l'Ontario
244 Viau Rd., Noelville ON P0M 2N0
Tel: 705-618-3403; *Fax:* 705-898-3403
info@olma.ca
olma.ca
Overview: A medium-sized provincial organization founded in 1966
Mission: To ensure a sound & renewable forest economy; To oversee lumber grading licenses & quality control at member sawmills in Ontario; To ensure market access within Northern America, Europe, & Japan
Affiliation(s): Canadian Lumber Standards Accreditation Board; American Lumber Standards Committee, Inc.
Membership: *Member Profile:* Ontario sawmills, planing mills, lumber remanufacturers, & MSR & Fj manufacturers; Ontario companies engaged in equipment manufacturing, & lumber sales & distribution
Activities: Training persons to classify lumber; Supervising the grading of lumber; Authorizing manufacturing facilities to mark pieces of lumber with the OLMA facsimile stamp; Mediating disputes between sellers & buyers of lumber with the OLMA stamp; Promoting trade & diversification; Improving access to markets for Canadian softwood lumber; Reviewing forestry issues & policies; Liaising with government
Chief Officer(s):
André G. Boucher, President/Chief Lumber Grading Inspector
aboucher@olma.ca
Awards:
• Ontario Lumber Manufacturers' Association Lumberjack Award
To recognize the outstanding lumberjack of the year

Ontario Lung Association (OLA)
#401, 18 Wynford Dr., Toronto ON M3C 0K8
Tel: 416-864-9911; *Fax:* 416-864-9916
Toll-Free: 888-344-5864
info@lungontario.ca
www.lungontario.ca
www.facebook.com/OntarioLungAssociation
twitter.com/OntarioLung
www.youtube.com/user/ONLungAssociation
Overview: A large provincial charitable organization founded in 1945 overseen by Canadian Lung Association
Mission: To provide lung health information & support to people affected by lung disease; To prevent & control chronic lung disease
Finances: *Funding Sources:* Donations; Fundraising; Sponsorships
Activities: Supporting lung health research; Providing education about asthma (Asthma Action Helpline) & chronic obstructive pulmonary disease (BreathWorks Program); Offering smoking cessation information; *Awareness Events:* I Love Lungs Race; The Amazing Pace; Tulip Day
Chief Officer(s):
George Habib, President & CEO, 416-864-9911 Ext. 237
ghabib@lungontario.ca

Canadian Associations / Ontario Maple Syrup Producers' Association (OMSPA)

Suresh Naraine, Chief Financial Officer, 416-864-9911 Ext. 263
snaraine@lungontario.ca
Tim Alcock, Vice-President, Operations, 416-864-9911 Ext. 249
talcock@lungontario.ca
Peter Glazier, Vice-President, Marketing, Development & Public Affairs, 416-864-9911 Ext. 251
pglazier@lungontario.ca
Publications:
• Asthma Action [a publication of the Ontario Lung Association]
Type: Newsletter
• Breathworks [a publication of the Ontario Lung Association]
Type: Newsletter

Belleville Office (Hastings & Prince Edward Counties)
#339, 110 North Front St. A3, Belleville ON K8P 0A6
Tel: 613-969-0323
www.on.lung.ca
Mission: To provide lung health resources in the Ontario counties of Hastings & Prince Edward
Chief Officer(s):
Lola McMurter, Coordinator, Special Events
lmcmurter@on.lung.ca

Brantford Office (Brant County)
410 Colborne St., Lower Level, Brantford ON N3S 3N6
Tel: 519-753-4682; *Fax:* 519-753-4667
brant@on.lung.ca
www.on.lung.ca
Mission: To provide lung health resources in Brant County, Ontario

Hamilton Office (Hamilton, Brant County, Niagara, Haldimand & Norfolk Counties, & Waterloo & Wellington Regions)
#255, 245 King George St., Brantford ON N3R 7N7
Tel: 905-383-1616
Toll-Free: 800-790-5527
hamilton@on.lung.ca
www.on.lung.ca
Mission: To provide resources about lung health to persons in Hamilton, Brant, Haldimand-Norfolk, Waterloo & Wellington, & Niagara areas

Kingston Office (Kingston & the Thousand Islands)
#339, 110 North Front St. A3, Belleville ON K8P 0A6
Tel: 613-545-3462
www.on.lung.ca
Mission: To serve the Ontario counties of Frontenac, Lennox, Addington, Leeds & Grenville
Chief Officer(s):
Lola McMurter, Coordinator, Volunteer & Fund Development
lmcmurter@on.lung.ca

London Office (Bluewater-Thames Valley)
#2, 639 Southdale Rd. East, London ON N6E 3M2
Tel: 519-453-9086; *Fax:* 519-453-9184
Mission: To serve Lambton, Elgin, London, Middlesex, & Oxford Counties
Chief Officer(s):
Lori Pallen, Regional Manager
lpallen@on.lung.ca

Ottawa Office (Ottawa, Renfrew County, & Cornwall Area)
#500, 2319 St. Laurent Blvd., Ottawa ON K1G 4J8
Tel: 613-230-4200; *Fax:* 613-230-5210
Mission: To provide service & support in Renfrew, Ottawa, Lanark, Prescott, Russell, Stormont, & Dundas & Glengarry Counties
Chief Officer(s):
Melanie Estable-Porter, Officer, Corporate & Community Development
melanie@on.lung.ca

Sault Ste Marie Office (Algoma Area)
514 Queen St. East, 1st Fl., Sault Ste Marie ON P6A 2A1
Tel: 705-256-2335; *Fax:* 705-256-1210
Mission: To serve the Algoma District
Chief Officer(s):
Grace Briglio, Coordinator, Volunteer & Fund Development
gbriglio@on.lung.ca

Stratford Office (Huron-Perth)
#105, 356 Ontario St., Stratford ON N5A 7X6
Tel: 519-271-7500; *Fax:* 519-271-7503
Mission: To serve Huron & Perth Counties
Chief Officer(s):
Deedee Herman, Area Manager
dherman@on.lung.ca

Toronto Office (Greater Toronto Area West)
#401, 18 Wynford Dr., Toronto ON M3C 0K8
Fax: 416-864-9916
Toll-Free: 888-344-5864
olalung@on.lung.ca
Mission: To serve the Halton, Dufferin, Peel, & York Region areas of Ontario

Windsor Office (Windsor-Essex & Chatham-Kent Area)
#210, 3041 Dougall Ave., Windsor ON N9E 1S3
Tel: 519-256-3433
Mission: To provide services to the Chatham-Kent & Windsor-Essex region
Chief Officer(s):
Julie Bortolotti, Coordinator, Volunteer & Fund Development
jbortolotti@on.lung.ca
• Windsor-Essex & Chatham-Kent Area Breathworks Support Group Newsletter
Type: Newsletter; *Frequency:* Monthly
Profile: Support & advice for patients with COPD & their caregivers

Ontario Maple Syrup Producers' Association (OMSPA)
275 Country Rd. 44, RR#4, Kemptville ON K0G 1J0
Tel: 613-258-2294; *Fax:* 613-258-0207
Toll-Free: 866-566-2753
admin@ontariomaple.com
www.ontariomaple.com
Overview: A small provincial organization founded in 1966
Mission: To promote Ontario maple products through research & education
Membership: 400+; *Fees:* $80 producer under 250 taps; $110 producer 250 or more taps; $110 associate; $30 affiliate;
Committees: Finance; Promotion; Research; Membership; Quality Assurance; Web Site Development
Chief Officer(s):
Rhonda Roantree, Office Administrator

Ontario Marathon Canoe & Kayak Racing Association (OMCKRA)
ON
info@omckra.com
www.omcra.ca
www.facebook.com/OntarioMarathonPaddling
Overview: A small provincial organization overseen by CanoeKayak Canada
Mission: To represent, promote & develop the sport of marathon canoe & kayak racing in Ontario.
Member of: CanoeKayak Canada
Publications:
• HUT! [a publication of the Ontario Marathon Canoe & Kayak Racing Association]
Type: Newsletter

Ontario Marine Operators Association *See* Boating Ontario

Ontario Masonry Contractors' Association (OMCA)
360 Superior Blvd., Mississauga ON L5T 2N7
Tel: 905-564-6622; *Fax:* 905-564-5744
cmc@canadamasonrycentre.com
www.canadamasonrycentre.com
Overview: A medium-sized provincial organization founded in 1971
Mission: To actively promote masonry in Ontario by providing technical & design assistance to professionals & help in the training of the labour force
Member of: Canadian Masonry Contractors' Association
Finances: *Funding Sources:* Membership dues
Staff Member(s): 7
Membership: 100-499; *Fees:* $460
Activities: *Library:* by appointment
Chief Officer(s):
John Blair, Executive Director

Ontario Massage Therapist Association *See* Registered Massage Therapists' Association of Ontario

Ontario Masters Athletics (OMA)
1185 Eglinton Ave. East, Toronto ON M3C 3C6
Tel: 416-426-4427; *Fax:* 416-426-7358
douglasj.smith@sympatico.ca
www.ontariomasters.ca
twitter.com/OntarioMasters
www.youtube.com/OntarioMasters
Previous Name: Ontario Masters Track & Field Association
Overview: A small provincial organization founded in 1973
Member of: Canadian Masters Athletic Association
Affiliation(s): Athletics Ontario; Athletics Canada
Membership: *Fees:* $40 individual; $60 family
Chief Officer(s):
Doug Smith, President
douglasj.smith@sympatico.ca
Karla Del Grande, Vice-President
karla.delgrande@bell.net

Ontario Masters Track & Field Association *See* Ontario Masters Athletics

Ontario Medical Association (OMA)
#900, 150 Bloor St. West, Toronto ON M5S 3C1
Tel: 416-599-2580; *Fax:* 416-340-2944
Toll-Free: 800-268-7215
Other Communication: membership@oma.org
info@oma.org
www.oma.org
www.linkedin.com/company/ontario-medical-association
www.facebook.com/Ontariosdoctors
twitter.com/OntariosDoctors
www.youtube.com/user/OntMedAssociation
Overview: A large provincial organization founded in 1880 overseen by Canadian Medical Association
Mission: To represent the clinical, political, & economic interests of Ontario physicians; To promote an accessible, quality health-care system
Membership: 30,000+; *Member Profile:* Practicing physicians, residents, & students who are enrolled in one of Ontario's faculties of medicine
Activities: Advocating for the health of Ontarians; Promoting health care services throughout Ontario; Providing a continuing medical education program; Offering tools to manage an effective practice, such as legal advice & incorporation services
Chief Officer(s):
Tom Magyarody, Chief Executive Officer
Danielle Milley, Senior Advisor, Media Relations, 416-599-2580
danielle.milley@oma.org
Awards:
• Ontario Medical Student Bursary Fund
• Ontario Medical Foundation Elective Bursaries
• Student Leadership Development Subsidy Program
• OMA Medical Student Achievement Award
Publications:
• Ontario Medical Review [a publication of the Ontario Medical Association]
Type: Journal; *Editor:* Kim Secord
• Scrub-In [a publication of the Ontario Medical Association]
Type: Magazine; *Frequency:* 3 pa.; *ISSN:* 1923-953X
Profile: Contains medical student-generated content written for a student audience

Ontario Medical Students Association (OMSA)
c/o Ontario Medical Association, #900, 150 Bloor St. West, Toronto ON M5S 3C1
Tel: 416-599-2580
Toll-Free: 800-268-7215
www.omsa.ca
www.facebook.com/OntarioMedicalStudents
twitter.com/OMSAofficial
www.instagram.com/OMSAofficial
Overview: A medium-sized provincial organization founded in 1974 overseen by Ontario Medical Association
Mission: To represent the concerns & views of medical students in Ontario
Member of: Ontario Medical Association
Affiliation(s): Canadian Medical Association
Membership: 3,000; *Fees:* $22; *Member Profile:* Ontario medical students; *Committees:* Communications; Education; Wellness
Activities: Lobbying the provincial government on issues such as tuition & government assistance to lower income students; Working to ensure adequate postgraduate training positions in Ontario; Offering seminars & a mentorship program, through the Ontario Medical Association (mentor@oma.org)
Chief Officer(s):
Ali Damji, Co-Chair
chair@omsa.ca
Justin Cottrell, Co-Chair
co-chair@omsa.ca
Awards:
• Ontario Medical Student Bursary Fund

Ontario Mental Health Foundation
180 Bloor St. West, #UC101, Toronto ON M5S 2V6
Tel: 416-920-7721; *Fax:* 416-920-0026
www.omhf.on.ca
www.linkedin.com/company/ontario-mental-health-foundation

www.facebook.com/TheOMHF
twitter.com/the_omhf
Overview: A small provincial charitable organization
Mission: To promote the mental health of people in Ontario; To improve the diagnosis & treatment of mental illness
Staff Member(s): 3
Membership: *Committees:* Audit & Finance; Conflict of Interest; Executive
Activities: Providing research grants, fellowships, & studentships; Supporting the professional development of researchers; Disseminating the results of funded research
Chief Officer(s):
Andrea Swinton, Executive Director
andreas@omhf.on.ca
Lauren Edding-Lee, Acting Officer, Program
laurene@omhf.on.ca
Publications:
• Ontario Mental Health Foundation Annual Report
Type: Yearbook; *Frequency:* Annually

Ontario Military Vehicle Association (OMVA)
c/o Peter Simundson, 6929 Estoril Rd., Mississauga ON L5N 1N2
Overview: A small provincial organization founded in 1986
Mission: To promote the place in history of Canadian military vehicles
Affiliation(s): Military Preservation Association
Finances: *Funding Sources:* Membership fees
Membership: 230+; *Fees:* $25 Canadian members; $30 international members; *Member Profile:* Military vehicle enthusiasts
Activities: Preserving Canadian military vehicles; Participating in parades, shows, & festivals
Chief Officer(s):
Peter Simundson, President, 905-826-6138
psimundson@rogers.com

Ontario Milk Transport Association (OMTA)
#301, 660 Speedvale Ave. West, Guelph ON N1K 1E5
Tel: 519-766-1133; *Fax:* 519-766-7722
Overview: A medium-sized provincial organization founded in 1967 overseen by Ontario Trucking Alliance
Mission: Collect raw milk from Ontario farms & take it to processing plants in Ontario, Manitoba & Quebec
Membership: 60 companies; *Member Profile:* Transporters of milk
Chief Officer(s):
John Johnston, General Manager, 519-766-1133

Ontario Mineral Exploration Federation (OMEF) See Ontario Prospectors Association

Ontario Mining Association (OMA)
#1201, 5775 Yonge St., Toronto ON M2M 4J1
Tel: 416-364-9301; *Fax:* 416-364-5986
info@oma.on.ca
www.oma.on.ca
twitter.com/OntMiningAssoc
www.youtube.com/user/miningontario;
www.pinterest.com/ontminingassoc
Overview: A medium-sized provincial organization founded in 1920 overseen by Mining Association of Canada
Mission: To help improve the competitiveness of the Ontario mineral industry
Finances: *Funding Sources:* Membership fees
Staff Member(s): 7
Membership: 88; *Member Profile:* Companies involved in the mining industry; *Committees:* Aboringal Relations; Energy; Education & Outreach; Environment; Hoist Plant; Mining Rules; Safety & Training; Workers' Compensation & Occupational Health
Activities: *Awareness Events:* Ontario Mining Week, 1st week of May
Chief Officer(s):
Chris Hodgson, President

Ontario Minor Hockey Association (OMHA)
#3, 25 Brodie Dr., Richmond Hill ON L4B 3K7
Tel: 905-780-6642; *Fax:* 905-780-0344
omha@omha.net
www.omha.net
www.facebook.com/HometownHockey
twitter.com/HometownHockey
instagram.com/ontariominorhockey
Overview: A medium-sized provincial organization founded in 1935
Mission: To provide community-based minor hockey programming for men, women, & children; To monitor the safety of the game, from equipment to rules
Affiliation(s): Ontario Hockey Federation
Finances: *Funding Sources:* Membership fees; Sponsorships
Membership: *Committees:* AAA Zone; Annual General Meeting; Appeals; Competition with Overseas Teams; By-law & Regulations; Development & Playing Rules; Finance; Group Structure; Maintenance Trust; Manual & Forms; Nominations; Select & Local League; Tournaments
Activities: Providing development programs; Conducting seminars, coaches clinics, skills camps, & festivals; Initiating safety measures, such as the concussion awareness program, a mouthguard policy, & helmets for all on-ice personnel
Chief Officer(s):
Richard Ropchan, Executive Director, 905-780-2150
Martha Dickie, Manager, Membership Services, 905-780-2159
Ian Taylor, Director, Hockey Development, 905-780-2172
Meetings/Conferences:
• 2018 Ontario Minor Hockey Association AGM, June, 2018, ON
Scope: Provincial
Description: Addressing the business of the association, plus revisions to regulations, policies, & procedures for the upcoming season
Publications:
• Hometown Hockey [a publication of the Ontario Minor Hockey Association]
Type: Magazine; *Frequency:* Quarterly
• OHF & OMHA [Ontario Minor Hockey Association]: Your Memberhip Opportunities & Benefits
• OMHA [Ontario Minor Hockey Association] Insider
Type: Newsletter; *Frequency:* Weekly; *Editor:* Mark Dickie
• OMHA [Ontario Minor Hockey Association] Manual of Operations: By-law, Regulations, & Policies
Type: Manual
• OMHA [Ontario Minor Hockey Association] Participant Guide
Type: Guide; *Frequency:* Annually
Profile: Detailed information of interest to OMHA parents & players

Ontario Mission of the Deaf See Bob Rumball Foundation for the Deaf

Ontario Modern Language Teachers Association (OMLTA) / Association ontarienne des professeurs de langues vivantes (AOPLV)
PO Box 268, 71 George St., Lanark ON K0G 1K0
omlta@omlta.org
www.omlta.org
www.facebook.com/omlta
twitter.com/omlta
Overview: A small provincial organization founded in 1886
Mission: To represent French & international languages teachers in the province of Ontario; To advocate on behalf of language educators; To promote the benefits of learning languages
Membership: *Fees:* $25 regular; $20 retired
Activities: Providing members with professional development opportunities; Advocating on behalf of membership; Forging strong partnerships with similar organizations to foster communication & networking
Chief Officer(s):
Jennifer Rochon, President
Meetings/Conferences:
• Ontario Modern Language Teachers Association Spring Conference 2018, March, 2018, Toronto, ON
Scope: Provincial
Description: Professional development & networking opportunities for members; 2018 theme is "Many Voices, Many Stories"
Publications:
• Communication [a publication of the Ontario Modern Language Teachers Association]
Type: Newsletter; *Frequency:* 3 pa; *Price:* Free with OMLTA membership
Profile: A resource exclusive to OMLTA members; includes practical strategies for the language classroom, classroomresources, & professional news & updates

Ontario Modern Pentathalon Association
c/o Shaun LaGrange, 513428 - 2 Line Amaranth, RR#4, Orangeville ON L9W 2Z1
Tel: 519-940-3721
www.ompa.ca
Overview: A medium-sized provincial organization
Mission: To promote modern pentathalon
Membership: *Fees:* $65 competitive; $20 supporting; $15 coach
Chief Officer(s):
Shaun LaGrange, President
salagrange@sympatico.ca

Ontario Monument Builders Association (OMBA)
PO Box 37, 137 Queenston St., Queenston ON L0S 1L0
Tel: 905-262-1359
info@omba.com
www.omba.com
Overview: A medium-sized provincial organization
Mission: To further the interests of the monument industry; To maintain high standards of business ethics for association members
Membership: *Member Profile:* Monument manufacturers & builders in Ontario, who subscribe to a code of ethics, & who comply with all legislation & regulations
Activities: Promoting the monument industry; Liaising with government & similar organizations
Chief Officer(s):
Doug King, Executive Director
Publications:
• Ontario Monument Builders Association Members Directory
Type: Directory

Ontario Motor Coach Association (OMCA)
#505, 555 Burnhamthorpe Rd., Toronto ON M9C 2Y3
Tel: 416-229-6622; *Fax:* 416-229-6281
info@omca.com
www.omca.com
www.facebook.com/72333053744
Overview: A medium-sized provincial organization founded in 1929
Mission: To further the interests of member bus companies by all possible & available means; To promote & further the interest of the inter-city bus & motor coach tour industry
Finances: *Funding Sources:* Membership dues; services
Staff Member(s): 5
Membership: *Fees:* Schedule available; *Member Profile:* Bus operators, tour operators, tour service providers & bus products & services manufacturers; *Committees:* Tour Operator; Supplier; Bus Operator; Executive; Conference; Golf; Membership
Activities: *Library:*
Chief Officer(s):
Doug Switzer, President/CEO, 416-229-6622 Ext. 222
doug@omca.com
Ann Fairley, Executive Vice-President, 416-229-6622 Ext. 223
ann@omca.com

Ontario Motor Vehicle Industry Council (OMVIC) / Conseil ontarien de commerce des véhicules automobiles
#300, 65 Overlea Blvd., Toronto ON M4H 1P1
Tel: 416-226-4500; *Fax:* 416-226-3208
Toll-Free: 800-943-6002
www.omvic.on.ca
www.facebook.com/71125415550
twitter.com/OMVIC_Consumers
www.youtube.com/user/buywithconfidence
Overview: A medium-sized provincial licensing organization founded in 1997
Mission: To enforce the Motor Vehicle Dealers Act (MVDA); To act as the self-management body of the motor vehicle dealer industry in Ontario, in order to protect the rights of consumers; to maintain a fair & safe marketplace in Ontario; To advance professionalism within the motor vehicle industry
Staff Member(s): 55
Membership: 8,800 registered dealers + 22,000 registered salespersons; *Member Profile:* Registered motor vehicle salespersons & registered dealers in Ontario, who must abide by the rules & regulations established in Ontario's Motor Vehicle Dealers Act (MVDA)
Activities: Providing services to motor vehicle dealers & salespersons in Ontario, the provincial government, consumers, & stakeholders in the industry; Informing consumers
Chief Officer(s):
Nazreen Ali, President & Chair
Cliff Pilon, Secretary-Treasurer
Carl Compton, Executive Director
Publications:
• Consumer Line
Type: Guide; *Frequency:* Monthly; *Price:* Free
Profile: A guide for consumers to the motor vehicle dealer industry in Ontario, featuring timely information about the industry & practical tips

Canadian Associations / Ontario Municipal Administrators' Association (OMAA)

- The Dealer Standard (formerly The Registrar's Report)
Author: Brenda McIntryre & Rob Kirsic
Profile: Information for registered dealers & salespersons throughout Ontario
- OMVIC Annual Report & Business Plan
Type: Yearbook; *Frequency:* Annually
Profile: Summary of Council activities, accomplishments, finances, & goals, submitted to the Minister of Government Services for review & approval

Ontario Municipal Administrators' Association (OMAA)
14 Caledonia Terrace, Goderich ON N7A 2M8
Toll-Free: 855-833-6622
www.omaa.on.ca
Overview: A medium-sized provincial organization
Mission: To support, promote, & strengthen Ontario's municipal administrators
Membership: 200; *Fees:* $375
Activities: Organizing workshops, events, & webinars for Chief Administrative Officers
Chief Officer(s):
Gary Dyke, President
Awards:
- Long Service Recogniton Awards
Recognizes OMAA members for years of service in a head municipal administrator position
- Robert Baldwin Award
Awarded to individuals who have made significant contributions to Ontario's municipal & local government
- OMAA Bursary
Eligibility: Students interested in a career in local government; *Amount:* $5,000

Ontario Municipal Human Resources Association (OMHRA)
#307, 1235 Fairview St., Burlington ON L7S 2K9
Tel: 905-631-7171; *Fax:* 905-631-2376
customerservice@omhra.on.ca
www.omhra.ca
Previous Name: Ontario Municipal Personnel Association
Overview: A medium-sized provincial organization founded in 1963
Mission: To provide direction on issues of human resources management; To represent the interests of the association, related to legislation & policies
Finances: *Funding Sources:* Membership fees; Sponsorships
Staff Member(s): 2
Membership: 300; *Fees:* $325 populations less than 50,000; $425 populations more than 50,000; *Member Profile:* Ontario human resources professionals who are employed by municipalities, commissions, & local public sector boards
Activities: Facilitating the exchange of information from the field of human resources; Promoting education
Chief Officer(s):
Elizabeth Bourns, President
Louise Ann Riddell, Vice-President
Christine A. Ball, Executive Officer
christine.ball@omhra.ca
Meetings/Conferences:
- Ontario Municipal Human Resources Association 2018 Spring Conference, April, 2018, Hilton Hotel, Niagara Falls, ON
Scope: Provincial

Ontario Municipal Management Development Board *See* Ontario Municipal Management Institute

Ontario Municipal Management Institute (OMMI)
618 Balmoral Dr., Oshawa ON L1J 3A7
Tel: 905-434-8885; *Fax:* 905-434-7381
ommi@bellnet.ca
www.ommi.on.ca
Previous Name: Ontario Municipal Management Development Board
Overview: A small provincial organization founded in 1979
Mission: To enhance management skills in order to strengthen local government administration
Membership: 350; *Member Profile:* Local governments, including cities, towns, regions & municipalities
Activities: Providing educational workshops & seminars; Conducting training opportunities; Certifying qualified candidates with the Certified Municipal Manager designation (CMM); Liaising with other professional local government associations
Chief Officer(s):
Bill McKim, Executive Director
bill@ommi.on.ca
Sandra Barter, Administrative Coordinator

Awards:
- Excellence in Training
- Distinguished Service Award
Publications:
- Councillor Development Resource Manual
Type: Manual
- You & Your Local Government
Type: Handbook

Ontario Municipal Personnel Association *See* Ontario Municipal Human Resources Association

Ontario Municipal Social Services Association (OMSSA) / Association des services sociaux des municipalités de l'Ontario
#2500, 1 Dundas St West, Toronto ON M5G 1Z3
Tel: 416-646-0513; *Fax:* 416-979-4627
info@omssa.com
www.omssa.com
www.linkedin.com/company/ontario-municipal-social-services-association
www.facebook.com/theOMSSA
twitter.com/theOMSSA
Overview: A large provincial organization founded in 1950
Mission: To promote high standards of competency within the profession to ensure quality delivery of human services in communities; To improve social policies & programs in the areas of affordable housing, homelessness prevention, children's services, & social assistance; To act as the voice for Consolidated Municipal Service Managers in Ontario
Membership: *Member Profile:* Individuals who plan, manage, deliver, & fund social & community services in Ontario at the municipal level; *Committees:* Policy & Advocacy; Professional Development; Human Services Integration Steering
Activities: Offering professional development opportunities; Providing networking activities; Presenting awards; Engaging in advocacy activities; Disseminating information; Raising awareness of the importance of human services
Chief Officer(s):
Petra Wolfbeiss, Acting Executive Director, 416-795-1514
pwolfbeiss@omssa.org
Awards:
- Lifetime Achievement Award
Deadline: February 8
- Local Municipal Champions Award
Deadline: February 8
- Champion of Human Services Award
Deadline: February 8
- Patti Moore Human Services Integration Award
Deadline: February 8
Meetings/Conferences:
- Ontario Municipal Social Services Association Annual General Meeting 2018, 2018
Scope: Provincial
Publications:
- OMSSA This Week [a publication of the Ontario Municipal Social Services Association]
Type: Newsletter; *Frequency:* Weekly
Profile: OMSSA activities & initiatives
- Ontario Municipal Social Services Association Annual Report
Type: Yearbook; *Frequency:* Annually
Profile: Association acheivements & financial information

Ontario Municipal Tax & Revenue Association (OMTRA)
#119, 14845 - 6 Yonge St., Aurora ON L4G 6H8
webmaster@omtra.ca
www.omtra.ca
www.facebook.com/278364522173943
twitter.com/omtra1
Previous Name: Association of Municipal Tax Collectors of Ontario
Overview: A medium-sized provincial organization founded in 1967
Mission: To bring those persons in the municipal field of tax collecting into helpful association with each other; To promote improved standards of ethics & efficiency in tax collection methods & procedures; To consider, resolve, & recommend amendments to Provincial Acts which may improve the tax billing & collection administration; To encourage submissions & disseminate information of interest to its members; To encourage & assist in the development of educational training programs for collection personnel; To cooperate with other municipal associations; To foster good public relations
Membership: 277 Municipalities + 22 Associate
Chief Officer(s):

Connie Mesih, President
connie.mesih@mississauga.ca
Meetings/Conferences:
- Ontario Municipal Tax & Revenue Association 2018 Spring Seminar, 2018, ON
Scope: Provincial
- Ontario Municipal Tax & Revenue Association 2018 Fall Conference, 2018, ON
Scope: Provincial

Ontario Municipal Water Association (OMWA)
c/o Ed Houghton, 2593 Tenth Concession, Collingwood ON L9Y 3Y9
Tel: 705-443-8472; *Fax:* 705-443-4263
admin@omwa.org
www.omwa.org
Overview: A medium-sized provincial organization
Mission: To act as the voice of Ontario's public water authorities
Affiliation(s): Ontario Water Works Association (a section of the American Water Works Association)
Membership: 200+ public drinking water authorities in Ontario; *Fees:* Schedule available, based upon population; *Member Profile:* Ontario's public water supply authorities; *Committees:* Resolutions; Communications & Website; Annual Conference; Awards/Service Recognition/Bursary; Nominations; Government Affairs; Finance
Activities: Reviewing policy & legislative & regulatory issues; Liaising with government, agencies & associations to maintain safe & sustainable water sources; Lobbying to improve conditions; Promoting high standards of treatment, infrastructure & operations; Offering technical training for operating authorities, operators & owners of drinking water systems; Encouraging dissemination of information for public education; Joint conferences with the Ontario Water Works Association (OWWA)
Chief Officer(s):
Ed Houghton, Executive Director, 705-445-1800, Fax: 705-445-0791
ehoughton@omwa.org
Awards:
- Award of Exceptional Merit
- Don Black Award
- OMWA Industry Leadership Award
- OMWA Student Bursary
Deadline: November 15; *Amount:* $500 (4)
Publications:
- Councillors Handbook: Stewardship Responsibilities Under the Safe Drinking Water Act
Type: Handbook
- Ontario Municipal Water Association Members' Handbook
Type: Handbook

Ontario Museum Association (OMA) / Association des musées de l'Ontario
George Brown House, 50 Baldwin St., Toronto ON M5T 1L4
Tel: 416-348-8672; *Fax:* 416-348-0438
Toll-Free: 866-662-8672
www.museumsontario.ca
www.facebook.com/museumsontario
twitter.com/museumsontario
Overview: A medium-sized provincial charitable organization founded in 1972
Mission: To enhance museums as significant cultural resources in the service of Ontario society & its development
Member of: Canadian Museums Association
Affiliation(s): Ontario Heritage Alliance
Finances: *Annual Operating Budget:* $250,000-$500,000; *Funding Sources:* Ontario Ministry of Citizenship, Culture & Recreation; Dept. of Canadian Heritage; membership fees
Staff Member(s): 6
Membership: 650 individual + 225 institutional; *Fees:* Schedule available; *Committees:* Advocacy; Award of Merit; Computer Advisory; Conference; Finance; Human Resources; Membership & Public Affairs; Publications
Activities: Serves as an information resource concerning Ontario's museums; Advocates on behalf of museums & their supporters; Fosters professional standards through seminars & courses; Promotes public understanding of museums; *Library:* by appointment
Chief Officer(s):
Marie Lalonde, Executive Director
Meetings/Conferences:
- 2018 Ontario Museum Association Annual Conference, October, 2018, Kingston, ON
Scope: National

Ontario Music Educators' Association (OMEA)
ON
www.omea.on.ca
www.facebook.com/OMEAOntario
twitter.com/OMEAOntario
Overview: A small provincial organization founded in 1949
Mission: The Ontario Music Educators' Association (OMEA), a non-profit organization that represents music educators in Ontario.
Membership: *Member Profile:* Music educators in Ontario
Chief Officer(s):
David Gueulette, President
Meetings/Conferences:
• Ontario Music Educators' Association Counterpoint 2018, November, 2018, Hamilton, ON
Scope: Provincial
Publications:
• The Recorder
Type: Journal; *Frequency:* Quarterly

Ontario Music Festivals Association (OMFA)
17 Pinemore Cres., Toronto ON M3A 1W5
Toll-Free: 888-307-6632
mail@omfa.ca
www.omfa.ca
www.facebook.com/ONTMUSFEST
Overview: A medium-sized provincial organization overseen by Federation of Canadian Music Festivals
Mission: To promote the performance of classical music by Ontario's youth; To encourage knowledge of classical music
Member of: Federation of Canadian Music Festivals (FCMF)
Finances: *Funding Sources:* Membership fees; Sponsorships
Membership: 44 music festivals; *Member Profile:* Music festivals across Ontario
Activities: Providing educational opportunities for music students & teachers; Creating networking opportunities with people from other music festivals; Facilitating the exchange of information
Chief Officer(s):
Martha Gregory, President
pgtamf@gmail.com
Pam Allen, Festival Administrator

Ontario Mutual Insurance Association (OMIA)
350 Pinebush Rd., Cambridge ON N1T 1Z6
Tel: 519-622-9220; *Fax:* 519-622-9227
info@omia.com
www.omia.com
Previous Name: Purely Mutual Underwriters Association; Mutual Fire Underwriters Association
Overview: A small provincial organization founded in 1882
Mission: To assist mutual insurance companies to achieve excellence in service provision
Affiliation(s): Canadian Association of Mutual Insurance Companies
Membership: *Member Profile:* Mutual insurance companies in Ontario that provide home, business, farm, & automobile insurance; Associate members in other provinces
Activities: Providing educational & training opportunities; Offering support services to member companies

Ontario Muzzle Loading Association (OMLA)
433 Queen St., Chatham ON N7M 5K5
Tel: 519-352-0924; *Fax:* 519-352-4380
Overview: A small provincial organization founded in 1973
Activities: Posting results from provincial matches & the Soper event

Ontario Native Education Counselling Association (ONECA)
PO Box 220, 37A Reserve Rd., Naughton ON P0M 2M0
Tel: 705-692-2999; *Fax:* 705-692-9988
oneca@oneca.com
www.oneca.com
Overview: A small provincial organization founded in 1985
Mission: To promote Native People to aspire to meet their potential through the ongoing development and improvement of Native Counselling and Education services.
Chief Officer(s):
Cindy Fisher, President
cfisher@picriver.com
Awards:
• Colin Wasacase Scholarship
• Four Directions Scholarship
Meetings/Conferences:
• Ontario Native Education Counselling Association Annual Conference, May, 2018, Thunder Bay, ON
Scope: Provincial

Ontario Native Women's Association (ONWA)
PO Box 15-684, 150 City Rd., Fort William First Nation ON P7J 1J7
Tel: 807-577-1492; *Fax:* 807-623-1104
Toll-Free: 800-667-0816
www.onwa.ca
www.facebook.com/onwa7
twitter.com/_onwa_
Overview: A medium-sized provincial organization founded in 1972 overseen by Native Women's Association of Canada
Mission: To foster & promote the economic, social, cultural, & political well-being of First Nations & Métis women in Ontario; To represent Native women on issues that affect their lives
Finances: *Funding Sources:* Government of Ontario, Aboriginal Healing & Wellness Strategy
Membership: *Member Profile:* Aboriginal women in Ontario from more than 80 organizations
Activities: Providing programs & services to improve the lives of Native women, such as recreational activities, workshops, & referrals
Chief Officer(s):
Dawn Harvard, President

Ontario Nature
#612, 214 King St. West, Toronto ON M5H 3S6
Tel: 416-444-8419; *Fax:* 416-444-9866
Toll-Free: 800-440-2366
info@ontarionature.org
www.ontarionature.org
www.facebook.com/OntarioNature
twitter.com/ontarionature
www.youtube.com/user/ONNature
Previous Name: Federation of Ontario Naturalists
Overview: A large provincial charitable organization founded in 1931
Mission: To promote knowledge, understanding & respect for Ontario's natural heritage & commitment to its conservation & protection on the part of the FON membership, landowners, decision makers & the general public; To seek legislation, policies, practices & institutions which permanently protect Ontario's natural ecosystem & indigenous biodiversity, including the establishment of a comprehensive natural heritage system for Ontario with an enlarged system of parks & other protected areas linked by a network of existing & rehabilitated natural corridors
Affiliation(s): Coalition on the Niagara Escarpment; Conservation Council of Ontario; International Union for Conservation of Nature & Natural Resources; International Committee for Bird Preservation
Finances: *Annual Operating Budget:* $1.5 Million-$3 Million; *Funding Sources:* Private donations; membership dues; foundations
Staff Member(s): 24; 100 volunteer(s)
Membership: 30,000 individuals + 140 member groups; *Fees:* $50
Activities: *Library:* by appointment
Chief Officer(s):
Caroline Schultz, Executive Director

Ontario Naturopathic Association *See* Ontario Association of Naturopathic Doctors

Ontario Network for the Prevention of Elder Abuse *See* Elder Abuse Ontario

Ontario Network of Employment Skills Training Projects / Réseau ontarien des organismes pour le développement de l'employabilité (ROODE)
116 Industry St., Toronto ON M6M 4L8
Tel: 416-767-1679; *Fax:* 888-272-9642
events@onestep.on.ca
www.onestep.ca
Also Known As: ONESTEP
Overview: A medium-sized provincial charitable organization founded in 1982
Member of: Canadian Centre for Philanthropy
Affiliation(s): Canadian Association of Educators & Trainers Organization
Finances: *Annual Operating Budget:* $500,000-$1.5 Million
Staff Member(s): 4; 15 volunteer(s)
Membership: 95; *Fees:* Schedule available; *Member Profile:* Organization must be non-profit in operation for at least 2 years & provide employment-related supports &/or services using the community-based training model
Activities: Advocacy; professional development; research; policy development; systems change; *Speaker Service:* Yes; *Library:* Onestep Resource Centre; Open to public
Chief Officer(s):
Ed Kothiringer, Executive Director
Lorraine Katanik, Manager, Career & Resource Solutions

Ontario Neurotrauma Foundation (ONF)
#601, 90 Eglinton Ave. East, Toronto ON M4P 2Y3
Tel: 416-422-2228; *Fax:* 416-422-1240
info@onf.org
www.onf.org
twitter.com/OntNeurotrauma
Overview: A medium-sized provincial organization founded in 1998
Mission: To reduce the impact, incidence & prevalence of neurotrauma injuries, through knowledge creation, Research Capacity Building, & knowledge mobilization
Finances: *Annual Operating Budget:* $1.5 Million-$3 Million; *Funding Sources:* Ontario Ministry of Health; Partnerships
Staff Member(s): 10
Membership: *Committees:* Finance
Activities: Offering grants to those researching neurotrauma
Chief Officer(s):
Mimi Lowi-Young, Chair
Kent Bassett-Spiers, Chief Executive Officer
kent@onf.org

Ontario Non-Profit Housing Association (ONPHA)
#400, 489 College St., Toronto ON M6G 1A5
Tel: 416-927-9144; *Fax:* 416-927-8401
Toll-Free: 800-297-6660
mail@onpha.org
www.onpha.on.ca
www.linkedin.com/company/ontario-non-profit-housing-association
www.facebook.com/ONPHA
Overview: A medium-sized provincial organization founded in 1988
Mission: To build a strong non-profit housing sector in Ontario; To strive for excellence in non-profit housing management; To represent non-profit housing
Finances: *Funding Sources:* Membership dues; Sponsorships
Staff Member(s): 20
Membership: 700+ organizations (housing more than 400,000 people); *Member Profile:* Non-profit organizations throughout Ontario which house persons in rental units; Individuals & organizations that support non-profit housing
Activities: Promoting new, affordable, & supportive housing for people in need in Ontario; Liaising with government & other organizations; Preparing position papers; Developing policy alternatives; Providing training; Offering management advice
Chief Officer(s):
Marlene Coffey, Executive Director
marlene.coffey@onpha.org
Michelle Coombs, Manager, Member Services, 416-927-9144 Ext. 111
michelle.coombs@onpha.org
Sarah Fisch, Coordinator, Communications, 416-927-9144 Ext. 122
jacqueline.waters@onpha.org
Helen Harris, Coordinator, Policy & Research, 416-927-9144 Ext. 109
helen.harris@onpha.org
Awards:
• Sybil Frenette Outstanding Leadership Award
• Tenant Achievement Recognition Award
• Lifetime of Service Recognition
• ONPHA Innovation Award
• Award for Excellence
• Kathleen Blinkhorn Aboriginal Student Scholarship Fund
; *Amount:* $1,000 *Contact:* scholarships@onpha.org
Meetings/Conferences:
• Ontario Non-Profit Housing Association 2018 Annual Conference, General Meeting & Trade Show, October, 2018, Sheraton Centre, Toronto, ON
Scope: Provincial
Description: Featuring speakers, workshops, & company exhibitors
Contact Information: Coordinator, Conference & Events: Sunny Chen, E-mail: Sunny.Chen@onpha.org, Phone: 416-927-9144, ext. 126
Publications:
• Ontario Non-Profit Housing Association Annual Report
Type: Yearbook; *Frequency:* Annually

- Ontario Non-Profit Housing Association Member Directory
Type: Directory
- Ontario Non-Profit Housing Association Administrative Policy Handbook
Type: Handbook; *Price:* $90
- Ontario Non-Profit Housing Association Asbestos Management Plan
Type: Handbook; *Price:* $70
- Ontario Non-Profit Housing Association Financial Policies & Procedures Handbook
Type: Handbook; *Price:* $120
- Ontario Non-Profit Housing Association Governance & Corporate Practices Handbook
Type: Handbook; *Price:* $120
- Ontario Non-Profit Housing Association Human Resources Handbook
Type: Handbook; *Price:* $100
- Ontario Non-Profit Housing Association Maintenance Planning Handbook
Type: Handbook; *Price:* $120
- Ontario Non-Profit Housing Association Tenant Handbook & Disk
Type: Handbook; *Price:* $70
- Ontario Non-Profit Housing Association Integrated Pest Management in Housing
Type: Handbook; *Price:* $79
- Ontario Non-Profit Housing Association Residential Tenancies Act Handbook
Type: Handbook; *Price:* $75

Ontario Nonprofit Network
#300, 2 St. Clair Ave. East, Toronto ON M4T 2T5
Tel: 416-642-5786
info@theonn.ca
www.theonn.ca
www.linkedin.com/company/ontario-nonprofit-network
www.facebook.com/OntarioNonprofitNetwork
twitter.com/o_n_n
www.youtube.com/user/TheONNetwork
Overview: A medium-sized provincial organization
Mission: To represent the non-profit sector of Ontario; To develop & analyze policies; To address issues affecting non-profits & charities
Membership: *Committees:* Policy
Activities: Developing sector advancement strategies with groups & leaders; Sharing information through webinars, conferences, meetings, & resources; Representing non-profits to provincial ministries
Chief Officer(s):
Cathy Taylor, Executive Director
cathy@theonn.ca
Kim Gignac, Manager, Operations & Membership Services
admin@theonn.ca
Sarah Matsushita, Manager, Communications & Network Engagement
sarah@theonn.ca
Kate Browning, Manager, Business Development & Strategic Partnerships
kate@theonn.ca

Ontario Numismatic Association (ONA)
c/o Bruce Raszmann, PO Box 40033, Stn. Waterloo Square, 75 King St. South, Waterloo ON N2J 4V1
the-ona.ca
Overview: A small local organization founded in 1962
Member of: Royal Canadian Numismatic Association
Membership: 320+; *Fees:* $5 juniors; $15 regular members; $17 spouses; $20 clubs or associations; $450 individual life membership; *Member Profile:* Numismatic clubs or associations; Individuals, such as professional numismatists & collectors; Families; Juniors up to age 18
Activities: Conducting research; Disseminating information; *Library:* Ontario Numismatic Association Education Library; Not open to public
Chief Officer(s):
Paul Petch, President, 416-745-3067
president@ontario-numismatic.org
Len Trakalo, Secretary
secretary@ontario-numismatic.org
Bruce Raszmann, Treasurer & Chair, Membership, 519-745-3104
Meetings/Conferences:
- Ontario Numismatic Association's 56th Annual Convention 2018, April, 2018, Kitchener Holiday Inn, Kitchener, ON
Scope: Provincial

Description: Education program, dealer participation, business meetings, & networking events
Publications:
- The ONA Numismatist
Type: Newsletter; *Frequency:* Bimonthly; *Number of Pages:* 36
Profile: Educational articles & information about Ontario coin club activities, plus a special annual convention issue

Ontario Nurses' Association (ONA) / Association des infirmières et infirmiers de l'Ontario
#400, 85 Grenville St., Toronto ON M5S 3A2
Tel: 416-964-8833; *Fax:* 416-964-8864
Toll-Free: 800-387-5580
onamail@ona.org
www.ona.org
www.facebook.com/OntarioNurses
twitter.com/ontarionurses
www.youtube.com/OntarioNurses
Overview: A large provincial organization founded in 1973
Mission: To improve the socio-economic welfare of members
Member of: Canadian Federation of Nurses Unions; Canadian Labour Congress
Finances: *Funding Sources:* Membership dues
Membership: 60,000 + 234 locals
Activities: *Speaker Service:* Yes; *Library:* by appointment
Chief Officer(s):
Vicki McKenna, President
vickim@ona.org
Marie Kelly, CEO & Chief Administrative Officer
Hamilton Office
#2R, 2 King St. West, Dundas ON L9H 6Z1
Tel: 905-628-0850; *Fax:* 905-628-2557
Toll-Free: 866-928-3496
Kingston Office
#201, 4 Cataraqui St., Kingston ON K7K 1Z7
Tel: 613-545-1110; *Fax:* 613-531-9043
London Office
#109, 1069 Wellington Rd. South, London ON N6E 2H6
Tel: 519-438-2153; *Fax:* 519-433-2050
Toll-Free: 866-933-2050
Orillia Office
#126A, 210 Memorial Ave., Orillia ON L3V 7V1
Tel: 705-327-0404; *Fax:* 705-327-0511
Toll-Free: 866-927-0511
Ottawa Office
#211, 1400 Clyde Ave., Nepean ON K2G 3J2
Tel: 613-226-3733; *Fax:* 613-723-0947
Toll-Free: 866-523-0947
Sudbury Office
#203, 40 Larch St., Sudbury ON P5E 5M7
Tel: 705-560-2610; *Fax:* 705-560-1411
Toll-Free: 866-460-1411
Thunder Bay Office
#200, 1139 Alloy Dr., Thunder Bay ON P7B 6M8
Tel: 807-344-9115; *Fax:* 807-344-8850
Toll-Free: 866-744-8850
Timmins Office
Canadian Mental Health Association Bldg., #203, 330 - 2nd Ave., Timmins ON P4N 8A4
Tel: 705-264-2294; *Fax:* 705-268-4355
Toll-Free: 866-568-4355
Windsor Office
#220, 3155 Howard Ave., Windsor ON N8X 3Y9
Tel: 519-966-6350; *Fax:* 519-972-0814
Toll-Free: 866-972-0814

Ontario Nursing Home Association See Ontario Long Term Care Association

Ontario Occupational Health Nurses Association (OOHNA)
#605, 302 The East Mall, Toronto ON M9B 6C7
Tel: 416-239-6462; *Fax:* 416-239-5462
Toll-Free: 866-664-6276
administration@oohna.on.ca
www.oohna.on.ca
www.linkedin.com/groups/OOHNA-Ontario-Occupational-Health-Nurses-5148429
twitter.com/OOHNA1
Overview: A medium-sized provincial organization founded in 1971
Mission: To foster a climate of excellence, innovation & partnership enabling Ontario Occupational Health Nurses to achieve positive workplace health & safety objectives
Member of: Canadian Occupational Health Nurses Association

Finances: *Funding Sources:* Membership fees
Staff Member(s): 3
Membership: 800+; *Fees:* $456.95 regular; $197.75 associate $56.50 retired; *Member Profile:* RN's practising occupational health & safety
Activities: *Speaker Service:* Yes
Chief Officer(s):
Ken Storen, President
board@oohna.on.ca
Brian Verrall, Executive Director
Awards:
- Award of Excellence
- Pat Ewen Bursary Award
- Lifetime Achievement Award
Meetings/Conferences:
- 47th Ontario Occupational Health Nurses Association Annual Conference, 2018, ON
Scope: Provincial
Description: Theme: "Keeping Workers Well"

Ontario Opticians Association (OOA)
PO Box 23518, Stn. Dexter, 5899 Leslie St., Toronto ON M2H 3R9
Tel: 905-709-4141; *Fax:* 416-226-6879
Toll-Free: 877-709-4141
info@ontario-opticians.com
www.ontario-opticians.com
www.facebook.com/ontarioopticiansassociation
Overview: A small provincial organization founded in 1946
Mission: To advance & protect the profession of opticianry
Member of: Opticians Association of Canada (OAC)
Membership: 1,200; *Fees:* $150 + $7.50 GST; Free students (first year); $25 students (second year & beyond); *Member Profile:* Dispensing opticians in Ontario; Students; New graduates; Intern opticians; Optical industry affiliates
Activities: Engaging in lobbying activities; Liaising with government; Presenting awards; Providing educational opportunities for Ontario opticians; Promoting the profession of opticianry; *Library:* Ontario Opticians Association Distance Module Library; Open to public
Chief Officer(s):
Martin Lebeau, President
Awards:
- Optician of the Year
- Student Achievement Awards
- Annual Industry Award
Publications:
- Focus [a publication of the Ontario Opticians Association]
Type: Newsletter; *Price:* Free with Ontario Opticians Association membership
Profile: Local & national issues, business advice, member benefits, & upcoming events

Ontario Painting Contractors Association (OPCA)
#10, 7611 Pine Valley Dr., Woodbridge ON L4L 0A2
Tel: 416-498-1897; *Fax:* 416-498-6757
Toll-Free: 800-461-3630
info@opca.org
www.ontpca.org
Overview: A medium-sized provincial organization founded in 1976
Mission: To foster, develop & maintain unity & stability among members by acting as a bargaining agent; providing services & educational opportunities; acting as a liaison between industry groups; upholding & improving the standards of the industry; promoting the use of modern specifications; advancing an attitude of ethical responsibility & pride
Member of: Construction Employers Coordinating Council of Ontario; Council of Ontario Construction Associations; Ontario Construction Secretariat
Affiliation(s): Federation of Painting & Decorating Contractors of Toronto; Architectural Painting Specifications Services Ltd.
Finances: *Annual Operating Budget:* $250,000-$500,000; *Funding Sources:* Membership dues
Staff Member(s): 2; 14 volunteer(s)
Membership: 57; *Fees:* Schedule available; *Member Profile:* Unionized, commercial, industrial & institutional painting contractors
Activities: *Speaker Service:* Yes
Chief Officer(s):
Thomas Corbett, President
Andrew Sefton, Executive Director
andrew.sefton@ontpca.org

Ontario Paramedic Association (OPA)
PO Box 1628, Blind River ON P0R 1B0

Toll-Free: 888-672-5463
info@ontarioparamedic.ca
www.ontarioparamedic.ca
www.facebook.com/sendaparamedic
twitter.com/OntParamedic
vimeo.com/ontarioparamedic
Overview: A small provincial organization founded in 1996
Mission: To act as a voice for both professional & patient care issues; To advocate for improvements in patient care
Member of: Paramedic Association of Canada (PAC)
Finances: *Funding Sources:* Membership dues
Membership: *Member Profile:* Paramedics certified under the Ontario Ministry of Health; Individuals interested in the field of paramedicine; Paramedic students; Corporations & organizations involved in emergency medical services
Activities: Raising public awareness of the role of paramedics; Providing seminars & workshops; Offering networking opportunities; *Awareness Events:* EMS Week, May; National Paramedic Competition
Chief Officer(s):
Geoff MacBride, President
Publications:
• OPA [Ontario Paramedic Association] News
Type: Newsletter; *Accepts Advertising; Editor:* Elizabeth Anderson; *Price:* Free with Ontario Paramedic Association membership
Profile: Association newsletter contained in Canadian Emergency News

Ontario Parks Association (OPA)
7856 - 5th Line South, RR#4, Milton ON L9T 2X8
Tel: 905-864-6182; *Fax:* 905-864-6184
Toll-Free: 866-560-7783
opa@ontarioparksassociation.ca
www.ontarioparksassociation.ca
Overview: A medium-sized provincial charitable organization founded in 1936
Mission: To develop & protect parks & green spaces in Ontario
Finances: *Funding Sources:* Donations
Membership: *Fees:* $70 students & seniors; $130 individuals; $500 associates
Activities: Offering education to park professionals
Chief Officer(s):
Paul Ronan, Executive Director, 905-864-6182 Ext. 6730
paul@ontarioparksassociation.ca
Eric Trogdon, Executive Director
eric@opassoc.on.ca
Shelley May, Coordinator, Operations & Administration, 905-864-6182 Ext. 6710
opa@ontarioparksassociation.ca
Maureen Sinclair, President
msinclair@brantford.ca
Bill Harding, Vice-President
bhardin@toronto.ca
Meetings/Conferences:
• Ontario Parks Association 62nd Annual Education Forum, March, 2018, ON
Scope: Provincial
Description: Description Educational presentations of interest to park & green space managers
Publications:
• OPA [Ontario Parks Association] Playability Tool Kit: Building Accessible Playspaces
Type: Kit
Profile: Creating playspaces that are accessible to persons with disabilities
• Urban Parks in Ontario
Type: Book; *Author:* Dr. J.R. Wright
Profile: The evolution of parks & open space development

Ontario Percheron Horse Association Inc. (OPHA)
c/o Michelle Campbell, 2321 Cockshutt Rd., Waterford ON N0E 1Y0
Tel: 519-443-6399
Secretary@ontariopercherons.ca
www.ontariopercherons.ca
Overview: A small provincial organization overseen by Canadian Percheron Association
Mission: To promote the Percheron draft horse breed in Ontario
Finances: *Funding Sources:* Membership fees; Sponsorships
Membership: *Fees:* $10 juniors, 18 years & under as of January 1; $20 adults, with a Canadian address; $30 adults, with non-Canadian addresses; *Member Profile:* Percheron horse owners & enthusiasts from Canada & elsewhere; *Committees:* Annual Dinner; Futurity & Extravaganza Day; Percheron Newsletter; Website; Juniors
Activities: Offering programs, such as the junior showmanship program & a futurity program; Sponsoring shows, such as the Regional Percheron Show & the Provincial Percheron Show
Chief Officer(s):
Kim Davidson, President, 519-454-8734
Regina Baezner, 1st Vice-President
Dan Barron, 2nd Vice-President
Michelle Campbell, Secretary-Treasurer, 519-443-6399
Secretary@ontariopercherons.ca
Meetings/Conferences:
• Ontario Percheron Horse Association 2018 AGM, 2018, ON
Scope: Provincial
Publications:
• Ontario Percheron Horse Association Inc. Ontario Breeders Directory
Type: Directory
• Percheron Newsletter
Type: Newsletter; *Frequency:* Quarterly; *Editor:* Susan Davidson

Ontario Personal Support Worker Association (OPSWA)
Cambridge ON
Tel: 519-654-9878
admin@opswa.com
www.opswa.com
www.facebook.com/OntarioPSWAssoc
twitter.com/OntarioPSWAssoc
instagram.com/OPSWA
Overview: A small provincial organization
Mission: To continuously strive to improve the professional status of the Personal Support Workers of Ontario through advocacy for excellence & consistency in training, services, working conditions & value to those they serve.
Membership: *Fees:* $20 student; $120 personal support worker
Chief Officer(s):
Miranda Ferrier, President

Ontario Pest Control Association *See* Structural Pest Management Association of Ontario

Ontario Petroleum Institute Inc. (OPI)
#104, 555 Southdale Rd. East, London ON N6E 1A2
Tel: 519-680-1620; *Fax:* 519-680-1621
opi@ontariopetroleuminstitute.com
ontariopetroleuminstitute.com
www.facebook.com/700315586681356
twitter.com/opi1963
Overview: A medium-sized provincial organization founded in 1963
Mission: To promote responsible exploration & development by Ontario's oil, gas, hydrocarbon storage & solution-mining industries
Finances: *Funding Sources:* Sponsorships
Membership: *Fees:* $45 student or retiree; $120 associate; $220 active; $850 sustaining; $1,200 sponsoring; *Member Profile:* Geologists in Ontario; Geophysicists; Explorationists; Producers; Contractors; Petroleum engineers; Companies involved in the oil & gas, hydrocarbon storage & solution mining industries
Activities: Liaising with government agencies; Disseminating information to members; Increasing public awareness of the importance of the industry in Ontario; *Library:* Ontario Oil, Gas, & Salt Resources Library
Chief Officer(s):
Hugh Moran, Executive Director
hughmoran@ontariopetroleuminstitute.com
Meetings/Conferences:
• Ontario Petroleum Institute 2018 57th Annual Conference & Trade Show, 2018
Scope: Provincial
Description: Presentation of papers about oil & natural gas exploration, production, & storage
• Ontario Petroleum Institute 2018 AGM, 2018
Scope: Provincial
Publications:
• Ontario Oil & Gas
Type: Magazine; *Accepts Advertising; Editor:* Carly Peters
Profile: Articles about the oil & gas industry & technical features
• Ontario Petroleum Institute Conference Proceedings
Frequency: Annually; *Price:* $50
Profile: Topics presented by guest speakers from around the world at the Institute's annual conference & trade show
• Ontario Petroleum Institute Membership Directory
Type: Directory; *Frequency:* Annually; *Accepts Advertising*
Profile: Listings & advertising are available to members of the Ontario Petroleum Institute only
• OPI [Ontario Petroleum Institute Inc.] Newsletter
Type: Newsletter; *Frequency:* Bimonthly; *Accepts Advertising;*
ISSN: 14802201
Profile: Membership updates, reports, conferences, & legislation information

Ontario Pharmacists' Association (OPA)
#600, 155 University Ave., Toronto ON M5H 3B7
Tel: 416-441-0788; *Fax:* 416-441-0791
Toll-Free: 877-341-0788
mail@opatoday.com
www.opatoday.com
Overview: A medium-sized provincial organization
Mission: To promote excellence in the practice of pharmacy & the wellness of patients; To act as the voice of pharmacists throughout Ontario
Finances: *Funding Sources:* Membership fees; Sponsorships
Membership: 7,200; *Member Profile:* Pharmacists throughout Ontario, who work in settings such as hospitals, long-term care facilities, community pharmacies, universities, & government; Pharmacists in training; *Committees:* Audit & Finance; Governance & Nominating; Human Resource & Compensation
Activities: Operating the Drug Information & Research Centre in Toronto; Providing continuing education; Advocating for pharmacists & their patients; Offering networking opportunities; *Speaker Service:* Yes
Chief Officer(s):
Dennis Darby, Chief Executive Officer
ddarby@opatoday.com
Amedeo Zottola, CFO & COO
azottola@opatoday.com
Allan H. Malek, Senior Vice-President, Professional Affairs
amalek@opatoday.com
Kristen Zamojc, Specialist, Events & Development
kzamojc@opatoday.com
Meetings/Conferences:
• Ontario Pharmacists Association Conference 2018, June, 2018, Deerhurst Resort, Huntsville, ON
Scope: Provincial
Attendance: 600
Publications:
• The Ontario Pharmacist
Type: Magazine; *Frequency:* Quarterly; *Accepts Advertising;*
Price: Free with Ontario Pharmacists' Association membership
Profile: Current issues of interest to Ontario's pharmacists & pharmacists in training

Ontario Philharmonic (OP)
PO Box 444, Oshawa ON L1H 7L5
Tel: 905-579-6711
contact@ontariophil.ca
www.ontariophil.ca
www.facebook.com/176411532317
Previous Name: Oshawa Symphony
Overview: A small local charitable organization founded in 1957 overseen by Orchestras Canada
Mission: To bring fine orchestral music to residents of Durham Region, Toronto, and the GTA
Member of: Orchestras Canada
Finances: *Funding Sources:* Municipal & provincial grants; Fundraising; Ticket sales; Donations; Sponsorship
Activities: *Library:*
Chief Officer(s):
Laura Vaillancourt, Executive Director, 905-706-5799
laura@ontariophil.ca
Marco Parisotto, Music Director
monica@marcoparisotto.com

Ontario Physical & Health Education Association (OPHEA)
#608, 1 Concorde Gate, Toronto ON M3C 3N6
Tel: 416-426-7120; *Fax:* 416-426-7373
Toll-Free: 888-446-7432
www.ophea.org
www.facebook.com/OpheaCanada
twitter.com/opheacanada
www.youtube.com/opheacanada
Overview: A medium-sized provincial organization
Mission: To support communities & schools to encourage healthy active living
Activities: Promoting physical activity, & health & physical literacy; Providing program supports to schools & communities; Forming partnerships; Engaging in advocacy activities
Chief Officer(s):
Lori Lukinuk, President
Chris Markham, Executive Director & CEO, 416-426-7126

Canadian Associations / Ontario Physiotherapy Association (OPA)

Awards:
• Ophea Award of Distinction
To recognize a leader in the advancement of active, healthy living opportunities for children & youth
• Ophea Award for Outstanding Contribution
To recognize a person or organization for contributions to the lives of children & youth in areas of health & physical education, promotion, advocacy, or community development
• Ophea School Community Award
To recognize a school community that has demonstrated excellence in successfully bringing together all members of the community
Publications:
• OPHEA [Ontario Physical & Health Education Association] Annual Report
Type: Yearbook; Frequency: Annually

Ontario Physiotherapy Association (OPA)
#210, 55 Eglinton Ave. East, Toronto ON M4P 1G8
Tel: 416-322-6866; Fax: 416-322-6705
Toll-Free: 800-672-9668
physiomail@opa.on.ca
www.opa.on.ca
www.linkedin.com/company/2385075
www.facebook.com/OntarioPT
twitter.com/ONTPhysio
www.youtube.com/user/OntarioPhysiotherapy
Overview: A medium-sized provincial organization founded in 1964 overseen by Canadian Physiotherapy Association
Mission: To act as a voice for the physiotherapy profession in Ontario; To ensure the provision of quality physiotherapy services to residents of Ontario
Member of: Canadian Physiotherapy Association
Finances: Funding Sources: Membership dues; Educational activities
Staff Member(s): 8
Membership: Member Profile: Physiotherapists registered with the College of Physiotherapists of Ontario; Support workers; Students
Activities: Liaising with provincial government ministries, such as the Ministry of Health & Long Term Care & the Ministry of Finance, as well as other professional & health care associations; Engaging in advocacy activities; Providing professional development opportunities; Developing resources for members; Increasing public awareness of the profession; Speaker Service: Yes
Chief Officer(s):
Dorianne Sauvé, Chief Executive Officer
dsauve@opa.on.ca
Wendy Smith, President
president@opa.on.ca
Sara Pulins, Manager, Marketing & Communications
spulins@opa.on.ca
Meetings/Conferences:
• InterACTION 2018: Ontario Physiotherapy Association Annual Conference, April, 2018, Marriott Toronto Airport Hotel, Toronto, ON
Scope: Provincial
Publications:
• Ontario Physiotherapy Association Annual Report
Type: Yearbook; Frequency: Annually
• Physiotherapy Today [a publication of the Ontario Physiotherapy Association]
Type: Newsletter; Frequency: Bimonthly; Price: Free with Ontario Physiotherapy Association membership

Ontario Physique Association (OPA)
ON
info@physiqueassociation.ca
www.bao.on.ca
www.facebook.com/ontario.physique
twitter.com/AroundtheOPA
www.flickr.com/photos/ontariophysique
Overview: A small provincial organization overseen by Canadian Bodybuilding Federation
Mission: To be the provincial governing body for the sport of amateur bodybuilding in Ontario
Member of: Canadian Bodybuilding Federation; International Federation of Bodybuilding
Membership: Fees: $100
Chief Officer(s):
Ron Hache, President
president@physiqueassociation.ca
Rudy Jambrosic, Vice President
westerndirector@physiqueassociation.ca
Angie Hache, Secretary-Treasurer, 705-694-4445
memberships@physiqueassociation.ca

Ontario Pinzgauer Breeders Association (OPBA)
c/o Terrylynn Scott, RR#1, Orton ON L0N 1N0
Tel: 519-855-4964; Fax: 519-855-4964
Overview: A small provincial organization
Mission: To facilitate the exhibition & sale of Pinzgauer cattle in Ontario; To develop interest in the breed
Membership: 1-99; Member Profile: Pinzgauer cattle breeders across Ontario
Chief Officer(s):
Terrylynn Scott, Secretary
david.scott1@sympatico.ca

Ontario Pioneers
21 Meadowland Dr., Brampton ON L6W 2R5
Tel: 905-451-5607; Fax: 905-453-3996
Overview: A small provincial organization overseen by TelecomPioneers of Canada
Chief Officer(s):
Sheila O'Donoghue, Manager
she.rob@sympatico.ca

Ontario Pipe Trades Council
#206, 400 Dundas St. East, Whitby ON L1N 3X2
Tel: 905-665-3500; Fax: 905-665-3400
info@optc.org
www.optc.org
www.facebook.com/pipetradescouncil
twitter.com/Pipe_Trades
Overview: A medium-sized provincial organization
Mission: To promote the many technical, commercial & environmental benefits of the Pipe Trades & maximize their use in the construction industry; to promote the interest of the plumbing, pipe fitting, sprinkler fitting & HVAC industry in the province of Ontario
Membership: 16 local unions
Chief Officer(s):
Neil McCormack, Business Manager

Ontario Plowmen's Association (OPA)
188 Nicklin Rd., Guelph ON N1H 7L5
Tel: 519-767-2928; Fax: 519-767-2101
Toll-Free: 800-661-7569
admin@plowingmatch.org
www.plowingmatch.org
www.facebook.com/internationalplowingmatchandruralexpo
Overview: A medium-sized provincial organization founded in 1913
Mission: To provide leadership to local plowing associations; To advance interest & involvement in agriculture by promoting new technologies, environmental & safety issues; To preserve the history of soil cultivation; To promote rural economic development
Member of: North American Farm Show Council
Finances: Annual Operating Budget: $250,000-$500,000; Funding Sources: Sale of space; gate admissions; sponsorships
Staff Member(s): 6; 200 volunteer(s)
Membership: 1,800 individual + 48 organizations; Fees: Schedule available; Member Profile: Farmers, agricultural community members & individuals interested in agriculture, conservation & rural resource management; Committees: Executive; Jr. Plowing; Management; Queen of the Furrow
Activities: Organizing branch meetings; Awareness Events: International Plowing Match & Rural Expo
Chief Officer(s):
Cathy Lasby, Executive Director
cathy@plowingmatch.org

Ontario Plumbing Inspectors Association (OPIA)
c/o Ursula Wengler, 22 Dalegrove Cres., Toronto ON M9B 6A7
www.opia.info
Overview: A medium-sized provincial organization founded in 1920
Mission: To promote uniform enforcement of plumbing regulations; To close liaison & interchange of ideas & knowledge between members of the OPIA & members of other associations; To provide education & training to members & the industry
Member of: World Plumbing Council
Affiliation(s): Ontario Ministry of Municipal Affairs, Building Branch
Finances: Annual Operating Budget: $50,000-$100,000; Funding Sources: Membership fees
14 volunteer(s)
Membership: 800; Fees: $70; Committees: Advisory; Auditors; Awards; Bulletin; Certification Review; Code Technical; Conference; Education; Election; Executive; Finance; Future Conference; Membership; Memorial; Nominations; Public Relations; Reciprocal Licensing; Resolutions; Special; Zone Meetings
Activities: CMX Show; CIPH Ex; Annual conference; Library: Not open to public
Chief Officer(s):
Jerry Monaco, President
Bryan Heyl, Vice-President
Ursula Wengler, Treasurer
Meetings/Conferences:
• Ontario Plumbing Inspectors Association 2018 Annual Meeting, June, 2018, ON
Scope: Provincial

Ontario Podiatric Medical Association (OPMA)
#900, 45 Sheppard Ave. East, Toronto ON M2N 5W9
Tel: 416-927-9111; Fax: 416-927-9111
Toll-Free: 866-424-6762
contact@opma.ca
www.opma.ca
www.facebook.com/756620137694740
Overview: A small provincial organization
Mission: To act as the voice of podiatry & podiatrists in Ontario; To advance the profession of podiatry in Ontario; To ensure timely access to high quality foot care services in Ontario in order to serve & protect the public
Member of: American Podiatric Medical Association, Inc., Region 5
Membership: Fees: Schedule available; Member Profile: Podiatrists (Doctors of Podiatric Medicine) in Ontario
Activities: Promoting the profession of podiatry in Ontario; Advocating on behalf of the profession; Liaising with government & stakeholders
Chief Officer(s):
Bruce Ramsden, President
Sheldon Freelan, Vice-President
Martin Brain, Secretary
Peter Higenell, Treasurer
Meetings/Conferences:
• 2018 Annual Ontario Podiatric Medical Association Conference, 2018, ON
Scope: Provincial

The Ontario Poetry Society (TOPS)
#710, 65 Spring Garden Ave., Toronto ON M2N 6H9
www.theontariopoetrysociety.ca
Overview: A small provincial charitable organization founded in 2000
Mission: To establish a democratic organization for members to unite in friendship for emotional support & encouragement in all aspects of poetry, including writing, editing, performing & publishing
Finances: Funding Sources: Membership fees; contest fees
Membership: Fees: $30; Member Profile: Poets or fans of poetry
Activities: Events held every other month in different cities throughout the province, including Ottawa, Sarnia & Toronto
Chief Officer(s):
Fran Figge, President
Mel Sarnese, Vice-President
Bunny Iskov, Treasurer
Joan Sutcliffe, Secretary
Awards:
• Annual Chapbook Contests Awards
• "No Matter What Shape Your Poem Is" Contest Award
• Ted Plantos Memorial Award
• The Second Time Around Poetry Contest Awards

Ontario Pollution Control Equipment Association (OPCEA)
6514 Mississauga Rd., #C, Mississauga ON L5N 1A6
Tel: 416-307-2185
opcea@opcea.com
www.opcea.com
Previous Name: Ontario Sanitation Equipment Association
Overview: A small provincial organization founded in 1970
Mission: To assist members in the promotion of their services & equipment in Ontario
Affiliation(s): Water Environment Association of Ontario
Finances: Funding Sources: Membership fees
Membership: 170+ companies; Fees: $536.75 privately owned Canadian companies; $310.75 non-qualifying CFIB companies; Member Profile: Ontario firms that manufacture or distribute

environmental & related equipment for the air & water pollution control marketplace
Chief Officer(s):
Max Rao, President
Robert Lee, Vice-President
Greg Jackson, Treasurer
Publications:
• Influents [a publication of the Ontario Pollution Control Equipment Association]
Type: Magazine; *Accepts Advertising; Editor:* Cole Kelman
Profile: A combined publication of the Ontario Pollution Control Equipment Association & the Water Environment Association of Ontario,featuring information about forthcoming trade shows & events
• OPCEA [Ontario Pollution Control Equipment Association] Membership Directory & Buyers Guide
Type: Directory; *Frequency:* Annually; *Accepts Advertising; Editor:* Steve Davey
Profile: Listings of member companies, with their products & services, distributed to the Ontario marketplace

Ontario Pork Producers' Marketing Board (OPPMB)
655 Southgate Dr., Guelph ON N1G 5G6
Tel: 519-767-4600; *Fax:* 519-829-1769
Toll-Free: 877-668-7675
comm@ontariopork.on.ca
www.ontariopork.on.ca
twitter.com/ontariopork
www.youtube.com/user/ontarioporkrecipes
Overview: A medium-sized provincial organization founded in 1946
Mission: To foster a vibrant business environment for pork producers
Membership: 1,284 farmers
Chief Officer(s):
Ken Ovington, General Manager
ken.ovington@ontariopork.on.ca
Stacey Ash, Manager, Communications & Consumer Marketing
stacey.ash@ontariopork.on.ca

Ontario Potato Board (OPB)
485 Washington St., Elora ON N0B 1S0
Tel: 519-846-5553; *Fax:* 519-846-8803
info@ontariopotatoes.ca
www.ontariopotatoes.ca
Merged from: Ontario Potato Growers Marketing Board; Fresh Potato Growers of Ontario
Overview: A medium-sized provincial organization founded in 1999
Mission: To provide consumers with high-quality potatoes
Activities: Providing information about potatoes, potato processing, storage, preparation, & nutrition
Chief Officer(s):
Kevin Brubacher, General Manager

Ontario Potters Association *See* Fusion: The Ontario Clay & Glass Association

Ontario Poultry Council *See* Poultry Industry Council

Ontario Powerlifting Association (OPA)
c/o Karen Maxwell, Registrar, 555 O'Brien Rd., Renfrew ON K7V 3Z3
info@ontariopowerlifting.org
www.ontariopowerlifting.org
www.facebook.com/OntarioPowerliftingAssociation
instagram.com/ontariopowerliftingassociation
Overview: A small provincial organization overseen by Canadian Powerlifting Union
Membership: *Fees:* $85 regular; $65 student/special athlete; $30 associate
Chief Officer(s):
Glyn Moore, President
mgmoore13@outlook.com

Ontario Prader-Willi Syndrome Association (OPWSA)
PO Box 73514, Toronto ON M6C 4A7
Tel: 416-481-8657; *Fax:* 416-981-7788
opwsa@rogers.com
www.opwsa.com
www.facebook.com/106828009519275
Overview: A small provincial charitable organization founded in 1982
Mission: To enhance the quality of life for individuals with Prader-Willi Syndrome
Affiliation(s): International Prader-Willi Syndrome Association

Finances: *Funding Sources:* Provincial Government
Membership: *Member Profile:* Individuals with PWS, their families, friends & concerned professionals
Activities: Counselling; referral & support services; medical information & resource linkage; province-wide parent groups; teaching seminars; on-site case consultation; client advocacy; *Library:* Open to public by appointment
Chief Officer(s):
Jessie Phillips, Family Services Coordinator
jessie.opwsa@gmail.com
Dan Yashinsky, Co-chair
dan_yashinsky@hotmail.com
Cathy Mallove, Co-chair
cmallove@sympatico.ca

Ontario Prepress Association *See* Digital Imaging Association

Ontario Principals' Council (OPC)
180 Dundas St. West, 25th Fl., Toronto ON M5G 1Z8
Tel: 416-322-6600; *Fax:* 416-322-6618
Toll-Free: 800-701-2362
admin@principals.ca
www.principals.ca
www.facebook.com/Ontario-Principals-Council
twitter.com/OPCouncil
Overview: A medium-sized provincial organization founded in 1998
Mission: To support the work of Ontario's principals & vice-principals to provide excellent leadership in the public education system
Finances: *Annual Operating Budget:* $3 Million-$5 Million; *Funding Sources:* Membership dues
Staff Member(s): 20
Membership: 5,500; *Fees:* $1133; *Member Profile:* Practising principals & vice-principals from publicly funded elementary & secondary schools across Ontario
Activities: Liaising with government & district school boards; Advocating for public education; Influencing education decision-making; Promoting the professional interests of members; Providing professional educational opportunities for principlas & vice-principals; Offering networking opportunities; *Speaker Service:* Yes
Chief Officer(s):
Ian McFarlane, Executive Director, 416-322-6600
imcfarlane@principals.ca
Bob Pratt, President, 416-322-6600
president@principals.ca
Peggy Sweeney, Senior Communications Consultant
psweeney@principals.ca
Awards:
• Honorary Life Membership
• Outstanding Contribution to Education Award
• Principals Award for Student Leadership
Publications:
• The Register
Type: Magazine; *Frequency:* 3 times yearly; *Accepts Advertising; Editor:* Peggy Sweeney; *Price:* Free with membership in the Ontario Principals' Council
Profile: Articles to build the professional capacity of principals & vice-principals

Ontario Printing & Imaging Association (OPIA)
#135, 3-1750 The Queensway, Toronto ON M9C 5H5
Tel: 905-602-4441; *Fax:* 905-602-9798
www.opia.on.ca
Overview: A medium-sized provincial organization
Mission: To provide leadership for a successful printing & imaging industry in Ontario
Affiliation(s): Canadian Printing Industries Association (CPIA); Printing Industries of America (PIA); Graphic Arts Technical Foundation (GATF)
Membership: *Committees:* Events; Government Affairs; Environment, Health & Safety; Human Resource Services; Membership
Activities: Providing technical advice; Facilitating the exchange of ideas; Offering print referral services
Chief Officer(s):
Dave Potje, Chair
Awards:
• Excellence in Print Awards

Ontario Processing Vegetable Growers
435 Consortium Ct., London ON N6E 2S8
Tel: 519-681-1875; *Fax:* 519-685-5719
opvg@opvg.org
www.opvg.org
Overview: A large provincial organization

Mission: To negotiate prices of crops on behalf of growers
Membership: 450
Chief Officer(s):
Francis Dobbelaar, Chairman, 519-627-2575
Meetings/Conferences:
• Ontario Processing Vegetable Industry Conference 2018, 2018, ON
Scope: Provincial

Ontario Professional Fire Fighters Association (OPFFA) / Association des pompiers professionnels de l'Ontario (ind.)
292 Plains Rd. East, Burlington ON L7T 2C6
Tel: 905-681-7111; *Fax:* 905-681-1489
www.opffa.org
Previous Name: Provincial Federation of Ontario Fire Fighters
Overview: A medium-sized provincial organization founded in 1997
Affiliation(s): International Association of Fire Fighters
Membership: *Member Profile:* Full-time professional fire fighters throughout Ontario; *Committees:* Education; Health & Safety & Section 21; Finance; Workplace Safety & Insurance Board; Occupational Disease; Pension; Legislative; Human Relations
Activities: Educating members to negotiate & administer collective agreements
Chief Officer(s):
Fred LeBlanc, President
Mark McKinnon, Executive Vice-President
Barry Quinn, Secretary-Treasurer
Jeff Braun-Jackson, Office Manager & Researcher
Awards:
• The Ed Hothersall Award
To recognize an individual who has displayed a dedication for service to their association & the community
• The Patrick J DeFazio Award
To recognize an individual who has contributed in the area of improving fire fighter health & safety
• The Joe Adamkowski Award
To recognize an individual who has demonstrated dedication & diligence within their own Local, the OPFFA, or the IAFF
Meetings/Conferences:
• Ontario Professional Fire Fighters Association 2018 Annual Legislative Conference, 2018, ON
Scope: Provincial
Description: An opportunity for representatoves from across Ontario to meet with MPPs to advocate on issues of concern
• Ontario Professional Fire Fighters Association 20th Annual Convention 2018, 2018
Scope: Provincial

Ontario Professional Foresters Association (OPFA)
#201, 5 Wesleyan St., Georgetown ON L7G 2E2
Tel: 905-877-3679; *Fax:* 905-877-6766
opfa@opfa.ca
www.opfa.ca
www.facebook.com/OntarioProfessionalForestersAssociation
Overview: A medium-sized provincial organization founded in 1957
Mission: To operate as a regulatory body for the practice of professional forestry in Ontario; To be committed to the development, management, conservation & sustainability of forest & urban forests
Finances: *Annual Operating Budget:* $100,000-$250,000; *Funding Sources:* Membership fees
Staff Member(s): 7
Membership: 850; *Fees:* Schedule available; *Member Profile:* Registered professional foresters in Ontario; *Committees:* Executive; Registration; Complaints; Discipline; Annual Conference; Competency Support; Editorial Board; Governance; Finance & Audit; Awards & Recognition; Nominations; Registration Appeals; Website; Forestry Practice Committees (Urban Forestry, Crown Land Foresty & Private Land Forestry)
Activities: *Speaker Service:* Yes
Chief Officer(s):
Fred Pinto, R.P.F, Executive Director
executive.director@opfa.ca
Susan Jarvis, R.P.F, Registrar
registrar@opfa.ca
Meetings/Conferences:
• Ontario Professional Foresters Association 2018 61st Annual Conference, 2018, ON
Scope: Provincial

Canadian Associations / Ontario Professional Planners Institute (OPPI) / Institut des planificateurs professionnels de l'Ontario

Ontario Professional Planners Institute (OPPI) / Institut des planificateurs professionnels de l'Ontario
#201, 234 Eglinton Ave. East, Toronto ON M4P 1K5
Tel: 416-483-1873; Fax: 416-483-7830
Toll-Free: 800-668-1448
info@ontarioplanners.ca
www.ontarioplanners.ca
www.linkedin.com/company/3068747
www.facebook.com/OntarioProfessionalPlannersInstitute
twitter.com/OntarioPlanners
www.youtube.com/user/OntarioPlanners
Overview: A medium-sized provincial organization founded in 1986 overseen by Canadian Institute of Planners
Mission: To act as the voice of Ontario's planning profession; To provide leadership on policies related to planning & development
Affiliation(s): Canadian Institute of Planners (CIP)
Finances: Annual Operating Budget: $1.5 Million-$3 Million; Funding Sources: Membership fees; Program & activity revenue
Staff Member(s): 9
Membership: 3,500 planners + 500 students; Fees: Schedule available; Member Profile: Practicing planners throughout Ontario; Students
Activities: Offering professional development courses; Preparing position statements, policy papers, & other documents of interest to planners; Presenting awards for excellence in planning
Chief Officer(s):
Andrea Bourrie, President
Mary Ann Rangam, Executive Director
executivedirector@ontarioplanners.ca
Robert Fraser, Director, Finance & Administration
finance@ontarioplanners.ca
Loretta Ryan, Director, Public Affairs
policy@ontarioplanners.ca
Brian Brophey, Registrar & Director, Member Relations
standards@ontarioplanners.ca
Awards:
• OPPI Excellence in Planning Awards
Awarded to OPPI members, corporations, or consortiums to acknowledge the year's best professional accomplishments in professional planning Deadline: April 15
Meetings/Conferences:
• Ontario Professional Planners Institute 2018 Symposium, October, 2018, Laurentian University, Sudbury, ON
Scope: Provincial
Publications:
• Ontario Planning Institute eNews
Type: Newsletter; Frequency: Monthly; Accepts Advertising
Profile: Ontario Professional Planners Institute activities & important dates
• Ontario Planning Journal [a publication of the Ontario Professional Planners Institute]
Type: Journal; Frequency: bimonthly; Accepts Advertising; Editor: Lynn Morrow; Price: Free with OPPI membership
Profile: Ontario Professional Planners Institute activities & planning issues

Ontario Progressive Conservative Party
59 Adelaide St. East, 4th Fl., Toronto ON M5C 1K6
Tel: 416-861-0020; Fax: 416-861-9593
Toll-Free: 800-903-6453
www.ontariopc.com
www.facebook.com/OntarioPC
twitter.com/OntarioPCParty
www.youtube.com/user/ontariopcparty
Also Known As: Ontario PC
Overview: A small provincial organization
Chief Officer(s):
Victor Fedeli, Interim Party Leader

Ontario Prospectors Association (OPA)
c/o Garry Clark, 1000 Alloy Dr., Thunder Bay ON P7B 6A5
Tel: 807-622-3284; Fax: 807-622-4156
Toll-Free: 866-259-3727
www.ontarioprospectors.com
Previous Name: Ontario Mineral Exploration Federation (OMEF)
Overview: A small provincial organization founded in 1987
Mission: To advance the interests of prospectors & the mineral exploration industry; To promote ethical standards among prospectors in Ontario; To ensure adherence by members to the code of conduct

Membership: 3,000; Committees: Audit; Membership; Symposium; Education; Land Use / Access; Issue Resolution; Communications; Policy; Finance
Activities: Engaging in lobbying activities; Designing prospector development initiatives; Providing information; Developing awareness of the industry; Offering networking opportunities; Presenting awards
Chief Officer(s):
Garry Clark, Executive Director
gjclark@ontarioprospectors.com
Publications:
• Building a Dialogue with Aboriginal Communities: A Guide for Junior Exploration Companies & Prospectors
Type: Guide
• The Explorationist [a publication of the Ontario Prospectors Association]
Type: Newsletter; Frequency: 10 pa
Profile: Information distributed to OPA members, associates, & government personnel about Ontario's mineral exploration scene
• Ontario Mining & Exploration Directory
Type: Directory
• The Ontario Prospector
Type: Magazine; Frequency: Semiannually; Accepts Advertising; Editor: Cindy Chan
Profile: Conference reports, feature articles, & buyers' guide

Ontario Provincial Police Association (OPPA)
119 Ferris Lane, Barrie ON L4M 2Y1
Fax: 705-721-4867
www.oppa.ca
Overview: A medium-sized provincial organization founded in 1954
Mission: To represent members in negotiations with the Ontario government; to promote safe & healthy work environments
Membership: 13,000; Member Profile: Civilian & uniform members of the Ontario Provincial Police; retirees; surviving family members
Chief Officer(s):
Jim Christie, President
Martin Bain, Vice-President

Ontario Provincial Trapshooting Association (OPTA)
ON
info@ontariotrap.com
www.ontariotrap.com
www.facebook.com/groups/OntarioTrap
Overview: A small provincial organization
Finances: Annual Operating Budget: Less than $50,000
Membership: 500-999
Chief Officer(s):
Neville Henderson, President
Pam Muma, Secretary-Treasurer

Ontario Psychiatric Association (OPA)
#100, 2233 Argentia Rd., Mississauga ON L5N 2X7
Tel: 905-813-0105; Fax: 905-826-4873
opa@eopa.ca
www.eopa.ca
www.linkedin.com/groups/4618836
www.facebook.com/146883128706932
twitter.com/OntPsychAssoc
Overview: A medium-sized provincial organization founded in 1956
Mission: To represent Ontario psychiatrists to government, universities & other associations; To promote high standards of professional development & practice; To promote the exchange of information; To advocate for people with mental disorders
Finances: Funding Sources: Membership dues
Membership: Fees: $50 first year member; $100 second year member/associate; $280 full; Member Profile: Psychiatrists in good standing; Students; Qualified medical practicioners in a related field; Committees: Advocacy; Continuing Education; Finance/Audit; Member Services/Communications; Nominations
Chief Officer(s):
Diana Kljenak, President

Ontario Psychological Association (OPA)
#403, 21 St. Clair Ave. East, Toronto ON M4T 1L8
Tel: 416-961-5552; Fax: 416-961-5516
opa@psych.on.ca
www.psych.on.ca
www.facebook.com/ONPsych
twitter.com/onpsych
Overview: A medium-sized provincial organization founded in 1947

Mission: To advance the practice & science of psychology in Ontario communities; To promote the highest ethical standards in the profession
Membership: Fees: $499; $195 first time member; $450 affiliate; $338 first time affiliate; $225 new graduate affiliate; $25 graduate student; $15 undergrad student; Member Profile: Psychologists who reside in Ontario; Committees: Audit & Finance; Auto Insurance; Communication & Member Services; Disaster Response Network; Diversity Interest Group; Early Career Psychology Interest Group; Executive; Governance; Ministry of Education Liaison; Planning & Policy Development; Prescription Authority; Primary Care Interest Group; Program Planning & Research; Section on Independent Practice; Section on Psychology in Education
Activities: Engaging in advocacy activities; Providing educational opportunities; Offering information to the public
Chief Officer(s):
Sylvain Roy, President
Janet Kasperski, Chief Executive Officer
Meetings/Conferences:
• Ontario Psychological Association 2018 Annual Conference, 2018
Scope: Provincial
Publications:
• Psychology Ontario
Type: Magazine

Ontario Public Buyers Association (OPBA)
OPBA Central Office, #361, 111 Fourth Ave., St. Catharines ON L2S 3P5
Tel: 905-682-2644
info@opba.ca
www.opba.ca
Overview: A medium-sized provincial organization founded in 1952
Mission: To promote the ethical & effective expenditure of public funds through the principles of professional procurement
Affiliation(s): National Institute of Governmental Purchasing, Inc.; Institute of Purchasing & Supply of Great Britain; International Federation of Purchasing & Materials Management
Finances: Annual Operating Budget: $100,000-$250,000; Funding Sources: Membership dues
Staff Member(s): 3; 20 volunteer(s)
Membership: 400 individual + 25 senior/lifetime; Fees: $259.90 individual; free for students; Committees: Professional Development; Communications; Legal; Newsletter; Technology; Professional Relations; Management Issues; Symposium; Benchmarking
Activities: Rents Mailing List: Yes; Library: OPBA Specification Library; Not open to public
Chief Officer(s):
Michelle Palmer, President, 519-741-2200 Ext. 7214
michelle.palmer@kitchener.ca
Tina Iacoe, Vice President, 905-546-2121 Ext. 2796
tina.iacoe@hamilton.ca
David Allan, Secretary
davidkallan@gmail.com
Michelle Rasiulis, Treasurer
michelle.rasiulis@oakville.ca

Ontario Public Health Association (OPHA) / Association pour la santé publique de l'Ontario
#502, 44 Victoria St., Toronto ON M5C 1Y2
Tel: 416-367-3313; Fax: 416-367-2844
admin@opha.on.ca
www.opha.on.ca
www.linkedin.com/company/ontario-public-health-association
www.facebook.com/opha1949
twitter.com/OPHA_Ontario
twitter.com/nutritionrc
Overview: A medium-sized provincial charitable organization founded in 1949 overseen by Canadian Public Health Association
Mission: To provide leadership on issues affecting public health in Ontario, such as preserving the environment, promoting disease prevention, narrowing health disparities & reducing poverty; To strengthen the influence of persons involved in public & community health across Ontario
Finances: Funding Sources: Membership fees; Sponsorships
Membership: 350; Fees: $85 students, retired persons; $150 individuals; $1,750 organizational member; Member Profile: Individuals & constituent societies interested in advancing public health
Activities: Providing education opportunities; Analyzing policy; Advocating for public health policies to improve the health of Ontarians; Liaising with governments; Partnering with other

organizations to address broader elements of public health issues
Chief Officer(s):
Ellen Wodchis, President
Pegeen Walsh, Executive Director
Barb Prud'homme, Coordinator
barbp@opha.on.ca
Meetings/Conferences:
• Ontario Public Health Association 2018 Annual Conference & General Meeting, 2018
Scope: Provincial
Description: A review of association bylaws, presentation of the annual report, & the appointment of the Board of Directors
Publications:
• Ontario Public Health Association E-Bulletin
Type: Newsletter; *Frequency:* Monthly
Profile: Current topics in public health & information about the association's workgroups & partnerships
• Public Health Today
Type: Magazine; *Price:* Free with membership in the Ontario Public Health Association

Ontario Public Interest Research Group (OPIRG) / Groupe de recherche d'intérêt public de l'Ontario
North Borden Building, #101, 563 Spadina Ave., Toronto ON M5S 2J7
Tel: 416-978-7770; *Fax:* 416-971-2292
opirg.toronto@utoronto.ca
www.opirg.org
Also Known As: OPIRG Provincial Network
Overview: A medium-sized provincial organization founded in 1973
Mission: To be committed to the struggle for social & environmental justice; To provide an alternative to the information provided by the academic community, government & business; To offer an analysis of environmental & social issues aimed at motivating change & placing issues in the broader social, economic & political perspective
Finances: *Annual Operating Budget:* $50,000-$100,000; *Funding Sources:* Student & community membership fees
Staff Member(s): 2; 50 volunteer(s)
Membership: 30,000; *Member Profile:* Grassroots student organizations comprised of invidiual campus chapters from universities in Ontario; *Committees:* Environment; Anti-Racism; Education; Global
Activities: Social & environmental justice activism; Community organizing & engagement; Radical research & popular education; *Speaker Service:* Yes; *Library:* by appointment
Chief Officer(s):
Sarom Rho, Director

OPIRG Brock
Brock University, Almuni Student Centre, #204, 500 Glenridge Ave., St Catharines ON L2S 3A1
Tel: 905-688-5555; *Fax:* 905-378-5701
info@opirgbrock.org
www.opirgbrock.org
www.facebook.com/opirgbrock
twitter.com/opirgbrock/
plus.google.com/115989504119091960180
Chief Officer(s):
Em (Matthew) Heppler, Coordinator, Promotions & Public Relations

OPIRG Carleton
Carleton University, 326 Unicentre, 1125 Colonel By Dr., Ottawa ON K1S 5B6
Tel: 613-520-2757; *Fax:* 613-520-3989
opirgadmin@gmail.com
www.opirg-carleton.org

OPIRG Guelph
University of Guelph, 1 Trent Lane, Guelph ON N1G 2W1
Tel: 519-824-2091; *Fax:* 519-824-8990
opirg@uoguelph.ca
www.opirgguelph.org
Chief Officer(s):
Mandy Hiscocks, Coordinator, Volunteer & Programming

OPIRG Kingston
Queens University, The Grey House, 51 Bader Lane, Kingston ON K7L 3N6
Tel: 613-533-3189
info@opirgkingston.org
www.opirgkingston.org
twitter.com/opirgkingston

OPIRG McMaster
McMaster University, MUSC 229, 1280 Main St. West, Hamilton ON L8S 4S4
Tel: 905-525-9140
opirg@mcmaster.ca
www.opirg.ca

OPIRG Peterborough
751 George St. North, 1st Fl., Peterborough ON K9H ET2
Tel: 705-741-1208
opirg@trentu.ca
www.opirgpeterborough.ca
Chief Officer(s):
Yolanda Jones, Coordinator

OPIRG Windsor
University Of Windsor, 252 Dillon Hall, Windsor ON N9B 3P4
Tel: 519-253-3000
opirg@uwindsor.ca
opirg.uwindsor.ca
Chief Officer(s):
Samina Yousuf Esha, President

OPIRG York
York University, C449 Student Centre, 4700 Keele St., Toronto ON M3J 1P3
Tel: 416-736-5724; *Fax:* 416-650-8014
opirgyork@gmail.com
www.opirgyork.ca
www.facebook.com/opirg.yorku
twitter.com/opirgyork

Waterloo PIRG (WPIRG)
Univ. of Waterloo, Student Life Centre, #2139, 200 University Ave. West, Waterloo ON N2L 3G1
Tel: 519-888-4882; *Fax:* 519-725-3093
info@wpirg.org
www.wpirg.org
Chief Officer(s):
Tammy Kovich, Coordinator, Programming & Volunteer Support
tammy@wpirg.org

Ontario Public Library Association (OPLA)
c/o Ontario Library Association, 2 Toronto St., 3rd Fl., Toronto ON M5C 2B6
Tel: 416-363-3388; *Fax:* 416-941-9581
Toll-Free: 866-873-9867
info@accessola.com
www.accessola.org
Overview: A medium-sized provincial organization founded in 1900
Mission: To foster the expansion & improvement of public library service in Ontario; To support public librarians throughout Ontario; To encourage standards & certification for public library workers
Member of: Ontario Library Association
Membership: *Member Profile:* Individuals & organizations interested in librarianship & in library & information service; *Committees:* Child & Youth Services; Readers' Advisory; Community-Led Libraries
Activities: Organizing professional development activities for public librarians in Ontario; Facilitating networking opportunities; Liaising with government
Chief Officer(s):
Jennifer La Chapelle, President
j.lachap@hotmail.com
Awards:
• James Bain Medallion
Awarded to a library board member who demonstrates outstanding leadership in governing a public Ontario library
• Lifetime Achievement Award
Presented to a library staff member who has demonstrated outstanding lifelong service to the profession
• Children's or Youth Services Librarian of the Year Award
Awarded to a children's or youth librarian who has made a positive impact on the profession
• Award for Leadership in Adult Readers' Advisory
Awarded to honour excellence in readers' advisory service to adults
• Advocacy in Action: Excellence in Children's or Teen Services Award
Awarded to an individual staff member/group of staff members that show excellence in working with children or youth
Meetings/Conferences:
• Ontario Public Library Association 2018 39th Annual General Meeting, 2018, ON
Scope: Provincial
Description: Featuring the introduction of the new council, as well as reports from the association's president, treasurer, & committees
Publications:
• HoOPLA [a publication of the Ontario Public Library Association]
Type: Newsletter; *Frequency:* Quarterly; *Editor:* Vanessa Holm
Profile: Association activities, public library news from around the province, & upcoming events

Ontario Public School Boards Association (OPSBA)
#1850, 439 University Ave., Toronto ON M5G 1Y8
Tel: 416-340-2540; *Fax:* 416-340-7571
webmaster@opsba.org
www.opsba.org
www.linkedin.com/company/ontario-public-school-boards'-association
twitter.com/OPSBA
www.flickr.com/photos/opsba
Previous Name: Association of Large School Boards of Ontario
Overview: A medium-sized provincial organization founded in 1988 overseen by Canadian School Boards Association
Mission: To represent Ontario's public school authorities & public district school boards; To advocate on behalf of the public school system in Ontario; To promote & enhance public education
Finances: *Funding Sources:* Sponsorships
Staff Member(s): 17
Membership: *Member Profile:* Representatives of public district school boards & public school authorities in Ontario
Activities: Developing policy positions & responses to government legislation & regulations; Providing input on legislation; Establishing partnerships with other organizations
Chief Officer(s):
Michael Barrett, President
Gail Anderson, Executive Director
Florenda Tingle, Executive Coordinator
Awards:
• Bernardine Yackman Award
• Jack A. MacDonald Award of Merit
• Fred L. Bartlett Memorial Award
• President's Award
• The Dr. Harry Paikin Award of Merit
• The Achievement Award / Award of Excellence
Meetings/Conferences:
• Ontario Public School Boards Association Public Education Symposium 2018, January, 2018, Sheraton Centre Hotel, Toronto, ON
Scope: Provincial
Contact Information: Contact, Conference & Event Planning: Susan Weinberg, Phone: 416-340-2540, ext. 128
• Ontario Public School Boards' Association Annual General Meeting 2018, May, 2018, Marriott on the Falls, Niagara Falls, ON
Scope: Provincial
Contact Information: Contact, Conference & Event Planning: Susan Weinberg, Phone: 416-340-2540, ext. 128
Publications:
• Ontario Public School Boards Association Annual Report
Type: Yearbook; *Frequency:* Annually

Ontario Public Service Employees Union (OPSEU) / Syndicat des employées et employés de la fonction publique de l'Ontario
100 Lesmill Rd., Toronto ON M3B 3P8
Tel: 416-443-8888; *Fax:* 416-443-9670
Toll-Free: 800-268-7376
opseu@opseu.org
www.opseu.org
www.facebook.com/OPSEU
twitter.com/OPSEU
www.youtube.com/user/OPSEUSEFPO
Previous Name: Civil Service Association of Ontario
Overview: A large provincial organization founded in 1911
Mission: To negotiate collective agreements; To conduct membership education; To lobby governments to maintain & improve public services; To defend the principle of social unionism by speaking out on public policy issues such as taxes, free trade, privatization, health care, social services, occupational health & safety, & employment equity
Member of: National Union of Public and General Employees
Affiliation(s): Canadian Labour Council; Ontario Federation of Labour
Membership: 130,000; *Member Profile:* Public sector workers; *Committees:* Provincial Francophone; Provincial Human Rights; Provincial Women's; Provincial Young Workers; Aboriginal; Audit; Central Political Action; Convention

Activities: *Awareness Events:* Injured Workers Day, June
Library: OPSEU Resource Centre; by appointment Not open to public
Chief Officer(s):
Warren (Smokey) Thomas, President
wthomas@opseu.org
Publications:
• Autumn View [a publication of Ontario Public Service Employees Union]
Type: Newsletter; *Frequency:* Quarterly
• In Solidarity [a publication of Ontario Public Service Employees Union]
Type: Newsletter; *Frequency:* Quarterly

Ontario Public Supervisory Officers' Association (OPSOA)
1123 Glenashton Dr., Oakville ON L6H 5M1
Tel: 905-845-7003; *Fax:* 905-845-2044
www.opsoa.org
Overview: A medium-sized provincial licensing organization founded in 1989
Mission: To achieve excellence in public education for the students of Ontario; To advance the cause of public education; To provide a distinctive voice for public supervisory officials in the province of Ontario; To further common interests in the cause of education in Ontario, by working collaboratively with other organizations & associations; To promote effective leadership through professional growth; To promote ethical practices among the members; To maintain a liaison with &, where appropriate, to advise the Ministry of Education & other partners on matters pertaining to education; To provide welfare, counselling, & advice for members
Finances: *Annual Operating Budget:* $250,000-$500,000
Staff Member(s): 4
Membership: 286; *Fees:* .85 of 1% of annual salary; *Member Profile:* Community of senior educational leaders of school districts
Chief Officer(s):
Joy Badder, Executive Director
Meetings/Conferences:
• Ontario Public Supervisory Officers' Association Annual Conference 2018, 2018, ON
Scope: Provincial

Ontario Public Transit Association (OPTA)
#200, 5063 North Service Rd., Burlington ON L7L 5H6
Tel: 416-229-6222; *Fax:* 416-969-8916
info@ontariopublictransit.ca
www.ontariopublictransit.ca
twitter.com/ON_PublicTrnsit
Previous Name: Ontario Community Transit Association
Overview: A medium-sized provincial organization founded in 1997
Mission: To strengthen & improve public transit services in Ontario; To ensure excellence & sustainability in public transit
Membership: *Fees:* Annual fees for transportation service providers sales based on operating budget or net sales, range from $560-$5,510; $560 for affiliates; *Member Profile:* Representatives of public transit systems; Health & social service agency transportation providers; Government representatives; Suppliers to the industry; Consultants
Activities: Engaging in advocacy activities; Sharing information; *Awareness Events:* Ontario Transit Expo (OTE) Conference & Trade Show
Chief Officer(s):
Kelly Paleczny, Chair
Vince Rodo, Vice Chair
Elly van der Made, Treasurer
Tony D'Alessandro, Secretary
Meetings/Conferences:
• Ontario Transportation Expo Conference & Trade Show 2018, April, 2018, International Plaza Hotel; International Centre, Hall 5, Toronto, ON
Scope: Provincial
Description: Conference and trade show organized by three partnering associations: the Ontario Motor Coach Association (OMCA), the Ontario Public Transit Association (OPTA) and the Ontario School Bus Assocation (OSBA)
Contact Information: 416-229-6622; info@ote.ca
Publications:
• OPTA [Ontario Public Transit Association] News
Type: Newsletter; *Frequency:* Quarterly
Profile: Association activities & upcoming events

Ontario Public Works Association (OPWA)
#22, 1525 Cornwall Rd., Oakville ON L6J 0B2
Tel: 647-726-0167; *Fax:* 289-291-6477
info@opwa.ca
opwa.ca
www.linkedin.com/groups/4147573/profile
www.facebook.com/OPWA1
www.youtube.com/user/apwatv?feature=watch
Overview: A medium-sized provincial organization overseen by Canadian Public Works Association
Mission: To promote professional excellence & public awareness through education, advocacy & the exchange of knowledge regarding public works in Ontario
Member of: American Public Works Association
Affiliation(s): American Public Works Association (APWA)
Membership: 630; *Member Profile:* Public works practitioners employed by the Federal & Provincial governments, municipalities, consulting engineers, utility companies, contractors & suppliers; *Committees:* Adovacy; Annual Conference; PWX Networking; Awards; Historical; IT Symposium; Membership; National Public Works Week; Communications; Education; Special Functions; Young Professionals
Chief Officer(s):
Terry Hardy, Executive Director, 647-726-0167, Fax: 289-291-6477

Ontario Puppetry Association
c/o Kerry Panavas, 52 Lamoreaux St., Hamilton ON L8R 1V1
www.onpuppet.ca
Overview: A small provincial charitable organization founded in 1956
Mission: To promote recognition of puppetry as art; to distribute information on all aspects; To assist in eventual formation of national puppet theatre
Member of: Toronto Theatre Alliance
Affiliation(s): UNIMA International
Membership: 40+; *Fees:* $15 student; $30 individual; $60 group; $350 lifetime; *Member Profile:* Puppeteers of different styles & at all levels of expertise
Activities: Offering professional development for artists
Chief Officer(s):
Jamie Ashby, President
Janna Munkittrick-Colton, Vice-President

Ontario Rainbow Alliance of the Deaf (ORAD)
c/o The 519 Community Centre, 519 Church St., Toronto ON M4Y 2C9
info@orad.ca
new2.orad.ca
www.facebook.com/176398609081793
www.twitter.com/OntarioRAD
www.youtube.com/ontariorad
Overview: A medium-sized provincial organization founded in 2001
Mission: Ontario Rainbow Alliance for the Deaf (ORAD) is a not for profit organization serving Deaf, deaf, deafened, hard of hearing and hearing people who are LGBTTIQQ2S* communities in the Province of Ontario.
Affiliation(s): Rainbow Alliance of the Deaf
Chief Officer(s):
Nicka Noble, Acting President/Vice-President
president@orad.ca

Ontario Real Estate Association (OREA)
99 Duncan Mill Rd., Toronto ON M3B 1Z2
Tel: 416-445-9910; *Fax:* 416-445-2644
Toll-Free: 800-265-6732
info@orea.com
www.orea.com
www.facebook.com/OREAinfo
twitter.com/oreainfo
www.youtube.com/OREAinfo
Overview: A large provincial organization founded in 1922
Mission: To represent the vocational interests of members; To advocate for a better working environment; To communicate with members & the public; To develop educational opportunities for the betterment of the real estate profession; To develop programs to assist members in providing quality services to the public; To develop & administer the educational courses required for registration to trade in real estate on behalf of The Real Estate Council of Ontario
Member of: The Canadian Real Estate Association; International Real Estate Association
Finances: *Funding Sources:* Membership dues; Education course fees
Staff Member(s): 100; 200 volunteer(s)
Membership: 64,240 individuals; *Fees:* Schedule available; *Member Profile:* Registered real estate brokers or salespeople belonging to local real estate boards; *Committees:* Arbitration & Ethics; Commercial; Finance/Audit; Governance; Government Relations; Marketing & Communication; Standard Forms; The Association Executive Advisory; Young Professionals Network
Activities: Operating the OREA Real Estate College
Chief Officer(s):
Tim Hudak, Chief Executive Officer
Meetings/Conferences:
• Ontario Real Estate Association 2018 Conference, 2018, ON
Scope: Provincial
Description: Educational & networking opportunities for current & future leaders in the real estate industry, plus the Ontario Real Estate Association Annual Assembly Meeting & elections

Ontario Recovery Group Inc. (ORG)
#1, 15 Keith Rd., Bracebridge ON P1L 0A1
Tel: 705-645-0033; *Fax:* 705-645-0017
Toll-Free: 866-356-0033
info@ontariorecoverygroup.com
www.ontariorecoverygroup.com
Also Known As: ORG Inc.
Overview: A small provincial organization founded in 1981
Mission: To promote harmony among members & competitors; to provide members with a means of exchanging information with respect to the towing & recovery industry; to encourage development of a professional approach; to sponsor, sanction & promote training courses; to develop & promote acceptable standards of equipment, facilities & drivers; to develop methods of regulation of standards for the industry; to provide all levels of government & law enforcement with a means of communication to the industry
Finances: *Annual Operating Budget:* Less than $50,000; *Funding Sources:* Membership dues
Staff Member(s): 2; 6 volunteer(s)
Membership: 38; *Fees:* $350; *Member Profile:* Heavy duty tow operators; *Committees:* Executive; Training
Activities: Heavy duty towing & recovery in Ontario; *Speaker Service:* Yes
Chief Officer(s):
Doug Nelson, Executive Director
doug@ptao.org

Ontario Recreation Facilities Association (ORFA)
#102, 1 Concorde Gate, Toronto ON M3C 3N6
Tel: 416-426-7062; *Fax:* 416-426-7385
Toll-Free: 800-661-6732
Other Communication: admin@orfa.com
info@orfa.com
www.orfa.com
Previous Name: Ontario Arenas Association Inc.
Overview: A medium-sized provincial organization founded in 1947
Mission: To provide leadership for the recreation facility profession in Ontario; To promote the professional operation of recreation facilities throughout the province
Membership: 4,000+; *Fees:* $145 individual; $695 group or corporate; $50 student; *Member Profile:* Individuals operate & manage recreation facilities in municipalities, First Nations communities, government agencies, educational institutions & in the private recreation sector; Businesses that support the recreation sector; *Committees:* Aquatics Technical Advisory; Arena Technical Advisory; Grounds Technical Advisory; EXPO Tradeshow; Refrigeration Technical Advisory
Activities: Promoting safe & accessible recreation facilities; Providing training & education programs, such as a program with the Canadian Red Cross - Ontario Zone, which leads to the professional designation, Certified Aquatic Professional (CAP); Presenting awards to recognize commitment to the recreation facility industry; *Awareness Events:* Parks & Recreation Month, Ontario *Library:* Facilities Library
Chief Officer(s):
Steve Hardie, RRFA, CIT, CPT, President & Chair
shardie@northperth.ca
John Milton, Chief Administrative Officer
jmilton@orfa.com
Remo Petrongolo, Director, Business Development
rpetrongolo@orfa.com
Terry Piche, RRFA, CIT, Director, Technical
tpiche@orfa.com
Hubie Basilio, Coordinator, Public Relations & Communications
hbasilio@orfa.com
Rebecca Russell, Facilities Librarian
library@orfa.com

Publications:
• Facility Forum [a publication of the Ontario Recreation Facilities Association Inc.]
Type: Newsletter; *Frequency:* Quarterly; *Accepts Advertising*
Profile: Information for government representatives, municipal chief building officials, municipal supervisors, facility managers, recreationdirectors, libraries, educational institutions, conservation authorities, & museum boards
• Ontario Recreation Facilities Association Inc. Members & Products / Services Directory
Type: Directory; *Frequency:* Annually
• ORFA [Ontario Recreation Facilities Association Inc.] E-News
Type: Newsletter
Profile: Issues & trends that affect the recreation facilities sector

Ontario Recreational Canoeing & Kayaking Association (ORCKA)
#209, 3 Concorde Gate, Toronto ON M3C 3N7
Tel: 416-426-7016; *Fax:* 416-426-7363
info@orcka.ca
www.orcka.ca
www.facebook.com/228950560506530
Previous Name: Canoe Ontario; Ontario Recreational Canoeing Association
Overview: A medium-sized provincial organization founded in 1975
Mission: To promote development of safe, competent & knowledgeable recreational paddlers
Finances: *Annual Operating Budget:* $100,000-$250,000; *Funding Sources:* Trillium Grant
Staff Member(s): 2
Membership: *Fees:* $42.20 - $141.25; *Member Profile:* Canoe, kayak instructors & recreational paddlers in Ontario; *Committees:* Safety; Promotion; Environment; Instructor Service; Membership
Activities: Canoeing in Ontario
Chief Officer(s):
Bruce Hawkins, President, 613-623-9950
bhawkins@orcka.on.ca

Ontario Refrigeration & Air Conditioning Contractors Association (ORAC)
#43, 6770 Davand Dr., Mississauga ON L5T 2G3
Tel: 905-670-0010; *Fax:* 905-670-0474
contact@oraca.ca
www.oraca.ca
Overview: A medium-sized provincial organization
Mission: To represent Ontario's contractor practitioners in the refrigeration & air conditioning trade; To enhance quality & efficiency in the industry to benefit customers
Membership: *Fees:* $1,500 initiation fee & $500 membership dues for provincial members; $1,500 initiation fee & $1,500 membership dues for associate members; *Member Profile:* Individuals, partnerships, & corporations in Ontario, who are engaged in selling, installing, repairing, & maintaining refrigeration & air conditioning equipment; Individuals, partnerships or corporations in Ontario, who provide materials, equipment, or training to the heating, ventilation, refrigeration & air conditioning industry
Activities: Liaising with government & other organizations that represent trade local, provincial, & national bodies; Managing a state of the art training centre; Educating the public about the profession
Chief Officer(s):
Dino Russo, President, 905-474-4449
dino@readair.com
David Sinclair, Vice-President, 416-465-7581
dsinclair@toromont.com
Mike Verge, Interim Managing Director, 905-670-0010 Ext. 102
mike.verge@orac.ca
Gregg Little, Treasurer, 905-569-8990
gregg@springbank.com
Meetings/Conferences:
• Ontario Refrigeration & Air Conditioning Contractors Association 2018 AGM, April, 2018, The Blue Mountains, ON
Scope: Provincial

Ontario Regional Common Ground Alliance (ORCGA)
#102, 545 North Rivermede Rd., Vaughan ON L4K 4H1
Tel: 905-532-9836
Toll-Free: 866-446-4493
office@orcga.com
www.orcga.com
www.linkedin.com/company/ontario-regional-common-ground-alliance
www.facebook.com/OntarioRegionalCGA
twitter.com/ORCGA
Overview: A small provincial organization
Mission: To ensure efficiency of, & limit damage to, the underground infrastructure of Ontario
Membership: 530; *Committees:* Best Practice; Education & Events; Reporting & Evaluation
Activities: Organizing damage prevention programs
Chief Officer(s):
Ian Munro, President & CEO
ian@orcga.com
Publications:
• Ear to the Ground [a publication of the Ontario Regional Common Ground Alliance]
Type: Magazine; *Frequency:* Biannually

Ontario Regional Poison Information Centre (ORPIC)
The Hospital for Sick Children, 555 University Ave., Toronto ON M5G 1X8
Tel: 416-813-5900
Toll-Free: 800-268-9017; *TTY:* 416-597-0215
www.ontariopoisoncentre.com
Overview: A small provincial organization founded in 1978
Mission: To provide telephone information & advice about exposures to poisonous substances; operates 24 hour, 7 day a week through local & toll free numbers
Member of: Canadian Association of Poison Control Centres
Activities: *Internships:* Yes
Chief Officer(s):
Lutfi Haj-Assaad, Director, Child Health Services

Ontario Registered Music Teachers' Association (ORMTA) / Association des professeurs de musique enregistrés de l'Ontario (APMEO)
PO Box 635, Timmins ON P4N 7G2
Tel: 705-267-1224; *Fax:* 705-264-0978
ormta@ntl.sympatico.ca
www.ormta.org
www.linkedin.com/groups/1798069/profile
www.facebook.com/223312484348113
twitter.com/ORMTA
www.youtube.com/user/TheORMTA
Overview: A medium-sized provincial organization founded in 1885
Member of: Canadian Federation of Music Teachers
Membership: 1,300; *Fees:* Schedule available; *Member Profile:* Music teachers
Activities: Music Writing Competition, March; *Awareness Events:* Canada Music Week, November; *Internships:* Yes
Chief Officer(s):
Ron Spadafore, Secretary-Registrar
Awards:
• ORMTA Provincial Instrumental Competition
• ORMTA Provincial Vocal Competition
• ORMTA Provincial Young Artist Competition
• ORMTA Music Writing Competition
• ORMTA Pedagogy Award
• ORMTA Contribution to Teaching Award
Meetings/Conferences:
• Ontario Registered Music Teachers' Association 2018 Convention, July, 2018, Infinity Convention Centre, Ottawa, ON
Scope: Provincial
Publications:
• NOTES [a publication of the Ontario Registered Music Teachers' Association]
Type: Magazine; *Frequency:* 3 pa; *Editor:* Patrick McCormick; *Price:* $12ORMTA members; $20 non-member (Canadian); $30 non-member (International)
Profile: Articles on pedagogical concepts & research, news on ORMTA activities & reviews of teaching materials

Ontario Research Council on Leisure (ORCOL) / Conseil Ontarien de Recherche en Loisir
c/o Recreation & Leisure Studies, Faculty of Applied Health Sciences, University of Waterloo, Waterloo ON N2L 3G1
ahsweb@healthy.uwaterloo.ca
www.orcol.uwaterloo.ca
Overview: A small provincial organization founded in 1975
Mission: To disseminate research about leisure & recreation, including culture, tourism, fitness, & sports
Membership: *Member Profile:* Researchers in the field of leisure from academe, government, & consultancies
Chief Officer(s):
Bryan Smale, President
Don Reid, Treasurer
Publications:
• Leisure / Loisir
Type: Journal; *Frequency:* Semiannually; *ISSN:* 1492-7713; *Price:* $40 students; $75 individuals; $100 institutions
Profile: Prepared in cooperation with the Canadian Association for Leisure Studies
• ORCOL [Ontario Research Council on Leisure] Symposium Proceedings
Profile: Abstracts of presentations made at the symposium

Ontario Residential Care Association *See* Ontario Retirement Communities Association

Ontario Respiratory Care Society (ORCS)
#401, 18 Wynford Dr., Toronto ON M3C 0K8
Tel: 416-864-9911; *Fax:* 416-864-9916
info@on.lung.ca
www.on.lung.ca
Overview: A medium-sized provincial charitable organization
Mission: To improve lung health through the provision of excellent interdisciplinary respiratory care
Finances: *Funding Sources:* Sponsorships
Membership: *Member Profile:* Persons involved in respiratory care, such as pulmonary function technologists, nurses, occupational therapists & physiotherapists, dietitians, & social workers; *Committees:* Provincial; Research & Fellowship; Editorial Board; Education; Membership & Program Promotion
Activities: Funding graduate education & research in respiratory care; Providing education & disseminating information for health care professionals; Offering professional expertise to the Ontario Lung Association & other interested groups
Chief Officer(s):
Bruce Cooke, Chair
George Habib, President & CEO
Awards:
• ORCS Research Grants
• ORCS Fellowship Awards
• Education Awards for Advanced Respiratory Practice
Publications:
• ORCS [Ontario Respiratory Care Society] Update
Type: Newsletter; *Frequency:* 3 pa; *Price:* Free with membership in the Ontario Respiratory Care Society
Profile: ORCS activities & respiratory articles
• Research Review [a joint publication of the Ontario Respiratory Care Society & the Ontario Thoracic Society]
Frequency: Annually; *Price:* Free with membership in the Ontario Respiratory Care Society
Profile: Highlights of researchers & their studies
• RHEIG [Respiratory Health Educators Interest Group] Connections
Frequency: 3 pa; *Price:* Free with membership in the Ontario Respiratory Care Society
Profile: Published by the Respiratory Health Educators Interest Group for members of the group

Ontario Restaurant, Hotel & Motel Association (ORHMA)
#8-201, 2600 Skymark Ave., Mississauga ON L4W 5B2
Tel: 905-361-0268; *Fax:* 905-361-0288
Toll-Free: 800-668-8906
info@orhma.com
www.orhma.com
www.linkedin.com/company/ontario-restaurant-hotel-&-motel-association
www.facebook.com/ORHMA
twitter.com/orhma
Previous Name: Ontario Hotel & Motel Association
Overview: A medium-sized provincial organization founded in 1999 overseen by Hotel Association of Canada Inc.
Mission: To foster a positive business climate for the hospitality industry in Ontario; To represent members before municipal & provincial governments
Staff Member(s): 9
Membership: 4,000+; *Fees:* Schedule available, based upon volume of sales for foodservice members, & number of rooms for accommodation members; $650 associate members; $185 s; *Member Profile:* Foodservice & accommodation establishments; Industry suppliers; Instructors & students
Activities: Liaising with government; Providing educational services
Chief Officer(s):
Steven Robinson, Chair
Tony Elenis, President & CEO, 905-361-0268
telenis@orhma.com

Canadian Associations / Ontario Retirement Communities Association (ORCA)

Fatima Finnegan, Director, Corporate Marketing & Business Development, 800-668-8906 Ext. 335
ffinnegan@orhma.com

Ontario Retail Farm Equipment Dealers' Association *See* Canada East Equipment Dealers' Association

Ontario Retail Lumber Dealers Association *See* Lumber & Building Materials Association of Ontario

Ontario Retirement Communities Association (ORCA)
#202, 2401 Bristol Circle, Oakville ON L6H 6P1
Tel: 905-403-0500; *Fax:* 905-829-1594
Toll-Free: 888-263-5559
info@orcaretirement.com
www.orcaretirement.com
twitter.com/ORCAhomes
www.youtube.com/user/ORCAhomes
Previous Name: Ontario Residential Care Association
Overview: A small provincial organization founded in 1977
Mission: To support high quality retirement communities throughout Ontario; To act as the voice of retirement communities in Ontario
Membership: 534 retirement residences; *Member Profile:* Retirement residences across Ontario
Activities: Setting operating standards; Conducting inspections; Accrediting Ontario-based retirement residences; Influencing public policy; Educating members; Enhancing public awareness
Chief Officer(s):
Laurie Johnston, Chief Executive Officer
Awards:
• Rick Winchell Resident of the Year Award
• The Award of Excellence
To honour leader in service excellence, quality, & innovation
Meetings/Conferences:
• Ontario Retirement Communities Association "Together We Care" Convention & Trade Show, April, 2018, Toronto Congress Centre, Toronto, ON
Scope: Provincial
Description: A gathering of retirement and long term care professionals.
Contact Information: www.together-we-care.com

Ontario Rett Syndrome Association (ORSA)
PO Box 50030, London ON N6A 6H8
Tel: 519-474-6877; *Fax:* 519-850-1272
www.rett.ca
www.facebook.com/OntarioRettSyndromeAssociation
twitter.com/OntarioRettSA
Overview: A small provincial charitable organization founded in 1991
Mission: To ensure that girls & women with Rett Syndrome are enabled to achieve their full potential & enjoy the highest quality of life within their community
Finances: *Annual Operating Budget:* $50,000-$100,000; *Funding Sources:* Donations; Nevada tickets; fundraising events
Staff Member(s): 7
Membership: 125; *Fees:* $30; *Member Profile:* Families & friends of women/girls with Rett Syndrome
Activities: Workshops; information; support; *Library:* Rett Syndrome Resource Centre Canada; by appointment Not open to public
Chief Officer(s):
Terry Boyd, President
Darcy Balak, Secretary
Scott Campbell, Coordinator, Membership
Meetings/Conferences:
• 2018 Ontario Rett Syndrome Association Conference, April, 2018, Holiday Inn, Toronto, ON
Scope: Provincial

Ontario Rheumatology Association (ORA)
#244, 12 - 16715 Yonge St., Newmarket ON L3X 1X4
Tel: 905-952-0698; *Fax:* 905-952-0708
admin@ontariorheum.ca
ontariorheum.ca
Overview: A small provincial organization founded in 2001
Mission: To represent Ontario Rheumatologists and promote their pursuit of excellence in Arthritis care in Ontario.
Affiliation(s): Canadian Rheumatology Association
Chief Officer(s):
Arthur Karasik, President
president@ontariorheum.ca
Meetings/Conferences:
• *Ontario Rheumatology Association 2018 Annual Meeting*, May, 2018, ON
Scope: Provincial

Ontario Rifle Association (ORA)
c/o ORA Membership Secretary, PO Box 22019, Stn. Elmwood Square, St Thomas ON H5R 6A1
oraatt@yahoo.ca
www.ontariorifleassociation.org
Overview: A medium-sized provincial organization founded in 1868
Affiliation(s): Dominion of Canada Rifle Association
Membership: *Fees:* $157 Probationary Basic; $182 Probationary ORA Membership with Associate DCRA; $257 Probationary ORA Membership with Full DCRA
Chief Officer(s):
Fazal Mohideen, Secretary
orafazal@bell.net

Ontario Ringette Association (ORA) / Association de ringuette de l'Ontario
#207, 3 Concorde Gate, Toronto ON M3C 3N7
Tel: 416-426-7204; *Fax:* 416-426-7359
admin@ontario-ringette.com
www.ontario-ringette.com
twitter.com/OntRingette
www.youtube.com/channel/UCWGddPSY6p6_X8wQqe1csPw
Overview: A medium-sized provincial organization founded in 1963 overseen by Ringette Canada
Mission: To promote fun, fitness, & friendship in a safe play environment; To be dedicated to quality performance & fair play opportunity for all ages
Member of: Ringette Canada
Membership: *Committees:* Officiating Development; Games & Tournament; Adult Development; Elite Development; Membership Services; Coaching Development; Sport Development; Rules Development
Chief Officer(s):
Keith Kaiser, President
president@ontario-ringette.com
Michael Beaton, Executive Director, 416-426-7205
ed@ontario-ringette.com
Karla Romphf, Director, Technical, 416-426-7206
tech@ontario-ringette.com
Rose Snagg, Coordinator, Administration, 416-426-7204
admin@ontario-ringette.com

Ontario Road Builders' Association (ORBA)
#1, 365 Brunel Rd., Mississauga ON L4Z 1Z5
Tel: 905-507-1107; *Fax:* 905-890-8122
info@orba.org
www.orba.org
www.facebook.com/OntarioRoadBuildersAssociation
twitter.com/onroadbuilders
Overview: A medium-sized provincial organization founded in 1926 overseen by Canadian Construction Association
Mission: To act as the voice of the Ontario road building industry; To maintain high standards in the road building industry & promote worker health & safety
Membership: 75+ road building contractors; 85+ associate members; *Fees:* Schedule available based upon annual civil contracting volume; *Member Profile:* Road building contractors across Ontario; Organizations that manufacture or supply products & services to the road building industry; *Committees:* Alternative Financing & Procurement; Area Maintenance Contractors Council; Audit; Contacts & Documents; Education; Environemnt; Grading; Membership; Municipal Affairs Council; Northern Affairs; Structures & Concrete; Transportation & Construction Equipment; Hot Mix Paving; Occupational Health & Safety; Infrastructure Transportation Committee & Metrolinx Infrastructure Council
Activities: Advocating for road building contractors throughout Ontario; Promoting the benefits of infrastructure investment; Providing education & training; Offering information & research
Chief Officer(s):
Geoffrey Stephens, President
Vince Aurilio, Executive Director, Ontario Asphalt Pavement Council, 905-507-1107 Ext. 230
vince@onasphalt.org
David Caplan, Chief Operating Officer, 416-300-4861 Ext. 224
david@orba.org
Andrew Hurd, Director, Policy & Stakeholder Relations, 905-507-1107 Ext. 223
andrew@orba.org
Meetings/Conferences:
• 91st Ontario Road Builders' Association 2018 Convention & Annual General Meeting, 2018, ON

Scope: Provincial
Description: Informative sessions of interest to members of the road building industry
Publications:
• ORBA [Ontario Road Builders' Association] Directory
Type: Directory; *Frequency:* Annually; *Price:* Free with Ontario Road Builders' membership
Profile: Member contact information, plus product & services information
• Road Builder Magazine
Type: Magazine; *Frequency:* Semiannually
Profile: Industry issues, new technology, & articles about member companies for Ontario Road Builders' Association members, Ministry of Transporation staff, as well as consulting engineers

Ontario Rock Garden Society
c/o Carol Clark, 88 Cottonwood Dr., Toronto ON M3C 2B4
info@onrockgarden.com
www.onrockgarden.com
Overview: A small provincial organization founded in 1984
Mission: To promote the study & cultivation of alpine & related garden plants & the creation of rock gardens
Member of: North American Rock Garden Society
Finances: *Annual Operating Budget:* Less than $50,000; *Funding Sources:* Membership fees; plant sales
Membership: 450; *Fees:* $25 individual; $30 family or overseas; $10 student
Activities: 10 meetings per year; spring & fall plant sales; seed exchange in Dec.; handbook listing members, gardens to visit, mail order & non-mail order services; *Speaker Service:* Yes; *Library*
Chief Officer(s):
Donna McMaster, Chair

Ontario Rodeo Association (ORA)
#3, 62 Gruhn St., Kitchener ON N2G 1S6
Tel: 519-954-4635
www.orarodeo.com
www.facebook.com/orarodeo
twitter.com/orarodeo
Overview: A small provincial organization founded in 1957
Mission: To promote rodeo in Ontario & produce a standard set of rules to be followed by the rodeo cowboys & rodeo producers & also, a set of rules to protect the stock used in rodeos from inhumane treatment
Membership: 375; *Fees:* $125 contestant, $93.75 contract; $31.25 associate
Activities: Seven standard events: Saddle Bronc Riding; Bareback Bronc Riding; Bull Riding; Calf Roping; Steer Wrestling; Team Roping & Ladies Barrel Racing; three optional events: Jr. Steer Riding & Ladies Breakaway Roping & Jr. Barrel Racing
Chief Officer(s):
Joe Scully, President
Earl Foster, Vice-President

Ontario Rowing Association (ORA)
#206, 19 Waterman Ave., Toronto ON M4B 1Y2
Tel: 416-759-8405
rowontarioadmin@rowontario.ca
www.rowontario.ca
www.facebook.com/ontariorowing
twitter.com/rowontario
Overview: A medium-sized provincial organization founded in 1970 overseen by Rowing Canada Aviron
Mission: To govern the sport of rowing in Ontario; To provide assistance to member clubs in the encouragement of competitive & recreational rowing; To maintain the principles of amateurism; To develop provincial rowing teams to represent Ontario at the Canada Games; To host an annual provincial rowing championship
Member of: Rowing Canada Aviron
Affiliation(s): Ontario Sport Council
Finances: *Funding Sources:* Membership dues; services; government grants; donations
Membership: 6,000 individuals; *Fees:* $1 non-rower; $3 highschool; $10 sport rower; $44 competitive rower; $275 club; *Member Profile:* Organized amateur rowing clubs in Ontario; *Committees:* Human Resources; Governance; Health & Safety; Finance; Nominating; RowOntario Coach Development
Activities: COAST (Club Operation Asset & Standards Tool)
Chief Officer(s):
Chris Waddell, President
Derek Ventor, Executive Director
derek@rowontario.ca

Ontario Rural Softball Association (ORSA)
c/o Secretary-Treasurer, 716029 - 18th Line, RR#1, Innerkip ON N0J 1M0
Tel: 519-469-3593
www.ontariororalsoftball.ca
Overview: A small provincial organization founded in 1931 overseen by Softball Ontario
Mission: To promote softball in rural districts, communities & small villages
Member of: Canadian Amateur Softball Association; Softball Ontario
Finances: *Funding Sources:* Sponsors; Partners; Government grants; Player/team fees
Chief Officer(s):
Earl Hall, President, 519-882-1599
Carl Littlejohns, Secretary-Treasurer
clittlejohnsorsa@live.ca

Ontario Safety League (OSL) / Ligue de sécurité de l'Ontario
#212, 2595 Skymark Ave., Mississauga ON L4W 4L5
Tel: 905-625-0556; *Fax:* 905-625-0677
info@osl.org
www.ontariosafetyleague.com
Overview: A medium-sized provincial licensing charitable organization founded in 1913
Mission: Safety through education with an emphasis on traffic & child safety
Affiliation(s): Canada Safety Council; Provincial Safety Leagues/Councils
Finances: *Annual Operating Budget:* $1.5 Million-$3 Million
Staff Member(s): 10
Membership: 300; *Fees:* $30-$300
Activities: Video production sales; courses for instructors of all vehicle types & road safety professionals; safety services for commercial fleets; *Speaker Service:* Yes; *Library:* OSL Film & Video Library; Not open to public
Chief Officer(s):
Brian J. Patterson, President & General Manager

Ontario Sailing / Association de voile de l'Ontario
#17, 70 Unsworth Dr., Hamilton ON L8W 3K4
Tel: 905-572-7245; *Fax:* 905-572-6056
Toll-Free: 888-672-7245
info@ontariosailing.ca
www.ontariosailing.ca
www.facebook.com/OntarioSailing
twitter.com/ontariosailing
Also Known As: Sail Ontario
Previous Name: Ontario Sailing Association
Overview: A medium-sized provincial organization founded in 1970 overseen by Sail Canada
Mission: To foster interest in sailing & to promote & encourage proficiency in the sport, particularly among young people in the province of Ontario; to promote sailboat racing events & to encourage the development of skills in sailboat handling & seamanship
Member of: Sail Canada
Affiliation(s): International Sailing Federation; Canadian Safe Boating Council
Finances: *Annual Operating Budget:* $500,000-$1.5 Million; *Funding Sources:* Membership fees; provincial government; corporate sponsorship; grants
Staff Member(s): 6; 25 volunteer(s)
Membership: 180 clubs/schools/associations; 10,000 families; 100,000 boaters
Chief Officer(s):
Glenn Lethbridge, Executive Director, 905-572-7245 Ext. 224
execdir@ontariosailing.ca

Ontario Sailing Association *See* Ontario Sailing

Ontario Sanitation Equipment Association *See* Ontario Pollution Control Equipment Association

Ontario School Bus Association (OSBA)
3075 Lenworth Dr., Mississauga ON L4X 2G3
Tel: 416-695-9965; *Fax:* 416-695-9977
info@osba.on.ca
www.osba.on.ca
Overview: A medium-sized provincial organization
Mission: To provide education, advocacy, & consultation services to persons involved in the school bus industry
Staff Member(s): 3
Membership: 100-499
Chief Officer(s):
Michele O'Bright, Director
mobright@osba.on.ca

Ontario School Counsellors' Association (OSCA)
PO Box 60, Hillsburgh ON N0B 1Z0
Tel: 519-800-0872; *Fax:* 519-800-0874
www.osca.ca
www.facebook.com/osca.acoso
twitter.com/OSCA_ACOSO
Overview: A medium-sized provincial organization founded in 1964
Mission: To provide progressive leadership & to support the work of school teacher-counsellors; committed to shaping a vision of the future through the development of specific initiatives which will influence the direction of change in programs & policies in Ontario
Staff Member(s): 6; 13 volunteer(s)
Membership: 1,500; *Fees:* $75 statutory/associate; $40 retired; *Committees:* Communication; Governance; Professional Development; Website
Chief Officer(s):
Joanne Brown, President
Awards:
• Olive Diefenbaker Award of Merit
• Russ Seltzer Award for Contribution to Counsellor Education in Ontario
 Deadline: September 15
• Twenty-Fifth Anniversary Award
 Deadline: September 15
• Certificate of Appreciation
 Deadline: September 15
• Marion Axford Award for Elementary Guidance
 Deadline: September 15
• Daryl L. Cook Peer Helping Award
 Deadline: September 15
• The Morgan D. Parmenter Memorial Award
 Deadline: September 15
• Career Education Citation
 Deadline: September 15
• Elmer Huff Award for Media Resources
 Deadline: September 15
• Frank Clute Award for Professional Research
 Deadline: September 15
• Howard R. Beattie Award for Professional Contribution
 Deadline: September 15
Meetings/Conferences:
• Ontario School Counsellors' Association Conference 2018, 2018
Scope: Provincial

Ontario School Library Association (OSLA)
c/o Ontario Library Association, 2 Toronto St., 3rd Fl., Toronto ON M5C 2B6
Tel: 416-363-3388; *Fax:* 416-941-9581
Toll-Free: 866-873-9867
info@accessola.com
www.accessola.org
Overview: A medium-sized provincial organization founded in 1972
Mission: To act as the voice of elementary & secondary school teacher-librarians in Ontario; To promote teacher-librarians as curriculum leaders; To support student success
Member of: Ontario Library Association
Membership: *Member Profile:* Teacher-librarians in Ontario; School board consultants
Activities: Advocating for the interests of teacher-librarians; Developing school libraries & school library programs; Providing continuing education; Promoting research related to school libraries
Chief Officer(s):
Melissa Jensen, President
meljensen@gmail.com
Awards:
• Teacher-Librarian of the Year
To recognize a teacher-librarian who has demonstrated leadership in the implementation of school library program
• Administrator of the Year
To recognize a school administrator who has influenced the development of school library information centres & school library programs
• Award for Special Achievement
To recognize individuals or organizations outside schools & school boards who have supported teacher-librarians & school library information centre development
• Technical Services Award
Awarded to the Ontario librarian, teacher-librarian, technician, library worker or department who has made a significant achievement to their institution/the profession as a whole in the area of technical services
Meetings/Conferences:
• Ontario School Library Association 2018 Annual General Meeting, 2018, ON
Scope: Provincial
Publications:
• The Teaching Librarian [a publication of the Ontario School Library Association]
Type: Newsletter; *Frequency:* 3 pa; *Editor:* Diana Maliszewski; *ISSN:* 1188-679X; *Price:* Free with OSLA membership; $36 without OSLA membership
Profile: Supports OSLA members in providing effective library programs & services; promotes library programming & curriculum development that furthers educational objectives

Ontario Seaplane Association
ON
Tel: 705-327-4730
doug@dougronan.com
www.dougronan.com/ontario
www.facebook.com/groups/213790595317592
Overview: A small provincial organization
Mission: To bring together seaplane pilots and enthusiasts
0 volunteer(s)
Membership: *Fees:* Free
Activities: Fly-ins; social events; fishing trips
Chief Officer(s):
Doug Ronan, President, 705-327-4730
doug@dougronan.com
Paul Armstrong, Vice President, 416-438-5985
paul-armstrong@rogers.com
Brain Wendt, Secretary, 847-971-6980
brwendt9@hotmail.com

Ontario Secondary School Teachers' Federation (OSSTF) / Fédération des enseignants des écoles secondaires de l'Ontario (FEESO)
60 Mobile Dr., Toronto ON M4A 2P3
Tel: 416-751-8300
Toll-Free: 800-267-7867
www.osstf.on.ca
www.facebook.com/osstfnews
twitter.com/osstf
www.youtube.com/user/OSSTF
Overview: A large provincial organization founded in 1919
Mission: To protect & enhance Ontario's public education system; To establish working conditions for members
Staff Member(s): 110
Membership: 60,000+; *Member Profile:* Ontario's English & French public high school teachers, occasional teachers, continuing education instructors, educational assistants, speech-language pathologists, psychologists, social workers, secretaries, & plant support personnel
Activities: Working with goverments, school boards, & parents to improve the public education system; Lobbying; Communicating with the media; Preventing the commercialization & privatization of educational institutions; Engaging in negotiations; Sponsoring professional conferences, workshops, & union training; *Library:* Ontario Secondary School Teachers' Federation Research Library
Chief Officer(s):
Paul Elliott, President & CEO
Harvey Bischof, Vice-President
Cindy Dubué, Vice-President
Pierre Côté, General Secretary
Earl Burt, Treasurer
Awards:
• OSSTF/FEESO Awards of Recognition for Members
• OSSTF/FEESO Awards for Non-Members
• OSSTF/FEESO Financial Assistance Awards for Further Education
• OSSTF/FEESO Grants in Support of Staff Development
Meetings/Conferences:
• Ontario Secondary School Teachers' Federation Annual Meeting of the Provincial Assembly (AMPA) 2018, March, 2018, Sheraton Centre Toronto, Toronto, ON
Scope: Provincial
Attendance: 500+
Publications:
• Education Forum [a publication of the Ontario Secondary School Teachers' Federation]
Type: Magazine; *Frequency:* 3 pa
Profile: A resource that explores the contemporary issues, events, trends, & personalities that shape education today

- Education Watch [a publication of the Ontario Secondary School Teachers' Federation]
Type: Newsletter; *Frequency:* 6 pa
Profile: Distributed to MPPS, some education stakeholders, & other decision makers; focuses on issues relevant to the union
- Ontario Secondary School Teachers' Federation Update
Type: Newsletter; *Frequency:* Monthly
Profile: News for all Ontario Secondary School Teachers' Federation members

Ontario Securities Commission (OSC)
20 Queen St. West, 20th Fl., Toronto ON M5H 3S8
Tel: 416-593-8314; *Fax:* 416-593-8122
Toll-Free: 877-785-1555; *TTY:* 866-827-1295
Other Communication: Whistleblower: 1-888-672-5553; www.officeofthewhistleblower.ca
inquiries@osc.gov.on.ca
www.osc.gov.on.ca
www.facebook.com/GetSmarterAboutMoney
twitter.com/OSC_News
Overview: A medium-sized provincial organization founded in 1928 overseen by Canadian Securities Administrators
Mission: To regulate securities trading in Ontario, through the administration of the Securities Act (Ontario) & the Commodity Futures Act (Ontario); To report to the Legislature, through the minister responsible for the administration of the Acts; To foster a fair & competitive securities market; To protect investors & market integrity
Member of: Canadian Securities Administrators
Finances: *Funding Sources:* Fees collected from market participants under the legislation
Activities: Offers the first paid whistleblower program by a securities regulator in Canada
Chief Officer(s):
Maureen Jensen, Chair & CEO
Leslie Byberg, Executive Director & CAO
Publications:
- Ontario Securities Commission Annual Report
Type: Report; *Frequency:* Annually
- OSC [Ontario Securities Commission] Investor News
Type: Newsletter; *Frequency:* Annually
- Statement of Priorities [a publication of the Ontario Securities Commission]
Type: Report; *Frequency:* Annually

Ontario Seed Corn Growers' Marketing Board *See* Seed Corn Growers of Ontario

Ontario Seed Growers Association (OSGA)
1 Stone Rd. West, Guelph ON N1G 4Y2
Tel: 519-826-4214; *Fax:* 519-826-4224
Toll-Free: 800-265-9751
Overview: A medium-sized provincial organization founded in 1953 overseen by Canadian Seed Growers' Association
Mission: To ensure the supply of genetically pure seed crop
Member of: Canadian Seed Growers Association
Affiliation(s): Ontario Soil & Crop Improvement Association
Finances: *Funding Sources:* Grower fees; Government
11 volunteer(s)
Membership: 1,200
Chief Officer(s):
Harold Rudy, Secretary
Harold.Rudy@ontariosoilcrop.org

Ontario Senior Games Association (OSGA)
#310, 3 Concorde Gate, Toronto ON M3C 3N7
Tel: 416-426-7031; *Fax:* 416-426-7226
Toll-Free: 800-320-6423
info@ontarioseniorgames.ca
www.ontarioseniorgames.ca
www.facebook.com/Ontario55plus
Overview: A medium-sized provincial organization
Mission: To provide physical & social activities to senior citizens
Membership: *Committees:* Rules
Chief Officer(s):
Gail Prior, President
president@ontarioseniorgames.ca
Geoffrey Johnson, Program Coordinator
geoff@ontarioseniorgames.ca

Ontario Sewer & Watermain Construction Association (OSWCA)
#300, 5045 Orbitor Dr., Unit 12, Mississauga ON L4W 4Y4
Tel: 905-629-7766; *Fax:* 905-629-0587
info@oswca.org
www.oswca.org
twitter.com/oswca1971
Overview: A medium-sized provincial organization
Mission: To represent sewer & watermain construction contractors throughout Ontario; To increase business opportunities for members
Membership: 700+ companies; *Committees:* Young Executives; Government Relations; Members Services; Marketing Initiatives; Education Program; Administration
Activities: Liaising with the Government of Ontario & its agencies; Increasing public awareness about the maintenance of water & wastewater systems in Ontario; Providing apprenticeship training & upgrading training; Informing members of industry developments
Chief Officer(s):
Giovanni Cautillo, Executive Director, 905-629-7766 Ext. 229
giovanni.cautillo@oswca.org
Patrick McManus, Manager, Stakeholder Relations and Services, 905-629-7766 Ext. 222
patrick.mcmanus@oswca.org
Daniela Polsoni, Office Coordinator, 905-629-7766 Ext. 221
daniela.polsoni@oswca.org
Publications:
- Ontario Sewer & Watermain Construction Association Membership Directory
Type: Directory; *Frequency:* Annually; *Accepts Advertising*
Profile: A buyers' guide for products & services used by sewer & watermain construction contractors, municipalities, utilities, & engineers
- Undergrounder [a publication of the Ontario Sewer & Watermain Construction Association]
Type: Magazine; *Frequency:* 3 pa; *Accepts Advertising*
Profile: Association business, industry issues, & regulatory updates available in print or digital editions

Ontario Shade Tree Council *See* Ontario Urban Forest Council

Ontario Sheep Association *See* Ontario Sheep Marketing Agency

Ontario Sheep Marketing Agency (OSMA)
130 Malcolm Rd., Guelph ON N1K 1B1
Tel: 519-836-0043; *Fax:* 519-836-2531
www.ontariosheep.org
Previous Name: Ontario Sheep Association
Overview: A medium-sized provincial organization founded in 1985
Mission: To represent all aspects of the sheep, lamb, & wool industry in Ontario; To improve the marketing of sheep & enhance producers' returns; To provide the public with safe, quality lamb & related products
Membership: *Member Profile:* All producers of sheep & wool in Ontario must register with the Ontario Sheep Marketing Agency
Activities: Advocating on behalf of sheep producers; Educating producers; Providing consumer education; Increasing public awareness of the industry; Developing promotional campaigns; Supporting research in the industry
Chief Officer(s):
Jennifer MacTavish, General Manager, 519-836-0043 Ext. 23
jmactavish@ontariosheep.org
Awards:
- Ontario Sheep Marketing Agency Scholorship
Publications:
- The Messenger
Type: Newsletter
Profile: Agency activities, industry news, & upcoming events

Ontario Sheet Metal & Air Handling Group *See* Ontario Sheet Metal Contractors Association

Ontario Sheet Metal Contractors Association (OSM)
#26, 30 Wertheim Ct., Richmond Hill ON L4B 1B9
Tel: 905-886-9627; *Fax:* 905-886-9959
shtmetal@bellnet.ca
www.osmca.org
Previous Name: Ontario Sheet Metal & Air Handling Group
Overview: A small provincial organization founded in 1967
Mission: To negotiate & administer all provincial collective agreements between OSM, the Ontario Sheet Metal Workers' & Roofers' Conference & the Sheet Metal Workers International Association.
Member of: National Trade Contractors Coalition of Canada
Membership: *Member Profile:* Contractors engaged in manufacturing, installing, servicing & maintaining of all sheet metal work associated with air handling systems & directly related processes
Chief Officer(s):
Kim Crossman, President, 416-663-4300, Fax: 416-663-4305
kimcrossman@dmcmechanical.com

Wayne Peterson, Executive Director

Ontario Shorthorn Association (OSA)
c/o Doug Brown, 212 Bassett Blvd., Whitby ON L1R 1G6
Tel: 905-431-8496
www.ontarioshorthorns.com
www.facebook.com/ontarioshorthorns
Overview: A small provincial organization
Mission: To preserve & promote the Shorthorn breed of cattle in Ontario
Member of: Canadian Shorthorn Association
Finances: *Annual Operating Budget:* Less than $50,000
Membership: 100; *Member Profile:* Shorthorn cattle owners
Activities: *Speaker Service:* Yes
Chief Officer(s):
Jamie Blenkiron, Vice-President
jamie.ellen@blenviewfarms.com

Ontario Shuffleboard Association (OSA)
PO Box 1690, Guelph ON N1H 6Z9
ontarioshuffleboard.com
Overview: A medium-sized provincial organization founded in 1964
Member of: Canadian Shuffleboard Congress
Chief Officer(s):
Rico Beaulieu, President
rick@ritewayaluminum.com

Ontario Sikh & Gurudwara Council (OSGC)
140 Rivalda Rd., Toronto ON M9M 2M8
info@osgc.ca
osgc.ca
www.facebook.com/OntarioSikhs
Overview: A small provincial organization
Mission: To fulfill the aspirations, along with the contemporary and broader needs, of the Skikh Community; To provide religious & social leadership; To raise awareness of Sikh philosophy, principles & heritage; To promote Sikh values & work as a liaison with similar organizations of different faiths
Membership: 62; *Fees:* $51 individual; $251 Gurdwaras; *Committees:* Nagar Kirtan; Religious Affairs; Medial Liason & Public Relations; Women Affairs; Youth Affairs
Chief Officer(s):
Bhupinder Singh, Chairperson
Kultar Singh, Vice Chairperson
Balkaran Singh, Secretary
Jagdev Singh, Treasurer

Ontario Simmental Association (OSA)
c/o Debbie Elliot, Line 26 #7062, RR#2, Staffa ON N0K 1Y0
Tel: 519-345-2785; *Fax:* 519-345-2779
ircc@nexicom.net
www.ontariosimmentalassociation.com
Overview: A small provincial organization founded in 1979
Mission: To represent & assist the breeders of Ontario in the development & marketing of Simmental
Member of: Canadian Simmental Association
Membership: *Fees:* $30 annual; $85 three-year; *Member Profile:* Breeder of Simmental cattle in Ontario
Activities: Shows & sales
Chief Officer(s):
Grace Oesch, Secretary
gravandale@netflash.net
Debbie Elliot, Treasurer
dje@djfarmscattle.com
Dan O'Brien, President
dan.obrien@sympatico.ca

Ontario Skeet Shooting Association (OSSA)
PO Box 96, Hampton ON L0B 1J0
Tel: 905-263-8174; *Fax:* 905-263-4870
info@ontarioskeet.com
www.ontarioskeet.com
Overview: A small provincial organization
Mission: To educate persons in the safe & efficient handling of shotguns; to encourage competition in shotgun target shooting; to promote the sport of skeet shooting in the province of Ontario
Member of: Shooting Federation of Canada; National Skeet Shooting Association
Finances: *Annual Operating Budget:* Less than $50,000
8 volunteer(s)
Membership: 165
Chief Officer(s):
Jennie Marsh, Secretary-Treasurer
Brad McRae, President

Ontario Sledge Hockey Association (OSHA)
ON
www.alpineontario.ca
www.facebook.com/467967866581968
twitter.com/OSHASledge
Overview: A medium-sized provincial organization
Mission: To oversee three regular season sledge hockey leagues
Member of: Ontario Hockey Federation; Hockey Canada
Membership: 20 clubs + 400 players; *Committees:* Rules
Chief Officer(s):
Dave Kisel, President, 905-560-8287
dkisel@bell.net

Ontario Small Urban Municipalities (OSUM)
c/o Association of Municipalities of Ontario, #801, 200 University Ave., Toronto ON M5H 3C6
Tel: 416-971-9856; *Fax:* 416-971-6191
Toll-Free: 877-426-6527
amo@amo.on.ca
www.osum.ca
Overview: A medium-sized provincial organization
Mission: To take matters which affect Ontario's small urban communities to the attention of the provincial & federal governments
Member of: Association of Municipalities of Ontario
Finances: *Funding Sources:* Sponsorships
Membership: 100-499; *Member Profile:* Small urban municipalities in Ontario
Activities: Providing a forum for both elected & appointed municipal officials of Ontario's small urban municipalities to exchange information
Chief Officer(s):
Paul Grenier, Chair, 905-788-2624
Jim Collard, Vice-Chair & Conference Chair, 905-658-1977
Larry McCabe, Administrative Member, OSUM Executive Committee, 519-524-8344, Fax: 519-524-7209
lmccabe@goderich.ca
Meetings/Conferences:
• Ontario Small Urban Municipalities 2018 65th Annual Conference & Trade Show, May, 2018, Niagara Falls, ON
Scope: Provincial
Attendance: 200+
Contact Information: Coordinator, Conference & Trade Show: Jim Collard, Phone: 905-468-3266, E-mail: collard@niagara.com

Ontario Soccer Association (OSA)
7601 Martin Grove Rd., Vaughan ON L4L 9E4
Tel: 905-264-9390; *Fax:* 905-264-9445
www.soccer.on.ca
www.facebook.com/TheOntarioSoccerAssociation
twitter.com/OSA_Tweeter
www.youtube.com/OSAVideoMaster
Overview: A medium-sized provincial organization founded in 1901 overseen by Canadian Soccer Association
Mission: To provide leadership & support for the advancement of soccer; To provide programs & services
Member of: Canadian Soccer Association
Staff Member(s): 39
Membership: 500,000 players; 70,000 coaches; 10,000 referees; *Committees:* Discipline & Appeals; Competitions; Information Management System Oversight; League Management; Referee Development; Technical Advisory; Women in Soccer; Rules Review; Audit; Executive; Finance; Governance; Human Resources; Nominations; Risk Management; Strategic Planning
Chief Officer(s):
Ron Smale, President
Lisa Beatty, Executive Director
lbeatty@soccer.on.ca

Ontario Society for Autistic Citizens *See* Autism Ontario

Ontario Society for Environmental Education (OSEE)
PO Box 587, Lakefield ON K0L 2H0
Tel: 705-652-0923
home.osee.ca
www.facebook.com/OS4EE
Overview: A small provincial organization
Mission: To develop a population that is aware of, & concerned about, the environment & its associated problems, & which has the knowledge, skills, attitudes, motivations & commitment to work individually & collectively toward solutions of current problems & the prevention of new ones (from UNESCO)
Finances: *Annual Operating Budget:* Less than $50,000
Staff Member(s): 2; 10 volunteer(s)
Membership: *Fees:* $40 individual; $20 student; $57 overseas; $300 corporate; *Member Profile:* Teachers & outdoor education leaders
Chief Officer(s):
Sherri Owen, President
sherri.owen@osee.ca
Meetings/Conferences:
• Ontario Society for Environmental Education EcoLinks Conference 2018, May, 2018, High Park, Toronto, ON
Scope: Provincial

Ontario Society for Environmental Management (OSEM)
85 Irondale Dr., Toronto ON M9L 2S6
Tel: 416-746-9076; *Fax:* 416-745-6761
Overview: A small provincial organization founded in 1976
Mission: To encourage the exchange of information on matters of environmental management through seminars, meetings, position papers, newsletter, etc.; to develop an interdisciplinary forum for information exchange with other professions; to help persons & institutions responsible for decisions affecting the environment to make & implement policy consistent with the Society's environmental management ethic; to encourage high standards of competence & ethics among environmental management practitioners; to encourage education in the field of environmental management; to encourage individuals to become environmental management practitioners
Membership: *Member Profile:* Open to those professionally involved in environmental management; potential members must have appropriate academic &/or professional credentials
Activities: Seminars; conferences
Chief Officer(s):
Sue Ruggero, Administrator

Ontario Society for the History of Nursing *See* Margaret M. Allemang Centre for the History of Nursing

Ontario Society for the Prevention of Cruelty to Animals (OSPCA)
16586 Woodbine Ave., Stouffville ON L4A 2W3
Tel: 905-898-7122; *Fax:* 905-853-8643
Toll-Free: 888-668-7722
info@ospca.on.ca
www.ontariospca.ca
www.facebook.com/OntarioSPCA
twitter.com/ontariospca
www.youtube.com/user/OntarioSPCA
Also Known As: Ontario Humane Society
Overview: A large provincial charitable organization founded in 1873 overseen by Canadian Federation of Humane Societies
Mission: To provide care & shelter for animals, especially pets; To enforce animal cruelty laws in the province; To investigate cruelty complaints; To carry out rescues & bring perpetrators to court; To advocate for humane laws; To promote humane education & public awareness of the humane treatment of animals; To operate a Wildlife Rehabilitation Centre in Midland, ON
Member of: World Society for the Protection of Animals; Canadian Federation of Humane Societies
Finances: *Annual Operating Budget:* Greater than $5 Million; *Funding Sources:* Fundraising; Public donations; Legacies
Activities: *Awareness Events:* Spay/Neuter Month, March; Adopt-a-Cat Month, June; Adopt-a-Dog Month, October; *Speaker Service:* Yes; *Library:* Open to public
Chief Officer(s):
Kate MacDonald, Chief Executive Officer
Connie Mallory, Chief Inspector
Alison Cross, Director, Marketing & Communications
Publications:
• Animals' Voice
Type: Magazine; *Frequency:* Quarterly

Alliston Branch (Affiliate)
Alliston & District Humane Society, PO Box 378, Beeton ON L0G 1A0
Tel: 705-458-9038; *Fax:* 705-435-2851
wendyh@idirect.com
www.allistonhumane.com

Arnprior Branch (Affiliate)
Arnprior & District Humane Society, 490 Didak Dr., Arnprior ON K7S 3H2
Tel: 613-623-0916
district.spca@bellnet.ca
www.arnpriorhumanesociety.ca

Barrie Branch
91 Patterson Rd., Barrie ON L4N 3V9
Tel: 705-728-7311; *Fax:* 705-728-7243
barrie@ospca.on.ca
www.barrie.ontariospca.ca
www.facebook.com/BarrieOSPCA
Chief Officer(s):
Melissa Bainbridge, Branch Manager

Brant County Branch (Affliate)
PO Box 163, 539 Mohawk Rd., Brantford ON N3T 5M8
Tel: 519-756-6620; *Fax:* 519-756-6910
reception@brantfordspca.com
www.brantfordspca.com
Chief Officer(s):
Robin Kuchma, Branch Manager

Bruce Grey Branch
16586 Woodbine Ave., RR#3, Newmarket ON L3Y 4W1
Tel: 888-668-7722; *Fax:* 905-853-8643
cruelty@ospca.on.ca

Cambridge & District Branch (Affiliate)
1650 Dunbar Rd., Cambridge ON N1R 8J5
Tel: 519-623-7722; *Fax:* 519-623-9442
spca@cambridgeweb.net
spca.cambridgeweb.net

Durham Region Branch (Affiliate)
1505 Wentworth St., Whitby ON L1N 0H9
Tel: 905-665-7430
humanedurham@auracom.com
www.humanedurham.com

Etobicoke Branch (Affiliate)
67 Six Point Rd., Toronto ON M8Z 2X3
Tel: 416-249-6100; *Fax:* 416-249-4118
info@etobicokehumanesociety.com
www.etobicokehumanesociety.com

Fort Erie Branch (Affiliate)
410 Jarvis St., Fort Erie ON L2A 2T1
Tel: 905-871-2461; *Fax:* 905-871-9746
forteriespca@bellnet.ca
www.forteriespca.org

Gananoque Branch (Affiliate)
Gananoque & District Humane Society, 85 Hwy. 32, RR#1, Gananoque ON K7G 2V3
Tel: 613-382-1512; *Fax:* 613-382-0333
humanesociety@bellnet.ca
www.ganhumanesociety.ca

Guelph Branch (Affiliate)
Guelph Humane Society, PO Box 684, 500 Wellington St. West, Guelph ON N1H 6L3
Tel: 519-824-3091; *Fax:* 519-824-3075
ghs-shelter@bellnet.ca
www.guelph-humane.on.ca

Hamilton / Burlington Branch (Affiliate)
Hamilton/Burlington SPCA, 245 Dartnall Rd., Hamilton ON L8W 3V9
Tel: 905-574-7722; *Fax:* 905-574-9087
info@hamiltonspca.com
www.hbspca.com
www.facebook.com/HBSPCA
twitter.com/hb_spca
www.youtube.com/user/TheHBSPCA;
www.pinterest.com/hamburspca

Huron County Branch
48 East St., Goderich ON N7A 1N3
Tel: 519-440-0250
huroncounty@ospca.on.ca
www.huroncounty.ontariospca.ca

Kawartha Lakes Branch (Affiliate) (HSKL)
c/o Humane Society of Kawartha Lakes, 107 McLaughlin Rd., Lindsay ON K9V 6K5
Tel: 705-878-4618; *Fax:* 705-878-5141
shelter.hskl@cogeco.net
www.hskl.ca
www.facebook.com/HumaneSocietyKawarthaLakes
twitter.com/pr_hskl
www.instagram.com/humanesocietyofkawarthalakes
Chief Officer(s):
Henny Venus, Executive Director

Kent Branch
405 Park Ave. East, Chatham ON N7M 3W4
Tel: 519-354-1713; *Fax:* 519-354-1716
kent@ospca.on.ca
www.kent.ontariospca.ca
www.facebook.com/ospca.kentbranch

Canadian Associations / Ontario Society for the Prevention of Cruelty to Animals (OSPCA)

Kingston Branch (Affliate)
Kingston Humane Society, 1 Binnington Ct., Kingston ON K7M 8M9
Tel: 613-546-1291; Fax: 613-546-3398
admin@kingstonhumanesociety.ca
www.kingstonhumanesociety.ca
www.facebook.com/10150127328310541

Kitchener-Waterloo Branch (Affiliate)
Kitchener-Waterloo Humane Society, 250 Riverbend Dr., Kitchener ON N2B 2E9
Tel: 519-745-5615
info@kwhumane.com
www.kwhumane.com
www.facebook.com/KitchenerWaterlooHumaneSociety
twitter.com/KWHumane
www.instagram.com/kwhumane
Chief Officer(s):
Jack Kinch, Executive Director
jack.kinch@kwhumane.com

Lanark Branch (Affiliate)
Lanark Animal Welfare Society, 253 Glenview Rd., Smiths Falls ON K7A 4S4
Tel: 613-283-9308; Fax: 613-283-0982
shelter@lanarkanimals.ca
www.lanarkanimals.ca
www.facebook.com/lanarkanimals
twitter.com/lawsshelter
Chief Officer(s):
Cheryl Griffen, Secretary
secretary.laws@gmail.com

Leeds & Grenville Branch
800 Centennial Rd., RR #4, Brockville ON K6V 5T4
Tel: 613-345-5520; Fax: 613-345-2169
leedsgrenville@ospca.on.ca
www.leedsgrenville.ontariospca.ca
www.facebook.com/ospcalgb
twitter.com/OSPCALG
Chief Officer(s):
Marianne Carlyle, Manager
mcarlyle@ospca.on.ca

Lennox & Addington Branch
156 Richmond Blvd. East, Napanee ON K7R 3Z7
Tel: 613-354-2492; Fax: 613-354-4802
lennoxaddington@ospca.on.ca
www.lennoxaddington.ontariospca.ca
www.facebook.com/ospca.lennoxaddingtonbranch
twitter.com/NapaneeOSPCA

Lincoln Branch (Affiliate)
Lincoln County Humane Society, 160 Fourth Ave., St Catharines ON L2R 6P9
Tel: 905-682-0767; Fax: 905-682-8133
myconnect@lchs.ca
www.lchs.ca
www.facebook.com/lincolncountyhumanesociety
twitter.com/lincolncountyhs
Chief Officer(s):
Kevin Strooband, Executive Director

London Branch (Affiliate)
London Humane Society, 624 Clarke Rd., London ON N5V 3K5
Tel: 519-451-0630; Fax: 519-451-8995
administration@londonhumane.ca
www.londonhumanesociety.ca
www.facebook.com/londonhumanesociety
twitter.com/londonhumanes

Midland & District Branch
15979 Highway 12 East, RR#1, Port McNicoll ON L0K 1R0
Tel: 705-534-4459; Fax: 705-534-4745
midland@ospca.org
www.midland.ontariospca.ca
www.facebook.com/MidlandOSPCA
twitter.com/OSPCAMidland
Chief Officer(s):
Caytlynn Croisier, Branch Manager

Muskoka Branch
PO Box 2804, Bracebridge ON P1L 1W5
Tel: 705-645-6225; Fax: 705-645-3382
muskoka@ospca.on.ca
www.muskoka.ontariospca.ca
www.facebook.com/muskoka.ospca
twitter.com/MuskokaOSPCA

Niagara Falls Branch (Affiliate)
Niagara Falls Humane Society, 6025 Chippawa Pkwy., Niagara Falls ON L2E 6X8
Tel: 905-356-4404; Fax: 905-356-7652
humane@nfhs.ca
www.nfhs.ca
www.facebook.com/NiagaraFallsHumaneSociety
twitter.com/nfhumanesociety

North Bay Branch (Affiliate)
North Bay & District Humane Society, 2060 Main St. West, North Bay ON P1B 8K5
Tel: 705-474-1251
info@northbayhumanesociety.ca
www.northbayhumanesociety.ca
www.facebook.com/nbHumaneSociety
twitter.com/nbhumanesociety
Chief Officer(s):
Daryl Vaillancourt, Executive Director
manager@northbayhumanesociety.ca

Northumberland Branch (Affiliate)
Northumberland Humane Society, 371 Ward St., Port Hope ON L1A 4A4
Tel: 905-885-4131; Fax: 905-885-8027
north1@eagle.ca
www.northumberlandhumanesociety.com
twitter.com/ShelteronWardSt

Oakville Branch (Affiliate)
Oakville & Milton Humane Society, 445 Cornwall Rd., Oakville ON L6J 7S8
Tel: 905-845-1551; Fax: 905-845-1973
shelter@omhs.ca
www.oakvillemiltonhumane.ca
www.facebook.com/OakvilleMiltonHumaneSociety
twitter.com/OakvilleHumane
www.instagram.com/oakvillemiltonhumane
Chief Officer(s):
Kim Millan, Executive Director

Ontario SPCA Centre Veterinary Hospital Spay/Neuter Services
16586 Woodbine Ave., Newmarket ON L3Y 4W1
Tel: 905-898-6112; Fax: 905-898-4321
Toll-Free: 888-668-7722
www.spayneuter.ontariospca.ca

Orangeville & District Branch
650 Riddell Rd., Orangeville ON L9W 5G5
Tel: 519-942-3140; Fax: 519-942-3678
orangeville@ospca.on.ca
www.orangeville.ontariospca.ca
www.facebook.com/OrangevilleSPCA
twitter.com/OrangevilleSPCA

Orillia Branch
467 West St. North, Orillia ON L3V 5G1
Tel: 705-325-1304; Fax: 705-325-1027
orillia@ospca.on.ca
www.orillia.ontariospca.ca
www.facebook.com/122372507786737
twitter.com/OrilliaSPCA
Chief Officer(s):
Carol Beard, Branch Manager
cbeard@ospca.on.ca

Ottawa Branch (Affiliate)
Ottawa Humane Society, 245 West Hunt Club Rd., Ottawa ON K23 1A6
Tel: 613-725-3166; Fax: 613-725-5674
ohs@ottawahumane.ca
www.ottawahumane.ca
www.facebook.com/OttawaHumane
twitter.com/ottawahumane
www.instagram.com/ottawahumane

Oxford-Elgin Branch
ON
Toll-Free: 888-668-7722

Peterborough Branch (Affiliate)
Peterborough Humane Society, 385 Landsdowne St. East, Peterborough ON K9L 2A3
Tel: 705-745-4722; Fax: 705-745-9770
info@ptbohs.com
www.peterboroughhumanesociety.ca
www.facebook.com/302384992539
www.twitter.com/twitter.com/HSpeterborough
Chief Officer(s):
Judy O'Brien, Executive Director
j.obrien@ptbohs.com

Provincial Education & Animal Centre
16586 Woodbine Ave., RR#3, Newmarket ON L3Y 4W1
Tel: 905-898-7122; Fax: 905-853-8643
peac@ospca.on.ca
www.peac.ontariospca.ca

Quinte Branch (Affiliate)
Quinte Humane Society, 527 Avonlough Rd., Belleville ON K8N 4Z2
Tel: 613-968-4673
qhs@quintehumanesociety.com
www.quintehumanesociety.com
www.facebook.com/quintehumanesociety2013
Chief Officer(s):
Frank Rockett, Executive Director
rockett@quintehumanesociety.com
Marja Smith, Shelter Manager
msmith@quintehumanesociety.com

Renfrew Branch
115 Woodcrest Dr., Pembroke ON K8A 6W4
Tel: 613-635-7508
renfrewcounty@ospca.on.ca
www.renfrewcounty.ontariospca.ca

Sarnia Branch (Affiliate)
Sarnia & District SPCA, 131 Exmouth St., Sarnia ON N7T 7W8
Tel: 519-344-7064; Fax: 519-344-2145
reception@sarniahumanesociety.com
www.sarniahumanesociety.com

Sault Ste. Marie Branch (Affiliate)
Sault Ste. Marie Humane Society, 962 Second Line East, Sault Ste Marie ON P6B 4K4
Tel: 705-949-3573; Fax: 705-949-0169
ssmhsinfo@shaw.ca
ssmhumanesociety.ca
www.facebook.com/153447011362291
twitter.com/ssmhs
www.youtube.com/user/SSMHumaneSociety

Scarborough Branch
Toronto ON
Toll-Free: 888-668-7722
www.sny.ontariospca.ca

Simcoe & District Branch (Affiliate)
Simcoe & District Humane Society, PO Box 193, 24 Grigg Dr., Simcoe ON N3Y 4L1
Tel: 519-428-9161; Fax: 866-817-1819
laf@s-dhs.ca
www.s-dhs.ca
www.facebook.com/simcoeanddistricthumanesociety
Chief Officer(s):
Cathie Hosken, Manager, Operations

Stormont, Dundas & Glengarry Branch
PO Box 52, 550 Boundary Rd., Cornwall ON K6H 5S3
Tel: 613-936-0072; Fax: 613-936-0137
sdg@ospca.on.ca
www.sdg.ontariospca.ca

Sudbury & District Branch
Collège Boréal, 21 Lasalle Blvd., Sudbury ON P3A 6B1
Tel: 705-566-9582; Fax: 705-566-6625
sudbury@ospca.on.ca
www.sudbury.ontariospca.ca
www.facebook.com/SudburyOSPCA
twitter.com/SudburySPCA
www.youtube.com/user/SudburyOSPCA;
www.instagram.com/ontariospca
Chief Officer(s):
Rachelle Lamoureux, Contact, Animal Centre

Thunder Bay Branch (Affiliate)
Thunder Bay & District Humane Society, 1535 Rosslyn Rd., Thunder Bay ON P7E 6W2
Tel: 807-475-8803; Fax: 807-475-8803
tbayhumane@gmail.com
www.tbayhumane.ca
www.facebook.com/189693437753647

Timmins Branch (Affiliate)
Timmins & District Humane Society, 620 Mahoney Rd., Timmins ON P4N 0H6
Tel: 705-264-1816; Fax: 705-264-3870
adoptions@timminshumanesociety.ca
www.timminshumanesociety.ca
www.facebook.com/TimminsHumaneSociety
Mission: To support animal adoptions & control
Chief Officer(s):
Alicia Santamaria, Manager
alicia.santamaria@timminshumanesociety.ca
Krystle Fletcher, Assistant Manager

Toronto Branch (Affiliate)
Toronto Humane Society, 11 River St., Toronto ON M5A 4C2
Tel: 416-392-2273; Fax: 416-392-9978
info@torontohumanesociety.com
www.torontohumanesociety.com
www.facebook.com/TorontoHumaneSociety
twitter.com/THS_tweet
www.instagram.com/toronto_humane_society
Chief Officer(s):
Barbara Steinhoff, Executive Director

Upper Credit Branch (Affiliate)
Upper Credit Humane Society, 5383 Trafalgar Rd., Erin ON N0B 1T0
Tel: 519-833-2287
infot@uppercredit.com
www.uppercredit.com
www.facebook.com/UpperCreditHumaneSociety
twitter.com/UpperCredit
Chief Officer(s):
Kaitlin Borque, Secretary

Welland Branch (Affiliate)
Welland & District Humane Society, 60 Provincial St., Welland ON L3B 5W7
Tel: 905-735-1552; Fax: 905-735-7414
Toll-Free: 888-222-0568
whs@wellandspca.org
wellandspca.com
www.facebook.com/WellandDistrictHumaneSociety
twitter.com/wellandspca

Windsor-Essex Branch (Affiliate)
Windsor-Essex County Humane Society, 1375 Provincial Rd., Windsor ON N8W 5V8
Tel: 519-966-5751; Fax: 519-966-1848
info@windsorhumane.org
www.windsorhumane.org
www.facebook.com/windsorhumane
twitter.com/windsorhumane
www.instagram.com/windsorhumane
Chief Officer(s):
Melanie Coulter, Executive Director
melanie@windsorhumane.org

Ontario Society of Artists (OSA)
#101, 1444 Queen St. East, Toronto ON M4L 1E1
Tel: 416-867-9448
info@ontariosocietyofartists.org
ontariosocietyofartists.org
Overview: A small provincial charitable organization founded in 1872
Mission: To preserve Ontario's artistic heritage & to enrich Canada's cultural life
Membership: Fees: $125; Member Profile: Professional visual artists
Activities: Members' shows; Open-juried shows; Educational programs
Chief Officer(s):
Tony Vander Voet, President
Mary Ng, Treasurer

Ontario Society of Chiropodists (OSC)
#100, 6700 Century Ave., Mississauga ON L5N 6A4
Tel: 905-567-3094; Fax: 905-567-7191
Toll-Free: 877-823-1508
info@ontariochiropodist.com
www.ontariochiropodist.com
Overview: A small provincial organization founded in 1985
Mission: To provide extensive & regular postgraduate education programs to ensure that the chiropodist remains a first rate foot care specialist
Membership: Fees: $452 full; $339 second year grad; $226 first year grad
Activities: Awareness Events: Foot Health Month, May; Speaker Service: Yes
Chief Officer(s):
Sarah Robinson, President

Ontario Society of Medical Technologists (OSMT)
#402, 234 Eglinton Ave. East, Toronto ON M4P 1K5
Tel: 416-485-6768; Fax: 416-485-7660
Toll-Free: 800-461-6768
osmt@osmt.org
www.osmt.org
www.linkedin.com/company/ontario-society-of-medical-technologists
www.facebook.com/217098608317170
twitter.com/osmt2011

Overview: A medium-sized provincial organization founded in 1963 overseen by Canadian Society For Medical Laboratory Science
Mission: To represent the professional interests of medical technologists & medical laboratory assistants/technicians in relations with government & the public; to provide continuing education & technical consulting services
Member of: Canadian Society for Medical Laboratory Science
Finances: Annual Operating Budget: $500,000-$1.5 Million; Funding Sources: Membership dues; Certification fees
Staff Member(s): 4; 50 volunteer(s)
Membership: 2,400; Fees: $135.60 active & subscriber; $108.48 inactive & affiliate; $27.12 student & retired; Member Profile: Medical laboratory technologists & medical laboratory assistants & technicians; Committees: MLA/T Certification; MLA/T Examination; Editorial; Professional Development; Membership Marketing & Communications; Finance; Bylaws; Conference; Nominations, Elections & Credentials
Activities: Working with stakeholders to represent laboratory professionals in the best way possible; Offering member services; Funding collaborative education; Organizing annual conferences & professional development opportunities; Awareness Events: National Medical Laboratory Week, April
Chief Officer(s):
Blanca McArthur, Executive Director, 416-485-6768 Ext. 25
bmcarthur@osmt.org
Awards:
• OSMT Trillium Award
Awarded to recognize significant contribution to the advancement of the OSMT and the profession of Medical Laboratory Technology in Ontario
• OSMT Richard Lafferty "Excellence in Writing" Award
Awarded to an individual who has made an ousttanding contribution to the OSMT Advocate magazine
• OSMT MLT Student Award
Awarded to a graduating full-time clinical year student who has achieved high academic status & who has demonstrated reliability, maturity, & a tireless attitude Eligibility: Graduating full-time clinical year student; Amount: $100
• OSMT Jim Braidwood Outstanding Professional Award
Awarded to a Medical Laboratory Technologist or Medical Laboratory Assistant/Technician who is highly regarded by professional colleagues for improving work life & professional practice
Meetings/Conferences:
• OSMT 2018 Annual General Meeting, September, 2018
Scope: National
• Advocate
Type: Magazine; Frequency: q.; Accepts Advertising; Editor: Blanca McArthur
Profile: The magazine features articles that pertain to medical technologists, including case studies & educational reports

Ontario Society of Nutrition Professionals in Public Health (OSNPPH) / La société ontarienne des professionelles et professionnels de la nutrition en santé publique
c/o Ontario Public Health Association, #1850, 439 University Ave., Toronto ON M5G 1Y8
info@osnpph.on.ca
www.osnpph.on.ca
twitter.com/RDsPubHealthON
Overview: A small provincial organization founded in 1977
Mission: To provide an official organization that will give nutrition personnel in public health a strong voice within public health & for commenting on public health issues
Member of: Ontario Public Health Association
Membership: Member Profile: Dietitians/nutritionists in public health departments/units
Activities: Annual Nutrition Exchange, 2-day conference
Chief Officer(s):
Rebecca Davids, Co-Chair
Heather Thomas, Co-Chair
Rachel Morgan, Coordinator, Communications

Ontario Society of Occupational Therapists (OSOT)
#210, 55 Eglinton Ave. East, Toronto ON M4P 1G8
Tel: 416-322-3011; Fax: 416-322-6705
Toll-Free: 877-676-6768
osot@osot.on.ca
www.osot.on.ca
www.linkedin.com/company/ontario-society-of-occupational-therapists
www.facebook.com/161471573904550
twitter.com/osotvoice

Overview: A medium-sized provincial organization founded in 1920
Mission: To promote & represent the profession of occupational therapy in the areas of government affairs, education, professional issues & public relations in Ontario
Affiliation(s): Canadian Association of Occupational Therapists
Finances: Annual Operating Budget: $250,000-$500,000
Staff Member(s): 4; 100 volunteer(s)
Membership: 3,800 individual; Fees: $211 full time; $142 part time; $108 non-practising; $105 associate; free for new graduates
Activities: Awareness Events: Occupational Therapy Month, Oct.; Rents Mailing List: Yes
Chief Officer(s):
Christie Benchley, Executive Director, 416-322-3011 Ext. 224
cbrenchley@osot.on.ca
Rob Linkiewicz, Manager, Operations, 416-322-3011 Ext. 231
rlinkiewicz@osot.on.ca
Seema Sindwani, Manager, Professional Development & Practice Support, 416-322-3011 Ext. 238
ssindwani@osot.on.ca
Awards:
• OT Research Fund Awards
• Honorary Life Membership
• Student Achievement Awards
• Volunteer Award
Meetings/Conferences:
• Ontario Society of Occupational Therapists Conference 2018, October, 2018, Sheraton Parkway Toronto North, Richmond Hill, ON
Scope: Provincial

Ontario Society of Periodontists (OSP)
#300, 1370 Don Mills Rd., Toronto ON M3B 3N7
Tel: 416-424-6632; Fax: 416-441-0591
Toll-Free: 855-336-8556
info@osp.on.ca
www.osp.on.ca
Overview: A medium-sized provincial organization
Mission: To be the official voice of Ontario periodontists; to serve the providers and recipients of periodontal care
Member of: Ontario Dental Association
Finances: Funding Sources: Membership dues
Membership: Fees: $150 active; $75 student to active; $0 student; Member Profile: Certified periodontal specialists in Ontario
Chief Officer(s):
Shari Bricks, Managing Director
shari@osp.on.ca
Stephen Gangbar, President
president@osp.on.ca

Ontario Society of Professional Engineers (OSPE)
#502, 4950 Yonge St., Toronto ON M2N 6K1
Tel: 416-223-9961; Fax: 416-223-9963
Toll-Free: 866-763-1654
Other Communication: Blog: blog.ospe.on.ca
info@ospe.on.ca
www.ospe.on.ca
www.linkedin.com/company/ontario-society-of-professional-engineers
www.facebook.com/OntarioSocietyOfProfessionalEngineers
twitter.com/O_S_P_E
www.youtube.com/OSPETV
Overview: A large provincial organization
Mission: To advance the interests of professional engineers in Ontario by advocating on behalf of engineers & the profession; To provide members with a sense of belonging & mutual support; To supply valued & innovative services; To offer quality professional training
Staff Member(s): 17
Membership: Fees: $169 professional; $99 professional (65+); $169 associate; $99 new graduate/intern; Schedule for student; Committees: Advocacy; Environment; Women in Engineering Advisory; Ontario Professional Engineers Awards; PEO Chapter Liaison; Social; Membership Advisory; mployer Salary Survey Advisory; Fee Schedule; Audit & Investments; Executive; Finance; Human Resources; Nominations; PEO/OSPE Joint Relations
Activities: Library: Reports Library
Chief Officer(s):
Karen Chan, P.Eng., MBA, President & Chair
Sandro Perruzza, Chief Executive Officer, 416-223-9961 Ext. 223
sperruzza@ospe.on.ca

Canadian Associations / Ontario Society of Psychotherapists (OSP)

John Moudakis, Manager, Professional Development & Career Services, 416-223-9961 Ext. 236
jmoudakis@ospe.on.ca
Baijul Shukla, Manager, Marketing & Membership, 416-223-9961 Ext. 222
bshukla@opse.on.ca
Awards:
• Gold Medal
• Engineering Medal for Excellence
• Engineering Medal for Management
• Engineering Medal for Research & Development
• Young Engineer Medal
• Professional Engineers Citizenship Award
• Engineering Project Award
Publications:
• Career Advantage [a publication of the Ontario Society of Professional Engineers]
Type: Newsletter; Frequency: q.
Profile: Includes information on courses, workshops, & other professional development programs
• Daily News Review [a publication of the Ontario Society of Professional Engineers]
Type: Newsletter; Frequency: Daily
Profile: Contains a daily round-up of political, economic, & professional news vital to the engineering industry
• Employer Salary Survey [a publication of the Ontario Society of Professional Engineers]
Type: Report; Frequency: Annually
• Employer's Edge [a publication of the Ontario Society of Professional Engineers]
Type: Newsletter; Frequency: Monthly
Profile: Designed for organizations that employ engineers
• OSPE [Ontario Society of Professional Engineers] Annual Report
Type: Report; Frequency: Annually
• OSPE [Ontario Society of Professional Engineers] Fee Guideline
Type: Report; Price: Free with OSPE membership; $20 without OSPE membership
Profile: A resource to help engineers determine fees for professional services
• OSPE [Ontario Society of Professional Engineers] Survey Summary Report
Type: Report
Profile: A summary of the National Engineering Compensation Survey; provides engineers & employers with a picture of hiring trends & compensation levels acrossall categories of the engineering profession
• Society Notes [a publication of the Ontario Society of Professional Engineers]
Type: Newsletter; Frequency: Monthly
Profile: Contains news & valuable information for members
• The Voice [a publication of the Ontario Society of Professional Engineers]
Type: Magazine; Frequency: q.
Profile: Formerly a print newsletter, The Voice is now a full-colour magazine

Ontario Society of Psychotherapists (OSP)
#1, 189 Queen St. East, Toronto ON M5A 1S2
Tel: 416-923-4050; Fax: 416-968-6818
mail@psychotherapyontario.org
psychotherapyontario.com
twitter.com/psychotherapyon
Overview: A small provincial organization
Mission: The Ontario Society of Psychotherapists is committed to the continuing development of ethically responsible and self-reflective psychotherapists
Membership: Committees: Ethics; Membership; PR; Professional Development
Chief Officer(s):
Christina Becker, President

Ontario Society of Safety Engineering See Canadian Society of Safety Engineering, Inc.

Ontario Society of Senior Citizens' Organizations (OSSCO) / La société des organisations des citoyens aînés de l'Ontario (COAAO)
#406, 333 Wilson Ave., Toronto ON M3H 1T2
Tel: 416-785-8570; Fax: 416-785-7361
Toll-Free: 800-265-0779
ocsco@ocsco.ca
www.ocsco.ca
Overview: A large provincial charitable organization founded in 1986
Mission: To improve the quality of life for Ontario's seniors by encouraging seniors' involvement in all aspects of society, by keeping them informed of current issues, & by focusing on programs to benefit an aging population
Finances: Funding Sources: Membership dues; grants; fundraising
Membership: 160 groups (500,000 individuals); Fees: Schedule available dependent on number of members or employees for organizations; $15 individual; $100 lifetime individual; Member Profile: Open to adults over 55 years of age; Committees: Bylaws; Finance & Revenue Generation; Communication & Membership; Education & Research; Human Resources
Activities: Education; alliances; information; referral & counselling; policy; outreach; special programs; drop-in; research; joint programs; self-help; volunteerism; speakers' bureau; Speaker Service: Yes; Library: Resource Centre; Open to public
Chief Officer(s):
Elizabeth Macnab, Executive Director
ed@ocsco.ca

Ontario Soil & Crop Improvement Association (OSCIA) / Association pour l'amélioration des sols et des récoltes de l'Ontario
1 Stone Rd. West, Guelph ON N1G 4Y2
Tel: 519-826-4214; Fax: 519-826-4224
Toll-Free: 800-265-9751
oscia@ontariosoilcrop.org
www.ontariosoilcrop.org
Overview: A medium-sized provincial organization founded in 1939
Mission: To communicate & facilitate the responsible management of soil, water, air, & crops
Membership: Member Profile: Farmers & persons involved in agriculture in Ontario; Committees: Nomination; Resolutions; Finance; Research; Membership; Constitution & Bylaws; Annual Meeting; Ontario Soil Management Research; Soil & Water Quality Sub-Committee; Waste Utilization Sub-Committee; Field Crops Sub-Committee; Ontario Corn; Ontario Weed; Ontario Cereal Crop; Ontario Forage Crops; Ontario Oil & Protein; Biosolids Utilization; Ontario Forage Council; Ontario Agri-Food Education; AGCare; Ontario Field Crops Research Coalition; Canada's Outdoor Farm Show; Ontario Agri-Food Technologies; Soil Conservation Council of Canada
Activities: Offering information about agricultural management practices; Networking with farmers
Chief Officer(s):
Harold Rudy, Executive Director, 519-826-4217
Julie Henderson, Administrator, Finance, 519-826-4221
Steven Nadeau, Administrator, Information Technology, 519-826-6059
Andrew Graham, Manager, Programs, 519-826-4216
John Laidlaw, Program Manager, Farm Business Management, 519-826-4218
Meetings/Conferences:
• Ontario Soil & Crop Improvement Association 2018 AGM, February, 2018, ON
Scope: Provincial
Description: An opportunity for farmers & persons involved in agriculture in Ontario to bring local views to give direction to the association
Publications:
• New Crops, Old Challenges: Tips & Tricks for Managing New Crops!
Number of Pages: 76
Profile: Crop profiles
• Ontario Soil & Crop Improvement Association Newsletter
Type: Newsletter; Frequency: Quarterly; Price: Free with Ontario Soil & Crop Improvement Association membership
• Rotational Grazing in Extensive Pastures
Type: Report
Profile: Discusses using rotational grazing to increase health of pastures, cattle & the environment.

Ontario Special Constable Association
ON
www.specialconstables.ca
www.facebook.com/ontariospecialconstableassociation
twitter.com/osca_est2008
www.instagram.com/ontspcassociation
Overview: A medium-sized provincial organization founded in 2008
Mission: To promote the interests of special constables in Ontario; To enforce & improve standards for special constables; To strengthen the roles of special constables in the law enforcement community
Membership: Fees: $15 associate; $35 individual; $150 organization; Member Profile: Actively serving special constables; Retired special constables & police/peace officers
Activities: Lobbying
Chief Officer(s):
David Moskowitz, President
president@specialconstables.ca

Ontario Special Olympics See Special Olympics Ontario

Ontario Speed Skating Association (OSSA)
PO Box 1179, Lakefield ON K0L 2H0
Tel: 705-652-9490; Fax: 705-652-1227
ossa@ontariospeedskating.ca
ontariospeedskating.ca
www.facebook.com/OntarioSpeedSkating
twitter.com/OSSA
www.flickr.com/photos/ontariospeedskating
Previous Name: Ice Skating Association of Ontario
Overview: A medium-sized provincial organization founded in 1981 overseen by Speed Skating Canada
Mission: To promote & develop the sport of speed skating in Ontario.
Member of: Speed Skating Canada
Finances: Funding Sources: Membership fee
Membership: Committees: Coaching; Marketing; Officials Development; Technical; Club & Membership Development; Fundraising; Personnel; Finance; Nominating
Activities: Speaker Service: Yes
Chief Officer(s):
Jacqueline Deschenes, Executive Director
executivedirector@ontariospeedskating.ca
Sarah Leslie, Manager, Sport Programs, 613-422-5210
sportmanager@ontariospeedskating.ca

Ontario Spondylitis Association (OSA)
18 Long Crescent, Toronto ON M4E 1N6
Tel: 416-694-5493
info@spondylitis.ca
spondylitis.ca
www.facebook.com/6562917242
Overview: A small provincial organization
Mission: To provide support, education & public awareness of the disease called Ankylosing Spondylitis
Member of: The Arthritis Society, Canadian Spondylitis Association
Finances: Funding Sources: Membership fees; donations
30 volunteer(s)
Membership: 300; Committees: Membership; Communications; Fundraising
Activities: Seminars; social events
Chief Officer(s):
Michael Mallinson, President

Ontario Sportfishing Guides' Association (OSGA)
4504 Trent Trail, Washago ON L0K 2B0
Tel: 705-689-3332; Fax: 705-689-1085
info@ontariofishcharters.ca
www.ontariofishcharters.ca
Previous Name: Ontario Charterboat Association
Overview: A small provincial organization founded in 1980
Mission: To monitor & participate in any regulation reform regarding sportfishing in the province; to lobby as a unified voice on behalf of its members, & serve as a network where members can promote & learn from each other.
Finances: Funding Sources: Membership fees
Membership: Fees: $100; Member Profile: Professional fishing charter boat operators & guides
Chief Officer(s):
George Watkins, Secretary

Ontario Square & Round Dance Federation (OSRDF)
88 Foxhollow Cres., London ON N6G 3R2
Tel: 519-472-1596
info@squaredance.on.ca
www.squaredance.on.ca
Overview: A medium-sized provincial organization founded in 1977 overseen by Canadian Square & Round Dance Society
Mission: To coordinate square, round, clog, & line dancing throughout Ontario
Finances: Funding Sources: Membership fees
Membership: Fees: $4 individuals; $6 organizations
Activities: Library: Not open to public
Chief Officer(s):
Wayne Hall, President
whall3@cogeco.ca

Ontario Standardbred Adoption Society (OSAS)
PO Box 297, 36 Main St. South, Campbellville ON L0P 1B0
Tel: 905-854-6099; *Fax:* 905-854-6100
osasadmin@bellnet.ca
www.osas.ca
Overview: A small provincial charitable organization founded in 1996
Mission: To aid in the adoption & relocation of retired Standardbred horses, as well as those no longer able to race, within Ontario.
Finances: *Funding Sources:* Fundraising; industry associations; donations
Staff Member(s): 1
Chief Officer(s):
Jim Evans, President
Anita TenBruggencate, Coordinator, Adoptions
anitaosas@bellnet.ca

Ontario Standardbred Improvement Association *See* Standardbred Breeders of Ontario Association

Ontario Steam & Antique Preservers Association (OSAPA)
PO Box 133, Stn. Main, Milton ON L9T 2Y3
Tel: 905-878-3114
www.steam-era.com
www.facebook.com/46132187050
Also Known As: Steam-Era
Overview: A small provincial organization founded in 1960
Mission: To promote interest in antiques & local history.
Membership: *Fees:* $25; $5 junior; *Member Profile:* Anyone interested in antique farm equipment; *Committees:* Antique cars/trucks; Antiques under grandstand; Antique Lawn tractors; Camping; Concessions; Gas Engines; Gas tractors; Membership; Souvenirs; Stationary steam; Steam engines; Trading post; Steam-Era Compound
Activities: Steam-era show
Chief Officer(s):
Brian Walsh, President
brian@realprocess.net

Ontario Steelheaders
PO Box 604, Brantford ON N3T 5T3
president@ontariosteelheaders.ca
www.ontariosteelheaders.ca
www.facebook.com/OntarioSteelheaders
twitter.com/ONSteelheaders
Overview: A small provincial organization
Mission: To improve access and habitat for migratory rainbow trout, provide young rainbow trout with suitable nursery habitat, provide relevent and appropriate input to government, agencies and other organizations, and to educate members and the public on relevent issues, conservation practices and proper angling techniques.
Membership: *Fees:* $30 individual; $35 family
Chief Officer(s):
Karl Redin, President, 519-756-3640

Ontario Stone, Sand & Gravel Association (OSSGA)
#103, 5720 Timberlea Blvd., Mississauga ON L4W 4W2
Tel: 905-507-0711; *Fax:* 905-507-0717
www.ossga.com
twitter.com/_OSSGA
Previous Name: Aggregate Producers' Association of Ontario
Overview: A medium-sized provincial organization founded in 1956
Finances: *Annual Operating Budget:* $250,000-$500,000; *Funding Sources:* Membership dues
Staff Member(s): 7
Membership: 200+ corporate
Chief Officer(s):
Moreen Miller, CEO
mmiller@ossga.com
Meetings/Conferences:
• Ontario Stone, Sand & Gravel Association 2018 Conference & Annual General Meeting, 2018, ON
Scope: Provincial

Ontario Streams
50 Bloomington Rd. West, Aurora ON L4G 3G8
Tel: 905-713-7399; *Fax:* 905-713-7361
www.ontariostreams.on.ca
Overview: A medium-sized provincial organization founded in 1995
Mission: To promote the conservation & rehabilitation of streams & wetlands, through education & community involvement

Chief Officer(s):
Doug Forder, General Manager
doug.forder@ontariostreams.on.ca

Ontario Students Against Impaired Driving / Élèves ontariens contre l'ivresse au volant
PO Box 3, #2B, 1015 Lakeshore Blvd. East, Toronto ON M4M 1B4
Toll-Free: 877-706-7243
www.osaid.org
www.facebook.com/OntarioStudentsAgainstImpairedDriving
twitter.com/OSAIDInc
Overview: A small provincial organization
Mission: To eliminate impaired driving through practical & positive peer education
Chief Officer(s):
Robin MacDonald, President
Matt John Evans, Executive Director

Ontario Summer Theatre Association (ASTRO)
c/o Theatre Ontario, #350, 401 Richmond St. West, Toronto ON M5V 3A8
Tel: 416-408-4556; *Fax:* 416-408-3402
info@summertheatre.org
www.summertheatre.org
www.facebook.com/514087251963959
twitter.com/summer_theatre
Also Known As: Summer Theatre Ontario
Overview: A small provincial organization founded in 1985
Mission: To act as an information & resource network for its members; To support the professional development of its members; To act as a liaison for its membership with arts & business organizations, the media & the community; To advocate for its membership with government, government agencies & other organizations; To undertake projects to increase awareness of the activities of its membership among the general public
Finances: *Funding Sources:* Membership fees
Membership: 21 theatres; *Member Profile:* Professional summer theatres
Activities: Promoting summer theatres in Ontario

Ontario Sustainable Energy Association (OSEA)
2 Champagne Dr., #C-9, Toronto ON M3J 0K2
admin@ontario-sea.org
www.ontario-sea.org
www.linkedin.com/company/ontario-sustainable-energy-association
www.facebook.com/ontariosea
twitter.com/ontariosea
www.youtube.com/ontariosea2009
Overview: A small provincial organization founded in 2002
Mission: To represent & serve municipalities, First Nations, institutions, businesses, cooperatives, farms & households; To support the work of local sustainable energy organizations
Finances: *Funding Sources:* Sponsorships; Donations
Staff Member(s): 6
Membership: *Fees:* $50 students/senior; $100 individuals; $500-$2,000 organizations; $5,000 benefactors
Activities: Engaging in advocacy activities, capacity building, & non-partisan policy work; Providing public outreach services
Chief Officer(s):
Janis Wilkinson, Interim Executive Director
Publications:
• Arts Revision Report: Renewables Without Limits [a publication of the Ontario Sustainable Energy Association]
Type: Report; *Price:* $1 + $13.50 shipping & handling, members; $10 +$13.50 S&H, non-members
Profile: A review of Ontario's Renewable Energy Standard Offer Program
• Community Power Financing Guidebook
Type: Manual; *Price:* $40 + $13.50 shipping & handling, members; $65 + $13.40 S&H, non-members
Profile: Contents include pre-development financing, land acquisition, legal contracting, permits & approvals, resource assessment, & community engagement
• The Community Power Guidebook
Type: Guide
Profile: A guide to the development of a community power project, from conception to commissioning
• Green Energy ACTion Kit
Type: Kit; *Price:* $10 + $13.50 shipping & handling, members; $20 + $13.40 S&H, non-members
Profile: Suggestions to help citizens advocate for green energy in Ontario

• Ontario Landowner's Guide to Wind Energy
Type: Guide; *Author:* Paul Gipe; James Murphy; *Price:* $10 + $13.50 shipping & handling, members; $20 + $13.50 S&H,non-members
Profile: A comprehensive manual for rural landowners & farmers who are interested in wind power
• Ontario Sustainable Energy Association E-Bulletin
Type: Newsletter; *Price:* Free with Ontario Sustainable Energy Association membership
Profile: Updates about the association & upcoming events
• OSEA [Ontario Sustainable Energy Association] Member Directory
Type: Directory
Profile: Contact information for members
• Permitting & Approvals Processes for CP Projects [a publication of the Ontario Sustainable Energy Association]
Type: Guide; *Price:* $40 + $13.50 shipping & handling, members; $65 + $13.50 S&H, non-members
Profile: An overview of the policy environment for biogas & wind projects in Ontario, of interest to municipal planners,project proponents, & the general public
• Powering Ontario Communities: Proposed Policy for Projects up to 10mw
Type: Study
Profile: Options to encourage small or community-owned renewable energy generation in Ontario
• Proposal for a Green Energy Act for Ontario
Profile: A proposal for renewable energy sources to protect the environment & to manage climate change
• Recommendations for Procuring Sustainable Energy: An Addendum to Renewables Without Limits
Profile: An update to recommendations from the Arts Revision Report: Renewable Without Limits
• Solar PV Community Action Manual
Type: Manual
Profile: Information for Canadian residents about residential-scale or small-scale commercial Solar PV installations, as well as related topics such as financing & home assessment
• Solar Thermal Community Action Manual
Type: Manual
Profile: Information for Canadians about residential-scale or small-scale commercial solar thermal installations, as well as the establishment of a community based organization

Ontario Table Soccer Association
ON
Toll-Free: 866-247-7702
www.ontariotablesoccer.com
Overview: A small provincial organization founded in 2002
Mission: To promote the sport of table soccer through hosting, sanctioning, & coordinating tournaments, events & clinics for players based in Ontario & to assist them in competing in national & international sanctioned events
Chief Officer(s):
Mario Recupero, Executive Director, 905-812-9994
director@ontariotablesoccer.com

Ontario Table Tennis Association (OTTA)
#110, 9140 Leslie St., Richmond Hill ON L4B 0A9
otta@ontariotabletennis.com
ontariotabletennis.com
www.facebook.com/TableTennisOntario
www.flickr.com/photos/135121071@N06/
Overview: A small provincial organization founded in 1934 overseen by Table Tennis Canada
Member of: Table Tennis Canada
Affiliation(s): International Table Tennis Federation
Membership: 500+; *Fees:* Schedule available
Chief Officer(s):
Attila Mosonyi, President
attila.mosonyi@gmail.com

Ontario Taekwondo Association
#500, 4560 Hwy 7 East, Markham ON L3R 1M5
Tel: 416-245-8582; *Fax:* 416-245-8582
otatkdinfo@gmail.com
www.taekwondo.on.ca
Overview: A medium-sized provincial organization
Chief Officer(s):
Hwa Sun Myung, President
otapresident@gmail.com
Hwan Yong Seong, Secretary General
masterseong@gmail.com

Ontario Teachers' Federation (OTF) / Fédération des enseignantes et des enseignants de l'Ontario (FEO)
#200, 1300 Yonge St., Toronto ON M4T 1X3
Tel: 416-966-3424; Fax: 416-966-5450
Toll-Free: 800-268-7061
www.otffeo.on.ca
www.facebook.com/otffeo
twitter.com/otffeo
Overview: A large provincial organization founded in 1944 overseen by Canadian Teachers' Federation
Mission: To represent the interests of all registered teachers in Ontario's publicly funded schools
Affiliation(s): Association des enseignantes et des enseignants franco-ontariens; Elementary Teachers' Federation of Ontario; Ontario English Catholic Teachers' Association; Ontario Secondary School Teachers' Federation
Finances: Annual Operating Budget: $1.5 Million-$3 Million
Membership: 160,000; Member Profile: Teachers in publicly-funded schools in Ontario
Activities: Advocating on behalf of its membership; Sponsoring the Ontario Teachers' Pension Plan, along with the Government of Ontario; Offering professional development opportunities; Speaker Service: Yes; Library: by appointment
Chief Officer(s):
Francine LeBlanc-Lebel, President
francine.leblanc-lebel@otffeo.on.ca
Rhonda Kimberley-Young, Secretary-Treasurer
rhonda.kimberley-young@otffeo.on.ca
Lindy Amato, Director, Professional Affairs
lindy.amato@otffeo.on.ca
Awards:
- OTFF / OTIP Teaching Awards
Presented in partnership with the Ontario Teachers Insurance Plan (OTIP); recognizes excellence in three categories: elementary school teacher, secondary school teacher & beginning teacher in their first five years of teaching
Meetings/Conferences:
- Ontario Teachers' Federation Annual General Meeting 2018, 2018, ON
Scope: Provincial
Contact Information: Administrator: Lavinia George, E-mail: lavinia.george@otffeo.on.ca
Publications:
- Ontario Teachers' Federation Annual Report
Type: Report; Frequency: Annually

Ontario Telecommunications Association See Independent Telecommunications Providers Association

Ontario Tender Fruit Producers Marketing Board
PO Box 100, Vineland ON L0R 2E0
Tel: 905-688-0990; Fax: 905-688-5915
info@ontariotenderfruit.ca
www.ontariotenderfruit.ca
www.facebook.com/OntarioTenderFruit
twitter.com/OntTenderFruit
Overview: A small provincial organization founded in 1979
Staff Member(s): 8
Membership: 500 grower members
Chief Officer(s):
Sarah Marshall, Manager

Ontario Tennis Association (OTA)
#200, 1 Shoreham Dr., Toronto ON M3N 3A7
Tel: 416-514-1100; Fax: 416-514-1112
Toll-Free: 800-387-5066
ota@tennisontario.com
www.tennisontario.com
www.facebook.com/OntarioTennisAssociation
twitter.com/TennisOntario
www.instagram.com/ontariotennisassociation
Previous Name: Ontario Lawn Tennis Association
Overview: A medium-sized provincial organization founded in 1918 overseen by Tennis Canada
Mission: To act as the provincial governing body for tennis in Ontario; To promote participation in tennis in Ontario; To create tennis opportunities for players of every level, from grassroots to national calibre athlete; To encourage the quest for excellence for all players
Member of: Tennis Canada
Finances: Funding Sources: Membership fees; Sponsorships; The Ontario Trillium Foundation
Membership: 220 clubs (55,000 youth & adult tennis players) + 2,200 individuals; Member Profile: Tennis clubs across Ontario, including private & commercial clubs, recreation departments, municipal parks, community clubs, & resorts
Activities: Offering professional development activities, such as clinics & tennis instructor courses; Coordinating the OTA Tennis Fair for clubs; Sanctioning tournaments; Providing guidance to clubs in the area of club management
Chief Officer(s):
Scott Fraser, President
James N. Boyce, Executive Director
jboyce@tennisontario.com
Andrew Chappell, Manager, Events
achappell@tennisontario.com
Peter Malcomson, Manager, Marketing
pmalcomson@tennisontario.com
Jay Neill, Manager, Membership
jneill@tennisontario.com
Awards:
- Ontario Tennis Association Distinguished Service Awards
Publications:
- Ontario Tennis [a publication of the Ontario Tennis association]
Type: Magazine; Frequency: Quarterly; Accepts Advertising
Profile: Junior development information, trade news, tournament reports, equipment information, health & lifestyle, tennis travel, & regional reports
- OTA Yearbook
Frequency: Annually; Accepts Advertising
Profile: An overview of the association's activities from the past year, plus recognition of provincial champions
- SPIN [a publication of the Ontario Tennis Association]
Type: Newsletter; Accepts Advertising
Profile: Junior development information, trade news, tournament reports, equipment information, health & lifestyle, tennis travel, & regional reports

Ontario Tenpin Bowling Association
3064 Tecumseh Dr., Burlington ON L7N 3M4
am@otba.ca
www.otba.ca
www.facebook.com/groups/800626176718495
Overview: A small provincial organization overseen by Canadian Tenpin Federation, Inc.
Mission: To oversee the sport of tenpin bowling in Ontario.
Member of: Canadian Tenpin Federation, Inc.
Membership: 16 associations
Chief Officer(s):
Charlotte Konkle, President
president@otba.ca
Della Trude, 1st Vice-President
1stVicePresident@otba.ca
Wayne Dubs, 2nd Vice-President
2ndVicePresident@otba.ca

Ontario Therapeutic Riding Association (OnTRA) / Association ontarienne d'équitation thérapeutique
47 Fairlane Rd., London ON N6K 3E3
president@ontra.ca
www.ontra.ca
Overview: A small provincial charitable organization founded in 1983
Mission: The Ontario Therapeutic Riding Association (OnTRA) promotes horseback riding as a form of therapy and sport for children and adults living with physical, cognitive, emotional, and/or behavioural challenges. OnTRA provides volunteers and therapeutic riding professionals with on-going information and training to ensure riders with disabilities receive the best possible therapy.
Member of: Canadian Therapeutic Riding Association; Ontario Equestrian Federation
Finances: Annual Operating Budget: Less than $50,000
2500 volunteer(s)
Membership: 250; Fees: $20 individual; $30 family; $12 junior; $300 lifetime
Activities: Competitions; promotion; educational clinic; grants; Used Equipment Program; Speaker Service: Yes
Awards:
- OnTRA Show Your Stuff! Grant
Eligibility: Current members of OnTRA Deadline: June; Amount: $2,500

Ontario Thoracic Society (OTS)
c/o Ontario Lung Association, #401, 18 Wynford Dr., Toronto ON M3C 0K8
Tel: 416-864-9911
olalung@on.lung.ca
www.on.lung.ca
Overview: A medium-sized provincial charitable organization founded in 1961
Mission: To promote respiratory health through medical research & education
Member of: Ontario Lung Association
Affiliation(s): Canadian Thoracic Society
Finances: Funding Sources: Lung Association
Membership: Fees: $95; Member Profile: Open to MD, Ph.D., or medical resident (student); Committees: Research Advisory
Activities: Research & education; Speaker Service: Yes; Library: Not open to public
Chief Officer(s):
Thomas Kovesi, Chair
Awards:
- Cameron C. Gray Fellowship in Respiratory Medicine

Ontario Tire Dealers Association
PO Box 516, 22 John St., Drayton ON N0G 1P0
Tel: 888-207-9059; Fax: 866-375-6832
www.otda.com
www.facebook.com/168955833458608
Overview: A medium-sized provincial organization
Mission: To represent members; To educate members in all areas that impact the continued growth of the tire industry
Affiliation(s): Tire Dealers Association of Canada; Tire Industry Association
Finances: Funding Sources: Membership fees; Fundraising
Membership: 50+; Fees: $214.70; Member Profile: Tire dealers in Ontario
Activities: Educating members; Promoting standards of ethics; Engaging in lobbying activities
Chief Officer(s):
Robert Bignell, Executive Director
bbignell@otda.com
Meetings/Conferences:
- Ontario Tire Dealers Association 2018 Winter Conference, 2018
Scope: Provincial
Publications:
- Ontario Tire Dealers Association Membership Directory
Type: Directory
Profile: Contact information about Ontario's tire professionals
- Trends [a publication of the Ontario Tire Dealers Association]
Type: Newsletter; Frequency: Quarterly; Accepts Advertising
Profile: Information for members about industry issues

Ontario Track & Field Association See Athletics Ontario

Ontario Track 3 Ski Association for the Disabled
#4, 61 Advance Rd., Toronto ON M8Z 2S6
Tel: 416-233-3872; Fax: 416-233-7862
Toll-Free: 877-308-7225
track3@track3.org
www.track3.org
www.facebook.com/OntarioTrack3
twitter.com/OntarioTrack3
Also Known As: Track 3
Overview: A small provincial charitable organization founded in 1972
Mission: To discover ability through the magic of snow sports.
450 volunteer(s)
Activities: Speaker Service: Yes
Chief Officer(s):
Naomi Schafler, Executive Director
Publications:
- On Track
Type: Newsletter; Frequency: Quarterly; Accepts Advertising

Ontario Traffic Council (OTC)
#208, 170 The Donway West, Toronto ON M3C 2G3
Tel: 647-346-4050; Fax: 647-346-4060
info@otc.org
www.otc.org
www.linkedin.com/groups/5071314/profile
twitter.com/ontariotraffic
Overview: A medium-sized provincial organization founded in 1950
Mission: To improve traffic conditions & traffic safety in municipalities of Ontario
Staff Member(s): 4
Membership: Member Profile: Made up of regions, cities, towns, counties and institutions from across Ontario that contribute to the OTC through their police services, elected representatives, traffic engineers and parking enforcement.; Committees: Active Transportation; Parking; Traffic Engineering; Traffic Training; Transportation Planning
Activities: Committees; Research & providing reports; Training programs
Chief Officer(s):

Marco D'Angelo, Executive Director
Nelson Cadete, President
Heide Schlegl, Vice President
Kimberly Rossi, Treasurer & Director of Enforcement
Adam Bell, Director, Engineering
John Crass, Director, Training
Scott Godwin, Operations Manager
Manoj Dilwaria, Director, Transportation Planning & Sustainability
Robyn Zutis, Director, Convention
Publications:
• OTC [Ontario Traffic Council] Radar
Type: E-Newsletter; *Frequency:* monthly.; *Number of Pages:* 1; *Price:* Free download
Profile: Contains information on upcoming courses, training opportunities & OTC committee meeting dates

Ontario Trail Riders Association (OTRA)
ON
Overview: A small provincial organization founded in 1970
Mission: To identify, develop, & preserve multi-use trails throughout Ontario
Affiliation(s): Ontario Trails Council; Ontario Equestrian Federation
Membership: 100-499; *Fees:* $30 single; $50 family; *Committees:* Trail Development; Government Relations; Public Relations; Trail Rides; Education
Chief Officer(s):
Helmut Hitscherich, President, 905-473-9329
helmuthit@gmail.com
Publications:
• The Rider [a publication of the Ontario Trail Riders Association]
Type: Newsletter; *Frequency:* Monthly; *Editor:* Ron Keeler
Profile: News & updates for association members

Ontario Trails Council (OTC) / Conseil des Sentiers de l'Ontario
PO Box 500, Deseronto ON K0K 1X0
www.ontariotrails.on.ca
www.facebook.com/OntarioTrails
twitter.com/ontrails
www.youtube.com/user/ontrails
Overview: A medium-sized provincial charitable organization founded in 1988
Mission: To promote the creation, development, preservation, management & use of an integrated, recreational, multi-seasonal trail network in Ontario; To show interest in all types of trails for non-motorized or motorized (where applicable) use in all seasons; To acquire & convert Ontario's abandoned railway rights-of-way to linear greenways for year-round recreational activities for the people of Ontario
Affiliation(s): Brant Waterways Foundation; Bruce Trail Conservancy; Bruce Trail Conservancy; Canadian Recreational Horse & Rider Association; Chatham Kent Trails Council; Collingwood Trails Network; Conservation Ontario; Credit Valley Conservation Foundation; Cycle Ontario; Durham Mountain Biking Association; Federation of Northern Ontario Municipalities; Georgian Cycle & Ski Trail Association; Greater Madawaska Trails Committee; Hamilton Burlington Trails Council; Hike Ontario; International Mountain Biking Association; Kawartha ATV Association; Keswick Beach Association; Kincardine Trail Association
Finances: *Annual Operating Budget:* Less than $50,000; *Funding Sources:* Membership fees; Corporate donations
Membership: 220 organizations, municipalities & conservation areas; *Fees:* $26.52 individual; $21.21 student; $109.27-$819.54 club/association + GST; *Member Profile:* Associations or clubs with interest in recreational trail acquisition, maintenance & use; individuals concerned with environment & trail recreation; municipalities; conservation areas
Activities: Library:
Chief Officer(s):
Patrick Connor, CAE, Executive Director, 613-396-3226
execdir@ontariotrails.ca
Paul Ronan, Chair, Education Program, 613-484-1140
courses@ontariotrails.ca
Meetings/Conferences:
• Ontario Trail Council Trailhead Ontario 2018, 2018, ON
Scope: Provincial
Publications:
• OTC [Ontario Trails Council] Newsletter
Type: Newsletter; *Frequency:* Monthly; *Price:* Free with membership in the Ontario Trails Council
Profile: Information about events, activities, & news from trails

Ontario Trial Lawyers Association (OTLA)
1190 Blair Rd., Burlington ON L7M 1K9
Tel: 905-639-6852; *Fax:* 905-639-3100
www.otla.com
Overview: A medium-sized provincial organization founded in 1990
Affiliation(s): Association of Trial Lawyers of America
Finances: *Funding Sources:* Membership dues; Conference fees; Advertising
Membership: 1,190; *Fees:* $125-$495
Activities: Providing a continuing legal education program; *Library:* Not open to public
Chief Officer(s):
Linda Langston, Executive Director
llangston@otla.com
Julia De Faria, Director, Finance & Administration
jdefaria@otla.com
Dianne Halcovitch, Director, Education & Events
dhalcovitch@otla.com
John Karapita, Director, Public Affairs
jkarapita@otla.com
Janie Hames, Coordinator, Membership Services
jhames@otla.com
Susanne Hasulo, Coordinator, Communications
shasulo@otla.com
Meetings/Conferences:
• Ontario Trial Lawyers Association 2018 Medical Malpractice Conference, February, 2018
Scope: Provincial
Description: Theme: "New Frontiers in Technology"

The Ontario Trillium Foundation / La Fondation Trillium de l'Ontario
800 Bay St., 5th Fl., Toronto ON M5S 3A9
Tel: 416-963-4927; *Fax:* 416-963-8781
Toll-Free: 800-263-2887; *TTY:* 416-963-7905
otf@otf.ca
www.otf.ca
www.facebook.com/ONTrillium
twitter.com/ONTrillium
www.youtube.com/user/trilliumfoundation1
Overview: A medium-sized provincial organization founded in 1982
Mission: To work with others to make strategic investments to build healthy & sustainable communities in Ontario
Finances: *Funding Sources:* Ontario government
330 volunteer(s)
Activities: *Library:* Resource Centre; Open to public by appointment
Chief Officer(s):
Andrea Cohen Barrack, Chief Executive Officer
corpoffice@otf.ca

Ontario Trucking Association (OTA)
555 Dixon Rd., Toronto ON M9W 1H8
Tel: 416-249-7401; *Fax:* 866-713-4188
www.ontruck.org
www.linkedin.com/groups/4783727/profile
www.facebook.com/202193323261162
twitter.com/OnTruck
www.youtube.com/user/ontruck
Overview: A medium-sized provincial organization founded in 1926 overseen by Canadian Trucking Alliance
Mission: To represent companies & industry suppliers; To provide political advocacy, education & information services to North American freight transport companies
Finances: *Funding Sources:* Membership fees
Membership: 1,700; *Member Profile:* Individuals from family-owned companies to publicly-traded conglomerates, including representatives from the for-hire carrier, private carrier, intermodal and supplier industries; *Committees:* Axle Weight; Credit; Education; Executive; Social/Labour; Tech./Ops; Convention; Dues; Membership; Insurance; Finance; Environmental Issues
Activities: Offering training courses & seminars; *Awareness Events:* Annual Spring Golf Tournament, May; *Speaker Service:* Yes
Meetings/Conferences:
• Truck World 2018, April, 2018, International Centre, Mississauga, ON
Scope: Provincial
Description: An event fully endorsed by the OTA; features new equipment, technology, & career opportunities for both carriers & suppliers

• 92nd Annual Ontario Trucking Association Convention & Executive Conference 2018, 2018, ON
Scope: Provincial
Publications:
• Ontario Trucking Association Buyers Guide
Profile: A directory of resources for freight transport industry members

Education Foundation (OTAEF)
555 Dixon Rd., Toronto ON M9W 1H8
Tel: 416-249-7401; *Fax:* 888-713-4188
info@otaef.com
www.otaef.com
twitter.com/OTAEFInfo
Mission: To further education for post-secondary students in Ontario who have links to the Ontario trucking industry
Chief Officer(s):
Betsy Sharples, Executive Director
Scott Smith, Chair
Scott Tilley, Vice-Chair
Peter Hodge, Sectretary-Treasurer

Ontario Umpires Association
ON
Tel: 905-791-0280
ontario_umpires@sympatico.ca
www.ontarioumpires.com
Overview: A small provincial organization
Mission: To provide officials for the games of baseball, softball, volleyball, flag football, hockey, basketball & soccer.
Affiliation(s): Ontario Sports Administration; Ontario Academy of Sports Officials; Sports Events International
Chief Officer(s):
Jim Cottrell, President

Ontario Undergraduate Student Alliance (OUSA)
#345, 26 Soho St., Toronto ON M5T 1Z7
Tel: 416-341-9948
info@ousa.ca
www.ousa.ca
www.facebook.com/98136969146
twitter.com/ousa
www.youtube.com/user/EducatedSolutions
Overview: A medium-sized provincial organization founded in 1992
Mission: The represent the interests of undergraduate students who attend Brock University, McMaster University, Queen's University, Trent University, Wilfrid Laurier University, the University of Waterloo & the University of Western Ontario
Staff Member(s): 5
Membership: 7 associations representing 140,000 students; *Committees:* Steering
Chief Officer(s):
Jen Carter, President
president@ousa.ca
Sean Madden, Executive Director
sean@ousa.ca

Alma Mater Society at Queen's University
John Deutsch University Centre, Queen's University, Kingston ON K7L 3N6
Tel: 613-533-2729; *Fax:* 613-533-3002
vpua@ams.queensu.ca
www.myams.org
Chief Officer(s):
Philip Lloyd, Vice-President, University Affairs

Brock University Students' Union
Student-Alumni Centre, 500 Glendridge Ave., St Catharines ON L2S 3A1
Tel: 905-688-5550
vpea@busu.net
www.busu.net
Drew Ursacki, Vice-President, External Affairs

Federation of Students, University of Waterloo (FEDS)
Student Life Centre, 200 University Ave. West, Waterloo ON N2L 3G1
Tel: 519-888-4567
vped@feds.uwaterloo.ca
www.feds.uwaterloo.ca
Chief Officer(s):
Stéphane Hamade, Vice President, Education

McMaster University Students Union (MSU)
1280 Main St. West, Hamilton ON L8S 4S4
Tel: 905-525-9140
vped@msu.mcmaster.ca
www.msu.mcmaster.ca
Chief Officer(s):

Canadian Associations / Ontario Underwater Council (OUC)

Rodrigo Narro-Perez, Vice President, Education
Trent in Oshawa Students Association (TOSA)
Trent University, #122, 55 Thornton Rd. South, Oshawa ON L1J 5Y1
Tel: 905-435-5102; *Fax:* 905-435-5101
vpua@tosa.ca
www.tosa.ca
Chief Officer(s):
Shawn Murphy, Vice President, University Affairs
University Students' Council at the University of Western Ontario
University of Western Ontario, London ON N6A 3K7
Tel: 519-661-3574; *Fax:* 519-661-2094
uscvpext@uwo.ca
www.usc.uwo.ca
Chief Officer(s):
Jen Carter, Vice President, External
Wilfrid Laurier University Students' Union
75 University Ave. West, Waterloo ON N2L 3C5
Tel: 519-884-0710
rcamman@wlu.ca
www.wlusu.com
Chief Officer(s):
Rick Camman, Vice President, University Affairs
rcamman@wlu.ca

Ontario Underwater Council (OUC)
#109, 1 Concorde Gate, Toronto ON M3C 3C6
Tel: 416-426-7033; *Fax:* 416-426-7280
ouc@underwatercouncil.com
www.underwatercouncil.com
www.facebook.com/groups/39720054237
Overview: A small provincial organization
Mission: To represent all divers in Ontario; to promote the sport of scuba diving
Staff Member(s): 1; 100 volunteer(s)
Membership: 2,600+; *Fees:* $20-$37 individual; $145 commercial; schedule for clubs
Chief Officer(s):
Ronald J. Bogart, President
ouc.president@underwatercouncil.com
Sasha Ilich, Director, Communications
communications@underwatercouncil.com
Awards:
• Ken Grant Memorial Trophy
• TINMAN Award
• Distinguished Service Award
• Executive Director's Trophy

Ontario Universities Athletics *See* Ontario University Athletics

Ontario University Athletics (OUA) / Sports universitaires de l'Ontario
#2, 3305 Harvester Rd., Burlington ON L7N 3N2
Tel: 905-635-5510; *Fax:* 905-635-5820
info@oua.ca
www.oua.ca
www.facebook.com/OntarioUniversityAthletics
twitter.com/ouasport
www.youtube.com/ouachampionsforlife;
www.instagram.com/ouasport
Previous Name: Ontario Universities Athletics
Overview: A small provincial organization founded in 1898
Mission: To provide leadership, stewardship & policy direction for university sport; To govern interuniversity sport competition in Ontario on behalf of member institutions
Member of: Canadian Interuniversity Sport
Finances: *Annual Operating Budget:* $250,000-$500,000
Staff Member(s): 8
Membership: 19 schools; 9,000 student athletes
Activities: *Awareness Events:* Women of Influence Luncheon, Nov.; *Internships:* Yes
Chief Officer(s):
Gord Grace, Chief Executive Officer, 905-635-7470
gord.grace@oua.ca
Publications:
• Uncovered [a publication of Ontario University Athletics]
Type: Magazine
Profile: Features season previews & student athlete profiles

Ontario University Registrars' Association (OUSA)
900 McGill Rd., Kamloops BC V2C 0C8
Tel: 250-828-5019
www.oura.ca

Overview: A medium-sized provincial organization founded in 1964 overseen by Association of Registrars of Universities and Colleges of Canada
Membership: *Member Profile:* Ontario university registrars, admissions, records, computer systems, recruitment, financial aid, graduate studies and other university personnel involved in registrarial work.
Chief Officer(s):
Lucy Bellissimo, President
Meetings/Conferences:
• Ontario University Registrars' Association 2018 Conference, February, 2018, Marriott Eaton Centre Hotel, Toronto, ON
Scope: Provincial
Description: Theme: "Collaborating in Changing Times"

Ontario Urban Forest Council (OUFC)
PO Box 32166, Stn. Harding Post Office, Richmond Hill ON L4C 9SC
Tel: 416-936-6735; *Fax:* 416-291-5709
info@oufc.org
www.oufc.org
www.facebook.com/oufc.org
twitter.com/oufc_canada
Previous Name: Ontario Shade Tree Council
Overview: A medium-sized provincial organization founded in 1964
Mission: To be dedicated to the the health of urban forests in the province of Ontario
Affiliation(s): Urban Forest Network
Finances: *Annual Operating Budget:* Less than $50,000
11 volunteer(s)
Membership: 189 corporate + 9 senior/lifetime + 55 individual; *Fees:* Student: $25; Individual: $75; Group/Corporate: $150; *Member Profile:* Arborists, foresters, lanscape architects, nurserymen, planners, municipalities, restoration specialists, enviornmentalists, conservation authorities, any other public individuals concerned about trees
Activities: Provide information; Provide volunteer speakers; Host educational displays; Offer educational workshops; Annual Urban Tree Conference & an AGM; *Speaker Service:* Yes
Chief Officer(s):
Peter Wynnyczuk, Executive Director

Ontario Veal Association
449 Laird Rd., Guelph ON N1G 4W1
Tel: 519-824-2942; *Fax:* 519-824-2534
info@ontarioveal.on.ca
www.ontarioveal.on.ca
twitter.com/OntarioVeal
Overview: A small provincial organization founded in 1990
Mission: To promote & enhance a viable & competitive Ontario veal industry through innovation, marketing, advocacy & education; to represent Ontario's veal producers as a progressive & dynamic organization that is dedicated to strategically & effectively addressing the needs of the industry through a responsible regulatory marketing system

Ontario Vegetation Management Association (OVMA)
4 Spruce Blvd., Acton ON L7J 2Y2
Tel: 905-805-2294; *Fax:* 519-853-0352
info@ovma.ca
www.ovma.ca
Overview: A small provincial organization founded in 1984
Membership: *Fees:* $90 individual; $300 corporate gold; $450 Corporate Platinum; *Member Profile:* Promotes environmentally safe vegetation management
Chief Officer(s):
Geoff Gordon, President

Ontario Veterinary Medical Association (OVMA)
#205, 420 Bronte St. South, Milton ON L9T 0H9
Tel: 905-875-0756; *Fax:* 905-875-0958
Toll-Free: 800-670-1702
info@ovma.org
www.ovma.org
www.facebook.com/onvetmedassoc
twitter.com/OnVetMedAssoc
www.youtube.com/user/TheOVMA
Overview: A medium-sized provincial organization founded in 1874 overseen by Canadian Veterinary Medical Association
Mission: To represent Ontario veterinarians in small animal, large animal & mixed practice as well as those employed in government, industry or other institutions; programs include government & public relations, humane veterinary practice, continuing education in veterinary science & practice management & direct services to members.

Finances: *Funding Sources:* Membership fees; events; advertising
Staff Member(s): 15
Membership: 4,400+; *Fees:* Schedule available; *Member Profile:* Veterinarians, Ontario
Chief Officer(s):
Doug Raven, CEO
draven@ovma.org
Melissa Carlaw, Manager, Communications & Public Relations
mcarlaw@ovma.org

Ontario Vintage Radio Association (OVRA)
ON
www.ovra.ca
Overview: A small provincial organization founded in 1970
Mission: To preserve Canada's radio history, literature & equipment; to serve as a forum for members to exchange information & continue the legacy of the original club.
Finances: *Funding Sources:* Membership fees
Activities: Auctions; flea markets of radio & related material; guest speakers; *Speaker Service:* Yes; *Library:* OVRA Library; by appointment Not open to public

Ontario Volleyball Association (OVA)
#111, 6 Scarsdale Rd., Toronto ON M3B 2R7
Tel: 416-426-7316; *Fax:* 416-426-7109
Toll-Free: 800-372-1568
info@ontariovolleyball.org
www.ontariovolleyball.org
www.facebook.com/OntarioVolleyball
twitter.com/ova_updates
www.youtube.com/user/ontariovolley;
www.instagram.com/ova_updates
Overview: A large provincial organization founded in 1929 overseen by Volleyball Canada
Mission: To lead in the promotion & development of volleyball in Ontario
Staff Member(s): 13
Membership: *Fees:* Schedule available; *Committees:* Train to Compete; Beach; Executive
Activities: *Internships:* Yes
Chief Officer(s):
Jo-Anne Ljubicic, Executive Director, 416-426-7414
jljubicic@ontariovolleyball.org
Awards:
• Doug Robbie Volunteer of the Year Award
• Diane Wood Special Achievement Award
• Achievement Award
• Recognition Award
• Mike Bugarski Male Coach of the Year Award
• Sandy Silver Female Coach of the Year Award
• Senior Development Coach of the Year Award
• Junior Development Coach of the Year Award
• Paul & Shelley Brownstein Builder Award
• Sylvia Jaksetic Female Official of the Year Award
• Officials' Committee Award of Merit
• Anton Furlani Achievement Award
• Corporate & Partner Awards
• Scarborough Solars Award
• Ken Davies Memorial Award
• Evelyn Holick Award
• Jason Senechal Memorial Award
• Child & Heese Trophy

Ontario Waste Management Association (OWMA) / Société ontarienne de gestion des déchets
#3, 2005 Clark Blvd., Brampton ON L6T 5P8
Tel: 905-791-9500; *Fax:* 905-791-9514
info@owma.org
www.owma.org
www.linkedin.com/company/ontario-waste-management-association
twitter.com/OWMA1
Overview: A medium-sized provincial organization founded in 1977
Mission: To act as the voice of the private sector waste industry in Ontario; To protect the enviroment by properly managing waste & recyclable materials
Membership: *Member Profile:* Private sector independent companies in Ontario which provide waste & recycling services; Associate members include equipment manufacturers, suppliers, legal firms, & consultants; *Committees:* Safety & Transportation; Waste Diversion & Recycling; Waste Transfer & Disposal; Organics Diversion; Resource Recovery
Activities: Monitoring & assessing regulatory & policy initiatives; Promoting new standards & regulatory policies to improve waste

management services; Providing information to members about government initiatives, waste management, & business issues
Meetings/Conferences:
• 2018 Ontario Waste Management Association Annual General Meeting, 2018, ON
Scope: Provincial

Ontario Water Garden Society *See* Greater Toronto Water Garden & Horticultural Society

Ontario Water Polo Association Incorporated (OWP) / L'Association de water polo d'Ontario
#206, 3 Concorde Gate, Toronto ON M3C 3N7
Tel: 416-426-7028; *Fax:* 416-426-7356
www.ontariowaterpolo.ca
Also Known As: Ontario Water Polo
Overview: A medium-sized provincial organization founded in 1967 overseen by Water Polo Canada
Member of: Water Polo Canada
Finances: *Annual Operating Budget:* $100,000-$250,000
Staff Member(s): 2; 100 volunteer(s)
Membership: 1,200 individual; *Fees:* Schedule available
Activities: *Speaker Service:* Yes
Chief Officer(s):
Kathy Torrens, Secretary
kathy.torrens@ontariowaterpolo.ca

Ontario Water Ski Association (OWSA)
#209, 3 Concorde Gate, Toronto ON M3C 3N7
Tel: 416-426-7092; *Fax:* 416-426-7378
office@wswo.ca
www.wswo.ca
www.facebook.com/waterskiwakeboardontario
twitter.com/wswo
Also Known As: Water Ski Wakeboard Ontario
Overview: A medium-sized provincial organization founded in 1976
Mission: To promote & develop the sport of water skiing through safety & instructional tournaments, courses & demonstrations
Member of: Water Ski & Wakeboard Canada
Finances: *Funding Sources:* Private; provincial grant
Staff Member(s): 1
Membership: *Fees:* $10 associate; $40 active; $100 family; $80 camp; $100 club/school; *Member Profile:* Individual & families involved in recreational &/or competitive water skiing, also water ski schools, camps & clubs
Activities: Watersport/waterski/wakeboard events & tournaments in Ontario; *Library:* by appointment
Chief Officer(s):
Paul Roberts, President
pwroberts@sympatico.ca
Awards:
• Water Ski Skill Awards

Ontario Water Well Association *See* Ontario Ground Water Association

Ontario Water Works Association (OWWA)
#100, 922 The East Mall Dr., Toronto ON M9B 6K1
Tel: 416-231-1555; *Fax:* 416-231-1556
Toll-Free: 866-975-0575
waterinfo@owwa.ca
www.owwa.com
www.linkedin.com/company/ontario-water-works-association
twitter.com/OWWA1
Overview: A medium-sized provincial organization
Mission: To protect public health through the delivery of safe, sufficient & sustainable drinking water in Ontario
Member of: American Water Works Association
Affiliation(s): Ontario Municipal Water Association; Ontario Water Works Equipment Association
Membership: 1,100+; *Member Profile:* Individuals employed by Ontario's municipal water systems sector, including hydrogeologists, scientists, engineers, chemists, managers & technicians; *Committees:* Climate Change; C-PAC; Conference Management; Continuing Education; Cross Connection Control; Distribution; Government Affairs; Groundwater; Joint OWWA / OMWA; Management; Membership; OWWA / WEAO Joint Asset Management; Publications; Small Systems; Source Water Protection; Training, Certification, & Safety; Treatment; University Forum; Water Efficiency; Water for People - Canada; Young Professionals; Youth Education
Activities: Improving technology, science & management; Influencing government policy; Providing education for members; *Library:* Ontario Water Works Association Library
Chief Officer(s):
Marcus Firman, President

Dan Huggins, Vice President
Nick Reid, Executive Director
Reg Russwurm, Secretary-Treasurer
Awards:
• The George Warren Fuller Award
Presented to a Section member for their distinguished service to the water supply field in commemoration of the sound engineering skill, brilliant diplomatic talent, and constructive leadership which characterized the life of George Warren Fuller.
• Norman J. Howard Award
Awarded to recognize proficiency in the design, construction, operation, maintenance, research or management of a municipal water supply.
• Operator's Meritorious Service Award
Recognizes commitment & long-term service by an operator
• Dr. Albert E. Berry Membership Award
Recognizes extraordinary contribution to membership promotion & OWWA activities
• Michael R. Provart Membership Award
Recognizes an Ontario university student (graduate or undergraduate) for excellence in his/her presentation at Ontario's Water Conference & Trade Show; *Amount:* $1,000
• Water Efficiency Awards
Awarded to recognize outstanding intitiatives in water efficiency in both the public & private sector
Meetings/Conferences:
• Ontario's Water Conference & Trade Show 2018, April, 2018, Niagara Falls, ON
Scope: Provincial
Attendance: 1,400+
Description: This annual industry highlight features a full slate of plenary and technical sessions focusing on the latest in technology and research affecting drinking water from source to tap. The Trade Show consistently has more than 100 exhibitors representing the manufacturers and suppliers of products and services for the water industry.
• Ontario's Water Conference & Trade Show 2019, May, 2019, Ottawa, ON
Scope: Provincial
Attendance: 1,400+
Description: This annual industry highlight features a full slate of plenary and technical sessions focusing on the latest in technology and research affecting drinking water from source to tap. The Trade Show consistently has more than 100 exhibitors representing the manufacturers and suppliers of products and services for the water industry.
Publications:
• Ontario Pipeline [a publication of the Ontario Water Works Association]
Type: Magazine; *Frequency:* Quarterly; *Accepts Advertising*
Profile: A joint publication of the Ontario Water Works Association, the Ontario Municipal Water Association, & the Ontario Water Works EquipmentAssociation

Ontario Waterpower Association (OWA)
#264, 380 Armour Rd., Peterborough ON K9H 7L7
Toll-Free: 866-743-1500
info@owa.ca
www.owa.ca
www.linkedin.com/company-beta/3216266
www.facebook.com/ONWaterpower
twitter.com/ONWaterpower
Overview: A medium-sized provincial organization founded in 2001
Mission: To promote the achievement of sustainable development & provide a source for quality information about waterpower that grows & enhances the competitiveness of the Ontario waterpower industry
Membership: 150+; *Member Profile:* Individuals or organizations associated with Ontario's waterpower industry, including generators, engineering firms, environmental consultants, project financing & insurance firms & First Nations communities
Chief Officer(s):
Paul Norris, President, 866-743-1500 Ext. 22
Janelle Bates, Manager, Conference & Events
Stephanie Landers, Advisor, Communications & Public Relations
Meetings/Conferences:
• 18th Annual Power of Water Canada Conference 2018, October, 2018, White Oaks Conference Resort, Niagara-on-the-Lake, ON
Scope: Provincial
Attendance: 400+
Description: The largest gathering of the hydroelectric sector in Canada; will feature a tradeshow with more than 60 exhibitors.

Contact Information: Manager, Conference & Events: Janelle Bates, E-mail: jbates@owa.ca, Phone: 1-866-743-1500, ext. 23
Publications:
• Ontario Waterpower Association Newsletter
Type: Newsletter; *Frequency:* Quarterly
Profile: News & updates for members

Ontario Weightlifting Association (OWA)
PO Box 14012, Stn. Glebe, Ottawa ON K1S 3T2
owamembership@gmail.com
www.onweightlifting.ca
www.facebook.com/OntarioWeightlifting
twitter.com/ONWeightlifting
www.youtube.com/user/ontarioweightlifting
Overview: A medium-sized provincial organization founded in 1968
Mission: To govern weightlifting in Ontario
Member of: Ontario Hockey Federation; Hockey Canada
Affiliation(s): Canadian Weightlifting Federation; Sport Alliance of Ontario; Sport4Ontario
Staff Member(s): 6
Membership: 36 clubs; *Fees:* $80 competitive; $50 introductory; $35 participation/coach/official; $2 volunteer
Chief Officer(s):
Moira Lassen, President
owapresident1@gmail.com

Ontario Wheelchair Sports Association (OWSA)
#101, 100 Sunrise Ave., Toronto ON M4A 1B3
info@owsa.ca
www.owsa.ca
www.facebook.com/WheelchairSportsON
twitter.com/WSA_Ontario
Overview: A medium-sized provincial organization founded in 1972
Mission: To provide sporting & recreational opportunities for athletes who compete in wheelchairs
Member of: Canadian Wheelchair Sports Association
Affiliation(s): Canadian Wheelchair Sports Association
Finances: *Funding Sources:* Provincial Government
Staff Member(s): 3
Chief Officer(s):
Ken Thom, President
kenthom@rogers.com
Laura Wilson, Executive Director
laura@owsa.ca

Ontario Women's Health Network (OWHN)
#301, 180 Dundas St. West, Toronto ON M5G 1Z8
Tel: 416-408-4840; *Fax:* 416-408-2122
Toll-Free: 877-860-4545
owhn@owhn.on.ca
www.owhn.on.ca
twitter.com/The_OWHN
Overview: A medium-sized local organization founded in 1997
Mission: To act as a network of individuals & organizations that promote women's health in Ontario
Chief Officer(s):
Christina Lessels, Coordinator, Research & Communications, 416-408-4840 Ext. 32

Ontario Women's Hockey Association (OWHA) / Association de hockey féminin de l'Ontario
225 Watline Ave., Mississauga ON L4Z 1P3
Tel: 905-282-9980; *Fax:* 905-282-9982
info@owha.on.ca
www.owha.on.ca
twitter.com/OWHAhockey
Overview: A medium-sized provincial organization founded in 1975
Mission: To provide & develop opportunities for girls & women to play female hockey in all aspects of female hockey; To foster & encourage leadership programs in all areas related to the development of female hockey in Ontario; To promote hockey as a game played primarily for enjoyment while also fostering sportsmanship
Member of: Hockey Canada
Chief Officer(s):
Fran Rider, President & Chief Executive Officer, 416-573-5447
fran@owha.on.ca
Pat Nicholls, Director, Operations, 416-571-9198
pat@owha.on.ca

Ontario Women's Justice Network (OWJN)
METRAC, 158 Spadina Rd., Toronto ON M5R 2T8
Tel: 416-392-3135; *TTY:* 877-558-5570
info@metrac.org

www.owjn.org
www.facebook.com/owjn.org
twitter.com/owjn
Overview: A medium-sized provincial organization founded in 1996
Mission: To demystify the legal system; to examine various justice issues; to provide legal information
Member of: National Association of Women & the Law
Membership: *Member Profile:* Violence against women organizations; community activists; researchers; students
Activities: Online legal resource for women's organizations & individuals working on issues related to justice & violence against women & children

Ontario Woodlot Association
RR#4, 275 County Rd. 44, Kemptville ON K0G 1J0
Tel: 613-258-0110; *Fax:* 613-258-0207
info@ont-woodlot-assoc.org
www.ont-woodlot-assoc.org
www.facebook.com/pages/Ontario-Woodlot-Association/237050606357425
Overview: A small provincial organization founded in 1992
Mission: To promote the wise & profitable use of Ontario's private land forest resource
Membership: 1,700; *Fees:* $40
Chief Officer(s):
Wade Knight, Executive Director
Pieter Leenhouts, President
David Sexsmith, Vice-President

Ontario Workers' Compensation Institute *See* Institute for Work & Health

Ontario Zoroastrian Community Foundation (OZCF)
Zoroastrian Religious and Cultural Centre (OZCF Centre), 1187 Burnhamthorpe Rd. East, Oakville ON L6H 7B3
Tel: 905-271-0366
www.ozcf.com
Overview: A small provincial charitable organization
Mission: To build 'Our Centre' by providing labour & expertise however possible
Membership: *Fees:* $100 family; $30 seniors; $65 single; $25 student; *Member Profile:* Zoroastrians living in Ontario; *Committees:* Communication/IT, Social & Entertainment, Facility Management, Finance, Lectures & Learning, Membership, Newsletter, Religious, Seniors, Sports, Youth
Activities: Religious education program for children; Zoroastrian Scouts; Seniors program; Cultural Kanoun for Farsi speakers; Lecture group; Library; Youth group; Committees for newly landed immigrants & others in need
Chief Officer(s):
Percy Dastur, President
percydastur@gmail.com

Ontario's Finest Inns & Spas
PO Box 9, 435 Turnberry St., Brussels ON N0G 1H0
Tel: 519-887-8383; *Fax:* 519-887-8192
Toll-Free: 800-340-4667
info@ontariosfinestinns.com
www.ontariosfinest.ca
Previous Name: Innkeepers of Ontario
Overview: A small provincial organization
Membership: *Member Profile:* Innkeepers, spa proprietors

Open Door Group
#300, 30 East 6 Ave., Vancouver BC V5T 1J4
Tel: 604-876-0770; *Fax:* 604-873-1758
Toll-Free: 866-377-3670
info@opendoorgroup.org
www.opendoorgroup.org
www.facebook.com/OpenDoorGroup
Previous Name: Arbutus Vocational Society; THEO BC
Overview: A medium-sized provincial charitable organization founded in 1976
Mission: To assist psychiatrically, emotionally & socially disadvantaged people to develop the necessary skills to lead more satisfying lives
Finances: *Funding Sources:* Provincial Government
Membership: 10 service centres
Chief Officer(s):
Tom Burnell, Chief Executive Officer
tom.burnell@opendoorgroup.org
Naomi Bullock, Executive Director, Program Management & Development
naomi.bullock@opendoorgroup.org
Alona Puehse, Executive Director, Corporate Development
alona.puehse@opendoorgroup.org

Christine Buchanan, Director, Diversity & Disability Services
christine.buchanan@opendoorgroup.org
Katrina Welsh, Director, Human Resources
katrina.welsh@opendoorgroup.org
Joey Alain, Director, Information Technology
joey.alain@opendoorgroup.org
Cora David, Financial Controller
cora.david@opendoorgroup.org

Chase & District Satellite Office
822B Shuswap Ave., Chase BC V0E 1M0
Tel: 250-679-8448; *Fax:* 250-679-8117
Gibsons Satellite Office
#25, 900 Gibsons Way, Gibsons BC V0N 1V8
Tel: 604-886-7729; *Fax:* 604-886-7759
Kamloops North Shore Office
795 Tranquille Rd., Kamloops BC V2B 3J3
Tel: 250-377-3670; *Fax:* 250-377-3695
Kamloops South Shore Office
#100, 275 Lansdowne St., Kamloops BC V2C 6H6
Tel: 250-434-9441; *Fax:* 250-434-9442
Lillooet Office
639B Main St., Lillooet BC V0K 1V0
Tel: 250-256-7758; *Fax:* 250-256-7768
Oliver Office
#D, 291 Fairview Rd., Oliver BC V0H 1T0
Tel: 250-498-2911; *Fax:* 250-498-2944
Osoyoos Satellite Office
#4, 9150 Main St., RR 2, Osoyoos BC V0H 1V2
Tel: 250-495-7731; *Fax:* 250-495-7797
Sechelt Office
PO Box 834, 5674 Cowrie St., Sechelt BC V0N 3A0
Tel: 604-885-3351; *Fax:* 604-885-3361
Vancouver Downtown Eastside - Hastings Office
134 East Hastings St., Vancouver BC V6A 1N4
Tel: 604-872-0770; *Fax:* 604-873-1758
Vancouver Downtown Eastside - VCC Office
#200, 250 West Pender St., Vancouver BC V6B 1S9
Tel: 604-872-0770; *Fax:* 604-873-1758

Open Harbour Refugee Association (OHRA)
#110, 1041 Wellington St., Halifax NS B3H 4P5
hello@openharbour.ca
www.openharbour.ca
www.facebook.com/openharbour
Overview: A small local organization
Mission: To provide assistance to refugee families settling in Halifax
Finances: *Funding Sources:* Fundraising
Chief Officer(s):
Richard Donald

"Open in Spirit to God" *See* Bukas Loob sa Diyos Covenant Community

Open Learning Agency *See* Open Learning at Thompson Rivers University

Open Learning at Thompson Rivers University (TRU-OL)
BC Centre for Open Learning, 900 McGill Rd., 4th Fl., Kamloops BC V2C 0C8
Tel: 250-852-7000
Toll-Free: 800-663-9711
student@tru.ca
www.tru.ca/distance.html
Previous Name: Open Learning Agency
Overview: A small provincial organization founded in 1988
Mission: To enhance the personal growth of individuals & their performance in society & in the workplace through the provision of high quality, flexible learning products, services & systems
Member of: Association of Community Colleges of Canada; Association of Universities & Colleges of Canada; Canadian Virtual University
Finances: *Funding Sources:* Provincial government
Activities: Open School; Open College; BC Open University; Knowledge Network; OLA Skills Centres; Learning Systems Institute; Canadian Learning Bank; International Credential Evaluation Service
Chief Officer(s):
Katherine Sutherland, Vice-Provost

Open Space Arts Society (OS)
510 Fort St., Victoria BC V8W 1E6
Tel: 250-383-8833; *Fax:* 250-383-8841
openspace@openspace.ca
www.openspace.ca

www.facebook.com/openspacevic
twitter.com/OpenSpaceVic
Overview: A small local organization founded in 1972
Mission: Open Space supports experimental artistic practices in all contemporary arts disciplines, acting as a laboratory for engaging art, artists, and communities.
Member of: Pacific Association of Artist-Run Centres; Canadian Museums Association; Canadian Conference for the Arts; Professional Arts Organizations of Greater Victoria
Finances: *Annual Operating Budget:* $100,000-$250,000; *Funding Sources:* Federal, provincial & regional government
Staff Member(s): 3; 5 volunteer(s)
Membership: 150; *Fees:* $15-$75; *Committees:* Community Relations Committee; Facility Committee; Human Resources Committee; Program Committee
Activities: Visual Arts; New Media; Interarts; New Music; Literary; *Internships:* Yes *Library:* Open Space Resource Centre
Chief Officer(s):
Helen Marzolf, Executive Director, 250-383-8833
director@openspace.ca
Ted Hiebert, Chair

OpenMedia Engagement Network
PO Box 21674, 1424 Commercial Dr., Vancouver BC V5L 5G3
Toll-Free: 844-891-5136
www.openmedia.org
www.facebook.com/openmediaorg
twitter.com/openmediaorg
Overview: A small local organization
Mission: To ensure that the Internet remains accessible, affordable, & free from surveillance
Activities: Educating the public about Internet-related issues; Organizing online & social media campaigns
Chief Officer(s):
Laura Tribe, Executive Director

Opéra Atelier (OA)
St. Lawrence Hall, 157 King St. East, 4th Fl., Toronto ON M5C 1G9
Tel: 416-703-3767; *Fax:* 416-703-4895
opera.atelier@operaatelier.com
www.operaatelier.com
www.facebook.com/466529060483
twitter.com/OperaAtelier
www.youtube.com/user/OperaAtelier
Also Known As: Atelier Theatre Society
Overview: A small local charitable organization founded in 1983
Mission: To produce opera, ballet, & drama from the 17th & 18th centuries; to educate and instruct young performers
Finances: *Annual Operating Budget:* $500,000-$1.5 Million; *Funding Sources:* Government; Corporations; Individual donations; Ticket sales
Staff Member(s): 12; 50 volunteer(s)
Membership: 35; *Fees:* $95-$285; *Member Profile:* Arts patrons
Activities: Opera performances; Conducting workshops for youth interested in opera
Chief Officer(s):
Alexandra Skoczylas, Executive Director
alex.skoczylas@operaatelier.com
Jeannette Lajeunesse Zingg, Co-Artistic Director/Choreographer
Marshall Pynkoski, Co-Artistic Director/Director
David Fallis, Resident Music Director
Trini Mitra, Director, Finance & Administration
trini.mitra@operaatelier.com

L'Opéra de Montréal (ODM) / Montréal Opera
260, boul de Maisonneuve ouest, Montréal QC H2X 1Y9
Tél: 514-985-2222
info@operademontreal.com
www.operademontreal.com
www.facebook.com/operademontreal
twitter.com/operademontreal
instagram.com/operademontreal
Aperçu: *Dimension:* petite; *Envergure:* locale; fondée en 1980
Mission: Afin de présenter des productions d'opéra de comparable qualité et originalité à ceux observés dans les plus grands opéras du monde; cherche la contribution du personnel de création de niveaux local et national; ainsi que d'inviter les meilleurs artistes de l'étranger; soutient l'émergence de nouveaux talents opéra canadienne
Affiliation(s): Professional Opera Companies of Canada; Opera America
Membre(s) du personnel: 33
Activités: Six productions d'opéra pour la saison; atelier lyrique; programme d'apprentissage; gala-bénéfice annuel; Signature

concert-bénéfice de l'événement; *Stagiaires:* Oui; *Service de conférenciers:* Oui
Membre(s) du bureau directeur:
Pierre Dufour, Directeur général
pdufour@operademontreal.com
Michel Beaulac, Directeur artistique
mbeaulac@operademontreal.com
Louis Bouchard, Directeur technique
lbouchard@operademontreal.com
Pierre Vachon, Directeur, Communications, communauté et éducation
pvachon@operademontreal.com

Opéra de Québec
1220, av Taché, Québec QC G1R 3B4
Tél: 418-529-4142; *Téléc:* 418-529-3735
www.operadequebec.com
www.facebook.com/operadequebec
twitter.com/operadequebec
Aperçu: Dimension: petite; *Envergure:* locale; fondée en 1983
Mission: Produire des spectacles d'opéra professionnels à Québec
Membre(s) du personnel: 7
Membre(s) du bureau directeur:
Gaston Déry, Président
Grégoire Legendre, Directeur général et artistique

Opera.ca
#6286, 2100 Bloor St. West, Toronto ON M6S 5A5
Tel: 416-591-7222
www.opera.ca
www.facebook.com/pages/Operaca/142045112454
twitter.com/opera_ca
Overview: A medium-sized national organization
Mission: To advance the interests of Canada's opera community; To create greater opportunity for opera audiences and professionals alike
Affiliation(s): Canadian Children's Opera Chorus; International Resource Centre for Performing Artists; National Arts Centre; Opera Canada; Opera in Concert; Saskatoon Opera; Théâtre Lyrichorégra 20; Toronto Operetta Theatre; Toronto Summer Music
Staff Member(s): 2
Membership: 13 opera companies; *Fees:* $75 individual; $250 affiliate; $300 business; $350 educational producing affiliate; $175 career services subscription
Chief Officer(s):
Christina Loewen, Executive Director
D. Liu, Coordinator, Membership & Communications
Publications:
• High Notes [a publication of Opera.ca]
Type: Newsletter; *Frequency:* Monthly

Operating Room Nurses Association of Canada (ORNAC) / Association des infirmières et infirmiers de salles d'opération du Canada
Toll-Free: 844-594-0052
info@ornac.ca
www.ornac.ca
www.facebook.com/491656354213298
twitter.com/ornacanada
Overview: A large national organization founded in 1983
Mission: To promote operating nursing for the betterment of surgical patient care
Member of: Canadian Nurses Association; International Federation of Perioperative Nurses (IFPN)
Membership: *Fees:* Schedule available; *Member Profile:* Perioperative RN
Activities: Professional & personal enhancement of operating room nurses; *Awareness Events:* OR Nurse Day, Nov.; *Speaker Service:* Yes
Chief Officer(s):
Heather Dow, Executive Director
Awards:
• Gloria Stephens Award for Excellence as an Educator of Perioperative Nursing
• RMAC Patient Safety Award
• ORNAC - Muriel Shewchuk Leadership Award
• Isabelle Adams Award for Excellence in Perioperative Nursing
• ORNAC / Johnson & Johnson Drake Thompson Writing Award
• Lorne Flower Memorial Award
• 3M Canadian Infection Prevention Champion Award
• Cardinal Health Research Grant
; *Amount:* $5,000
• ORNAC/Johnson & Johnson Medical Products Joint Bursary
Deadline: January 15

Meetings/Conferences:
• 26th Operating Room Nurses Association of Canada National Conference 2019, April, 2019, Halifax Convention Centre, Halifax, NS
Scope: National
Description: Theme: "Tides of Change, Oceans of Perioperative Excellence"
Publications:
• ORNAC Journal
Type: Journal; *Frequency:* Quarterly
Profile: Journal promotes professional perioperative nursing practice and provides its membership with relevant, practice-based information to apply in today's OR environment.

Operating Room Nurses Association of Nova Scotia (ORNANS)
NS
www.ornans.ca
Overview: A medium-sized provincial organization overseen by Operating Room Nurses Association of Canada
Mission: To address issues concerning nursing practice & standards; To provide educational opportunities to members; To promote the exchange of information among perioperative nurses
Membership: *Member Profile:* Registered Nurses in Nova Scotia who are engaged in operating room nursing or involved in the Perioperative setting
Activities: *Awareness Events:* Perioperative Nurses Week, November
Chief Officer(s):
Jennifer Radtke-Jardine, President
ornanspresident@gmail.com
Meetings/Conferences:
• Operating Room Nurses Association of Nova Scotia Annual General Meeting 2018, June, 2018, St. Francis Xavier University, Antigonish, NS
Scope: Provincial

Operating Room Nurses Association of Ontario (ORNAO)
ON
info@ornao.org
www.ornao.org
Overview: A medium-sized provincial organization overseen by Operating Room Nurses Association of Canada
Mission: To represent registered nurses working in the perioperative nursing field in Ontario
Membership: *Member Profile:* Registered Nurses in Ontario who are engaged in operating room nursing or involved in the Perioperative setting
Activities: *Awareness Events:* Perioperative Nurses Week, November
Chief Officer(s):
Linda Whyte, President, 416-864-6060 Ext. 2736
president@ornao.org

Operating Room Nurses of Alberta Association (ORNAA)
AB
info@ornaa.org
www.ornaa.org
Overview: A medium-sized provincial organization overseen by Operating Room Nurses Association of Canada
Mission: To ensure quality perioperative nursing practice; To promote the professional growth of members
Membership: *Member Profile:* Registered Nurses in Alberta who are engaged in operating room nursing or a member of CARNA who are involved in the perioperative setting
Activities: *Awareness Events:* Perioperative Nurses Week, November
Chief Officer(s):
Darlene Rikley, President
president@ornaa.org
Sandi Burton, Secretary
secretary@ornaa.org
Awards:
• Muriel Shewchuk Excellence in Leadership Award for Alberta
• The ORNAA Promising Star Award
Meetings/Conferences:
• Operating Room Nurses of Alberta Association AGM 2018, 2018, AB
Scope: Provincial

Operation Come Home
PO Box 53157, Ottawa ON K1N 1C5
Tel: 613-230-4663; *Fax:* 613-230-8223
Toll-Free: 800-668-4663
info@operationcomehome.ca
www.operationcomehome.ca
www.facebook.com/OperationComeHome
twitter.com/ochottawa
Previous Name: Operation Go Home
Overview: A medium-sized national charitable organization founded in 1971
Mission: To reunite runaway youth (aged 16 & up) with their families or to connect them with a safe environment off the streets
Finances: *Annual Operating Budget:* $250,000-$500,000; *Funding Sources:* Private; fundraising; corporate; service clubs
Staff Member(s): 8; 50 volunteer(s)
Activities: Spring Gala; Raceway; Steam Train; *Speaker Service:* Yes
Chief Officer(s):
Elspeth McKay, Executive Director

Operation Eyesight Universal
#200, 4 Parkdale Cres. NW, Calgary AB T2N 3T8
Tel: 403-283-6323; *Fax:* 403-270-1899
Toll-Free: 800-585-8265
www.operationeyesight.com
www.linkedin.com/company/operation-eyesight
www.facebook.com/OperationEyesightUniversal
twitter.com/OpEyesight
www.youtube.com/user/OpEyesightUniversal
Overview: A large international charitable organization founded in 1963
Mission: To eliminate avoidable blindness through the development & support of permanent, self-sustaining, quality blindness prevention & sight restoration programs for those people in greatest need
Member of: International Agency for the Prevention of Blindness
Affiliation(s): International Agency for the Prevention of Blindness; L.V. Prasad Eye Institute; Vision 2020
Finances: *Funding Sources:* Government of Canada
Activities: Gift of Sight Tour; *Speaker Service:* Yes
Chief Officer(s):
Brian Foster, Executive Director
Publications:
• SightLines [a publication of Operation Eyesight Universal]
Type: Newsletter; *Frequency:* Quarterly

Vancouver Regional Office
#200, 4 Parkdale Crescent NW, Calgary AB T2N 3T8
Tel: 403-283-6323; *Fax:* 403-270-1899
Toll-Free: 800-585-8265
vancouver@operationeyesight.ca
www.linkedin.com/company/operation-eyesight
www.facebook.com/OperationEyesightUniversal
twitter.com/OpEyesight
www.youtube.com/user/OpEyesightUniversal
Affiliation(s): Vision 2020; IAPB; L.V. Prasad Eye Institute; Optometry Givign Sight; Eyesight International; Seeing is Believing
Chief Officer(s):
Brian Foster, Executive Director
Rob Ohlson, Chair

Opération Gareautrain *See* Operation Lifesaver

Operation Go Home *See* Operation Come Home

Operation Go Home - Winnipeg Office *See* Resource Assistance for Youth

Operation Harvest Sharing
PO Box 522, 58 Buell St., Brockville ON K6V 5V7
Tel: 613-342-0605; *Fax:* 613-342-1713
info@oafb.ca
operationharvestsharing.ca
Also Known As: Brockville & Area Food Bank
Overview: A small local organization
Member of: Ontario Association of Food Banks
Chief Officer(s):
Myra Garvin, President

Operation Lifesaver (OL) / Opération Gareautrain
#901, 99 Bank St., Ottawa ON K1P 6B9
Tel: 613-564-8100; *Fax:* 613-567-6726
admin@operationlifesaver.ca
www.operationlifesaver.ca
www.facebook.com/oplifesaver
twitter.com/oplifesaver
www.youtube.com/user/OperationLifesaverCA
Overview: A small national organization founded in 1981

Mission: To create awareness by the general public of the potential hazards of rail/highway crossings; To improve drivers' & pedestrians' behaviour at these intersections; To inform the public of the dangers associated with trespassing on railway property; To reduce the number of accidents resulting in fatalities, injuries & monetary losses
Affiliation(s): olkids.ca; traintodrive.net
Finances: *Annual Operating Budget:* $250,000-$500,000; *Funding Sources:* Transport Canada; Railway Association of Canada
Staff Member(s): 2; 150 volunteer(s)
Activities: *Awareness Events:* OL Rail Safety Week, April
Chief Officer(s):
Sarah Mayes, National Director

Operation Mobilization Canada (OM)
84 West St., Port Colborne ON L3K 4C8
Toll-Free: 877-487-7777
info.ca@om.org
www.omcanada.org
www.facebook.com/omcanada
twitter.com/om_canada
Overview: A small international charitable organization founded in 1966
Mission: Missionary training movement operating in 80 countries with 6,000 people in program every year; mobilizes & trains young Protestant believers for mission fields.
Member of: Evangelical Fellowship of Canada; Canadian Council of Christian Charities
Finances: *Annual Operating Budget:* $1.5 Million-$3 Million
Staff Member(s): 25
Activities: *Speaker Service:* Yes; *Library*
Chief Officer(s):
Harvey Thiessen, Executive Director

Opération Nez rouge / Operation Red Nose
Maison Couillard, Université Laval, 2539, rue Marie-Fitzbach, Québec QC G1V 0A6
Tél: 418-653-1492; *Téléc:* 418-653-3315
Ligne sans frais: 800-463-7222
info@operationnezrouge.com
www.operationnezrouge.com
www.facebook.com/OperationNezrouge
twitter.com/ORNose
www.youtube.com/user/OperationNezrouge
Aperçu: *Dimension:* grande; *Envergure:* nationale; fondée en 1984
Mission: Service de chauffeur privé gratuit & bénévole offert pendant la période des Fêtes à tout automobiliste qui a consommé de l'alcool, ou qui ne se sent pas en état de conduire son véhicule
Membre de: Réseau de l'action bénévole du Québec; Chambre de commerce et d'industrie de la ville de Québec
Finances: *Budget de fonctionnement annuel:* $500,000-$1.5 Million; *Fonds:* Commanditaires; Articles promotionnels
Membre(s) du personnel: 10; 4000 bénévole(s)
Activités: Service de raccompagnement; Tournée Party sans Déraper; C'est Notre Tournée; Bouclez-la; *Stagiaires:* Oui; *Service de conférenciers:* Oui
Membre(s) du bureau directeur:
Jean-Philippe Giroux, Directeur général
jpgiroux@operationnezrouge.com
Monique Mailhot, Directrice, Administration et finances
mmailhot@operationnezrouge.com
Meetings/Conferences:
• Congrès annuel de l'Opération Nez rouge 2018, 2018
Scope: National

Operation Red Nose *Voir* Opération Nez rouge

Operation Springboard
#800, 2 Carlton St., Toronto ON M5B 1J3
Tel: 416-977-0089; *Fax:* 416-977-2840
info@springboardservices.ca
www.springboardservices.ca
www.linkedin.com/company/springboard-services
www.facebook.com/OperationSpringboard
twitter.com/OpSpringboard
www.youtube.com/user/OperationSpringbord
Also Known As: Springboard
Overview: A large provincial charitable organization founded in 1969
Mission: To design & provide services & programs that effectively reintegrate offenders into the community as *responsible individuals*; To develop crime prevention strategies; To promote community involvement in design & provision of services along with continuous effort to encourage understanding & support; To bring forward recommendations that will improve effectiveness of the criminal justice system.
Member of: Canadian Criminal Justice Association; American Corrections Association
Finances: *Annual Operating Budget:* Less than $50,000; *Funding Sources:* General public; corporations; foundations; government
Membership: *Committees:* Human Resources; Finance; Communication; Program; Executive; Nominating; Fundraising; Advisory Board; Audit; Innovation
Chief Officer(s):
Margaret Stanowski, Executive Director
Anna Peters, Director, Finance, IT & Facilities
Rafael Silver, Director, Organization & Business Development

  Aris Kaplanis Centre for Youth, Resource Room & Attendance Program
  2568 Lawrence Ave. East, Toronto ON M1P 2R7
  Tel: 416-615-0788
  Chief Officer(s):
  Mark Schuler, Supervisor
  Blue Jays Lodge
  51 Dawes Rd., Toronto ON M4C 5B1
  Tel: 416-698-0047; *Fax:* 416-698-0051
  Diversion Office - Old City Hall
  60 Queen St. West, Toronto ON M5H 2M4
  Tel: 416-214-2469
  Chief Officer(s):
  Liz Igoe, Supervisor
  Diversion Office - Scarborough Ct.
  1911 Eglinton Ave. East, Toronto ON M1L 4P4
  Tel: 416-755-1168
  Chief Officer(s):
  Nicole Howes, Diversion Counsellor
  Employment Services
  3195 Sheppard Avenue East, Fl. 1A, Toronto ON M1T 3K1
  Tel: 416-849-4421
  North Beaches Residence
  2305 Gerrard St. East, Toronto ON M4E 2E4
  Tel: 416-690-8001; *Fax:* 416-690-9646
  Terry Fox House
  230 Beverley St., Toronto ON M5T 1Z3
  Tel: 416-588-7706; *Fax:* 416-536-6676

Operative Plasterers' & Cement Masons' International Association of the US & Canada (AFL-CIO/CFL) - Canadian Office
Varette Bldg., #1902, 130 Albert St., Ottawa ON K1P 5G4
Tel: 613-236-0653; *Fax:* 613-230-5138
www.buildingtrades.ca
twitter.com/CDNTrades
www.youtube.com/user/Buildingtrades12
Also Known As: Building & Construction Trades Dept.
Overview: A medium-sized national organization
Mission: To represent the interests of those employed in the building, construction, fabrication & maintenance industry in Canada ensuring safe working conditions
Staff Member(s): 6
Membership: 500,000+
Activities: *Library:* by appointment Not open to public
Chief Officer(s):
Robert Blakely, Canadian Operating Officer, 613-236-0653 Ext. 22
rblakely@buildingtrades.ca

Opimian Society / La Société Opimian
#420, 5165, rue Sherbrooke ouest, Montréal QC H4A 1T6
Tel: 514-483-5551; *Fax:* 514-481-9699
Toll-Free: 800-361-9421
opim@opim.ca
www.opim.ca
twitter.com/opimianwineclub
Also Known As: Wine Society of Canada
Overview: A large national organization founded in 1973
Mission: To work as Canada's only national non-profit wine ordering co-operative
Member of: International Wine Clubs Association
Finances: *Funding Sources:* Membership fees
25 volunteer(s)
Membership: 20,000; *Fees:* $69 annual + $40 registration + applicable taxes
Chief Officer(s):
Lois-Anne Brebner, President
Paul Reimer, Vice-President

Opportunity For Advancement (OFA)
54 Wolseley St., 2nd Fl., Toronto ON M5T 1A5
Tel: 416-787-1481; *Fax:* 416-787-1500
info@ofacan.com
www.ofacan.com
Overview: A small local organization founded in 1974
Mission: To work with women in disadvantaged life situations; to promote women's economic self sufficiency; to build self-esteem, reduce social isolation, explore the roots of problem situations, learn & share information & skills, set new goals
Finances: *Funding Sources:* Regional government
Activities: Program delivery; social advocacy; *Internships:* Yes; *Speaker Service:* Yes

Opticians Association of Canada (OAC)
#2706, 83 Garry St., Winnipeg MB R3C 4J9
Tel: 204-982-6060; *Fax:* 204-947-2519
Toll-Free: 800-842-3155
canada@opticians.ca
www.opticians.ca
www.linkedin.com/company/opticians-association-of-canada
www.facebook.com/215512795151373
twitter.com/OACexecutiveDr
www.youtube.com/user/opticianstv
Overview: A medium-sized national organization
Finances: *Funding Sources:* Sponsorship
Staff Member(s): 6
Membership: *Fees:* $125; *Committees:* Advisory
Chief Officer(s):
Robert Dalton, Executive Director
rdalton@opticians.ca

Opticians Association of New Brunswick / Association des otpiciens du Nouveau-Brunswick
PO Box 6743, Stn. Brunswick Square, Saint John NB E2L 4S2
Tel: 506-642-2878; *Fax:* 506-642-7984
nbgdo@nbnet.nb.ca
www.opticiansnb.com
Previous Name: New Brunswick Guild of Dispensing Opticians
Overview: A small provincial licensing organization founded in 1976
Mission: To regulate the practice of opticianry in New Brunswick; To oversee education of candidates for licensing

Opticians of Manitoba (OOM)
#215, 1080 Portage Ave., Winnipeg MB R3G 3M3
Tel: 204-222-8404; *Fax:* 204-222-5296
Toll-Free: 855-346-3715
oom@optm.ca
www.opticiansofmanitoba.ca
www.facebook.com/1396718373891003
Overview: A small provincial organization founded in 1953
Mission: To protect the public through the self-regulation of the practice of Opticianry; To set standards of practice for the profession; To ensure that opticians practice safely & competently; To investigate concerns raised about registrants' practice
Membership: *Fees:* $75; *Committees:* Appointments/Nomination; Communication/Outreach; Complaints Resolution; Executive; Finance & Audit; Professional Relations; Registration; Standards of Practice
Chief Officer(s):
Carol Ellerbeck, Registrar
cellerbeck@opticians.ca
Publications:
• Opticians of Manitoba Newsletter
Type: Newsletter

Optimist International Canada (OIC)
Canadian Service Centre, #200, 5205, boul Metropolitain est, Montréal QC H1R 1Z7
Tel: 514-593-4401; *Fax:* 514-721-1104
Toll-Free: 800-363-7151
service@optimist.org
www.optimist.org
www.linkedin.com/groups/117333
www.facebook.com/optimistintl
twitter.com/optimistorg
www.youtube.com/user/OptimistIntl
Overview: A medium-sized national organization founded in 1919
Mission: To bring out the best in youth, their communities & themselves
Affiliation(s): Optimist International; Canadian Children's Optimist Foundation
Chief Officer(s):
Jacques Pelland, Senior Director

Option consommateurs
#440, 50, rue Sainte-Catherine ouest, Montréal QC H2X 3V4
Tél: 514-598-7288; *Téléc:* 514-598-8511
Ligne sans frais: 888-412-1313
info@option-consommateurs.org
www.option-consommateurs.org
www.facebook.com/option.consommateurs.fbp
twitter.com/OptionConso
Également appelé: ACEF - Centre
Nom précédent: Association coopérative d'économie familiale - Montréal (Centre)
Aperçu: *Dimension:* petite; *Envergure:* locale; Organisme sans but lucratif; fondée en 1983
Mission: Travailler à la défense et la promotion des droits des consommateurs
Membre de: Consumers International; Agence de la consommation en matière financière du Canada
Membre(s) du personnel: 27
Membre: *Montant de la cotisation:* 22$
Activités: Cours sur le budget, consultation budgétaire; service juridique; défense des droits aux consommateurs; information des consommateurs; recours collectifs; *Stagiaires:* Oui; *Service de conférenciers:* Oui
Membre(s) du bureau directeur:
Éliane Hamel, Directrice générale
ehamel@option-consommateurs.org

Options for Sexual Health (OPT)
3550 East Hastings St., Vancouver BC V5K 2A7
Tel: 604-731-4252; *Fax:* 604-731-4698
info@optbc.org
www.optionsforsexualhealth.org
www.facebook.com/optbc
twitter.com/optbc
Previous Name: Planned Parenthood Association of British Columbia
Overview: A medium-sized provincial charitable organization founded in 1963 overseen by Canadian Federation for Sexual Health
Mission: To promote optimal sexual health for all British Columbians by supporting reproductive choice, reducing unplanned pregnancy, & providing quality education, information & clinical services
Member of: United Way
Affiliation(s): International Planned Parenthood Federation
Finances: *Funding Sources:* Donations; memberships; grants; fees for service
Activities: Clinic & sexual health education services throughout British Columbia; pamphlets, manuals & publications, videos, teaching kits, fact sheets; *Library:* by appointment Not open to public
Chief Officer(s):
Michelle Fortin, Executive Director
Ashleigh Turner, Director, Communications
aturner@optbc.org

OPTIONS Sexual Health Association; Planned Parenthood Association of Edmonton *See* Compass Centre for Sexual Wellness

Options: Services to Communities Society
9815 - 140 St., Surrey BC V3T 4M4
Tel: 604-584-5811; *Fax:* 604-584-7628
info@options.bc.ca
www.options.bc.ca
www.facebook.com/OptionsCommunityServices
Overview: A small local organization founded in 1973
Mission: To empower individuals, support families & promote community health
Staff Member(s): 310; 200 volunteer(s)
Membership: 1-99
Activities: Family & child services; youth; women's services; housing & shelter; mental health; multicultural services; child care
Chief Officer(s):
Christine Mohr, Executive Director
  Newton Office
  13520 - 78 Ave., Surrey BC V3W 8J6
  Tel: 604-596-4321; *Fax:* 604-572-7413

Optometric Institute of Toronto *See* Vision Institute of Canada

Oral History Committee, Canadian Historical Association *See* Canadian Oral History Association

Orangeville & District Real Estate Board (ODREB)
228 Broadway Ave., Orangeville ON L9W 1K5
Tel: 519-941-4547
www.odreb.com
twitter.com/odrebrealtors
Overview: A small local organization founded in 1965 overseen by Ontario Real Estate Association
Member of: The Canadian Real Estate Association; Toronto Real Estate Board
Chief Officer(s):
David Grime, President

Oraynu Community for Secular Humanistic Judaism; Secular Jewish Association *See* Oraynu Congregation for Humanistic Judaism

Oraynu Congregation for Humanistic Judaism
#14, 156 Duncan Mill Rd., Toronto ON M3B 3N2
Tel: 416-385-3910
info@oraynu.org
www.oraynu.org
Previous Name: Oraynu Community for Secular Humanistic Judaism; Secular Jewish Association
Overview: A small local charitable organization founded in 1969
Mission: To integrate secular, humanistic Jewish ethics into members' daily lives
Affiliation(s): Society for Humanistic Judaism; Jewish Federation of Greater Toronto; Centre for Enhancement of Jewish Education; International Federation of Secular Humanistic Jews; International Institute for Secular Humanistic Jews; Leadership Conference of Secular Humanistic Jews
Finances: *Funding Sources:* Donations; Rasch Foundation; UJA Federation; Centre for Enhancement of Jewish Education
Activities: Providing information about Oraynu & Humanistic Judaism; Offering programs for youth; Providing cultural & social activities
Chief Officer(s):
Louise Sherman, President
Les Kelman, Secretary
Robert Horwitz, Treasurer
Roby Sadler, Manager, Office
Publications:
• The Shofar
Type: Newsletter; *Frequency:* Bimonthly; *Editor:* Sandi Horwitz
Profile: Upcoming events, board news, committee reports, & member information

Orchestra Toronto (OT)
5040 Yonge St., Toronto ON M2N 6R8
Tel: 416-467-7142
info@orchestratoronto.ca
orchestratoronto.ca
www.facebook.com/OrchestraToronto
twitter.com/OrchToronto
Previous Name: Bennington Heights Community Orchestra; East York Symphony Orchestra
Overview: A small local charitable organization founded in 1954
Mission: To provide affordable family entertainment, music education, & full repertoire in all its programs
Member of: Orchestras Canada
Finances: *Funding Sources:* Municipal & Provincial Arts Councils; Corporate & Individual Donations
Staff Member(s): 5
Membership: 66 musicians; *Committees:* Musician's
Activities: Providing a community volunteer symphony orchestra; Offering resources for motivated, dedicated musicians of all ages to rehearse & perform the complete orchestral repertoire; *Library:* Orchestra Toronto Library; Not open to public
Chief Officer(s):
Samantha Little, Executive Director
executive.director@orchestratoronto.ca
Kevin Mallon, Music Director
music.director@orchestratoronto.ca

Orchestras Canada (OC) / Orchestres Canada
PO Box 2386, Peterborough ON K9J 2Y8
Tel: 416-366-8834
Toll-Free: 877-809-7288
info@oc.ca
www.orchestrascanada.org
www.facebook.com/orchestrascanada
twitter.com/OrchCanada
Merged from: Association of Canadian Orchestras; Orchestras Ontario
Overview: A large national charitable organization founded in 1998
Mission: To strengthen Canada's orchestral community through leadership in advocacy, education, & professional development
Member of: Canadian Conference of the Arts
Affiliation(s): American Symphony Orchestra League; International Alliance of Orchestra Associations
Finances: *Annual Operating Budget:* $500,000-$1.5 Million; *Funding Sources:* Membership dues; conference; workshops; publication sales
Staff Member(s): 3
Membership: 170+; *Fees:* Based on annual revenues; *Member Profile:* Professional and semi-professional orchestras, music schools, & individuals who are involved with Canada's orchestral community; *Committees:* Government Communications; Marketing; Professional Development; Volunteer; Advocacy
Activities: Advocating on behalf of Canadian orchestras; Developing orchestras through education and leadership; Providing resources for members and supporters; *Internships:* Yes *Library:* Resource Centre; Music Library; by appointment Not open to public
Chief Officer(s):
Katherine Carleton, Executive Director, 416-366-8834 Ext. 1
katherine@oc.ca
Sarah Thomson, Administrator, 416-366-8834 Ext. 2
sarah@oc.ca
Krista Wodelet, Administrator, Communications
krista@oc.ca
Awards:
• Betty Webster Award
Awarded to an individual or organization that has made a sustained and significant contribution over a number of years to the Canadian orchestral community, with an emphasis on leadership, education and volunteerism. *Eligibility:* An individual or organization that has made a sustained contribution to the Canadian orchestral community, with a focus on education and volunteerism *Deadline:* May
Meetings/Conferences:
• 2018 Orchestras Canada National Conference, May, 2018, Calgary, AB
Scope: National
Contact Information: Executive Director: Katherine Carlton, E-mail: katherine@oc.ca

Orchestras Mississauga
Living Arts Centre, 4141 Living Arts Dr., 2nd Fl., Mississauga ON L5B 4B8
Tel: 905-615-4405; *Fax:* 905-615-4402
www.mississaugasymphony.ca
www.linkedin.com/company/mississauga-symphony-orchestra
www.facebook.com/207803209261897
twitter.com/MSymph
www.youtube.com/user/MississaugaSymph
Also Known As: Sinfonia Mississauga; Mississauga Philharmonic; Mississauga Symphony
Overview: A medium-sized local charitable organization founded in 1972 overseen by Orchestras Canada
Mission: To perform & promote orchestral music; to ensure its accessibility to all segments of the community
Member of: Orchestras Canada
Affiliation(s): Mississauga Board of Trade; Orchestras Canada; Mississauga Arts Council
Finances: *Funding Sources:* Government; Corporate & individual donations
Staff Member(s): 7
Activities: *Rents Mailing List:* Yes; *Library:* by appointment
Chief Officer(s):
Denis Mastromonaco, Music Director
Eileen Keown, General Manager

Orchestre civique des jeunes de Montréal *Voir* Orchestre symphonique des jeunes de Montréal

Orchestre de chambre de Montréal (OCM) / Montréal Chamber Orchestra (MCO)
#2001, 1, Place Ville Marie, Montréal QC H3B 2C4
Tél: 514-871-1224
info@mco-ocm.qc.ca
www.mco-ocm.qc.ca
www.linkedin.com/company/l%27orchestre-de-chambre-de-montr-al
www.facebook.com/Orchestredechambredemontreal
twitter.com/mcoocm
Aperçu: *Dimension:* petite; *Envergure:* locale; Organisme sans but lucratif; fondée en 1974 surveillé par Orchestras Canada
Mission: Se consacrer au répertoire pour ensemble de chambre & oeuvres canadiennes
Membre de: Orchestras Canada
Finances: *Budget de fonctionnement annuel:* $250,000-$500,000
Membre(s) du personnel: 4; 10 bénévole(s)

Canadian Associations / Orchestre Métropolitain

Membre: 32
Membre(s) du bureau directeur:
Natalia Boureaud, Executive Director
Wanda Kaluzny, Music Director

Orchestre de chambre McGill *See* McGill Chamber Orchestra

L'Orchestre des jeunes d'Ottawa *See* Ottawa Youth Orchestra Academy

Orchestre du Centre national des Arts *See* National Arts Centre Orchestra of Canada

Orchestre Métropolitain
#401, 486, rue Sainte-Catherine, Montréal QC H3B 1A6
Tél: 514-598-0870; *Téléc:* 514-840-9195
info@orchestremetropolitain.com
www.orchestremetropolitain.com
www.facebook.com/orchestremetropolitain
twitter.com/lemetropolitain
www.youtube.com/LeMetropolitain1
Nom précédent: Orchestre métropolitain du Grand Montréal
Aperçu: *Dimension:* petite; *Envergure:* locale; Organisme sans but lucratif; fondée en 1981 surveillé par Orchestras Canada
Mission: Apporter la musique classique à la communauté métropolitaine de Montréal
Membre de: Orchestres Canada
Affiliation(s): Commission scolaire de Montréal; Collège Regina Assumpta; Société pour les arts en milieux de santé
Membre(s) du personnel: 15
Membre: 60+
Activités: *Stagiaires:* Oui; *Bibliothèque:* Bibliothèque
Membre(s) du bureau directeur:
Jean R. Dupré, Directeur général, 514-598-0870 Ext. 24
jrdupre@orchestremetropolitain.com
Yannick Nézet-Séguin, Directeur artistique

Orchestre métropolitain du Grand Montréal *Voir* Orchestre Métropolitain

Orchestre national des jeunes Canada *See* National Youth Orchestra Canada

Orchestre symphonique d'Ottawa *See* Ottawa Symphony Orchestra Inc.

Orchestre symphonique de Laval
#203, 3235, boul Saint-Martin est, Laval QC H7E 5G8
Tél: 450-978-3666; *Téléc:* 450-661-6741
osl@osl.qc.ca
www.osl.qc.ca
www.facebook.com/OSLaval
twitter.com/OSLaval
Aperçu: *Dimension:* petite; *Envergure:* locale; Organisme sans but lucratif; fondée en 1984 surveillé par Orchestras Canada
Mission: Diffuser la musique classique et symphonique
Membre de: Orchestres Canada
Finances: *Fonds:* Sponsors individuels et corporatifs; Gouvernement
Membre(s) du personnel: 11
Activités:: *Bibliothèque:* Bibliothèque
Membre(s) du bureau directeur:
Marie-Pierre Rolland, Directrice générale
mprolland@osl.qc.ca
Alain Trudel, Directeur artistique

Orchestre symphonique de Longueuil
156, boul Churchill, Greenfield Park QC J4V 2M3
Tél: 450-466-6661; *Téléc:* 450-466-3331
info@osdl.ca
www.osdl.ca
www.linkedin.com/groups/Fondation-Orchestre-symphonique-Longueuil-4110883
www.facebook.com/OSDL.ca
twitter.com/Votre_OSDL
Aperçu: *Dimension:* petite; *Envergure:* locale; Organisme sans but lucratif surveillé par Orchestras Canada
Mission: Assurer la diffusion du grand répertoire classique et la promotion de l'excellence musicale en Montérégie
Membre de: Orchestres Canada
Membre(s) du personnel: 11
Membre(s) du bureau directeur:
Gilles Choquet, Directeur général, 450-466-6661 Ext. 221
Marc David, Directeur artistique

Orchestre symphonique de Montréal
1600, rue Saint-Urbain, Montréal QC H2X 0S1
Tél: 514-840-7400; *Téléc:* 514-842-0728
Ligne sans frais: 888-842-9951
www.osm.ca
www.facebook.com/OSMconcerts
www.youtube.com/user/OSMofficial
Aperçu: *Dimension:* petite; *Envergure:* locale; fondée en 1934 surveillé par Orchestras Canada
Mission: De diffuser, au plus large public possible, le répertoire mondial de la musique symphonique, & les artistes de niveau international; assumer son rôle social & institutionnel
Membre de: Orchestras Canada
Membre(s) du personnel: 55
Membre: *Comités:* Government Affairs; Sponsorship; Marketing; Fundraising and Fondation de l'OSM; Volunteer Association
Activités: *Stagiaires:* Oui; *Bibliothèque:* rendez-vous
Membre(s) du bureau directeur:
Madeleine Careau, Président Directeur Général
Kent Nagano, Directeur musical

Orchestre symphonique de Québec
#250, 437, Grande Allée est, Québec QC G1R 2J5
Tél: 418-643-8486
www.osq.org
www.facebook.com/orchestresymphoniquedequebec
twitter.com/osq_officiel
www.instagram.com/osq_officiel
Aperçu: *Dimension:* moyenne; *Envergure:* locale; Organisme sans but lucratif; fondée en 1903 surveillé par Orchestras Canada
Mission: Interpréter le répertoire symphonique; être le principal moteur de l'activité musicale de la région. L'OSM est reconnu comme un organisme de grande qualité, dynamique, accessible, et financièrement sain
Membre de: Orchestras Canada
Membre(s) du personnel: 19
Membre: 63
Membre(s) du bureau directeur:
Elizabeth Tessier, Présidente-directrice générale par intérim
Tristan Lemieux, Directeur musical

Orchestre symphonique de Sault Ste-Marie *See* Sault Symphony Association

Orchestre symphonique de Sherbrooke (OSS) / Sherbrooke Symphony Orchestra
135, rue Don Bosco nord, Sherbrooke QC J1L 1E5
Tél: 819-821-0227
Ligne sans frais: 866-821-0227
info@ossherbrooke.com
www.ossherbrooke.com
www.facebook.com/orchestresymphonique.desherbrooke
Aperçu: *Dimension:* petite; *Envergure:* locale; Organisme sans but lucratif; fondée en 1939 surveillé par Orchestras Canada
Mission: Faire connaître la musique symphonique dans la région et permettre aux musiciens de la région de jouer dans un orchestre professionnel
Membre de: Orchestres Canada
Affiliation(s): Conseil des Arts du Canada; Ville de Sherbrooke; Conseil des arts et des lettres Québec
Finances: *Fonds:* Conseil des arts et des lettres du Québec; Canadian Council for the Arts; Ville de Sherbrooke
Membre(s) du personnel: 6
Membre(s) du bureau directeur:
Nicolas Bélanger, Président Directeur Général
nicolasbelanger@ossherbrooke.com
Stéphane Laforest, Directeur artistique
stephanelaforest@ossherbrooke.com

Orchestre symphonique de Sudbury inc *See* Sudbury Symphony Orchestra Association Inc.

Orchestre symphonique de Trois-Rivières (OSTR)
CP 1281, Trois-Rivières QC G9A 5K8
Tél: 819-373-5340; *Téléc:* 819-373-6693
administration@ostr.ca
www.ostr.ca
www.facebook.com/127291994012065
www.youtube.com/user/OSTRofficiel
Aperçu: *Dimension:* petite; *Envergure:* locale; Organisme sans but lucratif; fondée en 1978 surveillé par Orchestras Canada
Mission: Poursuivre l'atteinte des objectifs inhérents à ses axes de développement: éducation, implication dans son milieu, diffusion de musique symphonique, création musicale et diffusion de nouveaux produits
Membre de: Conseil québécois de la musique; Orchestres Canada
Affiliation(s): Guilde des musiciens (AFM)
Finances: *Fonds:* Conseil des arts Canada; Conseil des arts et des lettres du Québec; Ville de Trois-Rivières
Membre(s) du personnel: 6
Activités: *Stagiaires:* Oui; *Service de conférenciers:* Oui; *Bibliothèque* Not open to public
Membre(s) du bureau directeur:
Natalie Rousseau, Directrice générale, 819-373-5340 Ext. 1002
direction@ostr.ca
Jacques Lacombe, Directeur artistique, 819-373-5340 Ext. 1006
directionartistique@ostr.ca

Orchestre symphonique des jeunes de Montréal (OSJM)
CP 83566, Succ. Garnier, Montréal QC H2J 4E9
Tél: 514-645-0311; *Téléc:* 514-524-9894
osjmontreal@gmail.com
www.osjm.org
www.facebook.com/OSJ.Montreal
twitter.com/osjm
Nom précédent: Orchestre civique des jeunes de Montréal
Aperçu: *Dimension:* petite; *Envergure:* locale; Organisme sans but lucratif; fondée en 1986 surveillé par Orchestras Canada
Mission: Présenter le jeune musicien de talent à un auditoire et lui fournir une expérience formative sous la supervision d'artistes reconnus; encourager et soutenir le choix d'une carrière musicale qui peut mener à un grand orchestre; promouvoir un intérêt dans les concerts et développer un soutien plus diversifié dans les activités de l'orchestre; fournir à l'entreprise privée l'occasion de participer plus activement dans une activité culturelle d'envergure et l'aider à faire apprécier son rôle dans la communauté
Membre de: Association des orchestres de jeunes du Québec (AOJQ); Orchestres Canada
Finances: *Fonds:* Ministère de la Culture et des communications du Québec
Membre: *Montant de la cotisation:* 250$; *Critères d'admissibilite:* Passer une audition annuelle; payer sa cotisation; s'engager à satisfaire les exigences des programmes
Activités: 3 concerts réguliers par saison; *Stagiaires:* Oui
Membre(s) du bureau directeur:
Anne-Marie Desbiens, Directrice générale

Orchestre symphonique des jeunes de Sherbrooke
CP 1536, Succ. Place de la Cité, Sherbrooke QC J1H 5M4
Tél: 819-566-1888
www.osjs.ca
www.facebook.com/153626511336448
Aperçu: *Dimension:* petite; *Envergure:* locale; Organisme sans but lucratif surveillé par Orchestras Canada
Mission: Fournir aux jeunes musiciennes et musiciens de Sherbrooke et de la région un milieu où ils pourront apprendre à faire de la musique d'ensemble, développer la maîtrise de leur instrument et perfectionner leur art dans un contexte de vie collective particulièrement enrichissante
Membre de: Orchestres Canada
Membre: *Critères d'admissibilite:* Les jeunes âgés de 8-25
Membre(s) du bureau directeur:
Hubert Tanguay-Labrosse, Directeur artistique

Orchestre symphonique des jeunes du West Island (OSJWI) / West Island Youth Symphony Orchestra (WIYSO)
CP 1028, Succ. Pointe-Claire, Pointe-Claire QC H9S 4H9
Tél: 514-912-5451
info@osjwi.qc.ca
www.osjwi.qc.ca
www.facebook.com/OSJWI
Aperçu: *Dimension:* petite; *Envergure:* locale; Organisme sans but lucratif; fondée en 1986 surveillé par Orchestras Canada
Mission: Permettre aux jeunes de 8-25 ans de jouer dans un orchestre regroupant tous les instruments sous la direction d'un chef professionnel
Membre de: Orchestres Canada
Affiliation(s): Association des orchestres de jeunes du Québec
Finances: *Fonds:* Subventions gouvernementales; Les dons individuels et corporatifs
Membre: 78; *Montant de la cotisation:* 300$ l'orchestre sénior; 200$ l'orchestre de la Relève; *Critères d'admissibilite:* Musiciens qui ont 8 à 25 ans
Membre(s) du bureau directeur:
Jackie Landry-Bigelow, Coordinatrice
Stewart Grant, Directeur artistique

Orchestre symphonique des jeunes Philippe-Filion
1200, boul des Hêtres, Shawinigan QC G9N 6V3
Tél: 819-539-6000
info@aosjpf.ca
www.aosjpf.ca
www.facebook.com/121002454597454

Aperçu: Dimension: petite; *Envergure:* locale; fondée en 1978 surveillé par Orchestras Canada
Mission: Offrir une formation orchestrale spécialisé pour jeunes musiciens.
Membre(s) du bureau directeur:
Michel Kozlovsky, Chef d'orchestre

Orchestre symphonique du Saguenay-Lac-St-Jean (OSSLSJ)
202, rue Jacques-Cartier est, Chicoutimi QC G7H 6R8
Tél: 418-545-3409; *Téléc:* 418-545-8287
info@lorchestre.org
www.lorchestre.org
www.facebook.com/151993804859233
twitter.com/orchestreSLSJ
www.youtube.com/channel/UCTPHtHRjL3-VnMomYcCRVNQ
Aperçu: Dimension: petite; *Envergure:* locale; Organisme sans but lucratif; fondée en 1979 surveillé par Orchestras Canada
Mission: Produire et diffuser des concerts professionnels à travers tout le Saguenay-Lac-Saint-Jean en regard des enjeux financiers et des structures d'accueil existantes. Ses qualités artistiques et administratives en constante évolution lui permettent d'exercer un leadership au sein des organismes musicaux régionaux, basé sur un partenariat serré avec le milieu, au service du développement de sa discipline et de sa communauté
Membre de: Orchestres Canada
Finances: *Fonds:* Conseil des Arts du Canada; Conseil des arts et lettres du Québec; Ville de Saguenay
Membre(s) du personnel: 7
Activités: La corporation gère sous une même administration les activités de l'Orchestre symphonique; l'Orchestre de chambre; le Quatuor Alcan; le Quintette à vent; le Choeur symphonique; l'Orchestre des jeunes; *Bibliothèque:* Musicothèque; rendez-vous
Membre(s) du bureau directeur:
Jacques Clément, Directeur artistique

Orchestre symphonique régional Abitibi-Témiscamingue
CP 2305, Rouyn-Noranda QC J9X 5A9
Tél: 819-762-0043
info@osrat.ca
www.osrat.ca
www.facebook.com/125183814205328
Également appelé: Société des Mélomanes
Aperçu: Dimension: petite; *Envergure:* locale; Organisme sans but lucratif; fondée en 1985 surveillé par Orchestras Canada
Mission: Diffusion de la musique classique et integration de la relève
Membre(s) du personnel: 6
Membre: *Montant de la cotisation:* Un don de 25$ ou plus; *Critères d'admissibilité:* Mélomane amateur
Membre(s) du bureau directeur:
Jacques Marchand, Directeur artistique

Orchestres Canada *See* Orchestras Canada

Orchid Society of Alberta
PO Box 31117, Stn. Namao Centre, Edmonton AB T5Z 3P3
info@orchidsalberta.com
www.orchidsalberta.com
Overview: A small provincial organization founded in 1976
Mission: To promote orchid gardening & share knowledge
Member of: Canadian Orchid Congress
Affiliation(s): American Orchid Society
Membership: *Fees:* $15 senior; $20 senior family; $25 single; $30 family
Chief Officer(s):
Darrell Albert, President
president@orchidsalberta.com

Orchid Society of Nova Scotia
c/o Ruth Ann Moger, 20 Christies Rd., Boutiliers Point NS B3Z 1S1
www.nsorchidsociety.com
www.facebook.com/101539916572332
Overview: A small local organization founded in 2010
Membership: *Fees:* $20 household; $10 student

Orchid Society of Royal Botanical Gardens
680 Plains Rd. West, Burlington ON L7T 1J1
osrbgorchidinfo@gmail.com
www.osrbg.ca
Overview: A small local organization founded in 1981
Mission: To provide education & information for its members & to help conserve orchid species

Membership: 100

Orchidophiles de Québec
Pavillon Envirotron, FSAA, Université Laval, #1246, 2480, boul Hochelaga, Québec QC G1V 0A6
www.orchidophilesdequebec.ca
www.facebook.com/Orchidophiles.de.Quebec
Aperçu: Dimension: petite; *Envergure:* locale; fondée en 1981
Membre: *Montant de la cotisation:* $35 individuel; $55 famille
Activités: *Bibliothèque:*
Membre(s) du bureau directeur:
Patricia Caris, Présidente
president@orchidophilesdequebec.ca

Order of Certified Pastoral Counsellors of America *See* Evangelical Order of Certified Pastoral Counsellors of America

Order of Malta - Canadian Association / Ordre de Malte - Association Canadienne
The Sovereign Military Order of Malta - Canadian Association, #302, 1247 Kilborn Pl., Ottawa ON K1H 6K9
Tel: 613-731-8897; *Fax:* 613-731-1312
smomca@bellnet.ca
www.orderofmaltacanada.org
Also Known As: Sovereign Military Hospitaller Order of St. John of Jerusalem of Rhodes & Malta - Canadian Association
Previous Name: Association of Canadian Knights of the Sovereign Military Order of Malta
Overview: A medium-sized national charitable organization founded in 1953
Mission: To act as a Roman Catholic religious, chivalric & charitable organization
Affiliation(s): Sovereign Military Order of Malta
Finances: *Annual Operating Budget:* $100,000-$250,000; *Funding Sources:* Donations
Staff Member(s): 1; 259 volunteer(s)
Membership: Over 12,500
Chief Officer(s):
Albert André Morin, President
Roman J Ciecwierz, Vice President
Publications:
• Epistula
Type: Newsletter

The Order of St. Lazarus
#100, 1435 Sanford Fleming Ave., Ottawa ON K1G 3H3
Tel: 613-746-5280; *Fax:* 613-746-3982
chancery@stlazarus.ca
www.stlazarus.ca
twitter.com/mhoslj
Overview: A small local organization
Staff Member(s): 2; 30 volunteer(s)
Membership: 400 individual
Chief Officer(s):
Peter A. S. Milliken, Grand Prior

Order of Sons of Italy in Canada
1375 Main St., Cambridge ON N1R 5S7
Tel: 905-388-9328; *Fax:* 905-383-9926
www.ordersonsofitalycanada.com
Overview: A small national organization founded in 1919
Mission: To assist the needy, the ill, and disabled through financial support, the provision of housing, and other support programs; To encourage the active participation of our members in the political, social and economic life of our community; to participate in programs combating discrimination, racism, and social injustice; To promote and preserve the Italian language, culture, and traditions in our country.
Finances: *Funding Sources:* Membership fees; sponsorships
Activities: Golden Lion Award; Ethnic Festival
Chief Officer(s):
Josie Cumbo, National President, 519-623-9993
Patsy Giammarco, National Administative Secretary, 905-892-3352

The Order of United Commercial Travelers of America (UCT)
Canadian Office, #300, 901 Centre St. North, Calgary AB T2E 2P6
Tel: 403-277-0745; *Fax:* 403-277-6662
Toll-Free: 800-267-2371
customerservice@uct.org
www.uct.org
www.linkedin.com/company/united-commercial-travelers
www.facebook.com/UCTinAction
www.youtube.com/UCTinaction
www.flickr.com/photos/uctinaction

Overview: A large international charitable organization founded in 1888
Mission: To provide members with affordable insurance & support through fraternal benefit & discount programs
Affiliation(s): American Special Hockey Association
Finances: *Annual Operating Budget:* $250,000-$500,000
Staff Member(s): 2
Membership: 70,000
Activities: *Awareness Events:* Join Hands Day, 1st Saturday in May
Chief Officer(s):
Tom Hoffman, President
Joseph Hoffman, CEO
Awards:
• Jack & Betty Heaston Memorial Scholarship, UCT Heaston Scholarship Program
  Deadline: March 15; *Amount:* $6,000 per year for four years
• Betty Y. Heaston Memorial Scholarship, UCT Heaston Scholarship Program
  Deadline: March 15; *Amount:* $3,000 per year for four years
• Jack Heaston Memorial Scholarship, UCT Heaston Scholarship Program
  Deadline: March 15; *Amount:* $3,000 per year for four years
• May E. Tisdale Scholarship Fund
  Eligibility: UCT members or children & grandchildren of living members *Deadline:* June 15

L'Ordinariat militaire Catholique Romain du Canada / Roman Catholic Military Ordinariate of Canada
USFC (O), Site Uplands, Édifice 469, Ottawa ON K1A 0K2
Tél: 613-990-7824; *Téléc:* 613-991-1056
carlone.l@forces.gc.ca
www.rcmilord.com
Aperçu: Dimension: petite; *Envergure:* nationale; Organisme sans but lucratif; fondée en 1987 surveillé par Canadian Conference of Catholic Bishops
Mission: Fournir une dimension spirituelle et morale à toutes les activités affectant le moral et le bien-être des membres catholiques des Forces canadiennes, leurs familles et les employés civils du Ministère de la Défense nationale
Membre de: La Conférence des évêques catholiques du Canada
Membre(s) du personnel: 3
Membre: 81,000+
Activités:; *Bibliothèque:* Centre d'entraînement des aumôniers de Borden
Membre(s) du bureau directeur:
Scott McCaig, C.C., Évêque diocésain
Donald Thériault, Évêque

Ordre de Malte - Association Canadienne *See* Order of Malta - Canadian Association

Ordre des acupuncteurs de Québec (OAQ)
#1106, 505, boul René-Lévesque ouest, Montréal QC H2Z 1Y7
Tél: 514-523-2882; *Téléc:* 514-523-9669
Ligne sans frais: 800-474-5914
info@o-a-q.org
www.o-a-q.org
Aperçu: Dimension: petite; *Envergure:* provinciale
Mission: Réglementer et de surveiller des activités professionnelles qui comportent des risques de préjudices pour le public
Membre(s) du bureau directeur:
Raymond Bourret, President
president@o-a-q.org

Ordre des administrateurs agréés du Québec (OAAQ)
#360, 1050, côte du Beaver Hall, Montréal QC H2Z 0A5
Tél: 514-499-0880; *Téléc:* 514-499-0892
Ligne sans frais: 800-465-0880
info@adma.qc.ca
www.adma.qc.ca
www.linkedin.com/company/1010422
www.facebook.com/OrdreAdmA
twitter.com/OrdreAdmA
Aperçu: Dimension: grande; *Envergure:* provinciale; Organisme sans but lucratif; Organisme de réglementation; fondée en 1973
Mission: Favorise auprès des professionnels de l'administration, l'innovation et l'atteinte d'un niveau de compétence supérieur pour qu'ils contribuent de façon proactive et dynamique au développement des entreprises et des organisations; Assure la protection du public en garantissant le respect des normes et standards professionnels en administration, en conformité avec le code de déontologie et par le biais des mécanismes prévus au code des professions;

Canadian Associations / Ordre des agronomes du Québec (OAQ)

Contribue à l'avancement de l'administration, discipline essentielle au développement social et économique du Québec
Affiliation(s): Institut des Auditeurs internes - Section Montréal (IAIM)
Finances: *Budget de fonctionnement annuel:* $1.5 Million-$3 Million
Membre(s) du personnel: 12; 125 bénévole(s)
Membre: 3 000; *Montant de la cotisation:* Barème; *Critères d'admissibilite:* Gestionnaires; *Comités:* Comité d'admission; Comité du Fonds d'indemnisation; Comité de la formation; Comité d'inspection professionnelle; Comité de révision; Comité de révision des demandes d'équivalence
Activités: Activités de formation et de développement professionnels; remise des permis; Activités régionales
Membre(s) du bureau directeur:
Francine Sabourin, Directrice générale
fsabourin@adma.qc.ca
Prix, Bourses:
• Fellow Adm.A.
• Fellow C.M.C.
• Prix Reconnaissance
• Prix Robert P. Morin
• Médaille des gouverneurs
• Mérite du CIQ
Meetings/Conferences:
• Ordre des administrateurs agréés du Québec Congrès 2018, 2018, QC
Scope: Provincial
Publications:
• Info Adm.A. [publication d'Ordre des administrateurs agréés du Québec]
Type: Bulletin

Ordre des agronomes du Québec (OAQ)
#810, 1001, rue Sherbrooke est, Montréal QC H2L 1L3
Tél: 514-596-3833; *Téléc:* 514-596-2974
agronome@oaq.qc.ca
www.oaq.qc.ca
Nom précédent: Corporation des agronomes du Québec
Aperçu: *Dimension:* moyenne; *Envergure:* provinciale; Organisme sans but lucratif; fondée en 1937
Mission: Assurer les utilisateurs de services agronomiques et les consommateurs de la compétence, du professionnalisme et de l'engagement des agronomes et ainsi favoriser le mieux-être de la société
Membre(s) du personnel: 14
Membre: 3,372; *Critères d'admissibilite:* Agronomes; *Comités:* Équivalences; Formation des agronomes; Inspection Professionnelle; Révision des décisions d'équivalences; Révision des décisions du bureau du syndic; Arbitrage des comptes; Admission; Formation Continue; Consultatif des prix de L'OAQ; Résolutions; Consultatif sur les pesticides; Consultatif sur la gestion des matières fertilisantes; Formation continue des agronomes; Consultatif sur les actes agronomiques en aménagement des sols
Membre(s) du bureau directeur:
René Mongeau, Président
rene.mongeau@oaq.qc.ca
Guillaume LaBarre, Directeur général
guillaume.labarre@oaq.qc.ca
Prix, Bourses:
• Prix Henri-C.Bois
Souligne la valeur inestimable du travail bénévole d'un agronome au sein de différents comités de l'OAQ
• Médaille de distinction agronomique
Décernée à un agronome pour souligner ses réalisations professionnelles exceptionnelles et son rayonnement au sein de la profession et de la collectivité
• Ordre du Mérite agronomique
Décerné à un agronome qui a rendu des services exceptionnels dans le domaine de l'agriculture ou pour la cause agronomique
• Mérite Spécial Adélard-Godbout
Reconnaît l'apport exceptionnel d'une entreprise, d'un organisme, d'un individu ou d'un groupe d'individus au développement de l'agriculture, de l'agronomie et/ou du secteur agroalimentaire québecois

Ordre des architectes du Québec (OAQ)
#200, 420, rue McGill, Montréal QC H2Y 2G1
Tél: 514-937-6168; *Téléc:* 514-933-0242
Ligne sans frais: 800-599-6168
info@oaq.com
www.oaq.com
www.facebook.com/133353596740232
twitter.com/OAQenbref
vimeo.com/user2657182

Aperçu: *Dimension:* moyenne; *Envergure:* provinciale; Organisme de réglementation; fondée en 1890
Mission: D'assurer la protection du public en régissant l'exercice de la profession d'architecte au Québec.
Affiliation(s): Institut royal d'architecture du Canada
Membre(s) du personnel: 21
Membre: 3,500; *Critères d'admissibilite:* Architectes; *Comités:* Admission; Formation continue; Inspection professionnelle; Discipline; Révision des plaintes; Concours; Techniques et bâtiments durables; Orientation des Prix d'excellence en architecture
Activités: *Stagiaires:* Oui
Membre(s) du bureau directeur:
Jean-Pierre Dumont, Directeur général
jpdumont@oaq.com
Prix, Bourses:
• Prix d'excellence en Architecture

Ordre des arpenteurs-géomètres du Québec (OAGQ) / Québec Land Surveyors Association
Iberville Quatre, #350, 2954 boul Laurier, Québec QC G1V 4T2
Tél: 418-656-0730; *Téléc:* 418-656-6352
Ligne sans frais: 800-243-6490
oagq@oagq.qc.ca
www.oagq.qc.ca
Aperçu: *Dimension:* moyenne; *Envergure:* provinciale; fondée en 1882 surveillé par Professional Surveyors Canada
Mission: La protection du public et le contrôle de la profession
Membre de: Association de géomatique municipale
Affiliation(s): Fédération des arpenteurs-géomètres du Québec
40 bénévole(s)
Membre: 1,000; *Montant de la cotisation:* 830$; *Critères d'admissibilite:* BAC en géomatique; Stage d'un an; Examens de l'Ordre; *Comités:* Arbitrage; Assurances et sinistres; Discipline; Examinateurs; Formation; Inspection; Réglementation; Révision; Stages; Syndic
Activités: Ateliers divers; *Stagiaires:* Oui; *Listes de destinataires:* Oui
Membre(s) du bureau directeur:
Pierre Tessier, Président
Meetings/Conferences:
• Ordre des arpenteurs-géomètres du Québec 50e Congrès, 2018, QC
Scope: Provincial

Ordre des audiologistes et des orthophonistes de l'Ontario
See College of Audiologists & Speech-Language Pathologists of Ontario

Ordre des audioprothésistes du Québec (OAQ)
#202-A, 11370, rue Notre-Dame est, Montréal QC H1B 2W6
Tél: 514-640-5117; *Téléc:* 514-640-5291
Ligne sans frais: 866-676-5117
oaq@ordreaudio.qc.ca
www.ordreaudio.qc.ca
Nom précédent: Corporation professionnelle des audioprothésistes du Québec
Aperçu: *Dimension:* petite; *Envergure:* provinciale
Mission: Protéger le public qui fait appel aux services professionnels d'un audioprothésiste
Membre: *Comités:* Administratif; inspection professionnelle; discipline; formation; formation continue; règlements; équivalence de diplôme; information; révision
Membre(s) du bureau directeur:
Sophie Gagnon, Présidente
sgagnon@ordreaudio.qc.ca

Ordre des chimistes du Québec (OCQ)
Place du Parc, #2199, 300, rue Léo-Pariseau, Montréal QC H2X 4B3
Tél: 514-844-3644; *Téléc:* 514-844-9601
information@ocq.qc.ca
www.ocq.qc.ca
www.facebook.com/1285160824849865
Aperçu: *Dimension:* moyenne; *Envergure:* provinciale; Organisme de réglementation; fondée en 1926
Mission: L'Ordre est une corporation professionnelle dont la raison d'être est la protection du public
Finances: *Budget de fonctionnement annuel:* $500,000-$1.5 Million
Membre(s) du personnel: 5; 120 bénévole(s)
Membre: 2 500; *Critères d'admissibilite:* Chimistes, biochimistes; Réglementations prévus par le code des professions (L.R.Q., chapitre C-26)
Membre(s) du bureau directeur:
Guy Collin, Président du Conseil d'administration

Ordre des chiropraticiens du Québec
7950, boul Métropolitain est, Montréal QC H1K 1A1
Tél: 514-355-8540; *Téléc:* 514-355-2290
Ligne sans frais: 888-655-8540
info@ordredeschiropraticiens.qc.ca
www.ordredeschiropraticiens.qc.ca
www.youtube.com/user/Ordrechirosqc
Aperçu: *Dimension:* petite; *Envergure:* provinciale; Organisme sans but lucratif; fondée en 1973
Mission: Organisme paragouvernemental qui assure la protection du public & octroie les permis de pratique; fondation de recherche chiropratique
Membre(s) du personnel: 5
Membre: *Critères d'admissibilite:* Docteur en chiropratique
Membre(s) du bureau directeur:
Pierre Paquin, Coordonnateur

L'Ordre des comptables professionels agréés du Québec
#800, 5, Place Ville Marie, Montréal QC H3B 2G2
Tél: 514-288-3256; *Téléc:* 514-843-8375
Ligne sans frais: 800-363-4688
info@cpaquebec.ca
cpaquebec.ca
www.linkedin.com/groups/3996221/profile
www.facebook.com/CPAquebec
twitter.com/CPAquebec
www.youtube.com/cpaquebec; www.instagram.com/cpaquebec
Également appelé: Ordre des CPA
Merged from: l'Ordre des CGA du Québec; l'Ordre des CMA du Québec
Aperçu: *Dimension:* grande; *Envergure:* provinciale; fondée en 2012 surveillé par Chartered Professional Accountants Canada
Mission: Tous les comptables professionnels du Québec sont regroupés au sein de l'Ordre des comptables professionnels agréés depuis le 2012
Membre de: Conseil interprofessionel du Québec
Membre: 39 000 membres & 5 000 candidats; *Critères d'admissibilite:* Détenir DESS, réussir examen final uniforme et completer un stage de 2 ans dans un cabinet d'expert-comptables; *Comités:* Audit; Évaluation des candidatures au titre de FCPA; Évaluation des demandes d'équivalence; Évaluation de la formation continue; Inspection professionnelle; Développement professionnel; Comptabilité publique; Évaluation de l'examen national; Révision; Vigie; Assurances; CPA en cabinet; CPA en entreprise; CPA dans la secteur public et parapublic; Programmes de formation professionnelle; Regroupements régionaux; Eessources humaines; Fonds d'indemnisation; Gouvernance; Réglementation; Orientations stratégiques; Arbitrage des comptes; Discipline
Activités: Formation professionnelle; formation continue; inspection professionnelle; *Stagiaires:* Oui
Membre(s) du bureau directeur:
Geneviève Mottard, CPA, CA, Président et chef de la direction
Jean-François Lasnier, FCPA, FCMA, Premier vice-président
Prix, Bourses:
• Prix Hommage
• Prix Excellence
• Prix des regroupements régionaux

Ordre des conseillers en ressources humaines agréés (CRHA)
#1400, 1200, av McGill Collège, Montréal QC H3B 4G7
Tél: 514-879-1636
Ligne sans frais: 800-214-1609
info@portailrh.org
www.portailrh.org
www.linkedin.com/groups?mostPopular=&gid=3233907
www.facebook.com/OrdreCRHACRIA
twitter.com/crha_quebec
Nom précédent: Association des professionnels en ressources humaines du Québec
Aperçu: *Dimension:* moyenne; *Envergure:* provinciale; fondée en 1934
Mission: De promouvoir l'importance stratégique de la gestion des ressources humaines dans la gestion des organisations ainsi que la promotion des nouveaux concepts et champs de développement qui caractérisent son évolution
Membre de: Conseil canadien des associations en ressources humaines/Canadian Council of Human Resources Associations
Membre: 9,000; *Critères d'admissibilite:* Gens qui sont dans les secteurs industriel et commercial, services et oublique et parapublique; *Comités:* Admissions; Révision; Inspection professionnelle; Conseil de discipline

Activités: Développement professionnel: colloques et compétences (40 par année); *Listes de destinataires:* Oui
Membre(s) du bureau directeur:
Florent Francoeur, Président-directeur général
Prix, Bourses:
• Concours Iris
• EXCALIBUR: Le tournoi universitaire canadien en ressources humaines
Promouvoir un enseignement de la gestion des ressources humaines dans les universités canadiennes préparant les étudiants au marché du travail; *Amount:* 3 000$; 2 250$; 1 500$

Ordre des conseillers et conseillères d'orientation du Québec (OCCOQ)
#520, 1600, boul Henri-Bourassa ouest, Montréal QC H3M 3E2
Tél: 514-737-4717; *Téléc:* 514-737-2172
Ligne sans frais: 800-363-2643
ordre@orientation.qc.ca
www.orientation.qc.ca
Nom précédent: Corporation professionnelle des conseillers et conseillères d'orientation du Québec
Aperçu: *Dimension:* moyenne; *Envergure:* provinciale; fondée en 1944
Mission: De veiller à ce que les services offerts par leurs membres sont de la plus haute qualité.
Membre(s) du personnel: 20
Membre: 2,458; *Montant de la cotisation:* 560$; *Comités:* Admissions par équivalence; Inspection professionnelle; Formation; Révision des plaintes; Arbitrage des comptes; Discipline
Membre(s) du bureau directeur:
Laurent Matte, Président
lmatte@orientation.qc.ca

Ordre des dentistes du Québec (ODQ)
#1640, 800, boul René-Lévesque ouest, Montréal QC H3B 1X9
Tél: 514-875-8511; *Téléc:* 514-393-9248
Ligne sans frais: 800-361-4887
www.odq.qc.ca
www.facebook.com/102225303175310
twitter.com/ordredentistes
www.youtube.com/webmestreodq
Aperçu: *Dimension:* grande; *Envergure:* provinciale; Organisme sans but lucratif; Organisme de réglementation; fondée en 1974
Mission: Assurer la qualité des services en médecine dentaire par le respect de normes élevées de pratique et d'éthique et de promouvoir la santé bucco-dentaire auprès de la population du Québec
Membre de: Conseil interprofessionnel du Québec
Affiliation(s): Association dentaire canadienne
Finances: *Budget de fonctionnement annuel:* $3 Million-$5 Million
Membre(s) du personnel: 46
Membre: 4 720
Activités: *Evénements de sensibilisation:* Mois de la santé bucco dentaire, avril; Journées dentaires internationales du Québec, mai; *Stagiaires:* Oui; *Listes de destinataires:* Oui
Membre(s) du bureau directeur:
Caroline Daoust, Directrice générale et secrétaire
Prix, Bourses:
• Prix Hommage
Contact: Nathalie Chasse, comité de sélection, nathalie.chasse@odq.qc.ca
• Prix Honneur
Meetings/Conferences:
• Journées dentaires internationales du Québec (JDIQ) 2018, May, 2018, QC
Scope: Provincial
Contact Information: Président, Comité d'organisation des JDIQ: Pierre Boudrias, Courriel: congres@odq.qc.ca
• Journées dentaires internationales du Québec (JDIQ) 2019, May, 2019, QC
Scope: Provincial
Contact Information: Président, Comité d'organisation des JDIQ: Pierre Boudrias, Courriel: congres@odq.qc.ca
• Journées dentaires internationales du Québec (JDIQ) 2020, May, 2020, QC
Scope: Provincial
Contact Information: Président, Comité d'organisation des JDIQ: Pierre Boudrias, Courriel: congres@odq.qc.ca

Ordre des denturologistes du Québec (ODQ)
395, rue du Parc-Industriel, Longueuil QC J4H 3V7
Tél: 450-646-7922; *Téléc:* 450-646-2509
Ligne sans frais: 800-567-2251
info@odq.com

www.odq.com
www.facebook.com/ordredesdenturologistesduquebec
Aperçu: *Dimension:* moyenne; *Envergure:* provinciale; fondée en 1974
Finances: *Budget de fonctionnement annuel:* $500,000-$1.5 Million
Membre(s) du personnel: 6
Membre: 966; *Comités:* Discipline; Formation continue; Formation des denturologistes; Inspection professionnelle; Pratique illégale; Révision
Activités: Protection du public; réception des plaintes par le syndic; *Stagiaires:* Oui
Membre(s) du bureau directeur:
Robert Cabana, Président
Monique Bouchard, Directrice générale et secrétaire

L'Ordre des diététistes de l'Ontario *See* College of Dietitians of Ontario

Ordre des ergothérapeutes de l'Ontario *See* College of Occupational Therapists of Ontario

L'Ordre des ergothérapeutes du Manitoba *See* College of Occupational Therapists of Manitoba

Ordre des ergothérapeutes du Québec (OEQ)
#920, 2021, av Union, Montréal QC H3A 2S9
Tél: 514-844-5778; *Téléc:* 514-844-0478
Ligne sans frais: 800-265-5778
ergo@oeq.org
www.oeq.org
Aperçu: *Dimension:* moyenne; *Envergure:* provinciale; Organisme sans but lucratif; Organisme de réglementation; fondée en 1974
Mission: Protéger le public; assurer la qualité d'ergothérapie; promouvoir l'accessibilité aux services d'ergothérapie; soutenir la pratique professionnelle et son évolution; favoriser le rayonnement de la profession
Finances: *Budget de fonctionnement annuel:* $500,000-$1.5 Million
Membre(s) du personnel: 19; 50 bénévole(s)
Membre: 4,100; *Montant de la cotisation:* 435$
Activités: Remise de prix et bourses annuels; *Evénements de sensibilisation:* Mois de l'ergothérapie en octobre
Membre(s) du bureau directeur:
Alain Bibeau, Président-directeur général
Louise Tremblay, Secrétaire générale
tremblayl@oeq.org
Prix, Bourses:
• Mention d'excellence
• Bourse de recherche Anne-Lang-Étienne Projet de maîtise
• Bourse de recherche Anne-Étienne Projet de doctorat
• Prix Nicole-Ébacher
• Prix Ginette-Théorêt
• Prix de l'OEQ

Ordre des évaluateurs agréés du Québec (OEAQ)
#450, 415, rue St-Antoine ouest, Montréal QC H2Z 2B9
Tél: 514-281-9888; *Téléc:* 514-281-0120
Ligne sans frais: 800-982-5387
oeaq@oeaq.qc.ca
www.oeaq.qc.ca
Aperçu: *Dimension:* moyenne; *Envergure:* provinciale; fondée en 1969
Mission: De réglementer la profession d'évaluation afin de s'assurer que le public reçoit le meilleur serviece réglementer la profession d'évaluation afin de s'assurer que le public reçoit le meilleur service
Membre(s) du personnel: 8
Membre: *Critères d'admissibilite:* Évaluateur immobilier; *Comités:* Révision; Inspection professionnelle; Admission; Formation continue; Formation
Membre(s) du bureau directeur:
Celine Viau, Secrétaire générale
cviau@oeaq.qc.ca

Ordre des Géologues du Québec
#900, 500, rue Sherbrooke ouest, Montréal QC H3A 3C6
Tél: 514-278-6220; *Téléc:* 514-844-7556
info@ogq.qc.ca
www.ogq.qc.ca
Aperçu: *Dimension:* moyenne; *Envergure:* provinciale; Organisme de réglementation
Mission: Pour régir la profession de géologue
Membre(s) du personnel: 3

Membre: *Comités:* Révision; Inspection professionnelle; Normes d'admission
Membre(s) du bureau directeur:
Alain Liard, Directeur général et secrétaire

Ordre des hygiénistes dentaires du Québec (OHDQ)
#1212, 1155, rue University, Montréal QC H3B 3A7
Tél: 514-284-7639; *Téléc:* 514-284-3147
Ligne sans frais: 800-361-2996
info@ohdq.com
www.ohdq.com
Aperçu: *Dimension:* moyenne; *Envergure:* provinciale; fondée en 1975
Membre(s) du personnel: 17
Membre: *Comités:* Administration; inspection professionnelle; discipline; formation des hygiénistes dentaires; syndic; révision; équivalences; révision des équivalences; exécutif; formation continue et professionnelle; publications; bourses; vérification
Membre(s) du bureau directeur:
Diane Duval, Présidente
Janique Ste-Marie, Directrice générale
jste-marie@ohdq.com
Prix, Bourses:
• Prix Sylvie de Grandmont
• Prix du Lecteur
• Bourse de Perfectionnement

Ordre des infirmières et infirmiers auxiliaires du Québec (OIIAQ)
531, rue Sherbrooke est, Montréal QC H2L 1K2
Tél: 514-282-9511; *Téléc:* 514-282-0631
Ligne sans frais: 800-283-9511
oiiaq@oiiaq.org
www.oiiaq.org
Nom précédent: Corporation professionnelle des infirmiers et infirmiers auxiliaires du Québec
Aperçu: *Dimension:* moyenne; *Envergure:* provinciale; fondée en 1974 surveillé par Canadian Council of Practical Nurse Regulators
Mission: Favoriser le développement professionnel des infirmières et infirmiers auxiliaires du Québec pour viser l'excellence dans l'exercice professionnel et tendre à une plus grande humanisation des soins
Membre de: Conseil interprofessionnel du Québec
Membre(s) du personnel: 24
Membre: 29 000+
Activités: *Bibliothèque:*
Membre(s) du bureau directeur:
Régis Paradis, Président et directeur général

Ordre des infirmières et infirmiers de l'Ontario *See* College of Nurses of Ontario

Ordre des infirmières et infirmiers du Québec (OIIQ)
4200, rue Molson, Montréal QC H1Y 4V4
Tél: 514-935-2501; *Téléc:* 514-935-1799
Ligne sans frais: 800-363-6048
www.oiiq.org
www.linkedin.com/company/ordre-des-infirmi-res-et-infirmiers-du-qu-bec
www.facebook.com/OIIQSante
twitter.com/OIIQ
www.flickr.com/photos/ordreinf/sets
Également appelé: Corporation professionnelle des infirmières et infirmiers du Québec
Aperçu: *Dimension:* grande; *Envergure:* provinciale; Organisme de réglementation; fondée en 1974
Mission: Assurer la protection du public; contrôler l'exercice de la profession par ses membres
Membre de: Conseil interprofessionnel du Québec (CIQ)
Finances: *Fonds:* Fondation de recherche en sciences infirmières du Québec (FRESIQ)
Membre: 73 000; *Critères d'admissibilite:* Détenir un permis d'exercice d'infirmière et être inscrit au Tableau des membres; *Comités:* Admission par équivalence; Admission par équivalence; Formation de l'IPS; Formation de l'IPS; Révision; Révision de l'examen des infirmières cliniciennes spécialisées; Révision de l'examen des IPS; Bourses du Fonds Patrimoine; Mise en candidature et de sélection Insigne du mérite de l'Ordre; Finances et de vérification; Inspection professionnelle; Examen pour la certification des infirmières cliniciennes spécialisées; Examen pour la certification des IPS; Discipline; Jeunesse provincial; Liés à l'examen professionnel
Activités: *Evénements de sensibilisation:* Congrès; Semaine de l'infirmière; Tournoi de golf; *Bibliothèque:* Centre de documentation; Bibliothèque publique
Membre(s) du bureau directeur:

Denise Brosseau, Directrice générale
Prix, Bourses:
- Prix Innovation clinique
- Prix Insigne du mérite de l'Ordre
- Bourses de baccalauréat, maîtrise, doctorat
- Prix Florence

Publications:
- Le Journal [publication d'Ordre des infirmières et infirmiers du Québec]

Type: Journal; *Frequency:* 5 fois par an

Ordre régional des infirmières et infirmiers du Bas-Saint-Laurent/Gaspésie-Iles-de-la-Madeleine
49, rue Saint-Jean-Baptiste ouest, Rimouski QC G5L 4J2
Tél: 418-725-3353; *Téléc:* 418-725-3350
oriibslg@cgocable.ca
www.oiiq.org/ordres/basStLaurent/
Membre(s) du bureau directeur:
Renée Rivière, Présidente

Ordre régional des infirmières et infirmiers de Québec
#102, 915, boul René-Lévesque ouest, Québec QC G1S 1T8
Tél: 418-527-2507; *Téléc:* 418-527-8621
oriiq03@globetrotter.net
www.oiiq.org/lordre/ordres-regionaux/quebec
Membre(s) du bureau directeur:
Nathalie Gauthier, Présidente
presidente.oriiq@globetrotter.net

Ordre régional des infirmières et infirmiers de Chaudière-Appalaches
69, rue Champagnat ouest, Lévis QC G6V 2B2
Tél: 418-835-1475; *Téléc:* 418-835-3587
oriica@videotron.ca
www.oiiq.org/lordre/ordres-regionaux/chaudiere-appalaches
Membre(s) du bureau directeur:
Ginette Bernier, Présidente
ginb55@videotron.ca

Ordre régional des infirmières et infirmiers de Mauricie/Centre-du-Québec (ORIIMCQ)
CP 955, 3910, rue Louis-Pinard, Trois-Rivières QC G9A 5K2
Tél: 819-374-1512; *Téléc:* 819-374-4150
oriimcq@cgocable.ca
www.oiiq.org/lordre/ordres-regionaux/mauriciecentre-du-quebec
Membre de: OIIQ
Membre(s) du bureau directeur:
Marie-Andrée Gauthier, Présidente
Lyne Campagna, Vice-Présidente
Nathalie Gélinas, Trésorier

Ordre régional des infirmières et infirmiers de l'Estrie
375, rue Argyll, Sherbrooke QC J1H 3H5
Tél: 819-346-6890; *Téléc:* 819-346-2077
oriie.csss-iugs@ssss.gouv.qc.ca
www.oiiq.org/lordre/ordres-regionaux/estrie
Membre(s) du bureau directeur:
Maryse Grégoire, Présidente

Ordre régional des infirmières et infirmiers de la Montérégie
Complexe Cousineau, #2300, 5245, boul Cousineau, Saint-Hubert QC J3Y 6J8
Tél: 450-462-4868
oriim@videotron.ca
www.oiiq.org/lordre/ordres-regionaux/monteregie
Membre(s) du bureau directeur:
Daniel Cutti, Président
dcutti@videotron.ca

Ordre régional des infirmières et infirmiers de Laurentides/Lanaudière
#100, 30, rue de Martigny, Saint-Jérôme QC J7Y 2E9
Tél: 450-436-6217; *Téléc:* 450-436-6610
Ligne sans frais: 877-436-6217
oriill@qc.aira.com
www.oiiq.org/lordre/ordres-regionaux/laurentideslanaudiere
Membre(s) du bureau directeur:
France Laframboise, Présidente

Ordre régional des infirmières et infirmiers de l'Outaouais
#160, 221, ch Freeman, Gatineau QC J8Z 1L3
Tél: 819-770-4121; *Téléc:* 819-770-3606
oriio@qc.aira.com
www.oiiq.org/lordre/ordres-regionaux/outaouais
Membre(s) du bureau directeur:
François-Régis Fréchette, Président
outaouais.president@gmail.com

Ordre régional des infirmières et infirmiers de Montréal/Laval
#120, 2120, rue Sherbrooke est, Montréal QC H2K 1C3
Tél: 514-343-3707; *Téléc:* 514-343-9070
oriiml@bellnet.ca
www.oiiq.org/lordre/ordres-regionaux/montreallaval
Membre(s) du bureau directeur:
Josée Breton, Présidente

Ordre régional des infirmières et infirmiers de la Côte-Nord
#222B, 690, boul Laure, Sept-Iles QC G4R 4K7
Tél: 418-968-1500
Ligne sans frais: 866-968-1500
www.oiiq.org/ordres/cote_nord/
Membre(s) du bureau directeur:
Marie Blanchet Legendre, Présidente
marie.legendre@cgocable.ca

Ordre régional des infirmières et infirmiers de Saguenay—Lac-Saint-Jean/Nord-du-Québec
Plaza II, CP 282, #2, 540, rue Sacré-Coeur ouest, Alma QC G8B 1M4
Tél: 418-662-5051; *Téléc:* 418-622-5052
Ligne sans frais: 866-662-5051
oriislsjnq@cgocable.ca
Membre(s) du bureau directeur:
Nancy Bouchard, Présidente
nancy.bouchard.csssj@ssss.gouv.qc.ca

Ordre régional des infirmières et infirmiers de l'Abitibi-Témiscamingue
#5, 210, av du Lac, Rouyn-Noranda QC J9X 4N7
Tél: 819-762-3768; *Téléc:* 819-762-3760
oriiat@tlb.sympatico.ca
www.oiiq.org/lordre/ordres-regionaux/abitibi-temiscamingue
Membre(s) du bureau directeur:
Danielle Gélinas, Présidente

Ordre des ingénieurs du Québec (OIQ)
Gare Windsor, #350, 1100, av des Canadiens-de-Montréal, Montréal QC H3B 2S2
Tél: 514-845-6141; *Téléc:* 514-845-1833
Ligne sans frais: 800-461-6141
info@oiq.qc.ca
www.oiq.qc.ca
www.linkedin.com/company/604039
www.facebook.com/oiq.qc.ca
twitter.com/OIQ
www.youtube.com/user/ordredesingenieurs
Aperçu: *Dimension:* grande; *Envergure:* provinciale; fondée en 1920 surveillé par Engineers Canada
Mission: Faire de la promotion et s'assurer de la qualité des services rendus à la société par les ingénieurs, individuellement et collectivement, en tant que membres d'un corps professionnel; Favoriser leur épanouissement professionnel et personnel; Contribuer au développement socio-économique de la société
Membre de: Engineers Canada
Affiliation(s): Conseil Interprofessionnel du Québec
600 bénévole(s)
Membre: 64 000+; *Montant de la cotisation:* 180$; *Comités:* Discipline; Admissions à l'Exercice; Inspection professionnelle; Révision; Arbitrage; Développement professionnel; Assurance responsabilité professionnelle; Finances et de vérification; Ressources Humaines; Surveillance des élections; Éthique des Administrateurs; Gouvernance et d'Éthique; Régionaux; La Formation et de Liaison CODIQ-OIQ-CRÉIQ; Sectoriels; Sélection pour la valorisation de l'Excellence
Activités: Préparation d'avis, mémoires et de documents professionnels; Organisation ou préparation à des conférences; Groupes de travail sur: la gestion des déchets solides, l'eau de consommation, le bilan technologique, l'analyse technologique des secteurs d'activité économique du Québec, le transfert de technologie, le génie-conseil; *Evénements de sensibilisation:* Journée de l'ingénieur(e); *Stagiaires:* Oui; *Service de conférenciers:* Oui; *Bibliothèque* Not open to public
Membre(s) du bureau directeur:
Kathy Baig, Président
Chantal Michaud, ing., Directrice générale
Claude Soucy, Directeur général adoint, Ressources humaines
Lorraine Godin, CPA-CA, Directrice, Administration-finances
Louis Tremblay, ing., Directeur, Affaires professionnelles
Luc Vagneux, CRIA, Directeur, Profession et communications
Prix, Bourses:
- Bourse Krashinsky
- Grand prix d'excellence
- Prix du Président au bénévolat
- Prix d'encouragement aux études supérieures

Meetings/Conferences:
- Ordre des ingénieurs du Québec Assemblée générale annuelle 2018, 2018, QC

Scope: Provincial

Publications:
- Bulletins aux membres [a publication of the Ordre des ingénieurs du Québec]

Type: Bulletin
- PLAN [a publication of the Ordre des ingénieurs du Québec]

Type: Revue

Abitibi-Témiscamingue
QC
www.oiq.qc.ca/fr/comites_regionaux/Abitibi-Temiscamingue
Membre(s) du bureau directeur:
Line Paquette, Coordonnatrice aux régions, 514-845-6141 Ext. 3174
lpaquette@oiq.qc.ca

Bas-Saint-Laurent—Gaspésie—îles-de-la-Madeleine
QC
Membre(s) du bureau directeur:
Pierre-Claude Gagnon, Président du comité régional
Line Paquette, Coordonnatrice aux régions, 514-845-6141 Ext. 3174
lpaquette@oiq.qc.ca

Côte-Nord
QC
www.oiq.qc.ca/fr/comites_regionaux/cote-nord
Membre(s) du bureau directeur:
Line Paquette, Coordonnatrice aux régions, 514-845-6141 Ext. 3174
lpaquette@oiq.qc.ca

Estrie
QC
www.oiq.qc.ca/fr/comites_regionaux/estrie
Membre(s) du bureau directeur:
Mohamed Ghazi Aissaoui, Président du comité régional
Julie Sageau, Contact, 514-845-6141 Ext. 3272
julie.sageau@oiq.qc.ca

Laval—Laurentides—Lanaudière
QC
www.oiq.qc.ca/fr/comites_regionaux/Laval-Laurentides-Lanaudiere
Membre(s) du bureau directeur:
Nathalie Martel, Présidente du comité régional
Julie Sageau, Contact, 514-845-6141 Ext. 3272
julie.saqeau@oiq.qc.ca

Mauricie—Centre-du-Québec
QC
www.oiq.qc.ca/fr/comites_regionaux/Centre-du-Quebec
Membre(s) du bureau directeur:
Louise Andy, Présidente du comité régional
Julie Sageau, Contact, 514-845-6141 Ext. 3272
julie.saqeau@oiq.qc.ca

Montérégie
QC
www.oiq.qc.ca/fr/comites_regionaux/monteregie
Membre(s) du bureau directeur:
Alexandre Vigneault, Président du comité régional
Valérie Bongain, Contact, 514-845-6141 Ext. 3142
vbongain@oiq.qc.ca

Montréal
QC
www.oiq.qc.ca/fr/comites_regionaux/montreal
Membre(s) du bureau directeur:
Vincent Carignan, Jr. président du comité
Valérie Bongain, Contact, 514-845-6141 Ext. 3142
vbongain@oiq.qc.ca

Outaouais
QC
www.oiq.qc.ca/fr/comites_regionaux/outaouais
Membre(s) du bureau directeur:
Luis Pablo Estable, Président
Julie Sageau, Contact, 514-845-6141 Ext. 3272
julie.sageau@oiq.qc.ca

Québec—Chaudière—Appalaches
QC
www.oiq.qc.ca/fr/comites_regionaux/quebec_chaudiere_appalaches
Membre(s) du bureau directeur:
Michaël Paquette, Président du comité regional
Valérie Bongain, Contact, 514-845-6141 Ext. 3412
vbongain@oiq.qc.ca

Saguenay—Lac-Saint-Jean
QC
www.oiq.qc.ca/fr/comites_regionaux/saguenay_lacsaintjean
Membre(s) du bureau directeur:
Félix Boudreault, Président
Valérie Bongain, Contact
vbongain@oiq.qc.ca

Ordre des ingénieurs forestiers du Québec (OIFQ)
#110, 2750, rue Einstein, Québec QC G1P 4R1
Tél: 418-650-2411; *Téléc:* 418-650-2168
oifq@oifq.com
www.oifq.com
www.linkedin.com/company-beta/8337438
www.facebook.com/OIFQc
twitter.com/oifqc
Aperçu: *Dimension:* moyenne; *Envergure:* provinciale; Organisme sans but lucratif; Organisme de réglementation; fondée en 1921
Mission: Assurer la protection du public; assurer la qualité des services rendus au public québécois; favoriser l'amélioration continue de l'expertise et de la compétence des ingénieurs forestiers; mettre en place des actions favorisant la durabilité de l'aménagement forestier pour le bénéfice de l'ensemble de la société
Membre de: Conseil interprofessionnel du Québec
Affiliation(s): Fédération canadienne des associations d'ingénieurs forestiers
Finances: *Budget de fonctionnement annuel:* $500,000-$1.5 Million
Membre: 2 260; *Montant de la cotisation:* 435$; *Critères d'admissibilite:* Diplôme universitaire de premier cycle en foresterie
Activités: *Service de conférenciers:* Oui
Membre(s) du bureau directeur:
Denis Villeneuve, Président

L'Ordre des massothérapeutes de l'Ontario *See* College of Massage Therapists of Ontario

Ordre des médecins vétérinaires du Québec (OMVQ)
#200, 800, av Ste-Anne, Saint-Hyacinthe QC J2S 5G7
Tél: 450-774-1427; *Téléc:* 450-774-7635
Ligne sans frais: 800-267-1427
www.omvq.qc.ca
Aperçu: *Dimension:* moyenne; *Envergure:* provinciale; Organisme sans but lucratif; Organisme de réglementation; fondée en 1902
Mission: Protection du public; contribuer à l'amélioration de la santé et du bien-être des animaux; formation des membres; maintien de la qualité des services vétérinaires
Finances: *Budget de fonctionnement annuel:* $500,000-$1.5 Million; *Fonds:* Cotisation annuelle
Membre(s) du personnel: 23
Membre: 1 940 actifs; *Montant de la cotisation:* 650$
Activités: *Evénements de sensibilisation:* Semaine de la vie animale, oct.
Membre(s) du bureau directeur:
Joël Bergeron, Président
Suzie Prince, Directrice générale/Secrétaire
suzie.prince@omvq.qc.ca
Publications:
• Revue Le Veterinarius [a publication of Ordre des médecins vétérinaires du Québec]
Type: Magazine; *Frequency:* 5 pa

Ordre des opticiens d'ordonnances du Québec (OOOQ)
#601, 630, rue Sherbrooke ouest, Montréal QC H3A 1E4
Tél: 514-288-7542; *Téléc:* 514-288-5982
Ligne sans frais: 800-563-6345
ordre@opticien.qc.ca
www.oodq.qc.ca
Aperçu: *Dimension:* moyenne; *Envergure:* provinciale; Organisme de réglementation; fondée en 1940 surveillé par Office des professions du Québec
Mission: Assurer la protection du public; contrôler l'exercice de la profession par ses membres
Membre de: National Accreditation Committee of Opticians
Affiliation(s): Conseil interprofessionnel du Québec (CIQ)
Membre(s) du personnel: 6
Activités: *Stagiaires:* Oui; *Listes de destinataires:* Oui
Membre(s) du bureau directeur:
Linda Samson, Présidente et directrice générale

Ordre des optométristes de l'Ontario *See* College of Optometrists of Ontario

Ordre des optométristes du Québec
#700, 1265, rue Berri, Montréal QC H2L 4X4
Tél: 514-499-0524; *Téléc:* 514-499-1051
Ligne sans frais: 888-499-0524
www.ooq.org
Aperçu: *Dimension:* moyenne; *Envergure:* provinciale; Organisme de réglementation
Mission: De réglementer la profession d'optométriste afin de s'assurer que le public reçoit la plus haute qualité de service
Membre(s) du personnel: 5
Membre: *Montant de la cotisation:* 194,91$ inactif; 1346,55$ actif; *Comités:* Exécutif; Gouvernance; Admission à l'exercice; Formation; Législation et réglementation; Enquête relatif aux affaires pénales; Exercice; Communications; Révision
Membre(s) du bureau directeur:
Marco Laverdière, Secrétaire et directeur général

Ordre des orthophonistes et audiologistes du Québec (OOAQ)
#601, 235, boul René-Levesque est, Montréal QC H2X 1N8
Tél: 514-282-9123; *Téléc:* 514-282-9541
Ligne sans frais: 888-232-9123
info@ooaq.qc.ca
www.ooaq.qc.ca
Aperçu: *Dimension:* moyenne; *Envergure:* provinciale; Organisme de réglementation; fondée en 1973
Mission: D'assurer la protection du public en regard du domaine d'exercice de ses membres, soit les troubles de la communication humaine; surveiller l'exercice professionnel des orthophonistes et des audiologistes et voir à favoriser l'accessibilité du public à des services de qualité; contribuer à l'intégration sociale des individus et à l'amélioration de la qualité de vie de la population québécoise
Membre(s) du personnel: 15
Membre: 2 518; *Critères d'admissibilité:* Maîtrise en orthophonie-audiologie; *Comités:* Admission; Inspection professionnelle; Discipline; Révision des plaintes; Révision des équivalences; Formation; Prix
Activités: Surveillance de l'exercice professionnel; favoriser l'accès aux services; amélioration de la qualité de vie; intégration sociale; *Bibliothèque:* Bibliothèque publique rendez-vous
Membre(s) du bureau directeur:
Louise Chamberland, Directrice générale
directiongenerale@ooaq.qc.ca

Ordre des pharmaciens du N.-B. *See* New Brunswick Pharmaceutical Society

Ordre des pharmaciens du Québec (OPQ)
#301, 266, rue Notre-Dame ouest, Montréal QC H2Y 1T6
Tél: 514-284-9588; *Téléc:* 514-284-3420
Ligne sans frais: 800-363-0324
ordrepharm@opq.org
www.opq.org
www.facebook.com/OrdredespharmaciensduQuebec
twitter.com/ordrepharmaQc
www.youtube.com/user/ordrepharmaciensqc
Aperçu: *Dimension:* moyenne; *Envergure:* provinciale; Organisme de réglementation; fondée en 1871 surveillé par National Association of Pharmacy Regulatory Authorities
Mission: Protection du public en matières de services pharmaceutiques
Membre de: Conseil canadien de l'Éducation permanente en pharmacie; Conseil interprofessionnel du Québec
Membre(s) du personnel: 50
Membre: *Montant de la cotisation:* Barème; *Critères d'admissibilite:* Détenteur d'un permis d'exercice de la pharmacie valide pour le Québec; *Comités:* Discipline; Révision; Arbitrage des compte; Enquête sur le contrôle de l'utilisation des médicaments; Admission à la pratique; Formation des pharmaciens; Réviseur de l'admission à la pratique; Inspection professionnelle; Veille sur les nouvelles pratiques liées aux développements technologiques; Attribution des prix; Gouvernance et d'éthique; Règlement sur l'exercice de la pharmacie en société; Déontologie; Étude des demandes de dispense des formations obligatoires; Vigie interordres; Ordre des pharmaciens du Québec / Collège des médecins du Québec
Activités: *Service de conférenciers:* Oui
Membre(s) du bureau directeur:
Bertrand Bolduc, Président
Manon Lambert, Directrice générale et secrétaire
Prix, Bourses:
• Prix Louis-Hébert

Ordre des physiothérapeutes de l'Ontario *See* College of Physiotherapists of Ontario

Ordre des Podiatres du Québec
#1000, 7151, rue Jean-Talon est, Anjou QC H1M 3N8
Tél: 514-288-0019; *Téléc:* 514-288-5463
Ligne sans frais: 888-514-7433
podiatres@ordredespodiatres.qc.ca
www.ordredespodiatres.qc.ca
Aperçu: *Dimension:* petite; *Envergure:* provinciale
Membre: 175; *Comités:* Révision; Formation; Inspection Professionelle; Équivalences; Formation Continue; Communications; Audit; Ressources Humaines
Membre(s) du bureau directeur:
Charles Faucher, Président
Martine Gosselin, Directrice générale

Ordre des psychoéducateurs et psychoéducatrices du Québec (OPP)
#510, 1600, boul Henri-Bourassa ouest, Montréal QC H3M 3E2
Tél: 514-333-6601; *Téléc:* 514-333-7502
Ligne sans frais: 877-913-6601
info@ordrepsed.qc.ca
www.ordrepsed.qc.ca
Aperçu: *Dimension:* moyenne; *Envergure:* provinciale; Organisme de réglementation
Mission: De réglementer la profession de psychoéducateurs afin de protéger le public et d'assurer la meilleure qualité de service possible est fournie
Membre(s) du personnel: 19
Membre: *Montant de la cotisation:* Barème; *Comités:* Exécutif; Admission par équivalence; Inspection professionnelle; Formation; Révision des plaintes; Discipline; Arbitrage des comptes; Affaires professionnelles
Membre(s) du bureau directeur:
Renée Verville, Directrice générale

L'Ordre des psychologues du Québec (OPQ)
#510, 1100, av Beaumont, Montréal QC H3P 3H5
Tél: 514-738-1881; *Téléc:* 514-738-8838
Ligne sans frais: 800-363-2644
info@ordrepsy.qc.ca
www.ordrepsy.qc.ca
Aperçu: *Dimension:* moyenne; *Envergure:* provinciale; fondée en 1962
Mission: Assurer la protection du public; contrôler l'exercice de la profession par ses membres; veiller à la qualité des services dispensés par ses membres; favoriser le développement de la compétence professionnelle, le respect des normes déontologiques et l'accessibilité aux services psychologiques
Affiliation(s): American Psychological Association
Membre(s) du personnel: 33
Membre: *Montant de la cotisation:* 622.02$; *Critères d'admissibilité:* Maîtrise en psychologie; *Comités:* Inspection professionnelle; Révision; Formation des psychologues; Équivalence; Rémunération; Vérification; Évaluation des demandes de permis de psychothérapeutes; Organismes accréditeurs en médiation familiale; Sélection des Prix de l'Ordre; Évaluation des demandes d'attestation de formation pour l'évaluation des troubles neuropsychologiques; Reconnaissance des activités de formation continue en psychothérapie; Révision des demandes de permis de psychothérapeutes; Révision des demandes d'attestation de formation pour l'évaluation des troubles neuropsychologiques
Activités: *Service de conférenciers:* Oui; *Listes de destinataires:* Oui
Membre(s) du bureau directeur:
Rose-Marie Charest, Présidente
presidence@ordrepsy.qc.ca

Ordre des Sages-Femmes de l'Ontario *See* College of Midwives of Ontario

Ordre des sages-femmes du Québec
#300, 4126, rue Saint-Denis, Montréal QC H2W 2M5
Tél: 514-286-1313
Ligne sans frais: 877-711-1313
info@osfq.org
www.osfq.org
Aperçu: *Dimension:* petite; *Envergure:* provinciale
Mission: Pour surveiller les pratiques des sages-femmes au Québec
Membre(s) du personnel: 4
Membre: *Comités:* Finances; Gouvernance; Lignes directrices; Inspection professionnelle; Syndique; Révision; Discipline; Surveillance de la pratique illégale; Formation continue; Formation; Étude pour la pratique en régions rurales et éloignées; Admission par équivalence; Médicaments, examens et analyses; Statistiques; Étude et enquête sur la mortalité et la morbidité périnatales

Membre(s) du bureau directeur:
Lorena Garrido, Directrice générale
lorena.garrido@osfq.org

Ordre des techniciens et techniciennes dentaires du Québec (OTTDQ)
#900, 500, rue Sherbrooke ouest, Montréal QC H3A 3C6
Tél: 514-282-3837; *Téléc:* 514-844-7556
www.ottdq.com
www.facebook.com/OTTDQ
Aperçu: *Dimension:* petite; *Envergure:* provinciale; Organisme de réglementation
Mission: De réglementer la profession des techniciens dentaires afin de protéger le public et d'assurer la meilleure qualité de service possible est fournie
Membre(s) du personnel: 3
Membre: *Comités:* Formation continue; Formation; Normes d'équivalences; Inspection professionnelle; Conciliation et arbitrage des comptes; Exercice illégal et usurpation de titre réservé; Conseil de discipline; Révisions des plaintes; Finances et régie interne
Membre(s) du bureau directeur:
Linda Carbone, Secrétaire

Ordre des technologues en imagerie médicale, en radio-oncologie et en élétrophysiologie médicale du Québec
#401, 6455, rue Jean-Talon, Saint-Léonard QC H1S 3E8
Tél: 514-351-0052
Ligne sans frais: 800-361-8759
www.otimroepmq.ca
Nom précédent: Ordre des technologues en radiologie du Québec
Aperçu: *Dimension:* moyenne; *Envergure:* provinciale; Organisme de réglementation; fondée en 1941
Mission: De surveiller l'exercice de la profession par ses membres, contribuer à leur développement professionnel & assurer au public des services de qualité en matière d'imagerie médicale & de radio-oncologies
Membre de: Canadian Association of Medical Radiation Technologists
Finances: *Fonds:* Les frais d'adhésion
Membre(s) du personnel: 22
Membre: 5,800; *Montant de la cotisation:* Barème; *Critères d'admissibilite:* Technologues qui travaillent dans le radiodiagnostic, la médecine nucléaire, la radio-oncologie et l'électrophysiologie médicale; *Comités:* Exécutif; Inspection professionnelle; Équivalences de diplôme et de formation; Discipline; Révision des plaintes; Formation; Développement professionnel; Relève; Magazine; Vérification; Examens; Révision des notes
Activités: Stagiaires: Oui; Listes de destinataires: Oui; Bibliothèque: Centre de doc
Membre(s) du bureau directeur:
Danielle Boué, Présidente
Meetings/Conferences:
• Ordre des technologues en imagerie médicale, en radio-oncologie et en élétrophysiologie médicale du Québec 44e Congrès 2018, May, 2018, Hilton Lac-Leamy, Gatineau, QC
Scope: Provincial

Ordre des technologues en radiation médicale de l'Ontario
See College of Medical Radiation Technologists of Ontario

Ordre des technologues en radiologie du Québec *Voir* Ordre des technologues en imagerie médicale, en radio-oncologie et en élétrophysiologie médicale du Québec

Ordre des technologues professionnels du Québec (OTPQ)
#505, 606, rue Cathcart, Montréal QC H3B 1K9
Tél: 514-845-3247; *Téléc:* 514-845-3643
Ligne sans frais: 800-561-3459
info@otpq.qc.ca
www.otpq.qc.ca
www.linkedin.com/groups/4134994/profile
www.facebook.com/TechnologuesProfessionnels
twitter.com/otpq
www.youtube.com/user/TechnologuePro1
Nom précédent: Corporation professionnelle des technologues professionnelles du Québec
Aperçu: *Dimension:* moyenne; *Envergure:* provinciale; fondée en 1927 surveillé par Canadian Council of Technicians & Technologists
Mission: Promouvoir et assurer la compétence des technologues professionnels dans l'intérêt public
Membre de: Conseil canadiens des techniciens et technologues

Finances: *Budget de fonctionnement annuel:* $500,000-$1.5 Million
Membre(s) du personnel: 9
Membre: 5 000; *Montant de la cotisation:* Barème; *Comités:* Admission; Discipline; Inspection professionnelle; Prix
Activités: Stagiaires: Oui; Listes de destinataires: Oui
Membre(s) du bureau directeur:
Denis Beauchamp, Directeur général et secrétaire, 514-845-3247 Ext. 107
Prix, Bourses:
• Technologue de l'année
• Bénévole de l'année
• Étudiant bénévole
• Mérite de l'innovation technologique

Ordre des traducteurs et interprètes agréés du Québec *Voir* Ordre des traducteurs, terminologues et interprètes agréés du Québec

Ordre des traducteurs, terminologues et interprètes agréés du Québec (OTTIAQ)
#1108, 2021, rue Union, Montréal QC H3A 2S9
Tél: 514-845-4411; *Téléc:* 514-845-9903
Ligne sans frais: 800-265-4815
info@ottiaq.org
www.ottiaq.org
Nom précédent: Ordre des traducteurs et interprètes agréés du Québec
Aperçu: *Dimension:* moyenne; *Envergure:* provinciale; Organisme sans but lucratif; fondée en 1992 surveillé par Canadian Translators, Terminologists & Interpreters Council
Mission: L'OTTIAQ assure la protection du public en octroyant les titres de traducteur agréé, de terminologue agréé et d'interprète agréé, en veillant au respect de son code de déontologie et des normes professionnelles et en mettant en ouvre les mécanismes prévus au Code des professions.
Membre de: Fédération internationale des traducteurs
Finances: *Budget de fonctionnement annuel:* $500,000-$1.5 Million
Membre(s) du personnel: 7; 100 bénévole(s)
Membre: 2150 société + 14 d'honneur + 447 adhérents + 1376 agréés; *Montant de la cotisation:* 150$ adhérents; 430$ agréés; *Critères d'admissibilite:* Traducteur; terminologue; interprète
Activités: Congrès annuel; Evénements de sensibilisation: Journée mondiale de la traduction, 30 sept.
Membre(s) du bureau directeur:
Johanne Boucher, Directrice générale
direction@ottiaq.org

Ordre des travailleurs sociaux et des techniciens en travail social de l'Ontario *See* Ontario College of Social Workers & Social Service Workers

Ordre des urbanistes du Québec (OUQ)
#410, 85, rue St-Paul ouest, Montréal QC H2Y 3V4
Tél: 514-849-1177; *Téléc:* 514-849-7176
info@ouq.qc.ca
www.ouq.qc.ca
www.facebook.com/666855766761080
Nom précédent: Ordre professionnel des urbanistes du Québec
Aperçu: *Dimension:* moyenne; *Envergure:* provinciale; fondée en 1963 surveillé par Canadian Institute of Planners
Mission: Assurer la protection du public dans l'exercice de la profession par ses membres et la promotion de la pratique de l'urbanisme au Québec
Membre: 700; *Montant de la cotisation:* 360$; *Comités:* Admission; Déontologie; Discipline; Formation Continue; Inspection Professionnelle
Membre(s) du bureau directeur:
Karina Verdon, Directrice générale, 514-849-1177 Ext. 23
kverdon@ouq.qc.ca
Meetings/Conferences:
• Congrès OUQ 2018, 2018, QC
Scope: Provincial
Publications:
• Urbanité [publication Ordre des urbanistes du Québec]
Type: Bulletin

Ordre professionnel de la physiothérapie du Québec (OPPQ)
#1000, 7151, rue Jean-Talon est, Anjou QC H1M 3N8
Tél: 514-351-2770; *Téléc:* 514-351-2658
Ligne sans frais: 800-361-2001
physio@oppq.qc.ca
www.oppq.qc.ca

Nom précédent: Ordre professionnel des physiothérapeutes du Québec; Corporation professionnelle des physiothérapeutes du Québec
Aperçu: *Dimension:* moyenne; *Envergure:* provinciale; fondée en 1973 surveillé par Canadian Alliance of Physiotherapy Regulators
Mission: Assurer la protection du public en surveillant l'exercice de la physiothérapie par ses membres et en contribuant à leur développement professionnel
Membre de: Alliance canadienne des organismes de réglementation de la physiothérapie; Association canadienne de physiothérapie
Finances: *Budget de fonctionnement annuel:* $500,000-$1.5 Million
Membre(s) du personnel: 27
Membre: 7 145; *Critères d'admissibilite:* Physiothérapeutes
Membre(s) du bureau directeur:
Denis Pelletier, Président
dpelletier@oppq.qc.ca
Claude Laurent, Directeur général et secrétaire
claurent@oppq.qc.ca

Ordre professionnel des diététistes Québec / Québec Professional Union of Dieticians
Tour Ouest, 550, rue Sherbrooke ouest, Montréal QC H3A 1B9
Tél: 514-393-3733; *Téléc:* 514-393-3582
Ligne sans frais: 888-393-8528
Nom précédent: Syndicat professionnel des diététistes
Aperçu: *Dimension:* moyenne; *Envergure:* provinciale; fondée en 1970
Membre: 1000; *Critères d'admissibilite:* Diététistes et nutritionnistes
Membre(s) du bureau directeur:
Claudette Péloquin-Antoun, Présidente

Ordre professionnel des inhalothérapeutes du Québec (OPIQ)
#721, 1440, rue Sainte-Catherine ouest, Montréal QC H3G 1R8
Tél: 514-931-2900; *Téléc:* 514-931-3621
Ligne sans frais: 800-561-0029
info@opiq.qc.ca
www.opiq.qc.ca
www.facebook.com/opiq.qc.ca
twitter.com/OPIQMEDSOC
Aperçu: *Dimension:* moyenne; *Envergure:* provinciale; Organisme sans but lucratif; fondée en 1969
Mission: Protection du public; surveillance de l'exercice professionnel de l'inhalothérapie
Affiliation(s): Alliance nationale des organismes de réglementation de la thérapie respiratoire
Membre(s) du personnel: 11
Membre: *Critères d'admissibilite:* Professionnel en santé cardio-respiratoire
Activités: Congrès annuel et Assemblée générale en automne; Stagiaires: Oui; Service de conférenciers: Oui
Membre(s) du bureau directeur:
Jocelyn Vachon, Présidente
Josée Prud'Homme, Directrice générale et secrétaire

Ordre professionnel des physiothérapeutes du Québec; Corporation professionnelle des physiothérapeutes du Québec *Voir* Ordre professionnel de la physiothérapie du Québec

Ordre professionnel des sexologues du Québec (OPSQ)
#300, 4126, rue Saint-Denis, Montréal QC H2W 2M5
Tél: 438-386-6777
Ligne sans frais: 855-386-6777
info@opsq.org
opsq.org
Aperçu: *Dimension:* petite; *Envergure:* provinciale; Organisme de réglementation
Mission: De réglementer la profession des sexologues afin de protéger le public et d'assurer la meilleure qualité de service possible est fournie
Membre(s) du personnel: 5
Membre: *Montant de la cotisation:* Barème
Membre(s) du bureau directeur:
Isabelle Beaulieu, Directrice générale et secrétaire de l'Ordre
isabelle.beaulieu@opsq.org

Ordre professionnel des technologistes médicaux du Québec (OPTMQ)
281, av Laurier est, Montréal QC H2T 1G2
Tél: 514-527-9811; *Téléc:* 514-527-7314
Ligne sans frais: 800-567-7763

info@optmq.org
www.optmq.org
Nom précédent: Corporation professionnelle des technologistes médicaux du Québec
Aperçu: *Dimension:* moyenne; *Envergure:* provinciale; Organisme de réglementation; fondée en 1973 surveillé par Canadian Society for Medical Laboratory Science
Mission: Protection du public en vérifiant la pratique des membres, en effectuant un contrôle lors de l'émission de permis, par la discipline et l'inspection professionnelle
Membre de: Conseil Interprofessionnel du Québec
Membre: *Montant de la cotisation:* 355,99$; *Comités:* Admission; Communications; Congrès; Développement professionnel; Jeunesse; Normes
Membre(s) du bureau directeur:
Doris Levasseur Bourbeau, Présidente
Alain Collette, Avocat, secrétaire et directeur général
acollette@optmq.org

Ordre professionnel des travailleurs sociaux du Québec (OPTSQ)
#520, 255, boul Crémazie est, Montréal QC H2M 1M2
Tél: 514-731-3925; *Téléc:* 514-731-6785
Ligne sans frais: 888-731-9420
info.general@optsq.org
www.optsq.org
www.facebook.com/OTSTCFQ
twitter.com/OTSTCFQ1
Aperçu: *Dimension:* moyenne; *Envergure:* provinciale; Organisme de réglementation; fondée en 1960
Mission: Assurer la protection du public par le contrôle de l'exercice de la profession, par la formation continue, et le développement professionnel.
Membre de: Canadian Association of Social Workers
Affiliation(s): Conseil interprofessionnel du Québec
Membre(s) du personnel: 44
Membre: *Critères d'admissibilité:* Diplôme universitaire en travail social; *Comités:* Exécutif; Révision; Révision en matière d'équivalences; Admissions et des équivalences; Inspection professionnelle; Formation; Formation Continue; Pratique Autonome; Médiation Familiale; Pratique de 'a thérapie conjugale et familiale; Enquête sur l'utilisation illégale des titres et l'exercice illégal de la profession; Éthique; Pratique en protection de la jeunesse; Jeunesse - secteur T.S.
Activités: *Service de conférenciers:* Oui
Membre(s) du bureau directeur:
Ghislaine Brosseau, Directrice générale

Ordre professionnel des urbanistes du Québec *Voir* Ordre des urbanistes du Québec

Ordres de réglementation des professionnels de la santé de l'Ontario *See* Federation of Health Regulatory Colleges of Ontario

Organic Crop Improvement Association - Alberta Chapter #1 *See* Alberta Organic Producers Association

Organic Crop Improvement Association - New Brunswick (OCIA-NB)
2002 Cedar Camp Rd., South Beach Kings NB E4E 5E7
Tel: 506-433-3935
ocianb@nbnet.nb.ca
Overview: A small provincial organization founded in 1987
Mission: To provide organic certification & crop improvement for New Brunswick farmers
Member of: OCIA International
Affiliation(s): New Brunswick Federation of Agriculture
Staff Member(s): 1; 12 volunteer(s)
Membership: *Fees:* $30; *Member Profile:* Growers both in New Brunswick & northern Maine
Chief Officer(s):
Susan Tyler, Administrator

Organic Producers Association of Manitoba Co-operative Inc. (OPAM)
PO Box 279, Miniota MB R0M 1M0
Tel: 204-567-3745; *Fax:* 204-567-3749
info@opam-mb.com
www.opam-mb.com
www.facebook.com/OPAMMB
Overview: A medium-sized provincial organization founded in 1988
Mission: To provide organic certification inspection service to farmers & processors; To teach & promote standards, methods, & techniques for growing, producing & processing organically grown products

Staff Member(s): 1; 20 volunteer(s)
Membership: 881; *Fees:* $25 individual
Activities: Marketing seminars; farm tours; production seminars; AGM

L'Organisation canadienne des physiciens médicaux *See* Canadian Organization of Medical Physicists

L'Organisation des musées militaires du Canada *See* Organization of Military Museums of Canada

Organisation mondiale des personnes handicapées *See* Disabled Peoples' International

Organisation montréalaise des personnes atteintes de cancer inc. *Voir* Organisation multiressources pour les personnes atteintes de cancer

Organisation multiressources pour les personnes atteintes de cancer (OMPAC)
3849, rue Sherbrooke est, Montréal QC H1X 2A3
Tél: 514-729-8833; *Téléc:* 514-729-5390
Ligne sans frais: 866-248-6444
Nom précédent: Organisation montréalaise des personnes atteintes de cancer inc.
Aperçu: *Dimension:* petite; *Envergure:* locale; Organisme sans but lucratif; fondée en 1981
Mission: Apporter aide et assistance aux personnes atteintes de cancer et à leurs proches en offrant des services d'écoute téléphonique, de rencontres individuelles et de groupe, de documentation et de référence, et des activités diverses
Finances: *Budget de fonctionnement annuel:* $250,000-$500,000; *Fonds:* Gouvernement; Centraide
Membre(s) du personnel: 6; 41 bénévole(s)
Membre: 130; *Montant de la cotisation:* $10 individu; *Critères d'admissibilité:* Personnes atteintes de cancer et leurs proches
Membre(s) du bureau directeur:
Colette Coudé, Directrice générale

Organisation nationale des femmes immigrantes et des femmes appartenant à une minorité visible du Canada *See* National Organization of Immigrant & Visible Minority Women of Canada

Organisation ontarienne pour la cybernétique en éducation *See* Educational Computing Organization of Ontario

Organisation pour le tourisme étudiant au Québec et Fédération québécoise d'ajisme *Voir* Fondation Tourisme Jeunesse

L'Organisation pour les carrières en environnement du Canada *See* Environmental Careers Organization of Canada

Organisation québécoise des personnes atteintes de cancer (OQPAC)
#100, 110 - 10e rue, Limoilou QC G1L 2M4
Tél: 418-529-1425; *Téléc:* 418-529-9714
info@oqpac.com
www.oqpac.com
www.facebook.com/99211283481
Aperçu: *Dimension:* petite; *Envergure:* provinciale; Organisme sans but lucratif; fondée en 1984
Membre: *Montant de la cotisation:* 10$
Membre(s) du bureau directeur:
Martin Côté, Directeur général

Organisme canadien de réglementation du commerce des valeurs mobilières *See* Investment Industry Regulatory Organization of Canada

Organisme communautaire des services aux immigrants d'Ottawa *See* Ottawa Community Immigrant Services Organization

Organisme d'autoréglementation du courtage immobilier du Québec (OACIQ) / Québec Real Estate Association
#2200, 4905, boul Lapinière, Brossard QC J4Z 0G2
Tél: 450-676-4800; *Téléc:* 450-676-5801
Ligne sans frais: 800-440-5110
www.oaciq.com
Aperçu: *Dimension:* grande; *Envergure:* provinciale
Mission: Protéger le public par l'encadrement des activités professionnelles de tous les courtiers et agents immobiliers exerçant au Québec
Membre: *Comités:* Éthique; évaluation du président et chef de la direction et du syndic; inspection; discipline; liaison; vérification et des finances; nominations; étude des infractions criminelles; congrès; formulaires; pratiques professionnelles

Activités: Séances de formation; examens de certification
Membre(s) du bureau directeur:
Serge Brousseau, Président du conseil

Organisme de développement d'affaires commerciales et économiques (ODACE)
924, rue King est, Sherbrooke QC J1G 1E2
Tél: 819-565-7991; *Téléc:* 819-565-3160
info@odace.quebec
www.odace.quebec
www.facebook.com/OdaceQuebec
Nom précédent: Chambre de commerce de Fleurimont
Aperçu: *Dimension:* petite; *Envergure:* locale; Organisme sans but lucratif; fondée en 1998
Mission: Assurer un développement économique prospère dans le grand Sherbrooke et générer des retombées sur l'ensemble du territoire de la ville de Sherbrooke
Membre(s) du personnel: 2
Membre: 350; *Montant de la cotisation:* Barème; *Critères d'admissibilite:* Gens d'affaires
Activités: Gala souper; déjeuner conférence
Membre(s) du bureau directeur:
Louis Longchamps, Directeur général

The Organization for Bipolar Affective Disorder (OBAD)
1019 - 7th Ave. SW, Calgary AB T2P 1A8
Tel: 403-263-7408
Toll-Free: 866-263-7408
obad@obad.ca
www.obad.ca
Overview: A medium-sized national charitable organization
Mission: To assist people affected directly or indirectly by bipolar disorder, depression, & anxiety
Chief Officer(s):
Kaj Korvela, Executive Director

Organization for Quality Education *See* Society for Quality Education

Organization of Book Publishers of Ontario *See* Ontario Book Publishers Organization

Organization of Canadian Nuclear Industries (OCNI)
#219, 1550 Kingston Rd., Pickering ON L1V 1C3
Tel: 905-839-0073; *Fax:* 905-839-7085
hello@ocni.ca
www.oci-aic.org
www.linkedin.com/company-beta/880494
www.facebook.com/623976057618324
twitter.com/theoci
www.youtube.com/user/OCINuclear
Previous Name: Organization of CANDU Industries
Overview: A medium-sized national organization founded in 1979
Mission: To promote the Canadian nuclear industry for the benefit of its members & to offer services that enable members to be successful in the domestic & global nuclear industry
Affiliation(s): Atomic Energy of Canada
Finances: *Annual Operating Budget:* Less than $50,000; *Funding Sources:* Membership dues
Staff Member(s): 3
Membership: 105; *Fees:* Schedule available; *Member Profile:* Manufacturing & engineering companies engaged in supply of goods & services for nuclear steam plants; *Committees:* Governance; Audit; Compensations & Performance; Elections & Nomination
Activities: *Awareness Events:* CNL Suppliers Day
Chief Officer(s):
Ron Oberth, President & CEO
ron.oberth@oci-aic.org

Organization of CANDU Industries *See* Organization of Canadian Nuclear Industries

Organization of Military Museums of Canada (OMMC) / L'Organisation des musées militaires du Canada
PO Box 2204, 2513 Beacon Ave., Sidney BC V8L 3S8
Tel: 250-654-0244
ommcinc2@gmail.com
www.ommcinc.ca
Overview: A medium-sized national charitable organization founded in 1967
Mission: To preserve the military heritage of Canada by encouraging the establishment & operation of military museums; To educate museum staff & cooperate with others having the same or similar purposes

Canadian Associations / Organization of Saskatchewan Arts Councils (OSAC)

Member of: Canadian Museums Association
Affiliation(s): Department of National Defence/Director of History & Heritage; Friends of the Canadian War Museum; Military Collectors Club of Canada
Finances: *Annual Operating Budget:* $100,000-$250,000; *Funding Sources:* Membership dues; DND support
Staff Member(s): 3; 10 volunteer(s)
Membership: 200+ individuals; 100+ museums; *Fees:* $40; *Member Profile:* Individuals & organizations with an interest in military museums, artifacts & history; *Committees:* Long-Range Planning; Bursary
Activities: Educating museum staff through lectures, discussions, workshops, visits, small education grants, publications & exhibits; *Speaker Service:* Yes; *Library:* Canadian War Museum Library; Not open to public
Chief Officer(s):
Léon Chamois, President
David Stinson, Secretary
Anne Lindsay-MacLeod, Vice President
Richard Ruggle, Treasurer

Organization of Saskatchewan Applied Economic Research
See Saskatchewan Economics Association

Organization of Saskatchewan Arts Councils (OSAC)
1102 - 8th Ave., Regina SK S4R 1C9
Tel: 306-586-1250; *Fax:* 306-586-1550
info@osac.ca
www.osac.ca
www.facebook.com/OSACsask
twitter.com/OSACsask
instagram.com/osacsask
Overview: A medium-sized provincial charitable organization founded in 1968
Mission: To assist the membership in their endeavors to develop, promote & present the visual arts &/or performing arts
Member of: SaskCulture Inc.
Finances: *Funding Sources:* Saskatchewan Lotteries; Sponsorship; Fundraising; Sask Arts Board; Donations; Canadian Heritage
Staff Member(s): 7
Membership: 50 full + 75 associate; *Fees:* $200 full; $30 associate; *Member Profile:* Arts councils & School centre associates
Activities: Offering concerts & showcases; Participating in community events; *Library:* Not open to public
Chief Officer(s):
Kevin Korchinski, Executive Director, 306-586-1220
kevin@osac.ca
Meetings/Conferences:
• Organization of Saskatchewan Arts Councils Showcase 2018, October, 2018, SK
Scope: Provincial

Orienteering Association of British Columbia (OABC)
1428 Edinburgh St., New Westminster BC V3M 2W4
www.orienteeringbc.ca
Overview: A small provincial organization
Member of: Sport BC; Orienteering Canada
Affiliation(s): Canadian Orienteering Federation (COF); Coaching Association of Canada
Activities: Offering technical coaching courses in orienteering; *Awareness Events:* National Orienteering Week
Chief Officer(s):
John Rance, President
rance1@shaw.ca

Orienteering Association of Nova Scotia (OANS)
5516 Spring Garden Rd., 4th Fl., Halifax NS B3J 1G6
Tel: 902-446-2295
info@orienteerings.ca
www.orienteerings.ca
Overview: A small provincial organization founded in 1971
Mission: To operate as the governing body for orienteering in Nova Scotia; To train & certify orienteering coaches, officials, & mapmakers
Member of: Canadian Orienteering Federation; Sport Nova Scotia
Membership: *Committees:* Mapping; Technical & Competition; Education; Promotion; Finance; Junior Development
Activities: Coordinating local club activities; Publishing event results; Promoting orienteering; Providing programs in map, compass, & wilderness navigation skills, introductory skills, & junior development; Preparing orienteering maps
Chief Officer(s):
Ashley Harding, President
ashleyaharding@hotmail.com
Ian Clark, Vice-President
clark@eastlink.ca
Dale Ellis, Treasurer
dale.ellis@ns.sympatico.ca

Orienteering New Brunswick (ONB)
c/o Robert Hughes, 69 Kingsclear Dr., Upper Kingsclear NB E3E 1R6
www.orienteering.nb.ca
www.facebook.com/OrienteeringNB
Overview: A small provincial organization founded in 1975
Mission: To promote, develop & encourage the sport & recreation of orienteering in New Brunswick
Member of: Canadian Orienteering Federation
Affiliation(s): International Orienteering Federation
Finances: *Annual Operating Budget:* Less than $50,000
Membership: *Fees:* $15 adult; $10 junior (under 20 years old); $50 family/group; *Member Profile:* Family groups; individuals; cadets & scouts
Activities: Competitive & recreational orienteering
Chief Officer(s):
Robert Hughes, Secretary
rustics@nb.sympatico.ca

Orienteering Ontario Inc.
ON
info@orienteeringontario.ca
www.orienteeringontario.ca
Also Known As: Ontario Orienteering Association, Inc.
Overview: A small provincial licensing organization founded in 1975
Mission: To encourage, promote & give leadership in all aspects of the sport of orienteering & associated activities at local, provincial & national levels
Member of: Canadian Orienteering Federation
Membership: *Fees:* Schedule available
Chief Officer(s):
Chris Laughren, President

Orienteering Québec (OQ) / Fédération québécoise de course d'orientation
QC
orientering_quebec@orienteringquebec.ca
www.orienteringquebec.ca
Overview: A small provincial charitable organization founded in 1967
Member of: Canadian Orienteering Federation (COF); International Orienteering Federation (IOF)
Affiliation(s): Ramblers Orienteering Club; Lou Garou Orienteering Club; Ottawa Orienteering Club
Finances: *Funding Sources:* Members
Activities: Organizing events; Posting event results; Coordinating club activities; mapping
Chief Officer(s):
Isabelle Robert, President
liriel@sympatico.ca
Paul Dubois, Vice-President
dubpaul@gmail.com
Bill Meldrum, Treasurer
bill.meldrum@videotron.ca
Publications:
• OQ Newsletter
Type: Newsletter; *Frequency:* Quarterly; *Price:* Free with memship in Orienteering Québec

Original Hockey Hall of Fame & Museum
Invista Centre, 1350 Gardiners Rd., 2nd Fl., Kingston ON K7L 4V6
Tel: 613-507-1943
info@originalhockeyhalloffame.com
www.originalhockeyhalloffame.com
www.facebook.com/207141552735961
twitter.com/ihhof43
Previous Name: International Hockey Hall of Fame & Museum; International Ice Hockey Federation Museum Inc.
Overview: A small local organization founded in 1943
Mission: The first sports hall of fame in Canada, the Hall features exhibits on the original six NHL teams, Kingston native Don Cherry & historic hockey artifacts
Finances: *Funding Sources:* Provincial government grants; special events; museum
Activities: *Awareness Events:* Historic Hockey Series, 1st Sat. in Feb.
Chief Officer(s):
Mark Potter, President
mpotter1@cogeco.ca
Larry Paquette, Vice-President
ihhof@kos.net

Orillia & District Chamber of Commerce
150 Front St. South, Orillia ON L3V 4S7
Tel: 705-326-4424; *Fax:* 705-327-7841
www.orillia.com
Overview: A small local organization founded in 1890
Mission: To operate as a cohesive force for business interests; To represent & promote Orillia & district businesses to government, community interest groups, businesses, & other Chambers of Commerce; To provide membership services
Affiliation(s): Canadian Chamber of Commerce
Finances: *Annual Operating Budget:* $500,000-$1.5 Million
Staff Member(s): 10
Membership: 600; *Fees:* $165
Chief Officer(s):
Susan Lang, Managing Director
Awards:
• Business Achievement Awards

Orillia & District Construction Association
PO Box 235, Orillia ON L3V 6J3
Tel: 705-326-1844
www.orilliaconstruction.ca
www.linkedin.com/company/2814901?trk=tyah&trkInfo=tas%3Aorillia%20const%2Cidx%3A-1-1
www.facebook.com/101221763341770?ref=ts&fref=ts
twitter.com/OrilliaConstruc
Overview: A small local organization founded in 1959
Finances: *Annual Operating Budget:* Less than $50,000; *Funding Sources:* Membership dues
Staff Member(s): 1; 11 volunteer(s)
Membership: 74 corporate; *Fees:* $295; $225 affiliate
Activities: Golf tournament; night at the Georgian Downs Raceway; boat cruise; family Xmas party; *Rents Mailing List:* Yes
Chief Officer(s):
Wayne Rowbotham, President

Orillia Youth Symphony Orchestra (OYSO)
c/o Mayumi Kumagai, 168 Parkview Ave., Orillia ON L3V 4M3
Tel: 702-241-9502
orilliayouthsymphonyorchestra@gmail.com
www.oyso.ca
www.facebook.com/OYSOrchestra
twitter.com/OrilliaOYSO
Overview: A small local charitable organization founded in 1982 overseen by Orchestras Canada
Mission: To offer youth 6-24 years of age to play in a symphonic orchestra; to participate in community events
Member of: Orchestras Canada
Finances: *Funding Sources:* Donations
Membership: *Fees:* $300 junior; $400 intermediate; $500 senior; *Member Profile:* Youth 6-24 years of age who are able to play a symphonic instrument and are interested in symphonic music
Activities: Performing at community events; Regular rehearsals
Chief Officer(s):
Mayumi Kumagai, Music Director

Orléans Chamber of Commerce / Chambre de commerce d'Orléans
#217W, 255 Centrum Blvd., Orléans ON K1E 3W3
Tel: 613-824-9137; *Fax:* 613-824-0090
www.orleanschamber.ca
twitter.com/orleanschamber
www.instagram.com/orleanschamber
Previous Name: Cumberland Chamber of Commerce
Overview: A small local organization founded in 1990
Mission: To act as a focal point for the business community on behalf of members with regard to business, social & political issues; To promote economic, environmental & social well-being of business community; To provide information & education on a variety of subjects of interest to members & community
Member of: Canadian Chamber of Commerce
Affiliation(s): National Capital Business Alliance
Finances: *Annual Operating Budget:* Less than $50,000; *Funding Sources:* Membership dues; luncheons/breakfasts
Staff Member(s): 1; 9 volunteer(s)
Membership: 226; *Fees:* $175-$495; *Committees:* Breakfast Club; Business Excellence Awards; Economic Development; Experience Orléans; Finance; Golf Tournament; Governance; Marketing & Communications; Membership

Activities: Organizing networking luncheons & events; Presenting guest speakers
Chief Officer(s):
Stella Ronan, Manager, Operations

Oro-Medonte Chamber of Commerce (OMCC)
148 Line 7 South, Oro ON L0L 2E0
Tel: 705-487-7337; *Fax:* 705-487-0133
info@oromedontecc.com
www.oromedontecc.com
www.facebook.com/142718922412363
twitter.com/OroMedonteCC
Overview: A small local organization
Mission: To advocate for business in the Oro-Medonte area; To improve the local economy
Member of: Ontario Chamber of Commerce
Membership: 200; *Fees:* $120; *Committees:* Advertising; Events & Fundraising
Activities: Providing networking & trade show opportunities; Providing business promotional items, such as flyers & business cards
Chief Officer(s):
George Wodoslawsky, President
Nadia Fitzgerald, Executive Director
Publications:
• Business / Membership Directory
Type: Directory; *Frequency:* Annually; *Accepts Advertising*
Profile: Contact information & description of services for members of Oro-Medonte Chamber of Commerce
• Chamber Newsletter
Type: Newsletter; *Frequency:* Monthly; *Accepts Advertising*; *Price:* Free for Oro-Medonte Chamber of Commerce members
Profile: Chamber activities, events, & updates from the Ontario Chamber of Commerce
• North Simcoe Community News
Frequency: Bimonthly; *Accepts Advertising*; *Editor:* Anna Proctor
Profile: Information & business opportunities for persons in Oro-Medonte & Severn townships
• Oro-Medonte Guide Map
Accepts Advertising

Oromocto & Area Chamber of Commerce
Oromocto Mall, PO Box 20124, Oromocto NB E2V 2R6
Tel: 506-446-6043; *Fax:* 506-446-6925
oromoctochamber@nb.aibn.com
www.oromoctochamber.com
Overview: A small local organization
Mission: To serve as the voice of the Oromocto area business community
Membership: 80+; *Fees:* $100
Activities: *Awareness Events:* Lunch & Learn Networking Event; Annual Awards Dinner
Chief Officer(s):
Beth Crowell, President

Oromocto & Area SPCA
111 D'Amours St., Oromocto NB E2V 0G5
Tel: 506-446-4107
orphans@oromoctospca.ca
oromoctospca.com
Overview: A small local charitable organization founded in 1973
Mission: To improve the welfare of animals through protection & advocacy
Affiliation(s): New Brunswick SPCA (NBSPCA)
Finances: *Funding Sources:* Membership fees; Donations; Fundraising
Staff Member(s): 4
Membership: *Fees:* $5 student; $10 adult; $25 family; $100 life members; *Member Profile:* Individuals who support the work of the SPCA
Activities: Providing shelter to animals; Finding homes for adoptable animals; Offering educational programs to promote responsible pet ownership & humane attitudes; *Awareness Events:* Pet Photos With Santa, Nov.; Christmas Tree Sale, Dec.
Chief Officer(s):
Tracy Marcotullio, Manager
Publications:
• Oromocto & Area SPCA Newsletter
Type: Newsletter; *Price:* Free for members
Profile: SPCA activities, information, profiles

Oromocto & Surrounding Area Food & Clothing Bank
101 D'Amours St., Oromocto NB E2V 0G5
Tel: 506-357-3461
ofb@nb.aibn.com
www.oromoctofoodbank.ca
www.facebook.com/oromoctofoodbank
Also Known As: Helpline Inc.
Previous Name: Oromocto Food & Clothing Bank
Overview: A small local charitable organization founded in 1987
Mission: To provide services to those in need in Oromocto & the surrounding area
Finances: *Funding Sources:* Donations
Activities: Accepting & distributing donations of food, clothing, & household items; Offering information about local support groups; Maintaining a job bank
Chief Officer(s):
Jane Buckley, Executive Director

Oromocto Food & Clothing Bank *See* Oromocto & Surrounding Area Food & Clothing Bank

Orphan Well Association (OWA)
#1000, 250 - 5th St. SW, Calgary AB T2P 0R4
Tel: 403-297-6416; *Fax:* 403-297-8981
www.orphanwell.ca
Overview: A small provincial organization founded in 2001
Mission: To manage & remediate abandoned upstream oil & gas orphan wells, pipelines, & facilities
Finances: *Funding Sources:* Orphan Fund Levy
Activities: Well abandonment operations & inspections; Pipeline abandonment operations; Decommissioning, winterizing, draining, cleaning, & securing facilities; Site reclamation
Chief Officer(s):
Lars De Pauw, Executive Director, 403-297-3398
lars.depauw@aer.ca
Patricia Payne, Director, Operations, 403-297-8555
pat.payne@aer.ca
Marcia Baker, Office Manager
marcia.baker@aer.ca

ORT Canada
c/o ORT Toronto, #604, 3101 Bathurst St., Toronto ON M6A 2A6
Tel: 416-787-0339; *Fax:* 416-787-9420
Toll-Free: 866-991-3045
info@ort-toronto.org
www.ortcanada.com
www.facebook.com/pages/ORT-Toronto/299243785455
Also Known As: Organization for Educational Resources & Technological Training
Overview: A medium-sized national organization founded in 1942
Mission: To fundraise in support of the worldwide vocational-training-school network of ORT.
Member of: World ORT
Finances: *Annual Operating Budget:* $250,000-$500,000
Staff Member(s): 3
Membership: 10,000+; *Fees:* $36
Chief Officer(s):
Janis Finkelstein, President
Lindy Meshwork, Executive Director

Montréal Office
#250, 5165, ch Queen Mary, Montréal QC H3W 1X7
Tel: 514-481-2787; *Fax:* 514-481-4119
info@ortmontreal.org
www.ortmontreal.org

Orthodox Church in America Archdiocese of Canada (OCA ADOC)
31 Lebreton St. North, Ottawa ON K1R 7H1
Tel: 613-233-7780; *Fax:* 613-233-1931
office@archdiocese.ca
www.archdiocese.ca
Also Known As: Orthodox Church in Canada
Previous Name: Russian Orthodox Greek Catholic Church (Metropolia)
Overview: A medium-sized international organization founded in 1902
Mission: A component of the Orthodox Church in America, an autocephalous (self-governing) church with territorial jurisdiction in Canada, the USA & Mexico; its doctrine & worship are those of the world-wide One Holy Catholic & Apostolic Church
Member of: Canadian Council of Churches; Churches of Manitoba; Orthodox Clergy Association of Québec
Membership: 10,000+
Chief Officer(s):
Irénée Rochon, Archbishop, Ottawa & the Archdiocese of Canada, 450-834-2870
bishopirenee@archdiocese.ca
Anatoliy Melnyk, Chancellor, 514-522-2801
montreal.sobor@gmail.com

Orthophonie et Audiologie Canada *See* Speech-Language & Audiology Canada

Orthotics Prosthetics Canada (OPC)
National Office, #202, 300 March Rd., Ottawa ON K2K 2E2
Tel: 613-595-1919; *Fax:* 613-595-1155
info@opcanada.ca
www.opcanada.ca
Previous Name: Canadian Association of Prosthetists & Orthotists
Merged from: Can. Ass'n for Prosthetics & Orthotics; Can. Board for Certification of Prosthetists & Orthotists
Overview: A medium-sized national organization founded in 1955
Mission: To promote high standards of patient care & professionalism in the prosthetic & orthotic profession throughout Canada; To represent members with government, related organizations, & the general public
Membership: 350+; *Fees:* $70 student; $105 associate/registered technician; $224 full; *Member Profile:* Canadian certified prosthetic & orthotic practitioners; Registered technical members; Associate members, such as suppliers, allied health professionals, or people associated with the prosthetic & orthotic field; Students; Retired persons
Activities: Encouraging continuing education, such as lectures & seminars; Providing educational materials, such as up-to-date medical research
Chief Officer(s):
Dan Mead, President
Dana Cooper, Executive Director
dana@opcanada.ca
Meetings/Conferences:
• Orthotics Prosthetics Canada 2018 National Conference, August, 2018, The Westin Hotel, Ottawa, ON
Scope: National

Osgoode Twp. Historical Society
PO Box 74, 7814 Lawrence St., Vernon ON K0A 3J0
Tel: 613-821-4062; *Fax:* 613-821-3140
manager@osgoodemuseum.ca
www.osgoodemuseum.ca
www.facebook.com/125725207465630
twitter.com/OsgoodeMuseum
Overview: A small local charitable organization founded in 1972
Mission: To promote, preserve & publicize history in the Township of Osgoode & to foster genealogical research
Member of: Ontario Historical Society
Affiliation(s): Ontario Geneology Society; Ontario Museum Association; Archives Association of Ontario
Finances: *Funding Sources:* Provincial, municipal grants; Heritage Ontario; Ontario Lotteries Corp.; City of Ottawa
Staff Member(s): 3
Membership: *Fees:* $15; *Member Profile:* Interest in local history
Activities: Open House; Heritage Day; Pioneer Day/Genorama/Outreach Community; *Library:* Museum Archives; Open to public
Chief Officer(s):
Gary Briggs, President
Ann Robinson, Administrator

Oshawa & District Coin Club
Oshawa ON
Tel: 905-728-1352
papman@bell.net
www.oshawacoinclub.com
Overview: A small local organization founded in 1960
Affiliation(s): Ontario Numismatic Association; Canadian Numismatic Association
Membership: *Fees:* $8
Activities: Providing education about coin & stamp collecting through monthly meetings
Chief Officer(s):
Sharon MacLean, President
Publications:
• The Numismatic Reporter [a publication of the Oshawa & District Coin Club]
Type: Newsletter

Oshawa & District Labour Council *See* Durham Regional Labour Council

Oshawa & District Real Estate Board *See* Durham Region Association of REALTORS

Oshawa / Clarington Association for Community Living See Community Living Oshawa / Clarington

Oshawa Historical Society
1450 Simcoe St. South, Oshawa ON L1H 8S8
Tel: 905-436-7624
membership@oshawamuseum.org
www.oshawahistoricalsociety.org
www.facebook.com/OshawaMuseum
twitter.com/oshawamuseum
Overview: A small local organization founded in 1957
Mission: To research, record, retain, & preserve historical information about Oshawa, Ontario; To provide historical research material, such as newspapers on microfilm, a photograph collection, & local history books
Finances: Funding Sources: Donations; Membership fees; City of Oshawa
Membership: Fees: $5 students; $20 individuals; $25 families & community organizations; $30 corporations; $300 life memberships
Activities: Administering the Oshawa Community Museum & Archives; Disseminating information about the history of the area through publications & presentations; Providing curriculum linked educational programs; Speaker Service: Yes; Library: Oshawa Community Museum & Archives Reference Library; Open to public
Chief Officer(s):
Laura Suchan, Executive Director
director@oshawamuseum.org
Publications:
• Historical Happenings
Type: Newsletter; Frequency: Quarterly; Price: Free e-newsletter for members of the Oshawa Historical Society; $5 hard copy format

Oshawa Symphony See Ontario Philharmonic

Oshawa/Clarington Chamber of Commerce See Greater Oshawa Chamber of Commerce

Oshawa-Durham Rape Crisis Centre (ODRCC)
PO Box 567, Stn. Main, Whitby ON L1N 5V3
Tel: 905-444-9672; Fax: 905-444-9277; Crisis Hot-Line: 905-668-9200
info@drcc.ca
www.drcc.ca
Overview: A small local charitable organization overseen by Canadian Association of Sexual Assault Centres
Mission: To provide counselling to those who are survivors of incest, sexual assault/sexual harassment
Affiliation(s): Ontario Coalition of Rape Crisis Centres
Finances: Annual Operating Budget: $250,000-$500,000
Staff Member(s): 6; 22 volunteer(s)
Activities: Counselling; crisis intervention; public education; volunteer training; children's program for sexual assault/abuse victims; Awareness Events: Take Back the Night; Library: Open to public by appointment

Oshawa-Whitby Kiwanis Music & Theatre Festival
PO Box 10017, 910 Dundas St. West, Whitby ON L1P 1P7
Tel: 905-430-1455
info@oshawawhitbykifest.ca
www.oshawawhitbykifest.ca
Also Known As: Kifest
Overview: A small local charitable organization founded in 1972
Mission: To organize an adjudicated event for youth to present their musical & theatrical talents; to encourage youth creativity
Member of: Ontario Music Festivals' Association
Finances: Funding Sources: Admissions; Donations; Sponsorships
Activities: Presenting an annual festival; Awarding scholarships
Chief Officer(s):
John Chave, Chair
Tina-Marie Schaaf, Festival Coordinator

Oshki Anishnawbeg Student Association
Confederation College, Student Union, PO Box 398, Thunder Bay ON P7C 4W1
Tel: 807-475-6314; Fax: 807-473-5160
succi.com/oasa
Previous Name: Confederation College Aboriginal Student Association
Overview: A small local organization
Mission: To provide a supportive environment that facilitates Indigenous inclusion in post-secondary education, fosters personal growth and furthers Indigenous contributions to Canadian society.

9 volunteer(s)
Chief Officer(s):
Mariah Wigwas, President
mwigwas@confederationc.on.ca

Osoyoos & District Arts Council
PO Box 256, 8713 Main St., Osoyoos BC V0H 1V0
Tel: 250-495-7968
jwhit@persona.ca
www.osoyoosarts.com
www.facebook.com/OsoyoosArtsCouncil
Overview: A small local charitable organization founded in 1981
Mission: To increase & broaden the opportunities for residents of Osoyoos & area to enjoy & participate in cultural activities
Member of: BC Arts Councils; BC Touring Council; Art Gallery of South Okanagan; Thompson/Okanagan Network of Arts Councils; Assembly of BC Arts Council
Finances: Annual Operating Budget: $50,000-$100,000; Funding Sources: Fundraising; government grants; donations; membership fees
70 volunteer(s)
Membership: 60; Fees: $10 individual; $15 non-profit group; $25 business; Committees: Art Gallery; Membership; Fundraising; Street Banner Project; Christmas Light-Up; Osoy Concerts
Activities: Operate art gallery; concert series; help coordinate community arts & cultural events; fundraising; provide street banners to town; Awareness Events: Arts & Culture Week
Chief Officer(s):
Sue Whittaker, President
swhit@persona.ca
Awards:
• Dorothy Fraser Award for Piano
Given to a student who obtains the highest marks in any Canadian Board Examination for the current year
• Christmas Light-Up Awards
Best Business; Best Residence; 2nd & 3rd for Best Residence
• Music Scholarships for Highest Marks
Grades I-III; Grades IV-VI; Grades VII & up
• Fine Arts Scholarships
Given to a graduating student who plans to continue his/her education in Fine Arts

Osoyoos Desert Society (ODS)
PO Box 123, Osoyoos BC V0H 1V0
Tel: 250-495-2470
Toll-Free: 877-899-0897
mail@desert.org
www.desert.org
Also Known As: Desert Centre, Osoyoos
Overview: A small local charitable organization founded in 1991
Mission: To conserve the endangered desert environment, featuring unique plants &animals, located in the south of British Columbia's Okanagan Valley
Finances: Funding Sources: Western Diversification Canada; McLean's Foundation; BC Gaming Commission; Citizen's Bank of Canada; Town of Osoyoos; Osoyoos Golf & Country Club
Membership: Fees: $20
Activities: Conducting research; Restoring the Antelope-brush ecosystem; Increasing public awareness; Providing education; Operating the Desert Centre; Speaker Service: Yes
Chief Officer(s):
Denise Eastlick, Executive Director
Publications:
• Desert Society News
Type: Newsletter; Price: Free for members
Profile: Society reports, upcoming events, species profiles, conservation updates, & volunteer news
• Native Plant Landscaping for The South Okanagan Similkameen
Type: Booklet; Number of Pages: 32; Author: Tamara Bonnemaison

Osoyoos Food Bank
6210 - 97th St., Osoyoos BC V0H 1V4
Tel: 250-495-6581; Fax: 250-495-8011
Overview: A small local organization overseen by Food Banks British Columbia
Member of: Food Banks British Columbia
Chief Officer(s):
Lu Ahrendt, Contact
rlahrendt@live.ca

Ostéoporose Canada See Osteoporosis Canada

Osteoporosis Canada / Ostéoporose Canada
#500, 1200 Eglinton Ave. East, Toronto ON M3C 1H9

Tel: 416-696-2663; Fax: 416-696-2673
Toll-Free: 800-463-6842
www.osteoporosis.ca
www.linkedin.com/company/2610844
www.facebook.com/osteoporosiscanada
twitter.com/OsteoporosisCA
www.youtube.com/osteoporosisca
Previous Name: Osteoporosis Society of Canada
Overview: A large national charitable organization founded in 1982
Mission: To encourage research into the prevention, diagnosis, & treatment of osteoporosis; To improve access to osteoporosis care & support
Member of: Canadian Coalition for Genetic Fairness
Finances: Funding Sources: Donations; Fundraising
Membership: Fees: $25; $45 outside Canada
Activities: Promoting awareness; Engaging in advocacy activities; Providing educational materials related to osteoporosis; Offering support groups; Speaker Service: Yes
Chief Officer(s):
Famida Jiwa, President & CEO
Publications:
• Osteoblast [a publication of Osteoporosis Canada]
Type: Newsletter; Frequency: 3 pa; Price: Free for members
Profile: Scientifically based information on osteoporosis & Osteoporosis Canada activities, for members & donors

Calgary - Alberta Chapter
Bldg. B8, Currie Barracks, #104, 2526 Battleford Ave. SW, Calgary AB T3E 7J4
Tel: 403-237-7022; Fax: 403-220-1727
alberta@osteoporosis.ca
Chief Officer(s):
Chloe Kilkenny, Contact

Dartmouth - Nova Scotia Chapter
#206, 44 - 46 Portland St., Dartmouth NS B2Y 1H4
Tel: 902-407-4053
novascotia@osteoporosis.ca
Chief Officer(s):
Charmaine Hollett, Chair

Hamilton - Hamilton-Burlington Chapter
75 MacNab St. South, Hamilton ON L8P 3C1
Tel: 905-525-5398; Fax: 905-577-0396
hamilton@osteoporosis.ca
Chief Officer(s):
Juanita Gledhill, Chair
• Osteoporosis Canada, Hamilton-Burlington Chapter Newsletter
Type: Newsletter; Frequency: Semiannually

Kelowna Chapter
PO Box 21072, Stn. Orchard Park, Kelowna BC V1Y 9N8
Tel: 250-861-6880
kelowna@osteoporosis.ca
Chief Officer(s):
Trish Gunning, Chair

Laval - Greater Montreal Chapter
274, rue Antoine Forestier, Laval QC H7M 6B9
Tel: 514-212-5549
Toll-Free: 800-977-1778
montreal@osteoporosis.ca

London - London & Thames Valley Chapter
PO Box 32017, London ON N5V 5K4
Tel: 519-457-0624; Fax: 519-457-0624
london-thamesvalley@osteoporosis.ca
Chief Officer(s):
Joanne Legros-Kelly, Chair

Mid-Island Chapter
110 Moss Ave., #B, Parksville BC V9P 1L5
Tel: 250-951-0243; Fax: 250-951-0343
mid-island@osteoporosis.ca
Chief Officer(s):
Lisa Leger, Chair

Mississauga Chapter
c/o/ #76, 6797 Formentera Ave., Mississauga ON L5N 2L6
Tel: 416-696-2663
mississauga@osteoporosis.ca
Chief Officer(s):
Bev Nickle, Chair
Elizabeth St. Onge, Chair

Moncton - Greater Moncton Chapter
Moncton NB
greatermoncton@osteoporosis.ca
Chief Officer(s):
Linda Hopper, Chair

Peterborough Chapter
PO Box 373, Stn. Main, Peterborough ON K9J 6Z3

Tel: 705-740-2776
peterborough@osteoporosis.ca
Chief Officer(s):
Heather Drysdale, Chair
Québec - Québec City Chapter
#100, 1200, av Germain-des-Prés, Québec QC G1V 3M7
Tél: 418-651-8661; *Téléc:* 418-650-3916
Ligne sans frais: 800-977-1778
sectiondequebec@osteoporosecanada.ca
Regina Chapter
90C Cavendish St., Regina SK S4N 5G7
Tel: 306-757-2663; *Fax:* 306-789-2663
regina@osteoporosis.ca
Chief Officer(s):
Sylvia Fiske, Chair
St. Catharines - Niagara Chapter
264 Welland Ave., St Catharines ON L2R 5P8
Tel: 905-685-1225
niagara@osteoporosis.ca
Chief Officer(s):
Phyllis Kerkhoven, Chair
Saskatoon Chapter
PO Box 25179, Stn. River Heights, Saskatoon SK S7K 8B7
Tel: 306-931-2663; *Fax:* 306-249-9065
saskatoon@osteoporosis.ca
Chief Officer(s):
Carole Young, Chair
Surrey / White Rock Chapter
#207, 1558 - 1st St., White Rock BC V4B 4B7
Tel: 604-538-2500
surrey-whiterock@osteoporosis.ca
Chief Officer(s):
Margaret Willson, Chair
Winnipeg - Manitoba Chapter
123 St. Anne's Rd., Winnipeg MB R2M 2Z1
Tel: 204-772-3498; *Fax:* 204-772-4200
manitoba@osteoporosis.ca
Chief Officer(s):
Cherylle Unryn, Chair

Osteoporosis Society of Canada *See* Osteoporosis Canada

Ostomy Canada Society
#210, 5800 Ambler Dr., Mississauga ON L4W 4J4
Tel: 905-212-7111; *Fax:* 905-212-9002
Toll-Free: 888-969-9698
info1@ostomycanada.ca
www.ostomycanada.ca
www.linkedin.com/company/united-ostomy-association-of-canada-inc-
www.facebook.com/OstomyCanada
twitter.com/OstomyCanada
www.youtube.com/user/ostomycanada
Previous Name: United Ostomy Association of Canada
Overview: A medium-sized national charitable organization founded in 1997
Mission: To assist all persons with gastrointestinal or urinary diversions, as well as their families & caregivers, by providing emotional & practical support & help, information & instruction
Affiliation(s): United Ostomy Association - USA
Finances: *Funding Sources:* Annual fundraising drive
Membership: *Fees:* $39 national; $42 international; $50 health care professional; $150 corporate; *Member Profile:* Member chapters; *Committees:* Advocacy; Finance & Fundraising; Governance; Marketing & Communication; Outreach
Activities: Operating 46 chapters across Canada; *Awareness Events:* World Ostomy Day; *Library:* by appointment
Chief Officer(s):
Ann Ivol, President
Carol Wells, Secretary
Meetings/Conferences:
• 16th Ostomy Canada Society National Conference, 2018
Scope: National

Ottawa & District Foster Parent Association *See* Foster Parents Association of Ottawa

Ottawa & District Labour Council (ODLC) / Conseil du travail d'Ottawa et du district
#500, 280 Metcalfe St., Ottawa ON K2P 1R7
Tel: 613-233-7820; *Fax:* 613-230-8404
www.ottawalabour.org
twitter.com/ottawalabour
Overview: A small local organization founded in 1872 overseen by Ontario Federation of Labour
Mission: To act as the voice of workers in the Ottawa area; To carry out the policies of the Canadian Labour Congress & the Ontario Federation of Labour in Ottawa
Affiliation(s): Ontario Federation of Labour (OFL); Amalgamated Transit Union; AFM; CAW; CUPE; CUPW; CUASA; CEP; Hospitality & Service Trades Union; IATSE; IBEW; OECTA; OPSEU; OSSTF; OCETF; ONG; PSAC; Service Employees International Union; Ottawa Steel Plate Feeders and Examiners; UBCJA; United Steelworkers
Membership: 55,000 workers from 90 unions; *Committees:* Political Municipal Affairs; Women's; Human Rights; Health, Safety & the Environment; International Solidarity; Education
Activities: Liaising with municipal governments; *Awareness Events:* Labour Day March; Day of Mourning, April 28

Ottawa Arts Council (OAC) / Conseil des arts d'Ottawa
Arts Ct., 2 Daly Ave., Ottawa ON K1N 6E2
Tel: 613-569-1387
info@ottawaartscouncil.ca
www.ottawaartscouncil.ca
www.facebook.com/OttawaArtsCouncil
twitter.com/CAOOttawa
Previous Name: Council for the Arts in Ottawa
Overview: A small local organization founded in 1982
Mission: To encourage & develop an appreciation for the arts in the Ottawa region
Finances: *Annual Operating Budget:* $50,000-$100,000
Membership: *Fees:* $10 student; $20 individual; $50 patron; $50-$150 arts group; $250 corporate; $1000 sponsorship patron
Chief Officer(s):
Peter Honeywell, Executive Director
peter@ottawaartscouncil.ca
Zoë Ashby, Creative Director
zoe@ottawaartscouncil.ca
Awards:
• Ottawa Arts Council Mid-Career Artist Award
• Victor Tolgesy Arts Award
• RBC Emerging Artist Award
• Business and the Arts Recognition Award

Ottawa Association of People Who Stutter (OAPWS)
Lakeside Gardens Centre, Britannia Park, 102 Greenview Ave., Ottawa ON K2B 5Z6
Tel: 613-226-7001
admin@oapws.ca
oapws.ca
Overview: A small local organization
Mission: A local support groups for people who stutter.

Ottawa Baptist Association (OBA)
249 Bronson Ave., Ottawa ON K1R 6H6
Tel: 613-235-7617
www.ottawabaptist.org
Overview: A small local organization founded in 1836 overseen by Canadian Baptists of Ontario and Quebec
Member of: Canadian Baptists of Ontario & Quebec
Affiliation(s): Canadian Baptist Ministries; Baptist World Alliance
Membership: 20 churches; *Member Profile:* Baptist churches in Ottawa
Chief Officer(s):
Hugh Willet, Executive Secretary
hwillett@sympatico.ca

Ottawa Builder's Exchange *See* Ottawa Construction Association

Ottawa Carleton Ultimate Association (OCUA)
#1, 875 Banks St., Ottawa ON K1S 3W4
Tel: 613-860-6282
info@ocua.ca
www.ocua.ca
www.facebook.com/ocua.ca
twitter.com/ocua
Overview: A medium-sized local organization founded in 1993
Mission: To promote ultimate & disc sports in the Ottawa-Carleton region
Staff Member(s): 3
Activities: Organizing & conducting the operations of leagues & tournaments; Operating a multi-field sports facility designed for ultimate
Chief Officer(s):
Christiane Marceau, Executive Director
ed@ocua.ca
Christopher Castonguay, Program Officer
christopher@ocua.ca
Nevan Sullivan, Program Officer, Youth & Junior
nevan@ocua.ca
Publications:
• Ultimate Happenings
Type: Newsletter; *Editor:* Catharina Israel
Profile: News about ultimate in Ottawa & league events & issues

Ottawa Centre for Research & Innovation; Ottawa Carleton Research Institute *See* Invest Ottawa

Ottawa Chamber of Commerce (OCC)
328 Somerset St. West, Ottawa ON K2P 0J9
Tel: 613-236-3631; *Fax:* 613-236-7498
www.ottawachamber.ca
www.facebook.com/ottawachamberofcommerce
twitter.com/ottawachamber
Previous Name: Ottawa-Carleton Board of Trade
Overview: A medium-sized local organization founded in 1857
Mission: To provide leadership in the community to enhance economic prosperity & quality of life
Member of: Ontario Chamber of Commerce; Canadian Chamber of Commerce
Finances: *Funding Sources:* Membership fees; Programs; Events; Services
50 volunteer(s)
Membership: 750; *Fees:* Schedule available; *Committees:* Ambassador Corps; Economic Development; Environment & Sustainability; Membership; Policy & Advocacy
Chief Officer(s):
Ian Faris, President & CEO, 613-236-3631 Ext. 125
ian.faris@ottawachamber.ca
Alexandra Walsh, Director, Membership Services, 613-236-3631 Ext. 127
alexandra.walsh@ottawachamber.ca
Kenny Leon, Director, Communications, 613-236-3631 Ext. 130
kenny.leon@ottawachamber.ca
Awards:
• Annual Business Achievement Award

Ottawa Chamber Orchestra (OCO)
2356 Keystone Court, Ottawa ON K1W 1A8
www.ottawachamberorchestra.ca
www.facebook.com/OttawaChamberOrchestra
twitter.com/OttChamberOrch
Overview: A small local charitable organization founded in 1992 overseen by Orchestras Canada
Mission: To share masterpieces of symphonic music with audiences from Ottawa & surrounding area
Finances: *Funding Sources:* Donations; Program advertisements
Membership: *Fees:* $175; *Member Profile:* Advanced music students, semi-professional musicians, serious amateur musicians from Ottawa & surrounding area
Chief Officer(s):
Donnie Deacon, Musical Director

Ottawa Chinese Community Services Centre (OCCSC)
#4004, 381 Kent St., Ottawa ON K2P 2A8
Tel: 613-232-4875; *Fax:* 613-235-5466
occsc@occsc.org
www.occsc.org
www.facebook.com/ottawachinese
twitter.com/chineseottawa
Overview: A small local charitable organization founded in 1975 overseen by Ontario Council of Agencies Serving Immigrants
Mission: To advance the full social & economic integration of newcomers into the mainsteam society in the Ottawa-Carleton region
Finances: *Funding Sources:* Citizenship & Immigration Canada; Ontario Ministry of Citizenship; City of Ottawa
Staff Member(s): 37
Membership: *Fees:* $10 regular; $5 senior; *Committees:* Personnel; Governance; Executive; Finance; Fundraising
Activities: Settlement & integration of newcomers; orientation workshops; counselling services; ESL classes; special needs groups; income tax filing services; job search workshop; mental health support
Chief Officer(s):
Sharon Kan, Executive Director
sharon.kan@occsc.org

Ottawa Coin Club *See* Ottawa Numismatic Society

Canadian Associations / Ottawa Community Immigrant Services Organization (OCISO) / Organisme communautaire des services aux immigrants d'Ottawa

Ottawa Community Immigrant Services Organization (OCISO) / Organisme communautaire des services aux immigrants d'Ottawa
959 Wellington St. West, Ottawa ON K1Y 2X5
Tel: 613-725-0202; *Fax:* 613-725-9054
info@ociso.org
www.ociso.org
twitter.com/intent/user?screen_name=OttawaOCISO
www.youtube.com/user/OCISOTV
Overview: A medium-sized local charitable organization founded in 1976
Mission: To enable newcomers & their families to fully participate in an open & welcoming Ottawa, through innovative services, community building & public engagement
Member of: Ontario Council of Agencies Serving Immigrants; Canadian Council for Refugees; Association of United Way Agencies; Local Agencies Serving Immigrants
Finances: *Annual Operating Budget:* $1.5 Million-$3 Million; *Funding Sources:* Government; United Way
Staff Member(s): 72; 278 volunteer(s)
Membership: 291; *Fees:* $25 individual; $30 not-for-profit; $65 other organization; $10 seniors/unwaged; *Member Profile:* Over 18 years old & supports our mission; *Committees:* Programs; Finance; Resource Development
Activities: Provides assistance to newcomers, agencies & institutions serving immigrants; Resettlement Service offers immigrants assistance with orientation to life in Canada, access to housing, education, employment & health services; individual advocacy; in-depth information sessions to groups on various themes; Counselling Service offers personal, family & crisis counselling; English language training in two locations; immigrant women's program; public education & communication program; vocational training program; *Awareness Events:* OCISO Gala; *Internships:* Yes; *Speaker Service:* Yes
Chief Officer(s):
Leslie Emory, Executive Director, 613-725-0202 Ext. 307

Ottawa Construction Association (OCA) / L'Association de la construction d'Ottawa
196 Bronson Ave., Ottawa ON K1R 6H4
Tel: 613-236-0488; *Fax:* 613-238-6124
oca@oca.ca
www.oca.ca
www.facebook.com/OttawaConstructionAssociation
twitter.com/ConstructionOtt
Previous Name: Ottawa Builder's Exchange
Overview: A small local organization founded in 1889 overseen by Canadian Construction Association
Mission: To act as the voice of the non-residential construction industry in Ottawa; To promote & maintain industry best practices & high ethical standards
Affiliation(s): Canadian Construction Association; Council of Ontario Construction Associations
Membership: 1,000+
Activities: Promoting suitable legislation that affects the construction industry; Providing networking opportunities; Offering education & training
Chief Officer(s):
John DeVries, President & General Manager
jdv@oca.ca
Publications:
• Who's Who - Buyers Guide
Type: Directory; *Frequency:* Annually; *Price:* Free for OCA members
Profile: Alphabetical & classified listings of members

Ottawa Council of Social Agencies *See* Social Planning Council of Ottawa

Ottawa District Minor Hockey Association (ODMHA)
#300, 1247 Kilborn Pl., Ottawa ON K1H 6K9
Tel: 613-224-3589; *Fax:* 613-224-4625
odmha@odmha.on.ca
www.odmha.on.ca
Overview: A medium-sized local organization founded in 1972
Mission: To promote minor hockey throughout the region
Member of: Hockey Canada
Membership: *Committees:* Development; Discipline & Appeals; Risk & Safety; Rules & Officials; Zoning & Constitution
Activities: *Speaker Service:* Yes; *Library:* Resource Centre; Open to public
Chief Officer(s):
Denis Dumais, President
denisdumais@sympatico.ca

Ottawa Duck Club (ODC)
841 Kinsgmere Ave., Ottawa ON K2A 3J8
www.ottawaduckclub.com
Overview: A small local organization founded in 1966
Mission: To actively improve the nesting habitat for waterfowl and other birds along the Ottawa River.
Membership: *Fees:* $20 individual; $25 family
Chief Officer(s):
Bill Bower, President, 613-824-9104
bigbuckbill@hotmail.com

Ottawa Economics Association (OEA)
PO Box 264, Stn. B, Ottawa ON K1P 6C4
Tel: 613-837-9415
www.cabe.ca/oea
twitter.com/OEAEconomics
Overview: A small local organization founded in 1975 overseen by Canadian Association for Business Economics
Mission: To organize programs of interest to members
Member of: Canadian Association for Business Economics
Finances: *Annual Operating Budget:* Less than $50,000
11 volunteer(s)
Membership: 300; *Fees:* $160 national; $35.40 new professionals; $35.40 retirees; $8.85 students; *Member Profile:* Economists & others with an interest in economics & economic policy
Activities: Luncheons with a public policy theme; Technical workshops; Speaker service; Annual conference
Chief Officer(s):
Brian Kingston, President, 613-288-3855
Jasmin Thomas, Treasurer, 613-233-0268

Ottawa Environmental Law Clinic *See* Ecojustice Canada Society

Ottawa Field-Naturalists' Club (OFNC)
PO Box 35069, Stn. Westgate, Ottawa ON K1Z 1A2
Tel: 613-722-3050
ofnc@ofnc.ca
www.ofnc.ca
Overview: A small local charitable organization founded in 1879
Mission: To promote the preservation & conservation of Canada's natural heritage
Membership: *Fees:* $40 individuals; $45 families; $20 students; *Member Profile:* Individuals who share an interest in nature; *Committees:* Awards; Birds; Conservation; Education & Publicity; Events; Finance; Fletcher Wildlife Garden Management; Macoun Club; Membership; Publications
Activities: Encouraging research in all fields of natural history
Chief Officer(s):
Diane Lepage, President
Awards:
• George McGee Service Award
• Conservation Award - Member
• Conservation Award - Non-Member
• Anne Hanes Natural History Award
• Mary Stuart Education Award
• President's Prize
• Honorary Member
Publications:
• Autobiography of John Macoun, Canadian Explorer & Naturalist, 1831-1920
Price: $10
• A Birder's Checklist of Ottawa
Price: $2
• The Canadian Field-Naturalist
Type: Journal; *ISSN:* 0008-3550
• Checklist of the Butterflies of the Ottawa District
Price: $2
• Larose Forest: A Guide with Species Lists
Price: $4
• Lichens of the Ottawa Region
Price: $5
• Trail & Landscape [a publication of the Ottawa Field-Naturalists' Club]
Type: Newsletter; *Frequency:* Quarterly; *Price:* Free for OFNC members
Profile: Club activities & articles on the natural history of the Ottawa Valley

Ottawa Flute Association (OFA) / Association des flûtistes d'Ottawa
Ottawa ON
www.ottawafluteassociation.com
Overview: A small local organization
Mission: To promote flute playing in Ottawa & the surrounding area
Membership: *Fees:* $20 youth; $40 adults; $100 corporate members; *Member Profile:* Professional & amateur flutists in the Ottawa region
Activities: Organizing classes & workshops; Arranging concerts & events; Providing flute choirs, flute fairs, & flute camps; *Library:* The OFA Library
Chief Officer(s):
Lindsay Foster, President
Publications:
• Ottawa Flute Association Newsletter
Type: Newsletter
Profile: OFA activities & upcoming events

Ottawa Food Bank / La banque d'alimentation d'Ottawa
1317 Michael St., Ottawa ON K1B 3M9
Tel: 613-745-7001; *Fax:* 613-745-7377
foodbank@ottawafoodbank.ca
www.ottawafoodbank.ca
www.facebook.com/OttawaFoodBank
twitter.com/OttawaFoodBank
www.youtube.com/ottawafoodbank
Overview: A small local charitable organization founded in 1984
Mission: To arrange for, collect, process, store, & distribute food to service agencies in the National Capital Region for delivery to the needy
Finances: *Funding Sources:* Donations; Corporate & individual sponsors
Staff Member(s): 23
Membership: *Committees:* Finance & Administration; Warehouse & Operations; Transportation; Communications & Development; Events; Agency Relations; Volunteering; Community Harvest
Activities: *Awareness Events:* Holiday Food Drive, December; Lunch Money Day
Chief Officer(s):
Michael Maidment, Executive Director
michael.maidment@ottawafoodbank.ca

Ottawa Fundraising Executives *See* Association of Fundraising Professionals

Ottawa Humane Society (OHS) / La Société protectrice des animaux d'Ottawa
245 West Hunt Club Rd, Ottawa ON K2E 1A6
Tel: 613-725-3166; *Fax:* 613-725-5674
ohs@ottawahumane.ca
ottawahumane.ca
www.facebook.com/OttawaHumane
twitter.com/ottawahumane
Previous Name: Humane Society of Ottawa-Carleton
Overview: A small local charitable organization founded in 1888
Mission: To provide leadership in the humane treatment of all animals; To give care to neglected, abused, exploited, stray, or homeless animals
Finances: *Annual Operating Budget:* Greater than $5 Million; *Funding Sources:* Donations
Membership: *Fees:* $15 juniors; $25 individuals; $35 schools; $40 families; $500 life memberships
Activities: Encouraging people to take responsibility for their animals, through humane education; Offering programs such as companion animals pet visiting & dog walking; Conducting cruelty investigations; *Awareness Events:* Summer Garden Harvest Party, August; Wiggle Waggle Walkathon, September
Chief Officer(s):
Bruce Roney, Executive Director
Natalie Pona, Manager, Communications, 613-725-3166 Ext. 261
Publications:
• A Legacy for the Animals
Type: Newsletter
Profile: Discussion of legacy giving options
• The OHS Volunteer Connection
Type: Newsletter; *Frequency:* Monthly; *Editor:* Christine Wheeler
Profile: Information for OHS volunteers
• The Ottawa Animal Advocate
Type: Newsletter; *Frequency:* Bimonthly
Profile: Updates on animal welfare in the Ottawa area
• Ottawa Humane Society Annual Report
Type: Yearbook; *Frequency:* Annually
• Our Best Friends
Type: Newsletter; *Frequency:* Quarterly; *Accepts Advertising*; *Editor:* Tara Jackson; *Price:* Free for OHS members

Ottawa Independent Writers (OIW) / Les écrivains indépendants d'Ottawa
PO Box 39016, Ottawa ON K1H 1A1

Tel: 613-841-0572
communicationsoiw@gmail.com
www.ottawaindependentwriters.com
www.linkedin.com/groups?gid=4680889
www.facebook.com/groups/ottawaindependentwriters
twitter.com/OIWgroup
Overview: A small local organization founded in 1986
Mission: To promote writing & writers in Ottawa; To act as the voice of Ottawa writers in areas of legislation, municipal activities, & grants; To provide assistance to writers
Finances: *Annual Operating Budget:* Less than $50,000; *Funding Sources:* Memberships
Staff Member(s): 9
Membership: 130; *Fees:* $30 students; $50 seniors; $75 adults; $135 families; *Member Profile:* All types of writers
Activities: Providing networking & learning opportunities; Offering advice regarding the business of writing, such as finding a publisher & marketing; Organizing monthly meetings, writing retreats, & Prose in the Park summer book fair; *Awareness Events:* Annual Fall Book Fair
Chief Officer(s):
Ian Shaw, President
deuxvoiliers@gmail.com
Bill Horne, Vice-President
wghorne@rogers.com
Darren Jerome, Treasurer
djerome11@gmail.com
Awards:
• Frank Hegyi Award for Emerging Authors
Deadline: January
Publications:
• Capital Letter [a publication of Ottawa Independent Writers]
Frequency: 4-5 pa; *Price:* Free with OIW membership
Profile: Compilation of OIW members' work
• Gems [a publication of Ottawa Independent Writers]
Type: Anthology; *Frequency:* Annually
Profile: Writing contributions from members
• Jewels [a publication of Ottawa Independent Writers]
Type: Anthology
Profile: Writing contributions from members
• OIW [Ottawa Independent Writers] Book Catalogue
Profile: Showcase of books written by OIW members
• OIW [Ottawa Independent Writers] Digest
Type: Newsletter; *Frequency:* Weekly; *Price:* Free with OIW membership
Profile: Information about writing

Ottawa Japanese Community Association Inc. (OJCA)
#B16, 2285 St. Laurent Blvd., Ottawa ON K1G 4Z4
Tel: 613-731-7939; *Fax:* 613-731-1367
ojca_ojcc@yahoo.ca
www.ottawajapanesecommunity.ca
www.facebook.com/ojcaojcc
Overview: A small local organization founded in 1976
Mission: To promote & maintain Japanese heritage in Ottawa
Member of: National Association of Japanese Canadians
Membership: *Fees:* $15 single; $20 family; $10 student/senior
Activities: Arts & Crafts; Cooking Class; Fundraisers

Ottawa Light Car Club *See* Motorsport Club of Ottawa

Ottawa Muslim Association (OMA)
251 Northwestern Ave., Ottawa ON K1Y 0M1
Tel: 613-722-8763
oma@ottawamosque.ca
www.ottawamosque.ca
Overview: A small local charitable organization
Mission: To foster unity among various Muslims; to promote better understanding of Muslims & Islam among Canadians of other faiths; to maintain cultural identity
Activities: Social services; seminars & conferences; *Library:* Open to public
Chief Officer(s):
Naeem Malik, President

Ottawa New Car Dealers Association
400 Slater St., Ottawa ON K1R 7S7
Tel: 613-241-7557
info@oncda.com
www.oncda.com
Overview: A small local organization

Ottawa Numismatic Society / Société numismatique d'Ottawa
PO Box 42004, RPO St. Laurent, Ottawa ON K1K 4L8
Info@ons-sno.ca
www.ons-sno.ca
Previous Name: Ottawa Coin Club
Overview: A small local organization founded in 1891
Member of: Royal Canadian Numismatic Association

Ottawa Orchid Society
221 Glebe Ave., Ottawa ON K1S 2C8
www.ottawaorchidsociety.com
www.facebook.com/196485693713178
Overview: A small local organization founded in 1978
Mission: To promote knowledge, development, improvement, & conservation of orchids
Membership: *Fees:* $25
Activities: Offering programs about the care of orchids; *Awareness Events:* Annual Orchid Show
Chief Officer(s):
Dave Cooper, President
Publications:
• Spike [a publication of the Ottawa Orchid Society]
Type: Newsletter; *Frequency:* Monthly; *Editor:* Aurora Richard

Ottawa Philatelic Society (OPS)
586 David Manchester Rd., Carp ON K0A 1L0
www.ottawaphilatelicsociety.org
Overview: A small local organization founded in 1891
Mission: To promote the study & history of stamps
Member of: Royal Philatelic Society of Canada; American Philatelic Society; American Topical Association
Membership: *Fees:* $40 full; $20 youth
Activities: *Library:* Ottawa Philatelic Society Library; Open to public
Chief Officer(s):
Tom Toomey, Contact
ttoomey@tiplimo.com

Ottawa Police Association (OPA)
#200, 141 Catherine St., Ottawa ON K2P 1C3
Tel: 613-232-9434; *Fax:* 613-232-1044
ottawapa@ottawapa.ca
www.ottawapa.ca
www.facebook.com/OttawaPoliceAssoc
twitter.com/OPA_President
Previous Name: Ottawa-Carleton Regional Police Association
Merged from: Ottawa Police Association; Nepean Police Association; Gloucester Police Association
Overview: A small local organization founded in 1948
Mission: To act as the voice for members at both the provincial & federal levels; To bargain collectively; To raise the standards of police services
Affiliation(s): Police Association of Ontario; Canadian Police Association
Membership: 1,900; *Member Profile:* Police officers; Civilian & Special Constable personnel
Activities: Providing moral support & financial assistance to members in accordance with the association's constitution
Chief Officer(s):
Matt Skof, President

Ottawa Rape Crisis Centre (ORCC)
PO Box 20206, Ottawa ON K1N 9P4
Tel: 613-562-2334; *Fax:* 613-562-2291; *TTY:* 613-562-3860; *Crisis Hot-Line:* 613-562-2333
orcc@orcc.net
www.orcc.net
www.facebook.com/OttawaRapeCrisis
twitter.com/ORCC_Tweets
Overview: A small local charitable organization founded in 1974
Mission: To end all forms of sexual violence to create a safe community; To provide education about sexual violence; To counsel & support those who have experienced sexual violence
Finances: *Funding Sources:* Donations
Membership: *Fees:* $25 annual; $250 lifetime; $50 annual organization; *Member Profile:* All members of the general public, regardless of gender identity, over the age of 18 are eligible for membership
Activities: Providing public education; Offering Girls Chat Groups in Ottawa high schools; Educating youth & children throught the project, Kids on the Block Teach About Sexual Abuse & Sexuality; Providing volunteer training
Chief Officer(s):
Sunny Marriner, Executive Director
sunny@orcc.net
Publications:
• ORCC [Ottawa Rape Crisis Centre] Newsletter
Type: Newsletter

Profile: Reports from Centre coordinators & current events affecting the Centre

Ottawa Real Estate Board (OREB) / Chambre d'immeuble d'Ottawa
1826 Woodward Dr., Ottawa ON K2C 0P7
Tel: 613-225-2240; *Fax:* 613-225-6420
Admin@oreb.ca
www.ottawarealestate.org
twitter.com/OREB1
Overview: A small local organization founded in 1921 overseen by Ontario Real Estate Association
Member of: The Canadian Real Estate Association
Finances: *Funding Sources:* Membership dues
Membership: 2,800; *Member Profile:* Registered brokers & salespeople

Ottawa Riverkeeper / Sentinelle Outaouais
#301, 1960 Scott St., Ottawa ON K1Z 8L8
Tel: 613-321-1120; *Fax:* 613-822-5258
Toll-Free: 888-953-3737
info@ottawariverkeeper.ca
www.ottawariverkeeper.ca
www.facebook.com/ottawa.riverkeeper
twitter.com/ottriverkeeper
www.instagram.com/ottawariverkeeper
Overview: A medium-sized local organization founded in 2001
Mission: To protect and promote the ecological health and diversity of the Ottawa River and its tributaries; To ensure swimmable, fishable, drinkable waterways
Finances: *Annual Operating Budget:* $250,000-$500,000
300 volunteer(s)
Activities: *Speaker Service:* Yes
Chief Officer(s):
Patrick Nadeau, Executive Director, 613-321-1120 Ext. 1007
pnadeau@ottawariverkeeper.ca

Ottawa Safety Council (OSC) / Conseil de sécurité d'Ottawa
#105, 2068 Robertson Rd., Nepean ON K2H 5Y8
Tel: 613-238-1513; *Fax:* 613-238-8744
info@ottawasafetycouncil.ca
www.ottawasafetycouncil.ca
www.facebook.com/OttawaSafetyCouncil
twitter.com/SafetyOttawa
Previous Name: Ottawa-Carleton Safety Council
Overview: A small local charitable organization founded in 1957
Mission: To assist the citizens of Ottawa to protect themselves & others from injury, property destruction due to accidents, & accidental death
Finances: *Annual Operating Budget:* $1.5 Million-$3 Million
Staff Member(s): 10
Activities: Providing safety programs, such as the school guard crossing program, the motorcycle training program, the Children's Safety Village, & a safety education outreach program; Offering a children's summer camp
Chief Officer(s):
Julie Vogt, Interim Executive Director, 613-238-1513 Ext. 223
julie.vogt@ottawasafetycouncil.ca
Publications:
• Ottawa Safety Council Newsletter
Type: Newsletter
Profile: Council reports & program updates

Ottawa South Community Association (OSCA)
Old Firehall, 260 Sunnyside Ave., Ottawa ON K1S 0R7
Tel: 613-247-4872
osca@oldottawasouth.ca
www.oldottawasouth.ca
www.facebook.com/oldottsouth
twitter.com/OldOttSouth
Overview: A small local organization
Mission: To improve the living conditions of Old Ottawa South
Membership: *Member Profile:* Residents of Old Ottawa South; *Committees:* Traffic; Planning & Zoning; Special Events; Program
Chief Officer(s):
Christy Savage, Executive Director

Ottawa Sports Hall of Fame Inc. (OSHOF) / Temple de la renommée des sports d'Ottawa
Heritage Bldg., Ottawa City Hall, 110 Laurier St. East, Ottawa ON K0A 1B0
ottawasportshalloffame@gmail.com
www.ottawasportshalloffame.com
www.facebook.com/195672987173454
twitter.com/OttawaSportsHoF

Overview: A small local organization founded in 1968
Mission: To preserve the history & development of sports in Ottawa
Finances: *Funding Sources:* Sponsorships
Membership: 200+ inductees
Activities: Recognizing individuals & teams who, through their achievements in or contributions to sport, have brought fame to Ottawa; *Awareness Events:* Induction Ceremony, May
Chief Officer(s):
Dave Best, Chair

Ottawa Symphony Orchestra Inc. (OSO) / Orchestre symphonique d'Ottawa
#250, 2 Daly Ave., Ottawa ON K1N 6E2
Tel: 613-231-7802; *Fax:* 613-231-3610
gm@ottawasymphony.com
www.ottawasymphony.com
www.facebook.com/ottawasymphony
twitter.com/ottawasymphony
Overview: A small local charitable organization founded in 1965 overseen by Orchestras Canada
Mission: To develop the highest possible artistic level of performance of symphonic repertoire among local musicians, local & Canadian soloists, Canadian music, partnership opportunities for performance with other local performing arts organizations, educational outreach opportunities for young audiences & young performers
Member of: Orchestras Canada
Finances: *Annual Operating Budget:* $500,000-$1.5 Million; *Funding Sources:* City of Ottawa; Ontario Arts Council; Trillium Foundation; Corporate & individual donations; Performance revenue
Staff Member(s): 3; 50 volunteer(s)
Membership: 500-999; *Fees:* Schedule available; *Member Profile:* Arts patrons
Activities: *Internships:* Yes
Chief Officer(s):
Vanessa Sutton, General Manager, 613-231-7802 Ext. 201
gm@ottawasymphony.com

Ottawa Tamil Seniors Association (OTSA)
605 Blair Rd., Ottawa ON K1G 7M3
info@ottawatamilseniors.com
www.ottawatamilseniors.com
www.facebook.com/ottawa.tamilseniors
Overview: A small local organization
Mission: To represent the interests of Tamil seniors in the Greater Ottawa region; To raise awareness of issues impacting the Tamil community; To promote & preserve Tamil language & culture in Canada
Membership: 180 individuals
Activities: Organizing cultural, recreational, & social activities & events; Helping members adapt to life in Canada; Working with officials & elected representatives

Ottawa Tourism / Tourisme Ottawa
#1800, 130 Albert St., Ottawa ON K1P 5G4
Tel: 613-237-5150; *Fax:* 613-237-7339
Toll-Free: 800-363-4465
info@ottawatourism.ca
www.ottawatourism.ca
www.facebook.com/visitottawa
twitter.com/Ottawa_Tourism
www.youtube.com/OttawaTourism
Previous Name: Ottawa Tourism & Convention Authority
Overview: A small local organization founded in 1972
Mission: To maximize the number of visits to Ottawa & Canada's Capital Region through effective marketing & communication programs; to help develop & promote awareness of the contribution of tourism in the community; to facilitate the development & promotion of the products, services & needs of members
Member of: Tourism Industry Association of Canada
Finances: *Annual Operating Budget:* Greater than $5 Million; *Funding Sources:* Membership fees; city government & 3% destination marketing fee
Staff Member(s): 28
Membership: 350; *Member Profile:* Hotels; attractions; festivals; restaurants; suppliers; *Committees:* Convention; Marketing; Convention; Rural Tourism; Membership; Travel Trade
Activities: Industry leadership, strategic direction & destination marketing of Ottawa
Chief Officer(s):
Noel Buckley, President & CEO

Ottawa Tourism & Convention Authority *See* Ottawa Tourism

Ottawa Twins' Parents Association *See* Multiple Birth Families Association

Ottawa Valley Curling Association (OVCA)
27 Veermeer Way, Ottawa ON K2K 2L9
webmaster@ovca.com
ottawavalleycurling.ca
www.facebook.com/ovcacurling
Overview: A small local organization founded in 1959 overseen by Canadian Curling Association
Mission: To foster curling in the Ottawa & St. Lawrence Valleys & Outaouais
Affiliation(s): Ladies Curling Association; Curling Quebec
Finances: *Annual Operating Budget:* Less than $50,000
Membership: 45 clubs; *Committees:* OVCA Ottawa Men's Bonspiel; OVCA Mixed Bonspiel; The Royal LePage OVCA Women's Fall Classic; JSI OVCA Junior SuperSpiel
Activities: Overseeing intermediate competitions between Eastern Ontario & Quebec; Offering instruction to new curlers
Chief Officer(s):
Elaine Brimicombe, President
elaine@ovca.com
Peter Smith, Coordinator, Events
ovca.eventscoordinator@hotmail.com
Awards:
• Ken Thain Award
Publications:
• OVCA [Ottawa Valley Curling Association] Newsletter
Type: Newsletter

Ottawa Valley Health Libraries Association (OVHLA) / Association des bibliothèques de santé de la Vallée d'Outaouais
c/o Canadian Agency for Drugs and Technologies in Health (CADTH), #600, 865 Carling Ave., Ottawa ON K1S 5S8
Tel: 613-226-2553
ovhla.chla-absc.ca
Merged from: Ottawa-Hull Health Libraries Association; OHA Region 9 chapter of the Ontario Health Libraries Assoc
Overview: A small local organization founded in 1994 overseen by Canadian Health Libraries Association
Mission: To support the provision of health library services throughout the Ottawa Valley and the Outaouais
Member of: Ontario Health Libraries Association (OHLA); Canadian Health Libraries Association (CHLA)
Finances: *Funding Sources:* Membership fees; Grants
Membership: *Fees:* $25 individual; $5 student; $40 institutional; *Member Profile:* Librarians; Library technicians
Chief Officer(s):
Alexandra Hickey, President
alexandra.hickey@cma.ca
Meetings/Conferences:
• Ottawa Valley Health Libraries Association Annual General Meeting 2018, 2018
Scope: Provincial

Ottawa Valley Historical Society (OVHS)
c/o Champlain Trail Museum, 1032 Pembroke St. East, Pembroke ON K8A 6Z2
Tel: 613-735-0517; *Fax:* 613-629-5067
pembrokemuseum@nrtco.net
champlaintrailmuseum.com/Ottawa_Valley_Historical_Society.html
Also Known As: Champlain Trail Museum & Pioneer Village
Overview: A small local charitable organization founded in 1958
Mission: To store & preserve historical artifacts from the Ottawa Valley area & to research & provide knowledge of these artifacts to the public
Membership: *Fees:* Schedule available
Activities: Operating the Champlain Trail Museum, including a school house, pioneer log home, church, train station, sawmill, & agricultural work sheds; Collecting & displaying historic artifacts of the Ottawa Valley; Organizing & maintaining research archives of the local area
Chief Officer(s):
Stephen Handke, President

Ottawa Valley Rock Garden & Horticultural Society
PO Box 9123, Stn. T, Ottawa ON K1G 3T8
info@ovrghs.ca
www.ovrghs.ca
Overview: A small local organization founded in 1992
Affiliation(s): North American Rock Garden Society, Ontario Horticultural Association
Membership: *Fees:* $20 individual, $25 family
Activities: Meetings held second Saturday of each month from Sept.-May at Woodroffe Campus of Algonquin College
Chief Officer(s):
Zandra Bainas, Co-President
president@ovrghs.ca
Margaret Don, Membership Secretary
membership@ovrghs.ca

Ottawa Valley Tourist Association (OVTA)
9 International Dr., Pembroke ON K8A 6W5
Tel: 613-732-4364; *Fax:* 613-735-2492
Toll-Free: 800-757-6580
info@ottawavalley.travel
www.ottawavalley.travel
www.facebook.com/ottawavalleytravel
twitter.com/theottawavalley
www.youtube.com/ottawavalleytravel
Overview: A medium-sized local organization
Mission: To promote Renfrew County as a prime tourist destination
Staff Member(s): 4
Membership: *Fees:* $60 artist/artisan; $95 allied; $125 event/festival; $200 regular; *Committees:* Membership
Activities: Tourism marketing
Chief Officer(s):
Alastair Baird, Manager
Chris Hinsperger, President, 613-628-2283

Ottawa West Office *See* Heart & Stroke Foundation of Ontario

Ottawa Youth Orchestra Academy (OYO) / L'Orchestre des jeunes d'Ottawa
#38, 2450 Lancaster Rd., Ottawa ON K1B 5N3
Tel: 613-233-9318; *Fax:* 613-233-5038
info@oyoa-aojo.ca
www.oyoa-aojo.ca
www.facebook.com/OttawaYouthOrchestraAcademy
twitter.com/oyoa_aojo
Also Known As: The Ottawa Youth Orchestra Academy
Previous Name: National Capital Music Academy
Overview: A small local charitable organization founded in 1988 overseen by Orchestras Canada
Mission: To provide high-quality orchestral training to youth in the Ottawa region
Member of: Orchestras Canada
Finances: *Funding Sources:* Tuition fees; Donations
Staff Member(s): 22
Membership: *Fees:* Schedule available
Activities: Performing concerts; Providing comprehensive music education through regular rehearsals and summer camps
Chief Officer(s):
John Gomez, Conductor

Ottawa-Carleton Board of Trade *See* Ottawa Chamber of Commerce

Ottawa-Carleton Children's Aid Society *See* Children's Aid Society of Ottawa

Ottawa-Carleton Council on Aging *See* The Council on Aging of Ottawa

Ottawa-Carleton Regional Police Association *See* Ottawa Police Association

Ottawa-Carleton Safety Council *See* Ottawa Safety Council

Ottawa-Hull Ice Carvers' Society *See* Canadian Ice Carvers' Society

Otter Valley Chamber of Commerce
PO Box 160, Straffordville ON N0J 1Y0
Tel: 519-550-0088
Overview: A small local organization
Member of: Canadian Chamber of Commerce
Membership: 41; *Fees:* $70
Chief Officer(s):
Val Donnell, President

Our Harbour / Le Havre
95, av Lorne, Saint-Lambert QC J4P 2G7
Tel: 450-671-9160; *Fax:* 450-671-9171
info@ourharbour.org
ourharbour.org
Overview: A small local charitable organization
Mission: To provide supportive, long-term housing; to provide life management support; to assist each resident's integration into society; to decrease risk of re-hospitalization; to educate the wider community about mental illness
Chief Officer(s):
Perveen Khokhar, Coordinator

Our Lady of Good Health Tamil Parish (OLGH)
Immaculate Heart of Mary Church, 131 Birchmount Rd., Toronto ON M1N 3J7
Tel: 416-264-6544
office@olghtamilparish.com
www.olghtamilparish.com
Overview: A small local charitable organization founded in 1987
Mission: To be a Roman Catholic Community that strives to preserve its Tamil cultural traditions, customs, values & language through faith
Affiliation(s): Archdiocese of Toronto
Finances: *Annual Operating Budget:* Less than $50,000
Chief Officer(s):
Arutapani Peter Gitararen, Father

Our Lady of The Prairies Foundation
PO Box 22076, Saskatoon SK S7H 5P1
info@ourladyfoundation.org
www.ourladyfoundation.org
Overview: A small national charitable organization founded in 1957
Mission: To nurture love & compassion; To achieve peace & freedom through prayers, words, & actions
Activities: Working with charitable organizations in the community; Distributing grants to registered Canadian charities with missions in Saskatchewan; Supporting spiritual, social, healing, educational, & environmental programs
Awards:
- Grant
Supports spiritual, healing, educational, social or environmental programs. *Eligibility:* A registered Canadian charity that carries on at 75% of their business in Saskatchewan.

Our Lady of the Rosary of Manaoag Evangelization Group
25 Mahoney Ave., Toronto ON M6M 2H5
Tel: 416-240-9249
Overview: A small local organization founded in 1989
Affiliation(s): Archdiocese of Toronto
Activities: Providing evangelization, faith formation & instruction, prayer, retreats, & pilgrimages
Chief Officer(s):
Teodora S. La Madrid, Contact

Our Place (Peel)
3579 Dixie Rd., Mississauga ON L4Y 2B3
Tel: 905-238-6916
info@ourplacepeel.org
www.ourplacepeel.org
Overview: A small local charitable organization founded in 1985
Mission: To provide emergency shelter & residential services for disadvantaged & homeless youth, from ages 16 to 21, in Peel Region
Finances: *Funding Sources:* Donations; Province of Ontario; Region of Peel; United Way
Staff Member(s): 10
Chief Officer(s):
Christy Upshall, Executive Director
cupshall@ourplacepeel.org

Out on the Shelf
10 Carden St., Guelph ON N1H 3A2
Overview: A small local organization
Mission: To provide resources to members of Guelph's LGBTQ community; To address the issues impacting LGBTQ people; To advocate for LGBTQ visibility
Activities: Organizing social gatherings; Offering education programs; *Library*
Chief Officer(s):
Amy Ellard-Gray, Chair

Outdoor Marketing Association of Canada *See* Out-of-Home Marketing Association of Canada

Outdoor Recreation Council of British Columbia (ORC)
47 West Broadway, Vancouver BC V5Y 1P1
Tel: 604-873-5546
outdoorrec@orcbc.ca
www.orcbc.ca
Overview: A medium-sized provincial charitable organization founded in 1976
Mission: To advise industry & government in the development & implementation of outdoor recreation & conservation plans for BC; to contribute to the coordination of regional outdoor recreation by assisting in the establishment of a provincial network of outdoor recreationists to address recreational use conflicts & to advise government & industry on local & regional needs for noncompetitive outdoor recreation; to encourage active participation by the residents of BC in outdoor recreation activities; to promote the quality & diversity of outdoor recreation opportunities in BC by working cooperatively with government, industry, business & the public.
Member of: Volunteer Vancouver; BC Environmental Network
Affiliation(s): Environmental Fund of BC
Finances: *Funding Sources:* Membership dues; fundraising; grants; foundations; donations
Staff Member(s): 1
Membership: 42 organizations; *Fees:* $84 non-voting; $156 voting; *Member Profile:* Voting - provincial outdoor non-profit recreation organization; non-voting organizations are not provincial in scope
Activities: *Library:* by appointment
Chief Officer(s):
Dennis Webb, Chair
Jeremy McCall, Executive Director

Outdoor Writers of Canada
PO Box 934, Cochrane AB T4C 1B1
Tel: 403-932-3585; *Fax:* 403-851-0618
outdoorwritersofcanada@shaw.ca
www.outdoorwritersofcanada.com
Overview: A small national organization founded in 1957
Mission: To promote high standards of craftsmanship in the portrayal of outdoor life
Membership: *Fees:* $40 student; $90 active & associate membership; $280 corporate; *Member Profile:* Professional communicators who specialize in the outdoor field, such as writers, photographers, artists, cinematographers, broadcasters, & government information officers; Corporate members that share the organization's goals; Students
Activities: Increasing appreciation of the outdoors
Chief Officer(s):
T.J. Schwanky, Executive Director
Meetings/Conferences:
- Outdoor Writers of Canada 2018 National Conference, 2018
Scope: National
Description: Craft improvement sessions for communicators with expertise in the outdoor field
Publications:
- Inside Outdoors
Type: Newsletter; *Frequency:* 6 pa
Profile: Happenings of Outdoor Writers of Canada, corporate news, craft improvement articles, & new markets

Outdoors Unlittered *See* Pitch-In Canada

Outlook & District Chamber of Commerce
PO Box 431, Outlook SK S0L 2N0
Tel: 306-867-9580; *Fax:* 306-867-9559
outlookchamber@gmail.com
outlookchamber.webs.com
www.facebook.com/outlookanddistrictchamberofcommerce
Overview: A small local organization
Finances: *Funding Sources:* Membership fees
Membership: 69; *Fees:* $50
Chief Officer(s):
Justin Turton, Executive President
jturton@sasktel.net
Ken Fehr, Executive Treasurer
ken.h.fehr@ca.pwc.com

Out-of-Home Marketing Association of Canada (OMAC) / Association marketing canadienne de l'affichage (AMCA)
#605, 111 Peter St., Toronto ON M5V 2H1
Tel: 416-968-3435; *Fax:* 416-968-6538
rcaron@omaccanada.ca
www.omaccanada.ca
www.linkedin.com/company-beta/2490361
www.facebook.com/1710234529188919
twitter.com/OMAC_AMCA
Previous Name: Outdoor Marketing Association of Canada
Overview: A small national organization founded in 2005
Mission: To promote the benefits & effectiveness of out-of-home media to advertisers & advertising agencies; To develop & implement new iniatives that serve as a resource to the industry to help increase the understanding of out-of-home media
Finances: *Funding Sources:* Membership fees
Staff Member(s): 4
Membership: 8
Activities: *Library:* Not open to public
Chief Officer(s):
Rosanne Caron, President, 416-968-3435 Ext. 108
rcaron@omac.comb.org
Jacques Major, Director, Marketing & Communications, 416-968-3435 Ext. 107
jmajor@omaccanada.ca

Outreach Literacy Program of the John Howard Society of Victoria / Haliburton / Simcoe & Muskoka *See* John Howard Society of Ontario

Outremangeurs Anonymes
312, rue Beaubien est, Montréal QC H2S 1R8
Tél: 514-490-1939
Ligne sans frais: 877-509-1939
reunions@outremangeurs.org
outremangeurs.org
Aperçu: *Dimension:* grande; *Envergure:* internationale; fondée en 1960
Mission: Aide les hommes et les femmes de maîtriser les problèmes ils ont avec la suralimentation

Outward Bound Canada
Centre for Green Cities, #404, 550 Bayview Ave., Toronto ON M4W 3X8
Fax: 705-382-5959
Toll-Free: 888-688-9273
info@outwardbound.ca
www.outwardbound.ca
www.linkedin.com/company/outward-bound-canada
www.facebook.com/outwardboundcanada
twitter.com/OutwardBoundCan
www.youtube.com/user/OutwardBoundCanada
Also Known As: Canadian Outward Bound Wilderness School
Overview: A small provincial charitable organization founded in 1976
Mission: To promote self-reliance, care & respect for others, responsibility to community & concern for the environment
Member of: Ontario Camping Association; Ontario Society for Training & Development; Association for Experiential Education; Council of Outdoor Educators of Ontario
Finances: *Annual Operating Budget:* $1.5 Million-$3 Million
Staff Member(s): 11; 20 volunteer(s)
Activities: Youth - 21-day Adventure courses available for 15-16 yrs. old & 22-day Voyageur programs for 17+ yrs.; Adults - courses vary from 7 - 24 days, including canoeing, sea-kayaking, hiking or dog-sledding & skiing; special courses for 50+ yrs., for women only & courses for managers & educators; leadership courses; *Internships:* Yes; *Speaker Service:* Yes
Chief Officer(s):
Sarah Wiley, Executive Director
sarah_wiley@outwardbound.ca

Ovarian Cancer Canada (OCC) / Cancer de l'ovaire Canada (COC)
#205, 145 Front St. East, Toronto ON M5A 1E3
Tel: 416-962-2700; *Fax:* 416-962-2701
Toll-Free: 877-413-7970
info@ovariancanada.org
www.ovariancanada.org
www.linkedin.com/company/728166
www.facebook.com/OvarianCancerCanada
twitter.com/OvarianCanada
www.youtube.com/OvarianCancerCanada
Previous Name: National Ovarian Cancer Association
Overview: A medium-sized national charitable organization founded in 1997
Mission: To support women & their families living with the disease; To raise awareness in the general public & with health care professionals; To fund research to develop reliable early detection techniques, improved treatments, & a cure
Member of: Canadian Coalition for Genetic Fairness
Finances: *Funding Sources:* Donations
Activities: Listen to the Whispers public education sessions; *Speaker Service:* Yes
Chief Officer(s):
Elisabeth Baugh, Chief Executive Officer
ebaugh@ovariancanada.org
Kelly Grover, Vice-President, National Programs & Partners
kgrover@ovariancanada.org
Troy Cross, Vice-President, Development & Marketing
tcross@ovariancanada.org
Sheila Smith, Vice-President, Finance & Administration
ssmith@ovariancanada.org
Janice Chan, Director, Communications
jchan@ovariancanada.org

Roxana Predoi, Director, HR & Operations
rpredoi@ovariancanada.org
Atlantic Regional Office (OCC)
1542 Queen St., Halifax NS B3J 2H8
Tel: 902-404-7070; Fax: 902-404-7071
Toll-Free: 866-825-0788
Chief Officer(s):
Emilie Chiasson, Regional Manager
echiasson@ovariancanada.org
Ontario Regional Office (OCC)
#205, 145 Front St. East, Toronto ON M5A 1E3
Tel: 416-962-2700; Fax: 416-962-2701
Toll-Free: 877-413-7970
Chief Officer(s):
Cailey Crawford, Regional Manager
ccrawford@ovariancanada.org
Pacific-Yukon Regional Office
#330, 470 Granville St., Vancouver BC V6C 1V5
Tel: 604-676-3431; Fax: 604-676-3435
Toll-Free: 800-749-9310
Chief Officer(s):
Tracy Kolwich, Regional Manager
tkolwich@ovariancanada.org
Quebec Regional Office
#260, 4950, rue Queen-Mary, Montréal QC H3W 1X3
Tel: 514-369-2972; Fax: 514-940-0158
Toll-Free: 888-369-2972
Chief Officer(s):
Monique Beaupré-Lazure, Regional Manager
mbeauprelazure@ovariancanada.org
Western Regional Office (OCC)
#105B, 1409 Edmonton Trail NE, Calgary AB T2E 3K8
Tel: 403-277-9449; Fax: 403-277-9919
Toll-Free: 866-591-6622
Chief Officer(s):
Tracy Kolwich, Regional Manager
tkolwich@ovariancanada.org

Overseas Book Centre See Canadian Organization for Development through Education

Owen Sound & District Association for the Mentally Retarded See Community Living Owen Sound & District

Owen Sound & District Chamber of Commerce
PO Box 1028, #266, 1051 2nd Ave. East, Owen Sound ON N4K 6K6
Tel: 519-376-6261; Fax: 519-376-5647
www.oschamber.com
www.linkedin.com/company/owen-sound-&-district-chamber-of-commerce
www.facebook.com/131296160275303
Overview: A small local organization founded in 1864
Mission: To be the voice of business committed to the enhancement of economic prosperity in Owen Sound & surrounding area
Member of: Ontario Chamber of Commerce; Canadian Chamber of Commerce
Finances: Funding Sources: Membership dues; fundraising
Staff Member(s): 2; 12 volunteer(s)
Membership: 450; Fees: Schedule available; Committees: Advocacy; Business Excellence Awards; Events; Marketing
Activities: Organizing & promoting events, meetings & presentations; Awareness Events: Awake @ 8; Golf Tournament; Business Excellence Awards
Chief Officer(s):
Peter Reesor, Chief Executive Officer
peter@oschamber.com

Owen Sound Family YMCA See YMCA Canada

Oxfam Canada
39 McArthur Ave., Ottawa ON K1L 8L7
Tel: 613-237-5236; Fax: 613-237-0524
Toll-Free: 800-466-9326
info@oxfam.ca
www.oxfam.ca
www.facebook.com/OxfamCanada
twitter.com/oxfamcanada
www.youtube.com/user/OxfamCanada
Overview: A large international charitable organization founded in 1963
Mission: To build solutions for the creation of a fair world, without poverty & injustice
Affiliation(s): Oxfam International
Finances: Funding Sources: Individual & institutional donations; Fundraising
Activities: Raising public awareness; Offering workshops & educational resources; Supporting organizations in oversees communities; Engaging in advocacy activities for just policies
Chief Officer(s):
Margaret Hancock, Chair
Don MacMillan, Treasurer
Publications:
- Oxfam Canada Annual Report
Type: Yearbook; Frequency: Annually
Saskatoon - Prairies Regional Office
#200, 416 - 21st St. East, Saskatoon SK S7K 0C2
Tél: 306-242-4097; Téléc: 306-665-2128
Toronto Regional Office & National Fundraising Office
#210, 410 Adelaide St. West, Toronto ON M5V 1S8
Tel: 416-535-2335; Fax: 416-537-6435
Toll-Free: 800-466-9326
toronto@oxfam.ca
British Columbia & Yukon Regional Office
#201, 343 Railway St., Vancouver BC V6A 1A4
Tel: 604-736-7678; Fax: 604-736-9646

Oxford Child & Youth Centre (OCYC)
912 Dundas St., Woodstock ON N4S 1H1
Tel: 519-539-0463; Fax: 519-539-7058
Toll-Free: 877-539-0463
info@ocyc.on.ca
www.ocyc.on.ca
Overview: A small local charitable organization founded in 1987
Mission: To provide a wide range of recreational & support services for children under 18
Finances: Funding Sources: Ministry of Community & Social Services; Ministry of Child & Youth Services
Chief Officer(s):
Marc Roberts, Executive Director
mroberts@ocyc.on.ca

Oxford County Geological Society
PO Box 20091, Woodstock ON N4S 8X8
Tel: 519-421-1700
oxford@ogs.on.ca
oxford.ogs.on.ca
Overview: A small local organization founded in 1977 overseen by Central Canadian Federation of Mineralogical Societies
Mission: To arouse interest & knowledge in all fields of earth sciences; to ensure that all age-group needs are considered
Member of: Canadian Central Federation Minerals Society
Finances: Funding Sources: Membership dues
Membership: Fees: $73.20
Activities: Workshops; seminars; monthly meetings meetings 2nd Friday of the month; guest speakers; Speaker Service: Yes; Library: by appointment

Oxford County Law Association
415 Hunter St., 3rd Fl., Woodstock ON N4S 4G6
Tel: 519-539-7711; Fax: 519-539-7962
Overview: A small provincial organization founded in 1893
Finances: Annual Operating Budget: $50,000-$100,000; Funding Sources: Law Society of Upper Canada; membership dues
Membership: 60; Member Profile: Lawyers
Activities: Library: Not open to public
Chief Officer(s):
Shabira Tamachi, Contact
stamachi@ocl.net

Oxford Family & Child Services See Children's Aid Society of Oxford County

Oxford Philatelic Society
PO Box 20113, Woodstock ON N4S 8X8
ward2221@rogers.com
www.oxfordphilsoc.com
Overview: A small local organization founded in 1949
Membership: 60+; Fees: $2 juniors; $10 adults
Activities: Conducting monthly meetings, featuring stamp news & views & guest speakers
Chief Officer(s):
Jim Watson, President
Betty Thomas, Membership Coordinator

Oxford Regional Labour Council
PO Box 1636, Woodstock ON N4S 0A8
oxfordlabourcouncil@gmail.com
www.oxfordlabourcouncil.ca
twitter.com/oxfordlabour
Overview: A small local organization founded in 1955
Mission: To promote & defend the interests of workers in the Oxford area
Affiliation(s): Canadian Labour Congress
Membership: 4 affiliates
Activities: Liaising with all levels of government; Assisting individuals with their concerns; Supporting groups; Contributing to charities in the community; Awareness Events: Day of Mourning Ceremony, April 28
Chief Officer(s):
Linda Leyten, President

Oxford/Middlesex/Elgin See Habitat for Humanity Canada

Oxford-Brant Association of Baptist Churches
ON
baptist.ca
Overview: A small local organization founded in 1896 overseen by Canadian Baptists of Ontario and Quebec
Member of: Canadian Baptists of Ontario & Quebec
Membership: 17 churches; Member Profile: Baptist churches in Oxford & Brant counties; Committees: Area ministry; Association Educational
Chief Officer(s):
David Partridge, Moderator

Oxygène
CP 85087, Gatineau QC J8P 7V2
Tél: 819-770-9794
cluboxygene@live.ca
www.cluboxygene.qc.ca
Aperçu: Dimension: petite; Envergure: locale
Mission: Pour fournir aux membres des activités de randonnée en plein air
Affiliation(s): La Fédération québécoise de la marche
Membre(s) du bureau directeur:
Suzanne Bisson-Girard, Présidente, Conseil d'administration

Oxy-jeunes
2020, rue de la Visitation, Montréal QC H2L 3C7
Tél: 514-728-6146
direction@oxy-jeunes.com
oxy-jeunes.com
www.facebook.com/page.oxyjeunes
www.youtube.com/user/oxyjeunes
Aperçu: Dimension: petite; Envergure: locale; fondée en 1981
Mission: Pour orienter les adolescents loin de décrochage scolaire, le suicide et la toxicomanie en utilisant diverses activités artistiques et ainsi renforcer l'estime de soi
Membre: Critères d'admissibilite: Jeunes de 12 à 17 ans
Activités: Spectacles; Concernts; Expositions; Ateliers de perfectionnement; Mentorat; Sorties
Membre(s) du bureau directeur:
Jovette Demers, Présidente, Conseil d'administration

Oyen & District Chamber of Commerce
PO Box 718, Oyen AB T0J 2J0
Tel: 403-664-1001
Overview: A small local organization
Member of: Alberta Chamber of Commerce

Pacific Asia Travel Association (Eastern Canada Chapter) (PATA)
13 Montalan Ave., Toronto ON M4J 1H3
Tel: 416-466-6552
www.pata.org
Overview: A medium-sized national organization
Mission: To enhance the growth, value & quality of Pacific Asia travel & tourism for the benefit of its membership
Finances: Funding Sources: Membership dues; project operations
Activities: Rents Mailing List: Yes
Chief Officer(s):
Karen Fawcett, Chair, 416-465-9185
karen.ian@sympatico.ca

Pacific Association of First Nations' Women
2017 Dundas St., Vancouver BC V5L 1J5
Tel: 604-872-1849; Fax: 604-872-1845
pafnw.ca
Also Known As: Pacific Association of First Nations' Women
Previous Name: Association of First Nations' Women; West Coast Professional Native Women's Association
Overview: A small local organization founded in 1981
Mission: To assist Aboriginal women & their families with health, education & social services issues
Member of: Council of Aboriginal Women of BC
Affiliation(s): Vancouver Aboriginal Council

Finances: *Funding Sources:* Canadian Heritage; Aboriginal Healing Foundation; Ministry of Health
Membership: *Fees:* $1; *Member Profile:* Aboriginal women
Activities: Monthly meetings; participation in cultural events; Christmas party; AGM; support & direct client services; Aboriginal Community Health Advocate; Aboriginal Women's Family Violence Prevention Training; Button Blanket Sharing Circles; Aboriginal Elder Women's Support Program; First Nations Advocate for GF Strong & Pearson Hospitals; *Library:* Small Resource Library
Chief Officer(s):
Joy Chalmers, Contact, Community Homecare Services Program
joy_bc@hotmail.com

Pacific Bluegrass Heritage Society (PBHS)
c/o The Anza Club, 3 West 8th Ave., Vancouver BC V5Y 1M8
pacificbluegrass@yahoo.ca
www.pacificbluegrass.ca
Overview: A small provincial licensing organization
Mission: To encourage education & participation in bluegrass music by the effective use of resources & volunteers
Affiliation(s): Canadian Music Centre
Membership: 200 individual; *Fees:* $20 individual; $30 family; *Member Profile:* Individual musicians, bands, families, supporters
Activities: Workshops, band showcase, picking sessions, summer festivals, Band of the Year Award
Chief Officer(s):
David Zaruba, President
davidzaruba@hotmail.com

Pacific Cinémathèque Pacifique (PCP)
#200, 1131 Howe St., Vancouver BC V6Z 2L7
Tel: 604-688-8202; *Fax:* 604-688-8204
info@thecinematheque.ca
www.thecinematheque.ca
www.facebook.com/theCinematheque
twitter.com/theCinematheque
Overview: A medium-sized provincial charitable organization founded in 1972
Mission: To promote the understanding of film & moving images in Canadian & international contexts; To foster critical media literacy through screenings, film tours, & educational services & resources
Member of: Alliance for Arts & Culture
Finances: *Annual Operating Budget:* $500,000-$1.5 Million; *Funding Sources:* Canada Council; City of Vancouver; provincial government
Staff Member(s): 14; 75 volunteer(s)
Membership: 13,000; *Fees:* $3
Activities: *Library:* Film Reference Library; by appointment
Chief Officer(s):
Jim Sinclair, Executive / Artistic Director
jim@theCinematheque.ca

Pacific Corridor Enterprise Council (PACE)
PO Box 3032, Vancouver BC V6B 3X5
Tel: 604-682-8278; *Fax:* 888-402-0708
pace@pacebordertrade.org
www.pacebordertrade.org
Overview: A medium-sized international organization founded in 1990
Mission: To build relationships through the production & dissemination of new information, the communication of information relevant to cross border business; To promote public policy that removes barriers to the free flow of capital, people goods & services across borders, & the facilitation of networking among members & the public/private sector
Finances: *Annual Operating Budget:* $50,000-$100,000
Staff Member(s): 2; 30 volunteer(s)
Membership: 150; *Fees:* $300-$700; *Committees:* Border Crossing; Transportation; Venture Capital
Activities: Seminars & conferences organized around specific & timely topics & featuring case studies from members & dialogue with professionals through panel discussions & roundtables; industry-specific working sessions & other events designed to bring together business people with common interests & problems; advises government of private sector perspective
Chief Officer(s):
K. David Andersson, Chair
Greg Boos, President

Pacific Immigrant Resources Society (PIRS)
#210, 3680 East Hastings St., Vancouver BC V5K 2A9
Tel: 604-298-5888; *Fax:* 604-289-7115
info@pirs.bc.ca
www.pirs.bc.ca
www.linkedin.com/company/pacific-immigrant-resources-society
www.facebook.com/163220843762811
twitter.com/PIRSVancouver
Overview: A small local charitable organization founded in 1975
Mission: To ensure that immigrant women & preschool children can participate actively in Canadian community life
Member of: Multicultural Societies & Service Agencies of BC
Membership: *Fees:* $5 student/senior; $10 individual; $25 non-profit organization; $50 business; $150 individual lifetime; *Committees:* Board Development; Fund Development; Personnel
Activities: ESL & ELSA; women's development; children's programs; volunteer programs
Chief Officer(s):
Gyda Chud, Chair
Jennifer McCarthy-Flynn, Executive Director

Pacific Independent Insurance Adjusters' Association
BC
www.ciaa-adjusters.ca
Overview: A small provincial organization overseen by Canadian Independent Adjusters' Association
Member of: Canadian Independent Adjusters' Association

Pacific Institute for Sport Excellence (PISE)
4371 Interurban Rd., Victoria BC V9E 2C5
Tel: 250-220-2510; *Fax:* 250-220-2501
info@pise.ca
www.pise.ca
www.facebook.com/PacificInstituteforSportExcellence
twitter.com/PISEworld
www.youtube.com/user/piseworld
Overview: A small provincial organization
Mission: To be a leader in high performance sport development, community programs, sport & exercise education & applied research & innovation
Membership: *Fees:* $65 per month; $175 four months; $460 annual
Chief Officer(s):
Robert Bettauer, CEO
rbettauer@piseworld.com

Pacific Institute for the Mathematical Sciences (PIMS)
University Of British Columbia, #4176, 22017 Main Mall, Vancouver BC V6T 1Z4
Tel: 604-822-3922; *Fax:* 604-822-0883
reception@pims.math.ca
www.pims.math.ca
twitter.com/pimsmath
Overview: A medium-sized local organization founded in 1998
Mission: To promote research in mathematics; To strengthen ties & collaboration between the mathematical scientists in the academic community, in the industrial & business sector, & in government; To enhance education & training in mathematical sciences; To broaden communication of mathematical ideas; To create strong mathematical partnerships & links within Canada & with organizations in other countries, focusing on the nations of the Pacific Rim
Affiliation(s): Mathematical Sciences Research Institute; University of Lethbridge; University of Regina; University of British Columbia
Finances: *Funding Sources:* Fundraising; Donations
Chief Officer(s):
Alejandro Adem, Director
adem@pims.math.ca
Publications:
• Pacific Institute for the Mathematical Sciences Newsletter
Type: Newsletter
• Pi in the Sky [a publication of the Pacific Institute for the Mathematical Sciences]
Type: Magazine; *Frequency:* Annually
• PIMS [Pacific Institute for the Mathematical Sciences] Magazine
Type: Magazine

Pacific Legal Education Association *See* PLEA Community Services Society of BC

Pacific Life Bible College
15030 - 66A Ave., Surrey BC V3S 2A5
Tel: 604-597-9082; *Fax:* 604-597-9090
Toll-Free: 877-597-7522
info@pacificlife.edu
pacificlife.edu
www.facebook.com/pacificlifebiblecollege
twitter.com/plbc
vimeo.com/channels/plbc
Merged from: Pacific Life Bible College; Christ College
Overview: A small national charitable organization founded in 1997
Member of: International Church of the Foursquare Gospel
Staff Member(s): 10
Membership: *Member Profile:* Applicants to the college must be born-again Christians actively involved in a church for a minimum of a full year prior to application.
Activities: *Library:* Wolf Memorial Library
Chief Officer(s):
Gerald Nussbaum, Interim President
gnussbaum@pacificlife.edu

Pacific Music Industry Association *See* Music BC Industry Association

Pacific National Exhibition
2901 East Hastings St., Vancouver BC V5K 5J1
Tel: 604-253-2311; *Fax:* 604-251-7753
info@pne.ca
www.pne.ca
www.facebook.com/PNE.Playland
twitter.com/pne_playland
www.youtube.com/user/pneclips
Also Known As: PNE
Overview: A small local organization
Activities: Organizing an annual summer fair, as well as shows, exhibits, amusement rides, concerts, sporting events, & cultural activities
Chief Officer(s):
Michael McDaniel, President & CEO
Jeff Strickland, Vice-President, Operations
Shelley Frost, Vice-President, Marketing
Peter Male, Vice-President, Sales
Stacy Shields, Vice-President, Human Resources

Pacific Northwest Library Association (PNLA)
c/o Candice Stenstrom, Public Library InterLINK, #158, 5489 Byrne Rd., Burnaby BC V5J 3J1
Tel: 604-437-8441; *Fax:* 604-437-8410
www.pnla.org
www.facebook.com/pnla.org
Overview: A medium-sized international organization
Mission: To strengthen library networks in the Pacific Northwest region; To provide support & opportunities for library workers
Membership: 200; *Member Profile:* Persons who work in, with, & for libraries in British Columbia, Alberta, Alaska, Idaho, Montana, & Washington
Activities: Providing educational opportunities; Offering the cultivation of leadership skills through the Pacific Northwest Library Association Leadership Institute; Providing forums for networking
Chief Officer(s):
Jenny Grenfell, President
Awards:
• Young Reader's Choice Award
Meetings/Conferences:
• Pacific Northwest Library Association 2018 Conference, August, 2018, Kalispell, MT
Scope: Provincial

Pacific Opera Victoria (POV)
925 Balmoral Rd., Victoria BC V8T 1A7
Tel: 250-382-1641; *Fax:* 250-382-4944
www.pov.bc.ca
Overview: A medium-sized local organization founded in 1975
Mission: To create a dynamic operatic experience, & to inspire audiences, artists & community
Member of: Opera America Inc.; Opera.ca
Finances: *Annual Operating Budget:* $100,000-$250,000
Staff Member(s): 10
Membership: 1-99
Activities: *Internships:* Yes
Chief Officer(s):
Timothy Vernon, Artistic Director

Pacific Peoples' Partnership (PPP)
#407, 620 View St., Victoria BC V8W 1J6
Tel: 250-381-4131; *Fax:* 250-388-5258
info@pacificpeoplespartnership.org
www.pacificpeoplespartnership.org
Previous Name: South Pacific Peoples Foundation
Overview: A small international organization founded in 1975

Canadian Associations / Pacific Post Partum Support Society (PPPSS)

Mission: To promote increased understanding of social justice, environment, development, health & other issues of importance to the people of the Pacific Islands; To support equitable, environmentally sustainable development & social justice in the region
Member of: Canadian Council for International Cooperation; British Columbia Council for International Cooperation
Affiliation(s): Nuclear Free & Independent Pacific Movement
Finances: Annual Operating Budget: $100,000-$250,000; Funding Sources: Membership dues; donors; sales; Canadian International Development Agency; professional service fees
Staff Member(s): 5; 15 volunteer(s)
Membership: 160; Fees: $35 regular; $45 family; $20 student; Member Profile: Supporter of SPPF's aims & objectives, Canadian citizen or a current resident of Canada, annual donation required; Committees: Program; Finance; Fundraising; Journal; Public Relations
Activities: Pacific Networking Conference; Awareness Events: One Wave Festival, September; Speaker Service: Yes; Library: Resource Centre; Open to public
Chief Officer(s):
April Ingham, Executive Director
director@pacificpeoplespartnership.org
Siobhan Powlowski, Deputy Director
deputy@pacificpeoplespartnership.org

Pacific Post Partum Support Society (PPPSS)
#200, 7342 Winston St., Burnaby BC V5A 2H1
Tel: 604-255-7955; Fax: 604-255-7588
Other Communication: Volunteer e-mail:
volunteer@postpartum.org
admin@postpartum.org
www.postpartum.org
www.facebook.com/120735171295360
twitter.com/postpartumbc
Overview: A small local charitable organization founded in 1984
Mission: To provide support for women affected by postpartum/perinatal distress, depression, & anxiety
Affiliation(s): United Way of the Lower Mainland
Finances: Annual Operating Budget: $100,000-$250,000; Funding Sources: City of Vancouver, Social Planning-Ministry of Children & Families; Simon Fraser Health Board
Staff Member(s): 9; 20 volunteer(s)
Membership: 105 individual; Fees: $10; Committees: Fundraising; Visibility; Outreach & Education; Personal
Activities: Weekly support groups for postpartum, depressed or anxious mothers; public education about PPD & its treatment; telephone helpline for families; community training for support people; presentations, booths, conferences, fairs & shows
Chief Officer(s):
Sheila Duffy, Director
Stace Dayment, Manager, Administration

Pacific Riding for Developing Abilities (PRDA)
1088 - 208 St., Langley BC V2Z 1T4
Tel: 604-530-8717; Fax: 604-530-8617
www.prda.ca
www.facebook.com/PRDALangley
Previous Name: Pacific Riding for Disabled Association
Overview: A small local charitable organization founded in 1973
Mission: To enhance the quality of life for people with a range of disabilities, providing therapeutic equestrian activities & educational opportunities.
Member of: Canadian Therapeutic Riding Association; Langley Chamber of Commerce; North American Riding for the Handicapped Association
Affiliation(s): Ishtar Transition Housing Society; Burnaby Association for Community Inclusion
Finances: Funding Sources: Donations; fundraising; United Way of the Lower Mainland
Staff Member(s): 8
Activities: Day camp; summer camp; horse shows; Speaker Service: Yes; Rents Mailing List: Yes; Library: Open to public
Chief Officer(s):
Michelle Ingall, Executive Director
  Chilliwack Branch
  47240 Greenhill Rd., Chilliwack BC V2R 4T2
  Tel: 604-858-2149
  Vancouver Branch
  c/o Southlands Riding Club, 7025 Macdonald St., Vancouver BC V6N 1G2
  Tel: 604-263-4817; Fax: 604-263-1281

Pacific Riding for Disabled Association See Pacific Riding for Developing Abilities

Pacific Salmon Commission
#600, 1155 Robson St., Vancouver BC V6E 1B5
Tel: 604-684-8081; Fax: 604-666-8707
info@psc.org
www.psc.org
Overview: A medium-sized international organization
Mission: The Pacific Salmon Commission is the body formed by the governments of Canada and the United States to implement the Pacific Salmon Treaty.
Staff Member(s): 27
Membership: Committees: Chinook; Chum; Coho; Data Sharing; Fraser River; Habitat & Restoration; Northern Boundary; Selective Fishery Evaluation; Transboundary; Finance & Administration; Scientific Cooperation
Chief Officer(s):
John Field, Executive Secretary
Susan Falinger, Canadian Commissioner
John McCulloch, Canadian Commissioner
Murray Ned, Canadian Commissioner
Bob Rezansoff, Canadian Commissioner

Pacific Salmon Foundation (PSF)
#300, 1682 West 7th Ave., Vancouver BC V6J 4S6
Tel: 604-664-7664; Fax: 604-664-7665
salmon@psf.ca
www.psf.ca
www.linkedin.com/company/pacific-salmon-foundation
www.facebook.com/PacificSalmonFoundation
twitter.com/PSF
www.youtube.com/user/SalmonFoundation
Overview: A small national organization founded in 1987
Finances: Funding Sources: Fundraising; Endowment income; Revenue from salmon conservation stamps
Staff Member(s): 10
Activities: Fund community salmon projects; manage comprehensive salmon recovery programs for priority watersheds; fund public awareness & educational programs pertaining to pacific salmon; fund critical research
Chief Officer(s):
Paul Kariya, Executive Director
Dianne Ramage, Director, Salmon Recovery
Chad Brealey, Director, Communications

Pacific Society of Nutrition Management (PSNM)
#3, 7488 Mulberry Pl., Burnaby BC V3N 5B4
info@psnm.net
www.psnm.net
Overview: A small local organization
Affiliation(s): Canadian Society of Nutrition Management
17 volunteer(s)
Membership: Fees: $55

Pacific Space Centre Society See H.R. MacMillan Space Centre Society

Pacific States-British Columbia Oil Spill Task Force
Environmental Emergencies Branch, BC Ministry of Environment, PO Box 9342, Stn. Prov Govt, 2975 Jutland Rd., 3rd Fl., Victoria BC V8W 9M6
Tel: 250-356-8383; Fax: 250-387-9935
www.oilspilltaskforce.org
Mission: The Pacific States-British Columbia Oil Spill Task Force was authorized by a Memorandum of Cooperation signed in 1989 by the Governors of Alaska, Washington, Oregon, & California & the Premier of British Columbia following the Nestucca & Exxon Valdez oil spills. These events highlighted their common concerns regarding oil spill risks & the need for cooperation across shared borders. In June 2001 a revised Memorandum of Cooperation was adopted to include the State of Hawaii & expand the focus to include spill preparedness & prevention. The Task Force provides a forum where Members can work with stakeholders from the Western US & Canada to implement regional initiatives that protect 56,660 miles of coastline from Alaska to California & the Hawaiian archipelago. Members are senior executives from environmental agencies with oil spill regulatory authority in the states of Alaska, Washington, Oregon, California & Hawaii & the Province of British Columbia. Oil spill program managers from each member agency comprise the Task Force's Coordinating Committee, which oversees activities & projects as authorized by the members when they adopt a Five Year Strategic Plan & Annual Work Plans. The Coordinating Committee convenes four times a year. Task Force members hold their Annual Meetings each summer, rotating locations among member jurisdictions.
Chief Officer(s):
Sarah Brace, Executive Coordinator, 206-409-3253
sarah@vedaenv.com

Pacific Urchin Harvesters Association (PUHA)
902 - 4th St., New Westminster BC V3L 2W6
Tel: 604-524-0322
info@puha.org
www.puha.org
www.facebook.com/153381171388169
twitter.com/puhaorg
Overview: A small local organization founded in 1994
Mission: To examine issues around the commercial dive fishery for Red Sea Urchins; To enhance the urchins' market profile & that of the Canadian seafood production industry in general
Chief Officer(s):
Mike Featherstone, President, 604-932-4559
president@puha.org
Ross Morris, Secretary-Treasurer, 604-524-0322
secretary@puha.org
Publications:
• Pacific Urchin Harvesters Association Newsletter
Type: Newsletter

Pacific Western Athletic Association (PACWEST)
BC
Tel: 250-740-6402; Fax: 250-740-6487
www.pacwestbc.ca
www.facebook.com/pacwestbc
twitter.com/pacwestbc
Previous Name: British Columbia Colleges Athletics Association
Overview: A small provincial organization
Mission: To govern intercollegiate sports in British Columbia
Member of: Canadian Collegiate Athletic Association
Affiliation(s): Atlantic Collegiate Athletic Association; Alberta Colleges Athletic Conference; Réseau du sport étudiant du Québec; Ontario Colleges Athletic Association
Activities: Soccer; volleyball; badminton; basketball; golf
Chief Officer(s):
Bruce Hunter, President
Jake McCallum, Vice-President, Administration, 604-323-5421

Packaging Association of Canada (PAC) / Association canadienne de l'emballage
#607, 1 Concorde Gate, Toronto ON M3C 3N6
Tel: 416-490-7860
pacinfo@pac.ca
www.pac.ca
www.linkedin.com/company/the-packaging-association
www.facebook.com/ThePackagingAssociation
Overview: A large national organization founded in 1950
Mission: To represent both users & suppliers on the strength of environmental & economic policy
Finances: Funding Sources: Membership dues; Activities
Staff Member(s): 9
Membership: 2,100+; Fees: Schedule available; Member Profile: Canadian packaging industry
Chief Officer(s):
James D. Downham, President & CEO, 416-646-4637
jdd@leaderlinx.com
Awards:
• The PAC Global Leadership Awards
Meetings/Conferences:
• Packaging Association of Canada Conference 2018, September, 2018, Montréal, QC
Scope: National
Contact Information: Director, National Events & Member Services: Lisa Abraham, E-mail: labraham@pac.ca, Phone: 416-646-4640
  Québec Office
  CP 43010, Succ. Vilamont, 1859, boul René-Laënnec, Laval QC H7M 6A1
  Tél: 514-990-0134
  quebec@pac.ca
  Chief Officer(s):
  Mary Ann Gryn, Coordinatrice, Chapitre du Québec, 514-990-0134

Paddle Alberta
PO Box 71039, Stn. Silversprings, Calgary AB T3B 5K2
Tel: 403-247-0083; Fax: 866-477-8791
Toll-Free: 877-388-2722
info@paddlealberta.org
www.paddlealberta.org
www.facebook.com/PaddleAlbertaSociety
twitter.com/PaddleAlberta
Overview: A small provincial organization
Mission: To promote safety & sustainability in recreational canoeing & kayaking in Alberta.
Member of: Paddle Canada

Membership: *Committees:* Safety & Touring; Education; Environment
Chief Officer(s):
Karla Handy, Coordinator, Program Services

Paddle Canada (PC) / Pagaie Canada
PO Box 126, Stn. Main, Kingston ON K7L 4V6
Tel: 613-547-3196; *Fax:* 613-547-4880
Toll-Free: 888-252-6292
info@paddlecanada.com
www.paddlecanada.com
www.facebook.com/paddlecanada
twitter.com/paddlecanada
www.youtube.com/user/PaddleCanada
Previous Name: Canadian Recreational Canoeing Association
Overview: A large national licensing charitable organization founded in 1971
Mission: To promote all forms of recreational paddling to Canadians of diverse abilities, culture or age; To advocate for a healthy natural environment; To develop an appreciation for the canoe & the kayak
Affiliation(s): Active Living Alliance for Canadians with a Disability; Girl Guides of Canada
Finances: *Funding Sources:* Membership fees; Donations; Program delivery; Sponsorships
80 volunteer(s)
Membership: 1,700; *Fees:* Schedule available; *Committees:* Canoeing Program Development; River Kayaking Program Development; Sea Kayaking Program Development; Stand Up Paddleboarding Program Development; Bill Mason Scholarship; Environment; Marketing; Membership; PaddleSmart; Program Coordination; Safety; Waterwalker Film Festival
Activities: Reviewing park management plans, hydroelectric developments & timber management plans; Promoting waterway conservation through the Waterwalker Film Festival; Providing educational programs; Increasing environmental awareness; *Awareness Events:* National Paddling Week, June 6-15
Chief Officer(s):
Graham Ketcheson, Executive Director
graham@paddlecanada.com
Awards:
• Bill Mason Memorial Scholarship Fund
Scholarship to a Canadian student enrolled in outdoor recreational or environmental studies at a Canadian college or university; *Amount:* $1,000 awarded annually
Publications:
• Current Strokes [a publication of Paddle Canada]
Type: Newsletter

Paddle Manitoba
PO Box 2663, Winnipeg MB R3C 4B3
info@paddle.mb.ca
www.paddle.mb.ca
www.facebook.com/373524412660987
twitter.com/paddlemanitoba
Previous Name: Manitoba Recreational Canoeing Association
Overview: A small provincial charitable organization founded in 1988
Mission: To promote safe canoeing & kayaking in the province.
Member of: Paddle Canada
Affiliation(s): Manitoba Paddling Association
Finances: *Funding Sources:* Membership fees; tuition fees; fundraising
Membership: *Fees:* $30 individual; $40 family/affiliate; $50 instructor
Activities: Canoe & kayak instruction (flatwater & moving water); information presentations; resource pamphlets; *Speaker Service:* Yes; *Library:* Resource Centre; Not open to public
Chief Officer(s):
Chris Randall, President
president@paddle.mb.ca

Paddle Newfoundland & Labrador
PO Box 2, Stn. C, St. John's NL A1C 5H4
paddle.nl@gmail.com
www.paddlenl.ca
Previous Name: Newfoundland Paddling Club
Overview: A small provincial organization
Mission: To promote paddle sports in Newfoundland & Labrador
Member of: Paddle Canada
Membership: *Fees:* $20 individual; $50 associate; $25 family
Activities: *Awareness Events:* Annual Retreat, May
Chief Officer(s):
Alan Goodridge, President

Pagaie Canada *See* Paddle Canada

Pagan Federation International - Canada (PFI)
PO Box 986, Tavistock ON N0B 2R0
Nuhyn@paganfederation.org
ca.paganfederation.org
Overview: A small national organization founded in 1998
Mission: To provide information on & counter misconceptions about Paganism; To work for the rights of Pagans to worship freely & without censure
Publications:
• Pagan Dawn
Type: Magazine

Pain Society of Alberta (PSA)
132 Warwick Rd., Edmonton AB T5X 4P8
Tel: 780-457-5225; *Fax:* 780-475-7968
info@painsocietyofalberta.org
painsocietyofalberta.org
Overview: A medium-sized provincial organization
Mission: To provide support for patients & health care professionals in Alberta who are concerned with pain management & treatment
Chief Officer(s):
Dawn Petit, President
Glyn Smith, Administrator
glyn@painsocietyofalberta.org
Meetings/Conferences:
• Pain Society of Alberta 12th Annual Conference, October, 2018, Banff, AB
Scope: Provincial

Pakistan Canada Association of Calgary
#507, 4656 Westwinds Dr. NE, Calgary AB T3J 3Z5
Tel: 403-285-5606
www.pcacalgary.ca
Overview: A small local organization founded in 1975
Mission: To represent Canadians of Pakistani heritage living in Calgary & its surrounding areas; To foster understanding, harmony, & good relations between the Pakistani-Canadian community & other communities in Canada; To advocate for inclusion in social, cultural, & educational programs within the Pakistani community as well as Canadian society
Member of: National Federation of Pakistani Canadians Inc.
Finances: *Annual Operating Budget:* Less than $50,000
Membership: 100-499; *Fees:* $20 single; $25 family; $10 student/senior
Activities: *Awareness Events:* National Days of Pakistan & Canada
Chief Officer(s):
Azam Khaloo, President
Tariq Khan, General Secretary

Pakistan Canada Association of Edmonton (PCAE)
9226 - 39 Ave. NW, Edmonton AB T6E 5T9
Tel: 780-463-7233; *Fax:* 780-469-8346
contactus@pcaedmonton.ca
www.pcaedmonton.ca
Overview: A small local organization founded in 1973
Mission: To generate goodwill & understanding among ethnic & mainstream communities; To provide support to new immigrants through language courses & cultural programs open to all
Finances: *Funding Sources:* Community
Membership: *Fees:* $5; *Member Profile:* Pakistani Canadian or any sympathiser of association objectives
Activities: *Speaker Service:* Yes; *Rents Mailing List:* Yes; *Library*
Chief Officer(s):
Habib Fatmi, Chair
president@pcaedmonton.com

Pakistani Canadian Cultural Association of British Columbia (PCCA-BC)
8356 - 146 St., Surrey BC V3S 9K1
Tel: 604-603-5972
info@pccabc.ca
www.pccabc.ca
www.facebook.com/PCCA.BC
Overview: A small local organization
Mission: To promote harmony & friendship among Pakistanis & other Canadians; To help new immigrants in the process of settlement & integration; To promote & embrace multiculturalism
Member of: National Federation of Pakistani Canadians Inc.
Activities: *Awareness Events:* Independence Day of Pakistan, Aug. 14; *Speaker Service:* Yes; *Library*
Chief Officer(s):
Farukh Syed, President

Palais Montcalm
Bureau des arts et de la culture, 995, Place D'Youville, Québec QC G1R 3P1
Tél: 418-641-6220; *Téléc:* 418-691-5171
Ligne sans frais: 877-641-6040
info@palaismontcalm.ca
www.palaismontcalm.ca
www.facebook.com/palaismontcalm
twitter.com/PalaisMontcalm
www.youtube.com/user/PalaisMontcalmQuebec
Aperçu: *Dimension:* petite; *Envergure:* locale
Mission: Pour faire fonctionner un centre de culture et de promouvoir les arts
Membre(s) du personnel: 16
Membre: *Comités:* Programmation; Gouvernance et nomination; Financement; Ressources humaines; Budget et d'audit
Membre(s) du bureau directeur:
Sylvie Roberge, Directrice générale
sylvie.roberge@palaismontcalm.ca

Palliative Care Association of Alberta *See* Alberta Hospice Palliative Care Association

Palliative Manitoba (HPCM)
2109 Portage Ave., Winnipeg MB R3J 0L3
Tel: 204-889-8525; *Fax:* 204-888-8874
Toll-Free: 800-539-0295
info@manitobahospice.mb.ca
palliativemanitoba.ca
www.facebook.com/palliativemanitoba
twitter.com/PalliativeMB
Previous Name: Hospice & Palliative Care Manitoba
Overview: A medium-sized provincial charitable organization founded in 1983
Mission: To champion the development of hospice palliative care for the people of Manitoba through education, information, advocacy & support to service delivery
Member of: Canadian Hospice Palliative Care Association
Finances: *Annual Operating Budget:* $250,000-$500,000; *Funding Sources:* Donations; Foundation grants; Fundraising; United Way
Staff Member(s): 8; 275 volunteer(s)
Membership: 200 individuals; 60 agencies; *Fees:* $45 Individual; $100 Agency
Activities: Providing a Community Hospice Volunteer Program & Volunteer Education Programs; *Awareness Events:* Celebrate Life Breakfast, April; Hike for Hospice, May; Poinsettias for the Holidays, December; *Speaker Service:* Yes; *Library:* Open to public
Chief Officer(s):
Mary Williams, Executive Director
mwilliams@manitobahospice.mb.ca
Lynda Wolf, President
Bob Brennan, Treasurer
Kelly Morris, Vice-President
Meetings/Conferences:
• Palliative Manitoba 27th Annual Provincial Conference, September, 2018, Victoria Inn & Conference Centre, Winnipeg, MB
Scope: Provincial
Attendance: 400+
Description: Theme: "Keep It Simple"
Publications:
• Hospice & Palliative Care Manitoba Annual Report
Type: Yearbook; *Frequency:* Annually
Profile: Highlights of the year plus financial statements
• The Hospice Companion
Type: Newsletter; *Frequency:* Semiannually; *Price:* Free with membership in Hospice & Palliative Care Manitoba
Profile: Information about volunteering, upcoming events, news from regions, & membership news

Palliser Wheat Growers Association *See* Western Canadian Wheat Growers

The Palyul Foundation of Canada
c/o Orgyan Osal Cho Dzong Buddhist Temple & Retreat Centre, 1755 Lingham Lake Rd., Madoc ON K0K 2K0
www.palyulcanada.org
www.facebook.com/Palyul.Canada
twitter.com/OrgyanDzong
Overview: A small local charitable organization founded in 1981
Mission: Dedicated to the preservation & advancement of the teachings of the Nyingma lineage of Vajrayana Buddhism
Activities: Classes on Buddhism, meditation, ritual practices; retreats; empowerments; celebration of Buddhist holy days & festivals

Pamiqsaiji Association for Community Living
PO Box 708, Rankin Inlet NU X0C 0G0
Tel: 867-645-2542; *Fax:* 867-645-2543
pamiqad@qiniq.com
Overview: A small provincial charitable organization overseen by Nunavummi Disabilities Makinnasuaqtiit Society
Mission: To provide support for adults with intellectual disabilities
Member of: Canadian Association for Community Living

Pan American Hockey Federation (PAHF)
c/o Ian Baggott, Field Hockey Canada, 3800 Wesbrook Mall, Vancouver BC V6S 2L9
info@panamhockey.org
www.panamhockey.org
www.facebook.com/PanAmHockey
twitter.com/PanAmHockey
www.youtube.com/user/PAHFvideo;
instagram.com/panamhockey
Overview: A large international organization founded in 1955
Mission: To be the governing continental federation for all field hockey in the Pan American region
Member of: International Hockey Federation
Finances: *Annual Operating Budget:* $100,000-$250,000; *Funding Sources:* Grants; Membership dues; Tournament fees; International Hockey Federation; Sponsorship
Membership: 30 national associations; *Member Profile:* National association recognized by national olympic committees & the International Hockey Federation; *Committees:* Appointments; Athletes; Competitions; Development; Media & Communications; Medical; Umpiring
Activities: Organizing international hockey tournaments; organizing instructional courses
Chief Officer(s):
Alberto Budeisky, President
Mary Cicinelli, Honorary Treasurer
mary.cicinelli@panamhockey.org
Renata Carneiro, Managing Director
renata.carneiro@panamhockey.org
Awards:
• Honorary Life Member
To honour long-time contribution by a member of the Board
• Order of Merit
To recognize Pan American Hockey Federation board or committee members who have served for ten years or more & made a significant contribution
• President's Award
To recognize a shorter-term contribution to the development of hockey

Pancreatic Cancer Canada Foundation
#508, 36 Eglinton Ave. West, Toronto ON M4R 1A1
Tel: 416-548-8077
Toll-Free: 888-726-2269
info@pccf.ca
www.pancreaticcancercanada.ca
www.facebook.com/PanCanCanada
twitter.com/pancancercanada
www.instagram.com/pancreaticcancercanada
Overview: A small national charitable organization founded in 2006
Mission: To eliminate pancreatic cancer; To improve survival rates of pancreatic cancer patients; To enhance the lives of individuals & families affected by pancreatic cancer
Activities: Raising awareness about risk factors, symptoms, & treatment options; Promoting research into pancreatic cancer detection & treatment; Offering resources & support to pancreatic cancer patients & their families; Advocating for increased funding of scientific projects & research; *Awareness Events:* Pancreatic Cancer Awareness Month, Nov.
Chief Officer(s):
Michelle Capobianco, Executive Director
Amanda Jodoin, Director, Marketing & Communications
Amy Lewis, Director, Strategic Partnerships
Joy Wagner, Director, Philanthropy & Donor Engagement
Jessica Stewart, Office Manager

Paper & Paperboard Packaging Environmental Council (PPEC)
#3, 1995 Clark Blvd., Brampton ON L6T 4W1
Tel: 905-458-0087; *Fax:* 905-458-2052
ppec@ppec-paper.com
www.ppec-paper.com
www.linkedin.com/company/2516029
Overview: A medium-sized national organization founded in 1990
Mission: To represent member companies to various levels of government, as well as to environmental & consumer interest groups
Affiliation(s): American Forest & Paper Association; Fibre Box Association; Association of Independent Corrugated Converters (AICC)
Membership: *Member Profile:* Packaging mills, and packaging converters
Chief Officer(s):
John Mullinder, Executive Director

Paper Packaging Canada *See* Canadian Corrugated Containerboard Association

Parachute
#300, 150 Eglinton Ave. East, Toronto ON M4P 1E8
Tel: 647-776-5100
Toll-Free: 888-537-7777
info@parachutecanada.org
www.parachutecanada.org
www.linkedin.com/company/parachute—-leaders-in-injury-prevention
www.facebook.com/parachutecanada
twitter.com/parachutecanada
Merged from: Safe Kids Canada; Safe Communities Canada; SMARTRISK; ThinkFirst Canada
Overview: A medium-sized national charitable organization founded in 2012
Mission: To promote effective strategies to prevent unintentional injuries; to build partnerships & uses a comprehensive approach to advance safety & reduce the burden of injuries to Canada's children & youth
Affiliation(s): The Hospital for Sick Children
Finances: *Annual Operating Budget:* Greater than $5 Million; *Funding Sources:* Corporate donations
Staff Member(s): 35
Membership: 4,000+; *Committees:* Parachute Expert Advisory
Activities: *Library:* Not open to public
Chief Officer(s):
Louise Logan, President & CEO

Paradise Hill Chamber of Commerce
c/o Village of Paradise Hill, PO Box 270, Paradise Hill SK S0M 2G0
Tel: 306-344-2206
www.paradisehill.ca
Overview: A small local organization
Member of: Saskatchewan Chamber of Commerce
Chief Officer(s):
George Palen, President

Paralympic Sports Association (Alberta) (PSA)
#305, 11010 101 St., Edmonton AB T5H 4B9
Tel: 780-439-8687; *Fax:* 780-432-0486
info@parasports.net
www.parasports.net
www.linkedin.com/company/paralympic-sports-association
www.facebook.com/PSASports
twitter.com/Sports_PSA
Overview: A medium-sized provincial charitable organization founded in 1965
Mission: To provide sports & recreation programs for people with physical disabilities
Affiliation(s): Wheelchair Sports Alberta
Staff Member(s): 2
Membership: *Fees:* $20 individual; $40 family; *Member Profile:* Persons with physical disabilities
Activities: *Speaker Service:* Yes
Chief Officer(s):
Amy MacKinnon, Executive Director
executivedirector@parasports.net
Amy Hayward, Coordinator, Programs
programs@parasports.net

Paralympics PEI Inc. *See* ParaSport & Recreation PEI

Paramedic Association of Canada
#201, 4 Florence St, Ottawa ON K2P 0W7
Tel: 613-836-6581; *Fax:* 613-836-6581
Toll-Free: 844-836-6581
info@paramedic.ca
www.paramedic.ca
www.linkedin.com/company/3173844
www.facebook.com/PACParamedic
twitter.com/PAC_Paramedic
plus.google.com/b/114891282468589944660
Overview: A medium-sized national organization founded in 1988
Mission: To represent the public & practitioner nationally on health related paramedic issues; To lobby government & to speak to the media; To establish national communications network for all practitioners
Affiliation(s): Ambulance Paramedics of British Columbia; Alberta College of Paramedics; Saskatchewan College of Paramedics; Paramedic Association of Manitoba; Ontario Paramedic Association; Association Professionnelle des Paramédics du Québec; Paramedic Association of New Brunswick; Paramedic Association of Newfoundland & Labrador
Membership: 14,000; *Fees:* $100 member at large; *Committees:* Certification; Government & Media Relations; Practitioner Protection
Activities: Developed the National Occupational Competency Profiles, Canadian Paramedic Standards; established the Canadian EHS Research Consortium
Chief Officer(s):
Chris Hood, President
Dwayne Forsman, Sec.-Treas.
Pierre Poirier, Executive Director

Paramedic Association of Manitoba (PAM)
#230, 530 Century St., Winnipeg MB R3H 0Y4
Fax: 866-222-6471
Toll-Free: 866-726-1210
info@paramedicsofmanitoba.ca
www.paramedicsofmanitoba.ca
www.facebook.com/262118083807029
twitter.com/PAM_manitoba
Overview: A small provincial organization founded in 2001
Mission: To promote excellence in pre-hospital emergency health care & excellence in the profession of paramedicine
Member of: Paramedic Association of Canada
Membership: *Fees:* $100 full; $55 associate; $200 corporate
Chief Officer(s):
Jodi Possia, Chair
chairman@paramedicsofmanitoba.ca
Christy Beazley, Director, Public Relations
cbeazley@paramedicsofmanitoba.ca

Paramedic Association of New Brunswick (PANB) / L'Association des paramédics du Nouveau-Brunswick
298 Main St., Fredericton NB E3A 1C9
Tel: 506-459-2638; *Fax:* 506-459-6728
Toll-Free: 888-887-7262
info@panb.ca
www.panb.ca
twitter.com/PANB_Paramedic
Overview: A small provincial organization
Mission: To develop & promote the highest ethical, educational, & clinical standards for all levels of Prehospital Care Professionals in New Brunswick
Member of: Paramedic Association of Canada
Membership: *Committees:* Executive; Complaints; Disipline & Fitness to Practice; Admin & Finance; Legislation; Policy Review; Public Relations; Honours & Awards
Chief Officer(s):
Chris Hood, Executive Director/Registrar
chris.hood@panb.ca
Chantale Hayes, Assistant Registrar/Office Manager
chantale.hayes@panb.ca

Paramedic Association of Newfoundland & Labrador (PANL)
PO Box 8086, St. John's NL A1B 3M9
Toll-Free: 855-561-3698
contact_us@panl.ca
www.panl.ca
Overview: A small provincial organization founded in 2005
Mission: To improve prehospital patient care in Newfoundland & Labrador
Member of: Paramedic Association of Canada
Membership: *Fees:* $20 full/associate; $15 student

ParaSport & Recreation PEI
Royalty Center House Of Sport, #123, 40 Enman Cres., Charlottetown PE C1E 1E6
Tel: 902-368-4540; *Fax:* 902-368-4548
info@parasportpei.ca
www.parasportpei.ca
www.facebook.com/141822665843254
twitter.com/ParaSportPEI
Previous Name: Paralympics PEI Inc.

Overview: A small provincial charitable organization founded in 1974
Mission: To ensure the ample provision of sport & recreation opportunities for persons who are physically challenged
Member of: Canadian Blind Sport Association; Canadian Association for Disabled Skiing; Canadian Wheelchair Sports Association
Affiliation(s): The JoyRiders Therapeutic Riding Association of PEI Inc.; The Canadian Council of the Blind - Prince County and Queensland Chapters; The Abegweit Club of Summerside; G.E.A.R. (Getting Everyone Accessibly Riding)
Finances: *Funding Sources:* Province of PEI; City of Charlottetown; business sector; community & service clubs; fundraising
Staff Member(s): 2
Activities: Demonstrations; presentations; sport/recreation events; *Speaker Service:* Yes; *Library:* Open to public
Chief Officer(s):
Tracy Stevenson, Executive Director
tracy@parasportpei.ca
Awards:
• ParaSport & Recreation PEI School Award, ParaSport & Recreation PEI
Eligibility: Must be enrolled in the PEI School System, have a physical disability, and is active in sport/recreation programs at the community or school level. *Deadline:* June; *Amount:* $25 for elementary students; $50 for intermediate students; $75 for high school students
• ParaSport & Recreation PEI Scholarships, ParaSport & Recreation PEI
Eligibility: Applicants with a physical disability that are entering university/college in the ensuing year. *Deadline:* June; *Amount:* 2 scholarships for $500

ParaSport Ontario
3701 Danforth Ave., Toronto ON M1N 2G2
Tel: 416-426-7187
info@parasportontario.ca
www.parasportontario.ca
twitter.com/parasport_ont
www.instagram.com/parasportontario
Previous Name: Sport for Disabled - Ontario; Paralympics Ontario
Overview: A medium-sized provincial charitable organization founded in 1981
Mission: To provide support to all members of the disability community, regardless of age or stage in life, to participate in sport programs & activities to enhance physical function & quality of life
Affiliation(s): ParaGolf Ontario; Ontario Cerebral Palsy Sports Association
Staff Member(s): 3
Membership: 1,800+
Activities: "Try Me" Program; Equipment Rental Program; Connecting people with disabilities with parasports & sports clubs; *Speaker Service:* Yes
Chief Officer(s):
Jeff Tiessen, Executive Director, 416-426-7186
jeff@parasportontario.ca

Parasports Québec
4545, av Pierre-de Coubertin, Montréal QC H1V 0B2
Tél: 514-252-3108; *Téléc:* 514-254-9793
info@parasportsquebec.com
www.parasportsquebec.com
www.facebook.com/367668269915613
Nom précédent: Association québécoise des sports en fauteuil roulants
Aperçu: *Dimension:* moyenne; *Envergure:* provinciale; Organisme sans but lucratif; fondée en 1983
Mission: Favoriser un accès à la pratique sportive en fauteuil roulant à tous les niveaux de performance pour le bénéfice des personnes ayant une limitation physique
Membre de: Canadian Wheelchair Sports Association
Finances: *Budget de fonctionnement annuel:* $250,000-$500,000
Membre(s) du personnel: 5; 25 bénévole(s)
Membre: 350; *Montant de la cotisation:* Barème
Activités: *Service de conférenciers:* Oui
Membre(s) du bureau directeur:
Donald Royer, Président

Parcelles de tendresse
CP 582, Chibougamau QC G8P 2Y8
Tél: 418-748-3753
Aperçu: *Dimension:* petite; *Envergure:* locale
Membre(s) du bureau directeur:
Lisa Fradette Caron, Présidente

Parcs et loisirs de l'Ontario *See* Parks & Recreation Ontario

PARD Therapeutic Riding (PARD)
PO Box 1654, Peterborough ON K9J 5S4
Tel: 705-742-6441
pardtherapeuticriding@gmail.com
www.pard.ca
www.facebook.com/PARDTherapeuticRiding
Previous Name: Peterborough Association for Riding for the Disabled
Overview: A small local charitable organization
Mission: Provides the benefits of riding to people with disabilities.
Member of: Canadian Therapeutic Riding Association; Ontario Therapeutic Riding Association
Activities: Horseback riding instruction as a form of therapeutic & social recreation for physically, emotionally, developmentally challenged individuals
Chief Officer(s):
Kathy Carruthers, Program Coordinator

Parent Action on Drugs (PAD)
#121, 7 Hawksdale Rd., Toronto ON M3K 1W3
Tel: 416-395-4970; *Fax:* 866-591-7685
Toll-Free: 877-265-9279
pad@parentactionondrugs.org
www.parentactionondrugs.org
www.facebook.com/ParentActionOnDrugs
twitter.com/PAD_Ontario
Overview: A small provincial charitable organization founded in 1983
Mission: To address issues of substance use among youth through outreach, prevention, education & parent support; enhances the capacity of parents, youth & communities to promote an environment that encourages youth to make informed choices
Member of: HC Link
Staff Member(s): 8
Activities: Peer education programs for youth (CBC: Challenges, Beliefs & Changes; WWW: What's With Weed); Resources for parents & professionals
Chief Officer(s):
Diane Buhler, Executive Director
pad@sympatico.ca
Publications:
• PAD Parent & COmmunity Handbook
Profile: Facts on tobacco, alcohol, cannabis and other drugs

Parent Cooperative Preschools International (PCPI)
8725 Westport Dr., Niagara Falls ON L2H 0A2
Tel: 905-374-6605
enquiries@preschools.coop
www.preschools.coop
www.facebook.com/parentcooperatives
plus.google.com/118022490917296587831
Previous Name: American Council of Co-operative Preschools
Overview: A medium-sized international organization founded in 1962
Mission: To promote the family & community; to strengthen & expand the parent cooperative movement & community appreciation of parent education for adults & preschool education for children; to promote desirable standards for program, practices & conditions in parent cooperative preschools & encourage continuing education for parents, teachers & directors; to promote interchange of information among parent cooperative nursery schools, kindergartens & other parent-sponsored preschool programs; to cooperate with family living, adult education & early childhood educational organizations in the interest of more effective service relationships with parents of young children; to study & promote legislation designed to further the health & well-being of children & families
Finances: *Annual Operating Budget:* Less than $50,000; *Funding Sources:* Membership fees; fundraising
Membership: 50,000+; *Fees:* $40 individual; $50 school/group; $200 council; $40 library; $100 sponsor; $500 individual life; *Committees:* Advisors; Awards; Katharine Whiteside Taylor Bursary; Becky Allen Fund; Marika Townshend Travel Grants
Chief Officer(s):
Mariah Battiston, Co-President
mariahbattiston@shaw.ca
Lesley Romanoff, Co-President
lesley@romanoffstudio.com

Parent Finders Ottawa
PO Box 21025, Stn. Ottawa South, Ottawa ON K1S 5N1
Tel: 613-730-8305; *Fax:* 613-730-0345
pfncr@yahoo.com
parentfindersottawa.ca
www.facebook.com/pages/Parent-Finders-Ottawa/120530528033309
twitter.com/ParentFinders
Overview: A small national organization
Mission: To assist adult adoptees/foster persons & birth relatives to obtain background information from adoption files kept in social services departments; To assist in search & reunion; To promote a feeling of openness about the adoption experience & a better understanding about the longing for a reunion between adult adoptees & birth relatives
Affiliation(s): American Adoption Congress; International Soundex Reunion Register
Finances: *Annual Operating Budget:* Less than $50,000; *Funding Sources:* Registration fees
Staff Member(s): 4; 4 volunteer(s)
Membership: 59,101; *Fees:* $25; *Member Profile:* Must be of legal age - 18 or 19 as applies in each province; *Committees:* Legislative; Freedom of Information
Activities: Canadian Adoption Reunion Register; lobbying; government social services; *Library:* Open to public by appointment
Chief Officer(s):
Patricia McCarron, President

Parent Support Services Society of BC (PSSS)
#204, 5623 Imperial St., Burnaby BC V5J 1G1
Tel: 604-669-1616; *Fax:* 604-669-1636
Toll-Free: 877-345-9777
office@parentsupportbc.ca
www.parentsupportbc.ca
www.facebook.com/ParentSupportBC
twitter.com/PSS_BC
www.youtube.com/user/ParentSupportBC
Previous Name: BC Parents in Crisis Society
Overview: A medium-sized provincial charitable organization founded in 1974
Mission: To promote parent support circles to help parents & guardians learn positive parenting skills & receive emotional support
Member of: Federation of Child & Family Services of BC
Finances: *Funding Sources:* Ministry for Children & Families; United Way; Private donations; Membership dues; Government grants
Staff Member(s): 9
Membership: *Fees:* $5-$35 volunteer; $35 individual; $100 agency; *Member Profile:* Any person above the age of consent who subscribes to the vision, mission, & values of the society
Activities: *Internships:* Yes
Chief Officer(s):
Carol Madsen, Executive Director, 604-669-1616 Ext. 102
cmadsen@parentsupportbc.ca
Awards:
• Bill McFarland Award
Eligibility: A group or individual that has displayed outstanding devotion to the prevention of child abuse

Central Island Office
PO Box 86, Nanoose Bay BC V9P 9J9
Tel: 250-468-9658; *Fax:* 250-468-9668
Toll-Free: 877-345-9777
parent@telus.net
www.parentsupportbc.ca/central-island
Chief Officer(s):
Sandi Halvorson, Program Manager

Prince George Office
PO Box 21106, RPO Spruceland, Prince George BC V2M 2A5
Tel: 250-962-0600
Toll-Free: 877-345-9777
parentnorth@shaw.ca
www.parentsupportbc.ca/prince-george
Chief Officer(s):
Jessica Turner, Program Coordinator

Victoria Office
PO Box 31075, RPO University Heights, Victoria BC V8N 6J3
Tel: 250-384-8042; *Fax:* 250-384-8043
psscoordinator@shaw.ca
www.parentsupportbc.ca/victoria
Chief Officer(s):
Annie Lavack, Program Coordinator

Parenting Education Saskatchewan
#306, 506 - 25th St. East, Saskatoon SK S7K 4A7
Tel: 306-934-2095; *Fax:* 306-934-2087
parent.educ@sasktel.net
www.parenteducationsask.ca
Overview: A medium-sized provincial organization founded in 1992
Mission: To link parenting services across the province & provide support & information to those facilitating or organizing parent support/education services
Member of: Canadian Association of Family Resource Programs (FRP Canada)
Chief Officer(s):
Bev Digout, Coordinator

Parents & Friends of Lesbians & Gays (Parents FLAG) *See* PFLAG Canada Inc.

Parents as First Educators (PAFE)
PO Box 84556, Toronto ON M6S 4Z7
Tel: 416-763-7233
pafe4you@gmail.com
www.p-first.com
www.facebook.com/pafe4
twitter.com/PAFE4
Overview: A medium-sized provincial organization
Mission: To ensure Ontario Catholic school board trustees are promoting Catholic teachings & to make parents aware of the work trustees are doing
Membership: 15,000

Parents for Children's Mental Health (PCMH)
PO Box 20004, St Catharines ON L2N 7W7
Tel: 416-220-0742
Toll-Free: 855-254-7264
admin@pcmh.ca
www.pcmh.ca
www.facebook.com/PCMHOntario
twitter.com/PCMHontario
Overview: A small provincial organization founded in 1994
Mission: To provide a voice for children & families in Ontario who are affected by mental health problems
Chief Officer(s):
Michele Sparling, Chair
Sarah Cannon, Executive Director

Parents of Multiple Births Association of Canada Inc. *See* Multiple Births Canada

Parents of the Handicapped of Southeastern Alberta *See* Bridges Family Programs Association

Parents partenaires en éducation (PPE)
435 rue Donald, #B-204, Ottawa ON K1K 4X5
Tél: 613-741-8846; *Téléc:* 613-741-7322
Ligne sans frais: 800-342-0663
www.ppeontario.ca
www.facebook.com/ppeontario
twitter.com/ppeontario
www.youtube.com/reseauppe
Nom précédent: Fédération des associations de parents francophones de l'Ontario
Aperçu: Dimension: grande; *Envergure:* provinciale; Organisme sans but lucratif; fondée en 1940
Mission: Travailler en étroite collaboration avec ses partenaires en éducation, outiller les parents dans leur rôle de partenaires en éducation et agir comme porte-parole provincial des parents; promouvoir l'excellence de l'éducation de langue française et l'épanouissement global des enfants francophones
Membre de: Association canadienne d'éducation de langue française; Commission nationale des parents francophones; Regroupement des organismes francophones en éducation
Finances: *Budget de fonctionnement annuel:* $250,000-$500,000; *Fonds:* Gouvernementale; Cotisation; Revenus autonomes
Membre(s) du personnel: 2; 14 bénévole(s)
Membre: 395; *Montant de la cotisation:* 75$; *Critères d'admissibilite:* Parents qui ont choisi d'offrir à leurs enfants une éducation de langue française publique ou catholique en Ontario
Activités: Appui aux parents; formation; animation; conférence; ateliers; ressources web; *Service de conférenciers:* Oui
Membre(s) du bureau directeur:
Louis Kdouh, Président
presidence@ppeontario.ca
Sylvie Ross, Directrice générale
dg@ppeontario.ca

Prix, Bourses:
- Programme de certificat de reconnaissance de PPE
- Fonds Marguerite Yamasaki
- Prix de la CNPF
Ce prix offert par la Commission nationale des parents francophones (CNPF)
Meetings/Conferences:
- Parents partenaires en éducation congrès et assemblée générale annuelle 2018, 2018, ON
Scope: Provincial
Contact Information: Directrice générale: Sylvie Ross, Courriel: dg@ppeontario.ca
Publications:
- Bulletin de PPE [publication Parents partenaires en éducation]
Type: Bulletin

Parents-secours du Québec inc. (PSQI)
#203, 17, rue Fusey, Trois-Rivières QC G8T 2T3
Tél: 819-374-5541
Ligne sans frais: 800-588-8173
info@parentssecours.ca
www.parentssecours.ca
www.facebook.com/262687173759603
www.youtube.com/user/ParentsSecours
Aperçu: Dimension: moyenne; *Envergure:* provinciale; fondée en 1976 surveillé par Block Parent Program of Canada Inc.
Mission: Parents-Secours du Québec inc. (PSQI) est un organisme à but non lucratif qui assure la sécurité et la protection des enfants et des aînés-es en offrant un réseau de foyers-refuges sécuritaires tout en contribuant à promouvoir la prévention par l'information et l'éducation.
Membre de: Block Parent Program of Canada Inc.
Membre(s) du bureau directeur:
Pierre Chalifoux, Directeur général
Prix, Bourses:
- Le bouton MÉRITE
Eligibility: Personnes qui habiter au Québec et ont contribué d'une manière marquante à la création, à la promotion ou au perfectionnement du programme Parents-Secours
Publications:
- Infolettre [a publication of Parents-secours du Québec inc.]
Type: Newsletter

Parents-Unis Lanaudière
#320, 144, rue St-Joseph, Joliette QC J6E 5C4
Tél: 450-755-6755; *Téléc:* 450-755-1773
Ligne sans frais: 844-662-6755
pul@parentsunis.org
www.parentsunis.org
Aperçu: Dimension: petite; *Envergure:* locale; Organisme sans but lucratif; fondée en 1985
Mission: Entraide à toute personne impliquée dans une situation incestueuse ou sexuellement abusive; contrer l'inceste et l'agression sexuelle à l'égard des enfants; aider les victimes et les parents touchés par ce problème
Finances: *Budget de fonctionnement annuel:* $100,000-$250,000; *Fonds:* Gouvernement
Membre(s) du personnel: 3; 30 bénévole(s)
Membre: 50; *Montant de la cotisation:* $1; *Critères d'admissibilite:* Toute personne de plus 18 ans ayant un intérêt pour la problématique de l'agression sexuelle envers les enfants
Activités: Stagiaires: Oui; *Service de conférenciers:* Oui
Membre(s) du bureau directeur:
Catherine Pelletier, Directrice générale
dg@parentsunis.org

Paris & District Chamber of Commerce
PO Box 130, Paris ON N3L 3E7
Tel: 226-208-1159
info@pariscoc.ca
www.pariscoc.ca
Overview: A small local organization
Mission: To enhance the quality of life in the Paris community; To help members to thrive
Membership: 105; *Fees:* $125
Chief Officer(s):
Joanne Forrest, President
Hayley Williams, Coordinator

Park People
City Builder's Lab, #119, 401 Richmond St. West, Toronto ON M5V 3A8
Tel: 416-583-5776
parkpeople.ca
www.facebook.com/ParkPeopleTO
twitter.com/Park_People
www.instagram.com/parkppl

Overview: A small local charitable organization
Mission: To build, expand & enhance sustainable city parks; To encourage community development through the improvement of parks & public spaces
Activities: Conducting research on park planning solutions; Encouraging community engagement with respect to park & public space planning & design; Offering park development programs & services
Chief Officer(s):
Dave Harvey, Executive Director

Parkdale Community Information Centre (PCIC)
1303 Queen St. West, Toronto ON M6K 1L6
Tel: 416-393-7689; *Fax:* 416-532-6531
info@pcic.ca
www.pcic.ca
Overview: A small local charitable organization founded in 1976
Mission: To establish & maintain in Parkdale a central, comprehensive, up-to-date & indexed collection of information about services & resources; To provide such information to anyone requiring it & to assist residents of Parkdale to find services or resources appropriate to their needs; To be active in identifying duplication & gaps or deficiencies in services or resources, to bring these to attention of appropriate organizations & assist community to fill gaps in services or resources whenever possible
Affiliation(s): Association of Community Information Centres in Ontario; Federation of Community Information Centres in the Greater Toronto Area; Ontario Council of Agencies Serving Immigrants
Finances: *Annual Operating Budget:* $100,000-$250,000; *Funding Sources:* United Way; City of Toronto
Staff Member(s): 3
Membership: 1-99; *Fees:* $5 regular; $3 seniors; $25 agency; *Member Profile:* Individuals who live or work in Parkdale
Activities: Youth outreach; community outreach
Chief Officer(s):
Cassandra Wong, Executive Director

Parkdale Community Legal Services
1266 Queen St. West, Toronto ON M6K 1L3
Tel: 416-531-2411; *Fax:* 416-531-0885
mailbox@parkdalelegal.org
www.parkdalelegal.org
www.facebook.com/parkdalelegal
twitter.com/parkdalelegal
www.flickr.com/photos/59309375@N05
Overview: A small local charitable organization founded in 1971
Member of: Association of Community Legal Clinics of Ontario
Affiliation(s): Legal Aid Ontario; Osgoode Hall Law School
Finances: *Annual Operating Budget:* $500,000-$1.5 Million
Staff Member(s): 20; 14 volunteer(s)
Membership: 1-99
Activities: Free legal advice & representation to Parkdale residents; *Internships:* Yes; *Library:* Not open to public

Parkdale Focus Community Project
#103, 1497 Queen St. West, Toronto ON M6R 1A3
Tel: 416-536-1234
www.stchrishouse.org/adults/alcohol-drug-pre-pro
Overview: A small local organization founded in 1991
Member of: St. Christopher House
Activities: Family & youth programs; drug, alcohol & injury prevention programs; early intervention programs; educational workshops; outreach to high-risk groups; *Awareness Events:* Drug Awareness Week

Parkdale Intercultural Association (PIA)
1257 Queen St. West, Toronto ON M6K 1L5
Tel: 416-536-4420; *Fax:* 416-538-3831
pia@piaparkdale.com
www.piaparkdale.com
Overview: A small local charitable organization founded in 1977
Mission: To provide settlement programs & services to refugees & immigrants; To foster an equitable & sustainable community in Parkdale
Member of: Ontario Council of Agencies Serving Immigrants
Finances: *Annual Operating Budget:* $500,000-$1.5 Million
Staff Member(s): 16; 16 volunteer(s)
Membership: 57; *Fees:* $5 individual; $10 family; $25 corporate
Activities: Language Instruction for Newcomers to Canada (LINC); programs & activities celebrating diversity, multiculturalism, & anti-racism; community development projects; partnerships & collaborations

Parkdale Neighbourhood Land Trust
c/o Parkdale Activity Recreation Centre, 1499 Queen St. West, Toronto ON M6R 1A3
info@pnlt.ca
www.pnlt.ca
www.facebook.com/ParkdaleCommunityLandTrust
Overview: A small local organization founded in 2010
Mission: To protect the social, cultural, & economic diversity of Toronto's Parkdale neighbourhood
Staff Member(s): 1
Activities: Acquiring land & leasing it to non-profit partners who can provide affordable housing & open space
Chief Officer(s):
Joshua Barndt, Coordinator, Development
joshuabarndt@pnlt.ca

Parkinson Alberta Society (PAS)
Westech Building, #102, 5636 Burbank Cres. SE, Calgary AB T2H 1Z6
Tel: 403-243-9901; *Fax:* 403-243-8283
Toll-Free: 800-561-1911
info@parkinsonalberta.ca
www.parkinsonalberta.ca
www.facebook.com/281448621909497
twitter.com/ParkinsonAB
www.youtube.com/user/ParkinsonAlberta
Overview: A small provincial charitable organization founded in 1981 overseen by Parkinson Society Canada
Mission: PAS is dedicated to helping people and families of Southern Alberta who live with Parkinson's and related disorders
Staff Member(s): 17
Membership: Fees: $25 individual; *Member Profile:* Anyone with interest in learning about Parkinson's
Activities: Golf Tournament, July; *Awareness Events:* SuperWalk for Parkinsons, Sept.; *Internships:* Yes; *Speaker Service:* Yes
Chief Officer(s):
John Petryshen, CEO
jpetryshen@parkinsonalberta.ca
Publications:
• Parkinson Pulse
Type: Newsletter
  Edmonton Office
  #102, 11748 Kingsway Ave., Edmonton AB T2G 0X5
  Tel: 780-425-6400; *Fax:* 780-425-6425
  Grande Prairie Office
  #103, 10901 - 100 St., Grande Prairie AB T8V 2M9
  Tel: 780-882-6640
  Chief Officer(s):
  Kristeva Dowling, Coordinator, Client Services
  KDowling@parkinsonalberta.ca
  Lethbridge Office
  St. John's Ambulance Building, 1254 - 3 Ave. South, Lethbridge AB T1J 0J9
  Tel: 403-317-7710; *Fax:* 403-327-2820
  Chief Officer(s):
  Brian Treadwell, Coordinator, Client Services
  btreadwell@parkinsonalberta.ca
  Medicine Hat Office
  United Way of South Eastern Alberta, #101, 928 Allowance Ave. SE, Medicine Hat AB T1A 3G7
  Tel: 403-526-5521; *Fax:* 403-526-5244
  Chief Officer(s):
  Beth Metcalf, Coordinator, Client Services
  bmetcalf@parkinsonalberta.ca
  Red Deer Office
  The Lending Cupboard Society, 5406D - 43 St., Red Deer AB T4P 1C9
  Tel: 403-346-4463
  Chief Officer(s):
  Marilynne Herron, Coordinator, Client Services
  mherron@parkinsonalberta.ca

Parkinson Canada
#316, 4211 Yonge St., Toronto ON M2P 2A9
Tel: 416-227-9700; *Fax:* 844-440-8963
Toll-Free: 800-565-3000
info@parkinson.ca
www.parkinson.ca
www.facebook.com/parkinsoncanada
twitter.com/parkinsoncanada
Previous Name: Parkinson Foundation of Canada
Overview: A small national organization founded in 1965
Mission: To raise funds for research into the causes & treatment of Parkinsons; to provide services which support Parkinsonians & their families; to disseminate information about the condition to individuals & organizations across Canada
Member of: Neurological Health Charities Canada; Health Partners; Canadian Coalition for Genetic Fairness
Finances: Annual Operating Budget: Greater than $5 Million; *Funding Sources:* Individual giving, Corporate and Foundation support, Events, Government, support from regional partners, investment income
Staff Member(s): 26
Membership: 15,000; *Fees:* $25; *Committees:* National Advocacy; Research Policy; Scientific Advisory; Finance; Audit
Activities: Programs, services, support and education about Parkinson's disease and related conditions (MSA, PSP) for public and health professionals.; *Awareness Events:* Parkinson's Awareness Month, April; Parkinson's Canadian Open Championships, Oct.; *Internships:* Yes; *Library:* Open to public by appointment
Chief Officer(s):
Joyce Gordon, President & CEO
Marina Joseph, Director, Marketing & Communication
communications@parkinson.ca
Meetings/Conferences:
• Parkinson Canada 2018 Annual General Meeting, 2018
Scope: National
Publications:
• ParkinsonPost
Type: Newsletter; *Frequency:* 5 pa; *Editor:* Marina Joseph
Profile: An online subscription for Canada's Parkinson's community, distributed 5 times per year.

Parkinson Foundation of Canada *See* Parkinson Canada

Parkinson Society British Columbia (PSBC)
#600, 890 West Pender St., Vancouver BC V6C 1J9
Tel: 604-662-3240; *Fax:* 604-687-1327
Toll-Free: 800-668-3330
info@parkinson.bc.ca
www.parkinson.bc.ca
www.facebook.com/191326604220827
twitter.com/ParkinsonsBC
www.youtube.com/user/ParkinsonSocietyBC
Overview: A medium-sized provincial organization founded in 1969 overseen by Parkinson Society Canada
Staff Member(s): 10
Membership: Fees: $25 individual
Chief Officer(s):
Jean Blake, CEO
jblake@parkinson.bc.ca

Parkinson Society Canada - Central & Northern Ontario Region *See* Parkinson Society Central & Northern Ontario

Parkinson Society Canada - Manitoba Region *See* Parkinson Society Manitoba

Parkinson Society Canada - Southwestern Ontario Region *See* Parkinson Society Southwestern Ontario

Parkinson Society Central & Northern Ontario
#321, 4211 Yonge St., Toronto ON M2P 2A9
Tel: 416-227-1200; *Fax:* 416-227-1520
Toll-Free: 800-565-3000
info.cno@parkinson.ca
www.cno.parkinson.ca
www.facebook.com/101248525517
twitter.com/ParkinsonCNO
Previous Name: Parkinson Society Canada - Central & Northern Ontario Region
Overview: A small local organization overseen by Parkinson Society Canada
Finances: Annual Operating Budget: Greater than $5 Million
Staff Member(s): 14
Membership: Committees: Research Policy; National Advocacy; Medical Advisory
Chief Officer(s):
Debbie Davis, CEO
debbie.davis@parkinson.ca

Parkinson Society Manitoba
#7, 414 Westmount Dr., Winnipeg MB R2J 1P2
Tel: 204-786-2637
Toll-Free: 866-999-5558
parkinson@mymts.net
www.parkinsonmanitoba.ca
www.facebook.com/ParkinsonSocietyManitobaSuperwalk2013
Previous Name: Parkinson Society Canada - Manitoba Region
Overview: A medium-sized provincial organization overseen by Parkinson Society Canada
Chief Officer(s):
Howard Koks, CEO
howard.koks@parkinson.ca
  Brandon/Westman Office
  Scotia Towers, #228, 1011 Rosser Ave., Brandon MB R7A 0L5
  Tel: 204-726-1702

Parkinson Society Maritime Region (PSMR) / Société Parkinson - Region Maritime (SPRM)
#150, 7071 Bayers Rd., Halifax NS B3L 2C2
Tel: 902-422-3656; *Fax:* 902-422-3797
Toll-Free: 800-663-2468
psmr@parkinsonmaritimes.ca
www.parkinsonmaritimes.ca
www.facebook.com/parkinsonmaritimes
twitter.com/psmr
www.youtube.com/channel/UCo1IYTO_WaeyIOiUhkrnjXg
Overview: A small provincial charitable organization overseen by Parkinson Society Canada
Mission: To give information to people with Parkinson & their family, children & caregivers
Finances: Funding Sources: Private donations, events, SuperWalk
Activities: Support groups; Physiotherapy Clinic; Speaker series; *Awareness Events:* Parkinson SuperWalk; *Internships:* Yes; *Speaker Service:* Yes; *Library:* Open to public
Chief Officer(s):
Jim Horwich, Chair
Robert Shaw, Regional CEO

Parkinson Society Newfoundland & Labrador
The Viking Bldg., #305, 136 Crosbie Rd., St. John's NL A1B 3K3
Tel: 709-574-4428; *Fax:* 709-754-5868
Toll-Free: 800-567-7020
parkinson@nf.aibn.com
www.parkinsonnl.ca
facebook.com/ParkinsonSocietyNewfoundlandAndLabrador
twitter.com/Parkinsons_NL
Overview: A medium-sized provincial organization overseen by Parkinson Society Canada
Chief Officer(s):
Derek Staubitzer, Executive Director

Parkinson Society of Eastern Ontario / Société Parkinson de l'est de l'Ontario
#1, 200 Colonnade Rd., Ottawa ON K2E 7M1
Tel: 613-722-9238; *Fax:* 613-722-3241
psoc@toh.on.ca
www.parkinsons.ca
twitter.com/ParkinsonEastOn
Previous Name: Parkinson Society Ottawa
Overview: A small local organization founded in 1978 overseen by Parkinson Society Canada
Mission: To improve the lives of individuals & families affected by Parkinson's disease
Affiliation(s): Parkinson Society of Canada
Staff Member(s): 4
Membership: 700 individual; *Fees:* $30 individual; $375 lifetime
Activities: Speaker Service: Yes; *Library:* Open to public
Chief Officer(s):
Alan Muir, Manager, Resource Development
alan.muir@parkinson.ca
Ginette Trottier, Coordinator, Community Development
Publications:
• The Parkinson Paper
Type: Newsletter; *Frequency:* Quarterly

Parkinson Society Ottawa *See* Parkinson Society of Eastern Ontario

Parkinson Society Québec *Voir* Société Parkinson du Québec

Parkinson Society Saskatchewan (PSS)
610 Duchess St., Saskatoon SK S7K 0R1
Tel: 306-933-4481; *Fax:* 888-775-1402
Toll-Free: 888-685-0059
saskatchewan@parkinson.ca
www.parkinsonsaskatchewan.ca
Overview: A medium-sized provincial charitable organization founded in 1972 overseen by Parkinson Society Canada
Mission: To provide education & support services in Saskatchewan to ease the burdens of people living with Parkinson's disease & their families; To support research to find a cure for Parkinson's disease
Member of: Parkinson Society Canada / Société Parkinson Canada

Canadian Associations / Parkinson Society Southwestern Ontario

Finances: *Funding Sources:* Donations
Activities: Providing informative resources; Hosting special educational events; Increasing public awareness through displays; Collaborating with movement disorder clinics; Offering clinical & peer counselling services; Providing support, information, & referral by phone; *Awareness Events:* Annual Fall Lecture by Movement Disorder Specialist; *Speaker Service:* Yes; *Library:* SPDF Resource Lending Library
Chief Officer(s):
Travis Low, Executive Director
traivs.low@parkinson.ca

Parkinson Society Southwestern Ontario
Meadowbrook Business Park, #117, 4500 Blakie Rd., London ON N6L 1G5
Tel: 519-652-9437; *Fax:* 519-652-9267
Toll-Free: 888-851-7376
info@parkinsonsociety.ca
www.parkinsonsociety.ca
www.facebook.com/parkinsonsociety
twitter.com/ParkinsonSWO
Previous Name: Parkinson Society Canada - Southwestern Ontario Region
Overview: A small local organization overseen by Parkinson Society Canada
Finances: *Funding Sources:* Charity
Staff Member(s): 4
Membership: *Fees:* $30
Activities: Support services; Education & awareness; Advocacy; *Awareness Events:* Parkinson Awareness Month, April; Parkinson Superwalk; Parkinson Cut-A-Thon
Chief Officer(s):
Chris Maciejowski, President
Joanne Bernard, Manager, Administration

Parkland Community Living & Supports Society
6010 - 45 Ave., Red Deer AB T4N 3M4
Tel: 403-347-3333; *Fax:* 403-342-2677
www.parklandclass.org
Also Known As: Parkland CLASS
Overview: A small local charitable organization founded in 1960
Mission: To improve the quality of life of disabled children & adults through individual choice, rights, & dignity
Member of: Alberta Association for Community Living
Affiliation(s): Alberta Association of Rehabilitation Centres
Staff Member(s): 600
Membership: 400; *Member Profile:* Adult with disabilities, their parents &/or adult siblings

Parkland Crisis Centre & Women's Shelter
PO Box 651, Dauphin MB R7N 2V4
Tel: 204-622-4626; *Fax:* 204-622-4625; *Crisis Hot-Line:* 877-977-0007
pkndcris@mymts.net
www.parklandcrisiscentre.ca
Overview: A small local organization founded in 1982
Mission: To provide short & long-term counselling for women & children, support & parenting groups, resource & referral information, advocacy & education; To provide shelter to women & their children who are fleeing abusive relationships
Member of: Manitoba Association of Women's Shelters, Inc.
Staff Member(s): 18; 20 volunteer(s)
Membership: 1-99
Activities: Emergency shelter for women & their children; support groups; child & youth program; referrals to other agencies; follow-up services; *Awareness Events:* Domestic Violence Awareness Month, Nov.; *Speaker Service:* Yes; *Library:* by appointment
Chief Officer(s):
Kari Prawdzik, Executive Director

Parkland Food Bank
PO Box 5213, 105 Madison Cres., Spruce Grove AB T7X 3A3
Tel: 780-962-4565
www.parklandfoodbank.org
www.facebook.com/PrklndFoodBank
Overview: A small local charitable organization founded in 1985 overseen by Food Banks Alberta Association
Mission: To address the needs of hunger by providing food to those in need
Member of: Food Banks Alberta Association
Finances: *Annual Operating Budget:* Less than $50,000; *Funding Sources:* Donations
Chief Officer(s):
Sheri Ratsoy, Executive Director
sheri@parklandfoodbank.org

Parkland Humane Society *See* Red Deer & District SPCA

Parkland Music Festival
Stony Plain AB
www.parklandmusicfestival.org
Overview: A small local organization
Affiliation(s): Canadian Federation of Music Festivals; Alberta Music Festival Association
Chief Officer(s):
RJ Chambers, Chair, Syllabus, 780-919-9132
rj@parklandmusicfestival.org
Gillian Brinston-Kurschat, Adjudicator Contact, 780-237-0248
gillian@parklandmusicfestival.org

Parks & Recreation Ontario (PRO) / Parcs et loisirs de l'Ontario
#302, 1 Concorde Gate, Toronto ON M3C 3N6
Tel: 416-426-7142; *Fax:* 416-426-7371
pro@prontario.org
www.prontario.org
www.facebook.com/PROntario
twitter.com/prontario
Overview: A large provincial organization founded in 1984 overseen by Canadian Parks & Recreation Association
Mission: To enhance the quality of life, health & well-being of people, their communities & their environments; To advocate provincially for parks & recreation issues; To provide networking as well as multi-discipline professional development opportunities
Finances: *Annual Operating Budget:* $500,000-$1.5 Million; *Funding Sources:* Self-funding through programs; provincial grants for special projects; membership dues
Membership: 5,200; *Fees:* Schedule available; *Member Profile:* Individual; student; corporate
Activities: Recreation - An Essential Service; *Library*
Chief Officer(s):
Cathy Denyer, CEO, 416-426-7143
cdenyer@prontario.org
Awards:
• ProAwards Program
Recognizes individuals & organizations who have contributed to the advancement of parks & recreation in Ontario, in 3 sections: member, community & special awards
• Hugh Clydesdale Bursary
Awarded to promising female parks & recreation students or practitioners in Ontario to further their education; *Amount:* up to $2,000
• Bob Secord Student Leadership Award
• President's Award of Distinction
To recognize the capabilities of students in writing a research paper on parks & recreation; *Amount:* $100
• Excellence in Design Award
To recognize the capabilities of students in writing a research paper on parks & recreation; *Amount:* $100
• Innovation Award
To recognize the capabilities of students in writing a research paper on parks & recreation; *Amount:* $100
• Emerging Leader Award
To recognize the capabilities of students in writing a research paper on parks & recreation; *Amount:* $100
Meetings/Conferences:
• Parks & Recreation Ontario Educational Forum & Trade Show 2018, 2018, ON
Scope: Provincial

Parksville & District Association for Community Living (PDACL)
PO Box 578, 118 McMillan St., Parksville BC V9P 2G6
Tel: 250-248-2933; *Fax:* 250-248-4774
www.pdacl.ca
Previous Name: District 69 Association for the Disabled
Overview: A medium-sized local organization founded in 1959
Mission: To help enhance the lives of people with disabilities.
Member of: British Columbia Association for Community Living
Finances: *Funding Sources:* Provincial government
Membership: *Committees:* Fundraising; Joint Building; Personnel; Finance; Communications Advisory; Policy & Procedures; Self Advocates
Activities: Providing support services to adults with developmental disabilities
Chief Officer(s):
Barb Read, Executive Director
execdirector@pdacl.ca

Parksville & District Chamber of Commerce
PO Box 99, Parksville BC V9P 2G3
Tel: 250-248-3613; *Fax:* 250-248-5210
info@parksvillechamber.com
www.parksvillechamber.com
www.facebook.com/parksvillechamber
twitter.com/parksvillechmbr
www.youtube.com/user/ParksvilleChamber1
Overview: A small local organization founded in 1978
Member of: BC Chamber of Commerce; Canadian Chamber of Commerce
Staff Member(s): 5
Membership: 480+; *Committees:* Advocacy; Communication; Economic Development; Membership; Business Initiatives
Activities: *Speaker Service:* Yes; *Rents Mailing List:* Yes
Chief Officer(s):
Kim Burden, Executive Director
Linda Tchorz, Manager, Member Services
Lynda Schneider, Bookkeeper
Patti Lee, Manager, Visitor Centre

Parksville & District Rock & Gem Club
PO Box 812, Parksville BC V9P 2G8
Tel: 250-248-6177
www.pdrockandgem.org
www.facebook.com/ParksvilleRockandGem
Previous Name: 69'ers Club of Coombs
Overview: A small local organization
Mission: To promote the study & collecting of gems, rocks, & minerals
Member of: British Columbia Lapidary Society (BCLS); Gem & Mineral Federation of Canada (GMFC)
Membership: *Member Profile:* Persons in the Parksville area of British Columbia who have an interest in rocks, minerals, gems, & lapidary
Activities: Hosting meetings; Organizing field trips; Offering information about geology, rockhounding, & lapidary to members; *Library:* Parksville & District Rock & Gem Club Library; Not open to public
Chief Officer(s):
Marion Barclay, Contact

Parksville Golden Oldies Sports Association (PGOSA)
PO Box 957, Parksville BC V9P 2G9
mail@pgosa.org
www.pgosa.org
Overview: A small local organization founded in 1993
Mission: To provide physical activities to citizens of Parksville over 55.
Membership: *Fees:* $15; *Member Profile:* People over 55
Chief Officer(s):
Bruan Ball, President, 250-240-0007
parksville.pgosa.executive@gmail.com

Parliamentary Centre / Le Centre parlementaire
#1000, 66 Slater St., Ottawa ON K1P 5H1
Tel: 613-237-0143; *Fax:* 613-235-8237
parlcent@parl.gc.ca
www.parlcent.org
www.linkedin.com/company/parliamentarycentre
www.facebook.com/parliamentarycentre
twitter.com/paricent
Previous Name: Parliamentary Centre for Foreign Affairs & Foreign Trade
Overview: A medium-sized national charitable organization founded in 1968
Mission: To strengthen legislatures through continuous learning & innovation in parliamentary development, mutual sharing & practical parliamentary experience, & the provision of advisory services
Finances: *Annual Operating Budget:* $500,000-$1.5 Million; *Funding Sources:* Contracts with House of Commons & Senate; World Bank
Staff Member(s): 6
Membership: 1-99
Activities: Offering assessment, strategic planning, capacity building, knowledge exchange, research, networking, & professional development services; Developing parliamentary support projects & programs; *Internships:* Yes
Chief Officer(s):
Jean-Paul Ruszkowski, President & CEO, 613-237-0143 Ext. 303
jean-paul.ruszkowski@parl.gc.ca
Petra Andersson-Charest, Director, Programs, 613-237-0143 Ext. 324
petra.andersson@parl.gc.ca

Ivo Balinov, Director, Partnerships & Program Development, 613-237-0143 Ext. 310
partnerships@parlcent.org
Lola Giraldo, Director, Operations, 613-237-0143 Ext. 311
lola.giraldo@parl.gc.ca

Parliamentary Centre for Foreign Affairs & Foreign Trade See Parliamentary Centre

Parlimage CCF
561, rue Canning, Montréal QC H3J 2R1
Tél: 514-288-1400; *Téléc:* 514-288-1400
comm@parlimageccf.qc.ca
www.parlimageccf.qc.ca
Nom précédent: Parlimage Inc.
Aperçu: *Dimension:* petite; *Envergure:* nationale; Organisme sans but lucratif; fondée en 1978
Mission: Centre de formation et de consultation en communications, cinéma, vidéo, télévision; offrir des formations professionnelles spécifiques à tous les aspects de la communication et de la production audio-visuelle, par des professionnelles pratiquants les métiers
Membre de: Association de recherche en communication du Québec
Finances: *Budget de fonctionnement annuel:* $250,000-$500,000
Membre(s) du personnel: 11
Membre: 1-99; *Montant de la cotisation:* 75$
Activités: Cours et formation en: Comptabilité de production; Assistance à la réalisation film; Tournage et montage vidéo; Prise de son; Étapes de la post-production; Recherchiste radio; Montage AVID; Régie ciné-vidéo-pub; Doublage-postsynchronisation; Direction de production vidéo; Scripte au cinéma, etc.; *Stagiaires:* Oui; *Service de conférenciers:* Oui
Prix, Bourses:
• Prix du leadership chambre de commerce Montréal métropolitain

Parlimage Inc. *Voir* Parlimage CCF

PARN Your Community AIDS Resource Network (PARN)
#302, 159 King St., Peterborough ON K9J 2R8
Tel: 705-749-9110; *Fax:* 705-749-6310
Toll-Free: 800-361-2895; *TTY:* 705-749-9110
getinformed@parn.ca
www.parn.ca
www.facebook.com/PARNStaff
twitter.com/PARN4Counties
Previous Name: Peterborough AIDS Resource Network
Overview: A small local charitable organization founded in 1987 overseen by Canadian AIDS Society
Mission: To support people HIV-infected & HIV-affected
Member of: Canadian AIDS Society; Ontario AIDS Network
Finances: *Funding Sources:* Donations; Ontario Ministry of Health & Long Term Care; Public Health Agency of Canada; United Way of Peterborough & District; City of Peterborough
Staff Member(s): 9
Activities: Promoting health; Engaging in advocacy activities; Providing education; Organizing support groups; Raising awareness of AIDS issues; *Library:* PARN Resource Centre
Chief Officer(s):
Kim Dolan, Executive Director
John Lyons, Chair
John Curtis, Treasurer
Publications:
• PARN News
Type: Newsletter; *Frequency:* Quarterly; *Accepts Advertising Profile:* Thematic issues, such as Hepatitis C, testing, harm reduction, & disclosure

Parrainage civique Montréal / Citizen Advocacy Montreal
#422, 4450, rue St-Hubert, Montréal QC H2J 2W9
Tél: 514-843-8813
info@parrainagemontreal.org
www.parrainagemontreal.org
www.facebook.com/parrainagemontreal
www.youtube.com/channel/UC_1ID2tsWNKvrH4_16AAdxg
Aperçu: *Dimension:* petite; *Envergure:* locale; Organisme sans but lucratif; fondée en 1979
Mission: Vise l'intégration des personnes ayant une déficience intellectuelle
Affiliation(s): Regroupement des Parrainages Civique du Québec

Finances: *Budget de fonctionnement annuel:* $100,000-$250,000; *Fonds:* Gouvernement; Centraide
Membre(s) du personnel: 4; 150 bénévole(s)
Membre: 100-499
Activités: *Stagiaires:* Oui
Membre(s) du bureau directeur:
Philippe Latreille, Président
Johanne Téodori, Directrice générale
direction@parrainagemontreal.org

Parrot Association of Canada (PAC)
637316 St. Vincent Township, RR#1, Meaford ON N4L 1W5
Fax: 450-887-1832
www.parrotscanada.org
Overview: A small national organization founded in 1994
Mission: To promote high standards in the keeping of parrots by educating the public & the media; To monitor, report on & influence the actions of government at all levels as they pertain to parrots; To promote professionalism in psittacine aviculture by establishing an aviary certification program & by providing services that will encourage cooperation in parrot breeding; To support parrot related research & conservation projects
Member of: Avicultural Advancement Council of Canada
Affiliation(s): Golden Triange Parrot Club; Parrot Club of Manitoba; PIJAC
Finances: *Annual Operating Budget:* Less than $50,000; *Funding Sources:* Membership dues; donations
15 volunteer(s)
Membership: 130; *Fees:* Schedule available; *Member Profile:* People who have a pet parrot; parrot breeders; avian veterinarians; bird curators of zoos; hobbyists
Activities: MAP - Model Aviary Program, a service provided to members to show that their aviary meets a high set of standards set to ensure the well-being, health & protection of the parrots in their care; *Speaker Service:* Yes
Chief Officer(s):
Mark Koenig, President, 519-699-5656
Chris Holoboff, Vice-President, 416-868-0878
Publications:
• The PAC [Parrot Association of Canada] Journal
Type: Journal; *Frequency:* Quarterly

Parrsboro & District Board of Trade
PO Box 297, Parrsboro NS B0M 1S0
Tel: 902-254-3266
info@pdbot.ca
pdbot.ca
Overview: A small local organization
Member of: Atlantic Canada Chamber of Commerce
Finances: *Funding Sources:* Membership fees; fund raising; town grant
20 volunteer(s)
Membership: *Fees:* $55-$125 business; $25 individual
Chief Officer(s):
Doug Wilson, President
Carry Goodwin, Secretary

Parrsborough Shore Historical Society
PO Box 98, 1155 Whitehall Rd., Parrsboro NS B0M 1S0
Tel: 902-254-2376
ottawa.house@ns.sympatico.ca
www.ottawahousemuseum.ca
Overview: A small local charitable organization founded in 1977
Mission: To collect, preserve & celebrate the social & cultural history of the Parrsboro Shore; To operate the historic Ottawa House by-the-Sea Museum
Finances: *Annual Operating Budget:* Less than $50,000; *Funding Sources:* Provincial government; Donations; Fundraising
Staff Member(s): 1; 15 volunteer(s)
Membership: 150 individual; *Fees:* $12 individual
Activities: *Library:* Ottawa House Genealogy Room; Open to public
Chief Officer(s):
Colin Curleigh, Chair
Susan Clarke, Facility Manager

Parry Sound & Area Association of REALTORS
47A James St., Parry Sound ON P2A 1T6
Tel: 705-746-4020; *Fax:* 705-746-2955
psreb@vianet.on.ca
www.parrysoundrealestateboard.ca
Previous Name: Parry Sound Real Estate Board
Overview: A small local organization founded in 1969 overseen by Ontario Real Estate Association
Mission: To set a high standard of practice & ethics for its members so that they may better serve the public

Member of: Canadian Real Estate Association; Ontario Real Estate Association
Membership: 100

Parry Sound Area Chamber of Commerce
21 William St., Parry Sound ON P2A 1V2
Tel: 705-746-4213
info@parrysoundchamber.ca
www.parrysoundchamber.ca
Overview: A small local organization founded in 1897
Mission: To support its members by providing them with networking opportunities, government services, education & marketing services
Member of: Canadian Chamber of Commerce; Ontario Chamber of Commerce
Membership: 375; *Fees:* $259.90 1-3 employees; $384.20 4-10 employees; $497.20 11+ employees; *Committees:* Advocacy & Economic Development; Lifestyle & Membership; Tourism
Chief Officer(s):
Andrew Ryeland, President
Heather Murch, Manager, Member Services

Parry Sound Friendship Centre
13 Bowes St., Parry Sound ON P2A 2K7
Tel: 705-746-5970; *Fax:* 705-746-2612
postmaster@parrysoundfriendshipcentre.com
www.parrysoundfriendshipcentre.com
Overview: A medium-sized local organization founded in 1966
Member of: National Association of Friendship Centres; Ontario Federation of Indian Friendship Centres
Finances: *Funding Sources:* Secretary of State; National Association of Friendship Centres; Ministry of Health; Casino Rama
Activities: *Speaker Service:* Yes; *Library:* Marion Rice Memorial Library
Chief Officer(s):
Gail Hall, Executive Director

Parry Sound Real Estate Board *See* Parry Sound & Area Association of REALTORS

Partage Humanitaire
#219, 435, boul Curé-Labelle, Laval QC H7V 2S8
Tél: 450-681-1536; *Téléc:* 450-681-3484
info@partagehumanitaire.ca
www.partagehumanitaire.ca
Aperçu: *Dimension:* petite; *Envergure:* locale; Organisme sans but lucratif; fondée en 1971
Mission: A pour but de meubler la solitude et valoriser les aînés vivant en établissement et c'est par le biais de loisirs spécialement adaptés à leurs besoins, que sont rejoints ces gens trop souvent oubliés
Membre(s) du bureau directeur:
Gilles Leduc, Président
Marie Bouchart d'Orval, Directrice générale
mariebdorval@partagehumanitaire.ca

Partenaires en recherche *See* Partners in Research

Le Partenariat canadien pour la santé des enfants et l'environnement *See* Canadian Partnership for Children's Health & Environment

Partenariat communauté en santé (PCS)
#328, 302, rue Strickland, Whitehorse YT Y1A 2K1
Tél: 867-668-2663; *Téléc:* 867-668-3511
pcsyukon@francosante.ca
www.francosante.org
Aperçu: *Dimension:* petite; *Envergure:* provinciale; fondée en 2003 surveillé par Société santé en français
Mission: Favorise l'offre de services de santé en français
Membre(s) du bureau directeur:
Sandra St-Laurent, Directrice

Partenariat pour des environnements intérieurs sains *See* Healthy Indoors Partnership

Parti Castor du Canada *See* Beaver Party of Canada

Parti Communiste du Canada *See* Communist Party of Canada

Parti communiste du Canada (marxiste-léniniste) *See* Communist Party of Canada (Marxist-Leninist)

Parti communiste du Québec (PCQ)
5359 av du Parc, #C, Montréal QC H2V 4G9
Courriel: pcq@cpc-pcc.ca
www.particommunisteduquebec.ca
www.facebook.com/pcq1965

Aperçu: *Dimension:* petite; *Envergure:* provinciale; fondée en 1965
Mission: Unifier avec la classe ouvrière et les couches populaires pour que s'installe le pouvoir populaire dans le but de construire le socialisme
Affiliation(s): Solidarité populaire Québec; Ligue des droits et libertés
Membre: *Critères d'admissibilité:* Adhérer au programme et aux statuts du PCQ
Activités: *Stagiaires:* Oui
Membre(s) du bureau directeur:
Pierre Fontaine, Chef

Parti communiste révolutionnaire (PCR) / Revolutionary Communist Party (RCP)
1918, rue Frontenac, Montréal QC H2K 2Z1
Tél: 514-563-1487
info@pcr-rcp.ca
www.pcr-rcp.ca
Aperçu: *Dimension:* petite; *Envergure:* provinciale; fondée en 2009
Mission: Créer un nouveau parti communiste révolutionnaire qui dirigera la lutte pour renverser le système capitaliste pourri dans lequel nous vivons, mettre fin à toute forme d'exploitation et d'oppression et conduire la société vers le socialisme et le communisme
Finances: *Budget de fonctionnement annuel:* Moins de $50,000
Activités: *Service de conférenciers:* Oui; *Bibliothèque*

Parti conservateur du Canada *See* Conservative Party of Canada

Parti de l'héritage du Canada *See* Christian Heritage Party of Canada

Parti libéral de l'Ile du Prince Édouard *See* Liberal Party of Prince Edward Island

Parti libéral de Terre-Neuve et du Labrador *See* Liberal Party of Newfoundland & Labrador

Le Parti Libéral du Canada *See* The Liberal Party of Canada

Parti libéral du Canada (Colombie-Britannique) *See* The Liberal Party of Canada (British Columbia)

Parti libéral du Canada (Ontario) *See* Liberal Party of Canada (Ontario)

Parti libéral du Québec (PLQ) / Québec Liberal Party (QLP)
254, rue Queen, Montréal QC H3C 2N8
Tél: 514-288-4364; *Téléc:* 514-288-9455
Ligne sans frais: 800-361-1047
info@plq.org
www.plq.org
www.facebook.com/liberalquebec
twitter.com/LiberalQuebec
www.youtube.com/PartiLiberalduQuebec
Aperçu: *Dimension:* moyenne; *Envergure:* provinciale surveillé par The Liberal Party of Canada
Membre(s) du bureau directeur:
Philippe Couillard, Chef du Parti

Parti Marijuana *See* Marijuana Party

Parti marxiste-léniniste du Québec (PMLQ)
CP 61, Succ. C, Montréal QC H2L 4J7
Tél: 514-522-5872
bureau@pmlq.qc.ca
www.pmlq.qc.ca
Aperçu: *Dimension:* petite; *Envergure:* provinciale
Membre: *Montant de la cotisation:* Schedule available
Membre(s) du bureau directeur:
Pierre Chénier, Chef du Parti, 514-970-1867

Le Parti Progressiste-Conservateur de Nouveau-Brunswick *See* Progressive Conservative Party of New Brunswick

Parti Progressiste Canadien *See* Progressive Canadian Party

Parti québécois (PQ)
#150, 1200, av Papineau, Montréal QC H2K 4R5
Tél: 514-526-0020; *Téléc:* 514-526-0272
Ligne sans frais: 800-363-9531
info@pq.org
www.pq.org
www.facebook.com/lepartiquebecois
twitter.com/PartiQuebecois
www.instagram.com/partiquebecois

Aperçu: *Dimension:* grande; *Envergure:* provinciale; fondée en 1968
Mission: Réaliser démocratiquement la souveraineté du Québec pour s'épanouir comme peuple francophone, pour ne plus être minoritaire, pour mettre fin au gaspillage, pour se doter d'une politique économique qui répond aux intérêts du Québec; donner au Québec une place dans le monde
Membre(s) du personnel: 15; 5000 bénévole(s)
Membre: 90 000; *Comités:* Action politique des femmes; Jeunes; Écologie et environnement; Relations internationales et ethnoculturelles
Membre(s) du bureau directeur:
Jean-François Lisée, Chef

Parti Socialiste du Canada *See* Socialist Party of Canada

Parti Vert d'Ontario *See* The Green Party of Ontario

Parti vert du Canada *See* Green Party of Canada

Parti Vert du Nouveau Brunswick *See* Green Party of New Brunswick

Parti Vert du Québec (PVQ) / Green Party of Québec
#208, 6575, av Somerled, Montréal QC H4V 1T1
Tél: 514-612-3365
info@pvq.qc.ca
www.pvq.qc.ca
www.facebook.com/partivert
twitter.com/partivertqc
Aperçu: *Dimension:* moyenne; *Envergure:* provinciale surveillé par Green Party of Canada
Membre(s) du bureau directeur:
Alex Tyrrell, Chef

Partners FOR the Saskatchewan River Basin (PFSRB)
402 - 3rd Ave. South, Saskatoon SK S7K 3G5
Tel: 306-665-6887; *Fax:* 306-665-6117
Toll-Free: 800-567-8007
partners@saskriverbasin.ca
www.saskriverbasin.ca
www.facebook.com/SKRiverBasin
Overview: A small local charitable organization founded in 1993
Mission: To promote watershed sustainability through awareness, linkages & stewardship
Finances: *Annual Operating Budget:* $250,000-$500,000
Staff Member(s): 2; 50 volunteer(s)
Membership: 110; *Fees:* $25 individual/family; $50-$10,000 corporations/organizations based on budget; *Member Profile:* Individuals & organizations from all sectors of society & all the geographic areas of the basin - Alberta, Saskatchewan & Manitoba
Activities: Watershed monitoring; low water landscaping; storm drain marking; basin-wide stewardship program; aquatic restoration projects; integrated research; ecotourism development & marketing; watershed stewardship program for children
Chief Officer(s):
Lis Mack, Manager
Doug Porteous, Managing Partner
Sue Bouchard, Communications Officer
Awards:
• Fred Heal Conservation Award
Publications:
• The River Current [a publication of Partners FOR the Saskatchewan River Basin]
Type: Newsletter; *Frequency:* 3 pa

Partners for Youth
535 Beaverbrook Ct., #B-10, Fredericton NB E3B 1X6
Tel: 506-462-0323; *Fax:* 506-462-0328
Toll-Free: 888-739-1555
info@partnersforyouth.ca
partnersforyouth.ca
www.facebook.com/partnersforyouthNB
twitter.com/pfyouthnb
Overview: A small provincial organization
Mission: To help underpriviledged youth through programs that encourage learning & help to foster self-esteem
Staff Member(s): 9
Chief Officer(s):
John Sharpe, Chief Executive Officer

Partners in Research (PIR) / Partenaires en recherche
#120, 100 Collip Circle, London ON N6G 4X8
Tel: 519-433-7866
info@pirweb.org
www.pirweb.org
www.facebook.com/VirtualResearcherOnCall
twitter.com/vroccanada
Also Known As: London Citizens for Medical Research
Overview: A medium-sized national charitable organization founded in 1988
Mission: To promote the value of all aspects of health research, including the wise & humane use of animals when necessary; To educate the public about means to achieve the control & cure of disease processes (including the history & potential of health research), providing literature & audio-visual information at no cost
Staff Member(s): 7
Activities: Education about the history, promise & potential of health research for humans & animals; Virtual Researcher On Call (VROC) program; *Library:* Not open to public
Chief Officer(s):
Brent Peltola, Executive Director, 519-433-7841
bpeltola@pirweb.org
Awards:
• Biomedical Science Ambassador Award

Partners International
#56, 8500 Torbram Rd., Brampton ON L6T 5C6
Tel: 905-458-1202; *Fax:* 905-458-4339
Toll-Free: 800-883-7697
info@partnersinternational.ca
www.partnersinternational.ca
twitter.com/PartnersIntlCan
www.youtube.com/user/partnerscanada
Previous Name: China Native Evangelistic Crusade
Overview: A small local charitable organization founded in 1963
Mission: To partner Canadians with indigenous Christian ministries to spread the Word of God
Member of: Canadian Council of Christian Charities
Chief Officer(s):
Kevin McKay, President, 905-458-1202 Ext. 227
kevin.mckay@partnersinternational.ca

The Pas & District Chamber of Commerce
PO Box 996, 1559 Gordon Ave., The Pas MB R9A 1L1
Tel: 204-623-7256; *Fax:* 204-623-2589
tpchamber@mailme.ca
www.thepaschamber.com
Overview: A small local charitable organization founded in 1913
Mission: To promote local businesses & help them grow
Member of: Manitoba Chambers of Commerce; Canadian Chamber of Commerce
Finances: *Funding Sources:* Membership fees; Trade show; Sales
Staff Member(s): 1
Membership: 133
Chief Officer(s):
Shirley Barbeau, Office Manager

The Pas Arts Council Inc.
PO Box 1409, The Pas MB R9A 1L2
Tel: 204-623-7035
thepasartscouncil@gmail.com
thepasarts.blogspot.ca
Overview: A small local charitable organization
Mission: To promote arts & culture in our community through education & live performance
Member of: Manitoba Arts Network
Finances: *Annual Operating Budget:* Less than $50,000; *Funding Sources:* Local & provincial government grants
12 volunteer(s)
Membership: 1-99; *Fees:* $10 individual; $15 group

Pas de la rue
CP 284, Succ. C, 1575, boul René-Lévesque est, Montréal QC H2K 4K1
Tél: 514-526-1699; *Téléc:* 514-526-1411
www.pasdelarue.org
www.facebook.com/366730670033857
www.youtube.com/user/lepasdelarue
Aperçu: *Dimension:* petite; *Envergure:* locale
Mission: Pour apporter soutien et assistance aux personnes sans-abri, âgé de 55 ans et plus
Membre(s) du personnel: 7
Activités: Tables ronde; Soirées cinéma; Sorties; Dîners mensuels
Membre(s) du bureau directeur:
Sebastien Payeur, Directeur
direction@pasdelarue.org

Jean Paul Pratte, Président, Conseil d'administration

The Pas Friendship Centre Inc.
PO Box 2638, The Pas MB R9A 1M3
Tel: 204-627-7500; *Fax:* 204-623-4268
tpfc@mts.net
Overview: A small local organization
Chief Officer(s):
Ron Chief, Executive Director

Pasadena Chamber of Commerce
c/o Town of Pasadena, 18 Tenth Ave., Pasadena NL A0L 1K0
Tel: 709-686-2075; *Fax:* 709-686-2507
info@pasadena.ca
www.pasadena.ca/chamber.html
Overview: A small local organization

La Passerelle - Intégration et Développement Économique
2, rue Carlton, Mezzanine ouest, Toronto ON M5B 1J3
Tél: 416-934-0558; *Téléc:* 416-934-0590
info@passerelle-ide.com
www.paserelle-ide.com
www.facebook.com/lapasserelleide
twitter.com/Passerelle_IDE
www.youtube.com/user/passerelleide/videos
Également appelé: La Paserelle-I.D.É
Aperçu: *Dimension:* petite; *Envergure:* locale
Mission: Pour répondre aux besoins d'intégration et économiques des francophones dans la Région du Grand Toronto (RGT)
Activités: Fournir des services d'intégration; Hotlines téléphoniques; Classes, stages, et le placement; Opportunités de réseautage
Membre(s) du bureau directeur:
Léonie Tchatat, Directrice générale

Passons à l'action Canada *See* Pitch-In Canada

Pastel Artists Canada
995 Southcote Rd., RR#2, Ancaster ON L9G 3L1
info@pastelartists.ca
pastelartists.ca
Also Known As: Pastel Artists.Ca
Previous Name: Pastel Artists of Ontario, Canada
Overview: A small national organization founded in 1989
Mission: To represent Canadian artists who use pastels in the creation of works of fine art
Member of: International Association of Pastel Societies
Affiliation(s): Pastel Artists of Eastern Canada
Membership: *Member Profile:* Pastel painters
Chief Officer(s):
Ruth Rodgers, President
rodgers.ruth@gmail.com

Pastel Artists of Ontario, Canada *See* Pastel Artists Canada

Patent & Trademark Institute of Canada *See* Intellectual Property Institute of Canada

The Paterson Foundation
1918 Yonge St., Thunder Bay ON P7E 6T9
www.patersonfoundation.ca
Overview: A small national charitable organization founded in 1970
Mission: To assist educational, religious & cultural, charitable, non-profit registered organizations with particular interest in health care & relief work
Chief Officer(s):
Donald C. Paterson, President

PATH Canada *See* HealthBridge Foundation of Canada

Pathways Abilities Society
123 Franklyn Rd., Kelowna BC V1X 6A9
Tel: 250-763-4387; *Fax:* 250-763-4488
ed@pathwayskelowna.ca
www.pathwayskelowna.ca
www.facebook.com/PathwaysKelowna
Merged from: Kelowna & District Society for Community Living; Kelowna Community Sevelopment Society
Overview: A small local organization
Chief Officer(s):
Gail Meier, President
Meetings/Conferences:
• Pathways Abilities Society Annual General Meeting 2018, 2018
Scope: Local

Publications:
• Pathways Abilities Society Newsletter
Type: Newsletter; *Frequency:* q.

Pathways to Education Canada
439 University Ave., 16th Fl., Toronto ON M5G 1Y8
Tel: 416-646-0123; *Fax:* 416-646-0122
Toll-Free: 877-516-0123
info@pathwayscanada.ca
www.pathwaystoeducation.ca
www.linkedin.com/company/pathways-to-education-canada
www.facebook.com/pathwaystoeducationcanada
twitter.com/PathwaysCanada
Overview: A large national charitable organization founded in 2001
Mission: To assist youth in low-income communities graduate high school & transition into post-secondary education opportunities
Staff Member(s): 46
Membership: Over 10,000 students & alumni
Activities: Providing academic, financial, & social support programs for youth through community-based programming
Chief Officer(s):
Sue Gillespie, President & CEO
Quinn Bingham, Chief Development Officer
Rosie Yeung, Vice-President, Finance
Konrad Glogowski, Director, Research & Evaluation
Colleen Ryan, Director, Marketing & Communications

Pathways to Education - Halifax-Spryfield
Chebucto Connections, 531 Herring Cove Rd., Halifax NS B3R 1X3
Tel: 902-477-0964; *Fax:* 902-477-8984
www.pathwaysspryfield.ca
Chief Officer(s):
Adrianna MacKenzie, Director, Program
ccda.mackenzie@bellaliant.com

Pathways to Education - Hamilton
North Hamilton Community Health Centre, 438 Hughson St. North, Hamilton ON L8L 4N5
Tel: 905-523-6719
pathways@nhchc.ca
www.nhchc.ca

Pathways to Education - Kingston
Kingston Community Health Centres, #6, 263 Weller Ave., Kingston ON K7K 2V4
Tel: 613-507-7107
www.kchc.ca
Chief Officer(s):
Wendy Vuyk, Program Director, 613-507-7107 Ext. 2018
wendyv@kchc.ca
Lisa Lund, Coordinator, Tutoring & Mentoring, 613-507-7107 Ext. 2109
lisal@kchc.ca

Pathways to Education - Kitchener
Mosaic Counselling & Family Services, 400 Queen St. South, Kitchener ON N2G 1W7
Tel: 519-743-6333
www.mosaiconline.ca
Chief Officer(s):
Sanjida Khan, Contact
skhan@mosaiconline.ca

Pathways to Education - Montréal-Verdun
Toujours Ensemble, 601, 2e av, Montréal QC H4G 2W7
Tel: 514-761-7867
www.toujoursensemble.org
Chief Officer(s):
Luc Mantha, Acting Program Director
lmantha.passeport@gmail.com

Pathways to Education - Ottawa
Pinecrest-Queensway Community Health Centre, 1365 Richmond Rd., Ottawa ON K2B 6R7
Tel: 613-820-4922
www.pqchc.com/youth/pathways-to-education
Chief Officer(s):
Dawn Lyons, Program Manager
d.lyons@pqchc.com

Patients Canada
PO Box 68, #2010, 65 Queen St. West, Toronto ON M5H 2M5
Tel: 416-900-2975
communications@patientscanada.ca
www.patientscanada.ca
www.facebook.com/patientscanada
Previous Name: Patients' Association of Canada
Overview: A medium-sized national charitable organization

Mission: To bring changes & improvements to health care policy & delivery in Canada; To represent patients in health care decision-making
Finances: *Funding Sources:* Donations; grants
Activities: Meetings; forums; research; resources for patients
Chief Officer(s):
Michael Decter, Chair
Awards:
• The Patients' Choice Awards
Patients can nominate their physicians for this award.

Patients' Association of Canada *See* Patients Canada

Patinage Canada *See* Skate Canada

Patinage de vitesse Canada *See* Speed Skating Canada

Patinage Québec
4545, av Pierre-de Coubertin, Montréal QC H1V 0B2
Tél: 514-252-3073; *Téléc:* 514-252-3170
patinage@patinage.qc.ca
www.patinage.qc.ca
www.facebook.com/patinageqc
Aperçu: *Dimension:* grande; *Envergure:* provinciale; fondée en 1969
Mission: Rendre accessible à tous, les programmes de Patinage Canada, que ce soit par amour, par plaisir ou pour atteindre l'excellence; a l'unisson, nous contribuons ainsi à l'avancement de notre sport.
Membre(s) du personnel: 10
Membre: 40 000
Membre(s) du bureau directeur:
Any-Claude Dion, Directrice générale, 514-252-3073 Ext. 3550
acdion@patinage.qc.ca
Prix, Bourses:
• Bénévole par excellence
• Médaillés québécois
• Temple de la renommée
• Trophée Josée-Chouinard

Patrimoine et Culture du Portage
655, rte du Fleuve, Notre-Dame-du-Portage QC G0L 1Y0
Tél: 418-862-7333
www.notredameduportage.org
Aperçu: *Dimension:* petite; *Envergure:* locale; fondée en 2007
Mission: Patrimoine et Culture du Portage est un organisme sans but lucratif dont la mission consiste à promouvoir la protection et la mise en valeur du patrimoine naturel et culturel de Notre-Dame-du-Portage, soutenir les activités culturelles et aider les enfants ayant des besoins spéciaux.
Membre(s) du bureau directeur:
Aubert Ouellet, Président

Patrimoine Huntingville
150, rue McKay, North Hatley QC J0B 2C0
Tel: 819-842-3102
huntingville@gmail.com
Overview: A small local organization founded in 1995
Chief Officer(s):
Terry Skeats, President

Patronato INAS (Canada)
PO Box 201, #205, 1263 Wilson Ave., Toronto ON M3M 3G2
Tel: 416-240-1844; *Fax:* 416-240-1785
inascanadatoronto@bellnet.ca
www.canada.inas.it
Also Known As: Instituto Nazionale di Assistenza Sociale
Previous Name: INAS (Canada)
Overview: A medium-sized international organization founded in 1972
Mission: To assist people in matters related to pensions, both nationally & internationally
Affiliation(s): Labour Council of Metropolitan Toronto
Finances: *Annual Operating Budget:* $250,000-$500,000;
Funding Sources: Italian government
Membership: 15,000; *Member Profile:* Pensioners
Activities: Pension services; *Speaker Service:* Yes

Calgary Office
201-A, 4th St. NE, Calgary AB TZE 3S1
Tel: 403-277-2772

Edmonton Office
9111 - 110 Ave., Edmonton AB T5H 4J9
Tel: 780-421-9559; *Fax:* 780-429-1984

Guelph Office
PO Box 872, 127 Feguson St., Guelph ON N1H 6M6
Tel: 519-837-2822
inascanadaguelph@bellnet.ca

Hamilton Office
#500, 105 Main St. East, Hamilton ON L8N 1G6
Tel: 905-529-8989; Fax: 905-529-2776
inascanadahamilton@bellnet.ca

La Salle Office
#303, 8190, boul Newman, La Salle QC H8N 1X9
Tél: 514-903-5004

London Office
120 Clarke Side Rd., London ON N5W 5E1
Tel: 519-455-7950

Mississauga Office
#101, 195 Forum Dr., Mississauga ON L4Z 3M9
Tel: 905-507-3189; Fax: 905-507-4826
inascanadamississauga@bellnet.ca

Montréal Office
505, rue Jean Talon est, Montréal QC H2R 1T6
Tel: 514-844-0010; Fax: 514-844-5174
inasquebec@qc.aira.com

Saint Leonard Office
#305, 8370, boul Lacordaire, Saint Leonard QC H1R 3Y6
Tél: 514-326-7262; Téléc: 514-326-1882
c.daniello@inas.it

Sarnia Office
#601-B, 546 North Christina St., Sarnia ON N7T 5W6
Tel: 519-542-8890; Fax: 519-542-5599

Winnipeg Office
88 Sherbrooke St., Winnipeg MB R3C 2B3
Tel: 204-284-0663

Woodbridge Office
#204, 7700 Pine Valley Dr., Woodbridge ON L4L 2X4
Tel: 905-856-9926; Fax: 905-856-4310
inascanadawoodbridge@bellnet.ca

Patrouille canadienne de ski See Canadian Ski Patrol

Patrouille de ski St-Jean
651, 6e rue ouest, Chibougamau QC G8P 2T8
Tél: 418-748-7162
Aperçu: Dimension: petite; Envergure: locale
Membre(s) du bureau directeur:
Fabien Belleau, Président, 418-770-8447
Sébastien d'Amboise, Vice-Président, 418-809-6059

Pauktuutit Inuit Women of Canada
#520, 1 Nicholas St., Ottawa ON K1N 7B7
Tel: 613-238-3977; Fax: 613-238-1787
Toll-Free: 800-667-0749
info@pauktuutit.ca
www.pauktuutit.ca
www.facebook.com/pauktuutit
twitter.com/Pauktuutit
Also Known As: Inuit Women Association of Canada
Overview: A medium-sized national charitable organization founded in 1984
Mission: To raise awareness of the needs of Inuit women; To promote the participation of Inuit women in matters relating to social, cultural & economic developments at the community, regional & national levels
Affiliation(s): Inuit Tapirisat of Canada; Nunavut Implementation Commission
Finances: Annual Operating Budget: $250,000-$500,000; Funding Sources: Government
Staff Member(s): 10
Membership: Member Profile: Inuit women in Canada
Activities: Advocating for the rights of Inuit women & children; Working towards the improvement of social, economic & political conditions for Inuit women; Offering resources pertaining to Inuit culture & values; Encouraging collaboration between Inuit women & other Aboriginal people; Speaker Service: Yes; Library: by appointment
Chief Officer(s):
Rebecca Kudloo, President

PAVED Arts
424 - 20th St. West, Saskatoon SK S7M 0X4
Tel: 306-652-5502
www.pavedarts.ca
www.facebook.com/pavedarts
twitter.com/PAVEDArts
www.instagram.com/pavedarts
Previous Name: Paved Arts New Media Inc.; Photographers Gallery Society Inc.
Overview: A small provincial charitable organization founded in 1971
Mission: To advance knowledge & practices in the arts community, in fields such as photography, audio, video, electronic & digital; To help artists & independent producers make & exhibit thier work
Finances: Annual Operating Budget: $250,000-$500,000; Funding Sources: Saskatchewan Arts Board; Canada Council for the Arts; Saskatchewan Arts Board; SaskLotteries; Saskatchewan Motion Potion Association; SaskCulture
Staff Member(s): 5; 40 volunteer(s)
Membership: 100-499; Fees: $25 Student/Underemployed; $50 Producing; $100 Institutional; Committees: Archive/Resource Centre; Exhibitions; Programming; Fundraising
Activities: Offer training & professional development for media arts; Bring examples of art into the community for exposure through gallery exhibitions & public screenings; Library: Open to public by appointment
Chief Officer(s):
Alex Rogalski, Executive Director, 306-652-5502 Ext. 2
executive@pavedarts.ca
David LaRiviere, Artistic Director, 306-652-5502 Ext. 1
artistic@pavedarts.ca
Lenore Maier, Technical Coordinator, 306-652-5502 Ext. 3
technical@pavedarts.ca
Devin McAdam, Production Manager, 306-652-5502 Ext. 3
production@pavedarts.ca

Paved Arts New Media Inc.; Photographers Gallery Society Inc. See PAVED Arts

Pavillion Marguerite de Champlain
PO Box 51535, Stn. Taschereau, Greenfield Park QC J4V 3N8
Tel: 450-656-1946; Fax: 450-656-6548
info@pavillonmarguerite.com
pavillonmarguerite.com
Overview: A small local organization
Mission: Pour aider les femmes et leurs enfants échapper à des relations abusives et pour les aider à rester loin de l'abus
Activities: Interventions; Sensbilisation; Groupes mères; Activités pour les enfants

Pax Natura Society for Rehabilitation of the Deaf
11460 - 60th Ave. NW, Edmonton AB T6H 1J5
Tel: 780-434-1671; Fax: 780-435-7788; TTY: 780-434-1671
Overview: A small local charitable organization founded in 1975
Mission: To administer & employ its property, assets & rights for the purpose of promoting or aiding in the promotion of programs to benefit the deaf community
Finances: Funding Sources: Provincial government; Private & government grants; Donations
Membership: Member Profile: Voting - deaf community; associate - family members, supporters, professionals from hearing community
Activities: Camp; Retreat; Counselling; Work events/work experience; Education; Outdoor/conservation; Recreation; Library: Not open to public
Chief Officer(s):
R.A. Bauer, Executive Director
Awards:
• G.W. Sutherland Memorial Scholarship
Eligibility: Deaf student, any age
• E.L. Palate Memorial Scholarship
Eligibility: Deaf student in post-secondary education

PBA Society of Alberta
#206, 10544 - 106th St., Edmonton AB T5H 2X6
Tel: 780-448-9692; Fax: 780-448-9698
Toll-Free: 855-541-4703
admin@pba-canada.org
Overview: A small provincial organization founded in 1980 overseen by PBA Society of Canada
Mission: To promote, organize & coordinate the educational activities of members
Member of: PBA Society of Canada
Staff Member(s): 1
Activities: Professional designation; annual convention; Errors & Omissions Insurance for members
Chief Officer(s):
Margo Desmarais, President, 780-492-5524

PBA Society of Atlantic
#206, 10544 - 106th St., Edmonton AB T5H 2X6
Toll-Free: 855-541-4703
admin@pba-canada.org
Overview: A small provincial organization founded in 2003 overseen by PBA Society of Canada
Mission: To promote, organize & coordinate the educational activities of members
Member of: PBA Society of Canada
Staff Member(s): 1
Membership: Fees: $575 regular; $325 associate; Member Profile: Professional accountants
Activities: Professional designation; annual convention; Errors & Omissions Insurance for members
Chief Officer(s):
Mark Reid, President, 506-832-7964

PBA Society of Canada
#206, 10544 - 106th St., Edmonton AB T5H 2X6
Toll-Free: 855-541-4703
www.pba-canada.org
www.facebook.com/PBACanada
Previous Name: Registered Professional Accountants Association of Canada
Overview: A small national organization founded in 1980
Mission: To develop & support professional accountant members; To advance the accounting profession in Canada
Membership: Member Profile: Professionals with two years of work experience in accounting, & who meet educational requirements
Activities: Professional designation; career centre
Chief Officer(s):
Angel Meinecke, President

PBA Society of Ontario
#206, 10544 - 106th St., Edmonton AB T5H 2X6
Toll-Free: 855-541-4703
admin@pba-canada.org
Overview: A small provincial organization overseen by PBA Society of Canada
Mission: To promote, organize & coordinate the educational activities of members
Member of: PBA Society of Canada
Membership: Fees: $450; Member Profile: Professional accountants
Activities: Professional designation; annual convention; Errors & Omissions Insurance for members
Chief Officer(s):
Alan Doody, President, 416-492-8662

Peace & Environment Resource Centre
PO Box 4075, Stn. E, 174 First Ave., Ottawa ON K1S 5B1
Tel: 613-230-4590
info@perc.ca
www.perc.ca
www.facebook.com/OttawaPERC
twitter.com/perc_ott
Overview: A small local charitable organization
Mission: To ensure peaceful, equitable, healthy, & sustainable local & global communities
Finances: Funding Sources: Donations; Fundraising
Activities: Developing community projects; Organizing workshops & events; Library: Peace & Environment Resource Centre Library; Open to public
Publications:
• The Peace & Environment News
Type: Newsletter; Price: Free
Profile: Information about critical issues for Canada & the world

Peace Arch Community Services See Sources Foundation

Peace Area Riding for the Disabled (PARDS)
8202 - 84 St., Grande Prairie AB T8X 0L6
Tel: 780-538-3211; Fax: 780-538-3683
info@pards.ca
www.pards.ca
Overview: A small local charitable organization founded in 1984
Mission: To enhance the lives of individuals with disabilities through "equine assisted therapy"; To promoten physical, emotional, intellectual & social growth for individuals with disabilities through therapeutic riding services; To build a community that embraces differences & supports growth & success for all of its members
Member of: Canadian Therapeutic Riding Association
Staff Member(s): 8
Activities: Summer camp
Chief Officer(s):
Jennifer Douglas, Executive Director

Peace Brigades International (Canada) (PBI)
323 Chapel St., Ottawa ON K1N 7Z2
Tel: 613-237-6968
info@pbicanada.org
www.pbicanada.org
www.facebook.com/pbicanada
twitter.com/pbicanada

Overview: A small international charitable organization founded in 1981
Mission: To explore & implement non-violent approaches to peacekeeping & support for basic human rights; to provide protective accompaniment & peace education training in Colombia, Indonesia, & Mexico
Affiliation(s): Canadian Peace Alliance
Finances: *Funding Sources:* Donations
Staff Member(s): 3
Activities: Non-violence & peace education workshops; *Speaker Service:* Yes; *Library:* Peace Brigades International (Canada) Library; Open to public
Chief Officer(s):
Meaghen Simms, Executive Director

Peace Country Beef & Forage Association (PCGFA)
PO Box 3000, Fairview AB T0H 1L0
Tel: 780-835-6799; *Fax:* 780-835-6628
www.peacecountrybeef.ca
Overview: A small local organization founded in 1982 overseen by Agricultural Research & Extension Council of Alberta
Mission: To demontrate new forage varieties & technology
Member of: Agricultural Research & Extension Council of Alberta
Staff Member(s): 3
Membership: 175; *Fees:* $25
Chief Officer(s):
Conrad Dolen, President
Liisa Vihvelin, Manager
lvihvelin@gprc.ab.ca
Akim Omokanye, Coordinator, Research
aomokanye@gprc.ab.ca
Publications:
• Forage Facts [a publication of the Peace Country Beef & Forage Association]
Type: Newsletter

High Prairie Office
PO Box 2803, 5226 - 53 Ave., High Prairie AB T0G 1E0
Tel: 780-523-4033; *Fax:* 780-523-6569
Member of: Agricultural Research & Extension Council of Alberta

Peace Curling Association (PCA)
PO Box 265, Grande Prairie AB T8V 3A4
Tel: 780-532-4782; *Fax:* 780-538-2485
peaccurl@telusplanet.net
www.peacecurl.org
Overview: A small local organization
Member of: Alberta Curling Federation; Canadian Curling Association
Finances: *Annual Operating Budget:* Less than $50,000; *Funding Sources:* Casino
Staff Member(s): 1

Peace Parkland Naturalists
PO Box 1451, Grande Prairie AB T8V 4Z2
info@peaceparklandnaturalists.ca
www.peaceparklandnaturalists.ca
www.facebook.com/208279709282869
www.flickr.com/photos/peaceparklandnaturalists
Overview: A small local organization founded in 1990
Mission: To promote awareness & appreciation of the natural history of the Peace Region of northwestern Alberta
Member of: Federation of Alberta Naturalists
Finances: *Annual Operating Budget:* Less than $50,000
Membership: 40; *Fees:* $10 individual; $15 family
Activities: Field trips; meetings
Chief Officer(s):
Margot Hervieux, Contact
Publications:
• The Hooter [a publication of the Peace Parkland Naturalists]
Type: Newsletter
• Kleksun Hill: A Discovery Guide [a publication of the Peace Parkland Naturalists]
Type: Book; *Author:* Margot Hervieux; *Price:* $6

Peace Region Internet Society (PRIS)
#1, 929 - 106th Ave., Dawson Creek BC V1G 2N8
Tel: 250-782-5128; *Fax:* 250-782-2459
Toll-Free: 800-768-3311
Other Communication: Fort St. John Phone: 250-785-8877
pris@pris.ca
portal.pris.ca
Overview: A small local organization founded in 1994
Mission: To provide affordable Internet access for individuals, businesses, & organizations in the Peace Region of British Columbia
Chief Officer(s):
Monte Bentley, President
Aaron Lamacchia, Executive Director
Angie Collins, Office Manager

Peace River & District Chamber of Commerce
PO Box 6599, 9309 - 100 St., Peace River AB T8S 1S4
Tel: 780-624-4166; *Fax:* 888-525-4423
www.peaceriverchamber.com
www.facebook.com/peaceriverchamber
twitter.com/pr_chamber
www.instagram.com/pr_chamber
Previous Name: Peace River Board of Trade
Overview: A small local organization founded in 1920
Mission: To promote & enhance the private enterprise in Peace River
Finances: *Funding Sources:* Municipal government; membership fees
Staff Member(s): 2
Membership: 214; *Fees:* $225
Chief Officer(s):
Shelly Shannon, President
George Brothers, General Manager
manager@peaceriverchamber.com

Peace River Alaska Highway Tourism Association *See* Northern Rockies Alaska Highway Tourism Association

Peace River Board of Trade *See* Peace River & District Chamber of Commerce

Peace Valley Environment Association (PVEA)
PO Box 6062, Fort St John BC V1J 4H6
pvea@shaw.ca
www.peacevalley.ca
twitter.com/SavePeaceValley
Overview: A small local organization
Mission: To protect and defend the natural environment of the Peace Valley area of British Columbia
Membership: *Fees:* $10

Peacebuild: The Canadian Peacebuilding Network
c/o Peggy Mason, Chair, #406, 575 Byron Ave., Ottawa ON K2A 1R7
Tel: 613-241-3446; *Fax:* 613-241-4846
info@peacebuild.ca
www.peacebuild.ca
www.facebook.com/Peacebuild1
twitter.com/Peacebuild1
www.youtube.com/user/peacebuild
Previous Name: Canadian Peacebuilding Coordinating Committee
Overview: A small national organization
Mission: To engender greater coherence & effectiveness in building peace through fostering collaboration & coordination amongst diverse stakeholders in Canada, & partners overseas
Finances: *Funding Sources:* The Canadian Partnerships Program, International Development Research Centre (IDRC)
Membership: *Fees:* $10 student; $50 individual; $100 coalition; $200 organization
Activities: Working Groups: Small Arms; Children & Conflict; Gender & Peacebuilding; Conflict Prevention; Peace Operations
Chief Officer(s):
Silke Reichrath, Coordinator

Peace-Laird Regional Arts Council (PLRAC)
PO Box 337, Hudson's Hope BC V0C 1V0
Tel: 250-783-9351
tacsote@pris.ca
www.peaceliardarts.org
Overview: A small local charitable organization founded in 1989
Mission: To assist with the promotional growth of the arts community in the Peace-Laird; involved in promoting, encouraging, offering help & guidance, & coordinating all the communities in the region
Member of: Assembly of BC Arts Councils; Canadian Conference of the Arts; BC Touring Council
Finances: *Annual Operating Budget:* $50,000-$100,000; *Funding Sources:* Regional & provincial government
Staff Member(s): 1; 10 volunteer(s)
Membership: 20; *Fees:* $35 or $15 every member group; *Member Profile:* Made up of members from Arts Councils within each community
Activities: Grants include activity & special events; arts collection, training & assistance; arts development
Chief Officer(s):
Patricia Markin, Chair
Awards:
• HRT Collection Award

Peachland Chamber of Commerce
5684 Beach Ave., Peachland BC V0H 1X6
Tel: 250-767-2422
peachlandchamber@gmail.com
www.chamberpeachland.com
www.facebook.com/chamberpeachland
twitter.com/PeachlandChambe
Overview: A small local organization founded in 1999
Mission: To encourage & strengthen business activity through the collective actions of its members for the benefit of the community at large
Member of: BC Chamber of Commerce; Canadian Chamber of Commerce
Finances: *Funding Sources:* Membership dues; municipal
Membership: *Fees:* Schedule available
Chief Officer(s):
Patrick Van Minsel, Executive Director

Peachland Food Bank
6490 Keyes Ave., Peachland BC V0H 1X0
Tel: 250-767-3312
Overview: A small local organization overseen by Food Banks British Columbia
Member of: Food Banks British Columbia
Chief Officer(s):
Judy Bedford, Contact

PEDVAC Foundation (PEDVAC)
12 Church St., Port Elgin NB E4M 2C9
Tel: 506-538-7638; *Fax:* 506-538-7638
pedvacfoundation@nb.aibn.com
www.pedvac.com
Previous Name: Port Elgin District Voluntary Action Group Inc.
Overview: A small local organization founded in 1988
Mission: To enable individuals & groups to create, maintain & extend throughout the community an improved quality of life
Member of: Association of Food Banks & C.V.A.'s for New Brunswick; Canadian Association of Food Banks; Laubach Literacy Canada & New Brunswick
Finances: *Annual Operating Budget:* $100,000-$250,000; *Funding Sources:* Government grants; fundraising; donations
Staff Member(s): 5; 200 volunteer(s)
Activities: After School Homework Assistance Program; Hot School Lunch Program; Food Bank; Tax Return Preparation for Seniors & Low Income Individuals; Used clothing & household goods boutique
Chief Officer(s):
Val MacDermid, Executive Director
Awards:
• Milton F. Gregg Conservation Award
• New Brunswick Family Award

Peel Committee Against Woman Abuse (PCAWA)
PO Box 45070, Mississauga ON L5G 1C9
Tel: 905-823-3441; *Fax:* 905-823-9695
pcawa@pcawa.org
www.pcawa.org
www.linkedin.com/company/2882034
www.facebook.com/321162981322389
twitter.com/PCAWA1
www.youtube.com/user/PCAWA
Overview: A small local organization founded in 1984
Mission: To promote a comprehensive & effective response to woman abuse in the region of Peel
Finances: *Funding Sources:* United Way; Region of Peel; Government of Ontario; Neighbours, Friends and Families

Peel Dufferin Catholic Services *See* Catholic Family Services of Peel Dufferin

Peel Family Services
#501, 151 City Centre Dr., Mississauga ON L5B 1M7
Tel: 905-270-2250; *Fax:* 905-270-2869; *TTY:* 905-270-7357
fsp@fspeel.org
www.fspeel.org
www.facebook.com/pages/Family-Services-of-Peel/163434633676036
twitter.com/fspeelca
Also Known As: Family Services of Peel

Canadian Associations / Peel HIV/AIDS Network

Overview: A medium-sized local charitable organization founded in 1971 overseen by Family Service Ontario
Mission: To provide support & community services to families in the Peel region.
Member of: Family Service Canada; Ontario Association of Credit CounsellingServices
389 volunteer(s)
Chief Officer(s):
Chuck MacLean, Executive Director

Peel HIV/AIDS Network
#1, 160 Traders Blvd., Mississauga ON L4Z 3K7
Tel: 905-361-0523; *Fax:* 905-361-1004
Toll-Free: 866-896-8700
www.phan.ca
www.facebook.com/PeelHIVAIDSNetwork
twitter.com/phanpeel
www.flickr.com/photos/31432883@N05/
Overview: A small local organization
Staff Member(s): 9
Membership: *Fees:* $10
Chief Officer(s):
Phillip Banks, Executive Director
phillipb@phan.ca

Peel Law Association (PLA)
#160, 7755 Hurontario St., Brampton ON L6W 4T1
Tel: 905-451-2924; *Fax:* 905-451-3137
Toll-Free: 866-228-0235
www.plalawyers.ca
Overview: A small local organization founded in 1947
Mission: To promote, protect & advance the interests of its members by providing resources to enhance the practice of law
Staff Member(s): 2; 15 volunteer(s)
Membership: 500-999; *Fees:* Schedule available; *Member Profile:* Lawyers in good standing with the Law Society of Upper Canada with offices in Peel; *Committees:* Executive; Financial; Personnel; Membership; Strategic Planning; Governance; Key Objectives; Social Activities
Activities: *Speaker Service:* Yes; *Library:* Not open to public
Chief Officer(s):
Eugene Bhattacharya, President

Peel Multicultural Council (PMC)
6630 Turner Valley Rd., Mississauga ON L5N 2P1
Tel: 905-819-1144; *Fax:* 905-542-3950
pmc@peelmc.com
www.peelmc.com
www.linkedin.com/company-beta/2823166
www.facebook.com/peelmulticulturalcouncil
www.youtube.com/peelpmc
Overview: A small local charitable organization founded in 1977 overseen by Ontario Council of Agencies Serving Immigrants
Mission: To promote a harmonious multicultural society by increasing communication & by building bridges of understanding between ethocultural groups, institutions & the community; To facilitate the settlement & integration of newcomers to Canada
Affiliation(s): Parks & Recreation Mississauga; Parks & Recreation Brampton
Finances: *Annual Operating Budget:* $250,000-$500,000
Staff Member(s): 9; 98 volunteer(s)
Membership: 150 groups + 350 individuals; *Fees:* $10 individual; $20 group; *Committees:* Housing; Membership; Advocacy; Public Relations; Cultural & Social; Personnel
Activities: Public education on race relations, equity, settlement of immigrants; ESL classes; Community development; *Library:* Open to public
Chief Officer(s):
Naveed Chaudhdry, Executive Director
Raj Jhajj, President
Atma Gill, Vice President
Baljinder Sekhon, Secretary
Eric Wen, Treasurer

Peel Music Festival
PO Box 70083, Stn. Fletcher's Creek, Brampton ON L7A 0N6
Tel: 647-282-7335
admin@peelmusicfestival.ca
www.peelmusicfestival.ca
Overview: A small local organization founded in 1927
Mission: A music competition for young performers, the festival is a not-for-profit organization run by volunteer music teachers.
Member of: Ontario Music Festivals Association Inc.
Finances: *Funding Sources:* Ontario Trillium Foundation

Peel Regional Labour Council (BMDLC)
PO Box 173, Stn. A, #403, 989 Derry Rd. East, Mississauga ON L5T 2J8
Tel: 905-696-8882; *Fax:* 905-696-7355
Other Communication: Legacy Site: www.bmdlc.ca
www.prlc.ca
www.facebook.com/172725789474737
Previous Name: Brampton-Mississauga & District Labour Council
Overview: A small local organization founded in 1962 overseen by Ontario Federation of Labour
Member of: Canadian Labour Congress
Finances: *Annual Operating Budget:* Less than $50,000; *Funding Sources:* Per capita tax from affiliates
12 volunteer(s)
Membership: 25,000; *Member Profile:* Affiliated local unions; *Committees:* Political Action; Affiliation; Events/Education
Activities: *Awareness Events:* Day of Mourning, April 28; Labour Day, Sept. 1
Chief Officer(s):
Jim McDowell, President

Peel Regional Police Association (PRPA) / Association des policiers de la région de Peel
10675 Mississauga Rd., Brampton ON L7A 0B6
Tel: 905-846-0615; *Fax:* 905-846-0649
admin@peelpa.on.ca
www.peelpa.on.ca
www.linkedin.com/company/peel-regional-police
twitter.com/PeelPoliceMedia
Overview: A medium-sized local organization founded in 1974
Mission: To represent the uniform & civilian members of Ontario's Peel Regional Police; To promote the mutual interests of members; To elevate the standards of police services
Finances: *Funding Sources:* Banquet hall rental fees; Store sales
Staff Member(s): 2
Membership: 2,700; *Member Profile:* Uniform & civilian members of the Peel Regional Police
Activities: Supporting charities
Chief Officer(s):
Paul Black, President
pblack@peelpa.on.ca
Mike Sharp, Chief Administrative Officer
msharp@peelpa.on.ca

PeerNetBC
#408, 602 West Hastings St., Vancouver BC V6B 1P2
Tel: 604-733-6186
info@peernetbc.com
www.peernetbc.com
www.linkedin.com/company/peernetbc
www.facebook.com/PeerNetBC
twitter.com/PeerNetBC
Previous Name: Self-Help Resource Association of British Columbia
Overview: A medium-sized provincial charitable organization founded in 1986
Mission: To promote peer support approaches that build the capacity of individuals, & therefore communities, to become healthy, responsive & self-determining
Finances: *Funding Sources:* Provincial government; Foundations; Membership dues
Staff Member(s): 5
Membership: *Member Profile:* Individuals interested in & supportive of self-help/mutual aid
Activities: Central resource centre & self-help library; Group development & facilitator training; Public education & outreach; Production of annual directory of self-help groups; Self-help/community development; Information & referral service; Youth outreach & facilitator training; *Library:* SHRA Resource Centre; Open to public
Chief Officer(s):
Romi Chandra Herbert, Co-Executive Director
Iris Yong Pearson, Co-Executive Director

P.E.E.R.S. Alliance
161 St. Peter's Rd., Charlottetown PE C1A 5P7
Tel: 902-566-2437
info@peersalliance.ca
www.peersalliance.ca
www.facebook.com/PEERSALLIANCE
twitter.com/PEERSAlliance
Previous Name: AIDS PEI
Overview: A small provincial charitable organization founded in 1990 overseen by Canadian AIDS Society
Mission: To educate Islanders on sexual health, drug use, HIV, Hepatitis C, & sexually transmitted & blood borne infections; To support persons affected by HIV or Hepatitis C; To promote social programs for LGBTQ+ youth; To support new options for treatment & diagnosis
Member of: Prince Edward Island Literacy Alliance Inc.
Finances: *Funding Sources:* Health Canada; donations; fundraising
Staff Member(s): 2
Membership: *Member Profile:* People living with HIV/AIDS; community groups; individuals; clergy
Activities: *Speaker Service:* Yes; *Library*
Chief Officer(s):
Cybelle Rieber, Executive Director
director@peersalliance.ca
Angele DesRoches, Program Coordinator
outreach@peersalliance.ca

PEERS Victoria Resource Society
#1, 744 Fairview Rd., Victoria BC V9A 4V1
Tel: 250-388-5325; *Fax:* 250-388-5324
info@peers.bc.ca
peers.bc.ca
www.facebook.com/PeersVictoria
twitter.com/@peersvictoria
Overview: A small local organization
Mission: PEERS is a non-profit society established by former sex workers and community supporters and is dedicated to the empowerment, education and support of sex workers, by working to improve their safety and working conditions, assisting those who desire to leave the sex industry, increasing public understanding and awareness of these issues, and promoting the experiential voice.
Activities: Education; outreach programs
Chief Officer(s):
Marion Little, Executive Director
ed@peers.bc.ca

P.E.I. Cattlemen's Association *See* Prince Edward Island Cattle Producers

PEI Cricket Association (PEI-CA)
PE
Other Communication: Alt. E-mail: peicricketcoach@gmail.com
cricketPEI@gmail.com
www.cricketpei.com
www.facebook.com/375538377835
twitter.com/CricketPEI
Overview: A small provincial organization founded in 2010 overseen by Cricket Canada
Mission: To promote the development of cricket in Prince Edward Island.
Member of: Cricket Canada
Membership: 100; *Fees:* $20
Chief Officer(s):
Sarath Chandrasekere, President
Cyril Roy, Secretary

PEI Field Hockey Association
40 Enman Cres., Charlottetown PE C1A 1E6
Tél: 902-368-4110; *Téléc:* 902-368-4548
Ligne sans frais: 800-247-6712
sports@sportpei.pe.ca
Aperçu: *Dimension:* moyenne; *Envergure:* provinciale surveillé par Field Hockey Canada
Membre(s) du bureau directeur:
Barb Carmichael, President, 902-566-4056
bcarmichael@eastlink.ca

PEI Music Festival Association *See* Prince Edward Island Kiwanis Music Festival Association

PEI People First
81 Prince St., Charlottetown PE C1A 4R3
Tel: 902-892-8989
www.facebook.com/312960685412957
Overview: A small provincial charitable organization overseen by People First of Canada
Mission: To encourage self-advocacy among individuals labelled with an intellectual disability
Activities: Organizing social events; Providing information & resources for members

PEI Powerlifting Association (PEIPLA)
PE
www.peipowerlifting.ca
Overview: A small provincial organization founded in 1996 overseen by Canadian Powerlifting Union

Member of: Canadian Powerlifting Union
Affiliation(s): Canadian Powerlifting Union; International Powerlifting Federation
Membership: *Fees:* $70 regular; $40 high school; *Committees:* Fundraising; Competition & Promotion; Selection & Grant
Chief Officer(s):
John MacDonald, President
john@peipowerlifting.ca

PEI Real Estate Brokers Association *See* Prince Edward Island Real Estate Association

PEI Roadbuilders Association *See* Prince Edward Island Road Builders & Heavy Construction Association

PEI Sailing Association (PEISA)
c/o Ellen MacPhail, PO Box 6708, York Point PE C0A 1H0
save@waveskills.ca
www.peisailing.ca
Also Known As: Sail Prince Edward Island
Overview: A medium-sized provincial organization overseen by Sail Canada
Mission: The PEI Sailing Association is a volunteer organization that promotes sailing in the province of Prince Edward Island, Canada. As the provincial chapter of the Canadian Sailing Association the PEI Sailing Association provides support and training to anybody interested in learning to sail or expanding their sailing.
Member of: Sail Canada
Chief Officer(s):
Ellen McPhail, Executive Director

PEI Shellfish Association
PO Box 82, Ellerslie PE C0B 1J0
Tel: 902-831-3374
peishellfish@pei.aibn.com
www.naturallywild.ca
twitter.com/shellfishpei
Overview: A small provincial organization
Mission: To represent the interests of quahog, clam, & oyster fishers in PEI; To advance the shell fishing & oyster industry; To promote research & organize projects dedicated to oyster shellfish improvement
Activities: Conducting oyster enhancement projects
Chief Officer(s):
Kenneth Arsenault, President

PEI Special Olympics *See* Special Olympics Prince Edward Island

PEI Teacher-Librarians' Association (PEITLA)
c/o Carrie St. Jean, PO Box 6500, Glen Stewart Primary School, Charlottetown PE Cl1 8B5
Overview: A small provincial organization
Mission: To represent Teacher-Librarians in PEI
Chief Officer(s):
Carrie St. Jean, President

PEI Tuberculosis League *See* Prince Edward Island Lung Association

Pelham Historical Society
PO Box 903, Fonthill ON L0S 1E0
Overview: A small local organization founded in 1975
Affiliation(s): Ontario Historical Society
Chief Officer(s):
Robert Young, President
Mary Lamb, Collections Coordinator
mblamb@sympatico.ca

Pemberton & District Chamber of Commerce
PO Box 370, Pemberton BC V0N 2L0
Tel: 604-894-6477; *Fax:* 604-894-5571
info@pembertonchamber.com
www.pembertonchamber.com
twitter.com/pemchamber
Overview: A small local organization founded in 1932
Mission: To promote the commercial, industrial, agricultural & welfare of Pemberton & the surrounding area
Member of: Vancouver Coast & Mountains Tourism Region; B.C. Chamber of Commerce; Tourism Pemberton
Affiliation(s): Vancouver Board of Trade
Finances: *Annual Operating Budget:* Less than $50,000; *Funding Sources:* Membership dues; fundraising; grants
Staff Member(s): 2; 2 volunteer(s)
Membership: 149; *Fees:* $170-$210 business; $65 individual/non-profit; *Committees:* Visitor Centre; Design Review; Business Development; Events; Tourism Pemberton; Fundraising
Activities: Maintaining the Visitor Centre; Promoting & organizing events including barn dances, golf tournaments, dinners & workshops
Chief Officer(s):
Garth Phare, President
Shirley Henry, Secretary-Treasurer

The Pembina Institute
219 - 19 St. NW, Calgary AB T2N 2H9
Tel: 403-269-3344; *Fax:* 403-269-3377
www.pembina.org
ca.linkedin.com/company/pembina-institute
www.facebook.com/pembina.institute
twitter.com/pembina
www.instagram.com/pembinainstitute
Overview: A medium-sized provincial charitable organization founded in 1985
Mission: To develop & promote public policy & educational programs which protect the environment & encourage environmentally sound resource management strategies; to implement a conserver society
Finances: *Funding Sources:* Project grants; Fee-for-service contracts; Sponsorship; Donations
Staff Member(s): 40
Activities: Major program areas include Environmental Education & Publishing (teacher professional development; national environmental education resource cataloguing service; curricular materials for schools; classroom presentations & student workshops; community adult environmental education courses); Research, Development & Promotion of Environmental Policy (analyzing & developing municipal, provincial & federal energy-related environmental policy, as well as policy related to other conservation & recycling issues; *Speaker Service:* Yes; *Library:* Open to public by appointment
Chief Officer(s):
Glen R. Murray, Executive Director
Andrew Aziz, Director, Communications, 647-217-7967
andrewa@pembina.org
 Edmonton Office
 #300, 9804 Jasper Ave., Edmonton AB T5J 0C5
 Tel: 780-229-3154; *Fax:* 403-269-3377
 Toronto Office
 #600, 920 Yonge St., Toronto ON M4W 3C7
 Tel: 647-478-9563; *Fax:* 403-269-3377
 Vancouver Office
 #610, 55 Water St., Vancouver ON V6B 1A1
 Tel: 604-874-8558; *Fax:* 403-269-3377

Pembroke & Area Chamber of Commerce *See* Upper Ottawa Valley Chamber of Commerce

Pembroke & District Association for Community Living *See* Community Living Upper Ottawa Valley

Pembroke Area Field Naturalists (PAFN)
375 Doran St., Pembroke ON K8A 4N3
www.pafn.on.ca
Overview: A small local charitable organization founded in 1983
Member of: Federation of Ontario Naturalists
Finances: *Annual Operating Budget:* Less than $50,000; *Funding Sources:* Donations; fundraising
Membership: 50; *Fees:* $15 individual; $20 family; $10 student/senior
Activities: Conducting bird & insect counts; Organizing public field trips focused on biodiversity in the region; Holding educational presentations
Chief Officer(s):
Leo Boland, Vice-President
leoboland@pafn.on.ca

Pembroke District Construction Association (PDCA)
1145 Pembrooke St. West, Pembroke ON K8A 7R4
Tel: 613-732-7311
Overview: A small local organization founded in 1960
Chief Officer(s):
Ken Day, Contact

Pembroke Kiwanis Music Festival
PO Box 1093, Pembroke ON K8A 6Y6
Tel: 613-735-7773
www.pembrokekiwanis.org
Overview: A small local organization founded in 1948
Affiliation(s): Kiwanis Club of Pembroke
Finances: *Annual Operating Budget:* Less than $50,000
80 volunteer(s)
Membership: 20
Activities: Kiwanis Music Festival
Chief Officer(s):
Lloyd Koch, President, Kiwanis Pembroke
Susan Fisher, Secretary
fisher@nrtco.net

Pembroke Symphony Orchestra
PO Box 374, Pembroke ON K8A 6X6
Tel: 613-587-4826
pembrokesymphony.org
Overview: A small local charitable organization overseen by Orchestras Canada
Mission: To provide members with the opportunity to perform classical and modern music in an orchestral setting; To share orchestral music with the listening public
Member of: Orchestras Canada
Finances: *Funding Sources:* Provincial government; corporate & individual donations
Membership: *Fees:* $75; $30 student
Chief Officer(s):
Angus Armstrong, Music Director
Gail Marion, President
bluroom@nrtco.net

Pender Harbour & District Chamber of Commerce
Madeira Park, PO Box 265, Madeira Park BC V0N 2H0
Tel: 604-883-2561; *Fax:* 604-883-2561
Toll-Free: 877-873-6337
chamber@penderharbour.ca
www.penderharbour.ca
Overview: A small local organization founded in 1928
Member of: BC Chamber of Commerce
Finances: *Annual Operating Budget:* Less than $50,000; *Funding Sources:* Membership dues
Staff Member(s): 1; 5 volunteer(s)
Membership: 87; *Fees:* Schedule available
Activities: Operates the Pender Harbour Information Centre, Information & Tourist Sign Boards
Chief Officer(s):
Leonard Lee, President

Pender Island Chamber of Commerce
PO Box 164, 4605 Bedwell Harbour Rd., Pender Island BC V0N 2M0
Tel: 250-999-6371
info@penderislandchamber.com
www.penderislandchamber.com
www.facebook.com/155758237803188
twitter.com/penderchamber
Overview: A small local organization
Mission: To promote local businesses
Chief Officer(s):
Mamie Hutt Temoana, President

Pender Island Field Naturalists (PIFN)
3822 Pirates Rd., Pender Island BC V0N 2M2
www.pendernaturalists.ca
www.facebook.com/penderislandfieldnaturalsts
Overview: A small local organization
Mission: To raise awareness & strengthen appreciation of nature
Membership: 1-99; *Fees:* $25; *Member Profile:* Birding & botany enthusiasts

Peninsula Field Naturalists (PFN)
PO Box 23031, Stn. Carlton, St Catharines ON L2R 7P6
Tel: 905-892-2566
info@peninsulafieldnats.com
peninsulafieldnats.com
Overview: A small local charitable organization founded in 1954
Mission: To promote the enjoyment of nature through environmental appreciation & conservation; to encourage wise use & conservation of natural resources; to promote environmental protection
Member of: Ontario Nature
Finances: *Funding Sources:* Membership fees
Membership: *Fees:* $10 student; $25 adult; $35 family; *Member Profile:* Interest in natural history
Activities: Outdoor natural history walks; annual park clean-up; annual bird & plant inventories
Chief Officer(s):
Bob Highcock, President

The Pennsylvania German Folklore Society of Ontario
c/o York Chapter, 10292 McCowan Rd., Markham ON L3P 3J3

Tel: 905-640-3906; Fax: 905-640-9394
www.pennsylvania-german-folklore-society.com
Overview: A small provincial organization founded in 1951
Mission: To research, record, interpret history of the Town of Markham
Finances: Annual Operating Budget: Less than $50,000
Membership: 250; Fees: $13 single; $20 family
Chief Officer(s):
Ralph Shantz, President

Pension Investment Association of Canada (PIAC) / Association canadienne des gestionnaires de fonds de retraite
#123, 20 Carlton St., Toronto ON M5B 2H5
Tel: 416-640-0264
www.piacweb.org
Overview: A medium-sized national organization founded in 1977
Mission: To promote the financial security of pension fund beneficiaries through sound investment policy & practices
Finances: Annual Operating Budget: $250,000-$500,000; Funding Sources: Membership fees
Membership: 130 pension funds; Fees: Schedule available; Member Profile: Pension fund employees who have investment responsibilities at their respective pension funds/organizations
Chief Officer(s):
Peter Waite, Executive Director
Awards:
• Chuck Harvie Award
• Terry Staples Award

Pentathlon Alberta
AB
info@pentathlonalberta.com
www.pentathlonalberta.com
Previous Name: Alberta Modern Pentathlon Association
Overview: A small provincial organization
Mission: To develop world-class athletes while promoting & developing the sport in Alberta.
Member of: Canadian Modern Pentathlon Association
Membership: 4 local clubs/groups
Chief Officer(s):
Connie Olsen, President, 403-703-4951

Pentathlon Canada
c/o Shaun LaGrange, 513428 - 2nd Line, Amaranth ON L9W 0S4
Tel: 519-940-3721; Fax: 450-458-1746
www.pentathloncanada.ca
www.facebook.com/PentathlonCanada
Previous Name: Canadian Modern Pentathlon Association
Overview: A medium-sized national charitable organization
Mission: To promote Modern Pentathlon in Canada
Affiliation(s): Union internationale de pentathlon moderne et biathlon
Membership: 2,000
Chief Officer(s):
Shaun LaGrange, President
president@pentathloncanada.ca
Bob Noble, Vice-President

Pentecostal Assemblies of Canada (PAOC) / Assemblées de la Pentecôte du Canada (APDC)
2450 Milltower Ct., Mississauga ON L5N 5Z6
Tel: 905-542-7400; Fax: 905-542-7313
Toll-Free: 800-779-7262; TTY: 800-855-0511
info@paoc.org
www.paoc.org
www.facebook.com/ThePAOC
twitter.com/thepaoc
www.youtube.com/paoctube
Overview: A large national charitable organization founded in 1919
Mission: To glorify God by making disciples everywhere by proclaiming & practising the gospel of Jesus Christ in the power of the Holy Spirit to establish local congregations & to train spiritual leaders
Affiliation(s): World Pentecost; Pentecostal/Charismatic Churches of North America; Pentecostal World Fellowship; World Assemblies of God Fellowship; Focus on the Family; Canadian Foodgrains Bank; Pentecostal European Mission; Seeds International; VisionLEDD; Canadian Council of Christian Charities; Every Home for Christ; Evangelical Missiological Society; Evangelical Fellowship of Canada; Canadian Children's Ministries Network; Canadian Bible Society; Family Life Ministries; Society of Pentecostal Studies

Finances: Annual Operating Budget: Greater than $5 Million; Funding Sources: Local churches; individuals
Staff Member(s): 50
Membership: 1,100 churches, 3,500 pastors representing 236,000 parishoners; Committees: General Executive; Administrative; International Missions; Audit; Credentials
Activities: Task Force; Work Force; Volunteers in Mission; Short-Term Missions; Volunteers in Special Assignment; ERDO (Emergency Relief & Development Overseas); Child Care Plus; Library: The PAOC Archives; Open to public by appointment
Chief Officer(s):
David Wells, General Superintendent
David Hazzard, General Secretary Treasurer
Murray Cornelius, Executive Director, International Missions
Meetings/Conferences:
• 2018 Biennial Conference of the Pentecostal Assemblies of Canada, 2018
Scope: National
Publications:
• Testimony [a publication of Pentecostal Assemblies of Canada]
Type: Magazine; Frequency: Bimonthly; Editor: Stephen Kennedy; Price: $2.50

Alberta & Northwest Territories Office
Vanguard College, 12140 - 103 St. NW, 2nd Fl., West Wing, Edmonton AB T5G 2J9
Tel: 780-426-0018; Fax: 780-420-1318
abnwt.com
Chief Officer(s):
Ken Solbrekken, District Superintendent

British Columbia & Yukon District Office
20411 Douglas Cres., Langley BC V3A 4B6
Tel: 604-533-2232; Fax: 604-533-5405
info@bc.paoc.org
www.bc.paoc.org
www.facebook.com/bcydist
twitter.com/bcydist
www.flickr.com/photos/bcydnet
Chief Officer(s):
Ken Russell, District Superintendent

Eastern Ontario District Office
PO Box 337, Cobourg ON K9A 4K8
Tel: 905-373-7374; Fax: 905-373-1911
info@eod.paoc.org
www.eod.paoc.org
Chief Officer(s):
Craig Burton, District Superintendent

Manitoba & Northwest Ontario District Office
187 Henlow Bay, Winnipeg MB R3Y 1G4
Tel: 204-940-1000; Fax: 204-940-1009
paoc.net
Chief Officer(s):
Jim S. Poirier, District Superintendent

Maritime District Office
PO Box 1184, Truro NS B2N 5H1
Tel: 902-895-4212; Fax: 902-897-0705
maritimepaoc.org
twitter.com/MaritimePAOC
Chief Officer(s):
Kevin Johnson, District Superintendent

Québec District Office
839, rue La Salle, Longueuil QC J4K 3G6
Tel: 450-442-2732; Fax: 450-442-3818
info@dq.paoc.org
www.dqpaoc.org
Chief Officer(s):
Michel Bisaillon, District Superintendent

Saskatchewan District Office
1303 Jackson Ave., Saskatoon SK S7H 2M9
Tel: 306-683-4646; Fax: 306-683-3699
www.skpaoc.com
www.youtube.com/channel/UCFXk7ls11W2p0NNYarBwBkQ
Chief Officer(s):
John Drisner, District Superintendent

Western Ontario District Office
3214 South Service Rd., Burlington ON L7N 3J2
Tel: 905-637-5566; Fax: 905-637-7558
reception@wodistrict.org
www.wodistrict.org
Chief Officer(s):
Lorrie Gibbons, District Superintendent

The Pentecostal Assemblies of Newfoundland & Labrador (PAONL)
PO Box 8895, Stn. A, 57 Thorburn Rd., St. John's NL A1B 3T2

Tel: 709-753-6314; Fax: 709-753-4945
info@paonl.ca
www.paonl.ca
www.facebook.com/252330011920
twitter.com/paonl
Overview: A medium-sized provincial charitable organization founded in 1911
Mission: To promote evangelism, world missions, famine relief, & education
Affiliation(s): Pentecostal Fellowship of North America
Finances: Annual Operating Budget: $1.5 Million-$3 Million
Staff Member(s): 13
Membership: 40,000
Activities: Internships: Yes; Speaker Service: Yes; Library: by appointment
Chief Officer(s):
Terry W. Snow, General Superintendent

Penticton & District Community Arts Council (PDCAC)
220 Manor Park Ave., Penticton BC V2A 2R2
Tel: 250-492-7997; Fax: 250-492-7969
info@pentictonartscouncil.com
www.pentictonartscouncil.com
www.facebook.com/Penticton.council
twitter.com/PentictonArtCou
Also Known As: Leir House Cultural Centre
Overview: A medium-sized local organization founded in 1960
Mission: To increase & broaden the opportunities for public enjoyment of & participation in cultural activities; to help co-ordinate the work & programmes of cultural groups; to act as a clearing house for information on cultural projects & activities
Member of: Assembly of BC Arts Councils
Finances: Funding Sources: Rentals; grants; fundraising
Staff Member(s): 2
Membership: 240; Fees: $15 individual; $25 family; $35 group; $45 business; $100 corporate; Member Profile: Local arts groups & societies; individuals & families; businesses
Chief Officer(s):
Eric Hanston, President
Sharon Lawrence, Office Administrator

Penticton & District Community Resources Society (PDCRS)
330 Ellis St., Penticton BC V2A 4L7
Tel: 250-492-5814; Fax: 250-492-7572
info@pdcrs.com
www.pdcrs.com
www.linkedin.com/company/penticton-&-district-community-resources-society
www.facebook.com/PdcrsCounsellingServices
Overview: A small local organization founded in 1966
Mission: To help people achieve their maximum independence & potential through effective & efficient delivery of services
Member of: BC Association for Community Living; Child Welfare League; Federation of Child & Family Services; United Community Services Coop.
Finances: Annual Operating Budget: $3 Million-$5 Million
Staff Member(s): 70; 20 volunteer(s)
Membership: 25; Fees: $2
Activities: After-School Program; child care resource & referral; community services office; family enhancement programs; FAS/FAE Project; Hand In Hand Infant/Toddler Centre; handyDART service; Little Trimphs Pre-School; parenting after separation; Penticton Alternate School; Penticton Family Centre; Penticton Paper Shuffle; Reconnect; residential services; sexual abuse treatment program; special services to children; supported child care; The Club; Lazy Lizard Fair; Awareness Events: Community Living Month
Chief Officer(s):
Tanya Behardien, Executive Director

Penticton & District Multicultural Society See South Okanagan Immigrant & Community Services

Penticton & District Society for Community Living (PDSCL)
180 Industrial Ave. West, Penticton BC V2A 6X9
Tel: 250-493-0312; Fax: 250-493-9113
admin@pdscl.org
www.pdscl.org
Overview: A small local charitable organization founded in 1958
Mission: Serves vulnerable persons & families with physical or developmental disabilites &/or economic disadvantages; provides community based day & residential supports, affordable housing, outreach services & education

Member of: British Columbia Association for Commmunity Living
Finances: *Annual Operating Budget:* $3 Million-$5 Million
Staff Member(s): 50; 25 volunteer(s)
Membership: 22; *Fees:* $5
Chief Officer(s):
Tony Laing, Executive Director

Penticton & Wine Country Chamber of Commerce
553 Vees Dr., Penticton BC V2A 8S3
Tel: 250-492-4103
admin@penticton.org
www.penticton.org
www.facebook.com/200338503334345
twitter.com/PentChamber
Overview: A medium-sized local organization founded in 1907
Member of: BC Chamber of Commerce; Canadian Chamber of Commerce
Finances: *Funding Sources:* Membership dues; publishing; sponsorship; provincial & municipal government
Staff Member(s): 4
Membership: *Fees:* Schedule available based on number of employees; *Committees:* Membership; Communications; Government Relations; Business Excellence Awards; Executive; Finance
Activities: *Rents Mailing List:* Yes; *Library*
Chief Officer(s):
Brandy Maslowski, Executive Director
Jason Cox, President

Penticton Geology & Lapidary Club
Penticton BC
pentictongeologyandlapidary@gmail.com
www.pentictongeologyandlapidary.blogspot.ca
Overview: A small local organization founded in 1959
Affiliation(s): British Columbia Lapidary Society
Activities: Hosting monthly meetings; *Awareness Events:* Penticton Geology & Lapidary Club Gem Show
Chief Officer(s):
Donna Carpenter, Secretary

People First Nova Scotia
568A Prince St., Truro NS B2N 1G3
Tel: 902-893-3033
Toll-Free: 877-454-3860
pfns2014@gmail.com
www.peoplefirstns.ca
Overview: A small provincial charitable organization overseen by People First of Canada
Mission: To promote equality for individuals who have been labelled with an intellectual disability; To promote & encourage self-advocacy among labelled individuals; To educate the community on issues affecting labelled individuals
Activities: Providing leadership development training; Offering presentation & speech preparation services; Working in conjunction with government & other community groups to promote change
Chief Officer(s):
Cindy Carruthers, Coordinator
Meetings/Conferences:
• People First Nova Scotia Annual General Meeting & Conference 2018, 2018, NS
Scope: Provincial

Annapolis Chapter
NS
Chief Officer(s):
Donnie MacLean, President

Halifax / Dartmouth Chapter
NS
Tel: 902-444-9202
Chief Officer(s):
Terry Wilson, President

Kings County Chapter
NS
Tel: 902-678-1458
Chief Officer(s):
Tammy Hiltz, President

Shelbourne Chapter
NS
Chief Officer(s):
Gillian Harris, President

Truro Chapter
NS
Tel: 902-843-0402
Chief Officer(s):
Heather Mackenzie, President

Windsor Chapter
PO Box 292, 100 King St., Windsor NS B0N 2T0
windsorpf@hotmail.com
www.nsnet.org/windsorpeoplefirst
Chief Officer(s):
Donna Sparks, President, 902-472-2839

Yarmouth Chapter
NS
Chief Officer(s):
Randy Muise, President
Joan Paquette, Contact, 902-742-5596

People First of Canada (PFC) / Personnes d'abord du Canada
#20, 226 Osborne St. North, Winnipeg MB R3C 1V4
Tel: 204-784-7362; *Fax:* 204-784-7364
info@peoplefirstofcanada.ca
www.peoplefirstofcanada.ca
www.facebook.com/PeopleFirstofCanada
twitter.com/PeopleFirstCA
www.youtube.com/user/PeoplefirstofCanada
Previous Name: National People First
Overview: A medium-sized national charitable organization founded in 1981
Mission: To educate the public on issues faced by persons with intellectual disabilities; To promote equality; To work toward the deinstitutionalization of persons with intellectual disabilities
Membership: *Member Profile:* Individuals who have been labeled with an intellectual disability, who have lived in an institution or group home, &/or have received services for individuals who have been labeled with an intellectual disability
Activities: Increasing awareness of issues encountered by people with intellectual disabilities, such as discrimination, segregation, unemployment, & poverty; Providing information, education, training; Advocating for persons labelled with intellectual disabilities
Chief Officer(s):
Shelley Fletcher, Executive Director
sfletcher@peoplefirstofcanada.ca
Meetings/Conferences:
• People First of Canada 2018 27th Annual General Meeting & Conference, 2018
Scope: National
Description: A meeting for People First representatives from across Canada, featuring the presentation of awards

People First of Manitoba
AB
Overview: A small provincial organization overseen by People First of Canada
Mission: To promote & educate the community about the values of inclusion; To assist individuals labelled with a disability in living a full & inclusive life
Activities: Hosting social events; Disseminating information

People First of Newfoundland & Labrador
#5A, Limerick Pl., St. John's NL A1B 2H2
peoplefirst@nl.rogers.com
www.peoplefirstnl.ca
Overview: A small provincial organization overseen by People First of Canada
Mission: To educate the public about issues that affect individuals labelled with a disability; To encourage self-advocacy among labelled individuals
Activities: Participating in local, provincial, & national projects; Organizing social events & film screenings; Disseminating information to the community

People First of Ontario
#4, 2495 Parkedale Ave., Brockville ON
Tel: 613-213-3214; *Fax:* 613-345-4092
info@peoplefirstontario.ca
www.peoplefirstontario.com
www.facebook.com/peoplefirstontario
twitter.com/people1ontario
www.youtube.com/user/PeopleFirstofCanada
Overview: A small provincial charitable organization founded in 1982 overseen by People First of Canada
Mission: To promote equality for all persons; To foster & encourage self-advocacy; To teach members about the rights, abilities, & strengths of individuals labelled with a disability
Activities: Providing peer support activities & leadership development skills workshops; Advocating for rights & freedoms
Chief Officer(s):
Richard Ruston, President
rruston2@cogeco.ca

Reina Soltis, Coordinator
reina.peoplefirston@gmail.com
Meetings/Conferences:
• People First of Ontario Annual General Meeting 2018, 2018, ON
Scope: Provincial

Peterborough Chapter
223 Aylmer St., Peterborough ON K9J 3K3
peoplefirstptbo@gmail.com
www.peoplefirstptbo.ca
www.facebook.com/150380531706324
Chief Officer(s):
Daniel Lombardi, President, 705-743-2412 Ext. 536

People First Society of Yukon
PO Box 31478, Whitehorse YT Y1A 6K8
Tel: 867-667-4606; *Fax:* 867-668-8169
peoplefirstyukon@hotmail.com
www.facebook.com/PeopleFirstSocietyOfYukon
Overview: A small provincial organization overseen by People First of Canada
Mission: To encourage self-advocacy among individuals labelled with an intellectual disability
Activities: Hosting social events; Disseminating information to promote awareness
Meetings/Conferences:
• People First Society of Yukon Annual General Meeting 2018, 2018, YT
Scope: Provincial

People for Education (P4E)
641 Bloor St. West, Toronto ON M6G 1L1
Tel: 416-534-0100; *Fax:* 416-536-0100
info@peopleforeducation.ca
www.peopleforeducation.ca
www.facebook.com/peopleforeducation
www.twitter.com/Anniekidder
Overview: A medium-sized provincial charitable organization
Mission: People for Education is an independent organization working to support public education in Ontario's English, Catholic and French schools.
Chief Officer(s):
Annie Kidder, Executive Director
annie@peopleforeducation.ca
Meetings/Conferences:
• People for Education Annual Conference 2018, 2018
Scope: International

People with AIDS Foundation See Toronto PWA Foundation

People's Alliance of New Brunswick
#118, 527 Dundonald St., Fredericton NB E3B 1X6
Tel: 506-455-3015
info@peoplesalliance.ca
www.peoplesalliance.ca
www.facebook.com/AGNBPANB
twitter.com/PANB_AGNB
Overview: A small provincial organization
Membership: *Fees:* $10
Chief Officer(s):
Kris Austin, Party Leader
krisaustin@peoplesalliance.ca

People's Law School
#150, 900 Howe St., Vancouver BC V6Z 2M4
Tel: 604-331-5400; *Fax:* 604-331-5401
info@publiclegaled.bc.ca
www.publiclegaled.bc.ca
www.linkedin.com/company/2024453?trk=tyah
www.facebook.com/peopleslawschool
twitter.com/PLSBC
www.youtube.com/user/plsbc
Overview: A small provincial organization founded in 1972
Mission: To make law & the legal system understandable & accessible to residents of British Columbia
Member of: Public Legal Education Association of Canada
Affiliation(s): Battered Women's Support Center; BC Center for Elder Advocacy and Support; Bully Free BC; Clicklaw; BC Chamber of Commerce; CourtHouse Libraries; Immigrant Public Legal Education and Information Consortium (IPC); Justice Education Society; The Law Foundation of British Columbia; British Columbia Ministry of Justice; Notary Foundation; PovNet; Public Legal Education Association of Canada (PLEAC); Public Legal Education and Information Working Group (PLEIWG); Tenant Resource and Advisory Centre (TRAC); Vancouver Community Network (VCN)
Staff Member(s): 6

Activities: Publishing & distributing plain language legal information in multiple formats such as print, online books, fact sheets & video; Offering public legal education through hands-on workshops, lectures & Justice Theatre; Providing referral services as well as a reading & resource room for the public; *Awareness Events:* Legal@Lunch; Public Legal Aid in the Community
Chief Officer(s):
Terresa Augustine, Executive Director

People's Memorial Society *See* People's Memorial Society of BC & Vancouver Island Memorial Society

People's Memorial Society of BC & Vancouver Island Memorial Society
PO Box 505, Stn. Main, Vernon BC V1T 9Z9
Fax: 250-558-3552
Toll-Free: 800-661-3358
info@peoplesmemorialsocietybc.com
www.peoplesmemorialsocietybc.com
Previous Name: People's Memorial Society
Overview: A small local organization founded in 1991
Membership: 15,000; *Fees:* $10 lifetime

People's Senate Party *See* Unparty: The Consensus-Building Party

People, Words & Change (PWC) / Monde des mots
Heartwood House, #202, 404 MacArthur Ave., Ottawa ON K1K 1G8
Tel: 613-234-2494; *Fax:* 613-241-4170
dee@pwc-ottawa.ca
pwc-ottawa.ca
www.facebook.com/PeopleWordsChange
Overview: A small local charitable organization founded in 1978
Mission: To teach adults to read & write in English
Member of: Ottawa-Carleton Coalition for Literacy; Heartwood House; Community Literacy of Ontario
Finances: *Annual Operating Budget:* $100,000-$250,000; *Funding Sources:* Government; donations
130 volunteer(s)
Membership: 275; *Member Profile:* Interest in literacy
Activities: *Library:* Not open to public
Chief Officer(s):
Dee Sullivan, Executive Director & Education Counsellor
Julie Oliveria, Education Counsellor
Susan Chabot, Computer Instructor

Peretz Centre for Secular Jewish Culture
6184 Ash St., Vancouver BC V5Z 3G9
Tel: 604-325-1812; *Fax:* 604-325-2470
info@peretz-centre.org
www.peretz-centre.org
Previous Name: Vancouver Peretz Institute; Vancouver Peretz Shule
Overview: A small local organization founded in 1945
Mission: To preserve Jewish secular humanistic culture & thought; To provide a broad range of educational & cultural programs for all ages, with secular humanist Yidishkayt at the core
Affiliation(s): International Federation of Secular Humanistic Jews; Congress of Secular Jewish Organizations; Jewish Federation of Greater Vancouver
Finances: *Funding Sources:* Membership fees; Donations; Banquet hall, auditorium, & meeting room rentals
Membership: *Fees:* $65 students & seniors; $120 individuals; $160 single parent families; $230 families; *Member Profile:* Persons with Jewish family ties in the Greater Vancouver area
Activities: Offering classes for children, in Jewish heritage, tradition, & culture, to help them develop their Jewish identity; Providing B'nai (Bar / Bas) Mitzvah classes & Yiddish classes; Organizing an Yiddish Reading Circle; Coordinating a seniors' group; Offering bursaries; Administrating the Vancouver Jewish Folk Choir; Operating a Kirman English & Yiddish Library; *Library:* The Kirman Library at the Peretz Centre
Chief Officer(s):
Gene Homel, President
Publications:
• Peretz Papers
Type: Newsletter; *Frequency:* Bimonthly
Profile: Executive reports & notices of upcoming events

Performing Arts BC
PO Box 1484, Stn. A, Comox BC V9M 8A2
Tel: 250-493-7279
festival@bcprovincials.com
www.bcprovincials.com
Previous Name: BC Association of Performing Arts Festivals
Overview: A medium-sized provincial organization founded in 1964 overseen by Federation of Canadian Music Festivals
Membership: 34 performing arts festivals
Activities: Provincial level performing arts festival

Periodical Marketers of Canada (PMC)
South Tower, #1007, 175 Bloor St. East, Toronto ON M4W 3R8
Tel: 416-968-7547; *Fax:* 416-968-6281
info@periodical.ca
www.periodical.ca
Overview: A medium-sized national organization founded in 1942 overseen by Book & Periodical Council
Mission: To represent Canadian wholesalers; To promote Canadian magazines
Member of: Book & Periodical Council
Finances: *Funding Sources:* Grants
Membership: *Member Profile:* Canadian wholesalers of periodicals
Activities: Sponsoring National Magazine Awards
Chief Officer(s):
Ray Argyle, Executive Director
rargyle@periodical.ca
Awards:
• Authors Award
• Book of the Year Award
• Authors Award for Leadership
• Canadian Letters Award

Periodical Writers Association of Canada *See* Professional Writers Association of Canada

Perioperative Registered Nurses Association of British Columbia (PRNABC)
4774 Hill Ave., Prince George BC V2M 0A5
www.prnabc.ca
Overview: A medium-sized provincial organization overseen by Operating Room Nurses Association of Canada
Mission: To promote quality perioperative nursing; To provide educational & professional development opportunities
Membership: *Member Profile:* Registered Nurses in British Columbia who are engaged in operating room nursing or members of the College of Registered Nurses (CRNBC) who are involved in the Perioperative setting & are interested in promoting the purpose of PRNABC
Activities: *Awareness Events:* Perioperative Nurses Week, November
Chief Officer(s):
Catherine Kruger, President
Leenta Nel, Treasurer

Personal Computer Club of Toronto
34 Ravenal St., Toronto ON M6N 3Y7
membership@pcct.org
www.pcct.org
Overview: A small local organization
Finances: *Annual Operating Budget:* Less than $50,000
50 volunteer(s)
Membership: 300; *Fees:* $65
Activities: General & S.I.G. meetints
Chief Officer(s):
Cristina Enretti-Zoppo, President, 416-925-8570
president@pcct.org

Personnel Association of Ontario *See* Human Resources Professionals Association

Personnel professionnel des services aux étudiants *See* Professional Student Services Personnel

Personnes d'abord du Canada *See* People First of Canada

Persons Living with AIDS Network of Saskatchewan Inc.
PO Box 7123, Saskatoon SK S7K 4J1
Tel: 306-373-7766; *Fax:* 306-374-7746
Toll-Free: 800-226-0944
plwa@sasktel.net
www.aidsnetworksaskatoon.ca
Also Known As: PLWA Network of Saskatchewan
Overview: A small provincial charitable organization founded in 1987 overseen by Canadian AIDS Society
Mission: To provide & operate support & social activities for persons diagnosed with HIV disease, as well as their families, friends & partners
Member of: Saskatoon Interagency Council on STD's & AIDS; Canadian Centre for Philanthropy
Finances: *Annual Operating Budget:* $100,000-$250,000; *Funding Sources:* Donations; fundraising; Saskatchewan Dept. of Health
Staff Member(s): 2; 9 volunteer(s)
Membership: 170; *Member Profile:* Persons infected/affected by HIV/AIDS
Activities: *Awareness Events:* World AIDS Day, Dec.; Red Ribbon Campaign, Nov; Jump for AIDS, Aug; *Speaker Service:* Yes; *Library:* The Tracie Wood Memorial Library; Not open to public

Perth & District Chamber of Commerce
66 Craig St., Perth ON K7H 1Y5
Tel: 613-267-3200; *Fax:* 613-267-6797
welcome@perthchamber.com
perthchamber.com
www.facebook.com/perthchamber
twitter.com/perthchamber
Previous Name: Perth Chamber of Commerce
Overview: A small local organization founded in 1889
Mission: To promote economic development & prosperity for the enrichment of the community
Affiliation(s): Canadian Chamber of Commerce; Ontario Chamber of Commerce
Finances: *Annual Operating Budget:* $50,000-$100,000
Staff Member(s): 2; 2 volunteer(s)
Membership: 350; *Fees:* $85-$356; *Committees:* Corporate Image; Economic Development; Festival of the Maples; Golf Tournament; Membership; Visitor Guide
Chief Officer(s):
Amber Hall, Manager

Perth Chamber of Commerce *See* Perth & District Chamber of Commerce

Peruvian Horse Association of Canada (PHAC)
Lyalta AB T0J 1Y0
Tel: 403-935-4435; *Fax:* 403-935-4774
www.phac.ca
Overview: A medium-sized national charitable organization founded in 1974
Mission: To assure registration of Pure Peruvian Paso Horses & to keep members informed of changes
Membership: *Fees:* $15 aficionado; $45 owner-breeder
Activities: *Rents Mailing List:* Yes
Chief Officer(s):
Gus McCollister, Executive Secretary
gusmccollister@efirehose.net

Ontario Peruvian Horse Association
c/o Lyn Knell, 354 Carnrike Rd., RR#2, Consecon ON K0K 1T0
Tel: 613-849-0740
Chief Officer(s):
Luis Fiallos, President
luis@peruvianpaso.ca
Lyn Knell, Contact
lyn@peruvianpaso.ca

Peruvian Horse Club of Alberta
PO Box 41, Site 1, RR#3, Rocky Mountain House AB T4T 2A3
Tel: 403-510-8090
www.peruvianpasosalberta.com
Chief Officer(s):
Kim Sheridan, President
kim@stoneridgeperuvians.com

Peruvian Horse Club of BC
PO Box 214, Armstrong BC V0E 1B0
Chief Officer(s):
Rob Sjodin, President

Pest Management Association of Alberta (PMAA)
6729 - 99 St., Edmonton AB
pmaa@telus.net
www.pmaapestworld.com
Previous Name: Structural Pest Management Association of Alberta
Overview: A small provincial organization
Mission: To improve & maintain standards of pest management services in the province
Member of: Canadian Pest Management Association; National Pest Management Association Inc.
Membership: *Fees:* $385
Chief Officer(s):
Tom Schultz, Treasurer, 780-466-8535
edexterm@telusplanet.net
Eric Schuster, Secretary

Pesticide Education Network
web.ncf.ca/bf250/pen.html
Overview: A small local organization
Finances: *Annual Operating Budget:* Less than $50,000
20 volunteer(s)
Membership: 1-99
Activities: Reduction of pesticide use within urban areas; *Speaker Service:* Yes
Chief Officer(s):
John Sankey, Contact
johnsankey@ncf.ca

Pet Food Association of Canada (PFAC) / Association des fabricants d'aliments pour animaux familiers du Canada
PO Box 35570, 2528 Bayview Ave., Toronto ON M2L 2Y4
Tel: 416-447-9970; *Fax:* 416-443-9137
www.pfac.com
Overview: A medium-sized national organization founded in 1970
Mission: To provide association members with a unified voice on issues that affect the pet food industry in Canada
Membership: *Member Profile:* Representatives from all areas of the Canadian pet food industry, including ingredient suppliers, manufacturers, packagers, & companies that market pet food sold in Canada; *Committees:* Regulatory affairs; Public relations
Activities: Providing recommendations about the Canadian pet food industry & shaping policies; Liaising with government, media, industry, & consumers; Offering networking opportunities; Providing information about the pet food industry

Pet Industry Joint Advisory Council (PIJAC)
#14, 1010 Polytek St., Ottawa ON K1J 9H9
Tel: 613-730-8111; *Fax:* 613-730-9111
Toll-Free: 800-667-7452
info@pijaccanada.com
www.pijaccanada.com
www.linkedin.com/company/3202482
www.facebook.com/PIJACCanada
twitter.com/pijaccanada
Also Known As: PIJAC Canada
Overview: A large national organization founded in 1988
Mission: To promote the highest level of pet care for all sectors of the Canadian pet industry; To support research into the best attainable pet care; To engage in legislation & regulation affecting the Canadian pet industry at all levels of government; To promote the humane treatment of animals
Finances: *Annual Operating Budget:* $500,000-$1.5 Million; *Funding Sources:* Membership dues & event revenue
Staff Member(s): 8
Membership: 550; *Fees:* Schedule available; *Member Profile:* Pet & pet supply retailers; Groomers, breeders, & vet clinics; Pet supply manufacturers; Individuals who are not in the pet industry & align with PIJAC values; *Committees:* Nominating; Executive; Education; Membership; Events
Activities: Advocating for pet industry representation; Providing online education programs, seminars, & events; Ensuring animals receive proper care according to the needs of the species
Chief Officer(s):
Louis McCann, President & CEO
executiveoffice@pijaccanada.com
Rénald Sabourin, Assistant Executive Director
operations@pijaccanada.com
Susan Dankert, Manager, Communications
communications@pijaccanada.com
Meetings/Conferences:
• Pet Industry Joint Advisory Council Western Canadian Pet Industry Trade Show 2018, April, 2018, Richmond Olympic Oval, Richmond, BC
Scope: Provincial
Description: A trade show providing visitors with the opportunity to explore the BC pet market
• Pet Industry Joint Advisory Council ExpoZoo 2018, August, 2018, Centrexpo Drummondville, Drummondville, QC
Scope: Provincial
Description: A trade show providing visitors with the opportunity to explore the Québec pet market
• Pet Industry Joint Advisory Council National Pet Industry Trade Show 2018, September, 2018, International Center, Mississauga, ON
Scope: National
Description: A trade show providing exhibitors with the opportunity to meet new clients & explore the Canadian pet industry

Pet Therapy Society of Northern Alberta
14620 - 111 Ave., Edmonton AB T5M 2P4
Tel: 780-413-4682; *Fax:* 780-440-3341
info@pettherapysociety.com
www.pettherapysociety.com
www.facebook.com/PetTherapySociety
Overview: A small local organization founded in 1994
Mission: To provide animal assisted therapy & pet visitation programs; To provide competent & compassionate support/services to grieving pet owners; To initiate or participate in new programs involving the human animal bond in response to proven needs in the community
Activities: Pet Loss Support Line: 780-418-1949

Peter Gilgan Foundation
TD Bank Tower, PO Box 97, #5500, 66 Wellington St. West, Toronto ON M5K 1G8
info@petergilganfoundation.org
www.petergilganfoundation.org
Overview: A small local charitable organization
Mission: To support causes in the areas of children, youth, & families, as well as environmental protection & international development
Activities: Organizing the Tour de Bleu cycling event
Chief Officer(s):
Peter Gilgan, Founder

Peterborough & District Labour Council
PO Box 1928, 246 Romaine St., Peterborough ON K9J 7X7
Tel: 705-868-7352
ptbolabour@gmail.com
www.ptbolabour.ca
www.facebook.com/ptbolabour
twitter.com/ptbolabour
Overview: A small local organization overseen by Ontario Federation of Labour
Membership: 38 locals; 6,000 members
Chief Officer(s):
Marion Burton, President
marionburton@nexicom.net

Peterborough & the Kawarthas Association of Realtors Inc. (PKAR)
PO Box 1330, 273 Charlotte St., Peterborough ON K9J 7H5
Tel: 705-745-5724; *Fax:* 705-745-9377
info@peterboroughrealestate.org
www.peterboroughrealestate.org
www.linkedin.com/company/peterborough-and-the-kawarthas-association-of-realtorsr-inc-
www.facebook.com/PtboRealtors
twitter.com/pkarrealestate
Previous Name: Peterborough Real Estate Board Inc.
Overview: A small local organization overseen by Ontario Real Estate Association
Member of: The Canadian Real Estate Association
Finances: *Funding Sources:* Membership dues; Services; Programs
Membership: 470
Chief Officer(s):
Mike Heffernan, President

Peterborough & the Kawarthas Tourism
1400 Crawford Dr., Peterborough ON K9J 6X6
Tel: 705-742-2201; *Fax:* 705-742-2494
Toll-Free: 800-461-6424
info@thekawarthas.net
www.thekawarthas.net
www.facebook.com/TheKawarthas
twitter.com/pktourism
www.pinterest.com/pktourism
Previous Name: Peterborough Kawartha Tourism & Convention Bureau
Overview: A small local organization founded in 1982
Mission: To help market the Peterborough area to visitors
Member of: Tourism Industry Association of Canada
Membership: 400
Activities: *Speaker Service:* Yes

Peterborough AIDS Resource Network *See* PARN Your Community AIDS Resource Network

Peterborough Association for Riding for the Disabled *See* PARD Therapeutic Riding

Peterborough Chamber of Commerce *See* Greater Peterborough Chamber of Commerce

Peterborough Field Naturalists (PFN)
PO Box 1532, Peterborough ON K9J 7H7
info@peterboroughnature.org
www.peterboroughnature.org
www.facebook.com/PeterboroughFieldNaturalists
twitter.com/PtboNature
Overview: A small local charitable organization founded in 1940 overseen by Ontario Nature
Mission: To promote the enjoyment of nature through environmental appreciation & conservation; To encourage wise use & conservation of natural resources & environmental protection
12 volunteer(s)
Membership: 200; *Fees:* $25 single; $30 family/couple; $15 student; *Committees:* Advocacy; Harper Park
Activities: Monthly meetings with guest speakers; Outings & field trips; Community education & advocacy; Research
Chief Officer(s):
Edward Vale, President, 705-741-3641
tedandmarion@sympatico.ca
Martin Parker, Secretary, 705-742-1524
mparker19@cogeco.ca
Publications:
• The Orchid [a publication of Peterborough Field Naturalists]
Type: Newsletter; *Frequency:* 9 pa

Peterborough Historical Society (PHS)
270 Brock St., Peterborough ON K9H 2P9
Tel: 705-740-2600
info@peterboroughhistoricalsociety.ca
www.peterboroughhistoricalsociety.ca
Overview: A small local organization founded in 1897
Mission: To preserve & promote the cultural & architectural history of Peterborough, Ontario
Finances: *Funding Sources:* Peterborough Community Futures Development Corporation; Federal Economic Development Agency for Southern Ontario; Donations; Fundraising
Membership: *Fees:* $40 individuals; $50 families; $15 students
Activities: Operating the Hutchison House Living History Museum; Hosting public meetings with presentation on local history; Erecting historical plaques
Chief Officer(s):
Don Willcock, President
Linda Chandler, Corresponding Secretary
Paul Lumsden, Treasurer
Awards:
• Heritage Awards
Presented annually to a member of the community
• History Awards
Presented annually to deserving high school students
Publications:
• Peterborough Historical Society Bulletin
Type: Newsletter; *Frequency:* Monthly; *Price:* Free with membership in the Peterborough Historical Society
Profile: Articles of historical interest & upcoming events

Peterborough Kawartha Tourism & Convention Bureau *See* Peterborough & the Kawarthas Tourism

Peterborough Law Association
470 Water St., Peterborough ON K9H 3M3
Tel: 705-742-9341; *Fax:* 705-742-6173
library@peterboroughlaw.org
www.peterboroughlaw.org
Overview: A small local organization founded in 1879
Member of: Law Society of Upper Canada
Staff Member(s): 1
Membership: 120
Activities: *Library:* by appointment
Chief Officer(s):
Laura Dobbie, Contact

Peterborough Numismatic Club
1230 Water St., Peterborough ON K9J 6Z5
Tel: 705-295-4734
Also Known As: Peterborough Coin Club
Overview: A small local organization founded in 1951
Mission: To promote the collection & study of coins & paper money
Member of: Ontario Numismatic Association; Royal Canadian Numismatic Association
Finances: *Annual Operating Budget:* Less than $50,000; *Funding Sources:* Annual dues; Meeting fees
Membership: 25; *Fees:* $10
Activities: Holding monthly meetings
Chief Officer(s):
Colin Caldwell, President, 705-742-0114

Randy McQuaid, Vice-President
rusty.mcquaid@nexicom.net

Peterborough Police Association (PPA) / Association de la police de Peterborough
c/o Headquarters, Peterborough Lakefield Community Police,
PO Box 2050, 500 Water Street, Peterborough ON K9J 7Y4
Tel: 705-876-1122; *Fax:* 705-743-1540
Toll-Free: 888-876-1122
www.facebook.com/149692195114005
Overview: A small local organization

Peterborough Real Estate Board Inc. *See* Peterborough & the Kawarthas Association of Realtors Inc.

Peterborough Social Planning Council (PSPC)
Peterborough Square, 360 George St. North, Lower Level,
Peterborough ON K9H 7E7
Tel: 705-743-5915
www.pspc.on.ca
Overview: A small local organization founded in 1977
Mission: To facilitate citizen participation in forming strong, healthy, & just communities in the City & County of Peterborough, Ontario; To act as a catalyst for positive social change; To promote social justice
Finances: *Funding Sources:* Donations; Fundraising
Staff Member(s): 2
Membership: *Committees:* Advisory
Activities: Conducting social research; Analyzing social policy; Providing information & public education about social issues & trends; Partnering with other organizations; Implementing community plans
Chief Officer(s):
Brenda Dales, Executive Director
Dawm Berry Merriam, Research & Policy Analyst

Peterborough Symphony Orchestra (PSO)
PO Box 1135, Peterborough ON K9J 7H4
Tel: 705-742-1992
info@thepso.org
www.thepso.org
www.facebook.com/Peterborough.Symphony.Orchestra
twitter.com/thepso
Overview: A small local charitable organization founded in 1967 overseen by Orchestras Canada
Mission: To perform & develop excellence in symphonic music that will enrich, stimulate & attract the widest possible audience by presenting quality orchestral music to the people of Peterborough & beyond
Member of: Orchestras Canada
Affiliation(s): Peterborough Chamber of Commerce
Finances: *Funding Sources:* Ticket revenue; Ontario Arts Council; City of Peterborough; Individual & corporate donations
Staff Member(s): 3
Membership: 44
Activities: *Internships:* Yes; *Speaker Service:* Yes; *Library:* PSO Music Library; Not open to public
Chief Officer(s):
Deanna Guttman, Executive Director, 705-775-4515
deanna@thepso.org
Michael Newnham, Music Director

Petite ligue Canada *See* Little League Canada

Petites-Mains
7595, boul St-Laurent, Montréal QC H2R 1W9
Tél: 514-738-8989; *Téléc:* 514-738-6193
info@petitesmains.com
www.petitesmains.com
www.facebook.com/PetitesMainsMtl
twitter.com/PetitesMains
Aperçu: *Dimension:* petite; *Envergure:* locale; fondée en 1994
Mission: Petites-Mains a pour mission de venir en aide aux gens, surtout les femmes immigrantes, monoparentales, sans revenu et prestataires de l'Assistance-Emploi. Il aide ces femmes à sortir de leur isolement, à échanger avec d'autres, à apprendre un métier, à intégrer le marché du travail et à vivre en dignité dans la société.
Membre(s) du personnel: 14
Membre(s) du bureau directeur:
Nahid Aboumansour, Directrice générale

Petits frères des pauvres
4624, rue Garnier, Montréal QC H2L 3S7
Tél: 514-527-8653; *Téléc:* 514-527-7162
Ligne sans frais: 866-627-8653
info@petitsfreres.ca
www.petitsfreres.ca
www.facebook.com/LesPetitsFreres
Aperçu: *Dimension:* moyenne; *Envergure:* internationale; fondée en 1962
Mission: Pour connecter les seniors avec les jeunes afin de les faire sortir de l'isolement et d'avoir la compagnie
Activités: Activité de collecte de fonds
Membre(s) du bureau directeur:
Luc Villeneuve, Président, Conseil d'administration

Petroleum Accountants Society of Canada (PASC)
PO Box 4520, Stn. C, #400, 1040 - 7 Ave. SW, Calgary AB T2T 5N3
Tel: 403-262-4744; *Fax:* 403-244-2340
info@petroleumaccountants.com
www.petroleumaccountants.com
www.linkedin.com/groups/Petroleum-Accountants-Society-Canada-3814298
Overview: A medium-sized national organization founded in 1950
Mission: To contribute to the long term success of the Canadian petroleum industry by staying abreast of the constantly changing needs of the industry & striving to satisfy those needs
Member of: Council of Petroleum Societies of North America
Finances: *Annual Operating Budget:* $50,000-$100,000; *Funding Sources:* Membership dues
Staff Member(s): 1; 70 volunteer(s)
Membership: 260+ from more than 160 energy companies; *Fees:* $100 regular; $20 student; *Member Profile:* Accounting, auditing, finance or economics employees with organizations associated with the petroleum or natural gas industry; *Committees:* Education; Emerging Issues; Joint Venture Audit; Joint Interest Research; Material Inventory; Member Services
Activities: Professional development, continuing education, standards & information; *Library:* Open to public by appointment
Chief Officer(s):
Josh Molcak, President
josh.molcak@paramountres.com
Tracy Kozak, Treasurer
tracy.kozak@baytex.ab.ca

Petroleum Industry Training Service *See* Enform

Petroleum Research Atlantic Canada (PRAC) *See* Petroleum Research Newfoundland & Labrador

Petroleum Research Newfoundland & Labrador
Baine Johnston Centre, #101, 1 Church Hill, St. John's NL A1C 3Z7
Tel: 709-738-7916; *Fax:* 709-738-7922
www.pr-ac.ca
Previous Name: Petroleum Research Atlantic Canada (PRAC)
Overview: A small local organization founded in 1999
Mission: To facilitate research & technology development & deliver value to members on behalf of the offshore oil & gas industry of Newfoundland & Labrador
Membership: *Member Profile:* Representatives from the oil & gas industry in Newfoundland & Labrador
Activities: Identifying opportunities; Developing proposals; Funding & managing projects
Chief Officer(s):
David Finn, Chief Operating Officer, 709-738-7917
dave.finn@petroleumresearch.ca
Tony Woolridge, Manager, Research & Development Program, 709-738-7912
tony.wpoolridge@petroleumresearch.ca
Susan Hunt, Manager, Research & Development Program, 709-738-7904
susan.hunt@petroleumresearch.ca
Metzi Prince, Manager, Research & Development Delivery, 709-738-7919
metzi.prince@petroleumresearch.ca
Matilda Maddigan, Manager, Office, 709-738-7916
matilda.maddigan@petroleumresearch.ca

Petroleum Services Association of Canada (PSAC)
#1150, 734 - 7 Ave. SW, Calgary AB T2P 3P8
Tel: 403-264-4195; *Fax:* 403-263-7174
Toll-Free: 800-818-7722
info@psac.ca
www.psac.ca
www.linkedin.com/groups/PSAC-Working-Energy-4706150
www.facebook.com/WorkingEnergy
twitter.com/workingenergy
www.youtube.com/user/PSACCanada
Overview: A large national organization founded in 1981
Mission: To lead responsible Canadian energy services, supply & manufacturing in the upstream petroleum industry
Membership: 230 companies; *Fees:* Schedule available; *Member Profile:* Petroleum services industry companies; *Committees:* Corporate Finance; Education Fund; Health & Safety; Human Resources; Special Events; Transportation Issues; Manufacturing; Oilwell Perforators' Safety Training & Advisory; Well Testing
Activities: Engaging in lobbying activities; Providing educational opportunities
Chief Officer(s):
Mark Salkeld, MBA, President & CEO
msalkeld@psac.ca
Elizabeth Aquin, CAE, Senior Vice-President
eaquin@psac.ca
Patrick J. Delaney, MBA, CRSP, Vice-President, Health & Safety
pdelaney@psac.ca
Meetings/Conferences:
• Petroleum Services Association of Canada 2018 Annual General Meeting, 2018
Scope: National
Description: At the end of October each year, the Petroleum Services Association of Canada Annual Report is released, in conjunction with the Annual General Meeting & the Canadian Drilling Activity Forecast
Publications:
• Canadian Drilling Activity Forecast
Type: Yearbook; *Frequency:* Annually
Profile: Five years of historical data, plus forecasts for the coming year across Canada
• FAST-Line [a publication of the Petroleum Services Association of Canada]
Type: Newsletter; *Frequency:* Biweekly
Profile: Association news & upcoming events
• Petroleum Services Association of Canada Membership Directory
Type: Directory
Profile: Contact information for association members
• Petroleum Services Association of Canada Annual Report
Type: Yearbook; *Frequency:* Annually
Profile: A review of the association's activities, released at the end of each October in conjunction with the Canadian Drilling Activity Forecast & the Annual GeneralMeeting
• Petroleum Services News [a publication of the Petroleum Services Association of Canada]
Type: Magazine; *Frequency:* Quarterly; *Accepts Advertising*
Profile: Covering issues of importance to the upstream oil & gas industry
• Total Compensation Survey [a publication of the Petroleum Services Association of Canada]
Type: Yearbook; *Frequency:* Annually
Profile: An analysis of current salary & benefits practices in the petroleum service, supply, & manufacturing industry
• Well Cost Study
Type: Study
Profile: Geological, technical, & financial data on wells drilled across Canada

Petroleum Tank Management Association of Alberta (PTMAA)
#980, 10303 Jasper Ave., Edmonton AB T5J 3N6
Tel: 780-425-8265; *Fax:* 780-425-4722
Toll-Free: 866-222-8265
ptmaa@ptmaa.ab.ca
www.ptmaa.ab.ca
Overview: A medium-sized provincial licensing charitable organization founded in 1994
Mission: To offer programs to enhance the management of petroleum storage tank systems in Alberta
Activities: Monitoring new storage tank installations; Inspecting existing storage tank installations; Investigating accidents & incidents
Chief Officer(s):
Mark Tse, Chair

Petroleum Technology Alliance Canada (PTAC)
Chevron Plaza, #400, 500 - 5th Ave. SW, Calgary AB T2P 3L5
Tel: 403-218-7700; *Fax:* 403-920-0054
info@ptac.org
www.ptac.org
twitter.com/PTACCalgary
Overview: A medium-sized national organization
Mission: To facilitate innovation, technology transfer & research & development in the upstream oil & gas industry
Membership: *Fees:* Schedule available
Activities: *Library:* PTAC Knowledge Centre; Not open to public

Chief Officer(s):
Soheil Asgarpour, President, 403-218-7701
sasgarpour@ptac.org
Katie Blanchett, Manager, Operations, 403-218-7714
kblanchett@ptac.org

Petrolia Discovery
PO Box 1480, 4281 Discovery Line, Petrolia ON N0N 1R0
Tel: 519-381-5979; *Fax:* 519-882-4209
petroliadiscovery@outlook.com
www.petroliadiscovery.com
www.facebook.com/ThePetroliaDiscoveryFoundationInc
Overview: A small national charitable organization founded in 1980
Mission: To provide information about Petrolia's oil heritage
Activities: Maintaining historical displays; Organizing programs for schools

PFLAG Canada Inc.
251 Bank St., 2nd Fl., Ottawa ON K2P 1X3
Fax: 888-959-4128
Toll-Free: 888-530-6777
inquiries@pflagcanada.ca
www.pflagcanada.ca
www.facebook.com/PFLAGCA
twitter.com/pflagcanada
Also Known As: Parents, Families & Friends of Lesbians & Gays
Previous Name: Parents & Friends of Lesbians & Gays (Parents FLAG)
Overview: A medium-sized national charitable organization founded in 2003
Mission: To support individuals with questions & concerns about sexual orientation or gender identity; To make Canada a more accepting place for persons of all gender identities & sexual orientations
Finances: *Funding Sources:* Donations
Membership: *Fees:* Free
Activities: Providing education & resources about gender identity & sexual orientation; Offering peer support; *Internships:* Yes; *Speaker Service:* Yes
Chief Officer(s):
Bev Belanger, President
president@pflagcanada.ca
Donny Potts, Vice-President
donnypotts@pflagcanada.ca
Daniel Snoek, Treasurer
treasurer@pflagcanada.ca
Tanya Dawson, Secretary
secretary@pflagcanada.ca
Louis Duncan-He, Director, Marketing
Steven Keddy, Director, Communications
stevenkeddy@pflagcanada.ca
Ross Wicks, Director, Governance
rwicks@pflagcanada.ca

Abbotsford Chapter
Abbotsford BC
Tel: 604-217-4616
abbotsfordbc@pflagcanada.ca
Chief Officer(s):
Kristie Johnson, Contact

Alberni Chapter
4345 Glenside Rd., Port Alberni BC V9Y 5W9
Tel: 250-723-3540
Chief Officer(s):
Pat Messenger, Contact

Barrie Chapter
Barrie ON
Tel: 705-725-9748
barrieon@pflagcanada.ca
Chief Officer(s):
Deborah Batt, Contact

Belleville - Quinte Chapter
1600 Thorpe Rd. RR#2, Odessa ON K0H 2H0
Tel: 613-386-1922
region3a@plfagcanada.ca
Chief Officer(s):
Eric Hargreaves, Contact

Brandon - Brandon / Westman Chapter
c/o Sexuality Education Resource Centre, 719 Rosser Ave., Brandon MB R7A 0K8
Tel: 204-727-0417
Chief Officer(s):
Laura Crookshanks, Contact

Bridgewater Chapter
107 Pleasant St., Bridgewater NS B4V 1N3
Toll-Free: 888-530-6777
bridgewtrns@pflagcanada.ca
Chief Officer(s):
Philip Lauren, Regional Director

Brockville Chapter
PO Box 194, 34 Buell St., Brockville ON K6V 5V2
Tel: 613-640-2273
brockvilleon@pflagcanada.ca
sites.google.com/site/pflagcanadabrockville/
www.facebook.com/PFLAGBrockville
Chief Officer(s):
Lori Taylor, Contact

Calgary Chapter
439 Tuscany Ridge Height NW, Calgary AB T3L 3B6
Tel: 403-695-5791
calgaryab@pflagcanada.ca
Chief Officer(s):
Sean Alley, Contact

Campbell River Chapter
Campbell River BC
crpflag@hotmail.com
Chief Officer(s):
Yvonne Buxton, Contact

Carleton Place/Lanark Chapter
11358 Hwy. 15, RR#3, Smiths Falls ON K7A 4S4
Tel: 613-283-2055
grandpa@magma.ca
Chief Officer(s):
Jim MacGregor, Contact

Cornwall Chapter
3523 Besner Rd., St Isidore ON K0C 2B0
Tel: 613-524-4085
Toll-Free: 877-874-4424
Chief Officer(s):
Lorna Cunningham, Regional Director
Lornacr@gmail.com

Cranbrook Chapter
2617 - 3rd St. South, Cranbrook BC V1C 4W4
Tel: 250-426-6558
cranbrookbc@pflagcanada.ca
Chief Officer(s):
Earl Waugh, Contact

Edmonton Chapter
c/o Institute for Sexual Minority Studies & Services, Univ. of Alberta, #7, 104 Education North, Edmonton AB T6G 2G5
Tel: 780-248-1971
Chief Officer(s):
Tamara Gartner, Contact
gartner1@ualberta.ca

Fenelon Falls Chapter
67 Fells Point Rd., RR#1, Fenelon Falls ON K0M 1N0
Tel: 705-887-6830
Chief Officer(s):
Carol Milroy, Contact
carol_milroy@hotmail.com

Fredericton Chapter
Fredericton NB
Toll-Free: 888-530-6777
Chief Officer(s):
Philip Lauren, Regional Director

Halifax Chapter
PO Box 223, Shearwater NS B0J 3A0
Toll-Free: 888-530-6777
halifaxns@pflagcanada.ca
Chief Officer(s):
Philip Lauren, Regional Director

Halton Region Chapter
87 - 5th Concession Rd. East, Waterdown ON L0R 2H1
Tel: 289-895-8933
Chief Officer(s):
Joanne Stacey, Contact

Kamloops Chapter
#17, 481 Monarch Ct., Kamloops BC V2E 2P1
Tel: 250-851-9385
kamloopsbc@pflagcanada.ca
Chief Officer(s):
Judy Lusk, Contact

Kimberley Chapter
2617 - 3rd St. South, Cranbrook BC V1C 4W4
Tel: 780-427-1087
kimberleybc@pflagcanada.ca

Chief Officer(s):
Melanie Wilson, Contact

Kindersley Chapter
PO Box 754, Kindersley SK S0L 1S0
Tel: 306-463-4381
dewhyley@sasktel.net

Kingston Chapter
#202, 298 Guthrie Dr., Kingston ON K7K 7B9
Tel: 613-766-1444
KingstonON@pflagcanada.ca
www.facebook.com/pflagkingston
Chief Officer(s):
Stephen Hartley, Contact

Kitchener - Guelph & Kitchener / Waterloo Chapter
ON
Tel: 888-530-6777

Lethbridge & Area Chapter
Lethbridge AB
lethbridgeab@pflagcanada.ca
Chief Officer(s):
Dino H. Beganovic, Regional Director
vp@pflagcanada.ca

London Chapter
170 Tarbart Terrace, London ON N6H 3B2
Tel: 519-319-6934
Chief Officer(s):
Joanne King, Contact

Medicine Hat & Area Chapter
Medicine Hat AB
Tel: 403-581-4923
www.facebook.com/pflagcanadamedicinehat

Middleton Chapter
Middleton NS
Tel: 888-530-6777
middletonns@pflagcanada.ca
www.pflagcanada.ca/middleton.html
Chief Officer(s):
Philip Lauren, Regional Director

Miramichi Chapter
#2, 117 Dolan Ave., Miramichi NB E1V 1C3
Toll-Free: 888-530-6777
Chief Officer(s):
Philip Lauren, Regional Director

Moncton Chapter
Moncton NB
Tel: 506-875-1220
monctonnb@pflagcanada.ca
www.pflagcanada.ca/moncton
Chief Officer(s):
Steven Brown, Contact

Montréal Chapter
Montréal QC
Tel: 514-561-0462
region5b@pflagcanada.ca
Chief Officer(s):
Karan Singh, Contact

Moose Jaw Chapter
Moose Jaw SK
Toll-Free: 888-530-6777
Chief Officer(s):
Dino Beganovic, Regional Director
vp@pflagcanada.ca

Muskoka Chapter
ON
Toll-Free: 866-843-6369
muskokaon@pflagcanada.ca
Chief Officer(s):
Sara Hay, Contact

Niagara Chapter
417 Bunting Rd., St Catharines ON L2M 3Z1
Tel: 905-937-0202
www.pflagcanada.ca/niagara
Chief Officer(s):
Cathy Mackenzie, Contact

Oshawa - Durham Region / Oshawa Chapter
PO Box 30555, 438 King St. West, Oshawa ON L1J 8L8
Tel: 905-231-0533
Inquiries@pflagdurhamregion.com
Chief Officer(s):
Tanya Shaw-White, President
President@PFLAGDurhamRegion.com

Ottawa Chapter
PO Box 71028, 174 Bank St., Ottawa ON K2P 2L9

Toll-Free: 888-530-6777
contact@pflagottawa.ca
www.pflagottawa.ca
Chief Officer(s):
Darrell Comeau, Contact
Peel Region Chapter
ON
Tel: 905-602-4082
Toll-Free: 888-530-6777
peelon@pflagcanada.ca
Mission: To support persons with concerns about gender identity or sexual orientation in Brampton, Caledon, & Mississauga
Chief Officer(s):
Stephen Hartley, Contact
President@pflagcanada.ca
Peterborough Chapter
PO Box 115, Warsaw ON K0L 3A0
Tel: 705-749-9723
pflagpeterborough@hotmail.com
pflagpeterborough.com
Chief Officer(s):
Dianne McKay, Volunteer Co-ordinator
Prince Albert Chapter
Comp. 42, Site 28, RR#5, Prince Albert SK S6V 5R3
Tel: 306-764-5150
pralbertsk@pflagcanada.ca
Chief Officer(s):
Lynne Delorme, Contact
Prince George Chapter
#12, 1475 Queensway St., Prince George BC V2L 1L4
Tel: 250-640-1874
prgeorgebc@pflagcanada.ca
www.pflagcanada.ca/princegeorge.html
Chief Officer(s):
Rory Allen, Contact
Regina Chapter
3720 Queens Gate, Regina SK S4S 7J1
Tel: 306-533-3965
reginask@pflagcanada.ca
Chief Officer(s):
Francine Proulx-Kenzle, Contact
fproulxkenzle@yahoo.ca
Richmond Hill - York Region Chapter
333 Crosby Ave., Richmond Hill ON L4C 2R5
Tel: 888-905-5428
pflagyork@yahoo.ca
www.pflagyork.ca
Sackville - Sackville NB / Amherst NS Chapter
14 Devon Ave., Sackville NB E4L 3W2
Tel: 506-536-4245
sacknb-amns@pflagcanada.ca
Chief Officer(s):
Janet Hammock, Contact
Saint John Chapter
27 Wasson Ct., Saint John NB E2K 2K6
Tel: 506-648-9227
www.pflagcanada.ca/saintjohn.html
Chief Officer(s):
Mack MacKenzie, Contact
St. John's Chapter
St. John's NL
Tel: 709-722-5791
stjohnsnl@pflagcanada.ca
Affiliation(s): AIDS Committee of Newfoundland & Labrador; Planned Parenthood Newfoundland & Labrador; Egale Canada; Canadians for Equal Marriage
Chief Officer(s):
Tony Braithwaite, Contact
Salt Spring Island Chapter
Salt Spring Island BC
Tel: 250-537-7773
Chief Officer(s):
Jill Simpson, Contact
Sarnia - Sarnia / Bluewater Chapter
1059 Willa Dr., Sarnia ON N7S 1T1
Tel: 519-344-8246
sarnia-bwon@pflagcanada.ca
Chief Officer(s):
Ruth Lambert, Contact, 519-337-2992
Saskatoon Chapter
2209 McKinnon Ave. South, Saskatoon SK S7J 1N5
Tel: 306-491-3484
saskatoonsk@pflagcanada.ca

Chief Officer(s):
Fran Forsberg, Contact
Sault Ste Marie Chapter
Sault Ste Marie ON
Tel: 705-777-0496
Chief Officer(s):
Susan Meades, Contact
ssmarieon@pflagcanada.ca
Stoney Creek - Hamilton Chapter
45 Glen Cannon Dr., Stoney Creek ON L8G 2Z6
hamiltonon@pflagcanada.ca
Sussex Chapter
Sussex NB
Tel: 506-672-6072
sussexnb@pflagcanada.ca
Chief Officer(s):
Joanne Jones, Contact
Sydney Chapter
c/o PLAG Contact, Family Place Resource Centre, 714 Alexandra St., Sydney NS B1S 2H4
Toll-Free: 888-530-6777
sydneyns@pflagcanada.ca
Chief Officer(s):
JoAnne Fitzgerald, Contact
Thunder Bay Chapter
Thunder Bay ON
Tel: 807-767-2447
thunderbayon@pflagcanada.ca
Timmins Chapter
Timmins ON
Tel: 705-268-0706
timminson@pflagcanada.ca
Chief Officer(s):
Julie DeMarchi, Contact
Toronto Chapter
200 Wolverleigh Blvd., Toronto ON M4C 1S2
Tel: 416-406-1727
office@pflagtoronto.org
www.torontopflag.org
www.facebook.com/TorontoPFLAG
twitter.com/torontopflag
Chief Officer(s):
Anne Creighton, President
Vancouver Chapter
Vancouver BC
Tel: 604-626-5667
info@pflagvancouver.com
www.pflagvancouver.com
www.linkedin.com/groups/PFLAG-Canada-1443017
www.facebook.com/PFLAGVancouver
twitter.com/PFLAGCanada
Victoria Chapter
1834 Newton St., Victoria BC V8R 2R4
Tel: 250-385-9462
victoriabc@pflagcanada.ca
Chief Officer(s):
Dino Beganovic, Regional Director
vp@pflagcanada.ca
Windsor Chapter
Windsor ON
Tel: 519-978-2777
windsoron@pflagcanada.ca
Chief Officer(s):
Karen McMahon, Contact
Windsor, Nova Scotia Chapter
Windsor NS
Tel: 888-530-6777
windsorns@pflagcanada.ca
Chief Officer(s):
Philip Lauren, Regional Director
Winnipeg Chapter
PO Box 66, Victoria Beach MB R0E 2C0
Tel: 204-981-9342
winnipegmb@pflagcanada.ca
Chief Officer(s):
Dino Beganovic, Regional Director
vp@pflagcanada.ca
Woodstock Chapter
119 Jules Dr., Woodstock NB E7M 1Z2
Toll-Free: 888-530-6777
Chief Officer(s):
Philip Lauren, Regional Director

Yarmouth Chapter
60 Vancouver St., Yarmouth NS B5A 2P5
Tel: 902-742-3542
Chief Officer(s):
Jaqi Sutherland-Allan, Contact
jsutherland-allan@swndha.nshealth.ca
Yorkton - East Central Chapter
72 Newfield Pl., Yorkton SK S3N 2M9
Tel: 306-782-0113
axios@sasktel.net
Chief Officer(s):
Andy Piasta, Contact

Pharmaceutical Advertising Advisory Board
#300, 1305 Pickering Pkwy., Pickering ON L1V 3P2
Tel: 905-509-2275; Fax: 905-509-2486
info@paab.ca
www.paab.ca
www.linkedin.com/groups/2104835
twitter.com/thepaab
www.youtube.com/channel/UCPVb7A-APEe03jXGU4uqrNw
Overview: A small national organization
Mission: To review health care product communication
Chief Officer(s):
Ray Chepesiuk, Commissioner

Pharmacists' Association of Newfoundland & Labrador (PANL)
#203, 85 Thorburn Rd., St. John's NL A1B 3M2
Tel: 709-753-7881; Fax: 709-753-8882
Toll-Free: 866-753-7881
email@panl.net
www.panl.net
www.facebook.com/pharmacistsnewfoundlandandlabrador
twitter.com/PANLupdates
Overview: A small provincial organization founded in 2003
Mission: To improve the profession of pharmacy throughout Newfoundland & Labrador; To support members in the the provision of quality services to the people of Newfoundland & Labrador; To advance the professional, economic, & social well-being of pharmacists
Finances: *Funding Sources:* Membership fees; Sponsorships
Membership: *Member Profile:* Pharmacists licensed to practice in Newfoundland & Labrador; Pharmacies in Newfoundland & Labrador; Non-practicing pharmacists (retired persons & those taking a leave of absence); Persons employed directly or indirectly in the profession of pharmacy; Students; *Committees:* Awards; Conference; Economics; Finance; Government Relations; Hospital Advisory; Public & Professional Relations
Activities: Promoting the profession of pharmacy in Newfoundland & Labrador; Advocating for pharmacists; Presenting continuing education programs; Providing industry information to members; Offering a new pharmacist mentorship program; Organizing networking opportunities; *Awareness Events:* Pharmacist Awareness Week
Chief Officer(s):
Glenda Power, Executive Director
gpower@panl.net
Tammy Brenton, Office Manager
tbrenton@panl.net
Meetings/Conferences:
• 2018 Pharmacists' Association of Newfoundland & Labrador Annual Conference, 2018
Scope: Provincial
Description: Educational sessions & networking opportunities
Publications:
• Newfoundland & Labrador Pharmacist Directory
Type: Directory
Profile: Pharmacists, their practice sites, & contact information
• Newfoundland & Labrador Pharmacy Directory
Type: Directory
Profile: Listings of pharmacies in the province & contact information
• Pharmacists' Association of Newfoundland & Labrador Newsletter
Type: Newsletter; *Frequency:* 7 pa; *Accepts Advertising; Price:* Free with membership in the Pharmacists' Association of Newfoundland & Labrador

Pharmacists' Association of Saskatchewan, Inc. (PAS)
#202, 2629 - 29th Ave., Regina SK S4S 2N9
Tel: 306-359-7277; Fax: 306-352-6770
info@skpharmacists.ca
www.skpharmacists.ca

www.facebook.com/saskatchewanpharmacists
twitter.com/PAS_SK
Overview: A small provincial organization
Mission: To advance the profession of pharmacy in Saskatchewan; To act as the voice of pharmacists throughout Saskatchewan; To protect the interests of pharmacists
Staff Member(s): 5
Membership: *Fees:* Schedule available; *Member Profile:* Practicing pharmacists across Saskatchewan; Students; Retired members; *Committees:* Governance; Audit & Finance; Compensation; Economics; Professional Practice; Conference; Members Services; Awards
Activities: Engaging in advocacy activities on behalf of the profession; Presenting professional development sessions; Offering assistance & advice on professional issues; Providing access to malpractice insurance
Chief Officer(s):
Christine Hrudka, Chair
chris@pharmacyfirst.ca
Dawn Martin, Executive Director
dawn.martin@skpharmacists.ca
Myla Wollbaum, Director, Professional Practice
myla.wollbaum@skpharmacists.ca
Publications:
• PAS It On
Type: Bulletin; *Price:* Free with memberships in the Pharmacists' Association of Saskatchewan, Inc.
Profile: Vital issues for Saskatchewan pharmacists

Pharmacological Society of Canada; Canadian Society for Clinical Pharmacology *See* Canadian Society of Pharmacology & Therapeutics

Pharmacy Association of Nova Scotia (PANS)
#225, 170 Cromarty Dr., Dartmouth NS B3B 0G1
Tel: 902-422-9583; *Fax:* 902-422-2619
pans@pans.ns.ca
pans.ns.ca
www.facebook.com/PharmacyNS
twitter.com/pharmacyns
www.youtube.com/pharmacyassocns
Overview: A small provincial organization founded in 1979
Mission: To advance the professional, academic, & commercial aspects of pharmacy & pharmacists throughout Nova Scotia; To represent the interests of Nova Scotia's pharmacists; To improve public health in Nova Scotia
Finances: *Funding Sources:* Membership fees; Sponsorships
Membership: *Member Profile:* Pharmaceutical chemists & certified dispensers in Nova Scotia; Students enrolled in the School of Pharmacy at Dalhousie University; International pharmacy graduates; Corporate members
Activities: Engaging in advocacy activities; Liaising with governments; Disseminating information to assist members in pharmacy management; Offering educational opportunities; *Awareness Events:* Pharmacy Awareness Week
Chief Officer(s):
Allison Bodnar, CEO
abodnar@pans.ns.ca
Meetings/Conferences:
• Nova Scotia Pharmacy Conference 2018, October, 2018, Holiday Inn, Truro, NS
Scope: Provincial
Description: Educational sessions on topics of interest to pharmacists in Nova Scotia
Publications:
• The Pharmacist
Type: Newsletter; *Frequency:* Quarterly
Profile: Updates distributed to all pharmacists in Nova Scotia
• Pharmacy Association of Nova Scotia Annual Report
Type: Yearbook; *Frequency:* Annually

The Pharmacy Examining Board of Canada (PEBC) / Le Bureau des examinateurs en pharmacie du Canada (BEPC)
717 Church St., Toronto ON M4W 2M4
Tel: 416-979-2431; *Fax:* 416-599-9244
pebcinfo@pebc.ca
www.pebc.ca
Overview: A large national organization founded in 1963
Mission: To establish qualifications for pharmacists; To provide for examinations of those qualifications
Membership: *Member Profile:* Registration by examination
Chief Officer(s):
Kendra Townsend, President
Janet MacDonnell, Vice-President

Pharmacy Technician Society of Alberta (PTSA)
PO Box 52134, Edmonton AB T6G 2T5
info@pharmacytechnicians.ab.ca
www.pharmacytechnicians.ab.ca
www.facebook.com/ptsa.ca
twitter.com/ThePTSA
Overview: A small provincial organization founded in 2008
Mission: To represent pharmacy technicians in Alberta; To optimize pharmacy services; To promote professionalism among pharmacy technicians
Finances: *Funding Sources:* Membership fees; Sponsorships
Membership: *Fees:* $31.50 students & pharmacy assistants; $42 associate members; $52.50 full members; *Member Profile:* Pharmacy technicians, who live in Alberta; Associate members are pharmacy technicians who do not live in Alberta & pharmacy industry representatives; Support personnel in pharmacies, who are not pharmacy technicians; Students, enrolled in a pharmacy technician training program; *Committees:* Newsletter; Web Page; Conference Planning; Continuing Education Events - Calgary Area; Continuing Education Events - Edmonton Area; Continuing Education Events - Grande Prairie Area; Certification
Activities: Upholding a Code of Ethics; Providing continuing education; Communicating through social media
Chief Officer(s):
Teresa Hennessey, President
Rhonda Bodnarchuk, Vice-President
Crystal Schultz, Secretary
Kim Fehr, Treasurer
Kristi Rein, Director, Promotions
Amanda Mann, Director, Education
Publications:
• Techs In Touch
Type: Newsletter
Profile: Current issues & regulation information for members

Philanthropic Foundations Canada (PFC) / Fondations philanthropiques Canada (FPC)
#1220, 615, boul René-Lévesque ouest, Montréal QC H3B 1P5
Tel: 514-866-5446; *Fax:* 514-866-5846
info@pfc.ca
pfc.ca
Overview: A medium-sized national charitable organization founded in 1999
Mission: To encourage public policies that promote philanthropy; to increase awareness of philanthropy & provide opportunities for foundations to learn from one another
Membership: 112 (foundations); *Member Profile:* Canadian grantmakers, including private & public foundations, charities & corporations
Chief Officer(s):
Hilary Pearson, President & CEO
hpearson@pfc.ca
Liza Goulet, Director, Research & Member Services
lgoulet@pfc.ca

Philharmonique Portugais de Montréal *Voir* Filarmónica Portuguesa de Montreal

Philippine Association of Manitoba, Inc. (PAM)
88 Juno St., Winnipeg MB R3A 1J1
Tel: 204-772-7210
Overview: A small provincial organization
Mission: To serve the needs of Filipino newcomers & the established Filipino community in Manitoba
Member of: Asian Heritage Society of Manitoba
Membership: *Member Profile:* Members of the Filipino community in Manitoba
Activities: Sponsoring English as a Second Language programs

Phobies-Zéro
CP 5681, Sainte-Julie QC J3E 1X5
Tél: 450-922-5964; *Téléc:* 450-922-5935
admin@phobies-zero.qc.ca
www.phobies-zero.qc.ca
Aperçu: *Dimension:* petite; *Envergure:* provinciale; fondée en 1991
Mission: Aider les gens avec leurs troubles anxieux en leur faisant comprendre leurs problèmes et en leur montrant les moyens de faire face à leur anxiété
Membre(s) du personnel: 6
Membre: *Montant de la cotisation:* 20$ par membre; *Critères d'admissibilite:* Toute personne qui souffre d'un trouble anxieux
Membre(s) du bureau directeur:
Ginette Gonthier, Directrice
ggonthier@phobies-zero.qc.ca

Phoenix Community Works Foundation (PCWF)
330 Bloor St. West, Toronto ON M5S 3A7
Tel: 416-964-3388
info@pcwf.ca
www.pcwf.ca
Overview: A medium-sized national charitable organization founded in 1973
Mission: To assist in the development of a healthy community by encouraging creativity; To promote educational programs relating to the emotional, intellectual & physical well-being of individuals & society; To foster studies & experimental projects related to the physical & social environments; To promote studies & programs in area of emotional health
Staff Member(s): 3
Activities: Community development in the areas of arts, education, environment, mental health; *Speaker Service:* Yes
Chief Officer(s):
Larry Rooney, Executive Director
Awards:
• The Chap-Book Award
Awarded for the best poetry chap-book in English, published in Canada; entries must be from 10-48 pages in length; *Amount:* $1,000

Photo Marketing Association International - Canada (PMAI)
PO Box 81191, Ancaster ON L9G 4X2
Tel: 905-304-8800; *Fax:* 905-304-7700
Toll-Free: 800-461-4350
www.pmai.org/content.aspx?id=21982
Overview: A medium-sized national organization founded in 1924
Mission: To disseminate timely information while providing market research & business improvement products & services that contribute to increased profitability & business growth for its membership
Staff Member(s): 1
Membership: 1,200; *Fees:* Schedule available; *Member Profile:* Voting - must be in photo & imaging retailing or processing; non-voting - manufacturing, distributing & supply side of the photo & imaging industry
Activities: Professional development seminars; Certification programs; trade shows; *Library:* Resource Centre; Open to public
Chief Officer(s):
Bob Moggach, Director of Canadian Activities
bmoggach@pmai.org

Photographes Professionnels du Canada *See* Professional Photographers of Canada

Photographic Historical Society of Canada (PHSC)
PO Box 11703, 4335 Bloor St. West, Toronto ON M9C 2A5
Tel: 416-691-1555; *Fax:* 416-693-0018
info@phsc.ca
www.phsc.ca
www.facebook.com/PHSCPhotographicHistoricalSocietyofCanada
Overview: A small national charitable organization founded in 1974
Mission: To facilitate the sharing of photographic knowledge; To help research & preserve Canada's photographic heritage
Finances: *Annual Operating Budget:* $50,000-$100,000; *Funding Sources:* Membership fees; Fairs; Auction; Donations
20 volunteers)
Membership: 300; *Fees:* $35 Canada; $45 US/International; *Member Profile:* Individuals; Collectors; Researchers; Libraries; Archives; Museums; Companies in the photographic industry; *Committees:* Executive
Activities: Spring & fall photo fairs; Spring photo auction; Public displays & presentations; Monthly meetings; *Library:* by appointment Not open to public
Chief Officer(s):
Clint Hyrorijiw, President
Awards:
• Research Grant
Presented annually to a current PHSC member for original research into Canada's photographic history; *Amount:* $500
• Publication Grant
Awarded to aid the publication, in book or monograph form, of original research into Canada's photographic history; *Amount:* Up to $1,000
• Kodak Canada Student Award
Presented annually for the best student paper on original research into any aspect of Canadian photographic history; *Amount:* $500 first prize, $250 second prize

Canadian Associations / Physical & Health Education Canada / Éducation physique et santé Canada

Publications:
- Photographic Canadiana
Type: Journal; *Frequency:* Quarterly; *Editor:* Robert Lansdale

Physical & Health Education Canada / Éducation physique et santé Canada
#301, 2197 Riverside Dr., Ottawa ON K1H 7X3
Tel: 613-523-1348; *Fax:* 613-523-1206
Toll-Free: 800-663-8708
info@phecanada.ca
www.phecanada.ca
www.facebook.com/PHECanada
twitter.com/PHECanada
Also Known As: PHE Canada
Previous Name: Canadian Physical Education Association; Canadian Association for Health, Physical Education, Recreation, & Dance
Overview: A large national charitable organization founded in 1933
Mission: To promote quality school health programs & the healthy development of Canadian children & youth
Membership: *Member Profile:* Principals, teachers, public health professionals, & recreation leaders from across Canada; *Committees:* Dance Education; Health Promoting Schools & Health Education; Intramurals & After School; Leadership; Physical Education & Physical Literacy
Activities: Advocating for quality, school-based physical & health education; Offering professional learning experiences; Creating networking opportunities
Chief Officer(s):
Melanie Davis, Executive Director & CEO, 613-523-1348 Ext. 225
melaniedavis@phecanada.ca
Jodie Lyn-Harrison, Chief Administrative Officer, 613-523-1348 Ext. 223
jodielynharrison@phecanada.ca
Jordan Burwash, Director, 613-523-1348 Ext. 229
jordanburwash@phecanada.ca
Stephanie Talsma, Director, 613-523-1348 Ext. 236
stephanietalsma@phecanada.ca
Marim Moreland, Manager, 613-523-1348 Ext. 227
marimmoreland@phecanada.ca
Awards:
- R. Tait McKenzie Award of Honour
To recognize Canadians who have made a significant impact on physical education, health promotion, recreation, & dance
- North American Society Fellowship Award
To recognize outstanding professionals within the professions of health education, physical education, recreation, sport, & dance
- PHE Canada Student Award
To recognize outstanding undergraduate student leadership in the field of physical & health education
- Dr. Andy Anderson Young Professional Award
To recognize one person in each province for exemplary work in the profession
- Health Promoting School Champion Award
Recognizing an individual, group or organization for their work with the Health Promoting School approach
- Research Council Emerging Scholar Award
- Quality Daily Physical Education Award
- National Award for Teaching Excellence in Physical Edcuation
- National Award for Teaching Excellence in Health Edcuation
- Legacy Fund Grants
Meetings/Conferences:
- Physical & Health Education Canada 2018 National Conference, May, 2018, Whistler, BC
Scope: National
Publications:
- In Touch Newsletter [a publication of the Physical & Health Education Canada]
Type: Newsletter
- phénEPS-PHEnex Journal [a publication of the Physical & Health Education Canada]
Type: Journal
Profile: Research, position papers, reviews & critical essays
- Physical & Health Education Journal
Type: Journal; *Frequency:* Quarterly
Profile: School physical education programs, quality school health programs, ready-to-use activities, resource reviews, & teaching strategies

Physical & Health Educators of Manitoba
#319, 145 Pacific Ave., Winnipeg MB R3B 2Z6
Tel: 204-925-5786
phemb@sportmanitoba.ca
www.phemanitoba.ca

Also Known As: PHE Manitoba
Previous Name: Manitoba Physical Education Teachers Association
Overview: A small provincial organization
Mission: To promote physical & health education in schools across Manitoba
Affiliation(s): Manitoba Teacher's Society
Membership: *Fees:* $25 full; $15 student/retired/associate
Chief Officer(s):
Ray Agostino, President
Meetings/Conferences:
- Physical & Health Educators of Manitoba 2018 Manitoba Teachers Society Professional Development Day, October, 2018, MB
Scope: Provincial

Physical Culture Association of Alberta
Percy Page Centre, 11759 Groat Rd., Edmonton AB T5M 3K6
Tel: 780-415-1744
physicalculturealberta@gmail.com
www.physicalculture.ca
Overview: A small provincial organization
Mission: To promote mental & physical well-being for all, using Physical Culture methods
Staff Member(s): 1
Membership: 7,000; *Fees:* $10; *Member Profile:* Children, teens, adults, older adults, seniors, pre/post-natal, post-cardiac, diabetics, & the physically & mentally challenged
Activities: Exercise to music; Training programs; Fitness classes
Chief Officer(s):
Lesley McEwan, Executive Director

Physical Education in British Columbia (PE-BC)
c/o British Columbia Teachers' Federation, #100, 550 West 6th Ave., Vancouver BC V5Z 4P2
Tel: 604-871-2283; *Fax:* 604-871-2286
www.bctf.ca/pebc
www.facebook.com/PhysicalEducationBC
Previous Name: British Columbia Physical Education Provincial Specialist Association
Overview: A medium-sized provincial organization overseen by British Columbia Teachers' Federation
Mission: To provide leadership, advocacy, & resources for teachers of physical education
Member of: British Columbia Teachers' Federation
Chief Officer(s):
Lisa Manzini, President

Physical Medicine Research Foundation *See* Canadian Institute for the Relief of Pain & Disability

Physicians for a Smoke-Free Canada / Médecins pour un Canada sans fumée
134 Caroline Ave., Ottawa ON K1Y 0S9
Tel: 613-297-3590; *Fax:* 613-728-9049
psc@nospamsmoke-free.ca
www.smoke-free.ca
Overview: A medium-sized national organization founded in 1985
Mission: To address tobacco issues; To promote reduced smoking & prevent tobacco-caused illness
Finances: *Funding Sources:* Health Canada; Membership dues
Staff Member(s): 1
Membership: 1,500
Chief Officer(s):
Atul Kapur, President
James Walker, Secretary-Treasurer

Physicians for Global Survival (Canada) (PGS) / Médecins pour la survie mondiale (Canada)
30 Cleary Ave., Ottawa ON K2A 4A1
Tel: 613-233-1982
pgsadmin@web.ca
www.pgs.ca
www.facebook.com/PhysiciansforGlobalSurvival
www.youtube.com/user/pgsottawa
Previous Name: Canadian Physicians for the Prevention of Nuclear War
Overview: A small international charitable organization founded in 1980
Mission: Committed to the abolition of nuclear weapons, the prevention of war, the promotion of non-violent means of conflict resolution & social justice in a sustainable world
Affiliation(s): International Physicians for the Prevention of Nuclear War (IPPNW)
Finances: *Funding Sources:* Contributions

Staff Member(s): 2
Membership: *Fees:* $120 physicians; $60 supporters; $25 student; *Member Profile:* Open to members of the medical profession & the general public
Activities: Education for the abolition of nuclear war; recommendations of measures, both national & international, which will help to prevent war; campaigning for limits on the free trade in arms; discussion of the impact of militarism on human health & environment; works toward the elimination of land mines; Greening of Hospitals & Health Care Facilities project; *Awareness Events:* Abolition of Nuclear Weapons Day, Aug. 6; *Speaker Service:* Yes; *Library:* Open to public by appointment
Chief Officer(s):
Juan Carolos Chirgwin, President

Physicians Services Inc. Foundation
#1006, 5160 Yonge St., Toronto ON M2N 6L9
Tel: 416-226-6323; *Fax:* 416-226-6080
psif@psifoundation.org
www.psifoundation.org
www.facebook.com/pages/PSI-Foundation/471879289534738
twitter.com/PSIFoundation
Also Known As: P.S.I. Foundation
Overview: A small provincial charitable organization founded in 1970
Mission: To promote charitable & educational purposes related to health, science & practice of medicine & healing arts
Finances: *Annual Operating Budget:* $1.5 Million-$3 Million
Staff Member(s): 5
Membership: *Member Profile:* Composed of physicians representing each of the 75 medical societies in Ontario, the Ontario Medical Association, & six other persons appointed by the Board for their interest in the foundation's activities; *Committees:* Executive; Governance; Finance; Grants
Chief Officer(s):
Samuel Moore, Executive Director
Awards:
- Health Research Grant
- Resident Research Grant

Physiotherapy Alberta - College + Association
Dorchester Bldg., #300, 10357 - 109 St., Edmonton AB T5J 1N3
Tel: 780-438-0338; *Fax:* 780-436-1908
Toll-Free: 800-291-2782
info@physiotherapyalberta.ca
www.physiotherapyalberta.ca
www.linkedin.com/company/physiotherapy-alberta—-college-association
www.facebook.com/PTAlberta
twitter.com/PTAlberta
www.youtube.com/user/PTAlberta
Previous Name: College of Physical Therapists of Alberta
Overview: A medium-sized provincial licensing organization founded in 1985 overseen by Canadian Alliance of Physiotherapy Regulators
Mission: To protect the public by the regulation of the practice of physical therapy
Member of: Canadian Alliance of Physiotherapy Regulators; Canadian Physiotherapy Association
Affiliation(s): Alberta Federation of Regulated Health Professions
Finances: *Annual Operating Budget:* $1.5 Million-$3 Million; *Funding Sources:* Membership dues
Staff Member(s): 9
Membership: 2,382; *Fees:* $750 active; $86 non-regulated; $115 corporations; *Member Profile:* Members must have completed an approved program of physical therapy; *Committees:* Competence; Registration; Conduct
Activities: Registration; Practice Standard; Complaint Resolution; Manpower Utilization; Communication; Government Relations; Governance
Chief Officer(s):
Dianne Millette, Registrar, 780-702-5353
dmillette@physiotherapyalberta.ca
Publications:
- PT Alberta [a publication of Physiotherapy Alberta - College + Association]
Type: Newsletter

Physiotherapy Association of British Columbia (PABC)
#402, 1755 West Broadway, Vancouver BC V6J 4S5
Tel: 604-736-5130; *Fax:* 604-736-5606
Toll-Free: 888-330-3999
office@bcphysio.org
www.bcphysio.org

www.facebook.com/bcphysio
twitter.com/bcphysio
www.youtube.com/user/BCPhysio
Overview: A medium-sized provincial organization founded in 1927 overseen by Canadian Physiotherapy Association
Mission: To provide leadership & direction to the physiotherapy profession; To foster excellence in practice, education & research
Member of: Canadian Physiotherapy Association
Finances: *Funding Sources:* Membership dues; Educational activities
Staff Member(s): 3
Membership: 2,100; *Fees:* Schedule available
Chief Officer(s):
Kevin Evans, Chief Executive Officer
kevin@bcphysio.org
Emira Mears, Director, Strategic Communications
communications@bcphysio.org
Tracy Stewart, Manager, Communications
tracy@bcphysio.org
Fiona Chiu, Manager, Knowledge
librarian@bcphysio.org
Sheana Lehigh, Manager, Education
education@bcphysio.org
Kimberley Payne, Office Administrator

Physiotherapy Association of Yukon (PAY)
Whitehorse YT
Overview: A medium-sized provincial organization overseen by Canadian Physiotherapy Association
Mission: To unite members of the profession
Member of: Canadian Physiotherapy Association
Finances: *Funding Sources:* Membership dues; educational activities
Membership: 30+
Activities: *Awareness Events:* National Physiotherapy Month, April 20 - May 20
Chief Officer(s):
Liris Smith, President
smithco@northwestel.net
Publications:
• Yukon Council of Canadian Physiotherapy Association Newsletter
Type: Newsletter; *Frequency:* a.

Physiotherapy Education Accreditation Canada (PEAC) / Agrément de l'enseignement de la physiothérapie au Canada (EPAC)
#26, 509 Commissioners Rd. West, London ON N6J 1Y5
Tel: 226-636-0632; *Fax:* 778-724-0669
info@peac-aepc.ca
www.peac-aepc.ca
Previous Name: Accreditation Council for Canadian Physiotherapy Academic Programs
Overview: A medium-sized national licensing organization founded in 2000
Mission: To provide leadership in maintaining the quality of physiotherapy education in Canada through a comprehensive accreditation program
Member of: Association of Accrediting Agencies of Canada (AAAC); The Canadian Council of Physiotherapy University Programs
Affiliation(s): Accreditation of Interprofessional Health Education (AIPHE)
Membership: 10
Chief Officer(s):
Sharon Switzer-McIntyre, President
Kathy Davidson, Executive Director
kathy.davidson@peac-aepc.ca
Publications:
• Peer Review Team Handbook
Type: Handbook; *Number of Pages:* 49
Profile: Includes the responsibilities of the peer review team members, a detailed schedule for the on-site accreditation review, & information about the final meeting & the written report
• Program Accreditation Handbook
Type: Handbook; *Number of Pages:* 50
Profile: Information about the accreditation of physiotherapy education programs in Canada, for physiotherapy education program faculty & staff who are preparing for accreditation review, membersof the accreditation Peer Review Team teams, university administrators, & members of the public

Pickering & Ajax Citizens Together for the Environment (PACT)
ON

Overview: A small local organization founded in 1987
Mission: To protect the environment in the Pickering/Ajax area, especially with reference to waste management issues
Member of: Ontario Environmental Network
Finances: *Funding Sources:* Fundraising
Activities: *Speaker Service:* Yes
Awards:
• High School Awards
Eligibility: Eight top students moving on to environmental subjects

Pickering Naturalists
PO Box 304, Pickering ON L1V 2R6
pnclub@pickeringnaturalists.org
www.pickeringnaturalists.org
Overview: A small local organization founded in 1977
Mission: To promote the study of nature & the environment; To raise awareness of nature; To encourage nature conservation
Member of: Federation of Ontario Naturalists
Finances: *Funding Sources:* Membership dues
Membership: *Fees:* $21 individual; $25 family; $250 life
Publications:
• Pickering Naturalist [a publication of Pickering Naturalists]
Type: Newsletter; *Frequency:* Quarterly
Profile: Nature articles & information on upcoming events.

Picton United Church County Food Bank
12 Chapel St., Picton ON K0K 2T0
Tel: 613-476-8516
pictonunitedchurch@bellnet.ca
pictonunitedchurch.ca/fbank.html
Previous Name: Picton United Church Food Bank
Overview: A small local charitable organization founded in 1984
Member of: Ontario Association of Food Banks
Finances: *Annual Operating Budget:* Less than $50,000; *Funding Sources:* Donations
20 volunteer(s)

Picton United Church Food Bank *See* Picton United Church County Food Bank

Pictou County Centre for Sexual Health
Bridgeview Square, 115 MacLean St., New Glasgow NS B2H 4M5
Tel: 902-695-3366
pcsexualhealth@hotmail.com
www.facebook.com/163306117043105
Overview: A small local charitable organization founded in 1979
Mission: To provide comprehensive & accessible sexual & reproductive health services to men & women of all ages in Pictou County
Member of: Planned Parenthood Nova Scotia
Finances: *Funding Sources:* Provincial government; United Way
Activities: *Library:* Open to public

Pictou County Chamber of Commerce
#3C, 115 MacLean St., New Glasgow NS B2H 4M5
Tel: 902-755-3463
info@pictouchamber.com
www.pictouchamber.com
www.linkedin.com/company/pictou-county-chamber-of-commerce
www.facebook.com/173337132712998
twitter.com/PCChamberCommer
Overview: A medium-sized local organization founded in 1983
Mission: To distinguish itself as the pre-eminent voice of business in our region
Member of: Atlantic Provinces Chamber of Commerce; Nova Scotia Chamber of Commerce; Canadian Chamber of Commerce
Membership: *Fees:* Schedule available based on number of employees
Activities: *Internships:* Yes; *Speaker Service:* Yes; *Library:* Business Service Centre; Open to public
Chief Officer(s):
Jack Kyte, Executive Director

Pictou County Historical Society
86 Temperance St., New Glasgow NS B2H 3A7
Tel: 902-752-5583
pictoucounty@ns.sympatico.ca
www.parl.ns.ca/csmuseum/historicalsociety.htm
Overview: A small local organization founded in 1964
Mission: To operate & manage Carmichael Stewart House Museum, property owned by the Town of New Glasgow
Affiliation(s): NS Museums
Membership: 200 individual; *Fees:* $10 individual

Chief Officer(s):
Fergie MacKay, President

Picture Butte & District Chamber of Commerce
PO Box 517, Picture Butte AB T0K 1V0
Tel: 403-732-4302
Overview: A small local organization

Pier 21 Society
1055 Marginal Rd., Halifax NS B3H 4P6
Tel: 902-425-7770; *Fax:* 902-423-4045
Toll-Free: 855-526-4721
info@pier21.ca
www.pier21.ca
www.facebook.com/210412625764977
twitter.com/pier21
www.youtube.com/Pier21Museum
Overview: A small national charitable organization
Mission: To preserve & share information about the Canadian immigration experience through history
Finances: *Funding Sources:* Donations; Gift shop sales; Sponsorships; Rental services
Staff Member(s): 49
Activities: Operating the national museum of immigration at Pier 21; Offering reference services on topics such as immigration, nautical history, World War II, & genealogy at the Soctiabank Research Centre; *Library:* Scotiabank Research Centre; Open to public
Chief Officer(s):
Tung Chan, Chair
Marie Chapman, Chief Executive Officer
Monica MacDonald, Manager, Research, 902-425-7770 Ext. 278
mmacdonald@pier21.ca
Cailin MacDonald, Manager, Communication
cmacdonald@pier21.ca

Pigeon Lake Regional Chamber of Commerce (PLRCC)
Box 6, Site 6, RR#2 Westerose, Westerose AB T0C 2V0
Tel: 780-586-6263
www.pigeonlakechamber.ca
Overview: A small local charitable organization founded in 1988
Mission: To build an economic base for permanent & seasonal residence that will provide services for tourists, while maintaining environmental characteristics & quality of life; To promote the commercial, industrial, social, & civic interests of the community
Affiliation(s): Alberta Chambers of Commerce
Finances: *Annual Operating Budget:* Less than $50,000; *Funding Sources:* Fundraising; Membership fees
Staff Member(s): 1; 70 volunteer(s)
Membership: 106; *Fees:* $120 + GST
Activities: Organizing dinner meetings & forums; *Library:* Tourist Booth; Open to public

PIJAC Canada / Conseil consultatif mixte de l'industrie des animaux de compagnie
#14, 1010 Polytek, Ottawa ON K1J 9H9
Tel: 613-730-8111; *Fax:* 613-730-9111
Toll-Free: 800-667-7452
information@pijaccanada.com
www.pijaccanada.com
www.linkedin.com/company/pijac-canada
Also Known As: Pet Industry Joint Advisory Council of Canada
Overview: A medium-sized national organization founded in 1988
Mission: To ensure the highest level of pet care attainable & a guarantee of a fair & equitable representation for all facets of the Canadian pet industry.
Member of: International Pet Advisory Council
Affiliation(s): PIJAC International
Finances: *Annual Operating Budget:* $500,000-$1.5 Million; *Funding Sources:* Membership fees; trade show revenues
Staff Member(s): 7; 20 volunteer(s)
Membership: 350 corporate; *Fees:* Schedule available; *Member Profile:* Working in the Pet Industry
Activities: Certified Companion Animal Specialist Program; Safe Handling of Pets Information Campaign; National Pet Industry Trade Shows; *Speaker Service:* Yes; *Library:* Open to public by appointment
Chief Officer(s):
Louis McCann, President & CEO, 613-730-8111 Ext. 112
executiveoffice@pijaccanada.com
Rénald Sabourin, Assistant Executive Director, 613-730-8111 Ext. 116
operations@pijaccanada.com

Pillar Nonprofit Network
251 Dundas St., 2nd Fl., London ON N6A 6H9
Tel: 519-433-7876; *Fax:* 519-435-0227
www.pillarv.com
www.facebook.com/Pillar.Nonprofit.Network
twitter.com/PillarNN
www.youtube.com/user/pillarnonprofit
Also Known As: Pillar - Voluntary Sector Network
Overview: A small local charitable organization founded in 2001
Mission: To strengthen & leverage the impact of the nonprofit sector for a civic & just society
Finances: *Annual Operating Budget:* $50,000-$100,000
Staff Member(s): 2; 50 volunteer(s)
Membership: 125; *Fees:* $50 individual; $50-$300 corporate; *Committees:* Training; Technology; Research; Marketing; Policy; Special Events
Activities: Volunteer referral; policy input; training; networking; raising awareness of the voluntary sector; *Library:* Open to public
Chief Officer(s):
Michelle Baldwin, Executive Director
mbaldwin@pillarnonprofit.ca

Pilot Mound & District Chamber of Commerce
Tel: 204-873-2591
chamberofcommerce@pilotmound.com
www.pilotmound.com
Overview: A small local organization
Mission: To promote the businesses & community of Pilot Mound
Member of: Manitoba Chamber of Commerce
Finances: *Annual Operating Budget:* Less than $50,000; *Funding Sources:* Fundraising
Staff Member(s): 1
Membership: 69; *Fees:* $15 individual; $30 business; *Committees:* Housing; Promotion; Development; Smorg

Pilot Parents
c/o Community Living Toronto, 8 Spadina Ave., Toronto ON M5R 2S7
Tel: 416-968-0650
Overview: A small local charitable organization founded in 1982
Mission: To provide emotional support & understanding to parents of children with developmental handicaps; to provide information about developmental handicaps & the services available for parents & children
Affiliation(s): Toronto Association for Community Living
Finances: *Annual Operating Budget:* $50,000-$100,000; *Funding Sources:* United Way
Staff Member(s): 1; 40 volunteer(s)
Membership: 90 individual
Activities: Individual parent-to-parent partnerships; workshops; support groups; social events to connect parents with other parents

Pin Collectors' Club *Voir* Club des collectionneurs d'épinglettes Inc.

Pinawa Chamber of Commerce
PO Box 544, Pinawa MB R0E 1L0
www.pinawachamber.com
Overview: A small local organization
Mission: To represent local businesses
Membership: 44; *Fees:* $60
Chief Officer(s):
Steffen Bunge, President
president@pinawachamber.com

Pincher Creek & District Chamber of Commerce
Ranchland Mall, PO Box 2287, #4, 1300 Hewetson Ave., Pincher Creek AB T0K 1W0
Tel: 403-627-5199
www.pincher-creek.com
www.facebook.com/219210741437000
twitter.com/PC_Chamber
Previous Name: Pincher Creek & District Chamber of Economic Development
Overview: A small local organization founded in 1972
Mission: To enhance the economic & social well-being of the area
Member of: Alberta Chamber of Commerce
Finances: *Funding Sources:* Membership fees; Town; Municipal District

Pincher Creek & District Chamber of Economic Development *See* Pincher Creek & District Chamber of Commerce

Pincher Creek Allied Arts Council
696 Kettles St., Pincher Creek AB T0K 1W0
Tel: 403-627-5272; *Fax:* 403-627-1559
lebelpc@gmail.com
www.pinchercreekarts.com
Overview: A small local charitable organization
Mission: To promote & advance arts education in Pincher Creek & to restore & preserve the Lebel Mansion Historic Site
Member of: Alberta Municipal Association for Culture
Affiliation(s): Heritage Canada
Finances: *Annual Operating Budget:* $50,000-$100,000; *Funding Sources:* Donations
Staff Member(s): 1
Membership: 130; *Fees:* $15 single; $20 family
Chief Officer(s):
Sharon Polski, Administrator

Pincher Creek Humane Society (PC SPCA)
PO Box 2647, 1068 Kettles St., Pincher Creek AB T0K 1W0
Tel: 403-627-5191; *Fax:* 403-627-1406
pchs@toughcountry.net
www.pinchercreekhumanesociety.org
www.facebook.com/142406202447008
Previous Name: Pincher Creek Society for the Prevention of Cruelty to Animals
Overview: A small local charitable organization founded in 1998
Mission: To educate the public about responsible pet ownership; To foster a sense of community in caring fo & dealing with lost or unwanted animals; To ensure a safe environment for lost or unwanted animals; To advocate for & ensoure animals are spayed or neutered; To return animals to their owners & to find caring homes for unwanted animals; to promote positive public awareness & acceptance of the Society; To ensure kind, efficient, cost-effective & humane euthanasia; To seek public & corporate sponsorship to ensure financial support & viability of the Society; To develop & encourage volunteers to participate in self-growth, self-expression & a positive volunteer experience
Affiliation(s): Alberta SPCA
Finances: *Annual Operating Budget:* Less than $50,000; *Funding Sources:* Municipal government; fundraising
Staff Member(s): 1; 5 volunteer(s)
Membership: 1-99

Pincher Creek Society for the Prevention of Cruelty to Animals *See* Pincher Creek Humane Society

Pine Tree Potters Guild
PO Box 28586, Aurora ON L4G 6S6
Tel: 905-727-1278
www.pinetreepotters.ca
www.facebook.com/pinetreepottersguild
Overview: A small local organization founded in 1979
Mission: To preserve & advance ceramic arts.
Chief Officer(s):
Sara Stevens, President

Pink Triangle Services; Association of Lesbians, Gays & Bisexuals of Ottawa *See* Kind Space

The Pioneer Association of Ontario *See* Ontario Historical Society

Pioneer Clubs Canada Inc.
3350 South Service Rd., Burlington ON L7N 3M6
Tel: 905-681-2883
Toll-Free: 800-465-5437
www.pioneerclubs.org
www.facebook.com/pioneerclubs
Also Known As: Pioneer Girls/Pioneer Boys
Overview: A large national licensing charitable organization founded in 1974
Mission: To serve God by assisting churches & other ministries in helping children & youth make Christ Lord in every aspect of life
Affiliation(s): Canadian Council of Christian Charities
Finances: *Annual Operating Budget:* $250,000-$500,000
Staff Member(s): 9
Membership: 216 institutional; 16,000 individual; *Fees:* $12 child
Activities: *Speaker Service:* Yes
Publications:
• Pioneer Clubs Canada Inc. Leadership eNewsletter
Type: Newsletter

Pioneer Women Organization of Canada Inc. *See* Na'amat Canada Inc.

Pipe Line Contractors Association of Canada (PLCAC)
#201, 1075 North Service Rd. West, Oakville ON L6M 2G2
Tel: 905-847-9383; *Fax:* 905-847-7824
plcac@pipeline.ca
www.pipeline.ca
Overview: A medium-sized national organization founded in 1954
Mission: To represent contractors in labour relations matters & to establish training courses for the development of Canadian workers in special pipeline consturction skills
Membership: 41 regular members; 92 associate members; 19 honorary members; *Member Profile:* Employers engaged in contacting for the construction, installation & maintenance of piplines; Corporations or individuals engages in manufacturing, supplying & transporting material for the construction & maintenance of piplines; *Committees:* Convention Planning; Education & Training; Executive; Membership & Promotion; National Labour Relations; Negotiating - Distribution; Negotiating - Mainline; Negotiating - Maintenance; Pipeline Standards; Safety
Activities: Establishing training courses; Reviewing legislation
Chief Officer(s):
Neil G. Lane, Executive Director
Kellie Gamble, Manager, Labour Relations
Lianne Appleby, Communications & Memeber Services
Awards:
• Pipe Line Contractors Association of Canada Student Award Program
• The Jack Cressey Future Leader Award
• The Wayne E. McArthur Memorial Award
Meetings/Conferences:
• Pipe Line Contractors Association of Canada 2018 64th Annual Convention, 2018
Scope: National
Description: A program about the special pipeline construction industry, including various speakers & the association's annual general meeting
Contact Information: Contact: Neil Lane, Phone: 905-847-9383
Publications:
• Canadian Pipeliner [a publication of the Pipe Line Contractors Association of Canada]
Type: Newsletter; *Frequency:* 4 pa
Profile: News, industry information, & upcoming events
• PLCAC [Pipe Line Contractors Association of Canada] Membership Directory
Type: Directory; *Frequency:* Annually
Profile: Featuring membership profiles & contact information

Pitch-In Canada (PIC) / Passons à l'action Canada
PO Box 45011, RPO Ocean Park, White Rock BC V4A 9L1
Tel: 604-536-4726; *Fax:* 604-535-4653
Toll-Free: 877-474-8244
pitch-in@pitch-in.ca
www.pitch-in.ca
www.facebook.com/pitchin.canada
twitter.com/@pitch_in_canada
Previous Name: Outdoors Unlittered
Overview: A medium-sized national charitable organization founded in 1967
Mission: To improve communities & the enviornment by providing programs to reduce, re-use, recycle, & properly manage & dispose waste
Affiliation(s): Clean World International; Clean up the World
Finances: *Funding Sources:* Donations; Sponsorships; Grants; Fees for service; Merchandising of materials
Activities: Working with all levels of government & other organizations; *Awareness Events:* National Pitch-In Week
Library: Pitch-In Canada Resource Centre
Chief Officer(s):
Misha Cook, Executive Director, 877-474-8244 Ext. 1
misha@pitch-in.ca
Erika Tibbe, Marketing & Program Coordinator
erika@pitch-in.ca

Pittsburgh Historical Society
211 Gore Rd., Kingston ON K7L 5H6
Tel: 613-483-8527
Overview: A small local organization founded in 1976
Mission: To create & maintain community awareness & interest in the heritage of Pittsburgh Township; To meet regularly for the presentation & discussion of papers; To encourage research & documentation; To encourage the establishment of a historical museum; To encourage the identification & conservation of historic sites within the township
Member of: Ontario Historical Society

Finances: *Annual Operating Budget:* Less than $50,000; *Funding Sources:* Membership fees
Membership: *Fees:* $10
Activities: Meetings; publications; exhibitions; plaques; presentations
Chief Officer(s):
Sheila Nichol, President

Pius X Secular Institute *Voir* Institut Séculier Pie X

Pivot Legal Society
121 Heatley Ave., Vancouver BC V6A 3E9
Tel: 604-255-9700; *Fax:* 604-255-1552
www.pivotlegal.org
www.facebook.com/PivotLegalSociety
twitter.com/pivotlegal
Overview: A small local organization
Mission: To use the law to address the root causes of social exclusion & poverty; To pressure authorities in order to shift society's values toward equality & inclusivity
Staff Member(s): 7
Activities: Lobbying for legislative reforms; Addressing poverty- and discrimination-related issues through communication; Creating opportunities for people from diverse backgrounds to understand the root causes of poverty & the issues surrounding poverty; *Internships:* Yes
Chief Officer(s):
Katrina Pacey, Executive Director
katrina@pivotlegal.org
Publications:
• BC's Residential Tenancy System- 13 Recommendations for Change [a publication of the Pivot Legal Society]
Type: Report; *Number of Pages:* 12
• Blueprint for an Inquiry [a publication of the Pivot Legal Society]
Type: Report; *Number of Pages:* 55; *Author:* Darcie Bennett et al.
• The Case for Heroin-Assisted Treatment in Canada [a publication of the Pivot Legal Society]
Type: Report; *Number of Pages:* 7
• Imagining Courts that Work for Women Survivors of Violence [a publication of the Pivot Legal Society]
Type: Report; *Number of Pages:* 66; *Author:* Darcie Bennett
• Moving to Minimum Force: Police Dogs & Public Safety in British Columbia [a publication of the Pivot Legal Society]
Type: Report; *Number of Pages:* 30; *Author:* Douglas King
Profile: A study evaluating the prevalence of Police Service Dog (PSD) bites and how PSDs fit intothe Canadian National Police Use of Force Framework (NUFF)
• My Work Should Not Cost Me My Life [a publication of the Pivot Legal Society]
Type: Report; *Number of Pages:* 21
• Throwing Away the Keys: The human and social cost of mandatory minimum sentences [a publication of the Pivot Legal Society]
Type: Report; *Number of Pages:* 43; *Author:* Darcie Bennett & Scott Bernstein
• Zoned Out [a publication of the Pivot Legal Society]
Type: Report; *Number of Pages:* 5; *Author:* Darcie Bennett & Scott Bernstein

Place Benoît Bon Courage Community Centre *Voir* Centre Communautaire Bon Courage De Place Benoît

Place Vermeil
#206, 2600, rue Ontario est, Montréal QC H2K 4K4
Tél: 514-251-7822
info@placevermeil.org
placevermeil.org
Aperçu: *Dimension:* petite; *Envergure:* locale; fondée en 1974
Mission: Pour aider les personnes âgées lutte contre l'isolement et de devenir indépendant
Membre: *Montant de la cotisation:* 6$
Activités: Art plastique; chant choral; cours de langue Italienne; atelier photo; éveil musical; clinique d'impôts
Membre(s) du bureau directeur:
Annie Boilon, Directrice générale

Placentia Area Chamber of Commerce (PACC)
1 O'Reilly St., Placentia NL A0B 2Y0
Tel: 709-227-0003
www.placentiachamber.ca
Previous Name: Argentia Area Chamber of Commerce
Overview: A small local organization
Member of: Canadian Chamber of Commerce
Staff Member(s): 2
Membership: *Fees:* $100
Chief Officer(s):

Gerry Sullivan, President
Eugene Collins, Executive Director

Plan Canada
#300, 245 Eglinton Ave. East, Toronto ON M4P 0B3
Tel: 416-920-1654; *Fax:* 416-920-9942
Toll-Free: 800-387-1418
info@plancanada.ca
plancanada.ca
www.linkedin.com/company/plan-canada
www.facebook.com/PlanCanada
twitter.com/PlanCanada
www.youtube.com/user/plancanadavideos
Previous Name: Foster Parents Plan Canada
Overview: A large international charitable organization founded in 1968
Mission: To help children, their families, & communities in developing countries; To raise funds through sponsorship program & implement programs in health, education, & community development overseas
Member of: Canadian Council for International Cooperation
Membership: *Member Profile:* Sponsorship fee; *Committees:* Finance, Audit & Compensation; Governance & Nominating; Program & Planning
Activities: *Internships:* Yes
Chief Officer(s):
Caroline Riseboro, President & CEO

Le plan nord-américain de gestion de la sauvagine *See* North American Waterfowl Management Plan

Planetary Association for Clean Energy, Inc. (PACE) / Société planétaire pour l'assainissement de l'énergie
#1001, 100 Bronson Ave., Ottawa ON K1R 6G8
Tel: 613-236-6265; *Fax:* 613-235-5876
paceincnet@gmail.com
pacenet.homestead.com
Overview: A medium-sized international charitable organization founded in 1976
Mission: To facilitate the discovery, research, development, demonstration & evaluation of clean energy systems
Finances: *Annual Operating Budget:* $100,000-$250,000; *Funding Sources:* Membership fees; donations
Staff Member(s): 2; 10 volunteer(s)
Membership: 3,600 in 60 countries; *Fees:* $50
Activities: Electromagnetic bioaffect, analyses & abatement; monitors unclean developments; peer review of new technologies; books, databases & technical reports; *Internships:* Yes; *Speaker Service:* Yes; *Library:* Planetary Association for Clean Energy Library; by appointment
Chief Officer(s):
Andrew Michrowski, President

Planned Lifetime Advocacy Network (PLAN)
#260, 3665 Kingsway, Vancouver BC V5R 5W2
Tel: 604-439-9566; *Fax:* 604-439-7001
www.plan.ca
www.facebook.com/JoinPLAN
twitter.com/plannedlifetime
www.youtube.com/user/PLANvids
Overview: A small local organization
Mission: To help families with disabled relatives plan for their future
Affiliation(s): PLAN Toronto; Thunderbay Family Network; PLAN Edmonton; Lethbridge Association for Community Living; PLAN Calgary; Lifetime Networks Ottawa; Planned Lifetime Networks; LifeSPAN; PLAN Okanagan; Regina RDACL PLAN; Family Link; PLAN of Arizona
Membership: *Member Profile:* Families with disabled relatives
Chief Officer(s):
Tim Ames, Executive Director
tames@plan.ca
Adam Trombley, Manager, Communications & Member Engagement

Planned Parenthood - Newfoundland & Labrador Sexual Health Centre (NLSHC)
203 Merrymeeting Rd., St. John's NL A1C 2W6
Tel: 709-579-1009; *Fax:* 709-726-2308
Toll-Free: 877-666-9847
info@nlsexualhealthcentre.org
www.nlsexualhealthcentre.org
www.facebook.com/PlannedParenthoodNL
twitter.com/NLSexualHealth
Overview: A medium-sized provincial organization founded in 1972 overseen by Canadian Federation for Sexual Health

Mission: To promote positive sexual health attitudes & practices throughout Newfoundland & Labrador; To support & respect individual choice
Member of: Coalition Against the Sexual Exploitation of Youth
Finances: *Funding Sources:* Fundraising; Donations
Staff Member(s): 3
Activities: Providing information & education to assist people to make informed sexual health choices; Offering workshops for schools, youth, & community groups, & agencies; Partnering with other community organizations; Promoting preventive health care & responsible sexual practices; Offering support groups; Counselling; Providing medical clinics & exams for women & men; *Awareness Events:* National Day Against Homophobia, May; Annual 5 km Run For Respect, August; Take Back The Night, September; *Speaker Service:* Yes; *Library:* Newfoundland & Labrador Sexual Health Centre Resource Library
Chief Officer(s):
Angie Brake, Executive Director
Publications:
• The Messenger
Type: Newsletter; *Frequency:* Semiannually; *Price:* Free with NLSHC membership
Profile: Centre reports, informative articles. & upcoming activities

Planned Parenthood Association of British Columbia *See* Options for Sexual Health

Planned Parenthood Banff; Banff YWCA Community Resource Centre *See* YWCA of Banff Programs & Services

Planned Parenthood Bridgewater *See* Sexual Health Centre Lunenburg County

Planned Parenthood Cape Breton *See* Cape Breton Centre for Sexual Health

Planned Parenthood Centre (Regina) *See* Planned Parenthood Regina

Planned Parenthood Manitoba *See* Sexuality Education Resource Centre Manitoba

Planned Parenthood Metro Clinic *See* Halifax Sexual Health Centre

Planned Parenthood Montréal *See* Sexual Health Network of Québec Inc.

Planned Parenthood of Toronto (PPT)
36B Prince Arthur Ave., Toronto ON M5R 1A9
Tel: 416-961-0113; *Fax:* 416-961-2512
ppt@ppt.on.ca
www.ppt.on.ca
www.facebook.com/PPToronto
twitter.com/PPofTO
www.youtube.com/user/PlannedParenthoodTO
Overview: A small local charitable organization founded in 1961
Mission: To provide accessible & inclusive services which promote healthy sexuality & informed decision-making to the people of the city of Toronto
Member of: Canadian Federation for Sexual Health; United Way Toronto
Finances: *Annual Operating Budget:* $1.5 Million-$3 Million; *Funding Sources:* Membership fees; donations; United Way Toronto
Staff Member(s): 30; 140 volunteer(s)
Membership: *Fees:* $10 general; $20 organization; $5 student; *Member Profile:* Individuals living in Toronto who are 18 and over; Corporations
Activities: Programming for women, teens, young men, & young parents; anti-homophobia education; community based research
Chief Officer(s):
Sarah Hobbs-Blyth, Executive Director

Planned Parenthood Ottawa (PPOC) / Planning des naissances d'Ottawa
#403, 2197 Riverside Dr., Ottawa ON K1H 7X3
Tel: 613-226-3234; *Fax:* 613-226-8955
ppottawa@ppottawa.ca
www.ppottawa.ca
www.facebook.com/285360338462
twitter.com/knowppo
Overview: A small local charitable organization founded in 1964
Mission: To offer education, couselling, & referral services to assist & support people making informed sexual & reproductive health choices
Member of: Planned Parenthood Federation of Canada
Affiliation(s): Planned Parenthood Ontario

Finances: *Funding Sources:* Government; United Way; City of Ottawa: Peoples Services; Program fees; Sponsorship
Staff Member(s): 4
Activities: Providing sexual health information & support; Offering teen outreach support; Providing community education; *Speaker Service:* Yes; *Library:* Dorothea Palmer Ferguson Resource Library; Open to public
Chief Officer(s):
Catherine Macnab, Executive Director, 613-226-3234 Ext. 301
director@ppottawa.ca

Planned Parenthood Regina
1431 Victoria Ave., Regina SK S4P 0P4
Tel: 306-522-0902
admin.ppr@accesscomm.ca
www.plannedparenthoodregina.com
Previous Name: Planned Parenthood Centre (Regina)
Overview: A small local organization founded in 1986
Mission: To provide education, counselling & medical services in the areas of sexuality, birth control & family planning
Finances: *Funding Sources:* Regina Health District; community grants; corporate & individual donations
Activities: Birth Control Centre

Planned Parenthood Saskatoon Centre *See* Sexual Health Centre Saskatoon

Planned Parenthood Society of Hamilton *See* Health Initiatives for Youth Hamilton

Planned Parenthood Waterloo Region (PPWR)
#500, 151 Frederick St., Kitchener ON N2H 2M2
Tel: 519-743-9360; *Fax:* 519-743-6710
director@ppwr.on.ca
www.ppwr.on.ca
www.facebook.com/ppwaterloo
Overview: A small local charitable organization founded in 1971
Mission: To promote healthy & responsible sexuality throughout the human life cycle
Member of: Planned Parenthood Federation of Canada
Finances: *Annual Operating Budget:* $100,000-$250,000; *Funding Sources:* Private donations; foundation grants
Staff Member(s): 11
Activities: *Speaker Service:* Yes; *Library:* Sexuality Resource Centre; Open to public
Chief Officer(s):
Lyndsey Butcher, Executive Director
director@ppwr.on.ca

Planning & Land Administrators of Nunavut (PLAN)
NU
Tel: 867-360-7705; *Fax:* 867-360-7142
Overview: A small provincial organization founded in 2004 overseen by National Aboriginal Lands Managers Association
Staff Member(s): 1
Chief Officer(s):
Troy Beaulieu, Chair
gjoalands@qiniq.com

Planning des naissances d'Ottawa *See* Planned Parenthood Ottawa

The Planning Forum *See* Strategic Leadership Forum

Planning Institute of British Columbia (PIBC)
#1750, 355 Burrard St., Vancouver BC V6C 2G8
Tel: 604-696-5031; *Fax:* 604-696-5032
Toll-Free: 866-696-5031
info@pibc.bc.ca
www.pibc.bc.ca
Overview: A medium-sized provincial organization founded in 1958 overseen by Canadian Institute of Planners
Mission: To promote orderly use of land, buildings & natural resources; to maintain high standard of professional competence; to protect rights & interests of those engaged in planning profession
Staff Member(s): 2
Membership: 1,500; *Fees:* Schedule available; *Member Profile:* Professional working in the planning industry & planning students; *Committees:* Executive; Membership; Education; Communications; Mentorship; Awards; Professional Practice Review
Chief Officer(s):
Andrew Young, President
andrew.young@pibc.bc.ca
Dave Crossley, Executive Director
dave.crossley@pibc.bc.ca

Meetings/Conferences:
• Planning Institute of British Columbia 2018 Annual Conference, May, 2018, Victoria Conference Centre, Victoria, BC
Scope: Provincial

Plant Biology Research Institute *Voir* Institut de recherche en biologie végétale

Plant Engineering & Maintenance Association of Canada (PEMAC)
#402, 6 - 2400 Dundas St. West, Mississauga ON L5K 2R8
Fax: 905-823-8001
Toll-Free: 877-532-7255
admin@pemac.org
www.pemac.org
Overview: A medium-sized national licensing organization founded in 1989
Mission: To be recognized as a nationwide centre of excellence in plant engineering & maintenance; To form positive & constructive links with industry & service sectors, in support of local & nationwide developments & productivity; To deliver strongly identifiable services & commitments across the range of disciplines embraced by the association; to educate & introduce new concepts; To provide representation at all government levels; To provide career enhancement & networking opportunities; To promote research in the field of plant engineering & maintenance
Affiliation(s): Annex Business Media; Canadian Institute for Nondestructive Evaluation; Canadian Network of Asset Managers; Canadian Association for University Continuing Education; Global Forum on Maintenance & Asset Management
Finances: *Funding Sources:* Membership fees; website; colleges
Membership: *Member Profile:* Maintenance professionals & practitioners
Activities: Certification Program, MMP - Maintenance Management Professional; *Speaker Service:* Yes; *Library:* by appointment Not open to public
Chief Officer(s):
Rob Lash, President
Awards:
• Annual Sergio Guy Memorial Award

Plast Ukrainian Youth Association of Canada
516 The Kingsway, Toronto ON M9A 3W6
Tel: 416-763-2186; *Fax:* 416-763-2186
plast@plastcanada.ca
www.plast.ca
www.facebook.com/pages/Plast-Toronto/135071499928751
Also Known As: PLAST
Overview: A small national charitable organization founded in 1948
Mission: To encourage Ukrainian Canadian youth to develop into conscious & responsible citizens
Finances: *Funding Sources:* Government
Activities: Offering camps & scout programs; Holding meetings & assemblies

The Platinum Party of Employers Who Think & Act to Increase Awareness
PO Box 8068, Stn. Main, Victoria BC V8W 3R7
Tel: 250-483-7717
www.platinumparty.org
Also Known As: Platinum Party
Overview: A small provincial organization
Mission: To ensure that the Government of British Columbia has in place the procedures necessary to maintain a legitimate position of authority over the commercial sector in BC
Chief Officer(s):
Espavo Sozo, Interim Party Leader
treasurer@platinumparty.org

Playwrights Guild of Canada (PGC)
#350, 401 Richmond St. West, Toronto ON M5V 3A8
Tel: 416-703-0201; *Fax:* 416-703-0059
info@playwrightsguild.ca
www.playwrightsguild.ca
twitter.com/PGuildCanada
Previous Name: Playwrights Union of Canada
Overview: A medium-sized national organization founded in 1972
Mission: To encourage Canadian playwriting; To publish, promote & distribute Canadian plays; To provide current information of Canadian plays & their authors; To offer copyright protection; To promote the study & appreciation of Canadian plays; To safeguard freedom of expression on the stage

Member of: Association of Canadian Publishers; Literary Press Group; Canadian Conference of the Arts
Finances: *Annual Operating Budget:* $250,000-$500,000; *Funding Sources:* Canada Council; provincial, municipal & city government; 45% earned revenue
Staff Member(s): 3; 23 volunteer(s)
Membership: 500; *Fees:* $155 full; $75 associate; $35 individual supporting; $100 institutional; $65 senior; *Member Profile:* Canadian citizens or landed immigrants with one play produced or revived within the past ten years, either as an Equity production or an equivalent production; *Committees:* Contracts; Copyright; Women's Caucus
Activities: Releasing several plays each year; Organizing special cultural events such as playwrights' cabarets; Offering touring programs; Managing reading rooms in more than 10 countries; Administration of amateur performance rights; Forwarding royalties from scripts; *Rents Mailing List:* Yes; *Library:* Drama Reading Room; Open to public
Chief Officer(s):
Robin Sokoloski, Executive Director
robin@playwrightsguild.ca

Playwrights Theatre Centre
#202, 739 Gore Ave., Vancouver BC V6A 2Z9
Tel: 604-685-6228
plays@playwrightstheatre.com
www.playwrightstheatre.com
www.facebook.com/playwrightstheatre
twitter.com/ptc_playwrights
Overview: A small local organization
Mission: To develop new Canadian plays; To provide support to experienced, emerging, & aspiring playwrights from across the country through dramaturgy, workshops, writers' groups and other programs
Staff Member(s): 5
Membership: 192; *Fees:* $25
Chief Officer(s):
Heidi Taylor, Artistic & Executive Director, 604-685-6228 Ext. 1
heidi@playwrightstheatre.com

Playwrights Union of Canada *See* Playwrights Guild of Canada

Playwrights' Workshop Montréal (PWM)
#240, 5337, boul St-Laurent, Montréal QC H2T 1S5
Tel: 514-843-3685
info@playwrights.ca
www.playwrights.ca
www.facebook.com/PlaywrightsWorkshopMontreal
twitter.com/pwmontreal
Overview: A small local charitable organization founded in 1963
Mission: To support the development of playwrights & contemporary work for the stage; To advance the artistry of all levels of professional theatre artists; To develop & disseminate work
Finances: *Funding Sources:* Donations
Staff Member(s): 5
Membership: *Fees:* Schedule available
Chief Officer(s):
Delphine Hervot, President
Chris Gobeil, Treasurer
Emma Tibaldo, Artistic Director
emma@playwrights.ca
Molly Maguire, General Manager
mollym@playwrights.ca

PLEA Community Services Society of BC (PLEA)
3894 Commercial St., Vancouver BC V5N 4G2
Tel: 604-871-0450; *Fax:* 604-871-0408
info@plea.bc.ca
www.plea.ca
www.linkedin.com/company/1185502
www.facebook.com/PLEAServicesBC
twitter.com/plea_bc
Previous Name: Pacific Legal Education Association
Overview: A medium-sized local charitable organization founded in 1979
Mission: To provide justice, counselling, mentoring, residential care, & support services, with a particular emphasis on young offenders & at-risk children & youth
Member of: Community Legal Services Employers Association; United Community Services Group
Finances: *Annual Operating Budget:* Greater than $5 Million; *Funding Sources:* Provincial government; charitable donations
Staff Member(s): 346; 250 volunteer(s)
Membership: 25
Chief Officer(s):

Tim Veresh, Executive Director
Michelle Hawco, Director, Human Resources & Finance
Mike Jeffreys, Senior Director, Programs

Plum Coulee & District Chamber of Commerce
PO Box 392, Plum Coulee MB R0G 1R0
Tel: 204-829-2317; *Fax:* 204-829-2319
rmofrhineland.com
Overview: A small local organization
Mission: To promote & support businesses in the community
Finances: *Annual Operating Budget:* Less than $50,000
8 volunteer(s)
Membership: 34; *Fees:* $75; *Committees:* Heritage; Millennium; Centennial; Foundation; Sports
Activities: *Awareness Events:* Plum Fest, every 3rd week-end in August
Chief Officer(s):
Moira Porte, President

Plumbing Officials' Association of British Columbia (POABC)
2328 Hollyhill Pl., Victoria BC V8N 1T9
Tel: 250-361-0342; *Fax:* 250-385-1128
bhusband@victoria.ca
www.bcplumbingofficials.com
Overview: A medium-sized provincial organization
Chief Officer(s):
Brian Husband, President

Point d'appui, centre d'aide et de prévention des agressions à caractère sexuel de Rouyn-Noranda (CAPACS)
CP 1274, Rouyn-Noranda QC J9X 6E4
Tél: 819-797-0101; *Téléc:* 819-797-0102
info@pointdappui.org
www.pointdappui.org
Aperçu: *Dimension:* petite; *Envergure:* locale; fondée en 1983
Mission: Service d'urgence, aide, support et écoute auprès des femmes agressées sexuellement; sensibilisation et prévention dans la communauté; relation d'aide individuelle et de groupe; collaboration avec les organismes du milieu (policiers, hôpitaux, etc)
Affiliation(s): Regroupement québécois des Calacs; Association canadienne des centres contre le viol
Finances: *Budget de fonctionnement annuel:* $50,000-$100,000; *Fonds:* Gouvernement provincial
Membre(s) du personnel: 2; 16 bénévole(s)
Membre: 30
Activités: *Evénements de sensibilisation:* Journée d'action contre la violence sexuelle, 3e vendredi de sept.
Membre(s) du bureau directeur:
Carmen Dion, Bénévole-militante

Pointe-au-Baril Chamber of Commerce
PO Box 67, Pointe-au-Baril-Station ON P0G 1K0
Tel: 705-366-2331
Also Known As: Information Booth
Overview: A small local licensing organization
Mission: To offer the travelling public the best accomodations in the area
Member of: Ontario Chamber of Commerce
Affiliation(s): Rainbow County Travel Association
Finances: *Funding Sources:* Membership fees

Poison & Drug Information Service
Foothills Medical Centre, 1403 - 29th St. NW, Calgary AB T2N 2T9
Tel: 403-944-6900
Toll-Free: 800-332-1414
www.albertahealthservices.ca/5423.asp
Also Known As: PADIS
Previous Name: Alberta Poison Centre
Overview: A small provincial organization
Mission: To provide information & advice on poisons, medications, & chemicals
Member of: Canadian Association of Poison Control Centres
Chief Officer(s):
Ryan Chuang, Associate Medical Director

Polanie-Polish Song & Dance Association
3015 - 15 St. NE, Calgary AB T2E 7L8
Tel: 403-287-7336
info@polanie.ca
www.polanie.ca
Overview: A small local organization founded in 1977
Mission: To present the richness of Polish folklore in a stylized artistic adaptation

Membership: 45
Chief Officer(s):
Sandro Barbosa, Artistic Director
artisticdirector@polanie.ca

Polarettes Gymnastics Club
4061 - 4th Ave., Whitehorse YT Y1A 1H1
Tel: 867-668-4794
info@polarettes.org
www.polarettes.org
Overview: A small provincial organization
Mission: To promote recreational & competitive gymnastics programs to Yukon residtents. Physical address: 16 Duke St., Whitehorse, YT Y1A 4M2.
Activities: Toddler Movement program (18 months); competitive programs start from 6-8 years old
Chief Officer(s):
Kimberly Jones, Head Coach

Police Association of Nova Scotia (PANS) / Association des policiers de la Nouvelle-Écosse
#2, 1000 Windmill Rd., Dartmouth NS B3B 1L7
Tel: 902-468-7555; *Fax:* 902-468-2202
Toll-Free: 888-468-2798
www.pansguide.com
Overview: A medium-sized provincial organization
Chief Officer(s):
David W. Fisher, CEO
dfisher@accesscable.net

Police Association of Ontario (PAO) / Association des policiers de l'Ontario
#302, 1650 Yonge St., Toronto ON M4T 2A2
pao@pao.ca
www.pao.ca
www.facebook.com/PoliceAssociationofOntario
Overview: A large provincial organization founded in 1944
Mission: To act as the official voice & representative body for Ontario's front line police personnel; To represent & support Ontario police associations
Member of: Canadian Police Association
Finances: *Annual Operating Budget:* $500,000-$1.5 Million; *Funding Sources:* Membership dues
Staff Member(s): 4
Membership: 18,000 individual + 53 organizations
Activities: *Library:* Not open to public
Chief Officer(s):
Stephen Reid, Executive Director, 416-487-9367, Fax: 416-487-3170
Meetings/Conferences:
• 27th Annual Police Employment Conference, February, 2018, Sheraton Parkway, Richmond Hill, ON
Scope: Provincial
Description: Labour relations

Police Brotherhood of the Royal Newfoundland Constabulary Association (Ind.) *See* Royal Newfoundland Constabulary Association

Police Martial Arts Association Inc. (PMAA)
PO Box 7303, Sub. #12, 162 Trites Rd., Top Fl., Riverview NB E1B 4T9
Tel: 506-387-5126; *Fax:* 506-387-5126
pmaa1@nb.sympatico.ca
www.policemartialarts.org
Also Known As: Riverview Karate Studio
Overview: A small international organization founded in 1993
Mission: To provide a forum for members from 34 nations for instructional technical development, information resources, officer safety & public concerns
Member of: World Head of Family Sokeship Council; Kam Lung Kempo Karate
Finances: *Annual Operating Budget:* Less than $50,000
Staff Member(s): 2; 20 volunteer(s)
Membership: 2,306; *Fees:* US$40 North America; US$50 International; *Member Profile:* Law enforcement officers - martial arts participants; *Committees:* Global Use of Force Research Committee
Activities: *Awareness Events:* Youth Intervention Initiative
Chief Officer(s):
Doug Devlin, Co-Founder
Foster MacLeod, Co-Founder

Police Sector Council (PSC) / Conseil sectoriel de la police (CSP)
#303, 1545 Carling Ave., Ottawa ON K1Z 8P9

Tel: 613-729-2789
info@policecouncil.ca
www.policecouncil.ca
twitter.com/PoliceCouncil
Overview: A medium-sized national organization founded in 2004
Mission: Improving the ways in which human resource planning & management support police operations & enhance police service in communities across Canada
Finances: *Funding Sources:* Federal government
Membership: *Committees:* Competency Based Management (CBM) Framework Steering; Leadership Framework; Recruit Training Comparative Analysis: E-Learning; HR Diagnostic; Sector Scanning
Chief Officer(s):
Geoff Gruson, Executive Director, 613-729-2789, Fax: 613-729-9691
ggruson@policecouncil.ca

Polio Québec
#219A, 3500 boul Décarie, Montréal QC H4A 3J5
Tél: 514-489-1143
Ligne sans frais: 877-765-4672
association@polioquebec.org
www.polioquebec.org
Également appelé: Polio Quebec Association
Aperçu: *Dimension:* moyenne; *Envergure:* provinciale; fondée en 1985
Mission: D'aider toutes les personnes atteintes par la polio et de sensibiliser la population en général sur tous les aspects de la polio, incluant la prévention
Affiliation(s): L'Institut et Hôpital Neurologiques de Montréal; Le centre de réadaptation MAB-Mackay; Confédération des organismes de personnes handicapées du Québec (COPHAN); L'Association multi-ethnique pour l'intégration des personnes handicapées (AMEIPH); Le Carrefour familial des personnes handicapées (Québec)
Finances: *Budget de fonctionnement annuel:* $50,000-$100,000
Membre: 640; *Montant de la cotisation:* $20
Activités: *Evénements de sensibilisation:* World Polio Awareness Month, October; *Stagiaires:* Oui
Membre(s) du bureau directeur:
Daniel Montmarquette, Président
Stewart Valin, Vice-président

Polio Regina
825 McDonald St., Regina SK S4N 2X5
polio@accesscomm.ca
nonprofits.accesscomm.ca/polio
Overview: A small local organization
Mission: To provide support & information to those who suffer & have suffered from polio.
Membership: *Fees:* $10 single; $15 family
Chief Officer(s):
Wilf Tiefenbach, President

Polish Alliance of Canada (PAC)
c/o Mississauga Branch, 3060 Eden Oak Cres., Mississauga ON L5L 5V2
Tel: 905-569-7139
www.polishalliance.ca
Merged from: Society of Mutual Aid "Sons of Poland"; Society of St. Stanislaus; Progressuve Polish Union
Overview: A small national organization founded in 1907
Mission: To promote Polish history, culture & interests
Affiliation(s): Polish Women Circle, Youth Groups, PAC-Mutual Aid Societ; Canadian Polish Congress; Canadian Polish Millennium Fund; Polish Canadian Womens Federation; Polish Combatants Association of Canada; Association of Polish Engineers in Canada; Polish National Union of Canada; Polish Scouting Association in Canada; Polish Teachers Association of Canada
Membership: *Committees:* Litigation; Audit
Chief Officer(s):
Robert Zawierucha, President
president@polishalliance.ca

Polish Army Veterans Association of America
783 College St., Toronto ON M6G 1C5
Tel: 416-606-8678
www.paderewskipark.org
Overview: A small local organization
Affiliation(s): Polish Army Veterans Association of America
Membership: 1-99; *Member Profile:* Polish veterans

Polish Canadian Women's Federation
ON

info@federacjapolek.ca
www.federacjapolek.ca
Overview: A medium-sized national organization founded in 1956
Mission: To preserve Polish culture in Canada & bring women of Polish heritage together
Member of: Canadian Polish Congress Head Executive Board; Canadian National Council of Women; World Polish Women's Federation
Chief Officer(s):
Ewa L. Zadarnowski, President, 613-739-8663, Fax: 613-739-8663
ewazadar@hotmail.com

Polish Combatants Association (SPK)
206 Beverley St., Toronto ON M5T 1Z3
www.spkcanada.com
Overview: A small local charitable organization founded in 1950
Member of: National Council of Veteran Associations
Membership: 3,000; *Member Profile:* WWII veterans
Activities: *Speaker Service:* Yes
Chief Officer(s):
Andrzej M. Ruta, President

Polish Combatants Association - Winnipeg
1364 Main St., Winnipeg MB R2W 3T8
Tel: 204-589-7638; *Fax:* 204-589-7638
Other Communication: Pub Phone: 204-586-6223
www.pcaclub13.com
Also Known As: Polish Combatants Association Club #13
Overview: A small local organization
Activities: *Library:* SPK Library
Chief Officer(s):
Elizabeth Pazerniuk, Club Manager
Krysia (Christine) Kovach, Contact
ckovach@pembinatrails.ca

Polish National Catholic Church of Canada *See* St. John's Cathedral Polish Catholic Church

Polish National Union of Canada
71 Judson St., Toronto ON M8Z 1A4
www.polishnationalunion.ca
Overview: A small national organization
Chief Officer(s):
Bartlomiej Habrowski, President

Polish North American Trucking Association
#6, 2550 Goldenridge Rd., Mississauga ON L4X 2S3
contact@pnata.org
www.pnata.org
www.facebook.com/pnata.org
Overview: A medium-sized national organization founded in 1999
Mission: To help European truckers with work advancement in Canada, including partnership development, acquiring information, obtaining work permits & qualified drivers, & process management
Membership: *Fees:* $25-$50; *Member Profile:* Trucking companies
Activities: Providing networking opportunities & information; Holding monthly meetings; Offering education & training
Chief Officer(s):
Mike Lotakow, President
Publications:
• Trucker(ski) Magazine [a publication of the Polish North American Trucking Association]
Type: Magazine; *Editor:* Beata Szczerba

Polish Society in Canada *See* Canadian Polish Society

Polish Teachers Association in Canada / Zwiazek Nauczycielstwa Polskiego w Kanadzie
3055 Lakeshore Blvd. West, Toronto ON M8V 1K6
Tel: 416-532-2876
zg@znp.ca
www.znp.ca
Overview: A small national organization
Chief Officer(s):
Maria Walicka, President
rwalicki@cogeco.ca

Polish-Canadian Coin & Stamp Club "Troyak"
Toronto ON
Tel: 416-258-1651
info@troyakclub.com
www.troyakclub.com
Overview: A small local organization
Mission: To promote the collection of Polish coins, paper money & stamps.
Member of: Ontario Numismatic Association; Greater Toronto Area Philatelic Alliance
Chief Officer(s):
Wieslaw Grzesicki, Vice-President

Polish-Jewish Heritage Foundation of Canada
#61, 396 Woodsworth Rd., Toronto ON M2L 2T9
www.pjhftoronto.ca
Overview: A small local organization founded in 1988
Mission: To preserve the unique heritage of Polish Jews & to actively foster better understanding & cooperation between Polish & Jewish communities in Canada
Chief Officer(s):
Peter Jassem, Chair

Montréal Chapter
PO Box 284, Stn. Côte-Saint-Luc, Montréal QC H4V 2Y4
aga.kozanecka@gmail.com
www.polish-jewish-heritage.org
Chief Officer(s):
Jolanta Duniewicz, President

Pollination Guelph
18 Karen Ave., Guelph ON N1G 2N9
pollinationguelph@gmail.com
www.pollinationguelph.ca
www.facebook.com/PollinationGuelph
twitter.com/PollinateGuelph
www.instagram.com/pollinateguelph
Overview: A small local charitable organization
Mission: To conserve & develop pollinator habitat; To promote pollinators & raise awareness of their impact on environmental sustainability
Finances: *Funding Sources:* Donations
Activities: Offering resources on pollinators & pollination; Promoting research on pollinators & their habitats; Organizing & participating in community events; Advocating for policies that address the importance of pollination
Chief Officer(s):
Victoria MacPhail, Co-Chair & Director, Publicity & Outreach
Clare Irwin, Co-Chair, Secretary & Treasurer

Pollution Control Association of Ontario *See* Water Environment Association of Ontario

The Pollution Probe Foundation (PPF)
#200, 150 Ferrand Dr., Toronto ON M3C 3E5
Tel: 416-926-1907; *Fax:* 416-926-1601
Toll-Free: 877-926-1907
Other Communication: Donations E-mail: donations@pollutionprobe.org
pprobe@pollutionprobe.org
www.pollutionprobe.org
www.linkedin.com/company/989805
www.facebook.com/PollutionProbe
twitter.com/PollutionProbe
Also Known As: Pollution Probe
Overview: A medium-sized national charitable organization founded in 1969
Mission: A registered Canadian charity which seeks to define environmental problems through research; to promote understanding through education & to press for practical solutions through advocacy. The organization is non-partisan & works collaboratively with government agencies, other non-profit organizations, & private business to engage key issues & find solutions
Member of: Canadian Environmental Network; Canadian Renewable Energy Alliance
Affiliation(s): Clean Air Network; Ontario Clean Air Alliance
Finances: *Annual Operating Budget:* $250,000-$500,000; *Funding Sources:* Individual & corporate charitable donations; foundation grants; publication sales; government grants
Staff Member(s): 16; 20 volunteer(s)
Membership: 100 corporate donors + 50 institutional
Activities: Programme areas include: Air, Water, Energy, Climate Change, Environment & Child Health, Mercury, Environmental Policy Development; *Awareness Events:* Clean Air Campaign & Commute
Chief Officer(s):
Ingrid Thompson, Chief Executive Officer
ithompson@pollutionprobe.org
Steve McCauley, Senior Director, Policy
Richard Carlson, Director, Energy Exchange & Energy Policy
rcarlson@pollutionprobe.org
Stephanie Thorson, Director, Human Health

Pommes de terre Nouveau-Brunswick *See* Potatoes New Brunswick

Ponoka & District Chamber of Commerce
PO Box 4188, 4205 Highway 2A, Ponoka AB T4J 1R6
Tel: 403-783-3888; *Fax:* 403-783-3886
chamberp@telus.net
www.ponokalive.ca
twitter.com/ponokaChamber
Overview: A small local charitable organization
Mission: To stimulate business & economic growth in Ponoka
Member of: Alberta Chamber of Commerce; Canadian Chamber of Commerce
Finances: *Annual Operating Budget:* $50,000-$100,000; *Funding Sources:* Membership dues; events
Staff Member(s): 2; 15 volunteer(s)
Membership: 185; *Fees:* Schedule available; *Member Profile:* Business professionals
Activities: Organizing trade fairs & events; Offering information; *Library:* Open to public
Chief Officer(s):
Andrew Middleton, President
Kori Hart, Vice-President

Ponoka Food Bank
4612 - 50th St., Ponoka AB T4J 1S7
Tel: 403-783-5910
Overview: A small local organization founded in 1984 overseen by Food Banks Alberta Association
15 volunteer(s)
Chief Officer(s):
Violet Smith, Contact

Pontiac Chamber of Commerce
131A, rue Victoria, Shawville QC J0X 2Y0
Tel: 819-647-2312
Toll-Free: 855-647-2312
info@pontiacchamberofcommerce.ca
www.pontiacchamberofcommerce.ca
www.facebook.com/CommercePontiac
Overview: A small local organization
Mission: To promote economic development in the Pontiac area
Member of: Canadian Chamber of Commerce
Membership: *Fees:* $100-$500; *Committees:* Partnership; Planning; Strategic
Chief Officer(s):
Mireille Alary, President

Pontifical Mission Societies
2219 Kennedy Rd., Toronto ON M1T 3G5
Tel: 416-699-7077; *Fax:* 416-699-9019
Toll-Free: 800-897-8865
mission@missionsocieties.ca
www.missionsocieties.ca
www.facebook.com/pontificalmissionsocieties
twitter.com/pmstoronto
www.youtube.com/user/WorldMissionTV
Overview: A medium-sized international charitable organization founded in 1922
Mission: Comprised of four missionaries: Holy Childhood Association; Propagation of the Faith (SPF); St. Peter the Apostle (SPA); Pontifical Missionary Union (PMU) and aim to provide mission awareness, evangelization and charitable works throughout the world
Affiliation(s): Holy Childhood Association; Propagation of the Faith (SPF); St. Peter the Apostle (SPA); Pontifical Missionary Union (PMU)
Finances: *Funding Sources:* Donations
Staff Member(s): 8
Chief Officer(s):
Osei Alex, National Director

Pool & Hot Tub Council of Canada (PHTCC) / Conseil canadien des piscines et spas
5 MacDougall Dr., Brampton ON L6S 3P3
Tel: 905-458-7242; *Fax:* 905-458-7037
Toll-Free: 800-879-7066
office@poolcouncil.ca
www.poolcouncil.ca
www.facebook.com/273144795787
Previous Name: National Spa & Pool Institute of Canada
Overview: A medium-sized national organization founded in 1959
Mission: To promote the image & sales of the pool, spa & hot tub industry throughout Canada; To promote & enhance consumer awareness of the industry's products; To encourage & promote increased health & safety standards within the industry;

To support efforts to improve pool, hot tub & spa equipment facilities, services & products; &, generally, to promote & advance the common interests of members
Member of: Canadian Association of Exposition Managers; Canadian Society of Association Executives
Finances: *Annual Operating Budget:* $500,000-$1.5 Million; *Funding Sources:* Membership dues; trade show
Staff Member(s): 2
Membership: 360; *Fees:* Schedule available; *Member Profile:* In pool & spa trade or related trade; *Committees:* Promotion & Marketing; Technical & Standards; Training & Education
Activities: Industry training & education; Advocacy; Safety Promotion; Networking; Conferences; *Library*
Chief Officer(s):
Robert Wood, National Executive Director
rwood@poolcouncil.ca
Awards:
• Awards of Design Excellence
Meetings/Conferences:
• 2018 Canadian Pool & Spa Conference & Expo, 2018
Description: The conference features seminars & courses, as well as the expo
Contact Information: www.poolcouncil.ca
  Alberta Chapter
  6349 - 76 Ave. NW, Edmonton AB T6B 0A7
  Tel: 780-466-4428; *Fax:* 780-466-4091
  Chief Officer(s):
  Rodney Taylor, President
  pools@telusplanet.net
  Atlantic Chapter
  c/o R&R Pools, 1949 St Margaret's Bay Rd., Timberlea NS B3T 1C3
  Tel: 902-876-2773; *Fax:* 902-876-1167
  info@rrpools.ca
  Chief Officer(s):
  Kara Redden, President
  info@rrpools.ca
  British Columbia Interior Chapter
  ken@sunshinepools.ca
  British Columbia Island Chapter
  gary@calaisspas-billiards.com
  Central Ontario Chapter
  Eastern Ontario Chapter
  Niagara Chapter
  roland@linerwerx.com
  Prairie Chapter
  MB
  Toronto Chapter
  Toronto ON
  ngray@nspd.net
  Western Ontario Chapter
  markus@forestcitypools.com

POPIR-Comité logement (St-Henri, Petite Bourgogne, Ville Émard, Côte St-Paul)
4017, rue Notre-Dame ouest, Montréal QC H4C 1R3
Tél: 514-935-4649; *Téléc:* 514-935-4067
info@popir.org
popir.org
twitter.com/lepopir
Aperçu: Dimension: petite; *Envergure:* locale
Membre(s) du personnel: 7
Membre(s) du bureau directeur:
Antoine Morneau-Sénéchal, Organisateur Communautaire
antoine.ms@popir.org

Poplar Council of Canada (PCC) / Conseil du peuplier du Canada
c/o Canadian Forest Service, 5320 - 122 St., Edmonton AB T6H 3S5
Tel: 780-430-3843; *Fax:* 780-435-7356
poplar@poplar.ca
www.poplar.ca
www.facebook.com/163419440417089
Overview: A medium-sized national organization founded in 1977
Mission: Committed to the wise use, conservation & sustainable management of Canada's poplar resources
Affiliation(s): Canadian Forest Service
Finances: *Funding Sources:* Government
Membership: *Fees:* $550 corporate; $15 student; $35 individual; *Member Profile:* Forest industry, universities, government
Activities: Workshops, projects
Chief Officer(s):
Raju Soolanayakanahally, Chair
raju.soolanayakanahally@agr.gc.ca

Porc NB Pork
#302, 259 Brunswick St., Fredericton NB E3B 1G8
Tel: 506-458-8051; *Fax:* 506-453-1985
info@porcnbpork.nb.ca
www.porcnbpork.nb.ca
Previous Name: New Brunswick Hog Marketing Board
Overview: A small provincial organization founded in 1951
Affiliation(s): Canadian Pork Council
Staff Member(s): 3
Membership: 75 individual
Chief Officer(s):
Linda Volpé, Chair

Porcupine Prospectors & Developers Association
PO Box 234, Timmins ON P4N 7H9
ppda@ntl.sympatico.ca
www.porcupineprospectors.com
Overview: A small local organization
Mission: To represent the interests of mineral explorationists in the Porcupine District of Northeastern Ontario
Membership: *Fees:* $60 individual; $50-$1000 corporate
Chief Officer(s):
Dean Rogers, President
Robert Calhoune, Secretary

Pork Nova Scotia
Perennia Innovation Park, 60 Research Dr., Bible Hill NS B6L 2R2
Tel: 902-895-0581; *Fax:* 902-893-7063
info@porknovascotia.ca
porknovascotia.ca
Overview: A small provincial organization founded in 1952
Mission: To provide the most economical allocation & sale of live hogs & to represent the special needs & concerns of the pork industry in Nova Scotia
Affiliation(s): Canadian Pork Council
Finances: *Annual Operating Budget:* $250,000-$500,000
Staff Member(s): 125
Membership: 250 individual; *Member Profile:* To create the most favorable environment possible for the production & marketing of pork in Nova Scotia & to assist in maximizing returns for N.S. producers
Chief Officer(s):
Terry Beck, Chair, 902-765-2018

Pork Producers Association of Newfoundland & Labrador
PO Box 9, Point Leamington NL A0H 1Z0
Tel: 709-484-3371; *Fax:* 709-484-3771
Overview: A small provincial organization
Chief Officer(s):
Roosevelt Thompson, Contact
roosevelt@nf.sympatico.ca

Port Alberni & District Labour Council (PADLC)
3940 Johnston Rd., Port Alberni BC V9Y 5N5
Tel: 250-724-7966; *Fax:* 250-724-0677
Overview: A small local organization overseen by British Columbia Federation of Labour
Mission: To promote the interests of affiliates in Port Alberni, British Columbia & the surrounding area; To advance the economic & social welfare of workers
Affiliation(s): Canadian Labour Congress (CLC)
Activities: Presenting educational opportunities; Recognizing the annual Day of Mourning, for workers who have suffered workplace illness, injury, or death; Organizing public forums surrounding local labour issues
Chief Officer(s):
Kelly Drybrough, President, 250-723-6352

Port Alberni Association for Community Living (PAACL)
3008 - 2nd Ave., Port Alberni BC V9Y 1Y9
Tel: 250-724-7155; *Fax:* 250-723-0404
admin@paacl.ca
www.paacl.ca
www.facebook.com/696933320344399
Overview: A small local organization founded in 1957
Membership: *Fees:* $5
Chief Officer(s):
Craig Summers, Executive Director

Port Alberni Friendship Center
3555 - 4 Ave., Port Alberni BC V9Y 4H3
Tel: 250-723-8281; *Fax:* 250-723-1877
www.pafriendshipcenter.com
Overview: A small local organization
Mission: To support the community by providing culturally based programs & services
Staff Member(s): 18; 50 volunteer(s)
Membership: 100; *Fees:* $2
Activities: Counselling; parenting programs; childhood development; family support; literacy programs; legal advocates; early intervention program
Chief Officer(s):
Cyndi Stevens, Executive Director
cstevens@pafriendshipcenter.com

Port Clements Historical Society
PO Box 417, Port Clements BC V0T 1R0
Tel: 250-557-4576; *Fax:* 250-557-4576
www.portclementsmuseum.com
Also Known As: Port Clements Museum
Overview: A small local charitable organization founded in 1985
Mission: To collect, catalogue, preserve & display marine history items & artifacts of Queen Charlotte Islands history relating to logging, mining, homesteading
Finances: *Annual Operating Budget:* Less than $50,000; *Funding Sources:* Grant; BC Heritage Trust; Skeena-Queen Charlotte Regional District; Village of Port Clements
Staff Member(s): 1; 7 volunteer(s)
Membership: 16; *Fees:* $10 voting; $1 non-voting; $5 senior
Activities: *Library:* Documentation Centre & Archives; by appointment

Port Colborne Community Association for Research Extension
92 Charlotte St., Port Colborne ON L3K 3E1
Tel: 905-834-3629; *Fax:* 905-835-6600
Toll-Free: 888-370-8738
portcares@portcares.ca
www.portcares.on.ca
www.facebook.com/363577343725445
twitter.com/PortCares
Also Known As: PORT CARES
Overview: A small local charitable organization founded in 1986
Mission: To facilitate efforts to improve the quality of life for the residents of Port Colborne & region by undertaking initiatives & responding to identified community needs
Member of: Port Colborne/Wainfleet Chamber of Commerce
Finances: *Annual Operating Budget:* $500,000-$1.5 Million; *Funding Sources:* Government; Foundation grants; Donations; Fundraising
Staff Member(s): 35; 60 volunteer(s)
Membership: 90; *Fees:* $25 individual; $20 senior; $50 charity; $100 corporate; *Member Profile:* Residents of Port Colborne & district who subscribe to the principles & objectives of Port Cares; *Committees:* Board of Directors; Fundraising; Advisory; Youth Justice; Auction
Activities: *Library:* Open to public
Chief Officer(s):
Christine Clark Lafleur, Executive Director
christine.clarklafleur@portcares.ca

Port Colborne District Association for Community Living, Inc. *See* Community Living Port Colborne-Wainfleet

Port Colborne-Wainfleet Chamber of Commerce
76 Main St. West, Port Colborne ON L3K 3V2
Tel: 905-834-9765; *Fax:* 905-834-1542
office@pcwchamber.com
www.pcwchamber.com
www.facebook.com/118999308131584
twitter.com/PCWChamber
Overview: A small local organization founded in 1902
Mission: To promote the commercial, industrial, agricultural, educational & civic interests of Port Colborne & Wainfleet; To work for sound legislation & efficient administration of municipal, regional, provincial & federal governments
Member of: Niagara Regional Chambers of Commerce; Ontario Chamber of Commerce
Finances: *Funding Sources:* Membership dues; fundraising
Membership: *Fees:* Schedule available; *Member Profile:* Businesses & members of community
Activities: Golf Tournament, Meet the Reps Barbecue, Information Seminars; Training Sessions; Networking Events; Annual General Meeting; *Speaker Service:* Yes; *Library:* Open to public

Port Dover Board of Trade
PO Box 239, 19 Market St. West, Port Dover ON N0A 1N0

Tel: 519-583-1314; Fax: 519-583-3275
info@portdover.ca
www.portdover.ca
www.facebook.com/PortDoverBoardOfTrade
Overview: A small local organization founded in 1912
Mission: To improve the social & economic welfare of community
Finances: *Annual Operating Budget:* $100,000-$250,000; *Funding Sources:* Membership dues; festivals
Staff Member(s): 1
Membership: 235; *Fees:* $100-150; *Member Profile:* Business owners & community residents
Activities: Perch Derby; Dragon Boat Festival; Fish Fest; Summer Festival; Christmas Fest; free Sunday concerts in the park
Chief Officer(s):
Adam Veri, President

Port Elgin & District Chamber of Commerce *See* Saugeen Shores Chamber of Commerce

Port Elgin District Voluntary Action Group Inc. *See* PEDVAC Foundation

Port Hardy & District Chamber of Commerce
PO Box 249, 7250 Market St., Port Hardy BC V0N 2P0
Tel: 250-949-7622; Fax: 250-949-6653
Toll-Free: 866-427-3901
phccadm@cablerocket.com
www.porthardychamber.com
www.facebook.com/porthardychamber
twitter.com/visitporthardy
statigr.am/visitporthardy
Also Known As: Port Hardy Chamber of Commerce & Visitor Centre
Overview: A small local organization founded in 1975
Member of: BC Chamber of Commerce
Finances: *Funding Sources:* Membership fees
Staff Member(s): 3
Membership: *Fees:* Schedule available
Activities: *Library:* Open to public
Chief Officer(s):
Todd Landon, President
Carly Pereboom, Executive Director
manager@porthardychamber.com

Port Hardy Harvest Food Bank
PO Box 849, 7135 Market St., Port Hardy BC V0N 2P0
Tel: 250-902-0332; Fax: 250-902-0613
harvest9@telus.net
Overview: A small local charitable organization overseen by Food Banks British Columbia
Mission: The agency provides food to the needy in the local area.
Member of: Food Banks British Columbia
Chief Officer(s):
Suzanne Talitzaine, Contact

Port Hastings Historical Society
24 Hwy. 19, Port Hastings NS B9A 1M1
Tel: 902-625-1295
porthastingsmuseum@gmail.com
porthastingsmuseum.ca
Overview: A small local charitable organization founded in 1978
Mission: To collect, preserve, study, exhibit & interpret those objects that will best serve to illustrate the founding, settlement & development of the Strait area
Member of: Federation of the Nova Scotian Heritage; Council of Nova Scotia Archives; Iona Connection; Canadian Museums Association
Finances: *Funding Sources:* Nova Scotia Museum; fundraising; donations
Activities: *Library:* Genealogy Records; Open to public by appointment

Port Hawkesbury Chamber of Commerce *See* Strait Area Chamber of Commerce

Port Hope & District Chamber of Commerce
58 Queen St., Port Hope ON L1A 3Z9
Tel: 905-885-5519; Fax: 905-885-1142
info@porthopechamber.com
www.porthopechamber.com
www.linkedin.com/groups?gid=3675771
www.facebook.com/phchamber
Overview: A small local organization
Mission: To be dedicated to Port Hope's economic development & prosperity

Membership: *Fees:* Schedule available; *Committees:* Governance; Business & Education; Policy & Advocacy; Special Events; Membership Development; Young Professionals; Technology & Innovation
Activities: *Awareness Events:* Golf Tournament, Sept.
Chief Officer(s):
Doug Blundell, President, 905-269-7130
Bree Nixon, Manager
bnixon@porthopechamber.com
Awards:
• Business Excellence Awards
Publications:
• Port Hope & District Chamber of Commerce Newsletter
Type: Newsletter

Port Hope/Cobourg & District Association for Community Living *See* Community Living West Northumberland

Port McNeill & District Chamber of Commerce
PO Box 129, Port McNeill BC V0N 2R0
Tel: 250-230-9952
portmcneillchamber@gmail.com
www.portmcneill.net
Overview: A small local organization
Mission: To promote & improve trade & commerce & the economic, civic, & social welfare of the district
Member of: Tourism BC; BC Chamber of Commerce; Canadian Chamber of Commerce
Finances: *Annual Operating Budget:* Less than $50,000
Staff Member(s): 1
Membership: 100; *Fees:* $100-$200 business; $50 non-profit; $25 senior/student; *Committees:* Tourism; Primary Resources; Education; Retail/Services Sector; Membership; Website
Activities: Operating the Port McNeill Info Centre
Chief Officer(s):
Gaby Wickstrom, President
Cheryl Jorgenson, Manager

Port Moody Heritage Society
2734 Murray St., Port Moody BC V3H 1X2
Tel: 604-939-1648; Fax: 604-939-1647
info@portmoodymuseum.org
portmoodymuseum.org
www.facebook.com/Portmoodyheritagesociety
twitter.com/pomomuseum
www.instagram.com/pomomuseum
Also Known As: Port Moody Station Museum
Previous Name: Port Moody Historical Society
Overview: A small local charitable organization founded in 1969
Mission: To collect, preserve, display, research & educate regarding local artifacts
Finances: *Annual Operating Budget:* $50,000-$100,000
Staff Member(s): 3; 60 volunteer(s)
Membership: 150; *Fees:* $10 individual; $15 family; $75 corporate; $500 lifetime
Activities: Operating Port Moody Station Museum & archives; Library
Chief Officer(s):
Jim Millar, Executive Director
jim@portmoodymuseum.org
Publications:
• Tracks in Time: Port Moody's First 100 Years
Type: Book; *Accepts Advertising; Number of Pages:* 192; *Price:* $40 plus tax

Port Moody Historical Society *See* Port Moody Heritage Society

Port Moody Rock & Gem Club
300 Ioco Rd., Port Moody BC V3H 5M9
info@portmoody.rocks
www.portmoody.rocks
Overview: A small local organization founded in 1978
Member of: Port Moody Arts Centre Society; ArtsConnect; British Columbia Lapidary Society; Gem & Mineral Federation of Canada
Membership: *Fees:* $25 individuals; $45 families; *Member Profile:* Persons in the Port Moody British Columbia area who are interested in geology & the earth sciences as well as the hobbies of rock hunting, faceting, & lapidary
Activities: Offering weekly lapidary & faceting workshops; Hosting monthly meetings, except in July, August, & December; Arranging field trips; *Awareness Events:* Annual Rock & Gem Show, October
Chief Officer(s):
Andrew Danneffel, President, 604-323-4273

Port Morien Wildlife Association
c/o Robert Boutilier, 36 Second St., Birch Grove NS B1B 1L5
Tel: 902-577-6117
www.facebook.com/groups/40196002717
Overview: A small local organization
Mission: To promote responsible fishing, trapping, & hunting in order to conserve resources & maintain a healthy ecosystem
Membership: *Fees:* $10
Chief Officer(s):
Robert Boutilier, President

Port Renfrew Chamber of Commerce
PO Box 39, Port Renfrew BC V0S 1K0
Tel: 250-858-7665
www.renfrewchamber.com
Overview: A small local organization
Mission: To promote business in the area
Finances: *Annual Operating Budget:* $100,000-$250,000
9 volunteer(s)
Membership: 75; *Fees:* $80-$135
Chief Officer(s):
Dan Hager, President

Port Sydney/Utterson & Area Chamber of Commerce
#4, 15 South Mary Lake Rd., Port Sydney ON P0B 1L0
Tel: 705-385-1117; Fax: 705-385-9753
www.portsydneycoc.com
www.facebook.com/182339001818525
Overview: A small local organization
Mission: To support the business community
Member of: Canadian Chamber of Commerce; Ontario Chamber of Commerce
Membership: 100-499; *Fees:* Schedule available
Activities: Offering resources, advertising opportunities & networking events; Engaging in advocacy
Chief Officer(s):
Karen MacInnes, President

Portage & District Arts Council (PDAC)
11 - 2nd St. NE, Portage la Prairie MB R1N 1R8
Tel: 204-239-6029; Fax: 204-239-1472
pdac@mts.net
www.portageartscentre.ca
Previous Name: Portage La Prairie & District Arts Council
Overview: A small local charitable organization founded in 1977
Mission: To provide the opportunity for exposure & education in the arts; to stimulate & develop cultural projects & activities; to act as a clearinghouse for information on cultural projects & activities; to foster an interest & pride in the cultural heritage of the community; to interpret work of cultural groups to the community; to bring to the attention of the civic, provincial & federal authorities the cultural needs of the community
Member of: Manitoba Association of Community Arts Councils Inc.
Staff Member(s): 2; 130 volunteer(s)
Membership: 400 individual + 23 group/corporate + 2 lifetime; *Fees:* $20 student; $25 adult; $45 family; $55 group; *Committees:* Exhibition; Art Rental; Touring
Activities: Art classes; workshops; dance classes; art studios; monthly art exhibits & receptions; gallery events; members meetings; *Awareness Events:* Celebration of the Arts, May 9; Dance Recital, April 12; Art Craft Market, Nov. 2
Chief Officer(s):
Jazz de Montigny, Executive Director

Portage & District Chamber of Commerce *See* Portage la Prairie & District Chamber of Commerce

Portage Friendship Centre Inc. (PFC)
20 - 3rd St. NE, Portage la Prairie MB R1N 1N4
Tel: 204-239-6333; Fax: 204-856-2470
info@ptgfc.org
www.ptgfc.org
www.facebook.com/PortageFriendshipCentre
Previous Name: Portage La Prairie Friendship Centre
Overview: A small local organization founded in 1966
Staff Member(s): 12
Membership: *Fees:* $2
Chief Officer(s):
Jacqueline Stasiuk, President
Shirley Bernard, Executive Director
s_bernard@ptgfc.org

Portage Industrial Exhibition Association
PO Box 278, Portage la Prairie MB R1N 3B5

Tel: 204-857-3231; Fax: 204-239-1701
portagex@mts.net
www.portageex.com
Also Known As: Portage X
Overview: A small local organization founded in 1872
Mission: To assist in providing educational & social activities related to the agricultural industry in the community
Member of: Western Canada Fairs Association
Affiliation(s): Canadian Association of Exhibitions; Manitoba Association of Agricultural Societies
Finances: *Annual Operating Budget:* $50,000-$100,000; *Funding Sources:* Provincial government; fundraising activities; donations
Staff Member(s): 2; 60 volunteer(s)
Membership: 156 institutional

Portage La Prairie & District Arts Council *See* Portage & District Arts Council

Portage la Prairie & District Chamber of Commerce
56 Royal Rd. North, Portage la Prairie MB R1N 1V1
Tel: 204-857-7778; Fax: 204-856-5001
info@portagechamber.com
www.portagechamber.com
www.facebook.com/PortageLaPrairieDistrictChamberOfCommerce
Previous Name: Portage & District Chamber of Commerce
Overview: A medium-sized local charitable organization founded in 1889
Mission: To foster an environment which will enhance the commercial development of the district
Member of: Manitoba Chamber of Commerce
Affiliation(s): Canadian Chamber of Commerce
Finances: *Funding Sources:* Membership dues; events
Membership: 205; *Fees:* Schedule available based on number of employees; *Committees:* Welcome; Communication
Activities: Central Manitoba Trade Fair; Santa's Parade of Lights; Best Business Awards; Agriculture Appreciation Evening; *Library:* Resource Centre; Open to public
Chief Officer(s):
Dave Omichinski, President, 204-856-2704, Fax: 204-856-2710
Cindy McDonald, Executive Director

Portage La Prairie Friendship Centre *See* Portage Friendship Centre Inc.

Portage La Prairie Real Estate Board
39 Royal Rd., Portage la Prairie MB R1N 1T9
Tel: 204-857-4111
Overview: A small local organization overseen by Manitoba Real Estate Association
Member of: The Canadian Real Estate Association

Portage Plains United Way
PO Box 953, 20 Saskatchewan Ave. East, Portage la Prairie MB R1N 3C4
Tel: 204-857-4440; Fax: 204-239-1740
info@portageplainsuw.ca
www.portageplainsuw.ca
www.facebook.com/353759031400503
twitter.com/PortagePlainsUW
Overview: A small local charitable organization founded in 1968 overseen by United Way of Canada - Centraide Canada
Mission: To unite the community & enhance the quality of life for those in need
Finances: *Annual Operating Budget:* Less than $50,000; *Funding Sources:* Manitoba Lotteries
Staff Member(s): 2; 200 volunteer(s)
Membership: 15 agencies; *Committees:* Executive; Finance; Allocations; Special Events; Campaign
Activities: *Speaker Service:* Yes
Chief Officer(s):
Mandy Dubois, Executive Director
Jennifer Sneesby, Office Manager

Portfolio Management Association of Canada (PMAC)
#1210, 155 University Ave., Toronto ON M5H 3B7
Tel: 416-504-1118; Fax: 416-504-1117
info@portfoliomanagement.org
www.portfoliomanagement.org
www.linkedin.com/company/portfolio-management-association-of-canada
twitter.com/PMACnews
Previous Name: Investment Counsel Association of Canada
Overview: A medium-sized provincial organization founded in 1952
Mission: To represent the Investment Counsel & portfolio managers in Canada; To advocate high standards of unbiased portfolio management in the interest of investors
Membership: *Committees:* Practices & Standards; AGM; Industry, Regulation & Tax; Member Services; Public Relations & Liaisons; Operation Heads' Network; Compliance Officers' Network
Activities: Offering member networking services; Increasing public awareness of investment counselling & its benefits; Liaising with securities regulators & other government agencies
Chief Officer(s):
Katie Walmsley, President
kwalmsley@portfoliomanagement.org
Alex Stephen, Manager, Member Services
astephen@portfoliomanagement.org

Portuguese Assocation of Canada *See* Associaça Portuguesa Do Canadà

Portuguese Canadian Seniors Foundation
5455 Imperial St., Burnaby BC V5J 1E5
Tel: 604-873-2979; Fax: 604-873-2974
www.pcsf.ca
www.youtube.com/user/THEPCSF
Overview: A small local organization founded in 1987
Membership: 1,600
Chief Officer(s):
Maria Viegas Guerreiro, President

Portuguese Club of London
134 Falcon St., London ON N5W 4Z1
Tel: 519-453-4330
info@portuguesecluboflondon.com
www.portuguesecluboflondon.com
www.facebook.com/PortugueseClubLondon
twitter.com/PtClubLdn
Overview: A small local organization founded in 1976 overseen by Ontario Council of Agencies Serving Immigrants
Mission: To provide assistance, information, & orientation to the Portuguese-speaking communities to ensure full participation in Canadian society & equal access to service respecting uniqueness of their culture & tradition; To assist the Portuguese community in integration with new social, cultural, & political environment
Finances: *Annual Operating Budget:* $50,000-$100,000
Staff Member(s): 3; 30 volunteer(s)
Membership: 550; *Fees:* $50 individual; $100 family; *Committees:* Personnel; Social
Activities: Counselling; educational workshops
Chief Officer(s):
Durvalina Teodoro, President

Portuguese Interagency Network (PIN)
pin002000@yahoo.com
portugueseintnetwork.tripod.com
Overview: A small provincial charitable organization founded in 1978
Finances: *Annual Operating Budget:* Less than $50,000
Staff Member(s): 1; 42 volunteer(s)
Membership: 40; *Fees:* $10 individual; $20 agency; *Member Profile:* Individuals & agencies who are concerned with the provision of services to Portuguese speaking Canadians in Ontario; *Committees:* Elderly; Youth; Health; Fundraising
Activities: Community development; needs assessment; public education; consulting body; information & referral centre

posAbilities Association of BC
#240, 4664 Lougheed Hwy., Burnaby BC V5C 5T5
Tel: 604-299-4001; Fax: 604-299-0329
info@posAbilities.ca
www.posabilities.ca
www.facebook.com/posAbilitiesCA
twitter.com/posAbilitiesCA
Previous Name: Mainstream Association for Proactive Community Living
Overview: A small local organization founded in 1968
Finances: *Annual Operating Budget:* Greater than $5 Million
Staff Member(s): 700; 60 volunteer(s)
Membership: 100; *Fees:* $5; *Member Profile:* Parents; selfadvocates; professionals
Activities: Accredited housing; day programs; recreation; socialization; *Awareness Events:* Annual Art Show, Oct.
Chief Officer(s):
Fernando Coelho, CEO
Celso A. A. Boscariol, President

A Post Psychiatric Leisure Experience (APPLE)
Bronson Center, 211 Bronson Ave., Ottawa ON K1R 6H5
Tel: 613-238-1209; Fax: 613-238-5806
contact_apple@hotmail.com
www.appledropin.com
www.facebook.com/appledropin
Overview: A small local organization founded in 1981
Mission: To enhance the quality of life for their members by offering support & activities; to prevent hospitalization of their members
Membership: 350; *Fees:* Free; *Member Profile:* Former & current mental health patients

Post Traumatic Stress Disorder Association
93 Dufferin Ave., Toronto ON N6A 1K3
Tel: 604-525-7566; Fax: 604-525-7586
info@ptsdassociation.com
ptsdassociation.com
Overview: A small provincial charitable organization
Mission: To empower individuals suffering from Post Traumatic Stress Disorder through education, linkages with appropriate services, facilitation of research and discovery into the causation.
Chief Officer(s):
Roméo A. Dallaire, O.C., C.M.M., G, Honorary Chair
Ute Lawrence-Fisher, President & Founder

Positive Living BC
803 East Hastings St., Vancouver BC V6A 1R8
Tel: 604-893-2200; Fax: 604-893-2251
Toll-Free: 800-994-2437
info@positivelivingbc.org
www.positivelivingbc.org
www.facebook.com/positivelivingbc
twitter.com/pozlivingbc
Previous Name: British Columbia Persons with AIDS Society
Overview: A small provincial charitable organization founded in 1986
Mission: To empower persons in British Columbia who live with HIV/AIDS
Member of: CAS; CAAN; Red Road HIV/AIDS Society; BC Health Coalition; Canadian HIV/AIDS Legal Network
Finances: *Annual Operating Budget:* $3 Million-$5 Million; *Funding Sources:* Donations; Fundraising
Staff Member(s): 32; 238 volunteer(s)
Membership: 5,700+; *Fees:* Free; *Member Profile:* Persons in British Columbia living with AIDS & HIV disease; *Committees:* Board & Volunteer Development; Community Representation & Engagement; Communications & Education; Health Promotion; Membership Development; Support Services
Activities: Engaging in advocacy activities (E-mail: advdesk@positivelivingbc.org); Providing support services (E-mail: support@positivelivingbc.org); Offering information about treatment; Conducting prison outreach services (E-mail: pop@positivelivingbc.org); Providing educational opportunities; Organizing awareness campaigns; Promoting health & wellness; *Awareness Events:* AccodAIDS, Apr.; AIDS Walk for Life, Sept.; Red Ribbon Breakfast, Nov.; *Internships:* Yes; *Speaker Service:* Yes
Chief Officer(s):
Neil Self, Chair
Tom McAulay, Vice-Chair
Awards:
• AccolAIDS Awards
Categories include science, research, & technology, the hero award, philanthropy, innovative programs & services, social, political, & community action, the media award, & health promotion & harm reduction
Publications:
• British Columbia Persons with AIDS Society Annual Report
Type: Yearbook; *Frequency:* Annually
• British Columbia Persons with AIDS Society HIV/AIDS eNewslist
Type: Newsletter; *Frequency:* Weekly
• eScoop [a publication of Positive Living BC]
Type: Newsletter; *Frequency:* Bimonthly
• Living+ [a publication of Positive Living BC]
Type: Magazine
Profile: Current issues encountered by those infected & affected by HIV/AIDS
• Positive Living Manual
Type: Manual
Profile: Information for BCPWA members, interested individuals, PWAs, AIDS service organizations, & health care workers

Positive Living North: No kheyoh t'sih'en t'sehena Society (PLN)
#1, 1563 - 2nd Ave., Prince George BC V2L 3B8
Tel: 250-562-1172; *Fax:* 250-562-3317
Toll-Free: 888-438-2437
www.positivelivingnorth.ca
www.facebook.com/103410213083441
Previous Name: Prince George AIDS Prevention Program; AIDS Prince George; Prince George AIDS Society
Overview: A small local organization founded in 1992 overseen by Canadian AIDS Society
Mission: To provide services to people live with HIV & their families; 75 per cent of PLN's clients are of Aboriginal descent
Staff Member(s): 29
Activities: Fire Pit Cultural Centre; social support; advocacy; crisis intervention; personal & group support; support for substance abuse issues; support team services; health information; grief & loss support; education & prevention services; *Awareness Events:* AIDS Walk for Life, Sept.; Smithers Camera Project
Chief Officer(s):
Vanessa West, Executive Director
Publications:
• Common Threads [a publication of Positive Living North]
Type: Newsletter; *Frequency:* Quarterly

Positive Women's Network (PWN)
#614, 1033 Davie St., Vancouver BC V6E 1M7
Tel: 604-692-3000; *Fax:* 604-684-3126
Toll-Free: 866-692-3001
pwn@pwn.bc.ca
www.pwn.bc.ca
www.facebook.com/Positivewomensnetwork
twitter.com/pwn_bc
Overview: A small local charitable organization founded in 1989 overseen by Canadian AIDS Society
Mission: Challenging HIV, Changing Women's Lives
Member of: Pacific AIDS Network; Canadian HIV/AIDS Legal Network
Finances: *Annual Operating Budget:* $250,000-$500,000; *Funding Sources:* ACAP; Provincial Health Services Authority; donations
Staff Member(s): 11
Membership: *Fees:* Free; *Member Profile:* Women living with HIV/AIDS
Activities: Support programs; drop-in centre; food bank; retreats; lunch program; support groups; education; health promotion resources; *Awareness Events:* AIDS Walk, Sept.
Chief Officer(s):
Marcie Summers, Executive Director
marcies@pwn.bc.ca

Positive Youth Outreach (PYO)
399 Church St., 4th Fl., Toronto ON M5B 2J6
Tel: 416-340-8484
pyo@actoronto.org
www.actoronto.org/home.nsf/pages/positiveyouthoutreach
Overview: A small local organization founded in 1990 overseen by Canadian AIDS Society
Mission: To provide education, support, advocacy & referral to all youth living with HIV/AIDS regardless of the mode of transmission
Member of: AIDS Committee of Toronto; Ontario AIDS Network
Finances: *Funding Sources:* Ontario Ministry of Health
Activities: Support & discussion groups; workshop; peer support; community outreach; leadership development; *Speaker Service:* Yes

Postal History Society of Canada (PHSC)
PO Box 562, Stn. B, Ottawa ON K1P 5P7
phscdb@postalhistorycanada.net
www.postalhistorycanada.net
Previous Name: Postal History Society of Ontario
Overview: A medium-sized national organization founded in 1972
Mission: To promote the study of postal history of Canada
Affiliation(s): American Philatelic Society; British North America Philatelic Society
Finances: *Annual Operating Budget:* Less than $50,000
Membership: 700 institutional; *Fees:* $15 e-membership; $35 regular membership
Activities: Online database of provincial post offices; *Library:* by appointment
Chief Officer(s):
Chris Green, Contact

Postal History Society of Ontario *See* Postal History Society of Canada

Postpartum Depression Association of Manitoba (PPDAM)
MB
info@ppdmanitoba.ca
www.ppdmanitoba.ca
Overview: A small provincial organization
Mission: PPDAM is committed to helping Manitoba families get connected with the help dealing with postpartum depression or related illnesses through education, awareness and resources.

Post-Polio Awareness & Support Society of BC (PPASS/BC)
#222, 2453 Beacon Ave., Sidney BC V8L 1X7
Tel: 250-655-8849; *Fax:* 250-655-8859
ppass@ppassbc.com
www.ppassbc.com
Overview: A medium-sized provincial charitable organization founded in 1986
Mission: To develop awareness, communication & education between society & community; To disseminate information concerning research & treatment about Post-Polio Syndrome; To support polio survivors other than through direct financial aid
Finances: *Annual Operating Budget:* $50,000-$100,000; *Funding Sources:* Membership fees; donations; bingo
Membership: 1,950; *Fees:* $20 BC resident; $25 others; *Member Profile:* Polio survivors & their friends; *Committees:* Public Relations
Activities: Special Water Exercise Program; *Speaker Service:* Yes; *Library:* Open to public
Chief Officer(s):
Joan Toone, President

Post-Polio Network Manitoba Inc. (PPN-MB)
c/o SMD Self-Help Clearinghouse, 825 Sherbrook St., Winnipeg MB R3A 1M5
Tel: 204-975-3037; *Fax:* 204-975-3027
postpolionetwork@gmail.com
www.postpolionetwork.ca
Overview: A small provincial charitable organization founded in 1986
Mission: To serve as a support group & information centre for polio survivors throughout Manitoba, especially those suffering from post-polio syndrome; To acquaint the medical community & those responsible for government services as to the nature & extent of the problems associated with the late effects of polio
Member of: Society of Manitobans with Disabilities
Affiliation(s): Polio Canada; SMD - Fostering Growth & Clearinghouse of Self-Help Organizations
Finances: *Funding Sources:* Membership fees; bequests; Grey Cup tickets
Membership: *Fees:* $15; *Member Profile:* Polio survivors; their families; health care professionals; *Committees:* Programming; Publicity; Funding; Privacy & Fire Safety; Phoning
Activities: *Library:* SMD Library; Not open to public
Chief Officer(s):
Cheryl Currie, President
Donna Remillard, Treasurer
Estelle Boissonneault, Secretary

Potato Growers of Alberta (PGA)
6008 - 46 Ave., Taber AB T1G 2B1
Tel: 403-223-2262; *Fax:* 403-223-2268
pga@albertapotatoes.ca
www.albertapotatoes.ca
www.facebook.com/174598775914665
twitter.com/AlbertaPotatoes
www.youtube.com/user/albertapotatoes
Previous Name: Alberta Potato Marketing Board
Overview: A small provincial licensing organization founded in 1968
Mission: To create success in Alberta's potato industry by supporting sustainable production, marketing, development & cooperation
Member of: Canadian Horticultural Council; Alberta Food Processors Association; Canadian Produce Marketing Association
Affiliation(s): Calgary Produce Marketing Association; Canadian Snack Foods Association
Finances: *Annual Operating Budget:* $500,000-$1.5 Million
Staff Member(s): 6; 27 volunteer(s)
Membership: 150; *Fees:* $50; *Member Profile:* Commercial/seed/table growers; *Committees:* Alberta Crop Insurance; Alberta Seed Potato Grower; Negotiating; Research; Table Fresh
Activities: Promoting & researching potatoes & potato products; policy development for potato farmers; *Awareness Events:* Potato Month, Feb.; *Speaker Service:* Yes
Chief Officer(s):
Terence Hochstein, Executive Director

Potatoes New Brunswick / Pommes de terre Nouveau-Brunswick
PO Box 7878, Grand Falls NB E3Z 3E8
Tel: 506-473-3036; *Fax:* 506-473-4647
gfpotato@potatoesnb.com
www.potatoesnb.com
www.facebook.com/newbrunswickpotatoes
Previous Name: New Brunswick Potato Agency
Overview: A medium-sized provincial organization founded in 1979
Mission: To work in close collaboration with industry partners in advocating, coordinating, promoting, negotiating, & leading growth & development of New Brunswick potato producers
Member of: Canadian Horticultural Council
Membership: 400 individual
Chief Officer(s):
Joe Brennan, Chair
Matt Hemphill, Executive Director
Robert Corriveau, Director, Finance
Gisele Beardsley, Bookkeeper & Translator
Meetings/Conferences:
• New Brunswick Potato Conference & Trade Show 2018, 2018, NB
Scope: Provincial
Description: An event for New Brunswick potato growers & interested stakeholders to present happening in the industry
Contact Information: E-mail: gfpotato@potatoesnb.com
Grand Falls
PO Box 7878, Grand Falls NB E3Z 3E8
Tel: 506-473-3036; *Fax:* 506-473-4647
gfpotato@potatoesnb.com
www.potatoesnb.com
www.facebook.com/newbrunswickpotatoes
twitter.com/POTATOESNB
Chief Officer(s):
Matt Hemphill, Executive Director

Pouce Coupe & District Museum & Historical Society
PO Box 83, 5006 - 49 St., Pouce Coupe BC V0C 2C0
Tel: 250-786-5555
pcmuseum@pris.ca
www.facebook.com/209995319062226
Overview: A small local charitable organization founded in 1972
Mission: To collect artifacts, pioneer histories & displays in order to preserve heritage of Pouce Coupe & district
Member of: BC Museums Association
Finances: *Annual Operating Budget:* Less than $50,000; *Funding Sources:* Government grants; museum fundraising
12 volunteer(s)
Membership: 20; *Fees:* $5
Activities: Monthly meetings; fundraising; community events

Poultry Industry Council (PIC)
483 Arkell Rd., Puslinch ON N0B 2J0
Tel: 519-837-0284; *Fax:* 519-837-3584
pic@poultryindustrycouncil.ca
www.poultryindustrycouncil.ca
twitter.com/PoultryIndCou
Previous Name: Ontario Poultry Council
Overview: A medium-sized provincial organization
Mission: To foster life-long learning programmes for members of the poultry industry; To foster research initiatives
Staff Member(s): 3
Membership: 250; *Fees:* $150 individual; $400 corporate; *Committees:* Fundraising; Research; Special Events; Communications
Activities: Poultry Health Conference; London Poultry Show
Chief Officer(s):
Keith Robbins, Executive Director

Powell River & District Labour Council
6239 Walnut St., Powell River BC V8A 4K4
Tel: 604-483-9800; *Fax:* 604-483-3369
Overview: A small local organization
Chief Officer(s):
Ron Van't Schip, President
skippies@shaw.ca

Powell River & District United Way
PO Box 370, #205, 4750 Joyce Ave., Powell River BC V8A 5C2

Tel: 604-485-2791
admin@unitedwayofpowellriver.ca
www.unitedwayofpowellriver.ca
www.facebook.com/322827261966
twitter.com/PRUnitedway
Overview: A small local charitable organization founded in 1976 overseen by United Way of Canada - Centraide Canada
Finances: *Annual Operating Budget:* $100,000-$250,000; *Funding Sources:* Donations
29 volunteer(s)
Membership: 11
Chief Officer(s):
Ashley Hull, President
hullashley@gmail.com

Powell River Chamber of Commerce
6807 Wharf St., Powell River BC V8A 2T9
Tel: 604-485-4051
office@powellriverchamber.com
www.powellriverchamber.com
www.facebook.com/188501364559861
Overview: A medium-sized local licensing organization founded in 1933
Member of: British Columbia Chamber of Commerce; Canadian Chamber
Staff Member(s): 2
Activities: To promote & enhance trade, commerce & the civil well-being of the Powell River communities; *Library:* Open to public
Chief Officer(s):
Jack Barr, President
Kim Miller, General Manager
Awards:
• Horizon Business Awards

Powell River Lapidary Club
2544 Dixon Rd., Powell River BC V8A 5C1
Tel: 604-487-0444
Overview: A small local organization
Affiliation(s): British Columbia Lapidary Society; Gem & Mineral Federation of Canada
Membership: *Member Profile:* Persons in the Powell River region of British Columbia who are interested in the hobbies of lapidary & wire wrapping
Activities: Hosting monthly meetings
Chief Officer(s):
Belinda Fogarty, President, 604-485-2141

Powell River Sunshine Coast Real Estate Board
PO Box 307, Powell River BC V8A 5C2
Tel: 604-485-6944; *Fax:* 604-485-6944
Overview: A small local organization overseen by British Columbia Real Estate Association
Chief Officer(s):
Geri Powell, Board Administrator

Power Workers' Union (PWU)
244 Eglinton Ave. East, Toronto ON M4P 1K2
Tel: 416-481-4491; *Fax:* 416-481-7115
Toll-Free: 800-958-8798
pwu@pwu.ca
www.pwu.ca
Overview: A large provincial organization founded in 1944
Affiliation(s): Canadian Union of Public Employees; Canadian Labour Congress; Ontario Federation of Labour; Labourers International Union of North America; Canadian Union of Skilled Workers
Staff Member(s): 31
Membership: 15,000-49,999; *Member Profile:* Individuals who work in the power production industry in Ontario
Chief Officer(s):
Mel Hyatt, President
mhyatt@pwu.ca
Andrew Clunis, Vice President, Sector 1
aclunis@pwu.ca
Jeff Parnell, Vice President, Sector 2
jparnell@pwu.ca
Tom Chessell, Vice President, Sector 3
tchessell@pwu.ca

Prader-Willi Syndrome Association of Alberta
9006 - 120 St. NW, Edmonton AB T6G 1X7
Tel: 780-459-1959
Other Communication: 403-217-8587 (Calgary); 403-340-1057 (Red Deer)
www.pwsaa.ca
Also Known As: PWSA of AB

Overview: A small provincial charitable organization founded in 1986
Mission: To advocate for individuals affected by Prader-Willi Syndrome; To improve the quality of life for affected individuals
Affiliation(s): Canadian Prader-Willi Syndrome Association
Finances: *Funding Sources:* Donations; Fundraising; Membership fees
Membership: *Fees:* $20 families; *Member Profile:* Parents, relatives, & support workers of individuals affected by Prader-Willi Syndrome
Activities: Raising awareness & knowledge of Prader-Willi Syndrome; *Awareness Events:* Prader-Willi Syndrome Association of Alberta Walk-a-thon, June
Chief Officer(s):
Lise Dunn, Contact, Edmonton
lisedunn@shaw.ca
Brooke Gibson, Contact, Calgary
brookergibson@gmail.com
Jill Hockin, Contact, Red Deer
reddeerbean@shaw.ca
Publications:
• Prader-Willi Syndrome Association of Alberta Newsletter
Type: Newsletter
Profile: Association reports, stories, & events

Pragmora
#107, 283 Danforth Ave., Toronto ON M4K 1N2
Tel: 416-778-6142
pragmora@pragmora.com
www.pragmora.com
www.facebook.com/pragmora
twitter.com/pragmora
Overview: A small international organization
Mission: To achieve peace through the development of pragmatic, non-violent solutions to armed & violent conflicts around the world
Activities: *Speaker Service:* Yes
Chief Officer(s):
Glenys Babcock, President
Guy Charlton, Vice-President
Salim Binbrek, Secretary
Adam Jackson, Treasurer

Prairie Agricultural Machinery Institute (PAMI)
PO Box 1150, 2215 - 8th Ave., Humboldt SK S0K 2A0
Tel: 306-682-5033; *Fax:* 306-682-5080
Toll-Free: 800-567-7264
humboldt@pami.ca
www.pami.ca
www.linkedin.com/company/2603883
www.facebook.com/PAMIMachinery
twitter.com/PAMI_Machinery
Overview: A medium-sized local charitable organization founded in 1974
Mission: To serve manufacturers & farmers in Manitoba & Saskatchewan's agricultural sector through applied research, development, & testing
Affiliation(s): Manitoba Ministry of Agriculture, Food, & Rural Initiatives; Saskatchewan Ministry of Agricultue
Finances: *Funding Sources:* Fee-for-service work; Government
Staff Member(s): 45
Activities: *Library:* Prairie Agricultural Machinery Institute Research Library
Chief Officer(s):
David Gullacher, President & CEO
Publications:
• Direct Seeding Manual: A Farming System for the New Millennium
Price: $50 Manitoba, Saskatchewan, & Alberta; $55 elsewhere
• The Rancher's Guide to Elk & Bison Handling Facilities
Type: Book; *Number of Pages:* 35; *Price:* $20 Canada; $25 international
• The Stockman's Guide to Range Livestock Watering from Surface Sources
Type: Book; *Number of Pages:* 36; *Price:* $10 Canada; $12 international
Profile: Includes a workbook
Portage la Prairie
PO Box 1060, 390 River Rd., Portage la Prairie MB R1N 3C5
Tel: 204-857-4811; *Fax:* 204-239-7124
portage@pami.ca
Chief Officer(s):
Harvey Chorney, Vice-President, Manitoba Operations

Prairie Apparel Market
PO Box 55065, Stn. Dakota Crossing, Winnipeg MB R2N 0A8

Tel: 204-973-3256; *Fax:* 204-947-0561
Overview: A medium-sized provincial organization overseen by Canadian Association of Wholesale Sales Representatives
Mission: To sell women's & children's apparel
Chief Officer(s):
Dan Kelsch, President
dkelsch@mymts.net

Prairie Conservation Forum
c/o Southern Region, Alberta Environment, 200 - 5th Ave. South, 2nd Fl., Lethbridge AB T1J 4L1
Tel: 403-381-5562; *Fax:* 403-382-4428
info@albertapcf.org
www.albertapcf.org
Overview: A small local organization
Mission: Conservation of native prairie & parkland environments in Alberta
Activities: Alberta Prairie Conservation Action Plan
Chief Officer(s):
Bill Dolan, Chair
bill.dolan@gov.ab.ca

Prairie Fruit Growers Association (PFGA)
PO Box 2430, Altona MB R0G 0B0
Tel: 204-324-5058; *Fax:* 204-324-5058
pfga@xplornet.com
www.pfga.com
Overview: A small local organization founded in 1974
Mission: To educate members, access quality planting stock, direct research & develop markets
Member of: North American Berry Association
Finances: *Annual Operating Budget:* $100,000-$250,000
Staff Member(s): 1
Membership: 115; *Fees:* $195

Prairie Implement Manufacturers Association; PIMA - Agricultural Manufacturers of Canada *See* Agricultural Manufacturers of Canada

Prairie Music Alliance *See* Western Canadian Music Alliance

Prairie Osteopathic Association
1603 - 20 Ave NW, Calgary AB T2M 1G9
Tel: 403-282-7165; *Fax:* 403-289-8269
Overview: A small provincial organization
Affiliation(s): Canadian Osteopathic Association
Chief Officer(s):
C.E. (Ted) Findlay, President

Prairie Provinces Forestry Association *See* Manitoba Forestry Association Inc.

Prairie Region Halfway House Association (PRHHA)
PO Box 45007, Stn. Inglewood, Calgary AB T2G 5H7
prhha.net
Overview: A small provincial organization overseen by Regional Halfway House Association
Mission: To help offenders reintegrate themselves into society
Member of: Region Halfway House Association
Chief Officer(s):
Pamela Gaudette, Executive Director, 403-969-4967
pam@prhha.net

Prairie Rock & Gem Society (PRGS)
2467 Swayze Cres., Regina SK S4V 1A4
Tel: 306-529-9834
www.prairierockandgem.info
Overview: A small provincial organization founded in 1955
Mission: To promote rockhounding & lapidary
Member of: Gem & Mineral Federation of Canada
Membership: *Member Profile:* Persons of all ages who like rocks & the hobby of lapidary
Activities: Hosting monthly meeting from September to June; Offering a fully equipped workshop; Organizing field trips; Providing educational programs; *Awareness Events:* Prairie Rock & Gem Society Annual Show & Sale *Library:* Prairie Rock & Gem Society Resource Library
Chief Officer(s):
Joan Riemer, Contact, 306-545-7111
jriemer@myaccess.ca

Prairie Saengerbund Choir Association
4823 Claret St. NW, Calgary AB T2L 1B9
Tel: 403-284-3731; *Fax:* 403-284-1470
Overview: A medium-sized local charitable organization founded in 1977
Mission: To share, enhance, encourage & celebrate German musical heritage

Finances: *Funding Sources:* Grants; self support
Membership: *Member Profile:* German choirs in the prairie provinces in Canada
Activities: Organizing biennial song festival of Prairie choirs (German)
Awards:
• 25 Year Member of the Choir
• Singer of the Year

Prairie Theatre Exchange (PTE)
Portage Place, #Y300, 393 Portage Ave., 3rd Fl., Winnipeg MB R3B 3H6
Tel: 204-942-7291; *Fax:* 204-942-1774
www.pte.mb.ca
www.facebook.com/423687680006
twitter.com/PrairieTheatre
Overview: A medium-sized provincial charitable organization founded in 1972
Mission: To operate a professional theatre of high calibre for the entertainment & edification of a broad spectrum of people; To operate a school to encourage appreciation of theatre & to provide accessible, high quality, innovative drama education; To support the development of new plays; To foster theatre arts-related endeavours of others through use of our facilities & expertise; To manage one or more community theatre arts centres
Member of: Professional Association of Canadian Theatres; Canadian Actors' Equity Association; Canadian Conference of the Arts; Cultural Human Resources Council
Affiliation(s): Canadian Institute of Theatre Technology
Finances: *Annual Operating Budget:* $500,000-$1.5 Million; *Funding Sources:* Earned revenue; Canada Council; Manitoba Arts Council; fundraising; City of Winnipeg; The Winnipeg Foundation; individual & corporate donations
Staff Member(s): 17; 180 volunteer(s)
Membership: 3,800; *Member Profile:* Subscribers; Donors; Volunteers; Students (or parents) of PTE school; *Committees:* Executive; Finance; Special Events; Fundraising
Activities: Conducting a theatre & film school for ages 6 & up; Offering outreach services; Producing 5 adult plays & 1 play for youths
Chief Officer(s):
Dwayne Marling, President
Tracey Loewen, General Manager
generalmgr@pte.mb.ca

Prairie West Historical Society Inc.
PO Box 910, 946 - 2nd St. SE, Eston SK S0L 1A0
Tel: 306-962-3772
Overview: A small local charitable organization founded in 1981
Mission: To educate & entertain visitors with the history of the Eston area; To collect, preserve, organize, & exhibit artifacts
Finances: *Funding Sources:* Donations; Grants
Activities: Operating a museum, consisting of a restored farmhouse, the Lovedale Schoolhouse, the Acadia school barn, & a Homesteader's shack, with artifacts, photographs, & documentation from the local area; Providing heritage programs for students; Offering research services; *Library:* Prairie West Historical Society Archives; Open to public by appointment

Prairieaction Foundation
#300, 2303 - 4 St. SW, Calgary AB T2S 2S7
Toll-Free: 877-926-8129
info@prairieaction.ca
www.prairieaction.ca
Overview: A small provincial charitable organization
Mission: To support & disseminate research into violence & abuse solutions; To promote anti-violence & anti-abuse education & awareness programs; To support the Research & Education for Solutions to Violence & Abuse (RESOLVE) research network
Activities: Offering grant programs; Funding research projects in all prairie provinces
Awards:
• Youth Leadership Award
Awarded to groups of young people who raise awareness about abuse & violence as well as promote safe relationships in their schools & communities *Deadline:* November

Presbyterian Church in Canada (PCC) / Église presbytérienne au Canada
50 Wynford Dr., Toronto ON M3C 1J7
Tel: 416-441-1111; *Fax:* 416-441-2825
Toll-Free: 800-619-7301
presbyterian.ca
www.facebook.com/pcconnect
twitter.com/pcconnect
youtube.com/presvideo
Overview: A large national organization founded in 1875
Mission: To proclaim the love & good news of Jesus Christ through words & actions
Member of: The Canadian Council of Churches; World Alliance of Reformed Churches; World Council of Churches; Action By Churches Together; Ecumenical Advocacy Alliance
Finances: *Funding Sources:* Congregations
Membership: 125,509; *Member Profile:* Presbyteries; Congregations; Communicants on roll; Ministers; *Committees:* Assembly Council; Committee to Advise with the Moderator
Activities: *Library:* Knox College & Presbyterian College Libraries; Open to public
Chief Officer(s):
Stephen Kendall, Principal Clerk, General Assembly Office, 416-441-1111 Ext. 227
skendall@presbyterian.ca
Don Muir, Deputy Clerk, General Assembly Office, 416-441-1111 Ext. 223
dmuir@presbyterian.ca
Frances Hogg, Secretary, General Assembly Office, 416-441-1111 Ext. 224
fhogg@presbyterian.ca
Oliver Ng, CFO & Treasurer, Financial Services, 416-441-1111 Ext. 316
ong@presbyterian.ca
Matthew Goslinkski, Coordinator, Life & Mission Agency, 416-411-1111 Ext. 247
mgoslinski@presbyterian.ca
Awards:
• Presbyterian Woman of Faith Award
To recognize the courageous and faithful work of women within the church. *Eligibility:* Any woman who is or has been part of The Presbyterian Church in Canada; Lay, elders, diaconal ministers or ordained clergy
Publications:
• Presbyterian Record [a publication of Presbyterian Church in Canada]
Type: Magazine; *Editor:* Andrew Faiz

Prescott & Russell Association for Community Living *See* Valoris for Children & Adults of Prescott-Russell

Prescott Board of Trade; Prescott Chamber of Commerce; Prescott and District Chamber of Commerce *See* South Grenville Chamber of Commerce

Prescott Group
3430 Prescott St., Halifax NS B3K 4Y4
Tel: 902-454-7387; *Fax:* 902-453-0275
Other Communication: Human Resources e-mail:
prescotthr@eastlink.ca
prescottgroup@eastlink.ca
prescottgroup.ca
www.facebook.com/337804192957428
twitter.com/PrescottGroupNS
Overview: A small local organization
Mission: To provide work skills & employment opportunities to adults with intellectual disabilities, in order to build independence
Member of: Halifax Adult Services Society; DIRECTIONS Council for Vocational Services Society
Finances: *Funding Sources:* Donations; sponsors; government
Activities: Operates the Atlantic Bag, Fireside Kitchen & Prescott Mailing Services businesses
Chief Officer(s):
Mona Reeves, Chair
Susan Slaunwhite, Executive Director

Préservation du bois Canada *See* Wood Preservation Canada

La presse canadienne *See* The Canadian Press

La Presse spécialisée du Canada *See* Canadian Business Press

Presse universitaire canadienne *See* Canadian University Press

Preventative Social Services Association *See* Family & Community Support Services Association of Alberta

Préventex - Association paritaire du textile
1936, rue Rossignol, Brossard QC J4X 2C6
Tél: 450-671-6925; *Téléc:* 450-671-9267
www.preventex.qc.ca
Nom précédent: Association paritaire pour la santé et la sécurité du travail - Textiles primaires
Aperçu: *Dimension:* moyenne; *Envergure:* provinciale; fondée en 1983
Mission: Amener les employeurs et les travailleurs du secteur à prendre charge activement de la prévention des accidents du travail et des maladies professionnelles
Membre(s) du personnel: 8
Activités: Formation; information; conseil et assistance technique; hygiène industrielle; ergonomie; *Service de conférenciers:* Oui
Membre(s) du bureau directeur:
François Lauzon, Co-président
Daniel Vallée, Co-président

Prevention CDN/NDG
5319, av Notre-Dame-de-Grâce, Montréal QC H4A 1L2
Courriel: info@preventionndg.org
www.preventionndg.org
Aperçu: *Dimension:* petite; *Envergure:* locale; fondée en 1988
Mission: To offer human resources as well as tools to increase their quality of life, at home, in the borough as well as in the community in general, focusing on crime prevention & environmental issues.

PRIDE - People to Reduce Impaired Driving Everywhere (Ontario) *See* MADD Canada

Pride Centre of Edmonton
10608 - 105 Ave., Edmonton AB T5H 0L2
Tel: 780-488-3234; *Fax:* 780-482-2855
exec@pridecentreofedmonton.org
www.pridecentreofedmonton.org
www.facebook.com/34126834504
twitter.com/yegpridecentre
Previous Name: Gay & Lesbian Community Centre of Edmonton
Overview: A small local organization founded in 2004
Mission: To provide a place where gay men, lesbians, bisexuals & transgendered may meet together in peace & harmony; to provide peer support to individuals in need in a lesbian, gay, bisexual & transgendered community; to act when requested as education & information resource for any person; to foster sense of community among gay men, lesbians, bisexual women & men & transgendered
Finances: *Funding Sources:* Fundraising; membership dues
Staff Member(s): 3
Activities: Edmonton Gay & Lesbian Archives; *Speaker Service:* Yes; *Library*
Chief Officer(s):
Mickey Wilson, Executive Director

Pride of Israel
59 Lissom Cres., Toronto ON M2R 2P2
Tel: 416-226-0111; *Fax:* 416-226-0128
office@prideofisraelshul.org
www.prideofisraelshul.org
Overview: A small local organization founded in 1905
Finances: *Funding Sources:* Donations
Activities: Offering a Kosher Food Bank; Providing Jewish educational programming
Chief Officer(s):
Steven Bloom, Chair
chairman@prideofisraelshul.org
Sean Gorman, Rabbi
rabbi@prideofisraelshul.org
Bonnie Moatti, Coordinator, Membership
Publications:
• Shabbat Matters [a publication of Pride of Israel]
Type: Newsletter; *Accepts Advertising*
Profile: Articles & forthcoming activities
• Shul Matters [a publication of Pride of Israel]
Type: Newsletter; *Accepts Advertising*
Profile: Articles & forthcoming activities

The Primate's World Relief & Development Fund (PWRDF) / Le fonds du Primat pour le secours et le développement mondial
Anglican Church of Canada, 80 Hayden St., Toronto ON M4Y 3G2
Tel: 416-924-9192; *Fax:* 416-924-3483
Toll-Free: 866-308-7973
Other Communication: www.flickr.com/photos/45005153@N07
pwrdf@pwrdf.org
www.pwrdf.org
www.facebook.com/111501932203731
twitter.com/PWRDF
www.youtube.com/user/PWRDF

Overview: A small international charitable organization founded in 1959
Mission: To connect Anglicans in Canada to communities around the world in dynamic partnerships to advance development, to respond to emergencies, to assist refugees, and to act for positive change
Member of: Canadian Council for International Cooperation; Action by Churches Together (ACT)
Affiliation(s): Canadian Council of Churches
Finances: Annual Operating Budget: Greater than $5 Million; Funding Sources: Anglican Church contributions
Staff Member(s): 16; 2000 volunteer(s)
Activities: Library: Resource Centre - Anglican Church of Canada; Open to public
Chief Officer(s):
Fred Hiltz, Archbishop & Primate
Will Postma, Executive Director
wpostma@pwrdf.org

Prince Albert & District Association of Realtors
615 Branion Dr., Prince Albert SK S6V 2R9
Tel: 306-764-8755; Fax: 306-763-0555
pareb@sasktel.net
www.princealbertrealtors.ca
Previous Name: Prince Albert Real Estate Board
Overview: A small local organization founded in 1959 overseen by Saskatchewan Real Estate Association
Mission: To support realtors in the Prince Albert Real Estate community.
Member of: The Canadian Real Estate Association
Staff Member(s): 1
Membership: 11
Activities: Internships: Yes
Chief Officer(s):
Candy Marshall, Executive Officer

Prince Albert & District Chamber of Commerce
3700 - 2nd Ave. West, Prince Albert SK S6W 1A2
Tel: 306-764-6222; Fax: 306-922-4727
chamberpa@sasktel.net
www.princealbertchamber.com
www.facebook.com/PrinceAlbertandDistrictChamberOfCommerce
twitter.com/ChamberPA
Overview: A small local organization founded in 1887
Mission: To enhance the economic & social conditions of Prince Albert & area
Member of: Regional Economic Development Alliance; Tourism & Convention Bureau; Saskatchewan Outfitters Association
Affiliation(s): Canadian Chamber of Commerce; Saskatchewan Chamber of Commerce
Finances: Annual Operating Budget: $100,000-$250,000; Funding Sources: Membership dues; fundraising
Staff Member(s): 3
Membership: 489; Fees: Schedule available; Committees: Finance; Government & Affairs; Human Resources; Investment & Growth; Membership
Chief Officer(s):
Gordon Jahn, Chair
Larry Fladager, CEO

Prince Albert & District Labour Council
107 - 8th St. East, Prince Albert SK S6V 0V8
Tel: 306-763-2303
palabourcouncil@sasktel.net
Overview: A small local organization overseen by Saskatchewan Federation of Labour
Mission: To promote the interests of affiliates in Prince Albert, Saskatchewan, & the surrounding district; To advance the economic & social welfare of workers
Affiliation(s): Canadian Labour Congress (CLC)
Activities: Organizing rallies to voice concerns of local workers; Liaising with local elected officials to present workers' issues; Presenting educational opportunities; Raising awareness about occupational health & safety; Organizing events, such as a ceremony on the International Day of Mourning for Workers Killed and Injured on the Job
Chief Officer(s):
Craig Thebaud, President, 306-764-0194
craigthebaud@gmail.com

Prince Albert Exhibition Association (PAEX)
PO Box 1538, 815 Exhibition Dr., Prince Albert SK S6V 5T1
Tel: 306-764-1711; Fax: 306-764-5246
paex@sasktel.net
www.paexhibition.com
www.facebook.com/paexhibition
twitter.com/pa_exhibition
Previous Name: Lorne Agricultural & Industrial Society
Overview: A small local charitable organization founded in 1883
Mission: To engage in activities which reflect the non-profit organization's motto, "Where Town & Country Meet"
Affiliation(s): Saskatchewan Association of Agricultural Societies & Exhibitions (SAASE)
Finances: Funding Sources: Sponsorships
Activities: Hosting a summer fair; Awareness Events: Summer Fair
Chief Officer(s):
Shirley Collins, Manager
Brandi Slywka, Administrator & Event Coordinator

Prince Albert Gliding & Soaring Club (PAG&SC)
219 Scissons Ct., Saskatoon SK S7S 1B7
Tel: 306-789-1535; Fax: 306-792-2532
soar@soar.sk.ca
www.soar.sk.ca/pagsc
Overview: A small local organization founded in 1986
Mission: To foster the sport of soaring
Affiliation(s): Soaring Association of Saskatchewan; Soaring Association of Canada
Finances: Funding Sources: Annual membership dues; Launch fees; Glider rental fees
Membership: 15; Fees: $85 youth; $170 regular
Activities: Promoting the sport of soaring; Providing flying activities; Offering flight instruction
Chief Officer(s):
Keith Andrews, President, 306-249-1859

Prince Albert Indian & Métis Friendship Centre See Indian & Metis Friendship Centre of Prince Albert

Prince Albert Model Forest Association Inc. (PAMF)
PO Box 2406, Prince Albert SK S6V 7G3
Tel: 306-953-8921; Fax: 306-763-6456
www.pamodelforest.sk.ca
Overview: A small provincial organization founded in 1992
Mission: To work towards sustainable forest management through development & testing of new forest management tools, sharing our successes, developing linkages & expanding the PAMF partnership
Member of: Saskatchewan Forestry Association; Canadian Model Forest Network; International Model Forest Network
Affiliation(s): University of Saskatchewan; University of Regina
Finances: Annual Operating Budget: $250,000-$500,000; Funding Sources: Canadian Forest Service; partners; grants
Staff Member(s): 2
Membership: Committees: Science & Technology; Communications & Outreach; Beyond our Boundaries; Planning & Operations
Activities: Applied research in sustainable forestry; technology transfer of research findings; Library: PAMF Reference Library; Open to public
Chief Officer(s):
Susan Carr, General Manager
susan.carr@sasktel.net

Prince Albert Real Estate Board See Prince Albert & District Association of Realtors

Prince Albert Tourism & Convention Bureau Inc. See Tourism Prince Albert

Prince County Hospital Foundation (PCHF)
PO Box 3000, 65 Roy Boates Ave., Summerside PE C1N 2A9
Tel: 902-432-2547; Fax: 902-432-2551
info@pchcare.com
www.pchcare.com
www.facebook.com/PCHFoundation
twitter.com/PCHFoundation
Overview: A medium-sized local charitable organization
Mission: To raise money for Prince County Hospital in order to keep up with medical equipment needs
Finances: Funding Sources: Donations; Fundraising
Staff Member(s): 4
Activities: Awareness Events: Grassroots & Cowboys Fundraiser, September; Women's Golf Classic Fundraiser, September; Lights for Life Fundraiser, December
Chief Officer(s):
Heather Matheson, Managing Director
hematheson@ihis.org
Bevan Woodacre, Officer, Communications
bdwoodacre@ihis.org
Lisa Schurman-Smith, Manager, Finance & Administration
leschurman@ihis.org
Kelly Arsenault, Administrator, Database
kmarsenault@ihis.org

Prince Edward Association for Community Living See Community Living Prince Edward (County)

Prince Edward County Arts Council (PECAC)
PO Box 6180, Picton ON K0K 2T0
Tel: 613-476-8767
info@pecartscouncil.org
www.pecartscouncil.org
Overview: A small local charitable organization founded in 1979
Mission: To enrich the life of the community by encouraging artists & artisans & their work & by promoting our arts community both as an important part of the fabric of life in the county & beyond its shores
Membership: Fees: Schedule available
Activities: Maker's Hand, Nov.; Art in the County, June/July; Jazz Festival, Aug.; Music Festival, Sept.; Awareness Events: Art in the County, June; Clic Photo Show, July; The Maker's Hand, October

Prince Edward County Chamber of Tourism & Commerce (PECCTAC)
116 Main St., Picton ON K0K 2T0
Tel: 613-476-2421; Fax: 613-476-7461
Toll-Free: 800-640-4717
www.pecchamber.com
www.facebook.com/PECChamber
Overview: A small local organization
Mission: To support members; To interact with policy makers & address issues affecting members; To promote a strong economic environment; To encourage economic development
Affiliation(s): Bay of Quinte Tourist Council; Business Improvement Area Association; Canadian Chamber of Commerce; Ontario Chamber of Commerce; Picton Business Improvement Association; Prince Edward County Federation of Agriculture; Wellington & District Business Association
Membership: 300; Fees: $150; $100 non-profit
Chief Officer(s):
Emily Cowan, Executive Director

Prince Edward Historical Society
c/o Prince Edward County Archives, 261 Main St., Wellington ON K0K 3L0
pehistsoc.wordpress.com
www.facebook.com/PrinceEdwardHistoricalSociety
twitter.com/PEHistSoc
Overview: A small local organization founded in 1899
Mission: To promote & preserve the history of the county
Member of: Archives Association of Ontario
Membership: Fees: $20 individual; $30 family
Chief Officer(s):
Steve Ferguson, President

Prince Edward Island Alpine Ski Association
PO Box 2026, Charlottetown PE C1A 7N7
Tel: 902-368-4110; Fax: 902-368-4548
Toll-Free: 800-247-6712
sports@sportpei.pe.ca
www.sportpei.pe.ca
Overview: A medium-sized provincial organization overseen by Sport PEI

Prince Edward Island Amateur Baseball Association See Baseball PEI

Prince Edward Island Amateur Boxing Association
PE
Overview: A medium-sized provincial organization overseen by Canadian Amateur Boxing Association
Member of: Canadian Amateur Boxing Association

Prince Edward Island Aquaculture Alliance (PEIAA)
101 Longworth Ave., 1st Fl., Charlottetown PE C1A 5A9
Tel: 902-368-2757; Fax: 902-626-3954
peiaqua@aquaculturepei.com
www.aquaculturepei.com
Merged from: PEI Cultured Mussel Growers Association, Island Oyster Growers Group & the PEI Finfish Association
Overview: A medium-sized provincial organization founded in 1998
Mission: To provide focus for the Prince Edward Island aquaculture industry; To enhance industry prosperity through its development as an effective world competitor
Member of: Canadian Aquaculture Industry Alliance

Finances: *Annual Operating Budget:* $100,000-$250,000; *Funding Sources:* Government; industry
Staff Member(s): 3
Membership: 130+; *Fees:* $100 seed; $250 supplier; $1000 supporting; $75 associate; *Member Profile:* Mussel, oyster, clam & finfish culturists in PEI; Companies that supply goods & services to these industries
Activities: Co-Host of International PEI Shellfish Festival; Co-Host of Great Atlantic Shellfish Exchange
Chief Officer(s):
Peter Warris, Coordinator, Research & Development
rd@aquaculturepei.com
Sharon Gilbank, Manager, Accounts & Officer
peiaqua@aquaculturepei.com
Publications:
• Soundings [a publication of the Prince Edward Island Aquaculture Alliance]
Type: Newsletter; *Frequency:* Quarterly

Prince Edward Island Association for Community Living (PEIACL)
13A Myrtle St., Stratford PE C1B 1P4
Tel: 902-393-3507
familysupport@peiacl.org
www.peiacl.org
www.facebook.com/PEIACL
twitter.com/PEIACL
www.youtube.com/channel/UCR951HZ9Ah9xD6VjYTsb8mQ
Overview: A medium-sized provincial charitable organization founded in 1955 overseen by Canadian Association for Community Living
Mission: To work on behalf of individuals with an intellectual disability & their families; To empower families to increase options available to Islanders with an intellectual disability
Member of: Canadian Association for Community Living; Prince Edward Island Literacy Alliance
Staff Member(s): 3
Membership: *Fees:* Free
Activities: *Speaker Service:* Yes; *Library:* PEI ACL Resource Library; Open to public
Chief Officer(s):
Bridget Cairns, Executive Director
executivedirector@peiacl.org

Prince Edward Island Association for Newcomers to Canada (PEI ANC)
49 Water St., Charlottetown PE C1A 1A3
Tel: 902-628-6009; *Fax:* 902-894-4928
www.peianc.com
Overview: A medium-sized provincial organization founded in 1993
Mission: To provide immigrants to Prince Edward Island with short-term settlement services & community integration programs
Member of: Prince Edward Island Literacy Alliance Inc.
Finances: *Funding Sources:* Citizenship & Immigration Canada; Service Canada; Government of Prince Edward Island; Health Canada
Activities: Increasing cross-cultural awareness; Providing public education programs; Offering training & resources to service providers & government departments; Conducting life skills training for immigrants; Engaging in advocacy activities; *Speaker Service:* Yes; *Library:* PEI ANC Resource Library
Chief Officer(s):
Craig Mackie, Executive Director
Myra Thorkelson, President
Dan Doran, Secretary-Treasurer
Publications:
• PEI ANC [Prince Edward Island Association for Newcomers to Canada] Annual Report
Type: Yearbook; *Frequency:* Annually

Prince Edward Island Association of Exhibitions (PEIAE)
Royalty Centre, PO Box 2000, #237, 40 Enman Cres., Charlottetown PE C1E 1E6
Tel: 902-368-4848; *Fax:* 902-368-5651
peiexhibitions@gov.pe.ca
peiae.ca
www.facebook.com/PEIAE
twitter.com/peiexhibitions
Overview: A small provincial licensing organization founded in 1973
Member of: Canadian Association of Fairs & Exhibitions; Intl. Association of Fairs & Exhibitions
Finances: *Annual Operating Budget:* $250,000-$500,000
Staff Member(s): 2
Membership: 1-99
Chief Officer(s):
Adele Moore, Executive Director

Prince Edward Island Association of Family Resource Programs
c/o Family Place, 75 Central St., Summerside PE C1N 3L2
Tel: 902-436-1348; *Fax:* 902-888-3954
familyplace@eastlink.ca
Overview: A medium-sized provincial organization
Chief Officer(s):
Laura Quinn Graham, Contact

Prince Edward Island Association of Medical Radiation Technologists (PEIAMRT)
60 Riverside Dr., Charlottetown PE C1A 8T5
peiamrt@gmail.com
www.peiamrt.com
Overview: A small provincial organization founded in 1982 overseen by Canadian Association of Medical Radiation Technologists
Mission: To act in accordance with the Public Health Act, "Radiation Safety Regulations"; To promote excellence in health care
Membership: *Member Profile:* Persons from Prince Edward Island who are involved in the following professions: nuclear medicine, magnetic resonance, radiation therapy, & radiological technology (including bone mineral densitometry, computed tomography, & mammography)
Activities: Offering continuing professional development; Providing public education; Partnering with allied health professionals to meet goals
Chief Officer(s):
Tyler Ferrish, President
tjferrish@ihis.org
Susan Colwill, Registrar
Meetings/Conferences:
• PEI Association of Medical Radiation Technologists 2018 AGM & Education Day, 2018, PE
Scope: Provincial

Prince Edward Island Association of Optometrists (PEIAO)
PO Box 1812, Charlottetown PE C1A 7N5
Tel: 902-566-4418; *Fax:* 902-566-4694
peiregistrar@peisympatico.ca
www.peioptometrists.ca
Previous Name: Prince Edward Island Optometrical Association
Overview: A medium-sized provincial organization founded in 1922 overseen by Canadian Association of Optometrists
Mission: To promote the professional interests of optometrists in Prince Edward Island Association; To improve optometrists' proficiency
Membership: *Member Profile:* Optometrists in Prince Edward Island
Activities: Encouraging continuing education for optometrists in Prince Edward Island; Disseminating information about optometry; Collaborating with other optometry associations & professional bodies
Chief Officer(s):
Jayne Toombs, President
Susan Judson, Vice-President
Alanna Stetson, Secretary
Joe E. Hickey, Treasurer

Prince Edward Island Association of Social Workers (PEIASW) / Association des travailleurs sociaux de l'Ile-du-Prince-Édouard
81 Prince St., Charlottetown PE C1A 4R3
Tel: 902-368-7337; *Fax:* 902-368-7180
contact@peiasw.ca
peiasw.ca
Overview: A small provincial organization overseen by Canadian Association of Social Workers
Mission: To acknowledge & promote the work of social workers in Prince Edward Island; To advance the social work profession throughout the province, to ensure well-being for residents
Member of: Canadian Association of Social Workers
Membership: *Member Profile:* Social workers in Prince Edward Island
Activities: *Awareness Events:* Social Work Month, March
Chief Officer(s):
Kelly MacWilliams, President

Prince Edward Island Association of the Appraisal Institute of Canada *See* The Appraisal Institute of Canada - Prince Edward Island

Prince Edward Island Automobile Dealers Association
PO Box 22004, Charlottetown PE C1A 9J2
Tel: 902-566-3639; *Fax:* 902-368-7116
peiada@eastlink.ca
Overview: A small provincial organization
Member of: Canadian Automobile Dealers Association
Chief Officer(s):
Lisa Doyle-MacBain, Manager

Prince Edward Island Badminton Association
c/o Sport PEI, PO Box 302, 40 Enman Cres., Charlottetown PE C1N 7K7
Tel: 902-368-4262; *Fax:* 902-368-4548
badm.pei@gmail.com
badmintonpei.weebly.com
Also Known As: Badminton PEI
Overview: A small provincial organization founded in 1987 overseen by Badminton Canada
Mission: To promote & develop badminton in Prince Edward Island
Activities: Organizing tournaments
Chief Officer(s):
Nancy MacKinnon, President

Prince Edward Island Baseball Umpires Association (PEIBUA)
PE
Tel: 902-367-0564
peibua@gmail.com
www.peibua.com
Overview: A small provincial organization
Mission: To represent certified amateur baseball umpires in the province of PEI.
Activities: *Library:* Open to public
Chief Officer(s):
Kent Walker, Supervisor of Officials
kentwalker019@gmail.com
Awards:
• Mutual Official of the Year Award
• Senior Official of the Year Award
• Junior Official of the Year Award

Prince Edward Island Beekeepers' Cooperative Association
4686 Rte. 17, Montague PE C0A 1R0
Tel: 902-651-8405
Overview: A small provincial organization
Mission: To promote beekeeping throughout Prince Edward Island; To provide education & information to members
Membership: *Member Profile:* Beekeepers from Prince Edward Island
Activities: Undertaking regional studies related to bees, beeswax, honey, & pollen
Chief Officer(s):
John Burhoe, President

Prince Edward Island Building & Construction Trades Council
326 Patterson Dr., Charlottetown PE C1A 8K4
Tel: 902-894-4269
Overview: A small provincial organization
Member of: AFL-CIO
Chief Officer(s):
Blair MacKinnon, President

Prince Edward Island Business Women's Association (PEIBWA)
#25, 25 Queen St., Charlottetown PE C1A 4A2
Tel: 902-892-6040; *Fax:* 902-892-6050
Toll-Free: 866-892-6040
office@peibwa.org
www.peibwa.org
www.linkedin.com/company-beta/2715049
www.facebook.com/PEIBWA
twitter.com/peibwa
www.instagram.com/peibwa
Overview: A medium-sized provincial organization
Mission: To assist women in business & help them to succeed by providing services & programs
Member of: Prince Edward Island Literacy Alliance Inc.
Membership: 420; *Fees:* $25 student; $78.75 small business; $157.50 business; $262.50 patron

Chief Officer(s):
Hannah Bell, Executive Director
hannah@peibwa.org
Shannon Pratt, Program Manager
shannon@peibwa.org

Prince Edward Island Canoe Kayak Association
RR#4, Alliston, Montague PE C0A 1R0
Tel: 902-962-3883; *Fax:* 902-962-3883
www.facebook.com/235534456533194
Overview: A small provincial organization overseen by CanoeKayak Canada
Member of: CanoeKayak Canada
Chief Officer(s):
Justin Richard Batten, President
justin.heidi@windsinc.com

Prince Edward Island Cattle Producers (PEICP)
420 University Ave., Charlottetown PE C1A 7Z5
Tel: 902-368-2229; *Fax:* 902-367-3082
cattlemen@eastlink.ca
www.peicattleproducers.com
Previous Name: P.E.I. Cattlemen's Association
Overview: A medium-sized provincial organization founded in 1976
Mission: To support the beef industry in Prince Edward Island; To ensure a responsible production of safe, quality beef; To foster a profitable industry
Member of: Canadian Cattlemen's Association (CCA)
Finances: *Funding Sources:* Mandatory levies; Membership fees
Membership: 550+; *Fees:* Levies collected by processing facilities or a $5 membership fee; *Member Profile:* Prince Edward Island beef producers
Activities: Representing the beef industry in Prince Edward Island; Providing education
Chief Officer(s):
Peter Verleun, Chair
Rinnie Bradley, Executive Director
Justin Lawless, Coordinator, Atlantic Verified Beef Program
Brian Morrison, Secretary-Treasurer
Publications:
• Beef Newsletter
Type: Newsletter
Profile: Timely information for Prince Edward Island's beef producers
• PEI Cattle Producers Annual Report with Financial Statements
Type: Yearbook; *Frequency:* Annually

Prince Edward Island Cerebral Palsy Association Inc.
PO Box 22034, Charlottetown PE C1A 9J2
Tel: 902-892-9694; *Fax:* 902-628-8751
info@peicpa.com
www.peicpa.com
Also Known As: Cerebral Palsy Association of PEI
Overview: A small provincial charitable organization founded in 1953
Mission: To promote individuals with cerebral palsy & their abilities; To advocate for individuals with cerebral palsy; To provide resources, activities & services
Member of: United Way of PEI; Atlantic Cerebral Palsy Asociation
Activities: *Speaker Service:* Yes; *Library:* by appointment

Prince Edward Island Certified Organic Producers Co-op
PO Box 1776, #110, 420 University Ave., Charlottetown PE C1A 7Z5
Tel: 902-894-9999
Toll-Free: 866-850-9799
www.organicpei.com
www.facebook.com/organicpei
Overview: A medium-sized provincial organization founded in 2002
Mission: To increase organic production, research and market development; invite growers into the organic industry and promote and educate Islanders about organic food.
Membership: 34; *Fees:* $25; *Member Profile:* Certified organic agriculture producers
Activities: Farmers Market
Chief Officer(s):
Fred Dollar, President

Prince Edward Island Chiropractic Association (PEICA)
#280, 119 Kent St., Charlottetown PE C1A 1N3
Tel: 902-892-4454; *Fax:* 902-892-4454
dtownchiro@pei.aibn.com
Overview: A small provincial organization overseen by Canadian Chiropractic Association
Mission: To represent the chiropractic profession in Prince Edward Island; To advance the chiropractic profession in the province; To encourage high standards of service; To protect the residents of Prince Edward Island from unqualified individuals acting as chiropractors
Membership: *Member Profile:* Chiropractors in Prince Edward Island
Activities: Raising public awareness of the chiropractic profession in Prince Edward Island; Encouraging continuing education
Chief Officer(s):
Christopher McCarthy, Registrar

Prince Edward Island College of Physiotherapists (PEICP)
PO Box 20078, Charlottetown PE C1A 9E3
Fax: 902-739-3051
contact@peicpt.com
www.peicpt.com
Overview: A small provincial licensing organization overseen by Canadian Alliance of Physiotherapy Regulators
Mission: To regulate the practice of physiotherapy on Prince Edward Island, in accordance with the provincial legislation, "Physiotherapy Act"; To protect the public by ensuring competent & ethical practice
Member of: Canadian Alliance of Physiotherapy Regulators
Membership: *Fees:* $250
Activities: Setting standards of care for physiotherapists; Registering physiotherapists

Prince Edward Island Colt Stakes Association
c/o PEI Harness Racing Industry Association, #204A, 420 University Ave., Charlottetown PE CIA 7L1
Tel: 902-569-1682; *Fax:* 902-569-1827
peracing@eastlink.ca
Previous Name: Prince Edward Island Harness Racing Club
Overview: A small provincial organization founded in 1934
Member of: Prince Edward Island Harness Racing Industry Association
Finances: *Funding Sources:* Prince Edward Island governments
Activities: Sponsoring the Prince Edward Island Colt Stakes, the oldest standardbred stakes races in Canada; Sponsoring a summer camp for children; Forming a history committee to document the history of the association & to arrange a permanenet historical exhibit
Chief Officer(s):
Wayne Pike, Executive Director, PEI Harness Racing Industry Association

Prince Edward Island Convention Partnership; Meetings Prince Edward Island; Prince Edward Island Convention Bureau See Meetings & Conventions Prince Edward Island

Prince Edward Island Council of People with Disabilities (PEICOD)
Landmark Plaza, #2, 5 Lower Malpeque Rd., Charlottetown PE C1E 1R4
Tel: 902-892-9149; *Fax:* 902-566-1919
Toll-Free: 888-473-4263
peicod@peicod.pe.ca
www.peicod.pe.ca
www.facebook.com/PEICOD
Overview: A small provincial charitable organization founded in 1974
Mission: To improve the quality of life of people with disabilities on PEI
Member of: Prince Edward Island Literacy Alliance Inc.
Finances: *Funding Sources:* Provincial & federal governments; United Way
Activities: Accessibility guides; Sourcebook; Employment Counselling & Services Program; information & referral; advocacy; Computer Recycle Program; Snoezelen Room - recreational environment for children with disabilities; *Speaker Service:* Yes; *Library:* Open to public
Chief Officer(s):
Marcia Carroll, Executive Director

Prince Edward Island Crafts Council (PEICC)
PO Box 20071, Stn. Sherwood, Charlottetown PE C1A PE3
Tel: 902-892-5152; *Fax:* 902-628-8740
info@peicraftscouncil.com
peicraftscouncil.com
www.facebook.com/peicraftscouncil
twitter.com/PECraftsCouncil
Overview: A small provincial organization founded in 1965
Mission: To promote the making & acceptance of quality handcrafted items through the provision of programs & services
Member of: Canadian Crafts Federation; Canadian Conference of the Arts
Finances: *Funding Sources:* Provincial government; projects; The Island Craft Shop
Membership: *Fees:* Schedule available
Activities: The Islands Crafts Shop; scholarships; workshops; Craft Fair; Loan Program; equipment rental; handcraft bags
Chief Officer(s):
Suzanne Scott, President
Laura Cole, Executive Director

Prince Edward Island Curling Association (PEICA)
40 Enman Cres., Charlottetown PE C1E 1E6
Tel: 902-368-4208; *Fax:* 902-368-4548
info@peicurling.com
www.peicurling.com
www.facebook.com/peicurling
twitter.com/peicurling
Overview: A medium-sized provincial organization overseen by Canadian Curling Association
Mission: To advance & promote curling as a competitive & recreational sport in Prince Edward Island
Affiliation(s): Sports PEI, Curl Atlantic
Chief Officer(s):
Amy Duncan, Executive Director
aduncan@sportpei.pe.ca

Prince Edward Island Dietetic Association (PEIDA)
c/o Prince Edward Island Dietitians Registration Board, PO Box 362, Charlottetown PE C1A 7K7
peidietitians@gmail.com
www.peidietitians.ca
www.facebook.com/peidieteticassociation
Overview: A small provincial organization founded in 1965 overseen by Dietitians of Canada
Mission: To promote, encourage & improve the status of dietitians & nutritionists in the province of PEI; To promote & increase the knowledge & proficiency of its members in all matters relating to nutrition & dietetics; To promote public awareness
Finances: *Annual Operating Budget:* Less than $50,000
Activities: *Rents Mailing List:* Yes
Chief Officer(s):
Doreen Pippy, President

Prince Edward Island Draft Horse Association (PEIDHA)
PE
info@peidrafthorse.com
peidrafthorse.com
Overview: A small provincial organization
Mission: To promote draft horses in Prince Edward Island
Membership: 1-99
Activities: Participating in shows; Providing information about draft horses
Chief Officer(s):
Chris MacGillivray, President
president@peidrafthorse.com
Ron Newcombe, Vice-President
vice.president@peidrafthorse.com
Dianne Delaney, Secretary
secretary@peidrafthorse.com

Prince Edward Island Eco-Net (PEIEN)
#216, 40 Enman Cres., Charlottetown PE C1E 1E6
Tel: 902-566-4170; *Fax:* 902-566-4037
network@eastlink.ca
www.facebook.com/peieconet
Also Known As: Prince Edward Island Environmental Network
Overview: A medium-sized provincial organization founded in 1990 overseen by Canadian Environmental Network
Mission: To promote communication & cooperation among ENGO's (Environmental NGO's) & between ENGO's & governments; to provide referral services; to coordinate workshops & conferences; to provide consultations; to publish & distribute information
Finances: *Annual Operating Budget:* Less than $50,000
Membership: 29; *Fees:* $25
Activities: *Speaker Service:* Yes; *Library*
Chief Officer(s):
Matthew McCarville, Executive Director

Canadian Associations / Prince Edward Island Federation of Agriculture (PEIFA)

Prince Edward Island Federation of Agriculture (PEIFA)
#110, 420 University Ave., Charlottetown PE C1A 7Z5
Tel: 902-368-7289; *Fax:* 902-368-7204
www.peifa.ca
www.facebook.com/peifederationofagriculture
Overview: A medium-sized provincial organization founded in 1941 overseen by Canadian Federation of Agriculture
Mission: To provide a united voice for Island farmers
Finances: *Annual Operating Budget:* $100,000-$250,000
Staff Member(s): 4
Membership: 500-999
Chief Officer(s):
Mary Robinson, President
Robert Godfrey, Executive Director

Prince Edward Island Federation of Foster Families
281 Kent St., Charlottetown PE C1A 1P4
Tel: 902-963-3888; *Fax:* 902-963-3888
Overview: A small provincial charitable organization
Mission: To provide support & information to families in West Prince region involved in providing foster care.
Chief Officer(s):
Wendi James Poirier, President
wenp@live.ca

Prince Edward Island Federation of Labour / Fédération du travail de l'Ile-du-Prince-Édouard
326 Patterson Dr., Charlottetown PE C1A 8K4
Tel: 902-368-3068
peifed@pei.aibn.com
www.peifl.ca
Overview: A medium-sized provincial organization founded in 1964 overseen by Canadian Labour Congress
Member of: Prince Edward Island Literacy Alliance Inc.
Chief Officer(s):
Carl Pursey, President

Prince Edward Island Fencing Association (PEIFA)
c/o Sport PEI, PO Box 302, 40 Enman Cres., Charlottetown PE C1A 7K7
Tel: 902-368-4110; *Fax:* 902-386-4548
Toll-Free: 800-247-6712
sports@sportpei.pe.ca
people.upei.ca/fencing/main.htm
Overview: A small provincial organization overseen by Canadian Fencing Federation
Mission: To promote & develop the sport of fencing in PEI
Member of: Sport PEI
Membership: *Fees:* $25 student; $200 regular
Chief Officer(s):
Phil Stewart, Contact, 902-566-1073
pstewart@pei.sympatico.ca

Prince Edward Island Fishermen's Association Ltd. (PEIFA)
#102, 420 University Ave., Charlottetown PE C1A 7Z5
Tel: 902-566-4050; *Fax:* 902-368-3748
Other Communication: Alt. URL: www.tastepeilobster.ca
adminpeifa@pei.eastlink.ca
www.peifa.org
Also Known As: PEI Fishermen's Association
Overview: A small provincial organization
Mission: To represent fishermen across Prince Edward Island; To act as a single, united voice on behalf of Island fishers on industry issues
Membership: *Fees:* $105; *Member Profile:* Prince Edward Island fishers from the following Locals: Central Northumberland Strait Fishermen's Association (CNSFA), Eastern Kings Fishermen's Association (EKFA), North Shore Fishermen's Association (NSFA), Prince County Fishermen's Association (PCFA), Southern Kings & Queens Fishermen's Association (SKQFA), & Western Gulf Fishermen's Association (WGFA)
Activities: Liaising with government; Facilitating networking opportunities; Collaborating with fisher organizations in other provinces
Chief Officer(s):
Craig Avery, President, 902-887-3883
hcraigavery@gmail.com
Ian MacPherson, Manager
managerpeifa@pei.eastlink.ca

Prince Edward Island Five Pin Bowlers Association Inc.
c/o Sport PEI, PO Box 302, Charlottetown PE C1A 7K7
Tel: 902-368-4110; *Fax:* 902-368-4548
Toll-Free: 800-247-6712
sports@sportpei.pe.ca
www.sportpei.pe.ca
Overview: A medium-sized provincial organization founded in 1981

Prince Edward Island Flying Association
250 Brackley Point Rd., Charlottetown PE C1A 6Y9
Tel: 902-368-3008
www.facebook.com/PEIFlying
Overview: A small provincial organization founded in 1983
Membership: *Fees:* $48.15 single; $58.85 family
Publications:
• PEI Flying Association Newsletter
Type: Newsletter

Prince Edward Island Forest Improvement Association (PEIFIA)
RR#1, York-Covehead PE C0A 1P0
Tel: 902-672-2114
Previous Name: Prince Edward Island Silvicultural Contractors Association
Overview: A medium-sized provincial organization overseen by Canadian Forestry Association
Finances: *Annual Operating Budget:* Less than $50,000
Staff Member(s): 1; 17 volunteer(s)
Membership: *Fees:* $40 individual; $30 associate
Activities: Umbrella organization of PEI forest-related groups
Chief Officer(s):
Wanson Hemphill, Contact
wm.hemphill@pei.sympatico.ca

Prince Edward Island Forestry Training Corp.
Covehead Rd., RR#1, York PE C0A 1P0
Tel: 902-672-2114
Overview: A small provincial organization
Chief Officer(s):
Wanson Hemphill, General Manager

Prince Edward Island Funeral Directors & Embalmers Association
PO Box 540, Kensington PE C0B 1M0
Tel: 902-836-3313; *Fax:* 902-836-4461
Overview: A small provincial organization founded in 1958
Mission: To ensure professional services of the highest standards
Affiliation(s): Funeral Service Association of Canada
Membership: *Member Profile:* Funeral directors & embalmers in Prince Edward Island

Prince Edward Island Genealogical Society Inc. (PEIGS)
PO Box 2744, Charlottetown PE C1A 8C4
peigs_queries@yahoo.ca
www.peigs.ca
Overview: A small provincial charitable organization founded in 1976
Mission: To encourage & promote the study of family history in PEI; to collect & preserve local genealogical & historical records & materials; to foster education in genealogical research
Member of: Canadian Federation of Genealogical & Family History Societies
Affiliation(s): Genealogy Institute of the Maritimes
Membership: *Fees:* $25

Prince Edward Island Gerontological Nurses Association (PEIGNA)
PE
www.cgna.net/PEIGNA.html
Overview: A medium-sized provincial organization founded in 2004 overseen by Canadian Gerontological Nursing Association
Mission: To promote a high standard of nursing care & related health services for older adults; To enhance professionalism in the practice of gerontological nursing
Activities: Offering professional networking opportunities; Providing professional development; Advocating for comprehensive services for older adults; Supporting research related to gerontological nursing; Promoting gerontological nursing to the public
Chief Officer(s):
Elaine E. Campbell, President
eecampbell@ihis.org

Prince Edward Island Golf Association (PEIGA)
PO Box 51, Charlottetown PE C1A 7K2
Tel: 902-393-3293
peiga@peiga.ca
www.peiga.ca
www.facebook.com/PEIGolfAssociation
twitter.com/PEIGolfAssoc
Overview: A small provincial organization founded in 1971 overseen by Golf Canada
Mission: To be the governing body of amateur golf in the province
Staff Member(s): 1; 32 volunteer(s)
Chief Officer(s):
Brenda McIlwaine, President
Ron MacNeill, Executive Director

Prince Edward Island Ground Water Association
PO Box 857, RR#2, Cornwall PE C0A 1H0
Tel: 902-675-2360; *Fax:* 902-675-2360
Overview: A small provincial organization
Mission: To promote the protection of ground water in Prince Edward Island
Activities: Encouraging education about ground water resources
Chief Officer(s):
Watson MacDonald, Contact

Prince Edward Island Harness Racing Club *See* Prince Edward Island Colt Stakes Association

Prince Edward Island Harness Racing Industry Association (PEIHRIA)
#204A, 420 University Ave., Charlottetown PE C1A 7Z5
Tel: 902-569-1682; *Fax:* 902-569-1827
peracing@isn.net
www.peiharnessracing.com/hria.html
Overview: A small provincial organization founded in 1999
Mission: To establish the financial stability & future viability of Prince Edward Island's harness racing industry; To provide a unified approach to the industry & sport of harness racing; To advance the interests of the industry to contribute to the social & economic well-being of Prince Edward Island
Affiliation(s): Maritime Development Council
Staff Member(s): 1
Membership: *Member Profile:* Organizations within the harness racing industry in Prince Edward Island & the Maritimes, such as the Atlantic Standardbred Breeders Association, the Maritime Breeders Association, the Prince Edward Island Standardbred Horseowners Association, & the Prince Edward Island Colt Stakes Association; *Committees:* Finance; Purse Pool; Stakes; Atlantic Classic Sale; Classification
Activities: Advocating on behalf of the harness racing industry on Prince Edward Island; Providing a forum for the exchange of information for the industry; Monitoring practices on the part of owners, trainers, drivers, grooms, & officials; Liaising with the Maritime Provinces Harness Racing Commission; Proposing changes to harness racing in order to attract new supporters
Chief Officer(s):
Wayne Pike, Executive Director
Earl Smith, President
Tom Clark, Vice-President
Eldred Nicholson, Secretary
Blair Campbell, Treasurer

Prince Edward Island Hockey Association *See* Hockey PEI

Prince Edward Island Hockey Referees Association
c/o Hockey PEI, 40 Enman Cres., Charlottetown PE C1A 7K7
Tel: 902-367-8373
Overview: A medium-sized provincial organization
Member of: Hockey PEI; Hockey Canada

Prince Edward Island Hog Commodity Marketing Board
#209, 420 University Ave., Charlottetown PE C1A 7Z5
Tel: 902-892-4201; *Fax:* 902-892-4203
peipork@hotmail.com
www.peipork.pe.ca
twitter.com/porkisyummy
www.youtube.com/user/SwineTV
Overview: A small provincial organization
Mission: To provide information to the pork production industry of Prince Edward Island; To voice the concerns of hog farmers
Membership: *Member Profile:* Hog farmers on Prince Edward Island
Activities: Pursuing off-Island markets for hogs; Liaising with the provincial government
Chief Officer(s):
Tim Seeber, Executive Director
Paul Larsen, Chair

Prince Edward Island Home & School Federation Inc. (PEIHSF)
PO Box 1012, 40 Enman Cres., Charlottetown PE C1A 7M4
Tel: 902-620-3186; *Fax:* 902-620-3187
Toll-Free: 800-916-0664
peihsf@edu.pe.ca
peihsf.ca
www.facebook.com/peihsf
twitter.com/peihsf
Overview: A medium-sized provincial organization founded in 1953 overseen by Canadian Home & School Federation
Mission: To improve standards of education in the province
Member of: Prince Edward Island Literacy Alliance Inc.
Staff Member(s): 1
Membership: *Committees:* Finance & Human Resources; Meeting Planning; Resolutions & Policy
Activities: Organizing annual meeting
Chief Officer(s):
Lisa MacDougall, President
president@peihsf.ca
Shirley Smedley Jay, Executive Director

Prince Edward Island Humane Society (PEIHS)
PO Box 20022, 309 Sherwood Rd., Charlottetown PE C1A 9E3
Tel: 902-892-1190; *Fax:* 902-892-3617
Other Communication: After Hours Animal Welfare Emergency Phone: 902-892-1191
info@peihumanesociety.com
www.peihumanesociety.com
www.facebook.com/peihumanesociety
twitter.com/peihs
Overview: A medium-sized provincial charitable organization founded in 1974 overseen by Canadian Federation of Humane Societies
Mission: To promote & provide the humane treatment of animals recognizing that each is deserving of moral concern
Member of: Canadian Federation of Humane Societies (CFHS)
Finances: *Annual Operating Budget:* $250,000-$500,000; *Funding Sources:* Donations; Fundraising
Staff Member(s): 13; 100 volunteer(s)
Membership: *Member Profile:* Interest in & love for animals, concern for animal welfare issues
Activities: Facilitating animal adoption & rescue; Investigating possible instances of inhumane treatment to animals; Offering pet therapy & animal control; *Speaker Service:* Yes
Chief Officer(s):
Marla Somersall, Executive Director
msomersall@peihumanesociety.com
Beckie MacLean, Manager, Shelter
bmaclean@peihumanesociety.com

Prince Edward Island Institute of Agrologists (PEIIA)
PO Box 2712, Charlottetown PE C1A 8C3
info@peiia.ca
www.peiia.ca
www.facebook.com/PEIInstituteofAgrologists
twitter.com/PEIAgrologists
Overview: A small provincial organization overseen by Agricultural Institute of Canada
Mission: To safeguard the public by ensuring its members are qualified & competent to provide knowledge & advice on agriculture & related areas
Finances: *Funding Sources:* Membership fees
Membership: *Fees:* Schedule available; *Committees:* Agrologist in Training; Membership; Program; Publicity; Honours & Awards; Nominations; Agrologists Canada
Activities: Providing professional certification & development opportunities; *Internships:* Yes
Chief Officer(s):
Paul MacDonald, Registrar
pxmacdonald@gov.pe.ca
Awards:
• Recognition Award
• Outstanding Agrologist Award

Prince Edward Island Karate Association (PEIKA)
c/o Dawn Brown, 131 Blue Heron Lane, Cornwall PE C0A 1H0
www.karatepei.ca
Also Known As: Prince Edward Island Karate Association
Overview: A small provincial organization founded in 1971 overseen by Karate Canada
Mission: To teach, train & coach karate & allied physical arts; to teach physical culture generally; to promote the principles & teaching of the sport of karate & to work toward the advancement of the sport in conjunction with all other groups throughout Canada; to arrange matches, contests & competitions of every nature relating to karate & to offer or grant & contribute towards judges, awards & distinctions; to provide conditional assistance on the approval of the Executive of the Association
Member of: Karate Canada; Sport PEI
Finances: *Annual Operating Budget:* Less than $50,000
Chief Officer(s):
Dawn Brown, President
dawn.brown@pei.sympatico.ca

Prince Edward Island Kiwanis Music Festival Association
c/o Diane Campbell, Administrator, 227 Keppoch Rd., Stratford PE C1B 2J5
Tel: 902-569-2885
www.peikiwanismusicfestival.ca
Previous Name: PEI Music Festival Association
Overview: A medium-sized provincial charitable organization founded in 1946 overseen by Federation of Canadian Music Festivals
Mission: To make possible performances of young & older musicians in a semi-professional atmosphere; To adjudicate using professionals; & to encourage performance & study in music
Affiliation(s): West Prince Music Festival; East Prince Music Festival; Queens County Music Festival; Kings County Music Festival
Finances: *Annual Operating Budget:* $50,000-$100,000
10 volunteer(s)
Membership: 50
Chief Officer(s):
Diane Campbell, Provincial Administrator
ddcampbell@eastlink.ca

Prince Edward Island Lawn Bowling Association
Sport PEI, PO Box 302, Charlottetown PE C1A 7K7
Tel: 902-368-4110; *Fax:* 902-368-4548
Toll-Free: 800-247-6712
sports@sportpei.pe.ca
Overview: A small provincial organization overseen by Bowls Canada Boulingrin
Mission: To provide guidance to bowlers and all people interested in the sport. They wish to assit in the growth and development of Lawn Bowling on PEI Island, they wish to promote and encourage fair play in the sport at club level and at National lvel, they wish to develop leadership and to provide oppourtunities for development in the field of coaching, umpiring, and administration. They also provide interesting tournaments and events throughout the playing season.

Prince Edward Island Literacy Alliance *See* Prince Edward Island Literacy Alliance Inc.

Prince Edward Island Literacy Alliance Inc.
Sherwood Business Centre, PO Box 20107, 161 St. Peters Rd., Charlottetown PE C1A 9E3
Tel: 902-368-3620; *Fax:* 902-368-3269
Toll-Free: 866-827-3620
www.peiliteracy.ca
www.facebook.com/PEILiteracyAlliance
twitter.com/PEILiteracy
www.youtube.com/user/LiteracyPEI
Previous Name: Prince Edward Island Literacy Alliance
Overview: A small provincial charitable organization founded in 1990
Mission: To improve literacy levels on Prince Edward Island
Finances: *Funding Sources:* Donations; Sponsorships; Office of Literacy & Essential Skills of HRSDC; PEI Department of Education; PGI Golf Tournament for Literacy
Membership: *Member Profile:* Provincial & national organizations with an interest in literacy
Activities: Raising public awareness about literacy; Providing information & referrals; Presenting workshops on topics such as study skills; Offering tutoring programs for youth; Liaising with other organizations to create partnerships; Advising government & educational institutions about programs & services; Conducting research; Producing fact sheets; Awarding bursaries & scholarships; *Awareness Events:* PGI Golf Tournament for Literacy; Family Literacy Day, Jan.; International Adult Learners' Week, April
Chief Officer(s):
Jinny Greaves, Executive Director
Publications:
• Family Literacy Things to Do
• A Guide to Social Assistance in PEI
Type: Book; *Author:* Norman Finlayson
• Instructor's Manual
Type: Book; *Author:* Karen Chandler & Ruth Rogerson
• Live & Learn
Type: Newsletter; *Frequency:* Quarterly
Profile: Alliance project news, events, announcements, & awards
• The New Adventures of Word Monster - Volumes 1 & 2
Author: Erin Casey & Brian Stevens
• PEI Literacy Alliance Annual Report
Type: Yearbook; *Frequency:* Annually
• Promoting Family Literacy in PEI: A Strategic Plan for Family Literacy in PEI

Prince Edward Island Lung Association
81 Prince St., Charlottetown PE C1A 4R3
Tel: 902-892-5957
Toll-Free: 888-566-5864
info@pei.lung.ca
www.pei.lung.ca
www.facebook.com/196098560534899
twitter.com/PEI_Lung
Previous Name: PEI Tuberculosis League
Overview: A small provincial charitable organization founded in 1936 overseen by Canadian Lung Association
Mission: To improve the respiratory health of Islanders through education, advocacy & research; To raise funds to support medical research
Finances: *Funding Sources:* Donations; Fundraising; Sponsorships
Staff Member(s): 3
Activities: Promoting lung health in Prince Edward Island; Helping people to stop smoking through the Provincial Cessation Program (QuitCare)
Chief Officer(s):
Joanne Ings, Executive Director
jings@pei.lung.ca

Prince Edward Island Marketing Council
PO Box 1600, Charlottetown PE C1A 7N3
Tel: 902-569-7575; *Fax:* 902-569-7745
Overview: A small provincial organization
Mission: To administer the Natural Products Marketing Act under which commodity boards & groups
Finances: *Annual Operating Budget:* $50,000-$100,000
Staff Member(s): 2
Membership: 8 individual
Chief Officer(s):
Ian MacIssac, Secretary & General Manager
ijmacissac@gov.pe.ca

Prince Edward Island Massage Therapy Association
PO Box 1882, Charlottetown PE C1A 7N5
Fax: 902-368-7281
Toll-Free: 866-566-1955
www.peimta.com
Overview: A medium-sized provincial organization
Mission: To raise the awareness of all Islanders on the benefits of therapeutic massage
Membership: 39; *Fees:* $25; *Member Profile:* Registered Massage Therapists
Chief Officer(s):
Jennifer White, President
president@peimta.com

Prince Edward Island Museum & Heritage Foundation (PEIMHF) / Le Musée et la fondation du patrimoine de l'Ile-du-Prince-Édouard
2 Kent St., Charlottetown PE C1A 1M6
Tel: 902-368-6600; *Fax:* 902-368-6608
mhpei@gov.pe.ca
www.peimuseum.com
www.facebook.com/124989037532122
twitter.com/PEIMUSEUM
Also Known As: PEI Museum
Overview: A medium-sized provincial charitable organization founded in 1970
Mission: To study, preserve, interpret & protect the human & natural heritage of PEI
Member of: Heritage Canada; Canadian Heritage; Canadian Museums Association; PEI Museums Association
Finances: *Annual Operating Budget:* $500,000-$1.5 Million; *Funding Sources:* Federal & provincial government; endowment; book sales; admissions
Staff Member(s): 20; 50 volunteer(s)
Membership: 500; *Fees:* $40.25 individual; $57.50 family; $34.50 senior/student; *Committees:* Government House; Institute for Architectural Studies

Canadian Associations / Prince Edward Island Numismatic Association

Activities: Offering public & children's programs; *Internships:* Yes; *Speaker Service:* Yes
Chief Officer(s):
David L. Keenlyside, Executive Director
dlkeenlyside@gov.pe.ca
Mary Paquet, Business Administrator
mmpaquet@gov.pe.ca
Nora J. Young, Executive Assistant
njyoung@gov.pe.ca
Awards:
• PEI Museums Heritage Annual Heritage Awards
Publications:
• The Island Magazine [a publication of the Prince Edward Island Museum & Heritage Foundation]
Type: Magazine; *Frequency:* Biannually; *Editor:* Boyde Beck
Profile: Provides information about Island history, genealogy & natural heritage

Prince Edward Island Numismatic Association
Charlottetown PE
Also Known As: PEI Coin Club
Overview: A small provincial organization founded in 1964
Affiliation(s): The Royal Canadian Numismatic Association
Membership: *Fees:* $15
Activities: Hosting regular meetings at Colonel Gray Senior High School

Prince Edward Island Nurses' Union (PEINU) / Syndicat des infirmières de l'Ile-du-Prince-Édouard
10 Paramount Dr., Charlottetown PE C1E 0C7
Tel: 902-892-7152; *Fax:* 902-892-9324
Toll-Free: 866-892-7152
office@peinu.com
www.peinu.com
twitter.com/PEINursesUnion
vimeo.com/user2758462
Overview: A medium-sized provincial organization founded in 1974
Mission: To regulate employment relations between nurses & employers through collective bargaining & negotiation of written contracts with employers implementing progressively better conditions of employment
Affiliation(s): Canadian Federation of Nurses Unions; Canadian Labour Congress
Finances: *Funding Sources:* Membership dues
Membership: 1,200 individuals in 8 locals; *Fees:* Schedule available; *Member Profile:* Employment in job classification covered by collective agreement; *Committees:* Constitution & Resolutions; Finance; Grievance; Nominations; Public Relations; Benefits Insurance; Civil Service Superannuation Fund; Education Fund
Activities: *Library:*
Chief Officer(s):
Mona O'Shea, President
Kendra Gunn, Executive Director

Prince Edward Island Occupational Therapy Society (PEIOTS)
c/o Manon Gallant, PO Box 6600, Charlottetown PE C1A 8T5
www.peiot.org
www.facebook.com/1674912579412289
twitter.com/PEIOTSociety
Overview: A small provincial organization
Mission: To represent occupational therapists in Prince Edward Island
Member of: Canadian Association of Occupational Therapists
Membership: 1-99
Activities: Promoting the profession; Supporting professional development; Providing networking opportunities
Chief Officer(s):
Katie Verhulst, Spokesperson

Prince Edward Island Office of the Superintendent of Securities
Shaw Bldg., PO Box 2000, 95 Rochford St., 4th Fl., Charlottetown PE C1A 7N8
www.gov.pe.ca/securities
Overview: A medium-sized provincial organization overseen by Canadian Securities Administrators
Mission: To foster fair & efficient capital markets; to protect investors
Member of: Canadian Securities Administrators
Chief Officer(s):
Steve Dowling, Superintendent, Securities

Prince Edward Island Optometrical Association *See* Prince Edward Island Association of Optometrists

Prince Edward Island Pharmacists Association
PO Box 24042, Stratford ON C1B 2V5
Tel: 902-367-7080
peipharm@gmail.com
www.peipharm.info
www.facebook.com/193958177311345
Overview: A small provincial organization
Mission: To support & advance the role of the pharmacist in Prince Edward Island
Finances: *Funding Sources:* Membership fees; Sponsorships
Activities: Promoting the profession of pharmacy in Prince Edward Island; Negotiating with government
Chief Officer(s):
Erin MacKenzie, Executive Director
Publications:
• Prince Edward Island Pharmacists Association Newsletter
Type: Newsletter
Profile: Information for members, supporters, & friends of the association

Prince Edward Island Pharmacy Board (PEIPB)
PO Box 89, 20454 Trans Canada Hwy., Crapaud PE C0A 1J0
Tel: 902-658-2780; *Fax:* 902-658-2528
info@pepharmacists.ca
www.pepharmacists.ca
Overview: A small provincial licensing organization founded in 1983 overseen by National Association of Pharmacy Regulatory Authorities
Mission: To prescribe qualifications, grant authorization & monitor adherence to established standards, so as to promote high standards & safeguard the public with regard to pharmaceutical service
Member of: Canadian Council on Continuing Education in Pharmacy
Affiliation(s): National Association of Pharmacy Regulatory Authorities
Finances: *Funding Sources:* Licensing fees
Staff Member(s): 2
Membership: *Member Profile:* Successful completion of degree program for pharmacists from recognized college of pharmacy; current competency, as demonstrated by such examination as Board may administer upon applicant's payment of prescribed fee; *Committees:* Investigations/Complaints; CE/Competence Assessment; Pharmacy Endowment Board - Dalhousie; Practice Experience - Dalhousie; Examinations; Standards for Long Term Care Facilities; Administration By Injection/Immunization; Standards of Practice for Pharmacists Prescribing; PhIP Advisory; Methadone Maintenance
Activities: *Internships:* Yes
Chief Officer(s):
Alicia McCallum, Chair
almccall@dal.ca
Michelle Wyand, Registrar
mwyand@pepharmacists.ca
Rachel Lowther-Doiron, Administrative Assistant
rlowtherdoiron@pepharmacists.ca

Prince Edward Island Physiotherapy Association (PEI CPA)
PE
www.physiotherapy.ca/Atlantic-Branches/Prince-Edward-Island
Overview: A medium-sized provincial organization overseen by Canadian Physiotherapy Association
Mission: To provide leadership & direction to the physiotherapy profession; To foster excellence in practice, education & research
Member of: Canadian Physiotherapy Association
Finances: *Funding Sources:* Membership dues; Educational activities
Chief Officer(s):
Trish Helm Neima, Contact

Prince Edward Island Police Association (PEIPA)
PE
www.peipolice.com
Overview: A medium-sized provincial organization
Mission: To help members of the community become more familiar with the Prince Edward Island Police force; To promote the public's role in crime prevention; To support Youth Development; To speak for Prince Edward Island's municipal police officers
Membership: *Member Profile:* Members of the Prince Edward Island Municipal Police
Chief Officer(s):
Ron MacLean, Corporal, President
Jason Blacquiere, Vice-President West
John Flood, Vice-President East
Publications:
• Annual Crime Prevention Guide
Type: Magazine; *Frequency:* Annual; *Editor:* Fenety Marketing Services; *Price:* Free
Profile: Distributed to schools, libraries & public facilities in order to educated public on potential hazards & risks.

Prince Edward Island Poultry Meat Commodity Marketing Board *See* Chicken Farmers of Prince Edward Island

Prince Edward Island Professional Librarians Association *See* Association of Prince Edward Island Libraries

Prince Edward Island Rape & Sexual Assault Centre (PEIRSAC)
PO Box 1522, 1 Rochford St., Charlottetown PE C1A 7N3
Tel: 902-566-1864; *Fax:* 902-368-2957
Toll-Free: 866-566-1864
admin@peirsac.org
www.peirsac.org
Overview: A small provincial charitable organization founded in 1981
Mission: To ensure that the people of Prince Edward Island are safe from sexual violence; To support abuse & sexual assault survivors
Finances: *Funding Sources:* Donations; Fundraising; PEI Provincial Government
Activities: Offering support, information, & counselling (902-368-8055) telephone service; Providing individual & group therapy; Accompanying persons to police stations & hospitals; Liasing with other community groups; Engaging in advocacy activities, such as representation on the Premier's Family Violence Prevention Action Committee & the PEI Child Sexual Abuse Prevention Advisory Committee; Offering public education; *Awareness Events:* Golf Against Assault Tournament
Chief Officer(s):
Sigrid Rolfe, Organizational Coordinator

Prince Edward Island Real Estate Association (PEIREA)
75 St. Peter's Rd., Charlottetown PE C1A 5N7
Tel: 902-368-8451; *Fax:* 902-894-9487
office@peirea.com
www.peirea.com
Previous Name: PEI Real Estate Brokers Association
Overview: A small provincial organization founded in 1964
Mission: To promote the real estate profession; to provide information & services to members, & to the public
Member of: The Canadian Real Estate Association
Finances: *Annual Operating Budget:* $250,000-$500,000
Membership: 230
Chief Officer(s):
Mary Jane Webster, President
Ritchie Simpson, Secretary-Treasurer

Prince Edward Island Recreation & Facilities Association *See* Recreation Prince Edward Island

Prince Edward Island Rifle Association (PEIPRA)
PO Box 160, Charlottetown PE C1A 7K4
Tel: 902-672-2773
peipra.ca/PEIPRA
Overview: A small provincial organization founded in 1861
Member of: Dominion of Canada Rifle Association
Finances: *Annual Operating Budget:* Less than $50,000; *Funding Sources:* Macdonald Stewart Foundation; local business; investment interest
Membership: 10; *Fees:* Adult: $130-$230; Under 25: $80-$100; *Committees:* Ammunition; Match; Publicity; Social
Activities: Annual prize matches
Chief Officer(s):
Ian Hogg, Director, Finance & Public Relations
irhogg@edu.pe.ca

Prince Edward Island Right to Life Association
PO Box 1988, Charlottetown PE C1A 7N7
Tel: 902-894-5473
www.peirighttolife.ca
Overview: A small provincial charitable organization founded in 1974
Mission: To value & promote respect for human life, from conception to natural death; To act as a unified voice for life issues
Finances: *Funding Sources:* Donations
Activities: Increasing awareness of respect for life in all its stages; Providing educational projects

Publications:
• PEI Right to Life News: "Life Sanctuary"
Type: Newsletter; *Frequency:* Semiannually; *Editor:* B. Connolly; A. Annema; M. Dykeman
Profile: Organizational reports, conferences, & related news

Prince Edward Island Road Builders & Heavy Construction Association
PO Box 1901, #223, 40 Enman Cres., Charlottetown PE C1A 7N5
Tel: 902-894-9514; *Fax:* 902-894-9512
info@peirb.ca
www.peirb.ca
Previous Name: PEI Roadbuilders Association
Overview: A medium-sized provincial organization founded in 1962 overseen by Canadian Construction Association
Mission: To be a strong, effective voice in the heavy construction industry
Member of: Atlantic Roadbuilders Association; Transportation Association of Canada
Finances: *Annual Operating Budget:* $50,000-$100,000
Staff Member(s): 2
Membership: 100+; *Member Profile:* Contractors & suppliers in the road & heavy construction industry; *Committees:* Asphalt Producer's Group; Bursary & FW Curtis Memorial Scholarship; CCA Representative; Education & Training; Environment & Specifications; Membership; Negotiated Prices & Rental Rates; Pipe, Structure, Site Services; Public Relations, Civil Infrastructure Council Corporation; Safety; Snow; Principals' Group; Treasurer
Chief Officer(s):
Steve Campbell, President
Meetings/Conferences:
• Price Edward Island Road Builders & Heavy Construction Association 2018 56th Annual General Meeting, February, 2018, PE
Scope: Provincial

Prince Edward Island Roadrunners Club
c/o Sport PEI, 40 Enman Cres., Charlottetown PE C1E 1E6
peiroadrunners.pbworks.com
Overview: A small provincial organization founded in 1977
Mission: The PEI RoadRunners Club is an organization whose objective is to promote & encourage running as a sport & healthful exercise. The Club welcomes all runners, regardless of ability & attempts to meet the needs of competitive & recreational runners.
Membership: *Fees:* $20 individual; $30 family
Chief Officer(s):
Janet Norman-Bain, President

Prince Edward Island Rugby Union (PEIRU)
10 Kenwood Circle, Charlottetown PE C1E 1Z8
peirugbyunion@gmail.com
peirugbyunion.com
twitter.com/PEIRugbyUnion
Also Known As: PEI Rugby Union
Overview: A medium-sized provincial organization overseen by Rugby Canada
Mission: To promote rugby in Prince Edward Island
Member of: Rugby Canada
Finances: *Funding Sources:* Membership fees; Gate receipts; Government; Sponsorship
Membership: *Committees:* Provincial team coordination; Youth Development; Women's Development; Official's Development; Newsletter; Summer League; Host Event
Chief Officer(s):
Alex Field, President

Prince Edward Island School Athletic Association (PEISAA)
#101, 250 Water St., Summerside PE C1N 1B6
Tel: 902-438-4846; *Fax:* 902-438-4884
www.peisaa.pe.ca
Overview: A medium-sized provincial organization overseen by School Sport Canada
Mission: Supporting sports including but not exclusive to, badminton, softball, wrestling, golf, cross country, curling, and volleyball, in PEI.
Member of: School Sport Canada
Chief Officer(s):
Trevor Bridges, Chair
Rick MacKinnon, Coordinator
Gerald MacCormack, Secretary-Treasurer

Prince Edward Island Senior Citizens Federation Inc. (PEISCF)
#214, 40 Enman Cres., Charlottetown PE C1E 1E6
Tel: 902-368-9008; *Fax:* 902-368-9006
Toll-Free: 877-368-9008
peiscf@pei.aibn.com
www.peiscf.com
Overview: A small provincial organization founded in 1972
Mission: To advance the education opportunities for seniors on PEI; to improve the quality of life for seniors by advising government & other decision making bodies regarding seniors' concerns; to improve the quality of life for seniors; to increase societal understanding of seniors & the aging process through positive role modelling
Finances: *Annual Operating Budget:* Less than $50,000; *Funding Sources:* Membership fees; fundraising
Staff Member(s): 3
Membership: 2,500; *Member Profile:* 50 years & over
Activities: *Speaker Service:* Yes
Chief Officer(s):
Linda Jean Nicholson, Executive Director

Prince Edward Island Sheep Breeders Association
PE
peisheepbreeders.weebly.com
Overview: A small provincial organization
Affiliation(s): Canadian Sheep Federation; Canadian Sheep Breeders' Association
Chief Officer(s):
Trent Coles, Treasurer

Prince Edward Island Shorthorn Association
PE
Overview: A small provincial organization
Member of: Canadian Shorthorn Association

Prince Edward Island Silvicultural Contractors Association
See Prince Edward Island Forest Improvement Association

Prince Edward Island Snowboard Association
Charlottetown PE
Tel: 902-326-9305
www.facebook.com/SnowboardPEI
Also Known As: Snowboard PEI
Overview: A small provincial organization overseen by Canadian Snowboard Federation
Mission: To be the provincial governing body of competitive snowboarding in Prince Edward Island
Member of: Canadian Snowboard Federation
Chief Officer(s):
Zak Likely, Contact
zak.likely@gmail.com

Prince Edward Island Soccer Association (PEISA)
40 Enman Cres., Charlottetown PE C1E 1E6
Tel: 902-368-6251; *Fax:* 902-569-7693
admin@peisoccer.com
www.peisoccer.com
www.facebook.com/197098723677560
twitter.com/peisoccerassoc
Overview: A medium-sized provincial organization founded in 1979 overseen by Canadian Soccer Association
Mission: To promote & regulate soccer in PEI; to provide competitive opportunities for members.
Member of: Canadian Soccer Association; Sport PEI
Finances: *Annual Operating Budget:* $250,000-$500,000
Staff Member(s): 1
Membership: 6,000 individual + 14 clubs; *Fees:* Schedule available
Chief Officer(s):
Peter Wolters, Executive Director
Jonathan Vos, Technical Director
jvos@peisoccer.com

Prince Edward Island Society for Medical Laboratory Science (PEIMLS)
PO Box 20061, Stn. Sherwood, 161 St. Peters Rd., Charlottetown PE C1A 9E3
peismls.com
www.facebook.com/320495861437823
twitter.com/peismls
Overview: A medium-sized provincial organization founded in 1953 overseen by Canadian Society for Medical Laboratory Science
Mission: To promote, maintain & protect professional identity & interests of medical laboratory technologist & of the profession; to promote development of continuing education; to provide information on current developments in medical laboratory technology
Activities: Career expos; education days; *Awareness Events:* National Medical Laboratory Week, April
Chief Officer(s):
Carolyn McCarville, President
Andrea Dowling, Vice-President
Gerard Fernando, Treasurer
Awards:
• Dr. John Craig Award of Merit
Recipient represents importance of education & professionalism
Eligibility: Registered technologist, member of association but not part of executive

Prince Edward Island Speech & Hearing Association (PEISHA)
PO Box 20076, Charlottetown PE C1A 9E3
www.peispeechhearing.ca
Overview: A small provincial organization
Mission: To promote the study, research, discussion & dissemination of information concerning the process of human communication in speech & hearing; To encourage the development & improvement of skills in the diagnosis & treatment of human communication disorders
Member of: Canadian Association of Speech-Language Pathologists & Audiologists
Finances: *Funding Sources:* Professional dues; workshops
Membership: 35; *Fees:* $100; *Committees:* Public Relations; Membership; Workshop; Legislation; Advocacy
Activities: *Awareness Events:* Speech & Hearing Month, May; *Internships:* Yes; *Library*
Chief Officer(s):
Jennifer Bartlett-Bitar, President

Prince Edward Island Speed Skating Association
See Speed Skate PEI

Prince Edward Island Sports Hall of Fame
See Prince Edward Island Sports Hall of Fame & Museum Inc.

Prince Edward Island Sports Hall of Fame & Museum Inc.
40 Enman Cres., Charlottetown PE C1E 1E6
Tel: 902-368-4547
publicrelations@sportpei.pe.ca
www.peisportshalloffame.ca
www.facebook.com/210800825622110
Previous Name: Prince Edward Island Sports Hall of Fame
Overview: A small provincial charitable organization founded in 1968
Finances: *Funding Sources:* Fees; events; admissions; fundraising events; government grants; sponsorships
Membership: 150+ inductees
Activities: *Library:*
Chief Officer(s):
Nick Murray, Executive Director

Prince Edward Island Square & Round Dance Clubs
The Charlotte Twirlers, 1 Avonlea Dr., Charlottetown PE C1C 1C8
Tel: 902-566-4307
www.csrds.ca/pei
Overview: A small provincial organization
Member of: Canadian Square & Round Dance Society
Chief Officer(s):
Ron Doyle, Contact
Joyce Doyle, Contact

Prince Edward Island Standardbred Horseowners' Association
c/o PEI Harness Racing Industry Association, #204A, 420 University Ave., Charlottetown PE C1A 7Z5
Tel: 902-569-1682; *Fax:* 902-569-1827
peracing@eastlink.ca
Overview: A small provincial organization
Mission: To support & recognize standardbred horseowners on Prince Edward Island
Member of: Prince Edward Island Harness Racing Industry Association
Membership: *Member Profile:* Standardbred horseowners on Prince Edward Island
Activities: Presenting harness racing awards annually, such as Horse of the Year & Horseman of the Year
Chief Officer(s):
Wayne Pike, Executive Director, PEI Harness Racing Industry Association

Canadian Associations / Prince Edward Island Symphony Society (PEISO)

Prince Edward Island Symphony Society (PEISO)
PO Box 185, Charlottetown PE C1A 7K4
Tel: 902-892-4333
admin@peisymphony.com
www.peisymphony.com
www.facebook.com/PEISymphony
twitter.com/PEISymphony
Also Known As: PEI Symphony Orchestra
Overview: A small provincial charitable organization founded in 1968 overseen by Orchestras Canada
Mission: To establish & promote symphonic music; to further & foster appreciation of musical education; to promote the welfare of musicians; to give & arrange performances, entertainments & concerts; to employ teachers & instructors to inform the public & awaken interest
Member of: Orchestras Canada
Finances: *Funding Sources:* Corporate sponsorship; Corporate & individual donations; Fundraising; Canada Council
Staff Member(s): 3
Activities: *Library:*
Chief Officer(s):
Mark Shapiro, Music Director

Prince Edward Island Table Tennis Association (PEITTA)
c/o Sport PEI Inc., 40 Enman Cres., Charlottetown PE C1E 1E6
www.freewebs.com/peitta
Overview: A small provincial organization founded in 1965 overseen by Table Tennis Canada
Mission: To promote table tennis in PEI; to provide competitive opportunities for its members
Member of: Table Tennis Canada; Sport PEI Inc.
Affiliation(s): International Table Tennis Federation
Finances: *Annual Operating Budget:* Less than $50,000; *Funding Sources:* Provincial government; fundraising
10 volunteer(s)
Membership: 55-75; *Fees:* Schedule available; *Member Profile:* Table tennis players; *Committees:* Fundraising; Coaching
Activities: Hosts provincial championships, local tournaments & recreational games; *Internships:* Yes

Prince Edward Island Teachers' Federation (PEITF) / Fédération des enseignants de l'Ile-du-Prince-Édouard
PO Box 6000, Charlottetown PE C1A 8B4
Tel: 902-569-4157; *Fax:* 902-569-3682
Toll-Free: 800-903-4157
www.peitf.com
www.facebook.com/PEITF
twitter.com/PEITF
Overview: A medium-sized provincial organization founded in 1880 overseen by Canadian Teachers' Federation
Mission: To promote & support education as well as the professional & economic well-being of PEI teachers
Member of: Prince Edward Island Literacy Alliance Inc.
Finances: *Funding Sources:* Membership dues
Staff Member(s): 7
Membership: *Member Profile:* Employed as teacher (administrator) by school board in PEI; *Committees:* Annual Convention Planning; Awards, Grants & Projects; Constitution & By-laws; Curriculum, Professional Development & Teacher Education; Diversity/Equity; Economic Welfare; Ethics; Finance & Property; General Secretary Evaluation; Nomination; Pension; Personnel; Provinicial Public Relations; Student Services; Technology
Activities: *Library:* by appointment Not open to public
Chief Officer(s):
McLeod Bethany, President
bmacleod@peitf.com
Shaun MacCormac, General Secretary
smaccormac@peitf.com

Prince Edward Island Tennis Association
PO Box 302, 40 Enman Cres., Charlottetown PE C1A 7K7
Tel: 902-368-4985; *Fax:* 902-368-4548
tennisprinceedwardisland@gmail.com
www.tennispei.ca
www.facebook.com/286640596313
twitter.com/TennisPEI
Also Known As: Tennis PEI
Overview: A medium-sized provincial organization overseen by Tennis Canada
Mission: To promote the sport of tennis on PEI
Member of: Tennis Canada
Finances: *Funding Sources:* Government; Sponsors; Participants

Staff Member(s): 2; 20 volunteer(s)
Membership: 600; *Fees:* Schedule available
Activities: Offering clinics, tournaments, & other programs
Chief Officer(s):
Daniel Arseneault, President
daniel.arseneault@gmail.com
Meetings/Conferences:
• Prince Edward Island Tennis Association Annual General Meeting 2018, September, 2018, PE
Scope: Provincial

Prince Edward Island Trucking Sector Council (PEITSC)
#211, 420 University Ave., Charlottetown PE C1A 7Z5
Tel: 902-566-5563; *Fax:* 902-566-4506
info@peitsc.ca
www.peitsc.ca
www.facebook.com/peitsc
twitter.com/peitsc
www.youtube.com/user/peitruckingsc
Overview: A medium-sized provincial organization
Mission: To address human resources issues & opportunities in the Trucking Industry on Prince Edward Island & to provide a vehicle for effective industry participation in identifying & addressing issues related to workforce attraction & retention, career awareness, skills upgrading & training
Member of: Prince Edward Island Literacy Alliance Inc.
Chief Officer(s):
Jason Ling, Chair
Clinton Myers, Vice Chair

Prince Edward Island Underwater Council
PE
Overview: A small provincial organization
Mission: The PEI Underwater Council's mission is to help support & promote the sport of scuba diving in Prince Edward Island through safety, advocacy, cultural & environmental awareness, self-governance & education.

Prince Edward Island Union of Public Sector Employees / Syndicat de la fonction publique de l'Ile-du-Prince-Édouard
4 Enman Cres., Charlottetown PE C1E 1E6
Tel: 902-892-5335; *Fax:* 902-569-8186
Toll-Free: 800-897-8773
peiupse@peiupse.ca
www.peiupse.ca
Overview: A medium-sized provincial organization
Mission: To represent & advocate on behalf of its members in order to ensure safe & fair working conditions
Staff Member(s): 9
Membership: *Committees:* Constitution & Structure; Education; Finance; Membership Services & Communications; Occupational Health & Safety; Pension & Insurance; Public Relations & Recreation/Convention; Staff Relations
Chief Officer(s):
Debbie Bovyer, President
dbovyer@peiupse.ca

Prince Edward Island Vegetable Growers Co-op Association
PO Box 1494, 280 Sherwood Rd., Charlottetown PE C1A 7J7
Tel: 902-892-5361; *Fax:* 902-566-2383
peiveg@eastlink.ca
Overview: A small provincial organization founded in 1969
Finances: *Annual Operating Budget:* Greater than $5 Million
Staff Member(s): 25
Membership: 95; *Fees:* $1,000
Chief Officer(s):
Don Read, Manager

Prince Edward Island Veterinary Medical Association (PEIVMA)
PO Box 21097, Stn. 465 University Ave., Charlottetown PE C1A 9h6
Tel: 902-367-3757; *Fax:* 902-367-3176
admin.peivma@gmail.com
www.peivma.ca
Overview: A small provincial licensing organization founded in 1920 overseen by Canadian Veterinary Medical Association
Mission: To represent PEI veterinarians in small animal, large animal & mixed practice as well as those employed in government, industry or other institutions; to licence & regulate veterinarians in PEI
Membership: 160 individual; *Fees:* $625 regular; $312.50 short-term
Chief Officer(s):

Wade Sweet, President
Jenn Reid, Vice-President
Meetings/Conferences:
• 2018 Prince Edward Island Veterinary Medical Association AGM, 2018, Rodd Charlottetown Hotel, Charlottetown, PE
Scope: Provincial

Prince Edward Island Wildlife Federation
#103B, 420 University Ave., Charlottetown PE C1A 7Z5
Tel: 902-626-9699
www.facebook.com/145488672186392
Overview: A small provincial organization founded in 1906 overseen by Canadian Wildlife Federation
Mission: To foster sound management & wise use of the renewable resources of PEI; to assist & encourage the enforcement of those game laws which are in keeping with the objectives of the Federation & to strive for better management & game laws where & when necessary; to cooperate with government departments & related groups where interests are mutual; to educate membership & the public, with particular emphasis upon conservation & safety; to represent the interests & concerns of PEI sportsmen
Activities: Assists with the Central Queens, O'Leary Wildlife & Souris Wildlife Federations
Chief Officer(s):
Duncan Crawford, Contact

Souris & Area
PO Box 692, Souris PE C0A 2B0
Tel: 902-687-4115
sourisareawildlife@gmail.com
www.souriswil.com
www.facebook.com/109225502447602
twitter.com/SourisWildlife
Mission: To conserve, protect, & enhance wildlife habitat in eastern PEI

Prince Edward Island Women's Institute (PEIWI)
#105, 40 Enman Cres., Charlottetown PE C1E 1E6
Tel: 902-368-4860; *Fax:* 902-368-4439
wi@gov.pe.ca
www.peiwi.ca
www.facebook.com/PEIWomensInstitute
Overview: A small provincial organization overseen by Federated Women's Institutes of Canada
Mission: To help discover, stimulate & develop leadership among women; To assist, encourage & support women to become knowledgeable & responsible citizens; To ensure basic human rights for women & to work towards their equality; To be a strong voice through which matters of utmost concern can reach the decision makers; to network with organizations sharing similar objectives; To promote the improvement of agricultural & other rural communities & to safeguard the environment
Membership: 1,300
Chief Officer(s):
Jacquie Laird, President
Awards:
• Friend of Women's Institute Award
• Golden Book of Recognition
• Helen Herring Scholarship
Eligibility: A PEI student enrolled in the third year of a university program in Applied Human Sciences such as Foods & Nutrition & Family Studies/Sciences, Kinesology or a related discipline; *Amount:* $500
• Louise MacMillan Scholarship
; *Amount:* $100
• Premier's Craft Education Award
• Women in Agriculture Recognition Award
• WI Education Scholarship
; *Amount:* $500
Publications:
• Notes & News [a publication of the Prince Edward Island Women's Institute]
Type: Newsletter; *Frequency:* 4 pa.
• WI Institute News [a publication of the Prince Edward Island Women's Institute]
Type: Newsletter; *Frequency:* Monthly

Prince George AIDS Prevention Program; AIDS Prince George; Prince George AIDS Society *See* Positive Living North: No kheyoh t'sih'en t'sehena Society

Prince George Alzheimer's Society
#202, 575 Quebec St., Prince George BC V2L 1W6
Tel: 250-564-7533; *Fax:* 250-564-1642
Toll-Free: 866-564-7533
Overview: A small local charitable organization founded in 1985

Mission: To provide information about Alzheimer's Disease in the Prince George, British Columbia area; To help people concerned with or facing dementia
Member of: Alzheimer Society British Columbia
Finances: *Funding Sources:* Donations
Activities: Offering early stage & family caregiver support groups; Providing education for people impacted by dementia; *Library:* Alzheimer Resource Centre; Open to public by appointment
Chief Officer(s):
Leanne Jones, Coordinator, Support & Education
ljones@alzheimerbc.org
Laurie De Croos, Coordinator, First Link
ldecroos@alzheimerbc.org

Prince George Backcountry Recreation Society (PGBRS)
PO Box 26, Stn. A, Prince George BC V2L 4R9
info@pgbrs.com
www.pgbrs.com
Overview: A small local organization founded in 1998
Mission: To promote and encourage safe non-motorized backcountry recreation in the Prince George region.
Member of: Federation of BC Naturalists
Chief Officer(s):
Duncan McColl, President

Prince George Brain Injured Group (PGBIG)
1237 - 4 Ave., Prince George BC V2L 3J7
Tel: 250-564-2447; *Fax:* 250-564-6928
Toll-Free: 866-564-2447
info@pgbig.ca
pgbig.ca
Overview: A small local organization founded in 1987
Mission: To provide assistance to adults whose lives have changed as a result of an acquired brain injury
Member of: Prince George United Way
Staff Member(s): 30
Chief Officer(s):
Alison Hagreen, Executive Director

Prince George Chamber of Commerce (PGCOC)
890 Vancouver St., Prince George BC V2L 2P5
Tel: 250-562-2454; *Fax:* 250-562-6510
chamber@pgchamber.bc.ca
www.pgchamber.bc.ca
www.linkedin.com/company/prince-george-chamber-of-commerce
www.facebook.com/PrinceGeorgeChamber
twitter.com/PGChamber1
www.youtube.com/channel/UCzQhi2Ttff84-IkN_Vb6NkQ
Overview: A medium-sized local organization founded in 1911
Mission: To enhance the quality of life in the community by fostering an environment that enables local businesses to thrive
Member of: BC Chamber of Commerce; Canadian Chamber of Commerce
Finances: *Annual Operating Budget:* $250,000-$500,000
Staff Member(s): 7; 35 volunteer(s)
Membership: 827; *Fees:* Schedule available; *Committees:* Advocacy; Communications; Service Delivery
Activities: *Speaker Service:* Yes; *Library:* Open to public
Chief Officer(s):
Christie Ray, CEO

Prince George Construction Association (PGCA)
3851 - 18th Ave., Prince George BC V2N 1B1
Tel: 250-563-1744; *Fax:* 250-563-1107
www.pgca.bc.ca
Overview: A small local organization founded in 1958
Mission: To establish & improve industry standards; to further fellowship & cooperation within the industry; To increase public awareness; To improve & standardize tendering & award practices; To disseminate information among members; To cooperate with other industry groups
Member of: BC Construction Association; Canadian Construction Association; Northern British Columbia Construction Association
Staff Member(s): 3; 500 volunteer(s)
Membership: 127 institutional; 25 associate; *Member Profile:* General & trade contractors, manufacturers, suppliers, allied service, professional associations
Activities: Chairman's Ball, Feb.
Chief Officer(s):
Brad Popoff, Chair
bpequity@shaw.ca
Rosalind Thorn, President

Prince George Native Friendship Centre
1600 - 3rd Ave., Prince George BC V2L 3G6
Tel: 250-564-3568; *Fax:* 250-563-0924
info@pgnfc.com
www.pgnfc.com
Overview: A small local organization founded in 1969
Mission: To serve the needs of Aboriginal people residing in the urban area; To improve the quality of life in the community as a whole
Membership: *Fees:* $1
Activities: Off-site services: Friendship Home, Ketso Yoh Men's Hostel, Reconnect Youth Services Drop-in/Downtown Youth Shelter; Prince George Aboriginal Head Start; Power of Friendship Aboriginal Head Start; Aboriginal Infant & Family Development Program; Native Art Gallery; Annual Pow Wow
Chief Officer(s):
Emma Palmantier, President
Joan Sutherland, Treasurer

Prince George Naturalists Club (PGNC) / Club de naturalistes de Prince George
PO Box 1092, Prince George BC V2L 4V2
pgnc@shaw.ca
pgnc.wordpress.com
www.facebook.com/pgnc
Overview: A small local organization founded in 1969
Mission: To promote the enjoyment of nature through environmental appreciation & conservation; To encourage wise use & conservation of natural resources & environmental protection.
Member of: Federation of BC Naturalists
Membership: *Fees:* $25 individual; $40 family
Activities: Monthly guest speakers; weekly field trips; birding; annual bird counts

Prince George Parents of Twins & Triplets Association (PGPOTTA)
7138 Harvard Cres., Prince George BC V2N 2V7
Tel: 250-640-6405
Other Communication: princegeorge@multiplebirthscanada.org
pgpotta@hotmail.com
www.multiplebirthscanada.org/~princegeorge
Overview: A small local organization founded in 1976 overseen by Multiple Births Canada
Mission: A support group for parents of multiple births.
Membership: *Fees:* $50

Prince George Recycling & Environmental Action Planning Society (REAPS)
PO Box 444, 1950 Gorse St., Prince George BC V2L 4S6
Tel: 250-561-7327; *Fax:* 250-561-7324
garden@reaps.org
www.reaps.org
www.facebook.com/REAPSPG
Overview: A small local organization founded in 1989
Mission: To educate the public on where & what can be recycled, how to compost & vermicompost, organic gardening, environmentally friendly alternatives, & promotion of the 5 R's (Rethink, Refuse, Reduce, Recycle & Reuse); To provide educational programs to schools, daycares, & committee groups
Member of: Recycling Council of British Columbia; Volunteer PG; Downtown Community Gardens
Finances: *Annual Operating Budget:* $100,000-$250,000; *Funding Sources:* Regional District Fraser Fort George; Dept. Fisheries & Oceans; City of Prince George
Staff Member(s): 2; 20 volunteer(s)
Membership: 61; *Fees:* $25 institutional; $8 student/individual; $15 family; *Committees:* EnhancePG, Recycling Council of BC; Civic Pride
Activities: Adopt-a-Worm Program; Salmonids in the Classroom Program; Workshops on gardening, composting, recycling; Earth Day Celebration; *Awareness Events:* Earth Day, April 22; Composting Week, May 5; Buy Nothing Day, November 3; *Internships:* Yes; *Speaker Service:* Yes
Chief Officer(s):
Terri McClymont, Executive Director
terri@reaps.org

Prince George Symphony Orchestra Society (PGSO)
2880 - 15 Ave., Prince George BC V2M 1T1
Tel: 250-562-0800; *Fax:* 250-562-0844
www.pgso.com
www.facebook.com/pgsymphony
twitter.com/pgsymphony
www.youtube.com/pgsymphony
Overview: A small local charitable organization founded in 1971 overseen by Orchestras Canada

Mission: To provide symphonic music for Prince George & region consistent with Prince George Symphony Orchestra artistic policy that facilitates artistic development of its players; to foster & facilitate positive community image & financial responsiblity so that a wide spectrum of musical experiences is offered to players & audiences alike
Member of: Orchestras Canada
Finances: *Funding Sources:* Box office; Sponsors; Individual & corporate donations; Government grants
Staff Member(s): 6
Membership: 48
Activities: *Library:* Not open to public
Chief Officer(s):
Jeremy Stewart, General Manager

Prince George United Way *See* United Way of Northern BC

Prince of Wales Northern Heritage Centre (PWNHC)
PO Box 1320, 4750 - 48th St., Yellowknife NT X1A 2L9
Tel: 867-767-9347; *Fax:* 867-873-0205
pwnhc@gov.nt.ca
www.pwnhc.ca
www.facebook.com/pwnhc
twitter.com/nrthrnheritage
www.instagram.com/northernheritage
Overview: A small provincial organization founded in 1979
Mission: To house the Central Museum operation of the Government of the Northwest Territories & the Northwest Territories Archives; To provide a broad range of heritage services; To preserve, promote, & portray the natural & human history of the Northwest Territories
Member of: Canadian Museums Association; Council of Canadian Archives
Finances: *Annual Operating Budget:* $3 Million-$5 Million
Staff Member(s): 18; 5 volunteer(s)
Membership: *Committees:* Acquisitions; Exhibits
Activities: Collections management; archives; exhibits; website; public programs; *Library:* NWT Archives Library; Open to public
Chief Officer(s):
Sarah Carr-Locke, Director
sarah_carr-locke@gov.nt.ca

Prince Rupert & District Chamber of Commerce (PRDCC)
#100, 515 3rd Ave., Prince Rupert BC V8J 1L9
Tel: 250-624-2296; *Fax:* 250-624-6105
info@princerupertchamber.ca
www.princerupertchamber.ca
www.facebook.com/PRDChamber
twitter.com/rueprtchamber
Overview: A small local organization founded in 1908
Mission: To promote & improve trade & commerce, economic, civil & social welfare of the City of Prince Rupert & District
Member of: BC Chamber of Commerce, Canadian Chamber of Commerce
Finances: *Annual Operating Budget:* $100,000-$250,000; *Funding Sources:* Membership dues; Christmas dinner; auction
Staff Member(s): 2; 200 volunteer(s)
Membership: 290; *Fees:* Based on number of employees; *Committees:* Business Excellence Awards; Communications; Finance; Gala; Golf Scramble; Member Initiatives; Policy; Rising Stars
Activities: Organizing membership meetings & speaker programs; *Awareness Events:* Business Excellence Awards *Library:* Visitor Information Centre; Open to public
Chief Officer(s):
Jamie Gerrie, Manager, Finance & Administration
jamie@princerupertchamber.ca
Simone Clark, Manager, Communications
simone@princerupertchamber.ca

Prince Rupert Association for Community Living
PO Box 442, Prince Rupert BC V8J 3R2
Tel: 250-624-5256; *Fax:* 250-627-7182
Overview: A small local organization
Member of: British Columbia Association for Community Living

Prince Rupert Fire Museum Society
200 - 1st Ave. West, Prince Rupert BC V8J 1A8
Tel: 250-624-2211; *Fax:* 250-624-3407
shirts@citytel.net
www.princerupertlibrary.ca/fire
Overview: A small local charitable organization founded in 1986
Finances: *Annual Operating Budget:* Less than $50,000
Activities: *Library:*

Prince Rupert Labour Council
867 Fraser St., Prince Rupert BC V8J 1R1
Tel: 250-627-8833; Fax: 250-627-8833
Overview: A small local organization overseen by British Columbia Federation of Labour
Mission: To advance the economic & social welfare of workers in the Prince Rupert area of British Columbia
Affiliation(s): Canadian Labour Congress (CLC)
Activities: Advocating for workers in the Prince Rupert area; Liaising with locally elected officials; Preparing presentations for Prince Rupert City Council, on workers' issues, such as pensions; Presenting educational opportunities for members; Marking the annual Day of Mourning for workers injured or killed on the job

Princess Margaret Cancer Foundation
700 University Ave., 10th Fl., Toronto ON M5G 1Z5
Tel: 416-946-6560; Fax: 416-946-6563
Toll-Free: 866-224-6560
info@thepmcf.ca
www.thepmcf.ca
www.facebook.com/thePMCF
twitter.com/thePMCF
www.youtube.com/user/PrincessMargaretHF
Overview: A small local charitable organization
Mission: To raise funds to support cancer research at the Princess Margaret Cancer Centre
Chief Officer(s):
Tom Ehrlich, Chair
Paul Alofs, President & CEO
Kenzie Broddy, Manager, Communications
kenzie.broddy@thepmcf.ca

Princess Patricia's Canadian Light Infantry Association
PO Box 10500, Stn. Forces, Edmonton AB T5J 4J5
Tel: 780-973-4011; Fax: 780-842-4106
secretary@ppliassoc.ca
ppcliassoc.ca
Also Known As: PPLIC Association
Overview: A medium-sized national charitable organization
Mission: To support the interests of the Regiment
Finances: Annual Operating Budget: Less than $50,000
Membership: 950; Fees: $20
Chief Officer(s):
Bud Hawkins, President, Manitoba/Northwest Ontario Branch

Princeton & District Chamber of Commerce
PO Box 540, 105 Hwy. 3 East, Princeton BC V0X 1W0
Tel: 250-295-3103; Fax: 250-295-3255
Overview: A small local organization founded in 1913
Member of: BC Chamber of Commerce; Canadian Chamber of Commerce
Finances: Funding Sources: Membership dues
Activities: Trade Show in May; Speaker Service: Yes; Library: Open to public

Princeton Community Arts Council
PO Box 281, Princeton BC V0X 1W0
Tel: 250-295-7588
princetonartscouncilbc@gmail.com
princetonarts.ca/Princeton_Arts.html
Overview: A small local organization founded in 1992
Mission: To promote & support community culture
Chief Officer(s):
Marjorie Holland, President

Printing & Graphics Industries Association of Alberta (PGIA)
PO Box 61229, RPO Kensington, Calgary AB T2N 4S6
Tel: 403-281-1421; Fax: 403-225-1421
info@pgia.ca
www.pgia.ca
Overview: A small provincial organization founded in 1987
Mission: To be committed to the advancement of a healthy, effective & ethical graphic arts industry by providing leadership in the development of imaged communications
Member of: Printing Industries of America
Finances: Annual Operating Budget: $50,000-$100,000; Funding Sources: Membership fees; Programs
8 volunteer(s)
Membership: 50 corporate; Fees: Schedule available; Member Profile: Printing company or supplier
Activities: Internships: Yes
Chief Officer(s):
Christoph Bruehl, President

Printing Equipment & Supply Dealers' Association of Canada (PESDA)
11 Alderbrook Place, Bolton ON L7E 1V3
Tel: 416-524-1954; Fax: 905-951-6374
www.pesda.com
Overview: A medium-sized national organization founded in 1975
Mission: To promote & advance the interests of the printing equipment, consumables & related services industries in Canada
Finances: Annual Operating Budget: $50,000-$100,000; Funding Sources: Trade show; membership dues
Staff Member(s): 2
Membership: 25 organizations
Chief Officer(s):
Richard Armstrong, President
Bob Kirk, General Manager
bkirk@pesda.com

Prison Fellowship Canada / Fraternite des prisons du Canada
#144, 5945 Airport Road, Mississauga ON L4V 1R9
Tel: 905-673-5867; Fax: 905-673-6955
Toll-Free: 844-618-5867
info@prisonfellowship.ca
www.prisonfellowship.ca
www.facebook.com/PrisonFellowshipCanada
twitter.com/ServingLifePFC
www.youtube.com/channel/UC6GV-_BVbJpuOoodh6P3XvA
Overview: A small national organization founded in 1980
Mission: To challenge, equip & serve the body of Christ in its ministry to prisoners, ex-prisoners, victims & their families; To promote the advancement of restorative justice
Member of: Prison Fellowship International
Chief Officer(s):
Stacey Campbell, Executive Director/CEO, 844-618-5867
Johathan Miller, National Director, Regional Development, 844-618-5867 Ext. 225
jmiller@prisonerfellowship.ca
Maria Hadzis, National Volunteer Coordinator, 844-618-5867 Ext. 222
maria@prisonfellowship.ca

Prisoners' HIV/AIDS Support Action Network (PASAN)
526 Richmond St. East, Toronto ON M5A 1R3
Tel: 416-920-9567; Fax: 416-920-4314
Toll-Free: 866-224-9978
www.pasan.org
Overview: A small national organization founded in 1991
Mission: Prisoners, ex-prisoners, organizations, activists & individuals working together to provide advocacy, education, & support to prisoners on HIV/AIDS, HCV & related issues
Staff Member(s): 11
Chief Officer(s):
Glen Brown, Interim Executive Director
glen@pasan.org

Private Capital Markets Association of Canada (PCMA)
First Canadian Place, #5700, 100 King St. West, Toronto ON M5X 1C7
Toll-Free: 877-363-3632
info@pcmacanada.com
www.pcmacanada.com
www.linkedin.com/groups/Exempt-Market-Dealers-Association-Canada-3431649?mostPopular=&gid=3431649
www.facebook.com/PCMACanada
twitter.com/PCMACanada
www.youtube.com/user/EMDACanada
Previous Name: Exempt Market Dealers Association of Canada; Limited Markets Dealers Association of Canada
Overview: A medium-sized national organization founded in 2002
Mission: The PCMA is focused on strengthening and growing the private capital markets to ensure robust capital raising opportunities across Canada.
Chief Officer(s):
Geoffrey Ritchie, Executive Director
geoffrey.ritchie@pcmacanada.com

Private Career Educational Council; Ontario Association of Career Colleges See Career Colleges Ontario

Private Forest Landowners Association (PFLA)
PO Box 48092, Victoria BC V8Z 7H5
Tel: 250-381-7565; Fax: 250-381-7409
Toll-Free: 888-634-7352
info@pfla.bc.ca
www.pfla.bc.ca
www.facebook.com/PFLABC?ref=ts
twitter.com/PFLABC
Overview: A medium-sized provincial organization founded in 1995
Mission: The Private Forest Landowners Association (PFLA) represents owners of private Managed Forest land in BC.
Chief Officer(s):
Rod Bealing, Executive Director
rod.bealing@pfla.bc.ca

Private Home Day Care Association of Ontario See Home Child Care Association of Ontario

Private Motor Truck Council of Canada (PMTC) / Association canadienne du camionnage d'entreprise (ACCE)
#5, 225 Main St. East, Milton ON L9T 1N9
Tel: 905-827-0587; Fax: 905-827-8212
Toll-Free: 877-501-7682
info@pmtc.ca
www.pmtc.ca
twitter.com/privatefleets
Overview: A medium-sized national organization founded in 1977
Mission: To provide forums for fleet operators and industry stakeholders to exchange views and resolve issues concerning the private motor truck sector
Member of: North American Private Truck Council
Affiliation(s): National Private Truck Council
Finances: Annual Operating Budget: $250,000-$500,000; Funding Sources: Seminars; social events; membership fees
Staff Member(s): 4
Membership: 400; Fees: $85-$1,620 principal; $1,000 associate; $220 additional; Member Profile: Private truck fleets or suppliers to same; private truck fleets operated by companies whose principal business is other than transportation, but use their own truck fleets to further their business
Activities: Seminars; annual conference; benchmarking and best practices survey; Awareness Events: National Vehicle Graphics Design Competition
Chief Officer(s):
Mike Millian, President, 519-932-0902
trucks@pmtc.ca
Awards:
• PMCT Awards Program
Awards include: Hall of Fame, Private Fleet Safety, Vehicle Graphics, Ontario Inspectors, Private top Fleet Employers & the President's Award
• PMTC Young Leaders Bursary Award
Award helps promote investment in the training needs of the future young leaders of the private trucking industry; Costs will be covered for the recipient to complete 2 of the 4 courses required of the eligible program Eligibility: Students enroled in a PMTC Logistics Management Graduate Program
• Fleet Safety Awards
Meetings/Conferences:
• Private Motor Truck Council of Canada 2018 Annual Conference, June, 2018, Crowne Plaza Fallsview, Niagara Falls, ON
Scope: National
Publications:
• The Counsellor [a publication of the Private Motor Truck Council of Canada]
Type: Magazine; Frequency: Quarterly
• NewsBriefs [a publication of the Private Motor Truck Council of Canada]
Type: Newsletter

Les Prix du Gouverneur Général pour les arts du spectacle See Governor General's Performing Arts Awards Foundation

Pro Bono Law Ontario (PBLO)
#110, 393 University Ave., Toronto ON M5G 1E6
Tel: 416-977-4448
Toll-Free: 855-255-7256
www.probonoontario.org
Overview: A small provincial organization founded in 2002
Mission: To broker partnerships & provide strategic guidance, training & tailored technical assistance to groups, law firms, & law associations that are dedicated to addressing the legal needs of low-income & disadvantaged individuals as well as the communities & charitable organizations that serve them
Activities: Volunteer Lawyers Service; South Asian Legal Clinic of Ontario; Child Advocacy Project; Lawyers for Aboriginal Arts

Project; Wills & Powers of Attorney Project; Community Economic Development Project
Chief Officer(s):
Lynn Burns, Executive Director
lynn@probonoontario.org

Pro Bono Québec
CP 55043, Succ. Notre-Dame, 11, rue Notre-Dame ouest, Montréal QC H2Y 4A7
Tél: 514-954-3434; *Téléc:* 514-954-3427
Ligne sans frais: 800-361-8495
info@probonoquebec.ca
www.probonoquebec.ca
www.facebook.com/150444894975367
twitter.com/probonoquebec
Aperçu: *Dimension:* moyenne; *Envergure:* provinciale; fondée en 2008
Mission: Pour fournir le coût des conseils juridiques gratuits ou faible pour la population déshéritée du Québec
Affiliation(s): Barreau du Québec; Justice Québec; Barreau de Montréal; Centre d'accès à l'information juridique; SOQUIJ
Membre(s) du bureau directeur:
Nancy Leggett-Bachand, Directrice générale
Alexander De Zordo, President, Conseil d'administraion

Pro Coro Canada
Birks Building, #309, 10113 - 104 St., Edmonton AB T5J 1A1
Tel: 780-420-1247
thechoir@procoro.ab.ca
www.procoro.ab.ca
www.facebook.com/procorocanada
twitter.com/ProCoroCanada
Previous Name: Pro Coro Society-Edmonton
Overview: A small local charitable organization founded in 1981
Member of: Alberta Choral Federation; Association of Canadian Choral Directors; Chorus America
Finances: *Annual Operating Budget:* $250,000-$500,000; *Funding Sources:* Federal, provincial & municipal government; private foundations; business & individuals production
Staff Member(s): 5; 100 volunteer(s)
Membership: 210 individual
Activities: Annual subscription concert series; regional performances; tours; caberet; *Library:* Pro Coro Music Library; by appointment
Chief Officer(s):
Michael Zaugg, Artistic Director & Conductor

Pro Coro Society-Edmonton *See* Pro Coro Canada

Pro Musica Society Inc. *Voir* Société Pro Musica Inc.

Probation Officers Association of Ontario (POAO)
#6245, 2100 Bloor St. West, Toronto ON M6S 5A5
www.poao.org
www.facebook.com/POAOntario
twitter.com/POAOntario
Overview: A small provincial organization founded in 1952
Mission: To represent the professional interests of the probation & parole Officers across the province; to provide representation on legislative issues to policy makers; to act as a forum for exchange of experience & information.
Membership: *Fees:* $197.75 full membership; $84.75 associate; $339 affliate
Activities: Symposiums with workshops & speakers
Chief Officer(s):
Elana Lamese, President
president@poao.org
Publications:
• The Monitor
Type: Newsletter; *Frequency:* Quarterly

Central Branch
Brampton ON
Tel: 905-456-4700
www.poao.org
Chief Officer(s):
Kerry Gray, Contact

Eastern Branch
Ottawa West Probation & Parole Services, 10A Hearst Way, Ottawa ON K2L 2P4
Tel: 613-270-8260; *Fax:* 613-270-8422
www.poao.org
Chief Officer(s):
Jamie Pearson, Chair

Midwest Branch
Stratford ON
Tel: 519-271-5220
www.poao.org

Chief Officer(s):
Anna Brenneman, Chair

Northeast Branch
Minden ON
Tel: 705-286-1489
www.poao.org
Chief Officer(s):
Terry Goodwin, Chair

Northwest Branch
Kenora Probation & Parole Office, 810 Robertson St., Kenora ON P9N 1S9
Tel: 807-468-2857
www.poao.org
Chief Officer(s):
Jane Van Toen, Chair

Southwest Branch
Chatham ON
Tel: 519-352-1243
www.poao.org
Chief Officer(s):
Jill Johns, Chair

Probe International (PI)
225 Brunswick Ave., Toronto ON M5S 2M6
Tel: 416-964-9223; *Fax:* 416-964-8239
Toll-Free: 800-263-2784
probeinternational@nextcity.com
journal.probeinternational.org
www.facebook.com/ProbeInternational
twitter.com/probeintl
Overview: A medium-sized international charitable organization founded in 1980
Mission: To educate Canadians about the environmental, social, & economic effects of Canada's aid & trade abroad; To monitor & expose the effects of projects financed by Canadian tax dollars (through international financial institutions, such as the World Bank & the Asian Development Bank, & through agencies such as CIDA & the Export Development Corp.) & by Canadian corporations
Member of: Energy Probe Research Foundation; Canadian Environmental Network
Affiliation(s): Environment Liaison Centre (International); International Organization of Consumers Unions; Energy Probe; Environment Probe; Consumer Policy Institute; Environmental Bureau of Investigation
Finances: *Annual Operating Budget:* $50,000-$100,000; *Funding Sources:* Private donations
Staff Member(s): 5
Activities: *Speaker Service:* Yes; *Library:* by appointment
Chief Officer(s):
Patricia Adams, Executive Director
patriciaadams@probeinternational.org

Procure Alliance
#110, 1320, boul Graham, Mont-Royal QC H3P 3C8
Tel: 514-341-3000
Toll-Free: 855-899-2873
info@procure.ca
www.procure.ca
www.facebook.com/PROCURE.ca
twitter.com/procureqc
www.youtube.com/user/procureqc
Also Known As: Alliance Procure
Overview: A medium-sized provincial charitable organization
Mission: To prevent, cure, & raise awareness about prostate cancer by providing research, education, & support
Finances: *Funding Sources:* Donations
Activities: Funding a bank of biological materials & data on prostate cancer; Organizing lectures & events; Maintaining a Prostate Cancer Support & Awareness Network in Quebec; Disseminating research & information on prostate cancer
Chief Officer(s):
Laurent Proulx, Executive Director

Product Care Association
105 West 3rd Ave., Vancouver BC V5Y 1E6
Tel: 604-592-2972; *Fax:* 604-592-2982
Toll-Free: 877-592-2972
contact@productcare.org
www.productcare.org
www.linkedin.com/company/3567005
www.facebook.com/ProductCare
twitter.com/Product_Care
Also Known As: ReGeneration
Overview: A medium-sized national organization founded in 1994

Mission: To manage product stewardship programs for household hazardous and special waste
Membership: 500+
Chief Officer(s):
Mark Kruschner, President
Publications:
• The Circular
Type: Newsletter

Producteurs d'oufs d'incubation du Canada *See* Canadian Hatching Egg Producers

Producteurs d'oufs du Canada *See* Egg Farmers of Canada

Les producteurs de lait du Québec (PLQ)
#415, 555, boul Roland-Therrien, Longueuil QC J4H 4G3
Tél: 450-679-0530; *Téléc:* 450-679-5899
plq@lait.qc.ca
www.lait.org
www.facebook.com/ProdLaitQc
twitter.com/ProdLaitQc
www.youtube.com/user/FPLQ
Nom précédent: Fédération des producteurs de lait du Québec
Aperçu: *Dimension:* grande; *Envergure:* provinciale; fondée en 1983
Mission: Défense et promotion des intérêts professionnels et sociaux des producteurs de lait et mise en marché du lait de la ferme
Membre de: Producteurs laitiers du Canada
Affiliation(s): Union des producteurs agricoles
Finances: *Budget de fonctionnement annuel:* Plus de $5 Million *Fonds:* Fonds de recherche
Membre: 14 syndicats; 5 856 fermes laitières; 12 000 producteurs et productrices de lait; *Critères d'admissibilite:* Producteurs de lait
Activités: *Service de conférenciers:* Oui
Membre(s) du bureau directeur:
Alain Bourbeau, Directeur général
Publications:
• Le producteur de lait québécois [publication de Producteurs de lait du Québec]
Type: Revue; *Frequency:* 10 fois par an

Producteurs de pommes du Nouveau-Brunswick *See* Apple Growers of New Brunswick

Les Producteurs de poulet du Canada *See* Chicken Farmers of Canada

Les Producteurs laitiers du Canada *See* Dairy Farmers of Canada

Producteurs Laitiers du Manitoba *See* Dairy Farmers of Manitoba

Producteurs laitiers du Nouveau-Brunswick *See* Dairy Farmers of New Brunswick

Les Productions DansEncorps Inc.
Centre Culturel Aberdeen, #14A, 140, rue Botsford, Moncton NB E1C 4X5
Tél: 506-855-0998; *Téléc:* 506-852-3401
dansencorps@bellaliant.com
www.dansencorps.ca
www.facebook.com/dansencorps
Aperçu: *Dimension:* moyenne; *Envergure:* provinciale; Organisme sans but lucratif; fondée en 1979
Mission: De contribuer au développement des arts au Nouveau-Brunswick
Finances: *Fonds:* Provinciaux et fédéraux
Activités: *Stagiaires:* Oui
Membre(s) du bureau directeur:
Chantal Cadieux, Directrice artistique

Produits alimentaires et de consommation du Canada *See* Food & Consumer Products of Canada

Professional Association of Canadian Theatres (PACT)
#555, 215 Spadina Ave., Toronto ON M5T 2C7
Tel: 416-595-6455; *Fax:* 416-595-6450
Toll-Free: 800-263-7228
info@pact.ca
www.pact.ca
www.facebook.com/pactpage
twitter.com/pacttweets
Also Known As: PACT Communications Centre
Previous Name: The League of Canadian Theatres

Overview: A large national charitable organization founded in 1976
Mission: To gain recognition & support for professional theatre in Canada; To support the development of Canadian theatre companies by sharing resources & knowledge; To develop working standards & relationships with theatre professionals through their associations; To inform & connect theatres across Canada through a communications network; To act as a major force in influencing cultural policy at all levels of government
Finances: *Funding Sources:* Membership fees; Government grants; Donations
Staff Member(s): 6; 36 volunteer(s)
Membership: 130+; *Fees:* Schedule available; *Member Profile:* Any not-for-profit organization that is engaged professionally in the creation of theatre in Canada; *Committees:* Advocacy; Artistic Practice; Cultural Diversity; Diversity; Executive; Finance; Governance; Labour Relations; Membership; Professional Development; Regional Advisory
Activities: Offering Human Resources program; Facilitating Professional Development program; Advocating for the well-being of its member theatres
Chief Officer(s):
Sara Meurling, Executive Director, 416-595-6455 Ext. 11
sara@pact.ca
Jeremy Stacey, Manager, Professional Development,
416-595-6455 Ext. 16
boomers@pact.ca
Meg Shannon, Manager, Membership & Communications,
416-595-6455 Ext. 15
megs@pact.ca
Awards:
• Mallory Gilbert Leadership Award
An individual who has demonstrated outstanding leadership within the Canadian theatre community.; *Amount:* $5,000
Publications:
• Artsboard [a publication of the Professional Association of Canadian Theatres]
Type: Newsletter; *Frequency:* s-m.
Profile: An information resource for PACT members that includes job postings, opportunities for professional development, and industry news
• impact! [a publication of the Professional Association of Canadian Theatres]
Type: Newsletter; *Frequency:* irregular
Profile: Long-form newsletter sharing insights from the PACT perspective

Professional Association of Foreign Service Officers (PAFSO) / L'Association professionnelle des agents du service extérieur (APASE)
#412, 47 Clarence St., Ottawa ON K1N 9K1
Tel: 613-241-1391; *Fax:* 613-241-5911
info@pafso-apase.com
www.pafso.com
www.linkedin.com/company/pafso-apase
www.facebook.com/pafso.apase
twitter.com/PafsoApase
Overview: A medium-sized national organization founded in 1965
Mission: To be the bargaining agent & the professional association for Canadian Foreign Service Officers
Staff Member(s): 9
Membership: 1,544
Chief Officer(s):
Ron Cochrane, Executive Director, 613-241-4396 Ext. 1
ron.cochrane@pafso-apase.com
Awards:
• Canadian Foreign Service Officer Award
Publications:
• bout de papier [a publication of Professional Association of Foreign Service Officers]
Type: Magazine; *Accepts Advertising*; *Price:* $16/year; $30/2-year

Professional Association of Internes & Residents of Newfoundland (PAIRN) / Association professionnelle des internes et résidents de Terre-Neuve
c/o Student Affairs, Health Sciences Complex, Memorial University, #2713, 300 Prince Philip Dr., St. John's NL A1B 3V6
Tel: 709-777-7118; *Fax:* 709-777-6968
pairn@mun.ca
www.pairn.ca
Overview: A small provincial organization overseen by Resident Doctors of Canada
Mission: To collaborate with local & national health care organizations to advocate on behalf of internes, resident physicians, & fellows of Newfoundland & Labrador; To advocate for the acknowledgement of the resident's role in medical education
Affiliation(s): Canadian Association of Internes & Residents; Newfoundland & Labrador Medical Association; Canadian Medical Association
Finances: *Funding Sources:* Membership fees
Membership: *Fees:* 1% of members' salary; *Member Profile:* Internes, residents, or fellows in any Newfoundland or Labrador hospital or its affiliate
Activities: Ensuring that resident physicians in Newfoundland & Labrador have input into health policy decisions that affect them; Helping members with situations during their residencies; Advising members on issues, such as contracts, benefits, education, & wellness; Participating in the community & donating to community organizations throughout Newfoundland & Labrador
Chief Officer(s):
Sarah Kean, President
Robert Mercer, Vice-President
Heather O'Reilly, Secretary
Erika Hansford, Treasurer
Awards:
• Dr. John G. Williams Clinical Teaching Award
To recognize the best clinical teacher of the year
• Lorimer Scholarship
To recognize non-academic qualities, such as patient support; *Amount:* $1,000

Professional Association of Residents & Internes of the Maritime Provinces *See* Professional Association of Residents in the Maritime Provinces

Professional Association of Residents & Interns of Manitoba (PARIM) / Association professionnelle des résidents et internes du Manitoba
Health Sciences Centre, 820 Sherbrook St., #GF132, Winnipeg MB R3A 1R9
Tel: 204-787-3673; *Fax:* 204-787-2692
parim.office@gmail.com
www.parim.org
Also Known As: PARI Manitoba
Overview: A small provincial organization founded in 1975 overseen by Resident Doctors of Canada
Mission: To represent the concerns of all residents & interns in Manitoba; To advocate for the well-being of residents & interns; To promote quality medical education & excellent patient care
Affiliation(s): Canadian Association of Internes & Residents
Membership: 400; *Member Profile:* Manitoba residents & interns who are receiving education & training at hospitals
Activities: Working to achieve optimal working conditions for physicians in training in Manitoba; Maintaining liaisons with other health care organizations in Manitoba; Raising public awareness about the roles of residents
Chief Officer(s):
Leslie Anderson, Co-President
Maha Haddad, Co-President
Jessica Burleson, Executive Director
jburleson@hsc.mb.ca

Professional Association of Residents in the Maritime Provinces (PARI-MP) / Association professionnelle des résidents des provinces maritimes
Halifax Professional Centre, #460, 5991 Spring Garden Rd., Halifax NS B3H 1Y6
Tel: 902-404-3597
Toll-Free: 877-972-7467
www.parimp.ca
Previous Name: Professional Association of Residents & Internes of the Maritime Provinces
Overview: A small provincial organization founded in 1969 overseen by Resident Doctors of Canada
Mission: To represent the interests of resident physicians who train at Dalhousie University; To improve the well-being & working conditions of residents in the Maritimes; To advocate on the behalf of residents
Affiliation(s): Canadian Association of Internes & Residents
Staff Member(s): 5
Membership: 540; *Member Profile:* Maritime residents who train at Dalhousie University & who are based in Halifax, Nova Scotia, Sydney, Nova Scotia, Moncton, New Brunswick, Fredericton, New Brunswick, & Saint John, New Brunswick
Activities: Organizing information seminars for Maritime resident physicians; Negotiating & enforcing the collective agreement; Arranging social events for residents; Adminstering an annual bursary program; Collaborating with other organizations for advocacy purposes
Chief Officer(s):
Philip Davis, President
Sandi Carew Flemming, Executive Director
sandi@parimp.ca
Publications:
• PARIscope
Type: Newsletter; *Frequency:* Quarterly
Profile: Association updates & information, plus upcoming events for members

Professional Association of Residents of Alberta (PARA) / Association professionnelle des résidents de l'Alberta
Garneau Professional Center, #340, 11044 - 82 Ave., Edmonton AB T6G 0T2
Tel: 780-432-1749; *Fax:* 780-432-1778
Toll-Free: 877-375-7272
para@para-ab.ca
www.para-ab.ca
www.facebook.com/ProfessionalAssociationofResidentPhysiciansofAB
twitter.com/para_ab
Overview: A medium-sized provincial organization founded in 1975 overseen by Resident Doctors of Canada
Mission: To represent physicians completing further training in residency programs; To promote excellence in education & patient care; To advocate for health care issues & for improvement in working conditions, salary, & benefits for resident physicians of Alberta
Affiliation(s): Canadian Association of Internes & Residents
Finances: *Funding Sources:* Membership dues
Staff Member(s): 5
Membership: *Member Profile:* Resident physicians of Alberta
Activities: Organizing information seminars & social events for residents in Alberta; Assisting residents who experience academic or professional difficulties or personal problems; Liaising with all levels of administration & government; Advocating for issues which affect residents; Preparing for & conducting contract negotiations on behalf of residents in Alberta; Enforcing the terms of contracts; Arranging payment for member life insurance & long term disability insurance
Chief Officer(s):
Catherine Cheng, President
Rob Key, Chief Executive Officer
rob.key@para-ab.ca
Kiersten Doblanko, Specialist, Communications
kiersten.doblanko@para-ab.ca

Professional Association of Residents of Ontario (PARO)
#1901, 400 University Ave., Toronto ON M5G 1S5
Tel: 416-979-1182; *Fax:* 416-595-9778
Toll-Free: 877-979-1183
paro@paroteam.ca
www.mypard.ca
Overview: A small provincial organization overseen by Resident Doctors of Canada
Mission: To improve the quality of life for young doctors training in Ontario; To advocate for acknowledgment of the resident's role in medical education; To ensure that patients receive excellent care
Member of: Resident Doctors of Canada
Membership: *Member Profile:* Residents who train in Ontario
Activities: Working to achieve optimal training & working conditons for residents throughout Ontario; Administering funds from the PARO Trust Fund for the welfare of residents
Chief Officer(s):
Robert Conn, CEO
Stephanie Kenny, President
Awards:
• PARO Excellence in Clinical Teaching Awards
To recognize excellent clinical teachers who train new physicians
• Lois H. Ross Resident Advocate Award
To recognize an individual who has advocated on behalf of residents & resident issues
• Residency Program Excellence Award
To recognize programs that create a positive environment to produce excellent clinicians
• Citizenship Awards for Medical Students
To recognize a medical student who has maintained an adquate

academic standing & who has contributed to the general welfare of fellow medical students
• Resident Teaching Awards
To recognize a resident at each university centre who provides outstanding clinical teaching experiences; *Amount:* $1,000
• Canadian Research Awards for Family Medicine Residents
Sponsored jointly by the PARO Trust Fund & The Royal College of Physicians & Surgeons of Canada, the award recognizes family medicine residents for original research
• Canadian Research Awards for Specialty Residents in the Divisions of Medicine & Surgery
Sponsored by the PARO Trust Fund, The Royal College of Physicians & Surgeons of Canada, & The Canadian Society for Clinical Investigation, the awards recognize original work by postgraduate trainees
• Travel Award for Clinical Educators
Eligibility: Faculty members who wish to visit another centre to improve his or her clinical teaching ability; *Amount:* $4,000

Professional Association of Volunteer Leaders Ontario (PAVRO)
2095 Nathaway Dr., Youngs Point ON K0L 3G0
Tel: 705-654-3261
pavro@pavro.on.ca
www.pavro.on.ca
Merged from: Ontario Association for Volunteer Administration; Ontario Directors of Volunteers in Healthcare
Overview: A small provincial organization founded in 1988
Mission: To lead the professional management of volunteer resources; To assist in the professional development of members
Affiliation(s): Ontario Directors of Volunteers in Hospitals
Finances: *Annual Operating Budget:* $50,000-$100,000; *Funding Sources:* Membership dues; fundraising; conference
20 volunteer(s)
Membership: 276; *Fees:* Schedule available; *Member Profile:* Individuals or organizations in the volunteer engagement field
Activities: *Speaker Service:* Yes
Chief Officer(s):
Judy Amyotte, Office Manager
Publications:
• ePowerline [a publication of the Professional Association of Volunteer Leaders Ontario]
Type: Newsletter; *Price:* Free with membership in PAVRO

Professional Convention Management Association - Canada West Chapter (PCMA)
BC
Tel: 604-647-7346
canadawest@pcma.org
www.pcma.org
Overview: A medium-sized international organization founded in 1957
Mission: To promote the convention management industry & provide education to its memebers
Membership: 233; *Member Profile:* Meetings industry professionals; suppliers; faculty members; students; *Committees:* Membership; Program
Activities: Educational seminars; networking opportunities with peers
Chief Officer(s):
Diana Reid, President
dreid@vancouverconventioncentre.com
Publications:
• Western News
Type: Newsletter; *Frequency:* Quarterly

Professional Council of Licensed Practical Nurses *See* College of Licensed Practical Nurses of Alberta

Professional Employees Association (Ind.) (PEA) / Association des employés professionnels (ind.)
#505, 1207 Douglas St., Victoria BC V8W 2E7
Tel: 250-385-8791; *Fax:* 250-385-6629
Toll-Free: 800-779-7736
www.pea.org
www.facebook.com/peaonline
twitter.com/pea_online
www.youtube.com/user/PEAblogger
Overview: A medium-sized provincial organization founded in 1974
Mission: To provide collective bargaining representation to professionals employed in the provincial public service & elsewhere in the BC public sector
Finances: *Annual Operating Budget:* $500,000-$1.5 Million; *Funding Sources:* Fees, grants, donations

Staff Member(s): 9
Membership: 2,500 (9 units)
Activities: *Library:*
Chief Officer(s):
Scott McCannell, Executive Director
smccannell@pea.org
Ben Harper, Communications Officer
bharper@pea.org

Professional Engineers & Architects of the Ontario Public Service *See* Professional Engineers Government of Ontario

Professional Engineers & Geoscientists Newfoundland & Labrador (PEGNL)
Baine Johnston Centre, PO Box 21207, #203, 10 Fort William Pl., St. John's NL A1A 5B2
Tel: 709-753-7714; *Fax:* 709-753-6131
main@pegnl.ca
www.pegnl.ca
Previous Name: Association of Professional Engineers & Geoscientists of Newfoundland
Overview: A medium-sized provincial licensing organization founded in 1952 overseen by Engineers Canada
Mission: To provide competent & ethical practice of engineering & geoscience in Newfoundland & Labrador; To ensure public confidence, sustainability, & stewardship of the professions; To provide leadership to enhance quality of life through the application & management of engineering & geoscience
Member of: Engineers Canada; Canadian Council of Professional Geoscientists
Finances: *Funding Sources:* Membership dues
200 volunteer(s)
Membership: 5,000; *Fees:* $224 individual; $564-1,031 corporate; $530 licensee; *Committees:* Registration; Limited License Assessment; Complaints Authorization; Disciplinary Panel; Nomination; Awards; Board Linkages; Compliance Advisory; Endowment Fund; Board of Directors; National Engineering & Geoscience Month; Environment; Envisioning
Activities: Administering The Engineers & Geoscientists Act in Newfoundland; *Awareness Events:* National Engineering Week; Science & Technology Week
Chief Officer(s):
Geoff Emberley, P.Eng., FEC, Chief Executive Offiver & Registrar, 709-753-7714 Ext. 108
gemberley@pegnl.ca
Mark Fewer, Chief Operating Officer & Deputy Registrar, 709-753-7714 Ext. 106
mfewer@pegnl.ca
Janet Bradshaw, P.Eng., FEC, Director, Professional Standards, 709-753-7714 Ext. 107
jbradshaw@pegnl.ca
Awards:
• Award for Merit
To recognize members who have made outstanding contributions to the profession &/or to the community
• Award for Service
Awarded to members who have served their profession diligently for many years & who have made substantial contributions to the Association & to the advancement of the professions
• Environmental Award
Recognizes the application of science, technology & engineering to human & resource environmental management in Newfoundland & Labrador
• Early Accomplishment Award
Given to members in recognition of exceptional achievement in the early years of an engineer's or geoscientist's professional career
• Community Service Award
Given to members in recognition of outstanding service & dedication to society
• Teaching Award

Professional Engineers for Public Safety Association (PEPSA)
4559.cupe.ca
Also Known As: CUPE 4559
Previous Name: The Professional Engineers Group of the Canadian Standards Association
Overview: A small national organization
Chief Officer(s):
Martin Buchanan, President
Pres4559@members.cupe.ca

Professional Engineers Government of Ontario
4711 Yonge St., 10th Fl., Toronto ON M2N 6K8

Tel: 416-784-1284; *Fax:* 416-784-1366
pego@pego.on.ca
www.pego.on.ca
Previous Name: Professional Engineers & Architects of the Ontario Public Service
Overview: A small provincial organization
Mission: The Professional Engineers Government of Ontario (PEGO) is a certified bargaining association representing Professional Engineers and Ontario Land Surveyors working directly for the Government of the Province of Ontario.

The Professional Engineers Group of the Canadian Standards Association *See* Professional Engineers for Public Safety Association

Professional Engineers Ontario (PEO)
#101, 40 Sheppard Ave. West, Toronto ON M2N 6K9
Tel: 416-224-1100; *Fax:* 416-224-9527
Toll-Free: 800-339-3716
www.peo.on.ca
www.linkedin.com/company/peo---professional-engineers-ontario
www.facebook.com/ProfessionalEngineersOntario
twitter.com/PEO_HQ
Previous Name: Association of Professional Engineers of Ontario
Overview: A large provincial licensing organization founded in 1922 overseen by Engineers Canada
Mission: To meet the needs of Ontario society by licensing & regulating the entire practice of professional engineering in an open, transparent, inclusive manner. There are 36 chapters across the province
Member of: Engineers Canada
Finances: *Funding Sources:* Membership fees
700 volunteer(s)
Membership: 70,000; *Fees:* Schedule available; *Committees:* Executive; Audit; Finance; Human Resources; Legislation; OSPE-PEO Joint Relations; Regional Councillors; Academic Requirements; Advisory Committee on Volunteers; Awards; Central Election & Search; Complaints; Complaints Review Councillor; Consulting Engineer Designation; Discipline; Education; Enforcement; Equity & Diversity; Experience Requirements; Fees Mediation; Government Liaison; Licensing; PEO-OAA Joint Liaison; Professional Standards; Registration; Regional; Volunteer Leadership Conference Planning
Activities: *Speaker Service:* Yes
Chief Officer(s):
Bob Dony, Ph.D., P.Eng., President
Gerard McDonald, P.Eng., MBA, Registrar, 416-840-1102
registrar@peo.on.ca
Scott Clark, LL.B., Chief Administrative Officer, 416-840-1126
sclark@peo.on.ca
Linda Latham, P.Eng., Deputy Registrar, Regulatory Compliance, 416-840-1076
llatham@peo.on.ca
Michael Price, P.Eng., MBA, Deputy Registrar, Licensing & Registration, 416-840-1060
mprice@peo.on.ca
Johnny Zuccon, P.Eng., Deputy Registrar, Tribunals & Regulatory Affairs, 416-840-1081
jzuccon@peo.on.ca
David Smith, Director, Communications, 416-840-1061
dsmith@peo.on.ca
Mehta Chetan, Director, Finance & PEO Controller, 416-840-1084
cmehta@peo.on.ca
Awards:
• The Engineering Medal
Established 1964; silver medal awarded to members of PEO who have made a substantial contribution to the technical side of the profession in any of its branches; awarded in the following categories: engineering, management, research & development; there is no limit to the number of medals that may be awarded each year
• V.G. Smith Award
Established 1962; awarded annually to a member of PEO who has achieved registration during the year by examination, with the highest standing of the candidates who have completed their examinations in that year
• S.E. Wolfe Thesis Award
Established 1965; awarded to a member who has passed at least one of the association examinations, & whose thesis has been awarded the highest mark of all those presented during the year
• The Professional Engineers Gold Medal
Established 1947; awarded to a member of PEO who has spent

Canadian Associations / Professional Engineers Ontario (PEO)

some years working in the profession & has subsequently given outstanding public service to the country in the federal, provincial, educational, charitable, or other fields; winner receives a gold medal & a citation
• The Professional Engineers Citizenship Award
Established 1970; awarded to members of PEO who have made a substantial contribution in such fields as education, the arts, medicine, law, & social service while maintaining their identity as professional engineers; there is no limit to the number of these awards made each year
• Order of Honour Award
An honorary society of PEO, the purpose of which is to recognize & honour those professional engineers & others who have rendered conspicuous service to the engineering profession in varying degrees & normally through the association; awards are made in three classes: Member, Officer, & Companion
• Fellow of Engineers Canada
• G. Gordon M. Sterling Engineering Intern Award
• The President's Award
Meetings/Conferences:
• Professional Engineers Ontario 96th Annual General Meeting 2018, 2018
Publications:
• Employer Salary Survey [a publication of the Professional Engineers Ontario]
Type: Report
• Engineering Dimensions [a publication of the Professional Engineers Ontario]
Type: Magazine; *Editor:* Jennifer Coombes
• Membership Salary Survey [a publication of the Professional Engineers Ontario]
Type: Report
• PEO [Professional Engineers Ontario] Practice Bulletins
Type: Bulletin
• Professional Engineers Ontario Annual Report
Type: Yearbook; *Frequency:* Annual

Algoma
ON
algoma@peo.on.ca
algoma.peo.on.ca
Chief Officer(s):
Sarah Ackert Ferguson, P.Eng., Chair
Matt Kirby, P.Eng., Vice-Chair

Algonquin
ON
algonquin@peo.on.ca
algonquin.peo.on.ca
Member of: Engineers Canada
Chief Officer(s):
Uditha Senaratne, P.Eng., Chair

Brampton
ON
info@peobrampton.ca
www.peobrampton.ca
www.facebook.com/190569797256
twitter.com/PEO_Brampton
Chief Officer(s):
Max Morrow, P.Eng., Chair
max.morrow@peobrampton.ca
Ravinder Panesar, P.Eng., Vice-Chair
ravinder.panesar@peobrampton.ca

Brantford
ON
brantford@peo.on.ca
brantford.peo.on.ca
Chief Officer(s):
Vicki Hilborn, Chair
Edgar Fernandez, Vice-Chair

Chatham-Kent
ON
chatham-kent@peo.on.ca
chathamkent.peo.on.ca
twitter.com/peochathamkent
Chief Officer(s):
Haris Ahmadzai, P.Eng., Chair
chatham-kent@peo.on.ca
Stuart Brandon, P.Eng., Vice-Chair

East Toronto
ON
easttoronto@peo.on.ca
easttoronto.peo.on.ca
twitter.com/EastTO_PEO
Chief Officer(s):
Arthur Sinclair, P.Eng., Chair
Larisse Nana, P.Eng., Vice-Chair

Etobicoke
ON
etobicoke@peo.on.ca
etobicoke.peo.on.ca
Chief Officer(s):
Andrew Demeter, P.Eng., Chair
George Dimitrov, P.Eng., Vice-Chair

Georgian Bay
ON
georgianbay@peo.on.ca
georgianbay@peo.on.ca
Chief Officer(s):
Vivender Adunuri, P.Eng., Chair
Rup Dhawan, P.Eng., Vice-Chair

Grand River
ON
granriver@peo.on.ca
grandriverpeo.ca
ca.linkedin.com/in/grandriverpeo
www.facebook.com/GrandRiverChapterPEO
twitter.com/grandriverpeo
Chief Officer(s):
Erica Lee Garcia, P.Eng., Chair
chair@grandriverpeo.ca
Jane Wilson, P.Eng., Vice-Chair
vicechair@grandriverpeo.ca

Hamilton-Burlington
ON
hamilton@peo.on.ca
hamilton.peo.on.ca
Chief Officer(s):
Julie Wedzinga, P.Eng., Chair
Matthew Minnick, P.Eng., Vice-Chair

Kingston
ON
kingston@peo.on.ca
kingston.pep.on.ca
Chief Officer(s):
Lionel Ryan, P.Eng., Chair

Kingsway
ON
kingsway@peo.on.ca
kingsway.peo.on.ca
www.facebook.com/PEOKingsway
twitter.com/PEOKingsway
Chief Officer(s):
George Ayer, P.Eng., Chair
Vasilj Petrovic, P.Eng., Vice-Chair

Lake-of-the-Woods/Atikokan
ON
lakeofthewoods@peo.on.ca
lakeofwoods.peo.on.ca

Lake Ontario
ON
lakeontario@peo.on.ca
www.peolakeontario.ca
twitter.com/peolakeontario
Chief Officer(s):
Karen Chan, P.Eng., Chair
Larry Westlake, P.Eng., Vice-Chair

Lakehead
ON
lakehead@peo.on.ca
lakehead.peo.on.ca
www.facebook.com/PEOLakehead
twitter.com/PEOLakehead
Chief Officer(s):
Zack White, P.Eng., Chair
Damien Ch'ng, P.Eng., Vice-Chair

Lambton
ON
lambton@peo.on.ca
www.peolambton.com
Chief Officer(s):
Phil Lasek, P.Eng., Chair
Hanne Hettinga, P.Eng., Vice-Chair

London
ON
london@peo.on.ca
london.peo.on.ca
Chief Officer(s):
Adriana Csiba, P.Eng., Chair

Mississauga
ON

Niagara
PO Box 30023, Stn. Ridley Square, 275 - 4 Ave., St Catharines ON L2S 4A1
niagara@peo.on.ca
niagara.peo.on.ca
Chief Officer(s):
Darlene Daigle, P.Eng., Chair

North Bay
ON
northbay@peo.on.ca
northbay.peo.on.ca
Chief Officer(s):
Karin Pratte, P.Eng., Chair
Lindsay Keats, P.Eng., Vice-Chair

Northern Regional Office
Lakehead University Campus, 955 Oliver Rd., #CBX-1022B, Thunder Bay ON
Tel: 807-343-8345
peonro@lakeheadu.ca
northernregionaloffice.peo.on.ca
Chief Officer(s):
Meilan Liu, P.Eng., Contact

Oakville
PO Box 60017, 300 North Service Rd. West, Oakville ON L6M 3H2
oakville@peo.on.ca
www.peo-oakvillechapter.ca
www.facebook.com/peooakvillechapter
twitter.com/PEOOakville
Chief Officer(s):
Len D'Elia, Chair
chair@peo-oakvillechapter.ca
Parisa Mahdian, Vice-Chair
vice-chair@peo-oakvillechapter.ca

Ottawa
1554 Carling Ave., #M004, Ottawa ON K1Z 7M4
ottawa@peo.on.ca
ottawa.peo.on.ca
Chief Officer(s):
Joseph Podrebarac, P.Eng., Chair
David Grant, P.Eng., FEC, Vice-Chair

Peterborough
ON
peterborough@peo.on.ca
peterborough@peo.on.ca
Chief Officer(s):
Arash Yazdani, P.Eng., Chair
Marcelo König Sarkis, P.Eng., Vice-Chair

Porcupine/Kapuskasing
ON
porcupinekap.peo.on.ca

Quinte
ON
quinte@peo.on.ca
quinte.peo.on.ca
twitter.com/PEOQuinte
Chief Officer(s):
Peter Zandbergen, P.Eng., Chair
Coellen Linkie, P.Eng., Vice-Chair

Scarborough
ON
scarborough@peo.on.ca
www.scarborough.peo.on.ca
Chief Officer(s):
Murad Hussain, P.Eng., Chair

Simcoe Muskoka
ON
simcoe-muskoka@peo.on.ca
pwo-simcoemuskoka.com
www.facebook.com/PEO.SimcoeMuskoka
twitter.com/peo_sm
Chief Officer(s):
Kevin Hughes, P.Eng., Chair
chair@peo-simcoemuskoka.com
Oday Wadee, P.Eng., Vice-Chair
chair@peo-simcoemuskoka.com

Sudbury
ON
sudbury@peo.on.ca
sudbury.peo.on.ca
Chief Officer(s):
Ronny Theiss, Chair

Sean Sennanyana, Vice-Chair
Temiskaming
ON
temiskaming@peo.on.ca
temiskaming.peo.on.ca
Thousand Islands
Unit P/Q, #132, 163 Ormond St., Brockville ON K6V 7E6
thousandislands@peo.on.ca
thousandislands.peo.on.ca
Chief Officer(s):
Graham Houze, P.Eng., Chair
Toronto Humber
PO Box 12526, Stn. Martinway Plaza, 415 The Westway, Toronto ON M9R 4C7
toronto-humber@peo.on.ca
tohumber.peo.on.ca
www.facebook.com/PEOTOHumber
twitter.com/PEOTOHumber
Chief Officer(s):
Bilal Sherazi, P.Eng., Chair
Manoj Shukla, Chair
Otto Zander, P.Eng., FEC, Vice-Chair
Upper Canada
ON
uppercanada@peo.on.ca
uppercanada.peo.on.ca
Chief Officer(s):
Steve Stang, P.Eng., Chair
Ted Naugler, P.Eng., Vice-Chair
West Toronto
ON
westtoronto@peo.on.ca
westtorontopeo.com
www.facebook.com/148953528500919
twitter.com/WestTorontoPEO
Chief Officer(s):
Catharine Hancharek, P.Eng., Chair
Ammar Nawaz, P.Eng., Vice-Chair
Western Regional Office
Spencer Engineering Building, University of Western Ontario, #2084, London ON N6A 5B8
Tel: 519-661-3764
wro@peo.on.ca
wro.peo.on.ca
Chief Officer(s):
Zachary Gouveia, Contact
Carolina Correa, Contact
Willowdale-Thornhill
ON
willowdale-thornhill@peo.on.ca
www.willowdalethornhill.peo.on.ca
www.linkedin.com/in/peowillowdalethonhill
www.facebook.com/peo.willowdalethornhillchapter
twitter.com/peowillowdale
Chief Officer(s):
Nick Shelton, P.Eng., Chair
nick.shelton@wtpeo.org
Amit Gupta, P.Eng., Vice-Chair
amit.gupta@wtpeo.org
Windor-Essex
ON
windsor-essex@peo.on.ca
windsoressex.peo.on.ca
www.linkedin.com/groups/PEO-WindsorEssex-5092970
www.facebook.com/PeoWindsorEssex
twitter.com/PEOWindsorEssex
Chief Officer(s):
Sardar Asif Khan, P.Eng., Chair
Radwan Tamr, P.Eng., Vice-Chair
York
PO Box 186, 7305 Woodbine Ave., Markham ON L3R 3V7
www.peoyork.com
www.facebook.com/PEO.York.Chapter
twitter.com/peoyork
Chief Officer(s):
Gordon Ip, P.Eng., FEC, Chair
chair@peoyork.com
Lui Tai, P.Eng., Vice-Chair
vicechair@peoyork.com

Professional Golfers' Assocation of British Columbia (PGA of BC)
#3280, 21331 Gordon Way, Richmond BC V6W 1J9
Tel: 604-303-6766; *Fax:* 604-303-6765
Toll-Free: 800-667-4653
info@pgabc.org
www.pgabc.org
www.facebook.com/pgabc
twitter.com/pgaofbc
www.youtube.com/user/pgaofbc
Previous Name: British Columbia Professional Golfers Association
Overview: A medium-sized provincial organization
Mission: To promote the game of golf and enhance all players' enjoyment of the sport.
Member of: Professional Golf Association
Finances: *Funding Sources:* Corporate sponsorship
Staff Member(s): 5
Membership: 650+; *Member Profile:* Individuals employed in the golf industry; *Committees:* Membership & Employment; Captain's; Education & Events; Long Range Planning & Grow the Game; Buying Show; Awards
Activities: PGA tournaments
Chief Officer(s):
Donald Miyazaki, Executive Director
donald@pgabc.org
Brian McDonald, President

Professional Golfers' Association of Canada / Association des golfeurs professionnels du Canada
13450 Dublin Line, RR#1, Acton ON L7J 2W7
Tel: 519-853-5450; *Fax:* 519-853-5449
Toll-Free: 800-782-5764
info@pgaofcanada.com
www.pgaofcanada.com
www.facebook.com/PGAofCanada
twitter.com/pgaofcanada
www.youtube.com/user/thepgaofcanada
Also Known As: PGA of Canada
Previous Name: Canadian Professional Golfers' Association
Overview: A medium-sized national organization founded in 1911
Mission: The Canadian Professional Golfer's Association is a member based non-profit organization representing golf professionals across Canada.
Finances: *Annual Operating Budget:* $500,000-$1.5 Million
Staff Member(s): 10
Membership: 3,500
Activities: *Rents Mailing List:* Yes; *Library:* Not open to public
Chief Officer(s):
Gary Bernard, Chief Executive Officer, 519-853-5450 Ext. 221
gary@pgaofcanada.com
Heather Bodden, Manager & Member Liaison, Operations, 519-853-5450 Ext. 260
heather@pgaofcanada.com

Professional Hockey Players' Association (PHPA)
3964 Portage Rd., Niagara Falls ON L2J 2K9
Tel: 289-296-5561; *Fax:* 289-296-4567
www.phpa.com
www.facebook.com/173409159401617
twitter.com/thephpa
instagram.com/thephpa
Overview: A small national organization founded in 1967
Staff Member(s): 12
Membership: 1,600+; *Member Profile:* All professional hockey players in the AHL & ECHL; *Committees:* Alumni Association; Workers' Compensation; Panel of Attorneys; Registered Agents Program; Career Enhancement Program; Membership Assistance Program
Awards:
• Curt Leichner Distinguished Member Award

The Professional Institute of the Public Service of Canada (PIPSC) / Institut professionnel de la fonction publique du Canada
250 Tremblay Rd., Ottawa ON K1G 3J8
Tel: 613-228-6310; *Fax:* 613-228-9048
Toll-Free: 800-267-0446
www.pipsc.ca
www.facebook.com/PIPSC.IPFPC/
twitter.com/PIPSC_IPFPC
www.youtube.com/user/PIPSCOMM/videos
Overview: A large national organization founded in 1920
Mission: To serve members by serving as their collective bargaining agent & by providing representational services
Staff Member(s): 100
Membership: 57,000; *Committees:* By-Laws & Policies; Elections; Executive Compensation; Finance; Human Rights in the Workplace; Member Services; Professional Recognition & Qualifications; Science Advisory
Activities: *Library:*
Chief Officer(s):
Debi Daviau, President
president@pipsc.ca
Edward Gillis, COO/Executive Secretary
egillis@pipsc.ca
Awards:
• Life Membership Award
• Institute Service Awards
Established 1970; not more than five awards (brass plaques) may be made annually to members of the Institute in any classification, or to persons ineligible for membership, for outstanding service to the Institute
• Citation Certificate
• President's Achievement Award
• Gold Medal
• Honorary Membership
Meetings/Conferences:
• The Professional Institute of the Public Service of Canada 99th Annual General Meeting 2018, 2018
Scope: International
Contact Information: Manager, Membership & Administration: Linda Martel, E-mail: lmartel@pipsc.ca; Phone: 613-228-6310, ext. 4854
Publications:
• Communications [a publication of the Professional Institute of the Public Service of Canada]
Type: Magazine; *Frequency:* Biannually

Alberta & Northwest Territories Regional Office
#1700, 10020 - 101A Ave., Edmonton AB T5J 3G2
Tel: 780-428-1347; *Fax:* 780-426-5962
Toll-Free: 800-661-3939
Chief Officer(s):
Grace Chychul, Regional Representative
gchychul@pipsc.ca

British Columbia & Yukon Regional Office
#2015, 401 West Georgia St., Vancouver BC V6B 5A1
Tel: 604-688-8238; *Fax:* 604-688-8290
Toll-Free: 800-663-0485
Chief Officer(s):
Ernie McLean, Regional Representative
emclean@pipsc.ca

Manitoba/Saskatchewan Regional Office
#700, 125 Garry St., Winnipeg MB R3C 3P2
Tel: 204-942-1304; *Fax:* 204-942-4348
Toll-Free: 800-665-0094
Chief Officer(s):
Grace Chychul, Regional Representative
gchychul@pipsc.ca

National Capital Region
250 Tremblay Rd., Ottawa ON K1G 3J8
Tel: 613-228-6310; *Fax:* 613-228-9048
Toll-Free: 800-267-0446
Chief Officer(s):
Nancy Lamarche, Regional Representative

Nova Scotia/New Brunswick/Newfoundland/Prince Edward Island Regional Office
#610, 1718 Argyle St., Halifax NS B3J 3N6
Tel: 902-420-1519; *Fax:* 902-422-8516
Toll-Free: 800-565-0727
Chief Officer(s):
Karyn Ladurantaye, Regional Representative
kladurantaye@pipsc.ca

Ontario Regional Office
#701, 110 Yonge St., Toronto ON M5C 1T4
Tel: 416-487-1114; *Fax:* 416-487-7268
Toll-Free: 800-668-3943
Chief Officer(s):
Marcia Kredentser, Regional Representative
mkredentser@pipsc.ca

Québec Regional Office
#2330, 1000, rue Sherbrooke ouest, Montréal QC H3A 3G4
Tél: 514-288-3545; *Téléc:* 514-288-0494
Ligne sans frais: 800-363-0622
Chief Officer(s):
Pierrette Gosselin, Regional Representative
gosselin@pipsc.ca

Professional Interior Designers Institute of Manitoba
137 Bannatyne Ave. East, 2nd Fl., Winnipeg MB R3B 0R3
Tel: 204-925-4625
pidim@shaw.ca
www.pidim.ca

Canadian Associations / Professional Locksmith Association of Alberta (PLAA)

Overview: A small provincial organization overseen by Interior Designers of Canada
Mission: To practice interior design in order to improve the lives of the public
Membership: 132; *Fees:* $26.25 student; $171.15 associate; $341.25 provisional; $622.91 professional; *Member Profile:* Interior designers & those interested in interior design

Professional Locksmith Association of Alberta (PLAA)
36 Sunridge Close, Airdrie AB T4B 2G6
Tel: 403-948-9997; *Fax:* 403-948-9997
Toll-Free: 877-765-7522
www.plaa.org
Overview: A small provincial organization founded in 1976
Mission: To promote public awareness of security matters; To promote training of members; To promote proper legislation for the security industry
Finances: *Annual Operating Budget:* $50,000-$100,000; *Funding Sources:* Membership fees; annual convention & trade show; newsletter ads
Membership: 296; *Fees:* $100 individual; $200 corporate
Activities: *Internships:* Yes
Chief Officer(s):
Dave Kennedy, Executive Director
Meetings/Conferences:
• Professional Locksmiths Association of Alberta Annual General Meeting 2018, January, 2018, Baymont Inn & Suites, Red Deer, AB
Scope: Provincial

Professional Organizers in Canada (POC)
468 Queen St. East, #LL-02, Toronto ON M5A 1T7
www.organizersincanada.com
www.linkedin.com/company/794301
www.facebook.com/professionalorganizerscanada
twitter.com/poccanada
www.pinterest.com/POCCanada
Overview: A small national organization founded in 1999
Mission: To provide a supportive environment for professional organizers; To promote networking, share ideas, encourage referrals, & increase public awareness of the field of professional organizing in Canada
Finances: *Annual Operating Budget:* $250,000-$500,000 20 volunteer(s)
Membership: 700; *Fees:* $107.50; *Member Profile:* Individuals who create customized solutions to increase the efficiency of any home, office or individual
Activities: *Speaker Service:* Yes
Chief Officer(s):
Stephanie Deakin, President
poc-president@organizersincanada.com
Susan Toth, Director, Finance & Administration
dir-finance@organizersincanada.com
Pearl Cluff, Director, Communications
dir-communications@organizersincanada.com

Professional Outfitters Association of Alberta *See* Alberta Professional Outfitters Society

Professional Petroleum Data Management Association (PPDM)
PO Box 22155, Stn. Bankers Hall, #860, 736 - 8th Ave. SW, Calgary AB T2P 4J5
Tel: 403-660-7817; *Fax:* 403-660-0540
info@ppdm.org
www.ppdm.org
www.linkedin.com/groups?home=&gid=146440
www.facebook.com/108325212519325?ref=ts
twitter.com/PPDMAssociation
Previous Name: Public Petroleum Data Model Association
Overview: A medium-sized national organization founded in 1991
Mission: To develop data management standards for the collection & exchange of data in the petroleum industry; To promote information standards
Membership: *Fees:* US$100 individual; free for students; based on revenue for corporate; *Committees:* Certification; Professional Development; Rules; Regulatory Data Standards
Activities: Increasing awareness of the value of data management; Providing training
Chief Officer(s):
Trudy Curtis, CEO
curtist@ppdm.org
Amanda Phillips, *Senior Operations Coordinator*
Elise Sommer, *Senior Community Development Coordinator*

Professional Photographers Association of British Columbia (PPABC) *See* Professional Photographers of Canada

Professional Photographers of Canada (PPOC) / Photographes Professionnels du Canada
209 Light St., Woodstock ON N4S 6H6
Tel: 519-537-2555; *Fax:* 519-537-5573
Toll-Free: 888-643-7762
www.ppoc.ca
Previous Name: Commercial & Press Photographers Association of Canada (CAPPAC)
Overview: A medium-sized national organization founded in 1946
Mission: To promote excellence in professional imaging; To elevate professional standards & ethics; To act as a voice for the photographic profession on legal matters & legislative issues
Affiliation(s): Professional Photographers Association of British Columbia (PPABC); Professional Photographers of Canada Alberta (PPOC-AB); Professional Photographers of Saskatchewan (PPOC-SK); Professional Photographers of Canada Manitoba (PPOC-MB); Professional Photographers of Ontario (PPO); Corporation des Maîtres Photographes du Quebec (CMPQ); Professional Photographers of Canada Atlantic (PPOC-Atlantic); Professional Government Military Photographers of Canada (PGMPC)
Membership: *Committees:* Accreditation; Archives; Bylaws; Convention Procedures Manual; Copyright; eContact; Education Project; Estimating Manual; Exhibition; Image Salon; Social Media; Speaker Registry; Student Program; Public Awareness; National Convention; Trade Liaison
Activities: Liaising with government agencies; Offering educational opportunities, such as seminars & practical workshops; Providing an accreditation program for members to earn an accreditation in a specific field; Facilitating networking opportunities; Offering annual print competitions; Providing a help line for photographers' questions in areas such as technical information; *Speaker Service:* Yes
Chief Officer(s):
Tanya Thompson, Executive Director, 888-643-7762, Fax: 519-537-5573
exec.director@ppoc.ca
Meetings/Conferences:
• Professional Photographers of Canada 2018 Canadian Imaging Conference & Expo, May, 2018
Scope: National
Description: An opportunity for the exchange of professional ideas
Publications:
• Convention Procedures Manual
Type: Manual; *Editor:* Carmen Matthews, MPA, F.
• Professional Photographers of Canada Magazine
Type: Magazine; *Frequency:* Bimonthly
Profile: Educational information & changing trends in photography

Photographes professionnels du Québec (PPDQ)
23, rue Frère André Daoust, Rigaud QC J0P 1P0
Tél: 438-397-8182
web@ppdq.ca
qc.ppoc.ca
www.facebook.com/PhotographesProfessionnelsduQuebec
twitter.com/PhotographesQc
www.youtube.com/user/cmpqadmin
Chief Officer(s):
Jean-François Perreault, Chair, 819-565-1165
info@jeanfrancoisperreault.ca

Professional Photographers of Canada - Atlantic Region
c/o Cindi-Lee Campbell, 9195 Rte. 102, Morrisdale NB E5K 4N3
Tel: 506-757-1198
at.ppoc.ca
Chief Officer(s):
Berni Wood, Chair, 302-566-1100
bwood@reelmedia.ca
• Developments
Type: Newsletter; *Accepts Advertising; Editor:* Susanne Hovey
Profile: Member profiles, articles, continuing education & upcoming events

Professional Photographers of Canada - British Columbia Region
PO Box 1329, 4543 - 201 St., Langley BC V3A 6M5
Tel: 604-857-1569; *Fax:* 604-857-1570
Toll-Free: 877-857-1569
contact@ppoc-bc.ca
ppoc-bc.ca
twitter.com/PPOC_BC
Affiliation(s): Professional Photographers of America
Chief Officer(s):
Renee Charboneau, Chair, British Columbia, 604-689-4337
chair@ppoc-bc.ca

Professional Photographers of Canada - Ontario Region
ON
Toll-Free: 888-643-7762
bureauduppoc@ppoc.ca
on.ppoc.ca
www.facebook.com/PPOC.ONTARIO
twitter.com/PPOC_Ontario
www.youtube.com/ppocontario
Member of: Professional Photographers of America
Chief Officer(s):
Jean Chartrand, Chair, 613-203-7334
jeanchartrand@gmail.com

Professional Photographers of Canada - Saskatchewan Region
SK
Toll-Free: 888-643-7762
sk.ppoc.ca
Affiliation(s): Professional Photographers of Canada
Chief Officer(s):
Theresa (Therri) Papp, Chair, 306-279-4937
SKdirector@ppoc.ca

Professional Photographers of Canadan - Alberta Region
AB
Toll-Free: 888-643-7762
ab.ppoc.ca
www.facebook.com/PPOC.Alberta.Public
Chief Officer(s):
Jill Shantz, Regional Director, 780-460-8690
ABdirector@ppoc.ca

Professional Photographers of Québec *Voir* Professional Photographers of Canada

Professional Property Managers Association Inc. (PPMA)
PO Box 2279, Stn. Main, Winnipeg MB R3C 4A6
Tel: 204-957-1224; *Fax:* 204-957-1239
info@ppmamanitoba.com
www.ppmamanitoba.com
Overview: A small provincial organization founded in 1984
Mission: To improve & advance the standards of the professional property management industry in Manitoba
Affiliation(s): Canadian Federation of Apartment Associations
Finances: *Funding Sources:* Membership dies 13 volunteer(s)
Membership: 74 principal; 134 associates; *Fees:* $400 associate; maximum $1200 principal; *Committees:* Awards; Education; Energy & Environmental; Ethics; Golf; Membership; Political Action; Program; Public Relations; Robert L. Simpson Memorial Scholarship; Safety & Security; Social; Trade Show & Conference
Activities: Monthly membership meetings; annual conference & trade show; annual golf tournament
Chief Officer(s):
Shirley Tillett, Executive Director
Mario Lopes, President
Awards:
• Member of the Year
• Associate Member of the Year
• Caretaker of the Year
• Community Service Lifetime Achievement
• Robert L. Simpson Memorial Scholarship Fund
Deadline: June; *Amount:* $1,000

Professional Student Services Personnel (PSSP) / Personnel professionnel des services aux étudiants
PSSP Bargaining Unit Office, 1501 Danforth Ave., Toronto ON M4J 5C3
Tel: 647-348-3351; *Fax:* 647-348-3352
pssp.on.ca
Overview: A small local organization
Chief Officer(s):
Olga DeMelo, President
president@pssp.on.ca

Professional Surveyors Canada / Géomètres professionnels du Canada
#101B, 900 Dynes Rd., Ottawa ON K2C 3L6
Tel: 613-695-8333
Toll-Free: 800-241-7200
www.psc-gpc.ca
Overview: A medium-sized national organization

Mission: To foster cooperation amongst surveyors in Canada; To advocate for an integrated Canadian surveying profession
Chief Officer(s):
Sarah Cornett, BSc, OLS, Executive Director

Professional Union of Government of Québec Physicians (Ind.) *Voir* Syndicat professionnel des médecins du gouvernement du Québec (ind.)

Professional Writers Association of Canada (PWAC)
#210, 2800 14th Ave., Markham ON L3R 0E4
Tel: 416-504-1645
operations@pwac.ca
www.pwac.ca
twitter.com/writersdotca
Previous Name: Periodical Writers Association of Canada
Overview: A small national charitable organization founded in 1976
Mission: The Professional Writers Association of Canada (PWAC) is an organization of writers in Canada whose members work in a variety of areas in non-fiction writing, including journalism, copywriting, report writing, speech writing, & B2B/B2C website content development. Their work can be found in print, online, & in many other media. PWAC protects & promotes the rights of non-fiction writers in Canada & helps freelancers build a strong network for professional & personal support. The organization is governed by a volunteer Board of Directors with representation from five regions in Canada (British Columbia, Prairies & the North, Ontario, Quebec, & Atlantic).
Membership: *Fees:* Scale; *Committees:* Awards; Communications; Digital Assets; Membership; Partnerships & Advocacy; Professional Development
Activities: Organizing professional development & social events for members; Holding a National Conference in conjunction with the Annual General Meeting; Circulating news, information, & market data on the industry through discussion boards, social media platforms, & a national newsletter
Chief Officer(s):
Christine Peets, President
president@pwac.ca
David Petrie, Chief Administrator
operations@pwac.ca

Professionnels en gestion de bénévoles du Canada *See* Volunteer Management Professionals of Canada

Professionnels en produits promotionnels du Canada *See* Promotional Product Professionals of Canada Inc.

Programme Action Réfugiés Montréal (ARM) / Refugee Action Montreal
#2, 1439, rue Sainte-Catherine ouest, Montréal QC H3G 1S6
Tél: 514-935-7799; *Téléc:* 514-935-9848
info@actionr.org
www.actionr.org
Aperçu: *Dimension:* petite; *Envergure:* internationale; Organisme sans but lucratif; fondée en 1994
Mission: Nous offrons des services qui permettent aux réfugiés de faire valoir leur droit d'asile et de refaire leur vie dans un nouveau milieu
Membre de: Canadian Council for Refugees; Table de Concertation des organismes de refugiés de Montréal
Finances: *Budget de fonctionnement annuel:* $100,000-$250,000; *Fonds:* Anglican Diocese of Montreal; Presbyterian Church in Canada
Membre(s) du personnel: 3; 40 bénévole(s)
Membre: 1-99
Activités: Parrainage; accompagnement; amitié-jumelage; intervention auprès des personnes détenues; *Bibliothèque*
Membre(s) du bureau directeur:
Paul Clarke, Directeur général
clarke@actionr.org

Programme d'aide aux membres du barreau (PAMBA)
#003, 315, boul René-Lévesque est, Montréal QC H2X 3P3
Tél: 514-286-0931
Ligne sans frais: 800-747-2622
aide@pamba.info
www.barreau.qc.ca
Aperçu: *Dimension:* petite; *Envergure:* provinciale; fondée en 1996
Mission: Pour aider les membres du Barreau du Québec qui souffrent de toxicomanie et de problèmes de santé mentale
Membre: *Critères d'admissibilite:* Membres du Barreau du Québec; Les conjoints des membres du Barreau; Étudiants d l'École du Barreau

Membre(s) du bureau directeur:
François Lajoie, Président, Conseil d'administraion

Programme Parents-Secours du Canada *See* Block Parent Program of Canada

Les programmes éducatifs JA Québec
#505, 300, rue du Saint-Sacrement, Montréal QC H2Y 1X4
Tél: 514-285-8944
info@jaquebec.org
www.jaquebec.com
www.linkedin.com/company/643829
www.facebook.com/JAQuebec
Également appelé: JA Québec
Aperçu: *Dimension:* moyenne; *Envergure:* provinciale; fondée en 1962
Mission: Diffusion de programmes d'éducation économique pour étudiants du secondaire et du collégial
Membre de: Junior Achievement of Canada
250 bénévole(s)
Membre(s) du bureau directeur:
Sylvie Tremblay, Présidente/directrice générale
stremblay@jaquebec.org

Progressive Canadian Party / Parti Progressiste Canadien
218 Twyford St., Ottawa ON K1V 0V9
Tel: 613-738-8946
www.pcparty.org
Overview: A small national organization
Staff Member(s): 5
Membership: *Fees:* $10
Chief Officer(s):
Sinclair M. Stevens, Leader

Progressive Conservative Association of Prince Edward Island
PO Box 578, 30 Pond St., #B, Charlottetown PE C1A 7L1
Tel: 902-628-8679; *Fax:* 902-628-6428
Toll-Free: 800-859-4221
info@peipcparty.ca
peipc.ca
www.facebook.com/peipcparty
twitter.com/PEIPCParty
Also Known As: PEI PC Party
Overview: A small provincial organization
Mission: To form a government that is socially progressive
Membership: *Fees:* $5 senior/youth; $10 individual; $25 family; *Member Profile:* Citizens of Prince Edward Island age 14 & older
Chief Officer(s):
James Aylward, Party Leader

Progressive Conservative Party of Canada, Canadian Alliance Party; Canadian Conservative Reform Alliance *See* Conservative Party of Canada

Progressive Conservative Party of Manitoba
23 Kennedy St., Winnipeg MB R3C 1S5
Tel: 204-594-4080
pcmanitoba@pcmanitoba.com
www.pcmanitoba.com
www.facebook.com/PCManitoba
twitter.com/PC_Manitoba
Also Known As: PC Manitoba
Overview: A small provincial organization
Staff Member(s): 5
Chief Officer(s):
Brian Pallister, Party Leader

Progressive Conservative Party of New Brunswick / Le Parti Progressiste-Conservateur de Nouveau-Brunswick
336 Regent St., Fredericton NB E3B 3X4
Tel: 506-453-3456; *Fax:* 506-444-4713
Other Communication: www.scribd.com/PCNBCA
info@pcng.org
www.pcnb.ca
www.facebook.com/PCNBca
twitter.com/pcnbca
Overview: A large provincial organization
Staff Member(s): 21
Membership: 55 institutional; 20,000 individual; *Fees:* $10
Chief Officer(s):
Blaine Higgs, Party Leader
blaine.higgs@gnb.ca
Rick Lafrance, President
rick.lafrance@pcnb.org

Stephen Smith, Executive Director
stephen.smith@pcnb.org

Progressive Conservative Party of Saskatchewan
72 High St. East, Moose Jaw SK S6H 0B8
Tel: 306-693-7572; *Fax:* 306-693-7580
pcsask@sasktel.net
www.pcsask.ca
www.facebook.com/1041656712574805
twitter.com/PC_Saskatchewan
plus.google.com/109797344778550107038
Also Known As: PC Saskatchewan
Overview: A small provincial organization
Staff Member(s): 5
Chief Officer(s):
Rick Swenson, Party Leader

Progressive Housing Society
7836 - 6th St., Burnaby BC V3N 3N2
Tel: 604-522-9669; *Fax:* 604-522-4081
info@progressivehousing.net
www.progressivehousing.net
www.facebook.com/progressivehousingsociety
twitter.com/PHS604
Overview: A small local organization
Chief Officer(s):
Jaye Robertson, Executive Director
jrobertson@progressivehousing.net

Project 10 *See* Projet 10

Project Adult Literacy Society (PALS)
#41, 9912 - 106 St., Edmonton AB T5K 1C5
Tel: 780-424-5514; *Fax:* 780-425-5176
palsedmonton@gmail.com
palsedmonton.blogspot.ca
Also Known As: PALS
Overview: A small local charitable organization founded in 1979
Mission: To offer literacy programs for adults in Edmonton
Affiliation(s): Laubach Literacy of Canada
Activities: Offering ESL, literacy, & math tutoring & classes
Chief Officer(s):
Shirley Sandul, Executive Director

Project Chance
3950, boul Cavendish, Montréal QC H4B 2N3
Tel: 514-934-6199
Overview: A small local organization
Mission: To offer social housing for single mothers, from ages 18 to 30, who are pursuing full-time post-secondary education
Activities: Providing parenting workshops, a food bank, & after-school programs

Project Genesis
4735, ch de la Côte-Sainte-Catherine, Montréal QC H3W 1M1
Tel: 514-738-2036; *Fax:* 514-738-6385
genese.qc.ca
Overview: A small local organization
Mission: Community group that provides community organization, advocacy, and education, as well as legal advice involving tenant rights, debt & bankruptcy, family law, and immigration
Staff Member(s): 16
Chief Officer(s):
Michael Chervin, Executive Director

Project Peacemakers
745 Westminster Ave., Winnipeg MB R3G 1A5
Tel: 204-775-8178; *Fax:* 204-784-1339
info@projectpeacemakers.org
www.projectpeacemakers.org
www.facebook.com/108617822532248
twitter.com/ProjectPeacmkrs
www.youtube.com/user/peacemakers
Overview: A small international charitable organization founded in 1983 overseen by Project Ploughshares
Mission: Project Peacemakers is a group of people working for peace from a faith perspective. Its activities are varied, from peace delegations in war zones to educational forums on such issues as child soldiers & violent video games.
Member of: Project Ploughshares
Affiliation(s): Canadian Centre for Arms Control & Disarmament; Manitoba Environmental Network; Mennonite Central Committee; Peace Alliance Winnipeg; Manitoba Japanese-Canadian Citizens Association
Finances: *Annual Operating Budget:* Less than $50,000; *Funding Sources:* Member donations; church grants
Staff Member(s): 2; 30 volunteer(s)

Membership: 200; *Fees:* $25 one year; $40 two years; $8 low income
Activities: Concerts; film festivals; protests; witness-for-peace delegations; forums; *Speaker Service:* Yes; *Library:* Open to public
Publications:
• Peace Projections
Type: Newsletter; *Frequency:* Quarterly

Project Ploughshares
140 Westmont Rd. North, Waterloo ON N2L 3G6
Tel: 519-888-6541; *Fax:* 519-888-0018
plough@ploughshares.ca
www.ploughshares.ca
www.facebook.com/206928856016444
twitter.com/ploughshares_ca
Overview: A medium-sized international organization founded in 1976
Mission: Ecumenical peace agency of the Canadian Council of Churches that identifies, develops & advances approaches that build peace & prevent war
Member of: Canadian Council for International Cooperation; Canadian Centre for Philanthropy
Affiliation(s): Canadian Council of Churches; Conrad Grebel College
Finances: *Annual Operating Budget:* $500,000-$1.5 Million; *Funding Sources:* Donations 60%; grants 39.5%; other 0.5%
Staff Member(s): 8
Membership: 9 sponsoring churches + 8,000 individuals; *Member Profile:* Representatives from sponsoring churches; *Committees:* Governing
Activities: Research (collects & analyzes information on a wide range of issues related to militarism, security & development); publications; policy development & education (staff often serve as public speakers or media commentators & testify at parliamentary hearings) public conferences, workshops, works in Canada & internationally; *Internships:* Yes; *Speaker Service:* Yes; *Library:* Open to public
Chief Officer(s):
Debbie Hughes, Assistant, 519-888-6541 Ext. 24302
dhughes@ploughshares.ca

Project READ Literacy Network Waterloo-Wellington (PRLN)
124 Sydney St. South, 3rd Fl., Kitchener ON N2G 3V2
Tel: 519-570-3054; *Fax:* 519-570-9510
info@projectread.ca
www.projectread.ca
www.facebook.com/ProjectREADLitNetwork
twitter.com/ProjectREADWW
Overview: A small local charitable organization founded in 1988
Mission: To provide coordination, advocacy, referrals & support to & for literacy, literacy providers & students; To enhance the effective & efficient provision of literacy services to meet the needs in Waterloo-Wellington
Member of: Kitchener-Waterloo Chamber of Commerce; Ontario Literacy Coalition; Movement for Canadian Literacy
Affiliation(s): Ontario Literacy Coalition
Finances: *Annual Operating Budget:* $100,000-$250,000; *Funding Sources:* National government; provincial government; donations
Staff Member(s): 4; 14 volunteer(s)
Membership: 30; *Fees:* $60 institutional; $15 individual; *Member Profile:* Organizations & individuals concerned with literacy in the community; *Committees:* Waterloo Literacy Services Planning Committee; Wellington Literacy Services Planning Committee
Activities: Public awareness; information & referral to literacy programs; literacy assessments; professional development of literacy workers; literacy service planning; *Awareness Events:* International Literacy Day, Sept. 8; Family Literacy Day, Jan. 27; *Speaker Service:* Yes; *Library:* PRLN Literacy Resources Library; Open to public
Chief Officer(s):
Jane Tuer, Executive Director
jane@projectread.ca

Project Share
#2, 4129 Stanley Ave., Niagara Falls ON L2E 7H3
Tel: 905-357-5121; *Fax:* 905-357-0143
info@projectshare.ca
www.projectshare.ca
www.facebook.com/projectsharenf
twitter.com/ProjectSHARE_NF
www.instagram.com/projectshare_nf
Overview: A small local charitable organization founded in 1991
Mission: To assist these residents of Niagara Falls who live below the poverty line with basic needs in a proactive manner
Member of: Ontario Association of Food Banks
Affiliation(s): Food Banks Canada
Finances: *Annual Operating Budget:* $250,000-$500,000; *Funding Sources:* City of Niagara Falls; United Way; provincial government; donations
Staff Member(s): 12; 240 volunteer(s)
Activities: Subsidy programs; food bank; clothing; community garden; transportation; workshops
Chief Officer(s):
Diane Corkum, Executive Director

Projet 10 (P10) / Project 10
1575, rue Amherst, Montréal QC H2L 3L4
Tel: 514-989-0001
questions@p10.qc.ca
www.p10.qc.ca
www.facebook.com/P10montreal
twitter.com/p10_mtl
www.instagram.com/p10_mtl
Overview: A small local organization founded in 1991
Mission: To provide advocacy, education, & services to support the personal, social, sexual, & mental well-being of lesbian, gay, bisexual, transgender, transsexual, two-spirit, intersexed, & questioning youth; To empower youth at individual, community, & institutional levels; To support oppressed groups & individuals
Member of: Trans Health Network; L'Asterisk
Finances: *Annual Operating Budget:* $50,000-$100,000; *Funding Sources:* Government; Fundraising
Staff Member(s): 2; 20 volunteer(s)
Membership: 24
Activities: Offering drop-in services, listening lines, individual support & accompaniment, & gender affirming accessories; Engaging in advocacy; *Internships:* Yes
Chief Officer(s):
Otto Vicé, Co-Coordinator
coordoprojet10@gmail.com
Sarah Butler, Co-Coordinator
sarah@p10.qc.ca

Projet d'Intervention auprès des mineurs-res prostitués-ées (PIAMP)
CP 907, Succ. C, 3736, rue St-Hubert, Montréal QC H2L 4V2
Tél: 514-284-1267; *Téléc:* 514-284-6808
piamp@piamp.net
piamp.net
Aperçu: *Dimension:* petite; *Envergure:* locale; Organisme sans but lucratif
Mission: Fournit de l'aide et de soutien à la famille et les amis concernés par la prostitution.
Activités: Consultation, médiation, banque alimentaire

Le Projet Faim *See* The Hunger Project Canada

Projet T.R.I.P.
#2520, 2000, rue Pathenais, Montréal QC H2K 3S9
Tél: 514-596-5711; *Téléc:* 514-596-7722
projet_trip@yahoo.ca
projet-trip.org
Aperçu: *Dimension:* petite; *Envergure:* locale
Mission: Pour éviter les problèmes de toxicomanie entre les 12 à 20 ans dans le centre-sud de Montréal et de promouvoir une meilleure qualité de vie

Projets pour une agriculture écologique *See* Ecological Agriculture Projects

Prologue aux arts de la scène *See* Prologue to the Performing Arts

Prologue to the Performing Arts / Prologue aux arts de la scène
#413, 15 Case Goods Lane, Toronto ON M5A 3C4
Tel: 416-591-9092; *Fax:* 416-591-2023
Toll-Free: 888-591-9092
info@prologue.org
www.prologue.org
www.facebook.com/PrologueToThePerformingArts
twitter.com/Prologuearts
www.youtube.com/user/prologueadmin
Also Known As: Prologue
Overview: A small local charitable organization founded in 1966
Mission: To bring diverse performing art experiences into schools & communities
Affiliation(s): BC Touring Council; Festival Events Ontario; CAPACOA
Finances: *Annual Operating Budget:* $1.5 Million-$3 Million; *Funding Sources:* Ontario Arts Council; City of Toronto; Canada Council
Staff Member(s): 6; 16 volunteer(s)
Membership: 1-99; *Fees:* $25 institutional; *Committees:* Program; Fundraising; Marketing
Activities: Prologue showcases
Chief Officer(s):
Mel Hurst, Chair
Awards:
• Lieutenant Governor's Award
• Paula Award
To enable a work for young audiences by one or more Prologue artists and companies to be brought to completion.

Promoting Awareness of RSD & CRPS in Canada (PARC)
PO Box 21026, St Catharines ON L2M 7X2
Tel: 905-934-0261
www.rsdcanada.org/parc
Also Known As: PARC
Overview: A small national charitable organization
Mission: To support persons with CRPS, type 1 & 2 (Reflex Sympathetic Dystrophy & Causalgia), their families, & medical professionals who treat CRPS
Finances: *Funding Sources:* Donations
Membership: *Fees:* $35 deluxe memberships; $25 regular memberships
Activities: Providing education & information for persons with CRPS, the public, & the health care community; Funding research; Organizing support groups
Publications:
• PARC [Promoting Awareness of RSD & CRPS in Canada] Pearl
Type: Newsletter; *Frequency:* Quarterly
Profile: Articles by professionals, latest research, coping techniques, resources, & upcoming conferences

ProMOTION Plus
#194, 71 West 2nd Ave., Vancouver BC V5Y 0J7
Tel: 604-333-3475; *Fax:* 604-629-2651
info@promotionplus.org
www.promotionplus.org
www.linkedin.com/in/promotion-plus-bb466136
www.facebook.com/promotionp
twitter.com/@ProMOTION_Plus
Overview: A small provincial organization founded in 1990
Mission: To promote equity & opportunity for British Columbian women in sport
Affiliation(s): Sport BC
Finances: *Funding Sources:* BC Ministry of Community; Sport & Cultural Development; 2010 Legacies Now; BC Gaming Commission; Government of Canada
Membership: *Fees:* $20 students; $35 adults; $75 organizations
Activities: Annual recognition program
Chief Officer(s):
Sue Griffin, Chair
Alison Hart, Administrative Manager

Promotional Product Professionals of Canada Inc. / Professionnels en produits promotionnels du Canada
#202, 455, boul Fénelon, Montréal QC H9S 5T8
Tel: 514-489-5359; *Fax:* 800-489-8741
Toll-Free: 866-450-7722
info@promocan.com
www.promocan.com
www.facebook.com/PPPC.ca
twitter.com/PPPCInc
www.youtube.com/user/pppcinc
www.flickr.com/photos/pppc/sets/
Also Known As: PPPC
Previous Name: Promotional Products Association of Canada; Specialty Advertising Association of Canada; Specialty Advertising Counselors of Canada
Overview: A medium-sized national organization founded in 1956
Mission: To advance the promotional products industry; To act as the voice of the predominant advertising medium in Canada
Affiliation(s): Canadian Professional Sales Association (CPSA); Incentive Marketing Association (IMA); National Advertising Benevolent Society (NABS)
Staff Member(s): 12
Membership: 1,700+; *Member Profile:* Suppliers; Distributors; *Committees:* Awards; Education & Certification; Events; Finance & Administration; Governance; Information Technology;

Marketing & Industry; Member Relations; Publications & Advertising; Recruitment
Activities: Providing seminars & workshops for members, which lead to industry professional certifications; Offering online education towards Certified Advertising Specialist (CAS) & Master Advertising Specialist (MAS) certification; *Speaker Service:* Yes
Chief Officer(s):
Edward Ahad, President & Chief Executive Officer
ed@pppc.ca
Gladys Kasp, Manager, Communications & Planning
gladys@pppc.ca
Maria Pimentel, Manager, Accounting
maria@pppc.ca
Melanie Gallagher, Coordinator, Member Services
melanie@pppc.ca
Mara Welch, Coordinator, Events
shows@pppc.ca
Tiffany Moniz, Coordinator, Marketing & Communications
tiffany@pppc.ca
Awards:
• Promotional Product Professionals of Canada Image Award
To recognize the most creative campaigns using promotional products & programs by distributor & supplier member companies
• Promotional Product Professionals of Canada Distributor of the Year
• Promotional Product Professionals of Canada Supplier of the Year
• Promotional Product Professionals of Canada Supplier Customer Service Representative of the Year
• Promotional Product Professionals of Canada Supplier Sales Representative of the Year
• Promotional Product Professionals of Canada Distributor Sales Representative of the Year
• Promotional Product Professionals of Canada Multi-Line Agency of the Year
• Promotional Product Professionals of Canada Best Catalogue of the Year
• Promotional Product Professionals of Canada Best Website of the Year
• Promotional Product Professionals of Canada Scholarship
Eligibility: A student enrolled in a full-time sales, marketing, business, management, or related program at a Canadian college or university *Deadline:* May; *Amount:* $1,500
Meetings/Conferences:
• Promotional Product Professionals of Canada 2018 National Convention, February, 2018, The International Centre, Mississauga, ON
Scope: National
Description: Educational seminars, business meetings, roundtable discussions, networking events, plus a trade show with over 600 exhibitors
Publications:
• Idea Book [a publication of the Promotional Product Professionals of Canada]
Type: Yearbook; *Frequency:* Annually
Profile: Promotional product ideas from suppliers, for distributors
• PPPC Echo [a publication of the Promotional Product Professionals of Canada]
Type: Newsletter; *Frequency:* Irregular
Profile: Contains industry news & updates
• Promotional Product Professionals of Canada Membership Directory
Type: Directory; *Frequency:* Annually; *Price:* Free with Promotional Product Professionals of Canada membership
Profile: A roster of current members in Canada & the United States, with contact information, product listings, sales policies, supplier advertisements &associaiton information

Promotional Products Association of Canada; Specialty Advertising Association of Canada; Specialty Advertising Counselors of Canada *See* Promotional Product Professionals of Canada Inc.

Property Owners League of Montréal *Voir* Ligue des propriétaires de Montréal

Prospect Human Services
915 - 33 St. NE, Calgary AB T2A 6T2
Tel: 403-273-2822; *Fax:* 403-273-0090
info@prospectnow.ca
www.prospectnow.ca
Previous Name: Rehabilitation Society of Calgary
Overview: A small local organization
Mission: To identify situations where groups face challenges with full participation; To develop services & supports for individuals & employers
Activities: Providing work search resources & strategies; Offering employment placement supports for persons having difficulty finding a job due to mental health illness or issues; Providing support to individuals with disabilities to obtain & maintain paid employment
Chief Officer(s):
Alexi Davis, Director, Employment Services
alexi.davis@prospectnow.ca
Caroline Stewart, Director, Human Resources
Lorne York, Director, Finance

Prospectors & Developers Association of Canada (PDAC) / Association canadienne des prospecteurs & entrepreneurs
135 King St. East, Toronto ON M5C 1G6
Tel: 416-362-1969; *Fax:* 416-362-0101
info@pdac.ca
www.pdac.ca
www.linkedin.com/company/prospectors-and-developers-association-of-canada-pdac
www.facebook.com/thePDAC
twitter.com/the_pdac
Overview: A medium-sized national organization founded in 1932
Mission: To protect & promote the interests of the Canadian mineral exploration & development sector
Finances: *Funding Sources:* Membership fees
Staff Member(s): 24
Membership: 6,000 individuals + 950 corporate members; *Member Profile:* Individuals, such as professional geoscientists, mining executives, prospectors, developers; geological consultants, & those working in the drilling, financial, investment, legal, & other related fields; Students; Corporate members, such as producing companies, junior non-producing exploration companies, & non-mining companies; *Committees:* Aboriginal Affairs; Audit; Awards; Convention Planning; Corporate Social Responsibility; Education; Environment; Executive; Finance & Taxation; Geosciences; Health & Safety; Human Resources Development; International; Lands & Regulations; Membership; Nomination; Public Affairs, Securities
Activities: Compiling statistics; Providing information; Offering continuing education; Engaging in advocacy activities; Providing networking opportunities; *Speaker Service:* Yes; *Library:* Not open to public
Chief Officer(s):
Andrew Cheatle, Executive Director, 416-362-1969 Ext. 222
Lisa McDonald, Chief Operations Officer, 416-362-1969 Ext. 223
Cameron Ainsworth-Vincze, Senior Manager, Communications, 416-362-1969 Ext. 234
Lesley Williams, Manager, Aboriginal Affairs & Resource Development, 416-362-1969 Ext. 294
Awards:
• Bill Dennis Award, PDAC Annual Awards
Awarded to an individual who has made a significant mineral discovery or an important contribution to the prospecting & exploration industry
• Environmental & Social Responsibility Award, PDAC Annual Awards
Awarded to honour an individual or organization that demonstrates initiative & leadership in preserving the natural environment during an exploration program
• Distinguished Service Award, PDAC Annual Awards
Recognizes an individual who has: made a substantial contribution to mineral exploration over a sustained period, dedicated substantial time & effort to the PDAC, or made outstanding contributions to the mineral industry in the field of finance, geology, or research
• Skookum Jim Award, PDAC Annual Awards
Awarded to an individual who has demonstrated exceptional achievement in an Aboriginal-run service business for the Canadian mining industry
• Viola R. MacMillan Award, PDAC Annual Awards
Honours an individual or company that demonstrates leadership in management & financing
• Thayer Lindsley Award for International Mineral Discoveries, PDAC Annual Awards
Awarded to recognize an individual or a team of explorationists who have made a recent significant mineral discovery anywhere in the world
• GAC-PDAC Logan Student Prize, PDAC Student Awards
Awarded to recognize an undergraduate student to support their advancement in geoscience studies; *Amount:* $5,000
• Canadian Mineral Indsutry Education Foundation Award, PDAC Student Awards
Eligibility: A university student who has completed the first year of a Canadian university program & is studying Geology, Geological or Mining Engineering, Mineral Processing, or Metallurgy *Deadline:* February 24; *Amount:* $1,000 per school term until graduation
• Mary-Claire Ward Geoscience Award, PDAC Student Awards
Awarded to encourage & support a graduate student in Canada whose thesis is focused on mapping & the geological history of Canada *Deadline:* December; *Amount:* $5,000
Meetings/Conferences:
• Prospectors & Developers Association of Canada (PDAC) 2018 Convention, March, 2018, Metro Toronto Convention Centre, Toronto, ON
Scope: International
Attendance: 23,000+
Description: A four-day event that attracts more than 900 exhibitors & 22,000 attendees from 125 countries to participate in short courses, technical sessions, & networking opportunities
Contact Information: Director, Convention: Nicole Sampson, Phone: 416-362-1969, ext. 226, E-mail: nsampson@pdac.ca
Publications:
• Communiqué [a publication of the Prospectors & Developers Association of Canada]
Frequency: Irregular
Profile: Each occasional publication deals with a particular topic related to exploration & development
• Core [a publication of the Prospectors & Developers Association of Canada]
Type: Magazine; *Frequency:* 3 pa; *Editor:* Cameron Ainsworth-Vincze
Profile: Industry news & events
• eNews [a publication of the Prospectors & Developers Association of Canada]
Type: Newsletter; *Frequency:* Irregular
Profile: Association news & important dates
• Prospectors & Developers Association of Canada Annual Report
Type: Report; *Frequency:* a.

Prosserman Jewish Community Centre
4588 Bathurst St., Toronto ON M2R 1W6
Tel: 416-638-1881; *Fax:* 416-636-5813
www.prossermanjcc.com
www.facebook.com/theprossermanjcc
twitter.com/prossermanjcc
Previous Name: Bathurst Jewish Community Centre
Overview: A small local organization
Mission: To provide social, educational, cultural, health and wellness programs rooted in Jewish values, and offers a variety of facilities & courses, including: fitness centre, culinary arts studio, media studio, courses in visual arts, dance, music, Jewish learning program, day camps, daycare.
Staff Member(s): 27
Membership: *Fees:* $45 senior; $50 single; $100 family
Chief Officer(s):
Jennifer Appleby-Goosen, Program Director
jennifer@srcentre.ca

Prostate Cancer Canada (PCC) / Fondation canadienne de recherche sur le cancer de la prostate
2 Lombard St., 3rd Fl., Toronto ON M5C 1M1
Tel: 416-441-2131; *Fax:* 416-441-2325
Toll-Free: 888-255-0333
info@prostatecancer.ca
www.prostatecancer.ca
www.linkedin.com/company/prostate-cancer-canada
www.facebook.com/prostatecancercanada
twitter.com/ProstateCancerC
www.instagram.com/prostatecancerc
Previous Name: Prostate Cancer Research Foundation of Canada
Overview: A small national organization founded in 1999
Mission: To raise funds for research into the causes, cure & prevention of prostate cancer by engaging Canadians through awareness, education, & advocacy
Member of: Prostate Cancer Alliance of Canada
Affiliation(s): Canadian Urological Association
Finances: *Annual Operating Budget:* $1.5 Million-$3 Million
Staff Member(s): 15; 100 volunteer(s)
Membership: 1-99
Activities: Organizing & participating in fundraising activities; *Awareness Events:* National Prostate Cancer Awareness Week, 3rd. week in Sept.

Chief Officer(s):
Ted Nash, Chair
Vacant, President & CEO
Stuart Edmonds, Vice President, Research, Health Promotion & Survivorship
Awards:
• Research Grants

Prostate Cancer Research Foundation of Canada See Prostate Cancer Canada

Prosthetics & Orthotics Association of British Columbia (POABC)
PO Box 30594, Stn. Brentwood Mall, #47A, 4567 Lougheed Hwy., Burnaby BC V5C 2A0
info@poabc.ca
www.poabc.ca
www.facebook.com/poabc.ca
Overview: A small provincial organization founded in 1974 overseen by Orthotics Prosthetics Canada
Mission: To promote quality patient care & professionalism in the field of prosthetics & orthotics in British Columbia
Membership: *Member Profile:* Individuals in British Columbia involved in the prosthetic & orthotic field
Activities: Representing members throughout British Columbia; Encouraging continuring education for members
Chief Officer(s):
Scott Hedlund, President
Randy Kramer, Vice-President
Gord Dillon, Secretary
Travis Finlayson, Treasurer

Protected Areas Association of Newfoundland & Labrador (PAA)
PO Box 1027, Stn. C, St. John's NL A1C 5M3
Tel: 709-726-2603
paa@nf.aibn.com
Overview: A small provincial charitable organization founded in 1989
Mission: To promote the establishment of a provincial network of reserves that preserve representative portions of all eco-regions & protect biodiversity; To promote sound ecological practices that support sustainable development
Member of: Newfoundland & Labrador Environment Network
Affiliation(s): World Wildlife Fund Canada; Canadian Parks & Wilderness Society
Finances: *Annual Operating Budget:* $100,000-$250,000
Staff Member(s): 4; 45 volunteer(s)
Membership: 500; *Fees:* $20 individual; *Member Profile:* People interested in conservation of nature, wilderness; *Committees:* Lac Joseph-Atikonak; Main River
Activities: Issue-related public meetings; *Awareness Events:* Benefit Concert, Nov.

Protestant Children's Home See Family Day Care Services (Toronto)

Provancher Society of Natural History of Canada Voir Société Provancher d'histoire naturelle du Canada

Province of Québec Rifle Association (PQRA) / Association de tir de la province de Québec (ATPQ)
973, rue Turcotte est, Thetford Mines QC G1J 5K3
info@pqra.org
www.pqra.org
twitter.com/atpq
Overview: A small provincial organization founded in 1869
Mission: To promote marksmanship training & competition especially at long range; To provide extensive cadet program; To organize & run cadet provincial championships
Member of: Dominion of Canada Rifle Association; Shooting Federation of Canada
Finances: *Funding Sources:* Membership fees
Activities: Long Range Target Shooting; Black Powder Long Range; Service Rifle Matches; Cadet Shooting Programs
Chief Officer(s):
Robert Fortier, President

Provincial & Territorial Public Library Council (PTPLC) / Conseil provincial et territorial des bibliotheques (CPTBP)
www.ptplc-cptbp.ca
Overview: A small provincial organization founded in 1978
Mission: To act as a forum in which provincial & territorial public libraries can share experience, information, & resources; To serve as a point of contact between national library organizations & the federal government

Publications:
• Early Literacy Storytimes for Preschoolers in Public Libraries [a publication of the PTPLC]
Type: Report; *Author:* Heather McKend; *ISBN:* 978-1-55471-479-7
• Sound Practices in Library Services to Aboriginal Peoples [a publication of the PTPLC]
Type: Report; *Author:* Mary Cavanagh

The Provincial Agricultural Fairs Association See British Columbia Association of Agricultural Fairs & Exhibitions

Provincial Animal Shelter See Nova Scotia Society for the Prevention of Cruelty to Animals

Provincial Association of CBDCs See Atlantic Association of CBDCs

Provincial Association of Home Builders of Québec Voir Association provinciale des constructeurs d'habitations du Québec inc.

Provincial Association of Resort Communities of Saskatchewan (PARCS)
PO Box 52, Elbow SK S0H 1J0
Tel: 306-545-6253; *Fax:* 306-854-4412
parcs@sasktel.com
www.parcs-sk.com
Overview: A medium-sized provincial organization founded in 1986
Mission: To promote the interests of resort communities in Saskatchewan; To promote fair & equitable policies & procedures for all resort communities
Finances: *Annual Operating Budget:* Less than $50,000; *Funding Sources:* Membership dues; grants
Staff Member(s): 2; 30 volunteer(s)
Membership: 200; *Fees:* $50-$550 active member; $200 associate; $100 affiliate; $25 individual
Activities: *Library:* by appointment
Chief Officer(s):
Shirley Gange, President, 306-982-3311
hgange@sasktel.net
Lynne Saas, Contact, Member Servivces, 306-854-4658
parcs@sasktel.net

The Provincial Autism Centre See Autism Nova Scotia

Provincial Black Basketball Association (PBBA)
PO Box 2702, Halifax NS B3J 3P7
Tel: 902-452-0682
pbba.blackbasketball@gmail.com
www.blackbasketball.ca
Overview: A medium-sized provincial organization founded in 1972
Mission: To promote basketball within the African Canadian community in Nova Scotia & across the country.
Chief Officer(s):
Carl Gannon, President
gannoncs@eastlink.ca

Provincial Building & Construction Trades Council of Ontario
#401, 75 International Blvd., Toronto ON M9W 6L9
Tel: 416-679-8887; *Fax:* 416-679-8882
info@ontariobuildingtrades.com
www.ontariobuildingtrades.com
Also Known As: Provincial Building Trades Council
Overview: A medium-sized provincial organization founded in 1959
Mission: To give construction workers a collective voice in the workplace; To ensure that workers are well-trained to meet industry needs; To promote healthy & safe working conditions with decent wages, pensions & benefits
Affiliation(s): International Foundation of Employee Benefit Plans - Building Trades Department
Finances: *Annual Operating Budget:* $250,000-$500,000
Staff Member(s): 2
Membership: 150,000 workers; *Member Profile:* Union members who work in the following constuction industry sectors: Industrial, Commercial & Institutional (ICI), Electrical Power Systems (EPSCA), Residential, Heavy Engineering, Roads, Sewers & Watermains, Pipelines
Chief Officer(s):
Patrick J. Dillon, Business Manager

Provincial CGIT Board of BC
c/o Janice Grinnell, 13780 Hill Rd., Ladysmith BC V9G 1G7

Tel: 250-245-4016
grinncon@nanaimo.ark.com
www.cgit.ca
Also Known As: Canadian Girls in Training - British Columbia
Previous Name: National CGIT Association - BC Provincial Board
Overview: A small provincial organization

Provincial Collective Bargaining Council See New Brunswick Nurses Union

Provincial Council of Women of Manitoba Inc. (PCWM)
#204, 825 Sherbook Ave., Winnipeg MB R3A 1M5
Tel: 204-992-2751
pcwm@mymts.net
pcwmanitoba.ca
www.facebook.com/thepcwm
Overview: A medium-sized provincial organization founded in 1949
Mission: To empower all women to work towards improving the quality of life for women, families & society through a forum of member organizations & individuals
Affiliation(s): National Council of Women of Canada
Finances: *Annual Operating Budget:* Less than $50,000
30 volunteer(s)
Membership: 28 institutional; 50 individual; *Fees:* $40 federate; $20 individual
Activities: Resolutions & briefs to the provincial government

Provincial Dental Board of Nova Scotia
#102, 1559 Brunswick St., Halifax NS B3J 2G1
Tel: 902-420-0083; *Fax:* 902-492-0301
Toll-Free: 866-326-1046
info@pdbns.ca
www.pdbns.ca
Overview: A small provincial licensing organization
Mission: To protect the public in the delivery of dental care through licensure & regulation
Membership: *Committees:* Complaints; Disicipline; Mandatory Continuing Dental Education; Dental Practice Review
Chief Officer(s):
Martin Gillis, Registrar

Provincial Exhibition of Manitoba
115 - 10th St., Brandon MB R7A 4E7
Tel: 204-726-3590; *Fax:* 204-725-0202
Toll-Free: 877-729-0001
info@provincialexhibition.com
www.provincialexhibition.com
www.facebook.com/provincial.exhibition
twitter.com/ProvincialEx
Overview: A medium-sized provincial organization founded in 1882
Mission: To showcase agriculture; To link urban & rural regions through education & awareness while providing entertainment, community pride & economic enhancement to the region
Member of: Canadian Association of Fairs & Exhibitions
Staff Member(s): 8
Membership: *Fees:* $10; *Member Profile:* Individuals who have purchased a share from the Provincial Exhibition of Manitoba office
Activities: Organizing three annual fairs: Royal Manitoba Winter Fair, Manitoba Summer Fair, Manitoba Agricultural Exhibition
Chief Officer(s):
Ron Kristjansson, General Manager, 204-726-3590 Ext. 1001
ronkristjansson@provincialexhibition.com
Awards:
• Royal Manitoba Winter Fair Awards
Prizes given in various categories for best of show for agricultural products, animals & crops; several equestrian events offer prizes for best in competition
Meetings/Conferences:
• Provincial Exhibition of Manitoba Royal Manitoba Winter Fair & Tradeshow 2018, March, 2018, Keystone Centre, Brandon, MB
Scope: Provincial
• Provincial Exhibition of Manitoba Royal Manitoba Summer Fair 2018, June, 2018, MB
Scope: Provincial
• Provincial Exhibition of Manitoba Agricultural Exhibition (Ag Ex) 2018, October, 2018
Scope: Provincial

Provincial Farm Women's Association
149 Brookfield Rd., St. John's NL A1E 6J4
Tel: 709-368-2458; *Fax:* 709-364-1421
Overview: A small local organization

Chief Officer(s):
Michelle Lester, Contact

Provincial Federation of Ontario Fire Fighters See Ontario Professional Fire Fighters Association

Provincial Fitness Unit of Alberta (AFLCA)
Percy Page Bldg., 11759 Groat Rd., 3rd Fl., Edmonton AB T5M 3K6
Tel: 780-492-4435; Fax: 780-455-2264
Toll-Free: 866-348-8648
info@provincialfitnessunit.ca
www.provincialfitnessunit.ca
www.facebook.com/provincialfitnessunitalberta
twitter.com/AbFitnessUnit
Previous Name: Alberta Fitness Leadership Certification Association
Overview: A medium-sized provincial organization founded in 1984
Member of: National Fitness Leadership Advisory Council; National Fitness Leadership Alliance
Staff Member(s): 6
Membership: 1,000-4,999; Fees: Member Profile: Fitness leader or trainer
Activities: Certifications in fitness training; Internships: Yes
Chief Officer(s):
Katherine MacKeigan, Executive Director
katherine.mackeigan@ualberta.ca

Provincial French Immersion & Francophone Programme Teachers' Association Voir Association Provinciale des Professeurs d'Immersion et du Programme Francophone

Provincial Health Ethics Network
Guardian Bldg., #507, 10240 - 124 St., Edmonton AB T5N 3W6
Tel: 780-447-1180; Fax: 780-447-1181
Toll-Free: 800-472-4066
middleton@phen.ab.ca
www.phen.ca
Overview: A small provincial organization
Mission: To provide resources on addressing ethical issues related to health; To facilitate informed & reasoned ethical decision-making
Staff Member(s): 5
Membership: 500; Fees: $0; Member Profile: Anyone interested in bioethics
Chief Officer(s):
Amy Middleton, Programming Director
middleton@phen.ab.ca
Al-Noor Nenshi Nathoo, Executive Director
nathoo@phen.ab.ca
Publications:
• Health Ethics Today
Type: Magazine; Frequency: Semiannually
Profile: Periodical covering bioethics topics
• PHEN Communiqué
Type: Newsletter; Frequency: Monthly
Profile: Regarding bioethics events & programs

Provincial Intermediate Teachers' Association
BC
www.pita.ca
www.facebook.com/108078755947920
Overview: A small provincial organization
Member of: BC Teachers' Federation
Membership: 1,000; Fees: $15 TOC and Student Teacher; $25 BCTF Active Members; $65 Subscriber
Chief Officer(s):
Elaine Jaltema, President
president@pita.ca
Meetings/Conferences:
• Provincial Intermediate Teachers' Association Fall Conference, 2018
Scope: Provincial
• Provincial Intermediate Teachers' Association Annual Whistler Conference, April, 2018, Whistler Hilton Resort, Whistler, BC
Scope: Provincial

Provincial Medical Board of Nova Scotia See College of Physicians & Surgeons of Nova Scotia

Provincial Nurse Educator Interest Group (PNEIG)
c/o First Stage Enterprises, #109, 1 Concorde Gate, Toronto ON M3C 3N6
Tel: 416-426-7234
secretary@pneig.ca
www.pneig.ca
Overview: A medium-sized provincial organization
Mission: To promote the professional development of Ontario nurse educators through continuing education resources; To foster & encourage an interest in the role of nurse educator as a career choice; To share & support the vision & mission of the Registered Nurses Association of Ontario (RNAO)
Member of: Registered Nurses Association of Ontario
Affiliation(s): American Nurses Association; Canadian Association of Schools of Nursing; Canadian Nurses' Association; Canadian Nursing Students' Association; College of Nurses of Ontario; Council of Ontario University Programs in Nursing; International Council of Nurses; Ontario Nurses Association; Registered Practical Nurses Association of Ontario; The Registered Nurses' Foundation of Ontario
Finances: Funding Sources: Membership dues
Staff Member(s): 10
Membership: 700+; Fees: $20; free for undergraduate nursing students; Member Profile: Ontario nurses & nursing students
Activities: Providing a support & communication network for nurse educators in Ontario; Providing professional development opportunities for members; Advocating for support & retention strategies to employ nurse educators & promote high quality care
Chief Officer(s):
Priya Herne, President
phern@tegh.on.ca
Mary Guise, Coordinator, Membership & Services
guisem@mcmaster.ca
Awards:
• PNEIG Educational Scholarship
• PNEIG Research Award
Eligibility: PNEIG members pursuing nursing education at the Graduate or Doctoral level
Publications:
• Provincial Nurse Educator Interest Group Newsletter
Type: Newsletter; Frequency: Monthly
Profile: Contains member news & course dates

Provincial Staff Nurses Committee See United Nurses of Alberta

Provincial Towing Association (Ontario) (PTAO)
65 Keith Rd., Bracebridge ON P1L 0A1
Tel: 705-646-0536; Fax: 705-645-0017
Toll-Free: 866-582-0855
www.ptao.org
www.facebook.com/234988159852788
Also Known As: Provincial Towing Association
Overview: A medium-sized provincial organization founded in 1998
Mission: To inform its members of revelant news regarding the industry; To set standards for its members; To represent its members at all levels of government
Finances: Annual Operating Budget: $50,000-$100,000; Funding Sources: Membership dues
Staff Member(s): 2; 9 volunteer(s)
Membership: Fees: $350; Member Profile: Towing companies within Ontario
Activities: Speaker Service: Yes
Chief Officer(s):
Doug Nelson, Executive Director
doug@ptao.org
Meetings/Conferences:
• The Provincial Towing Association 20th Annual Tow Show, 2018
Description: The Trade & Tow Show features training sessions, the PTAO general meeting, competitions & the awards banquet

Provincial Water Polo Association See Water Polo Nova Scotia

Provincial Women's Softball Association of Ontario (PWSAO)
c/o Registrar, 50 Capri St., Thorold ON L2V 4S8
Tel: 905-227-7574; Fax: 905-227-3574
info@ontariopwsa.com
www.ontariopwsa.ca
www.facebook.com/OntarioPWSA
twitter.com/OntarioPWSA
Overview: A medium-sized provincial organization founded in 1931 overseen by Softball Ontario
Mission: To support & advance women softball players in Ontario
Member of: Canadian Amateur Softball Association; Softball Ontario
Finances: Funding Sources: Sponsors; Partners; Government grants; Player/team fees
Membership: Committees: Annual General Meeting; Awards Banquet; Bids (Provincial/National); Canada Games/Talent ID; Draw Book; Eastern Canadian Liaison; Fundraising; Insurance (Associated Teams, Third Party & PWSA Teams); Rules & Constitution; Scholarship; Skills Camp; Travel Permits; House League Select; LTPD - Colour Your Dream
Chief Officer(s):
Debbie Malisani, Chair & President, 905-564-3533
littlehands1@rogers.com
Debbie DeMoel, Registrar
jondeb50@cogeco.ca

Provincial Youth Council Voir Conseil jeunesse provincial (Manitoba)

Provision Coalition
#205, 100 Stone Rd. West, Guelph ON N1G 5L3
Tel: 519-822-2042
www.provisioncoalition.com
www.linkedin.com/company/5132043
twitter.com/ProvisionC
Overview: A medium-sized national organization
Mission: To ensure that Canadian food & beverage manufacturers make food sustainably for the benefit of the public & the environment; To serve as the voice of the food & beverage manufacturing industry on issues relating to sustainability
Membership: 16 associations
Activities: Offering resources & tools through a food & beverage manufacturing sustainability management system; Developing tools & programs that will help food & beverage manufacturers adopt sustainable practices; Library
Chief Officer(s):
Cher Mereweather, Executive Director
cmereweather@provisioncoalition.com
Meena Hassanali, Director, Industry Programs
mhassanali@provisioncoalition.com
Brett Wills, Director, SMS Support Program
bwills@provisioncoalition.com
Holly Hendershot, Manager, Communications
hhendershot@provisioncoalition.com

Provost & District Chamber of Commerce
PO Box 637, Provost AB T0B 3S0
Tel: 780-753-6643
provost.ca/economic-development/chamber-of-commerce
Overview: A small local organization

Psoriasis Society of Canada / Société psoriasis du Canada
National Office, PO Box 25015, Halifax NS B3M 4H4
Fax: 902-443-2073
Toll-Free: 800-656-4494
www.psoriasissociety.org
Overview: A medium-sized national charitable organization founded in 1983
Mission: To provide programs & services to people who suffer from psoriasis in Canada; to encourage formation of support groups where individual sufferers may share experiences & exchange information; to provide facts about psoriasis to medical community, general public & teaching profession; to promote & encourage research directed towards treatment & cure for psoriasis
Affiliation(s): International Federation of Psoriasis Associations
Finances: Funding Sources: Membership fees; donations
Membership: Fees: $25, $35 outside of Canada
Activities: Awareness Events: National Psoriasis Awareness Month & Walk, Oct.
Chief Officer(s):
Judy Misner, President

Psychological Association of Manitoba (PAM) / Association des psychologues du Manitoba
#253, 162-2025 Corydon Ave., Winnipeg MB R3P 0N5
Tel: 204-487-0784; Fax: 204-489-8688
pam@mymts.net
www.cpmb.ca
Overview: A small provincial licensing organization founded in 1966
Mission: To provide screening & examination of candidates &, if eligible, registration as a psychologist; to protect the public from fraudulent services & provide referral to & liaison with psychologists
Finances: Annual Operating Budget: $50,000-$100,000
Membership: Fees: Schedule available; Member Profile: Psychologists practicing in Manitoba; Committees: Registration & Membership; Complaints; Inquiry; Examinations; Publications; Standards; Legislative Review

Canadian Associations / Psychological Association of Prince Edward Island (PAPEI)

Chief Officer(s):
John Arnett, President
Alan Slusky, Registrar

Psychological Association of Prince Edward Island (PAPEI)
PE
www.peipsychology.org/papei
Overview: A small provincial organization
Finances: *Funding Sources:* Membership fees; workshops
Membership: 20; *Fees:* $60
Chief Officer(s):
Nadine DeWolfe, Ph.D., President
Awards:
• Elizabeth Fox Percival PAPEI Professional Award
• PAPEI Humanitarian Award
• PAPEI Convocation Award to Outstanding UPEI Psychology Major
• PAPEI Science Fair Award

Psychologists Association of Alberta (PAA)
#103, 1207 - 91 St. SW, Edmonton AB T6X 1E9
Tel: 780-424-0294; *Fax:* 780-423-4048
Toll-Free: 888-424-0297
www.psychologistsassociation.ab.ca
www.facebook.com/169589246436220
Overview: A medium-sized provincial licensing organization founded in 1960
Mission: To enhance & promote the profession of psychology
Staff Member(s): 5
Membership: *Fees:* $310 full; $95 provisional; $190 affiliate/out-of-province; $40 student; *Member Profile:* Registered psychologists & psychology students; *Committees:* Awards Adjudicating; Awards Nominating; Fees; Public Education; Psychologically Healthy Workplace; School Psychology; Continuing Education; Executive Director Evalution
Activities: *Rents Mailing List:* Yes
Chief Officer(s):
Bonnie Rude-Weisman, President
Judi Malone, Acting Executive Director
judim@paa-ab.ca

Psychology Association of Saskatchewan
PO Box 4528, Regina SK S4P 3W7
info@psychsask.ca
psychsask.ca
twitter.com/PsychSask
Overview: A small provincial organization
Mission: To represent the interests of its members & to further & promote interest in psychology
Member of: Council of Provincial Associations of Psychologists
11 volunteer(s)
Membership: *Fees:* $190 full; $100 afiiliate; $50 student; *Member Profile:* Registered psychologists & psychology students
Activities: Spring Institute & AGM
Chief Officer(s):
Kristi Wright, President

Psychosocial Rehabilitation Canada / Réadaptation Psychosociale Canada (RPS)
323 Victoria St., Kingston ON K7L 3Z2
Fax: 705-456-9786
Toll-Free: 866-655-8548
registrar@psrrpscanada.ca
www.psrrpscanada.ca
Also Known As: PSR Canada/RPS Canada
Overview: A small national charitable organization founded in 2002
Mission: To achieve full community participation of persons with mental health issues; To promote the principles & practice of psychosocial rehabilitation through practice standards, education, quality, outcome measures, advocacy & public policy
Affiliation(s): International Association of Psychosocial Rehabilitation Services; Ontario Federation of Community Mental Health & Addictions Programs; Association québécoise pour la readaptation psychosociale; Psychosocial Rehabilitation Manitoba, BC, Atlantic Region, Ont.
Finances: *Annual Operating Budget:* Less than $50,000; *Funding Sources:* Membership fees; conference revenue
25 volunteer(s)
Membership: 300; *Fees:* $90.40-180.80 individual; $339-$3,390 organizations; *Member Profile:* Adherence to principles of PSR in service delivery; *Committees:* Membership; Certification; Affiliation; Publicity; Website; Newsletter
Activities: Conferences; Chapter building; Membership development; Public awareness; Advocacy; Certification of PSR Practitioners
Chief Officer(s):
John Higenbottam, President, 604-527-5314
higenbottamj@douglascollege.ca

Public Accountants Council for the Province of Ontario / Conseil des experts-comptables de la province de l'Ontario
#901, 1200 Bay St., Toronto ON M5R 2A5
Tel: 416-920-1444; *Fax:* 416-920-1917
Toll-Free: 800-387-2154
generalinquiries@pacont.org
www.pacont.org
Also Known As: Public Accountants Council
Overview: A medium-sized provincial licensing organization founded in 1950
Finances: *Annual Operating Budget:* $1.5 Million-$3 Million; *Funding Sources:* Licence fees
Membership: 1-99; *Member Profile:* Institute of Chartered Accountants of Ontario; Certified General Accountants of Ontario; Society of Management Accountants of Ontario; *Committees:* Audit; Governance
Chief Officer(s):
Michael Bryant, Chair
Shoba Khetrapal, Vice-Chair

The Public Affairs Association of Canada (PAAC) / Association des affaires publiques du Canada
c/o John Capobianco, Fleishman-Hillard Canada Inc., #1500, 33 Bloor St. East, Toronto ON M4W 3H1
Tel: 416-645-8182; *Fax:* 416-361-2447
info@publicaffairs.ca
www.publicaffairs.ca
www.linkedin.com/groups/Public-Affairs-Association-Canada-PAAC-4790500
twitter.com/PAAC84
Overview: A medium-sized national organization founded in 1984
Mission: To improve the professionalism of members to enhance the relations of members' organizations with their publics
Finances: *Funding Sources:* Membership fees
Membership: *Fees:* $56.50 student; $282.50 indvidual; $1130 corporate
Activities: Seminars; conferences; workshops; *Rents Mailing List:* Yes
Chief Officer(s):
John Capobianco, President
john.capobianco@fleishman.ca
Jennifer Dent, Events Chair
jennifer.e.dent@gsk.com
Stephen Andrews, Secretary-Treasurer
sandrews@blg.com
Rick Hall, Vice-President
rickhall@rickhallpr.com

Public Health Association of British Columbia (PHABC)
#210, 1027 Pandora Ave., Victoria BC V8V 3P6
Tel: 250-595-8422; *Fax:* 250-595-8622
staff@phabc.org
www.phabc.org
Overview: A medium-sized provincial organization founded in 1953 overseen by Canadian Public Health Association
Mission: To constitute a special resource in BC for the betterment & maintenance of the population's health at the community & personal level
Finances: *Funding Sources:* Membership dues; project grants
Membership: 500; *Fees:* $50 individual; $30 student; *Committees:* Governance; Capacity Building; PARC; Public Engagement
Activities: BC Healthy Communities Network
Meetings/Conferences:
• Public Health Association of British Columbia 2018 Early Years Conference, January, 2018, Vancouver, BC
Scope: Provincial
Description: Theme: "Strengthening Resilience in Today's World: Leading with Kindness & Understanding"

Public Health Association of Nova Scotia (PHANS)
PO Box 33074, Halifax NS B3L 4T6
www.phans.ca
Overview: A small provincial charitable organization overseen by Canadian Public Health Association
Mission: To build public health capacity & to make progress on the determinants of health in Nova Scotia
Affiliation(s): Canadian Public Health Association
Membership: *Fees:* $20 students & retired persons; $40 regular members; *Member Profile:* Persons interested in health & health issues in Nova Scotia
Activities: Advocating for policy change on issues that affect health; Liaising with government departments & voluntary agencies; Increasing professional & public awareness of health issues; Providing education; Offering networking opportunities; Delivering updates on health policy issues

The Public Interest Advocacy Centre (PIAC) / Centre pour la défense de l'intérêt public
#1204, 1 Nicholas St., Ottawa ON K1N 7B7
Tel: 613-562-4002
piac@piac.ca
www.piac.ca
Overview: A medium-sized national charitable organization founded in 1976
Mission: To provide legal services to groups & individuals addressing public interest issues of broad concern who would not otherwise have access to such services; The centre's special interests are telecommunications, energy, transportation, broadcasting, privacy, technical services & consumer protection
Member of: National Association of State Utility Consumer Advocates; Consumers International
Staff Member(s): 6
Membership: 900 individuals; 7 organizations
Chief Officer(s):
John Lawford, Executive Director & General Counsel

Public Legal Education Association of Canada (PLEAC)
Overview: A small national organization founded in 1987
Finances: *Funding Sources:* Membership dues
Membership: 26; *Fees:* $25 non-voting; $50 individual; $300 organization; $301-$500 sustaining; $500 patron; *Member Profile:* Agencies carrying out public legal education activities

Public Legal Education Association of Saskatchewan, Inc. (PLEA Sask.)
#500, 333 - 25th St. East, Saskatoon SK S7K 0L4
Tel: 306-653-1868; *Fax:* 306-653-1869
plea@plea.org
www.plea.org
Overview: A medium-sized provincial organization founded in 1980
Mission: To provide the public with information regarding the law
Member of: Public Legal Education Association of Canada
Staff Member(s): 8
Membership: *Fees:* $20
Activities: *Speaker Service:* Yes; *Library:* Public Legal Education Association of Saskatchewan Library; Open to public
Chief Officer(s):
Heather Jensen, President
Joel Janow, Executive Director

Public Legal Education Society of Nova Scotia *See* Legal Information Society of Nova Scotia

Public Legal Information Association of Newfoundland (PLIAN)
Tara Place, #227, 31 Peet St., St. John's NL A1B 3W8
Tel: 709-722-2643; *Fax:* 709-722-0054
Toll-Free: 888-660-7788
info@publiclegalinfo.com
www.publiclegalinfo.com
twitter.com/PLIAN_NL
Overview: A small provincial organization founded in 1984
Mission: To provide plain language legal information to the general public of Newfoundland, in both official languages, through a telephone enquiry line, public speaking engagements, publications, & a lawyer referral service
Member of: Public Legal Information Association of Canada
Finances: *Annual Operating Budget:* $100,000-$250,000; *Funding Sources:* Justice Canada; Newfoundland Dept. of Justice; Law Foundation of Newfoundland
Staff Member(s): 4; 3 volunteer(s)
Membership: 30
Activities: *Speaker Service:* Yes
Chief Officer(s):
Kevin O'Shea, Executive Director

Public Petroleum Data Model Association *See* Professional Petroleum Data Management Association

Public School Boards' Association of Alberta (PSBAA)
#12, 10227 - 118 St., Edmonton AB T5K 2V4
Tel: 780-479-8080; *Fax:* 780-477-1892
Toll-Free: 800-661-4605
gensec@public-schools.ab.ca
www.public-schools.ab.ca
www.facebook.com/publicschoolsAB
twitter.com/PublicSchoolsAB
Overview: A medium-sized provincial organization founded in 1989
Mission: To ensure the continuation & constant improvement of a universally accessible system of public education which is locally governed, student centred & challenging; To provide constructive leadership, represented by effective strategies, advocacy & communication; To work with others, wherever possible, for the good of public education
Member of: Canadian Education Association
Finances: *Annual Operating Budget:* $250,000-$500,000; *Funding Sources:* Membership fees
Staff Member(s): 5
Membership: 28; *Fees:* $2,000 + component determined by student enrollment; *Member Profile:* Public school boards in Alberta
Activities: Political advocacy on behalf of public school education; data gathering & analysis; leadership & community development; Spring assembly; AGM; *Speaker Service:* Yes
Chief Officer(s):
Cathy Hogg, President
president@public-schools.ab.ca

Public Service Alliance of Canada (PSAC) / Alliance de la Fonction publique du Canada (AFPC)
233 Gilmour St., Ottawa ON K2P 0P1
Tel: 613-560-4200
Toll-Free: 888-604-7722
www.psacunion.ca
www.facebook.com/psac.national
twitter.com/psacnat
www.youtube.com/psacafpc
Overview: A large national organization founded in 1966
Mission: To unite all workers in a single democratic organization; To obtain for all public service employees the best standards of compensation & other conditions of employment & to protect the rights & interests of all public service employees; To maintain & defend the right to strike
Member of: Canadian Labour Congress
Affiliation(s): Public Services International
Finances: *Annual Operating Budget:* Greater than $5 Million
Staff Member(s): 300
Membership: 17 components + 1,219 locals + 180,000 individual; *Member Profile:* The majority of members work for the federal government & its agencies.
Activities: *Library:* PSAC Library
Chief Officer(s):
Robyn Benson, National President
Chris Aylward, National Executive Vice-President
Sharon DeSousa, Regional Executive Vice-President, Ontario
Marianne Hladun, Regional Executive Vice-President, Prairies
Magali Picard, Regional Executive Vice-President, Québec
Jamey Mills, Regional Executive Vice-President, British Columbia
Jack Bourassa, Regional Executive Vice-President, North
Greg McGillis, Regional Executive Vice-President, National Capital Region
Colleen Coffey, Regional Executive Vice-President, Atlantic
Atlantic Branch
#301, 287 Lacewood Dr., Halifax NS B3M 3Y7
Tel: 902-445-0925; *Fax:* 902-443-8291
revp-atl@psac-afpc.com
www.psacatlantic.ca
Chief Officer(s):
Jeannie Baldwin, Regional Executive Vice-President, Atlantic
British Columbia Branch
#302, 5238 Joyce St., Vancouver BC V5R 6C9
Tel: 604-760-0191; *Fax:* 604-430-0194
Toll-Free: 866-811-7700
revp-bc@psac-afpc.com
www.psacbc.com
Chief Officer(s):
Bob Jackson, Regional Executive Vice-President, BC
Calgary Branch
Hillhurst Professional Building, #302, 301 - 14 St. NW, Calgary AB T2N 2A1
Tel: 403-270-6555; *Fax:* 403-270-6591
Toll-Free: 800-641-8914
Charlottetown Branch
614 North River Rd., #D, Charlottetown PE C1E 1K2
Tel: 902-892-5481; *Fax:* 902-892-6407
Edmonton Branch
First Edmonton Place, #670, 10665 Jasper Ave., Edmonton AB T5J 3S9
Tel: 780-423-1290; *Fax:* 780-429-2278
Halifax Branch
Park West Centre, #301, 287 Lacewood Dr., Halifax NS B2M 3Y7
Tel: 902-443-3541; *Fax:* 902-443-8291
Kingston Branch
City Place 1, #412, 1471 John Counter Blvd., Kingston ON K7M 8S8
Tel: 613-542-7322; *Fax:* 613-542-7387
London Branch
#U-11, 480 Sovereign Rd., London ON N6M 1A4
Tel: 519-659-1124; *Fax:* 519-659-1132
Moncton Branch
30 Englehart St., #G, Dieppe NB E1A 8H3
Tel: 506-857-4220; *Fax:* 506-857-9792
National Capital Region Branch
15 Holland Ave., Main Fl., Ottawa ON K1Y 4T2
Tel: 613-256-0438; *Fax:* 613-234-6209
revp-national-capital@psac-afpc.com
www.psac-ncr.com
Chief Officer(s):
Larry Rousseau, Regional Executive Vice-President, National Capital Region
Northern Branch
Building 1412, Sikituuq Court, PO Box 220, Iqaluit NU X0A 0H0
Tel: 867-979-7430; *Fax:* 867-979-5517
Toll-Free: 866-268-7097
revp-north@psac-afpc.com
psacnorth.com
Chief Officer(s):
Jack Bourassa, Regional Executive Vice-President, North
Ontario Branch
#608, 90 Eglinton Ave. East, Toronto ON M4P 2Y3
Tel: 416-485-3558; *Fax:* 416-485-8607
Toll-Free: 800-354-9086
revp-ont@psac-afpc.com
ontario.psac.com
Chief Officer(s):
Sharon DeSousa, Regional Executive Vice-President, Ontario
Ottawa Branch
15 Holland Ave., Main Fl., Ottawa ON K1Y 4T2
Tel: 613-560-2560; *Fax:* 613-234-6209
Prairies Branch
#460, 175 Hargrave St., Winnipeg MB R3C 3R8
Tel: 204-956-4625; *Fax:* 204-943-0652
revp-prairies@psac-afpc.com
prairies.psac.com
Chief Officer(s):
Marianne Hladun, Regional Executive Vice-President, Prairies
Regina Branch
#200, 2445 - 13 Ave., Regina SK S4P 0W1
Tel: 306-757-3575; *Fax:* 306-569-8425
St. John's Branch
#105, 33 Pippy Pl., St. John's NL A1B 2X3
Tel: 709-726-6453; *Fax:* 709-726-1821
Saskatoon Branch
#5, 511 - 1st Ave. North, Saskatoon SK S7K 1X5
Tel: 306-244-3033; *Fax:* 306-664-2016
Section de Gatineau
Place du Centre, #310, 200, promenade du Portage, Gatineau QC J8X 4B7
Tel: 819-777-4647; *Fax:* 819-777-9407
Section de Montréal
#1104, 5800, rue Saint-Denis, Montréal QC H2S 3L5
Tél: 514-875-7100; *Téléc:* 514-875-8399
Ligne sans frais: 800-642-8020
Section de Québec
#130, 5050, boul des Gradins, Québec QC G2J 1P8
Tél: 418-666-6500; *Téléc:* 418-666-6999
Ligne sans frais: 800-566-6530
Section provinciale du Québec
#1104, 5800, rue Saint-Denis, Montréal QC H2S 3L5
Tél: 514-875-2690; *Téléc:* 514-868-1678
vper-que@psac-afpc.com
www.afpcquebec.com
Chief Officer(s):
Magali Picard, Regional Executive Vice-President, Québec
Sudbury Branch
#500A, 10 Elm St., Sudbury ON P3C 5N3
Tel: 705-674-6907; *Fax:* 705-674-8652
Toll-Free: 800-354-9134
Thunder Bay Branch
#109, 1205 Amber Dr., Thunder Bay ON P7M 6M4
Tel: 807-345-8442; *Fax:* 807-344-0704
Toronto Branch
#608, 90 Eglinton Ave. East, London ON M4P 2Y3
Tel: 416-485-3558; *Fax:* 416-485-8607
Toll-Free: 800-354-9086
PSAC_Toronto_Mail@psac-afpc.com
Vancouver Branch
#200, 5238 Joyce St., Vancouver BC V5R 6C9
Tel: 604-430-5631; *Fax:* 604-430-0451
Toll-Free: 800-663-1655
Vancouver Satellite Office
#300, 5238 Joyce St., Vancouver BC V5R 6C9
Tel: 604-430-5761; *Fax:* 604-431-6727
Victoria Branch
#210, 1497 Admirals Rd., Victoria BC V9A 2P8
Tel: 250-953-1050; *Fax:* 250-953-1066
Toll-Free: 866-953-1050
Whitehorse Branch
#100, 2285 - 2 Ave., Whitehorse YT Y1A 1C9
Tel: 867-667-2331; *Fax:* 867-633-5347
Winnipeg Branch
#460, 175 Hargrave St., Winnipeg MB R3C 3R8
Tel: 204-947-1601; *Fax:* 204-943-0652
Yellowknife Branch
PO Box 637, 4916 - 49 St., Yellowknife NT X1A 2N4
Tel: 867-873-5670; *Fax:* 867-873-4295
Toll-Free: 800-661-0870

Public Services Health & Safety Association (PSHSA)
#1800, 4950 Yonge St., Toronto ON M2N 6K1
Tel: 416-250-2131; *Fax:* 416-250-7484
Toll-Free: 877-250-7444
www.pshsa.ca
www.linkedin.com/company/public-services-health-and-safety-association
twitter.com/pshsaca
www.instagram.com/pshsa
Previous Name: Education Safety Association of Ontario; Municipal Health & Safety Assn; Ontario Safety Assn. for Community & Healthcare
Overview: A small provincial organization founded in 2010
Mission: To reduce workplace risks & prevent occupational injuries & illness; To offer occupational health & safety resources to public sector workers & employers
Affiliation(s): Health & Safety Ontario
Finances: *Annual Operating Budget:* $1.5 Million-$3 Million
Membership: 9,000+ organizations; 1.2 million individuals; *Member Profile:* Public service sector organizations; *Committees:* Municipal & Community Affairs; Community & Healthcare; Education & Culture
Activities: Access to sector-specific advisory councils; onsite courses; safety audit services; safety resource materials; statistical data; interactive electronic communications; *Library:* by appointment
Chief Officer(s):
Ron Kelusky, President & CEO

Public Works Association of British Columbia (PWABC)
#102, 211 Columbia St., Vancouver BC V6A 2R5
Toll-Free: 877-356-0699
info@pwabc.ca
www.pwabc.ca
www.facebook.com/pubworksassocbc
twitter.com/PWABCupdates
Overview: A medium-sized provincial organization overseen by Canadian Public Works Association
Mission: To advance the public works profession by promoting excellence & public awareness through education, advocacy & the exhance of knowledge
Member of: American Public Works Association
Membership: *Fees:* $164 individual; Corporate: $403.00 for Heritage, $1683 for Prestige, $7991 for Crown

Canadian Associations / Pugwash & Area Chamber of Commerice

Activities: *Awareness Events:* Public Works Week
Chief Officer(s):
Deryk Lee, President, 250-361-0467
Gregory Wightman, Vice President, 250-828-3508
Karen Stewart, Secretary/Treasurer, 604-695-7403
Awards:
• Awards to Individuals
Women's Public Works Ambassador Award, Outstanding Public Works Employee Award, Dedicated Service Awards, PWABC Manager of the Year Award, PWABC Professional - Dedicated Service Award & Emerging Leader of the Year Award
• Awards to Municipalities
Project of the Year Award, Public Works Week - Community Celebration Award (Population d,000), Public Works Week - Community Celebration Award (Population 100,000) & Innovations Award
• PWABC Scholarship for Further Training
Eligibility: Members only
• $1000 Education Scholarship
Meetings/Conferences:
• Public Works Association of BC 2018 Technical Conference & Trade Show, 2018, BC
Scope: Provincial

Pugwash & Area Chamber of Commerice
PO Box 239, Pugwash NS B0K 1L0
Tel: 902-243-2275
info@pugwash.biz
pugwash.biz
www.facebook.com/pugwashbiz
Overview: A small local organization founded in 2007
Mission: To support Pugwash & area businesses
Member of: Canadian Chamber of Commerce; Atlantic Chamber of Commerce
Chief Officer(s):
Lee Fleming, Manager, Member Services

Pulaarvik Kablu Friendship Centre
PO Box 429, Rankin Inlet NU X0C 0G0
Tel: 867-645-2600; *Fax:* 867-645-2538
recept_pkfcmain@qiniq.com
www.pulaarvik.ca
Previous Name: Sappujjijit Friendship Centre
Overview: A small local organization founded in 1973
Member of: National Association of Friendship Centres
Staff Member(s): 3
Activities: Workshops, programs & projects aimed at education, health & well-being of people of the community
Chief Officer(s):
Marianne Taparti, Chair
George Dunkerley, Executive Director

Pulp & Paper Centre
University of British Columbia, 2385 East Mall, Vancouver BC V6T 1Z4
Tel: 604-822-8560
ppc-info@ubc.ca
www.ppc.ubc.ca
Previous Name: Canadian Pulp & Paper Network for Innovation in Education & Research; Mechanical Wood-Pulps Network
Overview: A medium-sized provincial organization
Mission: To act as a university-industry partnership for innovation & education; To house inter-disciplinary, cross-faculty post-graduate research programs relevant to the pulp & paper industry
Affiliation(s): FPInnovations; PAPIER
Membership: *Member Profile:* UBC faculty & students involved in teaching & research for the pulp & paper industry; Members of the manufacturing, utilities & supplier industries, as well as consultants & government agencies
Chief Officer(s):
Mark Martinez, Director, 604-822-8564
martinez@chbe.ubc.ca
George Soong, Safety & Operations Officer, Building/Technical Inquiries, 604-822-2530
gsoong@mail.ubc.ca
Chitra Arcot, Coordinator, Communications, 604-827-2117
chitra.arcot@ubc.ca
Publications:
• Canadian Pulp & Paper Network for Innovation in Education & Research Newsletter
Type: Newsletter; *Frequency:* Semiannually
Profile: Papier's recent activities, such as meetings & award presentations

Pulp & Paper Employee Relations Forum
c/o Westcott Consulting, 6627 Westcott Rd., Duncan BC V9L 6A4
Tel: 250-748-9445; *Fax:* 888-273-7148
westcot@telus.net
paperforum.com
Overview: A medium-sized national organization
Mission: To act primarily as a research & information service for the industry; to service the pulp & paper industry in job evaluation, benefit & pension plan administration & trusteeship, contract interpretation & any other matters relating to labour relations
Chief Officer(s):
Fred Oud, Executive Director

Pulp & Paper Products Council (PPPC)
#1000, 1200, av McGill College, Montréal QC H3B 4G7
Tel: 514-861-8828; *Fax:* 514-866-4863
general@pppc.org
www.pppc.org
Overview: A medium-sized international organization
Mission: To collect & provide market data & intelligence on the pulp, newsprint, printing, & writing papers sectors; the PPPC operates out of Montréal, Brussels, Beijing, & Delhi
Staff Member(s): 25
Membership: 72 corporate
Activities: *Awareness Events:* International Pulp Week, May
Publications:
• Monthly Flash Reports [a publication of the Pulp & Paper Products Council]
Type: Newsletter; *Frequency:* Monthly

Pulp & Paper Technical Association of Canada (PAPTAC) / Association technique des pâtes et papiers du Canada
#1070, 740, rue Notre-Dame ouest, Montréal QC H3C 3X6
Tel: 514-392-0265; *Fax:* 514-392-0369
tech@paptac.ca
www.paptac.ca
Previous Name: Canadian Pulp & Paper Association - Technical Section
Overview: A medium-sized national organization founded in 1915
Mission: To provide means for the interchange of knowledge & expertise among its members; to improve the skill levels & effectiveness of present & future employees through training & education; to provide technical & practical information on pulp & paper manufacture & use
Finances: *Funding Sources:* Membership fees; Events
Chief Officer(s):
Greg Hay, Executive Director, 514-392-6964
ghay@paptac.ca
Publications:
• Journal of Pulp and Paper Science (JPPS)
Type: Journal; *Frequency:* Quarterly

Pulp, Paper & Woodworkers of Canada (PPWC)
#201, 1184 - West 6 Ave., Vancouver BC V6H 1A4
Tel: 604-731-1909; *Fax:* 604-731-6448
Toll-Free: 888-992-7792
www.ppwc.ca
www.facebook.com/PulpPaperandWoodworkersofCanada
www.youtube.com/user/PPWCUnion
Overview: A medium-sized national organization founded in 1963
Mission: To ensure fair working conditions for its members
Affiliation(s): Confederation of Canadian Unions
Staff Member(s): 1
Chief Officer(s):
Arnold Bercov, President
abercov@ppwc.ca

Pumphouse Theatres Society
2140 Pumphouse Ave. SW, Calgary AB T3C 3P5
Tel: 403-263-0079; *Fax:* 403-237-5357
www.pumphousetheatres.ca
www.facebook.com/154210604615247
twitter.com/PumphouseTS
Also Known As: Pumphouse Theatre
Overview: A small local charitable organization founded in 1972
Mission: To provide a theatrical performance facility that is consistent with the heritage character of the site & to encourage, develop & maintain community theatre in Calgary
Member of: Professional Association of Canadian Theatres; Canadian Institute for Theatre Technology
Affiliation(s): Theatre Alberta; Calgary Professional Arts Alliance
Finances: *Annual Operating Budget:* $250,000-$500,000; *Funding Sources:* Municipal government; corporate sponsorship; individual donations
Staff Member(s): 11; 100 volunteer(s)
Membership: 40 individual; *Fees:* $20
Activities: One Act Play Festival; drama day camps; fall & winter drama classes; *Speaker Service:* Yes
Chief Officer(s):
Karen Almadi, President & Secretary
Scott McTavish, Executive Director
exec@pumphousetheatre.ca

Purchasing Management Association of Canada - Québec Institute *Voir* Corporation des approvisionneurs du Québec

Purebred Sheep Breeders Association of Nova Scotia
PO Box 550, Truro NS B2N 5E3
www.sheepnovascotia.ns.ca
Overview: A small provincial organization founded in 1980
Mission: To improve the quality of purebred sheep in Nova Scotia; To advance breeders' interests & speak on their behalf when necessary
Member of: Canadian Sheep Breeders Association
Finances: *Funding Sources:* Membership fees; commission on annual breeding stock sale
Membership: 40 individual; *Fees:* $30 first family member, $20 each additional family member
Chief Officer(s):
Andrew Hebda, President

Purebred Swine Breeders' Association of Canada *See* Canadian Swine Breeders' Association

Purely Mutual Underwriters Association; Mutual Fire Underwriters Association *See* Ontario Mutual Insurance Association

Qalipu Mi'kmaq First Nations Band
3 Church St., Corner Brook NL A2H 6J3
Tel: 709-634-0996; *Fax:* 709-639-3997
Toll-Free: 800-561-2266
qalipu.ca
Overview: A small provincial organization overseen by Congress of Aboriginal Peoples
Chief Officer(s):
Annie Randell, Chief Executive Officer
arandell@qalipu.ca

Qikiqtani Inuit Association (QIA)
Igluvut Building, 2nd Fl., PO Box 1340, Iqaluit NU X0A 0H0
Tel: 867-975-8400; *Fax:* 867-979-3238
Toll-Free: 800-667-2742
info@qia.ca
www.qia.ca
www.facebook.com/QikiqtaniInuit
twitter.com/Qikiqtani_Inuit
www.instagram.com/Qikiqtani_Inuit
Overview: A small local organization founded in 1975
Mission: To represent approximately 14,000 Inuit in Nunavut's Qikiqtani (Baffin) Region
Staff Member(s): 37
Chief Officer(s):
Navarana Beveridge, Executive Director
nbeveridge@qia.ca
Sima Sahar Zerehi, Director, Communications
szerehi@qia.ca
Hagar Idlout-Sudlovenick, Director, Social Policy
hidlout-sudlovenick@qia.ca
Scott Wells, Director, Finance
swells@qia.ca

QMI *See* QMI - SAI Global

QMI - SAI Global
#200, 20 Carlson Ct., Toronto ON M9W 7K6
Tel: 416-401-8700; *Fax:* 416-401-8650
Toll-Free: 800-465-3717
www.qmi.com
Also Known As: Quality Management Institute
Previous Name: QMI
Overview: A small provincial organization founded in 1984
Mission: The management systems registrar evaluates business processes against ISO or industry standards
Member of: CSA Group
Affiliation(s): Accredited by the American National Standards Institute - Registrar Accreditation Board of the USA (ANSI-RAB), the Standards Council of Canada (SCC), entidada mexicana de

acreditacion a.c. (EMA), & the International Automotive Oversight Bureau (IAOB)
Activities: Registering manufacturing & service organizations to a wide range of ISO & industry standards for quality & environmental systems; Increasing knowledge & understanding of standards by offering a variety of training courses; *Library:* Standards Library
Chief Officer(s):
Peter Granat, CEO
Publications:
• QMI Brief
Type: Newsletter; *Frequency:* 3 pa
Profile: News about management systems & registration, plus information on the automotive, aerospace, forestry, & environment sectors

Montréal
#605, 1, av Holiday, Pointe-Claire QC H9R 5N3
Tel: 514-426-3432
Toll-Free: 888-723-7755

Vancouver
PO Box 36002, 10991 No. One Rd., Richmond BC V7E 1S0
Tel: 778-297-5524; *Fax:* 778-297-1694
Toll-Free: 800-268-7321

Western Canada
Toll-Free: 800-268-7321

Qu'Appelle Valley Friendship Centre (QVFC)
PO Box 240, Fort Qu'Appelle SK S0G 1S0
Tel: 306-332-5616; *Fax:* 306-332-5091
admin@qvfc.ca
www.qvfc.ca
Overview: A small local charitable organization founded in 1980
Mission: To provide support & direct services to the Aboriginal community; To strive to bridge the gap between Aboriginal people & society at large, through assisting in the process of social interaction, sharing of cultures & the educating of harmonious working relationships between all communities & cultures
Affiliation(s): Friendship Centres of Saskatachewant; National Friendship Centre
Staff Member(s): 10
Activities: Personal services; housing & employment services; sustenance, maintenance & basic services; referral services; legal services; youth programs
Chief Officer(s):
Rob Donison, Executive Director
rdonison@qvfc.ca

Quad County Support Services (QCSS)
PO Box 65, 195 Wellington St., Wardsville ON N0L 2N0
Tel: 519-693-4812; *Fax:* 519-693-7055
qcssfundraising01@gmail.com
www.facebook.com/193422024035687
Overview: A small local charitable organization founded in 1963
Mission: To encourage the acceptance of all people by fostering a lifestyle that lends itself to the betterment of everyone in the community, safeguarding the rights & responsibilities of all individuals
Member of: Community Living Ontario
Finances: *Annual Operating Budget:* $500,000-$1.5 Million; *Funding Sources:* Ministry of Community & Social Services; municipal grants
Staff Member(s): 32; 14 volunteer(s)
Membership: 20; *Fees:* $5; *Member Profile:* Parents; advocates; family
Chief Officer(s):
William Shurish, Executive Director
Bonnie Campbell, President

Quadra Island Food Bank
PO Box 242, Heriot Bay BC V0P 1H0
Tel: 250-285-3888
Overview: A small local organization overseen by Food Banks British Columbia
Member of: Food Banks British Columbia
Chief Officer(s):
Teresa Tate, Contact
teresa_tate@yahoo.com

Quaker Aboriginal Affairs Committee (QAAC)
c/o Canadian Friends Service Committee, 60 Lowther Ave., Toronto ON M5R 1C7
Tel: 416-920-5213; *Fax:* 416-920-5214
quakerservice.ca
Also Known As: Quaker Committee for Native Concerns
Overview: A small national charitable organization founded in 1976
Mission: Support for Aboriginal fights & justice, public education & campaigns
Member of: Canadian Friends Service Committee
Affiliation(s): Aboriginal Rights Coalition
Activities: *Internships:* Yes
Chief Officer(s):
Jennifer Preston, Program Coordinator
jennifer@quakerservice.ca

Quakers Fostering Justice (QFJ)
c/o Canadian Friends Service Committee, 60 Lowether Ave., Toronto ON M5R 1C7
Tel: 416-920-5213; *Fax:* 416-920-5214
qfj@quakerservice.ca
quakerservice.ca/our-work/justice
Overview: A small national organization founded in 1975
Mission: To build caring community without need for prisons; to explore alternatives to prison based on economic, social justice & fulfillment of human needs; to foster awareness within & outside Quaker community of roots of crime & violence in society; to reach & support prisoners, guards, victims & families
Member of: Church Council on Justice & Corrections; Coalition for Gun Control; Canadian Friends Service Committee; Canadian Criminal Justice Association; Victim Offender Mediation Association
Affiliation(s): Alternatives to Violence Project - Canada
Finances: *Funding Sources:* Private donations
Activities: Workshops; seminars; conferences
Chief Officer(s):
Tasmin Rajotte, Program Coordinator

Qualicum Beach Chamber of Commerce
PO Box 159, 124 West 2nd Ave., Qualicum Beach BC V9K 1S7
Tel: 250-752-0960
chamber@qualicum.bc.ca
www.qualicum.bc.ca
www.facebook.com/QBChamber
twitter.com/qbchamber
instagram.com/QualicumBeachVIC
Overview: A small local organization founded in 1927
Mission: To promote local trade & commerce; To enhance to economic, civic & social well-being of the community; To represent a unified voice through which businesses & professional people can work together to build a strong & vibrant business climate
Member of: BC Chamber of Commerce; Tourism Vancouver Island
Affiliation(s): Oceanside Tourism Association
Finances: *Funding Sources:* Town of Qualicum Beach; membership fees; fundraising events
Staff Member(s): 4
Membership: 300; *Fees:* $225 regular; $125 non profit/affiliate/second business/individual
Activities: *Library:* Business Information Centre; Open to public
Chief Officer(s):
Oura Giakoumakis, Chair
Evelyn Clark, CEO
Awards:
• Three $750 scholarships each year to students from Kwalikum Secondary
Publications:
• Qualicum Beach Chamber of Commerce Eflash
Type: Newsletter

Qualifications Evaluation Council of Ontario / Le Conseil ontarien d'évaluation des qualifications
#308, 1300 Yonge St., Toronto ON M4T 1X3
Tel: 416-323-1969
Toll-Free: 800-385-1030
www.qeco.on.ca
Overview: A medium-sized provincial organization founded in 1969
Mission: To provide & to objectively administer the evaluation of teacher qualifications for salary purposes.
Affiliation(s): AEFO; ETFO; OECTA
Membership: *Member Profile:* Teachers
Chief Officer(s):
Sam Hammond, President
Ken Collins, Executive Director

Quality in Lifelong Learning Network (QUILL)
PO Box 1148, #202, 200 McNabb St., Walkerton ON N0G 2V0
Tel: 519-881-4655; *Fax:* 519-881-4638
Toll-Free: 800-530-6852
execdir.quill@gmail.com
www.quillnetwork.ca
www.facebook.com/QUILLNetwork
Also Known As: QUILL Learning Network
Previous Name: Queensbush Initiatives for Literacy & Learning Inc.
Overview: A small local charitable organization founded in 1995
Mission: To support & promote learning activities in Bruce, Grey, Perth & the Georgian Triangle
Member of: Essential Skills Ontario; Community Literacy of Ontario; Learning Networks of Ontario
Finances: *Annual Operating Budget:* $50,000-$100,000; *Funding Sources:* Ministry of Training, Colleges & Universities
Staff Member(s): 2
Membership: 45; *Fees:* $15 individual; $30 associate; $35 organization; *Member Profile:* Literacy programs & interested community members; *Committees:* Nominating
Activities: Ensures quality literacy programs for learners; provides training for literacy & upgrading providers; raises public awareness & promotes action on literacy issues; provides referral service; *Speaker Service:* Yes; *Library:* QUILL Network Resources
Chief Officer(s):
Debera Flynn, Executive Director
execdir@quillnetwork.ca
Awards:
• QUILL Network Recognition Awards

Québec Aboriginal Tourism Corporation *Voir* Société touristique des Autochtones du Québec

Québec Amateur Netball Federation *Voir* Fédération de Netball du Québec

Québec Anglophone Heritage Network (QAHN) / Reseau du Patrimoine Anglophone du Québec
#400, 257, rue Queen, Lennoxville QC J1M 1K7
Tel: 819-564-9595; *Fax:* 819-564-6872
Toll-Free: 877-964-0409
home@qahn.org
www.qahn.org
Overview: A small provincial organization founded in 2000
Mission: To operate as a non-profit, non-partisan umbrella organization to help advance knowledge of the history & culture of English-speaking society in Québec
Member of: Quebec Community Groups Network; Fédération des sociétés d'histoire du Québec
Finances: *Annual Operating Budget:* $50,000-$100,000
Staff Member(s): 2; 100 volunteer(s)
Membership: 150+; *Fees:* $20-30
Activities: *Library:* Open to public

Québec Angus Association
217 rte Adams, Durham-Sud QC J0H 2C0
Tél: 418-784-2311
quebecangus@live.ca
www.quebecangus.ca
Aperçu: *Dimension:* petite; *Envergure:* provinciale
Membre de: Canadian Angus Association
Membre(s) du bureau directeur:
Cynthia Jackson, Secrétaire, 819-588-2311

Québec Anxiety, Depressive & Bipolar Disorder Support Association *Voir* Revivre - Association Québécoise de soutien aux personnes souffrant de troubles anxieux, dépressifs ou bipolaires

Québec Association for Community Living / Québec Institute for Intellectual Disability *Voir* Association du Québec pour l'intégration sociale / Institut québécois de la déficience intellectuelle

Québec Association for ICT Freelancers *Voir* Association québécoise des informaticiennes et informaticiens indépendants

Quebec Association for Parents of Visually Impaired Children *Voir* Association québécoise des parents d'enfants handicapés visuels

Québec Association of Baptist Churches
6215, boul Côte St-Luc, Montréal QC H3X 2H3
Tel: 514-483-4302
associationbaptistcq@gmail.com
www.quebecbaptist.org
Also Known As: Eastern Association
Overview: A small provincial organization founded in 1887
Mission: To help churches carry out their services & goals
Member of: Canadian Baptists of Ontario & Quebec

Membership: 19 churches; *Member Profile:* Baptist churches in Quebec
Chief Officer(s):
Brian Berry, Moderator
bberry@videotron.ca

Québec Association of Energy Managers *Voir* Association québécoise pour la maîtrise de l'énergie

Québec Association of Export Trading Houses *Voir* Association des maisons de commerce extérieur du Québec

Québec Association of Fire Chiefs *Voir* Association des chefs en sécurité incendie du Québec

Québec Association of Independent Journalists *Voir* Association des journalistes indépendants du Québec

Québec Association of Independent Schools (QAIS) / Association des écoles privées du Québec
3635, av Atwater, Montréal QC H3H 1Y4
Tel: 514-483-6111; *Fax:* 514-483-0865
Toll-Free: 866-909-6111
www.qais.qc.ca
Overview: A medium-sized provincial organization founded in 1965 overseen by Canadian Accredited Independent Schools
Mission: To promote collaboration, provide services that further educational leadership & advocate for independent English language education in Quebec on behalf of its member schools.
Membership: 25 schools
Activities: *Rents Mailing List:* Yes
Chief Officer(s):
Holly Hampson, Executive Director
hollyhampson@qais.qc.ca

Quebec Association of Insolvency & Restructuring Professionals (QAIRP) / Association québécoise des professionnels de la réorganisation et de l'insolvabilité (AQPRI)
c/o Tremblay & Compagnie Syndices et Gestionnaires Ltée, 582, boul Saguenay est, Chicoutimi QC G7H 1L2
Tel: 418-549-5642; *Fax:* 418-549-5829
conseilsyndic.com
Previous Name: Association québécoise des professionnels d'insolvabilité
Overview: A small provincial organization overseen by Canadian Association of Insolvency & Restructuring Professionals
Mission: Promouvoir la pratique de l'administration de l'insolvabilité et l'intérêt public en ce domaine
Member of: Canadian Association of Insolvency & Restructuring Professionals
Finances: *Funding Sources:* Cotisations; séminaires
Chief Officer(s):
Charles Tremblay, President
ctremblay@tremblaycie.com

Québec Association of International Cooperation *Voir* Association québécoise des organismes de coopération internationale

Québec Association of Marriage & Family Therapy (QAMFT) / Association québécoise pour la thérapie conjugale et familiale
#200, 360, av Victoria, Westmount QC H3Y 2L5
Tel: 514-949-5688
Overview: A medium-sized provincial organization
Mission: To promote understanding, research & education in the field of couple & family therapy & to ensure that public needs are met by practitioners of the highest quality
Member of: American Association for Marriage & Family Therapy
Finances: *Funding Sources:* Membership dues
Staff Member(s): 1; 8 volunteer(s)
Membership: 135; *Member Profile:* M.A. or Ph.D. in psychology or social work
Chief Officer(s):
Andrew Sofin, President
asofin@qamft.org

Québec Association of Mennonite Brethren Churches *Voir* Association des Églises des frères mennonites du Québec

Québec Association of Naturopathic Medicine (QANM) / Association de medecine naturapathique du Québec (AMNQ)
1173, boul du Mont Royal ouest, Montréal QC H2V 2H6
Tel: 514-755-6629
info@qanm.org
qanm.org
www.linkedin.com/groups/AMNQ-QANM-4267434
www.facebook.com/amnq.qanm
twitter.com/amnq_qanm
Overview: A small provincial organization founded in 1995
Affiliation(s): Canadian Association of Naturopathic Doctors
Staff Member(s): 4
Membership: 6
Chief Officer(s):
André Saine, DC, ND, President

Québec Association of Pharmacy Owners *Voir* Association québécoise des pharmaciens propriétaires

Québec Association of Protestant School Boards *See* Québec English School Boards Association

Québec Association of Teachers of French as a Second Language *Voir* Association québécoise des enseignants de français langue seconde

Québec Ball Hockey Association (QBHA) / Association de Hockey-Balle du Québec (AHBQ)
2890, boul Dagenais ouest, Laval QC H7P 1T1
Tel: 450-963-9346; *Fax:* 450-622-4466
info@ahbq.com
www.qbha.com
www.facebook.com/AHBQ.QBHA
twitter.com/AHBQ_QBHA
Overview: A small provincial organization
Mission: To promote & organize ball hockey in Québec & across the country
Member of: Canadian Ball Hockey Association; International Street & Ball Hockey Federation; Hockey Canada

Québec Basketball Federation *Voir* Fédération de basketball du Québec

Québec Bio-Industries Business Network *Voir* BIOQuébec

Québec Black Medical Association
#180, 2021 av Atwater, Montréal QC H3H 2P2
Tel: 514-937-8822
www.qbma.ca
Overview: A medium-sized provincial organization
Mission: The Québec Black Medical Association aims to enable young people from the Black community to pursue careers as health professionals and to advance medical practice and research in Quebec.
Chief Officer(s):
Edouard Tucker, President

Québec Board of Black Educators (QBBE)
#310, 3333 boul Cavendish, Montréal QC H4B 2M5
Tel: 514-481-9400; *Fax:* 514-481-0611
qbbe@videotron.ca
www.qbbe.org
www.facebook.com/qbbe.ca
Overview: A medium-sized local organization founded in 1968
Mission: To promote the development of educational services for Black Youth & other youth between the ages of 5 to 25 who reside in the Greater Montreal area
Chief Officer(s):
Phylicia Burke, Contact
Clarence Bayne, President

Québec Brewers Association *Voir* Association des brasseurs du Québec

Québec Building Envelope Council *Voir* Conseil de l'enveloppe du bâtiment du Québec

Québec Camping Association *Voir* Association des camps du Québec inc.

Québec Celiac Foundation *Voir* Fondation québécoise de la maladie coeliaque

Québec Cerebral Palsy Association *Voir* Association de paralysie cérébrale du Québec

Québec Chess Federation *Voir* Fédération québécoise des échecs

Québec City & Area Tourism & Convention Board *Voir* Office du tourisme et des congrès de Québec

Québec City Summer Festival *Voir* Festival d'été de Québec

Québec Coalition for Orphan Diseases *Voir* Regroupement québécois des maladies orphelines

Québec Command *Voir* The Royal Canadian Legion

Québec Commercial Certification Office Inc. *Voir* L'Office de Certification Commerciale du Québec Inc.

Québec Community Newspaper Association (QCNA) / Association des journaux régionaux du Québec (AJRQ)
#207, 189, boul Hymus, Pointe Claire QC H9R 1E9
Tel: 514-697-6330; *Fax:* 514-697-6331
info@qcna.qc.ca
www.qcna.org
Previous Name: Association of Québec Regional English Media
Overview: A medium-sized provincial organization founded in 1980 overseen by Canadian Community Newspapers Association
Mission: To promote Québec community English media; To serve as clearinghouse for information; To promote good journalism among members; To enhance the role of the media as social catalysts; To represent members to pertinent government departments; To interact with other provincial & national newspaper associations in Canada; To help members better their financial condition
Affiliation(s): Conseil de la presse du Québec
Finances: *Annual Operating Budget:* $250,000-$500,000; *Funding Sources:* Federal government; advertising commissions surplus; membership fees
Staff Member(s): 3; 8 volunteer(s)
Membership: 30; *Fees:* $150; *Member Profile:* Newspaper enterprises that serve Québec's English-speaking community; *Committees:* By-laws; Editorial; Nomination; Awards
Activities: Offering member services, including advertising clearing & monitoring, promotions & marketing, networking & expertise, workshops, general meetings, & telephone information services; Advocating for communities' right to information in their language; Community building through media support; *Speaker Service:* Yes; *Rents Mailing List:* Yes
Chief Officer(s):
Richard Tardif, Executive Director
richard.tardif@qcna.qc.ca

Québec Competitive Festival of Music / Festival de concours du Québec
136, av Duke-of-Kent, Pointe-Claire QC H9R 1X9
Tel: 514-398-4535; *Fax:* 514-398-8061
Previous Name: Québec Competitive Music Festival
Overview: A medium-sized provincial organization overseen by Federation of Canadian Music Festivals
Chief Officer(s):
Tom Davidson, Provincial Administrator
thomas.davidson@mcgill.ca

Québec Competitive Music Festival *See* Québec Competitive Festival of Music

Québec Council on Tobacco & Health *Voir* Conseil québécois sur le tabac et la santé

Québec Crafts Council (Ind.) *Voir* Conseil des métiers d'art du Québec (ind.)

The Quebec Cricket Federation Inc. *Voir* La Fédération Québécoise du Cricket Inc.

Québec Cycling Sports Federation *Voir* Fédération québécoise des sports cyclistes

Québec Dairy Council Inc. *Voir* Conseil des industriels laitiers du Québec inc.

Québec dans le monde
#600, 355, rue Saint-Joseph est, Québec QC G1K 3B4
Tél: 418-659-5540; *Téléc:* 418-659-4143
info@quebecmonde.com
www.quebecmonde.com
twitter.com/Quebec_Monde
Également appelé: Association Québec dans le monde
Nom précédent: Alliance Champlain
Aperçu: *Dimension:* moyenne; *Envergure:* provinciale; Organisme sans but lucratif; fondée en 1983
Mission: Faire connaître le Québec et sa spécificité culturelle dans le monde; éditer des ouvrages de référence (annuaires, bottins, répertoires) sur le Québec
Finances: *Budget de fonctionnement annuel:* $100,000-$250,000; *Fonds:* Cotisations des membres; vente des produits d'édition; abonnements aux périodiques
Membre(s) du personnel: 3; 15 bénévole(s)
Membre: 1 200 membres québécois; *Montant de la cotisation:* 50$ individu; 75$ collectif

Activités: Édite 20 annuaires et répertoires sur le Québec et ses ressources; gère 30 listes informatisés sur le Québec totalisant 40,000 entreprises ou organismes parmi les plus importants du Québec; *Listes de destinataires:* Oui
Publications:
• AGENDA [a publication of Québec dans le monde]
Type: Magazine; *Frequency:* 3 fois par an
Profile: Les événements publics à venir au Québec
• QUÉBEC Info [a publication of Québec dans le monde]
Type: Bulletin électronique; *Frequency:* 6 fois par an
Profile: Principaux développements du Québec

Québec Dart Association Inc. *Voir* Association de Dards du Québec inc.

The Québec Drama Federation (QDF) / Fédération dramatique du Québec
#807, 460, rue Sainte-Catherine ouest, Montréal QC H3B 1A7
Tel: 514-875-8698
Toll-Free: 877-875-7863
qdf@quebecdrama.org
www.quebecdrama.org
www.facebook.com/quebecdramafederation
twitter.com/quebecdramafed
Overview: A small provincial charitable organization founded in 1972
Mission: To encourage & support English-language theatre in predominantly francophone Québec; to offer leadership in the promotion & development of professional theatre artists, companies & organizations; to offer consultation & advocacy services, as well as professional training & promotion
Member of: Conseil québécoise du théâtre; In Kind Canada
Affiliation(s): Canadian Conference of the Arts; Association of Drama Educators of Québec; Professional Association of Canadian Theatres; Québec Community Groups Network; Academie québécoise du théâtre
Finances: *Annual Operating Budget:* $50,000-$100,000; *Funding Sources:* Provincial government; Federal government; municipal government; regional government
Staff Member(s): 4; 22 volunteer(s)
Membership: 225; *Fees:* $15-$150; *Member Profile:* Theatre companies; individuals; artists; educators; students
Activities: *Library:* Not open to public
Chief Officer(s):
Jane Needles, Executive Director
Anne Clark, President

Québec Employers Council *Voir* Conseil du patronat du Québec

Quebec English Literacy Alliance (QELA)
PO Box 3542, #236, 410, rue St-Nicholas, Montréal QC H2Y 2P5
Tel: 450-242-2360; *Fax:* 450-242-2543
Toll-Free: 866-942-7352
info@qela.qc.ca
qela.qc.ca
Overview: A medium-sized provincial organization founded in 1997
Mission: To be the unified voice of Quebec English literacy providers nationally & provincially
Staff Member(s): 3
Membership: 25
Activities: Networking, training & information-sharing activities; advancement of literacy in the province
Chief Officer(s):
Louise Quinn, Executive Director
lquinn@qela.qc.ca

Québec English School Boards Association (QESBA) / Association des commissions scolaires anglophones du Québec (ACSAQ)
#515, 1410, rue Stanley, Montréal QC H3A 1P8
Tel: 514-849-5900; *Fax:* 514-849-9228
Toll-Free: 877-512-7522
qesba@qesba.qc.ca
www.qesba.qc.ca
twitter.com/qesba
Previous Name: Québec Association of Protestant School Boards
Overview: A medium-sized provincial charitable organization founded in 1929 overseen by Canadian School Boards Association
Mission: To represent English school boards in Québec
Finances: *Annual Operating Budget:* $500,000-$1.5 Million; *Funding Sources:* Membership dues
Staff Member(s): 3

Membership: 9 English school boards; 178 school trustees
Activities: Advocacy; research & analysis; professional development
Chief Officer(s):
Marcus Tabachnick, Executive Director

Québec Environment Foundation *Voir* Fondation québécoise en environnement

Québec Environmental Law Centre *Voir* Centre québécois du droit de l'environnement

Québec Esperanto Society *Voir* Société québécoise d'espéranto

Québec Eye Bank Foundation *Voir* Fondation de la banque d'yeux du Québec inc.

Québec Family History Society (QFHS) / Société de l'histoire des familles du Québec
PO Box 7156, Stn. Pointe Claire-Dorval, 15, av Donegani, Pointe-Claire QC H9R 4S8
Tel: 514-695-1502; *Fax:* 514-695-3508
qfhs@bellnet.ca
www.qfhs.ca
Overview: A medium-sized provincial charitable organization founded in 1977
Mission: To promote genealogy & genealogical research in Québec (particularly English & Protestant records); To collect & preserve books, manuscripts & other related material
Member of: Québec Anglophone Heritage Network
Affiliation(s): International Federation of Family History Societies
Finances: *Annual Operating Budget:* Less than $50,000; *Funding Sources:* Membership dues; book sales & research
20 volunteer(s)
Membership: 130 institutional + 800 individual; *Fees:* $40 institutional; $75 individual; $75 family; *Member Profile:* Individuals interested in finding out information about ancestors who lived in Quebec, Canada, the United States, the British Isles, Western Europe or elsewhere in the world; *Committees:* Cemetery Transcription
Activities: Monthly lectures; Workshops, seminars & conferences; *Library*
Chief Officer(s):
Gary Schroder, President
Jackie Billingham, Executive Secretary

Québec Farmers' Association (QFA)
#255, 555, boul Roland-Therrien, Longueuil QC J4H 4E7
Tel: 450-679-0540; *Fax:* 450-463-5291
qfa@upa.qc.ca
www.quebecfarmers.org
www.facebook.com/groups/306871089363565
twitter.com/quebecfarmers
Overview: A medium-sized provincial organization founded in 1957
Mission: To defend the rights of the English-speaking agricultural community within the province of Québec.
Member of: Quebec Community Groups Network
Staff Member(s): 2
Membership: 3,000; *Fees:* $68.99; *Member Profile:* Québec's English-speaking farmers & rural citizens
Chief Officer(s):
Dougal Rattray, Executive Director
Andrew McClelland, Director, Communications

Québec Federation for Autism *Voir* Fédération québécoise de l'autisme

Québec Federation of General Practitioners *Voir* Fédération des médecins omnipraticiens du Québec

Québec Federation of Home & School Associations Inc. (QFHSA) / Fédération des associations foyer-école du Québec Inc.
#560, 3285, boul Cavendish, Montréal QC H4B 2L9
Tel: 514-481-5619; *Fax:* 514-481-5610
Toll-Free: 888-808-5619
info@qfhsa.org
www.qfhsa.org
www.facebook.com/QFHSA
Previous Name: Québec Federation of Protestant Home & School Associations
Overview: A medium-sized provincial charitable organization founded in 1944 overseen by Canadian Home & School Federation

Mission: To provide facilities for the bringing together of members of Home & School Associations for discussion of matters of general interest & to stimulate cooperative effort; To assist in forming public opinion favorable to reform & advancement of the education of the child; to develop between educators & the general public such a united effort as shall secure for every child the highest advantage in physical, mental, moral & spiritual education; To raise the standard of home & national life; To maintain non-partisan, non-commercial, non-racial & non-sectarian organization
Affiliation(s): Center for Literacy
Finances: *Funding Sources:* Membership fees
Staff Member(s): 2; 20 volunteer(s)
Membership: 5,000+ families in 80+ member organizations; *Fees:* Schedule available; *Member Profile:* Home & school associations, parents, educational professionals, individuals with an interest in maintaining education standards in the province; *Committees:* Rights; Education; Membership; Literacy; Administration/Office Services/Hiring; Finance; Constitution/By-Laws/Standing Rules; Nominations; Annual General Meeting Planning; Fall Conference Planning; Communications (Editorial); Resolutions/Policy; Executive
Activities: Facilitating workshops on parenting & child-related issues; Providing resources to parents in schools; Organizing annual Fall Leadership Conference & an AGM; *Speaker Service:* Yes; *Library:* Open to public by appointment
Chief Officer(s):
Brian Rock, President
president@qfhsa.org
Awards:
• Lewis Peace Prize
• Leslie N. Buzzell Award
Awarded to a home & school member who has given outstanding service at the provincial level
• Gordon Paterson Award
Awarded to an outstanding educator who has encouraged parent participation in the educational process
• Pat Lewis Humanitarian Award

Québec Federation of Labour *Voir* Fédération des travailleurs et travailleises du Québec

Quebec Federation of Laryngectomees *Voir* Fédération québécoise des laryngectomisés

Quebec Federation of Managers & Professional Salaried Workers (CNTU) *Voir* Fédération des professionnèles

Quebec Federation of Policemen (Ind.) *Voir* Fédération des policiers et policières municipaux du Québec (ind.)

Quebec Federation of Professional Employees in Education *Voir* Fédération des professionnelles et professionnels de l'éducation du Québec

Québec Federation of Professional Firefighters *Voir* Syndicat des pompiers et pompières du Québec (CTC)

Quebec Federation of Protestant Home & School Associations *See* Québec Federation of Home & School Associations Inc.

Québec Federation of Residents (Ind.) *Voir* Fédération des médecins résidents du Québec inc. (ind.)

Quebec Federation of Senior Citizens *Voir* Réseau FADOQ

Québec Federation of the Blind Inc. (QFB) / Fédération des aveugles du Québec inc.
7010, rue Sherbrooke ouest, Montréal QC H4B 1R3
Tel: 514-484-9232
qfb@ssss.gouv.qc.ca
qfb.ca
Overview: A small provincial charitable organization founded in 1970
Finances: *Funding Sources:* Donations; Fundraising
Membership: 100-499

Québec Federation of University Professors *Voir* Fédération québécoise des professeures et professeurs d'université

Quebec Fish and Seafood Marketing Association *Voir* Association québécoise de commercialisation de poissons et de fruits de mer

Québec Fish Processors Association *Voir* Association québécoise de l'industrie de la pêche

Québec Food Retailers' Association *Voir* Association des détaillants en alimentation du Québec

Canadian Associations / Québec Lawn Bowling Federation / Fédération de Boulingrin du Québec

Québec Forestry Industry Council *Voir* Conseil de l'industrie forestière du Québec

Québec Furniture Manufacturers Association Inc. *Voir* Association des fabricants de meubles du Québec inc.

Québec Gardens Association *Voir* Association des jardins du Québec

Québec Golf Federation *Voir* Fédération de golf du Québec

Québec Golf Superintendents Association *Voir* Association des surintendants de golf du Québec

Québec Government Employees' Union (Ind.) *Voir* Syndicat de la fonction publique du Québec inc. (ind.)

Québec Gymnastics Federation *Voir* Fédération de gymnastique du Québec

Québec Handball Association *Voir* Balle au mur Québec

Québec Harvest *Voir* Moisson Québec

Québec Institute of Floor Covering *Voir* Fédération québécoise des revêtements de sol

Québec Interprofessional Council *Voir* Conseil interprofessionnel du Québec

Québec Jewellers' Corporation *Voir* Corporation des bijoutiers du Québec

Québec Land Surveyors Association *Voir* Ordre des arpenteurs-géomètres du Québec

Quebec Landlords Association *Voir* Association des propriétaires du Québec inc.

Québec Lawn Bowling Federation / Fédération de Boulingrin du Québec
QC
www.bowlsquebec.com
Overview: A medium-sized provincial organization overseen by Bowls Canada Boulingrin

Quebec Lawyers Abroad *Voir* Avocats Hors Québec

Québec Lesbian Network *Voir* Réseau des lesbiennes du Québec

The Québec LGBT Chamber of Commerce *Voir* Chambre de commerce LGBT du Québec

Québec Liberal Party *Voir* Parti libéral du Québec

Québec Library Association (QLA) / Association des bibliothécaires du Québec (ABQLA)
PO Box 26717, Stn. Beaconsfield, 50, boul St-Charles, Montréal QC H9W 6G7
Tel: 514-697-0146; *Fax:* 514-697-0146
www.abqla.qc.ca
www.linkedin.com/groups/5071380/profile
www.facebook.com/124766477552846
twitter.com/ABQLA
Overview: A medium-sized provincial organization founded in 1932
Mission: To promote the role of library & information specialists in the greater Québec community; To foster & encourage the exchange of information on library-related issues; To strengthen relationships with national, provincial, & local library associations
Finances: *Funding Sources:* Membership dues
Membership: *Fees:* Schedule available; *Member Profile:* Librarians & information professionals, related personnel, & supporters throughout Québec
Activities: Facilitating workshops, speaker sessions, & social events; Hosting an annual conference
Chief Officer(s):
Leticia Cuenca, President
Awards:
• Anne Galler Award for Outstanding Library Service
Awarded to recognize an individual who has enriched librarianship in Québec *Deadline:* April
• Student Scholarship
Eligibility: Current ABQLA student members completing a Masters or Diplôme d'études collégiales (DEC) in a dedicated library or information studies program *Deadline:* February; *Amount:* $1,000
• Professional Development Awards
Two grants available; awarded to allow recipients to participate in a professional development opportunity relevant to their profession *Deadline:* February; *Amount:* $1,000

Meetings/Conferences:
• 86e Congrès annuel de l'Association des bibliothécaires du Québec 2018, 2018, QC
Scope: Provincial
Publications:
• ABQLA [Québec Library Association] Bulletin
Type: Journal; *Frequency:* 3 pa; *Editor:* Sandra Bebbington; *ISSN:* 0380-7150
Profile: Book reviews, library-related issues, new technologies
• Québec Library Association Membership Directory
Type: Yearbook; *Frequency:* a.
• Québec Library Association: A Historical Overview/L'Association des bibliothécaires de Québec: un survoi historique
Type: Report; *Number of Pages:* 32; *Author:* Rosemary Cochrane & Peter McNally; *ISSN:* 0969-7803; *Price:* $20 Canada; $25 US; $30 rest of world

Québec Liquor Board Store & Office Employees Union (Ind.) *Voir* Syndicat des employé(e)s de magasins et de bureau de la Société des alcools du Québec (ind.)

Québec Liquor Board's Union of Technical & Professional Employees (Ind.) *Voir* Syndicat du personnel technique et professionnel de la Société des alcools du Québec (ind.)

Québec Lung Association (QLA) / Association pulmonaire du Québec (APQ)
#104, 6070, rue Sherbrooke est, Montréal QC H1N 1C1
Tel: 514-287-7400; *Fax:* 514-287-1978
Toll-Free: 888-768-6669
info@pq.poumon.ca
www.pq.poumon.ca
www.facebook.com/poumon.qc
twitter.com/AssoPulmonaireQ
www.youtube.com/user/PoumonAPQ
Overview: A medium-sized provincial charitable organization founded in 1938 overseen by Canadian Lung Association
Mission: To provide resources in Québec about lung cancer, chronic obstructive pulmonary disease, sarcoidosis, tuberculosis, asthma, chronic bronchitis, sleep apnea, pneumonia, & emphysema
Member of: World Health Organization; International Union against Tuberculosis & Lung Disease; American Lung Association; European Lung Association
Finances: *Funding Sources:* Donations; Fundraising; Sponsorships
Membership: *Fees:* $10 support group; $25 associate member; $50 voting member; *Committees:* Scientific
Activities: Supporting respiratory health research; Providing education about respiratory illness; Offering support groups for persons affected by lung disease; Organizing events to raise funds; *Awareness Events:* Triathlon: One Breath, One Life
Chief Officer(s):
Dominique Massie, Executive Director, 514-975-5382 Ext. 224
dominique.massie@pq.poumon.ca
Raymond Jabbour, Chief Financial Officer & Director, Direct Marketing & Information Technology, 514-975-5382 Ext. 226
Mathieu Leroux, Admisor, Development & Communications, 514-975-5382 Ext. 235
mathieu.leroux@pq.poumon.ca
Publications:
• Le Bulletin de l'association pulmonaire du Québec
Type: Newsletter; *Editor:* Louis P. Brisson; *ISSN:* 0843-381X
Profile: Respiratory health information, plus donation news
• Le Rapport annuel de l'association pulmonaire du Québec
Type: Yearbook; *Frequency:* Annually

Québec Maple Syrup Producers Federation *Voir* Fédération des producteurs acéricoles du Québec

Québec Master Roofers Association *Voir* Association des maîtres couvreurs du Québec

Québec Medical Association *Voir* Association médicale du Québec

Quebec Mineral Exploration Association *Voir* Association de l'exploration minière de Québec

Québec Mining Association *Voir* Association minière du Québec

Quebec Motorcyclist Federation *Voir* Fédération motocycliste du Québec

Québec Native Women Inc. *Voir* Femmes autochtones du Québec inc.

Quebec Network for Social Inclusion of the Deaf & Hard of Hearing *Voir* Réseau québécois pour l'inclusion social des personnnes sourdes et malentendantes

Quebec Oil and Gas Association *Voir* Association pétrolière et gazière du Québec

Quebec Oil Heating Association *Voir* Association québécoise du chauffage au mazout

Québec Optometric Association *Voir* Association des optométristes du Québec

Quebec Paraplegics Association *Voir* Moelle Épinière et Motricité Québec

Québec Press Council *Voir* Conseil de presse du Québec

Québec Produce Growers Association *Voir* Association des producteurs maraîchers du Québec

Québec Produce Marketing Association *Voir* Association québécoise de la distribution de fruits et légumes

Québec Professional Union of Dieticians *Voir* Ordre professionnel des diététistes Québec

Québec Provincial Association of Teachers *Voir* Association provinciale des enseignantes et enseignants du Québec

Québec Provincial Police Association *Voir* Association des policières et policiers provinciaux du Québec

Quebec Psoriasis Alliance *See* Alliance Québécoise du Psoriasis

Québec Psychiatrists' Association *Voir* Association des médecins-psychiatres du Québec

Québec Public Health Association *Voir* Association pour la santé publique du Québec

Québec Public Interest Research Group - McGill / Groupe de recherche d'intérêt public du Québec - McGill
3647, rue Université, 3e étage, Montréal QC H3A 2B3
Tél: 514-398-7432; *Téléc:* 514-398-8976
info@qpirgmcgill.org
qpirgmcgill.org
www.facebook.com/QPIRG.GRIP.McGill
twitter.com/qpirgmcgill
Également appelé: QPIRG-McGill
Aperçu: *Dimension:* petite; *Envergure:* locale
Mission: To work on social justice & environmental issues
Membre: *Critères d'admissibilite:* Students; *Comités:* Conflict Resolution & Complaints

Quebec Racquetball Association *Voir* Association québécoise de racquetball

Québec Raptor Rehabilitation Network *Voir* Union québécoise de réhabilitation des oiseaux de proie

Québec Real Estate Association *Voir* Organisme d'autoréglementation du courtage immobilier du Québec

Québec Regional Tourist Associations Inc. *Voir* Associations touristiques régionales associées du Québec

Québec Restaurant Association *Voir* Association des restaurateurs du Québec

Québec Road Builders & Heavy Construction Association *Voir* Association des constructeurs de routes et grands travaux du Québec

Quebec Rugby Union *Voir* Fédération de rugby du Québec

Québec Shooting Federation *Voir* Fédération québécoise de tir

Québec Shorthorn Association / Club Shorthorn du Québec
QC
Overview: A small provincial organization
Member of: Canadian Shorthorn Association
Chief Officer(s):
Ray Dempsey, Contact

Québec Simmental Association (QSA) / Association Simmental du Québec (ASQ)
530, rte 239, Saint-Germain QC J0C 1K0

Tel: 819-395-4453; Fax: 819-395-4453
info@simmentalquebec.ca
www.simmentalquebec.ca
Overview: A small provincial organization founded in 1981
Mission: To promote the Québec Simmental breeding programs to the market, purebred as well as commercial, within the province of Québec & abroad
Member of: Canadian Simmental Association
Finances: *Annual Operating Budget:* Less than $50,000; *Funding Sources:* Canadian Simmental Association; Comité Conjoint des Races de Boucherie
6 volunteer(s)
Membership: 135; *Fees:* $34.19 annual; $227.90 lifetime; *Member Profile:* Purebred Simmental cattle breeders
Chief Officer(s):
Sylvain Lambert, President, 450-789-2188
Publications:
• Simmental du Québec

Québec Snowboard Association *Voir* Association Québec Snowboard

Quebec Society for Disabled Children *Voir* Société pour les enfants handicapés du Québec

Québec Society for the Defense of Animals *Voir* Société québécoise pour la défense des animaux

Québec Society for the Protection of Plants *Voir* Société de protection des plantes du Québec

Quebec Society of Comparitive Law *Voir* Association québécoise de doit comparé

Québec Society of Lipidology, Nutrition & Metabolism Inc. (QSLNM) / Société québécoise de lipidologie, de nutrition et de métabolisme (SQLNM)
2705, boul Laurier, Sainte-Foy QC G1V 4G2
Tel: 418-656-4141; Fax: 418-654-2145
sqlnm@crchul.ulaval.ca
www.lipidologie.qc.ca
Overview: A small provincial charitable organization founded in 2000
Mission: To promote training, education & research in lipidology, nutrition, metabolism & cardiovascular health
Finances: *Annual Operating Budget:* $50,000-$100,000
Membership: 632; *Fees:* Free; *Member Profile:* Scientists; physicians; lipidologists
Chief Officer(s):
Pierre Julien, PhD, President
pierre.julien@crchul.ulaval.ca
Awards:
• Prix des fondateurs
• Prix des meilleures affiches

Québec Special Olympics *Voir* Jeux Olympiques Spéciaux du Québec Inc.

Québec Square & Round Dance Clubs *See* Border Boosters Square & Round Dance Association

Quebec Technology Association *Voir* Association québécoise des technologies

Québec Thistle Council Inc. / Le Conseil Québécois du Chardon Inc.
#703, 3495, rue de la Montagne, Montréal QC H3G 2A5
Tel: 514-982-4525
www.thistlecouncil.com
Also Known As: Auld Alliance in Canada
Overview: A small provincial charitable organization founded in 1991
Mission: To promote & maintain Scottish culture & traditions in the Province of Québec & in particular, Montréal, through the organization, sponsorship & coordination of Scottish cultural activities & events
Finances: *Annual Operating Budget:* Less than $50,000; *Funding Sources:* Private
10 volunteer(s)
Membership: 15
Activities: Auld Alliance Awards Dinner & Ceilidh
Chief Officer(s):
Mildred Benoit, Contact
mildredbenoit@hotmail.ca

Québec Trotting & Pacing Society *Voir* Association Trot & Amble du Québec

Québec Trucking Association Inc. *Voir* Association du camionnage du Québec inc.

Québec Union of Firefighters (CLC) *Voir* Syndicat des pompiers et pompières du Québec (CTC)

Québec Union of Health Professionals & Technicians *Voir* Syndicat des professionnels et des techniciens de la santé du Québec

Québec University Students' Federation *Voir* Fédération étudiante universitaire du Québec

Quebec Urban Transit Association *Voir* Association du transport urbain du Québec

Quebec Urological Association *Voir* Association des urologues du Québec

Québec Water Bottlers' Association *Voir* Association des embouteilleurs d'eau du Québec

Québec Welsh Pony & Cob Association *See* Association des Poneys Welsh & Cob au Québec

Québec Winter Carnival *Voir* Carnaval de Québec

Québec Women's Institutes (QWI)
177, Rg Ste-Anne, Saint-Chrysostome QC J0S 1G0
Toll-Free: 877-781-9293
info@qwi.la
www.qwi.la
www.facebook.com/QuebecWomensInstitute
Overview: A medium-sized provincial organization founded in 1911 overseen by Federated Women's Institutes of Canada
Mission: To help discover, stimulate & develop leadership among women; To assist, encourage & support women to become knowledgeable & responsible citizens; To ensure basic human rights for women & to work toward their equality; To be a strong voice through which matters of utmost concern can reach the decision makers; To promote the improvement of agricultural & other rural communities & to safeguard the environment
Affiliation(s): Associated Country Women of the World
Finances: *Annual Operating Budget:* Less than $50,000; *Funding Sources:* Membership dues; fundraising
Membership: 630 individuals in 14 counties & 52 branches; *Committees:* Operations; Scholarships; Resolutions & Cairn Restoration; QWI Essay Competition; Finances & Reports; Health & Community Living; Handicraft & Essay; Publicity; Agriculture
Chief Officer(s):
Norma Sherrer, President
npsherrer@hotmail.com
Pat Clarke, Treasurer
qwitreasurer@yahoo.ca
Awards:
• Erland Lee Award of Appreciation

Québec Wrestling Association *Voir* Fédération de lutte olympique du Québec

Québec Writers' Federation (QWF) / Fédération des Écrivaines et Écrivains du Québec
#3, 1200, av Atwater, Montréal QC H3Z 1X4
Tel: 514-933-0878
admin@qwf.org
www.qwf.org
Merged from: Québec Society for the Promotion of English Language Literature; Federation of English Writers of QC
Overview: A small provincial charitable organization founded in 1998
Mission: To encourage & support English-language writing in Québec to ensure a lasting place for English literature in the province's cultural scene.
Finances: *Funding Sources:* Corporation, government & individual donations
Staff Member(s): 2
Membership: *Fees:* $25; *Member Profile:* Professional & emerging writers; anyone interested
Activities: Writing workshops; literary readings; festival; short story competition in collaboration with CBC Radio; mentorship program; *Library:* Documentation Centre; by appointment
Chief Officer(s):
David Homel, President
Lori Schubert, Executive Director
Awards:
• QWF Prizes
Established 1988; awards five annual prizes of $2,000 each to honour literary excellence: The A.M. Klein poetry prize, The Hugh MacLennan fiction prize, Mavis Gallant prize for non-fiction, The McAuslan First Book Award & Translation award
Eligibility: Book by Québec author; 6 categories - fiction, non-fiction, poetry, 1st book, translation, children/young adult; *Amount:* 6 awards of $2000 each

Québec Young Farmers *Voir* Les Clubs 4-H du Québec

Québec-Labrador Foundation (Canada) Inc. (QLF (Canada)) / Fondation Québec Labrador du (Canada) inc.
#341, 606, rue Cathcart, Montréal QC H3B 1K9
Tel: 514-395-6020; Fax: 514-395-4505
qlf@qlf.org
www.qlf.org
www.facebook.com/318481021355
twitter.com/QLFNews
www.instagram.com/qlfphotos
Overview: A small national charitable organization founded in 1969
Mission: To promote local leadership & assist in improvement of human conditions in northern New England, Eastern Québec, & Canadian Atlantic provinces; To conserve cultural heritage & natural resources of region; To conduct scientific research; To enrich educational experience of Canadian & US students
Affiliation(s): Atlantic Centre for the Environment
Finances: *Annual Operating Budget:* $500,000-$1.5 Million
Staff Member(s): 17
Membership: 4,000 individual; 50 institutional
Chief Officer(s):
Elizabeth Alling, President & CEO
Awards:
• Sounds Conservancy Grants Program
• Caring for the Earth Award

Queen Charlotte Islands Arts Council *See* Haida Gwaii Arts Council

Queen Elizabeth Hospital Foundation
PO Box 6600, 60 Riverside Dr., Charlottetown PE C1A 8T5
Tel: 902-894-2425; Fax: 902-894-2433
info@qehfoundation.pe.ca
www.qehfoundation.pe.ca
www.facebook.com/QEHFoundation
twitter.com/QEHFoundation
Also Known As: QEH Foundation
Overview: A small local charitable organization
Mission: To receive donations on behalf of the Queen Elizabeth Hospital & utilize those funds in order to improve the quality of care at the Queen Elizabeth Hospital
Finances: *Funding Sources:* Donations
Staff Member(s): 10
Chief Officer(s):
Tracey Comeau, Chief Executive Officer
tacomeau@qehfoundation.pe.ca

The Queen of Puddings Music Theatre Company
The Case Good Warehouse, Bldg. 74, Studio 206, 55 Mill St., Toronto ON M5A 3C4
Tel: 416-203-4149; Fax: 416-203-8027
queenofpuddings@bellnet.ca
www.queenofpuddingsmusictheatre.com
www.facebook.com/queenofpuddings
Overview: A small local charitable organization
Mission: Queen of Puddings has consistently produced provocative, dramatic presentations that have challenged the parameters of the opera genre. The company works solely with Canadian artists.
Chief Officer(s):
Dairine Ni Mheadhra, Artistic Director
dairine@queenofpuddingsmusictheatre.com
John Hess, Artistic Director

Queen's University Faculty Association (QUFA) / Association des professeurs de l'Université Queen's
Queen's University, 9 St. Lawrence Ave., Kingston ON K7L 3N6
Tel: 613-533-2151; Fax: 613-533-6171
qufa2@queensu.ca
www.qufa.ca
www.facebook.com/qufapage
twitter.com/qufatweet
Overview: A small local organization founded in 1951
Mission: To act as the certified bargaining agent for Queen's University faculty members; To promote the interests of the Queen's University academic staff
Membership: 1,200; *Member Profile:* Queen's University faculty, librarians, & archivists; *Committees:* Executive; Joint Committee to Administer the Agreement; Finance; Grievance; Nominations & Elections; Political Action & Communications; Staff Relations; Benefits Oversight; Anomalies Fund;

Employment Systems Review; Intellectual Property; Merit & Career Development / Compensation; Budget Analysis Sub-Committee; Constitutional Review Sub-Committee; Equity Sub-committee; Fund for Scholarly Research & Creative Work & Professional Development Sub-Committee; Teaching Assessment Sub-Committee; Pension Ad hoc; Negotiators for the Employees Group Ad hoc; Past President's Ad hoc; Website Ad hoc
Activities: Promoting a positive, equitable working environment for Queen's University academic staff; Offering workshops for members
Chief Officer(s):
Paul Young, President
Paul Young, Vice-President
Monika Holzschuh Sator, Secretary
Ken Ko, Treasurer
Marvin Baer, Chief Negotiator
mgb1@post.queensu.ca
Elaine Berman, Administrative Officer, 613-533-3033
qufa@queensu.ca
Phil Goldman, Grievance Officer, 613-533-6241
goldmanp@post.queensu.ca
Publications:
• QUFA Voices
Type: Newsletter; *Frequency:* every 2 months; *Editor:* Robert G. May
Profile: QUFA news, opinions, & events

Queen's University International Centre (QUIC)
Queen's University, John Deutsch University Centre, 87 Union St., Kingston ON K7L 3N6
Tel: 613-533-2604; *Fax:* 613-533-3159
quic.queensu.ca
www.facebook.com/quic.queensu.ca
twitter.com/quic
www.youtube.com/user/quicatqueens
Previous Name: International Centre
Overview: A small international organization founded in 1961
Mission: To focus primarily on the university constituency with program links into the broader Kingston community
Member of: Canadian Bureau for International Education; Canadian Association of College & University Student Services; NAFSA: Association of International Educators
Finances: *Annual Operating Budget:* $250,000-$500,000; *Funding Sources:* Queen's University; Ed & Anna Churchill Foundation
Staff Member(s): 10; 300 volunteer(s)
Membership: 2,000-3,000; *Committees:* International Centre Council
Activities: *Library:* International Resource Library
Chief Officer(s):
Jyoti Kotecha, Director

Queens Association for Supported Living (QASL)
44 Pleasant St., Milton NS B0T 1P0
Tel: 902-354-2723; *Fax:* 902-354-2262
info@qasl.ca
www.qasl.ca
Overview: A small local organization founded in 1969
Mission: To improve the quality of life for individuals with disabilities
Member of: DIRECTIONS Council for Vocational Services Society
Activities: Residential services; integration programs; vocational programs, including Penny Lane Enterprises & Riverbank General Store

Queens County Fish & Game Association
PO Box 1598, Liverpool NS B0T 1K0
Tel: 902-354-4991
Overview: A small local organization
Mission: To promote the conservation of fish & wildlife
Chief Officer(s):
David Dagley, Secretary

Queens County Historical Society
PO Box 1078, 109 Main St., Liverpool NS B0T 1K0
Tel: 902-354-4058; *Fax:* 902-354-2050
www.queenscountymuseum.com
www.facebook.com/QueensCountyHistoricalSociety
Overview: A small local organization founded in 1929
Mission: To collect, preserve & display the human & natural history of Queens County, Nova Scotia
Member of: Federation of the Nova Scotian Heritage
Finances: *Funding Sources:* Provincial & regional government
Membership: *Fees:* $10 single; $12 family

Activities: *Library:* Thomas Raddall Research Centre; Open to public

Queensbush Initiatives for Literacy & Learning Inc. *See* Quality in Lifelong Learning Network

Queer Ontario
Community Centre, 519 Church St., Toronto ON M4Y 2C9
info@queerontario.org
queerontario.org
twitter.com/queerontario
Previous Name: Coalition for Lesbian & Gay Rights in Ontario; Coalition for Gay Rights in Ontario
Overview: A medium-sized provincial organization founded in 1975
Mission: To question, challenge & reform the laws, institutional practices & social norms that regulate queer people; to fight for accessibility, recognition & pluralism; to use social media & other tactics to engage in political action, public education & coalition-building
Finances: *Funding Sources:* Donations
Activities: Monthly meetings; social media discussions; Pressing Issues survey
Chief Officer(s):
Richard Hudler, Chair

Quest Centre Community Initiatives
PO Box 550, 3581 Concession Dr., Glencoe ON N0L 1M0
Tel: 519-287-2726; *Fax:* 519-287-3804
quest_centre@yahoo.com
www.quest-centre.com
Also Known As: The Quest Centre
Overview: A small local organization founded in 1999
Member of: CSAE
Finances: *Annual Operating Budget:* $100,000-$250,000; *Funding Sources:* United Way; Fundraisers; Thames Valley District School Board
Staff Member(s): 1; 1 volunteer(s)
Membership: *Committees:* Government information & forms; computer courses; children's programs
Activities: Employment councilling; Correspondance courses; First Aid & CPR training; Beginner computer taining; Workshops
Chief Officer(s):
Shirley Slaats, Manager

Quest Residential & Support Services *See* Quest Support Services Inc.

Quest Support Services Inc.
PO Box 1201, Stn. Main, Lethbridge AB T1J 4A4
Tel: 403-381-9515; *Fax:* 403-320-6555
www.questsupport.com
twitter.com/QuestLethbridge
Previous Name: Quest Residential & Support Services
Overview: A small local organization founded in 1993
Mission: To provide services for people with developmental disabilities, community based agencies
Finances: *Funding Sources:* Persons with Developmental Disabilities (PDD) provincial funding program
Chief Officer(s):
Michael Tamura, Owner

Quesnel & District Arts Council (QDCAC)
500 North Star Rd., Quesnel BC V2J 5P6
www.quesnelarts.ca
Overview: A small local organization founded in 1973
Mission: To increase & broaden opportunities for the region's citizens to enjoy & participate in arts, culture & heritage activities
Finances: *Annual Operating Budget:* Less than $50,000
Chief Officer(s):
Bernice Heinzelman, Contact
bheinzel@quesnelbc.com

Quesnel & District Association for the Mentally Handicapped *See* Quesnel Community Living Association

Quesnel & District Chamber of Commerce
335 East Vaughan St., Quesnel BC V2J 2T1
Tel: 250-992-7262
qchamber@quesnelbc.com
quesnelchamber.com
www.facebook.comm/10150128152340257
Overview: A small local organization founded in 1910
Mission: To undertake those policies & programs established annually that will effectively promote Quesnel & District in a manner improving trade, commerce & the welfare of its citizens; To create & maintain a cooperative enterprise of business people helping one another

Member of: BC Chamber of Commerce; Canadian Chamber of Commerce; Better Business Bureau
Staff Member(s): 1
Membership: *Fees:* Schedule available based on number of full-time employees
Activities: Small Business Week; Business Excellence; Professional Assistants Luncheon; monthly guest speakers; workshops; fair; *Library:* Open to public
Chief Officer(s):
William Lacy, President
Amber Gregg, Manager
Awards:
• Business Excellence Awards
Publications:
• Quesnel & District Chamber of Commerce Newsletter
Type: Newsletter

Quesnel & District Child Development Centre Association (QDCDCA)
488 McLean St., Quesnel BC V2J 2P2
Tel: 250-992-2481; *Fax:* 250-992-3439
www.quesnelcdc.com
www.facebook.com/quesnel.childdevelopmentcentre
Overview: A small local charitable organization founded in 1976
Mission: To assist local children by providing intervention programs which facilitate their physical, social, emotional, communicative & intellectual development
Affiliation(s): BC Association for Child Development & Intervention
Finances: *Annual Operating Budget:* $500,000-$1.5 Million; *Funding Sources:* Provincial Government
Staff Member(s): 23; 40 volunteer(s)
Membership: 20 individual; *Fees:* $1 individual
Activities: *Awareness Events:* Telethon, last Sun. in Oct.
Chief Officer(s):
Corrina Norman, President

Quesnel & District Labour Council (QDLC)
PO Box 4245, Quesnel BC V2J 3J3
Tel: 250-992-7725
qdlc@telus.net
Overview: A small local organization founded in 1975 overseen by British Columbia Federation of Labour
Mission: To act as the voice for working people of the Quesnel area of British Columbia
Affiliation(s): Canadian Labour Congress (CLC)
Activities: Promoting the interests of local affiliated unions; Hosting monthly meeting to share information about issues affecting unions & their membership; Raising awareness of workers' issues; Organizing rallies related to local labour issues; Providing local labour news

Quesnel Community Living Association (QCLA)
658 Doherty Dr., Quesnel BC V2J 1B9
Tel: 250-992-7774; *Fax:* 250-992-6651
roy@qcla.ca
qcla.ca
Previous Name: Quesnel & District Association for the Mentally Handicapped
Overview: A small local charitable organization founded in 1959
Member of: British Columbia Association for Community Living
Finances: *Funding Sources:* Bingo; membership dues
Membership: *Fees:* $5
Chief Officer(s):
Joan Calihou, President

Quesnel Naturalists
c/o Lorna Schley, 128 Lindsey St., Quesnel BC V2J 3E3
www.bcnature.ca
Overview: A small local organization
Mission: To promote the enjoyment of nature through environmental appreciation & conservation; To encourage wise use & conservation of natural resources & environmental protection.
Member of: Federation of BC Naturalists
Membership: 40; *Fees:* $20 single; $25 family
Chief Officer(s):
Lorna Schley, Contact
lschley@quesnelbc.com

Quesnel Tillicum Society Friendship Centre
319 North Fraser Dr., Quesnel BC V2J 1Y9
Tel: 250-992-8347; *Fax:* 250-992-5708
www.quesnel-friendship.org
www.facebook.com/QuesnelTillicum
twitter.com/QuesnelTillicum
Overview: A small local charitable organization founded in 1971

Mission: To improve the quality of life & to meet the needs of First Nations & other people who are faced with adjusting to the social, economic & cultural lifestyle of the community
Member of: National Association of Friendship Centres
Activities: Referral; Outreach; Youth worker
Chief Officer(s):
Tony Goulet, Executive Director
tony.goulet@qnfc.bc.ca

Quetico Foundation
#216, 642 King St. West, Toronto ON M5V 1M7
Tel: 416-941-9388; *Fax:* 416-941-9236
office@queticofoundation.org
www.queticofoundation.org
www.facebook.com/QueticoFoundation
Overview: A small provincial charitable organization founded in 1954
Mission: To preserve wilderness areas of Ontario, particularly Quetico Provincial Park, for recreation & scientific use
Finances: *Annual Operating Budget:* $100,000-$250,000; *Funding Sources:* Endowment & donations
Staff Member(s): 1; 20 volunteer(s)
Membership: 34 trustees & trustees Emeriti; *Fees:* $40
Activities: Scientific research, education & public awareness, liaison; *Internships:* Yes *Library:* John B. Ridley Research Library; Open to public
Chief Officer(s):
Glenda McLachlan, Executive Director
Publications:
• The Quetico
Type: Newsletter; *Frequency:* Quartley

Quickdraw Animation Society (QAS)
#201, 351 - 11 Ave. SW, Calgary AB T2R 0C7
Tel: 403-261-5767; *Fax:* 403-261-5644
Other Communication: Digital Coordinator e-mail:
digital@quickdrawanimation.ca
email@quickdrawanimation.ca
www.quickdrawanimation.ca
www.facebook.com/quickdrawanimation
twitter.com/GIRAFFEST
vimeo.com/quickdrawanimation
Overview: A small international charitable organization founded in 1984
Mission: To promote the study of animation & to encourage the production of independent animated films; to provide the general public with all types of animated film, particularly works that are innovative & independently produced; to establish & maintain a production facility for the discussion, study & production of independent animated film; to provide lectures, workshops & courses on all aspects of animation for the professional development of artists as well as for public education & appreciation of animation; to establish & maintain a resource centre on animation & related subjects; to facilitate the production of independent animated films & to extend this opportunity to all interested individuals
Member of: Alberta Media Arts Alliance Society; Association Internationale du Film d'Animation (ASIFA); Independent Media Arts Alliance
Finances: *Annual Operating Budget:* $100,000-$250,000; *Funding Sources:* Alberta Foundation for the Arts; The Canada Council; Calgary Region Arts Foundation
Staff Member(s): 4; 50 volunteer(s)
Membership: 172 individual; *Fees:* $50 producing; $25 associate; $30 youth; *Member Profile:* Interest in the production & appreciation of animation as an artistic medium; *Committees:* Programming; Library; Production; Promotion
Activities: *Library:*
Chief Officer(s):
Kim Walton, President
Evangelos Diavolitsis, Executive Director
director@quickdrawanimation.ca
Awards:
• Members' Awards

Quidi Vidi Rennie's River Development Foundation (QVRRDF)
Nagle's Place, St. John's NL A1B 2Z2
Tel: 709-754-3474; *Fax:* 709-754-5947
info@fluvarium.ca
www.fluvarium.ca
Overview: A small local organization founded in 1985
Mission: To promote responsible environmental stewardship; To raise awareness of the nature of freshwater systems; To provide leadership in urban watershed management; To operate The Fluvarium as a public centre for environmental education
Member of: Hospitality Newfoundland & Labrador; St. John's Board of Trade; Newfoundland & Labrador Environmental Industry Association
Finances: *Annual Operating Budget:* $250,000-$500,000; *Funding Sources:* Admission fees; building rentals; catering services; corporate & private donations; fundraising
Staff Member(s): 7; 100 volunteer(s)
Membership: 200; *Fees:* $30.00; *Member Profile:* Friends of Rennie's River; *Committees:* Development; Education; Facilities & Operations; Finance; Science & Exhibitions
Activities: Environmental education; tourism; restoration & habitat enhancement; *Awareness Events:* River Dance, March; Duck Race, Sept.; Fish Fry, August
Chief Officer(s):
Deborah Picco Garland, Executive Director

Quinte - Saint Lawrence Building & Construction Trades Council
Kingston ON
Overview: A small local organization
Mission: To act as a trade union in the Quinte, Saint Lawrence region
Activities: Supporting local organizations
Chief Officer(s):
Bill Pearse, President

Quinte & District Association of REALTORS Inc.
PO Box 128, 51 Cannifton Rd. North, Cannifton ON K0K 1K0
Tel: 613-969-7873; *Fax:* 613-962-1851
ExecOfficer@Quinte-mls.com
www.quinte-mls.com
twitter.com/quinte_REALTORS
Previous Name: Quinte & District Real Estate Board
Overview: A small local organization founded in 1977 overseen by Ontario Real Estate Association
Member of: The Canadian Real Estate Association; Ontario Real Estate Association; Real Estate Council of Ontario
Membership: 370
Chief Officer(s):
Jamie Troke, President

Quinte & District Real Estate Board *See* Quinte & District Association of REALTORS Inc.

Quinte Arts Council (QAC)
PO Box 22113, 36 Bridge St. East, Belleville ON K8N 5A2
Tel: 613-962-1232; *Fax:* 613-962-7163
qac@quinteartscouncil.org
www.quinteartscouncil.org
www.facebook.com/QuinteArtsCouncil
twitter.com/QAC1967
Overview: A small local charitable organization founded in 1967
Mission: To develop, integrate & promote a creative culture & artistic opportunities in our community; to raise awareness for the value of creativity & artistic expression within our community through programs & services that engage & nurture artists
Member of: Visual Arts Ontario; CARFAC; Canadian Association of Gift Planners; Canadian Centre for Philanthropy
Affiliation(s): Ontario Arts Council
Finances: *Annual Operating Budget:* $100,000-$250,000
Staff Member(s): 5; 400 volunteer(s)
Membership: 500; *Fees:* $30 community friends; $40 artists/groups; $50 business; $5 student; *Committees:* Executive; Strategic Planning; Awards & Bursaries; Fundraising & Finance; Programming
Activities: Kids' Playhouse Performing Arts Series; Desjardins Concerts; Ear Candy Music Festival; Festival of Trees; Expressions; *Internships:* Yes; *Speaker Service:* Yes; *Library:* Resource Area; Open to public
Chief Officer(s):
Carol Feeney, Executive Director
feeney@quinteartscouncil.org
Awards:
• Eugene Lang Memorial Bursary
• Hugh P. O'Neill Bursary
• The Arts Recognition Awards
• QAC Student Bursaries
• QAC Arts & Education Fund - Performing Arts
• QAC Arts & Education Fund - Visual Arts

Quinte Beekeepers' Association (QBA)
c/o Liz Corbett, 762 Clearview Rd., RR#2, Stirling ON K0K 3E0
Tel: 613-398-8422
Overview: A small local organization
Mission: To promote the beekeeping industry in the Quinte area; To educate & assist local beekeepers
Member of: Ontario Beekeepers' Association
Membership: *Member Profile:* Beekeepers of the Quinte region of Ontario
Activities: Hosting meetings for members; Offering networking opportunities for beekeepers to exchange information; Mentoring persons new to beekeeping; Educating the public about beekeeping; Presenting displays about beekeeping & honey; Establishing a cooperative beeyard; Participating in the creation of renewed sustainable communities
Chief Officer(s):
Liz Corbett, President
ebcorbett@yahoo.ca

Quinte Construction Association (QCA)
54 Station St., Belleville ON K8N 2S5
Tel: 613-962-2877; *Fax:* 613-962-0268
qca@on.aibn.com
www.quinteconstructionassociation.ca
Overview: A small local organization founded in 1948
Staff Member(s): 1; 10 volunteer(s)
Membership: 100; *Fees:* $450-$585
Activities: Annual golf tournament; curling day; education & safety training
Chief Officer(s):
Barbara Tebworth, Office Manager

Quinte Immigrant Services
PO Box 22141, Belleville ON K8N 5V7
Tel: 613-968-7723; *Fax:* 613-968-2597
info@quinteimmigration.ca
www.quinteimmigration.ca
www.facebook.com/125213660887946
twitter.com/Qimmigration
Overview: A small local organization founded in 1986 overseen by Ontario Council of Agencies Serving Immigrants
Mission: To prevent & relieve distress experienced by immigrants in Canada; To assist immigrants in locating affordable housing, furnishings, & other related items; To locate agencies & services to meet needs of immigrants; To cooperate & collaborate with & assist other organizations concerned with general welfare of immigrants to Canada
Member of: United Way; Ontario Trillium Foundation
Finances: *Annual Operating Budget:* $100,000-$250,000; *Funding Sources:* Federal & provincial government; United Way; fundraising
Staff Member(s): 5; 155 volunteer(s)
Membership: 46; *Fees:* $10 individual; $15 organizational; *Committees:* Financial; Special Projects; Policies & Personnel; Recruitment
Activities: Settlement programs; language orientation; host program; community support; economic development; interpretation & translation; public education; *Awareness Events:* Stop Racism, March 21; *Internships:* Yes; *Library:* by appointment
Chief Officer(s):
Orlando Ferro, Executive Director
oferro@quinteimmigration.ca
Nancy Sayeau, Financial & Programs Manager
accounting@quinteimmigration.ca

Quinte Labour Council
114 Victoria Ave., Belleville ON K8N 2A8
Tel: 613-848-7190
Overview: A small local organization overseen by Ontario Federation of Labour
Mission: To meet the on-going needs of organized & unorganized workers & to improve their quality of life in the workplace, in the home & in the community
Membership: 4,000; *Committees:* Education; Fundraising; Political Action
Activities: *Awareness Events:* Day of Mourning, April 28; *Speaker Service:* Yes
Awards:
• Loyalist College Bursary

Quinte Symphony
c/o Quinte Arts Council, PO Box 22113, Belleville ON K8N 2Z5
Tel: 613-962-7430
info@quintesymphony.com
www.quintesymphony.com
www.facebook.com/quintesymphony
twitter.com/quintesymphony
Previous Name: Eastern Ontario Concert Orchestra
Overview: A small local charitable organization founded in 1960 overseen by Orchestras Canada
Mission: Committed to enriching the Quinte community by actively promoting an appreciation of Classical & Canadian orchestral music

Canadian Associations / Quinte Therapeutic Riding Association (QUINTRA)

Member of: Quinte Arts Council, Belleville & District Chamber of Commerce, Volunteer & Information Centre
Finances: *Funding Sources:* Grants; Sponsors; Ticket sales; Advertising; Donations; Fundraising
Membership: 50
Activities: Four to five concerts per season; *Speaker Service:* Yes; *Library:* Not open to public
Chief Officer(s):
Dan Tremblay, Music Director

Quinte Therapeutic Riding Association (QUINTRA)
173 McGee Rd., RR#2, Stirling ON K0K 3E0
Tel: 613-395-4472
www.quintra.org
Overview: A small local charitable organization founded in 1985
Mission: To offer therapeutic horseback-riding sessions to disabled children & young adults to maximize the disabled person's physical & mental capabilities; To improve disabled young people's self-confidence & the ability to cope with everyday living
Member of: Canadian Therapeutic Riding Association; Ontario Therapeutic Riding Association
Affiliation(s): United Way of Quinte
Finances: *Funding Sources:* Donations; Bingos; United Way Quinte
Activities: *Speaker Service:* Yes
Chief Officer(s):
Barb Davis, Contact, 613-395-2990
barbara.davis@sympatico.ca

Quinte West Chamber of Commerce (QWCC)
97 Front St., Trenton ON K8V 4N6
Tel: 613-392-7635; *Fax:* 613-392-8400
Toll-Free: 800-930-3255
info@quintewestchamber.ca
www.quintewestchamber.ca
www.linkedin.com/groups?mostPopular=&gid=3774934
www.facebook.com/QWChamber
twitter.com/qwchamber
Previous Name: Trenton & District Chamber of Commerce
Overview: A small local organization founded in 1886
Mission: To promote business growth & prosperity for the local economy through effective leadership
Member of: Ontario Chamber of Commerce; Canadian Chamber of Commerce
Finances: *Annual Operating Budget:* $250,000-$500,000; *Funding Sources:* Membership fees
Staff Member(s): 3; 15 volunteer(s)
Membership: 405; *Fees:* $100 individual; $190-$500 corporate; *Member Profile:* Businesses; *Committees:* Court Affairs; Advocacy
Activities: Providing business services & tourism information; *Awareness Events:* Quinte BUsiness Week, Oct.
Chief Officer(s):
Cindy Dow, President
Suzanne Andrews, Manager
manager@quintewestchamber.ca
Publications:
• Business to Business Directory [a publication of the Quinte Chamber of Commerce]
Type: Directory; *Frequency:* Annual

Quintiles IMS Canada
16720, rte Transcanadienne, Kirkland QC H9H 5M3
Tel: 514-428-6000; *Fax:* 514-428-6086
www.quintileims.com
Previous Name: IMS Health Canada
Overview: A small national organization founded in 1960
Mission: To provide business intelligence & strategic consulting services for the pharmaceutical & health care industries
Chief Officer(s):
Murray Aitken, Executive Director

RA Stamp Club
2451 Riverside Dr., Ottawa ON K1H 7X7
Tel: 613-733-5100; *Fax:* 613-736-6238
racentre@racentre.com
www.racentre.com
Overview: A small local organization
Member of: The Recreation Association
Finances: *Annual Operating Budget:* Less than $50,000; *Funding Sources:* Membership fees
Membership: *Member Profile:* Local stamp collectors
Activities: Club meetings & shows; *Awareness Events:* MINIEX, Feb.; ORAPEX National Stamp Show, May
Chief Officer(s):
Tosha Rhodenizer, CEO & General Manager, RA Centre

Racquetball Canada
145 Pacific Ave., Winnipeg MB R3B 2Z6
www.racquetball.ca
twitter.com/RBallCanada
Previous Name: Canadian Racquetball Association
Overview: A medium-sized national charitable organization founded in 1972
Mission: To promote racquetball as a sport & physical activity; To provide leadership by developing & coordinating services & programs designed to meet the needs of the racquetball community
Member of: International Racquetball Federation
Affiliation(s): Canadian Sport Council; Canadian Olympic Association; Coaching Association of Canada
Finances: *Funding Sources:* Government; Membership dues; Sponsorships
50 volunteer(s)
Membership: 5 life + 700 individual + 350 club + 8 provincial associations (incl. 18,000 members); *Fees:* $1,500 life; $25 individual; $50 club; *Member Profile:* Individual resident in Canada or Canadian citizen involved in the sport of racquetball at any level of structured activity; *Committees:* National Team; Coaching; Sport Science; Tournament; Ranking; Officiating; Junior Development; Membership; Ways & Means; Wheelchair; Women
Activities: *Awareness Events:* National Championship Week, May; *Speaker Service:* Yes; *Rents Mailing List:* Yes
Chief Officer(s):
Cheryl Adlard, Executive Director
Publications:
• Canadian Racquetball
Type: Magazine; *Price:* Free with Racquetball Canada membership
• Racquetball Canada Newsletter
Type: Newsletter; *Frequency:* Monthly
Profile: Team information, administration news, coaching, awards, & events

Racquetball Manitoba Inc.
145 Pacific Ave., Winnipeg MB R3B 2Z7
Tel: 204-925-5666; *Fax:* 204-925-5703
racquetballmb.ca
Overview: A small provincial organization founded in 1974 overseen by Racquetball Canada
Mission: To promote racquetball as a sport & a physical activity throughout the Province of Manitoba; To provide leadership by developing & coordinating services & programs designed to meet the needs of the racquetball community
Member of: Racquetball Canada; Sport Manitoba
Staff Member(s): 1; 50 volunteer(s)
Membership: 600; *Fees:* $25 adult; $10 juniors/students

Racquetball Ontario (RO)
51 Springgarden Cres., Stoney Creek ON L8J 2S5
www.racquetballontario.ca
twitter.com/Rball_Ontario
Overview: A medium-sized provincial organization overseen by Racquetball Canada
Member of: Racquetball Canada
Membership: *Fees:* $25 individual; $50 family; $100 event coordinator
Chief Officer(s):
Greg Doricki, President
Peter Fisher, Director, Development
Tanya Hodgin, Director, Memberships
Sue Swaine, Director, Coaching

Racquetball PEI
c/o Sport PEI, 40 Enman Cres., Charlottetown PE C1E 1E6
Overview: A small provincial organization overseen by Racquetball Canada
Member of: Racquetball Canada

Radiation Safety Institute of Canada / Institut de radioprotection du Canada
Head Office & National Education Centre, #300, 165 Avenue Rd., Toronto ON M5R 3S4
Tel: 416-650-9090; *Fax:* 416-650-9920
Toll-Free: 800-263-5803
info@radiationsafety.ca
www.radiationsafety.ca
www.linkedin.com/company/radiation-safety-institute-of-canada
www.facebook.com/143472245714096
twitter.com/RSICanada
Previous Name: Canadian Institute for Radiation Safety
Overview: A medium-sized national charitable organization founded in 1981
Mission: To be an independent source for knowledge about radiation safety in the environment, the community, & the workplace
Activities: Providing information about radiation & radiation safety
Chief Officer(s):
Steve Horvath, President & Chief Executive Officer
Laura Boksman, Chief Scientist
Bruce Sylvester, Chief Financial Officer
Natalia Mozayani, Executive Director
Tara Hargreaves, Scientist & Coordinator, Training
Maria Costa, Administrative Assistant, Communications
   National Laboratories
   #102, 110 Research Dr., Saskatoon SK S7N 3R3
   Tel: 306-975-0566; *Fax:* 306-975-0494
   www.radiationsafety.ca

Radio Advisory Board of Canada (RABC) / Conseil consultatif canadien de la radio
#811, 116 Albert St., Ottawa ON K1P 5G3
Tel: 613-230-3261
Toll-Free: 888-902-5768
www.rabc-cccr.ca
twitter.com/RABC_CCCR
Previous Name: Canadian Radio Technical Planning Board
Overview: A medium-sized national organization founded in 1944
Mission: To consult & advise Industry Canada on behalf of industry on the development, management, & regulation of radio services in Canada
Finances: *Funding Sources:* Membership fees; grant
Membership: *Fees:* Schedule available; *Member Profile:* Generally non-profit associations of commercial companies, both operating & manufacturing; technical societies; amateur users, or any group concerned with radio spectrum use; a number of federal & provincial government bodies are also members; *Committees:* Broadcasting; Electromagnetic Compatibility; Mobile & Personal Communications; Fixed Wireless Communications; Events Planning
Chief Officer(s):
David Farnes, General Manager
david@rabc-cccr.ca

Radio Amateur Québec inc. (RAQI)
4545, av Pierre-de-Coubertin, Montréal QC H1V 0B2
Tél: 514-252-3012; *Téléc:* 514-254-9971
admin@raqi.ca
www.raqi.ca
Aperçu: *Dimension:* moyenne; *Envergure:* provinciale; fondée en 1951
Membre(s) du personnel: 2; 200 bénévole(s)
Membre: 4 500; *Montant de la cotisation:* 35$
Activités:: *Bibliothèque:* Bibliothèque publique rendez-vous
Membre(s) du bureau directeur:
Jacques Savard, Directeur général

Radio Amateurs du Canada inc. *See* Radio Amateurs of Canada Inc.

Radio Amateurs of Canada Inc. (RAC) / Radio Amateurs du Canada inc.
#217, 720 Belfast Rd., Ottawa ON K1G 0Z5
Tel: 613-244-4367
Toll-Free: 877-273-8304
www.rac.ca
Previous Name: Canadian Amateur Radio Federation
Overview: A medium-sized national organization founded in 1993
Mission: To act as coordinating body of amateur radio organizations in Canada, liaison agency between members & other amateur organizations in Canada & other countries, coordinating & advisory agency between members & industry Canada; to promote interests of amateur radio operators through program of technical & general education in amateur matters
Membership: *Fees:* Schedule available; *Committees:* Administration & Finance; Membership Services; Youth Education; VHF/UHF Band Planning; MF/HF Band Planning; Microwave Band Planning; Antenna Structures; ARISS Technical; ARRL Contest Advisory; ARRL DXAC
Chief Officer(s):
Geoff Bawden, President
ghbawden@gmail.com
Sukwan Widajat, Corporate Secretary
va3wid@rac.ca

Radio Starmaker Fund
#302, 372 Bay St., Toronto ON M5H 2W9

Tel: 416-597-6622; *Fax:* 416-597-2760
Toll-Free: 888-256-2211
www.starmaker.ca
Overview: A medium-sized national organization
Mission: To provide funding for Canadian musicians, bands & labels that have achieved a proven "track record" with previous work
Affiliation(s): Canadian Association of Broadcasters
Chief Officer(s):
Chip Sutherland, Executive Director
chipsutherland@starmaker.ca

Radio Television Digital News Association (Canada) (RTDNA Canada) / Association canadienne des directeurs de l'information en radio-télévision
#300, 1201 West Pender St., Vancouver BC V6E 2V2
Tel: 604-681-2153
admin@rtdnacanada.com
www.rtdnacanada.com
www.linkedin.com/groups/1800955
www.facebook.com/RTDNA.CAN
twitter.com/RTDNA_Canada
Also Known As: Association of Electronic Journalists
Previous Name: Radio Television News Directors' Association (Canada)
Overview: A small national organization founded in 1961
Mission: To represent electronic & digital journalists & news managers in Canada; To act as a progressive voice in the Canadian broadcast news industry; To foster education, professional development & recognition while encouraging active dialogue within its membership
Affiliation(s): Radio-Television News Directors Association International
Finances: *Annual Operating Budget:* $100,000-$250,000
15 volunteer(s)
Membership: 400; *Fees:* Schedule available; *Member Profile:* Radio, television & online news directors, producers, executives, reporters, educators, & students; *Committees:* Awards; Diversity; Ethics; Membership; Sponsorship
Activities: Offering annual awards for industry excellence; Holding an annual conference
Chief Officer(s):
Ian Koenigsfest, President
president@rtdnacanada.com
Leya Duigu, Manager
Awards:
• Radio Television Digital News Association (Canada) Network Awards
• Radio Television Digital News Association (Canada) Regional Awards
• Radio Television Digital News Association (Canada) National Awards
• Radio Television Digital News Association (Canada) Lifetime Achievement Award
• Radio Television Digital News Association (Canada) President's Award
Meetings/Conferences:
• Radio Television Digital News Association (Canada) National Conference 2018, 2018, Sheraton Centre Toronto Hotel, Toronto, ON
Scope: National

Radio Television News Directors' Association (Canada) *See* Radio Television Digital News Association (Canada)

Radiocomm Association of Canada *See* Canadian Wireless Telecommunications Association

Radios Rurales Internationales *See* Farm Radio International

Radisson & District Chamber of Commerce *See* Riverbend District Chamber of Commerce

Radium Hot Springs Chamber of Commerce
PO Box 225, Radium Hot Springs BC V0A 1M0
Tel: 250-347-9331; *Fax:* 250-347-9127
Toll-Free: 888-347-9331
chamber@RadiumHotSprings.com
www.RadiumHotSprings.com
www.facebook.com/Tourism.Radium
www.youtube.com/tourismradium
Previous Name: Columbia Valley Chamber of Commerce; Invermere Business Committee; Fairmont Business Association; Windermere Board of Trade
Overview: A small local organization founded in 1956
Mission: To promote & support quality, ethical business as well as facilitate growth for responsible commercial development in Radium Hot Springs & area
Member of: BC Chamber of Commerce
Finances: *Funding Sources:* Government; fund raising; corporate
Membership: *Fees:* $260; *Member Profile:* Businesses
Activities: Providing Internet access, visitor information, retail store & interpretive centre; *Library:* Open to public
Chief Officer(s):
Kent Kebe, Manager
manager@radiumhotsprings.com

Radius Child & Youth Services
60 Lakeshore Rd. West, Oakville ON L6K 1E1
Tel: 905-825-3242; *Fax:* 905-825-3276
Toll-Free: 855-744-9001
info@radiuschild-youthservices.ca
www.radiuschild-youthservices.ca
www.linkedin.com/company/radius-child-&-youth-services
www.facebook.com/RadiusChildandYouthServices
twitter.com/RadiusChild_Yth
Previous Name: Halton Trauma Centre
Overview: A small local organization founded in 1983
Mission: To provide clinical assessment & treatment services to children, adolescents, & families affected by child abuse
Chief Officer(s):
Darryl Hall, Executive Director
Alison Purvis, Director, Human Resources & Operations

Radville Chamber of Commerce
PO Box 799, Radville SK S0C 2G0
Tel: 306-869-2610
Overview: A small local organization

Railway Association of Canada (RAC) / Association des chemins de fer du Canada (ACFC)
#901, 99 Bank St., Ottawa ON K1P 6B9
Tel: 613-567-8591; *Fax:* 613-567-6726
rac@railcan.ca
www.railcan.ca
twitter.com/RailCanada
www.youtube.com/user/racmain
Overview: A large national organization founded in 1917
Mission: To promote the commercial viability & the safe & efficient operation of the Canadian railway industry; To act on behalf of, or work jointly with, member companies to promote public policy & regulation that provides equitable treatment between shipping modes; To provide factual information about the railway industry for the public, government & industry members, To provide the views of the industry on public policy issues.
Affiliation(s): Association of American Railroads
Finances: *Annual Operating Budget:* Greater than $5 Million; *Funding Sources:* Members fees
Staff Member(s): 23
Membership: 50+ companies; *Fees:* $2,000 minimum; *Member Profile:* Railway companies operating in Canada; *Committees:* Policy; Accounting; Finance; Human Resources; Safety & Operations Management; Taxation
Activities: Rule making; Advocacy; Communications; Liaison; Industry support & training; Equipment securement workshop
Chief Officer(s):
Michael Bourque, President & CEO, 613-564-8090
Gérald Gauthier, Vice-President, Public & Corporate Affairs, 613-564-8106
geraldg@railcan.ca
Publications:
• Interchange [a publication of the Railway Association of Canada]
Type: Magazine; *Frequency:* q.; *Accepts Advertising*; *Number of Pages:* 54; *Editor:* Alex Paterson; *ISBN:* 978-1-927520-05-5; *Price:* Free download
Profile: Information, news and stories about the railway sector in Canada
• Locomotive Emissions Monitoring Program [a publication of the Railway Association of Canada]
Type: Report; *Frequency:* a.; *Number of Pages:* 53; *Price:* Free download
Profile: Information concerning the emissions of greenhouse gases and criteria air contaminants from locomotives operating in Canada
• Railway Association of Canada Rail Trends
Type: Report; *Frequency:* a.; *Number of Pages:* 32; *ISBN:* 978-1-927520-05-5; *Price:* Freedownload
Profile: RACA's annual report on the performance of Canada's freight and passenger railway sector; contains a 10-year review of financial and statistical results

The Rainbow Alliance
c/o OPSEU, 100 Lesmill Rd., Toronto ON M3B 3P8
Tel: 416-443-8888
Toll-Free: 800-268-7376
pride@opseu.org
www.opseu.org/committees/rainbow.htm
Overview: A small local organization overseen by Ontario Public Service Employees Union
Mission: To provide representation & support to lesbian, gay, bisexual & transgendered members of OPSEU
Activities: *Awareness Events:* World AIDS Day, December 1; International Day Against Homophobia & Transphobia, May 17
Chief Officer(s):
Robert Hampsey, Chair

Rainbow Association of Canadian Artists (Spectra Talent Contest)
Toronto ON
www.spectrashowcase.com
Overview: A small national organization founded in 2012
Mission: A community encouraging amateur artistic expression regardless of cultural background, sexual orientation &/or gender identity
Staff Member(s): 15
Membership: *Committees:* Talent Recruitment; Fundraising & Sponsorship
Chief Officer(s):
Paul Bellini, Chair
Ralph Hamelmann, Director
producer@spectrashowcase.com

Rainbow Resource Centre
170 Scott St., Winnipeg MB R3L 0L3
Tel: 204-474-0212; *Fax:* 204-478-1160
Toll-Free: 855-437-8523
www.rainbowresourcecentre.org
www.facebook.com/RainbowResourceCentre
twitter.com/RainbowResCtr
www.instagram.com/rainbowresourcecentre
Also Known As: Gays for Equality
Previous Name: Campus Gay Club (University of Manitoba)
Overview: A small local charitable organization founded in 1972
Mission: To work toward an equal & diverse society, free of homophobia & discrimination, by encouraging visibility & fostering health & self-acceptance through education, support, resources & outreach
Finances: *Annual Operating Budget:* $100,000-$250,000; *Funding Sources:* Donations from individuals & organizations
Staff Member(s): 16; 45 volunteer(s)
Membership: 200; *Fees:* $25; *Committees:* Education; Advocacy; Law Reform; Management
Activities: Workshops; lectures; anti-homophobia training; peer support; counselling; *Library:* Rainbow Resource Centre Library; Open to public
Chief Officer(s):
Mike Tutthill, Executive Director

The Rainbow Society *See* The Dream Factory

The Rainbow Society of Alberta
6604 - 82nd Ave., Edmonton AB T6B 0E7
Tel: 780-469-3306; *Fax:* 780-469-2935
www.rainbowsociety.ab.ca
www.facebook.com/therainbowsocietyofalberta
twitter.com/RainbowSociety
Overview: A small provincial charitable organization founded in 1986
Mission: To grant the wishes of Alberta children between the ages of three years & eighteen who have been diagnosed with a chronic or life-threatening illness
Member of: Volunteer Centre of Edmonton & Calgary
Affiliation(s): The Rainbow Society Inc.
Staff Member(s): 5
Chief Officer(s):
Craig Hawkins, Executive Director
Calgary
PO Box 1153, Stn. M, Calgary AB T2P 2K9
Tel: 403-252-3891; *Fax:* 403-254-5183
Chief Officer(s):
Sharon Francis, Fund Development Manager
sharonf@rainbowsociety.ab.ca
Grande Prairie Office
PO Box 21069, Grande Prairie AB T8V 6W7
Tel: 780-882-4855; *Fax:* 888-415-9474
Chief Officer(s):

Teri Clarke, Regional Manager, Northern Alberta
teric@rainbowsociety.ab.ca

Rainy Hills Historical Society
PO Box General Delivery, Iddesleigh AB T0J 1T0
Tel: 403-898-2443
Also Known As: Rainy Hills Pioneer Exhibits
Overview: A small local organization founded in 1965
Mission: To preserve history of the area
Finances: *Funding Sources:* Grants; donations; fundraising
Membership: 30; *Fees:* $1; *Committees:* Historical Society
Activities: *Library:* Archives; by appointment

Rainy River & District Chamber of Commerce
PO Box 458, Atwood Ave., Rainy River ON P0W 1L0
rrdcoc@gmail.com
rainyriverchamber.ca
twitter.com/RainyRiverChamb
Overview: A small local organization
Mission: To promote business & commerce in Rainy River & the surrounding area
Member of: Northwestern Ontario Associated Chambers of Commerce
Membership: 39; *Fees:* $110; $60 associate
Chief Officer(s):
Paul Carousol, President

Rainy River Beekeepers' Association
c/o Richard Neilson, RR#1, Stratton ON P0W 1N0
Tel: 807-487-2387; *Fax:* 807-483-1217
Overview: A small local organization
Mission: To educate & inform beekeepers in the Rainy River area
Member of: Ontario Beekeepers' Association
Membership: *Member Profile:* Apiarists from the Rainy River area of Ontario
Chief Officer(s):
Richard Neilson, President, 807-487-2387

Rainy River District Municipal Association (RRDMA)
ON
www.noma.on.ca
Overview: A small local organization founded in 1908
Mission: To consider matters of general interest to the members & to take united action as required to promote their interests; To promote the free exchange of information; To petition for the enactment of legislation advantageous to the members
Member of: Northwestern Ontario Municipal Association
Affiliation(s): Kenora District Municipal Association & Thunder Bay District Municipal League
Finances: *Annual Operating Budget:* Less than $50,000; *Funding Sources:* Membership fees
Staff Member(s): 1
Membership: 10 incorporated municipalities; *Fees:* Per capita; *Member Profile:* Municipalities in Rainy River District
Chief Officer(s):
Peggy Johnson, Secretary-Treasurer

Ralliement national des Métis *See* Métis National Council

Ralph Thornton Centre
765 Queen St. East, Toronto ON M4M 1H3
Tel: 416-392-6810
info@ralphthornton.org
www.ralphthornton.org
www.youtube.com/user/ralphthorntoncentre
Overview: A medium-sized local charitable organization founded in 1980
Mission: To create a supportive environment in which the Riverdale community responds to issues and needs.
Finances: *Annual Operating Budget:* $500,000-$1.5 Million
Staff Member(s): 4; 150 volunteer(s)
Chief Officer(s):
Paula Fletcher, President
John Campey, Executive Director

Ramara & District Chamber of Commerce
2297 Hwy. 12, Brechin ON L0K 1B0
Tel: 705-484-2141
info@ramarachamber.com
www.ramarachamber.com
Overview: A small local organization
Mission: To serve, support & promote members & the community
Membership: 83; *Fees:* $95
Chief Officer(s):
Roger Selman, President

Ranch Ehrlo Society
Pilot Butte Campus, PO Box 570, Pilot Butte SK S0G 3Z0
Tel: 306-781-1800; *Fax:* 306-757-0599
inquiries@ranchehrlo.ca
www.ehrlo.com
www.facebook.com/RanchEhrlo
twitter.com/RanchEhrlo
www.youtube.com/user/ranchehrlo1
Previous Name: Saskatchewan Council on Children & Youth
Overview: A medium-sized provincial charitable organization
Mission: To provide a range of quality assessment, treatment, education & support services that improve the social & emotional functioning of children & youth
Chief Officer(s):
Andrea Brittin, President & CEO

Randonnées plein air du Québec
4545, rue Pierre-de-Coubertin, Montréal QC H1V 0B2
Tél: 514-252-3330; *Téléc:* 514-253-5537
info@randopleinair.com
randopleinair.com
Aperçu: *Dimension:* petite; *Envergure:* locale
Mission: D'encourager et d'organiser des activités de conditionnement physique en plein air
Membre(s) du bureau directeur:
Nicole Beauvais, Présidente, Conseil d'administration

Randonneurs du Saguenay
CP 8116, Chicoutimi QC G7H 5B5
randonneursdusaguenay.qc.ca
Aperçu: *Dimension:* petite; *Envergure:* locale; Organisme sans but lucratif; fondée en 1982
Mission: D'organiser des activités de randonnée et la raquette pour découvrir la région du Lac-St-Jean Saguenay
Affiliation(s): Fédération Québécoise de la Marche
Membre: *Montant de la cotisation:* 20$ Individuelle; 30$ Famille
Activités: Randonnée pédestre; Kayak; *Evénements de sensibilisation:* Assemblée générale annuelle (avril)
Membre(s) du bureau directeur:
Louis Langevin, Président, Conseil d'administration

Ranfurly & District Recreation & Agricultural Society
PO Box 162, 5119 - 49th St., Ranfurly AB T0B 3T0
Tel: 780-658-2114
Overview: A small local organization
Activities: Hosting community events, such as the Annual Summer Fair & Horseshow

Rape Crisis Centre Timmins *See* Timmins & Area Women in Crisis Support & Information Centre on Violence Against Women

Rare Breeds Canada (RBC)
RR#1, Nesbitt MB R0K 1P0
Tel: 204-573-8204
rbc@rarebreedscanada.org
www.rarebreedscanada.org
www.facebook.com/288297957875508
twitter.com/rarebreedsca
Overview: A medium-sized national charitable organization founded in 1986
Mission: To make Canadians more aware of their agricultural heritage; through education & niche marketing involve them in conserving endangered breeds of farm livestock & poultry
Affiliation(s): Canadian Coalition for Biodiversity
Finances: *Annual Operating Budget:* Less than $50,000; *Funding Sources:* Membership dues
Staff Member(s): 1; 20 volunteer(s)
Membership: 600; *Fees:* $35 individual; $50 family; $100 corporate
Activities: *Speaker Service:* Yes
Chief Officer(s):
Andy Sproston, Director, 905-309-4984
andy.sproston@yahoo.com

Island Heritage Livestock
c/o Margaret Thomson, Chair, 1432 North Beach Rd., Salt Spring Island BC V8K 1B2
Tel: 250-537-4669
www.islandsheritagelivestock.com
Chief Officer(s):
Wynnie Konkle, Contact
olderbonz@shaw.ca

Raspberry Industry Development Council (RIDC)
#265, 32160 South Fraser Way, Abbotsford BC V2T 1W5
Tel: 604-854-8010; *Fax:* 604-854-6050
council@bcraspberries.com
bcraspberries.com
www.facebook.com/raspberryindustrydevelopmentcouncil
twitter.com/bcraspberries
www.flickr.com/photos/bcraspberries
Previous Name: British Columbia Raspberry Industry Council
Overview: A small provincial organization founded in 1999
Mission: To promote the interests of raspberry growers
Member of: British Columbia Chamber of Commerce
Finances: *Annual Operating Budget:* $100,000-$250,000; *Funding Sources:* Membership levy fee; government; private donations & membership fees
Staff Member(s): 1
Membership: 277; *Member Profile:* Produce over 1 ton of raspberries; *Committees:* Labour; Research; Environment

Rassemblement canadien pour l'alphabétisation *See* Canadian Literacy & Learning Network

Rassemblement des bibliothèques publiques du Lac-Saint-Jean et Saguenay-Lac-Saint-Jean *Voir* Réseau BIBLIO du Saguenay-Lac-Saint-Jean

Rassemblement pour l'alphabétisation de la communauté urbaine de Toronto *See* Metro Toronto Movement for Literacy

Raymond Chamber of Commerce
PO Box 1435, Raymond AB T0K 2S0
Tel: 403-330-9057
www.facebook.com/146864378801811
Overview: A small local licensing organization
Member of: Alberta Chamber of Commerce
Finances: *Funding Sources:* Membership dues
Activities: *Awareness Events:* Annual Awards Banquet, April; Free Pancake Breakfast, July; Old Fashioned Christmas, Dec.

Rayons de Soleil pour enfants *See* Sunshine Dreams for Kids

RBC Fondation *See* RBC Foundation

RBC Foundation / RBC Fondation
Royal Bank Plaza, South Tower, #950, 200 Bay St., Toronto ON M5J 2J5
Tel: 416-974-3113; *Fax:* 416-955-7800
www.rbc.com/community-sustainability/community
Previous Name: Royal Bank of Canada Charitable Foundation
Overview: A medium-sized national organization founded in 1993
Finances: *Funding Sources:* RBC Financial Group
Activities: RBC After School Project; RBC Blue Water Project; RBC Children's Mental Health Project; RBC Emerging Artists Project; RBC Learn to Play Project; RBC Play Hockey; RBC Olympians Program
Chief Officer(s):
Gayle Longley, Contact
gayle.longley@rbc.com

RCMP Civilian Search & Rescue Civilian Search Dog Program; RCMP Civilian Search Dog Association *See* Canadian Search Dog Association

Re:Sound Music Licensing Company
#900, 1235 Bay St., Toronto ON M5R 3K4
Tel: 416-968-8870; *Fax:* 416-962-7797
info@resound.ca
www.resound.ca
www.linkedin.com/company-beta/1387508
www.facebook.com/resoundmlc
twitter.com/ReSoundMLC
Previous Name: The Neighbouring Rights Collective of Canada
Overview: A medium-sized national organization
Mission: To obtain fair compensation for artists & record companies for their performance rights
Staff Member(s): 18
Chief Officer(s):
Ian MacKay, President
Arif Ahmad, Vice President & General Counsel

Reach Canada
400 Coventry Rd., 3rd Fl, Ottawa ON K1K 2C7
Tel: 613-236-6636; *Fax:* 613-236-6605
Toll-Free: 800-465-8898; *TTY:* 613-236-9478
reach@reach.ca
www.reach.ca
www.facebook.com/ReachCanada
twitter.com/reachcanada1
Previous Name: Reach Equality & Justice for People with Disabilities; Resource, Education & Advocacy Centre for the Handicapped
Overview: A small local organization founded in 1981

Mission: To provide legal referral services & educational programs for people with disabilities
Membership: *Committees:* Education; Cabaret
Activities: *Awareness Events:* Reach Annual Auction, Oct.; Minto Run for Reach, April; *Speaker Service:* Yes
Chief Officer(s):
Renette Sasouni, President

Reach Equality & Justice for People with Disabilities; Resource, Education & Advocacy Centre for the Handicapped *See* Reach Canada

Reach for the Rainbow
20 Torlake Cres., Toronto ON M8Z 1B3
Tel: 416-503-0088; *Fax:* 416-503-0485
info@reachfortherainbow.ca
www.reachfortherainbow.ca
www.facebook.com/ReachForTheRainbow
twitter.com/RFTRCharity
www.youtube.com/RFTRCharity
Overview: A small provincial charitable organization founded in 1983
Mission: To offer integrated recreational & respite programs for disabled children within the province of Ontario
Staff Member(s): 20
Chief Officer(s):
David Neal, Executive Director
dneal@reachfortherainbow.ca
Lisa Carty, Chair

Réadaptation Psychosociale Canada *See* Psychosocial Rehabilitation Canada

Reading Council for Literacy Advance in Montréal (RECLAIM) / Conseil pour l'enseignement de la lecture aux analphabètes de Montréal
1001, rue Lenoir, #A2-10, Montréal QC H4C 2Z6
Tel: 514-369-7835
www.reclaimliteracy.ca
Overview: A small local charitable organization founded in 1980
Mission: To provide free, confidential, individualized literacy instruction to adults in the Greater Montréal area; to provide one-to-one tutoring & computer-assisted instruction, using trained volueers; to raise the public's awareness of literacy issues, & carrying out literacy-related projects, including family literacy
Member of: Literacy Volunteers of Québec; Québec Literacy Alliance
Affiliation(s): Laubach Literacy of Canada
Finances: *Annual Operating Budget:* $250,000-$500,000
Staff Member(s): 6; 270 volunteer(s)
Membership: 300; *Fees:* $20
Activities: *Speaker Service:* Yes
Chief Officer(s):
Margaret Suttie, President
Joy Fyckes, Executive Director
joy@reclaimliteracy.ca

Real Estate Board of Greater Vancouver
2433 Spruce St., Vancouver BC V6H 4C8
Tel: 604-730-3000; *Fax:* 604-730-3100
Toll-Free: 800-304-0565
www.rebgv.org
www.facebook.com/rebgv
twitter.com/rebgv
www.youtube.com/user/rebgv
Overview: A small local organization overseen by British Columbia Real Estate Association
Chief Officer(s):
Robert K. Wallace, CEO

Real Estate Board of the Fredericton Area Inc. (FREB)
544 Brunswick St., Fredericton NB E3B 1H5
Tel: 506-458-8163; *Fax:* 506-459-8922
www.frederictonrealestateboard.com
Overview: A small local organization founded in 1963 overseen by New Brunswick Real Estate Association
Mission: To serve the needs of its' members by providing cost effective tools, services & information necessary to foster professionalism
Member of: The Canadian Real Estate Association; New Brunswick Real Estate Association
Affiliation(s): Mortgage Lenders Association
Finances: *Annual Operating Budget:* $250,000-$500,000
Staff Member(s): 2
Membership: 280+

Chief Officer(s):
Bradley Thomas, President, 506-452-7295
Sharon Watts, Executive Officer, 506-458-8163
freb01@rogers.com

Real Estate Council of Alberta (RECA)
#350, 4954 Richard Rd. SW, Calgary AB T3E 6L1
Tel: 403-228-2954; *Fax:* 403-228-3065
Toll-Free: 888-425-2754
info@reca.ca
www.reca.ca
www.facebook.com/150222881696865
twitter.com/RECA
www.youtube.com/user/RECAAdmin
Overview: A medium-sized provincial organization founded in 1995
Mission: To protect consumers; To provide services that enhance & improve the industry & the business of industry professionals
Finances: *Annual Operating Budget:* Greater than $5 Million
Membership: 12 council members; *Committees:* Audit & Finance; Governance; Hearings
Chief Officer(s):
Bob Myroniuk, Executive Director
Publications:
• Annual Report of the Real Estate Council of Alberta
Type: Yearbook; *Frequency:* Annually
Profile: Messages from the chair & executive director, education, financial statements, & officers
• The Regulator [a publication of the Real Estate Council of Alberta]
Type: Newsletter; *Frequency:* Monthly
Profile: News from the Council

Real Estate Council of British Columbia (RECBC)
#900, 750 West Pender St., Vancouver BC V6C 2T8
Tel: 604-683-9664; *Fax:* 604-683-9017
Toll-Free: 877-683-9664
info@recbc.ca
www.recbc.ca
Overview: A medium-sized provincial organization founded in 1958
Mission: Protects the public interest by assuring the competency of real estate licensees and ensuring their compliance with the Real Estate Services Act. The Council is accountable to and advises government on industry issues and encourages public confidence, by impartially setting and enforcing standards of conduct, education, competency and licensing for real estate licensees in the province.
Finances: *Annual Operating Budget:* Greater than $5 Million
Staff Member(s): 26
Membership: 16; *Committees:* Education; Real Estate Services Act; Rental Property Management; Strata Management; Trading Services
Chief Officer(s):
Robert O. Fawcett, Executive Officer

Real Estate Council of Ontario (RECO)
West Tower, #1200, 3300 Bloor St. West, Toronto ON M8X 2X2
Tel: 416-207-4800; *Fax:* 416-207-4820
Toll-Free: 800-245-6910
info@reco.ca
www.reco.on.ca
Overview: A medium-sized provincial organization
Mission: To administer the regulatory requirements of the real estate industry as set down by the Government of Ontario; To protect consumers & members through a fair & safe & informed marketplace
Membership: *Committees:* Appeals; Audit; By-laws; Discipline; Education; Finance; Governance; Insurance; Premium Stabilization
Chief Officer(s):
Kate Murray, CEO

Real Estate Institute of British Columbia
#1750, 355 Burrard St., Vancouver BC V6C 2G8
Tel: 604-685-3702; *Fax:* 604-685-1026
Toll-Free: 800-667-2166
info@reibc.org
www.reibc.org
www.linkedin.com/company/real-estate-institute-of-british-columbia
www.facebook.com/REIBC
twitter.com/THE_REIBC
Overview: A medium-sized provincial organization founded in 1960

Mission: To advance the highest standards of education, knowledge, professional development & business practice in all sectors of the real estate industry
Finances: *Annual Operating Budget:* $250,000-$500,000
Staff Member(s): 3; 100 volunteer(s)
Membership: 1,600; *Fees:* $546 professional; $273.13 associate; $72.82 retired; *Committees:* Audit; Golf; Governance; Nominating; Professional Conduct; Standards & Practice
Chief Officer(s):
Brenda Southam, Executive Officer
bsoutham@reibc.org
Maggie Hill, Coordinator, Development
mhill@reibc.org

Real Estate Institute of Canada (REIC) / Institut canadien de l'immeuble (ICI)
#208, 5407 Eglinton Ave. West, Toronto ON M9C 5K6
Tel: 416-695-9000; *Fax:* 416-695-7230
Toll-Free: 800-542-7342
infocentral@reic.com
www.reic.ca
www.linkedin.com/company/real-estate-institute-of-canada
www.facebook.com/reicnational
twitter.com/reicnational
Previous Name: Canadian Institute of Realtors
Overview: A large national organization founded in 1955
Mission: To advance opportunities for persons involved in real estate; To offer certification & designation for real estate professionals
Finances: *Annual Operating Budget:* $500,000-$1.5 Million
Staff Member(s): 9; 2000 volunteer(s)
Membership: 2,000; *Fees:* $439; *Member Profile:* Real estate industry professionals in Canada bound by the Institute's Code of Professional Standards; *Committees:* Professional Standards; Audit; Liaison; Awards; Chapter Review; Bylaws
Activities: Offering certification courses & resources
Chief Officer(s):
Maura McLaren, Executive Director, 416-695-9000 Ext. 300
maura.mclaren@reic.com
Lesley Lucas, Director, Education & Business Development, 416-695-7457
lesley.lucas@reic.ca
Britny Rodé, Coordinator, Marketing & Communications, 416-695-9000 Ext. 290
britny.rode@reic.com
Shelley Barfoot-O'Neill, Director, Admissions & Membership, 416-695-9000 Ext. 260
shelley.oneill@reic.com
Awards:
• J.A. Weber Award
• Association of the Year Award
• W.P.J. McCarthy Corporate Citizen of the Year Award
• REIC Community Services Award
• Chapter Initiative of the Year Award
• Don Hill Award
• Chapter Administrator of the Year Award
• Patrick J. Harvey Memorial Award
• Murray Bosley Sales and Leasing Member of the Year Award
• Longley Condominiums Real Estate Management Member of the Year Award
• REIC Finance Member of the Year Award
• Bentall Kennedy Literary Award
• Bentall Kennedy Excellence Award
• REIC Emeritus Award
Meetings/Conferences:
• Real Estate Institute of Canada 2018 Annual Conference & Annual General Meeting, May, 2018, Montréal, QC
Scope: National
Description: A gathering of real estate professionals to participate in professional development programs, listen to guest speakers, & to network with industry experts, colleagues, & suppliers
Contact Information: Coordinator, Events: Natalie Wallace, E-mail: natalie.wallace@reic.com, Phone: 416-695-9000, ext. 270

Alberta - Calgary Chapter
c/o Erika Holter, PO Box 4520, Stn. C, Calgary AB T2T 5N3
Tel: 403-244-4487; *Fax:* 403-244-2340
calgary@reic.com
www.reic.ca/ABOUT-US/Chapters/Calgary
Chief Officer(s):
Erika Holter, Administrator
Alberta - Edmonton Chapter
Stony Plain AB

Tel: 780-453-9368; Fax: 780-451-6613
www.reic.ca/ABOUT-US/Chapters/Edmonton
Chief Officer(s):
Sharon Radford, Administrator
sharondr@telusplanet.net
British Columbia - Greater Vancouver Chapter
Vancouver BC
Tel: 604-600-8579
www.reic.ca/greatervancouver
Chief Officer(s):
Joyce D'Souza, Administrator
British Columbia Chapter - The Real Estate Institute of British Columbia
#1750, 355 Burrard St., Vancouver BC V6C 2G8
Tel: 604-685-3702; Fax: 604-685-1026
Toll-Free: 800-667-2166
info@reibc.org
www.reibc.org
www.linkedin.com/company/real-estate-institute-of-british-columbia
www.facebook.com/REIBC
twitter.com/THE_REIBC
www.youtube.com/channel/UCbRtDtvKYpiEW44GPE49KjA
Chief Officer(s):
Andrea Fletcher, President, 604-763-2188
Brenda Southam, Executive Officer, 604-685-3702 Ext. 104
bsoutham@reibc.org
Maggie Hill, Coordinator, 604-685-3702 Ext. 103
mhill@reibc.org
Manitoba Chapter
PO Box 544, Stn. Main, Winnipeg MB R3C 2J3
Tel: 204-415-5711; Fax: 204-339-7261
admin@reim.ca
www.reic.ca/ABOUT-US/Chapters/Manitoba/About-Us
Chief Officer(s):
Shirley Tillett, Administrator
Nova Scotia Chapter
c/o Stacy C. Wentzell, Harbourside Realty Ltd., 3476 Dutch Village Rd., Halifax NS B3N 2R9
Tel: 902-444-7301; Fax: 902-422-0556
www.reic.ca/ABOUT-US/Chapters/Nova-Scotia
Chief Officer(s):
Matthew Pendlebury, President, 902-420-0599
mpendlebury@montrosemortgage.com
Rémy St-Pierre, Administrator, 902-426-3604 Ext. 6686
rstpierr@cmhc-schl.gc.ca
Alice Galpin-Nicholson, Secretary, 902-420-6005
galpinam@gov.ns.ca
Theresa Salsman, Treasurer, 902-464-7784
tdawson@citigroup.ns.ca
Ontario - Ottawa Chapter
c/o Patricia Riccio, #803, 1568 Merivale Rd., Ottawa ON K2G 5Y7
Tel: 613-565-7342
ottawa@reic.com
www.reic.ca/chapters/ottawa
Chief Officer(s):
Debbie MacEwen, Administrator
Ontario - Toronto Chapter
c/o Beth MacKenzie, Taylor Enterprises, #310, 2175 Sheppard Ave. East, Toronto ON M2J 1W8
www.reic.ca/ABOUT-US/Chapters/Toronto
Chief Officer(s):
Beth McKenzie, Administrator, 416-491-2886 Ext. 248
beth@associationconcepts.ca
Québec Chapter
256, ch Grande-Côte, Rosemère QC J7A 1J2
Tel: 450-430-4207
www.reic.ca/about-us/chapters/Quebec
Chief Officer(s):
Serge Rivet, Président
remax@heleneetserge.com
Saskatchewan Chapter
c/o Sara Lawrence, Administrator, PO Box 653, Weyburn SK S4H 2K7
reisk@accesscomm.ca
www.reic.ca/ABOUT-US/Chapters/Saskatchewan
Chief Officer(s):
Sara Lawrence, Administrator

Real Property Association of Canada
TD North Tower, PO Box 147, #4030, 77 King St. West, Toronto ON M5K 1H1
Tel: 416-642-2700; Fax: 416-642-2727
Toll-Free: 855-732-5722
info@realpac.ca
www.realpac.ca
www.linkedin.com/company/realpac
www.facebook.com/111245762249174
twitter.com/realpac_news
www.youtube.com/user/REALpacVideos
Also Known As: REALpac
Previous Name: Canadian Institute of Public & Private Real Estate Companies
Overview: A medium-sized national organization
Mission: To represent the real estate industry's point of view to government at all levels on legislative & regulatory matters
Finances: Annual Operating Budget: $500,000-$1.5 Million
Staff Member(s): 10
Membership: 89 corporate; Member Profile: Owners & developers of real estate assets with value in excess of $100 million CDN; Committees: Capital Markets; Corporate Responsibility & Sustainability; Financial Best Practices; Fund Management; Human Resources; Research Advisory
Activities: Internships: Yes
Chief Officer(s):
Michael Brooks, Ph.D., Chief Executive Officer
mbrooks@realpac.ca
Carolyn Lane, Vice-President, Membership, Marketing & Communications
clane@realpac.ca

REAL Women of Canada / Vraies femmes du Canada
PO Box 8813, Stn. T, #403, 116 Albert St., Ottawa ON K1G 3J1
Tel: 613-236-4001; Fax: 613-236-7203
www.realwomenofcanada.ca
www.facebook.com/REALWomenofCanada
Overview: A small national organization founded in 1983
Finances: Annual Operating Budget: $50,000-$100,000
Membership: 55,000; Fees: $25 individual/family; $30 group
Activities: Speaker Service: Yes

Realtors Association of Edmonton
14220 - 112 Ave., Edmonton AB T5M 2T8
Tel: 780-451-6666; Fax: 780-452-1135
Toll-Free: 888-674-7479
www.ereb.com
www.facebook.com/REALTORSAssociationOfEdmonton
twitter.com/RAEinfo
Overview: A small local organization founded in 1909 overseen by Alberta Real Estate Association
Member of: Alberta Real Estate Association; The Canadian Real Estate Association
Membership: Fees: $415; Member Profile: Realtors in the Edmonton area
Chief Officer(s):
Michael Thompson, President & CEO, 780-453-9340
Ron Hutchinson, Executive Vice-President

REALTORS Association of Grey Bruce Owen Sound (RAGBOS)
517 - 10 St., Lower Level, Hanover ON N4N 1R4
Tel: 519-364-3827
www.ragbos.ca
Previous Name: Grey Bruce Real Estate Board; Grey Bruce Owen Sound Real Estate Board
Overview: A small local organization founded in 2000 overseen by Ontario Real Estate Association
Mission: To provide a web-based multiple listing service for its members
Member of: The Canadian Real Estate Association
Finances: Funding Sources: Membership fees
Membership: 360+
Activities: Speaker Service: Yes
Chief Officer(s):
Dawn Lee McKenzie, President, 519-422-1170

Realtors Association of Lloydminster & District
#203, 5009 - 48 St., Lloydminster AB T9V 0H7
Tel: 780-875-6939; Fax: 780-875-5560
lloydreb@telus.net
rald.realtyserver.com
Previous Name: Lloydminster Real Estate Board
Overview: A small local organization overseen by Alberta Real Estate Association
Member of: Canadian Real Estate Assn.; Saskatchewan Real Estate Assn.; Alberta Real Estate Assn.

Realtors Association of South Central Alberta (RASCA)
PO Box 997, 3 Royal Rd. East, Brooks AB T1R 1B8
Tel: 403-793-1666
www.facebook.com/115618335134095
Overview: A small local organization overseen by Alberta Real Estate Association
Member of: Alberta Real Estate Association; The Canadian Real Estate Association
Chief Officer(s):
Karen Bertamini, President

reBOOT Canada
#1, 2450 Lawrence Ave. East, Toronto ON M1P 2R7
Tel: 416-534-6017; Fax: 416-534-6083
rose@rebootcanada.ca
www.rebootcanada.ca
Overview: A small national charitable organization founded in 1995
Mission: Refurbishes old computers received from individual & corporate donors & distributes them, free of charge, to other charitable organizations
Chief Officer(s):
Nicholas Brinckman, Executive Director
nick@rebootcanada.ca

Receivables Insurance Association of Canada (RIAC) / Association canadienne de l'assurance comptes clients
122 Bagot St., Cobourg ON K9A 3G1
Tel: 613-794-6683
receivablesinsurancecanada.com
www.linkedin.com/company/3165607
www.facebook.com/ReceivablesInsuranceCanada
twitter.com/RcvblsInsCanada
www.youtube.com/user/RcvblsInsCanada
Overview: A small national organization
Mission: To promote the business opportunity for receivables insurance to Canadian insurance brokers, the banking industry & businesses engaged in domestic trade & exporting
Staff Member(s): 2
Membership: 7 insurers + 5 specialist brokers + 2 industry associates + 4 regular members; Fees: $200 regular; $1,000 regional broker/corporate/industry member; $2,500 active specialist broker member; $5,000 licensed insurer & EDC member
Chief Officer(s):
Mark Attley, President
mark.attley@receivablesinsurancecanada.com

Receivables Management Assocation of Canada Inc. / Association Canadienne de la Gestion de Créances Inc.
#440, 141 Adelaide St. West, Toronto ON M5H 3L5
Fax: 905-671-1579
Toll-Free: 855-690-7047
info@rmacanada.org
www.rmacanada.org
Overview: A medium-sized national organization
Mission: To bring the concerns of those involved in accounts receivable to those in charge, in order to improve daily operations, as well as to bring more attention and development to the industry
14 volunteer(s)
Membership: 52; Fees: Affiliate Membersip $295; Full Membership for companies with 10+ employees) $750; Full Membership for companies with under 10 employees $460
Activities: Educational sessions; Round table discussions; Annual general meeting
Chief Officer(s):
Mark Ball, President, Board of Directors
Steve Sheather, Vice President, Board of Directors
Scott Coffin, Secretary, Board of Directors
Elliot Ocopnick, Treasurer, Board of Directors

Reception House Waterloo Region
#201, 675 Queen St. South, Kitchener ON N2M 1A1
Tel: 519-743-2113
www.receptionhouse.ca
www.facebook.com/ReceptionHouseWR
Overview: A small local organization founded in 1988 overseen by Ontario Council of Agencies Serving Immigrants
Mission: To provide initial temporary accommodation, orientation & locate permanent accommodation for newly arrived government-sponsored refugees; To assist them with initial settlement needs

Finances: *Annual Operating Budget:* $100,000-$250,000; *Funding Sources:* Federal government
Staff Member(s): 8; 5 volunteer(s)
Chief Officer(s):
Carl Cadogan, Executive Director

Recherches amérindiennes au Québec
6742, rue Saint-Denis, Montréal QC H2S 2S2
Tél: 514-277-6178
www.recherches-amerindiennes.qc.ca
www.facebook.com/reamqu
Aperçu: *Dimension:* moyenne; *Envergure:* provinciale; fondée en 1971
Mission: Diffuser des informations sur les populations amérindiennes
10 bénévole(s)
Membre: 180 institutionnel; 270 individu
Membre(s) du bureau directeur:
Pierre Trudel, Président
Robert Lanari, Vice-président
Isabelle Bouchard, Secrétaire
François Girard, Trésorier

Recreation & Parks Association of New Brunswick Inc. See Recreation New Brunswick

Recreation & Parks Association of the Yukon (RPAY)
4061 - 4th Ave., Whitehorse YT Y1A 1H1
Tel: 867-668-3010; *Fax:* 867-668-2455
rpay@klondiker.com
www.rpay.org
facebook.com/goRPAY
twitter.com/RPAY1
Overview: A medium-sized provincial organization founded in 1993
Mission: To promote, encourage and foster the growth and development of all areas of recreation throughout the Yukon Territory.
Staff Member(s): 4
Membership: *Fees:* $15 individual; $50 associate/community
Chief Officer(s):
Ian Spencer, President
Anne Morgan, Executive Director

The Recreation Association / L'Association récréative
2451 Riverside Dr., Ottawa ON K1H 7X7
Tel: 613-733-5100; *Fax:* 613-736-6238
racentre@racentre.com
www.racentre.com
twitter.com/RACentreOttawa
Also Known As: RA Centre
Overview: A large national organization founded in 1941
Mission: To provide quality leisure & lifestyle activities to the membership
Finances: *Annual Operating Budget:* Greater than $5 Million; *Funding Sources:* Membership dues; program revenue; special projects revenue
Staff Member(s): 70; 500 volunteer(s)
Membership: 27,000; *Fees:* $33-$57
Activities: 100+ programs & services in health, fitness, recreation & leisure
Chief Officer(s):
Tosha Rhodenizer, CEO
trhodenizer@racentre.com
Kelly Shaw-Swettenham, Director, Membership, Recreation, Sports & Fitness Services, 613-736-6227
kshawswettenham@racentre.com
Publications:
• The Recreation Association E-News & Offers
Type: Newsletter

Recreation Facilities Association of British Columbia (RFABC)
PO Box 112, Powell River BC V8A 4Z5
Toll-Free: 877-285-3421
info@rfabc.com
www.rfabc.com
Overview: A medium-sized provincial organization founded in 1948
Mission: To promote safe & successful operating standards for community centres, swimming pools, arenas, stadiums, & parks in British Columbia; To encourage professionalism among recreation facility operators
Membership: *Fees:* $42,50 retired persons; $42.86 students; $107 practitioners & interested individuals; $500 facilities or agencies; *Member Profile:* Practitioners, who work in the field of recreation & parks in British Columbia; Students, attending a full-time program in a post secondary institution; Individuals, who are interested in the purpose of the association; Associate members, who are engaged in a business related to recreation facilities; Facilities, or agencies & communities involved in the operations of parks & recreation facilities
Activities: Supporting recreation facility operators in British Columbia; Promoting education of recreation facility operators; Offering courses for members, such as pool operators & arena ice makers; Facilitating the exchange of ideas among members; Providing access to employment opportunities; *Library:* RFABC Resource Library; Not open to public
Chief Officer(s):
Lori Blackman, Executive Director
lori@rfabc.com
Steve McLain, President
smclain@fortstjohn.ca
Karin Carlson, Secretary/Treasurer
kcarlson@fortstjohn.ca
Chante Patterson-Elden, Chair, Marketing
celden@dawsoncreek.ca
Awards:
• RFABC Associates' Scholarship
Meetings/Conferences:
• Recreation Facilities Association of BC 2018 Annual Conference, April, 2018, Delta Grand Okanagan Resort & Conference Centre, Kelowna, BC
Scope: Provincial
Description: Theme: "70 Years, Building for the Future"
Publications:
• Facility to Facility
Frequency: Quarterly; *Price:* Free with membership in the Recreation Facilities Association of British Columbia
• RFABC Communiqué
Type: Newsletter; *Frequency:* Bimonthly; *Price:* Free with membership in the Recreation Facilities Association of British Columbia

Recreation New Brunswick
70 Melissa St., Fredericton NB E3A 6W1
Tel: 506-459-1929; *Fax:* 506-450-6066
info@recreationnb.ca
www.recreationnb.ca
www.facebook.com/RecreationNB
twitter.com/RecreationNB
www.instagram.com/recreationnb
Previous Name: Recreation & Parks Association of New Brunswick Inc.
Overview: A medium-sized provincial organization founded in 1987 overseen by Canadian Parks & Recreation Association
Mission: To develop a professional organization for members; To enhance the image of recreation to government & the general public; To develop liaisons with other recreation groups; To affect legislation in the field of recreation & parks
Finances: *Annual Operating Budget:* $100,000-$250,000
Membership: *Fees:* $20 student; $62 individual; $165 associate; $330-$703 municipal; $294 corporate
Activities: Annual conference & awards; Resource centre; Membership directory; Workshops & counsellors conference; Canoe School; Career videos for high schools
Chief Officer(s):
Chris Gallant, Executive Director
cgallant@recreationnb.ca
Michelle DeCourcey, Coordinator, Project Development
mdecourcey@recreationnb.ca
Peter Morrison, Coordinator, Training & Services
pmorrison@recreationnb.ca

Recreation Newfoundland & Labrador
PO Box 8700, St. John's NL A1B 4J6
Tel: 709-729-3892; *Fax:* 709-729-3814
info@recreationnl.com
www.recreationnl.com
www.facebook.com/453370901173112
Previous Name: Newfoundland & Labrador Parks & Recreation Association
Overview: A medium-sized provincial organization founded in 1971 overseen by Canadian Parks & Recreation Association
Mission: To promote, foster & develop recreation; to provide a full range of services to enrich the concept of leisure throughout Newfoundland & Labrador; to enable individual citizens to improve their quality of life.
Affiliation(s): Provincial/Territorial parks & recreation associations
Finances: *Funding Sources:* Membership fees; services; government grants; corporate
Staff Member(s): 5
Membership: *Fees:* Schedule available; *Member Profile:* Municipalities, communities, individuals, non-profit groups, students or businesses interested or involved in recreation
Activities: Playground Training Workshops; *Library:* Not open to public
Chief Officer(s):
Dawn Sharpe, President
dawnsharpe12@gmail.com
Gary Milley, Executive Director
garymilley@recreationnl.com
Awards:
• Bridging the Gap
Presented annually to recognize efforts of volunteers who have made a significant contribution to the development of recreational opportunities for persons with a diability in an integrated setting
• Ebert J. Broomfield Memorial Scholarship
Established in 1989; presented annually on a rotation basis between Eastern, Central, Western & Northern regions to a student based on academic achievement, atheltic participation & community involvement
• Pitcher Plant Award
Presented annually to recognize outstanding efforts in the development of recreation & leisure services in Newfoundland & Labrador
• Cy Hoskins Award
Presented annually to a full-time recreation practitioner who has made significant contributions to the growth & development of parks, recreation & leisure services

Recreation Nova Scotia (RNS)
#309, 5516 Spring Garden Rd., Halifax NS B3J 1G6
Tel: 902-425-1128; *Fax:* 902-422-8201
www.recreationns.ns.ca
www.linkedin.com/company/recreation-nova-scotia
www.facebook.com/RecreationNovaScotia
twitter.com/recreations
Overview: A medium-sized provincial charitable organization founded in 1998 overseen by Canadian Parks & Recreation Association
Mission: To build healthier futures through programs & services that promote the benefits of recreation
Member of: Volunteer Canada; Sport Nova Scotia; Active Living Alliance for Canadians with Disability; NS Council for the Family
Finances: *Annual Operating Budget:* $500,000-$1.5 Million; *Funding Sources:* Membership fees; provincial & federal government; fundraising
Staff Member(s): 6
Membership: *Fees:* Schedule available; *Member Profile:* Municipal recreation directors; community group volunteers; community development associations; individuals; students; business; elected officials; *Committees:* Recreation Matters Campaign; HIGH FIVE; Membership Services; Inclusion; Conference; Education; Training
Activities: NS Volunteer Training Workshop; Liability Insurance Program for community groups; lottery for community groups; awards program; social marketing campaign; advocacy; conference; special events; *Library:* Open to public
Chief Officer(s):
Rhonda Lemire, Executive Director
rlemire@recreationns.ns.ca
Rae Gunn, President
coordinator@activepictoucounty.ca
Awards:
• Bluenose Achievement Award
• Mayflower Community Cooperation Award
• Rick Hansen Award
• Professional Achievement Award
• Provincial Volunteer Week Awards

Recreation Prince Edward Island
40 Enman Cres., Charlottetown PE C1E 1E6
Tel: 902-892-6445; *Fax:* 902-368-4548
info@recreationpei.ca
www.recreationpei.ca
www.youtube.com/user/RecPEI
Also Known As: Recreation PEI
Previous Name: Prince Edward Island Recreation & Facilities Association
Overview: A small provincial organization
Finances: *Funding Sources:* Canadian Parks & Recreation Association (CPRA)
Chief Officer(s):

Canadian Associations / Recreation Vehicle Dealers Association of Canada (RVDA) / Association des commerçants de véhicules récréatifs du Canada

Kim Meunier, President
kmeunier@town.cornwall.pe.ca
Beth Grant, Executive Director

Recreation Vehicle Dealers Association of Canada (RVDA) / Association des commerçants de véhicules récréatifs du Canada
#145, 11331 Coppersmith Way, Richmond BC V7A 5J9
Tel: 604-718-6325; Fax: 604-204-0154
info@rvda.ca
www.rvda.ca
www.facebook.com/RVDAofCanada
Overview: A medium-sized national licensing organization founded in 1986
Mission: To promote professionalism in the RV industry through educational programs & events; To present the views of the industry to government & the general public
Affiliation(s): Recreation Vehicle Dealers Association of America
Finances: Annual Operating Budget: $250,000-$500,000; Funding Sources: Membership dues
Staff Member(s): 3; 20 volunteer(s)
Membership: 700; Committees: Funding; Education; Program Development; Marketing
Activities: Speaker Service: Yes
Chief Officer(s):
Eleonore Hamm, President, 604-718-6325
eleonorehamm@rvda.ca

Atlantic Recreation Vehicle Dealers Association (ARVDA)
PO Box 142, #502, 5657 Spring Garden Rd., Halifax NS B3J 3R4
Tel: 902-425-2445; Fax: 902-425-2441
association@pathfinder-group.com
www.arvda.ca
Chief Officer(s):
John K. Sutherland, Executive Director
jsutherland@pathfinder-group.com

Recreation Vehicle Dealers Association of Alberta
10561 - 172 St. NW, Edmonton AB T5S 1P1
Tel: 780-455-8562; Fax: 780-453-3927
Toll-Free: 888-858-8787
rvda@rvda-alberta.org
www.rvda-alberta.org
Chief Officer(s):
Dan Merkowsky, Executive Vice President
dan@rvda-alberta.ca

Recreation Vehicle Dealers Association of British Columbia (RVDABC)
#195B, 1151 - 10th Ave. SW, Salmon Arm BC V1E 1T3
Tel: 778-489-5057; Fax: 778-489-5097
joan@rvda.bc.ca
www.rvda.bc.ca
Chief Officer(s):
Joan Jackson, Executive Director
joan@rvda.bc.ca

Recreation Vehicle Dealers Association of Manitoba
#503, 386 Broadway, Winnipeg MB R3C 3R6
Tel: 204-975-8219; Fax: 204-947-9767
info@mbrvda.ca
www.manitobarvda.com
Chief Officer(s):
Geoff Powell, Executive Director

Recreation Vehicle Dealers Association of Québec
#324, 300, Saint-Sacrement, Montréal QC H2Y 1X4
Tel: 514-338-1471; Fax: 514-335-6250
Toll-Free: 866-338-1471
info@acrvq.org
www.acvrq.com
Chief Officer(s):
Nesly Dieudonné, Controller

Recreational Aircraft Association (RAA) / Réseau aéronefs amateur
22 - 4881 Fountain St. North, Breslau ON N0B 1M0
Tel: 519-648-3030
Toll-Free: 800-387-1028
raa@raa.ca
www.raa.ca
Previous Name: Experimental Aircraft Association of Canada
Overview: A medium-sized national organization founded in 1983
Mission: To provide a liaison between Transport Canada, MD-RA Inspection Services, Enforcement & builders and flyers of recreational aircraft
Affiliation(s): Recreational Aviation Foundation
Finances: Annual Operating Budget: $100,000-$250,000; Funding Sources: Membership dues
Staff Member(s): 1; 150 volunteer(s)
Membership: 2,000; Fees: $59.99 individual; $74.58 family; Member Profile: Individuals who enjoy building and flying plans recreationally; Committees: 12 regional
Activities: Fly-ins across Canada; Speaker Service: Yes
Chief Officer(s):
Gary Wolf, President, 519-648-3030
garywolf@rogers.com
Wayne Hadath, Treasurer
whadath@rogers.com
Meetings/Conferences:
• Recreational Aircraft Association 86th Annual Fly-In, July, 2018, Midland, ON
Description: Pancake breakfast; BBQ lunch; Camping; Aircraft displays
Publications:
• The Recreational Flyer [a publication of the Recreational Aircraft Association Canada]
Type: Magazine; Frequency: s-m.; Accepts Advertising; Number of Pages: 42; Editor: George Gregory; Price: Mailed to members; Free download
Profile: Articles on members' aircraft & building endeavours, technical tips, news & other articles relevant to building, owning & flying recreationally in Canada

Recreational Canoeing Association BC (RCABC)
1755 East 7th Ave., Vancouver BC V5N 1S1
Tel: 250-592-4170
sec@bccanoe.com
www.bccanoe.com
Overview: A small provincial organization founded in 1984
Member of: Paddle Canada
Finances: Annual Operating Budget: Less than $50,000; Funding Sources: Membership dues; government
16 volunteer(s)
Membership: 350; Fees: $20; $45 instructor; Committees: Course Standards; Conservation & Access
Activities: Canoe instruction & standards
Chief Officer(s):
Kari-Ann Thor, President, 604-253-5410
Tony Shaw, Secretary, 250-468-7955

Recycling Council of Alberta (RCA)
PO Box 23, Bluffton AB T0C 0M0
Tel: 403-843-6563; Fax: 403-843-4156
info@recycle.ab.ca
www.recycle.ab.ca
www.facebook.com/RecyclingCouncilOfAlberta
twitter.com/3RsAB
Overview: A medium-sized provincial charitable organization founded in 1987
Mission: To promote & facilitate waste reduction, recycling, & resource conservation in Alberta
Membership: Fees: Fee based upon sales for corporations & small businesses; Fee based upon population for municipalities & regional waste authorities; Member Profile: Corporations; Small Businesses; Institutions; Governments; Municipalities; Regional Waste Authorities; Not-for-Profit Organizations; Individuals; Committees: Leadership & Advocacy; Small & Rural Communities; Communications; Indstrial, Commercial, & Institutional Sector Issues
Activities: Facilitating the exchange of information between environmental groups, governments, industries, & consumers; Providing public education campaigns; Encouraging research in the recycling of waste materials; Awareness Events: Waste Reduction Week, October; Speaker Service: Yes
Chief Officer(s):
Jason London, President
Sharon Howland, Vice-President
Maegan Lukian, Secretary
Anne Auriat, Treasurer
Meetings/Conferences:
• Recycling Council of Alberta 2018 Waste Reduction Conference, September, 2018, The Banff Centre for Arts and Creativity, Banff, AB
Scope: Provincial
Description: Presentations, exhibits, & networking opportunities. Held jointly with the Conference on Canadian Stewardship.
Contact Information: info@recycle.ab.ca
Publications:
• Connector [a publication of the Recycling Council of Alberta]
Type: Newsletter
Profile: RCA activities, member profiles, & success stories

• Enviro Business Guide
Type: Directory
Profile: Contact information & descriptions of businesses

Recycling Council of British Columbia (RCBC)
#10, 119 West Pender St., Vancouver BC V6B 1S5
Tel: 604-683-6009; Fax: 604-683-7255
Toll-Free: 800-667-4321
Other Communication: hotline@rcbc.bc.ca
rcbc@rcbc.bc.ca
www.rcbc.ca
www.facebook.com/RecyclingBC
twitter.com/RecyclingBC
Overview: A medium-sized provincial charitable organization founded in 1974
Mission: To promote the principles of zero waste; To decrease British Columbia's environmental footprint
Finances: Funding Sources: Sponsorships; Donations
Membership: Fees: Schedule available; Member Profile: Individuals & corporations that support environmental sustainability
Activities: Conducting research; Providing information services; Participating in community-based events & activities; Establishing public policy positions; Awareness Events: Waste Reduction Week
Chief Officer(s):
Brock Macdonald, Chief Executive Officer, 604-683-6009 Ext. 307
brock@rcbc.bc.ca
Anna Rochelle, Director, Finance, 604-683-6009 Ext. 302
anna@rcbc.bc.ca
Harvinder Aujala, Manager, Information Services, 604-683-6009 Ext. 313
harv@rcbc.bc.ca
Ben Ramos, Manager, Member Services, 604-683-6009 Ext. 314
ben@rcbc.bc.ca
Awards:
• RCBC Environmental Awards
Awarded to recognize the contributions that individuals make toward the preservation of British Columbia's environment; includes categories for the private & public sectors, non-profit groups, educators, & individual or corporate innovators
Meetings/Conferences:
• Recycling Council of British Columbia 44th Annual Zero Waste Conference 2018, May, 2018, Whistler, BC
Scope: Provincial
Contact Information: Manager, Member Services: Ben Ramos, Phone: 604-683-6009, ext. 314, Email: conference@rcbc.ca
Publications:
• Best Practices for Multi-Family Food Scraps Collection
Type: Report; Number of Pages: 18; Author: Jordan Best
Profile: Topics include barriers in the multi-family sector, materials collected, collection details, containers & liners, education & outreach, & incentives & policies
• Examining the Waste-to-Energy Option
Type: Report; Number of Pages: 24; Author: Jordan Best
Profile: A background paper examining environmental performance & compatibility with zero waste principles
• On the Road to Zero Waste: Priorities for Local Governments
Type: Report; Number of Pages: 16
Profile: Guidance for municipal & regional governments across British Columbia
• Organics Working Group Report: Recommendations for Residential Collection
Type: Report; Number of Pages: 16
Profile: Recommendations developed by the Organics Working Group to service single family homes
• Recycling Council of British Columbia Annual Report
Type: Yearbook; Frequency: Annually
Profile: Featuring the executive director's report, the auditor's report, & organizational information

Recycling Council of Manitoba; Resource Conservation Manitoba Inc. See Green Action Centre

Recycling Council of Ontario (RCO) / Conseil du recyclage de l'Ontario
#225, 215 Spadina Ave., Toronto ON M5T 2C7
Tel: 416-657-2797
Toll-Free: 888-501-9637
rco@rco.on.ca
www.rco.on.ca
www.facebook.com/372107118725
twitter.com/RCOntario

Overview: A medium-sized provincial charitable organization founded in 1978
Mission: To inform & educate society about the generation & avoidance of waste; To encourage recycling & the efficient use of resources
Finances: *Funding Sources:* Donations; Sponsorships
Membership: *Fees:* Schedule available based upon annual gross sales for businesses & population for municipalities; *Member Profile:* Businesses; Municipalities; Communities; Educational organizations; Individuals; Students; Families; *Committees:* Executive/Finance; Membership/Communications; Policy/Advocacy; Program Development; Events
Activities: Liaising with all levels of government, environmental organizations, & industry; Designing & facilitating short-term projects in response to market needs; Hosting knowledge sessions to disseminate information; *Awareness Events:* Waste Reduction Week in Ontario; Waste Free Lunch Challenge
Chief Officer(s):
Jo-Anne St. Godard, Executive Director, 416-657-2797 Ext. 3
joanne@rco.on.ca
Diane Blackburn, Manager, Events, 416-657-2797 Ext. 4
diane@rco.on.ca
Meirav Even-Har, Program Manager, Waste Diversion Certification Program, 416-657-2797 Ext. 8
meirav@rco.on.ca
Awards:
• RCO Awards Program
Meetings/Conferences:
• Recycling Council of Ontario 2018 Annual General Meeting & Policy Forum, 2018, ON
Scope: Provincial
Contact Information: Manager, Events: Diane Blackburn, E-mail: events@rco.on.ca, Phone: 416-657-2797, ext. 4
Publications:
• Recycling Council of Ontario Annual Report
Type: Yearbook; *Frequency:* Annually
Profile: Operational highlights of the council

Red Deer & District Allied Arts Council
#111, 4818 - 50 St., Red Deer AB T4N 4A3
Tel: 403-348-2787
info@reddeerartscouncil.ca
www.reddeerartscouncil.ca
www.facebook.com/reddeerartscouncil
twitter.com/RDArtsCouncil
Previous Name: Red Deer Allied Arts Council
Overview: A small local organization founded in 1964
Mission: To foster & encourage participation of young people & adults in the arts; to stimulate interest & appreciation of the arts in general
Membership: *Fees:* $15 student; $30 individual; $50 group; *Member Profile:* Interest & willingness to encourage the arts in central Alberta
Activities: Art gallery; artist and youth education; support to local artists and groups; scholarship programs; *Internships:* Yes; *Speaker Service:* Yes; *Rents Mailing List:* Yes
Chief Officer(s):
Diana Anderson, Coordinator

Red Deer & District Community Foundation (RDDCF)
Mid City Plaza, 4805 - 48 St., Red Deer AB T4N 1S6
Tel: 403-341-6911; *Fax:* 403-341-4177
info@rddcf.ca
www.rddcf.ca
twitter.com/rddcf
www.youtube.com/user/rddcf
Overview: A small local organization founded in 1989
Mission: To strengthen the quality of life in the Red Deer area by growing a legacy through the development of endowment funds, fostering collaboration & partnerships, responding to community needs & promoting innovation
Member of: Community Foundations of Canada
Finances: *Funding Sources:* Individual & corporate contributions
Staff Member(s): 3
Chief Officer(s):
Kristine Bugayong, CEO
Joanne Packham, Chair
Rhonda Elder, Vice-Chair

Red Deer & District SPCA
4505 - 77 St., Red Deer AB T4P 2J1
Tel: 403-342-7722; *Fax:* 403-341-3147
office@reddeerspca.com
www.reddeerspca.com
www.facebook.com/233609360018185
twitter.com/RedDeerSPCA
www.instagram.com/reddeerspca;
www.pinterest.com/reddeerspca
Previous Name: Parkland Humane Society
Overview: A small local charitable organization founded in 1970 overseen by Canadian Federation of Humane Societies
Mission: To care for & protect companion animals & promote humane treatment of animals & responsible pet ownership
Member of: Alberta Society for the Prevention of Cruelty to Animals; Red Deer Chamber of Commerce; Canadian Federation of Humane Societies
Finances: *Funding Sources:* United Way; Municipal grants
Staff Member(s): 20
Membership: *Fees:* $20 single; $25 family; $100 corporate
Chief Officer(s):
Tara Hellewell, Executive Director

Red Deer Action Group
#202, 4805 - 48 St., Red Deer AB T4N 1S6
Tel: 403-343-1198; *Fax:* 403-343-8945
rdag@telus.net
www.rdactiongroup.ca
Previous Name: Red Deer Action Group for the Physically Disabled
Overview: A small local charitable organization founded in 1976
Mission: To work toward providing a better quality of life for people with disabilities
Affiliation(s): Alberta Committee for Citizens with Disabilities
Finances: *Annual Operating Budget:* Less than $50,000
Staff Member(s): 2; 25 volunteer(s)
Membership: 75 individual; *Fees:* $10 individual
Chief Officer(s):
Jean Stinson, President

Red Deer Action Group for the Physically Disabled *See* Red Deer Action Group

Red Deer Allied Arts Council *See* Red Deer & District Allied Arts Council

Red Deer Chamber of Commerce
3017 Gaetz Ave., Red Deer AB T4N 5Y6
Tel: 403-347-4491; *Fax:* 403-343-6188
rdchamber@reddeerchamber.com
www.reddeerchamber.com
www.linkedin.com/groups?gid=2518693
www.facebook.com/109831038638
twitter.com/RedDeerChamber
Overview: A medium-sized local organization founded in 1894
Mission: To promote a thriving environment by advocating for Red Deer & area members on issues affecting business in the community
Member of: Alberta Chamber of Commerce; Canadian Chamber of Commerce
Finances: *Funding Sources:* Membership dues; trade shows; seminars
Staff Member(s): 7
Membership: *Fees:* Schedule available based on number of employees
Activities: *Rents Mailing List:* Yes; *Library:* by appointment
Chief Officer(s):
Bradley Williams, President
Tim Creedon, Executive Director

Red Deer City Soccer Association
6905 Edgar Industrial Dr., Red Deer AB T4P 3R2
Tel: 403-346-4259; *Fax:* 403-340-1044
office@rdcsa.com
www.rdcsa.com
www.facebook.com/RedDeerCitySoccerAssociation
twitter.com/RDCSA
Overview: A small local organization overseen by Alberta Soccer Association
Member of: Alberta Soccer Association
Staff Member(s): 2
Chief Officer(s):
Joan Van Wolde, Administrator
Ado Sarcevic, Manager, Soccer Operations
asarcevic@rdcsa.com

Red Deer Danish Canadian Club (RDDCC)
PO Box 173, Red Deer AB T4N 5E8
Tel: 403-783-4734
rddcc.com
Overview: A small local organization founded in 1959
Member of: Federation of Danish Associations in Canada
Chief Officer(s):
Pernille Nielsen, President
apernille@live.com

Red Deer Food Bank Society
#12, 7429 - 49 Ave., Red Deer AB T4P 1N2
Tel: 403-342-5355; *Fax:* 403-346-1551
rdfoodbank@hotmail.com
www.linkedin.com/RedDeerFoodbank
www.facebook.com/RedDeerFoodbank
twitter.com/RedDeerFoodBank
Overview: A small local organization founded in 1984
Mission: To feed the hungry; To promote human dignity; To help prevent the senseless waste of food; To develop community awareness of poverty issues; To intervene with policy makers on behalf of those in need
Member of: Food Banks Alberta
Finances: *Annual Operating Budget:* $100,000-$250,000; *Funding Sources:* Public donations
Staff Member(s): 8; 40 volunteer(s)
Membership: 43; *Fees:* $100; *Committees:* Advocacy; Finance
Activities: *Speaker Service:* Yes
Chief Officer(s):
Fred R. Scaife, Executive Director
Alice Kolisnyk, Deputy Director

Red Deer Landlord & Tenant Services *See* Volunteer Red Deer

Red Deer Native Friendship Society
4808-51 Ave., Red Deer AB T4N 4H3
Tel: 403-340-0020; *Fax:* 403-324-1610
anfca.com/friendship-centres/red-deer
Overview: A small local organization founded in 1984 overseen by Alberta Native Friendship Centres Association
Mission: To inform the community of the problems experiences by Aboriginal people living in urban areas, & to work with the community to resolve these problems where possible; To provide a medium for the development of Aboriginal Leadership in the community; To promote friendship & understanding between Aboriginal & Non-Aboriginal people; To preserve & promote Aboriginal Culture & Heritage within the community; To assist Aboriginal people to use & derive advantages from services & facilities & to improve generally the lives of Aboriginal people; To establish organizational leadership, management effectiveness & responsive program planning & delivery in addressing the issues facing the Native community
Member of: Alberta Native Friendship Centres Association
Chief Officer(s):
Lianne Hazell, Executive Director
lhazell@rdnfs.com

Red Deer River Naturalists (RDRN)
PO Box 785, Red Deer AB T4N 5H2
Tel: 403-347-8200; *Fax:* 403-347-8200
rd.rn@hotmail.com
www.rdrn.fanweb.ca
Previous Name: Alberta Natural History Society
Overview: A small local charitable organization founded in 1906
Mission: To foster increased knowledge, understanding & appreciation of natural history; to support conservation measures dealing with environment, wildlife & natural resources; to cooperate with other clubs & organizations having similar views & objectives
Member of: Federation of Alberta Naturalists
Affiliation(s): Canadian Nature Federation
Finances: *Annual Operating Budget:* Less than $50,000; *Funding Sources:* Membership fees; donations; grants
300 volunteer(s)
Membership: 300 individual; *Fees:* $15 individual; $20 family; *Committees:* Habitat Preservation
Activities: Field trips; Habitat Steward Program; educational programs; species counts
Chief Officer(s):
Don Wales, President

Red Deer Symphony Orchestra
Culture Services Centre, 3827 - 39th St., Red Deer AB T4N 0Y6
Tel: 403-340-2948
reddeersymphony@telus.net
www.rdso.ca
www.facebook.com/reddeersymphony
twitter.com/RedDeerSymphony
Overview: A small local charitable organization founded in 1987 overseen by Orchestras Canada
Mission: To provide nationally-recognized, quality symphonic music to central Alberta; To encourage an appreciation for the performance and development of symphonic music in central

Alberta
Member of: Orchestras Canada
Finances: *Annual Operating Budget:* $100,000-$250,000; *Funding Sources:* Corporate & individual sponsors; Online funfraising; Membership fees
Staff Member(s): 5
Membership: 1-99; *Fees:* Schedule available
Activities: Performing concerts; Operating education & outreach programs
Chief Officer(s):
Chandra Kastern, Executive Director
Claude Lapalme, Music Director

Red Lake & District Association for Community Living
PO Box 906, Red Lake ON P0V 2M0
Tel: 807-727-2828; *Fax:* 807-727-1102
Also Known As: Harmony Centre For Community Living
Previous Name: Red Lake & District Association for the Mentally Retarded
Overview: A small local charitable organization founded in 1975
Member of: Community Living Ontario
Activities: Provides support to disabled individuals
Chief Officer(s):
Margaret Kudlowsky, Executive Director

Red Lake & District Association for the Mentally Retarded
See Red Lake & District Association for Community Living

Red Lake District Chamber of Commerce
PO Box 430, 137 Howey St., Red Lake ON P0V 2M0
Tel: 807-727-3722; *Fax:* 807-727-3285
redlakechamber@shaw.ca
www.facebook.com/redlakechamber
Overview: A small local organization
Mission: To promote & improve trade & commerce & the economy, civic & social welfare of the district
Member of: Northwestern Ontario Associated Chambers of Commerce
Membership: *Fees:* Schedule available
Activities: Organizing & promoting trade show & other community events
Chief Officer(s):
Colin Knudsen, President
LaMar Weaver, Vice-President
Cathy Majewski, Second Vice-President
Awards:
• Business Program Award Bursary
; *Amount:* $500

Red Lake Indian Friendship Centre (RLIFC)
PO Box 244, Red Lake ON P0V 2M0
Tel: 807-727-2847; *Fax:* 807-727-3253
www.rlifc.ca
Previous Name: District Indian Youth Club
Overview: A small local charitable organization founded in 1964
Mission: To provide a gathering place for the Aboriginal community in the Red Lake, Ontario region; To promote economic development for Aboriginal people
Member of: Ontario Federation of Indian Friendship Centres
Finances: *Funding Sources:* Donations
Activities: Offering counselling & referral services; Organizing social, recreational, & cultural activities; Working with government official & local service agencies; Engaging in advocacy activities; Providing programs in areas such as prenatal nutrition, fetal alcohol spectrum disorder, child nutrition, & life long care

Red River Apiarists' Association (RRAA)
PO Box 16, RR#5, Winnipeg MB R2C 2Z2
Tel: 204-612-2337
www.beekeepingmanitoba.com
Also Known As: Beekeeping Manitoba
Overview: A small local organization founded in 1963
Mission: To provide members with continuing education in beekeeping skills & to provide a forum for the exchange of beekeeping ideas; To increase public awareness of the value of beekeeping
Finances: *Annual Operating Budget:* Less than $50,000; *Funding Sources:* Membership fees
Membership: 1-99; *Fees:* $25
Activities: Monthly meetings; field day tours; Honey Show; Convention/Symposium; *Library*
Chief Officer(s):
John Speer, Treasurer

Red River Exhibition Association
Red River Exhibition Park, 3977 Portage Ave., Winnipeg MB R3K 2E8
Tel: 204-888-6990; *Fax:* 204-888-6992
www.redriverex.com
www.facebook.com/redriverex
twitter.com/redriverex
www.youtube.com/user/redriverex
Overview: A small local organization founded in 1951
Mission: To enhance the lives of the people of Manitoba by showcasing their talents, abilities & achievements to each other & the world
Member of: Canadian Association Fairs & Exhibitions; International Association Fairs & Exposition; Manitoba Association of Agricultural Societies
Finances: *Annual Operating Budget:* $500,000-$1.5 Million
Staff Member(s): 8; 300 volunteer(s)
Membership: 100-499
Activities: *Awareness Events:* Red River Exhibition; Heart of the Continent Fair
Chief Officer(s):
Garth Rogerson, CEO
garth.rogerson@redriverex.com
Awards:
• Bob Lang Memorial Scholarship

Red Road HIV/AIDS Network (RRHAN)
#61-1959 Marine Dr., North Vancouver BC V7P 3G1
Tel: 778-340-3388; *Fax:* 778-340-3328
info@red-road.org
www.red-road.org
twitter.com/RRHAN
Overview: A small national organization founded in 1999
Mission: The Red Road HIV/AIDS Network works to reduce or prevent the spread of HIV/AIDS; improve the health and wellness of Aboriginal people living with HIV/AIDS; and increase awareness about HIV/AIDS and establish a network which supports the development and delivery of culturally appropriate, innovative, coordinated, accessible, inclusive and accountable HIV/AIDS programs and services
Finances: *Funding Sources:* First Nations & Inuit Health, Health Canada; Public Health Agency of Canada; First Nations Health Authority; private organizations
Membership: *Fees:* $50 full; $25 associate; $5 individual
Activities: Workshops, conferences; support groups
Chief Officer(s):
Kim Louie, Executive Director
klouie@red-road.org
Heidi Standeven, Provincial Coordinator
hstandeven@red-road.org
Publications:
• Bloodlines Magazine
Type: Magazine
Profile: a forum in which Aboriginal Persons Living with HIV/AIDS can share their personal experiences, discuss issues affecting them, offer advice and suggestions to their peers.
• Red Road Aboriginal HIV/AIDS Resource Directory
Type: Directory; *Frequency:* Semi-Annually

Redvers Chamber of Commerce
PO Box 249, Redvers SK S0C 2H0
Tel: 306-452-8844
redverschamberofcommerce@gmail.com
www.redvers.ca
Overview: A small local organization
Mission: To promote local businesses
Membership: 42
Activities: *Awareness Events:* Redvers AgEx & Bull Congress, April
Chief Officer(s):
Kim Krainyk, Contact

Redwater & District Chamber of Commerce
PO Box 322, Redwater AB T0A 2W0
Tel: 780-217-7496
Overview: A small local organization
Affiliation(s): Alberta Chamber of Commerce; Canadian Chamber of Commerce

ReelWorld Film Festival
#300, 438 Parliament St., Toronto ON M5A 3A2
Tel: 416-598-7933
www.reelworld.ca
www.facebook.com/ReelWorld.Film.Festival.Toronto
twitter.com/ReelWorldFilm
www.youtube.com/ReelWorldFestival;
www.flickr.com/photos/reelworldfilm
Overview: A medium-sized local organization founded in 1999
Mission: To present a culturally & racially diverse film festival showcasing films & music videos, & to connect filmmakers with producers, acquisitions personnel & distributors through The RealWorld Foundation.
Chief Officer(s):
Moe Jiwan, Chair & Treasurer
Tonya Lee Williams, Founder, Executive Director & Head, Programming

Reena
927 Clark Ave. West, Thornhill ON L4J 8G6
Tel: 905-889-6484; *Fax:* 905-889-3827
info@reena.org
www.reena.org
www.facebook.com/ReenaFoundation
twitter.com/ReenaFoundation
Previous Name: Reena Foundation
Overview: A medium-sized local charitable organization founded in 1975
Mission: To integrate developmentally disabled people towards independent living within community, with emphasis on Judaic programming
Affiliation(s): Jewish Federation of Greater Toronto
Finances: *Funding Sources:* Provincial government; community fundraising
Activities: Developing programs for children, adults, & seniors with developmental disabilities; *Speaker Service:* Yes
Chief Officer(s):
Lorne Sossin, Chair
Bryan Keshen, President & CEO
bkeshen@reena.org

Reena Foundation *See* Reena

Reflet Salvéo
#202B, 1415 Bathurst St., Toronto ON M5R 3H8
Tél: 647-345-5502; *Téléc:* 647-345-5520; *TTY:* 800-855-0511
info@refletsalveo.ca
www.refletsalveo.ca
www.facebook.com/pagerefletsalveo
twitter.com/refletsalveo
Aperçu: *Dimension:* petite; *Envergure:* locale
Mission: Assurer que les francophones ont un accès égal à des soins de santé de qualité, en français, indépendamment de l'origine, la race, l'orientation, ou le statut
Finances: *Fonds:* Gouvernement provincial
Membre(s) du personnel: 4
Activités: Promouvoir les services de santé à la communauté francophone; Soutenir les fournisseurs de services dans leurs efforts pour offrir des services en français; Travailler avec des groupes communautaires locaux afin de concevoir des programmes de soins de santé de qualité pour les francophones; *Stagiaires:* Oui
Membre(s) du bureau directeur:
Gilles Marchildon, Directeur général, 647-345-5502 Ext. 222
gillesm@refletsalveo.ca
Publications:
• Infolettre [publication de Reflet Salvéo]
Type: Bulletin

Reflexology Association of Canada (RAC) / Association canadienne de réflexologie
#304, 414 Graham Ave., Winnipeg MB R3C 0L8
Tel: 204-477-4909; *Fax:* 204-477-4955
Toll-Free: 877-722-3338
memberservices@reflexolog.org
www.reflexologycanada.ca
Overview: A medium-sized national organization founded in 1976
Mission: To set & maintain high standards among practising reflexologists; To advance quality training; To develop an effective referral system across Canada
Staff Member(s): 5
Activities: *Speaker Service:* Yes
Chief Officer(s):
Judy Carey, Executive Director
Mary Jardine, President

The Reformed Church of Québec. *Voir* L'Église Réformée du Québec

The Reformed Episcopal Church of Canada - Diocese of Western Canada & Alaska (RECWCAN)
Victoria BC
rec-canada.com

Overview: A small national licensing charitable organization founded in 1874
Mission: To reach out to those outside the existing congregation; establish new churches; assist congregations within the Diocese; receive congregations wishing to affiliate with the Reformed Episcopal Church; ordain candidates into the ministry
Affiliation(s): Common Cause Network
Finances: *Annual Operating Budget:* Less than $50,000; *Funding Sources:* Offerings; bequests; church assessments
Staff Member(s): 2
Membership: 300; *Fees:* Church offerings
Activities: Douglas House Retirement Home Ministry; Victoria Prayer Counselling; Healing Rooms; *Internships:* Yes; *Speaker Service:* Yes; *Library:* Diocesan Office Library; by appointment
Chief Officer(s):
Charles W. Dorrington, Bishop Ordinary
recwcan@islandnet.com

Refreshments Canada; Canadian Bottlers of Carbonated Beverages; Canadian Soft Drink Association *See* Canadian Beverage Association

Refrigeration Service Engineers Society (Canada) (RSES Canada)
PO Box 3, Stn. B, Toronto ON M9W 5K9
Tel: 905-842-9199
Toll-Free: 877-955-6255
www.rsescanada.com
Overview: A medium-sized national organization founded in 1952
Mission: To lead all segments of the HVAC industry by providing superior educational & training programs; to create an environment that encourages maximum member participation in the development & decision process of the Society
Member of: Refrigeration Service Engineers Society - International
Finances: *Annual Operating Budget:* $50,000-$100,000; *Funding Sources:* Membership dues; educational seminars
2 volunteer(s)
Membership: 2,200; *Fees:* $125; *Committees:* Awards; Budget & Finance; Bulletin Committee; CFC Training; Commercial Membership; Conference Liaison; Education; Mary Syer Memorial Education Fund; Membership & Welfare; Past Presidents Council; Strategic Planning Committee
Activities: Education program
Chief Officer(s):
Denis Hebert, President, 506-857-3233
denis.hebert@bellaliant.net
Nick Reggi, Secretary, 905-842-9199
dreggi@cogeco.ca

Refugee Action Montreal *Voir* Programme Action Réfugiés Montréal

Refugee Research Network (RRN)
4700 Keele St., 8th Fl., Toronto ON M3J 1P3
Tel: 416-736-2100
www.refugeeresearch.net
www.facebook.com/RefugeeResearchNetwork
twitter.com/refugeeresearch
www.youtube.com/user/refugeeresearch
Overview: A large international organization
Mission: To contribute to the improvement of the well-being of refugees and forced migrants around the world by expanding our awareness of refugee issues and forced migration; To improve communication within & between academic, policy-making and practice sectors in the Global South and North; To engage in alliance-building in the development of national & international policy frameworks and humanitarian practices affecting refugees & forced migrants
Chief Officer(s):
Michele Millard, Project Coordinator, 416-736-2100 Ext. 30391
mmillard@yorku.ca
Susan McGrath, Principal Investigator, 416-736-2100 Ext. 66662
smcgrath@yorku.ca

Regina & District Chamber of Commerce
2145 Albert St., Regina SK S4P 2V1
Tel: 306-757-4658; *Fax:* 306-757-4668
info@reginachamber.com
www.reginachamber.com
www.facebook.com/ReginaChamber
twitter.com/ReginaChamber
www.youtube.com/ReginaChamber
Overview: A small local organization founded in 1886
Mission: To enhance the business community of Regina by actively promoting economic growth & providing a collective voice for the benefit of our members
Affiliation(s): Canadian Chamber of Commerce; Saskatchewan Chamber of Commerce
Finances: *Funding Sources:* Membership fees; programs
Staff Member(s): 9
Membership: *Fees:* Schedule available
Activities: Festival of Lights; programs; services; trade shows; networking; lobbying; Paragon Awards; Business to Business Expo; *Internships:* Yes; *Rents Mailing List:* Yes
Chief Officer(s):
John Hopkins, CEO
jhopkins@reginachamber.com
Nadia Williamson, Chair

Regina & District Food Bank Inc.
445 Winnipeg St., Regina SK S4R 8P2
Tel: 306-791-6533; *Fax:* 306-347-0884
info@reginafoodbank.ca
www.reginafoodbank.ca
twitter.com/ReginaFoodBank
Overview: A medium-sized local charitable organization founded in 1982
Mission: To work in co-operation with others to meet the needs of the hungry in the Regina & district community; To promote an understanding of the issues of poverty & hunger; To facilitate a multi-dimensional holistic approach to those in need, including education, awareness & life skills training; To advocate on behalf of those in need
Member of: Canadian Association of Food Banks
Finances: *Annual Operating Budget:* $3 Million-$5 Million
Staff Member(s): 13; 350 volunteer(s)
Membership: *Fees:* Any taxable donation; *Committees:* Finance & Audit; Governance; Nominations
Activities: Distributing food; Offering education & support programs that address issues of hunger & food insecurity
Chief Officer(s):
Steve Compton, CEO
Publications:
• Regina & District Food Bank Annual Report
Type: Report; *Frequency:* Annually

Regina & District Labour Council (RDLC)
2709 - 12th Ave., #E, Regina SK S4T 1J3
Tel: 306-757-7076
Overview: A medium-sized local organization overseen by Saskatchewan Federation of Labour
Mission: To advance the economic & social welfare of workers in Regina & the surrounding region; To engage in political activity at the municipal level
Affiliation(s): Canadian Labour Congress (CLC)
Membership: 25,560; *Member Profile:* Nineteen unions & forty locals from Regina & the surrounding region
Activities: Increasing the council's affiliate base; Promoting the interests of affiliates; Liaising with the city council to discuss issues of importance to affilitates; Hosting an annual Day of Mourning Ceremony to recognize workers killed on the job; Ensuring that occupational health & safety laws are enforced; Supporting local causes to make the community a better place to work & live; Establishing the Janice Bernier Endowment Fund for long-term food sustainability with the United Way; Coordinating lobbies in Regina ridings

Regina Coin Club (RCC)
PO Box 174, Regina SK S4P 2Z6
Tel: 306-352-2337
info@reginacoinclub.com
www.reginacoinclub.com
www.facebook.com/ReginaCoinClub
twitter.com/ReginaCoinClub
Overview: A small local organization founded in 1953
Mission: To provide numismatic knowledge & good fellowship
Affiliation(s): Canadian Numismatic Association; American Numismatic Association
Finances: *Annual Operating Budget:* Less than $50,000; *Funding Sources:* Coin shows & sales
12 volunteer(s)
Membership: 140; *Fees:* $20 family; $15 regular; $5 junior; *Committees:* Social; Spring & Fall Coin Show
Activities: Meetings; coin shows; CoinHawks Club for kids

Regina Community Foundation *See* South Saskatchewan Community Foundation Inc.

Regina Exhibition Association Ltd. (REAL)
PO Box 167, 1700 Elphinstone St., Regina SK S4P 2Z6
Tel: 306-781-9200; *Fax:* 306-565-3443
Toll-Free: 888-734-3975
info@evrazplace.com
www.evrazplace.com
Overview: A medium-sized local organization founded in 1884
Mission: To provide a forum for the pursuit of excellence in agriculture & other selected fields of endeavour through the management & development of the facilities & grounds of Exhibition Park; To organize, promote & present agriculture, education, sports & entertainment facilities of & for the betterment of the people of the community & the province of Saskatchewan
Member of: Saskatchewan Association of Agricultural Societies & Exhibitions
Affiliation(s): Canadian Association of Fairs & Exhibitions; International Association of Fairs & Exhibitions
Finances: *Annual Operating Budget:* Greater than $5 Million
Staff Member(s): 160; 650 volunteer(s)
Membership: 100-499
Activities: Organizing events including Western Canada Farm Progress Show, Buffalo Days & "Taste of Spring" Food & Beverage Show
Chief Officer(s):
Mark Allan, President & CEO
Denise Wanner, Director, Corporate Governance & Corporate Office

Regina Gliding & Soaring Club
PO Box 4093, Regina SK S4P 3W5
Tel: 306-536-4119
fly@soar.regina.sk.ca
www.soar.regina.sk.ca
Overview: A small local organization
Member of: Soaring Association of Canada; soaring Association of Saskatchewan
Membership: *Fees:* $55-$390

Regina Humane Society Inc.
PO Box 3143, Regina SK S4P 3G7
Tel: 306-543-6363; *Fax:* 306-545-7661; *Crisis Hot-Line:* 306-543-6363
info@reginahumane.ca
www.reginahumanesociety.ca
www.facebook.com/reginahumane
twitter.com/reginahumane
www.instagram.com/reginahumanesociety
Overview: A medium-sized local charitable organization founded in 1965 overseen by Canadian Federation of Humane Societies
Mission: To provide care & shelter for animals; To encourage the humane treatment of animals
Member of: Saskatchewan Society for the Prevention of Cruelty to Animals
Finances: *Funding Sources:* City of Regina; Fundraising
200 volunteer(s)
Membership: 8,000; *Fees:* $5 junior; $15 senior; $25 single; $35 family; $200 lifetime; *Committees:* Board; Promotions; Education; Management; Policy; Philosophy
Activities: Providing Animal shelters; Conducting animal cruelty investigations; Offering education; Providing lost & found services; *Library:* Open to public
Chief Officer(s):
Louise Yates, President

Regina Immigrant Women Centre (RIWC)
1801 Toronto St., Regina SK S4P 1M7
Tel: 306-359-6514; *Fax:* 306-522-9959
info@reginaiwc.ca
www.reginaiwc.ca
www.facebook.com/reginaiwc.ca
twitter.com/ReginaIWC
Also Known As: Immigrant, Refugee & Visible Minority Women of Saskatchewan Inc.
Previous Name: Immigrant Women of Saskatchewan
Overview: A small local organization
Mission: To provide a forum for immigrant women in Saskatchewan to voice their needs & concerns; To provide support & services to immigrant women
Member of: United Way; Multicultural Council of Saskatchewan
Affiliation(s): Regina Multicultural Council
Finances: *Funding Sources:* Municipal, provincial & federal government; Saskatchewan Literacy Commission; Saskatchewan Lotteries
Staff Member(s): 4; 15 volunteer(s)
Membership: 500-999; *Fees:* $5; *Member Profile:* Any immigrant or ethno-racial woman living in Regina

Canadian Associations / Regina Multicultural Council (RMC)

Activities: Drop-in centre; research; information & referral services; educational, recreational & social services; translation services
Chief Officer(s):
Neelu Sachdev, Executive Director
neelu@reginaiwc.ca
Navjeet Parmar, Manager, Finance
navjeet@reginaiwc.ca
Kirandeep Bhullar, Manager, Programs
kirandeep@reginaiwc.ca

Regina Multicultural Council (RMC)
2054 Broad St., Regina SK S4P 1Y3
Tel: 306-757-5990; *Fax:* 306-352-1977
admin.rmc@sasktel.net
reginamulticulturalcouncil.ca
www.facebook.com/RMCMosaic
twitter.com/RMCMosaic
www.instagram.com/mosaicyqr
Overview: A medium-sized provincial charitable organization founded in 1965
Mission: To promote recognition of cultural diversity in Saskatchewan; To recognize, foster & promote the development of multilingualism & to promote positive cross-cultural relations
Affiliation(s): SaskCulture
Finances: *Annual Operating Budget:* $250,000-$500,000
Membership: 50 member groups; 50,000 individuals
Activities: Continuing Education scholarship; Information for new residents; Multicultural festival; *Awareness Events:* Bringing a Little Mosaic to You; *Library:* by appointment
Chief Officer(s):
John Findura, Interim President
Holly Paluck, Secretary

Regina Musicians' Association
2835B - 13 Ave., #G, Regina SK S4T 1N6
Tel: 306-352-1337; *Fax:* 306-359-6558
rma.446@sasktel.net
www.reginamusicians.wordpress.com
www.facebook.com/reginamusicians
Also Known As: AFM Local 446
Overview: A small local organization founded in 1912
Mission: To improve welfare & working conditions for professional musicians
Member of: American Federation of Musicians of the United States & Canada
Affiliation(s): Canadian Conference of Musicians; Canadian Labour Congress; Saskatchewan Federation of Labour
Finances: *Annual Operating Budget:* $50,000-$100,000; *Funding Sources:* Membership dues; fines; assessments
Staff Member(s): 1
Membership: 300+; *Fees:* $154
Activities: Annual charity fundraiser featuring showcase of bands; *Speaker Service:* Yes
Chief Officer(s):
Brian Sklar, President
Alan Denike, Secretary/Treasurer

Regina Orchid Society (ROS)
Regina SK
www.reginaorchidsociety.com
Overview: A small local organization
Mission: To promote orchid gardening & help with the conservation of orchids
Member of: Canadian Orchid Congress
Membership: *Fees:* $20 single; $30 family

Regina Peace Council
Regina SK
Overview: A small local organization founded in 1949
Mission: To help work for world peace & disarmament; To support victims of war & injustice
Member of: Canadian Peace Congress
Affiliation(s): World Peace Council; Canadian Peace Alliance; Regina Coalition for Peace & Disarmament; Saskatchewan Coalition Against Racism
Membership: 20 individual; *Committees:* Editorial Board; Solidarity
Chief Officer(s):
Ed Lehman, President

Regina Philatelic Club
PO Box 1891, Regina SK S4P 3E1
Overview: A small provincial organization founded in 1910

Regina Policemen Association Inc. / Association des agents de police de la ville de Regina
2168 McIntyre St., Regina SK S4P 2R7
Tel: 306-569-2991; *Fax:* 306-522-0053
rpaoffice@reginapoliceassociation.ca
www.reginapoliceassociation.ca
Overview: A small local organization
Mission: To represent the interests of police officers in Regina
Affiliation(s): Saskatchewan Federation of Police Officers; Canadian Police Association
Staff Member(s): 1
Membership: 560
Chief Officer(s):
Casey Ward, President

Regina Regional Opportunities Commission (RROC)
1925 Rose St., Regina SK S4P 3P1
Tel: 306-789-5099; *Fax:* 306-352-1630
Toll-Free: 800-661-5099
info@reginaroc.com
www.reginaroc.com
www.linkedin.com/in/reginaroc
www.facebook.com/ReginaRoc
twitter.com/ReginaRoc
www.youtube.com/user/thereginaroc
Merged from: Tourism Regina Convention & Visitor Bureau; Regina Regional Economic Development Authority
Overview: A medium-sized local organization founded in 2009
Mission: To promote tourism in Regina; To support industry growth & diversification through development
Member of: Tourism Industry Association of Canada
Finances: *Funding Sources:* Municipal government; Saskatchewan Tourism
Staff Member(s): 11
Chief Officer(s):
John Lee, President & CEO
Kim Exner, Director, Corporate Services

Regina Symphony Orchestra (RSO)
2424 College Ave., Regina SK S4P 1C8
Tel: 306-791-6395; *Fax:* 306-586-2133
info@reginasymphony.com
reginasymphony.com
www.facebook.com/reginasymphony
twitter.com/ReginaSymphony
Overview: A small local charitable organization founded in 1908 overseen by Orchestras Canada
Mission: To promote & enhance the performance & enjoyment of live orchestral music in Regina & southern Saskatchewan & contribute to the cultural life of the city, province & nation
Member of: Orchestras Canada
Affiliation(s): Saskatchewan Arts Alliance
Finances: *Funding Sources:* Canada Council; Saskatchewan Arts Board; City of Regina; Individual & corporate donations
Staff Member(s): 9
Activities: Performing concert series; Facilitating education and outreach programs for youth and community members; *Library:* Not open to public
Chief Officer(s):
Tanya Derksen, Executive Director, 306-791-6393
tderksen@reginasymphony.com
Victor Sawa, Music Director

Regina Therapeutic Recreation Association (RTRA)
c/o Sandra Procyk, 1150 Broadway Ave., Regina SK S4P 4V3
regina_tra@hotmail.com
nonprofits.accesscomm.ca/rtra
Overview: A small local organization
Mission: To provide professional development, education, & support to recreation practitioners & students in any vocational setting in Regina & surrounding area
Membership: *Fees:* $20; *Committees:* Membership; Issues; Education; Bursary
Chief Officer(s):
Angela Strelioff, Chair
rec.mutchmor@sasktel.net

Regina Therapeutic Riding Association (RTRA)
PO Box 474, Regina SK S4P 3A2
Tel: 306-530-0794
ReginaTRA@sasktel.net
rtra.ca
www.facebook.com/reginatherapeuticridingassociation
Overview: A small provincial charitable organization founded in 1992
Mission: To provide medically supervised horseback riding lessons for individuals with special needs.

Chief Officer(s):
John Van Knoll, Chair

Regina Transition Women's Society
Regina SK
Tel: 306-757-2096; *Crisis Hot-Line:* 306-569-2292
info@reginatransitionhouse.ca
www.reginatransitionhouse.ca
Also Known As: Regina Transition House
Overview: A small local organization founded in 1975
Mission: To provide shelter, education, support, counselling & advocacy for women & children fleeing any form of abuse by operating a safe temporary shelter with a supportive environment offering a range of services
Member of: Provincial Association of Transition Houses & Services of Saskatchewan
Finances: *Funding Sources:* Provincial Government; United Way; City of Regina
Activities: Safe shelter; 24-hour counselling; 24-hour crisis line; Children's program; Referral & advocacy for clients
Chief Officer(s):
Maria Hendrika, Executive Director
maria@reginatransitionhouse.ca

Regional Halfway House Association (RHHA) / Association régionale des maisons de transition
ON
halfwayhouses.ca
Overview: A medium-sized national organization
Mission: To help offenders reintegrate themselves into society

The Regional Health Authorities of Manitoba (RHAM)
#2, 203 Duffield St., Winnipeg MB R3J 0H6
Tel: 204-833-1720; *Fax:* 204-940-2042
www.rham.mb.ca
Previous Name: Manitoba Health Organizations
Overview: A medium-sized provincial organization founded in 1998 overseen by Canadian Healthcare Association
Mission: To establish programs that help to improve Manitoba health authorities
Finances: *Funding Sources:* Membership fees; service fees
Staff Member(s): 5
Membership: *Member Profile:* Regional health authorities
Activities: *Rents Mailing List:* Yes
Chief Officer(s):
Gayle Hryshko, Interim Executive Director
ghryshko@wrha.mb.ca
Debbie St. Amant, Coordinator, Finance & Administration
dstamant@rham.mb.ca

Regional HIV/AIDS Connection
#30, 186 King St., London ON N6A 1C7
Tel: 519-434-1601; *Fax:* 519-434-1843
Toll-Free: 866-920-1601
info@hivaidsconnection.ca
www.hivaidsconnection.ca
www.facebook.com/189146047805897
twitter.com/_RHAC
www.youtube.com/user/AIDSLondon
Previous Name: AIDS Committee of London
Overview: A small local organization founded in 1985 overseen by Canadian AIDS Society
Mission: To bring people together in partnership to provide leadership in education, support & advocacy to meet the challenge of HIV/AIDS; To create an atmosphere of trust which enables people living with & affected by HIV/AIDS to make informed choices; To serve the counties of Perth, Huron, Lambton, Elgin, Middlesex, & Oxford.
Member of: Ontario AIDS Network
Finances: *Funding Sources:* Provincial & federal ministries of health; fundraising
Staff Member(s): 21
Activities: HIV/AIDS prevention services to those at risk of infection (harm reduction materials, Counterpoint Needle Exchange, Outreach initiatives, educational resources); support services to those with HIV (counselling, practical supports, food program, volunteer assistance); awareness campaigns; *Speaker Service:* Yes; *Library*
Chief Officer(s):
Brian Lester, Executive Director, 519-434-1601 Ext. 243
blester@hivaidsconnection.ca
Mana Khami, President

Regional Occupation Centre Foundation
Regional Occupation Centre, 3 MacQuarrie Dr. Ext., Port Hawkesbury NS B9A 3A3

Tel: 902-625-0132; Fax: 902-625-5344
www.rocsociety.ca/Foundation
Also Known As: ROC Foundation
Overview: A small local charitable organization founded in 2009
Mission: To raise funds to support the mission & objectives of the Regional Occupation Centre Society
Finances: Funding Sources: Donations; fundraisers
Activities: Awareness Events: Harvest Moon Craft Market; Rock for the ROC Bonspiel; Abilities in Disabilities - Bike Run

Regional Occupation Centre Society
3 MacQuarrie Dr., Port Hawkesbury NS B9A 3A3
Tel: 902-625-0132; Fax: 902-625-5344
www.rocsociety.ca
Also Known As: ROC Society
Overview: A small local organization founded in 1975
Mission: To support individuals with disabilities through vocational & community programs
Member of: DIRECTIONS Council for Vocational Services Society
Activities: Vocational work, including woodworking, baking, recycling, mowing contracts & crafts; community activites, including swimming, dance & Special Olympics
Chief Officer(s):
Tom Gunn, President

Regional Solicitors' Association of Ontario See Municipal Law Departments Association of Ontario

Régionale Ringuette Rive-Sud
QC
www.ringuetterivesud.com
www.facebook.com/RegionaleRinguetteRiveSud
twitter.com/RinguetteRRS
instagram.com/regionale_rsud
Aperçu: Dimension: petite; Envergure: provinciale surveillé par Ringuette-Québec
Membre de: Ringuette-Québec
Membre(s) du bureau directeur:
Clémence Duchesneau, Présidente
clemdu@hotmail.com

Registered Deposit Brokers Association (RDBA)
#614, 55 Cedar Pointe Dr., Barrie ON L4N 5R7
Tel: 705-730-7599; Fax: 705-730-0477
Toll-Free: 866-261-6263
headoffice@rdba.ca
www.rdba.ca
Previous Name: Federation of Canadian Independent Deposit Brokers
Overview: A large national organization founded in 1987
Mission: To represent interests of deposit clients & independent deposit brokers
Membership: Fees: $112 affiliate; $725 deposit broker

Registered Insurance Brokers of Ontario (RIBO)
PO Box 45, #1200, 401 Bay St., Toronto ON M5H 2Y4
Tel: 416-365-1900; Fax: 416-365-7664
Toll-Free: 800-265-3097
www.ribo.com
Overview: A medium-sized provincial licensing organization founded in 1981
Mission: To regulate the licensing, professional competence, ethical conduct, & insurance related financial obligations of all independent general insurance brokers in the province
Activities: Licensing & examinations; resources for brokers
Chief Officer(s):
Doug Grahlman, President
dgrahlman@chatsworthinsurance.ca
Beth Pearson, Vice-President
bethp@apont.ca
Patty Crawford, Secretary
pattycrawford@rogers.com
Norma Hitchlock, Treasurer
norma@marshinsurance.com
Jeff Bear, Chief Executive Officer
jeff@ribo.com
Publications:
• Principal Broker Handbook [a publication of the Registered Insurance Brokers of Ontario]
Type: Handbook
Profile: Regulatory requirements & guidelines
• RIBO [Registered Insurance Brokers of Ontario] Bulletin
Type: Newsletter

Registered Massage Therapists' Association of British Columbia (RMTBC)
#180, 1200 West 73rd Ave., Vancouver BC V6P 6G5
Tel: 604-873-4467; Fax: 604-873-6211
Toll-Free: 888-413-4467
info@rmtbc.ca
www.rmtbc.ca
www.facebook.com/MTABC
twitter.com/RMTBC
www.youtube.com/user/MTABCVideo
Overview: A small provincial organization founded in 1983
Mission: To develop & advance the massage therapy profession in BC through education, promotion, empowerment & representation
Finances: Funding Sources: Membership dues
Staff Member(s): 8
Membership: Fees: Schedule available
Chief Officer(s):
Brenda Locke, Executive Director
locke@rmtbc.ca
Joseph Lattanzio, President
joseph@rmtbc.ca

Registered Massage Therapists' Association of Ontario (RMTAO)
#704, 1243 Islington Ave., Toronto ON M8X 1Y9
Tel: 416-979-2010; Fax: 416-979-1144
Toll-Free: 800-668-2022
info@rmtao.com
www.rmtao.com
twitter.com/RMTAO
Previous Name: Ontario Massage Therapist Association
Overview: A medium-sized provincial organization founded in 1936
Mission: To advocate on behalf of all masssage therapists in Ontario; To ensure public access to the services of massage therapists; To encourage high standards for massage therapists
Finances: Funding Sources: Membership fees; Advertising; Sponsorships
Membership: Fees: Schedule available; Member Profile: Registered massage therapists in Ontario; Students of massage therapy
Activities: Creating networking opportunities with professional colleagues; Providing access to technical & clinical information about massage therapy; Offering learning opportunities; Liaising with the government & the College of Massage Therapists of Ontario; Increasing awareness of massage therapy & massage therapists as health professionals
Chief Officer(s):
Andrew Lewarne, Exec. Director and Chief Exec. Officer, 416-979-2010 Ext. 301
andrew@rmtao.com
Jill Haig, Manager, Operations, 416-979-2010 Ext. 303
jill@rmtao.com
Laura Fixman, Contact, Communications & Member Services, 416-979-2010 Ext. 100
laura@rmtao.com
Meetings/Conferences:
• Registered Massage Therapists' Association of Ontario (RMTAO) Education Conference 2018, 2018, ON
Scope: Provincial

Registered Nurses Association of British Columbia See College of Registered Nurses of British Columbia

Registered Nurses Association of Nova Scotia See College of Registered Nurses of Nova Scotia

The Registered Nurses Association of the Northwest Territories & Nunavut (RNANT/NU)
PO Box 2757, Yellowknife NT X1A 2R1
Tel: 867-873-2745; Fax: 867-873-2336
info@rnantnu.ca
www.rnantnu.ca
www.facebook.com/www.rnantnu.ca
Previous Name: Northwest Territories Registered Nurses Association
Overview: A medium-sized provincial licensing organization founded in 1975 overseen by Canadian Nurses Association
Mission: To promote & ensure competent nursing practice for the people of the NWT
Member of: Canadian Nurses Association
Finances: Funding Sources: Membership fees
Staff Member(s): 5
Membership: 1,339; Member Profile: Registered nurses in NWT and Nunavut; Committees: Registration; NP Practice; RN Practice; Professional Conduct; Newsletter
Chief Officer(s):
Donna Stanley-Young, Executive Director, 867-873-2745 Ext. 24
ed@rnantnu.ca
Meetings/Conferences:
• Registered Nurses Association of the Northwest Territories & Nunavut Annual General Meeting 2018, 2018
Scope: Provincial
Publications:
• Connections [a publication of the Registered Nurses Association of the Northwest Territories & Nunavut]
Type: Newsletter; Frequency: 3 pa.; Editor: Elizabeth Cook; Pat Nymark
Profile: Nursing news & events

Registered Nurses' Association of Ontario (RNAO) / L'Association des infirmières et infirmiers autorisés de l'Ontario
158 Pearl St., Toronto ON M5H 1L3
Tel: 416-599-1925; Fax: 416-599-1926
Toll-Free: 800-268-7199
www.rnao.ca
www.facebook.com/RNAOHomeOffice
twitter.com/rnao
www.youtube.com/RNAOVideo
Overview: A large provincial organization founded in 1925 overseen by Canadian Nurses Association
Mission: To promote excellence in nursing practice; To advocate the role of nursing in empowering the people of Ontario to achieve & maintain their optimal health; To provide membership-centred services
Finances: Annual Operating Budget: Greater than $5 Million; Funding Sources: Membership fees; conference fees; educational workshops
Staff Member(s): 30
Membership: 35,000; Fees: $285.19; Member Profile: Registered to practise in province of Ontario
Chief Officer(s):
Carol Timmings, RN, BScN, MEd, President
Doris Grinspun, RN, MSN, PhD, L, Chief Executive Officer
Awards:
• Chapter of the Year
• Interest Group of the Year
• Leadership Award in Political Action
• Leadership Award in Nursing Administration
• Leadership Award in Nursing Education
• Award of Merit
• Leadership Award in Nursing Research
• Leadership Award in Nursing Education (Academic)
• President's Award for Leadership in Clinical Nursing Practice
Meetings/Conferences:
• Registered Nurses' Association of Ontario Annual General Meeting 2018, 2018
Scope: Provincial
• Registered Nurses' Association of Ontario 7th Annual Nurse Executive Leadership Academy, June, 2018, Old Mill Toronto, Toronto, ON
Scope: Provincial
Description: The program features expert faculty from policy, practice and academic settings, providing up-to-date insights for knowledge and competence in governance, policy formulation, evidence-based accountability and leadership.
Publications:
• Registered Nurses' Journal
Type: Journal; Frequency: 6 pa; Editor: Kimberley Kearsey

Registered Practical Nurses Association of Ontario (RPNAO)
Bldg. 4, #200, 5025 Orbitor Dr., Mississauga ON L4W 4Y5
Tel: 905-602-4664; Fax: 905-602-4666
Toll-Free: 877-602-4664
info@rpnao.org
www.rpnao.org
www.facebook.com/RPNAO
twitter.com/rpnao
Overview: A medium-sized provincial organization founded in 1958
Mission: Dedicated to decisions that enhance professional practical nursing
Member of: Ontario Hospital Association; Ontario Association of Non-Profit Homes & Services for Seniors; Canadian Practical Nurses Association
Finances: Funding Sources: Membership fees; education & training revenue
Staff Member(s): 14

Membership: 32,000+; *Fees:* Schedule available; *Member Profile:* RPN with current certificate of registration from College of Nurses; practical nurse student; retired RPN
Activities: Engaging in collective bargaining; *Awareness Events:* Registered Practical Nurses Day, May
Chief Officer(s):
Dianne Martin, RPN, RN, BScN, Executive Director, 905-602-4664 Ext. 226
dmartin@rpnao.org
Beth McCracken, RPN, CAE, Nursing Practice & Outreach Specialist, 905-602-4664 Ext. 227
bmccracken@rpnao.org
Pia Ramos-Javellana, BSc., CGA, Director, Finance, 905-602-4664 Ext. 239
pjavellana@rpnao.org
Publications:
• Registered Practical Nursing Journal
Type: Journal; *Frequency:* Quarterly

Registered Professional Accountants Association of Canada *See* PBA Society of Canada

Registered Professional Foresters Association of Nova Scotia (RPFANS)
PO Box 1031, Truro NS B2N 5G9
Tel: 902-893-0099
contact@rpfans.ca
www.rpfans.ca
Overview: A medium-sized provincial organization founded in 1999
Mission: To improve the holistic management of forest resources in Nova Scotia
Membership: *Member Profile:* Professional foresters in Nova Scotia; Foresters-in-training & students
Activities: Disciplining members who fail to comply with the code of ethics; Ensuring that the public receives proper forest management advice; Encouraging further education
Chief Officer(s):
Roger Aggas, Registrar
John Ross, President
Mike Brown, Treasurer
Meetings/Conferences:
• Registered Professional Foresters Association of Nova Scotia 2018 Annual General Meeting, 2018
Scope: Provincial
Description: A business meeting for Nova Scotia's professional foresters
Publications:
• Forest Steward [a publication of the Registered Professional Foresters Association of Nova Scotia]
Type: Newsletter
Profile: Contents include the message from the president & news from the association & forestry sector

Registered Psychiatric Nurses Association of Alberta *See* College of Registered Psychiatric Nurses of Alberta

Registered Psychiatric Nurses Association of British Columbia *See* College of Registered Psychiatric Nurses of British Columbia

Registered Psychiatric Nurses Association of Manitoba *See* College of Registered Psychiatric Nurses of Manitoba

Registered Psychiatric Nurses Association of Saskatchewan (RPNAS)
2055 Lorne St., Regina SK S4P 2M4
Tel: 306-586-4617; *Fax:* 306-586-6000
www.rpnas.com
Overview: A large provincial licensing organization founded in 1948
Mission: To regulate psychiatric nursing as a distinct profession
Finances: *Funding Sources:* Membership licensing fees
Staff Member(s): 4
Chief Officer(s):
Mike Clory, Director, Operations
Kim Clory, Office Administrator
Awards:
• Baccalaureate Level Program Scholarship
; *Amount:* $1,000
• Master's Level Program Scholarship
; *Amount:* $1,000
• Doctorate Level Program Scholarship
; *Amount:* $2,000
• RPN Bursary
; *Amount:* $500

• Psychiatric Nursing Program Student Year II Terrence B. Christiansen Memorial Bursary
; *Amount:* $200
• Psychiatric Nursing Program Student Year III Joyce P. Long Memorial Bursary
; *Amount:* $300
• Psychiatric Nursing Student Year III Bursary
; *Amount:* $300
• RPN Award - in Recognition of Performance in Nursing
Deadline: April 6

Registered Veterinary Technologists & Technicians of Canada (RVTTC)
PO Box 961, Kemptville ON K0G 1J0
Tel: 613-215-0619
Toll-Free: 844-626-0796
beta.rvttcanada.ca
www.facebook.com/RVTTC
Previous Name: Canadian Association of Animal Health Technologists & Technicians
Overview: A medium-sized national organization founded in 1989
Mission: To provide coordination & resources to support members in the delivery of animal health care services
Member of: International Veterinary Nurses & Technicians Association (IVNTA)
Affiliation(s): Canadian Veterinary Medical Association; National Association of Veterinary Technicians in America (NAVTA)
Finances: *Funding Sources:* Provincial association fees; Corporate sponsorship
Membership: *Committees:* Professional Development; Veterinary Technician Testing; CVMA Animal Health Technology / Veterinary Technician Program Accreditation; CVMA Professional Development
Activities: Facilitating communication links; Providing informational updates; Lobbying to protect & promote the profession; Coordinating national & provincial activities; Promoting Doggone Safe, a national dog bit prevention program; *Awareness Events:* Veterinary Technician Week; Animal Health Week
Chief Officer(s):
Heather Quilty, President
Shannon Brownrigg, Executive Director
Meetings/Conferences:
• Registered Veterinary Technologists & Technicians of Canada 2018 Annual General Meeting, 2018
Scope: National

Regnum Christi Movement
c/o Legionaries of Christ, 19119 Hwy. 2, RR#1, Cornwall ON K6H 5R5
Tel: 613-931-1600
cornwallbm@arcol.org
www.regnumchristi.org/en
www.facebook.com/regnumchristi.english
twitter.com/RegnumChristiEn
www.youtube.com/regnumchristi
Overview: A small international charitable organization founded in 2004
Mission: To love Christ, serve others, & build the Church
Affiliation(s): Archdiocese of Toronto; Legionaries of Christ
Finances: *Funding Sources:* Donations
Membership: *Member Profile:* Catholic young people, adults, deacons, & diocesan priests who wish to experience Christ's love & spread it to others; Members are active in service to the Church
Activities: Leading Christian lives; Taking apostolic action, in cooperation with bishops & parish priests; Providing faith instruction, prayer groups, religious books, & renewal programs; Offering programs, such as Familia, for families to learn & live their Catholic faith, Challenge youth programs, for girls, Catholic Kids Net of Canada Vacation Bible Schools, Conquest Boys' youth programs, Father & Son programs, Compass programs, for university students, & missions, for young people & families
Publications:
• Mission
Type: Newsletter
Profile: Features, news, & events for members of Regnum Christi, their families & friends, & supporters

Regroupement de Bouches à Oreilles (RBO)
#1, 317, rue Lanctôt, Chibougamau QC G8P 2P5
Tél: 418-748-2239; *Téléc:* 418-748-2761
bouchesaoreilles@yahoo.ca
www.abc02.org

Aperçu: Dimension: petite; *Envergure:* locale; fondée en 1983
Mission: Formation de base: compter, lire, écrire
Membre(s) du bureau directeur:
Isabelle Lamontagne, Coordonnatrice

Regroupement de parents de personnes ayant une déficience intellectuelle de Montréal
#911, rue Jean-Talon est, Local 227A, Montréal QC H2R 1V5
Tél: 514-255-3064; *Téléc:* 514-255-3635
www.rppadim.com
Aperçu: Dimension: petite; *Envergure:* locale; Organisme sans but lucratif
Mission: Défendre les droits des personnes ayant une déficience intellectuelle
Membre de: Parents de personne ayant déficience intellectuelle
Affiliation(s): Association du Québec pour l'intégration sociale
Membre(s) du personnel: 14; 10 bénévole(s)
Membre: 300; *Montant de la cotisation:* Parents stimulants, 3$ par semaine; loisirs 150$ par 10 samedis (automne/hiver); 75$ par semaine (été)
Activités: Parents stimulants (0 à 5 ans) et Activités loisirs (15 ans et plus)
Membre(s) du bureau directeur:
Marcel Faulkner, Directeur
marcelfaulkner@rppadim.com

Regroupement des Aidantes et Aidants Naturel(le)s de Montréal (RAANM)
#002, 1150, boul Saint-Joseph est, Montréal QC H2J 1L5
Tél: 514-374-1056; *Téléc:* 514-374-3040
Aperçu: Dimension: petite; *Envergure:* locale
Membre: *Montant de la cotisation:* 5$ individuel; 15$ corporatif; $50 beinfaiteur
Membre(s) du bureau directeur:
Josée Côté, Directrice générale

Regroupement des artistes en arts visuels du Québec (ind.) (RAAV)
460, rue Sainte-Catherine ouest, Montréal QC H3B 1A7
Tél: 514-866-7101; *Téléc:* 514-866-9906
raav@raav.org
www.raav.org
www.facebook.com/RAAVQc
Aperçu: Dimension: petite; *Envergure:* provinciale; fondée en 1989 surveillé par Canadian Artists' Representation
Mission: Représentation collective des intérêts socio-économiques et professionnels des artistes des arts visuels
Finances: *Budget de fonctionnement annuel:* $250,000-$500,000; *Fonds:* Conseil des arts et des lettres du Québec
Membre(s) du personnel: 6; 30 bénévole(s)
Membre: 1 480; *Critères d'admissibilite:* Artiste professionnel en arts visuels
Activités: Défense collective des artistes; conseils représentation officielle; *Stagiaires:* Oui
Membre(s) du bureau directeur:
Manon Pelletier, Présidente
Hélène Rochette, Vice-présidente
Christian Bédard, Directeur

Regroupement des associations de personnes traumatisées craniocérébrales du Québec (RAPTCCQ) / Coalition of Associations of Craniocerebral Trauma in Quebec
220, av du Parc, Laval QC H7N 3X4
Tél: 514-274-7447; *Téléc:* 514-274-1717
info@raptccq.com
www.raptccq.com
www.facebook.com/RAPTCCQ
Aperçu: Dimension: petite; *Envergure:* provinciale; fondée en 1999 surveillé par Brain Injury Association of Canada
Mission: Pour soutenir les personnes vivant avec une lésion cérébrale au Québec
Membre(s) du personnel: 1
Membre: 13 associations; *Critères d'admissibilite:* Associations de traumatisme cranio-cérébral au Québec
Activités: Engaging in advocacy activities on behalf of persons who live with the consequences of brain injury in Québec; Educating the public about brain injuries; Encouraging cooperation between member associations; Facilitating the exchange of information among members; Supporting members' projects
Membre(s) du bureau directeur:
Nicole Tremblay, Présidente
Denis Veilleux, Vice-Président
Pascal Brodeur, Secrétaire et trésorier

Guy Lemieux, Directeur

Regroupement des associations forestières régionales du Québec Voir Association forestières du sud du Québec

Regroupement des assureurs de personnes à charte du Québec (RACQ)
c/o Huis Clos Limitée, #1501, 1445, rue Stanley, Montréal QC H3A 3T1
Tél: 514-282-2207; *Téléc:* 514-282-2214
Aperçu: *Dimension:* petite; *Envergure:* provinciale; fondée en 1995
Mission: Regrouper les compagnies d'assurance à charte québécoise et agir comme porte-parole pour promouvoir leurs intérêts
Membre: *Critères d'admissibilite:* Compagnie d'assurance de personnes à charte québécoise
Membre(s) du bureau directeur:
Jean La Couture, Président-directeur général

Regroupement des Auberges du Coeur Voir La Fondation des Auberges du coeur

Regroupement des aveugles et amblyopes du Montréal métropolitain (RAAMM)
#101, 5225, rue Berri, Montréal QC H2J 2S4
Tél: 514-277-4401; *Téléc:* 514-277-8961
info@raamm.org
www.raamm.org
Aperçu: *Dimension:* petite; *Envergure:* locale; fondée en 1975
Mission: Faire la défense des droits pour les gens avec une déficience visuelle et fournir le service d'aide bénévole
Membre(s) du personnel: 8
Membre: *Montant de la cotisation:* 10$ par membre régulier; 20$ par membre associé; 50$ par membre affinitaire; *Critères d'admissibilite:* Toute personne qui est aveugle ou ambloyope et qui vie dans la région de Montréal
Membre(s) du bureau directeur:
Pascale Dussault, Directrice générale
direction@raamm.org

Regroupement des centres d'amitié autochtone du Québec (RCAAQ)
#100, 85, boul Maurice-Bastien, Wendake QC G0A 4V0
Tél: 418-842-6354; *Téléc:* 418-842-9795
Ligne sans frais: 877-842-6354
infos@rcaaq.info
www.rcaaq.info
www.facebook.com/RCAAQ
twitter.com/rcaaq
www.youtube.com/rcaaq
Aperçu: *Dimension:* moyenne; *Envergure:* nationale; Organisme sans but lucratif; fondée en 1976 surveillé par National Association of Friendship Centres
Mission: Etre la voix provinciale des centres existants ou en voie de développement et de leurs communautés; appuyer ses membres dans l'atteinte de leurs objectifs; favoriser leur concertation et les représenter collectivement pour qu'ils remplissent au mieux leur mandat
Membre(s) du personnel: 12
Membre(s) du bureau directeur:
Tanya Sirois, Directrice générale

Regroupement des éditeurs canadiens-français (RECF)
#402, 450, rue Rideau, Ottawa ON K1N 5Z4
Tél: 613-562-4507; *Téléc:* 613-562-3320
Ligne sans frais: 888-320-8070
info@recf.ca
www.recf.ca
www.facebook.com/RECF.ca
twitter.com/RECF_
Aperçu: *Dimension:* moyenne; *Envergure:* nationale; Organisme sans but lucratif; fondée en 1989
Mission: Former une plate-forme d'échanges et un front commun pour mener des actions concertées pertinentes à l'ensemble des éditeurs canadiens-français, tant sur le plan des politiques que de la promotion, la distribution et le développement de marchés
Membre de: Fédération culturelle canadienne-française
5 bénévole(s)
Membre: 1-99; *Montant de la cotisation:* 100$; *Critères d'admissibilite:* Éditeurs
Membre(s) du bureau directeur:
Marc Haentjens, Président
Serge Patrice Thibodeau, Vice-Président

Catherine Voyer-Léger, Directrice générale
dg@recf.ca
Safiatou Ali, Administratrice
admin@recf.ca
Anne Molgat, Secrétaire
Brigitte Bergeron, Trésorière

Regroupement des femmes de la Côte-de-Gaspé
189, rue Jacques-Cartier, Gaspé QC G4X 2P8
Tél: 418-368-1929; *Téléc:* 418-368-6697
michemingaspe@globetrotter.uil
Aperçu: *Dimension:* petite; *Envergure:* locale
Mission: Promotion de la condition féminine; défense des droits des femmes; formations sur mesure pour les femmes; démarche d'autonomie
Affiliation(s): Regroupement des centres de femmes du Québec
Finances: *Budget de fonctionnement annuel:* $50,000-$100,000; *Fonds:* Provincial government
Membre(s) du personnel: 3; 30 bénévole(s)
Membre: 99; *Montant de la cotisation:* $3
Membre(s) du bureau directeur:
Carmen Boulay, Secrétaire

Regroupement des jeunes chambres de commerce du Québec (RJCCQ)
#1100, 555, boul René-Lévesque ouest, 11e étage, Montréal QC H2Z 1B1
Tél: 514-933-7595
info@rjccq.com
www.rjccq.com
www.linkedin.com/groups?home=&gid=2161090
www.facebook.com/rjccq
twitter.com/RJCCQ
www.youtube.com/user/RJCCQ
Nom précédent: Regroupement des jeunes gens d'affaires du Québec
Aperçu: *Dimension:* petite; *Envergure:* locale; fondée en 1992
Mission: Le RJCCQ soutient un réseau de jeunes chambres de commerce et d'ailes jeunesse à travers le Québec, représentant plus de 8 000 jeunes professionnels, cadres, travailleurs autonomes et entrepreneurs âgés de 18 à 40 ans.
Membre(s) du personnel: 3
Membre: 8,000 individuelles + 34 chambres de commerce
Membre(s) du bureau directeur:
Julie Labrecque, Présidente-directrice générale
Virginie Leblanc, Chargée de projets

Regroupement des jeunes gens d'affaires du Québec Voir Regroupement des jeunes chambres de commerce du Québec

Regroupement des Marocains au Canada (RMC)
3005, boul Cartier ouest, Laval QC H7V 1J3
Tél: 450-681-2133
info@rmc-canada.org
www.rmc-canada.org
www.facebook.com/rmc.marocains.canada
plus.google.com/+Rmc-canadaOrg
Aperçu: *Dimension:* moyenne; *Envergure:* nationale; fondée en 1994
Mission: Promouvoir la fraternité entre les membres de la communauté marocaine au Canada; préserver son identité musulmane
Membre: *Montant de la cotisation:* 25$ membre; 10$ étudiant
Membre(s) du bureau directeur:
Lahcen Baissi, Président

Regroupement des offices d'habitation du Québec (ROHQ)
#170, 1135, Grande Allée ouest, Québec QC G1S 1E7
Tél: 418-527-6228; *Téléc:* 418-527-6382
Ligne sans frais: 800-463-6257
rohq@rohq.qc.ca
www.rohq.ca
Nom précédent: Association des offices municipaux d'habitation du Québec
Aperçu: *Dimension:* petite; *Envergure:* provinciale; Organisme sans but lucratif; fondée en 1972
Mission: Représenter, informer, former des offices municipaux d'habitations du Québec
Membre de: Réseau Habitat et Francophonie
Membre(s) du personnel: 8
Membre: *Comités:* Gouvernance et orientations stratégiques; Consultatif de formation; retraite; Paritaire de l'assurance collective
Activités: Congrès; rencontres régionales, *Service de conférenciers:* Oui

Membre(s) du bureau directeur:
Denis Robitaille, Directeur général
denis.robitaille@rohq.qc.ca

Regroupement des organismes de bassins versants du Québec (ROBVQ)
#106, 870, av de Salaberry, Québec QC G1R 2T9
Tél: 418-800-1144; *Téléc:* 418-780-6666
info@robvq.qc.ca
www.robvq.qc.ca
twitter.com/mclerc
www.youtube.com/user/lesobvduquebec
Aperçu: *Dimension:* petite; *Envergure:* provinciale; fondée en 2001
Mission: Le Regroupement des organismes de bassins versants du Québec (ROBVQ) est un organisme à but non lucratif créé et reconnu par le ministère du Développement durable, de l'Environnement et de la Lutte contre les changements climatiques du Québec comme étant son interlocuteur privilégié pour la mise en place de la gestion intégrée de l'eau par bassin versant au Québec.
Membre: 40; *Critères d'admissibilite:* Organismes de bassins versants du Québec
Membre(s) du bureau directeur:
Marie-Claude Leclerc, Directrice générale
mcleclerc@robvq.qc.ca
Publications:
• Tempo
Type: Newsletter; *Frequency:* 6 pa
Profile: Le bulletin de liaison Tempo du ROBVQ vise à diffuser l'information relative aux programmes, projets et dossiers en cours du ROBVQ. Il permet aussi de mettre en lumière certaines initiatives ou projets d'envergure entrepris par les organisations de bassin versant membres du ROBVQ.

Regroupement des personnes vivant avec le VIH-sida de Québec et la région
#100, 190 O'Connor St., Ottawa ON K2P 2R3
Tél: 613-230-3580; *Téléc:* 613-563-4998
casinfo@cdnaids.ca
www.facebook.com/aidsida
twitter.com/CDNAIDS
Aperçu: *Dimension:* petite; *Envergure:* locale; fondée en 1990 surveillé par Canadian AIDS Society
Mission: Regrouper les personnes vivant avec le VIH/sida
Finances: *Budget de fonctionnement annuel:* Moins de $50,000
Membre(s) du personnel: 5; 11 bénévole(s)
Membre: *Montant de la cotisation:* $100-$2,000, calculated based on member organization's annual budget; *Critères d'admissibilite:* 73

Regroupement des professionnels de la construction Richelieu Yamaska Voir Association de la Construction Richelieu Yamaska

Regroupement des professionnels de la danse du Québec Voir Regroupement québécois de la danse

Regroupement des Sourds de Chaudière-Appalaches (RSCA)
1294, ch Filteau, Saint-Nicolas QC G7A 2L7
Tél: 418-831-3723; *Téléc:* 418-831-3723; *TTY:* 418-831-3723
rsca@globetrotter.net
www.facebook.com/834524883229339
Nom précédent: Association des Sourds de Beauce
Aperçu: *Dimension:* petite; *Envergure:* locale; Organisme sans but lucratif; fondée en 1982
Mission: Travailler à l'amélioration des conditions de vie des personnes sourdes et malentendantes; les regrouper; les représenter et les supporter afin qu'elles aient accès et reçoivent tous les services auxquels elles ont droit et ce, dans leur langue respective; défense de droits
Membre de: Centre québécois de la déficience auditive; Regroupement des associations de personnes handicapées région Chaudière-Appalaches; Coallitions Sida des sourds du Québec
Finances: *Budget de fonctionnement annuel:* Moins de $50,000; *Fonds:* Agence de santé et des services sociaux
Membre(s) du personnel: 6; 15 bénévole(s)
Membre: 85; *Montant de la cotisation:* 15$ membre actif; 12$ membre associé; 10$ membre partenaire
Activités: Conférences portant sur des thèmes touchant la surdité des enfants; distribution de dépliants; cours de Langue des signes Québécoise; rencontres d'information; conférences; activités mensuelles; accueil et référence; rencontres individuelle pour aider le Sourd dans différentes sphères de la vie

Canadian Associations / Regroupement pour l'intégration dans la communauté de Rivière-des-Prairies

Membre(s) du bureau directeur:
Michel Laurent, Directeur

Regroupement des universités de la francophonie Hors-Québec *Voir* Association des universités de la francophonie canadienne

Regroupement pour l'intégration dans la communauté de Rivière-des-Prairies
3418, Place Désy, Laval QC H7P 3J2
Tél: 450-629-0096; *Téléc:* 450-629-1726
ropphl.free.fr/ricrp.htm
Aperçu: *Dimension:* petite; *Envergure:* locale.
Mission: Promouvoir et défendre les droits des personnes ayant une déficience intellectuelle et leur famille; améliorer les conditions de vie des personnes ayant une déficience intellectuelle. Soutien aux parents et aux personnes ayant une déficience intellectuelle; rédaction de dossiers et de mémoires
Affiliation(s): Association du Québec pour l'intégration sociale
Membre: *Critères d'admissibilite:* Personnes ayant une déficience intellectuelle et leur famille

Regroupement pour l'intégration sociale de Charlevoix (RISC)
#301, 367, rue St-Étienne, La Malbaie QC G5A 1M3
Tél: 418-665-7811
rischarlevoix@hotmail.com
Aperçu: *Dimension:* petite; *Envergure:* locale; Organisme sans but lucratif; fondée en 1990
Mission: Regrouper les parents d'enfants ayant une déficience intellectuelle; offrir du support, de l'entraide, de l'info, quant aux droits et intérêts de leurs enfants; favoriser la concertation avec les organismes communautaires, les établissements du réseaux, pour mieux répondre aux familles; sensibiliser la population face à la différence; informer les familles sur l'entraide et formation, la documentation et les services existants; proposer des activités culturelles, sociales et éducatives aux membres et leurs familles
Affiliation(s): Association du Québec pour l'intégration sociale
Finances: *Budget de fonctionnement annuel:* Moins de $50,000
Membre(s) du personnel: 1; 7 bénévole(s)
Membre: 26; *Montant de la cotisation:* 5$ par famille par année; *Critères d'admissibilite:* Famille avec un ou plusieurs enfants handicapés, trouble d'apprentissage, retard de développement
Activités: Semaine Québécoise de la déficience intellectuelle; social pour les jeunes; sorties familiales; rencontres d'échange; sensibilisation; intégration; *Événements de sensibilisation:* Semaine Québécoise en déficience intellectuelle, mars

Regroupement pour la surveillance du nucléaire *See* Canadian Coalition for Nuclear Responsibility

Regroupement pour la Trisomie 21 (RT21)
#1A, 3250 boul Saint-Joseph est, Montréal QC H1Y 3G2
Tél: 514-850-0666
info@trisomie.qc.ca
www.trisomie.qc.ca
www.linkedin.com/company/regroupement-pour-la-trisomie-21
www.facebook.com/trisomie
twitter.com/Trisomie21QC
Aperçu: *Dimension:* petite; *Envergure:* provinciale
Mission: Favoriser le plein développement des personnes ayant une trisomie 21
Membre(s) du bureau directeur:
Geneviève Labrecque, Directrice générale
genevievelabrecque@trisomie.qc.ca

Regroupement Pour-Valorisation
430, rue Principale est, Farnham QC J2N 1L8
Tél: 450-293-0066
Aperçu: *Dimension:* petite; *Envergure:* locale; fondée en 2001
Mission: Promouvoir le patrimoine religieux; d'établir des liens entre les différentes églises et de créer des partenariats avec des organisations oecuméniques
Membre(s) du bureau directeur:
Michel Goudoury, Propriétaire

Regroupement provincial des maisons d'hébergement et de transition pour femmes victimes de violence conjugale
CP 55005, Succ. Notre-Dame, 11, rue Notre-Dame ouest, Montréal QC H2Y 4A7
Tél: 514-878-9134; *Téléc:* 514-878-9136
info@maisons-femmes.qc.ca
www.maisons-femmes.qc.ca
www.facebook.com/RMFVVC
Aperçu: *Dimension:* petite; *Envergure:* locale; fondée en 1979

Mission: Venir en aide aux femmes victimes de violence conjugale et leurs enfants, par tous les moyens jugés nécessaires et appropriés; 51 maisons membres
Finances: *Budget de fonctionnement annuel:* $250,000-$500,000; *Fonds:* Gouvernement provincial
Membre(s) du personnel: 4; 1 bénévole(s)
Membre: 48 associés

Regroupement québécois de la danse (RQD)
#440, 3680, rue Jeanne-Mance, Montréal QC H2X 2K5
Tél: 514-849-4003; *Téléc:* 514-849-3288
Autres numéros: www.flickr.com/photos/rqd
info@quebecdanse.org
www.quebecdanse.org
www.facebook.com/quebecdanse
twitter.com/quebecdanse
www.youtube.com/user/quebecdanse
Nom précédent: Regroupement des professionnels de la danse du Québec
Aperçu: *Dimension:* moyenne; *Envergure:* nationale; Organisme sans but lucratif; fondée en 1984
Mission: Promouvoir, encourager et soutenir le développement artistique, social et économique des danseurs, chorégraphes et de tout intervenant professionnel de la communauté de la danse au Québec
Membre de: Conférence canadienne des arts; Coalition québécoise des arts de la scène; Les Arts et La Ville; Le mouvement pour les arts et les lettres
Affiliation(s): Agora de la danse; Regroupement québécois des créateurs professionnels
Finances: *Budget de fonctionnement annuel:* $250,000-$500,000
Membre(s) du personnel: 8
Membre: 500; *Montant de la cotisation:* Barème; *Critères d'admissibilite:* Individu - formation complétée; deux ans d'expérience; Organisme - organismes de création, production, diffusion établies au Québec; *Comités:* Formation; Interprétation; c/prd (création/production/diffusion)
Activités: *Service de conférenciers:* Oui
Membre(s) du bureau directeur:
Fabienne Cabado, Directrice générale

Regroupement québécois des maladies orphelines (RQMO) / Québec Coalition for Orphan Diseases
l'Institut de recherches cliniques de Montréal (IRCM), 110, av des Pins ouest, Montréal QC H2W 1R7
Tél: 514-987-5659
administration@rqmo.org
www.rqmo.org
www.facebook.com/139256366104757
twitter.com/maladorphelines
www.youtube.com/user/RQMOMalOrph
Aperçu: *Dimension:* petite; *Envergure:* provinciale; Organisme sans but lucratif; fondée en 2010
Mission: Améliorer la recherche, le financement, et la sensibilisation concernant les maladies rares au Québec
Finances: *Fonds:* Donations
Membre: *Montant de la cotisation:* 10$ individuel; 40$ association
Activités: Fournir aux patients et aux familles des renseignements et des ressources; Organiser un répertoire de ressources; Fournir de l'information sur les médicaments; *Événements de sensibilisation:* jour de maladie rare, février
Membre(s) du bureau directeur:
Gail Ouellette, Directrice générale

Regroupement québécois des organismes pour le développement de l'employabilité (RQuODE)
#202, 533, rue Ontario est, Montréal QC H2L 1N8
Tél: 514-721-3051; *Téléc:* 514-721-9114
inforquode@rquode.com
www.rquode.com
Aperçu: *Dimension:* moyenne; *Envergure:* provinciale; fondée en 1987
Mission: Favoriser l'intégration au travail des personnes éprouvant des difficultés sur le plan de l'emploi en regroupant et soutenant les organismes communautaires spécialisés en développement de l'employabilité
Finances: *Budget de fonctionnement annuel:* $100,000-$250,000; *Fonds:* Développement des ressources humaines du Canada
Membre(s) du personnel: 1
Membre: 54 membres qui sont répartis dans 11 des 17 régions du Québec; *Montant de la cotisation:* 600$
Activités: *Listes de destinataires:* Oui
Membre(s) du bureau directeur:
Valérie Roy, Directrice générale
vroy@rquode.com

Regroupement QuébecOiseaux
4545, av Pierre-de Coubertin, Montréal QC H1V 0B2
Tél: 514-252-3190; *Téléc:* 514-251-8038
Ligne sans frais: 888-647-3289
info@quebecoiseaux.org
www.quebecoiseaux.org
Nom précédent: Association québécoise des groupes d'ornithologues
Aperçu: *Dimension:* moyenne; *Envergure:* provinciale; Organisme sans but lucratif; fondée en 1981
Mission: Favoriser le développement du loisir ornithologique; promouvoir l'étude des oiseaux; veiller à leur protection et à celle de leurs habitats
Finances: *Budget de fonctionnement annuel:* $100,000-$250,000
Membre(s) du personnel: 4; 13 bénévole(s)
Membre: 6 000; *Montant de la cotisation:* Barème; *Critères d'admissibilite:* Toute personne intéressée par l'observation des oiseaux
Activités: Banques de données; *Stagiaires:* Oui
Membre(s) du bureau directeur:
Jean-Sébastien Guénette, Directeur général

Rehabilitation Society of Calgary *See* Prospect Human Services

Rehabilitation Society of Southwestern Alberta
Ability Resource Centre, 1610 - 29th St. North, Lethbridge AB T1H 5L3
Tel: 403-329-3911; *Fax:* 403-329-3581
staff@rehab.ab.ca
www.abilityresource.ca
Overview: A small local charitable organization
Mission: To support adults living with disabilities & provide them with a means of accessing opportunities; to facilitate personal growth; to promote inclusion
Activities: Operates the JobLinks Employment Centre & the Ability Resource Centre
Chief Officer(s):
Guy McNab, President
Paige McCann Sauter, Executive Director
paige@rehab.ab.ca
JobLinks Employment Centre
416 - 8th St. South, Lethbridge AB T1J 2J7
Tel: 403-317-4550; *Fax:* 403-317-4552
joblinks@rehab.ab.ca
www.job-links.ca

REHOBOTH Christian Ministries
3920 - 49th Ave., Stony Plain AB T7Z 2J7
Tel: 780-963-4044; *Fax:* 780-963-3075
provincial_admin@rehoboth.ab.ca
rehoboth.ab.ca
Also Known As: Christian Association for the Mentally Handicapped of Alberta
Overview: A medium-sized provincial charitable organization founded in 1976
Mission: To convey God's love to persons with disabilities through support, advocacy & public education, & by providing opportunities for personal growth & meaningful participation in society
Member of: Alberta Council of Disability Services; Canadian Centre for Philanthropy
Affiliation(s): Christian Stewardship Services
Finances: *Annual Operating Budget:* Greater than $5 Million; *Funding Sources:* Provincial government; membership fees; donations; church offerings
Staff Member(s): 535; 950 volunteer(s)
Membership: 4,600; *Fees:* $10; *Member Profile:* Everybody accepting their mission statement; *Committees:* Regional Advisory
Activities: Residential, vocational & recreational support for individuals who live with disabilities; summer camp program; fundraising golf tournament; *Internships:* Yes
Chief Officer(s):
Ron Bos, Executive Director
ron.bos@rehoboth.ab.ca
Calgary Branch
#20, 3740 - 27 St. NE, Calgary AB T1Y 5E2
Tel: 403-250-7333; *Fax:* 403-250-7148
calgary_region@rehoboth.ab.ca
Coaldale Branch
PO Box 1312, Coaldale AB T1M 1N1

Tel: 403-345-5199; *Fax:* 403-345-3483
coaldale_region@rehoboth.ab.ca
Grande Prairie Branch
#1063 - 3, 9899 - 112 Ave, Grande Prairie AB T8V 7T2
Tel: 780-532-5611; *Fax:* 780-532-5642
grandeprairie@rehoboth.ab.ca
Stony Plain Branch
3920 - 49th Ave., Stony Plain AB T7Z 2J7
Tel: 780-968-4315; *Fax:* 780-968-4318
stonyplain@rehoboth.ab.ca
Three Hills Branch
117 - 4th Ave. South, Three Hills AB T0M 2A0
Tel: 403-443-2239; *Fax:* 403-443-2399
threehills_region@rehoboth.ab.ca

Rehtaeh Parsons Society
NS
rehtaehparsons.ca
www.facebook.com/angelrehtaehofficial
twitter.com/angelrehtaeh
Overview: A small national organization founded in 2014
Mission: To prevent sexual assault & cyber-harassment; to raise awareness of suicide & mental health; to support victims & engage in public education of healthy relationships
Finances: *Funding Sources:* Donations
Activities: Outreach to schools, youth groups, assault centres, & community members; funding other non-profits with similar mandates; pursuing reforms in education, healthcare, & law enforcement.
Chief Officer(s):
Glen Canning, Co-founder
Leah Parsons, Co-founder

Reinforcing Steel Institute of Ontario (RSIO)
PO Box 30104, RPO New Westminster, Thornhill ON L4J 0C6
Tel: 416-239-7746; *Fax:* 416-239-7745
rsio@rebar.org
www.rebar.org
Overview: A small provincial organization
Mission: To promote reinforced concrete as a building material
Membership: 36

Reinsurance Research Council (RRC) / Conseil de recherche en réassurance (CRR)
#1, 189 Queen St. East, Toronto ON M5A 1S2
Tel: 416-968-0183; *Fax:* 416-968-6818
mail@rrccanada.org
www.rrccanada.org
Overview: A small national organization founded in 1973
Mission: Represents the majority of professional reinsurers registered in Canada; conducts research into all lines of property/casualty reinsurance, presents the views of its members where appropriate, and provides liaison with governments, the primary insurance market, & other interested parties; promotes high standards of service and ethical business practices; develops and maintains cordial relations among members and with kindred associations and the public
Finances: *Funding Sources:* Membership dues
Membership: 19 corporate; *Member Profile:* Licenced reinsurers; *Committees:* Executive; Finance; Underwriting Research
Chief Officer(s):
Anthony Laycock, General Manager

Relance jeunes et familles
2700, rue de Rouen, Montréal QC H2K 1N1
Tél: 514-525-1508
info@relance.org
www.relance.org
Aperçu: *Dimension:* petite; *Envergure:* locale
Mission: Pour aider les enfants défavorisés et leur famille aient des chances égales en offrant des ateliers éducatifs pour les familles et les activités de loisirs pour les enfants
Membre(s) du personnel: 19
Membre(s) du bureau directeur:
Benoit DeGuire, Directeur général
direction@relance.org

Religious Freedom Council of Christian Minorities *See* The Bible Holiness Movement

The Renascent Centres for Alcoholism & Drug Addiction
Lillian & Don Wright Family Health Centre, 38 Isabella St., Toronto ON MR7 1N1
Tel: 416-927-1202; *Fax:* 416-927-0331
Toll-Free: 866-232-1212
info@renascent.ca
www.renascent.ca
www.linkedin.com/company/renascent
www.facebook.com/RenascentCanada
twitter.com/renascentcanada
Also Known As: Renascent
Overview: A small local charitable organization founded in 1970
Mission: To facilitate prevention, education & recovery from addiction to alcohol & other drugs through a continuum of programs & services with equitable access
Finances: *Annual Operating Budget:* $3 Million-$5 Million
Staff Member(s): 80; 150 volunteer(s)
Membership: 1-99
Activities: Operating treatment centres; Facilitating recovery & rehab services; Offering drug & alcohol prevention education; *Internships:* Yes; *Speaker Service:* Yes
Chief Officer(s):
Patrick Smith, Chief Executive Officer
Publications:
• Renascent Annual Report
Type: Report; *Frequency:* Annually

Renewable Industries Canada
#450, 55 Murray St., Ottawa ON K1N 5M3
Tel: 613-594-5528; *Fax:* 613-594-3076
www.ricanada.org
www.linkedin.com/company/860794
www.facebook.com/RenewCan
twitter.com/RenewCan
Also Known As: RICanada
Previous Name: Canadian Renewable Fuels Association
Overview: A medium-sized national organization founded in 1984
Mission: To promote renewable fuel development & usage
Finances: *Funding Sources:* Membership dues
Staff Member(s): 3
Membership: 35; *Fees:* Schedule available; *Member Profile:* Representatives from all levels of the ethanol & biodiesel industries
Activities: Liaising with government; Promoting policy initiatives advantageous to ethanol & biodiesel fuel development; Increasing awareness of ethanol & biodiesel; Conducting research; *Speaker Service:* Yes
Chief Officer(s):
Andrea Kent, President
a.kent@ricanada.org
William Meyer, Manager, Communications & Stakeholder Relations
w.meyer@ricanada.org

Renfrew & Area Chamber of Commerce
161 Raglan St. South, Renfrew ON K7V 1R2
Tel: 613-432-7015; *Fax:* 613-432-8645
info@renfrewareachamber.ca
www.renfrewareachamber.ca
Overview: A small local organization
Mission: To be the recognized voice of business committed to improving the economy of Renfrew & area
Member of: Canadian Chamber of Commerce
Finances: *Funding Sources:* Town grant; membership fee
Staff Member(s): 1
Membership: 120; *Committees:* Tourism; Industrial Lumber Baron Festival; Year Book
Chief Officer(s):
Kent Tubman, President
Awards:
• Citizen of the Year
• Business Achievement Award

Renfrew & District Association for the Mentally Retarded *See* Community Living Renfrew County South

Renfrew & District Food Bank
163 Argyle St. South, Renfrew ON K7V 2X9
Tel: 613-433-9216
Overview: A small local organization
Member of: Ontario Association of Food Banks

Renfrew & District Historical Society
PO Box 554, Renfrew ON K7V 4B1
Tel: 613-432-7015
museum@renfrewmuseum.ca
www.renfrewmuseum.ca
Overview: A small local charitable organization
Mission: To operate McDougall Mill Museum
Member of: Ontario Museum Association; Ontario Historical Association; Chamber of Commerce
Affiliation(s): Ottawa Valley Travel Association

Renfrew County Child Poverty Action Network (CPAN)
130 Pembroke St. West, Pembroke ON K8A 5M8
Tel: 613-735-2374; *Fax:* 613-735-2378
Toll-Free: 800-465-1870
cpan@phoenixctr.com
www.renfrewcountycpan.ca
www.facebook.com/childpovertyactionnetwork
twitter.com/RenfrewCPAN
Overview: A small local organization founded in 2000
Mission: CPAN is involved with a number of activities related to the elimination of child poverty and minimizing the effect that poverty has on children living in Renfrew County.
Membership: 450 individuals; 61 agencies and organizations

Renfrew County Law Association
#1211, 297 Pembroke St. East, Pembroke ON K8A 3K2
Tel: 613-732-4880; *Fax:* 613-732-2262
rcla@bellnet.ca
www.rcla.on.ca
Overview: A small local organization
Activities: *Library:* County Courthouse Library
Chief Officer(s):
Michael March, President

Renfrew County Real Estate Board (RCREB)
197 Pembroke St. East, Pembroke ON K8A 3J6
Tel: 613-735-5840; *Fax:* 613-735-0405
www.renfrewcountyrealestateboard.com
www.facebook.com/RCREB
Overview: A small local organization founded in 1975 overseen by Ontario Real Estate Association
Mission: To promote standard practices among its members in order to unify & strengthen their abilities
Member of: The Canadian Real Estate Association; Ontario Real Estate Association
Membership: 160
Chief Officer(s):
Sue Martin, Executive Officer
eo@rcreb.com

Renfrew County United Way
224 Pembroke St. West, Pembroke ON K8A 5N2
Tel: 613-735-0436; *Fax:* 613-735-2663
Toll-Free: 888-592-2213
info@renfrewcountyunitedway.ca
www.renfrewcountyunitedway.ca
www.facebook.com/182315931870874
Merged from: United Way/Centraide of the Upper Ottawa Valley Inc. and The Deep River District United Way
Overview: A small local charitable organization founded in 1971 overseen by United Way of Canada - Centraide Canada
Mission: To identify & address the needs of our community by organizing the resources of community members to care for one another
Affiliation(s): Arnprior Community Council; Upper Ottawa Valley Chamber of Commerce; Pembroke Downtown Development Commission
Finances: *Funding Sources:* Donations
Membership: *Member Profile:* Non-profit organization, health & social services
Activities: Star-light Night Golf; 24-hour Ball Marathon
Chief Officer(s):
Shelley Rolland-Porucks, Chair
Gail Logan, Executive Director

Renfrew Family & Child Services *See* Family & Children's Services of Renfrew County

Rental Association of Canada *See* Canadian Rental Association

Rental Owners & Managers Society of British Columbia; Apartment Owners & Property Managers Association of Vancouver Island *See* LandlordBC

Reorganized Church of Jesus Christ of Latter Day Saints (Canada) *See* Community of Christ - Canada East Mission

Repaire jeunesse Dawson *See* Boys & Girls Clubs of Québec

Repaire jeunesse de Moncton *See* Boys & Girls Clubs of New Brunswick

Canadian Associations / Research & Development Institute for the Agri-Environment / Institut de recherche et de développement en agroenvironnement (IRDA)

Répertoire canadien des psychologues offrant des services de santé *See* Canadian Register of Health Service Psychologists

Research & Development Institute for the Agri-Environment / Institut de recherche et de développement en agroenvironnement (IRDA)
270, rue Einstein, Québec QC G1P 3W8
Tel: 418-643-2380; *Fax:* 418-644-6855
info@irda.qc.ca
www.irda.qc.ca
www.facebook.com/irdaqc
twitter.com/irda_qc
www.linkedin.com/company/2570365
Overview: A medium-sized national organization founded in 1998
Mission: To contribute to the sustainable development of agriculture, through research, knowledge acquisition, & transfer activities
Staff Member(s): 100
Activities: Publishing fact sheets, research reports, scientific papers, & technology transfer papers
Chief Officer(s):
Pierre Lemieux, President, Board
Georges Archambault, President & CEO
georges.archambault@irda.qc.ca
Stéphane P. Lemay, Director, Research & Development
stephane.lemay@irda.qc.ca
Publications:
• Agrosolutions Express [a publication of the Research & Development Institute for the Agri-Environment]
Type: Newsletter; *Frequency:* Monthly
Profile: French only; information on new projects, new publications & upcoming activities

Research & Education Foundation of the College of Family Physicians of Canada *See* Foundation for Advancing Family Medicine of the College of Family Physicians of Canada

Research Council Employees' Association (Ind.) (RCEA) / Association des employés du conseil de recherches (ind.) (AECR)
PO Box 8256, Stn. Alta Vista Terminal, Ottawa ON K1G 3H7
Tel: 613-746-9341; *Fax:* 613-745-7868
office@rcea.ca
www.rcea.ca
Overview: A medium-sized local organization founded in 1966
Mission: To act as the certified bargaining agent for six groups and categories and represents the majority of NRC employees, which are: AD (Administrative Support) Group, AS (Administrative Services) Group, CS (Computer Systems Administration) Group, OP (Operational) Category, PG (Purchasing and Supply) Group, and TO(Technical) Category.
Member of: National Joint Council
Finances: *Funding Sources:* Membership dues
Staff Member(s): 6
Membership: 1,600
Chief Officer(s):
Cathie Fraser, President
cathie@rcea.ca

Réseau ACCESS Network
#203, 111 Elm St., Sudbury ON P3C 1T3
Tel: 705-688-0500
Toll-Free: 800-465-2437
aainfo@reseauaccessnetwork.com
www.accessaidsnetwork.com
Also Known As: Réseau ACCESS Network HIV/Hepatitis Health & Social Services Services
Previous Name: AIDS Committee of Sudbury; Access AIDS Committee
Overview: A small local organization founded in 1989 overseen by Canadian AIDS Society
Mission: To serve the needs of HIV positive individuals living in Algoma, Sudbury, & Manitoulin.
Affiliation(s): Canada Helps; Ontarion Aboriginal HIV/AIDS Strategy; Sudbury Action Centre for Youth; HAVEN Program

Réseau ACTION TI
Tour Ouest, #355, 550, rue Sherbrooke ouest, Montréal QC H3A 1B9
Tél: 514-840-1240; *Téléc:* 514-840-1243
info@actionTI.com
www.actionti.com
www.linkedin.com/groups/90428
www.facebook.com/ActionTI
twitter.com/ActionTI
www.youtube.com/reseauactionti
Nom précédent: Fédération de l'informatique du Québec
Aperçu: *Dimension:* moyenne; *Envergure:* provinciale
Mission: De regrouper et de mobiliser les acteurs du secteur des technologies de l'information au Québec; de créer des occasions de rassemblement et aide à l'amélioration des connaissances et des compétences; de souligner la qualité des réalisations et de contribuer à valoriser les TI au Québec.
Membre(s) du personnel: 10
Membre: 2,300; *Montant de la cotisation:* Barème
Membre(s) du bureau directeur:
Patrice-Guy Martin, Président-directeur général, 514-840-1255
pgmartin@actionti.com

Réseau aéronefs amateur *See* Recreational Aircraft Association

Reseau Biblio de l'Abitibi-Témiscamingue Nord-du-Québec
20, av Québec, Rouyn-Noranda QC J9X 2E6
Tél: 819-762-4305; *Téléc:* 819-762-5309
info@reseaubiblioatnq.qc.ca
mabiblio.quebec
www.facebook.com/335729189842131
www.youtube.com/user/Mouvi1
Aperçu: *Dimension:* petite; *Envergure:* locale; fondée en 1985
Mission: Promotion du livre et de la lecture en Abitibi-Témiscamingue; promotion des bibliothèques
Membre de: Association des bibliothèques publiques du Québec
Membre(s) du personnel: 10
Membre: *Critères d'admissibilite:* Bibliothèque publique
Membre(s) du bureau directeur:
Louis Dallaire, Directeur général
louis.dallaire@reseaubiblioatnq.qc.ca

Réseau BIBLIO de la Côte-Nord
59, rue Napoléon, Sept-Iles QC G4R 5C5
Tél: 418-962-1020
biblio@reseaubibliocn.qc.ca
www.reseaubibliocn.qc.ca
Aperçu: *Dimension:* petite; *Envergure:* locale
Mission: Promouvoir les bibliothèques publiques; concertation dans des dossiers concernant les bibliothèques publiques; faire connaître nos services
Membre(s) du personnel: 5
Membre(s) du bureau directeur:
Jean-Roch Gagnon, Directeur général
jrgagnon@reseaubibliocn.qc.ca

Réseau BIBLIO du Québec
c.o Jacques Côté, 3189, rue Albert-Demers, Charny QC G6X 3A1
Tél: 418-867-1682; *Téléc:* 418-867-3434
www.reseaubiblioduquebec.qc.ca
Aperçu: *Dimension:* grande; *Envergure:* provinciale; fondée en 1984
Mission: Le Réseau BIBLIO du Québec est un regroupement national qui vise à unir les ressources des Réseaux BIBLIO régionaux pour maintenir et développer leur réseau de bibliothèques et de les représenter auprès des diverses instances sur des dossiers d'intérêts communs.
Membre: *Comités:* Comité de liaison/MCC; Comité de liaison/BAnQ; Comité de communication
Membre(s) du bureau directeur:
Jacques Côté, Secrétaire général
jacques.cote@crsbp.net

Réseau BIBLIO du Saguenay-Lac-Saint-Jean (RBSLSJ)
100, rue Price ouest, Alma QC G8B 4S1
Tél: 418-662-6425; *Téléc:* 418-662-7593
Ligne sans frais: 800-563-6425
info@reseaubiblioslsj.qc.ca
www.mabibliotheque.ca/saguenay-lac-saint-jean/fr/index.aspx
www.facebook.com/reseaubiblioSLSJ
twitter.com/reseaubiblio
Nom précédent: Rassemblement des bibliothèques publiques du Lac-Saint-Jean et Saguenay-Lac-Saint-Jean
Aperçu: *Dimension:* petite; *Envergure:* locale; fondée en 1981
Mission: Promouvoir les bibliothèques publiques; concertation dans des dossiers concernant les bibliothèques publiques; faire connaître nos services
Membre(s) du personnel: 9
Activités: Service régional d'animation
Membre(s) du bureau directeur:
Sophie Bolduc, Directrice générale
sbolduc@reseaubiblioslsj.qc.ca

Réseau canadien d'éducation et de communication relatives à l'environnement *See* Canadian Network for Environmental Education & Communication

Réseau canadien d'information sur le patrimoine *See* Canadian Heritage Information Network

Réseau canadien d'info-traitements sida *See* Canadian AIDS Treatment Information Exchange

Réseau canadien de DÉC *See* Canadian CED Network

Le Réseau canadien de l'arthrite *See* Canadian Arthritis Network

Réseau canadien de l'eau *See* Canadian Water Network

Réseau canadien de l'environnement *See* Canadian Environmental Network

Réseau canadien des associations nationales d'organismes de réglementation *See* Canadian Network of National Associations of Regulators

Réseau canadien des centres de toxicologie *See* Canadian Network of Toxicology Centres

Réseau canadien des subventionneurs en environnement *See* Canadian Environmental Grantmakers' Network

Réseau canadien du cancer du sein *See* Canadian Breast Cancer Network

Réseau Canadien en Obésité *See* Canadian Obesity Network

Réseau canadien pour l'innovation en éducation *See* Canadian Network for Innovation in Education

Le Réseau canadien pour la conservation de la flore *See* Canadian Botanical Conservation Network

Réseau canadien pour les essais VIH *See* Canadian HIV Trials Network

Réseau canadien pour les musiques nouvelles *See* Canadian New Music Network

Réseau Canadien pour les soins respiratoires *See* Canadian Network for Respiratory Care

Réseau canadien sur les maladies génétiques *See* Canadian Genetic Diseases Network

Réseau communautaire Chebucto *See* Chebucto Community Net

Réseau d'Action des Femmes Handicapées du Canada *See* DisAbled Women's Network of Canada

Réseau d'action et de communication pour le développement international / Alternatives Action & Communication Network for International Development
#300, 3720, av du Parc, Montréal QC H2X 2J1
Tél: 514-982-6606; *Téléc:* 514-982-6122
Ligne sans frais: 800-982-6646
www.alternatives.ca
www.facebook.com/AlternativesMtl
twitter.com/alternativesMTL
www.youtube.com/alternativesngo
Aperçu: *Dimension:* petite; *Envergure:* internationale; Organisme sans but lucratif
Mission: Pour soutenir les organisations communautaires qui travaillent à transformer leur environnement social, économique, politique et écologique au Canada et à l'étranger
Finances: *Fonds:* Dons; revenus auto-générés
Membre(s) du personnel: 10
Membre: *Montant de la cotisation:* 120$ partisan; 60$ régulier, 36$ chômeurs/étudiants
Activités: Formation et aide financière; lutter contre l'appauvrissement et l'exclusion sociale; aider les immigrants; *Stagiaires:* Oui; *Service de conférenciers:* Oui; *Listes de destinataires:* Oui
Membre(s) du bureau directeur:
Ronald Cameron, Président
Michel Lambert, Directeur général

Réseau d'aide aux personnes seiles et itinérantes de Montréal (RAPSIM)
#204, 105, rue Ontario est, Montréal QC H2X 1G9

Tél: 514-879-1949; Téléc: 514-879-1948
rapsim@qc.aira.com
www.rapsim.org
Aperçu: *Dimension:* petite; *Envergure:* locale
Mission: Pour aider les personnes sans-abri à avoir accès aux services de santé et les services sociaux et de réduire le niveau de pauvreté à Montréal
Membre: 95; *Critères d'admissibilite:* Organismes communautaires
Membre(s) du bureau directeur:
Pierre Gaudreau, Coordonnateur
pierre.gaudreau@qc.aira.com

Le Réseau d'enseignement francophone à distance du Canada (REFAD)
CP 47542, Succ. Plateau Mont-Royal, Montréal QC H2H 2S8
Tél: 514-284-9109; Téléc: 514-284-9363
refad@sympatico.ca
www.refad.ca
twitter.com/_refad
Aperçu: *Dimension:* moyenne; *Envergure:* nationale; Organisme sans but lucratif; fondée en 1988
Mission: Favoriser la collaboration entre les personnes et les organisations intéressées par l'enseignement à distance en français; rassembler en réseau les établissements qui ont recours à la formation à distance en français; appuyer et compléter d'autres réseaux d'enseignement à distance existant déjà à travers le Canada; promouvoir et accroître la qualité et la quantité des programmes et des cours offerts dans la francophonie canadienne.
Finances: *Budget de fonctionnement annuel:* $50,000-$100,000
Membre: 27 instiutionnels + 16 individuels; *Montant de la cotisation:* 2 000$ institutionnel; 250$ individuel
Activités: Finance des programmes d'éducation d'envergure pancanadienne; organise un colloque annuel; publie différents ouvrages
Membre(s) du bureau directeur:
Caroll-Ann Keating, Présidente
Alain Langlois, Directeur général

Réseau de cellules souches *See* Stem Cell Network

Réseau de développement économique et d'employabilité Ontario
880, promenade Taylor Creek, Ottawa ON K1C 1T1
Tél: 613-590-2493; Téléc: 613-590-2494
communications@rdee-ont.ca
www.rdee-ont.ca
Également appelé: RDÉE Ontario
Aperçu: *Dimension:* petite; *Envergure:* provinciale
Mission: Optimise le potentiel économique des communautés francophones et acadiennes
Membre de: Réseau national de développement économique francophone
Membre(s) du bureau directeur:
Daniel Sigouin, Directeur général

Réseau de la coopération du travail du Québec
#200, 3188, ch Sainte-Foy, Québec QC G1X 1R4
Tél: 418-651-0388; Téléc: 418-651-3860
www.reseau.coop
Également appelé: RESEAU
Aperçu: *Dimension:* petite; *Envergure:* provinciale
Mission: De promouvoir le développement des coopératives au Québec
Membre: *Critères d'admissibilite:* Coop de tracailleurs; coop de solidarité; coop de travailleurs actionnaires

Réseau de la Santé Sexuelle du Québec inc. *See* Sexual Health Network of Québec Inc.

Réseau de Santé en Français au Nunavut (SAFRAN)
CP 1516, Iqaluit NU X0A 0H0
Tél: 867-222-2107
resefan.nu@gmail.com
www.resefan.ca
Aperçu: *Dimension:* petite; *Envergure:* provinciale; fondée en 2004 surveillé par Société santé en français
Mission: Contribuer à l'amélioration de la santé des francophones du Nunavut
Membre(s) du bureau directeur:
Carine Chalut, Directrice générale

Réseau des cégeps et des collèges francophones du Canada (RCCFC)
#1015, 130, rue Slater, Ottawa ON K1P 6E2
Tél: 613-241-0430; Téléc: 613-241-0457
Ligne sans frais: 888-253-2486
rccfc.ca
Aperçu: *Dimension:* moyenne; *Envergure:* nationale; fondée en 1995
Mission: Le Réseau des cégeps et des collèges francophones du Canada a pour mission d'établir un véritable partenariat entre les établissements d'enseignement collégial francophones du Canada. Il constitue un réseau d'entraide, de promotion et d'échanges lié au développement de l'enseignement collégial en français au Canada tout en favorisant l'utilisation des technologies de l'information et des communications.
Finances: *Budget de fonctionnement annuel:* $1.5 Million-$3 Million
Membre(s) du personnel: 2
Membre: 61
Membre(s) du bureau directeur:
Laurier Thibault, Directeur général
dg@rccfc.ca

Réseau des femmes aînées *See* The Older Women's Network

Réseau des femmes d'affaires du Québec inc. (RFAQ) / Business Women's Network
#200, 476, rue Jean-Neveu, Longueuil QC J4G 1N8
Tél: 514-521-2441
Ligne sans frais: 800-332-2683
info@rfaq.ca
www.rfaq.ca
www.facebook.com/RFAQc
twitter.com/ReseauRFAQ
www.youtube.com/user/RFAQinc
Aperçu: *Dimension:* moyenne; *Envergure:* provinciale; fondée en 1981
Mission: Afin d'encourager et de promouvoir les femmes à devenir des leaders dans les instances sociales, politiques et économiques
Finances: *Budget de fonctionnement annuel:* $250,000-$500,000
Membre(s) du personnel: 6
Membre: 2,000; *Montant de la cotisation:* 100$ autres provinces/hors Canada; 125$ étudiant; 195$ OBNL; 225$ régulier
Membre(s) du bureau directeur:
Ruth Vachon, Présidente/Directrice générale, 514-521-5119 Ext. 113
rvachon@rfaq.ca
Publications:
• Cellule Express
Type: Bulletin; *Frequency:* hebdomadaire; *Accepts Advertising*
Profile: Bulletin officiel de l'RFAQ; comprend les dates importantes et nouvelles
• Les Propos
Type: Bulletin; *Frequency:* irrégulier
Profile: Caractéristiques des profils de membres du RFAQ
• RFAQ Bulletin des activités
Type: Bulletin; *Frequency:* hebdomadaire
Profile: Une liste des activités prévues par les sections régionales de la RFAQ

Réseau des femmes du sud de l'Ontario / Network of French Speaking Women of South Ontario
Serres #102, College Glendon, 2295, av Bayview, Toronto ON M4N 3M6
Tél: 416-487-6794; Téléc: 416-487-6794
Ligne sans frais: 800-387-8603
reseaudesfemmes@on.aibn.com
Également appelé: SOS-femmes; Institut de leadership social et communautaire des femmes
Aperçu: *Dimension:* petite; *Envergure:* provinciale; Organisme sans but lucratif; fondée en 1982
Mission: Améliorer les conditions de vie des femmes francophones
Membre(s) du personnel: 5; 8 bénévole(s)
Membre: 500; *Montant de la cotisation:* $10
Activités: *Stagiaires:* Oui

Réseau des femmes exécutives *See* Women's Executive Network

Réseau des lesbiennes du Québec (RLQ) / Québec Lesbian Network
#110, 2075, rue Plessis, Montréal QC H2L 2Y4
Tél: 438-929-6928; Téléc: 514-528-9708
rlqln.info@gmail.com
rlq-qln.algi.qc.ca
www.facebook.com/RLQQLN
Aperçu: *Dimension:* petite; *Envergure:* provinciale; fondée en 1996

Réseau des SADC du Québec *Voir* Réseau des SADC et CAE

Réseau des SADC et CAE (SADC)
#530, 979, av de Bourgogne, Québec QC G1W 2L4
Tél: 418-658-1530; Téléc: 418-658-9900
www.sadc-cae.ca
twitter.com/ReseauSADCCAE
Également appelé: Sociétés d'aide au développement des collectivités & Centre d'aide aux entreprises
Nom précédent: Réseau des SADC du Québec
Aperçu: *Dimension:* moyenne; *Envergure:* provinciale; Organisme sans but lucratif; fondée en 1995
Mission: Soutenir les efforts de regroupement des SADC (Sociétés d'aide au développement des collectivités) et des CAE (Centres d'aide aux entreprises) du Québec; il veille à leurs intérêts et procure des services qui facilitent le développement de ses membres; au cours des années, les SADC et CAE sont devenus de véritables experts en développement local et régional
Finances: *Budget de fonctionnement annuel:* Moins de $50,000
Membre(s) du personnel: 400; 1350 bénévole(s)
Membre: 67; *Critères d'admissibilite:* Sociétés d'investissement (financement d'entreprises et accompagnement personnalisé)
Membre(s) du bureau directeur:
Hélène Deslauriers, Directrice générale

CAE Beauce-Chaudière inc
595-J, 93 av, Beauceville QC G5X 1J3
Tél: 418-774-2022; Téléc: 418-774-2024
caebci@sogetel.net
www.caebeauce.com
Membre(s) du bureau directeur:
Johanne Jacques, Directrice générale
johanne.jacques@caebeauce.com

CAE Capital
#200, 270, boul Sir-Wilfrid-Laurier, Beloeil QC J3G 4G7
Tél: 450-446-3650; Téléc: 450-446-3806
info@caers.ca
www.caers.ca
Membre(s) du bureau directeur:
Michel Aubin, Directeur général
m.aubin@caecapital.com

CAE de Drummond
#475, 230, rue Brock, Drummondville QC J2C 1M3
Tél: 819-474-6477; Téléc: 819-474-5944
www.caedrummond.ca
Membre(s) du bureau directeur:
Errold Mayrand, Directeur général
errold.mayrand@caedrummond.ca

CAE Haute-Montérégie
Parc industriel E.L. Farrar, 700, rue Lucien-Beaudin, Saint-Jean-sur-Richelieu QC J2X 5M3
Tél: 450-357-9800; Téléc: 450-357-9583
info@caehm.com
www.caehm.com
Membre(s) du bureau directeur:
Édouard Bonaldo, Directeur général
edouard.bonaldo@caehm.com

CAE Haute-Yamaska et région inc.
#102, 90, rue Robinson sud, Granby QC J2G 7L4
Tél: 450-378-2294; Téléc: 450-378-7370
info@caehyr.com
www.caehyr.com
Membre(s) du bureau directeur:
Isabelle Brochu, Directeur général
i.brochu@caehyr.com

CAE LaPrade Trois-Rivière inc.
#300, 370, rue des Forges, Trois-Rivières QC G9A 2H1
Tél: 819-378-6000; Téléc: 819-378-2019
info@caelaprade.com
www.caelaprade.com
Membre(s) du bureau directeur:
Claude Lavergne, Directrice générale
jbouliane@caelaprade.com

CAE Memphrémagog inc
#206, 146, rue Principale ouest, Magog QC J1X 2A5
Tél: 819-843-4342; Téléc: 819-843-4393
www.caememphre.com
Membre(s) du bureau directeur:
Louise Paradis, Directrice générale
louisep@caememphre.com

CAE Montmagny-L'Islet
191, ch des Poirier, Montmagny QC G5V 4L2

Canadian Associations / Réseau des SADC et CAE (SADC)

Tél: 418-248-4815; Téléc: 418-248-4836
info@caeml.qc.ca
www.caeml.qc.ca
www.facebook.com/643623969022048
Membre(s) du bureau directeur:
Gilles Boulet, Directeur général
gboulet@caeml.qc.ca

CAE Rive-Nord
13035, rue Brault, Mirabel QC J7J 1P3
Tél: 450-437-0999; Téléc: 450-437-2080
info@caebl.ca
www.caebl.ca
www.facebook.com/256764761066491
twitter.com/CAERiveNord
Membre(s) du bureau directeur:
Renée Courchesne, Directrice générale
rcourchesne@caebl.ca

CAE Val-St-François
745, rue Gouin, Richmond QC J0B 2H0
Tél: 819-826-6571; Téléc: 819-826-6281
info@caevsf.com
www.caevsf.com
Membre(s) du bureau directeur:
Marc Ducharme, Directeur général

Eeyou Economic Group
CP 39, 12, rue Poplar, Waswanipi QC J0Y 3C0
Tél: 819-753-2560; Téléc: 819-753-2568
info@eeyoueconomicgroup.ca
www.eeyoueconomicgroup.ca
www.facebook.com/eeyoueconomicgroup
twitter.com/EEG_CFDC
Membre(s) du bureau directeur:
David Neeposh, Directeur général
dneeposh@eeyoueconomicgroup.ca

Nunavik Investment Corporation
CP 789, Kuujjuaq QC J0M 1C0
Tél: 819-964-1872; Téléc: 819-964-1497
Membre(s) du bureau directeur:
Martha Gordon, Directeur général
marthag@tamaani.ca

SADC Abitibi-Ouest
#202, 80, 12e av est, La Sarre QC J9Z 3K6
Tél: 819-333-3113; Téléc: 819-333-3132
sadc_abitibi@ciril.qc.ca
www.sadcao.com
Membre(s) du bureau directeur:
Thérèse Grenier, Directrice générale
tgrenier@sadcao.com

SADC Achigan-Montcalm inc.
104, rue St-Jacques, Saint-Jacques QC J0K 2R0
Tél: 450-839-9218; Téléc: 450-839-7036
info@sadc.org
www.sadc.org
Membre(s) du bureau directeur:
Claude Chartier, Directeur général
chartierc@sadc.org

SADC Arthabaska-Érable inc.
#101, 975, boul Industriel est, Victoriaville QC G6T 1T8
Tél: 819-758-1501; Téléc: 819-758-7971
sadc_ae@ciril.qc.ca
www.sadcae.ca
www.facebook.com/551798181594341
Membre(s) du bureau directeur:
Jean-François Girard, Directeur général
jfgirard@sadcae.ca

SADC Baie-des-Chaleurs
122, boul Perron ouest, New Richmond QC G0C 2B0
Tél: 418-392-5014; Téléc: 418-392-5425
sadc_chaleurs@ciril.qc.ca
www.sadcbc.ca
Membre(s) du bureau directeur:
Lyne Lebrasseur, Directrice générale
llebrasseur@sadcbc.ca

SADC Barraute-Senneterre-Quévillon inc
CP 308, 674, 11e av, Senneterre QC J0Y 2M0
Tél: 819-737-2211; Téléc: 819-737-8888
sadc_bsq@ciril.qc.ca
www.sadcbsq.ca
Membre(s) du bureau directeur:
Marc Hardy, Directeur général
mhardy@ciril.qc.ca

SADC Bellechasse-Etchemins
CP 158, 494-B, rue Principale, Saint-Léon-de-Standon QC G0R 4L0
Tél: 418-642-2844; Téléc: 418-642-5316
info@sadcbe.qc.ca
www.sadcbe.qc.ca
Membre(s) du bureau directeur:
Marie-Claire Larose, Directrice générale
mclarose@sadcbe.qc.ca

SADC Centre-de-la-Mauricie
812, av des Cèdres, Shawinigan QC G9N 1P2
Tél: 819-537-5107; Téléc: 819-537-5109
info@sadccm.ca
www.sadccm.ca
Membre(s) du bureau directeur:
Simon Charlebois, Directeur général
scharlebois@sadccm.ca

SADC Chibougamau-Chapais inc
#1, 600 - 3e rue, Chibougamau QC G8P 1P1
Tél: 418-748-6477; Téléc: 418-748-6160
sadc.administration@lino.com
www.sadccc.ca
Membre(s) du bureau directeur:
Annie Potvin, Directrice générale
sadc.dg@lino.com

SADC Côte-Nord inc.
#205, 456, av Arnaud, Sept-Iles QC G4R 3B1
Tél: 418-962-7233; Téléc: 418-968-5513
Ligne sans frais: 877-962-7233
info@sadccote-nord.org
www.sadccote-nord.org
www.linkedin.com/groups/SADC-CôteNord-4316537
www.facebook.com/254939334588954
twitter.com/SADCCoteNord
Membre(s) du bureau directeur:
Soraya Zarate, Directrice générale
szarate@sadccote-nord.org

SADC d'Antoine-Labelle
#4, 636, rue de la Madone, Mont-Laurier QC J9L 1S9
Tél: 819-623-3300; Téléc: 819-623-7300
info@sadcal.com
www.sadcal.com
www.facebook.com/sadcal
Membre(s) du bureau directeur:
Benoit Cochet, Directeur général
bcochet@sadcal.com

SADC de Autray-Joliette
#500, 550, rue Montcalm, Berthierville QC J0K 1A0
Tél: 450-836-0990; Téléc: 450-836-2001
Ligne sans frais: 877-777-0990
info@masadc.ca
masadc.ca
Membre(s) du bureau directeur:
Jocelyn de Grandpré, Directeur général
jdegrandpre@MaSADC.ca

SADC de Charlevoix
#208, 11, rue Saint-Jean-Baptiste, Baie-Saint-Paul QC G3Z 1M1
Tél: 418-435-4033; Téléc: 418-435-4050
sadc_charlevoix@ciril.qc.ca
www.sadccharlevoix.ca
Membre(s) du bureau directeur:
Pascal Harvey, Directeur général
p.harvey@sadccharlevoix.ca

SADC de Gaspé
CP 5012, #200, 15, rue Adams, Gaspé QC G4X 1E5
Tél: 418-368-2906; Téléc: 418-368-3927
sadcgasp@globetrotter.net
www.sadcgaspe.ca
www.facebook.com/sadc.degaspe
Membre(s) du bureau directeur:
Mario Cotton, Directeur général
mcotton@ciril.qc.ca

SADC de l'Amiante
725, boul Frontenac ouest, Thetford Mines QC G6G 7X9
Tél: 418-338-4531; Téléc: 418-338-9256
sadc_amiante@ciril.qc.ca
www.sadcamiante.com
Membre(s) du bureau directeur:
Luce Dubois, Directrice générale
dg@sadcamiante.com

SADC de la Haute-Gaspésie
Édifice des Monts, 10G, boul Sainte-Anne ouest, 1e étage, Sainte-Anne-des-Monts QC G4V 1P3
Tél: 418-763-5355; Téléc: 418-763-2933
info@sadchautegaspesie.com
sadchautegaspesie.com
www.facebook.com/SADCdelaHauteGaspesie
Membre(s) du bureau directeur:
Richard Marin, Directeur général
rmarin@sadchautegaspesie.com

SADC de la MRC de Maskinongé
#100, 871, boul Saint-Laurent est, Louiseville QC J5V 1L3
Tél: 819-228-5921; Téléc: 819-228-0497
pcloutier@ciril.qc.ca
www.sadcmaskinonge.qc.ca
www.linkedin.com/company/5011533
twitter.com/SADCMaskinonge
plus.google.com/113296207301131382242
Membre(s) du bureau directeur:
Julie Lemieux, Directrice générale
jlemieux@sadcmaskinonge.qc.ca

SADC de la MRC de Rivière-du-Loup
#101, 646, rue Lafontaine, Rivière-du-Loup QC G5R 3C8
Tél: 418-867-4272; Téléc: 418-867-8060
info@sadcmrcrivieredulop.ca
www.rivieredulop.ca/sadc
www.facebook.com/La.Vraie.Vie.MRCRDL
Membre(s) du bureau directeur:
Gilles Goulet, Directeur général

SADC de la Neigette inc.
#101, 79, rue De l'Évêché, Rimouski QC G5L 1X7
Tél: 418-735-2514; Téléc: 418-723-5879
info@sadcneigette.ca
www.sadcneigette.ca
www.facebook.com/sadcneigette
Membre(s) du bureau directeur:
Yvan Collin, Directeur général
ycollin@sadcneigette.ca

SADC de la région d'Acton inc.
#101, 1545, rue Peerless, Acton Vale QC J0H 1A0
Tél: 450-546-3239; Téléc: 450-546-3619
sadcacton@cooptel.qc.ca
www.sadcacton.qc.ca
Membre(s) du bureau directeur:
Éric Thubodeau, Directeur général
ericthibodeau@cooptel.qc.ca

SADC de la région de Matane
#312, 235, av St-Jérôme, Matane QC G4W 3A7
Tél: 418-562-3171; Téléc: 418-562-1259
sadcmat@globetrotter.net
www.sadc-matane.qc.ca
www.facebook.com/SADCMatane
Membre(s) du bureau directeur:
Annie Fournier, Directrice générale
afournier@ciril.qc.ca

SADC de Lotbinière
#100, 153, boul Laurier, Laurier-Station QC G0S 1N0
Tél: 418-596-3300; Téléc: 418-728-3345
Ligne sans frais: 866-596-3300
sadc_lotbiniere@ciril.qc.ca
www.sadclotbiniere.qc.ca
www.facebook.com/SADClotbiniere
Membre(s) du bureau directeur:
Sylvie Drolet, Directrice générale
sdrolet@ciril.qc.ca

SADC de Papineau inc.
565, av de Buckingham, Gatineau QC J8L 2H2
Tél: 819-986-1747; Téléc: 819-281-0303
Ligne sans frais: 888-986-7232
info@sadcpapineau.com
www.sadcpapineau.ca
www.facebook.com/sadcpapineau
Membre(s) du bureau directeur:
Mélissa Bergeron, Directeur général
mebergeron@sadcpapineau.ca

SADC de Rouyn-Noranda
161, av Murdoch, Rouyn-Noranda QC J9X 1E3
Tél: 819-797-6068; Téléc: 819-797-0096
info@sadcrn.ca
www.sadcrn.ca
www.facebook.com/105328519513571
Membre(s) du bureau directeur:
Jocelyn Lévesque, Directrice générale
jocelyn.levesque@sadcrn.ca

SADC de Témiscouata
#202, 3, rue Hôtel-de-Ville, Témiscouata-sur-le-Lac QC G0L 1X0

Canadian Associations / Réseau des SADC et CAE (SADC)

Tél: 418-899-0808; *Téléc:* 418-899-0808
sadctemis@videotron.ca
www.sadctemiscouata.com
Membre(s) du bureau directeur:
Serge Ouellet, Directeur
sergeouellet@ciril.qc.ca

SADC des Basques inc.
400-3, rue Jean Rioux, Trois-Pistoles QC G0L 4K0
Tél: 418-851-3172; *Téléc:* 418-851-3171
sadc_basques@ciril.qc.ca
www.sadcbasques.qc.ca
www.facebook.com/223623494391230
Membre(s) du bureau directeur:
Yvanho Rioux, Directeur général
yrioux@ciril.qc.ca

SADC des Îles-de-la-Madeleine
#203, 735, ch Principal, Cap-aux-Meules QC G4T 1G8
Tél: 418-986-4601; *Téléc:* 418-986-4874
sadc_iles@ciril.qc.ca
www.sadcim.qc.ca
www.facebook.com/sadcdesiles
Membre(s) du bureau directeur:
Daniel Gaudet, Directeur général
dgaudet@ciril.qc.ca

SADC des Laurentides
#230, 1332, boul Sainte-Adèle, Sainte-Adèle QC J8B 2N5
Tél: 450-229-3001; *Téléc:* 450-229-6928
Ligne sans frais: 888-229-3001
info@sadclaurentides.org
www.sadclaurentides.org
twitter.com/SADCL_DD
Membre(s) du bureau directeur:
Sylvie Bolduc, Directrice générale
sbolduc@sadclaurentides.org

SADC des Sources
309, rue Chassé, Asbestos QC J1T 2B4
Tél: 819-879-7147; *Téléc:* 819-879-5188
info@sadcdessources.com
www.sadcdessources.com
Membre(s) du bureau directeur:
Marc Grimard, Directeur général
mgrimard@sadcdessources.com

SADC du Fjord inc.
#101, 613, rue Albert, La Baie QC G7B 3L6
Tél: 418-544-2885; *Téléc:* 418-544-0303
courrier@sadcdufjord.qc.ca
www.sadcdufjord.qc.ca
Membre(s) du bureau directeur:
André Nepton, Directeur général
anepton@sadcdufjord.qc.ca

SADC du Haut-Saguenay
328, rue Gagnon, Saint-Ambroise QC G7P 2R1
Tél: 418-672-6333; *Téléc:* 418-672-4882
sadc@videotron.ca
www.sadchs.qc.ca
www.facebook.com/212354118628
Membre(s) du bureau directeur:
André Boily, Directeur général

SADC du Haut-Saint-François
47, rue Angus nord, East Angus QC J0B 1R0
Tél: 819-832-2447; *Téléc:* 819-832-1831
Ligne sans frais: 877-473-7232
sadc_haut-saint-francois@ciril.qc.ca
www.sadchsf.qc.ca
Membre(s) du bureau directeur:
Danielle Simard, Directrice générale
dsimard@ciril.qc.ca

SADC du Haut-Saint-Maurice inc.
290, rue St-Joseph, La Tuque QC G9X 3Z8
Tél: 819-523-4227; *Téléc:* 819-523-5722
info-sadchsm@ciril.qc.ca
www.sadchsm.qc.ca
Membre(s) du bureau directeur:
Chantal Fortin, Directeur général

SADC du Rocher-Percé
129, boul René-Lévesque ouest, #S-101, Chandler QC G0C 1K0
Tél: 418-689-5699; *Téléc:* 418-689-5556
sadc@globetrotter.qc.ca
www.sadcrp.ca
Membre(s) du bureau directeur:
Andreé Roy, Directrice générale
aroy@ciril.qc.ca

SADC du Suroît-Sud
#203, 50, rue Jacques-Cartier, Salaberry-de-Valleyfield QC J6T 4R3
Tél: 450-370-3332; *Téléc:* 450-370-4448
info@sadc-suroitsud.org
www.sadc-suroitsud.org
www.facebook.com/sadc.dusuroitsud
twitter.com/SADCSS
www.youtube.com/user/sadcdusuroitsud
Membre(s) du bureau directeur:
Robert Lafrance, Directeur Général

SADC du Témiscamingue
7B, rue des Oblats nord, Ville-Marie QC J9V 1H9
Tél: 819-629-3355; *Téléc:* 819-629-2793
sdt@temiscamingue.net
www.lasdt.com
www.facebook.com/sdt.temis
Membre(s) du bureau directeur:
Guy Trépanier, Directeur général

SADC Harricana inc.
550, 1e av ouest, Amos QC J9T 1V3
Tél: 819-732-8311; *Téléc:* 819-732-2240
sadc@sadc-harricana.qc.ca
www.sadc-harricana.qc.ca
www.facebook.com/439503636123429
Membre(s) du bureau directeur:
Éric Laliberté, Directeur générale
elaliberte@sadc-harricana.qc.ca

SADC Haute-Côte-Nord inc.
#200, 459, rte 138, Les Escoumins QC G0T 1K0
Tél: 418-233-3495; *Téléc:* 418-233-2485
sadchcn@ciril.qc.ca
www.sadchcn.com
Membre(s) du bureau directeur:
Léna St-Pierre, Directrice générale
lstpierre@ciril.qc.ca

SADC Kamouraska
#100, 901 - 5e rue, La Pocatière QC G0R 1Z0
Tél: 418-856-3482; *Téléc:* 418-856-5053
sadck@sadckamouraska.com
www.sadckamouraska.com
www.facebook.com/1403247896598126
Membre(s) du bureau directeur:
Brigitte Pouliot, Directrice générale
bpouliot@sadckamouraska.com

SADC La Mitis
#101, 1534, boul Jacques-Cartier, Mont-Joli QC G5H 2V8
Tél: 418-775-4619; *Téléc:* 418-775-5504
sadc_mitis@ciril.qc.ca
www.sadcmitis.ca
Membre(s) du bureau directeur:
Benoît Thériault, Directeur général
btheriault@sadcmitis.ca

SADC Lac-Saint-Jean Ouest inc.
#203, 915, boul St-Joseph, Roberval QC G8H 2M1
Tél: 418-275-2531; *Téléc:* 418-275-5787
sadc@sadclacstjeanouest.com
www.sadclacstjeanouest.com
www.linkedin.com/company/sadc-lac-st-jean-ouest-inc.
www.facebook.com/152811554739548
twitter.com/SADCLacStJeanO
Membre(s) du bureau directeur:
Serge Desgagné, Directeur général
sdesgagne@sadclsjo.com

SADC Lac-Saint-Jean-Est inc.
#101, 65, rue Saint-Joseph sud, 1e étage, Alma QC G8B 6V4
Tél: 418-668-3148; *Téléc:* 418-668-6977
www.sadc.lacstjean.qc.ca
Membre(s) du bureau directeur:
Daniel Deschênes, Directeur général
ddeschenes@sadc.lacstjean.qc.ca

SADC Manicouagan
#101, 810, rue Bossé, Baie-Comeau QC G5C 1L6
Tél: 418-295-7232; *Téléc:* 418-295-7233
solution@sadcmanic.ca
sadcmanic.ca
www.facebook.com/185152361597283
Membre(s) du bureau directeur:
Martin Ouellet, Directeur général
mouellet@sadcmanic.ca

SADC Maria-Chapdelaine
#107, 1500, rue des Érables, Dolbeau-Mistassini QC G8L 2W7
Tél: 418-276-0405; *Téléc:* 418-706-6061
sadc@sadcmaria.qc.ca
www.sadcmaria.qc.ca
Membre(s) du bureau directeur:
Jean-François Laliberté, Directeur général
labertejf@sadcmaria.qc.ca

SADC Matagami
CP 910, 180, Place du Commerce, Matagami QC J0Y 2A0
Tél: 819-739-2155; *Téléc:* 819-739-4271
fcossette@ciril.qc.ca
www.sadcdematagami.qc.ca
Membre(s) du bureau directeur:
François Cossette, Directeur général
fcossette@ciril.qc.ca

SADC Matapédia inc.
#401, 123, rue Desbiens, 4e étage, Amqui QC G5J 3P9
Tél: 418-629-4474; *Téléc:* 418-629-5530
sadcmatapedia@ciril.qc.ca
www.sadcmatapedia.com
www.facebook.com/sadcdelamatapedia
twitter.com/SADCMATAPEDIA
Membre(s) du bureau directeur:
Guy Côté, Directeur général
gcote@ciril.qc.ca

SADC Matawinie inc.
1080, rte 343, Saint-Alphonse-Rodriguez QC J0K 1W0
Tél: 450-883-0717; *Téléc:* 450-883-2006
sadc@matawinie.qc.ca
www.matawinie.qc.ca
Membre(s) du bureau directeur:
Michel Clément, Directeur général
mclement@matawinie.qc.ca

SADC Nicolet-Bécancour inc.
#102, 19205, boul des Acadiens, Bécancour QC G9H 1M5
Tél: 819-233-3315; *Téléc:* 819-233-3338
sadc_nicolet@ciril.qc.ca
www.sadcnicoletbecancour.ca
www.facebook.com/137821253004427
www.youtube.com/user/sadcnicoletbecancour
Membre(s) du bureau directeur:
Steve Brunelle, Directeur général
sbrunelle@sadcnicoletbecancour.ca

SADC Pierre-De Saurel
#220, 26, Place Charles-De Montmagny, Sorel-Tracy QC J3P 7E3
Tél: 450-746-5595; *Téléc:* 450-746-1803
sadc@bellnet.ca
www.soreltracyregion.net/sadc
Membre(s) du bureau directeur:
Sylvie Pouliot, Directrice générale
sadcdp@bellnet.ca

SADC Pontiac CFDC
CP 425, 1409, rte 148, Campbell's Bay QC J0X 1K0
Tél: 819-648-2186; *Téléc:* 819-648-2226
info@sadcpontiac.ca
www.sadc.commercepontiac.ca
www.facebook.com/SADCPontiac
Membre(s) du bureau directeur:
Rhonda Perry, Directrice générale
rhonda.perry@sadcpontiac.ca

SADC Portneuf
#201, 120, rue Armand-Bombardier, Donnacona QC G3M 1V3
Tél: 418-286-4422; *Téléc:* 418-285-3281
sadc_portneuf@ciril.qc.ca
www.sadcportneuf.qc.ca
Membre(s) du bureau directeur:
Guy Beaulieu, Directeur général
guybeaulieu@sadcportneuf.qc.ca

SADC région de Coaticook
#140, 38, rue Child, Coaticook QC J1A 2B1
Tél: 819-849-3053; *Téléc:* 819-849-7393
info@sadccoaticook.ca
www.sadccoaticook.ca
www.facebook.com/157109334304594
twitter.com/SADCCoaticook
Membre(s) du bureau directeur:
Joanne Beaudin, Directrice générale
direction@sadccoaticook.ca

SADC région de Mégantic
4336, rue Laval, Lac-Mégantic QC G6B 1B8
Tél: 819-583-5332; *Téléc:* 819-583-5957
sadc_megantic@ciril.qc.ca
www.sadcmegantic.ca

Membre(s) du bureau directeur:
Ginette Isabel, Directrice générale
SADC Vallée de la Batiscan
390, rue Goulet, Saint-Stanislas QC G0X 3E0
Tél: 418-328-4200; *Téléc:* 418-328-4201
sadcvb@cgocable.ca
www.sadcvb.ca
Membre(s) du bureau directeur:
Gilles Mercure, Directeur général
gmercure.sadcvb@cgocable.ca
SADC Vallée-de-l'Or
#1200, 1740, ch Sullivan, Val-d'Or QC J9P 7H1
Tél: 819-874-3676; *Téléc:* 819-874-3670
info@sadcvdo.com
www.sadcvdo.ca
Membre(s) du bureau directeur:
Francis Dumais, Directeur général
fdumais@ciril.qc.ca
SADC Vallée-de-la-Gatineau
#210, 100, rue Principale sud, Maniwaki QC J9E 3L4
Tél: 819-449-1551; *Téléc:* 819-449-7431
Ligne sans frais: 866-449-1551
info@sadc-vg.ca
www.sadc-vg.ca
Membre(s) du bureau directeur:
Pierre Monette, Directeur général

Réseau des services d'archives du Québec (RAQ)
a/s Archives nationales du Québec à Montréal, #5.27.1, 535, av Viger est, Montréal QC H2L 2P3
Tél: 514-864-9213
archiviste.conseil.raq@gmail.com
archivisteraq.com
www.facebook.com/293550674109606
twitter.com/reseauraq
Aperçu: *Dimension:* moyenne; *Envergure:* provinciale; fondée en 1986 surveillé par Canadian Council of Archives
Mission: Promouvoir le développement et la mise en valeur des archives historiques; favoriser l'échange et la mise en commun d'information, d'expérience et de ressources; devenir un instrument de consultation et un groupe de pression reconnu des divers intervenants des milieux archivistiques
Membre: *Montant de la cotisation:* Barème; *Critères d'admissibilite:* Organismes du Québec qui conserve, traite ou rend accessible des archives historiques
Activités: Programmes coopératifs de subventions pour la conservation des archives
Membre(s) du bureau directeur:
Theresa Rowat, Présidente
Meetings/Conferences:
• Réseau des services d'archives du Québec (RAQ) Assemblée générale annuelle 2018, 2018, QC
Scope: Provincial
  Réseau de diffusion des archives du Québec (RDAQ)
  a/s Archives nationales du Québec à Montréal, #5.27.1, 535, av Viger est, Montréal QC H2L 2P3
  Tél: 514-864-9213
  rdaq@banq.qc.ca
  rdaq.banq.qc.ca
  Mission: Le RDAQ permet la recherche d'archives québécoises ainsi que la mise en valeur des expositions virtuelles créées par les centres d'archives québécois.

Réseau des services de santé en français de l'Est de l'Ontario
#300, 1173, ch Cyrville, Ottawa ON K1J 7S6
Tél: 613-747-7431; *Téléc:* 613-747-2907
Ligne sans frais: 877-528-7565
reseau@rssfe.on.ca
www.rssfe.on.ca
Aperçu: *Dimension:* petite; *Envergure:* locale; fondée en 1998 surveillé par Société santé en français
Mission: Améliorer l'offre active et l'accès à un continuum de services de santé de qualité en français
Membre(s) du personnel: 11
Membre(s) du bureau directeur:
Jacinthe Desaulniers, Directrice générale
jdesaulniers@rssfe.on.ca

Réseau du mieux-être francophone du Nord de l'Ontario
CP 270, 469, rue Bouchard, Sudbury ON P3E 2K8
Tél: 705-674-9381
Ligne sans frais: 866-489-7484
www.reseaudumieuxetre.ca

www.facebook.com/rmefno
twitter.com/rmefno
Aperçu: *Dimension:* petite; *Envergure:* provinciale surveillé par Société santé en français
Mission: Favorisant l'offre de services de santé en français
Membre(s) du bureau directeur:
Diane Quintas, Directrice générale
dquintas@rmefno.ca

Reseau du Patrimoine Anglophone du Québec *See* Québec Anglophone Heritage Network

Réseau du patrimoine de Gatineau et de l'Outaouais
CP 1970, Succ. Hull, Gatineau QC J8X 3Y9
Tél: 819-205-5586
info@reseaupatrimoine.ca
www.reseaupatrimoine.ca
www.facebook.com/250399575001907
twitter.com/RPatrimoineG
Aperçu: *Dimension:* petite; *Envergure:* locale
Mission: La promotion et la préservation durables du patrimoine de Gatineau et de l'Outaouais
Membre: 10
Membre(s) du bureau directeur:
Nathalie Barbe, Directrice générale

Réseau du patrimoine franco-ontarien (RPFO)
267, rue Dalhousie, Ottawa ON K1N 7E3
Tél: 613-729-5769; *Téléc:* 613-729-2209
Ligne sans frais: 866-307-9995
www.rpfo.ca
www.facebook.com/RPFO.projets
twitter.com/RPFO_projets
Nom précédent: Société franco-ontarienne d'histoire et de généalogie
Aperçu: *Dimension:* moyenne; *Envergure:* provinciale; fondée en 1981
Mission: Permettre à ses membres de découvrir le patrimoine franco-ontarien par l'entremise de l'histoire et de la généalogie
Finances: *Fonds:* Ministère de la culture de l'Ontario; La Fondation Trillium
Membre(s) du personnel: 2
Membre: 1,000-4,999; *Critères d'admissibilite:* Professionnels retraités; *Comités:* Exécutif; Administration; Chaînon; Prix Décarie-Marier; Bourses Jean-Roch-Vachon; Restructuration
Activités: Recherches; Publications; Rencontres; Colloques; *Evénements de sensibilisation:* Semaine du patrimoine (février); *Stagiaires:* Oui; *Bibliothèque:* rendez-vous
Membre(s) du bureau directeur:
Soukaïna Boutiyeb, Directrice générale
dg@rpfo.ca
Prix, Bourses:
• Prix du patrimoine Roger-Bernard
  Jean-Nicolet
  327, av Dudley, North Bay ON P1B 7A4
  Tél: 705-495-2242
  jeannicolet@rpfo.ca
  Membre(s) du bureau directeur:
  André Tardif, Président
  Joseph-Marie-Couture
  CP 445, Longlac ON P0T 2A0
  Tél: 807-876-2671
  josephmariecouture@rpfo.ca
  Membre(s) du bureau directeur:
  Monique Rousseau, Présidente
  La Pionnière du Sud-Ouest (Belle Rivière)
  CP 1021, 2489, ch François, Windsor ON N8W 4T3
  Tél: 519-254-5721
  lapionniere@rpfo.ca
  Membre(s) du bureau directeur:
  Claire Grondin, Présidente
  La Vieille Branche
  CP 1344, Hearst ON P0L 1N0
  Tél: 705-372-1496
  lavieillebranche@rpfo.ca
  Membre(s) du bureau directeur:
  Claire Payeur, Présidente
  Niagara
  50, The Boardwalk, Welland ON L3B 6J1
  Tél: 905-734-7260
  duniagara@rpfo.ca
  Membre(s) du bureau directeur:
  Madeleine Boilard, Présidente

Réseau du sport étudiant du Québec (RSEQ)
4545, av Pierre-de-Coubertin, Montréal QC H1V 0B2

Tél: 514-252-3300; *Téléc:* 514-254-3292
info@rseq.ca
rseq.ca
www.facebook.com/RSEQ1
twitter.com/RSEQ1
Nom précédent: Fédération québécoise du sport étudiant
Aperçu: *Dimension:* moyenne; *Envergure:* provinciale; Organisme sans but lucratif; fondée en 1988 surveillé par School Sport Canada
Mission: Favoriser les actions éducatives dans le domaine de l'activité physique et sportive que se donne le milieu de l'éducation dans le but de contribuer, et cela dans les trois ordres d'enseignement, au développement intégral des élèves, des étudiantes et des étudiants du Québec
Membre de: Sport Scolaire Canada; Canadian Colleges Athletic Association
Finances: *Budget de fonctionnement annuel:* Plus de $5 Million
Membre(s) du personnel: 28
Membre: *Critères d'admissibilite:* Établissements scolaires, collégiaux et universitaires
Activités: *Stagiaires:* Oui
Membre(s) du bureau directeur:
Gustave Roel, Président-directeur général, 514-252-3300 Ext. 3600
groel@rseq.ca

Réseau du sport étudiant du Québec Abitibi-Témiscamingue (RSEQAT)
QC
Ligne sans frais: 866-626-2047
at.rseq.ca
Également appelé: RSEQ Abitibi-Témiscamingue
Nom précédent: Association régionale du sport étudiant de l'Abitibi-Témiscamingue
Aperçu: *Dimension:* petite; *Envergure:* locale; Organisme sans but lucratif; fondée en 1969
Mission: Regrouper sur le plan du sport étudiant les représentants des différentes institutions d'enseignement de la région de l'Abitibi-Témiscamingue; stimuler l'intérêt et favoriser le développement du sport étudiant dans cette région
Membre de: Réseau du sport étudiant du Québec
Finances: *Fonds:* Gouvernement provincial
Membre: 1-99
Membre(s) du bureau directeur:
Alain Dubois, Président

Réseau du sport étudiant du Québec Cantons-de-l'Est
5182, boul Bourque, Sherbrooke QC J1N 1H4
Tél: 819-864-0792
oaudet@ce.rseq.ca
ce.rseq.ca
Également appelé: RSEQ Cantons-de-l'Est
Aperçu: *Dimension:* petite; *Envergure:* locale
Membre de: Réseau du sport étudiant du Québec
Membre(s) du bureau directeur:
Paul Deshaies, Président

Réseau du sport étudiant du Québec Chaudière-Appalaches (RSEQ-QCA)
762, rue Jacques-Berthiaume, Québec QC G1V 3T1
Tél: 418-657-7678; *Téléc:* 418-657-1367
sportetudiant.qc.ca
www.facebook.com/RSEQQCA
twitter.com/RSEQ_QCA
www.instagram.com/rseqqca
Également appelé: RSEQ Chaudière-Appalaches
Nom précédent: Association régionale du sport étudiant de Québec et Chaudière-Appalaches
Aperçu: *Dimension:* petite; *Envergure:* locale
Mission: Organisme à but non-lucratif qui regroupe l'ensemble des institutions d'enseignement des régions de Québec et de Chaudière-Appalaches
Membre de: Réseau du sport étudiant du Québec
Membre(s) du personnel: 15
Membre(s) du bureau directeur:
Julie Dionne, Directrice générale, 418-657-7678 Ext. 202
jdionne@qca.rseq.ca
Prix, Bourses:
• Prix d'excellence

Réseau du sport étudiant du Québec Côte-Nord
#146, 40, rue Comeau, Sept-Iles QC G4R 4N3
Tél: 418-964-2888; *Téléc:* 418-968-4033
cote-nord.rseq.ca

Également appelé: RSEQ Côte-Nord
Nom précédent: Association régionale du sport étudiant de la Côte-Nord
Aperçu: *Dimension:* petite; *Envergure:* locale
Mission: Regrouper sur le plan du sport étudiant, les différentes commissions scolaires, institutions privées et institutions collégiales de la Côte-Nord; stimuler l'intérêt et favoriser le développement du sport étudiant; définir les politiques générales du sport étudiant; promouvoir l'établissement des programmes; coordonner et sanctionner les différentes compétitions du sport étudiant; organiser des stages de perfectionnement; établir les règlements que doivent régir les différentes compétitions du sport étudiant; homologuer les records établis lors des compétitions du sport étudiant
Membre de: Réseau du sport étudiant du Québec
Membre(s) du bureau directeur:
Brigitte Leblanc, Présidente
Cindy Hounsell, Directrice Générale
chounsell@cote-nord.rseq.ca

Réseau du sport étudiant du Québec Est-du-Québec
60, rue de L'Evêché ouest, #J-201, Rimouski QC G5L 4H6
Tél: 418-723-1880; *Téléc:* 418-722-0457
rseq-eq.com
www.facebook.com/RSEQEstDuQuebecviesaine
Également appelé: RSEQ Est-du-Québec
Nom précédent: Association régionale du sport étudiant de l'Est du Québec
Aperçu: *Dimension:* petite; *Envergure:* locale; fondée en 1989
Mission: Favoriser la réalisation de l'ensemble des actions éducatives par l'activité physique et particulièrement le sport en vue de contribuer au développement intégral des étudiants des niveaux primaire, secondaire et collégial dans la région Est du Québec.
Membre de: Réseau du sport étudiant du Québec
Finances: *Budget de fonctionnement annuel:* $250,000-$500,000; *Fonds:* Unité régionale de loisir et de sport de Québec
Membre(s) du personnel: 2; 25 bénévole(s)
Membre: 28; *Critères d'admissibilite:* Institutions scolaires
Activités: *Stagiaires:* Oui
Membre(s) du bureau directeur:
Marc Boudreau, Directeur, 418-722-0457 Ext. 2539
marcboud@cegep-rimouski.qc.ca

Réseau du sport étudiant du Québec Lac Saint-Louis
2900, rue Lake, Dollard-des-Ormeaux QC H9B 2P1
Tél: 514-855-4230; *Téléc:* 514-685-4643
www.arselsl.qc.ca
www.facebook.com/rseqlsl
twitter.com/RSEQ_LSL
Également appelé: RSEQ Lac Saint-Louis
Nom précédent: Association régionale du sport étudiant Lac Saint-Louis
Aperçu: *Dimension:* petite; *Envergure:* locale
Mission: Réseau du sport étudiant du Québec Lac Saint-Louis est un organisme sans but lucratif qui regroupe l'ensemble des institutions d'enseignement affiliées de la région Lac Saint-Louis
Membre de: Réseau du sport étudiant du Québec
Membre(s) du bureau directeur:
Karine Mayrand, Directrice générale, 514-855-4230 Ext. 6524
kmayrand@lsl.rseq.ca

Réseau du sport étudiant du Québec Laurentides-Lanaudière
401, boul du Domaine, Sainte-Thérèse QC J7E 4S4
Tél: 450-419-8786; *Téléc:* 450-419-8892
ll.rseq.ca
Également appelé: RSEQ Laurentides-Lanaudière
Nom précédent: Association régionale du sport étudiant Laurentides-Lanaudière
Aperçu: *Dimension:* petite; *Envergure:* locale; Organisme sans but lucratif
Mission: Favoriser la réalisation de l'ensemble des actions éducatives par l'activité physique et particulièrement le sport en vue de contribuer au développement intégral des étudiants des niveaux primaire, secondaire et collégial dans la région Laurentides-Lanaudière
Membre de: Réseau du sport étudiant du Québec
Membre(s) du bureau directeur:
Jacinthe Lussier, Directrice générale
jacinthe.lussier@cssmi.qc.ca

Réseau du sport étudiant du Québec Montérégie
c/o École secondaire Gérard-Filion, 1330, boul Curé-Poirier ouest, Longueuil QC J4K 2G8
Tél: 450-463-4055; *Téléc:* 450-463-4229
info@monteregie.rseq.ca
monteregie.rseq.ca
www.facebook.com/RseqMonteregie
twitter.com/RSEQMRG
www.youtube.com/channel/UCUPxwmcQY63heCqnGv8WqaQ
Également appelé: RSEQ Montérégie
Aperçu: *Dimension:* petite; *Envergure:* locale
Membre de: Réseau du sport étudiant du Québec
Membre(s) du bureau directeur:
Sylvie Cornellier, Directrice Générale, 450-463-4055 Ext. 102
scornellier@monteregie.rseq.ca

Réseau du sport étudiant du Québec Montréal
6875, rue Jarry est, Montréal QC H1P 1W7
Tél: 514-645-6923; *Téléc:* 514-354-8632
secretariat@montreal.rseq.ca
www.rseqmontreal.com
www.facebook.com/RSEQMontreal
www.youtube.com/user/RSEQMontreal
Également appelé: RSEQ Montréal
Nom précédent: Association régionale du sport étudiant de Montréal
Aperçu: *Dimension:* petite; *Envergure:* locale; Organisme sans but lucratif; fondée en 1989
Mission: Regrouper les associations régionales de sport scolaire, de sport collégial et de sport universitaire de l'Ile de Montréal et les représenter; développer et soutenir des réseaux de compétition régionaux en concertation avec les autres partenaires; offrir des stages de formation et de perfectionnement de cadres en étroite collaboration avec une fédération de sport donnée; participer à la programmation développée par leur instance provinciale; déléguer des officiers auprès des instance provinciales du sport en milieu d'éducation; développer une approche du sport en milieu d'éducation pour chacun des niveaux d'enseignement et développer des programmes en conséquence; promouvoir la pratique de l'activité physique et du sport en milieu d'éducation; coopérer dans le respect des valeurs éducatives avec les organismes intéressés au développement de l'activité physique et du sport
Membre de: Réseau du sport étudiant du Québec
Finances: *Fonds:* Gouvernement provincial
Membre(s) du personnel: 5
Membre: *Critères d'admissibilite:* Personnel du monde de l'éducation
Activités: Ligues; championnats; stages de perfectionnement pour entraOneurs, officiels et arbitres; *Stagiaires:* Oui
Membre(s) du bureau directeur:
Jacques Desrochers, Directeur général, 514-645-6923 Ext. 2
jdesrochers@montreal.rseq.ca

Réseau du sport étudiant du Québec Outaouais
Complexe Branchaud-Brière, #201, 499, boul Labrosse, Gatineau QC J8P 4R1
Tél: 819-643-6663; *Téléc:* 819-643-6665
www.arseo.qc.ca/ARSEO.php
www.facebook.com/RseqOutaouais
Également appelé: RSEQ Outaouais
Aperçu: *Dimension:* petite; *Envergure:* locale
Membre de: Réseau du sport étudiant du Québec
Membre(s) du bureau directeur:
Hélène Boucher, Directrice générale, 819-643-6663 Ext. 205
helene.boucher@arseo.qc.ca

Réseau du sport étudiant du Québec Saguenay-Lac St-Jean
CEGEP de Chicoutimi, 534, rue Jacques Cartier est, Chicoutimi QC G7H 1Z6
Tél: 418-543-3532; *Téléc:* 418-693-0503
saglac.rseq.ca
Également appelé: RSEQ Saguenay-Lac St-Jean
Nom précédent: Association régionale du sport étudiant du Saguenay-Lac St-Jean
Aperçu: *Dimension:* petite; *Envergure:* locale; Organisme sans but lucratif; fondée en 1974
Mission: Favoriser la réalisation de l'ensemble des actions éducatives dans le domaine de l'activité physique et particulièrement du sport en vue de contribuer au développement intégral des élèves et étudiants de niveaux primaire, secondaire, collégial et universitaire dans la région du Saguenay-Lac St-Jean
Membre de: Réseau du sport étudiant du Québec
Finances: *Fonds:* Gouvernement provincial
Membre: 16; *Critères d'admissibilite:* Écoles privées; commissions scolaires; CÉGEPS; universités
Activités: Manifestations sportives régionales et provinciales; perfectionnement; *Stagiaires:* Oui; *Service de conférenciers:* Oui
Membre(s) du bureau directeur:
Éric Benoît, Directeur général, 418-543-3532 Ext. 1214
ebenoit@saglac.rseq.ca

Réseau du sport étudiant du Québec, secteur Mauricie
260, rue Dessureault, Trois-Rivières QC G8T 9T9
Tél: 819-693-5805; *Téléc:* 819-693-1189
mauricie.rseq.ca
www.facebook.com/rseqmauricie
twitter.com/rseq_mauricie
Également appelé: RSEQ Mauricie
Nom précédent: Association régionale du sport étudiant de la Mauricie
Aperçu: *Dimension:* petite; *Envergure:* locale
Mission: Réseau du sport étudiant du Québec, secteur Mauricie, est un organisme sans but lucratif qui regroupe les institutions d'enseignement situées sur le territoire de la Mauricie et sur la rive sud du fleuve Saint-Laurent, jusqu'à l'autoroute 20
Membre de: Réseau du sport étudiant du Québec
Membre(s) du bureau directeur:
Micheline Guillemette, Directrice générale, 819-693-5805 Ext. 6543
mguillemette@mauricie.rseq.ca

Réseau écologique du Manitoba inc. *See* Manitoba Eco-Network Inc.

Réseau Enfants Retour Canada *Voir* Enfant-Retour Québec

Réseau environnement
#750, 255, boul Crémazie est, Montréal QC H2M 1L5
Tél: 514-270-7110; *Téléc:* 514-270-7154
Ligne sans frais: 877-440-7110
info@reseau-environnement.com
www.reseau-environnement.com
www.linkedin.com/company-beta/2382510
www.facebook.com/reseauenvironnement
twitter.com/Reseau_Envt
Nom précédent: Association québécoise des techniques de l'environnement
Aperçu: *Dimension:* moyenne; *Envergure:* provinciale; Organisme sans but lucratif; fondée en 1959
Mission: Regrouper des entreprises spécialisées dans la gestion des déchets commerciaux, industriels et des services municipaux reliés à l'environnement; Assurer l'avancement des technologies et de la science, la promotion des expertises et le soutien des activités en environnement
Membre: 364 corpratif
Membre(s) du bureau directeur:
Stéphanie Myre, Présidente-directrice générale
smyre@reseau-environnement.com
Mario Laplante, Directeur général adjointé
mlaplante@reseau-environnement.com
Josianne Lafantaisie, Coordonnatrice principale, Communications et relations publiques
jlafantaisie@reseau-environnement.com
Romy Regis, Coordonnatrice, Événements
rregis@reseau-environnement.com
Lyne Dubois, Merlicom, 514-935-3830 Ext. 227
ldubois@merlicom.com
Mihaela Sandor, Comptable, 514-935-3830 Ext. 237
msandor@reseau-environnement.com

Réseau environnemental du Nouveau-Brunswick *See* New Brunswick Environmental Network

Réseau FADOQ / Québec Federation of Senior Citizens
4545, av Pierre-de Coubertin, Montréal QC H1V 0B2
Tél: 514-252-3017
Ligne sans frais: 800-544-9058
info@fadoq.ca
www.fadoq.ca
www.facebook.com/reseaufadoq
www.youtube.com/user/ReseauFADOQ
Également appelé: FADOQ
Nom précédent: Fédération de l'âge d'or du Québec
Aperçu: *Dimension:* grande; *Envergure:* provinciale; Organisme sans but lucratif; fondée en 1970
Mission: Promouvoir un concept positif du vieillissement; encourager le maintien et l'amélioration de la qualité de vie et de l'autonomie des aînés; initier et soutenir l'organisation d'activités physiques et de loisirs; redonner aux aînés une nouvelle fierté en les revalorisant à leurs propres yeux comme à ceux de la

Canadian Associations / Réseau Femmes Québec (RFQ)

société; remettre entre les mains des aînés la gestion de leurs affaires
Membre de: Fédération internationale des associations des personnes âgées; Association internationale francophone des aînés; Fédération internationale du vieillissement
Affiliation(s): Association québécoise de gérontologie; Conseil canadien de développement social; Réseau canadien des aînés (One Voice); l'Assemblée des aîné(e)s francophones du Canada
Membre(s) du personnel: 20; 1500 bénévole(s)
Membre: 350,000 individus; 830 clubs; 16 regroupements régionaux; *Montant de la cotisation:* 30$; *Critères d'admissibilité:* Etre âgé de 50 ans et plus
Activités: *Evénements de sensibilisation:* Journée nationale des aînés, oct.; *Stagiaires:* Oui; *Service de conférenciers:* Oui; *Listes de destinataires:* Oui; *Bibliotheque:* Bibliotheque
Membre(s) du bureau directeur:
Maurice Duport, Président
Danis Prud'homme, Directeur général

Région Abitibi-Témiscamingue
33B, rue Gable ouest, SS#11, Rouyn-Noranda QC J9X 2R3
Tél: 819-768-2142; *Téléc:* 819-768-2144
fadoqat@tlb.sympatico.ca
www.fadoqat.ca
Membre(s) du bureau directeur:
Monic Roy, Directrice régionale

Région Bas St-Laurent (FADOQ)
474, rue des Étudiants, Pohénégamook QC G0L 1J0
Tél: 418-893-2111; *Téléc:* 418-893-7878
fadoqbsl@bellnet.ca
www.fadoqbsl.ca
Membre de: Tables de concertation des aînés
Affiliation(s): La Fédération des aînées et aînés francophones du Canada; Le Centre d'aide et de luttre contre les agesssions à caractère sexuel du KRTB; Le Conseil québécois du loisir; Le Regroupement Loisir Québec; La Table de concertation des aînés du Bas St-Laurent; La Table de concertation multisectorielle pour les aînéEs du Témiscouata; L'Unité Régionale de Loisir et de Sport du Bas-Saint-Laurent
Membre(s) du bureau directeur:
Guy Genest, Président

Région Centre-du-Québec
#110, 59, rue Monfette, Victoriaville QC G6P 1J8
Tél: 819-752-7876; *Téléc:* 819-752-7630
Ligne sans frais: 800-828-3344
fadoq.info@cdcbf.qc.ca
www.fadoq-qdc.ca
Membre(s) du bureau directeur:
Annie Belcourt, Directrice générale

Région Côte-Nord
#107, 859, rue Bossé, Baie-Comeau QC G5C 3P8
Tél: 418-589-7870; *Téléc:* 418-589-7871
Ligne sans frais: 800-828-3344
fadoqcn@globetrotter.net
www.fadoqcote-nord.ca
Membre(s) du bureau directeur:
Marie-Bois Turcotte, Présidente

Région Estrie
#102, 288, rue Marquette, Sherbrooke QC J1H 1M2
Tél: 819-566-7748; *Téléc:* 819-566-7263
Ligne sans frais: 800-828-3344
infos@fadoqestrie.ca
www.fadoqestrie.ca
Membre(s) du bureau directeur:
Martine Grégoire, Directrice générale

Région Gaspésie Iles-de-la-Madeleine
189, rue Jacques-Cartier, Gaspé QC G4X 2P8
Tél: 418-368-4715; *Téléc:* 418-368-4310
info@fadoq.ca
www.fadoqgim.ca
Membre(s) du bureau directeur:
François Lapierre, Président

Région Ile de Montréal
#215, 7378, rue Lajeunesse, Montréal QC H2R 2H8
Tél: 514-271-1411; *Téléc:* 514-271-1640
info@fadoqmtl.org
www.montreal.fadoq.ca
www.facebook.com/fadoqmontreal
twitter.com/FadoqMontreal
Membre(s) du bureau directeur:
Ghislain Bilodeau, Président

Région Lanaudière
626, boul Manseau, Joliette QC J6E 3H6
Tél: 450-759-7422; *Téléc:* 450-759-8279
info@fadoqlanaudiere.ca
www.fadoqlanaudiere.org
Membre(s) du bureau directeur:
Danielle Perreault, Directrice général

Région Laurentides
#201, 499, rue Charbonneau, Mont-Tremblant QC J8E 3H4
Tél: 819-429-5858; *Téléc:* 819-429-6850
Ligne sans frais: 800-828-3344
info@fadoqlaurentides.org
www.fadoqlaurentides.org
Membre(s) du bureau directeur:
Micheline Chalifour, Présidente

Région Laval
#218, 1450, boul Pie-X, Laval QC H7V 3C1
Tél: 450-686-2339; *Téléc:* 450-686-4845
Ligne sans frais: 800-828-3344
info@fadoqlaval.com
www.fadoqlaval.com
Membre(s) du bureau directeur:
Andrée Vallée, Directrice générale

Région Mauricie
1325, rue Brébeuf, Trois-Rivières QC G8Z 1Z9
Tél: 819-374-5774; *Téléc:* 819-374-8850
Ligne sans frais: 800-828-3344
www.fadoq-mauricie.com
Membre(s) du bureau directeur:
Ginette Lapointe, Directrice générale

Région Outaouais
CP 12009, Gatineau QC J8T 0C3
Tél: 819-777-5774; *Téléc:* 819-205-0787
Ligne sans frais: 800-828-3344
admin@fadoqoutaouais.qc.ca
www.fadoqoutaouais.qc.ca
Membre(s) du bureau directeur:
Lise Desaulniers, Présidente

Région Richelieu-Yamaska
2775, av Bourdage nord, Saint-Hyacinthe QC J2S 5S3
Tél: 450-774-8111; *Téléc:* 450-774-6161
Ligne sans frais: 800-828-3344
info@fadoqry.ca
www.fadoqry.ca
Membre(s) du bureau directeur:
Claude Leblanc, Directeur général

Région Rive-Sud-Suroît
6A, ch du Grand-Bernier sud, Saint-Jean-sur-Richelieu QC J3B 4P8
Tél: 450-347-0910; *Téléc:* 450-347-6385
Ligne sans frais: 800-828-3344
fadoq@fadoqrrss.org
www.fadoqrrss.org
Membre(s) du bureau directeur:
Denise Charest, Directrice générale
denise.charest@fadoqrrss.org

Région Saguenay - Lac-St-Jean - Ungava
414, rue Collard ouest, Alma QC G8B 1N2
Tél: 418-668-4795; *Téléc:* 418-668-0265
Ligne sans frais: 800-828-3344
reception@fadoqsaglac.com
www.fadoqsaglac.com
Membre(s) du bureau directeur:
Patrice St-Pierre, Directeur général
direction@fadoqsaglac.com

Régions de Québec et Chaudière-Appalaches
CP 8832, Succ. Sainte-Foy, Sainte-Foy QC G1V 3V9
Tél: 418-650-3552; *Téléc:* 418-650-1659
Ligne sans frais: 800-828-3344
info@fadoq-quebec.qc.ca
www.fadoq-quebec.qc.ca
Membre(s) du bureau directeur:
Gérald Lépine, Directeur général
glepine@fadoq-quebec.qc.ca

Réseau Femmes Québec (RFQ)
#134, 911, rue Jean-Talon est, Montréal QC H2R 1V5
Tél: 514-484-2375
Aperçu: *Dimension:* moyenne; *Envergure:* provinciale
Affiliation(s): Réseau Hommes Québec
Membre(s) du bureau directeur:
Ruth Vachon, Présidente

Réseau franco-santé du Sud de l'Ontario (RFSSO)
CP 90057, 1000, rue Golf Links, Ancaster ON L9K 0B4
Tél: 416-413-1717
Ligne sans frais: 888-549-5775
www.francosantesud.ca
www.facebook.com/RFSSO
twitter.com/RFSSO
Aperçu: *Dimension:* petite; *Envergure:* provinciale; fondée en 2004 surveillé par Société santé en français
Mission: Contribue au développement des services de santé en français
Membre(s) du bureau directeur:
Julie Lantaigne, Directrice générale
jlantaigne@francosantesud.ca

Réseau HEC Montréal
3000, ch de la Côte-Sainte-Catherine, Montréal QC H3T 2A7
Tél: 514-340-6000; *Téléc:* 514-340-6411
www.hec.ca/diplome/reseau
www.linkedin.com/company/hec-montreal
www.facebook.com/HECMontreal
twitter.com/HEC_Montreal
www.youtube.com/HECMontreal;
www.flickr.com/photos/hecmontreal
Également appelé: Association des diplômés HEC Montréal
Nom précédent: Association des diplômés de l'École des hautes Études commerciales
Aperçu: *Dimension:* grande; *Envergure:* locale; Organisme sans but lucratif; fondée en 1921
Mission: Contribuer au développement socio professionnel de ses membres; établir des relations amicales; promouvoir les intérêts de l'école des HEC; relier les promotions et utiliser ces rapports au profit du commerce, de l'industrie et de la finance; étendre les connaissances des membres sur les recherches du commerce et de la finance dans les divers programmes
Finances: *Budget de fonctionnement annuel:* $1.5 Million-$3 Million
Membre(s) du personnel: 5; 150 bénévole(s)
Membre: 51 000+ diplômés; *Montant de la cotisation:* 85$ diplômés réguliers; *Critères d'admissibilite:* Diplômés de l'École des hautes études commerciales de Montréal; *Comités:* AGA; Entre-Vues du Réseau HEC; Ce qu'il me reste à vous dire; Rendez-vous annuel des diplômés; Prix Relève d'Excellence; Activités du Comité Jeunes (Rencontres d'un leader, 6@8 ...); Retrouvailles; Section de l'Outaouais; Section de Québec; Section de Toronto; Section de New York; International; HEC Conjuguée au féminin
Activités: Assemblée générale; tournoi de golf; Gala du commerce
Membre(s) du bureau directeur:
Michel Patry, Directeur
Hélène Desmarais, Chef de la direction
Prix, Bourses:
• Prix Relève d'Excellence du Réseau HEC Montréal Reconnaît les réalisations exceptionnelles des diplômés HEC Montréal de 35 ans ou moins

Réseau Hommes Québec (RHQ)
Centre Jean-Marie Gauvreau, #134, 911, rue Jean-Talon est, Montréal QC H2R 1V5
Tél: 514-276-4545
Ligne sans frais: 877-908-4545
rhquebec.ca
www.facebook.com/114381705296554
Aperçu: *Dimension:* grande; *Envergure:* provinciale; fondée en 1992
Mission: Organisme sans but lucratif; a pour mission d'entretenir un réseau de groupes autogérés d'écoute, de parole & d'entraide aux hommes
Affiliation(s): Réseau Hommes Belgique; Réseau Hommes France; Réseau Hommes Romandie; Réseau Femmes Québec
Membre(s) du bureau directeur:
Éric Maisonneuve, Président
Léo-Paul Provencher, Directeur général intérimaire

Réseau indépendant des diffuseurs d'événements artistiques unis (RIDEAU)
1550, boul Saint-Joseph est, Montréal QC H2J 1M7
Tél: 514-598-8024; *Téléc:* 514-598-8353
admin@rideau-inc.qc.ca
www.rideau-inc.qc.ca
Aperçu: *Dimension:* moyenne; *Envergure:* provinciale; fondée en 1978
Mission: Favoriser la diffusion des arts de la scène
Membre de: Chambre de Commerce du Québec
Membre: 145; *Montant de la cotisation:* $150-$900; *Critères d'admissibilite:* Diffuseurs de spectacles
Membre(s) du bureau directeur:
Julie-Anne Richard, Directrice générale
direction@rideau-inc.qc.ca

Christiane Verroeulst, Directrice administrative
cverroeulst@rideau-inc.qc.ca
Marie-Pier Pilote, Responsable, Projets et développement numérique
projets@rideau-inc.qc.ca
Manuel Bouchard, Coordonnateur, Services aux membres et communications
mbouchard@rideau-inc.qc.ca

Réseau international pour la diversité culturelle See International Network for Cultural Diversity

Réseau juridique canadien VIH/sida See Canadian HIV/AIDS Legal Network

Réseau national d'action EM/FM encéphalomyélite myalgique/fibromyalgie See National ME/FM Action Network

Réseau national pour la santé mentale See National Network for Mental Health

Réseau ontarien des organismes pour le développement de l'employabilité See Ontario Network of Employment Skills Training Projects

Réseau pour le développement de l'alphabétisme et des compétences (RESDAC)
#205, 235 ch Montréal, Ottawa ON K1L 6C7
Tél: 613-749-5333; Téléc: 613-749-2252
Ligne sans frais: 888-906-5666
info@resdac.net
www.resdac.net
www.facebook.com/128384640568102
Aperçu: Dimension: petite; Envergure: nationale; fondée en 1991
Mission: Promouvoir l'alphabétisation en français au Canada; assurer une concertation des intervenantes en alphabétisation en français au Canada.
Membre(s) du personnel: 6
Membre: 13
Activités: Stagiaires: Oui; Service de conférenciers: Oui; Bibliothèque: Bibliothèque publique rendez-vous
Membre(s) du bureau directeur:
Normand Lévesque, Directeur général
directiongenerale@resdac.net
Isabelle Salesse, Présidente
presidence@resdac.net
Donald Desroches, Vice-président

Réseau Québec-France
4295, rue Chauveau, Sherbrooke QC J1L 1P1
Tél: 819-566-2379
www.quebecfrance.org
Aperçu: Dimension: moyenne; Envergure: internationale; fondée en 1971
Mission: Faire connaître, comprendre et apprécier la France aux Québécois et le Québec en France; participer au développement de l'amitié et de la coopération entre les deux principales communautés francophones du monde
Affiliation(s): Fédération France-Québec/francophonie
Finances: Budget de fonctionnement annuel: $250,000-$500,000
Membre(s) du personnel: 5
Membre: 16 associations
Activités: Stagiaires: Oui; Bibliothèque: Bibliothèque publique
Membre(s) du bureau directeur:
André-P. Robert, Président

Réseau québécois de l'asthme et de la MPOC (RQAM)
Institut universitaire de cardiologie et de pneumologie de Québec, 2723, ch Sainte-Foy, #U-3771, Québec QC G1V 4G5
Tél: 418-650-9500; Téléc: 418-650-9391
Ligne sans frais: 877-441-5072
info@rqam.ca
qww.rqam.ca
Aperçu: Dimension: petite; Envergure: provinciale
Mission: De fournir un soutien aux professionnels travaillant dans l'asthme dans le secteur de la santé et de leurs patients
Membre: Montant de la cotisation: 30$; Comités: Scientifique
Membre(s) du bureau directeur:
Jean Bourbeau, Président

Réseau québécois des groupes écologistes (RQGE)
454, av Laurier est, Montréal QC H2J 1E7
Tél: 514-587-8194
info@rqge.qc.ca
www.rqge.qc.ca
www.facebook.com/Reseau.quebecois.des.groupes.ecologistes
twitter.com/InfoRQGE
www.youtube.com/user/RQgroupesecologistes
Aperçu: Dimension: petite; Envergure: provinciale; Organisme sans but lucratif; fondée en 1982 surveillé par Canadian Environmental Network
Mission: Pour recueillir de services et d'information pour les groupes écologiques du Québec; aider les groupes à communiquer entre eux
Membre(s) du personnel: 3
Membre: 80
Activités: Service de conférenciers: Oui
Membre(s) du bureau directeur:
Stéphane Gingras, Président
presidence@rqge.qc.ca
Bruno Massé, Coordonnateur général
coordo@rqge.qc.ca

Réseau québécois des OSBL d'habitation (RQOH)
#102, rue Fullum, Montréal QC H2K 0B5
Tél: 514-846-0163; Téléc: 514-846-3402
Ligne sans frais: 866-846-0163
info@rqoh.com
www.rqoh.com
www.facebook.com/ReseauQuebecoisOsblHabitation
twitter.com/RQOH_
Aperçu: Dimension: moyenne; Envergure: provinciale
Mission: Pour représenter les organismes de logement à but non lucratif; Pour répondre aux besoins de logement des personnes vulnérables et exclus de la province
Membre: 8 fédérations régionales qui représentent 1,200 organismes; Critères d'admissibilite: Organismes sans but lucratif d'habitation (OSBL-H)
Activités: Représenter les fédérations régionales d'OSBL d'habitation du Québec; Garantir que les intérêts de groupes de logements communautaires sont protégés
Membre(s) du bureau directeur:
Isabelle Leduc, Présidente
administration@chambreclerc.org
Stéphan Corriveau, Directeur général
direction@rqoh.com
Meetings/Conferences:
• Réseau québécois des OSBL d'habitation 2018 Congrès national sur le logement et l'itinérance, 2018, QC
Scope: Provincial
Publications:
• Bulletin Le Réseau [publication Réseau québécois des OSBL d'habitation]
Type: Bulletin
Profile: Nouvelles et information pour les membres

Bas-St-Laurent, de la Gaspésie & des Iles (FOHBGI)
CP 391, Rivière-du-Loup QC G5R 5Y9
Tél: 418-867-5178
fohbgi@rqoh.com
www.fohbgi.rqoh.com

Laval, Laurentides & Lanaudière (FLOH)
260A, boul Cartier ouest, Laval QC H7N 6K7
Tél: 450-662-6950; Téléc: 450-662-0399
Ligne sans frais: 888-662-0399
info@floh.qc.ca
www.floh.rqoh.com
twitter.com/FLOH_OSBL

Mauricie - Centre-du-Québec (FROHMCQ)
1160, Terrasse Turcotte, Trois-Rivières QC G9A 5C6
Tél: 819-697-3004; Téléc: 514-846-3402
Ligne sans frais: 866-846-0163
frohmqc@habitations.qc.ca
www.frohmqc.rqoh.com
Membre(s) du bureau directeur:
Richard Maziade, Président

Montérégie & de l'Estrie (FROHME)
311, rue McLeod, Châteauguay QC J6J 2H8
Tél: 450-201-0786; Téléc: 450-699-7014
info@frohme.org
www.frohme.rqoh.com
Membre(s) du bureau directeur:
Robert Boivin, Président

Montréal (FOHM)
2310, boul de Maisonneuve est, Montréal QC
Tél: 514-527-6668; Téléc: 514-527-7388
info@fohm.org
www.fohm.rqoh.com
www.facebook.com/FOHMtl
Membre(s) du bureau directeur:
Claudine Laurin, Directrice générale

Outaouais (ROHSCO)
28, rue Caron, Gatineau QC J8Y 1Y7
Tél: 819-205-3485; Téléc: 819-205-1223
info@rohsco.com
www.rohsco.rqoh.com
Membre(s) du bureau directeur:
Stéphanie Rajotte, Directrice générale

Québec, Chaudière-Appalaches (FROHQC)
#290, 245, rue Soumande, Québec QC G1M 3H6
Tél: 418-614-2495; Téléc: 418-614-1541
Ligne sans frais: 877-499-9656
reception@frohqc.com
www.frohqc.rqoh.com

Saguenay, Lac St-Jean, Chibougamau, Chapais & Côte-Nord (FROH)
208, rue Côté, Laterrière QC G7N 1L4
Tél: 418-402-0504; Téléc: 418-678-2794
Ligne sans frais: 877-402-0504
froh@rqoh.com
www.froh.rqoh.com
Membre(s) du bureau directeur:
Nancy Brisson, Présidente

Réseau québécois pour l'inclusion social des personnnes sourdes et malentendantes (ReQIS) / Quebec Network for Social Inclusion of the Deaf & Hard of Hearing
#202, 2494, boul Henri-Bourassa est, Montréal QC H2B 1T9
Tél: 514-278-8703; Téléc: 514-278-8238; TTY: 514-278-8704
administration@reqis.org
www.requis.org
Nom précédent: Centre québécois de la déficience auditive
Aperçu: Dimension: petite; Envergure: provinciale; Organisme sans but lucratif; fondée en 1975
Mission: • l'amélioration de la qualité de vie et à la défense des droits des personnes sourdes et malentendantes, signeures et oralistes
Membre de: Confédération des organismes de personnes handicapées du Québec
Activités: Service de conférenciers: Oui; Listes de destinataires: Oui

Réseau régional du l'industrie biologique du Canada atlantique See Atlantic Canadian Organic Regional Network

Réseau Santé - Nouvelle-Écosse
#222, 2 rue Bluewater, Bedford NS B4B 1G7
Tél: 902-222-5871
reseau@reseausante.ca
www.reseausante.ca
www.facebook.com/reseausantenouvelleecosse
twitter.com/ReseauSanteNE
Aperçu: Dimension: petite; Envergure: provinciale surveillé par Société santé en français
Mission: Promouvoir et d'améliorer l'accessibilité en français aux services de santé et de mieux-être de qualité
Membre(s) du bureau directeur:
Jeanne-Françoise Caillaud, Directrice générale

Réseau santé albertain
#304A, 8627, rue Marie-Anne-Gaboury, Edmonton AB T6C 3N1
Tél: 780-466-9816
info@reseausantealbertain.ca
www.reseausantealbertain.ca
www.facebook.com/162905357095396
twitter.com/inforsab
www.youtube.com/user/reseausantealbertain
Aperçu: Dimension: petite; Envergure: provinciale surveillé par Société santé en français
Membre(s) du bureau directeur:
Pauline Légaré, Directrice générale par intérim
pauline.legare@reseausantealbertain.ca

Réseau Santé en français de la Saskatchewan (RSFS)
#220, 308 4e av Nord, Saskatoon SK S7K 2L7
Tél: 306-653-7445; Téléc: 306-664-6447
www.rsfs.ca
www.facebook.com/rsfsaskatchewan
Aperçu: Dimension: petite; Envergure: provinciale; fondée en 2003 surveillé par Société santé en français
Mission: D'assurer un meilleur accès à des programmes et services sociaux et de santé en français
Membre(s) du bureau directeur:
Frédérique Baudemont, Directrice générale, 306-229-4069
rsfs@shaw.ca

Réseau Santé en français I.-P.-É
CP 58, 48, ch Mill, Wellington PE C0B 2E0
Tél: 902-854-7444; *Téléc:* 902-854-7255
info@santeipe.ca
www.santeipe.ca
www.facebook.com/RSFIPE
Aperçu: Dimension: petite; *Envergure:* provinciale surveillé par Société santé en français
Mission: Améliorer l'accès à des programmes et services de santé de qualité en français
Membre: 19
Membre(s) du bureau directeur:
Élise Arsenault, Directrice
elisearsenault@gov.pe.ca

Réseau santé en français Terre-Neuve-et-Labrador
Centre scolaire et communautaire des Grads-Vants, #233, 65 ch Ridge, St. John's NL A1B 4P5
Tél: 709-575-2862; *Téléc:* 709-722-9904
reseausante@fftnl.ca
www.francotnl.ca
Aperçu: Dimension: petite; *Envergure:* provinciale surveillé par Société santé en français
Mission: Améliorer l'offre de services de santé en français
Membre(s) du bureau directeur:
Roxanne Leduc, Contact

Réseau Tara Canada (Québec)
CP 156, Succ. Ahuntsic, Montréal QC H3L 3N7
Ligne sans frais: 888-886-8272
medias@taraquebec.org
www.taraquebec.org
www.facebook.com/ShareInternationalCanada
Également appelé: Réseau Tara; Tara Québec
Aperçu: Dimension: petite; *Envergure:* locale; Organisme sans but lucratif; fondée en 1985
Mission: Répandre le message de l'Enseignant universel Maitreya, le Christ, dirigeant de la Hiérarchie spirituelle de la planète
Membre de: Tara Canada
Affiliation(s): Partage International Canada; Tara Canada Network Association
Finances: Budget de fonctionnement annuel: Moins de $50,000
6 bénévole(s)
Membre: 400
Activités: Meditation; Conférence; *Service de conférenciers:* Oui; *Bibliothèque:* rendez-vous

Réseau Technoscience
4545, av Pierre-de Coubertin, Montréal QC H1V 0B2
Tél: 514-252-3027; *Téléc:* 514-252-3152
info@technoscience.ca
www.technoscience.ca
Nom précédent: Conseil de développement du loisir scientifique
Aperçu: Dimension: moyenne; *Envergure:* provinciale; Organisme sans but lucratif; fondée en 1968
Mission: La promotion d'activités scientifiques, particulièrement chez les jeunes
Membre de: Regroupement Loisir Québec; Fondation Science Jeunesse Canada
Finances: Budget de fonctionnement annuel: $500,000-$1.5 Million
Membre(s) du personnel: 9; 20 bénévole(s)
Membre: 1-99
Membre(s) du bureau directeur:
Roland Grand'Maison, Directeur général

Réseau TNO Santé en français
CP 1325, 5016, 48 rue, Yellowknife NT X1A 2N9
Tél: 867-920-2919; *Téléc:* 867-873-2158
santetno@franco-nord.com
www.reseautnosante.ca
twitter.com/SanteTno
Aperçu: Dimension: petite; *Envergure:* provinciale surveillé par Société santé en français
Mission: Contribuer à l'amélioration de l'accès à des services de santé de qualité en français
Membre(s) du bureau directeur:
Audrey Fournier, Coordonnatrice

Le réseau Toucher Thérapeutique de l'Atlantique *See* Atlantic Therapeutic Touch Network

Resident Doctors of British Columbia
#2399, 650 West Georgia St., Vancouver BC V6B 4N7
Tel: 604-876-7636
Toll-Free: 888-877-2722
info@residentdoctorsbc.ca
www.residentdoctorsbc.ca
www.facebook.com/ResidentDoctorsBC
twitter.com/ResidentDocsBC
Overview: A medium-sized provincial organization overseen by Resident Doctors of Canada
Mission: To bargain collectively on behalf of residents in British Columbia; To foster the personal well-being of members
Affiliation(s): Canadian Association of Internes & Residents
Finances: Funding Sources: Union dues
Membership: 1,300+; *Member Profile:* All residents of British Columbia become members of PAR-BC upon commencement of employment; *Committees:* Advocacy; Awards Selection; Communications; Distributed Medical Education; Executive; Finance; Governance; Health & Wellness; Negotiations
Activities: Promoting the educational concerns of residents in British Columbia; Advocating for members' interests; Liaising with government; Preparing position papers
Chief Officer(s):
David Kim, President
Gagandeep Dhaliwal, Vice-President
Boluwaji Ogunyemi, Director, Communications
Clark Funnell, Director, Finance
Pria Sandhu, Executive Director
Brandi MacLean, Office Administrator
Awards:
• Dr. Patricia Clugston Memorial Award For Excellence in Teaching
To recognize clinical faculty for their contributions to the continuing medical education of residents
• Residents' Advocate Award
To recognize an individual who advocates on behalf of residents to improve their well-being
• Award of Merit
To recognize a resident physician whose achievements reflect the aims of the Professional Association of Residents of British Columbia

Resident Doctors of Canada (RDoC)
#412, 151 Slater St., Ottawa ON K1P 5H3
Tel: 613-234-6448; *Fax:* 613-234-5292
communications@residentdoctors.ca
www.residentdoctors.ca
www.facebook.com/ResidentDoctorsCAN
twitter.com/residentdoctors
Previous Name: Canadian Association of Internes & Residents
Overview: A medium-sized national organization founded in 1973
Mission: To improve the quality of medical education & professionalism for resident physicians in Canada
Affiliation(s): Royal College of Physicians & Surgeons of Canada; College of Family Physicians of Canada; Canadian Medical Association; Federation of Medical Licensing Authorities of Canada
Membership: 7,500; *Member Profile:* Resident physicians in Newfoundland & Labrador, the Maritime provinces, Ontario, Manitoba, Saskatchewan, Alberta, & British Columbia; *Committees:* Awards; Executive; Finance, Audit & Risk; Governance & Nominating; Practice; Regional Networking; Training; Wellness
Activities: Collaborating with other national health organizations; Developing national policies
Chief Officer(s):
Kimberly Williams, President
Irving Gold, Executive Director
irving@residentdoctors.ca
Todd Coopee, Manager, Communications
tcoopee@residentdoctors.ca
Maryan McCarrey, Manager, Policy & Research
mmccarrey@residentdoctors.ca
Publications:
• Resident Doctors of Canada Annual Report
Type: Report; *Frequency:* Annually

Residential Construction Council of Ontario (RESCON)
#13, 25 North Rivermede Rd., Vaughan ON L4K 5V4
Tel: 905-760-7777; *Fax:* 905-760-7718
Toll-Free: 866-531-1608
www.rescon.ws
Overview: A small local organization
Mission: To represent the Ontario Residential Contractors Construction Association during labour reltations negotiations, as well as in matters regarding health & safety, WSIB, training & education
Membership: Committees: Technical; Marketing & Membership; Training & Education; Health & Safety

Resilient Flooring Contractors Association of Ontario (RFCAO)
70 Leek Cres., Richmond Hill ON L4B 1H1
Tel: 416-499-4000; *Fax:* 416-499-8752
info@resilientflooring.ca
www.resilientflooring.ca
Overview: A medium-sized provincial organization founded in 1954
Mission: To advance the interests of members; To promote & implement trade practices & regulations; To negotiate among & between members of the corporation
Finances: Annual Operating Budget: Less than $50,000
10 volunteer(s)
Membership: 44
Chief Officer(s):
Eric Babiak, President
ebabiak@live.ca

Réso Santé Colombie Britannique (RSCB)
#201, 2929, rue Commercial, Vancouver BC V5N 4C8
Tél: 604-629-1000
info@resosante.ca
www.resosante.ca
www.linkedin.com/company/résosanté-colombie-britannique
www.facebook.com/resosante
twitter.com/resosante
Aperçu: Dimension: petite; *Envergure:* provinciale; fondée en 2003 surveillé par Société santé en français
Mission: Promouvoir des services de la santé et du bien-être en français en Colombie-Britannique
Membre(s) du bureau directeur:
Benjamin Stoll, Directeur général
bstoll@resosante.ca

RESOLVE: Research & Education for Solutions to Violence & Abuse
#108, Isbister Building, University of Manitoba, Winnipeg MB R3T 2N2
Tel: 204-474-8965; *Fax:* 204-474-7686
resolve@umanitoba.ca
www.umanitoba.ca/resolve
Overview: A small provincial organization
Chief Officer(s):
Cyndi Porcher, Office Manager

Resorts Ontario
29 Albert St. North, Orillia ON L3V 5J9
Tel: 705-325-9115; *Fax:* 705-325-7999
Toll-Free: 800-363-7227
escapes@resorts-ontario.com
www.resortsofontario.com
www.facebook.com/ResortsofOntario
twitter.com/ResortsOntario
www.youtube.com/user/ResortsofOntario
Also Known As: Association of Tourist Resorts of Ontario
Overview: A medium-sized provincial organization founded in 1942
Mission: To serve & promote the collective interests of resorts, lodges & inns of Ontario
Finances: Funding Sources: Membership fees
Membership: 100+
Chief Officer(s):
Grace Sammut, Executive Director
grace@resortsofontario.com

Resource and Intervention Center for Men Sexually Abused during their Childhood *Voir* Centre de ressources et d'intervention pour hommes abusés sexuellement dans leur enfance

Resource Assistance for Youth (RAY)
125 Sherbrooke St., Winnipeg MB R3C 2B5
Tel: 204-783-5617; *Fax:* 204-775-4988
info@rayinc.ca
www.rayinc.ca
www.linkedin.com/company/3040355
www.facebook.com/raywinnipeg
twitter.com/raywinnipeg
www.youtube.com/user/RaYWinnipeg
Previous Name: Operation Go Home - Winnipeg Office
Overview: A small local organization overseen by Operation Come Home
Mission: To improve the lives of homeless youth & help them reintegrate into society.

Staff Member(s): 17
Chief Officer(s):
Kelly Holmes, Executive Director
kelly@rayinc.ca

Resource Centre on Non-Violence *Voir* Centre des ressources sur la non-violence inc

Resource Efficient Agricultural Production (REAP Canada)
PO Box 125, Stn. Centennial Centre CCB13, #21, 111, rue Lakeshore, Sainte-Anne-de-Bellevue QC H9X 3V9
Tel: 514-398-7743; *Fax:* 514-398-7972
info@reap-canada.com
www.reap-canada.com
Also Known As: Sustainable Farming
Overview: A medium-sized national charitable organization founded in 1988
Mission: To improve farm profits & productivity while minimizing adverse health & environmental effects
Affiliation(s): Canadian Organic Growers; Ecological Farmers Association of Ontario
Staff Member(s): 5
Membership: *Fees:* $25 individual; $100 organization
Activities: Sustainable farming research into biomass energy on farm sustainable agriculture research for carbon dioxide reduction; *Speaker Service:* Yes; *Library:* by appointment
Chief Officer(s):
Roger Samson, Executive Director

Resource Industry Suppliers Association (RISA)
1002 - 7 St., Nisku AB T9E 7P2
Tel: 780-489-5900; *Fax:* 780-489-6262
risa@resourcesuppliers.com
www.resourcesuppliers.com
www.linkedin.com/company/resource-industry-suppliers-association
www.facebook.com/RISA.012
twitter.com/RISACan
Overview: A medium-sized national organization
Mission: To source project information & contracts from members of the energy, mining, forest & bio-products industries
Membership: *Fees:* $450
Chief Officer(s):
Kerri McTaggart, MBA, Executive Director
kerri@resourcesuppliers.com

Respiratory Therapy Society of Ontario (RTSO) / Société de la thérapie respiratoire de l'Ontario
#440, 160-2 Country Court Blvd., Brampton ON L6W 4V1
Tel: 647-729-2717; *Fax:* 647-729-2715
Toll-Free: 855-297-3089
office@rtso.ca
www.rtso.ca
Overview: A medium-sized provincial organization founded in 1972 overseen by Canadian Society of Respiratory Therapists
Mission: To represent & advance the professional interests of Ontario's respiratory therapists; To develop & maintain standards of practice for respiratory therapy
Membership: *Fees:* Schedule available; *Member Profile:* Respiratory therapists in Ontario; *Committees:* Student Affairs; Research; Community RT
Activities: Engaging in advocacy activities; Promoting respiratory therapy in Ontario; Supporting educational opportunities; Providing public education on respiratory health; Supporting research
Chief Officer(s):
Kyle Davies, President
Mike Keim, Treasurer
Publications:
• Airwaves
Type: Newsletter; *Price:* Free with RTSO membership
Profile: Society reports, events, & information plus articles

Responsible Dog Owners of Canada (RDOC)
9 Liette Crt., RR1, Kemptville ON K0G 1J0
Tel: 613-206-6885
inquiries@responsibledogowners.ca
www.responsibledogowners.ca
Overview: A medium-sized national organization founded in 1999
Mission: To promote responsible dog ownership and public safety through education and support, cultivate respect for the rights and privileges of all members of society, both dog-owning and non-dog owning, encourage and foster recognition of the contribution that canines make in society through companionship, service/assistance and therapy and assemble a strong network of responsible dog owners to ensure the restoration and preservation of a dog-friendly society.
Membership: *Fees:* $20 single/family; $10 student/senior; $35 non-profit; $50 corporate
Chief Officer(s):
Candice O'Connell, Chair
coconnell@responsibledogowners.ca

Responsible Gambling Council (Ontario) (RGC(O)) / Le Conseil ontarien pour le jeu responsable
#205, 411 Richmond St. East, Toronto ON M5A 3S5
Tel: 416-499-9800; *Fax:* 416-499-8260
www.responsiblegambling.org
www.linkedin.com/company/responsible-gambling-council
twitter.com/RGCouncil
www.youtube.com/user/RGCouncilCanada
Previous Name: Canadian Foundation on Compulsive Gambling (Ontario)
Overview: A small provincial charitable organization founded in 1983
Mission: To increase awareness of compulsive gambling among families, community & service club leaders; To support research into the causes & treatment
Affiliation(s): Responsible Gambling Council of Canada
Finances: *Funding Sources:* Ministry of Health; Ontario Lottery & Gaming Corporation
Staff Member(s): 35
Membership: *Committees:* Governance & Nominating; Strategic Directions; Audit
Activities: *Speaker Service:* Yes; *Library:* Open to public
Chief Officer(s):
Robin Boychuk, Chair
Jon E. Kelly, Chief Executive Officer, 416-490-2060
jonk@rgco.org

Responsible Investment Association (RIA)
#300, 215 Spadina Ave., Toronto ON M5T 2C7
Tel: 416-461-6042
staff@riacanada.ca
riacanada.ca
www.linkedin.com/company/responsible-investment-association
www.facebook.com/ResponsibleInvestmentAssociation
twitter.com/riacanada
Previous Name: Social Investment Organization
Overview: A medium-sized national organization founded in 1989
Mission: To take a leadership role in coordinating the responsible investing (RI) agenda in Canada; to raise public awareness of RI in Canada; to reach out to other groups interested in RI; to provide information on RI to members & the public
Staff Member(s): 4
Membership: 100-499; *Fees:* $15,000 sustaining; $5,500 associate; $1,000 pension fund; $350 financial advisor & consultant; $300 organizational; *Member Profile:* Asset management companies; investment fund companies; financial advisors; investors
Activities: *Internships:* Yes; *Speaker Service:* Yes; *Rents Mailing List:* Yes
Chief Officer(s):
Deb Abbey, Chief Executive Officer
deb@riacanada.ca
Wendy Mitchell, Financial Coordinator
wendy@riacanada.ca
Dustyn Lanz, Director, Research & Communications
dustyn@riacanada.ca
Meetings/Conferences:
• Responsible Investment Association 2018 Conference, June, 2018, Hyatt Regency Toronto, Toronto, ON
Scope: National

Ressources Saint-Jean-Vianney
CP 21036, Succ. Jacques Cartier, Longueuil QC J4J 5J4
Tél: 450-646-8690
direction@rsjv.org
rsjv.org
Aperçu: *Dimension:* petite; *Envergure:* locale
Mission: Pour aider les personnes défavorisées en leur offrant des activités sociales ainsi que des activités éducatives
Activités: Magasin-partage; Clinique d'impôts; Activités familiales; Activités pour les enfants
Membre(s) du bureau directeur:
Benjamin Sirois-Caouette, Directeur
Annelies Van Laer, Présidente, Conseil d'administration

Restaurants Canada
1155 Queen St. West, Toronto ON M6J 1J4
Tel: 416-923-8416; *Fax:* 416-923-1450
Toll-Free: 800-387-5649
info@restaurantscanada.org
www.restaurantscanada.org
www.linkedin.com/company/canadian-restaurant-and-foodservices-association
www.facebook.com/RestaurantsCanada
twitter.com/RestaurantsCA
www.instagram.com/restaurantscanada
Previous Name: Canadian Restaurant & Foodservices Association
Overview: A large national organization founded in 1944
Mission: To create a favourable business environment & deliver tangible value to members in all sectors of Canada's foodservice industry
Finances: *Funding Sources:* Membership dues; Trade shows; Sale of materials; Corporate sponsors
Staff Member(s): 5
Membership: 30,000; *Fees:* Schedule available, based upon sales volume; *Member Profile:* Foodservice or restaurant establishment or supplier to industry
Activities: Engaging in government affairs; Providing specialized training programs, information, & resources; Organizing trade shows & industry events; *Library:* Resource Centre; by appointment Not open to public
Chief Officer(s):
Shanna Munro, President & CEO
Sheryl Ross, Chief Financial Officer
Joyce Reynolds, Executive Vice-President, Government Affairs
Troy Taylor, Vice-President, Operations
Christopher Barry, Director, Membership Development & Engagement
Meetings/Conferences:
• Restaurants Canada Show 2018, February, 2018, Enercare Centre, Toronto, ON
Scope: National
Attendance: 13,000+
Description: An event featuring culinary demonstrations, seminars, workshops, presentations, more than 700 exhibitors, & numerous networking opportunities for members of Canada's foodservice sector
Atlantic Canada Office
#201, 5121 Sackville St., Halifax NS B3J 1K1
Tel: 902-425-0061; *Fax:* 902-422-1161
Toll-Free: 877-755-1938
Chief Officer(s):
Luc Erjavec, Vice-President, Atlantic Canada
lerjavec@restaurantscanada.org
Manitoba-Saskatchewan Office
201 Portage Ave., 18th Fl., Winnipeg MB R3B 3K6
Tel: 204-926-8557; *Fax:* 204-926-8687
Toll-Free: 877-926-8557
Chief Officer(s):
Dwayne Marling, Vice-President, Manitoba-Saskatchewan
dmarling@restaurantscanada.org
Québec Office
#2400, 1000, de la Gauchetière ouest, Montréal QC H3B 4W5
Tel: 514-448-2154; *Fax:* 514-448-5154
Chief Officer(s):
Jean Lefebvre, Vice-President, Quebec
jlefebvre@restaurantscanada.org
Western Canada Office
PO Box 12125, #2410, 555 West Hastings St., Vancouver BC V6B 4N6
Tel: 604-685-9655; *Fax:* 604-685-9633
Toll-Free: 866-300-7675
Chief Officer(s):
Mark von Schellwitz, Vice-President, Western Canada
mvonschellwitz@restaurantscanada.org

Restigouche County Society for the Prevention of Cruelty to Animals
165 Baybreeze Dr., Dalhousie NB E8C 1E4
Tel: 506-684-4396
restspca@nb.aibn.com
restigouchecountyspca.7p.com
www.facebook.com/RestigoucheCountySpca
Also Known As: Restigouche County SPCA
Overview: A small local organization
Member of: Canadian Federation of Humane Societies
Staff Member(s): 5
Membership: *Fees:* $5 student/senior; $10 individual; $25 family; $100 life
Chief Officer(s):

Kathy Vautour, Manager

Restigouche County Volunteer Action Association Inc. (RCVAA) / L'Association d'Action Communautaire Bénévole du Restigouche
PO Box 1007, 13 Aberdeen St. NE, Campbellton NB E3N 3H4
Tel: 506-753-2252; *Fax:* 506-753-6403
rcvaa@nb.aibn.com
Overview: A small local organization founded in 1983
Activities: Providing food, clothing, & furniture bank for residents of Restigouche County
Chief Officer(s):
Rachelle Ouellette, Executive Director

Retail Advertising & Marketing Club of Canada (RAC)
#800, 1881 Yonge St., Toronto ON M4S 3C4
Tel: 416-495-6826; *Fax:* 416-922-8011
Toll-Free: 877-790-4271
www.raccanada.ca
Overview: A medium-sized national organization founded in 1987
Mission: To provide a forum for retail advertising & marketing professionals to meet, discuss vital issues, explore trends, exchange ideas & address business needs
Affiliation(s): RAMA Chicago
Finances: *Annual Operating Budget:* $100,000-$250,000; *Funding Sources:* Membership fees; dinner fees
Staff Member(s): 3; 29 volunteer(s)
Membership: 150+; *Fees:* $97 individual; $184-$383 corporate; *Member Profile:* Advertising executives & their suppliers; *Committees:* Education; Events; Executive; Marketing & Communications; Membership; Sponsorship
Activities: Hosting speaker & dinner events that allow retail marketing professionals to exchange ideas & develop business strategies
Chief Officer(s):
Lisa Tompkins, Chair

Retail Council of Canada (RCC) / Conseil canadien du commerce de détail
#800, 1881 Yonge St., Toronto ON M4S 3C4
Tel: 416-467-3777; *Fax:* 416-922-8011
Toll-Free: 888-373-8245
info@retailcouncil.org
www.retailcouncil.org
www.linkedin.com/company/retail-council-of-canada
www.facebook.com/retailcouncil
twitter.com/RetailCouncil
www.youtube.com/user/RetailCouncil
Overview: A large national organization founded in 1963
Mission: To be the best at delivering the services our retail members value most; To serve, promote & represent the diverse needs of Canada's retailing industry to the highest standards of quality
Affiliation(s): Canadian Health Food Association; Footwear Council of Canada; Le Conseil quebeçois du commerce de rétail; Retail Merchants' Association of Alberta; Retail Merchants' Association of Manitoba
Membership: 45,000 companies; *Fees:* Schedule available; *Member Profile:* Retailers of all sizes across Canada; *Committees:* Alberta Labour Supply Task Force; Audit; CFO Network; Commitment to Parents; eCommerce Council; Environment; Executive; Human Resources; Independent Retailer Advisory Board; Loss Prevention; Ontario Business Sector Working Group; Payments; Public Affairs Forum; Regional Advisory Networks; Responsible Sourcing; Retail General Counsel Roundtable; Safety Group
Activities: *Speaker Service:* Yes; *Library:* by appointment Not open to public
Chief Officer(s):
Peter Higgins, Chair
Diane J. Brisebois, CAE, President & CEO
djbrisebois@retailcouncil.org

   Western Office
   #209, 1730 West 2nd Ave., Vancouver BC V6J 1H6
   Tel: 604-736-0368
   Toll-Free: 800-663-5135
   Chief Officer(s):
   Mark Startup, Vice-President, 604-730-5252
   mstartup@retailcouncil.org

Retail Council of Québec *Voir* Conseil québécois du commerce de détail

Rethink Breast Cancer
50 Carroll St., Toronto ON M4M 3G3
Tel: 416-920-0980
hello@rethinkbreastcancer.com
www.rethinkbreastcancer.com
www.facebook.com/RethinkBreastCancer
twitter.com/rethinktweet
www.youtube.com/user/rethinkbreastcancer1
Overview: A medium-sized national charitable organization
Mission: To help young people concerned about & affected by breast cancer
Finances: *Funding Sources:* Donations; Fundraising; Corporate support
Membership: *Committees:* Rethink Scientific Advisory
Activities: Providing support groups & breast cancer education; Supporting medical research; Increasing awareness of breast cancer; *Awareness Events:* Annual Little Sweetheart Ball; Urban Après Ski; Rethink Romp
Chief Officer(s):
Mary-Jo DeCoteau, Executive Director
mj@rethinkbreastcancer.com
Publications:
• Upfront
Type: Newsletter; *Frequency:* Quarterly
Profile: Information about upcoming events

The Retired Teachers of Ontario (RTO) / Les Enseignants et enseignantes retraités de l'Ontario (ERO)
#300, 18 Spadina Rd., Toronto ON M5R 2S7
Tel: 416-962-9463; *Fax:* 416-962-1061
Toll-Free: 800-361-9888
info@rto-ero.org
www.rto-ero.org
www.facebook.com/rto.ero
twitter.com/rto_ero
www.youtube.com/erorto
Previous Name: Superannuated Teachers of Ontario
Overview: A medium-sized provincial organization founded in 1968
Mission: To promote the interests of persons in receipt of a pension under the Ontario Teachers' Pension Act
Member of: Canadian Association of Retired Teachers
Finances: *Funding Sources:* Membership fees
Staff Member(s): 17
Membership: 69,000+; *Fees:* $53; *Member Profile:* Persons in receipt of a pension under the Ontario Teachers' Pension Act; *Committees:* Audit; Communications; Health Services & Insurance; Member Services; Nominating; Political Advocacy; Pension Retirement & Concerns; Project - Service to Others
Activities: Services available to members only
Chief Officer(s):
Howard Braithwaite, Executive Director
hbrathwaite@rto-ero.org

Retirement Planning Association of Canada (RPAC) / Association des planificateurs de retraite du Canada (APRC)
RPAC National Office, #600, 3660 Hurontario St., Mississauga ON L5B 3C4
Fax: 647-723-6457
Toll-Free: 866-933-0233
info@retirementplanners.ca
www.retirementplanners.ca
Overview: A small national organization founded in 1980
Finances: *Funding Sources:* Sponsorships
Membership: *Fees:* $173.25 individuals; $467.25 corporations; *Member Profile:* Financial planners; Lifestyle advisors; Retirement planners; Human resources personnel; Counsellors; Educators
Activities: Offering educational programs & networking opportunities; Providing information on retirement planning in Canada to the general public
Chief Officer(s):
Robert Jeffrey, Administrator
Publications:
• RPAC [Retirement Planning Association of Canada] Newsletter
Type: Newsletter; *Frequency:* Semiannually; *Price:* Free for RPAC members

Revelstoke Arts Council (RAC)
PO Box 1931, 320 Wilson St., Revelstoke BC V0E 2S0
Tel: 250-814-9325
info@revelstokeartscouncil.com
revelstokeartscouncil.com
www.facebook.com/revelstoke.arts.council
Overview: A small local organization
Mission: To promote the visual & performing arts in Revelstoke
Affiliation(s): Assembly of British Columbia Arts Councils
Activities: Overseeing the local art group, art gallery, concert series, community band, theatre company, women's writing group; Supporting community arts festivals, such as the Summer Street Festival & the Mountain Arts Festival
Chief Officer(s):
Carol Palladino, President
Garry Pendergast, Executive Director

Revelstoke Chamber of Commerce
PO Box 490, 301 Victoria Rd. West, Revelstoke BC V0E 2S0
Tel: 250-837-5345
Toll-Free: 800-487-1493
revelstokechamber.com
www.facebook.com/revelstokechamber
twitter.com/RevyChamber
Overview: A small local organization founded in 1895
Mission: To promote the progress & development of Revelstoke & region in order to make it a better place to live & work
Member of: BC Rockies Tourism Association; BC Chamber of Commerce; Kootenay Rockies Tourism
Finances: *Funding Sources:* Membership dues; municipal; Ministry of Small Business, Tourism & Culture; gift shop
Staff Member(s): 4
Activities: *Internships:* Yes *Library:* Business Information Center; Open to public
Chief Officer(s):
Judy Goodman, Executive Director

Revelstoke Community Connections Food Bank
c/o Community Connections, PO Box 2880, 314 - 2nd St. East, Revelstoke BC V0E 2S0
Tel: 250-837-2920; *Fax:* 250-837-2909
plarson@community-connections.ca
Overview: A small local organization
Mission: To meet the immediate food needs of people in the community of Revelstoke; To work towards long term solutions to hunger & poverty
Finances: *Funding Sources:* Donations
Activities: Coordinating free food distribution
Chief Officer(s):
Patti Larson, Contact

Revelstoke Women's Shelter Society
PO Box 1150, Revelstoke BC V0E 2S0
Tel: 250-837-4382; *Fax:* 250-837-4386; *Crisis Hot-Line:* 250-837-1111
revelstokewomensshelter.com
Overview: A small local organization founded in 1985
Mission: To offer support, assistance, information & referrals in a courteous & compassionate manner that respects the dignity, privacy, cultural & diversity of women (& their children) who are victims of abuse
Finances: *Funding Sources:* Provincial government; private donations; fundraising
Membership: *Member Profile:* Women & children suffering from abuse
Activities: Advocacy; Outreach; Transporation; Accompaniment; Referrals; Awareness; Promotion of prevention strategies
Chief Officer(s):
Nelli Richardson, Executive Director

Revivre
5140, rue St-Hubert, Montréal QC H2J 2Y3
Tél: 514-783-4873; *Téléc:* 514-529-3081
Ligne sans frais: 866-738-4873
revivre@revivre.org
revivre.org
www.facebook.com/173729222663452
twitter.com/revivre_org
Aperçu: *Dimension:* petite; *Envergure:* locale
Mission: Pour offrir aux personnes souffrant de maladies mentales et de leurs familles avec l'appui
Membre: *Montant de la cotisation:* 30$ Individuelle; 50$ Famille; 100$Assoié
Activités: Ateliers; Conférences
Membre(s) du bureau directeur:
Jean-Rémy Provost, Directeur général
Guy Latraverse, Président, Conseil d'administration

Revivre - Association Québécoise de soutien aux personnes souffrant de troubles anxieux, dépressifs ou bipolaires / Québec Anxiety, Depressive & Bipolar Disorder Support Association
5140, rue Saint-Hubert, Montréal QC H2J 2Y3

Tél: 514-529-3081; *Téléc:* 514-529-3083
Ligne sans frais: 866-738-4873
revivre@revivre.org
www.revivre.org
www.linkedin.com/company/revivre
www.facebook.com/revivre.org
twitter.com/revivre_org
Également appelé: Association des dépressifs et maniaco-dépressifs
Nom précédent: Association québécoise des cyclothymiques
Aperçu: *Dimension:* petite; *Envergure:* provinciale; Organisme sans but lucratif; fondée en 1983
Mission: Diffuser de l'information sur les troubles anxieux, dépressifs et bipolaires; favoriser le diagnostic et la prise en charge des personnes atteintes de ces maladies; supporter les personnes atteintes et leurs proches; briser l'isolement de ces personnes; partager notre expertise avec les professionnels et autres intervenants du milieu de la santé
Membre de: Association des professionnels en gestion philantropique
Affiliation(s): Réseau alternatif et communautaire des organismes en santé mentale
Finances: *Budget de fonctionnement annuel:* $250,000-$500,000
Membre: 850; *Montant de la cotisation:* 30$ individus; 50$ famille; 100$ professionnels; *Critères d'admissibilite:* Personnes atteintes; proches; professionnels de la santé
Activités: Ligne d'écoute, d'information et de références; groupes d'entraide; conférences relation d'aide individuelle; internet; centre de documentation; *Evénements de sensibilisation:* Journée Dépistage de la Dépression, oct.; *Bibliothèque:* rendez-vous
Membre(s) du bureau directeur:
Martin Enault, Président
Jean-Rémy Provost, Directeur général

Revolutionary Communist Party *Voir* Parti communiste révolutionnaire

Rexdale Community Legal Services (RCLC)
Woodbine Centre, #24, 21 Panorama Ct., Toronto ON M9V 4E3
Tel: 416-741-5201; *Fax:* 416-741-6540
www.rexdalecommunitylegalclinic.ca
Overview: A small local charitable organization founded in 1971
Mission: To provide legal advice & referrals to all Northern Etobicoke residents; to provide legal representation to low-income community residents in certain areas of law
Finances: *Annual Operating Budget:* $500,000-$1.5 Million
Activities: Library:
Chief Officer(s):
Jayne Mallin, Director, Legal Services
Italica Battiston, Director, Administration

Rexdale Community Microskills Development Centre *See* Community Microskills Development Centre

Rexdale Women's Centre (RWC)
#309, 925 Albion Rd., Toronto ON M9V 1A6
Tel: 416-745-0062; *Fax:* 416-745-3995
admin@rexdalewomen.org
www.rexdalewomen.org
www.linkedin.com/company/rexdale-women's-centre
www.facebook.com/rexdalewomencentre
Overview: A small local charitable organization founded in 1982 overseen by Ontario Council of Agencies Serving Immigrants
Mission: To provide support for high-need women & their families living in the Greater Toronto Area; To assist women to become self-sufficient, financially secure, safe, healthy, & socially active
Finances: *Funding Sources:* Donations
Membership: *Fees:* $2 client; $5 unemployed individuals & students; $10 employed individuals; $20 organizations
Activities: Facilitating access to resources & community services; Providing programs, such as violence prevention services, settlement services, English language classes, & family support services; Collaborating with other organizations; *Awareness Events:* Walk 4 Change
Chief Officer(s):
Fatima Filippi, Executive Director

RÉZO
CP 246, Succ. C, Montréal QC H2L 4K1
Tél: 514-521-7778; *Téléc:* 514-521-7665
www.rezosante.org
www.facebook.com/REZOsante
twitter.com/rezosante
www.youtube.com/REZOsante

Nom précédent: Action Séro Zéro
Aperçu: *Dimension:* petite; *Envergure:* locale; fondée en 1991
Mission: Développer et coordonner des activités d'éducation et de prévention du VIH-sida et des autres ITSS dans un contexte de promotion de la santé sexuelle auprès des hommes gais, bisexuels et hommes ayant des relations sexuelles avec d'autres hommes de Montréal.
Membre(s) du bureau directeur:
Robert Rousseau, Directeur général, 514-521-7778 Ext. 227
robertrousseau@rezosante.org

Rhinoceros Party
125, rang des Bouleaux, Saint-Donat QC G0K 1L0
Tel: 581-624-2530
Overview: A small national organization
Chief Officer(s):
Sébastien Corriveau, Leader

Rhythmic Gymnastics Alberta (RGA)
c/o Percy Page Centre, 11759 Groat Rd., Edmonton AB T5M 3K6
Tel: 780-427-8152; *Fax:* 780-427-8153
Toll-Free: 800-881-2504
rga@rgalberta.com
www.rgalberta.com
Previous Name: Alberta Rhythmic Sportive Gymnastics Federation
Overview: A medium-sized provincial organization founded in 1979
Mission: To foster & encourage participation & the development of excellence in rhythmic gymnastics
Member of: Gymnastics Canada Gymnastique
Finances: *Annual Operating Budget:* $100,000-$250,000
Staff Member(s): 2; 100 volunteer(s)
Membership: 800; *Fees:* Schedule available; *Member Profile:* Children 5-18; Active adults/coaches 16-80
Activities: Provincial Gymnastrada; National & international competitions & events; *Speaker Service:* Yes

Rhythmic Gymnastics Manitoba Inc. (RGM)
145 Pacific Ave., Winnipeg MB R3B 2Z6
Tel: 201-925-5738
rhythmic@sportmanitoba.ca
www.rgmanitoba.com
Previous Name: Manitoba Rhythmic Sportive Gymnastics Association
Overview: A medium-sized provincial organization founded in 1985
Mission: To support & promote rhythmic gymnastic programs
Affiliation(s): Sport Manitoba; Rhythmic Gymnastics Canada; Gymnastics Canada; International Gymnastics Federation; Canadian Sport Centre - Manitoba; Coaching Manitoba; Gymnastics Manitoba
Membership: 8 clubs in the Winnipeg & Eastman regions
Activities: Hosting performing & competitive events; Posting event results; Providing programs to the rhythmic gymnastics community in Manitoba, such as the long term athlete development program & training for gymnastics coaches, & judges; Promoting standards for programs
Awards:
• Heather Willoughby Trophy
Awarded to the club with the highest total of all-around scores at the Provincial Championships
• Diana Juchnowski Trophy
Awarded to the top Provincial Stream individual gymnast with the highest all-around score
• Zlatica Stauder Trophy
Awarded to the individual gymnast who scores the highest in the competition in the single event
• Emelia Reddy Trophy
Awarded to the National Stream group that achieves the highest score of the competition
• Thelma Kojima Trophy
Awarded to the Provincial Stream group that achieves the highest score of the competition
• Coach of the Year Awards
Awarded to recognize 3 outstanding coaches (one from each program: Recreational, Provincial & National)
• The Royals Apprentice Coach Award
• Zdravka Tchonkova Coach of the Year
Meetings/Conferences:
• Rhythmic Gymnastics Manitoba 2018 AGM, 2018, MB
Scope: Provincial

Richard Eaton Singers (RES)
11759 Groat Rd. NW, Edmonton AB T5M 3K6

Tel: 780-428-3737; *Fax:* 780-428-3736
info@richardeatonsingers.com
www.richardeatonsingers.com
Previous Name: University Singers
Overview: A small local charitable organization founded in 1951
Mission: To foster the appreciation, study, & performance of choral music
Finances: *Funding Sources:* Donations; Sponsorships
Membership: *Committees:* The RES Educational Outreach Committee
Activities: Presenting performances; Offering the RES Education Program to high school students; *Library:* The Richard Eaton Singers Music Library
Chief Officer(s):
Leonard Ratzlaff, Music Director & Conductor

Richard III Society of Canada
c/o 156 Drayton Ave., Toronto ON M4C 3M2
richardiii@cogeco.ca
home.cogeco.ca/~richardiii/
twitter.com/RichardIIICA
Overview: A small local organization founded in 1966
Mission: To promote research into the life & times of Richard III to secure a re-assessment of the material relating to this period & this monarch's role in English history.
Member of: Richard III Society (UK)
Finances: *Funding Sources:* Membership fees
Membership: *Fees:* $65 regular; $55 senior/student
Activities: Medieval Banquet in Oct.; *Library:* Buyers' Library; by appointment Not open to public

Richard Ivey Foundation
#400, 11 Church St., Toronto ON M5E 1W1
Tel: 416-867-9229; *Fax:* 416-601-1689
info@ivey.org
www.ivey.org
Overview: A medium-sized local charitable organization founded in 1947
Mission: To pursue & support excellence by making grants that will improve the well-being of Canadians
Activities: Participating in the Conserving Canada's Forests program, by providing support to national or provincial charitable environmental organizations
Chief Officer(s):
Rosamond Ivey, Chair
Richard W. Ivey, Secretary-Treasurer
Bruce Lourie, President

Richelieu International (RI)
#25, 1010 rue Polytek, Ottawa ON K1J 9J1
Tél: 613-742-6911; *Téléc:* 613-742-6916
Ligne sans frais: 800-267-6525
international@richelieu.org
www.richelieu.org
www.linkedin.com/company/richelieu-international?trk=company_name
www.facebook.com/277906642896
twitter.com/Le_Richelieu
www.youtube.com/watch?v=7pqgbohjM6A
Aperçu: *Dimension:* petite; *Envergure:* internationale; fondée en 1944
Mission: A pour mission l'épanouissement de la personalité de ses membres & au développement de leurs aptitudes personnelles & collectives; la promotion de la langue française; aider la jeunesse
Finances: *Budget de fonctionnement annuel:* $250,000-$500,000; *Fonds:* Cotisation des membres
Membre(s) du personnel: 4; 20 bénévole(s)
Membre: 4 000 individus; *Montant de la cotisation:* 60$ individu
Membre(s) du bureau directeur:
Laurier Thériault, Directeur général
lauriertheriault@hotmail.com
Denis Daigle, Directeur administratif
denis@richelieu.org

Richibouctou chambre de commerce *See* Kent Centre Chamber of Commerce

Richmond Agricultural Society
PO Box 1210, 6121 Perth St., Richmond ON K0A 2Z0
Tel: 613-838-3420; *Fax:* 613-838-3933
richmondfair@sympatico.ca
www.richmondfair.ca
www.facebook.com/pages/Richmond-Fair/273996526030979
Overview: A small local charitable organization founded in 1841 overseen by Ontario Association of Agricultural Societies

Canadian Associations / Richmond Caring Place Society (RCPS)

Mission: To promote agricultural awareness to the community by hosting a Fall Agricultural Fair
Member of: Society of Composers, Authors & Music Publishers of Canada
Affiliation(s): Canadian Association of Fairs & Exhibitions; Ontario Association of Agricutural Societies
Finances: *Annual Operating Budget:* $250,000-$500,000; *Funding Sources:* Federal, provincial & regional government; local businesses, individuals
Staff Member(s): 2; 450 volunteer(s)
Membership: 400 individual; *Fees:* $10 individual; *Member Profile:* To promote agricultural awareness to the community; *Committees:* Over 30, Livestock, Homecraft, Kiddyland, Entertainment, 4-H, Advertising, Consessions
Activities: Richmond Fair, Sept.; livestock shows; fundraising events
Chief Officer(s):
Dale Greene, General Manager/Secretary

Richmond Board of Trade *See* Richmond Chamber of Commerce

Richmond Caring Place Society (RCPS)
#140, 7000 Minoru Blvd., Richmond BC V6Y 3Z5
Tel: 604-279-7000; Fax: 604-279-7008
admin.caringplace@shaw.ca
www.richmondcaringplace.ca
Overview: A small local organization founded in 1994
Mission: RCPS operates Richmond Caring Place, a facility that serves as one convenient location housing several, non-profit, community service agencies. The agencies have common access to meeting rooms & can collaborate on programs with ease due to proximity. Agencies include: Alzheimer Society of BC; Canadian Cancer Society; Canadian Hemochromatosis Society; BC Centre for Ability; Richmond Hospice Association; & more. RCPS is a registered charity, BN: 130560139RR0001.
Finances: *Funding Sources:* Government, corporate, private donations
Membership: 13 agencies; *Member Profile:* Non-profit, social service agencies
Chief Officer(s):
Gary M. Hagel, Chair

Richmond Chamber of Commerce
North Tower, #202, 5811 Cooney Rd., Richmond BC V6X 3M1
Tel: 604-278-2822; Fax: 604-278-2972
rcc@richmondchamber.ca
www.richmondchamber.ca
www.linkedin.com/company/1026185
www.facebook.com/RichmondChamberCommerce
twitter.com/richmondchamber
www.youtube.com/user/RichmondchamberBC
Previous Name: Richmond Board of Trade
Overview: A medium-sized local organization founded in 1910
Mission: To support & represent the interests of business in the city on behalf of its membership; to promote, enhance & improve trade & commerce, & the economic, civic & social well-being of Richmond; to support & communicate to all levels of government the informed opinion & positions of policy of its members on key local, provincial & national issues
Member of: BC Chamber of Commerce; Canadian Chamber of Commerce
Affiliation(s): Tourism Richmond; Sister Chamber - Kent, Washington
Staff Member(s): 7
Membership: 1,150; *Fees:* Schedule available; *Committees:* Policy Advisory; Transportation Advisory; International Business; Membership; Communications
Activities: *Speaker Service:* Yes; *Library:* Business Resource Centre Library
Chief Officer(s):
Matt Pitcairn, President & CEO
mpitcairn@richmondchamber.ca

Richmond Chinese Community Society
#205, 8271 Westminster Hwy., Richmond BC V6X 1A7
Tel: 604-270-7222; Fax: 604-270-7252
www.rccs.ca
www.facebook.com/rccsinfo
Overview: A small local charitable organization founded in 1989
Mission: To promote the inclusion of the Chinese community in decision making for the city of Richmond; To help Chinese-Canadians integrate into Canadian society
Finances: *Funding Sources:* Membership fees; Donations; Fundraising
Membership: *Fees:* Schedule available

Activities: Offering information & educational seminars to Richmond's Chinese community; Providing service groups & organizations with suggestions & concerns from Richmond's Chinese community; Organizing services, programs, & activities, including dance, yoga, calligraphy, Chinese brush painting, & Tai Chi & Yuanji classes; Promoting volunteerism

Richmond Club of Toronto
655 Chiswick Line, Powassan ON P0H 1Z0
Tel: 416-640-1002
www.richmondclub.com
Overview: A small local organization
Affiliation(s): Chapters in New York & London
Activities: Every two months 50 fund managers, stock brokers & analysts attend a complementary lunch, held at various private clubs; 2-3 undervalued, high growth companies are showcased at each event
Chief Officer(s):
Scott Barber, President
sbarber@richmondclub.com
Greg Beckett, Director
greg.beckett@richmondclub.com

Richmond Community Orchestra & Chorus *See* Richmond Orchestra & Chorus Association

Richmond County Disabled Association (RCD)
PO Box 379, Petit de Grat NS B0E 2L0
Tel: 902-226-1353
Overview: A small local organization
Affiliation(s): Nova Scotia League For Equal Opportunities
Finances: *Funding Sources:* Grants
Chief Officer(s):
Kenneth L. David, Contact

Richmond County Historical Society (RCHS) / Société historique du comté de Richmond
1161, rte 243, Melbourne QC J0B 2B0
Tel: 819-826-1332
www.richmondcountyhistoricalsociety.com
Overview: A small local charitable organization founded in 1962
Mission: To preserve & organize historical documents of the County of Richmond & adjacent areas
Finances: *Funding Sources:* Donations; Fundraising; Museum admission fees
Membership: 200+
Activities: Operating a museum, with guided tours to visitors, schools, & other organizations; Maintaining archives, such as cemetery indexes, original newspapers, photographs, & maps, for use by researchers; *Library:* Archives o Richmond County Historical Society; Open to public by appointment

Richmond Delta Youth Orchestra
PO Box 26064, Stn. Central, Richmond BC V6Y 3V3
Tel: 604-365-3584
admin@rdyo.ca
www.rdyo.ca
www.facebook.com/deltayouthorchestra
twitter.com/rdyorchestra
Previous Name: Delta Symphony Society
Overview: A small local charitable organization founded in 1971 overseen by Orchestras Canada
Mission: To encourage young musicians to excel through education and performance; To provide a comprehensive and balanced musical education as a member of an ensemble; To promote an understanding and appreciation of orchestral music in the community at large
Member of: Orchestras Canada
Finances: *Funding Sources:* Tuition fees; Individual & corporate sponsorships; Donations
Staff Member(s): 4
Activities: Performing regular concerts; Providing weekly rehearsals; Facilitating master classes, workshops and weekend retreats; *Library:* by appointment
Chief Officer(s):
Stephen Robb, Music Director

Richmond Food Bank Society (RFB)
#100, 5800 Cedarbridge Way, Richmond BC V6X 2A7
Tel: 604-271-5609
info@richmondfoodbank.org
www.richmondfoodbank.org
www.facebook.com/RichmondFoodBank
Overview: A small local charitable organization founded in 1993 overseen by Food Banks British Columbia
Mission: To distribute free food to low-income Richmond residents; to assist food bank clients to break from the despair of poverty; to encourage responsibility & to maximize participation in the community
Member of: Food Banks British Columbia; Food Banks Canada; Richmond Chamber of Commerce; Richmond Community Services Advisory Council; Volunteer Richmond
Finances: *Annual Operating Budget:* $100,000-$250,000; *Funding Sources:* Donations
Staff Member(s): 3; 120 volunteer(s)
Membership: 1-99; *Member Profile:* Past & present board members
Activities: Nutrition demonstrations; distribute food & books (food for the body & for the mind); *Awareness Events:* Richmond Rotary Walk for the Richmond Food Bank; *Speaker Service:* Yes
Chief Officer(s):
Margaret Hewlett, Coordinator
margaret@richmondfoodbank.org

Richmond Gem & Mineral Club *See* Richmond Gem & Mineral Society

Richmond Gem & Mineral Society
c/o Richmond Cultural Centre, 7700 Minoru Gate, Richmond BC V6Y 1R9
Tel: 604-278-5141
www.richmondbclapidary.wordpress.com
Previous Name: Richmond Gem & Mineral Club
Overview: A small local organization
Affiliation(s): British Columbia Lapidary Society; Gem & Mineral Federation of Canada
Activities: Hosting monthly meetings; Arranging workshops; *Awareness Events:* Annual Gem Show
Chief Officer(s):
Darlene Howe, Contact, 604-274-4893
darhowe1@gmail.com
Meetings/Conferences:
• Richmond Gem & Mineral Society 57th Annual Show & Sale 2018, 2018, Richmond, BC
Scope: Local
Description: Features vendors selling gems, minerals & related items
Publications:
• Pebble Press [a publication of the Richmond Gem & Mineral Society]
Type: Newsletter; *Editor:* George Howe
Profile: Features important dates & society news for members

Richmond Hill Arts Council *See* Arts Richmond Hill

Richmond Hill Chamber of Commerce (RHCOC)
376 Church St. South, Richmond Hill ON L4C 9V8
Tel: 905-884-1961; Fax: 905-884-1962
info@rhcoc.com
www.rhcoc.com
www.linkedin.com/groups?mostPopular=&gid=1443337
www.facebook.com/RHCOC
twitter.com/RHChamber
www.youtube.com/user/richmondhillchamber
Overview: A medium-sized local organization founded in 1970
Mission: To foster a business enviornment that enhances the success of our members & improves the quality of life in Richmond Hill
Member of: Canadian Chamber of Commerce; Ontario Chamber of Commerce
Affiliation(s): Toronto Board of Trade
Finances: *Funding Sources:* Membership fees; events
Staff Member(s): 4
Membership: *Fees:* Schedule available; *Committees:* Business Awards; Golf; Government Affairs/Advocacy; Membership Services; RHYPE; Women in Business
Activities: *Rents Mailing List:* Yes
Chief Officer(s):
Bryon Wilfert, Chair
Elio Fulan, Executive Director

Richmond Hill Naturalists (RHN)
PO Box 33217, Stn. Harding Post Outlet, Richmond Hill ON L4C 9S3
Tel: 905-883-3047
Other Communication: trips@rhnaturalists.ca
membership@rhnaturalists.ca
www.rhnaturalists.ca
twitter.com/RHNaturalists
Overview: A small local organization founded in 1955
Mission: To encourage interest in natural history; To preserve natural areas; To discover & appreciate the natural world
Membership: *Fees:* $25 students; $30 individuals; $35 families

Activities: Offering field trips; Arranging programs on nature topics
Chief Officer(s):
Marianne Yake, President, 905-883-3047
president@rhnaturalists.ca
Gene Denzel, Treasurer
treasurer@rhnaturalists.ca
Publications:
• The RHN [Richmond Hill Naturalists] Bulletin
Type: Newsletter; *Frequency:* 9 pa; *Accepts Advertising; Editor:* Denise Potter; *Price:* Free with Richmond Hill Naturalists membership
Profile: Organization activities, nature news, & forthcoming events

Richmond Hill Symphony *See* York Symphony Orchestra Inc.

Richmond Multicultural Community Services (RMCS)
#210, 7000 Minoru Blvd., Richmond BC V6Y 3Z5
Tel: 604-279-7160; *Fax:* 604-279-7168
info@rmcs.bc.ca
www.rmcs.bc.ca
www.facebook.com/richmondmulticulturalcommunityservices
twitter.com/rmcs_1985
Previous Name: Richmond Multicultural Concerns Society
Overview: A small local charitable organization founded in 1986
Mission: To achieve inter-cultural harmony in the Richmond area; To identify & meet the needs of Richmond's ethno-cultural community
Activities: Assisting newcomers to the Richmond area; Providing information & referrals to citizens, immigrants & refugees; Increasing awareness of multiculturalism, through activities such as cross cultural understanding workshops; Liaising with government & other organizations; Offering group programs, such as the senior group & the women self-help group; Providing ESL conversation classes
Chief Officer(s):
Parm Grewal, Executive Director, 604-279-7160 Ext. 7161
parm@rmcs.bc.ca
Parm Grewal, Executive Director, 604-279-7160 Ext. 7161
parm@rmcs.bc.ca
Publications:
• Richmond Multicultural Concerns Society Newsletter
Type: Newsletter; *Price:* Free with RMCS membership
Profile: Information for RMCS members

Richmond Multicultural Concerns Society *See* Richmond Multicultural Community Services

Richmond Orchestra & Chorus Association
#130, 10691 Shellbridge Way, Richmond BC V6X 2W8
Tel: 604-276-2747; *Fax:* 604-270-3644
www.roca.ca
www.facebook.com/484458910322
Previous Name: Richmond Community Orchestra & Chorus
Overview: A small local organization founded in 1986 overseen by Orchestras Canada
Mission: To build community connections and enrich the Richmond cultural scene by performing orchestral & choral music; To nurture musical talent and provide community service
Member of: Orchestras Canada
Finances: *Funding Sources:* Individual & corporate donations; Government grants
Membership: 100; *Member Profile:* Orchestra & chorus members; *Committees:* Finance; Education & Outreach; Fundraising; Program Planning; Board Development; Membership; Marketing
Chief Officer(s):
Paul Dufour, Administrator

Richmond Orchid Club
Richmond Public Library, #100, 7700 Minoru Gate, Richmond BC V6Y 1R8
www.richmondorchidclub.com
www.facebook.com/richmond.orchid.club
Overview: A small local organization founded in 2007
Mission: To provide information to orchid enthusiasts
Member of: Canadian Orchid Congress
Chief Officer(s):
Elizabeth Markus, President

Richmond Society for Community Living (RSCL)
#170, 7000 Minoru Blvd., Richmond BC V6Y 3Z5
Tel: 604-279-7040; *Fax:* 604-279-7048
info@rscl.org
www.rscl.org
www.facebook.com/125201840847163
Overview: A small local organization founded in 1982
Member of: Inclusion BC
Finances: *Funding Sources:* Donations; Ministry for Children & Family Development; Community Living BC
Membership: *Fees:* $10 individual; $15 family; $100 individual (lifetime); $150 family (lifetime); *Member Profile:* Infants & children with special needs; Adults with developmental disabilities
Activities: Offering workshops on topics such as positive parenting & autism; Producing brochures on subjects such as infant development & support child development; Increasing public understanding of the rights of people with disabilities; *Awareness Events:* RSCL Annual Family Picnic, August; Benefit of Possibilities, November; Annual Children's Christmas Party, December
Chief Officer(s):
Janice Barr, Executive Director, 604-279-7043, *Fax:* 604-279-7058
jbarr@rscl.org
Publications:
• Richmond Society for Community Living Newsletter
Type: Newsletter; *Frequency:* 3 pa.

Rick Hansen Foundation
#300, 3820 Cessna Dr., Richmond BC V7B 0A2
Tel: 604-295-8149; *Fax:* 604-295-8159
Toll-Free: 800-213-2131
info@rickhansen.com
www.rickhansen.com
wwww.facebook.com/rickhansenfdn
twitter.com/RickHansenFdn
wwww.youtube.com/user/RickHansenFdn
Overview: A medium-sized national charitable organization founded in 1988
Mission: To improve the quality of life of people with spinal cord injury; To create more accessible & inclusive communities; to advance research
Finances: *Annual Operating Budget:* Greater than $5 Million; *Funding Sources:* Donations; Fundraising: Corporate partnerships
Activities: Offering programs such as the ambassador program (mrsmith@rickhansen.com) & the school program (nearley@rickhansen.com); Liaising with government; Increasing awareness of spinal cord injury; Creating inclusive play spaces for children with physical disabilities; *Awareness Events:* Rick Hansen Wheels In Motion, June; Annual Rick Hansen Fishing Challenge, June; Rick Hansen Sturgeon Classic, October
Chief Officer(s):
Lyall Knott, Co-Chair
Rick Hansen, Chief Executive Officer
George Gaffney, Co-Chair
Eric Watt, Treasurer
Publications:
• In Motion: The Rick Hansen Foundation Newsletter
Type: Newsletter; *Frequency:* Quarterly
Profile: Donation information, related news stories, possibilities, & solutions

Rideau Chamber of Commerce
PO Box 247, Manotick ON K4M 1A3
Tel: 613-692-6262
drvmc2003@yahoo.com
rideauchamber.com
Overview: A small local organization
Mission: To drive business growth
Affiliation(s): Ontario Chamber of Commerce
Finances: *Funding Sources:* Membership fees
10 volunteer(s)
Membership: 105; *Fees:* $85
Activities: Providing student job bank & business referral services; Organizing trade show & other events
Chief Officer(s):
Victoria Clarke, President

Rideau Environmental Action League (REAL)
PO Box 1061, Smiths Falls ON K7A 5A5
Tel: 613-283-9500
info@realaction.ca
www.realaction.ca
twitter.com/RideauEnvActL
Overview: A medium-sized local organization founded in 1989
Mission: To conduct community-wide environmental projects and promote environmental improvements within the Town of Smiths Falls and Lanark, Leeds and Grenville Counties.
Membership: *Fees:* $15 individual/schools; $20 family; $5 student; $25 associate; $50 corporate
Chief Officer(s):
Larry Manson, President

Rideau Trail Association (RTA)
PO Box 15, Kingston ON K7L 4V6
Tel: 613-545-0823
info@rideautrail.org
www.rideautrail.org
www.facebook.com/343658645521
Overview: A small local charitable organization founded in 1971
Mission: To preserve & maintain a hiking trail from Kingston to Ottawa
Member of: Hike Ontario
Finances: *Funding Sources:* Donations
Activities: Hiking, cross-country skiing, & snowshoeing
Awards:
• End-to-End
; *Amount:* Certificate & badge for those completing the trail
• Outstanding Service Award
Annually for each club
• Winter End-to-End
; *Amount:* Certificate & badge for those completing the trail
Publications:
• Rideau Trail Association E-Letter
Type: Newsletter; *Frequency:* Biweekly; *Price:* Free with RTA membership
• Rideau Trail Association Newsletter
Type: Newsletter; *Frequency:* Quarterly; *Price:* Free with RTA membership
Profile: Hiking articles & club activities
• The Rideau Trail Guidebook
Number of Pages: 109; *Editor:* Ernie Trischuk; *ISBN:* 0-9693759-7-2; *Price:* $25.50 members; $39.95 non-members
Profile: Maps & trail directions & descriptions

    Central Rideau Trail Club
    PO Box 213, Perth ON K7H 3E4
    Tel: 613-264-8338

    Ottawa Rideau Trail Club
    PO Box 4616, Stn. E, Ottawa ON K1S 5H8
    Tel: 613-860-2225

Rideau Valley Conservation Authority (RVCA)
PO Box 599, 3889 Rideau Valley Dr., Manotick ON K4M 1A5
Tel: 613-692-3571; *Fax:* 613-692-0831
Toll-Free: 800-267-3504
info@rvcf.ca
www.rvca.ca
www.facebook.com/108941882522595
twitter.com/RideauValleyCA
www.flickr.com/photos/64684563@N08
Overview: A large local organization
Mission: To advocate for clean water, natural shorelines & sustainable land use throughout the Rideau Valley watershed
Finances: *Annual Operating Budget:* Greater than $5 Million; *Funding Sources:* Grants; User fees; Donations; Fundraising
Staff Member(s): 65
Membership: 30 municipalities
Chief Officer(s):
Sommer Casgrain-Robertson, General Manager
sommer.casgrain-robertson@rvca.ca
Diane Downey, Director, Communications
diane.downey@rvca.ca
Publications:
• Around the Rideau [a publication of the Rideau Valley Conservation Authority]
Type: Newsletter; *Frequency:* bi-m.
Profile: Provides environmental information for municipalities in the Rideau Valley
• Rideau Valley Conservation Authority Annual Report
Type: Report; *Frequency:* a.
• Watershed Briefs [a publication of the Rideau Valley Conservation Authority]
Type: Newsletter
Profile: Newsletter for municipal councillors

Rideau Valley Field Naturalists (RVFN)
PO Box 474, Perth ON K7H 3G1
rvfn.colmar176.ca
Overview: A small local organization founded in 1983
Mission: To promote the enjoyment of nature through environmental appreciation & conservation; To encourage the wise use & conservation of natural resources; to promote environmental protection

Canadian Associations / Rideau Valley Soaring

Member of: Federation of Ontario Naturalists; World Wildlife Federation; Canadian Nature Federation
Finances: *Annual Operating Budget:* Less than $50,000; *Funding Sources:* Membership fees
12 volunteer(s)
Membership: 96; *Fees:* $5 student; $20 individual; $30 family/institution; *Committees:* Flora & Fauna; Outings
Activities: Monthly meetings except July & August; mall displays; educational outings; bird identification; clinics; bird, mammal & amphibian monitoring; *Library*
Chief Officer(s):
Murray Hunt, Treasurer, 613-264-9273
mkhunt@ripnet.com

Rideau Valley Soaring
PO Box 1164, Manotick ON K4M 1A9
Tel: 613-366-8208
club.pres@rvss.ca
rvss.ca
www.facebook.com/200156480081876
twitter.com/rvssca
Overview: A small local organization
Member of: Soaring Association of Canada
Affiliation(s): Gatineau Gliding Club; Montreal Soaring Club
Membership: *Fees:* $715 adult ($506 for additional spouse); $375 junior; $345 youth; $546 tow pilot/self launch
Chief Officer(s):
George Domaradzki, President & Chief Flight Instructor
club.pres@rvss.ca

Rideau-St. Lawrence Real Estate Board
#12, 1275 Kensington Pkwy., Brockville ON K6V 6C3
Tel: 613-342-3103; *Fax:* 613-342-1637
rideau@bellnet.ca
boards.mls.ca/rideau
Previous Name: Central St. Lawrence Real Estate Board
Overview: A small local organization founded in 1954 overseen by Ontario Real Estate Association
Finances: *Funding Sources:* Membership dues
Membership: 216

Ridge Meadows Association of Community Living (RMACL)
11641 - 224th St., Maple Ridge BC V2X 6A1
Tel: 604-467-8700; *Fax:* 604-467-8767
info@rmacl.org
www.rmacl.org
Overview: A small local organization founded in 1958
Mission: To assist children & adults with developmental disabilities in the Maple Ridge & Pitt Meadows area to live & work in their home & community
Member of: British Columbia Association for Community Living
Finances: *Funding Sources:* Donations; United Way of the Lower Mainland
Activities: Providing children's services, community support services, residential services, & vocational programs
Chief Officer(s):
Danette Kugler, Chief Executive Officer

Ridgetown & South East Kent Chamber of Commerce
PO Box 522, Ridgetown ON N0P 2C0
Tel: 519-359-6597
ridgetownchamber@gmail.com
www.ridgetown.com
Overview: A small local charitable organization
Mission: To promote business & tourism in Ridgetown
Finances: *Funding Sources:* Membership fees
Membership: 60; *Fees:* Schedule available
Chief Officer(s):
Charlie Mitton, President

The Right to Die Network of Canada *See* The Right to Die Society of Canada

The Right to Die Society of Canada (RTDSC) / Société Canadienne pour le Droit de Mourir (SCDM)
145 Macdonell Ave., Toronto ON M6R 2A4
Tel: 416-535-0690
Toll-Free: 866-535-0690
info@righttodie.ca
www.righttodie.ca
Previous Name: The Right to Die Network of Canada
Overview: A small national organization founded in 1991
Mission: To work with legislators, policy makers & the public to expand the range of humane options for people who are suffering intolerably from incurable conditions & who want a self-directed dying; to work with sufferers to expand their awareness of the options that are legal & may be appropriate for them
Finances: *Funding Sources:* Membership fees; donations
Membership: 400; *Fees:* $30 single; $40 family/couple; *Member Profile:* Must be over 18 years of age
Activities: *Speaker Service:* Yes
Chief Officer(s):
Ruth von Fuchs, President & Secretary

Right to Life Association of Newfoundland & Labrador *See* Newfoundland & Labrador Right to Life Association

The Right to Life Association of Toronto & Area
#302, 120 Eglinton Ave. East, Toronto ON M4P 1E2
Tel: 416-483-7869
www.righttolife.to
www.facebook.com/righttolifeto
Also Known As: Toronto Right to Life Association
Overview: A small local charitable organization founded in 1971
Mission: To uphold the right to life as the basic human right on which all others depend; to provide information & services to that end
Affiliation(s): Life Canada
Finances: *Funding Sources:* Donations
Membership: *Fees:* $10 student/senior; $20 adult; $25 family; *Committees:* Communications; Fundraising; Public Outreach
Activities: *Speaker Service:* Yes; *Library:* Resource Centre; Open to public
Publications:
• The Right to Life Association of Toronto Newsletter
Type: Newsletter; *Frequency:* Quarterly

Right to Play
Thomson Bldg., PO Box 64, #1900, 65 Queen St. West, Toronto ON M5H 2M5
Tel: 416-498-1922; *Fax:* 416-498-1942
info@righttoplay.com
www.righttoplay.com
www.linkedin.com/company/right-to-play
www.facebook.com/RightToPlayCAN
twitter.com/RighttoPlayCAN
www.youtube.com/user/RightToPlayCan
Previous Name: Olympic Aid
Overview: A medium-sized international charitable organization founded in 2002
Mission: Educating and empowering children and youth to use sport and play to overcome the effects of poverty, conflict and disease in disadvantaged communities.
Finances: *Funding Sources:* Donations
Activities: PLAY program, resource development, training; *Internships:* Yes
Chief Officer(s):
Johann Koss, President & CEO

Right to Quiet Society
#359, 1985 Wallace St., Vancouver BC V6R 4H4
Tel: 604-222-0207
info@quiet.org
www.quiet.org
Also Known As: Society for Soundscape Awareness & Protection
Overview: A small national organization founded in 1982
Mission: To promote awareness of the increasing problem of noise pollution & the dangers of noise to our physical, emotional & spiritual well-being; to work for noise abatement through regulation & enforcement & by encouraging responsible behaviour; to foster recognition of the right to quiet as a basic human right
Finances: *Annual Operating Budget:* Less than $50,000
6 volunteer(s)
Membership: 280; *Fees:* $12 individual; $18 family; $6 low income; $25 non-profit; $50 business
Activities: *Awareness Events:* International Noise Awareness Day, April
Chief Officer(s):
Hans Schmid, President

Rimbey Chamber of Commerce
PO Box 87, 5025 50 Ave., Rimbey AB T0C 2J0
Tel: 403-392-6521
rimbeychamber@gmail.com
www.rimbeychamberofcommerce.com
Overview: A small local organization
Mission: To strengthen Rimbey's business & economic community
Member of: Alberta Chamber of Commerce; Canadian Chamber of Commerce
Finances: *Funding Sources:* Local government; membership fees
Membership: 63; *Fees:* $75-$350
Activities: Providing resources, promotions, events, seminars, & meetings for members
Chief Officer(s):
Carrie Vaartstra, Executive Director

Rimbey Fish & Game Association
PO Box 634, Rimbey AB T0C 2J0
Tel: 403-843-3858
Other Communication: Campground Reservation Phone: 403-843-6931
www.rimbeyfishandgame.com
Overview: A small local organization
Member of: Alberta Fish & Game Association
Finances: *Annual Operating Budget:* Less than $50,000
Membership: 104; *Fees:* $29 family; $19 regular; $18 associate; $12 youth under 18
Activities: Fish & Game annual awards & trophies
Chief Officer(s):
Daryl Hunt, President, 403-843-6466

Rimbey Historical Society
PO Box 813, 5620 - 51 St., Rimbey AB T0C 2J0
Tel: 403-843-2004
paskapoo@telus.net
www.paskapoopark.com
Overview: A small local charitable organization founded in 1963
Mission: To preserve the heritage of the Rimbey region of Alberta
Finances: *Funding Sources:* Alberta Museums Association
Membership: *Fees:* $10
Activities: Maintaining the Pas-Ka-Poo Historical Park museums & historic buildings & the Smithson International Truck Museum
Publications:
• Over the Years: A History of the Rimbey Area
Type: Book; *Editor:* Rimbey History Book Committee

Ringette Alberta
Percy Page Centre, 11759 Groat Rd., 2nd Fl., Edmonton AB T5M 3K6
Tel: 780-451-1750; *Fax:* 780-415-1749
www.ringettealberta.com
www.facebook.com/ringettealberta
twitter.com/ringettealberta
www.youtube.com/channel/UCx0Yyv-lwy-mZJPFUPf8xZQ
Overview: A medium-sized provincial organization overseen by Ringette Canada
Mission: To provide ringette services to its members
Member of: Ringette Canada
Staff Member(s): 4
Chief Officer(s):
David Myers, Executive Director
david@ringettealberta.com

Ringette Association of Saskatchewan (RAS) / Association de ringuette de Saskatchewan
1860 Lorne St., Regina SK S4P 2L7
Tel: 306-780-9432; *Fax:* 306-780-9460
www.ringettesask.com
twitter.com/RingetteSask
Overview: A medium-sized provincial organization founded in 1976 overseen by Ringette Canada
Mission: To develop, promote, communicate, & administer programs, policies & procedures which will enhance the development & participation of coaches, players, officals, volunteers, & administrators from all levels throughout Saskatchewan
Member of: Sask Sport
Finances: *Funding Sources:* Saskatchewan Lotteries; Corporate sponsorships; Membership fees
Staff Member(s): 2
Activities: Coaching & officiating clinics; Providing player development camps; Organizing provincial championships
Chief Officer(s):
Jodi Lorenz, President
Crystal Gellner, Executive Director
executivedirector@ringettesask.com
Keith Doering, Director, Technical
technicaldirector@ringettesask.com

Ringette Canada (RC) / Ringuette Canada
#201, 5510 Canotek Rd., Ottawa ON K1J 9J4

Tel: 613-748-5655; Fax: 613-748-5860
Other Communication: www.flickr.com/photos/7738799@N02
ringette@ringette.ca
www.ringette.ca
twitter.com/ringettecanada
www.youtube.com/ringettecanada
Overview: A large national organization founded in 1975
Mission: To formulate, publish & administer national policies beneficial to the sport; To enforce laws & regulations governing ringette; To encourage ringette participants to strive for excellence in teamwork, team spirit & team discipline
Member of: International Ringette Federation
Finances: *Annual Operating Budget:* $1.5 Million-$3 Million; *Funding Sources:* Membership fees; Federal government; Corporate sponsorships
Staff Member(s): 7
Membership: *Member Profile:* Provincial or territorial ringette associations; *Committees:* Coach Development; Officials Development; High Performance; National Ringette League
Activities: Organizing the Canadian Ringette Championships; *Library:* Resource Centre; Not open to public
Chief Officer(s):
Natasha Johnston, Executive Director
natasha@ringette.ca
Frances Losier, Director, High Performance & Events
frances@ringette.ca
Nathalie Muller, Director, Technical
nathalie@ringette.ca
Anik Desjardins, Office Manager
anik@ringette.ca
Alayne Martel, Contact, Media & Public Relations
alayne@ringette.ca
Awards:
• Cara Brown Scholarship Award
• Agnes Jacks Scholarship Award

Ringette New Brunswick (RNB) / Ringuette Nouveau-Brunswick
487 rte La Vallée, Memramcook NB E4K 3C7
Tel: 506-851-5641
www.ringette-nb.com
twitter.com/RingetteNB
Also Known As: New Brunswick Ringette Association
Overview: A small provincial organization overseen by Ringette Canada
Mission: To ensure the well-being & development of ringette athletes in New Brunswick
Activities: Consulting with the Province of New Brunswick Wellness, Culture, & Sport; Providing direction in areas such as athlete development, officiating, coaching, & technical issues; Organizing coaching & officiating clinics; Establishing standards for bench staff
Chief Officer(s):
Chantal Poirier, Manager, Program
cpoirierRNB@hotmail.com

Ringette Nova Scotia
5516 Spring Garden Rd., 4th Fl., Halifax NS B3J 1G6
Tel: 902-425-5450; *Fax:* 902-425-5606
ringette@sportnovascotia.ca
www.ringette.ns.ca
www.facebook.com/ringettenovascotia
twitter.com/RingetteNS
Overview: A small provincial organization founded in 1973 overseen by Ringette Canada
Mission: To promote, develop & administer the sport of ringette within Nova Scotia
Member of: International Ringette Federation
Finances: *Annual Operating Budget:* Less than $50,000; *Funding Sources:* Provincial Sport & Recreation Commission 20 volunteer(s)
Membership: 800; *Fees:* Schedule available; *Committees:* Canada Winter Games; Fundraising; Provincial Teams; Strategic Plan
Activities: *Awareness Events:* Ringette Week, Feb. *Library:* Resource Library; by appointment
Chief Officer(s):
Lainie Wintrup, Executive Director
Publications:
• Ringette Nova Scotia Newsletter
Type: Newsletter
Profile: News & updates for members

Ringette PEI (RPEI)
40 Enman Cres., Charlottetown PE C1A 7K7
Tel: 902-368-6570
ringettepei.ca
www.facebook.com/ringettepei
twitter.com/RingettePEI
Also Known As: Prince Edward Island Ringette Association
Overview: A small provincial organization founded in 1982 overseen by Ringette Canada
Mission: To promote ringette throughout PEI
Activities: Offering officiating clinics, coaching courses & related resources; Providing tournament & championship information
Chief Officer(s):
Valerie Vuillemot, Executive Director
vvuillemot@sportpei.pe.ca
Michael James, President
mjames@islandtelecom.com
Steve Campbell, Vice-President
steve@curranandbriggs.com
Breanne MacInnis, Treasurer
bemacinnis@gmail.com

Ringuette 96 Montréal-Nord-Est
QC
Tél: 514-644-0153
ringuette96mn@hotmail.com
www.ringuette96mtlnord.com
www.facebook.com/1426672734232724
Aperçu: *Dimension:* petite; *Envergure:* provinciale surveillé par Ringuette-Québec
Membre de: Ringuette-Québec
Membre: *Montant de la cotisation:* Barème
Membre(s) du bureau directeur:
Sylvie Horth, Président

Ringuette Boucherville
490, ch du Lac, Boucherville QC J4B 6X3
Courriel: info@ringuetteboucherville.com
www.ringuetteboucherville.com
www.facebook.com/1460659494210802
www.youtube.com/channel/UCrhUtjVgaP9vNRmEeFxmVLA
Aperçu: *Dimension:* petite; *Envergure:* provinciale surveillé par Ringuette-Québec
Membre de: Ringuette-Québec
Membre: *Critères d'admissibilite:* Filles de 4 ans et plus
Membre(s) du bureau directeur:
Sylvain St-Cyr, Président

Ringuette Bourrassa-Laval-Lanaudière
QC
www.ringuettebll.com
Aperçu: *Dimension:* petite; *Envergure:* provinciale surveillé par Ringuette-Québec
Membre de: Ringuette-Québec

Ringuette Canada *See* Ringette Canada

Ringuette de la Capitale
#316, 1311, rue des Loisirs, Québec QC
Tél: 418-877-3000
ca@ringuettedelacapitale.com
www.ringuettedelacapitale.com
www.facebook.com/ringuettedelacapitale
Aperçu: *Dimension:* petite; *Envergure:* provinciale surveillé par Ringuette-Québec
Membre de: Ringuette-Québec
Membre: 4 équipes
Membre(s) du bureau directeur:
Steve Caron, Présidente, 418-655-8759
steven.caron@carons.ca

Ringuette Nouveau-Brunswick *See* Ringette New Brunswick

Ringuette St-Hubert
CP 29542, 5950, boul Cousineau, Saint-Hubert QC J3Y 9A9
Courriel: ringuette@ringuette-st-hubert.com
www.ringuette-st-hubert.com
Aperçu: *Dimension:* petite; *Envergure:* provinciale surveillé par Ringuette-Québec
Membre de: Ringuette-Québec
Membre(s) du bureau directeur:
David Létouneau, Président
Davidletourneau.cma@gmail.com

Ringuette St-Hyacinthe
CP 40502, Saint-Hyacinthe QC J2R 1K8
Courriel: info@ringuettesth.com
www.ringuettesth.com
www.facebook.com/ringuettesthyacinthe
Aperçu: *Dimension:* petite; *Envergure:* provinciale surveillé par Ringuette-Québec
Membre de: Ringuette-Québec
Membre: *Montant de la cotisation:* Barème

Ringuette-Québec
4545, av Pierre-de Coubertin, Montréal QC H1V 0B2
Tél: 514-252-3085; *Téléc:* 514-254-1069
ringuette@ringuette-quebec.qc.ca
www.ringuette-quebec.qc.ca
www.facebook.com/139856822762458
twitter.com/ringuetteqc
www.youtube.com/channel/UChlZmg35-zhVgQBkgru8k7g
Aperçu: *Dimension:* petite; *Envergure:* provinciale surveillé par Ringette Canada
Membre de: Ringuette-Canada
Membre(s) du bureau directeur:
Jocelyne Fortin, Président
jocfortin@videotron.ca

Ripple Rock Gem & Mineral Club
PO Box 6, Campbell River BC V9W 4Z9
info@ripplerockgemandmineralclub.com
www.ripplerockgemandmineralclub.com
Overview: A small local organization founded in 1989
Mission: To increase knowledge of rocks & minerals; To promote lapidary arts
Member of: British Columbia Lapidary Society; Gem & Mineral Federation of Canada
Membership: *Fees:* $15 individuals; $25 families; *Member Profile:* People from Campbell River & the surrounding area of British Columbia who are interested in gems & minerals
Activities: Hosting monthly meetings, except July & August; Organizing field trips & camps; Providing workshops for people to learn lapidary arts; *Awareness Events:* Ripple Rock Gem & Mineral Show *Library:* Ripple Rock Gem & Mineral Club Library
Chief Officer(s):
Linda Henderson, President
Publications:
• The Bugle [a publication of The Ripple Rock Gem & Mineral Club]
Type: Newsletter; *Frequency:* Monthly
Profile: Information about club activities, upcoming events, & member profiles

Risk & Insurance Management Society Inc. (RIMS)
c/o Darius Delon, RIMS Canada Council, Mount Royal University, 4825 Mount Royal Gate SW, Calgary AB T3E 6K6
rcc@rimscanada.ca
www.rimscanada.ca
www.facebook.com/RIMSorg
twitter.com/RIMSCdaCouncil
Also Known As: RIMS Canada (A Standing Committee of RIMS)
Previous Name: American Society of Insurance Management
Overview: A large international organization founded in 1950
Mission: To advance the practice of risk management in Canada
Finances: *Funding Sources:* Membership fees; Conferences
Membership: 950+ individual members + 380+ corporate members; *Fees:* Free for students; $125 educational/retired; $575 associate/corporate; *Member Profile:* Risk managers; Vendors or service providers; Risk management or insurance related professors; Students; Retired persons; *Committees:* National Conference; National Education; Communications & External Affairs
Activities: Providing professional educational courses & workshops; Offering career services; *Speaker Service:* Yes
Chief Officer(s):
Darius Delon, Chair
Meetings/Conferences:
• RIMS (Risk & Insurance Management Society Inc.) 2018 Annual Conference & Exhibition, April, 2018, San Antonio, TX
Scope: International
Description: A gathering of risk professionals from around the world to share experiences
• RIMS (Risk & Insurance Management Society Inc.) Canada 2018 Conference, September, 2018, St. John's, NL
Scope: National
Description: An annual risk management conference & exhibition held in the autumn for risk managers & the vendor community
Publications:
• RIMS [Risk & Insurance Management Society Inc.] Canada Newsletter
Type: Newsletter; *Frequency:* Irregular

Canadian Associations / Riverbend District Chamber of Commerce

Profile: Activities & news from RIMS Canada Council & its subcommittees
• Risk Professionals Directory [a publication of the Risk & Insurance Management Society Inc.]
Type: Directory

British Columbia Chapter (BCRIMA)
Vancouver BC
britishcolumbia.rims.org
Mission: To improve & promote risk management in British Columbia; To encourage the development of members
Chief Officer(s):
Vilma Zanchettin, President
Jeff Schaafsma, Vice-President & RCC Liaison
Janiece Brown, Secretary
Dan Heaman, Treasurer & RIMS Delegate
Gloria Gao, Director

Canadian Capital Region Chapter
Ottawa ON
canadiancapital.rims.org
Mission: To promote the discipline of risk management throughout eastern Ontario
Chief Officer(s):
Rachel Steen, Vice-President
Brigitte Cayer, Secretary
John Lammey, Treasurer

Manitoba Chapter (MaRIMS)
Winnipeg MB
manitoba.rims.org
Mission: To promote all aspects of risk management in Manitoba
Chief Officer(s):
Tim Lucko, President
Cindy Bauer, Vice-President
Stacie Dheilly, Secretary
Beverley Duthoit, Treasurer
Valerie Barber, Assistant Secretary & Director, Membership
• MaRIMS Newsletter [a publication of the Risk & Insurance Management Society Inc. - Manitoba Chapter]
Type: Newsletter; *Editor:* John Rislahti
Profile: Manitoba chapter activities & forthcoming programs

Maritime (New Brunswick, Nova Scotia, & Prince Edward Island) Chapter
Stellarton NB
maritime.rims.org
Chief Officer(s):
Stephen Trueman, President
Andrea Cameron, Vice-President
Dee Vipond, Secretary
Trevor Gonnason, Treasurer
Vanessa MacLean, Contact, Membership

Newfoundland & Labrador Chapter (NALRIMS)
St. John's NL
newfoundlandlabrador.rims.org
Chief Officer(s):
Gail Cullen, President
Gordon Payne, Vice-President & RIMS Delegate
Patrick Ryan, Secretary, Treasurer & Webmaster

Northern Alberta Chapter (NARIMS)
Sherwood Park AB
Tel: 780-400-2025
northernalberta.rims.org
Leatherland Angela, President

Ontario Chapter (ORIMS)
PO Box 1021, 66 Wellington St. West, Toronto ON M5K 1P2
ontario.rims.org
Chief Officer(s):
Paul Provis, Vice-President, 416-865-8411, *Fax:* 416-868-0701
pprovis@oxforproperties.com
Agata Jamroz, Secretary, 416-955-7681, *Fax:* 416-955-7621
agata.jamroz@rbc.com
Mark Cosgrove, Treasurer, 416-592-4487, *Fax:* 416-592-4775
mark.cosgrove@opg.com
Sandra Alwazani, Contact, Public Relations & External Affairs, 416-736-2100 Ext. 22922, *Fax:* 416-736-5815
alwazani@yorku.ca
Joseph Costello, Contact, Membership, 416-345-5019, *Fax:* 416-345-6266
joe.costello@hydroone.com
• PULSE
Type: Newsletter; *Frequency:* Irregular; *Accepts Advertising*;
Editor: Suzanne M. Barrett
Profile: Activities of the Ontario chapter, including educational workshops & seminars & social functions, as well as industry news

Québec Chapter (QRIMA)
CP 1102, Succ. B, Montréal QC H3B 3K9
Courriel: agraq.qrima@gmail.com
www.agraq.org
Chief Officer(s):
Michel Pontbriand, Président
Stephane Cossette, 1er Vice-président & Trésorier
• InfoRisque [a publication of the Risk & Insurance Management Society Inc. - Québec Chapter]
Type: Newsletter; *Editor:* Ginette Demers
Profile: Updates on chapter activities & announcements of upcoming programs

Saskatchewan Chapter (SKRIMS)
c/o David Jackson, Saskatchewan School Boards Association, #400, 2222 - 13th Ave., Regina SK S4P 3M7
Tel: 306-569-0750
saskatchewan.rims.org
Mission: To promote the discipline of risk management; To encourage a competitive insurance marketplace
Chief Officer(s):
David Jackson, President
djackson@saskschoolboards.ca
Randy Besse, Vice-President, Program, 306-775-6757
rbesse@sgi.sk.ca
David Boehm, Vice-President & Secretary, South, 306-787-0835
david.boehm@gov.sk.ca
Merv Dahl, Vice-President, North, 306-966-8753
merv.dahl@usask.ca
Marnie McCallum, Treasurer, 306-787-1440
marnie.maccallum@gov.sk.ca

Southern Alberta Chapter (SARIMS)
c/o Darius Delon, Mount Royal University, 4825 Mount Royal Gate SW, Calgary AB T3E 6K6
Tel: 403-440-6196
southernalberta.rims.org
Mission: To promote awareness & understanding of risk management
Chief Officer(s):
Darius Delon, President
ddelon@mtroyal.ca
Rob Groves, Vice-President & Treasurer, 403-500-2455, *Fax:* 403-298-1483
rob.groves@cssd.ab.ca
Lynne Kulchitsky, Secretary, 403-220-5719, *Fax:* 403-282-2765
lynne.kulchitsky@ucalgary.ca
Curtis Desiatnyk, Director, Membership, 403-440-5574, *Fax:* 403-440-8927
cdesiatnyk@mtroyal.ca

Riverbend District Chamber of Commerce
PO Box 397, Radisson SK S0K 3L0
Tel: 306-827-4801; *Fax:* 306-827-2218
riverbendchamber.weebly.com
Previous Name: Radisson & District Chamber of Commerce
Overview: A small local organization
Mission: To promote & strengthen trade, commerce & business in the Riverbend District
Chief Officer(s):
Gerald Wiebe, President

Riverdale Immigrant Women's Centre (RIWC)
1326 Gerrard St. East, Toronto ON M4L 1Z1
Tel: 416-465-6021; *Fax:* 416-465-3224
reception.riwc@gmail.com
www.riwc.ca
www.facebook.com/RiverdaleImmigrantWomensCentre
Overview: A small local organization founded in 1982 overseen by Ontario Council of Agencies Serving Immigrants
Mission: To support Asian & South Asian women & their families; To empower immigrant women
Membership: *Fees:* $10 new members & renewals; $25 organizations
Activities: Providing workshops on topics such as settlement issues, violence against women, legal issues, ESL, & health issues; Offering counselling support services; Assisting newcomers to Canada with employment services
Publications:
• Background & Model for Parent-Child Resource Centre
Author: Laura Jones
• Celebrating Women, Aging, & Cultural Diversity

• Child Family Resources
Author: Laura Jones
• ELT Community Based Mode for Language Training
Type: Report; *Author:* Baktygul Ismailova
• Mawan Thandian Chawan: A Parenting Manual for Community Workers & Activists Working with South Asian Survivors of Wife Abuse
Type: Manual
• A Tribute to Grassroots Organizing For Women's Health: Cases From Around the World
Author: S. Torres, P. Khosla, N. Leedham
• Violence Against Women Training Manual
Type: Manual; *Author:* Anna Willats & Jaswant Kaur
• Ward 30: Broadview-Greenwood Environmental Scan
Author: Laura Jones

Rivers & District Chamber of Commerce
PO Box 795, Rivers MB R0K 1X0
Tel: 204-328-7316
riverschamber@gmail.com
riversdaly.ca/chamber-of-commerce/
Overview: A small local organization founded in 1908
Mission: To encourage growth in Rivers & district by supporting existing businesses & encouraging new businesses
Member of: Manitoba Chamber of Commerce
Finances: *Annual Operating Budget:* Less than $50,000;
Funding Sources: Craft sale; Town of Rivers; Fundraisers
Staff Member(s): 1; 10 volunteer(s)
Membership: 28; *Fees:* $10-$100, based on number of employees; *Committees:* Crafty; Christmas; Downtown Promo
Activities: Organizing events including home & craft sale & Santa parade
Chief Officer(s):
Jean Young, Contact

Riverton & District Chamber of Commerce
PO Box 238, Riverton MB R0C 2R0
Tel: 204-378-2376
www.rivertoncanada.com
Overview: A small local organization
Chief Officer(s):
Clif Evans, Chair
cbevans@mymts.net

Riverton & District Friendship Centre
PO Box 359, 53 Laura Ave., Riverton MB R0C 2R0
Tel: 204-378-2800; *Fax:* 204-378-5705
rdfc@mymts.net
www.rivertonfc.com
Overview: A small local charitable organization founded in 1981
Mission: To provide a meeting place for individuals & community groups of different cultures; To create fellowship between the native members of the Riverton area
Member of: Manitoba Association of Friendship Centres
Affiliation(s): National Association of Friendship Centres; National Aboriginal Health Organization
Staff Member(s): 4
Activities: Delivering a youth drop-in program; Promoting health & prevention; Providing resources; Offering a social network; Providing regular community & family activities; Assisting Aboriginals with employment placements, in a program entitled, Partners for Careers; Helping native people to settle in Riverton; Providing a referral service to governments & agencies; Liaising with other community organizations; *Library:* Riverton & District Friendship Centre Seniors Resource Centre
Chief Officer(s):
Tanis Grimolfson, Executive Director

Robert L. Conconi Foundation
#380, 1050 Homer St., Vancouver BC V6B 2W9
Tel: 604-568-4064; *Fax:* 888-519-2539
info@conconi.org
www.conconi.org
www.linkedin.com/company/robert-l-conconi-foundation
www.facebook.com/robertlconconifoundation
twitter.com/ConconiFndn
Overview: A small provincial charitable organization founded in 2003
Mission: To aid organizations in the areas of health, poverty, education, & the arts; To empower people throughout British Columbia
Chief Officer(s):
Sanja Simic, Executive Director
sanja@conconi.org

Robert Sauvé Occupational Health & Safety Research Institute *Voir* Institut de recherche Robert-Sauvé en santé et en sécurité du travail

Robin Hood Association for the Handicapped
141 Broadway Blvd., Sherwood Park AB T8H 2A4
Tel: 780-467-7140; *Fax:* 780-449-2028
info@robinhoodassoc.com
www.robinhoodassoc.com
www.facebook.com/135479853139658
Overview: A medium-sized local charitable organization founded in 1963
Mission: To assist individuals with disabilities to achieve their personal best
Member of: Alberta Council of Disability Services (ACDS)
Finances: *Funding Sources:* Donations
Staff Member(s): 400
Activities: Offering programs for children, such as early childhood development, early intervention, family support services, & a summer program; Providing services to adults, such as the Centre for Learning day program, community access, residential services, resources, & transportation

Roblin & District Chamber of Commerce
PO Box 160, 147 Main St., Roblin MB R0L 1P0
Tel: 204-937-3194
rdcoc@mts.net
www.roblinmanitoba.com/index.php?pageid=BUSCOC
Overview: A small local organization
Mission: To improve economic development in the area
Member of: Manitoba Chambers of Commerce
Finances: *Annual Operating Budget:* Less than $50,000; *Funding Sources:* Membership dues
Staff Member(s): 1; 15 volunteer(s)
Membership: 85; *Fees:* Schedule available; *Committees:* Event
Activities: Organizing & promoting events including trade shows, craft shows, parades & Christmas Bonus Promotion; *Library:* Open to public
Chief Officer(s):
Kevin Arthur, President

Robson Street Business Association (RSBA)
#412, 1155 Robson St., Vancouver BC V6E 1B5
Tel: 604-669-8132; *Fax:* 604-669-0181
info@robsonstreet.ca
www.robsonstreet.ca
www.facebook.com/RobsonStreet
twitter.com/RobsonStreet
instagram.com/robsonstreet
Overview: A small local charitable organization founded in 1991
Mission: To promote the businesses on Robson St.
Member of: Business Improvement Association British Columbia; Tourism Vancouver
Finances: *Annual Operating Budget:* $100,000-$250,000; *Funding Sources:* Property tax levies
Staff Member(s): 2; 20 volunteer(s)
Membership: 200; *Member Profile:* Merchants & property owners

Rocanville & District Museum Society Inc.
PO Box 490, Rocanville SK S0A 3L0
Tel: 306-645-2113
rocanvillemuseum@gmail.com
rocanvillemuseum.wix.com
Overview: A small local charitable organization founded in 1964
Mission: To gather & display artifacts from the area so as to preserve for all time the historical beginnings & progress of this & surrounding communities
Member of: Saskatchewan Museums Association
Affiliation(s): Rocanville Recreation Board
Finances: *Funding Sources:* Museum gallery grant; fundraising
Activities: Displays; demonstrations of threshing, oat rolling, wheat gristing on Museum Day; guided tours available on request; *Library:* Documentation Centre; by appointment
Chief Officer(s):
Ray Behrns, President

Rocky Mountain House & District Chamber of Commerce
PO Box 1374, 5406 - 48 St., Rocky Mountain House AB T4T 1B1
Tel: 403-845-5450; *Fax:* 403-845-7764
Toll-Free: 800-565-3793
rmhcofc@rockychamber.org
www.rockychamber.org
Overview: A small local charitable organization

Mission: To develop strategic initiatives to promote & enhance the growth of economic development
Affiliation(s): AB Chamber of Commerce; Canadian Chamber of Commerce
Finances: *Annual Operating Budget:* $100,000-$250,000; *Funding Sources:* Memberships; projects
Staff Member(s): 3; 18 volunteer(s)
Membership: 360+; *Fees:* Schedule available; *Committees:* Administration & Finance; Membership; Development; Communication & Promotion; Municipal Partnering; Downtown Enhancement
Activities: Advocating at the municipal, provincial, & federal levels; Organizing annual banquet & trade show; *Speaker Service:* Yes; *Library:* Business Resource Centre; Open to public by appointment
Chief Officer(s):
Colleen Dwyer, President
Cindy Taschuk, Executive Director

Rocky Mountain Naturalists
PO Box 791, Cranbrook BC V1C 4J5
www.kootenaynaturalists.org/rocky
Overview: A small local charitable organization founded in 1985
Mission: To promote the enjoyment of nature through environmental appreciation & conservation; to encourage the wise use & conservation of natural resources & environmental protection
Member of: Federation of BC Naturalists
Membership: 40; *Fees:* $20 individual; $25 family
Activities: Field trips; study nights; conservation projects
Chief Officer(s):
Greg Ross, Contact
gsross@shaw.ca

Rocky Native Friendship Society
PO Box 1927, 4917 - 52 St., Rocky Mountain House AB T4T 1B4
Tel: 403-845-2788; *Fax:* 403-845-3093
www.friendshipcentre.shawbiz.ca
www.facebook.com/147332261987888
Overview: A small local organization founded in 1975 overseen by Alberta Native Friendship Centres Association
Mission: To create a healthy & supportive community to empower Aboriginal people in the Rocky Mountain House area; To strengthen Aboriginal cultural awareness
Member of: Alberta Native Friendship Centres Association
Affiliation(s): Alberta Native Friendship Centres Association
Activities: Offering services in early intervention, addictions, & for youth; Providing programs, such as Aboriginal Neighborhood Place & the Family Literacy Program; Advocating on behalf of clients for respectful & appropriate treatment
Chief Officer(s):
Helge Nome, President
Douglas Bonaise, Vice-President
Tani Amarook, Treasurer
Merle White, Executive Director

Rogersville Chamber of Commerce *Voir* Chambre de commerce de Rogersville

Roller Sports Canada / Sports à roulettes du Canada
1 Bancroft Cres., Whitby ON L1R 2E6
Tel: 905-666-9343
rollersports@hotmail.com
rollersports.ca
Previous Name: Canadian Federation of Amateur Roller Skaters
Overview: A small national organization
Chief Officer(s):
Wayne Burret, President
wayneburrett@rogers.com

Roman Catholic Military Ordinariate of Canada *Voir* L'Ordinariat militaire Catholique Romain du Canada

Romanian Children's Relief
12 Homedale Dr., Toronto ON M1V 1M2
Tel: 416-292-3688
romanianchildrensrelief@rogers.com
www.rcr.org
Previous Name: Association for Democracy in Romania
Overview: A small international charitable organization founded in 1990
Mission: To provide relief supplies to selected orphanages, asylums & hospitals in Romania
Finances: *Annual Operating Budget:* Less than $50,000
45 volunteer(s)

Membership: 1-99
Activities: Collecting & sending goods to selected orphanages (1-2 times a year)
Chief Officer(s):
Flavia Cosma, Chair

Romanian Orthodox Deanery of Canada
PO Box 4023, Stn. Main, Regina SK S4P 3R9
www.roea.org
Overview: A small national organization
Mission: The Romanian Orthodox Episcopate of America is grouped geographically into 7 deaneries & the Deanery of Canada is one of them, with 30 parishes across the country. It is non-profit, registered charity, BN: 888289642RR0001.
Member of: Romanian Orthodox Episcopate of America; Orthodox Church in America
Chief Officer(s):
Cosmin Vint, Parish Preist, Fort Qu'appelle, 306-332-1554
John Bujea, Ph.D., Contact, Fort Qu'appelle, 306-584-8943
eljohn2@accesscomm.ca

Ronald McDonald Children's Charities of Canada *See* Ronald McDonald House Charities of Canada

Ronald McDonald House Charities of Canada (RMHC) / Oeuvres pour enfants Ronald McDonald du Canada
1 McDonald's Place, Toronto ON M3C 3L4
Tel: 416-446-3493; *Fax:* 416-446-3588
Toll-Free: 800-387-8808
rmhc@ca.mcd.com
www.rmhccanada.ca
www.facebook.com/RMHCCanada
Previous Name: Ronald McDonald Children's Charities of Canada
Overview: A medium-sized national charitable organization founded in 1982
Mission: To help children in need by improving the physical & emotional quality of life for children with serious illnesses, disabilities &/or chronic conditions, allowing them to lead happier, healthier & more productive lives
Staff Member(s): 7
Membership: 14; *Member Profile:* Ronald McDonald Houses
Chief Officer(s):
Cathy Loblaw, President & CEO
cathy.loblaw@ca.mcd.com
Roxanna Kassam-Kara, Director, Marketing & Communications
roxanna.kassamkara@ca.mcd.com
Kelly Glover, Coordinator
kelly.glover@ca.mcd.com

Ronald McDonald House Toronto
240 McCaul St., Toronto ON M5T 1W5
Tel: 416-977-0458; *Fax:* 416-977-8807
info@rmhtoronto.ca
www.rmhtoronto.ca
www.linkedin.com/company/ronald-mcdonald-house-toronto
www.facebook.com/RMHCToronto
twitter.com/RMHToronto
Also Known As: Toronto Children's Care Inc.
Previous Name: Children's Oncology Care of Ontario Inc.
Overview: A small local charitable organization founded in 1981
Mission: To provide a home & support services for out-of-town families whose children are receiving treatment in Toronto hospitals for serious illness
Finances: *Annual Operating Budget:* $500,000-$1.5 Million; *Funding Sources:* Public
Staff Member(s): 10; 105 volunteer(s)
Membership: 30 board; *Fees:* $10
Activities: Child Life Program; Play Program; Summer Fun; Support & Courtesy Services; Family Room Program; *Speaker Service:* Yes
Chief Officer(s):
Sally Ginter, Chief Executive Officer
sginter@rmhctoronto.ca
Anita Price, Office Manager
aprice@rmhctoronto.ca

Roncesvalles Macdonell Residents' Association (RMRA)
c/o 49 Fermanagh Ave., Toronto ON M6R 1M1
info@rmra-to.org
www.rmra-to.org
Overview: A small local organization founded in 1973
Mission: To preserve & promote the community
Membership: *Fees:* $10 waged; $5 unwaged
Chief Officer(s):

Brian Torry, Co-Chair
Norman Kolasky, Co-Chair

La Ronge & District Chamber of Commerce
PO Box 1493, La Ronge SK S0J 1L0
chamber@laclarongechamber.ca
www.laclarongechamber.ca
Overview: A small local organization
Mission: To stimulate economic growth in the area through the promotion of trade & commerce; To represent members & businesses of all types
Member of: Saskatchewan Chamber of Commerce; Canadian Chamber of Commerce
Finances: *Annual Operating Budget:* Less than $50,000; *Funding Sources:* Membership dues
Membership: 79; *Fees:* Schedule available; *Committees:* Resource Development & Construction; Retail; Tourism
Chief Officer(s):
Matthew Klassen, President
Lynnette Merriman, Treasurer

Roofing Contractors Association of British Columbia (RCABC)
9734 - 201st St., Langley BC V1M 3E8
Tel: 604-882-9734
roofing@rcabc.org
www.rcabc.org
Also Known As: RCABC Educational Foundation
Overview: A medium-sized provincial organization founded in 1958 overseen by Canadian Roofing Contractors' Association
Mission: To provide continuing education for roofing contractors, their workers & interested others; to represent the roofing contracting industry in its relationships with legislative & regulating bodies; to work closely with affiliate organizations & liaison groups in advancing the professionalism of roofing contracting; to provide a forum for the interaction of members; to encourage high standards of professional conduct among roofing contractors; to develop a comprehensive body of knowledge about roofing management & technology; to disseminate ideas & knowledge to members & others; to monitor new products & systems; to work for cooperation & greater understanding between contracting, inspection, manufacturing & supply segments of the roofing industry
Member of: Canadian Roofing Contractors' Association
Affiliation(s): International Federation of Roofing Contractors
Finances: *Annual Operating Budget:* $1.5 Million-$3 Million; *Funding Sources:* Membership dues; government funding; administration fees
Staff Member(s): 15
Membership: 119 corporate; *Member Profile:* Professional roofers, suppliers, manufacturers; *Committees:* Associates; Education & Training; Entertainment; Ethics; Inspection; Membership; Nominating; Roofing Industry Safety Council; Technical
Activities: Third party labour & material guarantees; training; professional development; *Library:* Open to public by appointment
Chief Officer(s):
Bryan L. Wallner, Chief Executive Officer
bwallner@rcabc.org
Awards:
• Klaus Thiel Educational Endowment Fund

Roofing Contractors Association of Manitoba Inc. (RCAM)
1447 Waverley St., Winnipeg MB R3T 0P7
Tel: 204-783-6365; *Fax:* 204-783-6446
office@rcam.ca
www.rcam.ca
Overview: A small provincial organization founded in 1966 overseen by Canadian Roofing Contractors' Association
Member of: Canadian Roofing Contractors' Association
Finances: *Funding Sources:* Membership fees
Membership: 27
Chief Officer(s):
Marian Davidson Boles, Executive Director

Roofing Contractors Association of Nova Scotia (RCANS)
7 Frederick Ave., Mount Uniacke NS B0N 1Z0
Tel: 902-866-0505; *Fax:* 902-866-0506
Toll-Free: 888-278-0133
contact@rcans.ca
www.rcans.ca
Overview: A small provincial organization founded in 1965 overseen by Canadian Roofing Contractors' Association
Mission: To promote quality workmanship in the commerical, industrial & institutional roofing industry; to encourage training for roofers
Member of: Canadian Roofing Contractors' Association
Affiliation(s): Construction Association of Nova Scotia
Membership: 14 companies; *Member Profile:* Roofing companies; suppliers; manufacturers
Chief Officer(s):
Paula Webber, President, 902-662-3250, Fax: 902-662-2016

Rosaries for Canadian Forces Abroad
Overview: A small national organization
Mission: Providing military support by making & donating Rosaries to members of the Canadian Forces serving abroad
Affiliation(s): Archdiocese of Toronto
Membership: *Member Profile:* Any person who wishes to assist in the making or distribution of Rosaries for Canadian Forces deployed abroad may join the private Catholic lay apostolate
Activities: Making Rosaries in parish guilds, led by a guild leader

The Rosary Apostolate, Inc.
1208 Warden Ave., Toronto ON M1R 2R3
www.rosaryapostolate.com
Overview: A small local charitable organization founded in 1997
Mission: To lead children, youth, & families to Jesus through Mary
Finances: *Funding Sources:* Donations
Membership: *Member Profile:* Individuals, who are practising Catholics, are devoted to Mary & her rosary, & who respect & love children; Volunteers, who cater to the schools in their parishes as rosary visitors; Rosary visitors teach children by praying the Rosary & the Act of Consecration
Activities: Forming parish prayer groups for evangelization through prayer; Conducting school visits to pray the rosary with children in Catholic schools; Providing director workshops & regional meetings; Recruiting, screening, & training rosary visitors; Outlining themes & meditations for rosary visitors; Offering annual retreats
Chief Officer(s):
Marilina Cinelli, Spiritual Director
Publications:
• The Rosary Apostolate Newsletter
Type: Newsletter

Rose & Max Rady Jewish Community Centre (RJCC)
123 Doncaster St., Winnipeg MB R3M 0S3
Tel: 204-477-7510; *Fax:* 204-477-7530
inquiry@radyjcc.com
radyjcc.com
www.facebook.com/radyjcc
twitter.com/radyjcc
www.youtube.com/user/radyjcc
Also Known As: RADY JCC
Previous Name: Jewish Community Centre of Winnipeg
Overview: A small local charitable organization founded in 1919
Mission: To foster & encourage a welcoming community where Jewish culture & values can flourish; To strengthen communal & familial relationships between members; To encourage healthy & active lifestyles in the community at large
Member of: Jewish Community Centers Association of North America
Affiliation(s): Canadian Council of Jewish Community Centres; Association of Jewish Center Professionals; Manitoba Camping Association; Folk Arts Council of Winnipeg
Finances: *Annual Operating Budget:* $1.5 Million-$3 Million; *Funding Sources:* Program & membership generated; United Way; Jewish Federation of Winnipeg/Combined Jewish Appeal
Staff Member(s): 36; 200 volunteer(s)
Membership: 6,500; *Fees:* Schedule available
Activities: Offering fitness, aquatics, recreation, & sport programs; Facilitating day camps; Providing child care services; Offering recreational programs for seniors; Providing cultural enrichment workshops; *Internships:* Yes *Library:* Kaufman-Silverberg Resource Centre
Chief Officer(s):
Elliott Garfinkel, President

Rose Society of Ontario *See* Canadian Rose Society

Rosetown & District Chamber of Commerce
PO Box 744, Rosetown SK S0L 2V0
Tel: 306-882-1300
rosetownchamber@gmail.com
www.rosetownchamber.com
Overview: A small local organization
Mission: To represent Rosetown & area's business community in matters related to economic growth & development
Finances: *Annual Operating Budget:* Less than $50,000
Membership: 100-499; *Fees:* Schedule available
Chief Officer(s):
Kimiko Shimoda, President

Ross Township Historical Society of Whitewater Region; Ross Township Historical Society *See* Whitewater Historical Society

Rossburn & District Chamber of Commerce
PO Box 579, Rossburn MB R0J 1V0
Tel: 204-859-0050; *Fax:* 204-859-3313
rossburn.chamber@live.ca
Overview: A small local organization
Mission: To enhance & promote established businesses & encourage new businesses to come to Rossburn
Member of: Manitoba Chamber of Commerce
Finances: *Annual Operating Budget:* Less than $50,000
20 volunteer(s)
Membership: 49; *Fees:* $50; *Committees:* Membership; Events; Promotions; Welcome to Rossburn & Area
Activities: Organizing Annual Summer Festival Parade, Christmas Lighting Contest, Welcome Baskets & other events; *Awareness Events:* Welcome to Rossburn
Chief Officer(s):
Tony White, President

Rotary Club of Stratford Charitable Foundation
PO Box 21135, Stratford ON N5A 7V4
Tel: 519-273-6297
request@rotarystratford.com
www.rotarystratford.com
Overview: A small local charitable organization founded in 1922
Member of: Rotary International
Membership: 100-499
Chief Officer(s):
James Corkery, Contact

The Rotary Club of Toronto
Fairmont Royal York Hotel, 100 Front St. West, Toronto ON M5J 1E3
Tel: 416-363-0604
office@rotarytoronto.on.ca
www.rotarytoronto.com
Overview: A medium-sized local charitable organization founded in 1913
Mission: To encourage & foster the ideal of service as a basis of worthy enterprise through fellowship among members, ethical behaviour in business, service to the community, & the advancement of international understanding & peace; To improve the lives of the most vulnerable in the Toronto community
Affiliation(s): Rotary of International
Finances: *Annual Operating Budget:* $250,000-$500,000
Staff Member(s): 2; 240 volunteer(s)
Membership: 240; *Fees:* $2,280
Activities: Fundraising; granting activities; funding local projects; *Speaker Service:* Yes
Chief Officer(s):
Pat Neuman, President

Rotman Institute for International Business (RIIB)
University of Toronto, 105 St. George St., Toronto ON M5S 3E6
Tel: 416-978-5781
riib@utoronto.ca
www.rotman.utoronto.ca
Previous Name: Institute for Policy Analysis
Merged from: Institute for Policy Analysis; Institute for International Business
Overview: A medium-sized national organization founded in 2008
Mission: RIIB merges the former Institute for Policy Analysis & the Institute for International Business, & focusses on research on the global business environment, enterprise decision making in the global economy, & the urban service economy.
Affiliation(s): University of Toronto
Finances: *Annual Operating Budget:* $100,000-$250,000; *Funding Sources:* Grants; contracts; donations
Staff Member(s): 3
Membership: 1-99
Activities: *Library:* Not open to public
Chief Officer(s):
Wendy Dobson, Co-Director
dobson@rotman.utoronto.ca

Ig Horstman, Co-Director, Prof. of Economics
lhorstmann@rotman.utoronto.ca

La Route Celtique See The Celtic Way

Row Nova Scotia
5516 Spring Garden Rd., 4th Fl., Halifax NS B3J 1G6
Tel: 902-425-5450
rowing@rowns.ca
www.rowns.ca
www.facebook.com/RowNovaScotia
twitter.com/RowNovaScotia
Overview: A medium-sized provincial organization overseen by Rowing Canada Aviron
Mission: To govern the sport of rowing in Nova Scotia
Member of: Rowing Canada Aviron
Finances: Funding Sources: Sport Fund; Athlete Assistance; KidSport; Individual Coach Initiative; Row Nova Scotia Coach Fund; Individual Official Fund
Chief Officer(s):
Peter Webster, President
Patrick Thompson, PSO Administrative Coordinator, 902-425-5450 Ext. 357
rowing@rowns.ca
Publications:
• Row Nova Scotia Newsletter
Type: Newsletter; Frequency: Quarterly

Rowing British Columbia
#155, 3820 Cessna Dr., Richmond BC V7B 0A2
Tel: 604-273-4769; Fax: 888-398-5818
Toll-Free: 877-330-3638
admin@rowingbc.ca
www.rowingbc.ca
www.facebook.com/rowingbc
twitter.com/rowing_bc
Also Known As: Rowing BC
Overview: A medium-sized provincial organization founded in 1987 overseen by Rowing Canada Aviron
Mission: To govern the sport of rowing in British Columbia
Member of: Rowing Canada Aviron
Membership: Fees: $10 Sport; $20 Competetive; $50 Organization; Member Profile: Community, secondary & post-secondary educational rowing clubs; Committees: Umpire; Regatta Review Working Group; National Rowing Championships-Canada Cup Organizing; Regatta; Awards & Recognition
Chief Officer(s):
Susan Wilkinson, President
David Calder, Executive Director
exdirector@rowingbc.ca
Meetings/Conferences:
• Rowing British Columbia Annual General Meeting 2018, 2018
Scope: Provincial
Publications:
• Rowing British Columbia Newsletter
Type: Newsletter

Rowing Canada Aviron (RCA) / Association Canadienne d'Aviron Amateur
#321, 4371 Interurban Rd., Victoria BC V9E 2C5
Tel: 877-722-4769; Fax: 250-220-2503
rca@rowingcanada.org
www.rowingcanada.org
www.facebook.com/rowingcanada
twitter.com/rowingcanada
www.youtube.com/user/RowingCan
Also Known As: Canadian Amateur Rowing Association
Previous Name: The Canadian Association of Amateur Oarsmen
Overview: A large national organization founded in 1880
Mission: To encourage the formation of rowing clubs & provincial associations; To encourage the organization of national regattas; To define & to maintain the principles of amateurism in all competitions; To organize, develop, & select national rowing teams to represent Canada internationally
Member of: Canadian Olympic Committee; Canadian Paralympic Commmittee; Fédération internationale des sociétés d'aviron
Finances: Funding Sources: Sport Canada; Sponsors
Staff Member(s): 12
Membership: Fees: $700 rowing association; $500 associate organization & special association; $400 rowing club; Committees: Governance Review; Executive
Chief Officer(s):
Carol Purcer, President

Terry Dillion, Chief Executive Officer
tdillion@rowingcanada.org
Awards:
• Club - "Outstanding Achievement of the Year" Award
• Coach of the Year Award
• Long Service Awards
• Lifetime Achievement Award
• Volunteer of the Year Award
• Umpire of the Year Award
• Tony Zasada Memorial Fund Award
• Jack Nicolson Coaching Bursary
• Centennial Medal
• Award of Merit / Prix du mérite
• The President's Award / Le Prix Du Président
Meetings/Conferences:
• 2018 Rowing Canada Aviron National Conference & Semi-Annual Meeting, January, 2018, Chelsea Hotel, Toronto, ON

Rowing New Brunswick Aviron (RNBA)
PO Box 30047, Stn. Prospect Plaza, Fredericton NB E3B 0H8
president@rowingnb.ca
www.rowingnb.ca
Also Known As: Rowing NB Aviron
Overview: A medium-sized provincial organization overseen by Rowing Canada Aviron
Mission: To govern the sport of rowing in New Brunswick
Member of: Rowing Canada Aviron
Meetings/Conferences:
• 2018 Rowing New Brunswuck Aviron Annual General Meeting, 2018

Rowing Newfoundland
41 Cabot Rd., Conception Bay South NL A1W 4C5
Tel: 709-834-1581
Previous Name: Newfoundland Rowing Association
Overview: A small provincial organization overseen by Rowing Canada Aviron
Mission: To govern the sport of rowing in Newfoundland
Member of: Rowing Canada Aviron

Rowing PEI
c/o Daphne Dumont, Macnutt & Dumont Law Office, PO Box 965, 57 Water St., Charlottetown PE C1A 7M4
rowingpei@gmail.com
rowingpei.ca
Overview: A medium-sized provincial organization founded in 2010 overseen by Rowing Canada Aviron
Mission: To govern the sport of rowing in Prince Edward Island
Member of: Rowing Canada Aviron
Membership: Fees: $330
Chief Officer(s):
Daphne Dumont, President

Royal Academy of Dance Canada
#601, 1210 Sheppard Ave. East, Toronto ON M2K 1E3
Tel: 416-489-2813; Fax: 416-489-3222
Toll-Free: 888-709-0895
info@radcanada.org
www.radcanada.org
www.facebook.com/RoyalAcademyofDanceCanada
twitter.com/radcanada
Also Known As: RAD Canada
Overview: A small national organization founded in 1920
Mission: To provide dance education & training
Affiliation(s): Royal Academy of Dance
Finances: Annual Operating Budget: $1.5 Million-$3 Million; Funding Sources: Membership dues; Corporate sponsors; corporate and individual donations
Staff Member(s): 8
Membership: 14,000+; Fees: $110-170; Member Profile: Full and Affiliate memberships
Activities: Offering professional development courses
Chief Officer(s):
Clarke MacIntosh, National Director, Canada
cmacintosh@radcanada.org

Royal Agricultural Winter Fair Association (RAWF) / Foire agricole royale d'hiver
The Ricoh Coliseum, 100 Prince's Blvd., Toronto ON M6K 3C3
Tel: 416-263-3400
info@royalfair.org
www.royalfair.org
www.facebook.com/royalfair
twitter.com/THERAWF
theroyalagriculturalwinterfair.tumblr.com
Also Known As: Royal Winter Fair

Overview: A medium-sized national charitable organization founded in 1922
Mission: To promote excellence in agricultural & equestrian activities through world class competition, exhibitions & education
Member of: Canadian Association of Fairs & Exhibitions
Finances: Funding Sources: Sponsors; government; gate admissions; advertising
Activities: Internships: Yes
Chief Officer(s):
Sandra G. Banks, Chief Executive Officer
Awards:
• Performance Horse Awards
35 divisions & classes offer prizes; Leading International Rider is the highest honour in the horse show
• Breeding Horse Awards
17 sections award prizes in this category
• Agricultural Awards
Grand Champion is the highest honour in the following categories: dairy, beef, sheep, goats, swine, market livestock, field crops, vegetables, honey & maple, poultry, jams/jellies/pickles, dairy products, square dancing, fiddling, fleece wool, rabbits, & eight youth activities
Meetings/Conferences:
• The Royal Agricultural Winter Fair 2018, November, 2018, Exhibition Place, Toronto, ON
Scope: International
Description: The Royal is the largest combined indoor agricultural fair and international equestrian competition in the world.
Contact Information: www.royalfair.org

Royal Alberta United Services Institute (RAUSI)
c/o Mewata Armouries, 801 - 11 St., Calgary AB T2P 2C4
Tel: 403-265-6628; Fax: 403-265-8347
rausi@telus.net
www.rausi.ca
Overview: A small provincial organization founded in 1920
Mission: To support H.M. forces, regular, reserve & cadet
Member of: The Federation of Military & United Services Institutes of Canada
Finances: Annual Operating Budget: Less than $50,000
Staff Member(s): 1; 16 volunteer(s)
Membership: 200; Fees: $20-$85
Activities: Library: Open to public
Chief Officer(s):
Gord Leek, CD, President

Royal Arch Masons of Canada
361 King St. West. 2nd Fl., Hamilton ON L8P 1B4
Tel: 905-522-5775; Fax: 905-522-5099
office@royalarchmasons.on.ca
www.royalarchmasons.on.ca
Overview: A small national organization
Chief Officer(s):
Melvyn J. Duke, Grand Scribe E.

Royal Architectural Institute of Canada (RAIC) / Institut royal d'architecture du Canada
#330, 55 Murray St., Ottawa ON K1N 5M3
Tel: 613-241-3600; Fax: 613-241-5750
Toll-Free: 844-856-7242
info@raic.org
www.raic.org
www.linkedin.com/in/raicirac
www.facebook.com/theraic.irac
twitter.com/RAIC_IRAC
Overview: A medium-sized national organization founded in 1907
Mission: To represent Canadian architects nationally & internationally; To foster public awareness & appreciation of architecture; To engage in architectural research & education; To lobby government on architectural issues
Staff Member(s): 9
Membership: 4,800; Fees: Schedule available; Member Profile: Registered architects; Architectural graduates; Intern architects; Full-time architecture faculty members of a university; Committees: Awards; Communications; Executive; Festival Renewal; Finance; Practice Support; Professional Development
Activities: Engaging in advocacy & public outreach; Providing architectural resources; Internships: Yes; Library: Not open to public
Chief Officer(s):
Jody Ciufo, Executive Director Ext. 206
jciufo@raic.org

Canadian Associations / Royal Astronomical Society of Canada (RASC) / Société royale d'astronomie du Canada

Awards:
- RAIC Student Medal

Available to a student in each Canadian University School of Architecture in the graduating class for the degree of Bachelor of Architecture *Eligibility:* Sudents graduating from a School of Architecture at a Canadian university who have attained academic excellence or demonstrated proficiency through their final design project or thesis
- RAIC Gold Medal

Established 1930; gold medals awarded annually in recognition of a person of science or letters related to architecture & the arts, in addition to an architect, for great achievement & contribution to the architectural profession *Eligibility:* Individuals who have made significant contributions to Canadian architecture through architectural theory, practice, design, research, or education

Publications:
- RAIC [Royal Architectural Institute of Canada] Annual Report

Type: Report; *Frequency:* Annually

Royal Astronomical Society of Canada (RASC) / Société royale d'astronomie du Canada

#203, 4920 Dundas St. West, Toronto ON M9A 1B7
Tel: 416-924-7973; *Fax:* 416-924-2911
Toll-Free: 888-924-7272
www.rasc.ca
www.facebook.com/theRoyalAstronomicalSocietyofCanada
twitter.com/rasc
Overview: A medium-sized national licensing charitable organization founded in 1868
Mission: To promote the advancement of astronomy across Canada
Finances: *Funding Sources:* Membership dues; publication sales
Membership: 4,500; *Fees:* Schedule available; *Committees:* Awards; Constituttion; Education & Public Outreach; Finance; History; Information Technology; Light-Pollution; Membership & Development; Nominating; Observing; Publications
Activities: Telescope viewings; workshops; speakers; mall displays; *Awareness Events:* International Astronomy Week, April; *Library:* Open to public by appointment
Chief Officer(s):
James Edgar, President
Randy Attwood, Executive Director
Awards:
- The Plaskett Medal

Presented jointly with CASCA for an outstanding doctoral thesis
- Simon Newcomb Award

Established 1978; trophy awarded annually for the best article on astronomy, astrophysics or space sciences submitted by a member of the society during the year
- Chant Medal

Established 1940 in appreciation of the great work of the late Prof. C.A. Chant in furthering the interests of astronomy in Canada; silver medal is awarded no more than once a year to an amateur astronomer resident in Canada on the basis of the value of the work which he/she has carried out in astronomy & closely allied fields of original investigation
- Service Award Medal

Established 1959; bronze medal presented to members who have performed outstanding service to a Centre or to the National Society
- Ken Chilton Prize

Established 1977; plaque awarded annually to an amateur astronomer resident in Canada, in recognition of a significant piece of work carried out or published during the year

Publications:
- Journal

Frequency: Bimonthly; *Editor:* Jay Anderson
Profile: Welcomes articles on Canadian astronomers and current activities of the RASC and its Centres, research and review papers by professional and amateur astronomers, and articles of a historical, biographical,or educational nature of general interest to the astronomical community
- Obersver's Handbook

Frequency: Annually; *ISSN:* 0080-4193
Profile: The material in the Handbook is of interest to professional and amateur astronomers, scientists, teachers at all levels, students, science writers, campers, Scout and Guide leaders, as well asinterested general readers

Belleville Centre
c/o Greg Lisk, 11 Robert Dr., Trenton ON K8V 6P2
info@rascbelleville.ca
rascbelleville.ca

Calgary Centre
PO Box 20282, #250, 300 - 5th Ave. SW, Calgary AB T2P 4J3
Tel: 403-237-7827
calrascsec@telus.net
calgary.rasc.ca
www.facebook.com/164753350226370
twitter.com/CalgaryRASC
Chief Officer(s):
Jason Nishiyama, President

Centre de Québec
2000, boul Montmorency, Québec QC G1J 5E7
Tel: 418-660-2815
sracquebec@gmail.com
www.src-quebec.org
Chief Officer(s):
Guy Campeau, Président
president@astro-caaq.org

Charlottetown Centre
PO Box 1734, Charlottetown PE C1A 7N4
PE_Centre@rasc.ca
www.rasccharlottetown.ca
twitter.com/peiastronomy
Chief Officer(s):
Clair Perry, President
Brian Gorveatt, Vice-President

Edmonton Centre
c/o Telus World of Science, 11211 - 142 St., Edmonton AB T5M 4A1
Chief Officer(s):
Sherry Campbell, President
edm.president@edmontonrasc.com
Peter Hall, Vice-President
edm.vicepresident@edmontonrasc.com

Halifax Centre
PO Box 31011, Halifax NS B3K 5T9
Tel: 902-252-9453
www.halifax.rasc.ca
Chief Officer(s):
Paul Heath, President
pheath@eastlink.ca
Wes Howie, 1st Vice-President
firstvp@lightimages.org
Karl Penney, 2nd Vice-President

Hamilton Centre
2266 Lakeshore Rd. West, Oakville ON L6L 1G8
Tel: 905-689-0266
astronomers@hamiltonrasc.ca
www.hamiltonrasc.ca
www.facebook.com/271133892909573?fref=ts
Chief Officer(s):
Gary Colwell, President
president@hamiltonrasc.ca

Kingston Centre
c/o 76 Colebrook Rd., RR#1, Kingston ON K0K 3N0
Tel: 613-377-6029
kingston@rasc.ca
kingston.rasc.ca
www.facebook.com/pages/RASC-Kingston-Centre/161721290520084
Chief Officer(s):
Kim Hay, President
Kevin Kell, Treasurer

Kitchener/Waterloo Centre
#3-127, 133 Weber St. North, Waterloo ON N2J 3G9
Tel: 519-576-5301
kw-rasc-sec@sympatico.ca
kw.rasc.ca
www.facebook.com/AstronomyinKitchenerWaterloo
Chief Officer(s):
Gerald Bissett, President, 519-747-1275
president@kw.rasc.ca
Ognian Kabranov, 1st Vice-President
kabranov@hotmail.com
Marvin Warkentin, 2nd Vice-President
mwarkentin@rogers.com

London Centre
PO Box 842, Stn. B, London ON N6A 4Z3
info@rasclondon.ca
www.rasclondon.ca
Chief Officer(s):
Rick Saunders, President
prez@rasclondon.ca

Mississauga Centre
PO Box 98011, 2126 Burnhamthorpe Rd., Mississauga ON L5L 5V4
Tel: 416-894-4629
inquiries@mississauga.rasc.ca
www.mississauga.rasc.ca
Chief Officer(s):
Leslie Strike, President
pres@mississauga.rasc.ca
Andrew Opala, Vice-President
vpres@mississauga.rasc.ca

Montréal Centre - Centre francophone de Montréal
7110, 8e av, Montréal QC H2A 3C4
Tél: 514-808-6219
info@lasam.ca
www.lasam.ca
twitter.com/lasamontreal
www.youtube.com/profile?user=lasamontreal

Montréal Centre - English
PO Box 39061, Montréal QC H3B 0B2
info@rascmontreal.org
www.rascmontreal.org
www.facebook.com/pages/RASC-Montreal-Centre/120104748051743
Chief Officer(s):
Morrie Portnoff, President

New Brunswick Centre
70 Ian St., Saint John NB E2J 3K7
Tel: 506-696-6071
president@nb.rasc.ca
www.nb.rasc.ca
www.facebook.com/RASC.NB
twitter.com/RASCNB
Chief Officer(s):
Curt Nason, President
president@nb.rasc.ca

Niagara Centre
c/o Dr. Brian Pihack, 4245 Portage Rd., Niagara Falls ON L2E 6A2
www.astronomyniagara.com
www.facebook.com/rascniagara
Chief Officer(s):
Brian Pihack, President
drbgpdc@on.aibn.com
Brian Pihack, Vice-President
drbgpdc@on.aibn.com

Okanagan Centre
Kelowna BC
www.ocrasc.ca
Chief Officer(s):
Colleen O'Hare, President, 250-763-3573
chohare@shaw.ca

Ottawa Centre
PO Box 33012, 1363 Woodroffe Ave., Nepean ON K2C 3Y9
Tel: 613-830-3381
codale0806@rogers.com
www.ottawa-rasc.ca

Prince George Centre
7365 Tedford Rd., Prince George BC V2N 6S2
Tel: 250-964-3600
rascpg@telus.net
www.pgrasc.org
Chief Officer(s):
Bob Nelson, Vice-President
bob.nelson@shaw.ca

Regina Centre
PO Box 20014, Stn. Cornwall Centre, Regina SK S4P 4J7
Tel: 306-751-0128
regina.rasc.ca
Chief Officer(s):
Chris Beckett, President
Mike O'Brien, Vice-President

St. John's Centre
206 Frecker Dr., St. John's NL A1E 5H9
Tel: 709-745-2903
info@stjohnsrasc.ca
www.stjohnsrasc.ca
Randy Dodge, Secretary
randy@mun.ca

Sarnia Centre
Sarnia ON
mr_scope2@hotmail.com
sites.google.com/site/rascsarnia/home

Saskatoon Centre
PO Box 317, RPO University, Saskatoon SK S7N 4J8
Tel: 306-373-3902
skstars@shaw.ca
www.usask.ca/rasc
Chief Officer(s):
Jim Gorkoff, President
jgorkoff@yahoo.ca

Sunshine Coast Centre
PO Box 577, Sechelt BC V0N 3A0
Tel: 778-458-2666
cuhulain@telus.net
sunshinecoastastronomy.wordpress.com
www.facebook.com/pages/Sunshine-Coast-Astronomy-Club/2
15347841270
twitter.com/CoastRASC
Chief Officer(s):
Michael Bradley, President
Adrian Payne, Vice-President

Thunder Bay Centre
286 Trinity Cres., Thunder Bay ON P7C 5V6
Tel: 807-475-3406
www.tbrasc.org
Chief Officer(s):
Brendon Roy, President

Toronto Centre
c/o Ontario Science Centre, 770 Don Mills Rd., Toronto ON M3C 1T3
Tel: 416-724-7827
secretary@toronto.rasc.ca
rascto.ca
www.facebook.com/rascto
twitter.com/rasctc
Chief Officer(s):
Charles Darrow, President

Vancouver Centre
PO Box 19115, 2302 West Fourth Ave., Vancouver BC V6K 4R8
rasc-vancouver.com
Chief Officer(s):
Mark Eburne, President
president@rasc-vancouver.com
Suzanna Nagy, Vice-President
vp@rasc-vancouver.com

Victoria Centre
c/o Nelson Walker, 3836 Pitcombe Pl., Victoria BC V8N 4B9
Tel: 250-477-4820
secretary@victoria.rasc.ca
victoria.rasc.ca
Chief Officer(s):
Nelson Walker, President, 250-477-4820
president@victoria.rasc.ca

Windsor Centre
1508 Greenwood Rd., Kingsville ON N9Y 2V7
Tel: 519-969-8552
www.rascwindsor.com
Chief Officer(s):
Rick Marion, President
rmarion@mdirect.net
Matt McCall, Education Director, 519-984-3572
edu_director@outlook.com

Winnipeg Centre
PO Box 2694, Winnipeg MB R3C 4B3
Tel: 204-956-2830
www.winnipeg.rasc.ca
twitter.com/WinnipegRASC

Royal Bank of Canada Charitable Foundation *See* RBC Foundation

Royal Botanical Gardens (RBG) / Les jardins botaniques royaux
680 Plains Rd. West, Hamilton ON L7T 4H4
Tel: 905-527-1158; *Fax:* 905-577-0375
Toll-Free: 800-694-4769
www.rbg.ca
www.facebook.com/140038459379746
twitter.com/RBGCanada
www.youtube.com/user/royalbotanicalgarden
Overview: A medium-sized local organization founded in 1932
Mission: To be recognized in Canada & throughout the world for its unique contribution to the collection, research, exhibition, & interpretation of the plant world & for the development of public understanding & appreciation of the relationship between the plant world, humanity, & the rest of nature
Member of: American Association of Botanical Gardens; Archives Association of Ontario; Canadian Museum Association; Museum Trustee Association
Finances: *Annual Operating Budget:* Greater than $5 Million; *Funding Sources:* Ministry of Citizenship, Culture & Recreation
Staff Member(s): 37; 400 volunteer(s)
Membership: 7,500; *Fees:* $50 single; $70 dual; $25 youth; $750+ corporate
Activities: Over 150 programs a year for all ages including gardening, plant care, art, cooking, environmental awareness & wildlife; over 30 public festivals/events; RBG is open year-round & receives approx. 500,000 visitors annually; 5 garden areas: Arboretum, Laking Garden, Rock Garden, Hendrie Park, Mediterannean Greenhouse; *Speaker Service:* Yes
Chief Officer(s):
Mark C. Runciman, CEO

Royal Canadian Academy of Arts (RCA) / Académie royale des arts du Canada
#375, 401 Richmond St. West, Toronto ON M5V 3A8
Tel: 416-408-2718; *Fax:* 416-408-2286
rcaarts@interlog.com
www.rca-arc.ca
www.facebook.com/canada.rca.arc
Overview: A medium-sized national charitable organization founded in 1880
Mission: To celebrate the achievements of visual artists across Canada; To encourage emerging artists; To facilitate the exchange of ideas about visual culture for the benefit of all Canadians
Member of: Canadian Conference of the Arts
Affiliation(s): National Gallery of Canada; Royal Academy, England
Finances: *Annual Operating Budget:* $100,000-$250,000; *Funding Sources:* Membership dues; Friends & corporate donations
Staff Member(s): 2
Membership: 700; *Fees:* $200; *Member Profile:* Canadian visual artists in all disciplines; *Committees:* Management; Council; Finance; Exhibition; National Nominations; Trust Fund; Friends' Events
Activities: Advocating for the rights of artists in Canada; Offering mentorship programs; Implementing special projects that represent the achievements of members; *Speaker Service:* Yes; *Library:* Open to public by appointment
Chief Officer(s):
Lina Jabra, Executive Director
Awards:
• RCA/C.D. Howe Scholarship for Art & Design
Eligibility: Graduating undergraduate students from professional Canadian art & design colleges & universities who are seeking further studies or professional development
• RCA Medal
Eligibility: Individuals who have contributed to the promotion of RCA's goals or the social, financial or professional advancement of the visual art & design community
Meetings/Conferences:
• Royal Canadian Academy of Arts 2018 138th Annual General Assembly, 2018
Scope: National
Publications:
• RCA [Royal Canadian Academy of Arts] News
Type: Newsletter
Profile: Information about the events, projects & exhibitions involving members

Royal Canadian Air Force Association *See* Air Force Association of Canada

Royal Canadian Armoured Corps Association
17 Mandel Crescent, Toronto ON M2H 1B8
www.rcaca.org
Overview: A small national organization
Chief Officer(s):
David Stones, President

Royal Canadian Army Service Corps Association-(Atlantic Region) (RCASC Atlantic)
PO Box 435, 175 Main Street East, Stewaicke NS B0N 2J0
www.rcasc-atlantic.org
Overview: A small local organization
Membership: 224; *Fees:* $10; *Member Profile:* Maritimers who served in the RCASC
Chief Officer(s):
Doug Horsman, President

Royal Canadian Artillery Association (RCAA)
1346 Mitchell Dr., Victoria BC V8S 4P8
Tel: 250-385-7922
www.rcaa-aarc.ca
Overview: A small national charitable organization founded in 1876
Mission: Promotion of the efficiency & welfare of the RRCA & all matters pertaining to the defence of Canada
Member of: Conference of Defense Associations
Finances: *Annual Operating Budget:* Less than $50,000
22 volunteer(s)
Membership: 350; *Fees:* $30; *Member Profile:* Serving & retired members
Activities: *Speaker Service:* Yes
Chief Officer(s):
James L. Brazill, President
Awards:
• The Lieutenant-Colonel Jack de Hart, MC CD Bursary
Eligibility: For junior officers; Successful completion of Phase 2 of the Reserve Entry Scheme Officers
• The Master Gunner E.M. Evoy, MM & Bar Bursary
Eligibility: For NCMs

Royal Canadian College of Organists (RCCO) / Collège royal canadien des organistes (CRCO)
#202, 204 St. George St., Toronto ON M5R 2N5
Tel: 416-929-6400; *Fax:* 416-929-2265
info@rcco.ca
www.rcco.ca
www.facebook.com/RCCO.ca
twitter.com/RCCO_CRCO
Overview: A medium-sized national licensing charitable organization founded in 1909
Mission: To promote a high standard of organ playing, choral directing, church music & composition; to hold examinations in organ playing, choir directing, theory & general knowledge of music; to encourage recitals; to increase the understanding among church musicisans, authorities & the public of matters relating to church music
Member of: Canadian Conference of the Arts
Finances: *Funding Sources:* Membership fees
Staff Member(s): 4
Membership: *Fees:* Schedule available; *Member Profile:* Professional & non-professional organists, choirmasters, students & all who support the aims & objectives; *Committees:* Competitions; Conventions; Professional Development; Examinations; Historic Organs; Honorary Awards; Membership; Music Publications; Religious Denominations Liaison; Professional Support; Scholarships & Bursaries; Finance & Administration; Development; By-Laws
Activities: *Library:* by appointment
Chief Officer(s):
Elizabeth Shannon, Executive Director
execdirector@rcco.ca
Awards:
• Distinguished Service Award
• Award of Excellence

The Royal Canadian Geographical Society (RCGS) / La Société géographique royale du Canada (SGRC)
#200, 1155 Lola St., Ottawa ON K1K 4C1
Tel: 613-745-4629; *Fax:* 613-744-0947
rcgs@rcgs.org
www.rcgs.org
www.facebook.com/theRCGS
twitter.com/RCGS_SGRC
Overview: A large national organization founded in 1929
Mission: To impart a broader knowledge of Canada, including its environmental, economic, & social challenges, as well as it natural & cultural heritage
Finances: *Funding Sources:* Membership fees; Donations
Activities: Presenting education programs through the education committee, Canadian Geographic Education; Conducting research; *Speaker Service:* Yes
Chief Officer(s):
John Geiger, Chief Executive Officer, 613-745-4629 Ext. 158
geiger@rcgs.org
Gilles Gagnier, Chief Operating Officer, 613-745-4629 Ext. 140
gagnier@canadiangeographic.ca
Catherine Frame, Vice-President, Finance & Administration, 613-745-4629
frame@canadiangeographic.ca
Awards:
• Camsell Medal
To recognize individuals who have given outstanding service to The Royal Canadian Geographical Society

Canadian Associations / Royal Canadian Institute (RCI)

- 3M Environmental Innovation Award
Presented by The Royal Canadian Geographical Society & 3M Canada to recognize individuals who contribute to the restoration & protection of the environment
- The Massey Medal
Awarded annually for outstanding achievement in the exploration, development, or description of the geography of Canada
- The Gold Medal
To recognize an achievement of one or more individuals in the field of geography, or a significant national or international event
- Geographic Literacy Award
To honour the contributions of a Canadian geography educator
- Research Grants
  Deadline: February
- The Martin Bergmann Medal
To recognizes achievement for "excellence in Arctic leadership and science."

Meetings/Conferences:
- The Royal Canadian Geographical Society College of Fellows Annual Dinner 2018, 2018
Scope: National
Description: A gathering of Society members, featuring the approval of the audited financial statement, a guest speaker, & the presentation of awards

Publications:
- Canadian Geographic
Type: Magazine; Frequency: 10 pa; ISSN: 1182-3895
Profile: Subscription includes 4 issues of Canadian Geographic Travel
- géographica
Type: Magazine
Profile: The Royal Canadian Geographical Society's French publication
- Royal Canadian Geoographical Society Annual Report
Type: Yearbook; Frequency: Annually
Profile: Featuring the Society's audited financial statements

Royal Canadian Golf Association See Golf Canada

Royal Canadian Institute (RCI)
#H7D, 700 University Ave., Toronto ON M5G 1X6
Tel: 416-977-2983; Fax: 416-962-7314
royalcanadianinstitute@sympatico.ca
www.royalcanadianinstitute.org
www.facebook.com/481071185037
twitter.com/RCI_Canada
www.youtube.com/RCIonline
Overview: A medium-sized national charitable organization founded in 1849
Mission: To increase public understanding of science; to create an environment in which science can flourish & be appreciated
Membership: Fees: $20 senior/student; $30 individual; $500 lifetime
Activities: Sunday afternoon public science lectures
Chief Officer(s):
Helle Tosine, President
John W. Johnston, Treasurer

The Royal Canadian Legion (RCL) / La Légion royale canadienne
Dominion Command, 86 Aird Place, Ottawa ON K2L 0A1
Tel: 613-591-3335; Fax: 613-591-9335
Toll-Free: 888-556-6222
info@legion.ca
www.legion.ca
www.facebook.com/CanadianLegion
twitter.com/RoyalCdnLegion
www.youtube.com/user/RCLDominionCommand
Overview: A large national organization founded in 1925
Mission: To serve veterans, ex-military & military members, their families, communities & Canada
Affiliation(s): Royal Commonwealth Ex-Services League
Finances: Annual Operating Budget: Greater than $5 Million; Funding Sources: Membership dues
Staff Member(s): 48
Membership: 360,000, including 40,000 Ladies' Auxiliary members; Fees: Schedule available; Committees: Veterans' Services; Legion Seniors; Membership; Sports; Remembrance & Poppy; Ceremonies; Financial Advisory; Investment; Staff Pension; Dominion Convention; National Defence; Appeals; Planning & Administration; Canadian Unity; Canvet Publications; Public Relations; Youth
Activities: Veterans & ex-service member assistance; veterans disability pension plan application processing; youth programs; seniors program; National Track & Field Championships & Clinic; Canadian Unity Program; Member Sports Program; Community Sports Program; Pilgrimages; Awareness Events: Remembrance & Poppy Campaign, Nov. 11; Speaker Service: Yes; Library

Chief Officer(s):
Larry Murray, Grand President
Tom Eagles, Dominion President
Mark Barham, Dominion Treasurer
Bradley Kenneth White, Dominion Secretary
Awards:
- Poppy Trust Fund Bursaries
- Meritorious Service Medal
- Meritorious Service Award
- Palm Leaf Award

Meetings/Conferences:
- The Royal Canadian Legion 47th Dominion Convention 2018, August, 2018, Winnipeg, MB
Scope: International
Contact Information: Phone: 888-556-6222

Publications:
- Chaplain's Manual [a publication of the Royal Canadian Legion]
Type: Report
- Ritual, Awards & Protocol Manual [a publication of the Royal Canadian Legion]
Type: Report

Alberta & NWT Command
2020 - 15th St. NW, Calgary AB T2M 3N8
Tel: 403-284-1161; Fax: 403-284-9899
office@abnwtlegion.com
www.abnwtlegion.com

British Columbia/Yukon Command
#101, 17618 - 58 Ave., Surrey BC V3S 1L3
Tel: 604-575-8840; Fax: 604-575-8820
Toll-Free: 888-261-2211
info@legionbcyukon.ca
www.legionbcyukon.ca
www.facebook.com/LegionBCYukon
twitter.com/LegionBCYukon
www.youtube.com/user/BCYukonCommandRCL
Chief Officer(s):
Inga Kruse, Executive Director
inga.kruse@legionbcyukon.ca
Angus Stanfield, President

Direction du Québec
#410, 1000, rue Saint-Antoine ouest, Montréal QC H3C 3R7
Tél: 514-866-7491; Téléc: 514-866-6303
Ligne sans frais: 877-401-7111
info@qc.legion.ca
www.qc.legion.ca
Chief Officer(s):
Norman Shelton, Président

Manitoba & Northwest Ontario Command
563 St. Mary's Rd., Winnipeg MB R2M 3L6
Tel: 204-233-3405; Fax: 204-237-1775
mblegion@mbnwo.ca
www.mbnwo.ca
Chief Officer(s):
Dawn Golding, Executive Director
dgolding@mbnwo.ca

New Brunswick Command
490 Douglas Ave., Saint John NB E2K 1E7
Tel: 506-634-8850; Fax: 506-633-4836
Toll-Free: 866-320-8387
legion@nbnet.nb.ca
www.nb.legion.ca
Chief Officer(s):
Rick Love, President

Newfoundland & Labrador Command
PO Box 5745, St. John's NL A10 5X3
Tel: 709-753-6666; Fax: 709-753-5514
Toll-Free: 888-335-6666
www.legionnl.ca
twitter.com/legionnlca
Chief Officer(s):
Brenda Slaney, Contact
bslaney@nfld.net

Nova Scotia/Nunavut Command
Burnside Business Park, 61 Gloria McCluskey Ave., Dartmouth NS B3B 2Z3
Tel: 902-429-4090; Fax: 902-429-7481
Toll-Free: 877-809-1145
info@ns.legion.ca
www.ns.legion.ca
Chief Officer(s):
Ronald T. Trowsdale, Command President

Ontario Command
89 Industrial Pkwy. North, Aurora ON L4G 4C4
Tel: 905-841-7999; Fax: 905-841-9992
Toll-Free: 888-207-0939
info@on.legion.ca
www.on.legion.ca
Chief Officer(s):
Bruce Julian, President

Prince Edward Island Command
161 St. Peters' Rd., Charlottetown PE C1A 5P6
Tel: 902-892-2161; Fax: 902-368-8853
royalcanadianlegion@pei.aibn.com
www.peilegion.com
Chief Officer(s):
Wayne Pike, Provincial Service Officer

Saskatchewan Command
3079 - 5th Ave., Regina SK S4T 0L6
Tel: 306-525-8739; Fax: 306-525-5023
sasklegion@sasktel.net
www.sasklegion.ca
Chief Officer(s):
Cherilyn Cooke, Executive Director

Royal Canadian Military Institute (RCMI)
426 University Ave., Toronto ON M5G 1S9
Tel: 416-597-0286; Fax: 416-597-6919
Toll-Free: 800-585-1072
info@rcmi.org
www.rcmi.org
Overview: A medium-sized national organization founded in 1890
Mission: To promote the navy, army & air force art, science, literature & interests; promotion of good fellowship & esprit de corps amongst the officers of the various branches of the services; to maintain of a clubhouse for the accommodation, recreation, enlightenment, convenience & entertainment of its members.
Membership: Member Profile: 60% military & former service personnel who have been or were commissioned officers; 40% associates of professional status
Activities: Library: by appointment
Chief Officer(s):
Chris Corrigan, Executive Director
ccorrigan1@cogeco.ca

Royal Canadian Mounted Police Veterans' Association / Association des anciens de la Gendarmerie royale du Canada
1200 Vanier Pkwy., Ottawa ON K1A 0R2
Tel: 613-993-8633; Fax: 613-993-4353
Toll-Free: 877-251-1771
rcmp.vets@rcmp-grc.gc.ca
www.rcmpvetsnational.ca
Previous Name: Royal Northwest Mounted Police Veterans Association
Overview: A medium-sized national charitable organization founded in 1924
Finances: Annual Operating Budget: $50,000-$100,000; Funding Sources: Membership dues; grants
Membership: 6,000; 30 divisions across Canada; Member Profile: One year service in RCMP or associated services
Meetings/Conferences:
- Royal Canadian Mounted Police Veterans Association 2018 Annual General Meeting, May, 2018, Best Western Plus Winnipeg Airport Hotel, Winnipeg, MB
Scope: National

Royal Canadian Naval Benevolent Fund (RCNBF) / Caisse de bienfaisance de la marine Royale Canadienne
#9, 6 Beechwood Ave., Ottawa ON K1L 8B4
Tel: 613-236-7389; Fax: 613-236-8830
Toll-Free: 888-557-8777
rcnbf@rcnbf.com
www.rcnbf.ca
www.facebook.com/493640407445184
Overview: A medium-sized national organization founded in 1945
Mission: To relieve distress & promote the well-being of individuals who have served in the Naval Forces of Canada & their dependants
Finances: Funding Sources: Donations & investments
Staff Member(s): 2
Membership: 46
Chief Officer(s):

Nancy Brady, Office Administrator
Western Committee
CFB Esquimalt, PO Box 17000, Stn. Forces, Victoria BC V9A 7N2
Tel: 250-383-6264

Royal Canadian Numismatic Association (RCNA)
#432, 5694 Hwy. 7 East, Markham ON L3P 1B4
Tel: 647-401-4014; Fax: 905-472-9645
info@rcna.ca
www.rcna.ca
Previous Name: Canadian Numismatic Association
Overview: A medium-sized national organization founded in 1950
Mission: To encourage & promote education in the science of numismatics, through the study of coins, paper money, medals, tokens, & all other numismatic items, with special emphasis on material pertaining to Canada
Membership: Fees: $16.50 juniors; $35 regular & corporate members; $44 families; $50 international members; $595 life membership; Member Profile: Persons interested in coin collecting / numismatics; Clubs, societies, libraries, & other non-profit organizations
Activities: Providing advocacy for the hobby; Offering educational seminars & RCNA junior programs; Library: Royal Canadian Numismatic Association Lending Library
Chief Officer(s):
Kevin McCann, Chair, Membership
canadian@coinoisseur.com
Meetings/Conferences:
• Royal Canadian Numismatic Association 2018 Convention, August, 2018, Hilton Mississauga, Mississauga, ON
Scope: National
Description: An annual event, presenting an education symposium, a bourse & display, business meetings, award presentations, plus social & networking activities
Contact Information: E-mail: info@rcna.ca
Publications:
• Canadian Numismatic Association E-Bulletin
Type: Newsletter; Price: Free
Profile: Numismatic personalities, coin club activities, sources of information, upcoming events, Canadian numismatic issues, tips for collectors, & RCNA news
• The CN Journal
Type: Journal; Frequency: 10 pa; Accepts Advertising; Editor: Dan Gosling (dan@gosling.ca); Price: Free with membership in the The Royal Canadian Numismatic Association
Profile: Papers written by accomplished Canadian numismatists
• A Half Century of Advancement in Numismatics
Type: Book; Number of Pages: 148; Editor: Stan Clute

The Royal Canadian Regiment Association (RCR)
c/o 1st Battalion, Victoria Barracks, PO Box 9999, Stn. Main, Petawawa ON K8H 2X3
Tel: 613-687-5511; Fax: 613-588-5932
thercr.ca
Overview: A medium-sized national organization
Mission: To perpetuate the close bonds of comradeship and esprit de corps created by members of The Royal Candian Regiment; To preserve the memory of those who have died in service; To assist the sick, wounded and needy who have served in the Regiment; To assist widows and children of deceased members; To maintain the Regiments's memorials and develop its history.
Membership: Fees: $25
Chief Officer(s):
Jim MacInnis, Chair
Randy Kemp, A/Vice-President, 613-687-8194
rjkemp11@gmail.com
Awards:
• Bursaries
Three bursaries given to eligible family members; Amount: $1,000

Royal City Field Naturalists
#903, 1219 Harwood St., Vancouver BC V6E 1S5
Tel: 604-609-0679
Overview: A small local organization
Mission: To promote the enjoyment of nature through environmental appreciation & conservation; to encourage wise use & conservation of natural resources & environmental protection
Member of: Federation of BC Naturalists
Membership: 12; Fees: $25
Chief Officer(s):

Gareth Llewellyn, Contact
gllew@telus.net

Royal College of Dental Surgeons of Ontario
6 Crescent Rd., Toronto ON M4W 1T1
Tel: 416-961-6555; Fax: 416-961-5814
Toll-Free: 800-565-4591
info@rcdso.org
www.rcdso.org
Also Known As: RCDS of Ontario
Overview: A large provincial licensing organization founded in 1868
Mission: To operate as the governing body for dentists in Ontario; To protect the public's right to quality dental services by providing leadership to the dental profession in self-regulation
Finances: Annual Operating Budget: Greater than $5 Million; Funding Sources: Membership fees
Membership: 9,300 individual; Member Profile: Mandatory membership under Regulated Health Professional Act of government of Ontario; Committees: Audit; Inquiries, Complaints & Reports; Discipline; Executive; Finance, Property & Administration; Fitness to Practise; Legal & Legislation; Professional Liability Program; Patient Relations; Quality Assurance; Registration
Activities: Registration of Dentists/Specialists in Ontario; handling complaints; discipline; Rents Mailing List: Yes
Chief Officer(s):
Irwin W. Fefergrad, Registrar
Ronald Yarascavitch, President
Kevin Marsh, Director, Communications
kmarsh@rcdso.org
Publications:
• Dispatch [a publication of the Royal College of Dental Surgeons of Ontario]
Type: Magazine; Frequency: Quarterly

Royal College of Dentists of Canada (RCDC) / Collège Royal des Chirurgiens Dentistes du Canada
#2404, 180 Dundas St. West, Toronto ON M5G 1Z8
Tel: 416-512-6571; Fax: 416-512-6468
office@rcdc.ca
www.rcdc.ca
Overview: A medium-sized national organization founded in 1965
Mission: To provide examinations for dental sciences & for nationally recognized dental specialties in Canada
Staff Member(s): 9
Membership: Member Profile: A Fellow in the Royal College of Dentists of Canada is a dentist who has achieved the following: graduation from a post-graduate program; completion of the National Dental Specialty Examination; a Fellowship diploma; association with a specialty recognized by the Canadian Dental Association; payment of fees; & good ethical standing in the profession; Committees: Examinations; Credentials; Nomination
Chief Officer(s):
Christopher Robinson, President
Adel Kauzman, Vice-President
Peter McCutcheon, Executive Director & Secretary
James Posluns, Treasurer
Benjamin Davis, Examiner-in-Chief
Lori Gottlieb, Director, Engagement
Catalina Ponce de Leon, Manager, Registration
Meetings/Conferences:
• Royal College of Dentists of Canada 2018 Annual General Meeting, 2018
Scope: National
Publications:
• Royal College of Dentists of Canada Bulletin
Type: Yearbook; Frequency: Annually
Profile: Produced each year following Convocation
• Royal College of Dentists of Canada Communiqué
Type: Newsletter; Frequency: every six weeks

The Royal College of Physicians & Surgeons of Canada (RCPSC) / Le Collège royal des médecins et chirurgiens du Canada (CRMCC)
774 Echo Dr., Ottawa ON K1S 5N8
Tel: 613-730-8177; Fax: 613-730-8830
Toll-Free: 800-668-3740
feedback@royalcollege.ca
www.royalcollege.ca
www.facebook.com/TheRoyalCollege
twitter.com/Royal_College
Overview: A large national charitable organization founded in 1929
Mission: To oversee the medical education of specialists in Canada; To set the highest standards in postgraduate medical education, through national certification examinations & lifelong learning programs; To promote sound health policy
Affiliation(s): Canadian Medical Association; College of Family Physicians of Canada; Association of Canadian Medical Colleges; National Specialty Societies; Federation of Medical Licensing Authorities of Canada
Finances: Funding Sources: Membership dues; credentials & examination fees; donations
Membership: 47,216 fellows & residents; Fees: $895 fellows practicing in Canada; $670 fellows practicing outside Canada; $225 long term fellows; Member Profile: Certification in medical specialty with application for admission to fellowship; Committees: Executive; Awards; Ethics; Fellowship Affairs; Financial Reporting & Risk Oversight; Governance; Health & Public Policy; Nominating; Specialty Education
Activities: Certification of specialists; continuing professional development; health policy; Internships: Yes Library: Roddick Room; by appointment Not open to public
Chief Officer(s):
Andrew Padmos, CEO
Awards:
• Medical Education Research Grant
To support research in the field of postgraduate medical education or continuing professional development; Amount: $5,000-$50,000
• Detweiler Travelling Fellowships
To enable six Fellows to visit medical centres in Canada or abroad to study or gain experience in the use or application of new knowledge or techniques, or to further the pursuit of a project relevant to clinical practice or research; Amount: Up to $25,000
• Robert Maudsley Fellowship for Studies in Medical Education
To increase the number & quality of professionally trained medical educators in Canada by providing training in the science of medical education; Amount: $40,000 per year of study to a maximum of two years
• Royal College/Associated MEdical Services CanMEDS Research Development Grant
; Amount: Up to $25,000
• KJR Wightman Award for Research in Ethics
; Amount: $1,000
• Charles Peter W. Warren History of Medicine Essay Prize
; Amount: $1,500
• Duncan Graham Award for Outstanding Contribution to Medical Education
; Amount: $1,000
• International Collaboration Award
• International Residency Educator of the Year Award
• International Resident Leadership Award
• James H. Graham Award of Merit
• Kristin Sivertz Resident Leadership Award
• Program Administrator Award for Innovation & Excellence
• Program Director of the Year Award
• Regional Mentor of the Year
• Regional Prix d'excellence - Specialist of the Year
• Royal College Accredited CPD Provider Innovation Awards
• Royal College/Associated Medical Services DOnald R. Wilson Award
• Royal College Dr. Thomas Dignan Indigenous Health Award
• Royal College Teasdale-Corti Humanitarian Award
Meetings/Conferences:
• Royal College of Physicians & Surgeons of Canada 2018 Annual General Meeting, 2018
Scope: National

The Royal Commonwealth Society of Canada (RCS) / La Société royale du Commonwealth du Canada
c/o RCS Ottawa, PO Box 8023, Stn. T, Ottawa ON K1G 3H6
www.rcs.ca
www.facebook.com/RCSCanada
twitter.com
Overview: A medium-sized national organization founded in 1868
Mission: A charitable, non-partisan organization which promotes knowledge of the Commonwealth & its member countries; fosters unity in diversity in matters of common concern; promotes international understanding, cooperation & peace; upholds the best traditions of the Commonwealth
Activities: National Student Commonwealth Conference; Canadian Regional Student Commonwealth Conference; libraries & reading rooms; publications; professorships, fellowships; information services
Chief Officer(s):

Norman Macfie, Chair
British Columbia Mainland Branch
#816, 402 West Pender St., Vancouver BC V6B 1T6
Tel: 604-683-3201
Chief Officer(s):
Shawn M. Wade, President
shawnmwade@hotmail.com
Montréal Branch
235, rue Sherbrooke ouest, Montréal QC H2X 1X8
Tel: 514-281-6718; *Fax:* 450-656-7621
Chief Officer(s):
Judith Elson, President
jelson@rsb.qc.ca
Newfoundland Branch
16 Osbourne St., St. John's NL A1B 1X8
Tel: 709-753-6472; *Fax:* 709-738-5679
newfoundland@rcs.ca
Chief Officer(s):
Norman Macfie, Chair
nmacfie@nl.rogers.com
Nova Scotia Branch
PO Box 153, Chester NS B0J 1J0
Tel: 902-275-2358
chesteragu@eastlink.ca
Chief Officer(s):
Heather Mackinnon, President
Ottawa Branch
PO Box 8023, Stn. T, Ottawa ON K1G 3H6
rcs.bytown@gmail.com
rcs-ottawa.ca
Chief Officer(s):
Peter Meincke, President
peter.meincke@bell.net
Prince Edward Island Branch
6 Sunset Dr., Charlottetown PE C1A 7S9
rcs.pei@gmail.com
Chief Officer(s):
David Ashby, Chair
dashby@islandtelecom.com
Toronto Branch
1849 Lincoln Green Close, Mississauga ON L5K 1C4
Tel: 905-823-2819
rcstoronto1@gmail.com
www.facebook.com/theroyalcommonwealthsocietycanada
Chief Officer(s):
Andrew McMurtry, President
Andrew_McMurtry@alumni.unwo.ca
Vancouver Island
#4-2525 Oakville Ave., Sidney BC V8L 1V9
Tel: 250-544-1120
vancouverisland@rcs.ca
Winnipeg Branch
#1602, 277 Wellington Cres., Winnipeg MB R3M 3V7
Tel: 204-488-0167
Chief Officer(s):
Murray Burt, President
burt@mts.net

Royal Conservatory Orchestra
273 Bloor St. West, Toronto ON M5S 1W2
Tel: 416-408-2824; *Fax:* 416-408-5025
www.rcmusic.ca
Overview: A small local charitable organization overseen by Orchestras Canada
Mission: To develop individuals' potential through leadership in music & the arts
Member of: The Royal Conservatory of Music
Affiliation(s): The Glenn Gould School
Membership: *Member Profile:* Students
Activities: Four concert season featuring world-class guest conductors; *Library:* Not open to public
Chief Officer(s):
Michael M. Koerner, Chancellor

Royal Danish Guards Association of Western Canada
c/o Svend Aage Storm, 109 Hawkside Mews NW, Calgary AB T3G 3K9
Tel: 403-285-4457
www.garderforening.dk/wcgf.html
Overview: A small local organization founded in 1944
Membership: *Member Profile:* Individuals who have served in the Danish Royal Guards Regiment
Activities: Hosting regular meetings
Chief Officer(s):
Svend Aage Storm, Vice-President
xxsstorm.p@gmail.com
Jens Lind, President
xxjenslind@telus.net
Publications:
• Garderbladet
Type: Newsletter; *Frequency:* 11 pa; *Price:* Free with Royal Danish Guards Association of Western Canada membership
Profile: Information for association members

Royal Heraldry Society of Canada / Société royale héraldique du Canada
PO Box 8128, Stn. T, Ottawa ON K1G 3H9
secretary@heraldry.ca
www.heraldry.ca
Previous Name: Heraldry Society of Canada
Overview: A small national charitable organization founded in 1966
Mission: To maintain, foster & develop the heraldic traditions of Canadians by: increasing public awareness of heraldry & the society; advocating with governments for the protection & proper use of heraldry in Canada; advising the Canadian Heraldic Authority on matters of mutual concern
Affiliation(s): Commonwealth Heraldry Board
Membership: *Fees:* $25 student; $60 institution; $75 regular; *Committees:* Bylaws; Editorial Board; Education; Heraldic Arts; Honours & Awards; Investment; Library & Archives; Marketing; Membership; Periodicals; Special Publications; Special Projects; Roll of Arms; Gift Planning & Donations
Activities: *Internships:* Yes; *Library:* by appointment
Chief Officer(s):
David E. Rumball, President
president@heraldry.ca
Edward McNabb, 1st Vice-President
first_vice@heraldry.ca
Vicken Koundakjian, 2nd Vice-President
second_vice@heraldry.ca

Royal Life Saving Society Canada *See* Lifesaving Society

Royal Manitoba Theatre Centre (MTC)
174 Market Ave., Winnipeg MB R3B 0P8
Tel: 204-956-1340; *Fax:* 204-947-3741
Toll-Free: 877-446-4500
www.royalmtc.ca
www.facebook.com/MTCwinnipeg
twitter.com/MTCWinnipeg
Overview: A medium-sized provincial charitable organization founded in 1957
Mission: To study, practice & promote all aspects of the dramatic arts, with particular emphasis on professional production
Member of: Professional Association of Canadian Theatres (PACT); Canadian Institute for Theatre Technology
Finances: *Annual Operating Budget:* Greater than $5 Million; *Funding Sources:* Canada Council; Manitoba Arts Council; City of Winnipeg; The Winnipeg Foundation
Staff Member(s): 29; 450 volunteer(s)
Activities: *Awareness Events:* Master Playwright Festival; Winnipeg Fringe Theatre Festival; *Internships:* Yes; *Library:* by appointment
Chief Officer(s):
Steven Schipper, Artistic Director
Camilla Holland, Executive Director

Royal New Brunswick Rifle Association Inc. (RNBRA)
13 Curtis St., Fredericton NB E3A 8W3
Tel: 506-453-7724
info@rnbra.ca
www.rnbra.ca
Overview: A small provincial organization founded in 1866
Mission: To promote marksmanship in New Brunswick
Affiliation(s): National Firearms Association; Dominion of Canada Rifle Association; Firearms Canada; 30 New Brunswick clubs
Chief Officer(s):
Gordon Holloway, President
president@rnbra.ca

Royal Newfoundland Constabulary Association (RNCA) / Association de la gendarmerie royale de Terre-Neuve
125 East White Hills Rd., St. John's NL A1A 5R7
Tel: 709-739-5946; *Fax:* 709-739-6276
office@rnca.ca
www.rnca.ca
Previous Name: Police Brotherhood of the Royal Newfoundland Constabulary Association (Ind.)
Overview: A small provincial organization founded in 1970
Mission: To improve benefits & working conditions for police officers; to improve public safety & strive to create a positive relationship between the police & the community they protect
Finances: *Annual Operating Budget:* $250,000-$500,000
Staff Member(s): 1
Membership: 380 non-commissioned ranks; *Fees:* $783.07
Chief Officer(s):
Tim Buckle, President
Warren Sullivan, 1st Vice-President
Albert Gibbons, 2nd Vice-President

Royal Northwest Mounted Police Veterans Association *See* Royal Canadian Mounted Police Veterans' Association

The Royal Nova Scotia Historical Society (RNSHS)
PO Box 2622, Halifax NS B3J 3P7
RoyalNSHS@gmail.com
www.rnshs.ca
Overview: A small provincial charitable organization founded in 1878
Mission: To promote an understanding & appreciation of Nova Scotia's history & cultural development; to encourage the preservation of published & archival materials & artifacts; to read papers pertaining to Nova Scotia's history at meetings of the society; to publish selected papers in the society's periodical
Member of: Heritage Canada; Federation of Nova Scotian Heritage
Affiliation(s): Genealogical Association of Nova Scotia
Finances: *Annual Operating Budget:* Less than $50,000; *Funding Sources:* Membership fees & subscription sales
14 volunteer(s)
Membership: 280; *Fees:* $25; *Member Profile:* Amateur & professional historians
Activities: Lecture series; *Internships:* Yes
Chief Officer(s):
David Sutherland, President
Publications:
• Journal of the Royal Nova Scotia Historical Society
Type: Journal; *Accepts Advertising; Editor:* Brian Cuthbertson; *ISSN:* 1193-9451; *Price:* Included with membership
Profile: Artciles on Nova Scotia history; book reviews on publications pertaining to Nova Scotia history

The Royal Philatelic Society of Canada (RPSC) / La Société royale de philatélie du Canada (SRPC)
St Clair Post Office, PO Box 69080, Toronto ON M4T 3A1
Tel: 416-921-2077; *Fax:* 416-921-1282
Toll-Free: 888-285-4143
info@rpsc.org
www.rpsc.org
Previous Name: Canadian Philatelic Society
Overview: A small national organization founded in 1887
Mission: To promote the hobby of stamp collecting; To use stamps & postal history in education for youths & adults
Member of: Fédération internationale de philatélie
Finances: *Annual Operating Budget:* $50,000-$100,000
Staff Member(s): 2; 24 volunteer(s)
Membership: 2,200; *Fees:* Schedule available; *Member Profile:* Anyone interested in stamp collecting; *Committees:* Chapter & Affiliates; Convention; CSDA Dealer; Ethics; Facebook/Social Media; 50-Year Club; Finance; Historian/Archives; International; Membership Recruitment & New Collector Coordinator; Membership Reporting; Nationa & Regional Judging Program; Nominating; RPSC National Exhibits; Sevices francophones; Youth Commission
Activities: *Speaker Service:* Yes; *Library:* Harry Sutherland Philatelic Library
Chief Officer(s):
James R. Taylor, President
president@rpsc.org
Ed Kroft, Vice President
vp1@rpsc.org
Publications:
• The Canadian Philatelist [a publication of The Royal Philatelic Society of Canada]
Type: Journal; *Frequency:* 6 pa.; *Editor:* Tony Shaman

The Royal Society of Canada (RSC) / La Société royale du Canada
Walter House, 282 Somerset West, Ottawa ON K2P 0J6
Tel: 613-991-6990; *Fax:* 613-991-6996
www.rsc.ca
www.linkedin.com/pub/the-royal-society-of-canada-rsc/23/592/418

www.facebook.com/RSC.SRC
twitter.com/rsctheacademies
www.youtube.com/user/RSCSRC1
Also Known As: Canadian Academy of the Sciences & Humanities
Overview: A medium-sized national charitable organization founded in 1882
Mission: To promote learning & research in the arts, humanities & sciences in Canada; in its role as a National Academy, to draw on the breadth of knowledge & expertise of its members to recognize & honour distinguished accomplishments; to advise on the state of scholarship & culture across Canada; to inform the public on noteworthy social, scientific & ethical questions of the day; it is organized into three academies covering the arts & humanities, the social sciences, & the natural & applied sciences
Finances: *Funding Sources:* Membership dues; endowments; government; corporate
Staff Member(s): 5
Membership: 2000 fellows; *Member Profile:* Fellows are elected by their peers on the basis of distinction in their field; *Committees:* Promotion of Women in Scholarship; Freedom of Scholarship
Activities: *Library:* Open to public
Chief Officer(s):
Darren Gilmour, Executive Director
dgilmour@rsc-src.ca
Awards:
• A.G. Huntsman Award
To recognize excellence of research & outstanding contribution to marine sciences
• Alice Wilson Award
Awarded to three women of outstanding academic qualifications in the Arts & Humanities, Science or Social Sciences who are entering a career in scholarship at the postdoctorate level; *Amount:* $1,000
• Bancroft Award
Awarded to encourage & recognize instruction & research in geology
• Centenary Medal
Awarded to recognize outstanding contributions to the objectives of the RSC
• Flavelle Medal
Awarded to recognize outstanding achievement in biological science
• Ursula Franklin Award in Gender Studies
Awarded to recognize contributions to furthering the understanding of issues concerning gender
• Henry Marshall Tory Medal
Awarded to recognize outstanding research in any branch of chemistry, astronomy, math, physics, or an allied science
• Innis-Gérin Medal
Awarded to recognize a distinguished or sustained contribution to the literature of the social sciences
• J.B. Tyrrell Historical Medal
Awarded to honour outstanding work relating to the history of Canada
• Jason A. Hannah Medal
Awarded to recognize an important Canadian publication in the history of medicine; *Amount:* $1,500
• John L. Synge Award
Awarded to acknowledge outstanding research in any branch of mathematical science
• Konrad Adenauer Research Award
Created to promote academic collaboration between Canada & Germany; awarded annually to a Canadian scholar in the humanities or social sciences. Recipient is invited to carry out a research project of her/his choice in Germany, in collaboration with German colleagues; project can last six to twelve months & can be divided into several segments.; *Amount:* 50,000 Euros + travel costs to Germany
• Lorne Pierce Medal
Awarded to honour achievement in critical or imaginative literature written in either English or French
• McLaughlin Medal
Awarded to honour important research of sustained excellence in medical science
• McNeil Medal
Awarded with support from McNeil Consumer Healthcare to recognize a candidate who has demonstrated outstanding ability to promote & communicate science to students & the Canadian public; *Amount:* $1,500
• Miroslaw Romanowski Medal
Awarded for significant contributions to the resolution of scientific aspects of environmental problems; *Amount:* $3,000 + annual lecture series

• Pierre Chaveau Medal
Awarded for a distinguished contribution to knowledge in the humanities
• Rutherford Memorial Medals
Awarded for outstanding research in physics and in chemistry
• Sir John William Dawson Medal
Awarded for outstanding research in subjects of interest to the RSC
• Willet G. Miller Medal
Awarded for outstanding research in any branch of earth sciences
Meetings/Conferences:
• Royal Society of Canada Annual General Meeting 2018, 2018
Scope: National
Publications:
• Royal Society of Canada Annual Report
Type: Report; *Frequency:* Annually
• Royal Society of Canada e-Newsletter
Type: Newsletter; *Frequency:* Bimonthly
• Royal Society of Canada Membership Guides
Type: Guide
Profile: A series of five guides created to assist those seeking to nominate new Fellows & to describe the ways in which institutional members can benefit from membership
• Royal Society of Canada Report to the Fellowship
Type: Report; *Frequency:* Annually

Royal United Services Institute - Vancouver Society (RUSI)
2025 West 11th Ave., Vancouver BC V6J 2C7
secretary@rusivancouver.ca
www.rusivancouver.ca
Overview: A small local organization founded in 1921
Member of: The Federation of Military & United Services Institutes of Canada
Finances: *Funding Sources:* Membership fees
20 volunteer(s)
Membership: 150; *Fees:* $20; *Member Profile:* Army, Naval, Airforce, RCMP officers; *Committees:* Defence Research; Program; Membership/Welfare
Activities: *Speaker Service:* Yes
Chief Officer(s):
Jim Stanton, President

Royal United Services Institute of Regina (RUSIR)
1660 Elphinstone St., Regina SK S4T 3N1
Tel: 306-757-8405; *Fax:* 306-522-2556
rusirom@accesscomm.ca
www.rusiregina.ca
Overview: A small provincial charitable organization
Mission: To support the enhancement of national security & national defence policies by the government, & a capable Canadian Armed Forces
Member of: The Federation of Military & United Services Institutes of Canada (FMUSIC); Conference of Defence Associations
Affiliation(s): The Crow's Nest
Membership: *Fees:* $200 yearly; $70 yearly, out of town/province/country; $120 yearly, members of the Canadian Forces; *Member Profile:* Serving & retired officers from the Canadian & Commonwealth Forces, the Royal Canadian Mounted Police (RCMP), & allied nations; *Committees:* Library; Trust Fund; Administration; Military Events and Membership; Warning Order; Social
Activities: *Library:* The Royal United Services Institute of Regina Library; by appointment
Chief Officer(s):
Brad Hrycyna, President
Eddie Matthews, Managing Director

Royal United Services Institute of Vancouver Island (RUSI-VI)
Bay Street Armoury, #414, 715 Bay St., Victoria BC V8T 1R1
usiviccda@yahoo.ca
www.rusiviccda.org
Overview: A small local organization founded in 1927
Mission: To support the enhancement & maintenance of the Canadian Armed Forces, with adequate troops, training, & equipment, & of effective national defence policies by the government
Membership: 200+; *Fees:* $30 individuals; $40 families; *Member Profile:* Serving & retired officers from the Canadian & Commonwealth Forces, the Royal Canadian Mounted Police (RCMP), & allied nations
Activities: Hosting regular meetings; Presenting awards
Chief Officer(s):

E.S. Fitch, OMM, CD, President
Publications:
• RUSI: Newsletter of the Royal United Services Institute of Vancouver Island
Type: Newsletter; *Frequency:* Quarterly; *Editor:* Capt (Ret.) LE (Skip) Triplett
Profile: Information for members of the Royal United Services Institute of Vancouver Island

Royal University Hospital Foundation (RUHF)
#1626, 103 Hospital Dr., Saskatoon SK S7N 0W8
Tel: 306-655-1984
info@ruhf.org
www.ruhf.org
www.facebook.com/RoyalUniversityHospitalFoundation
twitter.com/RUHFoundation
www.youtube.com/channel/UCUu4nSywH8WtF7lQHZVgFTQ
Overview: A small local charitable organization founded in 1983
Mission: To help provide additional funds for the Royal University Hospital, a university teaching hospital
Finances: *Funding Sources:* Donations; Corporations
Staff Member(s): 6
Chief Officer(s):
Arla Gustafson, CEO

Royal Winnipeg Ballet (RWB)
380 Graham Ave., Winnipeg MB R3C 4K2
Tel: 204-956-0183; *Fax:* 204-943-1994
Toll-Free: 800-667-4792
customerservice@rwb.org
www.rwb.org
www.facebook.com/RWBallet
twitter.com/RWBallet
instagram.com/rwballet
Also Known As: Canada's Royal Winnipeg Ballet
Overview: A medium-sized local charitable organization founded in 1939
Mission: To enrich the human experience by teaching, creating & performing outstanding dance
Affiliation(s): Association of Cultural Executives; Canadian Conference of the Arts; Canadian Arts Presenting Association; Council for Business & the Arts in Canada; Dance USA; International Society for the Performing Arts
Finances: *Funding Sources:* Government, corporate & private
Staff Member(s): 178
Membership: *Committees:* Audit; Governance; Evaluation & Compensation; Nominations
Chief Officer(s):
David Reid, Chair
André Lewis, Artistic Director
Meetings/Conferences:
• 2018 Royal Winnipeg Ballet Ball, April, 2018, Winnipeg, MB
Scope: Local

RP Research Foundation - Fighting Blindness *See* The Foundation Fighting Blindness

The Rubber Association of Canada *See* Tire and Rubber Association of Canada

La rue des femmes / Herstreet
1050, rue Jeanne-Mance, Montréal QC H2Z 1L7
Tél: 514-284-9665; *Téléc:* 514-284-6570
www.laruedesfemmes.org
www.linkedin.com/company/2742443
www.facebook.com/PourLaRueDesFemmesHerstreet
twitter.com/laruedesfemmes
Aperçu: *Dimension:* petite; *Envergure:* locale; Organisme sans but lucratif
Mission: Offre des soins curatifs et préventifs aux femmes en état d'itinérance ou d'y sombrer
Finances: *Fonds:* Donations
Activités: Maison Olga; Centre Dahlia
Membre(s) du bureau directeur:
Léonie Couture, Directrice générale
lcouture@laruedesfemmes.org
Publications:
• Le Porte-Voix [un publication de La rue des femmes]
Type: Bulletin

Rug Hooking Guild of Nova Scotia (RHGNS)
c/o Gail Feetham, 52 Greendale Ct., Timberlea NS B3T 1J6
Tel: 902-576-2894
www.rhgns.com
Overview: A small provincial organization

Canadian Associations / Rugby Canada

Mission: To promote excellence & participation in the craft; to preserve its history; to promote public awareness through exhibits & publicity
Membership: *Fees:* $35; $50 outside Canada; *Committees:* Awards; Heritage; Magazine; Nominating; Publicity; School
Chief Officer(s):
Joyce LeMoine, President
lemoinejoyce@yahoo.ca

Rugby Canada
#110, 30 East Beaver Creek Rd., Richmond Hill ON L4B 1J2
Tel: 905-707-8998
info@rugbycanada.ca
www.rugbycanada.ca
www.facebook.com/RugbyCanada
twitter.com/rugbycanada
Previous Name: Canadian Rugby Union
Overview: A medium-sized national organization founded in 1974
Mission: To be the national governing body for the sport of rugby in Canada.
Membership: *Member Profile:* Official rugby teams in Canada
Activities: Player development; youth clinics
Chief Officer(s):
Tim Powers, Chair
tpowers@rugbycanada.ca
Allen Vansen, Chief Executive Officer, 905-707-8998 Ext. 225
avansen@rugbycanada.ca
Myles Spencer, Chief Operating Officer, 905-707-8998 Ext. 238
mspencer@rugbycanada.ca

Rugby Manitoba
145 Pacific Ave., Winnipeg MB R3B 2Z6
Tel: 204-925-5664
www.rugbymanitoba.com
Overview: A medium-sized provincial organization overseen by Rugby Canada
Mission: To govern rugby in Manitoba
Member of: Rugby Canada
Staff Member(s): 1
Chief Officer(s):
Brad Hirst, Executive Director
executivedirector@rugbymanitoba.com

Rugby Ontario
#201, 111 Railside Rd., Toronto ON M3A 1B2
Tel: 647-560-4790; *Fax:* 647-560-4790
info@rugbyontario.com
www.rugbyontario.com
www.facebook.com/RugbyOntario
twitter.com/rugbyontario
Overview: A medium-sized provincial organization founded in 1949 overseen by Rugby Canada
Affiliation(s): Canadian Rugby Union
Finances: *Annual Operating Budget:* $1.5 Million-$3 Million
Staff Member(s): 8
Membership: 10,827; *Member Profile:* Athletes, coaches, officials, administrators; *Committees:* Coaching; Executive
Chief Officer(s):
David Butler, Chair
chairman@rugbyontario.com
Michael Brown, Chief Executive Officer
mbrown@rugbyontario.com
Larissa Mankis, Chief Operating Officer
lmankis@rugbyontario.com

Ruiter Valley Land Trust (RVLT) / Fiducie foncière Vallée de Ruiter
PO Box 462, Mansonville QC J0E 1X0
info@valleeruiter.org
valleeruiter.org
Overview: A small local charitable organization founded in 1987
Mission: To acquire & protect forest land
Affiliation(s): Nature Conservancy of Canada
Membership: *Fees:* $25 individual; $40 family; $100 patron; $250 corporation; $450 steward; $1000 benefactor
Activities: *Speaker Service:* Yes
Chief Officer(s):
Marie-Claire Planet, President

Rumble Productions Society
1422 William St., Vancouver BC V5L 2P7
Tel: 604-662-3395; *Fax:* 604-630-7294
info@rumble.org
rumble.org
www.facebook.com/rumbleproductions
twitter.com/RumbleTheatre

Overview: A small local charitable organization founded in 1990
Mission: To research, develop & produce new & found works for the theatre & other media; to create work through a spirit of community & interdisciplinary collaboration; to initiate & produce events that foster communication, cooperation & exchange between artists of various disciplines locally, nationally & internationally
Member of: Vancouver Cultural Alliance; Vancouver Professional Theatre Alliance; Vancouver Dance Centre
Finances: *Funding Sources:* Province; Progress Lab 1422; British Columbia Arts Council; Canada Council for the Arts; City of Vancouver; Private donors
Staff Member(s): 4
Activities: *Internships:* Yes
Chief Officer(s):
Becky Low, Managing Producer

Rural Advancement Foundation International *See* ETC Group

Rural Education & Development Association *See* Alberta Community & Co-operative Association

Rural Municipal Administrators' Association of Saskatchewan (RMAA)
PO Box 130, Wilcox SK S0G 5E0
Tel: 306-732-2030; *Fax:* 306-732-4495
rmaa@sasktel.net
www.rmaa.ca
Previous Name: Rural Municipal Secretary-Treasurers' Association of Saskatchewan
Overview: A medium-sized provincial organization founded in 1955
Mission: To address the needs of rural administrators in Saskatchewan
Affiliation(s): Saskatchewan Association of Rural Municipalities
Finances: *Funding Sources:* Membership fees; Sponsorships
Membership: *Member Profile:* Practising rural municipal administrators, assistant administrators, secretary-treasurers & assistant secretary-treasurers in Saskatchewan; Associate members include non-practising rural municipal administrators & secretary-treasurers; Honorary life members; *Committees:* Forms & Computer Programs; Curling; Salary Negotiations; Local Government Administration Program; Seminars / Workshops / Guest Speakers; Board of Examiners; Disciplinary; Municipal Employees' Pension Plan; Golfing; Executive & Finance; Wine & Cheese Reception; Convention Sponsors / Door Prizes; Rural Advisory to SAMA; Professional Development; Enhanced Benefits; Resolutions; Humanitarian Services; Board of Reference; Council Mediation; Career Promotion; RMAA Home Page; Workshop; Ex-Officio to S.A.R.M.
Activities: Coordinating the certification of rural municipal administrator in Saskatchewan; Providing professional development activities; Carrying out disciplinary measures regarding professional practice
Chief Officer(s):
Kevin Ritchie, Executive Director
Tim Leurer, President
rm366@sasktel.net

Rural Municipal Secretary-Treasurers' Association of Saskatchewan *See* Rural Municipal Administrators' Association of Saskatchewan

Rural Ontario Municipal Association (ROMA)
#801, 200 University Ave., Toronto ON M5H 3C6
Tel: 416-971-9856; *Fax:* 416-971-6191
Toll-Free: 877-426-6527
www.roma.on.ca
twitter.com/share
Overview: A medium-sized provincial organization
Mission: The Rural Ontario Municipal Association (ROMA) is the rural arm of the Association of Municipalities of Ontario (AMO).
Member of: Association of Municipalities of Ontario
Finances: *Funding Sources:* Membership fees; Sales of services & products; Sponsorships
Membership: 100-499; *Member Profile:* Ontario rural municipalities; Related non-profit organizations & private corporations
Activities: Developing policy positions; Reporting on issues; Liaising with the Ontario provincial government; Informing & educating the media & the public; Marketing services to the municipal sector
Chief Officer(s):
Ron Eddy, Chair
ron.eddy@brant.ca
Meetings/Conferences:
• 2018 ROMA Annual Conference, January, 2018, Sheraton Centre Hotel, Toronto, ON
Scope: Provincial
• 2019 ROMA Annual Conference, January, 2019, Sheraton Centre Hotel, Toronto, ON
Scope: Provincial
• 2020 ROMA Annual Conference, January, 2020, Sheraton Centre Hotel, Toronto, ON
Scope: Provincial
• 2021 ROMA Annual Conference, January, 2021, Sheraton Centre Hotel, Toronto, ON
Scope: Provincial

Rushnychok Ukrainian Folk Dancing Association (RUFDA)
PO Box 85529, Stn. Main, Saskatoon SK S7L 6K6
rushnychok@gmail.com
www.rushnychokukrainiandance.com
Overview: A small local organization
Mission: To provide an opportunity to learn & develop the art of Ukrainian dance in a safe & friendly environment
Affiliation(s): AUDA Alberta Ukrainian Dance; SUDA Saskatchewan Ukrainian Dance
Finances: *Annual Operating Budget:* Less than $50,000
Staff Member(s): 10; 60 volunteer(s)
Membership: 70 student; *Fees:* $205 student

Russell & District Chamber of Commerce
PO Box 155, Russell MB R0J 1W0
Tel: 204-773-2456
chamber@mrbgov.com
www.russellbinscarth.com
Overview: A small local organization
Mission: To promote the economics of trade & commerce, & improve the quality of community life
Finances: *Annual Operating Budget:* Less than $50,000; *Funding Sources:* Grants
Staff Member(s): 1
Membership: 111; *Committees:* Asessippi Parkland Tourism; Education & Training; Russell Beef & Barley; Welcome Wagon
Chief Officer(s):
Jennifer Seib, President

Russian Orthodox Church in Canada
10812 - 108 St., Edmonton AB T5H 3A6
Tel: 780-420-9945
www.orthodox-canada.com
Overview: A medium-sized national organization
Membership: 22 parishes
Chief Officer(s):
Iov Job, Bishop of Kashira
bishjob@telus.net

Russian Orthodox Greek Catholic Church (Metropolia) *See* Orthodox Church in America Archdiocese of Canada

RVDA of Québec *Voir* Association des commerçants de véhicules récréatifs du Québec

RX-7 Club of Toronto *See* Mazda Sportscar Owners Club

Ryerson Faculty Association (RFA) / Association des professeurs de Ryerson
Kerr Hall South, #KHS-46, 40 Gould St., Toronto ON M5B 2K3
Tel: 416-979-5186
rfa@ryerson.ca
www.rfa.ryerson.ca
Overview: A small local organization founded in 1969
Mission: To act as the certified bargaining agent for Ryerson University's full-time faculty; To advance post-secondary education in Canada
Member of: Canadian Association of University Teachers; Ontario Confederation of University Faculty Associations
Membership: 550; *Member Profile:* Full-time faculty of Ontario's Ryerson University; *Committees:* Representatives' Council; Executive; Grievance; Health & Safety; Equity Issues; Negotiating; Professional Affairs; Services
Chief Officer(s):
Anver Saloojee, President
Awards:
• RFA Scholarship Award
To recognize full time students, part-time students, & Aboriginal students; *Amount:* $2,500 each
Publications:
• Ryerson Faculty Association News Link

Type: Newsletter
Profile: Previously known as the Forum & the Bulletin, the periodic publication covers the association's activities & features reports from committees

S'affirmer Ensemble *See* Affirm United

Saanich Historical Artifacts Society (SHAS)
7321 Lochside Dr., Saanichton BC V8M 1W4
Tel: 250-652-5522
shas@shas.ca
www.shas.ca
Overview: A small local charitable organization founded in 1963
Mission: To collect, restore, display & demonstrate artifacts
Member of: Saanich Peninsula Chamber of Commerce; Victoria Tourist Bureau
Membership: *Fees:* $20 single; $30 family
Activities: Summer Fair; Fall Threshing; *Library:* Michell Building Library; Not open to public
Chief Officer(s):
Hopkins Dave, President

Saanich Native Heritage Society
PO Box 28, 7449 West Saanich Rd., Brentwood Bay BC V8M 1R3
Tel: 250-652-5980; *Fax:* 250-652-5957
saanichnativeheritage@hotmail.com
Overview: A small local organization
Chief Officer(s):
Adelynne Claxton, Contact
Publications:
• Sencoten: Legends & Stories
Type: Booklet; *Number of Pages:* 126; *ISBN:* 1-4251-0456-8
Profile: For use in the LAU, WELNEW Tribal School primary & intermediate levels

Saanich Peninsula Chamber of Commerce (SPCOC)
10382 Pat Bay Hwy., North Saanich BC V8L 5S8
Tel: 250-656-3616; *Fax:* 250-656-7111
info@peninsulachamber.ca
www.peninsulachamber.ca
www.linkedin.com/company/saanich-peninsula-chamber-of-commerce
www.facebook.com/Peninsula.Chamber
twitter.com/penchamber
Also Known As: Peninsula Chamber
Previous Name: Sidney & North Saanich Board of Trade
Overview: A small local organization founded in 1947
Mission: To represent the interests of businesses; To create an environment that allows for business sustainability
Member of: BC Chamber of Commerce
Finances: *Funding Sources:* Membership dues
Staff Member(s): 3
Membership: 300+; *Fees:* Schedule available
Activities: *Speaker Service:* Yes; *Rents Mailing List:* Yes; *Library:* Business Information Centre; Open to public
Chief Officer(s):
Craig Norris, President
Denny Warner, Executive Director
execdir@peninsulachamber.ca

Sackville Rivers Association (SRA)
PO Box 45071, Sackville NS B4E 2Z6
Tel: 902-865-9238; *Fax:* 902-864-3564
sackvillerivers@ns.sympatico.ca
www.sackvillerivers.ns.ca
Overview: A medium-sized local organization founded in 1988
Mission: To promote the preservation, restoration and enhancement of the Sackville River Watershed.
Membership: 200+; *Fees:* $10; $5 student
Chief Officer(s):
Damon Conrad, Contact

SADC région d'Asbestos *Voir* Réseau des SADC et CAE

Safe Schools Manitoba
c/o Mary T. Hall, Manitoba School Boards Association, 191 Provencher Blvd., Winnipeg MB R2H 0G4
Tel: 204-233-1595; *Fax:* 204-231-1356
www.safeschoolsmanitoba.ca
Overview: A medium-sized provincial organization
Mission: Safe Schools Manitoba is a partnership initiative of organizations committed to working together to enhance the safety of schools and communities in Manitoba
Finances: *Funding Sources:* Manitoba Education; Children and Youth Opportunities
Staff Member(s): 5
Chief Officer(s):
Mary T. Hall, Provincial Director
mhall@safeschoolsmanitoba.ca

Safe Workplace Promotion Services Ontario *See* Workplace Safety & Prevention Services

Safety Services Manitoba (SSM)
#3, 1680 Notre Dame Ave., Winnipeg MB R3H 1H6
Tel: 204-949-1085; *Fax:* 204-949-2897
Toll-Free: 800-661-3321
registrar@safetyservicesmanitoba.ca
www.safetyservicesmanitoba.ca
ca.linkedin.com/in/gotosafetyservicesmanitoba
www.facebook.com/SafetyServicesManitoba
twitter.com/SafetyServMB
Previous Name: Manitoba Safety Council
Overview: A medium-sized provincial licensing charitable organization founded in 1920
Mission: To prevent accidental injury or occupational illness in Manitoba by providing effective safety & health programs.
Finances: *Funding Sources:* Membership & course fees; fundraising
Staff Member(s): 10
Membership: *Fees:* $500 partner; $750 leader; *Committees:* Executive; Motorcycle; Seat Belt; Operation Lifesaver; Road Safety Conference; OHS Conference
Activities: *Awareness Events:* Conference & AGM; Annual Golf Classic; Operation Red Nose
Chief Officer(s):
Judy Murphy, President & CEO
Meetings/Conferences:
• Safety Services Manitoba Occupational Health & Safety Conference 2018, January, 2018, Victoria Inn Hotel & Convention Centre, Winnipeg, MB
Scope: Provincial

Safety Services New Brunswick (SSNB) / Services de Sécurité Nouveau-Brunswick
#204, 440 Wilsey Rd., Fredericton NB E3B 7G5
Tel: 506-458-8034; *Fax:* 506-444-0177
Toll-Free: 877-762-7233
info@safetyservicesnb.ca
www.safetyservicesnb.ca
www.facebook.com/motorcyclecourse
twitter.com/safetynb
Previous Name: New Brunswick Safety Council Inc.
Overview: A small provincial charitable organization founded in 1967
Mission: To promote traffic, occupational & public safety issues & practices through safety training courses & programs, educational material, public information, safety campaigns & conferences.
Member of: National Safety Council
Affiliation(s): Canada Safety Council
Finances: *Annual Operating Budget:* $250,000-$500,000; *Funding Sources:* Safety training & workshop fees; membership fees; donations; grants
Staff Member(s): 8; 50 volunteer(s)
Membership: 200; *Fees:* Schedule available; *Committees:* Financial; Operation Lifesaver
Activities: *Speaker Service:* Yes
Chief Officer(s):
Bill Walker, President & CEO, 506-444-0171
bill@ssnb.ca
Jim Arsenault, Director of OSH & Traffic Training, 506-444-0178
jim@ssnb.ca
Meetings/Conferences:
• Safety Services New Brunswick Health & Safety Conference 2018, 2018, NB
Scope: Provincial

Safety Services Newfoundland & Labrador
1076 Topsail Rd., Mount Pearl NL A1N 5E7
Tel: 709-754-0210; *Fax:* 709-754-0010
info@safetyservicesnl.ca
safetyservicesnl.ca
www.facebook.com/303428916390762
twitter.com/SafetyNL
Previous Name: Newfoundland & Labrador Safety Council
Overview: A medium-sized provincial organization
Mission: Safety Services Newfoundland Labrador is dedicated to the prevention of injuries and fatalities; represents all the major sectors of the province's industry, business, government departments, volunteer organizations and many individuals who have a personal interest in safety, both on and off the job.
Affiliation(s): Canada Safety Council

Safety Services Nova Scotia (SSNS)
#1, 201 Brownlow Ave., Dartmouth NS B3B 1W2
Tel: 902-454-9621; *Fax:* 902-454-6027
Toll-Free: 866-511-2211
www.safetyservicesns.com
www.facebook.com/SafetyNS
twitter.com/SafetyNS
Previous Name: Nova Scotia Safety Council; The Nova Scotia Highway Safety Council
Overview: A small provincial organization founded in 1958
Mission: To develop & provide quality safety & health services, education & training programs to improve the quality of life of Nova Scotians.
Affiliation(s): Canada Safety Council
Finances: *Funding Sources:* Membership; Courses; Provincial government
Staff Member(s): 9
Membership: *Fees:* $270 associate; $525 corporate; *Member Profile:* Members include Nova Scotian businesses, government departments, charitable agencies, families, & hospital & police services.
Activities: Informing members of injury trends, new legislation, or anything that may affect the health & safety of members, their coworkers, family, & friends; *Library*
Chief Officer(s):
Jackie Norman, Executive Director, 902-454-9621 Ext. 223
norman@safetyservicesns.ca
Publications:
• Safety Lines
Type: Newsletter; *Frequency:* Quarterly

Sagitawa Friendship Centre / Where the Rivers Meet
PO Box 5083, 10108 - 100 Ave., Peace River AB T8S 1R7
Tel: 780-624-2443; *Fax:* 780-624-2728
tracy-sagitawa@telus.net
anfca.com/friendship-centres/peace-river
Overview: A small local organization founded in 1964 overseen by Alberta Native Friendship Centres Association
Mission: To encourage respect & acceptance of all people; To enhance the quality of life of Aboriginal people in the Peace River area
Member of: Alberta Native Friendship Centres Association
Activities: Increasing awareness & understanding of Aboriginal people in the local community; Partnering with other community agencies, & providing community referrals; Providing culturally based programs, as guided by elders, to assist indigenous people to meet their full potential; Offering social development programming; Providing employment & health related services; Conducting language & literacy classes; Revitalizing Aboriginal culture
Chief Officer(s):
Tracy Zweifel, Executive Director

The Saidye Bronfman Centre for the Arts *See* Segal Centre for the Performing Arts at the Saidye

Sail Canada / Voile Canada
Portsmouth Olympic Harbour, 53 Yonge St., Kingston ON K7M 6G4
Tel: 613-545-3044; *Fax:* 613-545-3045
Toll-Free: 877-416-4720
sailcanada@sailing.ca
www.sailing.ca
www.facebook.com/SailCanada
twitter.com/SailCanada
Previous Name: Canadian Yachting Association
Overview: A medium-sized national charitable organization founded in 1931
Mission: To promote the sport of sailing in Canada
Affiliation(s): International Sailing Federation; International Sailing Schools Association
Finances: *Annual Operating Budget:* $1.5 Million-$3 Million
Staff Member(s): 12
Membership: 10 provincial associations; 255 clubs; 175 sailing schools; 30 class associations; 80,000 active members; over 1 million Canadian sailors; *Member Profile:* Members of member yacht club or persons with interest in sailing; *Committees:* Athlete Development; Audit; Finance; Governance; High Performance; Nominating; Offshore; Provincial; Racing Appeals; Racing Rules; Training & Certification
Activities: *Library:*
Chief Officer(s):
Todd Irving, President
president@sailing.ca
Ken Dool, Director, High Performance
ken@sailing.ca

Genevieve Manning, Office Manager
gen@sailing.ca

Sail Manitoba
#409, 145 Pacific Ave., Winnipeg MB R3B 2Z6
Tel: 204-925-5650
sailing@sportmanitoba.ca
sailmanitoba.com
www.facebook.com/200107080070072
twitter.com/SailManitoba
Previous Name: Manitoba Sailing Association Inc.
Overview: A small provincial organization founded in 1965 overseen by Sail Canada
Mission: To be the sport's provincial regulator
Member of: Sail Canada
Staff Member(s): 1
Membership: 1,000; *Committees:* Finance; Operations; Recreation; Training; Racing; Team
Chief Officer(s):
Max Desmarais, President

Sail Nova Scotia
5516 Spring Garden Rd., 4th Fl., Halifax NS B3J 1G6
Tel: 902-425-5450
office@sailnovascotia.ca
www.sailnovascotia.ca
www.facebook.com/sailnovascotia
Previous Name: Nova Scotia Yachting Association
Overview: A small provincial organization overseen by Sail Canada
Mission: To regulate the sport of sailing in Nova Scotia
Member of: Sail Canada; Sport Nova Scotia
Affiliation(s): Canadian Sport Centre
Chief Officer(s):
Frank Denis, Executive Director & Media Contact
Awards:
• Sailor of the Year
• Hal Davies Offshore Sailor of the Year
• Male Sailor of the Year
• Female Sailor of the Year
• Youth Sailor of the Year
• Regatta of the Year
• Official of the Year
• Volunteer of the Year
• Presidents' Award
Meetings/Conferences:
• Sail Nova Scotia Annual General Meeting 2018, February, 2018, Halifax, NS
Scope: Provincial
Publications:
• Sail Nova Scotia Newsletter
Type: Newsletter

SailNL
PO Box 23102, Stn. Churchill Sq., St. John's NL A1B 4J9
sailing.nl@gmail.com
www.sailnl.ca
www.facebook.com/sailnl.ca
Also Known As: Newfoundland & Labrador Sailing Association
Overview: A small provincial organization founded in 1966 overseen by Sail Canada
Mission: To regulate the sport of sailing in Newfoundland & Labrador
Member of: Sail Canada; Sport NL
Chief Officer(s):
Ryan Kelly, President
ryan.kelly033@gmail.com

Saint Elizabeth Health Care (SEHC) / Les soins de santé Sainte-Elizabeth
#300, 90 Allstate Pkwy., Markham ON L3R 6H3
Tel: 905-940-9655; *Fax:* 905-940-9934
Toll-Free: 800-463-1763; *TTY:* 800-855-0511
communications@saintelizabeth.com
www.saintelizabeth.com
www.linkedin.com/company/saint-elizabeth-health-care
www.facebook.com/SaintElizabethSEHC
twitter.com/stelizabethSEHC
www.youtube.com/user/SaintElizabethSEHC
Previous Name: Saint Elizabeth Visiting Nurses' Association of Ontario
Overview: A medium-sized provincial charitable organization founded in 1908
Mission: To serve the physical, emotional, & spiritual needs of *people in their homes & communities*
Member of: Nursing Best Practice Research Unit, through the RNAO & the University of Ottawa
Affiliation(s): Canadian Council on Health Services Accreditation
Finances: *Funding Sources:* Donations; Grants
Staff Member(s): 7000
Activities: Providing nursing, supportive care, rehabilitation, & specialty services, such as long-term care, mental health & addictions, & palliative care; Offering customized consulting services; Investing in research, education, & best practices; Presenting a driver assessment & training program, including DriveABLE & Driver Rehabilitation Services
Chief Officer(s):
Noreen Taylor, Chair
Shirlee Sharkey, President & CEO
Heather McClure, Treasurer
Don McCutchan, Secretary
Publications:
• Saint Elizabeth Health Care e-Newsletter
Type: Newsletter
• Saint Elizabeth Health Care Foundation Newsletter
Type: Newsletter
• SEHC [Saint Elizabeth Health Care] Research Activity Report
Type: Report
Profile: Highlights of research achievements

   Barrie - North Simcoe Muskoka Service Delivery Centre
   #104, 85 Ferris Lane, Barrie ON L4M 6B9
   Fax: 877-619-4033
   Toll-Free: 888-737-5055

   Cornwall - Eastern Counties Service Delivery Centre
   #5, 1916 Pitt St., Cornwall ON K6H 5H3
   Tel: 613-936-8668; *Fax:* 866-619-4059

   Hamilton - Hamilton, Niagara, Haldimand & Brant Service Delivery Centre
   1525 Stone Church Rd. East, Hamilton ON L8W 3P8
   Fax: 866-619-4062
   Toll-Free: 888-275-2299

   Kingston - South East Service Delivery Centre
   #410, 1471 John Counter Blvd., Kingston ON K7M 8S8
   Tel: 613-530-3400; *Fax:* 866-619-4063

   London - South West Service Delivery Centre
   #15, 1100 Dearness Dr., London ON N6E 1N9
   Tel: 519-668-2997; *Fax:* 866-619-4065

   Markham - Central Service Delivery Centre
   #201, 90 Allstate Pkwy., Markham ON L3R GH3
   Tel: 905-944-1743; *Fax:* 866-619-4074

   Mississauga - Peel Service Delivery Centre
   #5, 6745 Century Ave., Mississauga ON L5N 1V9
   Tel: 905-826-0854; *Fax:* 905-826-0854

   Ottawa - Champlain Service Delivery Centre
   #225, 30 Colonnade Rd., Ottawa ON K2E 7J6
   Tel: 613-738-9661; *Fax:* 877-619-4038

   Seaforth - Huron Service Delivery Centre
   87 Main St. South, Seaforth ON N0K 1W0
   Fax: 519-600-0105
   Toll-Free: 888-823-1626

   Thunder Bay - North West Service Delivery Centre
   #103, 920 Tungsten St., Thunder Bay ON P7B 5Z6
   Tel: 807-344-2002; *Fax:* 807-344-1999

   Toronto - Toronto Central Service Delivery Centre
   #600, 2 Lansing Sq., Toronto ON M2J 4P8
   Tel: 416-498-8600; *Fax:* 416-498-0213

   Whitby - Central East Service Delivery Centre
   1549 Victoria St. East, Whitby ON L1N 8R1
   Fax: 416-398-3206
   Toll-Free: 877-397-1035

   Windsor - Erie St. Clair Service Delivery Centre
   2473 Ouellette Ave., Windsor ON N8X 1L5
   Tel: 519-972-3895; *Fax:* 866-619-4073

   Woodstock - Oxford County Service Delivery Centre
   #5, 695 Canterbury Ave., Woodstock ON N4S 8W7
   Tel: 519-539-9807; *Fax:* 866-619-4070

Saint Elizabeth Visiting Nurses' Association of Ontario *See* Saint Elizabeth Health Care

Saint Francis Xavier Association of University Teachers / Association des professeurs de l'Université Saint-François-Xavier
St. Francis Xavier University, Old Municipal Bldg., PO Box 5000, #219, 42 West St., Antigonish NS B2G 2W5
Tel: 902-867-3368; *Fax:* 902-867-3747
stfxaut@stfx.ca
stfxaut.ca
Also Known As: St. FXAUT
Overview: A small local organization
Member of: Canadian Association of University Teachers
Finances: *Annual Operating Budget:* $100,000-$250,000
Membership: 300 individual
Chief Officer(s):
Peter McInnis, President

Saint John & District Labour Council (SJDLC)
2018 Lancaster Ave., Saint John NB E2M 2K9
Tel: 506-635-1541
Overview: A small local organization overseen by New Brunswick Federation of Labour
Activities: *Awareness Events:* Labour Day Parade, Sept.
Chief Officer(s):
Joseph Theriault, President, 506-721-0867

Saint John Alzheimer Society
152 Westmorland Rd., Saint John NB E2J 2E7
Tel: 506-634-8722; *Fax:* 506-648-9404
saintjohn@alzheimernb.ca
www.alzheimernb.ca
Overview: A small local charitable organization founded in 1983
Mission: To alleviate the personal & social consequences of Alzheimer disease & related dementia; to promote the search for a cause & cure
Member of: Alzheimer Society of New Brunswick
Activities: Caregiver Support Group; Early Stage Support Group; *Speaker Service:* Yes; *Library:* Resource Centre; Open to public

Saint John Board of Trade *See* Saint John Region Chamber of Commerce

Saint John Coin Club (SJCC)
c/o 37 Valley View Dr., Grand Bay NB E5X 1X1
www.sjcoinclub.com
Overview: A small local organization founded in 1959
Membership: 15
Chief Officer(s):
S. McCullough, Contact

Saint John Community Food Basket
215 Charlotte St., Saint John NB E2L 2K1
Tel: 506-652-2707; *Fax:* 506-658-9441
www.saintjohnfoodbasket.org
twitter.com/SJCFB
Overview: A small local charitable organization founded in 1984
Mission: The food bank serves the needs of the people of the inner city & South End of St. John.
Member of: New Brunswick Association of Food Banks; Food Banks Canada
Affiliation(s): Hestia House; Coverdale Center; Inner City Youth Ministry
Finances: *Funding Sources:* Donations; Churches
Chief Officer(s):
Carolyn Danells, Chair
cmdanells@rogers.com

Saint John Construction Association *See* Construction Association of New Brunswick

Saint John Deaf & Hard of Hearing Services, Inc (SJDHHS)
324 Duke St. West, Saint John NB E2M 1V2
Tel: 506-633-0599; *Fax:* 506-652-3382; *TTY:* 506-634-8037
sjdhhs@nb.sympatico.ca
www.sjdhhs.com
www.facebook.com/sj.dhhs
Overview: A small local charitable organization founded in 1979
Mission: To empower deaf, hard of hearing & late deafened people to live independent, productive lives with the same full access to services & opportunites as the hearing population
Member of: United Way
Finances: *Funding Sources:* Donations; United Way
Staff Member(s): 16
Membership: *Member Profile:* Deaf & hard of hearing
Activities: Mentorship Program; HARP, recycling program for hearing aids; interpreter services; speech reading courses; community education; deaf culture courses; Community Academic Services Program; life skills program; employability skills program; *Library*
Chief Officer(s):
Lynn LeBlanc, Executive Director

Saint John East Food Bank Inc.
105 Wilton St., Saint John NB E2J 1H6
Tel: 506-633-8298
Overview: A small local organization

Mission: To serve the community through our local churches by supplying food to the needy.
Chief Officer(s):
Valerie McNeil, President

Saint John Gallery Association
Saint John Arts Centre, 20 Peel Plaza, Saint John NB E2L 3G6
Tel: 506-633-4870
sjac@sjartscentre.ca
www.sjartscentre.ca
www.facebook.com/114375408575288
twitter.com/SJArtsCentre
Overview: A small local organization
Mission: To promote fine art in uptown Saint John
Staff Member(s): 5
Membership: 14; *Member Profile:* Galleries located in Saint John that sell & promote fine art & have scheduled exhibitions
Chief Officer(s):
Andrew Kierstead, Executive Director
director@sjartscentre.ca

Saint John Jeux Canada Games Foundation Inc. / La Fondation Jeux Canada Games Saint John, Inc.
206 King St. West, Saint John NB E2M 1S6
Tel: 506-634-1985
cdagamesapps@acmca.com
www.sjcanadagamesfoundation.ca
Overview: A small national charitable organization founded in 1986
Mission: To promote amateur athletics not only in New Brunswick, but across Canada, by providing funding for athletes, amateur athletic organizations, governing bodies, universities & others involved in the training & development of amateur athletes.
Chief Officer(s):
Jeff White, Chair

Saint John Jewish Historical Society
91 Leinster St., Saint John NB E2L 1J2
Tel: 506-633-1833; *Fax:* 506-642-9926
sjjhm@nbnet.nb.ca
personal.nbnet.nb.ca/sjjhm/
Overview: A small local charitable organization founded in 1986
Mission: To preserve the heritage of the Saint John Jewish community
Affiliation(s): Association for Canadian Jewish Studies; New Brunswick Historical Society; Association Museums New Brunswick; Canadian Heritage Information Network; Council of New Brunswick Archives
Finances: *Funding Sources:* Membership dues; government grant; private individuals; donations
Membership: *Member Profile:* Former Saint John residents; other interested individuals/groups
Activities: Jewish education outreach kits - Sabbath; Rosh Hashanah; Yom Kippur; Chanukah; Purim; Passover; Succot & Lifecycles (from the Cradle to the Grave); Chanukah Menoral Lighting; annual art exhibition; *Library:* Dr. Moses I. Polowin Memorial Library; Open to public by appointment

Saint John Law Society
Library, PO Box 5001, 110 Charlotte St., Saint John NB E2L 4Y9
Tel: 506-658-2542; *Fax:* 506-634-7556
sjlaw@nbnet.nb.ca
Overview: A small local organization
Activities: *Library:*

Saint John Naturalists' Club
PO Box 2071, Saint John NB E2L 3T5
saintjohnnaturalistsclub.org
Also Known As: sjnc
Overview: A small local organization founded in 1962
Affiliation(s): NatureNB (The New Brunswick Federation of Naturalists)
Membership: *Fees:* $20 individuals; $25 families; *Member Profile:* Individuals interested in the conservation, study, & enjoyment of nature in New Brunswick; *Committees:* Program; Social; Greenlaw Mountain Hawk Watch (GMHW); Point Lepreau Bird Observatory (PLBO)
Activities: Hosting monthly meeting at the New Brunswick Museum; Planning field trips; Administering the Point Lepreau Bird Observatory project
Chief Officer(s):
Charles Graves, President
president_at_saintjohnnaturalistsclub.org
Jan Riddell, Vice-President
Jeanne Finn-Allen, Secretary
Don MacPhail, Treasurer

Publications:
• Saint John Naturalists' Club Bulletin
Type: Newsletter
Profile: Information assembled by a different editor for each issue

Saint John Real Estate Board Inc.
#100, 55 Drury Cove Rd., Saint John NB E2K 2Z8
Tel: 506-634-8772; *Fax:* 506-634-8775
www.sjrealestateboard.ca
www.facebook.com/SaintJohnRealEstateBoard
twitter.com/SJ_REALTORS
Overview: A medium-sized local organization founded in 1962 overseen by New Brunswick Real Estate Association
Mission: To provide services to & set standards for members; To preserve & promote the MLS marketing system to benefit buyers & sellers of real estate property
Member of: The Canadian Real Estate Association
Finances: *Funding Sources:* Membership fees
Membership: 300; *Member Profile:* Realtors
Activities: *Library:* Not open to public
Chief Officer(s):
Sheila Henry, President

Saint John Region Chamber of Commerce
40 King St., Saint John NB E2L 1G3
Tel: 506-634-8111; *Fax:* 506-632-2008
info@TheChamberSJ.com
www.sjboardoftrade.com
twitter.com/TheChamberSJ
www.youtube.com/SJBoardofTrade1
Previous Name: Saint John Board of Trade
Overview: A medium-sized local organization
Mission: To serve as the voice of the businesses of the Saint John region
Finances: *Annual Operating Budget:* $500,000-$1.5 Million
Membership: 1,000+ businesses; *Fees:* Based on number of employees; *Committees:* Branding; Communications; Finance; Golf; Governance
Activities: Providing programs, services & networking opportunities for members
Chief Officer(s):
David Duplisea, CEO
dduplisea@TheChamberSJ.com

Saint John SPCA Animal Rescue
295 Bayside Dr., Saint John NB E2J 1B1
Tel: 506-642-0920; *Fax:* 506-634-6101
info@spcaanimalrescue.com
www.spcaanimalrescue.com
www.facebook.com/Saint.John.SPCA.Animal.Rescue
twitter.com/SPCAAR
Overview: A small local charitable organization founded in 1913
Mission: To provide rescue, care, & temporary shelter to stray & unwanted animals in the Saint John area
Finances: *Funding Sources:* Donations; Fundraising; Sponsorships; Membership fees; Services
2 volunteer(s)
Activities: Finding homes for animals; Educating residents of Saint John about humane treatment of animals, including information sessions at local schools; Providing humane euthanasia at owners' request; Conducting a seniors' program; Offering public tours; *Awareness Events:* Pets in the Park, including the Annual Dog Jog, July; "No Fleas" Flea Market; Be Kind To Animals Week, May
Chief Officer(s):
Melody McElman, President
Brad Melanson, Treasurer
Publications:
• ARL [Animal Rescue League] Shelter Speak
Type: Newsletter; *Frequency:* 3-4 pa; *Price:* Free with League membership
Profile: Fundraising & donation updates & League information

Saint John Symphony *See* Symphony New Brunswick

Saint John Visitor & Convention Bureau *See* Tourism Saint John

Saint Leonard's Society of Nova Scotia *See* St. Leonard's Society of Canada

Saint Mary's University Faculty Union (SMUFU) / Syndicat des professeurs de l'Université Saint Mary
Saint Mary's University, McNally Main 221, 923 Robie St., Halifax NS B3H 3C3

Tel: 902-496-8190; *Fax:* 902-496-8102
unionoffice@smufu.org
www.smufu.org
Overview: A small local organization founded in 1974
Mission: To promote & maintain harmonious relations between the university administration & its faculty & professional librarians
Member of: Canadian Association of University Teachers
Affiliation(s): Canadian Labour Congress; NS Federation of Labour
Finances: *Annual Operating Budget:* $50,000-$100,000
Staff Member(s): 1
Membership: 269 individuals; *Fees:* Schedule available; *Member Profile:* Faculty, full-time, teaching at least two courses & professional librarians
Chief Officer(s):
Marc Lamoureux, President
marc.lamoureux@smu.ca
Ron Russell, Vice-President
ron.russell@smu.ca

St. Albert & District Chamber of Commerce
71 St. Albert Trail, St. Albert AB T8N 6L5
Tel: 780-458-2833; *Fax:* 780-458-6515
chamber@stalbertchamber.com
www.stalbertchamber.com
www.facebook.com/stalbertchamber
twitter.com/StAlbertchamber
Previous Name: St Albert Chamber of Commerce
Overview: A small local organization founded in 1984
Mission: To be the voice of business in St. Albert
Member of: Alberta Chamber of Commerce; Canadian Chamber of Commerce
Finances: *Funding Sources:* Membership dues; farmers' market; trade show
Staff Member(s): 9
Membership: 900; *Fees:* Schedule available; *Committees:* Member Services; Pillar; Perron District Business; Chamber Building; Farmers' Market; Lifestyle Expo and Sale; Small Business Week; Snowflake Festiva; Business in Blue Jeans; Chamber Gala; Golf Tournament
Chief Officer(s):
Barry Bailey, Chair
Lynda Moffat, President & CEO
lynda@stalbertchamber.com

St Albert Chamber of Commerce *See* St. Albert & District Chamber of Commerce

St. Albert Family Resource Centre
#10A, 215 Carnegie Dr., St. Albert AB T8N 5B1
Tel: 780-459-7377; *Fax:* 780-459-7399
recpt@stalbertfrc.ca
www.stalbertfrc.ca
www.facebook.com/St.AlbertFRC
twitter.com/StAlbertFRC
www.instagram.com/stalbertfrc
Also Known As: St. Albert FRC
Previous Name: St. Albert Parents' Place
Overview: A small local organization founded in 1982
Mission: To provide informational resources, support & educational services to families in St. Albert, Alberta, & its surrounding communities; To advocate for policies & systems that support families' abilities to raise healthy children
Finances: *Funding Sources:* Government; Donations; Fundraising; Membership fees; Edmonton & Area Child & Family Services Authority; United Way Alberta Capital Region
Staff Member(s): 12
Activities: Offering educational courses, workshops, & support services through the Family Life Education & Family Support Programs; *Library*
Chief Officer(s):
Heather McKinnon, Operations Manager
opsmgr@stalbertfrc.ca
Publications:
• Parenting Resource Guide [a publication of the St. Albert Family Resource Centre]
Profile: Articles & advice for parents of children from birth to preschool

St. Albert Firefighters - Union Local 2130
PO Box 127, St Albert AB T8N 1N2
Tel: 780-458-0588
info@syncopatemedia.com
www.stalbertfirefighters.com
twitter.com/saffu2130
Overview: A small local organization

Membership: 100+
Chief Officer(s):
Warren Gresik, President
Tim Stewart, Vice President

St. Albert Fish & Game Association
St. Albert Community Hall, PO Box 158, 17 Perron St., St Albert AB T8N 1N3
Tel: 780-458-2015
Other Communication: Alternate Phone: 780-459-9581
phil123@telus.net
Overview: A small local organization
Mission: To encourage the wise use of the environment & wild life resources in the St. Albert area
Member of: Alberta Fish & Game Association

St. Albert Historical Society
PO Box 77012, Stn. Main, St Albert AB T8N 6C1
Tel: 780-459-5119
stalberthistorcalsociety.wordpress.com
www.facebook.com/stahs
Overview: A small local charitable organization founded in 1971
Mission: To provide public awareness of the history of St. Albert & district
75 volunteer(s)
Membership: 100+; *Fees:* $15 family; $10 individual; $5 senior/youth
Chief Officer(s):
Raymond Pinco, Chair
chair@StAlbertHistoricalSociety.ca

St. Albert Parents' Place *See* St. Albert Family Resource Centre

St. Albert Soccer Association (SASA)
61 Riel Dr., St. Albert AB T8N 3Z3
Tel: 780-458-8973; *Fax:* 780-458-8994
www.stalbertsoccer.com
Overview: A small local organization overseen by Alberta Soccer Association
Member of: Alberta Soccer Association
Staff Member(s): 5
Chief Officer(s):
Chris Spaidal, Executive Director, 780-458-8973 Ext. 127
chris@stalbertsoccer.com

St. Albert Stop Abuse Families Society *See* Stop Abuse in Families Society

St. Andrew's Charitable Foundation *See* St. Andrew's Society of Toronto

St. Andrew's Society of Montréal (SASM)
1195B, rue Sherbrooke ouest, Montréal QC H3A 1H9
Tel: 514-842-2030; *Fax:* 514-842-9848
info@standrews.qc.ca
standrews.qc.ca
www.facebook.com/214046318618928
Overview: A small local organization founded in 1835
Mission: To assist those less fortunate of Scottish birth or descent; to provide youth of Scottish ancestry in Québec with opportunities to advance their education through grants, scholarships & loans; to maintain & preserve Scottish traditions in the community by promoting historical, cultural, patriotic, social & sporting activities
Membership: *Fees:* $40 regular; $500 lifetime; *Committees:* Welfare; Scottish Culture; St. Andrew's Ball; Communications; Activities
Activities: *Library:*
Chief Officer(s):
G. Scot Diamond, President

St. Andrew's Society of Toronto
PO Box 94024, 3409 Yonge St., Toronto ON M4N 3R1
www.standrews-society.ca
www.linkedin.com/groups/4789060
www.facebook.com/StAndrewsSocietyOfToronto
Previous Name: St. Andrew's Charitable Foundation
Overview: A small local charitable organization
Mission: To assist immigrant Scots in Canada; To address aspects of Scottish heritage; To hold functions for the community
Affiliation(s): St. Andrew's Society of Toronto
Finances: *Annual Operating Budget:* Less than $50,000
40 volunteer(s)
Membership: 350
Activities: *Awareness Events:* Society Spring Dinner, May; Society Church Parade, November; St Andrew's Charity Ball, November

St. Andrews Chamber of Commerce
252 Water St., #C, St Andrews NB E5B 1B5
Tel: 506-529-3555
www.standrewsbythesea.ca
www.facebook.com/standrewsbythesea
Overview: A small local organization founded in 1968
Mission: To promote & improve trade & commerce & the economic, civic & social welfare of the district
Member of: Canadian Chamber of Commerce
Finances: *Annual Operating Budget:* $50,000-$100,000
Staff Member(s): 1
Membership: 120; *Fees:* $280
Chief Officer(s):
Jeff Holmes, President

St Anthony & Area Chamber of Commerce
PO Box 650, St Anthony NL A0K 4S0
Tel: 709-454-6667
stanthonyandareachamber@yahoo.ca
www.town.stanthony.nf.ca/chamber.php
Overview: A small local organization founded in 1978
Mission: To promote & improve trade & commerce & the economic, civic & social welfare of the district
Member of: Atlantic Provinces Chambers of Commerce
Finances: *Annual Operating Budget:* Less than $50,000
Staff Member(s): 1
Membership: 70; *Fees:* $100/year
Activities: Providing educational programs; Organizing & promoting events; Offering information & referrals
Chief Officer(s):
Agnes Patey, Coordinator, 709-454-3465

St Catharines & District Labour Council
124 Bunting Rd., St Catharines ON L2P 3G5
labourcouncil@gmail.com
www.labourcouncil.blogspot.com
Overview: A small local organization overseen by Ontario Federation of Labour

St. Catharines and District Builders Exchange *See* Council of Ontario Construction Associations

St Catharines Association for Community Living
79 Welland Ave., St Catharines ON L2R 2M8
Tel: 905-688-5222; *Fax:* 905-688-9926
administration@clstcatharines.ca
www.clstcatharines.ca
www.facebook.com/clstcatharines
Overview: A medium-sized local charitable organization
Mission: To help people with developmental disabilities live in a state of dignity & have the opportunity to participate effectively in society
Member of: Community Living Ontario
Finances: *Funding Sources:* Ministry of Community & Social Services, Ministry of Housing, United Way
Membership: *Fees:* Donation
Activities: *Library:* Resource Centre; Open to public by appointment
Chief Officer(s):
Al Moreland, Chief Executive Officer

St. Catharines Coin Club
PO Box 511, Thorold ON L2V 4W1
Overview: A small local organization

St. Catharines Indian Centre *See* Niagara Regional Native Centre

St Catharines Stamp Club
c/o David Hillier, 6 Northridge Ave., St Catharines ON L2T 2G5
Tel: 905-641-2318
www.stcatharinesstampclub.ca
Overview: A small local organization
Membership: *Fees:* $15 youth & seniors; $20 adults & families; *Member Profile:* Individuals interested in stamp collecting
Activities: Conducting meetings at Holy Cross School; *Library:* St Catharines Stamp Club Library
Chief Officer(s):
David Hillier, President
Jim Glen, Treasurer

St. Catharines Youth Orchestra *See* Niagara Youth Orchestra Association

St Catharines-Thorold Chamber of Commerce; St Catharines Chamber of Commerce *See* Greater Niagara Chamber of Commerce

St. Christopher House
588 Queen St. West, Toronto ON M6J 1E3
Tel: 416-504-3535; *Fax:* 416-504-3047
info@stchrishouse.org
www.stchrishouse.org
Overview: A small local charitable organization founded in 1912 overseen by Ontario Council of Agencies Serving Immigrants
Mission: To enable less advantaged individuals, families & groups in the community to gain greater control over their lives & within their community
Member of: United Way of Greater Toronto
Affiliation(s): Toronto Neighbourhood Centres; Canadian Association of Neighbourhood Services
Membership: *Fees:* Schedule available; *Member Profile:* Donors; volunteers; staff; program participants
Activities: *Speaker Service:* Yes

St. Christopher House Adult Literacy Program *See* West Neighbourhood House

St. Elias Chamber of Commerce
PO Box 5419, Haines Junction YT Y0B 1L0
Tel: 867-634-2916
kluaneridin@yknet.ca
Previous Name: Haines Junction Chamber of Commerce
Overview: A small local organization
Chief Officer(s):
Paula Pawlovich, President

The St. George's Society of Toronto
#306, 50 Baldwin St., Toronto ON M5T 1L4
Tel: 416-597-0220
admin@stgeorgesto.com
stgeorgesto.com
www.linkedin.com/company/3235027
www.facebook.com/89559883760
Overview: A medium-sized local organization founded in 1834
Mission: To provide a focal point for people of English sympathies; to hold up English institutions & traditions; to host functions, the financial proceeds of which fund a range of educational & benevolent traditions
Finances: *Funding Sources:* Charitable trust; Membership fees; Donations
Membership: *Fees:* $5 student; $25 under 30 & family member; $85 senior; $125 member; *Member Profile:* British roots or heritage; *Committees:* Investment; Charitable Trust; Education; Red Rose Ball; Membership; Events; Heritage
Activities: Raising money for charities through the society's annual Red Rose Ball, as well as other events; *Awareness Events:* Red Rose Ball to Celebrate St. George's Day, April
Chief Officer(s):
Michele McCarthy, President
Samuel Minniti, Executive Director
Danny Ramgobin, Treasurer

St. James Community Service Society *See* The Bloom Group

St. John Ambulance / Ambulance Saint-Jean
#400, 1900 City Park Dr., Ottawa ON K1J 1A3
Tel: 613-236-7461
Toll-Free: 888-840-5646
www.sja.ca
www.facebook.com/St.John.Ambulance.TO
twitter.com/sja_canada
www.youtube.com/channel/UCKqDpzz1BjDqUgImjquTC7w
Also Known As: The Priory of Canada of the Most Venerable Order of the Hospital of St. John of Jerusalem
Overview: A medium-sized international charitable organization founded in 1883
Mission: To enable Canadians to improve their health, safety & quality of life by providing training & community service. Courses in CPR, emergency first aid, & safety training are offered, as well as community service programs (medical first response, therapy dog services, emergency preparedness, youth programs), & first aid kits
Activities: Range of safety-oriented first aid courses; 4 levels of CPR training; specialized training for people working in high-risk occupations & remote areas; health promotion courses; community service; emergencies & disaster relief; 2 schools of paramedicine in Eastern Canada; *Library:* by appointment
Chief Officer(s):
Robert White, Chancellor
Jerry Rankin, Interim Chief Operating Officer
Awards:
• Life-saving Awards of the Order of St. John
Instituted in 1874, recognizes those who risk their lives in

unselfish acts of bravery & heroism when saving or attempting to save a life

Alberta Council
12304 - 118 Ave., Edmonton AB T5L 5G8
Tel: 780-452-6565
Toll-Free: 800-665-7114
ab.sjatraining.ca
Chief Officer(s):
Maureen Gray, Contact
maureen.gray@stjohn.ab.ca

British Columbia & Yukon Council
6111 Cambie St., 2nd Fl., Vancouver BC V5Z 3B2
Tel: 604-321-7242
Toll-Free: 866-321-2651
bc.sjatraining.ca
Chief Officer(s):
Sandy Gerber, Director, Marketing
sandy.gerber@bc.sja.ca

Federal District Council (Ottawa Area)
#101, 1050 Morrison Dr., Ottawa ON K2H 8K7
Tel: 613-722-2002; *Fax:* 613-722-7024
registrations@fd.sja.ca
Chief Officer(s):
Steven Gaetz, CEO

Manitoba Council
1 St John Ambulance Way, Winnipeg MB R3G 3H5
Tel: 204-784-7000; *Fax:* 204-786-2295
Toll-Free: 800-471-7771
info@mb.sja.ca
mb.sjatraining.ca
Chief Officer(s):
Richard Fetherston, Coordinator, Sales & Marketing
richard.fetherston@mb.sja.ca

New Brunswick Council
PO Box 3599, Stn. B, 200 Miles St., Fredericton NB E3A 5J8
Fax: 506-452-8699
Toll-Free: 800-563-9998
nb.sjatraining.ca
Chief Officer(s):
Lisa Murphy, Director, Operations
lisa.murphy@nb.sja.ca

Newfoundland Council
8 Thomas Byrne Dr., Mount Pearl NL A1N 0E1
Tel: 709-726-4200; *Fax:* 709-726-4117
Toll-Free: 800-801-0181
nl.sjatraining.ca
Chief Officer(s):
Glenda Janes, CEO, 709-757-3374
glenda.janes@nl.sja.ca

Nova Scotia/PEI Council
72 Highfield Park Dr., Dartmouth NS B3A 4X2
Tel: 902-463-5646; *Fax:* 902-469-9609
Toll-Free: 800-565-5056
ns.sjatraining.ca
Chief Officer(s):
Steven Gaetz, CEO

NWT & Nunavut Council
5023 - 51st St., Yellowknife NT X1A 1S5
Tel: 867-873-5658
info@mb.sja.ca
ntnu.sjatraining.ca
Chief Officer(s):
Richard Fetherston, Coordinator, Sales & Marketing
richard.fetherston@mb.sja.ca

Ontario Council
#800, 15 Toronto St., Toronto ON M5C 2E3
Tel: 416-923-8411; *Fax:* 416-923-4856
Toll-Free: 800-268-7581
ont.sjatraining.ca
Chief Officer(s):
Brian Cole, CEO
bcole@on.sja.ca

Québec Council
#10, 110, boul Crémazie ouest, Montréal QC H2P 1B9
Téléc: 514-842-4807
Ligne sans frais: 877-272-7607
medias@qc.sja.ca
Chief Officer(s):
Karoline Bergeron, Conseillère principale, Services à la collectivité

Saskatchewan Council
2625 - 3rd Ave., Regina SK S4T 0C8
Tel: 306-522-7226; *Fax:* 306-525-4177
Toll-Free: 888-273-0003
sk.sjatraining.ca
Chief Officer(s):
Michael Brenholen, Director, Operations
michael.brenholen@sk.sja.ca

Yukon Branch
128 Copper Rd., #C, Whitehorse YT Y1A 2Z6
Tel: 867-668-5001; *Fax:* 867-667-5050
yukon@yt.sja.ca

St. John's Board of Trade
PO Box 5127, 34 Harvey Rd., 3rd Fl., St. John's NL A1C 5V5
Tel: 709-726-2961; *Fax:* 709-726-2003
mail@bot.nf.ca
www.stjohnsbot.ca
www.linkedin.com/company/st.-john%27s-board-of-trade
www.facebook.com/stjohnsbot
twitter.com/stjohnsbot
www.youtube.com/user/StJohnsBoardofTrade
Overview: A medium-sized local organization founded in 1971
Mission: To act as the voice of St. John's businesses; To improve economic prosperity & quality of life in Newfoundland
Finances: *Funding Sources:* Membership fees; programs & projects
Staff Member(s): 12
Membership: 1,000; *Fees:* Based on number of employees; *Committees:* Ambassadors; Communications; Nominating; Policy; Treasurer
Activities: Advocating for policies that strengthen the economic environment of St. John's; *Awareness Events:* Annual Business Development Summit, January; Business Excellence Awards, December; *Speaker Service:* Yes
Chief Officer(s):
Nancy Healey, CEO
nhealey@bot.nf.ca

St. John's Cathedral Polish Catholic Church
186 Cowan Ave., Toronto ON M6K 2N6
Tel: 416-532-8249; *Fax:* 416-532-4653
Previous Name: Polish National Catholic Church of Canada
Overview: A small national organization
Member of: The Canadian Council of Churches
Finances: *Annual Operating Budget:* $100,000-$250,000
Membership: 300

St. John's Clean & Beautiful (SJCAB)
PO Box 908, 10 New Gower St., St. John's NL A1C 5M2
Tel: 709-570-0350; *Fax:* 709-754-3100
sjcab@cleanandbeautiful.nf.ca
www.cleanandbeautiful.nf.ca
Overview: A small local organization founded in 1992
Mission: To inspire community pride & action in St. John's to lead to a clean community
Affiliation(s): Keep America Beautiful, Inc. (KAB)
Activities: Increasing public awareness in the city's cleanliness; Encouraging community involvment; Promoting partnerships; Coordinating efforts for litter reduction; Planning beautification projects; Publishing brochures, such as the Litter Free Event Guide, the Graffiti Removal Guide, Are You Running a Dirty Business? & Beautiful Gardens & A Healthy Environment
Chief Officer(s):
Michelle Eagles, Chair

St. John's Francophone Community Association *Voir* L'Association communautaire francophone de St-Jean

St. John's Harbour ACAP *See* Northeast Avalon ACAP, Inc.

St. John's International Women's Film Festival (SJIWFF)
PO Box 984, Stn. C, St. John's NL A1C 5M3
Tel: 709-754-3141; *Fax:* 709-754-0049
info@womensfilmfestival.com
www.womensfilmfestival.com
www.linkedin.com/company/st-john%27s-international-women%27s-film-festival
www.facebook.com/womensfilmfestival
twitter.com/sjiwff
www.youtube.com/user/womensfilmfest
Overview: A medium-sized local organization founded in 1989
Mission: To promote international women filmmakers through the annual film festival
Finances: *Funding Sources:* Canadian Heritage; Canada Council for the Arts; CBC; Telefilm Canada; Gov't of Newfoundland & Labrador; Atlantic Canada Opportunities Agency
Membership: 4,000 participants
Activities: *Awareness Events:* Film Festival, Oct.
Chief Officer(s):
Noreen Golfman, Chair
Kelly Davis, Executive Director
kelly@womensfilmfestival.com
Awards:
• RBC Michelle Jackson Emerging Filmmaker Award

St. John's Kiwanis Music Festival
#210, 90 O'Leary Ave., St. John's NL A1B 2C7
Tel: 709-579-1523; *Fax:* 709-579-2007
kiwanismusicfest@nf.aibn.com
www.kiwanismusicfestivalsj.org
Overview: A small local organization
Mission: To stimulate in the citizens of Newfoundland a greater appreciation & understanding of good music; To discover & encourage musical talents in young & old
Activities: *Awareness Events:* Major festival, February-March
Chief Officer(s):
Mary Anne Tobin, Executive Secretary

St. John's Native Friendship Centre
716 Water St., St. John's NL A1E 1C1
Tel: 709-726-5902; *Fax:* 709-722-0874
www.sjnfc.com
twitter.com/St_Johns_NFC
Overview: A small local organization
Mission: To provide programs & services for Aboriginal people
Member of: National Association of Friendship Centres
Staff Member(s): 20
Membership: 200+; *Fees:* $1
Chief Officer(s):
Christopher Sheppard, Executive Director

St. John's Philatelic Society
St. John's NL
Overview: A small local organization
Mission: To encourage & promote all aspects of philately
Affiliation(s): British North America Philatelic Society
Finances: *Annual Operating Budget:* Less than $50,000
Membership: 62; *Fees:* $20 year; $12 subscription; *Member Profile:* Stamp collector
Activities: *Library:* by appointment

St. John's Rape Crisis & Information Centre *See* Newfoundland & Labrador Sexual Assault Crisis & Prevention Centre Inc.

St. Joseph's Healthcare Foundation
224 James St. South, Hamilton ON L8P 3A9
Tel: 905-521-6036; *Fax:* 905-577-0860
Toll-Free: 866-478-5037
info@stjoesfoundation.ca
www.stjoesfoundation.ca
www.facebook.com/stjosephshealthcarefoundation
twitter.com/stjoeshamilton
www.instagram.com/stjoeshamilton
Overview: A small local charitable organization founded in 1970
Mission: To raise money for St. Joseph's Healthcare Hamilton
Finances: *Annual Operating Budget:* Greater than $5 Million; *Funding Sources:* Donations; Fundraising
Activities: Around the Bay Road Race; Golf Tournament; Holiday Gala
Chief Officer(s):
Sera Filice-Armenio, President & CEO

St. Josephine Bakhita Black Heritage
6 Dewberry Dr., Markham ON L3S 2R7
Tel: 905-472-3337
Overview: A small national organization
Mission: To promote new evangelization in black heritage communities through devotion to St. Josephine Bakhita
Affiliation(s): Archdiocese of Toronto
Chief Officer(s):
Audrey Johnson, Contact

St. Lambert Choral Society *Voir* Société chorale de Saint-Lambert

St. Lambert Council for Seniors *Voir* Conseil du troisuème âge de Saint-Lambert

St. Lawrence Economic Development Council *Voir* Société de développement économique du Saint-Laurent

St. Lawrence Shipoperators *Voir* Armateurs du Saint-Laurent

St. Lawrence Valley Natural History Society (SLVNHS) / Société d'histoire naturelle de la vallée du St-Laurent (SHNVSL)
21125, ch Ste-Marie, Sainte-Anne-de-Bellevue QC H9X 3Y7
Tel: 514-457-9449; *Fax:* 514-457-0769
info@ecomuseum.ca
www.zooecomuseum.ca
Also Known As: Ecomuseum
Overview: A small local charitable organization founded in 1981
Mission: To foster an appreciation & understanding of the physical & biotic characters of the St. Lawrence Valley; To awaken public interest in the conservation of natural resources of the Valley; To stimulate interest in research on & development of renewable resources for the betterment of society
Member of: Canadian Association of Zoos & Aquariums
Affiliation(s): Canadian Nature Federation; Union québécoise pour la conservation de la nature
Finances: *Annual Operating Budget:* $500,000-$1.5 Million
Staff Member(s): 27; 100 volunteer(s)
Membership: 500-999; *Fees:* $50 individual; $120 family
Activities: *Speaker Service:* Yes
Chief Officer(s):
David Rodrigue, Executive Director
Caroline Bourque, Director, Operations & Finance
Pascal Laplante, Director, Education
Émilie Sénécal, Director, Communications

St. Leonard's Society of Canada (SLSC) / Société St-Léonard du Canada
Bronson Centre, #208, 211 Bronson Ave., Ottawa ON K1R 6H5
Tel: 613-233-5170; *Fax:* 613-233-5122
Toll-Free: 888-560-9760
info@stleonards.ca
www.stleonards.ca
www.facebook.com/SLSCanada
twitter.com/StLeonards_Can
Overview: A medium-sized national charitable organization founded in 1967
Mission: Committed to the prevention of crime through programs which promote responsible community living & safer communities
Member of: National Associations Active in Criminal Justice; Canadian Criminal Justice Association
Affiliation(s): Volunteer Ottawa; Imagine Canada; Canada Helps.org
Finances: *Annual Operating Budget:* $100,000-$250,000; *Funding Sources:* Donations; Membership; Grants
Staff Member(s): 3; 18 volunteer(s)
Membership: 12 affiliate agencies; *Fees:* Schedule available; *Committees:* Research & Development; Operations; Executive; External Relations; Executive Directors
Activities: Engaging in collaborative research on Community Corrections policy; Disseminating information through publications; Consulting with levels of government on legislative & policy issues; Operating LifeLine In-Reach program to assist individuals serving life sentences in Saskatchewan & Alberta
Chief Officer(s):
Elizabeth White, Executive Director
elizabeth@stleonards.ca
Awards:
• The Cody Award
• The Luxton Award
• The Libby Fund Award
• The Gallagher Award
• The John Braithwaite Award of Distinction
Publications:
• Community Connections [a publication of St. Leonard's Society of Canada]
Type: Newsletter; *Frequency:* 3 pa.
Profile: Provides information that affects the community, society news, & special event dates
• St. Leonard's Society of Canada Annual Report
Type: Report; *Frequency:* Annually

Larch Halfway House of Sudbury
238 Larch St., Sudbury ON P3B 1M1
Tel: 705-674-2887; *Fax:* 705-674-4312
www.stleonards.ca/slssudbury
Chief Officer(s):
Vince Marconato, Executive Director
vince@stleonards.ca

Maison "Crossroads" de la Société St-Léonard de Montréal
5262, rue Notre-Dame ouest, Montréal QC H4C 1T5
Tél: 514-932-7188; *Téléc:* 514-932-6668
maisoncrossroads@qc.aibn.com
maisoncrossroads.qc.ca
Chief Officer(s):
Michel Gagnon, Directeur executif

St. Leonard's Community Services of London & Region
405 Dundas St., London ON N6B 1V9
Tel: 519-850-3777; *Fax:* 519-850-1396
stleonards@slcs.ca
slcs.ca
Chief Officer(s):
Heather Lumley, Executive Director

St. Leonard's Home Trenton
1790 Hamilton Rd., RR #5, Trenton ON K8V 5P8
Tel: 613-392-7149; *Fax:* 613-392-3509
stleonardshome@cogeco.net
www.stleonards.ca/stleonards-trenton
Chief Officer(s):
Kelly Nolan, Executive Director

St. Leonard's House Peel
PO Box 2607, 1105 Queen St. East, Brampton ON L6T 5M6
Tel: 905-457-3611; *Fax:* 905-457-2314; *TTY:* 905-457-6650
info@slpp.ca
www.stleonardsplace.com
www.facebook.com/stleonardsplacepeel
twitter.com/StLeonardsPeel
Chief Officer(s):
Christopher McIntosh, Chief Executive Officer

St. Leonard's House Windsor
491 Victoria Ave., Windsor ON N9A 4N1
Tel: 519-256-1878; *Fax:* 519-256-4142
www.stleonardswindsor.com
www.facebook.com/953321014685182
Chief Officer(s):
Skip Graham, Executive Director

St. Leonard's Society of Hamilton
73 Robert St., Hamilton ON L8L 2P2
Tel: 905-572-1150; *Fax:* 905-572-9152
info@slsh.ca
www.slsh.ca
Chief Officer(s):
John T. Clinton, Executive Director

St. Leonard's Society of North Vancouver
312 Bewicke Ave., North Vancouver BC V7M 3B7
Tel: 604-980-3684; *Fax:* 604-980-5339
Chief Officer(s):
Wilma Douglas-Dungey, Executive Director
executive@slnv.org

St. Leonard's Society of Peterborough
458 Rubidge St., Peterborough ON K9J 7S4
Tel: 705-743-9351; *Fax:* 705-743-9975
Chief Officer(s):
Darrell Rowe, Executive Director
drowe@stleoptbo.ca

Shelter Nova Scotia
#101, 5506 Cunard St., Halifax NS B3K 1C2
Tel: 902-406-3631; *Fax:* 902-406-3477
www.shelternovascotia.com
www.facebook.com/ShelterNovaScotia
twitter.com/ShelterNS
Chief Officer(s):
Linda Wilson, Executive Director, 902-406-3631 Ext. 226
lindawilson@shelternovascotia.com

St. Leonard's Youth & Family Services Society (STLEO)
7181 Arcola Way, Burnaby BC V5E 0A6
Tel: 604-524-1511; *Fax:* 604-524-1510
www.stleo.ca
Overview: A medium-sized local charitable organization founded in 1967
Mission: To provide innovative high quality social services to the community; to be the most responsive forward moving agency in our field; to promote the development of skills & values which embrace the ideals of a healthy community
Member of: Federation of Child & Family Services
Finances: *Funding Sources:* Provincial government
Membership: *Member Profile:* People interested in well being of others
Activities: Child & family services, both residential & non-residential
Chief Officer(s):
Renata Aebi, Executive Director

St. Martins & District Chamber of Commerce
#2, 73 Main St., St Martins NB E5R 1B4
Tel: 506-833-2010
stmartinschamber@gmail.com
www.stmartinscanada.com
Overview: A small local organization
Mission: To promote business & improve quality of life in the community
Chief Officer(s):
Eric Bartlett, President
Jackie Bartlett, Secretary

St. Mary's Prayer Group
St. Mary's Roman Catholic Parish, 66A Main St. South, Brampton ON L6W 2C6
Tel: 905-451-2300
info@stmarysbrampton.com
stmarysbr.archtoronto.org
Overview: A small local organization
Affiliation(s): Archdiocese of Toronto
Membership: *Member Profile:* Open to everyone; Core members plan meetings & activities & gather for prayer
Activities: Offering healing masses, intercessory prayer, & Life in the Spirit seminars

St Mary's River Association (SMRA)
PO Box 179, 8404 #7 Hwy., Sherbrooke NS B0J 3C0
Tel: 902-522-2099; *Fax:* 902-522-2241
stmarysriver@ns.sympatico.ca
stmarysriverassociation.com
Overview: A small local charitable organization founded in 1979
Mission: To further in all ways possible the conservation, protection, propagation & perpetuation of the fishery in the St Mary's River & its tributaries in eastern Nova Scotia; to support & assist the efforts of the federal Department of Fisheries, the provincial Department of Fisheries, other government bodies & voluntary associations in any program to conserve & improve the fishery; to impress upon all concerned that the fresh & salt water fishery must be developed, harvested & protected in a spirit of cooperation, with each being dependent on the other for survival & each recognizing the need for conservation measures in this area; to work with the federal, provincial & municipal governments & the private sector in undertaking capital works programs which will enhance the fishery in the St Mary's River & tributaries
Member of: Atlantic Salmon Federation; Nova Scotia Salmon Association
Finances: *Annual Operating Budget:* $50,000-$100,000; *Funding Sources:* Private donations; industry donations; fundraising activities
Staff Member(s): 1
Membership: 273; *Fees:* $20 regular; $50 contributing; $200 corporate; $5 junior; $500 gold; $300 silver; $100 bronze; *Member Profile:* Anglers; conservationists; business; *Committees:* Newsletter; Membership; River Projects; Fundraising; Interpretive Centre
Activities: River habitat improvement; operation of interpretive centre; fundraising; newsletter; community events; Library

St. Patrick's Society of Richmond & Vicinity
Richmond QC
www.richmondstpats.org
Overview: A small local organization founded in 1877
Mission: To promote & celebrate the Irish culture in the Richmond area, the oldest Irish society in mainland Québec
Membership: *Fees:* $5 single; $10 family
Chief Officer(s):
Érika Lockwood, President, 819-826-3322

St Paul & District Chamber of Commerce
PO Box 887, 4802 - 50 Ave., St Paul AB T0A 3A0
Tel: 780-645-5820; *Fax:* 780-645-5820
www.stpaulchamber.ca
twitter.com/StpaulChamber
Overview: A small local organization founded in 1929
Mission: To represent & speak for the business, agricultural & professional community; To advance economic & social development; To strenghten the business environment in the area; To participate in community action
Affiliation(s): Alberta Chambers of Commerce
Finances: *Annual Operating Budget:* $50,000-$100,000; *Funding Sources:* Membership & grants
Staff Member(s): 1
Membership: 160; *Fees:* $105-$525; *Member Profile:* Businesses; individuals; non-profit organizations
Chief Officer(s):
Kevin Bernhardt, President

Linda Sallstrom, Executive Director

St. Paul Abilities Network (SPAN)
4637 - 45 Ave., St Paul AB T0A 3A3
Tel: 780-645-3441; *Fax:* 780-645-1885
Toll-Free: 866-645-3900
mail@spanet.ab.ca
stpaulabilitiesnetwork.ca
Overview: A small local organization founded in 1964
Mission: To lead through empowerment & excellence; believes that all individuals have the right to full participation in society, enjoying benefits, respect for preferences & individuality
Member of: Alberta Association for Community Living
Affiliation(s): Alberta Association of Rehabilitaion Centres; Elk Point Abilities Network
Activities: Many supports to families; *Library:* SPAN Library; Open to public
Chief Officer(s):
Tim Bear, Executive Director
tbear@spanet.ab.ca

St. Pierre Chamber of Commerce
PO Box 71, St Pierre Jolys MB R0A 1V0
Tel: 204-377-4384
sundowng@mts.net
www.stpierrejolys.com
Overview: A small local organization overseen by The Manitoba Chambers of Commerce
Mission: To organize & facilitate the economic development of the St. Pierre area
Finances: *Funding Sources:* Membership fees; advertising
Membership: 83; *Member Profile:* Businesses
Activities: *Library:* Centre bilingue
Chief Officer(s):
Robert Bruneau, President

St. Stephen Area Chamber of Commerce
73 Milltown Blvd., St Stephen NB E3L 1G5
Tel: 506-466-7703; *Fax:* 506-466-7753
chamber.ststephen@nb.aibn.com
www.ststephenchamber.com
Overview: A small local organization
Mission: To represent the St. Stephen area community in business matters
Affiliation(s): Atlantic Chamber of Commerce; Canadian Chamber of Commerce
Finances: *Annual Operating Budget:* Less than $50,000; *Funding Sources:* Membership dues
Staff Member(s): 1; 30 volunteer(s)
Membership: 100+; *Fees:* $25-$155; *Committees:* Business & Education Partnership; Dinner & Events; Finance; Membership & Member Services; Policy; Promotion & Development
Activities: Organizing & promoting events; *Awareness Events:* Business Gala Awards
Chief Officer(s):
Jeremy Barham, President

St. Stephen's Community House
91 Bellevue Ave., Toronto ON M5T 2N8
Tel: 416-925-2103
execassistant@sschto.ca
www.sschto.ca
www.facebook.com/St.StephensHouse
twitter.com/StStephensHouse
www.youtube.com/channel/UCZhnIUtPv8BSKAUxZFVl5Tw
Overview: A small local charitable organization founded in 1962 overseen by Ontario Council of Agencies Serving Immigrants
Mission: To help eliviate social problems through their programming
Staff Member(s): 200; 400 volunteer(s)
Activities: Provides professional mediation, coaching & consulting services; training in mediation communication & conflict management; *Internships:* Yes
Chief Officer(s):
Liane Regendanz, Executive Director

St Thomas & District Chamber of Commerce
#115, 300 South Edgeware Rd., St Thomas ON N5P 4L1
Tel: 519-631-1981; *Fax:* 519-631-0466
mail@stthomaschamber.on.ca
www.stthomaschamber.on.ca
Previous Name: St. Thomas Board of Trade
Overview: A medium-sized local organization founded in 1869
Mission: To serve as the voice of the business community & to work to ensure economic success in central Elgin county
Affiliation(s): Ontario Chamber of Commerce; Canadian Chamber of Commerce
Finances: *Funding Sources:* Membership dues; projects & activities
Staff Member(s): 3
Membership: 600 corporate + 1,200 individual; *Fees:* Schedule available; *Committees:* Executive Council; Member Services
Activities: Free Enterprise Dinner & Awards; *Awareness Events:* Annual Best Ball Open Golf Tournament, August; *Speaker Service:* Yes; *Rents Mailing List:* Yes; *Library*
Chief Officer(s):
Bob Hammersley, President & CEO
bob@stthomaschamber.on.ca
Awards:
- Chair's Award
- Bell Canada Communication Innovation Award
- Free Enterprise Award of Merit
- The Free Enterprise Master Award

St. Thomas Board of Trade *See* St Thomas & District Chamber of Commerce

St. Vincent & the Grenadines Association of Montreal Inc. (SVGAM) / L'Association St.Vincent et Grenadines de Montrèal Inc.
PO Box 396, Stn. Snowdon Station, Montréal QC H3X 3T3
Tel: 514-344-9924
www.svgamontreal.com
Overview: A small local organization
Chief Officer(s):
Alfred Dear, President, 514-364-3299

St. Walburg Chamber of Commerce
PO Box 501, St Walburg SK S0M 2T0
Tel: 306-248-4681
info@stwalburg.com
www.stwalburg.com
Overview: A small local organization
Member of: Saskatchewan Chamber of Commerce
Finances: *Annual Operating Budget:* Less than $50,000
Membership: 45; *Fees:* $25; *Member Profile:* Business owners
Chief Officer(s):
Ali Schmidt, President

SAIT Academic Faculty Association (SAFA) / Association des professeurs du SAIT
Senator Patrick Burns Bldg., SAIT Campus, #N201, 1301 - 16 Ave. NW, Calgary AB T2M 0L4
Tel: 403-284-8321; *Fax:* 403-284-0005
safa@sait.ca
www.safacalgary.com
Previous Name: SAIT Instructors Association
Overview: A small local organization founded in 1983
Mission: To foster standards of excellence in instruction; to carry on liaison with external organizations; to foster good relations between the Institute & the community; to promote & establish appropriate renumeration, fringe benefits & good working conditions
Member of: Alberta College-Institute Faculty Association
Affiliation(s): Canadian Association of College-Institute Faculty
Staff Member(s): 4
Membership: *Fees:* 1.2% of salary; *Member Profile:* Full-time & part-time instructors at SAIT; *Committees:* Negotiations; Dispute Resolution/Grievance
Chief Officer(s):
James McWilliams, President, 403-210-4056
james.mcWilliams@sait.ca
Kathie Dann, Administrator
kathie.dann@sait.ca

SAIT Instructors Association *See* SAIT Academic Faculty Association

Salers Association of Canada (SAC) / Association salers du Canada
5160 Skyline Way NE, Calgary AB T2E 6V1
Tel: 403-264-5850; *Fax:* 403-264-5895
info@salerscanada.com
www.salerscanada.com
Also Known As: Canadian Salers
Overview: A small national organization founded in 1974
Mission: To develop & register Salers cattle
Member of: Canadian Beef Breeds Council
Staff Member(s): 4
Membership: 62; *Member Profile:* Canadian Salers breeders
Activities: Promoting the Salers breed; Disseminating information about the breed at promotional booths at fairs & expositions, auction markets, bull test stations, & international trade events; Coordinating Salers sales & shows; Supporting young cattlemen & women
Chief Officer(s):
Gar Williams, President
gmwilliams@sasktel.net
Ray Depalme, Treasurer
raymondj@xplornet.com
Lois Chivilo, Registrar
Publications:
- Salers
Type: Magazine; *Frequency:* Semiannually; *Accepts Advertising;* *Price:* $17 / year Canada; $21 / year foreign
Profile: Articles about the breed & industry, executive & provincial reports, show & sale news, plus association announcements

Sales & Marketing Executives of Vancouver (SMEV)
Vancouver BC
Tel: 604-266-0090
vancouver@smei.org
www.smeivancouver.org
www.linkedin.com/groups/45880
www.youtube.com/smeiorg
Also Known As: SMEI Vancouver
Overview: A small local organization founded in 1946
Member of: Sales & Marketing Executives International
Finances: *Funding Sources:* Membership fees; fundraising
18 volunteer(s)
Membership: 152; *Fees:* $225 professional; $325 executive; *Member Profile:* CEO; marketing & sales executives; *Committees:* Membership; Breakfast; Advisory Council
Activities: Monthly meetings; keynote speakers; workshops & breakfasts
Chief Officer(s):
Bonnie Turner, Executive Director

Salesian Cooperators, Association of St. Benedict Centre
c/o St. Benedict Parish, 2194 Kipling Ave., Toronto ON M9W 4K9
Tel: 416-743-3830; *Fax:* 416-743-8884
connect@stbenedicts.ca
stbenedicts.ca/salesiancooperators.html
Also Known As: Don Bosco's Cooperators
Overview: A small local organization founded in 1876
Mission: To bring a priviledged attention to young people, especially those who are poorest, or victims of marginalization, exploitation, & violence
Affiliation(s): Archdiocese of Toronto
Finances: *Funding Sources:* Fundraising
Membership: *Member Profile:* Lay, mature adults & priest members, accompanied by SDB or FMA religious, form the lay apostolic association; Members must be accepted by the provincial council & make personal, public promises
Chief Officer(s):
Joe Conroy, Contact

La Salle & District Chamber of Commerce
10 A Principale St., La Salle MB R0G 0A2
Tel: 204-801-3492
lasallechamber@gmail.com
www.lasallechamber.ca
www.facebook.com/254436004642699
Overview: A small local organization founded in 1990
Mission: To promote local businesses & help them grow
Member of: Manitoba Chambers of Commerce
Staff Member(s): 1
Membership: 62; *Fees:* $60 individual/organization; $125 business; *Member Profile:* Local businesses
Chief Officer(s):
Allyson Demski, Office Manager

Salmo & District Chamber of Commerce
PO Box 400, 100 - 4th St., Salmo BC V0G 1Z0
Tel: 250-357-2596
salmoch@telus.net
discoversalmo.ca/Chamber.aspx
www.facebook.com/198963673452419
Overview: A small local organization
Mission: To support & promote businesses & the community
Membership: *Fees:* $70 business; $25 non-profit; $20 individual; $10 student/senior
Chief Officer(s):
Dave Reid, President

Salmo Community Resource Society (SCRS)
PO Box 39, Salmo BC V0G 1Z0

Canadian Associations / Salmon Arm - Salvation Army Food Bank

Tel: 250-357-2277; *Fax:* 250-357-2385
www.scrs.ca
Overview: A small local organization
Mission: Provides support for underpriviledged families & children
2 volunteer(s)
Chief Officer(s):
Maureen Berk, Executive Director
maureen@scrs.ca

Salmon Arm - Salvation Army Food Bank
PO Box 505, 191 - 2nd Ave., Salmon Arm BC V1E 4N6
Tel: 250-832-9194; *Fax:* 250-832-9148
Overview: A small local organization overseen by Food Banks British Columbia
Mission: To provide food and services to the needy in the Salmon Arm area.
Member of: Food Banks British Columbia
Chief Officer(s):
Matthew Juhasz, Contact

Salmon Arm & District Chamber of Commerce (SACC)
PO Box 999, #101, 20 Hudson Ave. NE, Salmon Arm BC V1E 4P2
Tel: 250-832-6247; *Fax:* 250-832-8382
Other Communication: Visitor Centre e-mail:
info@visitsalmonarm.com
admin@sachamber.bc.ca
www.sachamber.bc.ca
www.facebook.com/salmonarmchamber
Overview: A small local organization founded in 1909
Mission: To provide a business perspective within the Salmon Arm region; To stimulate prosperity by promoting tourism, identifying business opportunities, & encouraging new & existing businesses
Member of: BC Chamber of Commerce
Finances: *Annual Operating Budget:* $100,000-$250,000; *Funding Sources:* Membership dues; service fees
Staff Member(s): 2
Membership: 600; *Fees:* Based on number of employees; *Committees:* Forestry; Tourism; Manufacturing; Retail; Centennial; Events; Education; Membership; Scholarship
Activities: Providing special speakers & workshops; Organizing events including Business After Hours, golf tournament, community business awards, & trade shows
Chief Officer(s):
Corryn Grayston, General Manager

Salmon Arm Bay Nature Enhancement Society (SABNES)
PO Box 27, Salmon Arm BC V1E 4N2
Tel: 250-833-9717
sabnes.org@gmail.com
www.sabnes.org
Overview: A small local organization founded in 1986
Mission: To assist the Wildlife Branch of the provincial government with the development & operation of their management plan for the Salmon Arm foreshore as a Nature Conservancy & viewing area; To develop, operate & promote a system of walkways, viewing areas & interpretive facilities for scientific, educational, environmental protection & public viewing purposes; & to promote environmental awareness & assist in projects meeting that goal in the Salmon Arm area.
Finances: *Funding Sources:* Corporate sponsorship; Membership dues
Membership: *Fees:* $10 individual; $20 family; $50 sustaining individual; $100 sustaining family; $500 life membership; $50-2500 corporate membership
Chief Officer(s):
Mike Saul, Treasurer

Salmon Preservation Association for the Waters of Newfoundland (SPAWN)
93 West St., Corner Brook NL A2H 2Y6
Tel: 709-634-3012; *Fax:* 709-634-4091
Toll-Free: 866-634-3012
spawn@nl.rogers.com
www.spawn1.ca
Overview: A small local charitable organization founded in 1979
Mission: Works with Government to help improve the migrating numbers of salmon.
Member of: Salmonid Council of Newfoundland & Labrador
Affiliation(s): Atlantic Salmon Federation
Finances: *Annual Operating Budget:* $50,000-$100,000; *Funding Sources:* Auctions
Staff Member(s): 1; 300 volunteer(s)

Membership: 300; *Fees:* $25 Canadian member; US$30 American member; US$35 outside North America; *Member Profile:* Conservationists; *Committees:* Enhancement; Enforcement; Habitat; Dinner/Auction; Magazine
Activities: Conservation projects; data collection; *Library:* by appointment
Chief Officer(s):
Keith Cormier, President

Salmonid Association of Eastern Newfoundland (SAEN)
PO Box 29122, #8, 50 Pippy Pl., St. John's NL A1A 5B5
Tel: 709-722-9300; *Fax:* 709-722-9320
saen@nfld.com
www.saen.org
twitter.com/SAEN_NL
Overview: A small provincial organization founded in 1979
Mission: Dedicated to the preservation of Newfoundland's freshwater resources
Staff Member(s): 1
Membership: *Fees:* $20 individual; $50 corporate
Activities: Fly-tying; Moose stew; Rod building club; River talks
Chief Officer(s):
Don Hutchens, Office Manager
Scott Nightingale, President
scottn@nl.rogers.com

Salon du livre de Toronto et Festival des écrivains / Toronto French Book Fair
789, rue Yonge, Toronto ON M4W 2G8
Tél: 416-670-9847
info@salondulivredetoronto.ca
www.salondulivredetoronto.ca
www.facebook.com/SalonDuLivreDeToronto
twitter.com/SDLTO
Aperçu: Dimension: petite; *Envergure:* internationale; Organisme sans but lucratif; fondée en 1993
Mission: Promouvoir le livre d'expression française et les écrivains francophones, pour le bénéfice des francophones et francophiles de Toronto et d'ailleurs
Finances: *Fonds:* Subventions gouvernementales (50%)
Membre(s) du personnel: 1
Membre: *Critères d'admissibilite:* Écrivain, professeur, critique littéraire, libraire, bibliothécaire, éditeur, journaliste, etc.
Activités: Exposition de livres avec ventes; soirées littéraires; tables rondes; conférences, ateliers; animation jeunesse; spectacles; lancements et signatures de livres; *Evénements de sensibilisation:* Le Festival des écrivains
Membre(s) du bureau directeur:
Jacques Charette, Chargé de la logistique
Jacques.Charette@salondulivredetoronto.ca
Vlad Valéry, Président
Prix, Bourses:
• Prix Christine-Dumitriu-Van-Saanen
; *Amount:* 5 000$
• Prix du Consulat Général de France
Un voyage au Salon du livre de Paris

Salt Spring Community Centre Food Bank
268 Fulford Ganges Rd., Salt Spring Island BC V8K 2K6
Tel: 250-537-9971; *Fax:* 250-537-9974
connect@ssics.ca
www.saltspringcommunityservices.ca/foodbank
Overview: A small local organization founded in 1975
Mission: To provide food & services to the needy in the Salt Spring Island area
Finances: *Funding Sources:* Donations; Grants; United Way; Public Health Agency
Activities: Resources & referrals; Adult counselling; Child & youth; Community housing; Outreach; Community living; Early childhood; Food security; Seniors services; Psychiatric services
Chief Officer(s):
Annika Lund, Contact
alund@ssics.ca

Salt Spring Island Chamber of Commerce (SSI Chamber)
121 Lower Ganges Rd., Salt Spring Island BC V8K 2T1
Tel: 250-537-4223; *Fax:* 250-537-4276
Toll-Free: 866-216-2936
chamber@saltspringchamber.com
www.saltspringchamber.com
www.facebook.com/saltspringchamb
twitter.com/saltspringchamb
Also Known As: Salt Spring Island Chamber of Commerce & Visitor Centre
Overview: A small local organization founded in 1948

Mission: To create a thriving & sustainable business environment
Member of: Destination BC; Canadian Chamber of Commerce; Tourism Vancouver Island
Finances: *Annual Operating Budget:* $100,000-$250,000; *Funding Sources:* BC Ministry of Tourism; Tourism Vancouver Island
Staff Member(s): 1; 100 volunteer(s)
Membership: 300; *Fees:* Schedule available; *Committees:* Events; Membership; Tourism; Economic Development
Activities: *Awareness Events:* Sip & Savour Salt Spring; Salt Spring Blooms, April; Christmas on Salt Spring
Chief Officer(s):
Janet Clouston, Executive Director
janet@saltspringchamber.com

S.A.L.T.S. Sail & Life Training Society (SALTS)
451 Herald St., Victoria BC V8W 3N8
Tel: 250-383-6811; *Fax:* 250-383-7781
Toll-Free: 888-383-6811
info@salts.ca
www.salts.ca
www.facebook.com/saltsvictoria
twitter.com/saltsvictoria
Overview: A small provincial charitable organization founded in 1974
Mission: Christian organization that believes through the medium of sail training both spiritual & physical development is encouraged in each individual
Member of: Canadian Council of Christian Charities
Finances: *Annual Operating Budget:* $500,000-$1.5 Million; *Funding Sources:* Trainee fees; donations; membership fees; fundraising
Staff Member(s): 7; 40 volunteer(s)
Membership: 450 single & family; *Fees:* $50 single; $100 family; $200 corporate
Chief Officer(s):
Loren Hagerty, Executive Director

SalvAide
#411, 219 Argyle Ave., Ottawa ON K2P 2H4
Tel: 613-233-6215; *Fax:* 613-233-7375
info@salvaide.ca
www.salvaide.ca
www.facebook.com/163091010412408
twitter.com/salvaide
www.youtube.com/user/SalvAide
Overview: A small national organization founded in 1985
Mission: To foster economic & democratic development in El Salvador
Member of: Canadian Council for International Cooperation
Finances: *Annual Operating Budget:* $250,000-$500,000
Staff Member(s): 3
Membership: 1-99
Chief Officer(s):
René Guerra Salazar, Executive Director
director@salvaide.ca

The Salvation Army in Canada
Territorial Headquarters, Canada & Bermuda, 2 Overlea Blvd., Toronto ON M4H 1P4
Tel: 416-425-2111
Toll-Free: 800-725-2769
Other Communication: www.flickr.com/photos/salvationarmy
www.salvationarmy.ca
www.linkedin.com/company/the-salvation-army-in-canada
www.facebook.com/salvationarmy
twitter.com/salvationarmy
www.youtube.com/user/salvationarmy
Overview: A large international charitable organization founded in 1882
Mission: To preach the Gospel of Jesus Christ; To supply basic human needs; To provide personal counselling & undertake the spiritual & moral regeneration & physical rehabilitation of all persons in need who come within its sphere of influence regardless of race, colour, creed; sex or age
Member of: Evangelical Fellowship of Canada
Finances: *Annual Operating Budget:* $3 Million-$5 Million
Staff Member(s): 152
Membership: 311 Corps (congregations); 330+ social-service institutes across Canada
Activities: *Speaker Service:* Yes
Chief Officer(s):
Susan McMillan, Territorial Commander
Publications:
• Salvationist

Type: Magazine; *Frequency:* Monthly; *Price:* $30
Profile: Magazine informing readers about the mission and ministry of the Salvation Army in Canada and Bermuda.

Burnaby - British Columbia Division
#103, 3833 Henning Dr., Burnaby BC V5V 6N5
Tel: 604-299-3908; *Fax:* 604-291-0345
www.salvationarmy.ca/britishcolumbia
twitter.com/SalArmyBC

Edmonton - Alberta & Northern Territories Division
9618 - 101A Ave. NW, Edmonton AB T5H 0C7
Tel: 780-423-2111; *Fax:* 780-425-9081
www.salvationarmy.ca/alberta
www.facebook.com/SalvationArmyAB
twitter.com/tsaedmonton
www.youtube.com/user/TSAAlberta;
www.instagram.com/tsaalberta
Chief Officer(s):
Pam Goodyear, Divisional Secretary, Public Relations & Development
pam_goodyear@can.salvationarmy.org

Halifax - Maritime Division
330 Herring Cove Road, Halifax NS B3R 1V4
Tel: 902-455-1201; *Fax:* 902-455-0055
www.salvationarmy.ca/maritime
www.facebook.com/SAmaritime
twitter.com/SAmaritime
www.youtube.com/SAmaritime
Chief Officer(s):
Rhonda Harrington, Divisional Secretary
Rhonda_Harrington@can.salvationarmy.org

London - Ontario Great Lakes Division
371 King St., London ON N6B 1S4
Tel: 519-433-6106; *Fax:* 519-433-0250
www.salvationarmy.ca/ontariogreatlakes
www.linkedin.com/company/the-salvation-army-ontario-great-lakes-division
www.facebook.com/TSAOntarioGreatLakes
www.youtube.com/user/TSAOntarioGreatLakes
Chief Officer(s):
Patricia Phinney, Divisional Secretary, Public Relations & Development
pat_phinney@can.salvationarmy.org

Montréal - Québec Division
1655, rue Richardson, Montréal QC H3K 3J7
Toll-Free: 877-288-7441
www.armeedusalut-quebec.ca
www.linkedin.com/company/166406
www.facebook.com/armeedusalut
Chief Officer(s):
Brian Venables, Divisional Commander
brian_venables@armeedusalut.ca

Regina Office
T.B. Coombs Centre, 2240 - 13th Ave., Regina SK S4P 3M7
Tel: 306-757-1631; *Fax:* 306-955-1378
www.salvationarmy.ca/prairie
Chief Officer(s):
Andrew Doan, Contact, Media Inquiries, 306-757-3111 Ext. 3

St. John's - Newfoundland & Labrador Division
21 Adams Ave., St. John's NL A1C 4Z1
Tel: 709-579-2022
www.salvationarmy.ca/newfoundland
Chief Officer(s):
John Goulding, Contact
john_goulding@can.salvationarmy.org

Saskatoon Office
1027 - 8th St. East, Saskatoon SK S7H 0S2
Tel: 306-244-9111; *Fax:* 306-244-9115
www.salvationarmy.ca/prairie
Chief Officer(s):
Heather Hedstrom, Contact, 306-244-9144

Toronto - Ontario Central East Division
1645 Warden Ave., Toronto ON M1R 5B3
Tel: 416-321-2654; *Fax:* 416-321-8005
www.salvationarmy.ca/ontariocentraleast
www.facebook.com/tsatoronto
twitter.com/tsatoronto
Chief Officer(s):
Sandra Rice, Divisional Commander & Director, 416-321-2654 Ext. 103
sandra_rice@can.salvationarmy.org

Winnipeg - Prairie Division
#204, 290 Vaughan St., Winnipeg MB R3B 2N8
Tel: 204-975-1033; *Fax:* 204-946-9498
www.salvationarmy.ca/prairie
www.facebook.com/TSA.Prairie
twitter.com/tsaprairie
Chief Officer(s):
Brenden Roemich, Contact, 204-946-9177

Salvation Army Mt. Arrowsmith Community Ministries - Food Bank
PO Box 1874, 886 Wembley Rd., Parksville BC V9P 2H6
Tel: 250-248-8793; *Fax:* 250-248-8601
Also Known As: Parksville Food Bank
Overview: A small local organization overseen by Food Banks British Columbia
Member of: Food Banks British Columbia

The Salvation Army START Program
9919 MacDonald Ave., Fort McMurray AB T9H 1S7
Tel: 780-743-4135; *Fax:* 780-791-2909
sastart@shawcable.com
Also Known As: Support Today Achieves Results Tomorrow Program
Overview: A small local organization founded in 1983
Member of: ACDS
Affiliation(s): Alberta Association of Rehab Centres
Finances: *Annual Operating Budget:* $1.5 Million-$3 Million; *Funding Sources:* N.E. Regional Persons with Developmental Disabilities Board
Staff Member(s): 49
Membership: 49; *Fees:* $10
Chief Officer(s):
Alyson McAlister, Program Director
alyson.mcalister@shawcable.com
Hibbs Stephen, Corporal Officers
Elaine Hibbs, Corporal Officer

The Sam Sorbara Charitable Foundation
#800, 3700 Steeles Avenue West, Vaughan ON L4L 8M9
Tel: 905-850-6154; *Fax:* 905-850-6166
csorbara@sorbara.com
www.sorbara.com
Overview: A small local charitable organization
Membership: *Committees:* Directing
Chief Officer(s):
Christina Sorbara, Vice-President, Corporate Knowledge

Samaritan House Ministries Inc.
820 Pacific Ave., Brandon MB R7A 0J1
Tel: 204-726-0758
info@samaritanhouse.net
samaritanhouse.net
www.facebook.com/210774752373958
twitter.com/SHM_Brandon
Overview: A small local charitable organization founded in 1987
Mission: To provide support & services to at-risk populations - the homeless, those living in poverty, people with literacy challenges or persons leaving abusive relationships
50 volunteer(s)
Activities: *Internships:* Yes; *Speaker Service:* Yes
Chief Officer(s):
Thea Dennis, Executive Director

Samaritan's Purse Canada (SPC)
20 Hopewell Way NE, Calgary AB T3J 5H5
Tel: 403-250-6565; *Fax:* 403-250-6567
Toll-Free: 800-663-6500
info@samaritan.ca
www.samaritanspurse.ca
www.facebook.com/samaritanspurse.ca
twitter.com/spcanada
www.youtube.com/user/samaritanspursecan;
pinterest.com/spcanada
Also Known As: Operation Christmas Child
Overview: A large international charitable organization founded in 1973
Mission: To meet both physical & spiritual needs of people who are victims of war, poverty, natural disasters, disease & famine; To provide emergency relief & development programs, & medical projects
Member of: Canadian Council of Christian Charities
Affiliation(s): Samaritan's Purse USA
Finances: *Annual Operating Budget:* Greater than $5 Million; *Funding Sources:* Donations
Staff Member(s): 100; 1500 volunteer(s)
Activities: Operation Christmas Child packages; Turn on the Tap access to safe water program; *Internships:* Yes; *Speaker Service:* Yes
Chief Officer(s):
Franklin Graham, President & CEO
Fred Weiss, Executive Director

Sanctuary
25 Charles St. East, Toronto ON M4Y 1R9
Tel: 416-922-0628; *Fax:* 416-922-4961
info@sanctuarytoronto.ca
www.sanctuarytoronto.ca
Overview: A small local organization
Mission: To establish & develop a holistic, inclusive & healthy community for people who are homeless, people who run their own businesses, middle-aged, middle-class people, squeegee kids, university students & hardened street people
Finances: *Funding Sources:* Donations from churches, agencies & organizations
Staff Member(s): 15
Activities: Arts; Church; Drop-ins; Health clinic; Street outreach
Chief Officer(s):
Alan Beattie, Executive Director
alanb@sanctuarytoronto.ca

Sandbox Project
#1600, 30 Adelaide St. East, Toronto ON M5C 3H1
Tel: 416-554-2610
sandboxproject.ca
www.facebook.com/SandboxProject
twitter.com/sandboxcanada
Overview: A small local charitable organization
Mission: To make Canada a place that emphasizes healthy living, for the benefit of Canadian children
Membership: *Committees:* Governance; Finance; Injury Prevention; Building Healthy Bodies; Mental Health; Environment
Chief Officer(s):
Paul J. Brown, Chair

Sandford Fleming Foundation
University of Waterloo, #E2 3336, 200 University Ave. West, Waterloo ON N2L 3G1
Tel: 519-888-4008; *Fax:* 519-746-1457
sff@uwaterloo.ca
www.eng.uwaterloo.ca/~sff/
Overview: A small national organization
Mission: To encourage cooperation between industry & university in engineering education
Chief Officer(s):
Bettina Wahl, Office Manager

Santé Mentale pour Enfants Ontario *See* Children's Mental Health Ontario

Sappujjijit Friendship Centre *See* Pulaarvik Kablu Friendship Centre

Sar-El Canada
#315, 788 Marlee Ave., Toronto ON M6B 3K1
Tel: 416-781-6089; *Fax:* 416-785-7687
toronto@sarelcanada.org
www.sarelcanada.org
Also Known As: Canadian Volunteers for Israel
Overview: A small international organization founded in 1986
Mission: Facilitates volunteering in Israel
Finances: *Annual Operating Budget:* Less than $50,000
10 volunteer(s)
Membership: 1-99
Activities: 1,200 clients; *Speaker Service:* Yes
Chief Officer(s):
Len Berk, President

Montréal
1, careé Cummings, 5e étage, Montréal QC H3W 1M6
Tel: 514-735-0272
montreal@sarelcanada.org
Chief Officer(s):
Jack Bordan, Vice-President

Sargeant Bay Society (SBS)
PO Box 1486, Sechelt BC V0N 3A0
srgntbay.soc@gmail.com
www.sargbay.ca
Also Known As: Society for the Protection of Sargeant Bay
Overview: A small local charitable organization founded in 1978
Mission: To protect the natural habitat of Sargeant Bay & its watershed
Membership: *Fees:* $10; $25 for 3 years
Chief Officer(s):
Rand Rudland, President
Maggie Marsh, Secretary

Publications:
• Sargeant Bay Society Newsletter
Type: Newsletter

SARI Riding for Disabled *See* SARI Therapeutic Riding

SARI Therapeutic Riding
12659 Medway Rd., RR#1, Arva ON N0M 1C0
Tel: 519-666-1123; *Fax:* 519-666-1971
office@sari.ca
www.sari.ca
www.facebook.com/SARITherapeuticRiding
twitter.com/SARITherapeutic
www.youtube.com/channel/UCWEQ6cSSY89McQFCwwTxLow
Also Known As: Special Ability Riding Institute
Previous Name: SARI Riding for Disabled
Overview: A medium-sized local charitable organization founded in 1978
Mission: To provide opportunities for people with special needs to move towards greater independence & freedom by providing therapeutic riding & driving programs which meet individual needs; To balance safety & challenge to maximize opportunities for growth; To support contributions of participants, parents, volunteers & staff
Member of: Canadian Therapeutic Riding Association
Affiliation(s): Ontario Therapeutic Riding Association
Finances: *Funding Sources:* Individual & service club donations; fundraising events
200 volunteer(s)
Membership: 150; *Committees:* Fund Development; Human Resources; Program; Marketing & Communications
Activities: Summer equestrian program
Chief Officer(s):
Diane Blackall, Executive Director

Sarnia & District Humane Society
131 Exmouth St., Sarnia ON N7T 7W8
Tel: 519-344-7064; *Fax:* 519-344-2145
humanesocietyfd@ebtech.net
www.sarniahumanesociety.com
www.facebook.com/sarniahumanesociety
twitter.com/sarniahumane
Also Known As: Sarnia & District SPCA
Overview: A small local charitable organization founded in 1953
Affiliation(s): Ontario SPCA
Finances: *Annual Operating Budget:* $250,000-$500,000; *Funding Sources:* Municipal poundage fees; adoption fees; fundraising events; donations; bequests
Staff Member(s): 15; 50 volunteer(s)
Membership: 1,000; *Fees:* $15; *Committees:* Education; Fundraising
Activities: Provides animal pound service to local municipalities; performs cruelty investigations; educates public regarding humane treatment of animals through news media & classes for children; *Awareness Events:* People-Pet Walkathon; Tag Days; Bazaar; Garage Sale; Lottery
Chief Officer(s):
Tami Holmes, Manager
tholmes@ebtech.net

Sarnia & District Labour Council (SDLC)
900 Devine St., Sarnia ON N7T 1X5
Tel: 519-542-2375
sldc@bellnet.ca
sarniaanddistrictlabourcouncil.com
Overview: A small local organization founded in 1956 overseen by Ontario Federation of Labour
Mission: To promote the interests of its union local affiliates; To advance the economic & social welfare of workers; To aid the sale of union made goods & services
Affiliation(s): Chatham-Kent Labour Council; Ontario Federation of Labour; Canadian Labour Congress
Membership: 6,800; *Fees:* Schedule available; *Committees:* Political Action; Good & Welfare; Health & Safety; Environmental; Education
Activities: *Awareness Events:* Day of Mourning, April 28; Labour Day Parade, first Monday of September
Chief Officer(s):
Ted Hext, President

Sarnia Building Trades Council
1151 Confederation St., Sarnia ON N7S 3Y5
Tel: 519-344-4680; *Fax:* 519-344-4680
smwia539@cogeco.net
Overview: A small local organization
Member of: AFL-CIO
Chief Officer(s):
Jim Bradshaw, Contact

Sarnia Concert Association (SCA)
PO Box 2777, Sarnia ON N7T 7W1
www.sarniaconcertassociation.ca
Overview: A small local charitable organization founded in 1936
Mission: To bring musical entertainment to the Sarnia area through annual concert series
Finances: *Funding Sources:* Department of Canadian Heritage
20 volunteer(s)
Chief Officer(s):
Dave Nichols, President

Sarnia Lambton Chamber of Commerce
556 North Christina St., Sarnia ON N7T 5W6
Tel: 519-336-2400; *Fax:* 519-336-2085
info@sarnialambtonchamber.com
www.sarnialambtonchamber.com
www.facebook.com/sarnialambtonchamber
twitter.com/SarLamChamber
www.youtube.com/user/SarniaLambtonChamber
Overview: A small local organization
Mission: To address the needs of members & the Sarnia Lambton community
Staff Member(s): 6
Membership: 890; *Fees:* Schedule available; *Member Profile:* Business in good standing
Activities: Lobbying; *Rents Mailing List:* Yes
Chief Officer(s):
Shirley de Silva, President & CEO
sdesilva@sarnialambtonchamber.com

Sarnia Minor Athletic Association (SMAA)
Chaytor Building - Germain Park, PO Box 524, Sarnia ON N7T 7J4
Tel: 519-332-1896; *Fax:* 519-332-1569
smaa@ebtech.net
www.sarniaminorathletic.com
Overview: A small local organization founded in 1947
Mission: To instill the knowledge that accompanies minor sports participation in the athletes
Chief Officer(s):
Murray Rempel, President

Sarnia Rock & Fossil Club
www.sarnia.com/groups/srfc
Overview: A small local organization founded in 1966
Membership: *Member Profile:* Individuals interested in rocks, minerals, fossils, & lapidary
Activities: Hosting monthly meetings, including children's programs, at the Kinsmen Oakwood Club; Organizing field trips
Chief Officer(s):
Ivan McKay, Contact, 519-287-2506
i.mckay@sympatico.ca
Mary Rastall, Contact, 519-542-6830
rastalls@gmail.com
Wayne Wilcocks, Contact, 519-786-6072
dotw@eastlink.ca
Publications:
• The Narrow News
Type: Newsletter
Profile: Upcoming events & general interest articles

Sarnia-Lambton Chinese-Canadian Association *See* Chinese Canadian National Council

Sarnia-Lambton Environmental Association (SLEA)
1489 London Rd., Sarnia ON N7S 1P6
Tel: 519-332-2010; *Fax:* 519-332-2015
admin@slea.ca
www.sarniaenvironment.com
Previous Name: Lambton Industrial Society: An Environmental Co-operative
Overview: A small local organization founded in 1952
Mission: To be recognized by members, regulatory agencies & the community for excellence in promoting & fostering a healthy environment consistent with sustainable development
Membership: 18 companies; *Member Profile:* Industrial facilities operating in Lambton County
Activities: *Library:* Lending Library
Chief Officer(s):
Dean Edwardson, General Manager

Sarnia-Lambton Real Estate Board (SLREB)
555 Exmouth St., Sarnia ON N7T 5P6
Tel: 519-336-6871; *Fax:* 519-344-1928
www.mls-sarnia.com
www.facebook.com/152351484834475
Overview: A small local organization founded in 1944 overseen by Ontario Real Estate Association
Member of: The Canadian Real Estate Association
Membership: 229; *Member Profile:* Licensed to sell real estate in Ontario; employed by member office; completion of board orientation course; committed to leadership, optimism & services that are valued by its membership; *Committees:* Arbitration; Nominating; Education & Membership; Government Relations; Professional Standards; Communications & Public Relations; Social Media
Activities: *Library:*
Chief Officer(s):
David Burke, Executive Officer
dburke@fonenet.ca

Sartre Society of Canada *See* Society for Existential & Phenomenological Theory & Culture

Sasha's Legacy Equine Rescue
RR#1, Northbrook ON K0H 2G0
Tel: 613-336-1804
sler@mazinaw.on.ca
Overview: A small local organization
Mission: To take in abused, neglected & unwanted horses & ponies; To rehabilitate these animals & place them in loving adoptive homes
Finances: *Funding Sources:* Donations; Sponsorship

Sask Pork
#2, 502 - 45th St. West, Saskatoon SK S7L 6H2
Tel: 306-244-7752; *Fax:* 306-244-1712
info@saskpork.com
www.saskpork.com
Overview: A small provincial organization founded in 1998
Mission: To position the Saskatchewan pork industry as a preferred supplier of high quality, competitively priced pork products for the global market.
Staff Member(s): 5
Membership: *Committees:* Audit
Chief Officer(s):
Neil Ketilson, General Manager
nketilson@saskpork.com

Sask Sport Inc.
1870 Lorne St., Regina SK S4P 2L7
Tel: 306-780-9300; *Fax:* 306-781-6021
sasksport@sasksport.sk.ca
www.sasksport.sk.ca
Overview: A medium-sized provincial organization founded in 1972
Mission: To ensure the total development of amateur sport through the provincial sport governing bodies; to promote extensive participation towards excellence
Finances: *Annual Operating Budget:* $500,000-$1.5 Million; *Funding Sources:* Lotteries
Staff Member(s): 50; 13 volunteer(s)
Membership: 70 active & affiliate; *Fees:* Schedule available
Activities: *Library:* Resource Centre for Sport, Culture & Recreation
Chief Officer(s):
Kevin Gilroy, Chief Executive Officer

Sask Taekwondo
106 Franklin Ave., Yorkton SK S3N 2G4
Tel: 306-782-1272
taekwondosk@sasktel.net
www.saskwtf.ca
Also Known As: Sask. WTF
Overview: A small provincial organization founded in 1981
Mission: To govern the sport of Tae Kwon Do in Saskatchewan.
Member of: World Taekwondo Federation
Chief Officer(s):
Audrey Ashcroft, Executive Director, 306-621-9696

Saskatchewan 5 Pin Bowlers' Association (S5PBA)
#100, 1805 - 8th Ave., Regina SK S4R 1E8
Tel: 306-780-9412; *Fax:* 306-780-9455
bowling@sasktel.net
www.saskbowl.com/s5pba
Overview: A small provincial organization founded in 1980 overseen by Bowling Federation of Saskatchewan
Mission: To develop trust & harmony among member organizations; to assist in the development & promotion of the sport of bowling through the provision of stable funding
Member of: Canadian 5 Pin Bowlers' Association; Bowling Federation of Saskatchewan
Finances: *Annual Operating Budget:* $100,000-$250,000

Saskatchewan Abilities Council
2310 Louise Ave., Saskatoon SK S7J 2C7
Tel: 306-374-4448; Fax: 306-373-2665
provincialservices@abilitiescouncil.sk.ca
www.abilitiescouncil.sk.ca
www.linkedin.com/company/saskatchewan-abilities-council
www.facebook.com/saskatchewanabilitiescouncil
twitter.com/skabilitiesyqr
Also Known As: Easter Seals Saskatchewan
Previous Name: Saskatchewan Council for Crippled Children & Adults
Overview: A medium-sized provincial charitable organization founded in 1950 overseen by Easter Seals Canada
Mission: To enhance the independence & community participation of people of varying abilities in Saskatchewan
Membership: *Fees:* $10 minimum annual membership donation; *Member Profile:* Individuals who wish to support the services offered by the Saskatchewan Abilities Council
Activities: Providing vocational, rehabilitation, & recreational services; Operating Camp Easter Seal (campeasterseal@abilitiescouncil.sk.ca); Offering training & employment opportunities; Providing adaptive technology & special needs equipment; Offering special needs transportation; Operating the Farmers with Disabilities Program (farmerswithdisabilities@abilitiescouncil.sk.ca)
Chief Officer(s):
Ian Wilkinson, Executive Director

Regina Branch
825 McDonald St., Regina SK S4N 2X5
Tel: 306-569-9048; Fax: 306-352-3717
regina@abilitiescouncil.sk.ca
www.facebook.com/AbilitiesCouncilRegina

Saskatoon Branch
1410 Kilburn Ave., Saskatoon SK S7M 0J8
Tel: 306-653-1694; Fax: 306-652-8886
saskatoon@abilitiescouncil.sk.ca
www.facebook.com/saskatchewanabilitiescouncil

Swift Current Branch
1551 North Railway St. West, Swift Current SK S9H 5G3
Tel: 306-773-2076; Fax: 306-778-9188
swiftcurrent@abilitiescouncil.sk.ca
www.facebook.com/456001834498239
Chief Officer(s):
Jason Loewer, Regional Director
Sandra Brong, Senior Supervisor, Programs
sbrong@abilitiescouncil.sk.ca

Yorkton Branch
PO Box 5011, 162 Ball Rd., Yorkton SK S3N 3Z4
Tel: 306-782-2463; Fax: 306-782-7844
yorkton@abilitiescouncil.sk.ca
www.facebook.com/saskatchewanabilitiescouncilyorktonregion

Saskatchewan Aboriginal Land Technicians (SALT)
c/o Cowessess First Nation Lands & Resources Dept., PO Box 100, Cowessess SK S0G 5L0
Tel: 306-696-3121; Fax: 306-696-3121
Overview: A small provincial organization overseen by National Aboriginal Lands Managers Association
Staff Member(s): 1
Chief Officer(s):
Denise Pelletier, Director
denise.pelletier@cowessessfn.com

Saskatchewan Aboriginal Women's Circle Corporation
PO Box 1174, Yorkton SK S3N 2X3
Tel: 306-783-1228; Fax: 306-783-1771
sawcc@hotmail.com
Previous Name: Saskatchewan Native Women's Association
Overview: A small provincial organization founded in 1972 overseen by Native Women's Association of Canada
Mission: To walk in balance with guidance by the creator; to unite people together as healthy nations to ensure a better life for future generations
Staff Member(s): 7
Membership: *Fees:* $5; *Member Profile:* Council & member locals
Staff Member(s): 1; 1000 volunteer(s)
Membership: 6,500; *Fees:* Schedule available
Chief Officer(s):
Rhonda Kurbis, Executive Director

Saskatchewan Agricultural Graduates' Association Inc. (SAGA)
College of Agriculture, University of Saskatchewan, Rm 2D27, 51 Campus Dr., Saskatoon SK S7N 5A8
saga.uofs@usask.ca
www.saskaggrads.com
Overview: A small provincial licensing organization founded in 1935
Mission: To promote the social well-being of graduates of the School & College of Agriculture; to ensure close relationships among graduates & between the College & School, including faculty & students; to keep graduates informed of some of the most recent developments in various fields of agriculture; to cooperate with University of Saskatchewan Alumni Association in promoting interests of the University as a whole
Finances: *Annual Operating Budget:* Less than $50,000; *Funding Sources:* Membership fees
20 volunteer(s)
Membership: 2,000; *Fees:* $10 annually; $100 life
Activities: Annual reunion weekend
Chief Officer(s):
Jill Turner, President

Saskatchewan Agricultural Hall of Fame (SAHF)
2610 Lorne Ave. South, Saskatoon SK S7J 0S6
Tel: 306-931-4057
www.sahf.ca
Overview: A small provincial charitable organization founded in 1972
Mission: To honour Saskatchewan people who have contributed to the field of agriculture
Member of: Museums Association of Saskatchewan
Finances: *Annual Operating Budget:* Less than $50,000; *Funding Sources:* Agricultural companies & associations; SK Agriculture & Food grant
Staff Member(s): 1; 5 volunteer(s)
Membership: 23; *Fees:* $25; *Member Profile:* Interest in agriculture; *Committees:* Marketing & Publicity; Executive; Finance; Induction
Activities: *Awareness Events:* Annual Induction Ceremony, Aug.
Chief Officer(s):
Jack Hay, Chair
netherdale@sasktel.net
Valerie Pearson, Secretary

Saskatchewan Alzheimer & Related Diseases Association
See Alzheimer Society of Saskatchewan Inc.

Saskatchewan Amateur Speed Skating Association (SASSA)
2205 Victoria Ave., Regina SK S4P 0S4
Tel: 306-780-9400; Fax: 306-525-4009
sassa@sasktel.net
www.saskspeedskating.ca
www.facebook.com/SaskatchewanSpeedSkating
Previous Name: Saskatchewan Speed Skating Association
Overview: A medium-sized provincial organization overseen by Speed Skating Canada
Mission: Working together to develop & promote the sport of speed skating at all levels as a fun, competitive, healthy, family activity
Member of: Speed Skating Canada
Affiliation(s): Sask Sport Inc.
Finances: *Annual Operating Budget:* $100,000-$250,000; *Funding Sources:* Provincial government
Staff Member(s): 2; 650 volunteer(s)
Membership: 10 institutional; 200 student; 600 individual
Chief Officer(s):
Jordan St. Onge, Executive Director
Awards:
• Dave Thomson Memorial Fund
Awarded to provide financial support to Saskatchewan skaters training at the Calgary Oval. *Eligibility:* A Saskatchewan Amateur Speed Skating Association member named to the Saskatchewan Speed Skating Calgary Oval Program *Deadline:* April; *Amount:* $200
• Dr. Bernie Goplen Award
Awarded to provide financial support to Saskatchewan skaters training at the Calgary Oval. *Eligibility:* A Saskatchewan Amateur Speed Skating Association member who has advanced the sport through dedication & leadership, provided loyal service to the sport &/or fostered & promoted the highest ideals of sportsmanship among participating members

Saskatchewan Amateur Wrestling Association (SAWA)
510 Cynthia St., Saskatoon SK S7L 7K7
Tel: 306-975-0822; Fax: 306-242-8007
sk.wrestling@shaw.ca
www.saskwrestling.com
www.facebook.com/groups/253817611302960
twitter.com/SaskWrestling
Overview: A small provincial organization founded in 1972 overseen by Canadian Amateur Wrestling Association
Mission: To govern & promote the sport of wrestling in Saskatchewan
Finances: *Annual Operating Budget:* $250,000-$500,000; *Funding Sources:* Sasksport; lotteries
Staff Member(s): 1; 12 volunteer(s)
Membership: 700; *Fees:* $65 coach/official/patron/junior, senior, juvenile, cadet athlete; $45 bantam, pee wee, novice, freshie athlete; $15 non-competitive; *Committees:* High Performance; Development; Administration; Finance
Activities: Athlete assistance grants
Chief Officer(s):
Anna-Beth Zulkoskey, Executive Director

Saskatchewan Anti-Tuberculosis League *See* Saskatchewan Lung Association

Saskatchewan Applied Science Technologists & Technicians (SASTT)
363 Park St., Regina SK S4N 5B2
Tel: 306-721-6633; Fax: 306-721-0112
info@sastt.ca
www.sastt.ca
Previous Name: Society of Engineering Technicians & Technologists of Saskatchewan (SETTS)
Overview: A medium-sized provincial licensing organization founded in 1965 overseen by Canadian Council of Technicians & Technologists
Mission: To regulate the professional conduct of applied science technologists & certified technicians in Saskatchewan, in order to protect the public
Affiliation(s): Applied Science Technologists & Technicians of British Columbia; Association of Science & Engineering Technology Professionals of Alberta; Saskatchewan Applied Science Technologists and Technicians; Certified Technicians & Technologists Association of Manitoba; Ontario Association of Certified Engineering Technicians & Technologists; Ordre des technologues preofessionels du Quebec; New Brunswick Society of Certified Engineering Technicians & Technologists; Society of Certified Engineering Technicians & Technologists of Nova Scotia; Island Technology Professionals (PEI)
Finances: *Funding Sources:* Membership fees
Membership: *Fees:* $125 technician/technologist; $90 association; $0 student; *Member Profile:* Individuals who have a recognized level of post-secondary academic & practical training in a specialized applied science or engineering technology field in Saskatchewan
Activities: Increasing the knowledge of applied science technologists & certified technicians; Raising awareness & understanding of applied science technologists & certified technicians
Awards:
• ASET / SASTT Lloydminster Scholarship
To recognize a graduating student from a high school in the attendance area of The Lloydminster Bi-Provincial Chapter of ASET / SASTT, who plans to continue his or her education in applied science technology, information technology, or engineering technology *Deadline:* August 20; *Amount:* $500
• Outstanding Technical Achievement Award
To recognize excellence in professional life
• Outstanding Employer Award
To recognize outstanding technical achievement by employers of applied science & engineering technologists & technicians in Saskatchewan
• Merit Award
To recognize persons who have distinguished themselves in the service of the association
• Applied Research Project Award
To recognize the outstanding achievement of a graduating student *Deadline:* June 30
• SASTT Student Awards
To recognize students from recognized programs at Saskatoon's Kelsey Campus, Moose Jaw's Palliser Campus, & Regina's Wascana Campus; *Amount:* $250
Publications:
• Saskatchewan Applied Science Technologists & Technicians Salary Survey

Canadian Associations / Saskatchewan Archaeological Society (SAS)

Type: Survey; *Frequency:* Annually
Profile: Information distributed to all Saskatchewan Applied Science Technologists & Technicians members
• SASTT [Saskatchewan Applied Science Technologists & Technicians] Journal
Type: Journal; *Frequency:* Quarterly; *Accepts Advertising*
Profile: Technical articles, association news, & upcoming events

Saskatchewan Archaeological Society (SAS)
#1, 1730 Quebec Ave., Saskatoon SK S7K 1V9
Tel: 306-664-4124; *Fax:* 306-665-1928
saskarchsoc@sasktel.net
www.saskarchsoc.ca
ca.linkedin.com/pub/saskatchewan-archaeological-society/77/372/436
www.facebook.com/137032406371156
twitter.com/saskarchsoc
Overview: A medium-sized provincial charitable organization founded in 1963 overseen by Canadian Archaeological Association
Mission: To promote & conserve archaeology
Member of: Council of Affiliated Societies; Plains Anthropological Society; SaskCulture Inc.; Multicultural Council of Saskatchewan; Architectural Heritage Society of Saskatchewan
Affiliation(s): Society for American Archaeology; Plains Anthropological Society
Finances: *Annual Operating Budget:* $250,000-$500,000; *Funding Sources:* Saskatchewan Lotteries; Self-generated funds
Staff Member(s): 3; 20 volunteer(s)
Membership: 350; *Fees:* $20 student or senior; $25 active membership; $35 family, institutional, school, or chapter; $350 lifetime membership; $450 couple life membership; *Committees:* Advocacy; Archaeological Conservation; Awards; Education; Festivals & Special Events; Finance & Fundraising; Management; Member Funding; Membership / Publicity
Activities: Promoting & carrying out eduational programs such as a field school, workshops, & tours; *Library:* Saskatchewan Archaeological Society Resource Centre; Open to public by appointment
Chief Officer(s):
Tomasin Playford, Executive Director
saskarchsoc@sasktel.net
Belinda Riehl-Fitzsimmons, Business Administrator
Awards:
• William A. Marjerrison Award
• Honourary Life Membership
• Certificate of Appreciation
• Saskatchewan Archaeological Society Newsletter
Type: Newsletter; *Frequency:* Quarterly; *Editor:* Belinda Riehl-Fitzsimmons
Profile: The newsletter publishes articles on archeology, history & geology

Archaeological & Historical Society of West Central Saskatchewan
Eatonia SK
Tel: 306-967-2266
Chief Officer(s):
Ted Douglas, Contact
ted.al.douglas@sasktel.net

Eagle Creek Historical Society
Rosetown SK
Chief Officer(s):
Sharon Farrell, Contact
sharon.farrell@sasktel.net

Northwest Archaeological Society
North Battleford SK
Tel: 306-445-2549
Chief Officer(s):
Jeff Baldwin, Contact
jefflaw@sasktel.net

Regina Archaeological Society
Regina SK
reginaarchaeological.zzl.org

Saskatchewan Association of Professional Archaeologists (SAPA)
PO Box 8954, Saskatoon SK S7K 6S7
sapaexec@gmail.com
www.saskarchaeologist.org
Chief Officer(s):
Mike Markowski, President

Saskatoon Archaeological Society
PO Box 328, RPO University, Saskatoon SK S7N 4J8
Tel: 306-244-4650; *Fax:* 306-966-5640
saskatoon.archaeology@gmail.com
saskatoonarchaeologicalsociety.zzl.org
Chief Officer(s):
David Meyer, President

South West Saskatchewan Archaeological Society
Swift Current SK
Chief Officer(s):
Jim Worrell, Contact, 306-774-5255
jamesworrell@sasktel.net

Saskatchewan Archery Association (SAA)
c/o Gil Segovia, President, 335 Brooklyn Cres., Warman SK S0K 0A1
Tel: 306-370-0640
www.saskarchery.com
www.facebook.com/SaskatchewanArcheryAssociation
Overview: A small provincial organization overseen by Archery Canada Tir à l'Arc
Mission: To foster, to perpetuate & direct the practice of Archery in a spirit of good fellowship & sportsmanship.
Member of: Archery Canada Tir à l'Arc
Finances: *Annual Operating Budget:* $50,000-$100,000 20 volunteer(s)
Membership: 850; *Fees:* $45 adult; $25 youth (17 & under)
Chief Officer(s):
Gil Segovia, President
gil@segovia-sask.com
Publications:
• Saskatchewan Archery Association Newsletter
Type: Newsletter
Profile: News & updates for members

Saskatchewan Arts Board (SAB)
1355 Broad St., Regina SK S4R 7V1
Tel: 306-787-4056; *Fax:* 306-787-4199
Toll-Free: 800-667-7526
info@saskartsboard.ca
www.saskartsboard.ca
twitter.com/saskartsboard
Overview: A medium-sized provincial organization founded in 1948
Mission: To cultivate an environment in which the arts thrive for the benefit of everyone in Saskatchewan
Finances: *Annual Operating Budget:* $3 Million-$5 Million; *Funding Sources:* Provincial government
Staff Member(s): 13
Membership: 1-99; *Committees:* Aboriginal Advisor; Governance
Activities: *Library:* by appointment
Chief Officer(s):
Michael Jones, CEO
mjones@saskartsboard.ca
Gail Paul Armstrong, Director, Administration
gparmstrong@saskartsboard.ca

Saskatchewan Association for Community Living (SACL)
3031 Louise St., Saskatoon SK S7J 3L1
Tel: 306-955-3344; *Fax:* 306-373-3070
sacl@sacl.org
www.sacl.org
www.facebook.com/SaskACL
twitter.com/thesacl
www.youtube.com/SACL3031
Overview: A medium-sized provincial charitable organization founded in 1955 overseen by Canadian Association for Community Living
Mission: To enhance the lives of individuals with intellectual disabilities throughout Saskatchewan; To develop programs & services to meet the needs of people with intellectual disabilities
Member of: Canadian Association for Community Living
Finances: *Funding Sources:* Donations; Fundraising
Activities: Engaging in advocacy activities to support persons with disabilities & their families; Creating networking opportunities, through the SACL Family Network; Connecting people to community resources; *Awareness Events:* International Day of Persons with Disabilities, December *Library:* John Dolan Resource Centre; Open to public
Chief Officer(s):
Kevin McTavish, Executive Director, 306-955-3344 Ext. 129
Christina Martens-Funk, Director, Finance, 306-955-3344 Ext. 111
Connie Andersen, Director, Community Development, 306-955-3344 Ext. 126
Travis Neufeld, Manager, Communications & Marketing, 306-955-3344 Ext. 120
Nicole Graham, Coordinator, Youth Program & Family Network, 306-955-3344 Ext. 123
Publications:
• Dialect [a publication of the Saskatchewan Association for Community Living]
Type: Magazine; *Frequency:* Semiannually
Profile: Stories, informative articles, & branch news
• School to Life Transition Handbook [a publication of the Saskatchewan Association for Community Living]
Type: Handbook
Profile: Stories of successful transitions, & steps for transition from school to adult life

Saskatchewan Association for Multicultural Education (SAME)
2454 Atkinson St., Regina SK S4N 3X5
Tel: 306-780-9428
same@sk.sympatico.ca
Overview: A medium-sized provincial organization founded in 1984
Mission: To promote multicultual & anti-racist education throughout Saskatchewan; To raise awareness & acceptance of cultural diversity in the province; To respond to changes in multicultural policies & demographics; To address social justice issues
Finances: *Funding Sources:* Canadian Heritage; Saskatchewan Lotteries; SaskCulture; Multicultural Council of Saskatchewan
Activities: Collaborating with other organizations to further educational opportunities to learn more about other cultures; Supporting formal & informal multicultural & intercultural education; Organizing workshops & conferences to explore issues of racism; Fostering research & projects to increase recognition of cultural identity & equity; Providing resources & advice to assist teachers
Publications:
• Saskatchewan Cultural Profiles
Profile: A set of profiles identifying holidays & celebrations

Saskatchewan Association of Agricultural Societies & Exhibitions (SAASE)
PO Box 31025, Regina SK S4R 8R6
Tel: 306-565-2121; *Fax:* 306-565-2079
www.saase.ca
Overview: A medium-sized provincial organization founded in 1987
Mission: To provide the forum for exchange of ideas among Association members; to provide educational opportunities for members; to address relevant issues affecting members; to provide for district, board & provincial meetings of members; to promote fair & agricultural industry; to help promote & form new societies; to provide a liaison with the extension program of University of Saskatchewan; to assist governments & universities to reach their agricultural & educational objectives
Member of: Foundation for Animal Care Saskatchewan; International Association of Fairs & Exhibitions; Agriculture in the Classroom
Affiliation(s): Canadian Association of Fairs & Exhibitions
Membership: 76 organizations; *Fees:* $200 associate
Chief Officer(s):
Glen Duck, Executive Director
gduck.saase@sasktel.net

Saskatchewan Association of Architects (SAA)
200 - 642 Broadway Ave., Saskatoon SK S7N 1A9
Tel: 306-242-0733; *Fax:* 306-664-2598
www.saskarchitects.com
Overview: A medium-sized provincial licensing organization founded in 1906
Mission: To regulate the profession of architecture in Saskatchewan, in order to ensure the protection of the public interest; To advance the profession of architecture in the province; To ensure that high standards for practice & conduct are followed
Staff Member(s): 4
Membership: *Fees:* Schedule available; *Member Profile:* Registered architects; Non-practising architects; Students of architecture; Architectural interns; Retired architects; Corporations & firms; *Committees:* Communications; Education; Executive; Nominations; Practice
Activities: Providing continuing education programs
Chief Officer(s):
Janelle Unrau, Executive Director

Saskatchewan Association of Certified Nursing Assistants
See Saskatchewan Association of Licensed Practical Nurses

Saskatchewan Association of Chiropodists (SAC)
100 - 2nd Ave. NE, Moose Jaw SK S6H 1B8
Tel: 306-691-6405; *Fax:* 306-691-3608
asta@fhhr.ca
Also Known As: Podiatry Association of Saskatchewan
Overview: A small provincial organization founded in 1943
Mission: To participate in the improvement of podiatry; To increase the scope & availability of practitioners in Saskatchewan; To encourage continuing post-graduate education in order to keep up with current trends
Activities: Legislative changes to podiatry; Promote public awareness; Diabetes foot health; Regulation of the profession in Saskatchewan

Saskatchewan Association of Health Organizations (SAHO)
#500, 2002 Victoria Ave., Regina SK S4P 0R7
Tel: 306-347-1740; *Fax:* 306-347-1043
www.saho.ca
Overview: A small provincial charitable organization founded in 1993 overseen by Canadian Healthcare Association
Mission: To serve members through services, support, & programs
Finances: *Funding Sources:* Membership fees; Government grants; Fee-for-service revenue; Interest revenue
Membership: *Member Profile:* Saskatchewan health agencies
Activities: Providing education for boards & administrators; Assisting with collective bargaining & employee relations; Offering payroll services, group purchasing, benefits administration
Publications:
• Health Matters
Type: Magazine; *Frequency:* Quarterly
Profile: Issues in the health care system

Saskatchewan Association of Human Resource Professionals; Saskatchewan Council of Human Resource Associations See Chartered Professionals in Human Resources Saskatchewan

Saskatchewan Association of Insolvency & Restructuring Professionals (SAIRP)
c/o Deloitte Restructuring Inc., #5, 77 - 15 St. East, Prince Albert SK S6V 1E9
Tel: 306-763-7411; *Fax:* 306-763-0191
Previous Name: Saskatchewan Insolvency Practitioners Association
Overview: A small provincial organization overseen by Canadian Association of Insolvency & Restructuring Professionals
Member of: Canadian Association of Insolvency & Restructuring Professionals
Chief Officer(s):
Victoria Doell, President
vdoell@deloitte.ca

Saskatchewan Association of Landscape Architects (SALA)
PO Box 20015, Regina SK S4P 4J7
www.sala.sk.ca
Overview: A small provincial organization founded in 1980 overseen by Canadian Society of Landscape Architects
Mission: To promote, improve, & advance the profession of landscape architecture; To maintain standards of professional practice & conduct
Member of: Canadian Society of Landscape Architects
Membership: *Fees:* $430 full; $259.90 out-of-province; $100 associate and allied; $20 student; *Member Profile:* Landscape architects in Saskatchewan
Chief Officer(s):
Laureen Snook, President
president@sala.sk.ca
Awards:
• SALA Academic Award
Based on academic standing and qualities of character, leadership skills and participation in student and community activities. *Eligibility:* Resident of Saskatchewan; enrolled in relevant academic program; *Amount:* $1000
• Design Excellence Awards

Saskatchewan Association of Library Technicians, Inc. (SALT)
PO Box 24019, Saskatoon SK S7K 8B4
sasksalt@gmail.com
www.sasksalt.ca
www.facebook.com/sasksalt
Overview: A small provincial organization founded in 1976
Mission: To support library technicians throughout Saskatchewan
Finances: *Funding Sources:* Membership fees; Donations; Fundraising
Membership: *Fees:* $10 student/unemployed/retired; $25 regular members; $40 institutions; *Member Profile:* Institutions throughout Saskatchewan; Graduate library technicians; Librarians; Library clerks & assistants; Students; Persons interested in the development of libraries & library technology
Activities: Fostering the exchange of information among library technicians; Providing continuing education in library technology; Liaising with other library associations
Chief Officer(s):
Nicolle DeGagne, President
nicdegagne@hotmail.com
Elisabeth Eilinger, Secretary & Treasurer
elisabeth.eilinger@sasktel.net
Awards:
• Dorothy Roberts Scholarship
Deadline: January; *Amount:* $300
Meetings/Conferences:
• Saskatchewan Association of Library Technicians 2018 Annual General Meeting & Fall Workshops, 2018, SK
Scope: Provincial
Description: A business meeting, speakers, & networking opportunities for library technicians from Saskatchewan
Contact Information: E-mail: sasksalt@gmail.com

Saskatchewan Association of Licensed Practical Nurses (SALPN)
#700A, 4400 - 4th Ave., Regina SK S4T 0H8
Tel: 306-525-1436; *Fax:* 306-347-7784
Toll-Free: 888-257-2576
admin@salpn.com
www.salpn.com
Previous Name: Saskatchewan Association of Certified Nursing Assistants
Overview: A medium-sized provincial licensing organization founded in 1957 overseen by Canadian Council of Practical Nurse Regulators
Mission: To regulate Licensed Practical Nurses (LPNs) in Saskatchewan, in order to ensure public safety; To ensure that Saskatchewan's Licensed Practical Nurses provide professional nursing care; To maintain an efficient investigation & disciplinary process
Staff Member(s): 7
Membership: *Member Profile:* Graduates; Practising licensed practical nurses; Non-practising licensed practical nurses; Honourary members; *Committees:* Awards & Recognition; Counselling & Investigation; Discipline
Activities: Registering & issuing licenses to Licensed Practical Nurses; Ensuring ethical practice; Providing continuing education program
Chief Officer(s):
Kari Pruden, President
kpruden@salpn.com
Lynsay Nair, Executive Director
lnair@salpn.com
Cara Brewster, Registrar
cbrewster@salpn.com
Awards:
• LPN of Distinction Award
To recognize exemplary service to the public
• Mentorship Award
• Lifetime Achievement Award

Saskatchewan Association of Medical Radiation Technologists (SAMRT)
#218, 408 Broad St., Regina SK S4R 1X3
Tel: 306-525-9678; *Fax:* 306-525-9680
info@samrt.org
samrt.org
Previous Name: Saskatchewan Society of X-Ray Technicians
Overview: A small provincial organization founded in 1940 overseen by Canadian Association of Medical Radiation Technologists
Mission: To serve & protect the public by regulating the practice of the profession of medical radiation technology
Finances: *Annual Operating Budget:* $250,000-$500,000
Membership: 633; *Fees:* $100 students; $130 associate members; $150 restricted license; $355 active members (SAMRT license); $200 non-practicing members (SAMRT); *Member Profile:* Persons involved in the technological disciplines of nuclear medicine, radiology, radiation therapy, & magnetic resonance imaging; *Committees:* Discipline; Professional Conduct; Audit; Ownership Linkage; Awards; Nominations; Credentials; Professional Development; Professional Practice
Activities: Offering continuing educational opportunities to members; Providing public education about the profession
Chief Officer(s):
Peter Derrick, President
Bashir Jalloh, Vice-President
Chelsea Wilker, Executive Director
chelseawilker@samrt.org
Publications:
• SAMRT Newsletter
Type: Newsletter; *Frequency:* Quarterly
Profile: Reports from the Saskatchewan Association of Medical Radiation Technologists, upcoming seminars, plus updates on legislation & bylaws, health & safety, & professional practice

Saskatchewan Association of Naturopathic Practitioners (SANP)
2706 13th Ave., Regina SK S4T 1N7
Tel: 306-543-4325; *Fax:* 306-543-4330
info@sanp.ca
www.sanp.ca
www.facebook.com/SaskNDs
Overview: A small provincial licensing organization overseen by The Canadian Association of Naturopathic Doctors
Mission: To act as the governing body for naturopathic doctors in Saskatchewan; To license & regulate naturopathic physicians in the province; To ensure members are educated & trained according to strict standards
Membership: *Member Profile:* Licensed naturopathic doctors in Saskatchewan; *Committees:* Communications; Conference; Discipline; Examination/Continuing Education/Audit; Financial Audit; Legislative & Quality Assurance; Membership; Professional Conduct
Activities: Encouraging continuing medical education; Providing information about naturopathic medicine, from regulation to health topics; Resolving complaints about concerns with naturopathic physicians
Chief Officer(s):
Laura Stark, President
president@sanp.ca
Wendy Presant-Jahn, Vice-President
vicepresident@sanp.ca
Kathleen Fyffe, Secretary
secretary@sanp.ca
Jacqui Fleury, Treasurer, 306-373-5209
treasurer@sanp.ca
Vanessa DiCicco, Registrar
registrar@sanp.ca

Saskatchewan Association of Optometrists (SAO)
#108, 2366 Ave. C North, Saskatoon SK S7L 5X5
Tel: 306-652-2069; *Fax:* 306-652-2642
Toll-Free: 877-660-3937
admin@saosk.ca
optometrists.sk.ca
twitter.com/SaskEyecare
Previous Name: Saskatchewan Optometric Association
Overview: A medium-sized provincial licensing organization founded in 1909 overseen by Canadian Association of Optometrists
Mission: To license the delivery of optometric care in Saskatchewan; To regulate doctors of optometry throughout the province; To ensure excellence in the delivery of vision & eye health services across Saskatchewan; To enforce high standards of optometric eye care, in order to protect the public; To act as the voice of optometry in Saskatchewan
Membership: *Member Profile:* Licensed doctors of optometry; Students
Activities: Providing information about vision & eye health to the government, other health organizations, the public, & the media; Coordinating an occupational vision care program; Offering programs & services to promote optometry; *Speaker Service:* Yes; *Library:* Patient Education Library
Chief Officer(s):
Sheila Spence, Executive Director
ed@saosk.ca
Publications:
• Eye on SAO
Type: Newsletter; *Frequency:* Monthly; *Price:* Free with membership in the Saskatchewan Association of Optometrists

Saskatchewan Association of Prosthetists & Orthotists (SAPO)
c/o Orthotics Prosthetics Canada, #202, 300 March Rd., Ottawa ON K2K 2E2

Overview: A small provincial organization founded in 1999 overseen by Orthotics Prosthetics Canada
Mission: To represent the prosthetic & orthotic field in Saskatchewan
Membership: *Member Profile:* Individuals involved in the prosthetic & orthotic field throughout Saskatchewan
Activities: Promoting high standards of care & professionalism; Encouraging continuing education

Saskatchewan Association of Recreation Professionals (SARP)
88 Saskatchewan St. East, Moose Jaw SK S6H 0V4
Tel: 306-693-7277; *Fax:* 306-988-8839
office@sarponlin.ca
www.sarp-online.ca
www.facebook.com/165792676792454
Also Known As: Saskatchewan Recreation Society
Overview: A medium-sized provincial organization founded in 1970
Mission: To be committed to supporting & being the voice of professionals working in the field of recreation in Saskatchewan
Finances: *Funding Sources:* Saskatchewan Lotteries
Membership: *Fees:* $100 professional; $75 affiliate; $60 associate; $40 alumni; free for students
Activities: Offering professional development activities & networking; Developing professional standards
Chief Officer(s):
Nicole Goldsworthy, Chair
Awards:
• Education Assistance Grant
• Professional Development Grant
• The Roy Ellis Bursary
• Employer Professional Development Award
• Annual Achievement Award
Publications:
• Saskatchewan Association of Recreation Professionals Update Newsletter
Type: Newsletter; *Frequency:* 3 pa

Saskatchewan Association of Rehabilitation Centres (SARC)
111 Cardinal Cres., Saskatoon SK S7L 6H5
Tel: 306-933-0616; *Fax:* 306-653-3932
contact@sarcan.sk.ca
www.sarcsarcan.ca
www.facebook.com/487285284623365
twitter.com/sarc_sk
Overview: A medium-sized provincial charitable organization founded in 1968
Mission: To provide vision, leadership & support to agencies through advocacy, education, provision & development of employment opportunities
Member of: Saskatchewan Association of Rehabilitation Centres
Membership: 81
Activities: Network of organizations which provide vocational & residential services to persons with disabilites

Saskatchewan Association of Rural Municipalities (SARM)
2075 Hamilton St., Regina SK S4P 2E1
Tel: 306-757-3577; *Fax:* 306-565-2141
Toll-Free: 800-667-3604
sarm@sarm.ca
www.sarm.ca
Overview: A medium-sized provincial organization founded in 1905
Mission: To represent & advocate for rural municipal government in Saskatchewan
Membership: 296; *Member Profile:* Rural municipalities in Saskatchewan
Activities: Researching policies; Reviewing legislation; Providing employee benefits, municipal insurance, & fuel supply programs
Chief Officer(s):
Dale Harvey, Executive Director, 306-761-3721
dharvey@sarm.ca
David Marit, President
dmarit@sasktel.net
Meetings/Conferences:
• Saskatchewan Association of Rural Municipalities 2018 Annual Convention, March, 2018, Evraz Place, Regina, SK
Scope: Provincial
Attendance: 2,000
Publications:
• Rural Councillor

Type: Magazine; *Frequency:* Bimonthly; *Accepts Advertising*
Profile: Issues facing rural Saskatchewan

Saskatchewan Association of School Councils (SASC)
#301, 221 Cumberland Ave. North, Saskatoon SK S7N 1M3
Tel: 306-955-5723; *Fax:* 306-445-7707
sasc@sasktel.net
Previous Name: Saskatchewan Federation of Home & School Associations
Overview: A medium-sized provincial charitable organization founded in 1938 overseen by Canadian Home & School Federation
Mission: To enhance the education & general well-being of children & youth; To promote the involvement of parents, students, educators & the community at large in the advancement of learning & to act as a voice for parents; To promote effective communication between the home & the school; To encourage parents to participate in educational activities & decision making
Finances: *Funding Sources:* Government grant; Membership fees; Donations
Membership: *Member Profile:* Parents of school children
Activities: Offering leadership workshops, resources, & speaker sessions

Saskatchewan Association of Social Workers (SASW) / Association des travailleurs sociaux de la Saskatchewan
Edna Osborne House, 2110 Lorne St., Regina SK S4P 2M5
Tel: 306-545-1922; *Fax:* 306-545-1895
Toll-Free: 877-517-7279
sasw@accesscomm.ca
www.sasw.ca
Overview: A medium-sized provincial licensing organization founded in 1962
Mission: To conduct the work of a professional regulator; To act as the voice of social workers in Saskatchewan; To develop & maintain standards of knowledge, skill, conduct, & competence among members to serve & protect the public interest
Member of: Canadian Association of Social Workers (CASW); Association of Social Work Boards (ASWB)
Finances: *Funding Sources:* Membership dues
Membership: *Fees:* Schedule available; *Member Profile:* Individuals with a certificate, bachelor, master, or doctorate in social work; Students; *Committees:* Professional Conduct; Discipline; Standards of Practice; Public Relations; Student Award; Health Services; Social Justice; Practice Ethics; Education; Newsletter; Psychologists Act Task Team; Aboriginal Social Workers Task Team
Activities: Lobbying the Saskatchewan provincial government & others for improvement in the status & recognition of social workers; Offering continuing education opportunities; Providing a means for members to take action on social policy issues; *Awareness Events:* Social Work Week, March *Library:* Saskatchewan Association of Social Workers Library
Chief Officer(s):
Kirk Englot, President
Awards:
• SASW Student Awards
Presented to a Saskatchewan social work student in recognition of contributions to the community, beyond the immediate requirements of education & employment
• SASW Distinguished Service Award
To honour outstanding contributions in any area of social work practice
Meetings/Conferences:
• Saskatchewan Association of Social Workers 2018 Annual General Meeting & Provincial Conference, 2018, SK
Scope: Provincial
Description: A conference usually held each April at one of the association's branch locations
Publications:
• Saskatchewan Association of Social Workers Annual Report
Type: Yearbook; *Frequency:* Annually
• Saskatchewan Social Worker
Type: Newsletter; *Frequency:* 3 pa; *Accepts Advertising; Editor:* R. Yachiw (ryachiw@cr.gov.sk.ca); *Price:* Free with membership in the Saskatchewan Association of Social Workers
Profile: Current events & reports of the Saskatchewan Association of Social Workers, plus articles, the CASW section, & the University of Regina Faculty of Social Worksection

Saskatchewan Association of Speech-Language Pathologists & Audiologists (SASLPA)
#11, 2010 - 7th Ave., Regina SK S4R 1C2

Tel: 306-757-3990; *Fax:* 306-757-3986
Toll-Free: 800-757-3990
saslpa@sasktel.net
www.saslpa.ca
twitter.com/SASLPA
Overview: A small provincial licensing organization founded in 1957
Mission: To encourage public awareness, professional development & quality service in the fields of speech-language pathology & audiology in the province
Member of: Canadian Association of Speech-Language Pathologists & Audiologists
Finances: *Funding Sources:* Membership fees
Membership: *Fees:* $600 practicing; $480 non-practicing; $600 provisional; $50 retired; *Member Profile:* Practicing & non-practicing speech therapists; *Committees:* Registration & Membership; Legislation & Bylaws; Professional Conduct; Discipline; Professional Development; Audiology; Private Practice; Website
Activities: Provides information about communication disorders & appropriate treatment resources; identifies issues & concerns through discussions with consumer groups, governments departments & other associations; establishes minimum standards for practice; investigates concerns regarding members & services; assists consumers in advocating for speech, language & hearing services; sponsors workshops & seminars; *Awareness Events:* Speech & Hearing Month, May
Chief Officer(s):
Kathy Carroll, Executive Director
ed.saslpa@sasktel.net
Publications:
• Private Practice Directory [a publication of the Saskatchewan Association of Speech-Language Pathologists & Audiologists]
Type: Directory

Saskatchewan Association of the Appraisal Institute of Canada See The Appraisal Institute of Canada - Saskatchewan

Saskatchewan Association of Veterinary Technologists, Inc. (SAVT)
PO Box 346, Stn. University, Saskatoon SK S7N 4J8
Tel: 306-931-2957; *Fax:* 855-861-6255
Toll-Free: 866-811-7288
www.savt.ca
www.facebook.com/SaskVetTech
twitter.com/SaskVetTech
Overview: A small provincial licensing organization founded in 1984
Mission: To promote recognition of the profession, offer opportunities for educational advancement, improve animal health & welfare & support its members
Member of: Canadian Association of Animal Health Technologists & Technicians
Finances: *Funding Sources:* Membership dues
Membership: *Fees:* $0 student; $100 non practicing; $185 active; *Member Profile:* Graduate of a formal, approved course in animal health technology/veterinary technology; Student in an approved animal health technology/veterinary technology program; Associate member is an individual out of the province of Saskatchewan
Activities: Registering veterinary technologists in Saskatchewan; Promoting the profession through public relations; Communicating for the profession regarding legislation; Developing & maintaining a Code of Ethics
Chief Officer(s):
Nadine Schuelle, Executive Director
Nicole Wood, President
president@savt.ca
Awards:
• Award of Appreciation
• Award of Merit
• SAVT Bursary
Publications:
• SAVT Newsletter
Type: Newsletter; *Editor:* Nadine Schueller RVT

Saskatchewan Athletic Therapists Association (SATA)
309B Durham Dr., Regina SK S4S 4Z4
Tel: 306-291-6069
info@saskathletictherapy.ca
www.saskathletictherapy.ca
twitter.com/therapySK
Overview: A small provincial organization
Mission: To certify, regulate, & discipline athletic therapists in Saskatchewan in order to protect the public

Member of: Canadian Athletic Therapists Association; Athletic Therapists in Canada
Membership: *Member Profile:* Athletic therapists in Saskatchewan; *Committees:* Ethics; Insurance Billing
Chief Officer(s):
Nicole Renneberg, President
president@saskathletictherapy.ca

Saskatchewan Athletics
2020 College Dr., Saskatoon SK S7N 2W4
Tel: 306-664-6744; *Fax:* 306-664-6761
athletics@sasktel.net
www.saskathletics.ca
twitter.com/SaskAthletics
Overview: A small provincial organization overseen by Athletics Canada
Mission: Promotes the sport of athletics by facilitating the development & maintenance of effective programs which assists athletes, coaches, officials, & volunteers in a fair & positive environment
Member of: Athletics Canada
Finances: *Funding Sources:* Saskatchewan Lotteries; Athletics Canada; Sask Sport Inc.; Corporate sponsorships
Staff Member(s): 3
Chief Officer(s):
Alan Sharp, President
asharp@mail.gssd.ca
Bob Reindl, Executive Director
Janine Platana, Administrative Assistant

Saskatchewan Automobile Dealers Association (SADA)
610 Broad St., Regina SK S4R 8H8
Tel: 306-721-2208; *Fax:* 306-721-1009
info@saskautodealers.com
www.saskautodealers.com
Overview: A medium-sized provincial organization
Mission: To address issues faced by automobile & truck dealers; To advance the interests of members
Affiliation(s): Canadian Automobile Dealers Association
Membership: *Member Profile:* Franchised new automobile & truck dealers in Saskatchewan
Activities: Providing advocacy on behalf of members; Organizing fundraising events
Chief Officer(s):
Susan Buckle, Executive Director

Saskatchewan Badminton Association (SBA)
55 Dunsmore Dr., Regina SK S4R 7G1
Tel: 306-780-9368
saskbadminton@sasktel.net
www.saskbadminton.ca
www.facebook.com/SaskatchewanBadminton
Overview: A small provincial organization overseen by Badminton Canada
Mission: To develop & promote badminton in Saskatchewan
Staff Member(s): 1
Chief Officer(s):
Frank Gaudet, Executive Director

Saskatchewan Band Association (SBA)
34 Sunset Dr. North, Yorkton SK S3N 3K9
Tel: 306-783-2263; *Fax:* 866-221-1879
Toll-Free: 877-475-2263
sask.band@sasktel.net
www.saskband.org
www.facebook.com/saskband
Overview: A medium-sized provincial charitable organization founded in 1983 overseen by Canadian Band Association
Mission: To promote & support instrumental music in Saskatchewan; To act as a voice on issues that affect bands in Saskatchewan
Member of: Canadian Band Association
Finances: *Funding Sources:* Donations; Sponsorships; Saskatchewan Lotteries Trust Fund for Sport, Culture & Recreation; SaskCulture; Saskatchewan Arts Board
Membership: *Fees:* $10 students; $25 retired individuals; $50 regular individuals & organizations; $200 corporate members; *Member Profile:* Individuals in Saskatchewan who wish to further the development of bands; Students; Retired individuals; Organizations, such as school bands & community bands; Corporations
Activities: Supporting bands & band students in Saskatchewan; Providing learning & performance opportunities for performers; Engaging in advocacy activities for bands in schools & communities; Sponsoring band camps & festivals & mentorship programs; Facilitating networking opportunities; Liaising with similar organizations
Chief Officer(s):
Chad Huel, President
c.huel@rcsd.ca
Awards:
• Beverley Shore Memorial Scholarship
To recognize a volunteer who has made an outstanding contribution to band in Saskatchewan *Eligibility:* Saskatchewan students enrolled in their first year of Music Education, majoring in instrumental music at the University of Regina or University of Saskatchewan *Deadline:* September 30; *Amount:* $1,000
• Saskatchewan Band Association Distinguished Band Director Award
To recognize a band director in Saskatchewan who has made an outstanding contribution to band *Eligibility:* A director who has made a notable contribution to band in Saskatchewan *Deadline:* September 20
• Distinguished Saskatchewan Music Volunteer Award
To recognize a volunteer who has made an outstanding contribution to band in Saskatchewan *Eligibility:* A volunteer who has demonstrated an outstanding contribution to the band in the province
• Outstanding Administrator Award
To recognize a volunteer who has made an outstanding contribution to band in Saskatchewan *Eligibility:* A current school administrator who has made an outstanding contribution to the success of music education in Saskatchewan
Publications:
• Saskatchewan Band Association eNews
Type: Newsletter; *Frequency:* Weekly; *Accepts Advertising*
Profile: Information about association programs & serives, members, scholarships, plus forthcoming band festivals, camps, & seminars

Saskatchewan Baseball Association (SBA)
1870 Lorne St., Regina SK S4P 2L7
Tel: 306-780-9237; *Fax:* 306-352-3669
www.saskbaseball.ca
www.facebook.com/101500956741303 84
twitter.com/baseballsask
Overview: A medium-sized provincial organization founded in 1959 overseen by Baseball Canada
Mission: To provide quality baseball programs to interested participants at whatever level they may choose
Member of: Baseball Canada; International Baseball Association; Sask Sport; Western Canada Baseball Association
Finances: *Annual Operating Budget:* $250,000-$500,000; *Funding Sources:* Lottery proceeds
Staff Member(s): 3
Membership: 14,000; *Fees:* Schedule available
Chief Officer(s):
Mike Ramage, Executive Director

Saskatchewan Basketball *See* Basketball Saskatchewan

Saskatchewan Baton Twirling Association (SBTA)
510 Cynthia St., Saskatoon SK S7L 7K4
Tel: 306-975-0847; *Fax:* 306-242-8007
skbaton@shaw.ca
www.saskbaton.com
Also Known As: Sask Baton
Overview: A small provincial organization overseen by Canadian Baton Twirling Federation
Mission: To be the provincial governing body for the sport of baton twirling in Saskatchewan
Member of: Canadian Baton Twirling Federation
Finances: *Funding Sources:* Sask Sport Inc.; SaskTel
Chief Officer(s):
Theresa Porter, Chair
Brenda O'Connor, Sport Coordinator

Saskatchewan Bed & Breakfast Association (SBBA)
SK
Tel: 306-789-3259
bbsask@gmail.com
www.bbsask.ca
Previous Name: Saskatchewan Country Vacations Association
Overview: A small provincial organization founded in 1972
Mission: To provide marketing, information & networking programs to increase members' growth & success
Member of: Tourism Saskatchewan
Finances: *Annual Operating Budget:* $50,000-$100,000; *Funding Sources:* Membership fees
Staff Member(s): 1; 6 volunteer(s)
Membership: 80; *Fees:* $145; *Member Profile:* Accredited bed & breakfast & country vacation operators in Saskatchewan
Chief Officer(s):
Cathy Currey, Director

Saskatchewan Beekeepers Association (SBA)
PO Box 55, RR#3, Yorkton SK S3N 2X5
Tel: 306-743-5469; *Fax:* 306-743-5528
whowland@accesscomm.ca
www.saskbeekeepers.com
Overview: A small provincial organization founded in 1923
Mission: To support Saskatchewan's beekeeping industry; To represent the province's beekeeping industry at both the provincial & national levels
Affiliation(s): Canadian Honey Council (CHC)
Finances: *Funding Sources:* Donations; Sponsorships; Agriculture Council of Saskatchewan's (ACS) Canadian Agriculture Adaptation Program (CAAP)
Membership: 250+; *Fees:* $30 / year (minimum) or $0.35 / hive; $30 / year associates; *Member Profile:* Commercial & hobby beekeepers in Saskatchewan
Activities: Providing information & education to Saskatchewan beekeepers, on topics such as wildlife damage compensation; Offering an annual field day to focus on beekeeping issues & to showcase a local producer; Conducting research, on subjects such as pollination needs, mite control, & nectar production; Providing a bear fence subsidy program & a crop advance program; *Awareness Events:* Day of the Honey Bee, May; Honey Month, October
Chief Officer(s):
Calvin Parsons, President, 306-864-2632
Corey Bacon, Vice-President, 306-864-3774, Fax: 306-864-3260
Wink Howland, Secetary-Treasurer, 306-783-7046, Fax: 306-786-6001
Dennis Glennie, Coordinator, SBA Bear Fence Program
Meetings/Conferences:
• Saskatchewan Beekeepers Association 2018 Annual Convention, 2018, SK
Scope: Provincial
Description: Featuring speakers & research results
Publications:
• Saskatchewan Beekeepers Association Newsletter
Type: Newsletter; *Frequency:* Quarterly; *Accepts Advertising*;
Editor: Rhonda Baker
Profile: Association activities & executive reports

Saskatchewan Bison Association (SBA)
PO Box 31, Regina SK S4P 2Z5
Tel: 306-585-6304; *Fax:* 306-522-4768
saskbison@sasktel.net
Overview: A small provincial organization
Mission: To promote the bison industry; To encourage market development for bison products
Member of: Canadian Bison Association; Saskatchewan Food Processors Association
Activities: Administering research projects; *Awareness Events:* Annual Fall Production Sale; Annual Spring Premium Stock Show & Sale
Chief Officer(s):
Les Kroeger, President, 306-544-2869
leskro@sasktel.net
Publications:
• Saskatchewan Bison Association Newsletter
Type: Newsletter; *Frequency:* Quarterly

Saskatchewan Black Powder Association (SBPA)
PO Box 643, Saskatoon SK S7K 3L7
www.sbpa.ca
Overview: A small provincial organization founded in 1980
Mission: To provide a common voice for all Black Powder Shooters in the province; To encourage development of the old skills & trades related to Black Powder; & to co-ordinate activities of the Black Powder Shooters in the province
Member of: Shooting Federation of Canada
Finances: *Funding Sources:* Membership dues; Donations
Membership: *Fees:* $6 individual; $10 family; $25 associate member
Activities: *Library:* Not open to public

Saskatchewan Blind Sports Association Inc. (SBSA)
510 Cynthia St., Saskatoon SK S7L 7K7
Tel: 306-975-0888
Toll-Free: 877-772-7798
sbsa.sk@shaw.ca
www.saskblindsports.ca
Overview: A small provincial organization founded in 1978 overseen by Canadian Blind Sports Association Inc.
Mission: To assist persons who are blind or with visual impairment to achieve excellence in sport, satisfaction in

Canadian Associations / Saskatchewan Bodybuilding Association (SABBA)

recreation, independence, self-reliance & full community participation
Finances: *Annual Operating Budget:* $100,000-$250,000
Staff Member(s): 1; 250 volunteer(s)
Membership: 100-499; *Fees:* $10
Activities: *Awareness Events:* Run for Light
Chief Officer(s):
Glenn Hunks, Executive Director

Saskatchewan Bodybuilding Association (SABBA)
430 Willow Bay, Estevan SK S4A 2G4
Fax: 306-634-2272
www.sabba.net
www.facebook.com/groups/2436360746
twitter.com/Sk_Bodybuilding
Overview: A small provincial organization overseen by Canadian Bodybuilding Federation
Mission: To be the provincial governing body for the sport of amateur bodybuilding in Saskatchewan
Member of: Canadian Bodybuilding Federation; International Federation of Bodybuilding
Chief Officer(s):
Shawn Peters, Vice-President
shawn.peters79@gmail.com
Leigh Keess, Secretary-Treasurer, 306-634-2072
fitrnmom2@yahoo.ca

Saskatchewan Brain Injury Association (SBIA)
PO Box 3843, Saskatoon SK S4P 3Y3
Tel: 306-373-1555
Toll-Free: 888-373-1555
www.sbia.ca
www.facebook.com/SaskBrainInjury
twitter.com/SKBrainInjury
www.youtube.com/user/sbiaPrograms?feature=mhee
Previous Name: Saskatchewan Head Injury Association
Overview: A small provincial charitable organization founded in 1985 overseen by Brain Injury Association of Canada
Mission: To improve the quality of living for person living with an acquired brain injury, their families, & service providers throughout Saskatchewan; To provide support, information, & services to persons living with the effects of acquired brain injury
Finances: *Annual Operating Budget:* $250,000-$500,000; *Funding Sources:* Donations; Fundraising; Sponsorships
Membership: *Fees:* $10 individual; $15 family; $25 organization; *Member Profile:* Persons with an acquired brain injury, their families, & service providers in Saskatchewan
Activities: Advocating on behalf of persons in Saskatchewan with traumatic or acquired brain injury; Organizing survivor support groups; Offering information & educational programs; Increasing awareness of the effects & causes of acquired brain injury; Promoting prevention of brain injury, through educational seminars & materials; Referring persons to other organizations in the area when appropriate; *Awareness Events:* Brain Blitz Gala, May; Brain Boogie *Library:* SBIA Provincial Information / Resource Centre; Open to public
Chief Officer(s):
Gordon MacFadden, President
Glenda James, Executive Director
Publications:
• Connections [a publication of the Saskatchewan Brain Injury Association]
Type: Newsletter
Profile: Association activities & event reviews & announcements

Saskatchewan Broomball Association (SBA)
2205 Victoria Ave., Regina SK S4P 0S4
Tel: 306-780-9215; *Fax:* 306-525-4009
saskbroomball@sasktel.net
www.saskbroomball.ca
www.facebook.com/307730589864
Overview: A medium-sized provincial organization overseen by Ballon sur glace Broomball Canada
Mission: To promote multi-level programs to members & non-member groups in both competitive & recreational settings; to promote broomball within the province of Saskatchewan
Member of: Ballon sur glace Broomball Canada
Membership: *Fees:* Schedule available
Chief Officer(s):
Stacey Silzer, Executive Director

Saskatchewan Building Officials Association Inc. (SBOA)
PO Box 1671, Prince Albert SK S6V 5T2
Tel: 306-445-1733; *Fax:* 306-445-1739
membership@sboa.sk.ca
www.sboa.sk.ca

Overview: A small provincial organization founded in 1960
Member of: Alliance of Canadian Building Officials' Associations
Finances: *Funding Sources:* Membership dues; Conference registration
Membership: 500+; *Fees:* $40 active member; $400 government agency or corporation; $100 associate member; *Member Profile:* Persons engaged in the administration & enforcement of building statutes & regulations; Employees of municipal, provincial, or federal agencies or non-profit agencies concerned with building regulations; Persons, companies, or association with knowledge of any phase of building construction or materials
Chief Officer(s):
Dan Knutson, President
Todd Russell, Secretary-Treasurer
Publications:
• SBOA Newsletter
Type: Newsletter; *Editor:* Dale Wagner

Saskatchewan Camping Association (SCA)
3950 Castle Rd., Regina SK S4S 6A4
Tel: 306-586-4026; *Fax:* 306-790-8634
Overview: A medium-sized provincial organization founded in 1974 overseen by Canadian Camping Association
Mission: To promote the development of quality organized camping in Saskatchewan; To act as the voice for leaders of organized camps throughout Saskatchewan
Member of: Canadian Camping Association
Finances: *Funding Sources:* Sask Lotteries Trust Fund
Membership: *Member Profile:* Camps in Saskatchewan
Activities: Engaging in advocacy activities; Facilitating the sharing of ideas among camp leaders; Providing education for camp leaders
Chief Officer(s):
Donna Wilkinson, Executive Director, 306-586-4026
donnaw@sasktel.net
Meetings/Conferences:
• Saskatchewan Camping Association 2018 Annual General Meeting, 2018, SK
Scope: Provincial
Description: Featuring the election of the board of directors of the association
Publications:
• Saskatchewan Directory of Camps [a publication of the Saskatchewan Camping Association]
Type: Directory
Profile: Listings of camps that are members of the Saskatchewan Camping Association
• SCAN: The Saskatchewan Camping Association Newsletter
Type: Newsletter; *Accepts Advertising*; *Price:* Free with Saskatchewan Camping Association membership
Profile: News, issues, & articles of interest to the camping community of Saskatchewan

Saskatchewan Canoe Association *See* Canoe Kayak Saskatchewan

Saskatchewan Canola Development Commission
#212, 111 Research Dr., Saskatoon SK S7N 3R2
Tel: 306-975-0262; *Fax:* 306-975-0136
Toll-Free: 877-241-7044
info@saskcanola.com
www.saskcanola.com
Also Known As: SaskCanola
Overview: A medium-sized provincial organization founded in 1991
Mission: SaskCanola enhances canola producers' competitiveness and profitability through research, market development, extension, and policy development.
Affiliation(s): Canola Council of Canada
Finances: *Funding Sources:* Membership fees
Membership: *Member Profile:* Canola producers in Saskatchewan
Activities: Monitoring all areas of the canola growing industry; Liaising with governments & industry stakeholders on policy related issues; Developing policies in areas such as safety nets, transportation, biofuels, & biotechnology; Providing agronomic information & market trends to canola growers in Saskatchewan; Publishing statements on issues that affect canola growers throughout Saskatchewan
Chief Officer(s):
Catherine Folkersen, Executive Director, 306-975-6620, Fax: 306-975-0136
cfolkersen@saskcanola.com
Franck Groeneweg, Chair
franck@greenatlantic.com

Ellen Grueter, Manager
Market Development & Communications

Saskatchewan Cattle Breeders Association
PO Box 3771, Regina SK S4P 3N8
Tel: 306-757-6133; *Fax:* 306-525-5852
Overview: A small provincial organization
Mission: To encourage a general & constant improvement of cattle quality through cooperation with the federal & provincial Departments of Agriculture, the University of Saskatchewan & various fair associations
Affiliation(s): Saskatchewan Stock Growers Association; Canadian Western Agribition Association
Staff Member(s): 3; 25 volunteer(s)
Membership: 250; *Fees:* $10
Chief Officer(s):
Belinda Wagner, Sec.-Treas.

Saskatchewan Cerebral Palsy Association (SCPA)
2310 Louise Ave., Saskatoon SK S7J 2C7
Tel: 306-955-7272; *Fax:* 306-373-2665
saskcpa@shaw.ca
www.saskcp.ca
Overview: A medium-sized provincial charitable organization founded in 1985
Mission: To improve the quality of life of persons with cerebral palsy through a broad range of programs, education, support of research & the delivery of needed services to people with cerebral palsy & their families
Membership: 400; *Fees:* $15 association; $10 individual
Activities: Great Canadian Stationary Bike Race; *Speaker Service:* Yes; *Library*
Chief Officer(s):
Darren Tkach, President
Awards:
• Grant Program
• Scholarship Program

Saskatchewan CGIT Committee
c/o Heather Berriault, 1002 Victory Cres., Regina SK S4N 6X1
Tel: 306-789-3949
saskcgit@accesscomm.ca
saskatchewanCGIT.wordpress.com
twitter.com/sk_CGIT
Also Known As: Canadian Girls in Training - Saskatchewan
Previous Name: National CGIT Association - Saskatchewan Committee
Overview: A small provincial organization
Chief Officer(s):
Alice Monks, Co-Chair

Saskatchewan Chamber of Commerce
The Saskatchewan Chamber of Commerce, #1630, 1920 Broad St., Regina SK S4P 3V2
Tel: 306-352-2671; *Fax:* 306-781-7084
info@saskchamber.com
www.saskchamber.com
www.linkedin.com/company/saskatchewan-chamber-of-commerce
www.facebook.com/saskchamber
twitter.com/SaskChamber
www.youtube.com/user/SaskChamber
Overview: A medium-sized provincial organization
Mission: To act as the voice of business in Saskatchewan; To make Saskatchewan a better place for living, working, & investing; To promote commercial & industrial progress in Saskatchewan; To improve the competitiveness of Saskatchewan's economy
Staff Member(s): 8
Membership: *Fees:* Schedule available; *Member Profile:* Business & professional individuals in Saskatchewan; *Committees:* Environment; Finance; Human Resources; Investment & Growth; Youth Education & Training
Activities: Lobbying for business in Saskatchewan; Meeting with foreign delegations to create importing & exporting opportunities; Providing timely educational & informational programs; Offering economic analysis & market research services to members; Hosting conferences; Conducting surveys of businesses; Promoting sustainable economic development & social responsibility; *Library:* Research Library
Chief Officer(s):
Steve McLellan, CEO

Saskatchewan Charolais Association
PO Box 256, Hudson Bay SK S0E 0Y0
Tel: 306-865-3953; *Fax:* 306-865-3953
www.charolaisbanner.com/sca/

Overview: A small provincial organization
Mission: To educate and infrom those about the Charolais breed of cattle.
Affiliation(s): Saskatchewan Stock Growers Association
Chief Officer(s):
Orland Walker, President
diamondw@sasktel.net

Saskatchewan Cheerleading Association (SCA)
PO Box 31090, Regina SK S4R 8R6
Tel: 306-343-7221; *Fax:* 306-343-7229
sca.ca
www.facebook.com/SaskCheer
twitter.com/SaskCheer
Overview: A small provincial organization overseen by Cheer Canada
Mission: To promote & develop cheerleading in Saskatchewan.
Member of: Cheer Canada
Chief Officer(s):
Thomas Rath, President
president@sca.ca
Alissa Stewart, Executive Director
executivedirector@sca.ca

Saskatchewan Child Care Association *See* Saskatchewan Early Childhood Association

Saskatchewan Choral Federation (SCF)
1415B Albert St., Regina SK S4R 2R8
Tel: 306-780-9230
Toll-Free: 877-524-6725
www.saskchoral.ca
business.facebook.com/saskchoral?business_id=833016706769036
twitter.com/SKChoral
Overview: A small provincial organization founded in 1978
Mission: To promote the choral arts in Saskatchewan
Member of: Association of Canadian Choral Conductors; SaskCulture
Finances: *Annual Operating Budget:* $100,000-$250,000
Staff Member(s): 1
Membership: 5,280 associate + 160 individual + 148 choirs; *Fees:* $50 individual; $15 choir; *Member Profile:* Singer; conductor; *Committees:* Program; Finance; Personnel; Communications
Activities: Youth & adult choir camps; *Library:* by appointment
Chief Officer(s):
Denise Gress, Executive Director
gress@saskchoral.ca

Saskatchewan Coalition for Tobacco Reduction (SCTR)
1080 Winnipeg St., Regina SK S4R 8P8
Tel: 306-766-6327; *Fax:* 306-766-6945
Previous Name: Saskatchewan Interagency Council on Smoking & Health
Overview: A small provincial organization founded in 1975
Mission: To advocate, coordinate & educate to ensure a tobacco-free Saskatchewan for all its residents
Member of: Canadian Centre for Tobacco Control
Finances: *Funding Sources:* Grants
Chief Officer(s):
Lynn Greaves, Contact
sctr@rqhealth.ca

Saskatchewan College of Opticians
#13 - 350, 103 St. East, Saskatoon SK S7N 1Z1
Tel: 306-652-0769; *Fax:* 306-652-0784
office@scoptic.ca
www.scoptic.ca
Overview: A small provincial organization
Mission: To ensure that Saskatchewan opticians adhere to high standards of care; To improve the vision of the people of Saskatchewan
Membership: *Committees:* Conduct; Discipline
Chief Officer(s):
Deanne Oleksyn, President

Saskatchewan College of Paramedics (SCoP)
#202, 1900 Albert St., Regina SK S4P 4K8
Tel: 306-585-0145; *Fax:* 306-543-6161
Toll-Free: 877-725-4202
office@collegeofparamedics.sk.ca
www.collegeofparamedics.sk.ca
Overview: A small provincial organization
Member of: Paramedic Association of Canada
Staff Member(s): 5
Membership: *Fees:* $470 practicing; $100 restricted; $50 non practicing; *Committees:* Professional Conduct; Disciplinary Committee; Legislation & Bylaws; Education; Audit; Nominations; Executive
Activities: Licensing Emergency Medical Responders, Emergency Medical Technicians, Emergency Medical Technicians - Advanced, & Emergency Medical Technicians - Paramedics in Saskatchewan
Chief Officer(s):
Jacquie Messer-Lepage, Executive Director & Registrar
jmesserlepage@collegeofparamedics.sk.ca
Daniel Lewis, President
Jason Trask, Vice-President

Saskatchewan College of Pharmacists (SCP)
#700, 4010 Pasqua St., Regina SK S4S 7B9
Tel: 306-584-2292; *Fax:* 306-584-9695
info@saskpharm.ca
www.napra.ca/pages/Saskatchewan
Overview: A small provincial licensing organization founded in 1911 overseen by National Association of Pharmacy Regulatory Authorities
Mission: To regulate pharmacists, pharmacies, & drugs in Saskatchewan; To register pharmacists who meet the education & training qualifications specified in "The Pharmacy Act, 1996"; To issue permits to operate pharmacies
Member of: Canadian Council on Continuing Education in Pharmacy
Affiliation(s): Canadian Council on Continuing Education; Council of Pharmacy Registrars of Canada; National Association of Pharmacy Regulatory Authorities; PEBC; University of Saskatchewan; University of Regina
Membership: *Committees:* Audit; Complaints; Discipline; Finance: Professional Practice; Registration & Licensing Policies; Awards & Honours
Activities: Liaising with government; Publishing research reports, concept papers, & discussion papers
Chief Officer(s):
Spiro Kolitsas, President
Justin Kosar, Vice-President
Ray Joubert, Registrar
Awards:
• SCP Award of Merit
 Deadline: January 31 *Contact:* SCP Awards Committee, Fax: 306-584-9695; E-mail: info@saskpharm.ca
• SCP Presidential Citation
 Deadline: January 31 *Contact:* SCP Awards Committee, Fax: 306-584-9695; E-mail: info@saskpharm.ca
Publications:
• Reference Manual
Type: Manual
Profile: Standards, guidelines, & policy statements
• Saskatchewan College of Pharmacists Newsletter
Type: Newsletter
Profile: College information, executive reports, & upcoming training programs
• Saskatchewan College of Pharmacists Annual Report
Type: Yearbook; *Frequency:* Annually

Saskatchewan College of Physical Therapists (SCPT)
#102, 320 - 21st St. West, Saskatoon SK S7M 4E6
Tel: 306-931-6661; *Fax:* 306-931-7333
Toll-Free: 877-967-7278
www.scpt.org
Previous Name: Saskatchewan College of Physical Therapy
Overview: A small provincial licensing organization overseen by Canadian Alliance of Physiotherapy Regulators
Member of: Canadian Alliance of Physiotherapy Regulators
Staff Member(s): 2
Membership: *Fees:* $125 non practicing; $450 practicing
Chief Officer(s):
Lynn Kuffner, Acting Executive Director & Registrar
ed@scpt.org

Saskatchewan College of Physical Therapy *See* Saskatchewan College of Physical Therapists

Saskatchewan College of Podiatrists (SCOP)
2105 Retallack St., Regina SK S4T 2K5
Tel: 306-352-9091; *Fax:* 306-352-9124
registrar@scop.ca
www.scop.ca
Overview: A small provincial licensing organization founded in 2003
Mission: To regulate the practice of podiatry; Establish standards of practice; Establish educational requirements; Establish continuing education; Educate the public on the practice of podiatry
Membership: 26; *Member Profile:* Podiatrists; *Committees:* Executive; Legislation; Professional Conduct; Quality Assurance; NIRO; Website
Chief Officer(s):
Ata Stationwala, President
Axel Rohrmann, Registrar

Saskatchewan College of Psychologists (SCP)
1026 Winnipeg St., Regina SK S4R 8P8
Tel: 306-352-1699; *Fax:* 306-352-1697
skcp@sasktel.net
www.skcp.ca
Previous Name: Saskatchewan Psychological Association
Overview: A small provincial licensing organization
Mission: To protect the public by guiding & regulating the professional conduct of Saskatchewan psychologists
Membership: *Fees:* $800 practicing; $200 non-practicing; $100 corporation; *Committees:* Discipline; Nominations; Professional Conduct; Professional Practice & Ethics; Oral Examination; Registration
Chief Officer(s):
Karen Litke, President
Karen Messer-Engel, M.A., R.Psych., Executive Director & Registrar

Saskatchewan Commercial Egg Producers Marketing Board *See* Saskatchewan Egg Producers

Saskatchewan Community Theatre Inc. *See* Theatre Saskatchewan

Saskatchewan Conference of Mennonite Brethren Churches (SKMB)
#201, 401 - 3rd St. E, Saskatoon SK S7K 8B7
Tel: 306-652-2752
www.skmb.ca
Overview: A small provincial organization overseen by Canadian Conference of Mennonite Brethren Churches
Mission: To foster & encourage a movement of churches led by healthy leaders who spread God's values to friends, neighbours, and the world
Chief Officer(s):
Terrance Froese, Director, Ministry
Awards:
• Student Internship Grant
 Contact: Darlene Klassen, Regional Leadership Team, Phone: 1-866-772-2175
• Saskatchewan Conference of Mennonite Brethren Churches Bursary Program
 Contact: Darlene Klassen, Regional Leadership Team, Phone: 1-866-772-2175
Meetings/Conferences:
• Saskatchewan Conference of Mennonite Brethren Churches 72nd Annual Conference 2018, 2018
Scope: Provincial

Saskatchewan Construction Association (SCA)
320 Gardiner Park Court, Regina SK S4V 1R9
Tel: 306-525-0171
sca@scaonline.ca
www.scaonline.ca
www.facebook.com/SaskConstAssociation
twitter.com/webuildsk
Overview: A medium-sized provincial organization overseen by Canadian Construction Association
Mission: To provide industry leadership, encourage investment in Saskatchewan, grow opportunities for its members & maintain a stable oranization
Staff Member(s): 5
Membership: 1,300; *Member Profile:* Companies involved in construction work; *Committees:* Finance & Audit; Governance; HR & Compensation; Advisory Council
Chief Officer(s):
Mark Cooper, President
president@scaonline.ca
Amanda Thick, Director, Operations
amandat@scaonline.ca

> **Moose Jaw Construction Association**
> 610 - 1 Ave. NW, Moose Jaw SK S6H 3M6
> *Tel:* 306-693-1232; *Fax:* 306-694-1766
> mjca3@shaw.ca
> www.mjcaonline.ca
> **Chief Officer(s):**
> Brad Duncan, President
> droofing@sasktel.net

Prince Albert Construction Association (PACA)
70 - 17th St. West, Prince Albert SK S6V 3X3
Tel: 306-764-2789; *Fax:* 306-764-3443
pacon@sasktel.net
www.pacaonline.ca
Chief Officer(s):
Joe Yungwirth, President, 306-763-1907
• PACA Newsletter
Type: Newsletter; *Frequency:* Weekly
Profile: Up-to-date information for members

Regina Construction Association
1935 Elphinstone St., Regina SK S4T 3N3
Tel: 306-791-7422; *Fax:* 306-565-2840
info@rcaonline.ca
www.rcaonline.ca
twitter.com/BuildRegina
www.youtube.com/user/buildsask
Chief Officer(s):
Darlene South, Manager, Operations

Saskatoon Construction Association
532 - 2nd Ave. North, Saskatoon SK S7K 2C5
Tel: 306-653-1771; *Fax:* 306-653-3515
planroom@saskatoonconstruction.ca
www.saskatoonconstruction.ca
www.facebook.com/buildyxe
twitter.com/buildyxe
Chief Officer(s):
Chris Doka, President
chrisd@wrightconstruction.ca
Deb Laberswelier, Executive Director
deb@saskatoonconstruction.ca

Saskatchewan Construction Safety Association Inc. (SCSA)
498 Henderson Dr., Regina SK S4N 6E3
Tel: 306-525-0175; *Fax:* 306-525-1542
Toll-Free: 800-817-2079
scsainfo@scsaonline.ca
www.scsaonline.ca
www.linkedin.com/company/saskatchewan-construction-safety-association-scsa-
www.facebook.com/SCSAonline
twitter.com/scsaonline
Overview: A medium-sized provincial organization founded in 1995
Mission: To provide safety programs & servies to construction employers & employees in order to reduce human & financial loss associated with injuries in the construction industry
Finances: *Funding Sources:* Membership dues
Membership: *Fees:* $750 supporter; *Member Profile:* Saskatchewan companies with an active Workers' Compensation Board account within the construction rate group; Supporter members with accounts outside the construction rate group
Activities: Offering safety training courses on a variety of industry-related topics
Chief Officer(s):
Blake Schneider, Director, Operations
blakes@scsaonline.ca
Heidi Tiller, Coordinator, Human Resources
heidit@scsaonline.ca
Lara Abu-Ghazaleh, Coordinator, Publications & Communications
laraa@scsaonline.ca
Publications:
• Safety Advocate Newsletter [a publication of the Saskatchewan Construction Safety Association Inc.]
Type: Newsletter
• Saskatchewan Residential Safety Guide [a publication of the Saskatchewan Construction Safety Association Inc.]
Type: Booklet

Saskatchewan Co-operative Association (SCA)
1515 - 20th St. West, Saskatoon SK S7M 0Z5
Tel: 306-244-3702; *Fax:* 306-244-2165
sca@sask.coop
www.sask.coop
www.facebook.com/SaskCoopAssociation
twitter.com/coopnewssk
Overview: A medium-sized provincial organization
Mission: Provincial coalition of co-operatives, including credit unions, that collaborates to support & promote the co-operative model for community & economic development
Affiliation(s): Canadian Co-operative Association
Membership: *Member Profile:* Co-operatives & credit unions; *Committees:* Co-op Merit Awards Program; Co-op Classic; Co-operative Development; CMAP Nominations
Activities: Training; educational resources; youth seminars; advisory services; *Awareness Events:* Co-op Classic charity golf fundraiser; Annual Awards
Chief Officer(s):
Victoria Morris, Executive Director
victoria.morris@sask.coop
Publications:
• The Co-operative Spotlight
Type: Newsletter; *Frequency:* 8-10 pa

Saskatchewan Council for Archives & Archivists (SCAA)
#202, 1275 Broad St., Regina SK S4R 1Y2
Tel: 306-780-9414; *Fax:* 306-585-1765
scaa@sasktel.net
www.scaa.sk.ca
www.facebook.com/SCAArchivists
Overview: A small provincial organization founded in 1987 overseen by Canadian Council of Archives
Mission: To facilitate the development of the archival system in Saskatchewan; To develop standard archival policies & practices; To promote public awareness of the use of archives
Membership: 66; *Fees:* $110 staffed archives; $60 volunteer run archives; $55 development institution; $20 individual; *Member Profile:* Institutions & individuals that are involved with the maintenance of archival records
Activities: Offering workshops, educational programs, & networking opportunities; Providing an Archival Advisory Service to assist archives; Maintaining the Saskatchewan Archival Information Network, with information about holdings in the province; *Awareness Events:* Archives Week, Feb.
Chief Officer(s):
Sandy Doran, Executive Director
Jeremy Mohr, President
Cameron Hart, Archives Advisor
Meetings/Conferences:
• Saskatchewan Council for Archives & Archivists Annual General Meeting 2018, 2018, SK
Scope: Provincial
Publications:
• Outside the Box [a publication of the Saskatchewan Council for Archives & Archivists]
Type: Newsletter
Profile: Information for SCAA members

Saskatchewan Council for Crippled Children & Adults *See* Saskatchewan Abilities Council

Saskatchewan Council for Educators of Non-English Speakers (SCENES)
PO Box 486 Delaronde Rd., Saskatoon SK S7J 4A6
scenes@sasktel.net
Overview: A small provincial organization
Mission: To represent and express the professional concerns of those involved in English as a Second Language/Dialect (ESL/D) in Saskatchewan.
Finances: *Funding Sources:* government, corporate sponsors
Membership: *Fees:* $40 individual; $70 couples; $15 students; $100 institutional
Activities: Learning conferences

Saskatchewan Council for Exceptional Children (SCEC)
PO Box 403, 302 Brookside Ct., Warman SK S0K 4S0
Tel: 703-620-3660; *Fax:* 703-264-9494
Toll-Free: 888-232-7733; *TTY:* 866-915-5000
www.saskcec.ca
www.linkedin.com/company/2756373
www.facebook.com/cechqanitobacec
twitter.com/cecmembership
Overview: A medium-sized provincial organization overseen by Council for Exceptional Children
Chief Officer(s):
Linda Balon-Smith, President

Saskatchewan Council for International Co-operation (SCIC) / Conseil de la Saskatchewan pour la co-opération internationale
2138 McIntyre St., Regina SK S4P 2R7
Tel: 306-757-4669; *Fax:* 306-757-3226
scic@earthbeat.sk.ca
www.earthbeat.sk.ca
www.facebook.com/SaskCIC
www.twitter.com/saskCIC
www.youtube.com/user/SCICYouth
Overview: A medium-sized international charitable organization founded in 1974
Mission: To act as the umbrella organization for international development agencies in Saskatchewan; To distribute international development funds provided by the Government of Saskatchewan; To facilitate communications among member agencies in Saskatchewan and across Canada; To support cooperative government relations, public education, & fundraising
Member of: Canadian Council for International Cooperation
Staff Member(s): 6
Membership: 29; *Member Profile:* Local committees of churches, educational organizations, & international development agencies
Activities: Advocating on international issues; *Awareness Events:* International Development Week, Feb.
Chief Officer(s):
Jacqui Wasacase, Executive Director
director@earthbeat.sk.ca

Saskatchewan Council of Cultural Organizations *See* SaskCulture Inc.

Saskatchewan Council on Children & Youth *See* Ranch Ehrlo Society

Saskatchewan Country Vacations Association *See* Saskatchewan Bed & Breakfast Association

Saskatchewan Craft Council (SCC)
813 Broadway Ave., Saskatoon SK S7N 1B5
Tel: 306-653-3616; *Fax:* 306-244-2711
Toll-Free: 866-653-3616
saskcraftcouncil@sasktel.net
www.saskcraftcouncil.org
www.facebook.com/SaskatchewanCraftCouncil
twitter.com/skcraftcouncil
Overview: A medium-sized provincial charitable organization founded in 1975
Member of: SaskCulture Inc.; Saskatchewan Tourism
Affiliation(s): Canadian Crafts Federation
Finances: *Funding Sources:* Government
Staff Member(s): 9; 50 volunteer(s)
Membership: 414; *Fees:* $50 students or patrons; $100 organizations, professional craftspeople, or affiliated marketers; *Committees:* Exhibition; Markets; Publications; Curatorial
Activities: Operating Affinity Gallery & SCC Fine Craft Boutique; Organizing craft markets & exhibitions; Offering workshops & conferences; *Library:* Saskatchewan Craft Council Library; Not open to public

Saskatchewan Cricket Association (SCA)
Regina SK
www.saskcricket.com
www.facebook.com/SaskatchewanCricketAssociation
twitter.com/saskcricket
Overview: A small provincial organization founded in 1977 overseen by Cricket Canada
Mission: To be the provincial governing body of cricket in Saskatchewan.
Member of: Cricket Canada
Affiliation(s): Regina Cricket Association; Saskatoon Cricket Association
Membership: 2 associations
Chief Officer(s):
Azhar (Sam) Khan, President
Raza Naqvi, Secretary

Saskatchewan Cultural Exchange Society (SCES)
2431 - 8th Ave., Regina SK S4R 5J7
Tel: 306-780-9494; *Fax:* 306-780-9487
james@culturalexchnage.ca
culturalexchange.ca
twitter.com/TheExchangeClub
Overview: A medium-sized provincial charitable organization founded in 1977
Mission: To encourage interactive & diverse artistic experienes through creative programming in Saskatchewan
Member of: SaskCulture Inc.
Affiliation(s): Tourism Saskatchewan; Canadian Tourism Human Resource Council; Saskatchewan Fiddle Association
Finances: *Annual Operating Budget:* $250,000-$500,000; *Funding Sources:* Saskatchewan Trust; Provincial & federal governments; self-generated revenue
Staff Member(s): 6; 50 volunteer(s)

Membership: 425; *Fees:* $10; $50 organization; *Committees:* Club; Festival; Performing Arts
Activities: Workshop tour; Fiddle Camp; Live performances
Chief Officer(s):
John Kennedy, Executive Director
john@culturalexchange.ca

Saskatchewan Cultural Society of the Deaf
511 Main St. East, Saskatoon SK S7N 0C2
Overview: A small provincial organization
Chief Officer(s):
Laurie Eva-Miller, Acting President
le-miller1@shaw.ca

Saskatchewan Curling Association (SCA)
613 Park St., Regina SK S4N 5N1
Tel: 306-780-9202; *Fax:* 306-780-9404
Toll-Free: 877-722-2875
curling@curlsask.ca
curlsask.ca
www.facebook.com/Curlsask
twitter.com/curlsask
Also Known As: CurlSask
Overview: A small provincial organization overseen by Canadian Curling Association
Mission: To govern and promote the sport of curling in Saskatchewan.
Membership: *Committees:* Executive; Finance & Audit; Governance & Policy; Strategic Planning; Competition; Participation & Development
Chief Officer(s):
Ashley Howard, Executive Director, 306-780-9403
ashleyhoward@curlsask.ca

Saskatchewan Cycling Association
2205 Victoria Ave., Regina SK S4P 0S4
Tel: 306-780-9299; *Fax:* 306-525-4009
cycling@accesscomm.ca
www.saskcycling.ca
www.facebook.com/327882317318669
Overview: A small provincial organization overseen by Cycling Canada Cyclisme
Mission: To promote & enhance the Saskatchewan cycling experience while recognizing its benefits to the individual & society.
Member of: Cycling Canada Cyclisme
Finances: *Funding Sources:* Saskatchewan Lotteries
Staff Member(s): 2
Activities: *Speaker Service:* Yes; *Rents Mailing List:* Yes
Chief Officer(s):
Bob Cochran, Interim President

Saskatchewan Darts Association (SDA)
c/o Pat Copeman, 17 Eden Ave., Regina SK S7R 5M2
Tel: 306-949-5180
www.saskdarts.com
Overview: A small provincial organization overseen by National Darts Federation of Canada
Mission: To provide recreational & competitive opportunities for darts players of all levels in Saskatchewan
Member of: National Darts Federation of Canada
Chief Officer(s):
Elaine Walker, President, 306-651-0481
empearson@shaw.ca
Judy Cleaveley, Secretary, 306-865-2028
hbaccount@sasktel.net

Saskatchewan Deaf & Hard of Hearing Services Inc. (SDHHS)
2341 Broad St., Regina SK S4P 1Y9
Tel: 306-352-3323; *Fax:* 306-757-3252
Toll-Free: 800-565-3323
Other Communication: Video Phone: 306-352-3322
regina@sdhhs.com
www.sdhhs.com
www.facebook.com/SDHHSinc
twitter.com/SDHHSinc
Overview: A small provincial charitable organization founded in 1981
Mission: To promote independence of deaf, late deafened, & hard of hearing persons; To provide services for persons with a hearing loss in order to enhance their quality of life
Affiliation(s): Canadian Hard of Hearing Association; Canadian Association of the Deaf; Regina Association of the Deaf; Saskatchewan Institute of Applied Science & Technology; United Way; United Way of Regina; United Way of Saskatoon
Finances: *Funding Sources:* Donations; Sponsorships

Staff Member(s): 15
Membership: *Fees:* $5 individual; $15 organization; *Member Profile:* People who are deaf, late deafened, hard of hearing, or deaf blind; Professionals who work with these groups; Families & friends of those with hearing loss
Activities: Youth camp; Cmmunity service workers; Voational counselling; Discount Hearing Aid Battery Program; Computerized note taking; Interpreting services; *Awareness Events:* Annual Silent Walk
Chief Officer(s):
Nairn Gillies, Executive Director
Dale Birley, President
  Saskatoon Office
  #3, 511 - 1st Ave. North, Saskatoon SK S7K 1X5
  Tel: 306-665-6575; *Fax:* 306-665-7746
  Toll-Free: 800-667-6575
  saskatoon@sdhhs.com

Saskatchewan Deaf Sports Association (SDSA)
PO Box 932, Fort Qu'Appelle SK S0G 1S0
Overview: A small provincial charitable organization overseen by Canadian Deaf Sports Association
Mission: To foster sporting opportunities to members of the deaf & hard-of-hearing communities; To select & train deaf & hard-of-hearing athletes for international competitions
Member of: Canadian Deaf Sports Association
Affiliation(s): Regina Deaf Athletic Club; Saskatoon Deaf Athletic Club; Saskatchewan Sport Inc.
Finances: *Annual Operating Budget:* Less than $50,000; *Funding Sources:* Provincial subsidy; Sask. Lotteries; tickets sales; special events
10 volunteer(s)
Membership: 300-400; *Fees:* $25 adult; $5 adult (no championships); $75 organization
Chief Officer(s):
Kevin Goodfeather, President
nivek26@hotmail.com

Saskatchewan Dental Assistants' Association (SDAA)
PO Box 294, 603 - 3rd St., Kenaston SK S0G 2N0
Tel: 306-252-2769; *Fax:* 306-252-2089
sdaa@sasktel.net
www.sdaa.sk.ca
www.facebook.com/111269682301325
Overview: A small provincial organization overseen by Canadian Dental Assistants Association
Mission: To promote excellence in dental health care; To advance public protection through enforcement of regulations, education, ethical practice, & standardization
Activities: Advocating for the health & safety of dental assistants
Chief Officer(s):
Gillian Nault, President
Susan Anholt, Executive Director
Tracey Taylor, Coordinator, Professional Development
seminars.sdaa@sasktel.net
Awards:
• Past President's Plaque
• Honorary Life Membership
• Penny Waite Achievement Award
• The Marg Steckler Award of Excellence
• The Susan Anholt Mentorship Award
• SDAA General Merit Award
• SDAA Outstanding Academic Achievement
• Twenty-Five Year Service Awards
Publications:
• Accent on Assisting [a publication of the Saskatchewan Dental Assistants' Association]
Type: Newsletter

Saskatchewan Dental Hygienists' Association (SDHA)
#114, 3502 Taylor St. East, Saskatoon SK S7H 5H9
Tel: 306-931-7342; *Fax:* 306-931-7334
sdha@sasktel.net
www.sdha.ca
Overview: A small provincial organization
Staff Member(s): 1
Membership: 500+; *Committees:* Professional Conduct; Discipline; Continuing Competency
Chief Officer(s):
Kellie Watson, Executive Director

Saskatchewan Dental Therapists Association (SDTA)
PO Box 360, 2364 Proton Ave., Gull Lake SK S0N 1A0
Tel: 306-672-3699; *Fax:* 306-672-3619
sdta@sasktel.net
www.sdta.ca
Overview: A small provincial organization founded in 1974
Mission: Dedicated to improving & promoting oral health excellence for all, respecting diversity & individuality
Membership: *Fees:* $30 affiliate; $100 non-practicing; $377 public health preventative practice; $495 clinical restorative practice; *Committees:* Professional Conduct; Discipline; Executive; Credentials; Continuing Education/Bursary/Scholarship; Editorial; Community Oral Health; Conventions
Chief Officer(s):
Cindy G. Reed, Executive Director/Registrar/Sec.-Tres.
Loretta Singh, President

Saskatchewan Dietitians Association (SDA)
#17, 2010 - 7th Ave., Regina SK S4R 1C2
Tel: 306-359-3040; *Fax:* 306-359-3046
registrar@saskdietitians.org
www.saskdietitians.org
Overview: A small provincial licensing organization founded in 1958 overseen by Dietitians of Canada
Mission: To protect the public by registering competent dietitians; To set standards of practice; To uphold codes of conduct; To provide a framework for continuing competence, consisting of a self-assessment tool, a learning plan, & a quality assurance audit
Affiliation(s): Network of Interprofessional Regulatory Organizations; Alliance of Dietetic Regulatory Bodies
Membership: 300; *Member Profile:* A graduate from an accredited baccalaureate program, or a graduate from an accredited practical training program which may or may not be included in a degree; Graduates must have completed the Canadian Dietetic Registration Examination; *Committees:* Communication; Discipline; Finance; Legislation; Professional Conduct; Professional Standards; Registration
Activities: Investigating complaints; Recommending alternate dispute resolutions; Determining discipline
Chief Officer(s):
Laurel Leushen, President
Lana Moore, Registrar

Saskatchewan Diving
1870 Lorne St., Regina SK S4P 2L7
Tel: 306-780-9405; *Fax:* 306-781-6021
info@divesask.ca
www.saskdiving.ca
www.facebook.com/DIVESASK
twitter.com/divesask
Also Known As: Sask Diving Inc.
Overview: A small provincial organization
Mission: To develop & promote safe diving; To ensure that diving clubs operate with safety & integrity; To provide opportunities for self fulfillment & the pursuit of excellence
Member of: Diving Plongeon Canada
Finances: *Funding Sources:* Sask Lotteries
Staff Member(s): 3
Membership: *Member Profile:* Diving clubs; Individuals, such as coaches, athletes, officials, parents, & executive members
Activities: Ensuring coaches are trained through the National Coaching Certification Program
Chief Officer(s):
Karen Swanson, Executive Director
kswanson@divesask.ca

Saskatchewan Early Childhood Association (SECA)
1015 Railway Ave., Weyburn SK S4H 2V5
Tel: 306-842-1209; *Fax:* 306-842-1206
Toll-Free: 888-658-4408
www.seca-sk.ca
Previous Name: Saskatchewan Child Care Association
Overview: A medium-sized provincial organization founded in 1988
Mission: To support high quality early childhood care, development, & education throughout Saskatchewan; To advance professional development in the early learning & child care community
Affiliation(s): Canadian Child Care Federation
Finances: *Funding Sources:* Membership fees; Saskatchewan Ministry of Education; Sponsorships; Merchandise
Membership: *Fees:* $50 students & parents; $89 professionals & corporate members; $105 child care centres; *Member Profile:*

Professional early childhood educators; Full-time students; Parents; Child care centres; Corporate members involved in or interested in the field of early childhood education
Activities: Providing education, resources, research, services, & networking opportunities to early childhood educators across Saskatchewan; Promoting awareness of the early learning & child care community
Chief Officer(s):
Angie Stevenson, Chair
Genaya Wojcichowsky, Secretary
Awards:
• SECA Student Award
Meetings/Conferences:
• Saskatchewan Early Childhood Association 2018 Annual General Meeting, 2018, SK
Scope: Provincial
• Saskatchewan Early Childhood Association 2018 Excellence in Early Learning Conference, 2018, SK
Scope: Provincial
Description: A conference offering demonstration classrooms, peer to peer learning, & hands-on activities
Publications:
• Child Care Connections
Type: Magazine; *Frequency:* 3 pa; *Price:* Free with Saskatchewan Early Childhood Association membership

Saskatchewan Eco-Network (SEN)
535 - 8 St. East, Saskatoon SK S7K 0P9
Tel: 306-652-1275
info@econet.ca
www.econet.sk.ca
Overview: A small provincial organization founded in 1980 overseen by Canadian Environmental Network
Mission: To provide educational activities to develop an awareness of conservation & enhancement of the environment
Affiliation(s): Canadian Environmental Network
Staff Member(s): 2
Membership: 55; *Fees:* Schedule available; *Member Profile:* Non-profit, non-governmental organizations in Saskatchewan concerned with environmental issues
Activities: Promoting networking opportunities for members; Providing referrals for members, media, government personnel, & the public
Chief Officer(s):
Rick Morrell, Executive Director
Publications:
• Saskatchewan's Green Directory
Type: Directory
Profile: A project of the Saskatchewan Eco-Network, with assistance from the Saskatchewan Research Council & the Ministry of Environment, the directory presents information about green products forconsumers.
• SEN [Saskatchewan Eco-Network] Bulletin
Type: Newsletter; *Frequency:* Biweekly; *Price:* Free
Profile: News & events from across Saskatchewan

Saskatchewan Economic Development Association (SEDA)
PO Box 113, #202, 120 Sonnenschein Way, Saskatoon SK S7K 3K1
Tel: 306-384-5817; *Fax:* 306-384-5818
Toll-Free: 877-551-7332
seda@seda.sk.ca
www.seda.sk.ca
www.linkedin.com/in/saskecdevassoc
www.facebook.com/148408781882152
twitter.com/saskecdevassoc
Overview: A small provincial organization
Mission: To secure the economic future of Saskatchewan by helping communities to grow
Finances: *Funding Sources:* Membership fees
Membership: 100-499; *Fees:* Schedule available
Activities: Business Counts Saskatchewan program; online resources; education & training
Chief Officer(s):
Russ McPherson, President, 306-867-9557, *Fax:* 306-867-9559
russmcpherson@midsask.ca
Verona Thibault, Executive Director
verona.thibault@seda.sk.ca
Awards:
• SEDA Economic Development Awards of Excellence
Publications:
• SEDA [Saskatchewan Economic Development Association] Directory
Type: Directory

Saskatchewan Economics Association (SEA)
c/o Rahatjan Judge, Treasurer, 826 Ave. K south, Saskatoon SK S7M 2E8
sea@cabe.ca
www.cabe.ca/jmv3/index.php/cabe-chapters/oskaer
Previous Name: Organization of Saskatchewan Applied Economic Research
Overview: A small provincial organization founded in 2013 overseen by Canadian Association for Business Economics
Member of: Canadian Association for Business Economics
Membership: *Fees:* $35; *Member Profile:* All individuals & agencies who are: economic policy analysts; certified financial, management & accounting officials; economic development consultants; statisticians; banking officials; university officials; & students of economics
Chief Officer(s):
Aaron Murray, President, 306-535-0668
aamurray@accesscomm.ca
Rahatjan Judge, Treasurer, 306-202-0350

Saskatchewan Egg Producers
496 Hoffer Dr., Regina SK S4N 7A1
Tel: 306-924-1505; *Fax:* 306-924-1515
www.saskegg.ca
www.facebook.com/saskegg
twitter.com/SaskEgg
www.instagram.com/saskegg
Previous Name: Saskatchewan Commercial Egg Producers Marketing Board
Overview: A small provincial licensing organization founded in 1969
Affiliation(s): Egg Farmers of Canada
Activities: Providing educational information about egg production, nutrition, handling & storage, & safety
Chief Officer(s):
Cam Broten, Executive Director, 306-924-1503
Cailyn Jones, Coordinator, Producer Services, 306-924-1507
Publications:
• Saskatchewan Egg Producers Eggzine
Type: Newsletter
Profile: Nutritional information, facts, & recipes for eggs

Saskatchewan Elocution & Debate Association (SEDA) / Association d'élocution et des débats de la Saskatchewan
1860 Lorne St., Regina SK S4P 2L7
Tel: 306-780-9243; *Fax:* 306-781-6021
info@saskdebate.com
www.saskdebate.com
www.facebook.com/sask.debate
twitter.com/SaskDebate
Overview: A medium-sized provincial charitable organization founded in 1974
Mission: To foster debate & public speaking
Affiliation(s): Canadian Student Debating Federation; SaskCulture Inc.
Finances: *Funding Sources:* Saskatchewan Lotteries Trust Fund for Sport, Culture & Recreation
Staff Member(s): 2
Membership: *Member Profile:* Schools in Saskatchewan
Activities: *Library:* by appointment
Chief Officer(s):
Lorelie DeRoose, Executive Director

Saskatchewan Emergency Medical Services Association (SEMSA)
#105, 111 Research Dr., Saskatoon SK S7N 3R2
Tel: 306-382-2147; *Fax:* 306-955-5353
semsa@semsa.org
www.semsa.org
Overview: A medium-sized provincial organization founded in 1959
Mission: To strengthen & advance EMS in Saskatchewan by ensuring high-quality, accountable patient care
Membership: *Member Profile:* EMS employees in Saskatchewan; *Committees:* Executive; Member Services; Operations; Professional Development; Community Development
Chief Officer(s):
Larise Skoretz, Administrator
Gerry Schriemer, President
Meetings/Conferences:
• 2018 Saskatchewan Emergency Medical Services Association Convention & Trade Show, 2018, SK
Scope: Provincial
Description: An informative convention with a trade show that provides the opportunitiy for those working in emergency medicl services to meet with suppliers to discuss products & services
Contact Information: semsa@semsa.org

Saskatchewan Environmental Industry & Managers' Association (SEIMA)
2341 McIntyre St., Regina SK S4P 2S3
Tel: 306-543-1567; *Fax:* 306-543-1568
info@seima.sk.ca
www.seima.sk.ca
www.facebook.com/146987992039835
Previous Name: Saskatchewan Environmental Managers Association
Overview: A medium-sized provincial organization founded in 1994
Mission: To act as the voice of practitioners in Saskatchewan's environmental industry on environmental matters; To promote responsible environmental management in the province; To develop the environmental industry in Saskatchewan
Membership: *Fees:* $15 undergrad students; $50 graduate students; Schedule, based upon number of employees for corporate & associate members; *Member Profile:* Environmental managers from various industries in Saskatchewan, such as agriculture, mining, & forestry; Companies in Saskatchewan's environmental industry; Suppliers to Saskatchewan's environmental industry; Students; Researchers; Consultants; Public policy developers; *Committees:* Government Relations; Governance; Finance; Program; First Nations & Metis Relations; Membership
Activities: Engaging in advocacy activities; Liaising with governments; Providing access to current industry intelligence, such as environmental legislation & regulations, & potential opportunities; Offering professional development activities for Saskatchewan's environmental businesses & managers, such as seminars & conferences; Facilitating networking opportunities with industry colleagues, for the exchange of information & ideas; Presenting an Aboriginal Youth Career Fair; Conferences & trade shows; *Speaker Service:* Yes
Chief Officer(s):
Kathleen Livingston, Executive Director & COO
klivingston@seima.sk.ca
Al Shpyth, President
ashpyth@ecometrix.ca
Lenore Swystun, Vice-President
prairiewildconsulting@sasktel.net
Lois Miller, Treasurer
lmiller@traceassociates.ca
Cheryl Hender, Secretary
chender@innovationplace.com
Publications:
• Saskatchewan Environmental Industry & Managers' Association Member Directory & Buyer's Guide
Type: Directory; *Frequency:* Annually; *Price:* Free with membership in Saskatchewan Environmental Industry & Managers' Association
Profile: Information about Saskatchewan Environmental Industry & Managers' Association member businesses & their areas ofspecialization, to provide marketing support for its users throughout North American & Europe
• Saskatchewan Environmental Industry & Managers' Association Newsletter
Type: Nesletter

Saskatchewan Environmental Managers Association *See* Saskatchewan Environmental Industry & Managers' Association

Saskatchewan Environmental Society (SES)
PO Box 1372, Saskatoon SK S7K 3N9
Tel: 306-665-1915
info@environmentalsociety.ca
www.environmentalsociety.ca
www.linkedin.com/company/saskatchewan-environmental-society
www.facebook.com/environmentalsociety
twitter.com/skenvsociety
www.youtube.com/user/EnvironmentalSociety
Overview: A medium-sized provincial charitable organization founded in 1970
Mission: To maintain the integrity of Saskatchewan's forests, farmlands & natural prairie landscapes; To promote energy conservation & the development of renewable energy resources; To build sustainable communities, enhanced waste management, & enhanced water quality in the province's lakes & rivers
Member of: Canadian Renewable Energy Alliance

Finances: *Funding Sources:* Membership fees; Donations; Fundraising; Sponsorships
Staff Member(s): 8
Membership: *Fees:* $20; *Member Profile:* Individuals interested in environmental sustainability
Activities: Advocating for & supporting environmental groups; Communicating with membership through various outlets; Promoting public education & awareness regarding environmental sustainability; *Speaker Service:* Yes; *Library:* Saskatchewan Environmental Society Resource Centre
Chief Officer(s):
Allyson Brady, Executive Director
allysonb@environmentalsociety.ca
Peter Prebble, Director, Environmental Policy
peterp@environmentalsociety.ca
Angie Bugg, Coordinator, Energy Conservation
angieb@environmentalsociety.ca
Lynette Suchar, Coordinator, Communications
communications@environmentalsociety.ca
Publications:
• Environmental Resource [a publication of the Saskatchewan Environmental Society]
Type: Newsletter; *Frequency:* bi-m.; *Price:* Free with SES membership
Profile: Information about the society's involvement in environmental issues, plus upcoming events, for society members

Saskatchewan Families for Effective Autism Treatment (SASKFEAT)
PO Box 173, Shaunavon SK S0N 2M0
saskfeat@sasktel.net
www.saskfeat.com
www.facebook.com/SaskFEAT
Previous Name: Saskatchewan Society for the Autistic Inc.
Overview: A small provincial organization founded in 1976 overseen by Autism Society Canada
Mission: To act as a voice for the concerns & needs of parents & families of autistic children & individuals in Saskatchewan; To find the most effective treatment for autistic children & individuals
Affiliation(s): Autism Society Canada
Finances: *Funding Sources:* Donations; Sponsorships
Membership: *Member Profile:* Individuals interested in the objectives of the association, such as families & friends of individuals with autism, plus professionals who are concerned with the well-being of persons with autism
Activities: Supporting Saskatchewan individuals with autism spectrum disorders & their families
Chief Officer(s):
Arden C. Fiala, President
Kathy Chambers, Vice-President
Calvin Fiala, Secretary & Treasurer

Saskatchewan Federation of Home & School Associations
See Saskatchewan Association of School Councils

Saskatchewan Federation of Labour (SFL) / Fédération du travail de la Saskatchewan
#220, 2445 - 13th Ave., Regina SK S4P 0W1
Tel: 306-525-0197; *Fax:* 306-525-8960
www.sfl.sk.ca
www.facebook.com/SkFedofLabour
twitter.com/SKFedLabour
Overview: A large provincial organization overseen by Canadian Labour Congress
Mission: To act as Saskatchewan's voice of labour
Affiliation(s): 700+ locals throughout Saskatchewan
Membership: 95,000+ unionized workers; *Member Profile:* Members from 37 national & international unions; *Committees:* Aboriginal; Ad Hoc Committee on Trade; Apprentice; Balancing Work & Family; Collective Bargaining; Education; Enviroment; Health Care; Human Rights; Office & Administration Workers; Occupational Health & Safety; Pension & Benefits; Political Education; Shiftwork; Solidarity & Pride; Women's; Workers' Compensation; Youth
Activities: Speaking out on local, provincial, national, & international issues to support social & economic justice; Offering scholarships
Chief Officer(s):
Larry Hubich, President
l.hubich@sfl.sk.ca
Meetings/Conferences:
• Saskatchewan Federation of Labour 2018 62nd Annual Convention, 2018, SK
Scope: Provincial

Contact Information: Office Administration Contact: Kathy Abel, E-mail: k.abel@sfl.sk.ca

Saskatchewan Federation of Police Officers (SFPO)
SK
Tel: 306-539-0960
www.saskpolice.com
Overview: A medium-sized provincial organization
Mission: To advance police work as a profession; To support members in their police careers
Membership: 1,000+; *Member Profile:* Police personnel from six municipalities in Saskatchewan; Police associations from Regina, Saskatoon, Prince Albert, Moose Jaw, Weyburn, & Estevan
Activities: Supporting public relations programs; Instituting charitable programs; Maintaining philanthropic programs; Presenting recommendations to the Saskatchewan Police Commission; Liaising with government about police issues
Chief Officer(s):
Bernie Eiswirth, Executive Officer
beiswirth@saskpolice.com
Evan Bray, President
ebray@saskpolice.com
Jason Stonechild, Executive Vice-President
ebray@saskpolice.com
Meetings/Conferences:
• Saskatchewan Federation of Police Officers 2018 Annual Meeting, 2018, SK
Scope: Provincial
Description: The Executive Board reports on matters dealt with for & on behalf of members of the Federation at a meeting held each year between April 1st & May 31st

Saskatchewan Fencing Association (SFA)
c/o Marcia Coulic Salahub, Office Manager, 510 Cynthia St., Saskatoon SK S7L 7K7
Tel: 306-975-0823
saskfencing@shaw.ca
saskfencing.com
www.facebook.com/SaskFencingAssoc
twitter.com/SKFencingAssoc
Overview: A small provincial charitable organization overseen by Canadian Fencing Federation
Mission: To promote & develop the sport of fencing in Saskatchewan
Affiliation(s): Saskatchewan Sport
Finances: *Annual Operating Budget:* $100,000-$250,000; *Funding Sources:* Saskatchewan Sport; Fundraising
Staff Member(s): 14; 20 volunteer(s)
Membership: 300; *Fees:* Schedule available
Activities: Organizing competitions & training camps
Chief Officer(s):
Marcia Coulic-Salahub, Office Manager

Saskatchewan Field Hockey Association
1860 Lorne St., Regina SK S4P 2L7
Tel: 306-780-9256; *Fax:* 306-781-6021
sfha@sasktel.net
Overview: A small provincial organization overseen by Field Hockey Canada
Mission: To promote the sport of field hockey in Saskatchewan.
Member of: Field Hockey Canada

Saskatchewan Filmpool Co-operative
#301, 1822 Scarth St., Regina SK S4P 2G3
Tel: 306-757-8818; *Fax:* 306-757-3622
Other Communication:
plus.google.com/111287203811213570676
info@filmpool.ca
www.filmpool.ca
www.facebook.com/27856059701
www.youtube.com/user/FilmpoolProduction
Also Known As: Filmpool
Overview: A small provincial charitable organization founded in 1977
Mission: To support & encourage independent visionary filmmaking; to develop an awareness & appreciation of independent & indigenous film
Member of: Independent Media Arts Alliance; Saskatchewan Motion Picture Assoc.; SaskCulture; Sask Arts Alliance
Finances: *Annual Operating Budget:* $100,000-$250,000; *Funding Sources:* Saskatchewan Lotteries; Saskatchewan Arts Board; Canada Council; City of Regina; National Film Board
Staff Member(s): 3
Membership: 168; *Fees:* $70 full; $55 basic; $15 subscriber; *Committees:* Production; Workshops; Communications; Exhibitions; Membership; Fundraising

Activities: Film production equipment; production assistance funding; filmmaking workshops; screening; *Library*
Chief Officer(s):
Gordon Pepper, Executive Director
gm@filmpool.ca

Saskatchewan Food Processors Association (SFPA) / Association des manufacturiers de produits alimentaires de Saskatchewan
#389, 8B-3110 - 8th St. East, Saskatoon SK S7H 0W2
info@sfpa.sk.ca
www.sfpa.sk.ca
www.facebook.com/SaskFoodProcessors
Overview: A small provincial organization founded in 1990
Mission: To encourage the growth of the Saskatchewan food & beverage industry by assisting our members in meeting the needs of the consumer through the promotion of Saskatchewan-made products in & beyond our province
Membership: 200; *Fees:* $220: 1-24 employees; $440: 25-29 employees; $660: 50+ employees; 325 associate; *Member Profile:* Food & beverage companies located in Saskatchewan; companies that provide services to the food industry
Activities: "Premier" & "Taste of Spring" wine & food festivals; market development, export development, business development activities that assist the growth of companies within the Saskatchewan food industry
Chief Officer(s):
Kim Hill, Executive Director
kimhill@sfpa.sk.ca

Saskatchewan Forestry Association (SFA)
#139, 1061 Central Ave., Prince Albert SK S6V 4V4
Tel: 306-763-2189; *Fax:* 306-763-6456
info@whitebirch.ca
www.whitebirch.ca
Overview: A medium-sized provincial charitable organization founded in 1972 overseen by Canadian Forestry Association
Mission: To promote the wise use, protection, & management of forests, water, & wildlife in Saskatchewan
Affiliation(s): Canadian Forestry Association
Finances: *Funding Sources:* Membership fees; Donations; Sponsorships; Fundraising
Membership: *Fees:* Schedule available for corporations, based upon size; $15 students; $25 individuals; $35 families; *Member Profile:* Individuals, families, groups, & corporations who care about the future of Saskatchewan's forest resources
Activities: Delivering forest education materials & programming to schools & the public; Managing interpretive trails
Chief Officer(s):
Sindy Nicholson, President
Publications:
• TreeLines [a publication of the Saskatchewan Forestry Association]
Type: Newsletter; *Frequency:* Quarterly; *Editor:* Andrea Atkinson; *Price:* Free with membership in the Saskatchewan Forestry Association
Profile: Information about association activities & forestry industry issues, as well as a "Teacher's Corner" for educators

Saskatchewan Francophone Youth Association *Voir* Association jeunesse fransaskoise

Saskatchewan Freestyle Ski Incorporated
SK
saskfreestyle.ca
Also Known As: Sask Freestyle Ski Incorporated
Overview: A small provincial organization overseen by Canadian Freestyle Ski Association
Mission: To run programs developed by the Canadian Freestyle Ski Association.
Member of: Canadian Freestyle Ski Association
Chief Officer(s):
Kim Ryan, President
kimeryan64@gmail.com

Saskatchewan Friends of Schizophrenics *See* Schizophrenia Society of Saskatchewan

Saskatchewan Funeral Service Association *See* Funeral & Cremation Services Council of Saskatchewan

Saskatchewan Genealogical Society (SGS)
#110, 1514 - 11th Ave., Regina SK S4P 0H2
Tel: 306-780-9207
saskgenealogy@sasktel.net
www.saskgenealogy.com
www.facebook.com/216892188363312

Overview: A medium-sized international charitable organization founded in 1969
Mission: To provide assistance in researching family history throughout the world; to preserve heritage documents; to collect materials for study
Finances: *Annual Operating Budget:* $250,000-$500,000; *Funding Sources:* Sask Lotteries; Membership fees; Fundraising; Donations; Sponsorships
Staff Member(s): 4
Membership: 569; *Fees:* $50 individual; $25 student; $55 organization; $250 corporate; $1000 lifetime; *Committees:* Conference; Newspaper Publication; Summer Camp
Activities: Locating & recording burial sites in Saskatchewan through the Saskatchewan Cemetery Program; Maintaining the Saskatchewan Obituary File & the Saskatchewan Residents Index; Offering workshops & cerification courses; *Library:* Saskatchewan Genealogical Society Library; Open to public
Chief Officer(s):
Linda Dunsmore-Porter, Executive Director
Awards:
• Heritage Volunteer of the Year Award
Publications:
• Births, Deaths, Marriages from Regina Newspapers
• Change of Name - The Saskatchewan Gazette - 1917 to 1950
• R.C.M.P. Obituary Index 1933-1989
• Saskatchewan Genealogical Society Bulletin
Type: Journal; *Frequency:* Quarterly; *Price:* Free with SGS membership
Profile: Information about genealogical resources in Saskatchewan & across the world
• Saskatchewan Heritage Resources Directory
Type: Directory
Profile: Location & identification of heritage resources in Saskatchewan
• Tracing Your Aboriginal Ancestors in the Prairie Provinces
• Tracing Your Saskatchewan Ancestors

Battlefords Branch
RR#3, North Battleford SK S9A 2X4
Tel: 306-445-5425

Biggar Branch
PO Box 1103, Biggar SK S0K 0M0
Tel: 306-948-3638
www.biggargenealogy.wikifoundry.com
Chief Officer(s):
Rae Chamberlain, Contact
rwcambe@sasktel.net

Central Butte Branch
PO Box 298, Central Butte SK S0H 0T0
Tel: 306-796-2148
Chief Officer(s):
Joanne Berg, Contact
barry.berg@sasktel.net

Grasslands Branch
PO Box 272, Mankota SK S0H 2W0
Tel: 306-478-2314
Chief Officer(s):
Linda Calvin, Contact

Moose Jaw Branch
PO Box 154, Briercrest SK S0H 0K0
Tel: 306-799-2004
grcleave@sasktel.net
www.rootsweb.ancestry.com/~skmjbsgs
Chief Officer(s):
Marge Cleave, Contact
grcleave@sasktel.net

North-East Branch
PO Box 100, Melfort SK S0E 1A0
Tel: 306-752-4080
Chief Officer(s):
Ron Unger, Contact
r.a.unger@sasktel.net

Pangman Branch
PO Box 159, Ceylon SK S0C 0T0
Tel: 306-454-2400
Chief Officer(s):
Joyce Carleton, Contact
jlcarlson@sasktel.net

Pipestone Branch
PO Box 331, Maryfield SK S0G 3K0
Tel: 306-646-4952
Chief Officer(s):
Gerald Adair, Contact
gerry.pat@sasktel.net

Prince Albert Branch
PO Box 9, Prince Albert SK S6V 5R5
Tel: 306-764-3632
Chief Officer(s):
Jim Wilm, Contact
jameswilm@sasktel.net

Regina Branch
3633 Mason Ave., Regina SK S4S 0Z7
Tel: 306-789-5120
sgsregina@gmail.com
www.rootsweb.ancestry.com/~canrbsgs
Chief Officer(s):
Ian Brace, Contact

Saskatoon Branch
350 Acadia Dr., Saskatoon SK S7H 3V6
Tel: 306-229-2378
www.genealogysaskatoon.org
twitter.com/GenealogySBSGS
Chief Officer(s):
Rene Stock, Contact
rene@stockfamily.ca

Southeast Branch
PO Box 795, Carnduff SK S0C 0S0
Tel: 306-482-3378
Chief Officer(s):
Lynette Lang, Contact
cl.lang@sasktel.net

Swift Current Branch
819 - 9th Ave. NE, Swift Current SK S9H 2S7
Tel: 306-773-0280
Chief Officer(s):
Joanne Jensen, Contact
jensen@sasktel.net

West Central Branch
PO Box 472, Eston SK S0L 1A0
Tel: 306-962-3382
Chief Officer(s):
Verna Thompson, Contact
tomgra@sasktel.net

Weyburn Branch
PO Box 117, Creelman SK S0G 0X0
Tel: 306-361-1816
Chief Officer(s):
Lorna Bossenberry, Contact
bossenberry@sasktel.net
Ilene Johnston, Contact, 306-848-0941
ilenel@accesscomm.ca

Yorkton Branch
PO Box 177, Yorkton SK S3N 2V7
Tel: 306-782-7969
sgsyorkton.chapter.wordpress.com
Chief Officer(s):
Glenn Wiseman, Contact
gwiseman@accesscomm.ca

Saskatchewan German Council Inc. (SGC)
John V. Remai Centre, 510 Cynthia St., Saskatoon SK S7L 7K7
Tel: 306-975-0845; *Fax:* 306-242-8007
office@saskgermancouncil.org
www.saskgermancouncil.org
www.facebook.com/saskgermancouncil
twitter.com/saskgerman
Overview: A medium-sized provincial organization founded in 1984
Mission: To promote & preserve the culture, language, customs, traditions & interests of Saskatchewan people of German-speaking backgrounds
Member of: German-Canadian Congress
Staff Member(s): 3
Membership: 38 organizations; *Fees:* $15 individual/associate; $30 organization; $45 supporting
Activities: *Speaker Service:* Yes; *Library*
Chief Officer(s):
Sabine Doebel-Atchison, Executive Director
sabine@saskgermancouncil.org
Josephin Dick, President
Awards:
• Special Volunteer Awards

Saskatchewan Golf Association Inc.
510 Cynthia St., Saskatoon SK S7L 7K7
Tel: 306-975-0850; *Fax:* 306-975-0840
www.golfsaskatchewan.org
www.facebook.com/GolfSaskatchewan
twitter.com/GolfSK
Also Known As: Golf Saskatchewan
Merged from: Saskatchewan Golf Association; Canadian Ladies Golf Association of Saskatchewan
Overview: A large provincial organization founded in 1999 overseen by Golf Canada
Mission: To promote & maintain amateur golf in Saskatchewan by providing access to information & clinics on golf skills development, rules, handicapping, & etiquette
Staff Member(s): 3
Membership: *Fees:* $31.50 adult & junior club; $52.45 Golf SK Public Players Club
Activities: Providing provincial championships, scholarships, player clinics, rules workshops, & handicap clinics; *Internships:* Yes
Chief Officer(s):
Brian Lee, Executive Director, 306-975-0841
Candace Dunham, Manager, Programs & Member Services, 306-975-0850

Saskatchewan Government & General Employees' Union (SGEU) / Syndicat de la fonction publique de la Saskatchewan
1440 Broadway Ave., Regina SK S4P 1E2
Tel: 306-522-8571; *Fax:* 306-352-1969
Toll-Free: 800-667-5221
general@sgeu.org
www.sgeu.org
www.facebook.com/SGEU.SK
twitter.com/sgeu
www.youtube.com/user/SGEUtube
Overview: A medium-sized provincial organization
Mission: To represent & protect the interests of its members who work in the public sector in Saskatchewan
Member of: National Union of Public and General Employees
Finances: *Annual Operating Budget:* Greater than $5 Million; *Funding Sources:* Membership dues
Membership: 20,000+
Activities: *Library:* Resource Centre
Chief Officer(s):
Bob Bymoen, President
bbymoen@sgeu.org

Saskatchewan Graphic Arts Industries Association (SGAIA)
PO Box 7152, Saskatoon SK S7K 4J1
Tel: 306-373-3202; *Fax:* 306-373-3246
info@sgaia.ca
sgaia.ca
Merged from: Saskatoon Employing Printers Association; Employing Printers Association of Regina
Overview: A medium-sized provincial organization founded in 1960
Mission: To promote the interests of Saskatchewan's printing & allied industries; To increase the influence of graphic arts industry to the government & the general business community; To promote programs for the graphic arts industry at universities & technical institutions
Affiliation(s): Canadian Printing Industries Association; Printing Industries of America; Graphic Arts Technical Foundation
Membership: 27; *Fees:* Schedule available, based on sales ranges; *Member Profile:* Companies engaged in the production of printed materials for sale; Firms in the pre-press, binding & finishing sectors; Associate members are firms that sell equipment & operating supplies; *Committees:* Annual General Meeting; Environment, Publicity & Promotion; Government Affairs; Membership
Activities: Providing information about the graphic arts industry; Improving members' management skills; Developing programs & seminars on topics such as production, sales, & marketing; Assisting suppliers to serve the needs of the industry; Facilitating networking opportunities for the exchange of business ideas; Upholding a code of ethics to maintain a high standard of service & products offered
Chief Officer(s):
Don Breher, Executive Director, 306-373-3202, Fax: 306-373-3246
execdir@sgaia.ca

Saskatchewan Ground Water Association (SGWA)
PO Box 9434, Saskatoon SK S7K 7E9
Tel: 306-244-7551; *Fax:* 306-343-0001
teksmarts.com/skgwa
Previous Name: Saskatchewan Water Well Association
Overview: A small provincial organization

Mission: To act as the voice of the ground water industy throughout Saskatchewan; To promote the management of ground water throughout the province
Activities: Providing education about ground water
Chief Officer(s):
Kathleen Watson, Contact

Saskatchewan Gymnastics Association See Gymnastics Saskatchewan

Saskatchewan Handball Association (SHA)
SK
Tel: 306-584-8035
dkazymyra@cableregina.com
nonprofits.accesscomm.ca/sha
Overview: A small provincial organization
Mission: To promote & develop the sport of handball in Saskatchewan

Saskatchewan Head Injury Association See Saskatchewan Brain Injury Association

Saskatchewan Health Libraries Association (SHLA)
SK
shlasask@gmail.com
shla.chla-absc.ca
Overview: A medium-sized provincial organization founded in 1988 overseen by Canadian Health Libraries Association
Mission: To promote access to health care literature for physicians & allied health care staff
Membership: *Fees:* $30 individuals; $75 institutions
Chief Officer(s):
Lukas Miller, President
lukas.miller@usask.ca
Erin Langman, Secretary & Treasurer
erin.langman@saskpolytech.ca

Saskatchewan Heavy Construction Association (SHCA)
1939 Elphinstone St., Regina SK S4T 3N3
Tel: 306-586-1805; *Fax:* 306-585-3750
www.saskheavy.ca
www.facebook.com/SaskHeavy
twitter.com/saskheavy
www.youtube.com/user/saskheavy
Overview: A medium-sized provincial organization founded in 1919 overseen by Canadian Construction Association
Mission: To commit to the heavy construction industry by actively promoting quality, cost-effective & socially responsible services for the public & its members
Member of: Saskatchewan Construction Association
Affiliation(s): Alberta Roadbuilders & Heavy Construction Association; BC Roadbuilders & Heavy Construction Association; Canadian Construction Association; Heavy Construction Association of Saskatchewan; Manitoba Heavy Construction Association; Western Canada Roadbuilders & Heavy Construction Association
Finances: *Annual Operating Budget:* $500,000-$1.5 Million
Staff Member(s): 2; 15 volunteer(s)
Membership: 200+; *Committees:* Executive
Activities: Advocating & lobbying on behalf of members
Chief Officer(s):
Carmen Duncan, Chairman
Publications:
• Think BIG [a publication by the Saskatchewan Heavy Construction Association]
Type: Magazine

Saskatchewan Herb & Spice Association (SHSA)
PO Box 7568, Stn. Main, Saskatoon SK S7K 4L4
Tel: 306-694-4622
shsa@sasktel.net
www.saskherbspice.org
Overview: A small provincial organization
Mission: To support research, development & promotion of crops & products from yesterday & tomorrow for producers to processors to retails today
Membership: 300; *Fees:* $65 regular; $220 corporate; $540 corporate sponsorship
Activities: Member networking; annual member directory; public awareness; ongoing research of production & market promotion
Chief Officer(s):
Connie Kehler, Executive Director

Saskatchewan Hereford Association (SHA)
PO Box 713, Weyburn SK S4H 2K8
Tel: 306-842-6149; *Fax:* 306-842-0296
skhereford@sasktel.net
www.saskhereford.com
Overview: A small provincial organization founded in 1919
Mission: To promote Saskatchewan Herefords provincially, nationally & internationally
Member of: Canadian Hereford Association
Membership: 300
Chief Officer(s):
Doug Mann, President
w_mann@xplornet.ca
Marilyn Charlton, General Manager

Saskatchewan High Schools Athletic Association (SHSAA)
#1, 575 Park St., Regina SK S4N 5B2
Tel: 306-721-2151; *Fax:* 306-721-2659
shsaa@shsaa.ca
www.shsaa.ca
www.facebook.com/264860913591330
twitter.com/shsaasport
Overview: A medium-sized provincial organization founded in 1948 overseen by School Sport Canada
Mission: To use interschool athletics as a means for fostering positive opportunities for students
Member of: School Sport Canada
Staff Member(s): 4
Chief Officer(s):
Roger Morgan, President
morgan.roger@prairiesouth.ca
Kevin Vollet, Executive Director
k.vollet@shsaa.ca
Awards:
• Merit Award
• Service Awards

Saskatchewan History & Folklore Society Inc. (SHFS)
1860 Lorne St., Regina SK S4P 2L7
Tel: 306-780-9204; *Fax:* 306-780-9489
Toll-Free: 800-919-9437
shfs.fa@sasktel.net
www.shfs.ca
Overview: A medium-sized provincial organization founded in 1957
Mission: To encourage & promote the gathering, preservation & sharing of the history & folklore of Saskatchewan
Member of: Heritage Canada; Sask Culture
Affiliation(s): American Association for State & Local History
Finances: *Annual Operating Budget:* $100,000-$250,000
Staff Member(s): 2; 25 volunteer(s)
Membership: 500 individuals + 30 organizations; *Fees:* $30
Activities: Summer Motorcoach Tours; provides funding for permanent recognition of local historical events; Saskatchewan Historical Recognition Registry; Local History Marker Program; oral history training; Publish quarterly magazine "Folklore";
Library: Open to public
Chief Officer(s):
Finn Andersen, Executive Director
Publications:
• Folklore
Type: Magazine; *Frequency:* Quarterly; *Price:* Included with membership, or annual subscription for $21
Profile: Original manuscripts that contain Saskatechwan history. The magazine publishes stories about folklore & history, as well as poetry

Saskatchewan Hockey Association (SHA) / Association de hockey de la Saskatchewan
#2, 575 Park St., Regina SK S4N 5B2
Tel: 306-789-5101
www.sha.sk.ca
www.facebook.com/324377598563
twitter.com/sask_hockey
Overview: A medium-sized provincial organization founded in 1912 overseen by Hockey Canada
Mission: To administer the operation of amateur hockey in the Province of Saskatchewan; To foster & promote amateur hockey within the province & to assist in the promotion of amateur hockey outside the province; To promote, supervise & administer all competitions for amateur hockey within the jurisdiction of the SAHA
Member of: Hockey Canada
Finances: *Annual Operating Budget:* $1.5 Million-$3 Million
Staff Member(s): 10
Membership: 46,000

Chief Officer(s):
Kelly McClintock, General Manager
kellym@sha.sk.ca

Saskatchewan Home Based Educators (SHBE)
PO Box 8541, Saskatoon SK S7K 6K6
help_desk@shbe.info
www.shbe.info
Overview: A small provincial licensing charitable organization
Mission: Assist in creating a positive social network and a positive political environment for all those who choose home-based education.
Membership: *Committees:* Home Schooling; Special Needs Advisory Council; High School & Post-Secondary Advisory Council; Unschooling Advisory Council
Activities: Annual provincial information meetings
Meetings/Conferences:
• 27th Annual Saskatchewan Home Based Educators Convention, February, 2018, Queensbury Convention Center, Regina, SK
Scope: Provincial

Saskatchewan Home Builders' Association See Canadian Home Builders' Association - Saskatchewan

Saskatchewan Home Economics Teachers Association (SHETA)
Saskatoon SK
www.sheta.ca
Overview: A small provincial organization founded in 1969
Mission: To allow Home Economics teachers from across Saskatchewan to network & share ideas
Affiliation(s): Saskatchewan Teachers Federation
Membership: *Fees:* $30
Chief Officer(s):
Michelle Hardy, President
shetapresident@gmail.com
Awards:
• SHETA Undergraduate Award
Meetings/Conferences:
• 2018 Saskatchewan Home Economics Teachers Association Conference, 2018, SK
Scope: Provincial

Saskatchewan Horse Breeders Association
PO Box 3771, Regina SK S4P 3N8
Tel: 306-757-6133; *Fax:* 306-525-5852
sla@accesscomm.ca
Overview: A small provincial organization
Member of: Saskatchewan Livestock Association
Affiliation(s): Canadian Western Agribition Association

Saskatchewan Horse Federation (SHF)
2205 Victoria Ave., Regina SK S4P 0S4
Tel: 306-780-9449; *Fax:* 306-525-4041
shfadmin@sasktel.net
www.saskhorse.ca
www.facebook.com/SaskHorse
Overview: A medium-sized provincial organization founded in 1976
Mission: To work with other equestrian organizations in order to bring educational & recreational programs to the public.
Member of: Equine Canada
Affiliation(s): Sask Sport; Western College Veterinary Medicine; SK Agriculture & Food (SAF)
Finances: *Funding Sources:* Self-help; Saskatchewan Lotteries
Staff Member(s): 2
Membership: *Fees:* $50 adults; $35 junior; $120 family; $85-$225 clubs; *Member Profile:* Individuals; family; corporate; clubs; sustaining
Activities: Coaching certification; competition circuit; clinics; grants; rider certification; officials development; horse industry; member insurance; Horsin' Around raffle; Agribition; Youth Equestrian Games; Sask Horse Week
Chief Officer(s):
Pam Duckworth, Senior Administrator
pamduckworth@saskhorse.ca

Saskatchewan Hotel & Hospitality Association (SHHA)
#302, 2080 Broad St., Regina SK S4P 1Y3
Tel: 306-522-1664
Toll-Free: 800-667-1118
info@skhha.com
www.skhha.com
Previous Name: Hotels Association of Saskatchewan

Canadian Associations / Saskatchewan Independent Insurance Adjusters' Association

Overview: A medium-sized provincial organization overseen by Hotel Association of Canada Inc.
Chief Officer(s):
Glenn Weir, Chair, 306-529-5240
Jim Bence, Chief Executive Officer, 306-291-3031
Meetings/Conferences:
• The Saskatchewan Hotel & Hospitality Association Hotel & Hospitality Conference, 2018, SK
Scope: Provincial

Saskatchewan Independent Insurance Adjusters' Association
c/o Justin Braaten, Capital Claims Adjusters Ltd., 3500 - 13th Ave., Regina SK S4T 1P9
Fax: 866-725-4794
Toll-Free: 866-550-0516
www.ciaa-adjusters.ca
Overview: A small provincial organization overseen by Canadian Independent Adjusters' Association
Member of: Canadian Independent Adjusters' Association
Chief Officer(s):
Justin Braaten, President
justin@capitalclaims.ca

Saskatchewan Insolvency Practitioners Association *See* Saskatchewan Association of Insolvency & Restructuring Professionals

Saskatchewan Institute of Agrologists (SIA)
#29, 1501 - 8th St. East, Saskatoon SK S7H 5J6
Tel: 306-242-2606; *Fax:* 306-955-5561
info@sia.sk.ca
www.sia.sk.ca
www.linkedin.com/company/saskatchewan-institute-of-agrologists
www.facebook.com/sia.sk.ca
twitter.com/SKAgrologists
Overview: A small provincial organization founded in 1946
Mission: To promote and increase the knowledge, skill & proficiency of its members in the practice of agrology; Do all things that may be necessary, incidental or conducive to the usefulness of agrologists to the public; Protect the public in all matters relating to the gathering, analyzing and distributing of information respecting agrology; Ensure the proficiency and competency of agrologists
Member of: Agrology/Agronomes Canada
Finances: *Annual Operating Budget:* $500,000-$1.5 Million; *Funding Sources:* Membership dues
Staff Member(s): 4; 75 volunteer(s)
Membership: 1,300; *Fees:* $385; *Member Profile:* Agrologists; *Committees:* Act & Bylaw; Admissions & Registration; Executive; Professional Conduct; Discipline; Honours & Awards; Articling Program; Education; Issues; Nominations; Professional Development & Standards; Public Awareness & Communications; Student Relations
Chief Officer(s):
Al Schola, Executive Director & Registrar
  Northeast Branch
  northeastbranch@sia.sk.ca
  Chief Officer(s):
  Chad Bohachewski, President, 306-862-2522
  Northwest Branch
  northwestbranch@sia.sk.ca
  Chief Officer(s):
  Colleen Murphy, President, 306-480-5596
  Regina Branch
  reginabranch@sia.sk.ca
  Chief Officer(s):
  Barry Rapp, President, 306-692-1661
  Saskatoon Branch
  saskatoonbranch@sia.sk.ca
  Chief Officer(s):
  Adams Frimpong, President, 306-716-2135
  Southwest Branch
  southwestbranch@sia.sk.ca
  Chief Officer(s):
  Wyatt Burnett, President, 306-750-7822
  Yorkton Branch
  yorktonbranch@sia.sk.ca
  Chief Officer(s):
  Allana Lewchuk, President, 204-806-4042

Saskatchewan Institute of the Purchasing Management Association of Canada *See* Supply Chain Management Association - Saskatchewan

Saskatchewan Institute on Prevention of Handicaps *See* Saskatchewan Prevention Institute

Saskatchewan Interagency Council on Smoking & Health *See* Saskatchewan Coalition for Tobacco Reduction

Saskatchewan Intercultural Association Inc. (SIA)
#405, 1702 - 20th St. West, Saskatoon SK S7M 0Z9
Tel: 306-978-1818; *Fax:* 306-978-1411
info@saskintercultural.org
saskintercultural.org
www.facebook.com/saskintercultural
twitter.com/skintercultural
Previous Name: Saskatoon Multicultural Council
Overview: A small provincial charitable organization founded in 1964
Mission: To promote equal opportunity & fair treatment for everyone
Finances: *Funding Sources:* Sponsorships
Staff Member(s): 15
Membership: *Fees:* $20 individual; $50 group
Activities: Employment programs; Education programs; Equity & anti-racism programs; Performing arts programs; *Speaker Service:* Yes; *Library:* SIA Resource Centre; Open to public
Chief Officer(s):
Jess Hamm, Executive Director
jhamm@saskintercultural.org
Gabrielle Bouchard, Manager, Policy & Program
gbouchard@saskintercultural.org

Saskatchewan Joint Board Retail, Wholesale & Department Store Union (SJBRWDSU)
1233 Winnipeg St., Regina SK S4R 1K1
Tel: 306-569-9311; *Fax:* 306-569-9521
Toll-Free: 877-747-9378
rwdsu.regina@sasktel.net
www.rwdsu.sk.ca
Also Known As: RWDSU-Saskatchewan
Overview: A medium-sized provincial organization
Staff Member(s): 11
Membership: 6,000+
Chief Officer(s):
Garry Burkart, Secretary-Treasurer
gburkart@rwdsu.sk.ca
Awards:
• SJBRWDSU Scholarship
33 scholarships awarded to the children of RWDSU members, or to members themselves, who are enrolled in a university or vocational school as a full-time student

Saskatchewan Karate Association (SKA)
510 Cynthia St., Saskatoon SK S7L 7K7
Tel: 306-374-7333; *Fax:* 306-374-7334
sk.karate@shaw.ca
www.saskarate.com
Overview: A small provincial organization founded in 1977 overseen by Karate Canada
Mission: To be the provincial governing body for the sport of karate in Saskatchewan
Member of: Karate Canada
Activities: Insurance Benefits; Seminars; Provincial, National & International Tournaments; Althletic Development Program; Althete's Assistance Program
Chief Officer(s):
Dave Smith, President

Saskatchewan Katahdin Sheep Association Inc. (SKSA)
PO Box 548, Quill Lake SK S0A 3E0
Tel: 306-383-2861
www.saskkatahdinsheep.com
www.facebook.com/570204566350748
twitter.com/SaskKatahdin
Overview: A small provincial organization founded in 1993 overseen by Canadian Katahdin Sheep Association Inc.
Mission: To develop & advance the Katahdin sheep breed in Saskatchewan
Membership: 1-99; *Fees:* $10 junior members, age 15 & under; $25 senior members; *Member Profile:* Owners of Canadian registered Katahdin sheep in Saskatchewan; *Committees:* Show & Sale; New Producer Liaison
Activities: Distributing breed information; Preparing displays for various shows throughout the province; Creating networking opportunities with other sheep producers; Providing education, such as on-farm seminars & hands-on-training sessions; Showing sheep at events such as the Canadian Western Agribition
Chief Officer(s):
Jean L'Arrivee, President, 306-769-8981, Fax: 306-769-8916
cccranch@sasktel.net
Janette Mish, Vice-President, 306-429-2221, Fax: 306-429-2221
jmish@sasktel.net
Donna Schryver, Secretary, 306-383-2861
schryvers@sasktel.net
Donna Bruynooghe, Treasurer, 306-937-2041
dbruynooghe@highways.gov.sk.ca
Publications:
• News for Ewes
Type: Newsletter; *Frequency:* Quarterly; *Accepts Advertising*; *Editor:* Janette Mish
• Saskatchewan Katahdin Sheep Association Membership Directory
Type: Directory; *Price:* Free

Saskatchewan Lacrosse Association
2205 Victoria Ave., Regina SK S4P 0S4
Tel: 306-780-9216; *Fax:* 306-525-4009
Toll-Free: 844-780-9216
lacrosse@sasktel.net
www.sasklacrosse.net
www.facebook.com/SaskLacrosse
Also Known As: Sask Lacrosse
Overview: A medium-sized provincial organization overseen by Canadian Lacrosse Association
Mission: To promote & deliver lacrosse programs to the residents of Saskatchewan
Member of: Canadian Lacrosse Association; Sask Sport Inc.
Finances: *Annual Operating Budget:* $250,000-$500,000
Staff Member(s): 1; 10 volunteer(s)
Membership: 3,000; *Fees:* Schedule available
Chief Officer(s):
Shawn Williams, President
Bridget Pottle, Executive Director
ed@sasklacrosse.net
Chris Lesanko, Coordinator, Programs
programs@sasklacrosse.net

Saskatchewan Land Surveyors' Association (SLSA)
#230, 408 Broad St., Regina SK S4R 1X3
Tel: 306-352-8999; *Fax:* 306-352-8366
info@slsa.sk.ca
www.slsa.sk.ca
Overview: A small provincial licensing organization founded in 1910 overseen by Professional Surveyors Canada
Mission: To uphold the stewardship & standards of the legal survey profession in Saskatchewan; To regulate & govern members in the practice of professional land surveying & professional surveying; To ensure the competency of members; To administer the profession to protect the public
Membership: 95; *Member Profile:* Registered members of the association, who are licensed to practice as Saskatchewan land surveyors in Saskatchewan, in accordance with the provisions of the Land Surveyors & Professional Surveyors Act of Saskatchewan
Activities: Providing continuing education to licensed members; Investigating complaints from the public
Chief Officer(s):
Mike Waschuk, President
Carla Stadnick, Executive Director
Awards:
• I.W. Tweddell Memorial Award
Eligibility: A student land surveyor from Saskatchewan enrolled in a program that will result in a Certificate of Completion from The Canadian Board of Examiners for Professional Surveyors
Deadline: May 31; *Amount:* $1,250
Publications:
• SLSA [Saskatchewan Land Surveyors' Association] Corner Post
Type: Newsletter; *Frequency:* Quarterly; *Accepts Advertising*; *Editor:* Doug A. Bouck, SLS
Profile: Articles about surveying, in addition to regular features, such as the president's message & council highlights

Saskatchewan Landlords Association *See* Saskatchewan Rental Housing Industry Association

Saskatchewan Liberal Association
845 A McDonald St., Regina SK S4N 2X5
Fax: 613-235-7208
Toll-Free: 888-542-3725
saskatchewan@liberal.ca
saskatchewan.liberal.ca
www.facebook.com/LPC.SK
twitter.com/lpcsask

Also Known As: Saskatchewan Liberal Party
Overview: A medium-sized provincial organization overseen by The Liberal Party of Canada
Chief Officer(s):
Tara Jijian, Interim Leader

Saskatchewan Library Association (SLA)
#15, 2010 - 7th Ave., Regina SK S4R 1C2
Fax: 306-780-9447
www.saskla.ca
www.facebook.com/sasklibraryassociation
twitter.com/sklibrary
Overview: A small provincial charitable organization founded in 1914
Mission: To further the development of library services in Saskatchewan
Finances: *Funding Sources:* Membership fees; Donations; Sponsorships
Membership: *Fees:* Schedule available, based upon salary; *Member Profile:* Individuals, organizations, & institutions interested in library service & cultural activities in Saskatchewan
Activities: Supporting Saskatchewan library staff & libraries; Advocating for Saskatchewan libraries; Supporting continuing education; Providing information; Raising awareness of libraries; Coordinating programs; Promoting cooperation among libraries throughout the province; *Awareness Events:* Saskatchewan Library Week, October
Chief Officer(s):
Judy Nicholson, Executive Director, 306-780-9413
slaexdir@sasktel.net
Anne Pennylegion, Program Coordinator, 306-780-9409
slaprograms@sasktel.net
Awards:
• Saskatchewan Libraries Education Bursary
Awarded annually towards completion of a graduate degree program in Master of Library & Information Science *Eligibility:* Master of Library & Information Sciences students
• SLA Frances Morrison Award
Awarded for outstanding service to libraries
• Mary Donaldson Award of Merit
• SLA Continuing Education Workshop Grant
To support continuing education activities
• Maureen Woods Education Bursary
Awarded to promote the continued growth of professional librarianship in Saskatchewan; *Amount:* $5,000
Meetings/Conferences:
• Saskatchewan Library Association 2018 Annual Conference & Annual General Meeting, 2018, SK
Scope: Provincial
Contact Information: Saskatchewan Library Association, Phone: 306-780-9413, Fax: 306-780-9447, E-mail: slaprograms@sasktel.net
Publications:
• Saskatchewan Library Association Annual Report
Type: Yearbook; *Frequency:* Annually
• Saskatchewan Library Association Conference Handbook
Type: Handbook
Profile: Featuring conference planning information, such as finances, facilities, registration, programs, public relations, volunteers, & social events
• SLA [Saskatchewan Library Association] Governance Handbook
Type: Handbook
Profile: Featuring constitutions, by-laws, & policies
• SLAte [a publication of the Saskatchewan Library Association]
Type: Newsletter; *Frequency:* Monthly
Profile: News & important event dates for members

Saskatchewan Library Trustees' Association (SLTA)
c/o Nancy Kennedy, 79 Mayfair Cres., Regina SK S4S 5T9
Tel: 306-584-2495; *Fax:* 306-585-1473
www.slta.ca
www.facebook.com/sasklibrarytrusteesassoc
twitter.com/yourslta
Overview: A small provincial organization founded in 1942
Mission: To foster the development of libraries & library services throughout Saskatchewan
Finances: *Annual Operating Budget:* Less than $50,000
Membership: 756; *Fees:* $10; *Member Profile:* Library trustees from across Saskatchewan; Residents of Saskatchewan who support libraries; Administrative bodies responsible for public libraries
Activities: Facilitating the exchange of ideas & experiences among library board members; Cooperating with other associations of library trustees; Seeking improvements to legislation affecting libraries in Saskatchewan

Chief Officer(s):
Nancy Kennedy, Executive Director
njk@sasktel.net
Lorna Black, President
lornablack@nlsd113.ca
Sharon Armstrong, Vice-President
town.office.wynyard@sasktel.net
Meetings/Conferences:
• Saskatchewan Library Trustees' Association Annual General Meeting 2018, 2018
Scope: Provincial
Publications:
• The Trustee [a publication of the Saskatchewan Library Trustees Association]
Type: Newsletter; *Frequency:* 3 pa
Profile: Association updates, library news from around the province, & upcoming events

Saskatchewan Lions Eye Bank
Eye Dept., Saskatoon City Hospital, PO Box 447, Kipling SK S0G 2S0
www.eyebank.sklions.ca
Overview: A small provincial charitable organization founded in 1982
Mission: To promote corneal/eye donations after death to be used for transplantation to restore vision to people who have been rendered blind due to corneal injury, disease or degeneration
Member of: Eye Bank Association of America
Affiliation(s): CNIB
Finances: *Annual Operating Budget:* $50,000-$100,000; *Funding Sources:* Lions Clubs of Saskatchewan; provincial government
Staff Member(s): 3
Membership: 1-99
Activities: *Awareness Events:* National Donor Awareness Week, April
Chief Officer(s):
Garnet Davis, President
Awards:
• Garnet Davis Fellowship
; *Amount:* $500
• Cliff Worden Fellowship
; *Amount:* $1,000

Saskatchewan Literacy Network
#11, 2155 Airport Dr., Saskatoon SK S7L 6M5
Tel: 306-651-7288; *Fax:* 306-651-7287
Toll-Free: 888-511-2111
saskliteracy@saskliteracy.ca
saskliteracy.ca
www.facebook.com/SaskatchewanLiteracyNetwork
twitter.com/SkLitNet
www.youtube.com/user/SkLitNet
Overview: A small provincial charitable organization
Mission: To promote literacy in Saskatchewan
Member of: Movement for Canadian Literacy
Staff Member(s): 6
Membership: *Fees:* $70 organization; $25 individual; $5 learner
Activities: Implementing literacy projects in schools & in the community; Disseminating resources; Holding an annual general meeting; *Speaker Service:* Yes; *Library:* SLN Resource Centre; by appointment
Chief Officer(s):
Karen Danielson, Executive Director, 306-651-7283
Awards:
• Business Leadership in Literacy Award
• Professional Leadership in Literacy Award
• Volunteer Service Award
• Cameco Literacy Learning Award & Bursary
Meetings/Conferences:
• Saskatchewan Literacy Network Annual General Meeting 2018, 2018, SK
Scope: Provincial
Publications:
• e-News [a publication of the Saskatchewan Literacy Network]
Type: Newsletter
Profile: Contains resources, information, & literacy-related events in the province & nationally

Saskatchewan Livestock Association (SLA)
Canada Center Building, Evraz Place, PO Box 3771, Regina SK S4P 3N8
Tel: 306-757-6133; *Fax:* 306-525-5852
sla@accesscomm.ca
www.sasklivestock.com

Overview: A medium-sized provincial organization founded in 1075
Mission: To promote cooperation among the livestock organizations in Saskatchewan; To communicate opinions of livestock producers to government & other agencies; To encourage improvement in the production of livestock
Chief Officer(s):
Murray Andrew, Executive Director
Belinda Wagner, General Manager
Meetings/Conferences:
• Saskatchewan Beef Industry Conference 2018, January, 2018, Saskatoon Inn, Saskatoon, SK
Scope: Provincial
Description: An event organized by the Saskatchewan Livestock Association, Saskatchewan Cattlemen's Association, Saskatchewan Cattle Feeders Association, Saskatchewan Beef & Forage Symposium Committee, & the Saskatchewan Stock Growers Association
Contact Information: Shannon McArton, Conference Coordinator; Email: shannon.mcarton@sasktel.net; Phone: 306-731-7610, www.saskbeefconference.com

Saskatchewan Lung Association
Saskatoon Office, 1231 - 8 St. East, Saskatoon SK S7H 0S5
Tel: 306-343-9511; *Fax:* 306-343-7007
Toll-Free: 888-566-5864
info@sk.lung.ca
www.sk.lung.ca
www.facebook.com/LungSask
twitter.com/lungsk
www.youtube.com/user/LungAssociation1
Previous Name: Saskatchewan Anti-Tuberculosis League
Overview: A medium-sized provincial charitable organization founded in 1911 overseen by Canadian Lung Association
Mission: To improve respiratory health & overall quality of life; To advocate for support of education & research
Finances: *Funding Sources:* Donations; Sponsorships; Fundraising
Staff Member(s): 16
Membership: *Fees:* $25
Activities: Supporting & conducting research into respiratory health & disease; Providing educational programs; Offering the most current lung health information; Organizing sleep apnea support groups; Promoting the prevention of lung disease; Raising public awareness of the impact of respiratory diseases; Collaborating with other organizations to work toward lung health
Chief Officer(s):
Pat Smith, Chair
Karen Davis, Vice-Chair
Brian Graham, President & CEO
Jennifer Miller, Vice-President, Health Promotion
Sharon Kremeniuk, Vice-President, Development
Melissa Leib, Vice-President, Finance & Operations
Donna Crooks, Treasurer
Publications:
• Breathworks: COPD Newsletter
Type: Newsletter
Profile: Educational articles plus notices of forthcoming support group meetings
• Lung Association of Saskatchewan Annual Report
Type: Yearbook; *Frequency:* Annually
• Nightly Nezzz Newsletter
Type: Newsletter; *Frequency:* Quarterly
Profile: Information for persons with sleep apnea & their families

Saskatchewan Manitoba Galloway Association
PO Box 178, Petersfield MB R0C 2L0
Tel: 204-886-7851
Overview: A small provincial organization founded in 1969
Mission: To inform about and promote the breeding of the Galloway breed of cattle.
Member of: Canadian Galloway Association
Finances: *Funding Sources:* Membership dues
Membership: *Member Profile:* Farmer/rancher
Chief Officer(s):
Doug Noakes, Secretary
doogie992011@hotmail.com

Saskatchewan Martial Arts Association (SMAA)
PO Box 789, Melville SK S0A 2P0
Tel: 306-565-2266
saskamartialarts.ca
Overview: A small provincial organization
Mission: To be the provincial governing body for a variety of martial arts styles practiced in Saskatchewan
Member of: Sask Sport Inc.

Membership: *Fees:* $100 club
Chief Officer(s):
Tim Oehler, President
Stephen McLeod, Vice President

Saskatchewan Meat Processors' Association (SMPA)
RR#1, Wymark SK S0N 2Y0
Tel: 306-741-9886; *Fax:* 306-773-9067
smpa@sasktel.net
www.smpa.ca
Overview: A medium-sized provincial organization founded in 1945
Mission: To act as the spokesman for Saskatchewan meat processors, to represent the industry in Saskatchewan & to be responsive to the needs of its members
Membership: *Fees:* $150; *Member Profile:* Small industry, manufacturers & processors
Activities: *Rents Mailing List:* Yes
Chief Officer(s):
David Mumm, President

Saskatchewan Medical Association (SMA)
#201, 2174 Airport Dr., Saskatoon SK S7L 6M6
Tel: 306-244-2196; *Fax:* 306-653-1631
Toll-Free: 800-667-3781
sma@sma.sk.ca
www.sma.sk.ca
www.facebook.com/SMAdocs
twitter.com/SMA_docs
Overview: A medium-sized provincial organization founded in 1906 overseen by Canadian Medical Association
Mission: To represent physicians in Saskatchewan; To advance the professional, educational, & economic welfare of physicians in the province
Staff Member(s): 28
Membership: *Member Profile:* Saskatchewan physicians; *Committees:* Appointments & Awards; Rural & Regional Practice; Finance; Medical Compensation Review; Economics; Legislation & Policy; Payment Schedule Review; Intersectional Council; Primary Care; Council on Education & Quality Care; Physician Health Program; Specialist Recruitment & Retention; eHealth; Insurance
Activities: Engaging in advocacy activities; Promoting quality health care in Saskatchewan; Acting as the bargaining agent for fee-for-service physicians; Providing information about health care issues in Saskatchewan; Supporting continuing professional learning; Managing funds to offer programs such as bursaries & educational grants; Supporting physician health, through programs such as the Saskatchewan Physician Support Program
Chief Officer(s):
Intheran Pillay, President
Bonnie Brossart, Chief Executive Officer
Joanne Sivertson, Vice-President
Siva Karunakaran, Honourary Treasurer
Publications:
• SMA [Saskatchewan Medical Association] News
Type: Newsletter
Profile: Association issues & events

Saskatchewan Mining Association (SMA)
#1500, 2002 Victoria Ave., Regina SK S4P 0R7
Tel: 306-757-9505; *Fax:* 306-569-1085
info@saskmining.ca
www.saskmining.ca
twitter.com/SaskMiningAssoc
Overview: A small provincial organization founded in 1965 overseen by Mining Association of Canada
Mission: To ensure the safe & profitable development of mineral resources in Saskatchewan; To act as the voice of the mining industry throughout the province; To promote understanding of the development of mineral resources in Saskatchewan
Finances: *Funding Sources:* Membership fees
Membership: 50; *Member Profile:* Individuals & enterprises involved with mining & metallurgical industries; *Committees:* Safety; Public Awareness; Human Resources; Taxation; Environmental; Geotechnical
Activities: Liaising with both provincial & federal governments; Organizing research into matters such as industrial relations; Cooperating with similar organizations
Chief Officer(s):
Neil McMillan, President, 306-668-7505, Fax: 306-668-7500
Pamela Schwann, Executive Director, 306-757-9505, Fax: 306-569-1085
Meetings/Conferences:
• Saskatchewan Mining Association 52nd Annual General Meeting 2018, 2018, SK
Scope: Provincial
Publications:
• ORE [a publication of the Saskatchewan Mining Association]
Type: Magazine; *Frequency:* s-a.

Saskatchewan Motion Picture Industry Association (SMPIA)
Canada Saskatchewan Production Studios, #312, 1831 College Ave., Regina SK S4P 4V5
Tel: 306-780-9840
office@smpia.sk.ca
www.smpia.sk.ca
twitter.com/smpiaoffice
Overview: A medium-sized provincial organization founded in 1985
Mission: Committed to the intrinsic cultural & economic value of motion pictures;to work toward the creation & advancement of opportunities for the production, promotion & appreciation of motion pictures in Saskatchewan
Finances: *Annual Operating Budget:* $250,000-$500,000
Staff Member(s): 3; 50 volunteer(s)
Membership: 100-499; *Fees:* Schedule available; *Member Profile:* Individual, corporation or organization interested in Saskatchewan film, video & multimedia
Activities: *Library:* Not open to public
Chief Officer(s):
Lioz Bouganin, President
Max Berdowski, Executive Director
max@smpia.sk.ca
Publications:
• E-Buzzzz [a publication of the Saskatchewan Motion Picture Industry Association]
Type: E-Newsletter; *Frequency:* Weekly

Saskatchewan Municipal Hail Insurance Association (SMHI)
2100 Cornwall St., Regina SK S4P 2K7
Tel: 306-569-1852; *Fax:* 306-522-3717
Toll-Free: 877-414-7644
smhi@smhi.ca
www.smhi.ca
twitter.com/MunicipalHail
Overview: A medium-sized provincial organization founded in 1917
Mission: To provide spot-loss hail insurance coverage to Saskatchewan grain farmers at cost
Finances: *Annual Operating Budget:* Greater than $5 Million
Chief Officer(s):
Rodney Schoettler, Chief Executive Officer
rschoettler@municipalhail.ca
Mark Holfeld, Chief Operating Officer
mholfeld@municipalhail.ca

Saskatchewan Museums Association *See* Museums Association of Saskatchewan

Saskatchewan Music Educators Association (SMEA)
PO Box 632, Cudworth SK S0K 1B0
Tel: 306-256-7187
smea@sasktel.net
www.musiceducationonline.org/smea/smea.html
Overview: A small provincial organization founded in 1957
Mission: To promote the development of high standards of music & music education; To exchange information & ideas with those interested in music; To sponsor conventions, workshops, clinics & other means of musical development, information & education
Affiliation(s): Saskatchewan Teachers Federation; ISME; Canadian Music Educators Association; SaskCulture Inc.; Saskatchewan Arts Board; The Canadian Coalition for Music Education; Canadian Conference of the Arts; The National Symposium on Arts Educations; The Canada Council; The British Columbia MEA; The Alberta Music Association; The Manitoba MEA; The Ontario MEA; The New Brunswick MEA; The University of Sask. Music Department; The University of Regina Music Department; Brandon School of Music; The International Music Camp (North Dakota); The Conservatory of Music.; Saskatchewan Choral Federation
Chief Officer(s):
Val Kuemper, Executive Director
smea@sasktel.net

Saskatchewan Music Festival Association Inc.
PO Box 37005, Regina SK S4S 7K3
Tel: 306-757-1722; *Fax:* 306-347-7789
Toll-Free: 888-892-9929
sask.music.festival@sasktel.net
www.smfa.ca
twitter.com/SKMusicFestival
Overview: A medium-sized provincial charitable organization founded in 1908 overseen by Federation of Canadian Music Festivals
Mission: To provide a classical competitive music festival system of the highest standard at the local, provincial & national levels
Member of: Saskatchewan Council of Cultural Organizations
Staff Member(s): 2
Activities: *Library:*
Chief Officer(s):
Carol Donhauser, Executive Director
carol.smfa@sasktel.net

Saskatchewan Native Women's Association *See* Saskatchewan Aboriginal Women's Circle Corporation

Saskatchewan Nursery Landscape Association (SNLA)
c/o Landscape Alberta Nursery Trades Association, #200, 10331 - 178 St., Edmonton AB T5S 1R5
Toll-Free: 888-446-3499
www.snla.ca
Previous Name: Saskatchewan Nursery Trades Association
Overview: A medium-sized provincial organization overseen by Canadian Nursery Landscape Association
Mission: To encourage people in the landscaping industry to network in order to spread their wealth of knowledge among each other
Membership: 40; *Fees:* Schedule available
Chief Officer(s):
Leslie Cornell, President

Saskatchewan Nursery Trades Association *See* Saskatchewan Nursery Landscape Association

Saskatchewan Optometric Association *See* Saskatchewan Association of Optometrists

Saskatchewan Orchestral Association, Inc. (SOA)
4647 Pasqua St., Regina SK S4S 6B9
Tel: 306-529-7366
info@saskorchestras.com
www.saskorchestras.com
Overview: A medium-sized provincial organization founded in 1985 overseen by Orchestras Canada
Mission: To enhance the quality of life in Saskatchewan by helping to develop a thriving orchestral community
Member of: Orchestras Canada; SaskCulture; Saskatchewan Arts Alliance
Affiliation(s): SaskCulture; Saskatchewan Band Association; Saskatchewan Music Educators Association; Saskatchewan Choral Federation; Saskatchewan Music Festivals Association
Finances: *Annual Operating Budget:* $100,000-$250,000; *Funding Sources:* Membership fees; Saskatchewan Lotteries Trust Fund for Sport, Culture & Recreation (via SaskCulture)
Membership: *Fees:* $25; *Member Profile:* Interest in strings, orchestra, music
Activities: Supporting community-based programs through grants, bursaries, scholarships, sponsorships, & subsidies
Chief Officer(s):
Peter Sametz, Managing Consultant
Publications:
• Saskatchewan Orchestral Association, Inc. Newsletter
Type: Newsletter; *Frequency:* Irregular; *Accepts Advertising*

Saskatchewan Orchid Society (SOS)
PO Box 411, Saskatoon SK S7K 3L3
info@saskorchids.com
www.saskorchids.com
Overview: A small provincial organization founded in 1983
Mission: To promote orchid habitats & to provide a place for members to share knowledge amongst each other
Membership: 65; *Fees:* $25 single; $30 family
Chief Officer(s):
Cal Carter, President

Saskatchewan Organization for Heritage Languages Inc. (SOHL)
2144 Cornwall St., Regina SK S4P 2K7
Tel: 306-780-9275; *Fax:* 306-780-9407
sohl@sasktel.net
www.heritagelanguages.sk.ca
www.linkedin.com/in/sohl-sk-aa554151

www.facebook.com/sohl.sask
twitter.com/sohl_sk
Overview: A medium-sized provincial charitable organization founded in 1985
Mission: To promote & develop teaching of heritage languages in Saskatchewan; to act in advocacy capacity to make representation to government, institutions & boards regarding matters pertaining to heritage languages; to promote cooperation with & mutual support of provincial organizations with similar aims & objectives; to encourage inter-provincial & national liaison
Affiliation(s): SaskCulture
Finances: *Funding Sources:* Saskatchewan Lotteries
Staff Member(s): 3
Membership: 93; *Fees:* $25 regular; $10 associate
Activities: Providing programs & services for heritage language schools & multilingual organizations; Offering professional development opportunities, grants & bursaries; *Awareness Events:* Heritage Language Recognition Day
Chief Officer(s):
Tamara Ruzic, Executive Director
Awards:
• SOHL Scholarship for University of Calgary Certificate in Teaching International and Heritage Languages
Offered to heritage language teachers to obtain the online University of Calgary Teaching International and Heritage Languages (TIHL) Certificate *Eligibility:* Current regular or substitute teacher at a SOHL member school*Location:* University of Calgary *Deadline:* May 31
• SOHL Youth Heritage Instructor Helper Bursary
Eligibility: Heritage language student youth (age 18 and under) who work as instructor helpers at their respective heritage language schools & who have provided 50-70 hours of classroom assistance throughout the school year *Deadline:* September 15
• SOHL Language Camp Funding
Offered to acknowledge & encourage the use of language camps as a fun & educational experience for heritage language school students *Eligibility:* SOHL members who do not have a year-round language instruction program & want to organize a summer language camp *Deadline:* January 31
• SOHL Heritage Language Teaching Program Grant
Offered to provide financial assistance to SOHL member schools and multilingual organizations to help offset the costs of operating heritage language schools *Eligibility:* SOHL member schools and multilingual organizations who provide 70 hours of instruction to students throughout the regular school year & whose classes are held in a public facility *Deadline:* September 15

Saskatchewan Outdoor & Environmental Education Association (SOEEA)
PO Box 398, Craven SK S0G 0W0
www.saskoutdoors.org
www.facebook.com/SaskOutdoors-271057812846
Overview: A small provincial organization founded in 1972
Mission: To encourage educators & people who participate in outdoor education to teach & practise environmental responsibility
Affiliation(s): North American Association for Environmental Education
Membership: *Committees:* Communications Working Goup; Decision Makers Working Group; Education Working Group; Partners Working Group; Public & Families Working Group
Activities: Developing & evaluating education activities; Providing professional development workshops; Partnering with related organizations; Facilitating networking opportunities
Chief Officer(s):
Dennie Fornwald, President
denniefornwald@gmail.com
Leah Japp, Outreach Coordinator
soeeaoutreach@gmail.com
Awards:
• B.M. Melanson Award
To be presented periodically to an individual who has made an outstanding contribution to outdoor & environmental education in Saskatchewan; candidates shall be active participants in outdoor & environmental education in Saskatchewan; candidates need not be a member of SOEEA *Contact:* Yvette Crane
Meetings/Conferences:
• SaskOutdoors Annual General Meeting 2018, 2018, SK
Scope: Provincial
Publications:
• Envisage [a publication of the Saskatchewan Outdoor & Environmental Education Association]

Type: Newsletter; *Frequency:* Quarterly
Profile: Articles on topics such as educational strategies & instructional methods
• Green Teacher

Saskatchewan Outfitters Association (SOA)
PO Box 572, Stn. Main, Saskatoon SK S7K 3L6
Tel: 306-668-1388; *Fax:* 306-668-1353
soa@sasktel.net
www.soa.ca
Overview: A small provincial organization founded in 1967
Mission: Working together to promote & foster excellence in outfitting
Membership: 109
Chief Officer(s):
Brian Hoffart, President
baitmaster@sasktel.net

Saskatchewan Palliative Care Association
PO Box 37053, Regina SK S4S 7K3
Tel: 306-522-3232
Toll-Free: 888-614-8016
info@saskpalliativecare.org
www.saskpalliativecare.org
Overview: A medium-sized provincial charitable organization founded in 1991
Mission: To promote the philosophy & principles of palliative care through networking, education, advocacy & research; to improve quality of life for the dying
Member of: Canadian Palliative Care Association
Membership: *Fees:* $55 regular; $250 affiliate
Activities: Educational programs; grant disbursement; *Library:* Resource Library; Open to public
Chief Officer(s):
Jeff Christiansen, President
JChristiansen@speersfuneralchapel.com

Saskatchewan Parks & Recreation Association (SPRA)
#100, 1445 Park St., Regina SK S4N 4C5
Tel: 306-780-9231; *Fax:* 306-780-9257
Toll-Free: 800-563-2555
Other Communication: resourcecentre@spra.sk.ca
office@spra.sk.ca
www.spra.sk.ca
Overview: A medium-sized provincial charitable organization founded in 1962 overseen by Canadian Parks & Recreation Association
Mission: To stimulate & advance parks, recreation & leisure activities, facilities, & programs in Saskatchewan
Finances: *Funding Sources:* Lottery ticket sales
Membership: 600 organizations; *Fees:* Schedule available
Activities: *Speaker Service:* Yes; *Library:* Resource Centre for Sport, Culture & Recreation; Open to public
Meetings/Conferences:
• Saskatchewan Parks & Recreation Association 2018 Conference & AGM, October, 2018, SK
Scope: Provincial
Publications:
• DIRECTION [a publication of the Saskatchewan Parks & Recreation Association]
Type: Newsletter; *Accepts Advertising*; *Price:* Free with membership in the Saskatchewan Parks &Recreation Association
Profile: A newsmagazine with news, articles, stories, & funding opportunities

Saskatchewan Party
6135 Rochdale Blvd., Regina SK S4X 2R1
Tel: 306-359-1638; *Fax:* 306-359-9832
info@saskparty.com
www.saskparty.com
www.facebook.com/SaskParty
twitter.com/SaskParty
www.youtube.com/user/SaskatchewanParty
Overview: A small provincial organization founded in 1997
Membership: *Fees:* $5 youth; $10 regular
Chief Officer(s):
Brad Wall, Party Leader
brad.wall@saskparty.com

Saskatchewan Pattern Dance Association
SK
Tel: 306-374-9383
webmaster@patterndance-sk.ca
www.patterndance-sk.ca
Overview: A small provincial organization founded in 1989

Activities: *Library:* Instructional Video Library
Chief Officer(s):
Armand Bourassa, President
ab.bourassa@shaw.ca

Saskatchewan PeriOperative Registered Nurses' Group (SORNG)
SK
sorng@ornac.ca
Overview: A medium-sized provincial organization overseen by Operating Room Nurses Association of Canada
Mission: To promote & advance the perioperative nursing profession
Membership: *Fees:* $40 active; $25 associate; *Member Profile:* Registered Nurses in Saskatchewan who are engaged in operating room nursing or involved in the Perioperative setting.
Activities: *Awareness Events:* Perioperative Nurses Week, November
Chief Officer(s):
Margaret Farley, President
rfarley@accesscomm.ca

Saskatchewan Physical Education Association (SPEA)
PO Box 193, Harris SK S0L 1K0
Tel: 306-656-4423; *Fax:* 306-656-4405
spea@xplornet.com
www.speaonline.ca
www.facebook.com/speaonline
twitter.com/SPEA4
Overview: A small provincial organization founded in 1951
Mission: The Saskatchewan Physical Education Association is a provincial nonprofit incorporated organization that provides quality leadership, advocacy and resources for professionals in physical education and wellness in order to positively influence the lifestyles of Saskatchewan's children and youth.
Member of: PHE Canada, SPRA, STF, SHSAA, U of S, U of R,SHEA, In Motion
Affiliation(s): Physical Health Education Canada; Saskatchewan Parks & Recreation Association; Saskatchewan Teachers Federal PHE Canada; Saskatchewan Teachers' Federation
Finances: *Annual Operating Budget:* $100,000-$250,000; *Funding Sources:* Membership fees; Sask Lotteries Trust; Sponsorships
Staff Member(s): 1; 15 volunteer(s)
Membership: 485; *Fees:* $25 regular; $10 student; $15 retired teacher; *Member Profile:* Individuals with a professional interest in the teaching of physical education; *Committees:* Social Media, Journal Editor/Website, New Resources/Wellness, Curriculum, Advocacy/Mentorship, Membership Services, Regional Directors
Activities: *Library:* Not open to public
Chief Officer(s):
Holly Stevens, Executive Director
Cole Wilson, President
Awards:
• Paul Renwick Award
For an individual who has made an outstanding contribution to physical education in Saskatchewan; *Amount:* $200 (gift), $250 (honorarium)
• Local Initiative Award
For individuals, schools or school divisions for their contributions to physical education in their region *Eligibility:* Recipients do not have to be members of the SPEA *Deadline:* February; *Amount:* 5 awards of $25 *Contact:* Daunean Dash-Rewcastle, dauneandash@gmail.com
• SPEA Book Prizes
Presented to post-secondary students of kinesiology, health or education; *Amount:* $150
• SPEA Scholarships
Eligibility: Student must have at least 2 physical education credits and be enrolleged in first year studies in physical education, kinesiology, education, health studies, applied science & technology in Saskatchewan *Deadline:* June 30, annually; *Amount:* 2 awards of $700
• QDPE (Quality Daily Physical Education) Professional of the Year Award
Eligibility: Employee of QDPE school and involved in promoting QDPE; *Amount:* $25 *Contact:* Daunean Dash-Rewcastle, dauneandash@gmail.com
• SPEA Classroom QDPE Award
• SPEA Elementary School QDPE Award
• SPEA Secondary & Combined Elementary / Secondary School QDPE Award
Meetings/Conferences:
• Saskatchewan Physical Education Association Conference

2018, May, 2018, SK
Scope: Provincial
Description: Theme: "Moving Together: Embracing Possibilities"
Publications:
• On the Move
Type: Journal; *Frequency:* Semiannually; *Editor:* Jennifer Foley; *Price:* Free for members

Saskatchewan Physiotherapy Association (SPA)
#118, 1121 College Dr., Saskatoon SK S7N 0W3
Tel: 306-955-7265; *Fax:* 306-955-7260
www.saskphysio.org
www.facebook.com/saskphysio
twitter.com/saskphysio
Overview: A medium-sized provincial organization overseen by Canadian Physiotherapy Association
Mission: To provide leadership to the physiotherapy profession; To foster excellence in practice, education & research; To promote high standards of health in Saskatchewan
Member of: Canadian Physiotherapy Association
Finances: *Funding Sources:* Membership dues; Educational activities
Staff Member(s): 3
Membership: 400+
Chief Officer(s):
Chris Wiechnik, President
Lorna MacMillan, Executive Director

Saskatchewan Playwrights Centre (SPC)
#700, 601 Spadina Cres. East, Saskatoon SK S7K 3G8
Tel: 306-665-7707; *Fax:* 306-244-0255
www.saskplaywrights.ca
www.facebook.com/saskplaywrights
twitter.com/SaskPlaywrights
Overview: A small provincial organization founded in 1982
Mission: To develop playwrights
Staff Member(s): 1
Membership: *Fees:* $20 associate; $55 playwright
Activities: Presenting the Spring Festival of New Plays; Providing competitions, development services, & networking opportunities for playwrights
Chief Officer(s):
Andrew Johnston, Artistic Director & General Manager
andrew@saskplaywrights.ca

The Saskatchewan Poetry Society
3809 Regina Ave., Regina SK S4S 0H8
Tel: 306-586-5898
Overview: A small provincial organization founded in 1935
Mission: To further the writing of poetry in Saskatchewan
Membership: *Member Profile:* All members must live in Saskatchewan at the time of joining, but may retain membership if they later move to some other province; members agree to buy 6 books
Activities: Monthly meetings

Saskatchewan Powerlifting Association (SPA)
PO Box 42, North Weyburn SK S0C 1X0
Tel: 306-842-4299; *Fax:* 306-842-2682
saskpowerlifting@gmail.com
www.saskpowerlifting.ca
www.facebook.com/saskpowerlifting
Overview: A small provincial organization overseen by Canadian Powerlifting Union
Mission: To promote fitness & provide opportunities to weightlifting athletes.
Membership: 100+; *Fees:* $60 regular; $35 new/special; $10 referee; $2 associate
Chief Officer(s):
Ryan Fowler, President

Saskatchewan Prevention Institute (SPI)
1319 Colony St., Saskatoon SK S7N 2Z1
Tel: 306-651-4300; *Fax:* 306-651-4301
info@skprevention.ca
www.skprevention.ca
www.facebook.com/SaskatchewanPreventionInstitute
www.youtube.com/user/PreventionInstitute1
Previous Name: Saskatchewan Institute on Prevention of Handicaps
Overview: A small provincial charitable organization founded in 1980
Mission: To reduce the occurrence of disabling conditions in children
Member of: Saskatchewan Health Care Association; Canadian College of Health Service Executives
Finances: *Annual Operating Budget:* $250,000-$500,000

Staff Member(s): 22; 1 volunteer(s)
Activities: *Awareness Events:* FASD (Fetal Alcohol Spectrum Disorder) Awareness Day, Sept. 9; *Speaker Service:* Yes; *Library:* Open to public
Chief Officer(s):
Noreen Agrey, Executive Director, 306-651-4302
nagrey@skprevention.ca

Saskatchewan Pro Life Association (SPLA)
PO Box 27093, Stn. RPO Avonhurst, Regina SK S4R 8R8
Tel: 306-352-3480; *Fax:* 306-352-3481
Toll-Free: 888-842-7752
www.saskprolife.com
www.facebook.com/skProLife
twitter.com/SaskProLife
Overview: A small provincial charitable organization founded in 1974
Mission: To protect all human life from conception to natural death
Finances: *Annual Operating Budget:* $100,000-$250,000
Staff Member(s): 1; 2 volunteer(s)
Membership: 5,000-14,999; *Fees:* $25
Activities: *Library:* Open to public
Chief Officer(s):
Colette Stang, President

Saskatchewan Professional Fire Fighters Burn Unit Fund
c/o Brian Belitsky, 62 Milne Bay, Yorkton SK S3N 3Z8
Tel: 306-782-4290; *Fax:* 306-783-0109
burnfund@burnfund.ca
www.burnfund.ca
Overview: A small provincial organization founded in 1974
Mission: To raise and distribute funds to help Saskatchewan families of burn patients with treatment, care, and rehabilitations.
Affiliation(s): British Columbia Professional Fire Fighters Burn Fund
Finances: *Funding Sources:* private donations; corporate sponsorship
Chief Officer(s):
Kirby Benning, President

Saskatchewan Professional Planners Institute (SPPI)
2424 College Ave., Regina SK S4P 1C8
Tel: 306-584-3879; *Fax:* 306-352-6913
msteranka@sasktel.net
sppi.ca
www.facebook.com/SaskPlanning
twitter.com/SaskPlanning
Previous Name: Association of Professional Community Planners of Saskatchewan
Overview: A medium-sized provincial organization founded in 1963 overseen by Canadian Institute of Planners
Mission: To promote & maintain professionalism in planning field
Affiliation(s): Canadian Institute of Planners
8 volunteer(s)
Membership: 24 student + 78 individual + 11 non-resident; *Committees:* Program; Education; Membership
Activities: *Speaker Service:* Yes; *Rents Mailing List:* Yes
Chief Officer(s):
Marilyn Steranka, Executive Director, 306-584-3879, Fax: 306-352-6913
msteranka@sasktel.net
Bill Delainey, Secretary, 306-975-1663, Fax: 306-242-6965
Ryan Walker, Treasurer, 306-966-5664, Fax: 306-966-5680
Meetings/Conferences:
• 2018 Saskatchewan Professional Planners Institute Annual Conference, 2018
Scope: Provincial
Description: A meeting of planners & related professionals to share new ideas, enhance professional practice, network & socialize

Saskatchewan Provincial Mediation Board
#304, 1855 Victoria Ave., Regina SK S4P S72
Tel: 306-787-5408; *Fax:* 306-787-5574
Toll-Free: 877-787-5408
pmb@gov.sk.ca
www.saskatchewan.ca/pmb
Overview: A small provincial organization overseen by Credit Counselling Canada
Mission: To offer counselling & budget advice to persons who are experiencing personal debt difficulties
Affiliation(s): Government of Saskatchewan, Justice & Attorney General; Credit Counselling Canada

Staff Member(s): 3
Activities: Assisting debtors with problems such as property tax arrears & residential mortgage foreclosures; Arranging mediated debt repayment with creditors; Using legal rememdies for debt repayment, through the Bankruptcy & Insolvency Act; *Speaker Service:* Yes
Chief Officer(s):
Dale Beck, Chair, 306-787-2695
dale.beck@gov.sk.ca

Saskatchewan Provincial Rifle Association Inc. (SPRA)
PO Box 40, Mazenod SK S0H 2Y0
Tel: 306-354-7493
www.saskrifle.ca
Overview: A small provincial organization founded in 1885
Mission: The governing body for fullbore target rifle shooting in Saskatchewan & promotes the pursuit of excellence in marksmanship & the safe & responsible handling of firearms
Finances: *Funding Sources:* Membership dues; SaskSport Inc.
Membership: *Fees:* Schedule available
Chief Officer(s):
Keith Skjerdal, Match Director, 306-652-2065

Saskatchewan Psychiatric Association
Saskatoon SK
sask-psychiatrists.tripod.com
Overview: A small provincial organization
Mission: To increase psychiatric knowledge in Saskatchewan
Affiliation(s): Canadian Psychiatric Association
Finances: *Funding Sources:* Membership fees; Donations; Grants
Membership: *Member Profile:* Psychiatrists in Saskatchewan
Activities: Fostering research into the cause, treatment, & prevention of mental disorders; Engaging in advocacy activities; Liaising with government, universities & other medical associations

Saskatchewan Psychological Association *See* Saskatchewan College of Psychologists

Saskatchewan Public Health Association Inc.
PO Box 845, Regina SK S4P 3B1
mail@saskpha.ca
www.saskpha.ca
twitter.com/saskpha
Overview: A small provincial organization overseen by Canadian Public Health Association
Mission: To constitute a resource in Saskatchewan for the improvement & maintenance of health
Chief Officer(s):
Wanda Martin, President

Saskatchewan Publishers Group (SPG)
#324, 1831 College Ave., Regina SK S4P 4V5
Tel: 306-780-9808; *Fax:* 306-780-9811
info@saskbooks.com
www.skbooks.com
twitter.com/SaskBooks
Also Known As: SaskBooks
Overview: A medium-sized provincial organization founded in 1989
Mission: To promote the Saskatchewan book publishing industry; To provide a forum for sharing information & ideas; To speak for the common interests of its members; To undertake specific projects, programs & studies; To work closely with other publishing & cultural organizations across Canada
Member of: SaskCulture; Saskatchewan Arts Alliance
Affiliation(s): Association of Canadian Publishers
Finances: *Annual Operating Budget:* $250,000-$500,000; *Funding Sources:* Canada Council; Canada Book Fund; Creative Saskatchewan
Staff Member(s): 3; 13 volunteer(s)
Membership: 50; *Fees:* $300 full/non publisher; $150 associate; $100 supporting; *Member Profile:* Full - individuals & companies who publish original Canadian books as the primary function of their business & who have in print no fewer than 4 original Canadian titles & an ongoing publishing program of at least 1 title each year; no more than 25% of the publishing program may be authored by owners or employees of the company
Activities: Marketing Saskatchewan-published books; Providing professional development; Advocating on behalf of Saskatchewan-based book publishers; *Speaker Service:* Yes
Chief Officer(s):
Brenda Niskala, Executive Director
bniskala@saskbooks.com

Jillian Bell, Chief Financial Officer, 306-780-9809
jbell@saskbooks.com
Meetings/Conferences:
• Saskatchewan Publishers Group 2018 Annual Conference, June, 2018, Regina, SK
Scope: Provincial
Publications:
• Read Saskatchewan [a publication of Saskatchewan Publishers Group]
Type: Brochure; *Editor:* Jillian Bell
Profile: A catalogue featuring new & upcoming books

Saskatchewan Pulse Growers (SPG)
#207, 116 Research Dr., Saskatoon SK S7N 3R3
Tel: 306-668-5556; *Fax:* 306-668-5557
pulse@saskpulse.com
www.saskpulse.com
www.facebook.com/SaskPulse
twitter.com/SaskPulse
www.youtube.com/SaskPulse
Also Known As: Saskatchewan Pulse Crop Development Board
Overview: A medium-sized provincial organization founded in 1976
Mission: To develop the pulse crop industry in Saskatchewan
Member of: Pulse Canada
Finances: *Annual Operating Budget:* Greater than $5 Million; *Funding Sources:* Provincial government; Producer levy
Staff Member(s): 14
Membership: 18,000+; *Fees:* 1% levy of the value of the gross sale is deducted at the first point of sale or distribution; *Member Profile:* Growers of peas, lentils, chickpeas, beans
Chief Officer(s):
Carl Potts, Executive Director, 306-668-6676
cpotts@saskpulse.com
Rachel Kehrig, Director, Communications
rkehrig@saskpulse.com

Saskatchewan Racquetball Association (SRA)
SK
racquetballsask.com
www.facebook.com/SaskatchewanRacquetballAssociation
twitter.com/saskracquetball
Overview: A small provincial organization overseen by Racquetball Canada
Mission: To To promote the sport of racquetball throughout Saskatchewan.
Chief Officer(s):
Karla Drury, President
k.drury@sasktel.net
Tim Landeryou, Executive Director
ed.rballsask@gmail.com

Saskatchewan Reading Council
c/o Good Spirit School Div., Fairview Education Centre, 63 King St. East, Yorkton SK S3N OT7
Tel: 306-786-5500; *Fax:* 306-783-0355
Toll-Free: 866-390-0773
saskreading.com
Also Known As: Council No: CR150
Overview: A small provincial organization overseen by International Reading Association
Activities: *Library:* Professional Library
Chief Officer(s):
Karen Koroluk, President
k.koroluk@rcsd.ca
Meetings/Conferences:
• 48th Annual Saskatchewan Reading Conference 2018, 2018, SK
Scope: Provincial

Saskatchewan Ready Mixed Concrete Association Inc.; Prairie Ready Mixed Concrete Association *See* Concrete Sask

Saskatchewan Real Estate Association *See* Association of Saskatchewan Realtors

Saskatchewan Recording Industry Association (SRIA)
1831 College Ave., 3rd Fl., Regina SK S4P 4V5
Tel: 306-347-7735
Toll-Free: 800-347-0676
info@saskmusic.org
www.saskmusic.org
www.facebook.com/SaskMusic1
twitter.com/SaskMusic
Also Known As: SaskMusic
Overview: A medium-sized provincial organization founded in 1987
Mission: To develop & promote the music & sound recording industry of Saskatchewan
Member of: SaskCulture
Affiliation(s): Foundation to Assist Canadian Talent on Records; Canadian Recording Industry Association; Canadian Independent Record Production Association; Society of Composers, Authors & Music Publishers of Canada; Canadian Academy of Recording Arts & Sciences; Western Canadian Music Awards
Finances: *Funding Sources:* Sask Lotteries; Dept. of Culture, Youth & Recreation; Canadian Heritage; SOCAN; FACTOR; Astral Media
Staff Member(s): 6
Membership: *Fees:* $30 youth (19 and under); $50 individual; $75 band; $100 corporate/affiliate; *Member Profile:* Anyone related to the Saskatchewan music industry: musicians, studios, radio stations, graphic artists, etc.
Activities: Conference, festivals, workshops & other training, advocacy; *Awareness Events:* Beer Bacon Bands Festival, Jan.; StirCrazy Blues Festival, Feb.; *Internships:* Yes; *Speaker Service:* Yes; *Library:* SRIA Resource Library; by appointment
Chief Officer(s):
Mike Dawson, Executive Director
mike@saskmusic.org

Saskatchewan Registered Music Teachers' Association (SRMTA)
45 Martin St., Regina SK S4S 3W4
srmta@sasktel.net
www.srmta.com
Overview: A medium-sized provincial organization founded in 1938
Mission: To promote progressive ideas & methods in the teaching of music; to encourage systematic preparation in the art of teaching; to seek agreement among members about a high standard of musicianship
Member of: Canadian Federation of Music Teachers' Association
Affiliation(s): Saskatchewan Music Educators Association
Membership: *Fees:* $25 application fee; $138.40 individual
Chief Officer(s):
Laureen Kells, President
lkells@sasktel.net
Lynn Ewing, Vice President
lewing@sasktel.net

Battleford Branch
PO Box 241, Battleford SK S0M 0E0
Tel: 306-937-2305
Chief Officer(s):
Cathy Swerid, President
cathysw@sasktel.net
Diane Neil, Secretary
jdneil228@sasktel.net

East Central Branch
c/o Angel Liebrecht, PO Box 148, Lanigan SK S0K 2M0
Tel: 306-365-9989
Chief Officer(s):
Angel Liebrecht, Secretary
liebrecht.a@sasktel.net
Maureen Loeffelholz, President

Lloydminster Branch
PO Box 3012, Lloydminster AB S9V 1P4
Tel: 306-825-4168
dan2@telusplanet.net
Pamela Rollheiser, President
nprollheiser@bellevista.ca

Prince Albert Branch
303 - 25 Ave., Prince Albert SK S6V 4P5
Tel: 306-763-7382
Marilyn Lohrenz, President
wmlz@shaw.ca

Regina Branch
335 Orchard Cres. South, Regina SK S4S 5B8
Tel: 306-585-7810
Kimberly Engen, President
engenk@gmail.com
Marina Wensley, Secretary
wensleytm@sasktel.net

Saskatoon Branch
519 Steiger Way, Saskatoon SK S7N 4K2
Tel: 306-373-9739
Chief Officer(s):
Bonnie Nicholson, President
stephen.nicholson@shaw.ca
Michelle Aalders, Secretary
m.aalders@sasktel.net

Swift Current Branch
427 - 15 Ave. NE, Swift Current SK S9H 2X5
Tel: 306-773-1468
Chief Officer(s):
Lois Noble, Secretary
noble.one@sasktel.net

West Central Branch
PO Box 2024, Rosetown SK S0L 2V0
Tel: 306-882-3591
Chief Officer(s):
Claire Seibold, President
rcseibold@sasktel.net
Helen Barclay, Secretary
helen.barclay2@gmail.com

Yorkton Branch
385 Circlebrooke Dr., Yorkton SK S3N 3C5
Tel: 306-783-6858
Laurel Teichroeb, President
lteichroab@accesscomm.ca

Saskatchewan Registered Nurses' Association (SRNA)
2066 Retallack St., Regina SK S4T 7X5
Tel: 306-359-4200; *Fax:* 306-359-0257
Toll-Free: 800-667-9945
info@srna.org
www.srna.org
www.facebook.com/677297492316483
twitter.com/SRNAdialogue
Overview: A medium-sized provincial licensing organization founded in 1917 overseen by Canadian Nurses Association
Mission: To ensure competent, knowledge-based, & ethical nursing in Saskatchewan, for the protection of the public; To establish registration & licensure requirements
Finances: *Funding Sources:* Membership fees; Sponsorships
Staff Member(s): 15
Membership: *Committees:* Discipline; Education Approval; Legislation & Bylaws; Membership Advisory; Registration & Membership; Advisory; Investigations; General Information; Awards
Activities: Setting standards of practice of RNs & RN(NP)s; Approving nursing education programs & offering continuing education opportunities; Responding to complaints of professional incompetence or misconduct against nurses; Providing liability protection for nurses
Chief Officer(s):
Joanne Petersen, President
Carolyn Hoffman, Executive Director
choffman@srna.org
Awards:
• Life Membership
To honour members of the association who are retiring from registered nursing employment *Deadline:* February 1 *Contact:* Barb Fitz-Gerald, RN, Fax: 306-359-0183; E-mail: bfitz-gerald@srna.org
• Honorary Membership
Eligibility: A non-nurse, or a nurse registered outside of Saskatchewan *Deadline:* February 1 *Contact:* Barb Fitz-Gerald, RN, E-mail: bfitz-gerald@srna.org
• Memorial Book
Eligibility: Nominees must have held an SRNA practicing membership during their careers *Deadline:* February 1 *Contact:* Barb Fitz-Gerald, RN, E-mail: bfitz-gerald@sma.org
• Millennium Award: Jean Browne Award for Leadership in Nursing Practice
To recognize a registered nurse or group whose leadership has made an outstanding contribution to the profession
• Millennium Award: Nora Armstrong Award for Health Advocacy
To recognize a registered nurse or group who promote & advocate quality care or health policy
• Millennium Award: Jean Wilson Award for Employer of the Year
To recognize an individual or group who have demonstrated leadership in the provision of a positive work environment for registered nurses
• Millennium Award: Granger Campbell Award for Clinical Excellence
To recognize a registered nurse or group who has demonstrated clinical excellence in any practice setting

- Millennium Award: Effie Feeny Award for Nursing Research
To recognize a registered nurse or group who has made an outstanding contribution in nursing or health related research
- Millennium Award: Helen Walker Award for Innovation in Nursing
To recognize a registered nurse or group who developed & implemented methods to meet health care challenges
- Millennium Award: Elizabeth Van Valkenburg Award for Leadership in Nursing Education
To recognize a registered nurse or group who has made an outstanding contribution in the field of nursing education
- Millennium Award: Ruth Hicks Award for Student Leadership
To recognize a nursing student or group who made a significant contribution as a student leader or group
- Mentorship Award
To recognize an SRNA practicing member who exhibits exceptional mentoring abilities *Deadline:* February 1 *Contact:* Barb Fitz-Gerald, RN, E-mail: bfitz-gerald@srna.org

Publications:
- Employer Newsbulletin [a publication of the Saskatchewan Registered Nurses' Association]
Type: Newsletter; *Frequency:* Semiannually
Profile: Information about registration, licences, examination dates, bylaws, & resolutions
- Saskatchewan Registered Nurses' Association Annual Report
Type: Yearbook; *Frequency:* Annually
- SRNA [Saskatchewan Registered Nurses' Association] Newsbulletin
Type: Magazine; *Frequency:* Quarterly; *Accepts Advertising*; *Editor:* Shelley Svedahl; *ISSN:* 1494-76668; *Price:* $21.40 Canada; $30 international
Profile: Information for RNs about the association's activities, plus topical articles

Saskatchewan Rental Housing Industry Association (SRHIA)
#2, 333 - 4th Ave. North, Saskatoon SK S7K 2L8
Tel: 306-653-7149; *Fax:* 306-665-7548
srhia@shaw.ca
www.srhia.ca
Previous Name: Saskatchewan Landlords Association
Overview: A small provincial organization founded in 1994
Mission: To advocate on behalf of landlords & property managers
Member of: Canadian Federation of Apartment Associations
Activities: *Speaker Service:* Yes
Chief Officer(s):
Della Thomas, President

Saskatchewan Rowing Association (SRA)
510 Cynthia St., Saskatoon SK S7L 7K7
Tel: 306-975-0842; *Fax:* 306-242-8007
saskrowing@sasktel.net
www.saskrowing.ca
Overview: A medium-sized provincial organization founded in 1977 overseen by Rowing Canada Aviron
Mission: To promote & govern the sport of rowing in Saskatchewan
Member of: Sask Sport; Rowing Canada Aviron
Affiliation(s): Rowing Aviron Canada, Saskatchewan Sports Hall of Fame & Museum, Saskatchewan Coaches Association
Finances: *Funding Sources:* Sponsors; Merchandise
Activities: *Internships:* Yes; *Library:* Not open to public
Chief Officer(s):
Doug Zolinski, President
John Haver, Provincial Head Coach North
Garrett Mathiason, Provincial Head Coach South

Saskatchewan Rugby Union (SRU)
#213, 1870 Lorne St., Regina SK
Tel: 306-780-9353
www.saskrugby.com
www.facebook.com/SaskRugby
Overview: A small provincial charitable organization overseen by Rugby Canada
Mission: To encourage, promote, organize, administer & otherwise regulate the sport of Rugby Union Football in the province of Saskatchewan in accordance with the laws of the game in a safe & proper manner
Member of: Rugby Canada; Sask Sport
Finances: *Annual Operating Budget:* $100,000-$250,000
Staff Member(s): 1; 200 volunteer(s)
Membership: 2,500; *Fees:* Schedule available
Chief Officer(s):
Grant Cranfield, President

Saskatchewan Safety Council
445 Hoffer Dr., Regina SK S4N 6E2
Tel: 306-757-3197; *Fax:* 306-569-1907
sasksafety.org
www.facebook.com/sasksafetycouncil
twitter.com/SkSafetyCouncil
www.flickr.com/sasksafetycouncil
Overview: A small provincial organization founded in 1955
Mission: To inform the public in order that they are able to make sound decisions regarding their safety
Staff Member(s): 21
Membership: *Fees:* Schedule available
Chief Officer(s):
Harley P. Toupin, Chief Executive Officer
Dianne Wolbaum, Director, Operations

Saskatchewan Sailing Clubs Association (SSCA)
SK
sasksail@sasktel.net
www.sasksail.com
Overview: A small provincial organization overseen by Sail Canada
Mission: To regulate the sport of sailing in Saskatchewan
Member of: Sail Canada
Chief Officer(s):
L.P. Gagnon, President
lpgagnon@hotmail.fr
Mark Lammens, Technical Director & Coach, 306-975-0833
Awards:
- SSCA Sailor of the Year
- SSCA President's Award
- Debbie Holgate Volunteer of the Year

Saskatchewan School Boards Association (SSBA)
#400, 2222 - 13th Ave., Regina SK S4P 3M7
Tel: 306-569-0750; *Fax:* 306-352-9633
admin@saskschoolboards.ca
www.saskschoolboards.ca
www.facebook.com/saskschoolboards
twitter.com/saskschoolboard
Previous Name: Saskatchewan School Trustees Association
Overview: A medium-sized provincial organization founded in 1915 overseen by Canadian School Boards Association
Mission: To represent boards of education, including division boards, conseils scolaires, & local or district boards; To ensure advoacy, leadership & support for member boards by speaking as the voice for quality public education for all children; To offer opportunities for trustee development
Finances: *Annual Operating Budget:* Greater than $5 Million; *Funding Sources:* Membership dues; Fees for service
Staff Member(s): 23
Membership: 28; *Fees:* Schedule available
Activities: Providing information services & professional development opportunities; *Library:* Not open to public
Chief Officer(s):
Darren McKee, Executive Director, 306-569-0750 Ext. 140
dmckee@saskschoolboards.ca
Catherine Vu, Director, Corporate Services, 306-569-0750 Ext. 112
cvu@saskschoolboards.ca
Jill Welke, Director, Communications Services, 306-569-0750 Ext. 142
jwelke@saskschoolboards.ca
Meetings/Conferences:
- Saskatchewan School Boards Association Spring 2018 General Assembly, April, 2018, Hilton DoubleTree, Regina, SK
Scope: Provincial
Contact Information: Director, Communications: Jill Welke, E-mail: jwelke@saskschoolboards.ca, Phone: 306-569-0750, ext. 142
Publications:
- Saskatchewan School Boards Association Annual Report
Type: Report; *Frequency:* Annually
- The School Trustee [a publication of the Saskatchewan School Boards Association]
Type: Newsletter; *Frequency:* 5 pa.
Profile: Informs members & education sector partners about various advocacy & services provided on behalf of K-12 education in Saskatchewan

Saskatchewan School Library Association (SSLA)
c/o Saskatchewan Teachers' Federation, 2317 Arlington Ave., Saskatoon SK S7J 2H8
sasksla@gmail.com
www.ssla.ca
twitter.com/SaskSLA
www.pinterest.com/sasksla
Overview: A medium-sized provincial organization founded in 1959
Mission: To develop, improve, & promote school libraries in Saskatchewan in order to enhance student learning
Affiliation(s): Saskatchewan Teachers' Federation
Membership: *Fees:* Schedule available
Activities: Providing information about school library issues; Hosting learning events
Chief Officer(s):
Charlotte Raine, President
craine@mail.gssd.ca
Carol Preece, Treasurer/Membership
carol.preece@rbe.sk.ca
Awards:
- Dr. Alixe Hambleton Bursary
- Art Forgay Award of Recognition of Administrators
- Connie Acton Award of Merit
- John G. Wright Distinguished Service Award
Meetings/Conferences:
- Saskatchewan School Library Association Annual General Meeting 2018, 2018
Scope: Provincial
Description: An annual event for members with a new facilitator each year
Publications:
- The Medium [a publication of the Saskatchewan School Library Association]
Type: Journal
Profile: Professional development information, library programs, literacy articles, technology & resources for SSLA members

Saskatchewan School Trustees Association *See* Saskatchewan School Boards Association

Saskatchewan Sheep Breeders' Association
c/o Saskatchewan Sheep Development Board, 2213C Hanselman Ct., Saskatoon SK S7L 6A8
info@sksheepbreeders.ca
sksheepbreeders.ca
Also Known As: SaskCanada Sheep Industry Development Inc.
Overview: A small provincial organization founded in 1978
Mission: To promote the sheep industry, deal with significant issues & support each other in the raising of high caliber breeding sheep.
Member of: Canadian Sheep Breeders Association
Finances: *Funding Sources:* Donations; membership dues
Membership: *Fees:* $21
Chief Officer(s):
Clint Wiens, President

Saskatchewan Shorthorn Association
c/o Betty Wyatt, PO Box 1528, Carlyle SK S0C 0R0
Tel: 306-557-4664; *Fax:* 306-577-2106
www.saskshorthorns.com
Overview: A small provincial organization
Mission: To promote the breeding of shorthorn cattle in Saskatchewan.
Member of: Canadian Shorthorn Association
Affiliation(s): Saskatchewan Livestock Association; Saskatchewan Cattle Breeders; Saskatchewan Stockgrowers Association; Canadian Western Agribition
Membership: 32; *Member Profile:* Purebred shorthorn breeders in Saskatchewan
Activities: Canadian Western Agribition; National Shorthorn Show, Elite Shorthorn Sale; Autumn Alliance Sale; Sponsorship: involved in all 4H youth shows within Saskatchewan
Chief Officer(s):
Betty Wyatt, Secretary
gerrybetty@gmail.com
Arron Huber, President
huberdale@sasktel.net

Saskatchewan Ski Association - Skiing for Disabled (SASKI)
1860 Lorne St., Saskatoon SK S4P 2L7
Tel: 306-780-9236; *Fax:* 306-781-6021
www.saski.ca
Also Known As: SASKI - Skiing for Disabled
Overview: A medium-sized provincial organization founded in 1982 overseen by Canadian Association for Disabled Skiing
Mission: To promote all aspects of winter skiing in Saskatchewan, including alpine, biathlon, cross country & skiing for disabled, & to provide assistance to clubs & individual athletes, instruction & training, adaptive equipment, & a resource

library
Member of: Canadian Association for Disabled Skiing
Finances: *Funding Sources:* Provincial lotteries; occasional grants; bingos
Membership: 1,000-4,999
Activities: Alpine/cross country/biathlon/freestyle skiing; skiing for disabled; snowboarding
Chief Officer(s):
Pat Prokopchuk, Contact
prokr@sasktel.net

Saskatchewan Snow Vehicles Association *See* Saskatchewan Snowmobile Association

Saskatchewan Snowboard Association (SSA)
1860 Lorne St., Regina SK S4P 2L7
Tel: 306-867-8489
info@sasksnowboard.ca
sasksnowboard.ca
www.facebook.com/238209089572128
twitter.com/sasksnowboard
Overview: A small provincial organization founded in 2001 overseen by Canadian Snowboard Federation
Mission: To be the provincial governing body of competitive snowboarding in Saskatchewan
Member of: Canadian Snowboard Federation
Membership: *Fees:* $20 support; $20 coach; $25 athlete
Chief Officer(s):
Brent Larwood, President
brent@sasksnowboard.ca
Dave Woods, Coordinator, Sport Development
dave@sasksnowboard.ca

Saskatchewan Snowmobile Association (SSA)
PO Box 533, 221 Centre St., Regina Beach SK S0G 4C0
Tel: 306-729-3500
Toll-Free: 800-499-7533
sasksnow@sasktel.net
www.sasksnow.com
www.facebook.com/sask.snow
twitter.com/sasksnow
www.youtube.com/channel/UC5gfjL3DgXAl3Z7te4leEuA
Previous Name: Saskatchewan Snow Vehicles Association
Overview: A medium-sized provincial organization founded in 1971
Mission: To promote the benefits of snowmobiling & increase access & participation; To provide leadership & support to members; To establish & maintain safe, high quality trails; To provide support to club development
Member of: International Snowmobile Council; Canadian Council of Snowmobile Organizations
Finances: *Funding Sources:* Membership dues; Saskatchewan Lotteries
20 volunteer(s)
Membership: 5,000; *Fees:* Schedule available; *Committees:* Membership; Raffles; Rallies; Grants; Equipment; Safety; Trails
Awards:
• Diamonds in the Snow Awards Program
Recognizes significant contributions & dedication to snowmobiling in Saskatchewan.
Meetings/Conferences:
• Saskatchewan Snowmobile Association 2018 AGM, 2018, SK
Scope: Provincial
Description: Reports from the chairman, president & chief executive officer, & discussions about finances & association issues

Saskatchewan Soccer Association Inc. (SSA)
SaskSport Administration Bldg., 1870 Lorne St., Regina SK S4P 2L7
Tel: 306-780-9225; *Fax:* 306-780-9480
www.sasksoccer.com
www.facebook.com/SaskatchewanSoccer
twitter.com/SaskSoccerAssoc
www.youtube.com/SaskatchewanSoccer
Overview: A medium-sized provincial organization founded in 1906 overseen by Canadian Soccer Association
Member of: Canadian Soccer Association
Staff Member(s): 10; 12 volunteer(s)
Membership: 33,000
Activities: *Internships:* Yes
Chief Officer(s):
Doug Pederson, Executive Director, 306-780-9225 Ext. 4
d.pederson@sasksoccer.com

Saskatchewan Society for Education through Art (SSEA)
205A Pacific Ave., Saskatoon SK S7K 1N9
Tel: 306-975-0222
Overview: A small provincial organization
Mission: To promote the need for art education in Saskatchewan schools
Member of: Saskatchewan Council of Cultural Organizations

Saskatchewan Society for the Autistic Inc. *See* Saskatchewan Families for Effective Autism Treatment

Saskatchewan Society for the Prevention of Cruelty to Animals
519 - 45th St. West, Saskatoon SK S7L 5Z9
Tel: 306-382-7722; *Fax:* 306-384-3425
Toll-Free: 877-382-7722
info@sspca.ca
www.sspca.ca
www.facebook.com/SaskSPCA
twitter.com/SaskSPCA
Also Known As: Saskatchewan SPCA
Overview: A medium-sized provincial organization overseen by Canadian Federation of Humane Societies
Mission: To promote humane treatment of animals
Member of: Canadian Federation of Humane Societies
Staff Member(s): 10
Membership: *Fees:* $15 junior/senior; $25 single; $35 family; $50 individual/SPCA/humane society; $200 life; $250 business
Chief Officer(s):
Frances Wach, Executive Director, 306-382-4471

Saskatchewan Society of Medical Laboratory Technologists (SSMLT)
PO Box 3837, Regina SK S4P 3R8
Tel: 306-352-6791; *Fax:* 306-352-6791
Toll-Free: 877-334-3301
info@ssmlt.org
www.ssmlt.org
Overview: A medium-sized provincial licensing organization founded in 1983 overseen by Canadian Society for Medical Laboratory Science
Mission: To ensure the professional competence of its members, thus contributing to excellence in health care; To promote the nationally accepted standard of medical laboratory technology; To promote, maintain & protect the professional identity & interests of the medical laboratory technologist & of the profession; To support a national system of certification which meets the changing needs of medical laboratory services & which has credibility with employers, governments & academic institutions; To encourage eligible laboratory personnel to seek & maintain membership in the CSMLS & SSMLT & participate in society activities; To encourage & assist members to improve their knowledge & qualifications
Affiliation(s): Canadian Society for Medical Laboratory Science; International Association of Medical Laboratory Technologists
Finances: *Funding Sources:* Membership fees
Staff Member(s): 2
Membership: *Member Profile:* Practicing - working as a medical laboratory technologist; Non-practicing - not working; *Committees:* Counselling & Investigation; Education, Marketing & Development; Discipline; Regulatory Affairs; Nominations
Activities: *Library:* SSMLT Loan Library; Not open to public
Chief Officer(s):
Kim Deydey, Executive Director
exec.dir@ssmlt.org
Awards:
• MDS-Raymond LePage Scholarship
• Honorary Membership
• Special Recognition Award
• Wheatland Bounty Professional Development Grant
• Wheatland Bounty Professional Development Scholarship

Saskatchewan Society of Occupational Therapists (SSOT)
PO Box 9089, Saskatoon SK S7K 7E7
Tel: 306-956-7768; *Fax:* 306-242-7941
admin@ssot.sk.ca
www.ssot.sk.ca
Overview: A small provincial licensing organization founded in 1971
Mission: To register & maintain a current listing of individuals whom SSOT has approved to practise occupational therapy in Saskatchewan; to develop & enforce standards of practice; to facilitate the development & strengthening of the profession & of individual members by providing a network for formal & informal communication, by encouraging & providing opportunities for continuing education & research; to promote awareness of the profession & the society by representing the occupational therapy point of view during interactions with other health care professions, employers, educational institutions, government, the media, & special interest groups
Member of: Canadian Association of Occupational Therapists
Finances: *Annual Operating Budget:* $50,000-$100,000; *Funding Sources:* Membership fees
Staff Member(s): 2; 8 volunteer(s)
Membership: 230; *Fees:* $398 full-time member; *Member Profile:* Degree or equivalent in OT & completion of approved exams; *Committees:* Public Relations; Education; Professional Development Fund; Professional Conduct; Discipline; Credentials; Finance; Nominations; Awards; Legislative; AGM; Professional Practice; Government Affairs
Activities: *Rents Mailing List:* Yes
Chief Officer(s):
Coralie Lennea, Executive Director
ed@ssot.sk.ca
Awards:
• Outstanding Contributions to the Community
• Outstanding Contributions to Society
• Outstanding Contributions to the Profession
• Clinical Teaching Award
• Clinical Fieldwork Award

Saskatchewan Society of X-Ray Technicians *See* Saskatchewan Association of Medical Radiation Technologists

Saskatchewan Soil Conservation Association (SSCA)
PO Box 1360, Indian Head SK S0G 2K0
Tel: 306-695-4233; *Fax:* 306-695-4236
Toll-Free: 800-213-4287
info@ssca.ca
www.ssca.ca
Overview: A small provincial charitable organization founded in 1987
Mission: To improve the land & environment; To increase public awareness of soil conservation; To promote conservation production systems to Saskatchewan producers
Finances: *Funding Sources:* Donations; Federal-Provincial sustainable agriculture programs
Membership: 800; *Member Profile:* Farmers in Saskatchewan
Activities: Sharing soil conservation information
Chief Officer(s):
Tim Nerbas, President
tnerbas@ssca.ca
Marilyn Martens, Office Manager, 306-695-4233
Meetings/Conferences:
• 30th Annual Conference of the Saskatchewan Soil Conservation Association, January, 2018, Western Development Museum, Saskatoon, SK
Scope: Provincial
Description: Theme: "Soil Health In a New Climate"
Publications:
• Direct Seeding Manual
Type: Manual
Profile: Developed & published with the Prairie Agricultural Machinery Institute for Saskatchewan growers
• Prairie Soils & Crops eJournal
Type: Journal
Profile: Peer-reviewed information from the Saskatchewan Soil Conservation Association, Agriculture & Agri-Food Canada, & the University of Saskatchewan for prairie producers & agrologists
• Prairie Steward
Type: Newsletter; *Frequency:* 3 pa
Profile: Association news & technical articles for Saskatchewan Soil Conservation Association members

Saskatchewan Special Olympics Society *See* Special Olympics Saskatchewan

Saskatchewan Speed Skating Association *See* Saskatchewan Amateur Speed Skating Association

Saskatchewan Sports Hall of Fame & Museum (SSFHM)
2205 Victoria Ave., Regina SK S4P 0S4
Tel: 306-780-9232; *Fax:* 306-780-9427
sshfm@sasktel.net
www.sasksportshallofffame.com
www.facebook.com/SaskSportsHF
twitter.com/SaskSportsHF
www.youtube.com/channel/UC2j_-agyX9f2-xa5laFueXQ

Saskatchewan Square & Round Dance Federation

Overview: A small provincial charitable organization founded in 1966 overseen by Sask Sport Inc.
Mission: To recognize sport excellence, preserve sport history & educate the public on the contribution of sport to Saskatchewan's cultural fabric
Member of: Canadian Museums Association; Museums Association of Saskatchewan; Canadian Association for Sports Heritage; International Association of Sport Museums & Halls of Fame
Finances: *Annual Operating Budget:* $250,000-$500,000; *Funding Sources:* Lotteries & self-help
Staff Member(s): 4; 95 volunteer(s)
Membership: 1,450
Activities: Museum galleries, archives, research facilities; Induction dinner; Annual Hall of Fame Game (Football); *Speaker Service:* Yes; *Library:* by appointment
Chief Officer(s):
Sheila Kelly, Executive Director
skelly@sshfm.com
Brock Gerrard, Curator
bgerrard@sshfm.com

Saskatchewan Square & Round Dance Federation
SK
Tel: 306-932-4430
www.sksquaredance.ca
Overview: A medium-sized provincial organization founded in 1979 overseen by Canadian Square & Round Dance Society
Mission: To guide & promote Square & Round Dancing & Clogging throughout the province as recreation for people of all ages & in all walks of life to enjoy
Member of: Canadian Square & Round Dance Society
Finances: *Funding Sources:* National conventions; membership dues; Saskatchewan Lotteries
Chief Officer(s):
Lyal Waddington, Co-President
Carmel Waddington, Co-President

Saskatchewan Squash
214 Wickenden Cres., Saskatoon SK S7N 3X7
Tel: 306-280-4320
sasksquash@gmail.com
www.sasksquash.com
Overview: A medium-sized provincial organization overseen by Squash Canada
Member of: Squash Canada
Chief Officer(s):
Brad Birnie, Executive Director

Saskatchewan Stock Growers Association (SSGA)
Main Floor, Canada Centre Building, Evraz Place, PO Box 4752, Regina SK S4P 3Y4
Tel: 306-757-8523; *Fax:* 306-569-8799
skstockgrowers.com
Overview: A medium-sized provincial organization founded in 1913
Mission: To serve, protect, & advance the interests of the beef industry in Saskatchewan; To represent the cattle industry in Saskatchewan on the legislative front
Member of: Canadian Cattlemen's Association
Affiliation(s): Saskatchewan Prairie Conservation Action Plan (SK PCAP) Partnership
Finances: *Funding Sources:* Membership fees
Membership: *Fees:* $105 active/associate; $262.50-$525 affiliate; *Member Profile:* Active members are individuals engaged in livestock production in Saskatchewan; Affiliate members are groups that are engaged in livestock marketing; Associate members have an interest in the industry; *Committees:* Beef; Policy/Trade; Land Use; Promotional
Activities: Providing education; Engaging in research; Advocating on behalf of the beef industry
Chief Officer(s):
Chad MacPherson, General Manager
Harold Martens, President
mranchltd@shaw.ca
Awards:
• Stewardship Award
To recognize excellence & environmental stewardship in the ranching industry
Publications:
• Beef Business
Type: Magazine; *Frequency:* Bimonthly; *Accepts Advertising*; *Editor:* Jim Warren; *Price:* Included with SSGA membership *Profile:* Industry news, markets & trade, features, analysis & opinion, science & productions, association news & reports, & stewardship

Saskatchewan Swine Breeders' Association
c/o Saskatchewan Livestock Association, PO Box 3771, Regina SK S4P 3N8
Tel: 306-757-6133; *Fax:* 306-525-5852
sla@accesscomm.ca
Overview: A small provincial organization
Mission: To support improved swine breeding practices; to establish & maintain a recognized organization to represent & voice the concerns & interests of swine breeders in Saskatchewan; to foster better swine health & management practices
Member of: Purebred Swine Breeders' Association of Canada
Membership: *Member Profile:* Swine producers

Saskatchewan Table Tennis Association Inc. (STTA)
510 Cynthia St., Saskatoon SK S7L 7K7
Tel: 306-975-0835; *Fax:* 306-952-0835
sktta@shaw.ca
www.sktta.ca
www.facebook.com/ttsask
twitter.com/SKTableTennis
Overview: A small provincial organization overseen by Table Tennis Canada
Mission: To promote & govern the sport of table tennis in Saskatchewan.
Member of: Table Tennis Canada; Sask Sport
Affiliation(s): International Table Tennis Federation
Membership: 2,200; *Fees:* $185 club; $5.25 individual
Activities: *Rents Mailing List:* Yes
Chief Officer(s):
Jeffrey Woo, Executive Director

Saskatchewan Teachers' Federation (STF) / Fédération des enseignants et des enseignantes de la Saskatchewan
2317 Arlington Ave., Saskatoon SK S7J 2H8
Tel: 306-373-1660; *Fax:* 306-374-1122
Toll-Free: 800-667-7762
stf@stf.sk.ca
www.stf.sk.ca
twitter.com/SaskTeachersFed
www.youtube.com/channel/UClw3RFPZPxTzbldiTocbknA
Overview: A medium-sized provincial organization overseen by Canadian Teachers' Federation
Mission: To help provide the best possible education to children
Membership: 12,000; *Member Profile:* Teachers & students enrolled in teachers' college; *Committees:* Economic Services; Social & Political Advocacy; Professional Stewardship & Responsibility; Ethics; Collective Interests; Professional Competency
Activities: *Library:* Stewart Resource Centre; Open to public
Chief Officer(s):
Patrick Maze, President
stf.executive@stf.sk.ca
Gwen Dueck, Executive Director
stf.administrative@stf.sk.ca

Saskatchewan Tennis Association *See* Tennis Saskatchewan

Saskatchewan Trade & Export Partnership (STEP)
PO Box 1787, #320, 1801 Hamilton St., Regina SK S4P 3C6
Tel: 306-787-9210; *Fax:* 306-787-6666
Toll-Free: 888-976-7875
inquire@sasktrade.sk.ca
www.sasktrade.com
twitter.com/SaskTrade
www.youtube.com/user/SaskTrade
Overview: A medium-sized provincial organization founded in 1996
Mission: To work in partnership with Saskatchewan exporters & emerging exporters to maximize commercial success in global ventures; To deliver custom export solutions & market intelligence to member companies; To coordinate international development projects
Finances: *Funding Sources:* Private & public funding
Membership: 426
Activities: Providing market intelligence, international finance solutions, export education & marketing services; *Library:* Not open to public
Chief Officer(s):
Chris Dekker, President & Chief Executive Officer
Brad Michnik, Senior Vice President, Trade Development
Angela Krauss, Vice President, Marketing & Membership Development
Publications:
• STEP Global Newsletter
Type: Newsletter; *Frequency:* Quarterly

Saskatchewan Triathlon Association Corporation (STAC)
PO Box 32080, Saskatoon SK S4N 7L2
Tel: 306-519-1822; *Fax:* 800-319-4959
info@triathlonsaskatchewan.org
www.triathlonsaskatchewan.org
www.facebook.com/287275596696
twitter.com/SaskTriathlon
Overview: A small provincial organization overseen by Triathlon Canada
Mission: To be the provincial governing body of triathlon in Saskatchewan
Member of: Triathlon Canada
Membership: *Fees:* $45 adult; $20 youth; $90 family
Chief Officer(s):
Shawn Rempel, President
Lacey Schroeder, Vice President

Saskatchewan Trucking Association (STA)
103 Hodsman Rd., Regina SK S4N 5W5
Tel: 306-569-9696; *Fax:* 306-569-1008
Toll-Free: 800-563-7623
info@sasktrucking.com
www.sasktrucking.com
www.linkedin.com/company/saskatchewan-trucking-association
www.facebook.com/154582251242283
twitter.com/sasktrucking
Overview: A medium-sized provincial licensing organization founded in 1937 overseen by Canadian Trucking Alliance
Mission: To act as a representative of the truck transport industry in Saskatchewan
Affiliation(s): CTA Board of Directors; BC Trucking Association; Ontario Trucking Association; Quebec Trucking Association; Atlantic Provinces Association
Finances: *Funding Sources:* Membership fees; Sponsorship of programs
Membership: *Fees:* Schedule available; *Member Profile:* Trucking companies operating in or suppliers to the trucking industry in Manitoba
Activities: Advocacy; Publications; Training
Chief Officer(s):
Susan Ewart, Executive Director, 306-569-9696 Ext. 450
sewaart@sasktrucking.com
Awards:
• Shaw Tracking Service to Industry Award
• Cervus Equipment Peterbilt Dispatcher of the Year
• Volvo Driver of the Year
• STA Scholarship Program
To provide support with post-secondary education; special consideration given to candidates specializing in an area within the truck transport industry *Eligibility:* Must be a dependent of an employee of an STA member company *Deadline:* June 30; *Amount:* $3,000; $1,000 x2
Meetings/Conferences:
• Saskatchewan Trucking Association Annual General Meeting 2018, 2018, SK
Scope: Provincial
Contact Information: Executive Assistant: Cecilia Taylor, E-mail: ctaylor@sasktrucking.com

Saskatchewan Turkey Producers' Marketing Board (STPMB)
1438 Fletcher Rd., Saskatoon SK S7M 5T2
Tel: 306-931-1050; *Fax:* 306-931-2825
saskaturkey@sasktel.net
Overview: A small provincial organization
Mission: To manage the supply managed system in Saskatchewan, which includes negotiating the province's quota levels with the CTMA, negotiating price levels with local processors and developing a long-term strategic focus for Saskatchewan's turkey industry
Member of: Turkey Farmers of Canada
Finances: *Annual Operating Budget:* $250,000-$500,000; *Funding Sources:* Levy on production
Staff Member(s): 1
Membership: 12; *Fees:* $5
Chief Officer(s):
Rose Olson, Executive Director

Saskatchewan Underwater Council
PO Box 7651, Saskatoon SK S7K 4R4
Tel: 306-374-8341; *Fax:* 306-374-8341
executive@saskuc.com
www.saskuc.com
Overview: A small provincial organization

Mission: To represent those interested in underwater activities in Saskatchewan.
Membership: *Fees:* $30 single; $35 family
Activities: Newsletter; Diver Magazine; Information on Dive Sites
Chief Officer(s):
Clifford Lange, Contact, 306-374-8341
Publications:
• Buddylines Newsletter [a publication of the Saskatchewan Underwater Council]
Type: Newsletter; *Frequency:* a.; *Number of Pages:* 4; *Editor:* Justin Rings
Profile: News, profiles & information useful to members of the SUC; membership renewal information

Saskatchewan Union of Nurses (SUN) / Syndicat des infirmières de la Saskatchewan
2330 - 2nd Ave., Regina SK S4R 1A6
Tel: 306-525-1666; *Fax:* 306-522-4612
Toll-Free: 800-667-7060
regina@sun-nurses.sk.ca
www.sun-nurses.sk.ca
www.facebook.com/SUNnurses
twitter.com/sunnurses
www.youtube.com/user/sunaccnt
Overview: A medium-sized provincial organization founded in 1974
Mission: To advocate to protect the rights of members; To enhance the socio-economic & general welfare of members through collective bargaining, research, & education
Affiliation(s): Saskatchewan Federation of Labour; Canadian Labour Congress; Canadian Federation of Nurses Unions; Saskatchewan Registered Nurses' Association; Registered Psychiatric Nurses Association of Saskatchewan; Canadian Nurses Association
Finances: *Funding Sources:* Membership dues
Membership: 9,000
Chief Officer(s):
Tracy Zambory, President
tracy.zambory@sun-nurses.sk.ca
Donna Trainor, Executive Director
donna.trainor@sun-nurses.sk.ca

Saskatchewan Urban Municipalities Association (SUMA)
#200, 2222 - 13th Ave., Regina SK S4P 3M7
Tel: 306-525-3727; *Fax:* 306-525-4373
suma@suma.org
www.suma.org
Overview: A medium-sized provincial organization founded in 1906
Mission: To work to enhance urban life in Saskatchewan, by providing administrative & consultative services to members, a forum for the discussion & resolution of current issues, & a negotiating vehicle for improvements in legislation, financing & programs. SUMA provides information & training for aldermen & mayors, and group benefits for its members
Member of: Federation of Canadian Municipalities
Finances: *Funding Sources:* Membership fees
Staff Member(s): 14
Membership: 450 municipalities
Activities: Group Benefits; Group Purchasing; *Rents Mailing List:* Yes
Chief Officer(s):
Laurent Mougeot, CEO
lmougeot@suma.org
Sean McEachern, Director, Policy & Communication
smceachern@suma.org
Awards:
• Honourary, Meritorius, Life Awards
Meetings/Conferences:
• Saskatchewan Urban Municipalities Association 113th Annual Convention and Tradeshow 2018, February, 2018, Regina, SK
Scope: Provincial

Saskatchewan Veterinary Medical Association (SVMA)
#202, 224 Pacific Ave., Saskatoon SK S7K 1N9
Tel: 306-955-7862; *Fax:* 306-975-0623
svma@svma.sk.ca
www.svma.sk.ca
Overview: A small provincial licensing organization overseen by Canadian Veterinary Medical Association
Mission: To protect the public by ensuring the proficiency, competency & ethical behaviour of its members in the practice of veterinary medicine; to license veterinarians; to approve practices; to discipline members as required; to promote veterinary medicine by supporting the physical, personal & financial well-being of members through continuing education & professional interaction
Staff Member(s): 3
Membership: *Fees:* Schedule available
Chief Officer(s):
Judy Currie, Registrar & Secretary-Treasurer
jacurrie@svma.sk.ca
Sue Gauthier, Co-ordinator, Communications & Member Services
sgauthier@svma.sk.ca
Publications:
• SVMA News
Type: Newsletter; *Frequency:* Quarterly; *Accepts Advertising*; *Number of Pages:* 35

Saskatchewan Voice of People with Disabilities, Inc. (SVOPD)
#201, 2206 Dewdney Ave., Regina SK S4R 1H3
Tel: 306-569-3111; *Fax:* 306-569-1889
Toll-Free: 877-569-3111; *TTY:* 306-569-3111
voice@saskvoice.com
www.saskvoice.com
www.facebook.com/SaskVoice
Also Known As: Sask Voice
Previous Name: Saskatchewan Voice of the Handicapped
Overview: A medium-sized provincial charitable organization founded in 1973
Mission: To act as a voice for people with disabilities throughout Saskatchewan; To participate in the life of society without discrimination; To increase employment opportunities, accessible housing & tranportation, & family support services
Member of: Council of Canadians with Disabilities
Finances: *Annual Operating Budget:* $100,000-$250,000; *Funding Sources:* Donations; Fundraising; Grants; Social Services; CCD
Staff Member(s): 3; 5 volunteer(s)
Membership: *Fees:* $10; *Committees:* DISC, PIND, PIAT, DESK, SKF, IF
Activities: Advocating for services to assist people with disabilities in Saskatchewan; Raising awareness of the needs of people with disabilities & the Independent Living Model; Liaising with Disabled First Nation People & other groups with similar interests; Developing local chapters; *Awareness Events:* The United Nations International Day for Person with Disabilities, December 3 *Library:* Saskatchewan Voice of People with Disabilities Resource Library

Saskatchewan Voice of the Handicapped See Saskatchewan Voice of People with Disabilities, Inc.

Saskatchewan Volleyball Association
1750 McAra St., Regina SK S4N 6L4
Tel: 306-780-9250; *Fax:* 306-780-9288
Toll-Free: 800-321-1685
meta@saskvolleyball.ca
www.saskvolleyball.ca
www.facebook.com/saskvolleyball
twitter.com/saskvolleyball
www.instagram.com/saskvolleyball
Overview: A small provincial organization overseen by Volleyball Canada
Mission: To develop interest, participation & excellence in volleyball through the promotion & provision of quality services for all
Finances: *Annual Operating Budget:* $500,000-$1.5 Million; *Funding Sources:* Corporate sponsors
Staff Member(s): 9; 2200 volunteer(s)
Chief Officer(s):
Aaron Demyen, Executive Director, 306-780-9801
aaron@saskvolleyball.ca
Awards:
• Sask Volleyball Awards
Awarded in a variety of categories to honour excellence in sport, coaching, & service

Saskatchewan Wall & Ceiling Bureau Inc.
532 - 2 Ave. North, Saskatoon SK S7K 2C5
Tel: 306-359-3282; *Fax:* 306-569-0260
Overview: A small provincial organization overseen by Northwest Wall & Ceiling Bureau
Mission: To promote quality workmanship in Saskatchewan's wall & ceiling industry
Membership: *Member Profile:* Manufacturers, suppliers, & contractors involved in Saskatchewan's wall & ceiling industry
Activities: Offering networking opportunities for the exchange of information & experience
Chief Officer(s):
Eric Donnelly, President
edonnelly@westcor.ca

Saskatchewan Waste Reduction Council (SWRC)
The Two-Twenty, #208, 220 - 20th St. West, Saskatoon SK S7M 0W9
Tel: 306-931-3242; *Fax:* 306-955-5852
info@saskwastereduction.ca
www.saskwastereduction.ca
Overview: A medium-sized provincial charitable organization founded in 1991
Mission: To lead in addressing the underlying causes of waste by identifying opportunities, creating connections & promoting solutions.
Staff Member(s): 3
Membership: 150; *Fees:* Schedule available
Activities: *Awareness Events:* Waste Reduction Week; *Speaker Service:* Yes
Chief Officer(s):
Joanne Fedyk, Executive Director
joanne@saskwastereduction.ca
Martha Hollinger, Contact, Member Services & Administration
martha@saskwastereduction.ca
Awards:
• Waste Minimization Awards
Eligibility: Categories: Individual Adult, Youth/School, Corporate Leadership, Non-profit Organization, Municipality, Partnerships
Deadline: Feb.
Meetings/Conferences:
• Saskatchewan Waste Reduction Council Waste ReForum 2018, 2018
Scope: Provincial
Description: Workshops & sessions on environmental issues
Publications:
• SWRC Report

Saskatchewan Water & Wastewater Association (SWWA)
PO Box 7831, Stn. Mn, Saskatoon SK S7K 4R5
Tel: 306-761-1278
Toll-Free: 888-668-1278
office@swwa.ca
www.swwa.ca
www.facebook.com/SaskatchewanWaterAndWastewaterAssociation
twitter.com/SWWA_Office
Overview: A small provincial organization
Mission: Dedicated to the professional operation and maintenance of water & wastewater facilities in Saskatchewan
Membership: *Fees:* $60.50; *Member Profile:* People involved in the operation, maintenance & troubleshooting of water & wastewater systems in Saskatchewan
Activities: Hosting workshops & training sessions; Providing access to job opportunities; Publishing a newsletter; Providing certification through the Operator Certification Board
Chief Officer(s):
Tim Cox, President
t.cox@swiftcurrent.ca
Awards:
• Operator of the Year Award
Meetings/Conferences:
• Saskatchewan Water and Wastewater Association 2018 Tradeshow and Conference, November, 2018
Scope: National
• Saskatchewan Water and Wastewater Association 2019 Tradeshow and Conference, November, 2019
Scope: National
• Saskatchewan Water and Wastewater Association 2020 Tradeshow and Conference, November, 2020
Scope: National
Publications:
• The Pipeline [a publication of the Saskatchewan Water & Wastewater Association]
Type: Magazine; *Frequency:* Quarterly; *Accepts Advertising*
Profile: Latest association news; events in the province & elsewhere

Saskatchewan Water Polo Association See Water Polo Saskatchewan Inc.

Saskatchewan Water Ski Association See Water Ski & Wakeboard Saskatchewan

Saskatchewan Water Well Association *See* Saskatchewan Ground Water Association

Saskatchewan Weekly Newspapers Association (SWNA)
#14, 401 - 45th St. West, Saskatoon SK S7L 5Z9
Tel: 306-382-9683; *Fax:* 306-382-9421
Toll-Free: 800-661-7962
www.swna.com
www.facebook.com/sask.newspaper
twitter.com/swnainfo
Overview: A medium-sized provincial organization founded in 1913 overseen by Canadian Community Newspapers Association
Mission: To assist persons to issue press releases, buy advertising, & place classifieds in member newspapers in central Saskatchewan & the Northwest Territories
Staff Member(s): 8
Membership: 86; *Member Profile:* Weekly newspapers in the central part of Saskatchewan & the Northwest Territories
Activities: Offering a press monitor & clipping service
Chief Officer(s):
Steven Nixon, Executive Director, 306-382-9683 Ext. 301
Rob Clark, President
Louise Simpson, Treasurer & Office Manager, 306-382-9683 Ext. 308
Awards:
- Junior Citizen of the Week
- Better Newspapers Competition

Saskatchewan Wheelchair Sports Association (SWSA)
510 Cynthia St., Saskatoon SK S7L 7K7
Tel: 306-975-0824
info@swsa.ca
www.swsa.ca
www.facebook.com/182080694193
twitter.com/skwcsports
www.youtube.com/user/SKWheelchairSports
Overview: A small provincial organization founded in 1977
Mission: Dedicated to developing & supporting opportunities for children, teens & adults with disabilities to participate in the Association's sport, recreation & leisure time activities to the best of their abilities.
Member of: Canadian Wheelchair Sports Association
Membership: *Fees:* $20 individual; $40 family

Saskatchewan Wildlife Federation (SWF)
9 Lancaster Rd., Moose Jaw SK S6J 1M8
Tel: 306-692-8812; *Fax:* 306-692-4370
Toll-Free: 877-793-9453
sask.wildlife@sasktel.net
www.swf.sk.ca
www.facebook.com/SaskatchewanWildlifeFederation
twitter.com/saskwildlife
Overview: A medium-sized provincial charitable organization founded in 1929 overseen by Canadian Wildlife Federation
Mission: To promote the wise use & management of natural resources in Saskatchewan
Finances: *Funding Sources:* Membership fees; Donations; Fundraising
Membership: 30,000+
Activities: Advocating on behalf of members: *Awareness Events:* Great Canadian Shoreline Cleanup, September
Chief Officer(s):
Darrell Crabbe, Executive Director
Darren Newberry, Coordinator, Habitat Land Trust
Laurel Waldner, Coordinator, Education Program
Adam Matichuk, Coordinator, Fisheries Project
Darby Briggs, Coordinator, Communications
Awards:
- Gordon Lund Memorial Award
Awarded to an individual to recognize exceptional contributions to the conservation of fish & wildlife resources
- Clayton Young Memorial Award
Awarded to recognize volunteer efforts within the SWF
- Resource Management Conservation Award
Presented to a professional employee in the resource management or conservation field
- Ed Begin Conservation Award
Awarded to the SWF branch with the most outstanding conservation proect completed in the last year
- Bill McDonald Youth Conservationist of the Year Award
Awarded to a SWF youth member who has provided exceptional contributions to the conservation & enjoyment of Saskatchewan's fish & wildlife resources
- Murray Doell Award
Awarded to honour an outstanding youth at SWF Outdoor Conservation Camp
- Lorne Topley Memorial Stewardship Award
Presented to the individual, group, or family whose actions display excellence in wildlife land conservation, enhancement, & stewardship
Meetings/Conferences:
- Saskatchewan Wildlife Federation 89th Annual Convention 2018, February, 2018, Prince Albert, SK
Scope: Provincial
Description: A yearly gathering of members, featuring the presentation of awards

Elbow & District Wildlife Federation
c/o Village of Elbow, PO Box 8, 201 Saskatchewan St., Elbow SK S0H 1J0
Tel: 306-854-2277; *Fax:* 306-854-2229
recdirector@elbowsask.com
elbowsask.com
Member of: Saskatchewan Wildlife Federation

Moose Jaw Wildlife Federation
1396 - 3rd Ave. NE, Moose Jaw SK S6H 0A1
Tel: 306-693-4047
MJWildlife.Federation@gmail.com
sites.google.com/site/moosejawwildlife
Member of: Saskatchewan Wildlife Federation
Chief Officer(s):
Doreen Dodd, Contact, 306-692-4148
doreendodd@sasktel.net

Regina Wildlife Federation (RWF)
PO Box 594, Regina SK S4P 3A3
Tel: 306-359-7733
rwf1@accesscomm.ca
nonprofits.accesscomm.ca/rwf
Mission: The RWF is a non-profit wildlife conservation organization.
Member of: Saskatchewan Wildlife Federation
Chief Officer(s):
Gil White, President

Saskatoon Wildlife Federation
PO Box 32041, Saskatoon SK S7S 1N8
Tel: 306-242-1666; *Fax:* 306-933-0617
www.saskatoonwildlifefederation.com
www.facebook.com/SaskatoonWildlifeFederation
twitter.com/SaskWildlifeFed
Mission: Saskatoon Wildlife Federation is a non-profit organization committed to providing a clean welcoming enviroment for individuals who enjoy hunting, fishing and various other outdoor sports. The organization works closely with Ducks Unlimited and other groups to preserve wetlands and other wildspaces for habitat.
Member of: Saskatchewan Wildlife Federation

Weyburn Wildlife Federation
415 - 3 Ave. NW, Weyburn SK S4H 1R2
Tel: 306-842-7658
Member of: Saskatchewan Wildlife Federation

Saskatchewan Women's Institute (SWI)
SK
saskatchewan@fwic.ca
www.facebook.com/436313276575974
Overview: A medium-sized provincial organization founded in 1911 overseen by Federated Women's Institutes of Canada
Mission: To help discover, stimulate & develop leadership among women; To assist, encourage & support women to become knowledgeable & responsible citizens; To ensure basic human rights for women & to work towards their equality; To be a strong voice through which matters of the utmost concern can reach the decision makers; To promote the improvement of agricultural & other rural communities & to safeguard the environment
Member of: Associated Country Women of the World
Finances: *Funding Sources:* Membership fees; Fundraising

Saskatchewan Writers Guild (SWG)
PO Box 3986, Regina SK S4P 3R9
Tel: 306-757-6310; *Fax:* 306-565-8554
Toll-Free: 800-667-6788
info@skwriter.com
www.skwriter.com
www.facebook.com/skwritersguild
twitter.com/SKWritersGuild
Overview: A medium-sized provincial charitable organization founded in 1969
Mission: To promote excellence in writing by Saskatchewan writers; To advocate for Saskatchewan writers; To promote the teaching of Saskatchewan & Canadian literature & instruction in the art of writing at all levels of education; To improve public access to writers & their work; To develop professionalism in the business of writing; To improve the economic status of Saskatchewan writers
Member of: Saskatchewan Council of Cultural Organizations; Saskatchewan Arts Alliance
Finances: *Annual Operating Budget:* $500,000-$1.5 Million; *Funding Sources:* Government grants & membership fees
Staff Member(s): 9; 15 volunteer(s)
Membership: 450; *Fees:* $75 regular; $55 senior; $20 student; *Member Profile:* Writers & non-writers who have an interest in supporting Saskatchewan's literary scene
Activities: Organizing & promoting readings & school visits, workshops, provincial reading series, The Caroline Heath Memorial Lecture, Mentorship Program, Manuscript Evaluation Service, & Award Program; Administering Resident Writer Program, Saskatchewan Writers/Artists Colonies & Retreats, & The Writers' Assistance Fund (WAF); *Speaker Service:* Yes; *Library:* Ken Mitchell Library
Chief Officer(s):
Judith Silverthorne, Executive Director, 306-791-7742
edswg@skwriter.com
Tracy Hamon, Program Manager, 306-791-7743
programs@skwriter.com
Leah MacLean-Evans, Executive Assistant, 306-791-7740
Awards:
- The Cheryl & Henry Kloppenburg Award for Literary Excellence
Awarded to recognize Saskatchewan writers who have written a substantial body of literary work *Deadline:* June 30; *Amount:* $10,000 *Contact:* Tracy Hamon, Manager, Programs, E-mail: programs@skwriter.com; *Phone:* 306-791-7743
- City of Regina Writing Award
Awarded to a Regina writer to reward merit & to enable the writer to focus on a specific writing project *Deadline:* January; *Amount:* $4,500 *Contact:* Tracy Hamon, Manager, Programs, E-mail: programs@skwriter.com; *Phone:* 306-791-7743
- The Currie-Hyland Prize
Awarded to honour excellence in poetry by a high school writer living outside of Regina or Saskatoon *Contact:* Tracy Hamon, Manager, Programs, E-mail: programs@skwriter.com; *Phone:* 306-791-7743
- The Hyland Volunteer Award
Established to recognize the volunteer achievements of Saskatchewan Writers' Guild members *Deadline:* September *Contact:* Tracy Hamon, Manager, Programs, E-mail: programs@skwriter.com; *Phone:* 306-791-7743
- The Jerrett Enns Award
Contact: Tracy Hamon, Manager, Programs, E-mail: programs@skwriter.com; *Phone:* 306-791-7743
- The John V. Hicks Long Manuscript Award
Awarded to recognize excellence in unpublished book-length manuscripts of fiction, non-fiction, & poetry; each year, the competition is open to a different genre *Deadline:* June *Contact:* Tracy Hamon, Manager, Programs, E-mail: programs@skwriter.com; *Phone:* 306-791-7743
Meetings/Conferences:
- Saskatchewan Writers' Guild Annual General Meeting & Fall Conference 2018, October, 2018, Saskatoon, SK
Scope: Provincial
Publications:
- eBriefs [a publication of the Saskatchewan Writers' Guild]
Type: Newsletter; *Frequency:* Weekly; *Accepts Advertising*
Profile: An information resource for members; includes event dates & calls of interest
- Freelance [a publication of the Saskatchewan Writers' Guild]
Type: Newsletter; *Frequency:* bi-m.; *Accepts Advertising*; *Price:* Free with membership inthe Saskatchewan Writers' Guild
Profile: An information resource for members; includes writing resources, monthly literary events in Saskatchewan, & literary news & issues
- Grain [a publication of the Saskatchewan Writers' Guild]
Type: Magazine; *Frequency:* q.; *Accepts Advertising*; *Editor:* Adam Pottle; *Price:* $35.00 + GST
Profile: A literary magazine which publishes engaging & challenging work by Canadian & international writers & artists
- Spring [a publication of the Saskatchewan Writers' Guild]
Type: Magazine; *Frequency:* s-a.; *Accepts Advertising*; *Price:* Free with membership in the SWG; $10+ GST without membership
Profile: A publication that showcases new work from emerging Saskatchewan writers who have not yet been published in book-length form

- Windscript [a publication of the Saskatchewan Writers' Guild]
Type: Magazine; *Frequency:* a.; *Accepts Advertising; Price:* $5
Profile: A publication that showcases writing by high school students

Saskatchewan Youth in Care & Custody Network (SYICCN)
Cornwall Professional Building, #510, 2125 - 11th Ave., Regina SK S4P 3X3
Tel: 306-522-1533; *Fax:* 306-522-1507
Other Communication: Toll Free Youth Line: 1-888-528-8061
info@syiccn.ca
www.syiccn.ca
www.facebook.com/SYICCN
twitter.com/syiccninc
Overview: A medium-sized provincial organization overseen by Youth in Care Canada
Mission: To advocate for & support youth in or from government care or young offender systems in Saskatchewan; To ensure that youth in care or custody have a voice in their lives & communities
Staff Member(s): 4
Membership: *Member Profile:* Individuals between the ages of 14 & 24 who are in or from foster care or young offender systems in Saskatchewan
Activities: Working with regional departments of social services & foster family associations; Providing education & employment opportunities; Facilitating workshops
Chief Officer(s):
Stephanie Bustamante, Executive Director
Sarah Caldwell, Coordinator, Provincial Outreach
Darlene Domshy, Coordinator, Research

Saskatchewan/Manitoba Gelbvieh Association
PO Box 379, Hudson Bay SK S0E 0Y0
Tel: 306-865-2929; *Fax:* 306-865-2860
firriver@xolornet.com
Previous Name: Manitoba/Saskatchewan Gelbvieh Association
Overview: A small local organization
Member of: Canadian Gelbvieh Association
Membership: 39
Chief Officer(s):
Darcy Hrebeniuk, Contact

Saskatoon & District Chamber of Commerce *See* Greater Saskatoon Chamber of Commerce

Saskatoon & District Labour Council (SDLC)
#110B, 2103 Airport Dr., Saskatoon SK S7L 6W2
Tel: 306-384-0303
sdlc@sasktel.net
www.saskatoondlc.ca
www.facebook.com/SaskatoonDistrictLabourCouncil
Overview: A medium-sized local organization overseen by Saskatchewan Federation of Labour
Mission: To support local unions in Saskatoon & the surrounding area; To advance the economic & social welfare of workers
Activities: Hosting council meetings & activities to share information on issues that affect unions; Promoting interests of affiliates; Engaging in municipal political action; Presenting educational opportunities; Raising awareness of workplace injuries & deaths, & advocating for the strengthening & enforcing of health & safety rules; Organizing a commemorative service to mark the annual National Day of Mourning For Workers Killed or Injured On The Job; Networking with community organizations
Meetings/Conferences:
• 2018 Saskatoon & District Labour Council Annual General Meeting, February, 2018, Heritage Inn, Saskatoon, SK
Scope: Local

Saskatoon City Police Association (SCPA) / Association de la police de la ville de Saskatoon
PO Box 170, Saskatoon SK S7K 3K4
Tel: 306-652-5662
scpa@sasktel.net
www.spassoc.ca
Overview: A small local organization founded in 1926
Mission: To establish friendly relationship between all members of police department; To encourage & strengthen cooperation between Chief of Police, Board of Police Commissioners, members of police department, Saskatoon, & those charged with enforcement of law & order
Member of: Canadian Police Association; Saskatchewan Federation of Police Officers
Affiliation(s): Canadian Professional Police Association
Membership: 100-499

Chief Officer(s):
Wally Romanuck, Treasurer
Stan Goertzen, President

Saskatoon Civic Middle Management Association (SCMMA)
PO Box 151, Saskatoon SK S7K 3K4
scmma.org
Overview: A small local organization founded in 1996
Membership: 220+
Chief Officer(s):
Roger Bradley, President

Saskatoon Coin Club
PO Box 1674, Saskatoon SK S7K 3R8
info@saskatooncoinclub.ca
www.saskatooncoinclub.ca
Overview: A small local organization founded in 1960
Membership: *Fees:* Free

Saskatoon Community Foundation
#101, 308 - Fourth Ave. North, Saskatoon SK S7K 2L7
Tel: 306-665-1766; *Fax:* 306-665-1777
office@saskatooncommunityfoundation.ca
www.saskatooncommunityfoundation.ca
Previous Name: The Saskatoon Foundation
Overview: A small local charitable organization founded in 1970
Mission: To provide a significant & sustaining contribution to the quality of life in Saskatoon & area through stewardship, strategic grant making, & community leadership
Member of: Community Foundations of Canada
Finances: *Funding Sources:* Donations
Membership: *Committees:* Asset Development; Grants; Investment
Activities: *Speaker Service:* Yes
Chief Officer(s):
Carm Michalenko, Executive Director
director@saskatooncommunityfoundation.ca

Saskatoon Crisis Intervention Service
#103, 506 - 25th St. East, Saskatoon SK S7K 4A7
Tel: 306-664-4525; *Fax:* 306-664-1974; *Crisis Hot-Line:* 306-933-6200
info@saskatooncrisis.ca
www.saskatooncrisis.ca
Also Known As: Mobile Crisis
Overview: A small provincial organization founded in 1980
Mission: To respond to crisis situations: suicide intervention, child abuse & neglect, marriage & family problems, mental health crisis intervention, drug & alcohol abuse, seniors in distress & individual crisis counselling; response may be on the telephone, in the office or in the community
Finances: *Funding Sources:* United Way

Saskatoon Farmers' Markets (SFM)
414 Ave. B South, Saskatoon SK S7M 1M8
Tel: 306-384-6262
skfarm@sasktel.net
www.saskatoonfarmersmarket.com
Overview: A small provincial organization founded in 1975
Mission: To provide residents & visitors the best in local agricultural products, baking, prepared foods & crafts

Saskatoon Food Bank & Learning Centre
202 Ave. C South, Saskatoon SK S7M 1N2
Tel: 306-664-6565; *Fax:* 306-664-6563
office.admin@saskatoonfoodbank.org
www.saskatoonfoodbank.org
www.facebook.com/saskatoonfoodbank
twitter.com/yxeFoodBank
www.youtube.com/user/SaskatoonFoodBank
Also Known As: Grassroots Resource & Learning Centre
Overview: A small local charitable organization founded in 1984
Mission: To distribute emergency food hampers (through a referral system) to those who require them
Member of: Canadian Association of Food Banks
Finances: *Annual Operating Budget:* $250,000-$500,000; *Funding Sources:* donations
Staff Member(s): 7; 20 volunteer(s)
Membership: 60; *Fees:* $5 organization; $1 individual
Activities: Annual general meeting; open house; food hamper program; adult literacy classes; community kitchen; personal development workshops; *Library:* Open to public
Chief Officer(s):
Laurie O'Connor, Executive Director

The Saskatoon Foundation *See* Saskatoon Community Foundation

Saskatoon Heritage Society
PO Box 7051, Saskatoon SK S7K 4J1
saskatoonheritagesociety@gmail.com
www.saskatoonheritage.ca
Overview: A small local charitable organization founded in 1976
Mission: To promote awareness of the history & heritage of Saskatoon
Member of: Heritage Canada; SaskCulture; Saskatchewan Architectural Heritage Society
Finances: *Annual Operating Budget:* Less than $50,000
20 volunteer(s)
Activities: Heritage tours & visits; advocacy; historical research; President's New Year's Levee in Jan.; annual fundraising dinner in Feb.; AGM in May.
Chief Officer(s):
Adam Pollock, President

Saskatoon Indian & Métis Friendship Centre
168 Wall St., Saskatoon SK S7K 1N4
Tel: 306-244-0174; *Fax:* 306-664-2536
reception_SIMFC@shaw.ca
www.simfc.ca
www.facebook.com/groups/SIMFCUpcomingEvents
Overview: A small local organization
Mission: To improve the quality of life for Aboriginal people in the City of Saskatoon.
Member of: Charities; donations; corporate sponsorship; government
Activities: Youth Programs; Family Programs; Urban Aboriginal Strategy Project; Community Access Program; Muisc Lessons; Sports; Cultural Classes
Chief Officer(s):
Bill Mintram, Executive Director

Saskatoon Lapidary & Mineral Club
210 Braeshire Lane, Saskatoon SK S7B 1B2
Overview: A small local organization founded in 1961
Mission: To promote interest in minerals & lapidary in the Saskatoon Saskatchewan area
Activities: Hosting regular meetings

Saskatoon Multicultural Council *See* Saskatchewan Intercultural Association Inc.

Saskatoon Musicians' Association (SMA)
#304, 416 - 21st St. East, Saskatoon SK S7K 0C2
Tel: 306-477-2506; *Fax:* 306-665-5694
afm553@sasktel.net
www.facebook.com/SaskatoonMusiciansAssociation
Also Known As: Local 553 AFM
Overview: A small local organization founded in 1910
Mission: To promote the quality & standard of live music in the community
Member of: American Federation of Musicians
Affiliation(s): AFL - CIO/CLC
Finances: *Annual Operating Budget:* Less than $50,000; *Funding Sources:* Membership dues
Staff Member(s): 1
Membership: 230; *Fees:* $65 half year; $120 full year
Chief Officer(s):
Ross Nykiforuk, President
Vesti Hanson, Secretary/Treasurer

Saskatoon Open Door Society Inc. (SODS)
#100, 129 - 3 Ave. North, Saskatoon SK S7K 2H4
Tel: 306-653-4464; *Fax:* 306-653-7159
skopendoor@sods.sk.ca
www.sods.sk.ca
Overview: A small local charitable organization founded in 1980
Mission: To welcome & assist refugees & immigrants to become informed & effective participants in Canadian society; to involve the Saskatoon community in their hospitable reception & just acceptance
Affiliation(s): Saskatchewan Association of Immigrant Settlement & Integration Agencies; Association of Western Canada Immigrant Serving Agencies
Finances: *Annual Operating Budget:* Greater than $5 Million; *Funding Sources:* Federal & provincial governments; United Way; Foundations
Staff Member(s): 150; 300 volunteer(s)
Membership: 70; *Fees:* $10
Activities: Settlement Support; Family Support; Language Education; Daycare; Employment Services; Translatoin Services; *Speaker Service:* Yes
Chief Officer(s):
Beulah Gana, Executive Director
Haidah Amirzadeh, President

Saskatoon Parents of Twins & Triplets Organization (SPOTTO)
PO Box 25093, RPO River Heights, Saskatoon SK S7K 8B7
Tel: 306-384-4234
saskatoon@multiplebirthscanada.org
spotto.ca
Overview: A small local organization overseen by Multiple Births Canada
Mission: Supports the multiple birth community in and around the Saskatoon area.
Membership: Fees: $35
Activities: Chat & Play; Multiple Expectation Classes; Providing support to parents of twins & triplets
Chief Officer(s):
Tammy Desrosiers, Communication Coordinator
spotto.communications@gmail.com

Saskatoon Real Estate Board See Saskatoon Region Association of REALTORS

Saskatoon Region Association of REALTORS (SRAR)
1149 - 8 St. East., Saskatoon SK S7H 0S3
Tel: 306-244-4453; Fax: 306-343-1420
info@srar.ca
www.srar.ca
Previous Name: Saskatoon Real Estate Board
Overview: A medium-sized local organization founded in 1911 overseen by Saskatchewan Real Estate Association
Mission: To represent the real estate interests of its members & the public; to provide services & programs to enhance the professionalism, competency & effectiveness of its members; to advocate public policy towards improving the real estate market environment
Member of: The Canadian Real Estate Association
Finances: Annual Operating Budget: $500,000-$1.5 Million; Funding Sources: Membership dues
Staff Member(s): 8
Membership: 610; Committees: Arbitration; Education; Finance; Discipline; Professional Standards; Public Relations; Newspaper; Legislation; Political Action
Chief Officer(s):
Jason Yochim, Executive Officer
Darrin Sych, Director, Advertising

Saskatoon Senior Citizens Action Now Inc.
310 F Ave. South, Saskatoon SK S7M 1T2
Tel: 306-244-6408
Previous Name: Saskatoon Seniors Action Now Inc.
Overview: A small local charitable organization founded in 1972
Mission: To help develop positive quality of life for seniors & improve community environment for all
Affiliation(s): National Pensioners & Senior Citizens Federation

Saskatoon Seniors Action Now Inc. See Saskatoon Senior Citizens Action Now Inc.

Saskatoon Soaring Club
510 Cynthia St., Saskatoon SK S7L 7K7
saskatoonsoaringclub@gmail.com
www.soar.sk.ca/ssc
Overview: A small local organization
Mission: To promote the sport of gliding and soaring in Saskatoon.
Member of: Soaring Association of Canada

Saskatoon Society for the Prevention of Cruelty to Animals Inc.
5028 Clarence Ave. South, Grasswood SK S7T 1A7
Tel: 306-374-7387; Fax: 306-373-7912
info@saskatoonspca.com
www.saskatoonspca.com
www.facebook.com/TheSaskatoonSPCA
twitter.com/SaskatoonSPCA
Also Known As: Saskatoon SPCA
Overview: A small local organization founded in 1968
Mission: To work for the protection of all animals & to develop in the public at large a humane attitude toward all animal life; To promote the enactment of laws for the prevention of cruelty to & neglect of animals; To promote quality of life for companion animals through responsible stewardship, successful adoptions, education, & enforcement of the Animal Protection Act
Member of: Canadian Federation of Humane Societies; Volunteer Saskatoon; Saskatchewan Society for Fundraising Executives; Association of Fundraising Professionals
Finances: Annual Operating Budget: $500,000-$1.5 Million; Funding Sources: Fundraising; donations; city pound contract; shelter services
Staff Member(s): 25; 200 volunteer(s)
Membership: 400 individual; Fees: $25 individual; $40 family; $10 junior/senior; $100 corporate; $200 life
Activities: Humane Education; adoptions; lost & found; cruelty investigations; special events; Internships: Yes
Chief Officer(s):
Patricia Cameron, Executive Director
Marv Le Nabat, Manager, Operations
Tracie Seeley, Manager, Fund Development
Tricia McAuley, Coordinator, Fundraising

Saskatoon Symphony Society (SSO)
408 - 20 St. West, Saskatoon SK S7M 0X4
Tel: 306-665-6414
Toll-Free: 888-639-7770
marketing@saskatoonsymphony.org
saskatoonsymphony.org
www.facebook.com/18975919587
www.youtube.com/user/SaskatoonSymphonyMM
Also Known As: Saskatoon Symphony Orchestra
Overview: A small local charitable organization founded in 1931 overseen by Orchestras Canada
Mission: To promote, encourage & support symphonic & classical music in Saskatoon & elsewhere in Saskatchewan
Member of: Orchestras Canada; Saskatchewan Chamber of Commerce
Affiliation(s): Saskatchewan Arts Alliance
Finances: Funding Sources: Box office; Donations; Sponsorships; Grants
Staff Member(s): 11
Activities: Speaker Service: Yes; Library
Chief Officer(s):
Mark Turner, Executive Director
Eric Paetkau, Music Director

Saskatoon Youth Orchestra
PO Box 21108, Saskatoon SK S7H 5N9
Tel: 306-955-6336
info@syo.ca
syo.ca
www.facebook.com/SaskatoonYouthOrchestra
twitter.com/SaskYouthOrch
Overview: A small local charitable organization founded in 1958 overseen by Orchestras Canada
Mission: To provide young musicians in the Saskatoon area with an opportunity to improve their playing skills in a full orchestral ensemble; To enruch the cultural landscape of the city of Saskatoon and the province of Saskatchewan at large
Member of: Orchestras Canada
Finances: Funding Sources: Grants; Individual & corporate sponsorship
Staff Member(s): 3
Membership: Fees: $510 Youth Orchestra; $395 Saskatoon Strings (developmental group); Member Profile: Musicians 12-25 years old living in the Saskatoon area who also participate in their respective school music programs
Activities: Performing concerts; Holding regular rehearsals; Conducting workshops; Commissioning pieces from Canadian composers
Chief Officer(s):
Paul Sinkewicz, Executive Director
Richard Carnegie, Music Director
conductor@syo.ca
Bernadette Wilson, Music Director
sstrings@syo.ca

SaskCentral
PO Box 3030, 2055 Albert St., Regina SK S4P 3G8
Tel: 306-566-1200
Toll-Free: 866-403-7499
info@saskcentral.com
www.saskcentral.com
www.linkedin.com/company/saskcentral
twitter.com/SaskCentral
Overview: A small provincial organization founded in 1938 overseen by Canadian Credit Union Association
Mission: To provide leadership, services, & support to Saskatchewan's 49 credit unions
Member of: Canadian Credit Union Association
Membership: Member Profile: Credit unions in Saskatchewan
Activities: Offering services to credit unions in Saskatchewan, such as financial liquidity management, consulting, research, & development support; Working with government & regulators to create a business environment where credit unions will succeed; Promoting credit unions by presenting a positive public image
Chief Officer(s):
Keith Nixon, Chief Executive Officer
Debbie Lane, Exec. Vice-President & Chief People Officer, CU Solutions
Sheri Lucas, Exec. Vice-President, CFO & CRO
Meetings/Conferences:
• SaskCentral 2018 Annual General Meeting, 2018
Scope: Provincial
Publications:
• SaskCentral Annual Report
Type: Yearbook; Frequency: Annually

SaskCulture Inc.
#404, 2125 - 11th Ave., Regina SK S4P 3X3
Tel: 306-780-9284
saskculture.info@saskculture.sk.ca
www.saskculture.sk.ca
www.facebook.com/SaskCulture
twitter.com/SaskCulture
www.youtube.com/user/SaskCult
Previous Name: Saskatchewan Council of Cultural Organizations
Overview: A medium-sized provincial organization founded in 1997
Mission: To bring together organizations which work to further the course of culture
Member of: Canadian Centre of Philanthropy; Tourism Saskatchewan; Regina Chamber of Commerce; Saskatoon Chamber of Commerce; Saskatchewan Association of Rural Municipalities; Saskatchewan Urban Municipalities
Affiliation(s): Canadian Society of Association Executives
Finances: Annual Operating Budget: Greater than $5 Million; Funding Sources: Saskatchewan Lotteries Trust Fund for Sport, Culture & Recreation
Staff Member(s): 17
Membership: 137; Fees: $15 individual; $75 non-voting; $150 voting; Member Profile: Non-profit, cultural organizations, province-wide, local-based, mandated to provide cultural programs, services & information
Chief Officer(s):
Rose Gilks, General Manager, 306-780-9282
rgilks@saskculture.sk.ca
Diane Ell, Communications Manager, 306-780-9453
dell@saskculture.sk.ca

SaskTel Pioneers
21016 - 1st Ave., Regina SK S4P 3Y2
Tel: 306-777-2515; Fax: 306-777-2831
Toll-Free: 866-944-4442
sasktel.pioneers@sasktel.sk.ca
www.sasktelpioneers.com
twitter.com/sasktelpioneers
Also Known As: Chapter 59
Overview: A small provincial organization founded in 1995 overseen by TelecomPioneers of Canada
Chief Officer(s):
Darrell Liebrecht, Director
Darrell.Liebrecht@sasktel.sk.ca

Sauble Beach Chamber of Commerce
672 Main St., Sauble Beach ON N0H 2T0
Tel: 519-422-2457
manager@saublebeach.com
www.saublebeach.com
Overview: A small local organization founded in 1947
Mission: To protect the interests of area businesses
Member of: Canadian Chamber of Commerce; Ontario Chamber of Commerce
Finances: Annual Operating Budget: Less than $50,000; Funding Sources: Membership fees; sponsorship
20 volunteer(s)
Membership: 130; Fees: $150-$300; $100 associate
Activities: Organizing events such as Sauble Sandfest, Oktoberfest, Winterfest, Business Achievement Awards, & Canada Day Fireworks

Saugeen Shores Chamber of Commerce
559 Goderich St., Port Elgin ON N0H 2C4
Tel: 519-832-2332; Fax: 519-389-3725
Toll-Free: 800-387-3456
portelgininfo@saugeenshores.ca
www.saugeenshoreschamber.com
www.facebook.com/saugeenshorestourism
Previous Name: Port Elgin & District Chamber of Commerce
Overview: A small local organization

Mission: To promote business & commerce; To protect the business interests of the community
Membership: 413; *Fees:* $231.65; *Committees:* Advocacy & Economic Development; Festivals & Events/Resource Centre; Governance, Policy & Procedures; Management; Marketing & Promotions/Fundraising; Membership Services & Representation; Networking & Membership; Tourism Services
Chief Officer(s):
Joanne Robbins, General Manager

Sault Naturalists
PO Box 21035, 306 Northern Ave. East, Sault Ste Marie ON P6B 6H3
carrie@ginou.ca
soonats.pbworks.com
Overview: A small local organization
Mission: To promote the enjoyment of nature through environmental appreciation & conservation; to encourage wise use & conservation of natural resources
Member of: Federation of Ontario Naturalists
Affiliation(s): Canadian Nature Federation
Finances: *Annual Operating Budget:* Less than $50,000
30 volunteer(s)
Membership: *Fees:* $20 individual; $25 family; $10 student
Chief Officer(s):
Don Hall, President, 705-248-1834

Sault Ste. Marie Music Festival
c/o Algoma Conservatory of Music, 1520 Queen St. East, Sault Ste Marie ON P6A 2G4
Tel: 705-253-4373
algomaconservatory@algomau.ca
Previous Name: Kiwanis Music Festival
Overview: A small local organization founded in 1937

Sault Ste Marie & 49th Field Regt. RCA Historical Society
690 Queen St. East, Sault Ste Marie ON P6A 2A4
Tel: 705-759-7278; *Fax:* 705-759-3058
heritage@saultmuseum.com
www.saultmuseum.com
www.facebook.com/saultmuseum
www.youtube.com/user/saultmuseum
Also Known As: Sault Ste Marie Museum
Overview: A small local charitable organization founded in 1920
Mission: To preserve, interpret & exhibit the heritage of Sault Ste Marie
Member of: Ontario Historical Society; Ontario Musuem Association; Ontario Archive Association; Attractions Ontario; Canadian Heritage Information Network
Finances: *Annual Operating Budget:* $100,000-$250,000; *Funding Sources:* Provincial, municipal government
Staff Member(s): 4; 50 volunteer(s)
Membership: 200; *Fees:* $25 individual; $35 family; $12 seniors; $60 group/business
Activities: Sault Ste Marie Museum; *Library:* by appointment
Chief Officer(s):
Kim Forbes, Curator, 705-759-7278

Sault Ste Marie Chamber of Commerce (SSMCOC)
#1, 369 Queen St. East, Sault Ste Marie ON P6A 1Z4
Tel: 705-949-7152; *Fax:* 705-759-8166
info@ssmcoc.com
www.ssmcoc.com
www.facebook.com/ssmcoc
Overview: A small local organization founded in 1889
Mission: To be the recognized voice of business committed to the enhancement of economic prosperity in Sault Ste Marie
Member of: Canadian Chamber of Commerce; Ontario Chamber of Commerce
Finances: *Annual Operating Budget:* $100,000-$250,000; *Funding Sources:* Membership dues; fundraising
Staff Member(s): 5; 150 volunteer(s)
Membership: 680; *Fees:* Schedule available; *Committees:* Advocacy; Business Development & Education; Finance; Government Relations; Marketing & Communications
Activities: *Speaker Service:* Yes
Chief Officer(s):
Paul A. Johnson, President
Rory Ring, CEO
rory@ssmcoc.com

Sault Ste Marie Economic Development Corporation (SSMEDC)
99 Foster Dr., Sault Ste Marie ON P6A 5X6
Tel: 705-759-5432; *Fax:* 705-759-2185
Toll-Free: 866-558-5144
info@ssmedc.ca
www.sault-canada.com
www.facebook.com/76704661918
twitter.com/SaultEDC
www.youtube.com/user/SSMEDC
Overview: A small local organization founded in 1982
Mission: To create jobs in the municipality & business attraction to the city
Affiliation(s): Economic Developers Council of Ontario
Finances: *Annual Operating Budget:* Greater than $5 Million; *Funding Sources:* Municipal, provincial & federal government; Partnership contributions
Staff Member(s): 18
Membership: 1-99; *Committees:* Executive; Finance & Audit; Business Sault Ste. Marie Advisory; Tourism Sault Ste. Marie Management; Meetings, Conventions & Sports Tourism Product Team; Festivals & Events Product Team
Chief Officer(s):
Don Mitchell, President
Tom Dodds, Chief Executive Officer

Sault Ste Marie Musicians' Association
#216, 451 Queen St. East, Sault Ste Marie ON P6A 5N2
Tel: 705-254-2210; *Fax:* 705-253-2140
afm276@soonet.ca
saultmusicians.org
Also Known As: AFM Local 276
Overview: A small local organization founded in 1918 overseen by American Federation of Musicians of the United States & Canada (AFL-CIO/CLC)
Mission: Committed to raising industry standards and placing the professional musician in the foreground of the cultural landscape by negotiating fair agreements, protecting ownership of recorded music, securing benefits such as health care and pension, or lobbying legislators.
Affiliation(s): Fédération internationale des musiciens
Finances: *Annual Operating Budget:* Less than $50,000; *Funding Sources:* Membership dues; work dues; fines
Staff Member(s): 1; 6 volunteer(s)
Membership: 130; *Fees:* $115
Activities: *Rents Mailing List:* Yes
Chief Officer(s):
Paul Leclair, Sec.-Treas.

Sault Ste Marie Police Association / Association de la police de Sault-Ste-Marie
262 Queen St. East, Sault Ste Marie ON P6A 5M6
Tel: 705-949-7632
Overview: A small local organization

Sault Ste Marie Real Estate Board (SSMREB)
372 Albert St. East, Sault Ste Marie ON P6A 2J6
Tel: 705-949-4560; *Fax:* 705-949-5935
www.saultstemarierealestate.ca
www.facebook.com/SaultSteMarieRealEstateBoard
Overview: A small local organization overseen by Ontario Real Estate Association
Member of: The Canadian Real Estate Association
Membership: 176; *Member Profile:* Realtors
Chief Officer(s):
Andrea Gagne, Executive Officer

Sault Symphony Association / Orchestre symphonique de Sault Ste-Marie
864 Queen St. East, Sault Ste Marie ON P6A 2B4
Tel: 705-945-5337; *Fax:* 705-945-8865
saultsymphonyorchestra@gmail.com
www.saultsymphony.ca
www.linked.n.com/pub/sault-symphony-association/38/96a/bab
www.facebook.com/saultsymphony
twitter.com/SaultSymphony
Overview: A small local charitable organization founded in 1972 overseen by Orchestras Canada
Mission: To promote symphonic music in Sault Ste Marie, Ontario & the surrounding region
Member of: Orchestras Canada
Finances: *Funding Sources:* Grants; Corporate sponsors; Individual donations; Fundraising
Staff Member(s): 4; 50 volunteer(s)
Membership: 360
Activities: *Library:* Sault Symphony Association Music Library; Not open to public
Chief Officer(s):
Angela Rasaiah, President
John Wilkinson, Artistic Director

SauveTerre *See* Earthsave Canada

Save a Family Plan (SAFP)
c/o St. Peter's Seminary, 1040 Waterloo St., London ON N6A 3Y1
Tel: 519-672-1115; *Fax:* 519-672-6379
safpinfo@safp.org
www.safp.org
www.facebook.com/saveafamilyplan
twitter.com/SaveaFamilyPlan
Overview: A large international charitable organization founded in 1965
Mission: To implement sustainable family & community development programs in 5 states in India
Member of: Coalition for the Right of Children
Finances: *Annual Operating Budget:* $3 Million-$5 Million; *Funding Sources:* Businesses; groups; individual benefactors
Activities: Public engagement program including presentations, displays guest speakers
Chief Officer(s):
Marisa Thorburn, Executive Director
Lois Côté, President
Publications:
• Ektha (Unity) [a publication of Save a Family Plan]
Type: Newsletter

Save Ontario Shipwrecks (SOS)
PO Box 2389, Blenheim ON N0P 1A0
Tel: 519-676-4110; *Fax:* 519-676-7058
www.saveontarioshipwrecks.on.ca
Overview: A small provincial organization founded in 1981
Mission: To promote & preserve Ontario's marine heritage
Member of: Canadian Maritime Heritage Federation
Affiliation(s): Underwater Council
Finances: *Annual Operating Budget:* Less than $50,000
Membership: 350-400; *Fees:* $25 individual; $40 family/institution; $250 corporate; *Committees:* Data Base; Forum; Education; Membership; Promotion
Chief Officer(s):
Chris Phinney, President
cphinney@SaveOntarioShipwrecks.ca
Nicole AuCoin, Secretary
naucoin@rogers.com

Save Our Heritage Organization (SOHO)
PO Box 578, 96 Young St., Brighton ON K0K 1H0
Tel: 613-475-2144
info@proctorhousemuseum.ca
www.proctorhousemuseum.ca
Also Known As: Proctor House Museum
Overview: A small local charitable organization founded in 1970
Mission: To discover, protect & preserve any material which may help to establish or illustrate the history of the Brighton area
Member of: Ontario Museum Association
Affiliation(s): Ontario Heritage Association
Finances: *Funding Sources:* Grants; admissions; special events; membership fees; donations
Activities: Restores & maintains the Proctor House Museum, reconstruction & restoration of 19th century barn on original site of Proctor House barn, 2-4 theatre productions a year; *Awareness Events:* Applefest Celebrations, last weekend in Sept.; *Library:* Open to public by appointment

Save the Children Canada (SCC) / Aide à l'enfance - Canada
#300, 4141 Yonge St., Toronto ON M2P 2A8
Tel: 416-221-5501; *Fax:* 416-221-8214
Toll-Free: 800-668-5036
info@savethechildren.ca
www.savethechildren.ca
www.facebook.com/savethechildren.ca
twitter.com/SaveChildrenCan
www.youtube.com/savethechildrenCA
Merged from: Street Kids International
Overview: A large national charitable organization founded in 1919
Mission: To fight for children's rights; To deliver immediate & lasting improvements to children's lives worldwide in Canada, Africa, Asia, Latin America & the Caribbean, & the Middle East
Member of: Save the Children International; Canadian Council for International Cooperation
Finances: *Annual Operating Budget:* Greater than $5 Million; *Funding Sources:* Individual; corporate donations
Staff Member(s): 30
Membership: *Fees:* $50
Activities: Developing programs that focus on child participation, children & education, children & violence, child labour, children & health, children & emergencies, child poverty,

juvenile justice, children's rights, rural children, street kids, rural development, & child prostitution; *Internships:* Yes
Chief Officer(s):
Bill Chambers, President & CEO

Save Your Skin Foundation
#319, 3600 Windcrest Dr., North Vancouver BC V7G 2S5
Toll-Free: 800-460-5832
www.saveyourskin.ca
www.facebook.com/SaveYourSkinFoundation
twitter.com/saveyourskinfdn
www.youtube.com/channel/UCNlKKrfOJ0Gh4SKrEqYpuRw
Overview: A small provincial organization
Mission: To provide help & support to patients with skin cancer; To raise awareness about melanoma; To raise funds for research
Membership: *Committees:* Editing & Strategic Development; Strategic Development; Corporate Governance; Fundraising; Patient Advocacy; Medical Advisory
Chief Officer(s):
Kathy Barnard, President
kathy@saveyourskin.ca

Savoy Foundation Inc. / Fondation Savoy inc.
230, rue Foch, Saint-Jean-sur-Richelieu QC J3B 2B2
Tél: 450-358-9779; *Téléc:* 450-346-1045
epilepsy@savoy-foundation.ca
www.savoy-foundation.ca
Aperçu: *Dimension:* petite; *Envergure:* internationale; Organisme sans but lucratif; fondée en 1971
Mission: Recherche en épilepsie
Finances: *Budget de fonctionnement annuel:* $250,000-$500,000
Membre: *Comités:* Scientifique
Membre(s) du bureau directeur:
George Savoy, Président

Scadding Court Community Centre (SCCC)
707 Dundas St. West, Toronto ON M5T 2W6
Tel: 416-392-0335; *Fax:* 416-392-0340
www.scaddingcourt.org
www.facebook.com/people/Scadding-Court/100001939237499
twitter.com/scadding_court
Overview: A medium-sized local charitable organization founded in 1978
Mission: To support and foster the well being of individuals, families, and community groups by providing and encouraging both local and international opportunities for recreation, education, athletics, community participation and inclusive social interaction.
Finances: *Funding Sources:* Government
Staff Member(s): 16
Membership: *Fees:* Schedule available
Chief Officer(s):
Kevin Lee, Executive Director

Scandinavian Assemblies of God in the United STates of America, Canada & Foreign Lands *See* Independent Assemblies of God International - Canada

Scandinavian Home Society of Northwestern Ontario
147 Algoma St. South, Thunder Bay ON P7B 3B7
Tel: 807-345-7442
www.scandihs.com
Overview: A small local organization founded in 1923
Mission: To preserve & promote Scandinavian culture & heritage in Northwestern Ontario
Affiliation(s): Lutheran Community Care of Thunder Bay; Swedish Council of America
Finances: *Funding Sources:* Restaurant (The Scandinavian Home Café) operated by the society; Membership dues; Contributions
Membership: *Fees:* $15; *Committees:* Social; Fundraising; Membership; Personnel; Property Membership
Activities: *Library:* by appointment

Scandinavian Society of Nova Scotia
Box 31241, Gladstone RPO, Halifax NS B3K 5Y1
scansons@gmail.com
www.scandinaviansociety.ca
www.facebook.com/scandns
twitter.com/ScandNS
Overview: A small provincial organization founded in 1976
Mission: To foster interest in the culture & traditions of Scandinavian countries
Activities: Assisting Scandinavians who are new to Nova Scotia; Teaching about Scandinavian life; Organizing cultural activities
Chief Officer(s):
Lis Petersen-Banfield, President
scansons@gmail.com
Meetings/Conferences:
• Scandinavian Society of Nova Scotia 2018 Annual General Meeting, 2018, NS
Scope: Provincial
Description: The presentation of society reports, a summary of events from the previous year, & an award ceremony
Publications:
• Scandinavian Society of Nova Scotia Newsletter
Type: Newsletter; *Frequency:* Quarterly; *Price:*
marshallburgess@ns.sympatico.ca
Profile: Information for members about upcoming events & articles about Scandinavia

Scarboro Foreign Mission Society (SFM)
2685 Kingston Rd., Toronto ON M1M 1M4
Tel: 416-261-7135; *Fax:* 416-261-0820
Toll-Free: 800-260-4815
info@scarboromissions.ca
www.scarboromissions.ca
Also Known As: Scarboro Missions
Overview: A small international charitable organization founded in 1918
Mission: To promote evangelization & human development in a cross-cultural context
Member of: Canadian Council for International Cooperation
Staff Member(s): 11
Membership: *Member Profile:* Priests & lay missionaries
Activities: Overseas missions; *Library:* Archives; by appointment
Chief Officer(s):
Brian Swords, Moderator
bswords@scarboromissions.ca

Scarborough Arts Council (SAC)
1859 Kingston Rd., Toronto ON M1N 1T3
Tel: 416-698-7322; *Fax:* 416-698-7972
office@scarboroughharts.com
www.scarboroughharts.com
facebook.com/scarboroughharts
twitter.com/scararts
youtube.com/scarboroughharts
Previous Name: Arts Scarborough
Overview: A small local charitable organization founded in 1979
Mission: To develop all arts disciplines in Scarborough, Ontario; To link artists & the community
Finances: *Funding Sources:* Donations; Sponsorships; Toronto Culture; Ontario Arts Council; The Ontario Trillium Foundation
Membership: *Fees:* $25 subscription (newspaper); $30 students & seniors; $35 individuals; $45 families & groups with 10 members or less; $60 groups of more than 10
Activities: Serving artists, from young & emerging artists to senior & professional artists; Hosting exhibitions, such as the SAC Annual Juried Art Exhibition & Art in the Park; Arranging exhibition space for members at The Bluffs Gallery, Agincourt Public Library, & Cliffcrest Public Library; Providing sales opportunities for members; Offering an after-school program for young people, known as Scarborough C.A.R.E.S. (Community, Art, Recreation, & Education Services); Arranging workshops; Providing networking opportunities
Chief Officer(s):
Tim Whalley, Executive Director
ed@scarboroughharts.com
Awards:
• Youth Scholarship Awards for Art
To help talented youth in Scarborough & east Toronto develop their skills, expose their work, & receive recognition for their accomplishments
Publications:
• Surface & Symbol
Type: Newspaper; *Frequency:* Bimonthly
Profile: Informative articles about local arts

Scarborough Centre for Healthy Communities (SCHC)
#2, 629 Markham Rd., Toronto ON M1H 2A4
Tel: 416-642-9445
www.schcontario.ca
ca.linkedin.com/company/scarborough-centre-for-healthy-communities
www.facebook.com/ScarboroughCentreforHealthyCommunities
twitter.com/schcont
www.youtube.com/schcont
Overview: A medium-sized local charitable organization
Mission: To offer home support, transportation, medical, & family support programs for individuals & families
Finances: *Funding Sources:* United Way
Activities: Operating 38 integrated services across 11 sites
Chief Officer(s):
Janice Dusek, Chair & President

Scarborough Coin Club
c/o Dick Dunn, PO Box 562, Pickering ON L1V 2R7
Tel: 905-509-1146
cpms@idirect.com
Overview: A small local organization
Member of: Ontario Numismatic Association; Canadian Numismatic Association
Finances: *Funding Sources:* Membership fees
Membership: *Member Profile:* Coin & paper money collectors
Activities: Monthly meetings & annual show
Chief Officer(s):
Dick Dunn, Program Director

Scarborough Cricket Association (SCA)
ON
www.scarboroughcricket.ca
Overview: A small local organization founded in 1981
Mission: To oversee the game of cricket in Scarborough, Ontario.
Member of: West Indies Cricket Umpires Association
Chief Officer(s):
Sahaban Khan, President, 647-997-2483
Sahbaankhan1990@hotmail.com

Scarborough Historical Society
6282 Kingston Rd., Toronto ON M1C 1K9
Tel: 416-282-2710
info@scarboroughhistorical.ca
www.scarboroughhistorical.ca
www.facebook.com/scarborough.lookingback
Overview: A small local charitable organization founded in 1956
Mission: To preserve, study & stimulate an interest in the history of Scarborough
Affiliation(s): Ontario Historical Society
Finances: *Annual Operating Budget:* Less than $50,000
Staff Member(s): 1; 10 volunteer(s)
Membership: 400; *Fees:* $10; *Committees:* Archives & Research; Programme; Communications; Museum; Editorial; Finance
Activities: Historical research; *Speaker Service:* Yes; *Library:* Scarborough Archives; Open to public by appointment
Chief Officer(s):
Richard Schofield, Executive Secretary/Treasurer

Scarborough Muslim Association (SMA)
2665 Lawrence Ave. East, Toronto ON M1P 2S2
Tel: 416-750-2253; *Fax:* 416-750-1616
info@smacanada.ca
www.smacanada.ca
twitter.com/SMA_AbuBakrSid
Overview: A small local charitable organization founded in 1984

Scarborough Philharmonic Orchestra
#209, 3007 Kingston Rd., Toronto ON M1M 1P1
Tel: 416-429-0007
spo@spo.ca
www.spo.ca
www.linkedin.com/company/scarborough-philharmonic-orchestra
www.facebook.com/ScarboroughPhilharmonicOrchestra
twitter.com/SPOGreatMusic
www.youtube.com/user/SPOGreatMusic
Overview: A small local charitable organization founded in 1980 overseen by Orchestras Canada
Mission: To enrich the cultural life of Scarborough, through the promotion & presentation of high calibre musical performances; To develop a strong & financially viable organization
Member of: Orchestras Ontario, Orchestras Canada
Affiliation(s): Toronto Arts Council
Finances: *Funding Sources:* Individual & corporate sponsors; Provincial and municipal government grants
Staff Member(s): 7
Activities: *Library:* by appointment
Chief Officer(s):
Sue Payne, Executive Director
Ronald Royer, Music Director
info@ronaldroyer.com

Scarborough Women's Centre (SWC)
#245, 2100 Ellesmere Rd., Toronto ON M1H 3B7
Tel: 416-439-7111; Fax: 416-439-6999
ed@scarboroughwomenscentre.ca
www.scarboroughwomenscentre.ca
www.linkedin.com/company/scarborough-women's-centre?trk=fc_badge
www.facebook.com/scarboroughwomenscentre
twitter.com/scarbwomensctr
Overview: A small local organization founded in 1982
Mission: To provide information, education & support to women & girls
Member of: Toronto Board of Trade; Volunteer Toronto
Affiliation(s): Ontario Association of Women's Centres; Woman Abuse Council
Finances: Annual Operating Budget: $250,000-$500,000; Funding Sources: Provincial & regional government; fundraising
Staff Member(s): 8; 100 volunteer(s)
Membership: 300; Fees: $10 general; $5 student/senior; Member Profile: Women
Activities: Information, education, support for women in transition; Young women's outreach; Outreach to women with disabilities; Internships: Yes
Chief Officer(s):
Lynda Kosowan, Executive Director
ed@scarboroughwomenscentre.ca
Awards:
• Mayor's Community Safety Award

Scented Products Education & Information Association of Canada (SPEIAC)
scents@scentedproducts.ca
www.scentedproducts.ca
Overview: A medium-sized national organization
Mission: To disseminate information & provide education about scented products including fine fragrances, cosmetics, toiletries & scented household products
Affiliation(s): Allied Beauty Association; Canadian Association of Chain Drug Stores; Canadian Cosmetic, Toiletry & Fragrance Association; Canadian Fragrance Materials Association; Canadian Consumer Specialty Products Association; Direct Sellers Association; Advancing Canadian Self-Care; The Soap & Detergent Association of Canada

Schizophrenia Society of Alberta (SSA)
4809 - 48 Ave., Red Deer AB T4N 3T2
Tel: 403-986-9440; Fax: 403-986-9442
info@schizophrenia.ab.ca
www.schizophrenia.ab.ca
www.linkedin.com/groups/Schizophrenia-Society-Alberta-SSA-2604548/about
www.facebook.com/SchizophreniaSocietyofAlberta
twitter.com/SchizophreniaAB
Previous Name: Alberta Friends of Schizophrenics
Overview: A small provincial charitable organization founded in 1980 overseen by Schizophrenia Society of Canada
Mission: To support individuals with schizophrenia & related illnesses through education, public policy, research, & programs
Affiliation(s): Schizophrenia Society of Canada
Finances: Funding Sources: Membership fees; Donations; Fundraising; Sponsorships
Membership: 586+; Fees: $20-$25; Member Profile: People in Alberta with schizophrenia; Family members impacted by schizophrenia; Professionals whose focus is mental illness; Committees: Advocacy; Finance; Nominating; Bylaw
Activities: Offering information about schizophrenia & services in Alberta; Raising public awareness & understanding of schizophrenia; Providing education; Researching; Advocating for better services to persons who suffer from schizophrenia; Collaborating with other organizations; Awareness Events: Schizophrenia Society of Alberta Annual Open Minds Walk & Run Library: Schizophrenia Society of Alberta Library
Chief Officer(s):
Doug Race, Chair
Lesley Vaage, Vice-Chair
Shelley Stigter, Secretary
Publications:
• Opening Minds [a publication of the Schizophrenia Society of Alberta]
Type: Newsletter

Calgary & Area Chapter
#1120 - 53 Ave. NE, Bay 101A, Calgary AB T2E 6N9
Tel: 403-264-5161; Fax: 403-269-1727
Mission: To support persons with the illness of schizophrenia & family members in the Calgary area
Chief Officer(s):
Larry Fedun, Program Coordinator
lfedun@schizophrenia.ab.ca

Camrose & Area Chapter
#206, 5010 - 50 Ave., Camrose AB T4V 3P7
Tel: 780-679-4280
aholler@schizophrenia.ab.ca
Mission: To provide support for persons affected by schizophrenia & other related illnesses in the Camrose region

Edmonton & Area Chapter (SSAEA)
5215 - 87 St., Edmonton AB T6E 5L5
Tel: 780-452-4661; Fax: 780-482-3027
nnicholson@schizophrenia.ab.ca
Mission: To provide support & information to people affected by schizophrenia & related illnesses in the Capital Health Region & in communities in northern Alberta
• Grey Matters
Type: Newsletter; Frequency: Monthly; Price: Free with membership in the Schizophrenia Society of Alberta, Edmonton & Area Chapter
Profile: Information about local activities & groups involved with mental illness

Lethbridge & Area Chapter
234C - 12th St. B North, Lethbridge AB T1H 2K7
Tel: 403-327-4305; Fax: 403-328-0124
jhansen@schizophrenia.ab.ca

Medicine Hat & Area Chapter
526B - 3 St. SE, Medicine Hat AB T1A 0H3
Tel: 403-526-8515
wbonertz@schizophrenia.ab.ca
Mission: To provide support & information for family members & persons living with schizophrenia in the Medicine Hat region

Red Deer & Area Chapter
4811 - 48 St., Red Deer AB T4N 3T2
Tel: 403-342-5760; Fax: 403-342-4866
JLund@schizophrenia.ab.ca
Mission: To offer support & information to family members, & persons living with schizophrenia & other mental illness in Red Deer & area
Chief Officer(s):
Lyle McKellar, Chair
Don Simpson, Vice-Chair
Gary Lathan, Executive Director
Marion Weidner, Secretary
Roger Goodwin, Treasurer
Lana King Kottman, Coordinator, Education
lana@ssard.com
Chris Thomas, Coordinator, Programs & Services
chris@ssard.com
• Courage
Type: Newsletter; Frequency: Quarterly; Price: Free with Schizophrenia Society of Alberta, Red Deer Chapter, membership
Profile: Information about Red Deer area & provincial events

Schizophrenia Society of Canada (SSC) / Société canadienne de schizophrénie
#100, 4 Fort St., Winnipeg MB R3C 1C4
Tel: 204-786-1616; Fax: 204-783-4898
Toll-Free: 800-263-5545
info@schizophrenia.ca
www.schizophrenia.ca
www.facebook.com/SchizophreniaSocietyCanada
twitter.com/SchizophreniaCa
Previous Name: Canadian Friends of Schizophrenics
Overview: A medium-sized national charitable organization founded in 1979
Mission: To improve the quality of life for those affected by schizophrenia & psychosis; To advocate on behalf of individuals & families affected by schizophrenia for improved treatment & services
Finances: Funding Sources: Donations; Sponsorships; Public Health Agency of Canada
Staff Member(s): 2
Membership: Committees: Advocacy; By-Law Review
Activities: Contributing to public policy; Supporting & conducting research; Providing education about schizophrenia & psychosis; Offering support programs to individuals & families; Raising public awareness about schizophrenia & psychosis to reduce stigma & discrimination
Chief Officer(s):
Chris Summerville, D. Min, CPRP, Chief Executive Officer
chris@schizophrenia.ca
Awards:
• Bill Jefferies Family Member Award
To recognize family members of persons with schizophrenia who have made outstanding voluntary contributions towards the mission of the Schizophrenia Society of Canada Deadline: June 15 Contact: Viola MacKay, E-mail: info@schizophrenia.ca
• Flag of Hope Award for Schizophrenia
To recognize people with schizophrenia who have shown self-determination in their recovery process Deadline: June 15 Contact: Viola MacKay, E-mail: info@schizophrenia.ca
• Initiatives / Programs of Excellence Award
To recognize initiatives or programs implemented at the local or provincial levels that have made significant impacts on the quality of life of individuals & family members affected by schizophrenia Deadline: June 15 Contact: Viola MacKay, E-mail: info@schizophrenia.ca
• Media Award
To recognize individuals or organizations in the media who have have advanced the cause of schizophrenia Deadline: June 15 Contact: Viola MacKay, E-mail: info@schizophrenia.ca
• Michael Smith Award for Schizophrenia
To recognize researchers & clinicians who have supported people with schizophrenia & psychosis & their families Deadline: June 15 Contact: Viola MacKay, E-mail: info@schizophrenia.ca
• Outstanding Achievement Award
To recognize individuals or groups who have made an exceptional contribution to the cause & cure of schizophrenia Deadline: June 15 Contact: Viola MacKay, E-mail: info@schizophrenia.ca
• Outstanding Staff Award
To recognize a staff member who has made an outstanding contribution toward the mission of the Schizophrenia society of Canada Deadline: June 15 Contact: Viola MacKay, E-mail: info@schizophrenia.ca
Publications:
• A Future With Hope
Type: Newsletter; Frequency: 3 pa; Price: Free with membership in the Schizophrenia Society of Canada
Profile: Society activities, executive reports, & current issues
• Psychosis & Substance Use: A Booklet for Youth
Type: Booklet; Number of Pages: 6
• Rays of Hope
Type: Manual; Number of Pages: 268; ISBN: 0-9733913-0-8
Profile: A reference publication for families & caregivers of individuals with schizophrenia
• Reaching Out
Type: Kit
Profile: An awareness & learning resource for students in grades seven to twelve, including a video
• Respite Needs of People Living with Schizophrenia
Number of Pages: 80; Editor: Michelle Bergin; Heather Stuart
Profile: Results of a national survey of Schizophrenia Society of Canada members
• Schizophrenia & Substance Use: Information for Families
Type: Booklet; Number of Pages: 9
• Schizophrenia & Substance Use: Information for Consumers
Type: Booklet; Number of Pages: 7
• Schizophrenia & Substance Use: Information for Service Providers
Type: Booklet; Number of Pages: 7
• Schizophrenia in Canada: A National Report
Type: Report
Profile: Sections include understanding schizophrenia, stigma & discrinication, & solutions
• Schizophrenia Society of Canada Annual Report
Type: Yearbook; Frequency: Annually
• Schizophrenia: The Journey to Recovery, A Consumer & Family Guide to Assessment & Treatment
Type: Booklet; Number of Pages: 48; Author: Mary Metcalfe, M.S.; Editor: Deborah Kelly; Francine Knoops
Profile: A guide produced by the Schizophrenia Society of Canada & the CanadianPsychiatric Association
• Strengthening Families Together: Helping Canadians Live with Mental Illness
Type: Handbook; Number of Pages: 146; Editor: Edna Barker
Profile: A book for facilitators of the Stenghtening Families Together program

Schizophrenia Society of New Brunswick (SSNB)
PO Box 562, 130 Duke St., Miramichi NB E1V 3T7
Tel: 506-622-1595; Fax: 506-622-8927
ssnbmiramichi@nb.aibn.com
www.schizophreniasociety.nb.ca
Overview: A small provincial charitable organization founded in 1986 overseen by Schizophrenia Society of Canada
Member of: Schizophrenia Society of Canada
Chief Officer(s):

Barb Johnson, President
ssbj@rogers.com
Fredericton Chapter
Fredericton NB
Tel: 506-451-7770
www.schizophreniasociety.nb.ca/chapters/fredericton.htm
Moncton Chapter
178 Summer Ave., Moncton NB E1C 8A5
Tel: 506-384-8668; *Fax:* 506-854-7524
cormiergc@rogers.com
www.schizophreniasociety.nb.ca/chapters/moncton.htm
Saint John Chapter
55 Union St., Saint John NB E2L 5B7
ssbj@rogers.com
schizophreniasocietysj.wordpress.com

Schizophrenia Society of Newfoundland & Labrador
UB Waterford Hospital, PO Box 28029, 48 Kenmount Rd., St. John's NL A1B 1X0
Tel: 709-777-3335; *Fax:* 709-777-3224
info@ssnl.org
ssnl.org
www.facebook.com/171941232764
twitter.com/schizophreniaNL
Overview: A small provincial charitable organization overseen by Schizophrenia Society of Canada
Mission: To alleviate the suffering caused by schizophrenia
Member of: Schizophrenia Society of Canada
Activities: Partnership Education Program; Strengthening Families Together; Schizophrenia Awareness Days

Schizophrenia Society of Nova Scotia (SSNS)
#B-23, E.C. Purdy Building, PO Box 1004, Stn. Main, 300 Pleasant St., Dartmouth NS B2Y 3Z9
Tel: 902-465-2601; *Fax:* 902-465-5479
Toll-Free: 800-465-2601
ssns@bellaliant.com
www.ssns.ca
www.facebook.com/schizophrenia.society.ns
twitter.com/ssnsc
Previous Name: Nova Scotia Friends of Schizophrenics
Overview: A small provincial charitable organization founded in 1982 overseen by Schizophrenia Society of Canada
Mission: To alleviate the suffering caused by schizophrenia
Member of: Schizophrenia Society of Canada
Finances: *Annual Operating Budget:* $100,000-$250,000
Staff Member(s): 4; 20 volunteer(s)
Membership: 200; *Fees:* $15; *Committees:* Education; Advocacy; Fundraising; Public Awareness
Activities: *Awareness Events:* Walk the World for Schizophrenia, May & Sept.; *Speaker Service:* Yes; *Library:* Open to public
Chief Officer(s):
Diane MacDougall, Executive Director

Schizophrenia Society of Ontario (SSO) / Société de schizophrénie de l'Ontario
#302, 130 Spadina Ave., Toronto ON M5V 2L4
Fax: 416-449-8434
Toll-Free: 800-449-6367
www.schizophrenia.on.ca
www.facebook.com/SchizophreniaSocietyON
twitter.com/peace_of_minds
www.youtube.com/user/SSOOntario
Previous Name: Ontario Friends of Schizophrenics
Overview: A medium-sized provincial charitable organization founded in 1979 overseen by Schizophrenia Society of Canada
Mission: To improve the quality of life for families affected by schizophrenia, by offering support to them, & by promoting community awareness of the disease
Finances: *Funding Sources:* Fundraising; provincial government
Membership: *Fees:* $35 family; $50 associate; *Member Profile:* Friends & family of people suffering from schizophrenia; health professionals
Activities: Family support; public awareness & education; advocacy; fundraising for research; *Awareness Events:* Peace of Minds Yogathon, Feb.; National Schizophrenia & Psychosis Awareness Day, May; Hole Out for Hope Golf Tournament, June
Chief Officer(s):
Aamir Mian, Chair
Mary Alberti, Chief Executive Officer
malberti@schizophrenia.on.ca
Halton / Peel Region
136 Cross Ave., Main Fl., Oakville ON L6J 2W6
Tel: 905-338-2112; *Fax:* 905-338-2113
Chief Officer(s):
Marina Sue-Ping, Family & Community Coordinator
msue-ping@schizophrenia.on.ca
Hamilton/Niagara Region
#405, 20 Hughson St. South, Hamilton ON L8N 2A1
Tel: 905-523-7413; *Fax:* 416-449-8434
Chief Officer(s):
Cassandra Roach, Regional Coordinator
Ottawa Region
c/o ROH, 1145 Carling Ave., Ottawa ON K1Z 7K4
Tel: 613-722-6521; *Fax:* 613-729-8980
Chief Officer(s):
Sheila Deighton, Regional Coordinator Ext. 7775
sdeighton@schizophrenia.on.ca
Peterborough/Durham Region
#3, 421 Water St., Peterborough ON K9H 3L9
Tel: 705-749-1753; *Fax:* 705-749-6175
Chief Officer(s):
Allyson Susko, Regional Coordinator
asusko@schizophrenia.on.ca

Schizophrenia Society of Prince Edward Island (SSPEI)
PO Box 25020, Charlottetown PE C1A 9N4
Tel: 902-368-5850; *Fax:* 902-368-5467
schizophreniapei@pei.aibn.com
Overview: A small provincial charitable organization founded in 1984 overseen by Schizophrenia Society of Canada
Mission: To alleviate the suffering caused by schizophrenia
Member of: Schizophrenia Society of Canada
Activities: *Library:* Open to public

Schizophrenia Society of Saskatchewan (SSS)
PO Box 305, Stn. Main, Regina SK S4P 3A1
Tel: 306-584-2620; *Fax:* 306-584-0525
Toll-Free: 877-584-2620
sssprov@sasktel.net
www.schizophrenia.sk.ca
www.facebook.com/201415453215067
twitter.com/SZSask
www.youtube.com/user/SchizophreniaSask
Previous Name: Saskatchewan Friends of Schizophrenics
Overview: A small provincial charitable organization founded in 1982 overseen by Schizophrenia Society of Canada
Mission: The Society provides easily understood information on schizophrenia for concerned families. It works to increase public awareness of the illness with initiatives aimed at all age groups, & speaks on behalf of affected families. It is a registered charity, BN :894249861RR0001.
Member of: Schizophrenia Society of Canada
Finances: *Funding Sources:* Government & foundation grants; donations; bequests; United Way
Staff Member(s): 6
Activities: Raises funds for research; counselling; public education; family support groups; advocacy; *Speaker Service:* Yes; *Library:* Open to public
Chief Officer(s):
Anita Hopfauf, Executive Director
Vonni Widdis, President
Saskatoon Chapter
#219, 230 Ave. R South, Saskatoon SK S7M 2Z1
Tel: 306-374-2224; *Fax:* 306-477-5649

Schneider Office Employees' Association (SOEA) / Association des employés de bureau de Schneider (FCNSI)
PO Box 130, 321 Courtland Ave. East, Kitchener ON N2G 3X8
Tel: 519-741-5000; *Fax:* 519-749-7465
Toll-Free: 800-567-3212
schneider@cwa-scacanada.ca
Overview: A small local organization founded in 1983
Member of: Local 30009 TNG Canada/CWA
Finances: *Annual Operating Budget:* $50,000-$100,000
Membership: 150 + 1 local
Chief Officer(s):
Sandy Russell, President

School Counsellors' Association of Manitoba *See* Manitoba School Counsellors' Association

School Lunch Association
Macpherson School, 40 Newton Rd., St. John's NL A1C 4E1
Tel: 709-754-5323; *Fax:* 709-754-4520
sla@schoollunch.ca
www.schoollunch.ca
www.facebook.com/schoollunch.ca
Previous Name: School Lunch Association, Inc.
Overview: A small local charitable organization founded in 1989
Mission: To operate a non-stigmatizing meal program for primary & elementary school children regardless of their ability to pay
Finances: *Funding Sources:* Provincial government; donations; meal revenue
Staff Member(s): 5
Chief Officer(s):
Ken Hopkins, Executive Director
khopkins@schoollunch.ca

School Lunch Association, Inc. *See* School Lunch Association

School Milk Foundation of Newfoundland & Labrador (SMFNL)
27 Sagona Ave., Mount Pearl NL A1N 4P8
Tel: 709-364-2776
info@schoolmilkfdn.nf.net
www.schoolmilk.nl.ca
Previous Name: Newfoundland & Labrador School Milk Foundation
Overview: A medium-sized provincial organization founded in 1991
Mission: To increase the availability of milk throughout Newfoundland & Labrador schools; to increase the affordability of milk in all schools, so that cost does not become the reason for not drinking milk; to educate students, teachers, parents & the general public about the nutritional value of milk & the importance of it for a healthy lifestyle; to develop & implement interesting & educational campaigns to promote milk consumption in all schools; to create a lifelong milk drinking habit amongst children in the province
Affiliation(s): Canadian Public Health Association; Coalition for School Nutrition
Finances: *Funding Sources:* Dairy producers; processors; provincial government
Membership: *Member Profile:* Schools & K-12 students
Activities: *Speaker Service:* Yes

School Sport Canada (SSC) / Sport Scolaire Canada
c/o Saskatchewan High School Athletic Association, #1-575 Park St., Regina SK S4N 5B2
Tel: 306-721-2151
schoolsportcanada@gmail.com
www.schoolsport.ca
Overview: A large national organization founded in 1967
Mission: To be the national body for school sport in Canada; To promote positive sportsmanship, citizenship, & the development of student athletes through interscholastic sport
Affiliation(s): National Federation of High Schools (NFHS)
Membership: 12 member associations
Chief Officer(s):
Lyle McKellar, President
l.mckellar@shsaa.ca

School Sports Newfoundland & Labrador (SSNL)
PO Box 8700, 1296A Kenmount Rd., St. John's NL A1B 4J6
Tel: 709-729-2795; *Fax:* 709-729-2705
www.schoolsportsnl.ca
Previous Name: Newfoundland & Labrador High School Athletic Federation
Overview: A medium-sized provincial charitable organization founded in 1969 overseen by School Sport Canada
Mission: To organize, promote & govern all high school sports within the province; to assist student athletes in reaching their full physical, educational & social potential through participation & sportsmanship in interscholastic sports
Member of: School Sport Canada; National Federation of High Schools
Finances: *Annual Operating Budget:* $500,000-$1.5 Million; *Funding Sources:* Provincial government; Federal government; corporate sponsors; membership dues
Staff Member(s): 3; 700 volunteer(s)
Membership: 150 schools; *Fees:* Schedule available
Activities: School sports tournaments; *Internships:* Yes
Chief Officer(s):
Karen Richard, Executive Director
karen@sportnl.ca
Mike Ball, President
mikeball@nlesd.ca
Meetings/Conferences:
• School Sports Newfoundland & Labrador Annual General Meeting, 2018

Science Alberta Foundation *See* MindFuel

Science Atlantic / Science Atlantique
Dept. of Psychology & Neuroscience, Dalhousie University, PO Box 15000, Halifax NS B3H 4R2
Tel: 902-494-3421
admin@scienceatlantic.ca
www.scienceatlantic.ca
twitter.com/scienceatlantic
Previous Name: Atlantic Provinces Council on the Sciences; Atlantic Provinces Inter-University Committee on the Sciences
Overview: A medium-sized provincial organization founded in 1962
Mission: To advance science & technology through education & public awareness & the promotion of scientific literacy education & research throughout the region
Finances: *Annual Operating Budget:* $100,000-$250,000; *Funding Sources:* Membership dues
Staff Member(s): 2; 150 volunteer(s)
Membership: *Committees:* Aquaculture & Fisheries; Biology; Chemistry; Computer Science; Earth Science; Environment; Mathematics & Statistics; Physics & Astronomy; Psychology; Animal Care; Research Working Group
Activities: Student conferences in nine disciplines; speaker tours by notable scientists; awards for outstanding undergraduate research
Chief Officer(s):
David McCorquodale, Chair
david_mccorquodale@cbu.ca
Lois Whitehead, Executive Director
lois.whitehead@scienceatlantic.ca
Awards:
• Science Atlantic Science Communication Award
• Science Atlantic Undergraduate Research Award
Meetings/Conferences:
• Atlantic Universities Physics & Astronomy Conference (AUPAC) 2018, 2018
Scope: Provincial

Science Atlantique *See* Science Atlantic

Science et paix *See* Science for Peace

Science for Peace (SfP) / Science et paix
c/o University College, #045, 15 King's College Circle, Toronto ON M5S 3H7
Tel: 416-978-3606
sfp@physics.utoronto.ca
www.scienceforpeace.ca
www.facebook.com/science4peace
twitter.com/ScienceforPeace
www.youtube.com/user/Science4Peace
Overview: A small national charitable organization founded in 1981
Mission: To understand & act against forces of militarism, social injustice, & environmental destruction
Finances: *Funding Sources:* Membership fees; Donations
Membership: *Fees:* $20 student/unwaged; $60 regular; $100 sustaining; *Member Profile:* Natural & social scientists; Scholars in the humanities
Activities: Conducting research; Providing education services, such as public lectures & panel discussions; Publishing statements, essays, & books
Chief Officer(s):
Metta Spencer, President
president@scienceforpeace.ca
Margrit Eichler, Secretary
secretary@scienceforpeace.ca
Bill Browett, Treasurer
treasurer@scienceforpeace.ca
Bryan Eelhart, Office Coordinator
Publications:
• The Bulletin [a publication of Science for Peace]
Type: Newsletter; *Frequency:* Quarterly; *Price:* Free with membership in Science for Peace
Profile: Association activities & articles about issues of interest to members

Science Teachers' Association of Ontario (STAO) / Association des professeurs de sciences de l'Ontario (APSO)
PO Box 771, Dresden ON N0P 1M0
Fax: 800-754-1654
Toll-Free: 800-461-2264
info@stao.org
www.stao.org
twitter.com/staoapso
plus.google.com/u/0/communities/105551248505159738951
Overview: A small provincial organization founded in 1890
Mission: To promote excellence in the teaching of science throughout Ontario; To act as the voice of science educators in the province
Finances: *Funding Sources:* Membership fees; Corporate sponsors
Membership: *Fees:* $28.25 students/retired; $56.50 regular; *Member Profile:* Science educators in Ontario, from elementary & secondary schools, as well as colleges & universities; Students in a full time program at a faculty of education; Corporations; Exhibitors at the STAO/APSO annual conference; *Committees:* Conference; Elementary Curriculum; Executive; Promotions & Social Media; Safety; ScienceWorks; Secondary Curriculum; STAO Science Store; Volunteers; Website
Activities: Advocating for excellence in science education throughout Ontario; Supporting new teachers; Providing the ScienceWorks workshop series; Operating The Science Store; *Library:* STAO Virtual Library
Chief Officer(s):
Jocelyn Paas, President
Karen Dodds, Vice-President
Shelley Khaper, Treasurer
Awards:
• STAO / APSO Merit Award
To recognize excellence & leadership in science teaching *Deadline:* September 1 *Contact:* Chair of the STAO / APSO Awards Committee, Fax: 1-800-754-1654; E-mail: awards@stao.org
• STAO / APSO Service Award
To honour outstanding contributions to the association *Deadline:* September 1 *Contact:* Chair of the STAO / APSO Awards Committee, Fax: 1-800-754-1654; E-mail: awards@stao.org
• Irwin Talesnick Award for Excellence in the Teaching of Science
To recognize excellence in the teaching of science in Ontario *Deadline:* September 1 *Contact:* Chair of the STAO / APSO Awards Committee, Fax: 1-800-754-1654; E-mail: awards@stao.org
• Jack Bell Award for Leadership in Science Education
To honour outstanding & sustained leadership in science education in Ontario *Deadline:* September 1 *Contact:* Chair of the STAO / APSO Awards Committee, Fax: 1-800-754-1654; E-mail: awards@stao.org
• STAO / APSO Emeritus Award
To recognize leadership & excellence in the teaching of science during a career *Deadline:* September 1 *Contact:* Chair of the STAO / APSO Awards Committee, Fax: 1-800-754-1654; E-mail: awards@stao.org
• STAO / APSO Life Member Award
Deadline: September 1 *Contact:* Chair of the STAO / APSO Awards Committee, Fax: 1-800-754-1654; E-mail: awards@stao.org
Meetings/Conferences:
• Science Teachers' Association of Ontario 2018 Conference, 2018
Scope: Provincial
Publications:
• Crucible
Type: Magazine; *Frequency:* 5 pa; *Price:* Free with membership in the Science Teachers' Association of Ontario
Profile: Innovative approaches to science education, including a section entitled "Elements" about elementary science education
• Science Teachers' Association of Ontario Newsletter
Type: Newsletter; *Frequency:* Monthly
Profile: Science ideas, plus information about upcoming events & workshops
• Tips & Strategies for the Novice Science Teacher
Profile: Advice to assist beginning teachers

Science Writers & Communicators of Canada
PO Box 75, Stn. A, Toronto ON M5W 1A2
Toll-Free: 800-796-8595
www.sciencewriters.ca
www.facebook.com/SWCCanada
Previous Name: Canadian Science Writers' Association
Overview: A small national organization founded in 1971
Mission: To foster excellence in science communication; To increase public awareness of Canadian science & technology
Membership: 450+; *Fees:* $75 regular members; $35 students; *Member Profile:* Professional science communicators in all media, who communicate science & technology to non-specialist audiences
Activities: Providing networking opportunities for communications officers in science & technology institutions, media professionals, educators, & technical writers; Offering workshops & public meetings; Encouraging awareness of the need for science coverage
Chief Officer(s):
Tim Lougheed, President
Janice Benthin, Executive Director
Awards:
• Book Awards
• Data Journalism Award
• Prix d'excellence en journalisme des données de la Société statistique du Canada
• Science Journalism Award
• Science Communications Award
• Herb Lampert Emerging Journalist Award
Meetings/Conferences:
• Science Writers & Communicators of Canada 2018 Conference, April, 2018, Vancouver, BC
Scope: National

Sciences jeunesse Canada *See* Youth Science Canada

Scleroderma Association of British Columbia
PO Box 218, Stn. Delta Main, Delta BC V4K 3N7
Tel: 604-940-9343; *Fax:* 604-940-9346
Toll-Free: 888-940-9343
www.sclerodermabc.ca
www.facebook.com/scleroderma.bc
Overview: A small provincial charitable organization founded in 1984
Mission: To support, educate & keep informed those diagnosed with scleroderma (in skin form - localized, or in systemic form - systemic sclerosis); To raise research funds
Member of: Scleroderma Society of Canada
Membership: 450 patients; *Fees:* $20; *Member Profile:* Ages 9-89 all nationalities
Activities: Community support meetings; *Library*
Chief Officer(s):
Rosanne Queen, President
rq.sabc@telus.net

Scleroderma Canada
#202, 41 King William St., Hamilton ON L8R 1A2
Toll-Free: 866-279-0632
info@scleroderma.ca
www.scleroderma.ca
Overview: A small national charitable organization founded in 2000
Mission: To advance health care options & enrich the lives of those dealing with scleroderma through advocacy, research, education, & counsel
Staff Member(s): 3
Chief Officer(s):
Anna McCusker, Executive Director
anna@scleroderma.ca
Meetings/Conferences:
• 18th Annual National Scleroderma Conference 2018, 2018, Calgary, AB

The Scleroderma Society of Ontario (SSO)
Empire Times Bldg., #206, 41 King William St., Hamilton ON L8R 1A2
Tel: 905-544-0343
Toll-Free: 888-776-7776
www.sclerodermaontario.ca
Overview: A small provincial charitable organization
Mission: To promote public awareness; To advance patient wellness; To support research in Scleroderma
Member of: The Arthritis Society
Finances: *Annual Operating Budget:* $50,000-$100,000 50 volunteer(s)
Membership: 300; *Fees:* Schedule available; *Committees:* Board of Directors
Chief Officer(s):
Anna McCusker, Executive Director
anna@sclerodermaontario.ca

Scotia Chamber Players
6181 Lady Hammond Rd., Halifax NS B3K 2R9
Tel: 902-429-9467; *Fax:* 902-425-6785
admin@scotiafestival.ns.ca
www.scotiafestival.ns.ca
www.facebook.com/scotiafestivalofmusic
twitter.com/scotiafestival
www.youtube.com/user/scotiafestival
Also Known As: Scotia Festival of Music
Overview: A small local charitable organization founded in 1976 overseen by Orchestras Canada

Mission: To enhance the quality of music by producing an annual festival of world-class chamber music in study & performance for the benefit of musicians, students & audiences
Finances: *Funding Sources:* Halifax Regional Municipality; NS Government; Canada Council; Dept. of Canadian Heritage; NS Tourism
Staff Member(s): 4
Activities: Two-week chamber music festival annually
Chief Officer(s):
Christopher Wilcox, Managing Director

Scotia Fundy Mobile Gear Fishermen's Association
355 Main St., Yarmouth NS B5A 1E7
Tel: 902-742-6732; *Fax:* 902-742-6732
sfmobile@ns.sympatico.ca
Previous Name: Nova Scotia Fishermen Draggers Association
Overview: A small local organization
Staff Member(s): 1
Membership: *Member Profile:* Vessel owners in NS fishery
Chief Officer(s):
Brian Giroux, Executive Director

The Scots
PO Box 9410, Stn. A, Halifax NS B3K 5S3
Tel: 902-425-2445; *Fax:* 902-425-2441
info@thescots.ca
www.thescots.ca
Also Known As: The North British Society
Overview: A small provincial organization founded in 1768
Membership: 330; *Fees:* $32.50; *Member Profile:* Scottish descent, marriage, affiliation
Chief Officer(s):
J. William MacLeod, President

The Scots Society of Colchester
60 Eastmount Court, East Mountain NS B6L 2E8
Tel: 902-897-4712
enquiries@thescotsns.com
www.thescotsns.com
Also Known As: The Scots
Previous Name: The Scottish Society of Colchester
Overview: A small local organization founded in 1972
Mission: To revive & maintain an appreciation for Scottish music, dance, history, sport, & literature; To contribute to the story of Scotland in the 21st century; To reinforce Scottish culture's influence in the fabric of Nova Scotia & Canada at large
Affiliation(s): Colchester Highland Games & Gathering Society
Finances: *Annual Operating Budget:* Less than $50,000; *Funding Sources:* Membership; Fundraising; Donations
45 volunteer(s)
Membership: 45; *Fees:* $15; *Member Profile:* Scots from Nova Scotia; Nova Scotians interested in the preservation of early settler traditions
Activities: Hosting events & social gatherings, including Burns Suppers, St. Andrews Day Luncheon, Summer BBQs, & Hogmanay Get Togethers; Performing Scottish history re-enactments; Supporting local culture & heritage
Chief Officer(s):
James Finnie, President
jacobitejames@aol.com
Scott Whitelaw, Vice-President
scott@sugarmoon.ca

The Scott Mission
502 Spadina Ave., Toronto ON M5S 2H1
Tel: 416-923-8872; *Fax:* 416-923-1067
info@scottmission.com
www.scottmission.com
www.facebook.com/scottmission
twitter.com/TheScottMission
www.flickr.com/photos/thescottmission
Overview: A small local charitable organization founded in 1941
Mission: To provide support for homeless individuals, low-income families, & children & youth in Toronto
Member of: Canadian Council of Christian Charities; Evangelical Fellowship of Canada
Finances: *Annual Operating Budget:* Greater than $5 Million
Staff Member(s): 100; 5000 volunteer(s)
Activities: *Internships:* Yes; *Speaker Service:* Yes
Chief Officer(s):
Peter Duraisami, CEO

Scottish Rite Charitable Foundation of Canada
4 Queen St. South, Hamilton ON L8P 3R3
Tel: 905-522-0033; *Fax:* 905-522-3716
info@srcf.ca
www.srcf.ca
Overview: A medium-sized national charitable organization founded in 1964
Mission: To provide assistance through major grants in the physical/biological & socio/economic areas; To support research into the causes & treatment of intellectual impairment
Finances: *Annual Operating Budget:* $250,000-$500,000
Staff Member(s): 29
Membership: 26,000
Activities: *Speaker Service:* Yes; *Library:* Learning Centres for Children; Open to public
Chief Officer(s):
Gareth Taylor, President
James E. Ford, Secretary
Awards:
• Research Grants
To support biomedical research into intellectual impairment; to support research into the causes & cure of Alzheimer's Disease; *Amount:* $35,000
• Graduate Student Awards
To support research by Doctoral candidates into the causes, cure & treatment of intellectual impairment; *Amount:* $10,000
Publications:
• Clarion [a publication of The Scottish Rite Charitable Foundation of Canada]
Type: Magazine
• The Foundation Newsletter [a publication of The Scottish Rite Charitable Foundation of Canada]
Type: Newsletter
• The Scottish Rite Charitable Foundation of Canada Annual Report
Type: Report

Scottish Settlers Historical Society (SSHS)
201 Kensington Rd., Charlottetown PE C1A 5K9
Tel: 902-894-9885
Also Known As: PEI Scottish Settlers Historical Society
Overview: A small local organization founded in 1968
Mission: To restore & maintain Scottish historical sites such as cemeteries & to promote Scottish music, dancing & culture
Affiliation(s): Prince Edward Island Multicultural Council
Chief Officer(s):
Etta Anderson, President

The Scottish Society of Colchester See The Scots Society of Colchester

Scottish Studies Foundation Inc.
PO Box 45069, 2482 Yonge St., Toronto ON M4P 3E3
Tel: 416-699-9942
admin@scottishstudies.com
www.scottishstudies.com
twitter.com/ssfcanada
Overview: A small national charitable organization founded in 1984
Mission: To fund in perpetuity a Chair in Scottish Studies at the University of Guelph; to provide funding towards the Scottish Library Collection at the University of Guelph; to provide funds for graduate scholarships in Scottish Studies
Finances: *Annual Operating Budget:* $50,000-$100,000
Membership: 450; *Fees:* $30-99 member; $100-499 patron; $500+ benefactor & corporate sponsor
Chief Officer(s):
Catherine McKenzie Jansen, Membership Secretary
David Hunter, Contact
davidhunter@scottishstudies.com
Publications:
• International Review of Scottish Studies
Editor: G. Morton; *ISSN:* 0703-1580
Profile: Annual journal

Scout Environmental
30 Commercial Rd., Toronto ON M4G 1Z4
Tel: 416-922-2448
info@scoutenvironmental.com
www.scoutenvironmental.com
Previous Name: Summerhill Impact; Clean Air Foundation
Overview: A small national organization
Mission: To develop, implement, & manage public engagement programs & other strategic approaches that lead to measurable emission reductions, to improve air quality & protect the climate
Chief Officer(s):
Dan Lantz, CEO
Melanie Dailey, Managing Director

Scouts Canada / Scouts du Canada
National Office, 1345 Baseline Rd., Ottawa ON K2C 0A7
Tel: 613-224-5134
Toll-Free: 888-855-3336
helpcentre@scouts.ca
www.scouts.ca
www.linkedin.com/company/scouts-canada
www.facebook.com/scoutscanada
twitter.com/scoutscanada
www.youtube.com/scoutscanada
Also Known As: Boy Scouts of Canada
Previous Name: The Boy Scouts Association - Canadian General Council
Overview: A large national charitable organization founded in 1907
Mission: To contribute to the education of young people through a value system based on the Scout Promise & Law; To emphasize learning by doing, particularly in small groups, with outdoor activities as a learning resource
Member of: World Organization of the Scout Movement
Finances: *Annual Operating Budget:* $250,000-$500,000; *Funding Sources:* Membership fees; Donations; Fundraising
Staff Member(s): 275; 21,4 volunteer(s)
Membership: 88,453; *Member Profile:* Boys, girls, & youths, age 5-26
Activities: Offering programs such as Beaver Scouts (ages 5-7), SCOUTSabout (ages 5-10), Cub Scouts (ages 8-10), Scouts (ages 11-14), Venturer Scouts (ages 14-17), Extreme Adventure (ages 14-17), & Rover Scout (ages 18-26)
Chief Officer(s):
John Estrella, National Commissioner
jestrella@scouts.ca
Caitlyn Piton, National Youth Commissioner
cpiton@scouts.ca
Andrew Price, Executive Commissioner & CEO
aprice@scouts.ca
Valarie Dillon, Executive Director, Human Resources & Volunteer Services
vdillon@scouts.ca
Ian Mitchell, Executive Director, Field Services
imitchell@scouts.ca
John Petitti, Executive Director, Marketing & Communications
jpetitti@scouts.ca
Peter Valters, Executive Director, Business Services
pvalters@scouts.ca

British Columbia - Yukon Operations Centre
664 West Broadway, Vancouver BC V5Z 1G1
Tel: 604-879-5721; *Fax:* 604-879-5725
Toll-Free: 888-726-8876
bcy@scouts.ca
www.facebook.com/pccscouts
Chief Officer(s):
Alamin Pirani, Centre Exec. Director

Manitoba Council
c/o Prairie Service Centre, 2140 Brownsea Dr. NW, Calgary AB T2N 3G9
Toll-Free: 888-726-8876
manitoba@scouts.ca
Chief Officer(s):
Don MacDonald, Executive Director

Central Ontario Service Centre
#120, 10 Kodiak Cres., Toronto ON M3J 3G5
Tel: 416-490-6364; *Fax:* 416-490-6911
gtc@scouts.ca
www.gtc.scouts.ca
Chief Officer(s):
Danny Anckle, Centre Exec. Director

Chinook Council
2140 Brownsea Dr. NW, Calgary AB T2N 3G9
Tel: 403-283-4993
chinook@scouts.ca
chin.scouts.ca
www.linkedin.com/company/scouts-canada
www.facebook.com/chinook.scouts.ca
twitter.com/chinookscouts
www.youtube.com/scoutscanada
Chief Officer(s):
Doug MacDonald, Council Exec. Director
dmacdonald@scouts.ca

Voyageur Council
#200, 1345 Baseline Rd., Ottawa ON K2C 0A7
Tel: 613-225-2770; *Fax:* 613-225-2802
Toll-Free: 888-855-3336
easternontario@scouts.ca
Chief Officer(s):
Chris Blais, Executive Director

New Brunswick Council
PO Box 7034, RPO Brookside Mall, Fredericton NB E3A 0Y7
Tel: 506-847-9593; *Fax:* 506-847-9379
Toll-Free: 888-855-3336
info@nb.scouts.ca
nb.scouts.ca
www.facebook.com/ScoutsNB
twitter.com/ScoutsNB
Chief Officer(s):
Peter Biddle, Council Exec. Director

Newfoundland & Labrador Council
55 Karwood Dr., Paradise NL A1L 0L3
Tel: 709-722-0931
nlcouncil@scouts.ca
nfldlabrador.scouts.ca
www.linkedin.com/company/scouts-canada
www.facebook.com/NLScouts
twitter.com/NLScouts
www.youtube.com/scoutscanada
Chief Officer(s):
Jennifer Neary, Council Exec. Director

Northern Lights Council
14205 - 109 Ave., Edmonton AB T5N 1H5
Tel: 780-454-8561; *Fax:* 780-451-5333
Toll-Free: 800-480-2054
northernlights@scouts.ca
northernlights.scouts.ca
Chief Officer(s):
Doug MacDonald, Council Exec. Director
dmacdonald@scouts.ca

Northern Ontario Council
#200, 1345 Baseline Rd., Ottawa ON K2C 0A7
Tel: 613-225-2770; *Fax:* 613-225-2802
northernontario@scouts.ca
noc.scouts.ca
www.linkedin.com/company/scouts-canada
www.facebook.com/scoutscanada
twitter.com/scoutscanada
www.youtube.com/scoutscanada
Chief Officer(s):
Jon Wiersma, Council Exec. Director
jwiersma[at]scouts.ca

Nova Scotia Council
84 Thorne Ave., Dartmouth NS B3B 1Y5
Tel: 902-423-9227; *Fax:* 902-423-7989
Toll-Free: 800-557-7268
nsoffice@scouts.ca
nsc.scouts.ca
Chief Officer(s):
Peter Biddle, Council Exec. Director

Prince Edward Island Council
PO Box 533, 100 Upper Prince St., Charlottetown PE C1A 7L1
Tel: 902-566-9153; *Fax:* 902-628-6396
office@pei.scouts.ca
peic.scouts.ca
www.linkedin.com/company/scouts-canada
www.facebook.com/ScoutsPrinceEdwardIsland
twitter.com/#%21/scoutscanada
www.youtube.com/scoutscanada

Québec Council
#200, 265, av Dorval, Dorval QC H9S 3H5
Tel: 514-334-3004; *Fax:* 514-636-8773
infoqc@scouts.ca
que.scouts.ca
www.facebook.com/ScoutsCanada.QC
Chief Officer(s):
Jon Wiersma, Council Exec. Director

Saskatchewan Council
1313 Broadway Ave., Regina SK S4P 1E2
Tel: 306-757-3701; *Fax:* 306-584-3366
saskatchewan@scouts.ca
skc.scouts.ca
Chief Officer(s):
Don MacDonald, Council Exec. Director

Southwestern Ontario Administrative Centre
531 Windermere Rd., London ON N5X 2T1
Tel: 519-432-2646; *Fax:* 519-432-1677
Toll-Free: 866-568-7472
trishores@scouts.ca
Chief Officer(s):
Grant Ferron, Centre Exec. Director

Scouts du Canada *See* Scouts Canada

Screen Composers Guild of Canada (SCGC)
41 Valleybrook Dr., Toronto ON M3B 2S6
Tel: 416-410-5076; *Fax:* 416-410-4516
Toll-Free: 866-657-1117
info@screencomposers.ca
www.screencomposers.ca
www.linkedin.com/company/screen-composers-guild-of-canada
www.facebook.com/ScreenComposers
twitter.com/ScreenComposers
Overview: A small national organization founded in 1980
Mission: To improve the status & quality of music as it applies to film/tv/new media through education & the professional development of its members & the producing community; to represent & communicate the interests of its members to the music & film/tv/new media industries as well as other institutions; to collaborate with trade & industry associations with common interests; to represent all Canadian composers within the certified territories & producer entities detailed in our certification under the Canadian Status of the Artist Act, as the exclusive organization for collective negotiations
Staff Member(s): 4
Membership: *Fees:* $75 associate; $150 professional; $250 gold; *Member Profile:* Recent graduates with indsutry education seeking entry into the business; Industry employees with at least one professional on-screen composing credit
Activities: Facilitating member meetings, seminars, & workshops; Representing media composers' interests to government & industry
Chief Officer(s):
Maria Topalovich, Executive Director
maria@screencomposers.ca
Tonya Dedrick, Manager, Operations
tkdedrick@screencomposers.ca
Awards:
• SCGC Christopher Dedrick Award for Live Musicians in Media Soundtracks
Awarded to encourage & support the hiring & use of live musicians in the production of media music soundtracks
Eligibility: A Professional Member in good standing of the SCGC
Contact: Tonya Dedrick, Manager, Operations, E-mail: tkdedrick@screencomposers.ca
Publications:
• Spotting Notes [a publication of the Screen Composers Guild of Canada]
Type: Magazine; *Editor:* Craig McConnell
Profile: The e-magazine of the SCGC, offering member profiles, news, & events

ScreenScene-Film & Television for Young People *See* The Atlantic Film Festival Association

Scugog Chamber of Commerce
PO Box 1282, 237 Queen St., Port Perry ON L9L 1A0
Tel: 905-985-4971; *Fax:* 905-985-7698
Toll-Free: 877-820-3595
scugogchamber.ca
Overview: A small local organization founded in 1956
Mission: To promote the commercial, industrial, agricultural & civic interest of the Township of Scugog
Member of: Ontario Chamber of Commerce
Affiliation(s): Joint Chambers of Durham Region; Durham Network for Excellence; Tourism Durham; Tourist Association of Durham Region; Durham Home & Small Business Association
Finances: *Annual Operating Budget:* Less than $50,000; *Funding Sources:* Membership fees; sponsored events
Membership: 227; *Fees:* $170; *Member Profile:* Commercial, entrepreneurial, industrial, agricultural, business & professional people
Activities: Organizing & promoting events such as Canada Day event, Festival Days, Countryside Adventure, Santa Parade, & Business for Breakfast (monthly); *Rents Mailing List:* Yes
Chief Officer(s):
Julie Curran, Chair

Sculptors Society of Canada (SSC) / Société des sculpteurs du Canada
c/o Canadian Sculpture Centre, 500 Church St., Toronto ON M4Y 2C8
Tel: 647-435-5858
gallery@cansculpt.org
www.cansculpt.org
Also Known As: Canadian Sculpture Centre
Overview: A small national charitable organization founded in 1928
Mission: To promote Canadian sculpture; to provide encouragement to sculptors through public exhibitions & discussions in Canada & other countries
Affiliation(s): Canadian Museum Association; International Sculpture Centre; Ontario Museum Association; Carfac ON; Toronto Arts Council
Finances: *Funding Sources:* Membership fees; Private donations
Membership: 157; *Fees:* $150
Activities: *Rents Mailing List:* Yes; *Library:* SSC Resource/Documentation Centre; by appointment
Chief Officer(s):
Judi Michelle Young, President

Sculptors' Association of Alberta (SAA)
PO Box 11212, Stn. Main, Edmonton AB T5J 3K5
Tel: 780-718-0486
info@sculptorsassociation.ca
www.sculptorsassociation.ca
Overview: A small provincial organization founded in 1988
Mission: To encourage & to promote the creation & exhibition of sculpture; to provide means of communication & information exchange among sculptors; to promote public awareness & appreciation of sculpture & activities of sculptors in Alberta
Member of: Canada Craft Council
Finances: *Funding Sources:* Membership dues; ice carving
Membership: *Fees:* $30
Activities: *Speaker Service:* Yes; *Library:* Not open to public
Chief Officer(s):
Robert Woodbury, President
Erin DiLoreto, Administrator

Sea Shepherd Conservation Society (SSCS)
PO Box 48446, Vancouver BC V7X 1A2
Tel: 604-688-7325
canada@seashepherd.org
www.seashepherd.org
www.facebook.com/SeaShepherdVancouver
Overview: A medium-sized national organization founded in 1977
Mission: To investigate & document violations of international laws, regulations & treaties protecting marine wildlife species
Activities: Volunteers work as crew members aboard our ships to investigate & document any violations of international laws, treaties or regulations against marine wildlife & then enforce those laws; *Speaker Service:* Yes
Chief Officer(s):
Farley Mowat, International Chair

Sea to Sky Free-Net Association
Hotspot Community Resource Centre, PO Box 2676, Squamish BC V0N 3G0
Tel: 604-815-4142
hotspot@seatoskycommunity.org
www.seatoskycommunity.org
Overview: A small local organization
Mission: To build a local community information system for the Sea to Sky corridor; To work to ensure universal participation in the system & the internet through free public access & education

Seacoast Trail Arts Association
PO Box 235, Sheet Harbour NS B0J 3B0
Tel: 902-654-2696
Toll-Free: 877-654-2696
seasideinn@ns.sympatico.ca
seacoasttrailart.com
Overview: A small local organization founded in 2006
Mission: To celebrate, foster & promote the talent from the Eastern Shore of Nova Scotia.
Membership: 25; *Fees:* $10 associate/student; $20 regular
Chief Officer(s):
Pat Bennett, Contact

Seafarers' International Union of Canada (AFL-CIO/CLC) / Syndicat international des marins canadiens (FAT-COI/CTC)
#200, 1333, rue Saint-Jacques, Montréal QC H3C 4K2
Tel: 514-931-7859; *Fax:* 514-931-3667
siuofcanada@seafarers.ca
www.seafarers.ca
www.facebook.com/SIUofCanada
twitter.com/SIUCanada
Overview: A medium-sized international organization
Mission: To ensure its members safe & fair working conditions
Affiliation(s): Seafarers' International Union of North America (AFL-CIO); International Transport Workers' Federation
Staff Member(s): 9
Chief Officer(s):
James Given, President

Seafood Producers Association of Nova Scotia
#900, 45 Alderney Dr., Dartmouth NS B2Y 3Z6
Tel: 902-463-7790; *Fax:* 902-469-8294
spans@ns.sympatico.ca
Overview: A medium-sized provincial organization overseen by Fisheries Council of Canada
Chief Officer(s):
Roger C. Stirling, President

Seagull Foundation
PO Box 108, Pugwash NS B0K 1L0
Tel: 902-243-2416
Overview: A small local charitable organization
Mission: To protect significant wilderness areas; to support environmental education & conservation; to support Third World development projects; to support programs that create environmental awareness
Finances: *Annual Operating Budget:* Less than $50,000
Staff Member(s): 1; 2 volunteer(s)
Chief Officer(s):
Bonnie Bond, Chair

Sealant & Waterproofing Association (SWA)
70 Leek Cres., Richmond Hill ON L4B 1H1
Tel: 416-499-4000; *Fax:* 416-499-8752
info@swao.com
www.swao.com
Also Known As: Sealant & Waterproofing Association of Ontario
Merged from: Waterproofing & Caulking Contractors Association
Overview: A medium-sized national organization founded in 1989
Mission: To promote the exchange of ideas for the development of the highest standards & operating efficiency within the sealant & waterproofing industry
Member of: Toronto Construction Association
Finances: *Annual Operating Budget:* Less than $50,000; *Funding Sources:* Membership dues; industry funds
Staff Member(s): 2; 30 volunteer(s)
Membership: 25 contractors, 30 associate members, 19 allied professionals
Chief Officer(s):
Marla Cosburn, President
Charles Doke, Vice-President

Search & Rescue Volunteer Association of Canada (SARVAC)
24 McNamara Dr., Paradise NL A1L 0A6
Tel: 709-368-5533; *Fax:* 709-368-1298
Toll-Free: 866-972-7822
info@sarvac.ca
www.sarvac.ca
Overview: A small national charitable organization founded in 1996
Mission: A national voice for ground search and rescue volunteers in Canada to address issues of common concern, to develop consistency and promote standardization or portability of programs and volunteers and deliver initiatives that benefit and support all ground search and rescue volunteers in Canada as well as the general public.
Finances: *Funding Sources:* Donations
Membership: 13 associations

Seasons Centre for Grieving Children
38 McDonald St., Barrie ON L4M 1P1
Tel: 705-721-5437
Toll-Free: 855-721-5437
info@grievingchildren.com
www.grievingchildren.com
www.facebook.com/212724485448284
twitter.com/Seasons_Centre
Also Known As: Grieving Children Centre
Previous Name: Grieving Children at Seasons Centre
Overview: A small local charitable organization founded in 1995
Mission: To provide support & an understanding environment for children grieving a loved one
Finances: *Annual Operating Budget:* $250,000-$500,000
Staff Member(s): 4; 50 volunteer(s)
Membership: 185; *Member Profile:* Children & families who have experienced the death of someone they love
Activities: Community events; fundraising events; Healing Hearts Golf Tournament; Tender Hearts Valentines Dance; *Internships:* Yes; *Speaker Service:* Yes; *Library:* Resource Centre; by appointment
Chief Officer(s):
Rowley Ramey, Managing Director, 705-721-5437 Ext. 100
managingdirector@grievingchildren.com
Marcy Baldry, Director, Development, 705-721-5437 Ext. 303
marcy@grievingchildren.com
Joan Kennedy, Director, Program
joan@grievingchildren.com
Johanna Stockley, Office Manager, 705-721-5437 Ext. 101
johanna@grievingchildren.com

SeCan Association / Association SeCan
#400, 300 Terry Fox Dr., Kanata ON K2K 0E3
Tel: 613-592-8600; *Fax:* 613-592-9497
Toll-Free: 800-764-5487
seed@secan.com
www.secan.com
Overview: A small national organization founded in 1976
Mission: As Canada's Seed Partner, SeCan actively seeks partnerships which promote profitability in Canadian agriculture. SeCan is the largest supplier of certified seed to Canadian farmers with more than 1,000 members from coast to coast engaged in seed production, processing and marketing. They are a private, not-for-profit, member corporation with the primary goal of accessing and promoting leading genetics.
Finances: *Annual Operating Budget:* $1.5 Million-$3 Million
Staff Member(s): 10
Membership: 1,000; *Fees:* $525; *Committees:* Cereals, Oilseeds & Special Crops; Forage; Promotion; Liaison
Activities: *Library:*
Chief Officer(s):
Jeff Reid, General Manager, 613-592-8600 Ext. 227
jreid@secan.com

Sechelt & District Chamber of Commerce
PO Box 360, #102, 5700 Cowrie St., Sechelt BC V0N 3A0
Tel: 604-885-0662; *Fax:* 604-885-0691
sdcoc9@telus.net
www.secheltchamber.bc.ca
www.facebook.com/SecheltChamberofCommerce
twitter.com/SecheltChamber
Overview: A medium-sized local organization founded in 1947
Mission: To provide resources & services to members, including business information, community profiles, discounts & benefits plans, payroll services & networking opportunities
Member of: BC Chamber of Commerce
Finances: *Funding Sources:* Provincial & municipal governments; membership dues
Staff Member(s): 1
Membership: 174; *Fees:* Schedule available
Activities: *Speaker Service:* Yes; *Library:* Resource LIbrary; Open to public
Chief Officer(s):
Kim Darwin, President
kim-mortgage@telus.net
Colleen Clark, Executive Director
Awards:
• Good Citizen Award

Sechelt Marsh Protective Society *See* Sunshine Coast Natural History Society

Second Harvest Food Support Committee *See* Second Harvest

Second Harvest
#18, 1450 Lodestar Rd., Toronto ON M3J 3C1
Tel: 416-408-2594; *Fax:* 416-408-2598
email@secondharvest.ca
www.secondharvest.ca
www.facebook.com/SecondHarvestTO
twitter.com/2ndharvestto
www.youtube.com/user/SecondHarvestToronto?feature=mhee
Previous Name: Second Harvest Food Support Committee
Overview: A small local charitable organization founded in 1985
Mission: To help feed hungry people in the Toronto area
Member of: Ontario Association of Food Banks
Finances: *Funding Sources:* Fundraisers; Corporate & individual sponsors
Staff Member(s): 33
Activities: Buying & delivering fresh surplus food to people experiencing hunger; *Awareness Events:* Lunch Money Day, Feb.; Toronto Taste, June
Chief Officer(s):
Debra Lawson, Executive Director, 416-408-2594 Ext. 222
debral@secondharvest.ca
Publications:
• Fresh Connections [a publication of Second Harvest]
Type: Newsletter; *Frequency:* 4 pa

Second Story Women's Centre
PO Box 821, 18 Dufferin St., Lunenburg NS B0J 2C0
Tel: 902-543-1315; *Fax:* 902-640-3044
info@secstory.com
www.secstory.com
www.facebook.com/secstory?ref_type=bookmark
twitter.com/Sec_Story
Overview: A small local organization
Membership: *Fees:* $10 (waged); $2 (unwaged)
Chief Officer(s):
Jeanne Fay, Executive Co-ordinator
exec@secstory.com

Secours aux lépreux (Canada) inc. (SLC) / Leprosy Relief (Canada) Inc. (LR)
#305, 1805, rue Sauvé ouest, Montréal QC H4N 3H4
Tél: 514-744-3199; *Téléc:* 514-744-9095
Ligne sans frais: 866-744-3199
info@slc-lr.ca
www.slc-lr.ca
Aperçu: *Dimension:* petite; *Envergure:* internationale; Organisme sans but lucratif; fondée en 1961
Mission: Venir en aide médicalement et socialement aux personnes affectées par la lèpre.
Membre de: Federation internationale des associations de lutte contre la lèpre
Finances: *Budget de fonctionnement annuel:* $500,000-$1.5 Million
Membre(s) du personnel: 3; 4 bénévole(s)
Membre: 10; *Montant de la cotisation:* 10$
Membre(s) du bureau directeur:
Paul E. Legault, Président
Maryse Legault, Director
maryse.legault@slc-lr.ca
Marie Gilbert, Secretaire
Christiane Beauvois, Trèsorière

Secours Quaker Canadien *See* Canadian Friends Service Committee

Secrétariat des conférences intergouvernementales canadiennes *See* Canadian Intergovernmental Conference Secretariat

Secrétariat international des infirmières et infirmiers de l'espace francophone (SIDIIEF)
#142, 4200, rue Molson, Montréal QC H1Y 4V4
Tél: 514-849-6060; *Téléc:* 514-849-7870
info@sidiief.org
www.sidiief.org
www.linkedin.com/company/sidiief
www.facebook.com/SIDIIEF
twitter.com/SIDIIEF
Aperçu: *Dimension:* moyenne; *Envergure:* internationale
Mission: Promouvoir la contribution de la profession infirmière à la santé des populations
Membre: *Montant de la cotisation:* 58$ individu; 22$ étudiant; 185$ association; 490$ institution/établissement; *Critères d'admissibilite:* Association professionnelle; institution ou un établissement de santé ou d'enseignement; infirmière ou un infirmier, un professionnel de la santé
Membre(s) du bureau directeur:
Gyslaine Desrosiers, Présidente
Meetings/Conferences:
• Secrétariat international des infirmières et infirmiers de l'espace francophone 7e Congrès mondial, June, 2018, Bordeaux
Scope: International
Contact Information: www.congres-sidiief.org

Sectorial Association: Transportation Equipment & Machinery Manufacturing *Voir* Association sectorielle: Fabrication d'équipement de transport et de machines

The Secular Institute of Missionaries of the Kingship of Christ (SIM)
Other Communication: International: ism.cc@virgilio.it
andre.comtois28@gmail.com
www.simkc.org
Previous Name: Missionaires de la Royauté du Christ
Overview: A small local organization founded in 1919
Membership: 2,200

Seed Corn Growers of Ontario
825 Park Ave. West, Chatham ON N7M 5J6
Tel: 519-352-6710; *Fax:* 519-352-0526
scgo.ca
twitter.com/SeedCornOntario

Previous Name: Ontario Seed Corn Growers' Marketing Board
Overview: A medium-sized provincial organization founded in 1942
Mission: To work with the individual seed corn companies to negotiate production contracts that not only make growers competitive, but also provide incentives to produce excellent seed. Also works to ensure that growers are provided with the best information and programs to maintain and broaden their seed corn production skills.
Staff Member(s): 1
Membership: *Member Profile:* Seed corn producers
Chief Officer(s):
Chris Nanni, Contact
cnanni@scgo.ca

SEEDS Foundation
#400, 144 - 4th Ave. SW., Calgary AB T2P 3N4
Tel: 403-221-0884; *Fax:* 403-221-0876
Toll-Free: 800-661-8751
seeds@telusplanet.net
www.seedsfoundation.ca
ca.linkedin.com/pub/seeds-foundation/3a/909/44
www.facebook.com/117021191648133
Also Known As: Society, Environment & Energy Development Studies Foundation
Overview: A medium-sized national charitable organization founded in 1976
Mission: To provide educational support materials & professional assistance to teachers in the area of energy, environment & sustainable development; To work toward the development of a society which understands & is committed to actions leading to wise stewardship of resources, resource use & the environment
Affiliation(s): Connections Education Society
Finances: *Annual Operating Budget:* $250,000-$500,000; *Funding Sources:* Donations (industry, business); government (federal/provincial, less than 5%); sponsorships
Staff Member(s): 6; 19 volunteer(s)
Membership: 19; *Committees:* Education; Environment; Industry
Activities: Providing educational resources on the environment for high school students, such as the Energy Literacy Series, Habitat in the Balance & the Climate of Change Program; Creating the Connections & Green School leadership programs for elementary, junior high & high school students; Creating challenge programs & projects for students such as the Canadian Bird Challenge, the Canadian Water Conservation Challenge & the Environmental Writing Challenge; *Awareness Events:* Green School Celebrations; Annual Bird Challenge; *Speaker Service:* Yes
Chief Officer(s):
Corinne Craig, Executive Director, 403-663-2575
ccraig@seedsfoundation.ca

Seeds of Diversity Canada (SoDC) / Semences du patrimoine Canada
#1, 12 Dupont St. West, waterloo ON N2L 2X6
Tel: 226-600-7782
mail@seeds.ca
www.seeds.ca
Also Known As: Heritage Seed Program
Overview: A medium-sized national organization founded in 1984
Mission: To search out, preserve, perpetuate, study & encourage the cultivation of heirloom & endangered varieties of food crops
Affiliation(s): Rare Breeds Canada; Canadian Organic Growers
Finances: *Funding Sources:* Membership fees; grants
Staff Member(s): 2
Membership: 1,700; *Fees:* $35-$45
Activities: *Awareness Events:* Seedy Saturdays & Seedy Sundays
Chief Officer(s):
Bob Wildfong, Executive Director
Publications:
• Seeds of Diversity Magazine
Type: Magazine; *Accepts Advertising*

Segal Centre for the Performing Arts at the Saidye / Centre des arts Saidye Bronfman
5170, ch de la Côte-Sainte-Catherine, Montréal QC H3W 1M7
Tel: 514-739-2301; *Fax:* 514-739-9340
www.segalcentre.org
www.facebook.com/segalcentre
twitter.com/segalcentre
www.youtube.com/user/segalcentre

Previous Name: The Saidye Bronfman Centre for the Arts
Overview: A small local charitable organization founded in 1967
Mission: To provide cultural activities to all Montréal communities
Affiliation(s): YM-YWHA Montreal Jewish Community Centres
Activities: Cultural activities
Chief Officer(s):
Lisa Rubin, Artistic & Executive Director, 514-739-2301 Ext. 8310
lrubin@segalcentre.org
Jon Rondeau, General Manager, 514-739-2301 Ext. 8347
jrondeau@segalcentre.org

Seguin Arts Council
535 Tally-Ho Rd., RR#1, Rosseau ON P0C 1J0
Tel: 705-732-1985
info@seguinartscouncil.com
www.seguinartscouncil.com
Previous Name: Seguin Township Arts Council
Overview: A small local charitable organization founded in 1988
Mission: To represent & develop the arts in Seguin Township
Member of: Community Arts Ontario
Finances: *Funding Sources:* Donations; Grants; Membership dues
Membership: *Fees:* $25
Activities: Annual Art Tour & Crafts Sale; Comedy Night; Concerts; Artisan's Market & antiques
Chief Officer(s):
Barb Harding, President
Awards:
• Wendy Marsh Memorial Award

Seguin Township Arts Council *See* Seguin Arts Council

Seicho-No-Ie Toronto Centre
662 Victoria Park Ave., Toronto ON M4C 5H4
Tel: 416-690-8686; *Fax:* 416-690-3917
www.seicho-no-ie.org
Also Known As: Home of Infinite Growth
Previous Name: Seicho-No-Ie Canada Truth of Life Centre
Overview: A small national organization founded in 1963
Mission: Provides a place of worship for those who believe in the Seicho-No-Ie Humanity Enlightenment Movement, which says that all religions emanate from one universal god
Member of: Seicho-No-Ie (Canada)

Seicho-No-Ie Vancouver Centre
305 East 16th Ave., Vancouver BC V5T 2T7
Tel: 604-879-8116; *Fax:* 604-876-8083
snivancouver.blogspot.ca

Seicho-No-Ie Canada Truth of Life Centre *See* Seicho-No-Ie Toronto Centre

Self-Help Connection Clearinghouse Association
#800, 11 Akerley Blvd., Dartmouth NS B2Y 2R7
Tel: 902-466-2011; *Fax:* 902-404-3205
Toll-Free: 866-765-6639
www.selfhelpconnection.ca
Overview: A small local charitable organization founded in 1987
Mission: To enable Nova Scotians to improve control over their health by increasing their knowledge, skills & resources for individual & collective action
Member of: Canadian Network of Self-Help Centres; International Network of Mutual Help Centres
Affiliation(s): National Network for Mental Health; Canadian Coalition of Mental Health Resources
Finances: *Annual Operating Budget:* $100,000-$250,000
Staff Member(s): 6
Activities: Workshops; conferences; displays; *Library:* Open to public

Self-Help Resource Association of British Columbia *See* PeerNetBC

Self-Help Resource Centre (SHRC)
#307, 40 St. Clair Ave. East, Toronto ON M4T 1M9
Tel: 416-487-4355; *Fax:* 416-487-0344
Toll-Free: 888-283-8806
shrc@selfhelp.on.ca
www.selfhelp.on.ca
twitter.com/selfhelprc
Overview: A small local charitable organization founded in 1987
Mission: To promote self-help/mutual aid; to increase awareness about self-help/mutual aid in the community & among helping professionals; to facilitate the growth & development of self-help groups, networks & resources
Affiliation(s): Centre of Health Promotion; Canadian Health Network

Staff Member(s): 5
Activities: Information/referral service for over 500 self-help groups in the Greater Toronto area; coordination of self-help networks & organizations across the province; *Speaker Service:* Yes; *Library:* Open to public
Chief Officer(s):
Jennifer Poole, President
Mark Freeman, Executive Director

Selkirk & District Chamber of Commerce
City of Selkirk Civic Centre, 200 Eaton Ave., Selkirk MB R1A 0W6
Tel: 204-482-7176; *Fax:* 204-482-5448
info@selkirkbiz.ca
www.selkirkanddistrictchamber.ca
Overview: A small local organization founded in 1901
Mission: To promote the economic, civic, educational & cultural interests of the citizens of Selkirk & district & the furtherance of the development of resources
Member of: Manitoba Chamber of Commerce
Finances: *Annual Operating Budget:* Less than $50,000; *Funding Sources:* Membership dues
15 volunteer(s)
Membership: 180+; *Fees:* $30 individual; $50-$275 business; *Committees:* Black Friday; Communications; Events; Finance; Governance; History; Marketing; Membership; Partnerships; Planning; Training & Development
Chief Officer(s):
Sheri Skalesky, Executive Director

Selkirk Friendship Centre (SFC)
425 Eveline St., Selkirk MB R1A 2J5
Tel: 204-482-7525; *Fax:* 204-785-8124
www.facebook.com/144548738915132
Overview: A small local organization founded in 1968
Mission: Promotes the progress in the educational, social, ecomonic, social, athletic & cultural life of both Aboriginal & Non-Aboriginal peoples
Activities: Provides assistance in employment, housing, daycare, youth activities; Fosters cultural awareness

Semences du patrimoine Canada *See* Seeds of Diversity Canada

Semiahmoo Foundation
15306 - 24th Ave., Surrey BC V4A 2J1
Tel: 604-536-1242; *Fax:* 604-536-9507
www.semi-house-society.com
Overview: A medium-sized national charitable organization
Mission: To fund, support & enhance the programs & services offered by the Semiahmoo House Society
Affiliation(s): Semiahmoo House Society
Finances: *Funding Sources:* Donations; memberships; fundraising
Activities: *Awareness Events:* Purdy's Campaign, Dec.
Chief Officer(s):
Caite Bajwa, Administrative Coordinator
c.bajwa@shsbc.ca
Louise Tremblay, Director, Development
l.tremblay@shsbc.ca

Semiahmoo House Society (SHS)
15306 - 24th Ave., Surrey BC V4A 2J1
Tel: 604-536-1242; *Fax:* 604-536-9507
shs@shsbc.ca
www.semi-house-society.com
www.facebook.com/SemiahmooHouseSociety
twitter.com/SemiahmooHouse
Overview: A small local organization founded in 1976
Mission: To provide vocational, residential life skills support services to adults with a mental handicap; community integration, advocacy & housing
Member of: Inclusion BC
Affiliation(s): American Association on Mental Retardation; National Association for the Dually Diagnosed; The Association for the Severely Handicapped
Finances: *Annual Operating Budget:* Greater than $5 Million; *Funding Sources:* Provincial government
Staff Member(s): 250; 50 volunteer(s)
Membership: 160; *Member Profile:* Community individuals; *Committees:* Performance & Quality Improvement (PQI); Occupational Health & Safety; Labour Management
Activities: Programs & services include: Acquired Brain Injury; advocacy; adult day & work programs; programs for children & youth; recreation & leisure; family servies; respite support; Snoezelen room for relaxation; supported living options;

Awareness Events: Community Awareness Month, Oct.; *Speaker Service:* Yes
Chief Officer(s):
Doug Tennant, Executive Director

Senate Protective Service Employees Association (SPSEA) / Association des employés du Service de sécurité du Sénate (AESSS)
c/o Senate of Canada, 140 Wellington St., Ottawa ON K1A 0A4
Tel: 613-992-9265; *Fax:* 613-943-0032
Overview: A small local organization founded in 1978
Membership: 87

Seneca Centennial Committee *See* York-Grand River Historical Society

Senior Citizens' Central Council of Calgary *See* Calgary Seniors' Resource Society

Senior Link
3036 Danforth Ave., Toronto ON M4C 1N2
Tel: 416-691-7407; *Fax:* 416-691-8466
info@neighbourhoodlink.org
www.neighbourhoodlink.org/seniors
Overview: A small local charitable organization founded in 1975
Mission: To promote the independence & dignity of seniors in their own community
Member of: Ontario Non-Profit Housing Association; Ontario Association of Non-Profit Homes & Services for Seniors; Ontario Community Support Association
Finances: *Annual Operating Budget:* Greater than $5 Million
Staff Member(s): 60; 300 volunteer(s)
Membership: 165; *Member Profile:* 50 hours of volunteering
Activities: Home support, supportive housing, advocacy & counselling services all designed to help older adults keep their independence for as long as possible; *Internships:* Yes; *Speaker Service:* Yes
Chief Officer(s):
Judith Leon, Contact

Seniors Association of Greater Edmonton (SAGE)
15 Sir Winston Churchill Sq., Edmonton AB T5J 2E5
Tel: 780-423-5510; *Fax:* 780-426-5175
info@mysage.ca
www.mysage.ca
www.facebook.com/438132792913806
twitter.com/sageYEG
Previous Name: Society for the Retired & Semi-Retired
Overview: A medium-sized local charitable organization founded in 1970
Mission: To enhance the quality of life of older persons through service, innovation, & advocacy
Affiliation(s): United Way; Imagine Canada
Finances: *Annual Operating Budget:* $1.5 Million-$3 Million; *Funding Sources:* City of Edmonton; Community Services; Alberta Seniors; United Way; Donations; Memberships; Casino
112 volunteer(s)
Membership: *Fees:* $26.25 individual; $131.25 non-profit; $262.50 for-profit
Activities: *Awareness Events:* SAGE Awards *Library:* Heritage Library
Chief Officer(s):
Barb Burton, President
Karen McDonald, Executive Director

Seniors for Nature Canoe Club (SFNCC)
PO Box 94051, Stn. Bedford Park, Toronto ON M4N 3R1
info@sfncc.org
www.sfncc.org
Overview: A small local organization founded in 1985
Mission: To offer seniors the opportunity to canoe, camp, hike, ski & cycle
Member of: Federation of Ontario Naturalists
Finances: *Annual Operating Budget:* Less than $50,000; *Funding Sources:* Membership fees
12 volunteer(s)
Membership: 135 senior; *Fees:* $35; *Member Profile:* Over 55 years of age; able to help transport & steer canoes & to swim; *Committees:* Program & Training; Purchasing & Inventory; Membership; Social; Publicity & Newsletter
Activities: Canoeing, hiking, skiing, biking, camping trips
Chief Officer(s):
Paul Short, President

Seniors in Need
#102, 40 St. Clair West, Toronto ON M4V 1M2
Tel: 416-550-4850
www.seniorsinneed.ca
www.facebook.com/SeniorsInNeed
twitter.com/seniorsinneed
Overview: A medium-sized local charitable organization founded in 2011
Mission: A grassroots organization that connects concerns Canadians to impoverished seniors; Registered nonprofit sponsors submit the details of a senior in need to a database and donors can find and help a senior of their choosing.
Finances: *Funding Sources:* Seniors for Seniors
Chief Officer(s):
Peter D. Cook, Founder

Seniors Peer Helping Program
80 Lothian Ave., Toronto ON M8Z 4K5
Tel: 416-239-7252
Also Known As: Peer Helping Centre
Overview: A small local organization founded in 1981
Mission: To provide growth experience for older adults in group setting; to train seniors to help other seniors
Finances: *Funding Sources:* Fundraising
Membership: *Member Profile:* Individuals 55 years of age & over
Activities: Personal growth courses; "Time for Me" course; Growing Further; Peer helping training; monthly time grads get together
Chief Officer(s):
Mary Neale, Chair

Seniors Resource Centre *See* Seniors Resource Centre Association of Newfoundland & Labrador Inc.

Seniors Resource Centre Association of Newfoundland & Labrador Inc. (SRC NL)
243 Topsail Rd., St. John's NL A1E 2B4
Tel: 709-737-2333; *Fax:* 709-737-3717
Toll-Free: 800-563-5599
info@seniorsresource.ca
www.seniorsresource.ca
Previous Name: Seniors Resource Centre
Overview: A small provincial organization founded in 1990
Mission: To promote the independence & well being of older adults in Newfoundland & Labrador through the provision of information as well as various programs & services
Finances: *Annual Operating Budget:* $500,000-$1.5 Million; *Funding Sources:* Donations; Will bequests; Memorial gifts; Grants; Fundraising; Foundations; Sponsorships
Staff Member(s): 9; 425 volunteer(s)
Activities: Provincial Peer Support Volunteer Program; Friendly Visiting Program; Mall-Walkers Club; NL Network for the Prevention of Elder Abuse (NLNPEA); Information Referral Line; *Internships:* Yes; *Speaker Service:* Yes; *Library*
Publications:
• Seniors Pride [a publication of the Seniors Resource Centre Association of Newfoundland & Labrador Inc.]
Type: Magazine; *Frequency:* s-a.
• Seniors Resource Centre Association of Newfoundland & Labrador Inc. Newsletter
Type: Newsletter

Sensibilisation au cancer du sein *See* Breast Cancer Action

Sentier Urbain
#310, 1710, rue Beaudry, Montréal QC H2L 3E7
Tél: 514-521-9292; *Téléc:* 514-596-7093
info@sentierurbain.org
www.sentierurbain.org
www.facebook.com/115278308497487
twitter.com/sentierurbain
Aperçu: *Dimension:* petite; *Envergure:* locale; fondée en 1993
Mission: De mettre en ouvre des programmes respectueux de l'environnement dans la communauté
Membre(s) du bureau directeur:
Pierre Dénommé, Directeur général
direction@sentierurbain.org

Sentiers de l'estrie
5182, boul Bourque, Sherbrooke QC J1N 1H4
Tél: 819-864-6314; *Téléc:* 819-864-1864
marche@lessentiersdelestrie.qc.ca
www.lessentiersdelestrie.qc.ca
www.facebook.com/202589809771641
Aperçu: *Dimension:* petite; *Envergure:* locale
Mission: Pour promouvoir la marche en faisant les repérages en Estrie plus accessible

Sentinelle Outaouais *See* Ottawa Riverkeeper

Serbian National Shield Society of Canada
#303, 1900 Sheppard Ave. East, Toronto ON M2J 4T4
Tel: 416-496-7881; *Fax:* 416-493-0335
Also Known As: Voice of Canadian Serbs
Overview: A small national organization
Mission: To promote & inform about interests & heritage of Canadian Serbs
Member of: Canadian Ethnocultural Council
Chief Officer(s):
Diane Dragasevich, Contact

Serbian Orthodox Church - Orthodox Diocese of Canada
7470 McNiven Rd., RR#3, Campbellville ON L0P 1B0
Tel: 905-878-0043
Other Communication: 905-878-3438
epkanadska@gmail.com
www.istocnik.ca/en
Overview: A medium-sized national charitable organization founded in 1983
Mission: To serve the Serbian Orthodox community & teach the Orthodox faith & culture
Finances: *Annual Operating Budget:* $500,000-$1.5 Million; *Funding Sources:* Donations; parish taxes; dispensations
Staff Member(s): 23
Membership: 150,000; *Committees:* Diocesan Executive Board; Diocesan Assembly
Activities: *Library:* Serbian Orthodox Church: Holy Transfiguration; Open to public by appointment
Chief Officer(s):
Vasilije Tomic, Episcopal Deputy, 416-450-4555
o.bajo@rogers.com
Jovan Marjanac, Diocesan Secretary, 905-878-0043

Serena Canada
151 Holland Ave., Ottawa ON K1Y 0Y2
Tel: 613-728-6536
Toll-Free: 888-373-7362
sc@serena.ca
www.serena.ca
Overview: A small national charitable organization founded in 1955
Mission: To promote natural family planning methods based on information from a woman's body
Affiliation(s): International Federation for Family Life Promotion; Roman Catholic Church
Finances: *Funding Sources:* Provincial corporations; revenue from publication sales; donations
Activities: *Speaker Service:* Yes

Alberta Branch
131 Twin Brooks Cove NW, Edmonton AB T6J 6T1
Tel: 780-488-5221
Toll-Free: 866-488-5221
alberta@serena.ca

British Columbia Branch
2540 Tulip Cres., Abbotsford BC V2T 1R6
Tel: 604-677-4132
bc@serena.ca
bc.serena.ca
www.facebook.com/198824256810301
twitter.com/Serena_BC

Manitoba Branch
99 Cornish Ave., Winnipeg MB R3C 1A2
Tel: 204-783-0091; *Fax:* 204-774-7834
Toll-Free: 866-317-5362
manitoba@serena.ca
www.serenamb.ca
www.facebook.com/serenamanitoba
Chief Officer(s):
Linda Kuehn, Executive Director

New Brunswick Branch
NB
Tel: 506-759-9557
nb@serena.ca

Nova Scotia Branch
Antigonish NS
Tel: 902-863-5061
ns@serena.ca

Ontario Branch
151 Holland Ave., Ottawa ON K1Y 0Y2
Tel: 613-728-6536
Toll-Free: 888-373-7362
ontario@serena.ca

Québec Branch
6646, rue Saint-Denis, Montréal QC H2S 2R9

Tél: 514-273-7531; Téléc: 514-273-7532
Ligne sans frais: 866-273-7362
info@serena.ca
serena.ca/fr
www.facebook.com/serenaqc
twitter.com/SerenaQuebec
Saskatchewan Branch
PO Box 7375, Saskatoon SK S7K 4J3
Tel: 306-934-8223
Toll-Free: 800-667-1637
sask@serena.ca

Service à la famille chinoise du Grand Montréal / Chinese Family Service of Greater Montréal
987, rue Côté, 4e étage, Montréal QC H2Z 1L1
Tél: 514-861-5244; *Téléc:* 514-861-9008
famille.chinoise@qc.aibn.com
www.famillechinoise.qc.ca
Aperçu: Dimension: petite; *Envergure:* locale; Organisme sans but lucratif; fondée en 1976
Membre de: Chinese Canadian National Council
Affiliation(s): Centre Sino-Québec de la Rive-Sud
Membre(s) du personnel: 13; 150 bénévole(s)
Activités: Club des femmes; Services aux personnes âgées et Centre Man Sau; Camp pour les enfants; Projet jeu problématique: Oui; *Service de conférenciers:* Oui
Membre(s) du bureau directeur:
Xixi Li, Directrice générale

Service alimentaire et aide budgétaire de Charlevoix-Est
2215, boul de Comporté, La Malbaie QC G5A 1N6
Tél: 418-665-4197
servicealimentaire@videotron.ca
Également appelé: SAAB de Charlevoix-Est
Aperçu: Dimension: petite; *Envergure:* locale surveillé par Coalition des associations de consommateurs du Québec
Membre de: Coalition des associations de consommateurs du Québec (CACQ)

Service alimentaire et aide budgétaire de Charlevoix-Est
2215, boul de Comporté, La Malbaie QC G5A 1N6
Tél: 418-665-4197
servicealimentaire@videotron.ca
www.servicebudgetaire.ca
Également appelé: SAAB de Charlevoix-Est
Aperçu: Dimension: petite; *Envergure:* locale surveillé par Coalition des associations de consommateurs du Québec
Membre de: Coalition des associations de consommateurs du Québec (CACQ)

Service budgétaire communautaire de Jonquière
CP 42, 3971, rue du Vieux Pont, Jonquière QC G7X 7V8
Tél: 418-542-8904; *Téléc:* 418-542-1424
Autres numéros: Alt. courriel: maisondequartier@videotron.ca
servicebudgetairejonq@videotron.ca
www.maisondequartier.org
Également appelé: SBC de Jonquière
Aperçu: Dimension: petite; *Envergure:* locale; fondée en 1976 surveillé par Coalition des associations de consommateurs du Québec
Membre de: Coalition des associations de consommateurs du Québec (CACQ)

Service budgétaire et communautaire d'Alma inc. *Voir* Service budgétaire Lac-Saint-Jean-Est

Service budgétaire et communautaire de Chicoutimi inc (SBC)
2422, rue Roussel, Chicoutimi QC G7G 1X6
Tél: 418-549-7597; *Téléc:* 418-549-1325
sbc@vl.videotron.ca
servicebudgetaire.org
www.facebook.com/ecofripesroussel
Également appelé: SBC de Chicoutimi
Aperçu: Dimension: petite; *Envergure:* locale; Organisme sans but lucratif; fondée en 1980 surveillé par Coalition des associations de consommateurs du Québec
Mission: Aider les personnes dans leurs difficultés financières et aux prises avec les problèmes sociaux qui en découlent
Membre de: Coalition des associations de consommateurs du Québec (CACQ)
Membre(s) du personnel: 6; 54 bénévole(s)
Membre(s) du bureau directeur:
Marion Toucas, Directrice, 418-549-7597 Ext. 3
directionsbc@videotron.ca

Service budgétaire et communautaire de la MRC Maria-Chapdelaine
#304, 1230, boul Walberg, Dolbeau-Mistassini QC G8L 1H2
Tél: 418-276-1211
Également appelé: SBC de la MRC Maria-Chapdelaine
Aperçu: Dimension: petite; *Envergure:* locale surveillé par Coalition des associations de consommateurs du Québec
Membre de: Coalition des associations de consommateurs du Québec (CACQ)

Service budgétaire Lac-Saint-Jean-Est
CP 594, 415, rue Collard ouest, Alma QC G8B 5W1
Tél: 418-668-2148; *Téléc:* 418-668-2048
info@servicebudgetaire.com
www.servicebudgetaire.com
www.facebook.com/290779631041748
Nom précédent: Service budgétaire et communautaire d'Alma inc.
Aperçu: Dimension: petite; *Envergure:* locale; Organisme sans but lucratif; fondée en 1977 surveillé par Coalition des associations de consommateurs du Québec
Mission: Aider les individus et les familles à faibles et moyens revenus, à résoudre leur difficultés financières et les problèmes qui en découlent; prévenir l'endettement; informer les consommateurs et les consommatrices sur les lois et sur leurs droits; travailler sur différentes problématiques au niveau des habitudes de consommation et de leurs conséquences sur le budget, la santé, l'organisation familiale, etc.
Membre de: Coalition des associations de consommateurs du Québec (CACQ)
Finances: *Budget de fonctionnement annuel:* Moins de $50,000
Membre(s) du personnel: 4; 40 bénévole(s)
Membre: 100-499
Activités: Cours de budget et consommation; consultation budgétaire individuelle; fonds d'épargne et de prêt populaire; *Bibliothèque:* Centre de documentation au service budgétaire; Bibliothèque publique
Membre(s) du bureau directeur:
Sophie Racine, Coordonnatrice

Service budgétaire populaire de La Baie et du Bas Saguenay
864, rue de la Fabrique, La Baie QC G7B 2S8
Tél: 418-544-5611; *Téléc:* 418-544-5590
Autres numéros: Alt. courriel: sbcoorlabaie@royaume.com
s.budgetlabaie@royaume.com
sbudgetairelabaie.e-monsite.com
www.facebook.com/sblabaie
Également appelé: SBP de La Baie et du Bas Saguenay
Aperçu: Dimension: petite; *Envergure:* locale surveillé par Coalition des associations de consommateurs du Québec
Membre de: Coalition des associations de consommateurs du Québec (CACQ)

Service budgétaire populaire de St-Félicien
1211, rue Notre-Dame, Saint-Félicien QC G8K 1Z9
Tél: 418-679-4646; *Téléc:* 418-679-5902
info@servicebudgetaire.ca
www.servicebudgetaire.ca
www.facebook.com/servicebudgetaire.stfelicien
Également appelé: SBP de St-Félicien
Aperçu: Dimension: petite; *Envergure:* locale surveillé par Coalition des associations de consommateurs du Québec
Membre de: Coalition des associations de consommateurs du Québec (CACQ)
Membre(s) du bureau directeur:
Jean-Roch Laprise, Président

Service budgétaire populaire des Sources
599, boul Simoneau, Asbestos QC J1T 4G7
Tél: 819-879-4173; *Téléc:* 819-879-4173
info@sbpdessources.com
www.sbpdessources.com
Également appelé: SBP des Sources
Aperçu: Dimension: petite; *Envergure:* locale; fondée en 1981 surveillé par Coalition des associations de consommateurs du Québec
Membre de: Coalition des associations de consommateurs du Québec (CACQ)
Membre(s) du bureau directeur:
Véronique Poirier, Coordonnatrice
vpoirier@sbpdessources.com

Service canadien d'évaluation de documents scolaires internationaux *See* International Credential Assessment Service of Canada

Service d'aide au consommateur *Voir* Service de protection et d'information du consommateur

Service d'assistance canadienne aux organismes *See* Canadian Executive Service Organization

Service de conciliation en assurance de dommages *See* General Insurance OmbudService

Service de protection et d'information du consommateur (SPIC)
1852, av St-Marc, Shawinigan QC G9N 2H7
Tél: 819-537-1414; *Téléc:* 819-537-5259
Ligne sans frais: 800-567-8552
info@serviceconsommateur.org
www.serviceconsommateur.org
Nom précédent: Service d'aide au consommateur
Aperçu: Dimension: petite; *Envergure:* locale; fondée en 1974 inc.
Mission: Le Service d'aide au consommateur (SAC) est un organisme privé sans but lucratif voué à la promotion et à la défense des droits et intérêts des consommateurs.
Membre: *Montant de la cotisation:* 24$

Service des programmes d'études Canada *See* Curriculum Services Canada

Service familial catholique d'Ottawa *See* Catholic Family Service of Ottawa

Service familial de Sudbury (SFS) / Sudbury Family Service
c/o Sudbury Counselling Centre, 260, rue Cedar, Sudbury ON P3B 1M7
Tél: 705-524-9629; *Téléc:* 705-524-1530; *Crisis Hot-Line:* 705-675-4760
info@counsellingccs.com
www.counsellingccs.com
Aperçu: Dimension: petite; *Envergure:* locale; Organisme sans but lucratif; fondée en 1971 surveillé par Family Service Ontario
Mission: Amélioration de la qualité de vie et la résolution des problèmes psychosociaux des individus, des familles, des groupes & de la communauté
Affiliation(s): Conseil de Développement social
Membre(s) du personnel: 17
Activités: Counselling général; intervention contre la violence faite aux femmes; aide aux employés; *Evénements de sensibilisation:* Semaine nationale de la famille, oct.; *Bibliothèque:* Centre de ressources du SFS; rendez-vous
Membre(s) du bureau directeur:
Lynne Lamontagne, Directrice générale
llamontagne@counsellingccs.com

Service Intégration Travail Outaouais (SITO)
#400, 4, rue Taschereau, Gatineau QC J8Y 2V5
Tél: 819-776-2260; *Téléc:* 819-776-2988
info@sito.qc.ca
sito.qc.ca
Aperçu: Dimension: petite; *Envergure:* locale
Mission: Pour aider les immigrants à trouver un emploi
Membre(s) du personnel: 11
Membre: *Montant de la cotisation:* 5$
Membre(s) du bureau directeur:
Robert Mayrand, Directeur

Le Service juif d'information et de référence *See* Jewish Information Referral Service Montréal

Service Social International Canada *See* International Social Service Canada

Service universitaire canadien outre-mer (SUCO)
#210, 1453, rue Beaubien est, Montréal QC H2G 3C6
Tél: 514-272-3019; *Téléc:* 514-272-3097
Ligne sans frais: 866-357-0475
montreal@suco.org
www.suco.org
www.facebook.com/SUCO.solidarite.union.cooperation
twitter.com/SUCOInc
www.youtube.com/user/SUCOMontreal
Aperçu: Dimension: petite; *Envergure:* internationale; fondée en 1961
Mission: Promouvoir la solidarité directe entre les peuples en vue d'un développement durable pris en charge démocratiquement par les populations concernées
Affiliation(s): AQCI-Association québécoise des organismes de coopération internationale
Finances: *Fonds:* International Government
Membre(s) du personnel: 17
Membre(s) du bureau directeur:

Canadian Associations / Seton Portage/Shalalth District Chamber of Commerce

Richard Veenstra, Directeur général
richardveenstra@suco.org

Services à la famille - Canada *See* Family Service Canada

Services à la Famille - Kent *See* Family Service Kent

Services à la famille - Moncton, Inc *See* Family Service Moncton Inc.

Services à la famille - Ontario *See* Family Service Ontario

Services à la famille et à l'enfance du Nord Est de l'Ontario *See* North Eastern Ontario Family & Children's Services

Services canadiens d'assistance aux immigrants juifs *See* Jewish Immigrant Aid Services of Canada

Services d'évaluation pédagogique *See* Canadian Test Centre Inc.

Services de Sécurité Nouveau-Brunswick *See* Safety Services New Brunswick

Services familiaux catholiques de Toronto *See* Catholic Family Services of Toronto

Services pour femmes immigrantes d'Ottawa *See* Immigrant Women Services Ottawa

Seton Portage/Shalalth District Chamber of Commerce
PO Box 2067, Seton Portage BC V0N 3B0
Tel: 250-259-8268
Overview: A small local organization
Chief Officer(s):
Ray Klassen, Vice-President

Settlement Assistance & Family Support Services
#214, 1200 Markham Rd., Toronto ON M1H 3C3
Tel: 416-431-4847; *Fax:* 416-431-7283
reception@safss.org
www.safss.com
www.youtube.com/channel/UCElY8hHUthem2DooDwhj73A
Previous Name: South Asian Family Support Services
Overview: A small local organization
Mission: To offer linguistically & culturally appropriate services to newcomers
Staff Member(s): 21
Membership: *Fees:* $5 clients/volunteers; $10 individual; $50 organization; $100 corporation
Chief Officer(s):
Kazi Hoque, Executive Director

Seva Canada Society
#100, 2000 West 12th Ave., Vancouver BC V6J 2G2
Tel: 604-713-6622; *Fax:* 604-733-4292
Toll-Free: 877-460-6622
www.seva.ca
www.facebook.com/sevacanada
twitter.com/sevacanada
www.instagram.com/sevacanada
Previous Name: Seva Service Society
Overview: A small international charitable organization founded in 1982
Mission: To prevent blindness in developing countries through the implementation of local eye care programs
Member of: British Columbia Council for International Cooperation
Finances: *Annual Operating Budget:* $500,000-$1.5 Million
Staff Member(s): 5; 35 volunteer(s)
Membership: 4,000; *Committees:* Fundraising; Management; P.R. Events; International Opthalmology
Activities: Working in partnerships in Nepal, Tibet, India & Tanzania, to build eye care programs to eliminate avoidable blindness; *Awareness Events:* World Sight Day, 2nd Thu. of Oct.; *Speaker Service:* Yes; *Library:* by appointment
Chief Officer(s):
Penny Lyons, Executive Director
Ken Bassett, Director, Program
Deanne Berman, Director, Marketing & Communications
Christine Smith, Director, Development
Lisa Demers, Manager, Operations & Program
Awards:
• MPB Achievement Award
• Lewis Perinbaum Award for International Development

Seva Service Society *See* Seva Canada Society

Seventh Step Society of Canada
#2017, 246 Stewart Green SW, Calgary AB T3H 3C8
Tel: 403-650-1902
seventh@7thstep.ca
www.7thstep.ca
Overview: A small national organization founded in 1967
Mission: Self-help organization dedicated to help adult & young offenders to become useful & productive members of society; to provide follow-up to those who wish to use organization as means to maintain freedom
Membership: *Fees:* $5
Chief Officer(s):
Patrick Graham, Executive Director

Seventh-day Adventist Church in Canada (SDACC) / Église adventiste du septième jour au Canada
1148 King St. East, Oshawa ON L1H 1H8
Tel: 905-433-0011; *Fax:* 905-433-0982
Toll-Free: 800-263-7868
communication@adventist.ca
www.adventist.ca
Overview: A large national charitable organization founded in 1901
Mission: To provide strategic leadership, support & resources to conferences & national entities to achieve the goal of a shared vision
Finances: *Annual Operating Budget:* $3 Million-$5 Million; *Funding Sources:* Donations
Staff Member(s): 23
Membership: 375 churches + 66,907 individual members
Activities: Native Ministries; It Is Written Canada; Christian Record Services; Canadian University College; Kingsway College
Chief Officer(s):
Mark Johnson, President, 905-433-0011 Ext. 2086
johnson.mark@adventist.ca
Daniel Dragan Stojanovic, Secretary/Vice-President, Administration, 905-433-0011 Ext. 2083
stojanovic.dragan@adventist.ca
Ulysses Guarin, Treasurer/Vice-President, Finance, 905-433-0011 Ext. 2089
guarin.ulysses@adventist.ca
Publications:
• Canadian Adventist Messenger
Type: Magazine; *Frequency:* Monthly; *Accepts Advertising*; *Editor:* Stan Jensen
Profile: Church news & feature articles on spiritual topics.

Severn Sound Environmental Association (SSEA)
67 Fourth St., Midland ON L4R 3S9
Tel: 705-527-5166; *Fax:* 705-527-5167
sseainfo@midland.ca
www.severnsound.ca
Overview: A small local organization
Mission: To forge cooperative initiatives to address environmental issues by planning, designing, arranging funding and implementing environmental projects and promoting a sustainable Severn Sound community.
Membership: 9 municipalities
Chief Officer(s):
Keith Sherman, Executive Director, 705-527-5166 Ext. 206
ksherman@midland.ca

Sex Information & Education Council of Canada (SIECCAN) / Conseil d'information et éducation sexuelles du Canada
#400, 235 Danforth Ave., Toronto ON M4K 1N2
Tel: 416-466-5304
www.sieccan.org
Overview: A large national charitable organization founded in 1964
Mission: To ensure that all Canadians have access to sexual health information, education, & health services; To share knowledge & information with health professionals, policymakers, & educators
Finances: *Annual Operating Budget:* $50,000-$100,000; *Funding Sources:* Donations, Membership dues, Publication sales
Staff Member(s): 2; 13 volunteer(s)
Membership: 325 institutional + 30 student/senior/retiree + 550 individual; *Fees:* $35 individual; $60 organization
Activities: Disseminating information through scholarly publication; Developing sexual health resources for professional, student, & public audiences; Offering expert consultation & policy development expertise; *Speaker Service:* Yes; *Library:* Open to public by appointment
Chief Officer(s):
Alex McKay, Executive Director

Publications:
• Canadian Journal of Human Sexuality [a publication of the Sex Information & Education Council of Canada]
Type: Journal; *Frequency:* Quarterly; *Editor:* Alexander McKay; *ISSN:* 1188-4517
Profile: Contains articles from a variety of disciplines related to the study ofhuman sexuality; includes research reports, literature reviews, scholarly commentary, & letters to the editor

Sexsmith & District Chamber of Commerce
PO Box 146, Sexsmith AB T0H 3C0
Tel: 780-933-2044
sexsmithchamber@gmail.com
www.sexsmithchamber.com
Overview: A small local organization
Mission: To improve the economic environment of Sexsmith
Membership: 44
Chief Officer(s):
Shirley Roth, Contact

Sexual Assault Centre Kingston Inc. (SACCK)
PO Box 1461, Kingston ON K7L 5C7
Tel: 613-545-0762; *Fax:* 613-545-9744; *Crisis Hot-Line:* 877-544-6424
sack@sackingston.com
www.sackingston.com
www.facebook.com/100698016685171
twitter.com/sackingston
Overview: A small local charitable organization founded in 1978 overseen by Canadian Association of Sexual Assault Centres
Mission: To provide non-judgmental support & counselling to people who have been sexually assaulted
Member of: Ontario Coalition of Rape Crisis Centres
Finances: *Annual Operating Budget:* $500,000-$1.5 Million; *Funding Sources:* Ministry of the Attorney General; Ministry of Health; Queen's University; United Way; fundraising; United Way; Membership fees; Donations
Activities: 24-hour crisis line; counselling (individual & group); information & referral; public education; *Awareness Events:* Take Back the Night, Sept.; National Day of Remembrance & Action on Violence Against Women, Dec 6; *Internships:* Yes; *Speaker Service:* Yes; *Library:* Open to public
Chief Officer(s):
Kim Allen, Executive Director

Sexual Assault Centre London (SACL)
#5, 255 Horton St., 3rd Fl., London ON N6B 1L1
Tel: 519-439-0844; *Fax:* 519-439-9931
Toll-Free: 877-529-2272; *TTY:* 519-439-0690; *Crisis Hot-Line:* 519-438-2272
sacl@sacl.ca
www.sacl.ca
www.facebook.com/SACLondon
twitter.com/SACLondon
www.youtube.com/user/SACLondon
Overview: A small local charitable organization founded in 1975
Mission: To promote social & attitudinal changes toward sexual violence through public education, outreach & cooperative effort with other community groups; to provide services in a safe environment to survivors of sexual violence through peer support, counselling, advocacy & information
Affiliation(s): Ontario Coalition of Rape Crisis Centres; London Coordinating Committee to End Woman Abuse
Finances: *Funding Sources:* Ministry of the Attorney General; United Way; Ontario Trillium Foundation; City of London; Status of Women Canada; Sisters of St. Joseph
Activities: 24-hour crisis & support line; peer support services; accompaniment; public education; training programs for volunteers & staff; crisis intervention & stabilization; support groups for survivors; young women's support groups; therapy groups for adult survivors of child sexual abuse; *Speaker Service:* Yes; *Library:* Not open to public
Chief Officer(s):
Louise Pitre, Executive Director

Sexual Assault Centre of Edmonton (SACE)
#205, 14964 - 121A Ave., Edmonton AB T5V 1A3
Tel: 780-423-4102; *Fax:* 780-421-8734; *TTY:* 780-421-1482; *Crisis Hot-Line:* 780-423-4121
info@sace.ab.ca
www.sace.ab.ca
www.facebook.com/sacetalks
twitter.com/sacetalks
Overview: A small local charitable organization founded in 1976
Mission: To assist individuals affected by sexual abuse & assault; To encourage the community of Edmonton to take action against sexual violence

Finances: *Funding Sources:* United Way; Family & Community Support Services; Alberta Justice; Alberta Children's Services; Edmonton Community Foundation; Fundraising
Activities: Providing crisis intervention & counselling; Offering public education & information; Delivering a diversity outreach program; *Awareness Events:* National Day of Remembrance & Action on Violence Against Women, December 6
Chief Officer(s):
Mary Jane James, Executive Director

Sexual Assault Centre of Guelph *See* Guelph-Wellington Women in Crisis

Sexual Assault Crisis Centre of Essex County Inc. (SACC)
1770 Langlois Ave., Windsor ON N8X 4M5
Tel: 519-253-3100; *Fax:* 519-253-0175; *Crisis Hot-Line:* 519-253-9667
info@saccwindsor.net
www.saccwindsor.net
Previous Name: Windsor Sexual Assault Crisis Centre
Overview: A small local charitable organization founded in 1978 overseen by Canadian Association of Sexual Assault Centres
Member of: United Way of Windsor & Essex County
Finances: *Funding Sources:* Provincial government; Donations
Staff Member(s): 13; 15 volunteer(s)
Activities: Providing crisis intervention services; Counselling; Offering education; Engaging in advocacy activities

Sexual Assault Support Centre Ottawa (SASC)
PO Box 4441, Stn. E, Ottawa ON K1S 5B4
Tel: 613-725-2160; *Fax:* 613-725-9259; *TTY:* 613-725-1657; *Crisis Hot-Line:* 613-234-2266
info@sascottawa.com
sascottawa.com
www.facebook.com/SASCOttawa
twitter.com/SascOttawa
Overview: A small local charitable organization founded in 1983
Mission: To offer accessible, confidential support to female survivors of sexual violence; to offer a non-directive service; to encourage self-confidence & self-esteem; to increase public awareness; to offer training on the politics & effects of violence against women; to engage in political action to pressure for change in the structures & systems that contribute to the practice, maintenance, & tolerance of violence, oppression, discrimination & exploitation
Member of: Ontario Coalition of Rape Crisis Centres; Regional Coordinating Committee to End Violence Against Women
Staff Member(s): 9
Activities: Survivors of sexual violence groups; individual support; accompaniments (to hospital & police); public education; volunteer trainings; work with survivors of war & torture; Young Women at Risk Program; drop-in information sessions; 24-hour support line; fundraising; *Speaker Service:* Yes; *Library:* by appointment
Chief Officer(s):
Elizabeth Aldrich, Coordinator, Finance & Administration
admin@sascottawa.com

Sexual Assault Survivors' Centre - Sarnia-Lambton
#3, 189 Wellington St., Sarnia ON N7T 1G6
Tel: 519-337-3154; *Fax:* 519-337-0819
Toll-Free: 888-231-0536; *Crisis Hot-Line:* 519-337-3320
www.sexualassaultsarnia.on.ca
Overview: A small local organization founded in 1982 overseen by Canadian Association of Sexual Assault Centres
Member of: Ontario Coalition of Rape Crisis Centres
Finances: *Funding Sources:* Ministry of the Attorney General; Donations
Activities: 24-hour crisis line; Counselling; Public education; Information & referral; Advocacy; Rural & First Nation outreach; *Library:* Open to public

Sexual Health Centre for Cumberland County
PO Box 661, Amherst NS B4H 4B8
Tel: 902-667-7500; *Fax:* 902-667-0585
shccc@ns.aliantzinc.ca
www.amherstsexualhealth.ca
www.facebook.com/25778277501746
Previous Name: Cumberland County Family Planning Association
Overview: A small local organization founded in 1981
Mission: To promote informed, responsible attitudes toward healthy sexuality, & strives to reduce unwanted pregnancy & sexually transmitted diseases; to encourage parents' involvement in their children's sexuality education
Member of: Nova Scotia Association for Sexual Health; Canadian Federation for Sexual Health; United Way of Cumberland County
Affiliation(s): Planned Parenthood Federation of Canada
Finances: *Funding Sources:* Health Canada
Activities: Girl Power program; Go Girl website, www.forgirls.ca; *Speaker Service:* Yes; *Library:* Open to public

Sexual Health Centre Lunenburg County
48 Empire St., Bridgewater NS B4V 2L4
Tel: 902-527-2868
lunco.ns.sexualhealth@gmail.com
www.sexualhealthlunenburg.com
www.facebook.com/shclc
twitter.com/shclc
Previous Name: Planned Parenthood Bridgewater
Overview: A small local charitable organization founded in 1988
Mission: To ensure that information & services concerning human sexuality & fertility are available; To encourage informed, responsible attitudes toward sexuality from childhood to old age
Finances: *Funding Sources:* Nova Scotia Department of Health; fundraising
Membership: *Fees:* $10
Activities: Sex-positive; youth-positive; offers free condoms, pregnancy tests, counselling & information on sexuality issues; educational services; *Awareness Events:* Sexual & Reproductive Health Week, Feb.; Aids Awareness Week, Nov.
Chief Officer(s):
Jan Cressman, Co-Chair
Kendra Fevens, Co-Chair
Rhonda Haines, Officer, Finance
Jill Skinner, Secretary

Sexual Health Centre Saskatoon (PPSC)
210 - 2 Ave. North, Saskatoon SK S7K 2B5
Tel: 306-244-7989; *Fax:* 306-652-4034
info@shcsaskatoon.ca
www.sexualhealthcentresaskatoon.ca
Previous Name: Planned Parenthood Saskatoon Centre
Overview: A medium-sized local charitable organization founded in 1971 overseen by Action Canada for Sexual Health & Rights
Mission: To provide sexuality, contraception, & reproduction information, resources, & support services for members of the community
Finances: *Funding Sources:* Donations; fundraising
Membership: *Fees:* $5 student/unemployed; $10 individual; $15 family; $25 organization
Activities: *Library:* Open to public by appointment
Chief Officer(s):
Jillian Arkles Schwandt, Executive Director
admin@shcsaskatoon.ca

Sexual Health Network of Québec Inc. / Réseau de la Santé Sexuelle du Québec inc.
PO Box 22516, 5683, av Monkland, Montréal QC H4A 3T4
info@shnq.ca
www.shnq.ca
www.facebook.com/shnq.rssq
Previous Name: Planned Parenthood Montréal
Overview: A small local charitable organization founded in 1964
Mission: To advance sexual health
Membership: *Fees:* $35 full; $20 student
Chief Officer(s):
Laurie Betito, President

Sexual Violence Support & Information Centre of the Kawarthas *See* Kawartha Sexual Assault Centre

Sexuality Education Resource Centre Manitoba (SERC)
#200, 226 Osborne St. North, Winnipeg MB R3C 1V4
Tel: 204-982-7800; *Fax:* 204-982-7819
www.serc.mb.ca
www.facebook.com/sercmb
www.youtube.com/user/sercmbca
Previous Name: Planned Parenthood Manitoba
Overview: A medium-sized provincial organization founded in 1966 overseen by Canadian Federation for Sexual Health
Mission: To promote universal access to comprehensive, reliable information & services on sexuality & related health issues by fostering awareness, understanding, & support through education
Affiliation(s): Canadian Federation for Sexual Health; International Planned Parenthood Federation
Finances: *Annual Operating Budget:* $1.5 Million-$3 Million; *Funding Sources:* Government; United Way; Donations; Fee for service
Staff Member(s): 25
Activities: Facts of Life Program; Translation services; Pamphlets & fact sheets; Education & training; *Awareness Events:* Sexual & Reproductive Health Awareness Day, Feb.; *Speaker Service:* Yes; *Library:* SERC Lending Library; Not open to public
Chief Officer(s):
Holly Banner, Acting Executive Director
Brandon Office
1700 Pacific Ave., #C, Brandon MB R7A 7L9
Tel: 204-727-0417; *Fax:* 204-729-8364

SF Canada
c/o Judy McCrosky, 516 9th St. East, Saskatoon SK S7N 0B1
www.sfcanada.org
Overview: A small national organization founded in 1989
Mission: To foster growth of quality writing in the genre of speculative fiction
Membership: *Fees:* $30; *Member Profile:* Canadian writers of speculative fiction who have published for payment at least two short stories or three poems, or received a royalty advance for a novel; Editors who have been contracted for payment for a least one book or three issues of a magazine; Canadians with a professional interest in speculative fiction, such as publishers, librarians, & academics
Activities: Lobbying on behalf of Canadian writers; Promoting translation of Canadian speculative fiction; Arranging critique groups for members
Chief Officer(s):
Ira Nayman, President
Judy McCrosky, Secretary-Treasurer

Shaare Zion Congregation
5575, rue Côte-St-Luc, Montréal QC H3X 2C9
Tel: 514-481-7727; *Fax:* 514-481-1219
info@shaarezion.org
www.shaarezion.org
www.linkedin.com/company/shaare-zion-congregation
www.facebook.com/shaarezion
twitter.com/ShaareZion_MTL
www.youtube.com/user/shaarezionmtl/featured
Overview: A small local charitable organization founded in 1924
Affiliation(s): United Synagogue of Conservative Judaism
Staff Member(s): 10
Chief Officer(s):
David Moscovitch, Executive Director, 514-481-7727 Ext. 227
david.moscovitch@shaarezion.org
Lionel E. Moses, Rabbi, 514-481-7727 Ext. 228
rabbi@shaarezion.org

Shaarei Tefillah
Shaarei Tefillah Congregation, 3600 Bathurst St., Toronto ON M6A 2C9
Tel: 416-787-1631; *Fax:* 416-785-5378
www.shaareitefillah.com
Also Known As: Vaad Harabonim (Orthodox Rabbinical Council); Rabbinical Council of Ontario
Overview: A small local organization founded in 1982
Mission: To celebrate Judaism, community, family & the creation of lasting friendships
Finances: *Annual Operating Budget:* Less than $50,000
Membership: 40; *Fees:* $1,000 individual; $2,000 family
Chief Officer(s):
Harvey Mincer, President
Shmuli Soroka, Executive Director, 416-787-1631 Ext. 220
executivedirector@shaareitefillah.com

Shad Valley International
8 Young St. East, Waterloo ON N2J 2L3
Tel: 519-884-8844; *Fax:* 519-884-8191
info@shad.ca
www.shad.ca
www.linkedin.com/groups?mostPopular=&gid=2101
www.facebook.com/ShadValley
twitter.com/shadvalley
www.youtube.com/ShadValleyOfficial
Also Known As: Shad Valley
Previous Name: Canadian Centre for Creative Technology
Overview: A medium-sized national charitable organization founded in 1981
Mission: To advance the scientific & technological capabilities of youth, integrated with the development of their entrepreneurial spirit; To collaborate with education, business & other communities, both domestic & international, to provide exceptional development opportunities
Finances: *Annual Operating Budget:* $500,000-$1.5 Million

Staff Member(s): 8; 100 volunteer(s)
Membership: 13,000; *Fees:* $3,950
Activities: Shad Valley program involves 600+ outstanding senior high school students, some 200 corporate partners, & 12 Canadian universities each summer in an academic/co-op experience; *Speaker Service:* Yes
Chief Officer(s):
Barry Bisson, President, 519-884-8844 Ext. 227
president@shad.ca
Wendy Zufelt-Baxter, Vice President, Advancement, 519-884-8844 Ext. 229
wendy@shad.ca
Mary Hamoodi, Vice President, Finance & Operations, 519-884-8844 Ext. 225
maryh@shad.ca

Shag Harbour Incident Society
Shag Harbour UFO Museum, 5615 Hwy. 3, Shag Harbour NS B0W 3B0
Tel: 902-723-0127
shagharbour@gmail.com
www.shagharbourincident.wordpress.com
www.facebook.com/shagharbourUFO
twitter.com/ShagHarbour1967
Overview: A small local organization founded in 2006
Mission: To display information collected on the Shag Harbour UFO incident of 1967
Finances: *Funding Sources:* Donations
Activities: Maintaining the UFO Museum; Organizing annual UFO Festival; *Awareness Events:* UFO Festival, September
Chief Officer(s):
Laurie Wickens, President
lauriewickens@outlook.com

Shamattawa Crisis Centre
PO Box 126, Shamattawa MB R0B 1K0
Tel: 204-565-2551; *Fax:* 204-565-2544; *Crisis Hot-Line:* 204-565-2548
Previous Name: Shamattawa Shelter
Overview: A small local organization
Mission: To provide an emergency shelter for battered women & their children

Shamattawa Shelter *See* Shamattawa Crisis Centre

SHARE Agriculture Foundation
14110 Kennedy Rd., Caledon ON L7C 2G3
Tel: 905-838-0897; *Fax:* 905-838-0794
Toll-Free: 888-337-4273
info@shareagfoundation.org
www.shareagfoundation.org
www.facebook.com/119869878092172
twitter.com/shareagfoundatn
Also Known As: Sending Help and Resources Everywhere Agriculture Foundation
Overview: A medium-sized international organization founded in 1976
Mission: To help improve the quality of life for agriculturally impoverished communities worldwide
Finances: *Annual Operating Budget:* $500,000-$1.5 Million; *Funding Sources:* Canadian International Development Agency; Donations
Membership: *Committees:* Communications; Fundraising; Finance; Human Resources
Chief Officer(s):
Murray Brownridge, Chair
Les Frayne, Project Manager, Central America
Bob Thomas, Project Manager, South America
Publications:
• SHARE News [a publication of SHARE Agriculture Foundation]
Type: Newsletter

Share Family & Community Services Society
#200, 25 King Edward St., Coquitlam BC V3K 4S8
Tel: 604-540-9161; *Fax:* 604-540-2290
www.sharesociety.ca
www.facebook.com/sharefcs
twitter.com/SHAREFamily
instagram.com/sharesociety
Overview: A small local organization founded in 1972 overseen by Food Banks British Columbia
Mission: To act as a multi-service, non-profit agency providing a range of programs & social services to residents of Coquitlam, Port Coquitlam, Port Moody & surrounding communities
Member of: Food Banks British Columbia
Affiliation(s): Federation of Child & Family Services of BC

Finances: *Annual Operating Budget:* Greater than $5 Million; *Funding Sources:* Government; Grants; Fundraising; Program Fees
Staff Member(s): 126; 1695 volunteer(s)
Activities: Food bank; youth counselling; addiction counselling; settlement support services; ESL groups
Chief Officer(s):
Martin Wyant, Chief Executive Officer
martin.wyant@sharesociety.ca

Shareholder Association for Research & Education
#510, 1155 Robson St., Vancouver BC V6E 3R5
Tel: 604-408-2456
www.share.ca
www.facebook.com/sharecanada
twitter.com/share_ca
Also Known As: SHARE
Overview: A medium-sized national organization
Mission: To help institutional investors in Canada develop & implement responsible investment strategies in order to work towards a sustainable economy
Activities: Providing shareholder engagement & proxy voting services; Offering educational workshops, conferences, & resources; Advocating for policy reforms; Conducting research on environmental, social, & corporate governance issues
Chief Officer(s):
Peter Chapman, Executive Director
pchapman@share.ca
Amor Verdeflor-Alvarado, Office Administrator
averdeflor@share.ca
Jackie Cook, Director, Proxy Voting Research & Operations
jcook@share.ca
Shannon Rohan, Director, Responsible Investment
srohan@share.ca
Kevin Thomas, Director, Shareholder Engagement
kthomas@share.ca

ShareLife
ShareLife Trust, 1155 Yonge St., Toronto ON M4T 1W2
Tel: 416-934-3411; *Fax:* 416-934-3412
Toll-Free: 800-263-2595
slife@archtoronto.org
www.sharelife.org
www.facebook.com/ShareLifeCan
twitter.com/ShareLifeCan
Overview: A large international charitable organization founded in 1976
Mission: ShareLife is the Catholic Community's response to helping the whole community through Catholic agencies by effectively raising & allocating funds
Member of: International Catholic Stewardship Council
Affiliation(s): Canadian Centre for Philanthropy
Finances: *Annual Operating Budget:* $500,000-$1.5 Million
Membership: 34 organizations
Activities: *Awareness Events:* Kickoffs; *Speaker Service:* Yes
Chief Officer(s):
Arthur Peters, Executive Director, 416-934-3411 Ext. 559
arthurpeters@archtoronto.org
Awards:
• Bishop Michael Power Award
Eligibility: Individual or couple who have shown leadership, selflessness & financial generosity in supporting the mission of ShareLife
• Mother Delphine Award
Eligibility: Individual or couple who have actively volunteered with ShareLife

ShareOwner Education Inc.
#806, 4 King St. West, Toronto ON M5H 1B6
Tel: 416-595-9600; *Fax:* 416-595-0400
Toll-Free: 800-268-6881
customercare@shareowner.com
www.shareowner.com
Overview: A medium-sized national organization founded in 1987
Mission: To offer practical education & portfolio training to individual investors & investment clubs, so that they may invest successfully in quality growth stocks; To increase stock market literacy
Activities: Providing the ShareOwner's Stock Market Mentorship program
Chief Officer(s):
John Bart, Founder & Chief Mentor
Publications:
• Discover the Great Stocks to Buy [a publication of ShareOwner Education Inc.]

Type: Manual; *Price:* $49.95
Profile: Topics include developing judgments about a stock's prospects for future growth, methods for studying cyclical stocks, & tests to determine if a company's stock price is currently on sale
• Investing in Growth Stocks [a publication of ShareOwner Education Inc.]
Type: Manual; *Number of Pages:* 65
• Investment Club Starter Kit [a publication of ShareOwner Education Inc.]
Type: Kit; *Price:* $129.95
Profile: Kit includes the manual entitled, "Use a Club to Beat the Market", the current issue of "Top Stock Case Studies", & a set of record-keeping forms for the club
• Mentorship Manual [a publication of ShareOwner Education Inc.]
Type: Manual; *Price:* $49.95
Profile: Practical information for students about investing successfully in growth stocks over the longer term
• Stock Market Starter Kit [a publication of ShareOwner Education Inc.]
Type: Kit; *Price:* $195.95
Profile: Kit includes the "Investing in Growth Stocks" manual, a "Stock Study Guide" software licence for two months, a two month subscription to "Top Stock CaseStudies", & a two month subscription to a financial database of companies
• Top Stock Case Studies [a publication of ShareOwner Education Inc.]
Type: Magazine; *Frequency:* Bimonthly; *Price:* $169.95
Profile: Use of research resources to identify top stocks, updates on the growth & valuation images for companies, & case studies featuring exchange-traded funds
• Use a Club to Beat the Market [a publication of ShareOwner Education Inc.]
Type: Manual; *Number of Pages:* 93
Profile: A sample club constitution, duties of officers, examples of record-keeping forms, & a model education program

The Sharing Place - Orillia & District Food Bank
PO Box 743, 22 West St. South, Orillia ON L3V 6K7
Tel: 705-327-4273
www.sharingplaceorillia.org
www.facebook.com/sharingplaceorillia
twitter.com/TheSharingPlace
Overview: A small local charitable organization founded in 1988
Mission: To provide needed, nutritious food to people of all ages
Member of: Ontario Association of Food Banks
Finances: *Funding Sources:* Donations from individuals, organizations, & corporations
Chief Officer(s):
Chris Peacock, Executive Director

Shaunavon Arts Council
PO Box 358, Shaunavon SK S0N 2M0
Tel: 306-297-3882
Overview: A small local organization founded in 1977
Mission: To promote cultural & artistic opportunities for the community of Shaunavon & district
Member of: Organization of Saskatchewan Arts Council
Finances: *Annual Operating Budget:* Less than $50,000
35 volunteer(s)
Membership: *Fees:* $5

Shaunavon Chamber of Commerce
PO Box 1048, Shaunavon SK S0N 2M0
Tel: 306-297-7383
shaunavonchamber@hotmail.com
www.shaunavon.com/?p=980
Overview: A small local organization
Mission: To strengthen local businesses & the community
Member of: Saskatchewan Chamber of Commerce
Finances: *Annual Operating Budget:* Less than $50,000; *Funding Sources:* Membership dues; grants
Staff Member(s): 1
Membership: 75; *Fees:* $110
Chief Officer(s):
Joanne Gregoire, President
Kathy Wilkins, Vice-President

Shaunawan Ability Centre *See* Cypress Hills Ability Centres, Inc.

Shaw Festival
PO Box 774, 10 Queen's Parade, Niagara-on-the-Lake ON L0S 1J0

Tel: 905-468-2172; Fax: 905-468-3804
Toll-Free: 800-511-7429
www.shawfest.com
www.linkedin.com/company/248019
www.facebook.com/shawfestival
twitter.com/shawtheatre
www.youtube.com/theshawfestival
Also Known As: Shaw Festival Theatre Foundation
Overview: A medium-sized local charitable organization founded in 1963
Mission: To create intellectually challenging & entertaining theatre at an affordable price
Member of: Canadian Conference for the Arts; Professional Association of Canadian Theatres (PACT); Theatre Ontario
Affiliation(s): Canadian Institute for Theatre Technology
Finances: *Funding Sources:* Box Office; corporate & individual fundraising programs; federal & provincial funding 400 volunteer(s)
Membership: *Fees:* Schedule available; *Committees:* Shaw Boxing Evening; Shaw Shivaree; Festival Film Series; ShawFest!
Activities: Presenting theatre productions; Providing professional workshops, seminars, classes & costume rental; *Internships:* Yes; *Speaker Service:* Yes; *Library:* Open to public by appointment
Chief Officer(s):
Tim Carroll, Artistic Director
Tim Jennings, Executive Director

Shaw Rocket Fund
#210, 2421 - 37th Ave., Calgary AB T2E 6Y7
www.rocketfund.ca
www.facebook.com/rocketfund
twitter.com/RocketFund
Overview: A medium-sized national organization
Mission: To provide funding for children's programming
Finances: *Funding Sources:* Shaw Communications Inc., Shaw Pay Per View Ltd. & Shaw Direct
Chief Officer(s):
Annabel Slaight, Chair
Agnes Augustin, President & Treasurer

Sheena's Place
87 Spadina Rd., Toronto ON M5R 2T1
Tel: 416-927-8900; Fax: 416-927-8844
info@sheenasplace.org
www.sheenasplace.org
www.facebook.com/Sheenasplacesupport
twitter.com/sheenasplace
www.youtube.com/user/SheenasPlace
Overview: A small local organization
Mission: To offer hope & support for people with eating disorders
Staff Member(s): 7
Chief Officer(s):
Deborah Berlin-Romalis, Executive Director
dberlin-romalis@sheenasplace.org

Sheep Creek Arts Council (SCAC)
PO Box 277, 133 Sunset Blvd., Turner Valley AB T0L 2A0
Tel: 403-933-4020
info@sheepcreekarts.ca
www.sheepcreekarts.ca
Overview: A small local organization founded in 1958
Mission: To donate funds to local groups; To provide bursaries to secondary students in the arts
Affiliation(s): Camera Club; Sheep Creek Creative Writers; Sheep Creek Sketch Group
Finances: *Funding Sources:* Membership dues; Events
Membership: *Fees:* $10

Sheet Harbour & Area Chamber of Commerce & Civic Affairs
PO Box 239, Sheet Harbour NS B0J 3B0
sheetharbourchamber.com
Previous Name: Sheet Harbour & Area Chamber of Commerce; Sheet Harbour Board of Trade
Overview: A small local organization founded in 1935
Mission: To promote & drive the growth of the regional economy
Finances: *Annual Operating Budget:* Less than $50,000; *Funding Sources:* Membership fees
Membership: 84; *Fees:* $20 individual; $50 business; *Committees:* Waterfront Development
Chief Officer(s):
Robert Moser, President

Sheet Harbour & Area Chamber of Commerce; Sheet Harbour Board of Trade *See* Sheet Harbour & Area Chamber of Commerce & Civic Affairs

Sheet Metal Contractors Association of Alberta (SMCAA)
#203, 2725 - 12th St. NE, Calgary AB T2E 7J2
Tel: 403-250-7040; Fax: 403-735-5910
Toll-Free: 888-265-6665
wilma@smcaa.ca
www.smcaa.ca
twitter.com/smcaa1
Merged from: Edmonton Association of Sheet Metal Contractors; Calgary Air Conditioning & Sheet Metal Association
Overview: A small local organization founded in 2000
Mission: To collaborate with the municipal, provincial & federal governments in order to promote positive changes for the members of the Heating, Ventilation & Air Conditioning industry in Alberta
Member of: Sheet Metal & Air Conditioning Contractors' National Association
Finances: *Funding Sources:* Membership
Staff Member(s): 1; 10+ volunteer(s)
Membership: 150+; *Fees:* Schedule available; *Member Profile:* Contractors, suppliers & manufacturers in Alberta; *Committees:* Bylaw & Code of Ethics Review; Golf; Old-Timers; Programming
Activities: Working with local & provincial governments to modify codes, permits & standards of practice; Providing educational programs; Preparing information about the profession for participation in career fairs; Assisting employers with employee benefit programs & volume discounts; Organizing a variety of annual events including dinner meetings, golf tournaments, Christmas parties & conferences; *Library:* SMACNA Manuals
Chief Officer(s):
Ken Fulmer, Provincial President, 780-469-7791
Darcy Spicer, Treasurer
darcy@asmindustries.com
Wilma Agnew, Executive Director
Awards:
• Alberta Apprenticeship & Industry Training Scholarship *Eligibility:* Alberta residents that are registered as an apprentice in a trade & have passed their first or subsequent period apprenticeship & industry training exam*Location:* Alberta *Deadline:* June; *Amount:* $1,000 *Contact:* Alberta Scholarship Programs, Phone: 780-427-8640; E-mail: scholarships@gov.ab.ca

Shelburne & Area Chamber of Commerce
PO Box 1150, Shelburne NS B0T 1W0
Tel: 902-875-2384
shelburnechamber@gmail.com
www.shelburnechamber.ca
www.facebook.com/ShelburneAreaChamber
twitter.com/SACCNovaScotia
Overview: A small local organization
Mission: To strengthen the economy; To improve business
Membership: 70+
Chief Officer(s):
Elizabeth Rhuland, President
Ron Chute, Treasurer

Shelburne Arts Council *See* Dufferin Arts Council

Shelburne Association Supporting Inclusion (SASI)
PO Box 59, 151 Water St., Shelburne NS B0T 1W0
Tel: 902-875-1083; Fax: 902-875-1056
sasi@eastlink.ca
www.supportinginclusion.ca
Overview: A small local charitable organization founded in 1985
Mission: To improve the quality of life for individuals with disabilities & mental health difficulties through person-centred programs
Member of: DIRECTIONS Council for Vocational Services Society
Membership: *Committees:* Personnel; Finance
Activities: Products & services include: Shelburne Café, catering, tropies & engraving, baking & crafts/textiles
Chief Officer(s):
Martha Holmes, Chair
Publications:
• Shelburne Association Supporting Inclusion Newsletter *Type:* Newsletter

Shelburne County Genealogical Society
PO Box 248, Shelburne NS B0T 1W0
Tel: 902-875-4299
gencentre@ns.sympatico.ca
nsgna.ednet.ns.ca/shelburne
Overview: A small local charitable organization founded in 1987
Mission: To promote and encourage the study of family history in Shelburne County; to assist with research of Shelburne County Genealogy; to promote standards of accuracy, responsibility, and scholarly excellence among genealogists; to contribute to the Society's holdings through volunteer activities and donations in a manner compatible with the aims and purposes of the Society; and to encourage and assist in the publication of genealogical source material
Member of: Council of Nova Scotia Archives
Membership: *Fees:* $25 single; $30 family; $225 single (life); $300 family (life); $3 student; $15 institution
Activities: *Library:* Genealogy Centre; Open to public

Shelburne Historical Society
PO Box 39, Shelburne NS B0T 1W0
Tel: 902-875-3219; Fax: 902-875-4141
shelburne.museum@ns.sympatico.ca
www.historicshelburne.com
www.facebook.com/364893103570881
Overview: A small local charitable organization founded in 1948
Mission: To promote & encourage interest in the history of our town & county; to gather, preserve & disseminate data relating to the early history of the town & county; to operate museums; to build & sell traditional wooden boats
Member of: Federation of Nova Scotian Heritage
Affiliation(s): Nova Scotia Museum
Finances: *Annual Operating Budget:* $100,000-$250,000
Staff Member(s): 4; 60 volunteer(s)
Membership: 60; *Fees:* $10; *Committees:* Museums
Activities: Shelburne County Museum; Ross-Thomson House & Store Museum; Dory Shop Museum; Muir-Cox Shipbuilding Interpretive Centre; *Library:* Open to public

Shelter for Helpless Animals in Distress (SHAID)
#138, 450 LaHave St., Unit 17, Bridgewater NS B4V 4A3
Tel: 902-543-4849
shiadshelter@gmail.com
www.shaid.ca
www.facebook.com/ShaidTreeAnimalShelter
Overview: A small local organization founded in 1986
Mission: To provide shelter for animals & to help find them a permanent home
Member of: Canadian Federation of Humane Societies
Staff Member(s): 6
Membership: 136; *Fees:* $10
Activities: Yard sale & auction; cat show; dog walk; penny auction; open house; craft sale
Chief Officer(s):
Harold Rowsell, Manager

The Shelter Movers of Toronto
92 Strathcona Ave., Toronto ON M4K 1K6
info@sheltermovers.com
www.sheltermovers.com
www.facebook.com/sheltermovers
twitter.com/ShelterMovers
Overview: A small local charitable organization
Mission: To collaborate with shelters, victim service agencies, & law enforcement to provide moving services for individuals experiencing domestic violence
Chief Officer(s):
Marc Hull-Jacquin, Executive Director

The Shepherds' Trust
Catholic Pastoral Centre, #603, 1155 Yonge St., Toronto ON M4T 1W2
Tel: 416-934-3400; Fax: 416-934-3444
retiredpriests@archtoronto.org
www.shepherdstrust.org
Overview: A medium-sized local charitable organization founded in 1996
Mission: To assist elderly & disabled priests by raising awareness & funds; to provide retired priests with the financial resources to allow them to live a dignified life
Affiliation(s): Archdiocese of Toronto
Finances: *Annual Operating Budget:* Greater than $5 Million; *Funding Sources:* Donations
Membership: *Member Profile:* Retired Catholic priests; *Committees:* Collection
Chief Officer(s):
Brian Clough, Elected Representative, Board of Trustees
Ivan Philip Camilleri, Elected Representative, Board of Trustees
Marisa Rogucki, Coordinator, Retired Diocesan Priests

Publications:
- The Sheperds' Trust Newsletter
Type: Newsletter; *Frequency:* Annual

Sherbrooke Snow Shoe Club
1900, rue Prospect, Sherbrooke QC J1J 1K7
Tel: 819-565-0355
Overview: A small local organization founded in 1877
Mission: To promote the grand old Canadian tradition of snow shoeing & to provide an environment for socializing among the members of the community

Sherbrooke Symphony Orchestra *Voir* Orchestre symphonique de Sherbrooke

Sheridan Park Association (SPA)
PO Box 811, Mississauga ON L5J 2Z1
Tel: 905-823-7091; *Fax:* 905-823-4403
contact@sheridanpark.ca
www.sheridanpark.ca
Overview: A small local organization founded in 1965
Mission: To maintain the Sheridan Science & Technology Park
Membership: *Member Profile:* Companies located in the Sheridan Science & Technology Park
Chief Officer(s):
Richard Perrier, President
rperrier@suncor.com

Sherwood Park & District Chamber of Commerce
100 Ordze Ave., Sherwood Park AB T8B 1M6
Tel: 780-464-0801; *Fax:* 780-449-3581
Toll-Free: 866-464-0801
www.sherwoodparkchamber.com
www.facebook.com/586363191397226
twitter.com/shpkchamber
www.youtube.com/user/ChamberSherwoodPark
Overview: A small local organization founded in 1978
Mission: To promote free enterprise to enhance the community's economic, industrial, & civic environments
Member of: Alberta Chamber of Commerce; Canadian Chamber of Commerce
Finances: *Annual Operating Budget:* $250,000-$500,000; *Funding Sources:* Membership dues
Staff Member(s): 7
Membership: 1,225; *Fees:* $135-$685
Activities: Organizing events; Providing advertising services & business-related programs; Advocating; *Awareness Events:* Trade Fair & Sale
Chief Officer(s):
Todd Banks, Executive Director
tbanks@sherwoodparkchamber.com

Sherwood Park District Soccer Association
Millenium Pl., #131.2, 2000 Premier Way, Sherwood Park AB T8H 2G4
Tel: 780-449-1343; *Fax:* 780-464-5821
www.spdsa.net
www.facebook.com/416487478408692
twitter.com/SPDSASoccer
Overview: A small local organization founded in 1976 overseen by Alberta Soccer Association
Member of: Alberta Soccer Association; Federation Internationale de Football Association; Canada Soccer Association
Affiliation(s): Breton Soccer Association; Calmar Soccer Association; Devon Soccer Association; Leduc Soccer Association; Millet Soccer Association; New Sarepta Soccer Association; Pigeon Lake Soccer Association; Thorsby Soccer Association; Warburg Soccer Association; Wetaskiwin Soccer Association
Membership: 3,000 players in 10 associations; *Committees:* Human Resources; Bylaw Reviewl Financial Policy; IT
Chief Officer(s):
Debbie Ballam, General Manager
d.ballam@spdsa.net

Sherwood Park Fish & Game Association
PO Box 3098, Stn. Main, Sherwood Park AB T8A 2A6
Tel: 780-467-0085
info@spfga.org
www.spfga.org
Overview: A small local organization founded in 1962
Mission: To promote through education, lobbying and programs, the conservation and utilization of fish and wildlife and to protect and enhance the habitat they depend on.
Member of: Alberta Fish & Game Association
Affiliation(s): Canadian Wildlife Federation

Chief Officer(s):
Pat Harris, Contact

Shevchenko Scientific Society of Canada
516 The Kingsway, Toronto ON M9A 3W6
ntsh.ca@gmail.com
www.ntsh.ca
www.facebook.com/1594608770752854
twitter.com/NtshCanada
Overview: A large national organization founded in 1949
Mission: To promote scholarly research & publication; To advance education in the field of Ukrainian & Ukrainian Canadian studies
Membership: *Member Profile:* Individuals of all backgrounds with a passion for research & education
Activities: Organizing public lectures, conferences, symposia, seminars, & round tables; Providing scholarly information & resources to develop Ukrainian & Ukrainian Canadian scholarship
Chief Officer(s):
Daria Darewych, President
daria_darewych@hotmail.com
Awards:
- Shevchenko Scientific Society of Canada Research Grant; *Amount:* up to $5,000
- Scholarly Publications Support Program; *Amount:* up to $5,000

Meetings/Conferences:
- Shevchenko Scientific Society of Canada Annual Conference 2018, 2018
Scope: National

Shiatsu Therapy Association of Ontario (STAO)
#1056, 7B Pleasant Blvd., Toronto ON M4T 1K2
Tel: 416-923-7826
Toll-Free: 877-923-7826
info@shiatsuassociation.com
www.shiatsuassociation.com
Overview: A small provincial organization founded in 1983
Mission: To promote awareness of Shiatsu to the public, health care professionals, government agencies & insurance companies; to protect the integrity of the profession with high educational standards & dedication to safeguarding the welfare of the public through strict adherence by its members to the STAO code of conduct
Finances: *Annual Operating Budget:* Less than $50,000; *Funding Sources:* Membership fees
20 volunteer(s)
Membership: 170; *Fees:* Schedule available; *Member Profile:* Graduates of the 2,200 hr. Shiatsu course who have passed the STAO exams & paid the membership fee; *Committees:* Membership; Examinations; Complaints; Disciplines; Marketing; CST Violations; Telephone
Activities: Promotes awareness & educates the public, health care providers, government agencies & insurance companies about Shiatsu Therapy; provides referral service for Certified Shiatsu Therapists (CST); provides speakers, presentations & demonstrations on Shiatsu Therapy; pursues government regulation of Shiatsu Therapy; *Library:* Resource Centre
Chief Officer(s):
Carolyn Kozole, Administrator, 416-719-4590

Shibogama First Nations Council (SFNC)
PO Box 449, 81 King St., Sioux Lookout ON P0V 2T0
Tel: 807-737-2662; *Fax:* 807-737-1583
Toll-Free: 866-877-6057
www.shibogama.on.ca
Overview: A small local organization
Mission: To promote the economic and community development of the Aboriginal people of the Shibogama area; to initiate, support and manage projects and programs which improve the social, cultural, economic, educational, recreational, or spiritual life of members of the Shibogama First Nations; and to provide assistance to the First Nations of the Shibogama area with regard to program development and administration.
Chief Officer(s):
Margaret Kenequanash, Executive Director
margaretk@shibogama.on.ca

Shipbuilding Association of Canada; Canadian Maritime Industries Association *See* The Canadian Marine Industries and Shipbuilding Association

Shipping Federation of Canada / Fédération maritime du Canada
#326, 300, rue St-Sacrement, Montréal QC H2Y 1X4
Tel: 514-849-2325; *Fax:* 514-849-7973
Toll-Free: 877-534-7367
info@shipfed.ca
www.shipfed.ca
Overview: A large national organization founded in 1903
Mission: To represent and promote the interests of the owners, operators & agents of ships involved in Canada's world trade
Finances: *Funding Sources:* International shipping
Staff Member(s): 8
Membership: 83; *Member Profile:* Member companies involved in all sectors of the shipping industry; *Committees:* Customs; Dangerous Goods; EDI; Immigration; Pilotage; Railways; Tanker Safety
Activities: To protect members in all matters affecting the operation of shipping from & to Eastern Canada, the St. Lawrence River, the Great Lakes & Arctic ports; areas of concern include pilotage, pollution, navigation aids, port operations, port charges, & federal government legislation & regulation
Chief Officer(s):
Michael Broad, President, 514-849-2325 Ext. 228
mhbroad@shipfed.ca

Shipyard General Workers' Federation of British Columbia (CLC) / Fédération des ouvriers des chantiers navals de la Colombie-Britannique (CTC)
#130, 111 Victoria Dr., Vancouver BC V5L 4C4
Tel: 604-254-8204; *Fax:* 604-254-7447
office@bcshipyardworkers.com
www.bcshipyardworkers.com
Overview: A medium-sized provincial organization
Affiliation(s): Machinists, Fitters & Helpers Industrial Union #3, Marine Workers & Boilerworkers' Industrial Union #1, Shipwrights, Joiners & Caulkers' Industrial Union #9
Membership: 1,100 + 3 locals
Chief Officer(s):
George MacPherson, President
Quentin Del Vecchio, General Secretary

Shoal Lake & District Chamber of Commerce
PO Box 176, Shoal Lake MB R0J 1Z0
Tel: 204-759-2215
www.facebook.com/105015103013460
Overview: A small local organization
Mission: To represent members; To help grow the economy
Chief Officer(s):
Tracey Myhill, President

Shock Trauma Air Rescue Society (STARS)
PO Box 570, 1441 Aviation Park NE, Calgary AB T2E 8M7
Tel: 403-295-1811; *Fax:* 403-275-4891
Toll-Free: 888-797-8277
info@stars.ca
www.stars.ca
www.facebook.com/STARSairambulance
twitter.com/STARSambulance
Overview: A small provincial organization founded in 1986
Mission: With a fleet of helicopters, STARS provides pre-hospital mobile emergency medical care through its focus on service, communications, education, training, research and consultation with the communities it serves. Its charitable registration # is: 118781103RR0001.
Finances: *Funding Sources:* donations
Chief Officer(s):
Andrea Robertson, President & CEO
Publications:
- Horizons
Type: Newsletter; *Frequency:* 2 pa

Edmonton Base
#100, 1519 35 Ave. East, Edmonton AB T9E 0V6
Tel: 780-890-3131; *Fax:* 780-890-3180

Grande Prairie Base
10911 - 123 St., Grande Prairie AB T8V 7Z3
Tel: 780-830-7000; *Fax:* 780-830-7009

Shoe Manufacturers' Association of Canada (SMAC) / Association des manufacturiers de chaussures du Canada
#203, 90, rue Morgan, Baie d'Urfe QC H9X 3A8
Tel: 514-457-3436; *Fax:* 514-457-8004
Overview: A medium-sized national organization founded in 1919
Mission: To represent & serve Canadian footwear manufacturers; To protect the Canadian domestic shoe industry
Membership: *Member Profile:* Footwear manufacturers throughout Canada

Activities: Monitoring developments in the Canadian footwear industry; Advocating on behalf of Canadian footwear manufacturers; Fostering a fair & competitive marketplace
Chief Officer(s):
George P. Hanna, President
hanna@shoecanada.com

Sholem Aleichem Community Inc. (SAC)
PO Box C105, 123 Doncaster St., Winnipeg MB R3N 2B2
Tel: 204-896-0456
sacommunity@gmail.com
www.sholemaleichemcommunity.ca
Overview: A small local organization
Mission: To preserve Jewish tradition & culture; To offer a secular humanistic approach to Jewish traditions & practices
Affiliation(s): The Congress of Secular Jewish Organizations
Membership: *Fees:* $20 student; $30 individual; $50 family; *Member Profile:* Jewish people from Winnipeg, Manitoba; Individuals of non-Jewish backgrounds who wish to participate because of family connections, friendships, & personal interests
Activities: Fostering the application of humanistic values; Providing ethical training for children & educational programs for adults; Offering exposure to Jewish languages, arts, & culture; Organizing celebrations
Chief Officer(s):
Henry Shuster, Chair
Publications:
• Sholem Aleichem Community Newsletter
Type: Newsletter
Profile: Organization activities & forthcoming events

Shooting Federation of Canada (SFC) / Fédération de tir du Canada (FTC)
45 Shirley Blvd., Nepean ON K2K 2W6
Tel: 613-727-7483; *Fax:* 613-727-7487
info@sfc-ftc.ca
www.sfc-ftc.ca
Overview: A medium-sized national charitable organization founded in 1932
Mission: To represent firearms users in matters of legislation, shooting sports promotion, & program activities
Member of: International Shooting Sport Federation
Affiliation(s): Canadian Shooting Sports Association
Finances: *Funding Sources:* Sales; Donations; Government
Membership: 108 organizations; *Committees:* Coaching; National Officials Development; Commonwealth Games; Awards & Merits; High Performance
Activities: *Awareness Events:* National Smallbore Rifle Championships; National Trapshooting Championships; National Skeet Shooting Championships; *Library*
Chief Officer(s):
Pat Boulay, President
president@sfc-ftc.ca
Awards:
• Female Athlete of the Year
• Male Athlete of the Year
• Official of the Year
• Coach of the Year
• Ernie Sopsich Memorial Fund
• Eddy Mark Shaske Memorial Fund
• Jim O'Connor Memorial Award

Shooting Federation of Nova Scotia (SFNS)
PO Box 28023, Dartmouth NS B2W 6E2
www.sfns.info
Overview: A small provincial organization founded in 1972
Member of: Sport Nova Scotia
Affiliation(s): Shooting Federation of Canada
Finances: *Annual Operating Budget:* Less than $50,000
12 volunteer(s)
Membership: 1600

Shorthorn Breeders of Manitoba Inc.
PO Box 54, Gladstone MB R0J 0T0
Tel: 204-870-0089
www.manitobashorthorns.com
www.facebook.com/296215440444692
Overview: A small provincial organization
Member of: Canadian Shorthorn Association
Chief Officer(s):
Monty Thomson, President
monty@hatfieldclydesdales.com
Susan Armbruster, Secretary, 204-859-2088

Shuswap Area Family Emergency Society (SAFE)
PO Box 1463, Salmon Arm BC V1E 4P6
Tel: 250-832-9616; *Fax:* 250-832-9516
safesociety@shaw.ca
www.safesociety.ca
Overview: A small local organization founded in 1979
Mission: To end violence against women & children in the Shuswap; To provide temporary accommodation; To offer support counselling for women & their children who are/have experienced violence
Member of: BC Council for Families
Finances: *Funding Sources:* Regional & provincial governments; Donations
Activities: Women's emergency shelter; Children Who Witness Abuse Program; Stopping the Violence Program; Youth sexual exploitation posters; Community based victim assistance; Police based victim assistance; *Awareness Events:* International Women's Day, March

Shuswap Association for Community Living (SACL)
PO Box 153, #103 & #301, 371 Hudson Ave. NE, Salmon Arm BC V1E 4N3
Tel: 250-832-3885; *Fax:* 250-832-1076
www.shuswapacl.com
Overview: A small local organization
Mission: To provide services, support and housing for people with intellectual disabilities and their families.
Finances: *Funding Sources:* donations; BC government; grants; fundraising events
Staff Member(s): 3
Activities: Vocational programs; leisure activities; housing assistance
Chief Officer(s):
Jo-Anne Crawford, Executive Director, 250-832-3885 Ext. 1301

Shuswap Columbia District Labour Council (SCDLC)
PO Box 1230, Revelstoke BC V0E 2S0
Tel: 250-832-8509; *Fax:* 250-832-8059
scdlabourcouncil@gmail.com
www.facebook.com/SCDLabourCouncil
Overview: A small local organization overseen by British Columbia Federation of Labour
Mission: To advance the economic & social welfare of workers in British Columbia's Shuswap Columbia Regional District
Affiliation(s): Canadian Labour Congress (CLC)
Membership: *Member Profile:* Unions in the Revelstoke & Salmon Arm area of British Columbia
Activities: Advocating for workers' rights in the Shuswap Columbia Regional District of British Columbia; Liaising with locally elected officials; Raising awareness of issues affecting workers, such as health & safety; Ensuring that provincial labour laws are enforced; Hosting a ceremony on the annual Day of Mourning to pay tribute to workers who were injured or killed on the job; Supporting local community organizations; Providing community information about employment
Chief Officer(s):
Michelle Cole, President
sahmof2iam@hotmail.com
Awards:
• William S. King Scholarship Trust
Eligibility: A student entering post-secondary education to pursue a career working with people; *Amount:* $500 *Contact:* SCDLC & Revelstoke NDP Club

Shuswap District Arts Council
PO Box 1181, Salmon Arm BC V1E 4P3
Tel: 250-832-6807; *Fax:* 250-832-6807
www.shuswapartscouncil.bc.ca
Overview: A small local organization founded in 1971
Member of: Assembly of BC Arts Councils; Thompson Okanagan Network of Arts Councils; BC Arts in Education Council; Canadian Conference of the Arts
Finances: *Annual Operating Budget:* $50,000-$100,000; *Funding Sources:* Provincial & local governments; donations; membership fees; fundraising
Staff Member(s): 1
Membership: 139; *Fees:* $15 Individual; $35 Arts groups; $50 Corporate; *Member Profile:* Amateur arts groups & individuals
Activities: Artwaves, summer school of the Arts; Community street banner project; Wow! Wednesdays on the Wharf, free summer concert series
Chief Officer(s):
Tracey Kutschker, Executive Director

Shuswap Lakes Tourism Association *See* Shuswap Tourism

Shuswap Naturalists
1740 - 16 St. NE, Salmon Arm BC V1E 3Z7
info@shuswapnaturalists.org
www.shuswapnaturalists.org
Overview: A small local charitable organization founded in 1970
Mission: To promote the enjoyment of nature through environmental appreciation & conservation; to encourage wise use & conservation of natural resources & environmental protection.
Member of: Federation of BC Naturalists
Membership: *Fees:* $20 single; $30 family
Chief Officer(s):
Derek Beacham, President

Shuswap Rock Club
PO Box 235, Sorrento BC V0E 2W0
Tel: 250-955-6484
Overview: A small local organization
Member of: Lapidary, Rock & Mineral Society of British Columbia
Activities: Rockhounding in thompson, Shuswap areas
Chief Officer(s):
Sylvia Repnow, Contact
shuswaprockclub@gmail.com

Shuswap Tourism
PO Box 978, 781 Marine Park Dr. NE, Salmon Arm BC V1E 4P1
Tel: 250-833-5906
info@shuswaptourism.ca
www.shuswaptourism.ca
www.facebook.com/shuswaptourism
twitter.com/shuswaptourism
www.youtube.com/shuswaptourism
Previous Name: Shuswap Lakes Tourism Association
Overview: A small local organization founded in 1988
Mission: To promote the development of tourism by providing external & local marketing of the Shuswap Lakes Area
Member of: Thompson Okanagan Tourism Association
Finances: *Funding Sources:* Regional government
Membership: *Fees:* Free

Shwachman-Diamond Syndrome Canada
2152 Gatley Rd., Mississauga ON L5H 3L9
Toll-Free: 866-462-8907
info@shwachman.org
www.shwachman.org
www.facebook.com/shwachmandiamondcanada
Also Known As: SDS-Canada
Overview: A small national charitable organization
Mission: To raise funds to support research; to disseminate current medical information; to heighten awareness of SDS in the medical community to allow earlier diagnosis & treatment; to develop network of contacts & resources for people & families with SDS
Finances: *Funding Sources:* Corporate & individual donations; Fund raising
Chief Officer(s):
Zoé Nakata, President
Awards:
• PhD Fellowship
Awarded annually

Sicamous & District Chamber of Commerce
PO Box 346, #3, 446 Main St., Sicamous BC V0E 2V0
Tel: 250-836-0002; *Fax:* 250-836-4368
info@sicamouschamber.bc.ca
www.sicamouschamber.bc.ca
Overview: A small local organization
Mission: To stimulate economic, industrial, & social growth in the community
Finances: *Annual Operating Budget:* $50,000-$100,000; *Funding Sources:* Fundraising event; municipal fee for service
Staff Member(s): 2
Membership: 183 businesses; *Fees:* $125

Sickle Cell Association of Ontario (SCAO)
#205, 4610 Dufferin St., Toronto ON M3H 5S4
Tel: 416-789-2855; *Fax:* 416-789-1903
www.linkedin.com/company/2437730
www.facebook.com/SickleCellCanada
twitter.com/SCA_O
Overview: A small provincial charitable organization founded in 1981
Mission: To serve the community as a recognized voluntary agency that endeavors to optimize the quality of life for individuals & families with sickle cell disease
Finances: *Funding Sources:* Donations
Staff Member(s): 2

Canadian Associations / Sickle Cell Foundation of Alberta

Membership: Fees: $15-$35; *Committees:* Educational; Social Suport; Fundraising; Events; Public Policy
Activities: Public awareness; education, support groups; alternative methods of pain management; *Awareness Events:* World Sickle Cell Day, June; *Internships:* Yes; *Speaker Service:* Yes
Chief Officer(s):
Marie Boyd, Administrative Assistant

Sickle Cell Foundation of Alberta
PO Box 55041, Stn. New Knottwood, 1704 Millwoods Rd. SW, Edmonton AB T6K 3N0
Tel: 780-450-4943
scfoa@telus.ca
www.sicklecellfoundationofalberta.org
Overview: A small provincial organization
Mission: To promote awareness about sickle cell disorder in Alberta
Chief Officer(s):
Ekua Yorke, Founder & Coordinator

SIDA Moncton *See* AIDS Moncton

Sida Nouveau Brunswick *See* AIDS New Brunswick

Sidaction Mauricie
515, rue Ste-Cécile, Trois-Rivières QC G9A 1K9
Tél: 819-374-5740
information@sidactionmauricie.ca
www.sidactionmauricie.ca
Aperçu: Dimension: petite; *Envergure:* locale; Organisme sans but lucratif; fondée en 1990 surveillé par Canadian AIDS Society
Mission: Offrir des programmes d'éducation et de prévention au grand public et aux clientèles à risque, en collaboration avec les organismes gouvernementaux et communautaires qui oeuvrent aussi dans le domaine du Sida, et avec les personnes séropositives; l'organisme offre aussi un service de soutien aux personnes atteintes du VIH/Sida et à leurs proches
Membre de: Coalition des organismes communautaires québécois de lutte contre le Sida
Finances: Budget de fonctionnement annuel: Moins de $50,000
Membre: 1-99
Activités: Stagiaires: Oui; *Bibliothèque*
Membre(s) du bureau directeur:
Hélène Neault, Adjointe à la coordination

SIDALYS
3702, rue Ste-Famille, Montréal QC H2X 2L4
Tél: 514-842-4439; *Téléc:* 514-842-2284
sidasecours@hotmail.com
Nom précédent: Centre des services sida secours du Québec
Aperçu: Dimension: petite; *Envergure:* provinciale surveillé par Canadian AIDS Society
Membre de: Coalition des organismes communautaires québécois de lutte contre le sida (COCQ-SIDA)
Activités: Hébergement: Habitations Jean-Pierre Valiquette (appartements supervisés); Centre sida secours; Centre Amaryllis

Siding & Window Dealers Association of Canada (SAWDAC)
84 Adam St., Cambridge ON N3C 2K6
Tel: 519-651-2812; *Fax:* 519-658-4753
Toll-Free: 800-813-9616
info@sawdac.com
www.sawdac.com
Overview: A small national organization founded in 1988
Mission: To build consumer confidence in our association by delivering high standards of products, installations & business ethics

Sidney & North Saanich Board of Trade *See* Saanich Peninsula Chamber of Commerce

Sidney Lions Food Bank
PO Box 2281, Sidney BC V8L 3S8
Tel: 250-655-0679; *Fax:* 250-655-1130
fdbank@telus.net
www.sidneyfoodbank.com
Overview: A small local organization overseen by Food Banks British Columbia
Mission: To provide food & support to the needy
Member of: Food Banks British Columbia
Finances: Funding Sources: Donations
Chief Officer(s):
Beverley Elder, Administrator

Sierra Club of Canada (SCC) / Sierre club du Canada
#412, 1 Nicholas St., Ottawa ON K1N 7B7
Tel: 613-241-4611; *Fax:* 613-241-2292
Toll-Free: 888-810-4204
info@sierraclub.ca
www.sierraclub.ca
www.facebook.com/sierraclubcanada
twitter.com/SierraClubCan
www.youtube.com/sierraclubcanada
Overview: A medium-sized national charitable organization founded in 1992
Mission: To develop a diverse, well-trained grassroots network, working to protect the integrity of our global ecosystems; To focus on five overriding threats: loss of animal & plant species, deterioration of the planet's oceans & atmosphere, the ever-growing presence of toxic chemicals in all living things, destruction of our remaining wilderness, spiralling population growth & overconsumption
Member of: CANET; Green Budget Coalition; Canadian Renewable Energy Alliance
Affiliation(s): Common Front on the World Trade Organization
Finances: Annual Operating Budget: $500,000-$1.5 Million; *Funding Sources:* Foundations; Governments; Individual donors
Staff Member(s): 20
Membership: Fees: $50 regular; $25 student & senior/fixed income; $125 sustainer; $1,000 lifetime
Activities: Program Areas: Atmosphere & Energy; Health & Environment; Environmental Education; Protecting Biodiversity; Transition to a Sustainable Economy; *Internships:* Yes; *Rents Mailing List:* Yes
Chief Officer(s):
John Bennett, Executive Director
Anowara Baqi, CFO
Tania Beriau, Development Director
Daniel Spence, Director, Communications
Publications:
• The RIO Report [a publication of the Sierra Club of Canada]
Type: Annual Report; *Frequency:* Annually
• SCAN - Sierra Club of Canada Activist News
Type: Newsletter

Atlantic Chapter
#533, 1657 Barrington St., Halifax NS B3J 2A1
Tel: 902-444-3113
atlanticcanadachapter@sierraclub.ca
atlantic.sierraclub.ca
www.facebook.com/sierraatlanticcanada
twitter.com/SierraClubACC
www.youtube.com/sierraclubcanada
Chief Officer(s):
Gretchen Fitzgerald, Director, 902-444-3113
gretchenf@sierraclub.ca

British Columbia Chapter (SCBC)
#301, 2994 Douglas St., Victoria BC V8T 4N4
Tel: 250-386-5255
info@sierraclub.bc.ca
www.sierraclub.bc.ca
www.facebook.com/SierraClubBC
twitter.com/Sierra_BC
www.youtube.com/user/SierraClubofBC
Mission: To explore, enjoy & protect the country's forests, waters, wildlife & wilderness
Member of: Wild Salmon Coalition
Chief Officer(s):
Bob Peart, Executive Director, 250-386-5255 Ext. 249
bob@sierraclub.bc.ca

Ontario Chapter
Evergreen Brickworks, #402, 550 Bayview Ave., Toronto ON M4W 3X8
Tel: 647-336-8744
ontariochapter@sierraclub.on.ca
ontario.sierraclub.ca
Affiliation(s): Sierra Club - USA
Chief Officer(s):
Dan McDermott, Director

Prairie Chapter
10008 - 82nd Ave., 2nd Fl., Edmonton AB T6E 1Z3
Tel: 780-439-1160; *Fax:* 780-485-9640
prairiechapter@sierraclub.ca
prairie.sierraclub.ca
twitter.com/SCPrairie
www.youtube.com/user/sierraprairie?feature=mhum
Mission: Program areas: energy; health communities; protecting biodiversity; training & support
Chief Officer(s):
Eriel Deranger, Chapter Director

Québec Chapter
1222, rue MacKay, Montréal QC H3G 2H4
Tél: 514-651-5847
quebec@sierraclub.ca
quebec.sierraclub.ca
Chief Officer(s):
Claude Martel, Directeur
claudem@sierraclub.ca

Sierra Club of Eastern Canada *See* Sierra Club of Canada

Sierra Legal Defence Fund *See* Ecojustice Canada Society

Sierra Youth Coalition (SYC) / Coalition Jeunesse Sierra
#406, 1 Nicholas St., Ottawa ON K1N 7B7
Tel: 613-241-1615; *Fax:* 613-241-2292
Toll-Free: 888-790-7393
info@syc-cjs.org
www.syc-cjs.org
www.facebook.com/sierrayouthcoalition
twitter.com/sierrayouth
Overview: A medium-sized local organization overseen by Sierra Club of Canada
Mission: To empower young people to become active community leaders who contribute to making Canada a more sustainable society
Finances: Funding Sources: Donations; Membership dues
Membership: 80 colleges & universities; 50 high schools; *Fees:* $12; *Member Profile:* Sierra Club of Canada members 25 or under & students of any age
Chief Officer(s):
Gabriela Rappell, Acting National Director
director@syc-cjs.org

Sierre club du Canada *See* Sierra Club of Canada

SIGMA Canadian Menopause Society
#103, 1089 West Broadway, Vancouver BC V6H 1E5
Tel: 604-736-7267
info@sigmamenopause.com
www.sigmamenopause.com
twitter.com/sigmamenopause
Overview: A medium-sized national organization founded in 2008
Mission: To act as a group of family physicians, specialists & healthcare professionals interested in menopausal & postmenopausal health; To provide educational initiatives & information services to women going through menopause, in order to advance women's health
Membership: Fees: $105; *Member Profile:* Physicians, specialists & healthcare professionals
Chief Officer(s):
Elaine Jolly, OC, MD, FRCSC, President
Christine Derzko, MD, FRCS(C), Vice-President
Nesé Yuksel, B.Sc.Pharm, Pha, Secretary
Michael Fortier, MD, FRCS(C), Treasurer
Chui Kin Yuen, MD, FRCS(C), FA, Executive Director

Sign Association of Canada (SAC) / Association canadienne de l'enseigne (ACE)
#301, 216 Chrislea Rd., Woodbridge ON L4L 8S5
Tel: 905-856-0000; *Fax:* 905-856-0064
Toll-Free: 877-470-9787
info@sac-ace.ca
www.sac-ace.ca
Overview: A small national organization founded in 1954
Mission: To represent & support association members
Member of: International Sign Association (ISA)
Membership: Fees: Schedule available, based upon number of employees or annual gross sales to the sign industry in Canada; *Member Profile:* Sign manufacturing, installation, & maintenance companies; Sign industry suppliers & distributors & trade show exhibitors
Activities: Engaging in advocacy activities; Liaising with governments; Providing referrals to members; Offering educational seminars & training
Chief Officer(s):
Bob Bronk, Executive Director, 416-628-6609
bronk@sac-ace.ca
Perry Brooks, President
perry@sac-ace.ca
Publications:
• Sign Association of Canada Membership Directory
Type: Directory

Atlantic Provinces Chapter
c/o Mattatall Signs, 80 Ilsley Ave., Dartmouth NS B3B 1L3

Tel: 902-468-8222; Fax: 902-468-2451
Chief Officer(s):
Justin Boudreau, Chapter President
jboudreau@mattatall.com
British Columbia Chapter
c/o Colortec, 4175 McConnell Dr., Burnaby BC V5A 3J7
Tel: 604-420-1718; Fax: 604-420-2591
Chief Officer(s):
Carlene Schoock, Chapter President
carlene@colortec.ca
Ontario Chapter
c/o ND Graphics, #1, 55 Interchange Way, Concord ON L4K 5W3
Tel: 416-663-6416; Fax: 416-663-5629
www.signsontario.com
Chief Officer(s):
Fred Elkins, Chapter President
fred@sac-ace.ca
Québec Chapter
#313, 315, Place d'Youville, Montréal QC H2Y 0A4
Tél: 514-876-4176
aqie.ca
www.facebook.com/aqiequebec
www.youtube.com/channel/UCkbJ1tuPGgwNJMI3sBGac3g/
Chief Officer(s):
Denis Barbeau, Président, 450-691-4907
Mélanie Arsenault, Directrice administrative
Saskatchewan Chapter
c/o Wolfecroft Signs, 806A - 43 St. East, Saskatoon SK S7K 3V1
Tel: 306-244-7739; Fax: 306-244-7759
www.sasksignassoc.ca
Chief Officer(s):
Sheldon Rioux, Chapter President
sheldon@sac-ace.ca

Sign Language Interpreters of the National Capital (SLINC)
c/o The Canadian Hearing Society, #600, 2197 Riverside Dr., Ottawa ON K1H 7X3
info@slinc.ca
www.slinc.ca
Overview: A small local organization overseen by Association of Visual Language Interpreters of Canada
Mission: To promote & advance the interpreting profession in the National Capital Region of Canada
Member of: Association of Visual Language Interpreters of Canada (AVLIC)
Chief Officer(s):
Roxanne Whiting, President
president@slinc.ca

Signal Hill
PO Box 45076, RPO Langley Crossing, Langley BC V2Y 0C9
Tel: 604-532-0023; Fax: 604-532-0094
Toll-Free: 877-774-4625
www.thesignalhill.com
www.facebook.com/thesignalhill
twitter.com/TheSignalHill
www.youtube.com/thesignalhill
Overview: A small provincial charitable organization
Mission: To offer education about life issues, women's health, & human rights; To promote the value of human life
Finances: *Funding Sources:* Donations
Staff Member(s): 9
Membership: 11,463
Activities: Offering support to women & families with issues such as unplanned pregnancy, abortion, suicide, & euthanasia; Providing outreach resources
Awards:
• Cecelia Moore Award

Sikh Foundation of Canada
45 Mill St., Toronto ON M5A 3R6
Tel: 416-777-6697; Fax: 416-484-9656
info@sikhfoundationcanada.com
sikhfoundationcanada.com
twitter.com/sikhfdncanada
www.youtube.com/channel/UCkzU4L_9NQtAM3Mr-xrdVJQ
Overview: A small national organization founded in 1999
Mission: To educate & promote greater understanding & appreciation of Sikh history, art & culture among Sikh-Canadians & the community at large
Staff Member(s): 16
Membership: *Member Profile:* All activities open to the general public

Activities: Academic seminars; Rare book, art & culture displays; Film festival
Chief Officer(s):
Davindra Singh, Chairman
Dilprit Grewal, Vice Chairman
Awards:
• The Sikh Foundation Scholarship
Funding to support exceptional students from Ontario to pursue an academic degree at any Canadian University in any program area *Eligibility:* Be of Sikh faith; *Amount:* $5,000 x2

Sik-ooh-kotoki Friendship Society
1709 - 2nd Ave. South, Lethbridge AB T1J 0E8
Tel: 403-328-2414; Fax: 403-327-0087
sikooh@telusplanet.net
anfca.com/friendship-centres/lethbridge
Also Known As: Lethbridge Friendship Centre
Overview: A small local organization founded in 1969 overseen by Alberta Native Friendship Centres Association
Mission: To improve the quality of life for Aboriginal peoples in an urban environment by supporting self-determined activities which encourage equal access to, & participation in Canadian society & which respect & strengthen the increasing emphasis on Aboriginal cultural distinctiveness
Member of: Alberta Native Friendship Centres Association
Finances: *Funding Sources:* Federal & provincial government; Membership dues
Membership: 100-499
Chief Officer(s):
Yolande Weasel Head, Executive Director
yolande.ywh@shaw.ca

Silent Children's Mission
RR#1 16060 Concession 8, Schomberg ON L0G 1T0
Tel: 416-418-0314
silentchildrenca@yahoo.com
www.silentchildrensmission.com
Overview: A small international charitable organization
Mission: To serve impoverished children both internationally & in Canada
Affiliation(s): Archdiocese of Toronto; Canadian Food for Children
Chief Officer(s):
Joan Simone, Founder
Andrew Simone, Chair/Founder

Silent Voice Canada Inc.
#300, 50 St. Clair Ave. East, Toronto ON M4T 1M9
Tel: 416-463-1104; Fax: 416-778-1876; TTY: 416-463-3928
silent.voice@silentvoice.ca
www.silentvoice.ca
www.facebook.com/silentvoice.canada
twitter.com/silentvoiceca
Also Known As: Silent Voice
Overview: A small national charitable organization founded in 1975
Mission: To serve deaf children, deaf youth & adults & their families in the GTA; to improve communication & relationships between the deaf & hearing in families & in our community; to provide services in a sign language environment
Member of: Catholic Charities of the Archdiocese of Toronto
Finances: *Annual Operating Budget:* $500,000-$1.5 Million; *Funding Sources:* Catholic charities; City of Toronto; Individual & corporate donations
Staff Member(s): 11; 130 volunteer(s)
Membership: *Member Profile:* Deaf adults, youth, & their families; *Committees:* Fundraising; Risk/Policy; Governance; Strategic Plan
Activities: *Awareness Events:* Deaf Awareness Day, June; *Library:* by appointment
Chief Officer(s):
Kelly MacKenzie, Executive Director
k.mackenzie@silentvoice.ca
Mike Cyr, Director, Child & Family Services
mikecyr@silentvoice.ca

Silver Trail Chamber of Commerce
PO Box 268, Mayo YT Y0B 1M0
Tel: 867-332-1770
Overview: A small local charitable organization founded in 1977
Finances: *Annual Operating Budget:* Less than $50,000; *Funding Sources:* Government; local businesses
10 volunteer(s)
Membership: 20; *Fees:* $40; *Member Profile:* Local businesses
Activities: Promoting businesses in the region
Chief Officer(s):
Anne Leckie, Secretary

SIM Canada
10 Huntingdale Blvd., Toronto ON M1W 2S5
Tel: 416-497-2424; Fax: 416-497-2444
Toll-Free: 800-294-6918
info@sim.ca
www.sim.ca
www.facebook.com/SIMCANADA1
twitter.com/SIMCANADA1
www.youtube.com/simcanadavideo
Also Known As: Serving In Mission
Previous Name: Society for International Ministries
Overview: A small international organization founded in 1893
Mission: To evangelize the unreached & minister to human need
Finances: *Annual Operating Budget:* $3 Million-$5 Million
Staff Member(s): 30
Membership: 300
Activities: *Speaker Service:* Yes
Chief Officer(s):
John Denbok, Executive Director

Simcoe & District Chamber of Commerce
Chamber Plaza, 95 Queensway West, Simcoe ON N3Y 2M8
Tel: 519-426-5867; Fax: 519-428-7718
www.simcoechamber.on.ca
twitter.com/SimcoeChamber
Overview: A small local organization founded in 1888
Mission: To support public policies that encourage economic development; To promote business
Membership: 350; *Committees:* Economic Development; Education; Government Relations; Membership; Public Relations; Tourism
Chief Officer(s):
Ian Swinton, President
Yvonne Di Pietro, General Manager

Simcoe & District Real Estate Board
191 Queensway West, Simcoe ON N3Y 2M8
Tel: 519-426-4454; Fax: 519-426-9330
www.norfolk-mls.ca
www.facebook.com/sdreb
Overview: A small local organization overseen by Ontario Real Estate Association
Member of: Canadian Real Estate Association
Membership: 140

Simcoe County Historical Association (SCHA)
PO Box 144, Barrie ON L4M 4S9
www.simcoecountyhistory.ca
Previous Name: Simcoe County Pioneer & Historical Society
Overview: A small local organization founded in 1891
Mission: To preserve the past in the present for the future
Member of: Ontario Historical Society
Membership: *Fees:* $15 individual; $20 couple/family; *Member Profile:* Anyone interested in local history
Activities: Public meetings (8/yr); annual meeting; plaque unveilings
Chief Officer(s):
Deb Exel, Treasurer & Chair, Membership
deb@simcoecountyhistory.ca

Simcoe County Jewish Association (SCJA) See Am Shalom

Simcoe County Law Association (SCLA)
Court House, 114 Worsley St., Barrie ON L4M 1M1
Tel: 705-739-6569; Fax: 705-728-8136
simlawlib@bellnet.ca
www.scla.ca
Also Known As: County of Simcoe Law Association
Overview: A small local organization founded in 1890
Membership: 350; *Member Profile:* Lawyers in Simcoe County
Activities: *Library:* Simcoe County Law Library
Chief Officer(s):
Ted Chadderton, President

Simcoe County Literacy Network See Simcoe/Muskoka Literacy Network

Simcoe County Parents of Multiples
Barrie ON
Tel: 705-733-3022
Other Communication: bulletwin@hotmail.com
simcoe@multiplebirthscanada.org
Previous Name: Barrie Parents of Twins and More
Overview: A small local organization overseen by Multiple Births Canada
Mission: Offers support to parents of multiples (and parents-to-be).

Canadian Associations / Simcoe Muskoka Family Connexions

Membership: *Fees:* $40
Chief Officer(s):
Christina Chase-Nugent, Chair

Simcoe County Pioneer & Historical Society *See* Simcoe County Historical Association

Simcoe Muskoka Family Connexions
#7, 60 Bell Farm Rd., Barrie ON L4M 5G6
Tel: 705-726-6587; *Fax:* 705-726-9788
Toll-Free: 800-461-4236
www.simcoecas.com
Merged from: Children's Aid Society of Simcoe County; Family, Youth & Child Services of Muskoka
Overview: A medium-sized local organization
Mission: To provide guidance & counseling to families & protection for children
Finances: *Annual Operating Budget:* Greater than $5 Million
140 volunteer(s)
Chief Officer(s):
Susan Carmichael, Executive Director

Simcoe Women's Wellness Centre Corporation
#232, 80 Bradford St., Barrie ON L4N 6S7
Tel: 705-721-5875; *Fax:* 705-721-5729
swwc@csolve.net
www.angelfire.com/vt2/womenshelter
Overview: A small local charitable organization founded in 1989
Mission: To promote a natural self-help approach to women's physical & emotional well-being; to provide resources including books, workshops & presentations about women's health concerns; to provide a well connected referral service on a local, provincial & national scale
Activities: Workshops; seminars on women issues; *Library:* Open to public

Simcoe/Muskoka Literacy Network (SMLN)
#15, 575 West St. South, Orillia ON L3V 7N6
Tel: 705-326-7227
Toll-Free: 888-518-4788
simcoe.muskoka@literacynetwork.ca
literacynetwork.ca
Previous Name: Simcoe County Literacy Network
Overview: A small local charitable organization founded in 1994
Mission: To provide high-quality, basic skills training
Member of: Ontario Literacy Coalition; Community Literacy of Ontario; Movement for Canadian Literacy
Affiliation(s): Laubach Literacy Ontario
Staff Member(s): 2
Membership: *Member Profile:* Literacy & essential skills training provider within Simcoe County & Muskoka Region
Activities: Literacy services planning; Communications; Outreach & public education; Information & referral service; Clear language consultations; *Library:* Not open to public
Chief Officer(s):
Stephanie Hobbs, Executive Director
sahobbs@literacynetwork.ca
Shari Menard, Administrative Director
shari@literacynetwork.ca

Similkameen Chamber of Commerce
PO Box 490, Keremeos BC V0X 1N0
Tel: 250-499-5225
Overview: A small local organization
Finances: *Funding Sources:* Membership dues
Membership: 8

Similkameen Okanagan Organic Producers Association (SOOPA)
PO Box 577, Keremeos BC V0X 1N0
Tel: 250-499-5381; *Fax:* 250-499-5381
soopa@nethop.net
www.soopa.ca
Overview: A small local organization founded in 1985
Mission: To set & maintain high standards of organic food production; to encourage growers to develop their horticultural skills; to educate consumers & encourage other farmers to begin to use sustainable farming methods
Affiliation(s): Certified Organic Associations of BC
Finances: *Annual Operating Budget:* Less than $50,000
Staff Member(s): 1; 15 volunteer(s)
Membership: 41 certified + 5 transitional + 7 associate; *Fees:* $200 certified & transitional depending on size of farm; $50 associate
Chief Officer(s):
Julie Hinton, Administrator
Guy Villecourt, President

Simmental Association of British Columbia
c/o Jan Wisse, 49420 Yale Rd., Chilliwack BC V2P 6H4
Tel: 604-794-3684
www.simmental.com/bc.htm
Previous Name: British Columbia Simmental Association
Overview: A small provincial organization
Mission: To promote the breeding of Simmental cattle in BC.
Member of: Canadian Simmental Association
Chief Officer(s):
Jan Wisse, Secretary
Lorne Webster, President, 604-823-6797

The Simon Foundation for Continence Canada *See* The Canadian Continence Foundation

Simon Fraser Public Interest Research Group (SFPIRG)
#TC326, Simon Fraser University, Burnaby BC V5A 1S6
Tel: 778-782-4360
info@sfpirg.ca
www.sfpirg.ca
www.facebook.com/sfpirg
twitter.com/sfpirg
Also Known As: SFPIRG
Overview: A large local organization founded in 1981
Mission: To operate as a student funded & directed centre dedicated to environmental & social change
Affiliation(s): Simon Fraser University
Finances: *Annual Operating Budget:* $100,000-$250,000; *Funding Sources:* Student fees
Staff Member(s): 3
Membership: 30,000; *Fees:* Per semester: $3 full-time student; $1.50 part-time student; *Member Profile:* Students of Simon Fraser University, who support the centre through a small fee included in their tuition (students are free to opt out of this fee if they choose); *Committees:* Ancient Forests; Human Resources; Finance; Anti-Oppression; Grants
Activities: Forming Action Groups; Working closely with other student organizations on campus to achieve goals; Advocating for an inclusive & safe space through which to build community on campus; *Internships:* Yes *Library:* Social Justice Lending Library; Open to public
Chief Officer(s):
Craig Pavelich, Director, Communications
communications@sfpirg.ca
Kalamity Hildebrandt, Director, Research & Education
education@sfpirg.ca
Susan Chiv, Director, Administration
admin@sfpirg.ca

Simon Fraser Society for Community Living; Simon Fraser Society for Mentally Handicapped People *See* Kinsight

Simon Fraser University Faculty Association (SFUFA) / Association des professeurs de l'Université Simon Fraser
Simon Fraser University, 8888 University Dr., Burnaby BC V5A 1S6
Tel: 778-782-4676
sfufaea@sfu.ca
www.sfufa.ca
www.facebook.com/585479218143003
twitter.com/SFU_FA
Overview: A small local organization founded in 1965
Mission: To act as the professional association & collective bargaining agent for faculty, librarians & other staff at Simon Fraser University
Member of: Canadian Association of University Teachers; Confederation of Faculty Association of British Columbia
Membership: 500-999; *Committees:* Advisory; Equity; Renewal, Tenure & Promotion (RTP) Advisor; Chief Negotiator
Chief Officer(s):
Brian Green, Executive Director
brian_green@sfu.ca
Jennifer Scott, Officer, Member Services
jascott@sfu.ca
Melanie Lam, Office Manager

Single Parent Association of Newfoundland (SPAN)
PO Box 21421, 472 Logy Bay Rd., St. John's NL A1A 5G6
Tel: 709-738-3401; *Fax:* 709-738-3406
span@spanl.ca
www.envision.ca/webs/span
Overview: A medium-sized provincial charitable organization founded in 1987
Mission: To provide information & referral services to single parents; To offer support & assistance in crisis situations
Finances: *Funding Sources:* Government grants; Public donations
Staff Member(s): 9
Activities: Distributing clothing & food through an outlet; Organizing the Prom Dream Project for single parent families as well as the general public; Offering the Single Parent Employment Support Program; Providing peer support; Operating the Back to School Project to help school-age children of lower income, single parent families; Partnering with businesses & organizations to supply food & gifts at Christmastime; Offering parent effectiveness training; Publishing a cookbook of healthy, low-cost recipes; *Speaker Service:* Yes
Chief Officer(s):
Elaine Balsom, Executive Director
ebalsom@spanl.ca

Single Parents Association of Montréal *See* Single Persons Association of Montréal

Single Persons Association of Montréal / L'Association des Personnes Seules de Montréal (APS)
PO Box 3114, Stn. Lapierre, LaSalle QC H8N 3H2
Tel: 514-366-8600
spasource@bell.net
home.total.net/~spa
Also Known As: SPA Montréal
Previous Name: Single Parents Association of Montréal
Overview: A small local charitable organization founded in 1989
Mission: To support singles & single parents through a wide variety of social, sports & children's activities
Membership: 300; *Fees:* 30$; *Member Profile:* Single people 25 & older

Sioux Lookout Chamber of Commerce
PO Box 577, 11 First Ave. South, Sioux Lookout ON P8T 1A8
Tel: 807-737-1937; *Fax:* 807-737-1778
chamber@siouxlookout.com
www.siouxlookout.com
www.facebook.com/SLKTCC
twitter.com/SLKTCentre
Overview: A small local organization founded in 1919
Mission: To promote Sioux Lookout area business; To contribute to the economic & social development of the area
Member of: Northwestern Ontario Associated Chambers of Commerce
Staff Member(s): 1
Membership: 140
Chief Officer(s):
Alana Vincent, President

Sistering - A Woman's Place
962 Bloor St. West, Toronto ON M6H 1L6
Tel: 416-926-9762; *Fax:* 416-926-1932
info@sistering.org
www.sistering.org
Overview: A small local organization founded in 1981
Mission: Sistering is a women's organization that offers practical & emotional support through programs which enable them to take greater control over their lives. Guided by the principles of Anti-Racism/Anti-Oppression, Sistering works to change social conditions which endanger women's welfare
Finances: *Funding Sources:* Donations
Staff Member(s): 34
Activities: Drop-in centre & outreach program for homeless women; Services in English, Spanish & Mandarin
Chief Officer(s):
Sheryl Lindsay, Executive Director, 416-926-9762 Ext. 226

Sisters Adorers of the Precious Blood / Soeurs Adoratrices du Précieux Sang
301 Ramsay Rd., London ON N6G 1N7
Tel: 519-473-2499; *Fax:* 519-473-6590
www.pbsisters.on.ca
Overview: A small local charitable organization founded in 1861
Chief Officer(s):
Eileen Mary Walsh, General Superior
Carol Forhan, rpb, Formation Director
srcforhan@pbsisters.on.ca

Sisters of Charity of Halifax (SC)
215 Seton Rd., Halifax NS B3M 0C9
Tel: 902-406-8077; *Fax:* 902-457-3506
Toll-Free: 844-406-8114
communications@schalifax.ca
www.schalifax.ca
www.facebook.com/schalifax

Canadian Associations / Skate Canada / Patinage Canada

twitter.com/schalifax
www.instagram.com/schalifax
Overview: A small local organization founded in 1849
Mission: To develop a sensitivity to the oppressed through presence, prayer & ministry to others
Membership: 400
Chief Officer(s):
Carrie Flemming, Advancement Associate
advancement@schalifax.ca
Ruth Jeppesen, Director, Communications

Sisters of Saint Joseph of Pembroke (CSJ)
1127 Pembroke St. West, Pembroke ON K8A 5R3
Tel: 613-732-3694; *Fax:* 613-732-3319
infopembroke@csjcanada.org
www.csjcanada.org
Overview: A small local organization founded in 1921
Mission: The Sisters of St. Joseph of Pembroke are a group of fifty Roman Catholic women religious based in eastern Ontario
Staff Member(s): 30; 5 volunteer(s)
Membership: 1-99

Sisters of Saint Joseph of Peterborough (CSJ)
PO Box 566, Stn. Mount St. Joseph, 1555 Monaghan Rd., Peterborough ON K9J 6Z6
Tel: 705-745-1307; *Fax:* 705-745-1377
infoPeterborough@csjcanada.org
www.csjpeterborough.com
www.facebook.com/112521912120451
twitter.com/CSJCdn
Overview: A small local charitable organization founded in 1890
Mission: To respond to the poor & most needy, particularly where the need is not already met
Membership: 80

Sisters of Saint Joseph of Sault Ste Marie
2025 Main St. West, North Bay ON P1B 2X6
Tel: 705-474-3800; *Fax:* 705-495-3028
stephanie.romiti@gmail.com
www.csjssm.ca
Overview: A small local organization
Mission: Lives & works that all people may be united with God & with one another
Chief Officer(s):
Shirley Anderson, General Superior
sanderson@csjssm.ca

Sisters of Saint Mary of Namur *Voir* Soeurs de Sainte-Marie de Namur

Sisters of St. Benedict (OSB)
225 Masters Ave., Winnipeg MB R4A 2A1
Tel: 204-338-4601; *Fax:* 204-339-8775
stbens@mts.net
www.stbens.ca
Also Known As: Sisters of the Order of St. Benedict
Overview: A small provincial charitable organization founded in 1912
Mission: To witness Jesus Christ, through community life & prayer, contemplative living, hospitality, service to the people of God & stewardship of all God's gifts
Member of: Federation of St. Gertrude
Finances: *Funding Sources:* Donations
Staff Member(s): 35; 30 volunteer(s)
Membership: 33
Activities: Programs in spirituality, personal growth & a variety of retreats; *Library:* St. Benedict's Monastery Library; by appointment
Chief Officer(s):
Virginia Evard, Prioress

Sisters of the Child Jesus (SEJ) / Soeurs de l'Enfant-Jésus
318 Laval St., Coquitlam BC V3K 4W4
Tel: 604-939-7545
dbillesberger@shaw.ca
sistersofthechildjesus.ca
Also Known As: Sisters of Instruction of the Child Jesus
Overview: A small local charitable organization founded in 1667
Mission: To be a presence of love to the Father & to others for the definite purpose of awakening & deepening faith; To enable people to grow in the uniqueness of their person as created by God & to liberate themselves from all that prevents their being truly human; To bring hope & direction to contemporaries; To be at the service of the least favoured, the marginalized & those who have no voice in society
Chief Officer(s):

Catherine Machell, President
Denece Billesberger, Secretary & Treasurer

Sisters of the Sacred Heart of Ragusa / Suore del Sacro Cuore di Ragusa
1 Edward St., Welland ON L3C 5H2
Tel: 905-732-4542
sacredhe@hotmail.com
www.sacredheartsisters.ca
Overview: A small local charitable organization founded in 1889
Mission: To live an apostolic life in the church & society through the works of beneficence among the poor & needy; To instruct & educate youth; To collaborate in parish pastoral work, especially through the teaching of catechism
Membership: 500-999
Activities: Day care, schools, orphanages & retirement homes for the elderly; Parish work; Home visits; Missions; Nursing

Sivananda Ashram Yoga Camp
673 8e av, Val Morin QC J0T 2R0
Tel: 819-322-3226
Toll-Free: 800-263-9642
hq@sivananda.org
www.sivananda.org
www.facebook.com/SivanandaYogaCamp
twitter.com/sivanandacamp
Previous Name: Yoga Vedanta Centre
Overview: A small international charitable organization founded in 1963
Mission: To practice classical Indian yoga
Member of: International Sivananda Yoga Vedanta Centres
Finances: *Funding Sources:* Private donations
Activities: Daily classes; teachers' training course; Thai yoga massage certification course

Centre Sivananda de Yoga Vedanta de Montréal
5178, boul St-Laurent, Montréal QC H2T 1R8
Tél: 514-279-3545
montreal@sivananda.org
www.sivananda.org/montreal
www.facebook.com/sivanandayogamontreal

Sivananda Yoga Vedanta Centre
77 Harbord St., Toronto ON M5S 1G4
Tel: 416-966-9642
toronto@sivananda.org
www.sivananda.org/toronto
www.facebook.com/sivanandatoronto
twitter.com/sivanandatoronto

69'ers Club of Coombs *See* Parksville & District Rock & Gem Club

Sjögren's Syndrome Association *See* Association du Syndrome de Sjogren, Inc

Skate Canada / Patinage Canada
PO Box 15, #261, 1200 St. Laurent Blvd., Ottawa ON K1K 3B8
Tel: 613-747-1007; *Fax:* 613-748-5718
Toll-Free: 888-747-2372
info@skatecanada.ca
www.skatecanada.ca
www.facebook.com/skatecanada
twitter.com/SkateCanada
Also Known As: Canadian Figure Skating Association
Overview: A large national licensing charitable organization founded in 1914
Mission: To enable all Canadians to participate in skating throughout their lifetime for fun, fitness, & achievement
Member of: International Skating Union
Finances: *Funding Sources:* User fees; Television events; Marketing; Membership fees
Staff Member(s): 50
Membership: *Committees:* CEO Operational Review; Governance; External Relations; Membership Policy; Finance & Risk Management; Athlete Fund & Alumni; Officials Development; Coaching Development; Sections Coordinating; Hall of Fame & Heritage; High Performance Development; Officials Assignment & Promotion; Skating Programs Development; Strategic Planning Steering
Activities: *Speaker Service:* Yes
Chief Officer(s):
Debra Armstrong, CEO
Terry Sheahan, Senior Director, Marketing & Events
Jeff Patrick, Director, Corporate Services
Norm Proft, Director, Member Services
Mike Slipchuk, Director, High Performance

Alberta/NWT/Nunavut Section
11759 Groat Rd., Edmonton AB T5M 3K6

Tel: 780-415-0465; *Fax:* 780-427-1734
Toll-Free: 866-294-0663
info@skateabnwtnun.com
www.skateabnwtnun.com
www.facebook.com/skateabnwtnun
twitter.com/SkateAB_NWT_NUN
Chief Officer(s):
Jessica Crighton, Coordinator, Communications & Events
jessica@skateabnwtnun.ca

British Columbia/Yukon Section
#2, 6501 Sprott St., Burnaby BC V5B 3B8
Fax: 604-205-6962
Toll-Free: 888-752-8322
www.skatinginbc.ca
www.facebook.com/172540199441743
twitter.com/SkateBCYT
Chief Officer(s):
Ted Barton, Executive Director
ted.b@attglobal.net

Central Ontario Section
111 Snidercroft Rd., #A, Concord ON L4K 2J8
Tel: 905-760-9100; *Fax:* 905-760-9104
Toll-Free: 877-267-0081
www.skatecanada-centralontario.com
Chief Officer(s):
Gary B. Oswald, Executive Director
gary@skatecanada-centralontario.com

Eastern Ontario Section
PO Box 2209, 276 King St. West, Prescott ON K0E 1T0
Tel: 613-925-1441; *Fax:* 613-925-1314
administrator@skate-eos.on.ca
www.skate-eos.on.ca
www.facebook.com/114053658638501
Mission: EO administrates figure skating clubs in Ontario, southeast of a line from Severn Bridge to Point Alexander on the Ottawa River, following the Ontario border along the Ottawa River to the St. Lawrence River and Lake Ontario, to the eastern boundary of Ajax and north to Atherly and Severn Bridge. The section's clubs (90+) offer a variety of programs to their members (over 10,000): Learn to Skate & Recreational programs - CanSkate, CanPowerSkate; Figure Skating - STARSkate, CompetitiveSkate, Skating Development, CollegiateSkate; Adult Skating - AdultSkate; Synchronized Skating: Festival SynchroSkate. The clubs showcase their skaters with Carnivals, Ice Shows, and Exhibitions which are normally held at the end of the skating season. The section hosts competitions, offers seminars, clinics and camps for the skaters as well as training for coaches, judges & officials.
Chief Officer(s):
Barbara Hough, Office Administrator

Fédération de patinage artistique du Québec
4545, av Pierre-De-Doubertin, Montréal QC H1V 0B2
Tel: 514-252-3073; *Fax:* 514-252-3170
patinage@patinage.qc.ca
www.patinage.qc.ca
www.facebook.com/patinageqc
Chief Officer(s):
Any-Claude Dion, Directrice générale
acdion@patinage.qc.ca

Manitoba Section
145 Pacific Ave., Winnipeg MB R3B 2Z6
Tel: 204-925-5707; *Fax:* 204-925-5924
skate.admin@sportmanitoba.ca
www.mbskates.ca
Chief Officer(s):
Shauna Marling, Executive Director
skate.exec@sportmanitoba.ca

New Brunswick Section
#4, 299 Champlain St., Dieppe NB E1A 1P2
Tel: 506-855-1751; *Fax:* 506-855-1723
www.skatenb.org
Chief Officer(s):
Lise Auffrey-Arsenault, Executive Director
executivedirector@skatenb.org

Newfoundland/Labrador Section
1296A Kenmount Rd., Paradise NL A1L 1N3
Tel: 709-576-0509; *Fax:* 709-576-0549
skating@sportnl.ca
www.skating.nf.ca
twitter.com/SkateCanada_NL
Chief Officer(s):
Lori Brett, Executive Director

Canadian Associations / Skate Ontario

Northern Ontario Section
PO Box 130, #3, 6 Main St., Callander ON P0H 1H0
Tel: 705-752-4803; *Fax:* 705-752-5977
office@scno.net
www.scno.net
www.facebook.com/SkateCanadaNO
twitter.com/SkateCanadaNO
Chief Officer(s):
Traci Fong, Chair
chair@scno.net

Nova Scotia Section
5516 Spring Garden Rd., 4th Fl., Halifax NS B3J 3G6
Tel: 902-425-5450; *Fax:* 902-425-5606
skatecanadans@sportnovascotia.ca
www.skatecanada.ns.ca
Chief Officer(s):
Jill Knowles, Executive Director

Prince Edward Island Section
40 Enman Cres., Charlottetown PE C1E 1E6
Tel: 902-368-4985; *Fax:* 902-368-4548
skatecanadapei.ca
Chief Officer(s):
Mike Connolly, Executive Director
mconnolly@sportpei.pe.ca

Saskatchewan Section
2205 Victoria Ave., Regina SK S4P 0S4
Tel: 306-780-9245
sk.skate@sasktel.net
www.skatecanadasaskatchewan.com
Chief Officer(s):
Danielle Shaw, Executive Director

Western Ontario Section
237 Consortium Ct., London ON N6E 2S8
Tel: 519-686-0431; *Fax:* 519-686-0593
memberservice@skating-wos.on.ca
www.skating-wos.on.ca
www.facebook.com/SkateCanadaWesternOntario
Chief Officer(s):
Steve Scherrer, Chair
scherrer@rogers.com

Skate Ontario
#100, 2605 Skymark Ave., Mississauga ON L4W 4L5
Tel: 905-212-9991
www.skateontario.org
www.facebook.com/SkateOntario
twitter.com/SkateOntario
Also Known As: Ontario Figure Skating Association
Overview: A small provincial organization founded in 1982
Mission: To enable every citizen of the province to participate in skating through out his/her lifetime for fun &/or achievement
Membership: 75,000; *Member Profile:* Competitive & recreational skaters as well as coaches & officials; *Committees:* Events; Programs; Technical; Transition
Chief Officer(s):
Lisa Alexander, Executive Director

Skeena Valley Naturalists
1677 Lupine St., Terrace BC V8G 0G1
Tel: 250-798-2535
weena@telus.net
Overview: A small local organization
Membership: 10; *Fees:* $15
Activities: Birdwatching; *Awareness Events:* Christmas Bird Count
Chief Officer(s):
Judy Chrysler, Director

Skeptics Canada *See* Association for Science & Reason

Ski de fond Canada *See* Cross Country Canada

Ski de fond Nouveau-Brunswick *See* Cross Country New Brunswick

Ski de fond Québec
157-F, rue Principale, St-Sauveur QC J0R 1R6
Tél: 450-745-0858
info@skidefondquebec.ca
www.skidefondquebec.ca
www.facebook.com/skidefondquebec
twitter.com/skidefondquebec
www.youtube.com/user/skidefondquebec
Aperçu: *Dimension:* petite; *Envergure:* provinciale surveillé par Cross Country Canada
Membre de: Cross Country Canada
Membre(s) du bureau directeur:
Sylvie Halou, Directrice générale
sylviahalou@skidefondquebec.ca

Ski Hawks Ottawa (SHO)
Canadian Association for Disabled Skiing - National Capital Division, 1216 Bordeau Grove, Ottawa ON K1C 2M7
Tel: 613-222-7718
www.cads-ncd.ca/?page_id=183
Overview: A small local charitable organization founded in 1985
Mission: To promote safe & enjoyable skiing & boarding experiences for the visually impaired community
Member of: Canadian Association of Disabled Skiing - National Capital Division (CADS-NCD)
Finances: *Annual Operating Budget:* Less than $50,000; *Funding Sources:* Private; Registration fees
55 volunteer(s)
Membership: 1,000+; *Fees:* $30; *Member Profile:* Visually impaired skiers & snowboarders, aged 8 to 88, in all ability levels
Activities: Offering an alpine ski program for children, adults & seniors
Chief Officer(s):
Carolyn Mitrow, President
cmitrow@gmail.com

Ski Jumping Canada (SJC) / Canada Saut à Ski
#418, 305 - 4625 Varsity Dr. NW, Calgary AB T3A 0Z9
www.skijumpingcanada.com
www.facebook.com/SkiJumpingCanada
Overview: A small national organization
Mission: To be the national governing body for the sport of ski jumping in Canada, alongside Nordic Combined Ski Canada.
Chief Officer(s):
Tom Reid, Chair
tomreid@skijumpingcanada.com

Ski nautique et planche Canada *See* Water Ski & Wakeboard Canada

Ski Québec alpin (SQA)
4545, av Pierre-de Coubertin, Montréal QC H1V 3R2
Tél: 514-252-3089; *Téléc:* 514-252-5282
www.skiquebec.qc.ca
www.facebook.com/skiqcalpin
twitter.com/SkiQuebecAlpin
www.youtube.com/channel/UCVQGzGbkN8J3tuPQD5WXIOw
Également appelé: Cross Country Québec
Aperçu: *Dimension:* moyenne; *Envergure:* provinciale; fondée en 1967
Mission: D'organiser et de gérer le ski alpin et concours
Membre de: Cross Country Canada
Membre(s) du personnel: 7
Membre: *Comités:* Haute Performance; Officiels
Membre(s) du bureau directeur:
Daniel Paul Lavallée, Directeur général, 514-252-3089 Ext. 3564
daniel@skiquebec.qc.ca
Éric Préfontaine, Directeur athlétique, 514-252-3089 Ext. 3621
eprefontaine@skiquebec.qc.ca
Sylvie Grenier, Responsable, Services comptables, 514-252-3089 Ext. 3565
comptabilité@skiquebec.qc.ca
Anthony Lamour, Responsable, Communications et du service aux partenaires, 514-252-3090
alamour@skiquebec.qc.ca

Skills Canada *See* Skills/Compétences Canada

Skills Canada / Compétences Canada
#201, 294 Albert St., Ottawa ON K1P 6E6
Tel: 343-883-7545; *Fax:* 613-691-1404
Toll-Free: 877-754-5226
skillscompetencescanada.com
www.facebook.com/skillscanada
twitter.com/Skills_Canada
www.youtube.com/user/SkillsCanadaOfficial
Overview: A medium-sized national organization
Mission: Actively promotes careers in skilled trades and technologies to Canadian youth.
Member of: World Skills International
Finances: *Funding Sources:* Public & private sponsorship
Staff Member(s): 14
Chief Officer(s):
Shaun Thorson, Chief Executive Officer
shaunt@skillscanada.com

Skills for Change (SfC)
791 St. Clair Ave. West, Toronto ON M6C 1B7
Tel: 416-658-3101; *Fax:* 416-658-6292
www.skillsforchange.org
www.linkedin.com/company/skills-for-change
www.facebook.com/SkillsforChange
twitter.com/skillsforchange
www.youtube.com/user/skillsforchange
Overview: A small local charitable organization founded in 1983
Mission: To provide services & training to immigrants & refugees to enter the Canadian workplace; To provide information & assistance to internationally-qualified professionals to enable them to find employment in their area of specialization
Member of: ONESTEP; Canadian Centre for Philanthropy; Ontario Council of Agencies Serving Immigrants; Advocates for Community Based Training & Education for Women
Affiliation(s): Access to Professions & Trades; Women in Information Technology
Finances: *Annual Operating Budget:* $3 Million-$5 Million; *Funding Sources:* United Way Toronto; Federal, provincial & municipal governments
Staff Member(s): 45; 60 volunteer(s)
Membership: 60; *Fees:* $10 individual; $20 groups/organizations; $250 corporate; *Committees:* Finance; Human Resources; Real Estate/Planning; Risk Management; Fundraising; Governance; Marketing/Communications; Strategic Planning
Activities: *Awareness Events:* diversity@work, Nov. *Library:* Employment Resource Centre; Open to public
Chief Officer(s):
Surranna Sandy, CEO
ssandy@skillsforchange.org
Awards:
• Pioneers for Change Awards

Skills Unlimited (SKILLS)
201 Scott St., Winnipeg MB R3L 0L4
Tel: 204-474-2443
Overview: A small local charitable organization founded in 1962
Mission: To train & assist in finding employment for persons living with vocational disabilities
Affiliation(s): Winnipeg Chamber of Commerce
Activities: Centre of Learning providing quality vocational rehabilitation services; Skills Manufacturing, a private non-profit manufacturing facility employing handicapped people
Chief Officer(s):
Ron Fortier, Contact

Skills/Compétences Canada
#201, 294 Albert St., Ottawa ON K1P 6E6
Fax: 613-691-1404
Toll-Free: 877-754-5226
www.skillscanada.com
www.facebook.com/skillscanada
twitter.com/Skills_Canada
www.youtube.com/user/SkillsCanadaOfficial
Previous Name: Skills Canada
Overview: A medium-sized national organization founded in 1989
Mission: To encourage & support a coordinated approach in promoting skilled trades & technologies to Canadian youth
Staff Member(s): 15
Membership: 13 provincial/territorial organizations
Activities: *Awareness Events:* Canadian Skills Competition, May; World Skills Competition International, Aug.
Chief Officer(s):
John Oates, President
Shaun Thorson, Chief Executive Officer, 343-883-7545 Ext. 503
shaunt@skillscanada.com
Karine R. Dupuis, Director, Communications, 343-883-7545 Ext. 506
karined@skillscanada.com
Gail Vent, Director, Business Development, 343-883-7545 Ext. 507
gailv@skillscanada.com
Awards:
• Canadian Skills Competition
Awarded annually; is an olympic-style skills competition in over 40 skilled trades, technology & leadership contests, representing 6 industry sectors, designed to test skills required in technology & trade occupations; allows students access to newest technologies & communicate with industry experts who serve as mentors *Eligibility:* Students compete at the local, regional & provincial levels to win the right to represent their province at the national level; *Amount:* Gold, silver & bronze medals
Alberta
17424 - 111th Ave., Edmonton AB T5S 0A2
Tel: 780-702-6851; *Fax:* 780-429-0009
alberta@skillsalberta.com
www.skillsalberta.com

www.facebook.com/SkillsCanadaAlberta
twitter.com/skillsalberta
www.youtube.com/user/skillsalberta
Chief Officer(s):
Chris Browton, Executive Director, 780-910-6068
chrisb@skillscanada.com
British Columbia
3777 Kingsway, Vancouver BC V5H 3Z7
Tel: 604-432-4229; Fax: 604-433-1241
bc@skillscanada.com
www.skillscanada.bc.ca
www.facebook.com/28602593007
twitter.com/skillsbc
www.youtube.com/user/SkillsCanadaBC
Chief Officer(s):
Elaine Allan, Executive Director
Manitoba
#31, 1313 Border St., Winnipeg MB R3H 0X4
Tel: 204-927-0250; Fax: 204-927-0258
skillsmb@skillscanada.com
www.skillsmanitoba.ca
www.facebook.com/skillscanadamanitoba
twitter.com/SkillsManitoba
www.youtube.com/user/SkillsManitoba
Chief Officer(s):
Maria Pacella, Executive Director
mariapa@skillscanada.com
New Brunswick
#426, 527 Beaverbrook Ct., Fredericton NB E3B 1X6
Tel: 506-457-2762; Fax: 506-453-5317
newbrunswick@skillscanada.com
www.skillscanada.nb.ca
www.facebook.com/232663270114132
twitter.com/SkillsCanadaNB
Chief Officer(s):
Luc Morin, Executive Director
Newfoundland & Labrador
Town Square, 75 Barbour Dr., 2nd Fl., Mount Pearl NL A1N 2X3
Tel: 709-739-4172; Fax: 709-739-4198
newfoundland@skillscanada.com
www.skillscanada-nfld.com
www.facebook.com/skillscanadanewfoundlandandlabrador
twitter.com/Skills_NL
www.youtube.com/SkillsCanadaNL
Chief Officer(s):
Carole Ann Ryan, Executive Director
Northwest Territories
PO Box 1403, 5011 – 44th St., Yellowknife NT X1A 2P1
Tel: 867-873-8743; Fax: 867-873-8197
skillsnt@skillscanada.com
skillscanadanwt.org
www.facebook.com/skillsnt
twitter.com/skillsnt
www.youtube.com/user/skillsnt
Chief Officer(s):
Ali Kincaid, Executive Director
ali@skillscanadanwt.org
Nova Scotia
#7B, 800A Windmill Rd., Dartmouth NS B3B 1L1
Tel: 902-491-4640; Fax: 902-428-0112
info@skillsns.ca
skillsns.ca
www.facebook.com/SkillsNS
twitter.com/Skills_NS
www.youtube.com/channel/UCGwYvar8WCxD2neFGty8lSw
Chief Officer(s):
Robin Lorway, Acting Executive Director, 902-491-3598
robinlorway@skillsns.ca
Nunavut
PO Box 176, 501 Queen Elizabeth Way, Iqaluit NU X0A 0H0
Tel: 867-979-5281; Fax: 867-979-4380
www.skillsnunavut.ca
www.facebook.com/SkillsCanNu
twitter.com/skillsnunavut
Chief Officer(s):
Janis Devereaux, Executive Director, 867-979-5281 Ext. 1432
janisd@skillscanada.com
Ontario
#7A, 60 Northland Rd., Waterloo ON N2V 2B8
Tel: 519-749-9899; Fax: 519-749-6322
Toll-Free: 888-228-5446
info@skillsontario.com
www.skillsontario.com

www.facebook.com/skillsontario
twitter.com/skillsontario
www.youtube.com/user/SkillsOntario
Chief Officer(s):
Stephanie Roth, Director, Operations, 519-749-9899 Ext. 240
sroth@skillsontario.com
Prince Edward Island
140 Weymouth St., Charlottetown PE C1A 4Z1
Tel: 902-566-9352; Fax: 902-566-9505
www.skillscanada.pe.ca
www.facebook.com/skillscanadapei
Chief Officer(s):
Tawna MacLeod, Executive Director
tmacleod@hollandcollege.com
Compétences Québec
#30, 190, rue Dorchester, Québec QC G1K 9M6
Tel: 418-646-3534; Fax: 418-643-6336
info@competencesquebec.com
www.competencesquebec.com
www.facebook.com/competencesquebec
twitter.com/Competencesqc
Saskatchewan
2911D Cleveland Ave., Saskatoon SK S7K 8A9
Tel: 306-373-6035; Fax: 306-373-6036
www.skillscanadasask.com
www.facebook.com/418492594887726
twitter.com/SkillsCanSask
Chief Officer(s):
Al Gabert, Executive Director
alg@skillscanada.com
Yukon
108 Lambert St., Whitehorse YT Y1A 1Z2
Tel: 867-668-2736; Fax: 867-668-2704
skillscanada@northwestel.net
www.skillsyukon.com
www.facebook.com/SkillsCanadaYukon
twitter.com/SkillsCanadaYT
Chief Officer(s):
Tracy Erman, Executive Director

Skookum Jim Friendship Centre
3159 - 3rd Ave., Whitehorse YT Y1A 1G1
Tel: 867-633-7680; Fax: 867-668-4460
sjfcfriends@northwestel.net
www.skookumjim.com
www.facebook.com/skookumjimfriendshipcentre
vimeo.com/user5226474
Overview: A small local organization founded in 1962 overseen by National Association of Friendship Centres
Mission: Committed to a vision of bettering the spiritual, emotional, mental & physical well being of First Nations peoples, fostering the way of Friendship & understanding between people
Staff Member(s): 21
Activities: Diversion Program; Prenatal Nutrition Outreach Program; Recreation Program; Traditional Training Program; Urban Multipurpose Aboriginal Youth Centre
Chief Officer(s):
Marney Paradis, Executive Director, 867-633-7687
sjfcexecutive@northwestel.net

SkyWorks Charitable Foundation
566 Palmerston Ave., Toronto ON M6G 2P7
www.skyworksfoundation.org
www.linkedin.com/company/1174113
www.facebook.com/237837822956251
twitter.com/skyworksorg
Overview: A small national charitable organization founded in 1983
Mission: To operate as a non-profit educational documentary production organization; To produce documentary films that deal with contemporary social issues & are designed to encourage audiences to see the value of their own experiences & to take action on their own behalf
Finances: Annual Operating Budget: $250,000-$500,000
Staff Member(s): 3; 15 volunteer(s)
Activities: Producing documentaries to raise questions, stimulate discussion & encourage audience participation in social & community process; Speaker Service: Yes; Library: Film Library
Chief Officer(s):
Laura Sky, Executive Director
laurasky@skyworksfoundation.org

Slave Lake & District Chamber of Commerce
PO Box 190, Slave Lake AB T0G 2A0

Tel: 780-849-3222; Fax: 780-849-6894
sldcc@telus.net
www.slavelakechamber.com
www.facebook.com/793499557423063
Overview: A small local organization
Mission: To serve & promote area businesses through advocacy & facilitation
Member of: Alberta Chamber of Commerce
Finances: Funding Sources: Municipal grant; membership fees; projects
Staff Member(s): 1; 15 volunteer(s)
Membership: 130+; Fees: Schedule available
Chief Officer(s):
Laurie Renauer, Executive Director

Slave Lake Native Friendship Centre
416 - 6 Ave., Slave Lake AB T0G 2A2
Tel: 780-849-3039; Fax: 780-849-2402
Other Communication: Alt. E-mail: slnfced@gmail.com
slnfc2@gmail.com
anfca.com/friendship-centres/slave-lake
Overview: A small local organization founded in 1972 overseen by Alberta Native Friendship Centres Association
Mission: To be a leader in the community by implementing new programs/services that will serve the needs of the Aboriginal people in order to improve their self-reliance & well being
Member of: Alberta Native Friendship Centres Association
Chief Officer(s):
Jamie Linington, Executive Director

Sledge Hockey of Canada (SHOC)
c/o Hockey Canada, #N204, 801 King Edward Ave., Ottawa ON K1N 6N5
Tel: 613-562-5677; Fax: 613-562-5676
www.hockeycanada.ca
www.facebook.com/HCSledge
twitter.com/HC_Sledge
www.youtube.com/hcsledge
Overview: A small national organization
Mission: To promote & govern the sport of sledge hockey in Canada

Sleeping Children Around the World (SCAW)
28 Pinehurst Cres., Toronto ON M9A 3A5
Tel: 416-231-1841; Fax: 416-231-0120
Toll-Free: 866-321-1841
www.scaw.org
Overview: A small local charitable organization founded in 1970
Mission: To raise funds to provide bedkits for needy children in underdeveloped & developing countries (each bedkit consists of items such as a groundsheet, mattress, sheets, pyjamas, blanket or mosquito netting, sweater or other clothing, personal care items); 100% volunteer, both at its Canadian base & overseas
Chief Officer(s):
Linda Webb, Executive Director

Slocan District Chamber of Commerce (SDCC)
PO Box 448, New Denver BC V0G 1S0
chamber@slocanlake.com
slocanlakechamber.com
www.linkedin.com/groups?home=&gid=4726589
Overview: A small local organization founded in 1911
Mission: To represent & advocate on behalf of its members; To build a strong economy for the Slocan Lake district
Staff Member(s): 1
Membership: 147; Fees: $35 individual/non-profit; $60 business
Chief Officer(s):
Jessica Rayner, Manager

Slo-Pitch Ontario Association (SPO)
#7, 8 Hiscott St., St Catharines ON L2R 1C6
Tel: 905-646-7773; Fax: 905-646-8431
spoa@slopitch.org
www.slopitch.org
www.facebook.com/172816356093689
twitter.com/slopitchontario
www.youtube.com/user/slopitchontario
Overview: A medium-sized provincial organization founded in 1982 overseen by Softball Ontario
Mission: To institute & regulate slo-pitch softball in Ontario
Member of: Canadian Amateur Softball Association; Softball Ontario
Finances: Funding Sources: Sponsors; Partners; Government grants; Team fees
Membership: Fees: Schedule available; Member Profile: Slo-pitch teams & leagues in Ontario

Canadian Associations / Slow Food Canada

Chief Officer(s):
Tom Buchan, CEO
tbuchan@slopitch.org
Ron Hawthorne, President, 613-831-8393
rhawthorne@slopitch.info

Slow Food Canada
Toll-Free: 866-266-6661
info@slowfood.ca
www.slowfood.ca
www.facebook.com/slowfoodcanada
twitter.com/SlowFoodCanada
Overview: A small national organization founded in 1989
Mission: To protect pleasures of the table from the homogenization of modern fast food & life
Member of: Slow Food International
Membership: 18 convivia; 600+ members; *Fees:* $40-$310
Activities: Convivia in Alberta, British Columbia, Ontario, Québec, Nova Scotia & Yukon
Chief Officer(s):
Heather Pritchard, Chair

Small Business Association (SBA)
Ottawa ON
Tel: 613-627-4318
info@sba-canada.ca
sba-canada.ca
www.linkedin.com/company/small-business-association-canada
www.facebook.com/SBACanada
twitter.com/sbacanada
Previous Name: Home Business Association of the National Capital Region
Overview: A small local organization founded in 1996
Mission: To facilitate networking & reduce isolation; To facilitate self-education, business development, growth, & sustainability; To become a public voice for self-employed entrepreneurs in the area
Finances: *Annual Operating Budget:* Less than $50,000; *Funding Sources:* Membership fees; donations; sponsorship
Staff Member(s): 6; 22 volunteer(s)
Membership: 200+; *Fees:* $150; *Member Profile:* Self-employed & working from home or small office; *Committees:* Information Technology; Communications; Newsletter; Trade Show; Seminar; Public Relations; Membership
Activities: Seminars; trade shows; newsletters; networking breakfasts; mentoring program; *Speaker Service:* Yes

Small Business Centre (SBC)
316 Rectory St., 3rd Fl., London ON N5W 3V9
Tel: 519-659-2882; *Fax:* 519-659-7050
info@sbcentre.ca
www.sbcentre.ca
www.facebook.com/SBCLondon
twitter.com/sbclondon
www.youtube.com/user/SBCLondon
Overview: A small local organization founded in 1986
Mission: To actively contribute to the economonic development of London by supporting local entrepreneurs & small businesses
Finances: *Funding Sources:* Municipal, provincial & federal governments
Activities: Offering seminars, workshops, Summer Company program, SEED program, Ontario Works program, Self Employment Benefit program, & online resources; *Library:* Resource Centre
Chief Officer(s):
Steve Pellarin, Executive Director
spellarin@sbcentre.ca

Small Explorers & Producers Association of Canada *See* Explorers & Producers Association of Canada

Small Investor Protection Association (SIPA)
PO Box 24008, Stratford PE C1B 2V5
Tel: 416-614-9128
sipa.toronto@sipa.ca
www.sipa.ca
Overview: A small national organization founded in 1999
Mission: To advocate on behalf of small investors in Canada
Finances: *Funding Sources:* Membership fees; private donations
Membership: 600+
Activities: Reports & submissions to government & regulators; *Library:* SIPA Library; Open to public
Chief Officer(s):
Stan I. Buell, President

Publications:
• SIPA [Small Investor Protection Association] Sentinel
Type: Newsletter; *Frequency:* bi-m.

Small Water Users Association of BC
PO Box 187, Balfour BC V0G 1C0
Tel: 250-229-5704
smallwaterusers@shaw.ca
www.smallwaterusers.com
Overview: A small provincial organization founded in 2003
Mission: To foster cooperation & information sharing amongst small water systems throughout BC in order to improve system operations & reduce costs; To represent the interests & concerns of small water systems
Membership: 258; *Fees:* $35 basic fee (+$1 per connection); $90 affiliate
Chief Officer(s):
Denny Ross-Smith, Executive Director

Smart Commute
c/o Metrolinx, #600, 20 Bay St., Toronto ON M5J 2W3
Tel: 416-874-5900; *Fax:* 416-869-1794
info@smartcommute.ca
www.smartcommute.ca
www.facebook.com/SmartCommuter
twitter.com/SmartCommute
www.youtube.com/user/smartcommuteGTAH
Overview: A small local organization
Mission: To reduce the stress on our lives, roads & environment; to reduce traffic congestion & to take action on climate change through transportation efficiency
Finances: *Annual Operating Budget:* $500,000-$1.5 Million; *Funding Sources:* Transport Canada; Greater Toronto Area Municipalities
Membership: 100-499
Activities: *Awareness Events:* Bike to Work Day, May
Chief Officer(s):
Aubrey Iwaniw, Acting Manager
Aubrey.Iwaniw@metrolinx.com

Smart Serve Ontario
#105, 5405 Eglinton Ave. West, Toronto ON M9C 5K6
Tel: 416-695-8737; *Fax:* 416-695-0684
Toll-Free: 877-620-6082
info@smartserve.ca
www.smartserve.ca
www.facebook.com/SmartServeOntario
twitter.com/smartserve
Overview: A medium-sized provincial organization founded in 1995
Mission: To develop & deliver responsible server training to all individuals who serve alcohol beverages or work where alcohol beverages are served in the province of Ontario
Finances: *Funding Sources:* Government grants
Activities: Officially delivers the Responsible Beverage Service Training Program for the Ontario hospitality industry
Chief Officer(s):
Richard Anderson, Executive Director
Ellie Johnson, Manager, Operations

Smith-Ennismore Historical Society
PO Box 41, Bridgenorth ON K0L 1H0
Tel: 705-292-9430
sehs@sehs.on.ca
www.sehs.on.ca
Previous Name: Smith-Ennismore Township Historical Society
Overview: A small local charitable organization founded in 1983
Mission: To collect, preserve & exhibit material for the study of history & genealogy, especially the history & families of Smith-Ennismore-Lakefield; to locate & preserve historical sites in the area; to provide access to all available information to all ages; to assist families in research of their land & roots; to assist school students in research; to provide bus trips to historical sites & attractions in Central Ontario; to be involved & voice concern on environmental issues
Member of: Ontario Historical Society
Membership: *Fees:* $30 couple; $20 single
Activities: Monthly meetings; Jan. install new executive; *Library:* Smith-Ennismore Heritage Resource Centre
Awards:
• Community Citizen

Smith-Ennismore Township Historical Society *See* Smith-Ennismore Historical Society

Smithers Community Services Association (SCSA)
PO Box 3759, 3815-B Railway Ave., Smithers BC V0J 2N0

Tel: 250-847-9515
Toll-Free: 888-355-6222
general@scsa.ca
www.scsa.ca
www.facebook.com/298672643483861
Overview: A small local charitable organization founded in 1973
Mission: To provide services that enhance the quality of life; To promote equal opportunity for all people within the community
Member of: British Columbia Association for Community Living; BC Non-Profit Housing Association; BC Council for Families
Finances: *Annual Operating Budget:* $1.5 Million-$3 Million
Staff Member(s): 40; 100 volunteer(s)
Membership: 50; *Fees:* $2 annual; $20 lifetime
Chief Officer(s):
Corol Johnson, Chair
Cathryn Olmstead, Executive Director
colmstead@scsa.ca

Smithers District Chamber of Commerce
PO Box 2379, Smithers BC V0J 2N0
Tel: 250-847-5072; *Fax:* 250-847-3337
Toll-Free: 800-542-6673
info@smitherschamber.com
www.smitherschamber.com
Overview: A small local organization founded in 1923
Mission: To be the voice of business in the community; To lead members & provide services
Member of: BC Chamber of Commerce; Canadian Chamber of Commerce
Affiliation(s): Northern BC Tourism Association
Finances: *Annual Operating Budget:* $100,000-$250,000; *Funding Sources:* Membership fees; Fee for services; Tourism BC; HRDC
Staff Member(s): 2; 14 volunteer(s)
Membership: 9 individual + 196 corporate; *Fees:* Based on number of employees; *Committees:* Business Development; Finance; Operations; Member Services
Activities: *Library:*
Chief Officer(s):
Heather Gallagher, Manager
heather@smitherschamber.com

Smiths Falls & District Chamber of Commerce
Town Hall, 77 Beckwith St. North, Smiths Falls ON K7A 2B8
Tel: 613-283-1334; *Fax:* 613-283-4764
info@smithsfallschamber.ca
www.smithsfallschamber.ca
www.linkedin.com/company/2345454
www.facebook.com/SmithsFallsChambers
twitter.com/sfchambers
Overview: A small local organization
Staff Member(s): 3
Membership: 250; *Fees:* Schedule available
Chief Officer(s):
Rebecca White, Marketing Coordinator
Ashley Lennox, Office Co-ordinator

Smiths Falls & District Historical Society
11 Old Sly's Rd., Smiths Falls ON K7A 4T6
Tel: 613-283-6311
sfdhistoricalsociety@gmail.com
www.facebook.com/SmithsFallsDistrictHistoricalSociety
Overview: A small local organization founded in 1971
Member of: Ontario Historical Society
Finances: *Funding Sources:* Membership dues

Smoking & Health Action Foundation
#221, 720 Spadina Ave., Toronto ON M5S 2T9
Tel: 416-928-2900; *Fax:* 416-928-1860
toronto@nsra-adnf.ca
www.nsra-adnf.ca
twitter.com/nsra_adnf
Overview: A small local organization founded in 1974
Mission: To conduct public policy research & education designed to reduce tobacco-related disease & death
Finances: *Funding Sources:* Federal government
Staff Member(s): 10; 50 volunteer(s)
Chief Officer(s):
Lorraine Fry, Executive Director

Smoky Applied Research & Demonstration Association (SARDA)
PO Box 90, 701 Main St., Falher AB T0H 1M0
Tel: 780-837-2900; *Fax:* 780-837-8223
www.sarda.ca
www.facebook.com/225868234131536
twitter.com/SARDA6

Overview: A small local organization overseen by Agricultural Research & Extension Council of Alberta
Mission: To conduct agricultural research
Member of: Agricultural Research & Extension Council of Alberta
Membership: *Fees:* $50 individual; $100 corporate
Chief Officer(s):
Vance Yaremko, Manager
manager@sarda.ca
Shelleen Gerbig, Extension Coordinator
extension@sarda.ca
Khalil Ahmed, Coordinator, Research
research@sarda.ca
Publications:
• Back Forty [a publication of the Smoky Applied Research & Demonstration Association]
Type: Newsletter

Smoky Lake & District Chamber of Commerce
PO Box 635, Smoky Lake AB T0A 3C0
Tel: 780-656-3532; *Fax:* 866-898-2608
www.smokylakechamber.com
Overview: A small local organization
Mission: To promote business & the community
Membership: *Member Profile:* Small businesses
Activities: *Speaker Service:* Yes
Chief Officer(s):
Noel Simpson, Vice-President

Smoky River Regional Chamber of Commerce
PO Box 814, 11 Centre Ave. SW, Falher AB T0H 1M0
Tel: 780-837-8311
www.smokyriverchamber.ca
Overview: A small local organization
Mission: To promote businesses in the Smoky River region; To serve as the voice for local business; To stimulate community growth
Affiliation(s): Alberta Chamber of Commerce; Canadian Chamber of Commerce
Membership: 71
Chief Officer(s):
Val Viens, President

Snow Crab Fishermans Inc.
c/o Carter Hutt, RR#2, Alberton PE C0B 1B0
Tel: 902-853-3332
Overview: A small provincial organization
Chief Officer(s):
Carter Hutt, President

Snowboard Nova Scotia
#311, 5516 Spring Garden Rd., Halifax NS B3J 1G6
Tel: 902-425-5450; *Fax:* 902-425-5606
www.snowboardnovascotia.ca
www.facebook.com/SnowboardNovaScotia
Previous Name: Nova Scotia Snowboard Association
Overview: A small provincial organization overseen by Canadian Snowboard Federation
Mission: To be the provincial governing body of competitive snowboarding in Nova Scotia
Member of: Canadian Snowboard Federation; Sport Nova Scotia
Membership: *Fees:* $45
Chief Officer(s):
Deb Maclean, President
Kristin d'Eon, Technical Director
kristin@snowboardnovascotia.ca
Andrew Hayes, Administrative Coordinator, Provincial Sport Organization, 902-425-5450 Ext. 370
ahayes@sportnovascotia.ca

Snowboard Yukon
YT
info@snowboardyukon.com
www.snowboardyukon.com
Overview: A medium-sized provincial organization overseen by Canadian Snowboard Federation
Mission: To organize & sanction events, train athletes & coaches, form & administer teams for out of territory competitions, & represent Yukon riders in the Canadian Snowboard Federation.
Member of: Canadian Snowboard Federation

Snowmobilers Association of Nova Scotia (SANS)
5516 Spring Garden Rd., 4th Fl., Halifax NS B3J 3G6
Tel: 902-425-5450; *Fax:* 902-425-5606
www.snowmobilersns.com

Overview: A small provincial organization founded in 1976
Mission: To provide leadership & support to member snowmobile clubs so that they may enjoy quality recreational snowmobiling opportunities on a province-wide network of safe & well-developed snowmobile trails
Membership: 21 member clubs; *Member Profile:* Snowmobile clubs
Chief Officer(s):
Mike Eddy, General Manager, 902-425-5450 Ext. 360
Martha Dunlop, Manager, Finance & Administration, 902-425-5450 Ext. 324

Snowmobilers of Manitoba Inc.
2121 Henderson Hwy., Winnipeg MB R2G 1P8
Tel: 204-940-7533; *Fax:* 204-940-7531
info@snoman.mb.ca
www.snoman.mb.ca
www.facebook.com/SnomanInc
Also Known As: Snoman
Overview: A small provincial organization founded in 1975
Mission: To provide strong leadership & support to member clubs; to develop & maintain safe & environmentally responsible snowmobile trails; to further the enjoyment of organized snowmobiling throughout Manitoba
Affiliation(s): Canadian Council of Snowmobile Organizations
Finances: *Annual Operating Budget:* $500,000-$1.5 Million
Staff Member(s): 2; 2500 volunteer(s)
Membership: 2,500; *Fees:* $150
Chief Officer(s):
Yvonne Rideout, Executive Director
execdirector@snoman.mb.ca
Meetings/Conferences:
• Snowmobilers of Manitoba Inc. 2018 8th Annual Snoman Congress, November, 2018, Canad Inns Destination Centre, Winnipeg, MB
Scope: Provincial

Soaring Association of Canada (SAC) / Association canadienne de vol à voile (ACVV)
c/o COPA National Office, #903, 75 Albert St., Ottawa ON K1P 5E7
Tel: 613-236-4901; *Fax:* 613-236-8646
sacoffice@sac.ca
www.sac.ca
twitter.com/canglide
Overview: A medium-sized national organization founded in 1945
Mission: To promote, enhance & protect the sport of soaring in Canada; To provide information & services to the soaring community: licensing, medical requirements for glider pilots, aircraft certification, technical issues, courses & training, insurance plan, & services to clubs
Affiliation(s): Aero Club of Canada; International Gliding Commission of the Fédération Aéronautique Internationale
Finances: *Funding Sources:* Membership fees; Sales; Donations
40 volunteer(s)
Membership: 1,500 club affiliates; *Fees:* Schedule available; *Committees:* Air Cadets; Airspace; Archives/Historian; Contest Letters; FAI Awards; FAI Records; Fit Training & Safety; Free Flight; Insurance; Medical; Technical; Trophy Claims; World Contest; Flight Records
Activities: *Library:* by appointment Not open to public
Awards:
• Hank Janzen Trophy
• Roden Trophy
• Walter Piercy Award
• Stachow Wave Trophy
Publications:
• Free Flight [a publication of the Soaring Association of Canada]

Soaring Eagle Friendship Centre
PO Box 396, #2, 8 Gagnier St., Hay River NT X0E 1G1
Tel: 867-874-6581; *Fax:* 867-874-3362
soaringeaglefc@northwestel.net
www.facebook.com/SoaringEagleFriendshipCentre
Overview: A small local organization

Soccer New Brunswick
#2, 125 Russ Howard Dr., Moncton NB E1C 0L7
Tel: 506-830-4762; *Fax:* 506-382-5621
admin@soccernb.org
www.soccernb.org
www.facebook.com/SoccerNb
twitter.com/SoccerNB
Also Known As: Soccer NB

Overview: A medium-sized provincial organization founded in 1965 overseen by Canadian Soccer Association
Mission: To foster & promote the development & growth of the sport of soccer in New Brunswick & to assure equitable accessibility through quality programs
Member of: Canadian Soccer Association
Finances: *Annual Operating Budget:* $500,000-$1.5 Million; *Funding Sources:* Government; membership
Staff Member(s): 2; 9 volunteer(s)
Membership: 16,500
Chief Officer(s):
Younes Bouida, Executive Director & Director, Technical Development, 506-830-4762 Ext. 2
younes@soccernb.org

Soccer Nova Scotia (SNS)
210 Thomas Raddall Dr., Halifax NS B3S 1K3
Tel: 902-445-0265; *Fax:* 902-445-0258
admin@soccerns.ns.ca
www.soccerns.ns.ca
www.facebook.com/SoccerNovaScotia
twitter.com/SoccerNS
www.youtube.com/user/SoccerNovaScotia
Overview: A medium-sized provincial organization founded in 1913 overseen by Canadian Soccer Association
Mission: To promote the sport of soccer in Nova Scotia; To provide information & resources to aid player training, coaching education, & referee programs
Member of: Canadian Soccer Association
Membership: 27,000+ players; 2,500+ coaches; 700+ referees
Chief Officer(s):
Brad Lawlor, Executive Director
executivedirector@soccerns.ns.ca
Carman King, Officer, Referee Development
ref.services@soccerns.ns.ca

Social Development Council Ajax-Pickering; Ajax/Pickering Social Development Council *See* Community Development Council Durham

Social Ecology Research Group *Voir* Groupe de recherche en écologie sociale

Social Investment Organization *See* Responsible Investment Association

Social Justice Committee / Comité pour la justice sociale
1857, rue de Maisonneuve ouest, Montréal QC H3H 1J9
Tel: 514-933-6797; *Fax:* 514-933-9517
info@sjc-cjs.org
www.s-j-c.net
Overview: A small local charitable organization founded in 1975
Mission: To work in solidarity with people in a number of southern countries & with Canadian & international organizations in the search for a more just & sustainable socio-economic system; To raise awareness of Canadians about the root causes of poverty & injustice in the world & how they are connected to us; To suggest ways by which we can work in cooperation with southern popular organizations
Finances: *Annual Operating Budget:* $50,000-$100,000; *Funding Sources:* Canadian Development Agency; Members; General public
30 volunteer(s)
Membership: 100-499; *Member Profile:* Individuals who support the work of the Social Justice Committee financially or in other ways & who share a common concern to work for social change, particularly in the areas of human rights in Central America & socio-economic rights; Subscribers to the newsletter; Volunteers; *Committees:* Human Rights & Development; Debt & Environment; Resource Centre; Upstream Journal; Urgent Action Centre
Activities: *Speaker Service:* Yes; *Rents Mailing List:* Yes; *Library:* Open to public
Chief Officer(s):
Ernie Schibli, Co-Founder & President
Derek MacCuish, Executive Director & Editor, Upstream Journal
Philippe Tousignant, Coordinator, Education Program
Doug Miller, Secretary
Dalila Benchaouche, Treasurer

Social Justice Cooperative Newfoundland & Labrador
PO Box 5125, St. John's NL A1C 5V5
socialjusticecoopnl@gmail.com
www.sjcnl.ca

Canadian Associations / Social Planning & Research Council of BC (SPARC BC)

www.facebook.com/SocialJusticeNL
twitter.com/NLsocialjustice
Overview: A small provincial organization
Mission: To raise awareness on social justice issues that affect the community & the world; To advocate for social, economic, & political equality
Membership: *Fees:* $10; *Member Profile:* Citizens living in Newfoundland; Non-government organizations operating in Newfoundland
Activities: Leading public awareness campaigns; Conducting research
Chief Officer(s):
Marilyn Porter, Co-Chair
Bill Hynd, Co-Chair

Social Planning & Research Council of BC (SPARC BC)
4445 Norfolk St., Burnaby BC V5G 0A7
Tel: 604-718-7733; *Fax:* 604-736-8697
Toll-Free: 888-718-7794
info@sparc.bc.ca
www.sparc.bc.ca
Overview: A medium-sized provincial charitable organization founded in 1966
Mission: To promote the social, economic & environmental well-being of citizens & communities; to advocate the principles of social justice, equality & the dignity & worth of all people in our multicultural society; to conduct research & planning for public information, education & citizen participation in developing social policies & programs
Member of: Canadian Council on Social Development
Affiliation(s): Community Social Planning Network; BC Community Accessibility Network
Finances: *Funding Sources:* United Way; various project grants; membership fees; donations
Membership: *Fees:* $25 individual; $60 organization
Activities: Projects & programs: Parking permits for people with disabilities & advocacy on accessibility issues; education & social services; health; community economic development; income security/labour market policies; social planning/citizen participation; Social Development Research Program; Community Development Institute; *Speaker Service:* Yes; *Library:* by appointment
Chief Officer(s):
Lorraine Copas, Executive Director
lcopas@sparc.bc.ca
Irene Willsie, President

Social Planning & Research Council of Hamilton
#103, 162 King William St., Hamilton ON L8R 3N9
Tel: 905-522-1148; *Fax:* 905-522-9124
sprc@sprc.hamilton.on.ca
www.sprc.hamilton.on.ca
www.facebook.com/sprchamilton
twitter.com/sprchamont
Overview: A small local organization founded in 1961
Mission: To improve the quality of life for all citizens of Hamilton-Wentworth
Finances: *Funding Sources:* United Way; municipal government
Staff Member(s): 17
Membership: *Fees:* $100 corporate; $50 non-profit; $25 individual; $10 students/unemployed
Chief Officer(s):
Don Jaffray, Executive Director
Purdeep Sangha, President

Social Planning Council for the North Okanagan (SPCNO)
c/o Community Futures North Okanagan, 3105 - 33rd St., Vernon BC V1T 9P7
Tel: 250-540-8572
info@socialplanning.ca
www.socialplanning.ca
Previous Name: North Okanagan Social Planning Council
Overview: A small local charitable organization founded in 1969
Mission: To facilitate & coordinate community planning & development by encouraging communication & cooperation amongst social, educational & health services in the North Okanagan
Finances: *Funding Sources:* Provincial & municipal governments
Membership: *Member Profile:* Non-profit agencies, supportive individuals
Activities: Maintains a central information bureau & referral service; community services directory; volunteer bureau; community development; research; cancer prevention programs; *Library*
Chief Officer(s):
Annette Sharkey, Executive Director

Social Planning Council of Cambridge & North Dumfries
#14, 55 Dickson St., Cambridge ON N1R 7A5
Tel: 519-623-1713; *Fax:* 519-267-4016
admin@spccnd.org
www.spccnd.org
www.facebook.com/220130431457527
twitter.com/SPCCND
Overview: A small local charitable organization founded in 1989
Mission: To actively participate in building & strengthening our community through research, analysis, facilitation & education
Finances: *Funding Sources:* United Way; Ontario Trillium Foundation; City of Cambridge
Staff Member(s): 5
Activities: Community research & planning; Community development; Trend analyses; Policy analyses; Public education; Facilitation; *Library:* by appointment
Chief Officer(s):
Linda Terry, Executive Director

Social Planning Council of Kitchener-Waterloo
#300, 151 Frederick St., Kitchener ON N2H 2M2
Tel: 519-579-1096; *Fax:* 519-578-9185
Toll-Free: 877-579-3859
info@waterlooregion.org
www.waterlooregion.org
www.facebook.com/socialplanningcouncil
twitter.com/spcofkw
Overview: A small local charitable organization founded in 1966
Mission: To link services & people for the well-being of the community; to gather & manage comprehensive data on community needs & human services in Waterloo Region; to prepare & distribute information in meaningful & accessible ways to community citizens; to collaborate with others in developing a community which offers a desirable quality of life for all its citizens
Affiliation(s): Social Planning Network of Ontario; AIRS; Ontario Healthy Communities Coalition; InformCanada; InformOntario; Imagine Canada; Ontario Nonprofit Network
Finances: *Annual Operating Budget:* $250,000-$500,000; *Funding Sources:* Municipal Government; Regional Government; United Way; Publications; Fee for service
Staff Member(s): 7
Membership: 63 organizations; *Fees:* Schedule available; *Member Profile:* Community members & non-profit organziations; *Committees:* Board Development; Fundraising
Activities: Research & data management; Community information; Community building; *Library:* Open to public
Chief Officer(s):
Trudy Beaulne, Executive Director
spckw@waterlooregion.org
Malcolm Waisman, Treasurer
Fahima Anwar, President
Awards:
• Sponsor Youth Leadership Award
• Sponsor Neighbourhood Community Spirit Award

Social Planning Council of Ottawa (SPCO) / Conseil de planification sociale d'Ottawa
790 Bronson Ave., Ottawa ON K1S 4G4
Tel: 613-236-9300; *Fax:* 613-236-7060
office@spcottawa.on.ca
www.spcottawa.on.ca
Previous Name: Ottawa Council of Social Agencies
Overview: A small local charitable organization founded in 1928
Mission: To provide the residents of Ottawa-Carleton with the means to exercise informed leadership on issues affecting their social & economic well-being
Member of: United Way of Ottawa-Carleton
Affiliation(s): District Health Council; Ontario Social Development Council
Finances: *Funding Sources:* United Way; Municipal & provincial government; Various charitable organizations; User fees & contracts
Staff Member(s): 7; 91 volunteer(s)
Membership: *Fees:* $25 individual; $30 non-profit organization; $65 for profit organization; $200 10 year individual; $500 individual lifetime
Activities: *Library:* Open to public
Chief Officer(s):
Diane Urquhart, Executive Director
dianneu@spcottawa.on.ca

Social Planning Council of Peel
#209, 1515 Matheson Blvd. East, Mississauga ON L4W 2P5
Tel: 905-629-3044; *Fax:* 905-629-7773
info@spcpeel.com
www.spcpeel.com
twitter.com/SPCPeel
Overview: A small local charitable organization
Mission: To promotes social justice by facilitating citizen participation in the identification of social issues and in the planning and implementation of collaborative actions to address those issues.

Social Planning Council of Sudbury Region (SPC) / Conseil de planification sociale Region de Sudbury
30 Ste. Anne Rd., Sudbury ON P3C 5E1
Tel: 705-675-3894
info@spcsudbury.ca
www.spcsudbury.ca
www.linkedin.com/company/1704612
www.facebook.com/SPC.Sudbury
twitter.com/SPCSudburyED
www.youtube.com/user/foodshed2011
Overview: A small local organization founded in 1991
Mission: To engage the diverse groups of the Sudbury community in a non-biased & interactive planning process aimed at improving the quality of life in the community
Member of: Social Planning Network of Ontario; Ontario Social Development Council; Canadian Council on Social Development
Finances: *Funding Sources:* Municipal & provincial governments; Donations; Foundations
Staff Member(s): 7
Activities: Annual Options & Opportunities Employment Fair
Chief Officer(s):
Annette Reszczynski, Interim Executive Director

Social Planning Council of Winnipeg
#300, 207 Donald St., Winnipeg MB R3C 1M5
Tel: 204-943-2561; *Fax:* 204-942-3221
info@spcw.mb.ca
www.spcw.mb.ca
ca.linkedin.com/company/social-planning-council-of-winnipeg
twitter.com/spcw1919
Overview: A small local organization
Mission: To identify & define social planning issues, needs & resources in the community; to develop & promote policy & program options to policy-makers; to support community groups & the voluntary human service sector; to raise community awareness of social issues & human service needs, social policy options & service delivery alternatives; to serve as a link between the three levels of government & community neighbourhoods
Membership: *Fees:* $20 individual, $50 organization, $100 sustaining
Chief Officer(s):
Dennis Lewycky, Executive Director
dlewycky@spcw.mb.ca

Social Planning Toronto (SPT)
#1001, 2 Carlton St., Toronto ON M5B 1J3
Tel: 416-351-0095; *Fax:* 416-351-0107
info@socialplanningtoronto.org
www.socialplanningtoronto.org
www.linkedin.com/company/social-planning-toronto
www.facebook.com/SocialPlanningToronto
twitter.com/planningtoronto
plus.google.com/112933900589591472077
Overview: A small local organization
Mission: To promote community-based, social policy, planning & civic participation at both the local & city-wide levels through analysis & action-oriented research on social issues.
Finances: *Funding Sources:* City of Toronto; United Way; Ontario Trillium Foundation
Staff Member(s): 12
Membership: *Fees:* $5 students/seniors/unwaged; $25 individual; fee for organizations dependant on operating budget
Activities: Adversity Game; consulting services; custom research; fundraising resources; *Library:* Open to public
Chief Officer(s):
Winston Tinglin, Interim Executive Director, 416-351-0095 Ext. 260
wtinglin@socialplanningtoronto.org
Maria Serrano, Director, Operations
mserrano@socialplanningtoronto.org

Etobicoke Office
Applewood, The Shaver Homestead, #205, 450 The West Mall, Toronto ON M9C 1E9
Tel: 416-231-5499; *Fax:* 416-231-4608
Chief Officer(s):
Richard DeGaetano, Community Planner
rdegaetano@socialplanningtoronto.org

York/West Toronto Office
1652 Keele St., Toronto ON M6M 3W3
Tel: 416-652-9772; *Fax:* 416-652-7128
Chief Officer(s):
Yasmin Khan, Community Planner
kyasmin@socialplanningtoronto.org

Socialist Party of Canada (SPC) / Parti Socialiste du Canada
PO Box 31024, Victoria BC V8N 6J3
spc@worldsocialism.org
www.worldsocialism.org/canada
Overview: A small national organization founded in 1905
Mission: To promote the establishment of socialism - a system of society based upon the common ownership & democratic control of the means & instruments for producing & distributing wealth by & in the interest of society as a whole
Affiliation(s): World Socialist Movement
Finances: *Annual Operating Budget:* Less than $50,000; *Funding Sources:* Membership fees; donations
3 volunteer(s)
Membership: 20; *Fees:* $25; *Member Profile:* Agreement with Object & Declaration of Principles; *Committees:* General Administrative
Activities: *Speaker Service:* Yes; *Library:* by appointment
Chief Officer(s):
John Ayers, General Secretary
jpayers@sympatico.ca

Società Unita
1775 Islington Ave., Toronto ON M9P 3N2
Tel: 416-243-7319; *Fax:* 416-243-7319
info@teopoli.com
teopoli.com
twitter.com/teopoli
www.flickr.com/photos/60905934@N05
Also Known As: The United Society (The Mission)
Overview: A small local charitable organization founded in 1972
Mission: To promote peace, love, & unity, according to the Gospel & the teaching of the Roman Catholic Church
Affiliation(s): Archdiocese of Toronto
Finances: *Funding Sources:* Donations
Membership: *Member Profile:* Individuals, over the age of eighteen, who wish to follow the principles of peace, love, & unity, acccording to the Gospel & the teaching of the Roman Catholic Church
Activities: Encouraging religious & social activities for spiritual & moral growth; Providing assistance to the needy; Offering faith instruction, prayer groups, spiritual retreats, & spiritual pilgrimages; Operating the Teopoli Summer Experience for children at Teopoli, located in Muskoka; Providing a daily Catholic braoadcast on Radio Teopoli, with programming such as Jesus the Listener, & The Good Samaritan
Chief Officer(s):
Antonio Apruzzese, Director

Société Alzheimer Canada *See* Alzheimer Society Canada

Société Alzheimer d'Ottawa et Renfrew County *See* Alzheimer Society of Ottawa & Renfrew County

Société alzheimer du nouveau brunswick *See* Alzheimer Society of New Brunswick

Société Alzheimer Ontario *See* Alzheimer Society Ontario

Société Alzheimer Society Sudbury-Manitoulin (SASSM)
960B Notre Dame Ave., Sudbury ON P3A 2T4
Tel: 705-560-0603; *Fax:* 705-560-6938
Toll-Free: 800-407-6369
info@alzheimersudbury.ca
www.alzheimersudbury.ca
www.facebook.com/alzheimersmnbd
Overview: A small local organization founded in 1983
Member of: Alzheimer Canada
Affiliation(s): Alzheimer Society of Ontario
Finances: *Funding Sources:* Local Health Integration Network
75 volunteer(s)
Activities: *Awareness Events:* Awareness Dinner, January; *Speaker Service:* Yes; *Library:* Société Alzheimer Society Sudbury-Manitoulin Library; Open to public
Chief Officer(s):
Lorraine LeBlanc, Executive Director
lleblanc@alzheimersudbury.ca

Société anthroposophique au Canada *See* Anthroposophical Society in Canada

Société asiatique des partenaires Canada *See* South Asia Partnership Canada

Société bibliographique du Canada *See* Bibliographical Society of Canada

Société biblique canadienne *See* Canadian Bible Society

Société Canada-Japon de Montréal / Canada-Japan Society of Montréal
7375, rue Sagard, Montréal QC H2E 2S8
Tél: 514-721-0052
www.mtlinfo.ca/canada-japon
Aperçu: *Dimension:* petite; *Envergure:* locale; Organisme sans but lucratif; fondée en 1960
Mission: Faciliter les échanges entre les Canadiens et les Japonais
Membre: 157
Activités: Démonstrations et activités artistiques; conférenciers; excursions; rencontres sociales
Membre(s) du bureau directeur:
Alice Bolduc, Présidente

La Société canadienne d'Addison *See* The Canadian Addison Society

La société canadienne d'aérophilatélie *See* Canadian Aerophilatelic Society

Société canadienne d'agroéconomie *See* Canadian Agricultural Economics Society

Société canadienne d'allergie et d'immunologie clinique *See* Canadian Society of Allergy & Clinical Immunology

Société canadienne d'Anthropologie *See* Canadian Anthropology Society

Société canadienne d'apprentissage psychomoteur et de psychologie du sport *See* Canadian Society for Psychomotor Learning & Sport Psychology

Société canadienne d'astronomie *See* Canadian Astronomical Society

Société canadienne d'Athérosclérose, de Thrombose et de Biologie Vasculaire *See* Canadian Society of Atherosclerosis, Thrombosis & Vascular Biology

Société canadienne d'autisme *See* Autism Canada

La Société canadienne d'éducation comparée et internationale *See* The Comparative & International Education Society of Canada

Société canadienne d'éducation par l'art *See* Canadian Society for Education through Art

Société canadienne d'endocrinologie et métabolisme *See* Canadian Society of Endocrinology & Metabolism

Société canadienne d'enregistrement des animaux *See* Canadian Livestock Records Corporation

Société canadienne d'épidémiologie et de biostatistique *See* Canadian Society for Epidemiology & Biostatistics

Société canadienne d'esthétique *See* Canadian Society for Aesthetics

Société canadienne d'étude du dix-huitième siècle *See* Canadian Society for Eighteenth-Century Studies

Société canadienne d'études ethniques *See* Canadian Ethnic Studies Association

Société canadienne d'évaluation *See* Canadian Evaluation Society

Société canadienne d'hématologie *See* Canadian Hematology Society

Société canadienne d'histoire de l'Église *See* Canadian Society of Church History

Société canadienne d'histoire de l'église catholique - Section anglaise *See* Canadian Catholic Historical Association - English Section

Société canadienne d'histoire de l'Église Catholique - Section française (SCHEC) / Canadian Catholic Historical Association - French Section
SCHEC, Université du Québec à Trois-Rivières, 3351, boul des Forges, Trois-Rivières QC G9A 5H7
Tél: 819-376-5011; *Télec:* 819-376-5179
schec.cieq.ca
Aperçu: *Dimension:* petite; *Envergure:* nationale; fondée en 1933
Mission: Grouper les personnes intéressées à l'histoire de l'Église catholique au Canada; stimuler l'intérêt pour cette histoire dans le grand public; tenir des congrès annuels dans diverses régions du Canada afin de susciter un dialogue entre chercheurs participants et de promouvoir les travaux d'histoire régionale
Finances: *Budget de fonctionnement annuel:* Moins de $50,000
4 bénévole(s)
Membre: 150 individu; 100 institutionnel; *Montant de la cotisation:* 20$ étudiants; 40$ individu; 50$ institutionnel; *Critères d'admissibilite:* La Société compte des membres dans toutes les parties du Canada de même qu'en Europe et aux États-Unis; les membres peuvent être des individus, ou des institutions publiques ou privées, tels des dépôts d'archives, bibliothèques, diocèses, communautés religieuses
Membre(s) du bureau directeur:
Dominique Marquis, Président
Janie Théôret, Vice Président
Dominique Laperle, Secrétaire
Jean Roy, Trésorier

Société canadienne d'histoire de la médecine *See* Canadian Society for the History of Medicine

Société Canadienne d'Histoire et Philosophie des Sciences *See* Canadian Society for the History & Philosophy of Science

Société canadienne d'histoire orale *See* Canadian Oral History Association

Société canadienne d'indexation *See* Indexing Society of Canada

Société canadienne d'ingénierie des services de santé *See* Canadian Healthcare Engineering Society

Société canadienne d'oncologie chirurgicale *See* Canadian Society for Surgical Oncology

Société canadienne d'onomastique *See* Canadian Society for the Study of Names

Société canadienne d'opthalmologie *See* Canadian Ophthalmological Society

Société canadienne d'otolaryngologie et de chirurgie cervico-faciale *See* Canadian Society of Otolaryngology - Head & Neck Surgery

Société canadienne de bioéthique *See* Canadian Bioethics Society

Société canadienne de biologie végétale *See* Canadian Society of Plant Biologists

Société canadienne de cardiologie *See* Canadian Cardiovascular Society

Société canadienne de chimie *See* Canadian Society for Chemistry

Société canadienne de chirurgie plastique et esthétique *See* Canadian Society for Aesthetic Plastic Surgery

Société canadienne de chirurgie vasculaire *See* Canadian Society for Vascular Surgery

Société canadienne de cytologie *See* Canadian Society of Cytology

Société canadienne de Dupuytren *See* Canadian Dupuytren Society

Société canadienne de fertilité et d'andrologie *See* Canadian Fertility & Andrology Society

Société canadienne de génie agroalimentaire et de bioingénierie *See* Canadian Society for Bioengineering

Société canadienne de génie biomédical inc. *See* Canadian Medical & Biological Engineering Society

Société canadienne de génie chimique *See* Canadian Society for Chemical Engineering

Société canadienne de génie civil *See* Canadian Society for Civil Engineering

Société canadienne de génie mécanique *See* Canadian Society for Mechanical Engineering

Société canadienne de gériatrie *See* Canadian Geriatrics Society

Société canadienne de gestion de la nutrition *See* Canadian Society of Nutrition Management

Société canadienne de gestion en ingénierie *See* Canadian Society for Engineering Management

Société Canadienne de greffe de cellules souches hematopoietiques *See* Canadian Blood & Marrow Transplant Group

Société canadienne de l'asthme *See* Asthma Society of Canada

Société canadienne de l'énergie du sol *See* Earth Energy Society of Canada

Société canadienne de l'hémochromatose *See* Canadian Hemochromatosis Society

Société canadienne de l'hémophilie *See* Canadian Hemophilia Society

Société canadienne de l'ouïe *See* Canadian Hearing Society

Société canadienne de la pivoine *See* Canadian Peony Society

Société canadienne de la rétine *See* Canadian Retina Society

Société canadienne de la santé et de la sécurité, inc. *See* Canadian Society of Safety Engineering, Inc.

Société canadienne de la santé internationale *See* Canadian Society for International Health

Société canadienne de la science du sol *See* Canadian Society of Soil Science

Société canadienne de la sclérose en plaques *See* Multiple Sclerosis Society of Canada

Société canadienne de la sclérose en plaques (Division du Québec) (SCSP) / Multiple Sclerosis Society of Canada (Québec Division)
Tour Est, #1010, 550, rue Sherbrooke ouest, Montréal QC H3A 1B9
Tél: 514-849-7591; Téléc: 514-849-8914
Ligne sans frais: 800-268-7582
info.qc@mssociety.ca
www.mssociety.ca/qc
www.facebook.com/SocieteSPCanada
twitter.com/SocCanDeLaSP
www.youtube.com/SocieteSPCanada
Également appelé: SP - Québec
Aperçu: *Dimension:* moyenne; *Envergure:* provinciale; Organisme sans but lucratif; fondée en 1948
Mission: Soutenir la recherche sur la SP; offrir des services aux personnes atteintes de la maladie et à leurs familles; sensibiliser le public à la sclérose en plaques et maintenir les relations avec les gouvernements.
Membre de: Multiple Sclerosis Society of Canada
Affiliation(s): Fédération internationale de la sclérose en plaques
Membre: 8 000; *Critères d'admissibilite:* Personnes atteintes de SP et autres
Activités: 26 sections locales; *Evénements de sensibilisation:* Mois de la sensibilisation de la SP, mai; Marche de l'eSPoir; *Stagiaires:* Oui; *Service de conférenciers:* Oui; *Bibliothèque:* Centre de documentation; rendez-vous
Membre(s) du bureau directeur:
Louis Adam, Directeur général

La Société canadienne de la SLA *See* ALS Society of Canada

Société canadienne de mathématiques appliquées et industrielles *See* Canadian Applied & Industrial Mathematics Society

Société canadienne de médecine interne *See* Canadian Society of Internal Medicine

Société canadienne de médecine transfusionnelle *See* Canadian Society for Transfusion Medicine

Société canadienne de météorologie et d'océanographie *See* Canadian Meteorological & Oceanographic Society

Société canadienne de néphrologie *See* Canadian Society of Nephrology

Société canadienne de neurologie *See* Canadian Neurological Society

Société canadienne de neurophysiologistes cliniques *See* Canadian Society of Clinical Neurophysiologists

Société canadienne de nutrition *See* Canadian Nutrition Society

Société canadienne de pédiatrie *See* Canadian Paediatric Society

Société canadienne de peintres en aquarelle *See* Canadian Society of Painters in Water Colour

Société Canadienne de Perfusion Clinique *See* Canadian Society of Clinical Perfusion

Société Canadienne de Philosophie de l'Education *See* Canadian Philosophy of Education Society

Société canadienne de physiologie *See* Canadian Physiological Society

Société canadienne de physiologie de l'exercice *See* Canadian Society for Exercise Physiology

Société Canadienne de Phytopathologie *See* Canadian Phytopathological Society

Société canadienne de psychanalyse *See* Canadian Psychoanalytic Society

Société canadienne de psychologie *See* Canadian Psychological Association

Société canadienne de recherche opérationelle *See* Canadian Operational Research Society

Société canadienne de recherche sur le glaucome *See* Glaucoma Research Society of Canada

Société canadienne de recherches cliniques *See* Canadian Society for Clinical Investigation

Société canadienne de rhumatologie *See* Canadian Rheumatology Association

Société canadienne de schizophrénie *See* Schizophrenia Society of Canada

Société canadienne de science animale *See* Canadian Society of Animal Science

Société canadienne de science de laboratoire médical *See* Canadian Society for Medical Laboratory Science

Société canadienne de science horticole *See* Canadian Society for Horticultural Science

Société canadienne de sociologie *See* Canadian Sociological Association

Société canadienne de soins intensifs *See* Canadian Critical Care Society

Société canadienne de technologie chimique *See* Canadian Society for Chemical Technology

Société canadienne de télédétection *See* Canadian Remote Sensing Society

Société canadienne de thoracologie *See* Canadian Thoracic Society

Société canadienne de transplantation *See* Canadian Society of Transplantation

Société canadienne de zoologie *See* Canadian Society of Zoologists

Société canadienne des anesthésiologistes *See* Canadian Anesthesiologists' Society

Société canadienne des auteurs, compositeurs et éditeurs de musique *See* Society of Composers, Authors & Music Publishers of Canada

La société canadienne des auteurs, illustrateurs et artistes pour enfants *See* Canadian Society of Children's Authors, Illustrators & Performers

Société canadienne des biologistes de l'environnement *See* Canadian Society of Environmental Biologists

Société canadienne des biomatériaux *See* Canadian Biomaterials Society

Société canadienne des bovins Dexter *See* Canadian Dexter Cattle Association

Société Canadienne des Bovins Red Poll *See* Canadian Red Poll Cattle Association

Société Canadienne des bovins Welsh Black *See* Canadian Welsh Black Cattle Society

Société canadienne des chirurgiens plasticiens *See* Canadian Society of Plastic Surgeons

Société canadienne des clinico-chimistes *See* Canadian Society of Clinical Chemists

Société canadienne des collectionneurs de jouets *See* Canadian Toy Collectors' Society Inc.

Société canadienne des courtiers en douane *See* Canadian Society of Customs Brokers

Société canadienne des directeurs d'association *See* Canadian Society of Association Executives

La Société canadienne des directeurs de club *See* Canadian Society of Club Managers

Société canadienne des éleveurs de bovins Highland *See* Canadian Highland Cattle Society

La Société canadienne des éleveurs de chèvres *See* Canadian Goat Society

La société canadienne des éleveurs de moutons *See* Canadian Sheep Breeders' Association

Société canadienne des études bibliques *See* Canadian Society of Biblical Studies

Société canadienne des études classiques *See* Classical Association of Canada

Société Canadienne des études juives *See* Canadian Society for Jewish Studies

La Société canadienne des études mésopotamiennes *See* The Canadian Society for Mesopotamian Studies

Société canadienne des infirmières et infirmiers en opthalmologie *See* Canadian Society of Ophthalmic Registered Nurses

Société canadienne des médecins de soins palliatifs *See* Canadian Society of Palliative Care Physicians

Société canadienne des médecins gestionnaires *See* Canadian Society of Physician Executives

Société canadienne des microbiologistes *See* Canadian Society of Microbiologists

Société canadienne des pharmaciens d'hôpitaux *See* Canadian Society of Hospital Pharmacists

La Société canadienne des relations publiques *See* Canadian Public Relations Society Inc.

Société Canadienne des Sciences du Cerveau, du Comportement et de la Cognition *See* Canadian Society for Brain, Behaviour & Cognitive Science

Société canadienne des sciences pharmaceutiques *See* Canadian Society for Pharmaceutical Sciences

Société canadienne des technologistes en orthopedie *See* Canadian Society of Orthopaedic Technologists

Société canadienne des technologues en cardiologie inc. *See* Canadian Society of Cardiology Technologists Inc.

Societe canadienne des therapeutes de la main *See* Canadian Society of Hand Therapists

La Société canadienne des thérapeutes respiratoires *See* Canadian Society of Respiratory Therapists

Société canadienne du cancer *See* Canadian Cancer Society

Société canadienne du cheval Thoroughbred *See* Canadian Thoroughbred Horse Society

Société canadienne du sang *See* Canadian Blood Services

Société canadienne du sida *See* Canadian AIDS Society

Société Canadienne du Sommeil *See* Canadian Sleep Society

Société canadienne du syndrome d'Angelman *See* Canadian Angelman Syndrome Society

Société canadienne du syndrome de Down *See* Canadian Down Syndrome Society

Société canadienne Galloway *See* Canadian Galloway Association

Société Canadienne pour Biosciences Moléculaires *See* Canadian Society for Molecular Biosciences

Société canadienne pour l'étude de l'éducation *See* Canadian Society for the Study of Education

La Société canadienne pour l'étude de l'enseignement supérieur *See* Canadian Society for the Study of Higher Education

Société canadienne pour l'étude de l'éthique appliquée *See* Canadian Society for the Study of Practical Ethics

Société canadienne pour l'Étude de l'Homme Vieillissant *See* Canadian Society for the Study of the Aging Male

Société canadienne pour l'étude de la religion *See* Canadian Society for the Study of Religion

Société canadienne pour la conservation de la nature *See* The Nature Conservancy of Canada

Société canadienne pour la distribution de la Bible *See* The Bible League of Canada

La société canadienne pour la protection la nature en israël *See* Canadian Society for the Protection of Nature in Israel

Société canadienne pour la recherche nautique *See* Canadian Nautical Research Society

Société Canadienne pour le Droit de Mourir *See* The Right to Die Society of Canada

Société canadienne pour le traitement de la douleur *See* Canadian Pain Society

Société canadienne pour les études italiennes *See* Canadian Society for Italian Studies

Société canadienne pour les traditions musicales *See* Canadian Society for Traditional Music

Société canadienne-française de radiologie (SCFR)
CP 216, Succursdale Desjardins, Montréal QC H5B 1G8
Tél: 514-350-5148; *Téléc:* 514-350-5147
courrier@scfr.qc.ca
www.arq.qc.ca
Aperçu: Dimension: petite; *Envergure:* provinciale; Organisme sans but lucratif; fondée en 1928
Membre de: Fédération des médecins spécialistes du Québec
Finances: *Budget de fonctionnement annuel:* Moins de $50,000
Membre(s) du personnel: 1; 13 bénévole(s)
Membre: 550; *Montant de la cotisation:* 150$; *Critères d'admissibilite:* Tous les radiologistes du Québec
Activités: Développement professionnel continu des radiologues du Québec; *Stagiaires:* Oui; *Service de conférenciers:* Oui
Membre(s) du bureau directeur:
Bruno Morin, Président
Vahid Khairi, Secrétaire général
Prix, Bourses:
• Prix Albert-Jutras
; *Amount:* 1000$
• Prix Bernadette-Nogrady
• Prix d'Innovation et d'excellence Dr Jean-A.-Vézina
; *Amount:* 5000$
• Prix Personnalité SCFR
; *Amount:* 1000$

Société catholique de la Bible (SOCABI) / Catholic Bible Society
2000, rue Sherbrooke ouest, Montréal QC H3H 1G4
Tél: 514-925-4300
cbiblique@interbible.org
www.interbible.org/socabi
Aperçu: Dimension: moyenne; *Envergure:* nationale; Organisme sans but lucratif; fondée en 1940
Mission: Rendre la bible accessible au plus grand nombre de personnes possible, en facilitant la lecture et la compréhension
Membre de: Association canadienne des périodiques catholiques
Affiliation(s): World Catholic Federation for the Biblical Apostolate
Finances: *Budget de fonctionnement annuel:* $100,000-$250,000
Membre(s) du personnel: 6; 3 bénévole(s)
Membre: 130; *Montant de la cotisation:* 45$ tous les trois ans; *Critères d'admissibilite:* Implication dans la pastorale biblique; *Comités:* Administration; Financement
Activités: Service de librairie; conférences sur cassettes; cours par correspondance; cours d'initiation et formation; voyage en Israël; retraites; publication d'articles
Membre(s) du bureau directeur:
Dumais Marcel, Président
Christiane Cloutier-Dupuis, Vice-Président
Publications:
• Parabole
Type: Revue; *Frequency:* Bimensuel; *Editor:* Yves Guillemette, ptre
Profile: Revue bilique en ligne

Société chorale de Saint-Lambert / St. Lambert Choral Society
CP 36546, Saint-Lambert QC J4P 3S8
Tél: 450-878-0200
info.choeur.scsl@gmail.com
www.chorale-stlambert.qc.ca
www.facebook.com/239010928525
Aperçu: Dimension: petite; *Envergure:* locale; fondée en 1919
Mission: De promouvoir et de recueillir une appréciation pour la musique chorale
Membre(s) du bureau directeur:
Xavier Brossard-Ménard, Directeur artistique

Société collective de retransmission du Canada *See* Canadian Retransmission Collective

Société culturelle de la Baie des Chaleurs (SCBC)
CP 707, 45A, av. du Village, Campbellton NB E3N 1N5
Tél: 506-753-6494; *Téléc:* 506-753-7498
scbc@nb.aibn.com
www.scbc-campbellton.ca
www.facebook.com/scbc.campbellton
Aperçu: Dimension: petite; *Envergure:* locale; Organisme sans but lucratif; fondée en 1967
Mission: Faire rayonner la culture francophone et acadienne au Restigouche
Membre de: Conseil provincial des sociétés culturelles
Finances: *Fonds:* Patrimoine canadien
Membre(s) du personnel: 1; 20 bénévole(s)
Membre: *Montant de la cotisation:* 10$ (carte de membre)
Activités: Spectacles et ateliers culturels
Membre(s) du bureau directeur:
Conrad Bourque, Responsable de la programmation
Veronique Savoie-Levesque, Présidente

Société culturelle régionale Les Chutes (SCRLC)
215, rue Guimont, Grand Falls NB E3Y 1C7
Tél: 506-473-4329; *Téléc:* 506-473-9786
culturel@nb.aibn.com
www.societeculturelleregionaleleschutes.ca
Aperçu: Dimension: petite; *Envergure:* locale; Organisme sans but lucratif; fondée en 1986
Mission: Établir un réseau de communication et d'échange d'information dans le domaine culturel afin de promouvoir l'entente, la solidarité et le partage entre les communautés de la région des Chutes; favoriser le développement et l'épanouissement des artistes et artisans acadiens et francophones de la région des Chutes en mettant à leur disposition des informations sur les mécanismes de promotion et de diffusion de leur art; aider la personne dans sa démarche de perfectionnement culturel; appuyer et promouvoir les projets culturels, artistiques et artisanaux, et participer; maintenir des liens et favoriser des échanges avec d'autres organismes culturels de la province
Membre de: Conseil provincial des sociétés culturelles
Finances: *Budget de fonctionnement annuel:* Moins de $50,000; *Fonds:* Patrimoine canadien - Secrétariat à la Culture et au Sport
Membre(s) du personnel: 1; 15 bénévole(s)
Membre: 250; *Montant de la cotisation:* 6$ individu; 12$ famille
Activités: Foire du Cadeau; spectacles; cours; galerie d'art; *Evénements de sensibilisation:* Développement culturel
Membre(s) du bureau directeur:
Nicole Levesque, Présidente
Nelly Kako, Agente de développement

Société culturelle Sud-Acadie (SCSA)
CP 9056, Shédiac NB E4R 8W5
Tél: 506-860-0413
info@sudacadie.ca
www.sudacadie.ca
Aperçu: Dimension: petite; *Envergure:* locale; Organisme sans but lucratif; fondée en 1979
Mission: Promouvoir l'expression culturelle des acadiens et acadiennes de la région; planifier et réaliser des activités culturelles sur le territoire
Membre de: Conseil Provincial des sociétés culturelles
Finances: *Budget de fonctionnement annuel:* $50,000-$100,000
15 bénévole(s)
Membre: 1-99
Activités: Organisation et support aux activités culturelles
Membre(s) du bureau directeur:
Nathalie LeBlanc, Présidente
lanleb@rogers.com

Société d'adoption enfants du monde inc. *See* Children of the World Adoption Society Inc.

Société d'agriculture de Chicoutimi *Voir* Expo agricole de Chicoutimi

La Société d'aide à l'enfance des districts de Sudbury et de Manitoulin *See* Children's Aid Society of the Districts of Sudbury & Manitoulin

La Société d'aide à l'enfance Nipissing & Parry Sound *See* Children's Aid Society of the District of Nipissing & Parry Sound

Société d'animation du Jardin et de l'Institut botanique *Voir* Les Amis du Jardin botanique de Montréal

Société d'archéologie et de numismatique de Montréal / The Antiquarian & Numismatic Society of Montréal (ANSM)
280, rue Notre-Dame est, Montréal QC H2Y 1C5
Tél: 514-861-3708; *Téléc:* 514-861-8317
info@chateauramezay.qc.ca
www.chateauramezay.qc.ca
www.facebook.com/Chateau.Ramezay
twitter.com/chateauramezay
Également appelé: Musée du Château Ramezay
Aperçu: Dimension: petite; *Envergure:* locale; Organisme sans but lucratif; fondée en 1862
Mission: Conserver, mettre en valeur, et rendre accessible une collection axée principalement sur l'histoire de Montréal et du Québec et de mettre en oeuvre des activités et d'accueillir des manifestations liées de près à la vie culturelle de Montréal; préserver à des fins muséologiques et de conserver un édifice classé monument historique
Membre de: Association des musées canadiens; société des musées québécois
Finances: *Fonds:* Ministère de la Culture et des Communications; Conseil des arts de Montréal; Ville de Montréal
Membre: *Critères d'admissibilite:* Majorité de retraités
Activités: Expositions; concerts; programmes éducatifs; activités familiales; *Stagiaires:* Oui; *Bibliothèque:* Recherches de niveau supérieur; rendez-vous
Membre(s) du bureau directeur:
André Delisle, Directeur général, Château Ramezay
Prix, Bourses:
• Prix Mérite National
• Prix Orange
• Prix Coup d'État
• Prix Ulysse

Société d'Eczéma du Canada *See* Eczema Society of Canada

Société d'entomologie du Québec (SEQ)
Insectarium de Montréal, 4581, rue Sherbrooke est, Montréal QC H1X 2B2
Courriel: registraire@seq.qc.ca
www.seq.qc.ca

Aperçu: *Dimension:* petite; *Envergure:* provinciale; Organisme sans but lucratif; fondée en 1873
Mission: Promouvoir et soutenir l'intérêt et le développement de l'entomologie en matière de recherche, d'éducation et de conservation
Affiliation(s): Société d'entomologie du Canada
Finances: *Budget de fonctionnement annuel:* Moins de $50,000
15 bénévole(s)
Membre: 230; *Montant de la cotisation:* 40$; *Critères d'admissibilite:* Entomologiste
Membre(s) du bureau directeur:
Jade Savage, Président
presidence@seq.qc.ca

Société d'études socialistes *See* Society for Socialist Studies

Société d'histoire d'Amos
222, 1e av est, Amos QC J9T 1H3
Tél: 819-732-6070; *Téléc:* 819-732-3242
societe.histoire@cableamos.com
www.societehistoireamos.com
Aperçu: *Dimension:* petite; *Envergure:* locale; fondée en 1952
Mission: Étudier et faire connaître l'histoire des familles, paroisses, institutions et industries de la MRC d'Abitibi; rechercher, conserver et rendre accessibles les documents qui témoignent de cette histoire
Membre de: Conseil de la culture d'Abitibi-Témiscamingue; Fédération des sociétés d'histoire du Québec
Finances: *Budget de fonctionnement annuel:* Moins de $50,000
2 bénévole(s)
Membre: 102; *Montant de la cotisation:* $15 individuel; $20 famille, organisme, entreprise
Activités: Expositions de photos; ateliers; conférences; circuit d'interprétation historique
Membre(s) du bureau directeur:
Carmen Rousseau, Présidente

Société d'histoire d'Asbestos
347, boul St-Luc, Asbestos QC J1T 2W4
Tél: 819-879-2198
sochisasbestos@gmail.com
histoireasbestos.wix.com
Aperçu: *Dimension:* petite; *Envergure:* locale; fondée en 1995

Société d'histoire Danville-Shipton
CP 518, Danville QC J0A 1A0
Tél: 819-839-2094
Aperçu: *Dimension:* petite; *Envergure:* locale; fondée en 1994
Mission: Colliger des documents, publications et photographies reliés à l'histoire de la région de Danville-Shipton; créer des archives
Membre(s) du bureau directeur:
J. Gilles Geoffroy, Président

Société d'histoire de Beloeil - Mont-Saint-Hilaire (SHBMSH)
CP 85010, Mont-Saint-Hilaire QC J3H 5W1
Tél: 450-446-5826
info@shbmsh.org
www.shbmsh.org
www.facebook.com/161940913845022
Aperçu: *Dimension:* petite; *Envergure:* locale; Organisme sans but lucratif; fondée en 1971
Mission: Promouvoir les recherches sur l'histoire de Beloeil, Mont-Saint-Hilaire et de la région avoisinante dans le but d'instruire la population et diffuser le résultat de ses recherches
Affiliation(s): Fédération des sociétés d'histoire du Québec
Membre: 249; *Montant de la cotisation:* 10$ conjoint; 20$ étudiant; 40$ général; 60$ corporatif; *Critères d'admissibilité:* Personnes intéressées à l'histoire
Activités: Conférences; présence dans le centre commercial local; *Service de conférenciers:* Oui; *Bibliothèque:* Bibliothèque publique
Membre(s) du bureau directeur:
Alain Côté, Président

Société d'histoire de Coaticook
34, rue Main est, Coaticook QC J1A 1N2
Tél: 819-849-1023
info@societehistoirecoaticook.ca
www.societehistoirecoaticook.ca
Aperçu: *Dimension:* petite; *Envergure:* locale; fondée en 1995
Mission: Effectuer du collectage d'archives et de la recherche historique sur différents thèmes; faire de la conservation et de la restauration de documents historiques; établir un centre de documentation pluridisciplinaire et un fond d'archives et le rendre accessible à la population pour faciliter la recherche personnelle et collective; diffuser les recherches faites pour la société d'histoire
Activités: Recherches; conférences; déjeuners; expositions

Société d'histoire de Compton *See* Compton Historical Society

Société d'histoire de Georgeville *See* Georgeville Historical Society

Société d'histoire de Greenfield Park
129, rue Greenfield, Greenfield Park QC J4V 2J6
Tél: 450-671-5141
Aperçu: *Dimension:* petite; *Envergure:* locale
Mission: De promouvoir l'histoire de Greenfield Park

Société d'histoire de l'Outaouais inc. (SHO)
CP 1007, Succ. B, 855, boul de la Gappe, Gatineau QC J8X 3X5
Tél: 613-562-5825; *Téléc:* 613-562-5198
Aperçu: *Dimension:* petite; *Envergure:* locale; fondée en 1968
Mission: Promotion de l'histoire et du patrimoine régional
Membre de: Fédération des sociétés d'histoire du Québec
Finances: *Budget de fonctionnement annuel:* Moins de $50,000
10 bénévole(s)
Membre: 150; *Montant de la cotisation:* 20$
Activités: Visites commentées de divers secteurs historiques; remise de prix annuels du patrimoine; conférences
Membre(s) du bureau directeur:
Michel Prévost, President
prevost@uottawa.ca

Société d'histoire de la Côte-des-Neiges (SHCDN)
Centre communautaire de loisir de la Côte-des-Neiges, 5347, ch de la Côte-des-Neiges, Montréal QC H3T 1Y4
Tél: 514-342-6754
Aperçu: *Dimension:* petite; *Envergure:* locale; fondée en 1982
Mission: Promotion de l'histoire et du patrimoine
Membre de: Fédération des sociétés d'histoire du Québec
Activités: Visites; expositions; publications; documentation

Société d'histoire de la Haute Gaspésie
675, boul Ste-Anne ouest, Sainte-Anne-des-Monts QC G4V 1T9
Tél: 418-763-7871
genealogie@globetrotter.net
Aperçu: *Dimension:* petite; *Envergure:* locale; Organisme sans but lucratif; fondée en 1970
Mission: Mettre en valeur tout ce qui a trait à l'histoire, la généalogie, l'archéologie et au patrimoine local et régional dans Haute-Gaspésie
Membre de: Fédération québécoise des sociétés de généalogie; Fédération des sociétés d'histoire du Québec
Activités: Imprimerie; reliure; musée; généalogie; *Bibliothèque:* Bibliothèque SHAM; Bibliothèque publique
Membre(s) du bureau directeur:
Ghislain Lebeau, Contact

Société d'histoire de la Haute-Yamaska (SHHY)
135, rue Principale, Granby QC J2G 2V1
Tél: 450-372-4500
info@shhy.info
www.shhy.info
Nom précédent: Société historique de Shefford
Aperçu: *Dimension:* petite; *Envergure:* locale; Organisme sans but lucratif; fondée en 1967
Mission: Promotion de l'histoire régionale et nationale; protection du patrimoine; conservation des archives régionales; service de généalogie
Membre de: Association des archivistes de Québec; Regroupement des services d'archives agréés; Réseau des archives du Québec
Finances: *Budget de fonctionnement annuel:* $100,000-$250,000
Membre(s) du personnel: 2; 3 bénévole(s)
Membre: 100-499; *Montant de la cotisation:* 20$
Activités: *Bibliothèque:* Archives
Membre(s) du bureau directeur:
René Beaudin, Président

Société d'histoire de la MRC de l'Assomption (SHRMCLASS)
CP 3147, 270, boul l'Ange-Gardien, L'Assomption QC J5W 4M9
Tél: 450-589-0233; *Téléc:* 450-589-2910
shmrclca@gmail.com
www.histoirequebec.qc.ca/membre_details.asp?idM=250
Aperçu: *Dimension:* petite; *Envergure:* locale; fondée en 1986
Mission: Sensibiliser la population à l'histoire; regrouper des personnes intéressées à l'histoire, à la généalogie et au patrimoine; inventorier, colliger et conserver tous les ouvrages, les documents, les objets, les souvenirs, etc. pouvant servir à l'histoire de la région et les rendre accessibles; favoriser l'étude, la recherche et la publication sur l'histoire.
Membre de: Fédération des sociétés d'histoire du Québec; Fédération québécoise des sociétés de généalogie
Finances: *Budget de fonctionnement annuel:* Moins de $50,000
Membre: 160; *Montant de la cotisation:* 30$; 15$ 2e personne
Activités: Conférences mensuelles; expositions; *Bibliothèque:* Centre de documentation
Membre(s) du bureau directeur:
Yolanda Gingras, Secrétaire
Natalie Myall, Vice-présidente
Yollande Masse, Trésorière
Josée Dufour, Secrétaire

Société d'histoire de La Prairie-de-la-Magdeleine (SHLM)
249, rue Sainte-Marie, La Prairie QC J5R 1G1
Tél: 450-659-1393
info@shlm.info
www.shlm.info
Aperçu: *Dimension:* petite; *Envergure:* locale; Organisme sans but lucratif; fondée en 1972
Mission: A comme objectif principal la préservation, la mise en valeur et la diffusion du patrimoine local et régional
Membre de: Association des archivistes du Québec
Affiliation(s): Fédération des sociétés d'histoire du Québec; Réseau des Archives du Québec; Conseil culturel Montérégien
Membre(s) du personnel: 1
Membre: *Montant de la cotisation:* 30$ individuel; 50$ familial; *Critères d'admissibilite:* Intérêt pour l'histoire et la généalogie
Activités: Conférences; expositions; généalogie; visites guidées; archéologie; mise en marché d'un logiciel d'archives: ARCHI-LOG; *Service de conférenciers:* Oui; *Bibliothèque:* Archives; Bibliothèque publique
Membre(s) du bureau directeur:
Johanne Doyle, Coordonnatrice

Société d'histoire de la Rivière du Nord inc.
Maison de la culture Claude-Henri-Grignon, #206, 101, Place du Curé-Labelle, Saint-Jérôme QC J7Z 1X6
Tél: 450-436-1511; *Téléc:* 450-436-1211
courriel@shrn.org
www.shrn.org
Aperçu: *Dimension:* petite; *Envergure:* locale; Organisme sans but lucratif; fondée en 1980
Mission: Mettre en valeur le patrimoine de la MRC Rivière-du-Nord
Membre de: Fédération des sociétés d'histoires du Québec
Finances: *Budget de fonctionnement annuel:* Moins de $50,000
20 bénévole(s)
Membre: 35; *Montant de la cotisation:* 15$ individuel; 30$ bibliothèques/institutions; 100$ membre à vie
Activités: *Bibliothèque:* rendez-vous
Membre(s) du bureau directeur:
Suzanne Marcotte, Présidente

Société d'histoire de la Rivière Saint-Jean incorporée
715, rue Priestman, Fredericton NB E3B 5W7
www.franco-fredericton.com/shrsj
Aperçu: *Dimension:* petite; *Envergure:* locale; fondée en 1981
Mission: Regrouper les personnes qui s'intéressent à l'histoire, en particulier à l'histoire acadienne le long de la rivière Saint-Jean; découvrir, collectionner et publier tout ce qui peut contribuer à mieux faire connaître et à valoriser cette histoire
Membre: *Montant de la cotisation:* 15$ individuel; 35$ collectif/bienfaiteur; 150$ vie
Activités: Rencontres; recherches; conférences publiques; consultations en histoire et en généalogie
Membre(s) du bureau directeur:
Bernard-Marie Thériault, Président
teriobm@gmail.com

La Société d'histoire de la Rivière-du-Nord
#203, 101, place du Curé-Labelle, Saint-Jérôme QC J7Z 1X6
Tél: 450-436-1512; *Téléc:* 450-436-1211
courriel@shrn.org
www.shrn.org
Aperçu: *Dimension:* petite; *Envergure:* locale
Mission: Soir une référence et un interlocuteur incontournable en matière d'histoire, ayant pignon sur rue dans un bâtiment patrimonial chaleureux, animé par une équipe conviviale de bénévoles, de permanents et de multiples partenaires
Membre(s) du bureau directeur:
Linda Rivest, Directrice générale

Société d'histoire de la Seigneurie de Chambly (SHSC)
CP 142, 2445, av Bourgogne, Chambly QC J3L 4B1
Tél: 450-658-2666
shsc@societehistoirechambly.org
www.societehistoirechambly.org
Aperçu: Dimension: petite; *Envergure:* locale; Organisme sans but lucratif; fondée en 1979
Mission: Réunir des personnes intéressées par l'histoire de la seigneurie et la généalogie; faire des recherches pour mieux connaître cette histoire afin de diffuser soit par des conférences, la publication de cahiers et du bulletin Le Voltigeur
Affiliation(s): Fédération des sociétés d'histoire du Québec; Société d'histoire de la Vallée du Richelieu
Finances: *Budget de fonctionnement annuel:* Moins de $50,000; *Fonds:* Ministère de la Culture et des Communications, députée de Chambly
Membre(s) du personnel: 1; 20 bénévole(s)
Membre: 205; *Montant de la cotisation:* 6$ étudiants; 25$ aînés; 30$ adultes; 40$ couples aînés; 45$ couples; 100$ entreprises; *Comités:* Écriture; Recherche sur l'histoire de Chambly
Activités: Conférences; réunion de généalogie publication d'un cahier annuellement; prêt de livres, magasin d'archives; *Bibliothèque:* rendez-vous
Membre(s) du bureau directeur:
Paul-Henri Hudon, Président
Prix, Bourses:
• Concours d'histoire de la fondation Percy-W.-Foy
Décernés pour des travaux de recherche en histoire locale

Société d'histoire de la Seigneurie de Monnoir (SHSM)
1800, rue du Pont, Marieville QC J3M 1J8
Tél: 450-460-6767
www.societehistoireseigneuriemonnoir.com
Aperçu: Dimension: petite; *Envergure:* locale; fondée en 1982
Membre: *Montant de la cotisation:* 5$ étudiant; 20$ adulte; 30$ couple

Société d'histoire de Lachine
Maison du Brasseur, 2901, boul Saint-Joseph, Lachine QC H8S 4B7
Tél: 514-634-9508
shl@genealogie.org
www.genealogie.org/club/shl
Aperçu: Dimension: petite; *Envergure:* locale; Organisme sans but lucratif; fondée en 1993
Mission: Faire connaître le riche patrimoine de la ville de Lachine; répondre à des demandes d'information concernant l'histoire locale, le patrimoine et la généalogie; maintenir d'étroites liaisons avec le Musée de la ville de Lachine; collaborer avec d'autres organismes culturels
Membre de: Fédération des sociétés d'histoire du Québec
Activités: Conférences mensuelles; promenades historiques; expositions
Membre(s) du bureau directeur:
André Robichaud, Responsable

Société d'histoire de Longueuil (SHL)
255, rue Saint-Charles est, Longueuil QC J4H 1B3
Tél: 450-674-0349
shl@societedhistoirelongueuil.qc.ca
www.societedhistoirelongueuil.qc.ca
www.youtube.com/user/societehistoirelong
Aperçu: Dimension: petite; *Envergure:* locale; Organisme sans but lucratif; fondée en 1971
Mission: Inventaire de tous les sujets à caractère historique (généalogique, archéologique, folklorique) se rapportant au territoire qui faisait partie de la baronnie de Longueuil; constitution d'archives, écrites, sonores, photographiques; protection du patrimoine bâti;l'association fête son 35e anniversaire le 24 nov. 2006
Activités: Conférences, expositions, visites et marches guidées; publications de plusieurs volumes sur l'histoire de Longueuil; publication de 33 cahiers d'histoire totalisant plus de 1 000 pages inédites; *Bibliothèque:* Maison André-Lamarre; rendez-vous
Membre(s) du bureau directeur:
Bruno Racine, Président

Société d'histoire de Louiseville inc.
#24, 121, rang de la Petite-Rivière, Louiseville QC J5V 2H3
Tél: 819-228-9656; *Téléc:* 819-228-0627
histoirelouiseville@hotmail.com
Nom précédent: Société d'histoire et de généalogie de Louiseville inc
Aperçu: Dimension: petite; *Envergure:* locale; fondée en 1981
Membre de: Fédération des sociétés d'histoire du Québec
Membre: *Critères d'admissibilite:* Amateur et chercheur en histoire
Activités: Histoire régionale et généalogie; *Bibliothèque:* Bibliothèque publique
Membre(s) du bureau directeur:
Mathieu Deschênes, Président

Société d'histoire de Magog (SHM) / Magog Historical Society
95, rue Merry nord, #002&024, Magog QC J1X 2E7
Tél: 819-868-6779; *Téléc:* 819-868-4016
info@histoiremagog.com
www.histoiremagog.com
www.facebook.com/SocieteDhistoireDeMagog
Également appelé: Histoire Magog
Aperçu: Dimension: petite; *Envergure:* locale; fondée en 1988
Mission: La mission se définit par la volonté de cueillir, traiter et diffuser l'informatique sur l'ensemble des documents et des objects de valeur historique et patrimoniale relatifs à la vie de nos populations. S'accomplit par la cueillette, traitement et diffusion de fonds d'archives et de collections diverses; par la mise en oeuvre de moyens visant la défense et la promotion du patrimoine régional; par la production de documentation et d'instruments de recherche; par la réalisation d'activités de promotion de notre culture historique; par un service offert à tous ceux et celles que l'histoire et la recherche intéressent
Membre de: Fédération des sociétés d'histoire du Québec; Conseil de la Culture de l'Estrie; Réseau des archives du Québec; Conseil Canadien des Archives; Table des Archives de l'Estrie
Membre(s) du personnel: 1; 20 bénévole(s)
Membre: 100; *Montant de la cotisation:* 20$ individuel; 25$ familial; 10$ étudiant; 100$ à vie; 100$ corporatif; *Comités:* Financement; Recrutement; Informatique; Activités; Gestion des archives et affaires légales; Rédaction et relations avec les médias
Activités: Expositions; ventes photographiques; panneaux d'interprétation; publication d'articles, chroniques historiques, brochures, outils promotionnels; *Evénements de sensibilisation:* Journées Nationales de la Culture
Membre(s) du bureau directeur:
Paul-René Gilbert, Présidente
Pierre Rastoul, Coordonnateur

Société d'histoire de Missisquoi See Missisquoi Historical Society

Société d'histoire de Montarville (SHM)
1585, rue Montarville, Saint-Bruno-de-Montarville QC J3V 3T8
Tél: 450-653-3194
info@shmontarville.org
shmontarville.org
Aperçu: Dimension: petite; *Envergure:* locale; fondée en 1981
Mission: De préserver et de recherches sur l'histoire de Montarville
Membre: *Montant de la cotisation:* 20$ individuelle; 30$ famille
Activités: Exposition photo; assemblée générale annuelle; *Evénements de sensibilisation:* Exposition annuelle sur le 24 juin
Membre(s) du bureau directeur:
Bernard Guilbert, Président, Conseil d'administration

Société d'histoire de Rouyn-Noranda
CP 681, Rouyn-Noranda QC J9X 5C6
Tél: 819-762-2059
shrn08@hotmail.com
Aperçu: Dimension: petite; *Envergure:* locale; fondée en 1951

Société d'histoire de Sainte-Foy
CP 8586, Sainte-Foy QC G1V 4N5
Tél: 418-641-6301; *Téléc:* 418-641-6553
Aperçu: Dimension: petite; *Envergure:* locale; Organisme sans but lucratif; fondée en 1977
Mission: Faire connaître toutes les dimensions de l'histoire de l'ancienne ville de Sainte-Foy; sauvegarder les plus beaux éléments de son patrimoine
Membre de: Fédération des sociétés d'histoire du Québec
Finances: *Budget de fonctionnement annuel:* Moins de $50,000 10 bénévole(s)
Membre: 70; *Montant de la cotisation:* 20$; *Critères d'admissibilité:* Intérêt pour l'histoire locale; *Comités:* Archives; Archéologie
Activités: Conférences mensuelles; recherches; *Service de conférenciers:* Oui; *Bibliothèque:* Centre d'Archives; rendez-vous
Membre(s) du bureau directeur:
Jean-Yves Landry, Contact

Société d'histoire de Saint-Hubert
CP 24, Saint-Hubert QC J3Y 4T1
Tél: 450-676-5385
Aperçu: Dimension: petite; *Envergure:* locale; fondée en 1984

Société d'histoire de Saint-Tite
410, rue du Couvent, Saint-Tite QC G0X 3H0
Tél: 418-365-7273
Aperçu: Dimension: petite; *Envergure:* locale
Membre(s) du bureau directeur:
Gilles Barbeau, Président

Société d'histoire de Sherbrooke (SHS) / Historical Society of Sherbrooke
275, rue Dufferin, Sherbrooke QC J1H 4M5
Tél: 819-821-5406; *Téléc:* 819-821-5417
info@histoiresherbrooke.com
www.histoiresherbrooke.com/en
Aperçu: Dimension: petite; *Envergure:* locale; Organisme sans but lucratif; fondée en 1927
Mission: Gérer un service d'archives privées et un centre d'interprétation; recueillir et conserver les collections d'archives, de les compléter et de les rendre accessibles aux chercheurs; initier et encourager la recherche en histoire régionale; interpréter et diffuser les résultats; favoriser les échanges avec d'autres institutions
Finances: *Budget de fonctionnement annuel:* $250,000-$500,000; *Fonds:* Ville de Sherbrooke; gouvernement fédéral et québecois
Membre(s) du personnel: 4; 15 bénévole(s)
Membre: 350; *Montant de la cotisation:* 30$
Activités: Expositions; visites scolaires; publications; circuits à pied et en autobus; archives; *Bibliothèque:* Société d'histoire de Sherbrooke; Bibliothèque publique
Membre(s) du bureau directeur:
Josée Delage, Directrice
Hélène Liard, Archiviste

Société d'histoire de Sillery (SHS)
CP 47051, Succ. Sheppard, Québec QC G1S 4X1
Tél: 418-641-6664
shs@videotron.ca
www.histoiresillery.org
www.facebook.com/pages/Société-dhistoire-de-Sillery/501293813255528
Aperçu: Dimension: petite; *Envergure:* locale; Organisme sans but lucratif; fondée en 1985
Mission: Interesser ses membres et le public de la région à l'histoire de Sillery et à l'histoire régionale
Membre de: Fédération des sociétés d'histoire du Québec; Quebec Anglophone heritage Network (QAHN); Table de concertation des Sociétés d"histoire de la Ville de Québec
Finances: *Budget de fonctionnement annuel:* Moins de $50,000
Membre(s) du personnel: 2; 22 bénévole(s)
Membre: 185; *Montant de la cotisation:* 25$ (résident de la Ville de Québec); 35$ (non résident), 10$ (étudiant); *Comités:* Publication de La Charcotte (2 fois par année); Protection du patrimoine; Recherche et bibliothèque; Activités spéciales
Activités: Conférences; excursions; expositions; soupers-conférence; *Stagiaires:* Oui; *Service de conférenciers:* Oui
Membre(s) du bureau directeur:
Louis Vallée, Président, 418-264-9068
jlvallee@cec.montmagny.qc.ca

La Société d'histoire de Toronto (LSHT)
CP 93, 63, rue Wellesley est, Toronto ON M4Y 1G7
Tél: 416-534-1079
info@sht.ca
shtoronto.wordpress.com
www.flickr.com/photos/societedhistoire
Aperçu: Dimension: petite; *Envergure:* locale; Organisme sans but lucratif; fondée en 1984
Mission: Étudier et faire connaître l'histoire de l'Ontario et des franco-ontariens particulièrement celle de la région de Toronto; intéresser les chercheurs et le grand public à l'histoire régionale; encourager la recherche par la publication de travaux pertinents; veiller à la conservation de toutes les catégories de documents historiques écrits et non écrits
Membre de: Ontario Historical Society; Regroupement des Organismes du Patrimoine Franco-Ontarien
Affiliation(s): The Toronto Historical Board
Finances: *Budget de fonctionnement annuel:* Moins de $50,000 25 bénévole(s)
Membre: 100; *Montant de la cotisation:* 25$

Activités: Conférences; visites guidés; publications; recherche; réunions mensuelles 3e mercredi du mois; *Stagiaires:* Oui; *Service de conférenciers:* Oui
Membre(s) du bureau directeur:
Lisette Mallet, Présidente
Prix, Bourses:
• Prix Jean-Baptiste Rousseaux

Société d'histoire de Val-d'Or *Voir* Société d'histoire et de généalogie de Val-d'Or

Société d'histoire de Warwick
154B, rue St-Louis, Warwick QC J0A 1M0
Tél: 819-358-6261
histoire@cablovision.com
fr-fr.facebook.com/SocieteHistoireWarwick
Aperçu: *Dimension:* petite; *Envergure:* locale; Organisme sans but lucratif; fondée en 1973
Mission: Protéger les biens à caractères historiques de notre municipalité, les conserver et sensibiliser la population à la richesse du patrimoine
Membre de: Fédération des Sociétés d'Histoire du Québec
Finances: *Budget de fonctionnement annuel:* Moins de $50,000
10 bénévole(s)
Membre: 147; *Montant de la cotisation:* 10$
Membre(s) du bureau directeur:
André Moreau, Président

Société d'histoire de Weedon
209, rue des Érables, Weedon QC J0B 3J0
Tél: 819-877-2917
admin@histoiredeweedon.info
histoiredeweedon.info
Aperçu: *Dimension:* petite; *Envergure:* locale; Organisme sans but lucratif; fondée en 1981
Mission: Retrouver l'histoire la plus complète de notre village; créer une banque d'information
Membre de: La Fédération des sociétés d' histoire du Québec
Membre: *Critères d'admissibilite:* Bénévole; intéressé à faire de la recherche en histoire
Activités: Expositions de photos anciennes agrandies; remise annuelle de certificats à des familles centenaires; en 2006, activités spéciales à l'occasion du 25e anniversaire de la société
Membre(s) du bureau directeur:
Yves St-Pierre, Secrétaire
Lucie Vachon, Présidente

Société d'histoire des Iles-Percées (SHIP)
CP 234, Boucherville QC J4B 5J6
Tél: 450-449-0790
pages.videotron.com/ship/
Aperçu: *Dimension:* petite; *Envergure:* locale; fondée en 1972
10 bénévole(s)
Membre(s) du bureau directeur:
Suzanne G. Carignan, Présidente, 450-449-0790
sgcarignan@yahoo.ca

Société d'histoire des Mille-Iles *Voir* Société d'histoire et de généalogie des Mille-Iles

Société d'histoire des Six Cantons
1093-c, rue St-André, Acton Vale QC J0H 1A0
Tél: 450-546-2093
Aperçu: *Dimension:* petite; *Envergure:* locale; fondée en 1977
Mission: Regrouper les amateurs d'histoire régionale; étudier et diffuser les connaissances
Membre de: Fédération des sociétés d'histoire du Québec
Finances: *Budget de fonctionnement annuel:* Moins de $50,000
3 bénévole(s)
Membre: 60; *Montant de la cotisation:* 15$ individuel; 20$ familial; *Comités:* Toponymy; Genealogy
Activités: Expositions d'anciennes photographies, de vieux documents et d'artefacts; journée portes ouvertes dans les Archives; soirée d'identification d'objets patrimoniaux; *Bibliothèque:* rendez-vous
Membre(s) du bureau directeur:
Marie-Paule La Brèque, Présidente

Société d'histoire du Haut-Richelieu (SHHR)
CP 212, 203, rue Jacques-Cartier nord, Saint-Jean-sur-Richelieu QC J3B 6Z4
Tél: 450-358-5220
shhr@qc.aira.com
www.genealogie.org/club/shhr
Aperçu: *Dimension:* petite; *Envergure:* locale; Organisme sans but lucratif; fondée en 1979
Mission: Diffusion, conservation, protection de l'histoire et du patrimoine; gestion de la bibliothèque de généalogie et du centre d'archives privées
Affiliation(s): Fédération québécoise des sociétés de généalogie
Finances: *Budget de fonctionnement annuel:* Moins de $50,000
Membre(s) du personnel: 2; 6 bénévole(s)
Membre: 200; *Montant de la cotisation:* 25$; *Critères d'admissibilite:* Historien-généalogiste
Activités: Publications de livres historiques; conférences; *Bibliothèque:* Bibliothèque privée; Bibliothèque publique
Membre(s) du bureau directeur:
Nicole Poulin, Présidente

Société d'histoire du Lac-St-Jean/Maison des Bâtisseurs (SHL)
1671, ev du Pont Nord, Alma QC G8B 5G2
Tél: 418-668-2606; *Téléc:* 418-668-5851
Ligne sans frais: 866-668-2606
info@shlsj.org
www.shlsj.org
www.facebook.com/OdysseeDesBatisseurs
Aperçu: *Dimension:* petite; *Envergure:* locale; Organisme sans but lucratif; fondée en 1942
Mission: Acquérir, conserver, traiter et rendre accessible au public divers documents historiques et objets témoins de cette histoire, sur le territoire; diffuser et sensibiliser à la conservation et la mise en valeur par des publications de toutes natures et par la présentation d'expositions et d'interprétations à caractère historique, accessibles à l'ensemble de la population locale, régionale et touristique et ayant une qualité didactique et esthétique; éduquer par l'histoire et susciter l'intérêt pour la recherche, par la tenue d'activités pédagogiques et d'ateliers divers, et par le service de généalogie; protéger et aider à la conservation du patrimoine bâti par le SARP; favoriser le développement de services complémentaires qui augmentent l'autofinancement tout en respectant les orientations de la mission; provoquer et soutenir les initiatives du milieu en matière de sauvegarde, de restauration et de mise en valeur du patrimoine et de la culture régionale
Membre de: Fédération des sociétés d'histoire du Québec; Société des musées québécois
Affiliation(s): Société Musée Québec
Finances: *Budget de fonctionnement annuel:* $500,000-$1.5 Million; *Fonds:* Municipalité d'Alma
Membre(s) du personnel: 1; 10 bénévole(s)
Membre: 550; *Montant de la cotisation:* 25$ individuel; 15$ aîné; 15$ étudiant; 120$ collaborateur; 50$ associé; 600$ à vie; 40$ famille; *Comités:* Acquisitions; Finance; Généalogie; Projet
Activités: Musée; programme pédagogique; service d'archives; service d'aide à la rénovation patrimoniale; *Bibliothèque:* Bibliothèque du Service d'Archives; Bibliothèque publique
Membre(s) du bureau directeur:
Alexandre Garon, Directeur général

Société d'histoire du Témiscamingue
CP 1022, 8, rue Saint-Gabriel nord, Ville-Marie QC J0Z 3W0
Tél: 819-629-3533; *Téléc:* 819-629-2200
sht@cablevision.qc.ca
www.maisondufreremoffet.com
Aperçu: *Dimension:* petite; *Envergure:* locale; fondée en 1949
Finances: *Budget de fonctionnement annuel:* Moins de $50,000
Membre(s) du personnel: 1; 9 bénévole(s)
Membre: 180; *Montant de la cotisation:* 10$
Activités: *Listes de destinataires:* Oui
Membre(s) du bureau directeur:
Cécile Herbet

Société d'histoire et d'archéologie du Témiscouata
81, rue Caldwell, Cabano QC G0L 1E0
Tél: 418-854-2375; *Téléc:* 418-854-0416
Ligne sans frais: 866-242-2437
www.fortingall.ca/shatfr.php?id=109
Nom précédent: Société historique de Cabano, Inc.
Aperçu: *Dimension:* petite; *Envergure:* locale; fondée en 1967
Mission: Recherche et diffusion de l'histoire régionale; animation et gestion du site historique Fort Ingall
Membre de: La Société des musées québécois; Fédération des sociétés d'histoire du Québec
Finances: *Budget de fonctionnement annuel:* $100,000-$250,000
7 bénévole(s)
Membre: 64; *Montant de la cotisation:* 10$
Membre(s) du bureau directeur:
Martin Simard, Président

Société d'histoire et de généalogie de l'Ile Jésus (SHGIJ)
4300, boul Samson, Laval QC H7W 2G9
Tél: 450-681-9096; *Téléc:* 450-686-8270
info@shgij.org
www.shgij.org
Aperçu: *Dimension:* petite; *Envergure:* locale; Organisme sans but lucratif; fondée en 1963
Mission: Veiller à la préservation et à la diffusion du patrimoine lavallois, retracer et faire connaître notre histoire et stimuler le dynamisme des citoyens envers la généalogie
Membre de: Fédération des sociétés d'histoire du Québec; Réseau des Archives du Québec; Fédération des sociétés de généalogie du Québec
Membre(s) du personnel: 3
Membre: *Montant de la cotisation:* 10$ étudiant; 30$ particulier; 40$ famille; 60$ corporatif; 400$ membre à vie
Activités: Conférences et ateliers de généalogie; *Bibliothèque:* Centre de documentation
Membre(s) du bureau directeur:
Dominique Bodeven, Directrice générale

Société d'histoire et de généalogie de la Matapédia
24, promenade de l'Hôtel-de-Ville, Amqui QC G5J 3E1
Tél: 418-629-4242
shgmma@cgocable.ca
www.genealogie.org/club/shgm
Aperçu: *Dimension:* petite; *Envergure:* locale; Organisme sans but lucratif; fondée en 1989 surveillé par Fédération québécoise des sociétés de généalogie
Mission: Favoriser la recherche et la connaissance de l'histoire de notre région; se familiariser avec la généalogie; fournir les outils pour retracer nos ancêtres
Membre: 148; *Montant de la cotisation:* 30$ individuel; 40$ couple; 400$ membre à vie
Activités: *Service de conférenciers:* Oui
Membre(s) du bureau directeur:
René Pelletier, Président

Société d'histoire et de généalogie de Louiseville inc *Voir* Société d'histoire de Louiseville inc.

Société d'histoire et de généalogie de Matane (SHGM) / Matane Historical & Genealogical Society
382, rue du Rempart, Matane QC G4W 2T7
Tél: 418-562-9766; *Téléc:* 418-562-9766
shgm@genealogie.org
www.shgmatane.org
fr-fr.facebook.com/shg.matane
Aperçu: *Dimension:* petite; *Envergure:* locale; Organisme sans but lucratif; fondée en 1950
Mission: Contribuer à la sauvegarde et à la mise en valeur du patrimoine régional sous tous ses aspects
Finances: *Budget de fonctionnement annuel:* Moins de $50,000
20 bénévole(s)
Membre: 400; *Montant de la cotisation:* 25$ membre régulier; 35$ membre conjoint; 50$ membre corporations; 300$ membre à vie
Activités:; *Bibliothèque:* Bibliothèque publique
Membre(s) du bureau directeur:
Louis Audet, Président

Société d'histoire et de généalogie de Rivière-du-Loup (SHGRDL)
67, rue du Rocher, Rivière-du-Loup QC G5R 1J8
Tél: 418-867-6604
info@shgrdl.org
www.shgrdl.org
Aperçu: *Dimension:* petite; *Envergure:* locale; Organisme sans but lucratif; fondée en 1987
Mission: Organiser, promouvoir et patronner des activités et manifestations historiques, généalogiques et culturelles; organiser et tenir des conférences, réunions, assemblées et expositions pour la promotion et la vulgarisation de l'histoire et de la généalogie; recueillir et classer vieux documents, contrats, photos, cartes postales, cartes mortuaires ou autres
Membre de: Fédération des sociétés d'histoire du Québec; Fédération des sociétés de généalogie du Québec
Membre: *Montant de la cotisation:* 15$ membre associé; 30$ membre régulier; 50$ association; 525$ membre à vie
Activités: Soirée-conférence; déjeuner-conférence; publication de volumes historiques
Membre(s) du bureau directeur:
Gilles Dubé, Président
gildub2@videotron.ca

Société d'histoire et de généalogie de Saint-Casimir
CP 127, 510, boul de la Montagne, Saint-Casimir QC G0A 3L0
Courriel: shgsc@hotmail.com
www.genealogie.org/club/shgsc

Aperçu: *Dimension:* petite; *Envergure:* locale; Organisme sans but lucratif; fondée en 1996
Mission: Groupe les personnes intéressées à l'histoire et à la généalogie; publier, diffuser ou susciter la publication de tout article relatif à l'histoire familiale, municipale, régionale et à la généalogie
Membre de: Fédération québécoise des sociétés de généalogie
Finances: *Budget de fonctionnement annuel:* Moins de $50,000
Membre: 143; *Montant de la cotisation:* 10$ membre associé; 15$ membre principal; 250$ membre à vie
Activités:; *Bibliothèque:* Bibliothèque Jean-Charles-Magnan
Membre(s) du bureau directeur:
Léo-Denis Carpentier, Président

Société d'histoire et de généalogie de Salaberry (SHGS)
80, rue St-Thomas, Salaberry-de-Valleyfield QC J6T 4J1
Tél: 450-371-0632
shgs2011@hotmail.fr
www.shgs.suroit.com
www.facebook.com/311946960934
Aperçu: *Dimension:* petite; *Envergure:* locale; Organisme sans but lucratif; fondée en 1991
Mission: Réunir les personnes intéressées par l'histoire, la généalogie et le patrimoine; renseigner la population sur ces sujets; faire fonctionner et animer un centre de documentation; faciliter la recherche et publier les résultats des recherches effectuées
Membre de: Fédération des sociétés d'histoire du Québec; Fédération des sociétés de généalogie du Québec
Activités: Visites; atelier de généalogie; cours d'initiation à la généalogie; paléographie; conférences; *Bibliothèque:* Bibliothèque Armand-Frappier; Bibliothèque publique
Membre(s) du bureau directeur:
Marie Royal, Présidente
marie.royal@sympatico.ca

Société d'histoire et de généalogie de Shawinigan-sud (SHGSS)
CP 1431, Shawinigan QC G9P 4R2
Tél: 819-537-5390
info@histoireshawinigan.com
www.histoireshawinigan.com
Aperçu: *Dimension:* petite; *Envergure:* locale; Organisme sans but lucratif; fondée en 1987
Mission: Regrouper les personnes intéressées à l'histoire et au patrimoine naturel de Shawinigan-Sud, ainsi qu'à la généalogie des familles et/ou individus qui composent sa population; rechercher, acquérir, conserver ou connaître tous les documents, objects, biens ou immeubles rattachés à l'histoire locale et à la généalogie des personnes; diffuser les connaissances historiques et généalogiques; promouvoir les recherches sur l'histoire de Shawinigan-Sud et l'origine de ses familles
Affiliation(s): Fédération des sociétés d'histoire du Québec; Fédération québécoise des sociétés de généalogie
Activités: Salle de recherches historiques et généalogiques; rencontres culturelle; conférence; déjeuner-causerie; souper-reconnaissance excursion à caractère historique; ateliers de généalogie; *Bibliothèque*
Membre(s) du bureau directeur:
Monique Duvot, Présidente

Société d'histoire et de généalogie de Val-d'Or (SHGVD)
600, 7e rue, Val-d'Or QC J9P 3P3
Tél: 819-874-7469; *Téléc:* 819-825-3062
shvd@ville.valdor.qc.ca
www.telebecinternet.com/histoirevd
Nom précédent: Société d'histoire de Val-d'Or
Aperçu: *Dimension:* petite; *Envergure:* locale; Organisme sans but lucratif; fondée en 1976
Mission: Recueillir, conserver et diffuser la documentation concernant l'histoire de Val-d'Or et de l'Abitibi
Membre de: Fédération des sociétés d'histoire du Québec; Commission de développement culturel de Val-d'Or; Conseil de la Culture de l'Abitibi-Témiscamingue
Finances: *Budget de fonctionnement annuel:* $50,000-$100,000
Membre(s) du personnel: 2; 8 bénévole(s)
Membre: 90; *Montant de la cotisation:* 15$ invividul; 20$ famille; 50$ corporatif
Activités: Histoire et généalogie; publication de livres historiques; *Stagiaires:* Oui; *Service de conférenciers:* Oui; *Bibliothèque*
Membre(s) du bureau directeur:
Louiselle Alain, Présidente

Société d'histoire et de généalogie de Verdun
Centre culturel de Verdun, Salle Canadiana, 5955, av Bannantyne, Verdun QC H4H 1H6
Tél: 514-765-7174
shgv1@hotmail.com
www.ville.verdun.qc.ca/shgv
Aperçu: *Dimension:* petite; *Envergure:* locale; fondée en 1995
Mission: Diffuser et mettre en valeur le patrimoine naturel et culturel de la ville de Verdun
20 bénévole(s)
Membre: 100-499
Membre(s) du bureau directeur:
Gilles Lepage, Président

Société d'histoire et de généalogie des Mille-Iles
Musée Joseph-Filion, 6, rue Blainville est, Sainte-Thérèse QC J7E 1L6
Tél: 450-434-9090
info@shgmi.ca
www.shgmi.ca
Également appelé: Musée régional Joseph-Filion
Nom précédent: Société d'histoire des Mille-Iles
Aperçu: *Dimension:* petite; *Envergure:* locale; Organisme sans but lucratif; fondée en 1939
Mission: Mise en valeur du patrimoine photographique écrit et bâti
Membre de: Fédération des sociétés d'histoire du Québec
Affiliation(s): Société des musées québécois
Activités: Opération du Musée régional Joseph-Filion; *Service de conférenciers:* Oui; *Bibliothèque:* rendez-vous
Membre(s) du bureau directeur:
J.G. Gilles Charron, Président
gramar@videotron.ca

Société d'histoire et de généalogie des Pays-d'en-Haut, inc.
#27, 33, rue de l'Église, Saint-Sauveur QC J0R 1R0
Tél: 450-227-2669
shgph12@gmail.com
www.shgph.org
Aperçu: *Dimension:* petite; *Envergure:* locale
Membre: 597
Membre(s) du bureau directeur:
Pierre Gravel, Président

Société d'histoire et de généalogie des Quatre Lieux
1291, rang Double, Rougemont QC J0L 1M0
Tél: 450-469-2409
shgql@videotron.ca
www.quatrelieux.qc.ca
Aperçu: *Dimension:* petite; *Envergure:* locale; Organisme sans but lucratif; fondée en 1980
Mission: Valoriser l'importance de l'histoire, du patrimoine et de la généalogie auprès de la population. Acquérir, recevoir et conserver toute documentation sous divers formats, concernant l'histoire et le patrimoine des quatre municipalités et la généalogie de nos familles
Affiliation(s): Fédération des Sociétés d'histoire du Québec
Membre: 203; *Montant de la cotisation:* 30$ régulier; 10$ associé
Activités: Assemblées mensuelles; *Service de conférenciers:* Oui; *Bibliothèque*
Membre(s) du bureau directeur:
Gilles Bachand, Président
gbachand@videotron.ca
Lucette Lévesque, Secrétaire-trésorière
lucettelevesque@sympatico.ca

Société d'histoire et de généalogie Maria-Chapdelaine
1024, rue des Copains, Dolbeau-Mistassini QC G8L 3N5
Tél: 418-276-4989; *Téléc:* 418-276-8156
mariachapdelaine@histoireetgenealogie.com
www.histoireetgenealogie.com
www.facebook.com/213010725404771
Aperçu: *Dimension:* petite; *Envergure:* locale; Organisme sans but lucratif; fondée en 1988
Mission: Recueillir et conserver tous les types de documents ayant une valeur historique et concernant les municipalités de la MRC Maria-Champdelaine
Membre(s) du personnel: 2
Membre: *Montant de la cotisation:* 20$ individu; 30$ supporteur; 50$ corporatif; 500$ vie
Activités: Centre d'archive; bibliothèque d'histoire et de généalogie; gestion documentaire; Numérisation professionnelle de documents; gestion archivistique; ateliers de généalogie; recherche historique et généalogique sur Internet; entreposage de documents; *Bibliothèque:* Bibliothèque publique
Membre(s) du bureau directeur:
Steeve Cantin, Directeur général
scantin@histoireetgenealogie.com
Jean-Marc Mailloux, Président
maillouxjmarc@videotron.ca

Société d'histoire et de musée de Lennoxville-Ascot See
Lennoxville-Ascot Historical & Museum Society

Société d'histoire et généalogie du granit (SHGG)
CP 166, 252, rue Principale, Saint-Sébastien QC G0Y 1M0
Tél: 418-483-5473; *Téléc:* 819-652-2584
Autres numéros: Autre téléphone: 819-652-2285
shgssf@msn.com
www.shggranit.org
Aperçu: *Dimension:* petite; *Envergure:* locale; fondée en 2000
Mission: Recherches et documentation de l'histoire de la région. installés la région St-Sébastian
Membre de: Fédération histoire Québec; Fédération généalogie Québec
Finances: *Budget de fonctionnement annuel:* Moins de $50,000; *Fonds:* Publication de volumes et cotisations des membres
Membre: 85; *Montant de la cotisation:* 15$ pour 1 an
Activités: Promotion de la conservation du patrimoine; Promotion de la conservation du patrimoine; Publication de BMS locales.; *Service de conférenciers:* Oui; *Bibliothèque:* Centre Paul VI
Membre(s) du bureau directeur:
Gilles Blouin, Président
gblouin@tellambton.net

Société d'histoire naturelle de la vallée du St-Laurent See
St. Lawrence Valley Natural History Society

Société d'histoire régionale de Chibougamau (SHRC)
646, 3e rue, Chibougamau QC G8P 1P1
Tél: 418-748-3124; *Téléc:* 418-748-3324
info@shrcnq.com
www.shrcnq.com
www.facebook.com/720678961296885
Aperçu: *Dimension:* petite; *Envergure:* locale
Membre(s) du personnel: 3
Membre: 51; *Montant de la cotisation:* 20$ individu/organisme à but non lucratif; 30$ entreprise privée
Membre(s) du bureau directeur:
Pierre Pelletier, Président

Société d'histoire régionale de Lévis
9, rue Mgr-Gosselin, #R-1, Lévis QC G6V 6J7
Tél: 418-837-2050; *Téléc:* 418-837-2050
histoirelevis@shrl.qc.ca
www.shrl.qc.ca
www.facebook.com/SHRL76
Aperçu: *Dimension:* petite; *Envergure:* locale; Organisme sans but lucratif; fondée en 1976
Mission: Grouper toutes les personnes intéressées à l'histoire régionale de Lévis et désireuses de participer à des rencontres, des études, des recherches et autres activités en vue de mieux connaître et faire connaître l'histoire de la région de Lévis, autrefois connue et désignée comme étant "la Seigneurie de Lauzon"
Membre de: Fédération des sociétés d'histoire du Québec
Finances: *Budget de fonctionnement annuel:* Moins de $50,000; *Fonds:* Municipal
Membre(s) du personnel: 3; 10 bénévole(s)
Membre: 200+; *Montant de la cotisation:* 25$; *Critères d'admissibilite:* Intéressé à la petite histoire régionale; *Comités:* Bulletin; Informatique; Conférence
Activités: Quatre conférences durant l'année; *Bibliothèque:* rendez-vous
Membre(s) du bureau directeur:
Vincent Couture, Président
Gilbert Samson, Directeur général

Société d'histoire régionale Deux-Montagnes (SHRDM)
CP 91, Succ. Bureau chef, Saint-Eustache QC J7R 4K5
Courriel: info@shrdm.org
www.shrdm.org
www.facebook.com/shrdm2013
twitter.com/shrdm2013
Aperçu: *Dimension:* petite; *Envergure:* locale; Organisme sans but lucratif; fondée en 1961

Mission: Couvre la région de l'ancien comté de Deux-Montagnes, soit l'actuel territoire de la MRC de Deux-Montagnes et la MRC de Mirabel. Elle travaille activement à la diffusion de l'histoire de la région, à la sauvegarde et à la mise en valeur de son patrimoine bâti
Membre de: La Fédération des sociétés d'histoire du Québec; Conseil de la culture des Laurentides
Membre: *Montant de la cotisation:* 15$ individu; 25$ couple; 50$ corporatif
Activités: Conférences; publication de dépliants; panneau d'interprétation historique; expositions; brunch du patrimoine; rallye
Membre(s) du bureau directeur:
Vicki Onufriu, Présidente
Eric Poisson, Vice-pésident et trésorier
Prix, Bourses:
• Prix Claire-Yale
• Mérite scolaire

Société d'histoire St-Stanislas inc.
1480, rue Principale, Saint-Stanislas-de-Champlain QC G0X 3E0
Tél: 418-328-3255
www.saint-stanislas.ca/fr/societe-d-histoire_53.html
Aperçu: *Dimension:* petite; *Envergure:* locale; Organisme sans but lucratif; fondée en 1976
Mission: Recherche et diffusion de notre histoire et mise en valeur de notre patrimoine local
Membre de: Appartenance-Mauricie
Finances: *Fonds:* Conseil municipal de St-Stanislas; Caisse populaire de Moraine
Membre: *Critères d'admissibilite:* Personnes intéressées à l'histoire locale
Activités: Rencontres; brunch-récital annuel; expositions-photos; lancements de livres; compilations statistiques locales; aide aux généalogistes de partout; circuit patrimonial; *Bibliothèque:* Bibliothèque de la société d'histoire; Bibliothèque publique rendez-vous
Membre(s) du bureau directeur:
Ghislaine Brouillette, Présidente

Société d'horticulture de Saint-Lambert
600, av Oak, Saint-Lambert QC J4P 1T3
Tel: 450-671-4535
slhorticulturalsociety@yahoo.com
slhorticulturalsociety.org
Overview: A small local organization founded in 1894
Mission: Promouvoir l'étude et l'engagement dans des pratiques horticoles
Membership: *Fees:* 15$ individu; 25$ famille
Chief Officer(s):
Kevin Cuffling, Président, Conseil d'administration

Société d'horticulture et d'écologie de Boucherville (SOCHEB)
CP 302, Boucherville QC J4B 5J6
Tél: 450-641-8362; *Téléc:* 450-641-3013
socheb_boucherville@yahoo.ca
socheb.fsheq.org
Aperçu: *Dimension:* petite; *Envergure:* locale; fondée en 1996
Mission: Encourager des pratiques horticoles et aider à protéger l'environnement
Membre: *Montant de la cotisation:* 30$ individuelle; 50$ famille
Membre(s) du bureau directeur:
Olga Bosak, Présidente, Conseil d'administration

Société d'Horticulture et d'Écologie de Brossard (SHEB)
CP 50549, Succ. Carrefour Pelletier, Brossard QC J4X 2V7
Courriel: sheb.brossard@gmail.com
www.shbrossard.org
www.facebook.com/SHBrossard
Aperçu: *Dimension:* petite; *Envergure:* locale; fondée en 1981
Mission: D'offrir des conseils éducatifs sur le jardinage
Membre: *Montant de la cotisation:* 25$ personne ou couple
Membre(s) du bureau directeur:
Diane Doutre, Présidente, Conseil d'administration

Société d'Horticulture et d'Écologie de Longueuil (SHELI)
205, ch Chambly, Longueuil QC J4H 3L3
Tél: 450-646-2621
sheli_longueuil@yahoo.fr
sheli.ca
Aperçu: *Dimension:* petite; *Envergure:* locale; fondée en 1981
Mission: De promouvoir l'activité horticole et de préserver l'environnement

Membre: *Montant de la cotisation:* 20$
Activités: Conférences mensuellement; *Bibliothèque:* rendez-vous Not open to public
Membre(s) du bureau directeur:
Jean-René Gauthier, Président, Conseil d'administration

Société d'Horticulture et d'Écologie de Prévost (SHEP)
CP 611, Prévost QC J0R 1T0
Tél: 450-224-9252
shep.qc.com
Aperçu: *Dimension:* petite; *Envergure:* locale
Affiliation(s): Fédération des Sociétés d'horticulture et d'écologie du Québec
Activités: Conférences; voyages horticoles; ateliers
Membre(s) du bureau directeur:
Florence Frigon, Présidente

Société d'investissement jeunesse (SIJ)
#720, 615, boul René Lévesque ouest, Montréal QC H3B 1P5
Tél: 514-879-0558; *Téléc:* 514-879-0444
info-generales@sij.qc.ca
www.sij.qc.ca
Aperçu: *Dimension:* petite; *Envergure:* provinciale; Organisme sans but lucratif; fondée en 2001
Mission: La S.I.J. garantit des prêts aux entrepreneurs agés de 18 à 35 ans, qui désirent se lancer en affaires
Membre(s) du bureau directeur:
Hélène Desmarais, Présidente

La société de biophysique du Canada See Biophysical Society of Canada

Société de communication Atikamekw-Montagnais (SOCAM)
#600, 50, boul Chef Maurice-Bastien, 4e étage, Wendake QC G0A 4V0
Tél: 418-843-3873; *Téléc:* 418-845-4198
Ligne sans frais: 800-663-2611
socam@socam.net
www.socam.net
www.facebook.com/socam.net
Aperçu: *Dimension:* petite; *Envergure:* locale; fondée en 1983
Mission: Diffuser de l'information radiophonique en langue autochtone sur 14 communautés atikamekw, montagnaises et innu
Membre(s) du personnel: 13
Membre: 14 radios communautaires
Membre(s) du bureau directeur:
Florent Bégin, Directeur général
fbegin@socam.net

Société de conservation de la Baie de l'Isle-Verte
CP 151, 371, rte 132 est, L'Isle-Verte QC G0L 1K0
Tél: 418-898-2757
Aperçu: *Dimension:* petite; *Envergure:* locale; Organisme sans but lucratif; fondée en 1984
Mission: Mise en valeur de la réserve national de faune, patrimoine culturel, historique et naturel de l'Isle-Vertex; gestion de trois centres d'interprétation
Finances: *Fonds:* Gouvernement fédéral
Activités: Interprétation du marais salé, de la sauvagine et du baguage de la sauvagine; sentiers de randonnées pédestres

Société de Conservation du Patrimoine de Saint-François-de-la-Rivière-du-Sud inc.
534, ch Saint-François ouest, St-François-de-la-Rivière-du-Sud QC G0R 3A0
Tél: 418-259-7228; *Téléc:* 418-259-2056
patrimoine.st-franc@oricom.ca
www.patrimoinesaintfrancois.org
Aperçu: *Dimension:* petite; *Envergure:* locale; fondée en 1979
Mission: Prendre toute initiative, engager toute action propre à conserver les écrits, les imprimés, les objets, les organismes, les structures héritées du passé lointain ou récent
Membre: *Critères d'admissibilite:* Personnes intéressées à la conservation du patrimoine
Activités: Recherches historiques; publication de brochures, dépliants, guides
Membre(s) du bureau directeur:
Jacques Boulet, Président, 418-259-7805
apiboulet@videotron.ca

Société de coopération pour le développement international (SOCODEVI)
#160, 850, av Ernest-Gagnon, Québec QC G1S 4S2
Tél: 418-683-7225; *Téléc:* 418-683-5229
info@socodevi.org

www.socodevi.org
www.facebook.com/socodevi
twitter.com/socodevi
Aperçu: *Dimension:* moyenne; *Envergure:* internationale; Organisme sans but lucratif; fondée en 1985
Mission: Avec l'engagement de ses institutions membres, et par la mise en valeur de la formule coopérative ou d'autres formes associatives; contribue au développement durable des pays où elle intervient en ayant pour objectif que les populations se prennent en charge
Finances: *Budget de fonctionnement annuel:* Plus de $5 Million
Membre(s) du personnel: 200
Membre: 27 entreprises et organisations; *Critères d'admissibilite:* Coopératives et mutuelles
Activités: *Bibliothèque:* Not open to public
Membre(s) du bureau directeur:
Richard Lacasse, Directeur général
r.lacasse@socodevi.org
Luc Simard, Directeur, Administration, Finances et Ressources humaines
l.simard@socodevi.org

Société de criminologie du Québec (SCQ)
#38, 2000, boul Saint-Joseph est, Montréal QC H2H 1E4
Tél: 514-529-4391; *Téléc:* 514-529-6936
crimino@societecrimino.qc.ca
www.societecrimino.qc.ca
www.facebook.com/SocieteCrimino
twitter.com/societecrimino
Aperçu: *Dimension:* moyenne; *Envergure:* provinciale; fondée en 1960
Mission: De contribuer à l'évolution du système de justice pénale, de favoriser les échanges & les débats entre tous les intéressés à l'avancement de la justice pénale, & de favoriser & encourager la recherche
Affiliation(s): Canadian Criminal Justice Association
Finances: *Budget de fonctionnement annuel:* $50,000-$100,000
Membre: 425; *Montant de la cotisation:* 50$ pour 1 an; 90$ pour 2 ans; *Critères d'admissibilite:* Toute personne concernée par l'administration de la justice pénale
Activités:; *Bibliothèque:* Bibliothèque publique
Membre(s) du bureau directeur:
Caroline Savard, Directrice générale
caroline.savard@societecrimino.qc.ca

Société de développement des entreprises culturelles (SODEC)
#800, 215, rue Saint-Jacques, Montréal QC H2Y 1M6
Tél: 514-841-2200; *Téléc:* 514-841-8606
Ligne sans frais: 800-363-0401
info@sodec.gouv.qc.ca
www.sodec.gouv.qc.ca
www.facebook.com/SODEC.gouv.qc.ca
twitter.com/la_sodec
Aperçu: *Dimension:* grande; *Envergure:* provinciale; fondée en 1995
Mission: Soutient la production et la diffusion de la culture québécoise dans le champ des industries culturelles
Affiliation(s): Ministère de la culture et des communications
Finances: *Budget de fonctionnement annuel:* Plus de $5 Million
Membre(s) du personnel: 102
Activités: Gestion des programmes de soutien aux entreprises culturelle et cinéma
Membre(s) du bureau directeur:
Pierre Laporte, Président du conseil
Monique Simard, Présidente et chef de la direction
Publications:
• Société de développement des entreprises culturelles rapport annuel
Type: Newsletter
• VigiSODEC [a publication of the Société de développement des entreprises culturelles]
Type: Report

Société de développement des périodiques culturels québécois (SODEP)
#716, 460, rue Sainte-Catherine ouest, Montréal QC H3B 1A7
Tél: 514-397-8669; *Téléc:* 514-397-6887
info@sodep.qc.ca
www.sodep.qc.ca
www.facebook.com/sodep.qc.ca?ref=ts
twitter.com/cultureenrevues
Également appelé: Périodiques culturels québécois
Nom précédent: Association des Éditeurs de périodiques culturels québécois

Aperçu: Dimension: moyenne; *Envergure:* provinciale; fondée en 1978
Mission: Travailler à l'essor et au rayonnement des revues culturelles; établir et entretenir des liens avec le milieu de l'enseignement, les bibliothèques, les médias et les maisons de distribution; représenter et promouvoir les intérêts professionnels, éthiques et économiques des éditeurs; favoriser les échanges internationaux
Membre: 44; *Montant de la cotisation:* 250$; *Critères d'admissibilite:* Revues culturelles
Activités: Listes de destinataires: Oui
Membre(s) du bureau directeur:
Éric Perron, Président
Isabelle Lelarge, Vice-président
Francine Bergeron, Directrice générale
Josiane Ouellet, Secrétaire-trésorier

Société de développement économique du Saint-Laurent (SODES) / St. Lawrence Economic Development Council
271, rue de l'Estuaire, Québec QC G1K 8S8
Tél: 418-648-4572; *Téléc:* 418-648-4627
sodes@st-laurent.org
www.st-laurent.org
www.facebook.com/SodesQc
twitter.com/Sodesqc
Aperçu: Dimension: petite; *Envergure:* locale; Organisme sans but lucratif; fondée en 1985
Mission: Promouvoir le St-Laurent comme axe de développement; protéger les intérêts de la communauté maritime du St-Laurent et la représenter auprès des gouvernements; rassembler la communauté maritime du St-Laurent et mettre à sa disposition un forum d'échange et de concertation
Finances: Budget de fonctionnement annuel: $100,000-$250,000
Membre(s) du personnel: 4
Membre: 80; *Montant de la cotisation:* Barème; *Comités:* Développement; Environnement; Réglementation; Tourisme; Assurances; Fiscalité municipale
Activités: Journée Maritime Québécoise; Prix du Saint-Laurent; *Stagiaires:* Oui; *Service de conférenciers:* Oui
Membre(s) du bureau directeur:
Nicole Trépanier, Président
nicole.trepanier@st-laurent.org
Mélissa Laliberté, Directrice, Projets et affaires gouvernementales
melissa.laliberte@st-laurent.org
Ariane Charette, Chargée, Communications
ariane.charette@st-laurent.org
Marie-Pier Racine, Adjointe administrative
marie-pier.racine@st-laurent.org

Société de généalogie de Drummondville
555, rue des Écoles, Drummondville QC J2B 1J6
Tél: 819-474-2318
info@histoiredrummond.com
www.histoiredrummond.com
www.facebook.com/societehistoiredrummond
Également appelé: Société d'histoire de Drummondville
Aperçu: Dimension: petite; *Envergure:* locale; fondée en 1957
Mission: Réunir les amateurs de l'histoire régionale et encourager la recherche historique; promouvoir la conservation des monuments et sites historiques; organiser des conférences et expositions à portée historique; promouvoir la diffusion de l'histoire par des publications; organiser une bibliothèque de documents historiques
Membre de: Fédération des sociétés d'histoire du Québec; Chambre de Commerce du Comté de Drummond
Membre(s) du personnel: 2
Membre: 113; *Montant de la cotisation:* 12$ étudiant; 25$ individu; 35$ résident hors MRC; 100$ corporatif/vie
Activités: Conférences; expositions; services d'accueil et d'orientation de chercheurs; *Stagiaires:* Oui; *Service de conférenciers:* Oui; *Bibliothèque:* Archives
Membre(s) du bureau directeur:
Hélène Vallières, Directrice

Société de généalogie de l'Outaouais
855, boul de la Gappe, Gatineau QC J8T 8H9
Tél: 819-243-0888; *Téléc:* 819-568-5933
sgo@genealogieoutaouais.com
www.genealogieoutaouais.com
Aperçu: Dimension: moyenne; *Envergure:* locale; fondée en 1978

Mission: Promouvoir la généalogie; donner des cours d'initiation à la recherche généalogique et en paléographie; collaborer avec le centre régional des archives nationales du Québec à Hull pour maintenir une bibliothèque spécialisée en généalogie et en histoire de la région
Affiliation(s): Fédération québécoise des sociétés de généalogie
Membre: Montant de la cotisation: 35$ individu; 50$ couple; *Comités:* Reconnaissances
Activités: Ateliers et rencontres; *Événements de sensibilisation:* Semaine nationale de la généalogie, novembre; *Service de conférenciers:* Oui; *Bibliothèque:* Bibliothèque publique
Membre(s) du bureau directeur:
Suzanne Bigras, Présidente
suzanne_bigras@hotmail.com

Société de généalogie de la Beauce
#403, 250 - 18e rue ouest, Saint-Georges QC G5Y 4S9
Tél: 418-228-3509
sgbce@globetrotter.net
genealogie.beauce.voila.net
Aperçu: Dimension: petite; *Envergure:* locale; Organisme sans but lucratif; fondée en 1996
Mission: Aider les membres dans leurs recherches généalogiques
Membre de: Fédération québécoise des sociétés de généalogie; Société de généalogie de Québec
Finances: Budget de fonctionnement annuel: Moins de $50,000
Membre(s) du personnel: 3; 8 bénévole(s)
Membre: 40; *Montant de la cotisation:* 20 $
Activités: Rencontre aux 2 semaines pour aider les membres en recherche; *Bibliothèque:* Bibliothèque publique
Membre(s) du bureau directeur:
Jean Nicol Dubé, Président

Société de généalogie de la Jemmerais (SGLJ)
CP 82, Sainte-Julie QC J3E 1X5
Tél: 450-922-4466
sglj@genealogie.org
www.genealogie.org/club/sglj
Nom précédent: Club de généalogie de Sainte-Julie
Aperçu: Dimension: petite; *Envergure:* locale; Organisme sans but lucratif; fondée en 1994
Mission: Regrouper les personnes intéressées à la généalogie; faire connaître la généalogie et les activités connexes comme l'histoire, la paléographie, la démographie, la sociologie, l'héraldique; faire naître et soutenir l'intérêt de la population de la région pour la généalogie
Membre: Montant de la cotisation: 20$ membre principal; 10$ membre associé
Activités: Visite organisées; conférences; ateliers; réunions mensuelles; cours d'initiation a la généalogie
Membre(s) du bureau directeur:
Anita de Chantal, Présidente

Société de généalogie de la Mauricie et des Bois-Francs
#208, 1800, rue St-Paul, Trois-Rivières QC G9A 1J7
Tél: 819-376-2691
sgmbf@cgocable.ca
www.genealogie.org/club/sgmbf/sgmbf.htm
Aperçu: Dimension: petite; *Envergure:* locale; fondée en 1979
Membre de: Fédération québécoise des sociétés de généalogie
Finances: Budget de fonctionnement annuel: Moins de $50,000
Membre: 425; *Montant de la cotisation:* 30$
Activités:; *Bibliothèque:* rendez-vous
Membre(s) du bureau directeur:
Normand Houde, Président

Société de généalogie de Lanaudière
CP 221, Joliette QC J6E 3Z6
Tél: 450-756-1818
sgl@lanaudiere.net
www.sgl.lanaudiere.net
Aperçu: Dimension: petite; *Envergure:* locale; fondée en 1980
Mission: Regrouper en association les personnes intéressées à la généalogie et à la promotion de cet héritage
Membre de: la Fédération des sociétés d'histoire du Québec, la Fédération québécoise des sociétés de généalogie
Membre: Montant de la cotisation: 20$ étudiant; 40$ individuel; 75$ corporatif; 600$ membre à vie; *Comités:* Bibliothèque; Activités mensuelles; Finances; Registraire; Publications; Informatique; Sites Web
Membre(s) du bureau directeur:
Jacques Gauthier, Président

Société de généalogie de Longueuil
CP 21027, Succ. Jacques-Cartier, Longueuil QC J4J 5J4
Tél: 450-670-1869; *Téléc:* 450-670-1427
www.slongueuil.org
Aperçu: Dimension: petite; *Envergure:* locale; fondée en 1990
Mission: Regrouper les personnes intéressées à la recherche généalogique, à l'histoire des familles et à la petite histoire du Québec.
Membre de: Fédération québécoise des sociétés de généalogie
Membre: Montant de la cotisation: 35$
Activités: Recherches généalogiques; cours; conférences; ateliers
Membre(s) du bureau directeur:
Léandre Vachon, Président

Société de généalogie de Québec (SGQ)
CP 9066, Succ. Sainte-Foy, #3112, 1055, av du Séminaire, Québec QC G1V 4A8
Tél: 418-651-9127; *Téléc:* 418-651-2643
sgq@uniserve.com
www.sgq.qc.ca
www.facebook.com/553614701384842
Aperçu: Dimension: moyenne; *Envergure:* provinciale; Organisme sans but lucratif; fondée en 1961
Mission: Regrouper les personnes intéressées à promouvoir les recherches sur les histoires de familles des ancêtres et à répandre les connaissances généalogiques; favoriser la conservation des documents relatifs à la généalogie; être un lieu de conservation du patrimoine familial
Membre de: Fédération des sociétés de généalogie du Québec; Canadian Federation of Genealogical & Family Histories Societies Inc.
Finances: Budget de fonctionnement annuel: $50,000-$100,000 50 bénévole(s)
Membre: 1 500; *Montant de la cotisation:* 25$ membre associé; 50$ membre principal; *Comités:* Bibliothèque; Centre virtuel de documentation; Conférences; Édition et Publication; Formation; Héraldique; Informatique; L'Ancêtre; Portail et intranet; Registraire; Service à la clientèle; Service de recherche et d'entraide
Activités: Recherche en généalogie; formation; entraide; conférences; *Service de conférenciers:* Oui; *Bibliothèque:* Roland J. Auger Bibliothèque; rendez-vous
Membre(s) du bureau directeur:
Solange Talbot, Registraire

Société de généalogie de Saint-Eustache
Société de Généalogie de Saint-Eustache, 12, ch de la Grande-Côte, Saint-Eustache QC J7P 1A2
Tél: 450-974-5164
sgse@sgse.org
www.sgse.org
Aperçu: Dimension: petite; *Envergure:* locale; Organisme sans but lucratif; fondée en 1997
Mission: Faire connaître la généalogie à l'ensemble du territoire; regrouper toutes les personnes désireuses de partager leurs connaissances généalogiques et leur histoire de famille; publier des livres, revues, plaquettes historiques sur les familles de la région ou tout autre sujet d'intérêt pour les membres
Membre: Montant de la cotisation: 25$ individuel; 30$ famille/couple
Activités: Centre de recherches; rencontres culturelles; cours d'initiation à la généalogie
Membre(s) du bureau directeur:
Claudette Giraldeau, Présidente
Prix, Bourses:
• Prix Jacques-Labrie
Pour travaux généalogiques

Société de généalogie des Cantons de l'Est (SGCE)
275, rue Dufferin, Sherbrooke QC J1H 4M5
Tél: 819-821-5414
sgce@abacom.com
www.sgce.qc.ca
www.facebook.com/sgce.qc.ca
Aperçu: Dimension: moyenne; *Envergure:* locale; Organisme sans but lucratif; fondée en 1968
Membre de: Fédération québécoise des sociétés de généalogie
Finances: Budget de fonctionnement annuel: Moins de $50,000
Membre(s) du personnel: 1; 28 bénévole(s)
Membre: 400; *Montant de la cotisation:* 20$ membre associé et étudiant; 30$ membre hors Québec; 40$ membre principal; 600$ membre à vie; *Comités:* Adhésion; Assistance aux chercheurs; Bénévolat; Bibliothèque; Communications; Conférences; Ententes négociées; Entretien informatique; Évènements

spéciaux; Financement; Formation; Publications; Publicité; Site Internet
Activités: Recherches; publication de répertoires généalogiques; *Service de conférenciers:* Oui; *Bibliothèque:* Bibliothèque publique
Membre(s) du bureau directeur:
Nicole Leblanc, Présidente
Prix, Bourses:
• Prix Raymond Lambert
; *Amount:* 500$

Société de généalogie des Laurentides (SGL)
Bibliothèque C-E Garneau, 500, boul des Laurentides, Saint-Jérôme QC J7Z 4M2
Tél: 450-553-1182
info@sglaurentides.org
www.genealogie.org/club/sglaurentides/
Aperçu: *Dimension:* petite; *Envergure:* locale; Organisme sans but lucratif; fondée en 1984
7 bénévole(s)
Membre: 100; *Montant de la cotisation:* 35$ individuel; 55$ couple
Activités: Centre de recherches; cours d'initiation à la généalogie; conférences; visites historiques; banque de données; *Service de conférenciers:* Oui
Membre(s) du bureau directeur:
Guy Constantineau, Présidente

Société de généalogie du Saguenay, inc. (SGS)
899A, ch Sydenham, Chicoutimi QC G7H 2H4
Tél: 418-693-8266; *Téléc:* 418-698-1156
sgssaguenay@videotron.ca
sgsaguenay.ca/wp
Aperçu: *Dimension:* petite; *Envergure:* locale; Organisme sans but lucratif; fondée en 1979
Mission: Regrouper des personnes qui s'intéressent à la généalogie et à l'histoire de leur famille et favoriser des échanges entre elles; vulgariser les connaissances généalogiques et historiques par l'édition, les conférences, les cours, la recherche et la confection de documents; supporter les chercheurs locaux et régionaux en généalogie
Membre de: La Fédération québécoise des sociétés de généalogie
Finances: *Budget de fonctionnement annuel:* Moins de $50,000
Membre(s) du personnel: 1; 15 bénévole(s)
Membre: 250; *Montant de la cotisation:* 15$ étudiant; 35$ individu; 50$ couple; 400$ membre à vie; *Critères d'admissibilite:* Retraité et autres; *Comités:* Journal; Surveillance; Publicité; Informatique de la bibliothèque
Activités: Cours de généalogie; cours sur les logiciels de généalogie; *Evénements de sensibilisation:* Portes Ouvertes; *Bibliothèque:* Centre de Documentation; Not open to public
Membre(s) du bureau directeur:
Paul-Henri Croft, Président
croftph@videotron.ca

Société de généalogie et d'archives de Rimouski (SGAR)
110, rue de l'Évêché est, #L-120, Rimouski QC G5L 1X9
Tél: 418-724-3242
www.sghr.ca
Nom précédent: Société généalogique de l'est du Québec
Aperçu: *Dimension:* moyenne; *Envergure:* locale; Organisme sans but lucratif; fondée en 1979
Mission: Organiser, promouvoir et patronner des activités et manifestations généalogiques, historiques et culturelles; inventorier, protéger et étudier le patrimoine; organiser et tenir des conférences, réunions, assemblées et expositions pour la promotion et la vulgarisation de la généalogie
Membre de: Fédération québécoise des sociétés de généalogie; Fédération histoire Québec
Affiliation(s): Centre de généalogie francophone d'Amérique (CGFA)
Finances: *Budget de fonctionnement annuel:* Moins de $50,000
50 bénévole(s)
Membre: 22 sociétés; 30 membres à vie; 495 individu; 45 échanges divers; *Montant de la cotisation:* 20$ étudiant; 30$ individuel; 55$ couple; 600$ membre à vie
Activités: Atelier de généalogie, cours de généalogie; navigation sur internet; *Service de conférenciers:* Oui; *Bibliothèque:* Centre de recherche en généalogie; Bibliothèque publique
Membre(s) du bureau directeur:
Guy Bernier, Président
info@sghr.ca

Pierre Rioux, Vice-président
pierre_rioux@uqar.qc.ca
Claude-Carrier Fortin, Trésorier
clsy@cgocable.ca

Société de généalogie et d'histoire de la région de Thetford-Mines
671, boul Frontenac ouest, Thetford Mines QC G6G 1N1
Tél: 418-338-8591
sghrtm@cegepth.qc.ca
www.genealogie.org/club/sghrtm
www.facebook.com/genealogiethetford?ref=ts&fref=ts
Aperçu: *Dimension:* petite; *Envergure:* locale; Organisme sans but lucratif
Mission: Favoriser l'entraide des membres, la recherche sur la généalogie et l'histoire des ancêtres et des familles; permettre la diffusion des connaissances généalogiques par la publication de répertoires généalogiques
Membre: *Montant de la cotisation:* 25$ individuel; *Critères d'admissibilite:* Personnes intéressées à la généalogie et à l'histoire; *Comités:* Revue; Informatique; Publicité; Recherche
Activités: Rencontres; études; recherches; publication d'articles, brochures, répertoires; banques de données; conférences; visites guidées
Membre(s) du bureau directeur:
Pascal Binet, Président

Société de généalogie Gaspésie-Les Îles
CP 6217, 80, boul de Gaspé, Gaspé QC G4X 2R7
Tél: 418-368-6438; *Téléc:* 418-368-1535
genealogie.gaspe@gmail.com
www.genealogie.org/club/sggi
Aperçu: *Dimension:* petite; *Envergure:* locale; Organisme sans but lucratif; fondée en 1990
Mission: Regrouper les personnes désireuses de partager des connaissances; publier des recherches en généalogie; organiser des sessions d'études et de formation en généalogie
Membre de: Fédération des Sociétés Généalogiques du Québec
Finances: *Budget de fonctionnement annuel:* Moins de $50,000
Membre: 80; *Montant de la cotisation:* 20$
Membre(s) du bureau directeur:
Serge Ouellet, Président
ouellet.serge@cgocable.ca

Société de généalogie Saint-Hubert
3500, rue Grand Boulevard, Longueuil QC J4T 0A1
Tél: 450-445-0080
www.sgsh.org
Aperçu: *Dimension:* petite; *Envergure:* locale; Organisme sans but lucratif; fondée en 1989
Mission: Mieux connaître et faire connaître la généalogie; faire découvrir les outils de recherche généalogique; favoriser la publication des recherches généalogiques
Membre de: Fédération québécoise des sociétés de généalogie
Finances: *Budget de fonctionnement annuel:* Moins de $50,000
Membre: *Montant de la cotisation:* 25$ membre; 15$ conjoint
Activités: Bibliothèque:
Membre(s) du bureau directeur:
Pierre Decelles, Président

Société de l'Acadie du Nouveau-Brunswick (SANB)
#204, 702, rue Principale, Petit-Rocher NB E8J 1V1
Ligne sans frais: 888-722-2343
info@sanb.ca
www.sanb.ca
www.facebook.com/sanb.ca
twitter.com/SAcadieNB
Aperçu: *Dimension:* moyenne; *Envergure:* provinciale; Organisme sans but lucratif; fondée en 1973 surveillé par Fédération des communautés francophones et acadienne du Canada
Mission: La Société vise à unir tous les Acadiens et Acadiennes du Nouveau-Brunswick et les sensibiliser aux problèmes sociaux, économiques, culturels et politiques qu'ils doivent affronter; s'occuper de tout sujet ayant trait à la protection et la promotion des droits et à l'avancement des intérêts des Acadiens et Acadiennes du Nouveau-Brunswick; entretenir des liens aussi étroits que possible avec les groupements analogues des autres provinces canadiennes et de l'étranger
Affiliation(s): Société Nationale de l'Acadie
Finances: *Budget de fonctionnement annuel:* $500,000-$1.5 Million
Membre(s) du personnel: 8
Membre: 20 000+
Activités: *Stagiaires:* Oui; *Bibliothèque:* Centre de documentations

Membre(s) du bureau directeur:
Ali Chaisson, Directeur général
dg@sanb.ca

Société de l'aide à l'enfance d'Algoma *See* Children's Aid Society of Algoma

La Société de l'aide à l'enfance d'Ottawa *See* Children's Aid Society of Ottawa

Société de l'arthrite *See* Arthritis Society

Société de l'histoire des familles du Québec *See* Québec Family History Society

Société de la francophonie manitobaine (SFM)
#106, 147, boul. Provencher, Saint-boniface MB R2H 0G2
Tél: 204-233-4915; *Téléc:* 204-977-8551
Ligne sans frais: 800-665-4443
sfm@sfm-mb.ca
www.sfm.mb.ca
www.facebook.com/societe.franco.manitobaine
twitter.com/SocieteFM
Aperçu: *Dimension:* moyenne; *Envergure:* provinciale; Organisme sans but lucratif; fondée en 1968 surveillé par Fédération des communautés francophones et acadienne du Canada
Mission: Veiller à l'épanouissement de cette communauté
Membre: 35 organismes probinciaux; *Critères d'admissibilite:* Age de 16 ans ou plus, comprenant le français et désirant vivre en français au Manitoba
Activités: *Service de conférenciers:* Oui
Membre(s) du bureau directeur:
Christian Monnin, Président
Daniel Boucher, Directeur général

Société de la médecine rurale du Canada *See* Society of Rural Physicians of Canada

Société de la SLA du Québec *Voir* ALS Society of Québec

Société de la thérapie respiratoire de l'Ontario *See* Respiratory Therapy Society of Ontario

Société de leucémie et lymphome du Canada *See* The Leukemia & Lymphoma Society of Canada

Société de Microscopie du Canada *See* Microscopical Society of Canada

Société de mise en marché des métiers d'art inc. *Voir* Conseil des métiers d'art du Québec (ind.)

Société de musique des universités canadiennes *See* Canadian University Music Society

Société de pharmacologie du Canada *See* Canadian Society of Pharmacology & Therapeutics

Société de philosophie du Québec (SPQ)
CP 217, Succ. B, Montréal QC H3B 3J7
Tél: 514-987-3000; *Téléc:* 514-987-6721
info@laspq.org
www.laspq.org
www.facebook.com/307698586002894
twitter.com/SocietePhiloQC
Aperçu: *Dimension:* petite; *Envergure:* provinciale; fondée en 1974
Membre de: La FISP; l'ASPLF
Finances: *Budget de fonctionnement annuel:* Moins de $50,000
15 bénévole(s)
Membre: 100-499; *Montant de la cotisation:* 30-195
Membre(s) du bureau directeur:
Patrick Turmel, Président

Société de Promotion et de Diffusion des Arts et de la Culture (SPDAC)
Festival International Montréal en Arts, #211, 576, rue Sainte-Catherine est, Montréal QC H2L 2E1
Tél: 514-370-2269
Ligne sans frais: 877-522-4646
info@mtlenarts.com
mtlenarts.com
www.facebook.com/MtlenArts
twitter.com/mtlenarts
Aperçu: *Dimension:* moyenne; *Envergure:* locale
Mission: Organisme à but non lucratif qui favorise un rapprochement entre les communautés locales et les artistes; Le Festival International Montréal en Arts accueille plus de 250 artistes en arts visuels et métiers d'arts
Membre(s) du bureau directeur:

Stéphane Mabilais, Directeur général
stephanie@mtlenarts.com

Société de protection des animaux du Grand Moncton *See* Greater Moncton Society for the Prevention of Cruelty to Animals

Société de protection des forêts contre les insectes et maladies (SOPFIM)
1780, rue Semple, Québec QC G1N 4B8
Tél: 418-681-3381; *Téléc:* 418-681-0994
Ligne sans frais: 877-224-3381
www.sopfim.qc.ca
Aperçu: Dimension: petite; *Envergure:* provinciale; fondée en 1990
Mission: Protéger efficacement les forêts contre les insectes et les maladies, dans le respect de l'environnement, pour l'ensemble des utilisateurs et au bénéfice de toute la collectivité québécoise
Membre(s) du personnel: 12
Membre(s) du bureau directeur:
Jean-Yves Arsenault, Directeur général
j.arsenault@sopfim.qc.ca
Prix, Bourses:
• Bourse Wladimir-A.-Smirnoff
Octroyée à deux étudiants poursuivant leurs études universitaires dans le domaine de la lutte biologique contre les insectes ravageurs forestiers; *Amount:* Deux bourses de 5 000$

Société de protection des infirmières et infirmiers du Canada *See* Canadian Nurses Protective Society

Société de protection des plantes du Québec / Québec Society for the Protection of Plants
QC
Courriel: info@sppq.qc.ca
www.sppq.qc.ca
Aperçu: Dimension: petite; *Envergure:* provinciale; fondée en 1908
Mission: Vouée à la protection des plantes; regroupe des chercheurs universitaires et gouvernementaux, des agronomes, des biologistes, des ingénieurs forestiers, des technologues, des étudiants, ainsi que toute personne intéressée à la protection des plantes.
Membre: *Comités:* Promotion et recrutement; Bourses étudiantes; Futurs congrès; Nomenclature française des maladies des plantes du Canada; Phytoprotection; Fondation SPPQ; Congrès annuel; Les Échos phytosanitaires
Membre(s) du bureau directeur:
Sylvie Rioux, Présidente
sylvie.rioux@cerom.qc.ca
Vicky Toussaint, Secrétaire
vicky.toussaint@agr.gc.ca
Pierre-Antoine Thériault, Trésorier
tresorier@sppq.qc.ca
Prix, Bourses:
• Bourse annuelle
Pour encourager les étudiantes et les étudiants à poursuivre des études graduées dans le domaine de la protection des végétaux; *Amount:* 1 000$
• Prix W.E. Sackston
Pour la meilleure communication étudiante présentée lors de son congrès annuel

Société de recherche sur le cancer *See* Cancer Research Society

Société de sauvetage *See* Lifesaving Society

Société de schizophrénie de l'Ontario *See* Schizophrenia Society of Ontario

Société de Schizophrénie de la Montérégie *Voir* Le Centre de soutien en santé mentale - Montérégie

Société de Théorie et de Culture existentialises et phénoménologique *See* Society for Existential & Phenomenological Theory & Culture

Société de toxicologie du Canada *See* Society of Toxicology of Canada

Société dentaire du Nouveau-Brunswick *See* New Brunswick Dental Society

Société des archives historiques de la région de l'Amiante (SAHRA)
671, boul Frontenac ouest, Thetford Mines QC G6G 1N1
Tél: 418-338-8591; *Téléc:* 418-338-3498
archives@cegepth.qc.ca
www.sahra.qc.ca
Aperçu: Dimension: petite; *Envergure:* locale; fondée en 1985
Mission: Recueillir, classer, conserver et rendre accessible au public les archives régionales
Finances: *Budget de fonctionnement annuel:* $50,000-$100,000
Membre(s) du personnel: 2; 2 bénévole(s)
Membre(s) du bureau directeur:
Stéphane Hamann, Directeur-archiviste

Société des artistes canadiens *See* Society of Canadian Artists

Société des attractions touristiques du Québec (SATQ)
4545, av Pierre-de Coubertin, Montréal QC H1V 0B2
Tél: 514-252-3037; *Téléc:* 514-254-1617
Ligne sans frais: 800-361-7688
info@satqfeq.com
www.attractionsevenements.com
www.facebook.com/satq.feq
twitter.com/SATQFEQ
Aperçu: Dimension: petite; *Envergure:* provinciale; Organisme sans but lucratif; fondée en 1991
Membre(s) du personnel: 33
Activités: Promotion; formation; information; représentation; *Stagiaires:* Oui; *Listes de destinataires:* Oui
Membre(s) du bureau directeur:
Pierre-Paul Leduc, Directeur général, 514-252-3037 Ext. 3475
pierre-paul.leduc@satqfeq.com
Camille Trudel, Président
camille.trudel@sympatico.ca

Société des Auteurs de Radio, Télévision et Cinéma (SARTEC) / Society of Writers in Radio, Television & Cinema
1229, rue Panet, Montréal QC H2L 2Y6
Tél: 514-526-9196; *Téléc:* 514-526-4124
information@sartec.qc.ca
www.sartec.qc.ca
twitter.com/SARTEC_auteur
vimeo.com/user8816585
Nom précédent: Société des auteurs, recherchistes, documentalistes et compositeurs
Aperçu: Dimension: moyenne; *Envergure:* nationale; fondée en 1949
Mission: Regroupe les auteurs de langue française oeuvrant au Canada dans les domaines de la radio, de la télévision, du cinéma ou de l'audiovisuel; a pour objet l'étude, la défense et le développement des intérêts économiques, sociaux et moraux de ses membres
Affiliation(s): International Affiliation of Writers Guilds (IAWG)
Finances: *Budget de fonctionnement annuel:* $500,000-$1.5 Million
Membre(s) du personnel: 9
Membre: 1,300; *Montant de la cotisation:* 35$ stagiaire; 50$ associé; 85$ actif
Membre(s) du bureau directeur:
Yves Légaré, Directeur général
ylegare@sartec.qc.ca
Sylvie Lussier, Présidente

Société des auteurs, recherchistes, documentalistes et compositeurs *Voir* Société des Auteurs de Radio, Télévision et Cinéma

Société des canadiennes dans la science et la technologie *See* Society for Canadian Women in Science & Technology

Société des chefs, cuisiniers et pâtissiers du Québec (SCCPQ)
CP 47536, Succ. Plateau Mont-Royal, Montréal QC H2H 2S8
Tél: 514-528-1083; *Téléc:* 514-528-1037
bureau-national@sccpq.ca
www.sccpq.ca
www.facebook.com/sccpq
twitter.com/SCCPQ
www.youtube.com/user/sccpq
Également appelé: Société des chefs du Québec
Aperçu: Dimension: moyenne; *Envergure:* provinciale; Organisme sans but lucratif; fondée en 1953
Mission: Mise en valeur et émulation de la profession; reconnaissance professionnelle au niveau national
Finances: *Fonds:* Cotisations
Membre(s) du personnel: 1; 23 bénévole(s)
Membre: 800; *Montant de la cotisation:* 125$
Activités: Gala annuel, golf, salon, compétitions et concours
Membre(s) du bureau directeur:
René Derrien, Président national
rene.derrien@hotmail.com
Patrick Gérome, Secrétaire
patrick.gerome@baluchon.com

Société des chirurgiens cardiaques *See* Canadian Society of Cardiac Surgeons

Société des ciné amateurs canadiens *See* Society of Canadian Cine Amateurs

Société des collectionneurs d'estampes de Montréal (SCEM) / Montréal Print Collectors' Society (MPCS)
CP 324, Succ. NDG, Montréal QC H4A 3P6
www.mpcsscem.com
Aperçu: Dimension: petite; *Envergure:* locale; fondée en 1986
Mission: Regroupe des collectionneurs, des artistes et des marchands d'estampes anciennes et modernes
Membre: *Montant de la cotisation:* Individuel/le 60$, Couple 90$, Étudiant/e 30$
Activités: Huit conférences mensuelles; visites guidées aux musées; démonstrations de techniques

Société des communicateurs du Québec (SOCOM)
CP 48050, Québec QC G1R 5R5
Tél: 418-640-2512
info@socom.ca
www.socom.ca
www.facebook.com/socomqc
twitter.com/socomqc
Aperçu: Dimension: moyenne; *Envergure:* provinciale
Mission: La promotion et la défense des enjeux de l'industrie des communications
Membre: 650; *Montant de la cotisation:* 110$ individuel; 39$ étudiant/jeune professionnel; 245$ corporatif (pigiste et petite entreprise); 675$ corporatif régulier; *Critères d'admissibilite:* Professionnels des communications de la grande région de Québec; *Comités:* Événements; Formations
Membre(s) du bureau directeur:
Anne-Marie Boissonnault, Présidente

La Société des comptables professionnels du Canada *See* The Society of Professional Accountants of Canada

Société des denturologistes du Nouveau-Brunswick *See* New Brunswick Denturists Society

Société des designers d'intérieurs du Québec *Voir* Association professionnelle des designers d'intérieur du Québec

Société des designers graphiques du Canada *See* Society of Graphic Designers of Canada

Société des designers graphiques du Québec (SDGQ)
#106, 7255, rue Alexandra, Montréal QC H2R 2Y9
Tél: 514-842-3960; *Téléc:* 514-842-4886
Ligne sans frais: 888-842-3960
infodesign@sdgq.ca
www.sdgq.ca
www.linkedin.com/groups?gid=1927274
www.facebook.com/sdgq.ca
twitter.com/SDGQ
Aperçu: Dimension: petite; *Envergure:* provinciale; Organisme sans but lucratif; fondée en 1972
Membre: *Critères d'admissibilite:* Professionnels en design graphique
Membre(s) du bureau directeur:
Philippe Lamarre, Président

Société des Écoles d'éducation internationale *Voir* Société des écoles du monde du BI du Québec et de la francophonie

Société des écoles du monde du BI du Québec et de la francophonie (SEBIQ)
2000, rue Lasalle, Longueuil QC J4K 3J4
Tél: 450-679-6618; *Téléc:* 450-679-9682
sec@sebiq.ca
www.sebiq.ca
Nom précédent: Société des Écoles d'éducation internationale
Aperçu: Dimension: petite; *Envergure:* provinciale; Organisme sans but lucratif; fondée en 1988
Mission: Favoriser la mise en commun des ressources et assurer la cohésion et l'uniformité de ses exigences dans plus de 125 établissements primaires, secondaires et collégiaux d'éducation internationale au Québec
Affiliation(s): Organisation du Baccalauréat International

Finances: *Budget de fonctionnement annuel:* $500,000-$1.5 Million
Membre(s) du personnel: 7
Membre: 214; *Montant de la cotisation:* Barème; *Critères d'admissibilité:* Établissement scolaire primaire, secondaire, ou collégial; *Comités:* Varient selon les années
Activités: Perfectionnement du personnel des écoles; harmonisation de programmes internationaux au contexte québécois; rédaction de nouveaux programmes et de guides pédagogiques; délivrance d'un diplôme particulier
Membre(s) du bureau directeur:
Louis Bouchard, Président, 450-679-9682
louisbouchard@sebiq.ca
Pierre Duclos, Directeur général, 450-679-6618

Société des écrivains canadiens *Voir* Écrivains Francophones d'Amérique

Société des éleveurs de bovins canadiens See Canadian Cattle Breeders' Association

Société des Éleveurs de Chevaux Canadiens See Canadian Horse Breeders' Association

Société des établissements de plein air du Québec (SEPAQ)
Place de la Cité, Tour Cominar, #1300, 2640 boul Laurier, Québec QC G1V 5C2
Tél: 418-686-4875; *Téléc:* 418-643-8177
Ligne sans frais: 800-665-6527
inforeservation@sepaq.com
www.sepaq.com
twitter.com/reseausepaq
www.youtube.com/user/ReseauSepaq
Nom précédent: Société des parcs de sciences naturelles du Québec
Aperçu: *Dimension:* petite; *Envergure:* provinciale
Mission: D'administrer et de développer des territoires naturels et des équipements touristiques qui lui sont confiés en vertu de sa loi constitutive; d'assurer l'accessibilité, la mise en valeur et la protection de ces équipements publics pour le bénéfice de sa clientèle, des régions du Québec et des générations futures
Membre(s) du bureau directeur:
Raymond Desjardins, Président-directeur général

Société des gynécologues oncologues du Canada See Society of Gynecologic Oncologists of Canada

Société des ingénieurs professionnels et associés See Society of Professional Engineers & Associates

Société des Jeux de l'Acadie inc. (SJA)
#210, 702, rue Principale, Petit-Rocher NB E8J 1V1
Tél: 506-783-4207; *Téléc:* 506-783-4209
sja1@nbnet.nb.ca
www.jeuxdelacadie.org
www.facebook.com/societedesjeuxdelacadie
twitter.com/acajoux
www.youtube.com/user/AcajouxJeuxdelAcadie
Aperçu: *Dimension:* petite; *Envergure:* locale; Organisme sans but lucratif; fondée en 1981
Mission: Voir au maintien et au développement du Mouvement des Jeux de l'Acadie dans ses régions constituantes par l'entremise de rencontres sportives grâce à des ressources humaines, financières et des infrastructures adéquates
Membre de: Fondation des Jeux de l'Acadie inc.; Conseil économique du N.-B.; Sports N.-B.
Finances: *Budget de fonctionnement annuel:* $250,000-$500,000
Membre(s) du personnel: 4; 3500 bénévole(s)
Membre: 8; *Comités:* Développement sportif; Développement régional; Financement et Marketing
Activités: Programme Académie jeunesse; relations publiques, représentations et communications
Membre(s) du bureau directeur:
Mylène Ouellet-LeBlanc, Directrice générale
sjadg@nb.aibn.com

Société des musées québécois (SMQ)
CP 8888, Succ. Centre-Ville, Montréal QC H3C 3P8
Tél: 514-987-3264; *Téléc:* 514-987-3379
info@smq.qc.ca
www.musees.qc.ca
www.facebook.com/museesadecouvrir
twitter.com/museesdecouvrir
Nom précédent: Association des musées de la province de Québec (1973)
Aperçu: *Dimension:* moyenne; *Envergure:* provinciale; fondée en 1958
Mission: Au service du développement de la muséologie au Québec
Membre de: AMC; ICOM
Finances: *Budget de fonctionnement annuel:* $500,000-$1.5 Million; *Fonds:* Ministère de la Culture et des Communications du Québec; Tourisme Québec; Patrimoine canadien
Membre(s) du personnel: 11
Membre: 300 insitutionnel + 600 individu; *Montant de la cotisation:* barème 70$-$1500; *Comités:* Prix; Congrès; Comités AD HOC
Activités: Événements; congrès; formation et développement professionnel; informatisation des collections; *Stagiaires:* Oui
Membre(s) du bureau directeur:
Michel Perron, Directeur général
perron.michel@smq.qc.ca
Publications:
• Musées à découvrir
Price: $20
Profile: Décrit 300 musées, lieux d'interprétation et centres d'exposition du Québec

Société des obstétriciens et gynécologues du Canada See Society of Obstetricians & Gynaecologists of Canada

Société des orchidophiles de Montréal
CP 57, Succ. NDG, Montréal QC H4A 3P4
Courriel: info@orchidophilesmontreal.ca
orchidophilesmontreal.ca
www.facebook.com/136506563085346
Aperçu: *Dimension:* petite; *Envergure:* locale; fondée en 2011
Mission: Pour préserver les espèces d'orchidées menacées
Membre: *Montant de la cotisation:* $35 individuel; $45 par couple
Activités: *Bibliothèque:*
Membre(s) du bureau directeur:
André Poliquin, Président

Société des Orchidophiles de Windsor See Windsor Orchid Society

La société des organisations des citoyens aînés de l'Ontario See Ontario Society of Senior Citizens' Organizations

Société des ornithologistes du Canada See Society of Canadian Ornithologists

Société des parcs de sciences naturelles du Québec *Voir* Société des établissements de plein air du Québec

Société des professeurs d'histoire du Québec inc. (SPHQ)
#202, 1319, ch de Chambly, Longueuil QC J4J 3X1
Tél: 514-242-1645
sphq.recitus.qc.ca
Aperçu: *Dimension:* moyenne; *Envergure:* provinciale; fondée en 1962
Mission: De promouvoir l'enseignement et la didactique de l'histoire au Québec; diffusion de moyens didactiques par revue et congrès; réseaux d'échanges de matériel
Affiliation(s): Conseil pédagogique interdisciplinaire du Québec
Membre: *Montant de la cotisation:* 35$ étudiant(e)/retraité(e); 65$ enseignant(e); 75$ organisme/institution; *Critères d'admissibilite:* Regroupe des individus de l'ordre primaire, secondaire, collégial et universitaire ainsi que des organismes préoccupés par l'enseignement de l'histoire
Membre(s) du bureau directeur:
Raymond Bédard, Président
raymondbedard@hotmail.com

Société des sculpteurs de glace See Canadian Ice Carvers' Society

Société des sculpteurs du Canada See Sculptors Society of Canada

Société des techniciens et des technologues agréés du génie du Nouveau-Brunswick See New Brunswick Society of Certified Engineering Technicians & Technologists

Société des technologues en nutrition (STN)
CP 68568, Succ. Seugneuriale, 3333, rue du Carrefour, Québec QC G1C 0G7
Tél: 418-990-0309
info@stnq.ca
www.stnq.ca
ca.linkedin.com/groups/Société-technologues-nutrition-STN-4543978
Nom précédent: Association des techniciennes et techniciens en diététique du Québec
Aperçu: *Dimension:* moyenne; *Envergure:* provinciale; Organisme de réglementation; fondée en 1975
Mission: Signer des contrats collectifs de travail; surveiller la mise en application des conditions de travail des membres; promouvoir la défense et les intérêts économiques et professionnels des membres
Affiliation(s): Centrale des professionelles et professionels de la santé (CPS)
Membre: *Montant de la cotisation:* 55$ étudiant; 110$ régulier; *Critères d'admissibilite:* Signature d'une carte d'adhésion; paiement d'une première cotisation syndicale de 2$
Membre(s) du bureau directeur:
Sylvie Gignac, Présidente

Société des traversiers du Québec (STQ)
Bureau de la traverse, 250, rue Saint-Paul, Québec QC G1K 9K9
Tél: 418-643-2019; *Téléc:* 418-643-7308
Ligne sans frais: 877-787-7483
stq@traversiers.gouv.qc.ca
www.traversiers.com
Aperçu: *Dimension:* petite; *Envergure:* provinciale; fondée en 1971
Mission: Contribuer à la mobilité des personnes et des marchandises en assurant des services de transport maritime de qualité, sécuritaires et fiables, favorisant ainsi l'essor social, économique et touristique du Québec
Finances: *Budget de fonctionnement annuel:* Plus de $5 Million
Membre: 100-499
Membre(s) du bureau directeur:
Jocelyn Fortier, Présidente/directrice générale

Traverse Isle aux Grues-Montmagny
125, ch du Quai, L'Isle-aux-Grues QC G0R 1P0
Tél: 418-248-2379; *Téléc:* 418-248-9268

Traverse Isle-aux-Coudres-St-Joseph-de-la-Rive
1, ch de la Traverse, Isle-aux-Coudres QC G0A 3J0
Tél: 418-438-2743; *Téléc:* 418-438-2144
stq-iac@traversiers.gouv.qc.ca
Membre(s) du bureau directeur:
Christyan Dufour, Directeur

Traverse Matane-Baie-Comeau-Godbout
1410, rue Matane-sur-Mer, Matane QC G4W 3P5
Tél: 418-560-8616; *Téléc:* 418-560-8044
stq-matane@traversiers.gouv.qc.ca
Membre(s) du bureau directeur:
Greta Bédard, Directrice

Traverse Québec-Lévis
10, rue des Traversiers, Québec QC G1K 8L8
Tél: 418-643-8420; *Téléc:* 418-643-5178
stq-quebec@traversiers.gouv.qc.ca
Membre(s) du bureau directeur:
M. Jean Cantin, Directeur

Traverse Sorel-St-Ignace-de-Loyola
9, rue Élizabeth, Sorel-Tracy QC J3P 4G1
Tél: 450-742-3313; *Téléc:* 450-742-4307
stq-sorel@traversiers.gouv.qc.ca
Membre(s) du bureau directeur:
François Harvey, Directeur

Traverse Tadoussac-Baie-Ste-Catherine
98, rue du Bateau-Passeur, Tadoussac QC G0T 2A0
Tél: 418-235-4395; *Téléc:* 418-235-4357
stq-tadoussac@traversiers.gouv.qc.ca
Membre(s) du bureau directeur:
Carole Campeau, Directrice

La Société du Barreau du Manitoba See Law Society of Manitoba

Société du cancer du sein du Canada See Breast Cancer Society of Canada

Société du droit de reproduction des auteurs, compositeurs et éditeurs au Canada (SODRAC 2003) inc. (SODRAC) / Society for Reproduction Rights of Authors, Composers & Publishers Canada
Tour B, #1010, 1470, rue Peel, Montréal QC H3A 1T1
Tél: 514-845-3268; *Téléc:* 514-845-3401
Ligne sans frais: 888-876-3722
sodrac@sodrac.ca
www.sodrac.ca
Aperçu: *Dimension:* moyenne; *Envergure:* internationale; Organisme sans but lucratif; Organisme de réglementation; fondée en 1985

Mission: Émettre au nom de ses membres des autorisations (licences); percevoir les sommes qui leur sont dues à la suite de la reproduction de leurs oeuvres; s'occuper de l'intérêt général de ses membres, notamment par une fonction conseil et des représentations au plan politique quand il s'agit par exemple de la révision de la loi sur le droit d'auteur
Affiliation(s): Bureau international des sociétés gérant les droits d'enregistrement et de reproduction mécanique; Confédération internationale des sociétés d'auteurs et compositeurs
Finances: *Budget de fonctionnement annuel:* $1.5 Million-$3 Million
Membre(s) du personnel: 40
Membre: 6 000; *Critères d'admissibilite:* Auteurs, compositeurs, et éditeurs canadiens; ayant aussi des droits étrangers (France, Italie, Espagne, Brésil, Autriche, etc.); les membres canadiens de la SODRAC sont représentés partout à l'étranger via des ententes de représentation conclues avec ses sociétés soeurs
Activités: *Service de conférenciers:* Oui
Membre(s) du bureau directeur:
Jehan Valiquet, Président

Société du Musée historique du Comté de Compton See Compton County Historical Museum Society

Société du patrimoine de Boucherville
566, boul Marie-Victorin, Boucherville QC J4B 1X1
Tél: 450-449-0384; *Téléc:* 450-655-6577
secretaire@patrimoineboucherville.com
patrimoineboucherville.com
Aperçu: *Dimension:* petite; *Envergure:* locale; fondée en 1983
Mission: De promouvoir l'histoire et le patrimoine de Boucherville
Membre: *Montant de la cotisation:* 10$ individu; 25$ organisme à but non lucratif; 100$ société commerciale
Activités: *Evénements de sensibilisation:* Concert annuel (avril)
Membre(s) du bureau directeur:
Madeleine Parenteau, Présidente, Conseil d'administration

Société du syndrome de Turner See Turner's Syndrome Society

Société du timbre de Pâques de l'Ontario See Easter Seals Ontario

Société franco-ontarienne d'histoire et de généalogie Voir Réseau du patrimoine franco-ontarien

Société francophone de Victoria (SFV)
#200, 535 Yates St., Victoria BC V8W 2Z6
Tél: 250-388-7350; *Téléc:* 250-388-6280
Ligne sans frais: 888-388-7350
benevolat@francocentre.com
www.francocentre.com
www.facebook.com/francophonie.Victoria
Aperçu: *Dimension:* petite; *Envergure:* locale; Organisme sans but lucratif; fondée en 1941
Mission: Promouvoir, défendre et représenter les intérêts de la communauté francophone à Victoria et dans ses banlieues
Membre de: Fédération des francophones de la Colombie-Britannique
Membre: 100-499; *Critères d'admissibilite:* Francophone ou francophile
Activités: *Evénements de sensibilisation:* Les beaux jeudis; Festival de la Francophonie de Victoria
Membre(s) du bureau directeur:
Christian Francey, Directeur général
cfrancey@francocentre.com
Marylène Saumier Demers, Coordonnatrice culturel
marylenesd@francocentre.com
Randy Delisle, Responsable du secteur à l'emploi
rdelisle@francocentre.com
Valérie Dionne, Conseillère à l'emploi
vdionne@francocentre.com

Société généalogique canadienne-française (SGCF)
3440, rue Davidson, Montréal QC H1W 2Z5
Tél: 514-527-1010; *Téléc:* 514-527-0265
info@sgcf.com
www.sgcf.com
Aperçu: *Dimension:* moyenne; *Envergure:* internationale; Organisme sans but lucratif; fondée en 1943
Mission: Regrouper toutes les personnes désireuses de partager des connaissances généalogiques et leur histoire de famille par les conférences et la publication de travaux de recherche
Membre de: Fédération québécoise des sociétés de généalogie
Finances: *Budget de fonctionnement annuel:* $100,000-$250,000

Membre(s) du personnel: 1; 65 bénévole(s)
Membre: 3,700; *Montant de la cotisation:* 45$
Activités: *Evénements de sensibilisation:* Journées de la culture, oct.; *Service de conférenciers:* Oui; *Bibliothèque:* Maison de la Généalogie
Membre(s) du bureau directeur:
Richard Masson, Président
Lisa Bertrand, Vice Présidente
Suzanne Houle, Secrétaire
Bissonnette Yves, Trésorier
Prix, Bourses:
• Prix Archange-Godbout
Décerné à un chercheur pour l'ensemble de son oeuvre; *Amount:* 1000$
• Prix Percy-W.-Foy
Encourage et récompense le travail accompli par les généalogistes. Trois catégories: meilleur article publié dans la revue Mémoires; meilleur outil de recherche offert en don à la Société; meilleur ouvrage de recherche offert en don à la Société; *Amount:* 500$

Société généalogique de Châteauguay
25, boul Maple, Châteauguay QC J6J 3P7
Tél: 450-698-3082
www.societegenealogiquedechateauguay.com
Aperçu: *Dimension:* petite; *Envergure:* locale; fondée en 1998
Mission: Favoriser la recherche généalogique et l'entraide entre ses membres ainsi que la diffusion de l'histoire de la vie des ancêtres ou de leurs familles
Membre(s) du bureau directeur:
Marie-Paule Hallé, Trésorière

Société généalogique de l'est du Québec Voir Société de généalogie et d'archives de Rimouski

Société Généalogique du Nouveau-Brunswick Inc. See New Brunswick Genealogical Society Inc.

La Société géographique royale du Canada See The Royal Canadian Geographical Society

Société histoire de Mouillepied
Bibliothèque de Saint-Lambert, 490, rue Mercille, 2e étage, Saint-Lambert QC J4P 2L5
Tél: 450-466-3910
Aperçu: *Dimension:* petite; *Envergure:* locale
Mission: De préserver et de découvrir l'histoire de St-Lambert

Société historique acadienne de la Baie Sainte-Marie
Université Sainte-Anne, 1695 route 1, Pointe-De-L'ÉGlise NS B0W 1M0
Tél: 902-769-2114
Aperçu: *Dimension:* petite; *Envergure:* locale; Organisme sans but lucratif; fondée en 1972
Mission: Promouvoir les études et recherches sur l'histoire acadienne dans notre milieu; il s'agit des sites historiques, d'anciens établissements, de cimetières, d'églises, et d'écoles
Affiliation(s): Société acadienne de Clare
Finances: *Budget de fonctionnement annuel:* Moins de $50,000
Membre: 100; *Montant de la cotisation:* 7$ individu; 10$ couple; 2$ étudiant
Membre(s) du bureau directeur:
Marc Lavoie, Président

Société historique Alphonse-Desjardins (SHAD)
6, rue du Mont-Marie, Lévis QC G6V 1V9
Tél: 418-835-2090; *Téléc:* 418-835-9173
Ligne sans frais: 866-835-8444
shad@desjardins.com
www.desjardins.com/maisonalphonsedesjardins
www.facebook.com/MaisonAlphonseDesjardins
Également appelé: Maison Alphonse-Desjardins
Aperçu: *Dimension:* petite; *Envergure:* provinciale; Organisme sans but lucratif; fondée en 1979
Mission: Sauvegarder et mettre en valeur l'histoire et le patrimoine du Mouvement Desjardins et de son fondateur au bénéfice des générations actuelles et futures
Finances: *Budget de fonctionnement annuel:* $500,000-$1.5 Million; *Fonds:* Fédération des caisses Desjardins
Membre(s) du personnel: 14
Membre: 1-99
Activités: Visites guidées - gratuites à l'année; publication de plusieurs volumes sur Alphonse Desjardins et l'histoire du Mouvement Desjardins; *Service de conférenciers:* Oui
Membre(s) du bureau directeur:
Marie Boissonneault, Directrice
maire.boissonneault@desjardins.com

Société historique Cavelier-de-LaSalle / Cavelier de Lasalle Historical Society
13A, rue Strathyre, LaSalle QC H8R 3P5
Tél: 514-364-9955; *Téléc:* 514-364-9955
www.csmb.qc.ca/shcavelier
Aperçu: *Dimension:* petite; *Envergure:* locale; fondée en 1965
Mission: Diffusion de l'histoire locale, de la généalogie; organisation de conférences; défense du patrimoine
Affiliation(s): Fédération des sociétés d'histoire
Membre: *Montant de la cotisation:* 15$ individuel; 20$ familial; 5$ étudiant; 50$ corporatif; 150$ à bie; *Critères d'admissibilite:* Citoyen de la région de Montréal
Activités: Conférences, voyage ou excursion ou visite patrimoniale; *Bibliothèque:* Centre d'information; rendez-vous
Membre(s) du bureau directeur:
Cécile Duhamel, Président

Société historique d'Ottawa See Historical Society of Ottawa

Société historique de Bellechasse
8, av Commerciale, Saint-Charles-de-Bellechasse QC G0R 2T0
Tél: 418-887-3761
shb@shbellechasse.com
www.shbellechasse.com
Aperçu: *Dimension:* petite; *Envergure:* locale; Organisme sans but lucratif; fondée en 1985
Mission: Mettre en valeur l'histoire et le patrimoine de Bellechasse
Membre de: Fédération des sociétés d'histoire du Québec
Membre: 425+; *Montant de la cotisation:* 25$; 30$ familial; 45$ corporatif
Activités: Cours d'initiation en généalogie; *Service de conférenciers:* Oui; *Bibliothèque:* Bibliothèque généalogique BGI; rendez-vous
Membre(s) du bureau directeur:
Jean-Pierre Lamonte, Président

Société historique de Cabano, Inc. Voir Société d'histoire et d'archéologie du Témiscouata

Société historique de Charlesbourg
Maison Éphraïm-Bédard, 7655, ch Samuel, Charlesbourg QC G1H 7H4
Tél: 418-624-7745; *Téléc:* 418-624-7230
SHDC@live.ca
www.societe-historique-charlesbourg.org
Aperçu: *Dimension:* petite; *Envergure:* locale; Organisme sans but lucratif; fondée en 1983
Mission: Faire connaître l'histoire de Charlesbourg, mettre en valeur le patrimoin bâti et humain de Charlesbourg; offrir des services d'aide en généalogie et en informations cadastrales de Charlesbourg
Membre de: Fédération des sociétés d'histoire du Québec
Finances: *Budget de fonctionnement annuel:* Moins de $50,000; *Fonds:* Statuaire de l'arrondissement Charlesbourg de la ville de Québec
9 bénévole(s)
Membre: 135; *Montant de la cotisation:* 20$; *Critères d'admissibilite:* Résidents adultes de Charlesbourg
Activités: Conférences mensuelles de septembre à avril; expositions; bulletins; *Stagiaires:* Oui; *Bibliothèque*
Membre(s) du bureau directeur:
Jean Breton, Président

Société historique de Dorval / Dorval Historical Society
1335, ch du Bord-du-Lac, Dorval QC H9S 2E5
Tél: 514-633-4000
societehistoriquededorval.org
Aperçu: *Dimension:* petite; *Envergure:* locale; Organisme sans but lucratif; fondée en 1984
Mission: D'étudier et de préserver l'histoire de Dorval
Affiliation(s): Fédération des sociétés d'histoire du Québec
Membre: *Montant de la cotisation:* 10$ résidents et non-résidents; *Critères d'admissibilite:* Surtout résidents de Dorval; retraités; intéressés à l'histoire locale
Activités: Expositions; kiosques; réunions mensuelles; conférences; visites patrimoniales
Membre(s) du bureau directeur:
Michel Hébert, Président

Société historique de Gloucester See Gloucester Historical Society

Société historique de Joliette-De Lanaudière
CP 354, 585, rue Archambault, Joliette QC J6E 2W7

Tél: 450-867-3183
shjlanaudiere@videotron.ca
societedhistoire.connexion-lanaudiere.ca
Aperçu: *Dimension:* petite; *Envergure:* locale; Organisme sans but lucratif; fondée en 1929
Mission: Faire des recherches historiques; rassembler et conserver des documents pour l'histoire spécifique de ville de Joliette et de la région De Lanaudière; prot,ger le patrimoine par diverses interventions auprès des responsables des villes
Finances: *Budget de fonctionnement annuel:* Moins de $50,000
Membre: 52; *Montant de la cotisation:* 20$ individuel
Activités: Recherches; conférences; expositions; *Service de conférenciers:* Oui
Membre(s) du bureau directeur:
Claire L. Saint-Aubin, Présidente
Claude Amyot, Trésorier

Société historique de Kamouraska *Voir* Société historique de la Côte-du-Sud

La Société historique de l'Ontario *See* Ontario Historical Society

Société historique de la Côte-du-Sud
100, 4e av Painchaud, La Pocatière QC G0R 1Z0
Tél: 418-856-2104; *Téléc:* 418-856-2104
archsud@bellnet.ca
www.shcds.org
Nom précédent: Société historique de Kamouraska
Aperçu: *Dimension:* petite; *Envergure:* locale; fondée en 1948
Mission: Colliger et conserver tous les ouvrages, documents, objets, souvenirs, etc. pouvant servir à l'histoire de la région; regrouper les amateurs d'histoire régionale, afin de favoriser l'étude, la recherche et la publication; étudier, faire connaître et aimer notre histoire régionale; tirer de l'histoire régionale des leçons de fierté, d'attachement aux traditions et de vrai patriotisme qu'elle comporte
Membre de: Fédération des sociétés d'histoire du Québec
Finances: *Budget de fonctionnement annuel:* Moins de $50,000
9 bénévole(s)
Membre: 200; *Montant de la cotisation:* 10$ étudiant; 15$ régulier; 25$ institutionnel; 500$ et plus à vie; *Critères d'admissibilité:* 150
Activités: Journée d'histoire; *Événements de sensibilisation:* Journée d'histoire, sept.; *Bibliothèque:* Centre de documentation; Bibliothèque publique
Membre(s) du bureau directeur:
Gaétan Godbout, Président

Société historique de la Côte-Nord (SHCN)
2, Place La Salle, Baie-Comeau QC G4Z 1K3
Tél: 418-296-8228
shcn@globetrotter.net
www.shcote-nord.org
www.facebook.com/215657145115493
Aperçu: *Dimension:* petite; *Envergure:* locale; Organisme sans but lucratif; fondée en 1947
Mission: Est un organisme de conservation, de préservation et de diffusion du patrimoine nord-côtier; met à la disposition des chercheurs ses fonds, ses collections et publications
Affiliation(s): Groupe de préservation des vestiges subaquatiques de Manicouagan; Centre d'interprétation Le Bord du Cap de Natashquan
Finances: *Fonds:* Privé; Public
Membre(s) du personnel: 2
Membre: *Montant de la cotisation:* 30$
Activités: Généalogie; Archives; Exposition estivale; *Stagiaires:* Oui; *Service de conférenciers:* Oui; *Bibliothèque:* Bibliothèque Historique
Membre(s) du bureau directeur:
Catherine Pellerin, Directrice-archiviste
catherine.pellerin@shcote-nord.org
Marc Champagne, Président
marcus_spartacus@hotmail.com

Société historique de la région de Mont-Laurier (SHRML)
CP 153, 385, rue du Pont, Mont-Laurier QC J9L 3G9
Tél: 819-623-1900; *Téléc:* 819-623-7079
shghl@hotmail.ca
www.genealogie.org/club/shrml/
www.facebook.com/societedhistoire.deshauteslaurentides
Aperçu: *Dimension:* petite; *Envergure:* locale; Organisme sans but lucratif; fondée en 1975
Mission: Regrouper toutes les personnes qui s'intéressent à l'histoire, à la généalogie et au patrimoine de la région des Hautes-Laurentides

Membre de: Fédération des sociétés d'histoire du Québec; Réseau des archives du Québec
Membre(s) du personnel: 2
Membre: *Montant de la cotisation:* 30$ individu; 50$ couple; *Critères d'admissibilité:* Individus avec intérêt pour l'histoire et la généalogie
Activités: Circuits historiques guidés; publication de livres; recherches; expositions; *Bibliothèque:* Bibliothèque publique
Membre(s) du bureau directeur:
Suzanne Guénette, Responsable administrative
Prix, Bourses:
• Prix Méritas
Implication exceptionnelle dans le monde de l'histoire
• Prix Alfred-Gamelin
Sauvegarde du patrimoine bâti

Société historique de la Vallée de la Châteauguay
Centre SHVC, 72, rue Dalhousie, Huntingdon QC J0S 1H0
www.cvhs.ca
Aperçu: *Dimension:* petite; *Envergure:* locale; fondée en 1963
Mission: Soutenir la recherche et promouvoir le rayonnement et la conservation de l'histoire du sud-ouest du Québec
12 bénévole(s)
Membre: 200; *Montant de la cotisation:* 10$; *Critères d'admissibilité:* Tous ceux qui s'intéressent à l'histoire de la Vallée
Membre(s) du bureau directeur:
Connie McClintock Wilson

Société historique de la Vallée de la Gatineau *Voir* Gatineau Valley Historical Society

La Société historique de Nouvelle-Beauce (SHNB)
640, rue Notre-Dame sud, Sainte-Marie QC G6E 2W4
Tél: 418-387-7221; *Téléc:* 418-387-2454
museedelaviation@globetrotter.net
Aperçu: *Dimension:* petite; *Envergure:* locale; Organisme sans but lucratif; fondée en 1982
Mission: Promouvoir l'histoire des pionniers canadiens de langue française s'étant illustrés dans l'aviation civile au Québec. Maison Dupuis héberge le premier musée francophone de l'aviation civile en Amérique du Nord
Membre de: Conseil de la culture Chaudière Appalaches; Association touristique régionale de Chaudière Appalaches; Centre local de développement de la Nouvelle-Beauce
Finances: *Budget de fonctionnement annuel:* Moins de $50,000
10 bénévole(s)
Membre: 40; *Montant de la cotisation:* 10$; *Critères d'admissibilité:* Personnes intéressées à encourager la SHNB
Activités: *Bibliothèque:*

Société historique de Pubnico-Ouest
CP 92, 898 Hwy. 335, West Pubnico NS B0W 3S0
Tél: 902-762-3380; *Téléc:* 902-762-0726
musee.acadien@ns.sympatico.ca
www.museeacadien.ca
www.facebook.com/101935276541461
Aperçu: *Dimension:* petite; *Envergure:* locale; Organisme sans but lucratif; fondée en 1973
Mission: L'étude de l'histoire du peuple acadien, en particulier celle de Pubnico-Ouest et du comté Yarmouth; le maintien du musée et du centre de recherche; le maintien et la présentation des artifacts et des archives qui s'y retrouvent
Membre de: Federation of Nova Scotian Heritage
Affiliation(s): Community museums Nova Scotia
Finances: *Budget de fonctionnement annuel:* $50,000-$100,000
Membre(s) du personnel: 4; 50 bénévole(s)
Membre: 125; *Montant de la cotisation:* 10$
Activités: Gère musée et archives; conférences; réunions; visites guidées; soirée acadienne; expositions arts et métiers; *Bibliothèque:* Centre de recherche des archives "Père Clarence d'Entremont"

Société historique de Québec
#158, 6, rue de la Vieille-Université, Québec QC G1R 5X8
Tél: 418-694-1020
shq1@bellnet.ca
www.societehistoriquedequebec.qc.ca
www.facebook.com/157594394301478
Aperçu: *Dimension:* moyenne; *Envergure:* provinciale; Organisme sans but lucratif; fondée en 1937
Mission: Étudier et diffuser l'histoire de la ville de Québec et de sa région; relever et mettre en valeur le patrimoine de la même région
Finances: *Fonds:* Ville de Québec

Membre: *Montant de la cotisation:* Barème; *Critères d'admissibilité:* Professionnels; étudiants; curieux; personnes ayant un intérêt pour l'histoire et le patrimoine
Activités: Publie plusieurs "Cahiers d'Histoire", calendriers, textes de conférences et cartes imprimées; *Bibliothèque:* Bibliothèque publique
Membre(s) du bureau directeur:
Jean Dorval, Président
Jean-François Caron, Trésorier
Doris Drolet, Secrétaire

Société historique de Rivière-des-Prairies
9140, boul Perras, Montréal QC H1E 7E4
Courriel: info@societe-historique-rdp.org
www.societe-historique-rdp.org
Aperçu: *Dimension:* petite; *Envergure:* locale; Organisme sans but lucratif; fondée en 1993
Mission: Promouvoir l'histoire locale
Membre de: Fédération des sociétés d'histoire du Québec
Membre: *Montant de la cotisation:* 10$ individu; 15$ famille; *Critères d'admissibilité:* Intéressés à l'histoire et au patrimoine
Membre(s) du bureau directeur:
Louise Bernard, Présidente

Société historique de Saint-Boniface (SHSB)
340, boul. Provencher, Saint-Boniface MB R2H 0G7
Tél: 204-233-4888; *Téléc:* 204-231-2562
shsb@shsb.mb.ca
www.shsb.mb.ca
www.facebook.com/234786813250213
Également appelé: Centre du patrimoine
Aperçu: *Dimension:* petite; *Envergure:* provinciale; Organisme sans but lucratif; fondée en 1902
Mission: Conserver et promouvoir le patrimoine, fruit de la présence des francophones dans l'Ouest canadien et en particulier au Manitoba
Membre(s) du personnel: 6
Activités: Service d'archives; gestion de lieux historiques; *Bibliothèque:* Centre de documentation; Bibliothèque publique
Membre(s) du bureau directeur:
Gilles Lesage, Directeur général
glesage@shsb.mb.ca
Michel Lagacé, Président

Société historique de Saint-Henri
521, Place Saint-Henri, 3e étage, Montréal QC H4C 2S1
Tél: 514-933-1318
shsth@videotron.ca
www.saint-henri.com
fr-ca.facebook.com/SHSTH
Aperçu: *Dimension:* petite; *Envergure:* locale; fondée en 1977
Membre: *Montant de la cotisation:* 10$ individuel; 15$ familial; 150$ à vie

Société historique de Saint-Romuald (SHSR)
2321, ch du Fleuve, Saint-Romuald QC G6W 1X9
Tél: 418-834-3662
info@shstromuald.org
www.shstromuald.org
Aperçu: *Dimension:* petite; *Envergure:* locale; fondée en 1992
Mission: Protéger et mettre en valeur l'histoire et le patrimoine de St-Romuald
Membre de: Fédération des sociétés d'histoire du Québec
Finances: *Budget de fonctionnement annuel:* Moins de $50,000
Membre(s) du personnel: 3; 9 bénévole(s)
Membre: 170; *Montant de la cotisation:* 10$; *Comités:* Diffusion; Toponymie
Activités: Conférences, expositions, publications; *Service de conférenciers:* Oui
Membre(s) du bureau directeur:
Michel L'Hebreux, Président

Société historique de Shefford *Voir* Société d'histoire de la Haute-Yamaska

Société historique des Noirs de l'Ontario *See* Ontario Black History Society

Société historique du Canada *See* Canadian Historical Association

La Société historique du Cap-Rouge (SHCR)
4473, rue Saint-Félix, Québec QC G1Y 3A6
Tél: 418-641-6380; *Téléc:* 418-650-7505
info@shcr.qc.ca
www.shcr.qc.ca
Aperçu: *Dimension:* petite; *Envergure:* locale; Organisme sans but lucratif; fondée en 1974

Mission: Sensibiliser la population aux valeurs du patrimoine; faire connaître notre histoire et nos richesses patrimoniales
Affiliation(s): Fédération des société d'histoire du Québec
Membre: *Montant de la cotisation:* 15$ régulier; 20$ couple; 5$ étudiant; 50$ collectif; 20$ couple; 150$ à vie; *Comités:* Le Saint-Brieuc; Envois postaux et archives administratives; Archives iconographiques; Prix Joseph-Bell-Forsyth; Activités; Centenaire du Tracel; Table de concertation de la ville; Vérification
Activités: Conférences; excursions; page jointe; *Stagiaires:* Oui; *Service de conférenciers:* Oui; *Bibliothèque:* Bibliothèque publique rendez-vous
Membre(s) du bureau directeur:
Emmanuel Rioux, Président
Louise Mainguy, Vice-Présidente
Louise Cloutier, Secrétaire
Yvon Lirette, Trésorier

La Société historique du Comté de Brome *See* Brome County Historical Society

Société historique du comté de Richmond *See* Richmond County Historical Society

Société historique du Marigot inc *Voir* Société historique et culturelle du Marigot inc.

Société historique du Saguenay (SHS)
930, rue Jacques-Cartier est, Chicoutimi QC G7H 7K9
Tél: 418-549-2805; *Téléc:* 418-549-3701
shs@shistoriquesaguenay.com
www.shistoriquesaguenay.com
Aperçu: *Dimension:* moyenne; *Envergure:* locale; Organisme sans but lucratif; fondée en 1934
Mission: Colliger et conserver tout ce qui peut servir à la recherche sur un ou plusieurs aspects de la région du Saguenay-Lac-St-Jean; faire connaître et apprécier l'histoire régionale; assumer un leadership dans la conservation et la mise en valeur du patrimoine de la région
Membre de: Fédération des sociétés d'histoire du Québec
Finances: *Budget de fonctionnement annuel:* $50,000-$100,000
Membre(s) du personnel: 1; 7 bénévole(s)
Membre: 800; *Montant de la cotisation:* 30$ individuel; 40$ institution
Activités: Recherches (grille tarifaire); publications; reproductions; photocopies; conférences; veillées de Saguenayensia; *Événements de sensibilisation:* Semaine de la fierté régionale; Fête du Saguenay-Lac-Saint-Jean; *Service de conférenciers:* Oui; *Bibliothèque:* Bibliothèque publique
Membre(s) du bureau directeur:
Joëlle Hardy, Directeur général

Société historique et culturelle du Marigot inc.
440, ch de Chambly, Longueuil QC J4H 3L7
Tél: 450-677-4573; *Téléc:* 450-677-6231
shm@marigot.ca
marigot.ca
twitter.com/LeMarigot
Nom précédent: Société historique du Marigot inc
Aperçu: *Dimension:* petite; *Envergure:* locale; Organisme sans but lucratif; fondée en 1978
Mission: Promouvoir la protection du patrimoine
Membre de: Fédération des sociétés d'histoire du Québec
Finances: *Budget de fonctionnement annuel:* $50,000-$100,000; *Fonds:* Emploi-Québec; gouvernement fédéral et provincial
Membre(s) du personnel: 6; 8 bénévole(s)
Membre: 190; *Montant de la cotisation:* 20$ individus; 30$ familles; *Critères d'admissibilité:* Adulte
Activités: Conférences; visites guidées; café communautaire internet; *Service de conférenciers:* Oui; *Bibliothèque:* rendez-vous
Membre(s) du bureau directeur:
Michel Pratt, Président

Société historique et généalogique de Trois-Pistoles, inc. (SHGTP)
Salle Philippe-Renouf, Centre culturel de Trois-Pistoles, CP 1586, 145-A, rue de l'Aréna, Trois-Pistoles QC G0L 4K0
Tél: 418-851-2105
info@shgtp.org
shgtp.org
Aperçu: *Dimension:* petite; *Envergure:* locale; Organisme sans but lucratif; fondée en 1977
Mission: Colliger et conserver tout document pertinent à notre histoire locale et/ou régionale; promouvoir la généalogie locale et/ou régionale et celle des descendants des basques ayant immigré au Québec et en Acadie; maintenir et garder à jour une bibliothèque permettant la recherche généalogique et historique
Finances: *Budget de fonctionnement annuel:* Moins de $50,000
Membre(s) du personnel: 1; 10 bénévole(s)
Membre: 210; *Montant de la cotisation:* 20$ régulier; 10$ étudiant
Activités: *Service de conférenciers:* Oui
Membre(s) du bureau directeur:
Robert Létourneau, Président

Société historique Machault
134, boul Inter-Provincial, Pointe-à-la-Croix QC G0C 1L0
Tél: 418-788-5590
fr-ca.facebook.com/GouMic
Aperçu: *Dimension:* petite; *Envergure:* locale; Organisme sans but lucratif; fondée en 1983
Mission: Collectionner et conserver tous les ouvrages, objets, souvenirs pouvant servir à faire connaître le patrimoine de la Baie-des-Chaleurs; administre et exploite un centre d'interprétation historique
Membre de: Fédération des Sociétés d'histoire du Québec
Activités: Centre d'interpretation Maison Young - 1830; *Bibliothèque:* Centre d'information; rendez-vous

Société historique Pierre-de-Saurel inc. (SHPS)
6A, rue Saint-Pierre, Sorel-Tracy QC J3P 3S2
Tél: 450-780-5739; *Téléc:* 450-780-5743
histoire.societe@shps.qc.ca
www.shps.qc.ca
www.facebook.com/shpierre.de.saurel
Aperçu: *Dimension:* petite; *Envergure:* locale; Organisme sans but lucratif; fondée en 1970
Mission: Grouper en association les personnes intéressées à la recherche historique; encourager la recherche historique; intéresser le public à l'histoire locale et régionale; favoriser la conservation de document, d'objets, de lieux et d'édifices historiques; publier des études et des document d'ordre historique
Finances: *Budget de fonctionnement annuel:* $100,000-$250,000; *Fonds:* ANQ; Ville de Sorel-Tracy; RAQ
Membre: 100-499; *Montant de la cotisation:* 30$ régulier; 15$ étudiant; 50$ famille/associé/corporatif
Activités: Conférences; expositions; *Stagiaires:* Oui; *Bibliothèque*
Membre(s) du bureau directeur:
Pierre Potvin, Président

Société Huntington du Canada *See* Huntington Society of Canada

Société Huntington du Québec (SHQ) / Huntington Society of Québec (HSQ)
2300, boul René-Lévesque ouest, Montréal QC H3R 3R5
Tél: 514-282-4272
Ligne sans frais: 800-220-0226
shq@huntingtonqc.org
www.huntingtonqc.org
www.facebook.com/138147292892093
Aperçu: *Dimension:* petite; *Envergure:* provinciale; Organisme sans but lucratif; Organisme de réglementation; fondée en 1986 surveillé par Huntington Society Of Canada
Mission: Pour aider les personnes atteintes de la maladie de Huntington à faire face
Membre de: Huntington Society of Canada
Membre(s) du personnel: 4
Activités:; *Bibliothèque:* Bibliothèque publique rendez-vous
Membre(s) du bureau directeur:
Francine Lacroix, Directrice générale

Société internationale d'histoire de la médecine *See* International Society for the History of Medicine - Canadian Section

Société internationale de communication non-orale *See* International Society for Augmentative & Alternative Communication

Société internationale de droit du travail et de la sécurité sociale *See* International Society for Labour & Social Security Law - Canadian Chapter

Société internationale de recherches en chirologie inc. *See* International Society for Research in Palmistry Inc.

Société internationale des entreprises ÉCONOMUSÉ *Voir* Société internationale du réseau ÉCONOMUSÉE et Société ÉCONOMUSÉE du Québec

Société internationale du réseau ÉCONOMUSÉE et Société ÉCONOMUSÉE du Québec (SIRE) / International Economuseum Network Society
Maison Louis-S.-Saint-Laurent, 203, Grande-Allée est, Québec QC G1R 2H8
Tél: 418-694-4466; *Téléc:* 418-694-4410
info@economusees.com
www.economusees.com
www.facebook.com/SREQC
www.youtube.com/watch?v=jQJc3pT_qMg
Nom précédent: Société internationale des entreprises ÉCONOMUSÉ
Aperçu: *Dimension:* petite; *Envergure:* nationale; Organisme sans but lucratif; fondée en 1992
Mission: Conserver, développer et mettre en valeur les métiers et savoir-faire traditionnels selon le concept de l'économuséologie, en favorisant l'implantation d'entreprises ÉCONOMUSÉE à travers le pays, et ce, afin d'offrir au public un produit touristique et culturel de qualité
Finances: *Budget de fonctionnement annuel:* $500,000-$1.5 Million
Membre(s) du personnel: 6
Membre: 44; *Critères d'admissibilité:* Artisans
Membre(s) du bureau directeur:
Cyril Simard, Président directeur général
   Bureau de l'Atlantique
   #204, 25 Wentworth St., Dartmouth NS B2Y 2S7
   Tél: 902-446-3409
   Membre(s) du bureau directeur:
   Tom Young, Regional Director

Société John Howard du Canada *See* The John Howard Society of Canada

La Société la Croix-Rouge canadienne *See* Canadian Red Cross

Société littéraire et historique de Québec *See* Literary & Historical Society of Québec

Société Logique
3210, rue Rachel est, Montréal QC H1W 1A4
Tél: 514-522-8284; *Téléc:* 514-522-2659
info@societelogique.org
www.societelogique.org
www.linkedin.com/company/societelogique
www.facebook.com/societelogique
twitter.com/SocieteLogique
Aperçu: *Dimension:* petite; *Envergure:* provinciale; Organisme sans but lucratif; fondée en 1981
Mission: Promouvoir et intervenir dans le développement et la création d'environnements universellement accessibles
Affiliation(s): Confédération des organismes de personnes handicapées du Québec
Finances: *Budget de fonctionnement annuel:* $250,000-$500,000; *Fonds:* Gouvernement provincial
Membre(s) du personnel: 10
Membre: 32
Activités: Consultation en aménagement et la promotion du concept d'accessibilité; recherche; formation; gestion immobilière; *Service de conférenciers:* Oui
Membre(s) du bureau directeur:
Sophie Lanctôt, Directrice générale

Société Louis-Napoléon Dugal *Voir* Société Louis-Napoléon Dugal/Société Grande-Rivière

Société Louis-Napoléon Dugal/Société Grande-Rivière (SLND)
NB
Tél: 506-397-0930
sanbmc@nb.aibn.com
Nom précédent: Société Louis-Napoléon Dugal
Aperçu: *Dimension:* petite; *Envergure:* locale
Mission: Organisme qui prône un développement communautaire actif et positif. La Société Louis-Napoléon Dugal poursuit deux grands objectifs: Favoriser la vie en français au Madawaska & favoriser l'émancipation et l'épanouissement des francophones d'ici
Membre de: Société de l'Acadie du Nouveau-Brunswick (SANB)
Membre: 1,000-4,999
Membre(s) du bureau directeur:
Maxime Caron, Coordonnatrice

Société Makivik *See* Makivik Corporation

La societe Manitobaine de la SLA *See* ALS Society of Manitoba

Canadian Associations / Société nationale de l'Acadie (SNA)

Société mathématique du Canada *See* Canadian Mathematical Society

La Société Medicale Canadienne sur l'Addiction *See* Canadian Society of Addiction Medicine

Société médicale du Nouveau-Brunswick *See* New Brunswick Medical Society

La Société Mensa Canada *See* Mensa Canada Society

Société mondiale pour la protection des animaux *See* World Animal Protection

Société Napoléonienne Internationale *See* International Napoleonic Society

Société nationale de bienfaisance en publicité *See* National Advertising Benevolent Society

Société nationale de l'Acadie (SNA)
#403, 236, rue St-George, Moncton NB E1C 1W1
Tél: 506-853-0404; *Téléc:* 506-853-0400
info@snacadie.org
www.snacadie.org
Aperçu: Dimension: moyenne; *Envergure:* nationale; Organisme sans but lucratif; fondée en 1881
Mission: Mène différentes activités sur les scènes interprovinciales et internationales afin de promouvoir et de défendre les droits et intérêts du peuple acadien
Membre: 8 réguliers, 4 affiliés; *Critères d'admissibilite:* Associations; *Comités:* Stratégie promotion d'artistes acadiens sur la scène internationale; Congrès Mondial Acadien; Commission Odyssée Acadienne
Membre(s) du bureau directeur:
Martin Arseneau, Directeur, Comunications
Prix, Bourses:
• Prix Littéraire France Acadie
• Médaille Léger-Comeau

Société nucléaire canadienne *See* Canadian Nuclear Society

Société numismatique d'Ottawa *See* Ottawa Numismatic Society

La Société Numismatique de Québec
CP 56036, Québec QC G1P 4P7
Courriel: information@snquebec.ca
www.snquebec.ca
Aperçu: Dimension: petite; *Envergure:* provinciale; fondée en 1960
Mission: Regroupe des personnes d'origines variées et de situations diverses qui ont en commun leur intérêt pour la numismatique
Membre: *Montant de la cotisation:* 40$ régulier; 16$ internet; 53$ Etats-Unis; 81$ International
Activités: Bulletin; Réunions mensuelles; Exposition annuelle; Encan; *Bibliothèque*
Membre(s) du bureau directeur:
Daniel Lemire, Président
president@snquebec.ca

La Société numismatique de Vancouver *See* Vancouver Numismatic Society

Société Nunavummi Disabilities Makinnasuaqtiit *See* Nunavummi Disabilities Makinnasuaqtiit Society

Société ontarienne de gestion des déchets *See* Ontario Waste Management Association

Société ontarienne des arbitres et des régisseurs *See* Society of Ontario Adjudicators & Regulators

La société ontarienne des professionelles et professionnels de la nutrition en santé publique *See* Ontario Society of Nutrition Professionals in Public Health

La Société Opimian *See* Opimian Society

Société Parkinson - Region Maritime *See* Parkinson Society Maritime Region

Société Parkinson de l'est de l'Ontario *See* Parkinson Society of Eastern Ontario

Société Parkinson du Québec / Parkinson Society Québec
#1080, 550 rue Sherbrooke ouest, Montréal QC H3A 1B9
Tél: 514-861-4422
Ligne sans frais: 800-720-1307
info@parkinsonquebec.ca
www.parkinsonquebec.ca
www.facebook.com/parkinsonquebec
twitter.com/parkinsonquebec
Aperçu: Dimension: moyenne; *Envergure:* provinciale; Organisme sans but lucratif surveillé par Parkinson Society Canada
Membre(s) du personnel: 12
Membre(s) du bureau directeur:
Nicole Charpentier, Directrice générale
ncharpentier@parkinsonquebec.ca

Société Philatelique de Québec (SPQ)
CP 70076, Succ. Québec Centre, Québec QC G2J 0A1
Courriel: societe.philatelique.quebec@s-p-q.org
www.s-p-q.org
Aperçu: Dimension: petite; *Envergure:* provinciale; fondée en 1929
Membre: 150
Activités: *Service de conférenciers:* Oui
Membre(s) du bureau directeur:
André Lafond, Président

Société planétaire pour l'assainissement de l'énergie *See* Planetary Association for Clean Energy, Inc.

Société pour enfants doués et surdoués (Ontario) *See* Association for Bright Children (Ontario)

Société pour l'étude de l'architecture au Canada *See* Society for the Study of Architecture in Canada

Société pour l'Étude de l'Égypte Ancienne *See* Society for the Study of Egyptian Antiquities

Société pour la nature et les parcs du Canada *See* Canadian Parks & Wilderness Society

Société pour la nature et les parcs du Canada, Section Québec *Voir* Canadian Parks & Wilderness Society

Société pour la perfectionnement de l'enseignement de l'anglais, langue seconde, au Québec *See* Society for the Promotion of the Teaching of English as a Second Language in Quebec

Société pour les enfants handicapés du Québec (SEHQ) / Quebec Society for Disabled Children
2300, boul René-Lévesque ouest, Montréal QC H3H 2R5
Tél: 514-937-6171; *Téléc:* 514-937-0082
Ligne sans frais: 877-937-6171
sehq@enfantshandicapes.com
www.enfantshandicapes.com
www.facebook.com/enfantshandicapes
twitter.com/SEHQ
Aperçu: Dimension: moyenne; *Envergure:* provinciale; Organisme sans but lucratif; fondée en 1930 surveillé par Easter Seals Canada
Mission: Voué au bien-être des enfants handicapés et de leur famille; grâce aux contributions publiques qui lui sont versées et aux efforts conjugués de bénévoles et des permanents, la société offre des services directs et professionnels qui favorisent le développement personnel des enfants et leur intégration dans la communauté
Finances: *Budget de fonctionnement annuel:* $1.5 Million-$3 Million
Membre(s) du personnel: 65; 200 bénévole(s)
Membre: 1-99; *Montant de la cotisation:* Barème
Activités: *Evénements de sensibilisation:* Cabaret sur le Mont Royal, sept.; Classique Louis Coutu, sept.; Zone de Chute, sept.
Membre(s) du bureau directeur:
Ronald Davidson, Directeur général, 877-937-6171 Ext. 210
rdavidson@enfantshandicapes.com
Carolle Desjardins, Directrice, Financement, 877-937-6171 Ext. 232
cdesjardins@enfantshandicapes.com
Nicole Amzallag, Séjours de groupes et classes nature, 877-937-6171 Ext. 212
namzallag@enfantshandicapes.com

Camp Papillon
210, rue Papillon, Saint-Alphonse-Rodriguez QC J0K 2W0
Tél: 450-883-5642; *Téléc:* 450-883-5642
Ligne sans frais: 877-937-6172
Membre(s) du bureau directeur:
Sylvianne Renaud, Directeur, 450-883-5642
srenaud@enfantshandicapes.com

La Société pour les troubles de l'humeur du Canada *See* Mood Disorders Society of Canada

Société Pro Musica Inc. / Pro Musica Society Inc.
#201, 3505, rue Sainte Famille, Montréal QC H2X 2L3
Tél: 514-845-0532; *Téléc:* 514-845-1500
Ligne sans frais: 877-445-0532
concerts@promusica.qc.ca
www.promusica.qc.ca
www.facebook.com/societepromusica
twitter.com/promusicamtl
Également appelé: La Société Pro Musica
Aperçu: Dimension: petite; *Envergure:* nationale; Organisme sans but lucratif; fondée en 1948
Mission: Promouvoir et présenter à Montréal la plus belle musique de chambre par les meilleurs interprètes d'ici et d'ailleurs; dans la série TOPAZE, promouvoir et offrir aux jeunes familles de meilleures conditions pour assister aux concerts avec un atelier d'animation musicale pour les enfants
Finances: *Fonds:* Conseil des arts et lettres du Québec; Conseil des arts de Montréal
Membre(s) du personnel: 2
Membre: *Critères d'admissibilite:* Adultes et étudiants agées de 15 à 85 ans
Membre(s) du bureau directeur:
Richard Lupien, Président
Louise-Andrée Baril, Directrice artistique

Société professionnelle des auteurs et des compositeurs du Québec (SPACQ)
#901, 505, boul René-Lévesque ouest, Montréal QC H2Z 1Y7
Tél: 514-845-3739; *Téléc:* 514-845-1903
Ligne sans frais: 866-445-3739
info@spacq.qc.ca
www.spacq.qc.ca
www.facebook.com/213627294934
twitter.com/SPACQ
www.youtube.com/laspacq
Aperçu: Dimension: petite; *Envergure:* nationale; Organisme sans but lucratif; fondée en 1981
Mission: Défendre les droits et les intérêts moraux, professionnels et économiques des auteurs et des compositeurs, ainsi que les droits qui se rapportent aux oeuvres, auprès des autorités gouvernementales
Membre de: Confédération internationale des sociétés d'auteurs et compositeurs (CISAC)
Finances: *Budget de fonctionnement annuel:* $250,000-$500,000
Membre(s) du personnel: 5
Membre: 750; *Montant de la cotisation:* 75$; *Critères d'admissibilite:* Etre membre de la Société canadienne des auteurs, compositeurs et éditeurs de musique et/ou de la Société du droit de reproduction des auteurs, compositeurs et éditeurs du Canada
Activités: Ateliers de composition; *Stagiaires:* Oui; *Service de conférenciers:* Oui
Membre(s) du bureau directeur:
Pierre-Daniel Rheault, Directeur général, 514-845-3739 Ext. 222
pdrheault@spacq.qc.ca
Sébastien Charest, Responsable, Service aux membres, 514-845-3739 Ext. 221
scharest@spacq.qc.ca

La Société protectrice des animaux d'Ottawa *See* Ottawa Humane Society

Société protectrice des animaux du Nouveau-Brunswick *See* New Brunswick Society for the Prevention of Cruelty to Animals

Société Provancher d'histoire naturelle du Canada (SPHNC) / Provancher Society of Natural History of Canada
1400, rue de l'Aéroport, Québec QC G2G 1G6
Tél: 418-554-8636; *Téléc:* 418-831-8744
societe.provancher@gmail.com
www.provancher.qc.ca
Aperçu: Dimension: petite; *Envergure:* provinciale; Organisme sans but lucratif; fondée en 1919
Mission: Société visant la protection de milieux naturels et l'éducation en sciences naturelles
Membre de: Reseau de milieux naturels protégés du Québec; Nature Québec; Institut Québécois de la Biodiversité
Finances: *Budget de fonctionnement annuel:* $100,000-$250,000; *Fonds:* Cotisations des membres; dons; location de chalets
Membre(s) du personnel: 3; 25 bénévole(s)
Membre: 50 institutionnel; 1,500 individu; 30 associé; *Montant de la cotisation:* 70$ corporatif; 35$ famille; 30$ individu; *Critères d'admissibilite:* Amant de la nature, scientifiques

Activités: Visites guidées; inventaires fauniques; conférences sur la nature; location de chalets (Ile aux Basques); *Evénements de sensibilisation:* Marais Léon-Provancher, oct.
Membre(s) du bureau directeur:
Gilles Gaboury, Président
Eric-Yves Harvey, 1er Vice-Président
Louise Fortin, 2me Vice-Président
Michel Lepage, Secrétaire
André St-Hilaire, Trésorier
Elisabeth Bossert, Administratrice

Société psoriasis du Canada *See* Psoriasis Society of Canada

Société québécoise d'espéranto (SQE) / Québec Esperanto Society (QES)
6358A, rue de Bordeaux, Montréal QC H2G 2R8
www.esperanto.qc.ca
Également appelé: Esperanto-Societo Kebekia
Aperçu: *Dimension:* petite; *Envergure:* provinciale; Organisme sans but lucratif; fondée en 1983 surveillé par Esperanto Association of Canada
Mission: Faire connaître et aider à l'apprentissage de l'espéranto; organiser des rencontres et favoriser l'utilisation de la langue; présenter les avantages de la langue et le mouvement mondial
Affiliation(s): Universala Esperanto-Asocio
Membre: *Montant de la cotisation:* 25$
Activités: *Service de conférenciers:* Oui; *Bibliothèque:* Bibliothèque publique rendez-vous
Membre(s) du bureau directeur:
Normand Fleury, Président
Sylvano Auclair, Secrétaire-trésorier
silvano@esperanto.qc.ca

Société québécoise d'ethnologie (SQE)
CP 8683, Québec QC G1V 4N6
Tél: 418-922-8340
www.ethnologiequebec.org
www.facebook.com/ethnologiequebec
Aperçu: *Dimension:* petite; *Envergure:* provinciale; Organisme sans but lucratif; fondée en 1975
Mission: Regroupe des personnes, professionnelles ou non de l'ethnologie, et des organismes intéressés à l'ethnologie et à la mise en valeur des patrimoines matériels et immatériels à des fins culturelles, sociales et scientifiques
Membre de: Fédération des sociétés d'histoire du Québec; Centre de valorisation du patrimoine vivant
Finances: *Budget de fonctionnement annuel:* Moins de $50,000
Membre: 1-99; *Montant de la cotisation:* 30$ individu; 20$ étudiant; 125$ institution; *Critères d'admissibilite:* Ethnologues, historiens; *Comités:* Ciné-rencontres; Communications; Publications; Valorisation des porteurs de traditions
Prix, Bourses:
• Le prix Simone-Voyer

Société Québécoise de droit international (SQDI)
Université du Québec à Montréal, CP 8888, Succ. Centre-Ville, Montréal QC H2L 4Y2
Tél: 514-987-3000; *Téléc:* 514-987-0115
info@sqdi.org
www.sqdi.org
www.linkedin.com/groups?gid=4184707
www.facebook.com/SocieteQuebecoisedeDroitInternational
twitter.com/SQDI_RQDI
Aperçu: *Dimension:* moyenne; *Envergure:* provinciale; fondée en 1982
Mission: De rassembler les gens qui sont intéressés à en apprendre sur le droit international et à en discuter, ainsi que de promouvoir le droit international au Québec
Membre: Réguliers: 98; Étudiants: 301; Institutionels: 9
Activités: Conférences
Membre(s) du bureau directeur:
Olivier Delas, Président, Conseil d'administration
Publications:
• Revue québécoise de droit international
Type: Revue; *Frequency:* Semestrielle
Profile: Articles présentera des études, des commentaires et des critiques de livres sur le droit international

Société québécoise de gériatrie (SQG)
a/s Mme Carole Labrie, 375, rue Argyll, Sherbrooke QC J1J 3H5
Tél: 819-346-9196; *Téléc:* 819-829-7145
clabrie.csss-iugs@ssss.gouv.qc.ca
www.sqgeriatrie.org
Aperçu: *Dimension:* petite; *Envergure:* provinciale; Organisme sans but lucratif; fondée en 1985
Finances: *Budget de fonctionnement annuel:* Moins de $50,000
Membre: 250; *Montant de la cotisation:* 50$; *Critères d'admissibilite:* Médecins et résidents
Activités: Congrès annuel
Membre(s) du bureau directeur:
Tamas Fülöp, Président

Société québécoise de l'autisme *Voir* Fédération québécoise de l'autisme

Société québécoise de la rédaction professionnelle (SQRP)
CP 83539, Succ. Garnier, Montréal QC H2J 4E9
Tél: 514-990-0430
info@sqrp.org
www.sqrp.org
www.linkedin.com/company/soci-t-qu-b-coise-de-la-r-daction-professionnelle-sqrp-
www.facebook.com/172644542768672
Aperçu: *Dimension:* petite; *Envergure:* provinciale
Mission: Regrouper rédacteurs et rédactrices; établir des critères et évaluer la qualité de la rédaction des textes soumis; tenir un registre des membres; promouvoir la qualité de la rédaction et défendre les intérêts de la profession
Affiliation(s): INTECOM
Membre: *Montant de la cotisation:* Barème; *Critères d'admissibilite:* Examen d'agrément
Activités: *Service de conférenciers:* Oui
Membre(s) du bureau directeur:
Marie-Noël Pichelin, Présidente
Rozanne Boucher, Secrétaire

Société québécoise de la schizophrénie (SQS)
7401, rue Hochelaga, Montréal QC H1N 3M5
Tél: 514-251-4125; *Téléc:* 514-251-6347
Ligne sans frais: 866-888-2323
info@schizophrenie.qc.ca
www.schizophrenie.qc.ca
www.linkedin.com/company/soci-t-qu-b-coise-de-la-schizophr-nie
www.facebook.com/SQSchizophrenie
twitter.com/SQSchizophrenie
www.youtube.com/user/SQSchizophrenie1
Nom précédent: Association québécoise de la schizophrénie
Aperçu: *Dimension:* petite; *Envergure:* provinciale; Organisme sans but lucratif; fondée en 1989
Mission: Contribuer à l'amélioration de la qualité de vie des personnes touchées par la schizophrénie et les psychoses apparentées, par le biais d'activités éducatives et de soutien, de prévention et de sensibilisation publique, de participations aux politiques gouvernementales et de contributions à la recherche, et ce, partout au Québec
Membre de: Fédération des familles et amis de la personne atteinte de maladie mentale; Association canadienne pour la santé mentale; Regroupement des organismes communautaires en santé mentale de l'est de l'Ile de Montréal; Le RACOR
Finances: *Budget de fonctionnement annuel:* $250,000-$500,000; *Fonds:* Subvention provinciale (PSOC); dons; membership; commandites ciblées; fondations; levée de fonds
Membre(s) du personnel: 7; 20 bénévole(s)
Membre: 589; *Montant de la cotisation:* 10$ personne atteinte; 20$ membre individu; 25$ membre famille; 50$ membre corporatif; *Critères d'admissibilite:* Famille et amis des personnes souffrant de schizophrénie; *Comités:* Bourses; Candidature; Financement; Gouvernance
Activités: Soutien aux personnes; conférences mensuelles; Défi schizophrénie et infolettre; groupe d'entraide; activités sociales et de répit; programmes d'éducation; bourses d'études; centre de documentation; information, formation et sensibilisation publique; *Service de conférenciers:* Oui; *Bibliothèque:* Centre de documentation
Membre(s) du bureau directeur:
Francine Dubé, Directrice générale
fdube@schizophrenie.qc.ca
Ginette Comtois, Présidente
gcomtois@schizophrenie.qc.ca
Prix, Bourses:
• Bourses Je crois en moi
Eligibility: Personnes avec un diagnostic de schizophrénie ou de psychoses apparentées *Deadline:* août; *Amount:* 500$ à 1 000$
Meetings/Conferences:
• Société québécoise de la schizophrénie 2018 Conférences mensuelles, 2018, Montréal, QC
Scope: Provincial
Publications:
• Bulletin Défi schizoprénie [publication de Société québécoise de la schizophrénie]
Type: Infolettre
• Infolettre [publication de Société québécoise de la schizophrénie]
Type: Infolettre
• Mieux comprendre un premier épisode de psychose... pour mieux agir [publication de Société québécoise de la schizophrénie]
Type: Brochure
• Le pouvoir social de l'employeur [publication de Société québécoise de la schizophrénie]

Société québécoise de lipidologie, de nutrition et de métabolisme *See* Québec Society of Lipidology, Nutrition & Metabolism Inc.

Société Québécoise de Psilogie inc (SQP)
375, boul Henri Bourassa ouest, Montréal QC H3L 1P2
Tél: 514-337-8292
Aperçu: *Dimension:* petite; *Envergure:* internationale; Organisme sans but lucratif; fondée en 1986
Mission: Études, échanges, rencontres traitant de psilogie pour favoriser la recherche, l'expérimentation, la publication; susciter la coopération entre les disciplines scientifiques; recueillir et gérer les fonds pour la poursuite des activités
Finances: *Budget de fonctionnement annuel:* Moins de $50,000
Membre(s) du personnel: 10; 10 bénévole(s)
Membre: 3 institutionnel; 50 individu; 20 associé; *Montant de cotisation:* 20$; *Critères d'admissibilite:* Chercheur sur base scientifique
Activités:; *Bibliothèque:* rendez-vous Not open to public
Membre(s) du bureau directeur:
Philippe Mabilleau, Président et Porte-Parole

Société québécoise de psychologie du travail (SQPTO)
533, rue de l'Atlantique, Mont-Saint-Hilaire QC J3H 0E8
Tél: 514-842-8178; *Téléc:* 514-842-8178
Ligne sans frais: 888-842-8178
permanence@sqpto.ca
www.sqpto.ca
www.facebook.com/sqpto
twitter.com/SQPTO
Également appelé: Société québécoise de psychologie du travail et des organisations
Aperçu: *Dimension:* petite; *Envergure:* provinciale; fondée en 1994
Membre(s) du personnel: 1; 3 bénévole(s)
Membre: 300; *Montant de la cotisation:* 125$, 40$ étudiants
Activités: Conférences, colloques, activit@s de formation

Société québécoise de récupération et de recyclage
#411, 300, rue Sant-Paul, Québec QC G1K 7R1
Tél: 418-643-0394; *Téléc:* 418-643-6507
Ligne sans frais: 866-523-8290
info@recyc-quebec.gouv.qc.ca
www.recyc-quebec.gouv.qc.ca
www.linkedin.com/company/recyc-qu-bec
www.facebook.com/recycquebec
twitter.com/recycquebec
Également appelé: RECYC-QUÉBEC
Aperçu: *Dimension:* moyenne; *Envergure:* provinciale; Organisme sans but lucratif; fondée en 1990
Mission: Promouvoir, développer et favoriser la réduction, le réemploi, la récupération et le recyclage des contenants, d'emballages, de matières ou de produits ainsi que leur valorisation dans une perspective de conservation des ressources
Finances: *Budget de fonctionnement annuel:* Plus de $5 Million
Activités: Coordination des activités de mise en valeur; gestion intégrée des pneus hors d'usage; gestion de la consigne sur les contenants à remplissage unique de bière ou de boissons gazeuses; développement des marchés et technologies dans le domaine de la mise en valeur des matières résiduelles; R&D; information, sensibilisation et éducation; promotion des produits québécois à contenu recyclé; publication de répertoires, guides, études et fiches; campagne sur la récupération des contenants à remplissage unique consignés; *Evénements de sensibilisation:* Semaine québécoise de réduction des déchets; *Stagiaires:* Oui
Membre(s) du bureau directeur:
Dany Michaud, Président-directeur général
Anna Walkowiak, Vice-présidente, Innovation et développement
Bureau à Montréal
141, av du Président-Kennedy, 8e étage, Montréal QC H2X 1Y4

Canadian Associations / Société québécoise de science politique (SQSP)

Tél: 514-352-5002; *Téléc:* 514-873-6542
Ligne sans frais: 800-807-0678

Société québécoise de science politique (SQSP)
a/s du Département de science politique, Université du Québec, CP 8888, Succ. Centre-Ville, Montréal QC H3C 3P8
Tél: 514-987-3000; *Téléc:* 514-987-0218
sqsp@er.uqam.ca
www.sqsp.uqam.ca
Aperçu: *Dimension:* petite; *Envergure:* provinciale
Mission: Favoriser l'avancement de la recherche et de l'enseignement en science politique; soutenir la diffusion des connaissances sur les phénomènes politiques
Membre de: Social Science Federation of Canada
Membre: *Montant de la cotisation:* 50$ étudiante; 60$ étudiante conjointe; 140$ régulière; 170$ régulière conjointe; *Critères d'admissibilité:* Professeurs et chercheurs en science politique
Activités: Congrès; colloques; conférences
Membre(s) du bureau directeur:
Daniel Salée, Président

Société québécoise de spéléologie (SQS)
4545, av Pierre-de Coubertin, Montréal QC H1V 0B2
Tél: 514-252-3006; *Téléc:* 514-252-3201
Ligne sans frais: 800-338-6636
info-sqs@speleo.qc.ca
www.speleo.qc.ca
www.facebook.com/101303566664
www.youtube.com/SPELEOSQS
Aperçu: *Dimension:* moyenne; *Envergure:* provinciale; Organisme sans but lucratif; fondée en 1970
Mission: De favoriser le développement de la spéléologie ainsi que la préservation du milieu cavernicole et de son environnement.
Membre de: Conseil québécois du Loisir; Regroupement Loisir Québec; Corporation de développement économique de l'Est; Science pour tous
Activités: *Stagiaires:* Oui; *Bibliothèque:* Centre de documentation
Membre(s) du bureau directeur:
François Gélinas, Directeur général
fgelinas@speleo.qc.ca

Société québécoise des auteurs dramatiques (SoQAD)
3492, av Laval, Montréal QC H2X 3C8
Tél: 514-596-3705
info@aqad.qc.ca
www.aqad.qc.ca
Aperçu: *Dimension:* petite; *Envergure:* nationale; fondée en 1994
Mission: Défendre les intérêts matériels et moraux de ses mandants (auteurs lui ayant confié un mandat de gestion)
Affiliation(s): Association québécoise des auteurs dramatiques
Membre(s) du bureau directeur:
Marie-Eve Gagnon, Directrice générale
megagnon@aqad.qc.ca

Société québécoise des hostas et des hémérocalles (SQHH)
4101, rue Sherbrooke est, Montréal QC H1X 2B2
Tél: 514-868-3078
info@millettephotomedia.com
sites.google.com/site/hostaquebec
Aperçu: *Dimension:* petite; *Envergure:* provinciale
Membre: *Montant de la cotisation:* 39$ individu 43$ famille
Membre(s) du bureau directeur:
Réjean Millette, Président

Société québécoise des psychothérapeutes professionnels (SQPP)
CP 34, Succ. Ahuntsic, Montréal QC H3L 3N5
Tél: 514-990-3403
info@sqpp.org
www.sqpp.org
Aperçu: *Dimension:* petite; *Envergure:* provinciale; fondée en 1991
Mission: Un regroupement multidisciplinaire de psychothérapeutes qui sont des professionnels de la psychothérapie régis par un code de déontologie; possèdent une formation académique universitaire ou son équivalent et une solide formation à la psychothérapie; ont accompli une démarche psychothérapeutique approfondie
Membre: *Comités:* Communication externes; Assurances; Formation continue
Activités: santé mentale
Membre(s) du bureau directeur:
Andrée Thauvette-Poupart, Présidente

Société québécoise du dahlia
11, rue Bellerose, Dollard-des-Ormeaux QC H9G 2A7
Courriel: dahlia@videotron.qc.ca
www.sqdahlia.qc.ca
Aperçu: *Dimension:* petite; *Envergure:* locale; Organisme sans but lucratif; fondée en 1992
Mission: Regrouper les amateurs de dahlias et encourager la culture de cette plante; favoriser les échanges d'informations et de spécimens entre les membres
Affiliation(s): American Dahlia Society; Fédération des Sociétés d'horticulture et d'Écologie du Québec; Société Canadienne du Glaïeul
Finances: *Budget de fonctionnement annuel:* Moins de $50,000
Membre(s) du personnel: 9
Membre: 100-499; *Montant de la cotisation:* 20$; *Critères d'admissibilité:* Amateurs de dahlias et de beaux jardins
Activités: Expositions; conférences; salons annuels; *Service de conférenciers:* Oui
Membre(s) du bureau directeur:
François Lefebvre, Président

Société québécoise pour l'étude de la religion (SQÉR)
Université de Montréal, #490, 3333, ch Queen Mary, Montréal QC H3V 1A2
Tél: 514-343-6568; *Téléc:* 514-343-5738
www.facebook.com/319498958060192
Aperçu: *Dimension:* petite; *Envergure:* provinciale; fondée en 1989
Mission: Promouvoir la recherche, l'enseignement et la diffusion des connaissances dans les disciplines ayant pour objet l'étude de la religion
Membre: *Montant de la cotisation:* 50$ régulier; 25$ étudiant
Membre(s) du bureau directeur:
Patrice Brodeur, Président

Société québécoise pour la défense des animaux (SQDA) / Québec Society for the Defense of Animals (QSDA)
#102, 847, rue Cherrier, Montréal QC H2L 1H6
Tél: 514-524-1976
sqda1976@gmail.org
www.sqda.org
Aperçu: *Dimension:* moyenne; *Envergure:* provinciale; Organisme sans but lucratif; fondée en 1976 surveillé par Canadian Federation of Humane Societies
Mission: Faire connaître et respecter le monde animal par tous les moyens possibles; obtenir une législation modifiée pour la protection de toute espèce; Combattre la destruction de notre faune; exposer l'aberration de l'élevage intensif; Contrôler l'expérimentation animale
Affiliation(s): The World Society for the Protection of Animals - England; The Royal Society for the Prevention of Cruelty to Animals - England; The Canadian Federation of Humane Societies; Société nationale pour la défense des animaux - France
Membre: 500; *Montant de la cotisation:* 20$/an; 250$ bienfaiteur
Activités: *Evénements de sensibilisation:* Campagne annuelle de déménagement

Société royale d'astronomie du Canada *See* Royal Astronomical Society of Canada

La Société royale de philatélie du Canada *See* The Royal Philatelic Society of Canada

La Société royale du Canada *See* The Royal Society of Canada

La Société royale du Commonwealth du Canada *See* The Royal Commonwealth Society of Canada

Société royale héraldique du Canada *See* Royal Heraldry Society of Canada

Société Saint-Jean-Baptiste de Montréal (SSJBM)
82, rue Sherbrooke ouest, Montréal QC H2X 1X3
Tél: 514-843-8851; *Téléc:* 514-844-6369
info@ssjb.ca
www.ssjb.ca
www.facebook.com/SSJBM
twitter.com/ssjbm
www.youtube.com/user/ssjbmofficiel
Aperçu: *Dimension:* moyenne; *Envergure:* provinciale; fondée en 1834
Mission: Une société nationale qui participe de façon non partisane à l'évolution politique, sociale, économique et culturelle du Québec par ses actions, ses études, ses interventions et ses campagnes d'opinion
Membre de: Mouvement national des Québécoises et Québécois
Membre(s) du personnel: 14
Membre: 15 000; *Montant de la cotisation:* 10 $; *Comités:* Comité de la fête nationale de la Saint-Jean
Activités: La Fondation Ludger-Duvernay; La Fondation Prêt d'Honneur; Fondation Langelier; Service d'Entraide
Membre(s) du bureau directeur:
Guy Raynault, Directeur général, 514-843-8851 Ext. 224
graynault@ssjb.com
Prix, Bourses:
• Prix Séraphin-Marion
Créé en 1984; décerné à une personnalité qui défend les droits de la francophonie hors-Québec
• Prix André-Guérin
Créé en 1990; décerné à une personnalité canadienne-française qui s'illustre dans le domaine du cinéma et vidéo
• Prix Léon-Lortie
Established 1987; awarded for achievement in the area of pure & applied sciences
• Prix Chomedey-de-Maisonneuve
Créé en 1983; décerné à une personnalité dont les réalisations contribuent au rayonnement de Montréal
• Prix Maurice-Richard
Established 1979; $1,500 & a medal awarded annually to a French Canadian in recognition of outstanding achievement in sports & athletics in serving the higher interests of the French Canadian people
• Prix Calixa-Lavallée
Established 1959; $1,500 & a medal awarded annually to a French Canadian in recognition of outstanding achievement in music in serving the higher interests of the French Canadian people
• Prix Victor-Morin
Créé en 1962; décerné à une personnalité canadienne-française qui s'illustre dans le domaine des arts de la scène
• Prix Esdras-Minville
Créé en 1978; décerné à une personnalité canadienne-française qui s'illustre dans le domaine des sciences humaines
• Prix Bene Merenti De Patria
Créée en 1923, cette médaille souligne les mérites d'un compatriote ayant rendu des services exceptionnels à la patrie. La maquette est l'oeuvre d'un artiste qui a préparé les chars allégoriques de nos grands défilés pendant de nombreuses années; *Amount:* Médaille d'argent
• Prix Patriote de l'année
Décerné à une personnalité qui s'est distinguée dans la défense des intérêts du Québec et de la démocratie des peuples, en mémoire des Patriotes des années 1830; créé en 1975
• Prix Ludger-Duvernay
Le prix a été créé en 1944 afin de signaler les mérites d'un compatriote dont la compétence et le rayonnement dans le domaine intellectuel et littéraire servent les intérêts supérieurs de la nation québécoise; le prix est de 3 000 $, accompagne une médaille, et est attribué à tous les trois ans
• Prix Louis Philippe-Hébert
Créé en 1971; décerné à une personnalité canadienne-française qui s'illustre dans le domaine des arts plastiques
• Prix Olivar-Asselin
Established 1955; $1,500 & a medal awarded annually to a French Canadian in recognition of outstanding achievement in journalism in serving the higher interests of the French Canadian people

Société Saint-Jean-Baptiste du Centre du Québec
222, rue Saint-Marcel, Drummondville QC J2B 2E4
Tél: 819-478-2519; *Téléc:* 819-472-7460
Ligne sans frais: 800-943-2519
info@ssjbcq.quebec
www.ssjbcq.quebec
www.facebook.com/ssjbcq
Aperçu: *Dimension:* moyenne; *Envergure:* locale; Organisme sans but lucratif; fondée en 1944
Mission: Promouvoir le développement et l'unité du peuple québécois dans tous les aspects de la vie en société et dans ses intérêts les plus dignes en favorisant: son émancipation dans le domaine économique; son épanouissement dans le domaine culturel; sa réalisation dans le domaine politique; sa solidarité dans le domaine social; et, son perfectionnement dans le domaine spirituel

Affiliation(s): Mouvement national des québécois et québécoises
Finances: Budget de fonctionnement annuel: $500,000-$1.5 Million
Membre(s) du personnel: 6; 200 bénévole(s)
Membre: 30 000; *Montant de la cotisation:* 7$ individu
Activités: *Evénements de sensibilisation:* Francofête, mars; Concours J'affiche en français, mars
Membre(s) du bureau directeur:
Gisèle Denoncourt, Directrice générale
gdenoncourt@ssjbcq.quebec
Gabriel Lacombe, Directeur, Services administratifs
glacombe@ssjbcq.quebec
Prix, Bourses:
• Prix Lionel-Groulx
Promotion de l'histoire ou du patrimoine québécois
• Prix Raymond-Beaudet
Le dévouement et le nationalisme
• Prix Monseigneur-Parenteau
Engagement communautaire et socioculturel

La Société Saint-Pierre
CP 430, 15584 Cabot Trail, Cheticamp NS B0E 1H0
Tél: 902-224-2642; *Téléc:* 902-224-1579
lestroispignons@ns.sympatico.ca
www.lestroispignons.com
Également appelé: Les Trois Pignons
Aperçu: *Dimension:* petite; *Envergure:* locale; Organisme sans but lucratif; fondée en 1947
Mission: Vise à la conservation de notre héritage et à la promotion de l'aspect intellectuel, culturel, social et économique des Acadiens du Cap-Breton
Finances: *Budget de fonctionnement annuel:* $100,000-$250,000
Membre(s) du personnel: 3; 100 bénévole(s)
Membre: 215; *Montant de la cotisation:* 10$ individuel; 15$ famille; *Critères d'admissibilité:* Acadien/francophone
Activités:; *Bibliothèque:* Centre de généalogie
Membre(s) du bureau directeur:
Lisette Aucoin-Bourgeois, Directrice générale

Société Saint-Thomas-d'Aquin (SSTA)
5, av Maris Stella, Summerside PE C1N 6M9
Tél: 902-436-4881; *Téléc:* 902-436-6936
colette.aesenault@ssta.org
www.ssta.org
www.facebook.com/SaintThomasdAquin
twitter.com/commSSTA
Aperçu: *Dimension:* petite; *Envergure:* provinciale; Organisme sans but lucratif; fondée en 1919
Mission: Travailler pour que tout Acadien, Acadienne ou francophone puissent vivre et s'épanouir (individuellement et collectivement) en français à l'Ile-du-Prince-Édouard; regrouper les Acadiens, Acadiennes et francophones de l'Ile-du-Prince-Édouard au sein d'une même association; représenter ses membres auprès du gouvernement municipal, provincial et national; revendiquer leurs droits; établir et administrer un fonds devant servir d'aide financière aux étudiant(e)s acadiens, acadiennes et francophones de l'Ile-du-Prince-Édouard dans tous les secteurs; développer des relations amicales entre les Acadiens, Acadiennes et francophones de l'Ile-du-Prince-Édouard et les autres francophones du Canada et des pays étrangers
Affiliation(s): SNA-Société Nationale de l'Acadie; FCFA-Fédération des communautés francophones et acadienne du Canada
Finances: *Budget de fonctionnement annuel:* $100,000-$250,000; *Fonds:* Gouvernement fédéral
Membre(s) du personnel: 6; 50 bénévole(s)
Membre: 17 institutionnel; 2,000 individuel; *Montant de la cotisation:* $25 institutionnel; 30$ couple; $20 étudiant; $20 individuel
Activités: La SSTA gère le programme de bourses de la Fondation acadienne d'aide aux étudiants et étudiantes
Membre(s) du bureau directeur:
Jeannita Bernard, Directrice Générale par intérim
dg@ssta.org
Crystal Barriault, Contact
reception@ssta.org

Comité du Carrefour Isle-Saint-Jean
5, promenade Acadienne, Charlottetown PE C1C 1M2
Tél: 902-368-1895; *Téléc:* 902-566-5989
info@carrefourisj.org
www.carrefourisj.org
Membre(s) du bureau directeur:
Nathalie Arsenault, Directrice générale
nathalie@carrefourisj.org

Comité régional la Belle-Alliance ltée
5, av Maris Stella, Summerside PE C1N 6M9
Tél: 902-888-1681; *Téléc:* 902-888-1686
bellealliance@ssta.org
www.belle-alliance.ca
Membre(s) du bureau directeur:
Giselle Babineau, Présidente
gbjordan@edu.pe.ca

Le Conseil Rév. S.-E.-Perrey
119, ch DeBlois, rte 157, Tignish PE C0B 2B0
Tél: 902-882-0475; *Téléc:* 902-882-0482
info@seperrey.org
www.seperrey.org
Membre(s) du bureau directeur:
Monique Arsenault, Directrice
monique@seperrey.org

Conseil Acadien de Rustico
Centre acadien Grand Rustico, CP 5617, 2244, ch Church, Rustico PE C0A 1N0
Tél: 902-963-3252; *Téléc:* 902-963-3442
www.conseilacadien.com
www.facebook.com/conseilacadienrustico
twitter.com/CaRustico
Membre(s) du bureau directeur:
Andréa Deveau, Directrice générale
andrea.deveau@conseilacadienrustico.org

Conseil scolaire-communautaire Évangéline (CSCÉ)
CP 124, 1596, rte 124 Abram-Village, Wellington PE C0B 2E0
Tél: 902-854-2166; *Téléc:* 902-854-2981
reception@cscevangeline.ca
www.cscevangeline.ca
Membre(s) du bureau directeur:
Nick Arsenault, Directeur
direction@cscevangeline.ca

Le comité acadien et francophone de l'Est (CAFE)
CP 858, 95, rte 310, RR#4, Fortune PE C0A 2B0
Tél: 902-687-7179; *Téléc:* 902-687-7176
cafe@ssta.org
www.facebook.com/129025990447823
Membre(s) du bureau directeur:
Joyce Gill, Directrice générale

Société Santé en français (SSF)
223, rue Main, #L396, Ottawa ON K1S 1C4
Tél: 613-244-1889; *Téléc:* 613-244-0283
info@santefrancais.ca
www.santefrancais.ca
www.facebook.com/santefrancais
twitter.com/santefrancais
Aperçu: *Dimension:* moyenne; *Envergure:* nationale; fondée en 2002 surveillé par Fédération des communautés francophones et acadienne du Canada
Mission: Pour améliorer l'accès et la qualité des services de soins de santé en français au Canada
Affiliation(s): Réseau de santé en français de Terre-Neuve-et-Labrador; Réseau Santé en français I.-P.-É; Réseau Santé - Nouvelle-Écosse; Réseau-action Communautaire; Réseau-action Formation et recherche; Réseau-action Organisation des services; Société Santé et Mieux-être en français du Nouveau-Brunswick; Réseau francophone de santé du Nord de l'Ontario; Réseau santé en français du Moyen-Nord de l'Ontario; Réseau franco-santé du Sud de l'Ontario; Réseau des services de santé en français de l'Est de l'Ontario; Conseil communauté en santé du Manitoba; Réseau Santé en français de la Saskatchewan
Membre: 17 associations; *Critères d'admissibilité:* Les associations dont le but est d'améliorer les services de soins de santé en français, qui sont situés dans les provinces où la majorité ne parle pas français comme première langue
Membre(s) du bureau directeur:
Aurel Schofield, Président
Michel Tremblay, Directeur général, 613-244-1889 Ext. 230
m.tremblay@santefrancais.ca

Société Santé et Mieux-être en français du Nouveau-Brunswick (SSMEFFNB)
CP 1764, Moncton NB E1C 9X6
Tél: 506-389-3351; *Téléc:* 506-389-3366
ssmefnb@nb.aibn.com
www.ssmefnb.ca
www.facebook.com/SSMEFNB
twitter.com/SSMEFNB

Aperçu: *Dimension:* petite; *Envergure:* provinciale surveillé par Société santé en français
Membre(s) du bureau directeur:
Gilles Vienneau, Directeur général

Société spatiale canadienne *See* Canadian Space Society

Société statistique du Canada *See* Statistical Society of Canada

Société St-Jean-Baptiste Richelieu-Yamaska (SSBRY)
151, rue Robert, Saint-Hyacinthe QC J2S 4L7
Tél: 450-773-8535; *Téléc:* 450-773-8262
Ligne sans frais: 888-773-8535
ssjb@maskatel.net
www.ssjbry.org
www.facebook.com/ssjbry
Aperçu: *Dimension:* moyenne; *Envergure:* locale; fondée en 1946
Mission: Coordination de la fête nationale du Québec
Affiliation(s): Mouvement national des Québécois

Société St-Léonard du Canada *See* St. Leonard's Society of Canada

Société théologique canadienne *See* Canadian Theological Society

Société touristique des Autochtones du Québec (STAQ) / Québec Aboriginal Tourism Corporation
#220, 50, boul Maurice-Bastien, Wendake QC G0A 4V0
Tél: 418-843-5030
Ligne sans frais: 877-698-7827
info@tourismeautochtone.com
www.tourismeautochtone.com
www.facebook.com/TourismeAutochtoneQuebec
twitter.com/AutochtoneQC
www.youtube.com/user/TourismeAutochtone
Nom précédent: Société touristique Innu
Aperçu: *Dimension:* petite; *Envergure:* provinciale
Mission: Créer, au moyen du tourisme, des activités propices au développement social et économique des communautés autochtones
Membre(s) du personnel: 6
Membre: *Montant de la cotisation:* Barème; *Critères d'admissibilité:* Intervenants en tourisme des nations amérindiennes et inuites
Activités: Formation des ressources humaines en tourisme; banque d'informations; bulletins trimestriels; promotion et représentation du tourisme autochtone; commercialisation des produits
Membre(s) du bureau directeur:
Dave Laveau, Directeur général
dlaveau@tourismeautochtone.com

Société touristique Innu *Voir* Société touristique des Autochtones du Québec

Société zoologique de Montréal *See* Zoological Society of Montréal

Les Sociétés Canadiennes de Technologies Médicales *See* Canada's Medical Technology Companies

Society for Canadian Women in Science & Technology (SCWIST) / Société des canadiennes dans la science et la technologie
#311, 525 Seymour St., Vancouver BC V6B 3H7
Tel: 604-893-8657
esourcecentre@scwist.ca
www.scwist.ca
www.linkedin.com/groups?gid=1915550
www.facebook.com/167831516563792
twitter.com/SCWIST
Overview: A small national charitable organization founded in 1981
Mission: To promote equal opportunities for women in scientific, technical & engineering careers; to educate public about careers in science & technology particularly to improve social attitudes on the stereotyping of careers in science; to assist educators by providing current information on careers & career training in sciences & scientific policies
Staff Member(s): 1
Membership: *Fees:* $100 sustaining; $60 professional; $20 student/retired/unemployed; *Member Profile:* Interest in promoting women in science & technology; *Committees:* Communications; Events; Fundraising; Grants; IWIS; ms infinity; Volunteer

Canadian Associations / Society for Existential & Phenomenological Theory & Culture (EPTC) / Société de Théorie et de Culture existentialises et phénoménologique (TCEP)

Activities: 5-6 regular program meetings of various topics; collection of gender free science & mathematics examples of questions; Ms. Infinity & Hands On Math & Sciences held in May in community colleges & high schools throughout province; *Speaker Service:* Yes; *Library:* Resource Centre
Chief Officer(s):
Rosine Hage-Moussa, President

Society for Disability Arts & Culture *See* KickStart Disability Arts & Culture

Society for Educational Visits & Exchanges in Canada; Bilingual Exchange Secretariat & Visites interprovinciales *See* Experiences Canada

Society for Existential & Phenomenological Theory & Culture (EPTC) / Société de Théorie et de Culture existentialises et phénoménologique (TCEP)
www.eptc-tcep.net
Previous Name: Sartre Society of Canada
Overview: A small national organization founded in 1987
Affiliation(s): Humanities & Social Sciences Federation of Canada
Activities: Invites papers & panel proposals in which any aspects of existential or phenomenological theory or culture are discussed; for example, papers or panels proposals dealing with theoretical or cultural issues in relation to contributions made by authors such as Kierkegaard, Nietzsche, Husserl, Heidegger, Levinas, Malraux, Sartre, Camus, Merleau-Ponty, or Beauvoir, & their critics
Chief Officer(s):
John Duncan, Treasurer
Meetings/Conferences:
• Existential & Phenomenological Theory & Culture Conference 2018, May, 2018, University of Regina, Regina, SK

Society for International Ministries *See* SIM Canada

Society for Manitobans with Disabilities Inc. (SMD)
825 Sherbrook St., Winnipeg MB R3A 1M5
Tel: 204-975-3010; *Fax:* 204-975-3073
Toll-Free: 866-282-8041; *TTY:* 204-975-3083
info@smd.mb.ca
www.smd.mb.ca
Overview: A large provincial charitable organization founded in 1946 overseen by Easter Seals Canada
Mission: To promote the full participation & equality of people with disabilities: To provide a full range of rehabilitation services: To facilitate the development of a receptive & supportive environment
Affiliation(s): Autism Society Manitoba
Finances: *Funding Sources:* Provincial government; United Way; The March of Dimes; Easter Seals; fees
Activities: Providing a variety of services to children & adults with disabilities; *Speaker Service:* Yes; *Library:* Open to public

Central Regional Office
#100, 30 Stephen St., Morden MB R6M 2G5
Tel: 204-822-7412; *Fax:* 204-822-7413
Toll-Free: 800-269-5451; *TTY:* 204-822-7412
smd.mb.ca

Eastman Regional Office
#5, 227 Main St., Steinbach MB R5G 1Y7
Tel: 204-326-5336; *Fax:* 204-326-9762
Toll-Free: 800-497-8196; *TTY:* 204-346-3998
smd.mb.ca

Interlake Regional Office
382 Main St., Selkirk MB R1A 1T8
Tel: 204-785-9338; *Fax:* 204-785-9340
Toll-Free: 888-831-4213; *TTY:* 204-482-5638
smd.mb.ca

Northern Regional Office
#303, 83 Churchill Dr., Thompson MB R8N 0L6
Tel: 204-778-4277; *Fax:* 204-778-4461
Toll-Free: 888-367-0268; *TTY:* 204-778-4277
smd.mb.ca

Parkland Regional Office
#411, 27 - 2 Ave. SW, Dauphin MB R7N 3E5
Tel: 204-622-2293; *Fax:* 204-622-2260
Toll-Free: 800-844-2307; *TTY:* 204-622-2293
smd.mb.ca

SMD Self-Help Clearinghouse
825 Sherbrook St., Winnipeg MB R3A 1M5
Tel: 204-975-3010; *Fax:* 204-975-3073
Toll-Free: 866-282-8041; *TTY:* 204-975-3012
smd.mb.ca

Mission: To foster collaboration & advocacy to assist self-help organizations

Westman Regional Office
#140, 340 - 9th St., Brandon MB R7A 6C2
Tel: 204-726-6157; *Fax:* 204-726-6499
Toll-Free: 800-813-3325; *TTY:* 204-726-6157
smd.mb.ca

Wheelchair Services
1857 Notre Dame Ave., Winnipeg MB R3E 3E7
Tel: 204-975-3250; *Fax:* 204-975-3240
Toll-Free: 800-836-5551; *TTY:* 800-856-7934
wreception@smd.mb.ca
smd.mb.ca

Society for Mesopotamian Studies *See* The Canadian Society for Mesopotamian Studies

Society for Muscular Dystrophy Information International (SMDI)
PO Box 7490, Bridgewater NS B4V 2X6
Tel: 902-685-3961; *Fax:* 902-685-3962
smdi@auracom.com
www.nsnet.org/smdi
Overview: A medium-sized international charitable organization founded in 1983
Mission: To facilitate international contact by producing website, & publications (newsletters, books) & by the sharing of neuromuscular & disability information between those concerned with muscular dystrophy &/or allied disorders
Finances: *Funding Sources:* Donations; Membership dues
Membership: *Fees:* $25 individuals; $35 organizations

Society for Organic Urban Land Care (SOUL)
PO Box 281, 2530 Alberni Hwy., Coombs BC V0R 1M0
Tel: 250-386-7685
info@organiclandcare.org
www.organiclandcare.org
www.facebook.com/SOUL.Organic.Land.Care
Overview: A small national organization
Mission: SOUL was formed in response to the growing need for ecologically responsible land care practices. The mission is to promote and support organic practices in our communities through education, certification and standardization.
Membership: 100; *Fees:* $30 public/professional; $250 supporting
Chief Officer(s):
Michael Cowan, President

Society for Personal Growth
Edmonton AB
Tel: 780-468-9435
prh@prh-canada.org
prh-canada.com
Overview: A small local charitable organization founded in 1984
Mission: To provide effective tools to foster personal growth & the emergence of the inner self; to help couples improve communication & build harmony & unity together; to facilitate the growth of parents & enable them to understand their children so they can live & grow harmoniously; to improve the quality of life in groups & in the workplace; to provide a place to achieve these objectives
Finances: *Funding Sources:* Regional government; Client fees
Activities: Personality & Human Relations (PRH) workshops; Couples & parenting workshops

Society for Quality Education (SQE)
57 Twyford Rd., Toronto ON M9A 1W5
Tel: 416-231-7247; *Fax:* 416-237-0108
Toll-Free: 888-856-5535
info@societyforqualityeducation.org
www.societyforqualityeducation.org
www.facebook.com/SQEducation
twitter.com/SQESocQualEd
Previous Name: Organization for Quality Education
Overview: A small local charitable organization
Mission: To advance public & private education in Canada by disseminating authoritative information on educational governance & methodology.
Finances: *Funding Sources:* Foundations
Staff Member(s): 1
Activities: DVD on charter schools; Demonstration Remedial Reading Project; Comparison of Provincial Science Curricula; *Speaker Service:* Yes
Chief Officer(s):
Doretta Wilson, Executive Director
Malkin Dare, President, 519-884-3166

Society for Reproduction Rights of Authors, Composers & Publishers Canada *Voir* Société du droit de reproduction des auteurs, compositeurs et éditeurs au Canada (SODRAC 2003) inc.

The Society for Safe & Caring Schools & Communities
11010 - 142 St., Edmonton AB T5N 2R1
Tel: 780-822-1500
office@sacsc.ca
safeandcaring.wordpress.com
www.facebook.com/safeandcaring
twitter.com/safeandcaring
www.youtube.com/safecaring
Overview: A small provincial organization
Mission: To encourage school practices that model & reinforce socially responsible & respectful behaviours, so that learning & teaching can take place in a safe & caring environment
Staff Member(s): 8
Membership: *Fees:* Free
Chief Officer(s):
Bev Esslinger, President
Marni Pearce, Executive Director
mpearce@sacsc.ca

Society for Socialist Studies (SSS) / Société d'études socialistes (SÉS)
c/o Radhika Desai, Dept. of Political Studies, Univ. of Manitoba, 451 University College, Winnipeg MB R3T 2N2
admin@socialiststudies.ca
socialiststudies.ca
www.facebook.com/SocietyForSocialistStudies
Overview: A small national charitable organization founded in 1967
Mission: To create, foster, & publish academic & scholarly research & analysis in Canada, with emphasis on socialist, feminist, anti-racist, & ecological points of view
Member of: Humanities & Social Science Federation of Canada
Finances: *Funding Sources:* Membership fees
Membership: 350; *Fees:* $10 low income; $40 standard; $70 supporter; $100 sponsor; *Member Profile:* Membership includes any person underwriting the Society's purpose.; *Committees:* Canadian Federation of Humanities and Social Sciences Congress Programme Committee; Journal Editorial Committee
Activities: Organizes conferences, seminars, & workshops; publishes educational material; advances public education
Chief Officer(s):
Chris Hurl, Secretary
societyforsocialiststudies@gmail.com
Publications:
• Socialist Studies: Journal of the Society for Socialist Studies
Type: Journal

Society for Technology & Rehabilitation *See* Ability Society of Alberta

Society for the Preservation & Encouragement of Barber Shop Quartet Singing in America Inc. *See* Harmony Foundation of Canada

Society for the Preservation of Old Mills - Canadian Chapter (SPOOM)
PO Box 352, 93 Woolwich St., Breslau ON N0B 1M0
Tel: 519-633-5577
spoomer@sympatico.ca
www.hips.com/spoomcanada
Overview: A small national organization founded in 1999
Mission: To promote interest in old mills, their history, function & preservation
Affiliation(s): Society for the Preservation of Old Mills USA
Finances: *Annual Operating Budget:* Less than $50,000
Staff Member(s): 6
Membership: 100; *Fees:* $20; *Member Profile:* Anyone interested in old mills
Chief Officer(s):
Maryanne Szuck, Treasurer

Society for the Promotion of the Teaching of English as a Second Language in Quebec (SPEAQ) / Société pour la perfectionnement de l'enseignement de l'anglais, langue seconde, au Québec
6662, rue Saint-Denis, #C, Montréal QC H2S 2R9
Tel: 514-271-3700; *Fax:* 514-271-4587
speaq@speaq.qc.ca
www.speaq.qc.ca
Overview: A medium-sized provincial charitable organization founded in 1976

Mission: To unite individuals engaged or interested in the teaching of English as a second language in Quebec; To promote & develop the professional & economic interests of members; To ensure favourable conditions for the development of teaching English as a second language in Quebec//Promouvoir l'enseignement de l'anglais, langue seconde au Québec
Member of: Conseil pédagogique interdisciplinaire du Québec
Affiliation(s): Teachers of English to Speakers of Other Languages, Inc; Canadian Association of Second Language Teachers; Society for Educational Visits & Exchanges in Canada
Finances: *Annual Operating Budget:* $100,000-$250,000; *Funding Sources:* Patrimoine Canada
Staff Member(s): 1; 7 volunteer(s)
Membership: 800; *Fees:* $10-$20; *Member Profile:* Individuals involved with & interested in teaching English as a second language in Quebec
Activities: Conducting research to encourage developments in the teaching of English as a second language in Québec; Organizing conventions & events; *Awareness Events:* DEESL Colloquium; Intensig/Sugar Shack Smash; RASCALS Colloquium
Chief Officer(s):
Gwenn Gauthier, President
Monique Mainella, Vice President
Awards:
• SPEAQ Award
Eligibility: Members of SPEAQ who have made contributions to the ESL field through research, teacher training, publishing, organization of SPEAQ or ESL activities, or promotion of ESL issues
• Teacher of Merit Award
Eligibility: Teachers who have taught ESL at the elementary, secondary, college, university, or adult education levels
• SPEAQ Board of Directors Award
Meetings/Conferences:
• Society for the Promotion of the Teaching of English as a Second Language in Quebec 2018 46th Annual Convention, 2018, QC
Scope: Provincial
Description: Featuring presentations on language, award ceremonies, workshops & exhibits

Society for the Retired & Semi-Retired *See* Seniors Association of Greater Edmonton

Society for the Study of Architecture in Canada (SSAC) / Société pour l'étude de l'architecture au Canada (SEAC)
PO Box 2302, Stn. D, Ottawa ON K1P 5W5
ssac.seac@gmail.com
canada-architecture.org
www.flickr.com/photos/ssac_photos
Overview: A small national organization founded in 1974
Mission: To promote the study of Canadian architecture including an examination of both historical & cultural issues relating to buildings, districts, cities & the cultural landscapes; to encourage the collection & preservation of Canada's architectural records; to encourage preservation of the built environment
Affiliation(s): Society of Architectural Historians
Finances: *Annual Operating Budget:* $50,000-$100,000; *Funding Sources:* Membership dues; SSHRC
Membership: *Fees:* $35 student; $40 low income; $65 individual; $90 corporate; *Member Profile:* Individuals, organizations, institutions & corporations which have a particular interest in the study of architecture in Canada
Chief Officer(s):
Peter Coffman, President
Awards:
• Martin Eli Weil Award
Student essay competition on role of the built environment

Society for the Study of Egyptian Antiquities (SSEA) / Société pour l'Étude de l'Égypte Ancienne
PO Box 19004, Stn. Walmer, 360A Bloor St. West, Toronto ON M5S 3C9
Tel: 647-520-4339
info@thessea.org
www.thessea.org
www.facebook.com/SocietyfortheStudyofEgyptianAntiquities
Overview: A medium-sized international charitable organization founded in 1969
Mission: To stimulate interest in Egyptology; To assist with research & training in the field; To sponsor & promote archaeological expeditions to Egypt

Member of: Canadian Association of Learned Journals
Affiliation(s): Canadian Institute in Egypt; Canadian Mediterranean Institute
Finances: *Funding Sources:* Membership fees; Donations; SSHRC Aid to Research & Transfer Journals
Membership: *Fees:* $30 student; $45 associate; $60 full; $80 library/institution; *Member Profile:* Individuals; Students; Institutions; *Committees:* Hospitality; Fieldwork & Research; Fundraising; Publications; Scholars' Colloquium; Symposium; Bylaws & Policy; Finance
Activities: Annual symposium; Main lecture series (4); Mini-lecture series; *Library:* Not open to public
Chief Officer(s):
Lyn Green, National President
Calgary Chapter
3008 Utah Dr. NW, Calgary AB T2N 4A1
Tel: 403-282-2153
info@calgaryssea.ca
www.calgaryssea.ca
www.facebook.com/pages/Calgary-SSEA/280577115303717
Chief Officer(s):
Julius Szekrenyes, Chapter President
Chapitre de Montréal
CP 49022, Succ. Versailles, Montréal QC H1N 3T6
Tél: 514-353-4674; Téléc: 514-353-4674
info@sseamtl.org
www.sseamtl.org
www.facebook.com/sseamontreal
Chief Officer(s):
Brigitte Ouellet, President
Vancouver Chapter
Vancouver BC
vancouver@thessea.org
sseavancouver.wordpress.com
www.facebook.com/sseavancouver
twitter.com/VancouverSSEA
www.youtube.com/user/sseavancouver
Chief Officer(s):
Christine Johnston, Chapter President

Society for Treatment of Autism / Association canadienne pour l'obtention des services aux personnes autistiques
404 - 94 Ave. SE, Calgary AB T2J 0E8
Tel: 403-253-2291; Fax: 403-253-6974
Toll-Free: 888-301-2872
intake@sta-ab.com
www.sta-ab.com
Overview: A medium-sized national charitable organization founded in 1988
Mission: To ensure that a comprehensive range of services exists across Canada to meet the needs of individuals with autism & their families, & that autistic people are given the opportunity to achieve maximum independence & productivity within the community
Activities: Supporting existing service providing organizations; Assisting in the development of such groups; Initiating & developing services independently when necessary; Acting as an ongoing resource for those with an interest in autism & related disorders
Chief Officer(s):
Peter Johnson, Chair
Dave Mikkelsen, Executive Director
Nova Scotia - Society for Treatment of Autism
PO Box 392, 541 Charlotte St., Sydney NS B1P 6H2
Tel: 902-567-6441; Fax: 902-567-0425
autism@ns.sympatico.ca
www.nsnet.org/autismns
Saskatchewan - Autism Services
209 Fairmont Dr., Saskatoon SK S7M 5B8
Tel: 306-665-7013; Fax: 306-665-7011
www.autismservices.ca
www.facebook.com/pages/Autism-Services-of-Saskatoon/333195500114558
www.youtube.com/user/AutismSaskatoon
Mission: Provides treatment, educational, management and consultative services to people with autism and related disorders across Saskatchewan
Chief Officer(s):
Lynn Latta, Executive Director

Society of Bastet
327 Windmill Rd., Dartmouth NS B3A 1H7
info@societyofbastet.com
www.societyofbastet.com

Overview: A small local organization
Mission: To act as an accepting & inclusive community for alternative lifestyles & fetishists throughout Atlantic Canada
Finances: *Funding Sources:* Membership dues
Membership: *Fees:* $30
Activities: Operating a non-profit playspace; Offering classes & peer tutoring; Organizing social events

Society of Canadian Artists (SCA) / Société des artistes canadiens (SAC)
24 Lorindale Ave., Toronto ON M5M 3C2
Tel: 647-919-6864
info@societyofcanadianartists.com
www.societyofcanadianartists.com
www.facebook.com/SocietyofCanadianArtist
twitter.com/SocCanArtists
www.instagram.com/society_of_canadian_artists
Overview: A small national organization founded in 1957
Mission: To promote recognition of its member-artists through exhibitions, seminars, workshops, travelling shows
Finances: *Annual Operating Budget:* Less than $50,000; *Funding Sources:* Membership dues
10 volunteer(s)
Membership: 311; *Fees:* $95 Elected members, $45 Associates; *Member Profile:* Professional visual artists & associate members; *Committees:* Membership; Exhibitions; Publicity; Website
Activities: An annual juried members' show; annual juried open show
Chief Officer(s):
Ortansa Moraru, President
Peter Gough, Vice-President
petergough.art@bellaliant.net

Society of Canadian Cine Amateurs (SCCA) / Société des ciné amateurs canadiens
3 Wardrope Ave. South, Stoney Creek ON L8G 1R9
Tel: 905-662-4406
sccaonline.ca
Overview: A small national organization founded in 1968
Mission: To promote the arts & sciences of amateur film & video production; to foster & stimulate interest in amateur films & videos in Canada
Finances: *Annual Operating Budget:* Less than $50,000; *Funding Sources:* Membership fees; entry fees; donations
15 volunteer(s)
Membership: 130 + 12 clubs; *Fees:* $30; *Committees:* Executive; Honours; Nominations
Activities: *Speaker Service:* Yes; Library
Chief Officer(s):
Fred Briggs, President
pres@sccaonline.ca

Society of Canadian Ornithologists (SCO) / Société des ornithologistes du Canada (SOC)
C/O Lance Laviolette, Membership Secretary, 22350 County Rd. 10, RR #1, Glen Robertson ON K0B 1H0
www.sco-soc.ca
Overview: A medium-sized national charitable organization founded in 1983
Mission: To support research to understand & conserve Canadian birds; To represent Canadian ornithologists
Finances: *Funding Sources:* Membership fees; Donations
Membership: 357; *Fees:* $10 students; $25 regular members; $50 sustaining members; $500 life members; *Member Profile:* Amateur & professional ornithologists
Activities: Connecting with other professional ornithological societies; Disseminating information about the birds of Canada; Offering grants to study birds
Chief Officer(s):
Greg Robertson, President
greg.robertson@ec.gc.ca
Lance Laviolette, Membership Secretary
lance.laviolette@gmail.com
Awards:
• Jamie Smith Memorial Award
• Speirs Award
• Taverner Awards
• James L. Baillie Student Research Award
• Fred Cooke Student Research Award
Meetings/Conferences:
• International Ornithological Congress 2018, August, 2018, Vancouver, BC
Scope: International
Publications:
• Avian Conservation & Ecology

Canadian Associations / Society of Christian Schools in British Columbia (SCSBC)

Type: Journal
Profile: Published by the Society of Canadian Ornithologists / Société des ornithologistes du Canada & Bird Studies Canada
• Biology & Conservation of Forest Birds
Editor: A.W. Diamond; D.N. Nettleship
Profile: A series of manuscripts from a Society of Canadian Ornithologists / Société des ornithologistes du Canada meeting
• Picoides: Bulletin of the Society of Canadian Ornithologists / Bulletin de la Société des Ornithologistes du Canada
Type: Newsletter; *Editor:* Rob Warnock
Profile: President, committee, & meeting reports, announcements, award news, research articles, essays, book reviews, bird surveys, & conservation information

Society of Christian Schools in British Columbia (SCSBC)
Fosmark Centre, Trinity Western University, 7600 Glover Rd., Langley BC V2Y 1Y1
Tel: 604-888-6366; *Fax:* 604-888-2791
contact@scsbc.ca
www.scsbc.ca
Previous Name: Southwest British Columbia League of Christian Schools
Overview: A small provincial organization founded in 1976
Mission: To serve Christian schools in British Columbia; To seek support in the provision of Christian education; To develop policies & curriculum outlines & units
Affiliation(s): Christian Schools International (CSI); Christian Schools Canada (CSC); Christian Teachers Association of British Columbia; Christian Principals Association of British Columbia
Membership: 1-99; *Member Profile:* Christian school campuses & societies in British Columbia
Activities: Monitoring government policies & regulations regarding Christian schoools, & advising schools about government relations; Promoting Christian education throughout British Columbia; Offering workshops; Publishing resource handbooks; Assisting new Christian schools & expanding schools; Supporting digital learning; *Library:* Society of Christian Schools in British Columbia Resource Library
Chief Officer(s):
Ed Noot, Executive Director
ed.noot@scsbc.ca
Darren Spyksma, Director, Learning
darren.spyksma@scsbc.ca
Greg Gerber, Director, Learning
greg.gerber@scsbc.ca
Karen Bush, Designer, Creative Services
karen.bush@scsbc.ca
Meetings/Conferences:
• Society of Christian Schools in BC Leadership Conference & AGM, 2018
Scope: Provincial
• Society of Christian Schools in BC Business & Development Conference, March, 2018
Scope: Provincial
Description: Offers workshops & networking opportunities for staff members of Christian schools
Contact Information: busdev2018.scsbc.net
Publications:
• eBulletin
Type: Newsletter
Profile: Information, such as Ministry of Education updates, society policies, & forthcoming workshops & courses, sent regularly to member school board members, principals, curriculum coordinators, & preschooldirectors
• Educating for Life Today & Tomorrow: Resource Manual for High School Guidance
Type: Manual
• Educating toward Wisdom
Type: Booklet
Profile: A resource for curriculum leaders & administrators in Christian schools
• Educating with Heart & Mind: Principles for Curriculum in Christian Schools
Type: Booklet
Profile: A collection of biblical perspective statements
• For the Love of Your Child
Type: Booklet; *Number of Pages:* 20
Profile: Christian education information
• Good Teaching Comes from the Inside
Type: Booklet
Profile: Information for school leaders & teachers
• International Education Program: Student Coordinator Handbook
Type: Handbook
Profile: Information for schools initiating or restructuring an international student program
• La Joie de la langue française
Type: Booklet
Profile: A resource for both elementary & secondary French teachers
• Learning Together in the Middle
Type: Booklet
Profile: Renewing middle level education in Christian schools
• The Link
Type: Newsletter; *Frequency:* Quarterly
Profile: Information for Christian school, staff, & committee members, including new resources & school news & events
• Living, Loving, & Learning: A Kindergarten Handbook
Type: Handbook
Profile: A resource for kindergarten teachers in Christian schools
• Responding to a School Emergency
Type: Booklet
Profile: School emergency preparedness
• SCSBC Administrative Handbook
Type: Handbook
Profile: General guidelines to shape school policy & practice
• SCSBC Internal Control Checklist
Type: Booklet
Profile: Internal controls which may be suitable for SCSBC schools & other independent schools
• The SCSBC Language Arts Handbook
Type: Handbook
Profile: Fundamental principles for language arts education
• The SCSBC Visual Arts Activity Handbook
Type: Booklet
Profile: Direction for visual arts programs in Christian schools
• Serving All Children Well
Type: Booklet
Profile: Information for Christian educators

Society of Composers, Authors & Music Publishers of Canada (SOCAN) / Société canadienne des auteurs, compositeurs et éditeurs de musique
41 Valleybrook Dr., Toronto ON M3B 2S6
Tel: 416-445-8700; *Fax:* 416-445-7108
Toll-Free: 800-557-6226
socan@socan.ca
www.socan.ca
www.facebook.com/SOCANmusic
twitter.com/SOCANmusic
www.youtube.com/SOCANmusic
Merged from: Performing Rights Organization of Canada Ltd. (PROCAN); Composers, Authors & Publishers Association
Overview: A large national licensing organization founded in 1990
Mission: To administer the performing rights of members & of affiliated international organizations by licensing the use of music in Canada
Finances: *Annual Operating Budget:* Greater than $5 Million; *Funding Sources:* Music performance licence fees
Staff Member(s): 200
Membership: 122,000; *Fees:* $50 one-time fee for publishers only; *Member Profile:* Music composer, author &/or publisher; *Committees:* Executive Governance; Membership; Risk; Tariffs, Licensing, & Distribution; Government Affairs
Chief Officer(s):
Eric Baptiste, CEO
Andrew Berthoff, Chief Communications & Marketing Officer
Jeff King, Chief Operating Officer
Michael McCarty, Chief Membership Officer
Jennifer Brown, Senior Vice-President, Operations
Janice Scott, Vice-President, Information Technology
Gilles M. Daigle, General Counsel, Legal Services
Awards:
• Gordon F. Henderson/SOCAN Copyright Competition
Presented annually to a law student or articling lawyer for an essay on the subject of copyright & music *Deadline:* April; *Amount:* $2,000
• SOCAN Awards
Established 1990 for the purpose of recognizing SOCAN creators & their contribution to Canadian music; presented at the annual Awards Dinner; only SOCAN member writers, composers & music publishers are eligible
• SOCAN Awards for Young Composers
Total of $17,500 awarded to encourage & recognize the creative talents of upcoming Canadian composers; The Sir Ernest MacMillan Awards for compositions for no fewer than 13 performers; The Serge Garant Awards for compositions for a minimum of three performers; The Pierre Mercure Awards for solo or duet compositions; The Hugh Le Caine Awards for compositions realized on tape with electronic means; The Godfrey Ridout Awards for choral compositions of any variety
Atlantic Division
Queen Square, #802, 45 Alderney Dr., Dartmouth NS B2Y 2N6
Tel: 902-464-7000; *Fax:* 902-464-9696
Toll-Free: 800-707-6226
Chief Officer(s):
Tim Hardy, Executive, Member & Industry Relations
Québec Division
#500, 600, boul de Maisonneuve ouest, Montréal QC H3A 3J2
Tél: 514-844-8377; *Téléc:* 514-849-8446
Ligne sans frais: 800-797-6226
Chief Officer(s):
Geneviève Côté, Chief Québec Affairs Officer
West Coast Division
#504, 1166 Alberni St., Vancouver BC V6E 3Z3
Tel: 604-669-5569; *Fax:* 604-688-1142
Toll-Free: 800-937-6226

Society of Deaf & Hard of Hearing Nova Scotians (SDHHNS)
#805, 1888 Brunswick St., Halifax NS B3J 3J8
Tel: 902-422-7130; *Fax:* 902-492-8110; *TTY:* 902-422-7130
sdhhns@ns.sympatico.ca
www.sdhhns.org
www.facebook.com/SDHHNSCB
Overview: A small provincial organization founded in 1980
Mission: To provide services that meet the needs of Deaf, hard of hearing and late deafened people with dignity, integrity and respect.
Staff Member(s): 7
Membership: 58,000; *Fees:* $10 individual; $15 couple/family; $50 organization/business; $100 life; $150 life family; *Member Profile:* Deaf & hard of hearing people in Nova Scotia
Chief Officer(s):
Frank O'Sullivan, Executive Director
fosullivan@ns.sympatico.ca
Rosalind Wright, Regional Manager, Cape Breton-Sydney Office, 902-564-0003
rwright@ns.aliantzinc.ca

The Society of Energy Professionals
2239 Yonge St., Toronto ON M4S 2B5
Tel: 416-979-2709; *Fax:* 416-979-5794
Toll-Free: 866-288-1788
society@thesociety.ca
www.thesociety.ca
Overview: A medium-sized provincial organization founded in 1948
Mission: To represent employees of Ontario's electricity industry; To ensure the best working conditions for members
Member of: Canadian Council of Professionals; Professional Employees' Network
Affiliation(s): International Federation of Professional & Technical Engineers; Canadian Labour Congress / Congrès du travail du Canada; American Federation of Labour / Congress of Industrial Organizations, (AFL/CIO); UNI Global Union
Finances: *Funding Sources:* Membership dues
Membership: *Member Profile:* Professional members of the elctricity industry in Ontario, such as scientists, engineers, financial specialists & supervisors
Chief Officer(s):
Scott Travers, President, 416-979-2709 Ext. 5002
traverss@thesociety.ca
Michelle Johnston, Executive Vice-President, Policy, 416-979-2709 Ext. 5001
johnstonm@thesociety.ca
Andy D'Andrea, Executive Vice-President, Member Services, 416-979-2709 Ext. 3027
dandreaa@thesociety.ca
Rob Stanley, Executive Vice-President, Finance, 416-979-2709 Ext. 3019
stanleyr@thesociety.ca

Society of Engineering Technicians & Technologists of Saskatchewan (SETTS) *See* Saskatchewan Applied Science Technologists & Technicians

Society of Engineering Technologists of BC *See* Applied Science Technologists & Technicians of British Columbia

Society of Graphic Designers of Canada (GDC) / Société des designers graphiques du Canada
Arts Court, 2 Daly Ave., Ottawa ON K1N 6E2
Tel: 613-567-5400; *Fax:* 613-564-4428
Toll-Free: 877-496-4453
info@gdc.net
www.gdc.net
www.linkedin.com/groups/124328
www.facebook.com/GDCNational
twitter.com/GDCNational
Also Known As: Graphic Designers of Canada
Overview: A large national charitable organization founded in 1966
Mission: To maintain a defined, recognized & competent body of graphic designers; To promote high standards of graphic design for benefit of Canadian industry, commerce, public service & education
Affiliation(s): International Council of Graphic Design Associations; Societe des designers graphiques du Quebec; University and College Designers Association; Canadian Association of Professional Image Creators; Australian Graphic Design Association
Finances: *Annual Operating Budget:* Less than $50,000; *Funding Sources:* Membership dues; Corporate
Staff Member(s): 1; 200 volunteer(s)
Membership: 1,000; *Fees:* $200-$300 regular; $60 student; $250 affiliate; *Committees:* Partnerships; CGD Certification Board; Sustainability; GDC Foundation; Ethics
Activities: Offering student scholarships; *Rents Mailing List:* Yes
Chief Officer(s):
Johnathon Strebly, President
president@gdc.net
Melanie MacDonald, Executive Director
director@gdc.net
Awards:
• Veer Scholarship
• Adobe Scholarship
• Applied Arts Magazine Scholarship
• Ray Hrynkow Scholarship
• Canada Type Scholarship
Publications:
• GDC Journal [a publication of the Society of Graphic Designers of Canada]
Type: Journal

Alberta North Chapter
PO Box 11185, Stn. Main, Edmonton AB T5J 3K5
www.gdc.net/chapter/alberta-north
twitter.com/GDCABnorth
Chief Officer(s):
Amanda Schutz, President
president.abnorth@gdc.net

Alberta South Chapter
#31020, 112 - 4 St. NE, Calgary AB T2E 3R9
www.gdc.net/chapter/alberta-south
www.facebook.com/gdcabsouth
twitter.com/GDCABsouth
Chief Officer(s):
Naoko Masuda, President
president.absouth@gdc.net

Arctic Chapter
www.gdc.net/chapters/arctic.htm
www.facebook.com/GDCArctic
twitter.com/GDCArctic
instagram.com/gdcarctic
Chief Officer(s):
Mark Rutledge, President
president.arctic@gdc.net

Atlantic Chapter
www.gdc.net/chapter/atlantic
www.facebook.com/GDCAtlantic
twitter.com/GDCAtlantic
Chief Officer(s):
Paul Williams, President
president.atlantic@gdc.net

British Columbia Chapter (GDCBC)
www.gdc.net/chapter/bc
www.facebook.com/GDCBC
twitter.com/gdcbc
Chief Officer(s):
Jonathan Vaughn Strebly, President
president.bc@gdc.net

Manitoba Chapter
www.gdc.net/chapter/manitoba
www.facebook.com/gdcmb
twitter.com/gdcmb
Chief Officer(s):
Andrew Boardman, President
president.mb@gdc.net

Saskatchewan North Chapter
PO Box 24016, Saskatoon SK S7K 8B4
www.gdc.net/chapter/saskatchewan-north
www.facebook.com/gdcskn
twitter.com/gdcskn
Chief Officer(s):
Dave Nagy, President
president.skn@gdc.net

Saskatchewan South Chapter
www.gdc.net/chapter/saskatchewan-south
www.facebook.com/GDCSaskSouth
twitter.com/GDCSaskSouth
Chief Officer(s):
Rhea Leibel, President
president.sks@gdc.net

Vancouver Island Chapter
www.gdc.net/chapter/vancouver-island
www.facebook.com/GDCVancouverIsland
www.twitter.com/GDCVI
Chief Officer(s):
Aaron Heppell, President
president.vibc@gdc.net

Society of Gynecologic Oncologists of Canada (GOC) / Société des gynécologues oncologues du Canada
780 Echo Dr., Ottawa ON K1S 5R7
Tel: 613-730-4192; *Fax:* 613-730-4314
Toll-Free: 800-561-2416
www.g-o-c.org
Overview: A small national organization founded in 1980
Mission: To improve the care of women with gynecologic cancer; to raise standards of practice in gynecologic oncology & to encourage ongoing research
Finances: *Annual Operating Budget:* $100,000-$250,000; *Funding Sources:* Membership fees; donations
Staff Member(s): 1
Membership: 170; *Fees:* $50 or $200, depending on membership category; *Member Profile:* Gyn-oncologists, medical, radiation oncologists, pathologists, nurse specialists, residents in fellowship training program, residents in ob-gyn programs; *Committees:* Practice Guidelines; Programme; Membership; Education; Government Relations
Activities: GOC Professional Continuing Development Meeting; GOC AGM; *Awareness Events:* Run for Her Life, June
Chief Officer(s):
Dianne Miller, President
Walter Gotlieb, Sec.-Treas.
Meetings/Conferences:
• The Society of Gynecologic Oncology of Canada 18th Annual Continuing Professional Development Meeting, April, 2018, Sheraton Centre Toronto Hotel, Toronto, ON
Scope: National
• The Society of Gynecologic Oncology of Canada 39th Annual General Meeting, June, 2018, Victoria, BC
Scope: National

Society of Incentive & Travel Executives of Canada
#100, 6700 Century Ave., Mississauga ON L5N 6A4
Tel: 905-812-7483; *Fax:* 905-567-7191
office@sitecanada.org
www.sitecanada.org
Also Known As: SITE Canada
Overview: A small national organization
Mission: Worldwide organization of business professionals dedicated to the recognition & development of motivational & performance improvement strategies of which travel is a key component; it recognizes global cultural differences & practices in developing these strategies & serves as a prime networking & educational opportunity for its members
Finances: *Funding Sources:* Membership fees; registration fees; advertising; sponsorship
Staff Member(s): 2; 20 volunteer(s)
Membership: 135; *Fees:* US$450; *Member Profile:* Involvement in the incentive travel industry; *Committees:* Meetings; Membership; Newsletter; Seminars; Social
Activities: *Rents Mailing List:* Yes
Chief Officer(s):
Hayley Bishop, President, 416-443-969 Ext. 436
hbishop@wynfordtwg.com
Awards:
• Crystal Awards
Annual competition recognizing outstanding incentive travel programs worldwide
• Lifetime Achievement Award
Voted as appropriate by the Board of Directors in acknoledgment of exceptional service to the industry
• Member of the Year
Annual award that recognizes one site member for outstanding contributions in a given year
• Certified Incentive Travel Executive
Certification that recognizes professionals who have demonsrated their extensive knowledge of the industry & achieved its highest standard of excellence

Society of Internet Professionals (SIP)
#305, 120 Carlton St., Toronto ON M5A 4K2
Tel: 416-891-4937
info@sipgroup.org
www.sipgroup.org
www.linkedin.com/groups/Society-Internet-Professionals-SIP-15 09387
twitter.com/sipgroup
Overview: A small local organization founded in 1997
Mission: To represent the interests of internet professionals
Membership: *Fees:* $100 individual; *Member Profile:* Accredited internet professionals
Activities: Online university; Accredited Internet Professional (AIP) Accreditation & Certification Program; symposiums; workshops; trade shows; *Internships:* Yes; *Speaker Service:* Yes; *Library:* Internet Resource Centre; Not open to public
Chief Officer(s):
Max Haroon, President

Society of Kabalarians of Canada
1160 West 10th Ave., Vancouver BC V6H 1J1
Tel: 604-263-9551; *Fax:* 604-263-5514
Toll-Free: 866-489-1188
info1@kabalarians.com
www.kabalarians.com
Also Known As: Kabalarian Philosophy
Overview: A small international organization founded in 1963
Mission: To promote Kabalarian philosophy, which teaches a constructive way of life through the understanding of the Mathematical Principle, encouraging people to live a more progressive, constructive life.
Finances: *Funding Sources:* Donations; courses
Staff Member(s): 6
Activities: Public presentations, seminars, workshops; classes of study; *Speaker Service:* Yes; *Library:* Resource Centre; Open to public by appointment
Chief Officer(s):
Lorenda Bardell, President

Calgary
2618 Richmond Rd. SW, Calgary AB T3E 4M4
Tel: 403-246-0926
calgarycentre@kabalarians.com
www.kabalarians.com/calgary
Chief Officer(s):
Garett Willington, Representative
ronaye.willington@modelland.com

Edmonton
7764 - 83 Ave., Edmonton AB T6C 1A4
Tel: 780-466-7369
www.kabalarians.com/edmonton
Chief Officer(s):
Floyd Farrell, Representative

Society of Local Government Managers of Alberta
PO Box 308, 4629 - 54 Ave., Bruderheim AB T0B 0S0
Tel: 780-796-3836; *Fax:* 780-796-2081
www.clgm.net
Overview: A medium-sized provincial organization
Mission: To govern & promote the profession of municipal government managers
Membership: *Committees:* Communications; Discipline; Practice Review; Professional Development; Registration; Planning Committee for the Municipal Administration Leadership Workshop
Chief Officer(s):
Linda M. Davies, Executive Director/Registrar
linda.davies@shaw.ca

Society of Manufacturing Engineers - Canada Office (SME)
#312, 7100 Woodbine Ave., Markham ON L3R 5J2
Tel: 905-752-4415; Fax: 905-479-0113
Toll-Free: 888-322-7333
canadasales@sme.org
www.sme.org
www.facebook.com/SMEmfg
twitter.com/@SME_MFG
www.youtube.com/smeevents; www.instagram.com/sme_mfg
Overview: A medium-sized national organization
Mission: To acquire & distribute manufacturing knowledge to its members & the manufacturing community
Activities: Providing educational opportunities; Offering networking possibilities
Chief Officer(s):
Jeffrey M. Krause, Chief Executive Officer
Steve Prahalis, Vice-President, SME Studios & Canadian Operations
Publications:
• Journal of Manufacturing Processes
Type: Journal; Frequency: Semiannually; Editor: Shiv Kapoor; ISSN: 1526-6125
• Journal of Manufacturing Systems
Type: Journal; Frequency: Quarterly; Editor: Neil Duffie; ISSN: 0278-6125
Profile: Research in manufacturing at the systems level
• Manufacturing Engineering
Type: Magazine; Frequency: Monthly
• Manufacturing Letters
Type: Journal; Editor: Kornel F. Ehmann
• Procedia Manufacturing
Type: Journal; Editor: S.J. Hu

The Society of Notaries Public of British Columbia
PO Box 44, #1220, 625 Howe St., Vancouver BC V6C 2T6
Tel: 604-681-4516; Fax: 604-681-7258
Toll-Free: 800-663-0343
www.notaries.bc.ca
Overview: A medium-sized provincial organization founded in 1926
Mission: To ensure that its members provide high quality services to their clients
Staff Member(s): 9
Chief Officer(s):
G.W. Wayne Braid, Chief Executive Officer/Secretary, 604-681-4516, Fax: 604-681-7258
Akash Sablok, President

Society of Obstetricians & Gynaecologists of Canada (SOGC) / Société des obstétriciens et gynécologues du Canada
780 Echo Dr., Ottawa ON K1S 5R7
Tel: 613-730-4192; Fax: 613-730-4314
Toll-Free: 800-561-2416
info@sogc.com
www.sogc.org
www.facebook.com/sogc.org
twitter.com/SOGCorg
Overview: A medium-sized national organization founded in 1944
Mission: To promote excellence in the practice of obstetrics & gynaecology; To produce national clinical guidelines for medical education on women's health issues; To promote optimal, comprehensive women's health care
Membership: 3,000+; Fees: Schedule available; Member Profile: Gynaecologists; Obstetricians; Family physicians; Nurses; Nurse practitioners; Midwives; Allied health professionals; Students, enrolled in an undergraduate training program in a Canadian medical school, a family medical residency program, or a postgraduate training program in obstetrics & gynaecology; Committees: SOGC has over 50 committees, such as Aboriginal Health Initiatives; Canadian Paediatric & Adolescent Gynaecology & Obstetricians; Clinical Practice - Obstetrics; Clinical Practice - Gynaecology; Diagnostic Imaging; Ethics; Genetics; Infectious Disease; Reproductive Endocrinology Infertility; Maternal Fetal Medicine; RM Advisory; ALARM Committee; Junior Member; Maternal Fetal Medicine; Public Affairs Urogynaecology; Western Regional
Activities: Collaborating with other national & international organizations to improve health care; Providing continued professional development for physicians & health care providers, such as e-learning modules; Offering public education; Encouraging research; Engaging in advocacy activities; Presenting grants, awards, & fellowships
Chief Officer(s):
George Carson, President
Jennifer Blake, Chief Executive Officer
Publications:
• Health News [a publication of the Society of Obstetricians & Gynaecologists of Canada]
Type: Newsletter
Profile: SOGC media reports & health news
• Healthy Beginnings [a publication of the Society of Obstetricians & Gynaecologists of Canada]
Profile: A guide to pregnancy & childbirth
• Journal of Obstetrics & Gynaecology Canada (JOGC)
Type: Journal; Frequency: Monthly; Price: Free with membership in the Society ofObstetricians & Gynaecologists of Canada
Profile: A peer-reviewed journal of obstetrics, gynaecology, & women's health, featuring original research articles,case reports, & reviews
• Sex Sense [a publication of the Society of Obstetricians & Gynaecologists of Canada]
Profile: A guide to contraception
• SOGC [Society of Obstetricians & Gynaecologists of Canada] News
Type: Newsletter; Frequency: 10 pa
Profile: Society work & events, plus information about recent legislation & developments in women's health care
• What You Should Know About The Society of Obstetricians & Gynaecologists of Canada

Society of Ontario Adjudicators & Regulators (SOAR) / Société ontarienne des arbitres et des régisseurs
PO Box 22031, Stn. The Colonnade, Toronto ON M5S 1R0
Tel: 416-623-7454; Fax: 416-623-7437
information@soar.on.ca
soar.on.ca
www.linkedin.com/company/5355886
twitter.com/SOAR_News
Overview: A small provincial organization founded in 1993
Mission: To improve the administrative justice system
Affiliation(s): Canadian Council of Administrative Tribunals
Membership: Fees: Free; Member Profile: Chairs, members & executive staff of administrative justice system agencies; Committees: Education; Advocacy & Innovation
Activities: Training; Conferences; Development of manuals; Model policies & guidelines
Chief Officer(s):
Emanuela Heyninck, President
Daphne Simon, Executive Director

Society of Ontario Nut Growers (SONG)
979 Lakeshore Rd., RR#3, Niagara-on-the-Lake ON L0S 1J0
Tel: 519-740-6220
www.songonline.ca
Overview: A medium-sized provincial organization founded in 1972
Mission: To promote the interests of nut growers; To encourage scientific research in the breeding & culture of nut-bearing plants suited to Ontario conditions; To disseminate information on propagation techniques & cultural practices
Member of: Northern Nut Growers Association
Affiliation(s): Eastern Chapter Society of Ontario Nut Growers
Finances: Annual Operating Budget: Less than $50,000; Funding Sources: Membership fees; annual auction
5 volunteer(s)
Membership: 300; Fees: $17/yr; $45 - 3/yrs.; Member Profile: Individuals & organizations involved with the planting & promotion of nut trees
Activities: Offering meetings, technical presentations, nut tree auctions & research
Chief Officer(s):
Bernice Grimo, Treasurer

The Society of Professional Accountants of Canada (SPAC) / La Société des comptables professionnels du Canada
#1007, 250 Consumers Rd., Toronto ON M2J 4V6
Tel: 416-350-8145; Fax: 416-350-8146
Toll-Free: 877-515-4447
registrar@professionalaccountant.org
www.professionalaccountant.org
Overview: A medium-sized national organization founded in 1978
Mission: To provide ongoing education & to set qualifying standards, to ensure the professional competence of its members in the practice of accountancy
Finances: Annual Operating Budget: $50,000-$100,000
Membership: 300; Fees: $250; Member Profile: Individuals who have successfully completed mandatory accreditation examinations, adhered to the code of ethics, & provided evidence of at least three years of practical experience in accountancy
Activities: Professional development; employment referral service
Chief Officer(s):
William O. Nichols, President
president@professionalaccountant.org

Society of Professional Engineers & Associates (SPEA) / Société des ingénieurs professionnels et associés
#2, 2275 Speakman Dr., Mississauga ON L5K 1B1
Tel: 905-823-3606; Fax: 905-823-9602
www.spea.ca
Overview: A medium-sized national organization founded in 1974
Mission: To represent scientists, engineers, technologists, & tradespeople who work for Atomic Energy of Canada Limited (AECL) in Mississauga, Ontario & abroad
Membership: 850; Member Profile: Scientists, engineers, technologists, & tradespeople who work for Atomic Energy of Canada Limited (AECL) in Mississauga, Ontario & abroad
Chief Officer(s):
Michael Ivanco, President
Brian Girard, Chair, Membership
Vincent Tume, Secretary
Val Aleyaseen, Treasurer

Society of Public Insurance Administrators of Ontario (SPIAO)
c/o The Municipality Of Clarington, 40 Temperance St., Bowmanville ON L1C 3A6
info@spiao.ca
www.spiao.ca
Overview: A small provincial organization founded in 1976
Mission: To exchange knowledge & pursue matters dealing with risk & insurance management; to promote cooperation among all local government bodies which have interests in the field of risk & insurance management; to encourage development of educational training programs; to collect & disperse information
Membership: Fees: $125; Member Profile: Must work for any of three levels of government, board of education, library board, public utility, conservation authority or public housing authority
Activities: 2 one-day & 1 two-day workshops per year
Chief Officer(s):
Marie Endicott, President
Catherine Carr, Treasurer

Society of Rural Physicians of Canada (SRPC) / Société de la médecine rurale du Canada
PO Box 893, 269, rue Main, Shawville QC J0X 2Y0
Fax: 819-647-2485
Toll-Free: 877-276-1949
info@srpc.ca
www.srpc.ca
Overview: A small national organization founded in 1993
Mission: To provide equitable medical care for rural communities; to provide sustainable working conditions for rural physicians
Affiliation(s): Canadian Medical Association; World Organization of Rural Doctors
Finances: Funding Sources: Membership fees
Staff Member(s): 4
Membership: 3,000+; Fees: $390 individual; $100 associate; $50 retired; $20 resident; free - student; Member Profile: Rural M.D., medical student/resident; Committees: Emergency; Anesthesia; Nominations & Awards; Education; Specialist; Maternity Care; Rural Critical Care; International; Research; First Year in Practice
Activities: Speaker Service: Yes; Library: by appointment
Chief Officer(s):
John Soles, President
Lee Teperman, Administrative Officer
Meetings/Conferences:
• Society of Rural Physicians of Canada Rural and Remote 2018, April, 2018, St. John's, NL
Scope: National

Society of Saint Vincent de Paul *Voir* Conseil national Société de Saint-Vincent de Paul

Society of St. Vincent de Paul - Toronto Central Council
240 Church St., Toronto ON M5B 1Z2

Tel: 416-364-5577; *Fax:* 416-364-2055
Other Communication: Camp e-mail: campinfo@ssvptoronto.ca
info@ssvptoronto.ca
www.ssvptoronto.ca
Overview: A small local charitable organization founded in 1850
Mission: To live the Gospel message by assisting the poor with love, respect, justice, & joy; To administer special works, including women's shelters, recovery homes, homes for the developmentally & mentally disabled, & a camp for girls
Affiliation(s): Archdiocese of Toronto
Finances: *Funding Sources:* Donations
Membership: *Member Profile:* Individuals who are non-judgmental, compassionate, & giving, who wish to act on their faith by assisting those in need in this lay Catholic organization; Applicants must successfully complete the screening process, which includes a police check, references, & an interview; *Committees:* Advocacy; Addiction Recovery; Camp; Community Living; Election; Executive; Finance; Governance; Health & Safety; Prison Apostolate & Court Services; Resource; Shelter; Spirituality; Stores; Strategic Planning; Twinning
Activities: Delivering Christ's love, material assistance, respect, compassion, & hope to those in need; Offering home visitations; Operating the Marygrove Camp for girls; Providing housing & support to women in crisis; Supporting men & women recovering from addiction; Providing residential care for the developmentally handicapped; Offering low cost clothing; Supporting persons awaiting trial or in prison; Conducting members' conference meetings once or twice a month to grow in faith & to consult regarding ways to assist the needy
Chief Officer(s):
Louise Coutu, Executive Director
Joseph McCalmont, Director, Finance
Publications:
• Volunteer Opportunities Handbook
Type: Handbook
Profile: Description, with contact information, of volunteer opportunities in special works

Society of the Plastics Industry of Canada *See* Canadian Plastics Industry Association

Society of Toxicology of Canada (STC) / Société de toxicologie du Canada
PO Box 55094, Montréal QC H3G 2W5
stcsecretariat@mcgill.ca
www.stcweb.ca
www.facebook.com/societyoftoxicologyofcanada
Overview: A medium-sized national organization founded in 1964
Mission: To promote acquisition, facilitate dissemination & encourage utilization of knowledge in the science of toxicology
Affiliation(s): Canadian Federation of Biological Societies; International Union of Toxicology
Finances: *Funding Sources:* Membership fees
Membership: *Fees:* $100 regular; $30 retired/post-doctoral fellow/graduate student; *Member Profile:* Ordinary - qualified individual who has continuing professional interest in field of toxicology; associate - individual who has not satisfied requirement for ordinary membership; student - graduate student enrolled in postgraduate degree program with major emphasis on toxicology; *Committees:* Awards; Editorial/Newsletter; Education; Finance; Membership; Nominating; Science Policy; Scientific Program; Symposium; Web Site
Chief Officer(s):
Mike Wade, President
Veronica Atehortua, Information Executive Secretary
Meetings/Conferences:
• The Society of Toxicology of Canada 50th Annual Symposium 2018, 2018
Scope: National

Society of Translators & Interpreters of British Columbia (STIBC)
#400, 1501 West Broadway, Vancouver BC V6J 4Z6
Tel: 604-684-2940
www.stibc.org
www.linkedin.com/groups/135809
www.facebook.com/200542026628804
twitter.com/STIBC2012
Overview: A medium-sized provincial licensing organization founded in 1981 overseen by Canadian Translators, Terminologists & Interpreters Council
Mission: To promote the interests of translators & interpreters in BC; To serve the public by applying a Code of Ethics members must comply with, by setting & maintaining high professional standards through education & certification
Finances: *Annual Operating Budget:* $100,000-$250,000; *Funding Sources:* Membership dues
Staff Member(s): 2
Membership: 490; *Member Profile:* Persons with minimum 1 year experience as a translator or interpreter, and who have written & passed the Language Proficiency exam, the Admissions exam, & the Ethics exam
Chief Officer(s):
Michael Radano, Chief Executive Officer
michaelradano@stibc.org

Society of Trust & Estate Practitioners (STEP)
#700, 1 Richmond St. West, Toronto ON M5H 3W4
Tel: 416-491-4949; *Fax:* 416-491-9499
Toll-Free: 877-991-4949
stepcanada@step.ca
www.step.ca
Overview: A medium-sized national licensing organization
Mission: To promote trust & estate work as a profession
Membership: 18,500+ in 80 jurisdictions worldwide; *Member Profile:* Individuals working in the field of trusts & estates; *Committees:* Audit; Awards; Education; Governance; Member Services; National Conference; Nominations & Human Resources; Step Inside; Student Liaison; Trust & Estate Technical
Activities: Diploma covering major areas of estate planning (TEP designation)
Chief Officer(s):
Ian Worland, Chair, 604-631-1220, Fax: 604-683-6953
iworland@legacylawyers.ca
Publications:
• STEP [Society of Trust & Estate Practitioners] Journal
Type: Journal
• STEP [Society of Trust & Estate Practitioners] Insider
Type: E-Newsletter
• STEP [Society of Trust & Estate Practitioners] Directory & Yearbook
Type: Directory
• STEP [Society of Trust & Estate Practitioners] Marketing Brochures
Type: Brochures
Profile: Brochures include: Why Make a Trust? Why Make a Will? Why Make a Lasting Power of Attorney?
• Trust Quarterly Review
Type: Journal

Society of Urologic Surgeons of Ontario (SUSO)
#510, 3030 Lawrence Ave. East, Toronto ON M1P 2T7
Tel: 416-438-9948; *Fax:* 416-438-9590
executive@suso.ca
www.suso.ca
Overview: A small provincial organization
Mission: Dedicated to ensuring patient access to urological care with a commitment to excellence, education, research & sharing of information
Finances: *Funding Sources:* Sponsorships; Membership dues
Membership: *Fees:* $50 resident; $100 corresponding; $200 full; *Member Profile:* Doctors in a residency program in urology; Doctors registered with the Royal College of Physicians & Surgeons of Canada or the American Board of Urology
Chief Officer(s):
Allan Toguri, Executive Director

Society of Writers in Radio, Television & Cinema *Voir* Société des Auteurs de Radio, Télévision et Cinéma

Society Promoting Environmental Conservation (SPEC)
2060 Pine St., Vancouver BC V6J 4P8
Tel: 604-736-7732; *Fax:* 604-736-7115
admin@spec.bc.ca
www.spec.bc.ca
www.facebook.com/137945192900176
www.youtube.com/user/SPECbc
Overview: A medium-sized provincial charitable organization founded in 1969
Mission: To address environmental issues in British Columbia, with a focus on urban communities in the Lower Mainland & the Georgia Basin; To encourage policies that lead to urban sustainability
Finances: *Funding Sources:* Donations
Activities: Advocating for food safety & security; Providing public education programs; Reducing the use of hazardous pesticides
Chief Officer(s):
Rob Baxter, President
Oliver Lane, Coordinator
Meetings/Conferences:
• Society Promoting Environmental Conservation AGM 2018, 2018
Scope: Provincial
Publications:
• SPECTRUM [a publication of the Society Promoting Environmental Conservation]
Type: Newsletter
Profile: Society Promoting Environmental Conservation activities, news releases, upcoming events, & articles

Soeurs Adoratrices du Précieux Sang *See* Sisters Adorers of the Precious Blood

Soeurs de l'Enfant-Jésus *See* Sisters of the Child Jesus

Soeurs de Sainte-Marie de Namur / Sisters of Saint Mary of Namur
68, av Fairmont, Ottawa ON K1Y 1X5
Tél: 613-725-1510
www.ssmn.ca
Aperçu: *Dimension:* petite; *Envergure:* internationale; Organisme sans but lucratif; fondée en 1819
Finances: *Budget de fonctionnement annuel:* $250,000-$500,000
Membre: 1-99
Membre(s) du bureau directeur:
Françoise Sabourin, Supérieure provinciale
jeannettessmn@yahoo.fr
Suzanne Martineau, Secrétaire-trésorière
sr.suzannem@ssmn.ca

Soeurs de Saint-Joseph de Saint-Vallier *Voir* Congregation des Soeurs de Saint-Joseph de Saint-Vallier

Soeurs missionnaires de Notre-Dame des Anges / Missionary Sisters of Our Lady of the Angels
80, av Laurier est, Montréal QC H2T 1E5
Tél: 514-277-3686
mnda.canada@gmail.com
missionnaires-mnda.com
Aperçu: *Dimension:* petite; *Envergure:* internationale; Organisme sans but lucratif; fondée en 1922
Membre: 142
Activités: Nos activités sont de toutes sortes: service d'Église, évangélisation et catéchèse, soins des malades, enseignement et promotion de la femme.
Membre(s) du bureau directeur:
Fernande Leblanc, Contact

Softball Manitoba
#321, 145 Pacific Ave., Winnipeg MB R3B 2Z6
Tel: 204-925-5673; *Fax:* 204-925-5703
softball@softball.mb.ca
www.softball.mb.ca
Also Known As: Softball Manitoba
Overview: A small provincial organization founded in 1965 overseen by Canadian Amateur Softball Association
Mission: To promote & develop softball at all levels by providing leadership, programs & services
Member of: Canadian Amateur Softball Association
Membership: 15,000+ players & coaches; *Committees:* Finance; Facilities; Development; Umpire Development; Competition
Chief Officer(s):
Bill Finch, President

Softball NB Inc. (SNB) / Softball Nouveau-Brunswick Inc.
4242 Water St., Miramichi NB E1N 4L2
Tel: 506-773-5343; *Fax:* 506-773-5630
www.softballnb.ca
www.facebook.com/210596526327
twitter.com/softballnb
Also Known As: Softball New Brunswick
Overview: A medium-sized provincial organization founded in 1925 overseen by Canadian Amateur Softball Association
Mission: To foster, develop, promote & regulate the playing of amateur softball in New Brunswick
Member of: Canadian Amateur Softball Association
Finances: *Annual Operating Budget:* $50,000-$100,000
Staff Member(s): 1; 17 volunteer(s)
Membership: 350 teams; 225 officials
Activities: *Awareness Events:* Hall of Fame, 1st Sat. in June

Softball Newfoundland & Labrador
PO Box 21165, #115, 183 Kenmount Rd., St. John's NL A1A 5B2
Tel: 709-576-7231; *Fax:* 709-576-7049
softball@sportnl.ca
www.softballnl.ca
Overview: A small provincial organization overseen by Canadian Amateur Softball Association
Member of: Canadian Amateur Softball Association
Chief Officer(s):
Paul F. Smith, President

Softball Nouveau-Brunswick Inc. *See* Softball NB Inc.

Softball Nova Scotia
5516 Spring Garden Rd., 4th Fl., Halifax NS B3J 1G6
Tel: 902-425-5454; *Fax:* 902-425-5606
softballns@sportnovascotia.ca
www.softballns.ca
www.facebook.com/softballnovascotia
twitter.com/Softball_NS
Overview: A small provincial organization overseen by Canadian Amateur Softball Association
Mission: To be the provincial governing body for the sport of softball in Nova Scotia
Member of: Canadian Amateur Softball Association
Chief Officer(s):
Richie Connors, President
Caroline Crooks, Executive Director

Softball Ontario
3 Concorde Gate, Toronto ON M3C 3N7
Tel: 416-426-7150; *Fax:* 416-426-7368
info@softballontario.ca
www.softballontario.ca
www.facebook.com/SoftballOntario
twitter.com/SoftballOntario
Overview: A medium-sized provincial organization founded in 1971 overseen by Canadian Amateur Softball Association
Mission: To promote & develop the sport of softball for its athletes, officials & volunteers by providing programs & services at all levels of competitions
Member of: Canadian Amateur Softball Association
Affiliation(s): Provincial Women's Softball Association (PWSA); Ontario Amateur Softball Association (OASA); Ontario Rural Softball Association (ORSA); Slo-Pitch Ontario Association (SPOA)
Staff Member(s): 5
Membership: 5 associations; *Committees:* Finance; Coaching; Participation; Scorekeeping; Fast Pitch & Slo-Pitch Umpire
Chief Officer(s):
Wendy Cathcart, Executive Director
wcathcart@softballontario.ca

Softball Prince Edward Island (SPEI)
#203, 40 Enman Cres., Charlottetown PE C1E 1E6
Tel: 902-620-3549; *Fax:* 902-368-4548
softballpei@gmail.com
softballpei.com
www.facebook.com/SoftballPEI33
twitter.com/SoftballPEI
Also Known As: Softball PEI
Overview: A small provincial organization overseen by Canadian Amateur Softball Association
Mission: To be the provincial governing body for the sport of softball in Prince Edward Island
Member of: Canadian Amateur Softball Association
Activities: Umpire Program; Coaching & Athlete Development Program; Scorekeeping Program; Participation Program; Communication/Promotion; Resources
Chief Officer(s):
Chris Halliwell, President, 902-367-1600
crhalliwell@hotmail.com
Heather Drake, Executive Director
heathercdrake@icloud.com

Softball Québec
4545, av Pierre-de Coubertin, Montréal QC H1V 3R2
Tél: 514-252-3061; *Téléc:* 514-252-3134
softballqc@gmail.com
www.softballquebec.com
www.facebook.com/softballquebec
twitter.com/SoftballQuebec
Aperçu: *Dimension:* moyenne; *Envergure:* provinciale; Organisme sans but lucratif; fondée en 1970 surveillé par Canadian Amateur Softball Association
Mission: Promouvoir la pratique du softball sur le territoire du Québec; offrir aux athlètes, aux entraîneurs, aux officiels et aux administrateurs québécois un support technique et des services de qualité
Membre de: Canadian Amateur Softball Association
Membre(s) du personnel: 5
Membre: 30,000
Activités: Programmes de formation pour officiels et entraîneurs; ligues; compétitions; *Stagiaires:* Oui
Membre(s) du bureau directeur:
Chantal Gagnon, Directrice générale
cgagnon@loisirquebec.qc.ca
Michel Nero, Président
mikeump@hotmail.com

Softball Saskatchewan
2205 Victoria Ave., Regina SK S4P 0S4
Tel: 306-780-9235; *Fax:* 306-780-9483
Other Communication: Alternate Fax: 306-525-4009
info@softball.sk.ca
www.softball.sk.ca
Overview: A small provincial organization overseen by Canadian Amateur Softball Association
Mission: To make softball the number one choice for participation by athletes, coaches, parents and umpires.
Member of: Canadian Amateur Softball Association
Chief Officer(s):
Guy Jacobson, Executive Director
guy@softball.sk.ca
Jacqueline Eiwanger, Technical Director
jac@softball.sk.ca
Meetings/Conferences:
• Softball Saskatchewan Annual General Meeting 2018, 2018
Scope: Provincial
Publications:
• Softball Saskatchewan Newsletter
Type: Newsletter
Profile: Clinic dates, event dates & locations & AGM info

Softball Yukon
c/o Sport Yukon, 4061 - 4th Ave., Whitehorse YT Y1A 1H1
Tel: 867-667-4487
softball@sportyukon.com
www.softballyukon.com
Overview: A small provincial organization overseen by Canadian Amateur Softball Association
Member of: Canadian Amateur Softball Association
Chief Officer(s):
George Arcand, Executive Director
garcand@northwestel.net

Software Human Resource Council (Canada) Inc. *See* Information & Communications Technology Council of Canada

SOHO Business Group (SOHO)
#1, 1680 Lloyd Ave., North Vancouver BC V7P 2N6
Tel: 604-929-8250; *Fax:* 604-929-8214
Toll-Free: 800-290-7646
questions@soho.ca
www.soho.ca
www.linkedin.com/company/724477
www.facebook.com/SOHObusinessgroup?ref=ts
twitter.com/sohomarketing
Overview: A medium-sized national organization founded in 1996
Mission: To provide a positive experience to small & medium sized businesses by developing special benefits, programs, & events that focus on the growth & success of Canadian business & entrepreneurship
Finances: *Funding Sources:* Membership fees
10 volunteer(s)
Membership: 5,000+; *Fees:* Schedule available; *Member Profile:* Small or home-based businesses with fewer than 25 employees
Activities: Offering seminars & networking events; *Speaker Service:* Yes
Chief Officer(s):
Moe Somani, Founder & Chief Executive Officer

Soil Conservation Council of Canada (SCCC)
PO Box 733, Beausejour MB R0E 0C0
Tel: 204-792-2424
info@soilcc.ca
www.soilcc.ca
Overview: A medium-sized national charitable organization founded in 1987
Mission: To act as the voice of soil conservation in Canada
Finances: *Funding Sources:* Corporations; Government
Membership: *Fees:* $20-$5,000
Activities: Raising awareness about the causes of soil degradation; Presenting conservation issues to the government, private industry, producers, & the public; Delivering agriculture & environment programs for producers; Facilitating information exchange among researchers, government representatives, industry, & farmers; Partnering with similar organizations; *Awareness Events:* National Soil Conservation Week, April
Chief Officer(s):
Jim Tokarchuk, Executive Director, 204-792-2424
jimtokarchuk@soilcc.ca
Publications:
• Global Warming & Agriculture [a publication of the Soil Conservation Council of Canada]
Type: Fact Sheets

Les soins de santé Sainte-Elizabeth *See* Saint Elizabeth Health Care

Soins et éducation à la petite enfance Nouveau-Brunswick *See* Early Childhood Care & Education New Brunswick

SoinsSantéCAN *See* HealthCareCAN

Sojourn House
101 Ontario St., Toronto ON M5A 2V2
Tel: 416-864-9136
info@sojournhouse.org
www.sojournhouse.org
www.facebook.com/SojournHouseCA
twitter.com/SojournHouse
Overview: A small local charitable organization
Mission: To offer safe & supportive emergency shelter, in Toronto, Ontario, for refugees from around the world; To assist refugees in building secure & productive lives in Canada
Finances: *Funding Sources:* Donations; City of Toronto; Government of Canada
Membership: *Fees:* $10 individual; $25 non profit organization; $50 for profit organization
Activities: Providing supportive counselling; Helping refugees in the re-settlement process; Liaising with government & non-governmental agencies; Assisting persons in identifying & accessing educational & employment opportunities; Connecting persons to ethno-cultural communities; Offering cultural orientation to Toronto & Canada
Chief Officer(s):
Gloria Nafziger, President
Publications:
• Sojourn House Newsletter
Type: Newsletter

Solbrekken Evangelistic Association of Canada
PO Box 44220, RPO Garside, Edmonton AB T5V 1N6
Tel: 780-460-8444
max@maxsolbrekken.com
www.mswm.org
Also Known As: Max Solbrekken World Mission
Overview: A small national charitable organization founded in 1961
Mission: To promote the gospel
Affiliation(s): Christ the Healer Gospel Church (Saskatchewan); The House of Prayer, New Sarepta (Alberta)
Staff Member(s): 4; 6 volunteer(s)
Activities: Publishes Christian literature; Founded & sponsors orphanages, churhces & Ministry crusades; *Library:* Audio Sermons Library; Open to public
Chief Officer(s):
Max Solbrekken, President
Donna Solbrekken, Secretary

Solo Swims of Ontario Inc. (SSO)
c/o Greg Taylor, 32 Coxwell Cres., Brantford ON N3P 1Z1
www.soloswims.com
Overview: A small provincial organization founded in 1975
Mission: To promote safety in marathon swimming in Ontario
Finances: *Funding Sources:* Provincial government
Membership: *Committees:* Advisory
Chief Officer(s):
Greg Taylor, President
gwc.taylor@sympatico.ca

Somali Immigrant Women's Association (SIWA)
1735 Kipling Ave. West, Toronto ON M9R 2V8
Tel: 416-741-7492
www.siwa.on.ca
Overview: A medium-sized provincial organization founded in 1997

Mission: To enhance the lives of Somali Canadians & immigrants in Ontario by motivating its members to actively participate in social service programs & by preserving their culture
Finances: *Funding Sources:* Federal, provincial & metro governments; foundations; donations
Activities: Immigration counselling & advocacy; translation services; orientation & workshops; ESL classes with daycare; support groups; job training; housing, welfare & legal services referrals

Somenos Marsh Wildlife Society
PO Box 711, Duncan BC V9L 3Y1
Tel: 250-746-7032
info@somenosmarsh.com
www.somenosmarsh.com
Overview: A small local organization
Mission: To preserve wetland habitat in Somenos Basin; to build wildlife viewing facilities
Member of: Cowichan Watershed Council; BC Environmental Network; Canadian Nature Federation
Staff Member(s): 1; 30 volunteer(s)
Membership: 200; *Fees:* $20-$35
Chief Officer(s):
Paul Fletcher, President

Songwriters Association of Canada (SAC) / Association des auteurs-compositeurs canadiens
41 Valleybrook Dr., Toronto ON M3B 2S6
Tel: 416-961-1588; *Fax:* 416-961-2040
Toll-Free: 866-456-7664
sac@songwriters.ca
www.songwriters.ca
www.facebook.com/itallstartswithasong
twitter.com/songwritersofCa
www.youtube.com/songwriterscanada
Overview: A medium-sized national charitable organization founded in 1983
Mission: To protect & develop the creative & business environments for songwriters in Canada & around the world
Finances: *Funding Sources:* Canadian government; Heritage Canada; SOCAN
Staff Member(s): 5
Membership: 1,500; *Fees:* $60 regular; $30 students; $130 associate; *Member Profile:* Songwriters; composers; lyricists
Activities: Canadian song depository; song assessment service; songwriting workshops; songwriter showcases; songwriting competitions; Bluebird North Oct./Nov.; Date with a Tape; Song Stage; Songposium, Jan./Feb.; *Internships:* Yes; *Speaker Service:* Yes
Chief Officer(s):
Isabel Crack, Managing Director
isabel@songwriters.ca
Greg Johnston, President

Sonography Canada / Échographie Canada
PO Box 119, Kemptville ON K0G 1J0
Fax: 613-258-0899
Toll-Free: 877-488-0788
Other Communication: memberinfo@sonographycanada.ca
info@sonographycanada.ca
www.sonographycanada.ca
Merged from: Cnd. Assoc. of Registered Diagnostic Ultrasound Professionals & Cnd. Society of Diagnostic Medicial
Overview: A small national organization founded in 2014
Mission: The national voice for diagnostic medical sonographers in Canada
Membership: 1-99; *Fees:* $70; *Committees:* National Education Advisory Committee; CJMS Editorial Board; Awards Committee; Examinations Committee
Chief Officer(s):
Tom Hayward, Business Manager
THayward@sonographycanada.ca
Meetings/Conferences:
• Sonography Canada 2018 National Conference & Annual General Meeting, May, 2018, St. John's, NL
Scope: National
Publications:
• Canadian Journal of Medical Sonography
Type: Jounral; *Frequency:* Quarterly
Profile: CJMS is a combination of clinical and scientific content and is distributed to all members of Sonograhy Canada.

Sons of Scotland Benevolent Association
#801, 505 Consumers Rd., Toronto ON M2J 4V8
Tel: 416-482-1250; *Fax:* 416-482-9576
Toll-Free: 800-387-3382
info@sonsofscotland.com
www.sonsofscotland.com
Overview: A small local organization founded in 1876
Mission: Undertake & support activities which promote the elements of Scottish culture in Canada; honour the history & heritage of Scots in Canada; support & raise funds for charitable organizations; provide fraternal & insurance benefits for members
Finances: *Annual Operating Budget:* $500,000-$1.5 Million
Staff Member(s): 5
Membership: 4,490; *Fees:* $60
Chief Officer(s):
Robert Stewart, Executive Director

Sooke Chamber of Commerce
Seaview Business Centre, #1A, 6631 Sooke Rd., Sooke BC V9Z 0A3
Tel: 250-642-6112
info@sookeregionchamber.com
www.sookeregionchamber.com
Overview: A small local organization founded in 1948
Mission: To drive economic development in the region
Member of: BC Chamber of Commerce
Finances: *Annual Operating Budget:* Less than $50,000; *Funding Sources:* Membership dues
Membership: 205; *Fees:* $180-$300 business; $110 non-profit
Chief Officer(s):
Aline Doiron, Office Manager

Sooke Food Bank Society
2037 Shields Rd., Sooke BC V9Z 1E7
Tel: 250-642-7666
Overview: A small local organization

Sooke Philharmonic Society
PO Box 767, Sooke BC V9Z 1H7
Tel: 250-419-3569
info@sookephil.ca
www.sookephil.ca
www.facebook.com/sookephil
twitter.com/sookephil
Overview: A small local charitable organization overseen by Orchestras Canada
Mission: To promote & enhance the appreciation of music; to support & nurture musical talent in the community
Member of: Orchestras Canada
Affiliation(s): Sooke Philarhmonic Chorus
Finances: *Funding Sources:* Individual & corporate donations
Membership: 60+
Activities: Performing eight concerts per season; Conducting music workshops; *Awareness Events:* Don Chrysler Concerto Competition for Young Musicians; Celebration of Young Artists; Sooke Harbour Chamber Music Workshop
Chief Officer(s):
Norman Nelson, Music Director

Soroptimist Foundation of Canada
c/o Treasurer, 2455 Cunningham Blvd., Peterborough ON K9H 0B2
www.soroptimistfoundation.ca
Overview: A small national charitable organization founded in 1963
Mission: To provide bursaries, scholarships & fellowships to Canadian students & Canadian schools, colleges & universities for the advancement of education & in particular to further the appreciation of social needs, & the study of community, national & international problems
Affiliation(s): Soroptimist International of the Americas
Finances: *Annual Operating Budget:* $50,000-$100,000; *Funding Sources:* Donations; membership fees
5 volunteer(s)
Membership: 46 clubs; *Fees:* Schedule available
Activities: Soroptimist Grants for Females (only in Canada)
Chief Officer(s):
Elizabeth Jane (BJ) Gallagher, Chair
chair@soroptimistfoundation.ca
Sheryl Hopkins, Treasurer
treasurer@soroptimistfoundation.ca
Lori Roblesky, Secretary
secretary@soroptimistfoundation.ca
Awards:
• Grants for Women
; *Amount:* Four grants of $7,500 each
• Club Grants
; *Amount:* Seven grants of $1,000 each

SOS Children's Villages Canada / SOS Villages d'Enfants Canada
#240, 44 By Ward Market Square, Ottawa ON K1N 7A2
Tel: 613-232-3309
Toll-Free: 800-767-5111
info@soschildrensvillages.ca
www.soschildrensvillages.ca
www.facebook.com/105288666168351
www.youtube.com/user/soscanada1
Also Known As: SOS - Canada
Previous Name: Friends of SOS Children's Villages, Canada Inc.
Overview: A small international charitable organization founded in 1969
Mission: To assist SOS-Children's Villages in Canada & abroad through financial & operating support; to care for orphaned, abandoned & other children in need of long-term placement; to create opportunities for children to become happy, stable, responsible members of society
Member of: Canadian Child Welfare League
Affiliation(s): SOS-Kinderdorf International
Finances: *Funding Sources:* Direct mail; special events
Staff Member(s): 10
Activities: *Internships:* Yes; *Speaker Service:* Yes
Chief Officer(s):
Boyd McBride, President & CEO

SOS Villages d'Enfants Canada *See* SOS Children's Villages Canada

SOSA Gliding Club
PO Box 81, Rockton ON L0R 1X0
Tel: 519-740-9328
sosa@sosaglidingclub.com
www.sosaglidingclub.com
www.facebook.com/groups/2228522913
twitter.com/sosaglidingclub
Overview: A small local organization
Member of: Soaring Association of Canada

Sou'wester Coin Club
c/o Douglas B. Shand, PO Box 78, Shag Harbour NS B0W 3B0
info@souwestercoinclub.com
www.souwestercoinclub.com
Overview: A small local organization founded in 1992
Member of: Royal Canadian Numismatic Association
Chief Officer(s):
Douglas B. Shand, Contact

Soundstreams Canada
#302m 579 Richmond St. West, Toronto ON M5V 1Y6
Tel: 416-504-1282
info@soundstreams.ca
www.soundstreams.ca
www.facebook.com/soundstreams
twitter.com/soundstreams
instagram.com/soundstreams
Overview: A small national charitable organization founded in 1981
Mission: To foster & promote the development of 20th century music & music by Canadian composers, through the sponsorship of concerts, musical theatre works for young audiences, festivals & special events, recording projects, the commissioning of new works by Canadian composers & touring of Canadian artists
Member of: Opera Canada; Orchestras Canada; Choirs Ontario
Staff Member(s): 7
Membership: *Committees:* Advisory; Encore Executive
Chief Officer(s):
Ben Dietschi, Executive Director
Lawrence Cherney, Artistic Director

Sources Foundation
882 Maple St., White Rock BC V4B 4M2
Tel: 604-531-6226; *Fax:* 604-531-2316
info@sourcesbc.ca
www.sourcesbc.ca
www.linkedin.com/company/sources
www.facebook.com/SourcesCommunityResourceCentres
twitter.com/sourcesbc
www.youtube.com/user/SourcesCommunity
Also Known As: Sources White Rock/South Surrey Food Bank
Previous Name: Peace Arch Community Services
Overview: A small local organization founded in 1978 overseen by Food Banks British Columbia
Mission: To raise funds for Sources BC, a comprehensive community service organization operating a food bank, programs

for seniors, counselling services for youth & families, employment consultation
Member of: Food Banks British Columbia; British Columbians for Mentally Handicapped People
Activities: Training & workshops; counselling; food distribution
Chief Officer(s):
Harry White, President
David Young, Executive Director
dyoung@sourcesbc.ca

Souris & Glenwood Chamber of Commerce
PO Box 939, Souris MB R0K 2C0
Tel: 204-483-2070
sourischamber@gmail.com
www.facebook.com/SourisGlenwoodChamber
Overview: A small local organization
Mission: To promote & strengthen the community & economy
Affiliation(s): Manitoba Chamber of Commerce
Membership: 68
Activities: Improving the well-being of Souris & area economically, educationally & recreationally; *Library:* Open to public
Chief Officer(s):
Darci Semeschuk, President

Sous-Traitance Industrielle Québec (STIQ)
#900, 1080, côte du Beaver Hall, Montréal QC H2Z 1S8
Tél: 514-875-8789
Ligne sans frais: 888-875-8789
info@stiq.com
www.stiq.com
Aperçu: Dimension: moyenne; *Envergure:* provinciale; fondée en 1987
Membre: 700; *Critères d'admissibilite:* Aéronautique; énergie; ressources; transport
Membre(s) du bureau directeur:
Normand Voyer, Vice-président executive
nvoyer@stiq.com

South Asia Partnership Canada (SAP) / Société asiatique des partenaires Canada
c/o HCI, 877 Shefford Rd., Ottawa ON K1J 8H9
Tel: 613-828-0372
www.sapcanada.org
Overview: A small international organization founded in 1981
Mission: To build support for development of policies & programs for disadvantaged people in South Asia; To promote the sharing of ideas & resources among Canadians & organizations on development in South Asia
Finances: *Annual Operating Budget:* Less than $50,000
Membership: 28 institutional
Chief Officer(s):
Richard Harmston, Executive Director
rharmston@sapcanada.org

South Asian Centre of Windsor
#208, 225 Wyandotte St. West, Windsor ON N9A 5X1
Tel: 519-252-7447
info@southasiancentre.ca
www.southasiancentre.ca
Overview: A small local organization founded in 1986 overseen by Ontario Council of Agencies Serving Immigrants
Finances: *Funding Sources:* Private; federal & provincial government
Chief Officer(s):
Sushil Jain, President
sacw1968@gmail.com

South Asian Family Support Services *See* Settlement Assistance & Family Support Services

South Asian Women's Centre (SAWC)
#1, 800 Lansdowne Ave., Toronto ON M6H 4K3
Tel: 416-537-2276; *Fax:* 416-537-9472
info@sawc.org
www.sawc.org
www.facebook.com/groups/12015202364
Overview: A medium-sized local organization
Mission: To increase self-awareness of South Asian women; to empower women through development of social & cultural potential
Membership: *Member Profile:* South Asian women of all backgrounds & ages
Activities: Serves 14,000 women annually. Programs include: settlement programs, wellness group, seniors' group, student placement program, tax clinic, violence against women program & forced marriages & trafficking project

Chief Officer(s):
Kripa Sekhar, Executive Director
ksekhar@sawc.org

South Cariboo Chamber of Commerce
PO Box 2312, #2, 385 Birch Ave., 100 Mile House BC V0K 2E0
Tel: 250-395-6124; *Fax:* 250-395-8974
manager@southcariboochamber.org
www.southcariboochamber.org
Overview: A small local organization founded in 1978
Mission: To provide a united voice for business, committed to the enhancement of economic prosperity of the South Cariboo communities
Member of: BC Chamber of Commerce
Affiliation(s): Canadian Chamber of Commerce
Finances: *Annual Operating Budget:* Less than $50,000; *Funding Sources:* Membership dues
Staff Member(s): 1; 2 volunteer(s)
Membership: 130; *Fees:* Schedule available; *Member Profile:* Business owners; Individuals with interest in business
Activities: *Awareness Events:* Chamber of Commerce Week, Feb.; Small Business Week, Oct. *Library:* Business Information Centre; Open to public by appointment
Chief Officer(s):
Leon Chretien, Chair

South Central Committee on Family Violence, Inc. (SCCFV)
PO Box 389, Winkler MB R6W 4A6
Tel: 204-325-9957; *Fax:* 204-325-5889; *Crisis Hot-Line:* 877-977-0007
sccfv@genesis-house.ca
genesishouseshelter.ca
Also Known As: Genesis House
Overview: A small local charitable organization founded in 1983
Mission: To provide a confidential service which includes a shelter for abused women & their children, supportive residential & non-residential programs & prevention through public education to empower women & their children to make informed choices
Member of: Manitoba Association of Women's Shelters Inc.
Finances: *Funding Sources:* Provincial & federal governments; United Way; donations
Activities: Advocacy; Elder Abuse; Crisis & Long-Term Counselling; Follow-Up Service; Child Counselling; Support Groups; 2nd-Stage Housing; Referrals; Resource Centre; Speakers; Training; 24-hour Toll-Free Crisis Line; 24-hour Shelter for Abused Women & Their Children; *Library:* by appointment

South Coast District Labour Council
PO Box 127, Marystown NL A0E 2M0
Tel: 709-279-3274; *Fax:* 709-279-4351
Overview: A small local organization
Member of: Newfoundland & Labrador Federation of Labour
Chief Officer(s):
Julie Mitchell, President
juliemitchell279@hotmail.com

South Cowichan Chamber of Commerce (SCCC)
#368, 2720 Mill Bay Rd., Mill Bay BC V0R 2P1
Tel: 250-743-3566; *Fax:* 250-743-5332
www.southcowichanchamber.org
Overview: A small local organization founded in 1982
Mission: To promote & improve trade & commerce & the economic, civic & social welfare of the district
Member of: BC Chamber Executives; BC Chamber of Commerce
Finances: *Annual Operating Budget:* Less than $50,000; *Funding Sources:* Membership dues; map advertising sales; showcase booths; auction
30 volunteer(s)
Membership: 130; *Fees:* $180-$775; *Committees:* Administration; Fundraising; Business Promotion; Local Issues; Tourism; Membership Services
Activities: Maintaining Seasonal Info Centre; Presenting annual business showcase; Offering membership directory, map, auction, group insurance, & monthly meetings
Chief Officer(s):
Dave Shortill, President

South Delta Food Bank
5545 Ladner Trunk Rd., Delta BC V4K 1X1
Tel: 604-946-1967; *Fax:* 604-946-4944
info@ladnerlife.com
Overview: A small local organization overseen by Food Banks British Columbia

Member of: Food Banks British Columbia
Chief Officer(s):
Joe Vanessen, Coordinator

South Dundas Chamber of Commerce
PO Box 288, 91 Main St., Morrisburg ON K0C 1X0
Tel: 613-543-3982; *Fax:* 613-543-2971
www.southdundaschamber.ca
www.facebook.com/SouthDundasChamber
Previous Name: Morrisburg & District Chamber of Commerce
Overview: A small local organization
Mission: To promote growth in the community & local economy
Staff Member(s): 1
Membership: 61; *Fees:* Schedule available
Chief Officer(s):
Carl McIntyre, President

South East Asian Services Centre *See* Support Enhance Access Service Centre

South Eastern Alberta Archaeological Society *See* Archaeological Society of Alberta

South Essex Community Centre (SECC)
215 Talbot St. East, Leamington ON N8H 3X5
Tel: 519-326-8629; *Fax:* 519-326-1529
info@secc.on.ca
www.secc.on.ca
www.facebook.com/138831152979483
Overview: A medium-sized local organization founded in 1973
Mission: To preserve & improve the quality of life in the communities of South Essex by providing social planning &/or direct services to all individuals
Finances: *Funding Sources:* Federal, provincial & municipal governments; United Way; fundraising; donations; membership dues
Membership: *Fees:* $10; *Member Profile:* Resident of South Essex 18 yrs of age & over
Activities: *Speaker Service:* Yes; *Rents Mailing List:* Yes; *Library:* Resource Centre; Open to public
Chief Officer(s):
Colleen Pearse, Chair

South Etobicoke Community Legal Services (SECLS)
#210, 5353 Dundas St. West, Toronto ON M9B 6H8
Tel: 416-252-7218; *Fax:* 416-252-1474
secls@southetobicokelegal.ca
www.southetobicokelegal.ca
Overview: A small local charitable organization founded in 1982
Mission: To protect & promote the legal welfare of community members by offering services, unique to the community, through a network of volunteers & staff members, where language, financial hardship or disability will not act as barriers
Member of: Association of Community Legal Clinics of Ontario
Affiliation(s): Toronto Refugees Affairs Council; Federation of Metro Tenants Ontario Council of Agencies Serving Immigrants
Staff Member(s): 5
Activities: *Speaker Service:* Yes

South Fraser Child Development Centre; Lower Fraser Valley Cerebral Palsy Association *See* Centre for Child Development

South Grenville Chamber of Commerce
PO Box 2000, 107 King St. West, Prescott ON K0E 1T0
Tel: 613-213-1043
southgrenvillechamber@gmail.com
www.southgrenvillechamber.ca
www.facebook.com/southgrenvilletourism
twitter.com/SGrenTourism
Previous Name: Prescott Board of Trade; Prescott Chamber of Commerce; Prescott and District Chamber of Commerce
Overview: A small local organization founded in 1893
Mission: To promote member businesses
Member of: Canadian Chamber of Commerce; Ontario Chamber of Commerce
Membership: 150; *Fees:* $70 1-5 employees; $100 6-15 employees; $150 16-30 employees; $180 31-50 employees; $235 51+ employees
Activities: Supporting community events & projects
Chief Officer(s):
Penny Harland, Secretary

South Huron Chamber of Commerce
483 Main St. South, Exeter ON N0M 1S1
Tel: 226-423-3028
www.shcc.on.ca

Overview: A small local organization
Mission: To improve business & the community
Chief Officer(s):
Stephen Boles, President

The South Journalists Club See Human Rights & Race Relations Centre

South Lake Community Futures Development Corporation (SLCFDC)
183 The Queensway South, Keswick ON L4P 2A3
Tel: 905-476-1244; *Fax:* 905-476-9978
Toll-Free: 866-606-1244
www.southlakecfdc.org
www.facebook.com/158511384227435
twitter.com/SouthLakeCFDC
Previous Name: Georgina Association for Business
Overview: A small local organization founded in 2004
Mission: A not-for-profit community based organization providing a variety of small business and community economic development services within the towns of East Gwillimbury, Georgina as well as Brock Township.
Member of: Ontario Association of Community Futures Development Corporation
Staff Member(s): 5; 11 volunteer(s)
Chief Officer(s):
Carl Mount, Chair
Peter Budero, General Manager
pbudreo@bellnet.ca

South Lake Simcoe Naturalists
PO Box 1044, Sutton West ON L0E 1R0
Tel: 905-722-8021
www.slsn.ca
www.facebook.com/slsnaturalists
Overview: A small local organization founded in 1980
Mission: To protect the natural environment, particularly Lake Simcoe & its watersheds
Member of: Federation of Ontario Naturalists
Finances: *Annual Operating Budget:* Less than $50,000; *Funding Sources:* Federal & provincial governments; private
Membership: 100-499
Activities: Wildlife research; breeding bird census; South Lake Simcoe Wildlife Research Station (seasonal); lectures; outings; land use planning; *Internships:* Yes; *Speaker Service:* Yes
Chief Officer(s):
Paul Harpley, President

South Norwich Historical Society
PO Box 162, Otterville ON N0J 1R0
Tel: 519-879-6804
www.historicotterville.ca/info.shtml
Also Known As: Historic Otterville
Overview: A small local charitable organization founded in 1975
Mission: To encourage the discovery, collection & preservation of local history & buildings; to maintain a museum
Member of: Ontario Historical Society; Tourism Oxford
Finances: *Funding Sources:* Grants; fundraising
Activities: Operates an 1845 grist mill & 1881 Grand Trunk Railway Station; Motorcoach Tours of Otterville; *Awareness Events:* Welcome Back to Otterville, Nov.; Car Show, June; Country Fair, Sept.
Chief Officer(s):
Gail Lewis, Contact
glewis@execulink.com

South Okanagan Boundary Labour Council (SOBLC)
697 Martin St., Penticton BC V2A 5L5
Tel: 778-476-5771; *Fax:* 250-492-5540
soblc@shaw.ca
Overview: A small local organization
Mission: To act as the voice of union affiliates in the Penticton area of British Columbia; To advance the economic & social welfare of workers
Affiliation(s): Canadian Labour Congress (CLC)
Membership: 2,000; *Member Profile:* Members of unions from the South Okanagan region of British Columbia
Activities: Arranging events for International Workers' Day (May Day); Participating in the annual Day of Mourning for workers injured or killed on the job; Liaising with local council
Chief Officer(s):
Brent Voss, President
soblc@shaw.ca
Renee van Uden, First Vice-President
redeye39@hotmail.com
Terry Green, Treasurer
terlingreen@shaw.ca

Colleen Wiens, Treasurer

South Okanagan Chamber Of Commerce
PO Box 1414, 6237 Main St., Oliver BC V0H 1T0
Tel: 250-498-6321; *Fax:* 250-498-3156
Toll-Free: 866-498-6321
manager@sochamber.ca
www.sochamber.ca
www.facebook.com/south.ok.chamber
twitter.com/southokchamber
www.youtube.com/user/SouthOKChamber
Previous Name: Oliver & District Chamber of Commerce
Overview: A small local organization founded in 1947
Mission: To build & promote thriving & sustainable businesses
Member of: Thompson Okanagan Tourism Association; BC Chamber of Commerce; Canadian Chamber of Commerce
Finances: *Annual Operating Budget:* $100,000-$250,000
Staff Member(s): 2; 8 volunteer(s)
Membership: 180; *Fees:* Schedule available
Activities: Providing opportunities & resources for business growth & professional development; Representing the interests of local businesses; *Library:* Open to public
Chief Officer(s):
Denise Blashko, Executive Director

South Okanagan Immigrant & Community Services (SOICS)
508 Main St., Penticton BC V2A 5C7
Tel: 250-492-6299; *Fax:* 250-490-4684
admin@soics.ca
www.soics.ca
www.facebook.com/soics.penticton
Previous Name: Penticton & District Multicultural Society
Overview: A small local organization founded in 1976
Mission: To build a community based upon mutual respect & full participation of people of all backgrounds through education, client advocacy & community programs
Member of: Affiliation of Multicultural Societies & Service Agencies of BC
Finances: *Annual Operating Budget:* $250,000-$500,000; *Funding Sources:* Grants; fundraising; donations; projects
Membership: 1-99; *Fees:* $15
Activities: English Language Training; Settlement & Integration; Community Connections; Employment; Local Immigration Partnership; Welcoming Communities
Chief Officer(s):
Helen Greaves, President
Doug Holmes, Vice President

South Okanagan Real Estate Board (SOREB)
365 Van Horne St., Penticton BC V2A 8S4
Tel: 250-492-0626; *Fax:* 250-493-0832
www.soreb.org
www.facebook.com/151180668308444
twitter.com/soreb1
Overview: A small local organization founded in 1979 overseen by British Columbia Real Estate Association
Mission: To pursue excellence & professionalism in real estate, through quality education & high ethical standards; To protect the interest of the membership & the public
Member of: The Canadian Real Estate Association
Finances: *Funding Sources:* Membership fees
Membership: 300 realtors
Activities: *Library:* Not open to public

South Okanagan Similkameen Brain Injury Society (SOSBIS)
#2, 996 Main St., Penticton BC V2A 5E4
Tel: 250-490-0613; *Fax:* 250-490-3912
info@sosbis.com
www.sosbis.com
www.facebook.com/SOSBIS
Overview: A small local charitable organization
Mission: To assist survivors of acquired brain injuries & their families in achieving independence & quality of life; To prevent brain injuries
Finances: *Funding Sources:* United Way; Interior Health; Government of British Columbia; Donations
Staff Member(s): 10
Membership: *Member Profile:* Anyone living with the effects of acquired brain injury/stroke; anyone interested in supporting the purposes of the organization
Chief Officer(s):
Linda Sankey, Executive Director
Publications:
• Brain Waves [a publication of the South Okanagan Similkameen Brain Injury Society]

Type: Newsletter; *Frequency:* Quarterly
Profile: Organization news; upcoming events; stories; strategies to cope with acquired brain injury

South Okanagan Women in Need Society (SOWINS)
#303, 246 Martin St., Penticton BC V2A 5K3
Tel: 250-493-4366
Toll-Free: 800-814-2033
info@sowins.com
www.sowins.com
Overview: A small local charitable organization founded in 1981
Mission: To provide a secure haven, support & advocacy for women (& their children) who experience abuse; to work towards the prevention of violence/abuse in the South Okanagan area; to operate a Transition House which honours women & respects their experiences; to offer a supportive environment for women to explore their personal choices; to provide individual & community education & pre-employment services for eligibile abused women.
Affiliation(s): BC/Yukon Society of Transition Houses; Imagine Canada
Finances: *Funding Sources:* Provincial government; fundraising
Staff Member(s): 30; 100 volunteer(s)
Membership: *Fees:* $10 individual
Activities: Transition House; counselling for women in abusive relationships; children's group; Wings, secondhand store; *Speaker Service:* Yes
Chief Officer(s):
Debbie Scarborough, Executive Director

South Pacific Peoples Foundation See Pacific Peoples' Partnership

South Peace AIDS Council of Grande Prairie; Society of the South Peace AIDS Council See HIV North Society

South Peace Community Arts Council
PO Box 2314, Dawson Creek BC V1G 4H4
Tel: 250-782-1164; *Fax:* 250-782-8801
dcagchin@pris.ca
www.southpeacearts.ca
www.facebook.com/138320271866
Overview: A small local organization founded in 1969
Mission: To foster an interest and pride in the cultural heritage of the community by supporting and developing ongoing programs.
Member of: Assembly of BC Arts Councils
Chief Officer(s):
Melissa Holoboff, President
dcagchin@pris.ca

South Peace Community Resources Society (SPCRS)
PO Box 713, 10110 - 13th St., Dawson Creek BC V1G 4H7
Tel: 250-782-9174; *Fax:* 250-782-4167
Toll-Free: 866-712-9174
reception@spcrs.ca
www.spcrs.ca
www.facebook.com/spcrs.dawsoncreek
twitter.com/SPCRS
Overview: A small local charitable organization founded in 1974
Mission: To meet the social, educational & personal needs of the community by providing services that develop skills for living; To provide community & residential services; to meet the needs of children, youth & families, women who have experienced violence, victims of crime, adults with mental handicaps, children with special needs, couples & individuals experiencing trauma or difficulties in their life
Member of: British Columbia Association for Community Living; Federation of Child & Family Services; BC/Yukon Society of Transition Houses; BC Association for Specialized Victims Assistance Programs & Counselling
Finances: *Annual Operating Budget:* $3 Million-$5 Million
Staff Member(s): 80; 9 volunteer(s)
Membership: 50; *Fees:* $5; *Member Profile:* Victims of crime; victims of family violence; special needs children; adults with disabilities & their families
Activities: Family Day; National Child Day; Little Black Dress Affair fundraiser; Youth Day; Community Living Month; White Ribbon Campaign; *Awareness Events:* December 6 Memorial; Take Back the Night; Community Living Week; International Women's Day; Family Week; *Internships:* Yes; *Speaker Service:* Yes; *Library:* Professional Resources Child Development; Open to public by appointment
Chief Officer(s):
Stefan Pavlis, Executive Director

Canadian Associations / South Peel Naturalists' Club (SPNC)

South Peel Naturalists' Club (SPNC)
PO Box 69629, 109 Thomas St., Oakville ON L6J 7R4
www.southpeel.wordpress.com
www.facebook.com/southpeel
Overview: A small local organization founded in 1952
Mission: To promote the study, conservation, & enjoyment of nature
Member of: Federation of Ontario Naturalists
Affiliation(s): Canadian Nature Federation
Finances: *Annual Operating Budget:* Less than $50,000; *Funding Sources:* Membership fees; Donations
35 volunteer(s)
Membership: 200+; *Fees:* $30 individual; $40 family; $15 student
Chief Officer(s):
Mark Cranford, President
Publications:
• SPNC [South Peel Naturalists' Club] Newsletter
Type: Newsletter; *Frequency:* 5 pa

South Queens Chamber of Commerce
PO Box 1378, Liverpool NS B0T 1K0
Tel: 902-350-1826
www.southqueenschamber.com
www.facebook.com/191426127877
Overview: A small local organization
Mission: To strengthen trade & commerce; To improve the economic, civic, & social welfare of the area
Membership: 60+; *Fees:* $85; *Committees:* Governance; Policy
Chief Officer(s):
Barry Tomalin, President
Sherri Elliott, Treasurer
Mallory Plummer, Secretary

South Saskatchewan Community Foundation Inc.
3934 Gordon Rd., Regina SK S4S 6Y3
Tel: 306-751-4756; *Fax:* 306-751-4768
sscf@sasktel.net
www.sscf.ca
Previous Name: Regina Community Foundation
Overview: A small local charitable organization founded in 1969
Mission: Supports communities by managing & investing permanent endowment funds & donations & distributing the fund proceeds to charitable non-profit organizations
Member of: Community Foundations of Canada
Finances: *Annual Operating Budget:* $50,000-$100,000
Staff Member(s): 2
Membership: 1-99
Chief Officer(s):
Cindy Chamberlin, Manager, Donor Services & Administration

South Saskatchewan Youth Orchestra (SSYO)
PO Box 868, Lumsden SK S0G 3C0
Tel: 306-761-2576
www.ssyo.ca
www.facebook.com/ssyo.ca
twitter.com/SSYO4all
Overview: A small local charitable organization founded in 1977 overseen by Orchestras Canada
Mission: To provide orchestral training to young musicians in Southern Saskatchewan
Member of: Saskatchewan Orchestral Association; Orchestras Canada
Affiliation(s): Regina Symphony Orchestra
Finances: *Funding Sources:* Membership fees; Government grants; Corporate & private donations
Membership: *Fees:* $700; *Member Profile:* Residents of southern Saskatchewan who are between the ages of 12 and 26 and who study an orchestral instrument
Activities: Performing 4-5 concerts a year; Facilitating outreach programs; *Library:* Music Library
Chief Officer(s):
Alan Denike, Music Director

South Shore Chamber of Commerce
PO Box 127, Crapaud PE C0A 1J0
Tel: 902-437-2510
www.southshorechamberpei.ca
Overview: A small local organization
Mission: To promote business in the community
Member of: Saskatchewan Chamber of Commerce
Finances: *Annual Operating Budget:* $50,000-$100,000
25 volunteer(s)
Membership: 82; *Fees:* $25
Activities: Sponsoring events
Chief Officer(s):
Cathie Thomas, Administrator

South Shore Genealogical Society
PO Box 901, 97 Kaulbach St., Lunenburg NS B0J 2C0
Tel: 902-634-8263
www.ssgs.ca
Overview: A small local organization founded in 1979
Mission: To develop & provide genealogical information on the South Shore area (Lunenburg & Queens counties) of Nova Scotia
Member of: Canadian Council of N.S. Archives
Finances: *Annual Operating Budget:* Less than $50,000; *Funding Sources:* Membership fees; Grants for summer student
25 volunteer(s)
Membership: 350; *Fees:* $25 individual; $35 family
Activities: *Library:* Open to public
Chief Officer(s):
Cheryl Lamerson, President
cheryllamerson@bellaliant.net

South Shore Reading Council (SSRC)
#4, 279, rue Hubert, Greenfield Park QC J4V 1R9
Tel: 450-671-4375
info@ssrc.ca
ssrc.ca
Overview: A small local organization
Mission: To encourage English literacy among youth and adults, as well as to raise awareness about the levels of illiteracy rates to the public
Activities: Tutoring for adults; Lessons for children

South Shore Wildlife Association
1632 Camperdown Rd., Camperdown NS B4V 6S5
Tel: 902-543-2893
southshorewildlifeassociation@hotmail.ca
www.southshorewildlife.weebly.com
Overview: A small local organization
Mission: To promote recreational hunting & fishing through land & water conservation
Affiliation(s): Nova Scotia Federation of Anglers & Hunters
Membership: *Fees:* $12 ($5 for each additional member)
Activities: Supporting & participating in conservation events; Encouraging youth to become involved in outdoor activities through the development of programs, events, & presentations
Chief Officer(s):
Stephen Joudrey, President
Eugene Herman, Secretary & Treasurer

South Shuswap Chamber of Commerce
2405B Centennial Dr., Blind Bay BC V0E 1H2
Tel: 250-515-0002
membership@southshuswapchamber.com
www.southshuswapchamber.com
www.facebook.com/southshuswap.chamber
twitter.com/shuswapchamber
Overview: A small local organization founded in 1985
Mission: To stimulate business growth in the region
Member of: Canadian Chamber of Commerce; British Columbia Chamber of Commerce
Finances: *Annual Operating Budget:* Less than $50,000; *Funding Sources:* Membership fees; fundraising; grant
15 volunteer(s)
Membership: 100+; *Fees:* Schedule available
Activities: *Library:* Open to public
Chief Officer(s):
Karen Brown, General Manager
manager@southshuswapchamber.com

South Simcoe Community Information Centre
Town Square, PO Box 932, 39 Victoria St. East, Alliston ON L9R 1W1
Tel: 705-435-4900; *Fax:* 705-435-1106
contact@contactsouthsimcoe.ca
www.contactsouthsimcoe.ca
www.facebook.com/CONTACTCommunityServices
Overview: A small local organization founded in 1977 overseen by InformOntario
Mission: To work to create a community that is informed of available resources through the provision of information & referral, access to information technologies & partnership with others
Staff Member(s): 14
Chief Officer(s):
Liz Beattie, Co-Executive Director
Sandra Mawby, Co-Executive Director

South Stormont Chamber of Commerce
PO Box 489, Ingleside ON K0C 1M0
Tel: 613-537-8344
info@sscc.on.ca
www.sscc.on.ca
Overview: A small local organization
Mission: To improve social & economic development within the community
Membership: *Fees:* $75
Chief Officer(s):
Carol Delorme, President

South Surrey & White Rock Chamber of Commerce
#22, 1480 Foster St., White Rock BC V4B 3X7
Tel: 604-536-6844; *Fax:* 604-536-4994
admin@sswrchamber.ca
www.sswrchamberofcommerce.ca
www.facebook.com/293324054033157
twitter.com/SswrChamber
sswrchamber.tumblr.com
Overview: A small local organization founded in 1937
Mission: To promote business & economic growth on the peninsula
Member of: Canadian Chamber of Commerce
Affiliation(s): BC Tourism
Finances: *Funding Sources:* Provincial & local government; membership fees
Staff Member(s): 3
Membership: 600+
Activities: *Library:* Business Library; Open to public
Chief Officer(s):
Cliff Annable, Executive Director, 604-536-6844 Ext. 6
cliff@sswrchamber.ca

South Wellington Coin Society (SWCS)
c/o 273 Mill St. East, Acton ON L7J 1J7
info@southwellingtoncoinsociety.ca
www.southwellingtoncoinsociety.ca
Previous Name: Guelph Coin Club
Overview: A small local organization founded in 1997
Mission: To trade information on coins, medals, & tokens of interest to collectors; To increase awareness of Canadian history through numismatics
Affiliation(s): Ontario Numismatic Association; Canadian Numismatic Association; London Numismatic Society
Membership: *Fees:* $10 regular; $12 couple; $5 adolescent
Activities: Providing education through monthly meetings
Chief Officer(s):
Scott E. Douglas, President
Publications:
• SWCS [South Wellington Coin Society] Newsletter
Type: Newsletter
Profile: Club news & upcoming events

South West Community Care Access Centre
356 Oxford St. West, London ON N6H 1T3
Fax: 519-472-4045
Toll-Free: 800-811-5147; *TTY:* 519-473-9626
info-london@sw.ccac-ont.ca
healthcareathome.ca/southwest
Also Known As: South West CCAC
Overview: A small local charitable organization founded in 1970 overseen by InformOntario
Mission: Online directory of community & social services & resources for citizens of London & area
Affiliation(s): London Health Sciences Centre; Middlesex-London Health Unit; St. Joseph's Health Care (London)
Activities: Publications & printed resources; information technology; database of community services; community development, consultation & education
Chief Officer(s):
Sandra Coleman, CEO

South Western Alberta Teachers' Convention Association (SWATCA)
c/o Roxane Holmes, 1215 - 19 Ave., Coaldale AB T1M 1A4
Tel: 403-308-8761
www.swatca.ca
twitter.com/swatca
Overview: A small provincial organization
Membership: *Committees:* Conference; Displays; Evaluation; Social; Website; Recruitment
Chief Officer(s):
Kim Yearous, President

Southam Foundation *See* Alva Foundation

Southeast Asia-Canada Business Council
5294 Imperial St., Burnaby BC V5J 1E4
Tel: 604-439-0779; *Fax:* 604-439-0284
info@aseancanada.org
www.aseancanada.com
Also Known As: Association of Southeast Asian Nations-Canada Business Council
Previous Name: ASEAN-Canada Business Council
Overview: A medium-sized international organization founded in 1987
Mission: To assist Canadian companies, especially small & medium sized enterprises (SMEs), to enter or expand their presence in the ASEAN market
Staff Member(s): 3
Membership: 50; *Fees:* $750; *Committees:* Publicity & Promotions
Chief Officer(s):
Carmelita Salonga Tapia, President

Southeast Environmental Association (SEA)
41 Woods Islands Hill, Montague PE C0A 1R0
Tel: 902-838-3351; *Fax:* 902-838-0610
seapei.org
Overview: A medium-sized provincial organization founded in 1992
Mission: To protect, maintain, and enhance the ecology of south eastern Prince Edward Island for the environmental, social, and economic well being of area residents.
Chief Officer(s):
Jackie Bourgeois, Executive Director
Lawrence Millar, Chair

Southeast Georgian Bay Chamber of Commerce
45 Lone Pine Rd., Port Severn ON L0K 1S0
Tel: 705-756-4863; *Fax:* 705-756-4863
info@segbay.ca
www.segbay.ca
www.facebook.com/SEGBAY
Previous Name: Honey Harbour/Port Severn District Chamber of Commerce
Overview: A small local organization
Membership: *Fees:* $69
Chief Officer(s):
Marianne Braid, Manager

South-East Grey Support Services (SEGSS)
PO Box 12, 24 Toronto St., Flesherton ON N0C 1E0
Tel: 519-924-3339; *Fax:* 519-924-3575
www.southeastgreysupportservices.com
www.facebook.com/329076267124425
Overview: A small local organization founded in 1961
Mission: Provides and advocates for a full range of community-based services for individuals with intellectual disabilities including accommodation, employment, day program, planning and family supports.
Member of: Community Living Ontario
Finances: *Funding Sources:* MCSS
Publications:
• Grey Bruce Facilitation Network Newsletter [a publication of South-East Grey Support Services]
Type: Newsletter

Souther Ontario Newsmedia Guild; Southern Ontario Newspaper Guild See Unifor87-M

Southern African Jewish Association of Canada (SAJAC)
PO Box 87510, 300 John St., Thornhill ON L3T 7R3
Tel: 289-597-8610
sajacnews@rogers.com
www.primequadrant.com/Sajac
Also Known As: SAJAC Seniors
Overview: A small international organization founded in 1979
Mission: To provide a network for Jewish ex-South Africans (including Zimbabwe) to assist in the fields of job & accomodation searching, seniors, & immigrant resources
Membership: 100-499; *Member Profile:* Jewish people from Southern Africa now living in Toronto
Activities: Providing information & resources for all Jewish ex-South Africans
Chief Officer(s):
Colin Baskind, President
Thea Abramson, Chair, Social Committee
theabramson@yahoo.com
Publications:
• SAJAC [Southern African Jewish Association of Canada] News
Type: Newsletter; *Accepts Advertising*; *Editor:* Heather Super

Southern Alberta Brain Injury Society (SABIS)
#102, 2116 - 27th Ave. NE, Calgary AB T2E 7A6
Tel: 403-521-5212; *Fax:* 403-283-5867
sabis@sabis.ab.ca
www.sabis.ab.ca
www.facebook.com/226816920793215
twitter.com/SABISCalgary
Overview: A medium-sized local charitable organization founded in 1985
Mission: To promote lifelong support for persons with acquired brain injury, their families & support networks; To raise community awareness of brain injury; To assist persons with acquired brain injury to live as independently as possible
Finances: *Funding Sources:* Membership dues; Fundraising; Donations
Membership: *Fees:* $10 individuals; $15 families; $20 professionals & non-profit agencies; $100 corporate members; *Member Profile:* Survivors & families of brain injury; Individual adults, families, professionals, non-profit agencies, corporations
Activities: Advocating on behalf of persons affected by brain injury; Promoting services for persons affected by brain injury; Developing personalized systems of support during recovery; Providing emotional support to persons with brain injury & their family members; Organizing peer support groups; Raising awareness of acquired brain injury & its causes & effects; Encouraging the further development of services & programs to support individuals with brain injury; *Awareness Events:* Astrid's Walk 'n' Roll, June; Brain Injury Awareness Month, June; *Speaker Service:* Yes; *Library:* Multimedia Resource Centre; Not open to public
Chief Officer(s):
Natasha Bodei, Executive Director
natasha@sabis.ab.ca
Cheryl Sayward, Program Manager
cheryl@sabis.ab.ca
Publications:
• Southern Alberta Brain Injury Society Newsletter
Type: Newsletter; *Frequency:* Quarterly; *Price:* Free with membership in the Southern Alberta Brain Injury Society
• Southern Alberta Brain Injury Society Annual Report
Type: Yearbook; *Frequency:* Annually; *Price:* Free with membership in the Southern Alberta Brain Injury Society

Southern Alberta Community Living Association (SACLA)
401 - 21A St. North, Lethbridge AB T1H 6L6
Tel: 403-329-1525; *Fax:* 403-329-1435
admin@sacla.ca
www.sacla.ca
Overview: A small local organization
Mission: To provide innovative supports to people with developmental disabilities & their families
Member of: Alberta Association of Rehab Centres
Chief Officer(s):
Sue Manery, CEO
sue.manery@sacla.ca

Southern Alberta Curling Association (SACA)
#720, 3 St. NW, Calgary AB T2N 1N9
Tel: 403-246-9300; *Fax:* 403-246-9349
curling@saca.ca
www.saca.ca
Overview: A small local organization overseen by Canadian Curling Association
Mission: To encourage active participation for residents of all ages in our communities by helping member curling clubs offer a wide variety of programs. To assist in providing opportunities to participate in curling.
Chief Officer(s):
Brent Syme, General Manager
brent@saca.ca
Stasia Perkins, Director, Clubs & Competitions
stasia@saca.ca

Southern Alberta Health Libraries Association (SAHLA)
c/o Health Sciences Library, University of Calgary, 3330 University Dr. NW, Calgary AB T2N 4N1
sahla.chla-absc.ca
Overview: A small local organization overseen by Canadian Health Libraries Association
Mission: To promote good health information service in southern Alberta; To encourage cooperation & communication among members; To promote educational development
Membership: *Fees:* $15
Chief Officer(s):
Yongtao Lin, President
yongtao.lin@albertahealthservices.ca
Lorraine Toews, Secretary
ltoews@ucalgary.ca
Pamela Harrison, Treasurer
pamela.harrison@albertahealthservices.ca
Meetings/Conferences:
• Southern Alberta Health Libraries Association Annual General Meeting 2018, 2018, AB
Scope: Provincial

Southern Alberta Post Polio Support Society (SAPPSS)
7 - 11 St. NE, Calgary AB T2E 4Z2
Tel: 403-265-5041; *Fax:* 403-265-0162
Toll-Free: 866-265-5049
sappss@shaw.ca
www.polioalberta.ca/sappss
Overview: A small local organization founded in 1988
Mission: To bring awareness about Post Polio Syndrome to the Southern Alberta community; to provide support for polio survivors

Southern First Nations Secretariat (SFNC)
22361 Austin Line, Bothwell ON N0P 1C0
Tel: 519-692-5868; *Fax:* 519-692-5976
Toll-Free: 800-668-2609
reception@sfns.on.ca
www.sfns.on.ca
Previous Name: London District Chief's Council
Overview: A small local organization
Mission: To provide a broad range of advisory & information services, technical & administrative support, & coordination of regional initiatives for Aboriginal peoples in southwestern Ontario
Affiliation(s): Caldwell First Nation; Delaware First Nation; Munsee-Delaware First Nation; Oneida Nation; Kettle & Stoney Point First Nation; Aamjiwinaang First Nation; Chippewa of the Thames First Nation
Staff Member(s): 27
Activities: Post-secondary counselling; technical services; financial & administrative services
Chief Officer(s):
Shirley Miller, Program Coordinator
Mike George, Executive Director

Southern Georgian Bay Association of REALTORS
243 Ste. Marie St., Collingwood ON L9Y 2K6
Tel: 705-445-7295
info@sgbREALTORS.com
www.sgbrealtors.com
Merged from: Georgian Triangle Real Estate Board & Southern Georgian Bay Real Estate Association
Overview: A small local organization overseen by Ontario Real Estate Association
Mission: To deliver MLS & real estate services
Member of: The Canadian Real Estate Association
Staff Member(s): 5
Membership: 500
Chief Officer(s):
Sandy Raymer, Executive Officer

Southern Georgian Bay Chamber of Commerce / Chambre de Commerce de la Baie Georgienne Sud
208 King St., Midland ON L4R 3L9
Tel: 705-526-7884
info@sgbchamber.ca
southerngeorgianbay.ca
www.linkedin.com/pub/sgb-chamber-of-commerce/17/620/b95
www.facebook.com/132190703477140
twitter.com/sgbchamber
Merged from: Penetanguishene-Tiny Chamber of Commerce; Midland Chamber of Commerce
Overview: A small local organization founded in 2003
Mission: To drive commercial, professional, industrial, agricultural, economic, civic & social progress in the district
Finances: *Funding Sources:* Membership dues; Fundraising
Staff Member(s): 3
Membership: 483; *Fees:* Schedule available; *Committees:* Membership
Activities: Promoting tourism; Providing benefits & networking opportunities; Offering various communications networks to members; *Rents Mailing List:* Yes
Chief Officer(s):
Denise Hayes, General Manager
dhayes@sgbchamber.ca

Canadian Associations / Southern Interior Construction Association (SICA)

Penetanguishene Tourist Information Centre
(May-Oct.) Town Dock, 2 Main St., Penetanguishene ON L9M 2G2
Tel: 705-549-2232; *Fax:* 705-549-3743
ticinfo@penetanguishene.ca
www.penetanguishene.ca/en/discover/tourist-information-centre.asp
Chief Officer(s):
Heidi Husten, Coordinator, Events

Southern Interior Construction Association (SICA)
#104 - 151 Commercial Dr., Kelowna BC V1X 7W2
Tel: 250-491-7330; *Fax:* 250-491-3929
www.sicabc.ca
www.linkedin.com/company/southern-interior-construction-association
www.facebook.com/SICABC
twitter.com/sicabc
Overview: A small provincial organization
Mission: To promote excellence in the Southern Interior region's construction industry; To lead & represent members
Membership: 374; *Fees:* Schedule available
Activities: Offering educational courses & networking events; Providing construction resources; Providing access to BidCentral; Holding public meetings
Chief Officer(s):
Jason Henderson, Chief Executive Officer
jhenderson@sicabc.ca
Clifford Kshyk, Vice-President, Operations
ckshyk@sicabc.ca
Publications:
• SICA [Southern Interior Construction Association] Newsletter
Type: Newsletter
Profile: Information about industry events, courses, promotions, & issues
• SICA [Southern Interior Construction Association] Construction Review
Type: Magazine; *Frequency:* Biannually
Profile: Information about the southern interior region's construction industry & community

Southern Interior Local Government Association (SILGA)
c/o Alison Slater, 1996 Sheffield Way, Kamloops BC V2E 2M2
Tel: 250-374-3678; *Fax:* 250-374-3678
www.silga.ca
Previous Name: Okanagan Mainline Municipal Association; Okanagan Valley Municipal Association; Okanagan Valley Mayors & Reeves Association
Overview: A small local organization
Mission: To represent the municipalities & regional districts of the Okanagan Mainline area
Membership: 36 municipalities; *Member Profile:* Elected officials from cities, towns, villages, districts, & regional districts in south central British Columbia
Activities: Working on water treatment standards issues; Organizing workshops for members; Liaising with the provincial & federal governments
Chief Officer(s):
Harry Kroeker, President
Marg Spina, First Vice-President
Tim Pennell, Second Vice-President
Alison Slater, Executive Director
alislater@shaw.ca
Meetings/Conferences:
• Southern Interior Local Government Association 2018 Annual General Meeting & Convention, 2018
Scope: Local

Southern Kings & Queens Chamber of Commerce *See* Eastern Prince Edward Island Chamber of Commerce

Southern Kings & Queens Food Bank Inc.
PO Box 1137, Montague PE C0A 1R0
Tel: 902-838-4234
Overview: A small local organization founded in 1988
Mission: To collect food & distribute to clients in need
Finances: *Funding Sources:* Fundraising; donations
6 volunteer(s)
Membership: 7; *Fees:* $1
Chief Officer(s):
Lawrence Power, Manager

Southern Kings Arts Council (SKAC)
PO Box 212, Montague PE C0A 1R0
Tel: 902-583-2888
southernkingsartscouncil.blogspot.ca
www.facebook.com/people/Southern-Kings-Arts-Council/100002014478545
Overview: A small local organization founded in 1980
Mission: To encourage & promote arts activities in the community.
Finances: *Annual Operating Budget:* Less than $50,000
20 volunteer(s)
Membership: 25; *Fees:* $5 individual; $8 family; *Member Profile:* Any person interested in the arts who lives in the area
Chief Officer(s):
Tom Rath, Contact, 902-962-3426

Southern Ontario Cocaine Anonymous (CA)
c/o Southern Ontario Cocaine Anonymous, PO Box 19032, 360A Bloor St. West, Toronto ON M5S 3C9
Tel: 416-927-7858
Toll-Free: 866-622-4636
www.ca-on.org
Overview: A small local organization founded in 1987
Mission: To help members stay free from cocaine and all other mind-altering substances through the Twelve Step Recovery Program
Activities: Facilitating 12-Step Meetings & other events

Southern Ontario Orchid Society
PO Box 88, Zephyr ON L0E 1T0
Tel: 905-640-5643; *Fax:* 905-640-0696
info@soos.ca
www.soos.ca
www.facebook.com/SOOSOrchid
Overview: A small local organization
Membership: *Fees:* $25
Chief Officer(s):
Laura Leibgott, President
president@soos.ca

Southern Ontario Seismic Network (SOSN)
c/o University of Western Ontario, London ON N6A 5B7
Tel: 519-661-3605; *Fax:* 519-661-3198
www.gp.uwo.ca
Overview: A small provincial organization
Mission: To obtain information on the seismicity and seismic hazards of a region of southern Ontario in which a number of nuclear power facilities are located.
Member of: POLARIS Network; Canadian National Seismograph Network
Chief Officer(s):
R.F. Mereu, Administrator
rmereu@uwo.ca

Southern Ontario Thunderbird Club
296 Village Green Ave., London ON N6J 3Z6
Tel: 519-471-8657
sotbirdclub.org
Overview: A small local organization founded in 1979
Mission: To preserve & enjoy Ford Thunderbird
Finances: *Annual Operating Budget:* Less than $50,000; *Funding Sources:* Membership fees
Membership: 180; *Fees:* $35
Chief Officer(s):
Bob Ranick, Contact

Southwest British Columbia League of Christian Schools *See* Society of Christian Schools in British Columbia

Southwestern Nova Scotia Fish Packers Association *See* Nova Scotia Fish Packers Association

Southwestern Ontario Adult Literacy Network *See* Literacy Link South Central

Southwestern Ontario Archivists' Association *See* Archives Association of Ontario

Southwestern Ontario Beekeepers' Association
c/o Mike Dodok, 108 London Dr., Chatham ON N7L 5J1
Tel: 519-351-8338
Overview: A small local organization
Mission: To help beekeepers in southwestern Ontario achieve excellence
Member of: Ontario Beekeepers' Association
Membership: *Member Profile:* Beekeepers in southwestern Ontario
Activities: Offering workshops in beekeeping to educate members; Organizing meetings with guest speakers to inform members
Chief Officer(s):
Mike Dodok, President
dodoks@yahoo.ca
Publications:
• Southwestern Ontario Beekeepers' Association Newsletter
Type: Newsletter
Profile: Association information, such as upcoming meetings

Southwestern Ontario Gliding Association (SOGA)
#6981, 7179 - 3 Line, Arthur ON N0G 1A0
soga.ca
Previous Name: K-W Hang Gliding Club; Hang-On-Tario
Overview: A medium-sized provincial organization founded in 1979
Mission: To organize hang gliding space & time for its members
Membership: *Fees:* $25 associate; $250 full/tow
Chief Officer(s):
John Pop, Contact
jpop@golden.net

Southwestern Ontario Health Libraries & Information Network (SOHLIN)
c/o Carolynne Gabriel, Library, Middlesex London Health Unit, 50 King St., London ON N6A 5L7
sohlin.chla-absc.ca
Previous Name: Windsor Area Health Libraries Association; Windsor Hospitals Library Group
Overview: A small local organization founded in 1971 overseen by Canadian Health Libraries Association
Mission: To build communication lines among members; To provide opportunities for continued education & professional development
Member of: Canadian Health Libraries Association
Membership: *Fees:* $30 student; $40 first time members; $50 regular
Chief Officer(s):
Jill McTavish, President
jill.mctavish@lhsc.on.ca
Meetings/Conferences:
• Southwestern Ontario Health Libraries & Information Network Spring General Meeting 2018, 2018, ON
Scope: Provincial
• Southwestern Ontario Health Libraries & Information Network Fall General Meeting 2018, 2018, ON
Scope: Provincial

Soyfoods Canada *See* Canadian Soybean Council

SPANCAN
#100, 596 Kingston Rd. West, Ajax ON L1T 3A2
Tel: 905-428-0700; *Fax:* 905-428-0690
spancan@idirect.ca
www.spancan.com
Overview: A small national organization founded in 1999
Affiliation(s): Independent Lumber Dealers Cooperative
Staff Member(s): 4
Membership: 4; *Member Profile:* Home improvement retailers; wholesale distributor
Chief Officer(s):
Mike Daniels, General Manager
mike2@idirect.ca

Sparwood & District Chamber of Commerce
PO Box 1448, 141 Aspen Dr., Sparwood BC V0B 2G0
Tel: 250-425-2423
Toll-Free: 877-485-8185
administrator@sparwoodchamber.bc.ca
www.sparwoodchamber.bc.ca
www.facebook.com/SparwoodChamber
twitter.com/SprwdChmbr
www.youtube.com/channel/UCdVQtK—71Zi_qit0g3xqrQ
Overview: A small local organization founded in 1983
Mission: To sustain existing business, enhance business opportunities & improve the economic, social, ecological & cultural well-being of the community
Member of: Canadian Chamber of Commerce; BC Chamber of Commerce
Finances: *Funding Sources:* Membership dues; municipal & provincial governments
Staff Member(s): 3
Membership: *Fees:* $58.85 individual; sliding scale for businesses; *Member Profile:* Interest in community, business & or commerce
Activities: Business information & visitor information centre; *Awareness Events:* Coal Miner Days *Library:* Business Information Centre; Open to public by appointment
Chief Officer(s):
Marjorie Templin, President

Norma McDougall, Manager

SPCA de l'ouest du Québec See SPCA of Western Québec

SPCA of Western Québec / SPCA de l'ouest du Québec
659, rue Auguste-Mondoux, Gatineau QC J9J 3K2
Tel: 819-770-7722; *Fax:* 819-770-7444
ahspca@storm.ca
www.aylmer-hull-spca.qc.ca
Also Known As: Society for the Prevention of Cruelty to Animals of Western Québec (Aylmer, Hull)
Overview: A small local charitable organization founded in 1977
Mission: To care for lost, abandoned, & unwanted animals in the Outaouais
Member of: Canadian Federation of Humane Societies
Finances: *Annual Operating Budget:* $100,000-$250,000; *Funding Sources:* Donations
Staff Member(s): 5; 25 volunteer(s)
Membership: 60; *Fees:* 25$
Activities: Provides care & adoption program for lost & abandoned dogs, cats & rabbits in the Outaouais; partners with Petsmart (Merivale Rd., Ottawa) for adoptions
Chief Officer(s):
Guillaume Rousseau, Manager

SPEC Association for Children & Families
c/o Community Culture Center, #101, 327 - 3rd St. West, Brooks AB T1R 0E7
Tel: 403-362-5056; *Fax:* 403-362-5090
home@spec.ab.ca
www.spec.ab.ca
Also Known As: SPEC: Support, Prevent, Educate, Counsel
Overview: A small local organization founded in 1978
Mission: To assist children & families in the Brooks area of Alberta to be healthy, nurtured, & safe; To encourage growth & education, from newborns to adults
Finances: *Funding Sources:* Donations
Activities: Offering preventive services to children & families; Providing counselling & supportive services; Disseminating information, through the LINKS Community Information Centre; Coordinating programs, such as the Boys & Girls Club of Brooks & District, Parent LINK Centre, & Connections & Family Support Services
Chief Officer(s):
Scott Berry, Executive Director, 403-362-5056 Ext. 226
executive.director@spec.ab.ca
Maureen Andruschak, Director, Programs, 403-362-5056 Ext. 247

Special Education Association of British Columbia See Teachers of Inclusive Education - British Columbia

Special Interest Group on Computer Human Interaction (VanCHI)
PO Box 93672, Stn. Nelson Park, Vancouver BC V6E 4L7
Tel: 604-876-8985
chi-VanCHI@acm.org
www.sigchi.org
Overview: A small national organization overseen by Association for Computing Machinery
Mission: To provide a forum for discussion of all aspects of human-computer interaction; To advance education in human-computer interaction
Membership: *Member Profile:* Professionals, academics, & students who are interested in human-technology & human-computer interaction
Chief Officer(s):
Gerrit van der Veer, President
sigchi-president@acm.org
James Willock, Contact, Vancouver
Meetings/Conferences:
• Computer Human Interaction 2018 Conference: Human Factors in Computing Systems, April, 2018, Montréal, QC
Scope: International
• Computer Human Interaction 2019 Conference: Human Factors in Computing Systems, May, 2019, Glasgow
Scope: International
Publications:
• Association for Computing Machinery Transactions on Computer-Human Interaction
Type: Journal; *Editor:* Shumin Zhai
• Interactions
Type: Magazine; *Editor:* Richard Anderson & Jon Kolko
• SIGCHI Bulletin
Type: Newsletter; *Editor:* Mark Apperley

Special Needs Planning Group
70 Ivy Cres., Stouffville ON L4A 5A9
Tel: 905-640-8285; *Fax:* 905-640-8285
www.specialneedsplanning.ca
Overview: A small local charitable organization founded in 1997
Mission: To provide planning services for disabled persons & their families
Chief Officer(s):
Graeme S. Treeby, Contact
graemetreeby@sympatico.ca

Special Olympics Alberta (SOA)
Percy Page Centre, 11759 Groat Rd., Edmonton AB T5M 3K6
Tel: 780-415-0719; *Fax:* 780-415-1306
Toll-Free: 800-444-2883
info@specialolympics.ab.ca
www.specialolympics.ab.ca
www.facebook.com/specialolympicsalberta
twitter.com/SpecialOAlberta
Previous Name: Alberta Special Olympics Inc.
Overview: A medium-sized provincial charitable organization founded in 1980 overseen by Special Olympics Canada
Mission: To enrich the lives of Albertans with an intellectual disability, through sport
Finances: *Annual Operating Budget:* $500,000-$1.5 Million; *Funding Sources:* Donations; Grants; Fundraising events; Sponsorship
Staff Member(s): 12; 1500 volunteer(s)
Membership: 3,000 athletes; 32 affiliates throughout Alberta; *Member Profile:* Athletes with intellectual disabilities; *Committees:* Strategic Development; Volunteer Management; New Community Development; New Sport Programs; Sport Development; Provincial Games; Team AB
Activities: Offering 15 official sports for athletes; Providing training; *Awareness Events:* Law Enforcement Torch Run; Sports Celebrities Festival; *Speaker Service:* Yes
Chief Officer(s):
John Byrne, President & CEO
jbyrne@specialolympics.ab.ca
Awards:
• Coach of the Year
• Administrator of the Year
• 5, 10, 15, 20 Year Service Award

Special Olympics BC (SOBC)
#210, 3701 East Hastings St., Burnaby BC V5C 2H6
Tel: 604-737-3078; *Fax:* 604-737-3080
Toll-Free: 888-854-2276
info@specialolympics.bc.ca
www.specialolympics.bc.ca
www.facebook.com/specialolympicsbc
twitter.com/sobcsociety
Previous Name: British Columbia Special Olympics
Overview: A medium-sized provincial charitable organization founded in 1980 overseen by Special Olympics Canada
Mission: To provide individuals with intellectual disabilities the opportunity to participate in sporting events at the regional, provincial, national, or international levels
Member of: Special Olympics Canada
Affiliation(s): Special Olympics International
Finances: *Funding Sources:* Donations; fundraising events; sponsors
Staff Member(s): 17; 3300 volunteer(s)
Membership: 4,300
Activities: Operating in 54 communities in British Columbia; *Speaker Service:* Yes
Chief Officer(s):
Dan Howe, President & CEO, 604-737-3079
dhowe@specialolympics.bc.ca
Christina Hadley, Vice-President, Fund Development & Communications
chadley@specialolympics.bc.ca
Lois McNary, Vice-President, Sport
lmcnary@specialolympics.bc.ca
Josh Pasnak, Manager, Finance & Administration
jpasnak@specialolympics.bc.ca
Lauren Openshaw, Office Administrator
lopenshaw@specialolympics.bc.ca
Awards:
• Athletic Achievement Award
• Spirit of Sport Award
• Howard Carter Award
• Grassroots Coach Award
• President's Award
  Victoria
  PO Box 31121, Stn. University Heights, Victoria BC V8N 6J3
  Tel: 250-213-5467
  www.victoriaspecialolympics.com
  Chief Officer(s):
  Kim Perkins, Coordinator, Public Relations
  kim@kimperkins.ca
  Kristina D'Sa, Secretary
  specialo.kristinadsa@gmail.com

Special Olympics Canada (SOC) / Olympiques spéciaux Canada
#600, 21 St. Clair Ave. East, Toronto ON M4T 1L9
Tel: 416-927-9050; *Fax:* 416-927-8475
Toll-Free: 888-888-0608
info@specialolympics.ca
www.specialolympics.ca
www.facebook.com/SpecialOCanada
twitter.com/SpecialOCanada
www.youtube.com/specialocanada
Previous Name: Canadian Special Olympics Inc.
Overview: A large national organization founded in 1969
Mission: To provide sport training & competition for people with an intellectual disability, at local, regional, provincial, national & international levels, year round
Affiliation(s): Special Olympics International; The Order of United Commercial Travelers of America; The Sandbox Project
Finances: *Funding Sources:* Foundations; Corporate sponsors; Individual donations
2050 volunteer(s)
Membership: 42,565 children, youth & adults with intellectual disabilities; *Member Profile:* To improve the lives of Canadians with an intellectual disability through sport
Activities: Offering national & international games; Providing coaching development
Chief Officer(s):
Sharon Bollenbach, Chief Executive Officer, 416-927-9050 Ext. 4389
sbollenbach@specialolympics.ca

Special Olympics Manitoba (SOM)
#304, 145 Pacific Ave., Winnipeg MB R3B 2Z6
Tel: 204-925-5628; *Fax:* 204-925-5635
Toll-Free: 888-333-9179
som@specialolympics.mb.ca
www.specialolympics.mb.ca
www.facebook.com/SpecOManitoba
twitter.com/SpecOManitoba
www.instagram.com/specomanitoba
Previous Name: Manitoba Special Olympics
Overview: A small provincial charitable organization founded in 1980 overseen by Special Olympics Canada
Mission: To enrich the lives of Manitobans with an intellectual disability, through active participation in sport
Member of: Special Olympics Inc.
Finances: *Funding Sources:* Sport Manitoba; Various events
Staff Member(s): 14
Membership: *Fees:* $25 athlete
Activities: *Speaker Service:* Yes
Chief Officer(s):
Jennifer Campbell, President & CEO, 204-925-5632
jcampbell@specialolympics.mb.ca
Awards:
• Hall of Fame
• Sponsor of the Year
• Team of the Year
• Male Athlete of the Year
• Female Athlete of the Year
• Male Coach of the Year
• Female Coach of the Year
• Builder of the Year

Special Olympics New Brunswick
#103, 411 St. Mary's St., Fredericton NB E3B 8H4
Tel: 506-455-0404; *Fax:* 506-455-0410
infosonb@specialolympics.ca
www.specialolympicsnb.ca
www.facebook.com/specialolympicsnb
twitter.com/specialonb
Previous Name: New Brunswick Special Olympics
Overview: A small provincial charitable organization founded in 1979 overseen by Special Olympics Canada
Mission: To offer athletic programs to people with intellectual disabilites in New Brunswick
Staff Member(s): 3
Membership: *Member Profile:* Athletes between 2 & 88 with an intellectual disability
Chief Officer(s):

Canadian Associations / Special Olympics Newfoundland & Labrador

Josh Astle, Executive Director

Special Olympics Newfoundland & Labrador
87 Elizabeth Ave., St. John's NL A1B 1R6
Tel: 709-738-1923; *Fax:* 709-738-0119
Toll-Free: 877-738-1913
sonl@sonl.ca
www.sonl.ca
www.facebook.com/TeamSONL
twitter.com/SpecialONL
Previous Name: Newfoundland-Labrador Special Olympics
Overview: A small provincial charitable organization founded in 1986 overseen by Special Olympics Canada
Mission: To provide sport, fitness & recreation programs for individuals with an intellectual disability
Finances: *Annual Operating Budget:* $100,000-$250,000
Staff Member(s): 2; 250 volunteer(s)
Activities: *Awareness Events:* Provincial Winter & Summer Games
Chief Officer(s):
Trish Williams, Executive Director
trishw@sonl.ca

Special Olympics Northwest Territories (SONWT)
PO Box 1691, Yellowknife NT X1A 2N1
Tel: 867-446-2873
www.sonwt.ca
Previous Name: Northwest Territories Special Olympics
Overview: A small provincial organization founded in 1989 overseen by Special Olympics Canada
Mission: Special Olympics N.W.T. is the territorial sport governing body responsible for the delivery of sport for people with intellectual disabilities in the Northwest Territories.
Member of: Sport North; Special Olympics Canada
Finances: *Funding Sources:* Law Enforcement Torch Run, public donations, grants, corporate sponsors and special fundraising events.
Chief Officer(s):
Lynn Elkin, Executive Director
lynn@sonwt.ca

Special Olympics Nova Scotia (SONS)
#201, 5516 Spring Garden Rd., Halifax NS B3J 1G6
Tel: 902-429-2266; *Fax:* 902-425-5606
Toll-Free: 866-299-2019
www.sons.ca
www.facebook.com/SpecialONS
twitter.com/SpecialONS
instagram.com/SpecialONS
Previous Name: Nova Scotia Special Olympics
Overview: A small provincial charitable organization founded in 1978 overseen by Special Olympics Canada
Mission: Special Olympics is a non-profit organization dedicated to providing year-round sports training and athletic competition in a variety of Olympic-type sports for children and adults with an intellectual disability.
Staff Member(s): 4
Membership: 1,700 athletes
Chief Officer(s):
Mike Greek, President & CEO
greekmr@sportnovascotia.ca

Special Olympics Ontario (SOO)
#200, 65 Overlea Blvd., Toronto ON M4H 1P1
Tel: 416-447-8326; *Fax:* 416-447-6336
Toll-Free: 888-333-5515
www.specialolympicsontario.com
www.facebook.com/specialolympicsontario
twitter.com/soontario
www.youtube.com/specialolympicson
Previous Name: Ontario Special Olympics
Overview: A medium-sized provincial charitable organization founded in 1979 overseen by Special Olympics Canada
Mission: To provide sports training & competition for people with an intellectual disability through community-based programs
Member of: Special Olympics Canada
Finances: *Annual Operating Budget:* Greater than $5 Million; *Funding Sources:* Individual & corporate donations; Provincial government
Staff Member(s): 22; 9000 volunteer(s)
Membership: 19,000 athletes; *Member Profile:* Athletes 2 years of age or older with an intellectual disability; *Committees:* Finance; Marketing & Fundraising; Program Services
Activities: Offering 18 official sports; Providing network & support opportunities for families; Facilitating outreach & education programs to Special Olympics athletes and students across Ontario; *Internships:* Yes; *Speaker Service:* Yes
Chief Officer(s):
Glenn MacDonell, President & Chief Executive Officer, 416-447-8326 Ext. 225
glennm@specialolympicsontario.com
Linda Ashe, Vice-President, 416-447-8326 Ext. 220
lindaa@specialolympicsontario.com
Willie E, Manager, Accounting Services, 416-447-8326 Ext. 223
williee@specialolympicsontario.com
Lynn Miller, Manager, Marketing Services, 416-447-8326 Ext. 226
lynnm@specialolympicsontario.com
James Noronha, Manager, Program Services, 416-447-8326 Ext. 240
jamesn@specialolympicsontario.com

Special Olympics Prince Edward Island (SOPEI)
PO Box 822, #240, 40 Enman Cres., Charlottetown PE C1A 7L9
Tel: 902-368-8919
Toll-Free: 800-287-1196
sopei@sopei.com
www.sopei.com
www.facebook.com/Specialopei
twitter.com/Specialopei
www.youtube.com/channel/UCqsAGVtPqgIJeQRN_GeNOtw
Previous Name: PEI Special Olympics
Overview: A small provincial charitable organization founded in 1987 overseen by Special Olympics Canada
Mission: To provide sport, recreation & fitness for the intellectually disabled in PEI; To provide competititve opportunities for its members
Finances: *Annual Operating Budget:* $100,000-$250,000
Staff Member(s): 2; 75 volunteer(s)
Membership: 235; *Member Profile:* Athletes with an intellectual disability; *Committees:* Program; Board of Directors
Chief Officer(s):
Charity Sheehan, Executive Director
csheehan@sopei.com

Special Olympics Saskatchewan
353 Broad St., Regina SK S4R 1X2
Tel: 306-780-9247; *Fax:* 306-780-9441
Toll-Free: 888-307-6226
sos@specialolympics.sk.ca
www.specialolympics.sk.ca
www.facebook.com/SOSaskatchewan
twitter.com/SpecialOSask
www.youtube.com/user/SpecialOSk
Previous Name: Saskatchewan Special Olympics Society
Overview: A small provincial organization overseen by Special Olympics Canada
Mission: To enhance the lives of persons with intellectual disabilities through sport
Chief Officer(s):
Faye Matt, Chief Executive Officer, 306-780-9277
fmatt@specialolympics.sk.ca

Special Olympics Yukon (SOY) / Les Jeux Olympiques Spéciaux du Yukon
4061 4th Ave., Whitehorse YT Y1A 1H1
Tel: 867-668-6511; *Fax:* 867-667-4237
info@specialolympicsyukon.ca
www.specialolympicsyukon.ca
www.facebook.com/191453284318177
twitter.com/SpecialOYukon
Previous Name: Yukon Special Olympics
Overview: A medium-sized provincial organization founded in 1981 overseen by Special Olympics Canada
Mission: To provide a full continuum of sport apportunities for Yukoners with a mental disability
Affiliation(s): Special Olympics International
Staff Member(s): 3; 65 volunteer(s)
Membership: 100+; *Fees:* Schedule available; *Member Profile:* Individuals with a mental disability
Activities: *Awareness Events:* Sports Celebrities Dinner Auction; Golf Gala; Law Enforcement Torch Run
Chief Officer(s):
Serge Michaud, Executive Director
smichaud@specialolympicsyukon.ca
Brettanie Deal-Porter, Program Director
bdealporter@specialolympicsyukon.ca
Sylvia Anderson, Coordinator, Marketing & Development
sanderson@specialolympicsyukon.ca
Awards:
• Most Improved Athlete of the Year
• Volunteer of the Year
• Sportsman of the Year

Specification Writers Association of Canada *See* Construction Specifications Canada

Spectacle aérienne d'Abbotsford *See* Abbotsford International Air Show Society

Spectra Helpline
#402, 7700 Hurontario St., Brampton ON L6Y 4M3
Tel: 289-569-1200; *Fax:* 888-658-8577; *Crisis Hot-Line:* 905-459-7777
info@spectrahelpline.org
www.spectrahelpline.org
www.linkedin.com/company/spectra-community-support-services
www.facebook.com/SpectraHelpline
twitter.com/spectrasupport
Previous Name: Telecare Distress Centre Brampton
Overview: A small local charitable organization founded in 1973 overseen by Distress Centres Ontario
Mission: To provide a 24-hour-a-day telephone service to people in need; To aim to be a listening ministry, not a problem-solving, advice-giving institution
Affiliation(s): Telecare Teleministries of Canada Inc.; Life Line International
Finances: *Funding Sources:* Region of Peel; United Way of Peel Region; Trillium Foundation; Central West LHIN
Activities: Distress line; TeleCheck seniors program; Multilingual lines; Peel Postpartum Family Support; Reassurance program; *Speaker Service:* Yes
Chief Officer(s):
Alison Caird, Executive Director

Spectroscopy Society of Canada *See* Canadian Society for Analytical Sciences & Spectroscopy

Spectrum Society for Community Living
3231 Kingsway, Vancouver BC V5R 5K3
Tel: 604-323-1433; *Fax:* 604-321-4144
www.spectrumfriends.ca
www.facebook.com/SpectrumSociety
twitter.com/SSCLSpectrum
Overview: A medium-sized local organization founded in 1987
Mission: To provide disabled persons with services that enable them to function more productively & independently in the community
Affiliation(s): British Columbia Association for Community Living
Finances: *Funding Sources:* Federal & provincial government; Fundraising
Staff Member(s): 37
Activities: *Library:* by appointment
Chief Officer(s):
Ernest Baatz, Co-Director
ernie@spectrumsociety.org
Susan Stanfield, Co-Director
susan@spectrumsociety.org
Aaron Johannes, Co-Director
aaron@spectrumsociety.org

Speech & Hearing Association of Nova Scotia
PO Box 775, Stn. Halifax Central CRO, Halifax NS B3J 2V2
Tel: 902-423-9331
webmaster@shans.ca
www.shans.ca
www.facebook.com/SpeechAndHearing
twitter.com/SpeechHearingNS
Overview: A medium-sized provincial charitable organization
Mission: To allow audiology & speech language pathology professionals to pursue professional development in order to benefit the public
Affiliation(s): Canadian Association of Speech-Language Pathologists & Audiologists (CASLPA)
Finances: *Funding Sources:* Membership dues
Chief Officer(s):
Patricia Cleave, President
president@shans.ca

The Speech & Stuttering Institute
#2, 150 Duncan Mill Rd., Toronto ON M3B 3M4
Tel: 416-491-7771; *Fax:* 416-491-7215
info@speechandstuttering.com
www.speechandstuttering.com
www.facebook.com/speechandstuttering
twitter.com/SpchStutterInst
Previous Name: Speech Foundation of Ontario
Overview: A medium-sized provincial charitable organization founded in 1977

Mission: To provide treatment of & foster the development of innovative speech/language therapy programs; to support education & research in communication disorders
Finances: *Funding Sources:* Ministry of Health
Activities: Speech therapy groups; language therapy groups; consultation services; *Awareness Events:* Speech & Hearing Month, May; *Internships:* Yes; *Speaker Service:* Yes
Chief Officer(s):
Paul L'Heureux, Chair
Robert Kroll, Executive Director

Speech Foundation of Ontario *See* The Speech & Stuttering Institute

Speech Language Hearing Association of Alberta *See* Alberta College of Speech-Language Pathologists & Audiologists

Speech-Language & Audiology Canada (SAC) / Orthophonie et Audiologie Canada (OAC)
#1000, 1 Nicholas St., Ottawa ON K1N 7B7
Tel: 613-567-9968; *Fax:* 613-567-2859
Toll-Free: 800-259-8519
info@sac-oac.ca
www.sac-oac.ca
www.linkedin.com/groups/4226965/profile
www.facebook.com/sac.oac
twitter.com/sac_oac
www.youtube.com/channel/UCmg6LP26_eRR72hBEFfnRug
Previous Name: Canadian Association of Speech-Language Pathologists & Audiologists
Overview: A medium-sized national charitable organization founded in 1964
Mission: To support & represent the professional needs & development of speech-language pathologists & audiologists; To champion the needs of people with communication disorders
Affiliation(s): International Association of Logopedics & Phoniatrics; International Society of Audiology; International Communication Project
Finances: *Annual Operating Budget:* $1.5 Million-$3 Million; *Funding Sources:* Membership fees
Staff Member(s): 14
Membership: 6,000+; *Member Profile:* Masters degree in S-LP or AUD; *Committees:* Awards & Recognition; Clinical Certification Examination; Clinical Research Grants; Executive; Governance & Nomination; Scholarship; Standards & Ethics
Activities: *Awareness Events:* Speech and Hearing Month, May; *Speaker Service:* Yes
Chief Officer(s):
Joanne Charlebois, Chief Executive Officer, 613-567-9968 Ext. 262
joanne@sac-oac.ca
Phil Bolger, Chief Financial Officer
phil@sac-oac.ca
Jessica Bedford, Director, Communications & Marketing, 800-259-8519 Ext. 241
jessica@sac-oac.ca
Michelle Jackson, Manager, Professional Development, 800-259-8519 Ext. 244
michelle@sac-oac.ca
Awards:
• Isabel Richard Student Paper Award
Presented annually to two students, one in speech-language pathology & one in audiology, for outstanding research conducted in the course of their graduate program
• Student Excellence Awards
Presented to one outstanding student from each graduate program in speech-language pathology & audiology in Canada
• Promotions Awards
Presented to members or non-members who have contributed to the public awareness & understanding of human communication disorders in Canada
• National Certification Exam Award
• Eve Kassirer Award for Outstanding Professional Achievement
Presented to a member for his or her outstanding professional achievement in the areas of education, clinical services or administration at the national or international level
• Lifetime Achievement Award
Presented to an individual who is neither a speech-language pathologist nor an audiologist who has made significant contributions to the fields of speech-language pathology & audiology
• Mentorship Award
• Editor's Award
• Consumer Advocacy Award
• Award of Excellence for Interprofessional Collaboration

Meetings/Conferences:
• Speech-Language & Audiology Canada 2018 Annual General Meeting & Conference, May, 2018, Edmonton, AB
Scope: National
Publications:
• Canadian Association of Speech-Language Pathologists & Audiologists Communiqué
Type: Newsletter; *Frequency:* Quarterly; *ISSN:* 0842-1196
• The Canadian Journal of Speech-Language Pathology & Audiology (CJSLPA)
Type: Journal; *Frequency:* Quarterly; *Accepts Advertising*; *ISSN:* 1913-200X
• SAC [Speech-Language & Audiology Canada] Membership Directory
Type: Directory

Speed Skate New Brunswick
NB
speedskatenb@gmail.com
speedskatenb.ca
twitter.com/SpeedSkateNB
Previous Name: New Brunswick Speed Skating Association
Overview: A small provincial organization overseen by Speed Skating Canada
Mission: The association provides members with access to coaching & chances to compete. It serves as a hub for information on the sport & for members to network.
Member of: Speed Skating Canada
Chief Officer(s):
Joe Oliver, Chair

Speed Skate Nova Scotia
5516 Spring Garden Rd., Halifax NS B3J 1G6
Tel: 902-425-5450
info@speedskatens.ca
www.speedskatens.ca
twitter.com/SpeedSk8NS
Previous Name: Nova Scotia Speed Skating Association
Overview: A small provincial organization overseen by Speed Skating Canada
Member of: Speed Skating Canada
Chief Officer(s):
Brent Thompson, President
Meetings/Conferences:
• Speed Skate Nova Scotia Annual General Meeting 2018, 2018
Scope: Provincial

Speed Skate PEI
PO Box 383, Charlottetown PE C1A 7K7
info@speedskatepei.ca
www.speedskatepei.com
www.facebook.com/SpeedSkatePEI
twitter.com/SpeedSkatePEI
www.youtube.com/channel/UCwDjLpo01Om1QBMoZn5EQLw
Previous Name: Prince Edward Island Speed Skating Association
Overview: A small provincial organization overseen by Speed Skating Canada
Mission: Supporting the sport of speedskating in PEI.
Member of: Speed Skating Canada
Chief Officer(s):
Jeff Wood, President
president@speedskatepei.ca
Shirliana Bruce, Secretary
secretary@speedskatepei.ca
Awards:
• SSPEI Annual Awards Program
Honours excellence & development in various categories

Speed Skating Canada (SSC) / Patinage de vitesse Canada
House of Sport, RA Centre, 2451 Riverside Dr., Ottawa ON K1H 7X7
Tel: 613-260-3669
Toll-Free: 877-572-4772
ssc@speedskating.ca
www.speedskating.ca
www.facebook.com/SSC.PVC
twitter.com/SSC_PVC
www.youtube.com/user/SpeedSkatingCanada;
instagram.com/ssc_pvc
Overview: A medium-sized national organization founded in 1887
Mission: To develop & promote long & short track speed skating in Canada; To prepare athletes, coaches, officials, & volunteers to make contributions to speed skating & to Canada's image abroad through development & international programs
Affiliation(s): International Skating Union
Finances: *Funding Sources:* Government; Sport Canada; Canadian Olympic Association; Sponsorships; Membership
50 volunteer(s)
Membership: 10,000; *Member Profile:* Participants in competitive or recreational speed skating; *Committees:* High Performance - Short Track & Long Track; Competitions Development; Coaching Development; Officials Development; Nominations; Participant & Athlete Development Steering
Activities: *Internships:* Yes; *Speaker Service:* Yes
Chief Officer(s):
Susan Auch, Chief Executive Officer
sauch@speedskating.ca
Shawn Holman, Chief Sport Officer
sholman@speedskating.ca
Janice Dawson, ChPC, Director, Sport Development
jdawson@speedskating.ca
Cynthia Dunford, Director, Finance & Administration
cdunford@speedskating.ca
Patrick Godbout, Manager, Communications & Media Relations, 514-213-9897
pgodbout@speedskating.ca
Awards:
• SSC Awards
Includes: SSC Hall of Fame; René Marleau Official of the Year; Guy-Marcoux Officials Mentor Award; Officials Awards of Excellence; Coach of the Year; Coaches Awards of Excellence; Jean R. Dupré Award; John Hurdis Award; Jean Grenier Award; Gagné Family Award; Catriona Le May Doan Award; Jeremy Wotherspoon Award; Female short track skater of the year; Marc Gagnon Award; Rising Star for long track; Guy Daignault Award
• Athlete Awards
Includes: Skater of the Year - Long Track; Skater of the Year - Short Track; Rising Star Award; Honour Roll; Peter Williamson Trust Fund Bursary
• Coach Awards
Includes: Coach of the Year; Coaches Awards of Excellence
• Officials Awards
Includes: Guy-Marcoux Officials Mentor Award; Official of the Year; Officials Award of Excellence
Meetings/Conferences:
• Speed Skating Canada 2018 Annual General Meeting, 2018
Scope: National
Description: A gathering of the organization's Board of Directors, branches, & committees
Publications:
• Speed Skating Canada eNews
Type: Newsletter

Spina Bifida & Hydrocephalus Association of British Columbia (SBHABC)
4480 Oak St., Vancouver BC V6H 3V4
Tel: 604-878-7000; *Fax:* 604-677-6608
www.sbhabc.org
Previous Name: Lower Mainland Spina Bifida Association
Overview: A medium-sized provincial licensing charitable organization founded in 1977
Mission: To improve the quality of life of all individuals with spina bifida &/or hydrocephalus & their families, through awareness, education & research
Finances: *Annual Operating Budget:* $50,000-$100,000
Staff Member(s): 5
Membership: 250; *Fees:* $10; *Member Profile:* Adults, caregivers or families with a child with Spina Bifida &/or Hydrocephalus
Activities: *Awareness Events:* Spina Bifida Month, June; *Library:* Not open to public
Chief Officer(s):
Colleen Talbot, President
Meetings/Conferences:
• Spina Bifida & Hydrocephalus Association of BC 2018 Annual General Meeting, 2018, BC
Scope: Provincial

Spina Bifida & Hydrocephalus Association of Canada (SBHAC) / Association de spina-bifida et d'hydrocephalie du Canada
#647, 167 Lombard Ave., Winnipeg MB R3B 0V3
Tel: 204-925-3650; *Fax:* 204-925-3654
Toll-Free: 800-565-9488
info@sbhac.ca
www.sbhac.ca
www.facebook.com/167743789940812
Overview: A medium-sized national charitable organization founded in 1981

Mission: To improve the quality of life of all individuals with spina bifida &/or hydrocephalus & their families through awareness, education, advocacy & research; to reduce the incidence of neural tube defects
Member of: Canadian Coalition for Genetic Fairness
Affiliation(s): International Federation for Hydrocephalus & Spina Bifida
Finances: *Funding Sources:* Donations; Special Events
Staff Member(s): 3
Membership: 11 provincial member associations; *Fees:* $20 individual; or membership in provincial association
Activities: *Awareness Events:* Spina Bifida & Hydrocephalus Awareness Month, June; Hope Classic 2008, August *Library:* SBHAC Library; Open to public by appointment
Chief Officer(s):
Colleen Talbot, President
Awards:
• Two $1,000 bursaries per year
• Research Grants

Spina Bifida & Hydrocephalus Association of New Brunswick
1325 Mountain Rd., Moncton NB E1C 2T9
Tel: 506-857-9947
spinabifidanb@hotmail.com
Overview: A small provincial organization overseen by Spina Bifida & Hydrocephalus Association of Canada
Mission: To improve the quality of life of those persons who have spina bifida &/or hydrocephalus; to gather information on spina bifida & hydrocephalus & to disseminate it to all interested persons & organizations; to encourage research into the causes & to advance more effective treatment & care

Spina Bifida & Hydrocephalus Association of Northern Alberta (SBHANA)
PO Box 35025, 10818 Jasper Ave., Edmonton AB T5J 0B7
Tel: 780-451-6921; *Fax:* 888-881-7172
info@sbhana.org
www.sbhana.org
www.facebook.com/sbhana01
twitter.com/SBHANA1
www.youtube.com/user/TheSBHANA
Previous Name: Spina Bifida Association of Northern Alberta
Overview: A small local charitable organization founded in 1981
Mission: To enhance the lives of individuals & families affected by spina bifida &/or hydrocephalus through public awareness, education & research
Member of: Spina Bifida & Hydrocephalus Association of Canada; Alberta Disablility Forum; Albera Committee for Citizens with Disabilities
Finances: *Annual Operating Budget:* $100,000-$250,000
Staff Member(s): 2; 30 volunteer(s)
Membership: 250; *Fees:* $10; *Member Profile:* Parents/grandparents of children with spina bifida &/or hydrocephalus & adults affected with spina bifida &/or hydrocephalus; professionals; *Committees:* Social; Public Awareness; Fundraising; Newsletter; Education
Activities: Christmas party; June BBQ; parent support group; summer camp; *Awareness Events:* Spina Bifida and Hydrocephalus Month, June; *Speaker Service:* Yes; *Library:* Resource Centre; by appointment
Chief Officer(s):
Cindy Smith, President
Megan Gergatz, Program Manager
Awards:
• 2 Scholarships
Scholarship for secondary students; schlorship for graduate research in related areas for University of Alberta students; *Amount:* $1,000

Spina Bifida & Hydrocephalus Association of Nova Scotia (SBHANS)
15 Laura Dr., RR#4, Eastern Passage NS B3G 1K3
Tel: 902-679-1124
Toll-Free: 800-304-0450
info@sbhans.ca
www.sbhans.ca
Overview: A small provincial charitable organization founded in 1984 overseen by Spina Bifida & Hydrocephalus Association of Canada
Mission: To eliminate spina bifida & hydrocephalus in newborns by promoting preventative measures; To help individuals with spina bifida &/or hydrocephalus to reach their full potential by promoting independence & improved quality of life
Member of: Spina Bifida & Hydrocephalus Association of Canada

Membership: *Fees:* $10 individual/family
Activities: Newsletter; resource kits; fundraising events; funding programs for members with spina bifida & hydrocephalus
Awards:
• Special Needs Fund
Designed to alleviate some of the financial strain placed on parents of children with spina bifida & persons with spina bifida, when funds are not available from other sources *Eligibility:* Parents of children or persons with spina bifida &/or hydrocephalus; must be a member of Spina Bifida & Hydrocephalus Associaton of Nova Scotia or register at time of application
• Education Awards
To encourage & support students with spina bifida &/or hydrocephalus; to develop independence & responsibility for their future education; to assist students in pursuing higher education at university or other post secondary studies *Eligibility:* Canadian citizens who are residents of Nova Scotia who have spina bifida or hydrocephalus *Deadline:* April; *Amount:* $500
• Bike/Vehicle Fund
• Recreation Fund
Cape Breton Chapter
20 Deanna Dr., Glace Bay NS B1A 6Y1
Tel: 902-849-4401

Spina Bifida & Hydrocephalus Association of Ontario (SB&H)
PO Box 103, #1006, 555 Richmond St. West, Toronto ON M5V 3B1
Tel: 416-214-1056; *Fax:* 416-214-1446
Toll-Free: 800-387-1575
provincial@sbhao.on.ca
www.sbhao.on.ca
www.facebook.com/SpinaBifidaHydrocephalusOntario
twitter.com/SBH_Ontario
www.youtube.com/channel/UC3psi9zf8KapVIgJ9p0f1EQ?
Overview: A medium-sized provincial charitable organization founded in 1973
Mission: To build awareness & drive education, research, support, care & advocacy to help find a cure while working to improve the quality of life of all individuals with spina bifida &/or hydrocephalus
Affiliation(s): Spina Bifida & Hydrocephalus Association of Canada
Finances: *Annual Operating Budget:* $250,000-$500,000
Staff Member(s): 7; 1003 volunteer(s)
Membership: *Fees:* $20 individual; $30 family/professional/associate; $60 corporate; *Committees:* Education; Fundraising; Finance & Audit
Activities: Toll-free telephone line to access support & information; support programs; scholarships programs; research programs; information materials; "Kids on the Block" Awareness Program; Folic Acid Awareness Program; educational workshops & conferences; advocacy; public awareness programs; *Awareness Events:* Spina Bifida & Hydrocephalus Month, June; *Speaker Service:* Yes; *Library:* Resource Lending Library; Open to public
Chief Officer(s):
Elaine Wilson, Executive Director
ewilson@sbhao.on.ca
Awards:
• Dr. E. Bruce Hendrick Scholarship Program
• Luciana Spring Mascarin Bursary

Spina Bifida & Hydrocephalus Association of Prince Edward Island
PO Box 3332, Charlottetown PE C0A 1R0
Tel: 902-628-8875
Overview: A small provincial charitable organization overseen by Spina Bifida & Hydrocephalus Association of Canada
Chief Officer(s):
Lurlean Palmer, Contact
lurleanpalmer@eastlink.ca

Spina Bifida & Hydrocephalus Association of South Saskatchewan
PO Box 37115, Stn. Landmark, Regina SK S4S 7K3
Tel: 306-586-2222
regina@sbhac.ca
Overview: A small provincial organization
Mission: To improve the quality of life for those afflicted with spina bifida &/or hydrocephalus
Member of: Spina Bifida & Hydrocephalus Association of Canada
Finances: *Funding Sources:* Fundraising; donations
Activities: *Library:* Family Resource Centre

North Chapter
351 Kenderdine Rd., Saskatoon SK S7N 3S9
Tel: 306-249-1362
www.sbhasn.ca
Chief Officer(s):
Laurel Scherr, President
South Chapter
PO Box 37115, Regina SK S4S 7K3
Tel: 306-359-6049
regina@sbhac.ca
Mission: To improve the quality of life of all individuals with spina bifida and/or hydrocephalus and their families through awareness, education, advocacy and research, and to reduce the incidence of neural tube defects

Spina Bifida & Hydrocephalus Association of Southern Alberta (SBHASA)
PO Box 6837, Stn. D, Calgary AB T2P 2E9
www.sbhasa.ca
Previous Name: Spina Bifida Association of Southern Alberta
Overview: A small provincial charitable organization founded in 1981 overseen by Spina Bifida & Hydrocephalus Association of Canada
Mission: To raise awareness about spina bifida & hydrocephalus & to provide help to people & families who suffer from these conditions
Membership: *Fees:* $10
Chief Officer(s):
Minh Ho, President
minh.ho@plainsmidstream.com

Spina Bifida Association of Manitoba (SBAM)
#647, 167 Lombard Ave., Winnipeg MB R3B 0V3
Tel: 204-925-3653; *Fax:* 204-925-3654
manitoba.sbhao.ca
Overview: A small provincial charitable organization founded in 1965 overseen by Spina Bifida & Hydrocephalus Association of Canada
Mission: To provide resources & support to people & families suffering from spina bifida & hydrocephalus

Spina Bifida Association of Northern Alberta *See* Spina Bifida & Hydrocephalus Association of Northern Alberta

Spina Bifida Association of Southern Alberta *See* Spina Bifida & Hydrocephalus Association of Southern Alberta

Spinal Cord Injury (Prince Edward Island) (SCI-PEI)
40 Enman Cres., Charlottetown PE C1E 1E6
Tel: 902-370-9523
www.sci-pei.ca
www.facebook.com/166802903349902
Previous Name: Canadian Paraplegic Association (Prince Edward Island)
Overview: A small provincial organization founded in 1990 overseen by Spinal Cord Injury Canada
Activities: *Awareness Events:* SCI Month, May
Chief Officer(s):
Meagan MacKenzie, Executive Director
mmackenzie@sci-pei.ca

Spinal Cord Injury Alberta
#305, 11010 - 101 St., Edmonton AB T5H 4B9
Tel: 780-424-6312; *Fax:* 780-424-6313
Toll-Free: 888-654-5444
edmonton@sci-ab.ca
www.sci-ab.ca
www.facebook.com/SpinalCordInjuryAlberta?ref=hl
twitter.com/scialberta
www.youtube.com/cpaalberta
Previous Name: Canadian Paraplegic Association (Alberta)
Overview: A medium-sized provincial organization overseen by Spinal Cord Injury Canada
Finances: *Annual Operating Budget:* $3 Million-$5 Million
Staff Member(s): 40
Activities: Rehabilitation support & service coordination; Aboriginal Services, Information Service; Peer Program; Community Development
Chief Officer(s):
Teren Clarke, CEO
Publications:
• Spinal Columns
Type: Magazine; *Frequency:* Quarterly; *Accepts Advertising*; *Price:* $20
Profile: Articles on issues such as advocacy, transportation, employment, & relationships

Canadian Associations / Spinal Cord Injury Ontario

• Wheel-e
Type: Newsletter; Frequency: Monthly
Profile: Association events & announcements

Calgary
5211 - 4th St. NE, Calgary AB T2K 6J5
Tel: 403-228-3001; Fax: 403-229-4271
calgary@sci-ab.ca

Fort McMurray
Fort McMurray AB
Tel: 587-645-0771
fortmcmurray@sci-ab.ca
Chief Officer(s):
Stephanie Myrick, Regional Program Coordinator
stephanie.myrick@sci-ab.ca

Grande Prairie
10 Knowledge Way, Grande Prairie AB T8W 2V9
Tel: 780-532-3305; Fax: 780-539-3567
grandeprairie@sci-ab.ca

Lethbridge
53 Mount Sundance Rd. West, Lethbridge AB T1J 0B6
Tel: 403-327-7577; Fax: 403-320-0269
lethbridge@sci-ab.ca

Lloydminster
Lloydminster AB
Tel: 780-871-4542
lloydminster@sci-ab.ca

Medicine Hat
#26, 419 - 3rd St. SE, Medicine Hat AB T1A 0G9
Tel: 403-504-4001; Fax: 403-504-5172
medicinehat@sci-ab.ca

Red Deer
Red Deer AB
Tel: 403-341-5060; Fax: 403-343-1630
reddeer@sci-ab.ca

St. Paul
PO Box 653, St Paul AB T0A 3A0
Tel: 780-645-5116; Fax: 780-645-5141
stpaul@sci-ab.ca

Spinal Cord Injury British Columbia (BCPA)
780 Southwest Marine Dr., Vancouver BC V6P 5Y7
Tel: 604-324-3611; Fax: 614-326-1229
info@bcpara.org
sci-bc.ca
www.facebook.com/SpinalCordInjuryBC
twitter.com/sci_bc
www.youtube.com/user/BCParaplegic
Previous Name: British Columbia Paraplegic Association; Canadian Paraplegic Association
Overview: A medium-sized provincial organization founded in 1957 overseen by Spinal Cord Injury Canada
Member of: BC SCI Community Services Network
Finances: Funding Sources: Donations; Rick Hansen Man in Motion Foundation; BC Neurotrauma Initiative; Fundraising
Staff Member(s): 24
Membership: 1,500; Fees: $10
Activities: Providing rehabilitation services; Engaging in advocacy activities; Administering the Youth: Bridges to the Future program; Presenting information & educational opportunities; Offering employment services; Arranging peer support; Providing grants to people with spinal cord injuries & other physical disabilities & to researchers who focus on community based rehabilitation & quality of life enhancement
Chief Officer(s):
Edward Milligan, Chair
Chris McBride, Executive Director
cmcbride@sci-bc.ca
Marion Patsis, Manager, Finance & Human Resources
mpastis@sci-bc.ca
Publications:
• Comming into Focus: People Living with Spinal Cord Injury in BC
Type: Report
• Paragraphic
Type: Magazine; Frequency: Quarterly; Accepts Advertising; Price: Free for BCPA supporting members & community partners
Profile: BCPA programs, research information, personal profiles, & updates from the GF Strong Rehabilitation Centre

Prince George
777 Kinsmen Pl., Prince George BC V2M 6Y7
Tel: 250-563-6942; Fax: 250-563-6992
info@sci-bc.ca
Chief Officer(s):

Brandy Stiles, Coordinator, Peer Program
bstiles@sci-bc.ca

Spinal Cord Injury Canada / Lésions Médullaires Canada
#104, 720 Belfast Rd., Ottawa ON K1G 6M8
Tel: 416-200-5814
www.sci-can.ca
www.facebook.com/223239864405595
Also Known As: SCI Canada
Previous Name: Canadian Paraplegic Association
Overview: A medium-sized national charitable organization founded in 1945
Mission: To assist persons with spinal cord injuries & other physical disabilitieto to cope with the changes caused by their injury, to become independent & self-reliant, & to lead productive lives
Finances: Funding Sources: Donations; Human Resources & Social Development Canada, Office of Disability Issues; Corporate Partners
Activities: Offering the Self Advocacy Training Program; Counselling; Providing the National Peer Support Program; Participating in international development activities; Providing information about research, health, & assistive equipment; Fundraising
Chief Officer(s):
Bill Adair, Executive Director
bill@sci-can.ca
Publications:
• Canadian Paraplegic Association Annual Report [a publication of Spinal Cord Injury Canada]
Type: Yearbook; Frequency: Annually
• The Complete Incomplete Resource [a publication of Spinal Cord Injury Canada]
Price: $6
Profile: Resource dedicated to incomplete SCI
• Fire Safety for People with Disabilities [a publication of Spinal Cord Injury Canada]
Price: $22
Profile: Fire safety training kit for people with disabilities & seniors
• Life After Spinal Cord Injury [a publication of Spinal Cord Injury Canada]
Price: $30 non-members; $15 members
Profile: Information resource for persons with SCI & their family members
• Life Interrupted [a publication of Spinal Cord Injury Canada]
Type: Manual
Profile: Practical information for youth, between the ages of 12 & 21, with SCI
• Opening Doors to Rehabilitation [a publication of Spinal Cord Injury Canada]
Type: Manual
Profile: Information for professional counsellors who work with clients with mobility impairments
• Total Access [a publication of Spinal Cord Injury Canada]
Type: Magazine; Frequency: Semiannually; Price: $19.99 Canada; $25 International
Profile: Information for people with spinal cord injury & other physical disabilities
• Workforce Participation Survey of Canadians with Spinal Cord Injuries [a publication of Spinal Cord Injury Canada]
Type: Report

Spinal Cord Injury Newfoundland & Labrador (SCI NL)
PO Box 21284, #101, 396 Elizabeth Ave., St. John's NL A1A 5G6
Tel: 709-753-5901; Fax: 709-753-4224
Toll-Free: 877-783-5901
info@sci-nl.ca
sci-nl.ca
www.facebook.com/186403331430655
twitter.com/SCI_NL
www.youtube.com/user/CanParaplegicNL
Previous Name: Canadian Paraplegic Association - Newfoundland & Labrador
Overview: A medium-sized provincial organization overseen by Spinal Cord Injury Canada
Mission: To help people with spinal cord injuries and other mobility impairments to become self-reliant and independent
Staff Member(s): 6
Membership: Member Profile: Individuals with spinal cord injuries, mobility disabilities, & their family members
Chief Officer(s):

Michael Burry, Executive Director, 902-753-5901 Ext. 222
mburry@sci-nl.ca

Bay Roberts
PMC Professional Bldg., PO Box 1309, 25 Bareneed Rd., Bay Roberts NL A0A 1G0
Tel: 709-786-1442; Fax: 709-786-1441

Corner Brook
PO Box 764, 1 Lester Ave., Corner Brook NL A2H 6G7
Fax: 709-634-7395
Toll-Free: 877-634-0928

Gander
230 Airport Blvd., Gander NL A1V 1L7
Tel: 709-256-7077; Fax: 709-256-7047

Grand Falls - Windsor
4A Bayley St., Grand Falls-Windsor NL A2A 2T5
Tel: 709-489-8445

Happy Valley - Labrador Office
PO Box 848, Stn. B, 215 Hamilton River Rd., Happy Valley-Goose Bay NL A0P 1E0
Tel: 709-896-7057; Fax: 709-896-3716

Marystown
PO Box 1296, #245, 247 Villa Marie Dr., Marystown NL A0E 2M0
Tel: 709-279-2790; Fax: 709-279-0919
Toll-Free: 877-792-2790

Spinal Cord Injury Ontario
520 Sutherland Dr., Toronto ON M4G 3V9
Tel: 416-422-5644; Fax: 416-422-5943
Toll-Free: 877-422-1112
www.sciontario.org
www.facebook.com/sciontario.org
twitter.com/SCI_Ontario
www.youtube.com/user/SCIOntarioOrg
Also Known As: SCI Ontario
Previous Name: Canadian Paraplegic Association Ontario
Overview: A medium-sized provincial organization founded in 1979 overseen by Spinal Cord Injury Canada
Mission: To act as the voice of persons with spinal cord injury in Ontario
Membership: Committees: Governance & Nominating; Client Services Quality Management; Audit & Finance; Advocacy
Activities: Delivers non-medical services to people with disabilities; Helping people integrate into the community; Increasing employment opportunities; Providing information services
Publications:
• Outspoken!
Type: Magazine; Frequency: Quarterly; Price: Free with membership
Profile: CPA Ontario services & activities

Barrie Office
#111, 80 Bradford St., Barrie ON L4N 6S7
Tel: 705-726-4546; Fax: 705-726-5054
Toll-Free: 800-870-5670

Hamilton Office
North Regional Rehabilitation Centre, #B1-3, 300 Wellington St., Hamilton ON L8L 0A4
Tel: 905-383-0216; Fax: 905-383-5021

Kingston Office
PO Box 20105, Kingston ON K7P 2T6
Tel: 613-547-1391; Fax: 613-547-1393
Toll-Free: 866-220-7539

London Office
#3, 1111 Elias St., London ON N5W 5L1
Tel: 519-433-2331; Fax: 519-433-3987
Toll-Free: 866-433-9888

Mississauga/Halton; Peel/Dufferin Office
c/o 520 Sutherland Dr., Toronto ON M4G 3V9
Tel: 905-459-6965; Fax: 905-459-0283
Toll-Free: 866-287-1689

Muskoka Office
PO Box 327, Kearney ON P0A 1M0
Tel: 705-636-5827; Fax: 705-636-7223

Ottawa Office
#104, 720 Belfast Rd., Ottawa ON K1G 0Z5
Tel: 613-723-1033; Fax: 613-688-0373
• Spinal Columns: Ottawa Region Newsletter
Type: Newsletter; Accepts Advertising
Profile: Resources, upcoming events, & volunteer opportunities

Peterborough Office
PO Box 131, Warsaw ON K0L 3A0
Tel: 705-652-7496; Fax: 705-652-0786
Toll-Free: 888-643-2507

Sault St. Marie Office
260 Elizabeth St., Sault Ste Marie ON P6A 6J3
Tel: 705-759-0333; *Fax:* 705-759-0335
Toll-Free: 866-531-1513

Thunder Bay Office
1201 Jasper Dr., #B, Thunder Bay ON P7B 6R2
Tel: 807-344-3743; *Fax:* 807-344-9490
Toll-Free: 866-344-4159

Toronto - West Office
#306, 1120 Finch Ave., Toronto ON M3J 3H7
Tel: 416-241-1433; *Fax:* 416-241-2466

Waterloo-Wellington Office
PO Box 1881, 88 Wyndham St. North, Guelph ON N1H 7A1
Tel: 519-893-1267; *Fax:* 519-893-2585
Toll-Free: 888-893-1267

Windsor Office
c/o Tafour Campus, Hotel Dieu Grace Hospital, 1453 Prince Rd., Windsor ON N9C 3Z4
Tel: 519-253-7272; *Fax:* 519-253-7279

Spinal Cord Injury Saskatchewan
311 - 38th St. East, Saskatoon SK S7K 0T1
Tel: 306-652-9644; *Fax:* 306-652-2957
Toll-Free: 888-282-0186
saskatoon@canparaplegic.org
www.spinalcordinjurysask.ca
www.facebook.com/CPASaskatchewan
twitter.com/scisask
Previous Name: Canadian Paraplegic Association (Saskatchewan)
Overview: A medium-sized provincial organization overseen by Spinal Cord Injury Canada
Mission: To provide services to persons with spinal cord injury & other mobility impairments in Saskatchewan
Staff Member(s): 9
Activities: Offering the Provincial Peer Support Program; Providing information, on topics such as home modification; Consulting about accessibility; Counselling; Engaging in advocacy activities; Offering employment services; *Awareness Events:* Annual Wheel Challenge for Everyone
Chief Officer(s):
Lyn Brown, Executive Director
lbrown@canparaplegic.org

Regina
3928 Gordon Rd., Regina SK S4S 6Y3
Tel: 306-584-0101; *Fax:* 306-584-0008
Toll-Free: 877-582-4483
regina@canparaplegic.org
Chief Officer(s):
Blake Lamontagne, Coordinator, Client Service
blamontagne@canparaplegic.org

Spirit of Sport Foundation *See* True Sport Foundation

Spiritans, the Congregation of the Holy Ghost
34 Collinsgrove Rd., Toronto ON M1E 3S4
Tel: 416-691-9319; *Fax:* 416-691-8760
secretary@spiritans.com
www.spiritans.com
www.youtube.com/user/SpiritansTransCanada
Also Known As: Spiritans of TransCanada
Overview: A medium-sized national organization
Mission: Roman Catholic religious congregation specializing in education & mission
Membership: 3,000+
Chief Officer(s):
Paul McAuley, Provincial Bursar
bursar@spiritans.com
Publications:
• Spiritan
Type: Magazine; *Frequency:* q.; *Editor:* Fr. Patrick Fitzpatrick CSSp

Spiritual Science Fellowship/International Institute of Integral Human Sciences (SSF-IIIHS)
PO Box 1387, Stn. H, 1974, rue de Maisonneuve ouest, Montréal QC H3G 2N3
Tel: 514-937-8359; *Fax:* 514-937-5380
info@iiihs.org
www.iiihs.org
www.facebook.com/SSF.IIIHS
twitter.com/SSF_IIIHS
Overview: A small local charitable organization
Mission: To provide spiritual services, educational programs, & pastoral ministrations for persons, regardless of religious background, who desire to understand experiences of psyche & spirit, & to dedicate themselves to personal spiritual growth & psychic development, in an atmosphere of informed free-thought & enquiry
25 volunteer(s)
Membership: 10,000; *Fees:* $15; gifts
Activities: *Internships:* Yes; *Speaker Service:* Yes
Chief Officer(s):
Marilyn Z. Rossner

Spiritwood Chamber of Commerce
PO Box 267, Spiritwood SK S0J 2M0
Tel: 306-883-2426
Overview: A small local organization

Sport BC
#230, 3820 Cessna Dr., Richmond BC V7B 0A2
Tel: 604-333-3400; *Fax:* 604-333-3401
info@sportbc.com
sportbc.com
www.facebook.com/SportBC
twitter.com/SportBC
Overview: A medium-sized provincial organization founded in 1966
Mission: To provide leadership, direction, & support to member organizations in their delivery of sport opportunities to all British Columbians
Member of: Sport West
Finances: *Annual Operating Budget:* $1.5 Million-$3 Million; *Funding Sources:* Provincial Funding; Membership Fees; Corporate Support, Event & Fundraising; Fee for Services; All Sport Insurance; SBC Insurance Operations
Staff Member(s): 7
Membership: 80 Associations; *Fees:* Schedule available; *Member Profile:* Non-profit society sport organization with province-wide representation; *Committees:* Finance & Audit
Activities: Participation & Excellence; KidSport Fund; Leadership; Sport Promotion; Advocacy; Organizations Development; Athlete Voice; *Internships:* Yes; *Speaker Service:* Yes
Chief Officer(s):
Pete Quevillon, Director, KidSport BC
Rob Newman, President & CEO
rob.newman@sportbc.com
Awards:
• Community Sport Hero Awards
• President's Awards
• Athlete of the Year Awards

Sport Dispute Resolution Centre of Canada (SDRCC)
#950, 1080, Beaver Hall Hill, Montréal QC H2Z 1S8
Tel: 514-866-1245; *Fax:* 514-866-1246
Toll-Free: 866-733-7767
www.crdsc-sdrcc.ca
www.facebook.com/crdscsdrcc
Also Known As: ADRsportRED
Overview: A small national organization founded in 2004
Mission: To provide to the sport community a national alternative dispute resolution service for sport disputes
Chief Officer(s):
Allan J. Sattin, Chair
Marie-Claude Asselin, Executive Director
mcasselin@crdsc-sdrcc.ca

Sport for Disabled - Ontario; Paralympics Ontario *See* ParaSport Ontario

Sport interuniversitaire canadien *See* Canadian Interuniversity Sport

Sport Jeunesse / KidSport Québec
CP 1000, Succ. M, 4545, av Pierre-de Coubertin, Montréal QC H1V 3R2
Tél: 514-252-3114; *Téléc:* 514-254-9621
www.jeuxduquebec.com/Mes_premiers_Jeux-fr-13.php
Également appelé: Mes Premiers Jeux
Aperçu: *Dimension:* petite; *Envergure:* provinciale surveillé par KidSport Canada
Membre de: KidSport Canada; Sports Québec

Sport Manitoba
Sport for Life Centre, 145 Pacific Ave., Winnipeg MB R3B 2Z6
Tel: 204-925-5600; *Fax:* 204-925-5916
info@sportmanitoba.ca
www.sportmanitoba.ca
www.facebook.com/sportmb
twitter.com/SportManitoba
www.youtube.com/user/sportmanitoba
Previous Name: Manitoba Sports Federation Inc.
Overview: A large provincial organization founded in 1996
Mission: To create the best sport community in Canada through provision of resources to recognized sport organizations, enabling them to encourage participation in sport at all levels of skill & ability & to develop athletes of national & international calibre
Finances: *Funding Sources:* Provincial government
Staff Member(s): 45
Activities: Operating & overseeing the Sport for Life Centre; Coaching Manitoba; Sport Medicine Centre; Manitoba Sports Hall of Fame; KidSport Manitoba; Power Smart Manitoba Games; & Team Manitoba; *Awareness Events:* Polar Bear Dare; *Speaker Service:* Yes; *Library:* by appointment
Chief Officer(s):
Jeff Hnatiuk, President & CEO
jeff.hnatiuk@sportmanitoba.ca
Laurel Read, Director, Finance & Operations
laurel.read@sportmanitoba.ca
Evan Andrew, Director, Marketing
evan.andrew@sportmanitoba.ca
Awards:
• Athlete Assistance
• Coaching Manitoba Bursary
• Manitoba Foundation for Sports Scholarships
• Princess Royal Pan Am Scholarship
Publications:
• Sport for Life [a publication of Sport Manitoba]
Type: Newsletter

Sport Medicine & Science Council of Manitoba Inc.
145 Pacific Ave., Winnipeg MB R3B 2Z6
Tel: 204-925-5750; *Fax:* 204-925-5624
sport.med@sportmanitoba.ca
sportmed.mb.ca
twitter.com/smsc_mb
Overview: A small provincial organization
Mission: To meet the needs of Manitoba's sport, recreation and fitness communities through an organized cooperative forum of medical, paramedical and sport science provider groups
Activities: *Library:* Sport Medicine & Science Council of Manitoba Resource Library; Open to public
Chief Officer(s):
Russ Horbal, Presidnet

Sport Medicine Council of Alberta (SMCA)
Percy Page Centre, 11759 Groat Rd., Main Fl., Edmonton AB T5M 3K6
Tel: 780-415-0812; *Fax:* 780-422-3093
www.sportmedab.ca
twitter.com/SportMedAB
Overview: A medium-sized provincial licensing organization founded in 1983
Mission: To develop, promote & coordinate programs & services optimizing safe & healthful participation in sport & leisure activities for all Albertans
Member of: Sport Medicine
Membership: *Fees:* $50 subscriber; $265 corporate; *Member Profile:* Athletic therapists & teachers; sport physiotherapists; sport medicine physicians; sport scientists (including exercise physiologists, sport nutrition specialists, sport psychologists); teams; clubs
Activities: Athletic first aid courses; taping & strapping; sport nutrition courses; medical supply sales; kit rentals; speakers bureau; resource library; *Internships:* Yes; *Speaker Service:* Yes; *Library:* Not open to public
Chief Officer(s):
Steve Johnson, President
Barb Adamson, Executive Director
badamson@sportmedab.ca

Sport Medicine Council of British Columbia *See* SportMedBC

Sport New Brunswick / Sport Nouveau-Brunswick
#13, 900 Hanwell Rd., Fredericton NB E3B 6A2
Tel: 506-451-1320; *Fax:* 506-451-1325
director@sportnb.com
www.sportnb.com
twitter.com/SportNB
Also Known As: Sport NB
Overview: A medium-sized provincial charitable organization founded in 1968
Mission: To promote the development of amateur sport in New Brunswick through services, programs, advocacy
Member of: Canadian Council of Provincial Territorial Sport Federations

Finances: *Annual Operating Budget:* $250,000-$500,000; *Funding Sources:* Provincial government; membership fees; corporate sponsorship
Staff Member(s): 3
Membership: 68 organizations with 120,000 participants; *Fees:* Schedule available
Activities: *Awareness Events:* McInnes Cooper Dragon Boat Festival; *Internships:* Yes; *Speaker Service:* Yes; *Library:* by appointment
Chief Officer(s):
Darcy McKillop, Chief Executive Officer, 506-451-1327
director@sportnb.com
Sally Hutt, Coordinator, Programs
programs@sportnb.com

Sport Newfoundland & Labrador
PO Box 8700, 1296A Kenmount Rd., St. John's NL A1B 4J6
Tel: 709-576-4932; *Fax:* 709-576-7493
sportnl@sportnl.ca
www.sportnl.ca
www.facebook.com/sportnl
twitter.com/sportnl
Also Known As: Sport NL
Previous Name: Newfoundland & Labrador Amateur Sports Federation
Overview: A medium-sized provincial organization founded in 1972
Mission: To promote & advance amateur sport throughout Newfoundland & Labrador; to represent collective interests & goals of members; to provide various programs & services; to liaise & lobby with government, communities, media & other representative organizations; to provide direction & leadership on issues which affect members
Staff Member(s): 4
Membership: 45 provincial sport organizations; 70,000 individual
Chief Officer(s):
Troy Croft, Executive Director
troy@sportnl.ca

Sport North Federation
Don Cooper Building, PO Box 11089, 4908 - 49 St., Yellowknife NT X1A 3X7
Tel: 867-669-8326; *Fax:* 867-669-8327
Toll-Free: 800-661-0797
www.sportnorth.com
www.facebook.com/sportnorthfederation
twitter.com/SportNorth
www.youtube.com/user/SportNorthFederation
Previous Name: Northwest Territories Sport Federation
Overview: A small provincial organization founded in 1976 overseen by Athletics Canada
Mission: To represent NWT sports organizations
Member of: Athletics Canada
Staff Member(s): 10
Chief Officer(s):
Maureen Miller, President
mmiller@sportnorth.com
Doug Rentmeister, Executive Director
drent@sportnorth.com

Sport Nouveau-Brunswick *See* Sport New Brunswick

Sport Nova Scotia (SNS)
5516 Spring Garden Rd., 4th Fl., Halifax NS B3J 1G6
Tel: 902-425-5450; *Fax:* 902-425-5606
sportns@sportnovascotia.ca
www.sportnovascotia.ca
www.facebook.com/sportnovascotia
twitter.com/SportNovaScotia
Overview: A medium-sized provincial organization founded in 1974
Mission: To promote the development of amateur sport in Nova Scotia through services, programs, advocacy & technical consultation
Finances: *Annual Operating Budget:* $1.5 Million-$3 Million; *Funding Sources:* Membership; sponsors; government
Staff Member(s): 17; 15 volunteer(s)
Membership: 86 groups + 150,000 individuals; *Fees:* Schedule available
Chief Officer(s):
Jamie Ferguson, Chief Executive Officer, 902-425-5450 Ext. 315
jferguson@sportnovascotia.ca
Awards:
• RICOH Sport Awards Program

Sport Parachute Association of Saskatchewan
SK
Other Communication: Board of Directors, E-mail: bod@skydive.sk.ca
www.skydive.sk.ca
Overview: A small provincial organization overseen by Canadian Sport Parachuting Association
Member of: Canadian Sport Parachuting Association
Chief Officer(s):
Craig Skihar, President
stimpysplace@gmail.com
Jayson Pister, Vice-President
jay.pister@gmail.com

Sport PEI Inc.
PO Box 302, 40 Enman Cres., Charlottetown PE C1E 1E6
Tel: 902-368-4110; *Fax:* 902-368-4548
Toll-Free: 800-247-6712
Other Communication: Toll-Free Fax: 1-800-235-5687
sports@sportpei.pe.ca
www.sportpei.pe.ca
www.facebook.com/176050449103403
twitter.com/sportpei
Overview: A small provincial organization founded in 1973
Mission: To assist in the development & promotion of amateur sport in the province of Prince Edward Island; To offer services & programs to meet the needs of the membership
Finances: *Annual Operating Budget:* $100,000-$250,000; *Funding Sources:* Government; Private sector sponsorhips
Staff Member(s): 8; 15 volunteer(s)
Membership: 6 corporate + 39 active + 15 affiliate + 11 honorary; *Fees:* Schedule available; *Member Profile:* Provincial sport organizations; *Committees:* Administration; Fundraising; Marketing; Sport Development
Activities: Advising member associations; Acting in consultative capacity with member associations; Offering fundraising opportunities for amateur sport in PEI; *Internships:* Yes; *Library:* Open to public
Chief Officer(s):
Tracey Clements, President
Gemma Koughan, Executive Director
gkoughan@sportpei.pe.ca
Awards:
• Top Junior & Senior Male & Female Athletes of the Year
• Team, Coach, Administrator & Official of the Year
• Sport Scholarships
Awarded to four Island student athletes (two male & two female)
Eligibility: Island student athletes graduating from a Prince Edward Island high school, have excelled in sports during the school year, & have maintained strong academic standing
Deadline: May; *Amount:* $1,000 each
• Earl F. Smith Athletic Scholarship
Awarded to four Island student athletes (two male & two female)
Deadline: May; *Amount:* $1,000 each
Publications:
• Island Sports Scene [a publication of Sport PEI]
Type: Newsletter; *Frequency:* Monthly
Profile: Features association news & important dates

Sport Physiotherapy Canada (SPC)
#75, 2192 Queen St. East, Toronto ON M4E 1E6
Tel: 647-722-3461
info@sportphysio.ca
www.sportphysio.ca
www.facebook.com/sportphysiocanada
twitter.com/sportphysiocan
www.youtube.com/user/physiotherapycan
Previous Name: Sport Physiotherapy Division of the Canadian Physiotherapy Association
Overview: A small national organization founded in 1972
Mission: To promote professional development of members; To ensure high-quality health care for Canada's athletes
Member of: Canadian Physiotherapy Association; Sport Medicine Council of Canada
Membership: 1,200; *Member Profile:* Members can be physiotherapists, students, graduate / practising physiotherapists, or SPD-certified sport physiotherapists
Chief Officer(s):
Ashley Lewis, Executive Director
alewis@sportphysio.ca
Ereka Roach, Coordinator, Member Services
program@sportphysio.ca

Sport Physiotherapy Division of the Canadian Physiotherapy Association *See* Sport Physiotherapy Canada

Sport Scolaire Canada *See* School Sport Canada

Sport Yukon
4061 - 4 Ave., Whitehorse YT Y1A 1H1
Tel: 867-668-4236; *Fax:* 867-667-4237
news@sportyukon.com
www.sportyukon.com
www.facebook.com/sportyukon
twitter.com/sportyukon
www.youtube.com/channel/UCX5XUbz5y6XN3je1bDXU5ig
Overview: A small provincial organization
Mission: To promote the development of amateur sport in the Yukon through services, programs, advocacy
Staff Member(s): 2
Membership: 68 clubs; *Fees:* $210
Chief Officer(s):
Tracey Bilsky, Executive Director
tbilsky@sportyukon.com
Awards:
• Administrator of the Year
• Coach of the Year
• Team of the Year
• International Female Athlete of the Year
• International Male Athlete of the Year
• National Territorial Female Athlete of the Year
• National Territorial Male Athlete of the Year

SportAbility BC
780 Marine Dr. SW, Vancouver BC V6P 5YZ
Tel: 604-324-1411
sportinfo@sportabilitybc.ca
www.sportabilitybc.ca
www.facebook.com/sport.ability.3
twitter.com/SportAbilityBC
www.youtube.com/SportAbilityBC
Previous Name: Cerebral Palsy Sports Association of British Columbia
Overview: A medium-sized provincial charitable organization founded in 1976 overseen by Canadian Cerebral Palsy Sports Association
Mission: To provide sports & recreational opportunities for people with cerebral palsy, head injury, stroke & similar disabilities at the local, regional, provincial & national level; To provide access to appropriate programming for members including segregated & integrated opportunities
Affiliation(s): Sport BC
Finances: *Annual Operating Budget:* $250,000-$500,000; *Funding Sources:* Fundraising; Sport BC; Gaming; Donations
Staff Member(s): 5
Membership: *Fees:* $25 senior/individual/family; *Member Profile:* Physically disabled athletes, coaches, officials, volunteers
Activities: *Library:* by appointment
Chief Officer(s):
Ross MacDonald, Executive Director
rossm@sportabilitybc.ca

SportMedBC
#2350, 3713 Kensington Ave., Burnaby BC B5B 0A7
Tel: 604-294-3050; *Fax:* 604-294-3020
Toll-Free: 888-755-3375
info@sportmedbc.com
www.sportmedbc.com
www.facebook.com/sportmedbc
twitter.com/SportMedBC
www.youtube.com/user/SportMedBC
Previous Name: Sport Medicine Council of British Columbia
Overview: A small provincial organization founded in 1982
Mission: To support health & performance in British Columbia through sport & exercise
Finances: *Annual Operating Budget:* $100,000-$250,000; *Funding Sources:* Service fees; grants
Staff Member(s): 7
Membership: 275; *Fees:* Free
Activities: Injury Prevention; Athlete Development; Drug-free Sport
Chief Officer(s):
Robert Joncas, Executive Director, 604-294-3050 Ext. 102
executivedirector@sportmedbc.com

Sports à roulettes du Canada *See* Roller Sports Canada

Sports Car Club of British Columbia (SCCBC)
PO Box 3432, 33191 - 1 Ave., Mission BC V2V 4J5
Tel: 778-999-7769
marketing@sccbc.net
www.sccbc.net
www.facebook.com/147929071991449

Canadian Associations / Sports Laval

twitter.com/SCC_BC
www.youtube.com/user/BSpecRacing
Overview: A small provincial charitable organization founded in 1951
Mission: To organize safe road race competition; to promote safe road conduct & to foster sportsmanship
Finances: *Funding Sources:* Race entries; sponsors; membership dues
Membership: 300; *Fees:* $60 annually + $25 family members; $25 associate; *Committees:* Track Operations; Race Drivers; Executives
Chief Officer(s):
Steve Hocaluk, President
president@sccbc.net

Sports Laval
#221, 3235, St-Martin est, Laval QC H7E 5G8
Tél: 450-664-1917
info@sportslaval.qc.ca
sportslaval.qc.ca
www.facebook.com/jdq.laval
twitter.com/SportsLaval
Également appelé: RSEQ Laval
Merged from: Association régionale du sport étudiant de Laval; La Commission Sports Laval
Aperçu: *Dimension:* petite; *Envergure:* locale; fondée en 2003
Mission: Mettre en ouvre des actions permettant aux différents sports de prendre place dans les communautés urbaines et scolaires lavalloises
Membre de: Réseau du sport étudiant du Québec
Affiliation(s): Réseau du sport étudiant du Québec
Membre(s) du bureau directeur:
Martin Savoie, Directeur général, 450-664-1917 Ext. 204
martin@sportslaval.qc.ca

Sports universitaires de l'Ontario *See* Ontario University Athletics

Sports-Québec
4545, av Pierre-de Coubertin, Montréal QC H1V 3R2
Tél: 514-252-3114; *Téléc:* 514-254-9621
sports@sportsquebec.com
www.sportsquebec.com
www.facebook.com/sportsquebec
twitter.com/sportsquebec
Aperçu: *Dimension:* moyenne; *Envergure:* provinciale; Organisme sans but lucratif; fondée en 1988
Mission: Assurer la synergie de ses membres et de ses partenaires du système sportif québécois et du système sportif canadien pour favoriser le développement et l'épanouissement de l'athlète et la promotion de la pratique sportive
Membre de: Canadian Council of Provincial & Territorial Sport Federation
Membre: 900,000 personnes; *Critères d'admissibilite:* Ordinaires; Régionaux; Affinitaires
Activités: *Stagiaires:* Oui; *Bibliothèque:* Centre de documentation; Not open to public
Membre(s) du bureau directeur:
Alain Deschamps, Directeur général, 514-252-3114 Ext. 3621
adeschamps@sportsquebec.com
Isabelle Ducharme, Directrice, Programmes, 514-252-3114 Ext. 3624
iducharme@sportsquebec.com
Michelle Gendron, Coordonnatrice, Communications stratégiques, 514-252-3114 Ext. 3622
mgendron@sportsquebec.com

Springboard Dance
205 - 8th Ave. SE, 2nd Fl., Calgary AB T2G 0K9
Tel: 403-265-3230
springboardperformance.com
www.facebook.com/springboardYYC
twitter.com/springboardyyc
Overview: A small local charitable organization founded in 1988
Mission: To produce, create & perform intellectually & sensually stimulating modern dance
Affiliation(s): Alberta Dance Alliance; Canadian Dance Federation; Dance Current
Finances: *Funding Sources:* Government
Staff Member(s): 8
Activities: *Awareness Events:* Fluid Festival, October; *Internships:* Yes
Chief Officer(s):
Nicole Mion, Artistic Director & Curator
nicole@springboardperformance.com
Selina Clary, Managing Director
selina@springboardperformance.com

Springdale & Area Chamber of Commerce
PO Box 37, 393 Little Bay Rd., Springdale NL A0J 1T0
Tel: 709-673-3837
info@springdalechamber.com
www.springdalechamber.com
Overview: A small local organization
Mission: To bolster economic development in the area; To promote economic growth; To unify the business community
Membership: 36
Chief Officer(s):
Glenn Seabright, President
Cassandra Caines, Secretary

Springhill & Area Chamber of Commerce
PO Box 1030, Springhill NS B0M 1X0
Tel: 902-597-8614
www.springhillchamber.ca
Overview: A small local organization
Mission: To protect the interests of local businesses
Member of: Atlantic Provinces Chamber of Commerce
Membership: 37; *Fees:* $20 individual; $50 corporate
Chief Officer(s):
Marcie Meekins, Secretary

Springtide Resources
#220, 215 Spadina Ave., Toronto ON M5T 2C7
Tel: 416-968-3422; *Fax:* 416-968-2026
info@womanabuseprevention.com
www.springtideresources.org
www.facebook.com/springtide.resources
twitter.com/Springtide_VAW
Previous Name: Education Wife Assault
Overview: A small local charitable organization founded in 1978
Mission: To increase public awareness of the many aspects of violence against women & its effect on children; to change the social conditions that subject women to abuse by providing training & resources proactively.
Member of: Volunteer Centre of Toronto; Association of Fundraising Professionals; Council of Agencies Serving South Asians.
Affiliation(s): The National Action Committee on the Status of Women; Ontario Association of Interval & Transition Houses; Woman Abuse Council of Toronto
Finances: *Funding Sources:* Individual donors; foundations; churches; various levels of government.
Staff Member(s): 8
Membership: *Fees:* $25
Activities: Offering educational & training expertise; workshops & training programs; publications available in wide variety of languages; *Internships:* Yes; *Speaker Service:* Yes; *Library:* Open to public by appointment
Chief Officer(s):
Marsha Sfeir, Executive Director

SPRINT Senior Care
140 Merton St., 2nd Fl., Toronto ON M4S 1A1
Tel: 416-481-0669; *Fax:* 416-481-9829
info@sprintseniorcare.org
sprintseniorcare.org
www.linkedin.com/company/sprint-senior-peoples-resources-in-north-toronto-
www.facebook.com/SPRINT.Senior.Care
twitter.com/SPRINT_Sr_Care
www.youtube.com/user/sprintseniorcare
Overview: A small local charitable organization
Mission: To offer community support services to seniors & their families in North Toronto
Chief Officer(s):
Stacy Landau, Executive Director
Publications:
• SPRINT News
Type: Newsletter; *Frequency:* Monthly

Spruce City Wildlife Association (SCWA)
1384 River Rd., Prince George BC V2L 5S8
Tel: 250-563-5437; *Fax:* 250-563-5438
info@scwa.bc.ca
www.scwa.bc.ca
Overview: A medium-sized local organization founded in 1970
Mission: To perform environmental acts that improve the BC wilderness
Member of: BC Wildlife Federation
Membership: *Fees:* $50 individual; $60 family; $125 corporate; $40 student/senior
Chief Officer(s):
Jim Glaicar, President

Spruce Grove & District Chamber of Commerce
PO Box 4210, 99 Campsite Rd., Spruce Grove AB T7X 3B4
Tel: 780-962-2561; *Fax:* 780-962-4417
info@sprucegrovechamber.com
www.sprucegrovechamber.com
Overview: A small local charitable organization founded in 1963
Mission: To develop a positive environment for successful businesses to profit; To foster confidence, progress & success through the synergy of professionalism, cooperation, respect, astute vision & leadership
Member of: Alberta Chamber of Commerce; Canadian Chamber of Commerce
Finances: *Annual Operating Budget:* $100,000-$250,000
Staff Member(s): 2
Membership: 600; *Fees:* $100-$325
Activities: *Internships:* Yes; *Speaker Service:* Yes; *Rents Mailing List:* Yes; *Library:* Not open to public
Chief Officer(s):
Brenda Johnson, President & CEO
bjohnson@sprucegrovechamber.com
Devyn Smith, Office Administrator

Squamish & District Labour Committee (SDLC)
38161 - 2nd Ave., Squamish BC V0N 3G0
Tel: 604-815-0811; *Fax:* 604-815-0811
Overview: A small local organization overseen by British Columbia Federation of Labour
Mission: To support workers' rights, strong social programs, & a sustainable environment in the Squamish & District region of British Columbia
Affiliation(s): Canadian Labour Congress (CLC)
Activities: Engaging in municipal political action; Liaising with local mayors & council members; Providing labour news for the Squamish area; Organizing a Day of Mourning ceremony to honour workers injured or killed on the job

Squamish & Howe Sound Chamber of Commerce; Chamber of Commerce Serving Squamish, Britannia Beach & Furry Creek *See* Squamish Chamber of Commerce

Squamish Chamber of Commerce
Squamish Adventure Centre, #102, 38551 Loggers Lane, Squamish BC V8B 0H2
Tel: 604-815-4990
admin@squamishchamber.com
www.squamishchamber.com
www.facebook.com/SquamishChamberofCommerce
twitter.com/SquamishChamber
www.youtube.com/spiritofsquamish
Previous Name: Squamish & Howe Sound Chamber of Commerce; Chamber of Commerce Serving Squamish, Britannia Beach & Furry Creek
Overview: A small local charitable organization founded in 1934
Mission: To enhance the quality of life in the community by actively supporting business, economic growth & diversification
Member of: Canadian Chamber of Commerce; BC Chamber of Commerce
Finances: *Annual Operating Budget:* $250,000-$500,000; *Funding Sources:* Membership dues; fundraising; contracts
Staff Member(s): 3; 13 volunteer(s)
Membership: 400; *Fees:* $105-$470; *Committees:* Finance; Governance; Membership; Policy
Activities: Operating Visitors Info Centre; *Library:* Reference Library; Open to public
Chief Officer(s):
Louise Walker, Executive Director
louise@squamishchamber.com

Squamish Food Bank
PO Box 207, Garibaldi Highlands BC V0N 1T0
Tel: 604-815-4054
squamishfoodbank@gmail.com
www.squamishfoodbank.com
Overview: A small local charitable organization overseen by Food Banks British Columbia
Mission: To provide food to community members experiencing hardship
Member of: Food Banks British Columbia

Square & Round Dance Federation of Nova Scotia
c/o Gary & Dottie Welch, 415 Conrad Rd., Lawrencetown NS B2Z 1S3
Tel: 902-435-4544
www.chebucto.ns.ca
Overview: A small provincial organization founded in 1983 overseen by Canadian Square & Round Dance Society

Mission: To provide liaison between clubs & the provincial government; To suggest guidelines & provide an organizational framework for operating & coordinating activities of member clubs; To encourage cooperation in advertising, promoting & operating Square & Round Dance classes throughout the province of Nova Scotia; To support & supplement the work of the Association of Nova Scotia Square & Round Dance Teachers
Affiliation(s): Dance Nova Scotia
Membership: 20+ member clubs; *Fees:* Schedule available; *Member Profile:* Couples interested in square & round dancing
Chief Officer(s):
Dottie Welch, Secretary
dwelch@eastlink.ca

Squash Alberta (SA)
3415 - 3rd Ave. NW, Calgary AB T2N 0M4
Tel: 403-270-7344
Toll-Free: 877-646-6566
membership@squashalberta.com
www.squashalberta.com
www.facebook.com/squashab
twitter.com/SquashAB
Previous Name: Alberta Squash Racquets Association
Overview: A medium-sized provincial charitable organization founded in 1967 overseen by Squash Canada
Mission: To promote & facilitate the development of the sport of squash in Alberta
Member of: Squash Canada
Finances: *Annual Operating Budget:* $250,000-$500,000; *Funding Sources:* Membership dues; programs; government grants; Alberta Sport Connection
Staff Member(s): 2; 12 volunteer(s)
Membership: 1,850; *Fees:* $55 adult; $50 junior; $130 family
Chief Officer(s):
Grant Currie, President
currieg@shaw.ca
Tim Landeryou, Executive Director
tim@squashalberta.com
Arthur Hough, Coach, High Performance
arthur@squashalberta.com
Awards:
• Zac Ezekowitz Memorial Scholarship
Eligibility: Active U19 squash players *Deadline:* November; *Amount:* $1,000

Squash British Columbia
Vancouver Racquets Club, 4867 Ontario St., Vancouver BC V5V 3H4
Tel: 604-737-3084; *Fax:* 604-736-3527
info@squashbc.com
www.squashbc.com
www.facebook.com/squashbc
twitter.com/squashbc
www.instagram.com/squashbc
Overview: A medium-sized provincial organization overseen by Squash Canada
Mission: To promote the growth of squash by providing orderly development opportunities for athletes, & encouraging participation through a variety of programs & activities organized by Squash BC & its partners
Member of: Sport BC; Squash Canada
Membership: *Fees:* $44 individual; $20 young adult (19-24); $15 junior (under 18)
Activities: *Library:*
Chief Officer(s):
Christine Bradstock, Executive Director
executivedirector@squashbc.com

Squash Canada
20 Jamie Ave., 2nd Fl., Nepean ON K2E 6T6
Tel: 613-228-7724; *Fax:* 613-228-7232
info@squash.ca
www.squash.ca
www.facebook.com/squashcanada
twitter.com/squashcanada
www.instagram.com/squashcanada
Previous Name: Canadian Squash Racquets Association
Overview: A large national charitable organization founded in 1915
Mission: To develop athletes, coaches & officials in the sport of squash; To set standards for squash in Canada; To promote growth & development in the sport across the country
Member of: Canadian Olympic Committee; Coaching Association of Canada; Commonwealth Games Canada; Pan American Squash Federation; World Squash Federation
Finances: *Annual Operating Budget:* $500,000-$1.5 Million; *Funding Sources:* Government; Donations; Sponsorships; Events; Sales
Staff Member(s): 4; 150 volunteer(s)
Membership: 8,500; *Fees:* Schedule available; *Member Profile:* Provincial/territorial clubs & members; *Committees:* High Performance; Squash Canada Officiating; Governance Review; Finance & Audit; Junior Development; Doubles; Masters; Patrons Fund; Community Endowment Fund; Nominations; Competitions; Coaching; Canada Games; Doubles Competition; Doubles Officiating
Activities: Participating in national championships, as well as world championships & other international events; Providing coach & officials development; Marketing & promoting squash; Establishing & maintaining rules & regulations; *Internships:* Yes
Chief Officer(s):
Lolly Gillen, President
Dan Wolfenden, Executive Director, 613-228-7724 Ext. 201
Jamie Hickox, Director, Performance
performance@squash.ca
Britany Gordon, Manager, Programs, 613-228-7724 Ext. 202
britany.gordon@squash.ca

Squash Manitoba
145 Pacific Ave., Winnipeg MB R3B 2Z6
Tel: 204-925-5661; *Fax:* 204-925-5792
squash@sportmanitoba.ca
www.squashmb.org
twitter.com/squashmanitoba
Overview: A medium-sized provincial organization overseen by Squash Canada
Mission: To promote the game of squash in Manitoba; To establish & enforce rules & programs for all levels of play
Member of: Squash Canada
Affiliation(s): Brandon squash & athletic centre; Dauphin Squash Club; University of Winnipeg; Winnipeg Squash Racquet Club; Winnipeg Winter Club
Membership: *Fees:* $20
Chief Officer(s):
Lynn Colliou, Executive Director

Squash Newfoundland & Labrador Inc.
PO Box 21254, St. John's NL A1A 5B2
hongngee@gmail.com
www.hongngee.com/squashnl
Also Known As: Squash NL
Overview: A small provincial organization overseen by Squash Canada
Mission: To coordinate & promote the sport of squash in Newfoundland & Labrador.
Member of: Squash Canada

Squash Nova Scotia
PO Box 3010, Stn. Park Lane Centre, #401, 5516 Spring Garden Rd., Halifax NS B3J 3G6
Tel: 902-425-5450; *Fax:* 902-425-5606
www.squashns.ca
Overview: A medium-sized provincial organization overseen by Squash Canada
Mission: Fosters & promotes a squash community for players of all abilities from across the province to improve the profile of the sport & its enjoyment by its members.
Member of: Squash Canada
Finances: *Annual Operating Budget:* Less than $50,000
Membership: 100-499; *Fees:* $20 student; $25 adult
Chief Officer(s):
Alfred Seaman, President
alfieseaman@gmail.com

Squash Ontario
c/o Glendon College, Proctor Field House, #226, 2275 Bayview Ave., Toronto ON M4N 1J8
Fax: 416-426-7393
admin@squashontario.com
www.squashontario.com
www.facebook.com/SquashOntario
twitter.com/SquashOntario
Overview: A medium-sized provincial organization founded in 1976 overseen by Squash Canada
Mission: To act as the governing body for the sport of squash in Ontario; To develop & promote the sport of squash across Ontario; To provide an environment in which the sport of squash can thrive; To meet the needs of present & potential players
Membership: *Committees:* Junior Advisory; High Performance; Masters'
Activities: Developing squash players, from beginners to elite athletes, as well as teams, coaches, & officials; Establishing & maintaining technical standards
Chief Officer(s):
Janice Lardner, President
board@squashontario.com
Jamie Nicholls, Executive Director, 416-426-7202
jmnicholls@squashontario.com
Lauren Sachvie, Coordinator, Programs, 416-426-7201
programs@squashontario.com
Awards:
• Mark Sachvie Coaching Achievement Award
To recognize outstanding coaches in Ontario
• Simon Warder Officiating Achievement Award
• Jim Mason Fair Play Award
• Corporate Achievement Award
• Outstanding Achievement Award

Squash PEI
PE
Overview: A small provincial organization overseen by Squash Canada
Mission: To promote squash in PEI; to provide competitive opportunities for members
Member of: Squash Canada; Sport PEI Inc.

Squash Québec
4545, av Pierre-de Coubertin, Montréal QC H1V 0B2
Tél: 514-252-3062
info@sports-4murs.qc.ca
www.squash.qc.ca
www.facebook.com/SquashQuebec
Aperçu: *Dimension:* petite; *Envergure:* provinciale surveillé par Squash Canada
Mission: Promouvoir le développement du Squash au Québec en offrant différentes opportunités aux adeptes, tout en encourageant la participation sportive à travers un ensemble de services et de programmes
Membre de: Squash Canada
Finances: *Budget de fonctionnement annuel:* $50,000-$100,000
Membre(s) du personnel: 2; 20 bénévole(s)
Membre: 5,000-14,999
Activités: *Stagiaires:* Oui
Membre(s) du bureau directeur:
Michel Séguin, Directeur général

Squash Yukon
YT
squashyukon.yk.ca
Overview: A small provincial organization overseen by Squash Canada
Member of: Squash Canada

Standardbred Breeders of Ontario Association (SBOA)
PO Box 371, Rockwood ON N0B 2K0
Tel: 519-856-4431
www.standardbredbreeders.com
Previous Name: Ontario Standardbred Improvement Association
Overview: A small provincial organization
Mission: To advocate on behalf of breeders; to establish races; to educate breeders
Membership: *Fees:* $22.60
Activities: Annual banquet; holds races; regular column in Canadian Sportsman; New Owners Mentoring Program
Chief Officer(s):
Walter Perkinson, President
Aimee Adams, Secretary-Treasurer & Administrator
aimee@sboa.info
Awards:
• Breeders Awards

Standardbred Canada (SC)
2150 Meadowvale Blvd., Mississauga ON L5N 6R6
Tel: 905-858-3060; *Fax:* 905-858-3111
www.standardbredcanada.ca
www.facebook.com/standardbred.canada
twitter.com/TrotInsider
www.youtube.com/user/jporchak
Merged from: The Canadian Trotting Association; The Canadian Standardbred Horse Society
Overview: A medium-sized national organization founded in 1909
Mission: To encourage & develop the breeding of Standardbred Horses

Finances: *Annual Operating Budget:* $3 Million-$5 Million; *Funding Sources:* Membership & registration fees; horse sales
Staff Member(s): 45
Membership: 13,135; *Committees:* Executive; Audit; Breeders
Activities: *Rents Mailing List:* Yes; *Library:* Standardbred Canada Library; Open to public
Chief Officer(s):
Dan Gall, President & CEO
dgall@standardbredcanada.ca
Linda Bedard, Manager & Registrar, Member Services
lbedard@standardbredcanada.ca
Publications:
• Trot [a publication of Standardbred Canada]
Type: Magazine; *Editor:* Darryl Kaplan

Stanley Park Ecology Society (SPES)
PO Box 5167, Vancouver BC V6B 4B2
Tel: 604-257-6908; *Fax:* 604-257-8378
info@stanleyparkecology.ca
www.stanleyparkecology.ca
www.facebook.com/StanleyPkEcoSoc
twitter.com/StanleyPkEcoSoc
Overview: A small local organization founded in 1988
Mission: To encourage stewardship of our natural world through environmental education & action & by fostering awareness of the fragile balance that exists between urban populations & nature
Membership: *Fees:* $20 individual; $15 senior/junior/volunteer; $40 family
Chief Officer(s):
Patricia Thomson, Executive Director, 604-718-6523
exec@stanleyparkecology.ca

Stanstead Historical Society (SHS) / Musée Colby-Curtis
535, rue Dufferin, Stanstead QC J0B 3E0
Tel: 819-876-7322; *Fax:* 819-876-7936
Other Communication: archives@colbycurtis.ca
info@colbycurtis.ca
www.colbycurtis.ca
Also Known As: The Colby-Curtis Museum/Carrollcroft
Overview: A small local charitable organization founded in 1929
Mission: To collect, preserve & pass on a knowledge & appreciation of all the people who have ever called the Border Region home
Member of: Canadian Museums Association; Société des musées quebecois
Affiliation(s): Fédération des sociétés d'histoire du Québec
Finances: *Annual Operating Budget:* $250,000-$500,000
Staff Member(s): 9; 25 volunteer(s)
Membership: 417; *Fees:* $15 individual; $20 family; $300 life; *Member Profile:* Seniors, local people & Americans
Activities: Victorian Tea Room & Garden; Boutique; *Internships:* Yes; *Speaker Service:* Yes; *Library:* Stanstead Historical Society Library; by appointment
Chief Officer(s):
Sophie Cormier, Museum Director

Starbright Children's Development Centre
1546 Bernard Ave., Kelowna BC V1Y 6R9
Tel: 250-763-5100; *Fax:* 250-862-8433
Toll-Free: 877-763-5100
info@starbrightokanagan.ca
iwishimight.ca
www.facebook.com/iwishimight
www.pinterest.com/starbrightchild
Previous Name: Central Okanagan Child Development Association; Okanagan Neurological Association
Overview: A medium-sized local charitable organization founded in 1966
Mission: To support families in promoting the optimum development of children with challenges
Affiliation(s): British Colombia Association of Child Development Centres
Membership: *Member Profile:* Individuals; family; corporate
Activities: Speech; physiotherapy; occupational therapy; infant development; autism program
Chief Officer(s):
Rhonda Nelson, Executive Director

Starlight Children's Foundation Canada
#105, 1375, rte Transcanadienne, Dorval QC H9P 2W8
Toll-Free: 888-782-7947
info@starlightcanada.org
www.starlightcanada.org
www.linkedin.com/groups?gid=1414967
www.facebook.com/starlightcanada
twitter.com/StarlightCanada
www.youtube.com/CanadaStarlight
Overview: A medium-sized national charitable organization
Mission: To brighten the lives of seriously ill children & their families by providing both in-hospital & out-patient programs to enhance their ability to cope with the stress of illness
Chief Officer(s):
Brian J.H. Bringolf, Executive Director
brian.bringolf@starlightcanada.ca
Trevor Dicaire, Vice-President
trevor.dicaire@starlightcanada.org
Jeannie O'Regan, Vice-President, Special Events & Operations
jeannie.oregan@starlightcanada.org
Michele Vantrepote, Manager, Communications
Palermo Coronado, Coordinator, Finance
  British Columbia Chapter
  Odd Fellows' Hall, 1443 West 8th Ave., Vancouver BC V6H 1C9
  Tel: 604-742-0272; *Fax:* 604-742-0274
  infovancouver@starlightcanada.org
  Chief Officer(s):
  Heather Burnett, Regional Coordinator
  heather@starlightcanada.org
  Calgary Chapter
  8 Mount Norquay Gate SE, Calgary AB T2Z 2L3
  Tel: 403-457-0344; *Fax:* 403-457-0384
  Toll-Free: 800-880-1004
  infocalgary@starlightcanada.org
  Chief Officer(s):
  Laura Stow, Regional Coordinator
  laura.stow@starlightcanada.org
  Montréal Chapter
  105, 1375, rte Transcanadienne, Dorval QC H9P 2W8
  Tel: 514-288-9474; *Fax:* 514-287-0635
  Toll-Free: 888-782-7947
  starlight@starlightquebec.org
  www.starlightquebec.org
  Chief Officer(s):
  Brian J.H. Bringolf, Executive Director
  brian@starlightquebec.org

Start Right Coalition for Financial Literacy
PO Box 384, Pembroke ON K8A 6X6
Tel: 613-638-4313
Overview: A small local organization founded in 1998
Mission: To improve the financial literacy skills of youth ages 15 to 24
Activities: Seminars to youth; website resources; newsletter; *Speaker Service:* Yes
Chief Officer(s):
Michael Gulliver, Contact

Start2Finish
1295 North Service Rd., Burlington ON L7R 4M2
Tel: 905-319-1885; *Fax:* 905-319-3413
Toll-Free: 888-320-8844
info@start2finishonline.org
start2finishonline.org
www.facebook.com/Start2FinishOnline
twitter.com/EmpowrKids4Life
www.youtube.com/user/START2FINISHonline
Previous Name: Kidsfest
Overview: A small local organization founded in 2000
Mission: To provide the most vulnerable school children in grades 1 to 6 in Canada with school supplies, hygiene items & gift certificates for school clothing & shoes
Staff Member(s): 6
Activities: KidsFest Festival to raise money for our activities; annual dinner & auction; Spring Break - Reading Week; *Internships:* Yes; *Speaker Service:* Yes
Chief Officer(s):
Tracey Brophy, Chair
Brian Warren, CEO & Founder

Startup Canada
#300, 56 Sparks St., Ottawa ON K1P 5A9
Tel: 613-627-0787
hello@startupcan.ca
www.startupcan.ca
www.linkedin/groups/Startup-Canada-Campaign-3895252
www.facebook.com/startupcanada
twitter.com/Startup_Canada
youtube.com/user/StartupCanada;
flickr.com/photos/62463248@N06
Overview: A large national organization founded in 2012
Mission: To be a national, grassroots, non-profit organization dedicated to strengthening & enhancing Canada's entrepreneurial culture
250 volunteer(s)
Membership: 55,000 entrepreneurs + 400 partner organizations
Activities: Resources for Canadian entrepreneurs, including the Startup Connect network (www.startupconnect.ca)
Chief Officer(s):
Brenda Halloran, Chair
Victoria Lennox, Co-Founder & CEO
Cyprian Szalankiewicz, Co-Founder & Manager, Production

Station Arts Centre Cooperative
PO Box 1078, Rosthern SK S0K 3R0
Tel: 306-232-5332; *Fax:* 306-232-5406
info@stationarts.com
www.stationarts.com
www.facebook.com/StationArts
Overview: A small local charitable organization founded in 1990
Mission: To promote the arts through education
Member of: Organization of Saskatchewan Arts Councils; Saskatchewan Arts Alliance; Saskatchewan Craft Council; Sask Culture; SK History & Folklore Society; Sask Tourism
Finances: *Annual Operating Budget:* $100,000-$250,000; *Funding Sources:* Federal & provincial grants; donations; rental; fundraising; tea room
Staff Member(s): 1; 50 volunteer(s)
Membership: 150; *Fees:* $15; *Committees:* Education; Fundraising; Maintenance; Performing; Tea Room; Theatre; Visual
Activities: Summer theatre; Christmas dinner concerts; winter concert series; spring concerts; juried art exhibits; tea room

Stationery & Office Equipment Guild of Canada Inc.; Stationers' Guild of Canada Inc. *See* Canadian Office Products Association

Statistical Society of Canada (SSC) / Société statistique du Canada
#209, 1725 St. Laurent Blvd., Ottawa ON K1G 3V4
Tel: 613-733-2662; *Fax:* 613-733-1386
Other Communication: admin@ssc.ca
info@ssc.ca
www.ssc.ca
Overview: A medium-sized national organization founded in 1977
Mission: To promote the development & use of statistics & probability; To ensure that decisions that affect society are based upon valid & appropriate statistics & interpretation; To encourage high standards for statistical education & practice
Membership: 900+; *Fees:* $15 students; $35 retired persons, spouses of regular members; $12510 regular membership; *Member Profile:* Canadian statisticians; *Committees:* Bilingualism; Election; Executive; Finance; Program; Publications; Accreditation; Accreditation Appeal; Awards; Award for Case Studies and Data Analysis; The Canadian Journal of Statistics Award; CRM-SSC Prize; Pierre Robillard Award; SSC Award for Impact of Applied & Collaborative Work; Student Presentation Award; Membership; Women in Statistics; Public Relations; Research; Statistical Education; AusCan Scholar; The Canadian Journal of Statistics Transition; Assessment of Meeting Arrangements; New Investigators; NSERC Liaison; Student Travel Awards
Activities: Increasing public awareness of the value of statistical thinking; Facilitating the exchange of ideas within the Canadian statistics community
Chief Officer(s):
John Brewster, President
president@ssc.ca
John J. Koval, Treasurer
treasurer@ssc.ca
Julie Trépanier, Executive Secretary
secretary@ssc.ca
Awards:
• CRM-SSC Prize
• Founder Recognition Award
• Honorary Members Award
• SSC Service Award
• SSC Gold Medalists Award
• Pierre-Robillard Award
• The Canadian Journal of Statistics Award
Meetings/Conferences:
• Statistical Society of Canada 2018 Annual Meeting, June, 2018, McGill University, Montréal, QC
Scope: National

- Joint Statistical Meetings 2018, July, 2018, Vancouver, BC
Scope: International
Description: Held jointly with the Statistical Society of Canada, American Statistical Association, the International Biometric Society (ENAR & WNAR), the International Chinese Statistical Association, the Institute of Mathematical Statistics, & the International Indian Statistical Association
Publications:
- The Canadian Journal of Statistics / La revue canadienne de statistique
Type: Journal; *Frequency:* Quarterly; *Editor:* George P.H. Styan & Paul Gustafson; *Price:* $260
Profile: Research articles of interest to the statistical community
- SSC Handbook / Manuel de la SSC
Type: Handbook; *Number of Pages:* 98; *Editor:* Paul Cabilio
- SSC Liaison
Type: Newsletter; *Frequency:* Quarterly; *Accepts Advertising*; *Editor:* Larry K. Weldon
Profile: Society reports, announcements, conferences, & employment opportunities
- Statistical Society of Canada Membership Directory
Type: Directory
- Statistics Surveys
Editor: Richard Lockhart

Status of Women Council of the Northwest Territories (SWC)
Northwest Tower, 4th Fl., PO Box 1320, Yellowknife NT X1A 2L9
Tel: 867-920-6177; *Fax:* 867-873-0285
Toll-Free: 888-234-4485
council@statusofwomen.nt.ca
www.statusofwomen.nt.ca
www.facebook.com/113623588652526
twitter.com/StatusofWomenNT
www.youtube.com/user/statusofwomennwt
Overview: A medium-sized provincial organization founded in 1990
Mission: To work towards equality for all NWT women, through public education & awareness, research, advocacy, community development, interagency cooperation, advice to government, & identification & development of opportunities for women
Member of: Status of Women Canada
Finances: *Annual Operating Budget:* $250,000-$500,000
Staff Member(s): 4
Membership: *Member Profile:* Represents all women through regional board members
Activities: *Awareness Events:* International Women's Day, March 8; Take Back the Night, Sept. 21; Family Violence Awareness Week, Oct.; *Library:* Open to public
Chief Officer(s):
Samantha Thomas, Executive Director, 867-920-8929
samantha@statusofwomen.nt.ca
Annemieke Mulders, Director, Program, Research & Advocacy, 867-920-8994
am@statusofwomen.nt.ca
Roxane Landry, Office Administrator
roxane@statusofwomen.nt.ca
Awards:
- Wise Woman Award

St-Boniface Chamber of Commerce *Voir* Chambre de commerce francophone de Saint-Boniface

Ste Rose & District Chamber of Commerce
PO Box 688, Ste Rose du Lac MB R0L 1S0
Tel: 204-447-2621; *Fax:* 204-447-3024
Overview: A small local organization founded in 1989
Mission: To represent & be the voice of the business community
Finances: *Annual Operating Budget:* Less than $50,000; *Funding Sources:* Membership dues; fundraising
Staff Member(s): 1
Membership: 57; *Fees:* $80 company; $25 single; *Committees:* Main Street; Citizen on Patrol

Steel Structures Education Foundation
#200, 3760 14th Ave., Markham ON L3R 3T7
Tel: 905-944-1390; *Fax:* 905-946-8574
info@ssef-ffca.ca
www.ssef-ffca.ca
Overview: A small national organization founded in 1985
Mission: To further the application & use of steel in structures, through education; to produce educational videos on steel construction, in English & French
Affiliation(s): Canadian Institute of Steel Construction; Canadian Steel Construction Council

Staff Member(s): 6
Membership: 22 institutional
Chief Officer(s):
David MacKinnon, Executive Director

Steelworkers Organization of Active Retirees (SOAR)
234 Eglinton Ave. East, 8th Fl., Toronto ON M4P 1K7
Tel: 416-487-1571; *Fax:* 416-482-5548
Toll-Free: 877-669-8792
info@usw.ca
www.usw.ca
Overview: A medium-sized national organization founded in 1985
Mission: To deal with the social, economic, educational, legislative & political developments & concerns of its members & spouses; to fight for the preservation of Social Security, Medicare, better health care protection, as well as for federal laws to better serve the elderly
Affiliation(s): United Steelworkers of America
Membership: *Fees:* $12
Chief Officer(s):
Doug MacPherson, National Coordinator
dmacpherson@usw.ca

Steinbach Arts Council (SAC)
PO Box 3639, 304 - 2nd Ave., Steinbach MB R0A 2A0
Tel: 204-346-1077; *Fax:* 204-346-9777
www.steinbachartscouncil.ca
Overview: A small local organization founded in 1979
Mission: To enhance our quality of life through the arts
Member of: Manitoba Association of Community Arts Councils Inc.
Finances: *Annual Operating Budget:* $100,000-$250,000
Staff Member(s): 4; 150 volunteer(s)
Membership: 300; *Fees:* $10 individual; $25 family; $30 affiliates; $100 corporate; *Member Profile:* Performing & visual artists & students; general public
Activities: Performing & visual arts in 60 programs as well as concert series; art & performing art programs
Chief Officer(s):
Cindi Rempel-Patrick, Executive Director
director@steinbachartscouncil.ca

Steinbach Chamber of Commerce
284 Reimer Ave., #D4, Steinbach MB R5G 0R5
Tel: 204-326-9566; *Fax:* 204-346-3638
info@steinbachchamber.com
www.steinbachchamber.com
www.facebook.com/SteinbachChamber
twitter.com/StbchChamber
Overview: A small local organization founded in 1954
Mission: To represent businesses in the area; To lead economic development & improve quality of life for the community
Member of: Manitoba Chamber of Commerce
Finances: *Annual Operating Budget:* Less than $50,000
Staff Member(s): 1
Membership: 313; *Fees:* Schedule available
Chief Officer(s):
Cameron Bergen, President
Linda Peters, Executive Director
lindap@steinbachchamber.com

Stem Cell Network (SCN) / Réseau de cellules souches
PO Box 611, 501 Smyth Rd., Ottawa ON K1H 8L6
Tel: 613-739-6674
info@stemcellnetwork.ca
www.stemcellnetwork.ca
www.facebook.com/CanadianStemCellNetwork
twitter.com/StemCellNetwork
vimeo.com/stemcellnetwork
Overview: A medium-sized national organization founded in 2001
Mission: To investigate the immense therapeutic potential of stem cells for the treatment of diseases currently incurable by conventional approaches
Member of: Networks of Centres of Excellence
Staff Member(s): 8
Membership: *Committees:* Research Management
Chief Officer(s):
Philip Welford, Executive Director
pwelford@stemcellnetwork.ca
Cate Murray, Director, Communications & External Affairs
catemurray@stemcellnetwork.ca

Shannon Sethuram, Director, Finance & Research Administration
ssethuram@stemcellnetwork.ca
Janetta Bijl, Director, Science
jbijl@stemcellnetwork.ca
Rebecca Cadwalader, Manager, Research & Training
rcadwalader@stemcellnetwork.ca

Step-By-Step Child Development Society
PO Box 47601, Stn. Blue Mountain, Coquitlam BC V3K 6T3
Tel: 604-931-1977
www.step-by-step.ca
Overview: A small local charitable organization founded in 1979
Mission: To provide preschool education to children requiring extra supports; To operate an equipment loans cupboard for children requiring specialized equipment; To provide physiotherapy & occupational therapy services to children; To provide outreach support services to neighbourhood child care centres; To promote inclusion of children needing extra supports
Member of: British Columbia Association Child Development & Rehabilitation
Finances: *Funding Sources:* User fees
Membership: *Member Profile:* Parents; early childhood professionals
Activities: Public education; early intervention; *Library:* Step-by-Step Community Resource Room; Open to public
Chief Officer(s):
Carla Arrano, Manager

Stephan G. Stephansson Icelandic Society
PO Box 837, Markerville AB T0M 1M0
Tel: 403-728-3006; *Fax:* 403-728-3225
Toll-Free: 877-728-3007
admin@historicmarkerville.com
www.historicmarkerville.com
Also Known As: Historic Markerville Creamery
Overview: A small local charitable organization founded in 1974
Mission: To preserve & interpret history; to promote culture & community fellowship
Member of: Alberta Museums Association
Affiliation(s): Canadian Museums Association; Icelandic National League
Finances: *Annual Operating Budget:* $100,000-$250,000; *Funding Sources:* Fundraising; bingos; casino; donations
Staff Member(s): 1; 60 volunteer(s)
Membership: 150; *Fees:* $10 individual; $20 family; *Committees:* Finance/Budget Process; Policy; Personnel; Fundraising; Icelandic National League; Membership; Icelandic Picnic/Fjallkona; Gift Shop; Coffee Shop; Newsletter; Sponsorship; Volunteer Appreciation; Cheer; Truck; Insurance; Special Request; Museums Alberta; Promotion; Volunteer Management
Activities: Owns & operates the historic Markerville Creamery & Fensala Hall; auction; Icelandic picnic; Cream Day; Pioneer Days; Volunteer Breakfast; Christmas in Markerville; *Awareness Events:* Cream Day, Aug. 12
Chief Officer(s):
Donna Nelson, President, 403-728-3438

Stephen Leacock Associates
PO Box 854, Orillia ON L3V 6K8
Tel: 705-835-3218; *Fax:* 705-835-5171
www.leacock.ca
www.facebook.com/148060321915484
twitter.com/leacockmedal
Overview: A small national organization founded in 1946
Mission: To honour & promote Stephen Leacock & his body of writing
Membership: *Fees:* $25 single; $35 family; *Committees:* Awards; Awards Dinner; Archives; Membership; Newspacket/Order of Mariposa; Planning; Publicity; Website & Social Media
Chief Officer(s):
Michael Hill, President
mghill@rogers.com
Awards:
- The Order of Mariposa
Awarded occasionally to someone who has contributed significantly to humour in Canada, in other than the written word
- Stephen Leacock Memorial Medal
Established 1946 to encourage the writing & publishing of humorous works in Canada; given annually for the best Canadian book of humour published in the preceding year; *Amount:* Winner receives the medal & a cash award of $10,000 donated by TD Canada Trust

Stephenville Chamber of Commerce *See* Bay St. George Chamber of Commerce

Stettler & District Chamber of Commerce *See* Stettler Regional Board of Trade & Community Development

Stettler Regional Board of Trade & Community Development
6606 - 50th Ave., Stettler AB T0C 2L2
Tel: 403-742-3181; *Fax:* 403-742-3123
Toll-Free: 877-742-9499
info@stettlerboardoftrade.com
www.stettlerboardoftrade.com
www.facebook.com/StettlerRegionalBoardofTrade
twitter.com/StettlerBOT
www.youtube.com/user/StettlerBoardofTrade
Previous Name: Stettler & District Chamber of Commerce
Overview: A small local charitable organization founded in 1905
Mission: To work together to improve & promote trade, commerce & tourism & the economic, civil & social welfare of the district
Member of: Alberta Chambers of Commerce
Staff Member(s): 3
Activities: AGM; Awards Banquet; Trade Show; Christmas Cash Cards Promotion; Santa Days; Tourist Information Centre
Chief Officer(s):
Matt Dorsett, President, 403-742-5600
Stacey Benjamin, Executive Director
s.benjamin@stettlerboardoftrade.com

Stewart Historical Society
PO Box 402, 703 Brightwell St., Stewart BC V0T 1W0
Tel: 250-636-2568
stewartbcmuseum@gmail.com
Also Known As: Stewart Museum Infocenter
Overview: A small local charitable organization founded in 1976
Member of: North By NorthWest Tourism Association
Membership: *Fees:* $15 family; $10 adult; $7 student; $100 lifetime

Stewart-Hyder International Chamber of Commerce
PO Box 306, Stewart BC V0T 1W0
Tel: 250-636-9224; *Fax:* 250-636-2199
Overview: A small local organization founded in 1984
Member of: BC Chamber of Commerce; Northern BC Tourism Association; Better Business Bureau of Mainland BC; Yellowhead Highway Association; Ketchikan Visitors Bureaux
Finances: *Annual Operating Budget:* Less than $50,000; *Funding Sources:* Membership dues; municipal government
Membership: 50; *Fees:* $25 individual; $35-100 business
Activities: *Speaker Service:* Yes

Stonewall & District Chamber of Commerce
PO Box 762, Stonewall MB R0C 2Z0
Tel: 204-467-8377
info@stonewallchamber.com
www.stonewallchamber.com
www.facebook.com/234810063371029
twitter.com/StonewallCoC
Overview: A small local organization
Mission: To represent businesses & associations of all sizes in Stonewall & District
Finances: *Annual Operating Budget:* Less than $50,000
5 volunteer(s)
Membership: 60; *Fees:* $122.50
Chief Officer(s):
Stephanie Duncan, Director
ads@stonewallteulontribune.ca

Stoney Creek Chamber of Commerce
21 Mountain Ave. South, Stoney Creek ON L8G 2V5
Tel: 905-664-4000; *Fax:* 905-664-7228
admin@chamberstoneycreek.com
www.chamberstoneycreek.com
www.linkedin.com/company/stoney-creek-chamber-of-commerce
www.facebook.com/chamberstoneycreek
twitter.com/CCStoneyCreek
www.youtube.com/ChamberStoneyCreek
Also Known As: Chambera Stoney Creek
Overview: A small local licensing organization founded in 1949
Mission: To grow businesses; To enhance & promote trade & commerce
Member of: Canadian Chamber of Commerce; Ontario Chamber of Commerce
Finances: *Annual Operating Budget:* $50,000-$100,000; *Funding Sources:* Membership dues
Staff Member(s): 1; 20 volunteer(s)
Membership: 400; *Fees:* $125-$300; *Member Profile:* Businesses in the area; *Committees:* Business Development; Citizen of the Year; Communications & Marketing; Governance; Strategic Planning
Activities: *Awareness Events:* Citizen of the Year, May
Chief Officer(s):
Arnold Strub, Executive Director

Stoney Creek Historical Society (SCHS)
PO Box 66637, Stoney Creek ON L8G 5E6
archives@stoneycreekhistorical.com
www.stoneycreekhistorical.ca
Overview: A small local charitable organization founded in 1908
Membership: *Fees:* $10 individual; $18 family; $25 business
Activities: Battle of Stoney Creek re-enactment; monthly meetings Sept.-June with guest speakers; field trips to historical points of interest; *Library:* Stoney Creek Historical Society Library; by appointment
Chief Officer(s):
Greg Armstrong, President
president@stoneycreekhistorical.ca

Stony Plain & District Chamber of Commerce
4815 - 44 Ave., Stony Plain AB T7Z 1V5
Tel: 780-963-4545; *Fax:* 780-963-4542
info@stonyplainchamber.ca
www.stonyplainchamber.ca
www.facebook.com/StonyPlainChamber
twitter.com/StonyChamber
Overview: A small local organization
Mission: To be a proactive leader & advocate for the promotion of business & community
Member of: Alberta Chamber of Commerce
Finances: *Annual Operating Budget:* $100,000-$250,000; *Funding Sources:* Membership dues; fundraising
Staff Member(s): 2; 20 volunteer(s)
Membership: 480+; *Fees:* Schedule available
Activities: Organizing events such as trade shows, garage sales, & mixers; Providing a community directory; *Awareness Events:* Networking Golf Tournament
Chief Officer(s):
Penny Gould, Executive Director

Stop Abuse in Families Society (SAIF)
#402, 22 Sir Winston Churchill Ave., St. Albert AB T8N 1B4
Tel: 780-460-2195; *Fax:* 780-460-2190
info@stopabuse.ca
www.stopabuse.ca
twitter.com/SAIFSociety
Previous Name: St. Albert Stop Abuse Families Society
Overview: A small local charitable organization founded in 1989
Mission: To provide services to adults in the St. Albert area of Alberta who are experiencing domestic abuse
Finances: *Funding Sources:* Membership fees; Donations; Grants; Fundraising
Staff Member(s): 10
Activities: Offering support groups & confidential counselling services to persons affected by family violence; Partnering with St. Albert Parents' Place Association & Merchant Consulting Services to offer New Directions, a program for children, youth, & mothers who have experienced or witnessed spousal abuse; Providing educational prevention programs to schools & community groups; Offering informational ressources to clients & the public; Engaging in advocacy activities on behalf of persons in abusive relationships; *Library:* St. Albert Stop Abuse Families Society Resource Center; Open to public
Chief Officer(s):
Craig Pilgrim, President
Doreen Slessor, Executive Director
Publications:
• SAIF Notes
Type: Newsletter
Profile: Society news & upcoming events

The Stop Community Food Centre
PO Box 69, Stn. E, Toronto ON M6H 4E1
Tel: 416-652-7867; *Fax:* 416-652-2294
general@thestop.org
www.thestop.org
Overview: A small local charitable organization
Activities: After-School Program; Bake Ovens & Markets; Community Advocacy; Community Cooking; Drop-In; Food Bank; Healthy Beginnings and Family Support; Sustainable Food Systems Education; Urban Agriculture
Chief Officer(s):
Rachel Gray, Executive Director, 416-652-7867 Ext. 223

Stormont, Dundas & Glengarry Historical Society
PO Box 773, Cornwall ON K6H 5T5
Tel: 613-936-0842; *Fax:* 613-936-0798
Overview: A small local charitable organization founded in 1920
Mission: To operate the local archives in the Cornwall Public Library & the United Counties Museum in the Wood House; to research, preserve, promote & inform the public about the history & archaeology of the counties of Stormont, Dundas & Glengarry for present & future generations
Affiliation(s): Ontario Historical Society
Finances: *Annual Operating Budget:* $100,000-$250,000; *Funding Sources:* Government & private
Staff Member(s): 2; 26 volunteer(s)
Membership: 150; *Fees:* $20
Activities: *Library:* Local History Room in the Cornwall Public Library; Open to public by appointment
Chief Officer(s):
Ian Bowering, Curator, The United Counties Museum

Stormont, Dundas & Glengarry Law Association
29 Second St. West, Cornwall ON K6H 1G3
Tel: 613-932-5411; *Fax:* 613-932-0474
Toll-Free: 866-830-9118
sdglaw@on.aibn.com
Overview: A small local organization founded in 1988
Member of: Law Society of Upper Canada
Staff Member(s): 1
Membership: 1-99
Activities: *Library:* Courthouse Library; Not open to public
Chief Officer(s):
Carolyn Goddard, Librarian

Storytellers of Canada / Conteurs du Canada
#201, 192 Spadina Ave., Toronto ON M5T 2C2
admin@storytellers-conteurs.ca
www.storytellers-conteurs.ca
www.facebook.com/210378645661591
twitter.com/storycanada
Overview: A small national organization
Mission: To promote storytelling across Canada; To support storytellers' work; To ensure the development of the art of storytelling
Membership: *Fees:* $45 individuals & organizations; *Member Profile:* Individuals & organizations across Canada who maintain & practice the oral tradition of storytelling
Activities: Advocating for storytellers; Facilitating communication among storytellers; Partnering with international storytelling organizations; Offering professional development opportunities; *Speaker Service:* Yes
Chief Officer(s):
Ruth Stewart-Verger, Co-President
president@sc-cc.com
Donna Stewart, Co-President
president@sc-cc.com
Anne Kaarid, Administrator, 519-372-0623
admin@sc-cc.com
Marva Blackmore, Secretary
secretary@sc-cc.com
Alan Auyeung, Treasurer
treasurer@sc-cc.com
Meetings/Conferences:
• Storytellers of Canada Conference 2018, July, 2018, Peterborough, ON
Scope: National
Description: Theme: "The Honour of One is the Honour of All"
Publications:
• Notice Board
Type: Newsletter; *Frequency:* Monthly; *Editor:* Heather Whaley; *Price:* Free with membership in Storytellers of Canada
Profile: Events, products, & opportunities of interest to storytellers
• Le Raconteur
Type: Newsletter; *Frequency:* 3 pa; *Editor:* Kathy Bennett; *Price:* Free with membership in Storytellers of Canada
Profile: News & information distributed to all members of Storytellers of Canada
• Storytellers of Canada - Conteurs du Canada Membership Directory
Type: Directory

The Storytellers School of Toronto *See* Storytelling Toronto

Storytelling Toronto
#173, 601 Christie St., Toronto ON M6G 4C7
Tel: 416-656-2445; *Fax:* 416-656-8510
admin@storytellingtoronto.org
www.storytellingtoronto.org

www.facebook.com/StorytellingToronto
twitter.com/storytellingTO
Previous Name: The Storytellers School of Toronto
Overview: A small local organization
Mission: To support creative work in the art of storytelling
Activities: Offers courses; promotes & subsidizes the work of storytellers in education; produces the Toronto Festival of Storytelling; *Awareness Events:* Legless Stocking; Toronto Storytelling Festival
Chief Officer(s):
Cristina Pietropaolo, Manager, Operations
Lorie Greisman, Financial Administrator
Awards:
• The Alice Kane Award
Eligibility: Supporters of Storytelling Toronto & members of Storytellers of Canada-Conteurs du Canada; *Amount:* $1,000
• The Anne Smythe Travel Grant
Eligibility: Supporters of Storytelling Toronto & members of Storytellers of Canada-Conteurs du Canada; *Amount:* $500
Publications:
• Pippin [a publication of Storytelling Toronto]
Type: Newsletter; *Frequency:* Quarterly

Strait Area Chamber of Commerce
The Professional Centre, #205, 609 Church St., Port Hawkesbury NS B9A 2X4
Tel: 902-625-1588; *Fax:* 902-625-5985
www.straitareachamber.ca
www.facebook.com/straitarea.chamber
twitter.com/StraitAreaCoC
Previous Name: Port Hawkesbury Chamber of Commerce
Overview: A small local organization founded in 1965
Mission: To promote & strengthen trade & commerce
Member of: Nova Scotia Chamber of Commerce
Affiliation(s): Atlantic Provinces Chamber of Commerce
Finances: *Funding Sources:* Membership revenue; fundraising
Staff Member(s): 1; 19 volunteer(s)
Membership: 130+; *Committees:* Communication & Membership; Fundraising & Events; Human Resources; Nominating; Policy & Governance
Chief Officer(s):
Amanda Mombourquette, Executive Director

Straits-St. Barbe Chamber of Commerce
c/o Straits-St. Barbe Community, PO Box 203, Plum Point NL A0K 4A0
Overview: A small local organization

Strategic Leadership Forum (SLF)
165 Thamesview Cres., St Marys ON N4X 1E1
Tel: 416-628-8262
membership@slftoronto.com
strategicleadershipforum.camp9.org
www.linkedin.com/company/strategic-leadership-forum
www.facebook.com/SLFToronto
twitter.com/Letstalkstrat
Previous Name: The Planning Forum
Overview: A medium-sized national organization founded in 1950
Mission: To provide our community of members with an independent & intellectually challenging forum that delivers practical insights & interactions on strategic management & leadership
Finances: *Annual Operating Budget:* $100,000-$250,000; *Funding Sources:* Membership fees; program fees; sponsorship revenue
Staff Member(s): 1; 24 volunteer(s)
Membership: 500; *Fees:* $295 executive; $175 academic; $1,180 corporate; *Member Profile:* Managers, directors, vice-presidents
Activities: Meetings: breakfast, luncheon, half-day, full-day & evening
Chief Officer(s):
Augustin Manchon, President

Stratford & District Chamber of Commerce
55 Lorne Ave. East, Stratford ON N5A 6S4
Tel: 519-273-5250; *Fax:* 519-273-2229
info@stratfordchamber.com
www.stratfordchamber.com
www.facebook.com/stratforddistrict.chamberofcommerce
twitter.com/stratfordchambr
Overview: A medium-sized local organization founded in 1860
Mission: To maintain & improve trade & commerce, conservation & good management of community resources; To promote the economic, commercial, industrial, tourist & convention, civic, agricultural & environmental welfare of the City of Stratford & the surrounding district
Member of: Ontario Chamber of Commerce; Canadian Chamber of Commerce
Affiliation(s): Chamber of Commerce Executives of Canada
Finances: *Funding Sources:* Membership dues & fundraising
Staff Member(s): 2; 16 volunteer(s)
Membership: 287; *Fees:* Schedule available; *Committees:* Membership Services; Legislative Action; Trade Show; Business Awards; Programs
Activities: Lobbying at all levels of government; Providing seminars, information, & publications
Chief Officer(s):
Brad Beatty, General Manager

Stratford & District Labour Council
PO Box 661, 182 King St., Stratford ON N5A 6V6
Tel: 519-273-0300; *Fax:* 519-273-1051
www.facebook.com/stratfordlabourcouncil
Overview: A small local organization founded in 1963 overseen by Ontario Fedearation of Labour
Member of: Ontario Federation of Labour

Stratford Area Association for Community Living *See* Community Living Stratford & Area

Stratford Coin Club
68 Galt Rd., Stratford ON N5A 7S6
info@stratfordcoinclub.ca
www.stratfordcoinclub.ca
Overview: A small local organization founded in 1960
Member of: Ontario Numismatic Association
Finances: *Annual Operating Budget:* Less than $50,000; *Funding Sources:* Membership dues; coin show
Membership: 100; *Fees:* Schedule available
Chief Officer(s):
Doug Hamilton, President
Darrell Nutt, Secretary
membership@stratfordcoinclub.ca
Bill Cousins, Treasurer
treasurer@stratfordcoinclub.ca

Stratford Musicians' Association, Local 418 of the American Federation of Musicians
PO Box 742, St Marys ON N4X 1B4
Tel: 519-301-2592
info@stratfordmusicians.org
www.stratfordmusicians.org
Overview: A small local organization founded in 1920
Mission: To unite the professional musicians in the jurisdiction who are eligible for membership; to provide services to members; to secure improved wages, hours, working conditions & other economic advantages; to establish terms & conditions for equitable & fair dealing among members
Affiliation(s): American Federation of Musicians of the United States & Canada
Finances: *Annual Operating Budget:* Less than $50,000; *Funding Sources:* Membership & work dues
Staff Member(s): 2
Membership: 160; *Fees:* $108 regular; *Member Profile:* Instrumentalists & vocalists
Activities: *Speaker Service:* Yes; *Library:* by appointment
Chief Officer(s):
Grant Heywood, President
Stephanie Martin, Acting Secretary/Treasurer

Stratford Tourism Alliance (STA)
47 Downie St., Stratford ON N5A 1W7
Tel: 519-271-5140; *Fax:* 519-273-1818
Toll-Free: 800-561-7926
hello@visitstratford.ca
www.visitstratford.ca
www.facebook.com/StratfordON
twitter.com/StratfordON
Previous Name: Tourism Stratford; Stratford & Area Visitors & Convention Bureau
Overview: A medium-sized local organization founded in 2007
Mission: To promote Stratford as a destination for leisure travelers & others; To improve the quality of life & local economy in Stratford; To provide services to members & offer information & guidance to visitors, convention planners, & media contacts about the advantages of Stratford & surrounding area as a destination
Affiliation(s): National Tour Association; Ontario Motor Coach Association
Finances: *Funding Sources:* Municipal taxation; membership dues
Staff Member(s): 5; 4 volunteer(s)
Membership: 1,000-4,999; *Committees:* Board of Directors; Executive; Finance; Governance
Activities: *Awareness Events:* Stratford Festival of Canada; *Library*
Chief Officer(s):
Kristin Sainsbury, Executive Director
ksainsbury@visitstratford.ca
Christina Phillips, Manager, Digital
cphillips@visitstratford.ca
Cathy Rehberg, Manager, Marketing
crehberg@visitstratford.ca
Publications:
• Savour Stratford Culinary Guide
Type: Brochure

Strathcona Archaeological Society *See* Archaeological Society of Alberta

Strathcona Christian Academy Society (SCA)
1011 Clover Bar Rd., Sherwood Park AB T8A 4V7
Tel: 780-467-4752
scasociety@spac.ca
www.scasociety.ca
Overview: A small local organization founded in 1980
Mission: To challenge students, through Christ-centred education & teach them to accept Jesus Christ as Savior & Lord in order to pursue a life of godly character, personal & academic excellence & service to others
Member of: Elk Island Public Schools
Affiliation(s): Sherwood Park Alliance Church
Finances: *Annual Operating Budget:* $3 Million-$5 Million; *Funding Sources:* Regional Government
Staff Member(s): 47; 120 volunteer(s)
Chief Officer(s):
Ken Ward, Chair
Liann Cross, Executive Assistant, 780-467-4752
scasociety@spac.ca

Strathcona Coin Discovery Group
c/o Ron Darbyshire, 4907 - 114 St., Edmonton AB T6H 3L5
Tel: 780-436-4335
coinguy@telus.net
Overview: A small local organization
Chief Officer(s):
Ron Darbyshire, Director

Strathcona Food Bank
255 Kaska Rd., Sherwood Park AB T8A 4E8
Tel: 780-449-6413
Overview: A small local charitable organization founded in 1983
Mission: To provide food and services to the needy in Strathcona.
69 volunteer(s)
Membership: 60

Strathcona Park Lodge & Outdoor Education Centre
PO Box 2160, Campbell River BC V9W 5C5
Tel: 250-286-3122; *Fax:* 250-286-6010
info@strathcona.bc.ca
www.strathcona.bc.ca
www.facebook.com/StrathconaParkLodge
twitter.com/strathconapark
www.youtube.com/user/strathconaparklodge
Also Known As: Canadian Outdoor Leadership Training Centre Ltd.
Overview: A medium-sized local organization founded in 1959
Mission: To teach the wonder, spirit & worth of people & the natural world through outdoor pursuits
Member of: Outdoor Recreation Council of British Columbia
Affiliation(s): Sea Kayak Guides Alliance of BC; Tourism Association of Vancouver Island
Finances: *Funding Sources:* Private
Activities: Kayaking; canoeing; sailing; ropes courses; rock climbing; mountaineering; hiking; backpacking; orienteering; wilderness ethics; survival; environmental education; *Library:* Open to public
Chief Officer(s):
Jamie Boulding, Executive Director
Christine Clarke, Executive Director

Strathmore & District Chamber of Commerce
PO Box 2222, 129 2nd Ave., Strathmore AB T1P 1K2
Tel: 403-901-3175; *Fax:* 403-901-3175
info@strathmoredistrictchamber.com
strathmoredistrictchamber.com
www.facebook.com/StrathmoreDistrictChamber
twitter.com/SDCOC

Overview: A small local organization founded in 1992
Mission: To advocate on behalf of its members
Membership: 87; *Fees:* Schedule available; *Member Profile:* Local businesses
Chief Officer(s):
Terri Kinsman, President

Strathroy & District Chamber of Commerce
137 Frank St., Strathroy ON N7G 2R8
Tel: 519-245-7620; *Fax:* 519-245-9422
info@sdcc.on.ca
www.sdcc.on.ca
Overview: A small local organization founded in 1940
Mission: To address the needs of businesses in the area
Member of: Canadian Chamber of Commerce; Ontario Chamber of Commerce
Membership: 250; *Fees:* $210 1-4 employees/non-profit; $265 5-8 employees; $320 9-15 employees; $320+ 16+ employees
Chief Officer(s):
Kathy Manness, General Manager

Street Haven at the Crossroads
87 Pembroke St., Toronto ON M5A 2N9
Tel: 416-967-6060; *Fax:* 416-924-6900
Toll-Free: 844-967-6060
fundraising@streethaven.com
www.streethaven.org
www.facebook.com/streethaven
twitter.com/StreetHaven
Overview: A small local charitable organization founded in 1965
Mission: To innovate & establish an integrated continuum of services which will improve the quality of life of women in need & bring creative solutions to their problems
Chief Officer(s):
Susan Keenan, President

Streetsville Historical Society (SHS)
PO Box 7357, Mississauga ON L5M 3G3
Tel: 905-814-5958; *Fax:* 413-513-6789
Overview: A small local charitable organization founded in 1970
Mission: To collect, preserve, & promote interest in the history of Streetsville, one of the principal pioneer villages which form the nucleus of Mississauga
Member of: Ontario Historical Society
Affiliation(s): Ontario Historical Society; City of Mississauga, Recreation & Parks Department
Finances: *Annual Operating Budget:* Less than $50,000; *Funding Sources:* Membership fees; Sale of publications; Provincial grant
9 volunteer(s)
Membership: 117; *Fees:* $10 single, $15 family or institution
Activities: Organizing displays at community fairs, such as Heritage Day; Hosting meetings throughout the year; *Speaker Service:* Yes; *Library:* SHS Archives; by appointment Not open to public
Chief Officer(s):
Malcolm Byard, President
mbyard@sympatico.ca
Bernice Cunningham, Vice President
bernice.two@hotmail.com
• SHS Bulletin
Type: Newsletter; *Frequency:* 4 times a year; *Editor:* Anne Byard

STRIDE
#26, 55 Ontario St. South, Milton ON L9T 2M3
Tel: 905-693-4252; *Fax:* 905-875-9262
stride@stride.on.ca
www.stride.on.ca
Also Known As: Supported Training & Rehabilitation in Diverse Environments
Overview: A small local organization
Chief Officer(s):
Anita Lloyd, Executive Director, 905-693-4252 Ext. 224
alloyd@stride.on.ca

Stroke Recovery Association of BC (SRABC)
#301, 1212 West Broadway, Vancouver BC V6H 3V1
Tel: 604-688-3603; *Fax:* 604-688-3660
Toll-Free: 888-313-3377
www.strokerecoverybc.ca
www.facebook.com/StrokeRecoveryBC
twitter.com/StrokeRecovBC
www.youtube.com/user/office814
Overview: A small provincial charitable organization founded in 1979
Mission: To encourage stroke survivors & their families as they adjust themselves to changes in their lives; To foster understanding of strokes within the community; To provide, through local Stoke Recovery branches throughout BC, a resource for stroke survivors living in the community
Membership: 1,000 individual; *Member Profile:* Stroke survivors, cargivers & volunteers
Activities: Supporting 40 community-based stroke recovery programs throughout BC; Providing two camps for stroke survivors & family members; Offering information; *Speaker Service:* Yes
Chief Officer(s):
Atul Gadhia, President
Awards:
• Phyllis Delaney Life After Stroke Awards

Stroke Recovery Association of Manitoba Inc.
247 Provencher Blvd., #B, Winnipeg MB R2H 0G6
Tel: 204-942-2880; *Fax:* 204-944-1982
admin@strokerecovery.ca
www.strokerecovery.ca
www.facebook.com/StrokeRecoveryMB
Overview: A small provincial organization overseen by Stroke Recovery Network
Mission: To help improve the lives of stroke victims & their families
Staff Member(s): 2
Membership: *Committees:* Policy/Planning; Personnel; Finance; Fund-Raising; Public Relations & Special Events; Membership
Chief Officer(s):
April Takacs, President
Diane O'Neil, Executive Director & Administrator

Stroll of Poets Society
c/o Writers Guild of Alberta, 11759 Groat Rd., Edmonton AB T5M 3K6
www.strollofpoets.com
Overview: A small local organization founded in 1991
Mission: To address the need to promote poetry as an art form
Membership: *Fees:* $25; $20 student
Activities: Stroll Anthology; e-poem; festivals; series of public recitations of poetry
Chief Officer(s):
John Leppard, President

Strome & District Historical Society (SAM)
PO Box 151, Strome AB T0B 4H0
Tel: 780-376-3688
Also Known As: Strome Museum; Sodbusters Archives Museum
Overview: A small local charitable organization founded in 1987
Mission: To preserve the history of Western Canada, Village of Strome & area
Member of: Alberta Museum Association
Affiliation(s): Alberta Historical Resource Foundation; Central Rural East Alberta Museums
Finances: *Annual Operating Budget:* Less than $50,000; *Funding Sources:* Donations; grants
50 volunteer(s)
Membership: 50; *Fees:* $5
Chief Officer(s):
Joan Brockhoff, Contact, 780-376-3546

Structural Innovation & Monitoring Technologies Resources Centre
Agricultural & Civil Engineering Building, University of Manitoba, #A250, 96 Dafoe Rd., Winnipeg MB R3T 2N2
Tel: 204-474-8506
info@simtrec.ca
simtrec.ca
Also Known As: SIMTReC
Previous Name: Intelligent Sensing for Innovative Structures (ISIS) Canada Research Network
Overview: A medium-sized national organization founded in 1995
Mission: To advance civil engineering in Canada to a world leadership position through the development & application of fibre-reinforced polymers & integrated intelligent fibre optic sensing technologies
Member of: Networks of Centres of Excellence
Finances: *Funding Sources:* NSERC
Membership: 100-499
Activities: *Speaker Service:* Yes
Chief Officer(s):
Donald Whitmore, Chair
donw@vectorgroup.com
Aftab Mufti, Director, 204-474-8506, Fax: 204-474-7519
aftab.mufti@umanitoba.ca

Structural Pest Management Association of Alberta *See* Pest Management Association of Alberta

Structural Pest Management Association of British Columbia (SPMABC)
c/o Integrated Pest Supplies, #108, 360 Edworthy Way, New Westminster BC V3L 5T8
Tel: 604-520-9900; *Fax:* 604-522-5557
Toll-Free: 800-465-5511
info@spmabc.com
www.spmabc.com
Overview: A small provincial organization
Member of: Canadian Pest Management Association
Membership: 54; *Fees:* $295-$420
Chief Officer(s):
Brett Johnston, President

Structural Pest Management Association of Ontario (SPMAO)
#300, 1370 Don Mills Rd., Toronto ON M3B 3N7
Tel: 866-957-7378
Fax: 866-957-7378
Toll-Free: 800-461-6722
spmao@pestworld.org
www.spmao.ca
Previous Name: Ontario Pest Control Association
Overview: A small provincial organization founded in 1950
Mission: To help their members obtain professional licenses & remain up to date on industry policies & practices
Member of: Canadian Pest Management Association; National Pest Management Association (U.S.); Urban Pest Management Council of Canada
Membership: 197; *Fees:* $425 active; $275 allied; $215 associate
Activities: Monthly meetings; annual conference; satellite meetings; *Library:* Not open to public
Chief Officer(s):
Greg Mulroney, Executive Coordinator
info@spmao.ca

Student Christian Movement of Canada (SCM) / Mouvement d'étudiant(e)s chrétien(ne)s
#200, 310 Dupont Street, Toronto ON M5R 1V9
Tel: 416-463-7622
info@scmcanada.org
scmcanada.org
www.facebook.com/scmcanada
twitter.com/scmcanada
Overview: A medium-sized national charitable organization founded in 1921
Mission: To be a national, ecumenical student organization that encourages members in theological & social reflection & in actions for social change
Member of: World Student Christian Federation
Finances: *Annual Operating Budget:* $50,000-$100,000
Staff Member(s): 2
Membership: 500; *Member Profile:* Groups at Canadian universities
Chief Officer(s):
Peter Haresnape, General Secretary

Central Region
c/o Ecumenical Chaplain, 1125 Colonel By Dr., Ottawa ON K1S 5B6
Tel: 613-520-4449
carleton@scmcanada.org
www.scmcanada.org/carleton
Chief Officer(s):
Tom Sherwood, Chaplain

Eastern Region
Memorial University Of Newfoundland, #4010, University Centre, St. John's NL A1C 5S7
Tel: 709-737-4376
mun@scmcanada.org
www.scmcanada.org/mun
Chief Officer(s):
Donna Lawrence, Chaplain

Western Region
PO Box 3015, Victoria BC V8W 3P2
Tel: 250-721-8338
victoria@scmcanada.org
www.scmcanada.org/victoria
Chief Officer(s):
Henri Lock, Chaplain

Student Legal Services of Edmonton
11036 - 88 Ave. NW, Edmonton AB T6G 0Z2

Tel: 780-492-2226; Fax: 780-492-7574
info@slsedmonton.com
www.slsedmonton.com
Overview: A small local charitable organization founded in 1971
Mission: As agents in Criminal & Civil Court, to provide free legal information & assistance to people who do not qualify for legal aid & are not able to afford a lawyer; legal research & education in issues of general community interest & concern; background work & suggestions for legal reform
Finances: *Annual Operating Budget:* $250,000-$500,000
250 volunteer(s)
Membership: *Committees:* Management
Chief Officer(s):
Neil Thomson, Executive Coordinator

Sturgeon Falls Literacy Alliance *See* Literacy Alliance of West Nipissing

Subuddhi Deri Dasi *See* Toronto's Hare Krishna Centre

Sudbury & District Association for Community Living *See* The City of Greater Sudbury Developmental Services

Sudbury & District Beekeepers' Association (SDBA)
Sudbury ON
Tel: 705-682-5925
www.sudburybeekeepers.com
www.facebook.com/1394362140801932
Overview: A small local organization founded in 1977
Mission: To serve beekeepers in the Sudbury area by helping them to develop their beekeeping skills
Member of: Ontario Beekeepers' Association
Membership: *Fees:* $15 senior; $20 adult; $25 family; *Member Profile:* Apiarists in the Sudbury district, from beginners to commercial operators
Activities: Educating the public about apiaries & apiculture through displays at places such as the local farmers' market; Providing workshops & presentations to assist beekeepers; Creating opportunities for beekeepers to network; Organizing meetings at the Lo-Ellen Park Secondary School in Sudbury; *Library:* Sudbury & District Beekeepers' Association Library
Chief Officer(s):
Wayne Leblanc, President
wleblanc@personainternet.com

Sudbury & District Labour Council
#209, 109 Elm St., Sudbury ON P3C 1T4
Tel: 705-674-1223
sdlc@persona.ca
sudburylabour.ca
www.facebook.com/215776655158327
twitter.com/sudburylabour
Overview: A small local organization founded in 1957 overseen by Ontario Federation of Labour
Chief Officer(s):
Jamie West, President

Sudbury Arts Council (SAC) / Conseil des arts de Sudbury
c/o AOE, 168 Elgin St., Sudbury ON P3E 3N5
Tel: 705-626-2787
sac.communicate@gmail.com
www.sudburyartscouncil.org
www.facebook.com/GuelphArtsCouncil
twitter.com/guelpharts
Overview: A small local charitable organization founded in 1974
Mission: To foster an environment that supports the arts at all levels; to enhance the quality of life adding to the vitality of the community by promoting an awareness & appreciation of the arts in all forms & to encourage the active pursuit of artistic excellence
Member of: Community Arts Ontario
Finances: *Funding Sources:* Government; fundraising
Staff Member(s): 1
Membership: 180; *Fees:* $20 regular/patron; $35 group; $50 business; *Member Profile:* Declared arts/culture interest
Activities: Promote arts & articulate relevance
Chief Officer(s):
Vicki Gilhula, President
vgilhula@gmail.com
Paddy O'Sullivan, Vice-President

Sudbury Community Service Centre Inc. / Centre de services communautaires de Sudbury
1166 Roy Ave., Sudbury ON P3A 3M6
Tel: 705-560-0430; *Fax:* 705-560-0440
Toll-Free: 800-685-1521
scsc@vianet.ca
www.sudburycommunityservicecentre.ca
www.youtube.com/channel/UCfXnydiEvAc1pf8QzXFbc1A
Overview: A small local charitable organization founded in 1972 overseen by Ontario Association of Credit Counselling Service
Mission: To provide support services to individuals with developmental disabilities & their families; To assist persons who are experiencing financial difficulties in the Greater Sudbury Area, as well as the Espanola & Parry Sound areas, through Credit Counselling Sudbury
Member of: Ontario Association of Credit Counselling Services
Finances: *Funding Sources:* Donations
Activities: Providing professional counselling services; Offering crisis management services for persons adapting to unexpected change; Providing case management services to help persons with developmental disabilities meet identified needs; Engaging in advocacy activities; Helping people resolve their debt & money management problems, through credit counselling, a Debt Management Program & negotiations with creditors; Teaching money management & budget planning skills

Sudbury Construction Association *See* Council of Ontario Construction Associations

Sudbury Family Service *Voir* Service familial de Sudbury

Sudbury Manitoulin Children's Foundation
PO Box 1264, Stn. B, 296 Larch St., Sudbury ON P3E 4S7
Tel: 705-673-2227; *Fax:* 705-673-8798
www.smcf.com
www.facebook.com/SudburyManitoulinChildrensFoundationSMCF
twitter.com/SMCF_1976
Overview: A small local charitable organization
Mission: To develop programs designed to assist children & families from the Sudbury-Manitoulin area
Activities: Bursary Program; Send-a-Kid-to-Camp program
Chief Officer(s):
Anne Salter Dorland, Executive Director
anne@smcf.com

Sudbury Real Estate Board
190 Elm St., Sudbury ON P3C 1V3
Tel: 705-673-3388; *Fax:* 705-673-3197
sreb@vianet.on.ca
www.sudburyrealestateboard.on.ca
Overview: A small local organization overseen by Ontario Real Estate Association
Mission: To keep its members informed in order to better serve their customers
Membership: 300
Chief Officer(s):
Pauline Pelangio, President

Sudbury Rock & Lapidary Society (SRLS)
c/o 3171 Romeo St., Val Caron ON P3N 1G5
rmineral@isys.ca
www.ccfms.ca/clubs/Sudbury
Overview: A small local organization founded in 1984
Mission: To promote rock, mineral, gem, & fossil collecting, & lapidary for both recreation & education
Member of: Central Canadian Federation of Mineralogical Societies
Membership: 85; *Fees:* $10 individual or family; *Member Profile:* Amateurs; Hobbyists; Professionals
Activities: Hosting monthly meetings from September to June; Offering courses in lapidary arts & silver smithing; Organizing field trips; *Awareness Events:* Annual Gem & Mineral Show, July
Library: Sudbury Rock & Lapidary Society Library
Chief Officer(s):
Roger Poulin, President, 705-897-6216
Ruth Debicki, Vice-President
Ed Debicki, Secretary, 705-522-5140
ed.debicki@sympatico.ca
Gil Benoit, Treasurer
Publications:
• Nickel Basin Rockhound
Type: Newsletter; *Frequency:* 10 pa; *Number of Pages:* 10; *Editor:* Erv Mantler; *Price:* Free with Sudbury Rock & Lapidary Society membership
Profile: Information for Sudbury Rock & Lapidary Society members, published from Septemer to June

Sudbury Stamp Club
1779 Graywood Dr., Sudbury ON P3A 5S5
Also Known As: Sudbury Philatelic Society
Overview: A small local organization founded in 1946
Mission: To educate ourselves about philatelic matters & provide a forum for exchange & purchase of stamps & stamp supplies
Membership: 20; *Fees:* $10
Chief Officer(s):
Biff Pilon, Contact

Sudbury Symphony Orchestra Association Inc. (SSO) / Orchestre symphonique de Sudbury inc
303 York St., Sudbury ON P3E 2A5
Tel: 705-673-1280; *Fax:* 705-673-1434
info@sudburysymphony.com
www.sudburysymphony.com
ca.linkedin.com/company/sudbury-symphony-orchestra
www.facebook.com/SudburySymphony
twitter.com/SudburySymphony
www.youtube.com/sudburysymphony
Overview: A small local charitable organization founded in 1953 overseen by Orchestras Canada
Mission: To provide the opportunity for a broad spectrum of the public in the Sudbury Region & surrounding area to attend a stimulating program of concerts; to maintain an environment & organization which encourages artistic responsibility & commitment; to attract & maintain private & public funding in order to achieve accessibility & continuity through financial stability; to increase the awareness & appreciation of music in the community; to provide a vehicle for the participation in & ongoing development of the performance of orchestral music; to increase the awareness, appreciation & performance of Canadian music in the community
Member of: SOCAN; Orchestras Canada
Finances: *Funding Sources:* Ontario Arts Council; City of Greater Sudbury; Individual & Corporate Donations
Staff Member(s): 4
Activities: Performing concert series; Facilitating a conservatory of music for students of all ages; Facilitating outreach programs for schools and community groups
Chief Officer(s):
Jennifer McGillivray, Executive Director

Sudbury Tourism
200 Brady St., Sudbury ON P3A 5P3
Toll-Free: 866-451-8525
sudburytourism@sudbury.ca
www.sudburytourism.ca
www.facebook.com/sudburytourism
twitter.com/sudburytourism
www.instagram.com/sudburytourism
Overview: A small local organization
Member of: Tourism Industry Association of Canada

Sudbury Youth Orchestra Inc.
PO Box 2241, Stn. A, Sudbury ON P3A 4S1
Tel: 705-566-8101
sudburyyouthorch@gmail.com
www.sudburyyouthorchestra.org
Previous Name: Cambrian Youth Orchestra
Overview: A small local charitable organization founded in 1972 overseen by Orchestras Canada
Mission: To foster an appreciation of orchestral music; to create opportunities for orchestral performance; to provide access to education & training in an orchestral setting for the youth of Sudbury & area
Member of: Orchestras Canada
Finances: *Funding Sources:* Government grants; Individual & corporate donations; Tuition fees
Membership: *Fees:* $90 per semester
Activities: Performing concerts; Providing comprehensive orchestral education for members
Chief Officer(s):
Jamie Arrowsmith, Music Director

Suicide Action Montréal (SAM)
2345, rue Bélanger, Montréal QC H2G 1C9
Tel: 514-723-3594; *Fax:* 514-723-3605
Toll-Free: 866-277-3553; *Crisis Hot-Line:* 514-723-4000
info@suicideactionmontreal.qc.ca
www.suicideactionmontreal.org
Overview: A small local charitable organization founded in 1984
Affiliation(s): Canadian Association for Suicide Prevention
Finances: *Annual Operating Budget:* $500,000-$1.5 Million
Staff Member(s): 24; 250 volunteer(s)
Membership: 260; *Member Profile:* Volunteers
Activities: Suicide prevention; bereaved; support group
Chief Officer(s):
Suzanne Carrière, President

Canadian Associations / Summer Street

Suicide Information & Education Centre *See* Centre for Suicide Prevention

Summer Street
72 Park St., New Glasgow NS B2H 5B8
Tel: 902-755-1745; *Fax:* 902-755-1956
www.summerstreet.ca
www.facebook.com/summerstr
twitter.com/SummStreet
Overview: A small local organization
Mission: To provide opportunities to people who have intellectual disabilities
Member of: DIRECTIONS Council for Vocational Services Society
Finances: *Funding Sources:* Donations
Staff Member(s): 39; 40 volunteer(s)
Activities: Vocational activities & services include: catering, conference rooms, trophies & awards, & mailing & packaging
Chief Officer(s):
John Potter, President
Bob Bennett, Executive Director
bob@summerstreet.ca

Summerhill Impact; Clean Air Foundation *See* Scout Environmental

Summerland Chamber of Commerce
PO Box 130, 15600 Hwy. 97, Summerland BC V0H 1Z0
Tel: 250-494-2686; *Fax:* 250-494-4039
membership@summerlandchamber.com
www.summerlandchamber.ca
www.facebook.com/161939953823991
twitter.com/SummerlandChmbr
www.youtube.com/user/scedt; instagram.com/visit_summerland
Previous Name: Summerland Chamber of Economic Development & Tourism
Overview: A small local organization founded in 2000
Mission: To act as a voice for business interests; To represent & promote Summerland & area businesses to governments, community interest groups, businesses, other chambers, & business groups in the Okanagan Valley & British Columbia; To provide a forum for business interaction & membership services to the business community
Member of: BC Chamber of Commerce
Affiliation(s): Thompson/Okanagan Tourism Association; Penticton & Wine Country Chamber of Commerce; South Okanagan Chamber of Commerce
Finances: *Annual Operating Budget:* $100,000-$250,000; *Funding Sources:* Municipal business license fees; Tourism BC Grant
Staff Member(s): 4; 7 volunteer(s)
Membership: 800+; *Member Profile:* Everyone with a business license in Summerland
Activities: Market Summerland; Sponsoring the visitor information centre; *Library:* Visitor Info Centre
Chief Officer(s):
Kelly Marshall, President
president@summerlandchamber.com
Christine Petkau, Executive Director
cpetkau@summerlandchamber.com
Awards:
- Business of the Year Award
- Rising Star Award
- Sustainability Leader Award
- Technology & Innovation Award
- Professional Services Excellence Award
- Trade Services Excellence Award
- Manufacturing/Industrial Excellence Award
- Retail Excellence Award
- Tourism & Hospitality Excellence Award
- Citizen/Volunteer of the Year
- Young Entrepreneur of the Year

Summerland Chamber of Economic Development & Tourism *See* Summerland Chamber of Commerce

Summerland Community Arts Council (SCAC)
PO Box 1217, Summerland BC V0H 1Z0
Tel: 250-494-4494; *Fax:* 250-494-0055
admin@summerlandarts.com
summerlandarts.com
Overview: A small local charitable organization founded in 1981
Mission: To promote & facilitate the awareness & appreciation of the arts in Summerland
Member of: Assembly of BC Arts Councils; Okanagan Mainline Regional Arts Councils
Affiliation(s): Corporation of Summerland
Finances: *Annual Operating Budget:* $50,000-$100,000; *Funding Sources:* Province of BC; Corporation of District of Summerland; activies
Staff Member(s): 1; 90 volunteer(s)
Membership: 100-499; *Fees:* Schedule available; *Member Profile:* Artists or friends of artists; *Committees:* Advocacy; Financial; Personnel; Art Centre; Arts Apprciation Award; Banner; Craft Sale; Entertainment; Finance; Gallery; Mainly Art Sale; Membership; Opportunities; Permanent Collection; Publicity; Art Reserve Fund; Summer Arts
Activities: Banner Program; entertainment series; art gallery; Mainly Arts Sale; summer arts program; bursaries; craft fair
Chief Officer(s):
David Finnis, President
Sharry Schneider, Vice-President
Awards:
- Arts Appreciation Award
- Member Group Grants
- Special Group Grants

Summerland Food Bank & Resource Centre
Summerland United Church, PO Box 20051, 13204 Henry Ave., Summerland BC V0H 1Z0
Tel: 778-516-0015
info@summerlandfoodbank.org
www.summerlandfoodbank.org
Overview: A small local charitable organization

Summerland Museum & Heritage Society
PO Box 1491, 9521 Wharton St., Summerland BC V0H 1Z0
Tel: 250-494-9395; *Fax:* 250-494-9326
info@summerlandmuseum.org
www.summerlandmuseum.org
www.facebook.com/summerlandmuseum
Overview: A small local charitable organization founded in 1964
Mission: To collect, preserve & promote Summerland's valuable heritage
Member of: B.C. Museums Association; Archives Association of B.C.
Finances: *Funding Sources:* Municipal & provincial government; fundraising; Heritage Canada
Staff Member(s): 2
Activities: *Library:* Archives; Open to public

Summerside & Area Minor Hockey Association (SAMHA)
PO Box 1454, Summerside PE C1N 4K4
info@summersideminorhockey.com
summersideminorhockey.com
Overview: A medium-sized local organization

Sun Ergos, A Company of Theatre & Dance
130 Sunset Way, Priddis AB T0L 1W0
Tel: 403-931-1527; *Fax:* 403-931-1534
Toll-Free: 800-743-3351
waltermoke@sunergos.com
www.sunergos.com
www.linkedin.com/company/sun.ergos-a-company-of-theatre-and-dance
www.facebook.com/SunErgosTheatreDance
twitter.com/sunergostheatre
www.youtube.com/user/sunergostheatre
Also Known As: Sun.Ergos
Overview: A small local charitable organization founded in 1977
Mission: To witness, maintain & develop the ethnocultural roots of theatre & dance, without prejudice of race, creed, sex, or cultural background, to celebrate the differences & recognize the similarities among all peoples; to provide the best possible theatre & dance within the urban & rural communities, nationally & internationally
Member of: Canadian Actors' Equity Association; Alliance of Canadian Cinema, Television & Radio Artists (ACTRA)
Affiliation(s): Western Arts Alliance; Arts Northwest; Montana Performing Arts Consortium; Arts Midwest; Arts Touring Alliance of Alberta; BC Touring; Wyoming Arts Alliance
Finances: *Annual Operating Budget:* $250,000-$500,000; *Funding Sources:* Performance fees; box office; grants; personal and corporate donations
Staff Member(s): 2
Membership: 150; *Fees:* $25+
Activities: 200-300 performances per year; residencies; workshops; master classes; *Speaker Service:* Yes; *Library:* Not open to public
Chief Officer(s):
Robert Greenwood, Artistic & Managing Director
bob.greenwood@sunergos.com
Dana Luebke, Artistic & Production Director
dana.luebke@sunergos.com

Sunbeam Sportscar Owners Club of Canada (SSOCC)
Overview: A small national organization founded in 1978
Finances: *Annual Operating Budget:* Less than $50,000; *Funding Sources:* Membership fees; advertising; regalia sales
Membership: 130; *Member Profile:* Owner or enthusiast of British "Rootes Group" production automobile of any year
Activities: *Library:* by appointment

Sunbury West Historical Society
110 Currie Lane, Fredericton Junction NB E5L 1X7
Tel: 506-368-2818
Also Known As: The Currie House Museum
Overview: A small local organization founded in 1986
Affiliation(s): Association of Museums of New Brunswick
Activities: Operates The Currie House, built in 1900; Meetings: Third Thursday of every month except Jul., Aug., Dec at 7:30 pm at Currie House; *Library:* by appointment

Sundre Chamber of Commerce
600 Main Ave. East, Sundre AB T0M 1X0
Tel: 403-638-3245
scoc@telus.net
www.sundrechamber.ca
www.facebook.com/sundrechamberofcommerce
twitter.com/sundrechamber
Overview: A small local organization
Mission: To promote & enrich trade & commerce & stimulate the economic, civil & social welfare of the district
Member of: Alberta Chamber of Commerce
Membership: 120; *Fees:* Schedule available
Chief Officer(s):
Mike Beaukaboom, President

Sunny South District Soccer Association
RR#8, Site 34, Comp 0, Lethbridge AB T1J 4P4
Tel: 403-894-2277
www.sunnysouthsoccer.com
Overview: A small local organization overseen by Alberta Soccer Association
Member of: Alberta Soccer Association
Staff Member(s): 2
Chief Officer(s):
Paul Anwender, Executive Director
paul.anwender@gmail.com

Sunrise Equestrian & Recreation Centre for the Disabled *See* Sunrise Therapeutic Riding & Learning Centre

Sunrise Therapeutic Riding & Learning Centre
6920 Concession 1, RR#2, Puslinch ON N0B 2J0
Tel: 519-837-0558; *Fax:* 519-837-1233
Other Communication: Barn office phone: 519-827-0558, ext. 30
info@sunrise-therapeutic.ca
www.sunrise-therapeutic.ca
www.facebook.com/224072694372280
Also Known As: Sunrise
Previous Name: Sunrise Equestrian & Recreation Centre for the Disabled
Overview: A small local charitable organization founded in 1982
Mission: To develop the full potential of children & adults with disabilites & lead them closer to independence through therapy, recreation, horse riding, life skills & farm related activity programme
Member of: Canadian Therapeutic Riding Association; Ontario Therapeutic Riding Association
Affiliation(s): Ontario's Promise
Finances: *Annual Operating Budget:* $250,000-$500,000; *Funding Sources:* Service clubs; Foundations; Industry; Corporate; Private; Golf tournament; Ride-a-thon
Staff Member(s): 18; 175 volunteer(s)
Membership: 250; *Fees:* $30; *Committees:* Finance; Fundraising; Public Relations/Marketing; Medical Advisory; Farm Management
Activities: Therapeutic riding; life skills program; Employment preparation courses for young adults with special needs; Therapeutic Riding Instructor Training School; integrated day camps; equestrian clinics; schooling shows; "Little Breeches" Club (4-7 years); education program for school groups (JK-3); monthly board & instructor meetings; Fall Open House; demonstrations at Royal Winter Fair; invitational horse shows; *Internships:* Yes *Library:* Resource Centre for Instructor School; by appointment Not open to public
Chief Officer(s):

Rob Vandebelt, Chief Executive Officer, 519-837-0558 Ext. 32
rob@sunrise-therapeutic.ca
Nikki Duffield, Program Director & Head Instructor,
519-837-0558 Ext. 29
nikkid@sunrise-therapeutic.ca
Lynne O'Brien, Manager, Operations & Volunteer, 519-837-0558 Ext. 31
lynne@sunrise-therapeutic.ca
Publications:
• Pony Express [a publication of the Sunrise Therapeutic Riding & Learning Centre]
Type: Newsletter; *Frequency:* Irregular
Profile: News & profiles on members

Sunshine Coast Arts Council (SCAC)
PO Box 1565, Sechelt BC V0N 3A0
Tel: 604-885-5412; *Fax:* 604-885-6192
sc_artscouncil@dccnet.com
www.suncoastarts.com/profiles/scartscouncil
www.facebook.com/sunshinecoastARTScouncil
Also Known As: Sunshine Coast Arts Centre
Overview: A small local charitable organization founded in 1966
Mission: To promote the arts on the Sunshine Coast; to increase & broaden the opportunities for public enjoyment of & participation in cultural activities
Member of: Assembly of Arts BC
Membership: *Fees:* $30 individual; $25 students/seniors; $35 family; $50 business/group; $100 corporate
Activities: 10-14 curated art exhibitions yearly; visual arts; performing arts; literary events; public garden; *Library:* Open to public
Awards:
• Anne & Philip Klein Visual Arts Award
Eligibility: Applicants must be active in the visual arts field, age 65 or older & a resident of Sunshine Coast. Artists whose began pursuing their field later in life are preferred.; *Amount:* $300
• Louise Baril Memorial Music Award
Eligibility: Advanced music students; *Amount:* $300
• Gillian Lowndes Award
Eligibility: Applicants must show growth, innovation & sustained achievement in their field of art; they must be currently pursuing the arts & a resident of Sunshine Coast

Sunshine Coast Community Services Society (SCCSS)
PO Box 1069, 5638 Inlet Ave., Sechelt BC V0N 3A0
Tel: 604-885-5881; *Fax:* 604-885-9493
sccssreception@sccss.ca
www.sccss.ca
Overview: A small local organization founded in 1974
Mission: To build strength in individuals, family & community by planning & providing a range of social services
Finances: *Annual Operating Budget:* $1.5 Million-$3 Million; *Funding Sources:* Provincial government; federal government; provincial & federal housing grants; donations; fundraising
Staff Member(s): 79; 60 volunteer(s)
Membership: 56; *Fees:* $5 individual; $100 organization
Activities: Services for children with special needs: paediatric occupational & physical therapy, infant development program, special services to children, supported child care, Variety Club Sunshine Coach, Kids in Motion Fund; Stopping the Violence: Yew Transition House, Thyme Second Stage program, Children who Witness Abuse, women's counselling service, women's support groups, Children's Sexual Abuse Treatment program; family & youth services: Project Parent, Nobody's Perfect, Parent-Tot Drop-In, & Parent support circles
Chief Officer(s):
Catherine Leach, Executive Director, 604-885-5881 Ext. 222
cleach@sccss.ca
Petra Haas, Director, Finance, 604-885-5881 Ext. 226
phaas@sccss.ca
Donna Hall, Director, Human Resources, 604-885-5881 Ext. 224
dhall@sccss.ca
Keely Halward, Director, Programs, 604-885-5881 Ext. 238
khalward@sccss.ca

Sunshine Coast Labour Council
PO Box 1391, Gibsons BC V0N 1V0
Tel: 604-886-2733; *Fax:* 604-886-7650
info@sclc.ca
www.sclc.ca
www.linkedin.com/in/sclc-clc-59126199
www.facebook.com/280412037266
twitter.com/sclabour
www.instagram.com/sun_coast_labour; www.pinterest.com/sclcc

Overview: A small local organization founded in 1986 overseen by British Columbia Federation of Labour
Mission: To defend the rights of workers on British Columbia's Sunshine Coast
Affiliation(s): Canadian Labour Congress (CLC)
Membership: *Member Profile:* Unions in British Columbia communities, such as Howe Sound, Jervis Inlet, Port Mellon, & Earls Cove
Activities: Supporting member unions on strike; Participating in rallies & protests; Raising awareness of workers' issues, such as women's equality, workplace safety, & harassment; Providing educational opportunities for members; Organizing an annual memorial service to recognize the Day of Mourning for workers injured or killed at work; Providing local labour news

Sunshine Coast Natural History Society (SCNHS)
PO Box 543, Sechelt BC V0N 3A0
sunshinecoastnature.blogspot.ca
Previous Name: Sechelt Marsh Protective Society
Overview: A small local organization founded in 1978
Member of: Federation of BC Naturalists
Finances: *Funding Sources:* Membership fees; municipal grant
Membership: 100; *Fees:* $30 single; $35 family
Activities: Monthly meetings; field trips; *Awareness Events:* Christmas Bird Count
Chief Officer(s):
Tony Greenfield, President
tony@whiskeyjacknaturetours.com

Sunshine Dreams for Kids / Rayons de Soleil pour enfants
#100, 300 Wellington St., London ON N6B 2L5
Tel: 519-642-0990; *Fax:* 519-642-1201
Toll-Free: 800-461-7935
info@sunshine.ca
www.sunshine.ca
www.linkedin.com/company/sunshine-foundation-of-canada
www.facebook.com/SunshineFound
twitter.com/SunshineFound
www.youtube.com/user/SunshineFound
Also Known As: The Sunshine Foundation of Canada
Overview: A medium-sized national charitable organization founded in 1987
Mission: To fulfill the dreams of children between the ages of three & nineteen who are challenged by a severe physical disability or life-threatening illness
Activities: *Awareness Events:* Annual Walk for Children's Dreams, June
Chief Officer(s):
Ed Holder, President

Suore del Sacro Cuore di Ragusa *See* Sisters of the Sacred Heart of Ragusa

Superannuated Teachers of Ontario *See* The Retired Teachers of Ontario

Superior Greenstone Association for Community Living (SGACL)
PO Box 970, 206 Hogarth Ave. West, Geraldton ON P0T 1M0
Tel: 807-854-0775; *Fax:* 807-854-1047
Toll-Free: 888-434-4409
sgacl@bellnet.ca
www.sgacl.ca
Previous Name: Nipigon, Red Rock & District Association for Community Living
Overview: A small local charitable organization founded in 1968
Mission: To help all persons live in a state of dignity, share in all elements of living in the community & have the opportunity to participate effectively
Member of: Community Living Ontario
Finances: *Funding Sources:* Ontario Ministry of Community & Social Services
Activities: *Awareness Events:* Flowers of Hope, March; Torch Run, Aug.

Superior International Junior Hockey League (SIJHL)
529 Dublin Ave., Thunder Bay ON P7B 5A1
Tel: 807-626-2316
sijhlmedia@gmail.com
www.sijhlhockey.com
www.facebook.com/SIJHL
twitter.com/SIJHL
Overview: A small local organization
Member of: Canadian Junior Hockey League
Membership: 6 teams

Chief Officer(s):
Ron Whitehead, President/Commissioner

Supply Chain Management Association (SCMA) / Association de la gestion de la chaîne d'approvisionnement (AGCA)
PO Box 112, #2701, 777 Bay St., Toronto ON M5G 2C8
Tel: 416-977-7111; *Fax:* 416-977-8886
Toll-Free: 888-799-0877
info@scmanational.ca
www.scmanational.ca
www.linkedin.com/groups/Supply-Chain-Management-Association-SCMA-2888933
www.facebook.com/scmanational
twitter.com/scmanational
Merged from: Purchasing Management Association of Canada; Supply Chain & Logistics Association of Canada
Overview: A medium-sized national licensing organization founded in 2010
Mission: To advance strategic supply chain management by providing training, education, & professional development for supply chain management professionals in Canada
Affiliation(s): Canadian Aboriginal & Minority Supplier Council; Canadian Chamber of Commerce; Canadian Public Procurement Council; Canadian Supply Chain Sector Council; International Federation of Purchasing & Supply Management; Network for Business Sustainability
Finances: *Funding Sources:* Membership dues
Staff Member(s): 14
Membership: 40,000+; *Fees:* Schedule available according to Institute &/or local District; *Member Profile:* Supply chain management professionals & enterprises in sectors including retail, manufacturing, transportation, distribution, government, natural resources, & service
Activities: Promoting standards of practice; Advocating for the profession; Developing partnerships; Providing networking opportunities
Chief Officer(s):
Cheryl Paradowski, President & CEO, 416-977-7111 Ext. 3125
cparadowski@pmac.ca
Cori Ferguson, Director, Public Affairs & Communications, 416-977-7111 Ext. 3129
cferguson@pmac.ca
Mike Whelan, Chair

Supply Chain Management Association - Alberta (SCMAAB)
Sterling Business Centre, #115, 17420 Stony Plain Rd., Edmonton AB T5S 1K6
Tel: 780-944-0355; *Fax:* 780-944-0356
Toll-Free: 866-610-4089
info@scmaab.ca
www.scmaab.ca
www.linkedin.com/groups?gid=4259963&trk=hb_side_g
www.facebook.com/332429763455410
twitter.com/SCMA_alberta
Previous Name: Alberta Institute Purchasing Management Association of Canada
Overview: A medium-sized provincial licensing organization founded in 1989 overseen by Supply Chain Management Association
Mission: To develop the profession by ensuring that professional status is accessible to all purchasing practitioners in the province; high standards of eligibility & professional conduct will be developed, maintained & enforced to enhance the profession & protect public interest in the province of Alberta
Finances: *Funding Sources:* Membership dues
Staff Member(s): 7
Membership: 1,650; *Fees:* $400; *Committees:* Registration; Practice Review; Discipline
Activities: *Speaker Service:* Yes; *Library:* Not open to public
Chief Officer(s):
Allan To, President
ato@scmaab.ca
Awards:
• Fellowship Award
• Corporate Partner Award

Supply Chain Management Association - British Columbia (SCMABC)
#300, 435 Columbia St., New Westminster BC V3L 5N8
Tel: 604-540-4494; *Fax:* 604-540-4023
Toll-Free: 800-411-7622
info@scmabc.ca
www.scmabc.ca
www.linkedin.com/groups/Supply-Chain-Management-Association

Canadian Associations / Supply Chain Management Association - Manitoba (SCMAMB)

n-SCMA-2888933/about
www.facebook.com/scmanational
twitter.com/scmabc
Previous Name: British Columbia Institute of the Purchasing Management Association of Canada
Overview: A small provincial licensing organization founded in 1920 overseen by Supply Chain Management Association
Mission: BC Institute PMAC is an incorporated, not-for-profit association that maintains a code of ethics for the profession to regulate quality & integrity.
Membership: 750; *Fees:* $370 regular; $75 student
Chief Officer(s):
Barrie Lynch, Executive Director, 604-540-4494 Ext. 104
exec@scmabc.ca
Ron Wiebe, President
Meetings/Conferences:
• 26th Supply Chain Management Association BC Education Conference, September, 2018, BC
Scope: Provincial

Supply Chain Management Association - Manitoba (SCMAMB)
#200, 5 Donald St., Winnipeg MB R3L 2T4
Tel: 204-231-0965; *Fax:* 204-233-1250
Toll-Free: 877-231-0965
info@scmamb.ca
www.scmamb.ca
www.linkedin.com/groups/SCMA-Manitoba-4546716
www.facebook.com/140785209269900
twitter.com/scmanational
Previous Name: Manitoba Institute of the Purhcasing Management Association of Canada; Purchasing Management Association of Canada - Manitoba Institute
Overview: A small provincial licensing organization overseen by Supply Chain Management Association
Mission: SCMAMB is committed to offering a professional development program coupled with networking opportunities to advance supply chain management.
Staff Member(s): 1
Membership: *Fees:* $410 regular; $45 student; $80 retired
Chief Officer(s):
Jay Anderson, President
Rick Reid, Executive Director

Supply Chain Management Association - New Brunswick (SCMANB)
#402, 527 Dundonald St., Fredericton NB E3B 1X5
Tel: 506-458-9414
info@scmanb.ca
www.scmanb.ca
www.linkedin.com/groups?about=&gid=2888933
www.facebook.com/NBPMI
twitter.com/scmanational
Previous Name: New Brunswick Purchasing Management Institute
Overview: A small provincial licensing organization overseen by Supply Chain Management Association
Mission: NBPMI is dedicated to being the leading source of education, training, & development in the field of purchasing & supply chain management. It provides members with networking opportunities & offers them training for a Supply Chain Management Professional (SCMP) designation.
Membership: 150; *Fees:* $365 regular; $0 student; *Member Profile:* Purchasing & supply management practioners, other business professionals, & students considering a career in the profession.
Activities: Training modules & interactive workshops
Chief Officer(s):
Ryan McPherson, President, 506-654-3280
president@scmanb.ca
Wendy Piercy, Administrator

Supply Chain Management Association - Newfoundland & Labrador (SCMANL)
PO Box 29011, Stn. Torbay Road, St. John's NL A1A 5B5
Tel: 709-778-4033; *Fax:* 709-724-5625
info@scmanl.ca
www.scmanl.ca
www.linkedin.com/groups?about=&gid=2888933
www.facebook.com/scmanational
twitter.com/scmanational
Previous Name: Newfoundland & Labradour Institute of the Purchasing Management Association of Canada
Overview: A small provincial licensing organization overseen by Supply Chain Management Association

Mission: To deliver education, training, & professional development programs in the province, so members may earn a Supply Chain Management Professional (SCMP) designation
Membership: *Fees:* $295 regular; $147.50 regular discounted; $65 retired; $40 student; *Member Profile:* From all sectors of the economy, including retail, manufacturing, transportation, distribution, government, natural resources & service
Chief Officer(s):
Shauna Clark, President
shaunak@nl.rogers.com

Supply Chain Management Association - Northwest Territories (SCMANWT)
PO Box 2736, Yellowknife NT X1A 2R1
Tel: 867-873-9324
info@scmanwt.ca
www.scmanwt.ca
Previous Name: Northwest Territories Institute of the Purchasing Management Association of Canada
Overview: A small provincial licensing organization overseen by Supply Chain Management Association
Mission: A non profit organization registered with the Societies Act in the Northwest Territories. They provide information and Education leading to a professional designation as a C.P.P. (Certified Professional Purchaser) the only accredited and legally recognized designation in the fields of Purchasing and Supply Management in Canada.
Membership: *Fees:* $350 regular; $175 regular discounted; $32 student; $52.50 retired
Chief Officer(s):
John Vandenberg, President

Supply Chain Management Association - Nova Scotia (SCMANS)
PO Box 21, Stn. CRO, Halifax NS B3J 2L4
Tel: 902-425-4029; *Fax:* 902-431-7220
info@scmans.ca
www.scmans.ca
www.linkedin.com/groups?about=&gid=2888933
www.facebook.com/140785209269900
twitter.com/scmanational
Previous Name: Nova Scotia Institute of the Purchasing Management Association of Canada
Overview: A small provincial licensing organization overseen by Supply Chain Management Association
Mission: NSIPMAC delivers education, training & professional development programs in the province, so members may earn a Supply Chain Management Professional (SCMP) designation.
Membership: *Fees:* $370 regular; *Member Profile:* From all sectors of the economy, including retail, manufacturing, transportation, distribution, government, natural resources & service.
Chief Officer(s):
Joe McKenna, President

Supply Chain Management Association - Ontario (SCMAO)
PO Box 64, #2704, 1 Dundas St. West, Toronto ON M5G 1Z3
Tel: 416-977-7566; *Fax:* 416-977-4135
Toll-Free: 877-726-6968
info@scmao.ca
www.scmao.ca
www.linkedin.com/groups?gid=5139410&trk=my_groups-b-grp-v
twitter.com/SCMAOnt
www.youtube.com/user/OIPMAC
Previous Name: Ontario Institute of the Purchasing Management Association of Canada
Overview: A small provincial licensing organization overseen by Supply Chain Management Association
Mission: The preeminent supply chain managemen organisation in Ontario, supporting a growing global SCM community of over 20,00 active members and program participants in meeting their professional and lifelong learning goals. Their programs taught by leading North American academics and professional trainers, are designed to build/enhance the professional competence and strategic perspective of practitioners at all levels of career progression, from entry-, to mid-, to senior/executive levels of functional responsibility.
Chief Officer(s):
Kelly Duffin, Executive Director Ext. 2136
kduffin@scmao.ca
Meetings/Conferences:
• 21st Supply Chain Management Association Ontario Annual Conference, 2018, ON
Scope: Provincial
Attendance: 400+

Supply Chain Management Association - Saskatchewan (SCMASK)
#221A, 3521 - 8th St. East, Saskatoon SK S7H 0W5
Tel: 306-653-8899; *Fax:* 306-653-8870
Toll-Free: 866-665-6167
info@scmask.ca
www.scmask.ca
www.linkedin.com/company/3549789
www.facebook.com/SCMASK
twitter.com/SCMASK
Previous Name: Saskatchewan Institute of the Purchasing Management Association of Canada
Overview: A small provincial licensing organization overseen by Supply Chain Management Association
Mission: To promote & improve supply management practices in the profession through education & raising the awareness of the supply management profession within Saskatchewan
Membership: 260; *Fees:* $450 regular; $225 regular discounted, student & retired; *Member Profile:* Supply chain management professionals
Activities: *Speaker Service:* Yes
Chief Officer(s):
Nicole Burgess, Executive Director
nburgess@scmask.ca

Support Enhance Access Service Centre (SEAS)
603 Whiteside Pl., Toronto ON M5A 1Y7
Tel: 416-362-1375; *Fax:* 416-362-4881
www.seascentre.org
www.youtube.com/user/SEASCentre
Previous Name: South East Asian Services Centre
Overview: A small local charitable organization founded in 1986
Mission: To promote individual well being, enhance family harmony and encourage community involvement in all walks of life through diverse programs, volunteer opportunities and community activities.
Member of: United Way
Activities: Community support service; family service; senior service; volunteer service; youth service
Chief Officer(s):
Rebecca Lee, Executive Director

Support Organization for Trisomy 18, 13 & Related Disorders
Toronto ON
Tel: 416-805-5736
www.trisomy.org
www.facebook.com/Trisomy18.Trisomy13.Awareness.SOFTrelatedDisorders
Also Known As: SOFT Canada
Overview: A small national licensing charitable organization founded in 1989
Mission: To offer support to families whose children are born with any of the following disorders: Trisomy, Partial Trisomy, Mosaic (not every cell), deletion of all or part of a chromosome, single gene disorders, any other disorder which produces serious, multiple birth defects
Affiliation(s): Easter Seals
Finances: *Annual Operating Budget:* Less than $50,000
Membership: 7,200 families; *Fees:* Schedule available; *Member Profile:* Families, friends or professionals associated with child with one of these disorders; (child may be alive or deceased);
Committees: Newsletter; Fundraising; Public Awareness; Professional Advisory; Information Services; Finance
Activities: Information about specific disorders; newsletters from Canada & the USA; access to an international database of children with rare disorders; *Speaker Service:* Yes
Chief Officer(s):
Satinder Sahota, Local Contact
satinder@sandalwoodpromos.com

Supporting Choices of People Edson (SCOPE)
4926 - 17 Ave., Edson AB T7E 1G4
Tel: 780-723-6100; *Fax:* 780-723-6100
scopel@telusplanet.net
Previous Name: Edson Association for the Developmentally Handicapped
Overview: A small local organization founded in 1974
Mission: To encourage the highest level of development of the individual; To promote normal opportunities for living in & integration within the community
Member of: Alberta Association for Community Living; Alberta Association of Rehabilitation Centres
Finances: *Annual Operating Budget:* $250,000-$500,000; *Funding Sources:* Government; fundraising
Staff Member(s): 21

Membership: 6; Fees: $5
Activities: Awareness Events: SCOPE Annual Telethon, Jan.

The Supreme Master Ching Hai Meditation Association of Ontario
Toronto ON
Tel: 416-503-0515
www.godsdirectcontact.org.tw
Overview: A small provincial organization
Mission: To promote the practice of meditation
Chief Officer(s):
Anita Kwok, Contact
anitawlkwok@gmail.com

Surety Association of Canada (SAC) / Association canadienne de caution
#709, 6299 Airport Rd., Mississauga ON L4V 1N3
Tel: 905-677-1353; Fax: 905-677-3345
surety@surety-canada.com
www.surety-canada.com
twitter.com/suretyincanada
www.youtube.com/suretyincanada
Overview: A small national organization founded in 1992
Mission: The Surety Association of Canada is committed to the continued development and use of surety products throughout all jurisdictions of Canada
Staff Member(s): 2
Membership: Member Profile: Major bonding companies, members from the insurance brokerage community, legal fraternity and other industry related entities.
Chief Officer(s):
Steven D. Ness, President
sness@suretycanada.com

Surrey Association for Community Living (SACL)
17687 - 56A Ave., Surrey BC V3S 1G4
Tel: 604-574-7481; Fax: 604-574-4731
admin@commliv.com
www.commliv.com
www.facebook.com/SurreyCommunityLiving
Previous Name: The Surrey Association for the Mentally Handicapped
Overview: A small local charitable organization founded in 1958
Mission: To provide services & support for individuals with special needs & their families & advocate on their behalf; to create an inclusive, safe & caring community that values dignity & choices through committed leadership & guidance
Member of: British Columbia Association for Community Living
Finances: Annual Operating Budget: $3 Million-$5 Million
Staff Member(s): 125; 50 volunteer(s)
Membership: 28; Committees: Audit & Policy Review; Governance; Monitoring
Activities: Library: Open to public
Chief Officer(s):
Coreen Windbiel, Executive Director
cwindbiel@commliv.com

The Surrey Association for the Mentally Handicapped See Surrey Association for Community Living

Surrey Board of Trade (SBOT)
#101, 14439 - 104 Ave., Surrey BC V3R 1M1
Tel: 604-581-7130; Fax: 604-588-7549
Toll-Free: 866-848-7130
info@businessinsurrey.com
www.businessinsurrey.com
www.linkedin.com/company/surrey-board-of-trade
www.facebook.com/SurreyBoardofTrade
twitter.com/SBofT
Previous Name: Surrey Chamber of Commerce
Overview: A small local organization founded in 1918
Mission: To provide advocacy, resources, experience & networking to members & fosters best business practices to ensure growth & prosperity of members
Member of: BC Chamber of Commerce; Canadian Chamber of Commerce
Finances: Funding Sources: Membership fees; events; sponsorship
Staff Member(s): 8
Membership: 1,900; Fees: Schedule available; Committees: Crime & Justice; Environment & Natural Resources; Finance & Taxation; Internationl Affaris; Social Policy; Transport & Infrastructure; Finance; Governance; Ambassador; Education; Networking Golf; Police Officer of the Year Awards; Surrey Business Excellence Awards; Innovation
Activities: Organizing monthly lunches & breakfasts, trade functions, forums, open houses & trade shows, & awards shows; Advocating; Providing networking, events, & workshops; Library: Business Resource Centre; Open to public
Chief Officer(s):
Anita Huberman, Chief Executive Officer
anita@businessinsurrey.com

Surrey Chamber of Commerce See Surrey Board of Trade

Surrey Food Bank
10732 City Pkwy., Surrey BC V3T 4C7
Tel: 604-581-5443; Fax: 604-588-8697
info@surreyfoodbank.org
www.surreyfoodbank.org
www.facebook.com/SurreyFoodBank
twitter.com/SurreyFoodBank
www.youtube.com/user/SurreyFoodBank
Overview: A small local charitable organization founded in 1983 overseen by Food Banks British Columbia
Mission: To help people help themselves by providing food hampers & alternatives to food lines such as community kitchens & food buying clubs
Member of: Food Banks British Columbia; Food Banks Canada; Surrey Chamber of Commerce
Affiliation(s): Better Business Bureau
Finances: Annual Operating Budget: $250,000-$500,000; Funding Sources: Public donations; foundation donations
Staff Member(s): 8; 75 volunteer(s)
Membership: 60; Fees: $5
Chief Officer(s):
Glen Slobodian, President

Surrey Symphony Society (SSS)
PO Box 39083, Stn. Panorama, #100, 15157 - 56th Ave., Surrey BC V3S 9A0
www.surreysymphony.com
www.facebook.com/surreysymphonysociety
twitter.com/SYOrchestra92
Also Known As: Surrey Youth Orchestra
Overview: A small local charitable organization founded in 1976 overseen by Orchestras Canada
Mission: To expand an appreciation of orchestral music among young musicians & to share this with the community through public performance
Member of: Orchestras Canada
Finances: Annual Operating Budget: Less than $50,000
Staff Member(s): 5; 8 volunteer(s)
Membership: 130 students; Fees: Schedule available
Activities: Weekly rehearsals; weekend workshops; public concerts; festival participation
Chief Officer(s):
Heather Christiansen, General Manager
gm.surreysymphony@gmail.com

Surrey-Delta Immigrant Services Society See DIVERSEcity Community Resources Society

Survivors of Abuse Recovering (SOAR)
PO Box 105, Kentville NS B4N 3V9
Tel: 902-679-7337
Toll-Free: 877-679-7627
info@survivorsofabuserecovering.ca
www.survivorsofabuserecovering.ca
Overview: A small local organization
Mission: To provide counselling service for survivors of childhood sexual abuse in Hants, Kings & Annapolis counties

SUS Foundation of Canada
620 Spadina Ave., Toronto ON M5S 2H4
www.susfoundation.ca
Also Known As: Cyc Foundation
Overview: A small national charitable organization founded in 1965
Mission: To fund educational & cultural projects
Member of: Ukrainian Self Reliance League of Canada
Affiliation(s): Ukrainian Self Reliance Associations
Finances: Funding Sources: Fundraising
Activities: Library: St. Vladimir Institute Library
Chief Officer(s):
William J. Strus, President

Sussex & District Chamber of Commerce
#2, 66 Broad St., Sussex NB E4E 5L2
Tel: 506-433-1845; Fax: 506-433-1886
sdcc@nb.aibn.com
sdccinc.org
www.facebook.com/157593137613881
Overview: A small local organization
Mission: To be a leading voice of business dedicated to enhancing opportunities for growth & development for our members & the community
Member of: Canadian Chamber of Commerce
Affiliation(s): Atlantic Provinces Chambers of Commerce
Finances: Annual Operating Budget: Less than $50,000; Funding Sources: Membership fees
Staff Member(s): 1
Membership: 100
Activities: Awareness Events: Kiwanis Home Show, April; Golf Tournament, Sept.; Community Awards Night Banquet, Oct.
Chief Officer(s):
Ivan Graham, President
Pam Kaye, Administrator

Sussex Sharing Club
PO Box 4196, 26 Eveleigh St., Sussex NB E4E 2N8
Tel: 506-433-6047
sussexsharingclub@nb.aibn.com
Overview: A small local charitable organization founded in 1986
Mission: To provide for those in need
Member of: Canadian Association of Food Banks; New Brunswick Association of Food Banks
Chief Officer(s):
Lois King, Administrator

Sustainability Project
2799 McDonald's Corners Rd., RR#3, Lanark ON K0G 1K0
Tel: 613-259-5022
sustain5@web.ca
www.sustainwellbeing.net
Also Known As: Guideposts for a Sustainable Future; Inviting Debate; 7th Generation Initiative
Overview: A small local organization founded in 1985
Mission: To collect, study, develop & teach ideas, information, technologies & customs that will help in the evolution of a sustainable society
Affiliation(s): Ontario Environment Network; Canadian Environmental Network; Sierra Club of Canada
Staff Member(s): 2
Activities: Life, Money & Illusion workshops
Chief Officer(s):
Mike Nickerson, Executive Director

Sustainable Buildings Canada (SBC) / Bâtiments Durables Canada
33 Longboat Ave., Toronto ON M5A 4C9
Tel: 416-752-3535
contact@sbcanada.org
www.sbcanada.org
www.linkedin.com/groups/3613714
www.facebook.com/SustBldgCan
twitter.com/SustBldgCan
Overview: A small national organization
Mission: To showcase to the world the Canadian cooperation that exists between the private sector & government, working together to implement innovative solutions to mitigate climate change, while serving the buildings industry
Chief Officer(s):
Michael Singleton, Executive Director

Sustainable Development Technology Canada (SDTC) / Technologies du développement durable Canada
#1850, 45 O'Connor St., Ottawa ON K1P 1A4
Tel: 613-234-6313; Fax: 613-234-0303
info@sdtc.ca
www.sdtc.ca
twitter.com/SDTC_TDDC
Overview: A medium-sized national organization founded in 2001
Mission: To create a healthy environment & a high quality of life for Canadians; To identify & fund technologies with strong competitive & environmental potential
Finances: Funding Sources: Government of Canada
Membership: Committees: Corporate Governance; Human Resources; Project Review; Audit
Chief Officer(s):
Jim Balsillie, Chair
Leah Lawrence, President & CEO
David Enns, Vice-President, Performance
Zoë Kolbuc, Vice-President, Partnerships
Ziyad Rahme, Vice-President, Investments
Publications:
• Sustainable Development Technology Canada Annual Report
Type: Yearbook; Frequency: Annually
• Sustainable Development Technology Canada Corporate Plan

Sustainable Kingston
184 Sydenham St., Kingston ON K7K 3M2
Tel: 613-544-2075
info@sustainablekingston.ca
sustainablekingston.ca
www.facebook.com/sustainablekingston
twitter.com/SustainableKtwn
www.pinterest.com/sustainablektwn/
Overview: A medium-sized local organization
Mission: Sustainable Kingston is a community-driven; non-profit organization that facilitates, connects and educates in order to drive initiatives as described in our city's Integrated Community Sustainability Plan (ICSP).
Chief Officer(s):
John Johnson, Executive Director
john@sustainablekingston.ca

Sustainable Urban Development Association (SUDA)
2637 Council Ring Rd., Mississauga ON L5L 1S6
Tel: 416-400-0553
mail@suda.ca
www.suda.ca
Overview: A medium-sized national organization
Mission: To foster a healthy natural environment by providing information about ways in which cities can become more efficient in the land, material, water and energy resources, and highly supportive of sustainable transportation.
Chief Officer(s):
John Banka, President

Svoboda Dance Festival Association
PO Box 664, North Battleford SK S9A 2Y9
Tel: 306-445-3732
Previous Name: Battlefords Dance Festival Association
Overview: A small local organization
Mission: To offer Ukranian dance instruction for all ages & skill levels
Chief Officer(s):
Marusia Kobrynsky, Co-President

Swampy Cree Tribal Council
PO Box 150, Hwy. 10 North, The Pas MB R9A 1K4
Tel: 204-623-3423; Fax: 204-623-2882
Toll-Free: 800-442-0459
www.swampycree.com
Overview: A small local organization founded in 1976
Mission: To vigorously pursue the object of fostering the social, economic & political well-being & development of member First Nations
Staff Member(s): 17
Membership: 12,000 individuals in 7 First Nations groups; *Member Profile:* First Nations groups in northwest central Manitoba
Activities: Providing administrative & service support to its members
Chief Officer(s):
Don Lathlin, Executive Director
don.lathlin@swampycree.com

Swan Hills Chamber of Commerce
PO Box 540, Swan Hills AB T0G 2C0
Tel: 780-333-5333
town@townofswanhills.com
www.townofswanhills.com
Overview: A small local organization
Mission: To support area businesses
Member of: Alberta Chamber of Commerce
Finances: *Annual Operating Budget:* Less than $50,000
Staff Member(s): 1; 10 volunteer(s)
Membership: 44; *Fees:* $15 homebase scale rate; *Committees:* Keyano Days; Tourist/Artists
Activities: Sponsoring events; Offering information on trade & business operations; *Awareness Events:* Keyano Days, last weekend in June; *Internships:* Yes; *Library:* Open to public
Chief Officer(s):
Janis Smith, Secretary

Swan Valley Chamber of Commerce
1500 Main St., Swan River MB R0L 1Z0
Tel: 204-734-3102
info@swanvalleychamber.com
www.swanvalleychamber.com
www.facebook.com/SwanValleyChamberOfCommerce
Overview: A small local organization
Mission: To promote local businesses & help them grow

Membership: *Committees:* Communications; Events; Executive; Membership; Retail/Promotion
Chief Officer(s):
Naomi Neufeld, President

The Swedish-Canadian Chamber of Commerce (SCCC)
#2109, 2 Bloor St. West, Toronto ON M4W 3E2
Tel: 416-925-8661
info@sccc.ca
www.sccc.ca
www.linkedin.com/groups/3401296
www.facebook.com/SwedishCanadianChamber
twitter.com/SwedishCanadian
Overview: A small international organization founded in 1965
Mission: To promote trade, commercial, cultural & social contacts between Sweden & Canada
Member of: European Union Chambers of Commerce in Toronto (Eurocit)
Finances: *Funding Sources:* Membership dues; events; sponsorship; advertising
Chief Officer(s):
Lennart P. Kleine, Chair

Sweet Adelines International - Westcoast Harmony Chapter
9574 - 160 St., Surrey BC V4N 2R6
membership@westcoastsings.com
www.westcoastsings.com
www.facebook.com/WestcoastHarmonyChorus
twitter.com/WestcoastSings
Overview: A small local charitable organization founded in 1965
Mission: To promote a capella, close harmony style singing for women, with high performance & competitive standards
8 volunteers
Activities: *Internships:* Yes
Chief Officer(s):
Anne Downton, Master Director

Swift Current & District Chamber of Commerce
145 - 1st Ave. NE, Swift Current SK S9H 2B1
Tel: 306-773-7268; Fax: 306-773-5686
info@swiftcurrentchamber.ca
www.swiftcurrentchamber.ca
www.linkedin.com/company/swift-current-&-district-chamber-of-commerce
Overview: A small local organization founded in 1908
Mission: To promote area businesses; To strengthen the business climate & local economy; To improve quality of life
Affiliation(s): Saskatchewan Chamber of Commerce; Canadian Chamber of Commerce
Finances: *Annual Operating Budget:* $100,000-$250,000; *Funding Sources:* Membership fees
Staff Member(s): 2; 20 volunteer(s)
Membership: 330; *Fees:* Schedule available
Activities: *Library:*
Chief Officer(s):
Clayton Wicks, CEO
ceo@swiftcurrentchamber.ca

Swift Current Agricultural & Exhibition Association
PO Box 146, 1700 - 17th Ave. SE, Swift Current SK S9H 3V5
Tel: 306-773-2944; Fax: 306-773-7015
swiftcurrentex@sasktel.net
www.swiftcurrentex.com
Overview: A small provincial charitable organization founded in 1938
Mission: To facilitate education, entertainment, exhibitions & agricultural programs for the cultural & economic benefits of the community
Member of: Saskatchewan Association of Agricultural Societies & Exhibitions
Finances: *Annual Operating Budget:* $500,000-$1.5 Million
Staff Member(s): 4; 500 volunteer(s)
Membership: 78; *Fees:* $5
Activities: Agricultural Fairs, Exhibitions, Livestock shows & sales, Trade shows
Chief Officer(s):
Donna Sagin, General Manager
Stuart Smith, President

Swift Current Creek Watershed Stewards (SCCWS)
PO Box 1088, Swift Current SK S9H 3X3
Tel: 306-778-5007; Fax: 306-778-5020
stewards@sccws.com
www.sccws.com
www.facebook.com/SwiftCurrentCreekWatershedStewards

Overview: A small local organization
Mission: To enhance water quality and stream health of the Swift Current Creek Watershed by promoting awareness and understanding among water users.
Chief Officer(s):
Arlene Unvoas, Executive Director

Swift Current United Way
Swift Current Business Centre, 145 1st Ave. NE, Swift Current SK S9H 2B1
Tel: 306-773-4828
unitedway@sasktel.net
www.swiftcurrentunitedway.ca
www.facebook.com/swiftunitedway
twitter.com/swiftunitedway
www.instagram.com/swiftunitedway
Overview: A small local organization overseen by United Way of Canada - Centraide Canada
Mission: To strengthen the social & economic conditions of the community; To improve the lives of all residents of Swift Current & Southern Saskatchewan
Chief Officer(s):
Stacey Schwartz, Executive Director

Swim Alberta
Percy Page Centre, 11759 Groat Rd., Edmonton AB T5M 3K6
Tel: 780-415-1780; Fax: 780-415-1788
office@swimalberta.ca
www.swimalberta.ca
www.facebook.com/swim.alberta
twitter.com/SwimAlberta
Overview: A medium-sized provincial organization founded in 1963 overseen by Swimming Canada
Mission: To maintain a progressive athletic / club development program & a high performance program
Member of: Swimming Natation Canada
Finances: *Funding Sources:* Membership fees; Sponsorships; Lottery
Staff Member(s): 4
Activities: *Speaker Service:* Yes; *Library:* Open to public
Chief Officer(s):
Dean Schultz, Interim President
president@swimalberta.ca
Cheryl Humphrey, Executive Director
chumphrey@swimalberta.ca

Swim BC
PO Box 1749, Garibaldi Highlands BC V0N 1T0
Tel: 604-898-9100; Fax: 604-898-9200
www.swim.bc.ca
facebook.com/SwimBC
twitter.com/swimbcstaff
Overview: A small provincial organization founded in 1974 overseen by Swimming Canada
Mission: To provide the opportunity, leadership & means for members to achieve excellence in all areas of the sport of swimming
Member of: Swimming Canada
Finances: *Annual Operating Budget:* $500,000-$1.5 Million; *Funding Sources:* Self-generated; provincial government
Staff Member(s): 4; 16 volunteer(s)
Membership: 8,000
Activities: *Library:*
Chief Officer(s):
Jerome Beauchamp, President
Mark Schuett, Executive Director
markschuett@swimbc.ca

Swim Manitoba *See* Swim-Natation Manitoba

Swim Nova Scotia (SNS)
5516 Spring Garden Rd., Halifax NS B3J 1G6
Tel: 902-425-5454; Fax: 902-425-5606
swimming@sportnovascotia.ca
www.swimnovascotia.com
Overview: A small provincial charitable organization overseen by Swimming Canada
Member of: Swimming Canada
Affiliation(s): AthletesCAN
Finances: *Annual Operating Budget:* $50,000-$100,000
Staff Member(s): 1; 20 volunteer(s)
Membership: 2,800
Activities: Swim competitions & fundraising events
Chief Officer(s):
Sue Jackson, President
suejack01@yahoo.com
Bette El-Hawary, Executive Director

Swim Ontario
#206, 3 Concorde Gate, Toronto ON M3C 3N7
Tel: 416-426-7220; *Fax:* 416-426-7356
info@swimontario.com
www.swimontario.com
www.facebook.com/117335688316744
twitter.com/SwimOntario
Overview: A medium-sized provincial organization founded in 1922 overseen by Swimming Canada
Member of: Swimming Canada
Staff Member(s): 5; 17 volunteer(s)
Membership: 10,000+ in 140+ clubs; *Committees:* Strategic Planning; Administration; Finance; Risk Management; Programme Policy
Activities: Learn-to-Swim; training for competitions & fitness
Chief Officer(s):
Eric Martin, President
ericmartin@rogers.com
John Vadeika, Executive Director
john@swimontario.com

Swim Saskatchewan
2205 Victoria Ave., Regina SK S4P 0S4
Tel: 306-780-9291; *Fax:* 306-525-4009
office@swimsask.ca
www.swimsask.ca
www.facebook.com/325400947571418
Overview: A medium-sized provincial organization overseen by Swimming Canada
Mission: To promote excellence through sport development, competition, education, training and strong member organizations.
Member of: Swimming Canada
Staff Member(s): 3
Chief Officer(s):
Susan Miazga, President
barrymiazga@sasktel.net
Marj Walton, Executive Director, 306-780-9238
marjwalton@swimsask.ca

Swim Yukon
4061 - 4th Ave., Whitehorse YT Y1A 1H1
swimyukon@gmail.com
sportyukon.com/member/swim-yukon
Overview: A medium-sized provincial organization
Mission: Swim Yukon is the Sport Governing Body for competitive swimming in the Yukon.
Member of: Sport Yukon
Affiliation(s): Swimming Canada
Activities: Swim meets
Chief Officer(s):
Michael McArthur, President

Swimming Canada / Natation Canada
307 Gilmour St., Ottawa ON K2P 0P7
Tel: 613-260-1348; *Fax:* 613-260-0804
natloffice@swimming.ca
www.swimming.ca
www.facebook.com/56320144853
twitter.com/SwimmingCanada
www.youtube.com/swimmingcanada;
instagram.com/swimmingcanada
Overview: A large national organization founded in 1909
Mission: To direct & develop competitive swimming in Canada; To represent Canada in international organizations & events
Affiliation(s): Aquatic Federation of Canada
Finances: *Funding Sources:* Membership fees; Corporate sponsorships; Sport Canada; Canadian Olympic Committee
21 volunteer(s)
Membership: Over 50,000
Activities: *Rents Mailing List:* Yes
Chief Officer(s):
Ahmed El-Awadi, Chief Executive Officer, 613-260-1348 Ext. 2007
aelawadi@swimming.ca
Larry Clough, Chief Financial Officer, 613-260-1348 Ext. 2008
lclough@swimming.ca
John Atkinson, Director, High Performance, 613-260-1348 Ext. 2006
jatkinson@swimming.ca
Brian Edey, Director, Operations, 613-260-1348 Ext. 2003
bedey@swimming.ca
Chris Wilson, Director, Marketing, 613-691-2975
cwilson@swimming.ca
Awards:
• Victor Davis Memorial Award

Annual awards from the Victor Davis Memorial Fund assist young Canadian swimmers to continue their training, education & pursuit of excellence at the international level of competition; recipients are determined by the Victor Davis Memorial Fund Awards Committee
• Female/Male Swimmer of the Year
Annual awards recognize best international swimmers in the following categories: 1) able-bodied athletes, 2) athletes with a disability, & 3) long distance competitors; each winner receives a plaque & gift
• Coach of the Year
Annual awards recognize coaches of swimmers in the following categories: 1) able-bodied athletes; 2) athletes with a disability, & 3) long distance competitors; each winner receives a plaque & gift
• Female/Male Para-swimmer of the Year
• Para-Coach of the Year
• Open Water Swimmer of the Year
• Open Water Coach of the Year
• President's Award
• Volunteer Contribution Award
• Volunteer of the Year

Swimming New Brunswick / Natation Nouveau-Brunswick
#13, 900 Hanwell Rd., Fredericton NB E3B 6A3
Tel: 506-451-1323; *Fax:* 506-451-1325
swimnb@nb.aibn.com
www.swimnb.ca
www.facebook.com/1401518450068316
twitter.com/SwimmingNB
Overview: A medium-sized provincial organization overseen by Swimming Canada
Member of: Swimming Canada
300 volunteer(s)
Membership: 668; *Fees:* $12-70; *Committees:* Nomination & Succession; Policy & Governance; Risk Management; Strategic Plan; Finance; Technical; Officials; Communication & Promotion; President's Council
Chief Officer(s):
David Frise, President
dfrise@gmail.com
Pat Ketterling, Executive Director

Swimming Newfoundland & Labrador
1296A Kenmount Rd., Paradise NL A1L 1N3
Tel: 709-576-7946; *Fax:* 709-576-7493
swimnl@sportnl.ca
www.swimnl.nfld.net
www.facebook.com/swimmingNL
twitter.com/SwimmingNL
www.youtube.com/user/SwimmingNL
Overview: A medium-sized provincial organization founded in 1974 overseen by Swimming Canada
Member of: Swimming Canada
Staff Member(s): 10
Chief Officer(s):
Joan Butler, President
joanb@mun.ca
Corina Hartley, Executive Director
swimnl@sportnl.ca

Swimming PEI *See* Swimming Prince Edward Island

Swimming Prince Edward Island
40 Enman Cres., Charlottetown PE C1E 1E6
Tel: 902-569-0583
Toll-Free: 800-247-6712
swimpei@sportpei.pe.ca
www.swimpei.com
Also Known As: Swim PEI
Previous Name: Swimming PEI
Overview: A small provincial charitable organization overseen by Swimming Canada
Member of: Swimming Canada
Finances: *Annual Operating Budget:* Less than $50,000
Staff Member(s): 1; 30 volunteer(s)
Membership: 200; *Fees:* $40; *Member Profile:* Ages 6-70; *Committees:* Finance; Coaching; Officials; Awards
Activities: Competitive swimming; swimming development; *Speaker Service:* Yes
Chief Officer(s):
Marguerite Middleton, Chief, Island Officials
memiddleton@gov.pe.ca

Swim-Natation Manitoba (SNM)
#209, 145 Pacific Ave., Winnipeg MB R3B 2Z6
Tel: 204-925-5778; *Fax:* 204-925-5624
swim@sportmanitoba.ca
www.swimmanitoba.mb.ca
twitter.com/Swim_Manitoba
Previous Name: Swim Manitoba
Overview: A medium-sized provincial organization founded in 1913 overseen by Swimming Canada
Mission: To produce fast swimmers & to make the experience a healthy, fun, exiting & rewarding adventure
Member of: Swimming Canada; Sport Manitoba
Finances: *Annual Operating Budget:* $250,000-$500,000
Staff Member(s): 3; 1500 volunteer(s)
Membership: 18 clubs + 1500 swimmers + 300 coaches + 1300 officials & volunteers; *Committees:* Advancement; Competition Hosting; Executive; Finance & Operations; Governance; Sport
Chief Officer(s):
Steve Armstrong, President
Mark Fellner, Executive Director
swim.ed@sportmanitoba.ca

Swiss Canadian Chamber of Commerce (Ontario) Inc. (SCCC)
756 Royal York Rd., Toronto ON M8Y 2T6
Tel: 416-236-0039; *Fax:* 416-551-1011
sccc@swissbiz.ca
www.swissbiz.ca
www.facebook.com/swiss.chamber
Overview: A medium-sized provincial organization founded in 1966
Mission: To assume a prominent role in promoting commercial, industrial & financial relations between Switzerland & Canada, with primary focus on membership in Ontario
Member of: Union of Swiss Chambers Abroad
Finances: *Funding Sources:* Annual dues; advertising in Info/Suisse
Membership: 88; *Fees:* Schedule available
Activities: Organizing luncheons, networking evening, golf tournament, annual black tie dinner dance, annual spousal dinner cruise; *Speaker Service:* Yes
Chief Officer(s):
Julien Favre, President

Swiss Canadian Chamber of Commerce (Québec) Inc. *Voir* Chambre de commerce Canado-Suisse (Québec) Inc.

Swiss Club Saskatoon
349 Carlton Dr., Saskatoon SK S7H 3P2
Tel: 306-665-6039
swissclubsaskatoon@hotmail.com
Overview: A small provincial organization founded in 1979
Mission: To provide opportunities for Canadians of Swiss background to speak Swiss languages & dialects
Chief Officer(s):
Elisabeth Eilinger, Contact

Sydenham Field Naturalists (SFN)
PO Box 22008, Wallaceburg ON N8A 5G4
www.sydenhamfieldnaturalists.ca
Overview: A small local charitable organization founded in 1985
Mission: To preserve wildlife, promote public interest, cooperate with others with similar interests, consider matters of environmental concern
Member of: Federation of Ontario Naturalists; Canadian Nature Federation; Carolinian Canada
Finances: *Funding Sources:* Bingo profits; private donations; grants
Membership: 35-40; *Fees:* $10 student; $15 single; $25 family
Activities: Field trips; planting of native shrubs/wildflowers; indoor meetings; wood lot acquisition
Chief Officer(s):
Denise Shephard, President

Sydney & Area Chamber of Commerce (SACC)
275 Charlotte St., Sydney NS B1P 1C6
Tel: 902-564-6453; *Fax:* 902-539-7487
www.sydneyareachamber.ca
www.facebook.com/sydneychamber
twitter.com/SydneyChamber
Overview: A small local organization
Mission: To promote local business; To foster economic development
Finances: *Funding Sources:* Membership fees
Staff Member(s): 2
Membership: 500; *Fees:* $199 bronze; $299 silver; $699 gold; $1499 platinum
Activities: *Internships:* Yes; *Speaker Service:* Yes
Chief Officer(s):

Adrian White, Executive Director
adrian@sydneyareachamber.ca

Sydney & Louisburg Railway Historical Society / Le Musée de chemin de fer de Sydney à Louisburg
S&L, 7330 Main Street, Louisbourg NS B1C 1P5
Tel: 902-733-2720
Also Known As: S&L Museum
Overview: A small local organization founded in 1973
Mission: To commemorate the history of the S&L Railway by preserving & displaying surviving artifacts & documents; To commemorate the people who worked for the S&L Railway; To explain the local & commercial history of the area which relates to the S&L Railway; To explain & commemorate the general themes of railway & transportation history & technology
Member of: Canadian Museums Association; Federation of Nova Scotia Heritage
Affiliation(s): Nova Scotia Museum
Membership: 250
Activities: Newsletter; Annual reunion the second Sunday in Septmeber; *Library:* Sydney & Louisburg Railway Historical Society Resource Centre; Open to public by appointment
Chief Officer(s):
William Bussey, President
Jean Bagnell, Secretary
Margie Cameron, Treasurer
Eugene Magee, Curator

Sylvan Lake Chamber of Commerce
PO Box 9119, Sylvan Lake AB T4S 1S6
Tel: 403-887-3048; Fax: 403-887-3061
info@sylvanlakechamber.com
www.sylvanlakechamber.com
www.facebook.com/SylvanLakeChamber
Overview: A small local organization
Mission: To promote & enhance the commercial, industrial, agricultural & civic environments of the Town of Sylvan Lake & district
Member of: Alberta Chamber of Commerce
Finances: *Funding Sources:* Town grants; fundraising
Membership: *Fees:* Schedule available
Chief Officer(s):
Denise Williams, Executive Director

Syme-Woolner Neighbourhood & Family Centre (SWNFC)
#3, 2468 Eglinton Ave. West, Toronto ON M6M 5E2
Tel: 416-766-4634; Fax: 416-766-8162
swoolner@symewoolner.org
www.symewoolner.org
Overview: A medium-sized local charitable organization founded in 1996
Mission: To create in the community a sense of belonging, to enable individuals, families and groups to support each other and build a better future.
Finances: *Funding Sources:* City of Toronto, United Way
Staff Member(s): 42
Chief Officer(s):
Mark Neysmith, Executive Director

Symphonie Nouveau-Brunswick See Symphony New Brunswick

Symphony New Brunswick / Symphonie Nouveau-Brunswick
Brunswick Square, 39 King St., Level III, Saint John NB E2L 4W3
Tel: 506-634-8379; Fax: 506-634-0843
symphony@nbnet.nb.ca
www.symphonynb.com
www.facebook.com/symphonynb
twitter.com/symphonynb
Previous Name: Saint John Symphony
Overview: A medium-sized provincial charitable organization founded in 1984 overseen by Orchestras Canada
Mission: To present high-quality, live orchestral & chamber music from all periods & to promote the appreciation of music through educational activities in New Brunswick
Member of: Orchestras Canada
Affiliation(s): American Federation of Musicians
Finances: *Annual Operating Budget:* $250,000-$500,000; *Funding Sources:* Canada Council; Province of NB; Individual & corporate donations
Staff Member(s): 4; 300 volunteer(s)
Membership: 500-999

Activities: Performing concert series in the New Brunswick area; Performing school outreach concerts; *Library:* Not open to public
Chief Officer(s):
Jennifer Grant, General Manager
Michael Newnham, Music Director

Symphony Nova Scotia (SNS)
Park Lane Mall, PO Box 218, #301, 5657 Spring Garden Rd., Halifax NS B3J 3R4
Tel: 902-421-1300; Fax: 902-422-1209
info@symphonyns.ca
www.symphonynovascotia.ca
www.linkedin.com/company/symphony-nova-scotia
www.facebook.com/SymphonyNovaScotia
twitter.com/SymphonyNS
www.youtube.com/user/SymphonyNovaScotia
Overview: A small provincial charitable organization founded in 1983 overseen by Orchestras Canada
Mission: To enhance the quality of life of the citizens of Nova Scotia through high quality, professionally performed orchestral music
Member of: Orchestras Canada
Finances: *Funding Sources:* Government; Corporate & individual donations; Ticket revenue
Staff Member(s): 13
Membership: 27
Activities: Classical, baroque & pops concerts; *Library*
Chief Officer(s):
Christopher Wilkinson, Chief Executive Officer, 902-421-1300 Ext. 222
ceo@symphonyns.ca
Bernhard Gueller, Music Director

Symphony on the Bay
#300, 1100 Burloak Dr., Burlington ON L7L 6B2
Tel: 905-526-6690
info@symphonyonthebay.ca
symphonyonthebay.com
www.facebook.com/119532624785141
twitter.com/SymphonyOnBay
www.youtube.com/channel/UC3N-Vqf9Yy304F5Q-mZ9IeQ
Previous Name: McMaster Symphony Orchestra; Greater Hamilton Symphony Association
Overview: A small local charitable organization founded in 1973 overseen by Orchestras Canada
Mission: To enrich the cultural life of the Hamilton & surrounding area by maintaining a full-size community symphony orchestra; to perform a wide repertoire of symphonic music, including works by Canadian composers; to make great symphonic music accessible to a larger public by offering attractive concert programs at affordable prices
Member of: Hamilton Volunteer Centre
Affiliation(s): Hamilton & Region Arts Council
Finances: *Funding Sources:* Government; Foundations; Corporate; Private; Fundraising
Staff Member(s): 5
Membership: 67; *Member Profile:* Audition for orchestra members
Activities: *Library:* by appointment Not open to public
Chief Officer(s):
Fonda Loft, President
Aaron Hutchinson, Orchestra Operations Manager
Andrea Armstrong, Personnel Manager

Synchro Alberta
The Percy Page Centre, 11759 Groat Rd., Edmonton AB T5M 3K6
Tel: 780-415-1789; Fax: 780-415-0056
www.synchroalberta.com
www.facebook.com/SynchroAlberta
Overview: A medium-sized provincial organization overseen by Synchro Canada
Member of: Synchro Canada
Staff Member(s): 2
Membership: 1200
Activities: Competitive & recreational meets
Chief Officer(s):
Jennifer Luzia, Executive Director
jluzia@synchroalberta.com

Synchro BC
#2002C, 3713 Kensington Ave., Burnaby BC V5B 0A7
Tel: 604-333-3640
www.synchro.bc.ca
www.facebook.com/Synchro-BC-213448205667190/?ref=hl

twitter.com/SynchroBC
www.youtube.com/channel/UCSpuYX-rsu9m6VJs6nKx-fA/feed
Overview: A medium-sized provincial licensing organization overseen by Synchro Canada
Mission: To foster & promote a fully integrated Synchronized Swimming Sport System throughout BC, which will offer opportunities for excellence at all levels of participation from Recreational to International
Member of: Synchro Canada
Finances: *Funding Sources:* Government; donations
Membership: 1,200; *Fees:* Schedule available
Activities: *Speaker Service:* Yes; *Rents Mailing List:* Yes
Chief Officer(s):
Annie Smith, Executive Director
ed@synchro.bc.ca
Kara Kalin Zader, Technical Director
td@synchro.bc.ca
Awards:
• Athlete Awards Program
Awarded to honour excellence among athletes in various categories.
• Club Development Award
• Coaching Awards
Awarded to recognize excellence in coaching, in various categories
• Officials Awards
Awarded to recognize excellence in officiating, in various categories
• Volunteer Awards
Awarded to recognize excellence in volunteering, in various categories

Synchro Canada
#401, 700 Industrial Ave., Ottawa ON K1G 0Y9
Tel: 613-748-5674; Fax: 613-748-5724
synchroinfo@synchro.ca
www.synchro.ca
www.facebook.com/synchrocanada
twitter.com/synchrocanada
www.youtube.com/synchrocanada
Previous Name: Canadian Amateur Synchronized Swimming Association
Overview: A medium-sized national charitable organization founded in 1968
Mission: To develop & operate the sport of synchronized swimming in Canada, through a variety of programs designed to develop athletes, coaches & officials
Staff Member(s): 7; 70 volunteer(s)
Membership: 5,000-14,999
Chief Officer(s):
Jackie Buckingham, Chief Executive Officer, 613-748-5674 Ext. 222
jackie@synchro.ca
Isabelle Lecompte, Manager, High Performance
isabelle@synchro.ca

Synchro Manitoba
145 Pacific Ave., Winnipeg MB R3B 2Z6
Tel: 204-925-5693; Fax: 204-925-5703
execdirector@synchromb.ca
www.synchromb.ca
Previous Name: Canadian Amateur Synchronized Swimming Association (Manitoba Section)
Overview: A small provincial organization founded in 1958 overseen by Synchro Canada
Mission: To promote, teach, foster, encourage, & improve, synchronized swimming in Manitoba; to regulate synchro swim in Manitoba in accordance with the constitution by-laws & rules
Member of: Synchro Canada
Affiliation(s): Manitoba Sports Federation
Staff Member(s): 2
Activities: *Library:* Resource Centre
Chief Officer(s):
Allison Gervais, Executive Director
execdirector@synchromb.ca

Synchro New Brunswick
436 Young St., Saint John NB E2M 2V2
Tel: 506-672-2399; Fax: 506-672-6020
www.synchronb.ca
Overview: A medium-sized provincial organization overseen by Synchro Canada
Member of: Synchro Canada

Synchro Newfoundland & Labrador
c/o Sport Newfoundland & Labrador, 1296-A Kenmount Rd., Paradise NL A1L 1N3

synchronl@hotmail.com
www.synchronl.com
www.facebook.com/synchronl
twitter.com/synchronl
Overview: A small provincial organization overseen by Synchro Canada
Member of: Synchro Canada
Chief Officer(s):
Jennifer Folkes, President, 709-368-1996

Synchro Nova Scotia
5516 Spring Garden Rd., 4th Fl., Halifax NS B3J 1G6
Tel: 902-426-5454; *Fax:* 902-425-5606
synchro@sportnovascotia.ca
www.sportnovascotia.ca
www.facebook.com/177261688979414
Overview: A medium-sized provincial organization overseen by Synchro Canada
Mission: To promote synchronized swimming throughout the province
Member of: Synchro Canada
Chief Officer(s):
Pam Kidney, Executive Director

Synchro PEI
c/o Sport PEI, 40 Enman Cres., Charlottetown PE C1E 1E6
synchropei.goalline.ca
Also Known As: PEI Synchronized Swimming Association
Overview: A small provincial organization overseen by Synchro Canada
Member of: Synchro Canada
Chief Officer(s):
Jodi Williams, President

Synchro Saskatchewan
#209, 1860 Lorne St., Regina SK S4P 2L7
Tel: 306-780-9227; *Fax:* 306-780-9445
synchro.sk@sasktel.net
www.synchrosask.com
Overview: A small provincial organization overseen by Synchro Canada
Mission: To promote & develop synchronized swimming in Saskatchewan
Member of: Synchro Canada; SaskSport
Finances: *Annual Operating Budget:* $100,000-$250,000;
Funding Sources: Saskatchewan Lottery Trust Fund
Staff Member(s): 3; 30 volunteer(s)
Membership: 1,200; *Fees:* Schedule available; *Committees:* Finance; Marketing; Technical; Competitions; Officials; Marketing; Grassroot Programming
Chief Officer(s):
Tanya Pohl, President
president@synchrosask.com
Kathleen Reynolds, Executive Director
ed@synchrosask.com
Awards:
• Recognition Awards Program
Awarded to recognize excellence in 3 categories: Athlete, Coach & Volunteer

Synchro Swim Ontario
128 Galaxy Blvd., Toronto ON M9W 4Y6
Tel: 416-679-9522; *Fax:* 416-679-9535
synchroontario.com
www.facebook.com/SynchroSwimOntario
twitter.com/SynchroONTARIO
Overview: A medium-sized provincial licensing organization overseen by Synchro Canada
Mission: To oversee synchronized swimming in Ontario, including varsity competiton, competitive clubs & community recreation programs; to develop, promote, support & regulate synchronized swimming through the implementation of an integrated sports system that is accessible to all Ontarians by providing opportunites for enjoyment & the pursuit of individual goals
Member of: Synchro Canada
Staff Member(s): 4
Membership: *Member Profile:* Athlete development at recreational through to elite levels; officials development; coach development; competition structures; *Committees:* Executive; Finance; High Performance; High Performance Hiring & Selection; Novice; Ontario Officials Management Team; Provincial Jury of Appeal; Technical Training & Development; Volunteer Management
Chief Officer(s):
Mary Dwyer, Executive Director, 416-679-9522 Ext. 222
mdwyer@synchroontario.com

Awards:
• Trillium Awards Program

Synchro Yukon Association
4061 - 4th Ave., Whitehorse YT Y1A 1H1
Tel: 867-668-7441
synchro_yukon@hotmail.com
sportyukon.com/member/synchro-yukon-association
Overview: A medium-sized provincial organization overseen by Synchro Canada
Mission: To promote the sport of Synchronized Swimming in the Yukon.
Member of: Synchro Canada; Sport Yukon
Chief Officer(s):
Lindsay Roberts, President

Synchro-Québec
4545, av Pierre-de Coubertin, Montréal QC H1V 0B2
Tél: 514-252-3087
Ligne sans frais: 866-537-3164
fnsq@synchroquebec.qc.ca
www.synchroquebec.com
www.facebook.com/synchro.quebec
twitter.com/synchroquebec
Nom précédent: Fédération de nage synchronisée
Aperçu: *Dimension:* moyenne; *Envergure:* provinciale; Organisme sans but lucratif surveillé par Synchro Canada
Mission: Planifier et supporter le développement de la nage synchronisée au Québec; administrer l'ensemble des compétitions qui se déroule au Québec; veiller au perfectionnement de ses entraîneurs, officiels et bénévoles
Membre de: Synchro Canada
Membre(s) du personnel: 4
Activités: *Stagiaires:* Oui
Membre(s) du bureau directeur:
Diane Lachapelle, Directrice générale
dlachapelle@synchroquebec.qc.ca

Syndicat Agriculture *See* Agriculture Union

Syndicat canadien de la fonction publique *See* Canadian Union of Public Employees

Le Syndicat canadien des employées et employés professionnels et de bureau *See* Canadian Office & Professional Employees Union

Syndicat catholique des ouvriers du textile de Magog *Voir* Syndicat des ouvriers du textile de Magog

Syndicat construction Côte-Nord (ind.) *Voir* Syndicat québécois de la construction

Syndicat de l'emploi et de l'immigration du Canada *See* Canada Employment & Immigration Union

Syndicat de la fonction publique de l'Alberta *See* Alberta Union of Provincial Employees

Syndicat de la fonction publique de l'Ile-du-Prince-Édouard *See* Prince Edward Island Union of Public Sector Employees

Syndicat de la fonction publique de la Nouvelle-Écosse *See* Nova Scotia Government & General Employees Union

Syndicat de la fonction publique de la Saskatchewan *See* Saskatchewan Government & General Employees' Union

Syndicat de la fonction publique du Québec inc. (ind.) (SFPQ) / Québec Government Employees' Union (Ind.)
5100, boul des Gradins, Québec QC G2J 1N4
Tél: 418-623-2424; *Téléc:* 418-623-6109
Ligne sans frais: 855-623-2424
communication@sfpq.qc.ca
www.sfpq.qc.ca
www.linkedin.com/company/syndicat-de-la-fonction-publique-du-qu-bec
www.facebook.com/SFPQ.Syndicat
twitter.com/SFPQ_Syndicat
www.youtube.com/user/SFPQ
Aperçu: *Dimension:* grande; *Envergure:* provinciale; fondée en 1962
Mission: Assurer la défense des intérêts économiques, politiques et sociaux des membres et le développement de leurs conditions de vie; faire la promotion des services publics comme moyen démocratique de répondre aux besoins de la population
Finances: *Budget de fonctionnement annuel:* $3 Million-$5 Million
Membre(s) du personnel: 105

Membre: 43 000 + 120 sections locales; *Comités:* Comité national des femmes; Comité national des jeunes
Activités: Recours; santé et sécurité au travail; assurances collectives; formation; publications de brochures, dépliants; *Bibliothèque:* Centre de documentation
Membre(s) du bureau directeur:
Lucie Martineau, Présidente général
Publications:
• Bulletin SFPQ Express [publication Syndicat de la fonction publique du Québec inc.]
Type: Bulletin
• Journal SFPQ [publication Syndicat de la fonction publique du Québec inc.]
Type: Journal

Abitibi - Témiscamingue - Nord du Québec
42, 7e rue, Rouyn-Noranda QC J9X 1Z7
Tél: 819-797-4254; *Téléc:* 819-797-4395
Ligne sans frais: 888-797-2844
alain.pomerleau@sfpq.qc.ca
www.sfpq.qc.ca/regions/abitibi-temiscamingue-nord-du-quebec
Membre(s) du bureau directeur:
Gabriel Bédard, Président régional, 819-797-4254
gabriel.bedard@sfpq.qc.ca

Bas Saint-Laurent - Côte Nord - Gaspésie et les Îles
159, rue St-Pierre, Matane QC G4W 2B8
Tél: 418-566-6591; *Téléc:* 418-566-8930
Ligne sans frais: 888-566-6591
nelson.carrier@sfpq.qc.ca
www.sfpq.qc.ca/regions/bas-laurent-gaspesie-cote-nord-les-iles
Membre(s) du bureau directeur:
Hélène Chouinard, Présidente régionale, 418-566-6591 Ext. 2002
helene.chouinard@sfpq.qc.ca

Centre du Québec-Estrie-Mauricie
2940, boul Lemire, Drummondville QC J2B 7J6
Tél: 819-475-0072; *Téléc:* 819-475-1188
Ligne sans frais: 800-561-5572
martine.charette@sfpq.qc.ca
www.monsyndicat.net
Membre(s) du bureau directeur:
Luc Légaré, Président régional, 819-475-0195
luc.legare@sfpq.qc.ca

Laurentides - Lanaudière - Outaouais
#204, 294, rue Labelle, 2e étage, Saint-Jérôme QC J7Z 5L1
Tél: 450-432-8800; *Téléc:* 450-432-0097
Ligne sans frais: 800-265-5693
rr5@sfpq.qc.ca
www.sfpq.qc.ca/regions/laurentides-lanaudiere-outaouais
Membre(s) du bureau directeur:
Sylvain Gendron, Président régional, 450-432-0011
sylvain.gendron@sfpq.qc.ca

Montérégie
#302, 3234 boul Taschereau, Greenfield Park QC J4V 2H3
Tél: 450-676-0357; *Téléc:* 450-676-0209
Ligne sans frais: 800-265-7445
normand.moreau@sfpq.qc.ca
www.sfpq.qc.ca/regions/monteregie
Membre(s) du bureau directeur:
Daniel Landry, Président régional
daniel.landry@sfpq.qc.ca

Montréal - Laval
#1005, 425, boul de Maisonneuve ouest, Montréal QC H3A 3G5
Tél: 514-844-4487; *Téléc:* 514-844-4619
sylvestre.jean-francois@sfpq.qc.ca
Membre(s) du bureau directeur:
Jean-François Sylvestre, Président régional

Québec - Chaudière-Appalaches
5100, boul des Gradins, Québec QC G2J 1N4
Tél: 418-623-9919; *Téléc:* 418-623-2286
Ligne sans frais: 800-382-6919
annie.dallaire@sfpq.qc.ca
www.sfpq.qc.ca/regions/quebec-chaudiere-appalaches
Membre(s) du bureau directeur:
Steve Dorval, Président régional, 418-623-9919 Ext. 101
steve.dorval@sfpq.qc.ca

Saguenay - Lac-St-Jean - Chibougamau - Charlevoix - Houte-Côte-Nord
2447, rue Saint-Dominique, Jonquière QC G7X 6K9
Tél: 418-548-5852; *Téléc:* 418-548-6777
Ligne sans frais: 800-561-5032
martine.duchesne@sfpq.qc.ca

Membre(s) du bureau directeur:
Brigitte Claveau, Présidente régionale, 418-548-5852
brigitte.claveau@sfpq.qc.ca

Syndicat de la relève agricole d'Abitibi-Témiscamingue
970, av Larivière, Rouyn-Noranda QC J9X 4K5
Tél: 819-762-0833; *Téléc:* 819-762-0575
abitibi-temiscamingue@upa.qc.ca
Aperçu: Dimension: petite; *Envergure:* locale
Membre de: Fédération de l'UPA d'Abitibi-Témiscamingue
Membre(s) du bureau directeur:
Simon Leblond, Président

Syndicat de professionnelles et professionnels du gouvernement du Québec (SPGQ) / Union of Professional Employees of the Québec Government
7, rue Vallière, Québec QC G1K 6S9
Tél: 418-692-0022; *Téléc:* 418-692-1338
Ligne sans frais: 800-463-5079
courrier@spgq.qc.ca
www.spgq.qc.ca
www.facebook.com/lespgq
twitter.com/spgq
www.youtube.com/spgqinformation
Aperçu: Dimension: grande; *Envergure:* provinciale; fondée en 1966
Finances: *Budget de fonctionnement annuel:* Plus de $5 Million
Membre(s) du personnel: 17
Membre: 20 000 + 35 sections locales; *Comités:* Électoral; surveillance; statuts et règlements; des femmes; griefs; classification, d'équité et de relativités salariales; avantages sociaux et de la retraite; santé et de sécurité du travail; d'information; d'action et de mobilisation; formation syndicale; personnes occasionnelles; sur la conciliation travail-famille; jeunes; régions
Activités: *Listes de destinataires:* Oui
Membre(s) du bureau directeur:
Richard Perron, Président
Francine Belleau, Secrétaire
Maurice Fortier, Directeur général
mfortier@spgq.qc.ca

Syndicat des Agents Correctionnels du Canada (CSN) (SACC-CSN) / Union of Canadian Correctional Officers (UCCO-CSN)
1601, av De Lorimier, Montréal QC H2K 4M5
Tel: 514-598-2263; *Fax:* 514-598-2943
Toll-Free: 866-229-5566
ucco-sacc@csn.qc.ca
www.ucco-sacc.csn.qc.ca
www.facebook.com/216852691687729
Overview: A medium-sized provincial organization founded in 1999
Chief Officer(s):
Kevin Grabosky, Président

Syndicat des agents de la paix en services correctionnels du Québec (SAPSCQ) / Union of Prison Guards of Québec
4906, boul Gouin est, Montréal QC H1G 1A4
Tél: 514-328-7774; *Téléc:* 514-328-0889
Ligne sans frais: 800-361-3559
support@sapscq.com
www.sapscq.com
Aperçu: Dimension: moyenne; *Envergure:* provinciale; Organisme sans but lucratif; fondée en 1982
Mission: Service syndical pour les agents de la paix en services correctionnels du Québec
Membre(s) du personnel: 4
Membre: 2,085 particuliers; *Montant de la cotisation:* Barème; *Critères d'admissibilite:* Etre agent de la paix en services correctionnels du Québec
Membre(s) du bureau directeur:
Mathieu Lavoie, Président national
Michel Désourdie, Vice Président
t.vallieres@sapscq.com
Jean-Pascal Bélisle, Secrétaire général

Syndicat des agents de maîtrise de Québectel (ind.) *Voir* Syndicat des agents de maîtrise de TELUS (ind.)

Syndicat des agents de maîtrise de TELUS (ind.) (SAMT) / TELUS Professional Employees Union (Ind.) (TPEU)
#605, 2, St-Germain est, Rimouski QC G5L 8T7

Tél: 418-722-6144; *Téléc:* 418-724-0765
info@samt.qc.ca
www.samt.qc.ca/apropos.php
Également appelé: SAMT - Section Locale 5144 du SCFP
Nom précédent: Syndicat des agents de maîtrise de Québectel (ind.)
Aperçu: Dimension: petite; *Envergure:* provinciale; fondée en 1980
Mission: La sauvegarde et la promotion des intérêts professionnels, scientifiques, économiques, sociaux, culturels et politiques de ses membres; faire bénéficier les membres et les travailleurs en général des avantages de l'entraide et des négociations collectives; obtenir pour ses membres un meilleur niveau de vie et de meilleures conditions de travail; représenter les membres auprès de l'employeur
Finances: *Budget de fonctionnement annuel:* $100,000-$250,000
12 bénévole(s)
Membre: 580; *Montant de la cotisation:* 1.5% du salaire brut; *Critères d'admissibilite:* Etre salarié, avoir rempli et signé une fiche d'adhésion, avoir été accepté par le comité exécutif; *Comités:* Conseil syndical; Comités: Exécutif; Relations de travail; Retraite; Sécurité; Évaluation des Emplois; Équité en Matière d'Emploi; Négociations
Membre(s) du bureau directeur:
Harold Morrissey, Président
Lynda Fortin, Secrétaire

Syndicat des agricultrices de la Beauce
225, rang St Charles, Notre-Dame-des-Pins QC G0M 1K0
Tél: 418-774-2330; *Téléc:* 418-774-2330
Aperçu: Dimension: petite; *Envergure:* locale; fondée en 1986
Affiliation(s): Fédération des agricultrices du Québec
15 bénévole(s)
Membre: 1-99
Membre(s) du bureau directeur:
Manon Poulin, Secrétaire

Syndicat des agricultrices de la Côte-du-Sud
#100, 1120 - 6e av, La Pocatière QC G0R 1Z0
Tél: 418-856-3044; *Téléc:* 418-856-5199
Ligne sans frais: 800-463-8001
edube@upa.qc.ca
www.agricultrices.com
Nom précédent: Syndicat des agricultrices de la région de la Côte-du-Sud
Aperçu: Dimension: petite; *Envergure:* locale; Organisme sans but lucratif; fondée en 1987
Mission: En relation avec la planification stratégique de la Fédération des agricultrices du Québec soit: représenter toutes les agricultrices; susciter des échanges entre agricultrices; développer une prise de conscience individuelle et collective en agriculture, de l'agricultrice; participer aux orientations de l'agricultrice de la province
Affiliation(s): Fédération des Agricultrices du Québec
Finances: *Budget de fonctionnement annuel:* Moins de $50,000
Membre: 60; *Montant de la cotisation:* 34 $
Membre(s) du bureau directeur:
Claire Lajoie, Présidente

Syndicat des agricultrices de la région de la Côte-du-Sud *Voir* Syndicat des agricultrices de la Côte-du-Sud

Syndicat des agricultrices de la région de Nicolet *Voir* Syndicat des agricultrices du Centre du Québec

Syndicat des agricultrices du Centre du Québec (SACQ)
179, rang 10, Durham-Sud QC J0H 2C0
Tél: 819-858-2091; *Téléc:* 819-858-2091
sacqcentreduquebec@hotmail.com
Nom précédent: Syndicat des agricultrices de la région de Nicolet
Aperçu: Dimension: petite; *Envergure:* locale; Organisme sans but lucratif; fondée en 1987
Mission: Regrouper toutes les agricultrices reconnues ou non; les représenter, les informer, les conscientiser à leur place dans l'agriculture
Affiliation(s): Fédération des agricultrices du Québec
Finances: *Budget de fonctionnement annuel:* Moins de $50,000; *Fonds:* Gouvernement provincial, fédéral
Membre(s) du personnel: 1; 50 bénévole(s)
Membre: 20 institutionnel; 200 individu; *Montant de la cotisation:* 30$; *Critères d'admissibilite:* Agricultrice impliquée sur la ferme; *Comités:* Agri-Elle

Activités: Quatre colloques annuels; Vidéo La Passion en 8 temps; *Evénements de sensibilisation:* Activité de formation; Forum, mars; Fête du 15e, avril
Membre(s) du bureau directeur:
Lucie Talbot, Présidente

Syndicat des conseillères et conseillers de la CSQ (SCC-CSQ)
#100, 320, rue Saint-Joseph est, Québec QC G1K 9E7
Tél: 418-649-8888; *Téléc:* 418-649-8800
Ligne sans frais: 877-850-0897
www.lacsq.org/la-csq
Aperçu: Dimension: petite; *Envergure:* provinciale; Organisme de réglementation; fondée en 1970
Mission: Défense des membres
Finances: *Budget de fonctionnement annuel:* $50,000-$100,000
Membre: 80; *Montant de la cotisation:* 1% du salaire; *Critères d'admissibilite:* Avocats, pédagogues, conseillers en relations de travail
Activités: Santé; sécurité; solidarité; sélection; relations du travail; perfectionnements
Membre(s) du bureau directeur:
Réjean Parent, Président

Syndicat des douanes et de l'immigration *See* Customs & Immigration Union

Syndicat des employé(e)s de l'impôt *See* Union of Taxation Employees

Syndicat des employé(e)s de magasins et de bureau de la Société des alcools du Québec (ind.) (SEMB SAQ) / Québec Liquor Board Store & Office Employees Union (Ind.)
1065, rue Saint-Denis, Montréal QC H2X 3J3
Tél: 514-849-7754; *Téléc:* 514-849-7914
Ligne sans frais: 800-361-8427
info@semb-saq.com
www.semb-saq.com
www.facebook.com/semb.saq
Aperçu: Dimension: moyenne; *Envergure:* provinciale; fondée en 1964
Membre(s) du bureau directeur:
Katia Lelièvre, Présidente

Syndicat des employé(e)s des affaires des anciens combattants *See* Union of Veterans' Affairs Employees

Syndicat des employé(es) de l'Université Laurentienne *See* Laurentian University Staff Union

Syndicat des employées de soutien de l'Université de Sherbrooke (SEESUS) / University of Sherbrooke Support Staff Union
Pavillon John-S.-Bourque, Université de Sherbrooke, #230, 2500, boul Université, Sherbrooke QC J1K 2R1
Tél: 819-821-7646; *Téléc:* 819-821-7627
seesus@usherbrooke.ca
www.seesus.ca
www.facebook.com/seesus
Aperçu: Dimension: moyenne; *Envergure:* locale; fondée en 1974
Affiliation(s): Syndicat canadien de la fonction publique
Finances: *Budget de fonctionnement annuel:* $250,000-$500,000
Membre(s) du personnel: 4
Membre: 1 100; *Montant de la cotisation:* 1.68% du salaire brut; *Critères d'admissibilite:* Etre salarié de l'Université de Sherbrooke; *Comités:* Activités sociales; Bien-être; Équité salariale; Exécutif syndical; Finances; Horaire variable; Information; Perfectionnement; Plan d'évaluation; Reconnaissance des acquis; Relations de travail
Membre(s) du bureau directeur:
Mélanie Cloutier, Présidente
melanie.cloutier@usherbrooke.ca

Syndicat des employées et employés de la fonction publique de l'Ontario *See* Ontario Public Service Employees Union

Syndicat des employées et employés nationaux *See* Union of National Employees

Syndicat des employés d'hôpitaux *See* Hospital Employees' Union

Syndicat des employés d'indemnisation (ind.) *See* Compensation Employees' Union (Ind.)

Syndicat des employés des postes et des communications See Union of Postal Communications Employees

Syndicat des employés du secteur public de la Nouvelle-Écosse (CCU) See Nova Scotia Union of Public & Private Employees (CCU)

Syndicat des employés du Solliciteur général See Union of Solicitor General Employees

Syndicat des employés du Yukon See Yukon Employees Union

Syndicat des employés en radio-télédiffusion de Télé-Québec (CSQ) / Télé-Québec Television Broadcast Employees' Union
c/o Télé-Québec, 1000, rue Fullum, Montréal QC H2K 3L7
Tél: 514-529-2805
sert@colba.net
Aperçu: Dimension: petite; Envergure: provinciale
Finances: Budget de fonctionnement annuel: $100,000-$250,000
Membre: 120 + 1 section locale; Critères d'admissibilite: Techniciens
Membre(s) du bureau directeur:
Sylvain Leboeuf, Président
sleboeuf@telequebec.tv

Syndicat des employés énergie électrique Québec, inc. Voir Syndicat des travaileurs énergie électrique nord

Syndicat des employés et employées des syndicats et des organismes collectifs du Québec (SEESOCQ)
2600, rue de la Jachère, Québec QC G1C 5J9
Courriel: information@seesocq.org
www.seesocq.org
Aperçu: Dimension: petite; Envergure: provinciale
Membre(s) du bureau directeur:
Richard Vennes, Président
presidence@seesocq.org
Ginette Boudreau, Trésorerie
tresorerie@seesocq.org
Myriam Lévesque, Secrétaire
secretaire@seesocq.org

Syndicat des enseignantes et enseignants Laurier See Laurier Teachers Union

Syndicat des enseignants de la Nouvelle-Écosse See Nova Scotia Teachers Union

Syndicat des fonctionnaires provinciaux et de service de la Colombie-Britannique See British Columbia Government & Service Employees' Union

Syndicat des infirmières de l'Ile-du-Prince-Édouard See Prince Edward Island Nurses' Union

Syndicat des infirmières de la Colombie-Britannique See British Columbia Nurses' Union

Syndicat des infirmières de la Saskatchewan See Saskatchewan Union of Nurses

Syndicat des infirmières de Terre-Neuve et du Labrador See Newfoundland & Labrador Nurses' Union

Syndicat des infirmières du Manitoba See Manitoba Nurses' Union

Syndicat des infirmières et infirmiers du Nouveau-Brunswick See New Brunswick Nurses Union

Syndicat des ouvriers du textile de Magog
15, rue David, Magog QC J1X 2Z2
Tél: 819-843-4420; Téléc: 819-843-3320
synditexmagog@qc.aira.com
Nom précédent: Syndicat catholique des ouvriers du textile de Magog
Aperçu: Dimension: petite; Envergure: locale
Publications:
• STEP Equipment Directory
Type: Directory
Profile: Available in Spanish & Russian
• STEP Newsletter
Type: Newsletter; Frequency: Quarterly

Syndicat des pompiers et pompières du Québec (CTC) (SPQ) / Québec Union of Firefighters (CLC)
#3900, 565, boul Crémazie est, Montréal QC H2M 2V6
Tél: 514-383-4698; Téléc: 514-383-6782
Ligne sans frais: 800-461-4698
www.spq-ftq.com
Nom précédent: Québec Federation of Professional Firefighters
Aperçu: Dimension: moyenne; Envergure: provinciale; fondée en 1945
Affiliation(s): FTQ
Membre(s) du bureau directeur:
Daniel Pépin, Président
dpepin@spq-ftq.com

Syndicat des producteurs de bois du Saguenay-Lac-Saint-Jean
3635, rue Panet, Jonquière QC G7X 8T7
Tél: 418-542-5666; Téléc: 418-542-4046
Ligne sans frais: 800-463-9176
info@spbsaglac.qc.ca
www.spbsaglac.qc.ca
Aperçu: Dimension: petite; Envergure: locale; Organisme sans but lucratif; fondée en 1955
Mission: La mise en marché; l'organisation du transport; l'aménagement; et la mise en application de programmes
Affiliation(s): Fédération des producteurs de bois du Québec
Finances: Budget de fonctionnement annuel: Plus de $5 MillionFonds: Gouvernement provincial
Membre(s) du personnel: 9; 65 bénévole(s)
Membre: 5 500; Montant de la cotisation: 25$
Membre(s) du bureau directeur:
Daniel Fillion, Directeur général

Syndicat des producteurs de chèvres du Québec (SPCQ)
555, boul Roland-Therrien, 4e étage, Longueuil QC J4H 4E7
Tél: 450-679-0540; Téléc: 450-463-5293
info@chevreduquebec.com
www.chevreduquebec.com
www.facebook.com/chevresduquebec.spcq
twitter.com/ChevreQC
Aperçu: Dimension: petite; Envergure: provinciale; fondée en 1982
Mission: Favoriser l'amélioration des revenus des producteurs caprins par le regroupement, la représentation et la défense des intérêts de l'ensemble des producteurs caprins du Québec; valoriser la profession des producteurs de chèvres; développer la production, la commercialisation et les marchés
Affiliation(s): Union des producteurs agricole
Finances: Fonds: Ministère de l'Agriculture, Pêcheries et Alimentation
Membre(s) du personnel: 3
Membre: Critères d'admissibilite: Producteurs de chèvres; Comités: Lait; Boucherie; Mohair
Activités: Représentation des producteurs de chèvres du Québec; Service de conférenciers: Oui; Listes de destinataires: Oui
Membre(s) du bureau directeur:
Robert Camden, Président
Anass Soussi, Directeur général

Syndicat des producteurs en serre du Québec (SPSQ)
#100, 555, boul Roland-Therrien, Longueuil QC J4H 3Y9
Tél: 450-679-0540
spsq@upa.qc.ca
www.spsq.info
www.facebook.com/SyndicatDesProducteursEnSerre
twitter.com/SPSQ1
Aperçu: Dimension: petite; Envergure: locale; Organisme sans but lucratif; fondée en 1974
Mission: Défendre les intérêts des producteurs en serre du Québec
Finances: Budget de fonctionnement annuel: $100,000-$250,000
Membre(s) du personnel: 1
Membre: 110; Montant de la cotisation: 170$ + superficie (m2) x 0,16$; Critères d'admissibilite: Producteur en serre
Membre(s) du bureau directeur:
Louis Dionne, Directeur général
ldionne@upa.qc.ca

Syndicat des professeures et professeurs de l'Université de Sherbrooke (SPPUS)
2500, boul Université, Sherbrooke QC J1K 2R1
Tél: 819-821-7656; Téléc: 819-821-7995
sppus@usherbrooke.ca
www.usherbrooke.ca/sppus
Aperçu: Dimension: petite; Envergure: locale; fondée en 1973
Mission: Voir à l'application de la convention collective; défendre les intérêts des membres
Affiliation(s): Fédération québécoise des professeures et professeurs d'universités
Finances: Budget de fonctionnement annuel: $250,000-$500,000
Membre(s) du personnel: 2
Membre: 450; Critères d'admissibilite: Professeur régulier; Comités: Comité de négociation; Conseil syndical
Membre(s) du bureau directeur:
Robert Tétrault, Secrétaire général
robert.tetrault@usherbrooke.ca

Syndicat des professeures et professeurs de l'Université du Québec à Chicoutimi (SPPUQAC)
555, boul de l'Université, #P2-1000, Chicoutimi QC G7H 2B1
Tél: 418-545-5378; Téléc: 418-545-6659
sppuqac@uqac.ca
www.uqac.ca/sppuqac
Aperçu: Dimension: petite; Envergure: provinciale; fondée en 1969
Membre de: Fédération québécoise des professeures et professeurs d'université
Finances: Budget de fonctionnement annuel: $100,000-$250,000
Membre(s) du personnel: 1; 5 bénévole(s)
Membre: 280; Critères d'admissibilité: Professeur(e)s
Membre(s) du bureau directeur:
Lison Bergeron, Secrétaire

Syndicat des professeures et professeurs de l'Université du Québec à Hull Voir Syndicat des professeures et professeurs de l'Université du Québec en Outaouais

Syndicat des professeures et professeurs de l'Université du Québec à Rimouski (SPPUQAR)
300, allée des Ursulines, #E230, Rimouski QC G5L 3A1
Tél: 418-724-1467; Téléc: 418-724-1559
sppuqar@uqar.ca
sppuqar.uqar.ca
Aperçu: Dimension: petite; Envergure: provinciale
Affiliation(s): Fédération québécoise des professeurs et professeures d'université; Comité de liaison intersyndical de l'Université du Québec; Cartel intersyndical des régimes de retraite et d'assurances collectives
Membre: Comités: Exécutif; Griefs; Paritaire de développement et d'assistance pédagogiques; D'accès des femmes à la carrière professorale; Réseau sur les assurances collectives; Retraite; Institutionnel de suivi de la politique environnementale; Relations professionnelles; Affaires universitaires; Travail sur la modification des questionnaires d'évaluation de l'enseignement
Membre(s) du bureau directeur:
Anne Giguère, Agente d'Administration
Mélanie Gagnon, Présidente

Syndicat des professeures et professeurs de l'Université du Québec en Outaouais (SPUQO) / University of Québec in Hull Faculty Union
Pavillon Lucien Brault, CP 1250, Succ. Hull, 101, rue Saint-Jean-Bosco, Hull QC J8X 3X7
Tél: 819-595-3900; Téléc: 819-773-1877
spuqo@uqo.ca
twitter.com/SPUQO
Nom précédent: Syndicat des professeurs et professeurs de l'Université du Québec à Hull
Aperçu: Dimension: petite; Envergure: locale; fondée en 1980 surveillé par Fédération québécoise des professeures et professeurs d'université
Mission: Protection des membres
Finances: Budget de fonctionnement annuel: $50,000-$100,000
Membre(s) du personnel: 1
Membre: 181; Montant de la cotisation: 1% du salaire; Critères d'admissibilite: Professeur, chercheur; Comités: Conseil exécutif; relations de travail
Membre(s) du bureau directeur:
Elmustapha Najem, Présidente

Syndicat des professeurs de l'État du Québec (ind.) (SPEQ) / Union of Professors for the Government of Québec (Ind.)
#1003, 2120, rue Sherbrooke est, Montréal QC H2K 1C3
Tél: 514-525-7979; Téléc: 514-525-4655
Ligne sans frais: 877-525-7979
info@speq.org
www.speq.org
Aperçu: Dimension: moyenne; Envergure: provinciale; fondée en 1965

Mission: Pour représenter les fonctionnaires enseignants salariés.
Membre: 900 + 21 sections locales
Membre(s) du bureau directeur:
Claude Tanguay, Président

Syndicat des professeurs de l'Université Laval / Laval University Faculty Union
Pavillon Louis-Jacques Casault, Université Laval, CP 2208, #3339, 2325, rue de l'Université, Québec QC G1K 7P4
Tél: 418-656-2955; *Téléc:* 418-656-5377
spul@spul.ulaval.ca
www.spul.ulaval.ca
Aperçu: Dimension: petite; *Envergure:* locale
Membre: 1 320
Membre(s) du bureau directeur:
Yves Lacouture, Président

Syndicat des professeurs de l'Université Saint Mary *See* Saint Mary's University Faculty Union

Syndicat des professeurs et des professeures de l'Université du Québec à Trois-Rivières
Pavillon Ringuet, CP 500, #1115, 3351, boul des Forges, Trois-Rivières QC G9A 5H7
Tél: 819-376-5011; *Téléc:* 819-376-5209
syndicat_professeurs@uqtr.ca
www.sppuqtr.ca
Aperçu: Dimension: petite; *Envergure:* locale; Organisme sans but lucratif; fondée en 1970
Membre de: Fédération québécoise des professeures et professeurs d'université
Finances: Budget de fonctionnement annuel: $100,000-$250,000
Membre(s) du personnel: 3
Membre: 346; *Critères d'admissibilite:* Ôtre professeur régulier de l'UQTR; *Comités:* services à la collectivité; affaires universitaires; préparation à la retraite relations de travail
Membre(s) du bureau directeur:
Pierre Baillargeon, Président
Denise Asselin, Secrétaire

Syndicat des professeurs et professeures de l'Université du Québec à Montréal (SPUQ)
Pavillon Hubert-Aquin, CP 8888, Succ. Centre-Ville, Montréal QC H3C 3P8
Tél: 514-987-6198; *Téléc:* 514-987-3014
spuq@uqam.ca
www.spuq.uqam.ca
Aperçu: Dimension: moyenne; *Envergure:* provinciale; fondée en 1971
Affiliation(s): Confédération des syndicats nationaux
Membre: 1 117
Membre(s) du bureau directeur:
Michèle Nevert, Présidente
nevert.michele@uqam.ca
Catherine Gosselin, Secrétaire générale
gosselin.catherine@uqam.ca
Mario Houde, Trésorier
houde.mario@uqam.ca

Syndicat des professionnelles et professionnels municipaux de Montréal (SPPMM)
#100, 281, rue Saint-Paul est, Montréal QC H2Y 1H1
Tél: 514-845-9646; *Téléc:* 514-844-3585
sppmm@sppmm.org
www.sppmm.org
Aperçu: Dimension: petite; *Envergure:* locale; fondée en 1965
Membre: 1 300; *Comités:* Assurances et les avantages sociaux; Communications; Caisse de retraite; Environnement et de la sécurité; Développement professionnel et productivité
Membre(s) du bureau directeur:
Gisèle Jolin, Présidente

Syndicat des professionnels et des techniciens de la santé du Québec (SPTSQ) / Québec Union of Health Professionals & Technicians
7595, boul St-Michel, Montréal QC H2A 3A4
Tél: 514-723-0422; *Téléc:* 514-723-5248
Ligne sans frais: 800-567-2022
secretariat@stepsq.org
stepsq.org
www.facebook.com/STEPSQ.org
twitter.com/STEPSQ
Aperçu: Dimension: moyenne; *Envergure:* provinciale; fondée en 1963

Mission: Défense des intérêts socio-économiques de ses membres
Affiliation(s): Centrale des professionnelles et professionnels de la santé
Membre(s) du personnel: 7
Membre: 2500; *Critères d'admissibilite:* Techniciens de la santé
Membre(s) du bureau directeur:
Nancy Corriveau, Présidente
nancy.corriveau@stepsq.org

Syndicat des ressources naturelles *See* Natural Resources Union

Syndicat des services du grain (CTC) *See* Grain Services Union (CLC)

Syndicat des services gouvernementaux *See* Government Services Union

Syndicat des technicien(ne)s et artisan(e)s du réseau français de Radio-Canada (ind.) (STARF) / CBC French Network Technicians' Union (Ind.)
1250, rue de la Visitation, Montréal QC H2L 3B4
Tél: 514-524-1100; *Téléc:* 514-524-6023
Ligne sans frais: 888-838-1100
secretariat@starf.qc.ca
www.starf.qc.ca
Aperçu: Dimension: moyenne; *Envergure:* nationale
Membre: *Comités:* Griefs nationaux; Supérieur inter-unités et comité mixte lettre d'entente 16; Formation; Conciliation travail; Harmonisation RC/PROFAC/STARF; Lettre d'entente 3; Équité en matière d'emplois
Membre(s) du bureau directeur:
Benoît Celestino, Président
bcelestino@starf.qc.ca
Marie-Lou Faille, Secrétaire-trésorière
mlfaille@starf.qc.ca

Syndicat des technologues en radiologie du Québec (STRQ) / Union of Radiology Technicians of Québec
#850, 1001, rue Sherbrooke est, Montréal QC H2L 1L3
Tél: 514-521-4469; *Téléc:* 514-521-0086
Aperçu: Dimension: moyenne; *Envergure:* provinciale; fondée en 1965
Mission: Étude, développement et la défense des intérêts professionnels, économiques, sociaux et éducatifs de ses membres et particulièrement la négociation et l'application de conventions collectives.
Membre de: Centrale des Professionnelles et Professionnels de la Santé
Finances: Budget de fonctionnement annuel: $500,000-$1.5 Million
Membre(s) du personnel: 3
Membre: 3 050 + 142 units; *Montant de la cotisation:* 1.4% du salaire; *Critères d'admissibilite:* 85% femmes

Syndicat des travailleurs énergie électrique nord (STEEN)
1640, rue Hamilton, Alma QC G8B 4Z1
Tél: 418-668-2560; *Téléc:* 418-668-7969
www.seeeq.qc.ca
www.facebook.com/syndicatsteen
Nom précédent: Syndicat des employés énergie électrique Québec, inc.
Aperçu: Dimension: petite; *Envergure:* locale; fondée en 1937
Membre(s) du bureau directeur:
Pierre Simard, Président
president@seeeq.qc.ca

Syndicat des travailleirs de l'environnement *See* Union of Environment Workers

Syndicat des travailleurs de la construction du Québec (CSD)
#300, 801 - 4e rue, Québec QC G1J 2T7
Tél: 418-522-3918; *Téléc:* 418-529-6323
info@csdconstruction.qc.ca
www.csdconstruction.qc.ca
www.facebook.com/csdconstruction
twitter.com/csdconstruction
www.youtube.com/user/LaCSDConstruction
Également appelé: CSD - Construction
Aperçu: Dimension: moyenne; *Envergure:* provinciale; fondée en 1972
Mission: Défendre et promouvoir les intérêts sociaux et économiques de ses membres
Affiliation(s): Centrale des syndicats démocratiques
Membre: *Critères d'admissibilite:* Travailleur en construction

Membre(s) du bureau directeur:
Daniel Laterreur, Président
Guy Terrault, Vice-président
Gilles C. Coulombe, Secrétaire

Syndicat des travailleurs du Nord *See* Union of Northern Workers

Syndicat des travailleurs et travailleuses des postes *See* Canadian Union of Postal Workers

Syndicat des travailleurs marins et de bacs de la Colombie-Britannique (CTC) *See* British Columbia Ferry & Marine Workers' Union (CLC)

Syndicat du Nouveau-Brunswick *See* New Brunswick Union

Syndicat du personnel technique et professionnel de la Société des alcools du Québec (ind.) (SPTP-SAQ) / Québec Liquor Board's Union of Technical & Professional Employees (Ind.)
905, rue de Lorimier, Montréal QC H2K 3V9
Tél: 514-873-5878; *Téléc:* 514-873-5896
intra.sptp-saq.ca
Aperçu: Dimension: petite; *Envergure:* provinciale; fondée en 1974
Finances: Budget de fonctionnement annuel: $100,000-$250,000
Membre: 691 + 1 section locale; *Comités:* Assurances, communication, conciliation famille-travail, développement durable, dotation, entraide, finances, horaire, mobilisation, partenariat, santé sécurité au travail
Membre(s) du bureau directeur:
Steve d'Agostino, Président
Patrick Bray, Vice-Président
Hélène Daneault, Directrice
Johanne Morrisseau, Directrice
Lisanne Racine, Directrice

Syndicat indépendant des briqueteurs et des maçons du Canada (CTC) *See* Bricklayers, Masons Independent Union of Canada (CLC)

Syndicat international des marins canadiens (FAT-COI/CTC) *See* Seafarers' International Union of Canada (AFL-CIO/CLC)

Syndicat interprovincial des ferblantiers et couvreurs, la section locale 2016 à la FTQ-Construction
#200, 8300, boul Métropolitain est, Anjou QC H1K 1A2
Tél: 514-374-1515; *Téléc:* 514-448-2265
Ligne sans frais: 866-374-1515
info@ftq2016.org
www.ftq2016.org
Nom précédent: Association nationale des ferblantiers et couvreurs, section locale 2020 (CTC)
Aperçu: Dimension: moyenne; *Envergure:* provinciale; fondée en 1982
Mission: Voir à la promotion et à la défense des intérêts économiques et sociaux des membres; assurer l'intégrité du métier de ferblantier et couvreur en défendant sa jurisdiction professionnelle et en assurant sa sécurité d'emploi; représenter les travailleurs, que leur travail soit effectué à l'intérieur du chantier de construction ou non; cultiver des sentiments de solidarité parmis les travailleurs; obtenir des améliorations dans les conditions de travail de ses membres
Membre de: Canadian Labour Congress
Affiliation(s): Fédération des travailleurs et travailleuses du Québec - Construction
Membre(s) du personnel: 9
Membre: *Critères d'admissibilite:* Détenir carte de compétence requise
Membre(s) du bureau directeur:
Dorima Aubut, Directeur provincial

Montréal
#203, 3730, boul Crémazie est, Montréal QC H2A 1B4
Tél: 514-374-1515

Québec
#150, 5000, boul des Gradins, Québec QC G2J 1N3
Tél: 418-624-2122; *Téléc:* 418-948-0798
Ligne sans frais: 866-624-2122
f.bouchard@ftq2016.org
Membre(s) du bureau directeur:
Gilles Caron, Président

Syndicat national de la santé *See* National Health Union

Syndicat national des cultivateurs *See* National Farmers Union

Syndicat national des employés de l'aluminium d'Alma inc.
Métallos local 9490, 830 rue des Pins ouest, Alma QC G8B 7R3
Tél: 418-662-7055; *Téléc:* 418-662-7354
www.staalma.org
Aperçu: *Dimension:* petite; *Envergure:* locale; fondée en 1943
Mission: Défense des membres
Membre de: Métallos local 9490
Membre(s) du personnel: 9
Membre: 871; *Montant de la cotisation:* 1.40%
Membre(s) du bureau directeur:
Patrice Harvey, Président

Syndicat national des employés de l'aluminium d'Arvida, inc.
1932, boul Mellon, Jonquière QC G7S 3H3
Tél: 418-548-4667; *Téléc:* 418-548-7942
www.sneaa.qc.ca
Aperçu: *Dimension:* petite; *Envergure:* locale; fondée en 1937
Membre: *Comités:* Comité de la condition féminine; Comité de la formation; Comité des retraités
Membre(s) du bureau directeur:
Alain Gagnon, Président

Syndicat professionnel de la police municipale de Québec
Voir Fraternité des Policiers et Policières de la Ville de Québec

Syndicat professionnel des diététistes *Voir* Ordre professionnel des diététistes Québec

Syndicat professionnel des homéopathes du Québec (SPHQ)
#106, 1600, av de Lorimier, Montréal QC H2K 3W5
Tél: 514-525-2037
Ligne sans frais: 800-465-5788
accueil@sphq.org
www.sphq.org
Aperçu: *Dimension:* petite; *Envergure:* provinciale; Organisme sans but lucratif; fondée en 1989
Affiliation(s): Fédération des professionnelles; Confédération des Syndicats Nationaux; Bureau fédéral des médecines alternatives; L'International Council for Homeopathy; Homéopathes de Terre Sans Frontières
Membre(s) du personnel: 1; 7 bénévole(s)
Membre: 300+; *Montant de la cotisation:* 350$; 60$ étudiants; *Critères d'admissibilite:* Professionnels de la santé autonomes pratiquant l'homéopathie
Activités: Semaine de l'homéopathie; conférences; programmes de formation

Syndicat professionnel des ingénieurs d'Hydro-Québec (SPIHQ) / Hydro-Québec Professional Engineers Union
#1400, 1255, boul Robert-Bourassa, Montréal QC H3B 3X1
Tél: 514-845-4239; *Téléc:* 514-845-0082
Ligne sans frais: 800-567-1260
spihq@spihq.qc.ca
www.spihq.qc.ca
Aperçu: *Dimension:* moyenne; *Envergure:* provinciale; fondée en 1964
Mission: Le Syndicat travaille pour la défense & le développement des intérêts économiques, sociaux & professionnels des membres
Finances: *Budget de fonctionnement annuel:* $500,000-$1.5 Million
Membre(s) du personnel: 3
Membre: 1 700
Membre(s) du bureau directeur:
Jacqueline Pilote, Chef administration, 514-845-4239 Ext. 112
chefadmin@spihq.qc.ca
Carole Leroux, Présidente, 514-845-4239 Ext. 103
president@spihq.qc.ca

Syndicat professionnel des ingénieurs de la Ville de Montréal et de la CUM *Voir* Syndicat professionnel des scientifiques à pratique exclusive de Montréal

Syndicat professionnel des médecins du gouvernement du Québec (ind.) (SPMGQ) / Professional Union of Government of Québec Physicians (Ind.)
1390, rue du Père-Jamet, Sainte-Foy QC G1W 3G5
Tél: 418-266-4670
Aperçu: *Dimension:* petite; *Envergure:* provinciale; Organisme sans but lucratif; Organisme de réglementation; fondée en 1966
Mission: Représenter les médecins à l'emploi du gouvernement du Québec
Activités: Relations de travail, bien-être des membres

Membre(s) du bureau directeur:
Christine Gagné, Présidente

Syndicat professionnel des scientifiques à pratique exclusive de Montréal (SPSPEM)
CP 96506, Succ. Montréal Gare Centrale, 895, rue de la Gauchetière ouest, Montréal QC H3B 5J8
Courriel: secretaire@spspem.org
www.spspem.org
Nom précédent: Syndicat professionnel des ingénieurs de la Ville de Montréal et de la CUM
Aperçu: *Dimension:* petite; *Envergure:* locale
Mission: Établir des relations de travail ordonnées entre l'employeur et les salariés, et entre les membres eux-mêmes; défendre et développer les intérêts économiques, sociaux, moraux et professionnels de ses membres
Membre: 200; *Critères d'admissibilite:* Ingénieur; arpenteur-géomètre; chimiste et médecin-vétérinaire à l'emploi de la ville de Montréal; société, organisme ou corporation accrédités
Membre(s) du bureau directeur:
André Émond, Président
president@spspem.org

Syndicat professionnel des scientifiques de l'IREQ (SPSI)
#2008, 210, boul Montarville, Boucherville QC J4B 6T3
Tél: 450-449-9630; *Téléc:* 450-449-9631
spsi@spsi.qc.ca
www.spsi.qc.ca
Aperçu: *Dimension:* petite; *Envergure:* locale
Membre: *Critères d'admissibilite:* Chercheurs et ingénieurs de l'Institut de recherche d'Hydro-Québec
Membre(s) du bureau directeur:
Michel Trudeau, Président

Syndicat québécois de la construction (SQC) / North Shore Construction Inc. (Ind.)
2121, av Sainte-Anne, Saint-Hyacinthe QC J2S 5H5
Tél: 450-773-8833; *Téléc:* 450-773-2232
Ligne sans frais: 888-773-8834
info@sqc.ca
www.sqc.ca
www.facebook.com/SyndicatQuebecoisConstruction
Nom précédent: Syndicat construction Côte-Nord (ind.)
Aperçu: *Dimension:* moyenne; *Envergure:* provinciale; fondée en 1975
Membre(s) du bureau directeur:
Sylvain Gendron, Président

Syndicates of Co-Ownership Association of Québec *Voir* Association des syndicats de copropriété du Québec

Syrian Canadian Council (SCC)
#100, 5000, rue Jean-Talon ouest, Montréal QC H4P 1W9
Tel: 514-207-5315
Other Communication: montreal@syriancanadiancouncil.ca
contact@syriancanadiancouncil.ca
syriancanadiancouncil.ca
www.facebook.com/Syrian.Canadian.Council
twitter.com/sccfreedom
Overview: A medium-sized national organization founded in 2011
Mission: SCC is a non-profit organization dedicated to empowering the Syrian Canadian community through active defense of human rights and civil liberty for all Syrians and Canadians
Membership: *Fees:* $40
London Office
#130, 1326 Huron St., London ON N5V 2E2
Tel: 519-852-6353
london@syriancanadiancouncil.ca
Toronto Office
#278, 2325 Hurontario St., Toronto ON L5A 4K4
gta@syriancanadiancouncil.ca
Vancouver Office
9040 No. 2 Rd., Richmond BC V7E 2C7
Tel: 778-987-0248
vancouver@syriancanadiancouncil.ca

Système informatisé sur les stagiaires post-MD en formation clinique *See* Canadian Post-MD Education Registry

The T. R. Meighen Foundation
#200, 12 Birch Ave., Toronto ON M4V 1C8
Tel: 416-413-1999; *Fax:* 416-413-0015
www.meighen.ca

Overview: A small provincial charitable organization founded in 1969
Mission: To encourage programs & initiatives that benefit at risk youth & families
Finances: *Funding Sources:* Private donations
Chief Officer(s):
Kate Pilgrim, Administrator
kpilgrim@meighen.ca

Taber & District Chamber of Commerce
4702 - 50 St., Taber AB T1G 2B6
Tel: 403-223-2265; *Fax:* 403-223-2291
taberchamber@gmail.com
destinationtaber.com
Overview: A small local organization
Mission: To promote the businesses & community of the Taber region of Alberta
Member of: Canadian Chamber of Commerce; Alberta Chamber of Commerce; Chinook Country Tourist Association
Finances: *Annual Operating Budget:* $100,000-$250,000; *Funding Sources:* Membership dues; fundraising; events
Staff Member(s): 1; 16 volunteer(s)
Membership: 200; *Fees:* $75+GST; *Committees:* Annual Dinner; Cornfest; Economic Development; Employee Review; Finance; Fundraising; Governmental Affairs & Policy; Member Services; Midnight Madness; Parade; Special Events
Activities: Organizing events such as Trade Show, Rodeo Daze, Cornfest, & Midnight Madness; Offering employment programs; Engaging in advocacy
Chief Officer(s):
Bruce Warkentin, President
Awards:
• Small Business of the Year
• Outstanding Business of the Year

Table d'Inter-Action du Quartier Peter-McGill
#215-216, 1857, de boul Maisonneuve ouest, Montréal QC H3H 1J9
Tél: 514-934-2280; *Téléc:* 514-934-1002
interaction_petermcgill@bellnet.ca
petermcgill.org
www.facebook.com/interactionduquartierpetermcgill
Nom précédent: Table du Quartier Peter-McGill
Aperçu: *Dimension:* petite; *Envergure:* locale; fondée en 2003
Mission: Promouvoir un sens d'appartenance au quartier et une participation active à la vie communautaire; créer un lieu de parole pour améliorer la qualité de vie dans le quartier
Membre(s) du bureau directeur:
Stéphane Febbrari, Coordinator

Table de concertation du faubourg Saint-Laurent
250, rue Ontario est, Montréal QC H2X 1H4
Tél: 514-288-0404; *Téléc:* 514-288-7643
info@faubourgstlaurent.ca
www.faubourgstlaurent.ca
Aperçu: *Dimension:* petite; *Envergure:* locale; fondée en 1995
Mission: D'informer les citoyens de St Laurent des changements dans la région, ainsi que de veiller à ce que les préoccupations des citoyens soient entendues par les parties concernées
Membre: 25; *Critères d'admissibilite:* Toute gens qui vie sue faubourg Saint-Laurent; Tout gens qui traille sue faubourg Saint-Laurent; tout groupe qui est impliqué dans des activités à caractère social, économique, éducatif ou culturel
Membre(s) du bureau directeur:
Christine Caron, Coordonnatrice, 514-288-0404, Fax: 514-288-7643
direction@faubourgstlaurent.ca

Table de développement de la production biologique
#100, 555, boul Roland-Therrien, Longueuil QC J4H 3Y9
Tél: 450-679-0530; *Téléc:* 450-670-4867
biologique@upa.qc.ca
Nom précédent: Fédération d'agriculture biologique du Québec
Aperçu: *Dimension:* petite; *Envergure:* provinciale; fondée en 1989
Membre: *Critères d'admissibilite:* Producteurs agricoles biologiques
Activités: Promotion générique; Développement de marchés; Information
Membre(s) du bureau directeur:
Gérard Bouchard, Président

Table des responsables de l'éducation des adultes et de la formation professionnelle des commissions scolaires du Québec (TRÉAQFP)
CP 75186, Succ. Cap-Rouge, Québec QC G1Y 3C7
Tél: 418-914-3977
www.treaqfp.qc.ca
Aperçu: *Dimension:* moyenne; *Envergure:* provinciale; fondée en 1975
Membre: 800
Membre(s) du bureau directeur:
Louise Dionne, Directrice générale
dionne.louise@treaqfp.qc.ca
Hélène Leduc, Agente, Développement en formation professionnelle, 418-747-0252
leduc.helene@treaqfp.qc.ca
Jaquis Gagnon, Agente, Développement en formation générale des adultes, 418-617-1165
gagnon.jaquis@treaqfp.qc.ca
Johanne Villeneuve, Agente, Bureau, 581-300-1253
villeneuve.johanne@treaqfp.qc.ca

Table du Quartier Peter-McGill *Voir* Table d'Inter-Action du Quartier Peter-McGill

Table jamésienne de concertation minière
958, 3e rue, Chibougamau QC G8P 1R6
Tél: 418-748-1141; *Téléc:* 418-748-6511
info@tjcm.ca
www.tjcm.ca
Aperçu: *Dimension:* petite; *Envergure:* locale
Mission: Maintenir et soutenir le développement de l'industrie minière en Eeyou Istchee Baie-James
Membre(s) du bureau directeur:
Régis Simard, Directeur général

La Table ronde nationale de l'électricité *See* National Electricity Roundtable

Table Tennis Canada / Tennis de Table Canada
18 Louisa St., Ottawa ON K1R 6Y6
Tel: 613-733-6272; *Fax:* 613-733-7279
ttcan@ttcan.ca
ttcan.ca
Previous Name: Canadian Table Tennis Association
Overview: A medium-sized national organization founded in 1937
Mission: To increase the popularity of the sport of table tennis through programs & activities; to increase participation in table tennis at all levels
Member of: International Table Tennis Federation
Affiliation(s): Sports Council of Canada; International Table Tennis Federation
Finances: *Annual Operating Budget:* $500,000-$1.5 Million; *Funding Sources:* Sponsorship; membership; government
Staff Member(s): 6
Membership: 20,000; *Committees:* Technical; Administrative
Activities: STIGA Canada Cup; Canadian Championships; Canadian Junior Championships; *Rents Mailing List:* Yes
Chief Officer(s):
Tony Kiesenhofer, Chief Executive Officer
tonyk@ttcan.ca
Brian Ash, Director, Marketing
brian@ttcan.ca

Table Tennis Yukon
4061 - 4th Ave., Whitehorse YT Y1A 1H1
Tel: 867-668-3358
sportyukon.com/member/table-tennis-yukon
Overview: A small provincial organization overseen by Table Tennis Canada
Mission: To promote the sport of Table Tennis in the Yukon.
Member of: Table Tennis Canada; Sport Yukon
Affiliation(s): International Table Tennis Federation
Chief Officer(s):
David Stockdale, President
stockdale@yknet.ca

Taekwondo Canada
#313A, 3 Concorde Gate, Toronto ON M3C 3N7
Tel: 416-426-7322; *Fax:* 416-426-7334
taekwondo-canada.com
www.facebook.com/Taekwondo.Canada
twitter.com/TKD_Canada
Overview: A medium-sized national organization
Mission: To develop, promote & govern the sport of Taekwondo in Canada.
Activities: National Championships
Chief Officer(s):
Kate Nosworthy, Chair
knosworthy@taekwondo-canada.com
Rebecca Khoury, Chief Executive Officer
ceo@taekwondo-canada.com

Taekwondo Manitoba
145 Pacific Ave., Winnipeg MB R3B 2Z6
Fax: 204-925-5703
secretary@taekwondomanitoba.ca
www.taekwondomanitoba.ca
Previous Name: Manitoba Tae Kwon-Do Association
Overview: A small provincial organization
Mission: To promote & govern the sport of Taekwondo in Manitoba.
Membership: *Committees:* Awards & Recognition; Finance; Membership; NCCP; Policy; Strategic Planning; Competition; Nominations; Referee

Tafelmusik Baroque Orchestra & Chamber Choir
Trinity-St. Paul's Centre, PO Box 14, 427 Bloor St. West, Toronto ON M5S 1X7
Tel: 416-964-9562; *Fax:* 416-964-2782
info@tafelmusik.org
www.tafelmusik.org
www.linkedin.com/company/tafelmusik-baroque-orchestra-and-chamber-choir
www.facebook.com/tafelmusik.org?ref=ts
twitter.com/tafelmusik
www.youtube.com/user/tafelmusik1979
Also Known As: Tafelmusik
Overview: A medium-sized local charitable organization founded in 1978 overseen by Orchestras Canada
Mission: Bringing baroque music to Toronto & the world, through concerts, recordings, & a music education programme
Member of: Orchestras Canada
Finances: *Annual Operating Budget:* $1.5 Million-$3 Million; *Funding Sources:* Provincial grants; Ticket and merchandise revenue; Donations
Staff Member(s): 21; 100 volunteer(s)
Membership: 800; *Fees:* Schedule available
Activities: Performing concert series; Facilitating artist training workshops and university programs; Providing free or low-cost concerts for elementary and high schools; *Internships:* Yes
Chief Officer(s):
William Norris, Managing Director, 416-964-9562 Ext. 225
wnorris@tafelmusik.org

Tahsis Chamber of Commerce
PO Box 278, 36 Rugged Mountain Rd., Tahsis BC V0P 1X0
Tel: 250-934-6425
www.villageoftahsis.com
www.facebook.com/tahsischamber
Overview: A small local organization founded in 1938
Mission: To promote village businesses & the community
Member of: BC Chamber of Commerce; Tourism Association of Vancouver Island
Finances: *Annual Operating Budget:* Less than $50,000; *Funding Sources:* Membership dues; sales; municipality
Staff Member(s): 3
Membership: 34; *Fees:* $25 individual; $50 business
Activities: Organizing & supporting community events; Maintaining Info Centre

Taiwan Entrepreneurs Society Taipei/Toronto
#213, 885 Progress Ave., Toronto ON M1H 3G3
Tel: 416-439-9778; *Fax:* 416-439-9515
testt@rogers.com
www.testt.com
Overview: A small local organization

Taiwan Trade Center, Vancouver
#1730, 650 West Georgia St., Vancouver BC V6B 4N8
Tel: 604-681-2787; *Fax:* 604-681-9886
vancouver@taitra.org.tw
vancouver.taiwantrade.com
Overview: A medium-sized international organization
Mission: To help Taiwanese businesses & manufacturers grow in the international market
Affiliation(s): Taiwan External Trade Development Council
Chief Officer(s):
Ruth R. H. Chang, Director

Taiwanese Canadian Cultural Society (TCCS)
8853 Selkirk St., Vancouver BC V6P 4J6
Tel: 604-267-0901; *Fax:* 604-267-0903
info@tccs.ca
www.tccs.ca
www.facebook.com/TCCSVan
Overview: A small local charitable organization founded in 1991
Mission: To educate & assist new immigrants; To contribute to multiculturalism; To introduce Taiwanese culture to Canadians
Member of: Taiwanese Canadian Cultural Society Collegiate Association
Affiliation(s): Multicultural Societies & Service Agencies of BC
Staff Member(s): 4; 100 volunteer(s)
Membership: 3,400 families; *Fees:* $60 family; $40 individual/senior/student; *Member Profile:* Taiwanese Canadian immigrants
Activities: Taiwanese Cultural Festival; Lunar New Year in Taiwan Celebration; *Library:* TCCS Library; Not open to public

Talent Agents & Managers Association of Canada (TAMAC)
PO Box 19597, Stn. Manulife, 55 Bloor St. West, Toronto ON M4W 3T9
info@tamac.ca
www.tamac.ca
Overview: A medium-sized national organization
Mission: To represent actors, writers, directors, craftspeople and other professionals in the entertainment industry; To address industry issues involving legislation & funding; To encourage constructive understanding & positive attitudes towards the entertainment industry
Finances: *Funding Sources:* Membership dues
Membership: 150
Chief Officer(s):
Sandra Gillis, President
president@tamac.ca

Tamil Eelam Society of Canada (TEOSC)
#1A, 1160 Birchmount Rd., Toronto ON M1P 2B8
Tel: 416-757-6043; *Fax:* 416-757-6851
ed@tesoc.org
www.tesoc.org
Also Known As: TESOC Multicultural Settlement Services
Overview: A medium-sized national organization founded in 1978
Mission: To provide opportunities & services to newcomers & immigrants from the Tamil community & other ethno cultures; To promote a smooth integration into Canadia by enhancing the lives of newcomers through programs designed for settlement, employment & personal growth
Finances: *Funding Sources:* Immigration, Refugees & Citizenship Canada

Tamil Writers' Association of Canada
4-2800 Eglinton Ave. East, Toronto ON M1J 2C8
Tel: 416-546-1394
ctamilwriters@gmail.com
www.facebook.com/665983446825550
Overview: A small national organization
Mission: To promote Tamil literature in Canada & around the world

Tansi Friendship Centre Society
PO Box 418, 5301 South Access Rd., Chetwynd BC V0C 1J0
Tel: 250-788-2996; *Fax:* 250-788-2353
reception@tansifcs.com
www.facebook.com/groups/181117091978465
Overview: A small local organization overseen by Food Banks British Columbia
Member of: Food Banks British Columbia

Taoist Tai Chi Society of Canada
Central Region, 134 Darcy St., Toronto ON M5T 1K3
Tel: 416-656-2110; *Fax:* 416-654-3937
fungloykok@taoist.org
www.taoist.org
www.facebook.com/flkttc
twitter.com/taoisttaichisoc
Overview: A medium-sized national organization founded in 1970
Mission: To make Taoist Tai Chi available to all &, through its teaching & practice, promote health improvement, cultural exchange & helping others
Member of: International Taoist Tai Chi Society
Finances: *Funding Sources:* Membership fees
Staff Member(s): 20
Membership: 15,000; *Fees:* $20; *Member Profile:* Open to everyone
Activities: *Awareness Events:* National Taoist Tai Chi Awareness Day, first Sat. after Labour Day

Atlantic Region
2029 North Park St., Halifax NS B3K 4B2
Tel: 902-422-8142; *Fax:* 902-422-1998
atlantic.office@taoist.org
www.atlantic.canada.taoist.org
Member of: International Taoist Tai Chi Society

Eastern Region
451, rue St-Jean, Longueuil QC J4H 2Y1
Toll-Free: 888-824-2441
region.est@taoist.org
www.taichitaoiste.org
Member of: Taoist Tai Chi Society of Canada

Pacific Region
588 East 15th Ave., Vancouver BC V6B 1L1
Tel: 604-681-6609; *Fax:* 604-681-6692
vancouver@taoist.org
www.pacific.canada.taoist.org
twitter.com/taoisttaichisoc
Member of: International Taoist Tai Chi Society
Chief Officer(s):
Tracey Hutchins, President

The International Centre
248305 5 Sideroad, Mono ON L9W 6L2
Tel: 905-941-5981; *Fax:* 905-941-4542
internationalcentre@taoist.org

Western Region
2310 - 24th St. SW, Calgary AB T5T 0G6
Tel: 403-240-4566; *Fax:* 403-240-4609
calgary@taoist.org
www.western.canada.taoist.org
Member of: International Taoist Tai Chi Society

Tara Canada Network Association
PO Box 15270, Vancouver BC V6B 5B1
Toll-Free: 888-278-8272
information@share-international.ca
www.taracanada.org/pp3
www.facebook.com/ShareInternationalCanada
Overview: A small national charitable organization
Mission: To provide information on the emergence of Maitreya, the World Teacher, & on transmission meditation, a specialized form of group meditation
Affiliation(s): Share International Canada
Activities: *Speaker Service:* Yes

Taras H. Shevchenko Museum & Memorial Park Foundation
1614 Bloor St. West, Toronto ON M6P 1A7
Tel: 416-534-8662; *Fax:* 416-535-1063
shevchenkomuseum@bellnet.ca
www.infoukes.com/shevchenkomuseum
Also Known As: Shevchenko Museum
Overview: A small local organization founded in 1952
Mission: To perpetuate the memory & humanist philosophy of Taras Hryhorovich Shevchenko (1814-1861), foremost poet, artist & revolutionary democrat of Ukraine, & to relate the conditions & contributions of the original Ukrainian immigration to Canada which began in 1891
Member of: Ontario Museum Association
Affiliation(s): Ontario Historical Society; Heritage Toronto
Finances: *Annual Operating Budget:* Less than $50,000
Staff Member(s): 1; 30 volunteer(s)
Membership: 1-99; *Committees:* Executive
Activities: AGM & monthly meetings; hosting visitors; special exhibitions; raising funds; Shevchenko's Birth, Museum Anniversary, March 9 & 10; *Speaker Service:* Yes; *Library:* Shevchenko Library; Open to public
Chief Officer(s):
Lyudmyla Pogoryelova, Director

Tarragon Theatre
30 Bridgman Ave., Toronto ON M5R 1X3
Tel: 416-531-1827
info@tarragontheatre.com
www.tarragontheatre.com
www.facebook.com/tarragontheatre
twitter.com/tarragontheatre
Overview: A small local charitable organization founded in 1971
Mission: To develop & produce new Canadian plays
Affiliation(s): Professional Association of Canadian Theatres
Staff Member(s): 22
Chief Officer(s):
James Buchanan, President
Richard Rose, Artistic Director
richard@tarragontheatre.com

Susan Moffat, Managing Director
susan@tarragontheatre.com

Taste of Nova Scotia
#240, 33 Ochterloney St., Dartmouth NS B2Y 4P5
Tel: 902-492-9291; *Fax:* 902-492-9286
Toll-Free: 800-281-5507
taste@tasteofnovascotia.com
www.tasteofnovascotia.com
www.facebook.com/TasteofNS
twitter.com/TasteofNS
www.youtube.com/user/TasteofNS
Overview: A small provincial organization
Mission: To promote its members & Nova Scotia as a leader in high quality culinary experiences.
Staff Member(s): 6
Membership: 140; *Member Profile:* Agricultural businesses; wineries; breweries; chocolate makers; meat & fish processors; jam & maple syrup producers & baked goods
Chief Officer(s):
Janice Ruddock, Executive Director
janice@tasteofnovascotia.com

Tavistock Chamber of Commerce
PO Box 670, Tavistock ON N0B 2R0
Tel: 519-301-2118
tavistockchamber@gmail.com
Overview: A small local organization
Mission: To promote & support the business community in Tavistock
Membership: 25; *Fees:* $150
Chief Officer(s):
Bob Routly, Secretary

TB Vets
1410 Kootenay St., Vancouver BC V5K 4R1
Tel: 604-874-5626
Toll-Free: 888-874-5626
information@tbvets.org
www.tbvets.org
www.facebook.com/tbvets
twitter.com/tbvets
plus.google.com/115497261163706842951
Overview: A medium-sized provincial charitable organization founded in 1945
Mission: Operates a key return service, with proceeds & donations going to respiratory disease research, treatments & education; annually sends out over 350,000 keytags to BC residents
Finances: *Funding Sources:* Donations; Sponsorships
Staff Member(s): 6
Chief Officer(s):
Eric Beddis, Chair
Kanys Merola, Executive Director
Publications:
• TB Vets e-newsletter
Type: Newsletter; *Frequency:* Quarterly

TD Friends of the Environment Foundation / Fondation des amis de l'environnement TD
TD Bank Tower, PO Box 1, 66 Wellington St., Toronto ON M5K 1A2
Toll-Free: 800-361-5333
tdfef@td.com
www.fef.td.com
Previous Name: Friends of the Environment Foundation
Overview: A medium-sized national charitable organization founded in 1990
Mission: To protect & preserve the Canadian environment
Finances: *Funding Sources:* Donations
Membership: 1,000+
Activities: Funding environmental projects across Canada; *Speaker Service:* Yes
Chief Officer(s):
Natasha Alleyne-Martin, Manager, National Programs
natasha.martin@td.com
Sarah Lawless-Ajibade, Regional Manager, Ontario North & East, Quebec and Atlantic Provinces, 613-783-4710
Sarah.Lawless-Ajibade@td.com
Mandip Kharod, Regional Manager, BC, Alberta, Yukon & Northwest Territories, Saskatchewan & Manito, 604-654-8832
mandip.kharod@td.com
Carolyn Scotchmer, Regional Manager, Greater Toronto Region & Western Ontario
Carolyn.Scotchmer@td.com

Tea Association of Canada (TAC) / Association du thé du Canada
#602, 133 Richmond St. West, Toronto ON M5H 2L3
Tel: 416-510-8647
info@tea.ca
www.tea.ca
www.facebook.com/teaassociationofcanada
twitter.com/Canadatea
Overview: A medium-sized national organization founded in 1991
Mission: To represent & advance the interests of Canada's tea industry to all levels of government in an effort to improve the conditions under which the industry operates & to promote better business relations between the industry's players
Finances: *Funding Sources:* Membership fees; events
Membership: 1-99; *Fees:* Schedule available; *Member Profile:* Tea producing countries; tea packers; importers; retailers; businesses involved with tea trade; people who have completed the tea sommelier program; students enrolled in the tea sommelier program; people who are considering going into the tea business
Activities: *Internships:* Yes
Chief Officer(s):
Louise Roberge, President

Teachers of Home Economics Specialist Association (THESA)
c/o G.W. Graham Middle-Secondary School, 45955 Thomas Rd., Chilliwack BC V2R 0B5
Tel: 604-847-0772; *Fax:* 604-824-0711
membership@thesa.ca
www.bctf.ca/thesa
www.facebook.com/groups/117646778348501
twitter.com/thesaorg
www.pinterest.com/thesaorg
Overview: A small provincial organization overseen by British Columbia Teachers' Federation
Member of: BC Teachers' Federation
Membership: *Fees:* Schedule available; *Member Profile:* Home Economics educators in BC
Chief Officer(s):
Paula Aquino, President
president@thesa.ca
Meetings/Conferences:
• Teachers of Home Economics Specialist Association (THESA) Conference 2018, 2018, Prince George, BC
Scope: Provincial

Teachers of Inclusive Education - British Columbia (TIE-BC)
w/o British Columbia Teachers' Federation, #100, 550 West 6th Ave., Vancouver BC V5Z 4P2
tiebcwebmanager@gmail.com
www.tiebc.com
Previous Name: Special Education Association of British Columbia
Overview: A small provincial organization overseen by British Columbia Teachers' Federation
Mission: To support teachers in providing quality education for students with special learning needs in British Columbia
Membership: *Fees:* Schedule available; *Member Profile:* Teachers interested in supporting students with special needs
Activities: Offering professional development opportunities
Awards:
• Hazel Davy Award
• Marg Csapo Student Scholarship
; *Amount:* $2,000
• Special Education Association Professional Development Scholarships
; *Amount:* 4 at $500
• Special Education Association Student Scholarships
Meetings/Conferences:
• Teachers of Inclusive Education - British Columbia 2018 Crosscurrents Conference, February, 2018, Sheraton Vancouver Airport Hotel, Richmond, BC
Scope: Provincial
Description: Sessions for regular & special education teachers, as well as administrators, teacher assistants, & parents

Teaching Support Staff Union (TSSU)
Academic Quadrangle, Simon Fraser University, #5129/5130, 8888 University Dr., Burnaby BC V5A 1S6
Tel: 778-782-4735
tssu@tssu.ca
www.tssu.ca

www.facebook.com/TSSU.ca
twitter.com/TSSU
Overview: A medium-sized local organization founded in 1978
Mission: To represent teaching support staff during collective bargaining agreements & in employee-employer conflicts.
Affiliation(s): Vancouver & District Labour Council
Finances: *Funding Sources:* Membership dues
Membership: *Member Profile:* Tutor markers; sessional instructors; language instructors & teaching assistants; *Committees:* Finanace; Internal Relations; Social Justice; Grievance; Membership Mobilization; Executive; Steward's; Contract; General Membership
Chief Officer(s):
Melissa Roth, Organizer

TEAL Manitoba
c/o Manitoba Teachers' Society, 191 Harcourt St., Winnipeg MB R3J 3H2
Tel: 204-888-7961
manitoba.teal@gmail.com
www.tealmanitoba.ca
Also Known As: Teachers of English as an Additional Language in Manitoba
Previous Name: TESL Manitoba
Overview: A medium-sized provincial organization overseen by TESL Canada Federation
Mission: To address the issues affecting EAL learners; To support professional development of members
Membership: *Fees:* $40-$50; $30 para-professional/assistant/volunteer; $25 student; *Member Profile:* Educators in Manitoba who are involved with or interested in English as an Additional Language
Activities: Networking; *Awareness Events:* Linguistic Diversity Workshops
Chief Officer(s):
Melanie Davlut, President
melanie.davlut@lrsd.net
Meetings/Conferences:
• TEAL Manitoba 2018 Conference, 2018, MB
Scope: Provincial
Description: Featuring presentations on EAL issues & professional development for EAL educators
Publications:
• TEAL [Teachers of English as an Additional Language] Manitoba Journal
Type: Journal; *Frequency:* 2 pa
Profile: Theoretical & practical articles on TEAL/TESL profession topics; reviews of EAL teaching materials; exercises, resources & news related to TEAL
• TEAL [Teachers of English as an Additional Language] Manitoba Newsletter
Type: Newsletter; *Frequency:* 3 pa
Profile: Newsletter discussing TEAL Manitoba events, as well as news & resources

Team Handball Ontario (THO)
Toronto ON
info@handballontario.com
www.handballontario.com
www.facebook.com/TeamHandballOntario
Overview: A medium-sized provincial organization
Mission: To represent team handball in Ontario
Membership: *Fees:* $200 full; $125 half season; $10 per drop in session; $25 social
Chief Officer(s):
Nick Cuddemi, President

TEAM of Canada Inc. (TEAM)
#372, 16 Midlake Blvd. SE, Calgary AB T2X 2X7
Toll-Free: 800-295-4160
info@teamcanada.org
www.teamcanada.org
www.facebook.com/125163240888381
twitter.com/team
instagram.com/teammissions
Also Known As: The Evangelical Alliance Mission of Canada Inc.
Overview: A medium-sized international charitable organization founded in 1969
Mission: To help churches send missionaries to establish reproducing churches among the nations, to the Glory of God
Member of: Canadian Council of Christian Charities
Finances: *Annual Operating Budget:* $1.5 Million-$3 Million
Staff Member(s): 6
Membership: 1-99

Activities: *Internships:* Yes; *Speaker Service:* Yes; *Library:* Resource Centre
Chief Officer(s):
Ralph Friebel, Chair
Scott Henson, International Director

Teamsters Canada (CLC) (TC)
#804, 2540, boul Daniel-Johnson, Laval QC H7T 2S3
Tél: 450-682-5521; *Téléc:* 450-681-2244
Ligne sans frais: 866-888-6466
info@teamsters.ca
www.teamsters-canada.org
www.facebook.com/TeamstersCanada
twitter.com/TeamstersCanada
www.instagram.com/teamsterscanada
Aperçu: *Dimension:* grande; *Envergure:* nationale; Organisme sans but lucratif; fondée en 1976
Mission: To create equality, security & fair opportunities in the workplace
Affiliation(s): International Brotherhood of Teamsters
Finances: *Budget de fonctionnement annuel:* Plus de $5 Million
Membre(s) du personnel: 24
Membre: 125 000; 32 sections locales; *Montant de la cotisation:* barème; *Critères d'admissibilite:* Individuals in the transportation, production, hospitality & service industries; *Comités:* Youth
Membre(s) du bureau directeur:
François Laporte, President
Ron Finley, Executive Assistant & National Rep., Western Region
Prix, Bourses:
• The James R. Hoffa Memorial Scholarship Fund
Deadline: March 31; *Amount:* $1,000-$10,000
Central Region
Airway Centre, Phase 1, #252, 5945 Airport Rd., 2nd Fl., Mississauga ON L4V 1R9
Tel: 905-678-6652; *Fax:* 905-678-6178
www.teamsters.ca
Membre(s) du bureau directeur:
Ken Dean, Representative
Western Region
#204, 1867 West Broadway, Vancouver BC V6J 4W1
Tel: 604-736-3517; *Fax:* 604-736-3518
Membre(s) du bureau directeur:
Grant Coleman, Organizer

Teamsters Canada Rail Conference (TCRC) / Conference ferroviaire de Teamsters Canada (CFTC)
#1710, 130 Albert St., Ottawa ON K1P 5G4
Tel: 613-235-1828; *Fax:* 613-235-1069
info@teamstersrail.ca
www.teamstersrail.ca
www.facebook.com/TeamstersRail
twitter.com/TeamstersRail
www.instagram.com/teamstersrail
Previous Name: Brotherhood of Locomotive Engineers
Overview: A medium-sized national organization
Mission: To act as a collective bargaining partner for rail industry workers in Canada
Staff Member(s): 1
Membership: 16,000 in 21 divisions; *Fees:* $15; *Member Profile:* Workers in the rail industry in Canada
Activities: *Library:* Teamsters Canada Rail Conference Library; Not open to public
Chief Officer(s):
Douglas Finnson, President
Roland Hackl, Vice President

Teamwork Children's Services International
5983 Ladyburn Cres., Mississauga ON L5M 4V9
Tel: 905-542-1047
www.teamworkchildrenservices.com
Overview: A small international charitable organization
Mission: To provide a safe environment for disadvantaged children in rural areas of Africa; To help children become productive citizens through the provision of physical & mental care, education, & vocational training
Finances: *Funding Sources:* Donations
Chief Officer(s):
Joel Chacha, Executive Director
jchacha@teamworkchildrenservices.com

TechConnex
#3, 1 Steelcase Rd. West, Markham ON L3R 0T3
www.techconnex.ca
www.linkedin.com/company/3351378

www.facebook.com/TechConnex
twitter.com/techconnex
Previous Name: York Technology Alliance
Overview: A small local organization founded in 1982
Mission: To provide a community for technology companies to connect & grow
Finances: *Funding Sources:* Sponsorships
Membership: *Fees:* Schedule available
Activities: Offering learning & networking opportunities
Chief Officer(s):
John Cameron, Executive Director, 905-415-4558 Ext. 102
Ryan Ellis, Director, Membership, 905-415-4558 Ext. 101
ryanellis@techconnex.ca
Kelley Phillips, Manager, Membership Development, 905-415-4558 Ext. 103
kelleyphillips@techconnex.ca

The technical society of the Canadian Nuclear Association (CNA) *See* Canadian Nuclear Society

Technion Canada
#206, 970 Lawrence Ave. West, Toronto ON M6A 3B6
Tel: 416-789-4545; *Fax:* 416-789-0255
Toll-Free: 800-935-8864
info@technioncanada.org
www.technioncanada.org
www.facebook.com/CanadianTechnion
Previous Name: Canadian Technion Society
Overview: A medium-sized national organization founded in 1943
Mission: To support Technion Israel Institute of Technology; to promote exchange of scientific information between Israel & Canada, scholarships, research, etc.
Staff Member(s): 7
Membership: 5,000; *Fees:* $100
Activities: *Speaker Service:* Yes
Chief Officer(s):
Marvin Ostin, National President
Cheryl Koperwas, National Executive Director
Edward Nagel, National Vice-President
Calgary Office
Tel: 403-238-5509
kaplanr@shaw.ca
www.technioncanada.org
Mission: To promote Canadian development and use of Technion educational facilities. The association supports those educators and scientists from Canada participating in Technion operations, as well as their Technion counter-parts involved in the exchange of scientific information and products of technical research and development.
Chief Officer(s):
Sandy Hurwitz, Director
Montréal Office
#3435, 6900, boul Décarie, Montréal QC H3X 2T8
Tel: 514-735-5541; *Fax:* 514-737-9222
montreal@technioncanada.org
www.technioncanada.org
Mission: To promote Canadian development and use of Technion educational facilities. The group supports those educators and scientists from Canada participating in Technion operations, as well as their Technion counter-parts involved in the exchange of scientific information and products of technical research and development.
Chief Officer(s):
Anne Kalles, Director

TechnoCentre éolien / Wind Energy TechnoCentre
70, rue Bolduc, Gaspé QC G4X 1G2
Tél: 418-368-6162; *Téléc:* 418-368-4315
info@eolien.qc.ca
www.eolien.qc.ca
Aperçu: *Dimension:* petite; *Envergure:* provinciale; fondée en 2000
Mission: Le TechnoCentre éolien a pour mission de contribuer au développement d'une filière industrielle éolienne québécoise, compétitive à l'échelle nord-américaine et internationale, tout en mettant en valeur la Gaspésie-Îles-de-la-Madeleine au cour de ce créneau émergeant de l'économie du Québec.
Membre(s) du bureau directeur:
Frédéric Côté, Directeur général
fcote@eolien.qc.ca
Meetings/Conferences:
• TechnoCentre éolien/ Wind Energy TechnoCentre 12th Colloque de l'industrie éolienne québécoise 2018, June, 2018, Carleton-sur-Mer, QC

Scope: Provincial
Attendance: 200

TECHNOCompétences
#350, 550, rue Sherbrooke ouest, Montréal QC H3A 1B9
Tél: 514-840-1237
www.technocompetences.qc.ca
www.linkedin.com/company/technocomp-tences/?-1803111
www.facebook.com/technocompetences
twitter.com/TECHNOCompetenc
www.youtube.com/user/technocompetences
Aperçu: *Dimension:* moyenne; *Envergure:* provinciale
Mission: Favoriser le développement de la main-d'oeuvre et de l'emploi dans le secteur des technologies de l'information et des communications
Membre(s) du bureau directeur:
Josée Lanoue, Directrice générale

Technologies du développement durable Canada *See*
Sustainable Development Technology Canada

Technoscience Estrie
195, rue Marquette, Sherbrooke QC J1H 1L6
Tél: 819-565-5062; *Téléc:* 819-565-4534
www.technoscienceestrie.ca
www.facebook.com/TechnoscienceEstrie
twitter.com/TechnoSEstrie
Nom précédent: Conseil du loisir scientifique de l'Estrie
Aperçu: *Dimension:* moyenne; *Envergure:* locale; fondée en 1980
Mission: Développer le loisir scientifique dans la région; encourager les carrières scientifiques chez les jeunes
Membre de: Réseau Technoscience
Finances: *Fonds:* Gouvernement régional
Membre(s) du personnel: 11
Membre: 26 institutionnel; 1 800 étudiant; 20 individu
Membre(s) du bureau directeur:
Marilou Pratte, Directrice générale
prattem@technoscienceestrie.ca
Valérie Bilodeau, Directrice adjointe
bilodeauv@technoscienceestrie.ca

TechNova
#308, 202 Brownlow Ave., Dartmouth NS B3B 1T5
Tel: 902-463-3236; *Fax:* 902-465-7567
Toll-Free: 866-723-8867
info@technova.ca
www.technova.ca
twitter.com/NSTechNova
Also Known As: Society of Certified Engineering Technicians & Technologists of Nova Scotia
Overview: A medium-sized provincial licensing organization founded in 1967 overseen by Canadian Council of Technicians & Technologists
Mission: To certify engineering & applied science technicians & technologists for the betterment of the public & the welfare of the environment
Finances: *Funding Sources:* Memberships
Staff Member(s): 2
Membership: 1,357; *Fees:* $165 active; $110 associate; $75 non-active/retired; *Member Profile:* Technicians & technologists; *Committees:* Awards; Bylaw Enforcement
Chief Officer(s):
Eric Jury, President
Joe Simms, Executive Officer

Tecumseh Community Development Corporation
1040 Degurse Dr., Sarnia ON N7T 7H5
Tel: 519-332-5151; *Fax:* 519-332-6196
Toll-Free: 888-433-1533
info@tcdc.on.ca
www.tcdc.on.ca
Overview: A small local organization
Mission: To make available financial & management services for the development of local First Nation economies
Affiliation(s): London District Chiefs Council
Finances: *Annual Operating Budget:* $250,000-$500,000
Staff Member(s): 5
Activities: *Library:* Seven Bands Community Futures Library; Open to public
Chief Officer(s):
Phyllis George, General Manager
phyllis@tcdc.on.ca

Tecumseh Historical Society *See* Naval Museum of Alberta Society

Tecumseth & West Gwillimbury Historical Society
PO Box 171, Bond Head ON L0G 1B0
Overview: A small local organization
Chief Officer(s):
Janine Harris-Wheatley, President

Tekeyan Armenian Cultural Association
825, rue Manoogian, Montréal QC H4N 1Z5
Tel: 514-747-6680; *Fax:* 514-747-6162
centretekeyan@bellnet.ca
Overview: A small local organization
Chief Officer(s):
Berge Manookian, Président

Tel-Aide Outaouais (TAO)
CP 7218, Succ. Vanier, Ottawa ON K1L 8E3
Tél: 819-776-2649; *Téléc:* 888-765-7040
administration@telaideoutaouais.ca
www.telaideoutaouais.ca
Aperçu: *Dimension:* petite; *Envergure:* locale; Organisme sans but lucratif; fondée en 1974
Mission: Offrir un service d'écoute téléphonique en français pour toute personne ayant besoin d'aide, de soutien et de référence; développer et offrir des services d'écoute en français pour la population de l'Outaouais et de l'Ontario; favoriser l'implication sociale de la communauté par le biais du bénévolat; sensibiliser et éduquer le public à la nécessité d'être à l'écoute des gens vivant dans la détresse; susciter et entretenir des partenariats avec des organismes du milieu de la santé et des services sociaux; promouvoir les services de Tel-Aide Outaouais auprès de la population
Membre de: Ontario Association of Distress Centres; Association québécois de suicidologie
Affiliation(s): Regroupement des organismes communautaires en santé mentale de l'Outaouais
Finances: *Budget de fonctionnement annuel:* $100,000-$250,000
Membre(s) du personnel: 4; 70 bénévole(s)
Membre: 10 doyen/membre à vie + 7 particuliers; *Montant de la cotisation:* 20$
Activités: *Stagiaires:* Oui; *Service de conférenciers:* Oui
Membre(s) du bureau directeur:
Jean-François Parent, Executive Director
direction@telaideoutaouais.ca

Telecare Distress Centre Brampton *See* Spectra Helpline

Telecommunications Employees Association of Manitoba (TEAM)
#200, 1 Wesley Ave., Winnipeg MB R3C 4C6
Tel: 204-984-9470; *Fax:* 204-231-2809
Toll-Free: 877-984-9470
team@teamunion.mb.ca
www.teamunion.mb.ca
www.facebook.com/teamunion161
twitter.com/teamunion161
Overview: A small provincial organization founded in 1972
Mission: To promote the interests of members; To advance the economic & social welfare of members
Membership: *Member Profile:* Management employees of the Manitoba Telephone System; *Committees:* Communications; Finance; Governance; Pay & Benefits; Grievance
Activities: Presenting TEAM scholarships
Chief Officer(s):
Misty Hughes-Newman, President
m.hughes-newman@teamunion.mb.ca
Mike Taylor, Vice President
mike.taylor@teamunion.mb.ca
Barb Hecko, Secretary
barb.hecko@teamunion.mb.ca
Tobias Theobald, Treasurer
tobias.theobald@teamunion.mb.ca
Awards:
• TEAM-IFPTE Local 161 Annual Scholarships
Eligibility: A TEAM member ($500), a TEAM member's dependent child ($1000) *Deadline:* October; *Amount:* $500 x4, $1000 x4

Telecommunities Canada Inc.
c/o President, #318, 210-1600 Kenaston Blvd., Winnipeg MB R3P 0Y4
www.tc.ca
Overview: A small national organization
Mission: To ensure that all Canadians are able to participate in community-based communications & electronic information services by promoting and supporting local community network initiatives; to represent & promote Canadian community networking movement at the national & international level
Chief Officer(s):
Clarice Leader, President
cleader@mb.e-association.ca

TelecomPioneers of Alberta
AB
Tel: 403-329-3462
Also Known As: Chapter 46
Overview: A small provincial organization overseen by TelecomPioneers of Canada
Chief Officer(s):
Stan Mills, Manager
stananddee@shaw.ca

TelecomPioneers of Canada
PO Box 880, Halifax NS B3J 2W3
Fax: 902-484-5189
Toll-Free: 888-994-3232
www.telecompioneers.ca
Overview: A medium-sized national organization overseen by TelecomPioneers
Mission: The TelecomPioneers of Canada is a network of current and former telecom industry employees, their partners and their families and are commited to improving the quality of life in Canada's communities.
Membership: *Fees:* $22
Chief Officer(s):
J. Michael Sears, President, 888-994-3232, Fax: 902-484-5189
Michael.sears@canadianpioneers.ca

Telemiracle/Kinsmen Foundation Inc.
2217C Hanselman Ct., Saskatoon SK S7L 6A8
Tel: 306-244-6400; *Fax:* 306-653-5730
www.telemiracle.com
www.facebook.com/Telemiracle
twitter.com/Telemiracle
Overview: A small local charitable organization
Mission: To provide special needs equipment & medical assistance to people in Saskatchewan
Chief Officer(s):
Cindy Xavier, Executive Director

Telephone Aid Line Kingston (TALK)
PO Box 1325, Kingston ON K7L 5C6
Tel: 613-531-8529; *Fax:* 613-531-3312; *Crisis Hot-Line:* 613-544-1771
director@telephoneaidlinekingston.com
www.telephoneaidlinekingston.com
www.facebook.com/telephoneaidlinekingston
Overview: A small local organization founded in 1973 overseen by Distress Centres Ontario
Mission: To provide telephone & support services, as well as community outreach & education, to meet the needs of the community
Finances: *Funding Sources:* Grants; Donations
Activities: *Speaker Service:* Yes; *Library*

Telephone Historical Centre (THC)
Prince of Wales Armouries Heritage Centre, PO Box 188, Stn. Main, 10440 108 Ave., Edmonton AB T5J 2J1
Tel: 780-433-1010; *Fax:* 780-426-1876
thc3@telus.net
www.telephonehistoricalcentre.com
www.facebook.com/149652501779810
Previous Name: Edmonton Telephone Historical Information Centre Foundation
Overview: A small local charitable organization founded in 1987
Mission: To achieve the acquisition, researching, organization, documentation, display & storage of historical materials relating to the telephone in Edmonton & development of telephone technology in general; To preserve artifact/archival materials for historic documentation of local technological change in the telephone industry; To serve as a research resource for scholars & students, & as educational tool for the public, employees in the telecommunications industry & school children
Member of: Alberta Museums Association; Canadian Museums Association; International Association of Transport & Communications Museums
Affiliation(s): Canadian Association of Science Centres; AMA; CMA; IATM
Finances: *Annual Operating Budget:* $50,000-$100,000; *Funding Sources:* Corporations; membership dues; fundraising; grants
Staff Member(s): 3; 25 volunteer(s)

Membership: 130; *Fees:* By donation; *Member Profile:* Retired industry professionals; *Committees:* Fundraising; Programs; Volunteer Coordination
Activities: Collects & exhibits telephone artifacts; school programs; antique telephone show; *Awareness Events:* Science & Technology Week; *Library:* Open to public by appointment

Télé-Québec Television Broadcast Employees' Union *Voir* Syndicat des employés en radio-télédiffusion de Télé-Québec (CSQ)

Television Bureau of Canada, Inc. (TVB) / Bureau de la télévision du Canada
#1005, 160 Bloor St. East, Toronto ON M4W 1B9
Tel: 416-923-8813; *Fax:* 416-413-3879
Toll-Free: 800-231-0051
tvb@tvb.ca
www.tvb.ca
twitter.com/TVB_CA
Also Known As: TVB of Canada Inc.
Overview: A medium-sized national organization founded in 1962
Mission: To promote sales, marketing & research of commercial television industry in Canada
Member of: Broadcast Executive Society; Broadcast Research Council
Affiliation(s): Television Bureau of Advertising - New York, USA
Finances: *Funding Sources:* Membership, research & event fees
Staff Member(s): 18
Membership: 150+; *Fees:* Based on advertising revenues; *Member Profile:* Television networks, stations & representative organizations; *Committees:* Sales; Research; Digital
Activities: *Library:* by appointment Not open to public
Chief Officer(s):
Rita Fabian, Chair
Theresa Treutler, President & CEO
Rhonda-Lynn Bagnall, Director, Telecaster Services
Duncan Robertson, Director, Media Insights & Research
  Montréal Branch Office
  7301, rue Beaubien est, Montréal QC H1M 3X3
  Tel: 514-284-0425
  tvb@bellnet.ca
  www.tvb.ca
  Chief Officer(s):
  Lyse Groleau, Senior Coordinator
  lgroleau@tvb.ca

TELUS Professional Employees Union (Ind.) *Voir* Syndicat des agents de maîtrise de TELUS (ind.)

The Tema Conter Memorial Trust
PO Box 265, King City ON L7B 1A0
Fax: 905-893-1574
Toll-Free: 888-288-8036
info@tema.ca
www.tema.ca
www.linkedin.com/groups/Heroes-Are-Human-Tema-Conter-1569977
www.facebook.com/HeroesAreHuman
twitter.com/TEMATrust
www.youtube.com/tematrust
Overview: A small local organization
Mission: To educate emergency care workers about critical incident stress & post-traumatic stress disorder
Staff Member(s): 10
Chief Officer(s):
Vince Savoia, Executive Director
Awards:
• The Tema Conter Memorial Award
To honor the memory of Tema Conter who was brutally raped & murdered in her Toronto apartment

Temagami & District Chamber of Commerce
PO Box 57, 7 Lakeshore Dr., Temagami ON P0H 2H0
Tel: 705-569-3344
Toll-Free: 800-661-7609
info@temagamiinformation.com
temagamiinformation.com
www.facebook.com/220034348098435
Overview: A small local organization founded in 1947
Mission: To promote businesses & the community of the Temagami area
Member of: Ontario Chamber of Commerce; Almaguin Nipissing Travel Association
Staff Member(s): 1
Membership: 1-99; *Fees:* $50-$125; $75 non-profit

Activities: Maintaining an information centre; Organizing events; Promoting business & tourism; *Library:* Temagami Public Library
Chief Officer(s):
Penny St. Germain, Treasurer

Temiskaming Cattlemen's Association (TCA)
RR#3, New Liskeard ON P0J 1P0
Overview: A small local organization
Mission: To provide dialogue between members & provincial agencies; To relay & discuss information on production, marketing & management; To direct & support promotion activities & policies
Member of: Ontario Cattlemen's Association
Staff Member(s): 1; 10 volunteer(s)
Membership: 150 individual

Temiskaming Environmental Action Committee (TEAC)
PO Box 541, New Liskeard ON P0J 1P0
Tel: 705-678-2404; *Fax:* 705-647-7511
Overview: A small local organization
Mission: To raise public awareness of environmental issues
Affiliation(s): Northwatch; Public Concern Temiskaming; Ontario Environmental Network
Activities: *Speaker Service:* Yes
Chief Officer(s):
Terry Graves, Contact

Temiskaming Law Association
PO Box 3020, 393 Main St., 2nd Fl., Haileybury ON P0J 1K0
Tel: 705-672-5655; *Fax:* 705-672-5070
temk-law@ntl.sympatico.ca
temk-law.wixsite.com/temisk-law-assoc
Overview: A small local organization
Mission: To serve lawyers from Temiskaming Shores & Kirkland Lake
Membership: 1-99
Activities: *Library:* Temiskaming Law Library
Chief Officer(s):
Shannon Wittmaack, Library Assistant

Temiskaming Multiple Births / Naissances multiples Temiskaming
PO Box 2331, New Liskeard ON P0J 1P0
Toll-Free: 866-228-8824
temiskaming@multiplebirthscanada.org
www.temiskamingmultiplebirths.com
Overview: A small local organization founded in 1985 overseen by Multiple Births Canada

Temiskaming Shores & Area Chamber of Commerce (TSACC)
PO Box 811, 883356 Hwy. 65 East, New Liskeard ON P0J 1P0
Tel: 705-647-5771; *Fax:* 705-647-8633
Toll-Free: 866-947-5753
info@tsacc.ca
www.tsacc.ca
www.facebook.com/Temiskaming.Shores.Area.Chamber
Previous Name: Tri-Town & District Chamber of Commerce
Overview: A small local organization
Member of: Ontario Chamber of Commerce
Staff Member(s): 2; 12 volunteer(s)
Membership: 235; *Fees:* $85-$345
Chief Officer(s):
Lois Weston-Bernstein, Executive Director
manager@tsacc.ca

Temple de la renommée des sports d'Ottawa *See* Ottawa Sports Hall of Fame Inc.

Temple de la renommée des sports du Canada *See* Canada's Sports Hall of Fame

Temple de la renommée olympique du Canada *See* Canadian Olympic Hall of Fame

Temple de la renommée sportive du N.-B. *See* New Brunswick Sports Hall of Fame

Temporomandibular Joint Society of Canada (TMJSC)
#7, 119 Henderson Ave., Thornhill ON L3T 2L3
Tel: 416-414-2445
tmjscanada@gmail.com
Overview: A small local organization founded in 2015
Mission: TJSC (Temporomandibular Joint Society of Canada) is devoted to furthering TMJ disease/disfunction /disorders

support, education, and awareness in Canada for both those afflicted and those who provide professional care for them.
Staff Member(s): 1; 1 volunteer(s)
Activities: *Speaker Service:* Yes; *Library*
Chief Officer(s):
Anita Frank, Executive Director, 416-414-2445
tmjscanada@gmail.com

Tennessee Walking Horse Association of Western Canada (TWHAWC)
c/o Ethel Mankow, Site 427, Box 1, Comp 4, RR#1, Drayton Valley AB T7A 2A1
www.twhawc.com
Overview: A small local organization founded in 1998
Mission: To promote the Tennessee Walking Horse breed in western Canada
Affiliation(s): Alberta Equestrian Federation; Tennessee Walking Horse Breeders' & Exhibitors' Association
Membership: *Fees:* $10 youth members; $25 single members; $40 family membership; *Member Profile:* Tennessee Walking Horse enthusiasts in western Canada
Activities: Sponsoring gaited clinics & shows; Organizing group trail rides; Arranging displays for local trade & equine fairs; Posting show results; Hosting regular membership meetings; Providing networking opportunities with other Walking Horse owners
Chief Officer(s):
Brent Bachman, President
bachman1@telusplanet.net
Lisa Adams, Vice-President
Koren LeVoir, Secretary
klmedia@shaw.ca
Ethel Mankow, Treasurer
mankow@live.com
Publications:
• Tennessee Walking Horse Association of Western Canada
Type: Newsletter
Profile: Issued every 2 months, featurring association activities & announcements

Tennis BC (TBC)
#204, 210 West Broadway, Vancouver BC V5Y 3W2
Tel: 604-737-3086; *Fax:* 604-737-3124
tbc@tennisbc.org
www.tennisbc.org
www.facebook.com/tennisbc
twitter.com/TennisBC
www.youtube.com/user/TennisBC1
Previous Name: British Columbia Tennis Association
Overview: A medium-sized provincial organization founded in 1978 overseen by Tennis Canada
Member of: Tennis Performance Association (TPA); Tennis Canada
Finances: *Funding Sources:* Government Sponsors; Tennis Canada; Sports Grants; Events; Member Clubs
Staff Member(s): 12
Membership: *Fees:* $46 adult; $27 junior
Activities: *Library:* Open to public
Chief Officer(s):
Roger Skillings, President
Mark Roberts, Chief Executive Officer, 604-737-3086 Ext. 9
mroberts@tennisbc.org
Meetings/Conferences:
• Tennis BC Annual General Meeting 2018, 2018, BC
Scope: Provincial

Tennis Canada
Aviva Centre, #100, 1 Shoreham Dr., Toronto ON M3N 3A6
Tel: 416-665-9777; *Fax:* 416-665-9017
Toll-Free: 877-283-6647
info@tenniscanada.com
www.tenniscanada.com
www.facebook.com/TennisCanada
twitter.com/TennisCanada
www.instagram.com/tennis_canada
Previous Name: Canadian Tennis Association
Overview: A large national organization founded in 1890
Mission: To stimulate participation & excellence in the sport at the local, provincial, national, & international levels; To provide encouragement, support, & leadership to organizations & individuals who seek to enhance the enjoyment, quality & image of Canadian tennis
Member of: International Tennis Federation; Canadian Olympic Association; Canadian Paralympic Committee; International Wheelchair Tennis Association
Finances: *Funding Sources:* Government

Membership: *Member Profile:* Provincial tennis associations
Activities: Holding a number of championships; programs for all ages & abilities; *Awareness Events:* Rogers Cup tournament; Davis Cup; Fed Cup; *Internships:* Yes
Chief Officer(s):
John LeBoutillier, Chair
Kelly D. Murumets, President & CEO
Hatem McDadi, Senior Vice-President, Tennis Development
Awards:
• Tennis Canada Excellence Awards
• Distinguished Service Awards
Publications:
• Tennis Canada Annual Report
Type: Yearbook; *Frequency:* Annually
Montréal
Uniprix Stadium, 285, rue Gary Carter, Montréal QC H2R 2W1
Tél: 514-273-1515; *Téléc:* 514-276-0070
Ligne sans frais: 866-338-2685

Tennis de Table Canada *See* Table Tennis Canada

Tennis Manitoba
#419, 145 Pacific Ave., Winnipeg MB R3B 2Z6
Tel: 204-925-5660; *Fax:* 204-925-5703
info@tennismanitoba.com
www.tennismanitoba.com
www.facebook.com/TennisManitoba
twitter.com/tennismanitoba
www.youtube.com/channel/UCXBmclr50I7GpGTP9u6UE3w
Also Known As: Manitoba Tennis Association
Overview: A medium-sized provincial organization founded in 1880 overseen by Tennis Canada
Mission: To stimulate participation & advancement in tennis by all Manitobans
Member of: Sport Manitoba; Tennis Canada
Finances: *Funding Sources:* Provincial government; Manitoba Lotteries; Private sponsors
Membership: *Fees:* Schedule available
Chief Officer(s):
Mark Arndt, Executive Director
mark@tennismanitoba.com

Tennis New Brunswick
PO Box 604, Fredericton NB E3B 5A6
Tel: 506-444-0885
tnb@tennisnb.net
www.tennisnb.net
www.facebook.com/TennisNewBrunswick
twitter.com/10sNB
Overview: A medium-sized provincial organization overseen by Tennis Canada
Mission: To be the body governing the sport of tennis in New Brunswick
Member of: Sport NB; Tennis Canada
Membership: *Fees:* Schedule available
Chief Officer(s):
Dana Brown, President
Mark Thibault, Executive Director

Tennis Newfoundland & Labrador
Greenbelt Tennis Club, 114 Newtown Rd., St. John's NL A1B 3A7
Tel: 709-722-3840
newfoundland.tenniscanada.com
www.facebook.com/TennisNFLD
twitter.com/tennisnfld
Previous Name: Newfoundland & Labrador Tennis Association
Overview: A medium-sized provincial organization overseen by Tennis Canada
Mission: To grow & promote the sport of tennis throughout Newfoundland & Labrador; To increase participation at levels consistent with the personal goals & aspirations of competitors in all age groups
Member of: Tennis Canada
Staff Member(s): 2
Chief Officer(s):
Nancy Taylor, President
Alan Mackin, Executive Director

Tennis Northwest Territories *See* Northwest Territories Tennis Association

Tennis Québec (TQ)
285, rue Gary-Carter, Montréal QC H2R 2W1
Tél: 514-270-6060; *Téléc:* 514-270-2700
courrier@tennis.qc.ca
www.tennis.qc.ca
www.facebook.com/tennisquebec270
www.youtube.com/user/tennisquebec
Nom précédent: Fédération québécoise de tennis
Aperçu: *Dimension:* moyenne; *Envergure:* provinciale; Organisme sans but lucratif; fondée en 1899 surveillé par Tennis Canada
Mission: Promotion et développement du tennis au Québec auprès de toutes les catégories d'âge et de tous les calibres
Membre de: Tennis Canada
Finances: *Budget de fonctionnement annuel:* $500,000-$1.5 Million
Membre(s) du personnel: 8; 30 bénévole(s)
Membre: 35 000; *Comités:* Table des entraîneurs; Commission des officiels; Commission d'enseignement
Activités: Tournée sports experts; *Stagiaires:* Oui; *Service de conférenciers:* Oui; *Bibliothèque:* Centre d'information; Bibliothèque publique rendez-vous
Membre(s) du bureau directeur:
Réjean Genois, Président
Jean François Manibal, Directeur général, 514-270-6060 Ext. 606
dg1@tennis.qc.ca

Tennis Saskatchewan
2205 Victoria Ave., Regina SK S4P 0S4
Tel: 306-780-9410; *Fax:* 306-525-4009
www.tennissask.com
Previous Name: Saskatchewan Tennis Association
Overview: A medium-sized provincial organization founded in 1976 overseen by Tennis Canada
Mission: To advance tennis throughout Saskatchewan by stimulating participation & excellence in the sport; To provide players throughout Saskatchewan with systematic opportunities to participate in tennis & to achieve a level of competence consistent with their abilities & aspirations, with particular emphasis on youth; To stage tennis events; To produce teams & athletes capable of winning national championships
Member of: Tennis Canada
Affiliation(s): Sask Sport Incorporated
Finances: *Funding Sources:* Saskatchewan Lotteries; Tennis Canada
Chief Officer(s):
Rory Park, Executive Director

Tennis Yukon Association
Whitehorse YT
Tel: 867-393-2621
tennisyukon@gmail.com
www.courtsidecanada.ca/communities/Yukon
Overview: A small provincial organization
Mission: To promote the sport of Tennis in the Yukon.
Chief Officer(s):
Stacy Lewis, President, 867-393-2621

The Teresa Group
#104, 124 Merton St., Toronto ON M4S 2Z2
Tel: 416-596-7703; *Fax:* 416-596-7910
info@teresagroup.ca
www.teresagroup.ca
www.facebook.com/120076698045376
twitter.com/TheTeresaGroup
Overview: A small local charitable organization founded in 1990 overseen by Canadian AIDS Society
Mission: Serves the needs of children & their families living with or affected by HIV/AIDS
Member of: Ontario AIDS Network; Canadian AIDS Society
Finances: *Annual Operating Budget:* $250,000-$500,000; *Funding Sources:* Government & the private sector; fundraising
Staff Member(s): 6
Activities: *Awareness Events:* Scotiabank Charity Challenge, Oct.; *Speaker Service:* Yes; *Library:* by appointment
Chief Officer(s):
Nicci Stein, Executive Director
Publications:
• Bye-Bye Secrets: A Book About Children Living With HIV or AIDS in their Family
Type: Book; *Number of Pages:* 36; *Price:* $14.95
Profile: The experiences of five girls, aged 8-12 years, who live with HIV/AIDS in their families.
• Early Intervention Programs for Children & Women Living with HIV & AIDS Leaflet
Type: Leaflet
Profile: Descriptions of the following: Pre-Natal, New Moms, Mom & Tots Groups, & The Formula Program
• Hopes, Wishes & Dreams: A Book of Art & Writing by Children Living with HIV/AIDS in their Family
Type: Book; *Number of Pages:* 40; *Price:* $14.95
Profile: Art, poetry & writings by children affected by HIV/AIDS
• How Do I Tell My Kids? A Disclosure Booklet About HIV/AIDS in the Family
Type: Booklet; *Number of Pages:* 48; *Price:* $5.00
Profile: A booklet for adults, designed to help with the process of telling their children that a family member has HIV.
• In Touch [a publication of The Teresa Group]
Type: Newsletter
• Programs & Services Booklet
Type: Brochure
Profile: This brochure outlines what The Teresa Group does.

Terrace & District Chamber of Commerce
3224 Kalum St., Terrace BC V8G 2N1
Tel: 250-635-2063; *Fax:* 250-635-4152
admin@terracechamber.com
www.terracechamber.com
Overview: A small local organization founded in 1927
Mission: To be the recognized voice of business committed to the enhancement & development of the economic well-being of the Terrace area
Member of: BC Chamber of Commerce; Canadian Chamber of Commerce; Terrace Tourism Society
Finances: *Annual Operating Budget:* $100,000-$250,000; *Funding Sources:* Membership dues; special projects
Staff Member(s): 2; 15 volunteer(s)
Membership: 373; *Fees:* Schedule available
Activities: *Library:* Resource Centre; Open to public
Chief Officer(s):
Erika Magnuson-Ford, Executive Director
executivedirector@terracechamber.com

Terrace & District Community Services Society (TDCSS)
#200, 3219 Eby St., Terrace BC V8G 4R3
Tel: 250-635-3178; *Fax:* 250-635-6319
info@tdcss.ca
www.tdcss.ca
www.facebook.com/TDCSS
twitter.com/TDCSS_
Overview: A small local organization founded in 1970
Member of: British Columbia Association for Community Living
Chief Officer(s):
Marilyn Lissimore, Executive Director

Terrazzo Tile & Marble Association of Canada (TTMAC) / Association canadienne de terrazzo, tuile et marbre
#8, 163 Buttermill Ave., Concord ON L4K 3X8
Tel: 905-660-9640; *Fax:* 905-660-0513
Toll-Free: 800-201-8599
association@ttmac.com
www.ttmac.com
Overview: A small national organization founded in 1944
Mission: To standardize terrazzo, tile, marble, & stone installation techniques, so that the industry will grow & proper; To support the hardsurface industry & its members
Finances: *Funding Sources:* Membership fees; Sponsorships
Membership: *Fees:* $145 - $405 professionals; $165 supplier & contractor branch offices; $3,000 affiliates; Schedule, based on volume, for contractors & suppliers; *Member Profile:* Professionals, such as architects, consultants, specifiers, designers, & engineers; Firms engaged in contracting to install terrazzo, tile, & stone products; Suppliers who sell or manufacture products, equipment, or services; Industry associations that want to be affiliated with Terrazzo Tile & Marble Association of Canada
Activities: Establishing guidelines; Promoting hardsurface products; Providing technical information to architects, specifiers, designers, & engineers; Testing; Conducting field inspections; Offering training opportunities; Providing networking occasions; *Library:* Terrazzo Tile & Marble Association of Canada Library
Chief Officer(s):
Elaine Cook, Eastern Editor, The Analyst
elaine@ttmac.com
Meetings/Conferences:
• Terrazzo Tile & Marble Association of Canada 2018 Convention, 2018
Scope: National
Publications:
• The Analyst
Type: Newsletter; *Frequency:* Bimonthly; *Accepts Advertising;*

Canadian Associations / Terrazzo, Tile & Marble Guild of Ontario, Inc. (TTMGO)

Editor: Len Tompkins
Profile: Terrazzo Tile & Marble Association of Canada developments, membership information, technical updates, business topics, training opportunities, & upcoming events
• Dimensional Stone Guide, Volume II
Type: Manual; *Price:* $150 members; $225 non-members
• Hard Surface Maintenance Guide
Type: Manual; *Price:* $10 members; $25 non-members
• Hardsurface
Type: Magazine; *Accepts Advertising*; *Editor:* Jeanne Fronda;
Price: Free for TTMAC members & architectural & design firms across Canada
Profile: Feature articles written by experts in the field, award information, & forthcoming events
• Terrazzo Installation Manual
Type: Manual; *Price:* $25 members; $45 non-members
• Tile Installation Manual
Type: Manual; *Price:* $25 members; $45 non-members
• TTMAC E-news
Type: Newsletter
Profile: Happenings in the industry & the Terrazzo Tile & Marble Association of Canada, distributed free to all members

Burnaby (Western Branch)
#108, 3650 Bonneville Pl., Burnaby BC V3N 4T7
Tel: 604-294-6885; *Fax:* 604-294-2406
association@ttmac.com
www.ttmac.com
www.linkedin.com/company/terrazzo-tile-&-marble-association-of-canada
www.facebook.com/444656588885871
twitter.com/TTMACCanada
www.youtube.com/user/TTMACCanada
Chief Officer(s):
Ashley Petelycky, Office Manager
ashley@ttmac.com

Terrazzo, Tile & Marble Guild of Ontario, Inc. (TTMGO)
#5, 30 Capstan Gate, Concord ON L4K 3E8
Tel: 905-660-5094; *Fax:* 905-660-5706
info@ttmgo.org
www.ttmgo.org
Overview: A small provincial organization founded in 1973
Member of: National Trade Contractors Coalition of Canada
Membership: 35 companies; *Member Profile:* Unionized contractors in Ontario specializing in the installation of terrazzo, tile & natural stone
Activities: Labour relations; operating the Terrazzo, Tile & Marble Trade School (TTMTS)
Chief Officer(s):
Rick Giacomini, President & Chair, Negotiations & Labour Relations

Terre sans frontières (TSF) / World Without Borders
#23, 399, rue des Conseillers, La Prairie QC J5R 4H6
Tél: 450-659-7717; *Téléc:* 450-659-2276
Ligne sans frais: 877-873-2433
tsf@terresansfrontieres.ca
www.terresansfrontieres.ca
www.linkedin.com/company/terre-sans-frontières
www.facebook.com/terresansfrontieres
www.youtube.com/user/TerreSansFrontieres
Merged from: Avions sans frontières; Prodeva
Aperçu: *Dimension:* petite; *Envergure:* internationale; Organisme sans but lucratif; fondée en 1981
Mission: Organisme de coopération internationale qui travaille dans la perspective de développement durable
Membre de: Canadian Council for International Cooperation
Affiliation(s): Association québécoise des organismes de coopération internationale (AQOCI)
Finances: *Budget de fonctionnement annuel:* Plus de $5 Million
Membre(s) du personnel: 14; 250 bénévole(s)
Membre: 121; *Montant de la cotisation:* 25$; *Comités:* Direction; Sélection de projets; Finances
Activités: Adduction d'eau et assainissement; éducation; transport aérien humanitaire; appui institutionnel; santé; agriculture; *Evénements de sensibilisation:* Journées Québécoises de la Solidarité Internationale; *Service de conférenciers:* Oui
Membre(s) du bureau directeur:
Jean Fortin, Directeur général

Les Terre-Neuviens français *Voir* La Fédération des francophones de Terre-Neuve et du Labrador

The Terry Fox Foundation / La Fondation Terry Fox
#150, 8960 University High St., Burnaby BC V5A 4Y6
Tel: 604-200-0541; *Fax:* 604-701-0247
Toll-Free: 888-836-9786
Other Communication: contact@terryfoxrun.org;
international@terryfox.org
national@terryfox.org
www.terryfoxrun.org
www.facebook.com/TheTerryFoxFoundation
twitter.com/TerryFoxCanada
www.youtube.com/terryfoxcanada
Also Known As: Terry Fox Run
Overview: A large national charitable organization founded in 1980
Mission: To maintain the vision & principles of Terry Fox while raising money for cancer research through the annual Terry Fox Run, memoriam donations & planned gifts. All money raised by the Foundation is distributed through the National Cancer Institute of Canada
Finances: *Annual Operating Budget:* Greater than $5 Million
Staff Member(s): 6
Activities: *Awareness Events:* Terry Fox Run, 2nd Sunday following Labour Day, Sept.; *Speaker Service:* Yes
Chief Officer(s):
Bill Pristanski, Chair
Judith Fox, International Director, 604-239-8576
international@terryfoxrun.org

Alberta/NWT/Nunavut Office
#D10, 6115 - 3rd St. SE, Calgary AB T2H 2L2
Tel: 403-212-1336; *Fax:* 403-212-1343
Toll-Free: 888-836-9786
Chief Officer(s):
Wendy Kennelly, Provincial Director
wendy.kennelly@terryfoxrun.org

British Columbia/Yukon Office
2669 Shaughnessy St., Port Coquitlam BC V3C 3G7
Tel: 604-464-2666; *Fax:* 604-464-2664
Toll-Free: 888-836-9786
bcyukon@terryfoxrun.org
Chief Officer(s):
Donna White, Provincial Director

International
#150, 8960 University High St., Burnaby BC V5A 4Y6
international@terryfoxrun.org
Chief Officer(s):
Rhonda Risenrough, International Director
Rhonda.risebrough@terryfox.org

Manitoba Office
1214 Chevrier Blvd., #A, Winnipeg MB R3T 1Y3
Tel: 204-231-5282; *Fax:* 204-321-5365
Toll-Free: 888-836-9786
mb@terryfoxrun.org
Chief Officer(s):
Tammy Ferrante, Provincial Director

New Brunswick/PEI Office
#493, 605 Prospect St., Fredericton NB E3B 6B8
Tel: 506-458-2618; *Fax:* 506-459-4572
Toll-Free: 888-836-9786
nbpei@terryfoxrun.org
Chief Officer(s):
Gwen Smith-Walsh, Provincial Director

Newfoundland & Labrador
#202, 835 Topsail Rd., Mount Pearl NL A1N 3J6
Tel: 709-576-8428; *Fax:* 709-747-7277
Toll-Free: 888-836-9786
nl@terryfoxrun.org
Chief Officer(s):
Heather Strong, Provincial Director

Nova Scotia Office
#203, 3600 Kempt Rd., Halifax NS B3K 4X8
Tel: 902-423-8131; *Fax:* 902-492-3639
Toll-Free: 888-836-9786
ns@terryfoxrun.org
Chief Officer(s):
Barbara Pate, Provincial Director

Ontario Office
#900, 1200 Eglinton Ave. Wast, Toronto ON M3C 1H9
Tel: 416-924-8252; *Fax:* 416-924-6597
Toll-Free: 888-836-9786
ontario@terryfoxrun.org
Chief Officer(s):
Martha McClew, Provincial Director

Québec Office
#207, 10, boul Churchill, Greenfield Park QC J4V 2L7
Tel: 450-923-9747; *Fax:* 450-923-8468
Toll-Free: 888-836-9786
qc@terryfoxrun.org
Chief Officer(s):
Peter Sheremeta, Provincial Director

Saskatchewan Office
1812 - 9th Ave. North, Regina SK S4R 7T4
Tel: 306-757-1662; *Fax:* 306-757-7422
Toll-Free: 888-836-9786
Chief Officer(s):
Heather Mackenzie, Provincial Director
heather.mackenzie@terryfoxrun.org

TESL Canada Federation (TESL Canada)
3751 - 21 St. NE, Calgary AB T2E 6T5
Tel: 403-538-7300; *Fax:* 403-538-7392
Toll-Free: 800-393-9199
info@tesl.ca
www.tesl.ca
Also Known As: Teaching English as a Second Language Canada Federation
Overview: A medium-sized national organization founded in 1978
Mission: To support the sharing of knowledge & experiences across Canada; To represents diverse interests in TESL nationally & internationally
Affiliation(s): Teachers of English to Speakers of Other Languages (TESOL); Société pour la promotion de l'enseignement de l'anglais (langue seconde) au Québec
Membership: *Fees:* Schedule available; *Committees:* Executive; Standards Advisory; Journal Advisory; Governance & Policy; Finance; Testing; Professional Development; Research & Dissemination; Settlement Language National Network
Activities: *Internships:* Yes
Chief Officer(s):
Sumana Barua, Executive Director
Ron Thomson, President

TESL Manitoba *See* TEAL Manitoba

TESL New Brunswick
16 Lamda Ave., Saint John NB E2J 0B6
www.teslnb.ca
www.facebook.com/teslnewbrunswick
twitter.com/TESL_NB
Overview: A small provincial organization overseen by TESL Canada Federation
Chief Officer(s):
Natalia Ribeiro, Treasurer

TESL Newfoundland & Labrador (TESL NL)
c/o ESL Program, Memorial University of Newfoundland, St. John's NL A1B 3X9
Tel: 709-737-8054; *Fax:* 709-737-8282
arts-srv.arts.mun.ca/tesl
Overview: A small provincial organization overseen by TESL Canada Federation
Member of: TESL Canada Federation
Affiliation(s): TESL Canada
Membership: $30; *Member Profile:* Teachers of English as a Second Language in Newfoundland & Labrador
Activities: Engaging in advocacy activities for ESL learners & issues; Offering professional development opportunities; Providing networking occasions; Sharing knowledge throughout the province; Hosting monthly meetings
Chief Officer(s):
Sonja Knutson, President
sknutson@mun.ca

TESL Nova Scotia (TESLNS)
PO Box 36068, Halifax NS B3J 3S9
teslnovascotia@gmail.com
tesl-nova-scotia.wikispaces.com
Also Known As: Teachers of English as a Second Language of Nova Scotia
Overview: A small provincial charitable organization founded in 1982 overseen by TESL Canada Federation
Mission: To advance communication & coordinating issues related to teaching English as a Second Language; To unify teachers & learners; To promote advocacy for ESL learners; To provide a forum for discussion & networking capabilities; To share knowledge in Nova Scotia
Member of: TESL Canada Federation
Finances: *Annual Operating Budget:* Less than $50,000
100 volunteer(s)
Membership: 100; *Fees:* $45; *Member Profile:* Teachers of adults, elementary & secondary learners

Activities: Annual conference; monthly board meetings; professional development meetings; newsletter
Chief Officer(s):
Andy de Champlain, President

TESL Ontario
#405, 27 Carlton St., Toronto ON M5B 1L2
Tel: 416-593-4243; *Fax:* 416-593-0164
Toll-Free: 800-327-4827
administration@teslontario.org
www.teslontario.net
www.linkedin.com/groups/TESL-Ontario-1813872
www.facebook.com/101601733235647
twitter.com/TESLOntario
Also Known As: Teachers of English as a Second Language Association of Ontario
Overview: A medium-sized provincial organization founded in 1972
Mission: To provide support for English as a Second Language educators in Ontario
Member of: TESOL International - Teachers of English to Speakers of Other Languages
Finances: *Annual Operating Budget:* $100,000-$250,000; *Funding Sources:* Membership fees
Staff Member(s): 8; 50 volunteer(s)
Membership: 4,500; *Fees:* Schedule available; *Member Profile:* ESL professionals, government bodies & learners; *Committees:* Accreditation Standards; Communications Advisory; Conference; Research; Social Content
Chief Officer(s):
Renate Tilson, Executive Director
James Papple, Chair
Meetings/Conferences:
• TESL Ontario 2018 46th Annual Conference, 2018, ON
Scope: Provincial
Publications:
• Contact [a publication of Teachers of English as a Second Language Association of Ontario]
Type: Magazine; *Frequency:* Quarterly
Profile: Articles on ESL conferences & research
• Membership Minutes [a publication of Teachers of English as a Second Language Association of Ontario]
Type: Newsletter
Profile: Information on TESL Ontario initiatives & resources
• TESL [Teachers of English as a Second Language Association] Ontario Annual Report
Type: Report; *Frequency:* Annually

TESL Prince Edward Island (TESL PEI)
c/o Webster Centre for Teaching & Learning, U of PEI, 550 University Ave., Charlottetown PE C1A 4P3
Tel: 902-566-6003
teslpei.ning.com
Overview: A small provincial organization overseen by TESL Canada Federation
Mission: To encourage & support the promotion of policies & programmes related to second language learning & teaching on Prince Edward Island
Member of: TESL Canada Federation
Finances: *Funding Sources:* TESL Canada; membership fees
Membership: 1-99; *Fees:* $32; *Member Profile:* Individuals & groups actively involved or interested in the teaching of English as a Second Lanaguage
Chief Officer(s):
Christina Perry, President
cperry@upei.ca

TESL Yukon
c/o E. Hurlburt, PO Box 5403, Haines Junction YT Y0B 1L0
dl1.yukoncollege.yk.ca/tesl
Overview: A small provincial organization founded in 1998 overseen by TESL Canada Federation
Membership: 16; *Member Profile:* Adults interested in English as a second language

Teslin Regional Chamber of Commerce
PO Box 181, Teslin YT Y0A 1B0
Overview: A small local organization

Tetra Society of North America
#318, 425 Carrall St., Vancouver BC V6B 6E3
Tel: 604-688-6464; *Fax:* 604-688-6463
Toll-Free: 877-688-8762
www.tetrasociety.org
Overview: A small national charitable organization founded in 1992

Mission: To link volunteer engineers & technicians with persons with disabilities to create custom assistive devices to help them achieve greater independence
Member of: Sam Sullivan Disability Foundation, Volunteer Vancouver
Finances: *Annual Operating Budget:* $100,000-$250,000
Staff Member(s): 2; 400 volunteer(s)
Membership: 1,000-4,999; *Member Profile:* Adults & children with disabilities
Activities: Monthly volunteer meetings; *Speaker Service:* Yes
Chief Officer(s):
Pat Tweedie, National Coordinator, Program
ptweedie@tetrasociety.org
Eric Molendyk, Coordinator, BC Chapter
eric@tetrasociety.org
Matthew Wild, Coordinator, Communications
matthew@disabilityfoundation.org
Awards:
• Gizmo Awards

Teulon Chamber of Commerce
PO Box 235, Teulon MB R0C 3B0
Tel: 204-886-3910
www.teulon.ca
Overview: A small local organization
Mission: To promote & support businesses & the community
Chief Officer(s):
Jan Lambourne, Chair
Linda Lamoureux, Secretary

Texada Island Chamber of Commerce
PO Box 249, Vananda BC V0N 3K0
Tel: 604-413-0994
Overview: A small local organization
Mission: To strengthen business & the community
Affiliation(s): British Columbia Chamber of Commerce; Canadian Chamber of Commerce
Chief Officer(s):
Karen May, President

Textile Federation of Canada *See* Canadian Textile Association

Thalassemia Foundation of Canada
338 Falstaff Ave., Toronto ON M6L 3E7
Tel: 416-242-8425; *Fax:* 416-242-8425
info@thalassemia.ca
www.thalassemia.ca
Overview: A small national charitable organization founded in 1982
Mission: To raise public awareness of Thalassemia; To raise money for Thalassemia research & treatment; To support families of children with Thalassemia
Chief Officer(s):
Helen Ziavras, President

Thalidomide Victims Association of Canada (TVAC) / Association canadienne des victimes de la thalidomide (ACVT)
#102, 7744, rue Sherbrooke est, Montréal QC H1L 1A1
Tel: 514-355-0811; *Fax:* 514-355-0860
Toll-Free: 877-355-0811
tvac.acvt@sympatico.ca
www.thalidomide.ca
Overview: A medium-sized national charitable organization founded in 1988
Mission: To monitor the drug thalidomide & to meet the needs of thalidomide survivors; To empower & enhance the quality of life of Canadians living with the effects of thalidomide
Affiliation(s): Council of Canadians with Disabilities; Canadian Centre for Philanthropy
Membership: *Member Profile:* Persons born disabled as a consequence of the drug thalidomide
Activities: *Speaker Service:* Yes; *Library:* TVAC Resource Library; by appointment
Chief Officer(s):
Mercedes Benegbi, Executive Director

Thames Region Ecological Association (TREA)
1017 Western Rd., London ON N6G 1G5
Tel: 519-672-5991; *Fax:* 519-645-0981
info@trea.ca
www.trea.ca
www.facebook.com/trealondon
twitter.com/TREAontario
www.youtube.com/user/londonbicyclefestiva
Overview: A small local charitable organization founded in 1986

Mission: Committed to educating ourselves & the community towards development of an ecologically responsible & sustainable future through awareness, reflection, caring & action
Member of: Grosvenor Lodge Resource Centre for Heritage & Environment
Affiliation(s): Urban League of London; London Composts
Finances: *Annual Operating Budget:* Less than $50,000; *Funding Sources:* Government; membership fees; Compost Day
Staff Member(s): 1; 40 volunteer(s)
Membership: 60 individual; *Fees:* $20 individual
Activities: TREATop; waste group; home cocmposting program; TREATalk, tree planting; pesticide group; London Bicycle Festival; *Speaker Service:* Yes
Chief Officer(s):
Anne Arnott, President

Thames Valley Trail Association Inc. (TVTA)
c/o Grosvenor Lodge, 1017 Western Rd., London ON N6G 1G5
Tel: 519-645-2845; *Fax:* 519-645-0981
tvta.ca
www.facebook.com/theTVTA
twitter.com/TVTA_London_Ont
Overview: A small local charitable organization founded in 1969
Mission: To promote hiking; to develop & maintain the Thames Valley Trail; to cooperate with other environmental groups
Member of: Hike Ontario
Finances: *Funding Sources:* Membership dues
Membership: *Fees:* $25 individual; $35 family; $20 senior; *Member Profile:* All ages with an interest in hiking & recreational walking
Activities: Trail follows north branch of Thames River from Kilworth, the parks of London through neat farmlands & stands of hardwood to historic St. Marys (100 km); *Awareness Events:* Hike Ontario Day; *Speaker Service:* Yes; *Library:* Grosvenor Lodge Library; Open to public
Chief Officer(s):
Ruth Hoch, Co-Chair
Murray Hamilton, Co-Chair
Dave Potten, Co-Chair

Théâtre Action (TA)
203, 255, ch Montréal, Ottawa ON K1L 6C4
Tél: 613-745-2322; *Téléc:* 613-745-1733
theatreaction@franco.ca
www.theatreaction.ca/fr
www.facebook.com/TheatreActionON
twitter.com/TheatreActionON
Aperçu: *Dimension:* petite; *Envergure:* locale; fondée en 1972
Mission: Oeuvrer au développement du théâtre en Ontario
Membre de: Réseau Ontario; Alliance culturelle de l'Ontario; Theatre Canada
Affiliation(s): Conseil des arts de l'Ontario, Ministère du patrimoine canadien, Ministère de l'Éducation de l'Ontario
Finances: *Fonds:* Gouvernement de l'Ontario
Membre(s) du personnel: 5; 150 bénévole(s)
Activités: Prix et bourses; programmes de formation; *Evénements de sensibilisation:* Festival Franco-ontarien de théâtre
Membre(s) du bureau directeur:
Pierre Simpson, Président
Prix, Bourses:
• Prix d'excellence artistique de Théâtre Action
; *Amount:* 1 000$
• Bourse d'études Théâtre Action
; *Amount:* 1 000$

Theatre Alberta Society
Percy Page Centre, 11759 Groat Rd., 3rd Fl., Edmonton AB T5M 3K6
Tel: 780-422-8162; *Fax:* 780-422-2663
Toll-Free: 888-422-8160
theatreab@theatrealberta.com
www.theatrealberta.com
www.facebook.com/TheatreAlberta
twitter.com/TheatreAlberta
Overview: A medium-sized provincial organization founded in 1985
Mission: To encourage the growth of theatre in Alberta through high quality support & training opportunities to theatre professionals, educators & community theatre practitioners
Finances: *Funding Sources:* Alberta Foundation for the Arts
Staff Member(s): 7
Activities: *Library:* Theatre Alberta Library; Not open to public
Chief Officer(s):
Keri Mitchell, Executive Director
keri@theatrealberta.com

Theatre Calgary
220 - 9 Ave. SE, Calgary AB T2G 5C4
Tel: 403-294-7440; *Fax:* 403-294-7493
subscriptions@theatrecalgary.com
www.theatrecalgary.com
www.facebook.com/theatrecalgary
twitter.com/theatrecalgary
www.youtube.com/user/TheatreCalgary
Overview: A small local organization
Mission: To produce classical & modern theatre for Calgary audiences
Staff Member(s): 41
Chief Officer(s):
Chad Newcombe, Chair
Shari Wattling, Interim Artistic Director

Théâtre de la Vieille 17
204, av King Edward, Ottawa ON K1N 7L7
Tél: 613-241-8562; *Téléc:* 613-241-9507
communications@vieille17.ca
www.vieille17.ca
www.facebook.com/LaVieille17
twitter.com/theatrev17
vimeo.com/user8318968
Aperçu: *Dimension:* petite; *Envergure:* locale; fondée en 1979
Mission: Créer et diffuser des spectacles pour la jeunesse et pour les adultes à l'échelle régionale, nationale et internationale
Membre(s) du personnel: 5
Membre(s) du bureau directeur:
Esther Beauchemin, Directrice artistique et générale
eb@vieille17.ca

Théâtre des épinettes
55, rue Laframboise, Chibougamau QC G8P 2S5
Tél: 418-748-4682
Aperçu: *Dimension:* petite; *Envergure:* locale
Membre(s) du bureau directeur:
Guy Lalancette, Responsable
glalancette@tlb.sympatico.ca

Théâtre du Nouvel-Ontario (TNO)
21, boul Lasalle, Sudbury ON P3A 6B1
Tél: 705-525-5606
tno@letno.ca
www.letno.ca
twitter.com/le_TNO
www.youtube.com/user/TheatreNouvel0ntario
Aperçu: *Dimension:* petite; *Envergure:* locale; fondée en 1971
Mission: Dédié à la création, à la dramaturgie franco-ontarienne et à l'accueil d'oeuvres principalement canadiennes
Membre(s) du personnel: 9
Activités: *Stagiaires:* Oui
Membre(s) du bureau directeur:
Geneviève Pineault, Directrice artistique
artistique@letno.ca

Théâtre du Trillium
#5, 109, rue Murray, Ottawa ON K1N 5M5
Tél: 613-789-7643; *Téléc:* 613-789-7641
comm@theatre-trillium.com
www.theatre-trillium.com
www.facebook.com/theatredutrillium
twitter.com/theatretrillium
www.youtube.com/theatredutrillium
Aperçu: *Dimension:* petite; *Envergure:* locale
Mission: Pour effectuer des productions théâtrales contemporaines
Membre(s) du personnel: 4
Activités: Trois productions grand public; laboratoire de mise en scène; spectacle pour adolescents
Membre(s) du bureau directeur:
Pierre Antoine Lafon Simard, Directeur artistique
artistique@theatre-trillium.com

Théâtre français de Toronto
#610, 21, rue College, Toronto ON M5G 2B3
Tél: 416-534-7303
www.theatrefrancais.com
www.facebook.com/Theatrefrancais
twitter.com/theatrefrancais
www.youtube.com/LeTheatreFrancaisTfT
Également appelé: TFT
Aperçu: *Dimension:* petite; *Envergure:* locale; Organisme sans but lucratif
Mission: Le Théâtre français de Toronto est un théâtre professionnel de langue française, de répertoire et de création. Il s'adresse à tous les amateurs de théâtre en français, tant les francophones que les francophiles : ce faisant, il contribue au développement culturel et pédagogique de la communauté de Toronto.
Théâtre français de Toronto is a professional French-language theatre presenting repertoire as well as new work. While appealing to all lovers of French-language theatre, it contributes to the cultural and educational development of Toronto's francophone community.
Finances: *Budget de fonctionnement annuel:* $500,000-$1.5 Million
Membre(s) du personnel: 11
Membre(s) du bureau directeur:
Joël Beddows, Directeur artistique
jbeddows@theatrefrancais.com
Ghislain Caron, Directeur administratif
gcaron@theatrefrancais.com

Théâtre l'Escaouette
170, rue Botsford, Moncton NB E1C 4X6
Tél: 506-855-0001; *Téléc:* 506-855-0010
escaouette@nb.aibn.com
www.escaouette.com
twitter.com/escaouette
www.youtube.com/user/escaouette
Aperçu: *Dimension:* petite; *Envergure:* locale; fondée en 1978
Mission: Pour effectuer productions acadiennes theatricial originaux
Finances: *Fonds:* Imperial Tobacco Canada
Membre(s) du personnel: 6
Membre(s) du bureau directeur:
Marcia Babineau, Direction artistique & codirection générale
marciababineau@nb.aibn.com

Théâtre la Catapulte
333, av King-Edward, Ottawa ON K1N 5E4
Tél: 613-562-0851; *Téléc:* 613-562-0631
communications@catapulte.ca
catapulte.ca
www.facebook.com/lacatapulte
twitter.com/LaCatapulte
Aperçu: *Dimension:* petite; *Envergure:* locale; fondée en 1992
Mission: Le Théâtre la Catapulte est une compagnie professionnelle de création, de production et de diffusion enracinée en Ontario français, proposant aux adolescents et au grand public des expériences théâtrales audacieuses et éclectiques nourries par la fougue de la relève et par des artistes établis. Il assure à ses productions une diffusion importante dans la région d'Ottawa-Gatineau et dans l'ensemble du Canada tout en cultivant sa relation avec ses publics.
Membre de: ATFC, Théâtre Action, ACT
Membre(s) du personnel: 5
Activités: *Stagiaires:* Oui
Membre(s) du bureau directeur:
Samuel Breau, Président
Jean Stéphane Roy, Directeur artistique
jsroy@catapulte.ca

Théâtre la Seizième
#266, 1555, 7e av Ouest, Vancouver BC V6J 1S1
Tél: 604-736-2616; *Téléc:* 604-736-9151
info@seizieme.ca
www.seizieme.ca
www.facebook.com/seizieme
twitter.com/seizieme
vimeo.com/seizieme
Aperçu: *Dimension:* petite; *Envergure:* locale; fondée en 1974
Mission: Promouvoir le théâtre professionnel francophone en Colombie-Britannique
Membre(s) du personnel: 4
Activités: Ateliers d' art dramatique
Membre(s) du bureau directeur:
Esther Duquette, Directrice générale et artistique
directionartistique@seizieme.ca

Theatre Network (1975) Society
8529 Gateway Blvd., Edmonton AB T6E 6P3
Tel: 780-453-2440; *Fax:* 780-453-2596
info@theatrenetwork.ca
theatrenetwork.ca
www.facebook.com/TheatreNetwork1975
twitter.com/Theatre_Network
www.youtube.com/user/TheatreNetworkEdm
Overview: A small local charitable organization founded in 1975
Mission: To promote original regional drama
Member of: Professional Association of Canadian Theatres (PACT)
Affiliation(s): Edmonton Arts Council
Staff Member(s): 16
Membership: *Committees:* Business Development & Outreach; Fundraising; Special Events/Projects; Building/Facility
Chief Officer(s):
Bradley Moss, Artistic Director
artisticdirector@theatrenetwork.ca

Theatre New Brunswick (TNB)
55 Whitting Rd., Fredericton NB E3B 5Y5
Tel: 506-460-1381; *Fax:* 506-453-9315
info@tnb.nb.ca
www.tnb.nb.ca
www.facebook.com/theatrenewbrunswick
twitter.com/TheatreNB
www.youtube.com/user/theatreNB
Overview: A medium-sized provincial charitable organization founded in 1969
Mission: To provide live professional theatre to the people of New Brunswick by touring & performing in nine centres throughout the province; To entertain by providing quality theatre & acting as a theatrical resource for playwrights, actors & young people interested in the field
Activities: Producing mainstage shows, as well as Young Company shows for schools across the province; Offering workshops & training through the Theatre School
Chief Officer(s):
Susan Ready, General Manager
generalmanager@tnb.nb.ca

Theatre Newfoundland Labrador
PO Box 655, Corner Brook NL A2H 6G1
Tel: 709-639-7238; *Fax:* 709-639-1006
www.theatrenewfoundland.com
www.facebook.com/71673366177
twitter.com/TheatreNL
Overview: A small provincial organization
Mission: To create & produce professional theatre which reflects the lives & diversity of the audiences on the province's west coast, extending to Labrador & across the island of Newfoundland
Staff Member(s): 6
Chief Officer(s):
Jeff Pitcher, Artistic Director

Theatre Nova Scotia (TNS)
1113 Marginal Rd., Halifax NS B3H 4P7
Tel: 902-425-3876; *Fax:* 902-422-0881
theatrens@theatrens.ca
www.theatrens.ca
www.facebook.com/TheatreNS
twitter.com/TheatreNS
Previous Name: Nova Scotia Drama League
Overview: A medium-sized provincial charitable organization founded in 1949
Mission: To provide services, training & resources to professional & amateur theatre community throughout Nova Scotia
Member of: International Amateur Theatre Association
Affiliation(s): Cultural Federation of NS; Professional Association of Canadian Theatres
Finances: *Funding Sources:* Government; Membership fees; fundraising
Staff Member(s): 6
Membership: *Fees:* $75 community theatre/affiliate group; $25 individual; $10 student; Schedule, based on operating budget, for professional theatre companies
Activities: Annual Robert Merritt Awards; Summer Theatre School Brochure; *Library:* Not open to public
Chief Officer(s):
Elizabeth Murphy, Chair
Nancy Morgan, Executive Director
Awards:
• Robert Merritt Awards Program
Honours excellence in theatre production in Nova Scotia in categories such as: Direction, Musical Direction, Original Score, Set Design, Sound Design & Performance.

Theatre Ontario
#350, 401 Richmond St. West, Toronto ON M5V 3A8
Tel: 416-408-4556; *Fax:* 416-408-3402
www.theatreontario.org
www.linkedin.com/company/theatre-ontario
www.facebook.com/theatreontario
twitter.com/theatreontario
Overview: A medium-sized provincial charitable organization founded in 1971

Mission: To promote the continued development of theatre arts & artists in Ontario; to support the continued development of vital & broadly accessible theatre training of the highest quality to all sectors of Ontario's theatre community; to encourage the continued development of high quality theatre & drama programs within the educational system of Ontario; to ensure that Ontario's community theatres & educators obtain access to the resources of professional theatre; to facilitate interaction & communication between community, educational & professional theatre
Member of: Association of Summer Theatres 'Round Ontario; Tourism Federation of Ontario; Toronto Association of Acting Studios; Acting & Modelling Information Service
Finances: *Annual Operating Budget:* $250,000-$500,000; *Funding Sources:* Ontario Arts Council; Toronto Arts Council; Ontario Trillium Foundation
Staff Member(s): 7; 5 volunteer(s)
Membership: 1,000+; *Fees:* $65 individual; $95 family (two people); $45 senior/student; $195 organization; *Member Profile:* People involved in the theatre community
Activities: Facilitating workshops & summer courses; Holding showcases; Disseminaing publications; *Awareness Events:* Theatre Ontario Festival, May; *Internships:* Yes; *Speaker Service:* Yes; *Library:* Resource Centre; Open to public
Chief Officer(s):
Bruce Pitkin, Executive Director, 416-408-4556 Ext. 11
bruce@theatreontario.org
Awards:
• Maggie Bassett Award
• Sandra Tulloch Award for Innovation in Arts & Culture
• Michael Spence Award for Contribution to Community Theatre
• Theatre Ontario Festival Awards
• Professional Theatre Training Program Grant
• Youth Theatre Training Program Grant
• International Creators Scholarship

Théâtre populaire d'Acadie (TPA)
#302, 220, boul St-Pierre ouest, Caraquet NB E1W 1A5
Tél: 506-727-0920; *Téléc:* 506-727-0923
Ligne sans frais: 800-872-0920
tpa@tpacadie.ca
www.tpacadie.ca
www.facebook.com/tpacadie
www.youtube.com/tpacadie1
Aperçu: *Dimension:* petite; *Envergure:* provinciale; Organisme sans but lucratif; fondée en 1974
Mission: Créer, produire, diffuser et faire rayonner le théâtre d'ici et d'ailleurs
Membre de: Association des théâtres francophones du Canada; Conseil économique du Nouveau-Brunswick
Membre(s) du personnel: 6
Membre(s) du bureau directeur:
Maurice Arsenault, Directeur artistique et général
maurice@tpacadie.ca

Theatre Saskatchewan
402 Broad St., Regina SK S4R 1X3
Tel: 306-352-0797; *Fax:* 306-569-7888
info@theatresaskatchewan.com
www.theatresaskatchewan.com
Previous Name: Saskatchewan Community Theatre Inc.
Overview: A medium-sized provincial organization founded in 1933
Mission: To strive to build a strong foundation for theatre which allows all people in Saskatchewan accessibility to live drama
Membership: 50+; *Fees:* $140 voting; $105 non-voting; $25+ associate; $10 subscription
Chief Officer(s):
Melissa Biro, Executive Director
melissa@theatresaskatchewan.com

Theatre Terrific Society
#430, 111 West Hastings St., Vancouver BC V6B 1H4
Tel: 604-222-4020; *Fax:* 604-669-2662
info@theatreterrific.ca
www.theatreterrific.ca
twitter.com/TheatreTerrific
www.youtube.com/user/theatreterrific
Overview: A small local charitable organization founded in 1985
Mission: To provide theatrical opportunities to people with disabilities
Member of: Alliance for Arts & Culture
Affiliation(s): Volunteer Vancouver; Greater Vancouver Professional Theatre Association
Finances: *Funding Sources:* Class fees; Corporate sponsors; Foundations; Government; Individuals
Staff Member(s): 1

Membership: *Fees:* $10
Activities: Providing courses in acting for people with mental & physical disabilities; Producing professional theatre productions featuring artists with physical & mental disabilities; Offering annual free day of acting classes; *Speaker Service:* Yes; *Library:* by appointment
Chief Officer(s):
Susanna Uchatius, Artistic Director

Théâtres associés inc. (TAI)
#405, 1908, rue Panet, Montréal QC H2L 3A2
Tél: 514-842-6361; *Téléc:* 514-842-9730
info@theatresassocies.ca
www.theatresassocies.ca
Aperçu: *Dimension:* petite; *Envergure:* provinciale; Organisme sans but lucratif; fondée en 1985
Mission: Se faire la voix d'institutions théâtrales francophones québécoises
Membre: 9; *Critères d'admissibilite:* Compagnie théatrale
Membre(s) du bureau directeur:
Louise Duceppe, Présidente
Christine Boisvert, Secrétaire

Théâtres unis enfance jeunesse (TUEJ)
#217, 911, rue Jean-Talon est, Montréal QC H2R 1V5
Tél: 514-380-2337
info@tuej.org
tuej.org
Aperçu: *Dimension:* petite; *Envergure:* provinciale; fondée en 1986
Mission: Défendre les intérêts des producteurs dans le domaine du théâtre pour la jeunesse
Membre de: Association québécoise des marionnettistes; Conseil Québécois du théâtre; Conseil québécois des Ressources humaines en Culture; RAPThéâtre
Affiliation(s): Conseil québécois du Théâtre; Academie québécoise du Théâtre; Les Arts et la Ville; Conseil Québécois des ressources humaines en culture; RAPThéâtre
Membre: 30 actifs et 8 autres; *Montant de la cotisation:* 300$; *Critères d'admissibilite:* Théâtre professionnel; *Comités:* Action politique; Succession; Petite jauge; Conseil québécois du théâtre (CQT) auxquels TUEJ participe
Membre(s) du bureau directeur:
Marc St-Jacques, Président
Pierre Tremblay, Directeur général

Thebacha & Wood Buffalo Astronomical Society (TAWBAS)
PO Box 1354, Fort Smith NT X0E 0P0
Tel: 867-872-0243
info@tawbas.ca
www.tawbas.ca
Overview: A small local organization founded in 2011
Mission: A collection of local amateur astronomers who have a passion for astronomy and space science and are eager to share, learn and teach others who may have similar interests.
Activities: Star gazing sessions; educational outreach programs
Chief Officer(s):
Peter Martselos, President
Richard Power, Economic Facilitator

Thebacha Chamber of Commerce
PO Box 628, Fort Smith NT X0E 0P0
info@thebachachamber.ca
www.fortsmith.ca/business/chamber-commerce
www.facebook.com/373651482728677
Overview: A small local organization founded in 2013
Mission: To protect the interests of businesses in Fort Smith & surrounding area
Chief Officer(s):
Janie Hobart, President

Them Days Inc.
PO Box 939, Stn. B, 3 Courte Manche, Happy Valley-Goose Bay NL A0P 1E0
Tel: 709-896-8531; *Fax:* 709-896-4970
administrator@themdays.com
www.themdays.com
www.facebook.com/themdaysinc
twitter.com/themdays
Overview: A small local charitable organization founded in 1975
Mission: To keep the history of Labrador alive by documenting & preserving the "old ways & early days" of Labrador
Member of: Association of Newfoundland & Labrador Archivists; Newfoundland & Labrador Genealogical Society
Staff Member(s): 2

Activities: Records, documents, researches & publishes the oral, visual & written history of Labrador; conducts special projects of research, translation, consultation, maintenance of an archival collection & production of publications on matters relating to Labrador history & culture; *Library:* Open to public by appointment
Chief Officer(s):
Daphne Fudge, Administrator

Therapeutic Ride Algoma
2627 Second Line West, Sault Ste Marie ON P6A 6K4
Tel: 705-759-9282
therapeuticridealgoma@hotmail.ca
www.ridealgoma.com
Overview: A small local organization
Member of: Canadian Therapeutic Riding Association
Chief Officer(s):
Bob Trainor, President

The Therapeutic Touch Network (Ontario) See The Therapeutic Touch Network of Ontario

The Therapeutic Touch Network of Ontario (TTNO)
#4, 290 The West Mall, 2nd Fl., Toronto ON M9C 1C6
Tel: 416-231-6824
ttno.membership@bellnet.ca
www.therapeutictouchontario.org
twitter.com/TTNOntario
Previous Name: The Therapeutic Touch Network (Ontario)
Overview: A small provincial licensing organization founded in 1994
Mission: To promote the practice & acceptance of Therapeutic Touch as developed by Dolores Krieger & Dora Kunz
Finances: *Funding Sources:* Members' fees; fundraising; donations
Membership: *Fees:* $55 general; $80 external; *Member Profile:* Health professionals, therapists, counsellors, clergy, educators, veterinarians & Lay People
Activities: TTNO Sponsored Practice Day, held throughout the year; Teacher Collective Days, held regionally; *Speaker Service:* Yes
Chief Officer(s):
Sharron Parrott, Chair
Awards:
• The Therapeutic Touch Network of Ontario Scholarship Fund
Publications:
• In Touch
Type: Newsletter

Theresians International - Canada
c/o Blessed Trinity Church, 3220 Bayview Ave., Toronto ON M2M 3R7
Tel: 905-763-7670
www.theresians.org
www.facebook.com/171787696166059
Also Known As: Theresians of Canada
Overview: A medium-sized international organization
Mission: To provide a nurturing, supportive, & spiritual environment for women
Affiliation(s): Archdiocese of Toronto
Finances: *Annual Operating Budget:* Less than $50,000
Chief Officer(s):
Camila C.D. Nowakowski, Contact
cnowakowski@rogers.ca

Thermal Environmental Comfort Association (TECA)
PO Box 73105, Stn. Evergreen RO, Surrey BC V3R 0J2
Tel: 604-594-5956; *Fax:* 604-594-5091
Toll-Free: 888-577-3818
training@teca.ca
www.teca.ca
Overview: A large provincial organization
Mission: To offer the residential heating, cooling & ventilation industry up-to-date training courses & a collective voice in local & provincial issues
Membership: 298; *Fees:* Schedule available
Chief Officer(s):
Katharine Czycz, President, 604-415-6487

Thermal Insulation Association of Alberta
#400, 1040 - 7 Ave. SW, Calgary AB T2P 3G9
Tel: 403-244-4487; *Fax:* 403-244-2340
info@tiaa.cc
www.tiaa.cc
Overview: A small provincial organization
Mission: To improve & elevate the technical & general knowledge of the mechanical insulation industry in Alberta,

promoting excellence in manufacture, application, & installation of all insulation products & materials
Member of: Thermal Insulation Association of Canada
Chief Officer(s):
Mark Travors, Provincial President
Meetings/Conferences:
• Thermal Insulation Association of Alberta 2018 Annual General Meeting, 2018, AB
Scope: Provincial

Thermal Insulation Association of Canada (TIAC) / Association Canadienne de l'Isolation Thermique (ACIT)
1485 Laperriere Ave., Ottawa ON K1Z 7S8
Tel: 613-724-4834; *Fax:* 613-729-6206
info@tiac.ca
www.tiac.ca
Overview: A medium-sized national organization
Member of: National Trade Contractors Coalition of Canada
Membership: 80 contractors + 30 suppliers/manufacturers; *Fees:* Schedule available; *Member Profile:* Members are engaged in the following areas: Drywall & Acoustic Installation; Thermal Insulation; Exterior Insulated Finishing Systems; Asbestos Removal; Drywall Taping & Plastering; Fireproofing Applications; Residential Steel Framing; & Mold Remediation
Activities: Programs include: Health and Safety Training; Computer Estimating; Foreman Upgrade Training Programs; & a WSIB Safety Group
Chief Officer(s):
Bob Fellows, President
bfellows@crossroadsci.com
Meetings/Conferences:
• Thermal Insulation Association of Canada 2018 Annual Conference, September, 2018, Fairmont Banff Springs, Banff, AB
Scope: National
• Thermal Insulation Association of Canada 2019 Annual Conference, August, 2019, Le Centre Sheraton Montréal, Montréal, QC
Scope: National
• Thermal Insulation Association of Canada 2020 Annual Conference, 2020, Whitehorse, YT
Scope: National
Publications:
• Membership Directory [a publication of Thermal Insulation Association of Canada]
Type: Directory; *Accepts Advertising*
• TIAC [Thermal Insulation Association of Canada] Times Magazine
Type: Magazine; *Frequency:* Quarterly

Thistletown Coin & Stamp Club *See* Mississauga-Etobicoke Coin Stamp & Collectibles Club

Thomas Sill Foundation Inc.
1350 B - 1 Lombard Pl., Winnipeg MB R3B 0X3
Tel: 204-947-3782; *Fax:* 204-956-4702
www.thomassillfoundation.com
Overview: A small provincial charitable organization founded in 1987
Mission: To provide grants to Manitoba-based registered charities that center on arts & culture, education, environment, health, heritage, or community well-being
Membership: 17
Activities: Teaching students in rural & northern Manitoba about the charitable sector through the Youth-in-Philanthropy project
Chief Officer(s):
Frank A. Wiebe, President

Thompson Chamber of Commerce
City Centre Mall, PO Box 363, Thompson MB R8N 1N2
Tel: 204-677-4155
Toll-Free: 888-307-0103
commerce@mts.net
www.thompsonchamber.ca
Overview: A small local organization founded in 1960
Mission: To promote the commercial, industrial & civic progress of the community
Member of: Manitoba Chamber of Commerce
Finances: *Annual Operating Budget:* Less than $50,000; *Funding Sources:* Membership dues; fundraising
Staff Member(s): 1; 50 volunteer(s)
Membership: 230; *Fees:* Schedule available
Activities: *Rents Mailing List:* Yes
Chief Officer(s):
Paula Yanko, Office Manager

Thompson Crisis Centre
PO Box 1226, Thompson MB R8N 1P1
Tel: 204-677-9668; *Fax:* 204-677-9042; *Crisis Hot-Line:* 800-442-0613
www.thompsoncrisiscentre.org
Overview: A medium-sized local organization founded in 1977
Mission: To provide immediate assistance through a walk-in facility & a 24-hour emergency telephone service; to provide a safe place for the women & their children who are victims of physical/emotional abuse; to provide services to women & their children needing longer term support
Activities: Emergency Program; Transition Program; 24-hour Crisis Line; Children's Program; Follow-up Program
Chief Officer(s):
Sue O'Brien, Chair

Thompson Okanagan Tourism Association (TOTA)
2280-D Leckie Rd., Kelowna BC V1X 6G6
Tel: 250-860-5999; *Fax:* 250-860-9993
Toll-Free: 800-567-2275
info@totabc.com
www.totabc.org/corporatesite
www.facebook.com/totabc
twitter.com/totamedia
www.youtube.com/user/thompsonokanagan
Previous Name: Okanagan Similkameen Tourism Association
Overview: A medium-sized local organization founded in 1963 overseen by Council of Tourism Associations of British Columbia
Mission: To represent & support all business & community tourism interests throughout the Thompson Okanagan
Member of: National Tour Association; American Bus Association
Finances: *Annual Operating Budget:* $500,000-$1.5 Million; *Funding Sources:* Private; provincial & federal government
Staff Member(s): 10; 2 volunteer(s)
Membership: 400; *Fees:* $100+; *Committees:* Experiences Development; Travel, Trade & Media; Regional Marketing; Industry Development; Community & Consortium
Chief Officer(s):
Glenn Mandziuk, CEO
ceo@totabc.com

Thompson Rivers University Faculty Association (TRUFA)
900 McGill Rd., Kamloops BC V2C 0C8
Tel: 250-374-3040; *Fax:* 250-374-6434
trufa@shawcable.com
trufa.tru.ca
Overview: A small local organization founded in 1974
Mission: To promote the professional standards set for its members at the university
Member of: Federation of Post-Secondary Educators of BC; Kamloops & District Labour Council
Affiliation(s): Canadian Association of University Teachers; British Columbia Federation of Labour; Canadian Labour Congress
Finances: *Funding Sources:* Membership dues
Membership: 650 faculty members; *Fees:* 1.5% of salary; *Committees:* Shop Stewards; Salary & Working Conditions; Human Rights; Status of Women; Equivalent Workload; Status of Non-Regular Faculty; Disability Management; Executive; Leave, Safety & Health; Education Policy; Pension Advocacy; Equity; Professional Development; Wellness; Consultative
Chief Officer(s):
Jason Brown, President
trufa-pres@shawcable.com
   Williams Lake
   #1015, 1250 Western Ave., Williams Lake BC V2G 1H7
   Tel: 250-392-8043
   Chief Officer(s):
   Barbara Bearman, Williams Lake Representative
   bbearman@tru.ca

Thompson Rivers University Open Learning Faculty Association (TRUFOLA)
www.truolfa.ca
Previous Name: Faculty Association of the Open Learning Agency
Overview: A small local organization
Chief Officer(s):
John O'Brien, President, 250-852-6962
jobrien@tru.ca

Thompson Valley Rock Club
Kamloops BC

tvrckamloops@gmail.com
www.tvrc.ca
Overview: A small local organization
Mission: To promote the collection of gemstones, mineral specimens, & other geological materials
Affiliation(s): British Columbia Lapidary Society; Gem & Mineral Federation of Canada
Membership: *Member Profile:* Rock hounding enthusiasts from Kamloops & the surrounding region
Activities: Hosting monthly meetings, except July & August; Providing workshops on topics such as cutting & polishing, wire wrapping, & faceting; Arranging field trips; *Speaker Service:* Yes
Publications:
• Chips & Chatter [a publication of the Thompson Valley Rock Club]
Type: Newsletter; *Price:* Free with membership in the Thompson Valley Rock Club

Thompson, Nicola, Cariboo United Way
177 Victoria St., Kamloops BC V2C 1Z4
Tel: 250-372-9933; *Fax:* 250-372-5926
Toll-Free: 855-372-9933
office@unitedwaytnc.ca
www.unitedwaytnc.ca
www.linkedin.com/company/thompson-nicola-cariboo-united-way
www.facebook.com/unitedwaytnc
twitter.com/unitedwaytnc
www.youtube.com/unitedwaytnc
Previous Name: United Way of Kamloops & Region
Overview: A small local organization founded in 1960 overseen by United Way of Canada - Centraide Canada
Mission: To enable all citizens to join in a community wide effort to fund & provide in consort with others, effective delivery of health & social services & programs in response to the needs of the community
Member of: United Way of Canada - Centraide Canada
Finances: *Annual Operating Budget:* $500,000-$1.5 Million; *Funding Sources:* Individual & corporate donations
Staff Member(s): 10; 800 volunteer(s)
Membership: 27 local service providers; *Fees:* $1 annually; *Committees:* Campaign Cabinet; Nominating; Advisory; Executive; Finance; GenNext Kamloops; Membership; Community Development; Women's Leadership Circle
Activities: Fundraising; Promoting community development & engagement; *Awareness Events:* Annual Golf Tournament, Aug.; Annual Kick Off Breakfast, Sept.; *Internships:* Yes; *Speaker Service:* Yes
Chief Officer(s):
Danalee Baker, Executive Director
danalee@unitedwaytnc.ca

Thorhild Chamber of Commerce
PO Box 384, Thorhild AB T0A 3J0
Tel: 780-699-3773
Overview: A small local organization
Membership: 29

Thornbury & District Chamber of Commerce *See* Blue Mountains Chamber of Commerce

Thorncliffe Neighbourhood Office
18 Thorncliffe Park Dr., Toronto ON M4H 1N7
Tel: 416-421-3054; *Fax:* 416-421-4269
info@thorncliffe.org
www.thorncliffe.org
Overview: A small local charitable organization overseen by Ontario Council of Agencies Serving Immigrants
Member of: Family Resource Association
Staff Member(s): 14
Membership: *Committees:* Finance; Human Resource; Board Recruitment
Chief Officer(s):
Jehad Aliweiwi, Executive Director
jaliweiwi@thorncliffe.org

Thorsby & District Chamber of Commerce
PO Box 197, Thorsby AB T0C 2P0
Tel: 780-903-1695
Overview: A small local organization
Activities: *Awareness Events:* Trade Fair; Customer Appreciation Night; Charity Golf Tournament
Chief Officer(s):
Mitch Williams, President

Thousand Islands Watershed Land Trust (TIWLT)
19 Reynolds Rd., Lansdowne ON K0E 1L0

Tel: 613-659-4824
info@tiwlt.ca
tiwlt.weebly.com
Overview: A small local organization founded in 2007
Mission: To permanently protect land in the Thousand Islands watershed region through acquisition or conservation agreements, and to achieve good land management through stewardship agreements and education.
Membership: Fees: $40-$100
Chief Officer(s):
Dann Michols, President

Three Hills & District Chamber of Commerce
PO Box 277, Three Hills AB T0M 2A0
Tel: 403-425-0086
info@threehillschamber.ca
threehillschamber.ca
Overview: A small local organization
Mission: To promote & improve commerce in the Three Hills District
Membership: 84
Activities: Awareness Events: Golf Tournament, Sept.; Small Business Week, Oct.; Moonlight Madness, Dec.
Chief Officer(s):
Tiffannie Patterson, President

The 3C Foundation of Canada / Fondation Canadienne des 3c
#200, 1 Hines Rd., Kanata ON K2K 3C7
Tel: 613-237-6690
info@3cfoundation.org
www.3cfoundation.org
www.facebook.com/GutTogether
Overview: A medium-sized national charitable organization founded in 1997
Finances: Funding Sources: Donations; fundraising
Membership: Member Profile: People living with Crohn's disease, colitis & colon cancer
Activities: The "IBDealing With It" program; Toilet Paper Flowers Campaign; Awareness Events: Gut Together, Oct.; Youth Gut Together; World IBD Day, May
Chief Officer(s):
Michele Hepburn, President
Awards:
• The Abbott IBD Scholarship Program

Threshold Ministries
National Ministry Centre, 105 Mountain View Dr., Saint John NB E2J 5B5
Tel: 506-642-2210; Fax: 506-657-8217
Toll-Free: 888-316-8169
hello@thresholdministries.ca
www.thresholdministries.ca
www.facebook.com/thresholdministries
twitter.com/thresholdmin
vimeo.com/thresholdministries
Overview: A medium-sized national charitable organization founded in 1929
Mission: To train and equip Evangelists to assist the Church in becoming missional in communicating the Gospel
Member of: Evangelical Fellowship of Canada
Affiliation(s): Anglican Church of Canada
Finances: Annual Operating Budget: $1.5 Million-$3 Million; Funding Sources: Individuals; churches; foundations
Staff Member(s): 12; 75 volunteer(s)
Membership: 70; Fees: none
Activities: Internships: Yes; Speaker Service: Yes; Library: Taylor College; Open to public
Chief Officer(s):
John W. Irwin, B.A., LLD, Chair
Shawn C. Branch, Dip.E.S., National Director
shawn.branch@thresholdministries.ca
Charles Harding, Communications
charles.harding@thresholdministries.ca
Shauna Hooper, Administrative Officer
shauna.hooper@thresholdministries.ca
Mike Hughes, Financial Officer
mike.hughes@thresholdministries.ca

Thunder Bay & District Labour Council
#1, 929 Fort William Rd., Thunder Bay ON P7B 3A6
Tel: 807-345-2621
Previous Name: Fort William Trades & Labour Council
Overview: A medium-sized local organization overseen by Ontario Federation of Labour
Finances: Funding Sources: Membership fees
Activities: Awareness Events: Day of Mourning, April

Thunder Bay Adventure Trails
PO Box 29190, Thunder Bay ON P7B 6P9
Toll-Free: 800-526-7522
tbat_den@hotmail.com
Overview: A medium-sized local organization founded in 1990
Mission: To groom & maintain 700 kilometres of snowmobile trails, from Thunder Bay to Shabaqua
Member of: North Superior Snowmobile Association (NOSSA)
Membership: Fees: $200-before Dec.1; $250-after Dec.1; $100-3-day permit; $140-7-day permit; $125-classic permit
Chief Officer(s):
Marcel Gauthier, Club Executive
Lloyd Chaykowski, Club Executive
Harold Harkonen, Club Executive
Bradley Pollock, Club Executive

Thunder Bay Amateur Hockey Association See Hockey Northwestern Ontario

Thunder Bay Beekeepers' Association
#228, 1100 Memorial Ave., Thunder Bay ON P7B 4A3
Tel: 807-476-0927
www.thunderbaybeekeepersassociation.ca
www.facebook.com/128459093838912
Overview: A small local organization
Mission: To share information about beekeeping in the Thunder Bay area
Member of: Ontario Beekeepers' Association
Membership: Fees: $25; Member Profile: Persons interested in apiculture in the Thunder Bay area
Activities: Promoting the beekeeping industry & educating the public in the Thunder Bay area by donating a bee journal to the Thunder Bay Public Library; Creating educational displays, such as the association's demo hive, at places such as the local country market, in order to show the public the basics of beekeeping & how the public can sustain the population; Presenting workshops to share beekeeping skills & Knowledge; Speaker Service: Yes
Chief Officer(s):
Chris Carolan, President
chris.carolan@me.com

Thunder Bay Chamber of Commerce (TBCC)
#102, 200 Syndicate Ave. South, Thunder Bay ON P7E 1C9
Tel: 807-624-2626; Fax: 807-622-7752
chamber@tbchamber.ca
www.tbchamber.ca
www.linkedin.com/company/thunder-bay-chamber-of-commerce
www.facebook.com/tbchamber
twitter.com/tbchamber
Overview: A medium-sized local organization founded in 1885
Mission: To serve the membership by providing leadership & influencing effective change for a healthy business environment
Affiliation(s): Northwestern Ontario Associated Chambers of Commerce; Ontario Chamber of Commerce; Canadian Chamber of Commerce
Finances: Annual Operating Budget: $500,000-$1.5 Million; Funding Sources: Membership dues & special events
Staff Member(s): 8; 250 volunteer(s)
Membership: 1,000+; Fees: Schedule available, based upon number of employees; Committees: Aboriginal Opportunities; Ambassadors; Education; Finance; Membership & Marketing; Policy & Advocacy; Quality Management
Activities: Internships: Yes; Speaker Service: Yes; Library: Office Library; Open to public
Chief Officer(s):
Charla Robinson, President
charla@tbchamber.ca
Awards:
• Business Excellence Awards
Honours excellence in small, medium, & large businesses
• Business Person of the Year Award
• Customer Service Award
• Environmental Stewardship Award
• Leadership in Diversity & Social Inclusion Award
• Looking Good Award
• New Business Excellence Award
• Not for Profit Excellence Award
• Quality of Life Award
• Strategic Partnership Award
• Tourism Partner Award
Meetings/Conferences:
• Thunder Bay Chamber of Commerce Annual General Meeting & Chair's Reception 2018, February, 2018, Thunder Bay, ON
Scope: Local

Thunder Bay Community Foundation
Ruttan Block, #17D, 4 Court St. South, Thunder Bay ON P7B 2W4
Tel: 807-475-7279; Fax: 807-684-0793
tbcf@tbaytel.net
www.tbcf.org
www.facebook.com/thunderbay.communityfoundation
twitter.com/@TBayCF
Previous Name: Thunder Bay Foundation
Overview: A small local charitable organization founded in 1971
Mission: To receive, maintain, manage, control & use donations for charitable purposes in the district of Thunder Bay to the benefit of children & youth services, alleviation of human suffering, & advancement of social work, education & cultural purposes
Member of: Community Foundations of Canada
Finances: Funding Sources: Donations
Membership: 1-99; Committees: Executive; Finance; Grants; Scholarships; Public Relations
Chief Officer(s):
Art Warwick, President
Rosy Brizi, Vice-President
Robert Mozzon, Secretary-Treasurer

Thunder Bay Counselling Centre
544 Winnipeg Ave., Thunder Bay ON P7B 3S7
Tel: 807-684-1880; Fax: 807-344-3782
Toll-Free: 888-204-2221
community@tbaycounselling.com
www.tbaycounselling.com
www.facebook.com/thunderbaycounsellingcentre
twitter.com/tbcounselling
Previous Name: Family Services Thunder Bay
Overview: A medium-sized local charitable organization founded in 1967 overseen by Ontario Association of Credit Counselling Services
Mission: To provide community based support services to individuals, couples, & families in the Thunder Bay area; To offer confidential counselling
Member of: Ontario Association of Credit Counselling Services; United Way of Thunder Bay
Finances: Funding Sources: Donations
Activities: Presenting courses on topics such as anger management, self-esteem, & stress reduction; Offering programs, such as Budgeting & Debt Management, & Employee Assistance Programs, featuring custom designed counselling solutions for businesses & employees; Disseminating promotional materials
Chief Officer(s):
Nancy Chamberlain, Executive Director
Publications:
• The Solution Source [a publication of the Thunder Bay Counselling Centre]
Type: Newsletter; Frequency: Quarterly; ISSN: 1481-2568
Profile: Issue topics include benefits of counselling, living with uncertainty, compassion fatigue, single parent families, & understanding teens & substance abuse

Thunder Bay District Municipal League (TBDML)
c/o Beth Stewart, 343 Parker Rd., Gillies Township, RR#1, Kakabeka Falls ON P0T 1W0
Tel: 807-476-0927; Fax: 807-622-8246
Overview: A small local organization founded in 1917
Mission: To improve services for its residents
Member of: Northwestern Ontario Municipal Association
Finances: Funding Sources: Municipal contributions
Membership: 19; Fees: Per capita; Member Profile: Municipalities dedicated to good local government
Chief Officer(s):
Larry Hebert, President
Beth Stewart, Secretary-Treasurer
bstewart@tbaytel.net

Thunder Bay Field Naturalists (TBFN)
PO Box 10037, Thunder Bay ON P7B 6T6
Tel: 807-474-6007
www.tbfn.net
Overview: A small local charitable organization founded in 1933
Mission: To promote the enjoyment of nature through environmental appreciation & conservation; to encourage wise use & conservation of natural resources; to promote environmental protection
Member of: Federation of Ontario Naturalists
Affiliation(s): Thunder Cape Bird Observatory
Finances: Annual Operating Budget: $50,000-$100,000; Funding Sources: Membership fees; donations; grants

Canadian Associations / Thunder Bay Historical Museum Society (TBHMS)

11 volunteer(s)
Membership: 200; *Fees:* $30 family; $25 single; $20 students/seniors; $350 life; *Member Profile:* Those interested in the study of nature & the environment; *Committees:* Nature Reserves; Bird Records; Peregrine Falcon Recovery; Bluebird Recovery
Activities: Adult & Junior Nature; oriented field trips; indoor lectures; *Speaker Service:* Yes
Chief Officer(s):
Brian McLaren, President
bmclaren@lakeheadu.ca
Rob Foster, Vice-President
rfoster@tbaytel.net

Thunder Bay Foundation *See* Thunder Bay Community Foundation

Thunder Bay Historical Museum Society (TBHMS)
425 Donald St. East, Thunder Bay ON P7E 5V1
Tel: 807-623-0801; *Fax:* 807-622-6880
info@thunderbaymuseum.com
www.thunderbaymuseum.com
Also Known As: Thunder Bay Museum
Overview: A small local charitable organization founded in 1908
Mission: To preserve, collect & interpret the heritage of Northwestern Ontario
Member of: Ontario Historical Society; Ontario Museum Association; Minnesota Historical Society; Canadian Museums Association
Finances: *Annual Operating Budget:* $250,000-$500,000
Staff Member(s): 6; 50 volunteer(s)
Membership: 1,000; *Fees:* $30 individual; $45 family; $100 business; $1,000 corporate; *Committees:* Publication; Programs & Plaques; Membership; Museum Development
Activities: Publications; lectures; craft classes; education; rotating exhibits; research services; outreach & extension; *Library:* Open to public by appointment
Chief Officer(s):
Tory Tronrud, Director

Thunder Bay Indian Friendship Centre (TBIFC)
401 North Cumberland St., Thunder Bay ON P7A 4P7
Tel: 807-345-5840; *Fax:* 807-344-8945
TBIFC@shawcable.com
www.tbifc.ca
Overview: A small local organization founded in 1964
Mission: To serve as a meeting place for the Native community in Thunder Bay, Ontario; To address issues that affect the lives of Native people
Member of: Ontario Federation of Indian Friendship Centres
Finances: *Funding Sources:* Donations
Membership: *Fees:* $1; *Member Profile:* Members of Aboriginal ancestry who live in Thunder Bay, Ontario; Corporations, partnerships, & other legal entities
Activities: Hosting seasonal feasts with the assistance of community elders; Providing programs & services such as the Children's Wellness Program, Anishnawbe Skills Development Program, Apatisiwin Employment Program, Aboriginal Healing & Wellness, the Urban Aboriginal Healthy Living Program, & the Life Long Care Program
Chief Officer(s):
Debbie Sault, President
Whitney Knott, Secretary
Audrey Fisher, Treasurer

Thunder Bay Law Association (TBLA)
125 Brodie St. North, Thunder Bay ON P7C 0A3
Tel: 807-344-3481; *Fax:* 807-345-9091
tbla@tbaytel.net
www.tbla.on.ca
Overview: A small local organization founded in 1905
Finances: *Funding Sources:* Membership fees; Law Society of Upper Canada
Membership: 200; *Committees:* Archives; Civil Liaison; Courthouse; Continuing Legal Education; Criminal Liaison; Electronic Resources; Family Liaison; Law Day; Law School Liaison; Library; Newsletter; Personnel; Real Estate; Social; Nominating; Public Service Awards; Judicial Complement
Activities: *Library:* District Courthouse Library; by appointment
Chief Officer(s):
Helen Heerema, Librarian
Gordon Fillmore, President

Thunder Bay Minor Football Association (TBMFA)
535 Chapples Dr., Thunder Bay ON P7C 2V7
Tel: 807-251-5052
www.tbmfa.com
www.facebook.com/tbmfa.knights
twitter.com/TBMFAKNIGHTS
Overview: A small local organization founded in 2013
Mission: To run a football program for boys & girls ages 7-13 in Thunder Bay
Chief Officer(s):
Rob Thompson, President
Sarah Kuzik, Secretary
spkuzik@shaw.ca

Thunder Bay Minor Hockey Association (TBMHA)
#101, 212 East Miles St., Thunder Bay ON
Tel: 807-346-4510; *Fax:* 807-346-4511
www.tbmha.com
Overview: A small local organization
Membership: *Committees:* Finance; Playing & Ice; Rules & Input; Grievance; Awards & Public Relations; Draft Committee; Harrassment & Abuse; Risk Management
Chief Officer(s):
Larry Busniuk, President

Thunder Bay Multicultural Association (TBMA)
17 North Court St., Thunder Bay ON P7A 4T4
Tel: 807-345-0551; *Fax:* 807-345-0173
Toll-Free: 866-831-1144
www.tbma.ca
Overview: A small local organization founded in 1972 overseen by Ontario Council of Agencies Serving Immigrants
Mission: To promote the concept of multiculturalism; to encourage cultural awareness, appreciation, & cooperation; to preserve cultural freedom, heritage, & cultural identity
Finances: *Funding Sources:* Federal government; provincial government; fundraising
Membership: *Member Profile:* Ethnocultural groups of region
Activities: Interpretation/translation; settlement services; community programs; newcomer services; educational materials; website; *Library:* Open to public

Thunder Bay Musicians' Association
1111 East Victoria Ave., Thunder Bay ON P7C 1B7
Tel: 807-622-1062; *Fax:* 807-622-3961
local591@tbaytel.net
www.afm.org/locals/info/number/591
Overview: A small local organization founded in 1970
Mission: To promote live music
Finances: *Annual Operating Budget:* Less than $50,000
Staff Member(s): 1
Membership: 286; *Fees:* $112
Chief Officer(s):
Garry Agostino, President

Thunder Bay Physical & Sexual Assault Crisis Centre *See* Thunder Bay Sexual Assault / Sexual Abuse Counselling & Crisis Centre

Thunder Bay Police Association (TBPA) / Association de la police de Thunder Bay
McIntyre Centre, PO Box 29035, Thunder Bay ON P7B 6P9
Tel: 807-344-8336
Overview: A small local organization
Member of: Police Association of Ontario
Membership: 325
Activities: Raising funds for service-oriented organizations in Thunder Bay, Ontario
Chief Officer(s):
Greg Stephenson, President

Thunder Bay Public Affairs - Visitors & Convention Department *See* Tourism Thunder Bay

Thunder Bay Real Estate Board
1135 Barton St., Thunder Bay ON P7B 5N3
Tel: 807-623-8422; *Fax:* 807-623-0375
info@thunderbay-mls.on.ca
www.thunderbay-mls.on.ca
www.facebook.com/286021454842003
Overview: A small local organization founded in 1971 overseen by Ontario Real Estate Association
Chief Officer(s):
Carol Ann Wesselius, President, 807-623-5011
carolannw@tbaytel.net

Thunder Bay Regional Arts Council (TBRAC)
#100, 105 South May St., Thunder Bay ON P7E 1B1
Tel: 807-623-6544; *Fax:* 807-623-2821
www.thunderbayculture.com
Overview: A small local charitable organization founded in 1982
Mission: To enrich the quality of life by promoting & encouraging the development of arts & cultural activities
Member of: Volunteer Thunder Bay; Community Arts Ontario
Finances: *Annual Operating Budget:* Less than $50,000
Staff Member(s): 1; 30 volunteer(s)
Membership: 150; *Fees:* $25-75; *Member Profile:* Artists; cultural organizations; arts supporters; *Committees:* Arts Alive; Mayor's Arts Luncheon; Website; Newsletter
Activities: Arts awareness; arts promotion; *Library:* Artist Resource Centre; Open to public
Chief Officer(s):
Janis Swanson, Office Administrator

Thunder Bay Sexual Assault / Sexual Abuse Counselling & Crisis Centre
385 Mooney St., Thunder Bay ON P7B 5L5
Tel: 807-345-0894; *Fax:* 807-344-1981; *Crisis Hot-Line:* 807-344-4502
tbcounselling@tbsasa.org
www.tbsasa.org
Previous Name: Thunder Bay Physical & Sexual Assault Crisis Centre
Overview: A small local organization overseen by Canadian Association of Sexual Assault Centres
Mission: To provide help & support to victims of sexual assault & their family that allows them to overcome their trauma
Member of: Ontario Federation of Mental Health & Addiction Program; Thunder Bay Chamber of Commerce
Finances: *Funding Sources:* Ontario Ministry of Health & Long-Term Care; Ontario Ministry of the Attorney General
Staff Member(s): 10

Thunder Bay Symphony Orchestra Association (TBSO)
PO Box 29192, Thunder Bay ON P7B 6P9
Tel: 807-474-2284; *Fax:* 807-622-1927
info@tbso.ca
www.tbso.ca
www.facebook.com/ThunderBaySymphonyOrchestra
twitter.com/tbayso
www.instagram.com/tbayso
Overview: A small local charitable organization founded in 1960 overseen by Orchestras Canada
Mission: To maintain & nurture a professional, regional orchestra of artistic integrity & excellence; to offer a variety of programs to enrich & encourage the widest possible audience; to support the development of local young musicians
Member of: Orchestras Canada
Finances: *Funding Sources:* Canada Council; City of Thunder Bay; Ticket sales; Ontario Arts Council; Individual & corporate donations
Staff Member(s): 11
Activities: *Library:* Music Library; Not open to public
Chief Officer(s):
Shannon Whidden, Executive Director, 807-474-2281
Arthur Post, Music Director

Thunderbird Friendship Centre
PO Box 430, 301 Beamish Ave. West, Geraldton ON P0T 1M0
Tel: 807-854-1060; *Fax:* 807-854-0861
Toll-Free: 888-854-1060
reception@thunderbirdfriendshipcentre.ca
Overview: A small local organization founded in 1971
Mission: To provide a meeting place for the Aboriginal & non-Aboriginal people of the Geraldton, Ontario area
Member of: Ontario Federation of Indian Friendship Centres
Activities: Offering cultural, educational, recreational, & social programs; Providing services in the areas of prenatal nutrition, healthy living, & career development
Chief Officer(s):
Karen Stephenson, Executive Director
karen.stephenson@thunderbirdfriendshipcentre.ca

Thyroid Foundation of Canada / La Fondation canadienne de la Thyroïde
PO Box 298, Bath ON K0H 1G0
Toll-Free: 800-267-8822
www.thyroid.ca
Overview: A medium-sized national charitable organization founded in 1980
Mission: To provide leadership to the fight against thyroid disease
Finances: *Funding Sources:* Health Canada; donations; membership fees
Membership: *Fees:* $25 regular; $20 student/senior; $30 family
Activities: Awareness Events: Thyroid Month, June
Chief Officer(s):

Donna Miniely, President
Rinda Hartner, Treasurer
Awards:
- Diana Meltzer Abramsky Research Fellowship
- Summer Student Scholarship

Tides Canada Foundation
#400, 163 Hastings St. West, Vancouver BC V6B 1H5
Tel: 604-647-6611
Toll-Free: 866-780-6611
info@tidescanada.org
www.tidescanada.org
www.linkedin.com/company/tides-canada
www.facebook.com/tidescanada
twitter.com/tidescanada
Overview: A small national charitable organization founded in 2000
Mission: To create partnerships with donors & charitable organizations to grow resources for social change & environmental stability
Member of: Canadian Environmental Grantmakers Network; Canadian Centre for Philanthropy
Finances: Annual Operating Budget: $500,000-$1.5 Million
Staff Member(s): 25
Chief Officer(s):
Ross McMillan, President & CEO

Toronto Office
#360, 215 Spadina Ave., Toronto ON M5T 2C7
Tel: 416-481-8652
Toll-Free: 866-843-3722

Yellowknife Office
#300, 4902 - 49 St., Yellowknife NT X1A 2P2
Tel: 867-988-1963
Toll-Free: 866-843-3722

Tiger Hills Arts Association Inc. (THAA)
McFeetors Centre, 103 Broadway St., Holland MB R0G 0X0
Tel: 204-526-2063; Fax: 204-526-2105
thaa@mymts.net
www.tigerhillsarts.com
www.facebook.com/tigerhillsarts
Overview: A small local charitable organization
Mission: To promote lifetime involvement in the visual, performing & literary arts through the development of a varied program of cultural activities in the Tiger Hills area
Member of: Manitoba Association of Community Arts Councils Inc.
Finances: Annual Operating Budget: $100,000-$250,000
Staff Member(s): 2; 200 volunteer(s)
Membership: 95; Fees: $15 individual; $30 family
Activities: Arts & cultural programs; Library
Chief Officer(s):
Catheryn Pedersen, Executive Director
Awards:
- Arts Career Scholarship
; Amount: $1,000
- Talent Search Scholarship
; Amount: $1,000

Tikinagan Child & Family Services
PO Box 627, 65 King St., Sioux Lookout ON P8T 1B1
Tel: 807-737-3466; Fax: 807-737-3543
Toll-Free: 800-465-3624
www.tikinagan.org
Previous Name: Tikinagan North Child & Family Services
Overview: A small local organization founded in 1984
Mission: To provide child protection services to First Nations communities
Member of: Association of Native Child & Family Services Agencies of Ontario
Finances: Annual Operating Budget: Greater than $5 Million; Funding Sources: Ministry of Community & Social Services
Staff Member(s): 100
Membership: 10
Chief Officer(s):
Thelma Morris, Executive Director

Tikinagan North Child & Family Services See Tikinagan Child & Family Services

Tilbury Chamber of Commerce
PO Box 1239, Tilbury ON N0P 2L0
Tel: 519-682-0202; Fax: 519-682-2391
tilburychamber@gmail.com
www.tilburychamber.com
www.facebook.com/217527424926762
twitter.com/TilburyOntario

Overview: A small local organization
Mission: To promote commercial business in the community; To improve commerce & industry
Member of: Ontario Chamber of Commerce
Finances: Annual Operating Budget: Less than $50,000; Funding Sources: Membership fees; donations
9 volunteer(s)
Membership: 120; Fees: $100-$350
Activities: Awareness Events: Tilbury Family Fest, June Library: Tilbury Odette Memorial Library; Open to public
Chief Officer(s):
Jay Dillon, President
Natalie Whittal, Executive Director

Tillicum Centre - Hope Association for Community Living
1166 - 7 Ave., Hope BC V0X 1L4
Tel: 604-869-2565; Fax: 604-869-2565
tillicum@telus.net
Previous Name: Hope Association for Community Living
Overview: A small local organization founded in 1964
Mission: To provide service to mentally & physically challenged adults in the community of Hope
Member of: British Columbia Association for Community Living
Finances: Annual Operating Budget: Less than $50,000
Activities: Life skills; recreation; academic activities

Tillicum Lelum Aboriginal Friendship Centre
774B Centre St., Nanaimo BC V9R 4Z6
Tel: 250-753-4417; Fax: 250-753-8122
www.tillicumlelum.ca
Overview: A small local organization
Mission: To provide programs & services designed to improve the quality of life for Aboriginal people
Chief Officer(s):
Grace Elliott-Nielsen, Executive Director

Tillsonburg & District Association for Community Living
96 Tillson Ave., Tillsonburg ON N4G 3A1
Tel: 519-842-9000; Fax: 519-842-7628
info@communitylivingtillsonburg.ca
www.communitylivingtillsonburg.ca
Overview: A small local organization
Mission: To work towards the inclusion of intellectually disabled people
Member of: Community Living Ontario
Chief Officer(s):
Doug Cooper, President

Tillsonburg & District Multi-Service Centre (TDMSC)
Livingston Centre, 96 Tillson Ave., Tillsonburg ON N4G 3A1
Tel: 519-842-9008; Fax: 519-842-4727
info@multiservicecentre.com
www.multiservicecentre.com
www.facebook.com/109475662455610
twitter.com/multisercen
Previous Name: Information Tillsonburg
Overview: A small local charitable organization founded in 1977
Mission: To provide human support resources
Staff Member(s): 7
Activities: Volunteer Recognition, May; Employee Recognition, summer/fall; Donor Recognition, Nov.; Speaker Service: Yes
Chief Officer(s):
Bill Hett, Executive Director & CEO
Maureen Vandenberghe, Coordinator, Communications & Development

Tillsonburg District Chamber of Commerce
20 Oxford St., Tillsonburg ON N4G 2G1
Tel: 519-688-3737
www.tillsonburgchamber.ca
www.linkedin.com/groups/5189753
www.facebook.com/175814389095607
twitter.com/TburgChamber
Overview: A small local organization founded in 1976
Mission: To promote & represent Tillsonburg's businesses & community
Finances: Annual Operating Budget: Less than $50,000
Membership: 115; Fees: Schedule available; Committees: Advocacy; Marketing & Communications; Program & Events
Chief Officer(s):
Andrew Burns, President
Suzanne Renken, CEO
suzanne@tillsonburgchamber.ca

Tillsonburg District Real Estate Board
#202, 1 Library Lane, Tillsonburg ON N4G 4W3
Tel: 519-842-9361; Fax: 519-688-6850
tburgreb@bellnet.ca
www.tburgreb.ca
Overview: A small local organization founded in 1968 overseen by Ontario Real Estate Association
Mission: To provide its members with the tools they need to best serve the public
Member of: The Canadian Real Estate Association; The Ontario Real Estate Association
Membership: 99
Chief Officer(s):
Frank Catry, President
frank.catry@century21.ca

Tim Horton Children's Foundation
RR#2, 264 Glen Morris Rd. East, St George ON N0E 1N0
Tel: 519-448-1248; Fax: 519-448-1415
Other Communication: Alt. E-mails: work@thcf.com; registrar@thcf.com
info@thcf.com
www.thcf.com
www.facebook.com/timhortonchildrensfoundation
Overview: A medium-sized national organization founded in 1975
Mission: Dedicated to fostering within children the quest for a brighter future
Activities: Operates 7 camps
Chief Officer(s):
Dave Newnham, President & Executive Director

Timberline Trail & Nature Club
701 - 105th Ave., Dawson Creek BC V1G 2K5
Tel: 250-782-7680
www.timberlinetrailandnature.com
www.facebook.com/timberlinetrailandnature
Overview: A small local organization founded in 1973
Mission: To promote the enjoyment of nature through environmental appreciation & conservation; To encourage wise use & conservation of natural resources & environmental protection
Member of: Federation of BC Naturalists
Membership: 15; Fees: $25
Chief Officer(s):
Meredith Thornton, Contact
mthorntnpris.ca

Timbres de Pâques Canada See Easter Seals Canada

Les Timbres de Pâques N.-B. See Easter Seals New Brunswick

Times Change Women's Employment Service
#1003, 365 Bloor St. East, Toronto ON M4W 3L4
Tel: 416-927-1900; Fax: 416-927-7212
women@timeschange.org
www.timeschange.org
www.facebook.com/timeschangeWES
twitter.com/CareersWomen
Overview: A small local charitable organization founded in 1974
Mission: To respond to the needs of women & the labour market through the provision of counselling, resources, & services
Member of: Ontario Council of Agencies Serving Immigrants
Finances: Funding Sources: Employment Ontario; Ontario Women's Directorate; United Way Toronto; Private donations
Staff Member(s): 10; 20 volunteer(s)
Membership: 150; Fees: $5 unemployed; $10 employed; Member Profile: Clients; Supporters
Activities: Providing group workshops in career planning & job search techniques; Offering individual educational counselling; Providing computers, by appointment, for practice or preparing cover letters & resumes; Arranging job matching & placement; Library: Times Change Women's Employment Service Resource Centre; Open to public by appointment
Chief Officer(s):
Katie Didyk, Coordinator, Marketing & Outreach
katie@timeschange.org

Timmins & Area Women in Crisis Support & Information Centre on Violence Against Women (TAWC)
355 Wilson Ave., Timmins ON P4N 2T7
Tel: 705-268-8380; Fax: 705-268-3332
info@tawc.ca

www.tawc.ca
www.facebook.com/TAWCTimmins
Previous Name: Rape Crisis Centre Timmins
Overview: A small local charitable organization founded in 1992
Mission: To assist survivors of sexual violence & to promote the establishment of social & political structures free of sexual violence & exploitation
Member of: Ontario Coalition of Rape Crisis Centres
Finances: *Annual Operating Budget:* $100,000-$250,000; *Funding Sources:* Ministry of the Attorney General; Ministry of Community & Social Services
Staff Member(s): 20; 12 volunteer(s)
Membership: *Member Profile:* Women 16 & over
Activities: Advocacy; counselling; crisis line; referrals; workshops; speakers; family court support; transitional housing support; women's shelter; *Awareness Events:* Take Back the Night March, Sept.; Sexual Assault Awareness Month, May; International Women's Day, March 8; *Internships:* Yes *Library:* Timmins & Area Women in Crisis Library; Open to public
Chief Officer(s):
Becky Mason, Contact, 705-268-8381
becky@tawc.ca

Timmins Chamber of Commerce / Chambre de commerce de Timmins
PO Box 985, 76 McIntyre Rd., Timmins ON P4N 7H6
Tel: 705-360-1900; *Fax:* 705-360-1193
info@timminschamber.on.ca
www.timminschamber.on.ca
www.linkedin.com/company/timmins-chamber-of-commerce
www.facebook.com/TimminsChamber
twitter.com/TimminsChamber
www.youtube.com/TimminsChamber
Overview: A small local organization founded in 1949
Mission: To encourage growth in our community by promoting business opportunities
Member of: Ontario Chamber of Commerce; Canadian Chamber of Commerce
Finances: *Funding Sources:* Membership dues; licence bureau; fundraising
Staff Member(s): 6
Membership: 800; *Fees:* Schedule available
Activities: Tourist Information Centre; Licensing Bureau (drivers & vehicles); Annual Dinner, fall; *Internships:* Yes
Chief Officer(s):
Kurt Bigeau, President
Keitha Robson, Chief Administrative Officer

Timmins Coin Club
c/o Randy Maass, PO Box 466, Timmins ON P4N 7E3
Overview: A small local organization
Chief Officer(s):
Randy Maass, President
nifinder@hotmail.com

Timmins Family Counselling Centre, Inc. / Centre de Counselling Familial de Timmins inc.
#310, 60 Wilson Ave., Timmins ON P4N 2S7
Tel: 705-267-7333; *Fax:* 705-268-6850
www.timminsfamilycounselling.com
Overview: A small local charitable organization founded in 1979
Mission: To provide high quality therapeutic services in regards to maintaining & improving the functioning of families, couples & the individual; aims to promote education & development in the community & intercedes for the client's rights with a goal of impro0ing the quality of life in Timmins & its surrounding areas
Staff Member(s): 10
Activities: Presentation to EAP clients; presentations in the community of Timmins & surrounding areas; *Internships:* Yes; *Speaker Service:* Yes; *Library:* by appointment
Chief Officer(s):
Nathalie Parnell, Executive Director

Timmins Family YMCA *See* YMCA Canada

Timmins Native Friendship Centre
179 Kirby Ave., Timmins ON P4N 1K1
Tel: 705-268-6262; *Fax:* 705-268-6266
reception@tnfc.ca
www.tnfc.ca
www.facebook.com/TimminsNativeFriendshipCentre
Overview: A small local organization
Mission: To provide a culturally sensitive, helpful environment for Aboriginal & non-Aboriginal people in Timmins, Ontario; To improve the quality of life for Aboriginal & non-Aboriginal people in the Timmins community
Member of: Ontario Federation of Indian Friendship Centres

Staff Member(s): 36
Activities: Offering programs in areas such as nutrition, literacy & basic skills, academic upgrading, & career development
Chief Officer(s):
Veronica Nicholson, Executive Director
vnicholson@tnfc.ca
Roseanne Ross, Director, Finance

Timmins Real Estate Board *See* Timmins, Cochrane & Timiskaming District Association of REALTORS

Timmins Symphony Orchestra
35 Pine St. South, 2nd Fl., Timmins ON P4N 7N2
Tel: 705-267-1006; *Fax:* 705-267-1006
info@timminssymphony.com
www.timminssymphony.com
www.facebook.com/TimminsSymphonyOrchestra
twitter.com/timminssymphony
Overview: A small local charitable organization founded in 1979 overseen by Orchestras Canada
Member of: Orchestras Canada
Finances: *Funding Sources:* Donations
Chief Officer(s):
Roy Takayesu, President
Matthew Jones, Music Director

Timmins, Cochrane & Timiskaming District Association of REALTORS
225 Algonquin Blvd. East, Timmins ON P4N 1B4
Tel: 705-268-5451; *Fax:* 705-264-6420
boards.mls.ca/timmins/
Previous Name: Timmins Real Estate Board
Overview: A small local organization overseen by Ontario Real Estate Association
Finances: *Annual Operating Budget:* $100,000-$250,000; *Funding Sources:* Membership dues
Staff Member(s): 2
Membership: 80

Tir-à-l'arc Moncton Archers Inc.
Moncton NB
Previous Name: Moncton Archers & Bowhunters Association
Overview: A small local organization founded in 1968
Mission: To enjoy the sport of archery & bowhunting; To promote saftey in each sport
Affiliation(s): New Brunswick Archery Association; Canadian Archery Association

Tire and Rubber Association of Canada (TRAC) / L'Association canadienne du pneu et du caoutchouc
260 Holiday Inn Dr., #A19, Cambridge ON N3C 4E8
Tel: 519-249-0366; *Fax:* 519-249-0401
info@tracanada.ca
www.tracanada.ca
Previous Name: The Rubber Association of Canada
Overview: A large national organization founded in 1920
Mission: To upgrade & maintain good industry/government working relations; To explore ways of improving industry competitiveness & efficiency; To promote safety in members' products, in their use & in the workplace; To promote expansion & profitability of Canadian rubber manufacturing units; To enhance standing of Canadian rubber industry worldwide; To provide members with industry marketing statistics
Finances: *Annual Operating Budget:* $250,000-$500,000; *Funding Sources:* Membership dues
Staff Member(s): 4
Membership: 24 corporate; *Fees:* Based on volume of product; *Member Profile:* Manufacturers of products made from rubber; suppliers; importers; *Committees:* Customs & Tariffs; General Rubber Products; Human Resources; Occupational Health & Safety; Workers' Compensation; Environment; Tire Statistical; Tire Technical; Scrap Tire
Activities: *Speaker Service:* Yes
Chief Officer(s):
Glenn Maidment, President
glenn@rubberassociation.ca

Tire Stewardship BC Association (TSBC)
PO Box 5366, 1627 Fort St., 4th Fl., Victoria BC V8R 6S4
Tel: 250-598-9112; *Fax:* 250-598-9119
Toll-Free: 866-759-0488
www.tsbc.ca
www.facebook.com/TiresBC
twitter.com/TiresBC
www.youtube.com/user/tiresbc
Overview: A small provincial organization founded in 2006

Mission: To manage the tire recycling program in British Columbia & ensure that tires are disposed of in environmentally responsible ways
Membership: *Committees:* Advisory
Chief Officer(s):
Don Blythe, Chair
Glenn Maidment, Secretary

Tisdale & District Chamber of Commerce
PO Box 219, 520 93rd Ave., Tisdale SK S0E 1T0
Tel: 306-873-4257
tisdalechamber@sasktel.net
tisdalechamber.ca
www.facebook.com/122558341262933
twitter.com/tisdalechamber
Overview: A small local organization
Mission: To promote & support businesses in the Tisdale area
Staff Member(s): 1; 12 volunteer(s)
Membership: 100; *Fees:* Schedule available; *Member Profile:* Local businesses
Activities: Organizing community events; Providing customer service training & community promotion
Chief Officer(s):
Rachelle Casavant, Executive Director

Title Insurance Industry Association of Canada (TIIAC) / Association canadienne des compagnies d'assurance titres (ACCAT)
PO Box 866, 31 Adelaide St. East, Toronto ON M5C 2K1
info@tiiac-accat.com
www.tiiac-accat.com
Overview: A small national organization
Mission: To represent the interests of the title insurance industry in Canada
Membership: 4 companies; *Member Profile:* Federally regulated title insurers
Activities: Education for members; advocation
Chief Officer(s):
Paul Zappala, President

Tobermory & District Chamber of Commerce
PO Box 250, 7420 Hwy. 6, Tobermory ON N0H 2R0
Tel: 519-596-2452; *Fax:* 519-596-2452
Other Communication: Visitor Information e-mail:
info@tobermory.com
chamber@tobermory.org
www.tobermory.org
Overview: A small local organization founded in 1977
Mission: To promote the trade & commerce of the business community; To encourage the economic, civic & social welfare of the district
Member of: Bruce County Tourism Association; Bruce Peninsula Tourist Association
Affiliation(s): Central Bruce Peninsula Chamber of Commerce; South Bruce Peninsula Chamber of Commerce; Manitoulin Chamber of Commerce; Manitoulin Tourism Association; Sauble Beach Chamber of Commerce
Finances: *Annual Operating Budget:* Less than $50,000; *Funding Sources:* Membership dues; municipal government; fundraising
Staff Member(s): 1; 45 volunteer(s)
Membership: 100; *Fees:* Schedule available
Chief Officer(s):
Kristen Buckley, President

Tofield & District Chamber of Commerce
PO Box 967, Tofield AB T0B 4J0
www.tofieldchamber.com
Overview: A small local organization
Mission: To advocate for businesses in the town of Tofield, Alberta & the surrounding area
Affiliation(s): Alberta Chambers of Commerce
Membership: 47
Activities: Participating in & sponsoring local events, such as the Sherwood Park Trade Show & the Small Business Week celebration
Chief Officer(s):
Greg Litwin, President
greg@lorenzteam.com
Jeff Edwards, Vice-President
jedwards@tofieldalberta.ca
Dan Hillyer, Secretary
danhillyer@gmail.com
Calvin Andringa, Treasurer
calvin.tofalliance@telus.net
Publications:
• Tofield & Area Business & Services Directory

Type: Directory
Profile: Detailed listings of local businesses

Tofield Historical Society
PO Box 1082, Tofield AB T0B 4J0
Tel: 780-662-3269
www.tofieldalberta.ca/recreation/attractions/museum
Also Known As: Tofield Museum
Overview: A small local organization founded in 1961
Member of: Museums Alberta
Finances: *Funding Sources:* Donations; grants; fundraising
Activities: Canada Day Open House; Strawberry Social, Aug.

Tofino-Long Beach Chamber of Commerce
PO Box 249, Tofino BC V0R 2Z0
Tel: 250-725-3153
info@tofinochamber.org
www.tofinochamber.org
www.facebook.com/tofinoChamber
twitter.com/tofinochamber
Overview: A small local charitable organization
Mission: To promote a healthy & responsible environment for businesses operating in or relocating to the Tofino region
Finances: *Annual Operating Budget:* $50,000-$100,000
Staff Member(s): 1; 10 volunteer(s)
Membership: 225; *Fees:* Schedule available
Activities: Organizing & supporting events such as the Pacific Rim Whale Festival, Clayoquot Shorebird Festival, Edge to Edge Marathon, & Clayoquot Oyster Festival
Chief Officer(s):
Jennifer Steven, President

Top of Lake Superior Chamber of Commerce
PO Box 402, Nipigon ON P0T 2J0
Tel: 807-887-3188
chamber@topoflakesuperior.com
www.topoflakesuperior.com
Overview: A small local organization founded in 1988
Mission: To build & sustain a strong economic environment in the area
Member of: Canadian Chamber of Commerce; Ontario Chamber of Commerce
Staff Member(s): 2
Membership: 96
Chief Officer(s):
Dan Bevilacqua, President

Toronto See Habitat for Humanity Canada

Toronto & District Square & Round Dance Association
c/o Bob & Betty Beck, 62 Tupper Dr., Thorold ON L2V 4C8
Tel: 905-227-7264
www.td-dance.ca
Overview: A small local organization founded in 1951
Mission: To promote, encourage & foster wider knowledge of square & round dancing; To provide for mutual exchange of philosophy & material pertaining to square & round dancing between callers, teachers, & leaders; To improve quality of square & round dancing; To encourage use of standards of uniformity relating to square & round dancing
Member of: Ontario Square & Round Dance Federation
Affiliation(s): Canadian Square & Round Dance Society
Finances: *Funding Sources:* Membership fees; dances; convention
Membership: *Fees:* $10; *Member Profile:* Individuals & clubs interested or engaged in square & round dancing
Activities: *Internships:* Yes; *Speaker Service:* Yes; *Library:* Resource Centre; by appointment
Chief Officer(s):
Sharron Hall, Co-President
president@td-dance.ca
Wayne Hall, Co-President
president@td-dance.ca

Toronto & York Region Labour Council
#407, 15 Gervais Dr., Toronto ON M3C 1Y8
Tel: 416-441-3663; *Fax:* 416-445-8405
council@labourcouncil.ca
www.labourcouncil.ca
www.facebook.com/LabourCouncil
twitter.com/torontolabour
Previous Name: Labour Council of Metropolitan Toronto & York Region
Overview: A medium-sized local organization overseen by Ontario Feeration of Labour
Chief Officer(s):
John Cartwright, President
jcartwright@labourcouncil.ca

Toronto Academy of Dentistry
#207, 970 Lawrence Ave. West, Toronto ON M6A 3B6
Tel: 416-967-5649; *Fax:* 416-967-5081
info@tordent.com
www.tordent.com
Overview: A small local organization founded in 1890
Mission: To provide leadership & service to both the profession & the community; To advance the art & science of dentistry; To promote the highest ideals of dental practice; To cultivate harmony & good fellowship among its fellows & among the members of the dental profession
Staff Member(s): 3
Membership: 1,800; *Member Profile:* Dentists
Chief Officer(s):
Lori O'Doherty, Executive Director

Toronto Action for Social Change
PO Box 73620, 509 St. Clair Ave. West, Toronto ON M6C 1C0
Tel: 416-651-5800
tasc@web.ca
www.homesnotbombs.ca/tasc.htm
Also Known As: Homes Not Bombs
Overview: A small local organization
Mission: Building community through non-violent action

Toronto Alliance for the Performing Arts (TAPA)
#350, 401 Richmond St. West, Toronto ON M5V 3A8
Tel: 416-536-6468; *Fax:* 416-536-3463
www.tapa.ca
www.facebook.com/torontoalliancefortheperformingarts
twitter.com/TAPA_TO
www.flickr.com/photos/torontotheatre
Previous Name: Toronto Theatre Alliance
Overview: A medium-sized local organization founded in 1980
Mission: To foster greater respect & support for the arts by advocating on behalf of Canadian theatre & dance, representing all cultural backgrounds, to government, supporters, & the general public; To provide services which enhance the artistic, technical, & administrative development of members
Affiliation(s): Professional Association of Canadian Theatres (PACT), Theatre Ontario
Finances: *Funding Sources:* Grants from Toronto Arts Council & Ontario Arts Council
Staff Member(s): 8; 80 volunteer(s)
Membership: 187 professional theatre, dance & opera companies; *Fees:* Schedule available
Activities: Operating ticket outlet in the downtown Toronto theatre district (TO Tix); Providing professional development workshops & seminars; *Internships:* Yes; *Rents Mailing List:* Yes
Chief Officer(s):
Jacoba Knaapen, Executive Director, 416-536-6468 Ext. 25
Alexis Da Silva-Powell, Manager, Corporate Partnerships & Membership, 416-536-6468 Ext. 30
Awards:
• Dora Mavor Moore Awards
Established 1979; celebrating excellence in Toronto theatre, 35 awards in large, medium & small theatre divisions, Theatre for Young Audiences & New Choreography
• Silver Ticket Award
; *Amount:* A lifetime of complimentary tickets to TAPA member company productions
• Audience Choice Award
• Pauline McGibbon Award For Unique Talents and Potential for Excellence
; *Amount:* $7,000
• Barbara Hamilton Memorial Award
; *Amount:* $1,000
• George Luscombe Mentorship Award
; *Amount:* $1,000
• The Leonard McHardy and John Harvey Award
; *Amount:* $1,000

Toronto Anglers See Toronto Sportsmen's Association

Toronto Animated Image Society (TAIS)
#102, 60 Atlantic Ave., Studio 9, Toronto ON M6K 1X9
Tel: 416-533-7889
tais.animation@gmail.com
www.tais.ca
www.facebook.com/TorontoAnimatedImageSociety
twitter.com/TAIS_Animation
Overview: A small local organization founded in 1984
Mission: To facilitate the growth of animation artists, craftsmen, & others interested in the art of animation through the sharing of ideas & information on animation; to be a support group for the individual as part of a pool of talent from which to draw
Membership: *Fees:* $40 individual; $150 studio
Chief Officer(s):
Madi Piller, President

Toronto Area Gays & Lesbians Phoneline & Crisis Counselling (TAGL)
PO Box 632, Stn. F, Toronto ON M4Y 2N6
Tel: 416-964-6600
Toll-Free: 877-964-6677
Overview: A small local charitable organization founded in 1975
Mission: To operate a telephone information & peer counselling line for gays & lesbians
Affiliation(s): Gay Lesbian & Bisexual Access Coalition
Finances: *Annual Operating Budget:* Less than $50,000
30 volunteer(s)
Membership: 1-99

Toronto Art Therapy Institute (TATI)
8 Prince Arthur Ave., 2nd Fl., Toronto ON M5R 1A9
Tel: 416-924-6221
torontoarttherapyassistant@gmail.com
www.tati.on.ca
Overview: A small local charitable organization founded in 1968
Mission: To train individuals who want to become art therapists; To use art therapy to promote growth & healing within communities
Affiliation(s): Lesley College, Cambridge, MA
Staff Member(s): 25
Membership: *Committees:* Academic; Admission
Activities: Training program; workshops & information meetings; *Library:* Not open to public
Chief Officer(s):
Debbie Anderson, Chair
Helene Burt, Executive Director
Awards:
• Martin Fischer Memorial Thesis Prize

Toronto Arts Council (TAC)
#200, 26 Grand Trunk Cres., Toronto ON MJ5 3A9
Tel: 416-392-6800; *Fax:* 416-392-6920
www.torontoartscouncil.org
www.linkedin.com/company/toronto-arts-council
www.facebook.com/torontoartscouncil
twitter.com/TorontoArts
Overview: A medium-sized local charitable organization founded in 1974
Mission: To support the development, accessibility & excellence of the arts in Toronto
Finances: *Annual Operating Budget:* Greater than $5 Million
Staff Member(s): 21; 29 volunteer(s)
Membership: *Member Profile:* Artists, art patrons, city councillors; *Committees:* Literary; Dance; Visual Arts/Media Arts; Music; Community Arts; Theatre
Activities: Offering grants to the city's artists & art organizations; *Library:* by appointment
Chief Officer(s):
Claire Hopkinson, Executive Director, 416-392-6802 Ext. 203
claire@torontoartscouncil.org
Beth Reynolds, Director of Grants, 416-392-6802 Ext. 206
beth@torontoartscouncil.org
Awards:
• TAC Grants Program
Awarded to support artistic excellence & innovation in the City of Toronto; supports arts disciplines & strategic arts initiatives

Toronto Arts Foundation (TAF)
#200, 26 Grand Trunk Cres., Toronto ON M5J 3A9
Tel: 416-392-6800; *Fax:* 416-392-6920
mail@torontoartscouncil.org
www.torontoartsfoundation.org
www.facebook.com/torontoartsfoundation
twitter.com/TorontoArts
Overview: A medium-sized local charitable organization founded in 1995
Mission: To create a Toronto-based repository for legacies & other gifts from individuals, families, corporations or trusts that wish to support the arts in Toronto
Finances: *Annual Operating Budget:* $250,000-$500,000
400 volunteer(s)
Membership: 5,300; *Member Profile:* Arts supporters in Toronto
Activities: Mayor's Arts Awards Lunch, Oct.
Chief Officer(s):
John McKellar, Chair
Michelle Parson, Office Manager, 416-392-6800 Ext. 200
michelle@torontoartscouncil.org

Claire Hopkinson, Director and CEO, 416-392-6802 Ext. 203
claire@torontoartscouncil.org
Awards:
• William Kilbourn Award
Awarded every second year to an individual performer, teacher, administrator, or creator in any arts discipline, including architecture & design, whose work is a celebration of life through the arts in Toronto; *Amount:* $5,000
• Muriel Sherrin Award
$10,000 cash prize presented to an artist or creator who has made a contribution to the cultural life ot Toronto through outstanding achievement in music. The recipient will also have participated in international initiatives, including touring, study abroad & artist exchanges. Awarded every second year
• Rita Davies Award
$5,000 cash prize presented to a Toronto artist, volunteer or administrator who has demonstrated creative leadership in the development of arts & culture in Toronto. Awarded every second year
• Margo Bindhardt Award
$10,000 cash prize presented every second year to Toronto artist or administrator whose leadership & vision, whether through their creative work or cultural activism, have had a significant impact on the arts in Toronto & for whom the cash prize will make a difference

Toronto Association for Business Economics Inc. (TABE)
PO Box 955, 31 Adelaide St. East, Toronto ON M5C 2K3
Tel: 647-693-7418
tabe@cabe.ca
www.cabe.ca/tabe
twitter.com/TABE_Economics
Overview: A small local organization founded in 1965 overseen by Canadian Association for Business Economics
Mission: To promote a better understanding of economic issues; To contribute to the professional development of members; To encourage the availability of economic information & to broaden awareness of business economics; To recognize achievement of business economists
Member of: Canadian Association for Business Economics
Finances: *Funding Sources:* Membership fees
Membership: *Fees:* $160 national; $80 local; $30 student
Activities: Luncheons; Workshops; Quarterly study sessions; *Speaker Service:* Yes; *Library:* Not open to public
Chief Officer(s):
Bonnie Lemcke, President, 416-325-8170

Toronto Association for Community Living *See* Community Living Toronto

Toronto Association for Democracy in China (TADC)
#407, 253 College St., Toronto ON M5T 1R5
Tel: 416-592-5406
www.tadc.ca
Overview: A small international organization founded in 1989
Finances: *Funding Sources:* Donations
Membership: 100-499; *Committees:* Lobbying; Education; Publicity
Activities: *Speaker Service:* Yes
Chief Officer(s):
Cheuk Kwan, Chair

Toronto Association for Learning & Preserving the History of WWII in Asia
#305, 85 Scarsdale Rd., Toronto ON M3B 2R2
Tel: 416-299-0111; *Fax:* 866-248-5290
www.torontoalpha.org
www.linkedin.com/company/1563278
www.facebook.com/torontoalpha
www.youtube.com/ALPHAtoronto
Overview: A small local organization
Mission: To achieve peace & reconciliation with the understanding of the history of World War II in Asia
Staff Member(s): 6
Chief Officer(s):
Flora Chong, Executive Director

Toronto Association of Acting Studios (TAAS)
c/o Theatre Ontario, #210, 215 Spadina Ave., Toronto ON M5T 2C7
Tel: 416-408-4556; *Fax:* 416-408-3402
info@theatreontario.org
www.torontoactingstudios.com
Overview: A small local organization founded in 1984
Mission: To offer a wide variety of high-quality approaches to the craft of acting & related theatrical skills

Membership: 31; *Fees:* $125
Chief Officer(s):
Vrenia Ivonoffski, Chair

Toronto Association of Law Libraries (TALL)
PO Box 1042, Stn. TDC, 77 King St. West, Toronto ON M5K 1P2
www.talltoronto.ca
www.facebook.com/TorontoAssociationOfLawLibraries
Overview: A small local organization founded in 1979
Mission: To represent & support members of the legal community in Toronto & the surrounding region
Membership: *Fees:* $34.65 students/retired/unemployed members; $52.50 general/associate members; *Member Profile:* Members of the Toronto & surrounding area legal community, representing corporate law libraries, law firms, law societies, court houses, academia, government, & legal publishers; *Committees:* Audit; Education; Election; Information Technology; Photographers Group; Publisher Liaison; Salary Survey; Union List
Activities: Informing members of new information sources & emerging technologies; Facilitating the exchange of ideas & information among Toronto area law libraries through the TALL Listserv; Developing continuing educational programs; Advocating for members; Conducting surveys of salaries & benefits in the Toronto region legal community; Providing an interlibrary loan list for members; Offering networking opportunities
Chief Officer(s):
Eve Leung, President
Robert Keshen, Vice-President
Meg Carruth, Secretary
Laura Chuang, Treasurer
Laura Knapp, Coordinator, Administration
talladminc@gmail.com
Publications:
• TALL Directory of Law Libraries
Type: Directory; *Frequency:* Annually; *Price:* Subscription based upon the size of an organization
Profile: Law library & personnel contact information, plus special subject collections & services provided to external users
• TALL Newsletter
Frequency: Quarterly; *Price:* Free with Toronto Association of Law Libraries membership
Profile: Communications for members of the Toronto Association of Law Libraries
• Toronto Association of Law Libraries Union List of Periodicals
Frequency: Biennially; *Price:* Free with Toronto Association of Law Libraries membership

Toronto Association of Synagogue & Temple Administrators
c/o Beth Tikvah Synagogue, 3080 Bayview Ave., Toronto ON M5N 5L3
Tel: 416-221-3433
Overview: A small local organization
Finances: *Annual Operating Budget:* Less than $50,000
Membership: 12; *Fees:* $50; *Member Profile:* Executive directors of synagogues & temples
Chief Officer(s):
Doris Alter, President
doris@bethtikvahtoronto.org

Toronto Association of Systems & Software Quality (TASSQ)
1489 Agnew Rd., Mississauga ON L5J 3G8
Tel: 905-822-6645
admin@toronto-assq.com
www.tassq.org
www.linkedin.com/groups/Toronto-Association-Systems-Software-Quality-981557
www.facebook.com/TASSQorg
twitter.com/TASSQ_Online
Overview: A small local organization founded in 1993
Mission: To promote quality assurance in the information technology industry
Membership: *Fees:* $100 individual; $500 corporate; $1200 media sponsorship; $2500 platinum media sponsorship
Chief Officer(s):
Joe Larizza, President

Toronto Autosport Club (TAC)
18759 Kennedy Rd., Sharon ON L0G 1V0
treasurer@torontoautosportclub.ca
www.torontoautosportclub.ca
Overview: A small local organization founded in 1956

Member of: Canadian Association of Rally Sport; Canadian Association Sport Clubs - Ontario Region; Rally Sport Ontario
Finances: *Annual Operating Budget:* Less than $50,000; *Funding Sources:* Membership fees; contract sports events 80 volunteer(s)
Membership: 80; *Fees:* $50; *Member Profile:* People who compete in car racing & rallying
Activities: Autosports; rallying-auto; racing-ice & autoslalom; *Speaker Service:* Yes
Chief Officer(s):
Rob McAuley, President
president@torontoautosportclub.ca
Publications:
• Fifth Gear [a publication of the Toronto Autosport Club]
Type: Newsletter; *Frequency:* Monthly; *Editor:* Nick Beck

Toronto Baptist Ministries
1585 Yonge St., Toronto ON M4T 1Z9
office@torontobaptistministries.com
www.torontobaptistministries.com
Overview: A small local organization overseen by Canadian Baptists of Ontario and Quebec
Mission: To support their member churches
Member of: Canadian Baptists of Ontario & Quebec
Membership: 100 churches; *Member Profile:* Baptist churches in the Greater Toronto Area

Toronto Bicycling Network
PO Box 279, #200, 131 Bloor St. West, Toronto ON M5S 1R8
Tel: 416-760-4191
Other Communication: Membership Inquiries, E-mail: membership@tbn.ca
info@tbn.ca
www.tbn.ca
twitter.com/TOBikeNetwork
Overview: A small local organization founded in 1983
Membership: 850; *Fees:* $70 family; $50 individual; $25 student
Activities: Leisure Wheeler Rides; Easy Roller Rides; Tourist & Short Tourist Rides; Sportif Rides; Country Cruise Rides; Snails & Spice Ride; cross-country skiing; in-line skating; ice skating & hiking
Chief Officer(s):
Ian Rankin, President
president@tbn.ca
Sandra Wong, Technical Director
sandra.wong@tbn.ca
Ed Weiss, Director, Communications
publicity@tbn.ca
Publications:
• Quick Release [a publication of the Toronto Bicycling Network]
Type: Newsletter; *Frequency:* 3 pa
Profile: News & updates for members

Toronto Biotechnology Initiative *See* Life Sciences Ontario

Toronto Blues Society (TBS)
#B04, 910 Queen St. West, Toronto ON M6J 1G6
Tel: 416-538-3885; *Fax:* 416-538-6559
Toll-Free: 866-871-9457
Other Communication: www.myspace.com/torontobluessociety
info@torontobluessociety.com
www.torontobluessociety.com
www.facebook.com/TorontoBluesSociety
twitter.com/TOBluesSociety
www.youtube.com/user/TorontoBluesSociety
Overview: A small local organization founded in 1985
Mission: To foster an appreciation & awareness of the blues as a musical form, thereby giving blues music a higher profile within the music industry & the larger community; to educate, inform & represent the interest of its members
Member of: Folk Alliance North America; Ontario Council of Folk Festivals; The Blues Foundation
Finances: *Annual Operating Budget:* $50,000-$100,000; *Funding Sources:* Toronto Arts Council; SOCAN Foundation; Ontario Arts Council
Staff Member(s): 1; 100 volunteer(s)
Membership: 600; *Fees:* $30 general; $45 charter; $65 family; $125 institutional; *Committees:* Executive; Internet; Programming; Newsletter; Volunteer
Activities: Maple Blues Awards; Women's Blues Revue; New Talent Search
Chief Officer(s):
Jordan Safer, Office Manager & Coordinator, Events

The Toronto Board of Trade *See* Toronto Region Board of Trade

Toronto Canada-China Friendship Association (TCCFA)
543 Markham St., Toronto ON M6G 2L6
www.tccfa.ca
Overview: A small international organization overseen by Federation of Canada-China Friendship Associations
Mission: To promote friendship between the people of Canada & China; to promote cultural, educational, scientific, athletic & other exchanges
Member of: Federation of Canada-China Friendship Associations
Membership: *Fees:* $15 senior/student; $25 individual; $35 family; $50 sustaining
Activities: Public meetings; culturals & social events; mentoring; dinners; learning tours to China
Chief Officer(s):
Michael Copeland, President
michael-copeland@rogers.com
Publications:
• TCCFA [Toronto Canada-China Friendship Association] Newsletter
Type: Newsletter

Toronto Cat Rescue
PO Box 41175, Stn. Rockwood, Mississauga ON L4W 5C9
Tel: 416-538-8592
info@torontocatrescue.ca
www.torontocatrescue.ca
www.facebook.com/TorontoCatRescue
twitter.com/TorontoCatRescu
Overview: A small local charitable organization founded in 1994
Mission: To help cats escape situations of abuse or neglect, or euthanasia at a pound
Finances: *Annual Operating Budget:* $500,000-$1.5 Million
500+ volunteer(s)
Chief Officer(s):
Heather Brown, Contact

Toronto Centre for Community Learning & Development (CCL&D)
269 Gerrard St. East, 2nd Fl., Toronto ON M5A 2G3
Tel: 416-968-6989; *Fax:* 416-968-0597
info@tccld.org
www.tccld.org
www.facebook.com/torontoccld
twitter.com/TorontoCCLD
Previous Name: East End Literacy
Overview: A small local organization founded in 1979
Mission: To encourage literacy skills, employability skills, independent living skills, & community capacity building
Staff Member(s): 11
Membership: *Committees:* Communications
Activities: Creating community engagement through innovative training; Offering programs, such as academic upgrading & the immigrant women integration program; Collaborating with other organizations to develop individual skills & community
Chief Officer(s):
Alfred Jean-Baptiste, Executive Director

Toronto CFA Society; Toronto Society of Financial Analysts *See* CFA Society Toronto

Toronto Chapter of the International Association of Printing House Craftsmen
#806, 170 - 6A The Donway West, Toronto ON M3C 2E8
Tel: 905-895-4141
www.iaphc.ca
Also Known As: Toronto IAPHC
Overview: A small local organization founded in 1921
Mission: To group people within the printing industry together, & to promote the industry
Member of: International Association of Printing House Craftsmen
Membership: *Member Profile:* Graphic arts
Activities: Monthly education meetings; golf tournament; dinner & dance
Chief Officer(s):
Bill Kidd, President
b.kidd@rogers.com

Toronto Child Psychoanalytic Program *See* Canadian Institute for Child & Adolescent Psychoanalytic Psychotherapy

Toronto Coin Club (TCC)
c/o 128 Silverstone Dr., Toronto ON M6V 3G7
info@torontocoinclub.ca
www.torontocoinclub.ca

Overview: A small local organization founded in 1936
Mission: To promote coin collecting & provide a discussion forum for its members
Member of: Royal Canadian Numismatic Association; Ontario Numismatic Association

Toronto Community Care Access Centre
#305, 250 Dundas St. West, Toronto ON M5T 2Z5
Tel: 416-506-9888; *Fax:* 416-506-0374
Toll-Free: 866-243-0061
feedback@toronto.ccac-ont.ca
healthcareathome.ca/torontocentral
ca.linkedin.com/company/toronto-central-community-care-access-centre
twitter.com/tcccac
www.youtube.com/torontoccac
Previous Name: Home Care Program for Metropolitan Toronto
Overview: A medium-sized local organization founded in 1964
Mission: To coordinate & deliver health & social care to all people in Metro Toronto who are sick or disabled; to enhance the quality of their lives & enable them to remain at home; to provide & coordinate an appropriate range of services to meet the diverse needs (health & social) of individuals & families
Member of: Canadian Home Care Association; Ontario Home Care Programs Association
Finances: *Annual Operating Budget:* Greater than $5 Million
Membership: *Committees:* Fiance; Audit; Quality; Governance
Activities: Nursing; physiotherapy; occupational therapy; speech pathology; social work services; homemaking; medical equipment; laboratory work; drugs; oxygen; transporation
Chief Officer(s):
Stacey Daub, CEO
William Yetman, Chair

Toronto Community Employment Services
#201, 2221 Yonge St., Toronto ON M4S 2B4
Tel: 416-488-0084; *Fax:* 416-488-3743
service@tces.on.ca
www.toronto-jobs.org
www.linkedin.com/company/toronto-community-employment-services
Previous Name: Immigrant Women's Job Placement Centre
Overview: A small local organization founded in 1978 overseen by Ontario Council of Agencies Serving Immigrants
Mission: To provide placement & employment services
Chief Officer(s):
Andrea de Shield, Chair

Toronto Community Foundation (TCF)
#1603, 33 Bloor St. East, Toronto ON M4W 3H1
Tel: 416-921-2035; *Fax:* 416-921-1026
info@tcf.ca
www.tcf.ca
Also Known As: TCF
Previous Name: Community Foundation for Greater Toronto
Overview: A medium-sized local charitable organization founded in 1983
Mission: To connect philanthropic individuals & families to charitable organizations in Toronto
Finances: *Annual Operating Budget:* Greater than $5 Million
Staff Member(s): 9
Membership: *Committees:* Community Initiatives; Finance & Audit; Governance; Investment; Social Impact Investment
Activities: TCF invests charitable gifts from donors into income-earning end owment funds, & makes grants from the earnings to support a range of charities
Chief Officer(s):
Aneil Gokhale, Director, Philanthropy, 416-921-2035 Ext. 212
Nicole Lilauwala, Development Coordinator, 416-921-2035 Ext. 217

The Toronto Consort
427 Bloor St. West, Toronto ON M5S 1X7
Tel: 416-966-1045; *Fax:* 416-966-1759
info@torontoconsort.org
www.torontoconsort.org
www.facebook.com/155552007809
www.youtube.com/thetorontoconsort
Overview: A small international charitable organization founded in 1972
Mission: To perform & promote music of the Middle Ages & the Renaissance
Finances: *Annual Operating Budget:* $250,000-$500,000
Staff Member(s): 5; 35 volunteer(s)
Membership: 300; *Fees:* $50-$1,000+
Activities: Concerts; Educational events; Recordings; Broadcasts

Toronto Council Fire Native Cultural Centre
439 Dundas St. East, Toronto ON M5A 2B1
Tel: 416-360-4350
cdo@councilfire.ca
www.councilfire.ca
Previous Name: Council Fire Native Cultural Centre
Overview: A small local organization founded in 1978
Mission: To provide cultural & social services to Aboriginal people
Membership: *Member Profile:* To provide counselling, material assistance & other direct services to First Nations people & to encourage & enhance spiritual & personal growth
Chief Officer(s):
Andrea Chrisjohn, Board Designate
andrea@cfis.ca

Toronto Council of Hazzanim (Cantors)
3080 Bayview Ave., Toronto ON M2N 6E1
Tel: 647-201-3956
info@torontohazzanim.com
www.torontohazzanim.com
www.facebook.com/hazzanim
Also Known As: Cantorial Clergymen of Ontario
Overview: A small local organization
Mission: To represent cantors from all denominations of Judaism; to provide funds for cantorial scholarships, Jewish music, etc.
Chief Officer(s):
Tibor Kovari, President

Toronto Cricket Umpires' & Scorers' Association (TCU&SA)
Toronto ON
www.tcuandsa.org
Overview: A small local organization
Mission: To train Canadian cricket umpires & scorers.
Chief Officer(s):
Saurabh Naik, President
presidenttcusa@gmail.com
Rohan Shah, Vice-President
rohans@rogers.com
Tushar Thakar, Secretary
secretarytcusa@gmail.com

Toronto Crime Stoppers
40 College St., 6th Fl., Toronto ON M5G 2J3
Tel: 416-808-7260; *Fax:* 416-808-7356
www.222tips.com
www.facebook.com/1800222TIPS
twitter.com/1800222TIPS
www.youtube.com/user/1800222TIPS
Overview: A small local organization
Mission: Partnership of the public, police & media that provides a program that enables people to assist the police anonymously to solve crimes & improve quality of life in the community
Activities: *Awareness Events:* Crime Stoppers Month, Jan.

Toronto Cultural Youth Orchestra *See* Canadian Sinfonietta Youth Orchestra

Toronto Curling Association (TCA)
#6A-1409, 170 The Donway West, Toronto ON M3C 2E8
Tel: 647-875-8906
general@torontocurling.com
www.torontocurling.com
www.facebook.com/torontocurling
twitter.com/torontocurling
Overview: A small local organization founded in 1964
Mission: To promote curling in the Greater Toronto Area
Finances: *Annual Operating Budget:* $50,000-$100,000; *Funding Sources:* Grants; Tournament entry fees
15 volunteer(s)
Membership: 24 clubs
Activities: Organizing curling games
Chief Officer(s):
Grace Bugg, President
grace.bugg@torontocurling.com

Toronto Cyclists Union *See* Cycle Toronto

Toronto Dance Theatre (TDT)
80 Winchester St., Toronto ON M4X 1B2
Tel: 416-967-1365; *Fax:* 416-963-4379
info@tdt.org
www.tdt.org
www.facebook.com/torontodancetheatre
twitter.com/TDTWinch
instagram.com/tdtwinch

Canadian Associations / Toronto District Beekeepers' Association (TDBA)

Overview: A small international charitable organization founded in 1968
Mission: To develop Canadian dance works of art; To perform nationally & internationally; To explore new ideas in choreographic expression while embracing the fresh & vital aspects of inherited traditions
Member of: Canadian Conference of the Arts; Canadian Dance Assembly; Toronto Theatre Alliance; PACT
Finances: *Funding Sources:* Municipal, federal & provincial governments; corporate; individuals; foundations
Staff Member(s): 23
Activities: Creating & performing original Canadian choreography; *Internships:* Yes
Chief Officer(s):
Andrea Vagianos, Managing Director
andrea@tdt.org
Christopher House, Artistic Director

Toronto District Beekeepers' Association (TDBA)
#005, 10350 Yonge St., Richmond Hill ON L4C 3K9
info@torontobeekeepers.org
www.torontobeekeepers.org
Overview: A small local organization founded in 1911
Mission: To assist beekeepers in the Toronto area; To improve the beekeeping industry
Member of: Ontario Beekeepers' Association
Membership: *Member Profile:* Professional & hobby apiarists in the Toronto area
Activities: Promoting the honey bee industry; Providing education about the industry; Liaising with the Ministry of Agriculture to share information; Organizing meetings with guest speakers, including research professors & manufacturers & suppliers of beekeeping equipment; Offering networking opportunities for beekeepers
Chief Officer(s):
André Flys, Contact
andreflys@sympatico.ca
Publications:
• Toronto District Beekeepers' Association Newsletter
Type: Newsletter; *Frequency:* Monthly
Profile: Association updates & meeting announcements

Toronto Downtown Jazz Society
82 Bleecker St., Toronto ON M4X 1L8
Tel: 416-928-2033; *Fax:* 416-928-0533
www.torontojazz.com
www.facebook.com/torontojazzfest
twitter.com/torontojazzfest
Overview: A small local charitable organization founded in 1987
Mission: To produce the Toronto Downtown Jazz Festival, as well as many other events & programs to further develop jazz talent & audience appreciation; To operate as a registered charity (No. 12969 0269 RR0001); To promote community involvement, artistic excellence, & outstanding production standards
Finances: *Funding Sources:* Donations
Chief Officer(s):
Howard Kerbel, CEO
Josh Grossman, Artistic Director

Toronto Endometriosis Network *See* The Endometriosis Network

Toronto Entertainment District Residental Association (TEDRA)
Toronto ON
info@torontoedra.ca
www.torontoedra.ca
www.facebook.com/TorontoEDRA
Overview: A small local organization founded in 2012
Mission: Engages local residents & businesses regarding concerns of area development, traffic congestion, government services, and circumstances that affect property values & quality of life.
Membership: *Member Profile:* Residents who inhabit Toronto's Entertainment District.
Chief Officer(s):
Mike Yen, Executive Director
mike@TorontoEDRA.ca

Toronto Entomologists Association (TEA)
c/o Chris Rickard, Treasurer, 16 Mount View Ct., Collingwood ON L9Y 5A9
info@ontarioinsects.org
www.ontarioinsects.org
Overview: A small local charitable organization founded in 1969
Mission: To maintain an interest in the insects, particularly the butterflies & moths of Ontario; To record life histories, changes in distribution, unusual records, etc., of Ontario butterflies & moths
Member of: Federation of Ontario Naturalists
Finances: *Annual Operating Budget:* Less than $50,000; *Funding Sources:* Membership fees; donations
Membership: 170; *Fees:* $15 student; $25 individual; $30 family; *Member Profile:* Amateur insect enthusiasts; professionals
Activities: Butterfly counts
Chief Officer(s):
Glenn Richardson, President
glennr@personainternet.com

Toronto Environmental Alliance (TEA)
#201, 30 Duncan St., Toronto ON M5V 2C3
Tel: 416-596-0660; *Fax:* 416-596-0345
tea@torontoenvironment.org
www.torontoenvironment.org
www.facebook.com/TOenviro
Overview: A small local organization founded in 1988
Mission: To bring together groups & individuals who share the common goal of making the communities of Greater Toronto area operate in an ecologically sustainable manner
Member of: Ontario Environmental Network
Finances: *Annual Operating Budget:* $250,000-$500,000
Staff Member(s): 7; 200 volunteer(s)
Membership: 8,000; *Fees:* Free; *Committees:* Water; Climate Change; Waste; Smog; Transit
Activities: *Library:* by appointment Not open to public
Chief Officer(s):
Franz Hartmann, Executive Director
franz@torontoenvironment.org

Toronto Esperanto-Klubo *See* Esperanto-Toronto

Toronto Fashion Incubator (TFI)
Exhibition Place, 285 Manitoba Dr., Toronto ON M6K 3C3
Tel: 416-971-7117; *Fax:* 416-971-6717
tfi@fashionincubator.com
www.fashionincubator.com
Overview: A medium-sized local organization founded in 1987
Mission: To provide business solutions to new & established members of the fashion industry in Toronto
Finances: *Funding Sources:* Sponsors
Activities: *Library:* TFI Resource Centre
Chief Officer(s):
David Dixon, President
Susan Langdon, Executive Director
Awards:
• The Suzanne Rogers Award for Most Promising New Label
; *Amount:* $30,000

Toronto Field Naturalists (TFN)
#1519, 2 Carlton St., Toronto ON M5B 1J3
Tel: 416-593-2656
office@torontofieldnaturalists.org
www.torontofieldnaturalists.org
www.facebook.com/TorontoFieldNaturalists
Overview: A medium-sized local charitable organization founded in 1923
Mission: To promote the enjoyment & preservation of nature; To raise public interest in natural history
Finances: *Funding Sources:* Membership fees; Donations
Membership: *Fees:* $20 youth; $30 single seniors; $40 adults & senior families; $50 families
Activities: Partnering with organizations such as Ontario Nature, Toronto Green Community, Toronto Parks & Recreation, & the Toronto & Region Conservation Authority; Engaging in advocacy activities; Organizing monthly talks by experts on natural history topics
Chief Officer(s):
Bob Kortright, President
Walter Weary, Secretary-Treasurer
Publications:
• Toronto Field Naturalist
Type: Newsletter; *Frequency:* 8 pa
Profile: Information about nature in Toronto, environmental issues, & the organization's upcoming activities

Toronto Film Society (TFS)
173B Front St. East, Toronto ON M5A 3Z4
Tel: 416-785-0335
info@torontofilmsociety.com
torontofilmsociety.org
www.facebook.com/pages/Toronto-Film-Society/138608787942
twitter.com/TorFilmSociety
www.youtube.com/channel/UCleKdJTKBEXiw97oC10mxjw
Overview: A small local charitable organization founded in 1948
Mission: To encourage & promote the study, appreciation & use of motion & sound pictures & television as educational & cultural factors in the city of Toronto, its vicinity & elsewhere; to encourage & promote motion & sound pictures through private showings of selected films of an artistic or experimental nature
Affiliation(s): British Film Institute; American Film Institute
Finances: *Funding Sources:* Membership fees
Membership: *Fees:* Schedule available; *Member Profile:* 18 years of age minimum
Activities: Screening of vintage sound & silent films; two weekend seminars; *Speaker Service:* Yes; *Library:* TFS Archives; by appointment
Chief Officer(s):
Barry Chapman, President

Toronto Financial Services Alliance (TFSA)
#1800, 55 University Ave., Toronto ON M5J 2H7
Tel: 416-933-6780; *Fax:* 416-933-6799
info@tfsa.ca
www.tfsa.ca
www.linkedin.com/company/toronto-financial-services-alliance
twitter.com/TFSAweb
Overview: A small local organization founded in 2001
Mission: To build Toronto's financial cluster into a "top ten" global financial services centre; to foster collaboration between the three levels of government, the financial services industry & academia.
Membership: 64; *Member Profile:* Government bodies, financial services companies & academic institutions
Activities: Operating the Centre of Excellence in Financial Services Education, & the Global Risk Institute in Financial Services
Chief Officer(s):
Jennifer Reynolds, President & CEO
Karen Tam, Chief Financial Officer
Sashya D'Souza, Senior Vice-President, Talent Initiatives
Matt Hobbs, Vice-President, Business Development & Marketing
Daniel Malik, Vice-President, Policy & Stakeholder Relations

Toronto Finnish-Canadian Seniors Centre
795 Eglinton Ave. East, Toronto ON M4G 4E4
Tel: 416-425-4134; *Fax:* 416-425-6319
reception@suomikoti.ca
www.suomikoti.ca
Also Known As: Suomi-Koti, Toronto
Overview: A small local organization founded in 1982
Mission: To provide multi-lingual care & services, housing & activities for the Finnish community
Finances: *Funding Sources:* Government; private
Membership: *Member Profile:* Individuals of Finnish descent
Activities: Exercise; pool; sauna; seniors' programs; outings
Chief Officer(s):
Juha Mynttinen, Administrator, 416-425-4134 Ext. 243

Toronto Free-Net (TFN)
#406, 600 Bay St., Toronto ON M5G 1M6
Tel: 416-204-9257; *Fax:* 416-273-2677
office@torfree.net
www.torfree.net
Also Known As: torfree.net
Overview: A small local organization founded in 1994
Finances: *Funding Sources:* Donations; service subscriptions
Staff Member(s): 12; 35 volunteer(s)
Membership: 50,000 registered
Activities: Community Network supplying ISP services on by-donation basis, tiered access plans including DSL high speed, IP, remote LAN administration, & cystom programming services; *Library:* Not open to public
Chief Officer(s):
Iain Calder, President & Manager

Toronto French Book Fair *Voir* Salon du livre de Toronto et Festival des écrivains

Toronto Gaelic Learners Association
43 Norbrook Cres., Toronto ON M9V 4P7
fios@torontogaelic.ca
www.torontogaelic.ca
Also Known As: CLUINN
Overview: A small provincial organization founded in 1995
Mission: To encourage education in the Scottish Gaelic language
Membership: *Member Profile:* Teachers & organizers of Scottish Gaelic language classes

Activities: Offering non-credit Scottish Gaelic language classes at St. Michael's College, University of Toronto; Presenting scholarships to students
Chief Officer(s):
Janice Chan, Contact

Toronto General & Western Hospital Foundation
R. Fraser Elliot Bldg., #5S-801, 190 Elizabeth St., Toronto ON M5G 2C4
Tel: 416-340-3935; *Fax:* 416-340-4864
Toll-Free: 877-846-4483
foundation@uhn.ca
www.tgwhf.ca
www.facebook.com/tgwhf
www.twitter.com/tgwhf
www.youtube.com/user/TGWHFoundation
Previous Name: Toronto Hospital Foundation
Overview: A small local charitable organization
Mission: To raise funds for research, education & the enhancement of patient care at University Health Network.
Chief Officer(s):
Tennys J.M. Hanson, President & CEO

Toronto Health Libraries Association (THLA)
c/o Raluca Serban, UHN - Toronto Rehabilitation Institute, 550 University Ave., Toronto ON M5G 2A2
secretary@thla.ca
thla.chla-absc.ca
Overview: A small local organization founded in 1965 overseen by Canadian Health Libraries Association
Mission: To promote the provision of quality library service to the health community; To encourage communication & cooperation among members & to foster their professional development; To consult & collaborate with other professional, technical & scientific organizations in matters of mutual interest
Affiliation(s): Ontario Hospital Association
Finances: *Funding Sources:* Membership dues
Membership: *Fees:* $25 individual; $15 student/retired/unemployed; *Member Profile:* Individuals & institutions interested in the goals of the association
Chief Officer(s):
Ashley Farrell, President
president@thla.ca
Meetings/Conferences:
• Toronto Health Libraries Association 2018 Annual General Meeting, 2018, Toronto, ON
Scope: Local

Toronto Hebrew Benevolent Society
#610, 333 Clark Ave. West, Toronto ON L4J 7K4
Tel: 905-889-3860
Overview: A small local organization
Mission: To support & meet the needs of members
Membership: 200
Chief Officer(s):
Charon Goldman, Financial Secretary

Toronto Historical Board *See* Heritage Toronto

Toronto Hospital Foundation *See* Toronto General & Western Hospital Foundation

Toronto Institute of Medical Technology *See* The Michener Institute for Applied Health Sciences

Toronto Insurance Conference (TIC)
#432, 157 Adelaide St. West, Toronto ON M5H 4E7
Tel: 416-410-4842; *Fax:* 866-746-3657
www.ticonf.com
Overview: A small local organization founded in 1918 overseen by Insurance Brokers Association of Canada
Mission: To provide a forum for commercial insurance brokerage firms in Toronto
Member of: Insurance Brokers Association of Canada (IBAC)
Membership: *Member Profile:* National & regional brokers located in Ontario
Activities: Member events; networking; *Awareness Events:* Black Tie Dinner, Nov.; Golf Classic Tournament, June
Chief Officer(s):
Michael Loeters, President
Sheila Reesor, Executive Director
Awards:
• Toronto Insurance Conference Scholarship Program Managed by the Insurance Institute of Ontario, the program offers financial assistance to applicants pursing full-time university undergraduate studies in Canada.; *Amount:* (3) $5,000

Toronto Insurance Women's Association (TIWA)
PO Box 861, 31 Adelaide St. East, Toronto ON M5C 2K1
www.tiwa.org
www.linkedin.com/groups/3224767
twitter.com/tiwatweets
Overview: A small local organization founded in 1960
Mission: To educate and assist its members in reaching their potential both professionally and personally, promote the spirit of friendship and service in the industry, and encourage and foster high ethical standards in business and social relations
Member of: Canadian Association of Insurance Women
Membership: *Fees:* $65 individual; scheule for corporate
Activities: Monthly dinner meetings; *Awareness Events:* Annual Wine & Cheese; Annual Golf Tournament
Chief Officer(s):
Sephora Sciara, President, 905-771-3205, Fax: 905-771-3410
sephora@tiwa.org

Toronto International Film Festival Inc. (TIFF)
TIFF Bell Lightbox, 250 King St. West, Toronto ON M5V 3K5
Tel: 416-599-8433
Toll-Free: 888-599-8433
customerrelations@tiff.net
www.tiff.net
www.facebook.com/TIFF
www.youtube.com/user/tiff
Overview: A medium-sized international charitable organization founded in 1976
Mission: To lead in creative & cultural discovery through the moving image
Finances: *Annual Operating Budget:* Greater than $5 Million; *Funding Sources:* Donations; Sponsorships
Staff Member(s): 600; 2000 volunteer(s)
Membership: *Fees:* $99 individual; $150 family/dual; $400 contributor; $600 principal; *Committees:* Sprockets Educational Advisory
Activities: Offering Cinematheque Ontario, a screening program of the classics of world cinema; Organizing Film Circuit, which provides films to formerly under-serviced areas; Coordinating Reel Talk, which offers preview screenings of films, followed by informal discussions; Providing specialized industry programming & project development; *Awareness Events:* Toronto International Film Festival, September; Sprockets Toronto International Film Festival for Children, April; Canada's Top Ten (a selection of the best Canadian films of the year)
Library: Film Reference Library
Chief Officer(s):
Lisa de Wilde, Chair

Toronto Japanese Association of Commerce & Industry
PO Box 104, #122, 20 York Mills Rd., Toronto ON M2P 2C2
Tel: 416-360-0235; *Fax:* 416-360-0236
office@torontoshokokai.org
www.torontoshokokai.org
Overview: A medium-sized local organization
Mission: To promote business relations between Canada & Japan through the activities of the members of the Japanese School of Toronto Shokokai Inc. (commonly known as the Hoshuko).
Membership: *Fees:* $700 + $170 per member regular; $350 + $85 per member associate; $200 individual
Activities: Business luncheons & information sessions; newsletter; New Year's reception; *Awareness Events:* Charity Golf Tournament, May
Chief Officer(s):
Tetsuo Komuro, President
Yukio Arita, Executive Director & Secretary

Toronto Jewish Film Society (TJFS)
c/o Miles Nadal Jewish Community Centre, 750 Spadina Ave., Toronto ON M5S 2J2
Tel: 416-924-6211; *Fax:* 416-924-0442
www.milesnadaljcc.ca
Overview: A small local charitable organization founded in 1978
Mission: Celebration of Jewish film; exposure of film artists; forum for promotion of Jewish film & relevant issues
Affiliation(s): Miles Nadal Jewish Community Centre
Membership: *Fees:* $100; $60 young adult
Activities: 8 Yearly screenings sold as a subscription series, includes speakers & Q&A session
Chief Officer(s):
Mark Clamen, Co-Chair
Shirley Kumove, Co-Chair
Esther Arbeid, Contact
esthera@mnjcc.org

Toronto Jewish Free Loan Cassa *See* Jewish Free Loan Toronto

Toronto Latvian Concert Association (TLK)
Tel: 416-512-7348
music.lv@sympatico.ca
www.torontolatvianconcerts.com
Overview: A small local charitable organization founded in 1959
Mission: To promote 4 concert season with Latvian performers & to provide an opportunity to hear music by composers of Latvian origin
Finances: *Annual Operating Budget:* Less than $50,000; *Funding Sources:* Subscription fees; ticket sale; donations
10 volunteer(s)
Membership: 300; *Fees:* $100 subscription to 4 concerts; $90 seniors; $45 students
Chief Officer(s):
Arvids Purvs, President

Toronto Law Office Management Association (TLOMA)
43 Daniel Ct., Markham ON L3P 4B8
Tel: 416-410-0979; *Fax:* 905-427-5115
www.tloma.com
Overview: A small local organization founded in 1968
Mission: To offer forum for legal administrators to learn about their industry
Membership: 420 individuals from over 225 law firms; *Fees:* $275; *Member Profile:* Law firm administrators
Activities: Education & professional development
Chief Officer(s):
Janice Rooney, President
janice.rooney@fmc-law.com

Toronto Lawyers Association (TLA)
Court House Library, 361 University Ave., 3rd Fl., Toronto ON M5G 3T1
Tel: 416-327-5700; *Fax:* 416-947-9148
library@tlaonline.ca
www.tlaonline.ca
www.linkedin.com/groups/4402002
www.facebook.com/TLAVoice
twitter.com/tlavoice
Previous Name: Metropolitan Toronto Lawyers Association; County of York Law Association
Overview: A small local organization founded in 1885
Mission: To provide lawyers with key services, timely & relevant information, education about issues & opportunities affecting members, & advocacy on behalf of the profession
Finances: *Annual Operating Budget:* $500,000-$1.5 Million; *Funding Sources:* Membership dues; library services
Staff Member(s): 6; 24 volunteer(s)
Membership: 1,000-4,999; *Fees:* $129.95; *Member Profile:* Lawyers; articling/LPP students; law school/law program students; law office administrators; retired lawyers; *Committees:* Advocacy; Awards, Functions & Events; Communications, Publications & Website; Education; Finance & Audit; Governance; Lawyers Feed the Hungry; Library; Membership; Young Lawyers
Activities: *Library:* County Court House Library; Open to public
Chief Officer(s):
Joan Rataic-Lang, Executive Director, 416-327-6012
jrataiclang@tlaonline.ca
Sandra Porter, Coordinator, Membership Services, 416-327-5702
sporter@tlaonline.ca

The Toronto Mendelssohn Choir
#404, 720 Bathurst St., Toronto ON M5S 2R4
Tel: 416-598-0422
admin@tmchoir.org
www.tmchoir.org
www.facebook.com/TMChoir
twitter.com/TMChoir
www.youtube.com/user/TOMendelssohnChoir
Overview: A small local charitable organization founded in 1894
Mission: To give Canadian audiences the experience of choral music
Finances: *Funding Sources:* Box office; donations; government; sponsorship
Staff Member(s): 6
Activities: Presenting choral performances; Providing educational & outreach programs; *Library:* by appointment
Chief Officer(s):
Cynthia Hawkins, Executive Director
manager@tmchoir.org

Toronto Montessori Institute (TMI)
8569 Bayview Ave., Richmond Hill ON L4B 3M7
Tel: 905-889-6882; Fax: 905-886-6516
tmi@tmsschool.ca
www.tmi.edu
Previous Name: Toronto Montessori Teacher Training Institute
Overview: A small local charitable organization founded in 1971
Mission: Engages in training Montessori teachers; competent in the curriculum, committed to working in a spirit of mutual respect, towards the fulfillment of each child's potential
Member of: Montessori Accreditation Council for Teacher Education
Affiliation(s): Canadian Council of Montessori Administrators
Finances: Annual Operating Budget: $500,000-$1.5 Million; Funding Sources: Student fees
Staff Member(s): 5
Chief Officer(s):
Nancy Coyle, Director
ncoyle@torontomontessori.ca

Toronto Montessori Teacher Training Institute See Toronto Montessori Institute

Toronto Musicians' Association (TMA)
#500, 15 Gervais Dr., Toronto ON M3C 1Y8
Tel: 416-421-1020; Fax: 416-421-7011
Toll-Free: 800-762-3444
info@tma149.ca
www.torontomusicians.org
www.facebook.com/146633580744
twitter.com/TMA149
Overview: A medium-sized local organization founded in 1887
Mission: To represent professional musicians in all facets of music in the greater Toronto area; To offer legal protection, assistance, & advice; To help musicians have a successful professional career
Member of: American Federation of Musicians
Finances: Funding Sources: Membership dues
Staff Member(s): 12
Membership: 3,500
Chief Officer(s):
Jim Biros, Executive Director, 416-421-1020 Ext. 235
jbiros@tma149.ca

Toronto Ornithological Club (TOC)
Toronto ON
info@torontobirding.ca
www.torontobirding.ca
Overview: A small local charitable organization founded in 1934
Mission: To afford opportunities for the meeting together of ornithologists at regular intervals for discussion; to facilitate cooperation in ornithological studies; to review & report on ornithological topics; to establish a liaison between members & visiting naturalists
Member of: Federation of Ontario Naturalists
Finances: Annual Operating Budget: Less than $50,000
Membership: 150+; Fees: $25; Committees: Outings; Records; Editorial; Archives; Conservation
Activities: Bird outings; High Park hawk watch; fall field day
Chief Officer(s):
Jeremy Hatt, Councillor, Membership
membership@torontobirding.ca

Toronto Paramedic Association
c/o Toronto Emergency Medical Services, 4330 Dufferin St., Toronto ON M3H 5R9
Tel: 416-410-9453
torontoparamedic.com
www.facebook.com/torontoparamedicassociation
twitter.com/tpanews
Overview: A small local organization founded in 1992
Mission: To support the paramedic community and focus on paramedic advancements in patient care.
Member of: Ontario Paramedic Association
Activities: Awareness Events: EMS Week, May

Toronto Parents of Multiple Births Association (TPOMBA)
#356, 1920 Ellesmere Rd., Toronto ON M1H 3G1
Tel: 416-760-3944
info@tpomba.org
www.tpomba.org
www.facebook.com/TorontoParentsOfMultipleBirthsAssociation
twitter.com/TPOMBA
plus.google.com/u/0/b/116137137302949869664
Previous Name: Toronto Parents of Twins Club
Overview: A small local organization founded in 1976
Mission: To provide guidance & help to adjust to multiple birth situations through educational meetings, support groups, social events for families & adults, & member services; to enable families to cope with their unique situation & therefore lead a full life
Membership: 500+; Fees: $42; Member Profile: Parents of twins, triplets, quads, quints & more
Activities: Awareness Events: New & Expectant Parents Nights; Toddler Nights; Library: by appointment Not open to public
Chief Officer(s):
Camille Kloppenburg, President

Toronto Parents of Twins Club See Toronto Parents of Multiple Births Association

Toronto Pig Save
Toronto ON
torontopigsave@gmail.com
www.torontopigsave.org
www.facebook.com/144171365639268
Overview: A small local organization founded in 2010
Mission: To advocate for animal equality & freedom; To bear witness to farmed animals as they are transported to slaughterhouses in Toronto; To promote plant-based vegan lifestyles
Activities: Holding vigils; Creating educational campaigns about animal agriculture
Chief Officer(s):
Anita Krajnc, Co-Founder

Toronto Police Accountability Coalition (TPAC)
#206, 401 Richmond St. West, Toronto ON M5V 3A8
Tel: 416-977-5097
info@tpac.ca
www.tpac.ca
Overview: A small local organization
Mission: To encourage debate about police issues & to make the police accountable to the public

Toronto Police Association (TPA) / Association de la police de Toronto
#200, 2075 Kennedy Rd., Toronto ON M1T 3V3
Tel: 416-491-4301; Fax: 416-494-4948
information@tpa.ca
www.tpa.ca
www.facebook.com/TPAca
twitter.com/TPAca
www.instagram.com/tpaca1
Previous Name: Metropolitan Toronto Police Association
Overview: A medium-sized local organization founded in 1956
Mission: To promote & advance the health, safety & economic well-being of the membership
Membership: 8,000+ uniform & civilian members
Chief Officer(s):
Mike McCormack, President
Dan Ross, Vice President

Toronto Press & Media Club
#101, 1755 Rathburn Rd. East, Mississauga ON L4W 2M8
info@torontopressclub.net
www.torontopressclub.net
www.facebook.com/TorontoPressAndMediaClub
Overview: A medium-sized provincial organization founded in 1882
Finances: Funding Sources: Membership dues; sponsorships; donations
Membership: Member Profile: Journalism; public relations; communications
Chief Officer(s):
Ed Patrick, President
Awards:
• National Newspaper Awards
Established 1949; awarded annually to print men & women employed regularly on the staffs of Canadian daily newspapers
• Canadian News Hall of Fame
Toronto Press Club is custodian of the Hall of Fame dedicated to those people who have contributed regularly to journalism as staffers
• Norman DePoe Memorial Scholastic Fund
A bursary awards program to students in the media

Toronto Professional Fire Fighters Association
39 Commissioners St., Toronto ON M5A 1A6
Tel: 416-466-1167; Fax: 416-466-6632
mail@torontofirefighters.org
www.torontofirefighters.org
twitter.com/tpffa
Overview: A small local organization
Chief Officer(s):
Ed Kennedy, President

Toronto Public Library Foundation
789 Yonge St., Toronto ON M4W 2G8
Tel: 416-393-7123; Fax: 416-397-5999
foundation@torontopubliclibrary.ca
tplfoundation.ca
www.facebook.com/tplfoundation
twitter.com/TPL_Foundation
www.youtube.com/tplfoundation
Overview: A medium-sized local charitable organization founded in 1997
Mission: To provide essential resources for the enhancement of Toronto Public Library & allocate funds to priority needs not supported by municipal funding.
Chief Officer(s):
Gillian Smith, Chair

Toronto Public Spaces Initiative (TPSI)
Toronto ON
info@publicspaces.ca
publicspaces.ca
www.facebook.com/254649407883843
twitter.com/TOpublicspace
Overview: A small local organization founded in 2001
Mission: Dedicated to enhancing public space through research, policy analysis, and service provision.
Chief Officer(s):
Jayme Turney, CEO

Toronto PWA Foundation (TPWAF)
200 Gerrard St. East, 2nd Fl., Toronto ON M5A 2E6
Tel: 416-506-1400; Fax: 416-506-1404
info@pwatoronto.org
www.pwatoronto.org
www.facebook.com/TorontoPWA
twitter.com/TPWA
Also Known As: Toronto People With AIDS Foundation
Previous Name: People with AIDS Foundation
Overview: A small local charitable organization founded in 1987 overseen by Canadian AIDS Society
Mission: To promote the health & well-being of all people living with HIV/AIDS by providing accessible, direct & practical services
Member of: Ontario AIDS Network
Finances: Annual Operating Budget: $500,000-$1.5 Million; Funding Sources: All levels of government; fundraising; private donations; honorarium
Staff Member(s): 15; 150 volunteer(s)
Membership: 1,000-4,999
Activities: Awareness Events: AIDS Awareness Week; Speaker Service: Yes; Library: Treatment Resource Centre; Open to public
Chief Officer(s):
Suzanne Paddock, Interim Executive Director
spaddock@pwatoronto.org

Toronto Railway Historical Association (TRHA)
#15, 255 Bremner Blvd., Toronto ON M5V 3M9
Tel: 416-214-9229
info@trha.ca
www.trha.ca
twitter.com/TORailwayMuseum
Overview: A small local charitable organization founded in 2001
Mission: To establish, develop & maintain the Toronto Railway Museum at the John Street Roundhouse
Affiliation(s): Toronto Locomotive Preservation Society; Canadian Railroad Historical Association
Finances: Funding Sources: Donations
Staff Member(s): 3; 50 volunteer(s)
Activities: Museum operation; miniature railway
Chief Officer(s):
Phil Spencer, President & CEO
Derek Boles, Chief Historian

Toronto Real Estate Board (TREB)
1400 Don Mills Rd., Toronto ON M3B 3N1
Tel: 416-443-8100
membership@trebnet.com
www.torontorealestateboard.com
www.linkedin.com/company/treb?trk=prof-following-company-logo
www.facebook.com/TorontoRealEstateBoard
twitter.com/TREBhome
www.youtube.com/TREBChannel; www.pinterest.com/trebhome

Overview: A large local organization founded in 1920 overseen by Ontario Real Estate Association
Member of: The Canadian Real Estate Association
Membership: 35,000; *Fees:* Schedule available; *Member Profile:* Specialists in industrial & commercial real estate, appraisals & property management registered under the Real Estate & Business Brokers Act
Activities: *Speaker Service:* Yes; *Library:* Resource Centre; Open to public by appointment
Chief Officer(s):
Mark McLean, President
Awards:
• Past President's Scholarship Program
Eligibility: Graduating high school students continuing to post-secondary education *Deadline:* June; *Amount:* 2 at $5,000 + 2 at $2,500 *Contact:* Christine Shallhorn, Contact, Education, Phone: 416-443-8000, ext. 8030; E-mail: cshallhorn@trebnet.com

Toronto Region Board of Trade
PO Box 60, 1 First Canadian Place, Toronto ON M5X 1C1
Tel: 416-366-6811; *Fax:* 416-366-2444
contactus@bot.com
www.bot.com
www.linkedin.com/company/toronto-board-of-trade
twitter.com/torontorbot
www.youtube.com/user/TorontoRBOT
Previous Name: The Toronto Board of Trade
Overview: A large local organization founded in 1845
Mission: To build a better community through business leadership by providing business services, advocating public policy positions, participating in community partnerships & facilitating economic & business development
Affiliation(s): World Trade Centre - Toronto
Finances: *Annual Operating Budget:* Greater than $5 Million; *Funding Sources:* Membership fees
Staff Member(s): 305
Membership: 10,500; *Fees:* Schedule available; *Committees:* Policy & Advocacy; Economic Development; Infrastructure; Municipal Performance; Liveability
Activities: *Speaker Service:* Yes; *Rents Mailing List:* Yes; *Library:* Worksite
Chief Officer(s):
Anne Sado, Chair
Janet (Jan) De Silva, President & CEO, 416-862-4542
Catherine Fels-Smith, CFO & COO, 416-862-4544
cfelssmith@bot.com
Jenny Basov, Senior Manager, Human Resources, 416-862-4517
jbasov@bot.com
Publications:
• OnBoard Magazine
Type: Magazine; *Frequency:* Quarterly
Profile: News, information and insights about issues and offerings that impact business in the Toronto region.
West End Office
#101, 91 Skyway Ave., Toronto ON M9W 6R5
Tel: 416-798-6811; *Fax:* 416-798-2499

Toronto Renaissance & Reformation Colloquium (TRRC)
c/o Germaine Warkentin, Victoria College, University of Toronto, #205, 73 Queen's Park Cres., Toronto ON M5S 1K7
www.crrs.ca
Overview: A small local organization founded in 1965
Affiliation(s): International Federation of Societies & Institutes for the Study of the Renaissance
Finances: *Annual Operating Budget:* Less than $50,000; *Funding Sources:* Membership fees
Staff Member(s): 2
Membership: 1-99; *Fees:* $12
Activities: Presents a lecture series; *Speaker Service:* Yes; *Library:* Centre for Renaissance & Reformation Studies
Chief Officer(s):
Germaine Warkentin, Director
g.warkentin@utoronto.ca

Toronto Renewable Energy Co-operative (TREC)
#240, 401 Richmond St. West, Toronto ON M5V 3A8
Tel: 416-977-5093; *Fax:* 416-306-6476
info@trec.on.ca
www.trec.on.ca
www.facebook.com/TRECcoop
twitter.com/TRECoop
Overview: A small local organization founded in 1998
Mission: To help create a world where people work together, pooling their resources, to benefit from a renewable energy economy
Member of: Canadian Renewable Energy Alliance
Affiliation(s): Toronto District School Board; Ontario Trillium Foundation; Ontario Power Authority Conservation Fund; Toronto Atmospheric Fund; Community Power Fund; Ontario Sustainable Energy Ass'n
Finances: *Funding Sources:* Donations
Activities: Community energy projects; interactive, hands-on education; Green City Bike Tours; Green Collar Career program; Our Power solar initiative; solar home tours; round table discussions; Bruce County wind energy co-operative project
Chief Officer(s):
David Cork, Managing Director, 416-977-5093 Ext. 2340
david@trec.on.ca
Mary Wagner, Manager, Finance, 416-977-5093 Ext. 2440
mary@trec.on.ca
Greg Goubko, Manager, Services, 416-977-5093 Ext. 2370
greg@trec.on.ca
Linda Varekamp, Manager, Operations & Communications, 416-977-5093 Ext. 2250
linda@trec.on.ca

Toronto Sheet Metal & Air Handling Group; Environmental Sheet Metal Association Toronto *See* Toronto Sheet Metal Contractors Association

Toronto Sheet Metal Contractors Association (TSMCA)
#26, 30 Wertheim Ct., Richmond Hill ON L4B 1B9
Tel: 905-886-9627; *Fax:* 905-886-9959
info@tsmca.org
www.tsmca.org
Previous Name: Toronto Sheet Metal & Air Handling Group; Environmental Sheet Metal Association Toronto
Overview: A medium-sized local organization
Mission: To address the needs of contractors involved in the manufacturing, installation, servicing, & maintenance of sheet metal work associated with air handling systems
Member of: Ontario Sheet Metal & Air Handling Group
Finances: *Annual Operating Budget:* $250,000-$500,000; *Funding Sources:* Collective Agreement Assessment
Staff Member(s): 5
Membership: 102 individuals
Chief Officer(s):
Darryl Stewart, Executive Director
dstewart@osmca.org

Toronto Sinfonietta
400 St. Clair Ave. East, Toronto ON M4T 1P5
Tel: 416-488-8057
info@torontosinfonietta.com
www.torontosinfonietta.com
www.facebook.com/147970791930326
Also Known As: Polish Canadian Society of Music
Overview: A small local charitable organization founded in 1990 overseen by Orchestras Canada
Affiliation(s): Oakham House Choir of Ryerson University
Chief Officer(s):
Matthew Jaskiewicz, Music Director, 416-763-8746
jaskiewicz@sympatico.ca

Toronto Soaring Club
ON
www.toronto-soaring.ca
www.facebook.com/TheTorontoSoaringClub
Overview: A small local organization
Member of: Soaring Association of Canada
Chief Officer(s):
David Cole, President
dmcole1212@gmail.com

Toronto Society of Model Engineers (TSME)
Toronto ON
tsmeexec@gmail.com
www.tsme.ca
Overview: A small local organization founded in 1933
Mission: To encourage the art & craft of model building in such areas as live steam locomotives, stationary engines, gas engines, ships, aircraft, clocks & models of all kinds
Membership: *Fees:* $35; *Member Profile:* Open to modellers, craftsmen & those with an interest in creating working models
Activities: Monthly meetings & special functions; participates in "Hobby Show" at International Centre in Nov.; *Library:* TSME Library; Not open to public

Awards:
• Herb Jordan Award

Toronto Sportsmen's Association (TSA)
#66, 2700 Dufferin St., Toronto ON M6B 4J3
Tel: 416-487-4477; *Fax:* 416-487-4478
info@torontosportsmens.ca
www.torontosportsmens.ca
Previous Name: Toronto Anglers
Overview: A small local organization founded in 1925
Mission: To promote fish restoration & conservation; to support outdoor enthusiasts in Toronto & Ontario.
Affiliation(s): Canadian Casting Federation; Ontario Fly & Bait Casting Association
Membership: *Fees:* Schedule available
Activities: Programs include archery, casting, handgun/rifle shooting & hunting groups; *Awareness Events:* Canadian Casting Championships

Toronto Symphony Orchestra (TSO)
#500, 145 Wellington St. West, Toronto ON M5J 1H8
Tel: 416-598-3375; *Fax:* 416-598-9522
contactus@tso.ca
www.tso.ca
www.facebook.com/torontosymphonyorchestra
twitter.com/TorontoSymphony
instagram.com/torontosymphony
Overview: A large local charitable organization founded in 1922 overseen by Orchestras Canada
Mission: To present concerts of both established & new music at the highest artistic standard possible, while recognizing audiences' needs; to play a role in the development of future musicians & audiences
Member of: Orchestras Canada
Finances: *Annual Operating Budget:* Greater than $5 Million; *Funding Sources:* Box office; Individual & corporate donations; Canada Council; Ontario Arts Council; City of Toronto
Staff Member(s): 38; 450 volunteer(s)
Membership: *Committees:* Volunteer; Young Leadership Council; Development and Donor Relations; Marketing; Finance; Patron Services
Activities: Performing concert series; Facilitating youth music education programs; *Awareness Events:* Mozart Festival; New Creations Festival; *Internships:* Yes *Library:* TSO Library; by appointment
Chief Officer(s):
Gary Hanson, Interim Chief Executive Officer
ghanson@tso.ca
Peter Oundjian, Music Director
Awards:
• TSYO Awards
Eligibility: TSYO member who demonstrates commitment to TSYO through leadership, attendance & punctuality, artistic excellence & professionalism *Contact:* Kendal Lander, klander@tso.ca

Toronto Symphony Youth Orchestra (TSYO)
212 King St. West, 6th Fl., Toronto ON M5H 1K5
Tel: 416-593-7769; *Fax:* 416-977-2912
www.tso.ca
www.facebook.com/TheTSYO
Overview: A small local charitable organization founded in 1974 overseen by Orchestras Canada
Mission: To provide a high-level orchestral experience for young musicians aged 22 and under; To encourage significant achievement for participants through education and performance
Member of: Orchestras Canada
Affiliation(s): Toronto Symphony Orchestra
Membership: *Member Profile:* Orchestral musicians 22 & under
Activities: Performing three full orchestra concerts per term; facilitating weekly rehearsals; Touring; *Library:* TSYO Library
Chief Officer(s):
Rachel Robbins, Manager, 416-593-7769 Ext. 372
rrobbins@tso.ca
Shalom Bard, Conductor
Awards:
• TSYO Awards
Eligibility: TSYO members who show an overall commitment to TSYO through good attendance & punctuality, leadership, professionalism, and artistic excellence *Contact:* Rachel Robbins, Manager, TSYO, Phone: 416-593-7769, ext. 372; Email: rrobbins@tso.ca

Toronto Theatre Alliance *See* Toronto Alliance for the Performing Arts

Canadian Associations / Toronto Transportation Society (TTS)

Toronto Training Board *See* Toronto Workforce Innovation Group

Toronto Transportation Society (TTS)
PO Box 5187, Stn. A, Toronto ON M5W 1N5
inquiries@torontotransportationsociety.org
www.torontotransportationsociety.org
Overview: A small local organization founded in 1973
Mission: To provide an association for persons interested in transportation by land, sea & air & to afford members facilities for discussion and exchange concerning these methods of transporation
Finances: Funding Sources: Membership fees
Membership: Fees: $30 Canadians; US$350 USA; $45-$50 international; *Member Profile:* Transportation enthusiasts with an interest in buses, streetcars, railways & subways
Activities: Hosting monthly meetings; Organizing a Memorabilia Night, featuring an auction of transit collections; Arranging charters using unique transit vehicles
Chief Officer(s):
Kevin Nichol, President
Richard Hooles, Vice-President
Robert Giles, Secretary
Robert Lubinski, Treasurer
Publications:
• Transfer Points [a publication of the Toronto Transport Society] *Type:* Newsletter; *Frequency:* 10 pa; *Editor:* Adam Zhelka; *Price:* Free with membership in the TorontoTransportation Society *Profile:* Transportation related news, historic articles, photographs & happenings in the Greater Toronto Area

Toronto Ukraina Sports Association
#75, 6 Point Rd., Toronto ON M8Z 2X3
Tel: 416-535-0681
postmaster@ukrainasports.com
www.ukrainasports.com
Overview: A small local organization founded in 1948
Mission: To promote an interest in sports among its members
Chief Officer(s):
Constantino Czoli, Contact
choli66@hotmail.com

Toronto Users Group for Power Systems
#850, 36 Toronto St., Toronto ON M5C 2C5
Tel: 905-607-2546
admin@tug.ca
www.tug.ca
www.facebook.com/TUG.Toronto
www.twitter.com/TUGPresident
Overview: A small local organization founded in 1985
Mission: To promote knowledge of IBM Power Systems
Finances: Funding Sources: Sponsorships
Membership: 350+ corporations
Activities: Hosting regular meetings for members
Chief Officer(s):
Léo Lefebvre, President
leo@tug.ca
Glenn Gundermann, Vice-President
ggundermann@tug.ca
Bob Lesiw, Vice-President
blesiw@gesco.ca
Jay Burford, Secretary
jburford@rogers.com
Kumar Rajendra, Treasurer
rajendra.kumar@aonbenfield.com
Publications:
• TUG [Toronto Users Group] Buzz
Type: Newsletter; *Price:* Free
Profile: Updates from the Toronto Users Group plus forthcoming events

Toronto Vegetarian Association (TVA)
17 Baldwin St., 2nd Fl., Toronto ON M5T 1L1
Tel: 416-544-9800
tva@veg.ca
www.veg.ca
www.facebook.com/torontoveg
twitter.com/torontoveg
instagram.com/torontoveg; pinterest.com/torontoveg
Overview: A small local charitable organization founded in 1945
Mission: To help Torontonians adopt & maintain a healthy, ethical & ecological vegetarian lifestyle
Member of: Vegetarian Union of North America; International Vegetarian Union
Finances: Annual Operating Budget: $100,000-$250,000; *Funding Sources:* Donations, advertising, exhibitor fees
Staff Member(s): 2; 300 volunteer(s)
Membership: 1,200; *Fees:* Donation min. $20
Activities: Awareness Events: Annual Vegetarian Food Festival, early Sept.; *Speaker Service:* Yes; *Library:* Resource Centre; Open to public
Chief Officer(s):
Diane Burgin, President & Treasurer

Toronto Women in Film & Television *See* Women in Film & Television - Toronto

Toronto Workforce Innovation Group (TWIG)
#350, 215 Spadina Ave., Toronto ON M5T 2C7
Tel: 416-934-1653; *Fax:* 416-934-1654
info@workforceinnovation.ca
www.workforceinnovation.ca
www.linkedin.com/groups?mostPopular=&gid=3160513
www.facebook.com/TOworkforce
twitter.com/TOworkforce
www.youtube.com/user/tworkforceinnovation
Previous Name: Toronto Training Board
Overview: A small local organization
Mission: To ensure that there are available workers for Toronto industries
Member of: Workforce Planning Ontario
Staff Member(s): 3
Chief Officer(s):
Karen Lior, Executive Director
karen@workforceinnovation.ca

Toronto Zoo
361A Old Finch Ave., Toronto ON M1B 5K7
Tel: 416-392-5929
www.torontozoo.com
www.facebook.com/TheTorontoZoo
Previous Name: Zoological Society of Metropolitan Toronto
Overview: A small local organization founded in 1969
Mission: To support the Toronto Zoo in its efforts to conserve species diversity through conservation, education, & research
Affiliation(s): Canadian Association of Zoos, Parks & Aquariums; American Association of Zoos, Parks & Aquariums; Canadian Centre for Philanthropy
Finances: Annual Operating Budget: $500,000-$1.5 Million; *Funding Sources:* Grants; Events; Corporate; Memberships; Bequests
Staff Member(s): 5; 45 volunteer(s)
Membership: 20,000; *Fees:* Schedule available; *Committees:* Executive; Finance; Sponsorship
Activities: Rents Mailing List: Yes
Chief Officer(s):
Raymond Cho, Chair
John Tracogna, Chief Executive Officer

Toronto's Hare Krishna Centre (ISKCON) / Subuddhi Deri Dasi
243 Avenue Rd., Toronto ON M5R 2J6
Tel: 416-922-5415; *Fax:* 416-922-1021
info@torontokrishna.com
iskcontoronto.blogspot.ca
twitter.com/TempleCouncil
Also Known As: ISKCON Toronto
Previous Name: International Society for Krishna Consciousness (Toronto Branch)
Overview: A medium-sized local charitable organization founded in 1966
Mission: To preach Krishna Consciousness around the world, following in the footsteps of the founder & spiritual master, His Divine Grace A.C. Bhaktivedanta Swami Prabhupada.
Finances: Annual Operating Budget: $3 Million-$5 Million; *Funding Sources:* Donations from congregations & festivals
Staff Member(s): 10; 20 volunteer(s)
Membership: 700 institutional; 2,000 individual; *Fees:* $1,100
Activities: Distribution of free food; taking care of seniors & youth; *Internships:* Yes; *Library:* Not open to public

The Toronto-Calcutta Foundation
2 Leland Ave., Toronto ON M8Z 2X5
www.toronto-calcutta.org
www.facebook.com/pages/Toronto-Calcutta-Foundation/191539797524369
twitter.com/torontocalc
www.youtube.com/user/TorCalFoundation#p/u
Overview: A small international charitable organization founded in 1988
Mission: To establish medical clinics for the improverished citizens of Calcutta, & of other cities of India; to establish schools for impoverished children in Calcutta, & in other cities of India; to protect animals & to provide for their welfare in Calcutta, & in other cities of India; to provide & to supervise developmental aid to alleviate the poverty of inhabitants of the provincial states in India, & of other countries of the Indian sub-continent
Membership: Fees: $25 regular; $100 five-year; $500 benefactor
Chief Officer(s):
Arun Palit, President
Tapan Mazumder, Secretary

Tottenham & District Horticultural Association
7563 Keennansville Rd., Tottenham ON L0G 1W0
Tel: 905-936-4711
www.gardenontario.org/site.php/tottenham
Also Known As: Tottenham Garden Club
Overview: A small local organization founded in 1974 overseen by Ontario Horticultural Association
Mission: To promote tree, shrub, & flower planting, community gardening, & outdoor beautification in Tottenham
Member of: Ontario Horticultural Association
50 volunteer(s)
Membership: 50; *Fees:* $15; *Committees:* Civic Beautification
Activities: Holding meetings on horticulture theory & practice; Organizing field trips, contests, & exhibitions; Disseminating horticultural information; Promoting therapeutic horticulture; Increasing awareness & interest in horticultural studies; Developing youth education & awareness efforts; *Awareness Events:* Plant & Bake Sale, May; Flower Shows; *Speaker Service:* Yes

Touch Football Ontario (TFO)
21 Bird Cres., Ajax ON L1S 5G3
Tel: 416-399-8792
Other Communication: touchfootballontario.wordpress.com
info@tfont.com
www.tfont.com
Overview: A medium-sized provincial organization
Mission: To organize touch football games among amateur teams in Ontario; to represent the sport within the province
Staff Member(s): 5
Membership: Member Profile: Touch football teams
Chief Officer(s):
Russ Henderson, President
president@tfont.com

Touchstones Nelson Museum of Art & History
502 Vernon St., Nelson BC V1L 4E7
Tel: 250-352-9813; *Fax:* 250-352-9810
info@touchstonesnelson.ca
www.touchstonesnelson.ca
www.facebook.com/touchstonesnelson
Previous Name: Nelson & District Museum, Archives, Art Gallery & Historical Society; Kootenay Museum Association & Historical Society
Overview: A small local charitable organization founded in 1955
Mission: To operate a community museum, archives, & public art gallery for Nelson & area
Member of: BC Museums Association; BC Historical Federation; Nelson & District Arts Council; Archives Association of BC; Heritage Federation of South Eastern BC
Affiliation(s): Canadian Museum Association; Nelson & District Chamber of Commerce
Finances: Funding Sources: Municipal & provincial government; donations; fundraising
Staff Member(s): 6
Membership: Fees: Schedule available
Activities: Art Gallery exhibitions; Historical exhibits; Public programs; *Library:* Nelson Museum Archives; Open to public
Chief Officer(s):
Astrid Heyerdahl, Executive Director
director@touchstonesnelson.ca

Tourette Syndrome Foundation of Canada (TSFC) / La Fondation canadienne du syndrome de Tourette
#245, 5955 Airport Rd., Mississauga ON L4V 1R9
Tel: 905-673-2255; *Fax:* 905-673-2638
Toll-Free: 800-361-3120
www.tourette.ca
www.youtube.com/TSFCanada
Also Known As: Tourette Canada
Overview: A large national charitable organization founded in 1976
Mission: To educate & increase public awareness about Tourette Syndrome
Member of: Canadian Brain Tissue Bank; Canadian Centre for Philanthropy; Volunteers Canada; Canadian Coalition for Genetic Fairness
Affiliation(s): Health Charities Council of Canada

Finances: *Funding Sources:* Membership dues; Fundraising programs & activities; Donations; Project funding
Membership: *Fees:* $45 individual; $65 family
Activities: *Awareness Events:* Trek for Tourette, March; *Speaker Service:* Yes; *Library:* Resource Centre; by appointment
Chief Officer(s):
Ramona Jennex, President
Awards:
• National Volunteer Awards
Meetings/Conferences:
• Tourette Syndrome Foundation of Canada 2018 National Conference, 2018
Scope: National
Publications:
• It's Your Move!
Type: Course
Profile: Personal development program aimed at helping youth with Tourette deal with their challenges
• Understanding Tourette Syndrome
Type: Handbook
Profile: Comprehensive information regarding Tourette Syndrome
• The Green Leaflet [a publication of the Tourette Syndrome Foundation of Canada]
Type: Newsletter; *Frequency:* 3 pa
• NewsFlash [a publication of the Tourette Syndrome Foundation of Canada]
Type: Newsletter
• Tourette Syndrome Foundation of Canada Annual Report
Type: Yearbook; *Frequency:* Annually
• Twitch Times [a publication of the Tourette Syndrome Foundation of Canada]
Type: Newsletter; *Frequency:* Monthly

Tourism Burlington
414 Locust St., Burlington ON L7S 1T7
Tel: 905-634-5594; *Fax:* 905-634-7220
Toll-Free: 877-499-9989
info@tourismburlington.com
www.tourismburlington.com
www.linkedin.com/groups?gid=4070362
www.facebook.com/TourismBurlington
twitter.com/burlingtontour
www.youtube.com/user/TourismBurlington
Also Known As: Burlington Visitor & Convention Bureau
Overview: A small local organization founded in 1988
Mission: To increase tourism, resulting in economic benefits through utilization of recreational, cultural, commercial & personal resources
Member of: Meeting Planners International; Tourism Industry Association of Canada
Finances: *Annual Operating Budget:* $250,000-$500,000; *Funding Sources:* Grants; co-op marketing; souvenir sales
Membership: *Committees:* Marketing
Activities: Tourism Awareness & Media Reception; Tourism Open House, June; *Library*
Chief Officer(s):
Pam Belgrade, Executive Director
Victor Szeverenyi, Chair
Awards:
• Tourism Ambassador Award

Tourism Calgary
#200, 238 - 11 Ave. SE, Calgary AB T2G 0X8
Tel: 403-263-8510; *Fax:* 403-262-3809
Toll-Free: 800-661-1678
www.visitcalgary.com
www.facebook.com/visitcalgary
twitter.com/calgary
www.instagram.com/tourismcalgary
Also Known As: Calgary Convention & Visitors Bureau
Previous Name: Calgary Tourist & Convention Bureau
Overview: A medium-sized local organization founded in 1957
Mission: A non-profit destination marketing organization, providing services to members to promote Calgary as a destination for travel industry professionals, as well as leisure & business travelers
Member of: Tourism Industry Association of Canada; Canadian Association of Convention & Visitor Bureaux; International Association of Convention & Visitors Bureaus; Western Association of Convention & Visitors Bureaus
Finances: *Annual Operating Budget:* $3 Million-$5 Million; *Funding Sources:* 46% public + 54% private
Staff Member(s): 32; 200 volunteer(s)
Membership: 600 institutional; 350 individual

Activities: White Hat Awards; Stampede Breakfast; Golf Tournament; *Library:* by appointment
Chief Officer(s):
Randy Williams, President & CEO

Tourism Canmore Kananaskis
PO Box 8608, #201, 802 8th St., Canmore AB T1W 2V3
Tel: 855-678-1295
www.tourismcanmore.com
www.facebook.com/TourismCanmore
twitter.com/TourismCanmore
Overview: A small local organization
Mission: To promote tourism in the Town of Canmore
Membership: *Fees:* Schedule available
Activities: *Awareness Events:* Canmore Nordic Festival, Nov.-Dec.

Tourism Cape Breton
PO Box 1448, Sydney NS B1P 6R7
Tel: 902-563-4636
Toll-Free: 888-562-9848
dcb@dcba.ca
www.cbisland.com
www.facebook.com/TourismCB
twitter.com/TourismCB
www.youtube.com/user/CBTourism
Previous Name: Cape Breton Tourist Association
Overview: A small local organization founded in 1996
Member of: Tourism Industry Association of Canada; Tourism Industry Association of Nova Scotia
Activities: Festivals & Events Line 1-888-562-9848 (May-Oct.)

Tourism Goderich
57 West St., Goderich ON N7A 2K5
Tel: 519-524-6600; *Fax:* 519-524-1466
Toll-Free: 800-280-7637
www.goderich.ca
Overview: A small local organization

Tourism Hamilton
The Lister Building, 28 James St. North, Ground Fl., Hamilton ON L8R 2K1
Tel: 905-546-2666; *Fax:* 905-546-2667
Toll-Free: 800-263-8590
tourism@hamilton.ca
www.tourismhamilton.com
www.facebook.com/TourismHamilton
twitter.com/tourismhamilton
www.youtube.com/user/HamiltonTourism
Previous Name: Greater Hamilton Tourism & Convention Services
Overview: A small local organization
Mission: To promote & increase the tourism & convention industries in Greater Hamilton
Member of: Tourism Industry Association of Canada; Canadian Society of Association Executives; Canadian Association of Visitor & Convention Bureaus; International Association of Visitor & Convention Bureaus
Staff Member(s): 12
Chief Officer(s):
Carrie Brooks-Joiner, Manager
carrie.brooks-joiner@hamilton.ca

Tourism Industry Association of British Columbia (TIABC)
#200, 948 Howe St., Vancouver BC V6Z 1N9
Tel: 604-685-5956
info@tiabc.ca
www.tiabc.ca
www.linkedin.com/company-beta/10019630
www.facebook.com/TourismIndustryAssociationBC
twitter.com/TIABC_CA
www.instagram.com/tiabc_ca
Also Known As: Tourism Industry Association of BC
Overview: A medium-sized provincial organization founded in 1991
Mission: To advocate for the interests of members to provincial & federal governments, businesses & media, in order to inform them of the opportunities & concerns of the tourism industry; To promote tourism in British Columbia
Staff Member(s): 4
Membership: *Member Profile:* Associations whose members are engaged in tourism-related services; *Committees:* Policy Development; Membership & Communications; Finance & Audit; Governance

Activities: Organizing a tourism industry conference; Preparing reports & strategies; Advising governments on tourism policy development; Chairing the the Air Issues Monitoring Consortium
Chief Officer(s):
Walt Judas, CEO, 778-953-0620
wjudas@tiabc.ca
Laura Plant, Manager, Communications & Membership Support, 778-788-3499
lplant@tiabc.ca

Tourism Industry Association of Canada (TIAC) / Association de l'industrie touristique du Canada (AITC)
#600, 116 Lisgar St., Ottawa ON K2P 0C2
Tel: 613-238-3883
info@tiac.travel
tiac-aitc.ca
www.facebook.com/TourismIndustryAssociationCanada
twitter.com/tiac_aitc
Overview: A large national organization founded in 1931
Mission: To enhance Canada's tourism industry by removing regulatory & legislative barriers to growth
Finances: *Annual Operating Budget:* $1.5 Million-$3 Million; *Funding Sources:* Membership dues
Staff Member(s): 15
Membership: 300 primary members; *Committees:* Policy; Conference; PTTIA; Rendez-Vous Canada
Activities: Talking with TIAC Forums; Issue Forum; Talking Tourism Symposium
Chief Officer(s):
Charlotte Bell, President & CEO, 613-238-8765
cbell@tiac-aitc.ca
Jennifer Taylor, Vice-President, Marketing & Member Relations, 902-698-0984
jtaylor@tiac-aitc.ca
Ken Ross, Vice-President, Events & Industry Services, 613-238-3885
kross@tiac-aitc.ca
Awards:
• Air Canada Business of the Year Award, TIAC Canadian Tourism Awards
Awarded to a tourism business that exemplifies industry best practices in operations
• VIA Rail Canada Community Outreach Award, TIAC Canadian Tourism Awards
Presented to the business or organization that makes the year's most notable contribution to devloping & enhancing social conditions in their community
• Metro Toronto Convention Centre Event of the Year Award, TIAC Canadian Tourism Awards
Awarded to an event that demonstrates best industry practices in its operations
• VISA Canada Innovator of the Year Award, TIAC Canadian Tourism Awards
Presented to the business or organization that develops the most innovative new tourism product that positively impacts the tourism industry as a whole
• Accor Hotels Marketing Campaign of the Year Award, TIAC Canadian Tourism Awards
Awarded to the organization that has implemented an outstanding tourism marketing initiative
• ITAC Aboriginal (Indigenous) Cultural Tourism Award, TIAC Canadian Tourism Awards
Awarded to recognize an Aboriginal tourism organization that demonstrates a commitment to the delivery of an authentic Aboriginal cultural tourism experience
• Diversey & Restaurants Canada Culinary Tourism Experience Award, TIAC Canadian Tourism Awards
• Hilton Worldwide Small or Medium-Sized Business of the Year Award, TIAC Canadian Tourism Awards
Presented to a tourism business with 20 employees or less that exemplifies industry best practices in its operations
• WestJet Social Media Initiative of the Year Award, TIAC Canadian Tourism Awards
Awarded to the tourism organization that has implemented an outstanding social media marketing campaign
• Transat Sustainable Tourism Award, TIAC Canadian Tourism Awards
Presented to an organization that has made a notable contribution to the practice of sustainable tourism in Canada
• Tourism HR Canada Employee of the Year Award, TIAC Canadian Tourism Awards
Awarded to a front-line employee who exemplifies professionalism, dedication, a positive attitude, & good quality of service

Canadian Associations / Tourism Industry Association of New Brunswick Inc. (TIANB) / Association de l'industrie touristique du Nouveau-Brunswick inc. (AITNB)

Tourism Industry Association of New Brunswick Inc. (TIANB) / Association de l'industrie touristique du Nouveau-Brunswick inc. (AITNB)
#440, 500 Beaverbrook Ct., Fredericton NB E3B 5X4
Tel: 506-458-5646; *Fax:* 506-459-3634
Toll-Free: 800-668-5313
info@tianb.com
www.tianb.com
www.facebook.com/tianb.aitnb
twitter.com/tianb_aitnb
Previous Name: Hospitality New Brunswick
Overview: A medium-sized provincial organization founded in 1978
Mission: To act as the provincial tourism & hospitality organization of New Brunswick, existing to fulfill the needs of its membership, in cooperation with both private & public sector partners; committed to be a representative, industry driven organization which provides leadership & direction, making tourism & hospitality the leading & most viably sustainable industry in New Brunswick
Member of: Tourism Industry Association of Canada; Hotel Association of Canada; Canadian Tourism Human Resource Council; Provincial Territorial Tourism Industry Association
Finances: *Annual Operating Budget:* $500,000-$1.5 Million
Staff Member(s): 10; 22 volunteer(s)
Membership: 600; *Fees:* Schedule available; *Member Profile:* Businesses having anything to do with the tourism industry in New Brunswick; *Committees:* Tourism strategy; National HR product quality; Emerit certification
Activities: Annual golf tournament, Sept.; *Awareness Events:* Annual meeting & conference, May; Provincial Tourism Awareness Week, June; *Library:* Open to public
Chief Officer(s):
Ron Drisdelle, Executive Director, 506-458-5646
Ron@tianb.com
Kathy Weir, President, 506-882-2349
Awards:
• TIANB Scholarship Program
• Business Recognition
• Pioneer Award

Tourism Industry Association of Nova Scotia (TIANS)
2089 Maitland St., Halifax NS B3K 2Z8
Tel: 902-423-4480; *Fax:* 902-422-0184
Toll-Free: 800-948-4267
information_central@tians.org
www.tians.org
www.facebook.com/tians.nsthrc
Overview: A medium-sized provincial organization founded in 1977
Mission: To lead, support, represent & enhance the Nova Scotia tourism industry
Member of: Tourism Industry Association of Canada; Canadian Tourism Human Resource Council
Affiliation(s): Innkeepers Guild of Nova Scotia; Adventure Tourism Association of Nova Scotia; Campground Owners Association of Nova Scotia; Metropolitan Area Tourism Association; Nova Scotia Bed & Breakfast Association
Finances: *Funding Sources:* Membership; projects
Staff Member(s): 11
Membership: *Fees:* Schedule available based on sales per year; *Member Profile:* Tourism industry services providers
Activities: Advocacy; Trend Applications; Long-term planning; seminars; Sustainable Tourism Project; NS Ecotourism Development Foundation; Standards & Certification; Tourism Careers for Youth; SuperHost Atlantic; It's Good Business; Accessible Service Nova Scotia; Discover Tourism Month; Career Awareness/Expos; Tourism/Hospitality Business Employment Inventory; festivals & events; *Internships:* Yes; *Speaker Service:* Yes; *Rents Mailing List:* Yes; *Library:* Business/Career Centre; Open to public
Chief Officer(s):
Darlene Grant Fiander, President
darlene@tourism.ca
Glenn Squires, Chair
James Miller, Secretary/Treasurer
Awards:
• Scholarship
Renewable for 2nd $1,000 based on performance awarded to Nova Scotia student choosing post-secondary tourism education; *Amount:* $1,000
• Scholarship
; *Amount:* $750

Tourism Industry Association of PEI (TIAPEI)
PO Box 2050, 25 Queen St., 3rd Fl., Charlottetown PE C1A 7N7
Tel: 902-566-5008; *Fax:* 902-368-3605
Toll-Free: 866-566-5008
webmaster@tiapei.pe.ca
www.tiapei.pe.ca
www.facebook.com/tiapei
twitter.com/tiapei
Overview: A small provincial organization
Mission: To represent tourism related businesses, associations, institutions, & individuals; to encourage tourism to & within PEI
Member of: Tourism Industry Association of Canada
Finances: *Annual Operating Budget:* $1.5 Million-$3 Million
Staff Member(s): 10
Activities: *Awareness Events:* Awards Gala & Tourism Conference (March); *Library:* Open to public
Chief Officer(s):
Kevin Mouflier, Chief Executive Officer
Meetings/Conferences:
• Tourism Industry Association of PEI 2018 Annual General Meeting, 2018

Tourism Industry Association of the NWT *See* Northwest Territories Tourism

Tourism Industry Association of the Yukon
#3, 1109 Front St., Whitehorse YT Y1A 5G4
Tel: 867-668-3331; *Fax:* 867-667-7379
info@tiayukon.com
www.tiayukon.com
www.facebook.com/232432356772503
Also Known As: TIA Yukon
Previous Name: Yukon Visitor's Association
Overview: A medium-sized provincial organization founded in 1972
Mission: To represent all sectors & businesses of the tourism industry in the Yukon; To encourage the increase & improvement of visitor facilities, services & attractions
Member of: Tourism Industry Association of Canada
Staff Member(s): 4
Membership: 270 corporate
Chief Officer(s):
Blake Rogers, Executive Director, 867-668-8021

Tourism Kelowna
#214, 1626 Richter St., Kelowna BC V1Y 2M3
Tel: 250-861-1515
Toll-Free: 800-663-4345
info@tourismkelowna.com
www.tourismkelowna.com
www.facebook.com/TourismKelowna
twitter.com/Tourism_Kelowna
www.youtube.com/user/TourismKelowna
Previous Name: Kelowna Visitor & Convention Bureau
Overview: A small local organization founded in 1990
Mission: To attract visitors by positioning Kelowna as a unique & diverse year-round destination for the benefit of our community
Staff Member(s): 13
Membership: *Member Profile:* Tourism businesses
Activities: Marketing & sales
Chief Officer(s):
Nancy Cameron, CEO
nancy@tourismkelowna.com

Tourism London
696 Wellington Rd. South, London ON N6C 4R2
Toll-Free: 800-265-2602
www.londontourism.ca
www.facebook.com/tourismlondon
twitter.com/tourism_london
www.youtube.com/tourismlondonontario
Overview: A small local organization founded in 1997
Mission: To promote London through co-operative partnerships as the tourism, sports tourism & meeting destination of choice resulting in positive economic impact on the city of London
Finances: *Funding Sources:* City of London; membership fees; co-op promotions; sponsorship
Activities: *Speaker Service:* Yes
Chief Officer(s):
Deb Harvey, President
dharvey@grandtheatre.com
Awards:
• Hotel & Food Services Scholarship
Location: Fanshawe College
• Tourism London Award

• Hospitality Scholarship
Location: Fanshawe College

Tourism Moncton / Tourisme Moncton
City Hall, City of Moncton, 655 Main St., Moncton NB E1C 1E8
Toll-Free: 800-363-4558
tourism@moncton.ca
tourism.moncton.ca
www.facebook.com/139158706094720
twitter.com/TourismMoncton
www.youtube.com/user/TourismMoncton;
flickr.com/photos/tourismmoncton
Overview: A small local organization
Mission: To position Moncton as the preferred visitor, convention & meeting destination in Atlantic Canada
Chief Officer(s):
Louise D'Amours, Manager, Destination Sales, 506-389-5913, Fax: 506-859-2629
louise.damours@moncton.ca

Tourism Nanaimo
104 Front St., Nanaimo BC V9R 5H7
Tel: 250-591-1551
Toll-Free: 800-663-7337
info@tourismnanaimo.com
tourismnanaimo.com
www.facebook.com/TourismNanaimo
twitter.com/TourismNanaimo
www.youtube.com/channel/UCNSBLKQoxvnLDliuzZ7T3Aw
Overview: A small local organization
Mission: To promote & enhance Nanaimo as a regional supply, service & accommodation base for the business & recreational traveller
Member of: Team Canada; American Bus Association; National Tour Association
Affiliation(s): Tourism Association of Vancouver Island; Tourism BC
Finances: *Funding Sources:* City of Nanaimo; provincial government; membership fees
Staff Member(s): 7
Activities: Destination marketing; operates city infocentre, convention sales; *Speaker Service:* Yes
Chief Officer(s):
Sasha Angus, CEO
sasha.angus@investnanaimo.com

Tourism Prince Albert
3700 - 2 Ave. West, Prince Albert SK S6W 1A2
Tel: 306-953-4385; *Fax:* 306-922-8687
Toll-Free: 877-868-7470
visitorpatourism@sasktel.net
www.princealberttourism.com
www.facebook.com/PrinceAlbertTourism
twitter.com/PAtourism
www.instagram.com/visitorpatourism
Previous Name: Prince Albert Tourism & Convention Bureau Inc.
Overview: A small local organization
Finances: *Annual Operating Budget:* $50,000-$100,000
Staff Member(s): 2
Membership: 1-99
Activities: *Library:* Open to public

Tourism Prince George
#101, 1300 - 1st Ave., Prince George BC V2L 2Y3
Tel: 250-562-3700; *Fax:* 250-564-9807
Toll-Free: 800-668-7646
tourismpg.com
www.facebook.com/tourismpg
twitter.com/TourismPG
www.youtube.com/user/TourismPrinceGeorge
Overview: A small provincial organization
Mission: To promote Prince George as a prime northern tourist destination; to help citizens & visitors in Prince George plan their vacations
Member of: Initiatives Prince George; Canadian Society of Association Executives; Canadian Sport Tourism Association
Affiliation(s): Northern BC Tourism Association; Yellowhead Highway Association
Finances: *Funding Sources:* Municipal government
Staff Member(s): 5
Chief Officer(s):
Erica Hummel, Chief Executive Officer, 250-649-3218
hummel@tourismpg.com

Tourism Red Deer (TRD)
#101, 4200 Hwy. 2, Red Deer AB T4N 1E3

Tel: 403-346-0180; *Fax:* 403-346-5081
info@tourismreddeer.net
www.tourismreddeer.net
www.facebook.com/tourismreddeer
twitter.com/VisitRedDeer
www.youtube.com/user/TourismRedDeer
Also Known As: Visit Red Deer
Overview: A small local organization founded in 1987
Mission: To develop & promote tourism in Red Deer in cooperation with industry partners
Member of: Tourism Industry Association of Canada; Canadian Association of Visitor & Convention Bureau
Finances: *Funding Sources:* City of Red Deer; membership dues; revenue from services & activities
Staff Member(s): 6
Membership: *Fees:* Schedule available; *Member Profile:* Interest in tourism industry in Red Deer
Chief Officer(s):
Liz Taylor, Executive Director
liz@tourismreddeer.com
RJ Steenstra, Chair
Awards:
• Red Hat Awards

Tourism Rockies *See* Kootenay Rockies Tourism

Tourism Saint John / Bureau de tourisme et de congrés de Saint John
PO Box 1971, Saint John NB E2L 4L1
Tel: 506-658-2990; *Fax:* 506-632-6118
Toll-Free: 866-463-8639
visitsj@saintjohn.ca
www.tourismsaintjohn.com
www.facebook.com/DiscoverSaintJohn
twitter.com/visitsaintjohn
www.youtube.com/user/discoversaintjohn
Previous Name: Saint John Visitor & Convention Bureau
Overview: A medium-sized local organization overseen by Tourism Industry Association of New Brunswick Inc.
Mission: To position Saint John as the premier all-season, visitor, meeting & event destination on New Brunswick's Bay of Fundy; to generate revenues & publicity for the city of Saint John & its tourism operators & businesses through increased visitation, service excellence & the provision of advice & partnering opportunities
Member of: Tourism Industry Association of Canada
Staff Member(s): 6
Membership: *Fees:* $75
Activities: Destination marketing & promotion
Chief Officer(s):
Ross Jefferson, Executive Director

Tourism Sarnia Lambton (TSL)
556 Christina St. North, Sarnia ON N7T 5W6
Tel: 519-336-3232; *Fax:* 519-336-3278
Toll-Free: 800-265-0316
info@tourismsarnialambton.com
www.tourismsarnialambton.com
www.facebook.com/tourismsarnialambton
www.youtube.com/user/VisitSarniaLambton?feature=watch
Previous Name: Convention & Visitors Bureau of Sarnia/Lambton
Overview: A small local organization founded in 2000
Mission: To promote tourism to Lambton County, creating economic value for the entire community
Member of: National Tour Association; American Bus Association; Ontario Motor Coach Association; Canadian Society of Association Executives
Finances: *Annual Operating Budget:* $500,000-$1.5 Million; *Funding Sources:* Municipal government; Chamber of Commerce; fundraising
Staff Member(s): 7; 100 volunteer(s)
Chief Officer(s):
Leona Allen, Office Administrator
Marlene Wood, General Manager
mwood@tourismsarnialambton.com

Tourism Saskatoon
#101, 202 Fourth Ave. North, Saskatoon SK S7K 0K1
Tel: 306-242-1206; *Fax:* 306-242-1955
Toll-Free: 800-567-2444
info@tourismsaskatoon.com
www.tourismsaskatoon.com
www.facebook.com/tourismsaskatoon
twitter.com/visitsaskatoon
www.instagram.com/visitsaskatoon
Also Known As: Saskatoon Visitor & Convention Bureau
Overview: A small local organization
Mission: To operate as Saskatoon's destination management organization, maximizing the economic benefit for Saskatoon through tourism
Member of: Tourism Industry Association of Canada
Affiliation(s): Tourism Saskatchewan
Finances: *Annual Operating Budget:* $500,000-$1.5 Million
Staff Member(s): 9; 20 volunteer(s)
Membership: 450+; *Fees:* $150-$1,400; *Member Profile:* All sectors in tourism industry
Chief Officer(s):
Todd Brandt, President & CEO
tbrandt@tourismsaskatoon.com

Tourism Simcoe County
Simcoe County Museum, 1151 Hwy. 26 West, Minesing ON L0L 1Y2
Toll-Free: 800-487-6642
tourism@simcoe.ca
discover.simcoe.ca
www.facebook.com/TourismSimcoeCounty
twitter.com/simcoecountytsc
Previous Name: Huronia Tourism Association
Overview: A small local organization founded in 1969
Mission: The association promotes & develops the tourism industry of Simcoe County & area.
Member of: Tourism Industry Association of Canada
Finances: *Funding Sources:* Membership dues; grants
Staff Member(s): 3
Membership: *Member Profile:* Tourism-based businesses
Activities: Brochure distribution program; border run program
Chief Officer(s):
Kathryn Stephenson, Manager, Tourism
kathryn.stephenson@simcoe.ca
Diana Coulson, Coordinator, Marketing & Communications
gayle.mckay@simcoe.ca

Tourism Stratford; Stratford & Area Visitors & Convention Bureau *See* Stratford Tourism Alliance

Tourism Thunder Bay
PO Box 800, 53 Water St. South, Thunder Bay ON P7C 5K4
Tel: 807-625-2564; *Fax:* 807-625-3789
Toll-Free: 800-667-8386; *TTY:* 807-622-2225
rtarnowski@thunderbay.ca
www.visitthunderbay.com
www.Facebook.com/visitthunderbay
twitter.com/visitthunderbay
Also Known As: City of Thunder Bay - Tourism Division
Previous Name: Thunder Bay Public Affairs - Visitors & Convention Department
Overview: A medium-sized local organization founded in 1970
Mission: To market Thunder Bay as a destination for individuals & groups
Member of: American Bus Association; National Tour Association
Finances: *Annual Operating Budget:* $500,000-$1.5 Million; *Funding Sources:* Municipality; Ontario Tourism
Staff Member(s): 5
Activities: Product development & training; visitor services; Marketing; Convention Services; *Awareness Events:* Doors Open Thunder Bay; Thunder Bay Children's Festival; Thunder Bay Blues Festival; *Internships:* Yes; *Speaker Service:* Yes
Chief Officer(s):
Paul Pepe, Tourism Manager, 807-625-3880
ppepe@thunderbay.ca
Rose Marie Tarnowski, Convention & Visitor Services Coordinator
rtarnowski@thunderbay.ca

Tourism Toronto (TCVA)
Toronto Convention & Visitors Association, PO Box 126, 207 Queen's Quay West, Toronto ON M5J 1A7
Tel: 416-203-2600; *Fax:* 416-203-6753
Toll-Free: 800-499-2514
Other Communication: hr@torcvb.com
toronto@torcvb.com
www.seetorontonow.com
www.facebook.com/visittoronto
twitter.com/seetorontonow
www.youtube.com/seetorontonow
www.instagram.com/seetorontonow
Also Known As: Toronto Convention & Visitors Association
Previous Name: Metropolitan Toronto Convention & Visitors Association
Overview: A large local organization founded in 1926
Mission: To promote Toronto as a convention & visitor destination; To position Toronto as one of the world's great cities & a year-round destination for leisure & business
Member of: Tourism Industry Association of Canada
Affiliation(s): International Association of Convention & Visitor Bureaux; Toronto Board of Trade; American Society of Association Executives
Finances: *Annual Operating Budget:* Greater than $5 Million
Staff Member(s): 65
Membership: 1,000; *Member Profile:* Located in or near Toronto; interested in accessing convention & visitor markets; *Committees:* Finance; Convention Services Council; Attractions Council; Public Relations; Marketing
Activities: *Internships:* Yes; *Speaker Service:* Yes; *Rents Mailing List:* Yes; *Library:* Information Centre; Open to public by appointment
Chief Officer(s):
Johanne R. Bélanger, President/CEO

Tourism Vancouver/Greater Vancouver Convention & Visitors Bureau
The Greater Vancouver Convention & Visitors Bureau, #210, 200 Burrard St., Vancouver BC V6C 3L6
Tel: 604-682-2222; *Fax:* 604-682-1717
VisitVancouver@tourismvancouver.com
www.tourismvancouver.com
www.facebook.com/insidevancouver
twitter.com/myvancouver
www.instagram.com/inside_vancouver
Overview: A large local organization founded in 1902
Mission: To lead the cooperative effort of positioning Greater Vancouver as a preferred travel destination in all targeted markets worldwide, thereby creating opportunities for member & community sharing of the resulting economic, environmental, social & cultural benefits
Member of: Tourism Industry Association of Canada; Council of Tourism Association of BC
Affiliation(s): Canadian Association of Convention & Visitors Bureaus
Finances: *Annual Operating Budget:* Greater than $5 Million
Staff Member(s): 80; 200 volunteer(s)
Membership: 1,000; *Fees:* $400+
Chief Officer(s):
Ty Speer, President/CEO
Dave Gazley, Vice-President, Meeting & Convention Sales, 604-631-2892
Ted Lee, CFO, 604-631-2807

Tourism Vernon
3004 39th Ave., Vernon BC V1T 3C3
Tel: 250-542-1415
Toll-Free: 800-665-0795
www.tourismvernon.com
www.facebook.com/Tourism.Vernon
twitter.com/tourismvernon
www.youtube.com/tourismvernon
Overview: A small local organization founded in 1991
Mission: To promote Vernon & the North Okanagan to the vacationing public
Affiliation(s): Greater Vernon Tourism Association
Finances: *Annual Operating Budget:* $100,000-$250,000
Staff Member(s): 2
Chief Officer(s):
Ange Chew, Manager, Tourism, 250-550-3649
achew@vernon.ca

Tourism Victoria/Greater Victoria Visitors & Convention Bureau
Administration Office, #200, 737 Yates St., Victoria BC V8W 1L6
Tel: 250-953-2033; *Fax:* 250-382-6539
Toll-Free: 800-663-3883
info@tourismvictoria.com
www.tourismvictoria.com
www.facebook.com/tourismvictoriafan
twitter.com/victoriavisitor
www.youtube.com/user/TourismVictoriaBC
Overview: A medium-sized local organization founded in 1974 overseen by Council of Tourism Associations of British Columbia
Mission: To oversee the development & promotion of the tourism industry in Greater Victoria
Member of: International Association of Convention & Visitors Bureaus
Finances: *Annual Operating Budget:* $3 Million-$5 Million; *Funding Sources:* Membership dues; government grants; fundraising; 2% hotel tax for external marketing

Membership: 750+; *Member Profile:* Must conform to municipal bylaws, applicable provincial & federal legislation; *Committees:* Sales & Marketing; Finance & Membership; Transportation
Activities: Marketing; convention sales & services; tour & travel; visitor services; tourism advocacy; *Speaker Service:* Yes; *Library*
Chief Officer(s):
Paul Nursey, President & CEO
Alan Paige, Vice-President, Strategy Management & CFO
Awards:
• Tourism Victoria Bursary

Tourism Windsor Essex Pelee Island
City Centre, #103, 333 Riverside Dr. West, Windsor ON N9A 5K4
Tel: 519-253-3616; *Fax:* 519-255-6192
Toll-Free: 800-265-3633
info@tourismwindsoressex.com
www.visitwindsoressex.com
www.facebook.com/visitwindsoressex
twitter.com/TWEPI
www.youtube.com/user/visitwindsoressex
Previous Name: Convention & Visitors Bureau of Windsor, Essex County & Pelee Island
Overview: A medium-sized local organization founded in 1980
Mission: To promote Windsor, Essex, Pelee Islnad as a tourist destination.
Member of: Tourism Industry Association of Canada; National Tour Association; American Bus Association
Staff Member(s): 14
Chief Officer(s):
Gordon Orr, Chief Executive Officer, 800-265-3633 Ext. 4334
gorr@tourismwindsoressex.com

Tourism Yorkton
PO Box 460, Yorkton SK S3N 2W4
Tel: 306-783-8707
tourismyorkton@sasktel.net
www.tourismyorkton.com
Overview: A small local organization founded in 1984
Mission: To promote, advance & encourage tourism, conventions, visitor & special events industry
Affiliation(s): Saskatchewan Tourism Authority
Activities: *Speaker Service:* Yes

Tourisme Abitibi-Témiscamingue
#100, 155, av Dallaire, Rouyn-Noranda QC J9X 4T3
Tél: 819-762-8181; *Téléc:* 819-762-5212
Ligne sans frais: 800-808-0706
info@tourisme-abitibi-temiscamingue.org
www.abitibi-temiscamingue-tourism.org
www.facebook.com/TourismeAbitibiTemiscamingue
twitter.com/tourismeAT
www.vimeo.com/atrat
Également appelé: Association touristique de l'Abitibi-Témiscamingue
Aperçu: *Dimension:* petite; *Envergure:* locale; Organisme sans but lucratif surveillé par Associations touristiques régionales associées du Québec
Mission: Promotion du tourisme en Abitibi-Témiscamingue
Membre de: ATR associées du Québec

Tourisme Baie-James (TBJ) / James Bay Tourism
CP 134, 1252, rte 167 sud, Chibougamau QC G8P 2K6
Tél: 418-748-8140; *Téléc:* 418-748-8150
Ligne sans frais: 888-748-8140
info@tourismebaiejames.com
www.tourismebaiejames.com
Aperçu: *Dimension:* petite; *Envergure:* locale; Organisme sans but lucratif surveillé par Associations touristiques régionales associées du Québec
Mission: Assure dans le cadre de ses responsabilités corporatives, des mandats en matière de concertation régionale, d'accueil, d'information, de signalisation, de promotion et de développement touristique
Finances: *Budget de fonctionnement annuel:* $250,000-$500,000
Membre(s) du personnel: 5; 11 bénévole(s)
Membre: 133; *Montant de la cotisation:* Barème
Membre(s) du bureau directeur:
Luc Letendre, Président

Tourisme Bas-Saint-Laurent
148, rue Fraser, 2e étage, Rivière-du-Loup QC G5R 1C8
Tél: 418-867-1272; *Téléc:* 418-867-3245
Ligne sans frais: 800-563-5268
info@bassaintlaurent.ca
bassaintlaurent.ca
www.facebook.com/tourismebassaintlaurent
Également appelé: Association touristique régionale du Bas-Saint-Laurent
Aperçu: *Dimension:* moyenne; *Envergure:* locale; Organisme sans but lucratif; fondée en 1978 surveillé par Associations touristiques régionales associées du Québec
Mission: Accueil, développement et promotion touristique
Finances: *Budget de fonctionnement annuel:* $500,000-$1.5 Million
Membre(s) du personnel: 8
Membre: 450; *Critères d'admissibilite:* Industrie touristique
Activités: *Stagiaires:* Oui
Membre(s) du bureau directeur:
Pierre Laplante, Directeur général
pierrelaplante@bassaintlaurent.ca

Tourisme Cantons-de-l'Est
20, rue Don-Bosco sud, Sherbrooke QC J1L 1W4
Tél: 819-820-2020; *Téléc:* 819-566-4445
Ligne sans frais: 800-355-5755
info@atrce.com
www.cantonsdelest.com
www.facebook.com/cantonsdelest
twitter.com/cantonsdelest
www.instagram.com/cantonsdelest
Également appelé: Association touristique des Cantons-de-l'Est
Aperçu: *Dimension:* moyenne; *Envergure:* locale; fondée en 1978 surveillé par Associations touristiques régionales associées du Québec
Mission: A pour mission de faire de la région des Cantons-de-l'Est une des meilleures destinations touristique du Québec en toutes saisons
Affiliation(s): Tourisme Québec
Finances: *Budget de fonctionnement annuel:* $3 Million-$5 Million; *Fonds:* Promotion coopérative
Membre(s) du personnel: 15
Membre: 525; *Montant de la cotisation:* 340$; *Comités:* Marketing; Club exportateur
Membre(s) du bureau directeur:
Alain Larouche, Directeur général
Francine Patenaude, Directrice, Marketing & développement

Tourisme Centre-du-Québec
20, boul Carignan ouest, Princeville QC G6L 4M4
Tél: 819-364-7177; *Téléc:* 819-364-2120
Ligne sans frais: 888-816-4007
info@tourismecentreduquebec.com
www.tourismecentreduquebec.com
www.linkedin.com/company/tourisme-centre-du-qu-bec
www.facebook.com/Tourismecentreduquebec
twitter.com/CentreduQuebec
www.youtube.com/TourismCentreduQc
Aperçu: *Dimension:* petite; *Envergure:* locale surveillé par Associations touristiques régionales associées du Québec
Membre(s) du personnel: 8
Membre(s) du bureau directeur:
Yves Zahra, Directeur général

Tourisme Chaudière-Appalaches (ATCA)
800, autoroute Jean-Lesage, Saint-Nicolas QC G7A 1E3
Tél: 418-831-4411; *Téléc:* 418-831-8442
Ligne sans frais: 888-831-4411
info@chaudiereappalaches.com
www.chaudiereappalaches.com
www.facebook.com/ChaudiereAppalaches
twitter.com/ChaudApp
Nom précédent: Association touristique Chaudière-Appalaches
Aperçu: *Dimension:* moyenne; *Envergure:* locale; Organisme sans but lucratif; fondée en 1976 surveillé par Associations touristiques régionales associées du Québec
Mission: Favoriser le développement et la promotion de l'industrie touristique de son territoire tout en contribuant à la réussite des entreprises qui en sont members
Finances: *Budget de fonctionnement annuel:* $500,000-$1.5 Million
Membre(s) du personnel: 10
Membre: 500; *Montant de la cotisation:* Barème
Activités: Promotion touristique
Membre(s) du bureau directeur:
Richard Moreau, Director général
rmoreau@chaudiereappalaches.com

Tourisme Côte-Nord
#304, 337, boul La Salle, Baie-Comeau QC G4Z 2Z1
Tél: 418-294-2876; *Téléc:* 418-294-2345
Ligne sans frais: 888-463-5913
info@cotenordqc.com
tourismecote-nord.com
Merged from: Association touristique régionale Manicouagan & Association touristique régionale de Duplessis
Aperçu: *Dimension:* moyenne; *Envergure:* locale; Organisme sans but lucratif; fondée en 1979 surveillé par Associations touristiques régionales associées du Québec
Mission: Regrouper efficacement, sur une base géographique et sectorielle, les diverses entreprises touristiques de la région; proposer un plan d'action annuel dans lequel sont déterminés les priorités, les programmes et les services offerts à ses membres
Finances: *Budget de fonctionnement annuel:* $250,000-$500,000
Membre(s) du personnel: 6
Membre: 220; *Comités:* Communication; Commercialisation
Membre(s) du bureau directeur:
Mario Leblanc, Directrice générale, 418-294-2876 Ext. 221
mleblanc@cotenordqc.com

Tourisme Gaspésie
1020, boul Jacques-Cartier, Mont-Joli QC G5H 0B1
Tél: 418-775-2223
Ligne sans frais: 877-775-2463
info@tourisme-gaspesie.com
www.tourisme-gaspesie.com
ca.linkedin.com/company/tourisme-gasp-sie
www.facebook.com/gaspesiejetaime
twitter.com/gaspesiejetaime
www.youtube.com/Gaspesiejetaime;
www.pinterest.com/gaspesiejetaime
Également appelé: Association touristique régionale de la Gaspésie
Aperçu: *Dimension:* moyenne; *Envergure:* locale; fondée en 1978 surveillé par Associations touristiques régionales associées du Québec
Mission: Orienter et favoriser la promotion, le développement et l'activité touristique dans le meilleur intérêt de la Gaspésie; promouvoir, organiser et coordonner divers programmes de promotion et de développement touristique ayant comme conséquence d'accroître la clientèle touristique et prolongation des séjours dans la Gaspésie
Membre de: Tourisme Québec
Finances: *Budget de fonctionnement annuel:* $500,000-$1.5 Million
Membre(s) du personnel: 7
Membre: 529
Membre(s) du bureau directeur:
Joëlle Ross, Directrice générale, 418-775-2223 Ext. 221

Tourisme Harricana *Voir* Maison du Tourisme

Tourisme Lanaudière
3568, rue Church, Rawdon QC J0K 1S0
Tél: 450-834-2535; *Téléc:* 450-834-8100
Ligne sans frais: 800-363-2788
info@lanaudiere.ca
www.lanaudiere.ca/fr
www.facebook.com/tourismelanaudiere
twitter.com/tourlanaud
www.instagram.com/tourismelanaudiere
Également appelé: Association touristique de Lanaudière
Aperçu: *Dimension:* moyenne; *Envergure:* locale; Organisme sans but lucratif; fondée en 1978 surveillé par Associations touristiques régionales associées du Québec
Mission: Faire la promotion, développement, commercialisation de l'offre touristiques de la région auprès des clientèles des différents marchés; Améliorer l'accueil & l'information touristique
Finances: *Budget de fonctionnement annuel:* $500,000-$1.5 Million
Membre(s) du personnel: 8
Membre: 360; *Montant de la cotisation:* Barème; *Critères d'admissibilité:* Organismes touristiques & municipalités
Activités: Développement et promotion touristique
Membre(s) du bureau directeur:
Évangéline Richard, Présidente

Tourisme Laurentides
14 142, rue de la Chapelle, Mirabel QC J7J 2C8
Tél: 450-436-8532; *Téléc:* 450-436-5309
Ligne sans frais: 800-561-6673
info-tourisme@laurentides.com
www.laurentides.com
www.facebook.com/TourismeLaurentides
twitter.com/TLaurentides
www.youtube.com/notredecor

Nom précédent: Association touristique des Laurentides
Aperçu: *Dimension:* moyenne; *Envergure:* locale; Organisme sans but lucratif; fondée en 1975 surveillé par Associations touristiques régionales associées du Québec
Mission: Unir tous les agents, corporations, corps publics et municipaux, associations et organismes, entreprises, oeuvrant dans le domaine touristique dans la région nord de Montréal; Orienter et favoriser le développement et l'activité touristique régionale dans le meilleur intérêt régional; Obtenir au nom de toute la région des interventions gouvernementales ou autres propres à favoriser son développement touristique
Membre de: Association de l'industrie touristique du Canada; National Tour Association
Finances: *Budget de fonctionnement annuel:* $1.5 Million-$3 Million
Membre(s) du personnel: 16
Membre: 752; *Montant de la cotisation:* 275$-2 900$; *Critères d'admissibilite:* Industrie touristique
Activités: Promotion et développement touristique régional; Service d'accueil; Information; Reservation

Tourisme Laval
480, promenade du Centropolis, Laval QC H7T 3C2
Tél: 450-682-5522; *Téléc:* 450-682-7304
info@tourismelaval.com
www.tourismelaval.com
www.facebook.com/tourismelaval
twitter.com/TourismeLaval
www.youtube.com/user/tourismelaval
Aperçu: *Dimension:* petite; *Envergure:* locale surveillé par Associations touristiques régionales associées du Québec
Mission: De promouvoir Laval comme destination touristique
Membre(s) du personnel: 11
Membre(s) du bureau directeur:
Geneviève Roy, Directrice générale
groy@tourismelaval.com
Yves Legault, Président
yves.legault@collegeletendre.qc.ca

Tourisme Mauricie
CP 100, Shawinigan QC G9N 8S1
Tél: 819-536-3334; *Téléc:* 819-536-3373
Ligne sans frais: 800-567-7603
info@tourismemauricie.com
www.tourismemauricie.com
www.facebook.com/tourismemauricie
twitter.com/mauricie
www.youtube.com/tourismemauricie
Également appelé: Association touristique régionale de la Mauricie
Aperçu: *Dimension:* moyenne; *Envergure:* locale; Organisme sans but lucratif; fondée en 1977 surveillé par Associations touristiques régionales associées du Québec
Mission: De promouvoir la ville de Maurice comme une destination touristique
Membre(s) du personnel: 11
Membre(s) du bureau directeur:
André Nollet, Directeur général
direction@tourismemauricie.com

Tourisme Moncton *See* Tourism Moncton

Tourisme Montérégie
#10, 8940, boul Leduc, Brossard QC J4Y 0G4
Tél: 450-466-4666; *Téléc:* 450-466-7999
Ligne sans frais: 866-469-0069
info@tourisme-monteregie.qc.ca
www.tourisme-monteregie.qc.ca
www.facebook.com/tourisme.monteregie
twitter.com/tourmonteregie
Également appelé: Association touristique régionale de la Montérégie
Aperçu: *Dimension:* moyenne; *Envergure:* locale; fondée en 1978 surveillé par Associations touristiques régionales associées du Québec
Finances: *Budget de fonctionnement annuel:* $1.5 Million-$3 Million
Membre(s) du personnel: 13
Membre: 378; *Comités:* Stratégique d'orientation marketing; Route des cidres; Route des vins; Cyclotourisme
Activités: *Stagiaires:* Oui; *Service de conférenciers:* Oui; *Listes de destinataires:* Oui
Membre(s) du bureau directeur:
Josée Juliener, Directrice générale
jjulien@tourisme-monteregie.qc.ca
François Trépanier, Directeur, Communications
ftrepanier@tourisme-monteregie.qc.ca

Tourisme Montréal/Office des congrès et du tourisme du Grand Montréal / Greater Montréal Convention & Tourism Bureau
CP 979, Montréal QC H3C 2W3
Tél: 514-873-2015; *Téléc:* 514-864-3838
Ligne sans frais: 877-266-5687
info@tourism-montreal.org
www.tourism-montreal.org
www.facebook.com/Montreal
twitter.com/montreal
www.youtube.com/user/TourismeMontreal
Également appelé: Tourisme Montréal
Aperçu: *Dimension:* moyenne; *Envergure:* locale; Organisme sans but lucratif; fondée en 1919 surveillé par Associations touristiques régionales associées du Québec
Mission: De promouvoir Montréal comme une destination touristique populaire
Membre de: Tourism Industry Association of Canada
Affiliation(s): Canadian Society of Association Executives
Membre: 750
Activités: *Stagiaires:* Oui; *Service de conférenciers:* Oui; *Bibliothèque*
Membre(s) du bureau directeur:
Yves Lalumière, Président et directeur général

Tourisme Ottawa *See* Ottawa Tourism

Tourisme Outaouais
103, rue Laurier, Gatineau QC J8X 3V8
Tél: 819-778-2222; *Téléc:* 819-778-7758
Ligne sans frais: 800-265-7822
info@tourisme-outaouais.ca
www.tourismeoutaouais.ca
www.facebook.com/tourismeoutaouais
twitter.com/TourOutaouais
www.youtube.com/tourismeoutaouais
Également appelé: Association touristique de l'Outaouais
Aperçu: *Dimension:* petite; *Envergure:* locale; fondée en 1981 surveillé par Associations touristiques régionales associées du Québec
Mission: Prospérité économique de la région par le développement et la promotion du produit touristique; structurer, organiser, orchestrer tout projet susceptible de générer des activités touristiques à retombées économiques importantes; assumer un accueil de qualité et une diffusion de l'information
Finances: *Budget de fonctionnement annuel:* $1.5 Million-$3 Million
Membre(s) du personnel: 22
Membre: 500; *Montant de la cotisation:* 150-1500; *Critères d'admissibilite:* Hébergement, plein air, restaurants, services professionnels, festivals, attractions touristiques
Activités: Gala des Grands Prix du Tourisme; *Evénements de sensibilisation:* Semaine Nationale du Tourisme
Membre(s) du bureau directeur:
France Bélisle, Directrice générale
fbelisle@tourisme-outaouais.ca

Tourisme Sherbrooke; Société de développement économique de la région sherbrookoise - Tourisme *Voir* Destination Sherbrooke

Tourisme Îles-de-la-Madeleine
128, ch Principal, Cap-aux-Meules QC G4T 1C5
Tél: 418-986-2245; *Téléc:* 418-986-2327
Ligne sans frais: 877-624-4437
info@tourismeilesdelamadeleine.com
www.tourismeilesdelamadeleine.com
www.facebook.com/tourismeilesdelamadeleine
twitter.com/ATRIM
www.youtube.com/TourismeIDM
Nom précédent: Association touristique des Iles-de-la-Madeleine
Aperçu: *Dimension:* moyenne; *Envergure:* locale surveillé par Associations touristiques régionales associées du Québec
Mission: Regrouper les entreprises de l'industrie touristique de l'archipel afin d'accroître les efforts de développement et de promotion
Finances: *Fonds:* Tourisme Québec
Activités: Salons consommateurs; bourses et foires professionnelles; tournées de presse; voyage de familiarisation; publicité; publication du guide touristique officiel et des brochures promotionnelles
Membre(s) du bureau directeur:
Michel Bonato, Directrice générale, 418-986-2245 Ext. 225
direction@tourismeilesdelamadeleine.com

Tournoi de Soccer de Victoriaville
CP 393, Victoriaville QC G6P 6T2
Tél: 819-752-2878
admin@soccervicto.com
www.soccervicto.com
Aperçu: *Dimension:* petite; *Envergure:* locale

Town of York Historical Society (TYHS)
260 Adelaide St. East, Toronto ON M5A 1N1
Tel: 416-865-1833; *Fax:* 416-865-9414
tfpo@total.net
www.townofyork.com
www.facebook.com/TOs1stPO
twitter.com/TOs1stPO
Also Known As: Toronto's First Post Office (TFPO)
Overview: A small local charitable organization founded in 1983
Mission: To research, interpret & promote the history of the Town of York & early Toronto, with emphasis on the role of postal service in communications of Upper Canada, & the surviving built environment
Member of: Ontario Museum Association; Canadian Museum Associations; Ontario Historical Society; Green Tourism Association; Attractions Ontario; Toronto Historical Association; Heritage Canada Foundation
Affiliation(s): La Société d'histoire de Toronto; Toronto Region, Architectural Conservancy; Cabbagetown Preservation Association
Finances: *Funding Sources:* Municipal & provincial government; postal retail outlet; donations; membership fees
Staff Member(s): 2
Membership: *Fees:* $25 single; $40 family; $250 life
Activities: Operates Toronto's First Post Office; exhibits; school tours; *Library:* Town of York Historical Association Library; by appointment
Chief Officer(s):
Janet Walters, Director/Curator, Toronto's First Post Office

Township of Clarence Minor Hockey Association (TCMHA)
PO Box 212, Clarence Creek AB K0A 1N0
clarencehockey.ca
Overview: A small local organization
Mission: To govern & promote minor hockey in Clarence
Chief Officer(s):
Linda Thompson, President
castorpresident@gmail.com

Townshippers' Association (TA) / Association des Townshippers
#100, 257, rue Queen, Sherbrooke QC J1M 1K7
Tel: 819-566-5717
Toll-Free: 866-566-5717
ta@townshippers.org
www.townshippers.qc.ca
twitter.com/townshippersTA
Overview: A medium-sized local organization founded in 1979
Mission: To promote the interests of the English-speaking community in the historical Eastern Townships; To strengthen the cultural identity of this community; To encourage the full participation of the English-speaking population in the community at large
Member of: Québec Community Groups Network; Québec Anglophone Heritage Network; Community Health & Social Services Network
Finances: *Annual Operating Budget:* $250,000-$500,000; *Funding Sources:* Canadian Heritage; membership fees; donations; diverse grants
Staff Member(s): 9; 100 volunteer(s)
Membership: 4,000; *Fees:* $15 individual; $25 family; $100 lifetime; *Member Profile:* English speakers in the historical Eastern Townships; *Committees:* Communications; Health & Social Services; Community & Culture; Membership; Townshippers of Tomorrow; Knowledge Base
Activities: *Awareness Events:* Townshippers' Day, Sept.; Outstanding Townshippers Banquet & AGM, June *Library:* Resource Centre; Open to public
Chief Officer(s):
Gerald Cutting, President
Rachel Hunting, Executive Director
Awards:
- Outstanding Townshippers Awards
- Townships Leaders of Tomorrow Awards

   Lac-Brome Office
   #3, 584, rue Knowlton, Lac-Brome QC J0E 1V0
   Tel: 450-242-4421; *Fax:* 450-242-5870
   Toll-Free: 877-242-4421

Toxics Watch Society of Alberta (TWS)
1-6328A - 104 St. NW, Edmonton AB T6H 2K9
Tel: 780-439-1912
www.toxwatch.ca
Overview: A small provincial organization founded in 1986
Mission: To promote reduction in the common use of toxic substances & zero discharge of toxic wastes; to ensure clean air & water & safe food for Albertans; to facilitate sustainable communities & environmental citizenship
Member of: Alberta Environmental Network; Canadian Environmental Network
Affiliation(s): Environmental Resource Centre; Tomorrow Foundation for a Sustainable Future
Activities: Public Information Service; *Library:* Resource Library; Open to public

T.P.U.G.
258 Lake Promenade, Toronto ON M8W 1B3
info@tpug.ca
www.tpug.ca
www.facebook.com/torontopetusersgroup
Also Known As: Toronto PET Users Group Inc.
Overview: A small local organization founded in 1978
Mission: To promote the effective use of Commodore computers
Finances: *Annual Operating Budget:* Less than $50,000
Membership: *Fees:* $15; *Member Profile:* Users of Commodore machines & operating systems

Trade Facilitation Office Canada / Bureau de promotion du commerce Canada
#300, 56 Sparks St., Ottawa ON K1P 5A9
Tel: 613-233-3925; *Fax:* 613-233-7860
Toll-Free: 800-267-9674
info@tfocanada.ca
www.tfocanada.ca
www.linkedin.com/company/tfo-canada
twitter.com/TFOcan
Also Known As: TFO Canada
Overview: A small international organization founded in 1980
Mission: To help improve the economic well-being of developing countries through increased integration into the global economy
Finances: *Funding Sources:* Government; international development agencies; private
Staff Member(s): 10; 2 volunteer(s)
Membership: 1-99
Activities: Provides free assistance to exporters from developing countries to find markets in Canada & to importers who wish to locate new sources of products from over 120 countries; provides training & related assistance in export marketing, trade policy & investment prospecting to developing & transition countries on a fee-for-service basis; *Internships:* Yes; *Speaker Service:* Yes
Chief Officer(s):
Brian Mitchell, Executive Director, 613-233-3925 Ext. 31

Traditional Archers Association of Nova Scotia
PO Box 353, Musquodoboit Harbour NS B0J 2L0
Overview: A small provincial organization
Mission: To support & promote archery in Nova Scotia
Chief Officer(s):
Roy MacInnis, Contact
roy.macinnis+TAANS@gmail.com

Traffic Injury Research Foundation (TIRF) / Fondation de recherches sur les blessures de la route
#200, 171 Nepean St., Ottawa ON K2P 0B4
Tel: 613-238-5235; *Fax:* 613-238-5292
Toll-Free: 877-238-5235
tirf@tirf.ca
www.tirf.ca
www.facebook.com/tirfcanada
twitter.com/tirfcanada
Overview: A medium-sized national charitable organization founded in 1964
Mission: To reduce traffic related deaths & injuries, through the design, promotion & implementation of prevention programs & policies based on sound research
Finances: *Annual Operating Budget:* $500,000-$1.5 Million; *Funding Sources:* Memberships; donations
Staff Member(s): 11
Membership: 100 corporate + 125 individual
Activities: Projects include: Distracted Driving; Drinking & Driving; Trends & Statistics; Trucks; Young & Novice Drivers; *Speaker Service:* Yes; *Library:* Resource Centre; Open to public
Chief Officer(s):
Robyn D. Robertson, President & CEO
Karen Bowman, Director, Marketing & Communications

Trager Canada
PO Box 28079, 1795 Henderson Hwy., Winnipeg MB R2G 4E9
Tel: 204-396-4747
Toll-Free: 888-724-3788
admin@trager.ca
www.trager.ca
Previous Name: Trager Practitioners of S. Central Ontario
Overview: A small national licensing organization founded in 1981
Mission: To support & encourage the expanding practice of the Trager Approach & Mentastics movement re-education in Canada
Member of: Trager International
Finances: *Annual Operating Budget:* Less than $50,000
Membership: 75; *Fees:* $225; *Member Profile:* Certified practitioners of Trager Psychophysical Integration & students
Activities: Provides information about Trager bodywork/movement education; referrals; *Speaker Service:* Yes

Trager Practitioners of S. Central Ontario *See* Trager Canada

Trail & District Chamber of Commerce
#200, 1199 Bay Ave., Trail BC V1R 4A4
Tel: 250-368-3144; *Fax:* 250-368-6427
www.trailchamber.bc.ca
Overview: A small local organization
Mission: To provide leadership in the growth of a progressive & financially strong community, by assisting members in improving their competitiveness
Member of: British Columbia Chamber of Commerce; British Columbia Rockies Tourist Association; Better Business Bureau
Finances: *Annual Operating Budget:* $100,000-$250,000; *Funding Sources:* Fee for service
Staff Member(s): 2
Membership: 210; *Fees:* Schedule available; *Member Profile:* Local businesses in Trail, British Columbia & the surrounding area; *Committees:* Membership; Greater Trail Community Events & Promotions; Special Events
Activities: Organizing business events & a trade show; *Library:* Open to public
Chief Officer(s):
Audry Durham, Executive Director

Trail & Ultra Running Association Of The Yukon (TURAY)
4061 - 4th Ave., Whitehorse YT Y1A 1H1
Tel: 867-668-4236; *Fax:* 867-667-4237
sportyukon.com
Overview: A small provincial organization
Chief Officer(s):
Nancy Thomson, President
nancy.thomson@cbc.ca

Trail Association for Community Living
PO Box 131, 1565B Bay Ave., Trail BC V1R 4L3
Tel: 250-368-3503; *Fax:* 250-368-5559
tacl@telus.net
www.taclkootenays.com
Overview: A small local organization
Mission: To help & support people with developmental disabilities, providing them with a higher quality of life
Member of: Kootenay Society for Community Living
Staff Member(s): 5
Membership: *Fees:* Schedule available
Chief Officer(s):
Nancy Gurr, Executive Director

Trail Riders of the Canadian Rockies
PO Box 6742, Stn. D, Calgary AB T2P 2E6
Tel: 403-874-4408
admin@trail-rides.ca
trailridevacations.com
www.facebook.com/189174017824540
Overview: A small national organization founded in 1923
Mission: To encourage travel on horseback through the Canadian Rockies; to foster the maintenance & improvement of old trails & the building of new trails; to promote good fellowship among those who visit & live in the Canadian Rockies; to encourage the appreciation of outdoor life & the study & conservation of mountain ecology; to assist in every way possible to ensure the preservation of the National Parks of Canada for the use & enjoyment of the public; to cooperate with other organizations with similar aims
Finances: *Funding Sources:* Ride sales; membership fees

Membership: *Fees:* $35
Chief Officer(s):
Robert Vanderzweerde, Secretary-Treasurer

Trail Riding Alberta Conference (TRAC)
PO Box 44, RR#4, Site 5, Lacombe AB T4L 2N4
Tel: 403-782-7363
office@trailriding.ca
www.trailriding.ca
www.facebook.com/299797026778773
Overview: A small provincial organization
Mission: To promote long-distance horse riding
Affiliation(s): Canadian Long Distance Riding Association
Finances: *Funding Sources:* Fundraising; membership fees; ride fees
Membership: 166
Activities: Three divisions: novice, intermediate & open; three categories within each: junior, lightweight & heavyweight.; *Speaker Service:* Yes; *Library:* Long Distance Info; Open to public
Chief Officer(s):
Ken Vanderwekken, President
Publications:
• Trail Riding Alberta Conference Handbook
Type: Guide

La Trame
CP 845, Succ. Desjardins, Montréal QC H5B 1B9
Tél: 514-374-0227
la.trame@hotmail.com
la-trame.ca
Aperçu: *Dimension:* petite; *Envergure:* locale
Mission: Regroupement pour lesbiennes dans le domaine des arts, de la culture et du loisir
Membre: *Montant de la cotisation:* 20$
Activités: Rencontres, expositions, sorties
Membre(s) du bureau directeur:
Mireille Robillard, Contact

Trans Canada Trail Foundation (TCTF) / Fondation du sentier transcanadian
#300, 321, rue de la Commune ouest, Montréal QC H2Y 2E1
Tel: 514-485-3959; *Fax:* 514-485-4541
Toll-Free: 800-465-3636
info@tctrail.ca
www.tctrail.ca
www.linkedin.com/company/trans-canada-trail
www.facebook.com/transcanadatrail
twitter.com/TCTrail
www.youtube.com/user/TheTransCanadaTrail
Overview: A medium-sized national charitable organization founded in 1992
Mission: To promote & coordinate the planning, designing & building of a continuous, shared-use recreation trail that winds its way through every Province & Territory
Finances: *Annual Operating Budget:* $250,000-$500,000; *Funding Sources:* Public donations
Staff Member(s): 11; 1 volunteer(s)
Membership: 2,500; *Fees:* $75-150
Activities: Trail-building; trail locators & signage; guidebooks & maps
Chief Officer(s):
Jane Murphy, National Director of Trail, 800-465-3636 Ext. 4355
jmurphy@tctrail.ca
Gay Decker, Director of Communications, 800-465-3636 Ext. 4350
gdecker@tctrail.ca
Amparo Jardine, Director of Development, 800-465-3636 Ext. 4349
AJardine@tctrail.ca

Trans Canada Yellowhead Highway Association (TCYHA)
77 Airport Rd., Edmonton AB T5G 0W6
Tel: 780-761-3800
members@yellowheadit.com
www.transcanadayellowhead.com
Previous Name: Yellowhead Highway Association
Overview: A small local organization founded in 1947
Mission: To improve highway infrastructure & promote tourism along the TransCanada/Yellowhead highway corridor
Finances: *Annual Operating Budget:* $100,000-$250,000
Staff Member(s): 3; 1 volunteer(s)
Membership: 390; *Member Profile:* Municipal, commercial, & corporate organizations & individuals; *Committees:* Marketing; Resources
Chief Officer(s):

Loranne Martin, President

Trans-Canada Advertising Agency Network (T-CAAN)
#300, 25 Sheppard Ave. West, Toronto ON M2N 6S6
Tel: 416-221-6984; *Fax:* 416-221-8260
bill@waginc.ca
www.tcaan.ca
Also Known As: T-CAAN
Overview: A medium-sized national organization founded in 1963
Mission: To serve & support its members in every type of marketing & communications endeavour; Focuses on advertising, communications, & marketing
Affiliation(s): Intermarket Agency Network (IAN)
Finances: *Annual Operating Budget:* Less than $50,000; *Funding Sources:* Membership fees
Membership: 24 corporate; *Fees:* $2000; *Member Profile:* Advertising agencies
Chief Officer(s):
Bill Whitehead, Managing Director
Meetings/Conferences:
• Trans-Canada Advertising Agency Network 56th Annual Conference, 2018
Scope: National
Publications:
• E-Tattler
Frequency: bi-monthly; *Editor:* Phil Chant
Profile: For members only

Trans-Himalayan Aid Society (TRAS)
#720, 999 West Broadway, Vancouver BC V5Z 1K5
Tel: 604-224-5133; *Fax:* 604-738-4080
tras@portal.ca
www.tras.ca
Overview: A small international organization founded in 1962
Mission: To help the people of the Himalayas to help themselves; to aid in poverty alleviation by giving basic health care, education for employment, skills, tools & basic inputs for agricultural development; to promote environmentally sound development by fostering understanding for conservation & ecologically sustainable development; to foster & strengthen the links between Canadians & the people of the Himalayas through non-government agencies
Staff Member(s): 1; 300 volunteer(s)
Membership: 375; *Fees:* $20
Chief Officer(s):
Armila C. Shakya, Office Manager

Transition House Association of Nova Scotia (THANS)
#215, 2099 Gottingen St., Halifax NS B3K 3B2
Tel: 902-429-7287; *Fax:* 902-429-0561
coordinator@thans.ca
www.thans.ca
www.facebook.com/transitionhouseassociationns
twitter.com/thans_ns
Overview: A medium-sized provincial organization founded in 1978
Mission: To provide transitional services to women (and their children) who are experiencing violence & abuse, including culturally relevant services to Mi'kmaw people
Chief Officer(s):
Pamela Harrison, Provincial Coordinator

Transitions
#100, 365 Carleton Dr., St Albert AB T8N 7L1
Tel: 780-458-7371; *Fax:* 780-460-7078
info@transitions-ab.org
www.transitions-ab.org
www.facebook.com/transitions.stalbert
twitter.com/Transitions_ab
Previous Name: Transitions Rehabilitation Association of St. Albert & District; St. Albert Association for People with Disabilities
Overview: A small local organization founded in 1978
Mission: To offer support services to individuals with developmental delays & disabilities of all ages & their families in St. Albert, Sturgeon County & Northwest Edmonton
Staff Member(s): 225
Activities: *Awareness Events:* Jump Start, Jan.; Roy Financial Mayor's Walk for Charity
Chief Officer(s):
Jim Dawson, President
Paul Fujishige, Executive Director

Transitions Rehabilitation Association of St. Albert & District; St. Albert Association for People with Disabilities
See Transitions

The Transplantation Society (TTS)
International Headquarters, #1401, 505, boul René-Lévesque ouest, Montréal QC H2Z 1Y7
Tel: 514-874-1717; *Fax:* 514-874-1716
info@tts.org
www.tts.org
Overview: A medium-sized international organization
Mission: To provide global leadership in transplantation; To develop the science & clinical practice
Membership: *Committees:* Education; Ethics; Finance; Journals; Medawar Prize; Membership; Section Presidents Liaison; Transplantation Science; Women in Transplantation
Activities: Providing continuing education; Offering guidance on the ethical practice
Chief Officer(s):
Nancy L. Ascher, President
Marcelo Cantarovich, Vice-President
Elmi Muller, Senior Treasurer
Jean-Pierre Mongeau, Executive Director
jp.mongeau@tts.org
Robert Colarusso, Director, Technologies
technologies@tts.org
Geneviève Leclerc, Director, Meetings
genevieve.leclerc@tts.org
Eugenia Siu, Coordinator, Registration & Administration
eugenia.siu@tts.org
Meetings/Conferences:
• 27th International Congress of The Transplantation Society 2018, 2018, Madrid
Scope: International
Publications:
• Transplantation: The Official Journal of The Transplantation Society
Type: Journal; *Frequency:* Semimonthly
Profile: Advances in transplantation, in areas such as cell therapy & islet transplantation, clinical transplantation, experimental transplantation,immunobiology & genomics, & xenotransplantation
• Tribune [a publication of The Transplantation Society]
Type: Newsletter; *Frequency:* 3 pa; *Editor:* Nancy K. Man
Profile: Society news, meeting reviews, & feature articles

Transport 2000 Canada *See* Transport Action Canada

Transport Action Canada
PO Box 858, Stn. B, #303, 211 Bronson Ave., Ottawa ON K1P 5P9
Tel: 613-594-3290; *Fax:* 613-594-3271
info@transport-action.ca
www.transport-action.ca
www.facebook.com/TransportAction/
twitter.com/transportaction
Previous Name: Transport 2000 Canada
Overview: A large national charitable organization founded in 1977
Mission: To seek sound public transportation policies, practices & services, especially modernized, intercity passenger rail and urban transit option; To inform Canadians of the need for a coherent national transport policy that recognizes conservation of resources must be a priority & access to good public transportation is a right of all Canadians; To press for the coordination of all transport services for the benefit of users; To maximize the use of the energy-efficient rail & marine modes for the shipment of freight
Affiliation(s): Transport 2000 International
Finances: *Annual Operating Budget:* $50,000-$100,000; *Funding Sources:* Donations
15 volunteer(s)
Membership: 1,500; *Fees:* $30
Activities: Research, public education & advocacy, representation of the consumer interests before federal, provincial, municipal public hearings & regulatory bodies, direction of consumer complaints to public carriers; *Speaker Service:* Yes; *Library:* Transport Action Canada Library; Open to public
Chief Officer(s):
Bruce Budd, President
Justin Bur, VP East
Peter Lacey, VP West
Tony Turrittin, Secretary
Klaus Beltzner, Treasurer
Bert Titcomb, Manager

Meetings/Conferences:
• Transport Action Canada 2018 Annual General Meeting, 2018
Publications:
• National Transport Newsletter [a publication of Transport Action Canada]
Type: Newsletter; *Frequency:* 4 pa; *Number of Pages:* 8; *Price:* Free Download
Profile: Includes news, information and updates relevant to the Canadian transport sector

Transportation Association of Canada (TAC) / Association des transports du Canada (ATC)
#401, 1111 Prince of Wales Dr., Ottawa ON K2C 3T2
Tel: 613-736-1350; *Fax:* 613-736-1395
Other Communication: services@tac-atc.ca
secretariat@tac-atc.ca
www.tac-atc.ca
www.linkedin.com/company/transportation-association-of-canada
www.facebook.com/tac2014atc
twitter.com/TAC_TranspAssn
Previous Name: Canadian Good Roads Association; Roads & Transportation Association of Canada
Overview: A large national organization founded in 1914
Mission: To promote the provision of safe, efficient, effective & environmentally sustainable transportation services in support of Canada's social & economic goals; To act as a neutral forum for the discussion of transportation issues & matters; To act as a technical focus in the highway transportation area
Finances: *Annual Operating Budget:* Greater than $5 Million; *Funding Sources:* Membership dues
Staff Member(s): 18; 800 volunteer(s)
Membership: 500+ corporate; *Fees:* Schedule available; *Member Profile:* Federal, provincial & territorial departments of transportation; municipalities; private sector firms; academic institutions & associations; *Committees:* Chief Engineers' Council; Education & Human Resources Development Council; Environment Council; Integrated Committee on Climate Change; Operating Information; Urban Transportation Council; World Road Association; Small Municipalities Task Force
Activities: *Library:* Transportation Information Services; by appointment
Chief Officer(s):
Sarah Wells, Executive Director, 613-736-1350 Ext. 229
swells@tac-atc.ca
Janet Wlodarczyk, Director, Finance & Administration, 613-736-1350 Ext. 254
mperuvemba@tac-atc.ca
Sandra Majkic, Director, Technical Programs, 613-736-1350 Ext. 228
smajkic@tac-atc.ca
Erica Andersen, Director, Member Services & Communications, 613-736-1350 Ext. 235
eandersen@tac-atc.ca
Awards:
• TAC Member Recognition Awards
Awarded annually to recognize contributions made by TAC members
• TAC Volunteer Recognition Awards
Awarded annually to recognize contributions made by TAC volunteers
• TAC Technical Excellence Awards
Awarded annually to recognize technical excellence among membership; categories include: Educational Achievement, Environmental Achievement, Road Safety Engineering & Sustainable Urban Transportation
• Canadian Transportation Awards Program (CTAP)
Transportation Person of the Year; Award of Excellence; Award of Achievement; Award of Academic Merit
• TAC Scholarships Program
TAC offers scholarships for graduate, undergraduate and college/CEGEP students
Meetings/Conferences:
• Transportation Association of Canada 2018 Conference & Exhibition, September, 2018, Saskatoon, SK
Scope: National
Description: Theme: "Innovation & Technology: Evolving Transportation"
Publications:
• Transportation Association of Canada Year in Review
Type: Report; *Frequency:* a.; *Number of Pages:* 15; *Price:* Free download
Profile: Provides information, news & a summary of events relevant to Canada's transportation sector

Trappers Association of Nova Scotia
355 Meister Rd., RR#2, New Ross NS B0J 2M0
info@trappersassociationofnovascotia.ca
www.trappersassociationofnovascotia.ca
Overview: A small provincial organization
Mission: To promote responsible trapping & fur harvesting
Membership: Fees: $20
Activities: Organizing educational resources, workshops, & forums on trapping
Chief Officer(s):
Gary Fisher, President
Meetings/Conferences:
• Trappers Association of Nova Scotia 2018 Annual Workshop & Convention, 2018
Scope: Provincial

Trauma Association of Canada (TAC) / Association canadienne de traumatologie
PO Box 8862, Halifax NS B3K 5M5
Fax: 902-850-2289
Toll-Free: 855-403-5463
info@traumacanada.org
www.traumacanada.org
twitter.com/TraumaCanada
Overview: A small national organization founded in 1984
Mission: To promote the highest standards of care for the injured patient; To encourage research & education related to trauma
Member of: Royal College of Physicians & Surgeons of Canada
Membership: Fees: $50 Canadian affiliate; $125 internaltional affiliate/member; Member Profile: Physicians; Surgeons; Allied health care professionals; Canadian community; Committees: Canadian Forces Medical Liason; Education; Guidelines; Injury Prevention/Surveillance; International Issues/Disasters; Nomination; Pediatrics; Publication; Research; Scientific Programme
Activities: Engaging in advocacy activities; Facilitating professional & community education in the field of injury prevention; Participating in community disaster response planning; Developing & maintaining a National Trauma Registry; Establishing guidelines for Trauma Centres
Chief Officer(s):
Paula Poirier, President
president@traumacanada.org
Tracey Taulu, Secretary
director2.secretary@traumacanada.org
Morad Hameed, Treasurer
director1.treasurer@traumacanada.org
Kate Mahon, Executive Director
exec.director@traumacanada.org
Meetings/Conferences:
• Trauma 2018, February, 2018, Hilton Toronto, Toronto, ON
Scope: National
Publications:
• Trauma Association of Canada Newsletter
Type: Newsletter; Frequency: Semiannually

Travel and Tourism Research Association (Canada Chapter) (TTRA)
#600, 116 Lisgar St., Ottawa ON K2P 0C2
Tel: 613-238-6378
info@ttracanada.org
www.ttracanada.ca
Overview: A medium-sized international organization founded in 1970
Mission: An association of tourism research and marketing professionals with Chapters in the U.S., Canada, Europe, and Asia.
Membership: 700 worldwide; Fees: $50 student; $225 standard; $370 premier; $600 professional organization
Chief Officer(s):
Kelly MacKay, President, 416-979-5000 Ext. 6700
k7mackay@ryerson.ca
Meetings/Conferences:
• Travel and Tourism Research Association Canada Conference 2018, September, 2018, Halifax, NS
Scope: National

Travel Health Insurance Association of Canada (THIA)
#300, 191 John St., Toronto ON M5T 1X3
info@thiaonline.com
www.thiaonline.com
twitter.com/thiaonline
Overview: A medium-sized national organization founded in 1998
Mission: To be the leading voice for travel insurance in Canada
Membership: 381 individuals; Fees: $125 individual; $525 corporate; Member Profile: Travel insurers, brokers, underwriters, re-insurers, emergency assistance companies, air ambulance companies & allied services in the travel insurance field
Activities: Seminars; annual conferences; continuing education sessions
Chief Officer(s):
Alex Bittner, President

Travel Industry Council of Ontario (TICO)
West Tower, #402, 2700 Matheson Blvd., Mississauga ON L4W 4V9
Tel: 905-624-6241; Fax: 905-624-8631
Toll-Free: 888-451-8426
tico@tico.ca
www.tico.ca
www.facebook.com/ticontario
www.youtube.com/user/ticoinfo
Overview: A medium-sized provincial organization
Mission: To promote a fair & informed marketplace where consumers can be confident in their travel purchases; To promote fair & ethical competition in the industry, support a Code of Ethics; To maintain & enforce programs that provide for consumer compensation in specific circumstances; To promote an expected level of education as a criterion for registration & encourage legislative & regulatory amendments aimed at industry professionalism & consumer confidence
Finances: Funding Sources: Registration fees
Staff Member(s): 25
Membership: 2,500 travel retailers & wholesalers; Committees: Audit; Executive; Business Strategy; Governance; Legislative & Regulatory Review; Complaints; Education Standards; Expanded Converage; Compensation Fund; Consumer Advisory
Chief Officer(s):
Michael Pepper, President & CEO
Publications:
• TICO [Travel Industry Council of Ontario] Talk
Type: Newsletter; Frequency: Quarterly
Profile: Information distributed to all Ontario registered travel retailers & travel wholesalers
• TICO [Travel Industry Council of Ontario] Education Standards Study Manual
Type: Manual
Profile: Every person in Ontario who works for a retail travel agency & sells travel services or provides travel advice to the public must meet TICO'seducation standards
• TICO [Travel Industry Council of Ontario] Annual Report
Type: Manual
Profile: An outline of activities, the performance of the council, & a financial report for each fiscal year

Travel Manitoba
21 Forks Market Rd., Winnipeg MB R3C 4T7
Tel: 204-927-7800
Toll-Free: 800-665-0040
www.travelmanitoba.com
www.facebook.com/TravelManitoba
twitter.com/travelmanitoba
www.youtube.com/TravelManitoba
Overview: A medium-sized provincial organization
Mission: To contribute to Manitoba's economic well-being by facilitating & supporting the growth & development of tourism in harmony with the environment & in partnership with all stakeholders
Finances: Annual Operating Budget: Greater than $5 Million
Staff Member(s): 32
Activities: Library: Industry, Trade & Tourism Business Library
Chief Officer(s):
Colin Ferguson, President & CEO
coferguson@travelmanitoba.com
Brigitte Sandron, Senior Vice-President, Strategy & Market Development
bsandron@travelmanitoba.com
Linda Whitfield, Vice-President, Marketing & Communications
lwhitfield@travelmanitoba.com

Travel Media Association of Canada (TMAC)
#602, 319 Merton St., Toronto ON M4S 1A5
Tel: 416-934-0599
info@travelmedia.ca
www.travelmedia.ca
www.facebook.com/travelmediaca
twitter.com/TravelMediaCA
Overview: A small national organization founded in 1994
Mission: To bring together travel media & tourism industry members to foster excellence, uphold ethical standards, & promote professional development
Finances: Annual Operating Budget: $50,000-$100,000
Staff Member(s): 1
Membership: 460; Fees: Schedule available; Member Profile: Journalists & industry dealing with travel; Committees: Awards; Communications; Conference; Finance; Governance & Nominations; Industry Membership; Media Membership; Membership Benefits; Professional Development; Social Media; Volunteer
Chief Officer(s):
Grant Fraser, President
gfraser@golf-management.org
Awards:
• Travel Media Association of Canada Awards
Honours members with the best travel writing and photography.; Amount: $1000 each
Meetings/Conferences:
• Travel Media Association of Canada 2018 Conference & AGM, 2018
Scope: National

Travellers' Aid Society of Toronto (TAS)
13 Mountalan Ave., Toronto ON M4J 1H3
Tel: 416-366-7788; Fax: 416-466-6552
TAID668@gmail.com
www.travellersaid.ca
Also Known As: Travellers'Aid
Overview: A small local charitable organization founded in 1903
Mission: To provide a base of needed information for travellers as well as shelter & other help in crisis situations
Member of: Tourism Toronto; Volunteer Centre of Toronto/Etobicoke; Green Tourism; Travellers Assistance Services of Toronto
Affiliation(s): Travellers Aid International
Finances: Annual Operating Budget: $50,000-$100,000; Funding Sources: Donations; government; corporations & individuals
Staff Member(s): 8; 185 volunteer(s)
Activities: Finding accommodation for travellers; Working with social agencies in assisting immigrants & refugees; Acting as a link between stranded travellers & social service agencies; Operating information booths at all terminals at the Lester B. Pearson Airport, Toronto Coach Terminal & Union Railway Station; Speaker Service: Yes

Treasury Management Association of Canada - British Columbia See Association for Financial Professionals - Vancouver

Treasury Management Association of Canada - Edmonton See Association for Financial Professionals - Edmonton

Treasury Management Association of Canada - Toronto
Toronto ON
Tel: 416-629-2871; Fax: 416-981-3282
admin@tmac-toronto.ca
tmac-toronto.ca
Also Known As: TMAC - Toronto
Overview: A small local organization founded in 1984 overseen by Association for Financial Professionals
Mission: To act as a resource & advocate for Canadian corporate treasurers
Member of: Association for Financial Professionals
Membership: 200; Fees: $502.85; Member Profile: Treasury professionals from mid-market corporations, crown corporations, banks, investment dealers, finance & trust companies, software vendors, management consultants & government organizations
Activities: Events; job postings
Chief Officer(s):
Linda Hartley, President
David Balmer, Vice-President/Treasurer
Vivien Hall-Cho, Administrator
Linda Baldwin, Communications Contact
linda.baldwin@scotiabank.com

Treaty & Aboriginal Land Stewards Association of Alberta (TALSAA)
c/o Piikani Nation, PO Box 70, Brocket AB T0K 0H0
Tel: 403-965-3807; Fax: 403-965-2214
Overview: A small provincial organization founded in 2000 overseen by National Aboriginal Lands Managers Association
Staff Member(s): 1
Chief Officer(s):
Lance Yellow Face, Contact

Treaty & Aboriginal Rights Research Centre of Manitoba Inc.
#300, 153 Lombard Ave., Winnipeg MB R3B 0T4
Tel: 204-943-6456; *Fax:* 204-942-3202
Also Known As: TARR Centre of Manitoba
Overview: A small local organization
Chief Officer(s):
Ralph Abramson, Contact

Tree Canada Foundation / Arbres Canada
#1, 470 Somerset St. West, Ottawa ON K1R 5J8
Tel: 613-567-5545; *Fax:* 613-567-5270
info@treecanada.ca
www.treecanada.ca
www.facebook.com/TreeCanada
twitter.com/TreeCanada
www.youtube.com/user/treecanada1
Overview: A small national organization founded in 1992
Mission: To provide education, technical support, resources & financial support through working partnerships to encourage Canadians to plant & care for trees in our urban & rural environment in an effort to help reduce the harmful effects of carbon dioxide emissions
Staff Member(s): 11
Activities: *Speaker Service:* Yes
Chief Officer(s):
Michael Rosen, President
mrosen@treecanada.ca
Awards:
• Awards
National tree-planting & tree-care program designed to offset the problem of global warming; provides technical advice & financial assistance to qualifying partners for certain planting costs & for buying trees; partners are expected to contribute cash &/or in-kind services *Eligibility:* Groups interested in tree-planting programs

T.R.E.E. Foundation for Youth Development / Fondation pour le développement de la jeunesse T.R.E.E.
#810, 5250, rue Ferrier, Montréal QC H4P 1L4
Also Known As: TREE
Overview: A small national charitable organization
Mission: To receive & maintain general & special funds & apply from time to time all or part thereof &/or the income from these funds, by making gifts, grants, contributions & donations, for charitable, educational or research purposes with relation to youth in general
Membership: 1-99
Chief Officer(s):
Peter L. Clement, Executive Director

Trees Winnipeg
1539 Waverley St., Winnipeg MB R3T 4V7
Tel: 204-832-7188; *Fax:* 204-986-4050
office@treeswinnipeg.org
www.treeswinnipeg.org
www.facebook.com/436910829692291
twitter.com/TreesWinnipeg
Previous Name: Coalition to Save the Elms
Overview: A medium-sized local charitable organization founded in 1992
Mission: To protect, preserve, & promote the urban forest & environment
Finances: *Funding Sources:* Donations
Membership: 10,000; *Fees:* $25 preferred; $15 regular/renewal
Activities: Providing public workshops; Organizing a treebanding program; *Awareness Events:* Arbor Day, June; Adopt-a-Tree Program; *Speaker Service:* Yes
Chief Officer(s):
Gerry Engel, President
Kerienne La France, Executive Director
Richard Westwood, Treasurer
Publications:
• Winnipeg Forest Watch Handbook
Type: Guide

Treherne Chamber of Commerce
c/o Municipality of Norfolk Treherne, PO Box 30, 215 Broadway St., Treherne MB R0G 2V0
Tel: 204-723-2044; *Fax:* 204-723-2719
info@treherne.ca
www.treherne.ca
www.facebook.com/NorfolkTreherne
Overview: A small local organization
Mission: To promote & support the businesses of the Municipality of Norfolk Treherne

Chief Officer(s):
Ross McKellar, President, 204-723-2532

Trent Hills & District Chamber of Commerce
PO Box 376, 51 Grand Rd., Campbellford ON K0L 1L0
Tel: 705-653-1551; *Fax:* 705-653-1629
Toll-Free: 888-653-1556
tourism@trenthillschamber.ca
www.trenthillschamber.ca
www.facebook.com/trenthillschamber
twitter.com/THchamber
Previous Name: Campbellford-Seymour Chamber of Commerce
Overview: A small local organization founded in 1921
Mission: To promote the commercial, industrial, agricultural, social, civic & tourism interests of the community
Finances: *Annual Operating Budget:* $50,000-$100,000; *Funding Sources:* Regional government
Staff Member(s): 3; 12 volunteer(s)
Membership: 190 individual; *Fees:* Schedule available
Chief Officer(s):
Nancy Allanson, Executive Director
nancy@trenthillschamber.ca

Trent Port Historical Society
55 King St., Trenton ON K8V 3V9
Tel: 613-394-1333
Overview: A small local charitable organization founded in 1980
Mission: To encourage research into area history; to promote public interest in history; to preserve artifacts, buildings & lands of historical significance to the area
Member of: Ontario Historical Society
Finances: *Funding Sources:* Donations; fundraising
Activities: Restoration of Trenton Town Hall - 1861 & Trent Port Museum
Chief Officer(s):
Shawn Ellis, President
trentonshawn@hotmail.com

Trent University Faculty Association (TUFA) / Association des professeurs de l'Université Trent
Champlain College, c/o TUFA Office, Peterborough ON K9J 7B8
Tel: 705-748-1011; *Fax:* 705-748-1651
tufa@trentu.ca
www.trentfaculty.ca
Overview: A small local organization founded in 1980
Mission: To protect & enhance the professional interests of the university faculty & librarians, especially ensuring that the collective agreement is properly administered; to ensure that members develop & practise their expertise & are rewarded suitably both in monetary & nonmonetary aspects
Affiliation(s): Canadian Association of University Teachers; Ontario Confederation of University Faculty Associations
Finances: *Annual Operating Budget:* $100,000-$250,000; *Funding Sources:* Membership dues
Staff Member(s): 1
Membership: 312; *Member Profile:* Fulltime, tenured, librarians & sessionals
Chief Officer(s):
Marcus Harvey, Executive Director

Trent Valley Association of Baptist Churches
ON
trentvalleybaptists@gmail.com
tvabaptist.wordpress.com
Overview: A small local organization overseen by Canadian Baptists of Ontario and Quebec
Member of: Canadian Baptists of Ontario & Quebec
Membership: *Member Profile:* Baptist churches in the Trent Valley Area
Chief Officer(s):
Clarke Dixon, Moderator, 905-372-5058
clarkedixon@me.com

Trenton & District Association for Community Living *See* Community Living Quinte West

Trenton & District Chamber of Commerce *See* Quinte West Chamber of Commerce

Trenton Art Club
c/o Dufferin Centre, 344 Dufferin Ave., Trenton ON K8V 5N1
Tel: 613-392-7743
Overview: A small local organization
Finances: *Funding Sources:* Fundraising
Chief Officer(s):
Amy Worrick, Treasurer

Trenton Care & Share Food Bank
38 Guelph St., Trenton ON K8V 4G4
Tel: 613-394-5551; *Fax:* 613-394-0508
caresharefoodbank@bellnet.ca
www.trentonfoodbank.ca
www.facebook.com/129719410433462?fref=ts
twitter.com/TrentonFoodBank
Also Known As: Trenton Foodbank
Overview: A small local organization founded in 1985
Member of: Ontario Association of Food Banks; Canadian Association of Food Banks
Staff Member(s): 1; 27 volunteer(s)
Chief Officer(s):
Al Teal, Manager

Trial Lawyers Association of British Columbia (TLABC)
#1111, 1100 Melville St., Vancouver BC V6E 4A6
Tel: 604-682-5343; *Fax:* 604-682-0373
Toll-Free: 888-558-5222
tla-info@tlabc.org
www.tlabc.org
www.linkedin.com/pub/tlabc-vancouver/23/7b5/b61
www.facebook.com/111199725596510
twitter.com/tla_bc
pinterest.com/tlabc2012/
Overview: A medium-sized provincial organization founded in 1980
Staff Member(s): 6
Membership: 910; *Fees:* Schedule available; *Member Profile:* Trial lawyers; *Committees:* Bylaws; Criminal Defence; Family Law; Finance; Jury Project; Legal Aid Action; Litigation; Membership; Nominations; Public Affairs; Rules; Seminar Planning; Strategic Planning; Wrongful Death Action
Activities: *Speaker Service:* Yes
Chief Officer(s):
Carla Terzariol, Executive Director & CEO

Triathlon British Columbia
PO Box 34098, Stn. D, Vancouver BC V6J 4M1
Tel: 604-736-3176; *Fax:* 604-736-3180
info@tribc.org
www.tribc.org
www.facebook.com/TriathlonBC
Also Known As: Triathlon BC
Overview: A small provincial organization overseen by Triathlon Canada
Mission: To be the provincial governing body of triathlon, duathlon, aquathon & winter triathlon in British Columbia
Member of: Triathlon Canada
Membership: *Fees:* $20 adult, coach or associate; $10 junior or youth; $35 members of a Triathlon BC affiliated club
Chief Officer(s):
Emily Vickery, Program Manager
Andrew Armstrong, Technical Coordinator

Triathlon Canada
#121, 1925 Blanshard St., Victoria BC V8T 4J2
Tel: 250-412-1795; *Fax:* 250-412-1794
info@triathloncanada.com
www.triathloncanada.com
www.facebook.com/148631098541373
twitter.com/TriathlonCanada
Previous Name: National Federation for the Sports of Triathlon, Duathlon & Aquathlon in Canada
Overview: A small national organization
Mission: To function as the National Federation for triathlon & duathlon in Canada, & to represent Canada internationally; to promote the triathlon & duathlon, both competitive & non-competitive in Canada; to encourage support of Triathlon Canada programmes by the public generally; to provide guidance, information & assistance to the provincial triathlon associations, zones & clubs in respect to these objects & in the development of programmes for competitive & non-competitive triathletes & duathletes; to affiliate all provincial associations to Triathlon Canada who are the Provincial Sports Governing Bodies, or who are in the process of becoming the Provincial Sports Governing Bodies in their province; to organize training courses for triathletes, duathletes, coaches & administrators to national & international standards; to promote other multi-disciplined endurance events & excluding the traditional decathlon, pentathlon, heptathlon, modern pentathlon & biathlon, which are part of existing National Federations
Chief Officer(s):
Tim Wilson, Chief Executive Officer
tim.wilson@triathloncanada.com

Chris Dornan, Manager, Communications, 403-620-8731
hpprchris@shaw.ca
Awards:
• Excellence Awards

Triathlon Manitoba
c/o Sport for Life Centre, #328, 145 Pacific Ave., Winnipeg MB R3B 2Z6
Tel: 204-925-5703
triathlon@sportmanitoba.ca
www.triathlon.mb.ca
www.facebook.com/TriathlonManitoba
twitter.com/MBTri
Overview: A small provincial organization overseen by Triathlon Canada
Mission: To be the provincial governing body of triathlon in Manitoba
Member of: Triathlon Canada; Sport Manitoba
Membership: *Fees:* $10 under 16 years; $25 youth (16-19 years); $50 full
Activities: Training; Races; Awards; Kids of Steel program
Chief Officer(s):
Angela Lloyd, Executive Director, 204-925-5636
triathlon.ed@sportmanitoba.ca

Triathlon New Brunswick
PO Box 22053, Stn. Landsdowne, Saint John NB E2K 4T7
Tel: 506-848-1144
www.trinb.ca
www.facebook.com/TriathlonNB
twitter.com/TriathlonNB
Also Known As: Triathlon NB
Overview: A small provincial organization overseen by Triathlon Canada
Mission: To be the provincial governing body of triathlon in New Brunswick
Member of: Triathlon Canada
Membership: *Fees:* $50
Chief Officer(s):
Garth Miller, President
garth39@fastmail.fm
Brittany Pye, Executive Director
executivedirector@trinb.ca
Althea Arsenault, Vice President
Althea.Arsenault@gnb.ca

Triathlon Newfoundland & Labrador
PO Box 872, Stn. C, St. John's NL A1C 5L7
admin@trinl.com
www.trinl.com
www.facebook.com/triathlon.nl
twitter.com/trinl
Also Known As: TriNL
Overview: A small provincial organization overseen by Triathlon Canada
Mission: To be the governing body for the sport of triathalon in Newfoundland & Labrador
Member of: Triathlon Canada
Affiliation(s): International Triathlon Union
Membership: *Fees:* $10 youth/one event; $20 adult
Chief Officer(s):
Rob Coleman, President
president@trinl.com

Triathlon Nova Scotia
5516 Spring Garden Rd., 4th Fl., Halifax NS B3J 1G6
Tel: 902-425-5450; *Fax:* 902-425-5606
triathlon@sportnovascotia.ca
triathlonnovascotia.ca
www.facebook.com/triathlonnovascotia
twitter.com/Triathlon_NS
www.instagram.com/triathlon_ns
Overview: A small provincial organization overseen by Triathlon Canada
Mission: To be the provincial governing body of triathlon in Nova Scotia
Member of: Triathlon Canada; Sport Nova Scotia
Membership: *Fees:* $45 adult or junior; $25 youth; $3 kids (per race)
Chief Officer(s):
Gregg Kerr, President
Wade McCallum, Vice President

Triathlon Price Edward Island
40 Enman Cres., Charlottetown PE C1E 1E6
triathlonpei@gmail.com
www.tripei.com
www.facebook.com/217742304907740
twitter.com/triathlonpei
Also Known As: Triathlon PEI
Overview: A small provincial organization founded in 2012 overseen by Triathlon Canada
Mission: To be the provincial governing body of triathlon in Prince Edward Island
Member of: Triathlon Canada
Chief Officer(s):
Jamie Nickerson, President

Triathlon Québec
4545, av Pierre-de Coubertin, Montréal QC H1V 3R2
Tél: 514-252-3121
www.triathlonquebec.org
www.facebook.com/132997480092478
twitter.com/triathlonquebec
Aperçu: *Dimension:* petite; *Envergure:* provinciale; fondée en 1985 surveillé par Triathlon Canada
Membre de: Triathlon Canada
Affiliation(s): Triathlon Canada
Finances: *Budget de fonctionnement annuel:* $250,000-$500,000
Membre(s) du personnel: 3; 20 bénévole(s)
Membre: 1 100
Activités: *Stagiaires:* Oui
Membre(s) du bureau directeur:
Marie-Eve Sullivan, Directrice générale, 514-252-3121 Ext. 4
msullivan@triathlonquebec.org

Tribuna Noastra *Voir* Fondation roumaine de Montréal

Tri-Cities Chamber of Commerce Serving Coquitlam, Port Coquitlam & Port Moody
1209 Pinetree Way, Coquitlam BC V3B 7Y3
Tel: 604-464-2716; *Fax:* 604-464-6796
info@tricitieschamber.com
www.tricitieschamber.com
www.linkedin.com/company/tri-cities-chamber-of-commerce
www.facebook.com/TriCitiesCoC
twitter.com/tricitiescoc
Previous Name: Chamber of Commerce Serving Coquitlam, Port Coquitlam, Port Moody
Overview: A small local organization
Mission: To support, educate, & promote business interests in the community
Member of: Canadian Chamber of Commerce; BC Chamber of Commerce
Finances: *Annual Operating Budget:* $100,000-$250,000
Staff Member(s): 3; 14 volunteer(s)
Membership: 900; *Fees:* Schedule available; *Committees:* Communications; Economic; Education; Event; Membership; Public Policy
Activities: Organizing & promoting business & community events
Chief Officer(s):
Michael Hind, CEO
michaelh@tricitieschamber.com

Tri-County Soccer Association
c/o Fran Glenn, President, 9904 - 109 St., Fort Saskatchewan AB T8L 2K2
tricounty.district@yahoo.ca
www.tricountysoccer.net
Overview: A small local organization overseen by Alberta Soccer Association
Member of: Alberta Soccer Association
Chief Officer(s):
Fran Glenn, President
tricouny.president@yahoo.ca

Tri-County Women's Centre
12 Cumberland St., Yarmouth NS B5A 3K3
Tel: 902-742-0085; *Fax:* 902-742-6068
Toll-Free: 877-742-0085
tcwc@tricountywomenscentre.org
www.tricountywomenscentre.org
Overview: A small local organization founded in 2002
Mission: To support, enrich & empower the lives of women in Nova Scotia

The Trident Mediation Counselling & Support Foundation
PO Box 8148, Canmore AB T1W 2T9
Tel: 403-678-2918; *Fax:* 732-601-2918
info@tridentfoundation.net
www.tridentfoundation.net
Also Known As: TRIDENT
Overview: A small local charitable organization founded in 1999
Mission: Covers the disciplines of social work, law, conflict management & education; focuses on policy & practice in social development, conflict management & training services
Finances: *Annual Operating Budget:* Less than $50,000
Staff Member(s): 2; 1 volunteer(s)
Membership: 11; *Fees:* Fee for service
Activities: Conflict management; mediation; on-line dispute resolution; public speaking; counselling; marriage & family therapy; consultancy; research & policy development; distance education; *Speaker Service:* Yes
Chief Officer(s):
Jennifer Geary, Contact

Trillium Automobile Dealers' Association (TADA)
85 Renfrew Dr., Markham ON L3R 0N9
Tel: 905-940-6232; *Fax:* 905-940-6235
Toll-Free: 800-668-6510
info@tada.ca
www.tada.ca
www.facebook.com/149581915142339
twitter.com/tada_gr
Merged from: Toronto Automobile Dealers' Association; Ontario Automobile Dealers' Association
Overview: A medium-sized provincial organization
Member of: Canadian Automobile Dealers Association
Membership: 340 Dealers; *Member Profile:* New franchise automobile dealers
Chief Officer(s):
Brenda Sachdev, Contact, 905-940-8421
brendas@tada.ca

Trillium Gift of Life Network
#900, 522 University Ave., Toronto ON M5G 1W7
Tel: 416-363-4001; *Fax:* 416-363-4002
Toll-Free: 800-263-2833
www.giftoflife.on.ca
www.linkedin.com/company/1426658
www.facebook.com/TrilliumGiftofLife
twitter.com/TrilliumGift
Previous Name: Multiple Organ Retrieval & Exchange Program of Ontario
Overview: A medium-sized provincial organization founded in 1988
Mission: To enable every Ontario resident to make an informed decision to donate organs & tissue; To support healthcare professionals in implementing their wishes; To maximize organ & tissue donation in Ontario in a respectful & equitable manner through education, research, services & support
Activities: Administering computer system that lists transplant patients & matches donated organs; Promoting public awareness; *Awareness Events:* Organ Donor Awareness Week; *Speaker Service:* Yes; *Library:* Not open to public
Chief Officer(s):
Ronnie Gavsie, President & CEO

Trillium Health Partners Foundation
Clinical & Administrative Bldg., 100 Queensway West, 5th Fl., Mississauga ON L5B 1B8
Tel: 905-848-7575; *Fax:* 905-804-7927
foundation@thp.ca
trilliumgiving.ca
www.facebook.com/TrilliumHealthPartnersFoundation
twitter.com/trilliumhealth
www.youtube.com/user/TrilliumHeroes
Merged from: Trillium Health Centre Foundation; Credit Valley Hospital Foundation
Overview: A small local charitable organization founded in 2013
Mission: To help raise funds for the Credit Valley Hospital, the Mississauga Hospital & the Queensway Health Centre in order to provide patients with improved health care services & to fund research
Staff Member(s): 32
Activities: Fundraising
Chief Officer(s):
Steve Hoscheit, President & CEO
Steve.Hoscheit@thp.ca

Trillium Party of Ontario
95 Cousins Dr., Aurora ON L4G 1B5
Tel: 289-319-1220; *Fax:* 905-953-9469
info@trilliumpartyontario.ca
www.trilliumpartyontario.ca
www.facebook.com/556310181202720
twitter.com/trilliumpartyON
Overview: A small provincial organization

Mission: To prioritize policies that will benefit the citizens of Ontario
Chief Officer(s):
Bob Yaciuk, Party Leader
bobyaciuk@trilliumpartyontario.ca
John Grant, Director, Political Operations

Trinity Historical Society Inc.
PO Box 8, Trinity NL A0C 2S0
Tel: 709-464-3599; *Fax:* 709-464-3599
info@trinityhistoricalsociety.com
www.trinityhistoricalsociety.com
www.facebook.com/thsoc
Overview: A small local organization founded in 1964
Mission: To operate the Trinity Museum, Green Family Forge, Lester-Garland House, the Cooperage & the Court House, Gaol & General Building

Tri-Town & District Chamber of Commerce *See* Temiskaming Shores & Area Chamber of Commerce

Trochu Chamber of Commerce
PO Box 771, Trochu AB T0M 2C0
Tel: 403-442-7980
Overview: A small local organization
Membership: *Fees:* $50
Chief Officer(s):
Laurie Klassen, President

Trois-Rivières Real Estate Board *Voir* Chambre immobilière de la Mauricie Inc.

Tropicana Community Services Organization
1385 Huntingwood Dr., Toronto ON M1S 3J1
Tel: 416-439-9009
www.tropicanacommunity.org
Overview: A small local organization founded in 1969 overseen by Ontario Council of Agencies Serving Immigrants
Mission: To work for the creation of a harmonious, multicultural society; to develop youth participation & leadership; to recruit & develop volunteers; to advocate & provide access to counselling for youth
Chief Officer(s):
Sharon Shelton, Executive Director

Trotskyist League of Canada / Ligue trotskyste du Canada
PO Box 7198, Stn. A, Toronto ON M5W 1X8
Tel: 416-593-4138
spartcan@on.aibn.com
www.icl-fi.org
Overview: A small national organization
Member of: International Communist League
Chief Officer(s):
John Masters, President

Troubles d'apprentissage - Association de l'Alberta *See* Learning Disabilities Association of Alberta

Troubles d'apprentissage - Association de l'Ontario *See* Learning Disabilities Association of Ontario

Troubles d'apprentissage - Association de la Colombie-Britannique *See* Learning Disabilities Association of British Columbia

Troubles d'apprentissage - Association de la Saskatchewan *See* Learning Disabilities Association of Saskatchewan

Troubles d'apprentissage - Association de Manitoba *See* Learning Disabilities Association of Manitoba

Troubles d'apprentissage - Association du Nouveau-Brunswick *See* Learning Disabilities Association of New Brunswick

La Troupe du Jour (LTDJ)
914, 20e rue Ouest, Saskatoon SK S7M 0Y4
Tél: 306-244-1040
ltdj.dreamhosters.com
www.facebook.com/LaTroupeDuJour
twitter.com/latroupedujour
Aperçu: *Dimension:* petite; *Envergure:* locale; fondée en 1985
Mission: Développement du théâtre francophone en Saskatchewan
Membre(s) du personnel: 5
Membre(s) du bureau directeur:
Denis Rouleau, Directeur artistique et général
artistique@latroupedujour.ca

Trout Unlimited Canada (TUC)
#160, 6712 Fisher St. SE, Calgary AB T2H 2A7
Tel: 403-221-8360; *Fax:* 403-221-8368
Toll-Free: 800-909-6040
tuc@tucanada.org
www.tucanada.org
www.facebook.com/TroutUnlimitedCanada
twitter.com/TUCanada1
www.youtube.com/user/TroutUnlimitedCanada
Overview: A small national charitable organization founded in 1972
Mission: To promote the conservation & wise use of trout & other coldwater fisheries & their watersheds, through the undertaking of habitat restoration & enhancement, research, management, & public education
Finances: *Annual Operating Budget:* $500,000-$1.5 Million
Staff Member(s): 10; 1000 volunteer(s)
Membership: 4,000; *Fees:* $30
Activities: Yellow Fish Road Program; Adopt a Trout; Aquatic Renwal Program; educational programs; *Library:* by appointment
Chief Officer(s):
Jeff Surtees, CEO, 403-221-8363
jsurtees@tucanada.org
Dean Orlando, CFO, 403-221-8373
DOrlando@tucanada.org

Trowel Trades Canadian Association, Local 100 (CLC) *Voir* Association canadienne des métiers de la truelle, section locale 100 (CTC)

Truck Loggers Association (TLA)
#725, 815 Hastings St. West, Vancouver BC V6C 1B4
Tel: 604-684-4291; *Fax:* 604-684-7134
contact@tla.ca
www.tla.ca
www.linkedin.com/company/the-truck-loggers-association
www.facebook.com/TruckLoggersAssociation
twitter.com/truckloggerBC
Overview: A medium-sized provincial organization founded in 1942
Affiliation(s): Pacific Logging Congress
Finances: *Annual Operating Budget:* $500,000-$1.5 Million
Staff Member(s): 5; 17 volunteer(s)
Membership: 600 institutional; *Member Profile:* TO give the independent loggers a collective voice in the changes taking place in society and the forest industry; To share information about newly developing logging machines, methods, and technology.
Chief Officer(s):
Dwight Yochim, Executive Director, 604-684-4291 Ext. 1
dwight@tla.ca
Meetings/Conferences:
• 75th Truck Loggers Association Convention & Trade Show, 2018
Scope: National

Truck Training Schools Association of Ontario Inc. (TTSAO)
#100, 1 Hunter St. East, Hamilton ON L8N 3W1
Fax: 905-704-1329
Toll-Free: 866-475-9436
ttsao@ttsao.com
www.ttsao.com
www.facebook.com/1557624047783648
twitter.com/TTSAOontario
www.youtube.com/channel/UC7O4v3yCiO3Mekvai0knznw
Overview: A small provincial licensing organization founded in 1992
Mission: To provide the trucking industry with the highest quality driver training programs for entry level individuals that earn & maintain public confidence, adhering to sound & ethical business practices
Affiliation(s): Ontario Trucking Association; Ministry of Education, Ministry of Transportation
Finances: *Annual Operating Budget:* $100,000-$250,000
Staff Member(s): 7
Membership: 75; *Fees:* Schedule available; *Member Profile:* Institutions that provide truck training services within Ontario, Canada
Activities: *Internships:* Yes
Chief Officer(s):
Yvette Lagrois, President
Robert Barclay, Vice President

Truckers Association of Nova Scotia (TANS)
#3, 779 Prince St., Truro NS B2N 1G7
Tel: 902-895-7447; *Fax:* 902-897-0487
Toll-Free: 800-232-6631
contact@tans.ca
www.tans.ca
www.facebook.com/TruckersAssociationNS
twitter.com/TruckersAssocNS
Overview: A medium-sized provincial organization founded in 1968
Mission: To promote all matters aiding in the development & improvement of the trucking industry and the allied trades in Nova Scotia, including social, recreational, benevolent, educational & charitable activities; To be the main proponent in gaining access to the provincial haul rates & beneficial changes to the contract specifications used by the contractors
Member of: The Transportation Sector of Voluntary Planning
Affiliation(s): Atlantic Provinces Trucking Association of Nova Scotia
Membership: *Member Profile:* Individuals involved in the trucking industry in Nova Scotia
Activities: Makes presentations to government & other regulatory bodies in relation to the economic welfare of the trucking industry
Chief Officer(s):
David MacKenzie, Chair, 902-295-0442, Fax: 902-622-1389
kilkare@gmail.com

Trucking Human Resources Canada (THRC)
#202, 16 Beechwood Ave., Ottawa ON K1L 8L9
Tel: 613-244-4800
info@truckingHR.com
truckinghr.com
www.linkedin.com/company-beta/10320679
twitter.com/truckinghr
Also Known As: Trucking HR Canada
Overview: A medium-sized national organization
Mission: To promote the provision of safe, secure, efficient & professional trucking services in Canada
Affiliation(s): CCA Truck Driver Training Ltd.; Capilano Truck Driver Training Institute; JVI Provincial Transportation & Safety Academy; Mountain Transport Institute Ltd.; Red Deer College; SK Driver Training Ltd.; Wheels On Ltd. / Training & Driver Training
Membership: *Committees:* Labour Market Information; Outreach; Foreign Credential Recognition; Gap; Professional Driver Recognition Program; Skills Upgrading
Activities: Conducting research; Training; Offering advice; Liaising with industry members
Chief Officer(s):
Angela Splinter, CEO
Publications:
• Industry in Motion: Canada's Trucking HR Newsletter
Type: Newsletter
Profile: Industry, government, & general information

True Sport Foundation / Fondation sport pur
#350, 955 Green Valley Cres., Ottawa ON K2C 3V4
Tel: 613-521-9533; *Fax:* 613-521-3134
info@truesport.ca
www.truesportfoundation.ca
Previous Name: Spirit of Sport Foundation
Overview: A small national charitable organization founded in 1993
Mission: To ensure that sport makes a positive contribution to Canadian society, to our athletes & to the physical & moral development of Canada's youth; to bring together leading organizations to promote, celebrate & recognize sporting excellence
Member of: Canadian Centre for Ethics in Sport; Athletics Canada
Finances: *Annual Operating Budget:* $250,000-$500,000
Staff Member(s): 3; 14 volunteer(s)
Membership: 1-99
Chief Officer(s):
Karri Dawson, Executive Director, 613-521-9533 Ext. 3213
kdawson@truesport.ca
Awards:
• Lyle Makosky Values & Ethics in Sport Fund

Truro & Area Outreach Project; Pictou County AIDS Coalition *See* The Northern AIDS Connection Society

Truro & Colchester Chamber of Commerce
605 Prince St., Truro NS B2N 1G2
Tel: 902-895-6328; *Fax:* 902-897-6641
oa@tcchamber.ca
www.trurocolchesterchamber.com
www.linkedin.com/profile/view?id=88974880

www.facebook.com/tdcoc
twitter.com/TruColCoC
Previous Name: Truro & District Chamber of Commerce
Overview: A medium-sized local charitable organization founded in 1890
Mission: To be the principal advocate for business in Truro & the Colchester Region in matters of economic, social & political importance
Member of: Nova Scotia Chamber; Atlantic Provinces Chamber; Canadian Chamber
Finances: *Annual Operating Budget:* $50,000-$100,000; *Funding Sources:* Membership dues
Staff Member(s): 2; 25 volunteer(s)
Membership: 300 corporate + 6 institutional + 4 senior/lifetime + 21 individual; *Fees:* Schedule available; *Member Profile:* Must do business in the community
Activities: Advocacy; networking; educational events; community events; Chamber Group Insurance Plan; Chamber Credit Card Discount Program; member-to-member discounts; *Awareness Events:* Home & Country Living Show; Chamber Golf Tournament; Annual General Banquet; *Library:* by appointment
Chief Officer(s):
Sherry Martell, Executive Director
Trish Petrie, Office Administrator
Awards:
• Chamber Business Person of the Year Award

Truro & District Chamber of Commerce *See* Truro & Colchester Chamber of Commerce

Truro Art Society
36 Arthur St., Truro NS B2N 4X9
truroartsociety.ca
Overview: A small local organization founded in 1969
Mission: To promote the arts in Truro & vicinity
Membership: *Fees:* $25 adult; $35 family; $10 student
Chief Officer(s):
Janice Stewart, President

Tuberous Sclerosis Canada Sclérose Tubéreuse (TSCST)
PO Box 35057, Essa Rd., Barrie ON L4N 5Z2
tscanadast@gmail.com
www.tscanada.ca
www.facebook.com/TSCanadaST
Overview: A small national charitable organization founded in 1990
Mission: To provide information & support to tuberous sclerosis patients & their families; To promote & improve professional & public awareness, education & research regarding this disease
Affiliation(s): Tuberous Sclerosis Alliance (USA); Tuberous Sclerosis Association (GB); Tuberous Sclerosis International (The Netherlands)
Finances: *Annual Operating Budget:* Less than $50,000; *Funding Sources:* Fundraising; donations
15 volunteer(s)
Membership: 150; *Fees:* $25
Activities: *Awareness Events:* Tuberous Sclerosis Awareness Month, May; *Library:* Not open to public
Chief Officer(s):
Cathy Evanochko, Co-Chair
Karen Shulist, Co-Chair

Tunisian Canadian Chamber of Commerce *Voir* Chambre de commerce Canado-Tunisienne

Tunnelling Association of Canada (TAC) / Association canadienne des tunnels
8828 Pigott Rd., Richmond ON V7A 2C4
Tel: 604-241-1297; *Fax:* 604-241-1399
admin@tunnelcanada.ca
www.tunnelcanada.ca
Overview: A medium-sized international organization
Mission: To promote Canadian tunnelling & underground excavation technologies; To represent the tunnelling community in matters of public & technical concern
Member of: Canadian Geotechnical Society
12 volunteer(s)
Membership: 350 individual, student & corporate members; *Fees:* $75 individual; $15 student; $25 retired; $500 corporate
Activities: Seminars; Field trips; Socials
Chief Officer(s):
Derek Zoldy, Secretary-Treasurer
secretary@tunnelcanada.ca
Rick Staples, President
president@tunnelcanada.ca

Meetings/Conferences:
• Tunnelling Association of Canada 2018 Annual Conference, 2018, ON
Scope: National

Turkey Farmers of Canada (TFC) / Les éleveurs de dindon du Canada (ÉDC)
Bldg. One, #202, 7145 West Credit Ave., Mississauga ON L5N 6J7
Tel: 905-812-3140; *Fax:* 905-812-9326
www.turkeyfarmersofcanada.ca
www.facebook.com/TastyTurkey
twitter.com/tastyturkey
Previous Name: Canadian Turkey Marketing Agency
Overview: A medium-sized national organization founded in 1974
Mission: To develop & strengthen the Canadian Turkey market through an effective supply management systems that stimulates growth & profitability for stakeholders
Member of: Canadian Federation of Agriculture
Affiliation(s): Further Poultry Processors Association of Canada; Canadian Poultry & Egg Processors Council
Finances: *Funding Sources:* Turkey producer levies
Chief Officer(s):
Mark Davies, Chair
Publications:
• CTMA Annual Report
Type: Yearbook; *Frequency:* Annually
Profile: Produced for the Federal Minister of Agriculture & Agri-Food, National Farm Products Council, & CTMA members
• Eye on the Industry
Frequency: Biweekly
Profile: Currents happenings & news related to the Canadian turkey industry
• Plume
Frequency: 4-6 pa
Profile: Current events, & industry issues, for all Canadian turkey producers, government, regulatory associations, & industry affiliates

Turkey Farmers of New Brunswick / Les Éleveurs de dindons du Nouveau-Brunswick
#103, 277 Main St., Fredericton NB E3A 1B1
Tel: 506-452-8103; *Fax:* 506-451-2121
nbturkey@nb.aibn.com
Previous Name: New Brunswick Turkey Marketing Board
Overview: A small provincial organization
Chief Officer(s):
Larry Slipp, Chair
Louis Martin, Secretary-Manager

Turkish Community Heritage Centre of Canada (TCHHC)
#35B, 234-10520 Yonge St., Richmond Hill ON L4C 3C7
Tel: 416-644-9909
info@TurkishCommunityCentre.org
www.turkishcommunitycentre.org
www.facebook.com/178208095522790?sk=info
twitter.com/tchcc
Overview: A small national charitable organization founded in 2007
Mission: Provides and maintains a community centre for the Canadian Turkish community.
Activities: Host seminars and cultural, educational and consulting events
Chief Officer(s):
Musabay Figen, President

Turks & Caicos Development Organization of Canada
3501, 50 Aurora Crt., Toronto ON M1W 2M6
Tel: 416-760-0908; *Fax:* 416-760-0908
www.turksandcaicoscanada.ca
Overview: A small international organization founded in 1987
Mission: To promote closer ties between Canada & the Turks & Caicos Islands & to assist Canadians interested in vacationing, investing, retiring, or starting a business in the Turks & Caicos Islands
Staff Member(s): 3
Membership: 735 individual
Chief Officer(s):
Ian A. Stuart, Vice-President & General Manager
ianstuart@turksandcaicoscanada.ca

Turner's Syndrome Society (TSS) / Société du syndrome de Turner
#9, 30 Clearly Ave., Ottawa ON K2A 4A1

Tel: 613-321-2267; *Fax:* 613-321-2268
Toll-Free: 800-465-6744
info@turnersyndrome.ca
www.turnersyndrome.ca
www.facebook.com/TurnerSyndromeSocietyOfCanada
Overview: A small national charitable organization founded in 1981
Mission: To improve the quality of life for individuals & families affected by Turner's Syndrome; to strive to accomplish this through providing public & professional awareness about the needs & concerns of individuals with Turner's Syndrome & their families through the development of communication networks to provide mutual support
Finances: *Funding Sources:* Government; direct mail; donations; fundraising
Membership: *Fees:* $15 student; $30 individual; $40 family; $50 health professional/institution
Activities: *Library:* by appointment
Chief Officer(s):
Krista Kamstra-Cooper, President

Tweed & Area Historical Society
PO Box 665, 40 Victoria St. North, Tweed ON K0K 3J0
Tel: 613-478-3989; *Fax:* 613-478-6457
tweedheritageinfo@on.aibn.com
Also Known As: Tweed Heritage Centre
Overview: A small local charitable organization founded in 1988
Mission: To research, document, preserve & promote the heritage (past, present, natural built) of the Tweed area.
Member of: Ontario Historical Society; Ontario Genealogical Society
Finances: *Annual Operating Budget:* $50,000-$100,000; *Funding Sources:* Donations; Grants; Fees
Staff Member(s): 1; 10 volunteer(s)
Membership: 37; *Fees:* $40 families; $25 individuals
Activities: Tours; research; local arts & crafts; Art Gallery; Museum; Archives, Genealogy; *Speaker Service:* Yes; *Library:* Tweed Heritage Centre; Open to public
Chief Officer(s):
Evan Morton, Curator

Tweed Chamber of Commerce
255 Metcalf St., Tweed ON K0K 3J0
Tel: 613-473-2151
info@tweedchamber.com
www.tweedchamber.com
Overview: A small local organization
Mission: To promote & develop a strong economic environment in Tweed & area
Membership: 52; *Fees:* $80; $40 non-profit
Chief Officer(s):
Roseann Trudeau, President

Twins Plus Association of Brampton
218 Ecclestone Dr., Brampton ON L6X 3P9
Tel: 905-799-4658
brampton@multiplebirthscanada.org
www.twinsplus.ca
www.facebook.com/MultipleBirthsBrampton
twitter.com/BramptonTwins
Overview: A small local organization overseen by Multiple Births Canada
Mission: A not-for-profit support and social group for expectant parents, parents and families of twins, triplets, or multiples living in Brampton, Caledon, Georgetown, Acton, Milton, Bolton, Orangeville and surrounding areas.
Membership: *Fees:* $30
Activities: *Library:*

Twins, Triplets & More Association of Calgary (TTMAC)
#16, 1215 Lake Sylvan Dr. SE, Calgary AB T2J 3Z5
Tel: 403-274-8703
info@ttmac.org
www.ttmac.org
Previous Name: Calgary Parents of Multiple Births Association
Overview: A small local organization founded in 1970
Mission: To improve & promote the health & well-being of expectant multiple birth families & families with multiple births
Finances: *Annual Operating Budget:* Less than $50,000
60 volunteer(s)
Membership: 500 families; *Fees:* Schedule available;
Committees: Breastfeeding Support; Health Support; Membership Services; Social, Resources & Zone Support
Activities: Prenatal classes; new parents info sessions; women's retreats; children's Halloween & Christmas parties;

BBQs; two playgroups; bi-annual sale; coffee parties; *Library:* by appointment

211 Ontario North
Victoria Mall, #38, 125 Syndicate Ave., Thunder Bay ON P7E 6H8
Tel: 807-624-1729
Toll-Free: 866-586-5638; *TTY:* 888-622-4651
info@lspc.ca
www.211OntarioNorth.ca
Overview: A small local organization founded in 2008 overseen by InformOntario
Mission: To provide accurate, up-to-date information on community services, organizations, clubs, events & activities; To assist organizations & the general public in accessing information & the resources they require & identify gaps in services; To work with individuals & groups to meet their needs & improve community well-being
Affiliation(s): A program of the Lakehead Social Planning Council
Finances: *Funding Sources:* Grants; donations; fundraising events; sale of services
Staff Member(s): 8
Membership: *Fees:* $20 individual; $40 organization
Chief Officer(s):
Kristen Tomcko, Supervisor

211 Southwest Ontario
#410, 400 City Hall Sq., Windsor ON N9A 7K6
Tel: 519-258-0247; *Fax:* 519-256-3311
Toll-Free: 866-686-0045; *TTY:* 866-488-9311
info@211southwestontario.ca
www.211ontario.ca
Previous Name: Information Windsor
Overview: A small local charitable organization founded in 1966
Mission: To provide leadership in the collection, management & dissemination of community service information for all consumers within the Greater Windsor region
Finances: *Funding Sources:* United Way/Centraide Windsor-Essex County; sale of publications, labels, lists, data sets
Activities: Help desk services; community online database; publications; list & label production; broadcast announcement service; data leasing; professional management services; educational programs for human service workers & call centres; Golf Drop Raffle Event, Aug.; *Speaker Service:* Yes; *Rents Mailing List:* Yes; *Library:* Open to public
Chief Officer(s):
Jennifer Tanner, Project Manager

Two Planks & a Passion Theatre Company (TP&aP)
PO Box 190, 555 Ross Creek Rd., Canning NS B0P 1H0
Tel: 902-582-3073; *Fax:* 902-582-7943
www.artscentre.ca
www.facebook.com/twoplanks.ca
twitter.com/rosscreek
www.youtube.com/user/rosscreektv
Overview: A small provincial organization founded in 1992
Mission: To develop & present high quality, professional theatre both regionally & nationally which reflects Canadian life, with strong roles for women; To develop & build an artistic centre in Canning, NS, accessible to both the local community & to artists of all disciplines & residencies
Member of: Professional Association of Canadian Theatres; Nova Scotia Professional Theatre Alliance
Affiliation(s): Playwrights Union of Canada
Finances: *Funding Sources:* Canada Council; NS Dept. of Education & Culture; NS Arts Council; Canadian Heritage; foundations
Membership: *Fees:* $15 individual; $25 family
Activities: Producing theatre productions & tours; Providing theatre workshops; Organizing fundraising & community events
Chief Officer(s):
Ken Schwartz, Artistic Director

Two/Ten Charity Trust of Canada Inc. / Deux/Dix
Thornhill Square, PO Box 87617, 298 John St., Thornhill ON L3T 7R3
Tel: 416-602-9668; *Fax:* 877-275-1040
info@twotencanada.com
www.twotencanada.com
Also Known As: Two/Ten Foundation of Canada
Overview: A small national charitable organization founded in 1989
Mission: To promote services to members of the Canadian footwear & allied industries
Member of: Two/Ten International Footwear Foundation
Finances: *Annual Operating Budget:* Less than $50,000; *Funding Sources:* Fundraising; corporate donations
Membership: 400; *Fees:* No fee; *Member Profile:* Shoe industry related; *Committees:* Bursary Program; Social Service Programs
Chief Officer(s):
Michelle Kofman, Executive Director

2-Spirited People of the First Nations (TPFN)
#105, 145 Front St. East, Toronto ON M5A 1E3
Tel: 416-944-9300; *Fax:* 416-944-8381
www.2spirits.com
www.facebook.com/2spiritsTO
www.instagram.com/2spirits_com
Previous Name: Gays & Lesbians of the First Nations
Overview: A medium-sized national charitable organization founded in 1989
Mission: To create a place where Aboriginal 2-Spirited people can grow & learn together as a community, fostering a positive, self-sufficient image, honouring our past & building a future; to work together toward bridging the gap between the 2-Spirited, Lesbian, Gay, Bisexual & Transgendered community & our Aboriginal identity
Member of: Ontario AIDS Network; Toronto Aboriginal Social Services Association; Canadian Aboriginal AIDS Network
Finances: *Funding Sources:* Ontario Ministry of Health; Health Canada; Aboriginal Healing & Wellness Strategy
Staff Member(s): 5; 80 volunteer(s)
Membership: 100+; *Fees:* Schedule available; *Member Profile:* Full (Aboriginal, Homosexual); Associate (non-Aboriginal); *Committees:* Aboriginal people living with HIV/AIDS; Communications; Finance; Fundraising; Membership; Personnel; 2 Spirit Women's
Activities: 2-Spirits HIV/AIDS education & prevention program; counselling; client support programs
Chief Officer(s):
Art Zoccole, Executive Director Ext. 222
art@2spirits.com

Tyndale St-Georges Community Centre / Centre Communautaire Tyndale St-Georges
870, careé Richmond, Montréal QC H3J 1V7
Tel: 514-931-6265; *Fax:* 514-931-1343
info@tyndalestgeorges.com
www.tyndalestgeorges.com
www.linkedin.com/in/tyndalestgeorges
www.facebook.com/tyndalecommunity
twitter.com/tyndalestgeorge
youtube.com/user/TyndaleStGeorges
Overview: A medium-sized local organization founded in 1927
Mission: To provide services to more than 2,000 members of the Little Burgundy community through programs extending from pre-school to adult development without regard to race or religious affiliation
Activities: The Richmond Square branch (careé Richmond) offers youth programming
Chief Officer(s):
Joseph D'Intino, Interim Executive Director
josephdintino@tyndalestgeorges.com
Publications:
• Tyndale St-Georges Community Centre Newsletter
Type: Newsletter
Profile: Published twice a year

Des Seigneurs Branch
753, rue des Seigneurs, Montréal QC H3J 1Y2
Tel: 514-989-2155; *Fax:* 514-935-1662
tsgad@tyndalestgeorges.com

U'mista Cultural Society
PO Box 253, Alert Bay BC V0N 1A0
Tel: 250-974-5403; *Fax:* 250-974-5499
Toll-Free: 800-690-8222
info@umista.ca
www.umista.org
www.facebook.com/Umista.Cultural.Society
Overview: A medium-sized local charitable organization founded in 1974
Mission: To collect, preserve & exhibit native artifacts of cultural, artistic & historic value to the Kwakwaka'wakw; to promote & foster carving, dancing, ceremonial & other cultural/artistic activities engaged in by the Kwakwaka'wakw; to collect, record & make available information & records relating to the language & history of the Kwakwaka'wakw; to promote, build & maintain facilities for carrying out the above aims; to recover from other institutions & individuals artifacts & records of cultural, artistic & historic value to the Kwakwaka'wakw
Member of: Canadian Museums Association; British Columbia Museums Association; First Nations Confederacy of Cultural Education Centres
Finances: *Funding Sources:* Federal & provincial government; private; sales
Membership: *Fees:* $20 Canadian individual; $35 Canadian family; $35 international individual; $70 international family; *Member Profile:* Ordinary membership open to any person who can trace ancestry to a member of any tribe of the Kwakwaka'wakw; persons eligible to become ordinary members become honourary members at age 65; persons not eligible to become ordinary members may become individual or family members upon payment of a small annual fee
Activities: The U'mista Cultural Centre disseminates cultural, historic & artistic information about the Kwakwaka'wakw by means of travelling exhibits, cooperation with researchers, distribution of films, participation in conferences & the distribution of newsletters, etc.; Language Retention Programs (including Kwak'wala language books & tapes, & an Oral History Project); Big House rebuilding; Potlatch Collection; *Speaker Service:* Yes; *Library:* Open to public

UBC Alumni Association
The Robert H. Lee Alumni Centre, 6163 University Blvd., Vancouver BC V6T 1Z1
Tel: 604-822-3313; *Fax:* 604-822-8928
Toll-Free: 800-883-3088
alumni.ubc@ubc.ca
www.alumni.ubc.ca
www.linkedin.com/groups/59693
www.facebook.com/ubcalumni
twitter.com/alumniubc
www.youtube.com/ubcalumni
Overview: A large provincial organization founded in 1946
Mission: To serve alumni, the university & its students by fostering communications, life-long relationships, networking & access to resources that enrich the lives of alumni & students while advancing the reputation of the university
Member of: Canadian Council for the Advancement of Education (CCAE); Council for Advancement & Support of Education (CASE)
Finances: *Annual Operating Budget:* $500,000-$1.5 Million; *Funding Sources:* Marketing of alumni services & programs; Travel programs; University grant
Staff Member(s): 38; 250 volunteer(s)
Membership: 225,000; *Member Profile:* Graduates of UBC; *Committees:* Board; Governance; Advocacy; Regional Networks; Marketing & Communications; Awards; Dinner; Young Alumni
Activities: Hosting reunion weekends; Providing career services; Offering discounts on services to members; Offering mentorship & networking opportunities for students
Chief Officer(s):
Jeff Todd, Executive Director, 604-454-4699
jeff.todd@ubc.ca
Awards:
• Alumni Award of Distinction, Alumni UBC Achievement Awards
Recognizes a UBC alumnus whose accomplishments have made an outstanding contribution to the community *Deadline:* January
• Faculty Community Service Award, Alumni UBC Achievement Awards
Recognizes a UBC faculty member who has demonstrated significant community services in areas other than teaching *Deadline:* January
• Future Alumnus Award, Alumni UBC Achievement Awards
Awarded to a UBC student who has excelled in leadership, academic success, or community service *Eligibility:* UBC students with no more than a Bachelor's degree completed *Deadline:* January
• Global Citizenship Award, Alumni UBC Achievement Awards
Awarded to an alumnus to recognize significant community or voluntary service that has garnered international recognition & made a difference on a global scale *Deadline:* January
• Honorary Alumnus Award, Alumni UBC Achievement Awards
Awarded to recognize outstanding contributions to the UBC community made by a non-UBC alumnus *Deadline:* January
• Volunteer Leadership Award, Alumni UBC Achievement Awards
Awarded to honour alumni who have contributed as a volunteer to the University or the Alumni Association over a sustained period *Deadline:* January
• Young Alumnus Award, Alumni UBC Achievement Awards
Awarded to a young alumnus whose accomplishments in the professional or public service sector inspire & lead other young alumni *Deadline:* January

Publications:
• Trek [a publication of UBC Alumni Association]
Type: Magazine; *Frequency:* Biannually; *Accepts Advertising;*
Editor: Vanessa Clarke

Ucluelet Chamber of Commerce (UCOC)
PO Box 428, 1604 Peninsula Rd., Ucluelet BC V0R 3A0
Tel: 250-726-4641; *Fax:* 250-726-4611
info@uclueletinfo.com
www.ucluelet.ca
Overview: A small local organization founded in 1947
Mission: To address the needs of businesses in the community; To strengthen the economy in the region
Member of: Tourism BC; BC Chamber of Commerce
Finances: *Annual Operating Budget:* $50,000-$100,000
Staff Member(s): 3
Membership: 110; *Fees:* $100-$250
Activities: Organizing & supporting events such as the Edge to Edge Marathon, Winter Festival, & Pacific Rim Whale Festival; *Library:* Business Library; Open to public
Chief Officer(s):
Sally Mole, Executive Director
smole@uclueletinfo.com

UJA Federation of Greater Toronto
4600 Bathurst St., Toronto ON M2R 3V2
Tel: 416-635-2883
info@jewishtoronto.com
www.jewishtoronto.com
www.facebook.com/UJAFederationToronto
twitter.com/UJAFederation
www.youtube.com/user/UJAFederation;
www.instagram.com/UJAFederation
Also Known As: United Jewish Appeal
Previous Name: The Jewish Federation of Greater Toronto
Overview: A large local charitable organization founded in 1994
Mission: To preserve & strengthen Jewish life in Toronto, Canada & Israel, through philanthropic, volunteer & professional leadership; The UJA is committed to social justice on behalf of the Jewish poor & vulnerable locally & internationally, to strengthening ties with Israel & its people, to supporting Israel's struggle to meet its social welfare needs, to combatting antisemitism in all its forms around the world, to nurturing shared values with Canadians of all faiths, to promoting Jewish education, to building a vibrant Jewish communal life. The following Pillars identify main areas of focus for UJA: Jewish Education & Identity; Strategic Planning & Community Engagement; Integrated Development; Operations & Corporate Relations; Business & Finance
Affiliation(s): Toronto Jewish Library; Board of Jewish Education; Committee for Yiddish; Holocaust Centre of Greater Toronto; Jewish Information Service of Greater Toronto; Ontario Jewish Archives; Bathurst JCC & Miles Nadal JCC; Jewish Family & Child Service; Hillel of Greater Toronto; Bernard Betel Centre for Creative Living; Jewish Immigrant Aid Services Toronto; Jewish Vocational Services Toronto, Jewish Russian Community Centre
Finances: *Funding Sources:* Corporate partners, Private donations
Activities: *Awareness Events:* Campaign for Our Jewish Future; Tomorrow Campaign
Chief Officer(s):
Adam Minsky, President & CEO
Publications:
• UJA Federation of Greater Toronto Annual Report
Type: Report; *Frequency:* Annually

Ukrainian Canadian Civil Liberties Association (UCCLA) / L'Association ukrainienne-canadienne des droits civils
PO Box 100, Stn. A, Ottawa ON K1N 8V1
media@uccla.ca
www.uccla.ca
www.facebook.com/TheUCCLA
twitter.com/UCCLA
Overview: A small national organization founded in 1984
Mission: To promote the interests of the Ukrainian Canadian community & educate the general public about the Ukrainian experience in Canada & about contemporary Ukrainian issues; to articulate & defend the civil liberties & human rights of Canadians of Ukrainian heritage & to provide objective information on Ukraine & Ukrainians to the media, government & general public
Finances: *Annual Operating Budget:* Less than $50,000
25 volunteer(s)

Membership: 1,000-4,999; *Member Profile:* Canadian Ukrainians
Activities: Publish occasional booklets for eductional purposes in English with Ukrainian & French abstracts; prepare & install historical markers relevant to Ukrainian history; *Speaker Service:* Yes
Chief Officer(s):
Roman Zakaluzny, Chair

Ukrainian Canadian Committee *See* Ukrainian Canadian Congress

Ukrainian Canadian Congress (UCC) / Congrès des ukrainiens canadiens
#203, 952 Main St., Winnipeg MB R2W 3P4
Tel: 204-942-4627; *Fax:* 204-947-3882
Toll-Free: 866-942-4627
ucc@ucc.ca
www.ucc.ca
www.linkedin.com/company/ukrainian-canadian-congress
www.facebook.com/ukrcancongress
twitter.com/ukrcancongress
www.youtube.com/user/UkrainianCanCongress
Previous Name: Ukrainian Canadian Committee
Overview: A large national charitable organization founded in 1940
Mission: To protect, promote & enhance cultural identity of Ukrainians throughout Canada & beyond; To maintain, develop & enhance Ukrainian culture & language as integral elements of Canada's multicultural mosaic; To encourage participation of Ukrainian Canadians in cultural, social, economic, & political life in Canada; To advance communication, understanding & mutual respect between Ukrainian Canadians & other ethnocultural communities; To foster sense of unity, cohesiveness & cooperation among member organizations
Member of: Canadian Ethnocultural Council; Ukrainian World Congress
Affiliation(s): Ukrainian Catholic Brotherhood; Ukrainian Self-Reliance Association (Orthodox); Ukrainian National Federation; League of Ukrainian Canadians; Ukrainian Canadian Foundation of Taras Shevchenko; Canada-Ukraine Foundation
Membership: 50+ organizations; *Fees:* Schedule available; *Member Profile:* Member organizations; *Committees:* Awards & Recognitions; Canada Ukraine Stakeholder Advisory Council; Finance; Fundraising; Governance; Immigration; Invictus Host; Museums, Archives & Research Institutions; National Religious Affairs; National Ukrainian Education; Ukraine Appeal; Ukrainian Canadian Arts Network
Activities: *Awareness Events:* Holodomor Awareness Week, November; *Internships:* Yes; *Library:* Open to public
Chief Officer(s):
Paul Grod, President
Awards:
• Shevchenko Medal Award
Recognizes individuals of Ukrainian and non-Ukrainian descent, as well as institutions and organizations, for their outstanding national contribution towards the development of the Ukrainian Canadian community
• Youth Leadership Award of Excellence
• Leadership Awards
Meetings/Conferences:
• Ukrainian Canadian Congress Triennal Congress 2019, 2019
Scope: National
Publications:
• Ukrainian Canadian Congress eNewsletter
Type: Newsletter; *Frequency:* Monthly
Profile: Association & world news
Alberta Provincial Council
#8, 8103 - 127 Ave., Edmonton AB T5C 1R9
Tel: 780-414-1624; *Fax:* 780-414-1626
uccab@shaw.ca
www.uccab.ca
www.facebook.com/UCCAPC
Chief Officer(s):
Barbara Hlus, President
British Columbia Provincial Council
Vancouver BC
www.infoukes.com/uccbc/
Mission: To protect & develop the Ukranian culture in BC
Montréal Branch
6175, 10e av, Montréal QC H1Y 2H5
Tel: 514-593-1000
www.uccmontreal.org
Chief Officer(s):
Zorianna Hrycenko-Luhova, President

Saskatchewan Provincial Council
4 - 2345 Ave. C North, Saskatoon SK S7L 5Z5
Tel: 306-652-5850; *Fax:* 306-665-2127
Toll-Free: 888-652-5850
uccspc@ucc.sk.ca
www.ucc.sk.ca
Chief Officer(s):
Slawko Kindrachuk, President
s.kindrachuk@ucc.sk.ca
Danylo Puderak, Executive Director
danylo.puderak@ucc.sk.ca
Toronto Branch
#208, 145 Evans Ave., Toronto ON M8Z 5X8
Tel: 416-323-4772
ucctoronto@bellnet.ca
www.ucctoronto.ca
Chief Officer(s):
Oksana Rewa, President
Nadia Sydorenko, Office Administrator

Ukrainian Canadian Foundation of Taras Shevchenko
#202, 952 Main St., Winnipeg MB R2W 3P4
Tel: 204-944-9128; *Fax:* 204-944-9135
Toll-Free: 866-524-5314
www.shevchenkofoundation.ca
www.facebook.com/ShevchenkoFoundation
Also Known As: Shevchenko Foundation
Overview: A medium-sized national charitable organization founded in 1963
Mission: To promote & advance Ukrainian culture in Canada
Member of: Ukrainian Canadian Congress
Finances: *Annual Operating Budget:* $250,000-$500,000; *Funding Sources:* Donations & bequests
Staff Member(s): 1
Membership: 1,000-4,999; *Committees:* Investment
Activities: Building & maintaining an endowment fund
Chief Officer(s):
Lesia Szwaluk, Executive Director
lesia@shevchenkofoundation.ca
Awards:
• Kobzar Literary Award
Eligibility: Canadian authors of narratives with Ukrainian Canadian themes *Deadline:* January; *Amount:* $25,000
Publications:
• Shevchenko Foundation Annual Report
Type: Report; *Frequency:* Annually

Ukrainian Canadian Research & Documentation Centre (UCRDC) / Centre canadien-ukrainien de recherches et de documentation
620 Spadina Ave., Toronto ON M5S 2H4
Tel: 416-966-1819; *Fax:* 416-966-1820
info@ucrdc.org
www.ucrdc.org
www.facebook.com/261703763950638
Overview: A small national charitable organization founded in 1986
Mission: To collect, store & promote information pertaining to Ukrainian historical events & Ukrainian Canadian experiences
Member of: Ukrainian Canadian Congress
Affiliation(s): St. Vladimir Institute
Finances: *Funding Sources:* Private donations; Sale of films & publications; Sponsorship
Activities: Organizing exhibits & film screenings; Collecting & preserving historical records; *Internships:* Yes *Library:* Research & Documentation Centre; by appointment
Chief Officer(s):
Jurij Darewych, Chair & President
Publications:
• Between Hitler & Stalin [a publication of the Ukrainian Canadian Research & Documentation Centre]
Type: Book; *Author:* Wsevolod W. Isajiw et al.; *Price:* $10
• The Extraordinary Lives of Ordinary Women: Oral History of the 20th Century" [a publication of the UCRDC]
Type: Book; *Number of Pages:* 835; *Editor:* Iroida Wynnyckyj; *Price:* $40
Profile: Contains 21 fully transcribed interviews with Ukrainian women who experienced events like WorldWars & the interwar period
• Famine-Genocide in Ukraine [a publication of the Ukrainian Canadian Research & Documentation Centre]
Type: Book; *Author:* Wsevolod W. Isajiw; *ISBN:* 978-0-921537-56-4; *Price:* $10
Profile: Presents an analysis of documents about the Ukrainian Famine that were found in Western & Russian archives

• Ukrainian Holocaust 1932-1933 [a publication of the Ukrainian Canadian Research & Documentation Centre]
Type: Book; *Author:* Yuri Mycyk; *Price:* $20
Profile: Written in Ukrainian; contains testimonies of Ukrainian Famine victims & witnesses

Ukrainian Canadian Social Services (Toronto) Inc
2445 Bloor St. West, Toronto ON M6S 1P7
Tel: 416-763-4982; *Fax:* 416-763-3997
toradmin@ucss.info
tor.ucss.info
www.facebook.com/1581507065420248
Overview: A small local charitable organization founded in 1960
Mission: To provide social services to individuals & families of Ukrainian background who experience language & cultural barriers
Affiliation(s): Ukrainian Canadian Social Services Inc. of Canada
Finances: *Funding Sources:* All levels of government; Donations; Fund raising
Staff Member(s): 4
Membership: 196 individual; 7 organizational; *Fees:* $25 individual; $50 organization; *Member Profile:* Any individual or Ukrainian-Canadian organization that supports the mission of the organization
Activities: Offering social & cultural services for community members; Facilitating programs for seniors & individuals requiring special assistance
Chief Officer(s):
Lidia Cymbaluk, Executive Director

Ukrainian Democratic Youth Association (ODUM)
3029 Bloor St. West, Toronto ON M8X 1C5
www.odum.org
Overview: A small local organization
Mission: To unite Ukrainian Canadians & other Ukrainians across North America
Activities: Organizing summer camps & community events

Ukrainian Fraternal Society of Canada (UFSC)
235 McGregor St., Winnipeg MB R2W 4W5
Tel: 204-568-4482; *Fax:* 204-589-6411
Toll-Free: 800-988-8372
info@ufsc.ca
www.ufsc.ca
Overview: A small national licensing organization founded in 1921
Member of: Canadian Fraternal Association
Finances: *Annual Operating Budget:* $250,000-$500,000
Staff Member(s): 1
Membership: 995; *Member Profile:* Ukrainian Canadians only; *Committees:* Donations; Scholarship
Activities: *Library:* by appointment
Chief Officer(s):
Boris Salamon, President
Donna Smigelsky, Manager
Awards:
• Provincial Scholarships
5 Annual provincial scholarships of $500
Meetings/Conferences:
• 25th Convention of the Ukrainian Fraternal Society of Canada, 2018
Scope: National

Ukrainian Genealogical & Historical Society of Canada (UGHSC)
PO Box 56, Blaine Lake SK S0J 0J0
Tel: 306-497-2770; *Fax:* 306-497-2770
ukrainiangenealogist@sasktel.net
ukrainiangenealogist.tripod.com
Also Known As: UGHS of Canada
Overview: A small national charitable organization founded in 1979
Mission: To encourage individuals & families to record their family tree; to research & collect family histories, genealogies & data pertinent to Ukraine's diasporas
Member of: Federation of Eastern European Family History Societies
Finances: *Annual Operating Budget:* Less than $50,000
42 volunteer(s)
Membership: 100-499
Activities: Library is mobile & visiting local events throughout North America; society is involved in "village identifying" 880 microfilms from Lviv, Ukraine; *Library:* Prosvita; Open to public by appointment
Chief Officer(s):
Walter Rusel, President

Ukrainian National Federation of Canada (UNF) / Fédération nationale Ukrainienne du Canada
#210, 145 Evans Ave., Toronto ON M8Z 5X8
Tel: 416-925-2770
info@unfcanada.ca
www.unfcanada.ca
www.facebook.com/unfcanada
Overview: A medium-sized national charitable organization
Mission: To unite Ukrainian Canadians while promoting good Canadian citizenship; To represent the interests & needs of the Ukrainian Canadian community; To inform Canadians about Ukrainian history & culture while strengthening the place of the Ukrainian community in Canadian society at large
Affiliation(s): Ukrainian War Veterans Association of Canada; Ukrainian Women's Organization of Canada (UWOC); Ukrainian National Youth Federation (UNYF)
Finances: *Funding Sources:* Donations
Membership: *Fees:* Schedule available, based upon branch; *Member Profile:* Individuals & organizations who share the beliefs & values of the Ukrainian National Federation
Activities: Offering educational & cultural programming; Offering children's day camps; Providing networking opportunities; *Library:* Open to public
Chief Officer(s):
Olya Grod, Executive Director

Ukrainian Orthodox Church of Canada (UOCC) / L'Église orthodoxe ukrainienne du Canada
Ecumenical Patriarchate, 9 St. John's Ave., Winnipeg MB R2W 1G8
Tel: 204-586-3093; *Fax:* 204-582-5241
Toll-Free: 877-586-3093
consistory@uocc.ca
www.uocc.ca
Overview: A large national organization founded in 1918
Membership: 120,000
Activities: *Speaker Service:* Yes; *Library:* Ukrainian Orthodox Church of Canada Library; Open to public by appointment
Chief Officer(s):
Metropolitan Yurij, Primate
metropolitan@uocc.ca
Taras Udod, Chancellor & Chair, Presidium
chancellor@uocc.ca
Publications:
• Visnyk/Herald [a publication of Ukrainian Orthodox Church of Canada]
Type: Newspaper
   Eastern Eparchy
   3281 Cindy Cres., Mississauga ON L4Y 3S7
   Tel: 905-206-9372; *Fax:* 905-206-9373
   uocceast@rogers.com
   uocceast.ca
   Western Eparchy
   11404 - 112 Ave., Edmonton AB T5G 0H6
   Tel: 780-455-1938; *Fax:* 780-454-5287
   admin@uocc-we.ca
   www.uocc-we.ca
   Chief Officer(s):
   Ilarion, Bishop, Edmonton & the Western Eparchy
   rudnyk1@telus.net

Ukrainian Self-Reliance League of Canada (CYC)
1027 North Service Rd., Stoney Creek ON L8E 5C8
Tel: 905-643-3250
www.usrl-cyc.org
Overview: A large national organization founded in 1927
Mission: To preserve Canadian heritage while advancing Ukrainian Canadian culture; To enhance the future growth of the Ukrainian Orthodox Church of Canada
Affiliation(s): Canadian Ukrainian Youth Association; Ukrainian Women's Association
Activities: Organizing workshops & educational opportunities; Communicating with membership through print material; Holding membership meetings
Chief Officer(s):
Peter Kondra, President
Meetings/Conferences:
• Ukrainian Self-Reliance League of Canada Biennial National Convention 2019, 2019
Scope: National

Ukrainian War Veterans Association of Canada (UWVA)
145 Evans Ave., Toronto ON M8Z 5X8
Tel: 416-925-2770
www.unfcanada.ca/uwva

Overview: A small national organization founded in 1928
Mission: To promote national unity & maintain Ukrainian identity; To support the Ukrainian National Federation of Canada
Affiliation(s): Ukrainian National Federation of Canada

Ukrainian Women's Association of Canada (UWAC)
10611 - 110 Ave. NW, Edmonton AB T5H 1H7
Tel: 780-465-5440; *Fax:* 780-425-3991
info@uwac-national.ca
www.uwac-national.ca
Overview: A large national organization founded in 1926
Mission: To support the continual growth of the Ukrainian Orthodox Church of Canada; To preserve, develop, & nurture Ukrainian heritage; To foster & encourage cooperation within Canadian society; To support education of Ukrainian Canadian youth in church schools, Ukrainian schools, & bilingual schools; To maintain the growth of the Ukrainian Museum of Canada of the UWAC
Membership: 1,300 in 45 branches
Activities: *Library:* Ukrainian Museum of Canada; Open to public
Chief Officer(s):
Lesia Perritt, President
Publications:
• Anniversary Cookbook [a publication of the Ukrainian Women's Association of Canada]
Type: Book
Profile: Traditional Ukrainian cookbook
• The Child's Companion [a publication of the Ukrainian Women's Association of Canada]
Type: Book; *Author:* Lilia Matwijiw Sorokowski
Profile: A pictorial prayer book
• Essays from the History of Ukrainian culture, Book I [a publication of the Ukrainian Women's Association of Canada]
Type: Book; *Author:* Savella Stechishin et al.
• Essays from the History of Ukrainian Culture, Book II [a publication of the Ukrainian Women's Association of Canada]
Type: Book; *Author:* Serhij Eremenko et al.
• Feast Days of the Orthodox Church [a publication of the Ukrainian Women's Association of Canada]
Type: Book; *Author:* Ivan Stus
• From Baba With Love [a publication of the Ukrainian Women's Association of Canada]
Type: Book
Profile: Traditional Ukrainian cookbook
• From Generation to Generation [a publication of the Ukrainian Women's Association of Canada]
Type: Book
Profile: Traditional Ukrainian cookbook
• A Half Century of Service to the Community [a publication of the Ukrainian Women's Association of Canada]
Type: Book; *Author:* Natalia Kohuska
Profile: A history of the Ukrainian Women's Association of Canada from 1926-1976
• Ukrainian Canadiana [a publication of the Ukrainian Women's Association of Canada]
Type: Book
• Ukrainian Daughter's Cookbook [a publication of the Ukrainian Women's Association of Canada]
Type: Book; *ISBN:* 0-919845-13-4
Profile: Traditional Ukrainian cookbook
• Ukrainian Embroidery Designs & Stitches [a publication of the Ukrainian Women's Association of Canada]
Type: Book; *Author:* Nancy Ruryk
   Toronto Branch
   145 Evans Ave., Toronto ON M8Z 5X8
   Tel: 416-253-6002
   www.unfcanada.ca/staff/toronto
   www.facebook.com/UkrainianWomensOrganizationOfCanada TorontoBranch

Ukrainian World Congress / Congrès mondial des ukrainiens
#207, 145 Evans Ave., Toronto ON M8Z 5X8
Tel: 416-323-3020; *Fax:* 416-323-3250
uwc@ukrainianworldcongress.org
www.ukrainianworldcongress.org
www.facebook.com/130772870318563
twitter.com/UWCongress
www.youtube.com/user/UkrWorldCongress/videos?view=0
Overview: A medium-sized international organization
Mission: To be an umbrella organization for Ukrainian associations outside Ukraine; To promote solidarity among Ukrainian people throughout the world; To cooperate with governments, organizations, & individuals to accomplish goals in the spirit of equality & justice

Finances: *Funding Sources:* Donations
Chief Officer(s):
Aleksandra Szubelak, Executive Administrator

Ukrainian Youth Association of Canada
9 Plastics Ave., Toronto ON M8Z 4B6
Tel: 416-537-2007; *Fax:* 416-516-4033
KY-Canada@CYM.org
cym.org/ca
www.facebook.com/CYM.Canada
Overview: A large national charitable organization
Mission: To encourage Ukrainian children & youth to discover their Ukrainian heritage; To promote Ukrainian traditions & language; To emphasize the development of Christian ethics & leadership skills
Membership: *Member Profile:* Ukrainian Canadian youth between the ages of 5 & 18
Activities: Organizing excursions, trips, athletic programs, & camps; Holding weekly membership meetings
Chief Officer(s):
Tamara Tataryn, President
Publications:
• Krylati [a publication of the Ukrainian Youth Association of Canada]
Type: Magazine; *Frequency:* Bimonthly; *Price:* $30
Profile: Information & articles for youth & counsellors
• Ukrainian Youth Association of Canada Newsletter
Type: Newsletter; *Frequency:* Quarterly
Profile: Association news & information

Edmonton Branch
9615 - 153 Ave., Edmonton AB T5E 6B1
uyaedm@gmail.com
archive.cym.org/ca/edmonton/
www.facebook.com/cym.edmonton
Chief Officer(s):
Yuri Broda, President

Montréal Branch
3260, rue Beaubien, Montréal QC H1X 3C9
Tel: 514-728-8816
montrealbulava@cym.org
archive.cym.org/ca/Montreal/index.asp
Chief Officer(s):
Michael Shwec, President

Ottawa Branch
911 Carling Ave., Ottawa ON K1Y 4E3
ottawa@cym.org
archive.cym.org/ca/ottawa/
Chief Officer(s):
Wolodymyr Usyk, President

Winnipeg Branch
77 Pritchard Ave., Winnipeg MB R2X 0E8
Tel: 204-586-2956
archive.cym.org/ca/winnipeg/
Chief Officer(s):
Irene Semaniuk, President

Ultimate Canada
4382 Shelbourne St., Vancouver BC V8N 3G3
Toll-Free: 888-691-1080
info@canadianultimate.com
www.canadianultimate.com
www.facebook.com/UltimateCanada
twitter.com/Ultimate_Canada
Previous Name: Canadian Ultimate Players Association
Overview: A medium-sized national charitable organization founded in 1993
Mission: To be the governing body for the sport of ultimate in Canada.
Finances: *Annual Operating Budget:* $50,000-$100,000; *Funding Sources:* Membership dues
Staff Member(s): 4; 50 volunteer(s)
Membership: 800; *Fees:* $30 junior; $55 regular
Activities: *Awareness Events:* Canadian National Championships; Canadian National University Championships
Chief Officer(s):
Danny Saunders, Executive Director
ed@canadianultimate.com
Publications:
• CUPA Connection
Type: Newsletter

Ultralight Pilots Association of Canada (UPAC) / Association canadienne des pilotes d'avions ultra-légers
907289 Township Rd. 12, RR#4, Bright ON N0J 1B0
Tel: 519-684-7628
info@upac.ca
www.upac.ca
www.facebook.com/groups/155979254430741/
Merged from: Ultralight Aircraft Association of Canada (UAAC) & Microlight Owners and Pilots of Canada (MOPAC)
Overview: A small national organization founded in 1986
Mission: To promote ultralight aviation in Canada and act as a representative voice for ultralight pilots in discussions with the federal government
Finances: *Annual Operating Budget:* Less than $50,000; *Funding Sources:* Membership fees
10 volunteer(s)
Membership: 500+; *Fees:* $50-$70; *Member Profile:* Interest in ultralight aviaton
Activities: Video library for members; *Library:* Ultralight Pilots Association of Canada Video Library; Not open to public
Chief Officer(s):
K. Lubitz, President
Publications:
• Light Flight (a publication of the Ultalight Pilots Association of Canada)
Type: Newsletter; *Frequency:* monthly
Profile: Information on current and proposed Transport Canada rules & regulations; tips on maintenance; information on ultalight activity acrossCanada

Uncles & Aunts at Large
11031 - 124 St. NW, Edmonton AB T5M 0J5
Tel: 780-452-5791; *Fax:* 780-453-6914
info@unclesatlarge.ab.ca
www.unclesatlarge.ab.ca
Overview: A small local organization founded in 1967
Mission: To provide mentoring services to children of single parent homes

Underwater Archaeological Society of British Columbia (UASBC)
c/o Vancouver Maritime Museum, 1905 Ogden Ave., Vancouver BC V6J 1A3
www.uasbc.com
vimeo.com/uasbc
Overview: A small provincial charitable organization founded in 1975
Mission: To promote the science of underwater archaeology; to conserve, preserve & protect the maritime heritage lying beneath our coastal & inland waters
Member of: Outdoor Recreation Council of British Columbia
Finances: *Funding Sources:* Membership dues; government; corporate
Activities: Archaeological site surveys, heritage awareness promotion; operates 4 chapters in Vancouver, Victoria, Kootenay & Okanagan; *Speaker Service:* Yes; *Library:* Archives; by appointment

Underwater Council of British Columbia (UCBC)
BC
underwatercouncil.bc@gmail.com
www.underwatercouncilbc.org
www.facebook.com/246182652097184
www.youtube.com/user/TheUCBC
Overview: A small provincial organization
Mission: To represent recreational divers in British Columbia
Membership: *Fees:* Free
Chief Officer(s):
Adam Taylor, President
Scott Meixner, Secretary

Underwriters' Laboratories of Canada (ULC) / Laboratoires des assureurs du Canada
7 Underwriters Rd., Toronto ON M1R 3A9
Tel: 416-757-3611; *Fax:* 416-757-8727
Toll-Free: 866-937-3852
customerservice@ulc.ca
www.ul.com
Overview: A medium-sized national organization founded in 1920
Mission: To support domestic governmental product safety regulations, & works with international safety systems to help further trade with adherence to local safety requirements.
Affiliation(s): Underwriters Laboratories Inc., Northbrook IL
Finances: *Funding Sources:* Fee for service
Activities: *Library:*
Chief Officer(s):
Keith E. Williams, President & CEO

Montréal Site
#330, 6505, rte Transcanada, Montréal QC H4T 1S3
Tél: 514-363-5941; *Téléc:* 514-363-7014
customerservice@ulc.ca

Ottawa Site
#400, 171 Nepean St., Ottawa ON K2P 0B4
Tél: 613-755-2729; *Téléc:* 613-231-5977
customerservice@ulc.ca

Vancouver Site
#130, 13775 Commerce Pkwy., Richmond BC V6V 2V4
Tel: 604-214-9555; *Fax:* 604-214-9550
customerservice@ulc.ca

Unemployed Help Centre (UHC)
6955 Cantelon Dr., Windsor ON N8T 3J9
Tel: 519-944-4900; *Fax:* 519-944-9184
uhc@uhc.ca
www.uhc.ca
www.facebook.com/UHC.Windsor
twitter.com/@uhc_
Overview: A small local charitable organization founded in 1977
Mission: To assist, inform & advise on problems related to being unemployed; to assist the unemployed in dealing with Canada Employment & Immigration, E.I.; Social Services & other appropriate community service agencies; to provide a phone-in service for the unemployed; to promote community projects that assist disadvantaged people; to offer relief to the poor; to solicit funds by way of donations, grants, bequests, lotteries & other similar methods
Member of: Ontario Association of Food Banks; Ontario Association of Help Centres
Finances: *Annual Operating Budget:* $1.5 Million-$3 Million; *Funding Sources:* Government grants; United Way; fundraising
Staff Member(s): 26; 25 volunteer(s)
Activities: Vocational Counselling; Literacy/Numeracy; Closure & Downsizing; On-the-job Training; Human Resources; Job Line; Food Bank; Income Tax; Pre-employment Preparation Services; Resource Centre; *Library:* Information Resource Centre; Open to public
Chief Officer(s):
Pamela Pons, Contact
Awards:
• Minister's Award of Excellence

UNICEF Canada / Comité UNICEF Canada
Canada Sq., #1100, 2200 Yonge St., Toronto ON M4S 2C6
Toll-Free: 800-567-4483
Other Communication: communityevents@unicef.ca
secretary@unicef.ca
www.unicef.ca
www.linkedin.com/company/unicef-canada
www.facebook.com/UNICEF-Canada
twitter.com/UNICEFLive
www.youtube.com/user/unicefcanada
Also Known As: Canadian UNICEF Committee
Overview: A large national charitable organization founded in 1955
Mission: To raise funds to help ensure the survival, growth & long term development of the world's children
Member of: UNICEF International
Finances: *Annual Operating Budget:* Greater than $5 Million; *Funding Sources:* General public; government grants
Staff Member(s): 62; 3276 volunteer(s)
Membership: 1,200; *Committees:* Communication; Education for Development; Direct Mail; Finance & Administration; International Program; Marketing; Youth
Activities: *Awareness Events:* UNICEF Fund Drive - Halloween, Oct. 31; National UNICEF Day, October 31; *Speaker Service:* Yes; *Library:* by appointment
Chief Officer(s):
Noella Milne, Chair
David Morley, President & CEO
Dave Spedding, Chief Operating Officer
Sharon Avery, Chief Development Officer
Meg French, Chief Int'l Programs & PA Officer

UNICEF Alberta
#140, 301 - 14th St. NW, Calgary AB T2N 2A1
Tel: 403-270-2857; *Fax:* 403-283-0115
Toll-Free: 800-819-0889
Chief Officer(s):
Holly Davidson, Regional Davidson

UNICEF Atlantic
#103, 11 Thornhill Dr., Dartmouth NS B3B 1R9
Tel: 902-422-6000; *Fax:* 902-425-3002
Toll-Free: 877-786-4233

Chief Officer(s):
John Humble, Regional Director
UNICEF British Columbia
#201, 3077 Granvile St., Vancouver BC V6H 3J9
Tel: 604-874-3666; *Fax:* 604-874-5411
Toll-Free: 800-381-4343
Chief Officer(s):
Shirley Kepper, Regional Director, British Columbia
UNICEF Ontario - Toronto
#1100, 2200 Yonge St., Toronto ON M4S 2C6
Tel: 416-482-4444; *Fax:* 416-482-8035
Toll-Free: 800-567-4483
Chief Officer(s):
Jacqueline Jones, Regional Director
UNICEF Carleton
1125 Colonel By Dr., Ottawa ON K1S 5B6
UNICEF Prairies
#323, 112 Market Ave., Winnipeg MB R3B 0P4
Tel: 204-477-4600; *Fax:* 204-477-4040
Toll-Free: 866-888-6088
Chief Officer(s):
Tricia Schers, Regional Director
UNICEF Québec - Montréal
#400, 4060, rue Sainte-Catherine ouest, Montréal QC H3Z 2Z3
Tel: 514-288-5134

Unifarm *See* Wild Rose Agricultural Producers

UNIFOR
205 Placer Ct., Toronto ON M2H 3H9
Tel: 416-497-4110
Toll-Free: 800-268-5763
communications@unifor.org
www.unifor.org
www.facebook.com/UniforCanada
twitter.com/UniforTheUnion
www.youtube.com/user/UniforCanada
Previous Name: National Automobile, Aerospace, Transportation & General Workers Union of Canada
Merged from: Canadian Auto Workers; Communications, Energy & Paperworkers Union of Canada
Overview: A large national organization founded in 2013
Mission: To improve the working conditions & general economic & social conditions of Canadian workers in the industries of: aerospace, mining, fishing, auto & specialty vehicle assembly, auto parts, hotels, airlines, rail, education, hospitality, retail, road transportation, health care, manufacturing, shipbuilding, & others
Affiliation(s): TCA-Quebec
Finances: *Funding Sources:* Membership dues
Staff Member(s): 200
Membership: 310,000+
Activities: *Library:* Not open to public
Chief Officer(s):
Jerry Dias, National President
president@unifor.org
Bob Orr, Secretary-Treasurer
bob.orr@unifor.org
Meetings/Conferences:
• UNIFOR 3rd Biennial Pride Conference, 2019
Scope: National
Contact Information: E-mail: communications@unifor.org, Phone: 416-497-4110

Chatham Office
200 Riverview Dr., Chatham ON N7M 5Z8
Tel: 519-354-5800
Toll-Free: 800-204-3121
chatham@unifor.org
Drummondville
Place Royale, #120, 1125, boul St-Joseph, Drummondville QC J2C 2C8
Tel: 819-478-0111
Toll-Free: 877-478-0111
drummondvilleoffice@unifor.org
Edmonton
#410, 10525 170 St. NW, Edmonton AB T5P 4W2
Tel: 780-448-5865
Toll-Free: 800-890-9608
alberta@unifor.org
Gatineau
#315, 259 boul St Joseph, Gatineau QC J8Y 3X8
Tel: 819-775-4472
infoquebec@unifor.org
Halifax Office
63 Otter Lake Crt., 2nd Fl., Halifax NS B3S 1M1
Tel: 902-455-9327
Toll-Free: 800-565-1272
halifax@unifor.org
Jonquière
#120, 2679 boul du Royaume, Jonquière QC G7S 5T1
Tel: 418-548-7075
Toll-Free: 800-268-4808
infoquebec@unifor.org
Kitchener
5 Executive Pl., Kitchener ON N2P 2N4
Tel: 519-893-4873
Toll-Free: 800-265-2884
kitchener@unifor.org
London Office
140 Pine Valley Blvd., London ON N6K 3X3
Tel: 519-649-2552
Toll-Free: 800-265-1891
london@unifor.org
Mississauga
#510, 5915 Airport Rd., Mississauga ON L4V 1T1
Tel: 905-678-0800
Toll-Free: 800-268-9040
unifor@unifor.org
Moncton
55 Highfield St., Moncton NB E1C 5N2
Tel: 506-857-8647
unifor@unifor.org
Montréal Office
#10100, 565, boul Crémazie est, Montréal QC H2M 2W1
Tel: 514-389-9223
Toll-Free: 800-361-0483
infoquebec@unifor.org
New Westminster
326 - 12th St., New Westminster BC V3M 4H6
Tel: 604-522-7911
Toll-Free: 800-665-3553
newwestminster@unifor.org
Ottawa
5 Gurdwara Dr., Ottawa ON K2E 7X6
Tel: 613-523-0434
Toll-Free: 800-982-2601
ottawa@unifor.org
Ottawa
301 Laurier Ave. West, Ottawa ON K1P 6M6
Tel: 613-230-5200
Toll-Free: 877-230-5201
unifor@unifor.org
Port Elgin Office (Family Education Centre)
c/o Family Education Centre, Bruce County Rd. 25, RR#1, 115 Shipley Ave., Port Elgin ON N0H 2C5
Tel: 519-389-3200
Toll-Free: 800-265-3735
confcentre@unifor.org
Québec Office
#275, 5000, boul des Gradins, Québec QC G2J 1N3
Tel: 418-624-5320
infoquebec@unifor.org
Regina
2365 - 13th Ave., Regina SK S4P 0V8
Tel: 306-777-0000
regina@unifor.org
St Catharines
#103, 25 Corporate Park Dr., St Catharines ON L2S 3W2
Tel: 905-687-1841
Toll-Free: 800-663-9983
stcatharines@unifor.org
St. John's
PO Box 922, Stn. C, #301, 55 Bond St., St. John's NL A1C 5L7
Tel: 709-753-7191
unifor@unifor.org
St. John's
NAPE Building, 330A Portugal Cove Pl., St. John's NL A1A 4Y5
Tel: 709-726-5667
unifor@unifor.org
Sarnia
900 Devine St., Sarnia ON N7T 1X5
Tel: 519-332-4102
unifor@unifor.org
Sudbury
2550 Richard Lake Dr., Sudbury ON P3G 0A3
Tel: 705-673-3661
unifor@unifor.org
Sydney
4 Hugh St., Sydney NS B1P 1V7
Tel: 902-562-3857
Toll-Free: 800-591-7523
sydney@unifor.org
Thunder Bay
#100, 979 Alloy Dr., Thunder Bay ON P7B 5Z8
Tel: 807-344-1122
Toll-Free: 866-832-1122
thunderbay@unifor.org
Trois Rivières
7080, rue Marion, Trois-Rivières QC G9A 6G4
Tel: 819-378-4696
infoquebec@unifor.org
Windsor Office
2345 Central Ave., 2nd Fl., Windsor ON N8W 4J1
Tel: 519-944-5866
Toll-Free: 800-465-0974
windsor@unifor.org
Winnipeg
1376 Grant Ave., 2nd Fl., Winnipeg MB R3M 3Y4
Tel: 204-489-0355
Toll-Free: 800-665-7492
winnipeg@unifor.org

Unifor87-M (SONG)
1253 Queen St. East, Toronto ON M4L 1C2
Tel: 416-461-2461; *Fax:* 416-461-5058
Toll-Free: 800-463-5797
info@unifor87m.org
unifor87m.org
www.facebook.com/unifor87m
twitter.com/unifor87m
Previous Name: Souther Ontario Newsmedia Guild; Southern Ontario Newspaper Guild
Overview: A small local organization
Member of: Communications, Energy & Paperworkers Union of Canada
Membership: *Member Profile:* Employees at newspapers, magazines, television & publishing houses
Chief Officer(s):
Paul Morse, President, 416-461-2461 Ext. 1
paul@unifor87m.org

UniforACL
c/o Unifor Local 2289, #100, 6300 Lady Hammond Rd., Halifax NS B3K 2R6
Tel: 902-425-2440; *Fax:* 902-422-4647
Toll-Free: 800-565-2289
unifor-acl.ca
Merged from: Telephone Employee's Union
Overview: A medium-sized provincial organization
Membership: 4 locals
Chief Officer(s):
Penny Fawcett, Chair
penny.fawcett@cep2289.ca

Uniform Law Conference of Canada (ULCC) / Conference pour l'harmonisation des lois au Canada (CHLC)
c/o 622 Hochelaga St., Ottawa ON K1K 2E9
Tel: 613-747-1695; *Fax:* 613-941-9310
conference@ulcc.ca
www.ulcc.ca
Overview: A small national organization founded in 1935
Mission: To facilitate & promote the harmonization & improvements to laws throughtout Canada by developing, at the request of the constituent jurisdictions, Uniform Acts, Model Acts, Statements of Legal Principles, Proposals to Change Laws & other documents deemed appropriate to meet the demands that are presented to it by the constituent jurisdictions from time to time
Finances: *Annual Operating Budget:* $50,000-$100,000
Staff Member(s): 1
Membership: 14; *Member Profile:* Canada, the Provinces & Territories are constituent jurisdictions of the Conference; *Committees:* Criminal Section; Civil Section
Activities: Annual Conference, research
Chief Officer(s):
C. Lynn Romeo, President
lynn.romeo@gov.mb.ca
Marie Bordeleau, Executive Director
Meetings/Conferences:
• Uniform Law Conference of Canada 2018 Conference, August,

Canadian Associations / L'Union culturelle des Franco-Ontariennes (UCFO)

2018, Delta Hotel, Québec, QC
Scope: National

Union canadienne des employés des transports *See* Union of Canadian Transportation Employees

L'Union culturelle des Franco-Ontariennes (UCFO)
#302, 450, rue Rideau, Ottawa ON K1N 5Z4
Tél: 613-741-1334; *Téléc:* 613-741-8577
Ligne sans frais: 877-520-8226
ucfo@on.aibn.com
www.unionculturelle.ca
Aperçu: *Dimension:* moyenne; *Envergure:* provinciale; Organisme sans but lucratif; fondée en 1936
Mission: Améliorer les conditions et les réalités sociales des femmes francophones de l'Ontario; faciliter l'épanouissement de la femme tout en favorisant son autonomie
Membre de: Réseau canadien de développement économique communautaire; Table féministe francophone de concertation provinciale de l'Ontario; Assemblée de la francophonie de l'Ontario
Membre: *Critères d'admissibilite:* 14 ans et plus; femme; francophone
Membre(s) du bureau directeur:
Madeleine Chabot, Présidente provinciale

Union des artistes (UDA) / Artists' Union
#1005, 5445, ave De Gaspé, Montréal QC H2T 3B2
Tél: 514-288-6682; *Téléc:* 514-285-6789
info@uda.ca
www.uda.ca
www.facebook.com/UnionDesArtistes
twitter.com/udaquebec
www.youtube.com/user/Uniondesartistes
Aperçu: *Dimension:* grande; *Envergure:* provinciale; fondée en 1937
Mission: Identification, étude, défense et développement des intérêts économiques, sociaux et moraux de ses membres
Membre de: Fédération internationale des acteurs
Finances: *Budget de fonctionnement annuel:* $3 Million-$5 Million
Membre(s) du personnel: 70
Membre: +12 000 membres actifs et stagiaires; *Montant de la cotisation:* 125$ + 2,5%; *Comités:* Comité permanent des femmes artistes interprètes; Comité permanent d'éthique; Comité permanent du secrétariat général; Comité du doublage; Comité sur les relations agents - artistes; Comité sur le cinéma autogéré (artisanal); Comité sur l'accessibilité au travail; Comité minorités ethniques; Comité du congrès; Comité du 75e anniversaire; Comité Variétés scène / Comité Variétés phonogramme; Comité consultatif sur la formation continue
Membre(s) du bureau directeur:
Sophie Prègent, Président
Sylvie Brousseau, Directrice générale

Union des Artistes (FIA) - Bureau de Québec (UDA)
#520, rue De Saint-Vallier est, Québec QC G1K 9G4
Tél: 418-523-4241; *Téléc:* 418-523-0168
Ligne sans frais: 877-523-4299
pcauffope@uda.ca
Aperçu: *Dimension:* petite; *Envergure:* locale

Union des Artistes (FIA) - Bureau de Toronto (UDA)
#200, 625 Church St., Toronto ON M4Y 2G1
Tél: 416-485-7670; *Téléc:* 416-485-9063
Ligne sans frais: 866-379-8643
scouture@uda.ca
Aperçu: *Dimension:* petite; *Envergure:* locale

Union des associations des professeurs des universités de l'Ontario *See* Ontario Confederation of University Faculty Associations

Union des consommateurs
#201, 7000, av du Parc, Montréal QC H3N 1X1
Tél: 514-521-6820; *Téléc:* 514-521-0736
Ligne sans frais: 888-521-6820
info@unionsdesconsommateurs.ca
uniondesconsommateurs.ca
www.facebook.com/uniondesconso
twitter.com/union_conso
Aperçu: *Dimension:* moyenne; *Envergure:* provinciale
Membre: *Critères d'admissibilite:* Associations coopératives d'économie familiale (ACEF), l'Association des consommateurs pour la qualité dans la construction (ACQC) ainsi que des membres individuels; *Comités:* Agroalimentation; Énergie; Finances personnelles et endettement; Politiques sociales et fiscales; Protection du consommateur; Santé; Télécom
Activités:; *Bibliothèque:* Centre de documentation
Membre(s) du bureau directeur:
France Latreille, Directrice
flatreille@uniondesconsommateurs.ca

Union des cultivateurs franco-ontariens (UCFO)
2474 rue Champlain, Clarence Creek ON K0A 1N0
Tél: 613-488-2929; *Téléc:* 613-488-2541
Ligne sans frais: 877-425-8366
info@ucfo.ca
www.ucfo.ca
www.facebook.com/UCFO.ca
Aperçu: *Dimension:* petite; *Envergure:* provinciale; Organisme sans but lucratif; fondée en 1929
Mission: Regrouper les franco-ontariens et les franco-ontariennes qui oeuvrent dans le secteur agricole; concerter pour la protection de nos droits; promouvoir nos intérêts; informer notre communauté; appuyer les institutions et groupements qui favorisent notre développement; développer notre sentiment et fierté; stimuler le développement social et économique des régions agricoles et rurales
Finances: *Budget de fonctionnement annuel:* $100,000-$250,000
Membre(s) du personnel: 5; 10 bénévole(s)
Membre: 500; *Montant de la cotisation:* 15$ membre régulier, 35$ membre auxiliaire; *Critères d'admissibilite:* Agriculteurs, agricultrices de l'Ontario
Activités: Formation agricole
Membre(s) du bureau directeur:
Marc Laflèche, Président
Simon Durand, Directeur exécutif
sdurand@ucfo.ca
Marc-André Tessier, Agent, Communication et développement du leadership
communication@ucfo.ca

Union des écrivaines et écrivains québécois (UNEQ)
3492, av Laval, Montréal QC H2X 3C8
Tél: 514-849-8540; *Téléc:* 514-849-6239
Ligne sans frais: 888-849-8540
ecrivez@uneq.qc.ca
www.uneq.qc.ca
www.facebook.com/152536222994
twitter.com/Ecrivains_QC
Aperçu: *Dimension:* moyenne; *Envergure:* provinciale; fondée en 1977
Mission: Élaborer des politiques et administrer des programmes en vue de favoriser le développement de la littérature québécoise et sa diffusion au Québec comme à l'étranger, en vue également de faire reconnaître la profession d'écrivain de telle sorte que les intérêts moraux, sociaux et économiques des auteurs soient respectés
Membre(s) du personnel: 8
Membre: 1,500 écrivains; *Montant de la cotisation:* 140$ titulaire; 115$ associé/adhérent; 100$ doyen titulaire/adhérent/associé; 50$ débutant; *Critères d'admissibilite:* Les membres doivent avoir publié au moins deux livres (d'au moins 48 pages, publiés par une maison d'édition reconnue et qu'ils appartiennent à l'un ou l'autre des genres suivants: le roman, le récit, la nouvelle; la poésie; le théâtre; l'essai), dont l'un doit être pendant les dix années précédentes; membres adhérents doivent avoir publié une oeuvre; *Comités:* Trans-Québec; Sur le numérique; Membres associés
Activités: Tournées-rencontres; tournées dans les écoles; parrainage; festival de la littérature; animation à la maison des écrivains; centre de documentation virtuel: www.litterature.org; *Bibliothèque:* Bibliothèque L'Île; Bibliothèque publique
Membre(s) du bureau directeur:
Danièle Simpson, Présidente
Francis Farley-Chevrier, Directeur général
ffc@uneq.qc.ca

Union des employés de la Défense nationale *See* Union of National Defence Employees

Union des municipalités du Nouveau-Brunswick *See* Union of Municipalities of New Brunswick

Union des municipalités du Québec (UMQ)
#680, 680, rue Sherbrooke ouest, Montréal QC H3A 2M7
Tél: 514-282-7700; *Téléc:* 514-282-8893
info@umq.qc.ca
www.umq.qc.ca
twitter.com/UMQuebec
Aperçu: *Dimension:* grande; *Envergure:* provinciale; Organisme sans but lucratif; fondée en 1919
Mission: Au bénéfice des citoyens, représenter les municipalités auprès du gouvernement et contribuer à l'efficience de gestion des municipalités
Membre de: Fédération canadienne des municipalités
Affiliation(s): Conseil du patronat du Québec; Fédération canadienne des municipalités
Finances: *Budget de fonctionnement annuel:* $3 Million-$5 Million
Membre(s) du personnel: 35
Membre: 300; *Montant de la cotisation:* 0,46$ per capita; *Critères d'admissibilite:* Toutes les municipalités du Québec
Activités: Formation des élus et des gestionnaires municipaux; *Stagiaires:* Oui; *Service de conférenciers:* Oui; *Listes de destinataires:* Oui; *Bibliothèque* Not open to public
Membre(s) du bureau directeur:
Jasmin Savard, Directeur général, 514-282-7700 Ext. 281
Martine Painchaud, Directrice, Relations Internationales
Diane Simard, Directrice/Secrétaire, Affaires juridiques

Union des municipalités régionales de comté et des municipalités locales du Québec *Voir* Fédération Québécoise des Municipalités

Union des pêcheurs des Maritimes (CTC) *See* Maritime Fishermen's Union (CLC)

Union des philatélistes de Montréal
Maison du citoyen, 7501, rue François-Perrault, Montréal QC H2A 1M1
Courriel: info@philatelie-upm.com
www.philatelie-upm.com
Aperçu: *Dimension:* petite; *Envergure:* locale; fondée en 1933
Membre de: Royal Philatelic Society of Canada

Union des producteurs agricoles (UPA)
#100, 555, boul Roland-Therrien, Longueuil QC J4H 3Y9
Tél: 450-679-0530
www.upa.qc.ca
www.facebook.com/pageUPA
twitter.com/upaqc
www.youtube.com/user/upa1972
Aperçu: *Dimension:* grande; *Envergure:* provinciale; fondée en 1924 surveillé par Canadian Federation of Agriculture
Mission: Promouvoir, défendre et développer les intérêts professionnels, économiques, sociaux et moraux des producteurs agricoles et forestiers, sans distinction de race, de nationalité, de sexe, de langue et de croyance
Membre: 42 000
Membre(s) du bureau directeur:
Marcel Groleau, Président général

Union des tenanciers de bars du Québec (UTBQ)
3800, rue Notre-Dame ouest, Montréal QC H4C 1P9
Tél: 514-937-0531
info@utbq.ca
utbq.ca
Aperçu: *Dimension:* petite; *Envergure:* provinciale; fondée en 2006
Mission: Représenter de façon active et responsable ses membres afin de défendre leurs droits en tant que tenanciers de bars
Membre: 683; *Critères d'admissibilite:* Les propriétaires de bars

Union géophysique canadienne *See* Canadian Geophysical Union

Union internationale pour les livres de jeunesse *See* International Board on Books for Young People - Canadian Section

Union mondiale des aveugles *See* World Blind Union

Union of British Columbia Indian Chiefs
#500, 342 Water St., Vancouver BC V6B 1B6
Tel: 604-684-0231; *Fax:* 604-684-5726
Toll-Free: 800-793-9701
ubcic@ubcic.bc.ca
www.ubcic.bc.ca
www.facebook.com/UBCIC
twitter.com/UBCIC
www.youtube.com/UBCIC
Overview: A medium-sized provincial organization founded in 1969
Mission: To settle land claims & Aboriginal rights in BC; To improve the social, economic, health, & education of Aboriginal people in BC; To provide a political voice for Aboriginal people in BC

Member of: Assembly of First Nations; World Council of Indigenous Peoples
Activities: *Library:* Open to public by appointment
Chief Officer(s):
Stewart Phillip, President

Union of British Columbia Municipalities (UBCM)
#60, 10551 Shellbridge Way, Richmond BC V6X 2W9
Tel: 604-270-8226; *Fax:* 604-270-9116
www.ubcm.ca
twitter.com/UBCM
Overview: A medium-sized provincial organization founded in 1905
Mission: To provide a common voice for local government
Member of: Federation of Canadian Municipalities
Finances: *Annual Operating Budget:* $500,000-$1.5 Million
Staff Member(s): 20
Membership: 161 municipalities + 29 regional districts; *Committees:* Community Economic Development; Community Safety; Convention; Environment; First Nations; Healthy Communities; Presidents; Resolutions
Activities: *Awareness Events:* Local Government Awareness Week, May; *Speaker Service:* Yes; *Library:* Open to public
Chief Officer(s):
Mary Sjostrom, President
Gary MacIsaac, Executive Director
gmacisaac@ubcm.ca
Marie Crawford, Associate Executive Director
mcrawford@ubcm.ca
Anna-Maria Wijesinghe, Manager, Member & Association Services
amwijesinghe@ubcm.ca
Awards:
• Community Excellence Awards
• Long Service Awards
Meetings/Conferences:
• Union of British Columbia Municipalities 2018 Annual Convention, September, 2018, Whistler Conference Centre, Whistler, BC
Scope: Provincial
• Union of British Columbia Municipalities 2019 Annual Convention, September, 2019, Vancouver Convention & Exhibition Centre, Vancouver, BC
Scope: Provincial

Union of Calgary Co-op Employees (UCCE)
420 - 35th Ave. NE, Calgary AB T1Y 5R8
Tel: 403-299-6700; *Fax:* 403-299-6710
reception@ucce.info
www.ucce.info
Also Known As: Calco Club
Overview: A small local organization
Mission: To represent members employed in occupations including trades, janitorial, clerical & technical positions in the field of retail grocery
Membership: *Committees:* Bargaining; Elections; Constitution; Finance; Health & Safety
Chief Officer(s):
Pat Rose, President
Shelley Winters, Vice President
Kim Revenco, Treasurer

Union of Canadian Correctional Officers *See* Syndicat des Agents Correctionnels du Canada (CSN)

Union of Canadian Transportation Employees (UCTE) / Union canadienne des employés des transports (UCET)
#702, 233 Gilmour St., Ottawa ON K2P 0P2
Tel: 613-238-4003; *Fax:* 613-236-0379
www.ucte.com
Overview: A medium-sized national organization overseen by Public Service Alliance of Canada
Mission: To represent members working in the public & private sectors of the Canadian transportation industry (ports, airports, NAV Canada, pilotage authorities, transportation companies, canals, the Dept. of Transport, lighthouses, ships and Canadian Coast Guard bases)
Affiliation(s): Public Service Alliance of Canada
Membership: 7,500 + 90 locals; *Member Profile:* Individuals in the public & private sectors of the Canadian transportation industry, inclduing ports, airports, NAV Canada, pilotage authorities, transportation companies, canals, the Dept. of Transport, lighthouses, ships & Canadian Coast Guard bases
Chief Officer(s):
Christine Collins, National President, 613-238-4003, Fax: 613-236-0379
collinc@psac-afpc.com
Darlene Brown, National VicePresident, 613-238-4003, Fax: 613-236-0379
brown@psac-afpc.com
Awards:
• D. Bennett/W. Weaver Memorial Scholarship
Eligibility: UCTE members who wish to attend the Labour College Residential Program *Deadline:* August 21; *Amount:* $5,000
• Gary Farrell Scholarship
Eligibility: UCTE members who wish to attend training in the area of Health & Safety, Workers Compensation, Duty to Accommodate, Labour Relations, Social Justice or Social Science *Deadline:* August 21
Meetings/Conferences:
• Union of Canadian Transportation Employees 18th Triennial Convention, 2020

Union of Energy, Mines & Resources Employees *See* Natural Resources Union

Union of Environment Workers (UEW) / Syndicat des travailleirs de l'environnement (STE)
2181 Thurston Dr., Ottawa ON K1G 6C9
Tel: 613-736-5533; *Fax:* 613-736-5537
www.uew-ste.ca
www.facebook.com/111345079011371
twitter.com/UEWCanada
Overview: A medium-sized national organization founded in 1972 overseen by Public Service Alliance of Canada
Mission: To protect their members by ensuring safe working conditions & fair wage rights & benefits
Staff Member(s): 4
Membership: 5,700 + 40 Locals; *Member Profile:* Employees in the departments of Environment, Fisheries and Oceans & the Canadian Forest Service; *Committees:* Staff Relations; By-Laws & Policies; Strategies & Planning; Honours and Awards; Environment; Finance & Planning; Collective Bargaining; Convention; Our Fish
Chief Officer(s):
Luc Paquette, Service Officer
Luc.paquette@uew-ste.ca

Union of Injured Workers of Ontario
2888 Dufferin St., Toronto ON M6B 3S6
Tel: 416-785-8787; *Fax:* 416-785-6390
Overview: A medium-sized provincial organization founded in 1974
Mission: To serve injured workers & their families in Ontario
Affiliation(s): Ontario Network of Injured Workers Groups
Finances: *Annual Operating Budget:* $100,000-$250,000; *Funding Sources:* Unions; government
Staff Member(s): 3; 25 volunteer(s)
Membership: 2,500; *Fees:* $30 optional
Activities: Advocacy, counselling, information & referrels
Chief Officer(s):
Philip Biggin, Executive Director
pbiggin@hotmail.com

Union of Municipalities of New Brunswick (UMNB) / Union des municipalités du Nouveau-Brunswick
#145, 9 Main St., Rexton NB E4W 2A6
Tel: 506-523-7991; *Fax:* 506-523-7992
umnb@nb.aibn.com
www.umnb.ca
Merged from: Association of the Villages of New Brunswick; Towns of New Brunswick Association
Overview: A medium-sized provincial organization founded in 1995
Mission: To unite the municipalities of New Brunswick through their respective councils into a body whose efforts shall be devoted to the achievement of the common good of all
Member of: Federation of Canadian Municipalities
Finances: *Annual Operating Budget:* $50,000-$100,000; *Funding Sources:* Membership dues
Staff Member(s): 1; 40 volunteer(s)
Membership: 60 municipalities; *Member Profile:* Municipalities in New Brunswick; *Committees:* Finance; Media Advisory; Protective Services; Resolutions/Policies/Constitution; Nominating; Personnel
Chief Officer(s):
Bev Gaston, President

Union of National Defence Employees (UNDE) / Union des employés de la Défense nationale (UEDN)
#700, 116 Albert St., Ottawa ON K1P 5G3
Tel: 613-594-4505; *Fax:* 613-594-8233
Toll-Free: 866-594-4505
www.unde-uedn.com
twitter.com/UNDEUEDN
www.youtube.com/channel/UCHq7kXfLm2OP2EpPj4L58DA
Overview: A medium-sized national organization overseen by Public Service Alliance of Canada
Mission: To represent the interests of their members & ensure safe working conditions for them
Membership: 18,000 + 80 locals
Chief Officer(s):
John MacLennan, National President

Union of National Employees (UNE) / Syndicat des employées et employés nationaux (SEN)
#900, 150 Isabella St., Ottawa ON K1S 1V7
Tel: 613-560-4364; *Fax:* 613-560-4208
Toll-Free: 800-663-6685
une-sen.org
www.facebook.com/Union.NE.Syndicat.EN
twitter.com/my_UNE
www.youtube.com/user/UnionNESyndicatEN
Overview: A medium-sized national organization overseen by Public Service Alliance of Canada
Mission: To protect their members by ensuring safe working conditions & fair wage rights & benefits
Staff Member(s): 24
Membership: 26,000; *Committees:* By-laws and Policies; Collective Bargaining; Communications, Education, Honours & Awards; Finance & Human Resources; Francophone; Locals & Membership; National Executive Disciplinary
Chief Officer(s):
Georges St-Jean, Acting Coordinator & Finance Officer
georges.stjean@une-sen.org

Union of Northern Workers / Syndicat des travailleurs du Nord
#200, 5112 - 52 St., Yellowknife NT X1A 3Z5
Tel: 867-873-5668; *Fax:* 867-920-4448
Toll-Free: 877-906-4447
hq@unw.ca
www.unw.ca
twitter.com/UNW_NWT
Previous Name: Northwest Territories Public Service Association
Overview: A medium-sized national organization overseen by Public Service Alliance of Canada
Mission: To represent the interests of its members in contract negotiatons & grievances
Staff Member(s): 13
Membership: 4,000 + 18 locals
Chief Officer(s):
Todd Parsons, President

Union of Nova Scotia Indians (UNSI)
47 Maillard St., Membertou NS B1S 2P5
Tel: 902-539-4107; *Fax:* 902-564-2137
rec@unsi.ns.ca
www.unsi.ns.ca
Overview: A medium-sized provincial organization founded in 1969
Mission: To promote welfare & progress of Native people in Nova Scotia; to liaise with all Native people on relevant issues; to defend & advise on Native rights; to cooperate with Native & non-Native agencies & organizations to the benefit of Nova Scotia Native people
Finances: *Annual Operating Budget:* $1.5 Million-$3 Million
Staff Member(s): 21
Membership: *Member Profile:* Individual who is registered as an Indian pursuant to the Indian Act
Chief Officer(s):
Joe B. Marshall, Executive Director

Union of Nova Scotia Municipalities (UNSM)
#1106, 1809 Barrington St., Halifax NS B3J 3K8
Tel: 902-423-8331; *Fax:* 902-425-5592
info@unsm.ca
www.unsm.ca
Overview: A medium-sized provincial organization founded in 1906
Mission: To represent the interests of municipalities on policy & program matters that fall within the Nova Scotia provincial jurisdiction
Member of: Federation of Canadian Municipalities

Canadian Associations / Union of Ontario Indians (UOI)

Finances: *Annual Operating Budget:* $250,000-$500,000; *Funding Sources:* Membership dues
Staff Member(s): 3; 20 volunteer(s)
Membership: 376 individual; *Member Profile:* Mayors, wardens & councillors
Activities: *Library:* by appointment
Chief Officer(s):
Betty MacDonald, Executive Director
bmacdonald@unsm.ca
Judy Webber, Event Planner/Financial Officer
jwebber@unsm.ca

Union of Ontario Indians (UOI)
Nipissing First Nation, 1 Miigizi Mikan, North Bay ON P1B 8J8
Tel: 705-497-9127; *Fax:* 705-497-9135
Toll-Free: 877-702-5200
info@anishinabek.ca
www.anishinabek.ca
www.facebook.com/AnishinabekNation
twitter.com/anishnation
www.youtube.com/user/AnishinabekNation
Also Known As: Anishinabek Nation
Overview: A large provincial organization founded in 1949
Mission: To represent 42 First Nations throughout the province of Ontario from Golden Lake in the east, Sarnia in the south, Thunder Bay & Lake Nipigon in the north
Finances: *Annual Operating Budget:* $3 Million-$5 Million
Staff Member(s): 24
Membership: 42 First Nations
Activities: *Speaker Service:* Yes; *Library:* Open to public
Chief Officer(s):
Patrick Madahbee, Grand Council Chief
Gordon Waindubence, Grand Council Elder

Union of Postal Communications Employees (UPCE) / Syndicat des employés des postes et des communications (SEPC)
#701, 233 Gilmour St., Ottawa ON K2P 0P2
Tel: 613-560-4342; *Fax:* 613-594-3849
sepc-upce@psac.com
www.upce.ca
Overview: A medium-sized national licensing organization overseen by Public Service Alliance of Canada
Mission: Represents Canada Post members employed in administrative, clerical, technical & professional capacities
Finances: *Annual Operating Budget:* $1.5 Million-$3 Million
Staff Member(s): 4
Membership: 2,900 + 24 locals
Chief Officer(s):
François Paradis, National President, 613-560-4425
paradif@psac.com

Union of Prison Guards of Québec *Voir* Syndicat des agents de la paix en services correctionnels du Québec

Union of Professional Employees of the Québec Government *Voir* Syndicat de professionnelles et professionnels du gouvernement du Québec

Union of Professors for the Government of Québec (Ind.) *Voir* Syndicat des professeurs de l'État du Québec (ind.)

Union of Radiology Technicians of Québec *Voir* Syndicat des technologues en radiologie du Québec

Union of Solicitor General Employees (USGE) / Syndicat des employés du Solliciteur général (SESG)
#603, 233 Gilmour St., Ottawa ON K2P 0P2
Tel: 613-232-4821; *Fax:* 613-232-3311
www.usge-sesg.com
Overview: A medium-sized national organization overseen by Public Service Alliance of Canada
Membership: 15,000 + 140 locals; *Committees:* National Health & Safety Advisory
Chief Officer(s):
Stan Stapleton, National President

Union of Spiritual Communities of Christ (USCC)
PO Box 760, Grand Forks BC V0H 1H0
Tel: 250-365-3613; *Fax:* 250-442-3433
iskrainfo@uscc.ca
iskra.ca
Overview: A small national organization founded in 1943
Mission: To be dedicated to the sustainability and enrichment of the Doukhobor Life-Concept based on the Law of God and the Teachings of Jesus Christ
Activities: Publish Iskra newsletter

Chief Officer(s):
Stephanie Swetlishoff, Editor
Barry Verigin, Editor
Publications:
• Iskra: Voice of the Doukhobors [a publication of the Union of Spiritual Communities of Christ]

Union of Taxation Employees (UTE) / Syndicat des employé(e)s de l'impôt (SEI)
#800, 233 Gilmour St., Ottawa ON K2P 0P2
Tel: 613-235-6704; *Fax:* 613-234-7290
www.ute-sei.org
www.facebook.com/UnionofTaxationEmployees
Overview: A medium-sized national organization founded in 1967 overseen by Public Service Alliance of Canada
Staff Member(s): 15
Membership: 27,000 + 51 locals; *Committees:* Bargaining; By-Laws; Call Centre; Communications; Employee Assistance Program; Equal Opportunities; Executive; Finance; Harassment; Health & Safety; Honours & Awards; National Union-Management; Political Action; Staffing; Technological Change; Workforce Adjustment
Chief Officer(s):
Robert Campbell, National President

Union of Veterans' Affairs Employees (UVAE) / Syndicat des employé(e)s des affaires des anciens combattants (SEAC)
#703, 233 Gilmour St., Ottawa ON K2P 0P2
Tel: 613-560-5460; *Fax:* 613-237-8282
uvae-seac.ca
Overview: A small national organization overseen by Public Service Alliance of Canada
Mission: To represent the interests of employees of Veterans' Affairs Canada
Membership: 2,600
Chief Officer(s):
Carl Gannon, National President
gannonc@psac.com

Union Paysanne
CP 899, Succ. Bureau Chef, Lachute QC J8H 4G5
Tél: 450-230-5046
paysanne@unionpaysanne.com
www.unionpaysanne.com
www.facebook.com/unionpaysanne
twitter.com/UnionPaysanne
Aperçu: *Dimension:* moyenne; *Envergure:* provinciale
Mission: A pour but de regrouper en une force collective organisée et représentative tous ceux qui sont en faveur d'une agriculture et d'une alimentation paysannes pour faire contrepoids au monopole de représentation syndicale et au puissant lobby de l'industrie agro-alimentaire et des promoteurs du libre échange en faveur d'un modèle industriel d'agriculture
Membre: *Montant de la cotisation:* 60$
Membre(s) du bureau directeur:
Benoit Girouard, Président

Union québécoise de réhabilitation des oiseaux de proie (UQROP) / Québec Raptor Rehabilitation Network
CP 246, Saint-Hyacinthe QC J2S 7B6
Tél: 450-773-8521; *Téléc:* 450-778-8125
info@uqrop.qc.ca
www.uqrop.qc.ca
www.facebook.com/166157060085717
Aperçu: *Dimension:* petite; *Envergure:* provinciale; fondée en 1987
Mission: Conservation des oiseaux de proie & de leurs habitats naturels par la réhabilitation d'oiseaux blessés & l'éducation du public
Membre(s) du personnel: 4
Membre: *Critères d'admissibilite:* Ornithologues
Activités: *Stagiaires:* Oui; *Service de conférenciers:* Oui
Membre(s) du bureau directeur:
Guy Fitzgerald, Président et directeur

Union québécoise des infirmières et infirmiers *Voir* Fédération de la santé du Québec - CSQ

Union québécoise du bison
#100, 555, boul Roland-Therrien, Longueuil QC J4H 3Y9
Tél: 450-679-0530; *Téléc:* 450-670-4867
www.bisonquebec.com
Aperçu: *Dimension:* petite; *Envergure:* provinciale
Membre de: Canadian Bison Association
Membre(s) du bureau directeur:

Jean-Luc Chouinard, President
jl_chouinard@videotron.ca

Union québécoise pour la conservation de la nature *Voir* Nature Québec

Unison Health & Community Services
1651 Keele St., Toronto ON M6M 3W2
Tel: 416-653-5400; *Fax:* 416-653-1696
unisonhcs.org
www.facebook.com/UnisonHCS
twitter.com/unisonhcs
www.youtube.com/user/UnisonHCS
Overview: A small local organization founded in 1973 overseen by Ontario Council of Agencies Serving Immigrants
Mission: To provide services to the public to help improve their lives
Finances: *Annual Operating Budget:* Greater than $5 Million
Staff Member(s): 226; 150 volunteer(s)
Membership: *Fees:* $1
Chief Officer(s):
Janak Jass, Chair

Unisphere (Cross-Cultural) Learner Centre *See* Unisphere Global Resource Centre

Unisphere Global Resource Centre
101 - 6 St. SE, Medicine Hat AB T1A 1G7
Tel: 403-529-2656
unispheregrc@gmail.com
nonprofit.memlane.com/unisphere
Previous Name: Unisphere (Cross-Cultural) Learner Centre
Overview: A small local charitable organization
Mission: To create a climate in which the sharing of cultures can be experienced & where vital global issues are discussed with openness; to provide a place for all peoples to develop as informed world citizens through sharing of ideas, experiences, & friendship; to identify & develop sensitive awareness to the values of all cultures through dialogue, with a view to cross-cultural enrichment; to work towards a better understanding of the essential inter-relatedness, culturally & economically, of all nations; to "think globally"
Member of: LEARN; MH Volunteerism in Action; Southeastern Alberta Racial & Community Harmony Society
Membership: *Fees:* $6 student/senior; $15 individual; $25 family; $40 organization
Activities: World Food Day; Spring Fundraiser; *Speaker Service:* Yes; *Library:* Open to public

UNITE HERE Canada
12836 146 St. NW, Edmonton AB T5L 2H7
Tel: 780-453-2607; *Fax:* 780-426-5098
info@uniteherecanada.ca
www.uniteherecanada.org
Merged from: UNITE; HERE
Overview: A large national organization
Mission: To organize & represent individuals who work in the hospitality, gaming, food service, manufacturing, textile, laundry, & airport industries
Membership: 50,000 in Canada; 250,000 total across the USA & Canada; *Member Profile:* Represents workers in: hotels, casinos, apparel & textile manufacturing, apparel distribution centers, apparel retail, industrial laundries, foodservice, airport concessions, & restaurants
Chief Officer(s):
Ian Robb, Canadian Director

Edmonton-Calgary Chapter
Local 47, 12836 - 146 St. NW, Edmonton AB T5L 2H7
Tel: 780-426-7890; *Fax:* 780-426-5098
info@local47.net
www.local47.net
Chief Officer(s):
Ian Robb, President & Administrator

Ottawa Chapter
893 Admiral Ave., Ottawa ON K1Z 6L6
Tel: 613-228-9991; *Fax:* 613-228-9909
Chief Officer(s):
Kevin Porter, President

Regina Chapter
Local 41, 320 Longman Cres., Regina SK S4N 6J7
Tel: 306-781-8157; *Fax:* 306-543-3856
Chief Officer(s):
Garry Whalen, President

Toronto Chapter
Local 75, OFL Bldg., #300, 15 Gervais Dr., Toronto ON M3C 1Y8

Tel: 416-384-0983; *Fax:* 416-384-0991
Toll-Free: 877-410-0707
info@unitherelocal75.org
www.unitherelocal75.org
twitter.com/UniteHere75
Ottawa Chapter
Local 261, #2, 200 Cooper St., Ottawa ON K2P 0G1
Tel: 613-238-8136; *Fax:* 613-238-5499
local261@aol.com
Chief Officer(s):
Karen Grella, Secretary-Treasurer
Vancouver & Vicinity Chapter
Local 40, #100, 4180 Lougheed Hwy., Burnaby BC V5C 6A7
Tel: 604-291-8211; *Fax:* 604-291-2676
Toll-Free: 800-663-1728
www.unitherelocal40.org
www.facebook.com/unitehere40
twitter.com/UniteHere40
Chief Officer(s):
Robert Demand, President
rdemand@unitehere.org
Shelly Ervin, Secretary-Treasurer
servin@local40union.com

United Appeal of Ottawa-Carleton *See* United Way/Centraide Ottawa

United Baptist Convention of the Maritime Provinces *See* Convention of Atlantic Baptist Churches

The United Brethren Church in Canada
501 Whitelaw Rd., Guelph ON N1K 1E7
Tel: 519-836-0180; *Fax:* 519-821-8385
www.ubcanada.org
Previous Name: Ontario Conference, Church of the United Brethren in Christ
Overview: A small national charitable organization founded in 1856
Mission: To organize groups of people into congregations to worship God; to make effective application of principles of righteousness in the Society
Member of: Church of the United Brethren in Christ, International
Affiliation(s): Evangelical Fellowship of Canada
Finances: *Annual Operating Budget:* $50,000-$100,000; *Funding Sources:* Donations
Staff Member(s): 1
Membership: 12 churches; *Fees:* Schedule available; *Member Profile:* Personal knowledge of God through faith in Christ; desire to live a life conforming to biblical principles
Activities: *Library:* At Emmanuel Bible College Library
Chief Officer(s):
Brian K. Magnus, Bishop
b_magnus@ubcanada.org

United Church of Canada (UCC) / L'Église Unie du Canada
#200, 3250 Bloor St. West, Toronto ON M8X 2Y4
Tel: 416-231-5931; *Fax:* 416-231-3103
Toll-Free: 800-268-3781
Other Communication: Voice Mail: 416-231-7680
info@united-church.ca
www.united-church.ca
www.linkedin.com/company/unitedchurchcda
www.facebook.com/UnitedChurchCda
twitter.com/UnitedChurchCda
www.youtube.com/unitedchurchofcanada
Overview: A large national charitable organization founded in 1925
Mission: To foster the spirit of unity in Canada
Member of: Canadian Council of Churches; World Council of Churches; Canadian Council for International Cooperation; World Methodist Council
Affiliation(s): United Church of Canada Foundation
Finances: *Annual Operating Budget:* Greater than $5 Million; *Funding Sources:* Voluntary givings; Sales; Bequests; Investment income; Foundation
Staff Member(s): 5000
Membership: 650,000; *Member Profile:* Baptism & profession of faith in Jesus Christ as Saviour & Lord
Activities: *Speaker Service:* Yes; *Library*
Chief Officer(s):
Jordan Cantwell, Moderator
Nora Sanders, General Secretary
nsanders@united-church.ca

Awards:
• Bill Lord Bursary in Continuing Education
• Agatha Kaasa Bursary Fund
Meetings/Conferences:
• The United Church of Canada 45th General Council 2018, 2018
Scope: National
Contact Information: Secretary: Nora Sanders, E-mail: nsanders@united-church.ca
Publications:
• Aujourd'hui Credo [publication de l'Église Unie du Canada]
Type: Magazine; *Frequency:* trimestriel; *Accepts Advertising*; *Price:* 25$ Canada; 35$ L'Europe; 48$ autres pays
• E-ssentials [a publication of the United Church of Canada]
Type: Newsletter; *Frequency:* Bimonthly
Profile: Offers essential news from the United Church of Canada, including general conference updates
• Gathering [a publication of the United Church of Canada]
Type: Magazine; *Frequency:* q.; *Accepts Advertising*; *Price:* $25.95 within Canada; $28.95 outside of Canada
• Mandate: United for God's Mission [a publication of the United Church of Canada]
Type: Magazine; *Frequency:* q.; *Accepts Advertising*; *Price:* $12.95
• The United Church Observer [a publication of the United Church of Canada]
Type: Magazine; *Frequency:* Monthly; *Accepts Advertising*; *Editor:* Jocelyn Bell; *Price:* $30/year within Canada; $40/year outside of Canada

Alberta & Northwest Conference
9911 - 48th Ave. NW, Edmonton AB T6E 5V6
Tel: 780-435-3995; *Fax:* 780-438-3317
coffice@anwconf.com
www.anwconf.com
www.facebook.com/albertanorthwestconference
Chief Officer(s):
Lynn Maki, Executive Secretary, 780-435-3995
lmaki@anwconf.com

All Native Circle Conference
367 Selkirk Ave., Winnipeg MB R2W 2M3
Tel: 204-582-5518; *Fax:* 204-582-6649
admin@ancc.united-church.ca
allnativecircleconference.com
www.facebook.com/allnativecircleconference
twitter.com/ANCC_Winnipeg
instagram.com/ancc_winnipeg
Chief Officer(s):
Nelson Hart, Representative
Marlene Lightning, Representative

Bay of Quinte Conference
25 Holloway St., Belleville ON K8P 1N8
Tel: 613-967-0150; *Fax:* 613-967-1934
Toll-Free: 888-759-2444
officeadmin@bayofquinteconference.ca
www.bayofquinteconference.ca
Chief Officer(s):
Bill Smith, Executive Secretary
execsec@bayofquinteconference.ca

British Columbia Conference
4383 Rumble St., Burnaby BC V5J 2A2
Tel: 604-431-0434; *Fax:* 604-431-0439
Toll-Free: 800-934-0434
reception@bc.united-church.ca
bc.united-church.ca
twitter.com/unitedbcconf
Chief Officer(s):
Doug Goodwin, Executive Secretary, 604-431-0434 Ext. 301
dgoodwin@bc.united-church.ca

Hamilton Conference
PO Box 100, Carlisle ON L0R 1H0
Tel: 905-659-3343; *Fax:* 905-659-7766
office@hamconf.org
www.hamconf.org
www.facebook.com/HamiltonConference
twitter.com/HamiltonConfere
Chief Officer(s):
Peter Hartmans, Executive Secretary
phartmans@hamconf.org

London Conference
PO Box 28039, 695 Riverside Dr., London ON N6H 5E1
Tel: 519-672-1930; *Fax:* 519-439-2800
office@londonconference.ca
www.londonconference.ca

www.facebook.com/556287354497545
www.youtube.com/channel/UCwXE33RTsKxV-isk-Ffr_CA
Chief Officer(s):
Cheryl-Ann Stadelbauer-Sampa, Executive Secretary, 519-672-1930 Ext. 101
c-a@londonconference.ca

Manitoba & Northwestern Ontario Conference
#1622-B, St. Mary's Rd., Winnipeg MB R2M 3W7
Tel: 204-233-8911; *Fax:* 204-233-3289
Toll-Free: 866-860-9662
office@confmnwo.mb.ca
www.mnwo.united-church.ca
www.facebook.com/mnwoconference
twitter.com/MNWOConference
www.youtube.com/user/UCCMNWOCONFERENCE
Chief Officer(s):
Shannon McCarthy, Executive Secretary, 204-333-8911 Ext. 231

Manitou Conference
319 McKenzie Ave., North Bay ON P1B 7E3
Tel: 705-474-3350; *Fax:* 705-497-3597
office@manitouconference.ca
manitouconference.ca
www.facebook.com/manitouconference
Chief Officer(s):
Will Kunder, Executive Secretary, 705-474-3350 Ext. 203
wkunder@manitouconference.ca

Maritime Conference
21 Wright St., Sackville NB E4L 4P8
Tel: 506-536-1334; *Fax:* 506-536-2900
info@marconf.ca
www.marconf.ca
www.facebook.com/329299033776135
twitter.com/maritimeconf
www.youtube.com/user/maritimeconference
Chief Officer(s):
David W. Hewitt, Executive Secretary, 506-536-1334 Ext. 1
dhewitt@marconf.ca

Newfoundland & Labrador Conference
320 Elizabeth Ave., St. John's NL A1B 1T9
Tel: 709-754-0386; *Fax:* 709-754-8336
unitedchurch@nfld.net
www.newlabconf.com
Chief Officer(s):
Faith March-McCuish, Executive Secretary

Saskatchewan Conference
418A McDonald St., Regina SK S4N 6E1
Tel: 306-721-3311; *Fax:* 306-721-3171
ucskco@sasktel.net
www.sk.united-church.ca
Chief Officer(s):
Bill Doyle, Executive Secretary
bdoyle@skconf.ca

Synode Montréal & Ottawa Conference
225, 50e av, Montréal QC H8T 2T7
Tel: 514-634-7015; *Fax:* 514-634-2489
www.synodemontrealetottawa.ca
www.facebook.com/163730530356996
twitter.com/MO_Conference
Chief Officer(s):
Rosemary Lambie, Executive Secretary, 514-634-7015 Ext. 24

Toronto Conference
65 Mayall Ave., Toronto ON M3L 1E7
Tel: 416-241-2677; *Fax:* 416-241-2689
Toll-Free: 800-446-4729
tco-office@united-church.ca
www.torontoconference.ca
www.facebook.com/196221203732363
twitter.com/TorontoConferen
Chief Officer(s):
David Allen, Executive Secretary, 416-241-2677 Ext. 6226
dallen@united-church.ca

United Church of Canada Foundation / Église Unie du Canada
#200, 3250 Bloor St. West, Toronto ON M8X 2Y4
Toll-Free: 866-340-8223
fdn@united-church.ca
www.unitedchurchfoundation.ca
Overview: A large national charitable organization founded in 2002
Mission: To help sustain the United Church of Canada
Affiliation(s): United Church of Canada
Finances: *Annual Operating Budget:* $3 Million-$5 Million

Staff Member(s): 3
Membership: *Committees:* Audit; Executive; Governance & Nominating; Investment; Joint Grants
Activities: Managing 40 endowments; grants & scholarships
Chief Officer(s):
David Armour, President, 416-231-5931 Ext. 2022
Sarah Charters, Senior Manager, 416-231-5931 Ext. 3410
Awards:
• Rowntree Scholarship
To promote, advance & encourage theological education
• McGeachy Senior Scholarship
To develop leaders for the United Church of Canada
• Davidson Trust Award
To acknowledge excellence of scholarship & theological teaching; *Amount:* $5,000
• Clifford Elliott Rural Ministry Award
To enable study at the Saskatoon Theological Union's Institute for Rural Ministry; *Amount:* $5,000
• Alfred J. Mitchell Trust
• James Robertson Memorial Trust
• Bill & Anna Jentzsch Endowment Bursary
• Victor Blatherwick Memorial Bursary
• Elizabeth White Bursary
• Seeds of Hope Fund
• The New Ministries Fund

United Conservative Association
4317 - 23B St. NE, Calgary AB T2E 7V9
Toll-Free: 888-465-2660
info@unitedconservative.ca
www.unitedconservative.ca
Also Known As: United Conservative Party (UPC)
Merged from: Progressive Conservative Association of Alberta; Wildrose Political Association
Overview: A large provincial organization
Finances: *Funding Sources:* Membership purchases; Donations
Membership: *Member Profile:* Pre-existing members of the Legacy Parties; residents of Alberta who support the principles of the UCP
Chief Officer(s):
Jason Kenney, Party Leader
Ed Ammar, Chair, Interim Joint Board

United County Beekeepers
QC
Tel: 514-630-6336
ucba@hotmail.ca
www.ucbabee.com
Overview: A small local organization
Mission: To assist beekeepers in the United County of Ontario by providing education & information
Member of: Ontario Beekeepers' Association
Membership: *Member Profile:* Apiarists in Ontario's United County
Chief Officer(s):
John McCraig, Contact

United Empire Loyalists' Association of Canada (UELAC)
Dominion Office, The George Brown House, #202, 50 Baldwin St., Toronto ON M5T 1L4
Tel: 416-591-1783
uelac@uelac.org
www.uelac.org
www.facebook.com/UELAC
twitter.com/uelac
Also Known As: UEL Association
Overview: A medium-sized national charitable organization founded in 1914
Mission: To unite together descendants of those families who, as a result of the American revolutionary war, sacrificed their homes in retaining their loyalty to the British Crown; to keep alive the knowledge of the early contributions of hundreds of thousands of Loyalists of many cultures, creeds & colours
Membership: 664; *Member Profile:* Descent from or interest in United Empire Loyalists
Activities: Educational Program; Loyalist Burial Sites; True Millennium Projects; Poetry-Essay Collections; *Library:* Reference Library

Abegweit Branch
873 Brush Wharf Rd., Vernon Bridge PE C0A 2E0
www.islandregister.com/uel.html
Chief Officer(s):
Dave Hunter, Genealogist
dhunter@islandregister.com

Bay of Quinte Branch
PO Box 647, Stirling ON K0K 3E0
Tel: 613-373-2632
1784@uel.ca
www.uel.ca
Chief Officer(s):
Janet Eggleton, Membership Secretary

Bicentennial Branch
1641 Tumbleweed Ct., Windsor ON N9G 3B9
membership.bicentennial@uelac.org
www.uelac.org/Bicentennial-UEL
Chief Officer(s):
Dan Griffin, Branch President
president.bicentennial@uelac.org

Calgary Branch
339 Whitefield Dr. NE, Calgary AB T1Y 5S2
www.uelac.org/calgary
Chief Officer(s):
Suzanne Davidson, President
s_e_davidson@hotmail.com

Chilliwack Branch
46486 Uplands Dr., Chilliwack BC V2R 4M5
ksdargatz@shaw.ca
www.uelac.org/Chilliwack
Chief Officer(s):
Shirley Dargatz, Contact

Col. Edward Jessup Branch
ON
www.uelac.org/ColEdwardJessup

Col. John Butler Branch
5 Elgin St., Thorold ON L2V 3B3
www.coljohnbutleruel.com
Chief Officer(s):
Rodney Craig, Genealogist

Edmonton Branch
PO Box 68029, Stn. Bonnie Doon, Edmonton AB T6C 4G0
www.ueledmonton.ca
Chief Officer(s):
Robert Rogers, President
president@ueledmonton.ca

Governor Simcoe Branch
#78, 24 Fundy Bay Blvd., Toronto ON M1W 3A4
Tel: 416-492-1623
www.uelgovsimcoe.org
Chief Officer(s):
Jo Ann Tuskin, Secretary & Genealogist
jmtuskin@sympatico.ca

Grand River Branch
PO Box 193, Port Rowan ON N0E 1M0
www.grandriveruel.ca
twitter.com/GrandRiverUELAC
Chief Officer(s):
Paul Smith, President, 226-401-2652
paulmar.smith@gmail.com

Nova Scotia Branch
PO Box 421, Halifax NS B3J 2P8
novascotia@uelac.org
www.uelac.org/NovaScotia
Chief Officer(s):
Carol Harding, Branch Genealogist
cmharding@bellaliant.net

Hamilton Branch
#409, 908 Mohawk Rd. East, Hamilton ON L8T 2R8
www.uel-hamilton.com
Chief Officer(s):
Pat Blackburn, President
Gloria Howard, Treasurer

Heritage Branch
383, av Clarke, Montréal QC H3Z 2E7
Tel: 514-937-3274
rwilkins@blg.com
Chief Officer(s):
Robert Wilkins, President

Kawartha Branch
ON
maplegrm@gmail.com
www.uelac.org/Kawartha
Chief Officer(s):
Robert C. McBride, President

Kingston Branch
PO Box 635, Kingston ON K7L 4X7
kingston.uelac@gmail.com
www.uelac.org/Kingston

Chief Officer(s):
Peter Milliken, President

Little Forks Branch
PO Box 67, Stn. Lennoxville, 5955 rte Gilbert Hyatt, Sherbrooke QC J1M 1Z3
Tel: 819-346-6746
Chief Officer(s):
Beverly Loomis, President

London & Western Ontario Branch
2 Lansdowne Park Cres., Komoka ON N0L 1R0
Tel: 519-641-1448
www.uelac.org/londonuel
Chief Officer(s):
Carol Childs, President

Manitoba Branch
120 Eugenie St., Winnipeg MB R2H 0X7
uelmanitoba@gmail.com
www.uelmanitoba.ca
Chief Officer(s):
Mary Steinhoff, Secretary

New Brunswick Branch
PO Box 484, Saint John NB E2L 3Z8
membership@uelac-nb.ca
www.uelac-nb.ca
Chief Officer(s):
Dave Laskey, President

Saskatchewan Branch
PO Box 331, Maryfield SK S0G 3K0
Tel: 306-646-4952
gerry.pat@sasktel.net
www.uelac.org/Saskatchewan
Chief Officer(s):
Gerald Adair, Branch Genealogist

St. Lawrence Branch
PO Box 607, 3 Augusta St., Morrisburg ON K0C 1X0
www.uelac.org/st-lawrence
Chief Officer(s):
Lorraine Reoch, President

Sir Guy Carleton Branch
PO Box 5104, 19 Colonnade Rd., Nepean ON K2C 3H5
carletonuel@hotmail.com
www.uelac.org/Carletonuel

Sir John Johnson Centennial Branch
QC
Tel: 450-293-6342
www.uelac.org/SirJohnJohnson
Chief Officer(s):
Michel Racicot, President
mracicot001@sympatico.ca

Thompson/Okanagan Branch
BC
www.uel-thompson-okanagan.ca
Chief Officer(s):
William Adams, President

Toronto Branch
#300, 40 Scollard St., Toronto ON M5R 3S1
Tel: 416-489-1783; *Fax:* 416-489-3664
info@ueltoronto.ca
www.ueltoronto.ca
Chief Officer(s):
Susan Ellsworth, Secretary

Vancouver Branch
6797 La Salle St., Vancouver BC V5S 3X4
vancouver@uelac.org
www.uelac.org/Vancouver
Chief Officer(s):
Diane Faris, President

Victoria Branch
1299 Lidgate Ct., Victoria BC V8Z 7E3
www.uelac.org/uelvictoria
Chief Officer(s):
Barry Curran, President

United Food & Commercial Workers Canada (UFCW CANADA)
#300, 61 International Blvd., Toronto ON M9W 6K4
Tel: 416-675-1104; *Fax:* 416-675-6919
ufcw@ufcw.ca
www.ufcw.ca
www.facebook.com/ufcwcanada
twitter.com/ufcwcanada
www.youtube.com/user/UFCWCanada
Overview: A large national organization
Mission: One of Canada's largest private sector unions

Membership: 197,000 + 143 locals
Chief Officer(s):
Paul Meinema, National President
pmeinema@ufcw.ca
Awards:
- Beggs-Dowling-Mathieu Scholarships Program
- Migrant Workers Scholarships Program

Atlantic Canada
220, 1550 Bedford Hwy., Bedford NS B4A 1E6
Tel: 902-832-1935; *Fax:* 902-832-0186
ufcw@eastlink.ca
Chief Officer(s):
Mark Dobson, Regional Director, Eastern Provinces

Quebec Council
#720, 1100, boul Crémazie est, Montréal QC H2P 2X2
Tel: 514-326-8822; *Fax:* 514-326-1226
Chief Officer(s):
Anouk Collet, Regional Director, Québec
anouk.collet@tuac.ca

Western Canada
PO Box 21056, Stn. Westwood Plateau, Coquitlam BC V3E 3P9
Tel: 604-269-3511; *Fax:* 604-909-1701
Chief Officer(s):
Nancy Quiring, Regional Director, Western Provinces
nancy.quiring@ufcw.ca

United Generations Ontario (UGO) / Générations Unies Ontario
#604B, 1185 Eglinton Ave. East, Toronto ON M3C 3C6
Tel: 416-426-7115; *Fax:* 416-426-7388
info@intergenugo.org
Overview: A small provincial charitable organization founded in 1993
Mission: To promote programs that bring young & old together in a spirit of cooperation, mutual support, shared affection & regard; to empower people to take a constructive part in the life of their own communities & to create a vital volunteer exchange in caring & sharing
Member of: Ontario Community Support Association; Canadian Centre for Philanthropy; Vanier Institute of the Family
Affiliation(s): Ontario Gerontological Association; Older Adults Association of Ontario; BC Council for Families; Canadian Health Network
Finances: *Funding Sources:* Membership dues; Canadian Living Foundation; Trillium; corporate sponsors
Membership: *Member Profile:* Interest &/or active in intergenerational activities
Activities: *Speaker Service:* Yes

United Independent Contractors' Group of Ontario *See* Merit OpenShop Contractors Association of Ontario

United Jewish Peoples' Order (UJPO)
c/o Maxine Hermolin, 585 Cranbrooke Ave., Toronto ON M6A 2X9
Tel: 416-789-5502; *Fax:* 416-789-5981
Other Communication: www.winchevskycentre.org
info@winchevskycentre.org
www.ujpo.org
www.facebook.com/WinchevskyCtr
Overview: A small local organization founded in 1926
Mission: To develop a secular approach to social & cultural matters, the Jewish heritage, & the Yiddish language; To promote peace & social justice in Canada & the world; To support universal human rights & gender & ethnic equality
Affiliation(s): Canadian Peace Alliance; Congress of Secular Jewish Organizations; North American Federation of Secular Humanistic Jews; International Institute of Secular Humanistic Jews
Activities: Sponsoring secular Jewish education & cultural groups
Chief Officer(s):
Maxine Hermolin, Executive Director
Publications:
- UJPO [United Jewish People's Order] News
Type: Newsletter; *Editor:* UJPO National Board of Directors
Profile: Regional reports, articles, & upcoming events

United Macedonians Organization of Canada (UMOC)
#214, 6A - 170 The Donway West, Toronto ON M3C 2E8
Tel: 647-558-9258
Other Communication: Alt. E-mail: united.macedonians.org@gmail.com
info@unitedmacedonians.org
www.unitedmacedonians.org
Overview: A medium-sized national organization founded in 1959
Mission: Uniting Canadians of Macedonian origin with the purpose of maintaining the Macedonian heritage & preserving it by passing it to the next generation
Member of: Canadian Ethnocultural Council; Canadian Cultural Council
Finances: *Annual Operating Budget:* Less than $50,000
Membership: 5,000; *Fees:* $20
Activities: Delchef Night, Feb.; *Awareness Events:* Ilinden Picnic (National Day), Aug. *Library:* Canadian Macedonian Historical Society Library
Chief Officer(s):
Mendo Bakalovski, President
Elizabeth Medichkov, Secretary

United Nations Association in Canada (UNAC) / Association canadienne pour les Nations Unies (ACNU)
#300, 309 Cooper St., Ottawa ON K2P 0G5
Tel: 613-232-5751; *Fax:* 613-563-2455
info@unac.org
www.unac.org
www.linkedin.com/company/1177974
www.facebook.com/canimunconference
twitter.com/UNACanada
www.flickr.com/photos/106512533@N07
Also Known As: UNA - Canada
Overview: A medium-sized international charitable organization founded in 1946
Mission: To study international problems & Canada's relationship to them as a member of the UN & its related agencies; To foster mutual understanding, goodwill & cooperation between the people of Canada & those of other countries, with the object of promoting peace & justice; To study possible courses of action in the field of international affairs; To work for support by the government & the people of Canada for desirable policies; To provide information on & stimulate public interest in the UN & its various agencies which have been established for direct or indirect promotion of international order, justice & security; To foster national commitment to principles of multilateralism & international cooperation
Affiliation(s): World Federation of United Nations Associations
Finances: *Annual Operating Budget:* $500,000-$1.5 Million; *Funding Sources:* Individual donations; corporate support; government grants
Staff Member(s): 12; 200 volunteer(s)
Membership: 100 corporate + 12,000 individual; *Fees:* Suggested minimum of $25
Activities: Projects include: Healthy Children, Healthy Communities; Model United Nations; United Nations Professional Placement Programme; *Awareness Events:* UN Day, Oct. 24; Canadian International Model United Nations Conference *Library:* Resource Centre; Open to public
Chief Officer(s):
Kathryn White, Executive Director
Awards:
- Pearson Peace Medal
Awarded to a Canadian who has contributed significantly to humanitarian causes

Calgary
PO Box 6593, Stn. D, Calgary AB T2Z 2M3
unac.calgary@gmail.com
calgary.unac.org
www.linkedin.com/company/unaccalgary
www.facebook.com/unaccalgary
twitter.com/unaccalgary
Chief Officer(s):
Michael Gretton, President

Edmonton
c/o C. Mensah, Grant MacEwan College, 10700 - 104 Ave., Edmonton AB T5J 4S2
Tel: 780-432-6531; *Fax:* 780-497-5308
edmonton@unac.org
www.edmonton.unac.org
www.facebook.com/unacedmonton
twitter.com/unacanadayeg

Greater Montréal Office
a/s #J-4350, Université du Québec à Montréal, CP 8888, Succ. Centre-Ville, Montréal QC H3C 3P8
Tél: 514-987-8743; *Téléc:* 514-987-0249
acnu@uqam.ca
Chief Officer(s):
Michèle Bertrand, Présidente

Hamilton
173 Dundurn St. South, Hamilton ON L8P 4K5
Tel: 905-527-0470
info@hamilton.unac.org
hamilton.unac.org
Chief Officer(s):
Brian Reid, President

Kootenay Region
PO Box 760, Grand Forks BC V0H 1H0
Tel: 250-442-8252; *Fax:* 250-442-3433

National Capital Region
#300, 309 Cooper St., Ottawa ON K2P 0G5
Tel: 613-232-5751; *Fax:* 613-563-2455
info@ncrb.unac.org
ncrb.unac.org

Prince George
Prince George BC
unacpg@gmail.com
Chief Officer(s):
Giulliana Tamblyn, President

Québec Office
c/o Institut Québécois des Hautes Études Internationales (IQHEI), #5458, Pavillon Charles-de-Koninck, Université Laval, Québec QC G1K 7P4
Courriel: infos@acnu-quebec.org
Chief Officer(s):
Daniel Atangana, Président

Quinte & District
221 Charles St., Belleville ON K8N 3M3
Tel: 613-966-3928; *Fax:* 613-966-3928
globalperspectives@cogeco.ca
Chief Officer(s):
Aruna Alexander, President

Saguenay/Lac-St-Jean
a/s UQAC, Département des sciences humaines, 555, boul de l'Université, Chicoutimi QC G7H 2B1
Tél: 418-545-5011; *Téléc:* 418-545-5012
jules_dufour@uqac.uquebec.ca
Chief Officer(s):
Jules Dufour, Président

St. John's
c/o Ian McMaster, 3 Ross Rd., Paradise NL A1A 1M2
unacnl@yahoo.ca
Chief Officer(s):
Lesley Herridge, Contact

Saskatoon
c/o John Parry, President, Saskatoon SK
Tel: 306-664-3698
johnparry@shaw.ca

Toronto Office
PO Box 26008, 2345 Yonge St., Toronto ON M4P 3E0
Tel: 416-467-4672
info@to.unac.org
to.unac.org
Chief Officer(s):
Ali Khachan, President, 416-467-4672

Vancouver Office
2305-867 Hamilton St., Vancouver BC V6B 6B7
Tel: 604-732-0448; *Fax:* 604-736-8963
unacvancouver@gmail.com
edmonton.unac.org
Chief Officer(s):
Chrystal Coleman, President
cc@chrystalcoleman.com

Victoria Office
c/o France Gilbert, #200, 535 Yates St., Victoria BC V8W 2Z6
Tel: 250-388-7350
unac.victoria@gmail.com
Chief Officer(s):
Nora Curry, Contact

Winnipeg Office
c/o Univ. of Winnipeg Library, 515 Portage Ave., Winnipeg MB R3B 2E9
Tel: 204-586-0173; *Fax:* 204-783-8910
unacwinnipeg@gmail.com
www.unacwinnipeg.ca

United Nations Educational, Scientific & Cultural Organization: Canadian Commission for UNESCO
PO Box 1047, 150 Elgin St., Ottawa ON K1P 5V8
Tel: 613-566-4414; *Fax:* 613-566-4405
Toll-Free: 800-263-5588
www.unesco.ca

Overview: A medium-sized international organization
Mission: To act as a forum for governments & civil society, & to mobilize the participation of Canadian organizations & committed individuals in UNESCO's mandated areas: education, natural & social sciences, culture & communication & information
Staff Member(s): 13
Membership: 330; *Member Profile:* Government department, institutions & individuals; *Committees:* Membership
Chief Officer(s):
Louise Filiatrault, Secretary General

United Nations Entity for Gender Equality & the Empowerment of Women - National Committee Canada
#502, 331 Cooper St., Ottawa ON K2P 0G5
Tel: 613-234-8252
info@unwomencanada.org
www.unwomencanada.org
www.facebook.com/unwomencanada
twitter.com/unwomencanada
Overview: A medium-sized international organization
Mission: To advance the status of women worldwide by working to make sure women have more rights, reducing AIDS & HIV transmission, ending violence against women & improving gender equality
Membership: *Fees:* $25 student; $50 individual; $1000 corporate; *Committees:* Public Relations; Social Media; Fundraising & Outreach; Newsletter; Communications; Executive Advisory
Chief Officer(s):
Almas Jiwani, President

United Nations Environment Programme - Multilateral Fund for the Implementation of the Montréal Protocol
#4100, 1000, de la Gauchetière ouest, Montréal QC H3B 4W5
Tel: 514-282-1122; *Fax:* 514-282-0068
secretariat@unmfs.org
www.multilateralfund.org
Overview: A medium-sized international organization
Mission: To assist developing countries party to the Montréal Protocol whose annual per capita consumption & production of Ozone Depleting Substances (ODS) is less than 0.3 Kg to comply with the control measures of the Protocol
Chief Officer(s):
Eduardo Ganem, Chief Officer

United Nations Environment Programme - Secretariat of the Convention on Biological Diversity
#800, 413, rue St-Jacques, Montréal QC H2Y 1N9
Tel: 514-288-2220; *Fax:* 514-288-6588
secretariat@biodiv.org
www.cbd.int
www.facebook.com/UNBiodiversity
twitter.com/cbdnews
www.youtube.com/user/chmcbd
Overview: A medium-sized international organization
Mission: The Convention on Biological Diversity was inspired by the world community's growing commitment to sustainable development. It represents a dramatic step forward in the conservation of biological diversity, the sustainable use of its components, and the fair and equitable sharing of benefits arising from the use of genetic resources.
Chief Officer(s):
Braulio Ferreira de Souza Dias, Executive Secretary, 514-287-7002
Braulio.Dias@cbd.int

United Nations High Commissioner for Refugees
#401, 280 Albert St., Ottawa ON K1P 5G8
Fax: 613-230-1855
Toll-Free: 877-232-0909
withyou@unhcr.ch
www.unhcr.ca
www.facebook.com/UNHCRCanada
twitter.com/UNHCRCanada
www.youtube.com/user/storytellingunhcr
Also Known As: UNHCR Canada
Overview: A medium-sized international organization
Mission: To monitor Canada's intake & treatment refugees; to create awareness about the status of refugees worldwide

United Native Friendship Centre (UNFC)
PO Box 752, Fort Frances ON P9A 3N1
Tel: 807-274-8541; *Fax:* 807-274-4110
Toll-Free: 877-496-9034
Other Communication: Aboriginal Headstart Phone: 807-274-7244
inquiry@unfc.org
www.unfc.org
Overview: A small local charitable organization founded in 1973
Mission: To enhance the lives of Native & non-Native peoples; to serve Aboriginal people with special services in the fields of social, educational, & cultural development while at the same time building a bridge of understanding between Native & non-Native people
Member of: Ontario Federation of Indian Friendship Centres
Staff Member(s): 34
Membership: *Fees:* $5 individual; $10 family
Activities: Operating a Family Resource/Youth Centre; Offering employment services; Facilitating support groups; *Library*
Chief Officer(s):
Sheila McMahon, Executive Director
smcmahon@unfc.org
Publications:
• UNFC [United Native Friendship Centre] Newsletter
Type: Newsletter
Profile: Features centre updates & event dates

> **Circle of Life Centre**
> 616 Mowat Ave., Fort Frances ON P9A 3N1

United Native Nations Society
#6, 534 Cedar St., Campbell River BC V9W 2V6
Tel: 250-287-9249
administration@unitednativenation510.com
www.unitednativenation510.com
Overview: A small local organization overseen by Congress of Aboriginal Peoples
Chief Officer(s):
Bill Williams, Contact

United Nurses of Alberta (UNA) / Infirmières unies de l'Alberta
#700, 11150 Jasper Ave. NW, Edmonton AB T5K 0C7
Tel: 780-425-1025; *Fax:* 780-426-2093
Toll-Free: 800-252-9394
provincialoffice@una.ab.ca
www.una.ab.ca
www.facebook.com/UnitedNurses
twitter.com/unitednurses
www.youtube.com/user/UnitedNursesAlberta
Previous Name: Provincial Staff Nurses Committee
Overview: A large provincial organization founded in 1977
Mission: To advance the social, economic & general welfare of nurses & other allied personnel
Member of: Canadian Labour Congress; Alberta Federation of Labour; Canadian Federation of Nurses Unions
Finances: *Funding Sources:* Membership dues
Membership: 30,000 + 170 locals
Activities: *Library:* Not open to public
Chief Officer(s):
Heather Smith, President
Awards:
• UNA Nursing Education Scholarship
Eligibility: Applicants must be related to a UNA member in good standing, complete an application form and write a short essay responding to the question "Over the past 35 years, how has the United Nurses of Alberta made a difference in the work lives of Alberta Nurses?" *Deadline:* October 15; *Amount:* $1,000 (11)

> **Southern Alberta Regional Office**
> #300, 1422 Kensington Rd. NW, Calgary AB T2N 3P9
> *Tel:* 403-237-2377; *Fax:* 403-263-2908
> *Toll-Free:* 800-661-1802
> calgaryoffice@una.ab.ca
> www.una.ab.ca
> **Chief Officer(s):**
> Heather Smith, President

United Ostomy Association of Canada *See* Ostomy Canada Society

United Senior Citizens of Ontario Inc. (USCO)
3033 Lakeshore Blvd. West, Toronto ON M8V 1K5
Tel: 416-252-2021; *Fax:* 416-252-5770
Toll-Free: 888-320-2222
office@uscont.ca
www.uscont.ca
www.facebook.com/uscont
twitter.com/USCONTseniors
Overview: A large provincial organization founded in 1961
Mission: To further the interests & promote the welfare of the senior population in Ontario; To provide for an exchange of ideas for member groups; To assist in the formation of senior citizens clubs
Finances: *Funding Sources:* Membership fees
Membership: *Fees:* $25 individual; $30 couple
Chief Officer(s):
Bernard Jordaan, President
Publications:
• The Voice [a publication of United Senior Citizens of Ontario]
Type: Newsletter

United Steelworkers Local 1-424
#100, 1777 - 3rd Ave., Prince George BC V2L 3G7
Tel: 250-563-7771; *Fax:* 250-563-0274
Toll-Free: 800-565-3641
usw1-424@telus.net
www.steelworkers1-424.ca
Also Known As: United Steelworkers Local 1-424
Previous Name: Northern Interior Wood Workers Association
Merged from: International Woodworkers of America (Canada); United Steelworkers of America
Overview: A small local organization founded in 1937
Chief Officer(s):
Frank Everitt, President
frank@usw1-424.ca
Brian O'Rourke, Financial Secretary
brian@usw1-424.ca

United Synagogue of Conservative Judaism, Canadian Region (USCJ)
1700 Bathurst St., Toronto ON M3J 2V5
Tel: 416-667-1717; *Fax:* 416-667-1881
Overview: A medium-sized provincial organization

United Synagogue Youth (USY)
1700 Bathurst St., Toronto ON M5P 3K3
Tel: 416-667-1717; *Fax:* 416-667-1881
ecrusy@uscj.org
www.ecrusy.org
Also Known As: ECRUSY
Overview: A medium-sized international organization
Mission: To offer opportunities to Jewish Youth to continue to strengthen their identification with Judaism and with the synagogue; To develop a programme based on personality development, needs, and interests of the Jewish teenager.
Staff Member(s): 1
Chief Officer(s):
Max Marmer, Director, Youth Activities
marmer@uscj.org

United Ukrainian Charitable Trust
2445 Bloor St. West, Toronto ON M6S 1P7
Tel: 416-763-4982; *Fax:* 416-763-3997
toradmin@ucss.info
Overview: A small local charitable organization
Mission: To provide financial assistance to Ukrainian institutions involved in charitable work & in cultural & educational programming in the Toronto area
Chief Officer(s):
Maria Tarnavskyj, President, Ukrainian Canadian Social Services (Toronto)

United Utility Workers' Association (UUWA)
1207 - 20 Ave. NW, Calgary AB T2M 1G2
Tel: 403-284-4521; *Fax:* 403-282-1598
info@uuwac.org
www.uuwac.org
Previous Name: Calgary Power Employees Association; TransAlta Employees' Association
Overview: A medium-sized national organization founded in 1943
Mission: To represent employees in the energy secotr
Membership: 1,400; *Member Profile:* Employees in the energy sector, such as meter readers, power line technicians, designers & administrators
Activities: Offering training courses
Chief Officer(s):
Mike Donnelly, Chief Executive Officer & Board Director
Grace Thostenson, Manager, Business
grace@uuwac.org

United Way Alberta Northwest
#213, 11330 106 St., Grande Prairie AB T8V 7X9
Tel: 780-532-1105
info@unitedwayabnw.org
www.unitedwayabnw.org
www.facebook.com/UnitedWayABNW

twitter.com/UnitedWayABNW
www.youtube.com/user/GrowUnitedBreakfast
Overview: A small local organization overseen by United Way of Canada - Centraide Canada
Mission: To change community conditions & improve the lives of people in need
Chief Officer(s):
Sheldon Rowe, Chair
Brenda Yamkowy, Executive Director
brenda@unitedwayabnw.org
Jodie Johnson, Director, Resource Development
resource@unitedwayabnw.org
Marnie Young, Director, Resource Development
resource@unitedwayabnw.org
Joanne Cousins, Administrator

United Way Central & Northern Vancouver Island
#9, 327 Prideaux St., Nanaimo BC V9R 2N4
Tel: 250-591-8731; *Fax:* 250-591-7340
info@uwcnvi.ca
www.uwcnvi.ca
www.linkedin.com/company/united-way-central-&-northern-vancouver-island
www.facebook.com/UWCNVI
twitter.com/UWCNVI
www.youtube.com/user/UnitedWayCNVI
Previous Name: United Way of Nanaimo & District
Overview: A small local charitable organization founded in 1958 overseen by United Way of Canada - Centraide Canada
Mission: To improve lives by engaging individuals & mobilizing collective action
Member of: Nanaimo & Ladysmith Chambers of Commerce
Finances: *Annual Operating Budget:* $250,000-$500,000; *Funding Sources:* Annual fundraising campaign; Donations; Sponsorship
Staff Member(s): 14; 25+ volunteer(s)
Membership: 1,000 voting members + 28 agencies
Activities: *Internships:* Yes
Chief Officer(s):
Signy Madden, Executive Director
signy@uwcnvi.ca
Publications:
• Younited [a publication of the United Way Central & Northern Vancouver Island]
Type: Newsletter; *Frequency:* irregular
Profile: An information resource for United Way donors, volunteers, & supporters

United Way Elgin-St. Thomas
#103, 10 Mondamin St., St Thomas ON N5P 2V1
Tel: 519-631-3171; *Fax:* 519-631-9253
www.stthomasunitedway.ca
www.facebook.com/UnitedWayElginStThomas
Previous Name: Elgin-St.Thomas United Way Services
Overview: A small local charitable organization founded in 1957 overseen by United Way of Canada - Centraide Canada
Mission: To be a leader in improving the quality of life for all people in Elgin County.
Member of: St. Thomas & District Chamber of Commerce; Canadian Association of Gift Planners
Finances: *Funding Sources:* Annual campaign; fundraising
Staff Member(s): 3
Activities: Fundraising on behalf of 23 member agencies; *Awareness Events:* Aylmer StairClimb, Nov.; Timken StairClimb for United Way, Nov.; *Speaker Service:* Yes
Chief Officer(s):
James Todd, President
Melissa Schneider, Campaign/Communications Coordinator

United Way for the City of Kawartha Lakes (UWVC)
50 Mary St. West, Lindsay ON K9V 2N6
Tel: 705-878-5081; *Fax:* 705-878-0475
office@ckl.unitedway.ca
www.ckl-unitedway.ca
www.facebook.com/UWCKL
twitter.com/unitedwayckl
Previous Name: United Way of Victoria County (UWVC)
Overview: A medium-sized local charitable organization founded in 1983 overseen by United Way of Canada - Centraide Canada
Mission: To promote the organized capacity of people & groups in the City of Kawartha Lakes to care for each other
Finances: *Annual Operating Budget:* $250,000-$500,000; *Funding Sources:* Private & corporate donations; fundraising; special events
Staff Member(s): 2

Membership: 1-99
Activities: *Speaker Service:* Yes
Chief Officer(s):
Penny Barton Dyke, Executive Director
pbartondyke@ckl.unitedway.ca

United Way of Amherst *See* United Way of Cumberland County

United Way of Barrie/South Simcoe *See* United Way of Greater Simcoe County

United Way of Belleville & District *See* United Way of Quinte

United Way of Brandon & District Inc.
Scotia Towers, 201 - 1011 Rosser Ave., Brandon MB R7A 0L5
Tel: 204-571-8929; *Fax:* 204-727-8939
office@brandonuw.ca
www.brandonuw.ca
www.facebook.com/UnitedWayBrandon
Also Known As: Brandon & District United Way
Overview: A small local organization founded in 1966 overseen by United Way of Canada - Centraide Canada
Staff Member(s): 3; 785 volunteer(s)
Activities: *Library:*
Chief Officer(s):
Cynamon Mychasiw, CEO

United Way of Burlington & Greater Hamilton
177 Rebecca St., Hamilton ON L8R 1B9
Tel: 905-527-4543; *Fax:* 905-527-5152
uway@uwaybh.ca
www.uwaybh.ca
www.facebook.com/unitedwaybh
twitter.com/UnitedWayBH
www.youtube.com/user/UnitedWayBH
Previous Name: United Way of Burlington, Hamilton-Wentworth
Overview: A small local charitable organization overseen by United Way of Canada - Centraide Canada
Mission: To empower a diverse community to achieve positive social development
Chief Officer(s):
Jeff Vallentin, CEO
   Burlington Office
   #107, 3425 Harvester Rd., Burlington ON L7N 3N1
   Tel: 905-635-3138; *Fax:* 905-632-1918
   uway@uwaybh.ca
   Chief Officer(s):
   Jeff Vallentin, CEO

United Way of Burlington, Hamilton-Wentworth *See* United Way of Burlington & Greater Hamilton

United Way of Calgary & Area
#600, 105 - 12 Ave SE, Calgary AB T2G 1A1
Tel: 403-231-6265; *Fax:* 403-355-3135
uway@calgaryunitedway.org
www.calgaryunitedway.org
www.linkedin.com/companies/united-way-of-calgary-and-area
www.facebook.com/calgaryunitedway
twitter.com/UnitedWayCgy
www.instagram.com/unitedwaycgy
Overview: A small local organization overseen by United Way of Canada - Centraide Canada
Mission: To invest in 250 programs offered by 130 agencies in Calgary, Airdrie, Cochrane, High River, Okotoks & Strathmore
Finances: *Annual Operating Budget:* Greater than $5 Million
Staff Member(s): 63; 1000 volunteer(s)
Membership: Over 50,000
Chief Officer(s):
Lucy Miller, President

United Way of Cambridge & North Dumfries
#2, 135 Thompson Dr., Cambridge ON N1T 2E4
Tel: 519-621-1030; *Fax:* 519-621-6220
www.uwcambridge.on.ca
www.facebook.com/UWCND
twitter.com/uwcambridge
www.youtube.com/user/UWcambridge
Overview: A small local charitable organization founded in 1940 overseen by United Way of Canada - Centraide Canada
Mission: To enhance the quality of life in Cambridge & North Dumfries by caring for & contributing to community needs
Finances: *Annual Operating Budget:* $1.5 Million-$3 Million; *Funding Sources:* Workplace campaign; corporate; individual
Staff Member(s): 10; 1200 volunteer(s)
Membership: 5,000-14,999; *Fees:* Donations
Activities: *Speaker Service:* Yes

Chief Officer(s):
Ron Dowhaniuk, CEO
ron@uwcambridge.on.ca

United Way of Canada - Centraide Canada
#900, 116 Albert St., Ottawa ON K1P 5G3
Tel: 613-236-7041; *Fax:* 613-236-3087
Toll-Free: 800-267-8221
info@unitedway.ca
www.unitedway.ca
ca.linkedin.com/company/united-way-centraide-canada
www.facebook.com/UnitedWayCentraide
twitter.com/UnitedWayCanada
www.youtube.com/UnitedWayofCanada
Also Known As: Centraide Canada - United Way of Canada
Overview: A large national charitable organization
Mission: To create opportunities for a better life for all; To inspire Canadians to make a lasting difference in their communities
Affiliation(s): United Way International
Finances: *Annual Operating Budget:* $3 Million-$5 Million; *Funding Sources:* Donations
Activities: Influencing public attitudes, systems, & policy; Strengthening social service networks; Engaging the community's financial resources & influence to create posititive change; *Library:* Not open to public
Chief Officer(s):
Jacline A. Nyman, President/CEO

United Way of Cape Breton
245 Charlotte St., Sydney NS B1P 6W4
Tel: 902-562-5226; *Fax:* 902-562-5721
www.unitedwaycapebreton.com
www.facebook.com/UnitedWayOfCapeBreton
Overview: A small local organization overseen by United Way of Canada - Centraide Canada
Mission: To improve the quality of life of Cape Breton's residents
Chief Officer(s):
Lynne McCarron, Executive Director

United Way of Central Alberta
4811 - 48th St., Red Deer AB T4N 1S6
Tel: 403-343-3900; *Fax:* 403-309-3820
info@caunitedway.ca
www.caunitedway.ca
Overview: A small local charitable organization founded in 1965 overseen by United Way of Canada - Centraide Canada
Mission: To improve lives & build community by engaging individuals & mobilizing collective action
Finances: *Funding Sources:* Corporate & individual donations
Staff Member(s): 7
Activities: *Speaker Service:* Yes
Chief Officer(s):
Robert J. Mitchell, Chief Executive Officer

United Way of Chatham-Kent County
PO Box 606, 425 McNaughton Ave. West, Chatham ON N7M 5K8
Tel: 519-354-0430; *Fax:* 519-354-9511
info@uwock.ca
uwock.ca
www.facebook.com/UnitedWayofChathamKent
twitter.com/UnitedWayCK
www.youtube.com/user/UnitedWayChathamKent
Previous Name: United Way of Kent County
Overview: A small local charitable organization founded in 1948 overseen by United Way of Canada - Centraide Canada
Mission: To build the organized capacity of people to care for one another
Finances: *Funding Sources:* Corporate donations; employee payroll deductions; individual gifts; special events
Staff Member(s): 13
Activities: AGM; kick-off event; fundraising; *Speaker Service:* Yes
Chief Officer(s):
Alison Patrick, President
Karen Kirkwood-Whyte, CEO

United Way of Cochrane-Timiskaming
PO Box 984, Timmins ON P4N 7H6
Tel: 705-268-9696
www.facebook.com/85026973282
Overview: A small local charitable organization founded in 1967 overseen by United Way of Canada - Centraide Canada
Mission: To promote the organized capacity of people to care for one another

Finances: *Annual Operating Budget:* $250,000-$500,000; *Funding Sources:* Donations
Staff Member(s): 2; 460 volunteer(s)
Membership: 100-499; *Committees:* Campaign; Citizen Review; Finance; Special Events
Activities: *Speaker Service:* Yes
Chief Officer(s):
Jennifer Gorman, Coordinator, Resource Development

United Way of Cornwall & District *See* United Way of Stormont, Dundas & Glengarry

United Way of Cumberland County
PO Box 535, #206, 16 Church St., Amherst NS B4H 4A1
Tel: 902-667-2203; *Fax:* 902-667-3819
www.amherst.unitedway.ca
Previous Name: United Way of Amherst
Overview: A small local organization overseen by United Way of Canada - Centraide Canada
Chief Officer(s):
Curt Gunn, President

United Way of Durham Region
345 Simcoe St. South, Oshawa ON L1H 4J2
Tel: 905-436-7377
Toll-Free: 866-463-6910
www.unitedwaydr.com
Overview: A small local organization founded in 1940 overseen by United Way of Canada - Centraide Canada
Mission: To strengthen the Durham region communities & improve the quality of life of its residents
Staff Member(s): 6
Activities: *Speaker Service:* Yes
Chief Officer(s):
Cindy Murray, Chief Executive Officer
Robert Howard, Director, Campaign & Communications
Karie Stephenson, Manager, Finance & Office
Michele Watson, Manager, Information Services Program
Jessica Hanson, Manager, Communications & Data
Barb Fannin, Coordinator, Community Investment

Ajax Office
Ajax ON
Tel: 905-686-0606

United Way of East Kootenay
PO Box 657, 930 Baker St., Cranbrook BC V1C 4J2
Tel: 250-426-8833; *Fax:* 250-426-5455
office@cranbrook.unitedway.ca
www.cranbrook.unitedway.ca
www.facebook.com/ourunitedway
Overview: A small local charitable organization founded in 1969 overseen by United Way of Canada - Centraide Canada
Mission: To ensure the effective raising & allocation of charitable funds for community based social services that are in the best interest of the community
Finances: *Annual Operating Budget:* Less than $50,000
Staff Member(s): 1; 30 volunteer(s)
Activities: *Awareness Events:* Day of Caring
Chief Officer(s):
Donna Brady Fields, Executive Director

United Way of Estevan
PO Box 611, Estevan SK S4A 2A5
Tel: 306-634-7375
admin@unitedwayestevan.com
www.unitedwayofestevan.com
www.facebook.com/unitedwayestevan
twitter.com/uwestevan
Overview: A small local organization founded in 1967 overseen by United Way of Canada - Centraide Canada
Mission: To strengthen the community
Membership: *Committees:* Banking; Community Building; Entertainment; Facilities; Finance & Allocations; Food Services; Fundraising; History; Phones & Cameras; Public Relations; Production; Raffle; Security
Chief Officer(s):
Christa Morhart, President

United Way of Fort McMurray
The Redpoll Centre, #200, 10010 Franklin Ave., Fort McMurray AB T9H 2K6
Tel: 780-791-0077
info@fmunitedway.com
fmunitedway.com
www.facebook.com/142299649181047
twitter.com/FMUnitedWay
www.youtube.com/user/fmunitedwaycampaign

Overview: A small local charitable organization founded in 1978 overseen by United Way of Canada - Centraide Canada
Mission: To provide effective support for social health & welfare services in the community of Fort McMurray
Finances: *Funding Sources:* Corporate & employee donations
Staff Member(s): 9
Membership: *Member Profile:* Registered charity; volunteer component
Chief Officer(s):
Ben Dutton, President
Diane Shannon, Executive Director
dshannon@fmunitedway.com
Russell Thomas, Director, Communications & Community Impact
communications@fmunitedway.com

United Way of Greater Moncton & Southeastern New Brunswick (UWGMSENB) / Centraide de la région du Grand Moncton et du Sud-Est du NB Inc. (CGMSENB)
22 Church St., #T210, Moncton NB E1C 0P7
Tel: 506-858-8600; *Fax:* 506-858-0584
office@moncton.unitedway.ca
www.gmsenbunitedway.ca
www.facebook.com/UnitedWayGMSENBCentraideGMSENB
twitter.com/unitedwaygmsenb
www.flickr.com/photos/unitedwaygmsenb
Previous Name: United Way/Centraide of the Moncton Region
Overview: A small local charitable organization founded in 1953 overseen by United Way of Canada - Centraide Canada
Mission: To strengthen Southeastern New Brunswick's communities
Finances: *Annual Operating Budget:* $100,000-$250,000
Staff Member(s): 9; 2000 volunteer(s)
Membership: 1-99
Chief Officer(s):
Debbie McInnis, Executive Director
dmcinnis@moncton.unitedway.ca

United Way of Greater Saint John Inc.
#301, 28 Richmond St., Saint John NB E2L 3B2
Tel: 506-658-1212; *Fax:* 506-633-7724
contactus@unitedwaysaintjohn.com
www.unitedwaysaintjohn.com
www.facebook.com/21724743048
twitter.com/SJUnitedWay
www.youtube.com/UnitedWaySJ
Overview: A small local charitable organization founded in 1958 overseen by United Way of Canada - Centraide Canada
Finances: *Annual Operating Budget:* $100,000-$250,000; *Funding Sources:* Corporate & individual donations
Staff Member(s): 4; 2000 volunteer(s)
Membership: 400 corporate + 25 institutional + 30,000 individual; *Fees:* Schedule available; *Committees:* Agency Relations Allocations; Public Relations/Marketing; Strategic Planning; Labour
Activities: *Speaker Service:* Yes
Chief Officer(s):
Wendy MacDermott, Executive Director
wendy@unitedwaysaintjohn.com

United Way of Greater Simcoe County
1110 Hwy. 26, Midhurst ON L9X 1N6
Tel: 705-726-2301; *Fax:* 705-726-4897
info@uwsimcoemuskoka.ca
www.unitedwaygsc.ca
www.facebook.com/UWSimcoeMuskoka
twitter.com/UWSimcoeMuskoka
www.youtube.com/user/UnitedWaySimcoeCty
Previous Name: United Way of Barrie/South Simcoe
Overview: A small local charitable organization founded in 1960 overseen by United Way of Canada - Centraide Canada
Mission: To improve quality of life & build community by helping those most in need
Member of: Barrie Chamber of Commerce
Finances: *Annual Operating Budget:* $500,000-$1.5 Million; *Funding Sources:* Community
Staff Member(s): 5; 400 volunteer(s)
Membership: 21 agencies; *Committees:* Allocations; Communications; Executive; Campaign Cabinet
Activities: Food for Thought; Simcoe County Alliance to End Homelessness; Partners for Success by Six; 211 Information; Training & Consulting Services; *Internships:* Yes; *Speaker Service:* Yes; *Library:* by appointment
Chief Officer(s):
Dale Biddell, CEO, 705-726-2301 Ext. 2033
dbiddell@uwsimcoemuskoka.ca

United Way of Guelph, Wellington & Dufferin
85 Westmount Rd., Guelph ON N1H 5J2
Tel: 519-821-0571; *Fax:* 519-821-7847
www.unitedwayguelph.com
www.linkedin.com/company/united-way-of-guelph-&-wellington
www.facebook.com/unitedwayguelph
twitter.com/uwguelph
Previous Name: Guelph & Wellington United Way Social Planning Council
Overview: A small local charitable organization founded in 1945 overseen by United Way of Canada - Centraide Canada
Mission: To meet the needs of the community & improve lives
Staff Member(s): 9; 750 volunteer(s)
Membership: *Committees:* Fund Distribution
Activities: *Library:* Open to public
Chief Officer(s):
Ken Dardano, Executive Director
ken@unitedwayguelph.com

United Way of Haldimand-Norfolk
PO Box 472, 45 Kent St. North, Simcoe ON N3Y 4L5
Tel: 519-426-5660; *Fax:* 519-426-0017
reception@unitedwayhn.on.ca
www.unitedwayhn.on.ca
www.facebook.com/UnitedWayofhn
twitter.com/UnitedWayofHN
Previous Name: Norfolk Community Chest
Overview: A small local charitable organization founded in 1946 overseen by United Way of Canada - Centraide Canada
Mission: To improve people's lives & to strengthen the community
Finances: *Annual Operating Budget:* $100,000-$250,000
Staff Member(s): 2; 500 volunteer(s)
Membership: 1,000-4,999; *Committees:* Campaign Planning; Administration; Allocations
Activities: Amazing Race, Aug.; Mini Putt Marathon, Sept.; *Speaker Service:* Yes
Chief Officer(s):
Brittany Burley, Executive Director
brittany.burley@unitedwayhn.on.ca

United Way of Halifax Region
Royal Bank Bldg., 46 Portland St., 7th Fl., Dartmouth NS B2Y 1H4
Tel: 902-422-1501; *Fax:* 902-423-6837
www.unitedwayhalifax.ca
www.linkedin.com/company/united-way-of-halifax-region
www.facebook.com/UnitedWayHalifaxRegion
twitter.com/UWHalifax
Previous Name: Metro United Way (Halifax-Dartmouth)
Overview: A medium-sized local charitable organization founded in 1924 overseen by United Way of Canada - Centraide Canada
Mission: To strengthen neighbourhoods & communities by providing programs & services that link people & resources, encourage participation & increase giving
Chief Officer(s):
Sara Napier, President & CEO
snapier@unitedwayhalifax.ca

United Way of Halton Hills
PO Box 286, Georgetown ON L7G 4Y5
Tel: 905-877-3066; *Fax:* 905-877-3067
office@unitedwayofhaltonhills.ca
www.unitedwayofhaltonhills.ca
Overview: A small local charitable organization founded in 1986 overseen by United Way of Canada - Centraide Canada
Mission: To provide leadership in the raising & allocation of funds to meet human needs & to improve social conditions in the community
Finances: *Annual Operating Budget:* Less than $50,000
Staff Member(s): 1; 300 volunteer(s)
Membership: 1-99; *Committees:* Campaign; House Tour
Chief Officer(s):
Janet Foster, Executive Director

United Way of Kamloops & Region *See* Thompson, Nicola, Cariboo United Way

United Way of Kent County *See* United Way of Chatham-Kent County

United Way of Kingston, Frontenac, Lennox & Addington
417 Bagot St., Kingston ON K7K 3C1

Tel: 613-542-2674; *Fax:* 613-542-1379
uway@unitedwaykfla.ca
www.unitedwaykfla.ca
www.facebook.com/unitedwaykfla
twitter.com/unitedwaykfla
www.youtube.com/unitedwaykfla
Overview: A small local charitable organization overseen by United Way of Canada - Centraide Canada
Mission: To strengthen the community by supporting social service & health agencies
Finances: *Annual Operating Budget:* $100,000-$250,000; *Funding Sources:* Annual campaign; endowment fund interest
Staff Member(s): 6; 1000 volunteer(s)
Membership: 1-99; *Fees:* Donation
Activities: Campaign kick-off; Fare for Friends; Country 96, 36-hour Radiothon; *Speaker Service:* Yes
Chief Officer(s):
Bhavana Varma, President & CEO
bvarma@unitedwaykfla.ca

United Way of Kitchener-Waterloo & Area
Marsland Centre, #801, 20 Erb St. West, Waterloo ON N2L 1T2
Tel: 519-888-6100
info@uwaykw.org
www.uwaykw.org
www.facebook.com/uwaykw
twitter.com/UnitedWayKW
www.youtube.com/user/UwayKW
Overview: A small local charitable organization founded in 1941 overseen by United Way of Canada - Centraide Canada
Mission: To improve quality of life in the community
Member of: Kitchener-Waterloo Chamber of Commerce
Finances: *Annual Operating Budget:* $3 Million-$5 Million; *Funding Sources:* Donations
Staff Member(s): 12; 3000 volunteer(s)
Membership: 25,000+; *Fees:* $10 donation; *Member Profile:* An individual who makes a financial donation of $10 or more; *Committees:* Campaign; Allocations; Admissions; Planned Giving; Finance/Human Resources; Nominating; Policy Development & Governance
Activities: *Internships:* Yes; *Speaker Service:* Yes
Chief Officer(s):
Ingrid Pregel, President
Jan Varner, CEO
jvarner@uwaykw.org

United Way of Lanark County
15 Bates Dr., Carleton Place ON K7C 4J8
Tel: 613-253-9074; *Fax:* 888-249-9075
www.lanarkunitedway.com
www.linkedin.com/company/united-way-of-lanark-county
www.facebook.com/UnitedWayLanarkCounty
twitter.com/UWLanarkCounty
Overview: A small local organization overseen by United Way of Canada - Centraide Canada
Mission: To mobilize people to strengthen the community & enact social change
Staff Member(s): 3
Chief Officer(s):
Fraser Scantlebury, Executive Director
fscantlebury@lanarkunitedway.com

United Way of Leeds & Grenville
PO Box 576, 42 George St., Brockville ON K6V 5V7
Tel: 613-342-8889; *Fax:* 613-342-8850
info@uwlg.org
www.uwlg.org
www.facebook.com/UnitedWayLG
www.youtube.com/user/UnitedWayLeedsGrenv
Overview: A small local licensing charitable organization founded in 1957 overseen by United Way of Canada - Centraide Canada
Mission: To unite people to improve quality of life & build healthy communities
Finances: *Annual Operating Budget:* $500,000-$1.5 Million
Staff Member(s): 2
Membership: 27; *Committees:* Allocations; Administrative; Long Range Planning; Policy & Procedures; Sub Allocation; Marketing & Publicity
Activities: *Speaker Service:* Yes; *Library:* Open to public
Chief Officer(s):
Melissa Hillier, Executive Director

United Way of Lethbridge & South Western Alberta
1277 - 3 Ave. South, Lethbridge AB T1J 0K3
Tel: 403-327-1700; *Fax:* 403-317-7940
together@lethbridgeunitedway.ca
www.lethbridgeunitedway.ca
www.facebook.com/unitedwaylethy
twitter.com/unitedwaylethy
Overview: A small local charitable organization overseen by United Way of Canada - Centraide Canada
Mission: To build a better community by organizing the capacity of people to care for one another
Finances: *Annual Operating Budget:* $100,000-$250,000; *Funding Sources:* Campaigns & special events
Staff Member(s): 3; 140 volunteer(s)
Membership: 3,000; *Fees:* $1; *Committees:* Budget Allocation; Nominating; Special Events; Community Development; Campaign
Chief Officer(s):
Jeff McLarty, Executive Director
jmclarty@lethbridgeunitedway.ca

United Way of London & Middlesex
409 King St., London ON N6B 1S5
Tel: 519-438-1721; *Fax:* 519-438-9938
www.unitedwaylm.ca
www.linkedin.com/company/unitedwaylm
www.facebook.com/unitedwaylm
twitter.com/unitedwaylm
Overview: A small local charitable organization founded in 1965 overseen by United Way of Canada - Centraide Canada
Mission: To exercise leadership in coordinating people & organizations to assist those in need in our community
Finances: *Annual Operating Budget:* $3 Million-$5 Million
Staff Member(s): 15; 3000 volunteer(s)
Membership: 985 corporate + 43,966 individual; *Fees:* $10 minimum donation; *Committees:* Community Services; Finance; Resource Development; Nominations; External Review; Executive
Activities: Annual fundraising campaign; *Speaker Service:* Yes
Chief Officer(s):
Kelly Ziegner, Chief Executive Officer
kziegner@unitedwaylm.ca
Suzanne Bembridge, Director, Finance & Operations
sbembridge@unitedwaylm.ca

United Way of Medicine Hat, Redcliff & District *See* United Way of South Eastern Alberta

United Way of Milton
PO Box 212, 1 Chris Hadfield Way, Milton ON L9T 4N9
Tel: 905-875-2550; *Fax:* 905-875-2402
campaign@miltonunitedway.ca
www.miltonunitedway.ca
www.linkedin.com/groups?gid=2558626
www.facebook.com/UnitedWayMilton
twitter.com/unitedwaymilton
www.youtube.com/unitedwaymilton
Overview: A small local charitable organization founded in 1982 overseen by United Way of Canada - Centraide Canada
Mission: To serve the people of the Milton area by working with recognized charitable agencies to ensure human services that enhance the quality of life in the community
Staff Member(s): 2; 150 volunteer(s)
Chief Officer(s):
Kate Holmes, CEO

United Way of Morden & District Inc.
PO Box 758, 379 Stephen St., Morden MB R6M 1A7
Tel: 204-822-6992
mordendistrictuw@gmail.com
www.unitedwaymorden.com
Overview: A small local organization overseen by United Way of Canada - Centraide Canada
Mission: To partner with charitable agencies & organizations to improve the lives of residents in Morden & the surrounding area
Finances: *Annual Operating Budget:* Less than $50,000; *Funding Sources:* Manitoba lotteries
Chief Officer(s):
Lisa Gander, President

United Way of Nanaimo & District *See* United Way Central & Northern Vancouver Island

United Way of Niagara Falls & Greater Fort Erie
7150 Montrose Rd., Niagara Falls ON L2H 3N3
Tel: 905-735-0490
www.unitedwayniagara.org
www.facebook.com/UnitedWayNiagara
twitter.com/UWNiagara
Overview: A small local charitable organization founded in 1942 overseen by United Way of Canada - Centraide Canada
Mission: To support the people in Fort Erie, Niagara Falls, Pelham, Port Colborne, Wainfleet, & Welland; To bring about positive change to the community
Staff Member(s): 3; 250 volunteer(s)
Chief Officer(s):
Tamara Coleman-Lawrie, Executive Director
tamara.coleman-lawrie@unitedwayniagara.org

United Way of North Okanagan Columbia Shuswap
3304 - 30th Ave., Vernon BC V1T 2C8
Tel: 250-549-1346; *Fax:* 250-549-1357
Toll-Free: 866-448-3489
unitedwaynocs@shaw.ca
www.unitedwaynocs.com
www.facebook.com/226411234037024
twitter.com/unitedwaynocs
Previous Name: North Okanagan United Way
Overview: A small local charitable organization founded in 1961 overseen by United Way of Canada - Centraide Canada
Mission: To promote a healthy, caring inclusive community; To strenghten our community's capacity to address social issues
Member of: Vernon Chamber of Commerce
Finances: *Funding Sources:* Donations; fundraising; payroll deductions; special events
Chief Officer(s):
Linda Yule, Executive Director

United Way of Northern BC
1600 - 3rd Ave., Prince George BC V2L 3G6
Tel: 250-561-1040; *Fax:* 250-562-8102
info@unitedwaynbc.ca
www.unitedwaynbc.ca
www.facebook.com/unitedwaynorthernbc
twitter.com/unitedwaynbc
Previous Name: Prince George United Way
Overview: A small local charitable organization founded in 1969 overseen by United Way of Canada - Centraide Canada
Mission: To promote the organized capacity of persons to care for one another through voluntarism, leadership & education; To ensure the effective raising & allocation of charitable funds for community-based social services; To foster the effective provision of services that are in the best interest of the community
Staff Member(s): 8
Activities: Volunteer Leadership Development to provide training & support to develop effective leadership of not-for-profit voluntary agencies
Chief Officer(s):
Russ Beerling, Chair
Roberta Squire, Chief Executive Officer
robertas@unitedwaynbc.ca

United Way of Oakville (UWO)
#200, 466 Speers Rd., Oakville ON L6K 3W9
Tel: 905-845-5571; *Fax:* 905-845-0166
info@uwoakville.org
www.uwoakville.org
www.linkedin.com/company/united-way-oakville
www.facebook.com/UnitedWayOakville
twitter.com/uwoakville
www.youtube.com/user/UnitedWayofOakville
Overview: A medium-sized local charitable organization founded in 1955 overseen by United Way of Canada - Centraide Canada
Mission: To bring people & resources together to strengthen the Oakville community
Finances: *Annual Operating Budget:* $3 Million-$5 Million; *Funding Sources:* Fundraising Campaign; leadership giving; sponsorship
Staff Member(s): 16; 200 volunteer(s)
Membership: *Committees:* Finance & Audit; Human Resources; Governance; Campaign Cabinet
Activities: Campaign Kick-Off; Annual Bathtub Race; Golf Tournament; Day of Caring; *Internships:* Yes; *Speaker Service:* Yes
Chief Officer(s):
John Armstrong, Chair
Brad Park, Chief Executive Officer
brad@uwoakville.org
Tara Neal, Office Administrator
tara@uwoakville.org

United Way of Oxford
#447 Hunter St., Woodstock ON N4S 4G7
Tel: 519-539-3851
info@unitedwayoxford.ca
www.unitedwayoxford.ca

www.facebook.com/UnitedWayOxford
twitter.com/UnitedWayOxford
www.youtube.com/channel/UCup-8AJZ2pJFCCeZbJ4t87w
Overview: A small local organization overseen by United Way of Canada - Centraide Canada
Mission: To build strong communities & help improve the lives of residents, especially those affected by poverty, mental health issues, or other social challenges
Member of: United Way of Ontario
Finances: *Annual Operating Budget:* $500,000-$1.5 Million
Staff Member(s): 4; 200 volunteer(s)
Membership: *Fees:* Donation
Activities: Fundraising; fund distribution
Chief Officer(s):
Kelly Gilson, Executive Director
kelly@unitedwayoxford.ca
Anne Wismer, Manager, Operations
anne@unitedwayoxford.ca

United Way of Peel Region
PO Box 58, #408, 90 Burnhamthorpe Rd. West, Mississauga ON L5B 3C3
Tel: 905-602-3650; *Fax:* 905-602-3651; *TTY:* 905-602-3653
www.unitedwaypeel.org
www.linkedin.com/company/657177
www.facebook.com/unitedwaypeel
twitter.com/Unitedwaypeel
www.youtube.com/user/unitedwaypeel
Overview: A large local charitable organization founded in 1967 overseen by United Way of Canada - Centraide Canada
Mission: To serve the communities of Mississauga, Brampton, & Caledon; To improve social conditions so that everyone can thrive; To provide a strong voice for social change that strengthens communities & improves lives
Finances: *Funding Sources:* Campaign pledges; donations; gifts in kind
Staff Member(s): 38; 2601 volunteer(s)
Membership: *Committees:* Alumni; Allocations; Finance & Audit; Governance; Nominations; Public Policy
Activities: Fair Share for Peel Task Force; *Awareness Events:* Campaign Kickoff; Lexus Golf Tournament; Roll Around Square One
Chief Officer(s):
Shirley Crocker, Vice-President, Finance & Administration
scrocker@unitedwaypeel.org
Cecelia Paolucci, Vice-President, Philanthropy
Anita Stellinga, Vice-President, Community Investment
astellinga@unitedwaypeel.org
Awards:
• Outstanding Agency Campaign Award
• Speakers Bureau Award
• Outstanding Joint Union-Management Campaign Award
• Leading the Way Campaign Award
• Outstanding Corporate Campaign Award
• Bank Branch Campaign of the Year
• Best National Campaign Award
• Employee Campaign Chair of the Year Award

United Way of Perth-Huron
32 Erie St., Stratford ON N5A 2M4
Tel: 519-271-7730; *Fax:* 519-273-9350
Toll-Free: 877-818-8867
info@perthhuron.unitedway.ca
www.perthhuron.unitedway.ca
www.linkedin.com/groups?gid=3966504
www.facebook.com/UWPH1
twitter.com/UnitedWayPH
www.youtube.com/user/UnitedWPH
Previous Name: United Way of Stratford-Perth
Overview: A small local charitable organization founded in 1967 overseen by United Way of Canada - Centraide Canada
Mission: To improve people's lives & meet the needs of the community by mobilizing agencies, individuals, & resources
Affiliation(s): Perth County Community Development Council; Local Voices
Finances: *Annual Operating Budget:* $250,000-$500,000; *Funding Sources:* Workplace campaigns; special events; individual donations
Staff Member(s): 3; 50 volunteer(s)
Membership: 17 organizations; *Member Profile:* Funded, not for profit agencies; *Committees:* Board of Directors; Campaign Cabinet; Program Review & Allocations
Activities: Fundraising & allocation to agencies; Building awareness of emerging community needs; *Awareness Events:* Kick-Off Luncheon; *Speaker Service:* Yes
Chief Officer(s):
Ryan Erb, Executive Director
rerb@perthhuron.unitedway.ca
Carolynne Champagne, Vice-President, Resource Development & Communications
cchampagne@perthhuron.unitedway.ca
Jeanine Clarke, Director, Finance & Property
jclarke@perthhuron.unitedway.ca
Susan Faber, Director, Communications & Community Information
sfaber@perthhuron.unitedway.ca

United Way of Peterborough & District
277 Stewart St., Peterborough ON K9J 3M8
Tel: 705-742-8839; *Fax:* 705-742-9186
office@uwpeterborough.ca
www.uwpeterborough.ca
www.facebook.com/15103169591
twitter.com/UnitedWayPtbo
Overview: A medium-sized local charitable organization founded in 1941 overseen by United Way of Canada - Centraide Canada
Mission: To improve lives & build community by engaging individuals & mobilizing collective action; to provide resources, services & programs for community leadership
Finances: *Annual Operating Budget:* $1.5 Million-$3 Million; *Funding Sources:* Community fundraising
Staff Member(s): 11
Membership: *Committees:* Agency & Community Services; Finance
Activities: Campaign kick-off, Sept.; fundraising; *Speaker Service:* Yes
Chief Officer(s):
Jim Russell, CEO
jrussell@uwpeterborough.ca

United Way of Pictou County
PO Box 75, 342 Stewart St., New Glasgow NS B2H 5E1
Tel: 902-755-1754; *Fax:* 902-755-0853
info@pictoucountyunitedway.ca
www.pictoucountyunitedway.ca
www.facebook.com/UWPictouCounty
twitter.com/UWPictouCo
Overview: A small local charitable organization founded in 1960 overseen by United Way of Canada - Centraide Canada
Mission: To strengthen communities by facilitating programs & services that link people & resources; encourage participation; increase giving
Staff Member(s): 2
Chief Officer(s):
Jessica Smith, Executive Director
jessica@pictoucountyunitedway.ca

United Way of Prince Edward Island / Centraide PEI
PO Box 247, 180 Kent St., 2nd Fl., Charlottetown PE C1A 7K4
Tel: 902-894-8202; *Fax:* 902-894-9643
Toll-Free: 877-902-4438
www.peiunitedway.com
www.facebook.com/peiunitedway
twitter.com/uwpei
www.youtube.com/channel/UCQAZJYD21v35hl9ggOoAJ9w
Overview: A small provincial charitable organization founded in 1962 overseen by United Way of Canada - Centraide Canada
Mission: To provide funds needed to meet community needs & build stronger communities
Finances: *Annual Operating Budget:* $500,000-$1.5 Million; *Funding Sources:* Corporate, individual donations
Staff Member(s): 3; 2300 volunteer(s)
Membership: 20,000; *Member Profile:* All donors; *Committees:* Board of Directors; Executive; Campaign Cabinet
Activities: *Speaker Service:* Yes
Chief Officer(s):
Carol O'Hanley, President
Andrea MacDonald, CEO
amacdonald@peiunitedway.com

United Way of Quinte
PO Box 815, Belleville ON K8N 5B5
Tel: 613-962-9531; *Fax:* 613-962-4165
www.unitedwayofquinte.ca
www.facebook.com/UnitedWayofQuinte
twitter.com/unitedwayquinte
Previous Name: United Way of Belleville & District
Overview: A small local charitable organization founded in 1959 overseen by United Way of Canada - Centraide Canada
Mission: To provide leadership in a collaborative endeavor with our member agencies & others to increase the capacity of our community to respond to human service needs
Member of: United Way Ontario
Finances: *Annual Operating Budget:* $1.5 Million-$3 Million; *Funding Sources:* Donations
Staff Member(s): 7
Activities: Fundraising; information & referral; monthly community forum
Chief Officer(s):
Danny Nickle, Chair
Judi Gilbert, Executive Director
jgilbert@unitedwayofquinte.ca
Tambra Patrick-MacDonald, Director, Finance & Administration
tmacdonald@unitedwayofquinte.ca

United Way of Regina
1440 Scarth St., Regina SK S4R 2E9
Tel: 306-757-5671; *Fax:* 306-522-7199
www.unitedwayregina.ca
www.facebook.com/UnitedWayRegina
twitter.com/unitedwayregina
www.instagram.com/unitedwayregina
Overview: A small local charitable organization founded in 1935 overseen by United Way of Canada - Centraide Canada
Mission: To mobilize individuals, agencies & resources to improve lives & strengthen the community
Finances: *Annual Operating Budget:* $1.5 Million-$3 Million; *Funding Sources:* Fundraising
Staff Member(s): 11; 3500 volunteer(s)
Membership: 37 funded agencies + 100 registered agencies; *Committees:* Allocations/Admissions; Campaign; Audit; Nominations; Resource Devlopment
Activities: AGM; Tribute Luncheon; *Awareness Events:* Day of Caring; Vital Link Dinner; *Speaker Service:* Yes; *Library:* Volunteer Regina Resource Centre; Open to public
Chief Officer(s):
Robyn Edwards-Bentz, CEO
redwardsbentz@unitedwayregina.ca
Tanya Murray, Director, Operations
tmurray@unitedwayregina.ca

United Way of St Catharines & District
63 Church St., #LC1, St Catharines ON L2R 3C4
Tel: 905-688-5050; *Fax:* 905-688-2997
office@stcatharines.unitedway.ca
www.unitedwaysc.ca
www.facebook.com/148938585140989
twitter.com/uwaysc
Overview: A small local charitable organization founded in 1953 overseen by United Way of Canada - Centraide Canada
Mission: To increase the organized capacity of people to care for one another
Finances: *Annual Operating Budget:* $500,000-$1.5 Million; *Funding Sources:* Fundraising
Staff Member(s): 10
Membership: 20,000; *Fees:* $10 donation or more
Activities: *Internships:* Yes; *Speaker Service:* Yes
Chief Officer(s):
Frances Hallworth, Executive Director
fhallworth@stcatharines.unitedway.ca

United Way of Sarnia-Lambton
PO Box 548, 420 East St. North, Sarnia ON N7T 6Y5
Tel: 519-336-5452; *Fax:* 519-383-6032
info@theunitedway.on.ca
www.theunitedway.on.ca
Overview: A small local charitable organization founded in 1959 overseen by United Way of Canada - Centraide Canada
Mission: To generate resources enabling the community to respond to human care priorities in Sarnia-Lambton
Finances: *Annual Operating Budget:* $250,000-$500,000; *Funding Sources:* Annual fall fundraising campaign
Staff Member(s): 5; 2000 volunteer(s)
Membership: 28 local agencies; *Committees:* Campaign Cabinet; Community Investment
Activities: *Speaker Service:* Yes
Chief Officer(s):
Dave Brown, Executive Director
dave@theunitedway.on.ca

United Way of Saskatoon & Area
#100, 506 - 25 St. East, Saskatoon SK S7K 4A7
Tel: 306-975-7700
office@unitedwaysaskatoon.ca
www.unitedwaysaskatoon.ca
www.facebook.com/UnitedWaySaskatoonAndArea
twitter.com/UnitedWayStoon

Overview: A small local organization overseen by United Way of Canada - Centraide Canada
Mission: To improve social conditions & build a strong community
Chief Officer(s):
Jocelyn Zurakowski, Interim CEO

United Way of Sault Ste Marie & District
7A Oxford St., Sault Ste Marie ON P6B 1R7
Tel: 705-256-7476; *Fax:* 705-759-5899
uwssm@ssmunitedway.ca
www.ssmunitedway.ca
www.facebook.com/unitedwaysault
Overview: A small local organization founded in 1957 overseen by United Way of Canada - Centraide Canada
Mission: To improve the health, well-being, & quality of life of individuals & families in the community; To fight against poverty & address community issues
Member of: Chamber of Commerce of Sault Ste Marie
Affiliation(s): United Way of Ontario; Regional Professional Advisory Council
Finances: *Annual Operating Budget:* $500,000-$1.5 Million; *Funding Sources:* 99% donations + 1% government
Staff Member(s): 5; 450 volunteer(s)
Membership: 23; *Fees:* Donation; *Committees:* Community Services; Volunteer Centre; Labour
Activities: Public assistance coordination; Charity Golf Scramble; Starlight Filmfest; Old Tyme Fair & Picnic, June; Annual Fall Campaign, Sept.-Nov.; *Speaker Service:* Yes; *Library:* Campaign & Volunteer Centre; by appointment
Chief Officer(s):
Gary Vipond, CEO

United Way of South Eastern Alberta
928 Allowance Ave., Medicine Hat AB T1A 7G7
Tel: 403-526-5544; *Fax:* 403-526-5244
www.utdway.ca
www.facebook.com/UnitedWaySEAB
twitter.com/UnitedWaySEAB
Previous Name: United Way of Medicine Hat, Redcliff & District
Overview: A small local organization overseen by United Way of Canada - Centraide Canada
Chief Officer(s):
Melissa Fandrick, Coordinator, Community Investment
communityinvestment@utdway.ca

United Way of Stormont, Dundas & Glengarry / Centraide de Stormont, Dundas & Glengarry
PO Box 441, Stn. Case Postale, Cornwall ON K6H 5T2
Tel: 613-932-2051; *Fax:* 613-932-7534
info@unitedwaysdg.com
www.unitedwaysdg.com
www.facebook.com/209841445745076
twitter.com/unitedwaysdg
Previous Name: United Way of Cornwall & District
Overview: A small local charitable organization founded in 1944 overseen by United Way of Canada - Centraide Canada
Mission: To improve lives & build community by supporting agencies, programs & services in the area
Finances: *Annual Operating Budget:* $50,000-$100,000; *Funding Sources:* Fundraising
Staff Member(s): 3; 500 volunteer(s)
Membership: 500-999
Activities: Variety of fundraisers to raise money to fund 18 agencies; *Speaker Service:* Yes
Chief Officer(s):
Nolan Quinn, President
Lori Greer, Executive Director
lori@unitedwaysdg.com
Stephanie Lalonde, Coordinator, Campaign & Communication
stephanie@unitedwaysdg.com

United Way of Stratford-Perth *See* United Way of Perth-Huron

United Way of the Alberta Capital Region
15132 Stony Plain Rd., Edmonton AB T5P 3Y3
Tel: 780-990-1000; *Fax:* 780-990-0203
united@myunitedway.ca
www.myunitedway.ca
www.facebook.com/myUnitedWay
twitter.com/myunitedway
www.youtube.com/uwacr
Overview: A large local charitable organization founded in 1941 overseen by United Way of Canada - Centraide Canada
Mission: To bring people & resources together to build caring, vibrant communities
Finances: *Funding Sources:* Donations

Activities: *Awareness Events:* United Way Campaign Kick Off, Sept. 22
Chief Officer(s):
Anne Smith, Secretary/Treasurer
Publications:
• WE Magazine [a publication of United Way of the Alberta Capital Region]
Type: Magazine

United Way of the Central Okanagan & South Okanagan/Similkameen
#202, 1456 St. Paul St., Kelowna BC V1Y 2E6
Tel: 250-860-2356; *Fax:* 250-868-3206
info@unitedwaycso.com
unitedwaycso.com
www.facebook.com/unitedwaycso
twitter.com/UnitedWayCSO
www.youtube.com/user/UnitedWayCSO
Overview: A medium-sized local charitable organization founded in 1950 overseen by United Way of Canada - Centraide Canada
Mission: To increase the organized capacity of people in our community to care for one another
Finances: *Funding Sources:* Donations
Staff Member(s): 6
Activities: September Kick-Off Breakfast; Golf Tournament; Drive-Thru Breakfast; Fundraising Campaign; Leadership Development Program; Volunteer Leadership Development Program; *Speaker Service:* Yes
Chief Officer(s):
Shelley Gilmore, Executive Director

United Way of the Fraser Valley (UWFV)
Sweeney Neighbourhood Centre, #208, 33355 Bevan Ave., Abbotsford BC V2S 0E7
Tel: 604-852-1234; *Fax:* 604-852-2316
Toll-Free: 888-251-7777
info@uwfv.bc.ca
www.facebook.com/unitedwayfraservalley
twitter.com/unitedwayfv
Overview: A small local charitable organization founded in 1985 overseen by United Way of Canada - Centraide Canada
Mission: To promote the organized capacity of people to care for one another
Member of: United Way of Canada; Abbotsford Chamber of Commerce; Chilliwack Chamber of Commerce
Finances: *Annual Operating Budget:* $500,000-$1.5 Million; *Funding Sources:* Donations; Government grants
Staff Member(s): 4; 200 volunteer(s)
Membership: 26; *Member Profile:* Charitable health & social service agencies; *Committees:* Executive; Campaign; Impact; Finance
Activities: Volunteer training; Fundraising; Developing communities; *Speaker Service:* Yes
Chief Officer(s):
Wayne Green, Executive Director
wayne@uwfv.bc.ca

United Way of the Lower Mainland
4543 Canada Way, Burnaby BC V5G 4T4
Tel: 604-294-8929; *Fax:* 604-293-0220
www.uwlm.ca
www.linkedin.com/groups?about=&gid=4196396
www.facebook.com/UnitedWayoftheLowerMainland
twitter.com/uwlm
www.youtube.com/user/UnitedWayVancouver
Overview: A small local organization overseen by United Way of Canada - Centraide Canada
Chief Officer(s):
Michael McKnight, President & CEO
michaelm@uwlm.ca

United Way of Trail & District
803B Victoria St., Trail BC V1R 3T3
Tel: 250-364-0999; *Fax:* 250-364-1564
www.traildistrictunitedway.com
Overview: A small local charitable organization founded in 1928 overseen by United Way of Canada - Centraide Canada
Mission: To raise funds which are allocated to 26 affiliated non-profit organizations
Finances: *Annual Operating Budget:* $100,000-$250,000; *Funding Sources:* Donations; fundraising
Staff Member(s): 1; 200 volunteer(s)
Membership: 3,000; *Fees:* $25; *Committees:* Budget; Publicity; Campaign; Nominating; Fundraising; Special Events
Activities: *Awareness Events:* Campaign Kickoff Event; *Library:* Open to public

Chief Officer(s):
Jodi LeSergent, President

United Way of Victoria County (UWVC) *See* United Way for the City of Kawartha Lakes

United Way of Windsor-Essex County
300 Giles Blvd. East, #A1, Windsor ON N9A 4C4
Tel: 519-258-0000; *Fax:* 519-258-2346
info@weareunited.com
www.weareunited.com
www.facebook.com/unitedway.windsoressex
twitter.com/UnitedWayWE
Overview: A small local charitable organization overseen by United Way of Canada - Centraide Canada
Mission: To bring people & resources together to improve the community
Staff Member(s): 25; 25 volunteer(s)
Membership: 15,000-49,999
Activities: *Speaker Service:* Yes
Chief Officer(s):
Lorraine Goddard, CEO
lgoddard@weareunited.com

United Way of Winnipeg / Winnipeg Centraide
580 Main St., Winnipeg MB R3B 1C7
Tel: 204-477-5360; *Fax:* 204-453-6198
info@unitedwaywinnipeg.mb.ca
www.unitedwaywinnipeg.ca
www.facebook.com/unitedwaywinnipeg
twitter.com/unitedwaywpg
www.youtube.com/user/uwaywinnipeg
Overview: A small local organization founded in 1965 overseen by United Way of Canada - Centraide Canada
Mission: To support & strengthen the organized capacity of people to care for one another
Staff Member(s): 30; 8000 volunteer(s)
Membership: 75,000; *Fees:* Donation
Activities: *Speaker Service:* Yes
Chief Officer(s):
Marilyn McLaren, Chair

United Way South Niagara (UWSN) / Centraide de Niagara Sud
Seaway Mall, 800 Niagara St., 2nd Fl, Welland ON L3C 5Z4
Tel: 905-735-0490; *Fax:* 905-735-5432
www.unitedwayniagara.org
www.facebook.com/UnitedWayNiagara
twitter.com/UWNiagara
Overview: A medium-sized local charitable organization founded in 1964 overseen by United Way of Canada - Centraide Canada
Finances: *Funding Sources:* Donations; Fundraising
Staff Member(s): 3
Activities: Distributing funds for programs & services; Contributing to community development
Chief Officer(s):
Tamara Coleman-Lawrie, Executive Director

United Way Toronto & York Region
26 Wellington St. East, 12th Fl., Toronto ON M5E 1S2
Tel: 416-777-2001; *Fax:* 416-777-0962; *TTY:* 866-620-2993
www.unitedwaytyr.com
www.linkedin.com/company/unitedwaytyr
www.facebook.com/unitedwaytyr
twitter.com/unitedwaytyr
instagram.com/unitedwaytyr
Previous Name: United Way Toronto; Red Feather United Appeal; United Way of Greater Toronto
Overview: A medium-sized local organization founded in 1956 overseen by United Way of Canada - Centraide Canada
Mission: To meet urgent human needs & improve social conditions by mobilizing the community's volunteer & financial resources in a common cause of caring
Finances: *Annual Operating Budget:* Greater than $5 Million; *Funding Sources:* Corporate & individual donations
Staff Member(s): 148; 2000 volunteer(s)
Membership: 126
Activities: Annual fundraising campaign on behalf of 200 agencies; Dragon Boat Race, Aug.; CN Tower Climb, Oct.; Scotiabank Rat Race, June; *Internships:* Yes; *Speaker Service:* Yes; *Library:* by appointment Not open to public
Chief Officer(s):
Vince Timpano, Chair
Daniele Zanotti, President & CEO
Awards:
• Spirit Awards

Given each year in the following categories: Spirit of Community; Student Campaign; Campaign Team; Joint Labour & Management Campaign; Leadership Campaign; Agency Campaign; & Employee Campaign.
• Thanks a Million Awards
• Bhayana Family Foundation Awards

United Way Toronto; Red Feather United Appeal; United Way of Greater Toronto *See* United Way Toronto & York Region

United Way/Centraide (Central NB) Inc.
#1A, 385 Wilsey Rd., Fredericton NB E3B 5N6
Tel: 506-459-7773; *Fax:* 506-451-1104
office@unitedwaycentral.com
www.unitedwaycentral.com
www.facebook.com/148382218531358
twitter.com/JessieUnitedWay
Previous Name: United Way/Centraide Fredericton Inc.
Overview: A small local charitable organization founded in 1960 overseen by United Way of Canada - Centraide Canada
Mission: To be a leader in helping to create & sustain a caring & healthy community
Finances: *Funding Sources:* Corporate; general public
Staff Member(s): 4
Activities: Fundraising; Community Need Survey; Allocation of Funds
Chief Officer(s):
Blair McLaughlin, President
Jeff Richardson, Executive Director
jeff@unitedwaycentral.com

United Way/Centraide Fredericton Inc. *See* United Way/Centraide (Central NB) Inc.

United Way/Centraide of the Moncton Region *See* United Way of Greater Moncton & Southeastern New Brunswick

United Way/Centraide Ottawa (UW/CO)
363 Coventry Rd., Ottawa ON K1K 2C5
Tel: 613-228-6700; *Fax:* 613-228-6730
info@unitedwayottawa.ca
www.unitedwayottawa.ca
www.linkedin.com/company/united-way-centraide-ottawa
www.facebook.com/unitedwayottawa
twitter.com/UnitedWayOttawa
www.youtube.com/user/unitedwayottawa
Previous Name: United Appeal of Ottawa-Carleton
Overview: A small local charitable organization founded in 1933 overseen by United Way of Canada - Centraide Canada
Mission: To bring people & resources together to build a strong, healthy, safe community for all; to build & support a network of high priority, results-oriented community services; to offer leadership in bringing the community together; to excel in fundraising; to invest resources & charitable funds in partnership with the community; to inform & engage community stakeholders
Finances: *Funding Sources:* Donations
Activities: *Speaker Service:* Yes
Chief Officer(s):
Michael Allen, President/CEO

United Way/Centraide Sudbury & District
#E6, 105 Elm St., Sudbury ON P3C 1T3
Tel: 705-560-3330
www.unitedwaysudbury.com
www.facebook.com/UWSudNip
twitter.com/UWSudNip
Overview: A small local charitable organization founded in 1982 overseen by United Way of Canada - Centraide Canada
Mission: To increase the organized capacity of people to care for one another through effective fundraising & allocation of these funds
Finances: *Funding Sources:* Donations
Staff Member(s): 15
Activities: *Speaker Service:* Yes
Chief Officer(s):
Michael Cullen, Executive Director
edirector@unitedwaysudbury.com

United World Colleges
Lester B. Pearson College of the Pacific, 650 Pearson College Dr., Victoria BC V9C 4H7
Tel: 250-391-2411
alumni@pearsoncollege.ca
www.pearsoncollege.ca
www.linkedin.com/groups?gid=49277&home=
www.facebook.com/PearsonUWC
twitter.com/PCUWC
www.youtube.com/user/PearsonUWC
Also Known As: Pearson College
Overview: A medium-sized international charitable organization founded in 1974
Mission: To encourage young people to become responsible citizens, politically & environmentally aware, committed to the ideals of peace, justice, understanding & cooperation, & to the implementation of these ideals through action & personal example
Member of: United World Colleges International
Finances: *Funding Sources:* Governments; corporations; foundations; individuals
Staff Member(s): 72
Membership: 200; *Fees:* All students attend on full scholarship; *Member Profile:* Students from over 100 countries are brought together after being competitively selected by committees in their own countries; they generally have completed the equivalent of 11 years of North American schooling & are between the ages of 16 & 18; *Committees:* Student selection committees are established in each province/territory & in 136 countries
Activities: *Internships:* Yes; *Speaker Service:* Yes; *Library:* by appointment Not open to public
Chief Officer(s):
David B. Hawley, Director

United Wushu Association of Ontario *See* WushuOntario

Unity & District Chamber of Commerce
PO Box 834, Unity SK S0K 4L0
Tel: 306-228-2688; *Fax:* 306-228-4229
www.townofunity.com
Overview: A small local organization
Mission: To support local businesses
Chief Officer(s):
Helena Long, President
Kristine Moon, Treasurer

Unity for Autism
PO Box 38066, 550 Eglinton Ave. West, Toronto ON M5N 3A8
Tel: 416-414-7726
info@unityforautism.ca
www.unityforautism.ca
www.facebook.com/324290850957490
Overview: A medium-sized national charitable organization
Mission: To provide support for individuals with autism & related disorders, as well as their families; To promote research on childhood autism
Finances: *Funding Sources:* Donations
Activities: Raising money for centers that provide programs & services for people with autism
Chief Officer(s):
Kathy Carsley, Founding Director
kathy@unityforautism.ca

Universal Negro Improvement Association of Montreal (UNIA)
2741, rue Notre-Dame, Montréal QC H3J 1N9
Tel: 514-846-0049
Overview: A small local organization

Universal Youth Foundation
#301, 2800 Hwy. 7, Concord ON L4K 1W8
Tel: 905-326-9732; *Fax:* 905-695-0801
info@universalyouthfoundation.org
www.universalyouthfoundation.org
Overview: A small international organization founded in 2005
Mission: To provide educational assistance to children & youth in need throughout the world by funding schools & teachers, with the goal of creating & inspiring a new generation of leaders
Chief Officer(s):
Mario Cortellucci, Founder & Chairman

Universités Canada *See* Universities Canada

Universities Art Association of Canada (UAAC) / Association d'art des universités du Canada (AAUC)
189 Mill Ridge Rd., Arnprior ON K7S 3G8
Tel: 613-622-5570; *Fax:* 613-622-0671
uaac@gozoom.ca
www.uaac-aauc.com
www.facebook.com/UAACAAUC
Overview: A small national organization founded in 1974
Mission: To provide a national voice for its membership
Member of: Humanities & Social Sciences Federation of Canada
Affiliation(s): Comité International d'histoire de l'art
Finances: *Annual Operating Budget:* Less than $50,000; *Funding Sources:* National government
Staff Member(s): 1
Membership: 50 institutional + 400 individual; *Fees:* $225 institutional; $55 student; $115 full; $80 unaffliate; *Member Profile:* Art historians & artists who teach in Canadian universities & colleges, independent scholars & other art professionals
Chief Officer(s):
Anne Whitelaw, President
anne.whitelaw@concordia.ca
Meetings/Conferences:
• 2018 Universities Art Association of Canada Conference, October, 2018, University of Waterloo, Waterloo, ON
Scope: National

Universities Canada (AUCC) / Universités Canada
#1710, 350 Albert St., Ottawa ON K1R 1B1
Tel: 613-563-1236; *Fax:* 613-563-9745
info@univcan.ca
www.univcan.ca
twitter.com/univcan
www.pinterest.com/univcan; www.youtube.com/user/auccweb
Previous Name: Association of Universities & Colleges of Canada
Overview: A large national charitable organization founded in 1911
Mission: To act as the voice of Canadian universities; To present a unified voice for higher education, research, & innovation
Finances: *Annual Operating Budget:* Greater than $5 Million; *Funding Sources:* Membership dues; Contract administration; Publication sales
Staff Member(s): 80
Membership: 97 universities; *Member Profile:* Canadian universities
Activities: Advocating for Canadian universities at the federal level; Providing a forum for university leaders to address challenges in higher education; Offering university information & scholarships for students; Foster networking & collaboration between member universities; *Library:* Information Centre; Not open to public
Chief Officer(s):
Paul Davidson, President/CEO, 613-563-1236 Ext. 232
president@univcan.ca
Helen Murphy, Assistant Director, Communications, 613-563-1236 Ext. 238
hmurphy@univcan.ca
Heather Cayouette, Manager, Higher Education Scholarships, 613-563-1236 Ext. 266
hcayouette@univcan.ca
Awards:
• L'Oreal Canada Scholarship for Women in Science
Eligibility: Female Canadian citizens or permanent residents who are starting or currently enrolled in research at the post-doctoral level, under the supervision of an academic supervisor; *Amount:* 2 at $20,000
• Multiple Sclerosis Society of Canada Scholarship Programs
Eligibility: Canadian citizens living & attending high school in the Greater Toronto Area who have at least an 85% average over the last 3 terms of available marks; students must be planning to enroll in full-time studies at a Canadian, American, or foreign university, specifically in science, technology, engineering, or math; *Amount:* 4 at $25,000
• Veterans Bursary Program
Eligibility: Veteran or veteran's spouse, child, grandchild, niece of nephew; applicant must be studying at the post-secondary level on a full- or part-time basis; *Amount:* $1,300 available per student
• Queen Elizabeth II Silver Jubilee Endowment Fund for Study in a Second Official Language
Eligibility: Canadian residents enrolled in the second or third year of their first bachelor program; candidates must have sufficient ability in their second official language to pursue their studies in that language; *Amount:* Up to 3 at $7,000
• C.D. Howe Scholarship
Eligibility: Residents of Thunder Bay or the former federal constituency of Port Arthur who have an 80% average in their last three terms of studies; applicants must be Canadian citizens or permanent residents of Canada; *Amount:* 2 at $5,500
• Conocophillips Canada Centennial
Eligibility: Canadian citizens or permanent residents of Canada who have a minimum average of 70% in the last academic year of studies & who have been nominated by an eligible institution from Alberta, BC, or Saskatchewan; applicants must be pursuing

oil & gas related studies or environmental/sustainable development studies; *Amount:* 4 at up to $5,000
• Vale Manitoba Operations Scholarship
Eligibility: Residents of Manitoba who are living in a community that is North of the 52nd parallel; applicants must be entering the first year or already enrolled in a bachelor degree or diploma program on a full-time basis & be available to accept a summer internship at Vale Manitoba Operations; *Amount:* 3 at $5,000 (Bachelor degree program) or $2,500 (diploma program)
• Fessenden-Trott Scholarship
Eligibility: Students who have completed the first year of their first bachelor degree program; *Amount:* 4 at $9,000
• Nexen Oil Sands Scholarship
Eligibility: Canadian citizens or permanent residents graduating from one of the following high schools: Bill Woodward School, Father Patrick Mercredi High School, Fort McMurray Composite High School, Frank Spragins High School, Holy Trinity High School; Westwood Community High School; applicants must be or have been a resident of one of the following communities: Anzac, Gregoire Lake Estates, Fort McMurray First Nation 468, Chard, Janvier, or Conklin; *Amount:* $2,500 (degrees, diplomas, or certificates); $750 (apprenticeships)
• Bayer CropScience Scholarship for Future Leaders in Agriculture
Eligibility: Canadian citizens or permanent residents who are entering the first year or currently enrolled full-time in an eligible agricultural bachelor degree program; eligible institutions are University of Alberta, University of Guelph, University of Saskatchewan, University of Lethbridge, University of Manitoba; *Amount:* 5 at $5,000
• Nordstrom Scholarship
Eligibility: Grade 11 students who live & attend high school in either Ontario or Alberta & have at least a 75% average over the last 3 semesters of available marks; *Amount:* 10 at $10,000 for a 4-year bachelor program
• Mattinson Scholarship Program for Students with Disabilities
Eligibility: Canadian citizens or permanent residents who are nominated by their eligible insitution; eligible students must be diagnosed with a documented permanent disability; *Amount:* 4 at $2,000
• C.D. Howe Memorial Foundation Engineering Award
Eligibility: Two male & two female candidates, nominated by the dean of engineering at their eligible institution, who have completed the first year of an engineering program & are entering their second year; *Amount:* 2 at $7,500
• Frank Knox Memorial Fellowship at Harvard University
Eligibility: Canadian citizens or permanent residents of Canada who have completed a first degree or higher degree at a Canadian university which is a member of Universities Canada; each applicant must also submit an application for admission directly to the Harvard graduate or professional school of her/his choice & be accepted into the program; *Amount:* Full tuition & mandatory health insurance fees for a 10-month academic year; 3 scholarships offered
• TD Scholarships for Community Leadership
Eligibility: Grade 12 students who demonstrate outstanding community leadership, possess the academic skills to successfully enter & complete college or university, & plan to attend post-secondary education in Canada; applicants must be Canadian citizens or permanent residents; *Amount:* 20 at $10,000 for tuition + $7,500 for living stipend, plus guaranteed summer employment
• Horatio Alger Canada Scholarship Program
Eligibility: Canadian citizens in their final year or high school with plans to attend a post-secondary institution following graduation, have a minumum grade percentage of 65, & demonstrate critical financial need; *Amount:* 80 at $5,000 + 5 at $10,000

University College of Cape Breton Faculty Association of University Teachers *See* Cape Breton University Faculty Association

University Counselling & Placement Association *See* Canadian University & College Counselling Association

University of Alberta Library & Information Studies Alumni Association (LISAA)
c/o School of Library and Information Studies, #3, 20 Rutherford South, Edmonton AB T6G 2J4
Tel: 780-492-4578; *Fax:* 780-492-2430
www.ualberta.ca
www.linkedin.com/grp/home?gid=4850476
www.facebook.com/UofA.LISAA
twitter.com/UAlbertaLISAA
Overview: A small provincial organization

University of Alberta Non-Academic Staff Association *See* Non-Academic Staff Association for the University of Alberta

University of Alberta South East Asian Students' Association (SEASA)
#SUB 040T, Basement, University of Alberta, Edmonton AB T6G 2R3
seasa@ualberta.ca
www.ualberta.ca/~seasa
Previous Name: Federation of Asian Students (FAS)
Overview: A small local organization founded in 1996
Mission: To unite & support southeast Asian students who attend the University of Alberta; To assist members to adapt in a Canadian environment
Finances: *Funding Sources:* Fundraising; Sponsorships
Membership: *Member Profile:* Full-time, part-time, & alumni Southeast Asian students of the University of Alberta; Individuals interested in the services of the association
Activities: Offering cultural, educational, recreational, & social activities; Promoting cultural awareness amongst students & the Edmonton community; Providing study buddies
Publications:
• South East Asian Students' Association Newsletter
Type: Newsletter; *Frequency:* Monthly
Profile: Association information for members each month from September to April

University of Alberta Students' Union
Students' Union Building, University of Alberta, #2-900, 8900 - 114 St. NW, Edmonton AB T6G 2J7
Tel: 780-492-4241; *Fax:* 780-492-4643
www.su.ualberta.ca
www.facebook.com/UAlbertaSU;
www.facebook.com/uasuevents
twitter.com/ualbertaSU
www.youtube.com/ualbertaSU
Overview: A medium-sized local organization
Chief Officer(s):
Nigel Brachi, Senior Manager, Marketing & Communications
marketing@su.ualberta.ca

University of British Columbia Faculty Association (UBCFA) / Association des professeurs de l'Université de la Colombie-Britannique
University of British Columbia, #112, 1924 West Mall, Vancouver BC V6T 1Z2
Tel: 604-822-3883; *Fax:* 604-222-0174
faculty.association@ubc.ca
www.facultyassoc.ubc.ca
Overview: A medium-sized local organization founded in 1920
Mission: To provide information and support in workplace issues; To advocate on behalf of it members on a wide variety of issues; To provide workshops and seminars.
Staff Member(s): 7
Membership: 3,200; *Member Profile:* Faculty members;
Committees: Bargaining Prepation; Librarians & Archivists; Member Services & Grievance; Okanagan Faculty; Sessional Faculty; Status of Women
Chief Officer(s):
Deena Rubuliak, Executive Director, 604-822-3301
deena.rubuliak@ubc.ca

University of British Columbia Symphony Orchestra
c/o School of Music, University of British Columbia, 6361 Memorial Rd., Vancouver BC V6T 1Z2
Tel: 604-822-3113; *Fax:* 604-822-4884
www.som.sites.olt.ubc.ca/student-ensembles/symphony-orchestra
www.facebook.com/UBCSO
twitter.com/ubcso
Also Known As: UBC Symphony Orchestra
Overview: A small local organization overseen by Orchestras Canada
Mission: To perform symphonic works from the 18th, 19th and 20th centuries
Membership: 90; *Member Profile:* University of British Columbia students
Activities: Performing concerts; Holding regular rehearsals
Chief Officer(s):
Jonathan Girard, Director

University of Calgary Faculty Association / Association des professeurs de l'Université de Calgary
Math Sciences, University of Calgary, #220, 2500 University Dr. NW, Calgary AB T2N 1N4

Tel: 403-220-5722; *Fax:* 403-284-1976
faculty.association@tucfa.com
www.tucfa.com
Overview: A medium-sized local organization
Mission: To promote and protect Faculty Interests; To represent the Faculty in the councils of the University; To provide information to members and to negotiate the Collective Agreement with the Board of Governors.
Member of: Canadian Association of University Teachers (CAUT); Confederation of Alberta Faculty Associations (CAFA)
Staff Member(s): 7
Membership: *Member Profile:* CAUT is a defender of academic freedom and works actively in the public interest to improve the quality and accessibility of post-secondary education in Canada; CAFA promotes the quality of education in the province and the well-being of Alberta universities and their academic staff.;
Committees: Election; Executive; Personnel; Joint Liaison
Chief Officer(s):
Sheila Miller, Executive Director
sheila.miller@tucfa.com

University of Guelph Food Service Employees Association (UGFSEA)
Drew Hall, University of Guelph, Guelph ON N1G 2W1
Tel: 519-824-4120; *Fax:* 519-837-9302
Previous Name: Hospitality Food Service Employees Association
Overview: A small local organization

University of Guelph Professional Staff Association / Association du personnel professionelle de l'Université de Guelph
University Centre, University of Guelph, #158, 50 Stone Rd. East, Guelph ON N1G 2W1
Tel: 519-824-4120
psa@uoguelph.ca
psa.uoguelph.ca
Previous Name: University of Guelphy Staff Association
Overview: A medium-sized local organization
Mission: To promote the interests of its members
Membership: *Fees:* $10.00/month; *Member Profile:* To promote career enhancement and development programs to members; To partecipate in the review and negotiation of salary and benefit improvements
Chief Officer(s):
Kent Percival, Chair, 519-824-4120 Ext. 56397
percival@uoguelph.ca

University of Guelphy Staff Association *See* University of Guelph Professional Staff Association

University of Lethbridge Faculty Association (ULFA) / Association des professeurs de l'Université de Lethbridge
#D620, 4401 University Dr., Lethbridge AB T1K 3M4
Tel: 403-329-2578; *Fax:* 403-329-2113
www.ulfa.ca
Overview: A small local organization founded in 1967
Mission: To ensure academic freedom of membership; To bargain collectively on behalf of membership
Member of: Canadian Association of University Teachers; Confederation of Alberta Faculty Associations
Finances: *Funding Sources:* Membership dues
Membership: 100-499; *Fees:* Mill rate multiplied by actual salary; *Committees:* Economic Benefits; Academic Welfare; Executive; Grievance
Chief Officer(s):
Brenda Rennie, Executive Director, 403-329-2328, Fax: 403-329-2113
rennie@uleth.ca
John Usher, President, 403-329-2759, Fax: 403-329-2038
john.usher@uleth.ca
Trevor Harrison, Vice-President, 403-329-2552, Fax: 403-329-2085
trevor.harrison@uleth.ca
Jon Doan, Secretary-Treasurer, 403-332-5208, Fax: 403-380-1839
jon.doan@uleth.ca
Awards:
• ULFA Academic Scholarship

University of Manitoba Faculty Association (UMFA) / Association des professeurs de l'Université du Manitoba
#100, 29 Dysart Rd., Winnipeg MB R3T 2M7

Tel: 204-474-8272; Fax: 204-474-7548
faum@umfa.ca
www.umfa.ca
Overview: A medium-sized local organization founded in 1965
Mission: To promote the well-being of the university community; to defend academic freedom; To promote the collective & individual interests of members
Member of: National Union of CAUT (NUCAUT), Manitoba Labour Federation (MFL)
Affiliation(s): Canadian Association of University Teachers (CAUT), Manitoba Organization of Faculty Associations (MOFA), National Union of CAUT (NUCAUT); Manitoba Labour Federation (MFL); Winnipeg Labour Council (WLC)
Finances: *Funding Sources:* Membership fees
Staff Member(s): 5
Membership: *Member Profile:* CLC advocates for human and civil rights, academic freedom and freedom of speech.The MFL is an important ally in lobbying the provincial government and in advocating for legislative amendments.; *Committees:* Collective Agreement; Status of Women; Board of Representatives; Reserve Fund; UMFA Staff Benefits; Workplace Health & Safety
Activities: Collective bargaining, Employee-employer relations, Higher Education Issues
Chief Officer(s):
Linda Guse, Executive Director
lguse@umfa.ca

University of Prince Edward Island Faculty Association (UPEIFA) / Association des professeurs de l'Université de l'Ile-du-Prince-Edouard
University of Prince Edward Island, Main Bldg., #315, 550 University Ave., Charlottetown PE C1A 4P3
Tel: 902-566-0438; Fax: 902-566-6043
upeifa@upeifa.org
www.upeifa.org
Overview: A small local organization founded in 1969
Mission: To encourage academic discussion among members; to provide full support for all activities; to maintain & improve quality & stature of members; to provide for student-faculty discussion on matters of mutual concern
Member of: Canadian Association of University Teachers
Finances: *Annual Operating Budget:* Less than $50,000
Membership: 230 individual; *Fees:* Schedule available; *Member Profile:* Full-time faculty of University of Prince Edward Island; part-time teaching faculty; *Committees:* Executive; Awards & Scholarships; Hessian Merit Award; Merit Award; Communications; Equity; Social; Research & Advocacy; Nominating; Health & Safety Steering; University Joint Benefits Advisory; Joint Benefits Management; UPEI Questions
Chief Officer(s):
Betty Jeffery, President

University of Québec in Hull Faculty Union *Voir* Syndicat des professeures et professeurs de l'Université du Québec en Outaouais

University of Regina Faculty Association (URFA) / Association des professeurs de l'Université de Regina
University of Regina, #122, Campion College, Regina SK S4S 0A2
Tel: 306-585-4378; Fax: 306-585-5208
urfa@uregina.ca
www.urfa.uregina.ca
Overview: A small local organization founded in 1977
Affiliation(s): Canadian Association of University Teachers (CAUT)
Finances: *Funding Sources:* Union dues
Membership: 500-999
Activities: *Library:*
Chief Officer(s):
Gary Tompkins, Chair
Chair.URFA@uregina.ca
Richard Buettner, Chair, Grievance
Grievance.URFA@uregina.ca
Mairin Barnabé, Officer, Member Services
Mairin.Barnabe@uregina.ca
Debbie Sagel, Professional Officer
Debbie.Sagel@uregina.ca

University of Saskatchewan Arts Council (USAC)
#488, Williams Bldg., Centre for Continuing & Distance Education, University of Saskatchewan, Saskatoon SK S7N 5C8
Tel: 306-966-5530
community.arts@usask.ca
ccde.usask.ca/uscad/usac
www.facebook.com/CCDEUniversityofSaskatchewan

Also Known As: U of S Arts Council
Overview: A small local charitable organization founded in 1993
Mission: To promote lifelong learning in the arts & culture
Member of: Organization of Saskatchewan Arts Councils
Finances: *Annual Operating Budget:* Less than $50,000; *Funding Sources:* Membership fees; special events; programs; grants
Staff Member(s): 2; 20 volunteer(s)
Membership: 250; *Fees:* $25 individual; $30 family; $15 student; *Member Profile:* Art students
Chief Officer(s):
Val Miles, Program Manager

University of Saskatchewan Faculty Association (USFA) / Association des professeurs de l'Université de la Saskatchewan
Education Bldg., University of Saskatchewan, #20, 28 Campus Dr., Saskatoon SK S7N 0X1
Tel: 306-966-5609; Fax: 306-966-8807
usfa@usaskfaculty.ca
www.usaskfaculty.ca
Overview: A medium-sized provincial organization founded in 1952
Mission: To attain highest standards of excellence through teaching, scholarship, & research; To encourage climate of freedom, responsibility & mutual respect
Affiliation(s): Saskatchewan Association of University Teachers; Saskatchewan Federation of Labour
Finances: *Funding Sources:* Membership dues
Staff Member(s): 4
Membership: 1,100; *Fees:* Mil rate of 8.5%; *Member Profile:* Full time faculty members; *Committees:* Negotiating; Executive; Committee on Committees; Trustees of the Contingency Trust Fund; Trustees of the VGLI Trust Fund; Communications; Constitutuin; External Relations; Financial Appeal; Grievance; Member Development; Planning & Assessment; University Administrative Practice; Status of Visible Minorities; Women's Issues; Charitable Donations; Collective Negotiating; Joint Benefits; Management of the Agreemen; Joint Grievance; Pension; Occupational Health
Chief Officer(s):
Tammy Stieb, Administrative Secretary
Tammy.Stieb@usask.ca
Doug Chivers, Chair
Publications:
• University of Saskatchewan Faculty Association Faculty Guide
Type: Guide
Profile: A guide to help answer questions of USFA members
• USFA [University of Saskatchewan Faculty Association] E-Letter
Type: Newsletter
Profile: Association news & issues

University of Sherbrooke Support Staff Union *Voir* Syndicat des employées de soutien de l'Université de Sherbrooke

University of the Fraser Valley Faculty & Staff Association (UFV FSA)
33844 King Rd., Abbotsford BC V2S 7M8
Tel: 604-854-4530; Fax: 604-853-9540
FSA.Info@ufv.ca
www.ufv-fsa.ca
Overview: A small local organization founded in 1977
Mission: To act as the official collective bargaining agent for the University of the Fraser Valley; To promote & protect the welfare of its membership
Staff Member(s): 2
Membership: 500-999; *Committees:* Finance; Contract; Communications; Labour & Management; Agreements; Job Classification Audit; Joint Professional Development; Occupational Health & Safety; Constitution Review; Status of Women; Human Rights & International Solidarity; Social
Chief Officer(s):
Sean Parkinson, President, 604-866-8918
sean.parkinson@ufv.ca
Tanja Rourke, Administrative Assistant, 604-854-4530 Ext. 4530
tanja.rourke@ufv.ca
Meetings/Conferences:
• University of the Fraser Valley Faculty & Staff Association 2018 Annual General Meeting, 2018, BC
Scope: Local
Contact Information: Administrator: Tanja Rourke, E-mail: tanja.rourke@ufv.ca, Phone: 604-854-4530, ext. 4530

University of the Philippines Alumni Association of Toronto (UPAA Toronto)
c/o Paulina Corpuz, 30 Minerva Ave., Toronto ON M1M 0C3

Tel: 647-477-8722
www.upaatoronto.org
Previous Name: U.P. Alumni Association in Metro Toronto
Overview: A small local organization founded in 1977
Mission: To facilitate communication among University of the Philippines alumni members in the Greater Toronto Area; To promote the interests of members; To offer programs that promote the personal & professional growth of members
Finances: *Funding Sources:* Membership fees; Charitable donations; Fundraising
Membership: *Fees:* $25 2 years; $50 5 years; *Member Profile:* Canadian residents who have earned at least 30 units of graduate education from the University of the Philippines; Residents of Canada who have earned a minimum of 60 units of post secondary education from the University of the Philippines; Canadian residents who are graduates of the University of the Philippines secondary school; Persons who are former faculty members or administrative staff of the University of the Philippines; Parents & spouses of regular members; Individuals who are members of other University of the Philippines alumni associations outside Ontario
Activities: Presenting educational activities; Hosting social & cultural events, such as reunions; Facilitating professional & business networking opportunities; Involving members in University of the Philippines activities; Posting jobs; Organizing discussion-forums on issues of interest to the Filipino & Canadian communities; Establishing a mentoring program for new immigrant alumni; Participating in social issues, such as protests against racism; Assisting disaster victims in the Philippines; Partnering with other organizations
Chief Officer(s):
Rose Tijam, President
Marlene Mogado, Vice-President
Rheea Liboro, Secretary
Alice Herrera, Treasurer
Marie Garingalao, Officer, Public Affairs & Communications
Awards:
• Most Outstanding UPAA Member Award
To honour exceptional alumni for remarkable achievements
• Most Outstanding UP Graduate Award
• University of the Philippines Alumni Association of Toronto Scholarship
Publications:
• University of the Philippines Alumni Association of Toronto Members' Directory
Type: Directory; *Price:* Free with membership in University of the Philippines Alumni Association of Toronto

University of Toronto Faculty Association (UTFA) / Association des professeurs de l'Université de Toronto
#419, 720 Spadina Ave., Toronto ON M5S 2T9
Tel: 416-978-3351; Fax: 416-978-7061
www.utfa.org
Overview: A medium-sized local organization founded in 1971
Mission: To promote the welfare of the current & retired faculty members & librarians of the University of Toronto, the University of St. Michael's College, the University of Trinity College, & Victoria University; To advance the interests of teachers, researchers & librarians in Canadian universities
Member of: Canadian Association of University Teachers
Affiliation(s): Ontario Confederation of University Faculty Associations
Staff Member(s): 7
Membership: 1,000-4,999; *Fees:* 0.75% of salary; $50/year retired members; *Member Profile:* University of Toronto academics & retired members; *Committees:* Salary, Benefit & Pensions; Grievance; Status of Women; Appointments; University & External Affairs; Teaching Stream; Librarians; Equity; Membership; Financial Advisory; Office Staff Relations; Nominating; Constitutional Review; Apportionment
Activities: *Library:* Not open to public
Chief Officer(s):
Scott Prudham, President, 416-978-4613
prudham@utfa.org
Cynthia Messenger, Vice-President, Grievances, 416-978-4640
cynthia.messenger@utoronto.ca

University of Toronto Institute for Aerospace Studies
Faculty of Applied Science & Engineering, 4925 Dufferin St., Toronto ON M3H 5T6
Tel: 416-667-7700; Fax: 416-667-7799
www.utias.utoronto.ca
Overview: A medium-sized national organization founded in 1949

Mission: UTIAS is a graduate studies & research institute, forming part of the faculty of Applied Science & Engineering at the University of Toronto
Affiliation(s): Canadian Aeronautics & Space Institute; Institute for Space & Terrestrial Science; Canadian Space Agency; Intelligent Sensing for Innovative Structures Canada
Staff Member(s): 55
Membership: 68
Activities: *Library:* University of Toronto Institute for Aerospace Studies Library
Chief Officer(s):
C.J. Damaren, Director, 416-667-7704, Fax: 416-667-7799
damaren@utias.utoronto.ca
P. Lavoie, Associate Director, Research, 416-667-7716, Fax: 476-667-7799
lavoie@utias.utoronto.ca
C.A. Steeves, Associate Director, Graduate Studies, 416-667-7710, Fax: 416-667-7799
csteeves@utias.utoronto.ca

University of Toronto Menorah Society *See* Hillel of Greater Toronto

University of Toronto Native Students Association (NSA)
First Nations House, Borden Building North, 563 Spadina Ave., 3rd Fl., Toronto ON M5S 2J7
Tel: 416-978-1042; *Fax:* 416-978-1893
nsa.exec@utoronto.ca
www.fnh.utoronto.ca
Overview: A small local organization
Mission: To create social & cultural networks of students through feasts, social gatherings, conferences and cultural events; to support events run through other students' organizations both in the university & in broader Canadian communities; to advocate on behalf of Indigenous issues in Canada.
Chief Officer(s):
Sarah Nanibush, Crane Clan Leader

University of Toronto Symphony Orchestra
Faculty of Music, University of Toronto, 80 Queen's Park Cres., Toronto ON M5S 2C5
Tel: 416-978-3750; *Fax:* 416-946-3353
performance.music@utoronto.ca
www.music.utoronto.ca
Overview: A small local organization overseen by Orchestras Canada
Finances: *Annual Operating Budget:* Less than $50,000
Membership: 1-99
Activities: *Library:* Not open to public
Chief Officer(s):
Uri Mayer, Conductor

University of Toronto, Faculty of Information Alumni Association (FIAA)
Claude T. Bissell Bldg., 140 St. George St., Toronto ON M5S 3G6
Tel: 416-978-3234; *Fax:* 416-978-5762
www.ischool.utoronto.ca
www.linkedin.com/groups/Faculty-Information-Alumni-Association-University-35853
www.facebook.com/iSchoolAlumniTO
twitter.com/iSchoolAlumniTO
Overview: A small local organization founded in 1929
Mission: To represent all the graduates of the Faculty of Information, University of Toronto
Affiliation(s): University of Toronto Alumni Association
Membership: 7,000; *Member Profile:* All are graduates of the Faculty of Information Sciences; *Committees:* Ask-an-Alum Mentoring; Bertha Bassam Lecture Event Planning; Grants & Awards; Job Shadowing; Social Events; Social Media & Website
Activities: *Internships:* Yes
Chief Officer(s):
Jeannie An, President
Awards:
• Student Conference/Research Grants
Eligibility: Masters students who have been invited to a conference to present a paper/poster session or participate as a speaker/panelist, or students who are conducting a clearly defined research project, supervised by a Faculty member; *Amount:* up to $500
• Professional Development Grant
Offered to support attendance at a conference or a professional development program; one grant awarded in the fall & one in the spring; *Amount:* 2 at $500

• Outstanding Alumni Award
Honours innovation or leadership in libraries, archives, museums or information management, professional organizations, research &/or the community at large *Deadline:* March
• Outstanding Student Contribution Award
Awarded to a Masters student who has made a significant contribution to Faculty life *Deadline:* April; *Amount:* $500

University of Victoria Faculty Association / Association des professeurs de l'Université de Victoria
#102 University House 2, University of Victoria, PO Box 3060, Stn. CSC, Victoria BC V8W 3R4
Tel: 250-721-7939; *Fax:* 250-721-8873
xdfa@uvic.ca
www.uvicfa.ca
www.linkedin.com/company/university-of-victoria-faculty-association
www.facebook.com/uvicfa
twitter.com/uvicfa
Also Known As: UVIC Faculty Association
Overview: A medium-sized local organization founded in 1979
Mission: To maintain & promote the professional & material status of members; To promote the welfare of the University of Victoria; To further the cause of higher education
Affiliation(s): Confederation of University Faculty Associations of BC; Canadian Association of University Teachers
Staff Member(s): 2
Membership: *Fees:* Schedule available; *Member Profile:* UVIC Faculty - full-time; librarians; *Committees:* Nominations & Elections; Equity; Constitution & Bylaws; Executive; Disability; Librarians; Senior Instructors; Advising & Dispute Resolution; Compensation & Benefits
Chief Officer(s):
Doug Baer, President
baer@uvic.ca
Jeff McKeil, Executive Director

University of Waterloo Staff Association (UWSA)
#3603, Davis Centre, 200 University Ave. West, Waterloo ON N2L 3G1
Tel: 519-888-4567
staffasc@uwaterloo.ca
www.adm.uwaterloo.ca/infostaf
www.linkedin.com/groups?gid=3741942
twitter.com/UWStaffAssoc
Overview: A small local organization
Chief Officer(s):
Carlos Mendes, President
Gail Spencer, Executive Manager
gspencer@uwaterloo.ca

University of Western Ontario Staff Association (UWOSA)
#255, University Community Centre, London ON N6A 3K7
Tel: 519-661-2111
mhay2@uwo.ca
www.uwosa.ca
Overview: A small local organization founded in 1967
Staff Member(s): 1; 40 volunteer(s)
Membership: 1,200; *Fees:* 1.25% gross earnings; *Member Profile:* Unionized administrative & technical staff
Chief Officer(s):
John Critchley, President
jcritchley@uwosa.ca
Karen Foullong, Vice-President
karen@uwosa.ca

University of Western Ontario Symphony Orchestra (UWOSO)
Faculty of Music, University of Western Ontario, Lambton Dr., London ON N6A 3K7
Tel: 519-661-2111
music@uwo.ca
www.music.uwo.ca
Overview: A small local organization founded in 1968 overseen by Orchestras Canada
Member of: Orchestras Canada
Finances: *Annual Operating Budget:* Less than $50,000
Staff Member(s): 2
Membership: 93
Activities: *Library:* UWO Music Library

University of Winnipeg Faculty Association (UWFA) / Association des professeurs de l'Université de Winnipeg
Sparling Hall, University of Winnipeg, #4M56, 515 Portage Ave., 3rd Fl., Winnipeg MB R3B 2E9
Tel: 204-786-9430; *Fax:* 204-774-3068
uwfa@uwinnipeg.ca
www.uwfa.ca
Overview: A small local organization founded in 1981
Member of: Canadian Association of University Teachers
Membership: 100-499; *Fees:* Mill rate; *Member Profile:* Continuing, tenured & probationary academic staff, librarians & academic staff on contract
Chief Officer(s):
Lisa McGifford, B.A., LLB, Executive Director
l.mcgifford@uwinnipeg.ca
Marissa Dudych, B.A., Administrative Assistant
ma.dudych@uwinnipeg.ca

University Settlement (USRC)
23 Grange Rd., Toronto ON M5T 1C3
Tel: 416-598-3444
universitysettlement.ca
ca.linkedin.com/in/university-settlement-8b815963
www.facebook.com/101047346739823
Overview: A small local organization founded in 1910 overseen by Ontario Council of Agencies Serving Immigrants
Mission: To help individuals & families obtain housing, employment, & wellness, with a focus on assisting newcomers to adapt to Canada
Affiliation(s): Toronto Association of Neighbourhood Services
Finances: *Annual Operating Budget:* $3 Million-$5 Million; *Funding Sources:* Government; United Way; Foundations
Staff Member(s): 150; 300 volunteer(s)
Activities: Operating four locations in Toronto; Offering social services
Chief Officer(s):
Patricia Jacobs, Executive Director, 416-598-3444 Ext. 222
patricia.jacobs@universitysettlement.ca
Publications:
• University Settlement Annual Report
Type: Report

University Singers *See* Richard Eaton Singers

Unparty: The Consensus-Building Party
5675 - 47 Ave., Delta BC V4K 1R5
Tel: 778-896-3571; *Fax:* 604-637-2189
www.unparty.ca
Also Known As: Unparty
Previous Name: People's Senate Party
Overview: A small provincial organization founded in 2011
Mission: To promote consensus government over adversarial party politics
Chief Officer(s):
Michael Donovan, Party Leader
mikedonovan2011@gmail.com

U.P. Alumni Association in Metro Toronto *See* University of the Philippines Alumni Association of Toronto

Upper Canada District Canadian Horse Breeders (UCD)
PO Box 179, Hillsburgh ON N0B 1Z0
Tel: 519-855-6498
info@ucdcanadianhorse.ca
www.ucdcanadianhorse.ca
Overview: A small provincial organization founded in 1988
Mission: To preserve & promote the Canadian horse, Canada's National Horse
Membership: *Fees:* $50 adult; $25 junior/supportive (non-voting) member; *Member Profile:* Owners & breeders of the Canadian horse from Ontario, & beyond the provincial borders
Activities: Addressing the concerns of members; Providing educational activities, such as clinics on topics such as show preparation & dressage; Educating the public about the heritage of the Canadian horse; Distributing information about the Canadian horse at events, such as The Royal Winter Fair; Hosting an annual general meeting early each year; Arranging The UCD Futurity & Show, a major Canadian horse show in Ontario in the fall; Organizing UCD Fun Days to enjoy the recreational aspects of the Canadian horse
Publications:
• Upper Canada District Canadian Horse Breeders Newsletter
Type: Newsletter; *Frequency:* Bimonthly
Profile: News from the board of directors, show results, member profiles, articles, & forthcoming events

Chief Officer(s):
Ron Marino, Director
marinoathome@hotmail.com

Upper Ottawa Valley Beekeepers' Association
c/o Murray Borer, RR#2, Renfrew ON K7H 2Z5
Tel: 613-432-3432
Overview: A small local organization
Mission: To serve members by disseminating information about beekeeping practices in the Upper Ottawa Valley; To promote the beekeeping industry locally
Membership: *Member Profile:* Apiarists in the Upper Ottawa Valley
Activities: Creating opportunities for member beekeepers to network
Chief Officer(s):
Murray Borer, President, 613-432-3432

Upper Ottawa Valley Chamber of Commerce
224 Pembroke St. West, Pembroke ON K8A 5N2
Tel: 613-732-1492
manager@uovchamber.com
www.upperottawavalleychamber.com
www.facebook.com/UOVCC
twitter.com/UOVCC
www.youtube.com/user/UOVCC
Previous Name: Pembroke & Area Chamber of Commerce
Overview: A small local organization founded in 1955
Mission: To promote commerce, the cooperation of tourist organizations, business & industry, consumers, government, agriculture & service groups; to give informed, responsible leadership in tourism, publicity, planning, education, civic action, beautification, special events & free enterprise
Member of: Canadian Chamber of Commerce; Ontario Chamber of Commerce; Ottawa Valley Tourist Association
Finances: *Funding Sources:* Membership dues; non-dues revenue
Membership: 308; *Fees:* Schedule available based on number of employees; *Committees:* Education; Communications/PR; Membership; Social Events; Awards Gala; Voice of Business; Policy & Procedures; Zoomer Entrepreneur Peer Group
Activities: Business improvement seminars; Business After Hours; annual golf tournament
Awards:
• Upper Ottawa Valley Chamber of Commerce Achievement Awards

Upper Thames River Conservation Authority
1424 Clarke Rd., London ON N5V 5B9
Tel: 519-451-2800; *Fax:* 519-451-1188
infoline@thamesriver.on.ca
www.thamesriver.on.ca
www.facebook.com/UpperThamesRiverConservationAuthority
twitter.com/UTRCAMarketing
www.youtube.com/user/UTRCA
Previous Name: Upper Thames River Conservation Foundation
Overview: A small local organization founded in 1947
Mission: To establish and undertake, in the area in which it has jurisdiction, a program designed to further the conservation, restoration, development and management of natural resources other than gas, oil, coal and minerals
Staff Member(s): 60; 6 volunteer(s)
Chief Officer(s):
Jane Boyce, Chair
Ian Wilcox, General Manager/Sec.-Treas.
wilcoxi@thamesriver.on.ca

Upper Thames River Conservation Foundation *See* Upper Thames River Conservation Authority

Urban Alliance on Race Relations (UARR)
#1001, 2 Carlton St., Toronto ON M5B 1J3
Tel: 416-703-6607; *Fax:* 416-703-4415
info@urbanalliance.ca
www.urbanalliance.ca
Overview: A medium-sized local charitable organization founded in 1975
Mission: To promote a stable & healthy multiracial environment in the community, by creating awareness of current issues, assisting institutions to develop solid policies & practices, & promoting full participation by the community to dismantle barriers to equal opportunity
Finances: *Annual Operating Budget:* Less than $50,000; *Funding Sources:* Donations; Municipal government; Foundations
Staff Member(s): 2; 50 volunteer(s)

Membership: 300; *Fees:* $10 general; $5 seniors, youth & unemployed; $500 corporate; $1000 life; *Committees:* Volunteer
Activities: Annual Employment Equity Forum & Career Fair; Anti-Racism Response Network; Seminars, workshops & conferences; Research studies; *Awareness Events:* Annual Golf Day; *Internships:* Yes; *Speaker Service:* Yes; *Library:* Open to public
Chief Officer(s):
Nigel Barriffe, President
Malika Mendez, Vice President
Ilaneet Goren, Secretary
Tam Goossen, Treasurer
Awards:
• Urban Alliance on Race Relations
Presented biennially
• President's Award
Presented biennially

Urban Development Institute Greater Edmonton Chapter
Birks Bldg., #324, 10113 - 104 St., Edmonton AB T5J 1A1
Tel: 780-428-6146; *Fax:* 780-425-9548
info@udiedmonton.com
www.udiedmonton.com
Overview: A small local organization founded in 1958
Chief Officer(s):
Rick Preston, Executive Director

Urban Development Institute of Canada (UDI) / Institut de développement urbain du Canada
200-602 West Hastings St., Vancouver BC V6B 1P2
Tel: 604-669-9585; *Fax:* 604-689-8691
www.udi.bc.ca
www.linkedin.com/company/urban-development-institute---pacific-region
www.facebook.com/UDIBC
twitter.com/udibc
www.youtube.com/UDIPacific; www.instagram.com/udibc
Overview: A large national organization
Mission: To promote wise, efficient & productive urban growth; To be an effective voice of the land development & property management industry at all levels of government; To serve as a forum for the exchange of knowledge, experience & research on land use planning & development
Finances: *Annual Operating Budget:* $500,000-$1.5 Million; *Funding Sources:* Membership dues
Staff Member(s): 10
Membership: 1,500 corporations; *Fees:* Schedule available
Activities: *Speaker Service:* Yes; *Library:* by appointment
Chief Officer(s):
Anne McMullin, President & CEO
amcmullin@udi.org
Jeff Fisher, Vice-President
jfisher@udi.org
Cheryl Ziola, Director, Communications
cziola@udi.org
Elsie Edillor, Manager, Finance
eedillor@udi.org

Capital Region
#101, 727 Fisgard St., Victoria BC V8W 1R8
Tel: 250-383-1072; *Fax:* 250-590-2039
udivictoria@udi.org
www.udicapitalregion.ca
Chief Officer(s):
Kathy Hogan, Executive Coordinator

Okanagan
#210, 1460 Pandosy St., Kelowna BC V1Y 1P3
Tel: 778-478-9649; *Fax:* 778-478-0393
udiokanagan@udi.org
www.udiokanagan.ca
Chief Officer(s):
Jennifer Dixon, Executive Coordinator

Urban Development Institute of Nova Scotia
#150, 1083 Queen St., Halifax NS B3H 1M2
Tel: 902-442-5017; *Fax:* 902-431-7220
udi@udins.ca
www.udins.ca
Also Known As: UDI of Nova Scotia
Overview: A medium-sized provincial organization
Mission: To represent the interests of the development industry & related professions
Membership: 50; *Fees:* $595 supplier & government; $895 associate; $1,195 builder; $1,495 developers; *Committees:* Technical; Membership; Finance; Public Relations/Communications

Chief Officer(s):
Ben Young, President

Urban Municipal Administrators' Association of Saskatchewan (UMAAS)
PO Box 730, Hudson Bay SK S0E 0Y0
Tel: 306-865-2261; *Fax:* 306-865-2800
umaas@sasktel.net
www.umaas.ca
Overview: A medium-sized provincial organization founded in 1974
Finances: *Annual Operating Budget:* Less than $50,000; *Funding Sources:* Membership; convention; donations
Membership: 350+; *Fees:* Schedule available; *Member Profile:* Local government administration certificate; employment in urban municipal government in Saskatchewan; *Committees:* Education; Discipline; Advisory; Administration; Convention
Chief Officer(s):
Richard Dolezsar, Executive Director
rdolezsar@sasktel.net

Urban Music Association of Canada (UMAC)
#210, 675 King St. West, Toronto ON M5V 1M9
Tel: 416-916-2874; *Fax:* 416-504-7343
umacgoturb@gmail.com
Overview: A small national organization founded in 1996
Mission: The Urban Music Association of Canada (UMAC) is the voice of Canada's urban entertainment scene. It is a member-driven, non-profit organization dedicated to building the domestic and international profile of Canadian urban music
Activities: Workshops, artist showcases, networking events
Chief Officer(s):
Will Strickland, President

Urban Native Indian Education Society *See* NEC Native Education College Society

Urology Nurses of Canada
c/o 62 Barrie St., Kingston ON K7L 3J7
membership@unc.org
www.unc.org
Overview: A small national organization
Mission: To promote the specialty of urologic nursing in Canada by promoting education, research & clinical practice.
Affiliation(s): Canadian Urological Association; Canadian Nurses' Association
Membership: *Fees:* $50 regular; $25 students; *Member Profile:* Nurses & other allied health care professionals; Corporations, foundations, & associations
Activities: Maintaining & promoting standards of care; Raising the profile of urologic nursing; Promoting communication among members
Chief Officer(s):
Gina Porter, President
president@unc.org
LuAnn Pickard, Secretary
secretary@unc.org
Nancy Carson, Treasurer
treasurer@unc.org
Awards:
• Editorial Award
$1,000 for written or co-editor of paper, article or editorial concerning urological nursing practice, education or research in one of the sub specialities of urodynamic, biofeedback, endourology, sexual health uro-oncology or incontinence; *Amount:* $1000
• Research Award
$1,000 towards research related to urological nursing practice or subspecialities of urodynamic, biofeedback, endourology, sexual health uro-oncology or incontinence; *Amount:* $1000
• Scholarship Award
$1,000 towards student enrolled in full or part time study related to the practice of nursing; *Amount:* $1000
Publications:
• Pipeline
Type: Newsletter; *Frequency:* Semiannually; *Editor:* Brenda Bonde

Calgary
Calgary AB

Edmonton
Chief Officer(s):
Elizabeth Smits, Contact
lizsmits@shaw.ca

Halifax
Halifax NS
Chief Officer(s):

Liette Connor, Contact
liette.connor@cdha.nshealth.ca
Kingston
Chief Officer(s):
Sylvia Robb, Contact
sylviamrobb@gmail.com
Montréal
Montréal QC
Chief Officer(s):
Raquel DeLeon, Contact
raquel.deleon@muhc.mcgill.ca
New Brunswick
Chief Officer(s):
Gina Porter, Contact
gina.porter@rogers.com
Newfoundland & Labrador
Chief Officer(s):
Sue Hammond, Contact
hammond_so@yahoo.ca
Ottawa
Chief Officer(s):
Susan Freed, Contact
freeds@teksavvy.com
Nancy Bauer, Secretary
Judy St. Germain, Treasurer
Toronto
Chief Officer(s):
Frances Stewart, Contact
bladderqueen@hotmail.com
Victoria
Chief Officer(s):
Jill Jeffery, Contact
jpjeffery@shaw.ca

USC Canada
#600, 56 Sparks St., Ottawa ON K1P 5B1
Tel: 613-234-6827; *Fax:* 613-234-6842
Toll-Free: 800-565-6872
info@usc-canada.org
www.usc-canada.org
www.facebook.com/78368904729
twitter.com/usccanada
www.youtube.com/user/USCCanada
Also Known As: Unitarian Service Committee of Canada
Overview: A medium-sized international charitable organization founded in 1945
Mission: Committed to enhancing human development through an international partnership of people linked in the challenge to reduce poverty
Member of: Canadian Council for International Cooperation
Finances: *Annual Operating Budget:* Greater than $5 Million; *Funding Sources:* Support from the general public; bequests; foundations & corporations; investment income; government
Staff Member(s): 22
Membership: 25; *Member Profile:* Individuals who support USC through volunteer or financial means; *Committees:* Finance; Executive; Programs
Activities: Communications/Media Program; Development Education Program to raise awareness about development issues & their impact on lives in Canada; Fundraising & Volunteer Programs; Overseas programs to work in partnership with people in the developing world to build self-reliant communities; *Speaker Service:* Yes; *Rents Mailing List:* Yes; *Library:* USC Canada Library; by appointment
Chief Officer(s):
Martin Settle, Co-Executive Director
Jane Rabinowicz, Co-Executive Director
Sheila Petzold, Director, Communications
Jeff de Jong, Director, International Programs
Faris Ahmed, Director, Policy & Campaigns
Brian McFarlane, Director, Fundraising

USC Canada
#600, 56 Sparks St., Ottawa ON K1P 5B1
Tel: 613-234-6827; *Fax:* 613-234-6842
Toll-Free: 800-565-6872
Other Communication: fundraising@usc-canada.org
info@usc-canada.org
usc-canada.org
www.facebook.com/usccanada
twitter.com/usccanada
www.instagram.com/usccanada
Overview: A large national charitable organization
Mission: USC Canada promotes vibrant family farms, strong rural communities, and healthy ecosystems around the world.

With engaged Canadians and partners in Africa, Asia, and Latin America, they support programs, training, and policies that strengthen biodiversity, food sovereignty, and the rights of those at the heart of resilient food systems - women, indigenous peoples, and small-scale farmers.
Staff Member(s): 26
Chief Officer(s):
Susan Walsh, Executive Director

Used Car Dealers Association of Ontario (UCDA)
230 Norseman St., Toronto ON M8X 6A2
Tel: 416-231-2600; *Fax:* 416-232-0775
Toll-Free: 800-268-2598
web@ucda.org
www.ucda.org
Overview: A medium-sized provincial organization founded in 1984
Mission: To enhance the image of the used car dealing industry through member education, consumer awareness of the benefits members provide & mediation of consumer-dealer disputes
Affiliation(s): International Auto Theft Investigators; National Independent Automobile Dealers Association
Finances: *Annual Operating Budget:* $1.5 Million-$3 Million; *Funding Sources:* Membership dues; Services
Staff Member(s): 19
Membership: 4,600+; *Fees:* $200; *Member Profile:* Registered motor vehicle dealers engaging in used vehicle sales in Ontario
Activities: *Speaker Service:* Yes
Chief Officer(s):
Steve Peck, President

Utility Contractors Association of Ontario, Inc. (UCA)
PO Box 762, Oakville ON L6K 0A9
Tel: 905-847-7305; *Fax:* 905-412-0339
bbrown@uca.on.ca
www.uca.on.ca
Overview: A medium-sized provincial organization founded in 1968
Mission: To negotiate & administer collective agreements with operating engineers & labourers in Ontario's utility sector
Membership: 10 contractor members + 34 associate (supplier) members; *Member Profile:* Contractors, engineers & labourers in Ontario's utility sector
Activities: Organizing networking events; Recognizing exellence in safety through the presentation of awards
Chief Officer(s):
Rene Beaudry, President
Barry Brown, Executive Director
bbrown@uca.on.ca
Glen Hansen, Treasurer
Meetings/Conferences:
• 2018 Utility Contractors Association of Ontario Convention, July, 2018, JW Marriott The Rosseau Muskoka Resort & Spa, Minett, ON
Scope: Provincial
Description: An event with guest speakers & networking activities for association members & their guests
Publications:
• The Conduit [a publication of the Utility Contractors Association of Ontario]
Type: Newsletter; *Frequency:* Semiannually
Profile: Association news, action dates, & industry information

Uxbridge & District Chamber of Commerce *See* Uxbridge Chamber of Commerce

Uxbridge Chamber of Commerce
PO Box 810, 2 Campbell Dr., Uxbridge ON L9P 0A3
Fax: 905-852-2632
info@uxcc.ca
www.uxcc.ca
www.linkedin.com/grp/home?gid=8288113
www.facebook.com/UxbridgeChamberofCommerce
Previous Name: Uxbridge & District Chamber of Commerce
Overview: A small local organization
Mission: Association exists to represent all businesses in Uxbridge Township
Membership: *Fees:* $175
Chief Officer(s):
Terry Barrett, President

Uxbridge Historical Centre
PO Box 1301, 7239 Conc. 6, Uxbridge ON L9P 1N5
Tel: 905-852-5854
museum@town.uxbridge.on.ca
www.uxbridgehistoricalcentre.com
www.facebook.com/uxbridgehistoricalcentre
twitter.com/UxbridgeMuseum
www.instagram.com/uxbridgehistoricalcentre
Previous Name: Uxbridge-Scott Museum & Archives
Overview: A small local organization founded in 1972
Mission: To collect, preserve & display artifacts, photographs, documents & buildings which record & illustrate the community & daily life of early & successive generations of residents of the Uxbridge-Scott area; To maintain, display & interpret this collection in a museum comprised of local historic buildings or replicas; To promote understanding of the local heritage & encourage research of local history & families, through educational programs, research, outreach & special events
Affiliation(s): Ontario Museum Assocation
Finances: *Annual Operating Budget:* $50,000-$100,000
Staff Member(s): 2; 20 volunteer(s)
Membership: *Fees:* $15 individual; $25 family; $125 patron; $250 sponsor; $500 partner
Activities: Steam Threshing & Heritage Days; *Library:* Archives; Open to public

Uxbridge-Scott Museum & Archives *See* Uxbridge Historical Centre

Vaccination Risk Awareness Network Inc. (VRAN)
PO Box 169, Winlaw BC V0G 2J0
info@vaccinechoicecanada.com
www.vran.org
www.facebook.com/330700720307290
twitter.com/vran_canada
Overview: A small national organization
Mission: To provide information about the potential risks & side-effects of vaccines; To foster a multi-disciplinary approach to child & family health; To uphold the right of persons to exercise informed consent
Finances: *Funding Sources:* Donations
Membership: *Fees:* Donation
Publications:
• Vaccination Risk Awareness Network Newsletter
Type: Newsletter; *Frequency:* 3 pa; *Price:* Free with membership in the Vaccination Risk Awareness Network
Profile: Information about the educational & outreach work of the organization

Vaccine & Infectious Disease Organization (VIDO)
University of Saskatchewan, 120 Veterinary Rd., Saskatoon SK S7N 5E3
Tel: 306-966-7465; *Fax:* 306-966-7478
info@vido.org
www.vido.org
Previous Name: Veterinary Infectious Disease Organization
Overview: A medium-sized international organization founded in 1975
Mission: To serve the livestock & poultry industry by conducting animal health related research; communicating livestock management techniques & information; facilitating the transfer of technology for international commercial development; to be recognized as an international biotechnology leader in the development of innovative vaccines & vaccine delivery systems, & to be a preferred partner in the development & commercialization of products for use by the food animal industry; to retain leaders in product discovery & strive for excellence in establishing partnerships at all levels of industry (producers, governments, universities, bio- pharmaceutical companies & other research institutions in the biopharmaceutical industry)
Finances: *Funding Sources:* Livestock & poultry industries; charitable foundations; federal & provincial granting donations
Activities: 50,000 square foot research facility; a 160 acre research farm; specific pathogen-free isolation facilities, & state of the art virology, bacteriology, biochemistry & immunology laboratories
Chief Officer(s):
Andrew Potter, Director & CEO

Val-d'Or Native Friendship Centre *Voir* Centre d'amitié autochtone de Val-d'Or

Valemount & Area Chamber of Commerce (VACC)
PO Box 690, Valemount BC V0E 2Z0
Tel: 250-566-0061; *Fax:* 250-566-0061
info@valemountchamber.com
www.valemountchamber.com
www.facebook.com/152151818151811
Overview: A small local organization

Mission: To promote local businesses through educational activities
Member of: BC Chamber of Commerce
Finances: *Funding Sources:* Donations; membership dues
Membership: *Fees:* $85 business; $47 associate
Chief Officer(s):
Christine Latimer, Chair

Valhalla Wilderness Society (VWS)
PO Box 329, New Denver BC V0G 1S0
Tel: 250-358-2333; *Fax:* 250-358-2748
info@vws.org
www.vws.org
Overview: A small local charitable organization founded in 1975
Mission: To raise awareness of environmental issues such as wildlife conservation & the protection of forests
Finances: *Funding Sources:* Donations
Membership: *Fees:* $10
Activities: Participating in advocacy activities; Working with scientists & researchers, such as forest ecologists, wildlife biologists, botanists, & hydrologists; Providing information about environmental issues; Working with Aboriginal people on issues of environmental & social justice
Publications:
• Valhalla Wilderness Society Year-End Newsletter
Type: Newsletter; *Frequency:* Annually; *Price:* Free with membership in the Valhalla Wilderness Society
Profile: A report to members about the society's campaigns & activities

VALID Association (VALID)
4843 - 49th St., Vegreville AB T9C 1K7
Tel: 780-632-2418; *Fax:* 780-632-3882
www.valid-assoc.org
Previous Name: Vegreville Association for Living in Dignity; Vegreville Association for the Handicapped
Overview: A small local charitable organization
Mission: To provide excellence in programs founded upon individual strengths & needs; to be a person-centered organization that believes in every individual's ability to succeed
Member of: Alberta Council of Disability Services
Finances: *Funding Sources:* Fundraising
Staff Member(s): 2
Membership: *Member Profile:* 18 years of age & older
Activities: Residential services; community support; community access program; employment preparation & placement; recycling program; second chance store; family intervention services; *Library:* Not open to public
Chief Officer(s):
Jody Nicholson, Executive Director
jody@valid-assoc.org

Valley Chamber of Commerce / Chambre de commerce de la Vallée
#200, 131 Pleasant St., Grand Falls NB E3Z 1G6
Tel: 506-473-1905; *Fax:* 506-475-7779
gfcocgs@nbnet.nb.ca
www.chambrevallee.ca
Previous Name: Grand Falls, Saint-André & Drummond Chamber of Commerce; Grand Falls & Region Chamber of Commerce
Overview: A small local organization
Mission: To support local businesses
Finances: *Annual Operating Budget:* Less than $50,000
Staff Member(s): 1; 16 volunteer(s)
Membership: 113
Chief Officer(s):
Christine Levesque, General Manager

Valley Family Resource Centre Inc.
#1, 110 Richmond St., Woodstock NB E7M 2N9
Tel: 506-325-2299; *Fax:* 506-328-8896
woodstock@frc-crf.com
frc-crf.com/woodstock
Previous Name: Atlantic Alliance of Family Resource Centres
Overview: A small local organization
Chief Officer(s):
Anne-Marie Hayes, Director

Valley Native Friendship Centre Society *See* Hiiye'yu Lelum Society House of Friendship

Valleyview & District Chamber of Commerce
PO Box 1020, Valleyview AB T0H 3N0
Tel: 780-524-4535
info@valleyviewchamber.ca
www.valleyviewchamber.ca
Overview: A small local organization
Mission: To focus on meeting the needs & expectations of businesses, industries, local consumers, & travellers in the Valleyview area
Membership: 39; *Fees:* $120 non-profit; $145 for profit; *Member Profile:* Local businesses
Chief Officer(s):
Justin Jasper, President

Valoris for Children & Adults of Prescott-Russell / Valoris pour enfants et adultes de Prescott-Russell
PO Box 248, 173, Old Hwy 17, Plantagenet ON K0B 1L0
Tel: 613-673-5148
Toll-Free: 800-675-6168
info@valorispr.ca
www.valorispr.ca
Previous Name: Prescott & Russell Association for Community Living
Overview: A small local organization
Mission: To provide support for vulnerable & underprivileged members of the United Counties of Prescott-Russell community
Member of: Community Living Ontario
Activities: Offering scholarships to children & students; Funding summer camp activities; Purchasing therapeutic & remedial equipment for physically disabled individuals
Chief Officer(s):
Gilles Barrette, President

Valoris pour enfants et adultes de Prescott-Russell *See* Valoris for Children & Adults of Prescott-Russell

The Van Horne Institute for International Transportation & Regulatory Affairs
#420, 715 - 5th Ave. SW, Calgary AB T2P 2X6
Tel: 587-430-0291
info@vanhorneinstitute.com
www.vanhorne.info
www.facebook.com/VanHorneInstitute
twitter.com/Van_Horne
Overview: A small international organization founded in 1991
Mission: To contribute to public policy development & education in the areas of transportation & regulated industries
Affiliation(s): University of Calgary; University of Alberta; Southern Alberta Institute of Technology
Finances: *Annual Operating Budget:* Less than $50,000; *Funding Sources:* Private sector
Staff Member(s): 4
Membership: 60; *Member Profile:* Government; industry; education; *Committees:* Centre for Transportation; Centre for Regulatory Affairs; Centre for Innovation & Communication
Activities: Transporation research & education; programs to assist in improving the efficiency & equity of transportation & regulated industries; *Speaker Service:* Yes; *Rents Mailing List:* Yes; *Library:* The Van Horne Institute Library; Open to public
Chief Officer(s):
Alex Phillips, President & CEO, 403-220-3967
pcwallis@ucalgary.ca
Bryndis Whitson, Director, Stakeholder Relations, 403-220-2114
bwhitson@ucalgary.ca
Publications:
• Van Horne Institute Annual Report
Type: Report; *Frequency:* a.; *Number of Pages:* 30; *Price:* Free download
Profile: Highlights, statistics & information relevant to individuals associated with the Van Horne Institute

Vancity Community Foundation
810 - 815 West Hastings St., Vancouver BC V6C 1B4
Tel: 604-877-7647; *Fax:* 604-709-6909
vcf@vancity.com
www.vancitycommunityfoundation.ca
twitter.com/vancitycommfdn
www.youtube.com/vancitycu
Overview: A small local charitable organization founded in 1989
Mission: To strengthen community well-being; To drive community change
Activities: Developing & supporting initiatives that advance social justice, financial inclusion, & environmental sustainability; Organizing & promoting learning events; Offering resources
Chief Officer(s):
Derek Gent, Executive Director
derek_gent@vancity.com
Nancy Melo, Manager, Administration
nancy_melo@vancity.com
Michelle Eggli, Manager, Communication & Engagement
michelle_eggli@vancity.com

Vancouver & District Labour Council (VDLC)
Maritime Labour Centre, #20, 1880 Triumph St., Vancouver BC V5L 1K3
Tel: 604-254-0703; *Fax:* 604-254-0701
office@vdlc.ca
www.vdlc.ca
www.facebook.com/vancouver.labourcouncil
Overview: A large local organization founded in 1889 overseen by British Columbia Federation of Labour
Mission: To act as the voice of the labour movement in Vancouver & the surrounding district
Affiliation(s): Canadian Labour Congress (CLC)
Membership: 65,000 workers; *Member Profile:* 118 affiliated local unions in the Greater Vancouver area
Activities: Promoting the interests of local affiliates; Assisting unions on strike; Organizing political action; Working for social justice
Chief Officer(s):
Joey Hartman, President
president@vdlc.ca

Vancouver & Lower Mainland Multicultural Family Support Services Society
#306, 4980 Kingsway, Burnaby BC V5H 4K7
Tel: 604-436-1025; *Fax:* 604-436-3267
againstviolence@vlmfss.ca
www.vlmfss.ca
Overview: A small local charitable organization founded in 1991
Mission: To prevent family violence; To offer assistance to immigrant & visible minority women & their families who are experiencing family violence
Finances: *Funding Sources:* Donations
Activities: Providing free & confidential counselling & support services; Offering educational programs & cultural sensitization presentations & workshops; Publishing anti-violence material; Providing referrals; Staging emergency interventions
Chief Officer(s):
Anna Foschi, Coordinator, Volunteers
Publications:
• Let's Talk: Families Across Cultures
Type: Manual
• Through the Eyes of a Child
Type: Manual
Profile: Manual for school personnel

Vancouver Aboriginal Friendship Centre Society (VAFCS)
1607 East Hastings St., Vancouver BC V5L 1S7
Tel: 604-251-4844; *Fax:* 604-251-1986
info@vafcs.org
www.vafcs.org
www.facebook.com/354262331330400
Overview: A small local charitable organization founded in 1963
Mission: To assist Aboriginal people making a transition to the urban community by providing social, cultural & recreational programs & services
Staff Member(s): 25; 6 volunteer(s)
Membership: 100-499; *Fees:* $1
Activities: *Internships:* Yes
Chief Officer(s):
John Webster, Chair

Vancouver Art Gallery Association (VAG)
750 Hornby St., Vancouver BC V6Z 2H7
Tel: 604-662-4700; *Fax:* 604-682-1086
customerservice@vanartgallery.bc.ca
www.vanartgallery.bc.ca
www.facebook.com/VancouverArtGallery
twitter.com/VanArtGallery
Overview: A small local organization founded in 1931
Mission: A place for people to meet to experience inspiration, meaning & pleasure through visual art
Affiliation(s): Canadian Museum Association; British Columbia Museums Association; American Federation of Arts
Finances: *Annual Operating Budget:* Greater than $5 Million; *Funding Sources:* Private; corporate; grants; foundations; government
Staff Member(s): 100; 300 volunteer(s)
Membership: 10,000; *Fees:* $35 student; $60 individual; $90 household; $40 senior; $60 senior couple
Activities: Exhibitions, children's programs, school tours & workshops; *Library:* Open to public
Chief Officer(s):
Bruce Wright, Chair, Board of Trustees
Kathleen Bartels, Director

The Vancouver Art Therapy Institute
1575 Johnston St., Vancouver BC V6H 3R9
Tel: 604-681-8284; *Fax:* 604-331-8262
info@vati.bc.ca
www.vati.bc.ca
Overview: A small local charitable organization founded in 1982
Mission: To train art therapists at the graduate level; To provide art therapy as a service; To educate the public about the efficiency of art therapy
Member of: Canadian Art Therapy Association; BC Art Therapy Association
Finances: *Annual Operating Budget:* $100,000-$250,000
Staff Member(s): 10
Membership: 1-99
Activities: Master of Counselling with Art Therapy Program; Advanced Diploma Program; *Internships:* Yes; *Library:* Not open to public
Chief Officer(s):
Tatjana Jansen, Executive Director

Vancouver Association for the Survivors of Torture (VAST)
2618 East Hastings St., Vancouver BC V5K 1Z6
Tel: 604-299-3539; *Fax:* 604-299-3523
Toll-Free: 866-393-3133
office@vast-vancouver.ca
www.vast-vancouver.ca
Overview: A small local charitable organization founded in 1986
Mission: To encourage & promote the well-being of people who have survived torture &/or political violence
Member of: Affiliation of Multicultural Societies & Service Agencies of BC; Canadian Council for Refugees; Vancouver Refugee Council; BC Human Rights Coalition; International Rehabilitation Council for Torture Victims
Affiliation(s): Vancouver Multicultural Society
Finances: *Annual Operating Budget:* $100,000-$250,000; *Funding Sources:* Membership fees; provincial & municipal government; United Nations; private donations
Staff Member(s): 7; 20 volunteer(s)
Membership: 1-99
Activities: *Awareness Events:* International Day in Support of Victims of Torture, June 26; *Internships:* Yes; *Speaker Service:* Yes; *Library:* by appointment
Chief Officer(s):
Christine Thomas, Executive Director

Vancouver Association of Law Libraries (VALL)
PO Box 48663, Stn. Bentall Centre, Vancouver BC V7X 1A3
www.vall.vancouver.bc.ca
twitter.com/VALLBC
Overview: A small local organization founded in 1988
Mission: To serve as a platform for information exchange & continuing education
Membership: *Fees:* $47 regular; free for students; *Member Profile:* Individuals working in or associated with law libraries; *Committees:* Program
Chief Officer(s):
Sarah Richmond, President
srichmond@ahbl.ca

Vancouver Ballet Society
Scotiabank Dance Theatre, 677 Davie St., Level 6, Vancouver BC V6B 2G6
Tel: 604-681-1525; *Fax:* 604-681-7732
vbs@telus.net
vancouverballetsociety.ca
www.facebook.com/VancouverBalletSocietyvbs
Overview: A medium-sized local charitable organization founded in 1946
Mission: To promote further interest in the art of classical ballet & contemporary dance through education, encouragement & assistance
Member of: Canadian Magazine Publishers Association; Volunteer Vancouver; BC Association of Magazine Publishers
Finances: *Funding Sources:* BC Arts Council; Vancouver Foundation; Canada Council; individuals
Staff Member(s): 4
Membership: *Fees:* $20 dance student; $40 individual; $50-$99 contributing; $100-$249 sustaining; *Member Profile:* Dance enthusiasts
Activities: Master Dance Classes; Spring Dance Seminar; *Library*
Chief Officer(s):
Maureen Allen, President

The Vancouver Board of Trade; World Trade Centre Vancouver *See* The Greater Vancouver Board of Trade

Vancouver Botanical Gardens Association *See* VanDusen Botanical Garden Association

Vancouver Chinatown Business Improvement Area Society (VCBIA)
106 Keefer St., Vancouver BC V6A 1X4
Tel: 604-632-3808; *Fax:* 604-632-3809
VCBIA@vancouver-chinatown.com
www.vancouver-chinatown.com
www.facebook.com/129549240480971
twitter.com/#!/chinatownfest
Previous Name: Vancouver Chinatown Merchants Association
Overview: A small provincial organization founded in 2000
Mission: To acquire best benefits for the Chinese merchants & the whole community
Member of: Vancouver Chinatown BIA Society
Affiliation(s): Tourism Vancouver
Finances: *Annual Operating Budget:* $250,000-$500,000; *Funding Sources:* Membership fees; fundraising
Staff Member(s): 3; 50 volunteer(s)
Membership: 230; *Fees:* $100
Activities: Vancouver Chinatown Night Market; Chinese New Year Parade

Vancouver Chinatown Merchants Association *See* Vancouver Chinatown Business Improvement Area Society

Vancouver Community College Faculty Association (VCCFA) / Association des professeurs de Collège Communautaire de Vancouver
#401, 402 Pender St. West, Vancouver BC V6B 1T6
Tel: 604-688-6210; *Fax:* 604-688-6219
info@vccfa.ca
www.vccfa.ca
Overview: A small local organization
Membership: 500-999
Chief Officer(s):
Frank Cosco, President, 604-838-9428

Vancouver Community Network (VCN)
#280, 111 West Hastings St., Vancouver BC V6B 1H4
Tel: 778-724-0826; *Fax:* 855-299-0647
Other Communication: Complaints e-mail: abuse@vcn.bc.ca
help@vcn.bc.ca
www.vcn.bc.ca
www.facebook.com/vcn.community
twitter.com/VCN_Community
Overview: A small local organization founded in 1993
Mission: To operate & promote a free, publicly accessible, non-commercial community computer utility in the Lower Mainland of BC which provides a public space on the Internet
Member of: BC Community Network Association
Finances: *Funding Sources:* Membership fees; project funding
Staff Member(s): 2; 50 volunteer(s)
Membership: 9,750 registered users; 2,700 members
Activities: Web community index; modem lines; public access terminals; training; *Internships:* Yes
Publications:
• VCN [Vancouver Community Network] Newsletter
Type: Newsletter

Vancouver Consultants
PO Box 48232, Stn. Bentall Centre, Vancouver BC V7X 1A1
Tel: 604-562-1746; *Fax:* 604-583-7132
mailbox@vancouverconsultants.com
www.vancouverconsultants.com
Overview: A small local organization founded in 2000
Mission: To provide a virtual directory of consultants in Vancouver; to facilitate & enhance opportunities for independent consultants & the market
Membership: *Fees:* Free basic; $9.95-$299.95 basic plus-platinum
Chief Officer(s):
Ian Marshall, Partner/Associate, 604-512-1265
ian@vancouverconsultants.com
Dave Schulte, Partner

Vancouver Cultural Alliance *See* BC Alliance for Arts & Culture

Vancouver East Cultural Centre *See* The Cultch

Vancouver Electric Vehicle Association (VEVA)
PO Box 3456, 349 West Georgia St., Vancouver BC V6B 3Y4
info@veva.bc.ca
www.veva.bc.ca
www.linkedin.com/groups?home=&gid=4741516
www.facebook.com/vancouverelectricvehicleassociation
twitter.com/vevabc
www.youtube.com/user/VEVAEVTV/
Overview: A small local organization founded in 1987
Mission: To promote the development of clean alternative transportation with a focus on electric vehicles
Membership: *Fees:* $25; $10 students
Chief Officer(s):
Bruce Stout, President
pres@veva.dhs.org
Robert Shaw, Treasurer
treasurer@veva.dhs.org

Vancouver Elementary School Teachers' Association (VESTA)
2915 Commercial Dr., Vancouver BC V5N 4C8
Tel: 604-873-8378; *Fax:* 604-873-2652
www.bctf.ca/vesta
Overview: A small local organization
Chief Officer(s):
Glen Hansman, President
gerry@vesta.ca

Vancouver Executives Association
#400, 601 West Broadway, Vancouver BC V5Z 4C2
Tel: 604-684-0660; *Fax:* 604-205-5490
exec@vanex.com
www.vanex.com
www.facebook.com/VancouverExecutivesAssociation
Also Known As: VANEX
Overview: A small local organization founded in 1920
Mission: To promote business & share ideas with trusted business leaders in a non-competitive environment
Member of: International Executives Association
Staff Member(s): 1
Membership: 60+
Chief Officer(s):
Linda Enns, Executive Director

Vancouver Foundation
#200, 475 West Georgia St., Vancouver BC V6B 4M9
Tel: 604-688-2204; *Fax:* 604-688-4170
info@vancouverfoundation.bc.ca
www.vancouverfoundation.bc.ca
www.facebook.com/VancouverFdn
twitter.com/vancouverfdn
Overview: A small national charitable organization founded in 1943
Mission: To fund special programs or capital projects of non-profit organizations in British Columbia; concerned with the mental, physical, moral, educational, & cultural well-being of residents of British Columbia
Staff Member(s): 52
Membership: *Committees:* Development; Distribution; Executive; Finance & Audit; Governance & Human Resources; Invesment
Chief Officer(s):
Kevin McCort, President & CEO

Vancouver Francophone Cultural Centre *Voir* Le Centre culturel francophone de Vancouver

Vancouver Grain Exchange
#100, 1111 Hastings St. West, Vancouver BC V6E 2J3
Tel: 604-685-0141; *Fax:* 604-681-4364
vge@bcmarine.org
Overview: A small local organization
Chief Officer(s):
Andrew Knapman, Contact

Vancouver Holocaust Centre Society - A Museum for Education & Remembrance (VHEC)
#50, 950 West 41st Ave., Vancouver BC V5Z 2N7
Tel: 604-264-0499
info@vhec.org
www.vhec.org
www.facebook.com/140874547755
twitter.com/VHolocaustCntr
Also Known As: Vancouver Holocaust Education Centre
Overview: A small provincial charitable organization founded in 1983
Mission: To provide educational programs, commemorative services, lecture series, exhibits, archives (documents & artifacts), oral history program; To maintain an education centre containing an archives & teaching museum
Member of: Canadian Museum Association; Association of Holocaust Organizations

Canadian Associations / Vancouver Humane Society (VHS)

Finances: Annual Operating Budget: $250,000-$500,000; *Funding Sources:* Membership fees, donations, grants
Staff Member(s): 10
Activities: *Library:* Open to public
Chief Officer(s):
P. Levinson, President
Nina Krieger, Executive Director

Vancouver Humane Society (VHS)
#303, 8623 Granville St., Vancouver BC V6P 5A2
Tel: 604-266-9744; *Fax:* 604-266-1311
info@vancouverhumanesociety.bc.ca
www.vancouverhumanesociety.bc.ca
www.facebook.com/VancouverHumaneSociety
twitter.com/vanhumane
Overview: A small local organization founded in 1987
Mission: To promote public awareness of animal welfare problems; to ensure & promote the fair & proper treatment of animals; to accept & solicit funds for education about animal welfare; to disburse funds for care & veterinary treatment of animals in need
Finances: Annual Operating Budget: $100,000-$250,000
Staff Member(s): 3; 27 volunteer(s)
Membership: 23 individual
Chief Officer(s):
Liberty Mulkani, President
Debra Probert, Executive Director
debra@vancouverhumanesociety.bc.ca

Vancouver International Children's Festival
#301, 601 Cambie St., Vancouver BC V6B 2P1
Tel: 604-708-5655
Other Communication: www.flickr.com/photos/vankidsfest
info@childrensfestival.ca
www.childrensfestival.ca
www.facebook.com/KidsFest
twitter.com/VICF
www.youtube.com/user/VanKidsFest
Previous Name: Canadian Institute of the Arts for Young Audiences
Overview: A small national charitable organization founded in 1975
Mission: To provide performing arts programs to young people in a festival environment; to encourage critical thinking & a lifelong interest in learning, the arts & cultural development
Member of: Vancouver Cultural Alliance; Canadian Children's Festival Association
Finances: Annual Operating Budget: $500,000-$1.5 Million; *Funding Sources:* Corporate; government; private sector; earned revenue; consulting
Staff Member(s): 9; 1400 volunteer(s)
Chief Officer(s):
Nicole Yeasting, Chair
Katharine Carol, Artistic & Executive Director

Vancouver Island Advanced Technology Centre (VIATeC)
777 Fort St., Victoria BC V8W 1G9
Tel: 250-483-3214
info@viatec.ca
www.viatec.ca
www.linkedin.com/company/149983
www.facebook.com/VIATeC
twitter.com/VIATeC
www.flickr.com/photos/viatec
Overview: A small local organization founded in 1989
Mission: To promote & enhance the development of the advanced technology industry on Vancouver Island; To be the first place contacted by people who require information or assistance related to the development or application of advanced technology; To act as liaison with industry, government & educational organizations to ensure that Vancouver Island's potential for growth in the advanced technology industry is fully realized
Affiliation(s): Canadian Advanced Technology Association
Staff Member(s): 5
Membership: 400; *Fees:* $20 student; $100 individual; $370 + $5 per employee organization; $2,625 sustaining; *Member Profile:* Persons, companies, organizations & agencies within Vancouver Island's advanced technology community
Activities: Information or assistance related to the development or application of advanced technology
Chief Officer(s):
Dan Gunn, CEO
dgunn@viatec.ca

Rob Bennett, COO
rbennett@viatec.ca

Vancouver Island Community Forest Action Network (VIC FAN)
PO Box 75, Port Renfrew BC V0S 1K0
forestaction@gmail.com
forestaction.wikidot.com
Overview: A small local organization
Mission: To defend & protect land; To challenge clearcut logging & unethical development on Indigenous land
Finances: Annual Operating Budget: Less than $50,000
Membership: 100-499
Activities: Public education & civil disobedience against clearcutting & other industrial deforestation

Vancouver Island Construction Association (VICA)
1075 Alston St., Victoria BC V9A 3S6
Tel: 250-388-6471; *Fax:* 250-388-5183
Toll-Free: 877-847-6471
Other Communication: communications@vicabc.ca
info@vicabc.ca
www.vicabc.ca
www.linkedin.com/company/vancouver-island-construction-association
www.facebook.com/VIConstructionAssoc
twitter.com/VICA_BC
Overview: A small local organization founded in 1912
Mission: To serve & promote the business life of members & the construction industry; To be the recognized voice & authority of Victoria's construction industry
Affiliation(s): British Columbia Construction Association; Canadian Construction Association
Finances: Annual Operating Budget: $250,000-$500,000
Staff Member(s): 3
Membership: 275; *Fees:* $1,400-$2,400 per company based on volume of business; $650 professional services/associate/public owner; $55 student/apprentice; *Member Profile:* ICI sectors; *Committees:* Civil Contractors; General Contractor; Membership; Standard & Practices; Trade Contractor; Training & Education Program Advisory; Under 40; Women in Construction
Activities: AGM; Christmas Lunch; golf tournament; educational seminars
Chief Officer(s):
Rory Kulmala, CEO
rorykulmala@vicabc.ca
Rosie Manhas, Director, Operations
rosiemanhas@vicabc.ca
Sarah Bartfai, Coordinator, Member Services & Events
memberservices.victoria@vicabc.ca
Kelly Marion, Coordinator, Marketing & Communications
kelly@vicabc.ca
Chenelle Falconer, Coordinator, Training & Education
chenelle@vicabc.ca

Nanaimo Office
#5, 1850 Northfield Rd., Nanaimo BC V9S 3B3
Tel: 250-388-6471
Toll-Free: 877-847-6471

Vancouver Island Crisis Society
PO Box 1118, Nanaimo BC V9R 6E7
Tel: 250-753-2495; *Fax:* 250-753-2475
Toll-Free: 877-753-2495; *Crisis Hot-Line:* 888-494-3888
info@vicrisis.ca
www.vicrisis.ca
www.facebook.com/vicrisis.ca
Overview: A small local charitable organization founded in 1970
Member of: British Columbia Crisis Line Association
Affiliation(s): Canadian Association of Suicide Prevention; American Association of Suicidology
Finances: Funding Sources: Municipal government; Provincial government; Private donations
Staff Member(s): 20; 40 volunteer(s)
Membership: 55; *Fees:* $20 individuals; *Member Profile:* Board members; Community members; Volunteers; *Committees:* Training Development
Activities: *Awareness Events:* Crisis Line Awareness Week, last week of arch

Vancouver Island Danish-Canadian Club
Nanaimo BC
Tel: 250-390-2388
www.facebook.com/VIDanishClub
Overview: A small local organization founded in 1989
Mission: To promote Danish culture
Member of: Federation of Danish Associations in Canada

Finances: Annual Operating Budget: Less than $50,000; *Funding Sources:* Membership fees; party tickets
10 volunteer(s)
Membership: 180; *Fees:* $15; *Member Profile:* Danish by birth, descent or marriage
Activities: 3 annual parties; cultural meetings

Vancouver Island Miniature Horse Club (VIMHC)
c/o Catherine Royle, 2918 Glen Eagles Rd., Shawnigan Lake BC V0R 2W1
Tel: 250-743-2755; *Fax:* 250-743-2785
bcminiaturehorseclubs.wordpress.com
Overview: A small local organization
Finances: Funding Sources: Sponsorships; Membership fees
Membership: *Fees:* $5 youth members under age 18; $25 adult members; $30 families; *Member Profile:* Miniature horse owners & breeders on Vancouver Island
Activities: Organizing meetings & educational activities for members; Hosting & participating in shows for miniature horses; Presenting awards
Chief Officer(s):
Catherine Royle, Treasurer
Publications:
• Vancouver Island Miniature Horse Club Newsletter
Type: Newsletter
Profile: Club activities, announcements, & upcoming events for members

Vancouver Island Prostate Cancer Research Foundation
#107, 1027 Pandora Ave., Victoria BC V8V 3P6
Tel: 250-920-0772
vip@viprostate.org
Overview: A small local charitable organization
Mission: To support prostate cancer patients, by finding better methods of treatment & increasing the quality of life for prostate cancer sufferers
Affiliation(s): Canadian Prostate Cancer Network
Membership: *Member Profile:* Prostate cancer patients, survivors, spouses & others

Vancouver Island Public Interest Research Group (VIPIRG)
University of Victoria, SUB Room B122, PO Box 3035, Stn. CSC, Victoria BC V8W 3P3
Tel: 250-472-4386
info@vipirg.ca
www.vipirg.ca
www.facebook.com/VIPIRG
twitter.com/VIPIRG
Overview: A medium-sized local organization
Mission: Combines original research on emerging social & environmental issues with education, advocacy & action for positive change; research is directly relevant to community; projects developed in partnership & consultations with other groups; research internship program, training workshops, resource library & other programming
Member of: BC Environmental Network; Canadian Centre for Policy Alternatives
Staff Member(s): 3
Membership: *Fees:* $3 full-time students; $1.50 part-time students; $2 graduate students; $10 community member; *Member Profile:* All University of Victoria students are automatically members & community members
Activities: Research projects leading to lobbying, education, activism & advocacy on emerging social justice & environmental issues; research internship program; *Internships:* Yes; *Speaker Service:* Yes; *Library:* VIPIRG Alternative Resource Library; Open to public
Chief Officer(s):
Meghan Jezewski, Internal Coordinator

Vancouver Island Real Estate Board (VIREB)
6374 Metral Dr., Nanaimo BC V9T 2L8
Tel: 250-390-4212; *Fax:* 250-390-5014
info@vireb.com
www.vireb.com
www.linkedin.com/pub/vancouver-island-real-estate-board/4a/926/332
www.facebook.com/vancouverislandrealestateboard
twitter.com/vireb
Overview: A small local organization founded in 1966 overseen by British Columbia Real Estate Association
Mission: To provide cost-effective tools, services & information necessary to foster professionalism & maintain the realtor's position as the primary focus in the real estate industry
Member of: The Canadian Real Estate Association

Finances: Annual Operating Budget: $1.5 Million-$3 Million; *Funding Sources:* Members monthly assessment
Staff Member(s): 13; 50 volunteer(s)
Membership: 1,000+; *Member Profile:* Licensed as realtor
Activities: Speaker Service: Yes; *Library:* Not open to public
Chief Officer(s):
Janice Stromar, President, 250-758-7653
jan@janandtom.com
Bill Benoit, CAE, CRAE, Executive Officer, 250-390-4212
bbenoit@vireb.com
Awards:
• REALTORS Care Awards

Vancouver Island Rock & Alpine Garden Society (VIRAGS)
PO Box 33012, 1907 Sooke Rd., Colwood BC V9B 1V0
www.virags.ca
www.facebook.com/939938976066394
Overview: A small local organization
Mission: To promote the growing & distribution of plants
Membership: *Fees:* $20
Activities: Field trips; garden shows

Vancouver Island Society for Disabled Artists
#304, 1550 Church Ave., Victoria BC V8P 2H1
Tel: 250-472-2917
Overview: A small local organization founded in 1995
Mission: To support artists with disabilities by creating an art gallery in Victoria British Columbia so artists can showcase their art work
Membership: *Fees:* $20
Chief Officer(s):
Garry Curry, President
Alistair Green

Vancouver Island Symphony
PO Box 661, Nanaimo BC V9R 5L9
Tel: 250-754-0177; *Fax:* 250-754-0165
info@vancouverislandsymphony.com
www.vancouverislandsymphony.com
www.facebook.com/vanislesymphony
twitter.com/vanislesymphony
Overview: A small local charitable organization founded in 1995 overseen by Orchestras Canada
Mission: To promote & present orchestra music in the Central Vancouver Island Region
Member of: Orchestras Canada
Finances: Funding Sources: Box office revenue; Government grants; Individual & corporate sponsors
Staff Member(s): 5
Activities: Performing concert series; Facilitating community outreach concerts; Partnering with local community groups; *Speaker Service:* Yes
Chief Officer(s):
Margot Holmes, Executive Director
Pierre Simard, Artistic Director
pierresnotes@hotmail.com

Vancouver Island University Faculty Association (VIUFA)
Building 360, #108, 900 Fifth St., Nanaimo BC V9R 5S5
Tel: 250-740-6339; *Fax:* 250-753-9713
www.viufa.ca
Overview: A small local organization
Member of: Federation of Post-Secondary Educators of British Columbia (FPSE)
Membership: *Committees:* Contract Negotiating; Personnel Stewards; Professional & Scholarly Development; Status of Women; Status of Non-Regular Faculty; Human Rights & International Solidarity
Chief Officer(s):
Marni Stanley
Manjeet Uppal, Vice-President
Johnny Blakeborough, Secretary-Treasurer
Judy Benner, Office Manager

Vancouver Island Vegan Association (VIVA)
Victoria BC
Tel: 250-216-0562
www.vancouverislandvegan.com
www.facebook.com/vancouverislandveganassociation
twitter.com/VanIsleVegan
www.instagram.com/vancouverislandvegan
Overview: A small local organization founded in 1980
Mission: To promote awareness of veganism on Vancouver Island
Finances: Funding Sources: Donations
Activities: Providing resources about veganism; Offering support services & mentor programs; *Awareness Events:* Vegtoria

Vancouver Japanese Gardeners Association
4291 Slocan St., Vancouver BC V5R 1Z2
Tel: 604-439-0348; *Fax:* 604-439-0348
vancouvervjga@gmail.com
www.vanjapangardeners.com
Overview: A small local organization
Mission: To promote & plant Japanese gardens throughout Vancouver
Membership: 64
Activities: Offering garden tours & workshops; Organizing social events for members through various clubs, including the Bonsai, Shigin, Karaoke, Heiseikai, & Golf clubs

Vancouver Jewish Film Centre Society (JFAS)
6184 Ash St., Vancouver BC V5Z 3G9
Tel: 604-266-0245; *Fax:* 604-266-0244
film@vjff.org
www.vjff.org
Previous Name: Vancouver Jewish Film Festival Society
Overview: A small local charitable organization founded in 1986
Mission: To provide Jewish cultural & heritage programs, exhibits & performances for the Jewish community & general public; To provide information on artists & performing groups; To maintain records on locally owned Judaica
Finances: Funding Sources: Donations; Programs; Fundraising; Government grants
Activities: Organizing & presenting the annual Vancouver Jewish Film Festival; Providing cultural programs & film screenings; *Speaker Service:* Yes; *Rents Mailing List:* Yes
Chief Officer(s):
Robert Albanese, Executive Director

Vancouver Jewish Film Festival Society *See* Vancouver Jewish Film Centre Society

Vancouver Maritime Museum
1905 Ogden Ave., Vancouver BC V6J 1A3
Tel: 604-257-8300; *Fax:* 604-737-2621
info@vancouvermaritimemuseum.com
www.vancouvermaritimemuseum.com
www.facebook.com/vanmaritime
twitter.com/vanmaritime
www.youtube.com/channel/UChBhyY0K-sOpAr32kQz306w
Overview: A small local organization founded in 1959
Mission: Canada's principal maritime museum on the Pacific, located in the heart of Canada's greatest part, Vancouver, at the gateway to the Pacific
Member of: Council of American Maritime Museums; International Congress of Maritime Museums; Canadian Museums Association; British Columbia Museums Association; Historic Naval Ships Association
Finances: Funding Sources: Municipal & provincial governments; private
Staff Member(s): 32; 62 volunteer(s)
Membership: *Fees:* $60 family; $40 individual; $35 senior
Activities: Educational Programs; Conferences; Exhibits; *Internships:* Yes; *Speaker Service:* Yes; *Rents Mailing List:* Yes; Library
Chief Officer(s):
Ken Burton, Executive Director
director@vancouvermaritimemuseum.com

Vancouver Moving Theatre (VMT)
PO Box 88270, Stn. Chinatown, 418 Main St., Vancouver BC V6A 4A4
Tel: 604-628-5672
vancouvermovingtheatre@shaw.ca
www.vancouvermovingtheatre.com
www.facebook.com/189986727692739
twitter.com/VanMovTheatre
Overview: A small local charitable organization founded in 1983
Mission: To develop a new form of interdisciplinary art influenced by the Pacific Rim culture of Vancouver; To present services & products to affirm the importance of art in questions of healing, humanity & the soul
Member of: Vancouver Professional Theatre Alliance; Vancouver Dance Centre; Vancouver Cultural Alliance
Finances: Funding Sources: City of Vancouver; provincial government; foundations
Activities: Presenting performances; Organizing workshops, demonstrations, & lectures; Providing articles & miscellaneous cultural services; *Speaker Service:* Yes; *Library:* by appointment
Chief Officer(s):
Savannah Walling, Artistic Director
Terry Hunter, Executive Director

Vancouver Multicultural Society (VMS)
1254 - West 7th Ave., Vancouver BC V6H 1B6
Tel: 604-731-4648
vmsbc@telus.net
www.vmsbc.com
Previous Name: Vancouver Multicultural Society of British Columbia
Overview: A small local charitable organization founded in 1974
Mission: To raise awareness of & conduct public education in cross-cultural relations & multiculturalism with the object of preserving & fostering cultural heritages; To advocate on issues related to multiculturalism, human rights, race relations, & cross-cultural understanding
Membership: *Fees:* $25 Youth/Senior; $30 Individual; $75 Non-profit Organization; $100 Corporate; *Member Profile:* Applications must be reviewed by Membership Committee Chairperson & accepted/not accepted at regular Board of Directors meetings
Chief Officer(s):
John Halani, President, 604-687-6631
jhalani@telus.net

Vancouver Multicultural Society of British Columbia *See* Vancouver Multicultural Society

Vancouver Museum Commission *See* Vancouver Museum Society

Vancouver Museum Society
1100 Chestnut St., Vancouver BC V6J 3J9
Tel: 604-736-4431; *Fax:* 604-736-5417
guestservices@museumofvancouver.ca
www.museumofvancouver.ca
www.facebook.com/MuseumofVancouver
twitter.com/Museumofvan
www.youtube.com/user/MuseumofVancouver
Previous Name: Vancouver Museum Commission
Overview: A small local charitable organization founded in 1894
Mission: To interpret the natural & cultural history of Vancouver including all its cultural constituents
Finances: Annual Operating Budget: $1.5 Million-$3 Million; *Funding Sources:* Federal; provincial; municipal; fundraising
Staff Member(s): 30; 200 volunteer(s)
Membership: 500; *Fees:* Schedule available
Activities: Bus tours; school programs; adult programs; *Speaker Service:* Yes; *Library:* by appointment
Chief Officer(s):
Greg Fruno, Director, Operations

Vancouver Musicians' Association (VMA)
#100, 925 West 8th Ave., Vancouver BC V5Z 1E4
Tel: 604-737-1110; *Fax:* 604-734-3299
Toll-Free: 800-644-2899
office@vma145.ca
www.vma145.ca
Overview: A medium-sized local organization founded in 1901
Mission: To unite professional musicians; To defend the interests of members; To ensure fair treatment & wages for professional musicians
Member of: American Federation of Musicians of the United States & Canada
Affiliation(s): Vancouver District Labour Council
Staff Member(s): 3
Membership: 1,900+; *Fees:* $141.50; *Member Profile:* Professional musicians
Chief Officer(s):
David G. Brown, President
dbrown@vma145.ca

Vancouver Natural History Society *See* Nature Vancouver

Vancouver New Music (VNM)
837 Davie St., Vancouver BC V6Z 1B7
Tel: 604-633-0861
info@newmusic.org
www.newmusic.org
www.facebook.com/vannewmusic
twitter.com/vannewmusic
Also Known As: Vancouver New Music Society
Overview: A medium-sized local charitable organization founded in 1973
Mission: To foster connections in the community to bring new music to a wider audience; To commission & premiere new work by Canadian composers; To produce music-theatre & electroacoustic music; To explore the interaction of

contemporary music with other disciplines
Member of: Alliance for Arts & Culture
Affiliation(s): Canadian Music Centre
Finances: *Annual Operating Budget:* $250,000-$500,000; *Funding Sources:* Government grants; Individual & corporate sponsorships
Staff Member(s): 7; 31 volunteer(s)
Membership: 183; *Fees:* Free with donation to society; *Committees:* Marketing & Communications; Volunteering; Publicity
Activities: Performing an annual concert series; Producing a biennial music theatre production, Facilitating lectures & workshops with visiting artists; *Library:* Musical Score Archive; by appointment
Chief Officer(s):
Giorgio Magnanensi, Artistic Director
Publications:
• Oscillations [a publication of the Vancouver New Music Society]
Type: Newsletter; *Frequency:* Monthly; *Accepts Advertising*; *Price:* Free with online subscription
Profile: An information resource containing new music listings for Vancouver and the lower mainland

Vancouver Numismatic Society (VNS) / La société numismatique de Vancouver
PO Box 38040, 968 West King Edward Ave., Vancouver BC V5Z 4L9
contactvns@gmail.com
www.vancouvernumismaticsociety.ca
Overview: A small local organization founded in 1955
Mission: To promote the collection & study of coins, tokens, medals & paper money
Member of: Canadian Numismatic Association
Affiliation(s): British Columbia Numismatic Association; Pacific Northwest Numismatic Association
Finances: *Annual Operating Budget:* Less than $50,000; *Funding Sources:* Membership fees & revenue from annual collectors' fair
Membership: 1-99; *Fees:* $15 adult; $5 junior; $20 family; *Member Profile:* Currency collectors
Activities: Monthly meetings for currency collectors; annual show to display & sell old & modern examples of currency; *Library:* Open to public by appointment

Vancouver Opera (VOA) / Association de l'opéra de vancouver
1945 McLean Dr., Vancouver BC V5N 3J7
Tel: 604-682-2871; *Fax:* 604-682-3981
online@vancouveropera.ca
www.vancouveropera.ca
www.linkedin.com/company/vancouver-opera
www.facebook.com/vancouveropera
twitter.com/VancouverOpera
www.youtube.com/user/vancouveropera
Previous Name: Vancouver Opera Association
Overview: A large local charitable organization founded in 1958
Mission: To share the power of opera with all who are open to receiving it, through superior performances & meaningful education programs for all ages
Member of: Opera America; Opera.ca
Finances: *Annual Operating Budget:* Greater than $5 Million; *Funding Sources:* Earned revenue; Fundraising; Government grants; Individual & corporate donations
Staff Member(s): 55; 117 volunteer(s)
Membership: 6,500; *Fees:* Subscription; donation; *Member Profile:* Subscribers & donors; *Committees:* Development; Marketing; Education; Artistic Administration; Music; Production
Activities: Performing 4 fully staged opera productions; Organizing and performing VO Ensemble performances in schools & the community; *Internships:* Yes *Library:* Music Library
Chief Officer(s):
Kim Gaynor, General Director
kgaynor@vancouveropera.ca
Jonathan Darlington, Music Director

Vancouver Opera Association *See* Vancouver Opera

Vancouver Orchid Society
PO Box 42025, Stn. Marpole, Vancouver BC V6B 6S6
info@vancouverorchidsociety.ca
www.vancouverorchidsociety.ca
Overview: A small local organization founded in 1946
Mission: To promote & widen knowledge of orchids
Membership: *Fees:* $20 students; $30 regular
Chief Officer(s):
Margaret Prat, President

Vancouver Paleontological Society (VanPS)
#12 8171 Steveson Hwy., Richmond BC V7A 1M4
www.vcn.bc.ca/vanps
Overview: A small local organization
Mission: To promote public awareness of our fossil heritage; to promote safe & responsible fossil collecting; to provide educational information about ancient life through field trips, presentations & displays; to bring together amateurs & professionals who share a common interest in fossils
Member of: BC Paleontological Alliance
Finances: *Annual Operating Budget:* Less than $50,000
Membership: 62; *Fees:* $35; *Member Profile:* Amateur & professional paleontologists
Activities: Monthly lectures; field trips
Chief Officer(s):
Jim Haggart, Chair
Jim.Haggart@NRCan-RNCan.gc.ca

Vancouver Peretz Institute; Vancouver Peretz Shule *See* Peretz Centre for Secular Jewish Culture

Vancouver Philharmonic Orchestra (VPO)
PO Box 27503, Stn. Oakridge, Vancouver BC V5Z 4M4
Tel: 604-878-9989
vancouver.philharmonic@gmail.com
www.vanphil.ca
www.linkedin.com/grps/Vancouver-Philharmonic-Orchestra-6709643
www.facebook.com/vancouverphilharmonic
Overview: A small local charitable organization founded in 1964 overseen by Orchestras Canada
Mission: To provide non-professional musicians with an opportunity to perform orchestral music with a full symphony orchestra; To train aspiring professional conductors and musicians; To inspire and entertain the Vancouver community through performance
Member of: Orchestras Canada
Finances: *Annual Operating Budget:* Less than $50,000; *Funding Sources:* Ticket sales; Grants; Corporate & individual donations; Fundraising
Staff Member(s): 5; 20 volunteer(s)
Membership: 1-99; *Fees:* $150 adult; $75 student/senior; *Member Profile:* Amateur and professional musicians who practice regularly and have played with orchestras at a university-equivalent level or higher
Activities: Performing five concerts a year; Organizing tri-annual Concerto Competition for Emerging Artists; *Internships:* Yes
Chief Officer(s):
Jin Zhang, Music Director

Vancouver Pro Musica Society
PO Box 78077, Stn. Grandview, Vancouver BC V5N 5W1
Tel: 604-688-6407
www.vancouverpromusica.ca
www.facebook.com/VanProMusica
twitter.com/vanpromusica
Overview: A small local charitable organization founded in 1984
Mission: To promote musical life in British Columbia by holding concerts
Finances: *Annual Operating Budget:* Less than $50,000; *Funding Sources:* Donations
10 volunteer(s)
Membership: 40; *Member Profile:* Vancouver-based composers active in various aspects of new music
Activities: Sonic Boom Concert Series (spring); Further East/Further West Concert Series (fall)
Chief Officer(s):
Fleur Sweetman, Administrator

Vancouver Professional Theatre Alliance *See* Greater Vancouver Professional Theatre Alliance

Vancouver Rape Relief & Women's Shelter
PO Box 21562, 1424 Commercial Dr., Vancouver BC V5L 5G2
Tel: 604-872-8212; *TTY:* 604-877-0958; *Crisis Hot-Line:* 604-877-8212
info@rapereliefshelter.bc.ca
www.rapereliefshelter.bc.ca
Overview: A small local charitable organization founded in 1973
Mission: To stop violence against woman; to give women survivors emotional support after a sexual assault; to house battered women & their children
Member of: Canadian Association of Sexual Assault Centres; BC/Yukon Transition House Society
Finances: *Annual Operating Budget:* $250,000-$500,000; *Funding Sources:* Provincial government; fundraising

Activities: 24 hour rape crisis centre; shelter for battered women; peer counselling; advocacy & accompaniment; support group; *Awareness Events:* Take Back the Night, Dec. 6 Memorial; *Speaker Service:* Yes; *Library:* by appointment

Vancouver Recital Society (VRS)
#304, 873 Beatty St., Vancouver BC V6B 2M6
Tel: 604-602-0363; *Fax:* 604-602-0364
vrs@vanrecital.com
vanrecital.com
www.facebook.com/vancouverrecitalsociety
twitter.com/vanrecital
www.youtube.com/user/vanrecital
Overview: A small local organization founded in 1980
Staff Member(s): 5
Chief Officer(s):
Jean Hodgins, President
Niamh Small, Director, Communications & Marketing
niamhsmall@vanrecital.com

Vancouver Second Mile Society
509 East Hastings St., Vancouver BC V6A 1P9
Tel: 604-254-2194; *Fax:* 604-254-2150
info@vsms.ca
www.vsms.ca
Overview: A small local organization
Mission: To address the wellness, recreational, educational, & social needs of low-income seniors in Vancouver; To provide programs & services that will enable seniors to become active members of the community; To provide support for seniors so that they can deal effectively with their own needs as well as the needs of others; To help members achieve self-sufficiency & personal fulfillment
Activities: Offering education & peer support; Providing information & referral services; Networking & establishing partnerships with other seniors' organizations; Organizing weekly events
Chief Officer(s):
Steve Chan, Executive Director

Vancouver Soaring Association
PO Box 3251, Vancouver BC V6B 3X9
Tel: 604-869-7211
vancouversoaring@gmail.com
vancouversoaring.com
www.facebook.com/148597568530530
twitter.com/vancouversoaring
www.flickr.com/photos/128138428@N03
Overview: A small local organization
Member of: Soaring Association of Canada

Vancouver Society of Financial Analysts *See* CFA Society Vancouver

Vancouver Society of Immigrant & Visible Minority Women (VSIVMW)
#204, 2534 Cypress St., Vancouver BC V6J 1Z2
Tel: 604-731-9108
Overview: A small local organization
Mission: To assist immigrant & visible minority women; To advocate & facilitate their empowerment; To create an awareness of their rights & to help them access equal opportunities in Canadian society; To serve as a voice for the concerns & issues facing immigrant & visible minority women, at grassroots & professional levels; To provide education, services, referrals, research, & advocacy; To promote multiculturalism & harmony for all cultures
Finances: *Annual Operating Budget:* $50,000-$100,000
Membership: 1-99
Activities: Referral services; workshops & seminars; sponsors research projects in area of needs of immigrant women; *Library:* Open to public

Vancouver Status of Women (VSW)
2652 East Hastings St., Vancouver BC V5K 1Z6
Tel: 604-255-6554; *Fax:* 604-255-7508
womencentre@vsw.ca
www.vsw.ca
Overview: A small local organization founded in 1971
Mission: To ensure that women participate fully in the social, political & economic life of our communities; To work for women's full equality in these areas by addressing barriers of patriarchy, racism, poverty, male violence against women, heterosexism, ablism, classism, imperialism & anti-Jewish oppression; all of which profoundly impact the lives of women
Affiliation(s): National Action Committee on the Status of Women

Finances: *Annual Operating Budget:* $100,000-$250,000; *Funding Sources:* Regional government
Staff Member(s): 7; 50 volunteer(s)
Membership: 50 institutional + 30 student + 300 individual; *Fees:* $1-$50 based on sliding scale
Chief Officer(s):
Patricia E. Aguilar-Zeleny, Coordinator

Vancouver Symphony Society (VSO)
#500, 833 Seymour St., Vancouver BC V6B 0G4
Tel: 604-876-3434; Fax: 604-684-9264
customerservice@vancouversymphony.ca
www.vancouversymphony.ca
www.linkedin.com/company/vancouver-symphony-orchestra
www.facebook.com/VSOrchestra
twitter.com/VSOrchestra
www.youtube.com/user/VancouverSymphony
Overview: A small local charitable organization founded in 1919 overseen by Orchestras Canada
Mission: Provides stewardship for the Vancouver Symphony Orchestra to achieve recognition as one of Canada's highest quality symphony orchestras; to perform at all times with artistic distinction & thereby enrich BC's quality of life; to expand the enjoyment & appreciation of the finest orchestral music of the past & present
Member of: Orchestras Canada
Finances: *Annual Operating Budget:* Greater than $5 Million; *Funding Sources:* Ticket sales; Individual & corporate donations; Fundraising; Federal & provincial government grants; Endowment funds
Staff Member(s): 107; 70 volunteer(s)
Membership: 1,000-4,999
Activities: Performing concert series; Offering quality music education programs for music students and educators; *Library:* VSO Library; Not open to public
Chief Officer(s):
Alan Gove, Acting President & Chief Executive Officer
Bramwell Tovey, Music Director

Vancouver TheatreSports League (VTSL)
1515 Anderson St., Vancouver BC V6H 3R5
Tel: 604-738-7013; Fax: 604-738-8013
mailto.services@vtsl.com
www.vtsl.com
www.facebook.com/VanTheatreSports
twitter.com/VanTheatreSport
Overview: A small local organization founded in 1980
Mission: To challenge & inspire the community by growing & exploring exceptional improv-based work
Staff Member(s): 14
Chief Officer(s):
Jay Ono, Executive Director
director@vtsl.com

Vancouver Women's Health Collective
29 West Hastings St., Vancouver BC V6B 1G4
Tel: 604-736-5262
vwhc.centre@gmail.com
www.womenshealthcollective.ca
Overview: A small local charitable organization founded in 1972
Mission: Raises awareness for women's health issues; provides information on women's health
Finances: *Funding Sources:* Donations; Membership Fees; Grants; Fundraising; Gaming revenue
Staff Member(s): 2
Membership: *Fees:* $10-25 individual; $50 organization
Chief Officer(s):
Caryn Duncan, Executive Director

Vancouver Youth Symphony Orchestra Society (VYSO)
3214 - 10 Ave. West, Vancouver BC V6K 2L2
Tel: 604-737-0714
vyso2@telus.net
www.vyso.com
www.facebook.com/VYSOmusicians
twitter.com/vyso1
Previous Name: Junior Symphony Society
Overview: A small local charitable organization founded in 1930 overseen by Orchestras Canada
Mission: To provide orchestral training & experience to music students in Greater Vancouver & the Lower Mainland from beginner to advanced level career student; To contribute to the cultural landscape of the local and provincial community by offering education and support to school & community groups
Member of: Orchestras Canada; Alliance for Arts & Culture

Finances: *Annual Operating Budget:* $100,000-$250,000; *Funding Sources:* Government; Corporate & private donations; Tuition fee; Concert revenue; Fundraising
Staff Member(s): 3; 200 volunteer(s)
Membership: 240; *Fees:* $20
Activities: Performing public concerts; Training young musicians between the ages of 8 & 14; *Library*
Chief Officer(s):
Roger Cole, Artistic Director
Holly Littleford, Orchestra Manager
vyso@telus.net

Vancouver, Coast & Mountains Tourism Region
#270, 1651 Commercial Dr., Vancouver BC V5l 3Y3
Tel: 604-739-9011; Fax: 604-739-0153
Toll-Free: 800-667-3306
info@vcmbc.com
www.604pulse.com
www.facebook.com/vcmbc
twitter.com/vcmbc
Overview: A small local organization founded in 1972 overseen by Council of Tourism Associations of British Columbia
Mission: To create tourist experineces for travellers
Finances: *Annual Operating Budget:* $1.5 Million-$3 Million
Staff Member(s): 10; 25 volunteer(s)
Membership: 3500
Activities: *Internships:* Yes; *Speaker Service:* Yes
Chief Officer(s):
Kevan Ridgway, President & CEO, 604-638-6930, Fax: 604-739-0153
kevan@vcmbc.com
Doleen Dean, Visitor Services
doleen@vcmbc.com

Vanderhoof & District Chamber of Commerce See
Vanderhoof Chamber of Commerce

Vanderhoof Chamber of Commerce
PO Box 126, 2353 Burrard Ave., Vanderhoof BC V0J 3A0
Tel: 250-567-2124; Fax: 250-567-3316
Toll-Free: 800-752-4094
info@vanderhoofchamber.com
www.vanderhoofchamber.com
www.facebook.com/119783441393384
twitter.com/VisitVanderhoof
Previous Name: Vanderhoof & District Chamber of Commerce
Overview: A small local organization
Mission: To provide a strong voice for the future of business, industry & the professional community
Member of: Canadian Chamber of Commerce
Affiliation(s): BC Chamber of Commerce
Staff Member(s): 2
Membership: *Fees:* Schedule available; *Committees:* Agriculture; Beautification; Bylaws & Policy; Education; Finance; Forestry; Future Planning; Nominating; Real Estate; Retail; Special Events; Tourism; Trade Show
Activities: *Awareness Events:* Pumpkin Walk, Oct.; Parade of Lights, Dec.; *Rents Mailing List:* Yes; *Library:* Open to public
Chief Officer(s):
Joe Von Doellen, President
Spencer Siemens, Executive Director
manager@vanderhoofchamber.com

VanDusen Botanical Garden Association (VBGA)
5251 Oak St., Vancouver BC V6M 4H1
Tel: 604-257-8335
volunteer@vandusen.org
www.vandusengarden.org
www.facebook.com/vandusenbotanicalgarden
Previous Name: Vancouver Botanical Gardens Association
Overview: A small local charitable organization founded in 1965
Mission: To support & promote VanDusen Gardens as an outstanding botanical garden; To act as a source & focus of excellence in botanical/horticultural plant conservation & education; To enhance & perpetuate the Garden as a place of beauty, pleasure & inspiration for all
Affiliation(s): American Association of Botanical Gardens & Arboretums
Finances: *Annual Operating Budget:* $500,000-$1.5 Million; *Funding Sources:* Membership fees; private donations; special events
Staff Member(s): 18; 1200 volunteer(s)
Membership: 9,000; *Fees:* Schedule available
Activities: *Library:* VanDusen Library
Publications:
• The Bulletin [a publication of the VanDusen Botanical Garden Association]
Type: Newsletter; *Frequency:* Quarterly

Vanier Institute of The Family (VIF) / Institut Vanier de la famille
94 Centrepointe Dr., Ottawa ON K2G 6B1
Tel: 613-228-8500; Fax: 613-228-8007
info@vanierinstitute.ca
www.vanierinstitute.ca
www.facebook.com/vanierinstitute
twitter.com/vanierinstitute
Overview: A medium-sized national charitable organization founded in 1965
Mission: To create awareness of, & to provide leadership on the importance & strengths of families in Canada, & the challenges families face in all their diverse structures; information from the institute's research, consultation & policy development is conveyed through advocacy, education & communications vehicles to elected officials, policymakers, educators, the media, the public & Canadian families themselves
Finances: *Annual Operating Budget:* $500,000-$1.5 Million; *Funding Sources:* Foundation; project funding
Staff Member(s): 8
Membership: *Committees:* Finance & Investment; Nominations; Special Events; Human Resources
Activities: *Speaker Service:* Yes
Chief Officer(s):
Nora Spinks, Chief Executive Officer
CEO@vanierinstitute.ca
David Northcott, Chair

Vanscoy & District Agricultural Society
PO Box 35, Vanscoy SK S0L 3J0
Tel: 306-493-2388; Fax: 306-956-3136
vanscoyag@gmail.com
sites.google.com/a/saase.ca/vanscoy-district-agricultural-society
www.facebook.com/145413282193512
Overview: A small local organization founded in 1983
Mission: To improve agriculture & the quality of life in the community by educating members & the community; To provide a community forum for discussion of agricultural issues; to encourage the conservation of natural resources
Member of: Saskatchewan Association of Agricultural Societies & Exhibitions
Finances: *Funding Sources:* Saskatchewan lotteries; fundraising
100 volunteer(s)
Membership: 200; *Fees:* $1
Activities: Rodeo; Taste of RM; Perennial Exchange; fair
Chief Officer(s):
Shelley Sowter, Administrator
Quinten Odnokon, President

Variety - The Children's Charity (Ontario)
3701 Danforth Ave., Toronto ON M1N 2G2
Tel: 416-699-7167; Fax: 416-699-5752; TTY: 416-699-8147
info@varietyvillage.on.ca
www.varietyvillage.ca
Previous Name: Variety Club of Ontario, Tent 28
Overview: A medium-sized provincial organization founded in 1945
Mission: To improve the quality of life for children with disabilities & to promote their integration into society
Member of: Variety Clubs International
Affiliation(s): Variety Village; Variety Ability Systems Inc.
Finances: *Annual Operating Budget:* Greater than $5 Million; *Funding Sources:* Events; private & corporate donations
Staff Member(s): 120
Membership: 5,644
Activities: Gold Heart Day Campaign; Blue Jay Kids Day; Sunshine Games; Sports Festival; Blue Jays Luncheon; Lieutenant Governor's Games
Chief Officer(s):
Karen Stintz, President & CEO
kstintz@varietyvillage.on.ca

Variety - The Children's Charity of BC
4300 Still Creek Dr., Burnaby BC V5C 6C6
Tel: 604-320-0505
Toll-Free: 800-310-5437
info@variety.bc.ca
www.variety.bc.ca
www.facebook.com/variety.bc.ca
twitter.com/VarietyBC
www.youtube.com/user/VarietyBC
Also Known As: Variety Club

Overview: A medium-sized provincial charitable organization founded in 1965
Mission: To raise funds throughout the province of B.C. for the benefit of B.C.'s children with special needs; To provide funds for capital costs; To create new centres or improve existing facilities & purchase specialized equipment
Member of: Variety Clubs International
Finances: *Funding Sources:* Special events & annual telethon
Membership: *Fees:* $75
Activities: Sunshine Coaches; Electro Limb Program; Talking Computers Program; Child Development Centres; Variety's Parks for Special Children; Outings for Variety's Kids; Variety B.C. Lifeline; grants to other organizations dedicated to helping children with special needs; *Awareness Events:* Annual "Show of Hearts" Telethon; Market & Auction; Boat for Hope; *Speaker Service:* Yes
Chief Officer(s):
Kristy Gill, Executive Director
kristy.gill@variety.bc.ca

Variety - The Children's Charity of Manitoba, Tent 58 Inc.
#2, 1313 Border St., Winnipeg MB R3H 0X4
Tel: 204-982-1050; *Fax:* 204-475-3198
admin@varietymanitoba.com
www.varietymanitoba.com
www.facebook.com/varietymanitoba
twitter.com/Varietymanitoba
www.youtube.com/user/varietymanitoba
Overview: A medium-sized provincial charitable organization founded in 1979
Member of: Variety International - The Children's Charity
Finances: *Annual Operating Budget:* $500,000-$1.5 Million; *Funding Sources:* Corporate support; Special events; Individual donations
Staff Member(s): 6
Activities: *Awareness Events:* Gold Heart Day, February
Chief Officer(s):
Jerry Maslowsky, Chief Executive Officer
Awards:
• Gold Heart Humanitarian of the Year Award

Variety Club of Northern Alberta, Tent 63
#1205 Energy Square, 10109 - 106th St., Edmonton AB T5J 3L7
Tel: 780-448-9544; *Fax:* 780-448-9289
Overview: A small local organization
Mission: Raises funds for the children of Northern Alberta who have disabilities or are disadvantaged
Chief Officer(s):
Sue McEachern, Executive Director

Variety Club of Ontario, Tent 28 *See* Variety - The Children's Charity (Ontario)

Variety Club of Southern Alberta
Calgary AB
Tel: 403-228-6168
info@varietyalberta.ca
www.varietyalberta.ca
www.facebook.com/VarietyAlberta
Overview: A small local charitable organization founded in 1982
Mission: To provide disabled & disadvantaged children with the means to enjoy quality life experiences; to support research for below the knee amputee children; to provide assistance & bursaries to children in special situations
Affiliation(s): Variety Children's Lifeline
Finances: *Funding Sources:* Membership dues; fundraising
Activities: Variety at Work; Special Celebrity Dinner & Dance; Calgary Stampeder Football Game; Variety Children's Holiday Toylift; Variety Children's Park

Vasculitis Foundation Canada (WGSG)
#446, 425 Hespeler Rd., Cambridge ON N1R 8J6
Toll-Free: 877-572-9474
contact@vasculitis.ca
www.vasculitis.ca
www.linkedin.com/groups?home=&gid=6526945
www.facebook.com/Vasc.Canada
twitter.com/Vasculitis_CND
plus.google.com/109006309123254946353
Also Known As: Wegener's Granulomatosis Support Group of Canada
Overview: A small national charitable organization founded in 1998
Mission: To provide emotional & informational support to patients with WG; to assist them & their families in understanding the disease & recovery process, to educate the public about WG, & to support research into the cause, control & cure of WG
Affiliation(s): Canadian Order of Rare Disorders (CORD); Wegeners Granulomatosis Association International
Finances: *Funding Sources:* Membership fees; Donations; Bequests
Membership: *Fees:* $20 CDN membership; $50 dual Mmbership; *Member Profile:* To encourage and support research efforts for the cause and cure for all forms of Vasculitis; To establish rapport with all known Vasculitis patients and try to alleviate the isolation of having an uncommon, life-threatening disease; To assist Vasculitis patients and their families with clinical information and coping strategies, to help them develop a strong and positive outlook.
Activities: *Awareness Events:* Annual Picnic
Chief Officer(s):
Jon Stewart, President

Vatnabyggd Icelandic Club of Saskatchewan Inc.
www.inlofna.org/Elfros/Vatnabyggd.html
Overview: A small provincial organization founded in 1981
Mission: To foster & promote good citizenship among people of Icelandic origin; to foster & promote knowledge of the Icelandic language, literature & other Icelandic cultural heritage
Member of: Icelandic National League of North America
Affiliation(s): Multicultural Council of Saskatchewan
Finances: *Funding Sources:* Membership fees; raffles; events; Multicultural Council of Saskatchewan
Membership: 210; *Fees:* $5 individual; $10 family
Chief Officer(s):
Christie Dalman, President, 306-554-2267
dalman@sasktel.net
Stella Stephanson, Secretary, 306-328-2077

Vaughan Chamber of Commerce (VCC)
#2, 25 Edilcan Dr., Vaughan ON L4K 3S4
Tel: 905-761-1366; *Fax:* 905-761-1918
info@vaughanchamber.ca
www.vaughanchamber.ca
www.facebook.com/vaughanchamberofcommerce
Overview: A medium-sized local organization founded in 1977
Mission: To be the voice of business; To promote & improve business in the City of Vaughan
Member of: Ontario Chamber of Commerce; Canadian Chamber of Commerce
Finances: *Annual Operating Budget:* $100,000-$250,000; *Funding Sources:* Membership fees; fundraising
Staff Member(s): 5; 60 volunteer(s)
Membership: 900; *Fees:* Schedule available; *Committees:* Government Relations; Marketing & Communications; Membership; Women's
Activities: Networking; Providing education & training
Chief Officer(s):
Brian Shifman, President & CEO
brian@vaughanchamber.ca
Lori Suffern, Office Manager
lori@vaughanchamber.ca
Awards:
• Business Achievement Awards

Vecova Centre for Disability Services & Research
3304 - 33 St. NW, Calgary AB T2L 2A6
Tel: 403-284-1121; *Fax:* 403-284-1146
info@vecova.ca
www.vecova.ca
www.linkedin.com/company/vecova
www.facebook.com/Vecova
twitter.com/Vecova
www.youtube.com/user/Vecovadisability
Previous Name: Vocational & Rehabilitation Research Institute
Overview: A large national charitable organization founded in 1966
Mission: To be leaders in innovative services & research that support persons with disabilities to live as contributing & valued members of the community
Member of: Alberta Association of Rehabilitation Centres
Affiliation(s): University of Calgary
Finances: *Funding Sources:* City of Calgary; donations; fundraising; Canada Mortgage & Housing
Activities: *Speaker Service:* Yes; *Library:* Dr. Randy Tighe Resource Centre; Open to public
Chief Officer(s):
Joan Lee, CEO
Ann-Marie Latoski, Chief Operating Officer
Yvonne Martodam, Chief Administrative Officer
Donovan Tymchyshyn, Chief Strategy Officer

Vegetable & Potato Producers' Association of Nova Scotia
See Horticulture Nova Scotia

Vegetable Growers' Association of Manitoba (VGAM)
PO Box 894, Portage la Prairie MB R1N 3C4
Tel: 204-857-4581; *Fax:* 204-239-0260
vgamveggies@hotmail.com
www.vgam.ca
Overview: A small provincial organization founded in 1953
Mission: To support Manitoba's vegetable growers
Member of: Canadian Horticultural Council
Finances: *Funding Sources:* Membership fees
Activities: Providing information to assist members
Chief Officer(s):
Todd Giffin, President

Vegetarians of Alberta Association (VOA)
9605 - 82 Ave., Edmonton AB T6C 0Z9
Tel: 780-439-8725
info@vofa.ca
www.vofa.ca
Overview: A small provincial organization founded in 1989
Mission: To promote & advance a vegetarian diet in North America based on the proven health, environmental, animal welfare & spiritual benefits
Member of: Alberta Environment Network Society
Affiliation(s): North American Vegetarian Society
Finances: *Annual Operating Budget:* Less than $50,000 25 volunteer(s)
Membership: 300 individual; *Fees:* $15 student & senior; $25 individual; $30 family; $150 life single; $175 life family; *Member Profile:* Open to anyone sympathetic to our goals
Activities: November cook-off competition; Edmonton Earth Day; speakers; *Internships:* Yes; *Speaker Service:* Yes; *Library:* VOA Resource Library; Open to public
Chief Officer(s):
Dayna McIntyre, President
Laura-Lynn Johnston, Vice-President

Vegreville & District Chamber of Commerce
PO Box 877, #106, 4925 - 50 Ave., Vegreville AB T9C 1R9
Tel: 780-632-2771; *Fax:* 780-632-6958
vegchamb@telus.net
www.vegrevillechamber.com
Overview: A small local organization founded in 1906
Mission: To build & perpetuate confidence in business enterprise to a level where, willingly & enthusiastically they risk resources to achieve economic success
Member of: Alberta Chambers of Commerce
Finances: *Funding Sources:* Membership fees; fundraising events
Staff Member(s): 1
Membership: 149; *Fees:* Schedule available based on number of employees; *Member Profile:* Retail; automotive; industry; professionals; *Committees:* Economic Development; Finance/Personnel; Publicity/Promotions/Tourism; Policy; Land Use/Town of Vegreville; Physician Attraction & Retention; Club Activities; Communities in Bloom
Activities: Fundraisers; Awards Night; Christmas Events
Chief Officer(s):
Darcie Sabados, President
Elaine Kucher, General Manager
Awards:
• Citizen of the Year
• Junior Citizen of the Year
• Senior Citizen of the Year
• Small Business Owner of the Year
• Farm Family of the Year

Vegreville Association for Living in Dignity; Vegreville Association for the Handicapped *See* VALID Association

Vehicle Information Centre of Canada *See* Insurance Bureau of Canada

Vela Microboard Association of British Columbia
#1, 5761 Glover Rd., Langley BC V3A 8M8
Tel: 604-539-2488; *Fax:* 604-539-2483
info@velacanada.org
www.velacanada.org
www.facebook.com/VelaCanada
Overview: A small local charitable organization
Mission: To offer people with developmental challenges subsidized housing in the Greater Vancouver area
Chief Officer(s):
Linda Perry, Executive Director

Velo Halifax Bicycle Club
PO Box 125, Dartmouth NS B2Y 3Y2
cycling@chebucto.ns.ca
www.velohalifax.com
Overview: A medium-sized local organization founded in 1974
Membership: *Fees:* $30
Chief Officer(s):
Terry Walker, President, 902-835-8045
teddymw@hotmail.com

Vélo New Brunswick
536 McAllister Rd., Riverview NB E1B 4G1
www.velo.nb.ca
www.facebook.com/VeloNB
Overview: A small provincial organization founded in 1993 overseen by Cycling Canada Cyclisme
Mission: To promote all aspects of the activity of bicycling, competitive & recreational, both on & off the road
Member of: Cycling Canada Cyclisme
Affiliation(s): Sport New Brunswick
Chief Officer(s):
Kelly Murray, President
Kelly.Murray@velo.nb.ca
Michelle Chase, Vice-President
Michelle.Chase@velo.nb.ca
Sheila Colbourne, Executive Director
Sheila.Colbourne@velo.nb.ca

Vélo Québec
Maison des cyclistes, 1251, rue Rachel est, Montréal QC H2J 2J9
Tél: 514-521-8356; *Téléc:* 514-521-5711
Ligne sans frais: 800-567-8356
www.velo.qc.ca
www.facebook.com/VeloQuebec
twitter.com/VeloQuebec
instagram.com/veloquebec
Aperçu: *Dimension:* moyenne; *Envergure:* provinciale; fondée en 1967
Mission: À promouvoir l'utilisation du vélo à travers le Québec
Membre: *Montant de la cotisation:* 41$
Activités: *Stagiaires:* Oui; *Service de conférenciers:* Oui
Membre(s) du bureau directeur:
Suzanne Lareau, Directrice générale

VeloNorth Cycling Club
68 Klondike Rd., Whitehorse YT Y1A 3M1
Tel: 867-668-3531
www.velonorth.ca
Overview: A small provincial organization
Mission: To encourage safe bicycle riding for sport, recreation & fitness.
Affiliation(s): Contagious Mountain Bike Club
Chief Officer(s):
McCann Mike, Chair
mike@velonorth.org
Bill Curtis, Treasurer
wcurtis@northwestel.net

Venezuelan Association for Canadian Studies / Asociación Venezolana de Estudios Canadienses
Apartado 3-F, Piso 3, Final Calle Chama, Mérida, Estado Mérida Venezuela
Overview: A small international organization founded in 1991
Mission: To foster an awareness of Canada; to promote the study of Canada & to contribute to the body of research in Canadian Studies
Activities: Nine Canadian Studies centres distributed in the different regions of Venezuela
Chief Officer(s):
Diego R. Zamvrano-Nieto, President
dzambran@cantv.net

Vera Perlin Society
PO Box 7114, 4 O'Leary Ave., St. John's NL A1E 3Y3
Tel: 709-739-6017; *Fax:* 709-739-5532
veraperlinsociety@nfld.net
www.veraperlinsociety.ca
Overview: A small local charitable organization founded in 1954
Mission: To secure & provide quality services & support for all individuals with developmental disabilities & their families in the St. John's & surrounding area, enabling them to participate in all areas of community living
Affiliation(s): Newfoundland Association for Community Living
Finances: *Funding Sources:* Regional government
Membership: 250 individual; *Fees:* $2 individual
Chief Officer(s):

Roger Downer, Executive Director

Vermilion & District Chamber of Commerce
4606 - 52 St., Vermilion AB T9X 0A1
Tel: 780-853-6593; *Fax:* 780-853-1740
vermilionchamber@gmail.com
www.vermilionchamber.ca
www.facebook.com/vermilionchamber
twitter.com/vermilchamber
Overview: A small local charitable organization founded in 1906
Mission: To improve the business community; To address issues affecting businesses
Member of: Alberta Chamber of Commerce; Canadian Chamber of Commerce
Finances: *Annual Operating Budget:* $100,000-$250,000; *Funding Sources:* Membership dues; fundraising
Staff Member(s): 2; 13 volunteer(s)
Membership: 200; *Fees:* Schedule available; *Member Profile:* Business people & others interested; *Committees:* Finance/Administration; Retail Promotions; Membership/Speakers; Economic Development; Hire-a-Student
Chief Officer(s):
Robert Ernst, President
Awards:
- Vermilion Chamber of Commerce Award

Vermilion Association for Persons with Disabilities *See* FOCUS

Vermilion Forks Field Naturalists
PO Box 2074, Princeton BC V0X 1W0
vffnbc@gmail.com
www.vffn.ca
Overview: A small local organization
Membership: 75; *Fees:* $30 individual; $40 family; $10 student
Activities: Organizing two field trips every month
Chief Officer(s):
Mary Masiel, President, 250-295-7154

Vernon BC Food Bank
3303 - 32 Ave., Vernon BC V1T 2M7
Tel: 250-549-4111
Overview: A small local charitable organization overseen by Food Banks British Columbia
Member of: Food Banks British Columbia; Salvation Army
Chief Officer(s):
Kristin Ford, Coordinator

Vernon Community Arts Council *See* Arts Council of the North Okanagan

Vernon Japanese Cultural Society (VJCS)
4895 Bella Vista Rd., Vernon BC V1H 1A1
Tel: 250-545-4162
vjcsannouncement@gmail.com
www.vjcs.org
Overview: A small local organization founded in 1940
Member of: National Association of Japanese Canadians
Membership: 150-200; *Fees:* $10 individual; $20 family
Activities: Providing Japanese classes; Organizing annual events including Autumn Bazaar, Christmas Concert for Children, Bon Odori, & Seniors' Dinner
Publications:
- Vernon Japanese Cultural Society Newsletter
Type: Newsletter

Vernon Jubilee Hospital Foundation
2101 - 32nd St., Vernon BC V1T 5L2
Tel: 250-558-1362; *Fax:* 250-558-4133
info@vjhfoundation.org
www.vjhfoundation.org
www.facebook.com/VJHFoundation
Overview: A small local charitable organization founded in 1981
Mission: To support & raise funds for Vernon Jubilee Hospital, as well as residential care facilities & community care programs
Staff Member(s): 3
Chief Officer(s):
Sue Beaudry, Director, Development, 250-558-1200 Ext. 1405

Vernon Lapidary & Mineral Club
c/o Vernon Community Arts Centre, 2704A Hwy. #6, Vernon BC V1T 5G5
www.vernonclub.rocks
Overview: A small local organization founded in 1959
Membership: *Fees:* $20 individuals; $30 families
Activities: Hosting monthly meetings, except July & August; Offering lapidary workshops to members; *Awareness Events:* Vernon Lapidary Show & Sale

Chief Officer(s):
Joy Gillies, Secretary

Vernon Women's Transition House Society
PO Box 625, Vernon BC V1T 6M6
Fax: 250-549-3347; *Crisis Hot-Line:* 250-542-1122
transition@telus.net
Overview: A small local organization founded in 1977
Mission: To provide temporary accommodation in a safe, supportive environment, to women & their children who have experienced abusive relationships; to provide information & referrals to appropriate counselling agencies & to provide a program for young unwed mothers, including support groups
Member of: British Columbia Federation of Child & Family Services
Finances: *Funding Sources:* Provincial government
Staff Member(s): 6; 6 volunteer(s)
Membership: 40 individual + 25 associate

Vert l'Aventure Plein Air
#204, 321, rue Père Marquette, Québec QC G1S 1Y9
Tél: 418-687-2396
vertlaventure@videotron.ca
vertlaventurepleinair.com
Aperçu: *Dimension:* petite; *Envergure:* locale
Mission: De réunir des gens qui aiment les activités de plein air et à organiser des randonnées
Activités: Randonnées; Voyages

Vertes boisées du fjord
#304, 129, rue Jacques Cartier est, Chicoutimi QC G7H 1Y4
Tél: 418-973-4261; *Téléc:* 418-543-7270
vertsboises@lvbf.org
www.lvbf.org
twitter.com/LVBFjord
Aperçu: *Dimension:* petite; *Envergure:* locale
Mission: De protéger et de préserver les forêts urbain dans la région du Saguenay
Membre: *Montant de la cotisation:* 10$
Membre(s) du bureau directeur:
Julien Petitclerc, Président, Conseil d'administration

Vêtement Québec *See* Apparel Quebec

Veterinary Infectious Disease Organization *See* Vaccine & Infectious Disease Organization

Vetta Chamber Music Society
PO Box 19148, 2302 4th Ave., Vancouver BC V6K 4R8
Toll-Free: 866-863-6250
www.vettamusic.com
twitter.com/VettaChamber
Overview: A small local organization
Member of: Vancouver Cultural Alliance
Chief Officer(s):
Joan Blackman, Artistic Director

VHA Home HealthCare
#600, 30 Soudan Ave., Toronto ON M4S 1V6
Tel: 416-489-2500; *Fax:* 416-482-8773
Toll-Free: 888-314-6622
www.vha.ca
www.facebook.com/VHAHomeHealthCare
twitter.com/VHACaregiving
www.youtube.com/user/VHAHomeHealthCare
Also Known As: Visiting Homemakers Association
Overview: A large local charitable organization founded in 1925
Mission: To be a leading not-for-profit provider of community-based, client-centred health & support services in the Greater Toronto Area
Member of: United Way
Finances: *Annual Operating Budget:* Greater than $5 Million
Staff Member(s): 1904
Chief Officer(s):
Carol Annett, President & CEO
Jennifer Blum, Chief Financial Officer

Via Prévention
#301, 6455, boul Jean-Talon est, Montréal QC H1S 3E8
Tél: 514-955-0454; *Téléc:* 514-955-0449
Ligne sans frais: 800-361-8906
info@viaprevention.com
www.viaprevention.com
www.facebook.com/Via-Prévention-419326141538058
twitter.com/ViaPrevention
Aperçu: *Dimension:* moyenne; *Envergure:* provinciale; fondée en 1982

Mission: Pour protéger les personnes qui travaillent dans les transports, de l'Entreposage et de l'environnement en leur donnant une formation en santé et sécurité routière
Membre(s) du personnel: 10
Membre(s) du bureau directeur:
Alain Lajoie, Directeur général

ViaSport
#1351, 409 Granville St., Vancouver BC V6C 1T2
Tel: 778-654-7542
Toll-Free: 800-335-7549
Other Communication: Toll-Free Fax: 1-888-316-3527
info@viasport.ca
www.viasport.ca
www.facebook.com/viaSportBC
twitter.com/ViaSportBC
www.youtube.com/user/viaSportBC
Overview: A medium-sized provincial organization
Mission: To provide the opportunity for participation in sports for all British Columbians, at every age & level of skill.
Activities: Funding & grants
Chief Officer(s):
Sheila Bouman, Chief Executive Officer
sheilab@viasport.ca
Michelle Tice, Director, Communications & Engagement
michellet@viasport.ca
Scott Stefani, Manager, Grants
scotts@viasport.ca
Awards:
- BC Ferries Sport Experience Program
- Northern BC Coaching & Officiating Development Fund
- Community Sport Program Development Fund
- Hosting BC Grant Program
- BC Sport Participation Program
- Bob Bearpark Coaching Bursary Awards
- Coaches BC Legacy Grants
- Professional Development Fund for Advancing Gender Equity in Sport
- #LeveltheField Inspiring Change Grant

Coaches ViaSport
#1000, 510 Burrard St., Vancouver BC V6C 3A8
Tel: 778-331-8642; *Fax:* 778-327-5199
Toll-Free: 800-335-3120
Coaches@ViaSport.ca
www.viasport.ca/coaches
Mission: To act as the provincial representative for coaches in British Columbia
Affiliation(s): Coaching Association of Canada
Chief Officer(s):
Eric Sinker, Manager, Coaching & Leadership Development
eric@viasport.ca

Victims of Violence (VOV)
#340, 117 Centrepointe Dr., Ottawa ON K2G 5X3
Tel: 613-233-0052; *Fax:* 613-233-2712
Toll-Free: 888-606-0000
vofv@victimsofviolence.on.ca
www.victimsofviolence.on.ca
www.facebook.com/205047429517768
twitter.com/victimsofviolen
Also Known As: Canadian Centre for Missing Children
Overview: A small provincial charitable organization founded in 1984
Mission: To provide long term support & guidance to victims of violent crime & their families; To provide aide to families of missing children
Affiliation(s): National Organization for Victim Assistance - Washington DC; RCMP Missing Children's Registry
Finances: *Annual Operating Budget:* Less than $50,000; *Funding Sources:* Fundraising; donations; memoriam donations
Staff Member(s): 5; 6 volunteer(s)
Membership: 1,000+; *Member Profile:* Concerned citizens
Activities: Victim assistance; Missing children services; Child protection & crime prevention programs; Referral program; *Speaker Service:* Yes; *Rents Mailing List:* Yes; *Library:* Research Library; Open to public by appointment
Chief Officer(s):
Gary Rosenfeldt, Executive Director

Victoria Association for Community Living *See* Community Living Victoria

Victoria Canada-China Friendship Association (VCCFA)
PO Box 5074, Victoria BC V8R 6N4
Tel: 250-882-5820
charlebois721@gmail.com
www.vccfa.net
www.facebook.com/334764179959851
Overview: A small international organization founded in 1965 overseen by Federation of Canada-China Friendship Associations
Mission: To foster friendship & understanding between the peoples of Canada & the peoples of China
Member of: Federation of Canada-China Friendship Associations
Affiliation(s): Chinese Peoples Association for Friendship with Foreign Countries
Activities: Dinner meetings; tours to China

Victoria Cool Aid Society
#101, 749 Pandora Ave., Victoria BC V8W 1N9
Tel: 250-383-1977; *Fax:* 250-383-1639
society@coolaid.org
www.coolaid.org
www.linkedin.com/company/victoria-cool-aid-society
www.facebook.com/VicCoolAid
twitter.com/VicCoolAid
www.youtube.com/VicCoolAid
Overview: A medium-sized local charitable organization founded in 1958
Mission: To provide shelter, housing & community health services to the most disadvantaged in the community
Finances: *Annual Operating Budget:* Greater than $5 Million
Staff Member(s): 145; 40 volunteer(s)
Membership: 1-99
Chief Officer(s):
Kathy Stinson, CEO

Victoria County Association for Community Living *See* Community Living Kawartha Lakes

Victoria County Historical Society
Old Gaol Museum, 50 Victoria Ave. North, Lindsay ON K9V 3T4
Tel: 705-324-3404
info@oldegaolmuseum.ca
www.oldegaolmuseum.ca
Overview: A small local charitable organization founded in 1957
Mission: To collect, preserve, exhibit, & publish information about the history of Ontario's County of Victoria
Finances: *Funding Sources:* Admission fees; Fundraising
Membership: *Fees:* $20 individual; $30 family; $100 corporate or patron
Activities: Operating the Olde Gaol Museum; Maintaining a gallery of historical portraits; Promoting study of the history of the County of Victoria; Hosting a speaker series
Chief Officer(s):
Mairi Bew, President
Publications:
- VCHS [Victoria County Historical Society] Newsletter
Type: Newsletter
Profile: Information about the speakers series, meetings, membership, & exhibits

Victoria County Humane Society *See* Ontario Society for the Prevention of Cruelty to Animals

Victoria County Society for the Prevention of Cruelty to Animals
2238 Rte. 109, Arthurette NB E7H 4C2
Tel: 506-356-1117
www.facebook.com/VictoriaCountySpca
Also Known As: Victoria County SPCA
Overview: A small local charitable organization
Member of: Canadian Federation of Humane Societies

Victoria Epilepsy & Parkinson's Centre Society
#202, 1640 Oak Bay Ave., Victoria BC V8R 1B2
Tel: 250-475-6677; *Fax:* 250-475-6619
help@vepc.bc.ca
www.vepc.bc.ca
twitter.com/VEPC
Overview: A small local charitable organization founded in 1983
Mission: To provide education & support services to those affected by epilepsy or Parkinson's Disease, individuals & family members; To promote excellence in care through collaboration with the health care community; To increase public understanding of these conditions & expand awareness & support of the services provided
Affiliation(s): Canadian Epilepsy Alliance
Finances: *Annual Operating Budget:* $250,000-$500,000; *Funding Sources:* United Way of Greater Victoria, Vndekerkhove Family Foundation, grants
Staff Member(s): 6; 200 volunteer(s)
Membership: 200 institutional + 800 individual; *Fees:* By donation; *Committees:* Parkinson's Advisory; Epilepsy Advisory
Activities: Support, knowledge, advocacy, public awareness; *Awareness Events:* Purple Day for Epilepsy, March 26; Parkinson's Month, April; *Speaker Service:* Yes; *Library:* Vandekerkhove Library; Open to public
Chief Officer(s):
Mira Laurence, Executive Director
mlaurence@vepc.bc.ca
Della Cronkrite, Office Manager
Shannon Oatway, Coordinator, Community Education & Awareness

Victoria Hospitals Foundation (VHF)
1952 Bay St., Victoria BC V8R 1J8
Tel: 250-519-1750; *Fax:* 250-519-1751
vhf@viha.ca
www.victoriahf.ca
www.facebook.com/VictoriaHF
twitter.com/ourvichospitals
Previous Name: Greater Victoria Hospitals Foundation
Overview: A small local charitable organization founded in 1989
Mission: To raise funds for Victoria's major hospitals: Victoria General & Royal Jubilee, which also serve the entire Vancouver Island
Affiliation(s): Vancouver Island Health Authority
Finances: *Funding Sources:* Donations; Foundations; Corporations; Fundraising
Staff Member(s): 15
Activities: Visions - annual fundraising event
Chief Officer(s):
Melanie Mahlman, President & CEO
Publications:
- InTouch [a publication of Victoria Hospitals Foundation]
Type: Newsletter; *Frequency:* Quarterly
Profile: Relays news about funding activities & priorities at the hospitals

Victoria International Development Education Association (VIDEA)
1200 Deeks Pl., Victoria BC V8P 5S7
info@videa.ca
www.videa.ca
www.linkedin.com/company/videa-victoria-international-development-education-association-
twitter.com/VIDEAvictoria
www.youtube.com/user/Videavids1
Overview: A small international charitable organization founded in 1977
Mission: To increase awareness of international development issues, particularly those affecting Third World countries
Member of: Canadian Council for International Cooperation
Affiliation(s): BC Council for International Cooperation
Finances: *Annual Operating Budget:* $100,000-$250,000
Staff Member(s): 3
Membership: 490 senior/lifetime; *Fees:* $15 students, low income, elderly; $25 individual; $50 organizational; *Committees:* Schools; Resource Centre; Public Programs; Personnel
Activities: *Internships:* Yes; *Speaker Service:* Yes; *Library:* Resource Centre; Open to public
Chief Officer(s):
Elvira Perrella, Chair
Lynn Thornton, Executive Director

Victoria Jazz Society
PO Box 39083, RPO James Bay, Victoria BC V8V 4X8
Tel: 250-388-4423; *Fax:* 250-388-4407
info@jazzvictoria.ca
jazzvictoria.ca
www.facebook.com/VicJazzSociety
twitter.com/VicJazzSociety
Overview: A small local organization founded in 1981
Mission: The Victoria Jazz Society is a professional arts organization committed to presenting the highest quality of jazz possible to our community, by presenting music in performance, with acclaimed musicians. The Victoria Jazz Society's primary activity is to produce two major multi-day music festivals in the summer, TD Victoria International JazzFest and the Vancouver Island Blues Bash, as well as a series of concerts from September to May, all featuring international, national and regional jazz artists.

Membership: *Fees:* $10 student; $15 senior; $25 individual; $40 couple/family
Chief Officer(s):
Darryl Mar, Artistic/Executive Director

Victoria Labour Council (VLC)
#219, 2750 Quadra St., Victoria BC V8T 4E8
Tel: 250-384-8331
vlc@victorialabour.ca
www.victorialabour.ca
Overview: A small local organization overseen by British Columbia Federation of Labour
Mission: To advance the economic & social welfare of workers in Victoria, British Columbia
Affiliation(s): Canadian Labour Congress (CLC)
Membership: *Member Profile:* Locals of national unions affiliated to the Canadian Labour Congress; *Committees:* Womens; Solidarity
Activities: Supporting local community organizations, such as the United Way; Providing local labour news; Engaging in municipal political action; Advocating for workers' issues, such as wages & safe working conditions; Organizing rallies for issues such as public services; Marking International Woman's Day; Participating in campaigns, such as Women's Economic Equality Campaign
Chief Officer(s):
Mike Eso, President
Stan Dzbik, Secretary-Treasurer
Robin Tosczak, Secretary

Victoria Lapidary & Mineral Society (VLMS)
PO Box 5114, Stn. B, Victoria BC V6R 6N3
vlms@vlms.ca
www.vlms.ca
Overview: A small local organization
Affiliation(s): British Columbia Lapidary Society; Gem & Mineral Federation of Canada
Finances: *Funding Sources:* Annual auction of used equipment & lapidary material
Membership: 100; *Fees:* $25 individuals; $35 couples; $40 families; *Member Profile:* Individuals with an interest in rocks, crystals, minerals, lapidary arts, or earth sciences in Victoria, British Columbia
Activities: Providing lapidary & silversmithing courses; Hosting monthly meetings with guest speakers; Planning field trips; *Awareness Events:* Rock & Gem Show *Library:* Victoria Lapidary & Mineral Society Library
Chief Officer(s):
Gilles Lebrun, Contact, Field Trips, 250-382-6119
Publications:
• Victoria Lapidary & Mineral Society Newsletter
Type: Newsletter; *Price:* Free, if e-mailed; $15 for mailing *Profile:* Information for VLMS members

Victoria Medical Society (VMS)
Eric Martin Pavillion, #190, 2334 Trent St., Victoria BC V8R 4Z3
Tel: 250-598-6021; *Fax:* 250-370-8274
administrator@victoriamedicalsociety.org
www.victoriamedicalsociety.org
Overview: A small local organization founded in 1895
Mission: To promote good health & act as an advocate on health issues; to promote good & appropriate medical practice in accord with the Code of Ethics; to promote the good name of medicine; to promote medical education; to promote fellowship & good relations within the profession & with the public; to help, as much as possible, any member in distress from any cause; to advocate for any doctor or group of doctors subjected to injustice; to mediate, when requested, in disputes & differences between local medical groups or individuals (mediation & advocacy does not apply to cases under the jurisdiction of the College of Physicians & Surgeons of BC); to cooperate with the BCMA, CMA & College of Physicians & Surgeons of BC
Affiliation(s): BC College of Physicians & Surgeons; BC Medical Association
Membership: 100-499; *Fees:* $135 ordinary; $25 associate (retired); *Member Profile:* Practicing & retired physicians
Activities: Education & social; annual dinner; Listerian Oration
Chief Officer(s):
C. Peter Innes, President
vicmedso@telus.net

Victoria Musicians' Association *See* Musicians' Association of Victoria & the Islands, Local 247, AFM

Victoria Native Friendship Centre (VNFC)
231 Regina Ave., Victoria BC V8Z 1J6
Tel: 250-384-3211; *Fax:* 250-384-1586
www.vnfc.ca
www.facebook.com/150790278331058
twitter.com/VNFCTWEET
Overview: A small local organization founded in 1969
Mission: To meet the needs of Native people in the greater Victoria area by providing them with services & information designed to enhance their traditional values
Member of: United Way; Association of Aboriginal Post-Secondary Institutions
Finances: *Funding Sources:* Federal, provincial & Aboriginal organizations; charitable foundations; corporations; local business
Staff Member(s): 68
Membership: *Fees:* $1
Activities: Wellness Clinic; Health services; family services; intervention programs
Chief Officer(s):
Bruce Parisian, Executive Director

Victoria Natural History Society
PO Box 5220, Stn. B, Victoria BC V8R 6N4
www.vicnhs.bc.ca
Overview: A small local organization founded in 1944
Mission: To stimulate active interest in natural history; to study & protect flora & fauna & their habitats
Member of: Federation of BC Naturalists
Affiliation(s): Canadian Nature Federation
Finances: *Funding Sources:* Membership fees
Membership: 750; *Fees:* $30 Regular; $35 Family; $25 senior; $20 student
Activities: Christmas Bird Count; *Speaker Service:* Yes; *Library:* Open to public
Chief Officer(s):
Darren Copley, President, 250-479-6622
dccopley@telus.net

Victoria Numismatic Society
PO Box 39028, Stn. James Bay Postal Outlet, Victoria BC V8V 4X8
victoriacoinclub@yahoo.ca
victoriacoinclub.webs.com
Overview: A small local organization founded in 1955
Mission: To promote coin & money collecting
Membership: *Fees:* $20; $15 junior

Victoria Orchid Society
1199 Tattersall Dr., Victoria BC V8P 1Y8
www.victoriaorchidsociety.ca
Overview: A small local organization
Membership: 153; *Fees:* $15 single; $20 family
Chief Officer(s):
Ingrid Ostrander, President
ifl@telus.net

Victoria Particular Council *See* Conseil national Société de Saint-Vincent de Paul

Victoria Peace Centre *See* Victoria Peace Coalition

Victoria Peace Coalition (VPC)
victoriapeacecoalition.org
www.facebook.com/victoriapeacecoalition
twitter.com/peace_victoria
Previous Name: Victoria Peace Centre
Overview: A small provincial organization founded in 2001
Mission: To raise awareness on a wide range of issues, such as Palestine, Iraq, & Missile Defence; To promote education through research & the publishing of brochures
Finances: *Annual Operating Budget:* Less than $50,000
20 volunteer(s)
Membership: 100-499
Activities: *Awareness Events:* Earth Walk, April; *Speaker Service:* Yes

Victoria READ Society
#201 & 202, 990 Hillside Ave., Victoria BC V8T 2A1
Tel: 250-388-7225; *Fax:* 250-386-8330
info@readsociety.bc.ca
www.readsociety.bc.ca
www.linkedin.com/company/703924
www.facebook.com/209661882291
twitter.com/READSociety
Also Known As: READ Learning Centre
Previous Name: Victoria Reading Evaluation & Development Society
Overview: A small local charitable organization founded in 1976
Mission: To help children & adults improve & upgrade their basic reading, writing & math skills in a supportive small class; also literacy, English as a Second Language
Member of: ASPECT; ELSA-Net; International Reading Association; Literacy BC; Volunteer Victoria
Finances: *Annual Operating Budget:* $500,000-$1.5 Million; *Funding Sources:* Federal government; provincial government; corporate sponsorship; fees for service; foundations
Staff Member(s): 23; 130 volunteer(s)
Membership: 30 individual; *Fees:* $10 individual; *Committees:* READ Festival; Bursary; Finance; Personnel; Fundraising
Activities: READ Festival - an annual "Poetry Bash" to benefit children's literacy programs; Bursary Fund program to subsidize tuition for children's programming; Scrabble Scramble for Literacy; Random Acts of Poetry
Chief Officer(s):
Carol J. Carman, Chair
Claire Rettie, Executive Director
crettie@readsociety.bc.ca

Victoria Reading Evaluation & Development Society *See* Victoria READ Society

Victoria Real Estate Board (VREB)
3035 Nanaimo St., Victoria BC V8T 4W2
Tel: 250-385-7766; *Fax:* 250-385-8773
info@vreb.org
www.vreb.org
Overview: A small local organization founded in 1921 overseen by British Columbia Real Estate Association
Mission: To promote & enhance the use of the real estate services that its members provide to the public
Member of: The Canadian Real Estate Association
Finances: *Annual Operating Budget:* $1.5 Million-$3 Million
Staff Member(s): 15
Membership: 1,153; *Member Profile:* Realtors
Activities: Continuing education; Leadership; *Library:* Resource Centre; Not open to public
Chief Officer(s):
David Corey, Executive Officer, 250-920-4658

Victoria Riding for Disabled Association *See* Victoria Therapeutic Riding Association

Victoria Society for Humanistic Judaism (VSHJ)
3636 Shelbourne St., Victoria BC V8P 4H2
Tel: 250-658-5836
info@vshj.ca
vshj.ca
Overview: A small local organization
Mission: To preserve Jewish heritage, culture, & customs within a non-theistic environment
Affiliation(s): Congress of Secular Jewish Organizations; Leadership Conference of Secular & Humanistic Jews; Canadian Jewish Congress
Membership: *Fees:* $100 single; $150 family; *Member Profile:* Persons of Jewish descent; Persons who wish to identify with the history, culture, & ethical values of Jewish people
Activities: Hosting meetings twice a month at the Jewish Community Centre in Victoria; Discussing topics relevant to Humanism; Providing educational programs for children; Offering life cycle events to members; Celebrating major Jewish holidays with secularly meaningful programs
Chief Officer(s):
Larry Gontovnick, President

Victoria Symphony Society
#610, 620 View St., Victoria BC V8W 1J6
Tel: 250-385-6515
boxoffice@victoriasymphony.ca
www.victoriasymphony.ca
www.linkedin.com/company/victoria-symphony
www.facebook.com/victoriasymphony
twitter.com/VicSymphony
Overview: A small local charitable organization founded in 1941 overseen by Orchestras Canada
Mission: To advance musical culture; to advance musical education among younger members of community; to encourage, foster, & promote performance of Canadian & other contemporary musicians
Member of: Orchestras Canada
Finances: *Annual Operating Budget:* $3 Million-$5 Million; *Funding Sources:* Government; Corporate & individual sponsors; Ticket revenue; Fundraising
Staff Member(s): 14; 150 volunteer(s)
Activities: *Library:* Music Library; Not open to public
Chief Officer(s):

Mitchell Krieger, Executive Director, 250-385-9771 Ext. 226
mitchell@victoriasymphony.ca
Tania Miller, Music Director

Victoria Therapeutic Riding Association (VTRA)
PO Box 412, Brentwood Bay BC V8M 1R3
Tel: 778-426-0506
vtra.ca
www.facebook.com/VictoriaTherapeuticRidingAssociation
twitter.com/VicTherapeutic
instagram.com/victherapeutic
Previous Name: Victoria Riding for Disabled Association
Overview: A small local charitable organization founded in 1982
Mission: To provide a therapeutic riding program for children & adults with disabilities to promote their physical, psychological, & social well-being
Member of: Canadian Therapeutic Riding Association
Affiliation(s): B.C. Therapeutic Riding Association; Horse Council of British Columbia; Volunteer Victoria; Canadian Therapeutic Riding Association's; Association of Fundraising Professionals
Finances: *Funding Sources:* Service club; fund-raising events; foundations
Staff Member(s): 4; 100 volunteer(s)
Membership: *Fees:* $20 individual; $200 life; $10 riders
Chief Officer(s):
Annie Brothwell, President
Audrey Cooper, Executive Director
Publications:
• The Stable Voice [a publication of Victoria Therapeutic Riding Association]
Type: Newsletter; *Frequency:* q.

Victoria Youth Empowerment Society
533 Yates St., Victoria BC V8W 1K7
Tel: 250-383-3514; *Fax:* 250-383-3812
office_manager@vyes.ca
www.vyes.ca
Merged from: Alliance Club; Association for Street Kids
Overview: A small local charitable organization founded in 1992
Mission: To assist youth to remove themselves from the high risk environment of the street & make the transition to healthier & more constructive life situations; To help youth make positive choices which will prevent involvement in at risk behaviour or connection with the street scene
Member of: Federation of Child & Family Services of BC; United Way
Finances: *Annual Operating Budget:* $1.5 Million-$3 Million; *Funding Sources:* Ministry of Social Services; Ministry of Health; United Way; churches; fun-raising; individual contributions
Staff Member(s): 60
Membership: *Fees:* $10
Activities: Souper Bowls; Mayor's Golf Classic Tournament; daytime/evening drop-in centre; information; referrals; advocacy; counselling; housing; outreach; workshops; employment

Victorian Order of Nurses for Canada (VON Canada) / Infirmières de l'Ordre de Victoria du Canada
#100, 2315 St. Laurent Blvd., Ottawa ON K1G 4J8
Tel: 613-233-5694; *Fax:* 613-230-4376
Toll-Free: 888-866-2273
national@von.ca
www.von.ca
www.linkedin.com/company/von-canada
www.facebook.com/VONCanada
twitter.com/VON_Canada
www.youtube.com/VONCanadaFD
Overview: A medium-sized national charitable organization founded in 1897
Mission: To be a leader in the delivery of innovative comprehensive health & social services; To influence the development of health & social policy in Canada; To meet rapidly changing social & external challenges
Finances: *Annual Operating Budget:* $1.5 Million-$3 Million
Staff Member(s): 5000; 9000 volunteer(s)
Activities: Offering a wide range of community health care solutions
Chief Officer(s):
Jo-Anne Poirier, President & CEO
Bill Smethurst, Chief Financial Officer

Victorian Studies Association of Western Canada
LLPA Department, Douglas College, University of Victoria, #2635, 700 Royal Ave., New Westminster BC V3M 5Z5
web.uvic.ca/vsawc
twitter.com/vsawc
Overview: A medium-sized local organization founded in 1972
Mission: To promote the interest & activity of scholars in the study of Victorian Britain & the British Empire & to promote a sense of a community among scholars in Western Canada, where distance often makes informal & frequent meetings with colleagues & access to major libraries difficult
Membership: *Fees:* $50 faculty; $30 students
Activities: Annual fall conference, Sept./Oct.
Chief Officer(s):
Ryan Stephenson, Contact
stephensonr@douglascollege.ca
Meetings/Conferences:
• Victorian Studies Association of Western Canada 2018 Conference, July, 2018, University of Victoria, Victoria, BC
Scope: National
Description: Theme: "The Body & the Page in Victorian Culture"

VideoFACT, A Foundation to Assist Canadian Talent *See* MuchFACT

Vidéographe
4550, rue Garnier, Montréal QC H2J 3S7
Tél: 514-521-2116; *Téléc:* 514-521-1676
info@videographe.qc.ca
www.videographe.qc.ca
www.facebook.com/124501969721
twitter.com/Videographe
Aperçu: *Dimension:* petite; *Envergure:* provinciale; fondée en 1971
Mission: Favoriser le développement de la pratique de la vidéo en soutenant autant les jeunes auteurs dans le cadre de la réalisation de leurs premières oeuvres, que les vidéastes professionnels dans la pratique et la reconnaissance de leur art; cette mission s'articule autour d'un triple mandat: faciliter l'accès à la production, à la création et à la recherche en arts médiatiques; soutenir la pratique professionnelle, notamment en assurant la distribution des oeuvres vidéographiques et une juste rétribution des droits aux artistes; permettre l'ouverture de marchés par le biais d'activités multiples en diffusion et de rencontres interactives
Membre de: Alliance de la vidéo et du cinéma indépendant; Conseil québécois des arts médiatiques; Culture Montréal
Finances: *Budget de fonctionnement annuel:* $500,000-$1.5 Million
Membre(s) du personnel: 8; 15 bénévole(s)
Membre: 263; *Montant de la cotisation:* 112,88$ individu; 225,75$ institution; *Comités:* Programmation; Co-Production
Activités: Stagiaires: Oui
Membre(s) du bureau directeur:
Etienne Desrosiers, Président
Fortner Anderson, Directeur général
fanderson@videographe.qc.ca

Vides Canada
178 Steeles Ave. East, Markham ON L3T 1A5
Tel: 416-803-3558
videscanada.ca
www.facebook.com/videscanada
www.flickr.com/photos/57388169@N05
Overview: A small international charitable organization founded in 1987
Mission: To improve the lives of underpriviledged children; to train volunteers & send them to developing countries in order to help the children who live there
Chief Officer(s):
Jeannine Landra, Director
jeanninefma@videscanada.ca

Vie autonome Canada *See* Independent Living Canada

VieCanada *See* LifeCanada

Vietnamese Association, Toronto (VAT)
1364 Dundas St. West, Toronto ON M6J 1Y2
Tel: 416-536-3611; *Fax:* 416-536-8364
www.vatoronto.ca
Overview: A small local charitable organization founded in 1972 overseen by Vietnamese Canadian Federation
Mission: To promote unity, fraternity, & mutual assistance among members of the community through social, educational, & cultural activites
Finances: *Annual Operating Budget:* $250,000-$500,000; *Funding Sources:* Federal, provincial & municipal government
Staff Member(s): 16; 30 volunteer(s)
Membership: *Fees:* $10
Activities: Settlement & adaptation programs; employment counselling; computer tutorials; tai chi; health & community workshops; *Awareness Events:* TET, Lunar New Year Festival
Chief Officer(s):
Manh Nguyen, Executive Director
manh@vatoronto.ca

Vietnamese Canadian Federation (VCF) / Fédération vietnamienne du Canada
2476 Regatta Ave., Ottawa ON K2J 5V6
Tel: 780-708-0876; *Fax:* 780-425-0799
lhnvc1980vcf@gmail.com
www.vietfederation.ca
www.facebook.com/vietnamesecanadian.centre
twitter.com/VietCdnCentre
www.flickr.com/photos/vietnamesecanadianfederationcentre
Previous Name: Canadian Federation of Vietnamese Associations of Canada
Overview: A medium-sized national licensing charitable organization founded in 1980
Mission: To provide focal point for activities of the Vietnamese community in the National Capital Region & across Canada; to serve as resource centre on Vietnamese culture & issues related to resettlement & integration of Vietnamese refugees & immigrants in Canada; to maintain solidarity among the Vietnamese associations across Canada; to harmonize their activities for a better achievement of their common objectives; to work for the preservation & development of Vietnamese culture & for the enrichment of Canadian culture; to foster the spirit of mutual help & community responsibility
Member of: World Federation of Vietnamese Associations Overseas
Affiliation(s): Canadian Ethnocultural Council
Finances: *Funding Sources:* Canadian Heritage; membership fees; Vietnamese community
Membership: *Member Profile:* Vietnamese community organizations
Activities: *Internships:* Yes; *Speaker Service:* Yes; *Library:* Vietnamese Canadian Centre; Open to public

Les Vieux Brachés de Longueuil
Centre Communcautaire Le Traint d'Union, 3100, rue Mosseau, Longueuil QC J4L 4P2
Tél: 450-647-1107
vieuxbranches@hotmail.com
cctu.ca
Aperçu: *Dimension:* petite; *Envergure:* locale; fondée en 1996
Mission: Pour faire discouveries, répondre aux questions et résoudre les problèmes concernant les ordinateurs
Membre: 200; *Montant de la cotisation:* 25$; *Critères d'admissibilite:* Les adultes qui ont 50 ou plus anées qui sont intéressés à en apprendre sur les ordinateurs
Activités: *Evénements de sensibilisation:* Dîner de Noël
Membre(s) du bureau directeur:
Robert Bujold, Président, Consil d'administration

Viking Economic Development Committee (VEDC)
PO Box 369, Viking AB T0B 4N0
Tel: 780-336-3466
info@viking.ca
www.townofviking.ca
Overview: A small local organization
Mission: To promote the community of Viking
Finances: *Funding Sources:* Town of Viking; fundraising
12 volunteer(s)
Membership: 12
Chief Officer(s):
Allan Harvey, Manager

Villa Charities Inc. (Toronto District)
901 Lawrence Ave. West, Toronto ON M6A 1C3
Tel: 416-789-7011; *Fax:* 416-789-3951
www.villacharities.com
Previous Name: Italian Canadian Benevolent Corporation (Toronto District)
Overview: A medium-sized provincial charitable organization founded in 1971
Mission: To develop social programs that enhace the lives of their senior members & promote Italian heritage
Affiliation(s): Villa Colombo Services for Seniors; Columbus Centre; VITA Community Living Services; Caboto Terrace; Casa DelZotto; Casa Abruzzo; Villa Colombo Vaughan Di Poce Centre
Membership: 8 organizations
Activities: *Library:* Alberto DiGiovanni Library; Not open to public
Chief Officer(s):
Aldo Cundari, Chair
Frank Chiarotto, Vice-Chair
Joseph Arcuri, Treasurer

Columbus Centre
901 Lawrence Ave. West, Toronto ON M6A 1C3
Tel: 416-789-7011; *Fax:* 416-789-3951
Chief Officer(s):
Karen Manarin, Chair
Pal Di Iulio, Executive Director
Mark DeVito, Administrator
Villa Colombo Services for Seniors
40 Playfair Ave., Toronto ON M6B 2P9
Tel: 416-789-2113; *Fax:* 416-789-5435
Chief Officer(s):
Nick Manocchio, President & Chair
Tracey Comeau, Executive Director
tcomeau@villacolombo.on.ca
Villa Colombo Vaughan - Di Poce Centre
10443 Hwy. 27, Vaughan ON L0J 1C0
Tel: 289-202-2222; *Fax:* 289-202-2000
Chief Officer(s):
Rina Tiberini, Chair
Valeria De Simone, Acting Administrator
VITA Community Living Services
4301 Weston Rd., Toronto ON M9L 2Y3
Tel: 416-749-6234; *Fax:* 416-749-1456
www.vitacls.org
Mission: To provide services to adults with developmental disabilities and dual diagnosis (developmental disability accompanied by a psychiatric diagnosis).
Affiliation(s): Mens Sana Families for Mental Health
Chief Officer(s):
Brian Naraine, President
Adam M. Smith, Executive Director, 416-749-6234 Ext. 240
asmith@vitacls.org

Village International Sudbury (VIS)
139 Durham St., Sudbury ON P3E 3M9
Tel: 705-524-2999
villageinternationalsudbury@hotmail.com
www.northernontario.org/vi
Overview: A small local organization founded in 1989
Mission: To support the development of community-based enterprises by importing products made by workers in developing countries
Member of: Global Education Centres of Ontario
Finances: *Annual Operating Budget:* $100,000-$250,000; *Funding Sources:* Crafts sale
Staff Member(s): 2; 25 volunteer(s)
Membership: 175; *Fees:* $10-$20

Villages internationaux d'enfants *See* Children's International Summer Villages (Canada) Inc.

Vilna & District Chamber of Commerce
PO Box 542, Vilna AB T0A 3L0
Tel: 780-636-3615
Overview: A small local organization
Affiliation(s): Alberta Chamber of Commerce; Canadian Chamber of Commerce

The Vimy Foundation / La Fondation Vimy
#726, 1470, rue Peel, Montréal QC H3A 1T1
Tel: 514-904-1007
info@vimyfoundation.ca
www.vimyfoundation.ca
twitter.com/vimyfoundation
Overview: A organization founded in 2005
Mission: To preserve & promote Canada's First World War legacy as symbolized with the 1917 victory at Vimy Ridge
Activities: Educational programs; souvenir items such as pins & medals; promoting greater recognition of Vimy Day; lobbying; *Awareness Events:* Vimy Day, April 9
Chief Officer(s):
Rick Hillier, Honorary Chair
Christopher Sweeney, Chair

Vinok Worldance
PO Box 4867, Edmonton AB T6E 5G7
Tel: 780-454-3739; *Fax:* 780-454-3436
www.vinok.ca
www.facebook.com/vinok.worldance
twitter.com/VinokWorldance
Overview: A small local organization founded in 1988
Mission: To present music & dances of the world to audiences all across Canada; To reflect world dance as a way of celebrating life & expressing through dance, music, song, & improvisation

Finances: *Funding Sources:* The Canada Council; The Alberta Foundation for the Arts; City of Edmonton; Edmonton Arts Council
Activities: Presenting theatre productions; Offering educational programs, workshops, & special event performances
Chief Officer(s):
Leanne Koziak, Artistic Director

Vintage Locomotive Society Inc.
c/o The Vintage Locomotive Society Inc., PO Box 33021, RPO Polo Park, Winnipeg MB R3G 3N4
Tel: 204-832-5259; *Fax:* 866-751-2348
info@pdcrailway.com
www.pdcrailway.com
www.facebook.com/The-Prairie-Dog-Central-Railway-194984377257515
Also Known As: Prairie Dog Central Steam Train
Overview: A small local charitable organization founded in 1968
Mission: To collect, restore & maintain steam locomotives & rolling stock of the early twentieth-century; To provide a source of historical information relating to the origin & past operation of acquired equipment & buildings
Finances: *Annual Operating Budget:* $250,000-$500,000
170 volunteer(s)
Membership: 170; *Fees:* $25 full; $15 junior; $40 family; *Committees:* Restoration-Locomotive; Restoration-Coaches; Painting; Sign Work; Public Relations; Advertising; Photography; Operations & Maintenance
Activities: *Speaker Service:* Yes
Chief Officer(s):
Paul Newsome, General Manager

Vintage Road Racing Association (VRRA)
c/o Yanie Veilleux, 570 RG Bellevue, Sainte-Victoire-de-Sorel QC J0G 1T0
Tel: 514-924-3615
Other Communication: Alt. E-mail: vrramembership@gmail.com
info@vrra.ca
www.vrra.ca
www.facebook.com/vrra.ca
twitter.com/VRRACANADA
Overview: A medium-sized national organization founded in 1980
Mission: To promote & maintain the sport & traditions of racing classic & vintage machines
Membership: *Fees:* $75 racing member; $30 non-racing member; *Member Profile:* Amateur & ex-professional racers; mechanics; bike builders; bike owners; racing fans
Activities: Races; newsletter
Chief Officer(s):
Miles Holden, President
elvisholden@icloud.com
Dominic Aubry, Vice-President
dominic413@hotmail.com
Yanie Veilleux, Membership Secretary
Awards:
• Rookie of the Year
• Most Improved Rider
• President's Award
• Most Meritorious Award
• Roger Beaumont Award
• Dorman Diesel Award
• Mary McCaw Award
• Sportsman of the Year Award
• Winner of the #1 Plate
• The Peter Sheppard Women's Trophy
• The John McCaw Memorial Sportsman Award
• Sidecar Trophy
• Castrol Cup
• HB Cycle Award
• Period 4 Formula 2 Trophy
• Steve Crover Award
Publications:
• The Baffled Muffler [a publication of the Vintage Road Racing Association]
Type: Newsletter

Vintners Quality Alliance (VQA)
#1601, 1 Yonge St., Toronto ON M5E 1E5
Tel: 416-367-2002; *Fax:* 416-367-4044
info@vqaontario.ca
www.vqaontario.ca
Also Known As: VQA Ontario
Overview: A medium-sized national organization founded in 1989

Mission: To establish standards of quality & designations for wines produced in Ontario
Finances: *Annual Operating Budget:* $250,000-$500,000
Staff Member(s): 4
Membership: 44 institutional
Chief Officer(s):
Laurie Macdonald, Executive Director
laurie.macdonald@vqaontario.ca
Katherina Radcliffe, Manager, Communications
katherina.radcliffe@vqaontario.ca

Viol-secours inc.
3293 - 1e av, Québec QC G1L 3R2
Tél: 418-522-2120; *Téléc:* 418-522-2130
info@violsecours.qc.ca
www.violsecours.qc.ca
Aperçu: *Dimension:* petite; *Envergure:* locale; Organisme sans but lucratif; fondée en 1976
Mission: Venir en aide à toute femme, adolescente ou enfant ayant subi une situation d'agression à caractère sexuel en offrant divers services: intervention téléphonique, accompagnement médico-légal et juridique, suivi individuel et de groupe
Affiliation(s): Regroupement québécois des CALACS

Virden & District Chamber of Commerce *See* Virden Community Chamber of Commerce

Virden Community Arts Council *See* Arts Mosaic

Virden Community Chamber of Commerce
PO Box 899, 425 - 6th Ave. South, Virden MB R0M 2C0
Tel: 204-851-1551
info@virdenchamber.ca
www.virdenchamber.ca
Previous Name: Virden & District Chamber of Commerce
Overview: A small local organization
Mission: To support & serve area businesses
Member of: Manitoba Chamber of Commerce
Affiliation(s): Virden Wallace Community Development Corp.; Virden Employment Skills Centre Inc.; Virden Agricultural Society; Virden Indoor Rodeo
Finances: *Annual Operating Budget:* Less than $50,000; *Funding Sources:* Membership dues; grants
16 volunteer(s)
Membership: 100; *Fees:* Schedule available; *Committees:* Budget; Constitution & Incorporation; Membership; Promotion; Sign; Special Events; Western Rodeo
Activities: Organizing & promoting spring & Christmas events
Chief Officer(s):
Dave Wowk, President

Viscount Cultural Council Inc. (VCC)
PO Box 186, 293 Mountain Ave., Neepawa MB R0J 1H0
Tel: 204-476-3232
Other Communication: VCCBoard1@gmail.com
viscount@mts.net
www.neepawavcc.ca
www.facebook.com/profile.php?id=100001507473370
Also Known As: Manawaka Gallery
Overview: A small local charitable organization founded in 1976
Mission: To enrich the leisure time of the citizens of Neepawa & the surrounding area by offering instruction in visual & performing arts & crafts by operating an art gallery & by bringing performing artists to the community
Member of: Manitoba Arts Network
Finances: *Annual Operating Budget:* $50,000-$100,000
Staff Member(s): 1; 12 volunteer(s)
Membership: 150-200; *Fees:* $10 student; $12 adult; $20 family; *Committees:* Exhibition; Performance; Craft Sale; Personnel; Program
Activities: Craft sale, Nov.; music lessons; dance lessons; workshops on quilting; drawing
Chief Officer(s):
Brenda Kryschuk, Administrator
Awards:
• VCC Art Award

Vision Institute of Canada (VIC)
#205, 4025 Yonge St., Toronto ON M2P 2E3
Tel: 416-224-2273; *Fax:* 416-224-9234
www.visioninstitutecanada.com
Previous Name: Optometric Institute of Toronto
Overview: A medium-sized national charitable organization founded in 1981
Mission: To improve the quality of vision care in the community; To provide eye & vision care to persons with special needs

Canadian Associations / Vision of Love Ministry - Canada

Finances: Funding Sources: Fundraising; corporate; OHIP billings
Activities: Internships: Yes; *Speaker Service:* Yes; *Library:* Bobier-Fisher-Lyle Vision Science Library; by appointment
Chief Officer(s):
Paul Chris, Executive Director
Catherine Chiarelli, Director, Clinical Services
Meetings/Conferences:
• Vision Institute of Canada 2018 Conference, 2018
Scope: National

Vision Mondiale *See* World Vision Canada

Vision of Love Ministry - Canada
ON
info@visionoflove.ca
www.visionoflove.ca
Also Known As: Vision 2000
Overview: A small provincial organization founded in 1996
Mission: To manifest God's love & enrich the local Catholic faith; To share time & musical & artistic talent at churches & Christian gatherings, especially within the Catholic Charismatic Renewal & lay organizations
Affiliation(s): Archdiocese of Toronto; Renewal Ministries CCRER/CCRSO; Radio Maria; Mission SOS - Toronto; Living Waters and Fr. Trevor Nathasingh - Trinidad; Multi-Cultural Christian Communities
Finances: *Funding Sources:* Sponsorships
Membership: 30+; *Member Profile:* Members are part of a Christian community of artists, who desire to live the contemplative Christian faith & serve with love, through music & the arts; Participants must acknowledge "Jesus Christ is Lord"
Activities: Providing music & worship with the arts for Catholic liturgies, renewal programs, pastoral groups, parishes, churches, & youth; Offering praise & worship music in a range of styles, such as rock, blues, jazz, folk, Gospel, Latin, & reggae; Producing CDs & DVDs; Tutoring; Providing Christian artwork
Chief Officer(s):
Danny Nelson, Contact
danny@visionoflove.ca

VISION TV
64 Jefferson Ave., Toronto ON M6K 1Y4
Tel: 416-368-3194; *Fax:* 416-368-9774
Toll-Free: 888-321-2567; *TTY:* 416-216-6311
www.visiontv.ca
www.facebook.com/visiontelevision
twitter.com/visiontv
Overview: A medium-sized national charitable organization founded in 1988
Mission: To air multi-faith, multicultural & family-oriented entertainment
Member of: Canadian Association of Broadcasters; North American Interfaith Network
Affiliation(s): North American Broadcasters Association
Finances: *Funding Sources:* Sale of airtime; Advertising; Cable fees
3 volunteer(s)
Chief Officer(s):
Znaimer Moses, Executive Producer

Visions of Science Network for Learning (VoSNL)
#300, 585 Dundas St. East, Toronto ON M5A 3B7
Tel: 416-266-6464
info@vosnl.org
www.vosnl.org
www.facebook.com/visionsofscience
twitter.com/visionsofsci
Overview: A small local charitable organization
Mission: To provide educational advancement opportunities in the science, technology, engineering, & mathematics (STEM) fields for low-income & marginalized youth
Activities: Offering STEM learning programs & initiatives; *Awareness Events:* Visionary Gala
Chief Officer(s):
Eugenia Duodu, Chief Executive Officer
eugenia@vosnl.org
Trisha Hosein, Manager, Programs
trisha@vosnl.org

Visual Artists Newfoundland & Labrador (VANL-CARFAC)
Devon House, 59 Duckworth St., St. John's NL A1C 1E6
Tel: 709-738-7303; *Fax:* 709-738-7304
Toll-Free: 877-738-7303
vanlcarfac@gmail.com

vanl-carfac.com
twitter.com/VisualArtistsNL
Overview: A small provincial organization overseen by Canadian Artists' Representation
Mission: To improve the socio-economic statuses of artists
Membership: *Committees:* Advocacy
Chief Officer(s):
Dave Andrews, Executive Director
Awards:
• The Long Haul Award
; *Amount:* $1,000 + lifetime membership
• The Large Year Award
; *Amount:* $1,000
• The Emerging Visual Artist Award
; *Amount:* $1,000
• The Kippy Goins Award
; *Amount:* Original artwork by Michael Pittman
• The Critical Eye Award
; *Amount:* $1,000

Visual Arts Nova Scotia (VANS)
1113 Marginal Rd., Halifax NS B3H 4P7
Tel: 902-423-4694; *Fax:* 902-422-0881
Toll-Free: 866-225-8267
vans@visualarts.ns.ca
www.visualarts.ns.ca
www.facebook.com/VisualArtsNovaScotia
twitter.com/visualartsns
Overview: A medium-sized provincial charitable organization founded in 1976
Mission: To promote a better understanding of arts & artists in Nova Scotia; to provide practical assistance to artists; to act in an advisory capacity to public & private interests
Member of: Canadian Conference of the Arts; Cultural Federations of Nova Scotia; Nova Scotia Cultural Network; Art Gallery of NS
Affiliation(s): Nova Scotia College of Art & Design; Visual Arts of Ontario; Canadian Conference of the Arts
Finances: *Funding Sources:* Fundraising; Membership; Programs; Grants
Staff Member(s): 3
Membership: *Fees:* $40 individual; $60 group; $75 corporate; $35 senior; $30 student; $55 family; $45 international; *Member Profile:* Working artists; art students; educators; critics; curators; galleries & corporate patrons
Activities: Exhibitions; Information; Slide Registry; Equipment Rentals; Workshops; *Library:* Video & Slide Library, Resource Centre; Open to public by appointment
Chief Officer(s):
Briony Carros, Executive Director
director@visualarts.ns.ca

Vitesse
#210, 359 Terry Fox Dr., Ottawa ON K2K 2E7
Tel: 613-254-9880; *Fax:* 613-254-9881
info@vitesse.ca
www.vitesse.ca
Also Known As: Re-Skilling Canada/Réorientation professionnelle Canada
Overview: A small provincial organization
Mission: Retrains & re-skills science & engineering graduates to take advantage of current & emerging opportunities in software engineering, photonics, bioinformatics, microelectronics, wireless communications, & related fields
Chief Officer(s):
Hamid Rahbar, President & CEO
hamid.rahbar@vitesse.ca

Vividata
Tel: 416-961-3205
info@vividata.ca
www.vividata.ca
Merged from: Print Measurement Bureau; NADbank
Overview: A medium-sized national organization founded in 2014
Mission: To conduct research on the topics of print readership, non-print media exposure, product usage & lifestyles.
Membership: 550+ companies; *Fees:* Schedule available
Activities: Conducting Canada-wide surveys; Delivering a database of consumer demographics
Chief Officer(s):
Donald Williams, Director, Research
donald@vividata.ca
Tosha Kirk, Manager, Client Services
tosha@vividata.ca

Vocational & Rehabilitation Research Institute *See* Vecova Centre for Disability Services & Research

Vocational Rehabilitation Association of Canada (VRA Canada)
PO Box 370, #3, 247 Barr St., Renfrew ON K7V 1J6
Fax: 613-432-6840
Toll-Free: 888-876-9992
www.vracanada.com
www.facebook.com/VRACanada
twitter.com/VRACanada
Previous Name: Canadian Association of Rehabilitation Professionals Inc.
Overview: A small national organization founded in 1970
Mission: To support members in promoting & providing vocational & pre-vocational rehabilitation services
Member of: Commission on Rehabilitation Counselor Certification
Affiliation(s): Canadian Association for Vocational Evaluation & Work Adjustment
Finances: *Funding Sources:* Membership fees
Membership: *Fees:* $275 associate; $325 professional; $200 new graduate; $137.50 student; *Member Profile:* Vocational rehabilitation professionals
Activities: *Rents Mailing List:* Yes
Chief Officer(s):
Tricia Gueulette, President
Meetings/Conferences:
• Vocational Rehabilitation Association of Canada 2018 National Conference, May, 2018, Four Points Hotel, Kingston, ON
Scope: National

Alberta Society
Calgary AB
vrac.ab@gmail.com
Chief Officer(s):
Shelley Langstaff, President

Atlantic Society
PO Box 757, 14 Weymouth Street, Charlottetown PE C1A 7L7
Tel: 902-569-7730; *Fax:* 902-368-6359
amaxwell@wcb.pe.ca
www.vraatlantic.com
Chief Officer(s):
Ann Maxwell, BBA, RRP, President

British Columbia Society
#102, 211 Columbia St., Vancouver BC V6A 2R5
Tel: 604-681-0296; *Fax:* 604-305-0424
office@vracanadabc.ca
www.vracanadabc.ca
Chief Officer(s):
Claire Benson-Mandl, President

Manitoba Society
VRAC Manitoba, c/o 299 Truro Street, Winnipeg MB R3J 2A2
Tel: 204-799-8842
kerrihiebert@mts.net
vracanada.com/manitoba.php
Chief Officer(s):
Kerri Hiebert, Contact

Ontario Society
#200, 411 Richmond St. East, Toronto ON M5A 3S5
Tel: 647-875-8046
office@vracanadaon.com
www.vracanadaon.com
Chief Officer(s):
Ravi Persaud, President

Saskatchewan Society
1440 Broadway Ave., Regina SK S4P 1E2
Tel: 306-522-8571
Chief Officer(s):
Rhonda Teichreb, Contact

Voice for Animals Humane Society
PO Box 68119, 162 Bonnie Doon Mall, Edmonton AB T6C 4N6
Tel: 780-490-0905; *Fax:* 780-922-5287
info@v4a.org
www.v4a.org
Also Known As: V4A
Previous Name: Voice for Animals Society
Overview: A small provincial organization founded in 1997
Mission: To raise awareness of animal cruelty issues through education, lobbying, speakers & peaceful protests
Member of: Zoocheck Canada
Affiliation(s): World Society for the Protection of Animals; Canadian Coalition for Farm Animals
Finances: *Annual Operating Budget:* Less than $50,000

30 volunteer(s)
Membership: 500; *Fees:* $20
Activities: Animal protection & advocacy
Chief Officer(s):
Tove Reece, Contact
treece@v4a.org

Voice for Animals Society *See* Voice for Animals Humane Society

VOICE for Hearing Impaired Children
#302, 177 Danforth Ave., Toronto ON M4K 1N2
Tel: 416-487-7719; *Fax:* 416-487-7423
Toll-Free: 866-779-5144; *TTY:* 416-487-7719
info@voicefordeafkids.com
www.voicefordeafkids.com
www.facebook.com/VOICEforHearingImpairedChildren
twitter.com/VOICE4DEAFKIDS
www.youtube.com/channel/UCtqS6zWzpmW9Tq6DRRbZubw
Overview: A small provincial charitable organization founded in 1972
Mission: To ensure that all hearing impaired children have the right to develop their ability to listen & speak & have access to services which will enable them to listen & speak
Member of: Canadian Society of Association Executives
Affiliation(s): Alexander Graham Bell Association
Finances: *Annual Operating Budget:* $250,000-$500,000; *Funding Sources:* Private - foundations, corporations, individuals, special events; Golf Tournament & Theatre Night
Staff Member(s): 4; 200 volunteer(s)
Membership: 1,000 individual; *Fees:* $65; *Member Profile:* Parents & professionals in support of deaf & hard of hearing children; *Committees:* Education; Health
Activities: Service provider for Ontario Infant Hearing Program; *Speaker Service:* Yes; *Library:* by appointment Not open to public

Voice of English-speaking Québec (VEQ) / La Voix des anglophones de Québec
Pavilion Jeffery Hale, #2141, 1270, ch Sainte-Foy, Québec QC G1S 2M4
Tel: 418-683-2366; *Fax:* 418-688-3273
info@veq.ca
www.veq.ca
www.facebook.com/VoiceofEnglishspeakingQuebec
twitter.com/VEQ_QC
Overview: A small provincial organization founded in 1981
Mission: To preserve & promote a dynamic English-speaking community in the Québec City & Chaudière-Appalaches regions
Finances: *Funding Sources:* Canadian Heritage's Official Languages Programme
Staff Member(s): 2; 50 volunteer(s)
Membership: 1,300+
Activities: Demographic research
Chief Officer(s):
Brigitte Wellens, Executive Director
Ellie Fleming, Manager, Operations

Voices for Children
#207, 12 Birch Ave., Toronto ON M4V 1C8
Tel: 416-489-5485; *Fax:* 416-489-5204
Toll-Free: 877-489-5485
info@voicesforchildren.ca
www.offordcentre.com/VoicesWebsite
Overview: A small provincial charitable organization
Mission: To speak up for children & youth in Ontario
Finances: *Funding Sources:* Child Development Institute; Margaret & Wallace McCain Family Foundation; Scotia Capital; Donations
Staff Member(s): 6
Chief Officer(s):
Cathy Vine, Executive Director
cathy@voicesforchildren.ca

Voices: Manitoba's Youth in Care Network
61 Juno St., 3rd Fl., Winnipeg MB R3A 1T1
Tel: 204-982-4956; *Fax:* 204-982-4950
Toll-Free: 866-982-4956
info@voices.mb.ca
www.voices.mb.ca
www.facebook.com/VoicesMB
twitter.com/VoicesMYICN
Overview: A medium-sized provincial organization founded in 1995 overseen by Youth in Care Canada
Mission: To advocate for & support youth in or from government care in Manitoba
Affiliation(s): Boys & Girls Clubs of Winnipeg

Staff Member(s): 4
Membership: *Member Profile:* Individuals between 12 & 30 years of age in or from government care in Manitoba
Activities: Raising awareness of the challenges youth-in-care face through public education; Working with child welfare professionals to improve system conditions; Providing outreach & support to youth who have recently come into care
Chief Officer(s):
Marie Christian, Program Director
maire@voices.mb.ca

Voile Canada *See* Sail Canada

Voitures anciennes du Québec inc. (VAQ)
#200, 270, boul Sir-Wilfred-Laurier, Beloeil QC J3G 447
Tél: 514-990-9111; *Téléc:* 450-464-5368
voituresanciennes@bellnet.ca
www.vaq.qc.ca
Aperçu: *Dimension:* moyenne; *Envergure:* provinciale; fondée en 1974
Mission: Préservation de la voiture ancienne au Québec.
Finances: *Budget de fonctionnement annuel:* $50,000-$100,000
Membre(s) du personnel: 1; 15 bénévole(s)
Membre: 2 000+; *Montant de la cotisation:* 59.95$
Activités: Expositions de voitures de collection durant la période estivales et publication d'un magazine mensuel de 56 pages en couleurs
Membre(s) du bureau directeur:
Léo Gravelle, Président
Marie-Pier Charest, Coordonnatrice

La Voix des anglophones de Québec *See* Voice of English-speaking Québec

Volkssport Association of Alberta (VAA)
PO Box 131, #3, 11 Bellerose Dr., St Albert AB T8N 5C9
Tel: 780-998-1033
walksalot2@shaw.ca
www.walkalberta.ca
Overview: A small provincial charitable organization founded in 1987
Mission: To promote fun, fitness, & friendship through physical activity, specifically walking
Finances: *Annual Operating Budget:* Less than $50,000
Membership: 100-499; *Committees:* Advertising & Publicity; Alberta Materials; Alberta Sanction; Booklet; Event Calendar; Event; Fundraising; Merchandise Sales; Newcomer Program; Newsletter; Public Relations & Communications; Refreshment/Social
Activities: Group walks; swimming, cycling, & skiing events
Chief Officer(s):
Glenda Palmer, President

Volkssport Association of British Columbia (VABC)
9350 Cinnamon Dr., Surrey BC V3V 1V2
Tel: 604-584-1900
vabc@volkssportingbc.ca
www.volkssportingbc.ca
Overview: A small provincial organization
Mission: To promote health, fitness, & friendship through stress-free exercise
Member of: Canadian Volkssport Federation
Affiliation(s): Victoria International Walking Festival Society
Membership: *Committees:* Sanction; Webpage; Materials; Publicity & Marketing
Activities: Group walks
Chief Officer(s):
Brenda Dudfield, President, 604-584-1900
dudfield@shaw.ca
Publications:
• Volkssporting BC [a publication of the Volksport Association of British Columbia]
Type: Newsletter; *Editor:* Janet Lewis

Volleyball Alberta
Percy Page Centre, 11759 Groat Rd., Edmonton AB T5M 3K6
Tel: 780-415-1703; *Fax:* 780-415-1700
info@volleyballalberta.ca
www.volleyballalberta.ca
www.facebook.com/VolleyballAlberta
twitter.com/volleyballab
www.youtube.com/channel/UCofbTw7zPP30PVt8pzDrPAw
Overview: A medium-sized provincial charitable organization founded in 1974 overseen by Volleyball Canada
Mission: To promote volleyball in Alberta; To provide competitive opportunities for members
Affiliation(s): Federation of Outdoor Volleyball Associations

Staff Member(s): 11
Membership: *Committees:* Athlete Development; Business Development; High Performance; Leadership; Nominations/Awards
Activities: *Internships:* Yes; *Rents Mailing List:* Yes
Chief Officer(s):
Terry Gagnon, Executive Director, 587-273-1513
tgagnon@volleyballalberta.ca

Volleyball BC
Harry Jerome Sports Centre, 7564 Barnet Hwy., Burnaby BC V5A 1E7
Tel: 604-291-2007; *Fax:* 604-291-2602
www.volleyballbc.org
www.facebook.com/volleyballbc
twitter.com/VolleyballBC
instagram.com/volleyballbc
Also Known As: British Columbia Volleyball Association
Overview: A medium-sized provincial organization founded in 1965 overseen by Volleyball Canada
Mission: To promote volleyball in British Columbia; To provide competitive opportunities for members
Staff Member(s): 17
Membership: *Committees:* Beach Players; Finance & Audit; Governance; High Performance; Nominations; Regional Development
Chief Officer(s):
Chris Densmore, Executive Director, 604-291-2007 Ext. 223
execdirector@volleyballbc.org
Chris Berglund, Director, Technical & High Performance, 604-291-2007 Ext. 222
cberglund@volleyballbc.org
Dave Brewin, Manager, Marketing & Communications, 604-291-2007 Ext. 226
communications@volleyballbc.org
Awards:
• Volleyball Excellence Awards
• Ray Lepp Scholarship
Award is offered to one female & one male athlete who meet eligibility criteria *Eligibility:* An individual committed to a year of eligibility for volleyball at a BC Athlete Assistance-funded post-secondary institution; eligible nominees must demonstrate significant potential & show promise to compete at the national team level; *Amount:* 2 at $1,000

Volleyball Canada (VC)
National Office, #1A, 1084 Kenaston St., Ottawa ON K1B 3P5
Tel: 613-748-5681; *Fax:* 613-748-5727
info@volleyball.ca
www.volleyball.ca
www.facebook.com/VolleyballCanada
twitter.com/VBallCanada
instagram.com/volleyballcanada
Also Known As: Canadian Volleyball Association
Overview: A large national charitable organization founded in 1953
Mission: To lead the growth of & excellence in the sport of volleyball for all Canadians
Affiliation(s): International Volleyball Federation; Canadian Olympic Association; Coaching Association of Canada
Finances: *Funding Sources:* Membership dues; Fundraising; Merchandise & publications sale; Government; Sponsorships
Staff Member(s): 28
Membership: *Member Profile:* Athletes, officials; *Committees:* Domestic Development; National Championships; Sitting Volleyball; High Performance Management; National Referee; Alumni & Awards; National Registration Systems Project Management; National Registration System Operation Group; Nominations & Elections; Finance & Audit; Legal; Ethics; External Relations
Activities: Offering National Championships for Indoor & Beach Volleyball & National Team Challenge Cup (for Provincial Teams); Providing coaching certification & education programs; Producing publications & videos; Coordinating international & national officials programs; Hosting international events; Marketing & promoting volleyball to the corporate community & the media; *Internships:* Yes; *Rents Mailing List:* Yes
Chief Officer(s):
Mark Eckert, President & CEO, 613-748-5681 Ext. 225
meckert@volleyball.ca
Jackie Skender, Director, Communications, 613-748-5681 Ext. 226
jskender@volleyball.ca
Linden Leung, Director, Finance & Operations, 613-748-5681 Ext. 223
linden@volleyball.ca

Canadian Associations / Volleyball New Brunswick

Lucie Leclerc, Office Manager, 613-748-5681 Ext. 236
lucie@volleyball.ca
Awards:
• Hall of Fame: Athlete, Builder, Coach, Referee, Team
Contact: Lucie Leclerc, Manager, National Office, E-mail: lucie@volleyball.ca

Volleyball New Brunswick
#13, 900 Hanwell Rd., Fredericton NB E3B 6A3
Tel: 506-451-1346; *Fax:* 506-451-1325
vnb@nb.aibn.com
www.vnb.nb.ca
www.facebook.com/volleyballnb
twitter.com/volleyballnb
www.instagram.com/volleyballnb
Also Known As: VNB
Overview: A medium-sized provincial organization overseen by Volleyball Canada
Mission: To promote volleyball in New Brunswick; To provide competitive opportunities for members
Staff Member(s): 2
Membership: *Fees:* Schedule available; *Committees:* Executive; Officials; Beach; Senior; Age Class; Female High Performance; Male High Performance; Coaching
Chief Officer(s):
Ryley Boldon, Executive Director
Rachelle Duguay, Coordinator, Programs, 506-878-3064
vnbcoordinator@nb.aibn.com

Volleyball Nova Scotia
5516 Spring Garden Rd., 4th Fl., Halifax NS B3J 1G6
Tel: 902-425-5606
vns@sportnovascotia.ca
www.volleyballnovascotia.ca
www.facebook.com/Volleyballnovascotia
twitter.com/volleyballNS
Overview: A medium-sized provincial organization founded in 1965 overseen by Volleyball Canada
Mission: To promote volleyball in Nova Scotia; To provide competitive opportunities for members
Staff Member(s): 3
Chief Officer(s):
Jason Trepanier, Executive Director, 902-425-5450 Ext. 322
vns@sportnovascotia.ca
Shane St-Louis, Director, Technical, 902-425-5450 Ext. 514
volleyballtd@sportnovascotia.ca

Volleyball Nunavut
PO Box 208, Iqaluit NU X0A 0H0
Tel: 250-718-8411; *Fax:* 250-984-7600
volleyballnunavut.ca
www.facebook.com/VolleyballNunavut
Overview: A medium-sized provincial organization founded in 1999 overseen by Volleyball Canada
Mission: To promote volleyball in Nunavut & provide programs throughout the territory
Member of: Sport & Recreation Nunavut
Finances: *Funding Sources:* Sport & Recreation Nunavut
Chief Officer(s):
Scott Schutz, Executive Director
scott@volleyballnunavut.ca

Volleyball Prince Edward Island
PO Box 302, Charlottetown PE C1A 7K7
Tel: 902-569-0583; *Fax:* 902-368-4548
Toll-Free: 800-247-6712
Other Communication: Toll Free Fax: 1-800-235-5687
www.volleyballpei.org
www.facebook.com/volleyballpei
Overview: A small provincial organization overseen by Volleyball Canada
Mission: To promote volleyball in PEI; To provide competitive opportunities for members
Affiliation(s): Sport PEI
Finances: *Funding Sources:* Government grants; Membership fees; Fund-raising
Membership: *Member Profile:* Coaches & players
Activities: *Rents Mailing List:* Yes
Chief Officer(s):
Cheryl Crozier, Executive Director, 902-569-0583
cgcrozier@sportpei.pe.ca

Volleyball Yukon
Sport Yukon Building, 4061 - 4th Ave., Whitehorse YT Y1A 1H1
Fax: 867-667-4237
volleyballyukon@gmail.com
www.volleyballyukon.com

Overview: A small provincial organization overseen by Volleyball Canada
Mission: To promote volleyball in the Yukon; To provide competitive opportunities for its members
Chief Officer(s):
D'Arcy Hill, Executive Director, 867-333-2424
darcy.j.hill@gmail.com

Vols d'espoir *See* Hope Air

Voluntas Dei Institute *Voir* Institut Voluntas Dei

Volunteer Alberta
Birks Bldg., #217, 10113 - 104 St., Edmonton AB T5J 1A1
Tel: 780-482-3300; *Fax:* 780-482-3310
Toll-Free: 877-915-6336
volab@volunteeralberta.ab.ca
www.volunteeralberta.ab.ca
Overview: A medium-sized provincial organization
Mission: Building the capacity of the voluntary sector by strategically connecting leaders, organizations, & networks to ensure Albertans are engaged in creating vibrant & progressive communities
Membership: *Fees:* $50 affiliate; $80 associate; $125 volunteer centre
Chief Officer(s):
Kim McClymont, President
Angela Keibel, Vice-President

Volunteer BC
c/o Volunteer Richmond Information Services, #190, 7000 Minoru Blvd., Vancouver BC V6Y 3Z5
Tel: 604-873-5877
volunteerbc@gmail.com
www.volunteerbc.bc.ca
twitter.com/volunteerbc
Overview: A medium-sized provincial organization
Mission: To strengthen the growth & development of voluntary action in British Columbia
Membership: *Fees:* $25 individual; $35 volunteer centres/voluntary organizations; *Member Profile:* Volunteer centres; provincial voluntary organizations; individuals
Chief Officer(s):
Lawrie Portigal, President
Stacy Ashton, Vice-President

Volunteer Bureau of Montreal *Voir* Centre d'action bénévole de Montréal

Volunteer Canada / Bénévoles Canada
#201, 309 Cooper St., Ottawa ON K2P 0G5
Tel: 613-231-4371; *Fax:* 613-231-6725
Toll-Free: 800-670-0401
info@volunteer.ca
volunteer.ca
www.facebook.com/VolunteerCanada
twitter.com/VolunteerCanada
www.youtube.com/VolunteerCanada
Previous Name: Canadian Association of Volunteer Bureaux Centres
Overview: A medium-sized national organization
Mission: To support volunteerism & civic participation through special projects & programs
Staff Member(s): 20
Membership: 1,200+ members; *Fees:* $125 individual/organization; $100 volunteer centre; $500 business
Activities: Canada Volunteerism Initiative; *Awareness Events:* National Volunteer Week, April; International Volunteer Day; International Volunteer Managers Day
Chief Officer(s):
Paula Speevak, President & CEO

Volunteer Central Society
#115, 4818 50 Ave., Red Deer AB T4N 4A3
Tel: 403-346-3710
info@volunteercentral.ca
www.volunteercentral.ca
www.linkedin.com/company/volunteer-red-deer
twitter.com/volcentral
www.instagram.com/volcentral
Also Known As: Volunteer Central
Overview: A small local charitable organization
Mission: To deliver volunteer services to non-profit & community service organizations
Finances: *Funding Sources:* Provincial government; corporate sponsors
Chief Officer(s):
Kay Kenny, Chair

Awards:
• VolunTeen Awards

Volunteer Centre of Charlotte County Inc.
PO Box 271, 199 Union St., St Stephen NB E3L 2X2
Tel: 506-466-4995; *Fax:* 506-465-0988
Overview: A small local organization
Member of: Canadian Association of Food Banks; Canadian Association of Volunteer Centres
Finances: *Funding Sources:* Donations
Staff Member(s): 2
Activities: Services for under-employed families

Volunteer Centre of Guelph/Wellington
#1, 46 Cork St. East, Guelph ON N1H 2W8
Tel: 519-822-0912; *Fax:* 519-822-1389
Toll-Free: 866-693-3318
info@volunteerguelphwellington.on.ca
www.volunteerguelphwellington.on.ca
www.linkedin.com/company/volunteer-centre-of-guelph-wellington
www.facebook.com/VolunteerGW
twitter.com/volunteergw
Previous Name: Guelph Information
Overview: A small local charitable organization founded in 2001 overseen by InformOntario
Mission: The Centre strives to build a vibrant, volunteer-based community. It offers programs to assist non-profit organizations find & maintain a force of capable volunteer workers.
Finances: *Funding Sources:* Federal, proviincial, municipal governments; foundations & corporations; public donations
Staff Member(s): 7
Membership: *Fees:* $83 individual; $94 agnecy affiliate; $193 agency
Activities: Leadership program for non-profit management; Community Information Guelph, a community news database to connect programs & volunteers; Snow Angels, to help senior/disabled people with snow removal; *Awareness Events:* National Volunteer Week; *Rents Mailing List:* Yes; *Library:* Volunteer Centre Resource Library; Open to public
Chief Officer(s):
Christine Oldfield, Executive Director, 519-822-0912 Ext. 222
coldfield@volunteerguelphwellington.on.ca

Volunteer Circle of the National Gallery of Canada / Cercle des bénévoles du Musée des beaux-arts du Canada
c/o National Gallery of Canada, PO Box 427, Stn. A, 380 Sussex Dr., Ottawa ON K1N 9N4
Tel: 613-990-0130
info@gallery.ca
www.gallery.ca/en/about/volunteers.php
Overview: A small national charitable organization founded in 1958
Mission: To raise funds for the National Gallery; to provide activities for members & to provide ancillary volunteer assistance to the Gallery
Member of: Canadian Museum Association
Finances: *Annual Operating Budget:* $50,000-$100,000
Staff Member(s): 1; 300 volunteer(s)
Membership: 100-499
Awards:
• Volunteer Awards
Given annually for 100 hrs., 500 hrs, 1,000 hrs, 2,000 hrs cumulative volunteer service

Volunteer Grandparents (VIP)
#203, 2101 Holdom Ave., Burnaby BC V5B 0A4
Tel: 604-736-8271; *Fax:* 604-294-6814
info@volunteergrandparents.ca
www.volunteergrandparents.ca
Also Known As: Volunteers for Intergenerational Programs Society
Previous Name: Volunteer Grandparents Society of Canada
Overview: A small local charitable organization founded in 1973
Mission: To support & encourage multigenerational relationships & the concept of extended family by matching screened volunteers (50+) with families with children between the age of 3-14
Member of: Volunteer Vancouver; BC Council of Families; Go Volunteer.ca
Affiliation(s): Volunteer Burnaby
Finances: *Annual Operating Budget:* Less than $50,000; *Funding Sources:* Provincial Gaming
Staff Member(s): 1; 100 volunteer(s)
Membership: 1-99; *Fees:* $5; *Committees:* Executive

Activities: Family Match Program; school grandparent program; ambassador program
Chief Officer(s):
Stephen Sjoberg, President

Volunteer Grandparents Society of Canada See Volunteer Grandparents

Volunteer Management Professionals of Canada (VMPC) / Professionnels en gestion de bénévoles du Canada (PGBC)
#1101, 60 Richmond St. East, Toronto ON M5C 1N8
www.vmpc.ca
Overview: A small national licensing organization founded in 1983
Mission: To work towards the advancement of the volunteer resources management profession
Finances: Funding Sources: Membership fees
25 volunteer(s)
Membership: 425; Fees: $80; Committees: Advocacy & Professional Standards; Communications; Fund Development; Membership; Professional Development
Chief Officer(s):
Bobby Hrehoruk, President
president@vmpc.ca
Meetings/Conferences:
• 2018 Volunteer Management Professionals of Canada National Conference, May, 2018, Winnipeg, MB
Scope: National

Volunteer Red Deer
Community Village, 4728 Ross St., Red Deer AB T4N 1X2
Tel: 403-346-4636; Fax: 403-340-8193
info@volunteerreddeer.ca
volunteerreddeer.ca
Previous Name: Red Deer Landlord & Tenant Services
Overview: A small local organization
Mission: To meet the needs of the citizens of Red Deer & Central Alberta through strengthening the non-profit sector
Finances: Funding Sources: Provincial government; municipal government
Chief Officer(s):
Bill Farr, Chair

Vonda Chamber of Commerce
c/o Vonda Hometown Insurance Brokers, PO Box 285, Vonda SK S0K 4N0
Tel: 306-221-0559
Overview: A small local organization

Voyageur Trail Association (VTA)
PO Box 20040, 150 Churchill Blvd., Sault Ste Marie ON P6A 6W3
Toll-Free: 877-393-4003
info@voyageurtrail.ca
www.voyageurtrail.ca
www.facebook.com/voyageurtrailassociation
Overview: A small local charitable organization founded in 1973
Mission: The Voyageur Trail Association remains today as a trail building and maintenance organization to a trail building-and-hiking organization with several public outings held throughout the year in various clubs
Member of: Hike Ontario
Affiliation(s): Great Lakes Forestry Research; Pukaskwa National Park; Lake Superior Provincial Park; Rainbow Falls Provincial Park; Nipigon River Recreational Trail; Charity Village
Finances: Funding Sources: Membership fees & donations
Membership: Fees: $30 family; $25 adult; $10 student
Activities: Trail follows the clear waters of North Channel to the cold granite coast of Lake Superior (640 km completed; 470+ km planned)
Chief Officer(s):
Gail Andrew, Treasurer
Susan Graham, President

Vrac environnement group d'action et de recherche en développement durable
7003, rue Hutchison, Montréal QC H3N 1Y9
Tél: 514-270-4049; Téléc: 514-270-8428
info@vracenvironnement.org
www.vracenvironnement.org
Aperçu: Dimension: petite; Envergure: locale; fondée en 2008
Mission: D'améliorer la qualité de vie des Montréalais et Montréalaises en favorisant des pratiques de développement durable
Membre(s) du bureau directeur:

Simon Racine, Directeur général
sracine@vracenvironnement.org

Vraies femmes du Canada See REAL Women of Canada

Vrais Copains See Best Buddies Canada

Vues d'Afrique (Les Journées africaines et créoles). Voir Vues d'Afriques - Les Journées du cinéma africain et créole

Vues d'Afriques - Les Journées du cinéma africain et créole (VA)
#3100, 100, rue Sherbrooke est, Montréal QC H2X 1C3
Tél: 514-284-3322; Téléc: 514-845-0631
www.vuesdafrique.org
www.facebook.com/vuesdafrique
Nom précédent: Vues d'Afrique (Les Journées africaines et créoles).
Aperçu: Dimension: petite; Envergure: internationale; Organisme sans but lucratif; fondée en 1984
Mission: Est une force dans l'action nationale et internationale pour le soutien des cultures comme outil de développement harmonieux des sociétés du Nord et du Sud; organiser des activités grand public qui contribuent à faire connaître les cultures africaines et créoles, et développer des partenariats entre le Canada et les pays du Sud dans le domaine des industries culturelles
Membre de: Conseil des festivals jumelés
Finances: Budget de fonctionnement annuel: $500,000-$1.5 Million
Membre(s) du personnel: 15; 150 bénévole(s)
Membre: 1-99
Activités: Festival de films, avril; Stagiaires: Oui; Bibliothèque: IMPAC; rendez-vous
Prix, Bourses:
• Prix de la communication interculturelle documentaire
• Prix Vues d'Afrique
• Prix ONF
• Bourse pour la meilleure production indépendante
• Prix de la communication interculturelle long métrage
• Prix de la communication interculturelle court métrage
• Prix Images de Femmes

Vulcan & District Chamber of Commerce
PO Box 385, Vulcan AB T0L 2B0
www.vulcanchamber.ca
www.facebook.com/VulcanChamber
twitter.com/VulcanDChamber
Also Known As: Vulcan Business Development & Tourism
Overview: A small local organization
Mission: To promote, educate & develop Vulcan & district businesses & their community
Member of: Alberta Chamber of Commerce
Finances: Annual Operating Budget: Less than $50,000; Funding Sources: Membership fees; fund-raising
30 volunteer(s)
Membership: 40; Fees: $75; Member Profile: New or existing businesses; Committees: Tourism; Economic Development
Activities: Organizing events; Offering benefit programs & resources; Speaker Service: Yes; Rents Mailing List: Yes; Library: Economic Development Centre
Chief Officer(s):
Dwayne Hill, Chair
Tony Scott, Vice-Chair

Vulcan & District Fish & Game Club
PO Box 301, Vulcan AB T0L 2B0
Tel: 403-485-6744
Overview: A small local organization
Member of: Alberta Fish & Game Association
Chief Officer(s):
Doug McIntyre, Treasurer

Vulcan Business Development Society (VBDS)
PO Box 1205, 110 - 1st Ave. South, Vulcan AB T0L 2B0
Tel: 403-485-4100; Fax: 403-485-3143
www.vulcanbusiness.ca
Overview: A small local organization
Mission: To assist the existing businesses in their development and to encourage new businesses.
Finances: Funding Sources: Membership fees; fund-raising
Chief Officer(s):
Gordon Nelson, President
Paul Taylor, Vice-President

The W. Garfield Weston Foundation
c/o George Weston Ltd., #2001, 22 St. Clair Ave. East, Toronto ON M4T 2S3

info@westonfoundation.org
www.westonfoundation.org
Overview: A medium-sized national charitable organization
Mission: Focuses on education (through a scholarship & bursary program), conservation (via habitat conservation projects through national organizations only), & trustee-initiated grants (for which applications are not accepted)

W. Maurice Young Centre for Applied Ethics (CAE)
University of British Columbia, #227, 6356 Agricultural Rd., Vancouver BC V6T 1Z2
Tel: 604-822-2772; Fax: 604-822-8627
www.ethics.ubc.ca
Previous Name: Centre for Applied Ethics
Overview: A small local organization founded in 1993
Mission: To conduct research on health care practices, new technologies & business & professional procedures
Finances: Annual Operating Budget: $50,000-$100,000
Membership: 1-99
Activities: Research projects
Chief Officer(s):
David Silver, Director
david.silver@ubc.ca

Wabamun District Chamber of Commerce Society
PO Box 300, Wabamun AB T0E 2K0
Tel: 780-892-4773
wabamun.chamber@xplornet.com
www.facebook.com/WDCoC
Overview: A small local organization
Mission: To promote the commercial, social, civic & economic communities of the area
Chief Officer(s):
Vicki Specht, President

Wainwright & District Chamber of Commerce
PO Box 2997, #203, 1006 - 4th Ave., Wainwright AB T9W 1S9
Tel: 780-842-4910; Fax: 780-842-6061
exec@wdchamber.com
www.wdchamber.com
Overview: A small local organization founded in 1959
Mission: To improve the businesses in the region; To promote economic development; To protect the interests of members
Member of: Alberta Chambers of Commerce
Staff Member(s): 1
Membership: 200+
Chief Officer(s):
Stephanie Evans, President
Kelsey Robinson, Executive Director

Wakaw & District Board of Trade
PO Box 188, Wakaw SK S0K 4P0
www.townofwakaw.com/boardoftrade.html
Overview: A small local organization
Mission: Group of local Business Owners who work together with various clubs and organizations to promote the Town of Wakaw and its business community
Chief Officer(s):
Laurianne Osmak, President & Secretary, 306-233-5330
Sandi Draude, Vice-President

Waldorf School Association of Kelowna
429 Collett Rd., Kelowna BC V1W 1K6
Tel: 250-764-4130; Fax: 250-764-4139
info@kelownawaldorf.org
www.kelownawaldorf.org
www.facebook.com/kelownawaldorfschool
Also Known As: Kelowna Waldorf School
Overview: A small local organization founded in 1981
Staff Member(s): 16; 20 volunteer(s)
Membership: 35 individual
Chief Officer(s):
Dana Bodnar, Administrator

Walker Lynch Foundation
72 Railside Rd., Toronto ON M3A 1A3
Tel: 416-449-5464; Fax: 416-449-9165
Overview: A small national charitable organization
Chief Officer(s):
Walker Lynch, Contact

Walker Mineralogical Club (WMC)
c/o Department of Natural History, Royal Ontario Museum, 100 Queens Park, Toronto ON M5S 2C6
walkermineralogicalclub@gmail.com
www.walkermineralogicalclub.org
Overview: A small local organization founded in 1937

Member of: Central Canadian Federation of Mineralogical Societies
Finances: *Funding Sources:* Fundraising
Membership: *Fees:* $15 students (ages 14-18); $30 singles; $40 families; *Committees:* Auction; Banquet; Field Trip
Activities: Hosting monthly meetings featuring guest speakers with expertise in mineralogy or geology; Organizing field trips; Arranging an annual mineral specimen auction
Publications:
• Walker Club SourceBook [a publication of the Walker Mineralogical Club]
Type: Handbook
Profile: Information about club activities for new members of the Walker Mineralogical Club
• The Walker Mineralogical Club Newsletter
Type: Newsletter; *Frequency:* Monthly
Profile: Articles about mineralogy

Walkerton & District Chamber of Commerce *See* Walkerton Business Improvement Area

Walkerton & District Community Support Services *See* Community Living Walkerton & District

Walkerton Business Improvement Area
PO Box 1344, 101 Durham St., Walkerton ON N0G 2V0
Tel: 519-881-3413; *Fax:* 519-881-4009
info@walkertonbia.ca
walkertonbia.ca
Previous Name: Walkerton & District Chamber of Commerce
Overview: A small local organization founded in 1956
Mission: To foster & develop trade & commerce, & the further improvement of the economic, civic & social welfare of our district
Member of: Ontario Chamber of Commerce; Ontario Business Improvement Association
Affiliation(s): Ontario Chamber of Commerce
Finances: *Funding Sources:* Membership fees
Staff Member(s): 2
Membership: 300; *Fees:* $150; *Committees:* Brockton's Buskers Festival; Doors Open Walkerton & Area; Media & Marketing; Promotions; Santa Claus Parade; Special Events
Activities: Business improvement; town beautification; tourist guide; Santa Parade; *Library:* Walkerton Tourist Information Centre
Chief Officer(s):
Christine Brandt, Chamber Manager
Dwayne Kaster, President
Trent Heipel, Vice-President

Walkley Centre / Association des familles unies de la rue Walkley
665, ch de la Côte-St-Luc, Montréal QC H4V 1G8
Tel: 514-872-1391
walkley.center@gmail.com
www.facebook.com/pages/Walkley-Center-Centre-Walkley/206990426007754
Overview: A small local organization
Mission: Community Centre serving families in the Notre-Dame-de-Grâce borough of Montréal

Wallaceburg & District Chamber of Commerce
152 Duncan St., Wallaceburg ON N8A 4E2
Tel: 519-627-1443; *Fax:* 519-627-1485
Toll-Free: 888-545-0558
info@wallaceburgchamber.com
www.wallaceburgchamber.com
www.facebook.com/WallaceburgDistrictChamber
twitter.com/Wburgchamber
Overview: A small local organization
Mission: To act as the voice of business in Wallaceburg & district; To promote local businesses
Membership: *Fees:* Schedule available
Chief Officer(s):
Karen Debergh, President
Publications:
• Wallaceburg & District Chamber of Commerce Newsletter
Type: Newsletter

Wallaceburg & District Council for the Arts *See* Wallaceburg Arts Council

Wallaceburg & District Historical Society, Inc.
505 King St., Wallaceburg ON N8A 1J1
Tel: 519-627-8962; *Fax:* 519-627-9859
wallaceburg.museum@kent.net
www.kent.net/wallaceburg-museum
Overview: A small local charitable organization founded in 1973
Mission: To collect, preserve, research, exhibit, & intrepret a collection of historical artifacts
Member of: Ontario Museums Association; Ontario Historical Society; Architectural Conservancy of Ontario; Wallaceburg Chamber of Commerce; Heritage Sarnia-Lambton
Finances: *Annual Operating Budget:* $100,000-$250,000
Staff Member(s): 3; 122 volunteer(s)
Membership: 221; *Fees:* $15 single; $20 family
Activities: Operates the Wallaceburg & District Museum; *Library:* Open to public

Wallaceburg & Sydenham District Association for Community Living *See* Community Living Wallaceburg

Wallaceburg Arts Council
PO Box 20077, Stn. James St., Wallaceburg ON N8A 5G1
Tel: 519-627-1607
Previous Name: Wallaceburg & District Council for the Arts
Overview: A small local charitable organization founded in 1980
Mission: To stimulate awareness & appreciation for the arts in Wallaceburg & district by organizing, promoting, & operating shows for local artists, sponsoring appearance of provincial on-tour performers, coordinating planned cultural events, raising funds for operation of the Council &/or events it will support or create, supporting local art & artists, sponsoring, organizing or promoting clinics & workshops for benefit of local artists
Affiliation(s): Ontario Arts Council
Finances: *Annual Operating Budget:* Less than $50,000
Membership: 50; *Member Profile:* Divided into 4 classes: artists (amateur or professional) - produce any work of art or craft; patrons - appreciate artistic endeavours produced by others; junior patrons - 16 years of age or under & appreciate artistic endeavours; sponsors - interests similar to the Council
Chief Officer(s):
Dave Babbitt, Contact, 519-627-9803

Walpole Island Heritage Centre
RR#3, Wallaceburg ON N8A 4K9
Tel: 519-627-1475; *Fax:* 519-627-1530
Also Known As: Nin-Da-Waab-Jig
Overview: A small local organization
Affiliation(s): Centre for Indigenous Environmental Resources
Chief Officer(s):
Joyce Johnson, Director
joyce.johnson@wifn.org

The War Amputations of Canada / Les Amputés de guerre du Canada
2827 Riverside Dr., Ottawa ON K1V 0C4
Tel: 613-731-3821; *Fax:* 613-731-3234
Toll-Free: 800-465-2677
communications@waramps.ca
www.waramps.ca
www.facebook.com/TheWarAmps
twitter.com/thewaramps
www.youtube.com/warampsofcanada
Also Known As: The War Amps
Overview: A medium-sized national charitable organization founded in 1919
Mission: To provide a wide range of assistance to all Canadian war amputees & child amputees; To promote the advancement of prosthetics through grants to facilities undertaking research in field of prosthetics
Member of: National Council of Veteran Associations
Activities: Child Amputee Program (CHAMP) financially assists child amputees & their families & provides counselling & pays travel & accommodation expenses to prosthetic centres; Key Tag Service provides employment & fund-raising capabilities to war amputees; Play Safe Program promotes child safety; Matching Mothers Program matches families whose children have similar amputations for purposes of counselling & information; Provides public awareness films about amputee sports & child safety, & Canada's military history; *Speaker Service:* Yes
Chief Officer(s):
David Saunders, Chief Operating Officer
Danita Chisholm, Executive Director, Communications

Warden Woods Community Centre
74 Firvalley Ct., Toronto ON M1L 1N9
Tel: 416-694-1138; *Fax:* 416-694-1161
www.wardenwoods.com
www.facebook.com/wardenwoodscc
twitter.com/WardenWoodsCC
www.flickr.com/photos/80046247@N07
Overview: A medium-sized local charitable organization founded in 1970
Mission: Warden Woods is a charitable community centre in Scarborough offering programmes to families, seniors, youth.
Finances: *Funding Sources:* United Way; Provincial & municipal government
300 volunteer(s)
Membership: *Fees:* $5
Chief Officer(s):
Ginelle Skerritt, Executive Director

Wasaga Beach Chamber of Commerce
PO Box 394, 550 River Rd. West, Wasaga Beach ON L9Z 1A4
Tel: 705-429-2247; *Fax:* 705-429-1407
Toll-Free: 866-292-7242
info@wasagainfo.com
www.wasagainfo.com
Overview: A small local organization founded in 1938
Mission: To promote & improve trade & commerce, as well as the economic, civic & social welfare of the district
Affiliation(s): Canadian Chamber of Commerce; Ontario Chamber of Commerce
Staff Member(s): 3
Membership: *Fees:* Schedule available
Activities: *Awareness Events:* Annual Business Awards
Chief Officer(s):
Trudie McCrea, Office Manager

Wasagaming Arts Council *See* Wasagaming Community Arts Inc.

Wasagaming Chamber of Commerce
PO Box 621, Onanole MB R0J 1N0
discoverclearlake@gmail.com
www.discoverclearlake.com
Overview: A small local organization
Mission: To help promote local businesses & their growth
Membership: 67
Chief Officer(s):
Scott Gowler, President
Bob Bickerton, Treasurer

Wasagaming Community Arts Inc.
PO Box 98, 110 Wasagaming Dr., Wasagaming MB R0J 2H0
Tel: 204-848-2993; *Fax:* 204-848-2993
Previous Name: Wasagaming Arts Council
Overview: A small local charitable organization founded in 1979
Mission: To provide a creative learning experience for children & adults; to develop in individuals an appreciation of nature & positive attitude toward the environment; to create meaningful work experience for students & volunteers; to interpret the work of cultural groups & to enlist public interest & understanding
Member of: Manitoba Association of Community Arts Councils Inc.
Affiliation(s): Wasagaming Chamber of Commerce
Finances: *Annual Operating Budget:* Less than $50,000
Staff Member(s): 4; 15 volunteer(s)
Membership: 1-99; *Committees:* Membership; Exhibitions; Gallery Shop; Building
Activities: Exhibitions; adult & youth workshops in the visual arts & crafts; children's arts/craft classes; community arts resource; *Internships:* Yes

Washademoak Region Chamber of Commerce
3359 Lower Cambridge Rd., Cambridge-Narrows NB E4C 4P9
Tel: 506-488-8091
Overview: A small local organization
Mission: To provide a forum that enables businesses to meet, exchange ideas, identify issues, & formulate plans of action to increase awareness & commerce for businesses within the region
Membership: 30; *Fees:* $30
Chief Officer(s):
David Craw, President

Waskesiu Chamber of Commerce
PO Box 216, Waskesiu Lake SK S0J 2Y0
Tel: 306-663-5140; *Fax:* 306-663-5448
wakesiuchamber@sasktel.net
www.waskesiulake.ca
Overview: A small local organization
Chief Officer(s):
George Wilson, Manager

Waswanipi Cree Model Forest
3 Rte 113, Waswanipi QC J0Y 3C0
Tel: 819-753-2900; *Fax:* 819-753-2904
Overview: A small local organization
Member of: Canadian Model Forest Network
Chief Officer(s):

Rhonda Oblin, General Manager

Watch Tower Bible & Tract Society of Canada
PO Box 4100, Georgetown ON L7G 4Y4
Tel: 905-873-4100; *Fax:* 905-873-4554
www.jw.org
Also Known As: Jehovah's Witnesses
Overview: A large national organization
Mission: To serve Jehovah's Witnesses in Canada
Membership: 8,340,982 (worldwide)
Chief Officer(s):
Kenneth Little, President
Publications:
• Awake! [a publication of Jehovah's Witness]
Type: e-Magazine; *Number of Pages:* 16; *Price:* Free download
Profile: Concerns everyday problems & helps to build confidence in God's promise of a peaceful & secure new world
• The Watchtower [a publication of Jehovah's Witness]
Type: e-Magazine; *Number of Pages:* 16; *Price:* Free download
Profile: Shows the significance of world events in the light of Bible prophecies, & helps to comfort people with the good news of God's Kingdom while promoting faith in JesusChrist

Water Environment Association of Ontario (WEAO)
PO Box 176, Milton ON L9T 4N9
Tel: 416-410-6933; *Fax:* 416-410-1626
weao@weao.org
www.weao.org
twitter.com/WEAOYP
Previous Name: Pollution Control Association of Ontario
Overview: A medium-sized provincial organization founded in 1971
Mission: To advance the water environment industry; To promote sound public policy
Member of: Water Environment Federation (WEF)
Affiliation(s): Canadian Water & Wastewater Association
Finances: *Funding Sources:* Membership fees; Sponsorships
Staff Member(s): 3; 150 volunteer(s)
Membership: 1,400; *Member Profile:* Technical & professional individuals committed to the preservation & enhancement of Ontario's water environment, such as scientists, operators, engineers, & students; Employees of consulting firms, industries, equipment manufacturers, municipalities, colleges & universities, & provincial & federal government agencies; *Committees:* Asset Management; Communications; Conference; Environmental, Health, Safety & Security; Government Affairs; New Professionals; Operations Challenge; Promotions & Events Planning; Public Education; Residuals & Biosolids; Water for People - Canada; Wastewater Collection Systems; Wastewater Treatment & Technology
Activities: Delivering services to members; Providing a forum for members to interact for educational & professional advancement; Increasing public understanding; Promoting careers in the water environment industry; *Library*
Chief Officer(s):
Julie Vincent, Executive Administrator, 416-410-6933 Ext. 2, Fax: 416-410-1626
julie.vincent@weao.org
Awards:
• Exemplary Biosolids Management Award
To recognize biosolids practitioners who go beyond the normal requirements in the practice of managing biosolids *Contact:* Water Environment Association of Ontario, PO Box 176, Milton, ON, L9T 4N9
• Geoffrey T. G. Scott Memorial Award
To honour outstanding leadership & inspiration in the water environment industry *Contact:* Water Environment Association of Ontario, PO Box 176, Milton, ON, L9T 4N9
• Golden Manhole Award
Contact: Water Environment Association of Ontario, PO Box 176, Milton, ON, L9T 4N9
• Service Awards
Contact: Water Environment Association of Ontario, PO Box 176, Milton, ON, L9T 4N9
• Outstanding New Professional Award
Contact: Water Environment Association of Ontario, PO Box 176, Milton, ON, L9T 4N9
• Water Environment Association of Ontario Scholarship
To recognize outstanding students in the water quality field in Ontario *Deadline:* October *Contact:* Water Environment Association of Ontario, E-mail: scholarship@weao.org
• Kelman Scholarship
To recognize outstanding students in the water quality field in Ontario; *Amount:* $500 *Contact:* Water Environment Association of Ontario, E-mail: scholarship@weao.org

Meetings/Conferences:
• Water Environment Association of Ontario 2018 Annual Conference, April, 2018, London, ON
Scope: Provincial
Description: A conference featuring technical sessions, a keynote speaker, a student program, an awards presentation, & networking opportunities
Publications:
• INFLUENTS [a publication of the Water Environment Association of Ontario]
Type: Magazine; *Frequency:* Quarterly; *Accepts Advertising*; *Editor:* Christine Hanlon
Profile: Features on current issues, educational articles, project profiles, people in the news, committee reports,events, & marketplace developments

Water Polo Canada (WPC)
1084 Kenaston St., #1A, Ottawa ON K1B 3P5
Tel: 613-748-5682; *Fax:* 613-748-5777
office@waterpolo.ca
www.waterpolo.ca
www.facebook.com/waterpolocanada
twitter.com/waterpolocanada
www.youtube.com/waterpolocanada
Also Known As: Canadian Water Polo Association
Overview: A medium-sized national organization founded in 1976
Mission: To promote growth in sport of water polo in Canada; to administer Canada's high performance programs (Olympics, Pan Am Games, etc.) in water polo
Affiliation(s): Aquatic Federation of Canada
Finances: *Funding Sources:* Government; sponsors; members
Staff Member(s): 15
Membership: *Member Profile:* Water polo participant or team
Activities: *Internships:* Yes
Chief Officer(s):
Martin Goulet, Executive Director, 613-748-5682 Ext. 322
mgoulet@waterpolo.ca

Water Polo New Brunswick (WPNB)
NB
waterpolonb.ca
Overview: A medium-sized provincial organization overseen by Water Polo Canada
Member of: Water Polo Canada
Chief Officer(s):
JC Besner, President
president@waterpolonb.ca

Water Polo Newfoundland (WPNL)
NL
waterpolonl.ca
Overview: A medium-sized provincial organization overseen by Water Polo Canada
Member of: Water Polo Canada

Water Polo Nova Scotia
c/o Sport Nova Scotia, #311, 5516 Spring Garden Rd., Halifax NS B3J 1G6
Tel: 902-425-5450; *Fax:* 902-425-5606
info@waterpolonovascotia.ca
waterpolons.ca
Previous Name: Provincial Water Polo Association
Overview: A small provincial organization founded in 2006 overseen by Water Polo Canada
Mission: To promote the sport of water polo in Nova Scotia
Member of: Water Polo Canada
Chief Officer(s):
Joey Postma, Chair

Water Polo Québec *Voir* Fédération de Water-Polo du Québec

Water Polo Saskatchewan Inc. (WPS)
1860 Lorne St., Regina SK S4P 2L7
Tel: 306-780-9260; *Fax:* 306-780-9467
admin@wpsask.ca
www.wpsask.ca
www.facebook.com/waterpolosask
Previous Name: Saskatchewan Water Polo Association
Overview: A small provincial organization overseen by Water Polo Canada
Member of: Water Polo Canada
Finances: *Funding Sources:* Saskatchewan Lotteries; self-help projects

Water Ski - Wakeboard Manitoba (WSWM)
#415, 145 Pacific Ave., Winnipeg MB R3B 2Z6
Tel: 204-925-5700; *Fax:* 204-925-5792
info@wswm.ca
www.wswm.ca
www.flickr.com/photos/wswm/sets/
Overview: A small provincial organization founded in 1956 overseen by Sport Manitoba
Mission: To meet the needs of all those interested in the sport of water skiing by providing the resources necessary to help them achieve their goals & to encourage fun, friendship, fitness & fair play for skiers at all ability levels
Member of: Water Ski & Wakeboard Canada
Finances: *Funding Sources:* Provincial grants
Membership: *Fees:* $35 regular; $75 family; $5 associate
Activities: Slalom, tricks and jump water skiing; barefoot water skiing; wakeboarding; adaptive skiing
Chief Officer(s):
Alanna Boudreau, Executive Director
Mark Mueller, President

Water Ski & Wakeboard Alberta (WSWA)
Percy Page Centre, 11759 Groat Rd., Edmonton AB T5M 3K6
Tel: 780-415-0088; *Fax:* 780-422-2663
Toll-Free: 866-258-2754
info@wswa.ca
www.wswa.ca
www.facebook.com/WaterSkiWakeboardAlberta
twitter.com/WaterskiWakeAB
Previous Name: Water Ski Alberta
Overview: A small provincial organization founded in 1967
Mission: To promote participation & excellence in the sport of water skiing & wakeboarding in Alberta
Member of: Alberta Sport Council; Water Ski & Wakeboard Canada
Affiliation(s): International Water Ski Federation
Finances: *Funding Sources:* Alberta government; fundraising (casinos) membership fees; program fees
Membership: 1,000; *Fees:* $40
Chief Officer(s):
Peter Peebles, President
peterpeebles@gmail.com
Kate McNeil, Executive Director
kate@wswa.ca

Water Ski & Wakeboard British Columbia (WSWBC)
PO Box 56011, 1511 Admiral's Rd., Victoria BC V9A 2P8
Toll-Free: 888-696-6677
info@wswbc.org
www.wswbc.org
twitter.com/WSWBC
Previous Name: BC Water Ski Association
Overview: A medium-sized provincial charitable organization founded in 1969
Mission: To promote organized towed water sports in British Columbia
Member of: Water Ski & Wakeboard Canada
Finances: *Funding Sources:* Government; advertising sales; fundraisings
Membership: 1,250; *Fees:* $40 active single; $80 family
Activities: Provincial championships; Protour; *Internships:* Yes
Chief Officer(s):
Kim McKnight, Executive Director
Shawn Shorsky, President, 250-479-7828
Awards:
• Kim de Macedo Skier Achievement Award
• Coach of the Year
• Official of the Year
• Curtis McDonell Memorial Trophy

Water Ski & Wakeboard Canada (WSWC) / Ski nautique et planche Canada
#22, 1554 Carling Ave., Ottawa ON K1Z 7M4
Tel: 613-526-0685; *Fax:* 613-701-0385
Toll-Free: 888-526-0685
info@wswc.ca
wswc.ca
www.facebook.com/wswcanada
twitter.com/wswc_canada
www.youtube.com/user/TheWSWCanada;
instagram.com/wswcanada
Previous Name: Canadian Water Ski Association
Overview: A medium-sized national charitable organization
Mission: To promote & organize competitive Canadian towed water sports
Finances: *Annual Operating Budget:* $500,000-$1.5 Million
Staff Member(s): 4

Membership: 4,500; Committees: Water Ski; Wakeboard; Barefoot; Adaptive Towed Water Sports; Athlete Development; Coaching; Safety; Waterways; Hall of Fame
Chief Officer(s):
Glenn Bowie, Chair
Jasmine Northcott, Chief Executive Officer
jasmine@wswc.ca

Water Ski & Wakeboard Saskatchewan (WSWS)
SK
Tel: 306-931-2901
info@wswsask.com
wswsask.com
www.facebook.com/wswsask
twitter.com/wswsask
Previous Name: Saskatchewan Water Ski Association
Overview: A small provincial organization
Mission: To promote & develop towed water spoorts in Saskatchewan
Member of: Water Ski & Wakeboard Canada; Sask Sport Inc.
Membership: Fees: $25 recreational; $30 competitive; $45 recreational family; $50 competitive family
Activities: All activity & advocacy related to towed water sports; tournaments
Awards:
- Male Athlete of the Year
- Female Athlete of the Year
- Rookie of the Year
- Wakeboarder of the Year
- Most Improved Skier of the Year
- Most Improved Wakeboarder

Water Ski Alberta See Water Ski & Wakeboard Alberta

Water Ski Wakeboard Nova Scotia
PO Box 97, Greenfield NS B0T 1E0
www.nswsa.com
www.facebook.com/waterskiwakeboardns
Previous Name: Nova Scotia Water Ski Association
Overview: A small provincial organization
Member of: Water Ski & Wakeboard Canada
12 volunteer(s)
Membership: 135; Fees: $25 single; $50 family
Chief Officer(s):
Blair O'Neill, President

WaterCan / Eau Vive
321 Chapel St., Ottawa ON K1N 7Z2
Tel: 613-230-5182; Fax: 613-230-0712
Toll-Free: 800-370-5658
info@watercan.com
www.watercan.com
www.facebook.com/watercan
twitter.com/WaterCanCharity
www.youtube.com/Watercancontest
Overview: A small international charitable organization founded in 1987
Mission: To support integrated water supply, sanitation, & hygiene promotion projects that assist rural communities & the urban poor in Africa
Member of: Canadian Water Resources Association; Canadian Water & Wastewater Association
Finances: Annual Operating Budget: $500,000-$1.5 Million; Funding Sources: Direct mail; special events; corporate donations; private donations; government grants; foundations
Staff Member(s): 7; 200 volunteer(s)
Membership: 1-99
Activities: Partnerships with local/indigenous organizations; technical training; knowledge networks in the international water & sanitation sector; education activities to raise awareness on the health & development benefits of clean water in the developing world; Awareness Events: World Water Day, March 22; Library: Open to public by appointment
Chief Officer(s):
George Yap, Executive Director
Bonnie Kirkwood, Administrative Assistant
Erinn Steringa, Coordinator, Communications & Development
George Yap, Program Director
Amyn Hyder Ali, Financial Officer

Waterford & Townsend Historical Society
PO Box 1308, Waterford ON N0E 1Y0
Overview: A small local organization
Membership: Fees: $25 individual; $30 family
Chief Officer(s):
Suzan Yates, President

Waterfront Regeneration Trust
#227, 4195 Dundas St. West, Toronto ON M8X 1Y4
Tel: 416-943-8080; Fax: 416-943-8068
info@wrtrust.com
www.waterfronttrail.org
Overview: A medium-sized local organization founded in 1988
Mission: To expand, promote and enhance the Waterfront Trail and Greenway of Lake Ontario and the St. Lawrence River.
Staff Member(s): 4
Chief Officer(s):
Marlaine Koehler, Executive Director
mk@wrtrust.com
David Crombie, Founding Chair

Waterloo Coin Society (WCS)
PO Box 40044, Stn. Waterloo Square, 75 King St. South, Waterloo ON N2J 4V1
Tel: 519-745-3104
www.waterloocoinsociety.com
Overview: A small local organization founded in 1959
Mission: To offer our members a monthly educational meeting in addition to the opportunity to buy, sell & evaluate their numismatic items
Member of: Ontario Numismatic Association; Royal Canadian Numismatic Association
Finances: Annual Operating Budget: Less than $50,000; Funding Sources: Membership dues; auction fees; show
Membership: 150; Fees: $10 Individual; $5 Junior; $15 Family
Activities: Monthly educational meeting; 40 lot numismatic auction; youth program; Library: WCS Library; by appointment
Chief Officer(s):
Ben Dettweiler, President
president@waterloocoinsociety.com
Chris Boyer, Vice-President
vicepresident@waterloocoinsociety.com

Waterloo Historical Society (WHS)
c/o Kitchener Public Library, 85 Queen St. North, Kitchener ON N2H 2H1
whs@whs.ca
www.whs.ca
www.facebook.com/waterloohs
twitter.com/waterloohs
Overview: A medium-sized local charitable organization founded in 1912
Mission: To strengthen recognition of the region's heritage; To promote heritage preservation
Affiliation(s): Ontario Historical Society; Waterloo Regional Heritage Foundation
Finances: Annual Operating Budget: Less than $50,000; Funding Sources: Membership; provincial government; Waterloo Regional Heritage Foundation
15 volunteer(s)
Membership: 300; Fees: $15 student; $30 adult/family; $35 international; Committees: Membership; Plaques; Programs; Publications
Activities: At least four public meetings per year; Speaker Service: Yes; Library: Open to public
Chief Officer(s):
Lesley Webb, President

Waterloo Regional Heritage Foundation (WRHF)
Regional Admin. Building, PO Box 9051, Stn. C, 150 Frederick St., 2nd Fl., Kitchener ON N2G 4J3
Tel: 519-575-4732; Fax: 519-575-4481
wrhf@regionofwaterloo.ca
www.wrhf.org
Overview: A small local organization founded in 1973
Mission: To act as funding & support umbrella for organizations throughout the Region of Waterloo to preserve its heritage
Member of: Heritage Canada
Finances: Annual Operating Budget: $100,000-$250,000; Funding Sources: Regional Municipality of Waterloo
Staff Member(s): 2
Membership: 18; Committees: Allocations & Finance; Communications; Heritage Advisory
Activities: Awareness Events: Heritage Day
Chief Officer(s):
Warren Stauch, Chair
Awards:
- Regional Award for Heritage Research
For M.A. or Ph.D. student, resident of, or registered at a university in, the Waterloo region

Waterloo Regional Labour Council (WRLC)
#203, 120 Ottawa St., Kitchener ON N2H 3K5
Tel: 519-743-8301; Fax: 519-743-9460
www.wrlc.ca
www.facebook.com/wrlabour
Overview: A small local organization founded in 1941 overseen by Ontario Federation of Labour
Staff Member(s): 1; 20 volunteer(s)
Membership: 15,000-49,999
Activities: Speaker Service: Yes
Chief Officer(s):
Marc Xuereb, President

Waterloo Regional Police Association / Association de la police de Waterloo
1128 Rife Rd., Cambridge ON N1R 5S3
Tel: 519-622-0771; Fax: 519-622-5194
info@wrpa.org
www.wrpa.org
Overview: A small local organization
Mission: To promote the interests of members & maintain interest in active membership
Chief Officer(s):
Bruce Tucker, President

Waterloo, Wellington, Dufferin & Grey Building & Construction Trades Council (WWDGBCTC)
#172, 55 Northfield Dr. East, Waterloo ON N2K 3T6
Tel: 519-503-2347; Fax: 519-579-4076
www.yourlocaltrades.ca
Previous Name: Kitchener-Waterloo Building & Construction Trades Council
Overview: A small local organization
Mission: To work together with local union contractors to build & work on construction projects
Member of: AFL-CIO
Affiliation(s): Provincial Building & Construction Trades Council of Ontario
Membership: 5,000+

Waterski & Wakeboard New Brunswick (NBWSWBA)
NB
info@nbwswba.com
www.nbwswba.com
Also Known As: NB Waterski
Overview: A small provincial organization
Mission: To promote organized pulled watersports in the province of New Brunswick.
Member of: Water Ski & Wakeboard Canada
Membership: Fees: $20 individual; $40 family

Waterton Natural History Association (WNHA)
PO Box 145, 117 Waterton Ave., Waterton Park AB T0K 2M0
Tel: 403-859-2624; Fax: 403-859-2624
www.facebook.com/WatertonNaturalHistoryAssociation
Overview: A small local charitable organization founded in 1983
Mission: To further the understanding & preservation of Waterton Lakes National Park; To develop programs & services that will enhance visitor experience & appreciation of Waterton Lakes National Park
Member of: Canadian Parks Partnership; Alberta Museums Association; Alberta Historical Society; Canadian Booksellers Association
Finances: Annual Operating Budget: $50,000-$100,000; Funding Sources: Fundraising
Staff Member(s): 10; 20 volunteer(s)
Membership: 395; Fees: $20 individual lifetime; $25 family lifetime
Activities: Museum upgrade

Waterton Park Chamber of Commerce & Visitors Association
PO Box 55, Waterton Park AB T0K 2M0
Tel: 403-859-2224; Fax: 403-859-2650
info@mywaterton.ca
www.mywaterton.ca
Overview: A small local organization
Mission: To promote local businesses
Chief Officer(s):
Rod Kretz, President

Watrous & District Chamber of Commerce
PO Box 906, Watrous SK S0K 4T0
Tel: 306-946-3353; Fax: 306-946-3966
Overview: A small local organization

Watrous Area Arts Council
102 - 3rd Ave. East, Watrous SK S0K 4T0

Tel: 306-946-1333
www.townofwatrous.com/artscouncil.htm
www.facebook.com/247519998694936
Overview: A small local charitable organization founded in 1979
Mission: To present performing & visual arts to the community of Watrous & surrounding areas
Member of: Organization of Saskatchewan Arts Councils
Finances: *Annual Operating Budget:* Less than $50,000
10 volunteer(s)
Membership: 1-99

Watson & District Chamber of Commerce
PO Box 686, Watson SK S0K 4V0
Tel: 306-287-3659; *Fax:* 306-287-3601
Overview: A small local organization

Watson Lake Chamber of Commerce
c/o Town Office, PO Box 590, 710 Adela Trail, Watson Lake YT Y0A 1C0
Tel: 867-536-8000; *Fax:* 867-536-7522
www.watsonlakechamber.com
Overview: A small local organization
Mission: To promote & enhance trade, commerce & economic development in Watson Lake
3 volunteer(s)
Membership: 37; *Fees:* $120; *Member Profile:* Local businesses
Chief Officer(s):
Rick Harder, President

Wawatay Native Communications Society
PO Box 1180, 16 - 5th Ave., Sioux Lookout ON P8T 1B7
Tel: 807-737-2951; *Fax:* 807-737-3224
Toll-Free: 800-243-9059
reception@wawatay.on.ca
www.wawataynews.ca
ca.linkedin.com/company/wawatay-native-communications-society
www.facebook.com/wawataynews
Also Known As: Wawatay News Online
Overview: A medium-sized national organization founded in 1974
Mission: To preserve & promote aboriginal languages & cultures with the use of modern technology in radio, television & newspaper
Member of: Nishnawbe-Aki Nation
Affiliation(s): Grand Council Treaty #3; Robinson-Superior Treaty Area
Membership: 49 first nations communities; *Member Profile:* 48 First Nations Communities of Nishnawbe-Aski Nation
Activities: *Internships:* Yes; *Speaker Service:* Yes; *Library:* Open to public
Chief Officer(s):
Lenny Carpenter, Publisher/Editor

Waypoint centre de soins de santé mentale *See* Waypoint Centre for Mental Health Care

Waypoint Centre for Mental Health Care / Waypoint centre de soins de santé mentale
500 Church St., Penetanguishene ON L9M 1G3
Tel: 705-549-3181
info@waypointcentre.ca
www.waypointcentre.ca
Overview: A small local organization founded in 2008
Mission: To provide psychiatric inpatient & outpatient services & mental health programs to individuals in Simcoe County, Dufferin County & Muskoka/Parry Sound
Finances: *Funding Sources:* Catholic Health Corporation of Ontario
Staff Member(s): 10
Chief Officer(s):
Betty Valentine, Chair
Carol Lambie, President & CEO

WE Charity
339 Queen St. East, Toronto ON M5A 1S9
Tel: 416-925-5894
info@we.org
www.wecharity.org
www.facebook.com/WEmovement
twitter.com/wemovement
www.youtube.com/WEMOVEMENT
Previous Name: Free the Children
Overview: A large international charitable organization founded in 1995
Mission: To free young people from the idea that they are powerless to bring about positive social change, to encourage them to act now to improve the lives of young people everywhere
Affiliation(s): Me to We
Finances: *Annual Operating Budget:* Greater than $5 Million
400 volunteer(s)
Membership: 100,000+
Activities: Education; peacebuilding & leadership; *Internships:* Yes; *Speaker Service:* Yes
Chief Officer(s):
Scott Baker, Executive Director
  Quebec Office
  #1635, 1, Place Ville Marie, Montréal QC H3B 2B6
  Tel: 514-878-3733
  Western Canada Office
  #300, 228 East Georgia St., Vancouver BC V6A 1Z7
  Tel: 604-875-8791

Webgrrls Canada
c/o Webgrrls International, #314, 119 West 72nd St., New York NY 10023 USA
Fax: 866-935-1188
Toll-Free: 888-932-4775
www.webgrrls.com
Overview: A medium-sized international organization
Mission: To serve as a learning & networking resource for women in & interested in new media & the internet
  Calgary
  www.webgrrls.com
  Nova Scotia
  NS
  www.webgrrls.com/novascotia/
  Vancouver
  Vancouver BC
  www.webgrrls.com/vancouver.ca

Welcome Friend Association (WFA)
PO Box 242, 76 Dawson St., Thessalon ON P0R 1L0
Fax: 705-998-2612
Toll-Free: 888-909-2234
Other Communication: rainbowcamp.ca
info@welcomefriend.ca
www.welcomefriend.ca
www.facebook.com/welcomefriendassociation
twitter.com/WelcomeFriend
Overview: A medium-sized national organization founded in 2009
Mission: To educate & promote awareness in society regarding gender, sexual identities, & expressions; To support individuals facing gender & sexual issues; To increase understanding of the queer community; To work towards a society that includes & respects all persons regardless of gender or sexual orientation
Finances: *Annual Operating Budget:* $50,000-$100,000
Staff Member(s): 1; 50 volunteer(s)
Activities: Operating Rainbow Camp for youth; Holding fundraisers; Offering seminars; *Speaker Service:* Yes
Chief Officer(s):
Harry Stewart, Chair
hstewart@welcomefriend.ca

Welcome Hall Mission *See* Mission Bon Accueil

Welfare Committee for the Assyrian Community in Canada
#102, 964 Albion Rd., Toronto ON M9V 1A7
Tel: 416-741-8836; *Fax:* 416-741-8836; *Crisis Hot-Line:* 416-742-5676
assyrianwelfare@aol.com
Previous Name: Assyrian Association
Overview: A small national charitable organization founded in 1989
Mission: To sponsor Assyrian refugees for admission into Canada; To provide support for the settlement of Assyrian refugees; To offer referrals & general information
Member of: Canadian Council for Refugees
Finances: *Annual Operating Budget:* $50,000-$100,000
Membership: 1-99

Welland & District Labour Council *See* Niagara Regional Labour Council

Welland County Law Association
102 East Main St., Welland ON L3B 3W6
Tel: 905-734-3174; *Fax:* 905-734-1883
Toll-Free: 866-455-6489
wcla@execulink.com
www.execulink.com/~wellaw
Overview: A small local organization
Staff Member(s): 1; 12 volunteer(s)
Membership: 150
Activities: *Library:* R. Boak Burns Law Library

Welland District Association for Community Living *See* Community Living Welland Pelham

The Welland/Pelham Chamber of Commerce / La Chambre de commerce de Welland/Pelham
32 East Main St., Welland ON L3B 3W3
Tel: 905-732-7515; *Fax:* 905-732-7175
www.wellandpelhamchamber.com
www.linkedin.com/company/welland-pelham-chamber-of-commerce
www.facebook.com/WellandPelhamChamber
www.youtube.com/user/WellandPelhamChamber
Overview: A small local organization founded in 1889
Mission: To represent members & businesses; To promote the community; To provide opportunities for business, trade & commerce growth
Finances: *Annual Operating Budget:* $100,000-$250,000
Membership: 350; *Fees:* Schedule available; *Committees:* Communications; Education; Member Services; Membership; Policy; Special Events
Activities: Lobbying
Chief Officer(s):
Jeff Neill, President
Dolores Fabiano, Executive Director
dolores@wellandpelhamchamber.com

Wellesley & District Board of Trade
c/o Wendy Sauder, Wellesley Service Centre, 1220 Queens Bush Rd., Wellesley ON N0B 2T0
Tel: 519-656-3494
wellesleyboardoftrade@gmail.com
wellesleyboardoftrade.com
Overview: A small local organization
Mission: To improve the economic & social welfare of the community; To strengthen the business climate in Wellesley & area
Member of: Canadian Chamber of Commerce; Ontario Chamber of Commerce
Membership: 21; *Fees:* $175 non-business; $250 business
Chief Officer(s):
Kim Heinmiller, President

Wellington County *See* Habitat for Humanity Canada

Wellington County Beekeepers' Association
Guelph ON
Tel: 519-787-2530
Overview: A small local organization
Mission: To promote apiculture education
Membership: *Member Profile:* Commercial & hobbyist beekeepers in Wellington County
Activities: Organizing regular meetings; Providing networking opportunities for local beekeepers; Teaching the proper care & maintenance of hives & correct harvesting techniques; Arranging delivery of beekeeping supplies for the group, such as polypropylene

Wellington County Historical Society (WCHS)
PO Box 5, Fergus ON N1M 2W7
www.wchs.ca
www.facebook.com/wellingtoncounty.historicalsociety
Overview: A small local charitable organization founded in 1928
Mission: To preserve, promote & publicize the history of Wellington County; To assist with the Wellington County Museum & Archives
Affiliation(s): Ontario Historical Society
Finances: *Annual Operating Budget:* Less than $50,000; *Funding Sources:* Membership fees; donations; local & provincial grants
Membership: 250; *Fees:* $20 Canada; $25 USA; *Committees:* Program & Publicity; Publications; Membership; Constitution; Historical Research & Records
Chief Officer(s):
Ron Hattle, President, 519-546-3450
Publications:
• Wellington County History [a publication of the Wellington County Historical Society]
Type: Journal; *Frequency:* Annually

Wellington Law Association
Court House, 74 Woolwich St., Guelph ON N1H 3T9

Tel: 519-763-6365; Fax: 519-763-6847
Toll-Free: 866-893-5220
lawlibwell@gmail.com
www.wellingtonlaw.org
Overview: A small local organization
Mission: To serve lawyers in Wellington County
Member of: Federation of Ontario Law Associations
Finances: *Annual Operating Budget:* $50,000-$100,000; *Funding Sources:* Provincial government; membership fees
Staff Member(s): 1
Membership: 151 individual
Activities: *Library:* Wellington Law Association Library; by appointment
Chief Officer(s):
John Kerr, Librarian

Wellington Waterloo Dufferin Health Library Network (WWDHLN)
ON
wwdhln-l@mailman.uwaterloo.ca
wwdhln.chla-absc.ca
Overview: A medium-sized local organization overseen by Canadian Health Libraries Association
Mission: To support & enhance the ability of its members to provide high quality knowledge information services to member organizations; To promote communication among members; To co-operate with other health library networks to promote the efficient delivery of service; To support health library development
Finances: *Funding Sources:* Membership dues
Membership: *Fees:* $50
Activities: Organizing & facilitating continuing education programs; Providing free reciprocal resource sharing between members
Chief Officer(s):
Tracy Morgan, President
tmorgan@gghorg.ca

Wells & District Chamber of Commerce
PO Box 123, Wells BC V0K 2R0
Tel: 250-994-2323; Fax: 250-994-3331
Toll-Free: 877-451-9355
wells.ca/profile/wells-district-chamber-commerce
twitter.com/mt_trails
Overview: A small local organization founded in 1936
Mission: To promote Wells, Barkerville & Bowron Lake business community
Member of: BC Chamber of Commerce
Activities: *Awareness Events:* Fred Wells Days

Wellspring Cancer Support Foundation / Fondation Wellspring pour les personnes atteintes de cancer
4 Charles St. East, Toronto ON M4Y 1T1
Tel: 416-961-1928; Fax: 416-961-3721
Toll-Free: 877-499-9904
www.wellspring.ca
www.facebook.com/WellspringCAN
twitter.com/wellspringCAN
www.youtube.com/user/WellspringCancer
Overview: A medium-sized provincial charitable organization
Activities: Five centres that provide emotional & psychological support, free of charge, to individuals & families living with cancer
Chief Officer(s):
John Philp, Chair
Christina Smith, CEO

Welsh Pony & Cob Association of Ontario (WPCAO)
c/o Paula Dalgarno, 125 Hazelwood Dr., Whitby ON L1N 3L7
Tel: 905-728-4802
WPCAO2014@gmail.com
wpcao.com
www.facebook.com/112049522224451
Overview: A small provincial organization overseen by Welsh Pony & Cob Society of Canada
Mission: To promote Welsh Ponies & Cobs in Ontario
Membership: *Fees:* $20 junior; $35 regular; $60 family; *Member Profile:* Welsh Ponies & Cob enthusiasts in Ontario
Activities: Offering networking opportunities; Supporting clinics; Operating the annual Canadian All Welsh Show; Holding the annual Champion of Champions competition; Providing an annual High Point Awards program; Offering information about the breed
Chief Officer(s):
Rose Reid, *President,* 905-260-2848
Alice McKeen, Vice-President, 905-786-1059
Jessica Figas, Secretary, 905-431-5620

Paula Dalgarno, Treasurer
Publications:
• Welsh Pony & Cob Association of Ontario Newsletter
Type: Newsletter; *Frequency:* Quarterly; *Editor:* Bev Fantauzzi
Profile: Information about Ontario events

Welsh Pony & Cob Society of Canada (WPCSC)
PO Box 119, Alliston ON L94 1T9
Tel: 705-435-3210; Fax: 705-435-5936
welshponyandcobsociety@bellnet.ca
www.welshponyandcob.org
Overview: A small international organization founded in 1979
Mission: To oversee the registration of Welsh ponies
Affiliation(s): Canadian Livestock Records Corporation
Membership: 400; *Fees:* $20 junior members, 18 years & under; $40 individuals, over age 18, as well as corporate members; $350 life members, over age 50; $500 life members; *Member Profile:* Individuals, companies, partnerships, associations, & syndicates interested in the Welsh pony breed in Canada, the United States, & Great Britain
Activities: Maintaining registration certificates & other official records of the society; Participating in shows
Chief Officer(s):
Mary Cork, President
Duane Stewart, Vice-President
Jennifer Parsons, Secretary
Ray Dabrowski, Treasurer, 416-431-7624, Fax: 416-431-9844
raydabrowski@rogers.com
Publications:
• Canadian Stud Book
Type: Book; *Frequency:* Annually
Profile: Details of every Welsh pony registered in Canada
• Welsh in Canada
Type: Magazine; *Frequency:* Quarterly; *Accepts Advertising*
Profile: Society meeting highlights, financial statements, transfer lists, awards, ratings, Welsh pony stories, farm & breeder profiles, & forthcoming events

Welsh Pony & Cob Society of Saskatchewan
c/o Alana Longman, PO Box 36, Harris SK S0L 1K0
Tel: 306-656-2051
Overview: A small provincial organization overseen by Welsh Pony & Cob Society of Canada
Mission: To promote the Welsh pony breed in Saskatchewam
Membership: *Member Profile:* Welsh pony breeders & other interested persons in Saskatchewan
Chief Officer(s):
Alana Longman, Contact
alana@ch-equestrian.com

The West Bend Community Association (TWBCA)
c/o Secretary, 33 Kenneth Ave., Toronto ON M6P 1J1
www.thewestbend.ca
Previous Name: Dundas West Residents Association
Overview: A small local organization
Mission: To help promote & improve the community of West Bend in Toronto
Membership: *Fees:* $10

West Central Forage Association (WCFA)
5009 45 Ave., Entwistle AB T0E 0S0
Tel: 780-727-4447; Fax: 780-727-4424
Toll-Free: 866-725-4447
info@westcentralforage.com
www.westcentralforage.com
www.facebook.com/westcentralforage
Overview: A small local organization founded in 1978 overseen by Agricultural Research & Extension Council of Alberta
Mission: To share knowledge, conduct applied research & extension activities, & demonstrate new agricultural technology & production practices
Member of: Agricultural Research & Extension Council of Alberta
Membership: *Fees:* $30
Chief Officer(s):
Melissa Freeman, General Manager
manager@westcentralforage.com
Fito Zamudio Baca, Manager, Forage & Livestock Program
forage@westcentralforage.com
Jessica Watson, Manager, Conservation AG/Extension Program
conservationag@westcentralforage.com
Publications:
• Forage Views [a publication of the West Central Forage Association]
Type: Newsletter; *Frequency:* Monthly

West Coast Amateur Musicians' Society (WCAMS)
5468 Walter Place, Burnaby BC V5G 4K3
Tel: 778-828-6007
info@wcams.ca
www.wcams.com
Overview: A small local charitable organization founded in 1981
Mission: To operate a summer music camp for adult amateur musicians & their families; To provide skills development (sight reading) sessions for chorus & orchestra; To provide workshops for singers & instrumentalists of all ages & all levels of ability
Finances: *Annual Operating Budget:* $50,000-$100,000
30 volunteer(s)
Membership: 250; *Fees:* $25; *Member Profile:* Amateur instrumentalists & singers; *Committees:* Fundraising; Publicity; Festival Operations; Workshops
Activities: West Coast Summer Music Festival; workshops; *Library:* Music Library; Not open to public
Chief Officer(s):
Sara Brusse, President
Claudia Morawetz, Vice-President

West Coast Book Prize Society
#901, 207 West Hastings St., Vancouver BC V6B 1H7
Tel: 604-687-2405; Fax: 604-687-2435
info@bcbookprizes.ca
www.bcbookprizes.ca
www.facebook.com/BCBookPrizes
twitter.com/bcbookprizes
pinterest.com/bcbookprizes
Overview: A small provincial organization founded in 1985
Mission: To celebrate writers from British Columbia through the BC Book Prizes; to bridge the gap between writing & publishing
Staff Member(s): 4
Membership: *Fees:* $20
Chief Officer(s):
Bryan Pike, Executive Director
bryan@rebuscreative.com
Awards:
• The Christie Harris Illustrated Children's Literature Prize, BC Book Prizes
• Dorothy Livesay Poetry Prize, BC Book Prizes
Awarded to the author of the best work of poetry; the writer must have lived in BC for three of the preceding five years
• The Sheila A. Egoff Children's Prize, BC Book Prizes
Awarded to the author of the best book for young people aged 16 & under; the author or illustrator must have lived in BC for three of the preceding five years
• The Bill Duthie Booksellers' Choice Prize, BC Book Prizes
Awarded for the best book in terms of public appeal, initiative, design, production & content; the book must have been published in BC
• The Roderick Haig-Brown Regional Prize, BC Book Prizes
Awarded to the author of the book that contributes most to the enjoyment & understanding of BC; the book may deal with any aspect of the province & should epitomize the BC experience
• The Ethel Wilson Fiction Prize, BC Book Prizes
Awarded to the author of the best work of fiction; the writer must have lived in BC for three of the preceding five years
• The Hubert Evans Non-Fiction Prize, BC Book Prizes
Awarded to the author of the best original non-fiction literary work (philosophy, belles lettres, biography, history, etc.); the writer must have lived in BC for three of the preceding five years
• Lieutenant Governor's Award of Literary Excellence, BC Book Prizes

West Coast Domestic Workers' Association (WCDWA)
#302, 119 West Pender St., Vancouver BC V6B 1S5
Tel: 604-669-4482; Fax: 604-669-6456
Toll-Free: 888-669-4482
info@wcdwa.ca
www.wcdwa.ca
Overview: A medium-sized local organization founded in 1986
Mission: To provide free legal assistance in the form of advocacy, support and counselling to live-in caregivers based in British Columbia
Staff Member(s): 5
Membership: 525; *Fees:* $25-$30
Chief Officer(s):
Natalie Drolet, Lawyer & Executive Director

West Coast Environmental Law (WCEL)
#200, 2006 West 10th Ave., Vancouver BC V6J 2B3
Tel: 604-684-7378; Fax: 604-684-1312
Toll-Free: 800-330-9235
admin@wcel.org

www.wcel.org
www.facebook.com/WCELaw
twitter.com/WCELaw
Overview: A medium-sized local charitable organization founded in 1974
Mission: To safeguard the environment through law; To help British Columbians access legal assistance to protect the environment
Finances: *Funding Sources:* Law Foundation of British Columbia & other foundations; Independent donations
Staff Member(s): 8
Activities: Publishing policy papers; Offering legal advice; *Library:* West Coast Environmental Law; Open to public
Chief Officer(s):
Jessica Clogg, Executive Director & Senior Counsel, 604-601-2501
jessica_clogg@wcel.org
Lucy Hough, Director, Development, 604-601-2509
lucy_hough@wcel.org
Todd Monge, Manager, Environmental Dispute Resolution Fund & Communications, 604-601-2503
todd_monge@wcel.org
Awards:
• Dr. Andrew Thompson Award
Meetings/Conferences:
• West Coast Environmental Law 2018 Annual General Meeting, 2018
Scope: Provincial
Description: The appointment of board members takes place each year
Publications:
• Legal e-Brief
Type: Newsletter; *Frequency:* Monthly
Profile: Information about topical environmental law issues, plus explanations of new & existing laws & policies
• West Coast Environmental Law Annual Report
Type: Yearbook; *Frequency:* Annually

West Coast Railway Association (WCRA)
PO Box 2790, Stn. Term., Vancouver BC V6B 3X2
Tel: 604-681-4403; *Fax:* 604-876-4104
Toll-Free: 800-722-1233
info@wcra.org
www.wcra.org
www.facebook.com/WCRHP
twitter.com/wcrhp
www.instagram.com/wcrhp
Overview: A small local charitable organization founded in 1961
Mission: To collect, preserve, restore, operate & exhibit artifacts relating to the history of railways, especially those of BC; The West Coast Railway Heritage Park in Squamish, BC develops educational exhibits on railway heritage for all age groups
Member of: Association of Rail Museums; Tourist Railroad Association
Finances: *Annual Operating Budget:* $500,000-$1.5 Million; *Funding Sources:* Tours; government grants; donations; fundraising; foundation
Staff Member(s): 12; 150 volunteer(s)
Membership: 1500; *Fees:* Schedule available; *Member Profile:* Interest in railways past & present; *Committees:* Museum; Tours; Collections; Motive Power; Children; Education
Activities: Develops & operates West Coast Railway Heritage Park in Squamish, BC;Houses a collection of 60+ locomotives, freight & passenger cars; Operates tour program, community events & a 'Polar Express' ride; *Speaker Service:* Yes; *Library:* West Coast Railway Association Archives; Open to public by appointment
Chief Officer(s):
Gerry Burgess, Executive Director
board@wcra.org

West Elgin Chamber of Commerce
PO Box 276, Rodney ON N0L 2C0
Tel: 519-785-0916
Overview: A small local organization overseen by Ontario Chamber of Commerce
Mission: To promote & improve trade & commerce, the economic, civil & social welfare of the district
Finances: *Funding Sources:* Membership fees
Membership: *Committees:* Membership; Downtown Improvement; Business & Education; Welcome; Tourism & Special Events; New Business Development
Activities: *Speaker Service:* Yes
Chief Officer(s):
Mike Madeira, President

West Elgin Historical & Genealogical Society
c/o Norma Schnekenburger, RR #3, Rodney ON N0L 2C0
Tel: 519-785-0177
Overview: A small local organization
Chief Officer(s):
Norma Schnekenburger, Contact

West Elgin Nature Club
230 Morden St., West Lorne ON N0L 2P0
Tel: 519-768-3313
westelginnatureclub@hotmail.com
www.facebook.com/125906937480017
Overview: A small local organization
Mission: To promote interest in the study, preservation, & appreciation of nature
Member of: Federation of Ontario Naturalists
Membership: *Fees:* $10 individual; $20 family

West Grey Chamber of Commerce
PO Box 671, 144 Garafraxa St. South, Durham ON N0G 1R0
Tel: 519-369-5750
westgreychamber@gmail.com
westgreychamber.ca
Previous Name: Durham & District Chamber of Commerce
Overview: A small local organization founded in 1978
Mission: To promote the town of Durham, as well as town events; To provide members with an opportunity to obtain insurance through the Ontario Chamber of Commerce
Member of: Ontario Chamber of Commerce
Affiliation(s): Durham Business Improvement Association
Finances: *Annual Operating Budget:* Less than $50,000; *Funding Sources:* Membership dues
Staff Member(s): 1; 8 volunteer(s)
Membership: 56; *Fees:* $100; *Committees:* Finance; Membership; Newsletter
Chief Officer(s):
Nella Monaco-Wells, President

West Hants Chamber of Commerce; Windsor Board of Trade *See* Avon Chamber of Commerce

West Hants Historical Society (WHHS)
PO Box 2335, 281 King St., Windsor NS B0N 2T0
Tel: 902-798-4706
whhs@ns.aliantzinc.ca
westhantshistoricalsociety.ca
www.facebook.com/141349919273121
Also Known As: West Hants Museum
Overview: A small local charitable organization founded in 1973
Mission: To collect, record, & preserve the history of West Hants; To initiate & promote programs to further historic interest in West Hants; To compile & publish local historical data from material collected; To collect, frame, catalogue & display photos of local historical interest; To develop display areas on specific subjects; To compile graveyard inscriptions
Member of: Federation of the Nova Scotian Heritage
Affiliation(s): Heritage Trust of Nova Scotia
Membership: *Fees:* $10 individual; $15 couple; $100 corporate
Activities: Operates Genealogy Centre; Heritage Banquet; Museum Day; *Library:* Open to public
Chief Officer(s):
Jeff Barrett, President
Garnet Clark, Vice-President
Isabel Palmeter, Secretary

West Island Black Community Association (WIBCA)
48C, 4e av sud, Roxboro QC H8Y 2M2
Tel: 514-683-3925; *Fax:* 514-683-7649
admin@wibca.org
www.wibca.org
www.facebook.com/wibca.montreal
twitter.com/WIBCAMontreal
Overview: A small local organization founded in 1982
Mission: To respond to the needs of the community; to help our young people achieve their highest potential
Membership: *Committees:* Cultural & Social; Education; Finance; Membership; Seniors'; Youth, Sports & Recreation

West Island Chamber of Commerce *Voir* Chambre de commerce de l'Ouest-de-l'Ile de Montréal

West Island Youth Symphony Orchestra *Voir* Orchestre symphonique des jeunes du West Island

West Kootenay District Labour Council
101 Baker St., Nelson BC V1L 4H1
Tel: 250-352-9223; *Fax:* 250-352-9223
wklc@telus.net
www.facebook.com/westkootenaylabourcouncil
Overview: A small local organization overseen by British Columbia Federation of Labour
Mission: To promote the interests of affiliates in the West Kootenay region of Birtitish Columbia; To advance the economic & social welfare of workers
Activities: Organizing a Day of Mourning ceremony, to pay tribute to workers injured or killed on the job; Participating in rallies; Supporting community organizations
Chief Officer(s):
Gay Mary, Contact

West Kootenay Naturalists Association
c/o Esther Brown, 415 Olivia Cres., Trail BC V1R 1A6
Tel: 250-368-3663
www.kootenaynaturalists.org
Overview: A small local organization founded in 1973
Mission: To promote the enjoyment of nature through environmental appreciation & conservation; to encourage wise use & conservation of natural resources & environmental protection.
Member of: Federation of BC Naturalists
Affiliation(s): Creston Valley Wildlife Management Area
Finances: *Funding Sources:* Donations; membership fees
Membership: *Fees:* $30 single; $46 family
Activities: Botany & ornithology hikes; scenic hikes, skiing/snow shoeing; trail maintenance; bird counts; Violin Lake Conservation Project; educational presentations; Waldie Island Heron Project
Chief Officer(s):
Peter Wood, President, 250-359-7107
Awards:
• Selkirk College Foundation Bursary

West Kootenay Regional Arts Council (WKRAC)
PO Box 103, #2, 619B Front St., Nelson BC V1L 5P7
Tel: 250-352-2421; *Fax:* 250-352-2420
Toll-Free: 800-850-2787
wkrac@telus.net
www.wkartscouncil.com
Overview: A small local charitable organization founded in 1980
Member of: Assembly of BC Arts Councils; BC Touring Council; Canadian Conference of the Arts; Columbia Kootenay Cultural Alliance
Finances: *Annual Operating Budget:* Less than $50,000; *Funding Sources:* Grant; BC Arts Council; Columbia Basin Trust
Staff Member(s): 1; 10 volunteer(s)
Membership: 12 community arts councils; *Fees:* $45; *Member Profile:* Arts councils & regional cultural organizations; *Committees:* Regional Events Producers
Activities: Workshops; advocacy; delivery agent for Columbia Basin Trust arts, culture & heritage funding sector; *Library:* Lending Library; by appointment
Chief Officer(s):
Krista Patterson, Executive Director

West Kootenay Women's Association
420 Mill St., Nelson BC V1L 4R9
Tel: 250-352-9916
info@nelsonwomenscentre.ca
www.nelsonwomenscentre.com
Also Known As: Nelson & District Women's Centre
Overview: A small local organization founded in 1974
Mission: To provide & promote educational & cultural activities to promote the status of women
Member of: West Kootenay Women's Council; VAWIR; Women't Health Council
Affiliation(s): National Action Committee on the Status of Women
Finances: *Annual Operating Budget:* $50,000-$100,000; *Funding Sources:* National & provincial government; private donations
Staff Member(s): 3; 25 volunteer(s)
Membership: 200 individual; *Fees:* $15-30 sliding scale
Activities: *Awareness Events:* Dec. 6 Memorial; Anti-Violence Prevention Week; Take Bak the Nigth *Library:* Women's Centre Library; Open to public
Chief Officer(s):
Maibrit Sorensen, Chair
Tasha Bassingthwaighte, Executive Director

West Lincoln Chamber of Commerce
PO Box 555, 288 Station St., Smithville ON L0R 2A0
Tel: 905-957-1606; *Fax:* 905-957-4628
www.westlincolnchamber.com

www.facebook.com/WestLincolnChamber
twitter.com/wlincolnchamber
Overview: A small local charitable organization founded in 1950
Mission: To strengthen the municipality industrially, commercially & economically
Member of: Canadian Chamber of Commerce
Finances: *Funding Sources:* Membership; events
Staff Member(s): 1
Membership: 103; *Member Profile:* Businesses
Activities: *Library:* Open to public
Chief Officer(s):
Ivan Carruthers, President
Pamela Haire, Administrator
Publications:
• West Lincoln Chamber of Commerce Newsletter
Type: Newsletter

West Lincoln Historical Society & Archives (WLHS)
PO Box 797, Smithville ON L0R 2A0
Tel: 905-957-0138
archives@wlhs.info
www.wlhs.info
Overview: A small local organization
Mission: To preserve & restore the Smithville train station
Membership: *Fees:* $10 individual; $15 family

West Muskoka Chamber of Commerce *See* Muskoka Lakes Chamber of Commerce

West Neighbourhood House
588 Queen St. West, 2nd Fl., Toronto ON M6J 1E3
Tel: 416-532-7586; *Fax:* 416-504-3047
info@westnh.org
www.westnh.org
www.facebook.com/StChristopherHouse
twitter.com/WestNHouse
Previous Name: St. Christopher House Adult Literacy Program
Overview: A small local organization founded in 1977
Mission: To provide various social leaning programs to children & adults
Affiliation(s): Metro Toronto Movement for Literacy; Ontario Literacy Coalition
Finances: *Funding Sources:* Municipal, provincial & federal government; Local businesses; Clubs; Foundations; Individual donors
Staff Member(s): 235; 1400 volunteer(s)
Chief Officer(s):
Maureen Fair, Executive Director

West Niagara Second Stage Housing & Counselling
PO Box 1115, 5032 King St., Beamsville ON L0R 1B0
Tel: 905-563-5548; *Fax:* 905-563-3197
admin@wnss.org
www.wnss.org
www.facebook.com/WNSSHousing
twitter.com/WNSSHousing
Overview: A small local charitable organization founded in 1998
Mission: To provide safe, low cost housing to women & children & provide them with the tools to progress to independent living
Staff Member(s): 5
Activities: Providing interim housing & counselling to women & their children leaving situations of family violence
Chief Officer(s):
Mary Shaw, President

West Nipissing Association for Community Living *See* Community Living West Nipissing

West Nipissing Chamber of Commerce / Chambre de commerce de Nipissing Ouest
200 Main St., Sturgeon Falls ON P2B 1P2
Tel: 705-753-5672; *Fax:* 705-580-5672
info@westnipissingchamber.ca
www.westnipissingchamber.ca
Overview: A small local organization founded in 1951
Mission: To promote businesses in West Nipissing & strengthen commerce
Staff Member(s): 2; 9 volunteer(s)
Membership: *Committees:* Advocacy & Lobbying; Agricultural Task Force; Business Awards; Business Development Workshop; Downtown Parking; Feast on the Farm; Golf Tournament; Marketing & Website; Revenue Generating; Study Steering; Youth Entrepreneurial Capacity
Chief Officer(s):
Patrick Keough, President
Jolene Greer, Project Manager
jolene.greer@westnipissingchamber.ca

West Ottawa Board of Trade
#140, 555 Legget Dr., Kanata ON K2K 2X3
Tel: 613-592-8343; *Fax:* 613-592-1157
info@westottawabot.com
www.westottawabot.com
www.facebook.com/WestOttawaBoT
twitter.com/WestOttawaBoT
www.youtube.com/user/KanataChamber
Previous Name: Kanata Chamber of Commerce
Overview: A small local organization founded in 1991
Mission: To help with the success of its members by providing leadership & information; To help create a positive business environment in the Nepean, Kanata, Goulbourn & West Carleton business community
Member of: Canadian Chamber of Commerce
Staff Member(s): 4
Membership: 473; *Fees:* $200 non-profit; $250 1-3 employees; $300 4-9 employees; $450 10-25 employees; $650 26-50 employees; $815 50+ employees; *Committees:* Economic & Business Development; Food & Wine Show; Communications; Membership; Business Advisory; Golf Tournament Organizing; People's Choice Business Awards Organizing
Activities: Providing information & networking opportunities
Chief Officer(s):
Rosemary Leu, Executive Director
rosemaryleu@westottawabot.com

West Region Tribal Council Cultural Education Centre
21 - 4th Ave. NW, Dauphin MB R7N 1H9
Tel: 204-638-8225; *Fax:* 204-638-8062
Overview: A small provincial organization

West Scarborough Neighbourhood Community Centre
313 Pharmacy Ave., Toronto ON M1L 3E7
Tel: 416-755-9215
www.wsncc.org
Overview: A small local organization
Mission: To provide neighbourhood programs & services designed to enhance the well-being of people in the context of their community, culture & environment
Member of: Boys & Girls Clubs of Ontario
Finances: *Annual Operating Budget:* $250,000-$500,000; *Funding Sources:* Government; United Way; donations
Staff Member(s): 32; 400 volunteer(s)
Membership: 5,000+

West Shore Arts Council (WSAC)
PO Box 28090, RPO Can West, Victoria BC V9B 6R8
Tel: 250-478-2286; *Fax:* 250-478-5591
info@westshorearts.org
www.westshorearts.org
Previous Name: Western Communities Arts Council
Overview: A small local organization founded in 1988
Mission: To encourage creative participation & excellence in visual & performing arts; to provide information & promote public interest; to bring the artistic needs of the community to the attention of governing authorities; to advocate arts education
Member of: Assembly of BC Arts Councils
Finances: *Annual Operating Budget:* Less than $50,000; *Funding Sources:* Membership; Donations; Government Grants
Staff Member(s): 1; 20 volunteer(s)
Membership: 125; *Fees:* $10 individual; $15 family, $20 groups; *Member Profile:* Individual, group/organizations involved in the Arts; *Committees:* Scholarship; Events; Funding
Activities: Monthly meetings, annual visual art show; periodic literary & music evenings events; trade shows; *Library:* by appointment
Chief Officer(s):
Gail Nash, President

West Shore Chamber of Commerce
2830 Aldwynd Rd., Victoria BC V9B 3S7
Tel: 250-478-1130; *Fax:* 250-478-1584
www.westshore.bc.ca
Overview: A small local organization founded in 1955
Mission: To promote a strong economic & social environment for Victoria's West Shore
Member of: BC Chamber of Commerce; Canadian Chamber of Commerce
Finances: *Funding Sources:* Membership dues; municipalities; auction; golf tournament
Staff Member(s): 4
Membership: 380+; *Fees:* Schedule available
Activities: *Awareness Events:* Fire Truck Parade, December; *Internships:* Yes; *Speaker Service:* Yes

Chief Officer(s):
Julie Lawlor, Executive Director
jlawlor@westshore.bc.ca

West Toronto Junction Historical Society (WTJHS)
c/o Annette Street Public Library, 145 Annette St., Lower Level, Toronto ON M6P 1P3
Tel: 416-763-3161
junctionhistorical@gmail.com
wtjhs.ca
twitter.com/WTJHS
Overview: A small local charitable organization founded in 1980
Mission: A non-profit, charitable, volunteer organization
Member of: Ontario Historical Society; Heritage Canada; Architectural Conservancy of Ontario (Toronto Region); Archives Association of Ontario; Toronto Historical Association
Finances: *Annual Operating Budget:* Less than $50,000; *Funding Sources:* Donations; grants; house tour; book sales
Staff Member(s): 1; 20 volunteer(s)
Membership: 477; *Fees:* $25 single; $30 family; *Member Profile:* Interest in local history
Activities: Walking tours; speakers & slideshows at meetings, research projects; exhibits; *Library:* Open to public
Publications:
• The Leader & Recorder [a publication of the West Toronto Junction Historical Society]
Type: Newsletter; *Frequency:* Quarterly

West Toronto Stamp Club
Fairfield Seniors' Centre, 80 Lothian Ave., Toronto ON M8Z 4K6
www.westtorontostampclub.org
Overview: A small local organization
Mission: To promote the hobby to collectors of all ages; To gain knowledge & experience in the various fields of the hobby; To acquire & dispose of postal material; To foster friendship among collectors
Staff Member(s): 5
Membership: 1,000-4,999
Activities: Holding monthly meetings (except July & August) as well as discussion & study groups; Organizing an annual exhibition & club auctions
Chief Officer(s):
Sid Mensinga, President
president@westtorontostampclub.org

West Vancouver Chamber of Commerce
2235 Marine Dr., West Vancouver BC V7V 1K5
Tel: 604-926-6614; *Fax:* 604-926-6647
info@westvanchamber.com
www.westvanchamber.com
www.linkedin.com/company/west-vancouver-chamber-of-commerce
www.facebook.com/WestVanChamber
twitter.com/westvanchamber
Overview: A medium-sized local organization
Mission: To promote, enhance, & facilitate business in the community
Finances: *Annual Operating Budget:* $250,000-$500,000; *Funding Sources:* Membership dues
Staff Member(s): 5
Membership: 380; *Fees:* Schedule available; *Member Profile:* Individuals & businesses directly engaged or interested in trade, commerce or the economic welfare of the District of West Vancouver; *Committees:* Executive; Advocacy; Membership; Events
Activities: Providing networking & educational opportunities for members through keynote speaker engagements; Offering member discount programs on services; Publicizing & promoting the business community; Advocating on behalf of members; *Speaker Service:* Yes
Chief Officer(s):
Leagh Gabriel, Executive Director, 604-926-6614
leagh@westvanchamber.com
Awards:
• West Vancouver Chamber of Commerce Excellence Awards
Eligibility: A West Vancouver Chamber of Commerce member located in West Vancouver or Bowen Island
Publications:
• West Vancouver Chamber of Commerce Newsletter
Type: Newsletter; *Frequency:* weekly
Profile: An information resource containing West Vancouver Chamber of Commerce news & events

West Vancouver Community Arts Council
1570 Argyle Ave., West Vancouver BC V7V 1A4

Tel: 604-925-7292; *Fax:* 604-922-8924
westvanartscouncil@shaw.ca
www.silkpurse.ca
Overview: A small local charitable organization founded in 1968
Mission: To champion the arts as fundamental to a vital community by encouraging an environment in which all the arts can be created, shared, & celebrated
Member of: Assembly of BC Arts Councils
Affiliation(s): West Vancouver Chamber of Commerce; Alliance of the Arts
Finances: *Annual Operating Budget:* Less than $50,000
Staff Member(s): 1; 55 volunteer(s)
Membership: 250; *Fees:* $35 family; $30 individual; $20 senior; $50 group
Activities: Music & Muffins-monthly concerts; Spoken Word award readings from the Canada Council-monthly; Cercle Francophone French readings; evening classical music concerts; *Internships:* Yes; *Speaker Service:* Yes
Chief Officer(s):
Sara Baker, Executive Director

West Vancouver Community Foundation
775 - 15th St., West Vancouver BC V7T 2S9
Tel: 604-925-8153; *Fax:* 604-925-8154
westvanfoundation@telus.net
www.westvanfoundation.com
www.facebook.com/westvanfoundation
Overview: A small local charitable organization founded in 1979
Mission: To improve the quality of life in West Vancouver; to assist organizations & people through grants & awards, with special emphasis on health, education, the arts, social services & West Vancouver's physical environment
Member of: Community Foundations of Canada
Finances: *Funding Sources:* Donations
Staff Member(s): 2
Activities: Fundraising event
Chief Officer(s):
Geoff Jopson, Chair
Delaina Bell, Executive Director
Awards:
• Gertrude Lawson Scholarship in Education
Awarded annually to a Grade 12 graduating student, orginarily a resident of West Vancouver, who is continuing wth studies in the field of Education at a post-secondary institution in BC *Eligibility:* Evidence of high academic standing & community service; *Amount:* $1,200
• Faris Family Scholarship
Awarded annually to a Grade 12 graduating student, ordinarily a resident of West Vancouver, who is planning to attend university in BC *Eligibility:* Must provide evidence of high academic standing & community service; *Amount:* $6,000 ($1,500/yr for 4 years)
• James A. Inkster Leadership Award
Presented annually to a West Vancouver Grade 12 graduating student who has shown leadership & enthusiasm for extra-curricular activities as well as a vigorous school spirit, academic performance is not a factor; *Amount:* $500
• Christina Lawson Scholarship in Music/Drama
Awarded annually to a Grade 12 graduating student, ordinarily a resident of West Vancouver, who will be involved in music/drama pursuits at a post-secondary institution in Canada or the United States; perference given to students in a Canadian institution *Eligibility:* Evidence of high academic standing & community service; *Amount:* $1,200
• Bradley T. Bowles Scholarship
Awarded annually to a West Vancouver Secondary Grade 12 graduating student continuing with post-secondary study *Eligibility:* Applicant must present evidence of superior athletic performance, high academic standing, leadership & school spirit as well as community service; *Amount:* $1,000
• West Vancouver Community Foundation Grant
Awarded annually *Eligibility:* To local non-profit projects or community programs with an emphasis on health, education, the arts, social services and the improvement of West Vancouver's physical environment. *Deadline:* Feb. 15, 2013

West Vancouver Municipal Employees Association (WVMEA) / Association des employés municipaux de Vancouver-Ouest
#118, 2419 Bellevue Ave., West Vancouver BC V7V 4T4
Tel: 604-925-7447; *Fax:* 604-926-7059
info@wvmea.com
www.wvmea.com
Overview: A small local organization

Mission: To maintain & protect working conditions & a just & reasonable scale of wages, salaries & benefits for WVMEA members
Staff Member(s): 3
Membership: 650+
Chief Officer(s):
Clive Mynott, President

The Wesleyan Church of Canada - Atlantic District *See* The Atlantic District of The Wesleyan Church

The Wesleyan Church of Canada - Central Canada District
#27, 3545 Centennial Road, Lyn ON K0E 1M0
Tel: 613-877-2087
Toll-Free: 877-862-4637
office.ccdwesleyan@gmail.com
www.ccdwesleyan.ca
Also Known As: The Wesleyan Methodist Church of Canada
Overview: A medium-sized national charitable organization founded in 1897
Mission: To create a context that produces healthy churches
Affiliation(s): Tyndale Seminary; World Hope International; World Relief Canada; Bethany Bible College; Outreach Canada; Evangelical Fellowship of Canada
Finances: *Annual Operating Budget:* $500,000-$1.5 Million; *Funding Sources:* District churches
Staff Member(s): 3
Membership: 1,736; *Member Profile:* Covenant members & community members in Ontario & Quebec
Activities: Camps; Church Planting; Emerging Regions; Friends for the Future; Missions; *Internships:* Yes
Chief Officer(s):
Peter Rigby, District Superintendent
peter.rigby@ccdwesleyan.ca
Daryl MacPherson, District Secretary
ccdsecretary@gmail.com
Sheldon Gilmer, District Treasurer
sheldon@blackscreek.ca

Westbank & District Chamber of Commerce *See* Greater Westside Board of Trade

Westcoast Association of Visual Language Interpreters (WAVLI)
PO Box 41542, 923 - 12th St., New Westminster BC V3M 6L1
www.wavli.com
www.facebook.com/wavli.britishcolumbia
twitter.com/WAVLI
Overview: A small local organization founded in 1987 overseen by Association of Visual Language Interpreters of Canada
Mission: Committed to advancing the profession of sign language interpretation & to ensuring that our members provide British Columbians with exceptional standards of practice
Member of: Association of Visual Language Interpreters of Canada (AVLIC)
Finances: *Funding Sources:* Membership fees; Fundraising
Membership: *Member Profile:* Sign language interpreters & those supporting goals of the association; *Committees:* Fundraising; Membership; Newsletter; Professional Development; Professional Standards; Public Relations; Technology
Chief Officer(s):
Caroline Tetreault, President
Brenda Carmichael, Vice-President

Western Association of Broadcast Engineers (WABE)
#319, 300, 8120 Beddington Blvd. NW, Calgary AB T3K 2A8
Tel: 403-630-4907; *Fax:* 403-295-3135
info@wabe.ca
www.wabe.ca
www.linkedin.com/company/651175
www.facebook.com/wabe.convention
twitter.com/WABE_Convention
Overview: A medium-sized local organization
Chief Officer(s):
Kathy Watson, Office Manager

Western Association of Broadcasters (WAB)
#507, 918 - 16th Ave. NW, Calgary AB T2M 0K3
Toll-Free: 877-814-2719
Other Communication: Toll-Free Fax: 1-877-814-2749
info@wab.ca
www.wab.ca
Overview: A medium-sized provincial organization

Mission: To represent private television & radio stations in Alberta, Saskatchewan & Manitoba.
Chief Officer(s):
Tom Newton, President
Meetings/Conferences:
• 84th Annual Western Association of Broadcasters Conference 2018, June, 2018, Banff, AB
Scope: Provincial

Western Ayrshire Club
Cobble Hill BC
Tel: 250-743-6192; *Fax:* 250-743-6190
Overview: A medium-sized provincial organization founded in 1928
Mission: To promote the breeding of Ayrshire cattle in British Columbia; to promote the dairy farming industry & the Ayrshire dairy cow as the most economical, productive, profitable & efficient dairy cow to the farmer
Member of: Ayrshire Canada
Chief Officer(s):
Olivier Balme, Director

Western Barley Growers Association (WBGA)
Agriculture Centre, 97 East Lake Ramp NE, Airdrie AB T4A 0C3
Tel: 403-912-3998; *Fax:* 403-948-2069
wbga@wbga.org
www.wbga.org
Overview: A medium-sized local organization founded in 1973
Mission: To provide farmers with an informed & effective voice in the agriculture industry of Western Canada
Membership: *Fees:* $200; *Member Profile:* Farmers; industry-related to agriculture; end users
Activities: *Rents Mailing List:* Yes
Chief Officer(s):
Doug Robertson, President
dougarob@gmail.com
Douglas McBain, Treasurer
dkmcbain@lincsat.com
Tom Hewson, Saskatchewan Vice-President
hewws@sasktel.net
Meetings/Conferences:
• Western Barley Growers Association 40th Annual Convention, March, 2018, Deerfoot Inn & Casino, Calgary, AB
Scope: Provincial
Description: Theme: "A New Era in Agriculture"

Western Board of Music *See* Conservatory Canada

Western Boreal Growth & Yield Association
c/o Renewable Resources, Room 861 GSB, University of Alberta, Edmonton AB T6G 2H1
Tel: 780-492-1879; *Fax:* 780-492-4323
wesbogy.ales.ualberta.ca
Also Known As: WESBOGY Association
Overview: A small local organization
Mission: To conduct research projects that help develop & disseminate growth & yield modeling technology for natural & regenerated stands growing in the boreal mixedwood region
Chief Officer(s):
Phil Comeau, Contact
phil.comeau@ualberta.ca
Mike Bokalo, Contact
mike.bokalo@ualberta.ca

Western Canada B&B Innkeepers Association *See* British Columbia Bed & Breakfast Innkeepers Guild

Western Canada Children's Wear Markets (WCCWM)
#245, 1868 Glen Dr., Vancouver BC V6A 4K4
Tel: 604-634-0909; *Fax:* 888-595-9360
www.wccwm.com
Overview: A small local organization founded in 1967 overseen by Canadian Association of Wholesale Sales Representatives
Mission: To provide showcases for children's & maternity goods
Member of: CAWS
Affiliation(s): WCCM
Finances: *Funding Sources:* Advertising; Markets
Membership: 18
Chief Officer(s):
Doug Fulton, President
doug@fultonsales.com

Western Canada Family Child Care Association of British Columbia (WCFCCA) *See* British Columbia Family Child Care Association

The Western Canada Group of Chartered Engineers (WCGCE)
www.wcgce.org
Overview: A medium-sized local organization founded in 1987
Mission: To provide a series of technical meetings & visits programs; to act as a liaison between local engineers & British engineering institutes
Affiliation(s): Institutions of Civil, Mechanical, Structural, Electrical & Chemical Engineers, London UK
Membership: 1,000 individual
Chief Officer(s):
Andrzej Nawrocki, Chair
David Harvey, Vice-Chair

Western Canada Irish Dancing Teachers Association (WCIDTA)
c/o Deirdre Penk-O'Donnell, Penk O'Donnell School of Irish Dance, Vancouver BC
Tel: 604-921-0700
www.wcidta.ca
Overview: A small provincial organization founded in 1964
Mission: To administer & regulate Irish dancing in British Columbia, Alberta, Saskatchewan, & Manitoba; To ensure the quality of competitive Irish dancing standards in the western Canadian region
Member of: An Coimisiun le Rinci Gaelacha (the governing body of Irish dancing); Irish Dancing Teachers Association of North America
Membership: *Member Profile:* Registered teachers (TCRG) & adjudicators (ADCRG) in British Columbia, Alberta, Saskatchewan, & Manitoba who are also members of the An Coimisiun le Rinci Gaelacha & the Irish Dancing Teachers Association of North America
Activities: Promoting Irish dancing throughout western Canada
Chief Officer(s):
Deirdre Penk-O'Donnell, Regional Director

Western Canada Roadbuilders & Heavy Construction Association
c/o Manitoba Heavy Construction Association, #3, 1680 Ellice Ave., Winnipeg MB R3H 0Z2
Tel: 204-947-1379; *Fax:* 204-943-2279
www.wcrhca.org
Overview: A medium-sized local organization founded in 1975 overseen by Canadian Construction Association
Mission: To represent four western provincial roadbuilders & heavy construction associations at the provincial & federal level
Affiliation(s): Roads & Transportation Association of Canada
Membership: 4 member associations; *Member Profile:* British Columbia Roadbuilders & Heavy Construction Association, Alberta Roadbuilders & Heavy Construction Association, Saskatchewan Heavy Construction Association, Manitoba Heavy Construction Association

Western Canada Theatre Company Society (WCT)
PO Box 329, 1025 Lorne St., Kamloops BC V2C 5K9
Tel: 250-372-3216; *Fax:* 250-374-7099
www.wctlive.ca
www.facebook.com/wctlive
twitter.com/wctlive
www.youtube.com/user/wctkamloops
Also Known As: Western Canada Theatre
Overview: A small provincial charitable organization founded in 1975
Mission: To provide the regional community with challenging professional theatre; To entertain, educate, enrich & interact with the cultural mosaic of its community; To promote & assist the performing arts through the provision of educational, theatrical & artistic opportunities & services & through the management & operation of facilities
Affiliation(s): Professional Association of Canadian Theatres
Finances: *Funding Sources:* Regional government; federal government; City of Kamloops; private donations; box office sales
Staff Member(s): 30
Activities: Producing 5 mainstage productions, as well as 2-4 second stage productions; *Internships:* Yes
Chief Officer(s):
Lori Marchand, Executive Director
lori@wctlive.ca

Western Canada Tire Dealers Association (WCTD)
PO Box 58047, Stn. Chaparral, Calgary AB T2X 3V2
Tel: 403-264-3179; *Fax:* 403-264-3176
www.wctd.ca
twitter.com/WestCanTire
Overview: A medium-sized local organization founded in 1962
Mission: To establish standards of excellence for members; To promote a professional image in the industry; To act as a unified voice in dealings with government agencies & equipment distributors; To inform members of advancements in products & services
Membership: 900+; *Fees:* $100; *Member Profile:* Independent tire dealers & retreaders from the Yukon, Northwest Territories, British Columbia, Alberta, Saskatchewan, Manitoba, & western Ontario; Manufacturers; Distributors; Exporters; Dealer support services
Activities: Maintaining standards of excellence for tire dealers; Providing a forum for members to discuss issues within the industry; Assisting members to develop beneficial business plans; Representing members on scrap tire boards across western Canada; Offering the Tire Certification Training Program to train employees, plus seminars on various subjects
Chief Officer(s):
Andy Nagy, Contact
andy@wctda.ca
Awards:
• Western Canada Tire Dealers Academic Scholarship
; *Amount:* 5 scholarships of $2,000 each *Contact:* Dan Harper, Chair, WCTD Scholarship Committee, Address: 948 Jim Common Dr. North, Sherwood Park, AB, T8H 1Y3
• WCTD Hall of Fame
To recognize individuals who have made outstanding contributions for the betterment of the industry
Publications:
• Tracker
Type: Newsletter; *Frequency:* 5 pa; *Accepts Advertising*
Profile: Informative stories, guest editorials from industry leaders, & special reports on issues, for small to medium-sized enterprises throughout western Canada

Western Canada Water (WCW)
PO Box 1708, 240 River Ave., Cochrane AB T4C 1B6
Tel: 403-709-0064; *Fax:* 403-709-0068
Toll-Free: 877-283-2003
member@wcwwa.ca
www.wcwwa.ca
Overview: A medium-sized local organization founded in 1948
Mission: To advance support for water professionals throughout western Canada
Affiliation(s): Alberta Water & Wastewater Operator Association (AWWOA); Manitoba Water & Wastewater Association (MWWA); Municipal Service & Suppliers Association (MSSA); Northern Territories Water & Waste Association (NTWWA); Saskatchewan Water & Wastewater Association (SWWA); Western Canada Water Environment Association (WCWEA)
Membership: 4,000; *Committees:* Alberta Provincial Council; Saskatchewan Provincial Council; Manitoba Provincial Council; Joint Operators; Conference Planning; Editorial
Activities: Offering education & training
Chief Officer(s):
Audrey Arisman, Executive Director, 403-709-0064, Fax: 403-709-0068
aarisman@wcwwa.ca
Meetings/Conferences:
• Western Canada Water 2018 70th Annual Conference & Exhibition, September, 2018, Winnipeg Convention Centre, Winnipeg, MB
Scope: Provincial
Attendance: 500+
Description: A technical program, a keynote speaker, & a trade show for delegates from Western Canada Water
Contact Information: Western Canada Water, Toll-Free Phone: 1-877-283-2003, Toll-Free Fax: 1-877-283-2007, E-mail: info@wcwwa.ca
• Western Canada Water 2019 71st Annual Conference & Exhibition, September, 2019, Shaw Conference Center, Edmonton, AB
Scope: Provincial
Attendance: 500+
Description: A technical program, a keynote speaker, & a trade show for delegates from Western Canada Water
Contact Information: Western Canada Water, Toll-Free Phone: 1-877-283-2003, Toll-Free Fax: 1-877-283-2007, E-mail: info@wcwwa.ca
• Western Canada Water 2020 72nd Annual Conference & Exhibition, September, 2020, Regina, SK
Scope: Provincial
Attendance: 500+
Description: A technical program, a keynote speaker, & a trade show for delegates from Western Canada Water
Contact Information: Western Canada Water, Toll-Free Phone: 1-877-283-2003, Toll-Free Fax: 1-877-283-2007, E-mail: info@wcwwa.ca
• Western Canada Water 2021 73rd Annual Conference & Exhibition, 2021, Winnipeg, MB
Scope: Provincial
Attendance: 500+
Description: A technical program, a keynote speaker, & a trade show for delegates from Western Canada Water
Contact Information: Western Canada Water, Toll-Free Phone: 1-877-283-2003, Toll-Free Fax: 1-877-283-2007, E-mail: info@wcwwa.ca
• Western Canada Water 2022 74th Annual Conference & Exhibition, September, 2022, Calgary, AB
Scope: Provincial
Attendance: 500+
Description: A technical program, a keynote speaker, & a trade show for delegates from Western Canada Water
Contact Information: Western Canada Water, Toll-Free Phone: 1-877-283-2003, Toll-Free Fax: 1-877-283-2007, E-mail: info@wcwwa.ca
Publications:
• Western Canada Water
Type: Magazine; *Frequency:* Quarterly; *Accepts Advertising*;
Editor: Terry Ross (terry@kelman.ca); *ISSN:* 1483-7730; *Price:* Free with Western Canada Water membership
Profile: Theme issues, plus regular departments such as the president's message, the calendar of events, going green, news from the field, the minister's forum, & a newproduct showcase
• Western Canada Water Member Newsletter
Type: Newsletter
Profile: Membership information & news about forthcoming events

Western Canada Wilderness Committee *See* Wilderness Committee

Western Canadian Association of Bovine Practitioners (WPABP)
226E Wheeler St., 2nd Fl., Saskatoon SK S7P 0A9
Fax: 306-956-0607
Toll-Free: 866-269-8387
info@wcabp.com
www.wcabp.com
Overview: A medium-sized national organization
Membership: 250+; *Fees:* $200 active; $16 student
Chief Officer(s):
Kerri-Rae Millar, President, 204-822-4333
kes113@mail.usask.ca
Meetings/Conferences:
• 2018 Western Canadian Association of Bovine Practitioners Conference, January, 2018, Calgary, AB
Scope: National

Western Canadian Miniature Horse Club (WCMHC)
c/o Charlene Bier, PO Box 1475, Vulcan AB T0L 2B0
www.wcmhc.ca
Overview: A small local organization founded in 1985
Mission: To encourage the breeding & exhibition of Canadian stock, as defined by the American Miniature Horse Association Standard of Perfection & the American Miniature Horse Registry Standard of Perfection; To develop & promote the miniature horse breed
Affiliation(s): American Miniature Horse Association (AMHA); American Miniature Horse Registry (AMHR)
Membership: *Fees:* $10 associate & youth members; $35 single memberships; $40 family memberships; *Member Profile:* Any person with an interest in the miniature horse breed; Members do not need to own a horse & do not need to live in western Canada
Activities: Presenting show results; Cooperating with other horse associations; Arranging exhibits about miniature horses; Providing showing & judges' clinics
Chief Officer(s):
Bill Clark, President
wcmhclub@gmail.com
Scott Rempel, Vice-President
rempel44@telus.net
Sonja Marinoske, Secretary
minirose@telusplanet.net
Charlene Bier, Treasurer
charlene@doubletreefarms.ca
Publications:
• WCMHC Newsletter
Type: Newsletter; *Editor:* Cindy Hunter; *Price:* Free with Western Canadian Miniature Horse Club membership

Western Canadian Music Alliance (WCMA)
#1, 118 Sherbrook St., Winnipeg MB R3C 2B4
Tel: 204-943-8485; *Fax:* 204-453-1594
info@breakoutwest.ca
breakoutwest.ca
www.facebook.com/breakoutwest
twitter.com/breakoutwest
instagram.com/breakoutwest
Previous Name: Prairie Music Alliance
Overview: A large local organization founded in 1999
Mission: The music industry associations of Manitoba, Alberta, and Saskatchewan work in tandem towards the shared vision of developing the infrastructure of the independent music industry in Western Canada.
Affiliation(s): Alberta Recording Industry Association; Saskatchewan Recording Industry Association; Manitoba Audio Recording Industry Association
Membership: 5 organizations
Activities: Prairie Music Week; Music Awards; *Awareness Events:* BreakOut West
Chief Officer(s):
Robyn Stewart, Executive Director
robyn@breakoutwest.ca
Awards:
• Western Canadian Music Awards
Annual Awards in the following categories: Recording Engineer of the Year, Record Producer of the Year, Recording Studio of the Year, Record Company of the Year, Publishing Company of the Year, Best Compilation Album of the Year, Best Album Design of the Year, Best Music Score of the Year, Best Music Video, Best Booking Agent, Manager of the Year, & Musician of the Year; also Annual Awards for Prairie artists in the following categories: People's Choice Award, Female/Male Recording Artist of the Year, Group Recording of the Year, Most Promising Artist, Best Pop/Light Rock, Best Rock/Heavy Metal, Best Alternative, Best Country, Best Blues/R&B/Soul, Best Roots/Traditional/Ethnic, Best Rap/Dance/Rhythm, Best Jazz, Best Classical Performance
Meetings/Conferences:
• Western Canadian Music Alliance BOW [Break Out West] Conference 2018, October, 2018, Kelowna, BC
Scope: Provincial

Western Canadian Opera Society
PO Box 5105, Vancouver BC V6B 4A9
Tel: 604-942-6646
info@operaclub.net
www.operaclub.net
Also Known As: The Opera Club
Overview: A small local charitable organization founded in 1974
Mission: To educate the public about opera through a series of illustrated lectures; one special annual lecture by a nationally known expert in Opera (Western Canadian Opera Lecture)
Membership: *Fees:* $45 individual; $85 double; *Member Profile:* Opera-goers & enthusiasts living in the Greater Vancouver, BC area
Activities: Eight monthly lectures; bus trips to operas outside Vancouver lower mainland; annual special lecture presented by expert in opera

Western Canadian Shippers' Coalition (WCSC)
31 Centennial Pkwy., Delta BC V4L 2C3
Tel: 604-943-8984; *Fax:* 604-943-8936
contact@westshippers.com
www.westshippers.com
twitter.com/Westshippers
www.youtube.com/user/Rhobot?feature=mhee
Overview: A medium-sized provincial organization
Member of: a
Membership: 21; *Member Profile:* Companies & associations involved in the transportation industry in western Canada
Chief Officer(s):
Ian May, Chair

Western Canadian Wheat Growers
3602 Taylor St. East, Bay 6A, Saskatoon SK S7H 5H9
Tel: 306-586-5866; *Fax:* 306-244-4497
Other Communication: Alt. Phone: 306-955-0356
info@wheatgrowers.ca
www.wheatgrowers.ca
Previous Name: Palliser Wheat Growers Association
Overview: A medium-sized national organization founded in 1970
Mission: To promote changes that improve the wheat industry for its members
Membership: *Fees:* $25 students; $238.10 farmers; $500 agribusiness; *Member Profile:* Wheat farmers in Western Canada
Chief Officer(s):
Blair Rutter, Executive Director, 204-256-2353, Fax: 204-256-2357
brutter@wheatgrowers.ca

Western Communities Arts Council *See* West Shore Arts Council

Western Convenience Store Association (WCSA)
AB
Tel: 778-987-4440
Toll-Free: 800-734-2487
andrew@conveniencestores.ca
www.thewcsa.com
www.linkedin.com/groups/Western-Convenience-Stores-Association-4191541
Overview: A medium-sized provincial organization overseen by Canadian Convenience Store Association
Mission: To represent convenience store retailers in Manitoba, Saskatchewan, Alberta, British Columbia, Yukon, Northwest Territories & Nunavut
Affiliation(s): Canadian Convenience Stores Association; Ontario Convenience Stores Association; Association Québécoise des dépanneurs en alimentation; Atlantic Convenience Stores Association
Finances: *Funding Sources:* Membership fees
Membership: *Member Profile:* Major convenience store companies; independent owners; food retailers; suppliers & wholesalers; gasoline & automotive product vendors
Chief Officer(s):
Andrew Klukas, President
andrew@conveniencestores.ca

Western Employers Labour Relations Association
#203, 27126 Fraser Hwy., Langley BC V4W 3P6
Tel: 604-857-5540; *Fax:* 604-857-5547
Previous Name: Metal Industries Association
Overview: A medium-sized local organization founded in 1967
Mission: To provide employee relations services for both union & non-union employers

Western Fair Association (WFA)
PO Box 7550, 316 Rectory St., London ON N5Y 5P8
Tel: 519-438-7203
Toll-Free: 800-619-4629
contact@westernfairdistrict.com
www.westernfairdistrict.com
www.facebook.com/westernfairdistrict
twitter.com/WesternFair
Overview: A small local charitable organization founded in 1867
Mission: To create unique experiences that build positive memories
Member of: International Association of Fairs & Expositions; Canadian Association of Fairs & Exibitions
Affiliation(s): Ontario Horse Racing Industry
Finances: *Annual Operating Budget:* Greater than $5 Million
Staff Member(s): 80; 175 volunteer(s)
Membership: 243; *Member Profile:* Agriculture, civic, city representatives & individuals
Activities: Presenting horse racing, IMAX-theatre, an annual fair, banquets, a 4 pad ice arena, & trade, consumer, & agricultural related shows
Chief Officer(s):
Hugh Mitchell, Chief Executive Officer

Western Fertilizer & Chemical Dealers Association *See* Canadian Association of Agri-Retailers

Western Forestry Contractors Association (WFCA)
#720, 999 West Broadway, Vancouver BC V5Z 1K5
Tel: 604-736-8660; *Fax:* 604-728-4080
Other Communication: Nelson Phone: 250-229-4380; Fax: 250-229-4366
info@wfca.ca
www.wfca.ca
Merged from: Consulting Foresters of British Columbia; Western Silviculture Contractors Association
Overview: A small provincial organization
Membership: 62; *Member Profile:* Contractors providing all levels of pre & post-harvest planning & implementation services to the forest industry
Activities: Focus is on the following areas: communications, business practices, forest policy, forestry consulting & safety
Chief Officer(s):
John Betts, Executive Director
Karline Mark-Eng, Administrative Secretary
admin@wfca.ca

Western Front Society
303 East 8th Ave., Vancouver BC V5T 1S1
Tel: 604-876-9343; *Fax:* 604-876-4099
admin@front.bc.ca
www.front.bc.ca
www.facebook.com/pages/Western-Front/164127636934501
twitter.com/western_front
Overview: A small local charitable organization founded in 1974
Mission: Artist-run centre that focuses on the production & presentation of new art
Member of: Pacific Association of Artist Run Centres; Museums Associations Canada; Alliance for Arts & Culture
Finances: *Annual Operating Budget:* $250,000-$500,000; *Funding Sources:* National, provincial & municipal government; private
Staff Member(s): 11; 60 volunteer(s)
Membership: 250 individual; *Fees:* $40 individual; $100 sustaining; *Member Profile:* Artists; patrons; litterati; *Committees:* Personnel; Budget; Access & Outreach; Building; Communications; Fund-raising
Activities: Offers programs of exhibition, performance art, video production, computer graphics, telecommunications, poetry, dance & music; through a residency program, local, national & international artists are invited to create new works in this interdisciplinary environment; *Internships:* Yes; *Library:* by appointment
Chief Officer(s):
Kate Armstrong, President
Caitlin Jones, Executive Director
caitlinjones@front.bc.ca

Western Grain Elevator Association
#440, 360 Main St., Winnipeg MB R3C 3Z3
Tel: 204-942-6835; *Fax:* 204-943-4328
wgea@mts.net
www.wgea.ca
Overview: A small local organization
Mission: To represent grain businesses operating in Canada
Staff Member(s): 3
Membership: 10 institutional; *Member Profile:* Major grain handling & sales companies
Chief Officer(s):
Wade Sobkowich, Executive Director

Western Grains Research Foundation (WGRF)
#306, 111 Research Dr., Saskatoon SK S7N 3R2
Tel: 306-975-0060; *Fax:* 306-975-0316
info@westerngrains.com
www.westerngrains.com
Overview: A medium-sized provincial organization founded in 1981
Mission: To fund & invest in agricultural research that benefits western Canadian crop producers; To give producers a voice in funding decisions; To encourage the long-term sustainability of crop research in western Canada
Staff Member(s): 8
Activities: Managing an endowment fund; Collecting wheat & barley check-off funds (deductions made on wheat & barley cash sales) & re-investing them into development & research
Chief Officer(s):
Garth Patterson, Executive Director, 306-975-2081
GarthPatterson@westerngrains.com
Publications:
• Western Grains Research Foundation Annual Report
Type: Report

Western Hockey League (WHL)
Father David Bauer Arena, 2424 University Dr. NW, Calgary AB T2N 3Y9
Tel: 403-693-3030; *Fax:* 403-693-3031
info@whl.ca
www.whl.ca
www.facebook.com/WHLHockey
twitter.com/theWHL
Overview: A medium-sized local organization founded in 1966
Mission: To remain the world's premiere major junior hockey league by continuing to provide the best player development & educational opportunities while enhancing the entertainment value of the game for our fan base
Member of: Canadian Hockey League
Staff Member(s): 12
Membership: Comprised of 22 hockey teams in Western Canada & the northwest United States

Canadian Associations / Western Independence Party of Saskatchewan (WIPSK)

Chief Officer(s):
Ron Robison, Commissioner

Western Independence Party of Saskatchewan (WIPSK)
PO Box 263, Endeavour SK S0A 0W0
Tel: 306-547-4738
Overview: A small provincial organization founded in 2003
Chief Officer(s):
Neil Fenske, Party Leader

Western Independent Adjusters' Association
c/o Doreen Lennon, Townsend & Leedham Adjusters Ltd., #200, 4245 - 97 St., Edmonton AB T6E 5Y7
Tel: 780-463-7776; *Fax:* 780-462-1280
www.ciaa-adjusters.ca
Overview: A small provincial organization overseen by Canadian Independent Adjusters' Association
Chief Officer(s):
Doreen Lennon, President
dlennon@tladjusters.com

Western Institute for the Deaf & Hard of Hearing (WIDHH)
2125 West 7th Ave., Vancouver BC V6K 1X9
Tel: 604-736-7391; *Fax:* 604-736-4381; *TTY:* 604-736-2527
info@widhh.com
www.widhh.com
www.facebook.com/92914429597
twitter.com/widhh
Also Known As: Western Institute
Overview: A small provincial charitable organization founded in 1956
Mission: To address the needs of the deaf, deafened & hard of hearing individuals by providing products, services & programs that work towards ensuring accessibility to their environment which is equal to that of the hearing public
Member of: United Way; Better Business Bureau
Staff Member(s): 39
Membership: *Fees:* $15; $100 life; *Member Profile:* Deaf & hard of hearing
Activities: Public displays; *Library*
Chief Officer(s):
Ruth Warick, President
Susan Masters, Executive Director
masters@widhh.com

Western Inter-College Conference (WICC) *See* Alberta Colleges Athletic Conference

Western Magazine Awards Foundation (WMAF)
#102, 211 Columbia St., Vancouver BC V6A 2R5
Tel: 604-945-3711
info@westernmagazineawards.ca
www.westernmagazineawards.ca
www.facebook.com/WesternMagazineAwards
twitter.com/WesternMagAward
Also Known As: The Westerns
Overview: A small local organization
Mission: To recognize exceptional work in the Western Canadian magazine industry.
Staff Member(s): 1
Chief Officer(s):
Jane Zatylny, President
Kate Cockerill, Executive Director
Awards:
• The Western Magazine Awards
Editorial excellence in western Canadian magazine writing, photography, illustration & art direction

Western Newfoundland Model Forest *See* Model Forest of Newfoundland & Labrador

Western Québec Literacy Council (WQLC) / Conseil d'alphabétisation de l'ouest du Québec
PO Box 266, 381, rte 148, Shawville QC J0X 2Y0
Tel: 819-647-3112; *Fax:* 819-647-3188
Toll-Free: 888-647-3112
info@wq-literacy.org
www.wq-literacy.org
www.facebook.com/199249413439491
Overview: A small local charitable organization founded in 1984
Mission: To give free lessons in reading, writing & mathematics, in English, to adults in the Western Québec region; to train volunteer tutors; to sensitize the public about the problem of illiteracy & to offer support to tutors & students
Affiliation(s): Literacy Volunteers of Québec; Laubach Literacy of Canada

Finances: Annual Operating Budget: $50,000-$100,000; *Funding Sources:* Provincial & federal government; private funding
Staff Member(s): 3; 100 volunteer(s)
Membership: 75 individual; *Fees:* $5 institutional; $5 individual; $5 associate
Chief Officer(s):
Marilee DeLombard, Executive Director
Norma J. DesRosiers, President

Western Red Cedar Lumber Association (WRCLA)
Pender Place 1, #1501, 700 West Pender St., Vancouver BC V6C 1G8
Tel: 604-891-1262; *Fax:* 604-687-4930
Toll-Free: 866-778-9096
www.wrcla.org
www.facebook.com/RealCedar
twitter.com/RealCedar
www.youtube.com/user/WRCLA
Overview: A small local organization founded in 1954
Mission: Trade association representing quality producers of Western Red Cedar lumber products in BC & the Pacific Northwest states; members are dedicated to producing quality siding, decking, paneling, outdoor & other specialty cedar products
Staff Member(s): 5
Membership: 29; *Fees:* Based on shipments; *Member Profile:* Producers of Western Red cedar

Western Refederation Party of BC; Western Independence Party of BC *See* British Columbia Refederation Party

Western Regional Advocacy Group Society (WRAGS)
#370, 3771 Jacombs Rd., Richmond BC V6V 2L9
Tel: 604-214-0613; *Fax:* 604-214-0614
Toll-Free: 866-949-7247
wrags@telus.net
www.wrags.net
Overview: A small local charitable organization founded in 1992
Mission: To offer free, used mattresses to individuals & groups in need
Chief Officer(s):
Stephen Pearce, President

Western Retail Lumber Association (WRLA)
Western Retail Lumber Association Inc., #1004, 213 Notre Dame Ave., Winnipeg MB R3B 1N3
Tel: 204-957-1077; *Fax:* 204-947-5195
Toll-Free: 800-661-0253
wrla@wrla.org
www.wrla.org
Overview: A medium-sized local organization founded in 1890
Mission: To serve & promote needs & common interests of lumber, building materials & hard goods industry on the Prairies
Membership: *Fees:* Schedule available
Chief Officer(s):
Gary Hamilton, Executive Director
Dwight Dixon, President
Meetings/Conferences:
• Western Retail Lumber Association 2018 Buying Show, January, 2018, Calgary, AB
Scope: Provincial
• Western Retail Lumber Association 2018 Prairie Showcase Buying Show & Convention, 2018
Scope: Provincial
Publications:
• The YardStick [a publication of the Western Retail Lumber Association]
Type: Magazine; *Frequency:* 6 pa

Western Silvicultural Contractors' Association (WSCA)
#720, 999 West Broadway, Vancouver BC V5Z 1K5
Tel: 604-736-8660; *Fax:* 604-738-4080
info@wsca.ca
www.wsca.ca
Overview: A medium-sized local organization founded in 1984
Mission: Dedicated to improving working conditions, quality of life and safety for all silviculture workers.
Finances: Annual Operating Budget: $50,000-$100,000
Staff Member(s): 2; 15 volunteer(s)
Membership: 75; *Fees:* $200 supplier; $1000 licensee; *Member Profile:* Silvicultural contractors
Chief Officer(s):
John Betts, Executive Director

The Western Stock Growers' Association (WSGA)
PO Box 179, #14, 900 Village Lane, Okotoks AB T1S 1Z6
Tel: 403-250-9121
office@wsga.ca
www.wsga.ca
www.facebook.com/WesternStockGrowers
Overview: A medium-sized local organization founded in 1896
Mission: To support & protect livestock growers by lobbying the government on existing legislation & proposed new legislation; Tto promote environmentally sound range management practices
Staff Member(s): 1
Membership: 1,200; *Fees:* $150-$500; *Member Profile:* Stockmen
Chief Officer(s):
Phil Rowland, President
Meetings/Conferences:
• Western Stock Growers' Association Annual General Meeting 2018, 2018
Scope: Provincial

Western Transportation Advisory Council (WESTAC)
#401, 899 Pender St. West, Vancouver BC V6C 3B2
Tel: 604-687-8691; *Fax:* 604-687-8751
infoservices@westac.com
www.westac.com
www.linkedin.com/company/2275285?trk=tyah
www.facebook.com/181099878620851
twitter.com/WESTAC
Overview: A small local organization founded in 1973
Mission: To advance Western Canadian economy through the improvement of the region's transportation systems
Finances: Annual Operating Budget: $500,000-$1.5 Million; *Funding Sources:* Membership fees; project fees; professional services fees
Staff Member(s): 4
Membership: 52 corporate; *Fees:* Revenue-related scale; *Member Profile:* Carriers; shippers; ports & terminals; labour unions; government
Activities: *Library:* Westenr Transportation Advisory Council Library; by appointment
Chief Officer(s):
Oksana Excell, President & CEO, 604-687-8691 Ext. 310
oexellwestac.com
Lisa Baratta, Director, Administration & Program Delivery
Jennifer Perih, Manager, Communications & Member Engagement
Phil Allmark, Intern, Transportation Analyst
Meetings/Conferences:
• Western Canada's Transportation Forum Spring 2018, May, 2018, Fairmont Hotel, Winnipeg, MB
Description: Members representing the shipper and service provider communities wil be encouraged to share information and insight to improve capacity and service
• Western Canada's Transportation Forum Fall 2018, 2018

Westerner Park
4847A - 19th St., Red Deer AB T4R 2N7
Tel: 403-343-7800; *Fax:* 403-341-4767
askus@westerner.ab.ca
www.westernerpark.ca
www.facebook.com/westernerpark
twitter.com/westernerpark
www.youtube.com/westernerpark
Also Known As: The Westerner Exposition Association
Overview: A small local charitable organization founded in 1891
Mission: To take a leadership role in providing superior services, programs, & events benefiting Central Alberta
Member of: Canadian Association of Fairs & Exhibitions; International Association of Fairs & Exhibitions
Staff Member(s): 22
Activities: Westerner Days Fair & Exposition; Agritrade Farm Expo
Chief Officer(s):
John Harms, Chief Executive Officer & General Manager, 403-309-0200
jharms@westerner.ab.ca

Westgen
PO Box 40, 6681 Glover Rd., Milner BC V0X 1T0
Tel: 604-530-1141; *Fax:* 604-534-3036
Toll-Free: 800-563-5603
www.westgen.com
Previous Name: BC Artificial Insemination Centre

Overview: A small provincial charitable organization founded in 1943
Mission: To provide Semex Alliance Genetics & other value-added products & services which enhance herd improvement to livestock producers in western Canada
Member of: Semex Alliance
Finances: *Annual Operating Budget:* Greater than $5 Million
Staff Member(s): 46
Membership: 1,400; *Fees:* $5; *Member Profile:* Dairy & beef producers in Western Canada
Chief Officer(s):
Brent Belluk, General Manager
gm@westgen.com
Darcie Kaye, Marketing Manager
dkaye@westgen.com

Westhaven-Elmhurst Community Association
7405, av Harley, Montréal QC H4B 1Y2
Tel: 514-872-6134
westhavencenter@hotmail.com
www.westhavenndg.com
www.facebook.com/WesthavenNDG
Overview: A small local organization founded in 1972
Mission: To offer recreational & social programs & activities to the community on a year-round basis

Westlock & District Chamber of Commerce
PO Box 5917, Westlock AB T7P 2P7
Tel: 780-349-4444
Overview: A small local organization
Member of: Alberta Chamber of Commerce
Finances: *Annual Operating Budget:* Less than $50,000; *Funding Sources:* Membership dues; fundraising
75 volunteer(s)
Membership: 78; *Fees:* $75 individual; $125 business; $15 senior/student; *Committees:* Agriculture; Economic Development; Fund-raising; Membership
Activities: Organizing events including Christmas Liteup; Offering Best Bloomin' Town in the West program; *Awareness Events:* Small Business Week; Seniors Week

Westmorland Historical Society (WHS)
4974 Main St., Dorchester NB E4K 2Z1
Tel: 506-379-6633
www.keillorhousemuseum.com
Overview: A small local organization founded in 1961
Mission: To preserve the past for the future

Westmount Historical Association (WHA) / Association historique de Westmount
Westmount Public Library, 4574, rue Sherbrooke ouest, Montréal QC H3Z 1G1
Tel: 514-989-5510
info@westmounthistorical.org
www.westmounthistorical.org
Overview: A small local charitable organization founded in 1944
Mission: To collect, preserve, & interpret the history of Westmount, Québec; To promote awareness of local history; To encourage research about local cultural & social development
Finances: *Funding Sources:* Donations; Membership fees
Membership: *Fees:* $20 individuals; $30 families; $100 patrons; $250 corporate
Activities: Presenting lectures on topics related to heritage; Offering walking tours of Westmount; *Library:* Westmount Historical Association Archives; Open to public by appointment
Publications:
• The Westmount Historian
Type: Newsletter; *Frequency:* Semiannually
Profile: Articles about the history of Westmount, Québec & association events

Weston Historical Society
1901 Weston Rd., Toronto ON M9N 3P1
Tel: 416-249-6663
westonhistoricalsociety@rogers.com
www.facebook.com/113972951953777
Overview: A small local organization

Westport & Rideau Lakes Chamber of Commerce
PO Box 157, Westport ON K0G 1X0
Tel: 613-273-2929; *Fax:* 613-273-2929
wrlcc14@gmail.com
www.therideaucalls.ca
twitter.com/WRLCC
Overview: A small local charitable organization founded in 1960
Mission: To support area businesses; To enhance economic prosperity in the community

Finances: *Annual Operating Budget:* Less than $50,000; *Funding Sources:* Membership fees; donations
12 volunteer(s)
Membership: 130; *Fees:* $125-$175; *Member Profile:* Local businesses & services
Chief Officer(s):
Marty Hawkins, Co-Chair
Ken Rose, Co-Chair

Westward Goals Support Services Inc.
PO Box 2292, Rocky Mountain House AB T4T 1B7
Tel: 403-845-2922; *Fax:* 403-845-2277
wwgoals@telusplanet.net
www.westwardgoals.ca
Overview: A small local organization founded in 1991
Mission: To assist mentally handicapped/brain injured persons in maximizing independence through supported programs; to offer residential support, community networking & outreach support for adults; to provide children with outreach & family support, including in-home support, rehabilitation aides & host family services
Finances: *Funding Sources:* Provincial government
Chief Officer(s):
Marla Hills, Executive Director

Wetaskiwin & District Association for Community Service (WDACS)
5211 - 54 St., Wetaskiwin AB T9A 1T2
Tel: 780-352-2241; *Fax:* 780-352-8558
info@wdacs.ca
www.wdacs.ca
Overview: A small local organization founded in 1964
Mission: To provide services to persons with disabilities thereby promoting quality of life, individual choices, respect, personal growth & development
Affiliation(s): Alberta Association of Rehabilitation Centres
Finances: *Funding Sources:* Regional government
Activities: Annual Pumpkin Ball
Chief Officer(s):
Marilyn Conner, Executive Director
m.conner@wdacs.ca
Lavern Buchert, President

Wetaskiwin Chamber of Commerce (WCC)
6420 - 50 St., Leduc AB T9E 7K9
Tel: 780-312-0657; *Fax:* 780-986-8108
info@wetaskiwinchamber.ca
www.wetaskiwinchamber.ca
twitter.com/WetaskChamber
Overview: A small local organization founded in 1929
Mission: To foster sustainable business development & growth in the Wetaskiwin area
Member of: Alberta Chamber of Commerce; Canadian Chamber of Commerce; Economic Developers Association of Alberta
Finances: *Annual Operating Budget:* $100,000-$250,000; *Funding Sources:* Business license revenue
Staff Member(s): 3
Membership: 688; *Fees:* $140-$400; *Committees:* Ambassadorship; Marketing; Policy; Strategic Planning; Technology; Tourism
Activities: *Speaker Service:* Yes; *Library*
Chief Officer(s):
Wayne Di Lallo, President
Allan Halter, Secretary
Joe Letourneau, Treasurer

Weyburn & District Labour Council
PO Box 1204, Weyburn SK S4H 2L5
Tel: 306-842-7938
Overview: A small local organization overseen by Saskatchewan Federation of Labour
Mission: To promote the interests of affiliates in Weyburn, Saskatchewan, & the surrounding area; To advance the economic & social welfare of workers
Affiliation(s): Canadian Labour Congress (CLC)
Activities: Presenting educational opportunities; Coordinating local campaigns & events, such as a ceremony on the annual Day of Mourning, for workers who have suffered workplace injury, illness or death; Promoting occupational health & safety; Supporting community organizations, such as the Envision Counselling & Support Centre
Chief Officer(s):
Wanda Bartlett, President
wbartlett@sasktel.net

Weyburn & District United Way
PO Box 608, Weyburn SK S4H 2K7
www.weyburnunitedway.com
Overview: A small local charitable organization overseen by United Way of Canada - Centraide Canada
Mission: To improve lives & strengthen the community
Finances: *Annual Operating Budget:* Less than $50,000; *Funding Sources:* Donations
Membership: 1-99
Chief Officer(s):
Sandra Alexander, Executive Director

Weyburn Agricultural Society
PO Box 699, Weyburn SK S4H 2K8
Tel: 306-842-4052; *Fax:* 306-842-1469
agsociety@accesscomm.ca
www.facebook.com/169526276432957
Overview: A small local charitable organization founded in 1908
Mission: To promote agriculture; To act as a liaison between the rural & urban population; To promote education on agriculture-related subjects
Member of: Saskatchewan Association of Agricultural Societies & Exhibitions
Affiliation(s): Western Canada Fairs; Canadian Association of Exhibitions
Finances: *Annual Operating Budget:* $50,000-$100,000
Staff Member(s): 1; 250 volunteer(s)
Membership: 36 senior/lifetime; 120 individual; *Fees:* Schedule available; *Member Profile:* Interest in agriculture; *Committees:* Attractions; Commercial; Hospitality; Gates; Horse; Cattle; 4H Youth; 4H Calf; Publicity
Activities: *Awareness Events:* Weyburn Agricultural Society Fair, July; Weyburn Rodeo, Aug.
Chief Officer(s):
Treva Tollefson, President

Weyburn Chamber of Commerce
11 - 3rd St. NE, Weyburn SK S4H 0W5
Tel: 306-842-4738; *Fax:* 306-842-0520
www.weyburnchamber.com
twitter.com/WeyburnChamber
Overview: A small local organization
Mission: To assume a leadership role in business & community growth by promoting programs designed to strengthen & expand the potential of business within the trading area; To enhance the general welfare & prosperity of the Weyburn area
Affiliation(s): Saskatchewan Chamber of Commerce
Finances: *Funding Sources:* Membership fees; special projects
Staff Member(s): 3
Membership: *Member Profile:* Local business & industry
Activities: Business Cleanup Competition; local promotions; parades; *Speaker Service:* Yes; *Rents Mailing List:* Yes
Chief Officer(s):
Rodney Gill, President
Awards:
• Golden Spike Award
Presented yearly to a member of the community who has contributed to growth & improvement by participating on volunteer committees
• Two scholarships a year
• Golden Sheaf Award
To recognize excellence in farming achievement & to help foster rural-urban understanding & consideration
• Golden Service Award

Weyburn Group Home Society Inc
Weyburn SK
Tel: 306-842-6686
wghs@sasktel.net
www.weyburngrouphomesociety.com
Overview: A small local organization
Mission: To provide residential support & other support services to adults with physical or developmental disabilities, long term psychiatric disorders, or acquired brain injuries in southeast Saskatchewan; To encourage independence & responsbility
Chief Officer(s):
Colin Folk, Executive Director

Weymouth Historical Society
c/o Maurine Mullen, RR#3, Weymouth NS B0W 3T0
Tel: 902-837-5185
Overview: A small local organization
Membership: 30 individual; *Fees:* $5 individual
Activities: Thursday teas held July-Sept.
Chief Officer(s):
Leota Lewis, President, 902-837-5185
Maurine Mullen, Secretary, 902-837-5593

Wheelchair Sports Alberta
11759 Groat Rd., Edmonton AB T5M 3K6
Tel: 780-427-8699
Toll-Free: 888-453-6770
wsa1@telus.net
www.abwheelchairsport.ca
www.facebook.com/WheelchairSportsAlberta
twitter.com/WSA_Alberta
Overview: A small provincial organization
Mission: To develop wheelchair sports throughout Alberta
Member of: Canadian Wheelchair Sports Association
Membership: *Fees:* $10 board/coach/official; $25 athlete; $30 family; *Member Profile:* Any athlete, club, official, coach or board member
Chief Officer(s):
Sharleen Edwards, Executive Director

Wheelchair Sports Association of Newfoundland & Labrador (WSANL)
NL
Overview: A small provincial organization
Member of: Canadian Wheelchair Sports Association

Where the Rivers Meet *See* Sagitawa Friendship Centre

Whistler Chamber of Commerce
#201, 4230 Gateway Dr., Whistler BC V0N 1B4
Tel: 604-932-5922; *Fax:* 604-932-3755
www.whistlerchamber.com
www.linkedin.com/company/whistler-chamber-of-commerce
www.facebook.com/whistlerchamber
twitter.com/whistlerchamber
www.youtube.com/channel/UCphpSBZQmhRux_-jalEtcwQ
Overview: A small local organization founded in 1966
Mission: To serve its members & promote the businesses of Whistler; To provide leadership in monitoring & directing the local economy; To lobby on behalf of business in Whistler; To provide Whistler businesses with networking opportunities; to provide training opportunities & recognition programs for employer/employees to ensure service excellence throughout the Resort
Member of: BC Chamber of Commerce
Finances: *Funding Sources:* Membership dues; municipal; sponsorships
Staff Member(s): 5
Membership: 630+; *Fees:* Schedule available
Activities: American Express Employee Recognition Program; Whistler Spirit Program; Canada Day; monthly luncheons; Business 2 Business; Women of Whistler; Whistler Card; *Library:* Open to public
Chief Officer(s):
Val Litwin, Chief Executive Officer
Grant Cousar, Chair

Whistler Food Bank
PO Box 900, Whistler BC V0N 1B0
Tel: 604-932-0113; *Fax:* 604-932-0599
foodbank@mywcss.org
Overview: A small local organization overseen by Food Banks British Columbia
Member of: Food Banks British Columbia
Chief Officer(s):
Sara Jennings, Coordinator, 604-935-7717

Whistler Resort Association (WRA)
4010 Whistler Way, Whistler BC V0N 1B4
Tel: 604-932-3928; *Fax:* 604-932-7231
Toll-Free: 888-869-2777
www.whistler.com
www.facebook.com/gowhistler
twitter.com/gowhistler
www.youtube.com/gowhistler
Also Known As: Tourism Whistler
Overview: A small local organization founded in 1979
Mission: To develop strategic partnerships, positioning Whistler as a preferred resort destination in all target markets; To successfully grow the business; To improve the value provided to stakeholders; To create a climate for growth & development of staff within the organization
Finances: *Annual Operating Budget:* Greater than $5 Million
Staff Member(s): 88
Membership: 6,000; *Fees:* Schedule available; *Member Profile:* Having a business in Whistler/owners of resort land
Chief Officer(s):
Suzanne Denbak, President

Whitby Chamber of Commerce (WCC)
128 Brock St. South, Whitby ON L1N 4J8
Tel: 905-668-4506; *Fax:* 905-668-1894
info@whitbychamber.org
www.whitbychamber.org
www.linkedin.com/company/whitby-chamber-of-commerce
www.facebook.com/93725729133
twitter.com/whitbychamber
Overview: A medium-sized local organization founded in 1928
Mission: To act as the recognized voice of business for Whitby; To support members & the community through advocacy, networking, education, communication, government liaison, value-added programs, & leadership opportunities
Member of: Canadian Chamber of Commerce; Ontario Chamber of Commerce
Finances: *Annual Operating Budget:* $250,000-$500,000; *Funding Sources:* Membership fees; Events
Staff Member(s): 2; 80 volunteer(s)
Membership: 800; *Fees:* Schedule available; *Committees:* Advocacy; Ambassadors; Membership; Young Entrepreneurs & Professional
Activities: Hosting an annual general meeting, monthly networking breakfasts, evening meetings, an annual golf tournament, the Monday Night Golf League, the Peter Perry Business Achievement Awards Gala, a President's Ball, & the Annual Mayor's Luncheon; Organizing training & mentoring programs
Chief Officer(s):
Brenda Bemis, Office Manager
brenda@whitbychamber.org
Awards:
• Peter Perry Award
• Scholarships
Two scholarships presented to children of Chamber members or children of employees of Chamber members in full time post secondary education program; *Amount:* $1,000
• Young Entrepreneur Achievement Award
• Business Achievement Award

Whitchurch-Stouffville Chamber of Commerce
6176 Main St., Stouffville ON L4A 2S5
Tel: 905-642-4227; *Fax:* 905-642-8966
www.stouffvillechamber.ca
www.facebook.com/100780059972589
Overview: A small local organization founded in 1977
Mission: To promote & improve trade & commerce & the economic, civic & social welfare of the district
Member of: Ontario Chamber of Commerce; Canadian Chamber of Commerce
Finances: *Annual Operating Budget:* $50,000-$100,000; *Funding Sources:* Membership dues; social events; golf tournament; trade show; event sponsorship
Staff Member(s): 3; 1 volunteer(s)
Membership: 205; *Fees:* Schedule available; *Member Profile:* Small & medium sized businesses; *Committees:* Events; Governance; Marketing; Membership
Activities: Hosting golf tournaments; Organizing networking events; *Library:* Tourist Information Centre
Chief Officer(s):
Danny Huang, Chair
Harry Renaud, Executive Director
Awards:
• Heritage Award
• Business of the Year
• Business Entrepreneur of the Year
• Corporate Citizen of the Year
• Young Entrepreneur

The White Ribbon Campaign
#603, 36 Eglinton Ave. West, Toronto ON M4R 1A1
Tel: 416-920-6684; *Fax:* 416-920-1678
Toll-Free: 800-328-2228
info@whiteribbon.ca
www.whiteribbon.ca
www.facebook.com/whiteribboncampaign
twitter.com/whiteribbon
Overview: A medium-sized national charitable organization founded in 1991
Mission: Men working to end men's violence against women; To bring about positive behaviour & attitude shifts that will contribute to ending violence against women through public education, advocacy activities & encouraging the efforts of men to gather men around the issue
Finances: *Annual Operating Budget:* $250,000-$500,000
Staff Member(s): 4
Membership: 1,000-4,999; *Fees:* $10
Activities: Education & Action Kit; workbook, lesson plans for educators; *Awareness Events:* White Ribbon Campaign, Nov. 25 - Dec. 6
Chief Officer(s):
Humberto Carolo, Executive Director

White River District Historical Society
PO Box 583, 200 Elgin St., White River ON P0M 3G0
Tel: 807-822-2657
heritagemuseum@bellnet.ca
www.heritagemuseumwhiteriver.ca
Overview: A small local organization
Member of: Ontario Museum Association
Finances: *Annual Operating Budget:* Less than $50,000
3 volunteer(s)
Membership: 40; *Fees:* $10 single; $20 family
Activities: Winnie's Hometown Festival; Perfect Pie Contest; Museum & Gift Shop

White Rock & Surrey Naturalists
Surrey BC
Overview: A small local charitable organization
Mission: To promote the enjoyment of nature through environmental appreciation & conservation; to encourage wise use & conservation of natural resources & environmental protection
Member of: Federation of BC Naturalists
Finances: *Annual Operating Budget:* Less than $50,000
42 volunteer(s)
Membership: 120; *Fees:* $27 single; $37 family; *Committees:* Conservation; Education
Activities: Natural history walks & hikes; conservation & education activities
Chief Officer(s):
Viveka Ohman, Contact, Christmas Bird Count
ohmanv@inspection.gc.ca
Lynn Pollard, Contact, Youth Program, 604-531-6307
jacquielynn@telus.net
Liz Walker, Contact
swalker3@shaw.ca

Whitecourt & District Chamber of Commerce
Synergy Business Centre, PO Box 1011, 4907 - 52 Ave., Whitecourt AB T7S 1N9
Tel: 780-778-5363; *Fax:* 780-778-2351
manager@whitecourtchamber.com
www.whitecourtchamber.com
www.facebook.com/whitecourtchamber
Overview: A medium-sized local organization founded in 1980
Mission: To promote trade & commerce & the economic, civic & social welfare of the district
Member of: Canadian Chamber of Commerce
Affiliation(s): Alberta Chamber of Commerce
Finances: *Funding Sources:* Membership fees; projects & promotions
Staff Member(s): 1
Membership: 240; *Fees:* Schedule available; *Member Profile:* Associations; Corporations; Societies; Partnerships or estates
Activities: Providing business information & resources; *Speaker Service:* Yes; *Library:* Chamber Resource Library; Open to public
Chief Officer(s):
Rand Richards, President

Whitecourt Fish & Game Association
PO Box 3, Whitecourt AB T7S 1N3
www.wfga.ca
Overview: A small local licensing charitable organization
Member of: Alberta Fish & Game Association
Affiliation(s): Alberta Bow Hunting Association
Finances: *Annual Operating Budget:* Less than $50,000
Membership: 100; *Fees:* $25 regular; $15 associate; $35 family; $25 range passes
Activities: Archery & gun ranges; hunter education; 3D archery shoots; birdhouse building
Chief Officer(s):
Rick Fetch, President
president@wfga.ca
Ron Brown, Vice-President
vicepresident@wfga.ca

Whitehorse Chamber of Commerce (WCC)
#101, 302 Steele St., Whitehorse YT Y1A 2C5
Tel: 867-667-7545; *Fax:* 867-667-4507
business@whitehorsechamber.ca
www.whitehorsechamber.ca
Overview: A medium-sized local organization founded in 1948

Mission: To promote & improve trade & commerce; to contribute to the economic, civic & social well-being of Whitehorse
Member of: Canadian Chamber of Commerce
Affiliation(s): Yukon Chamber of Commerce; Tourism Industry Association of Yukon
Finances: *Annual Operating Budget:* $100,000-$250,000; *Funding Sources:* Membership fees; fund-raising
Staff Member(s): 2
Membership: 400
Activities: Chamber luncheons; Business After Hours; Fair Exchange; Planter Box Program; lobbying on behalf of business community; *Rents Mailing List:* Yes
Chief Officer(s):
Rick Karp, President

Whitehorse Cross Country Ski Club
#200, 1 Sumanik Dr., Whitehorse YT Y1A 6J6
Tel: 867-668-4477
info.xcskiwhitehorse@gmail.com
www.xcskiwhitehorse.ca
Overview: A small provincial organization
Mission: To maintain high-quality ski trails & facilities, maintain a safe environment, ensure the long-term viability of the club & secure land tenure for the Yukon's trail system.
Membership: *Fees:* Schedule available
Chief Officer(s):
Miriam Lukszova, Club Manager
Jan Polivka, Operations Manager
grooming.xcskiwhitehorse@gmail.com

Whitehorse Glacier Bears Swim Club
c/o Sport Yukon, 4061 - 4th Ave., Whitehorse YT Y1A 1H1
Fax: 867-667-4237
whseglacierbears@yahoo.ca
www.whitehorseglacierbears.ca
www.facebook.com/569737653073155
Overview: A small local organization
Mission: To promote competitive swimming.

Whitehorse Minor Hockey Association (WMHA)
4061 - 4th Ave., Whitehorse YT Y1A 1H1
Tel: 867-393-4698; *Fax:* 867-667-4237
office@whitehorseminor.ca
www.whitehorseminorhockey.ca
Overview: A medium-sized provincial organization
Mission: Promotes and coordinates minor hockey leagues in Whitehorse.
Member of: Sport Yukon
Affiliation(s): Yukon Amateur Hockey Association
Membership: *Committees:* Policy & Discipline; Sponsorship/Grants; House League; Mustangs; Online Communications; Fundraising/Bingo/Cantina
Chief Officer(s):
Justin Halowaty, President
justin@ttlp.com
Richelle Bierlmeier, Vice-President, Operations
richelle99@gmail.com

Whitehorse Minor Soccer Association (WMS)
4061 - 4th Ave., Whitehorse YT Y1A 1H1
Tel: 867-667-2445
yukonsoccer@sportyukon.com
www.yukonsoccer.yk.ca/whitehorseminorsoccer.html
Overview: A medium-sized provincial organization founded in 1977
Member of: Sport Yukon
Chief Officer(s):
Cali Battersby, Sport Administrator

Whitehorse Women's Hockey Association (WWHA)
c/o Sport Yukon, 4061 - 4th Ave., Whitehorse YT Y1A 1H1
wwhayukon@gmail.com
whitehorsewomenshockey.com
www.facebook.com/whitehorsewomenshockeyassn
Overview: A small local organization founded in 1993
Mission: To administer women's hockey in Whitehorse.

Whitewater Historical Society
2022 Foresters Falls Rd., Foresters Falls ON K0J 1V0
Tel: 613-646-2622
info@rossmuseum.ca
www.rossmuseum.ca
Previous Name: Ross Township Historical Society of Whitewater Region; Ross Township Historical Society
Overview: A small local organization founded in 1985
Mission: To promote & preserve local history & collections of the Township of Whitewater Region
Finances: *Funding Sources:* Ontario Trillium Foundation; Ministry of Culture of Ontario; Donations
Membership: *Fees:* $10 individuals; $15 families
Activities: Operating the Ross Museum in Foresters Falls, which consists of the Ross House, the former Ross Township Fire Hall, a drive shed, & St. Aidan's Church; Organizing & maintaining the records of the Whitewater region for researchers; *Library:* Ross Museum Resource Centre; Open to public

Whitewater Ontario
411 Carnegie Beach Rd., Port Perry ON L9L 1B6
Tel: 905-985-4585; *Fax:* 905-985-5256
Toll-Free: 888-322-2849
info@whitewaterontario.ca
www.whitewaterontario.ca
www.facebook.com/whitewaterontario
Overview: A small provincial organization overseen by CanoeKayak Canada
Mission: Whitewater Ontario is the sport governing body in the province, & represents provincial interests within the national body CanoeKayak Canada.
Member of: CanoeKayak Canada
Membership: *Fees:* $30 adult; $15 junior; $30 family; $75 commercial
Chief Officer(s):
Jim Tayler, President

Whole Village
20725 Shaws Creek Rd., Caledon ON L7K 1L7
Tel: 519-941-1099
info@wholevillage.org
www.wholevillage.org
www.facebook.com/wholevillage
twitter.com/WholeVillageEco
www.youtube.com/watch?v=SUzdnR6dqwM&feature=plcp
Overview: A small local organization founded in 1996
Mission: To create an example of sustainable living
Member of: Ecovillage Network of Canada; Canadian Cohousing Network; Canadian Organic Growers
Affiliation(s): National Farmers Union; Ecological Farm Association of Ontario
Finances: *Annual Operating Budget:* $100,000-$250,000; *Funding Sources:* Membership fees; member loans; grants 55 volunteer(s)
Membership: 25; *Fees:* $10/month or $120/year; *Committees:* Legal/Financial; Communications; Education; Farm; Community Dynamics
Activities: Sustainable agriculture; green construction; community development; *Internships:* Yes; *Speaker Service:* Yes

Wiarton South Bruce Peninsula Chamber of Commerce
PO Box 68, #2, 402 William St., Wiarton ON N0H 2T0
Tel: 519-534-4545
info@wiartonchamber.ca
www.wiartonchamber.ca
www.facebook.com/visitwiarton
Also Known As: Wiarton & District Chamber of Commerce
Overview: A small local organization founded in 1991
Mission: To act as the collective voice of area businesses; To promote growth & prosperity of members in the community
Member of: Bruce Peninsula Tourism
Affiliation(s): Wiarton BIA
Membership: 83; *Fees:* Schedule available based on number of employees
Chief Officer(s):
Paul Deacon, President

Wiccan Church of Canada
The Occult Shop, 1373 Bathurst St., Toronto ON M5R 3J1
info@wcc.on.ca
www.wcc.on.ca
Overview: A small national organization founded in 1979
Mission: To assist practicing Wiccans in achieving a spiritual balance that brings them into true harmony with the Gods; To bring the non-Wiccan population an understanding that they are a positive, reputable & life-affirming religion & lifestyle; To acchieve for Wiccans the same rights & freedoms enjoyed by other more mainstream religions
Chief Officer(s):
Richard James, Priest
richard@wcc.on.ca

Wikimedia Canada
535, av Viger est, Montréal QC H2L 2P3
info@wikimedia.org
ca.wikimedia.org
www.facebook.com/WikimediaCAfr
twitter.com/WikimediaCA
Overview: A medium-sized national organization
Mission: To develop & distribute information & media for free in Canada
Chief Officer(s):
Benoit Rochon, President

Wikwemikong Anishinabe Association for Community Living
11 Fox Lake Rd., Wikwemikong ON P0P 2J0
Tel: 705-859-2147; *Fax:* 705-859-2147
Overview: A small local organization
Member of: Community Living Ontario
Chief Officer(s):
Jacqueline Hopkin, Director, Program
jhopkin_clwa@eastlink.ca

WIL Employment Connections
141 Dundas St., 4th Fl., London ON N6A 1G3
Tel: 519-663-0774; *Fax:* 519-663-5377
careerinformation@wil.ca
www.wil.ca
www.linkedin.com/company/676963
www.facebook.com/wilemploymentconnections
twitter.com/wilemployment
Previous Name: Women Immigrants of London
Overview: A small local organization founded in 1984
Mission: To offer employment help for new immigrants, the unemployed & employers
Member of: Ontario Network of Employment Skills Training Projects
Finances: *Funding Sources:* Federal; provincial; private sector
Staff Member(s): 51
Membership: *Committees:* Steering
Chief Officer(s):
Anne Langille, Executive Director

Wilberforce Project
PO Box 11479, Edmonton AB T5J 3K5
Tel: 780-421-7747; *Fax:* 888-492-9375
Toll-Free: 877-880-5433
office@wilberforceproject.ca
thewilberforceproject.ca
Previous Name: Alberta Pro Life Alliance Association
Overview: A small provincial organization founded in 1986
Mission: To educate Albertans on pro-life & pro-family issues; to mobilize citizens to effect changes in government policy relating to sanctity of life issues
Staff Member(s): 2
Membership: *Fees:* $25
Activities: *Library:* Open to public
Chief Officer(s):
Dale Bullock, President
Rosey Rosenke, Executive Director
Publications:
• The Rose
Type: Newsletter; *Frequency:* Quarterly

Wild Bird Care Centre (WBCC)
PO Box 11159, Nepean ON K2H 7T9
Tel: 613-828-2849; *Fax:* 613-828-2194
mojo@wildbirdcarecentre.org
www.wildbirdcarecentre.org
Overview: A medium-sized national organization founded in 1981
Mission: To assess, treat, and rehabilitate sick, orphaned, or injured wild birds before releasing them back to the wild.
Membership: *Fees:* $25 single; $40 family; $15 student/senior; $50 school; $100 business; $1000+ corporate/patron
Chief Officer(s):
Kathy Nihei, Founder

Wild Blueberry Association of North America (WBANA) / Association des bleuets sauvages de l'Amérique du Nord (ABSAN)
81 Woodmere Dr., Upper Kingsclear NB E3E 1T8
Tel: 506-363-3606
wildblueberries@gwi.net
www.wildblueberries.com
www.facebook.com/wildblueberries
twitter.com/wildbberries
www.instagram.com/wildblueberries

Overview: A medium-sized international organization founded in 1981
Mission: To extend awareness & promote use of wild blueberries on domestic & overseas markets
Finances: *Funding Sources:* Dues; government co-op programs
Activities: *Speaker Service:* Yes

Wild Blueberry Producers Association of Nova Scotia (WBPANS)
PO Box 119, 168 Dakota Rd., Debert NS B0M 1G0
Tel: 902-662-3306; *Fax:* 902-662-3284
wbpans@ns.aliantzinc.ca
www.nswildblueberries.com
Overview: A medium-sized provincial organization founded in 1970
Mission: To encourage the production & consumption of wild blueberries; to provide a viable & sustainable industry for Nova Scotia blueberry producers
Affiliation(s): Wild Blueberry Association of North America
Finances: *Funding Sources:* Membership dues; interest income
Membership: *Member Profile:* Must be a producer of wild blueberries
Awards:
• Scholarship
; *Amount:* $750

Wild Rose Agricultural Producers
5033 - 52 St., Lacombe AB T4L 2A6
Tel: 403-789-9151; *Fax:* 780-789-9152
Toll-Free: 855-789-9151
info@wrap.ab.ca
www.wrap.ab.ca
www.facebook.com/122046961202493
twitter.com/WildRoseGFO
Previous Name: Unifarm
Overview: A medium-sized provincial organization founded in 1996
Mission: To represent its members at the regional, provincial & national level for the benefit of agriculture; to create an atmosphere of cooperation & communication to ensure that areas of common concern among all producers are dealt with to the benefit of agriculture as a whole
Membership: 1,000-4,999; *Fees:* $140 producer; $65 associate
Chief Officer(s):
Sheryl Rae, Executive Director

Wild Rose Ball Hockey Association
Edmonton AB
wrbha@telus.net
www.wrballhockey.com
Overview: A small provincial organization
Member of: Canadian Ball Hockey Association
Chief Officer(s):
Connie Liosis, Executive Director

Wild Rose Draft Horse Association (WRDHA)
c/o Barb Stephenson, PO Box 96, Turner Valley AB T0L 2A0
Tel: 403-933-5765
www.wrdha.com
Overview: A small provincial organization founded in 1994
Mission: To act as a unified voice for the draft horse industry in Alberta
Membership: *Fees:* $20 single members; $25 family members; *Member Profile:* Draft horse enthusiasts in Alberta
Activities: Hosting events, such as 4-H Draft Horse Events, the Annual Wild Rose Draft Horse Sale, & the Alberta Draft Horse Improvement; Sponsoring other events, such as the Calgary Stampede; Offering a Wild Rose Draft Horse Futurity to showcase pedigreed Clydesdale, Percheron, Belgian, Suffolk, & Shire breeding stock; Posting show results; Providing educational programs
Chief Officer(s):
Barb Stephenson, Secretary
dbsteph@telusplanet.net
Awards:
• Wild Rose Draft Horse Association Youth Scholarship
Eligibility: Members of the Wild Rose Draft Horse Association between the ages of 15 & 21

Wild Rose Economic Development Corporation *See* Community Futures Wild Rose

Wilderness Canoe Association (WCA)
PO Box 91068, 2901 Bayview Ave., Toronto ON M2K 2Y6
Tel: 416-223-4646
info@wildernesscanoe.ca
www.wildernesscanoe.ca

Overview: A small local organization founded in 1973
Mission: Organization of individuals interested in wilderness travel, mainly by canoe, kayak, and backpacking and, in winter, by skis and snowshoes
Member of: Federation of Ontario Naturalists
Finances: *Annual Operating Budget:* Less than $50,000
Membership: 750; *Fees:* $35 single; $45 family
Activities: Winter pool training sessions; Paddle the Don River; year-round outings; *Awareness Events:* Wine & Cheese, Nov.; Paddlers' Club Night, Feb.
Chief Officer(s):
David Young, Chair
chair@wildernesscanoe.ca
Publications:
• Nastawgan Journal [a publication of the Wilderness Canoe Association]
Type: Journal; *Frequency:* Quarterly; *Editor:* Aleks Gusev

Wilderness Committee (WCWC)
46 East 6th Ave., Vancouver BC V5T 1J4
Tel: 604-683-8220; *Fax:* 604-683-8229
Toll-Free: 800-661-9453
info@wildernesscommittee.org
www.wildernesscommittee.org
www.facebook.com/wildernesscommittee
twitter.com/wildernews
www.instagram.com/wildernews
Previous Name: Western Canada Wilderness Committee
Overview: A large international charitable organization founded in 1980
Mission: To work for the protection of Canadian & the Earth's wilderness through research & education; To promote the principles which achieve ecologically sustainable communities
Finances: *Annual Operating Budget:* $1.5 Million-$3 Million; *Funding Sources:* Donations; Membership dues; Merchandise sales; Grants
Staff Member(s): 25; 300 volunteer(s)
Membership: 26,000; *Fees:* $35 individual (Canada); $50 international; $59 family
Activities: Research; education; slide shows; events; trailbuilding; speaking tours; conferences; media relations; *Speaker Service:* Yes; *Library:* by appointment
Chief Officer(s):
Beth Clarke, Director, Development & Program
Gwen Barlee, Director, Policy
Joe Foy, Director, National Campaign
Publications:
• Wilderness Committee Annual Report
Type: Report; *Frequency:* Annually

Manitoba Field Office
#3, 303 Portage Ave., Winnipeg MB R3B 2B4
Tel: 204-942-9292; *Fax:* 204-942-8214
contactmb@wildernesscommittee.org
www.wildernesscommittee.org/manitoba
www.facebook.com/WildernessCommitteeManitoba
twitter.com/WilderNewsMB
Chief Officer(s):
Eric Reder, Campaign Director

Toronto Office
#207, 425 Queen St. West, Toronto ON M5V 2A5
Tel: 416-849-6520

Vancouver Island - Mid-Island Office
PO Box 442, Qualicum Beach BC V9K 1S9
Tel: 250-752-6585
www.wildernesscommittee.org/mid_island
Chief Officer(s):
Annette Tanner, Contact

Victoria Office & Outreach Centre
#202, 3 Fan Tan Alley, Victoria BC V8W 3G9
Tel: 250-388-9292; *Fax:* 250-388-9223
vi_info@wildernesscommittee.org
www.wildernesscommittee.org/victoria

Wilderness Tourism Association (WTA)
PO Box 423, Cumberland BC V0R 1S0
Tel: 250-336-2862; *Fax:* 250-336-2861
admin@wilderness-tourism.bc.ca
www.wilderness-tourism.bc.ca
Overview: A small local organization founded in 1999
Mission: To protect a land base for the wilderness tourism industry
Finances: *Funding Sources:* Membership fees; Donations
Membership: 100-499; *Fees:* Schedule available; *Member Profile:* Wilderness tourism operators in British Columbia, such as businesses & community DMOs; Educational institutions; Industry suppliers
Activities: Engaging in advocacy activities; Providing education
Chief Officer(s):
Brian Gunn, President
Evan Loveless, Executive Director
Sam Purin, Director, Membership & Development
Jim DeHart, Secretary
Gilles Valade, Treasurer
Meetings/Conferences:
• Wilderness Tourism Association BC 2018 Annual General Meeting, 2018
Scope: Provincial
Description: Informative sessions & workshops about nature based tourism

Wilderness Tourism Association of the Yukon (WTAY)
#4, 1114 - 1st Ave., Whitehorse YT Y1A 1A3
Tel: 867-668-3369; *Fax:* 867-668-3370
info@wtay.com
wtay.com
Overview: A small provincial organization
Mission: To represent the wilderness & adventure tourism industry in the Yukon Territory, Canada; to provide marketing, advocacy, research, consultation, referral & education resources.
Affiliation(s): Yukon Wild
Membership: 68; *Fees:* $125; *Committees:* Environment; Legislation; Marketing; Research; Education
Chief Officer(s):
Felix Geithner, President

Wildlife Foundation of Manitoba; Fort Whyte Centre for Environmental Education *See* FortWhyte Alive

Wildlife Habitat Canada (WHC) / Habitat faunique Canada (HFC)
#247, 2039 Robertson Rd., Ottawa ON K2H 8R2
Tel: 613-722-2090; *Fax:* 613-722-3318
Toll-Free: 800-669-7919
admin@whc.org
www.whc.org
www.linkedin.com/company/wildlife-habitat-canada
www.facebook.com/WildlifeHCanada
twitter.com/WildlifeHCanada
Overview: A medium-sized national organization founded in 1984
Mission: To promote the conservation, restoration & enhancement of wildlife habitat to retain diversity, distribution & abundance of wildlife; To provide a funding mechanism for the conservation, restoration & enhancement of wildlife habitat in Canada; To foster coordination & leadership in the conservation, restoration & enhancement of wildlife habitat in Canada
Finances: *Annual Operating Budget:* $1.5 Million-$3 Million; *Funding Sources:* Donations; Revenue from products
Staff Member(s): 4; 1 volunteer(s)
Membership: *Committees:* North American Wetlands Conservation Council; North American Bird Conservation Initiative; Hunting & Angling Advisory Panel
Activities: Funding wildlife habitat conservation programs in Canada; *Rents Mailing List:* Yes
Chief Officer(s):
Cameron Mack, Executive Director, 613-722-2090 Ext. 224
cmack@whc.org
Julia Thompson, Program Manager, 613-722-2090 Ext. 266
jthompson@whc.org
Awards:
• Wildlife Habitat Canada Conservation Grants
Awarded to habitat conservation projects across Canada
Deadline: November
Publications:
• Wildlife Habitat Canada Annual Report
Type: Report; *Frequency:* Annually

Wildlife Haven Rehabilitation Centre
PO Box 165, 1053 Old Provincial Hwy. 59, Ile des Chênes MB R0A 0T0
Tel: 204-878-3740
www.wildlifehaven.ca
www.facebook.com/Wildlifehaven.ca
twitter.com/WildlifeHaven
www.instagram.com/wildlifehaven_mb
Previous Name: Manitoba Wildlife Rehabilitation Organization
Overview: A small provincial charitable organization founded in 1984

Mission: To maintain & preserve the province's wildlife; To receive & professionally handle injured & orphaned native wildlife; To promote public education in wildlife conservation & appreciation; To establish & maintain a Wildlife Rehabilitation Centre; To stimulate & conduct applied noninvasive research; To record data & preserve materials pertaining to rehabilitation & captive breeding of endangered species
Member of: International Wildlife Rehabilitation Council
Finances: *Annual Operating Budget:* $50,000-$100,000
Staff Member(s): 3; 40 volunteer(s)
Membership: 550; *Fees:* $50 family; $30 individual; $20 student; *Member Profile:* Individuals with an appreciation for wildlife & nature; all ages; *Committees:* Education; Fundraising; Relocation
Activities: Education; rehabilitation; *Internships:* Yes; *Speaker Service:* Yes

Wildlife Preservation Canada (WPC) / Conservation de la faune au Canada
RR#5, 5420 Hwy. 6 North, Guelph ON N1H 6J2
Tel: 519-836-9314
Toll-Free: 800-956-6608
admin@wildlifepreservation.ca
www.wildlifepreservation.ca
www.facebook.com/WildlifePreservationCanada
twitter.com/WPCWild911
Previous Name: Wildlife Preservation Trust Canada
Overview: A medium-sized national charitable organization founded in 1985
Mission: To save endangered animal species from extinction in Canada & internationally
Finances: *Annual Operating Budget:* $500,000-$1.5 Million
Membership: *Committees:* Conservation; Communications; Strategic Funding; Nominations
Activities: Providing training & outreach programs; Administering conservation grants
Chief Officer(s):
Elaine Williams, Executive Director
elaine@wildlifepreservation.ca
Ian Glen, President
Jessica Steiner, Recovery Biologist
Publications:
• Home on the Range [a publication of Wildlife Preservation Canada]
Type: Newsletter
Profile: Updates on the Eastern Loggerhead Shrike recovery program
• On the Edge [a publication of Wildlife Preservation Canada]
Type: Newsletter; *Frequency:* 3 pa
Profile: Information about recovery & conservation efforts of Wildlife Preservation Canada
• Wildlife Preservation Canada Annual Report
Type: Yearbook; *Frequency:* Annually
Profile: Financial highlights & donation information

Wildlife Preservation Trust Canada *See* Wildlife Preservation Canada

Wildlife Rescue Association of British Columbia (WRA)
5216 Glencarin Dr., Burnaby BC V5B 3C1
Tel: 604-526-2747; *Fax:* 604-524-2890; *Crisis Hot-Line:* 604-526-7275
info@wildliferescue.ca
www.wildliferescue.ca
www.facebook.com/WildlifeRescue
twitter.com/WRAofBC
Previous Name: Lower Mainland Wildlife Rescue Association
Overview: A medium-sized provincial charitable organization founded in 1979
Mission: To rehabilitate wildlife; To promote the welfare of wild animals in the urban environment
Membership: *Fees:* $15 students & seniors; $25 individuals; $35 families; $250 businesses & life memberships
Activities: Providing education & outreach services
Chief Officer(s):
Rose Hamilton, Senior Executive Consultant
Heather Gill, Administrator
Stefanie Broad, Coordinator, Volunteers
Johanna Thompson, Officer, Education
Yolanda Brooks, Manager, Communications
yolanda@wildliferescue.ca
Linda Bakker, Team Leader, Wildlife Rehabilitation
Janelle Stephenson, Coordinator, Care Centre
Publications:
• To the Rescue [a publication of the Wildlife Rescue Association of British Columbia]
Type: Newsletter; *Frequency:* 3 pa; *Accepts Advertising;* *Editor:* Yolanda Brooks
Profile: Educational information, success stories, care centre news, forthcoming events, donation information, campaigns, & avolunteer update from the association

Wildrose Polio Support Society
132 Warwick Rd. NW, Edmonton AB T5X 4P8
Tel: 780-428-8842; *Fax:* 780-475-7968
wpss@polioalberta.ca
www.polioalberta.ca/wildrose
Overview: A small local organization founded in 1999
Mission: To bring awareness about Post Polio Syndrome to the Southern Alberta community; to provide support for polio survivors
Membership: *Fees:* $15 individual; $25 couple; *Member Profile:* Polio survivors from Edmonton & northern Alberta; *Committees:* Events; Casino; Telephone; Outreach; Fundraising; Nominations; Newsletter; Membership; Web; Birthdays
Chief Officer(s):
Marleen Henley, President

Wilfrid Laurier University Faculty Association (WLUFA) / Association des professeurs de l'Université Wilfrid-Laurier
Wilfrid Laurier University, #114, 202 Regina St. North, Waterloo ON N2L 3C5
Tel: 519-884-1970; *Fax:* 519-888-9721
wlufa@wlu.ca
www.wlufa.ca
Overview: A small local organization founded in 1988
Member of: Ontario Confederation of University Faculty Associations; Canadian Association of University Teachers
Membership: 100-499
Chief Officer(s):
Sheila McKee-Protopapas, Executive Director, 519-884-1970 Ext. 2367
smckeeprotopapas@wlu.ca
Linda Watson, Senior Administrative Assistant, 519-884-1970 Ext. 2603
lwatson@wlu.ca

Wilfrid Laurier University Symphony Orchestra
Faculty of Music, 75 University Ave. West, Waterloo ON N2L 3C5
Tel: 519-884-0710; *Fax:* 519-884-5285
www.wlu.ca/academics/faculties/faculty-of-music/
Overview: A small local organization overseen by Orchestras Canada
Mission: To train music students to be musicians with solid knowledge of music theory & history,& competent performers
Member of: Canadian University Music Society; Association of Canadian Choral Conductors; Choirs Ontario
Membership: *Member Profile:* Faculty of music students
Chief Officer(s):
Paul Pulford, Conductor

William Morris Society of Canada (WMSC)
87 Government Rd., Toronto ON M8X 1W4
Tel: 416-233-7686
info@wmsc.ca
www.wmsc.ca
Overview: A small national charitable organization founded in 1981
Mission: To foster knowledge about the life & work of William Morris (1834-1896), the nineteenth-century English artist, writer, & craftsman
Affiliation(s): William Morris Society - Great Britain & US
Finances: *Annual Operating Budget:* Less than $50,000
15 volunteer(s)
Membership: 200; *Fees:* $50 individual; $65 dual; $25 student; $40 out-of-town
Activities: Lectures; tours; trips; symposia
Publications:
• The Canadian Society Newsletter [a publication of the William Morris Society of Canada]
Type: Newsletter; *Frequency:* s-a.
• The Journal [a publication of the William Morris Society of Canada]
Frequency: s-a.

William W. Creighton Youth Services
PO Box 10632, 1014 Oliver Rd., Thunder Bay ON P7B 6V1
Tel: 807-345-4456; *Fax:* 807-345-1635
www.creightonyouth.com
Overview: A small local organization
Mission: To provide youth justice services under the Child & Family Services Act & the Youth Criminal Justice Act
Staff Member(s): 23
Chief Officer(s):
Keith Zehr, Executive Director

Williams Lake & District Chamber of Commerce
1660 South Broadway, Williams Lake BC V2G 2W4
Tel: 250-392-5025
Toll-Free: 877-967-5253
info@williamslakechamber.com
www.williamslakechamber.com
www.facebook.com/williams.centre
Overview: A small local organization founded in 1949
Mission: To represent the business community by providing services, benefits, & leadership for positive growth
Affiliation(s): BC Chamber of Commerce; Canadian Chamber of Commerce; Cariboo Chilcotin Coast Tourism Association
Finances: *Funding Sources:* Municipal, provincial & federal government; private
Staff Member(s): 2
Membership: *Fees:* Schedule available
Activities: *Library:* Business Info Centre; Open to public
Chief Officer(s):
Angela Sommer, President
Claudia Blair, Executive Director
Awards:
• Business Excellence Awards

Williams Lake Field Naturalists
1305A Borland Rd., Williams Lake BC V2G 5K5
Tel: 250-392-7680
muskratexpress@midbc.com
www.williamslakefieldnaturalists.ca
Overview: A small local charitable organization
Mission: To promote the enjoyment of nature through environmental appreciation, education & conservation; To encourage wise use & conservation of natural resources & environmental protection; To administer the Scout Island Nature Centre in Williams Lake
Member of: Federation of BC Naturalists
Membership: *Fees:* $22 individual; $27 family
Activities: *Library:* Open to public
Chief Officer(s):
Fred McMechan, President

Williams Lake Stampede Association
PO Box 4076, Williams Lake BC V2G 2V2
Tel: 250-398-8388; *Fax:* 250-398-7701
Toll-Free: 800-717-6336
info@williamslakestampede.com
www.williamslakestampede.com
www.facebook.com/WilliamsLakeStampede
www.youtube.com/WilliamsLakeStampede
Overview: A small local organization
Chief Officer(s):
Fred Thomas, President

Willow Beach Field Naturalists (WBFN)
PO Box 421, Port Hope ON L1A 3Z3
info@willowbeachfieldnaturalists.org
www.willowbeachfieldnaturalists.org
Overview: A small local charitable organization founded in 1953
Mission: To protect & enhance the natural heritage of Northumberland County & surrounding areas; To develop & share knowledge of the area's natural heritage; To encourage the preservation, renewal, & enhancement of the area's natural heritage
Member of: Ontario Nature
Finances: *Annual Operating Budget:* Less than $50,000; *Funding Sources:* Membership fees; donations
Membership: 200; *Fees:* $25 individual; $35 family; *Member Profile:* Interest in all aspects of nature & conservation
Activities: Monthly meetings; outings; bird counts; breeding bird atlas
Publications:
• The Curlew [a publication of the Willow Beach Field Naturalists]
Type: Newsletter

Willowdale Community Legal Services
106, 245 Fairview Mall Dr., Toronto ON M2J 4T1
Tel: 416-492-2437
willowdalelegal.com
Overview: A small local organization overseen by Ontario Council of Agencies Serving Immigrants
Mission: To provide free legal advice, assistance and representation to low-income residents living in a specified area

Finances: *Funding Sources:* Legal Aid Ontario

Wilno Heritage Society
c/o Beverly A. Glofcheskie, PO Box 232, 6 Biernacki Mountain Rd., Barry's Bay ON K0J 1B0
heritage@wilno.org
www.wilno.org
Overview: A small local organization founded in 1998
Mission: To commemorate the past, recognize contributions by our ancestors; to support & augment existing Polish language studies for our students; to preserve the Kaszubian customs & traditions
10 volunteer(s)
Membership: *Fees:* $10 single; $15 family; $25 sponsor
Activities: Compiling genealogy of Polish Kashub Canadians; promoting Kashub language & culture; *Awareness Events:* Canadian Polish Kashub Festival, 1st Sat. in May
Chief Officer(s):
Peter Glofcheskie, President
peter.glofcheskie@gmail.com
Mike Coulas, Vice-President
Teenie Mask, Secretary
christinemask@hotmail.com
Ursula Jeffrey, Treasurer
ujeffrey@rogers.com

Wind Athletes Canada
PO Box 29047, Stn. Portsmouth, Kingston ON K7M 8W6
www.windathletes.ca
www.facebook.com/windathletes
twitter.com/windathletes
Overview: A medium-sized national organization
Mission: To promote the sport of sailing in Canada; to provide funding to the Canadian Sailing Team
Finances: *Funding Sources:* Fundraising
Activities: Training programs
Chief Officer(s):
John Curtis, President

Wind Energy TechnoCentre *Voir* TechnoCentre éolien

Windermere District Historical Society
PO Box 2315, Invermere BC V0A 1K0
Tel: 250-342-9769
wvmuseum@shaw.ca
www.windermerevalleymuseum.ca
www.facebook.com/WindermereValleyMuseum
Also Known As: Windermere Valley Museum & Archives
Overview: A small local charitable organization founded in 1965
Mission: To preserve & display pioneer artifacts & record local history
Member of: BC Museums Association; BC Heritage; BC Archives Association
Finances: *Annual Operating Budget:* Less than $50,000; *Funding Sources:* Admissions; membership dues; municipal grant
Staff Member(s): 2; 20 volunteer(s)
Membership: 120; *Fees:* $20; *Committees:* Displays; Acquisitions; Building
Activities: Historical displays; Heritage Day luncheons; historical talks, slides & videos; school programs & field trips; *Library:* Archives; Open to public

Windfall Ecology Centre
93A Industrial Pkwy. South, Aurora ON L4G 3V5
Tel: 905-727-0491; *Fax:* 905-727-0491
Toll-Free: 866-280-4431
Other Communication: Alt. phone: 416-465-6333
info@windfallcentre.ca
www.windfallcentre.ca
www.facebook.com/windfallcentre
twitter.com/windfallcentre
www.youtube.com/user/WindfallCentre
Overview: A medium-sized provincial organization founded in 1998
Mission: To educate & advocate in the areas of energy conservation, renewable energy production, water protection and leadership development.
Affiliation(s): Green Communities Canada; Ontario Trillium Foundation; Ontario Sustainable Energy Association; Ashoka; TD Friends of the Environment
Staff Member(s): 7
Activities: Programs for youth; First Nations joint projects; Well Aware and other water protection programs; Safe Routes to School, and ecoDriver; projects in wind energy, solar energy, and geothermal energy; Windfall Home Energy Assessment

program; *Awareness Events:* Windfall Ecology Festival, June; *Internships:* Yes
Chief Officer(s):
Brent Kopperson, Executive Director
Meetings/Conferences:
• Windfall Ecology Festival 2018, 2018
Scope: Local
Description: Electric vehicles, infrastructure development and practical information on how to incorporate electric mobility into your organization and strategy planning.
Contact Information: Email: festival@windfallcentre.ca

Windigo First Nations' Council
PO Box 299, 160 Alcona Dr., Sioux Lookout ON P8T 1A3
Tel: 807-737-1585; *Fax:* 807-737-3133
Toll-Free: 800-465-3621
www.windigo.on.ca
Overview: A small local organization
Mission: To develop programs & services that respond to the needs of the Band members within the six communities of the Windigo area; To negotiate with other levels of government on various aspects of First Nations' jurisdiction & control
Staff Member(s): 28
Chief Officer(s):
Frank McKay, CEO & Council Chair

Windsor & District Baseball Umpires Association (WDBUA)
Windsor ON
www.windsorumpires.ca
twitter.com/WDBUA
Also Known As: Windsor Umpires
Overview: A small local organization
Mission: To train, instruct & evaluate members.
Affiliation(s): Baseball Ontario; Baseball Canada; Sun Parlour Baseball Association
Chief Officer(s):
Matthew Tyler, President
president@windsorumpires.ca

Windsor & District Black Coalition of Canada
PO Box 1381, Stn. A, Windsor ON N9A 6R3
Tel: 519-252-2561
Overview: A small local organization founded in 1980
Mission: To see that the Black people of Windsor achieve full social, cultural, political & economic participation in the shaping of a humane society, & they benefit fully from this society; to eradicate all forms of racism & discrimination in Windsor & area
Member of: Federation of Race Relations Organizations
10 volunteer(s)
Membership: 350; *Fees:* $20 individual, $35 family; *Committees:* Fundraising; Program; Public Relations; Social Action
Activities: *Awareness Events:* Black History Month, Feb.; International Day for Elimination of Racial Discrimination, March 21

Windsor & District Labour Council
3450 Ypres Ave., Windsor ON N8W 5K9
Tel: 519-252-8281; *Fax:* 519-252-2906
wdlc_office@bellnet.ca
www.wdlc.ca
www.facebook.com/WindsorDistrictLC
twitter.com/WDLCWindsor
www.flickr.com/photos/122133224@N04/sets
Also Known As: CAW Local 44
Overview: A small local organization founded in 1986 overseen by Ontario Federation of Labour
Chief Officer(s):
Brian Hogan, President

Windsor Area Health Libraries Association; Windsor Hospitals Library Group *See* Southwestern Ontario Health Libraries & Information Network

Windsor Association for the Deaf (WAD)
c/o Shoppers Drug Mart, PO Box 28036, 500 Tecumseh Rd. East, Windsor ON N8X 2S2
deafwad@gmail.com
deafwad.weebly.com
www.facebook.com/deafwad
twitter.com/deafwad
pinterest.com/deafwad
Overview: A small local organization founded in 1959
Mission: Social & recreational activities for persons deafened or hard of hearing; provides social gatherings; offers special events & traveling sports tournaments; promotes the welfare of deaf

members, preserves Deaf Culture & ASL, offers social interaction between cultures, encourage the promotion of Deaf Awareness; offer workshops for deaf, hearing, & parents of deaf children & deaf parents of hearing children
Membership: *Fees:* $20 single; $10 student/senior
Chief Officer(s):
Gary Vassallo, President
wadpresident1@gmail.com
Michelle Walls-Carr, Vice-President
wasvicepresident2@gmail.com
Ken Brockway, Treasurer
wadtreasurer3@gmail.com

Windsor Association of Moldmakers *See* Canadian Association of Moldmakers

Windsor Catholic Family Service Bureau *See* Family Services Windsor-Essex Counselling & Advocacy Centre

Windsor Coin Club
#505, 5060 Tecumseh Rd. East, Windsor ON N8T 1C1
Tel: 519-735-0727
info@windsorcoinclub.com
www.windsorcoinclub.com
Overview: A small local organization founded in 1951
Membership: *Fees:* $15 regular; $12 seniors; free for children 16 & under
Chief Officer(s):
Brett Irick, President

Windsor Community Living Support Services *See* Community Living Windsor

Windsor Electrical Contractors Association
#202, 2880 Temple Dr., Windsor ON N8W 5J5
Tel: 519-974-3411; *Fax:* 519-974-9923
weca@meshgroup.ca
www.weca.ca
Overview: A small local organization
Mission: To foster & advance the interests of those who are engaged in any branch of the Electrical Construction Industry; To represent the members of the Association in any matters pertaining to the Electrical Construction Industry; To enter into such agreements as may appear to be in the best interests of the Electrical Construction Industry
Chief Officer(s):
Jim Kennedy, Executive Director
jkennedy@meshgroup.ca

Windsor Federation of Musicians
#307, 52 Chatham St., Windsor ON N9A 5M6
Tel: 519-258-2288; *Fax:* 519-258-9041
winfdmus@mnsi.net
www.afm.org/locals/info/number/566
Also Known As: Local 566 AFM
Overview: A small local organization founded in 1911
Member of: Federation of Musicians of the United States & Canada
Staff Member(s): 2
Membership: 300
Chief Officer(s):
Chris Borshuk, President

Windsor Islamic Association (WIA)
c/o Windsor Mosque, 1320 Northwood St., Windsor ON N9E 1A4
Tel: 519-966-2355
wia@windsormosque.com
www.wiao.org
www.facebook.com/windsormosque
twitter.com/myWIA
www.youtube.com/user/windsormosque
Overview: A medium-sized local organization founded in 1964
Affiliation(s): World Muslim League
Membership: 25,000; *Fees:* $100
Activities: Prayer, funeral & marriages services; Qura'an memorization; Arabic language lessons; Teachings about Islam; Live broadcast
Chief Officer(s):
Abdallah Shamisa, President
president@windsormosque.ca
Mirza Baig, Vice President
vicepresident@windsormosque.ca
Radwan Tamr, Secretary
secretary@windsormosque.ca
Hossam Behairy, Treasurer
treasurer@windsormosque.ca

Windsor Orchid Society / Société des Orchidophiles de Windsor
c/o Betty Levar, 1822 Chilver Rd., Windsor ON N8W 2T8
www.windsororchidsociety.ca
Overview: A small local organization
Membership: *Fees:* $20 single; $25 family; *Committees:* Archives; Budget; Conservation; Fundraising; Hospitality; Library; Membership; Newsletter; Photographer; Program; Raffles & Prizes; Special Orders & Supplies; Website; Welcoming; Winter Social
Chief Officer(s):
Deb Boersma, President

Windsor Police Association (WPA) / Association de la police de Windsor
548 Windsor Ave., Windsor ON N9A 1J5
Tel: 519-969-0510; *Fax:* 519-969-6064
windsorpa@cogeco.net
www.windsorpa.ca
Overview: A small local organization founded in 1967
Mission: To represent member's interests in regards to all aspects of their collective agreements with the Windsor Police Service Board & issues in general with policing in the community
Member of: Police Association of Ontario; Canadian Police Association
Chief Officer(s):
Ed Parent, Administrator
eparent@cogeco.net

Windsor Public Library Adult Literacy Program
850 Ouellette Ave., Windsor ON N9A 4M9
Tel: 519-255-6770; *Fax:* 519-255-7207; *TTY:* 519-252-4775
www.windsorpubliclibrary.com/?portfolio=adult-literacy
Previous Name: Windsor Volunteers for Literacy
Overview: A small local organization founded in 1980
Mission: To enable adults to achieve personal goals through literacy
Affiliation(s): Laubach Literacy of Canada
Finances: *Funding Sources:* Municipal government; Ministry of Training, Colleges & Universities
Activities: Offering one-on-one tutoring classes & classes focused on employment goals, reading, writing, numeracy & self-management skills; Offering adult literacy upgrading for the deaf

Windsor Sexual Assault Crisis Centre *See* Sexual Assault Crisis Centre of Essex County Inc.

Windsor Symphony Orchestra (WSO)
121 University Ave. West, Windsor ON N9A 5P4
Tel: 519-973-1238; *Fax:* 519-973-0764
Toll-Free: 888-327-8327
www.windsorsymphony.com
www.linkedin.com/company/windsor-symphony-orchestra
www.facebook.com/theWSO
twitter.com/WindsorSymphony
Overview: A medium-sized local charitable organization founded in 1947 overseen by Orchestras Canada
Mission: To enrich community life & serve as an educational resource through high quality live performance of orchestral music
Member of: Orchestras Canada
Finances: *Annual Operating Budget:* $500,000-$1.5 Million; *Funding Sources:* Ticket sales; Government grants; Community support; Special events; Volunteer association
Staff Member(s): 12; 150 volunteer(s)
Membership: 500; *Fees:* $65; *Committees:* Artistic Planning; Development; Education & Youth; Finance; Marketing; Outreach; Strategic Planning
Activities: Performing concert series; Providing education & outreach programs for schools & community groups; *Awareness Events:* Great-West Life Community Concert; Gift of Music Concerts; *Library:* by appointment
Chief Officer(s):
Sheila Wisdom, Executive Director, 519-973-1238 Ext. 19
swisdom@windsorsymphony.com
Robert Franz, Music Director

Windsor University Faculty Association (WUFA) / Association des professeurs de l'Université Windsor
Kerr House, 366 Sunset Ave., Windsor ON N9B 3P4
Tel: 519-253-3000; *Fax:* 519-977-6154
wufa@uwindsor.ca
www.wufa.ca
www.facebook.com/215414038490229
twitter.com/_WUFA
Overview: A small local organization founded in 1963
Mission: To act as the exclusive bargaining agent for all academic staff & librarians at the University of Windsor at any stages of their career whether it be employed on a permanent or limited term contract, full-time or sessional appointment, tenure-track or tenured, arriving or departing.
Affiliation(s): Canadian Association of University Teachers; Ontario Confederation of University Faculty Associations; National Union of the Canadian Association of University Teachers; Canadian Labour Congress
Membership: *Member Profile:* Professors; sessional instructors; librarians; *Committees:* Grievance; Health & Safety; Negotiating; Retirement & Benefits; Sessional; Status of Women, Diversity & Equity Action
Chief Officer(s):
Brian E. Brown, President
brown2v@uwindsor.ca

Windsor Volunteers for Literacy *See* Windsor Public Library Adult Literacy Program

Windsor Women Working with Immigrant Women (WWWWIW)
1368 Ouellette Ave., Windsor ON N8X 1J9
Tel: 519-973-5588; *Fax:* 519-973-1534
info@wwwwiw.org
www.wwwwiw.org
www.facebook.com/fivews.windsor
twitter.com/wwwwiw_org
Overview: A small local charitable organization founded in 1981 overseen by Ontario Council of Agencies Serving Immigrants
Mission: To help immigrant & refugee women & first generation Canadians to be full members of society; To welcome & support newcomers & first generation Canadians; To eliminate systemic barriers affecting immigrants & refugees; To offer services that address the needs of newcomers & first generation Canadians
Affiliation(s): Teachers of English as a Second Language; National Action Committee on the Status of Women
Finances: *Annual Operating Budget:* $50,000-$100,000
Staff Member(s): 10; 20 volunteer(s)
Membership: 1-99
Activities: LINC classes; Women's Circle; In-Depth, support & group counselling; citizenship class; support services; introduction to self-employment; child care
Chief Officer(s):
Sudip Minhas, Executive Director, 519-973-5588 Ext. 101
Philippine Ishak, Senior Manager, Administration, 519-973-5588 Ext. 102
Ying Ye, Senior Manager, Finance, 519-973-5588 Ext. 103
Olivia Brezeanu, Senior Manager, Employment Services, 519-973-5588 Ext. 201

Windsor/Essex County Parents of Multiple Births Association
7515 Forest Glade Dr., Windsor ON N8T 3P5
Tel: 519-948-5545
Other Communication: suppor@PombaWindsor.com
windsor.essex@multiplebirthscanada.org
www.pombawindsor.com
Overview: A small local organization overseen by Multiple Births Canada
Mission: To improve and promote the health and well-being of multiple birth families before, during and after pregnancy.
Membership: *Fees:* $40; *Member Profile:* Parents of twins, triplets and higher order multiples
Activities: *Library:*
Chief Officer(s):
Christine Prieur, Co-President
Valerie Hodgins, Co-President

Windsor-Essex *Voir* Réseau du patrimoine franco-ontarien

Windsor-Essex Children's Aid Society (WECAS)
1671 Riverside Dr. East, Windsor ON N8Y 5B5
Tel: 519-256-1171; *Fax:* 519-256-2739
foundation@wecas.on.ca
www.wecaf.on.ca
Overview: A small local organization founded in 1899
Mission: Dedicated to the well being & safety of every child by advocating for & partnering with our children, families & communities
Member of: Ontario Association of Children's Aid Societies
Finances: *Annual Operating Budget:* $100,000-$250,000
Activities: Summer camps; holiday assistance programs; independent living program; public education
Chief Officer(s):
Cheryl Sprague, Interim President

Windsor-Essex County Real Estate Board
3020 Deziel Dr., Windsor ON N8W 5H8
Tel: 519-966-6432; *Fax:* 519-966-4469
www.windsorrealestate.com
www.facebook.com/wecrealtors
twitter.com/wecrealtors
www.youtube.com/wecrealtors
Previous Name: Border Cities Real Estate Board
Merged from: Windsor Real Estate Board; South Essex Real Estate Board
Overview: A small local organization founded in 1918 overseen by Ontario Real Estate Association
Member of: Canadian Real Estate Association
Activities: *Library:* Not open to public
Chief Officer(s):
Norm Langlois, President, 519-734-5656
nlanglois3@cogeco.ca

Windsor-Essex Down Syndrome Parent Association
#206, 5060 Tecumseh Rd. East, Windsor ON N8T 1C1
Tel: 519-973-6486
www.upaboutdown.org
www.facebook.com/upaboutdown
Also Known As: Up About Down
Overview: A small local charitable organization founded in 1990
Mission: To enhance the lives of individuals with Down syndrome & their families; To provide positive & accurate information through advocacy & education thereby raising awareness throughout the community
Membership: *Member Profile:* Parents of children with Down syndrome
Chief Officer(s):
Suzanne Cyr, President

Windsor-Essex Regional Chamber of Commerce
2575 Ouellette Place, Windsor ON N8X 1L9
Tel: 519-966-3696; *Fax:* 519-966-0603
www.windsorchamber.org
www.linkedin.com/groups?home=&gid=2762020
www.facebook.com/125412597496221
twitter.com/WERCofC
Overview: A medium-sized local organization founded in 1876
Mission: To serve the business community of Windsor & district by providing networking opportunities, & by communicating positions & opinions on government policy & other issues on behalf of its membership
Member of: Ontario Chamber of Commerce; Canadian Chamber of Commerce; Better Business Bureau
Finances: *Funding Sources:* Membership fees
Staff Member(s): 10
Membership: 1,200; *Committees:* After Business; Business Excellence Awards; Finance & Taxation; Membership; Transportation
Activities: *Library:* Open to public
Chief Officer(s):
Jeffrey MacKinnon, Chair
Matt Marchand, President & CEO
mmarchand@windsoressexchamber.org

Windsor-Essex Therapeutic Riding Association (WETRA) / Association d'équitation thérapeutique Windsor-Essex
3323 North Malden Rd., RR#2, Essex ON N8M 2X6
Tel: 519-726-7682; *Fax:* 519-726-4403
info@wetra.ca
www.wetra.ca
www.facebook.com/wetraca
twitter.com/WETRA_
Overview: A small local charitable organization founded in 1969
Mission: To improve the quality of life of physically, emotionally, mentally challenged persons through equine related therapy
Member of: Canadian Therapeutic Riding Association
Affiliation(s): Ontario Therapeutic Riding Association
Finances: *Annual Operating Budget:* $100,000-$250,000; *Funding Sources:* United Way; Donations; Bingo
Staff Member(s): 12; 80 volunteer(s)
Membership: 200 riders
Activities: Offering therapeutic riding & horse shows; Hosting an open house, benefit horse show, & golf tournament; *Awareness Events:* Ride-a-Thon, March
Chief Officer(s):
Becky Mills, Executive Director

Wine Council of Ontario *See* Wine Country Ontario

Wine Country Ontario
PO Box 4000, 4890 Victoria Ave. North, Vineland ON L0R 2E0

Tel: 905-684-8070; Fax: 905-562-1993
info@winecountryontario.ca
winecountryontario.ca
www.facebook.com/WineCountryOntario
twitter.com/winecountryont
www.instagram.com/winecountryont
Previous Name: Wine Council of Ontario
Overview: A medium-sized provincial organization founded in 1974
Mission: A non-profit trade association which plays a leadership role in the marketing, promotion & future direction of the Ontario wine industry
Affiliation(s): VQA Wines of Ontario
Finances: *Annual Operating Budget:* $500,000-$1.5 Million; *Funding Sources:* Membership dues
Staff Member(s): 9
Membership: Represents 81 winery properties; *Fees:* $1,000 + marketing fee
Chief Officer(s):
Sylvia Augaitis, Executive Director, Marketing, 905-562-8070 Ext. 231
sylvia.augaitis@wmao.ca
Magdalena Kaiser, Director, Public Relations - Marketing & Tourism, 905-562-8070 Ext. 228
magdalena@wmoa.ca

Wine Writers' Circle of Canada
Toronto ON
www.winewriterscircle.ca
www.instagram.com/wwccanada
Overview: A small local organization founded in 1985
Mission: To provide a forum for information sharing, education, & maintenance of professional standards in the wine writer & educator professions
3 volunteer(s)
Membership: 29 individual; *Fees:* $150
Activities: *Rents Mailing List:* Yes
Chief Officer(s):
Dean Tudor, Treasurer
dtudor@ryerson.ca

Wings & Heros
PO Box 405, Beeton ON L0G 1A0
wingsandheros2017@gmail.com
www.wingsandheros.com
Also Known As: Mentors In Motion
Overview: A small national organization
Mission: To promote the concept of NetWeaving for business women; To help business women connect with people they can trust
Membership: *Fees:* $50

Winkler & District Chamber of Commerce
185 Main St., Winkler MB R6W 1B4
Tel: 204-325-9758; Fax: 204-325-8290
www.winklerchamber.com
www.facebook.com/600355936651723
twitter.com/winklerchamber
Overview: A small local organization founded in 1922
Mission: To represent the business community by providing & coordinating activities that support a vibrant business environment
Member of: Manitoba & Canadian Chamber of Commerce
Finances: *Annual Operating Budget:* $100,000-$250,000; *Funding Sources:* City of Winkler; Membership dues
Staff Member(s): 1; 18 volunteer(s)
Membership: 240; *Fees:* Schedule available, based upon number of employees
Chief Officer(s):
Ryan Hildebrand, President
ryan@edenhealthcare.ca
Tanya Chateauneuf, Executive Director, 204-325-9758 Ext. 102
director@winklerchamber.ca
Dianne Friesen, Manager, 204-325-9758 Ext. 100
admin@winklerchamber.com
Awards:
• P.W. Enns Business Awards

Winkler & District United Way
PO Box 1528, Winkler MB R6W 4B4
Tel: 204-325-6321
unitedwaywinkler@gmail.com
www.unitedwaywinkler.com
www.facebook.com/609225769188170
Overview: A small local organization overseen by United Way of Canada - Centraide Canada
Mission: To serve & improve the community

Chief Officer(s):
Lori Penner, President

Winnipeg Association of Non-Teaching Employees (WANTE) / Association des employés non enseignants de Winnipeg
#111, 1555 St. James St., Winnipeg MB R3H 1B5
Tel: 204-953-0250; Fax: 204-953-0259
wante@wante.org
www.wante.org
Overview: A small local organization
Mission: To act as a bargaining agent for members to help regulate relations between members & their employers
Membership: 1,700; *Member Profile:* Teaching support staff members; *Committees:* Executive & Council; Labour Education; Liaison; Social
Chief Officer(s):
Gale Hladik, President

Winnipeg Association of Public Service Officers (WAPSO) / Association des agents de services au public de Winnipeg
#2705, 83 Garry St., Winnipeg MB R3C 4J9
Tel: 204-925-4120; Fax: 201-925-4128
www.wapso.ca
www.facebook.com/WinnipegAssociationofPublicServiceOfficers
www.flickr.com/photos/112212984@N04
Overview: A medium-sized local organization founded in 1969
Mission: To represent the interests of its workers during collective bargaining; to ensure its members a high standard quality of work life.
Finances: *Funding Sources:* Membership dues
Staff Member(s): 6
Membership: *Member Profile:* Supervisory, professionals & administrative
Chief Officer(s):
Robert Young, Executive Director
Andrew Weremy, President
Alex Regiec, 1st Vice-President
Michael Robinson, 2nd Vice-President

Winnipeg Board of Trade *See* Winnipeg Chamber of Commerce

Winnipeg Branch *See* Manitoba Genealogical Society Inc.

Winnipeg Building & Construction Trades Council *See* Manitoba Building & Construction Trades Council

Winnipeg Centraide *See* United Way of Winnipeg

Winnipeg Chamber of Commerce (WCC) / Chambre de commerce de Winnipeg
#100, 259 Portage Ave., Winnipeg MB R3B 2A9
Tel: 204-944-8484; Fax: 204-944-8492
info@winnipeg-chamber.com
www.winnipeg-chamber.com
www.linkedin.com/company/the-winnipeg-chamber-of-commerce
www.facebook.com/WpgChamber
twitter.com/TheWpgChamber
www.youtube.com/wpgchamber;
www.instagram.com/wpgchamber
Previous Name: Winnipeg Board of Trade
Overview: A medium-sized local organization founded in 1873
Mission: To act as the voice of business in Winnipeg; To foster an environment in which Winnipeg businesses can proper
Finances: *Funding Sources:* Membership dues; Sponsorships
Staff Member(s): 21
Membership: 2,060+ companies, representing close to 90,000 employees; *Fees:* Schedule available, based upon number of full-time Winnipeg employees
Activities: Promoting Winnipeg businesses; Engaging in lobbying & advocacy activities
Chief Officer(s):
Dave Angus, President & Chief Executive Officer, 204-944-3300
dangus@winnipeg-chamber.com
Maxine Kashton, Vice-President, Finance & Operations, 204-944-3304
mkashton@winnipeg-chamber.com
Karen Weiss, Vice-President, Membership & Marketing, 204-944-3305
kweiss@winnipeg-chamber.com
Awards:
• The Winnipeg Chamber of Commerce Spirit of Winnipeg Awards
The following categories will be recognized for innovation: small businesses, with revenues less than $10 million; medium businesses, with revenues of $10-$75 million; large businesses, with revenues over $75 million; start-up businesses, that have been operating for under three years; not-for-profit organizations; & charities*Location:* Winnipeg, Manitoba *Deadline:* December *Contact:* Elizabeth Catacutan, Manager, Events, Phone: 204-944-3308, E-mail: ecatacutan@winnipeg-chamber.com
Publications:
• The Chamber Connected [a publication of the Winnipeg Chamber of Commerce]
Type: Newsletter; *Frequency:* bi-weekly; *Accepts Advertising*
Profile: Chamber happenings, policies, events, & new members
• Winnipeg Chamber Member Directory
Type: Directory; *Accepts Advertising*
Profile: A directory to connect users with trusted member companies of the Winnipeg Chamber of Commerce
• Winnipeg Chamber of Commerce Annual Report
Type: Yearbook; *Frequency:* Annually
Profile: A year-in-review summary in conjunction with the annual general meeting

Winnipeg Clinic Employees Association (WCEA)
Winnipeg MB
Overview: A small local licensing organization founded in 1981
Finances: *Annual Operating Budget:* Less than $50,000
Membership: 150; *Fees:* $5 biweekly; *Member Profile:* Medical support staff
Chief Officer(s):
Louise Torfason, President

Winnipeg Construction Association
1447 Waverly St., Winnipeg MB R3T 0P7
Tel: 204-775-8664; Fax: 204-783-6446
wca@winnipegconstruction.ca
www.winnipegconstruction.ca
twitter.com/wcanews
Also Known As: Manitoba Construction Association
Overview: A medium-sized local organization overseen by Canadian Construction Association
Mission: To encourage a high level of standards among the construction industry in Manitoba & to promote the industry as a whole
Member of: Canadian Construction Association
Membership: 700+; *Fees:* $2400 regular; $875 professional/associate; *Member Profile:* Commercial contractors & suppliers in Manitoba
Chief Officer(s):
Ronald Hambley, President

Winnipeg Executives Association (WEA)
#503, 386 Broadway Ave., Winnipeg MB R3C 3R6
Tel: 204-947-9766
weaadmin@wpgexecs.ca
www.wpgexecs.ca
Overview: A small local organization founded in 1923
Mission: To enhance, develop & promote business opportunities available to our members through networking & direct contacts with Winnipeg's business leaders in a spirit of fellowship & friendship
Finances: *Annual Operating Budget:* $100,000-$250,000; *Funding Sources:* Membership dues
Staff Member(s): 1
Membership: 125; *Fees:* $1,134; *Member Profile:* Owners; presidents; *Committees:* Membership; Programme; Attendance; Leads
Activities: Golf Days; Presidents Ball; Holiday Party; Associates Day; Spouse/Guest Day; Inspirational Day
Chief Officer(s):
Geoff Powell, Executive Director
gap@strauss.ca

Winnipeg Film Group (WFG)
#304, 100 Arthur St., Winnipeg MB R3B 1H3
Tel: 204-925-3456; Fax: 204-942-6799
info@winnipegfilmgroup.com
www.winnipegfilmgroup.com
Overview: A small local charitable organization founded in 1974
Mission: To enhance the art of film by providing equal opportunities to make, view & discuss film within a greater artistic & social community
Member of: Independent Film & Video Alliance; Artspace
Staff Member(s): 14
Membership: *Fees:* Schedule available; *Member Profile:* Independent filmmakers; *Committees:* Community Engagement; Finance; Board Development
Activities: Workshops; screenings; film production assistance; grants to filmmakers; distribution; promotion; *Library*
Chief Officer(s):

Cecilia Araneda, Executive Director
cecilia@winnipegfilmgroup.com

Winnipeg Foundation
#1350, One Lombard Pl., Winnipeg MB R3B 0X3
Tel: 204-944-9474; *Fax:* 204-942-2987
Toll-Free: 877-974-3631
info@wpgfdn.org
www.wpgfdn.org
www.facebook.com/wpgfdn
twitter.com/winnipegfdn
www.youtube.com/user/winnipegfoundation
Overview: A small local charitable organization founded in 1921
Mission: Community trust for charitable, educational & cultural purposes in Greater Winnipeg
Staff Member(s): 11
Chief Officer(s):
Richard L. Frost, CEO

Winnipeg Gliding Club (WGC)
PO Box 1255, Winnipeg MB R3C 2Y4
Tel: 204-735-2868
info@wgc.mb.ca
www.wgc.mb.ca
Overview: A small local organization
Mission: The Winnipeg Gliding Club is a non-profit organization dedicated to the promotion of gliding and soaring
Member of: Soaring Association of Canada
Membership: 70; *Fees:* $25-$450
Awards:
• The Cracked Head Award
Eligibility: Tow pilots

Winnipeg Harvest Inc.
1085 Winnipeg Ave., Winnipeg MB R3E 0S2
Tel: 204-982-3663; *Fax:* 204-775-4180
info@winnipegharvest.org
www.winnipegharvest.org
www.facebook.com/wpgharvest
twitter.com/WinnipegHarvest
www.youtube.com/user/WinnipegHarvestInc
Overview: A small local charitable organization founded in 1984
Mission: To collect & distribute food to feed those in our community who struggle to feed themselves & their families & to maximize public awareness of hunger while working towards long term solutions to hunger & poverty
Affiliation(s): Canadian Association of Food Banks
Finances: *Annual Operating Budget:* $500,000-$1.5 Million
Staff Member(s): 12; 200 volunteer(s)
Activities: Food Bank; Share Your Thanks, Oct.; Hunger Count, fall; *Speaker Service:* Yes; *Library:* Open to public
Chief Officer(s):
Jody Hecht, President

Winnipeg Humane Society (WHS)
45 Hurst Way, Winnipeg MB R3T 0R3
Tel: 204-982-2021; *Fax:* 204-663-9401
reception@winnipeghumanesociety.ca
www.winnipeghumanesociety.ca
www.facebook.com/WinnipegHumaneSociety
twitter.com/thewhs
www.instagram.com/whsanimals
Overview: A small local charitable organization
Mission: To protect animals from suffering & promoting their welfare & dignity
Member of: Canadian Federation of Humane Societies
Staff Member(s): 50; 250 volunteer(s)
Chief Officer(s):
Javier Schwersensky, CEO

Winnipeg Labour Council
#504, 275 Broadway Ave., Winnipeg MB R3C 4M6
Tel: 204-942-0522; *Fax:* 204-942-7396
info@winnipeglabour.ca
www.winnipeglabour.ca
www.facebook.com/WinnipegLabourCouncil
twitter.com/DaveSour
Overview: A small local organization
Chief Officer(s):
Dave Sauer, President
sauer@winnipeglabour.ca

Winnipeg Musicians' Association
#201, 180 Market Ave. East, Winnipeg MB R3B 0P7
Tel: 204-943-4803; *Fax:* 204-943-5029
wma190@mts.net
winnipegmusicians.ca
Also Known As: AFM Local 190
Overview: A small local organization founded in 1902
Member of: American Federation of Musicians of the United States & Canada
Staff Member(s): 2
Membership: 600; *Fees:* $170 yearly dues; $136 initiation fee; *Member Profile:* Professional musicians of Manitoba
Chief Officer(s):
Cornelius Godri, President
James Jay Harrison, Vice-President
Tony Cyre, Secretary-Treasurer

Winnipeg Ostomy Association (WOA)
#204, 825 Sherbrook St., Winnipeg MB R3A 1M5
Tel: 204-234-2022
woainfo@mts.net
www.ostomy-winnipeg.ca
Overview: A small local charitable organization founded in 1972 overseen by Canadian Ostomy Society
Mission: To assist people with ostomy & related surgeries in Winnipeg and the surrounding area
Finances: *Funding Sources:* Membership dues; donations
Membership: 280; *Fees:* $40
Chief Officer(s):
Lorrie Pismenny, President
Publications:
• Inside Out
Type: Newsletter; *Frequency:* 6 pa

Winnipeg Philatelic Society (WPS)
PO Box 1425, Winnipeg MB R3C 2Z1
post99@yahoo.com
www.wps.mb.ca
Also Known As: Winnipeg Stamp Club
Overview: A small local organization founded in 1900
Finances: *Funding Sources:* Membership dues
5 volunteer(s)
Membership: 160; *Fees:* $35; $25 senior; $20 spouse; $15 junior; $350 life
Activities: *Library:*
Publications:
• The Buffalo [a publication of the Winnipeg Philatelic Society]
Type: Newsletter; *Frequency:* 10 pa

Winnipeg Police Association (WPA) / Association de la police de Winnipeg
#70, 81 Garry St., Winnipeg MB R3C 4J9
Tel: 204-957-1579; *Fax:* 204-949-1674
info@wpa.mb.ca
www.winnipegpoliceassociation.ca
www.facebook.com/169240943135061
twitter.com/wpgwpa
pinterest.com/winnipegpolicea
Overview: A medium-sized local organization founded in 1972
Mission: To support its members & act as the bargaining agent in all contractual matters
Member of: Canadian Police Association
Affiliation(s): Manitoba Police Association; Alberta Federation of Police Associations; Calgary Police Association; Edmonton Police Association; British Columbia Federation of Police Officers; Vancouver Police Union; Winnipeg Police Credit Union; Winnipeg Police Service; New Brunswick Police Association; Police Association of Nova Scotia; Royal Newfoundland Constabulary Association; Durham Regional Police Association; Ontario Provincial Police Association; Ottawa Police Association; Peel Regional Police Association; Police Association of Ontario; Toronto Police Association; Montreal Police Brotherhood
Membership: 1,400+ individual; *Member Profile:* Police officers & support staff
Activities: *Speaker Service:* Yes
Chief Officer(s):
Mike Sutherland, President

Winnipeg Real Estate Board (WREB)
1240 Portage Ave., Winnipeg MB R3G 0T6
Tel: 204-786-8854; *Fax:* 204-784-2343
websupport@winnipegrealtors.ca
www.winnipegrealtors.ca
www.youtube.com/user/winnipegrealtors
Overview: A medium-sized local organization founded in 1903 overseen by Manitoba Real Estate Association
Mission: To serve members & to promote the benefits of organized real estate
Member of: The Canadian Real Estate Association
Affiliation(s): Winnipeg Chamber of Commerce
Finances: *Funding Sources:* Membership dues
Membership: *Member Profile:* Real estate salespeople & brokers
Activities: Citizens Hall of Fame; Housing Opportunity Partnership; *Library:* Not open to public
Awards:
• Citizens Hall of Fame
• Board Builders Awards
• Medallion Awards
• Rookie of the Year
• Community Services & Commercial Awards
• Member Recognition (25 year & 35 year)

Winnipeg Society of Financial Analysts *See* CFA Society Winnipeg

Winnipeg Symphony Orchestra Inc. (WSO)
555 Main St., Winnipeg MB R3B 1C3
Tel: 204-949-3999; *Fax:* 204-956-4271
www.wso.ca
www.facebook.com/WinnipegSymphony
twitter.com/WpgSymphony
www.youtube.com/WinnipegSymphony
Overview: A large local charitable organization founded in 1947 overseen by Orchestras Canada
Mission: To perform a wide variety of orchestral music including classical, contemporary, pop & children's music in Manitoba & Northwestern Ontario; To enrich the cultural landscape by engaging with the community
Member of: Orchestras Canada
Finances: *Annual Operating Budget:* Greater than $5 Million; *Funding Sources:* Federal, provincial & municipal governments; Corporate & individual donors; Ticket revenue
Staff Member(s): 44; 100 volunteer(s)
Membership: 5,000-14,999; *Committees:* Artistic Operations; Education & Community Engagement; Finance; Development; Sales & Audience Services; Marketing & Communications
Activities: Performing concert series; Facilitating an annual New Music Festival; Providing education & outreach initiatives for students & community groups; *Library:* Music Library; Not open to public
Chief Officer(s):
Trudy Schroeder, Executive Director
tschroeder@wso.mb.ca
Alexander Mickelthwate, Music Director
lmarks@wso.mb.ca

Winnipeg Tribal Council *See* Keewatin Tribal Council

Winnipeg Vegetarian Association (WVA)
PO Box 2721, Stn. Main, Winnipeg MB R3C 4B3
wva@ivu.org
www.ivu.org/wva
www.facebook.com/WinnipegVeg
twitter.com/WinnipegVeg
Overview: A small local organization founded in 1993
Mission: To foster & encourage vegetarianism through social & educational events
Member of: Vegetarian Union of North America
Affiliation(s): North America Vegetarian Society; American Vegan Society
Finances: *Annual Operating Budget:* Less than $50,000; *Funding Sources:* Membership fees
11 volunteer(s)
Membership: 150+; *Fees:* $10-$100 individual; $15-$150 family; $5-$50 senior/student; *Member Profile:* Vegetarian or interest in becoming vegetarian; *Committees:* Health Professionals; Restaurants
Activities: *Awareness Events:* World Vegetarian Day, Oct. 1; World Vegetarian Month, Oct.; National Nutrition Month, March; *Speaker Service:* Yes

Winnipeg Youth Orchestras
PO Box 273, Winnipeg MB R3C 2G9
Tel: 204-805-9961
admin@winnipegyouthorchestras.ca
www.winnipegyouthorchestras.ca
www.facebook.com/winnipegyouthorchestras
www.instagram.com/youth_orchestra
Also Known As: Junior Strings; Youth Concert Orchestra; Youth Symphony Orchestra
Previous Name: Manitoba Schools' Orchestra
Overview: A large local charitable organization founded in 1923 overseen by Orchestras Canada
Mission: To enable young musicians from Winnipeg to expand their musical abilities while playing in an ensemble setting
Member of: Orchestras Canada

Finances: *Funding Sources:* Individual & corporate donations; Government
Staff Member(s): 12
Chief Officer(s):
Tracey LeClair, Administrator

Winnipeg's Contemporary Dancers
#204, 211 Bannatyne Ave., Winnipeg MB R3B 3P2
Tel: 204-452-0229
wcd@mts.net
www.winnipegscontemporarydancers.ca
www.facebook.com/WpgContemps
twitter.com/WpgContemps
vimeo.com/wpgcontemps
Previous Name: Contemporary Dancers Canada
Overview: A small local charitable organization founded in 1964
Mission: To create a place on the local, national & international arts landscape that enables vital intersections, linkages & exchange among dance creators, dance interpreters, spectators and communities
Chief Officer(s):
Brent Lott, Artistic Director

WinSport Canada
88 Canada Olympic Rd. SW, Calgary AB T3B 5R5
Tel: 403-247-5452
info@coda.ca
www.winsportcanada.ca
www.facebook.com/CanadaOlympicPark
twitter.com/winsportcanada
www.youtube.com/channel/UCXyy8HyMGaBiVmAY-ZZVLsQ
Previous Name: Calgary Olympic Development Association
Overview: A small local organization founded in 1956
Mission: WinSport Canada is a not-for-profit association that develops & sustains the sporting facilities of Canada Olympic Park. It supports national sports organizations & subsidizes unique facilities used by top athletes & the public.
Member of: Calgary Society of Associations Executives
Affiliation(s): Canadian Olympic Committee; Canadian Paralympic Committee
Staff Member(s): 260; 200 volunteer(s)
Activities: Fundraising for Canada Wins, a winter sports institute
Chief Officer(s):
Robert (Bob) Hamilton, Chair
Barry Heck, President & CEO

Wireless Toronto
c/o Urban+Digital, #400, 215 Spadina Ave., Toronto ON M5T 2C7
Tel: 647-722-3567
hello@wirelesstoronto.ca
www.wirelesstoronto.ca
Overview: A small local organization
Mission: To expand wireless networking; To bring free wireless Internet access to Toronto's public spaces
Finances: *Funding Sources:* Donations; membership fees
Membership: *Fees:* $50

Wolastoqey Tribal Council Inc.
150 Cliffe St., 2nd Fl., Fredericton NB E3A 0A1
Tel: 506-459-6341
admin@wtci-nb.ca
www.wolastoqey.ca/wtc
Overview: A small local organization
Mission: To provide advisory services & assistance to the member First Nations
Membership: 4 First Nations; *Member Profile:* Madawaska Maliseet First Nation; Kingsclear First Nation; St. Mary's First Nation; The Oromocto First Nation
Activities: Aboriginal Skills & Employment & Training Strategy (ASETS) program
Chief Officer(s):
Shyla O'Donnell, Executive Director

Wolfville Historical Society
259 Main St., Wolfville NS B4P 1C6
Tel: 902-542-9775
randallhouse@outlook.com
www.wolfvillehs.ednet.ns.ca
Overview: A small local charitable organization founded in 1941
Mission: To operate the Randall House Museum
Membership: *Fees:* $10 youth/distance member; $20 individual; $30 family; $100 sustaining member/couple
Activities: *Library:* Wolfville Historical Society Photograph Archive; Open to public
Chief Officer(s):

Martin Hallett, President
John Whidden, Archivist
Publications:
• Wolfville Historical Society Newsletter
Type: Newsletter
Profile: News & events of the society

Wolverines Wheelchair Sports Association
10 Knowledge Way, Grande Prairie AB T8W 2V9
Tel: 780-402-3331; *Fax:* 780-402-3318
info@gpwolverines.com
www.gpwolverines.com
Overview: A small local organization founded in 1990
Mission: To provide people with disabilities the opportunity to engage in physcial & recreational activities.
Membership: *Fees:* Schedule available

The Women & Environments Education & Development Foundation *See* Women's Healthy Environments Network

Women Business Owners of Manitoba (WBOM)
#338, 23-845 Dakota St., Winnipeg MB R2M 5M3
Tel: 204-775-7981; *Fax:* 204-897-8094
info@wbom.ca
www.wbom.ca
www.facebook.com/WomenBusinessOwnersOfManitoba
twitter.com/WBOManitoba
instagram.com/WBOManitoba
Overview: A small provincial organization
Mission: To connect, support & inspire excellence amongst women in the entrepreneurial community in Manitoba
Membership: 165; *Fees:* $399 regular; $1,575 corporate; $399 friend
Activities: *Awareness Events:* Annual Golf Tournament
Chief Officer(s):
Lucy Camara, President
lcamara@olatechcorp.com
Tracy Ducharme, Vice-President
tracy@veritus.ca
Awards:
• Manitoba Woman Entrepreneur of the Year Award

Women Educating in Self-Defense Training (WEST)
Tel: 604-876-6390
wenlido.west@gmail.com
wenlido-west.webs.com
www.facebook.com/wenlido
Also Known As: Wenlido WEST
Overview: A small provincial organization founded in 1976
Affiliation(s): Women in Self-Defense Education
Finances: *Annual Operating Budget:* Less than $50,000
3 volunteer(s)
Membership: 20; *Fees:* $15
Activities: Teaching self-defense to women & their children; *Speaker Service:* Yes

Women Entrepreneurs of Saskatchewan Inc. (WE)
#108, 502 Cope Way, Saskatoon SK S7T 0G3
Tel: 306-477-7173; *Fax:* 306-477-7175
Toll-Free: 844-900-9375
info@wesk.ca
www.womenentrepreneurs.sk.ca
www.linkedin.com/company/1277529
www.facebook.com/WESK306
Overview: A medium-sized provincial organization founded in 1995
Mission: To provide programs & service to women who are considering a business, starting a business, or operating an existing business
Member of: Women's Enterprise Initiative
Affiliation(s): Western Economic Diversification Canada
8 volunteer(s)
Membership: 800; *Fees:* $125
Activities: Offering training & seminars & financing; *Library:* Resource Centre for Members; Open to public
Chief Officer(s):
Prabha Mitchell, CEO
Jennifer Smith, Officer, Finance
Katelyn Bruce, Officer, Marketing & Communications
Awards:
• Member of the Year
Publications:
• Connect [a publication of the Women Entrepreneurs of Saskatchewan Inc.]
Type: Newsletter
Profile: Information about the association plus training events & conferences across Saskatchewan

• Women Entrepreneurs of Saskatchewan Inc. Annual Report
Type: Yearbook; *Frequency:* Annually
Profile: Contents include financial statements & the auditor's report
Regina Office
100 - 1919 Rose St., Regina SK S4P 3P1
Tel: 306-359-9732; *Fax:* 306-359-9739
Toll-Free: 844-901-9375

Women Expanding Business Network of Lanark County
158 Herriott St., Carleton Place ON K7C 2A9
Tel: 613-253-1802
lanarkcountyweb@rogers.com
www.facebook.com/lanarkweb
Also Known As: WEB Network
Overview: A small local organization founded in 1998
Mission: To connect & educate business women in Lanark County
Staff Member(s): 1
Activities: Meetings; showcases; groups; keynote speakers
Chief Officer(s):
Lara LaFreniere, Owner

Women for Recreation, Information & Business (WRIB)
PO Box 1155, Stn. F, 50 Charles St. East, Toronto ON M4Y 2T8
wrib.ca@gmail.com
twitter.com/WRIB2
Overview: A small local organization founded in 1991
Mission: To provide social, business & informational networking environment for lesbians, bisexual, transsexual & transgendered women with common goals & interests
Membership: *Fees:* $36 single membership

Women Immigrants of London *See* WIL Employment Connections

Women in a Home Office
PO Box 369, #440, 10816 Macleod Trail South, Calgary AB T2J 5N8
Tel: 403-726-0785
Toll-Free: 800-615-7685
info@womeninahomeoffice.com
www.womeninahomeoffice.com
Overview: A small local organization founded in 2000
Mission: To support women working in a home based business &/or from a home office through network events, workshops, etc. on & off-line
Membership: *Fees:* $99; *Member Profile:* Chapters in Alberta, Manitoba & Ontario

Women in Capital Markets (WCM) / Les femmes sur les marchés financiers
#300, 37 Front St. East, Toronto ON M5E 1B3
Tel: 416-502-3614
info@wcm.ca
www.wcm.ca
www.linkedin.com/groups/1681457
www.facebook.com/WomenInCapitalMarkets
twitter.com/WCMCanada
Overview: A small national organization founded in 1995
Mission: To enable capital markets professionals to reach their greatest potential for success; to advance woment within Canadian financial services
Finances: *Funding Sources:* Founding firms; sponsors; membership dues
Membership: 1200+; *Member Profile:* Professionals working in Capital Markets; Students; *Committees:* Awards; Executive Coaching; External & Joint Events; High School Liaison; Marketing & Communications; Membership; Mentorship Program; PR; Professional Development; Return to Bay St.; Sponsorship; Socialnet; Women in Leadership; UniConnect; WCM Gala
Activities: Education & outreach; mentorship program
Chief Officer(s):
Mari Jenson, Chair
Camilla Sutton, President & CEO

Women In Crisis (Algoma) Inc. (WIC)
23 Oakland Ave., Sault Ste Marie ON P6A 2T2
Tel: 705-759-1230
Toll-Free: 877-759-1230
adminassist@wicalgoma.com
www.womenincrisis.ca
Also Known As: Oakland Place
Overview: A small local organization founded in 1979

Mission: To work towards the elimination of violence against women & their children; To provide a range of direct & indirect services for women who have or currently are experiencing abuse in their lives; To work within a feminist perspective to provide programs which facilitate the claiming of power by women
Affiliation(s): Ontario Association of Interval & Transition Houses
Finances: *Annual Operating Budget:* $500,000-$1.5 Million; *Funding Sources:* Provincial government; United Way; Ministry of Health
Staff Member(s): 38
Membership: *Committees:* MCSS; MDF Housing; United Way; Bequests/Donation
Chief Officer(s):
Norma Elliott, Director, Programs & Staff
nelliott@wicalgoma.com
Sharon Reid, Director, Community Relations & Finance
sreid@wicalgoma.com

Women in Film & Television - Toronto
#601, 110 Eglinton Ave. East, Toronto ON M4P 2Y1
Tel: 416-322-3430; *Fax:* 416-322-3703
wift@wift.com
www.wift.com
www.linkedin.com/groups/Women-in-Film-Television-Toronto-2908431
www.facebook.com/WIFT.Toronto
twitter.com/WIFT
vimeo.com/wift
Also Known As: WIFT-T
Previous Name: Toronto Women in Film & Television
Overview: A medium-sized provincial charitable organization founded in 1984
Mission: To provide year-round training programs, industry events, & professional awards for women & men in Canadian screen based media
Affiliation(s): Women in Film Chapters (worldwide)
Finances: *Annual Operating Budget:* $250,000-$500,000; *Funding Sources:* Membership fees; government; corporate; donations
Staff Member(s): 5; 50 volunteer(s)
Membership: 850; *Fees:* $148.75 full; $106.25 associate; $144.50 friend; $42.50 Senior/student; *Member Profile:* Open to all women working in any facet of the film & television industry residing in Ontario; Friend category for both women & men who don't qualify for other membership categories but wish to take part in WIFT-T's programs; *Committees:* Professional Development, Member Services, Special Events, Fundraising, Profile & Policy
Activities: Professional development workshops; monthy networking breakfasts; advanced training courses; annual awards gala; booths at industry events; *Library:* Resource Centre; by appointment Not open to public
Chief Officer(s):
Prentiss Fraser, Chair
Heather Webb, Executive Director
Awards:
• The Crystal Awards - Annual Outstanding Achievement Awards

Women in Film & Television Alberta (WIFTA)
c/o Luanne Morrow, Borden Ladner Gervais, #1000 Canterra Tower, 400 3rd Ave. SW, Calgary AB T2P 4H2
admin@wifta.ca
www.wifta.ca
www.linkedin.com/groups/4165901/profile
www.facebook.com/WIFTAlberta
twitter.com/WIFTAlberta
Also Known As: WIFT Alberta
Overview: A medium-sized provincial organization
Mission: To promote & assist the professional development, equitable treatment, recognition of achievements & the creation of new opportunities for professional women in the film, video, multimedia & television industries
Membership: *Fees:* $50 voting members; $10 student
Chief Officer(s):
Susan Feddena-Leonard, President, 780-827-2696

Women in Film & Television Vancouver (WIFTV)
Dominion Building, #306, 207 West Hastings St., Vancouver BC V6B 1H7
Tel: 604-685-1152; *Fax:* 604-685-1124
info@womeninfilm.ca
www.womeninfilm.ca
www.facebook.com/Womeninfilm
twitter.com/WIFTV
www.youtube.com/user/wiftv
Overview: A medium-sized provincial organization founded in 1989
Mission: To support, advance, promote & celebrate the professional development & achievements of women working in British Columbia's film, television, video & multimedia industries
Member of: Women in Film & Television International; Alliance for Arts & Culture
Finances: *Annual Operating Budget:* $100,000-$250,000
Staff Member(s): 2; 200 volunteer(s)
Membership: 750; *Fees:* $78.75-$157.50; *Member Profile:* Directors; writers; producers; actors; crew; *Committees:* Advocacy; Fundraising
Activities: Mentorship Program; Walking Talking Heads seminar; Career Cafe Seminars; Producers, Actors, Writers & Directors Workshops; Flash Forward; Film Festival for International Women's Day; Spotlight Gala; networking breakfasts; *Internships:* Yes; *Speaker Service:* Yes
Chief Officer(s):
Rachelle Chartrand, President
Michelle Billy Povill, Vice-President
Christine Larsen, Secretary
Awards:
• Spotlights Awards Gala
• Artistic Merit Award
• WIFVV Scholarships

Women in Food Industry Management (WFIM)
c/o ADM Milling Company, 7585 Danbro Cres., Mississauga ON L5N 6P9
admin@wfim.ca
www.wfim.ca
Overview: A small national organization founded in 1984
Mission: To build a network of contacts among women at the management level in the food industry, for the exchange of ideas & information of importance to the industry & the members; To promote & encourage personal growth of members
Membership: *Fees:* $135
Chief Officer(s):
Barbara Onyskow, Chair

Women of the Word - Toronto (WOW)
Maple ON
Tel: 416-453-0402
www.wowblessingstoronto.com
Overview: A medium-sized international organization
Mission: To inspire, teach, & help women grow in the Catholic community
Affiliation(s): Archdiocese of Toronto
Finances: *Annual Operating Budget:* Less than $50,000
Activities: Publishing the "Blessings" magazine
Chief Officer(s):
Mary Filangi, Contact
mary.filangi@sympatico.ca
Publications:
• Blessings [a publication of Women of the Word - Toronto] *Type:* Magazine

Women That Hunt
Hwy. 289, Brookfield NS B0N 1C0
Tel: 902-986-7010
info@womenthathunt.com
www.womenthathunt.com
www.facebook.com/womenthathunt
twitter.com/womenthathunt
www.instagram.com/womenthathunt
Overview: A small provincial organization
Mission: To educate & support women & youth with a passion for hunting, fishing, health & wellness, & the outdoors
Membership: *Fees:* $25 adult; $10 youth; $45 couple; $50 family
Activities: Organizing & participating in community events & seminars; Fundraising
Chief Officer(s):
Kelly Countway, Founding Member
Teresa Elliott, Founding Member
Sharleen Martell, Founding Member

Women Who Excel Inc. (WWE)
9 Woodbridge Rd., Hamilton ON L8K 3C6
Tel: 905-547-7135; *Fax:* 905-547-7135
Toll-Free: 800-363-0268
info@womenwhoexcel.com
www.womenwhoexcel.com
Overview: A small local organization founded in 1989
Mission: To promote women in business & to get more business
Member of: Oakville Chamber of Commerce; Burlington Chamber of Commerce; Hamilton Chamber of Commerce
Finances: *Funding Sources:* User fees; memberships; advertising
Membership: 52; *Fees:* $60; *Member Profile:* Women in home-based or small retail businesses; organizations; media; politics
Activities: Networking dinners, breakfasts, & bingos to find & make contacts with other women in the Hamilton-Wentworth & Halton Regions; mini trade shows; seasonal fashion shows; *Internships:* Yes; *Speaker Service:* Yes; *Rents Mailing List:* Yes; *Library:* Open to public by appointment
Chief Officer(s):
Christine Whitlock, President/Publisher

Women's & Gender Studies et Recherches Féministes (WGSRF)
c/o Elyse Cottrell, 131 Machar Ave., Thunder Bay ON P7B 2Y7
Other Communication: membership@wgsrf.com
generalinfo@wgsrf.com
www.wgsrf.com
Previous Name: Canadian Women's Studies Association / L'association canadienne des études sur les femmes (CWSA / ACÉF)
Overview: A small national organization founded in 1982
Mission: To foster & promote women's & gender studies as an academic field
Member of: Canadian Federation for the Humanities & Social Sciences
Finances: *Funding Sources:* Membership fees; Donations
Membership: *Fees:* $15 students & unwaged persons; $25 ind. (retired or low income); $70 ind. (waged under $100,000); $100 ind. (waged over $100,000); *Member Profile:* Women's & gender studies practitioners in Canada; Undergraduate & graduate students; Community activists; Policy researchers; *Committees:* Communications; Conference Abstract Adjudication; Conference Program; Graduate Essay Prize; Keynote Speaker; Outstanding Scholarship Prize; Undergraduate Essay Prize
Chief Officer(s):
Ilya Parkins, Secretary

Women's Art Association of Canada (WAAC)
23 Prince Arthur Ave., Toronto ON M5R 1B2
Tel: 416-922-2060
administration@womensartofcanada.ca
www.womensartofcanada.ca
Overview: A small national charitable organization founded in 1887
Mission: To provide scholarships for the arts through the following schools & colleges: The Royal Conservatory of Music of Toronto; The Ontario College of Art; The Faculty of Music, University of Toronto; The National Ballet School; Sheridan College
Membership: 7; *Fees:* $225 regular; $75 out of town/student
Activities: Fundraising events; art shows; recitals; *Library:* by appointment Not open to public

Women's Association of the Mining Industry of Canada
c/o Vi Andersen, President, 140 Shanty Bay Rd., Barrie ON L4M 1E3
scholarships@cogeco.ca
www.pdac.ca/wamic
Overview: A small national organization founded in 1921
Mission: To promote friendship among women whose interests are connected with the mining industry; to render service where possible to the mining industry or those connected therewith; & to participate in work which relates to the well-being of Canadian residents
Membership: 270 individual; *Fees:* $17 individual
Chief Officer(s):
Vi Andersen, President
Awards:
• National Geophysics Scholarship
Eligibility: Awarded annually to an undergraduate student who has attained the highest academic average on completion of third year in an accredited geophysics program at a qualified Canadian university *Deadline:* June 4; *Amount:* $1,000
• National Scholarship
Eligibility: Awarded annually to an undergraduate student enrolled in any of the above accredited programs at a qualified Canadian university who has attained the highest academic average on completion of third year *Deadline:* June 4; *Amount:* $1,000

Canadian Associations / Women's Business Network of Ottawa (WBN)

• The Wood Bursary
Eligibility: Awarded annually to third and fourth year undergraduate students who can demonstrate financial need and who are enrolled in an accredited mining related program in a Canadian university. This bursary can be continued through re-application providing the scholar maintains good academic standing and the need prevails *Deadline:* June 4; *Amount:* $6,000

Women's Business Network of Ottawa (WBN)
#200, 435 St. Laurent Blvd., Ottawa ON K1K 2Z8
Tel: 613-749-5975; *Fax:* 613-745-8753
info@womensbusinessnetwork.ca
www.womensbusinessnetwork.ca
www.linkedin.com/groups?gid=2967196
www.facebook.com/WBNOttawa
twitter.com/WBN_Ottawa
Overview: A small local organization founded in 1981
Mission: To be the leading vehicle for business women to build business relationships; achieve success; celebrate their accomplishments & have fun doing it
Finances: *Annual Operating Budget:* Less than $50,000
Staff Member(s): 1
Membership: 150; *Fees:* $220; *Member Profile:* Women business owners in commission sales or senior managers; *Committees:* Golf; Membership; Marketing & Communications; Events & Programming; Sponsorship
Activities: Monthly meetings; *Speaker Service:* Yes
Chief Officer(s):
Lynda Carter, President
lycarter@deloitte.ca
Awards:
• Business Woman of the Year
• Businesswoman's achievement award

Women's Canadian Historical Society of Ottawa *See* Historical Society of Ottawa

The Women's Centre
#229, 1515 Rebecca St., Oakville ON L6G 5G8
Tel: 905-847-5520; *Fax:* 905-847-7413
admin@haltonwomenscentre.org
www.haltonwomenscentre.org
www.facebook.com/TheWomensCentreofHalton
twitter.com/HalWomensCentre
www.flickr.com/photos/haltonwomenscentre
Also Known As: Halton Women's Centre
Overview: A small local organization founded in 1991
Mission: To make a positive difference in the lives of women in transition, crisis or distress

Women's Centre of Montréal *Voir* Centre des femmes de Montréal

Women's Centre of Montréal / Centre des femmes de Montréal
3585, rue St-Urbain, Montréal QC H2X 2N6
Tel: 514-842-1066; *Fax:* 514-842-1067
Other Communication: emploi@centredesfemmesdemtl.org
cfmwcm@centredesfemmesdemtl.org
www.centredesfemmesdemtl.org
Overview: A small local charitable organization founded in 1973
Mission: To provide front line services to women to promote their personal, social, psychological, & economic autonomy; To facilitate the integration of women into the labour market
Finances: *Funding Sources:* Donations
Membership: *Fees:* $5
Activités: Offering services in a number of languages, including English, French, Arabic, Spanish, & Creole; Providing workshops & presentations by employers; Offering a Community Internet Access Centre; Providing a professional clothing kiosk
Membre(s) du bureau directeur:
Johanne Bélisle, Executive Director
Publications:
• Women's Centre of Montréal Annual Report
Type: Yearbook; *Frequency:* Annually

Women's Enterprise Centre of Manitoba / Centre d'entreprise des femmes du Manitoba
#100, 207 Donald St., Winnipeg MB R3C 1M5
Tel: 204-988-1860; *Fax:* 204-988-1871
Toll-Free: 800-203-2343
wecinfo@wecm.ca
www.wecm.ca
www.linkedin.com/company/women's-enterprise-centre-of-manitoba
www.facebook.com/WomensEnterprise
twitter.com/wecmanitoba
www.instagram.com/wecmanitoba
Previous Name: Manitoba Women's Enterprise Centre
Overview: A small provincial organization founded in 1994
Mission: To assist Manitoba women to start or expand businesses; To raise awareness of entrepreneurship & self-employment as a career option for girls & women
Member of: Women Business Owner of Manitoba; Winnipeg Chamber of Commerce; Manitoba Chamber of Commerce
Staff Member(s): 12
Activities: Business seminars; business advice; loan program; *Speaker Service:* Yes
Chief Officer(s):
Sandra Altner, CEO

Women's Executive Network (WXN) / Réseau des femmes exécutives (RFE)
#502, 180 Bloor St. West, Toronto ON M5S 2V6
Tel: 416-361-1475; *Fax:* 416-361-1652
Toll-Free: 866-465-3996
Other Communication: Top 100 Inquiries:
top100@wxnetwork.com
membership@wxnetwork.com
www.wxnetwork.com
www.facebook.com/WXNevents
www.twitter.com/wxn
Overview: A medium-sized national organization founded in 1997
Mission: Dedicated to the advancement & recognition of executive-minded women in the workplace
Affiliation(s): Canadian Board Diversity Council
Staff Member(s): 16
Membership: 22,000 total; 18,500 in Canada; *Fees:* $150 individual; $6,650 corporate silver; $10,250 corporate gold; $16,275 corporate platinum
Activities: Locations in Canada, Ireland & the U.K.
Chief Officer(s):
Pamela Jeffery, Founder, 416-361-1475 Ext. 224
pjeffery@wxnetwork.com
Sherri Stevens, Chief Executive Officer, 416-361-1475 Ext. 229
sstevens@wxnetwork.com
Linsay Moran, Vice-President, Programs & Events, 416-361-1475 Ext. 226
lmoran@wxnetwork.com

Women's Healthy Environments Network (WHEN)
The Centre for Social Innovation, #400, 215 Spadina Ave., Toronto ON M5T 2C7
Tel: 416-928-0880; *Fax:* 416-644-0116
office@womenshealthyenvironments.ca
www.womenshealthyenvironments.ca
www.facebook.com/WHENonlinex
twitter.com/WHENonline
www.youtube.com/user/WHENwomen
Previous Name: The Women & Environments Education & Development Foundation
Overview: A medium-sized national charitable organization founded in 1994
Mission: To provide a forum for communication & to conduct research on issues relating to women in their environments of planning, health, ecology, workplace design, community development & urban & rural sociology & economy
Affiliation(s): National Action Committee on the Status of Women
Finances: *Funding Sources:* Government; Corporate; Private foundations
Staff Member(s): 1
Activities: *Speaker Service:* Yes; *Library:* WEED Resource Centre
Chief Officer(s):
Cassie Barker, Executive Director

Women's Institutes of Nova Scotia (WINS)
#207, 90 Research Dr., Bible Hill NS B6L 2R2
Tel: 902-843-9467; *Fax:* 902-896-7276
novascotiawi@eastlink.ca
www.gov.ns.ca/agri/wins
Overview: A medium-sized provincial organization founded in 1913 overseen by Federated Women's Institutes of Canada
Mission: To provide women with opportunities to enhance their lives through community service & involvement, education & leadership development
Member of: Federated Women's Institutes of Canada
Affiliation(s): Associated Country Women of the World
Finances: *Funding Sources:* Membership fees; Grants; Project funding

Women's Inter-Church Council of Canada (WICC) / Conseil oecuménique des chrétiennes du Canada
47 Queen's Park Cres. East, Toronto ON M5S 2C3
Tel: 416-929-5184; *Fax:* 416-929-4064
wicc@wicc.org
www.wicc.org
www.facebook.com/WICCanada
Overview: A medium-sized national organization founded in 1918
Mission: To encourage women to grow in ecumenism; To share their spirituality & prayer; To respond to national & international issues affecting women; To take action together for justice
Finances: *Funding Sources:* World Day of Prayer offerings
Membership: *Member Profile:* Representatives from the Anglican Church of Canada, the Canadian Baptist Ministries, the Christian Church (Disciples of Christ), the Evangelical Lutheran Church in Canada, the Mennonite Central Committee, the Presbyterian Church in Canada, the Religious Society of Friends, the Roman Catholic Church, the Salvation Army & the United Church of Canada; Membership is by appointment & election; *Committees:* Program; Communications; Membership & Nominating; Finance
Activities: Establishing the Ecumenical Network for Women's Justice; Preparing policy statements on issues such as racial justice & health care; Granting funds for a variety of projects that benefit women & children in Canada & around the world; Coordinating the Fellowship of the Least Coin program in Canada; Providing education, such as theology workshops; *Awareness Events:* World Day of Prayer
Chief Officer(s):
Catherine MacKeil, Executive Director
mackeil@wicc.org
Awards:
• World Day of Prayer Grant
Eligibility: Canadian ecumenical organizations; local women's groups in Canada; national & international organizations supporting local initiatives with & on behalf of women; denominational groups that have ecumenical outreach serving women within the wider community *Deadline:* March 1; *Amount:* $500-$5000
Meetings/Conferences:
• Women's Inter-Church Council of Canada 2018 Annual General Meeting, 2018
Scope: National
Publications:
• Riding the Waves
Type: Newsmagazine; *Frequency:* 3x/yr.
Profile: Updates on the work of the Women's Inter-Church Council of Canada, including results of project grants & forthcoming events; Bible study; Book review; Youth page; Issues important to women of faith

Women's International League for Peace & Freedom (WILPF)
www.wilpfvancouver.ca
Overview: A small international organization founded in 1915
Mission: To unite women throughout the world into a force working to put an end to war; To promote the participation of women in all aspects of international & regional disarmament & peace processes
Membership: *Fees:* $50
Activities: *Internships:* Yes
Chief Officer(s):
Marlene LeGates, President
mlegates33@gmail.com

Women's Legal Education & Action Fund (LEAF) / Fonds d'action et d'éducation juridiques pour les femmes (FAEJ)
#401, 260 Spadina Ave., Toronto ON M5T 2E4
Tel: 416-595-7170; *Fax:* 416-595-7191
Toll-Free: 888-824-5323
info@leaf.ca
www.leaf.ca
www.linkedin.com/company/women%27s-legal-education-and-action-fund-leaf-
www.facebook.com/LEAFFAEJ
twitter.com/LEAFNational
Overview: A medium-sized national charitable organization founded in 1985
Mission: To promote equality for women, primarily by using the gender equality provisions of the Canadian Charter of Rights & Freedoms; To sponsor test cases before the Canadian courts, human rights commissions & government agencies on behalf of women; To provide public education on the issue of gender equality

Staff Member(s): 16
Membership: 2,500
Activities: *Library:*
Chief Officer(s):
Michelle Bullas, Chair
Hailee Morrison, Executive Director, 416-595-7170 Ext. 225
h.morrison@leaf.ca
Kim Stanton, Legal Director, 416-595-7170 Ext. 223
k.stanton@leaf.ca
Crystal Daniel, Manager, Fund Development, 416-595-7170 Ext. 226
c.daniel@leaf.ca
Danielle Dewar, Manager, Communications & Media
d.dewar@leaf.ca
LEAF Halifax
Halifax NS
halifax@leaf.ca
LEAF Sudbury
Sudbury ON
sudbury@leaf.ca
Chief Officer(s):
Carol Stos, Contact
West Coast LEAF
#555, 409 Granville St., Vancouver BC V6C 1T2
Tel: 604-684-8772
Toll-Free: 866-737-7716
info@westcoastleaf.org
www.westcoastleaf.org
www.facebook.com/WestCoastLEAF
twitter.com/WestCoast_LEAF
Chief Officer(s):
Kasari Govender, Executive Director

Women's Missionary Society (WMS)
Tel: 416-441-1111
Toll-Free: 800-619-7301
www.wmspcc.ca
Overview: A medium-sized national organization overseen by Presbyterian Church in Canada
Mission: To encourage people of the Presbyterian Church in Canada to be involved in local & world mission
Member of: Presbyterian Church in Canada
Membership: *Member Profile:* Women who belong to the Presbyterian Church in Canada
Chief Officer(s):
Sarah Kim, Executive Director
skim@presbyterian.ca
Publications:
• Glad Tidings [a publication of the Women's Missionary Society] *Type:* Magazine; *Editor:* Colleen Wood

Women's Musical Club of Toronto (WMCT)
#203A, 56 The Esplanade, Toronto ON M5E 1A7
Tel: 416-923-7052
wmct@wmct.on.ca
www.wmct.on.ca
Overview: A small local charitable organization founded in 1899
Mission: To provide fine chamber music; to give a series of afternoon concerts of international standard; To award a number of scholarships & a triennial national career development award for young Canadian musicians
Finances: *Annual Operating Budget:* $50,000-$100,000
90 volunteer(s)
Membership: 420 individual; *Fees:* $165; *Member Profile:* By subscription for concert series; *Committees:* Concert; Membership; Finance; Career Development Award; Honourary Board Members
Activities: Annual "Music in the Afternoon" concert series; *Library:* Archives: housed at Toronto Reference Library, Special Collection; Open to public
Chief Officer(s):
Julia Smith, President
Awards:
• WMCT Career Development "Artist of the Year" Award
• WMCT Centennial Foundation Graduate Fellowship, Faculty of Music, University of Toronto
• Entrance Scholarship - Faculty of Music, University of Toronto
• WMCT Centennial Scholarship - Faculty of Music, University of Toronto
• Ottilie M. Gunning Memorial Scholarship - The Royal Conservatory

Women's Network PEI
PO Box 233, 40 Enman Cres., Charlottetown PE C1A 7K4
Tel: 902-368-5040; *Fax:* 902-368-5039
Toll-Free: 888-362-7373
www.wnpei.org
www.facebook.com/wnpei
Overview: A medium-sized provincial organization founded in 1984
Mission: To strengthen & support the efforts of PEI women to improve their status in society
Member of: National Action Committee on the Status of Women (NAC); Prince Edward Island Literacy Alliance Inc.
Finances: *Annual Operating Budget:* $100,000-$250,000; *Funding Sources:* Advertising; sales; subscriptions; fees; government; private donations
Staff Member(s): 4; 50 volunteer(s)
Membership: 270; *Fees:* $15
Activities: Referral service; project related work; *Internships:* Yes
Chief Officer(s):
Michelle MacCallum, Executive Director
michelle@wnpei.org

Women's Sexual Assault Helpline & Outreach Services *See* Women's Support Network of York Region

Women's Soccer Assocation of Lethbridge (WSAL)
4401 University Dr., Lethbridge AB T1K 3M4
Tel: 403-329-2232
www.losa.ca
twitter.com/wsal_soccer
Overview: A small local organization founded in 2001
Chief Officer(s):
Ilsa Wong, President

Women's Support Network of York Region (WSAH)
#109, 1110 Stellar Dr., Newmarket ON L3Y 7B7
Tel: 905-895-3646; *Fax:* 905-895-6542
Toll-Free: 800-263-6734
info@womenssupportnetwork.ca
www.womenssupportnetwork.ca
Also Known As: Women's Helpline
Previous Name: Women's Sexual Assault Helpline & Outreach Services
Overview: A small local charitable organization founded in 1992
Mission: To eliminate sexual violence
Affiliation(s): Ontario Coalition of Rape Crisis Centres
Finances: *Annual Operating Budget:* $250,000-$500,000; *Funding Sources:* Provincial government; United Way; Fund raising; Ontario Trillium Foundation
Staff Member(s): 7; 40 volunteer(s)
Membership: 1-99; *Committees:* Violence Against Women Coordinating Committee
Activities: Offering resources; *Awareness Events:* International Women's Day; Take Back the Night, Dec. 6; Sexual Assault Awareness & Prevention Month, May; *Speaker Service:* Yes; *Library:* Open to public

Wong Kung Har Wun Sun Association
303 Spadina Ave., Toronto ON M5T 2E6
Tel: 416-977-3426
Also Known As: Wong Association of Ontario
Overview: A small local organization
Mission: To provide support and assistance to recent immigrants from China.
Membership: *Member Profile:* Member of the Wong family.

Wood Buffalo Environmental Association (WBEA)
#100, 330 Thickwood Blvd., Fort McMurray AB T9K 1Y1
Tel: 780-799-4420
info@wbea.org
www.wbea.org
www.facebook.com/321509804531241
twitter.com/WBEA1
www.youtube.com/user/WoodBuffaloEnvAssoc?feature=watch
Overview: A small local organization
Mission: To provide state of the art air monitoring system that meets the needs of residents and stakeholders in the Wood Buffalo Region.
Membership: 28 corporate
Chief Officer(s):
Kevin Percy, Executive Director
Diane Phillips, President

Wood Buffalo Food Bank
10117 King St., Fort McMurray AB T9H 3J1
Tel: 780-743-1125; *Fax:* 780-743-9156
ea@woodbuffalofoodbank.com
www.woodbuffalofoodbank.com
www.facebook.com/woodbuffalofoodbank
twitter.com/wbfoodbank
Previous Name: Fort McMurray Food Bank
Overview: A small local charitable organization founded in 1983 overseen by Food Banks Alberta Association
Mission: To ensure food security for all persons in Wood Buffalo
Member of: Food Banks Alberta Association
Finances: *Annual Operating Budget:* $100,000-$250,000
Staff Member(s): 10; 35 volunteer(s)
Membership: 1-99
Activities: *Awareness Events:* Hunger Awareness Week, Sept.; Syncrude Food Drive, Nov.; *Speaker Service:* Yes
Chief Officer(s):
Arianna Johnson, Executive Director

Wood Energy Technology Transfer Inc. (WETT)
#1, 189 Queen St. East, Toronto ON M5A 1S2
Tel: 416-968-7718; *Fax:* 416-968-6818
Toll-Free: 888-358-9388
WETT@funnel.ca
www.wettinc.ca
Overview: A medium-sized national organization founded in 1993
Mission: To promote the safe & effective use of wood burning systems, WETT maintains a training program designed to confirm & recognize the knowledge & skills of practising wood energy professionals; to provide training to new people entering the industry; to provide training to non-industry professionals such as inspectors; to provide training to specialty audiences such as volunteer firefighters & carpenters in remote communities
Finances: *Annual Operating Budget:* $100,000-$250,000; *Funding Sources:* Membership dues; member services
Staff Member(s): 2
Membership: 1,400; *Fees:* $40-$75
Activities: Administers Wood Energy Technical Training Program for providers, installers, inspectors & cleaners of wood heat services
Chief Officer(s):
Anthony Laycock, Executive Director

Wood Manufacturing Council (WMC) / Conseil des fabricants de bois (CFB)
#302, 1390 Prince of Wales Dr., Ottawa ON K2C 3N6
Tel: 613-567-5511; *Fax:* 613-567-5411
wmc@wmc-cfb.ca
www.wmc-cfb.ca
www.facebook.com/pages/Wood-Manufacturing-Council/119407547397
twitter.com/careersinwood
Overview: A medium-sized national organization
Mission: To plan, develop & implement human resources strategies that support the long-term growth & competitiveness of Canada's advanced wood products manufacturing industry & meet the developmental needs of its workforce
Finances: *Funding Sources:* Federal government
Chief Officer(s):
Mike McClements, Chairman

Wood Pellet Association of Canada (WPAC)
PO Box 2989, 1877 Upper McKinnon Rd., Revelstoke BC V0E 2S0
www.pellet.org
Overview: A medium-sized national organization
Mission: The Wood Pellet Association of Canada is a member-driven organization advancing the interests of Canadian wood pellet producers.
Chief Officer(s):
Gordon Murray, Executive Director, 250-837-8821
gord@pellet.org

Wood Preservation Canada (WPC) / Préservation du bois Canada
#202, 2141 Thurston Dr., Ottawa ON K1G 6C9
Tel: 613-737-4337; *Fax:* 613-247-0540
www.woodpreservation.ca
Previous Name: Canadian Wood Preservers Bureau
Overview: A small national organization founded in 1988
Mission: To provide a quality assurance program for the treated wood industry
Finances: *Funding Sources:* Membership dues
Membership: *Member Profile:* Treated wood producers; consumer groups
Chief Officer(s):
Henry Walthert, Executive Director
henry@woodpreservation.ca

Woodgreen Community Centre
#100, 815 Danforth Ave., Toronto ON M4J 1L2

Tel: 416-645-6000
info@woodgreen.org
www.woodgreen.org
Overview: A small local organization founded in 1937 overseen by Ontario Council of Agencies Serving Immigrants
Mission: To promote self-sufficiency & reduce poverty
Finances: *Annual Operating Budget:* Greater than $5 Million; *Funding Sources:* United Way; government
Staff Member(s): 650; 1000 volunteer(s)
Membership: *Fees:* $20 or more donation
Chief Officer(s):
Brian Smith, President & CEO

Woodland Cultural Centre (WCC)
PO Box 1506, 184 Mohawk St., Brantford ON N3T 5V6
Tel: 519-759-2650; *Fax:* 519-759-2445
Toll-Free: 866-412-2202
museum@woodland-centre.on.ca
www.woodland-centre.on.ca
www.facebook.com/WoodlandCulturalCentre
twitter.com/woodlandcc
www.youtube.com/user/woodlandcc1972
Overview: A small local charitable organization founded in 1972
Mission: To preserve the values & practices of First Nation cultures through the storage & exhibits of First Nation National Treasures; to bring about acceptable positive change in our communities & in the interaction with western Euro-society; to provide a place where people can receive teachings & guidance from our First Nation existence; to instill pride in self, children & our existence as Nations in the world community
Member of: Mohawks of the Bay of Quinte; Mohawks of Wahta; Six Nations of the Grand River
Finances: *Annual Operating Budget:* $500,000-$1.5 Million
Staff Member(s): 20; 30 volunteer(s)
Membership: 25,000; *Member Profile:* First Nations Peoples; *Committees:* Education; Marketing
Activities: Museum; art gallery; library; First Nations languages; *Awareness Events:* Snowsnake Tournament, Jan/Feb.; Ancestors in the Archives, Feb & Sept.; Christmas Craft Fair, 1st Sat in Nov.; *Internships:* Yes; *Speaker Service:* Yes; *Library:* Woodland Culture Centre Library; Open to public
Chief Officer(s):
Janis Monture, Executive Director
jamonture@woodland-centre.on.ca
Paula Whitlow, Museum Director
pwhitlow@woodland-centre.on.ca
Virve Wiland, Library Technician
librarywoodland@yahoo.com

Woodstock & District Chamber of Commerce *See* Woodstock District Chamber of Commerce

Woodstock & District Developmental Services (WDDS)
212 Bysham Park Dr., Woodstock ON N4T 1R2
Tel: 519-539-7447; *Fax:* 519-539-7332
info@wdds.ca
www.wdds.ca
www.facebook.com/363364180390260
Overview: A small local charitable organization founded in 1959
Mission: To support lifelong opportunities for individuals & their families; To strive for independent living in the community through services, partnership & advocacy
Affiliation(s): Ontario Agencies Supporting Individuals with Special Needs
Finances: *Annual Operating Budget:* Greater than $5 Million
Staff Member(s): 200; 120 volunteer(s)
Membership: 74; *Fees:* $10 member; $1,000 life; *Member Profile:* Volunteers; parents; consumers; general public
Activities: Sport Celebrity Dinner; *Awareness Events:* Flower of Hope Campaign, May; Christmas Tea, Dec.
Chief Officer(s):
Janet Thomson, President
Kathy Straus, Chief Executive Officer
kstraus@wdds.ca
Kelly Christo, Director, Operations
kchristo@wdds.ca
Marrianna Correia, Director, Finance & Administration
mcorreia@wdds.ca
Deb Roloson, Coordinator, Community Development
droloson@wdds.ca

Woodstock Coin Club
PO Box 20128, Woodstock ON N4S 8X8
Tel: 519-537-5914
Overview: A small local organization
Member of: Royal Canadian Numismatic Association

Chief Officer(s):
John Tuffnail, President

Woodstock District Chamber of Commerce
476 Peel St., Woodstock ON N4S 1K1
Tel: 519-539-9411; *Fax:* 519-456-1611
info@woodstockchamber.ca
www.woodstockchamber.ca
www.facebook.com/WoodstockChamberOfCommerce
twitter.com/woodstockcoc
www.youtube.com/woodstockonchamber
Previous Name: Woodstock & District Chamber of Commerce
Overview: A small local organization
Mission: To support businesses in their efforts to be successful & grow
Membership: *Fees:* Schedule available
Chief Officer(s):
Martha Dennis, General Manager

Woodstock Field Naturalists
PO Box 20037, Stn. Woodstock Centre, Woodstock ON N4S 8X8
woodstockfnc@gmail.com
www.execulink.com/~wfnc
Overview: A small local organization founded in 1934
Mission: To promote the enjoyment of nature; to learn about natural history; To promote preservation of the environment through active participation in conservation projects
Member of: Federation of Ontario Naturalists
Membership: *Fees:* $20 individual; $25 family
Chief Officer(s):
Roger Boyd, President
rogeboyd@oxford.net

Woodstock-Ingersoll & District Real Estate Board
#6, 65 Springbank Ave. North, Woodstock ON N4S 8V8
Tel: 519-539-3616; *Fax:* 519-539-1975
admin@widreb.ca
woodstockingersolldistrictrealestateboard.com
www.facebook.com/widreb1
Overview: A small local organization founded in 1956 overseen by Ontario Real Estate Association
Member of: The Canadian Real Estate Association
Finances: *Funding Sources:* Membership dues
Membership: 200
Chief Officer(s):
Nicole Bowman, Executive Officer
nicole@widreb.ca

Woodview Mental Health & Autism Services
69 Flatt Rd., Burlington ON L7R 3X5
Tel: 905-689-4727; *Fax:* 905-689-2474
wcc@woodview.ca
woodview.ca
www.facebook.com/woodviewmha
twitter.com/WoodviewWLC
www.youtube.com/user/WoodviewMHA
Overview: A small local organization
Mission: To provide services & support to youth & adults with Autism Spectrum Disorder, in order to help them live more independently
Finances: *Annual Operating Budget:* Greater than $5 Million; *Funding Sources:* Provincial government; donations
Chief Officer(s):
Cindy l'Anson, Executive Director
cianson@woodview.ca

Woolwich Community Services (WCS)
5 Memorial Ave., Elmira ON N3B 2P8
Tel: 519-669-5139; *Fax:* 519-669-4210
wcs@execulink.com
www.woolwichcommunityservices.com
Overview: A small local organization founded in 1974 overseen by InformOntario
Mission: To help people find solutions to social, legal, health, government & environmental problems; To define unmet needs in the community & communicate with appropriate agencies or organizations about such needs; To initiate action toward solutions when appropriate agencies do not exist in the community, including direct assistance, organizing & coordinating
Activities: Thrift Store; Parent & Child Resource Centre; Growing Together; Family Violence Prevention; Care-Ring; Christmas Goodwill; Food Bank; support to Low German speaking Mennonites; Youth Centre; *Speaker Service:* Yes; *Library:* Kids & I Resource Centre; Open to public

The Workers' Educational Association of Canada
#205, 157 Carlton St., Toronto ON M5A 2K2
Tel: 416-923-7872; *Fax:* 416-923-7896
info@weacanada.ca
www.weacanada.ca
Also Known As: WEA Canada
Overview: A small national charitable organization founded in 1917
Mission: To promote lifelong education
Member of: International Federation of Worker Education Associations
Finances: *Annual Operating Budget:* $100,000-$250,000
Staff Member(s): 3; 25 volunteer(s)
Membership: 1-99; *Fees:* $15
Activities: *Library:* Resource Centre; by appointment
Chief Officer(s):
Wendy Terry, Administrator & Manager
Publications:
• Learning Curves
Type: Newspaper; *Frequency:* 8 pa; *Editor:* Deborah Visconti

Working Women Community Centre (WWCC)
533A Gladstone Ave., Toronto ON M6H 3J1
Tel: 416-532-2824; *Fax:* 416-532-1065
admin@workingwomencc.org
www.workingwomencc.org
www.linkedin.com/company/1357713
www.facebook.com/WorkingWomenCommunityCentre
twitter.com/workingwomencc
www.youtube.com/channel/UCnArFwwXd3I1sJJAuBAQwvQ
Overview: A small local charitable organization founded in 1975 overseen by Ontario Council of Agencies Serving Immigrants
Mission: To increase the self-sufficiency of Portuguese, Spanish-speaking & African women of Metro Toronto through the provision of settlement adaptation, education, language & citizenship acquisition, & general support; to break down employment barriers by meeting educational training needs of immigrant women; to act as a resource to the immigrant community & community at large in Metro Toronto
Affiliation(s): Portuguese Interagency Network; Hispanic Council; Advocates for Community-Based Training & Education
Membership: *Member Profile:* Immigrant women from communities served
Activities: Counselling; peer support groups; employment; seniors program; LINC-ESL; Computer classes; Ontario Works Placement; *Library:* Open to public
Chief Officer(s):
Marcie Ponte, Executive Director
marcie@workingwomencc.org
Lorraine Boucher, President

Workplace Safety & Prevention Services (WSPS)
Centre for Health & Safety Innovation, 5110 Creekbank Rd., Mississauga ON L4W 0A1
Tel: 905-614-1400; *Fax:* 905-614-1414
Toll-Free: 877-494-9777
customercare@wsps.ca
www.wsps.ca
www.linkedin.com/company/workplace-safety-&-prevention-services
www.facebook.com/workplacesafetyandpreventionservices
twitter.com/WSPS_NEWS
www.youtube.com/user/WSPSpromo
Previous Name: Safe Workplace Promotion Services Ontario
Merged from: Industrial Accident Prevention Association; Ontario Service Safety Alliance; Farm Safety Association
Overview: A large provincial organization founded in 2010
Mission: To meet the health & safety needs of businesses in the agricultural, manufacturing & service industries; To provide programs, products & services for the prevention of injury & illness
Affiliation(s): Amalgamated Industry Groups - Ceramics & Stone Accident Prevention Association; Chemical Industries Accident Prevention Association; Food Products Accident Prevention Association; Grain, Feed & Fertilizer Accident Prevention Association; Leather, Rubber & Tanners Accident Prevention Association; Metal Trades Accident Prevention Association; Printing Trades Accident Prevention Association; Textile & Allied Industries Accident Prevention Association; Woodworkers' Accident Prevention Association; High Tech; Offices & Related Services
Finances: *Funding Sources:* Ministry of Labour, WSIB employer premiums
Membership: 154,000 employers
Activities: *Library:* Information Centre; Open to public by appointment

Chief Officer(s):
Lynn Brownell, President & CEO
Meetings/Conferences:
• Partners in Prevention 2018 Health & Safety Conference & Trade Show, May, 2018
Scope: National
Description: Theme: "Shifting Landscapes in Health & Safety"
Publications:
• Network News [a publication of Workplace Safety & Prevention Services]
Type: Newsletter; *Frequency:* Monthly; *Price:* Free to members
Profile: Occupational health & safety news; notices & alerts on products, services & events
• WSPS [Workplace Safety & Prevention Services] Newsletter
Type: Newsletter; *Price:* Free to members
Profile: OHS news, updates, events, & product promotions

Workshop Council of Nova Scotia *See* DIRECTIONS Council for Vocational Services Society

World Accord
#1C, 185 Frobisher Dr., Waterloo ON N2V 2E6
Tel: 519-747-2215
Toll-Free: 800-525-3545
www.worldaccord.org
www.facebook.com/WorldAccord
twitter.com/worldaccord
www.instagram.com/worldaccord
Overview: A small international organization founded in 1980
Mission: To work with people & organizations at the local level to cultivate communities; To respond to needs & opportunities that recognize the worth & dignity of all
Finances: *Annual Operating Budget:* $500,000-$1.5 Million
Staff Member(s): 3
Activities: Implementing development projects & programs in Asia & Latin America; Organizing expeditions & monitoring trips; *Awareness Events:* Black & White Gala; *Internships:* Yes; *Speaker Service:* Yes
Chief Officer(s):
David Barth, Executive Director
dbarth@worldaccord.org
Isabelle Hachette, Program Coordinator
ihachette@worldaccord.org

World Amateur Muay Thai Association of Canada (WAMTAC)
164 Macatee Pl., Cambridge ON N1R 6Z8
Tel: 519-584-5426
info@wamtac.org
www.wamtac.org
Overview: A medium-sized national organization
Mission: To govern amateur muay thai in Canada
Affiliation(s): World Muay Thai Council; Olympic Committee of Asia; General Association of International Sports Federations
Membership: *Fees:* $500 club; $50 coach/athlete/official
Chief Officer(s):
Khan Phady, President

World Animal Protection (WSPA) / Société mondiale pour la protection des animaux
#960, 90 Eglinton Ave. East, Toronto ON M4P 2Y3
Tel: 416-369-0044; *Fax:* 416-369-0147
Toll-Free: 800-363-9772
info@worldanimalprotection.ca
www.worldanimalprotection.ca
www.facebook.com/WorldAnimalProtectionCanada
twitter.com/movetheworldca
www.instagram.com/worldanimalprotectioncanada
Previous Name: World Society for the Protection of Animals
Overview: A large international charitable organization founded in 1953
Mission: To promote effective means for the prevention of cruelty to, & relief of suffering of animals in any part of the world
Finances: *Annual Operating Budget:* $1.5 Million-$3 Million; *Funding Sources:* Donations
Staff Member(s): 9; 20 volunteer(s)
Membership: 900 member organizations in 150 countries; *Fees:* $25
Activities: Providing educational courses; Disseminating information; Financially supporting initiatives that help protect animals worldwide
Chief Officer(s):
Dominique Bellemare, President
Publications:
• News [a publication of World Animal Protection]
Type: Magazine; *Frequency:* s-a.
Profile: Full-length stories about the association's work to protect animals

World Anti-Doping Agency
Stock Exchange Tower, PO Box 120, #1700, 800, Place Victoria, Montréal QC H4Z 1B7
Tel: 514-904-9232; *Fax:* 514-904-8650
media@wada-ama.org
www.wada-ama.org
www.facebook.com/wada.ama
twitter.com/wada_ama
www.youtube.com/wadamovies
Overview: A medium-sized international organization founded in 1999
Mission: To promote & coordinate at international level the fight against doping in sport in all forms
Membership: *Committees:* Executive; Athlete; Education; Finance & Administration; Health, Medical & Research
Chief Officer(s):
Craig Reedie, President

World Association for Christian Communication (WACC) / Association mondiale pour la communication
308 Main St., Toronto ON M4C 4X7
Tel: 416-691-1999; *Fax:* 416-691-1997
info@waccglobal.org
www.waccglobal.org
www.linkedin.com/company/world-association-for-christian-communication-wacc-
https://www.facebook.com/WACCglobal
twitter.com/waccglobal
vimeo.com/waccglobal
Overview: A small international charitable organization founded in 1968
Mission: To promote communication as a basic human right through advocacy & communication; To promote open & diverse media; To strengthen communication networks to advance peace & justice
Member of: ACT Alliance, Canadian Church Press, ECOSOC
Finances: *Annual Operating Budget:* $3 Million-$5 Million; *Funding Sources:* Church-related sources; Non-governmental & governmental development agencies; Donations
Staff Member(s): 12; 2 volunteer(s)
Membership: 1600 worldwide; *Fees:* US$120 corporate; US$40 personal; US$10 student; *Member Profile:* Individuals, churches, church-related agencies, media producers, educational institutions, secular communication organizations, & persons who share WACC's mission
Activities: Facilitating communication-related projects; Providing seminars, workshops, & publications; Offering outreach programs worldwide; *Speaker Service:* Yes; *Library:* by appointment
Chief Officer(s):
Karin Achtelstetter, General Secretary
KA@waccglobal.org
Samuel W. Meshack, President
Publications:
• Media and Gender Monitor [a publication of the World Association for Christian Communication]
Type: Journal; *Frequency:* s-a.
Profile: Concerns of WACC's Media & Gender Justice Programme from varied perspectives
• Media Development [a publication of the World Association for Christian Communication]
Type: Journal; *Frequency:* Quarterly; *Author:* Dr. Philip Lee; *Price:* US$40 individual; US$50-US$75 libraries & institutions
Profile: Theory & practice of communication worldwide
• No-Nonsense Guides [a publication of the World Association for Christian Communication]
Number of Pages: 6
Profile: Different aspects of communication for practitioners & activists

World Association of Societies of Pathology and Laboratory Medicine (WASPaLM)
#310, 4 Cataraqui St., Kingston ON K7K 1Z7
Tel: 613-531-9210
info@waspalm.org
www.waspalm.org
www.facebook.com/192357901115161
Overview: A small international organization founded in 1947
Mission: To promote the teaching & practice of pathology & laboratory medicine throughout the world; To set education, research, & international quality standards; To foster collaboration among pathology & laboratory medicine societies; To facilitate the exchange of information among pathologists & laboratory scientists
Membership: 45 societies, colleges, or associations; *Committees:* Awards; Constitution & By-Laws; Education; Finance & Corporate Sponsors; International Liaison; Nominating; Policy, Guidelines & Advocacy; Publication & Informatics
Chief Officer(s):
Jagdish Butany, Secretary-Treasurer

World Blind Union / Union mondiale des aveugles
1929 Bayview Ave., Toronto ON M4G 3E8
Tel: 416-486-9698; *Fax:* 416-486-8107
info@wbu.ngo
www.worldblindunion.org
www.facebook.com/BlindUnion
twitter.com/BlindUnion
Overview: A medium-sized international organization founded in 1984
Mission: To speak on behalf of blind & partially sighted persons of the world, representing 285 million blind & visually impaired persons from 190 countries
Member of: Vision Alliance
Membership: 500+ organizations; *Committees:* Right to Read; Mobility & Transport; Technology; Human Rights & Advocacy; Employment; Development; Diversity; Languages Strategy; Finance; Policy Review; Constitution; Membership Fee; Resource Generation; Nominations; World Braille Council
Chief Officer(s):
Fredric Schroeder, President
president@wbu.ngo
Penny Hartin, Chief Executive Officer
penny.hartin@wbu.ngo
Ajai Kumar Mittal, Secretary General

World Border Organization
#1100, 343 Preston St., Ottawa ON K1S 1N4
www.borderpol.org
www.linkedin.com/company/borderpol
twitter.com/borderpol
Also Known As: BORDERPOL
Overview: A medium-sized international organization founded in 2003
Mission: To improve border safety & security through border management policies
Membership: *Member Profile:* Border security & travel management professionals & organizations
Activities: Offering resources, training & educational programs
Chief Officer(s):
Thomas Tass, Director General

World Council on City Data (WCCD)
#1103, 170 Bloor St. West, Toronto ON M5S 1T9
Tel: 416-966-2368; *Fax:* 416-966-0478
info@dataforcities.org
www.dataforcities.org
www.linkedin.com/company/world-council-on-city-data
www.facebook.com/WCCityData
twitter.com/wccitydata
Overview: A medium-sized international organization
Mission: To help build sustainable & successful cities through the provision of standardized data on city services & quality of life
Activities: Providing a standardized urban metrics platform
Chief Officer(s):
Patricia McCarney, President & CEO
Helen Ng, Executive Vice-President
James Patava, Director, Communications

World Energy Council - Canadian Member Committee *See* Energy Council of Canada

World Federalist Movement - Canada (WFMC)
#110, 323 Chapel St., Ottawa ON K1N 7Z2
Tel: 613-232-0647
www.wfmcanada.org
www.facebook.com/WorldFederalistMovementCanada
twitter.com/WFMCanada
Overview: A small national organization founded in 1948
Mission: Education, research, political support for strengthening the United Nations & rule of law in world affairs
Member of: Canadian Council for International Cooperation; Coalition for the International Criminal Court; International Civil Society Forum for Democracy; Canadian Peacebuilding Coordinating Committee; Canadian Network to Abolish Nuclear Weapons; Climate Action Network
Affiliation(s): World Federalist Movement

Finances: *Annual Operating Budget:* $100,000-$250,000
Staff Member(s): 3
Membership: 2,200; *Fees:* $200 contributor; $90 household; $60 individual; $15 limited income
Activities: *Speaker Service:* Yes; *Rents Mailing List:* Yes; *Library*
Chief Officer(s):
Walter Dorn, National President
Fergus Watt, Executive Director
ferguswatt@worldfederalistscanada.org
Monique Cuillerier, Director, Membership & Communications
monique@worldfederalistscanada.org
Awards:
• World Peace Award
• Hanna Newcombe Award
Recognizes an individual's service & contribution to the cause of world federalism over a lifetime

World Federation of Chiropractic (WFC) / La Fédération mondiale de chiropratique
#601, 160 Eglinton Ave. East, Toronto ON M4P 3B5
Tel: 416-484-9978; *Fax:* 416-484-9665
info@wfc.org
www.wfc.org
www.facebook.com/WorldFederationofChiropractic
Overview: A medium-sized international organization founded in 1988
Mission: To increase awareness of & access to chiropractic
Member of: Council of International Organizations of Medical Sciences (CIOMS)
Affiliation(s): World Health Organization (WHO)
Membership: *Committees:* Associate Membership; Policies & Procedures; Public Health
Chief Officer(s):
Richard Brown, Secretary-General

World Federation of Hemophilia (WFH) / Fédération mondiale de l'hémophilie (FMH)
#1010, 1425, boul René-Lévesque ouest, Montréal QC H3G 1T7
Tel: 514-875-7944; *Fax:* 514-875-8916
wfh@wfh.org
www.wfh.org
www.facebook.com/wfhemophilia
twitter.com/wfhemophilia
www.youtube.com/user/WFHcommunications
Overview: A medium-sized international licensing organization founded in 1963
Mission: To introduce, improve & maintain care for people with hemophilia & related blood disorders around the world
Affiliation(s): World Health Organization; International Society of Blood Transfusion; International Committee on Thrombosis & Haemostasis; International Society of Haematology; Société internationale de chirurgie orthopédique (SICOT)
Finances: *Annual Operating Budget:* Greater than $5 Million
Staff Member(s): 38
Membership: 127 countries; *Committees:* Data & Demographics; Dental; Epidemiological Research Program Steering; International External Quality Assessment Scheme; International Hemophilia Training Centre; Lab Sciences; Musculoskeletal; Nurses; Psychosocial; Treatment Product Safety, Supply & Access; von Willebrand Disease & Rare Bleeding Disorders
Activities: Health care development programs; humanitarian aid; data collection; public affairs; publications
Chief Officer(s):
Alain Baumann, Chief Executive Officer
Sarah Ford, Director, Strategy & Communications
sford@wfh.org

World Federation of Ukrainian Engineering Societies (WFUES)
27 Newell Ct., Toronto ON M9A 4T9
Tel: 416-235-2610; *Fax:* 416-240-9095
jgk@the-wire.com
Overview: A medium-sized international organization founded in 1973
Mission: To maintain Ukrainian engineering tradition & culture; To publish Ukrainian engineering news; To organize conferences & seminars on technical subjects; To exchange information on technology & facilitate technology transfer
Finances: *Annual Operating Budget:* Less than $50,000; *Funding Sources:* Membership fees
Staff Member(s): 4; 6 volunteer(s)
Membership: 5,000 individuals; *Fees:* Schedule available; *Member Profile:* Licensed professional engineer in respective country; *Committees:* Environmental; Educational; Social Events
Activities: *Speaker Service:* Yes
Chief Officer(s):
J.G. Kurys, President

World Federation of Ukrainian Women's Organizations (WFUWO)
#206, 145 Evans Ave., Toronto ON M8Z 5X8
Tel: 416-546-2491
info@wfuwo.org
www.wfuwo.org
Overview: A medium-sized national charitable organization founded in 1948
Mission: To represent women's organizations that work towards pursuing civic, religious, cultural, educational, & humanitarian goals for Ukrainian women; To support the dignity & integrity of women in Ukraine & Ukrainian women in other countries
Affiliation(s): Ukrainian World Congress; General Federation of Women's Clubs
Finances: *Annual Operating Budget:* Less than $50,000
Staff Member(s): 1; 10 volunteer(s)
Membership: 15,000-49,999; *Fees:* $150 institutional; $10 individual
Chief Officer(s):
O. Sushko, Chair
Meetings/Conferences:
• World Federation of Ukrainian Women's Organizations Annual General Meeting 2018, 2018
Scope: International

World Home Bible League *See* The Bible League of Canada

World Hypertension League (WHL)
415 Bass Lane, Corvallis MT 59828 USA
www.whleague.org
Overview: A large international organization founded in 1984
Mission: To promote the detection, control & prevention of arterial hypertension in populations; To assist national bodies by providing internationally applicable programs
Member of: International Society of Hypertension
Affiliation(s): Canadian Coalition for High Blood Pressure Prevention & Control; WHO
Finances: *Funding Sources:* Membership dues; grants
Membership: *Fees:* Schedule available; *Member Profile:* Must be a league, society or national body
Activities: Hypertension Management Audit Project; hypertension control in developing countries; international workshop on patient education; cooperative patient education project; conference every two years; *Awareness Events:* World Kidney Day, March; World Hypertension Day, May; *Speaker Service:* Yes; *Rents Mailing List:* Yes; *Library:* Open to public
Chief Officer(s):
Mark Niebylski, CEO
CEO@whleague.org
Publications:
• WHL [World Hypertension League] Newsletter
Type: Newsletter; *Frequency:* q.

World Inter-Action Mondiale; Ottawa-Hull Learner Centre *See* One World Arts

The World Job & Food Bank Inc. (WJFB)
#104, 820 - 10th St., Calgary AB T2P 2X1
Tel: 403-457-0416; *Fax:* 403-457-0493
info@wjfb.org
www.wjfb.org
Previous Name: Global Food Bank Association Inc.
Overview: A medium-sized international charitable organization founded in 1985
Mission: To alleviate poverty, chronic unemployment, disease, hunger, homelessness & the causes of same, in Canada & less developed countries
Member of: Council of Alberta NGOs
Finances: *Funding Sources:* Corporations; foundations & clubs; churches; general public
Activities: Jobs for the unemployed; hope for children; health care for families; food for the hungry; surplus food & goods for the poor; "Brown Bagging for Calgary Street Kids" program; has over 60 development projects in 15 developing countries; *Speaker Service:* Yes
Chief Officer(s):
Joseph Edison, CEO
jedison@wjfb.org
Linda Zhou, Director, International Programs

World Literacy of Canada (WLC) / Alphabétisation mondiale Canada
#281, 401 Richmond St. West, Toronto ON M5V 3A8
Tel: 416-977-0008; *Fax:* 416-977-1112
info@worldlit.ca
www.worldlit.ca
www.facebook.com/worldlit
twitter.com/WorldLit
www.youtube.com/user/worldliteracycanada
Overview: A medium-sized international charitable organization founded in 1955
Mission: To promote international development & social justice through support of community-based programs that emphasize adult literacy & non-formal education
Finances: *Funding Sources:* CIDA; private sector; donors
Staff Member(s): 4
Activities: KAMA Poetry Reading Series; *Awareness Events:* International Women's Day, March; The World on the Street, Sept.; *Internships:* Yes; *Speaker Service:* Yes
Chief Officer(s):
Ken Setterington, President
Jasmine Gill, Vice-President
Virginia Bosomworth, Secretary
Mamta Mishra, Executive Director
mamta@worldlit.ca

World Organization of Building Officials (WOBO)
155 Bearspaw Meadows, Calgary AB T3L 2M3
Tel: 403-239-2889; *Fax:* 403-547-4546
channan@telus.net
www.wobo-un.org
Overview: A medium-sized international organization founded in 1984
Mission: To improve the quality of life & resource optimization internationally, through the development, exchange & application of knowledge & experience, affecting the health, safety, welfare & usefulness of the built environment; To promote safeguards from potential hazards & to recommend solutions for preventing fire risks in existing buildings or buildings under construction; To promote the concept of standardizing construction training, materials, equipment & appliances; To promote the unification of legislation pertaining to the administration & enforcement of codes & standards; To update the development of technology
Member of: Habitat International Coalition
Affiliation(s): Special conservative status with the Economic & Social Council of the United Nations, the United Nations Industrial Development Organization, the United Nations Habitat Human Settlements Program, & the Department of Information of the United Nations
Finances: *Annual Operating Budget:* $50,000-$100,000; *Funding Sources:* Membership fees
Membership: 22 country members; 600 individual members; *Fees:* US$30 individuals; US$175 group; *Member Profile:* Individual members consist of individuals interested in codes related to construction, fire safety, property maintenance, development, land use, enforcement, administration, inspection, investigations, testing, designs, surveys, appraisals, education & other such disciplines connected therewith directly or indirectly; Group members consist of government units, agencies, departments, corporations, bureaus, professional institutes, associations & organizations, which administer, formulate, or enforce laws, codes or standards relating to construction, fire safety, property maintenance, development, land use, research, inspections, testing, designs, standards, investigations, surveys, manufacture or education.
Activities: *Internships:* Yes; *Speaker Service:* Yes
Chief Officer(s):
Omkar Nath Channan, Founding President & Governor

World Organization Ovulation Method Billings Inc.
1506 Dansey Ave., Coquitlam BC V3K 3J1
Tel: 604-936-4472; *Fax:* 604-936-5690
www.woomb.ca
Also Known As: WOOMB Canada Inc.
Overview: A small international organization founded in 1982
Mission: To teach fertility awareness & natural family planning
Affiliation(s): WOOMB International - Australia
Finances: *Funding Sources:* Donations
Membership: *Member Profile:* Trained teachers of OM Billings; natural family plannings; supportive individuals/groups
Activities: *Speaker Service:* Yes

World Potato Congress
Farm Centre, #101, 420 University Ave., Charlottetown PE C1A 7Z5
Tel: 902-368-8885; *Fax:* 902-628-2225
info@potatocongress.org
www.potatocongress.org
Also Known As: WPC Inc.

Overview: A small international organization founded in 1991
Mission: Dedicated to supporting the global growth and development of the potato
Staff Member(s): 1
Membership: *Member Profile:* Group of volunteer directors representing potato jurisdictions around the world; *Committees:* Intl. Advisory; Awards
Chief Officer(s):
Romain Cools, President

World Renew (CRWRC)
PO Box 5070, Stn. LCD 1, 3475 Mainway, Burlington ON L7R 3Y8
Tel: 905-336-2920
Toll-Free: 800-730-3490
info@worldrenew.net
www.worldrenew.net
www.facebook.com/worldrenew
twitter.com/worldrenew_net
www.youtube.com/c/SeeWorldRenew;
www.pinterest.com/worldrenew
Previous Name: Christian Reformed World Relief Committee
Overview: A large international charitable organization founded in 1962
Mission: To engage God's people in redeeming resources & developing gifts in collaborative activities of love, mercy, justice, & compassion
Member of: Canadian Foodgrains Bank; Canadian Council of Christian Charities; Canadian Council for International Cooperation.
Affiliation(s): Christian Reformed Church in North America
Finances: *Funding Sources:* Christian Reformed Churches; CIDA; Other denominations
Staff Member(s): 31
Membership: 15,000-49,999
Activities: *Awareness Events:* World Hunger Week, November; *Internships:* Yes; *Speaker Service:* Yes; *Library:* CRWRC Development Education Library; Open to public
Chief Officer(s):
Ida Mutoigo, Director, 905-336-2920 Ext. 4303
imutoigo@worldrenew.net
Peter Bulthuis, Director, Church Relations, 905-336-2920 Ext. 4237
pbulthuis@worldrenew.net
Kristen VanderBerg, Director, Communications & Media Relations, 905-336-2920 Ext. 4306
kvanderberg@worldrenew.net

World Sikh Organization of Canada (WSO)
1183 Cecil Ave., Ottawa ON K1H 7Z6
Tel: 416-904-9110
www.worldsikh.org
www.facebook.com/WSOCanada
twitter.com/WorldSikhOrg
Overview: A large international organization founded in 1984
Mission: To promote & protect the interests of Canadian Sikhs; To promote & advocate for the protection of human rights for all individuals, regardless of race, religion, gender, ethnicity & social & economic status
Affiliation(s): World Sikh Organization (International)
100 volunteer(s)
Membership: 15,000-49,999; *Fees:* $1,000 institutional; $10 student/associate; $100 individual
Activities: *Library:* World Sikh Organization of Canada Library; Open to public by appointment
Chief Officer(s):
Mukhbir Singh, President
Jasbir Kaur Randhawa, Senior Vice President
Rupinder Kaur Dhaliwal, Director, Administration
Jagdeep Singh Mann, Director, Finance

World Small Animal Veterinary Association (WSAVA)
72 Melville St., Dundas ON L9H 2A1
Tel: 905-627-8540
wsavasecretariat@gmail.com
www.wsava.org
www.linkedin.com/company/world-small-animal-veterinary-association
www.facebook.com/WSAVA
twitter.com/vetswsava
Overview: A medium-sized international organization founded in 1957
Mission: To advance the health & welfare of small companion animals worldwide through a collaborative global community of veterinary peers; To unite veterinary associations that share common goals; To create a unified standard of care for the benefit of animals & humankind
Finances: *Funding Sources:* Membership dues; Corporate sponsors
Membership: 96 associations; *Fees:* Schedule available, based upon members in association; *Member Profile:* Veterinary associations from all over the world which concerned with companion animal care; *Committees:* Vaccination Guidelines; Animal Wellness & Welfare; Congress Steering; Continuing Education; Financial Advisory; Global Nutrition; Global Pain; Hereditary Diseases; Leadership & Nomination; One Health; PR & Communications; Scientific Advisory
Activities: Engaging in research projects; Organizing annual WAVSA World Congress; Providing continuing education & professional development opportunities
Chief Officer(s):
Colin Burrows, President, 352-294-4401
burrowsc@ufl.edu
June Ingwersen, Administrator
wsavasecretariat@gmail.com
Awards:
• International Award for Scientific Achievement, WAVSA Annual Awards
• Global One Health Award, WAVSA Annual Awards
• Global Meritorious Service Award, WAVSA Annual Awards
• President's Award, WAVSA Annual Awards
• Excellence in Veterinary Healthcare Award, WAVSA Annual Awards
• Next Generation Award, WAVSA Annual Awards
• Henry Schein Cares International Veterinary Community Service Award, WAVSA Annual Awards
Meetings/Conferences:
• World Small Animal Veterinary Association Annual Congress 2018, September, 2018, Singapore
Scope: International
Contact Information: URL: www.wsava2018.com
Publications:
• Clinician's Brief [a publication of the World Small Animal Veterinary Association]
Type: Journal
Profile: Clinical publication featuring informative articles
• Journal of Small Animal Practice [a publication of the World Small Animal Veterinary Association]
Type: Journal; *Editor:* Nicholas Jeffery; *ISSN:* 1748-5827
Profile: Official scientific journal of the WSAVA; features papers from members
• World Small Animal Veterinary Association e-Bulletin
Type: Newsletter; *Frequency:* bi-m.
Profile: Features member news & event details

World Society for the Protection of Animals *See* World Animal Protection

World Trade Centre Atlantic Canada (WTCAC)
PO Box 955, Halifax NS B3J 2V9
Tel: 902-424-5054
info@tclns.com
wtcac.tradecentrelimited.com
Overview: A small international organization
Mission: To provide Atlantic Canadian companies with export trade training & assistance & give them access to the World Trade Centers Association network. It is operated by Trade Centre Ltd.
Member of: World Trade Centers Association
Affiliation(s): 300 World Trade Centres in 85 countries
Membership: 189
Chief Officer(s):
Scott Ferguson, President & CEO, Trade Centre Ltd.

World Trade Centre Montréal (WTCM)
#6000, 380, rue St-Antoine ouest, Montréal QC H2Y 3X7
Tél: 514-871-4002; *Téléc:* 514-849-3813
Ligne sans frais: 877-590-4040
wtcmontreal@ccmm.qc.ca
www.btmm.qc.ca/en/international
Également appelé: WTC Montréal
Aperçu: *Dimension:* moyenne; *Envergure:* nationale; Organisme sans but lucratif; fondée en 1984
Mission: Appuyer, former et conseiller les entreprises, associations, institutions et organismes de développement économiques dans leurs démarches sur les marchés internationaux
Membre de: World Trade Centre Association
Affiliation(s): Chambre de commerce du Montréal Metropolitain
Finances: *Fonds:* Développement économique Canada
Membre: 7,000
Activités: Missions commerciales; services de préparation à l'exportation; ateliers de formation en commerce international; *Listes de destinataires:* Oui
Membre(s) du bureau directeur:
Michel Leblanc, Président et chef de la direction
Lise Aubin, Vice-présidente, Exploitation & Administration

World University Service of Canada (WUSC) / Entraide universitaire mondiale du Canada (EUMC)
1404 Scott St., Ottawa ON K1Y 4M8
Tel: 613-798-7477; *Fax:* 613-798-0990
Toll-Free: 800-267-8699
wusc@wusc.ca
www.wusc.ca
www.linkedin.com/groups/2441658
www.facebook.com/wusc.ca
twitter.com/worlduniservice
www.youtube.com/wusceumc
Overview: A large international charitable organization founded in 1939
Mission: To foster human development & global understanding through education & training
Affiliation(s): Canadian Council for International Cooperation
Finances: *Annual Operating Budget:* Greater than $5 Million; *Funding Sources:* Overseas governments; international agencies
Staff Member(s): 60; 400 volunteer(s)
Membership: 4,000+; *Member Profile:* Universities & colleges; students; alumni; development workers
Activities: International seminars to give Canadian students personal exposure to issues & problems of development; through Local Committees, WUSC has sponsored more than 1200 student refugees from Africa, Central America, Asia & the Middle East since 1978; administers a variety of scholarship programs on behalf of the Government of Canada & a number of developing countries which bring pre-selected students from Latin America, Africa, the Caribbean & Asia for study or technical skills upgrading at universities & colleges in Canada; *Internships:* Yes; *Library*
Chief Officer(s):
Chris Eaton, Executive Director
ceaton@wusc.ca
Hao Zhang, Chief Financial Officer
Ravi Gupta, Director, International Services
Awards:
• Annual WUSC Alumni Award
To recognize the outstanding contribution of an individual who has demonstrated dedication and long-time commitment to the organization.

World Vision Canada (WVC) / Vision Mondiale
1 World Dr., Mississauga ON L5T 2Y4
Tel: 905-565-6100; *Fax:* 866-219-8620
Toll-Free: 866-595-5550
www.worldvision.ca
www.facebook.com/WorldVisionCan
twitter.com/worldvisioncan
www.youtube.com/WorldVisionCanada;
www.instagram.com/worldvisioncan
Overview: A large international charitable organization founded in 1950
Mission: To act as an international partnership of Christians that provides relief to children, families, & communities; To work towards overcoming poverty & injustice; To aid people regardless of religion, race, ethnicity, or gender
Member of: Canadian Council for International Cooperation; Ontario Council for International Cooperation
Affiliation(s): Evangelical Fellowship of Canada
Finances: *Annual Operating Budget:* Greater than $5 Million; *Funding Sources:* 89% private + 11% government
Staff Member(s): 500; 660 volunteer(s)
Membership: 100-499
Activities: Offering child sponsorship opportunities; Engaging in development projects; Providing emergency relief & rehabilitation; Fundraising; Mobilizing volunteers; Connecting people in need with local resources; *Awareness Events:* National 30-Hour Famine, April; *Internships:* Yes; *Speaker Service:* Yes; *Library:* Resource Centre; by appointment
Chief Officer(s):
Michael Messenger, President & CEO
Publications:
• ChildView [a publication of World Vision Canada]
Type: Magazine; *ISSN:* 0846-4278
• World Vision Canada Annual Report
Type: Report; *Frequency:* Annually
British Columbia Office
5951 No. 3 Rd., Richmond BC V6X 2E3

Tel: 604-295-4803

World Wildlife Fund - Canada (WWF-Canada) / Fonds mondial pour la nature
#410, 245 Eglinton Ave. East, Toronto ON M4P 3J1
Tel: 416-489-8800; *Fax:* 416-489-3611
Toll-Free: 800-267-2632
www.wwf.ca
www.facebook.com/WWFCanada
twitter.com/wwfcanada
www.youtube.com/wwfcanada
Overview: A large international charitable organization founded in 1967
Mission: To conserve wild animals, plants & habitats for their own sake & the long-term benefit of people; to protect the diversity of life on earth; to stop, & eventually reverse, the accelerating degradation of our planet's natural environment, & to help build a future in which humans live in harmony with nature
Affiliation(s): World Wide Fund for Nature (International)
Finances: *Annual Operating Budget:* Greater than $5 Million; *Funding Sources:* Individuals; corporate donations; government; foundations
Staff Member(s): 80
Membership: 64,000; *Fees:* Donation of $26 or more; *Committees:* Management
Activities: Endangered Species Recovery Fund; Marine, Forests & Trade Biodiversity; Arctic; *Awareness Events:* National Sweater Day, Feb.; Earth Hour, March; CN Tower Climb, April; *Rents Mailing List:* Yes
Chief Officer(s):
Alex Himelfarb, Chair
David Miller, President & CEO
Mary MacDonald, Chief Conservation Officer & Senior VP
Sara Oates, CFO & Vice-President, Finance & Administration
Jay Hooper, Vice-President, Development
Awards:
• Endangered Species Recovery Fund
Sponsors high-priority conservation projects to assist the recovery of endangered wildlife & their natural habitats. This program is under review *Eligibility:* Must be affiliated with a non-governmental organization or non-profit body with a mandate for conservation *Deadline:* January
• Endangered Spaces Campaign Local Action Fund
Sponsors site-specific, public awareness activities to advance protection of terrestrial & marine areas across Canada *Eligibility:* Must be affiliated with a non-governmental organization or non-profit body with a mandate for conservation *Deadline:* November *Contact:* Project Manager, Jarmila Becka Lee
Publications:
• World Wildlife Fund - Canada E-Newsletter
Type: Newsletter

Halifax
Duke Tower, #1202, 5251 Duke St., Halifax NS B3J 1P3
Tel: 902-482-1105; *Fax:* 902-487-1107

Inuvik
PO Box 1019, Inuvik NT X0E 0T0
Tel: 867-688-8678

Iqaluit
PO Box 1750, 318 Creekside Village, Iqaluit NU X0A 0H0
Tel: 416-489-8800
Toll-Free: 800-267-2632

Montréal
#340, 50, rue Sainte-Catherine ouest, Montréal QC H2X 3V4
Tél: 514-394-0008

Ottawa
#810, 275 Slater St., Ottawa ON K1P 5H9
Tel: 613-232-8706; *Fax:* 613-232-4181

Prince Rupert
PO Box 362, #3, 437 - 3rd Ave. West, Prince Rupert BC V8J 3P9
Tel: 250-624-3705; *Fax:* 250-624-3725
pacificmarine@wwfcanada.org

St. John's
Caledonia Place, #103, 40 Quidi Vidi Rd., St. John's NL A1A 1C1
Tel: 709-722-9453

Vancouver
#1588, 409 Granville St., Vancouver BC V6T 1T2
Tel: 604-678-5152; *Fax:* 604-678-5155

World Without Borders *Voir* Terre sans frontières

World's Poultry Science Association - Canadian Branch
Edmonton AB
sv1@ualberta.ca
www.facebook.com/WPSAcanada
Overview: A small national organization

Worldwide Association of Business Coaches (WABC)
c/o WABC Coaches Inc., PO Box 215, Saanichton BC V8M 2C3
www.wabccoaches.com
www.linkedin.com/groups?about=&gid=3262807
twitter.com/wabccoaches
Overview: A small international organization
Mission: To develop, advance & promote the emerging profession of business coaching, worldwide
Membership: *Fees:* US$195 individual affiliate; US$395 individual regular; *Committees:* Ethics & Integrity
Chief Officer(s):
Wendy Johnson, President/CEO

Worldwide Church of God Canada *See* Grace Communion International Canada

Worldwide Marriage Encounter
Toronto ON
Overview: A small local organization
Mission: To renew the sacraments of Matrimony & Holy Orders
Affiliation(s): Archdiocese of Toronto
Finances: *Funding Sources:* Donations
Membership: *Member Profile:* Persons who are validly married, & who have attended a Worldwide Marriage Encounter weekend experience in one of the seven secretariats (Africa, Asia, Europe, Latin America, Pacific, Canada, USA); Members become part of a pro-marriage movement in the Catholic Church
Activities: Programming for married couples, including enrichments, peer support, community activities, & social events

Worsley Chamber of Commerce
PO Box 181, Worsley AB T0H 3W0
Tel: 780-685-3943; *Fax:* 780-685-2115
Overview: A small local organization

Wrestling Nova Scotia
NS
www.wrestlingnovascotia.ca
Overview: A small provincial organization overseen by Canadian Amateur Wrestling Association

Wrestling PEI
c/o Sport PEI, PO Box 302, 40 Enman Crescent, Charlottetown PE C1A 7K7
Tel: 902-368-4262; *Fax:* 902-368-4548
sports@sportpei.pe.ca
www.wrestlingpei.ca
Overview: A small provincial organization overseen by Canadian Amateur Wrestling Association
Mission: To promote wrestling in PEI; to provide competitive opportunities for members
Member of: Wrestling Canada
Staff Member(s): 1
Activities: Canada Games; Provincials; Atlantics; Nationals
Chief Officer(s):
Glen Flood, Executive Director
gflood@sportpei.pe.ca

Writers Guild of Canada (WGC)
#401, 366 Adelaide St. West, Toronto ON M5V 1R9
Tel: 416-979-7907; *Fax:* 416-979-9273
Toll-Free: 800-567-9974
info@wgc.ca
www.wgc.ca
www.facebook.com/writers.guild.12
twitter.com/WGCtweet
Overview: A small national organization founded in 1991
Mission: To be the voice of professional Canadian screenwriters; To lobby on their behalf, protect their interests & raise the profile of screenwriters & screenwriting
Member of: International Affiliation of Writers Guilds
Affiliation(s): Coalition of Canadian Audio-Visual Unions; Canadian Screenwriters Collection Society
Finances: *Funding Sources:* Union member supported
Staff Member(s): 18
Membership: 2,200+; *Fees:* $350 initiation + $150 annual; *Member Profile:* Professional English-language screenwriters in Canada
Activities: Script Registration Service; Contract negotiation, administration & enforcement; Policy & lobbying on behalf of screenwriters
Chief Officer(s):
Jill Golick, President
j.golick@wgc.ca
Maureen Parker, Executive Director
m.parker@wgc.ca
Awards:
• Canadian Screenwriting Awards
Publications:
• Canadian Screenwriter [a publication of the Writers Guild of Canada]
Type: Magazine; *Frequency:* 3 pa

Writers' Alliance of Newfoundland & Labrador (WANL)
Haymarket Square, #208, 223 Duckworth St., St. John's NL A1C 6N1
Tel: 709-739-5215
Toll-Free: 866-739-5215
wanl@nf.aibn.com
wanl.ca
www.facebook.com/writersalliance
twitter.com/WANL
Overview: A small provincial organization founded in 1987
Mission: To enhance the quality of writing in Newfoundland & Labrador through such programmes as workshops, meetings, readings; to encourage & develop public awareness & appreciation for the work of writers in Newfoundland & Labrador
Member of: Access Copyright; Canadian Writers' Summit
Finances: *Funding Sources:* Federal, provincial & municipal government grants
Staff Member(s): 2
Membership: 400+; *Fees:* Free youth; $25 students/unemployed/retired; $55 adult; *Member Profile:* Writers & anyone interested in the writing/publishing industry
Activities: *Speaker Service:* Yes; *Library*
Chief Officer(s):
Alison Dyer, Executive Director
Awards:
• Provincial Book Awards
Poetry & Non-Fiction categories; *Amount:* $1,250 in each category

The Writers' Development Trust *See* The Writers' Trust of Canada

Writers' Federation of New Brunswick (WFNB)
#151, 527 Dundonald St., Fredericton NB E3B 1X5
Tel: 506-260-3564
info@wfnb.ca
www.wfnb.ca
www.facebook.com/writersfederation
twitter.com/WritersNB
Overview: A small provincial organization founded in 1983
Mission: To promote New Brunswick writing; to assist writers of New Brunswick at all stages of their development by providing services; to uphold the right to free artistic expression; to provide additional educational services to schools & libraries; to contribute to the enhancement of literary arts
Member of: CANCOPY
Finances: *Funding Sources:* Provincial government; sponsors; membership fees; Canada Council
Membership: 235 individual; *Member Profile:* Published amateur
Activities: Annual Literary Competition; manuscript reading service; Writers-in-Schools program; Literary Festival; *Library:* by appointment
Awards:
• The Sheree Fitch Prize
Open to youth, 14-18 years of age; entries will alternate between fiction & poetry; *Amount:* 1st - $150; 2nd - $100; 3rd - $50
• The Richards Prize
For a collection of short stories, a short novel, or a substantial portion of a longer novel; *Amount:* $400
• The Alfred G. Bailey Prize
For poetry manuscript not previously published; *Amount:* $400

Writers' Federation of Nova Scotia (WFNS)
1113 Marginal Rd., Halifax NS B3H 4P7
Tel: 902-423-8116; *Fax:* 902-422-0881
contact@writers.ns.ca
www.writers.ns.ca
www.facebook.com/WritersFedNS
twitter.com/WFNS

Overview: A medium-sized provincial charitable organization founded in 1975
Mission: To foster creative & professional writing; To provide advice & assistance to writers; To encourage greater public recognition of Nova Scotia writers
Affiliation(s): Cultural Federation of Nova Scotia; Writers' Trust; Access Copyright; Canadian Children's Book Centre; International Board on Books for Youth
Finances: *Annual Operating Budget:* $250,000-$500,000; *Funding Sources:* Federal & provincial government support; Fundraising; Earned income
Staff Member(s): 2; 100 volunteer(s)
Membership: 30 student + 20 senior/lifetime + 800 individual; *Fees:* $25 students; $60 general
Activities: Atlantic Writing Awards; Readings, workshops & mentorships; *Internships:* Yes; *Speaker Service:* Yes; *Library:* Open to public
Chief Officer(s):
Jonathan Meakin, Executive Director
director@writers.ns.ca
Robin Spittal, Officer, Communications & Development
programs@writers.ns.ca
Linda Hudson, Officer, Arts Education
wits@writers.ns.ca
Awards:
• Thomas H. Raddall Atlantic Fiction Prize
Honours the best fiction writing by an Atlantic Canadian writer; *Amount:* $10,000
• Evelyn Richardson Memorial Literary Trust Award
Award was established in 1978 to recognize outstanding work in non-fiction by a Nova Scotian writer (native or resident); *Amount:* $2,000
• Atlantic Poetry Prize
; *Amount:* $2,000

The Writers' Guild of Alberta (WGA)
Percy Page Centre, 11759 Groat Rd., Edmonton AB T5M 3K6
Tel: 780-422-8174; *Fax:* 780-422-2663
Toll-Free: 800-665-5354
mail@writersguild.ab.ca
www.writersguild.ab.ca
www.facebook.com/139496766118754
twitter.com/WritersGuildAB
Overview: A medium-sized provincial charitable organization founded in 1980
Mission: To provide a meeting ground & collective voice for the writers of Alberta; To promote excellence in writing in Alberta
Affiliation(s): Manitoba Writers' Guild; Federation of BC Writers; Saskatchewan Writers' Guild; Writers' Union of Canada; Newfoundland & Labrador Guilds; Periodical Writers' Association of Canada; League of Canadian Poets
Finances: *Annual Operating Budget:* $250,000-$500,000
Staff Member(s): 16
Membership: 500-999; *Fees:* $80 annually; $50 seniors; $40 low income; free for students; *Committees:* Awards; Annual General Meeting; Newsletter; Promote Alberta Writing; Professional Standards; Retreats; Workshop
Activities: *Awareness Events:* Alberta Book Awards Gala; *Library:* Open to public
Chief Officer(s):
Carol Holmes, Executive Director
cholmes@writersguild.ab.ca
Patricia MacQuarrie, President
Julie Sedivy, Vice-President
Awards:
• Annual Awards Program
Established 1982 to recognize excellence in writing by Alberta authors; published books may be entered in any of the following categories: Children's Literature (any genre), Drama, Novel, Non-Fiction, Poetry, Short Fiction, Best First Book; winners receive $1000 cash award

Calgary Office
505 - 21 Ave. SW, Calgary AB T2S 0G9
Tel: 403-265-2226
mail@writersguild.ca

The Writers' Trust of Canada
#600, 460 Richmond St. West, Toronto ON M5V 1Y1
Tel: 416-504-8222; *Fax:* 416-504-9090
Toll-Free: 877-906-6548
info@writerstrust.com
www.writerstrust.com
www.facebook.com/writerstrust
twitter.com/writerstrust
Previous Name: The Writers' Development Trust
Overview: A small national organization founded in 1976
Mission: Is a national charitable organization providing support to writers through various programs & awards; celebrates the talents & achievements of our country's writers; is committed to exploring & introducing to future generations the traditions that will enrich our common literary heritage & strengthen Canada's cultural foundations
Finances: *Funding Sources:* Business sponsors; individuals; government
Staff Member(s): 5
Membership: 1-99
Activities: Canada Book Day; Great Literary Dinner Party; Great Literary Awards; Politics & the Pen; Small Literary Dinner Parties; *Awareness Events:* Canada Book Week, April
Chief Officer(s):
Peter Kahnert, Chair
Don Oravec, Executive Director
doravec@writerstrust.com
Amanda Hopkins, Program Coordinator
ahopkins@writerstrust.com
Awards:
• The Thomas Raddall Atlantic Fiction Award
Presented in conjunction with the Writers' Federation of Nova Scotia to an Atlantic writer for a work of fiction published in the previous year; *Amount:* $5,000
• The W.O. Mitchell Literary Prize
Presented annually to a writer who has produced an outstanding body of work, has acted during his/her career as a "caring mentor" for writers *Eligibility:* Has published a work of fiction or had a new stage play produced during the three-year period specified for each competition; every third year the prize will be awarded to a writer who works in French*Location:* $15,000
• Vicky Metcalf Prize for Children's Literature
Awarded annually to an author of children's literature, either fiction, non-fiction, picture books or poetry, not for a single book, but for a body of work, unless, in the opinion of the jury, there is no author worthy of the award that year; *Amount:* $15,000
• Rogers Writers' Trust Fiction Prize
Annually to the author of the work of fiction published in the previous year that in the opinion of the judges, shows the best literary merit; *Amount:* $15,000
• McClelland & Stewart Journey Prize
Awarded annually to a new & developing writer; *Amount:* $10,000
• Matt Cohen Award
For a lifetime of distinguished work by a Canadian writer, working in either poetry or prose, writing in either French or English who has dedicated their life to writing as a primary pursuit; *Amount:* $20,000
• The Matt Cohen Award
; *Amount:* $20,000
• The Writers' Trust of Canada/McClelland & Stewart Journey Prize
; *Amount:* $10,000
• The Bronwen Wallace Memorial Award
Awarded annually to a Canadian writer under the age of 35 who is not yet published in book form; award alternates each year between poetry & short fiction; *Amount:* $1,000
• The Writers Trust of Canada's Shaughnessy Cohen Award for Political Writing
Sponsored by CTV awarded to a non-fiction book of outstanding literary merit that enlarges our understanding of contemporary Canadian political & social issues; *Amount:* $10,000
• The Drainie-Taylor Biography Prize
Awarded annually for the best work of biography, autobiography or personal memoir; *Amount:* $10,000
• The Timothy Findley Award
Awarded annually to a male Canadian writer for a body of work & in hope of future contributions; *Amount:* $15,000
• Pearson Writers' Trust Non-Fiction Prize
Awarded annually to the author of the work of non-fiction published in the previous year that, in the opinion of the judges, shows the best literary merit; *Amount:* $15,000
• The Marian Engel Award
Established 1986; awarded annually to a female Canadian writer, for a body of work & in hope of future contributions; *Amount:* $15,000
• The Vicky Metcalf Award for Children's Literature
; *Amount:* $15,000

The Writers' Union of Canada (TWUC)
#600, 460 Richmond St. West, Toronto ON M5V 1Y1
Tel: 416-703-8982; *Fax:* 416-504-9090
info@writersunion.ca
www.writersunion.ca
www.facebook.com/thewritersunionofcanada
twitter.com/twuc
Overview: A medium-sized national organization founded in 1973
Mission: To unite writers for the advancement of their common interests; To foster writing in Canada; To maintain relations with publishers; To exchange information among members; To safeguard the freedom to write & to publish; To advance good relations with other writers & their organizations in Canada & all parts of the world
Member of: Book & Periodical Council
Affiliation(s): Canadian Copyright Licensing Agency; Canadian Conference of the Arts; Cultural Human Resources Council
Finances: *Funding Sources:* Member dues; Canada Council; Ontario Arts Council; Ontario Ministry of Tourism, Culture & Recreation
Staff Member(s): 7
Membership: 2,000; *Fees:* $205; *Member Profile:* Canadian citizen or landed immigrant who has had a trade book published by a commercial or university press
Activities: Offering Writers in the Schools Program & National Public Readings Program; Providing manuscript & contract evaluation services; *Speaker Service:* Yes; *Library:* Not open to public
Chief Officer(s):
John Degen, Executive Director, 416-703-8982 Ext. 221
jdegen@writersunion.ca
Awards:
• Postcard Story Competition
; *Amount:* $500
• Writing for Children Competition
; *Amount:* $1,500
• Short Prose Competition for Developing Writers
; *Amount:* $2,500
• Postcard Story Competition
• Danuta Gleed Literary Award
Awarded to a Canadian writer for the best first collection of published short stories in the English language; *Amount:* $10,000

WTF Taekwondo Federation of British Columbia
#3, 511 Cottonwood Ave., Coquitlam BC V3J 2R4
Tel: 604-939-8232
wtfbccanada@gmail.com
taekwondobc.com
www.facebook.com/taekwondobc
Also Known As: BC Taekwondo Federation
Overview: A small provincial organization
Mission: To be the governing body of taekwondo in British Columbia; Sanctioned to send athletes to the Olympic Games, World Taekwondo Championships, World Junior Taekwondo Championships, World Cup Taekwondo Games, Pan-American Games, Canadian National Championships & Canadian Junior National Championships
Member of: WTF Taekwondo Canada; Sport BC
Affiliation(s): International Olympic Committee
Chief Officer(s):
Song Chul Kim, President, 604-430-5467
Tony Kook, Vice President, 604-986-5558
tkook@vancouvermartialarts.ca
Minku Chang, Secretary General, 604-541-9457
changstkd@hotmail.com

WushuCanada
2370 Midland Ave., #B25, Toronto ON M1S 5C6
Tel: 416-321-5913
info@wushucanada.com
wushucanada.com
www.facebook.com/pages/WushuCanada/211084358925927
twitter.com/WushuCanada
Previous Name: Confederation of Canadian Wushu Organizations
Overview: A small national organization
Mission: To promote & develop the Olympic sport of Wushu in Canada

WushuOntario
2370 Midland Ave., #B25-22, Toronto ON M1S 5C6
Tel: 416-321-5913
www.wushuontario.ca
Previous Name: United Wushu Association of Ontario
Overview: A small provincial organization founded in 1997
Mission: To govern & promote Wushu in Ontario

WWOOF Canada (WWOOF Canada)
4429 Carlson Rd., Nelson BC V1L 6X3

Tel: 250-354-4417
wwoofcan@shaw.ca
www.wwoof.ca
Also Known As: Willing Workers on Organic Farms, World Wide Opportunities on Organic Farms
Overview: A small national organization founded in 1985
Mission: WWOOF Aims to get firsthand experience of organic farming & gardening and to lend a helping hand wherever needed
Member of: WWOOF International Federation
Finances: *Annual Operating Budget:* Less than $50,000
Staff Member(s): 1; 2000 volunteer(s)
Membership: 20,000; *Fees:* $45
Activities: WWOOFing is a cultural exchange & a helping exchange; *Internships:* Yes

Wycliffe Bible Translators of Canada, Inc. (WBTC)
4316 - 10th St. NE, Calgary AB T2E 6K3
Tel: 403-250-5411; *Fax:* 403-250-2623
Toll-Free: 800-463-1143
info@wycliffe.ca
www.wycliffe.ca
www.facebook.com/WycliffeCanada
twitter.com/wycliffe_canada
www.youtube.com/wycliffecanada;
www.godtube.com/wycliffecanada
Also Known As: Wycliffe Canada
Overview: A large national charitable organization founded in 1968
Mission: To serve minority language groups worldwide by fostering an understanding of God's Word through Bible translation, while encouraging literacy, education & stronger communities
Member of: Wycliffe Global Alliance
Affiliation(s): Wycliffe Bible Translators International; Summer Institute of Linguistics; Canada Institute of Linguistics; Wycliffe Associates Canada
Finances: *Annual Operating Budget:* Greater than $5 Million; *Funding Sources:* Charitable donations
Staff Member(s): 400; 75 volunteer(s)
Membership: 400 individual
Activities: Overseas Bible translation & literacy programs; *Internships:* Yes; *Speaker Service:* Yes; *Library:* Resource Centre; Open to public
Chief Officer(s):
Roy Eyre, President
Jackie Buhler, Senior Vice-President, Operations
John Feniak, Vice-President, Administration
Publications:
• Prayer Alive [a publication of Wycliffe Bible Translators of Canada Inc.]
Type: Newsletter; *Frequency:* Quarterly
• Word Alive [a publication of Wycliffe Bible Translators of Canada Inc.]
Type: Magazine; *Frequency:* 3 pa; *Editor:* Dwayne Janke
Profile: Feature stories about the Bible translation movement
Eastern Region Office
#4, 14 Steinway Blvd., Toronto ON M9W 6M6
Tel: 416-675-6473
Toll-Free: 866-702-5273
toronto_office_canada@wycliffe.ca
Chief Officer(s):
Randall Mah, Representative, Ontario
randall_mah@wycliffe.ca
Western Canada Office
7600 Glover Rd., Langley BC V2Y 1Y1

Wynyard & District Chamber of Commerce
PO Box 508, Wynyard SK S0A 4T0
Tel: 306-554-3363; *Fax:* 306-554-3851
Overview: A small local organization
Finances: *Funding Sources:* Membership dues
Activities: *Speaker Service:* Yes

X Changes Artists' Gallery & Studios Society
#6E, 2333 Government St., Victoria BC V8T 4P4
Tel: 250-382-0442
www.xchangesgallery.org
Overview: A small local organization founded in 1981
Staff Member(s): 7; 20 volunteer(s)
Membership: 20 individual; *Fees:* $30 - annual

Xplor Canada Association
#100, 445 Apple Creek Blvd., Markham ON L3R 9X7
Toll-Free: 888-258-0335
info@xplorcanada.org
www.xplorcanada.org
www.linkedin.com/groups/1851072
twitter.com/Xplorcanada
Also Known As: Xplor
Overview: A small national organization founded in 1985
Mission: To provide an international forum to educate organizations & enable professionals to build & share knowledge concerning solutions, tools & processes for communicating customized information
Affiliation(s): Xplor International
Finances: *Funding Sources:* Membership dues; conference fees
Staff Member(s): 2; 35 volunteer(s)
Membership: 500; *Fees:* $25 USD student/retired; $99 USD associate; $199 USD professional individual; $895 USD professional company; $1,795 USD vendor; *Member Profile:* Organizations that develop & use the technology of the document systems industry
Activities: Electronic Document Professional certification (EDP); *Speaker Service:* Yes
Chief Officer(s):
Joanne Gore, President
jgore@avantisystems.com
Paul Abdool, Treasurer
paul.abdool@solimarsystems.com
Awards:
• Xplorer of the Year
• Innovator of the Year

Yamaska Literacy Council (YLC) / Conseil d'alphabétisation de Yamaska
#203, 505, rue South, Cowansville QC J2K 2X9
Tél: 450-263-7503; *Téléc:* 450-263-7209
Ligne sans frais: 866-337-7503
yamaskalit@endirect.qc.ca
www.yamaskaliteracy.ca
Aperçu: *Dimension:* petite; *Envergure:* locale; Organisme sans but lucratif
Mission: The Yamaska Literacy Council trains volunteers to help adults improve their literacy skills
Affiliation(s): Laubach Literacy of Canada-Québec; Literacy Volunteers of Québec; Québec English Literacy Alliance; The Literacy Foundation
Finances: *Budget de fonctionnement annuel:* $50,000-$100,000; *Fonds:* Regional government
Membre(s) du personnel: 2; 40 bénévole(s)
Membre: 1-99
Membre(s) du bureau directeur:
Martha Shufelt, President
Wendy Seys, Coordinator

Yarmouth & Area Chamber of Commerce (YCC)
PO Box 532, Yarmouth NS B5A 4B4
Tel: 902-742-3074; *Fax:* 902-749-1383
info@yarmouthchamberofcommerce.com
www.yarmouthchamberofcommerce.com
www.linkedin.com/groups?about=&gid=2910385
www.facebook.com/YarmouthNSChamber
Overview: A medium-sized local organization founded in 1892
Mission: To promote a positive economic & business climate in Yarmouth county
Member of: Canadian Chamber of Commerce; Atlantic Provinces Chamber of Commerce
Finances: *Funding Sources:* Membership dues; fee for service; magazine publications
Staff Member(s): 2
Membership: 200+; *Fees:* Schedule available; *Committees:* Transportation; AGM; Technology; Human Resources; Financial; Marketing & Promotions; Fundraising; Annual Business Awards
Chief Officer(s):
Chris Atwood, President
Neil Rogers, 1st Vice-President
Angie Greene, 2nd Vice-President
Awards:
• The Royal Bank Partners in Education Award

Yarmouth County Historical Society
22 Collins St., Yarmouth NS B5A 3C8
Tel: 902-742-5539; *Fax:* 902-749-1120
ycmuseum@eastlink.ca
yarmouthcountymuseum.ednet.ns.ca
www.facebook.com/92402018979
Also Known As: Yarmouth County Museum & Archives
Overview: A small local charitable organization founded in 1935
Mission: To collect and preserve historical data, records and objects of interest, to erect historical markers, and generally to promote interest in Yarmouth County history.
Member of: Federation of the Nova Scotian Heritage; Canadian Museums Association; Council of Nova Scotia Archives
Finances: *Annual Operating Budget:* $100,000-$250,000; *Funding Sources:* Membership dues; provincial government; gift shop
Staff Member(s): 2; 100 volunteer(s)
Membership: 385; *Fees:* $20 individual; $40 family
Activities: Historical programs; genealogy; *Speaker Service:* Yes; *Library:* Yarmouth County Museum Archives; Open to public
Chief Officer(s):
Nadine Gates, Director/Curator

Yarmouth Food Bank Society
390 Main St., Yarmouth NS B5A 2A3
Tel: 902-742-0918
Overview: A small local charitable organization founded in 1987
Member of: Nova Scotia Food Bank Association; Atlantic Alliance of Food Banks & C.V.A.'s
Finances: *Annual Operating Budget:* Less than $50,000; *Funding Sources:* Fundraising
Staff Member(s): 14; 14 volunteer(s)
Membership: 1-99; *Fees:* $100
Activities: Food drives; *Speaker Service:* Yes
Chief Officer(s):
Bill Carter, Contact

Yasodhara Ashram Society
PO Box 9, Kootenay Bay BC V0B 1X0
Tel: 250-227-9224; *Fax:* 250-227-9494
Toll-Free: 800-661-8711
info@yasodhara.org
www.yasodhara.org
Overview: A small international charitable organization founded in 1963
Mission: To maintain a centre for adults engaged in a life of spiritual intent; to provide instruction in & opportunities for religious & spiritual practice
Finances: *Annual Operating Budget:* $500,000-$1.5 Million
15 volunteer(s)
Membership: 125; *Fees:* $25
Activities: *Internships:* Yes; *Speaker Service:* Yes; *Library:* by appointment
Chief Officer(s):
Swami Lalitananda, President

The Yellow Dog Project
#5 4646 Riverside Dr., Red Deer AB T4N 6Y5
Tel: 403-342-0187
info@theyellowdogproject.com
www.theyellowdogproject.com
www.facebook.com/TheYellowDogProject
twitter.com/YellowDogProj
pinterest.com/yellowdogproj/
Overview: A small international organization
Mission: To educate the public and dog owners to identify dogs needing space, promote appropriate contact of dogs and assist dog parents to identify their dog as needing space.

Yellowhead Emergency Shelter for Women Society
PO Box 6401, Hinton AB T7V 1X7
Tel: 780-865-4359; *Fax:* 780-865-7151
Toll-Free: 800-661-0937; *Crisis Hot-Line:* 780-865-5133
yeswomen@shaw.ca
Overview: A small local organization
Mission: To offer temporary safe accommodation for abused women & their children & 24-hour telephone & walk-in counselling; To offer outreach & public education
Finances: *Funding Sources:* Provincial government

Yellowhead Highway Association See Trans Canada Yellowhead Highway Association

Yellowknife Association for Community Living (YKACL)
Abe Miller Bldg., PO Box 981, 4912 - 53 St., Yellowknife NT X1A 2N7
Tel: 867-920-2644; *Fax:* 867-920-2348
info@ykacl.ca
www.ykacl.ca
www.facebook.com/124566867584059
Overview: A small provincial charitable organization overseen by Canadian Association for Community Living
Mission: To promote the welfare of people with handicaps & their families; to lobby on behalf of people with developmental disabilities in the Northwest Territories; to ensure that every person in Northwest Territories has access to supports to live

with dignity & to participate in the community of his/her choice
Member of: Canadian Association for Community Living
Finances: *Funding Sources:* Canadian & GNWT governments
Staff Member(s): 28
Membership: *Fees:* $10
Activities: *Library:* Open to public
Chief Officer(s):
Lynn Elkin, Executive Director, 867-920-2644, Fax: 768-920-2348
ed@ykacl.ca
Janice McKenna, President
president@ykacl.ca
Anita Griffore, Vice-President

Yellowknife Chamber of Commerce
#21, 4802 - 50th Ave., Yellowknife NT X1A 1C4
Tel: 867-920-4944; *Fax:* 867-920-4640
admin@ykchamber.com
www.ykchamber.com
www.facebook.com/ykchamber
twitter.com/YKChamber
Overview: A medium-sized local organization founded in 1947
Member of: Canadian Chamber of Commerce; NWT Chamber of Commerce
Finances: *Annual Operating Budget:* $250,000-$500,000; *Funding Sources:* Membership & service fees
Staff Member(s): 2
Membership: *Fees:* Schedule available based on number of employees
Activities: Public awareness; business advocacy; Spring Trade Show; Small Business Week; *Speaker Service:* Yes; *Library:* by appointment
Chief Officer(s):
Daneen Everett, Executive Director

Yellowknife Real Estate Board
#201, 5204 - 50 Ave., Yellowknife NT X1A 1E2
Tel: 867-920-4624; *Fax:* 867-873-6387
boards.mls.ca/yellowknife
Overview: A small local organization
Member of: The Canadian Real Estate Association

Yellowknife Shooting Club (YKSC)
PO Box 2931, Yellowknife NT X1A 2R2
yellowknifeshootingclub.ca
Overview: A small local organization founded in 1961
Mission: Safe shooting of all types for firearms for sport & recreational purposes
Affiliation(s): NWT Federation of Shooting Sports; Shooting Federation of Canada; NRA
Membership: *Fees:* $170 individual; $280 family; $10 youth; *Member Profile:* Firearms owners & users
Activities: Caribou Carnival; Wolverine Days; fun shoot; media shoot; turkey shoot; Sight-In Days
Chief Officer(s):
Scott Cairns, President, 867-669-9220
Bud Rhyndress, Vice-President, 867-873-6209

YMCA ASK! & YMCA ASCC *See* ASK! Community Information Centre (LAMP)

YMCA Canada
#601, 1867 Yonge St., Toronto ON M4S 1Y5
Tel: 416-967-9622; *Fax:* 416-967-9618
www.ymca.ca
www.facebook.com/YMCACanada
twitter.com/YMCA_Canada
Also Known As: The National Council of Young Men's Christian Associations of Canada
Overview: A large national charitable organization founded in 1851
Mission: Dedicated to the growth of all persons in spirit, mind & body, & in a sense of responsibility to each other & the global community; fosters & stimulates the development of strong member associations & advocates on their behalf regionally, nationally & internationally
Affiliation(s): Canadian Centre for Philanthropy; Canadian Child Care Federation; Canadian Coalition for the Rights of Children; Canadian Council for International Cooperation; Canadian Council on Children & Youth; Canadian Recreational Canoeing Association; Coalition on National Voluntary Organizations; Conference Board of Canada; Huronia Tourism Association; National Fitness Leadership Advisory Committee; National Life Guard Service; National Voluntary Health Agencies; National Youth Serving Agencies; Partnership Africa Canada; Resorts Ontario; Royal Life Saving Society; Voluntary Sector Round Table

Finances: *Annual Operating Budget:* Greater than $5 Million
Staff Member(s): 21
Membership: 2.1 million participants annually; *Member Profile:* 42 YMCAs + 5 YMCA-YWCAs
Activities: Camps; Leadership development; Child care; Health & fitness programs; *Awareness Events:* YMCA Healthy Kids Day, May-June; *Library:* Not open to public
Chief Officer(s):
Dinsdale Peter, President & Chief Executive Officer
Flaherty Brenda, Chair
Awards:
- Fellowship of Honour
- YMCA Hall of Fame
- YMCA Canada Educational Awards

YMCA of Bockville & Area
345 Park St., Brockville ON K6V 5Y7
Tel: 613-342-7961; *Fax:* 613-342-8223
yba.ymca@brockville.ymca.ca
www.brockvilley.com
www.facebook.com/brockvilley
twitter.com/YMCABrockville
Chief Officer(s):
Diana Deakin-Thomas, Chief Executive Officer
ddeakin-thomas@brockvilley.com

YMCA of Western Ontario - Windsor
Central Park Athletics, 3400 Grand Marais Rd. E, Windsor ON N8W 1W7
Tel: 519-419-1267
windsor@ymca.ca
ymcawo.ca
www.facebook.com/ymcawindsor
twitter.com/yourYMCAWO
Chief Officer(s):
Soyuth Sok, Regional Manager, 519-245-6075 Ext. 222
ssok@ymcawo.ca

YMCA-YWCA of the National Capital Region
Taggart Family Y, 180 Argyle Ave., Ottawa ON K2P 1B7
Tel: 613-237-1320; *Fax:* 613-788-5052
www.ymcaywca.ca
www.facebook.com/ymcaywca
twitter.com/YMCAYWCA_Ottawa
www.youtube.com/user/ymcaywcaottawa
Chief Officer(s):
Bob Gallagher, President & Chief Executive Officer, 613-237-1320 Ext. 5025
bob.gallagher@ymcaywca.ca

YMCA of Northern Alberta - Edmonton
#200, 10211 - 105 St. NW, Edmonton AB T5J 1E3
Tel: 780-425-9622; *Fax:* 780-428-9469
northernalberta.ymca.ca
www.facebook.com/YMCAofNorthernAlberta
Chief Officer(s):
Nick Parkinson, President & CEO
nparkinson@edmonton.ymca.ca

YMCA of Owen Sound Grey Bruce
700 10th Street East, Owen Sound ON N4K 0C6
Tel: 519-376-0484; *Fax:* 519-376-0487
Toll-Free: 800-265-3711
membership@ymcaowensound.on.ca
www.ymcaowensound.on.ca
Chief Officer(s):
Maria Canton, President

YMCA of Timmins
376 Poplar Ave., Timmins ON P4N 4S4
Tel: 705-360-4381; *Fax:* 705-360-4382
info.timminsy@timmins.ymca.ca
timminsymca.org
Chief Officer(s):
Lacey Rigg, Chair

YMCA of Moose Jaw
220 Fairford St. East, Moose Jaw SK S6H 6H2
Tel: 306-692-0688; *Fax:* 306-694-5034
www.mjymca.ca
www.facebook.com/mjymca
Chief Officer(s):
Jeff Fox, Chief Executive Officer

YMCA of Greater Saint John
191 Churchill Blvd., Saint John NB E2K 3E2
Tel: 506-693-9622; *Fax:* 506-634-0783
admin@saintjohny.com
www.saintjohny.com
www.facebook.com/SaintJohnY
twitter.com/Y_SaintJohn
Chief Officer(s):

Shilo Boucher, President & Chief Executive Officer

YMCA of Okanagan
375 Hartman Rd., Kelowna BC V1X 2M9
Tel: 250-491-9622; *Fax:* 250-765-7962
info@ymca-ywca.com
www.ymcaokanagan.ca
Chief Officer(s):
Joni Metherell, Board Chair

YMCA-YWCA of Winnipeg
3550 Portage Ave., Winnipeg MB R3K 0Z8
Tel: 204-832-7002; *Fax:* 204-889-9002
info@ymcaywca.mb.ca
www.ywinnipeg.ca
www.facebook.com/ywinnipeg
twitter.com/YWinnipeg
www.youtube.com/user/YWinnipeg
Chief Officer(s):
Kent Paterson, President & Chief Executive Officer

YMCA of Simcoe/Muskoka - Barrie
22 Grove St. West, Barrie ON L4N 1M7
Tel: 705-726-6421; *Fax:* 705-726-0508
barrie@ymcaofsimcoemuskoka.ca
ymcaofsimcoemuskoka.ca

YMCA of Central East Ontario - Belleville
433 Victoria Ave., Belleville ON K8N 2G1
Tel: 613-966-9622; *Fax:* 613-962-9247
info@bellevilleymca.ca
www.bellevilleymca.ca
www.facebook.com/YMCAofCEO
Chief Officer(s):
David Allen, President & Chief Executive Officer
Ron Riddell, Regional General Manager

YMCA of Brandon
231 - 8th St., Brandon MB R7A 3X2
Tel: 204-727-5456; *Fax:* 204-726-0995
BRN-info@ymanitoba.ca
www.ymcabrandon.ca
Chief Officer(s):
Kerri Bridges, General Manager

YMCA Calgary
101 - 3 St. SW, 2nd Fl., Calgary AB T2P 4G6
Tel: 403-237-9622; *Fax:* 403-269-4661
www.ymcacalgary.org
www.facebook.com/ymcacalgary
Chief Officer(s):
Shannon Doram, President & Chief Executive Officer, 406-781-1655
shannon.doram@calgary.ymca.ca

YMCA of Cape Breton
399 Charlotte St., Sydney NS B1P 1E3
Tel: 902-562-9622; *Fax:* 902-564-2063
info@cbymca.com
www.cbymca.com
www.facebook.com/YMCAcapebreton
twitter.com/capebretonymca
Chief Officer(s):
Andre Gallant, Cheif Executive Officer
agallant@cbymca.com

YMCAs across Southwestern Ontario - Chatham—Kent
101 Courthouse Lane, Chatham ON N7L 0B5
Tel: 519-360-9622; *Fax:* 519-360-9629
ymcaswo.ca
www.facebook.com/chathamkentYMCA
twitter.com/chathamkenty
Chief Officer(s):
Kathi Lomas-McGee, Interim Cheif Executive Officer, 519-955-3432

YMCA of Greater Vancouver - Chilliwack
45844 Hocking Ave., Chilliwack BC V2P 1B4
Tel: 604-792-3371; *Fax:* 604-792-7298
chilliwack@gv.ymca.cag
gv.ymca.ca
twitter.com/ChilliwackYMCA
Chief Officer(s):
Stephen Butz, President & Chief Executive Officer

YMCA of Simcoe/Muskoka - Collingwood
200 Hume St., Collingwood ON L9Y 4E8
Tel: 705-445-5705; *Fax:* 705-445-7732
ymcaofsimcoemuskoka.ca
Chief Officer(s):
Rob Armstrong, CEO, 705-726-9622 Ext. 437

YMCA of Cumberland
PO Box 552, 92 Church St., Amherst NS B4H 4A1

Canadian Associations / YMCA Canada

Tel: 902-667-9112; Fax: 902-661-4692
info@cumberland.ymca.ca
www.ymcaofcumberland.com
www.facebook.com/YMCAofCumberland
Chief Officer(s):
Trina Clarke, Chief Executive Officer
trina.clarke@cumberland.ymca.ca

YMCA of Exploits Valley
13 Prices Ave., Grand Falls-Windsor NL A2B 1C9
Tel: 709-489-9622; Fax: 709-489-8404
www.exploitsvalleyymca.ca
www.facebook.com/exploitsvalleyymca
Chief Officer(s):
Caravan Amanda, Contact
amanda_caravan@exploitsvalley.ymca.ca

YMCA of Niagara - Fort Erie
1555 Garrison Rd., Fort Erie ON L2A 1P8
Tel: 905-871-9622; Fax: 905-871-9228
ymcaforterie@niagara.ymca.ca
www.ymcaofniagara.org
www.facebook.com/YMCANiagara

YMCA of Fredericton
570 York St., Fredericton NB E3B 3R2
Tel: 506-462-3000; Fax: 506-462-3007
www.ymcafredericton.nb.ca
www.facebook.com/FrederictonYMCA
twitter.com/FrederictonYMCA
Member of: Fredericton Chamber of Commerce
Chief Officer(s):
Jason Dickson, Chief Executive Officer

YMCA of Greater Halifax/Dartmouth
#306, 5670 Spring Garden Road, Halifax NS B3J 1H6
Tel: 902-423-4261
www.ymcahfx.ca
Chief Officer(s):
Brian Watson-Borg, CEO

YMCA of Greater Moncton
30 War Veterans Ave., Moncton NB E1C 0B3
Tel: 506-857-0606; Fax: 506-859-8198
info@ymcamoncton.com
www.ymcamoncton.ca
www.facebook.com/MonctonYMCA
Chief Officer(s):
Zane Korytko, Chief Executive Officer
zane.korytko@ymcamoncton.com

YMCAs of Quebec
1435, rue Drummond, 4e étage, Montréal QC H3G 1W3
Tel: 514-849-5331; Fax: 514-849-5863
contact@ymcaquebec.org
www.ymcaquebec.org
Chief Officer(s):
Stéphane Vaillancourt, President & Chief Executive Officer

YMCA of Greater Toronto
#300, 2200 Yonge St., Toronto ON M4S 2C6
Tel: 416-928-9622; Fax: 416-928-2030
Toll-Free: 800-223-8024
memberservices@ymcagta.org
www.ymcagta.org
www.facebook.com/YMCAGTA
twitter.com/ymcagta
www.youtube.com/user/ymcagta
Chief Officer(s):
Medhat Mahdy, President & Cheif Executive Officer

YMCA of Greater Vancouver
300 - 5055 Joyce Street, Vancouver BC V5R 6B2
Tel: 604-681-9622; Fax: 604-688-0220
info@gv.ymca.cag
gv.ymca.ca
Chief Officer(s):
Stephen Butz, President & Chief Executive Officer

YMCA-YWCA of Greater Vancouver Island
851 Broughton St., Victoria BC V8W 1E5
Tel: 250-386-7511; Fax: 250-380-1933
memberservices@vancouverislandy.com
vancouverislandy.com

YMCA of Hamilton/Burlington/Brantford
79 James St. South, Hamilton ON L8P 2Z1
Tel: 905-529-7102; Fax: 905-529-6682
hamilton.membership@ymcahbb.ca
www.ymcahbb.ca
Chief Officer(s):
Jim Commerford, President & Chief Executive Officer,
905-317-4919
jim_commerford@ymca.ca

YMCA of Western Newfoundland - Humber Community
PO Box 836, 2 Herald Ave., Corner Brook NL A2H 6H6
Tel: 709-639-9676; Fax: 709-634-9622
www.humbercommunityymca.ca
twitter.com/HumberCommunity
Chief Officer(s):
Christine Young, CEO

YMCA of Kingston
100 Wright Cres., Kingston ON K7L 4T9
Tel: 613-546-2647; Fax: 613-549-0654
contact@kingston.ymca.ca
www.kingston.ymca.ca
Chief Officer(s):
Mary Kloosterman, Cheif Executive Officer
mary_kloosterman@kingston.ymca.ca

YMCA of Lethbridge
515 Stafford Dr. South, Lethbridge AB T1J 2L3
Tel: 403-327-9622; Fax: 403-320-6475
admin@lethbridgeymca.org
www.lethbridgeymca.org
Chief Officer(s):
Jennifer Petracek-Kolb, Cheif Executive Officer,
403-327-9622
jennifer@lethbridgeymca.org

YMCA of Western Ontario - London
382 Waterloo St., London ON N6B 2N8
Tel: 519-667-3300; Fax: 519-433-8527
www.ymcawo.ca
www.facebook.com/CentreBranchYMCALondon
twitter.com/yourYMCAWO
Chief Officer(s):
Katie Payler, Regional Manager, 519-631-2418 Ext. 226

YMCA of Southwest Nova Scotia - Lunenburg County
75 High St., Bridgewater NS B4V 1V8
Tel: 902-543-9622; Fax: 902-543-6545
www.ymcalunenburgcounty.org
www.facebook.com/YMCALunenburgCounty
twitter.com/ymcalunenburg
Chief Officer(s):
Yvonne Smith, Chief Executive Officer
yvonne_smith@ymca.ca

YMCA of Medicine Hat
150 Ash Ave. SE, Medicine Hat AB T1A 3A9
Tel: 403-527-4426; Fax: 403-529-5702
www.medicinehatymca.ca
www.facebook.com/YMCAMH
twitter.com/MedicineHatYMCA
Chief Officer(s):
Sharon Hayward, Chief Executive Officer, 403-905-0102
sharon@medicinehatymca.ca

YMCA of Simcoe/Muskoka - Midland
Little Lake Park, PO Box 488, 560 Little Lake Park Rd.,
Midland ON L4R 4L3
Tel: 705-526-7828; Fax: 705-526-8735
ymcaofsimcoemuskoka.ca

YMCA of Niagara - St Catharines
43 Church Street, St Catharines ON L2R 7E1
Tel: 905-646-9622; Fax: 905-646-4213
ymcawalker@niagara.ymca.ca
www.ymcaofniagara.org
Chief Officer(s):
Stephen Butz, CEO

YMCA of Northeastern Ontario - North Bay
186 Chippewa St. West, North Bay ON P1B 6G2
Tel: 705-497-9622; Fax: 705-474-5116
www.ymcanorthbay.com
www.facebook.com/ymcanorthbay
Chief Officer(s):
Kim Kanmacher, Chief Executive Officer

YMCA of Northumberland
339 Elgin St. West, Cobourg ON K9A 4X5
Tel: 905-372-0161; Fax: 905-377-8940
www.ymcanorthumberland.ca
www.facebook.com/ymca.northumberland
Chief Officer(s):
Eunice Kirkpatrick, Executive Director, 905-372-9247 Ext. 242
eunice.kirkpatrick@nrt.ymca.ca

YMCA of Oakville
410 Rebecca St., Oakville ON L6K 1K7
Tel: 905-845-3417; Fax: 905-842-6792
customerservice@oakville.ymca.ca
www.ymcaofoakville.com
www.linkedin.com/company/ymca-of-oakville

www.facebook.com/YMCAOakville
twitter.com/YMCAOakville
Chief Officer(s):
Kyle Barber, President & Chief Executive Officer
kyleba@oakville.ymca.ca

YMCA of Simcoe/Muskoka - Orillia
300 Peter St. North, Orillia ON L3V 5A2
Tel: 705-325-6168; Fax: 705-325-0243
orillia@ymcaofsimcoemuskoka.ca
www.ymcaofsimcoemuskoka.ca

YMCA of Central East Ontario - Peterborough
123 Aylmer St. South, Peterborough ON K9J 3H8
Tel: 705-748-9622; Fax: 705-741-3719
kelly_wilson@ymca.ca
www.peterboroughymca.ca
www.facebook.com/YMCAofCEO
twitter.com/YMCA_of_Ptbo
Chief Officer(s):
David Allen, President & Chief Executive Officer

YMCA of Pictou County
2655 Westville Rd., New Glasgow NS B2H 5C4
Tel: 902-752-0202; Fax: 902-755-3446
frontdesk@pcymca.ca
www.pcymca.ca
www.facebook.com/YMCAPictouCounty
Chief Officer(s):
Dave MacIntyre, General Manager

YMCA of Northern BC - Prince George
PO Box 1808, 2020 Massey Dr., Prince George BC V2L 4V7
Tel: 250-562-9341; Fax: 250-564-2474
nbc.ymca.ca
www.facebook.com/NBCYMCA
twitter.com/NBCY
Chief Officer(s):
Amanda Alexander, Chief Executive Officer, 250-562-9341
Ext. 116
amanada.alexander@nbcy.org

YMCA of Regina
2400 - 13th Ave., Regina SK S4P 0V9
Tel: 306-757-9622; Fax: 306-525-5508
regina.ymca.ca
www.facebook.com/YMCARegina
Chief Officer(s):
John Bailey, Acting Chief Executive Officer, 306-757-9622
Ext. 214

YMCA of Newfoundland & Labrador
35 Ridge Rd., St. John's NL A1B 4P5
Tel: 709-726-9622; Fax: 709-576-0410
ymcanl.com
www.facebook.com/ymcanl
twitter.com/YMCAofNL
Chief Officer(s):
Jason Brown, President & Chief Executive Officer,
709-726-9622 Ext. 241
jbrown@ymcanl.com

YMCA of Western Ontario - St Thomas—Elgin
20 High St., St Thomas ON N5R 5V2
Tel: 519-631-2418; Fax: 519-631-4131
www.ymcawo.ca
www.facebook.com/StThomasYMCA
twitter.com/yourYMCAWO
Chief Officer(s):
Katie Payler, General Manager, 519-631-2418 Ext. 226
kpayler@ymcawo.ca

YMCAs across Southwestern Ontario - Sarnia—Lambton
1015 Finch Dr., Sarnia ON N7S 8G5
Tel: 519-336-9622; Fax: 519-336-7818
ymcaswo.ca
twitter.com/sarniay
Chief Officer(s):
Kathi Lomas-McGee, Interim Chief Executive Officer

YMCA of Saskatoon
25 - 22nd St. East, Saskatoon SK S7K 0C7
Tel: 306-652-7515; Fax: 306-652-2828
ymca@ymcasaskatoon.org
ymcasaskatoon.org
Chief Officer(s):
Dean Dodge, Chief Executive Officer,
ddodge@ymcasaskatoon.org, 306-652-7515 Ext. 226

YMCA of Sault Ste Marie
235 McNabb St., Sault Ste Marie ON P6B 1Y3
Tel: 705-949-3133; Fax: 705-949-3344
info@ssmymca.ca
www.sault.ymca.ca

Chief Officer(s):
Kim Caruso, CEO
kim.caruso@ssmymca.ca

YMCA of Stratford—Perth
204 Downie St. South, Stratford ON N5A 1X4
Tel: 519-271-0480; *Fax:* 519-271-0489
stratfordperthymca.com
twitter.com/YMCAstratfordCA
Chief Officer(s):
Mimi Price, Chief Executive Officer, 519-271-0480

YMCA of Northeastern Ontario - Sudbury
140 Durham St., Sudbury ON P3E 3M7
Tel: 705-673-9136; *Fax:* 705-675-8777
memberservices@sudbury.ymca.ca
www.sudbury.ymca.ca
www.facebook.com/YMCASudbury
twitter.com/ymcasudbury
Chief Officer(s):
Kim Kanmacher, Chief Executive Officer

YMCA of Northern Alberta - Wood Buffalo
Westwood Centre, 221 Tundra Dr., Fort McMurray AB T9H 4Z7
Tel: 780-790-9622; *Fax:* 780-743-4045
www.ymca.woodbuffalo.org
www.facebook.com/FortMcMurrayYmcaWoodbuffalo
twitter.com/YMCAWoodBuffalo
instagram.com/ymcawoodbuffalo
Chief Officer(s):
Nahanni Alma, Senior Director, Membership Sales & Service, 780-790-9622 Ext. 226
nahanni_alma@ymca.ca

YMCA of Yarmouth
PO Box 86, 275 Main St., Yarmouth NS B5A 4B1
Tel: 902-742-7181; *Fax:* 902-742-7676
denise_reid@ymca.ca
www.ymcayarmouth.net
www.facebook.com/YmcaYarmouth
Chief Officer(s):
Yvonne Smith, Chief Exeutive Officer
Yvonne_Smith@ymca.ca

YMCAs of Cambridge & Kitchener-Waterloo
#203, 460 Frederick Street, Kitchener ON N2H 2P5
Tel: 519-584-7479
ymcacambridge@ymca.ca
www.ymcacambridgekw.ca
Chief Officer(s):
Peter Sweeney, Chief Executive Officer, 519-584-7479 Ext. 200

YMCA-YWCA of Guelph
130 Woodland Glen Dr., Guelph ON N1G 4M3
Tel: 519-824-5150; *Fax:* 519-824-4729
contact@guelphy.org
www.guelphy.org
www.facebook.com/YGuelph
twitter.com/YGuelph
Chief Officer(s):
Geoff Vogt, Chief Executive Officer

YMCA-YWCA of Kamloops
400 Battle St., Kamloops BC V2C 2L7
Tel: 250-372-7725; *Fax:* 250-372-3023
dharris@kamloopsy.org
www.kamloopsy.org
Chief Officer(s):
Colin Reid, Chief Executive Officer, 250-376-9744 Ext. 108
colin.reid@kamloopsy.org

YMCA Immigrant & Community Services
256 Hespeler Rd., Cambridge ON N1R 3H3
Tel: 519-621-1621
newcomers@ckwymca.ca
www.ymcaimmigrantservices.ca
www.facebook.com/YMCAImmigrant
Previous Name: Cambridge Multicultural Centre
Overview: A small local organization founded in 1985 overseen by Ontario Council of Agencies Serving Immigrants
Mission: To promote integration of newcomers & first Canadians
Activities: Settlement; *Speaker Service:* Yes

YMCA of Belleville & Quinte *See* YMCA Canada

YMCA of Calgary *See* YMCA Canada

YMCA of Cambridge *See* YMCA Canada

YMCA of Edmonton *See* YMCA Canada

YMCA of Greater Victoria *See* YMCA Canada

YMCA of St. John's *See* YMCA Canada

YMCA Prince George *See* YMCA Canada

YMCA-YWCA de la région de la capitale nationale *See* YMCA Canada

Yoga Association of Alberta (YAA)
Percy Page Centre, 11759 Groat Rd., Edmonton AB T5M 3K6
Tel: 780-427-8776; *Fax:* 780-427-0524
yaa@yoga.ca
www.yoga.ca
www.facebook.com/yogaalberta
Overview: A small provincial charitable organization founded in 1976
Mission: To offer yoga activities to the public; to provide coordination & support to yoga enthusiasts
Finances: *Annual Operating Budget:* $250,000-$500,000; *Funding Sources:* Government grant
Staff Member(s): 7; 100 volunteer(s)
Membership: 1,200; *Fees:* $10 associate; $25 individual; $300 life; *Committees:* Teacher Training Program; Outreach
Activities: *Internships:* Yes; *Library:* Not open to public
Chief Officer(s):
Debbie Spence, Executive Director

Yoga Vedanta Centre *See* Sivananda Ashram Yoga Camp

Yonge Street Mission (YSM)
H.B Martin Family Centre for Urban Education, 306 Gerrard St. East, Toronto ON M5A 2G7
Tel: 416-929-9614; *Fax:* 416-929-7204
Toll-Free: 800-416-5111
info@ysm.ca
www.ysm.ca
www.facebook.com/YongeStreetMission
twitter.com/YSM_TO
Overview: A medium-sized local charitable organization founded in 1896
Mission: To bring God's peace, love & justice to people living with economic, social & spiritual poverty in Toronto
Finances: *Annual Operating Budget:* Greater than $5 Million; *Funding Sources:* Donations; churches; individuals; businesses; foundations; grants
Staff Member(s): 120; 4000 volunteer(s)
Activities: Recreation; Education; Social & family events; Relief; Housing; *Internships:* Yes; *Speaker Service:* Yes
Chief Officer(s):
Angela Draskovic, President & CEO
Angela Solomos, Chief Philanthropy Officer
Brent Mitchell, Mission Program Officer
Cliff Cline, Mission Administrative Officer

York and Metro Toronto Region *See* Junior Achievement of Canada

York Pioneer & Historical Society
PO Box 45026, 2482 Yonge St., Toronto ON M4P 3E3
Tel: 416-961-4420
www.yorkpioneers.org
Overview: A small provincial charitable organization founded in 1869
Mission: To unite descendants of those who immigrated to original county of York & others interested in preserving & perpetuating such historical recollections, incidents, documents & pictorial illustrations relating to early settlement of this district of Ontario
Member of: Ontario Historical Society
Finances: *Annual Operating Budget:* Less than $50,000
Staff Member(s): 1; 40 volunteer(s)
Membership: 7 corporate + 94 lifetime + 160 individual; *Fees:* Schedule available; *Committees:* Editorial; Eversley Church; Scadding Cabin; Program; Publicity
Activities: Operates Scadding Cabin Museum; *Library*
Chief Officer(s):
John Marshall, President

York Region Athletic Association (YRAA)
#1038, 44 Main St. South, Unionville ON L3R 2E4
Tel: 905-470-1551; *Fax:* 905-470-9092
www.yraa.com
twitter.com/yraa_news
Overview: A small local organization
Mission: To offer athletics in York Region high schools
Chief Officer(s):
Scot Angus, President
scot.angus@yrdsb.edu.on.ca

York Region Children's Aid Society
Kennedy Place, 16915 Leslie St., Newmarket ON L3Y 9A1
Tel: 905-895-2318; *Fax:* 905-895-2113
Toll-Free: 800-718-3850
www.yorkcas.org
Also Known As: York Region CAS
Previous Name: Children & Family Services for York Region
Overview: A small local charitable organization
Mission: To protect children & promote a safe, healthy & caring environment for them in partnership with a diverse community
Member of: Ontario Association of Children's Aid Societies
Finances: *Funding Sources:* Provincial government
Activities: Providing adoption & foster placement services; Investigating possible instances of child abuse & neflect; *Awareness Events:* Purple Ribbon Campaign for Child Abuse Prevention; *Speaker Service:* Yes
Chief Officer(s):
Colette Prévost, Executive Director

York Region Family Services (Markham)
#203, 4261 Hwy. 7, Unionville ON L3R 1L5
Tel: 905-415-9719; *Fax:* 905-415-9706
Toll-Free: 888-820-9986
www.fsyr.ca
Also Known As: FSYR Markham
Overview: A medium-sized local organization founded in 1968 overseen by Family Service Ontario
Mission: To assist people experiencing emotional, behavioural, relational &/or financial challenges through counselling, educational & assessment programs & services designed to improve functioning & coping skills in daily life
Member of: Ontario Psychological Association; Ontario Association of Credit Counselling Services
Affiliation(s): Canadian Register of Health Service Providers in Psychology; United Way of York Region
Membership: *Member Profile:* Psychologists & counselors
Activities: Annual meeting; community workshops; *Internships:* Yes; *Speaker Service:* Yes
Chief Officer(s):
Elisha Laker, Executive Director
elaker@fsyr.ca

York Region Law Association
50 Eagle St. West, 3rd Fl., Newmarket ON L3Y 6B1
Tel: 905-895-2018; *Fax:* 905-853-7678
Toll-Free: 866-221-8864
bdykstra@yorklaw.ca
www.yorklaw.ca
Overview: A small local organization
Staff Member(s): 5
Membership: *Committees:* Civil Litigation; Criminal Law; Family Law
Chief Officer(s):
Corinne Rivers, President
corinne@cmrlaw.ca

York Regional Police Association (YRPA) / Association régionale de la police de York
600 Stonehaven Ave., Newmarket ON L3X 2M4
Tel: 905-830-4947; *Fax:* 905-898-7282
yrpa@rogers.com
www.yrpa.on.ca
Overview: A small local organization founded in 1971
Member of: Police Association of Ontario; Canadian Police Association
Staff Member(s): 8
Membership: 2,200
Chief Officer(s):
John Miskiw, President

York Rose & Garden Society *See* Greater Toronto Rose & Garden Horticultural Society

York Soaring Association
Airfield, 7296, 5th Line, RR#1, Belwood ON N0B 1J0
Tel: 519-848-3621
www.yorksoaring.com
www.facebook.com/yorksa
Overview: A small local organization founded in 1961
Member of: Soaring Association of Canada
Finances: *Annual Operating Budget:* $250,000-$500,000
10 volunteer(s)
Membership: 100-499

Canadian Associations / York Symphony Orchestra Inc.

Activities: Soaring & gliding facilities; advanced training of glider pilots
Chief Officer(s):
Jim Fryett, President

York Symphony Orchestra Inc.
PO Box 355, Richmond Hill ON L4B 4R6
Tel: 416-410-0860; *Fax:* 416-410-0860
yorksymphonyorchestra@hotmail.com
www.yorksymphony.ca
www.facebook.com/pages/York-Symphony-Orchestra/292050064166541
twitter.com/yorksymphony
Previous Name: Richmond Hill Symphony
Overview: A small local charitable organization founded in 1961 overseen by Orchestras Canada
Mission: To provide musical enjoyment for audiences & musicians, with the goal of being recognized & supported throughout York Region
Affiliation(s): York Symphony Youth Orchestra
Finances: *Annual Operating Budget:* $50,000-$100,000; *Funding Sources:* Ticket revenue; Individual & corporate donations
Activities: *Speaker Service:* Yes; *Library*
Chief Officer(s):
Denis Mastromonaco, Music Director

York Technology Alliance *See* TechConnex

York University Faculty Association (YUFA) / Association des professeurs de l'Université York
240 York Lanes, 4700 Keele St., Toronto ON M3J 1P3
Tel: 416-736-5236; *Fax:* 416-736-5850
yufa@yorku.ca
www.yufa.ca
Overview: A medium-sized local organization founded in 1962
Mission: To promote the welfare of the university as an institution of higher learning & the welfare of academic staff including the regulation of employment relations between the University & its academic staff
Affiliation(s): Ontario Council of Faculty Associations; Canadian Association of University Teachers
Staff Member(s): 4
Membership: 1,400; *Member Profile:* Appointed to full-time teaching or librarian; *Committees:* Compensatrion; Pension; Equity; Grievance; Community Projects
Chief Officer(s):
Arthur Hilliker, President
Mary Kandiuk, Vice President Internal
Craig Heron, Vice President External

York University Staff Association / Association du personnel de l'Université York
East Office Bldg., 190 Albany Rd., 2nd Fl., Toronto ON M3J 1P3
Tel: 416-736-5109; *Fax:* 416-736-5519
yusapuy@yorku.ca
www.yusapuy.org
www.facebook.com/YorkUniversityStaffAssociation
www.youtube.com/user/CCUchannel
Also Known As: YusApuY
Overview: A medium-sized local organization founded in 1975
Member of: Equal Pay Coalition; York Community Coalition
Affiliation(s): Confederation of Canadian Unions
Finances: *Funding Sources:* Membership dues
Staff Member(s): 2
Membership: 2,500+; *Member Profile:* Clerical, technical, computer & laboratory staff; *Committees:* Bargaining; Communications; Constitution & Policy; Grievance; Grievance; Job Evaluation; Nominations; Health & Safety
Activities: *Speaker Service:* Yes; *Library:* Open to public
Chief Officer(s):
Giulio Malfatti, President

York-Grand River Historical Society
Caledonia ON
Previous Name: Seneca Centennial Committee
Overview: A small local organization founded in 1974
Mission: To support, encourage & facilitate the conservation, protection & promotion of the heritage of the community
Member of: Ontario Historical Society
Affiliation(s): Golden Horseshoe Antique Society
Finances: *Annual Operating Budget:* Less than $50,000; *Funding Sources:* Membership fees; Heritage Organization Development Grant
10 volunteer(s)
Membership: 30; *Fees:* $5; *Member Profile:* Interest in local history

Activities: Interested in putting up signs to mark former local sites

Yorkton & District Labour Council (YDLC)
180A Broadway St. West, Yorkton SK S3N 0M6
Tel: 603-621-8948
Overview: A small local organization overseen by Saskatchewan Federation of Labour
Mission: To promote the interests of affiliates in Yorkton, Saskatchewan & the surrounding region; To advance the economic & social welfare of workers
Affiliation(s): Canadian Labour Congress (CLC)
Activities: Presenting educational opportunities; Hosting a ceremony on the annual Day of Mourning for workers killed & injured on the job; Raising awareness of occupational health & safety; Supporting community organizations
Chief Officer(s):
Mary Ann Fererko, President, 306-783-2234
mfederko@sasktel.net

Yorkton & District United Way Inc.
180 Broadway St. West, #A, Yorkton SK S3N 0M6
Overview: A small local charitable organization founded in 1982 overseen by United Way of Canada - Centraide Canada
Mission: To unite & facilitate community fundraising; To strengthen the community
Finances: *Annual Operating Budget:* Less than $50,000
Activities: Community donations; *Awareness Events:* Helping Hand Campaign

Yorkton Chamber of Commerce
PO Box 1051, Yorkton SK S3N 2X3
Tel: 306-783-4368; *Fax:* 306-786-6978
info@yorktonchamber.com
www.chamber.yorkton.sk.ca
www.facebook.com/yorktonchamber
twitter.com/YorktonChamber
Overview: A small local organization founded in 1898
Mission: To represent the interests of business & encourage economic development
Member of: Canadian Chamber; City Economic Development Commission; Saskatchewan Chamber of Commerce
Affiliation(s): Saskatchewan Economic Developers Association
Finances: *Funding Sources:* Membership fees; sponsored Spring Trade show
Staff Member(s): 2
Membership: 450; *Committees:* Business Development; Communication; Executive; Public Policy
Activities: Business Awards Program; Dine-a-night
Chief Officer(s):
Joel Martinuk, President
keyadmin@keychev.com
Juanita Polegi, Executive Director
jpolegi@yorktonchamber.com
Awards:
• Celebrate Success Awards

Yorkton Film Festival (YFF)
49 Smith St. East, Yorkton SK S3N 0H4
Tel: 306-782-7077; *Fax:* 306-782-1550
info@yorktonfilm.com
www.yorktonfilm.com
Also Known As: Golden Sheaf Awards
Overview: A small local charitable organization founded in 1947
Member of: Saskatchewan Motion Picture Association
Staff Member(s): 2; 55 volunteer(s)
Membership: 189; *Fees:* $5
Activities: Canada's Golden Sheaf Awards Competition
Chief Officer(s):
Randy Goulden, Executive Director

Yorkton Friendship Centre
139 Dominion Ave., Yorkton SK S3N 1S3
Tel: 306-782-2822; *Fax:* 306-782-6662
Overview: A small local organization

Yorkton Real Estate Association Inc. (YREA)
41 Broadway St. West, Yorkton SK S3N 0L6
Tel: 306-783-3067; *Fax:* 306-782-3231
yrea@sasktel.net
Overview: A small local organization founded in 1969 overseen by Saskatchewan Real Estate Association
Mission: To promote a high level of professionalism among members by providing leadership in the real estate industry & in the community
Member of: The Canadian Real Estate Association

Finances: *Annual Operating Budget:* Less than $50,000; *Funding Sources:* Membership fees
Staff Member(s): 1
Membership: 30; *Fees:* Annual/quarterly/monthly; *Member Profile:* Brokers; Salespeople; Affiliate members; *Committees:* Education; Professional Standards; PAC; Public Relations; Nominating; Financial
Activities: Fundraising for Kidney Foundation, Yorkton Big Brothers & Big Sisters
Chief Officer(s):
Judy Pfeifer, Executive Officer
Ron Skinner, President
ronskinner@royallepage.ca

Yorkton Society for the Prevention of Cruelty to Animals Inc.
79 - 7th Ave. South, Yorkton SK S3N 3V1
Tel: 306-783-4080; *Fax:* 306-783-4080
Other Communication: After hours: 306-786-1799
www.facebook.com/241196172557900
Also Known As: Yorkton SPCA
Overview: A small local organization founded in 1977
Mission: To help find homes for animals in the shelter & to educate people so that they may become better pet owners
Member of: Canadian Federation of Humane Societies

Young Alberta Book Festival Society *See* Young Alberta Book Society

Young Alberta Book Society (YABS)
Percy Page Ctr., 2nd Fl., 11759 Groat Rd., Edmonton AB T5M 3K6
Tel: 780-422-8232
www.yabs.ab.ca
www.facebook.com/youngalbertabooksociety
twitter.com/YABStweet
Previous Name: Young Alberta Book Festival Society
Overview: A small provincial charitable organization founded in 1985
Mission: To foster literacy & a love of reading among young people in Alberta by providing access to Albertan literary artists & their work
Member of: Edmonton Arts Council; Professional Arts Coalition of Edmonton
Affiliation(s): Canadian Children's Book Centre
Finances: *Annual Operating Budget:* $250,000-$500,000; *Funding Sources:* Provincial Government; Municipal Government; Sponsorship; Donations
Staff Member(s): 2; 70 volunteer(s)
Membership: 250; *Fees:* $50
Activities: Taleblazers Festival, annual month-long tour of literary artists; Story Avenue, two day writing workshop for grades 5-7; WordPower, week-long series writing workshops in rural communities; *Library:* Canadian Children's Book Centre Collection; by appointment
Chief Officer(s):
Stephanie Gregorwich, Executive Director
Awards:
• Charles Allard Award
Teachers & librarians must explain the struggles they face when encouraging their students to read, & how a presentation from an author of their choice would benefit their students. The society selects 10 winners, who will receive a visit from that author. *Eligibility:* Teachers & librarians
• Martyn Godfrey Young Writers Award
Students must submit a 500 - 1500 word humour story or graphic novel. One winner in grade 4-6 and one winner in grade 7-9 is chosen to receive a visit from an anuthor, a selection of book & an e-reader *Eligibility:* Alberta students in grades 4 to 9

Young Bar Association of Montréal *Voir* Association du jeune barreau de Montréal

Young Guard *See* Hashomer Hatzair Canada

Young People's Theatre (YPT)
165 Front St. East, Toronto ON M5A 3Z4
Tel: 416-862-2222
online@youngpeoplestheatre.ca
www.youngpeoplestheatre.ca
www.linkedin.com/company/young-people's-theatre
www.facebook.com/YoungPeoplesTheatre
twitter.com/YPTToronto
www.youtube.com/user/YoungPeoplesTheatre
Previous Name: Lorraine Kimsa Theatre for Young People
Overview: A medium-sized local charitable organization founded in 1966

Mission: To make a positive impact on the intellectual, social, & emotional development of young people; To produce plays for young audiences; To operate a year-round drama school for youth
Finances: *Funding Sources:* Ticket sales; Donations; Corporate sponsorships
Staff Member(s): 43
Chief Officer(s):
Nancy J. Webster, Executive Director
Alexis Buset, Technical Director
Allen MacInnis, Artistic Director
Rick Banville, Director, Production
Jill Ward, Director, Education & Participation
Marilyn Hamilton, Director, Marketing

Your Life Counts (YLC)
Seaway Mall, #GG5B, 800 Niagara St. North, Welland ON L3C 5Z4
Tel: 289-820-5777
info@yourlifecounts.org
www.yourlifecounts.org
www.facebook.com/YourLifeCounts
twitter.com/yourlifecounts
www.youtube.com/user/YOURLIFECOUNTSTV
Overview: A small national charitable organization founded in 2000
Mission: Works with youth, families, veterans and emergency services in the battle against trauma, addictions and overwhelming life situations that may lead to thoughts of suicide.
Chief Officer(s):
Kevin Bolibruck, Chair

Your Political Party of BC (YPP)
313-2040 York Ave., Vancouver BC V6J 1E7
Tel: 604-805-3547; *Fax:* 604-939-5564
ypp@yppofbc.com
www.yourbc.ca
www.facebook.com/yppbc
twitter.com/yppofbc
www.instagram.com/yppofbc
Also Known As: Your Party
Overview: A small provincial organization
Mission: To advocate more transparency & accountability in government
Chief Officer(s):
James Filippelli, Party Founder & Leader

Youth Assisting Youth (YAY)
#401, 5734 Yonge St., Toronto ON M2M 4E7
Tel: 416-932-1919; *Fax:* 416-932-1924
Toll-Free: 877-932-1919
mail@yay.org
www.yay.org
www.linkedin.com/company/yay-iyouth-assisting-youth
www.facebook.com/thepeerproject
twitter.com/PeerProject
www.instagram.com/thepeerproject
Overview: A medium-sized local charitable organization founded in 1976
Mission: To implement Special Friend/Mentor program, matching mature, responsible youth (ages 16-29) with children (ages 6-15) experiencing social, emotional &/or cultural adjustment problems; To prevent delinquency by providing positive role models & friendship; To promote healthy growth & development of young people, strengthening families & responding to & supporting changing community needs
Finances: *Annual Operating Budget:* $500,000-$1.5 Million; *Funding Sources:* Government; United Way; corporations; foundations; service clubs; events; individuals; gaming
Staff Member(s): 18; 450 volunteer(s)
Membership: 70 corporate + 25 institutional + 450 volunteers; *Fees:* $25; *Committees:* Executive; Finance; Youth Leadership; Policy & Procedure; Fundraising; Information & Technology
Activities: *Internships:* Yes; *Speaker Service:* Yes
Chief Officer(s):
Sally Spencer, CEO
sspencer@yay.org

Youth Ballet & Contemporary Dance of Saskatchewan Inc. (YBCS) / Les ballets de la jeunesse Saskatchewan
1106 McNiven Ave., Regina SK S4S 3X3
Tel: 306-352-9908; *Fax:* 306-585-2565
ybcs@sasktel.net
www.youthballet.net
www.linkedin.com/company/youth-ballet-and-contemporary-dance-of-saskatchewan
www.facebook.com/368852441211
twitter.com/youthballet
Overview: A small provincial charitable organization founded in 1983
Mission: To enable the youth of Saskatchewan to develop to their highest potential in classical ballet & contemporary dance, by providing superior training & support; to enhance public appreciation of dance
Member of: Dance Saskatchewan; Dance & the Child International; Sask Culture; Sask Arts Alliance
Finances: *Funding Sources:* Grants; fundraising; school fees
Staff Member(s): 4
Chief Officer(s):
Michelle McMillan, Artistic Director
Brenda Bancescu, Executive Director

Youth Bowling Canada (YBC)
c/o Bowl Canada, #10A, 250 Shields Ct., Markham ON L3R 9W7
Tel: 905-479-1560; *Fax:* 905-479-8613
info@bowlcanada.ca
www.youthbowling.ca
www.facebook.com/youthbowlingcanada
twitter.com/ybcbowling
instagram.com/bowlcanada
Previous Name: National Youth Bowling Council
Overview: A small national organization founded in 1963 overseen by Bowling Proprietors' Association Of Canada
Mission: YBC is a program operating under the auspices of the Bowling Proprietors' Association of Canada (Bowl Canada), a not-for-profit organization comprised of 500 member centres across the country. The YBC league is divided in 5-pin & 10-pin, & further broken down in 3 age groups: bantam, junior & senior.
Membership: *Fees:* Schedule available

Youth Challenge International (YCI)
Centre for Social Innovation, 585 Dundas St. West, 3rd Fl., Toronto ON M5A 2B7
Tel: 416-504-3370; *Fax:* 416-504-3376
Toll-Free: 877-504-3370
info@yci.org
www.yci.org
www.facebook.com/yci.org
www.youtube.com/user/YCICanada
Overview: A small international charitable organization founded in 1989
Mission: To promote young people's active, responsible & continuing participation in the issues of local & global development; To promote & support the establishment of a YCI global network, with partners in developed & developing regions of the world; To foster increased international cooperation between individuals, communities, service organizations, governments & agencies by focusing expertise & materials upon locally identified problems in developing regions
Finances: *Annual Operating Budget:* $500,000-$1.5 Million; *Funding Sources:* Private sources; foundations; government
Staff Member(s): 13; 200 volunteer(s)
Membership: 100-499; *Committees:* Social Justice; Global Development Education
Activities: Offering a network of youth innovation spaces in developing countries through EQWIP HUBs; Providing the EMBRACE program to improve the lives of women & children in hard-to-reach areas of Cambodia, Myanmar, Rwanda, & the Philippines; Developing youth innovation programs
Chief Officer(s):
Bryan Cox, Executive Director

Youth Emergency Shelter Society of Edmonton See Youth Empowerment & Support Services

Youth Empowerment & Support Services (YESS)
9310 - 82 Ave., Edmonton AB T6C 0Z6
Tel: 780-468-7070; *Fax:* 780-466-1374
reception@yess.org
www.yess.org
www.facebook.com/YESSorg
twitter.com/YESSorg
www.youtube.com/user/YESSorg
Previous Name: Youth Emergency Shelter Society of Edmonton
Overview: A small local charitable organization founded in 1981
Mission: To provide food, shelter, clothing & support to youth at risk who have no other viable living alternatives or who are in immediate risk or jeopardy; To provide multiple services for troubled families & homeless youth, including mediation, counselling, advocacy & shelter
Member of: Alberta Association of Services for Children & Families; Association of Fundraising Professionals
Finances: *Annual Operating Budget:* $3 Million-$5 Million; *Funding Sources:* Provincial government; United Way; private donations; sponsorship
Staff Member(s): 85; 350 volunteer(s)
Membership: 200; *Fees:* $20
Activities: Offering short-term shelter through Nexus, as well as long-term residence through Graham's Place & Shanoa's Place; Providing medical care, addictions & mental health counselling, help with continuing education & housing resources, & other daytime programs through the Armoury Resource Centre; *Awareness Events:* Bacon Day; Annual General Meeting, June; Homeless for a Night, June; *Internships:* Yes; *Speaker Service:* Yes
Chief Officer(s):
Margo Long, Executive Director
margo.long@yess.org
Edward Gots, Manager, Finance
edward.gots@yess.org

Youth Flight Canada (YFC)
1028 Royal York Rd., Toronto ON M8X 2G4
www.youthflight.ca
Also Known As: Youth Flight Canada Education Fund
Previous Name: YouthFlightCanada
Overview: A small national charitable organization founded in 1995
Mission: To inspire, motivate, educate, & foster self-esteem within challenged & disadvantaged youth
Member of: Freedom's Wings Canada
Affiliation(s): Canadian Paraplegic Association, Ontario; K-W Access Ability
Finances: *Annual Operating Budget:* Less than $50,000; *Funding Sources:* Public & corporate donations; Ontario Trillium Foundation
40 volunteer(s)
Membership: 1-99
Activities: Flight programs for challenged & disadvantaged youth & adults; "Inspiration Flights" & pilot training for persons with disabilities: www.freedomswings.ca; flying scholarships for youth; *Internships:* Yes; *Speaker Service:* Yes
Chief Officer(s):
Charles Petersen, Chair
Virginia Thompson, Executive Director
Awards:
• YFC Soaring Bursary

Youth for Christ Canada
#308, 8047 - 199 St., Langley BC V2Y 0E2
Tel: 604-637-3400; *Fax:* 604-243-6992
Toll-Free: 800-899-9322
info@yfccanada.com
www.yfccanada.com
Overview: A medium-sized national organization
Mission: To impact every young person in Canada with the person, work & teachings of Jesus Christ & discipling them into the Church
Membership: 31 chapters + 300 Ministry Centres
Activities: Responsible, effective & culturally sensitive evangelism of youth, communicating & caring in ways that are relevant to this generation
Chief Officer(s):
Dave Brereton, National Director
Shirley Loewen, Office Manager

Youth in Care Canada (YICC)
PO Box 96, 223 Main St., Ottawa ON K1S 1C4
Tel: 613-327-4317
Toll-Free: 800-790-7074
info@youthincare.ca
www.youthincare.ca
www.facebook.com/youthincarecanada
twitter.com/youthincare
Previous Name: National Youth in Care Network
Overview: A medium-sized national charitable organization founded in 1985
Mission: To increase the awareness of the needs of youth in & from government care by researching the issues & presenting the results to youth, professionals & the general public through publications & speaking engagements; To provide emotional support to youth in or from government care & to guide the development of youth in care groups
Finances: *Funding Sources:* Government; Corporate; Foundation; Membership fees
Staff Member(s): 10

Canadian Associations / Youth in Care in Ontario

Membership: 70+ networks; *Fees:* $60 individual; $300 organization; $20 alumni (age 19-29); $30 alumni (age 30+); Free for youth 14-18; *Member Profile:* Any interested individuals or organizations may become members, but only those members from the child welfare system (ages 14-24) ghave voting privileges
Activities: Providing mentoring services; Connecting membership with scholarship & bursary opportunities; *Internships:* Yes; *Speaker Service:* Yes; *Rents Mailing List:* Yes; *Library:* Open to public
Chief Officer(s):
Mike McGuire, President
Awards:
• Ken Dryden Scholarship
Assists youth to complete an undergraduate university degree, who are currently or were previously in the care of the Canadian child welfare system

Youth in Care in Ontario
ON
youthcan@oacas.org
ontarioyouthcan.org
Also Known As: Ontario Youth Communication Advocacy Network (YouthCAN)
Overview: A medium-sized provincial organization overseen by Youth in Care Canada
Mission: To be the unifying voice for youth in care of Children's Aid Societies in the province of Ontario; To improve the quality of care for youth in Ontario's Child Welfare System
Membership: *Member Profile:* Youth in care of Children's Aid Societies across Ontario, and Children's Aid staff who work with them
Activities: Organize networking, skill building, education & leadership events; Annual conference; Provide advocacy & resources supporting youth in transition; Health coverage benefits for former youth in care
Chief Officer(s):
Patricia McMahon, Sec.-Treas.
Joyce Kehler, President
Awards:
• Clark Bursary Awards
Multi-year awards offered to young people pursuing post-secondary educational, employment or skills development programs that require financial assistance *Eligibility:* Upwards of 25 recipients per year; *Amount:* $3500 per year, for 4 years
Meetings/Conferences:
• YouthCAN's 12th Annual Conference, 2018
Description: So youth can enhance communication, teamwork & leadership skills; develop connections; expand educational & professional options & participate in speaker events, workshops & other activities

Youth Media Alliance (AMJ) / Alliance Médias Jeunesse (AET)
#106, 1400, boul René-Lévesque est, Montréal QC H2L 2M2
Tel: 514-597-5417
alliance@ymamj.org
www.ymamj.org
www.facebook.com/150380741707933
twitter.com/YMAMJ
www.youtube.com/alliancemediasjeunes
Previous Name: The Children's Broadcast Institute
Overview: A medium-sized national charitable organization founded in 1974
Mission: To promote the production & carriage of quality Canadian television programming for children; To ensure the development of critical viewing skills so that families are able to use media more effectively in the home; To promote awareness of the need to help young people make the most of their experience of television & other screen-based media
Finances: *Annual Operating Budget:* $250,000-$500,000; *Funding Sources:* Membership dues; Endowment Fund; project grants
Staff Member(s): 2
Membership: 100-499; *Fees:* $100 individual; $600-$3,000 organization; *Member Profile:* Among its members are parents, producers, educators, broadcasters, researchers, advertisers, writers & performers; *Committees:* Executive; Awards; Communications; Strategic Planning
Activities: Media Literacy Workshop Kit; professional development seminars; annual awards of excellence; research; publications; submissions & presentations; *Awareness Events:* Children's Television Festival (and Media); Prime Time Parent Workshop Kit; *Speaker Service:* Yes; *Library:* Open to public by appointment
Chief Officer(s):

Chantal Bowen, Executive Director
cbowen@ymamj.org
Awards:
• Awards of Excellence
For children's TV programs produced in Canada

Youth Now on Track Program (YNOT)
2300 Sheppard Ave. West, #LL17, Toronto ON M9M 3A2
Tel: 647-427-4989; *Fax:* 647-430-5814
info@ynotservices.org
www.ynotservices.org
Overview: A small local organization
Mission: To help youth who have had trouble with the law in the forms of prevention and intervention, in order to help these youth avoid such problems in the future
Membership: *Member Profile:* People ages 12 - 24 who have existing problems with the law
Activities: *Awareness Events:* Award & Fundraising Dinner (October); Family Day (December)

Youth Science Canada (YSC) / Sciences jeunesse Canada (SJC)
#213, 1550 Kingston Rd., Pickering ON L1V 1C3
Tel: 416-341-0040; *Fax:* 866-613-2542
Toll-Free: 866-341-0040
info@youthscience.ca
youthscience.ca
www.facebook.com/ysc.sjc
twitter.com/YouthScienceCan
www.youtube.com/user/YOUTHSCIENCECANADA
Previous Name: Youth Science Foundation Canada
Overview: A small national charitable organization founded in 1966
Mission: YSF assists Canadian youth to develop skills & knowledge for excellence in science & technology.
Finances: *Funding Sources:* Corporate; government agencies
Staff Member(s): 2
Membership: 100-499; *Fees:* $50 adult; $25 full-time post-secondary students; *Member Profile:* Members are those who support the development of youth science, technology, & innovation.
Activities: Provides programs to increase awareness & involvement of youth in science and technology; sets standards for scientific experimentation by young people; promotes the creation & support of science fairs; engages scientists, educators, parents, & leading public & private sector organizations in the development of a national science & technology network of Canadian youth; *Awareness Events:* Youth Science Month, March; Invent the Future, October; Canada-Wide Science Fair, May *Library:* Resource Centre; Not open to public
Chief Officer(s):
Reni Barlow, Executive Director
reni.barlow@youthscience.ca
Malcolm Butler, Chair
Mayur Gahdia, Treasurer
Jennifer Gerritsen, Secretary

Youth Science Foundation Canada *See* Youth Science Canada

Youth Singers of Calgary (YSC)
1371 Hastings Cres. SE, Calgary AB T2G 4C8
Tel: 403-234-9549; *Fax:* 403-234-9590
yscadmin@youthsingers.org
www.youthsingers.org
www.facebook.com/YouthSingersCalgary
twitter.com/YouthSingers
www.youtube.com/user/YouthSingersCalgary
Overview: A small local charitable organization founded in 1985
Mission: To develop & deliver a comprehensive choral program for young performers; To train students & young people in the performance of classical music, jazz, folk & contemporary music, musical theatre & dance
Member of: Alberta Choral Federation; Arts Touring Alliance; Canadian Choral Conductors Association
Affiliation(s): Calgary Chamber of Commerce
Finances: *Funding Sources:* Alberta Foundation for the Arts; Calgary Region Arts Foundation; corporate sponsors; individual dono
Staff Member(s): 9
Activities: *Internships:* Yes *Library:* Music Library
Chief Officer(s):
Shirley Penner, CEO & Artistic Director
shirl@youthsingers.org
Keith Heilman, Financial Administrator & Office Manager
keith@youthsingers.org

Youth Travel Foundation *Voir* Fondation Tourisme Jeunesse

Youth Without Shelter (YWS)
6 Warrendale Ct., Toronto ON M9V 1P9
Tel: 416-748-0110; *Fax:* 416-748-2169
communications@yws.on.ca
www.yws.on.ca/about-us/a-safe-haven
www.linkedin.com/company/2345421
www.facebook.com/ywstoronto
twitter.com/YWSToronto
www.youtube.com/user/YouthWithoutShelter
Overview: A small local charitable organization founded in 1986
Mission: Help youth aged 16 to 24 develop to their fullest potential by providing shelter and counselling.
Affiliation(s): Youth Empowerment & Support Services, Edmonton
12 volunteer(s)
Chief Officer(s):
Wendy Horton, Executive Director

YouthFlightCanada *See* Youth Flight Canada

YOUTHLINK
636 Kennedy Rd., Toronto ON M1K 2B3
Tel: 416-967-1773; *Fax:* 416-967-7515
info@youthlink.ca
www.youthlink.ca
www.facebook.com/YouthLinkTO
twitter.com/youthlinkto
Overview: A small local charitable organization founded in 1914
Mission: To support vulnerable youth in making positive life choices
Member of: Ontario Association of Children's Mental Health Centres
Finances: *Annual Operating Budget:* $1.5 Million-$3 Million; *Funding Sources:* Ministry of Community & Social Services; City of Toronto; Ontario Ministry of Health; United Way; Big Sister Thrift Shop; individuals; corporations
Staff Member(s): 60; 100 volunteer(s)
Membership: 250; *Fees:* $30 general; $10 youth; $100 friend; $250 patron; *Member Profile:* Volunteers come from a variety of backgrounds & disciplines including graduate students; former clients & community volunteers; *Committees:* Agency Operations; Social Advocacy; Client Services & Human Resources; Board
Activities: Individual, family & group counselling; school-based prevention programs & community education; case management & coordination of support services to young people with developmental disabilities & their families; residential & co-op programs; *Library:* Not open to public
Chief Officer(s):
Janice Hayes, Executive Director
Rick Dybvig, Director, Finance & Administration
Michael Tross, Director, Client Services
Denise Chan, Director, Human Resources
Awards:
• Big Sister Legacy Fund Bursary

North West Scarborough Youth Centre
3850 Finch Ave. East, Toronto ON M1T 3T6
Tel: 416-502-9293

Pathways to Education - Scarborough Village
#1, 3545 Kingston Rd., Toronto ON M1M 1R6
Tel: 647-351-0091; *Fax:* 647-351-0092

Yukon Aboriginal Sport Circle (YASC)
2166 - 2nd Ave., Whitehorse YT Y1A 4P1
Tel: 867-668-2840; *Fax:* 867-668-6577
aboriginalsport@yasc.ca
www.yasc.ca
www.facebook.com/343599029002109
twitter.com/yukonasc
Merged from: Yukon Aboriginal Sport Development Office Interim Steering Committee & YIGSC
Overview: A medium-sized provincial organization founded in 1990
Mission: The Yukon Aboriginal Sport Circle is a non-profit society dedicated to the advancement of Aboriginal recreation and sport in the Yukon through a variety of programs to increase participation and skill levels and to increase awareness.
Member of: Sport Yukon
Membership: *Member Profile:* The Yukon Aboriginal Sport Circle is a non-profit society dedicated to the advancement of Aboriginal recreation and sport in the Yukon.
Chief Officer(s):
Gael Marchand, Executive Director
ed@yasc.ca

Justin Ferbey, President

Yukon Aboriginal Women's Council
#202, 307 Jarvis St., Whitehorse YT Y1A 2H3
Tel: 867-667-6162; Fax: 867-668-7539
yawc@northwestel.net
Overview: A small provincial organization founded in 1983 overseen by Native Women's Association of Canada
Mission: To create equal opportunities for Aboriginal women by implementing programs aimed to improving their quality of life
Staff Member(s): 2

Yukon Agricultural Association
#203, 302 Steele St., Whitehorse YT Y1A 2E5
Tel: 867-668-6864; Fax: 867-393-3566
admin@yukonag.ca
www.yukonag.ca
Overview: A small provincial organization founded in 1974
Mission: To provide resources and opportunities to agricultural producers in the Yukon.
Staff Member(s): 2
Membership: Fees: $10; Member Profile: Agricultural producers in the Yukon
Chief Officer(s):
Mike Blumenschein, President
Bev Buckway, Executive Director

Yukon Amateur Boxing Association
YT
Overview: A small provincial organization overseen by Canadian Amateur Boxing Association
Mission: To govern the sport of boxing in the Yukon Territory.
Member of: Canadian Amateur Boxing Association

Yukon Amateur Hockey Association See Hockey Yukon

Yukon Amateur Radio Association (YARA)
PO Box 2703, Whitehorse YT Y1A 2C6
www.yara.ca
Overview: A small provincial organization founded in 1976
Mission: To represent all amateur radio operators in Yukon; To promote the exciting hobby of amateur radio; To be of service to the public in case of emergency
Member of: Radio Amateurs of Canada
Finances: Annual Operating Budget: Less than $50,000; Funding Sources: Yukon Government Emergency Measures; Yukon Lotteries
20 volunteer(s)
Membership: 25; Fees: $50; Member Profile: Amateur radio certificate; Committees: Nominating
Activities: Sport Yukon Klondike International Road Relay; Chilkat Bicycle Relay
Chief Officer(s):
Bob Melanson, President
Awards:
• Amateur of the Year

Yukon Amateur Speed Skating Association
4061 - 4th Ave., Whitehorse YT Y1A 1H1
Tel: 867-660-5347
www.shorttrack06.com
Also Known As: Whitehorse Rapids Speed Skating Club
Overview: A small provincial organization

Yukon Art Society (YAS)
#15, 305 Main St., Whitehorse YT Y1A 2B4
Tel: 867-667-4080; Fax: 867-667-4099
reception@artsunderground.ca
www.artsunderground.ca
www.facebook.com/ArtsUnderground
Also Known As: Arts Underground
Overview: A small local organization founded in 1970
Mission: To promote Yukon artists through shows & workshops
Finances: Annual Operating Budget: $50,000-$100,000; Funding Sources: Provincial government
Staff Member(s): 2; 25 volunteer(s)
Membership: 140 individual; Fees: $45 institutional; $15 student; $25 individual; $35 family; Member Profile: All walks of life from ages 12-87; Committees: Road Show; Auction
Activities: Arts in the Park Events; Rendezvous Show; Points of View Show; Artist of the Month Shows; workshops; Internships: Yes; Rents Mailing List: Yes; Library: Yukon Art Society Library; Open to public
Chief Officer(s):
Cass Collins, Contact, Exhibitions & Programs
programs@artsunderground.ca
Leslie Leong, Contact, Administration
admin@artsunderground.ca

Yukon Arts Centre (YAC)
PO Box 16, Whitehorse YT Y1A 5X9
Tel: 867-667-8575; Fax: 867-393-6300
www.yukonartscentre.com
www.facebook.com/YukonArtsCentre
twitter.com/YukonArtsCentre
Overview: A medium-sized provincial organization
Mission: To promote, stimulate & nurture the Arts throughout the Yukon; to create educational & developmental programmes, to maintain & manage the Yukon Arts Centre to the benefit of Yukon artists & audiences
Finances: Funding Sources: Provincial government
Chief Officer(s):
Patrick Michael, Chair
Deborah Bartlette, Vice-Chair

Yukon Association for Children & Adults with Learning Disabilities See Learning Disabilities Association of Yukon Territory

Yukon Association for Community Living (YACL)
#7, 4230 - 4 Ave., Whitehorse YT Y1A 1K1
Tel: 867-667-4606; Fax: 867-667-4606
yaclwhse@northwestel.net
www.ycommunityliving.com
www.facebook.com/YCommunityLiving
Overview: A medium-sized provincial organization founded in 1965 overseen by Canadian Association for Community Living
Mission: To promote the welfare of people with intellectual disabilities & their families; To ensure that every person in the Yukon has access to supports necessary to live with dignity & to participate fully in the community of his/her choice
Member of: Canadian Association for Community Living
Finances: Funding Sources: Federal, territorial & municipal government; Fundraising; National CACL; Yukon lotteries; United Way
Activities: Library: YACL Resource Library
Awards:
• Nicki Henry Award

Yukon Badminton Association
4061 - 4th Ave., Whitehorse YT Y1A 1H1
Tel: 867-393-4343
Overview: A small provincial organization overseen by Badminton Canada
Chief Officer(s):
Michael Muller, President, 867-393-4343
muller@northwestel.net

Yukon Broomball Association (YBA)
4061 - 4th Ave., Whitehorse YT Y1A 1H1
www.yukonbroomball.net
Previous Name: Yukon Broomball League
Overview: A medium-sized provincial organization overseen by Ballon sur glace Broomball Canada
Mission: To promote & facilitate Broomball in the Yukon Territory.
Member of: Ballon sur glace Broomball Canada; Sport Yukon
Membership: 1-99
Chief Officer(s):
Sheena Laluk, President

Yukon Broomball League See Yukon Broomball Association

Yukon Canoe & Kayak Club
YT
current@yckc.ca
www.yckc.ca
Overview: A small provincial organization founded in 1961
Membership: Fees: $20 adult; $10 child; $40 family
Activities: White water rafting; kayak polo
Chief Officer(s):
John Quinsey, President

Yukon Chamber of Commerce (YCC)
#205, 2237 - 2 Ave., Whitehorse YT Y1A 0K7
Tel: 867-667-2000; Fax: 867-667-2001
office@yukonchamber.com
www.yukonchamber.com
www.facebook.com/YukonChamberOfCommerceYukonCanada
Overview: A medium-sized provincial charitable organization founded in 1985
Mission: To create a climate conducive to a strong private sector economy by providing leadership & representation
Member of: Canadian Chamber of Commerce
Finances: Funding Sources: Territorial government; self-generated
Staff Member(s): 3
Membership: 163; Fees: Schedule available; Member Profile: Business sector & associations
Activities: Library: Canada Yukon Business Service Centre; Open to public
Chief Officer(s):
Peter Turner, President

Yukon Chamber of Mines (YCM)
3151B - 3rd Ave., Whitehorse YT Y1A 1G1
Tel: 867-667-2090; Fax: 867-668-7127
info@yukonminers.ca
www.yukonminers.ca
Overview: A medium-sized provincial organization founded in 1959
Mission: To provides services to members, with a focus on the mining industry; To promote responsible exploration & sustainable mining practices
Affiliation(s): Mining Association of Canada
Finances: Funding Sources: Membership fees; Government funding
Membership: 350; Fees: $50 individual; $120-$6000 other
Activities: Library: Open to public
Chief Officer(s):
Mark Ayranto, President
Hugh Kitchen, Vice President
Meetings/Conferences:
• 2018 Yukon Geoscience Forum & Trade Show, 2018
Scope: Provincial
Description: A conference for the mining & exploration industry, featuring technical events, short courses, & exhibits

Yukon Child Care Association (YCCA)
PO Box 31103, Whitehorse YT Y1A 5P7
Tel: 867-668-5130
ycca1974@gmail.com
www.yukonchildcareassociation.org
www.facebook.com/YukonCCA
twitter.com/YukonChildCare
Overview: A medium-sized provincial organization founded in 1974
Mission: To develop a high quality, universally accessible, & affordable child care system in the Yukon; To represent caregivers & families
Affiliation(s): Canadian Child Care Federation
Activities: Arranging inspections & enforcing regulations; Advocating on behalf of child care providers in the Yukon; Liaising with the territorial government; Encouraging parental involvement; Hosting child care conferences; Educating the public about child care
Chief Officer(s):
Cyndi Desharnais, President

Yukon Church Heritage Society (YCHS)
PO Box 5956, Whitehorse YT Y1A 5L7
Tel: 867-668-2555; Fax: 867-667-6258
logchurch@klondiker.com
www.oldlogchurchmuseum.ca
www.facebook.com/oldlogchurchmuseum
Also Known As: Old Log Church Museum
Overview: A small local charitable organization founded in 1982
Mission: To promote & preserve church history in the Yukon
Member of: Yukon Historical & Museums Association
Affiliation(s): Canadian Museums Association
Finances: Annual Operating Budget: $50,000-$100,000
Staff Member(s): 1; 8 volunteer(s)
Membership: 25; Fees: $15 student/senior; $20 adult; $30 family
Activities: Operates Old Log Church Museum; Daily tours & interpretive programs; Library: Yukon Church Heritage Society Archives; Open to public by appointment
Chief Officer(s):
Taryn Parker, Director/Curator
Linda Thistle, President

Yukon Conservation Society (YCS)
302 Hawkins St., Whitehorse YT Y1A 1X6
Tel: 867-668-5678; Fax: 867-668-6637
ycs@ycs.yk.ca
www.yukonconservation.org
Overview: A small provincial charitable organization founded in 1968
Mission: To pursue ecosystem well-being throughout the Yukon & beyond
Finances: Funding Sources: Membership fees; Donations
Membership: 400; Fees: $10 students; $25 individuals & corporate or business memberships; $40 families; Committees: Personnel Standing Committee; Executive Standing Committee;

Finance Standing Committee; Membership / Fundraising Standing Committee; Energy & Climate Change Working Group; Forestry Working Group; Habitat & Wildlife Working Group; Mining Working Group; Whitehorse Area Issues Working Group
Activities: Influencing environmental policy in the North; Providing environmental educational programs; Raising environmental awareness & the realization that human well-being is dependent upon fully functioning healthy ecosystems; *Library:* Yukon Conservation Society Library; Open to public by appointment
Chief Officer(s):
Karen Baltgailis, Executive Director
Georgia Greetham, Coordinator, Office
Sue Kemmett, Coordinator, Forestry
Anne Middler, Coordinator, Energy
Lewis Rifkind, Coordinator, Mining
Meetings/Conferences:
• Yukon Conservation Society 2018 Annual General Meeting, 2018, YT
Scope: Provincial
Publications:
• Walk Softly
Type: Newsletter; *Frequency:* Quarterly; *Editor:* Georgia Greetham; *Price:* Free with Yukon Conservation Society membership; $25 non-members
Profile: Information about current & upcoming issues & events

Yukon Contractors Association (YCA)
103A-103 Platinum Rd., Whitehorse YT Y1A 5M3
Tel: 867-335-0374; *Fax:* 867-668-3985
Overview: A medium-sized provincial organization

Yukon Council of Archives (YCA)
PO Box 31089, Whitehorse YT Y1A 5P7
Fax: 867-393-6253
yukoncnclarch@gmail.com
www.yukoncouncilofarchives.ca
Overview: A small provincial organization founded in 1986 overseen by Canadian Council of Archives
Mission: To facilitate the development of the archival system in the Yukon; To make recommendations about the system's operation & financing; To develop & facilitate implementation & management of programs to assist the archival community; To communicate archival needs & concerns to decision-makers, researchers, & the general public
Membership: *Fees:* Schedule available; *Member Profile:* Individuals & institutions engaged or interested in archival practice; *Committees:* Education; Membership
Chief Officer(s):
Derek Cooke, President
Publications:
• Yukon Council of Archives Newsletter
Type: Newsletter; *Frequency:* 3 pa
Profile: News & updates for members

Yukon Council on Aging (YCOA)
4061B - 4th Ave., Whitehorse YT Y1A 1H1
Tel: 867-668-3383
Toll-Free: 866-582-9707
ycoa@yknet.yk.ca
www.yukon-seniors-and-elders.org
Also Known As: Seniors Information Centre
Overview: A small provincial organization founded in 1977
Mission: The YCOA is a volunteer organization of Yukon seniors administered by a Board of Directors elected from its membership
Membership: *Fees:* $10; *Member Profile:* 55 years of age & older
Activities: Information workshops; home & yard maintenance program; rural yukon pension workshops; *Library:* Open to public
Chief Officer(s):
Connie Dublenko, President

Yukon Curling Association (YCA)
4061 - 4th Ave., Whitehorse YT Y1A 1H1
Tel: 867-668-7121; *Fax:* 867-667-4237
www.yukoncurling.ca
Overview: A small provincial organization founded in 1974 overseen by Canadian Curling Association
Affiliation(s): Watson Lake Curling Club; Mayo Curling Club
10 volunteer(s)
Membership: 1,000; *Member Profile:* Seniors; masters; adults; juniors; youth; little rockers
Chief Officer(s):
Laura Eby, Executive Director
executivedirector@yukoncurling.ca

Yukon Denturist Association
#1, 106 Main St., Whitehorse YT Y1A 2A7
Tel: 867-668-6818; *Fax:* 867-668-6811
Overview: A small provincial organization overseen by Denturist Association of Canada

Yukon Employees Union (YEU) / Syndicat des employés du Yukon
#201, 2285 - 2nd Ave., Whitehorse YT Y1A 1C9
Tel: 867-667-2331; *Fax:* 867-667-6521
Toll-Free: 888-938-2331
contact@yeu.ca
www.yeu.ca
www.facebook.com/YukonEmployeesUnion
twitter.com/YEUPSAC
www.youtube.com/user/YukonEmployeesUnion
Overview: A medium-sized provincial organization founded in 1965 overseen by Public Service Alliance of Canada
Mission: To obtain for all members the best possible standards of wages, salaries & other conditions of employment; To protect the interests, rights & privileges of all such employees
Staff Member(s): 7
Membership: 4,000 + 19 locals; *Committees:* Women's; Health & Safety; Visible Minority; Aboriginal Peoples; Pride; Access
Activities: *Library:*
Chief Officer(s):
Steve Geick, President
Laura Hureau, Executive Director

Yukon Family Services Association *See* Many Rivers Counselling & Support Services

Yukon Federation of Labour (YFL) / Fédération du travail du Yukon
#102, 106 Strickland St., Whitehorse YT Y1A 2J5
Tel: 867-456-8250; *Fax:* 867-668-3426
yfl@yukonfed.com
www.yukonfed.com
www.facebook.com/yukonworkers
twitter.com/yukonworkers
Overview: A medium-sized provincial organization founded in 1980 overseen by Canadian Labour Congress
Mission: To advocate on behalf of its memebers
Chief Officer(s):
Vikki Quocksister, President

Yukon Film Society (YFS)
212 Lambert St., Whitehorse YT Y1A 1Z4
Tel: 867-393-3456; *Fax:* 867-393-3456
yfs@yukonfilmsociety.com
www.yukonfilmsociety.com
Overview: A small provincial organization founded in 1984
Mission: To present independent and alternative media art works to Yukon audiences and to support the production and distribution of works by Yukon media artists.
Finances: *Funding Sources:* membership fees; rental fees; screenings
Staff Member(s): 2; 9 volunteer(s)
Membership: *Fees:* $30 production; $5 exhibition
Activities: Available Light Film Festival; Film screenings
Chief Officer(s):
Noel Sinclair, President
Zoë Toupin, General Manager

Yukon First Nations Culture & Tourism Association (YFNCT)
1 - 1109 Front St., Whitehorse YT Y1A 5G4
Tel: 867-667-7698
info@yfnct.ca
www.yfnct.ca
www.facebook.com/yfnct
Overview: A small provincial organization
Chief Officer(s):
Charlene Alexander, Executive Director
ed@yfnct.ca

Yukon Fish & Game Association (YFGA)
509 Strickland St., Whitehorse YT Y1A 2K5
Tel: 867-667-4263; *Fax:* 867-667-4273
yfga@klondiker.com
www.yukonfga.ca
www.facebook.com/yukonfga
www.flickr.com/photos/74103579@N03/
Overview: A medium-sized provincial organization founded in 1945 overseen by Canadian Wildlife Federation
Mission: To ensure the long-term management of fish, wildlife, & outdoor recreational resources in the Yukon; To improve wildlife habitat
Finances: *Funding Sources:* Membership fees; Donations; Sponsorships
Staff Member(s): 2
Membership: *Fees:* $30 individual; $35 family; $500 corporate & lifetime
Activities: Providing hunter education & ethics development; Promoting proper catch & release; Meeting with government regarding fish & wildlife issues; Promoting sportsmanship; Managing the Whitehorse Rapids fish ladder & tourist facility; Overseeing the operation of a salmon hatchery
Chief Officer(s):
Gord Zealand, Executive Director
yfgaexdir@klondiker.com
Publications:
• Outdoor Edge [a publication of the Yukon Fish & Game Association]
Type: Newsletter; *Frequency:* Bimonthly; *Accepts Advertising*;
Price: Free with Yukon Fish & Game Association membership
Profile: A publication sent to more than 450 households in the Yukon & throughout Canada

Yukon Foundation
PO Box 31622, Whitehorse YT Y1A 6L2
Tel: 867-393-2454
yukonfoundation@klondiker.com
www.yukonfoundation.com
Overview: A small provincial organization founded in 1980
Mission: To promote educational advancement and scientific or medical research for the enhancement of human knowledge; provide support intended to contribute to the mental, cultural and physical well-being of residents of Yukon; and promote the cultural heritage of Yukon.
Chief Officer(s):
Sophie Partridge, Executive Director

Yukon Freestyle Ski Association
4061 - 4th Ave., Whitehorse YT Y1A 1H1
Tel: 867-393-3369
www.yfsa.ca
www.facebook.com/239011292821887
Overview: A small provincial organization overseen by Canadian Freestyle Ski Association
Mission: To promote & facilitate freestyle skiing in the Yukon Territory.
Member of: Canadian Freestyle Ski Association; Sport Yukon

Yukon Golf Association
4061 - 4th Ave., Whitehorse YT Y1A 1H1
Tel: 867-633-3364; *Fax:* 867-393-3051
sportyukon.com/member/yukon-golf-association
Overview: A small provincial organization
Mission: The Yukon Golf Association is an organization that enhances opportunities for all Yukonners in their pursuit of excellence & in their enjoyment of participation.
Chief Officer(s):
Gordon Zealand, President
zealandg@northwestel.net

Yukon Green Party
PO Box 31603, Whitehorse YT Y1A 3R3
Tel: 867-633-3392; *Fax:* 867-633-3392
Other Communication: Courriel: partivertduyukon@gmail.com
yukongreenparty@gmail.com
www.yukongreenparty.ca
Overview: A small provincial organization overseen by Green Party of Canada
Membership: *Fees:* $20; $10 students/seniors
Chief Officer(s):
Frank de Jong, Party Leader

Yukon Gymnastics Association
4061 - 4th Ave., Whitehorse YT Y1A 1H1
Tel: 867-456-7896; *Fax:* 867-668-6922
yukongymnastic.com
Overview: A small provincial organization
Member of: Canadian Gymnastics Federation
Chief Officer(s):
Shannon Albisser, President
shannonalbisser@yahoo.ca

Yukon Historical & Museums Association (YHMA)
3126 - 3 Ave., Whitehorse YT Y1A 1E7
Tel: 867-667-4704; *Fax:* 867-667-4506
info@heritageyukon.ca

heritageyukon.ca
twitter.com/Yukonheritage
Overview: A medium-sized provincial charitable organization founded in 1977
Mission: To preserve & foster an appreciation of the Yukon's history & culture; to act as forum for other museum & heritage organizations in the region
Member of: Canadian Museums Association
Affiliation(s): Heritage Canada; BC Heritage Trust
Finances: *Funding Sources:* Membership fees; territorial & municipal governments
Membership: 44 individual + 28 institutional + 15 commercial; *Fees:* Schedule available; *Member Profile:* Interest in preserving & promoting heritage; *Committees:* Heritage Training Fund; Joint Marketing; Awards; Advocacy; Membership; Newsletter; Conference
Activities: Yukon Lifestyles program which involves oral history, photography & building documentation as ways of preserving & recording Yukon buildings; Historical Maps series; Heritage Lecture series; Heritage awards which honour contributions to the preservation of the Yukon heritage by individuals, organizations & businesses; *Library:* YHMA Reference Centre; by appointment
Chief Officer(s):
Nancy Oakley, Executive Director
Awards:
• YHMA Heritage Award

Yukon Horse & Rider Association (YHRA)
PO Box 31482, Whitehorse YT Y1A 6K8
yukonhorseandriderassociation@gmail.com
yukonhorseandrider.wordpress.com
www.facebook.com/186825158005753
Overview: A medium-sized provincial organization
Mission: The YHRA is dedicated to the sport of horseback riding in the Yukon Territory, Canada. The Association aims to encourage good horsemanship & help promote interest in the light horse industry.
Membership: 100+; *Fees:* $40 senior; $30 junior; $65 family; *Committees:* Events; Development
Meetings/Conferences:
• Yukon Horse & Rider Association AGM 2018, 2018
Scope: Provincial
Publications:
• Yukon Horse & Rider Association Newsletter
Type: Newsletter
Profile: News & updates for members

Yukon Indian Hockey Association (YIHA)
PO Box 31769, Whitehorse YT Y1A 6L3
Tel: 867-456-7294; *Fax:* 867-456-7290
yihahockey@gmail.com
www.yiha.ca
Overview: A medium-sized provincial organization founded in 1984
Mission: To establish a hockey league in the Yukon to enable Native athletes to compete with other Canadian Provinces & Territories in the sport.
Chief Officer(s):
Jeanie Dendys, President

Yukon Kennel Club
Whitehorse YT
Tel: 867-668-6960
YukonKennelClub@gmail.com
www.yukonkennelclub.com
www.facebook.com/YukonKennelClub
Overview: A small provincial organization
Member of: Canadian Kennel Club
Membership: *Fees:* $25

Yukon Law Foundation
PO Box 31789, Whitehorse YT Y1A 6L3
Tel: 867-667-7500; *Fax:* 867-393-3904
info@yukonlawfoundation.com
www.yukonlawfoundation.com
Overview: A small local organization founded in 1985
Mission: To maintain & manage a fund accumulated primarily from the interest on lawyers' trust accounts
Member of: Association of Canadian Law Foundation
Finances: *Annual Operating Budget:* $100,000-$250,000
Staff Member(s): 1; 6 volunteer(s)
Activities: *Library:* Law Library; Open to public
Chief Officer(s):
Deana Lemke, Executive Director
execdir@yukonlawfoundation.com

Yukon Learn Society (YLS)
2158 Second Ave., #B, Whitehorse YT Y1A 5N9
Tel: 867-668-6280; *Fax:* 867-633-4576
Toll-Free: 888-668-6280
community@yukonlearn.com
www.yukonlearn.com
www.facebook.com/YukonLearnSociety
Overview: A small provincial charitable organization founded in 1983
Mission: To provide adult literacy services; To promote literacy awareness; To be the voice representing & uniting literacy in the Yukon
Member of: Movement for Canadian Literacy
Finances: *Annual Operating Budget:* $100,000-$250,000
Staff Member(s): 4; 80 volunteer(s)
Membership: 128
Activities: *Awareness Events:* PGI Golf Tournament, June; International Literacy Day, Sept.; Yukon Literacy Week, Oct.; Family Literacy Day, Jan. *Library:* Yukon Learn Library; Open to public
Chief Officer(s):
Debbie Parent, Executive Director
Awards:
• Tutor of the Year
• Learner of the Year
• Volunteer of the Year

Yukon Liberal Party
PO Box 183, 108 Elliott St., Whitehorse YT Y1A 2C6
info@ylp.ca
www.ylp.ca
www.facebook.com/yukonliberals
twitter.com/YukonLiberal
Overview: A small provincial organization overseen by The Liberal Party of Canada
Chief Officer(s):
Sandy Silver, Leader
Devin Bailey, President
president@ylp.ca

Yukon Medical Association
5 Hospital Rd., Whitehorse YT Y1A 3H7
Tel: 867-393-8749
office@yukondoctors.ca
www.yukondoctors.ca
Overview: A medium-sized provincial organization overseen by Canadian Medical Association
Mission: A voluntary association of Yukon doctors; advocates on behalf of members; promotes professionalism in medical practice & accessibility to quality health care for Yukoners
Affiliation(s): British Columbia Medical Association
Chief Officer(s):
Ken Quong, President
yma@yukondoctors.ca

Yukon Mine Training Association (YMTA)
2099 - 2nd Ave., Whitehorse YT Y1A 1B5
Tel: 867-633-6463
Toll-Free: 877-986-4637
info@ymta.org
ymta.org
Overview: A medium-sized provincial organization
Mission: To maximize employment opportunities emerging from the growth of the mining and related resource sectors in the North for First Nations and other Yukoners.
Chief Officer(s):
P. Jerry Asp, Chair
Sascha Weber, Executive Director

Yukon Order of Pioneers (YOOP)
PO Box 31693, Whitehorse YT Y1A 6L3
Tel: 867-993-6441
yukon-seniors-and-elders.org/yukonorder/yukonorder.home.htm
Overview: A small provincial organization
Mission: To protect its members, & to unite those members in the strong tie of Brotherhood & to preserve the names of all Yukon Pioneers on its rolls & to collect & preserve the literature & incidents of the Order's history
Membership: *Member Profile:* Men over 20 years old in the Yukon Territory
Chief Officer(s):
Mark Castellarin, President

Yukon Orienteering Association (YOA)
4061 - 4th Ave., Whitehorse YT Y1A 1H1
Tel: 867-335-2287
info@yukonorienteering.ca
www.yukonorienteering.ca
Overview: A small provincial organization
Mission: To provide both friendly & quality competitive orienteering opportunities in Yukon, & encourage the development & growth of the sport of orienteering where possible
Member of: Canadian Orienteering Federation
Membership: *Fees:* $5; *Member Profile:* Male & female, 0-70 yrs old, enjoys outdoors
Activities: Kids Running Wild; Yukon Orienteering Team; Yukon Championships; clinics
Chief Officer(s):
Afan Jones, President
Bob Sagar, Vice-President
Publications:
• Legends [a publication of the Yukon Orienteering Association]
Type: Newsletter

Yukon Outdoors Club (YOC)
4061 - 4th Ave., Whitehorse YT Y1A 1H1
yukonoutdoorsclub@gmail.com
www.yukonoutdoorsclub.ca
Overview: A small provincial organization founded in 1980
Mission: To co-ordinate trips that promote the enjoyment of the outdoors.
Membership: *Fees:* $10 single; $15 family

Yukon Outfitters' Association (YOA)
#6, 103 Main St., Whitehorse YT Y1A 2C7
Tel: 867-668-4118; *Fax:* 867-668-4120
info@yukonoutfitters.net
www.yukonoutfitters.net
Overview: A small provincial organization
Mission: To conserve, maintain & enhance the Yukon wildlife & their habitat on a sustained basis for the benefit & pleasure of all Yukoners including hunters
Affiliation(s): Safari Club International; Foundation for North American Wild Sheep
Finances: *Annual Operating Budget:* $50,000-$100,000
Staff Member(s): 1; 18 volunteer(s)
Membership: 17; *Member Profile:* Yukon outfitters & associates
Activities: *Speaker Service:* Yes

Yukon Party
PO Box 2703 A-11, Whitehorse YT Y1A 2C6
Tel: 867-393-7104
www.yukonpartycaucus.ca
www.facebook.com/yukonparty
Overview: A small provincial organization founded in 2011
Finances: *Funding Sources:* Donations
Membership: *Fees:* $10
Chief Officer(s):
Stacey Hassard, Interim Party Leader

Yukon Prospectors' Association (YPA)
3151B - 3rd Ave., Whitehorse YT Y1A 1G1
www.yukonprospectors.ca
Overview: A small provincial organization
Mission: To promote and advocate for the mining industry and miners of the Yukon Territory
Chief Officer(s):
Mike Power, President

Yukon Public Legal Education Association (YPLEA)
Tutshi Building, #102, 2131 Second Ave., Whitehorse YT Y1A 1C3
Tel: 867-668-5297
Toll-Free: 866-667-4305
www.yplea.com
Overview: A medium-sized provincial organization founded in 1984
Mission: To provide free legal information to the public & promote greater accessibility to the legal system
Finances: *Annual Operating Budget:* $50,000-$100,000
Staff Member(s): 2; 7 volunteer(s)
Membership: *Fees:* $10
Activities: Operates Yukon Law Line; *Speaker Service:* Yes; Library
Chief Officer(s):
Carmen Gustafson, Executive Director
ypleayt@gmail.com

Yukon RCMP Veteran's Association
PO Box 314 63, Whitehorse YT Y1A 6K8
www.yukonrcmpvets.ca

Overview: A medium-sized provincial organization
Mission: To represent members' interests on pension and benefits issues, and provide a formal communications link to the RCMP
Chief Officer(s):
Helmer Hermanson, President

Yukon Real Estate Association
3 Bonanza Pl., Whitehorse YT Y1A 5M4
Tel: 867-633-5565; *Fax:* 867-667-7005
admin@yrea.ca
www.yrea.ca
Overview: A small provincial organization founded in 1977
Mission: To promote interest in marketing of real estate in all its aspects & to advance & improve relations of members of society with public
Member of: The Canadian Real Estate Association
Membership: 5 corporate

Yukon Registered Nurses Association (YRNA)
#204, 4133 - 4th Ave., Whitehorse YT Y1A 1H8
Tel: 867-667-4062; *Fax:* 867-668-5123
admin@yrna.ca
www.yrna.ca
www.facebook.com/190306321094679
twitter.com/YrnaExec
Overview: A medium-sized provincial licensing organization founded in 1993 overseen by Canadian Nurses Association
Mission: To establish & promote standards of practice for registered nurses; To regulate nursing practice & to advance professional excellence; To speak out on health care issues; To advocate for the development of healthy public policy in the interest of the public
Finances: *Funding Sources:* Membership fees
Staff Member(s): 2
Membership: *Fees:* $900 practising; $112 non-practising; $189 associate plus; $300 special practice; $52.50 student; *Committees:* Appeal; Audit; Complaints; Discipline; Education Approval; Education Fund Management; Finance; Nominations; Nurse Practitioner Advisory; Nurse Practitioner; Nursing Practice; Registration Advisory; Registration Appeal
Activities: *Library:* Open to public
Chief Officer(s):
Christina Sim, President
Mieke Leonard, Executive Director
exec.director@yrna.ca
Carrie Huffman, Registrar
registrar@yrna.ca
Erika Serviss-Low, Coordinator, Communications
Publications:
• Nurses' Notes [a publication of the Yukon Registered Nurses Association]
Type: Newsletter; *Frequency:* Quarterly

Yukon River Marathon Paddlers Association
4061 - 4th Ave., Whitehorse YT Y1A 1H1
Tel: 867-333-5628; *Fax:* 888-959-3846
info@yukonriverquest.com
www.yukonriverquest.com
www.facebook.com/186123281403836
Also Known As: Yukon River Quest
Overview: A small provincial organization
Mission: To govern the Yukon River Quest canoe & kayak race.
Membership: *Fees:* $20 regular; $100 lifetime
Activities: *Awareness Events:* Yukon River Quest, June
Chief Officer(s):
Harry Kern, President

Yukon Schools' Athletic Association (YSAA)
Sport Yukon Bldg., 4061 - 4th Ave., Whitehorse YT Y1A 1H1
Tel: 867-332-7081; *Fax:* 867-667-4237
ysaa.yukonschools.ca
Overview: A medium-sized provincial organization founded in 1996 overseen by School Sport Canada
Mission: To encourage participation of students in inter school athletics, emphasize interschool athletics as an integral part of the total educational process & plan, promote, supervise & administer a program of inter-school athletics in all approved competitions.
Member of: School Sport Canada
Chief Officer(s):
Jeff Cressman, President
jeff.cressman@yesnet.yk.ca
Vickie Dawe, Vice-President
vickie.dawe@yesnet.yk.ca
Ron Billingsley, Secretary/Treasurer
ron.billingsley@yesnet.yk.ca

Awards:
• Ben Sheardown Award for Coaching Excellence

Yukon Schutzhund Association
Whitehorse YT
yukon.schutzhund@gmail.com
www.facebook.com/yukonysa
Overview: A small provincial organization founded in 2002
Mission: To promote dog training for the sport of Schutzhund in the Yukon Territory.
Member of: German Shepherd Schutzhund Club of Canada

Yukon Shooting Federation
4061 - 4th Ave., Whitehorse YT Y1A 1H1
Tel: 867-667-6728
sportyukon.com/member/yukon-shooting-federation
Overview: A small provincial organization
Mission: To promote & facilitate air rifle & air pistol shooting in the Yukon Territory.
Member of: Sport Yukon
Activities: Junior Shooters Program
Chief Officer(s):
Lyle Thompson, President

Yukon Ski Division *See* Cross Country Yukon

Yukon Soccer Association
4061 - 4th Ave., Whitehorse YT Y1A 1H1
Tel: 867-633-4625; *Fax:* 867-667-4237
yukonsoccer@sportyukon.com
www.yukonsoccer.yk.ca
Overview: A small provincial organization overseen by Canadian Soccer Association
Mission: The Yukon Soccer Association is the sport governing body for the sport of soccer in the Yukon Territory. It is a volunteer based organization that coordinates & administers various programs devoted to the promotion & development of soccer.
Member of: Canadian Soccer Association
Chief Officer(s):
Cali Battersby, Sport Administrator
John MacPhail, Technical Director
jmac@sportyukon.com

Yukon Sourdough Rendezvous Society
4230 4th Ave., Whitehorse YT Y1A 1G7
Tel: 867-667-2148; *Fax:* 867-668-6755
info@yukonrendezvous.com
www.yukonrendezvous.com
www.facebook.com/YukonSourdoughRendezvous
twitter.com/yukonrendezvous
www.instagram.com/yukonrendezvous
Overview: A small local organization
Mission: Society that organizes the Yukon Sourdough Rendezvous festival
Chief Officer(s):
Dave Blottner, Executive Director

Yukon Special Olympics *See* Special Olympics Yukon

Yukon Speech-Language Pathology & Audiology Association (YSLPAA)
c/o 80 Falcon Dr., Whitehorse YT Y1A 6C7
yslpaa@gmail.com
Overview: A small provincial organization
Mission: Supports and represents the professional needs of speech-language pathologists, audiologists and supportive personnel in the Yukon.
Chief Officer(s):
Karen Rach, President

Yukon Teachers' Association (YTA) / Association des enseignantes et des enseignants du Yukon
2064 - 2 Ave., Whitehorse YT Y1A 1A9
Tel: 867-668-6777; *Fax:* 867-667-4324
Toll-Free: 866-668-2097
admin@yta.yk.ca
www.yta.yk.ca
Overview: A medium-sized provincial organization founded in 1955 overseen by Canadian Teachers' Federation
Mission: To promote & support public education; To represent the professional & economic needs of Yukon educators
Finances: *Funding Sources:* Fees & funding from employers
Staff Member(s): 6
Membership: *Member Profile:* Teachers; Assistants; Tutors; Native language instructors; *Committees:* Ethics
Chief Officer(s):

Jill Mason, President
pres@yta.yk.ca
Douglas Rody, General Secretary
gensec@yta.yk.ca
Awards:
• Mary Gartside Scholarship
• Elijah Smith Scholarship
• Doris Stanbraten Scholarship
• YTA 50th Anniversary Bursary
• Yukon Retired Teachers Alumni Scholarship
• The Alice Elston Award
Eligibility: Any person whose contributions the association or education warrants special recognition *Deadline:* February
Publications:
• YTA [Yukon Teachers' Association] Benefit Guide
Type: Guide
• YTA [Yukon Teachers' Association] Handbook
Type: Handbook
• YTA [Yukon Teachers' Association] Notes
Type: Newsletter; *Frequency:* Monthly

Yukon Territory Environmental Network
302 Hawkins St., Whitehorse YT Y1A 1X6
Tel: 867-668-5678; *Fax:* 867-668-6637
yukonenvironet@gmail.com
Previous Name: Nornet-Yukon
Overview: A small provincial organization overseen by Canadian Environmental Network
Chief Officer(s):
Susan Davis, Coordinator

Yukon Tourism Education Council (YTEC)
#C, 202 Strickland St., Whitehorse YT Y1A 2J8
Tel: 867-667-4733; *Fax:* 867-667-2688
yukontec@internorth.com
www.yukontec.com
Overview: A small provincial organization
Mission: To foster industry led development of a professional tourism workforce
Staff Member(s): 3
Activities: Providing education & training
Chief Officer(s):
Darlene Doerksen, Chief Executive Officer
Publications:
• Yukon Tourism Education Council Newsletter
Type: Newsletter; *Frequency:* Monthly

Yukon Trappers Association
175 Titanium Way, Whitehorse YT Y1A 0G1
Tel: 867-667-7091
yukonfur@yknet.ca
www.facebook.com/494095120650850
Overview: A small provincial charitable organization founded in 1972
Mission: To assist trappers in all aspects of the trapping & marketing of their furs
Finances: *Annual Operating Budget:* $100,000-$250,000; *Funding Sources:* Government contracts
Staff Member(s): 2; 6 volunteer(s)
Membership: 175; *Fees:* $30; $200 corporate
Activities: Retail store specializing in locally handcrafted products, as well as tanned fur; *Library:* Yukon Trappers Library; Open to public
Chief Officer(s):
Brian Melanson, President

Yukon Underwater Diving Association (YUDA)
YT
www.yukonweb.com/community/yuda
Overview: A small provincial organization
Mission: The Yukon Underwater Diving Association (YUDA) is a non-profit organization created by sport divers to promote the sport of underwater diving in the Yukon, Northern British Columbia & South East Alaska.
Chief Officer(s):
Allyn Lyon, President
alyon@yukon.net
Doug Davidge, Contact
ddavidge@yknet.yk.ca

Yukon Visitor's Association *See* Tourism Industry Association of the Yukon

Yukon Weightlifting Association
YT
yukonweightlift.weebly.com
Overview: A small provincial organization

Mission: To promote & facilitate competitive weightlifting in the Yukon Territory.
Member of: Sport Yukon
Chief Officer(s):
Kim Haehnel, President
frozenveggies@hotmail.com
Jeane Lassen, Development Coordinator
jeanelassen@gmail.com

YWCA Canada / Association des jeunes femmes chrétiennes du Canada
104 Edward St., 1st Fl., Toronto ON M5G 0A7
Tel: 416-962-8881; *Fax:* 416-962-8084
national@ywcacanada.ca
www.ywcacanada.ca
www.facebook.com/ywcacanada
twitter.com/YWCA_Canada
www.instagram.com/ywcacanada
Also Known As: Young Women's Christian Association of Canada
Overview: A large national charitable organization founded in 1893
Mission: To coordinate the YWCA movement in Canada, & advocate for the equity & equality rights of women; To raise awareness on the prevention of violence against women, end homelessness for women, & the need for universal, accessible & quality child care & economic equality
Affiliation(s): Selective: Canadian Policy Research Network; National Council of Women; National Youth Serving Organizations; Women's Future Fund; Canadian Centre for Philanthropy; National Action Committee on the Status of Women
Finances: *Annual Operating Budget:* $500,000-$1.5 Million; *Funding Sources:* Affiliation fees; donations; grants; sponsorships
Staff Member(s): 11; 50 volunteer(s)
Membership: 28 YWCA + 4 YMCA-YWCA Associations; *Fees:* Schedule available; *Committees:* Executive; Finance; International Cooperation; Nominating; Youth Engagement
Activities: Providing shelter & non-profit housing, childcare, & adult education; Offering long-term supportive housing, life-skills training, & youth services; *Awareness Events:* YWCA Week Without Violence, Oct.; Rose Button Campaign, Dec.; Women of Distinction Awards; *Internships:* Yes; *Speaker Service:* Yes; *Library:* by appointment
Chief Officer(s):
Maya Roy, Chief Executive Officer
mayaroy@ywcacanada.ca
Ann Decter, Director, Advocacy & Public Policy
adecter@ywcacanada.ca
Raine Liliefeldt, Director, Membership Services & Development
rliliefeldt@ywcacanada.ca

Community YWCA Muskoka
440 Ecclestone Dr., Bracebridge ON P1L 1Z6
Tel: 705-645-9827; *Fax:* 705-645-4804
www.ywcamuskoka.com
www.facebook.com/ywcamuskoka
twitter.com/YWCAMuskoka
Chief Officer(s):
Hannah Lin, Executive Director

YWCA Agvvik Nunavut
PO Box 237, 3118 Angel St., Iqaluit NU X0H 0H0
Tel: 867-979-4566; *Fax:* 867-979-0328
executivedirector@ywca-agvvik.ca

YWCA Niagara Region
183 King St., St Catharines ON L2R 3J5
Tel: 905-988-3528; *Fax:* 905-988-3739
info@ywcaniagararegion.ca
www.ywcaniagararegion.ca
www.facebook.com/YWCANiagaraRegion
twitter.com/YWCA_Niagara
Chief Officer(s):
Elisabeth Zimmermann, Executive Director, 905-988-3528 Ext. 3239
ezimmermann@ywcaniagararegion.ca

YWCA St. John's
#217, 31 Peet St., St. John's NL A1B 3W8
Tel: 709-726-9622; *Fax:* 709-576-0410
info@ywcastjohns.ca
www.ywcastjohns.ca
www.facebook.com/YWCAStJohns
twitter.com/YWCAYYT
Chief Officer(s):
Wendolyn Schlamp, Executive Director, 709-726-9922
wendolyn@ywcastjohns.ca

YWCA Banff
PO Box 520, 102 Spray Ave., Banff AB T1L 1A6
Tel: 403-762-3560; *Fax:* 403-762-3204
info@ywcabanff.ca
www.ywcabanff.ab.ca
www.facebook.com/YWCABanff
twitter.com/ywcabanff
Chief Officer(s):
Connie MacDonald, Chief Executive Officer

YWCA Brandon
148 - 11th St., Brandon MB R7A 4J4
Tel: 204-571-3680; *Fax:* 204-571-3687
ywcaadmin@wcgwave.ca
www.ywcabrandon.com
www.facebook.com/YWCABrandon
twitter.com/YWCABrandon
Chief Officer(s):
Karen Peto, Executive Director
kpeto@wcgwave.ca

YWCA Calgary
320 - 5th Ave. SE, Calgary AB T2G 0E5
Tel: 403-263-1550; *Fax:* 403-263-4681; *Crisis Hot-Line:* 403-266-0707
ywca@ywcalgary.ca
www.ywcalgary.ca
www.facebook.com/YWcalgary
twitter.com/YWcalgary
www.youtube.com/ywcaofcalgary
Chief Officer(s):
Sue Tomney, Chief Executive Officer

YWCA Durham
33 McGrigor St., Oshawa ON L1H 1X8
Tel: 905-576-6356; *Fax:* 905-576-0816; *Crisis Hot-Line:* 888-576-2997
info@ywcadurham.ca
www.ywcadurham.org
Chief Officer(s):
Tracey Burke, President

YWCA Edmonton
Empire Building, #400, 10080 Jasper Ave., Edmonton AB T5J 1V9
Tel: 780-423-9922; *Fax:* 780-488-6077
information@ywcaofedmonton.org
www.ywcaofedmonton.org
www.facebook.com/YWCAEdmonton
twitter.com/ywcaedmonton
www.flickr.com/photos/ywcaedmonton
Chief Officer(s):
Renee Oxley, President

YWCA Halifax
1233 Barrington St., 'W' Suite, Halifax NS B3J 1Y2
Tel: 902-423-6162; *Fax:* 902-444-3568
www.ywcahalifax.com
www.facebook.com/ywcahalifax
twitter.com/YWCAHalifax
www.youtube.com/user/YWCAHalifax
Chief Officer(s):
Miia Suokonautio, Executive Director, 902-423-6162 Ext. 2230
m.suokonautio@ywcahalifax.com

YWCA Hamilton
75 MacNab St. South, Hamilton ON L8P 3C1
Tel: 905-522-9922
www.ywcahamilton.org
www.facebook.com/YWCAHamilton
Chief Officer(s):
Denise Christopherson, Chief Executive Officer, 905-522-9922 Ext. 101
dchristopherson@ywcahamilton.org

YWCA Kitchener-Waterloo
153 Frederick St., Kitchener ON N2H 2M2
Tel: 519-576-8856; *Fax:* 519-576-0129
general@ywcakw.on.ca
www.ywcakw.on.ca
www.facebook.com/ywcakw
twitter.com/ywcakw
Chief Officer(s):
Patricia Polischuk, President

YWCA Lethbridge & District
604 - 8th St. South, Lethbridge AB T1J 2K1
Tel: 403-329-0088; *Fax:* 403-327-9112; *Crisis Hot-Line:* 403-320-1881
inquiries@ywcalethbridge.org
www.ywcalethbridge.org
www.facebook.com/ywcalethbridge
twitter.com/YWCALethbridge
Chief Officer(s):
Jennifer Lepko, Chief Executive Officer

YWCA Moncton
YW Jean E.S. Irving Centre for Women & Children, 135 Kendra St., Moncton NB E1C 9V9
Tel: 506-855-4349; *Fax:* 506-855-3320
info@ywcamoncton.com
www.ywcamoncton.com
www.facebook.com/ywcamoncton
twitter.com/ywcamoncton
www.ywcamoncton.tumblr.com
Chief Officer(s):
Jewell Mitchell, Executive Director
jmitchell@ywcamoncton.com

Y des femmes de Montréal
1355, boul René-Lévesque ouest, Montréal QC H3G 1T3
Tel: 514-866-9941; *Fax:* 514-866-4866
info@ydesfemmesmtl.org
www.ydesfemmesmtl.org
www.facebook.com/YWCA.Montreal
twitter.com/YWCA_mtl
www.youtube.com/user/YWCAMTL
Chief Officer(s):
Hélène Lépine, Présidente-directrice générale

YWCA Peterborough Haliburton
216 Simcoe St., Peterborough ON K9H 2H7
Tel: 705-743-3526; *Fax:* 705-745-4654; *TTY:* 705-743-4015; *Crisis Hot-Line:* 800-461-7656
info@ywcapeterborough.org
www.ywcapeterborough.org
www.facebook.com/ywcapeterborough
twitter.com/YWCAPtbo
Chief Officer(s):
Lynn Zimmer, Executive Director, 705-743-3526 Ext. 112
lzimmer@ywcapeterborough.org

YWCA Prince Albert
1895 Central Ave., Prince Albert SK S6V 4W8
Tel: 306-763-8571; *Fax:* 306-763-8165
ywcaprincealbert.ca
www.facebook.com/YwcaPrinceAlbert
Chief Officer(s):
Donna Brooks, Chief Executive Officer
donnabrooks.ywca@sasktel.net

YWCA Regina
1940 McIntyre St., Regina SK S4P 2R3
Tel: 306-525-2141; *Fax:* 306-525-2171
ywcaregina@ywcaregina.com
www.ywcaregina.com
Chief Officer(s):
Melissa Coomber-Bendtsen, Executive Director, 603-525-2141 Ext. 120
melissa@ywcaregina.com

YWCA St. Thomas-Elgin
16 Mary St. West, St Thomas ON N5P 2S3
Tel: 519-631-9800; *Fax:* 519-631-6411
Toll-Free: 800-461-0954
info@ywcaste.ca
www.ywcastthomaselgin.org
www.facebook.com/YWCAStThomas
twitter.com/YWCAStThomas
Chief Officer(s):
Laurie Intven, President

YWCA Saskatoon
510 - 25th St. East, Saskatoon SK S7K 4A7
Tel: 306-244-0944; *Fax:* 306-653-2468
info@ywcasaskatoon.com
www.ywcasaskatoon.com
www.facebook.com/ywcasaskatoon
twitter.com/YWCASaskatoon
Chief Officer(s):
Shannon Friesen, Cheif Executive Officer

YWCA Sudbury
370 St. Raphael St., Sudbury ON P3B 4K7
Tel: 705-673-4754; *Fax:* 705-688-1727
ywcasudbury.ca
Chief Officer(s):
Marlene Gorman, Executive Director, 705-673-4754 Ext. 222
m.gorman@ywcasudbury.ca

YWCA Thompson
39 Nickel Rd., Thompson MB R8N 0Y5
Tel: 204-778-6341; *Fax:* 204-778-5308
www.ywcathompson.ca

Chief Officer(s):
Kim Hicks, Executive Director
ywcaexdir@mymts.net

YWCA Metro Vancouver
535 Hornby St., Vancouver BC V6C 2E8
Tel: 250-895-5800; *Fax:* 604-684-9171
enquire@ywcavan.org
www.ywcavan.org
www.linkedin.com/company/ywca-metro-vancouver
www.facebook.com/YWCAMetroVancouver
twitter.com/YWCAVAN
www.youtube.com/user/YWCAVancouver
Chief Officer(s):
Janet Austin, Chief Executive Officer

YWCA NWT
#104, 4904 - 54 Ave., Yellowknife NT X1A 1H7
Tel: 867-920-2777; *Fax:* 867-873-9406; *Crisis Hot-Line:* 866-223-7775
info@ywcanwt.ca
www.ywcanwt.ca
www.facebook.com/ywcanwt
twitter.com/ywcanwt
Chief Officer(s):
Lyda Fuller, Executive Director

YWCA Québec
855, av Holland, Québec QC G1S 3S5
Tél: 418-683-2155; *Téléc:* 418-683-5526
info@ywcaquebec.qc.ca
www.ywcaquebec.qc.ca
www.facebook.com/ywcaquebec
twitter.com/ywcaqc
Chief Officer(s):
Katia de Pokomandy-Morin, Directrice générale
directiongenerale@ywcaquebec.qc.ca

YWCA Toronto
87 Elm St., Toronto ON M5G 0A8
Tel: 416-961-8100; *Fax:* 416-961-7739
Toll-Free: 888-843-9922
info@ywcatoronto.org
www.ywcatoronto.org
www.facebook.com/YWCA.TO
twitter.com/YWCAToronto
Chief Officer(s):
Heather McGregor, Chief Executive Officer

YWCA Cambridge
55 Dickson St., Cambridge ON N1R 7A5
Tel: 519-267-6444; *Fax:* 519-267-6440
ywcacambridge.ca
www.facebook.com/YWCACambridge
twitter.com/ywcacambridge
www.youtube.com/YMCAsofCandKW
Chief Officer(s):
Kim Decker, Executive Director

YWCA December 6 Fund of Toronto
87 Elm St., Toronto ON M5G 0A8
Tel: 416-961-8101; *Fax:* 416-961-7739
Toll-Free: 888-843-9922
dec6@ywcatoronto.org
www.dec6fund.ca
Overview: A small local organization founded in 1994
Mission: To raise money to help women build lives free of violence
Finances: *Funding Sources:* United Way; Canadian Women's Foundation; donations
Activities: Provide interest free loans to women fleeing abuse
Chief Officer(s):
Yvonne Avila, Registrar

YWCA Northeast Avalon *See* YWCA Canada

YWCA of Banff Programs & Services
PO Box 520, 102 Spray Ave., Banff AB T1L 1A6
Tel: 403-762-3560; *Fax:* 403-760-3202
info@ywcabanff.ca
www.ywcabanff.ca
www.facebook.com/YWCABanff
twitter.com/YWCABanff
Previous Name: Planned Parenthood Banff; Banff YWCA Community Resource Centre
Overview: A small local charitable organization founded in 1987
Mission: To provide safe, affordable housing & prevent family violence through education, programming, events, resource management & crisis intervention
Affiliation(s): Society Against Family Violence
Staff Member(s): 5

Membership: 100-499; *Fees:* $25/yr.; $50/3 yrs.
Activities: *Awareness Events:* Week Without Violence; International Women's Day; Walk a Mile in Her Shoes *Library:* YWCA of Banff Programs & Serives
Chief Officer(s):
Wendy Kuiper, President
Connie MacDonald, Chief Executive Director

YWCA of Peterborough, Victoria & Haliburton *See* YWCA Canada

YWCA of Vancouver *See* YWCA Canada

YWCA of Yellowknife *See* YWCA Canada

YWCA Westman Women's Shelter
148 - 11 St., Brandon MB R7A 4J4
Tel: 204-727-3644; *Fax:* 204-726-1793; *Crisis Hot-Line:* 877-977-0007
ywca2@wcgwave.ca
Overview: A small local charitable organization founded in 1978
Mission: To provide women with safe shelter, supportive counselling, advocacy, education & awareness of alternatives to violence
Finances: *Funding Sources:* Provincial government; United Way; grants; donations
Activities: *Speaker Service:* Yes

YWCAs of Cambridge & Kitchener-Waterloo *See* YWCA Canada

Zane Cohen Centre for Digestive Diseases Familial Gastrointestinal Cancer Registry (FGICR)
Mount Sinai Hospital, Zane Cohen Centre, PO Box 24, 60 Murray St., Toronto ON M5T 3L9
Tel: 416-586-4800; *Fax:* 416-586-5924
Toll-Free: 877-586-5112
zcc@mtsinai.on.ca
www.zanecohencentre.ca
Previous Name: Familial GI Cancer Registry
Overview: A small local organization founded in 1980
Mission: The Registry is an interdisciplinary program dedicated to the specialty care of families affected with rare forms of inherited colorectal cancer.
Publications:
• Network [a publication of the Familial Gastrointestinal Cancer Registry]
Type: Newsletter; *Editor:* Terri Berk

ZAP Montérégie
3205, boul Rome, Brossard QC J4Y 1R2
Tél: 514-800-0935
info@zapmonteregie.org
www.zapmonteregie.org
Aperçu: *Dimension:* petite; *Envergure:* locale
Mission: De fournir un accès à Internet sans fil public et gratuit aux utilisateurs d'unité portable dans la région de la Montérégie
Membre(s) du bureau directeur:
Hélène Picard, Coordonnatrice
Meetings/Conferences:
• ZAP Montérégie assemblée générale annuelle, 2018, QC
Scope: Local

Zeballos Board of Trade
c/o Village of Zeballos, PO Box 127, Zeballos BC V0P 2A0
Tel: 250-761-4229; *Fax:* 250-761-4331
adminzeb@recn.ca
www.zeballos.com
Overview: A small local organization founded in 1938
Member of: BC Chamber of Commerce
Finances: *Annual Operating Budget:* Less than $50,000; *Funding Sources:* Membership dues
4 volunteer(s)
Membership: 1-99

Zenon Park Board of Trade
PO Box 250, Zenon Park SK S0E 1W0
Tel: 306-767-2434; *Fax:* 306-767-2224
Overview: A small local organization

Zhahti Koe Friendship Centre
PO Box 209, Fort Providence NT X0E 0L0
Tel: 867-699-3801; *Fax:* 867-699-4355
Overview: A small local organization

ZOOCHECK Canada Inc.
788 1/2 O'Connor Dr., Toronto ON M4B 2S6
Tel: 416-285-1744
zoocheck@zoocheck.com

www.zoocheck.com
www.facebook.com/canadazoocheck
Overview: A small national charitable organization founded in 1984
Mission: Zoocheck works to improve wildlife protection in Canada and to end the abuse, neglect and exploitation of individual wild animals through: investigation & research; public education & awareness campaigns; capacity building initiatives; legal programs; legislative actions.
Finances: *Funding Sources:* Donations
Activities: *Speaker Service:* Yes; *Rents Mailing List:* Yes

Zoological Society of Manitoba *See* Assiniboine Park Conservancy

Zoological Society of Metropolitan Toronto *See* Toronto Zoo

Zoological Society of Montréal / Société zoologique de Montréal
#525, 1117, rue Sainte-Catherine ouest, Montréal QC H3B 1H9
Tel: 514-845-8317
contact@zoologicalsocietymtl.org
www.zoologicalsocietymtl.org
Overview: A small local organization founded in 1964
Mission: To promote & develop interest in & knowledge of wildlife; To encourage the study of biology & nature sciences; To encourage the protection of wildlife
Finances: *Funding Sources:* Fundrasing, donations, member dues
Membership: 500; *Fees:* $35 individual; $55 family
Activities: Field trips; monthly meetings; *Speaker Service:* Yes

Zoroastrian Associaton of Québec *See* L'Association Zoroastrianne du Québec

Zoroastrian Society of Ontario (ZSO)
3590 Bayview Ave., Toronto ON M2M 3S6
Tel: 416-225-7771
secretary@zso.org
www.zso.org
Overview: A small provincial charitable organization founded in 1971
Mission: Meeting the religious & cultural needs of the Zoroastrian community of Ontario
Affiliation(s): Federation of North American Zoroastrian Associations
Finances: *Annual Operating Budget:* $100,000-$250,000; *Funding Sources:* Membership fees; donations; investment income
Staff Member(s): 1; 200 volunteer(s)
Membership: 1,000; *Fees:* $70 family; $40 individual; $20 seniors & students; *Member Profile:* Zoroastrians living in Ontario; *Committees:* 15 sub-committees reporting to elected executive committee of 9
Activities: Religious & cultural, youth & seniors activities; Sponsors 100th Scout Group; *Library:* ZSO Library; by appointment
Chief Officer(s):
Russi Surti, President
president@zso.org
Dara Panthakee, Executive Vice President
evp@zso.org
Vispi Patel, Vice President
vp@zso.org
Anahita Ogra, Secretary
Meherab Chothia, Treasurer
Awards:
• Volunteer of the Year
4 volunteer awards given per year

Zurich & District Chamber of Commerce
PO Box 189, Zurich ON N0M 2T0
zurichontario.com
Overview: A small local organization founded in 1951
Mission: To serve as the voice of business, to promote and enhance economic prosperity and quality of life in Zurich.
Member of: Ontario Chamber of Commerce
Membership: 34; *Fees:* $35

Zwiazek Nauczycielstwa Polskiego w Kanadzie *See* Polish Teachers Association in Canada

Foreign Associations

Academic Pediatric Association (APA)
6728 Old McLean Village Dr., McLean VA 22101 USA
Tel: 703-556-9222; *Fax:* 703-556-8729
info@academicpeds.org
www.academicpeds.org
www.facebook.com/AcademicPeds
twitter.com/academicpeds
Overview: A large international organization
Mission: To improve the health of children & adolescents; To provide leadership in education of child health professionals; To engage in research & disseminate knowledge
Membership: *Fees:* $50 in-training; $170 non-physician; $320 physician
Chief Officer(s):
Jessica O'Hara, Executive Director
jessica@academicpeds.org
Stephanie Blyskal, Manager
stephanie@academicpeds.org
Jennifer Padilla, Manager
jennifer@academicpeds.org
Awards:
- Child Advocacy Award
- APA Public Policy & Advocacy Award
- Global Health Research Award
- Health Care Delivery Award
- Michael Shannon Award
- Teaching Program Award
- Research Award

Meetings/Conferences:
- Academic Pediatric Association 2018 Quality Improvement & Implementation Science Conference, May, 2018
Scope: International
- Pediatric Academic Societies' 2018 Annual Meeting, May, 2018, Toronto, ON
Scope: International
Description: An international meeting focussing on research in child health
Contact Information: Address: #7B, 3400 Research Forest Dr., The Woodlands, TX, 77381, USA; Phone: 346-980-9717
- Pediatric Academic Societies' 2019 Annual Meeting, April, 2019, Baltimore, MD
Scope: International
Description: An international meeting focussing on research in child health
Contact Information: Address: #7B, 3400 Research Forest Dr., The Woodlands, TX, 77381, USA; Phone: 346-980-9717
- Pediatric Academic Societies' 2020 Annual Meeting, May, 2020, Philadelphia, PA
Scope: International
Description: An international meeting focussing on research in child health
Contact Information: Address: #7B, 3400 Research Forest Dr., The Woodlands, TX, 77381, USA; Phone: 346-980-9717
- Pediatric Academic Societies' 2021 Annual Meeting, April, 2021, Vancouver, BC
Scope: International
Description: An international meeting focussing on research in child health
Contact Information: Address: #7B, 3400 Research Forest Dr., The Woodlands, TX, 77381, USA; Phone: 346-980-9717
- Pediatric Academic Societies' 2022 Annual Meeting, April, 2022, Denver, CO
Scope: International
Description: An international meeting focussing on research in child health
Contact Information: Address: #7B, 3400 Research Forest Dr., The Woodlands, TX, 77381, USA; Phone: 346-980-9717
- Pediatric Academic Societies' 2023 Annual Meeting, April, 2023, Washington, DC
Scope: International
Description: An international meeting focussing on research in child health
Contact Information: Address: #7B, 3400 Research Forest Dr., The Woodlands, TX, 77381, USA; Phone: 346-980-9717

Publications:
- Academic Pediatrics [a publication of the Academic Pediatric Association]
Type: Journal; *Frequency:* Bimonthly; *Editor:* Peter Szilagyi, MD, MPH; *Price:* Free with Academic Pediatric Association membership
Profile: The peer-reviewed publication is the official journal of the Academic Pediatric Association, featuring research &educational information for health professionals who care for children
- APA [Academic Pediatric Association] Focus
Type: Newsletter; *Frequency:* Bimonthly; *Price:* Free with Academic Pediatric Association membership

Académie européenne des sciences, des arts et des lettres (AESAL) / European Academy of Sciences, Arts & Humanities
60, rue Monsieur le Prince, Paris 75006 France
Téléc: 33-4-93-34-05-06
www.europeanacademysciencesartsandletters.com
Aperçu: *Dimension:* moyenne; *Envergure:* internationale; Organisme sans but lucratif; fondée en 1980
Mission: De coopérer bénévolements avec L'UNESCO dans ses domaines de compétence
Affiliation(s): Relation formelle avec l'UNESCO
Membre: *Critères d'admissibilite:* Personnalités choisies pour leur polyvalence, principalement au sein des Académies Nationales, et parmi les Lauréats des Grands Prix Internationaux, comme le Prix Nobel, le Prix Erasme
Membre(s) du bureau directeur:
Nicole D'Agaggio Lemaire, Secrétaire Perpétuelle
nilemaire@wanadoo.fr

Academy of Management (AOM)
PO Box 3020, Briarcliff Manor NY 10510-8020 USA
Tel: 914-326-1800; *Fax:* 914-326-1900
membership@aom.org
www.aom.org
www.linkedin.com/groups/102523
www.facebook.com/aomconnect
twitter.com/aomconnect
Overview: A large international organization founded in 1936
Mission: To create & disseminate knowledge about management & organizations
Membership: 17,719; *Member Profile:* Scholars from 114 nations
Chief Officer(s):
Nancy Urbanowicz, Executive Director
nurbanowicz@aom.org
Terese M. Loncar, COO
tloncar@aom.org
Marko Vukosavovic, CFO
mvukosavovic@aom.org
Matthew Suppa, CIO
msuppa@aom.org
Meetings/Conferences:
- Academy of Management 2018 Annual Meeting, August, 2018, Chicago, IL
Scope: International
Attendance: 10,000+
Description: Sharing of research and expertise in all management disciplines through distinguished speakers, competitive paper sessions, symposia, panels, workshops, & special programs for doctoral students
Contact Information: Director, Meetings & Conferences: Taryn Fiore, E-mail: tfiore@aom.org

Publications:
- Academy of Management Annals
Type: Book; *Frequency:* Annually
Profile: Advances in various management fields, with critical research reviews, for academic scholars in management & professionals in allied fields
- Academy of Management Annual Meeting Proceedings
Type: Yearbook; *Frequency:* Annually
- Academy of Management Journal (AMJ)
Type: Journal; *Frequency:* 6 pa; *Accepts Advertising*
Profile: Research for management scholars
- Academy of Management Learning & Education (AMLE)
Type: Journal; *Frequency:* Quarterly; *Accepts Advertising*
Profile: Issues in the fields of management learning & education for scholars, educators, program directors, deans at academic institutions, & practitioners in training &corporate education
- Academy of Management Member Directory
Type: Directory
- Academy of Management News
Type: Newsletter; *Frequency:* Quarterly
Profile: Association announcements, news, professional opportunities, & meetings
- Academy of Management Perspectives (AMP)
Type: Journal; *Frequency:* Quarterly; *Accepts Advertising*
Profile: Formerly the Academy of Management Executive, the journal features advances in management theory & research & articles about the process of managing an organization
- Academy of Management Review (AMR)
Type: Journal; *Frequency:* Quarterly; *Accepts Advertising*
Profile: Theory development, conceptual work, articles about organizations & their role in society, & reviews of literature

Action Mondiale des Parlementaires *See* Parliamentarians for Global Action

AdvaMed
#800, 701 Pennsylvania Ave. NW, Washington DC 20004-2654 USA
Tel: 202-783-8700; *Fax:* 202-783-8750
info@advamed.org
www.advamed.org
www.linkedin.com/company/79166
www.facebook.com/AdvaMed
twitter.com/advamedupdate
www.youtube.com/advamedupdate
Also Known As: Advanced Medical Technology Association
Overview: A small international organization
Mission: To promote procedures that encourage ethical practices & easier access to technology in the medical industry.
Staff Member(s): 75
Membership: 300 companies; *Member Profile:* Medical technology firms; professional service firms that support and directly benefit the medical industry; emerging growth companies
Chief Officer(s):
José E. Almedia, President/CEO

Aerospace & Electronic Systems Society (AESS)
3 Park Ave., 2nd Fl., New York NY 10016-5997 USA
Tel: 732-981-0060; *Fax:* 732-981-1721
customer-service@ieee.org
www.ieee-aess.org
www.facebook.com/IEEEAESS
twitter.com/IEEE_AESS
Overview: A medium-sized international organization founded in 1965 overseen by Institute of Electrical & Electronics Engineers Inc.
Finances: *Annual Operating Budget:* $500,000-$1.5 Million; *Funding Sources:* Membership dues; Conferences
100 volunteer(s)
Membership: 8,500; *Fees:* $25 for IEEE professional members; $13 for IEEE student members; $98.50 for society affiliate; *Member Profile:* IEEE members interested in the organization, systems engineering, design, development, & integration of complex systems for space, air, ocean, or ground environments; *Committees:* Formal Methods in System Design; Gyro & Accelerometer; Integrated Avionics; Radar; Satellite Navigation; Space Systems; System Engineering; Target Tracking & Sensor Fusion
Chief Officer(s):
Teresa Pace, President
teresapace@ieee.org
Publications:
- IEEE Transactions on Aerospace & Electronic Systems [publications of the Aerospace & Electronic Systems Society]
Type: Report; *Frequency:* q.; *Editor:* Lance Kaplan
Profile: A series of articles with aerospace or related applications
- Systems Magazine [a publication of the Aerospace & Electronic Systems Society]
Type: Magazine; *Editor:* Maria S. Greco
Profile: Publishes articles concerned with the various aspects of systems for space, air, ocean, or groundenvironments

AFCOM
910 West Chester Towne Centre Rd., West Chester OH 45069 USA
Tel: 714-997-9743; *Fax:* 714-997-9743
membership@AFCOM.com
www.afcom.com
www.linkedin.com/company/afcom
twitter.com/afcom
Previous Name: Association for Computer Operations Management
Overview: A large international organization founded in 1980
Mission: To enable data center professionals to share industry best practices by providing a forum for dissemination of criticial information; to provide education on key data center management issues; to provide the industry's most comprehensive insight & analysis in key areas affecting all data-intensive organizations & to be the most comprehensive & effective resource available to the overall data community
Finances: *Annual Operating Budget:* $500,000-$1.5 Million; *Funding Sources:* Membership dues; conference dues; trade show sales
Staff Member(s): 17

Membership: 2,500; *Fees:* US$300 individual; US$690 site; US$1,020 corporate; *Committees:* Membership advisory
Activities: *Library:* Data Center Institute
Chief Officer(s):
Tom Roberts, President, 513-322-1740
troberts@afcom.com
Joshua Ater, Manager, Marketing, 513-898-1253
jater@afcom.com
Erin Heekin, Manager, Accounts, 513-322-1550
erin.heekin@inetinteractive.com
Gina Jahn, Manager, Events, 714-643-8119
gjahn@afcom.com
Meetings/Conferences:
• AFCOM Data Center World Global Conference 2018, March, 2018, San Antonio, TX
Scope: International
Contact Information: URL: global.datacenterworld.com
Publications:
• Data Center Management [a publiction of AFCOM]
Type: Magazine

African Literature Association (ALA) / Association Africane de Literature
c/o Hobart & William Smith Colleges, 300 Pulteney St., Geneva NY 14456 USA
Tel: 315-781-3491; *Fax:* 315-781-3822
www.africanlit.org
www.facebook.com/AfricanLit
Overview: A medium-sized international organization founded in 1975
Mission: To promote the study & teaching of African literatures in their broad social, historical, & political dimensions; To aim for constructive interaction between scholars & artists, the worldwide understanding & appreciation of African literatures, & the continual refinement of the tools & methods of African literary study
Member of: African Studies Association
Finances: *Annual Operating Budget:* Less than $50,000; *Funding Sources:* Membership dues; Subscriptions
Staff Member(s): 1
Membership: 600; *Fees:* Schedule available; *Member Profile:* Scholars; teachers; writers; *Committees:* Awards; Caucus Liaison; Constitution & Policy; Elections; Finance; Issues & Human Rights, Publicity, Digital & Social Media; Publications; Conferences; Teaching & Research; Travel Grants
Activities: *Rents Mailing List:* Yes
Chief Officer(s):
James McCorkle, Director, 315-781-3491, Fax: 315-781-3822
mccorkle@hws.edu
Awards:
• Graduate Student Best Essay Award
Deadline: August *Contact:* Juliana Makuchi Nfah-Abbenyi, E-mail: jmphd@ncsu.edu
• Book of the Year Award - Creative Writing
Deadline: August *Contact:* Juliana Makuchi Nfah-Abbenyi, E-mail: jmphd@ncsu.edu
• Book of the Year Award - Scholarship
Deadline: August *Contact:* Juliana Makuchi Nfah-Abbenyi, E-mail: jmphd@ncsu.edu
• First Book Award - Scholarship
Deadline: August *Contact:* Juliana Makuchi Nfah-Abbenyi, E-mail: jmphd@ncsu.edu
• Best Article Award
Deadline: August *Contact:* Juliana Makuchi Nfah-Abbenyi, E-mail: jmphd@ncsu.edu
• Fonlon-Nichols Award
Deadline: October *Contact:* Juliana Makuchi Nfah-Abbenyi, E-mail: jmphd@ncsu.edu
• Distinguished Member Award
Deadline: October *Contact:* Juliana Makuchi Nfah-Abbenyi, E-mail: jmphd@ncsu.edu
Meetings/Conferences:
• African Literature Association 2018 Conference, May, 2018, Marriott Wardman Park, Washington, DC
Scope: International
Description: Theme: "The Environments of African Literature"
Publications:
• ALA [African Literature Association] Newsletter
Type: Newsletter; *Frequency:* s-a.; *ISSN:* 0146-4965
Profile: Provides a forum for matters of record to the Association
• Journal of the African Literature Association
Type: Journal; *Frequency:* s-a.; *Editor:* Abioseh Porter; *ISSN:* 2167-4736
Profile: Contains essays & reviews that reflect the range of materials, methodologies, & movements in African & African diaspora literatures

African Wildlife Foundation (AWF)
#120, 1400 Sixteenth St. NW, Washington DC 20036 USA
Tel: 202-939-3333; *Fax:* 202-939-3332
Toll-Free: 888-494-5354
africanwildlife@awf.org
www.awf.org
www.facebook.com/AfricanWildlifeFoundation
twitter.com/AWF_Official
www.youtube.com/AfricanWildlife
Overview: A large international organization
Mission: To promote conservation of Africa's wildlife & natural resources; To promote belief that the survival of African wildlife lies in a working knowledge of the relationship between man, his economics & his environment; To promote, establish & support grassroots & institutional programs in conservation education, wildlife management & training, & management of threatened conservation areas; To manage projects aimed at saving endangered species (eg. the African Elephant, Mountain Gorilla, Rhinoceros)
Staff Member(s): 120
Chief Officer(s):
Patrick J. Bergin, CEO
Kaddu Sebunya, President
Jeff Chrisfield, Chief Operating Officer

Agence internationale de l'énergie atomique *See* International Atomic Energy Agency

Agence spatiale européenne *See* European Space Agency

AIM Global (AIM)
One Landmark North, #203, 20399 Rte. 19, Cranberry Township PA 16066 USA
Tel: 724-742-4470; *Fax:* 724-742-4476
info@aimglobal.org
www.aimglobal.org
Previous Name: Automatic Identification Manufacturers
Overview: A small international charitable organization founded in 1972
Mission: To stimulate the understanding, adoption & use of AIM technology by providing timely, unbiased & commercial-free news & information
Staff Member(s): 2
Membership: 95; *Member Profile:* Providers & users of technologies, systems, & services that capture, manage & integrate accurate data into larger information management systems; *Committees:* Internet of Things; RFID Experts Group; Technical Symbologies; Unique Device Identification Initiative-AIM North America; UID Suppliers Alliance AIM North America
Activities: Sponsor of frontline solution shows; standards developer in Bar code & RFID; liaison member ISO SC31; *Speaker Service:* Yes
Chief Officer(s):
Mary Lou Bosco, Chief Operating Officer
marylou@aimglobal.org
Awards:
• Don Percival Award
• Richard R. Dilling Award

Air & Waste Management Association (A&WMA) / Association pour la prévention de la contamination de l'air et du sol
One Gateway Center, 420 Fort Duquesne Blvd., 3rd Fl., Pittsburgh PA 15222-1435 USA
Tel: 412-232-3444; *Fax:* 412-232-3450
Toll-Free: 800-270-3444
info@awma.org
www.awma.org
www.linkedin.com/company/445959
www.facebook.com/AirandWasteManagementAssociation
twitter.com/AirandWaste
Previous Name: Air Pollution Control Association
Overview: A large international organization founded in 1907
Mission: To improve environmental knowledge & decisions; To assist members in critical environmental decision making & professional development; To provide a neutral forum for exchanging information & developing networking opportunities; To increase public education & outreach
Member of: International Union of Air Pollution Prevention & Environmental Protection Associations
Affiliation(s): Canadian Prairie & Northern Section (www.cpans.org); Ontario Section (www.awma.on.ca); Québec Section (www.apcas.qc.ca); Ottawa Valley Chapter (www.awma-ovc.ca); Pacific Northwest International Section (www.pnwis.org)
Membership: 5,000+ in 65 countries; *Fees:* $35 students; $98 emeritus members; $98 young professional members; $195 individuals; $470-1,495 organizational members; *Member Profile:* Environmental professionals; *Committees:* Councils: Education; Sections & Chapters; Technical; Young Professionals
Chief Officer(s):
Brad Waldron, President
Stephanie Glyptis, Executive Director, 412-904-6006
sglyptis@awma.org
Awards:
• S. Smith Griswold Outstanding Air Pollution Control Official Award
• Frank A. Chambers Excellence in Air Pollution Control Award
Awarded to individuals who make an exceptional contribution to any technical aspect of air pollution control
• Richard Beatty Mellon Environmental Stewardship Award
Presented to a person who has made a civic contribution to a field related to the mission & objectives of the association
• Charles W. Gruber Association Leadership Award
• Lyman A. Ripperton Environmental Educator Award
Presented to teachers who inspire students to achieve excellence in professional & social endeavours; recipients are educators from some field related to the mission & objectives of the association
• Richard C. Scherr Award of Industrial Environmental Excellence
• Richard I. Stessel Waste Management Award
• Honorary A&WMA Membership
• Fellow A&WMA Membership
• Outstanding Young Professional Award
• JA&WMA Arthur C. Stern Award for Distinguished Paper
Meetings/Conferences:
• Air & Waste Management Association 111th Annual Conference & Exhibition 2018, June, 2018, Hartford, CT
Scope: International
Description: Theme: "Charting the Future: Environment, Energy & Health"
Publications:
• Air & Waste Management Association Membership Directory
Type: Directory
Profile: Contact information for members
• EM, The Magazine for Environmental Managers [a publication of the Air & Waste Management Association]
Type: Magazine; *Frequency:* Monthly; *Accepts Advertising*
Profile: Management, policy, & regulatory perspective; available digitally & by print-on-demand
• Journal of the Air & Waste Management Association
Type: Journal; *Frequency:* Monthly; *Editor:* S. Trivikrama Rao
Profile: Peer reviewed, technical environmental journal

Air Pollution Control Association *See* Air & Waste Management Association

Airports Council International - Asia-Pacific Region
Unit 13, 2/F, Airport World Trade Centre, 1 Sky Plaza Road, Hong Kong Intl. Airport, Hong Kong Hong Kong
Tel: 852-2180-9449
info@aci-asiapac.aero
www.aci-asiapac.aero
Also Known As: ACI Asia-Pacific
Overview: A medium-sized international organization founded in 1992
Mission: To foster cooperation among member airports & with other partners in world aviation, including governmental, airlines & aircraft manufacturing organizations; To provide the travelling public with an air transport system that is safe, secure, efficient & environmentally compatible
Member of: Airports Council International
Staff Member(s): 3
Membership: 104; *Fees:* Airports, dependent upon size; US$1,500 associates
Chief Officer(s):
Kerrie Mather, President

Alcoholic Beverage Medical Research Foundation (ABMRF)
#310, 1200-C Agora Dr., Bel Air MD 21014 USA
Toll-Free: 800-688-7152
info@abmrf.org
www.abmrf.org
www.linkedin.com/company/1137768
www.facebook.com/AlcoholResearch?ref=ts
twitter.com/AlcoholResearch
Also Known As: The Foundation for Alcohol Research

Overview: A small international organization founded in 1982
Activities: International conferences
Chief Officer(s):
Mack C. Mitchell, President
Lisa Hoffberger, Director, Development & Communications
Erin Teigen, Director, Research & Grants Programs

Alliance for Sustainability
Greenway Building, #100, 2801 - 21st Ave. South, Minneapolis MN 55407 USA
Tel: 612-250-0389
www.afors.org
twitter.com/AforSMN
Also Known As: International Alliance for Sustainable Agriculture
Overview: A medium-sized international charitable organization founded in 1983
Mission: Supporting ecologically sound, economically viable, socially just & humane projects on a personal, organizational & planetary level
Finances: *Annual Operating Budget:* Less than $50,000; *Funding Sources:* Membership; Foundations; Donors; Corporations; Religious groups; Fundraising; Revenue from public speaking, sale of publications, shirts, & buttons
Staff Member(s): 1; 5 volunteer(s)
Membership: 800; *Fees:* $25; *Member Profile:* Farmers; consumers; business & government leaders; environmentalists; educators & scientists
Activities: Facilitating seminars; Supporting projects overseas; Disseminating information; *Internships:* Yes; *Speaker Service:* Yes; *Library:* Sustainability Resource Center; Open to public
Chief Officer(s):
Sean Gosiewski, Program Director
sean@afors.org

Alliance for the Wild Rockies (AWR)
PO Box 505, Helena MT 59624 USA
Tel: 406-459-5936
wildrockies@gmail.com
allianceforthewildrockies.org
www.facebook.com/WildRockies
Overview: A medium-sized international organization founded in 1988
Mission: To protect wildlands & wildlife habitat in the Wild Rockies Bioregion, containing parts of Alberta, British Columbia, Montana, Idaho, Wyoming, Oregon, Washington; To protect threatened, endangered & sensitive species; To promote sound ecosystem protection & sustainable economic development; To promote ecosystem-based land management based on scientific principles
Finances: *Annual Operating Budget:* $250,000-$500,000; *Funding Sources:* Membership dues; fundraising; donations; foundations
Staff Member(s): 2; 10 volunteer(s)
Membership: 3,500 individual + 1,000 organizational
Activities: *Internships:* Yes
Chief Officer(s):
Michael Garrity, Executive Director

Alliance internationale de tourisme / International Touring Alliance
2 ch de Blandonnet, Geneva 1215 Switzerland
Tel: 41-22-544-4500; *Fax:* 41-22-544-4550
ait-admin@fia.com
www.ait-touringalliance.com
Overview: A small international organization founded in 1898
Mission: Represents motoring organizations & touring clubs around the world
Affiliation(s): Canadian Automobile Association
Membership: 117 member associations in 96 countries
Chief Officer(s):
Werner Kraus, President

Alliance of Foam Packaging Recyclers See EPS Industry Alliance

The Aluminum Association
#600, 1525 Wilson Blvd., Arlington VA 22209 USA
Tel: 703-358-2960; *Fax:* 703-358-2961
www.aluminum.org
www.facebook.com/AluminumAssociation?v=wall
twitter.com/AluminumNews
Previous Name: Aluminum Recycling Association
Overview: A small national organization
Mission: To enhance aluminum's position in a world of proliferating materials, increase its use as the "material of choice" remove impediments to its fullest use & assist in achieving the industry's environmental, societal, & economic objectives
Membership: *Member Profile:* Producers of primary aluminum, recyclers & semi-fabricated aluminum products, as well as suppliers to the industry
Chief Officer(s):
Heidi Biggs Brock, President
hbrock@aluminum.org

Aluminum Recycling Association See The Aluminum Association

Amalgamated Transit Union (AFL-CIO/CLC) (ATU) / Syndicat uni du transport (FAT-COI/CTC)
10000 New Hampshire Ave., Silver Spring MD 20903 USA
Tel: 301-431-7100; *Fax:* 301-431-7117
Toll-Free: 888-240-1196
www.atu.org
www.facebook.com/ATUInternational
twitter.com/ATUComm
www.youtube.com/user/stpatuorg
Overview: A medium-sized international organization
Mission: To maintain the benefits & interests of members of the U.S. and Canadian mass transit sector
Membership: *Member Profile:* Transit workers, including bus drivers, rail operators, mechanics, station attendants and other support personnel
Chief Officer(s):
Lawrence J. Hanley, President
Oscar Owens, International Secretary-Treasurer
Javier Perez, Jr, International Executive Vice President
Awards:
• The Oscars Financial Secretary Awards
Based on accuracy and punctuality of the officers' resports to the International and government agencies, including audit and monthly per capita reports.

Amateur Athletic Union (AAU)
PO Box 22049, Lake Buena Vista FL 32830 USA
Tel: 407-934-7200; *Fax:* 407-934-7242
Toll-Free: 800-228-4872
www.aausports.org
www.facebook.com/realaau
twitter.com/therealaau
www.youtube.com/therealaauvideo
Overview: A large national organization founded in 1888
Mission: To offer a lifelong progression of amateur sports programs for persons of all ages, races & creeds, thereby enhancing the physical, mental & moral development of amateur athletes; To promote good sportsmanship, good citizenship & safety
Finances: *Funding Sources:* Membership dues
1000 volunteer(s)
Membership: 650,000; *Fees:* Schedule available
Activities: Conducts programs & works with other sports organizations to benefit amateur athletes; conducts recognition programs for outstanding amateur athletes; publishes an extensive line of handbooks & brochures on individual sports; *Internships:* Yes; *Rents Mailing List:* Yes; *Library:* Not open to public
Chief Officer(s):
Roger Goudy, President
Awards:
• AAU James E. Sullivan Memorial Award
Honors an outstanding amateur athlete in the United States.

American Academy for Cerebral Palsy & Developmental Medicine (AACPDM)
#1100, 555 East Wells St., Milwaukee WI 53202 USA
Tel: 414-918-3014; *Fax:* 414-276-2146
info@aacpdm.org
www.aacpdm.org
www.facebook.com/aacpdm
twitter.com/aacpdm
Overview: A medium-sized international organization founded in 1947
Mission: To foster & stimulate education & research in cerebral palsy & developmental medicine for the welfare of patients & their families
Affiliation(s): Canadian Cerebral Palsy Association
Staff Member(s): 4
Membership: *Fees:* US$300 fellow; US$50 corresponding; US$40 trainee/student; *Committees:* Adapted Sports & Recreation; Advocacy; Awards; Communications; Complex Care; Education; International Affairs; Lifespan Care; Membership; Research; Scientific Program
Activities: *Library*
Chief Officer(s):
Unni Narayanan, President
Tracy Burr, Executive Director
tburr@aacpdm.org
Awards:
• AACPDM Research Grant
  Deadline: April
• International Scholarship
  Contact: Tracy Burr, tburr@aacpdm.org
• Student Scholarship
• AACPDM Mentorship Award
Meetings/Conferences:
• American Academy for Cerebral Palsy & Developmental Medicine 72nd Annual Meeting, October, 2018, Duke Energy Convention Center, Cincinnati, OH
  Scope: International
Publications:
• AACPDM [American Academy for Cerebral Palsy & Developmental Medicine] Newsletter
  Type: Newsletter; *Frequency:* Quarterly
• Developmental Medicine & Child Neurology [a publication of the American Academy for Cerebral Palsy & Developmental Medicine]
  Type: Journal
  Profile: Peer reviewed journal

American Academy of Arts & Sciences
Norton's Woods, 136 Irving St., Cambridge MA 02138 USA
Tel: 617-576-5000; *Fax:* 617-576-5050
www.amacad.org
www.facebook.com/americanacad
twitter.com/americanacad
www.youtube.com/americanacad
Overview: A small international organization founded in 1780
Mission: To conduct a series of multidisciplinary studies & projects
Member of: American Council of Learned Societies
Affiliation(s): International Institute of Applied Systems Analysis
Membership: 4,600 USA + 600 foreign honorary; *Fees:* Schedule available; *Member Profile:* Membership based on distinction in a given field or profession
Activities: The Committee on International Security Studies; Science & Global Security; Social Policy & American Institutions; Humanities & Culture; Education
Chief Officer(s):
Jonathan F. Fanton, President
Don M. Randel, Chair
Awards:
• Scholar-Patriot Award
• Francis Amory Prize
• Talcott Parsons Prize
• George & May Sarton Fellowship
• The Emerson-Thoreau Prize in Literature
• Humanistic Studies Award
• Rumford Prize

American Academy of Neurology (AAN)
201 Chicago Ave., Minneapolis MN 55415 USA
Tel: 612-928-6000; *Fax:* 612-454-2746
Toll-Free: 800-879-1960
memberservices@aan.com
www.aan.com
www.linkedin.com/groups/2386034
www.facebook.com/AmericanAcademyofNeurology
twitter.com/AANMember
www.youtube.com/AANChannel
Overview: A large international organization
Mission: To advance the art & science of neurology; To promote the best possible care for patients with neurological disorders
Membership: 20,000+; *Member Profile:* Medical specialists dedicated to improving the care of patients with neurological diseases; *Committees:* Disclosures; Archives; AAN Audit; AEI Audit; Board Planning; Bylaws; Committee on Sections; Editors-in-Chief; Education; Ethics, Law, & Humanities; Executive; Finance; Government Relations; Grievance; Investment; Journal Arbitration; Medical Economics & Management; Meeting Management; Membership; Nominations; Practice; Science
Activities: Advocating for ethical, high-quality neurological care; Providing professional education programs to physicians & allied health professionals; Supporting clinical & basic research in the neurosciences & related fields; Offering information to patients
Chief Officer(s):

Catherine M. Rydell, Executive Director & CEO
crydell@aan.com
Jason Kopinski, Deputy Executive Director
jkopinski@aan.com
Timothy Engel, Chief Financial Officer
tengel@aan.com
Angela Babb, Chief Communications Officer
ababb@aan.com
Chris Becker, Chief Business Development Officer
cbecker@aan.com
Lynee Koester, Project Manager, Health Policy
lkoester@aan.com
Meetings/Conferences:
• American Academy of Neurology 2018 70th Annual Meeting, April, 2018, Los Angeles, CA
Scope: International
Attendance: 12,000+
Description: Education, science, & practice programs & exhibits
Publications:
• AANnews [a publication of the American Academy of Neurology]
Type: Newsletter; *Frequency:* Monthly; *Price:* Free with American Academy of Neurology membership
Profile: American Academy of Neurology & practice information
• American Academy of Neurology Patient Education Series
Type: Books
Profile: Information & treatment options for patients & caregivers
• Continuum: Lifelong Learning in Neurology
Frequency: Bimonthly; *Editor:* Steven L. Lewis, MD
Profile: A self-study continuing medical education publication
• Neurology
Type: Journal; *Editor:* Robert A. Gross, MD, PhD, FAAN
Profile: The official scientific journal of the American Academy of Neurology, directed to physicians concerned with diseases & conditions of the nervous system
• Neurology Now
Type: Magazine; *Frequency:* Bimonthly
Profile: Updated & important information for neurology patients, families, & caregivers
• Neurology Today
Type: Newspaper; *Frequency:* Biweekly
Profile: Clinical, policy, research, & practice news, for neurologists

American Academy of Religion (AAR)
#300, 825 Houston Mill Rd. NE, Atlanta GA 30329-4205 USA
Tel: 404-727-3049; *Fax:* 404-727-7959
info@aarweb.org
www.aarweb.org
www.facebook.com/americanacademyofreligion
twitter.com/AARWeb
www.youtube.com/user/AAReligion
Overview: A medium-sized national charitable organization founded in 1909
Mission: To promote research, teaching & scholarship in the field of religion; To be dedicated to furthering knowledge of religion & religious institutions in all their forms & manifestations
Member of: American Council of Learned Societies
Staff Member(s): 16
Membership: 9,000+; *Fees:* US$55 student; US$15 international; US$55-$220 professional or retired; *Member Profile:* Teachers, scholars & other professionals in the field of Religion; *Committees:* Academic Relations; Executive; Finance; Graduate Student; International Connections; Nominations; Program; Publications; Public Understanding of Religion; Regions; Status of Racial & Ethnic Minorities in the Profession; Status of Women in the Profession; Teaching & Learning; Theological Education Steering Committee
Activities: Sustainability Task Force; Status of Lesbian, Gay, Bisexual & Transgendered Persons in the Profession; Awards for Excellence in the Study of Religion Book Award Juries; History of Religions Jury; Research Grants Jury; *Speaker Service:* Yes
Chief Officer(s):
John R. Fitzmier, Executive Director & Treasurer, 404-727-3049
jfitzmier@aarweb.org
Elizabeth Hardcastle, Coordinator, Service, 404-712-6654
ehardcastle@aarweb.org
Steve Herrick, Director, Educational Publishing
Awards:
• Book Awards
For scholarly publications that contribute to the study of religion
• Journalism Awards
For best in-depth reporting on topics related to religion
• Ray L. Hart Service Award

• Martin E. Marty Public Understanding of Religion Award
• AAR Award for Excellence in Teaching
• Religion and the Arts Award
• Annual Meeting Travel Grants
• Wabash Center For Teaching & Learning In Theology & Religion
• Regional Development Grants
Meetings/Conferences:
• American Academy of Religion 2018 Annual Meeting, 2018
Description: Meeting bringing together thousands of professors & students, authors & publishers, religious leaders & interested laypersons for academic sessions, meetings & workshops in the fields of religious studies & theology
Publications:
• In the Field
Type: Newsletter
Profile: Calls for papers, grant news, conference announcements, & other opportunities for scholars of religion
• Journal of the American Academy of Religion
Type: Journal; *Frequency:* Quarterly
Profile: Scholarly articles of world religious traditions & methodologies

American Anthropological Association (AAA)
#1301, 2300 Clarendon Blvd., Arlington VA 22201 USA
Tel: 703-528-1902; *Fax:* 703-528-3546
www.americananthro.org
www.linkedin.com/company/american-anthropological-association
www.facebook.com/AmericanAnthropologicalAssociation
twitter.com/AmericanAnthro
blog.aaanet.org
Overview: A medium-sized international organization founded in 1902
Mission: To represent professional anthropologists in the fields of cultural anthropology, biological & physical anthropology, archaeology, & linguistic anthropology
Member of: American Council of Learned Societies; Consortium of Social Science Associations; International Union of Anthropological & Ethnological Sciences; National Humanities Alliance; World Council of Anthropological Associations
Affiliation(s): World Council of Anthropological Associations
Finances: *Annual Operating Budget:* $3 Million-$5 Million
Staff Member(s): 22
Membership: 10,000; *Fees:* Schedule available; *Member Profile:* Persons with a professional or scholarly interest; *Committees:* Nominations; Finance; Annual Meeting Program; Awards; Association Operations; Scientific Communications; Public Policy; Ethics; Human Rights; Minority Issues in Anthropology; Status of Women in Anthropology
Activities: Publishing American Anthropology & Anthropology News, of 22 journals; Hosting Anthrosource, digital archive of the discipline; Providing career planning & professional development services; Developing education initiatives; Sponsoring a summer internship program & field school in ethnography & occupational therapy; Organizing research conferences; *Internships:* Yes; *Library:* Open to public by appointment
Chief Officer(s):
Ed Liebow, Executive Director
eliebow@americananthro.org
Elaine Lynch, Deputy Executive Director/CFO
elynch@americananthro.org
Awards:
• Franz Boas Award
• AIME Award
• McGraw Hill Award
• Textor Award
Meetings/Conferences:
• American Anthropological Association 2018 Annual Meeting, November, 2018, San Jose Convention Center, San Jose, CA
Scope: International
Contact Information: Director, Meetings & Conferences: Ushma Suvarnakar, Phone: 703-528-1902 ext. 1172
• American Anthropological Association 2019 Annual Meeting, November, 2019, Vancouver Convention Center, Vancouver, BC
Scope: International
Contact Information: Director, Meetings & Conferences: Ushma Suvarnakar, Phone: 703-528-1902 ext. 1172
• American Anthropological Association 2020 Annual Meeting, November, 2020, Cervantes Convention Center at America's Center, St. Louis, MO
Scope: International
Contact Information: Director, Meetings & Conferences: Ushma Suvarnakar, Phone: 703-528-1902 ext. 1172

• American Anthropological Association 2021 Annual Meeting, November, 2021, Baltimore Convention Center, Baltimore, MD
Scope: International
Contact Information: Director, Meetings & Conferences: Ushma Suvarnakar, Phone: 703-528-1902 ext. 1172
Publications:
• American Anthropologist [a publication of the American Anthropological Association]
Type: Journal
• Anthropology News [a publication of the American Anthropological Association]
Type: Magazine; *Frequency:* Bimonthly; *Editor:* Natalie Konopinski
Profile: News for the discipline of anthropology
• Open Anthropology [a publication of the American Anthropological Association]
Type: Journal

American Antiquarian Society (AAS)
185 Salisbury St., Worcester MA 01609-1634 USA
Tel: 508-755-5221; *Fax:* 508-753-3311
library@mwa.org
www.americanantiquarian.org
Overview: A small national organization founded in 1812
Mission: To maintain a research library of American history & culture in order to collect, preserve & make available for study the printed record of the United States; specializes in the American period to 1877
Member of: American Council of Learned Societies
Finances: *Annual Operating Budget:* Greater than $5 Million
Staff Member(s): 60; 5 volunteer(s)
Membership: 1,021; *Member Profile:* Contributions to advancement of historical scholarship in America
Activities: Public lectures & seminars on the history of the book & the copies related to the collections; grants & fellowships; research; public programs; *Library*
Chief Officer(s):
Sidney Lapidus, Chair
Ellen S. Dunlap, President

American Association for Justice (AAJ)
#200, 777 - 6th St. NW, Washington DC 20001 USA
Tel: 202-965-3500
Toll-Free: 800-424-2725
Other Communication: media.replies@justice.org
membership@justice.org
www.justice.org
www.linkedin.com/company/american-association-for-justice
www.facebook.com/JusticeDotOrg
twitter.com/JusticeDotOrg
Previous Name: Association of Trial Lawyers of America (ATLA); National Association of Claimants' Compensation Attorneys (NACCA)
Overview: A large international organization
Mission: To promote a fair & effective justice system; To support the work of attorneys
Membership: *Fees:* Schedule available
Chief Officer(s):
Linda Lipsen, CEO, 202-965-3500 Ext. 8305
linda.lipsen@justice.org
Anne Doohan, COO, 202-965-3500 Ext. 2837
anne.doohan@justice.org
Kathi Berge, CFO, 202-965-3500 Ext. 8244
kathi.berge@justice.org
Awards:
• AAJ Paralegal of the Year Award
• Steven J. Sharp Public Service Award
• Community Champion Award
• Johnnie L. Cochran Soaring Eagle Award
• Marie Lambert Award
• F. Scott Baldwin Award
• Tonahill Award
• Wiedemann & Wysocki Award
• Alia Herrera Memorial Scholarship
• The Richard D. Hailey Law Student Scholarship
• Trial Advocacy Scholarship
• Leesfield Scholarship
• Mike Eidson Scholarship
Meetings/Conferences:
• American Association for Justice 2018 Winter Convention, February, 2018, Grand Wailea, Maui, HI
Scope: International
• American Association for Justice 2018 Annual Convention, July, 2018, Denver Convention Center, Denver, CO
Scope: International

- American Association for Justice 2019 Winter Convention, February, 2019, Loews Miami Beach, Miami Beach, FL
Scope: International
- American Association for Justice 2019 Annual Convention, July, 2019, San Diego Convention Center, San Diego, CA
Scope: International
Publications:
- American Association for Justice Member Directory
Type: Directory
Profile: Directory listings of AAJ membership for public & AAJ members
- Law Reporters [a publication of the American Association for Justice]
Type: Newsletter; *Frequency:* Monthly; *Accepts Advertising*
Profile: Products Liability Law Reporter; Professional Negligence Law Reporter; Class Action Law Reporter; Motor Vehicle Law Reporter
- Trial [a publication of the American Association for Justice]
Type: Magazine; *Frequency:* Monthly; *Accepts Advertising*;
Price: Free with AAJ membership
Profile: Trial focuses on a specific theme each month, such as employment law, products liability, & medical negligence

American Association for the Advancement of Science (AAAS)
1200 New York Ave. NW, Washington DC 20005 USA
Tel: 202-326-6440
Other Communication: media@aaas.org; development@aaas.org
membership@aaas.org
www.aaas.org
www.facebook.com/AAAS.Science
twitter.com/AAAS
www.youtube.com/user/wwwAAASorg
Overview: A large national organization founded in 1848
Mission: To advance science, engineering, & innovation around the world to benefit all people; To provide a voice for science on societal issues
Affiliation(s): 262 affiliated societies & academies of science
Staff Member(s): 300
Membership: *Fees:* Schedule available; *Member Profile:* Open to all
Activities: Offering international programs; Providing science education; Publishing books & reports; Promoting the integrity of science & its responsible use in public policy; Facilitating communication among scientists, engineers, & the public; Raising public engagement with science & technology
Chief Officer(s):
Geraldine Richmond, Chair
Barbara A. Schaal, President
Rush D. Holt, Chief Executive Officer
David Evans Shaw, Treasurer
Awards:
- AAAS Philip Hauge Abelson Prize
- AAAS Award for International Scientific Cooperation
- AAAS Award for Public Understanding of Science and Technology
- AAAS Mentor Award
- AAAS Scientific Freedom and Responsibility Award
- AAAS Science Journalism Award
Meetings/Conferences:
- American Association for the Advancement of Science 2018 Annual Meeting, February, 2018, Austin, TX
Scope: International
Description: Information for scientists, engineers, educators, & policy-makers
Contact Information: Phone: 202-326-6450; Fax: 202-289-4021;
E-mail: meetings@aaas.org; Director, Meetings: Andrew Black, E-mail: ablack@aaas.org
- American Association for the Advancement of Science 2019 Annual Meeting, February, 2019, Washington, DC
Scope: International
Description: Information for scientists, engineers, educators, & policy-makers
- American Association for the Advancement of Science 2020 Annual Meeting, February, 2020, Seattle, WA
Scope: International
Description: Information for scientists, engineers, educators, & policy-makers
Publications:
- AAAS [American Association for the Advancement of Science] Annual Report
Type: Yearbook; *Frequency:* Annually
- AAAS [American Association for the Advancement of Science] Advances

Type: Newsletter
Profile: A members only newsletter with updates on American Association for the Advancement of Science research
- AAAS [American Association for the Advancement of Science] Policy Alert
Type: Newsletter; *Frequency:* Weekly
Profile: News about science policy
- Science [a publication of the American Association for the Advancement of Science]
Type: Journal; *Frequency:* Weekly; *Editor:* Bruce Alberts
Profile: Original scientific research & global news
- Science Books & Films [a publication of the American Association for the Advancement of Science]
Type: Journal
Profile: A critical review journal of educational materials for science teachers
- Science Roundup [a publication of the American Association for the Advancement of Science]
Type: Newsletter
Profile: A members only newsletter with updates on American Association for the Advancement of Science research & programs
- Science Signaling [a publication of the American Association for the Advancement of Science]
Type: Journal; *Frequency:* Weekly; *Editor:* Michael B. Yaffe, M.D., Ph.D; *ISSN:* 1937-9145
Profile: Information for experts & novices in cell signaling
- Science Translational Medicine [a publication of the American Association for the Advancement of Science]
Type: Journal; *Editor:* Katrina L. Kelner, Ph.D.
Profile: Information for basic translational, & clinical research practitioners & trainees

American Association for the Advancement of Slavic Studies (AAASS) *See* Association for Slavic, East European, & Eurasian Studies

American Association for Thoracic Surgery (AARS)
#4550, 500 Cummings Center, Beverly MA 01915 USA
Tel: 978-927-8330; *Fax:* 978-524-0498
www.aats.org
www.facebook.com/AATS1917
twitter.com/AATSHQ
Overview: A medium-sized international organization founded in 1917
Mission: To promote scholarship & scientific research in thoracic & cardiovascular surgery
Membership: 1,300+; *Member Profile:* Cardiothoracic surgeons from 37 countries
Activities: Offering continuing medical education
Chief Officer(s):
Thoralf M. Sundt, President
Meetings/Conferences:
- American Association for Thoracic Surgery 98th Annual Meeting, April, 2018, San Diego Convention Center, San Diego, CA
Scope: International
Description: Education in the field of thoracic & cardiovascular surgery, for cardiothoracic surgeons, physicians in related specialties, allied health professionals, fellows & residents in cardiothoracic & general surgical training programs, as well as medical students with an interest in cardiothoracic surgery
Publications:
- Journal of Thoracic & Cardiovascular Surgery
Type: Journal; *Editor:* Richard Weisel
Profile: Original articles about the chest, heart, lungs, & great vessels where surgical intervention is indicated
- Operative Techniques in Thoracic & Cardiovascular Surgery: A Comparative Atlas
Editor: J. William Gaynor
Profile: Technique-based articles in cardiovascular & thoracic surgery by renowned surgeons in the field
- Pediatric Cardiac Surgery Annual
Type: Journal; *Frequency:* Annually; *Editor:* Robert D.B. Jaquiss
Profile: Developments in pediatric cardiac surgery
- Seminars in Thoracic & Cardiovascular Surgery
Type: Journal; *Editor:* Harvey Pass; Todd Rosengart
Profile: Topics & issues faced by practising surgeons in clinical practice
- Thoracic Surgery News
Type: Newspaper; *Frequency:* 10 pa; *Editor:* Michael Liptay
Profile: News of general thoracic surgery, adult cardiac surgery, transplantation, & congenital heart disease

American Association of Bovine Practitioners (AABP)
PO Box 3610, #802, 3320 Skyway Dr., Auburn AL 36831-3610 USA
Tel: 334-821-0442; *Fax:* 334-821-9532
aabphq@aabp.org
www.aabp.org
Overview: A medium-sized international organization
Mission: To enhance the professional lives of international veterinarians; To improve the well-being of cattle; To help the economic success of cattle owners
Membership: *Member Profile:* International veterinarians engaged in the general field of bovine medicine or those who are interested in bovine medicine; Honorary members are persons who have made outstanding contributions to bovine practice; Veterinary students; *Committees:* Amstutz Scholarship; Animal Welfare; Beef Production Management; Biological Risk Management & Preparedness; Bovine Respiratory Disease; Food Quality, Safety, & Security; Distance Education; Information Management; Lameness; Milk Quality & Udder Health; Membership; Nutrition; Pharmaceutical & Biological Issues; Reproduction
Activities: Offering continuing education programs; Providing networking opportunities with fellow veterinarians; Improving career opportunities in bovine medicine; Increasing awareness of issues in the cattle industry; Promoting leadership on critical issues in the cattle business
Chief Officer(s):
Roger Saltman, President
M. Gatz Riddell, Executive Vice-President
mgriddell@aabp.org
Meetings/Conferences:
- The American Association of Bovine Practitioners 2018 Annual Conference, September, 2018, Phoenix, AZ
Scope: International
- The American Association of Bovine Practitioners 2019 Annual Conference, September, 2019, St. Louis, MO
Scope: International
- The American Association of Bovine Practitioners 2020 Annual Conference, September, 2020, Louisville, KY
Scope: International
- The American Association of Bovine Practitioners 2021 Annual Conference, September, 2021, Minneapolis, MN
Scope: International
- The American Association of Bovine Practitioners 2022 Annual Conference, September, 2022, Long Beach, CA
Scope: International
Publications:
- American Association of Bovine Practitioners Newsletter
Type: Newsletter; *Frequency:* Monthly; *Price:* Free with American Association of Bovine Practitioners membership
Profile: Updates from the association
- American Association of Bovine Practitioners Annual Membership Directory
Type: Directory; *Frequency:* Annually; *Price:* Free with American Association of Bovine Practitioners membership
- The Bovine Practitioner
Type: Journal; *Frequency:* Semiannually; *Accepts Advertising*;
Price: Free with American Association of Bovine Practitioners membership
- Proceedings of the American Association of Bovine Practitioners Annual Conference
Type: Yearbook; *Frequency:* Annually; *Price:* Free with American Association of Bovine Practitioners membership

American Association of Naturopathic Physicians (AANP)
#250, 818 - 18th St. NW, Washington DC 20006 USA
Tel: 202-237-8150; *Fax:* 202-237-8152
Toll-Free: 866-538-2267
member.services@naturopathic.org
www.naturopathic.org
www.linkedin.com/groups/1213117
www.facebook.com/theAANP
twitter.com/AANP
Overview: A small international organization
Mission: Represents licensed or licensable naturopathic physicians who are graduates of four-year, residential graduates programs
Affiliation(s): Canadian Association of Naturopathic Doctors; College of Naturopathic Doctors of Alberta; British Columbia Naturopathic Association; Manitoba Naturopathic Association; New Brunswick Association of Naturopathic Doctors; Newfoundland and Labrador Association of Naturopathic Doctors; Nova Scotia Association of Naturopathic Doctors;

Foreign Associations / American Association of Neuromuscular & Electrodiagnostic Medicine (AANEM)

Ontario Association of Naturopathic Doctors; Prince Edward Island Association of Naturopathic Doctors; Quebec Association of Naturopathic Medicine; Saskatchewan Association of Naturopathic Practitioners; Yukon Naturopathic Association
Membership: 2,000 (students & physicians)
Chief Officer(s):
Laura Farr, Executive Director, 202-849-6306
laura.farr@naturopathic.org
Awards:
• Physician of the Year
• Corporation of the Year
• President's Award
• Vis Award
Meetings/Conferences:
• American Association of Naturopathic Physicians 2018 Annual Conference, July, 2018, Town & Country Resort, San Diego, CA
Scope: International

American Association of Neuromuscular & Electrodiagnostic Medicine (AANEM)
2621 Superior Dr. NW, Rochester MN 55901 USA
Tel: 507-288-0100; *Fax:* 507-288-1225
aanem@aanem.org
www.aanem.org
www.facebook.com/AANEMorg
twitter.com/aanemorg
Overview: A medium-sized international organization founded in 1953
Mission: To advance neuromuscular, musculoskeletal, & electrodiagnostic medicine; To increase members' knowledge of neurophysiology, pathophysiology, instrumentation, & electrodiagnostic medicine; To improve the quality of patient care
Membership: 5,187; *Member Profile:* Physicians who diagnose & treat patients with disorders of the muscless & nerves
Activities: Liaising with other organizations; Providing educational programs; Encouraging research
Chief Officer(s):
Shirlyn A. Adkins, Executive Director
sadkins@aanem.org
Patrick Aldrich, Director, Finance
paldrich@aanem.org
Millie Suk, Director, Health Policy
msuk@aanem.org
Laurie Mona, Manager, Communications
lmona@aanem.org
Meetings/Conferences:
• American Association of Neuromuscular & Electrodiagnostic Medicine 2018 65th Annual Meeting, October, 2018, Gaylord National, Washington, DC
Scope: International
Publications:
• AANEM [American Association of Neuromuscular & Electrodiagnostic Medicine] News
Type: Newsletter; *Frequency:* Quarterly
Profile: Association activities, science in brief, legislative issues, & information about coding
• Muscle & Nerve
Type: Journal; *Accepts Advertising*; *ISSN:* 0148-639X
Profile: Readership includes neurologists, physiatrists, & physical & rehabilitative medical specialists

American Association of Opticians *See* American Optometric Association

The American Association of Petroleum Geologists (AAPG)
PO Box 979, 1444 South Boulder, Tulsa OK 74101-0979 USA
Tel: 918-584-2555; *Fax:* 918-560-2665
Toll-Free: 800-364-2274
postmaster@aapg.org
www.aapg.org
linkd.in/AAPG_Group
www.facebook.com/AAPGeologists
twitter.com/AAPG
www.youtube.com/AAPGweb
Overview: A small national organization
Affiliation(s): Canadian Society of Petroleum Geologists
Activities: *Library:* AAPG Library; Open to public
Chief Officer(s):
Richard (Rick) D. Fritz, Executive Director
Scott W. Tinker, President
Awards:
• Grants-in-Aid
Postgraduate research projects leading to the M.S. degree in geology, geophysics, engineering, environmental studies, earth sciences, chemistry, mineralogy or science for Canadian, landed immigrant or visa students *Amount:* $2,000 maximum

American Association on Intellectual & Developmental Disabilities (AAIDD)
#200, 501 - 3rd St. NW, Washington DC 20001 USA
Tel: 202-387-1968; *Fax:* 202-387-2193
admin@aaidd.org
aaidd.org
www.linkedin.com/groups/American-Association-on-Intellectual-Developmental-4286523
www.facebook.com/350322627779
twitter.com/_aaidd
www.youtube.com/user/aaiddvideos
Previous Name: American Association on Mental Retardation
Overview: A large international organization founded in 1876
Mission: To provide leadership in the field of intellectual & developmental disabilities throughout the world
Finances: *Funding Sources:* Membership fees; donations
Membership: 5,000 in the USA; present in 55 countries worldwide; *Fees:* $50 international electronic; $75 basic; $125 classic
Activities: Offering publications, webinars, e-learning & continuing professional education, & Supports Intensity Scale; Organizing annual conference
Chief Officer(s):
William Gaventa, MDiv, President
Margaret A. Nygren, EdD, Executive Director & CEO
mnygren@aaidd.org
Paul D. Aitken, CPA, Director, Finance & Administration
pdaitken@aaidd.org
Corinne Carpenter, Coordinator, Communications & Membership
ccarpenter@aaidd.org
Meetings/Conferences:
• 142nd American Association on Intellectual & Developmental Disabilities Annual Meeting, June, 2018, St. Louis, MO
Scope: International
Publications:
• American Journal on Intellectual & Developmental Disabilities
Type: Journal; *Frequency:* Bimonthly; *Editor:* Deborah Fidler; *ISSN:* 1944-7558
Profile: Scientific, scholarly & archival journal for original contributions of knowledge of intellectual disability, including its causes, treatment & prevention.
• Inclusion [a publication of the American Association on Intellectual & Developmental Disabilities]
Type: Journal; *Frequency:* Bimonthly; *Editor:* Michael Wehmeyer; Karrie Shogren; *ISSN:* 2326-6988
Profile: Peer-reviewed journal that discusses strategies that promote the inclusion ofpeople with intellectual & developmental disabilities in society.
• Intellectual & Developmental Disabilities
Type: Journal; *Frequency:* Bimonthly; *Editor:* James R. Thompson; *ISSN:* 1934-9556
Profile: Peer-reviewed journal of policy, practices & perspectives.

American Association on Mental Retardation *See* American Association on Intellectual & Developmental Disabilities

The American Astronautical Society (AAS)
#102, 6352 Rolling Mill Pl., Springfield VA 22152-2370 USA
Tel: 703-866-0020; *Fax:* 703-866-3526
aas@astronautical.org
www.astronautical.org
www.facebook.com/AmericanAstronauticalSociety
twitter.com/astrosociety
www.youtube.com/user/astrosociety
Overview: A medium-sized international organization founded in 1954
Mission: To promote professional support & interaction in astronautical sciences (rocketry, spaceflight, space medicine, international cooperation); To advance space activities; To provide a platform that allows members to exchange information, expand knowledge, & meet with leaders in their field
Member of: International Astronautical Federation
Finances: *Annual Operating Budget:* $500,000-$1.5 Million; *Funding Sources:* Membership dues; Donations; Revenue from conferences & publications
Staff Member(s): 2; 40 volunteer(s)
Membership: 1,400; *Fees:* $100 USD individual, affiliate; $50 USD retired; $45 teacher, student; $125 USD senior member; schedule corporate; *Member Profile:* Space professionals & enthusiasts; *Committees:* Space Flight Mechanics; Guidance & Control; International Programs; International Space Station Technical; History; Education; Space Surveillance
Activities: Organizing three general conferences & three technical conferences including Goddard Symposium, Van Braun Symposium, & ISS Conference; *Internships:* Yes
Chief Officer(s):
Lyn D. Wigbels, President
James Kirkpatrick, Executive Director, 703-866-0020
jkirkpatrick@astronautical.org
Diane Thompson, Executive Assistant, 703-866-0020
dthompson@astronautical.org
Awards:
• Space Entrepreneurship Award
• Space Life Sciences Award
• Sally Ride Education Award
• Earth Science & Applications Award
• Space Technology Award
• Advancement of International Cooperation Award
• Carl Sagan Memorial Award
• Lifetime Achievement Award
• Industrial Leadership Award
• John F. Kennedy Astronautics Award
• Eugene M. Emme Astronautical Literature Award
• Neil Armstrong Space Flight Achievement Award
• Space Flight Award
• Dirk Brouwer Award
• Ordway Award for Sustained Excellence in Spaceflight History
Meetings/Conferences:
• American Astronautical Society 2018 56th Robert H. Goddard Memorial Symposium, March, 2018, Greenbelt, MD
Scope: International
Publications:
• The Journal of Astronautical Sciences [a publication of the American Astronautical Society]
Type: Journal; *Frequency:* Quarterly; *Editor:* Kathleen C. Howell

American Bankers Association (ABA)
1120 Connecticut Ave. NW, Washington DC 20036 USA
Toll-Free: 800-226-5377
custserv@aba.com
www.aba.com
www.linkedin.com/company/american-bankers-association
www.facebook.com/AmericanBankersAssociation
twitter.com/ABABankingNews
www.youtube.com/user/AmericanBankersAssn
Overview: A medium-sized national organization
Mission: To represent banks of all sizes on issues of national importance for financial institutions & their customers
Chief Officer(s):
Jeff L. Plagge, Chair
Frank Keating, President & CEO

American Birding Association, Inc. (ABA)
PO Box 744, 93 Clinton St., #ABA, Delaware City DE 19706 USA
Tel: 302-838-3660; *Fax:* 302-838-3651
Toll-Free: 800-850-2473
member@aba.org
www.americanbirding.org
www.facebook.com/birders
twitter.com/aba
www.youtube.com/user/AmericanBirding
Overview: A large national organization founded in 1969
Mission: To provide leadership to field birders by increasing their knowledge, skills & enjoyment of birding & by contributing to bird conservation
Member of: Partners in Flight; American Bird Conservancy; Bird Conservation Alliance
Finances: *Annual Operating Budget:* $500,000-$1.5 Million
Staff Member(s): 18
Membership: 22,000; *Fees:* Schedule available
Activities: Providing youth education; Engaging in conservation programs; *Rents Mailing List:* Yes; *Library:* Open to public
Chief Officer(s):
Louis M. Morrell, Chair
Jeffrey A. Gordon, President
jgordon@aba.org
Awards:
• ABA Roger Tory Peterson Award Promoting the Cause of Birding
• ABA Chandler Robbins Award Education/Conservation
• ABA Claudia Wilds Award Distinguished Service
• ABA Robert Ridgway Award Publications in Field Ornithology
• ABA Ludlow Griscom Award Outstanding Contributions in Regional Ornithology
• ABA Betty Petersen Award for Conservation and Community
Publications:
• Birder's Guide [a publication of American Birding Association,

Inc.]
Type: Magazine; *Frequency:* Quarterly; *Editor:* Michael Retter
• Birding [a publication of American Birding Association, Inc.]
Type: Magazine; *Frequency:* s-m.; *Editor:* Ted Floyd
• North American Birds [a publication of American Birding Association, Inc.]
Type: Journal; *Price:* US $30 for members; US $32 fornon-members; $US 60 for libraries/corporations
Profile: Provides an overview of the changing panorama of North America's birdlife through regional reports & summaries

American Cave Conservation Association (ACCA)
PO Box 409, 119 East Main St., Horse Cave KY 42749 USA
Tel: 270-786-1466; *Fax:* 270-786-1467
acca@cavern.org
caveconservation.com
Also Known As: American Cave & Karst Center
Overview: A small international organization founded in 1977
Mission: To protect & preserve caves, karstlands & groundwater; to bring together information about cave & karst resources from across the nation & make it available to those who are working to protect these resources
Staff Member(s): 4
Membership: *Fees:* Regular: $25; Internation: $30; Student: $15; Family: $35, Supporter: $50; Sustainer: $100; Guarantor: $200; Benefactor: $500; Patron: $1000
Activities: Operates National Cave Management Training program & The American Cave Museum; provides outreach educational programs; constructs cave gates; *Library:* by appointment Not open to public
Chief Officer(s):
David G. Foster, Executive Director
acca@cavern.org
Publications:
• American Caves

American Chemistry Council (ACC)
700 Second St. NE, Washington DC 20002 USA
Tel: 202-249-7000; *Fax:* 202-249-6100
www.americanchemistry.com
www.linkedin.com/company/american-chemistry-council
www.facebook.com/ImpactChemistry
twitter.com/AmChemistry
Overview: A medium-sized national organization
Mission: To support members through advocacy, member engagement, political advocacy, communications & scientific research
Membership: *Member Profile:* Companies engaged in the business of chemistry
Activities: Conducting research & development activities
Chief Officer(s):
Calvin M. Dooley, President & CEO
Raymond J. O'Bryan, Chief Financial Officer & CAO
Dell Perelman, Chief of Staff & General Counsel
Nacole B. Hinton, Vice-President, Administration
Anne Kolton, Vice-President, Communications, 202-249-6500
Anne_Kolton@americanchemistry.com
Debra M. Phillips, Vice-President, Responsible Care & Value Chain Outreach
Steve Russell, Vice-President, Plastics Division
Robert J. Simon, Vice-President, Chemical Products & Technology & Chlorine Chemistry
Rudy Underwood, Vice-President, State Affairs & Public Mobilization
Michael P. Walls, Vice-President, Regulatory & Technical Affairs
Bryan Zumwalt, Vice-President, Federal Affairs
Meetings/Conferences:
• GlobalChem Conference & Exhibition 2018, February, 2018, Washington, DC
Scope: International
• American Chemistry Council 2018 Annual Meeting, June, 2018, Colorado Springs, CO
Scope: International

American College of Chest Physicians (ACCP)
2595 Patriot Blvd., Glenview IL 60062-2348 USA
Tel: 224-521-9800; *Fax:* 224-521-9801
Toll-Free: 800-343-2227
www.chestnet.org
Overview: A medium-sized international organization founded in 1935
Mission: To improve cardiopulmonary health & critical care worldwide; To promote the prevention & treatment of diseases of the chest
Membership: 19,000; *Member Profile:* USA & Canadian physicians, who are board-certified specialists in chest medicine, surgery, or critical care medicine, & who devote a major portion of their practice to diseases of the chest; International physicians, recognized in their community in disciplines related to chest medicine, surgery, or critical care medicine; Physicians who are interested in cardiopulmonary medicine or surgery, critical care, or related disciplines; Physicians-in-Training; Allied health members, such as nonphysician health professionals or administrators; *Committees:* Compensation; Council of Advisors; Diversity Task Force; Education; Council of NetWorks; Guidelines Oversight; Joint Finance Oversight; Membership; Nominating; Professional Standards; Scientific Presentations & Awards; Scientific Program; Social Media Work Group; Training & Transitions; Trainee Work Group
Activities: Providing educational opportunities; Encouraging research; Liaising with government agencies
Chief Officer(s):
Stephen J. Welch, Interim Chief Executive Officer
P. Stratton Davies, Chief Financial Officer & Sr. Vice-President
Jennifer Nemkovich, Chief Strategy Officer
Robert Musacchio, Senior Vice-President, Business Development
Nicole Augustyn, Senior Vice-President, Education
Sue Reimbold, Senior Vice-President, Marketing & Communications
Meetings/Conferences:
• American College of Chest Physicians Conference: CHEST 2018, October, 2018, San Antonio, TX
Scope: International
Description: Educational sessions, CME credits, clinical instruction, & networking opportunities for health professionals
Publications:
• ACCP [American College of Chest Physicians] Critical Care Medicine Board Review
ISBN: 978-0-916609-76-4
Profile: Review chapters developed to complement the American College of Chest Physicians Critical Care Medicine Board Review course,directed toward an audience of physicians in critical care & pulmonary medicine, emergency departments, anesthesiology, & surgery, as well as nurses & respiratory therapists
• ACCP [American College of Chest Physicians] Pulmonary Medicine Board Review
ISBN: 978-0-916609-77-1
Profile: A text covering current pulmonary literature & management strategies for critically ill patients, written for physicians & fellows incritical care pulmonary medicine, as well as advanced critical care nurse practitioners & respiratory therapy practitioners
• ACCP [American College of Chest Physicians] Sleep Medicine Board Review
ISBN: 978-0-916609-75-7
Profile: Review chapters of major topics from the American College of Chest Physicians Sleep Medicine Board Review course, intended for physiciansin sleep medicine, physicians in pulmonary medicine, neurologists, respiratory therapists, & nurses
• ACCP [American College of Chest Physicians] / AAP Pediatric Pulmonary Board Review
ISBN: 978-0-916609-85-6
Profile: Review chapters of major topics from the American College of Chest Physicians / American Academy of Pediatrics PediatricPulmonary Medicine Board Review course, of interest to pediatric pulmonologists, family physicians, pediatric intensivists, allergists, & general pediatricians
• CHEST [a publication of the American College of Chest Physicians]
Type: Journal; *Frequency:* Monthly; *Accepts Advertising*; *Editor:* Richard S. Irwin, MD, FCCP; *ISSN:* 0012-3692
Profile: Original research in the multidisciplinary specialties of chest medicine, of interest to specialists in pulmonology,critical care medicine, sleep medicine, thoracic surgery, cardiorespiratory interactions, & related specialists
• Chest Physician
Type: Newspaper; *Frequency:* Monthly; *Accepts Advertising*; *Editor:* Vera A. De Palo, MD, MBA, FCCP
Profile: News from chest medicine specialties, clinical information, American College of Chest Physicians activities, & updoming events

American Concrete Institute (ACI)
38800 Country Club Dr., Farmington Hills MI 48331-3439 USA
Tel: 248-848-3700; *Fax:* 248-848-3701
www.concrete.org
www.linkedin.com/company/american-concrete-institute
www.facebook.com/AmericanConcreteInstitute
twitter.com/concreteaci
www.youtube.com/user/AmericanConcreteInst;
instagram.com/concreteaci
Overview: A large international licensing organization founded in 1905
Mission: To gather & disseminate technical information relating to the design & construction of concrete & its properties
Finances: *Annual Operating Budget:* Greater than $5 Million
Staff Member(s): 96
Membership: 20,000 individuals in 120 countries; *Committees:* Many committees grouped into the following categories: Board; Certification; Convention; Educational; International; Student & Young Professional Activities; Technical
Activities: Offering 18 certification programs; Disseminating information through publications
Chief Officer(s):
Ronald G. Burg, Executive Vice-President
ron.burg@concrete.org
John C. Glumb, Senior Managing Director, Operations
john.glumb@concrete.org
Chris J. Darnell, Managing Director, Customer & Product Strategy
chris.darnell@concrete.org
Michael L. Tholen, Managing Director, Engineering & Professional Development
mike.tholen@concrete.org
Bernie Pekor, Director, International Business Development
bernie.pekor@concrete.org
Awards:
• ACI Foundation Awards
• ACI Chapter Awards
• Chapter Activities Award
• Student Fellowships & Scholarships Program
Meetings/Conferences:
• American Concrete Institute Spring 2018 Concrete Conference & Exhibition, March, 2018, Grand America & Little America, Salt Lake City, UT
Scope: International
Description: Theme: "Concrete Elevated"
Contact Information: Event Planner: Alexandria R. Prokic, E-mail: alex.prokic@concrete.org
• American Concrete Institute Fall 2018 Concrete Conference & Exhibition, October, 2018, Rio All-Suites Hotel & Casino, Las Vegas, NV
Scope: International
Contact Information: Event Planner: Alexandria R. Prokic, E-mail: alex.prokic@concrete.org
• American Concrete Institute Spring 2019 Concrete Conference & Exhibition, March, 2019, Quebec City Convention Centre & Hilton Quebec, Québec, QC
Scope: International
Contact Information: Event Planner: Alexandria R. Prokic, E-mail: alex.prokic@concrete.org
• American Concrete Institute Fall 2019 Concrete Conference & Exhibition, October, 2019, Duke Energy Convention Center & Hyatt Regency Cincinnati, Cincinnati, OH
Scope: International
Contact Information: Event Planner: Alexandria R. Prokic, E-mail: alex.prokic@concrete.org
• American Concrete Institute Spring 2020 Concrete Conference & Exhibition, March, 2020, Hyatt Regency O'Hare, Rosemont, IL
Scope: International
Contact Information: Event Planner: Alexandria R. Prokic, E-mail: alex.prokic@concrete.org
• American Concrete Institute Fall 2020 Concrete Conference & Exhibition, October, 2020, Raleigh Marriott, Raleigh, NC
Scope: International
Contact Information: Event Planner: Alexandria R. Prokic, E-mail: alex.prokic@concrete.org
• American Concrete Institute Spring 2021 Concrete Conference & Exhibition, March, 2021, Hilton & Marriott Baltimore, Baltimore, MD
Scope: International
Contact Information: Event Planner: Alexandria R. Prokic, E-mail: alex.prokic@concrete.org
• American Concrete Institute Fall 2021 Concrete Conference & Exhibition, October, 2021, Hilton Atlanta Downtown, Atlanta, GA
Scope: International
Contact Information: Event Planner: Alexandria R. Prokic, E-mail: alex.prokic@concrete.org
Publications:
• ACI [American Concrete Institute] Materials Journal
Type: Journal; *ISSN:* 0889-325X
• ACI [American Concrete Institute] Structural Journal
Type: Journal; *ISSN:* 0889-3241

Foreign Associations / American Council for an Energy-Efficient Economy (ACEEE)

- American Concrete Institute Certification Publications
Type: Guide
Profile: A series of documents designed to ensure that ACI Certification candidates have access to the technical materials used as resources to develop ACI Certification exams
- American Concrete Institute Educational Publications
Type: Guide
Profile: A series of documents that use ACI technical documents as a basis to disseminate information for a wider audience
- American Concrete Institute Handbooks & Manuals
Type: Guide
Profile: A series of handbooks that provide tools & guidance to the practitioner on applying design, construction, & inspection standards
- American Concrete Institute Technical Documents
Type: Guide
Profile: A series of documents that involve codes, specifications, guides, & reference manuals
- Concrete International [a publication of the American Concrete Institute]
Type: Magazine; *Frequency:* Monthly; *ISSN:* 0162-4075

Alberta Chapter
Edmonton AB
www.aci-alberta.org
Mission: To gather & disseminate technical information relating to the design & construction of concrete & its properties
Chief Officer(s):
Martin Maier, President
mmaier@islengineering.com

Atlantic Chapter
c/o Corey Boland, 845 Prospect St., Fredericton NB E3B 2T7
Tel: 506-457-3262; *Fax:* 506-452-0112
www.concrete.org
Chief Officer(s):
Corey Boland, President

British Columbia Chapter
1231 East 51st Ave., Vancouver BC V5X 1E9
Tel: 604-734-0184
www.acibc.ca
Chief Officer(s):
Darlene Lane, Secretary-Treasurer

Eastern Ontario & Quebec Chapter
PO Box 57501, Stn. Courville, Québec QC G1C YW3
Tel: 855-300-7803
info@aciquebec.com
www.aciquebec.com
Chief Officer(s):
Éric Bédard, Directeur général
eric.bedard@aciquebec.com

Manitoba Chapter
PO Box 1703, Winnipeg MB R3C 2Z6
e-mail: info@acimanitoba.ca
www.acimanitoba.ca
Chief Officer(s):
Marc Baril, President

Ontario Chapter
172 Bethridge Rd., Toronto ON M9W 1N3
www.aciontario.com
Chief Officer(s):
Alain Belanger, Secretary-Treasurer
abelanger@nca.ca

American Council for an Energy-Efficient Economy (ACEEE)
#600, 529 - 14th St. NW, Washington DC 20045-1000 USA
Tel: 202-507-4000; *Fax:* 202-429-2248
www.aceee.org
www.facebook.com/myACEEE
twitter.com/ACEEEdc
Overview: A medium-sized national organization founded in 1980
Mission: To advance energy-conserving technology & policies; To assist utilities & regulators in implementing cost-effective conservation programs; To support the adoption of comprehensive new policies for increasing energy efficiency; To analyse & promote technologies & policies for increasing vehicle fuel efficiency & reducing vehicle use; To help developing & Eastern European countries undertake energy efficiency programs
Activities: *Library:* American Council for an Energy-Efficient Economy Library
Chief Officer(s):
Steven Nadel, Executive Director, 202-507-4011
snadel@aceee.org

American Council for Québec Studies (ACQS)
c/o University of Maine, 213 Little Hall, Orono ME 04469 USA
e-mail: acqs2@maine.edu
www.southalabama.edu/acqs
Previous Name: Northeast Council for Québec Studies
Overview: A small international organization founded in 1981
Mission: To promote the study of Québec in the United States through the publication of its Québec Studies journal & the sponsorship of the biennial conference
Membership: *Fees:* US$100; *Member Profile:* American scholars & others with teaching, research, &/or business interests in Québec & French Canada, or with an active interest in Québec's history, literature, politics, language and culture.
Activities: Biennial conference
Chief Officer(s):
Sam Fisher, President
Meetings/Conferences:
- American Council for Québec Studies Biennial Conference, 2018

Publications:
- Québec Studies
Type: Journal

American Council of Learned Societies
633 Third Ave., New York NY 10017-6795 USA
Tel: 212-697-1505; *Fax:* 212-949-8058
www.acls.org
www.facebook.com/acls1919
twitter.com/acls1919
www.pinterest.com/acls1919; www.acls1919.tumblr.com
Overview: A large international organization founded in 1919
Mission: To represent American scholarship in the humanities & social sciences; To provide opportunities for innovation & advancement in the field
Finances: *Funding Sources:* Private grants, endowment income, annual subscriptions from university and college Associates, government contracts, individual gifts
Membership: 73; *Member Profile:* Scholarly organizations
Activities: Holding meetings & seminars; Facilitating commissions & working groups
Chief Officer(s):
Pauline Yu, President, 212-697-1505 Ext. 121
paulineyu@acls.org
Sandra Bradley, Director, Member Relations, 212-697-1505 Ext. 123
sbradley@acls.org
Matthew Goldfeder, Director, Fellowship Programs, 212-697-1505 Ext. 124
mgoldfeder@acls.org
Meetings/Conferences:
- American Council of Learned Societies Annual Meeting 2018, April, 2018, Sheraton Society Hill Hotel, Philadelphia, PA
Scope: International
Contact Information: Director, Member Relations: Sandra Bradley, E-mail: sbradley@acls.org, Phone: 212-697-1505, ext. 123
- American Council of Learned Societies Annual Meeting 2019, April, 2019, New York Marriott Downtown Hotel, New York, NY
Scope: International
Contact Information: Director, Member Relations: Sandra Bradley, E-mail: sbradley@acls.org, Phone: 212-697-1505, ext. 123

American Dialect Society (ADS)
Duke University Press, PO Box 90660, Durham NC 27708-0660 USA
Tel: 919-688-5134
Toll-Free: 888-651-0122
administrator@americandialect.org
www.americandialect.org
www.linkedin.com/groups?about=&gid=103237
www.facebook.com/americandialect
twitter.com/americandialect
Overview: A medium-sized national organization founded in 1889
Mission: To study the English language in North America
Member of: American Council of Learned Societies
Finances: *Funding Sources:* Membership dues
Membership: *Fees:* $60 regular; $25 student; *Member Profile:* Interest in the English language in North America & other languages as they interact with it
Activities: Publishes the journal American Speech; Sponsors sessions at the national conventions of the Dictionary Society of North America; Holds an annual meeting at the annual meeting of the Linguistic Society of America; *Rents Mailing List:* Yes
Chief Officer(s):
Jesse Sheidlower, President
Allan A. Metcalf, Executive Secretary
aallan@aol.com
Awards:
- Presidential Honorary Memberships for Outstanding Students

American Economic Association (AEA)
#305, 2014 Broadway, Nashville TN 37203 USA
Tel: 615-322-2595; *Fax:* 615-343-7590
aeainfo@vanderbilt.edu
www.aeaweb.org
twitter.com/AEAJournals
Overview: A medium-sized national organization founded in 1888
Mission: The encouragement of economic research, especially the historical & statistical study of the actual conditions of industrial life; the issue of publications on economic subjects; the encouragement of perfect freedom of economic discussion
Member of: American Council of Learned Societies
Affiliation(s): International Economic Association
Finances: *Annual Operating Budget:* $1.5 Million-$3 Million
Membership: 18,000 individual; *Fees:* Schedule available; *Committees:* Editorial Appointments; Audit; Budget & Finance; Oversight of Operations & Publishing; Economic Education; Economic Statistics; Government Relations; Honors & Awards; Status of Minority Groups in the Economics Profession; Status of Women in the Economics Profession; Nominating; Registry of Random Controlled Trial
Activities: *Rents Mailing List:* Yes
Chief Officer(s):
William D. Nordhaus, President
Peter L. Rousseau, Secretary-Treasurer
Regina H. Montgomery, Administrative Director
Awards:
- Distinguished Fellows
- John Bates Clark Medal
- Francis A. Walker Medal

Publications:
- AEJ: Applied Economics [a publication of the American Economic Association]
Type: Journal
- AEJ: Economic Policy [a publication of the American Economic Association]
Type: Journal
- AEJ: Macroeconomics [a publication of the American Economic Association]
Type: Journal
- AEJ: Microeconomics [a publication of the American Economic Association]
Type: Journal
- The American Economic Review [a publication of the American Economic Association]
Type: Journal
- The Journal of Economic Literature [a publication of the American Economic Association]
Type: Journal
- The Journal of Economic Perspectives [a publication of the American Economic Association]
Type: Journal

American Electroplaters & Surface Finishers Society *See* National Association for Surface Finishing

American Farmland Trust (AFT)
#600, 1150 Connecticut Ave. NW, Washington DC 20036 USA
Tel: 800-431-1499
info@farmland.org
www.farmland.org
www.linkedin.com/company/american-farmland-trust
www.facebook.com/AmericanFarmland
twitter.com/farmland
www.instagram.com/americanfarmlandtrust
Overview: A large national charitable organization founded in 1980
Mission: To stop the loss of productive farmland & to promote farming practices that lead to a healthy environment
Membership: 20,000; *Fees:* $25
Activities: Offering public education; Providing technical assistance in policy development; Engaging in farmland protection & sustainable agriculture projects
Chief Officer(s):
Ralph Grossi, Interim President, 202-378-1212
rgrossi@farmland.org
John Larson, Executive Director, Programs, 202-378-1219
jlarson@farmland.org

agva@agvausa.com
www.agvausa.com
www.facebook.com/171985806179829
Overview: A large national organization founded in 1939
Mission: To represent performing artists & stage managers for live performances in the variety field
Member of: Associated Actors & Artistes of America
Affiliation(s): AFL-CIO
Finances: *Funding Sources:* Membership dues
Staff Member(s): 20
Membership: 5,000+; *Fees:* Schedule available, based upon earnings; *Committees:* AGVA Sick & Relief Fund; Membership
Chief Officer(s):
Judy Little, Acting Executive President

American Hiking Society (AHS)
8605 Second Ave., Silver Spring MD 20910 USA
Tel: 301-565-6704
Toll-Free: 800-972-8608
info@americanhiking.org
www.americanhiking.org
www.facebook.com/AmericanHiking
twitter.com/AmericanHiking
www.instagram.com/americanhiking
Overview: A medium-sized international organization founded in 1977
Mission: To promote & protect foot trails & the hiking experience
Finances: *Annual Operating Budget:* $500,000-$1.5 Million
Staff Member(s): 8
Membership: 5,000+; *Fees:* Schedule available
Activities: Maintains a public information service to provide hikers & other trail users with facts regarding facilities, organizations, & how to make best use of trails while protecting the environment; work trips; Trails for All Americans project; National Trails Day; Winter Trails; Advocacy Week; *Awareness Events:* National Trails Day, June; *Rents Mailing List:* Yes

American Historical Association (AHA)
400 A St. SE, Washington DC 20003-3889 USA
Tel: 202-544-2422; *Fax:* 202-544-8307
info@historians.org
www.historians.org
www.linkedin.com/groups/3810333
www.facebook.com/AHAhistorians
twitter.com/ahahistorians
Overview: A medium-sized international organization founded in 1884
Mission: To promote historical studies, the collection & preservation of historical documents & artifacts, & the dissemination of historical research
Member of: American Council of Learned Societies
Affiliation(s): Comité international des sciences historiques
Finances: *Annual Operating Budget:* $3 Million-$5 Million
Staff Member(s): 22
Membership: 13,420 individual + 4,100 institutional; *Fees:* Schedule available; *Member Profile:* Interest in history; *Committees:* Advisory Committee on Disability; Affiliated Societies; Annual Meeting Program; Award & Prize; Committees; Contingent Faculty; Digital History Working Group; Finance; Gender Equity; Graduate & Early Career; Grant & Fellowship; Harmsworth Professorship; International Historical Activities; Investment; LGBTQ Status in the Profession; Local Arrangements; Minority Historians; Nominating; Professional Evaluation of Digital Scholarship by Historians; State Standards
Activities: *Rents Mailing List:* Yes
Chief Officer(s):
Tyler E. Stovall, President
aha@historians.org
Jim Grossman, Executive Director
jgrossman@historians.org
Awards:
• Book Awards & Prizes

American Hotel & Lodging Association (AHLA)
#600, 1201 New York Ave. NW, Washington DC 20005-3931 USA
Tel: 202-289-3100; *Fax:* 202-289-3199
Toll-Free: 888-743-2515
informationcenter@ahla.com
www.ahla.com
www.linkedin.com/pub/american-hotel-lodging-association/6/870/a22
www.facebook.com/hotelassociation
twitter.com/ahla
Previous Name: American Hotel & Motel Association
Overview: A small international organization
Mission: To provide national representation for the lodging industry with services including public relations, image management, education & training, research & information.
Affiliation(s): Ontario Hotel & Motel Association
Finances: *Funding Sources:* Membership dues; sponsorship
Staff Member(s): 26
Membership: 12,000+; *Fees:* Schedule available; *Member Profile:* Stakeholders in the lodging industry, including individual hotel property members, hotel companies, student and faculty members, and industry suppliers; *Committees:* Audit, Certification & Credentials; Communications; Sustainability; Executive; Financial Management; Food & Beverage; Governmental Affairs; Human Resrouces; Labor Relations; Lodging Industry Rating Advisory; Resort; Risk Management
Chief Officer(s):
John Fitzpatrick, Chair
Katherine Lugar, President & CEO
klugar@ahla.com

American Hotel & Motel Association *See* American Hotel & Lodging Association

American Humane Association (AHA)
#360, 1400 - 16th St. NW, Washington DC 20036 USA
Toll-Free: 800-227-4645
info@americanhumane.org
www.americanhumane.org
www.facebook.com/americanhumane
twitter.com/americanhumane
www.youtube.com/user/americanhumane
Overview: A large international organization founded in 1877
Mission: To prevent cruelty, abuse, neglect & exploitation of children & animals & to assure that their interests & well-being are fully, effectively & humanely guaranteed by an aware & caring society
Finances: *Annual Operating Budget:* $3 Million-$5 Million; *Funding Sources:* Individual contributions; foundation grants; state & federal contracts
Staff Member(s): 23
Membership: 2,000; *Fees:* $59 individual; $119 organization
Activities: Management workshops; fundraising; public relations; education/outreach; animal care facilities; cruelty investigation; *Awareness Events:* Be Kind to Animals Week; *Library:* by appointment
Chief Officer(s):
Robin R. Ganzert, President & CEO

American Industrial Hygiene Association (AIHA)
#777, 3141 Fairview Park Dr., Falls Church VA 22042 USA
Tel: 703-849-8888; *Fax:* 703-207-3561
www.aiha.org
www.linkedin.com/company/aiha
www.facebook.com/aihaglobal
twitter.com/AIHA
www.youtube.com/user/IHValue
Overview: A medium-sized international organization founded in 1939
Mission: To serve the needs of occupational & environmental health professionals; To achieve high professional standards; To promote certification of industrial hygienists
Staff Member(s): 61
Membership: 10,000; *Fees:* Schedule available; *Member Profile:* International occupational & environmental health & safety professionals, who practise industrial hygiene in industry, academic institutions, government, & independent organizations
Activities: Administering education programs; Operating laboratory accreditation programs based on high international standards; Providing networking opportunities; Engaging in advocacy activities
Chief Officer(s):
Lawrence Sloan, Chief Executive Officer
Meetings/Conferences:
• American Industrial Hygiene Conference & Exposition 2018, May, 2018, Philadelphia, PA
Scope: International
Publications:
• American Industrial Hygiene Association Member Directory
Type: Directory
• Journal of Occupational & Environmental Hygiene
Type: Journal; *Accepts Advertising*; *Editor:* Mark Nicas
Profile: A peer-reviewed publication to enhance the knowledge & practice of occupational & environmental hygiene & safety
• The Synergist
Type: Magazine; *Frequency:* Monthly; *Accepts Advertising*; *Editor:* Ed Rutkowski

American Federation of Labor & Congress of Industrial Organizations (AFL-CIO) / Fédération Américaine du travail et congrès des organisations industrielles (FAT-COI)

815 - 16th St. NW, Washington DC 20006 USA
Tel: 202-637-5000; Fax: 202-637-5058
www.aflcio.org
www.linkedin.com/company/afl-cio
www.facebook.com/aflcio
twitter.com/AFLCIO
www.youtube.com/user/AFLCIOvideos
Overview: A large international [organization]...
Membership: Open...
Activities:...

[American Federation of Musicians] of the United States [& Canada] (AFM) / Fédération [des musiciens] du Canada

Richard...
Eliz... 0036 United States
...

Overview: A large... national organization founded in [1896]
Mission: ...nal musicians in both Canada [& the U.S.; To negotiate] agreements, protect ownership of [rights & benefits]; To raise industry standards & [keep the musici]an in the foreground of the cultural [scene]
...
Member Profile: Professional musicians
...
[... Dr.], Toronto ON M3C 3E5
...
...org
...com/afm.org
...MusiciansUnion
...ace.com/afmorg
...be.com/user/MusiciansUnion
Chief Officer(s):
...nik, Canadian Vice-President
...@afm.org

American Fisheries Society (AFS)

5410 Grosvenor Lane, Bethesda MD 20814-2199 USA
Tel: 301-897-8616; Fax: 301-897-8096
www.fisheries.org
www.linkedin.com/company/american-fisheries-society
www.facebook.com/AmericanFisheriesSociety
twitter.com/AmFisheriesSoc
www.flickr.com/photos/americanfisheriessociety
Overview: A large international organization founded in 1870
Mission: To advance fisheries science & the conservation of renewable aquatic resources; To promote & evaluate the educational, scientific, & technological development & advancement of all branches of fisheries science & practice, including aquatic biology, engineering, economics, fish culture, limnology, oceanography, & technology; To gather & disseminate technical & other information on fish, fishing, fisheries, & all phases of fisheries science & practice; To encourage the teaching of all phases of fisheries science
Finances: Annual Operating Budget: $1.5 Million-$3 Million; Funding Sources: Donations; Grants; Membership fees; Publication sales
Staff Member(s): 24
Membership: 8,500+ fisheries & aquatic science professionals & students; Fees: $80 North America; $95 outside North America; Member Profile: Open to anyone interested in the progress of fisheries science & education & the conservation & management of fisheries resources; Committees: Arrangements; Award of Excellence; Board of Appeals; Board of Professional Certification; Budget & Finance; Continuing Education; Mail Ballot Tally; Membership; Membership Concerns; Names of Fishes; Names of Aquatic Invertebrates; Nominating; Program; Publications Overview; Resolutions; Resource Policy; Time & Place
Activities: Rents Mailing List: Yes
Chief Officer(s):
Ronald J. Essig, President, 413-253-8504
Douglas J. Austen, Executive Director, 301-897-8616 Ext. 208
dausten@fisheries.org
Awards:
• The Meritorious Service Award
Given to an individual for loyalty, dedication & meritorious service to the society over a long period of time, & for exceptional commitment to the society's programs, ideals, objectives, & long-term goals
• The Distinguished Service Award
Given in recognition of outstanding service to the society
• The AFS Award of Excellence
Given to recognize outstanding scientists in the fields of fisheries & aquatic biology
• The Carl R. Sullivan Fisheries Conservation Award
Given annually to an individual or organization, professional or non-professional, for outstanding contributions to the conservation of fishery resources
• Emerging Leaders Mentorship Award
• Meritorious Service Award
• Outstanding Chapter & Outstanding Student Subunit Award
• Presidents' Fishery Conservation Award
Presented annually, one or more awards if warranted, in one of two categories: (1) an AFS individual or unit or (2) a non-AFS individual or entity, for a singular accomplishment or activity that advances aquatic resource conservation at the regional or Society level
• William E. Ricker Resource Conservation Award
Given to any entity for a singular accomplishment or activity in resource conservation that is significant at the U.S., continental, or international level
• Excellence in Public Outreach
Awarded annually to an AFS member who goes "the extra mile" in sharing the value of fisheries science/research with the general public through the popular media & other communication channels
• The Emmeline Moore Prize
Meetings/Conferences:
• American Fisheries Society 148th Annual Meeting 2018, August, 2018, Atlantic City Convention Center, Atlantic City, NJ
Scope: International
• American Fisheries Society 149th Annual Meeting 2019, September, 2019, Reno, NV
Scope: International
• American Fisheries Society 150th Annual Meeting 2020, August, 2020, Columbus, OH
Scope: International
Publications:
• Journal of Aquatic Animal Health [a publication of the American Fisheries Society]
Type: Journal; Frequency: Quarterly; ISSN: 1548-8667
• Marine & Coastal Fisheries [a publication of the American Fisheries Society]
Type: Journal; Frequency: m.; ISSN: 0363-2415
• North American Journal of Aquaculture [a publication of the American Fisheries Society]
Type: Journal; Frequency: Quarterly; ISSN: 1548-8454
• North American Journal of Fisheries Management [a publication of the American Fisheries Society]
Type: Journal; Frequency: bi-m.; ISSN: 1548-8678
• Transactions of the American Fisheries Society
Type: Journal; Frequency: bi-m.; ISSN: 1548-8659

American Forest & Paper Association (AF&PA)

#700, 1101 K St. NW, Washington DC 20005 USA
Tel: 202-463-2700
info@afandpa.org
www.afandpa.org
www.linkedin.com//company/american-forest-&-paper-association
www.facebook.com/ForestandPaper
twitter.com/ForestandPaper
www.youtube.com/user/afandpa1
Previous Name: American Paper Institute
Overview: A large international organization founded in 1993
Mission: To act as a leading voice for the forest products industry
Membership: 157; Member Profile: Companies & associations that produce forest, paper, & wood products; Committees: North American Forest Carbon Standards; Environment Resource; Energy Resource; Air Quality; Printing-Writing; Timber Purchasers
Activities: Providing advice & counsel about the forest products industry; Operating a statistics program in the paper & packaging industry
Chief Officer(s):
Donna A. Harman, President & Chief Executive Officer
Samuel Kerns, Vice-President, Administration & CFO
Kathy Smith, Senior Manager, Meetings & Membership Services

American Foundry Society (AFS)

1695 North Penny Lane, Schaumburg IL 60173 USA
Tel: 847-824-0181; Fax: 847-824-7848
Toll-Free: 800-537-4237
www.afsinc.org
www.linkedin.com/groups/1796048
www.facebook.com/americanfoundrysociety
twitter.com/AmerFoundrySoc
Previous Name: American Foundrymen's Society
Overview: A medium-sized international organization founded in 1896
Mission: To promote the interests of the metalcasting industry before the legislative & executive branches of the federal government.
Member of: International Committee of Foundry Technical Association (CIATF)
Membership: 7,700; Fees: Schedule available; Member Profile: Metalcasting facilities, diecasters & industry suppliers
Activities: Speaker Service: Yes; Rents Mailing List: Yes; Library: Open to public
Chief Officer(s):
Doug Kurkul, Chief Executive Officer
dkurkul@afsinc.org

British Columbia Chapter
#15, 18503 - 97 Ave., Surrey BC V4N 3N9
Tel: 604-888-0181
www.afsbc.ca
www.linkedin.com/groups?homeNewMember=&gid=2259332
www.facebook.com/280931248600222
twitter.com/AFSBC
Chief Officer(s):
David Lalonde, Chair
dlalonde@almacg.ca

Manitoba Chapter
MB

Ontario Chapter
555 Bay St. North, Hamilton ON L8L 1H1
e-mail: afsontario@bell.net
afsontario.ca
Chief Officer(s):
John Papaionnou, Chair
Crystal Burkholder, Secretary-Treasurer

American Foundrymen's Society See American Foundry Society

American Galvanizers Association (AGA)

#108, 6881 South Holly Circle, Centennial CO 80112 USA
Tel: 720-554-0900; Fax: 720-554-0909
Toll-Free: 800-468-7732
aga@galvanizeit.org
www.galvanizeit.org
www.linkedin.com/company/american-galvanizers-association
www.facebook.com/galvanizeit
twitter.com/agagalvanizeit
www.youtube.com/user/AGAGalvanizeIt
Overview: A medium-sized national organization founded in 1935
Finances: Annual Operating Budget: $500,000-$1.5 Million
Staff Member(s): 9; 30 volunteer(s)
Membership: 125 corporate; Fees: Schedule available; Member Profile: Galvanizers & industry suppliers
Chief Officer(s):
Philip G. Rahrig, Executive Director
Awards:
• Excellence in Hot-Dip Galvanizing Annual Award
Meetings/Conferences:
• American Galvanizers Association 2018 Annual Conference, April, 2018, Westin LaPaloma, Tucson, AZ
Scope: National

American Guild of Variety Artists (AFL-CIO) (AGVA) / Guilde américaine des artistes de variétés (FAT-COI)

363 - 7 Ave., 17th Fl., New York NY 10001-3904 USA
Tel: 212-675-1003; Fax: 212-633-0097
Other Communication: Alternate E-mail: agvany@aol.com

agva@agvausa.com
www.agvausa.com
www.facebook.com/171985806179829
Overview: A large national organization founded in 1939
Mission: To represent performing artists & stage managers for live performances in the variety field
Member of: Associated Actors & Artistes of America
Affiliation(s): AFL-CIO
Finances: *Funding Sources:* Membership dues
Staff Member(s): 20
Membership: 5,000+; *Fees:* Schedule available, based upon earnings; *Committees:* AGVA Sick & Relief Fund; Membership
Chief Officer(s):
Judy Little, Acting Executive President

American Hiking Society (AHS)
8605 Second Ave., Silver Spring MD 20910 USA
Tel: 301-565-6704
Toll-Free: 800-972-8608
info@americanhiking.org
www.americanhiking.org
www.facebook.com/AmericanHiking
twitter.com/AmericanHiking
www.instagram.com/americanhiking
Overview: A medium-sized international organization founded in 1977
Mission: To promote & protect foot trails & the hiking experience
Finances: *Annual Operating Budget:* $500,000-$1.5 Million
Staff Member(s): 8
Membership: 5,000+; *Fees:* Schedule available
Activities: Maintains a public information service to provide hikers & other trail users with facts regarding facilities, organizations, & how to make best use of trails while protecting the environment; work trips; Trails for All Americans project; National Trails Day; Winter Trails; Advocacy Week; *Awareness Events:* National Trails Day, June; *Rents Mailing List:* Yes

American Historical Association (AHA)
400 A St. SE, Washington DC 20003-3889 USA
Tel: 202-544-2422; *Fax:* 202-544-8307
info@historians.org
www.historians.org
www.linkedin.com/groups/3810333
www.facebook.com/AHAhistorians
twitter.com/ahahistorians
Overview: A medium-sized international organization founded in 1884
Mission: To promote historical studies, the collection & preservation of historical documents & artifacts, & the dissemination of historical research
Member of: American Council of Learned Societies
Affiliation(s): Comité international des sciences historiques
Finances: *Annual Operating Budget:* $3 Million-$5 Million
Staff Member(s): 22
Membership: 13,420 individual + 4,100 institutional; *Fees:* Schedule available; *Member Profile:* Interest in history; *Committees:* Advisory Committee on Disability; Affiliated Societies; Annual Meeting Program; Award & Prize; *Committees:* Contingent Faculty; Digital History Working Group; Finance; Gender Equity; Graduate & Early Career; Grant & Fellowship; Harmsworth Professorship; International Historical Activities; Investment; LGBTQ Status in the Profession; Local Arrangements; Minority Historians; Nominating; Professional Evaluation of Digital Scholarship by Historians; State Standards
Activities: *Rents Mailing List:* Yes
Chief Officer(s):
Tyler E. Stovall, President
aha@historians.org
Jim Grossman, Executive Director
jgrossman@historians.org
Awards:
• Book Awards & Prizes

American Hotel & Lodging Association (AHLA)
#600, 1201 New York Ave. NW, Washington DC 20005-3931 USA
Tel: 202-289-3100; *Fax:* 202-289-3199
Toll-Free: 888-743-2515
informationcenter@ahla.com
www.ahla.com
www.linkedin.com/pub/american-hotel-lodging-association/6/870/a22
www.facebook.com/hotelassociation
twitter.com/ahla
Previous Name: American Hotel & Motel Association
Overview: A small international organization
Mission: To provide national representation for the lodging industry with services including public relations, image management, education & training, research & information.
Affiliation(s): Ontario Hotel & Motel Association
Finances: *Funding Sources:* Membership dues; sponsorship
Staff Member(s): 26
Membership: 12,000+; *Fees:* Schedule available; *Member Profile:* Stakeholders in the lodging industry, including individual hotel property members, hotel companies, student and faculty members, and industry suppliers; *Committees:* Audit, Certification & Credentials; Communications; Sustainability; Executive; Financial Management; Food & Beverage; Governmental Affairs; Human Resrouces; Labor Relations; Lodging Industry Rating Advisory; Resort; Risk Management
Chief Officer(s):
John Fitzpatrick, Chair
Katherine Lugar, President & CEO
klugar@ahla.com

American Hotel & Motel Association *See* American Hotel & Lodging Association

American Humane Association (AHA)
#360, 1400 - 16th St. NW, Washington DC 20036 USA
Toll-Free: 800-227-4645
info@americanhumane.org
www.americanhumane.org
www.facebook.com/americanhumane
twitter.com/americanhumane
www.youtube.com/user/americanhumane
Overview: A large international organization founded in 1877
Mission: To prevent cruelty, abuse, neglect & exploitation of children & animals & to assure that their interests & well-being are fully, effectively & humanely guaranteed by an aware & caring society
Finances: *Annual Operating Budget:* $3 Million-$5 Million; *Funding Sources:* Individual contributions; foundation grants; state & federal contracts
Staff Member(s): 23
Membership: 2,000; *Fees:* $59 individual; $119 organization
Activities: Management workshops; fundraising; public relations; education/outreach; animal care facilities; cruelty investigation; *Awareness Events:* Be Kind to Animals Week; *Library:* by appointment
Chief Officer(s):
Robin R. Ganzert, President & CEO

American Industrial Hygiene Association (AIHA)
#777, 3141 Fairview Park Dr., Falls Church VA 22042 USA
Tel: 703-849-8888; *Fax:* 703-207-3561
www.aiha.org
www.linkedin.com/company/aiha
www.facebook.com/aihaglobal
twitter.com/AIHA
www.youtube.com/user/IHValue
Overview: A medium-sized international organization founded in 1939
Mission: To serve the needs of occupational & environmental health professionals; To achieve high professional standards; To promote certification of industrial hygienists
Staff Member(s): 61
Membership: 10,000; *Fees:* Schedule available; *Member Profile:* International occupational & environmental health & safety professionals, who practise industrial hygiene in industry, academic institutions, government, & independent organizations
Activities: Administering education programs; Operating laboratory accreditation programs based on high international standards; Providing networking opportunities; Engaging in advocacy activities
Chief Officer(s):
Lawrence Sloan, Chief Executive Officer
Meetings/Conferences:
• American Industrial Hygiene Conference & Exposition 2018, May, 2018, Philadelphia, PA
Scope: International
Publications:
• American Industrial Hygiene Association Member Directory
Type: Directory
• Journal of Occupational & Environmental Hygiene
Type: Journal; *Accepts Advertising*; *Editor:* Mark Nicas
Profile: A peer-reviewed publication to enhance the knowledge & practice of occupational & environmental hygiene & safety
• The Synergist
Type: Magazine; *Frequency:* Monthly; *Accepts Advertising*; *Editor:* Ed Rutkowski
Profile: Information about the occupational & environmental health & safety fields & the industrial hygiene profession, including industry trends, government activities, technical information, &association news

American Institute of Plant Engineers *See* Association for Facilities Engineering

American Iron & Steel Institute (AISI)
#800, 25 Massachusetts Ave. NW, Washington DC 20001 USA
Tel: 202-452-7100; *Fax:* 202-463-6573
webmaster@steel.org
www.steel.org
www.facebook.com/AISISteel
twitter.com/aisisteel
www.youtube.com/user/AISIsteel
Overview: A small international organization
Mission: To advance steel as the material of choice and to enhance the competitiveness of member companies and the North American steel industry.
Membership: *Member Profile:* Producer companies - including integrated, electric furnace & reconstituted mills; associate companies - suppliers to or customers of the industry; affiliate organizations - downstream steel producers of products such as cold rolled strip, pipe & tube, coated sheet
Chief Officer(s):
Thomas J. Gibson, President & CEO

American Library Association (ALA)
50 East Huron St., Chicago IL 60611-2795 USA
Tel: 312-944-6780; *Fax:* 312-440-9374
Toll-Free: 800-545-2433
Other Communication: Member & Customer Service, E-mail: customerservice@ala.org
ala@ala.org
www.ala.org
www.linkedin.com/groups/40592/profile
www.facebook.com/AmericanLibraryAssociation
twitter.com/ALALibrary
www.instagram.com/americanlibraryassociation
Overview: A large international organization founded in 1876
Mission: To develop & improve library & information services & the profession of librarianship; To enhance learning; To ensure access to information for all
Membership: *Fees:* Schedule available; *Member Profile:* Individuals & organizations interested in library & information science & library service; *Committees:* Accreditation; Advisory; Appointments; Awards; Chapter Relations; Conference; Constitution & Bylaws; Diversity, Literacy & Outreach Services Advisory; Election; Human Resource Development & Recruitment Advisory; Information Technology Policy Advisory; Literacy; Membership; Nominating; Public & Cultural Programs Advisory; Research & Statistics; Rural, Native & Tribal Libraries; Scholarships & Study Grants; Training, Orientation & Leadership Development; Website Advisory
Activities: Promoting libraries & information services; Providing professional development opportunities, awards, bursaries, & scholarships; *Library:* ALA Library; Open to public
Chief Officer(s):
Keith Fiels, Executive Director, 800-545-2433 Ext. 1392
kfiels@ala.org
Mark Leon, Chief Financial Officer, 800-545-2433 Ext. 4261
mleon@ala.org
Cheryl Malden, Officer, Programs, 800-545-2433 Ext. 3247
cmalden@ala.org
Dan Hoppe, Associate Executive Director, Human Resources, 800-545-2433 Ext. 5063
dhoppe@ala.org
Awards:
• ALA Book, Print & Media Awards Program
Given by ALA & its member units to honour books, print & other media forms through a variety of awards; awarded to publications & the authors, illustrators & publishers who create them
• ALA Professional Recognition Awards Program
Given to individuals, groups or organizations that show outstanding leaderships in areas of importance to the mission & goals of the ALA
• ALA Grants & Fellowships Program
A variety of grants & fellowships that provide monetary support/funding for present or future activities; grants may be offered to support the implementation of new programs or to promote research in the profession. Grants can also be awarded to cover travel costs to conferences
• ALA Scholarships Program
The ALA & its units provide more than $300,000 annually for

Foreign Associations / American Guild of Variety Artists (AFL-CIO) (AGVA) / Guilde américaine des artistes de variétés (FAT-COI)

American Federation of Labor & Congress of Industrial Organizations (AFL-CIO) (AFL-CIO) / Fédération Américaine du travail et congrès des organisations industrielles (FAT-COI) (FAT-COI)
815 - 16th St. NW, Washington DC 20006 USA
Tel: 202-637-5000; Fax: 202-637-5058
www.aflcio.org
www.linkedin.com/company/afl-cio
www.facebook.com/aflcio
twitter.com/AFLCIO
www.youtube.com/user/AFLCIONow; www.pinterest.com/aflcio
Overview: A large international organization
Membership: 13,700,000 + 90 affiliated unions
Activities: Operating as one of the largest labour bodies in the United States
Chief Officer(s):
Richard Trumka, President
Elizabeth Shuler, Sec.-Tres.
Tefere Gebre, Executive Vice-President

American Federation of Musicians of the United States & Canada (AFL-CIO/CLC) (AFM) / Fédération des musiciens des États-Unis et du Canada (FAT-COI/CTC)
#600, 1501 Broadway, New York NY 10036 United States
Tel: 212-869-1330; Fax: 212-764-6134
www.afm.org
www.facebook.com/afm.org
twitter.com/The_AFM
Overview: A medium-sized international organization founded in 1896
Mission: To represent professional musicians in both Canada and the US; To negotiate fair agreements, protect ownership of recorded music & secure benefits; To raise industry standards & place the professional musician in the foreground of the cultural landscape
Staff Member(s): 9
Membership: 15,000; *Member Profile:* Professional musicians
Chief Officer(s):
Ray Hair, President
presoffice@afm.org

Canadian Office
#202, 150 Ferrand Dr., Toronto ON M3C 3E5
Tel: 416-391-5161
afmcan@afm.org
www.afm.org
www.facebook.com/afm.org
twitter.com/MusiciansUnion
www.myspace.com/afmorg;
www.youtube.com/user/MusiciansUnion
Chief Officer(s):
Bill Skolnik, Canadian Vice-President
bskolnik@afm.org

American Fisheries Society (AFS)
#110, 5410 Grosvenor Lane, Bethesda MD 20814-2199 USA
Tel: 301-897-8616; Fax: 301-897-8096
www.fisheries.org
www.linkedin.com/company/american-fisheries-society
www.facebook.com/AmericanFisheriesSociety
twitter.com/AmFisheriesSoc
www.flickr.com/photos/americanfisheriessociety
Overview: A large international organization founded in 1870
Mission: To advance fisheries science & the conservation of renewable aquatic resources; To promote & evaluate the educational, scientific, & technological development & advancement of all branches of fisheries science & practice, including aquatic biology, engineering, economics, fish culture, limnology, oceanography, & technology; To gather & disseminate technical & other information on fish, fishing, fisheries, & all phases of fisheries science & practice; To encourage the teaching of all phases of fisheries science
Finances: *Annual Operating Budget:* $1.5 Million-$3 Million; *Funding Sources:* Donations; Grants; Membership fees; Publication sales
Staff Member(s): 24
Membership: 8,500+ fisheries & aquatic science professionals & students; *Fees:* $80 North America; $95 outside North America; *Member Profile:* Open to anyone interested in the progress of fisheries science & education & the conservation & management of fisheries resources; *Committees:* Arrangements; Award of Excellence; Board of Appeals; Board of Professional Certification; Budget & Finance; Continuing Education; Mail Ballot Tally; Membership; Membership Concerns; Names of Fishes; Names of Aquatic Invertebrates; Nominating; Program; Publications Overview; Resolutions; Resource Policy; Time & Place
Activities: *Rents Mailing List:* Yes
Chief Officer(s):
Ronald J. Essig, President, 413-253-8504
Douglas J. Austen, Executive Director, 301-897-8616 Ext. 208
dausten@fisheries.org
Awards:
• The Meritorious Service Award
Given to an individual for loyalty, dedication & meritorious service to the society over a long period of time, & for exceptional commitment to the society's programs, ideals, objectives, & long-term goals
• The Distinguished Service Award
Given in recognition of outstanding service to the society
• The AFS Award of Excellence
Given to recognize outstanding scientists in the fields of fisheries & aquatic biology
• The Carl R. Sullivan Fisheries Conservation Award
Given annually to an individual or organization, professional or non-professional, for outstanding contributions to the conservation of fishery resources
• Emerging Leaders Mentorship Award
• Meritorious Service Award
• Outstanding Chapter & Outstanding Student Subunit Award
• Presidents' Fishery Conservation Award
Presented annually, one or more awards if warranted, in one of two categories: (1) an AFS individual or unit or (2) a non-AFS individual or entity, for a singular accomplishment or activity that advancces aquatic resource conservation at the regional or Society level
• William E. Ricker Resource Conservation Award
Given to any entity for a singular accomplishment or activity in resource conservation that is significant at the U.S., continental, or international level
• Excellence in Public Outreach
Awarded annually to an AFS member who goes "the extra mile" in sharing the value of fisheries science/research with the general public through the popular media & other communication channels
• The Emmeline Moore Prize
Meetings/Conferences:
• American Fisheries Society 148th Annual Meeting 2018, August, 2018, Atlantic City Convention Center, Atlantic City, NJ
Scope: International
• American Fisheries Society 149th Annual Meeting 2019, September, 2019, Reno, NV
Scope: International
• American Fisheries Society 150th Annual Meeting 2020, August, 2020, Columbus, OH
Scope: International
Publications:
• Journal of Aquatic Animal Health [a publication of the American Fisheries Society]
Type: Journal; *Frequency:* Quarterly; *ISSN:* 1548-8667
• Marine & Coastal Fisheries [a publication of the American Fisheries Society]
Type: Journal; *Frequency:* m.; *ISSN:* 0363-2415
• North American Journal of Aquaculture [a publication of the American Fisheries Society]
Type: Journal; *Frequency:* Quarterly; *ISSN:* 1548-8454
• North American Journal of Fisheries Management [a publication of the American Fisheries Society]
Type: Journal; *Frequency:* bi-m.; *ISSN:* 1548-8678
• Transactions of the American Fisheries Society
Type: Journal; *Frequency:* bi-m.; *ISSN:* 1548-8659

American Forest & Paper Association (AF&PA)
#700, 1101 K St. NW, Washington DC 20005 USA
Tel: 202-463-2700
info@afandpa.org
www.afandpa.org
www.linkedin.com//company/american-forest-&-paper-association
www.facebook.com/ForestandPaper
twitter.com/ForestandPaper
www.youtube.com/user/afandpa1
Previous Name: American Paper Institute
Overview: A large international organization founded in 1993
Mission: To act as a leading voice for the forest products industry
Membership: 157; *Member Profile:* Companies & associations that produce forest, paper, & wood products; *Committees:* North American Forest Carbon Standards; Environment Resource; Energy Resource; Air Quality; Printing-Writing; Timber Purchasers
Activities: Providing advice & counsel about the forest products industry; Operating a statistics program in the paper & packaging industry
Chief Officer(s):
Donna A. Harman, President & Chief Executive Officer
Samuel Kerns, Vice-President, Administration & CFO
Kathy Smith, Senior Manager, Meetings & Membership Services

American Foundry Society (AFS)
1695 North Penny Lane, Schaumburg IL 60173 USA
Tel: 847-824-0181; Fax: 847-824-7848
Toll-Free: 800-537-4237
www.afsinc.org
www.linkedin.com/groups/1796048
www.facebook.com/americanfoundrysociety
twitter.com/AmerFoundrySoc
Previous Name: American Foundrymen's Society
Overview: A medium-sized international organization founded in 1896
Mission: To promote the interests of the metalcasting industry before the legislative & executive branches of the federal government.
Member of: International Committee of Foundry Technical Association (CIATF)
Membership: 7,700; *Fees:* Schedule available; *Member Profile:* Metalcasting facilities, diecasters & industry suppliers
Activities: *Speaker Service:* Yes; *Rents Mailing List:* Yes; *Library:* Open to public
Chief Officer(s):
Doug Kurkul, Chief Executive Officer
dkurkul@afsinc.org

British Columbia Chapter
#15, 18503 - 97 Ave., Surrey BC V4N 3N9
Tel: 604-888-0181
www.afsbc.ca
www.linkedin.com/groups?homeNewMember=&gid=2259332
www.facebook.com/280931248600222
twitter.com/AFSBC
Chief Officer(s):
David Lalonde, Chair
dlalonde@almacg.ca

Manitoba Chapter
MB

Ontario Chapter
555 Bay St. North, Hamilton ON L8L 1H1
e-mail: afsontario@bell.net
afsontario.ca
Chief Officer(s):
John Papaionnou, Chair
Crystal Burkholder, Secretary-Treasurer

American Foundrymen's Society *See* American Foundry Society

American Galvanizers Association (AGA)
#108, 6881 South Holly Circle, Centennial CO 80112 USA
Tel: 720-554-0900; Fax: 720-554-0909
Toll-Free: 800-468-7732
aga@galvanizeit.org
www.galvanizeit.org
www.linkedin.com/company/american-galvanizers-association
www.facebook.com/galvanizeit
twitter.com/agagalvanizeit
www.youtube.com/user/AGAGalvanizeIt
Overview: A medium-sized national organization founded in 1935
Finances: *Annual Operating Budget:* $500,000-$1.5 Million
Staff Member(s): 9; 30 volunteer(s)
Membership: 125 corporate; *Fees:* Schedule available; *Member Profile:* Galvanizers & industry suppliers
Chief Officer(s):
Philip G. Rahrig, Executive Director
Awards:
• Excellence in Hot-Dip Galvanizing Annual Award
Meetings/Conferences:
• American Galvanizers Association 2018 Annual Conference, April, 2018, Westin LaPaloma, Tucson, AZ
Scope: National

American Guild of Variety Artists (AFL-CIO) (AGVA) / Guilde américaine des artistes de variétés (FAT-COI)
363 - 7 Ave., 17th Fl., New York NY 10001-3904 USA
Tel: 212-675-1003; Fax: 212-633-0097
Other Communication: Alternate E-mail: agvany@aol.com

study in a master's degree in library and information studies from an ALA accredited program, or for a master's degree in school library media program that meets ALA curriculum guidelines
• ALA Youth Media Awards Program
Honour children's & young adult authors & illustrators
Meetings/Conferences:
• American Library Association 2018 Midwinter Meeting & Exhibits, February, 2018, Denver, CO
Scope: International
Description: A library & information service meeting presenting speakers, discussion groups, exhibits, & committee meetings
• American Library Association 2018 Annual Conference, June, 2018, New Orleans, LA
Scope: International
Description: A conference providing speakers, educational programs, committee meetings, & exhibits related to library & information services
• American Library Association 2019 Midwinter Meeting & Exhibits, January, 2019, Seattle, WA
Scope: International
Description: A library & information service meeting presenting speakers, discussion groups, exhibits, & committee meetings
• American Library Association 2019 Annual Conference, June, 2019, Washington, DC
Scope: International
Description: A conference providing speakers, educational programs, committee meetings, & exhibits related to library & information services
• American Library Association 2020 Midwinter Meeting & Exhibits, January, 2020, Philadelphia, PA
Scope: International
Description: A library & information service meeting presenting speakers, discussion groups, exhibits, & committee meetings
• American Library Association 2020 Annual Conference, June, 2020, Chicago, IL
Scope: International
Description: A conference providing speakers, educational programs, committee meetings, & exhibits related to library & information services
• American Library Association 2021 Midwinter Meeting & Exhibits, January, 2021, Indianapolis, IN
Scope: International
Description: A library & information service meeting presenting speakers, discussion groups, exhibits, & committee meetings
• American Library Association 2021 Annual Conference, June, 2021, Chicago, IL
Scope: International
Description: A conference providing speakers, educational programs, committee meetings, & exhibits related to library & information services
Publications:
• American Libaries [a publication of the American Library Association]
Type: Magazine; *Frequency:* 6 pa; *Accepts Advertising*; *ISSN:* 0002-9769; *Price:* Free with payment of American Library Association dues
Profile: Topics include association & international news, conference highlights, professional development opportunities, advocacy, intellectualfreedom, legislation, & technology
• Book Links
Type: Magazine; *Frequency:* Quarterly
Profile: A quarterly supplement to Booklist, with articles & thematic bibliographies of interest to youth librarians, school library media specialists, teachers, reading specialists, & curriculum coordinators
• Booklist [a publication of the American Library Association]
Type: Magazine; *Accepts Advertising*
Profile: Reviews of books, media. & reference sources for collection development
• Guide to Reference
Profile: An annotated guide to reference sources, organized by academic discipline
• Library Technology Reports
Type: Newsletter; *Accepts Advertising*
Profile: The most recent information about library technology

American Lung Association (ALA)
#1150, 55 West Wacker Dr., Chicago IL 60601 USA
Toll-Free: 800-548-8252
www.lung.org
www.facebook.com/lungusa
twitter.com/lungassociation
www.youtube.com/user/americanlung
Overview: A large international charitable organization founded in 1904
Mission: To prevent lung disease & promote lung health
Affiliation(s): American Thoracic Society
Finances: *Funding Sources:* Donations; Grants
Chief Officer(s):
Harold P. Wimmer, National President & CEO
Laura Scott, National Chief Financial Officer
Sue Swan, National Chief Development Officer

American Management Association (AMA)
1601 Broadway, New York NY 10019 USA
Tel: 877-566-9441; *Fax:* 518-891-0368
customerservice@amanet.org
www.amanet.org
www.linkedin.com/company/american-management-association
www.facebook.com/176633092380292
twitter.com/amanet
www.youtube.com/user/AmericanManagement
Overview: A large international organization founded in 1923
Mission: To advance the skills of individuals in order to drive business success
Staff Member(s): 750
Membership: 70,000
Chief Officer(s):
Edward T. Reilly, President & CEO

American Marketing Association (AMA)
130 East Randolph St., 22nd Fl., Chicago IL 60601 USA
Tel: 312-542-9000; *Fax:* 312-542-9001
www.ama.org
www.linkedin.com/company/american-marketing-association
www.facebook.com/AmericanMarketing
twitter.com/AMA_Marketing
Overview: A medium-sized international organization founded in 1937
Mission: To urge & assist the personal & professional development of members; To advance the science & ethical practice of the marketing discipline
Finances: *Annual Operating Budget:* $3 Million-$5 Million; *Funding Sources:* Membership fees; publications; conferences
Staff Member(s): 60
Membership: 30,000; *Fees:* Schedule available
Activities: *Library* Open to public
  British Columbia Chapter (BCAMA)
  #200, 420 West Hastings St., Vancouver BC V6B 1L1
  Tel: 604-564-1262
  info@bcama.com
  www.bcama.com
  www.linkedin.com/company/bcama
  www.facebook.com/bcama
  twitter.com/BCAMA
  www.youtube.com/user/bcamamarketing
  Chief Officer(s):
  Sarah Finstad, President
  Toronto Chapter
  c/o Managing Matters, #202, 720 Spadina Ave., Toronto ON M5S 2T9
  Tel: 416-944-9529
  contact@ama-toronto.com
  www.ama-toronto.com
  www.linkedin.com/groups?gid=72166
  www.facebook.com/AMAToronto
  twitter.com/amatoronto
  Mission: To increase the impact and value of marketing to its members and helps connect its members to Toronto marketing and business professionals and the world's largest marketing community, the American Marketing Association.
  Chief Officer(s):
  Craig Lund, President

American Medical Association
#39300, 330 North Wabash Ave., Chicago IL 60611-5885 USA
Tel: 312-464-4430
Toll-Free: 800-621-8335
www.ama-assn.org
www.linkedin.com/company/american-medical-association
www.facebook.com/AmericanMedicalAssociation
twitter.com/AmerMedicalAssn
plus.google.com/+americanmedicalassociation
Overview: A large international organization founded in 1847
Mission: To achieve better health through improved delivery of care
Membership: *Fees:* Schedule available
Activities: Advocating for physicians; Offering medical education & career planning opportunities
Chief Officer(s):
James L. Madara, CEO
Awards:
• Nathan Davis Awards for Outstanding Government Service
Spotlights legislators, public health officials, researchers and state and local executives who put health care at the forefront of their civic efforts.
• Joan F. Giambalvo Memorial Scholarship
To advance the progress of women in the medical profession and strengthening the ability of the AMA to identify and address the needs of women physicians and medical students.
• Distinguished Service Award
• Citation for Distinguished Service
• AMA Medal of Valor
• Scientific Achievement Award
• Benjamin Rush Award for Citizenship & Community Service
• President's Citation for Service to the Public
• Dr. William Beaumont Award in Medicine
• AMA Foundation Award for Health Education
• Isaac Hays, MD and John Bell, MD Award for Leadership in Medical Ethics & Professionalism
• Medical Executive Lifetime Achievement Award
• Medical Executive Meritorious Achievement Award
• Community Service Award
• Young at Heart Award
Publications:
• JAMA [The Journal of the American Medical Association]
Type: Journal

American Musicological Society (AMS)
20 Cooper Sq., 2nd Fl., New York NY 10003 USA
Tel: 212-992-6340; *Fax:* 212-995-4022
Toll-Free: 877-679-7648
ams@ams-net.org
www.ams-net.org
www.facebook.com/AMS.musicology
twitter.com/AMS_musicology
www.youtube.com/user/amsformusicology
Overview: A large international organization founded in 1934
Mission: To advance research in the various fields of music as a branch of learning & scholarship
Member of: American Council of Learned Societies
Affiliation(s): International Musicological Society
Finances: *Funding Sources:* Membership dues; Endowments; Gifts
Staff Member(s): 3
Membership: 3,600 individual + 1,200 institutional; *Fees:* Schedule available; *Member Profile:* Persons with an interest in the advancement of research in various fields of music; *Committees:* Annual Meeting; Committees; Communications; Development; Membership & Professional Development; Awards; Nominating; Publications; AMS-MLA Joint RISM; Chapter Activities; Career-Related Issues; Cultural Diversity; Graduate Education; History of the Society; Obituaries; Technology; Finance; Travel Grants; Women & Gender
Chief Officer(s):
Robert Judd, Executive Director
rjudd@ams-net.org
Katie VanDerMeer, Office Manager
kvandermeer@ams-net.org
Awards:
• The Alfred Einstein Award
Musical article of exceptional merit by a scholar in the early stages of his/her career
• The Noah Greenberg Award
For outstanding performance projects
• The Otto Kinkeldey Award
For outstanding work of musicological scholarship (senior scholar)
• Lewis Lockwood Award
For outstanding work of musicological scholarship (early stages)
• Claude V. Palisca Award
For outstanding edition or translation
• Thomas Hampson Award
To honour research & publication in Classic Song
• Music in American Culture Award
Awarded to honour outstansing scholarship in music of the United States
• Paul Pisk Award
For outstanding paper at annual meeting by graduate student
• H. Colin Slim Award
For outstanding article in musicology (senior scholar)
• Ruth A. Solie Award
For outstanding collection of essays
• Robert M. Stevenson Award
For outstanding scholarship in Iberian music

Foreign Associations / American Numismatic Society (ANS)

- Philip Brett Award
For oustanding work in gay, lesbian, bisexual, and transgender/transsexual studies
Meetings/Conferences:
- American Musicological Society Annual Meeting 2018, 2018
Scope: International
Publications:
- AMS [American Musicological Society] Newsletter
Type: Newsletter; *Frequency:* Semiannually; *Editor:* James Parsons
- Journal of the American Musicological Society
Type: Journal; *Frequency:* 3 pa; *Accepts Advertising; Editor:* Joy H. Calico; *ISSN:* 0003-0139; *Price:* $47 per issue
Profile: One of the premier journals in the field of publishing scholarship from all fields of musical inquiry from historical musicology, critical theory,music analysis, iconography & organology, to performance practice, aesthetics & hermeneutics, ethnomusicology, gender & sexuality, & popular music

New York - St. Lawrence Chapter
c/o Dan School of Drama & Music, Queen's University, 39 Bade Lane, Kingston ON K7L 3N6
www.ams-nyssl.blogspot.ca
Chief Officer(s):
Colleen Renihan, Secretary-Treasurer

American Newspaper Guild *See* The Newspaper Guild (AFL-CIO/CLC)

American Numismatic Society (ANS)
75 Varick St., 11th Fl., New York NY 10013 USA
Tel: 212-571-4470; *Fax:* 212-571-4479
info@numismatics.org
www.numismatics.org
www.facebook.com/AmericanNumismaticSociety
twitter.com/ANSCoins/
www.instagram.com/americannumismaticsociety
Overview: A large national organization founded in 1858
Member of: American Council of Learned Societies
Affiliation(s): Commission internationale de numismatique; Fédération internationale de la médaille
Finances: *Annual Operating Budget:* $500,000-$1.5 Million
Staff Member(s): 15; 7 volunteer(s)
Membership: 1,875 individual + 112 institutional; *Fees:* Schedule available; *Member Profile:* Individuals or institutions with a serious interest in numismatics
Activities: *Internships:* Yes; *Library:* The Francis D. Campbell Library
Chief Officer(s):
Sydney Martin, President
Ute Wartenberg Kagan, Executive Director
Natalie Jordan, Director, Finance & Administration, 212-571-4470 Ext. 121
Awards:
- Huntington Medal Award
- Saltus Medal Award
Meetings/Conferences:
- American Numismatic Society Annual Meeting 2018, October, 2018
Scope: International
Contact Information: Director, Development: Eshel Kreiter, E-mail: ekreiter@numismatics.org, Phone: 212-571-4470, ext. 130
Publications:
- American Journal of Numismatics
Type: Journal; *Editor:* Oliver Hoover; *ISSN:* 1053-8356; *Price:* $75
- American Numismatic Society Annual Report
Type: Report; *Frequency:* Annually

American Optometric Association (AOA)
243 North Lindbergh Blvd., 1st Fl., St. Louis MO 63141-7881 USA
Tel: 314-991-4100; *Fax:* 314-991-4101
Toll-Free: 800-365-2219
aoa@aoa.org
www.aoa.org
www.linkedin.com/company/american-optometric-association
www.facebook.com/American.Optometric.Association
twitter.com/aoaconnect
www.youtube.com/user/aoaweb
Previous Name: American Association of Opticians
Overview: A large international organization founded in 1898
Mission: To advance the quality, availability & accessibility of eye, vision & related health care; To represent the profession of optometry; To enhance & promote the independent & ethical decision making of its members; To assist doctors of optometry in practicing successfully in accordance with the highest standards of patient care
Member of: World Council of Optometry
Affiliation(s): Canadian Association of Optometrists
Finances: *Funding Sources:* Membership dues
Membership: 39,000; *Member Profile:* Active members generally are doctors of optometry; they become members of AOA only through membership in an affiliated (state) optometric association
Activities: *Awareness Events:* Save Your Vision Month, March; Diabetes Awareness Month, Nov.; *Internships:* Yes; *Rents Mailing List:* Yes; *Library:* Open to public
Chief Officer(s):
Christopher J. Quinn, President
CJQuinn@aoa.org
Awards:
- Young Optometrist of the Year
Recognizes those individuals (who have been active prctice less than 10 years) who show leadership skills when serving their profession, patients & community
- Apollo Award
Recognizes individuals, organizations or institutions who have performed a signigicant public service for the visual welfare of others
- Distinguished Service
Recognizes an individual doctor of optometry who has distinguished him/herself within the profession for unusually significant contributions & outstanding achievements contributing to the advancement for the profession of optometry
- Optometrist of the Year
Recognizes the deserving individual doctor of optometry for performance of outstanding services on behalf of the profession & to the visual welfare of the public
Publications:
- Optometry [a publication of the American Optometric Association]
Type: Journal; *Frequency:* Monthly

American Ornithological Society (AOS)
1400 South Lake Shore Dr., Chicago IL 60605 USA
Tel: 312-883-4670
info@americanornithology.org
www.americanornithology.org
twitter.com/AmOrnith
Merged from: American Ornithologists' Union; Cooper Ornithological Society
Overview: A medium-sized national organization founded in 2016
Mission: To promote & advance the scientific study of birds
Membership: 3,000; *Fees:* Schedule available; *Committees:* Audit; Bird Collections; Bylaws; Communications; Conservation; Early Professionals; Early Professional Awards; Ethics; Finance; History; International Affairs; Investing Trustees; Local Arrangements; Meeting Coordination; Membership; Memorials; Publications; Research Awards; Science Arbitration; Senior Professional Awards; Service Awards; Student Affairs; Student Membership Awards; Student & Postdoc Travel & Presentation Awards
Activities: Offering mentoring services to students; Presenting awards for excellence in research; Holding annual meetings; Supporting regional events; Co-sponsoring Birds of North America
Chief Officer(s):
Melinda Pruett-Jones, Executive Director
mpruettjones@americanornithology.org
Crystal Ruiz, Administrator
cruiz@americanornithology.org
Awards:
- William Brewster Memorial Award
- Elliott Coues Award
- Lloye & Alden Miller Research Award
- Ralph W. Schreiber Conservation Award
- Marion Jenkinson AOU Service Award
- Peter R. Stettenheim Service Award
- James G. Cooper Young Professional Award
- Ned K. Johnson Young Investigator Award
- Harry R. Painton Award
- Katma Award
Publications:
- The Auk: Ornithological Advances [a publication of the American Ornithological Society]
Type: Journal; *Frequency:* Quarterly
Profile: Information about bird species
- The Condor: Ornithological Applications [a publication of the American Ornithological Society]
Type: Journal; *Frequency:* Quarterly
Profile: Publishes original research & assessments

American Paper Institute *See* American Forest & Paper Association

American Philological Association *See* Society for Classical Studies

American Planning Association (APA)
#750 West, 1030 15th St. NW, Washington DC 20005-1503 USA
Tel: 202-872-0611; *Fax:* 202-872-0643
customerservice@planning.org
www.planning.org
www.linkedin.com/groups?gid=116818
www.facebook.com/AmericanPlanningAssociation
twitter.com/APA_Planning
www.youtube.com/user/AmericanPlanningAssn
Overview: A large national organization founded in 1909
Mission: To provide members with systematic ways to work on problems in common & to affect national planning policies
Finances: *Annual Operating Budget:* $3 Million-$5 Million
Staff Member(s): 66
Membership: 29,000
Activities: Bringing sound planning principles to the protection, management or conservation of environmental, natural & energy resources, as well as national forests & public lands; *Rents Mailing List:* Yes; *Library:* APA Library; by appointment
Chief Officer(s):
James Drinan, Executive Director
Ann Simms, COO & CFO
Harriet Bogdanowicz, Chief Communications Officer
Deene Alongi, Director, Meetings & Conferences
Awards:
- Judith McManus Price Scholarship
Eligibility: Undergraduate or graduate planning students; Women and minority (African American, Hispanic American, or Native American) students enrolled in an approved Planning Accreditation Board (PAB) planning program who are citizens of the United States, intend to pursue careers as practicing planners in the public sector, and are able to demonstrate a genuine financial need *Deadline:* April 30*Amount:* $2,000 - $4,000
- Charles Abrams Scholarship
Eligibility: A student who is enrolled in a graduate planning program leading to a master's degree in one of the five schools at which Charles Abrams taught and who has been nominated by the program's department chair. *Deadline:* April 30
Meetings/Conferences:
- American Planning Association Policy & Advocacy Conference 2018, September, 2018, Washington, DC
Scope: International
Publications:
- The Commissioner [a publication of the American Planning Association]
Profile: Features practical resources for planning commissioners, board members, & elected officials
- JAPA [The Journal of the American Planning Association]
Type: Journal; *ISSN:* 0194-4363
Profile: Features planning research, commentaries, & book reviews
- PAS Memo [a publication of the American Planning Association]
Profile: An information resource for Planning Advisory Service subscribers
- Planning Magazine [a publication of the American Planning Association]
Type: Magazine; *ISSN:* 2162-4577
- Zoning Practice [a publication of the American Planning Association]
; *ISSN:* 1548-0135
Profile: Features updates on latest trends in local land-use controls

American Political Science Association (APSA)
1527 New Hampshire Ave. NW, Washington DC 20036-1206 USA
Tel: 202-483-2512; *Fax:* 202-483-2657
apsa@apsanet.org
www.apsanet.org
www.linkedin.com/company/american-political-science-association
www.facebook.com/likeAPSA
twitter.com/apsatweets
www.youtube.com/user/APSAvideos
Overview: A large national organization founded in 1903

Mission: To provide members with services to facilitate research, teaching, & professional development
Member of: American Council of Learned Societies; Consortium of Social Science Associations; National Humanities Alliance
Affiliation(s): International Political Science Association
Finances: *Funding Sources:* Membership dues; fees; sales; endowments; grants
Staff Member(s): 24
Membership: 13,000 individual + 3,000 institutional; *Fees:* Schedule available; *Member Profile:* Interest in political science; *Committees:* Academic & Professional Development; Annual Meeting; Awards; Centennial Center; Congressional Fellowship Program; Council; Governance; International; Publications; Status
Activities: Programs: International Exchange, Congressional Fellowship, Graduate Minority Fellowship; Projects: Task Forces, Minority Identification; The Ralph Bunche Summer Institute for Black Undergraduates
Chief Officer(s):
David Lake, President
Steven Rathgeb Smith, Executive Director
smithsr@apsanet.org
Betsy Super, Senior Director, Research & Development
bsuper@apsanet.org
Amanda Meyers, Manager, Research & Development
ameyers@apsanet.org
Dan Gibson, Director, Communications & Marketing
dgibson@apsanet.org
Awards:
- Dissertation Awards
- Paper & Article Awards
- Book Awards
- Career Awards
- Frank J. Goodnow Award

Meetings/Conferences:
- American Political Science Association 114th Annual Meeting 2018, August, 2018, Boston, MA
Scope: International
- American Political Science Association 115th Annual Meeting 2019, August, 2019, Washington, DC
Scope: International
- American Political Science Association 116th Annual Meeting 2020, September, 2020, San Francisco, CA
Scope: International

Publications:
- American Political Science Review [a publication of the American Political Science Association]
Type: Journal; *Frequency:* Quarterly; *Editor:* Thomas Koenig; *ISSN:* 0003-0554
- Perspectives on Politics [a publication of the American Political Science Association]
Type: Journal; *Frequency:* Quarterly; *Editor:* Jeffrey C. Isaac; *ISSN:* 1541-0986
Profile: Features important scholarly topics, ideas, & innovations to promote discussion
- PS: Political Science & Politics [a publication of the American Political Science Association]
Type: Journal; *Frequency:* Quarterly; *ISSN:* 1049-0965
Profile: Features news & scholarly essays on the discipline

American Psychological Association (APA)
750 - 1st St. NE, Washington DC 20002-4242 USA
Tel: 202-336-5500
Toll-Free: 800-374-2721; *TTY:* 202-336-6123
executiveoffice@apa.org
www.apa.org
www.linkedin.com/groups/58284
www.facebook.com/AmericanPsychologicalAssociation
twitter.com/apa
plus.google.com/+americanpsychologicalassociation
Overview: A large international organization founded in 1892
Mission: To advance psychology as a science, profession & as a means of promoting human welfare
Member of: American Council of Learned Societies
Finances: *Annual Operating Budget:* Greater than $5 Million; *Funding Sources:* Membership dues; publications
Staff Member(s): 500
Membership: 129,595 members & affiliates; *Fees:* Schedule available; *Member Profile:* Must have doctoral degree based in part upon a psychological dissertation or based on other evidence of proficiency in psychological scholarship; *Committees:* Aging; Animal Research & Ethics; APA Fellows; Children, Youth & Families; Continuing Education; Disability Issues in Psychology; Division/APA Relations; Early Career Psychologists; Education & Training Awards; Election; Ethics; Ethnic Minority Affairs; Finance; Human Research; International Relations in Psychology; Professional Practice & Standards; Psychology in the Public Interest Awards; Psychological Tests & Assessment; Rural Health; Scientific Awards; Sexual Orientation & Gender Diversity; Socioeconomic Status; Women in Psychology
Activities: An extensive range of publications; *Rents Mailing List:* Yes; *Library:* by appointment
Chief Officer(s):
Arthur C. Evans, CEO
Meetings/Conferences:
- American Psychological Association 2018 Conference, April, 2018, Washington, DC
Scope: International
Description: Theme: "Technology, Mind, & Society"

American Public Gardens Association (APGA)
351 Longwood Rd., Kennett Square PA 19348 USA
Tel: 610-708-3010; *Fax:* 610-444-3594
info@publicgardens.org
www.publicgardens.org
www.linkedin.com/company/american-public-gardens-association
www.facebook.com/publicgardens
twitter.com/publicgardens
www.youtube.com/user/americapublicgardens
Overview: A medium-sized international organization founded in 1940
Mission: To support North American botanical gardens & arboreta, public horticultural organizations, their staff & trustees by: promoting the value of botanical gardens, arboreta & public horticultural organizations involved in the display, study & conservation of plants for public benefit; setting, promoting & recognizing professional standards; facilitating the exchange of information; advocating the collective interests of the association's members; promoting membership services
Finances: *Annual Operating Budget:* $250,000-$500,000; *Funding Sources:* Membership dues; meetings; publication sales
Staff Member(s): 8
Membership: 2,400; *Fees:* $65 student/individual; $125 non-affiliated individual; institutional dues based on operating budget; *Member Profile:* Anyone who works or volunteers for public gardens, zoos, horticultural societies, arboreta or historic house gardens; *Committees:* Awards; Plant Collections Network; Program Selection
Activities: *Internships:* Yes; *Rents Mailing List:* Yes; *Library:* by appointment
Chief Officer(s):
Casey Sclar, Executive Director, 610-708-3010
csclar@publicgardens.org
Publications:
- The Public Garden
Profile: Quarterly Magazine

American Public Works Association (APWA)
#1400, 1200 Main St., Kansas City MO 64105-2100 USA
Tel: 816-472-6100; *Fax:* 816-472-1610
Toll-Free: 800-848-2792
apwa@apwa.net
www.apwa.net
www.facebook.com/AmericanPublicWorksAssociation
twitter.com/apwatweets
www.youtube.com/apwatv
Overview: A large international organization founded in 1938
Mission: To provide high quality public works, goods & services
Affiliation(s): Canadian Public Works Association
Finances: *Annual Operating Budget:* Greater than $5 Million; *Funding Sources:* Membership dues; Federal grants; Products
Staff Member(s): 50; 250 volunteer(s)
Membership: 26,000; *Fees:* Schedule available; *Member Profile:* Public agencies, private sector companies & individuals engaged in public works services; *Committees:* Transportation; Solid Waste; Water Resources; Engineering & Technology; Management & Leadership; Emergency Management; Fleet Services; Facilities & Grounds; Utility & Public Right of Way
Chief Officer(s):
Scott Grayson, Executive Director, 816-595-5209
sgrayson@apwa.net
Teresa Hon, Manager, Board Operations & Governance, 816-595-5224
thon@apwa.net

American Rhododendron Society (ARS)
PO Box 525, Niagara Falls NY 14304 USA
Tel: 416-424-1942; *Fax:* 905-262-1999
www.rhododendron.org
Overview: A small international charitable organization
Mission: To encourage interest in and to disseminate information about the genus Rhododendron.
Finances: *Annual Operating Budget:* Less than $50,000; *Funding Sources:* Membership dues; plant sales
50 volunteer(s)
Membership: 400; *Fees:* $35; *Member Profile:* Growers of rhododendrons
Activities: Bulletins; flower shows; plant sales
Chief Officer(s):
Laura Grant, Executive Director
lauragrant@arsoffice.org

American Rivers
#1400, 1101 - 14th St. NW, Washington DC 20005 USA
Tel: 202-347-7550
feedback@americanrivers.org
www.americanrivers.org
www.facebook.com/AmericanRivers
twitter.com/AmericanRivers
www.instagram.com/americanrivers
Previous Name: American Rivers Conservation Council
Overview: A medium-sized national organization founded in 1973
Mission: To preserve & restore America's river systems; To foster a river stewardship ethic
Finances: *Annual Operating Budget:* $1.5 Million-$3 Million
Staff Member(s): 25; 7 volunteer(s)
Activities: Policy manuals; *Internships:* Yes; *Speaker Service:* Yes
Chief Officer(s):
William Robert (Bob) Irvin, President

American Rivers Conservation Council *See* American Rivers

American Society for Aesthetic Plastic Surgery (ASAPS)
c/o Renato Saltz, M.D., FACS, 5445 South Highland Dr., Salt Lake City UT 84117 USA
Tel: 801-274-9500; *Fax:* 801-274-9515
Toll-Free: 888-272-7711
Other Communication: media@surgery.org
findasurgeon@surgery.org
www.surgery.org
Overview: A medium-sized international organization founded in 1967
Mission: To advance the science, art, & safe practice of aesthetic plastic surgery among qualified plastic surgeons
Membership: 2,400; *Member Profile:* Plastic surgeons from the United States, certified by the American Board of Plastic Surgery; Plastic surgeons from Canada certified in plastic surgery by the Royal College of Physicians & Surgeons of Canada; Plastic surgeons from several other countries, who specialize in cosmetic plastic surgery
Activities: Providing both medical & public education; Advocating for patients; Publishing annual statistics; *Speaker Service:* Yes
Chief Officer(s):
Renato Saltz, President
rsaltz@saltzplasticsurgery.com
Jeffrey M. Kenkel, Vice-Presidnet
James A. Matas, Treasurer
Leo R. McCafferty, Secretary
Adeena Babbitt, Manager, Media Relations, 212-921-0500, Fax: 212-921-0011
media@surgery.org
Meetings/Conferences:
- American Society for Aesthetic Plastic Surgery 2018 Annual Meeting, 2018
Scope: International
Publications:
- Aesthetic Surgery Journal
Type: Journal; *Accepts Advertising*; *Editor:* Foad Nahai, MD; *ISSN:* 1090-820X
Profile: A peer-reviewed international journal which focuses on scientific developments & clinical techniques in aesthetic surgery
- Beautiful Choice Newsletter
Type: Newsletter

American Society for Bone & Mineral Research (ASBMR)
#800, 2025 M St. NW, Washington DC 20036-3309 USA
Tel: 202-367-1161; *Fax:* 202-367-2161
Other Communication: Publications E-mail:
jbmroffice@wiley.com
asbmr@asbmr.org

Foreign Associations / American Society for Environmental History (ASEH)

www.asbmr.org
www.facebook.com/ASBMR
twitter.com/ASBMR
Overview: A medium-sized international organization
Mission: To promote study in the field of bone & mineral metabolism
Membership: 4,000; *Member Profile:* Clinical & experimental scientists involved in the study of bone & mineral metabolism; Physicians; Other healthcare practitioners; *Committees:* Advocacy/Science Policy; Development; Diversity in Bone & Mineral Research Subcommittee; Ethics Advisory; Finance; Membership Engagement & Education; Professional Practice; Publications; Women in Bone & Mineral Research; Young Investigator Subcommittee
Activities: Engaging in advocacy activities; Interacting with government agencies & related societies
Chief Officer(s):
Jane Cauley, President
Ann L. Elderkin, Executive Director
Douglas Fesler, Associate Executive Director
Deborah Kroll, Director, Development
Brenda Malottke, Director, Finance
Amanda Darvill, Director, Marketing & Communications
Katie Duffy, Director, Publications
Lauren Taggart, Manager, Operations
Angela Cangemi, Manager, Programs
Meetings/Conferences:
• American Society for Bone & Mineral Research 2018 Annual Meeting, September, 2018, Palais des Congrès de Montréal, Montréal, QC
Scope: International
Description: Plenary & poster sessions, panel discussions, & networking events
Publications:
• ASBMR [American Society for Bone & Mineral Research] e-news
Type: Newsletter; *Frequency:* Monthly
Profile: Information from the American Society for Bone & Mineral Research, including upcoming events, grant announcements, membership benefits, committee & task force highlights, & program updates
• Journal of Bone & Mineral Research
Type: Journal; *Accepts Advertising; Editor:* Juliet E. Compston
Profile: Up-to-date basic & clinical research in the pathophysiology & treatment of bone & mineral disorders
• Primer on the Metabolic Bone Diseases & Disorders of Mineral Metabolism
Type: Primer; *Editor:* Clifford Rosen, M.D.; *Price:* A free copy & on-line access for American Society for Bone & Mineral Research members
Profile: A resource for scientists & students seeking an overview of the bone & mineral field, as well as for clinicians who care for patients with disorders of bone & mineral metabolism

American Society for Environmental History (ASEH)
Interdisciplinary Arts & Sciences Program, University of Washington, PO Box 358436, 1900 Commerce St., Tacoma WA 98402-3100 USA
Tel: 206-465-0630
director@aseh.net
www.aseh.net
www.facebook.com/78043136293
www.youtube.com/watch?v=ewX25rVu0EY
Overview: A small international charitable organization founded in 1977
Mission: To promote interdisciplinary study of past environmental change; to promote the study of environmental history in all disciplines
Member of: American Council of Learned Societies
Affiliation(s): International Consortium of Environmental History Organizations
Membership: *Committees:* Executive; Nominating; Diversity; Outreach; Conference Site Selection; Publications; Education; Conference Program; Conference Local Arrangements; George Perkins Marsh Prize; Alice Hamilton Prize; Rachel Carson Prize; Leopold-Hidy Prize; H-Evironment
Chief Officer(s):
Gregg Mitman, President
Awards:
• Leopold-Hidy Prize for Best Article in Environmental History
• Alice Hamilton Prize for Best Article, Outside the journal, Environmental History
• Rachel Carson Prize for Best Dissertation in Environmental History
• George Perkins March Prize for Best Book in Environmental History
Publications:
• ASEH [American Society for Environmental History] News
Type: Newsletter; *Frequency:* Quarterly
• Environmental History
Type: Journal
Profile: Published jointly with the Forest History Society

American Society for Information Science & Technology (ASIS&T)
#850, 8555 - 16th St., Silver Spring MD 20910 USA
Tel: 301-495-0900; *Fax:* 301-495-0810
Other Communication: membership@asis.org
asis@asis.org
www.asis.org
www.facebook.com/asist.org
twitter.com/asist_org
Overview: A small international organization founded in 1937
Mission: To advance the information sciences & related applications of information technology by providing focus, opportunity, & support to information professionals & organizations
Member of: American Library Association
Staff Member(s): 8
Membership: 4,000; *Fees:* US$140 regular; US$40 student; US$70 retired; US$800 corporate; US$650 institutional; US$65 Entry/Transitional Professionals; *Member Profile:* Information professionals; *Committees:* Executive; Budget & Finance; Awards & Honors; Constitution & Bylaws; Information Science Education; International Relations; Leadership; Membership; Nominations; Communications & Publications; Standards
Chief Officer(s):
Harry W. Bruce, President
harryb@uw.edu
Richard B. Hill, Executive Director
rhill@asis.org
Janice Hatzakos, Director, Finance & Administration
jan@asis.org

American Society for Legal History (ASLH)
c/o Western Michigan University, 4301 Friedmann Hall, Kalamazoo MI 49008-5334 USA
Fax: 269-387-4651
www.aslh.net
Overview: A small international organization founded in 1956
Mission: To promote study, research & publication in the worldwide history of law & legal institutions
Member of: American Council of Learned Societies
Affiliation(s): American History Association
Finances: *Funding Sources:* Membership dues; donations; advertisements; mailing lists
Membership: *Fees:* Schedule available; *Committees:* Conferences & the Annual Meeting; Cromwell Prizes; Documentary Preservation; Finance; Graduate Student Outreach; Honours; Willard Hurst Memorial Fund; Local Arrangements; Membership; Paul L. Murphy Award; Nominating; Kathryn T. Preyer Memorial; Annual Meeting Program; Projects & Proposals; Publications; John Phillip Reid Book Award; Research Fellowships & Awards; Surrency Prize; Sutherland Prize
Activities: Publishes, in conjunction with UNC press, monograph series "Studies in Legal History"; *Rents Mailing List:* Yes
Chief Officer(s):
Rebecca J. Scott, President-Elect
Michael Grossberg, President
grossber@indiana.edu
Sally Hadden, Secretary
sally.hadden@wmich.edu
Publications:
• Law and History Review
Editor: David S. Tanenhaus; *ISSN:* 0738-2480
Profile: Journal, issued three times per year

American Society for Parenteral & Enteral Nutrition (ASPEN)
#412, 8630 Fenton St., Silver Spring MD 20910 USA
Tel: 301-587-6315; *Fax:* 301-587-2365
aspen@nutritioncare.org
www.nutritioncare.org
www.linkedin.com/company/american-society-for-parenteral-&-enteral-nutrition-a-s-p-e-n-
www.facebook.com/nutritioncare.org
twitter.com/aspenweb
Overview: A medium-sized international organization founded in 1976
Mission: To advance the science & practice of nutrition support therapy; To improve patient care
Staff Member(s): 17
Membership: 5,500+; *Fees:* Schedule available; *Member Profile:* Individuals from around the world who are involved in the provision of clinical nutrition therapies, such as dietitians, physicians, nurses, pharmacists, & other health professionals
Chief Officer(s):
Debra BenAvram, Chief Executive Officer
debrab@nutritioncare.org
Colleen Harper, Chief Operating Officer
colleenh@nutritioncare.org
Fatema Gharzai, Director, Membership & Marketing
fatemag@nutritioncare.org
Publications:
• Journal of Parenteral & Enteral Nutrition
Type: Journal; *Frequency:* Bimonthly; *Accepts Advertising; Price:* Free with membership in the American Society for Parenteral & EnteralNutrition
Profile: Original peer-reviewed studies about basic & clinical research in the field of nutrition & metabolic support
• Nutrition in Clinical Practice
Type: Journal; *Frequency:* Bimonthly; *Accepts Advertising; Price:* Free with membership in the American Society for Parenteral & Enteral Nutrition
Profile: Multidisciplinary peer-reviewed articles for the clinical practice professional

American Society for Quality (ASQ)
PO Box 3005, 600 Plankinton Ave. North, Milwaukee WI 53203 USA
Tel: 414-272-8575; *Fax:* 414-272-1734
Toll-Free: 800-248-1946
help@asq.org
www.asq.org
www.linkedin.com/company/asq
www.facebook.com/ASQ
twitter.com/ASQ
www.youtube.com/user/ASQhq
Overview: A large international organization founded in 1946
Mission: To advance learning, quality improvement, & knowledge exchange to improve business results, & to create better workplaces & communities worldwide
Finances: *Annual Operating Budget:* Greater than $5 Million
Staff Member(s): 225; 600 volunteer(s)
Membership: 150,000 individual & corporate; *Fees:* $29 student; $99 associate; $159 full; *Committees:* Technical Forums/Divisions: Quality Management; Aviation, Space & Defense; Automotive; Chemical & Process Industries; Electronics & Communications; Textile & Needle Trades; Food, Drug, & Cosmetics; Inspection; Biomedical; Energy & Environmental; Statistics; Human Development & Leadership; Software; Customer-Supplier; Service Industries; Quality Audit; Health Care; Measurement Quality; Design & Construction; Education; Advanced Manufacturing; Community Quality Councils; Government; Product Safety & Liability Prevention; Reliability; Six Sigma; Teamwork & Participation
Activities: Providing instruction, home study classes, & courses taught by highly qualified instructors from business, industry, & academia; *Speaker Service:* Yes; *Library:* Quality Information Center; Open to public
Chief Officer(s):
Bill Troy, Chief Executive Officer
wtroy@asq.org
Meetings/Conferences:
• American Society for Quality 2018 World Conference on Quality & Improvement, April, 2018, Seattle, WA
Scope: International

Edmonton Section
Edmonton AB
e-mail: info@asqedmonton.org
www.asqedmonton.org
Chief Officer(s):
Atheer Jawad, Chair
chair@asqedmonton.org

Kitchener Section
Kitchener ON
www.asqkitchener.org
Mission: To create awareness of the need for quality, to promote research & development of standards, and to provide educational opportunities to ensure product and service excellence.
Chief Officer(s):

Jane Martin, Chair
chair@asqkitchener.org
London Section
London ON
www.asqlondon.on.ca
Chief Officer(s):
Keith Harasyn, Chair
Nova Scotia Section
NS
www.asq411.org
Chief Officer(s):
Christopher Anstey, Chair
Saskatchewan Section
Saskatoon SK
e-mail: info@asqsask.org
www.facebook.com/pages/ASQ-Saskatchewan/105726962829232
Toronto Section
Toronto ON
e-mail: webmaster@asqtoronto.org
www.asqtoronto.org
Mission: To function as a volunteer resource for learning, networking, & fellowship for members, organizations, & the community interested in & with a passion for Quality
Chief Officer(s):
Rogerio Boaventura, Chair
chair@asqtoronto.org
Vancouver Section
Vancouver BC
www.asq.bc.ca
www.linkedin.com/groups?gid=3789010
twitter.com/ASQVancouver
vimeo.com/asqvancouver
Chief Officer(s):
David Muncaster, Chair
chair@asq.bc.ca
Windsor Section
Windsor ON
www.asqwindsor.ca

American Society for Theatre Research (ASTR)
#252, 1000 Westgate Dr., St. Paul MN 55114 USA
Tel: 651-288-3429; Fax: 651-290-2266
info@astr.org
www.astr.org
twitter.com/ASTRtweets
Overview: A medium-sized international organization founded in 1956
Mission: To promote the cause of theatre as a field for serious scholarly study & research
Member of: American Council of Learned Societies
Affiliation(s): International Federation for Theatre Research
Finances: Annual Operating Budget: $50,000-$100,000
Staff Member(s): 1
Membership: 750 individual; Fees: $145 individual; $95 contingent faculty/independent scholar; $65 retired; $50 student; Member Profile: Students; professors; independent scholars of theatre; Committees: Awards; Conferences; Nominating
Activities: Rents Mailing List: Yes
Chief Officer(s):
Eric Ewald, Executive Director
erice@astr.org
Awards:
• Errol Hill Award
Awarded for the most outstanding work on African-American theatre
• Barnard Hewitt Award
Given in conjuction with the University of Illinois for the best book in theatre history to be published by a North American or on a North American topic
• Gerald Kahan Scholars Prize
Given for the best article by an emerging scholar
• Biennial Sally Banes Publication Prize
• Selma Jeanne Cohen Conference Presentation Award
• Distinguished Scholar Award
Publications:
• Theatre Survey
Type: Journal; Frequency: 3 pa; Editor: Nicholas Ridout
Profile: Theatre history journal

American Society of Association Executives (ASAE)
1575 I St. NW, Washington DC 20005 USA
Tel: 202-371-0940; Fax: 202-371-8315
Toll-Free: 888-950-2723
Other Communication: Main Phone: 202-626-2723
ASAEservice@asaecenter.org
www.asaecenter.org
Overview: A large national organization founded in 1920
Mission: To advance the value of voluntary associations to society & to support the professionalism of the individuals who lead them
Finances: Annual Operating Budget: Greater than $5 Million
Staff Member(s): 140; 37 volunteer(s)
Membership: 21,000 executives + 9,300 organizations
Activities: Internships: Yes; Rents Mailing List: Yes; Library
Chief Officer(s):
Scott D. Wiley, Chair
John Graham, President & CEO
jgraham@asaecenter.org
Awards:
• The Key Award
Honours a CEO who has demonstrated exceptional leadership skills Deadline: April 1
• The Professional Performance Award
Honours top-level executives for their contributions Deadline: April 1
• The Academy of Leaders Award
Awarded to industry partners & consultants who have supported the association community in an outstanding way Deadline: April 1
Publications:
• AMC Connection [a publication of American Society of Association Executives]
Type: Newsletter; Frequency: q.
• Association Law & Policy [a publication of American Society of Association Executives]
Type: Newsletter; Frequency: Monthly
• Associations Now [a publication of American Society of Association Executives]
Type: Magazine; Frequency: Monthly
• Communication News [a publication of American Society of Association Executives]
Type: Newsletter; Frequency: s-m.
• Component Relations [a publication of American Society of Association Executives]
Type: Newsletter; Frequency: s-m.
• Consultants Connection [a publication of American Society of Association Executives]
Type: Newsletter; Frequency: q.
• Dollars & Cents [a publication of American Society of Association Executives]
Type: Newsletter; Frequency: s-m.
• Executive IdeaLink [a publication of American Society of Association Executives]
Type: Newsletter; Frequency: s-m.
• Global Link [a publication of American Society of Association Executives]
Type: Newsletter; Frequency: s-m.
• Government Relations [a publication of American Society of Association Executives]
Type: Newsletter; Frequency: s-m.
• Marketing Insights [a publication of American Society of Association Executives]
Type: Newsletter; Frequency: s-m.
• Meetings & Expositions [a publication of American Society of Association Executives]
Type: Newsletter; Frequency: s-m.
• Membership Developments [a publication of American Society of Association Executives]
Type: Newsletter; Frequency: q.
• Professional Development Forum Online [a publication of American Society of Association Executives]
Type: Newsletter; Frequency: q.
• TechnoScope [a publication of American Society of Association Executives]
Type: Newsletter; Frequency: s-m.

American Society of Colon & Rectal Surgeons
#550, 85 West Algonquin Rd., Arlington Heights IL 60005 USA
Tel: 847-290-9184; Fax: 847-427-9656
ascrs@fascrs.org
www.fascrs.org
www.linkedin.com/company/the-american-society-of-colon-and-rectal-surgeons
www.facebook.com/fascrs
twitter.com/fascrs_updates
Overview: A medium-sized international organization
Mission: To advance the science & practice of the treatment of patients with diseases & disorders that affect the colon, rectum, & anus
Membership: 3,500+; Member Profile: Colon & rectal surgeons & other professionals; Committees: Awards; Bylaws; Clinical Practice Guidelines; Continuing Education; CREST; Finance & Management; Fundamentals of Rectal Cancer Surgery; Healthcare Economics; History of ASCRS; International; Membership; New Technologies; Operative Competency Evaluation; Professional Outreach; Program; Public Relations; Quality Assessment & Safety; Rectal Cancer Coordinating; Regional Society; Residents; Self-Assessment; Social Media; Video-Based Education; Website; Young Surgeons
Activities: Assuring high quality research; Promoting education for the prevention & management of disorders of the colon, rectum, & anus
Chief Officer(s):
Patricia L. Roberts, MD, President
David A. Margolin, MD, Vice-President
Tracy L. Hull, MD, Secretary
Neil H. Hyman, MD, Treasurer
Meetings/Conferences:
• American Society of Colon & Rectal Surgeons 2018 Annual Scientific Meeting, May, 2018, Omni Nashville Hotel, Nashville, TN
Scope: International
Attendance: 1,500+
Description: Courses, workshops, symposia, lectures, & scientific sessions for surgeons
Publications:
• ASCRS [American Society of Colon & Rectal Surgeons] News
Type: Newsletter; Frequency: Semiannually
Profile: Information from the society of interest to its members

American Society of Echocardiography (ASE)
#310, 2100 Gateway Centre Blvd., Morrisville NC 27560 USA
Tel: 919-861-5574; Fax: 919-882-9900
ase@asecho.org
www.asecho.org
www.linkedin.com/groups/55219
www.facebook.com/asecho
twitter.com/ase360
www.youtube.com/user/AmericanSocietyofEch
Overview: A medium-sized international organization founded in 1975
Mission: To promote excellence in cardiovascular ultrasound & its application to patient care
Membership: 16,000+; Fees: Schedule available; Member Profile: Heart & circulation ultrasound specialists, such as physicians, scientists, lab managers, sonographers & retirees who live in the United States, Canada, & Mexico; International specialists; Medical & sonogrpahy students; Committees: Advocacy; Awards; CME; Bylaws & Ethics; Education; FASE; Finance, Strategy & Development; Guidelines and Standards; Industry Relations; Information Technology; Management/Executive; Membership Steering; Nominating; Research; Research Awards; Scientific Sessions Program
Activities: Providing education; Engaging in advocacy activities; Encouraging research
Chief Officer(s):
Allan Klein, President
president@asecho.org
Robin Wiegerink, Chief Executive Officer
rwiegerink@asecho.org

American Society of Heating, Refrigerating & Air Conditioning Engineers (ASHRAE)
1791 Tullie Circle NE, Atlanta GA 30329 USA
Tel: 404-636-8400; Fax: 404-321-5478
Toll-Free: 800-527-4723
ashrae@ashrae.org
www.ashrae.org
www.facebook.com/106136469528
twitter.com/ashraenews
www.youtube.com/user/ASHRAEvideo
Overview: A medium-sized international organization founded in 1894
Mission: To advance heating, ventilation, air conditioning & refrigeration; To promote a sustainable environment through research, standards writing, publishing & continuing education.
Staff Member(s): 32
Membership: 54,000; Fees: $196 Regular/Student/Associate; $52 Affiliate; Committees: Advocacy; Finance; Nominating; Planning; Society Rules; Membership Promotion; Research Promotion; Chapter Technology Transfer; Student Activities; Conferences & Expositions; Young Engineers in ASHRAE; Honors & Awards; Publishing & Education; Historical; Certification; Electronic Communications; Professional Development; Handbook; Publications; Research Administration;

Environmental Health; Standards; Refrigeration; Technical Activities
Chief Officer(s):
William Bahnfleth, President
Jeff H. Littleton, Executive Vice President
Awards:
• ASHRAE Engineers Grant-in-Aid
Graduate level studies in the areas of heating, cooling, refrigeration, air conditioning, energy conservation, air quality
Deadline: February *Amount:* $6,000 US; 12 awards available
Contact: Manager of Research, ASHRAE
Meetings/Conferences:
• American Society of Heating, Refrigerating and Air-Conditioning Engineers 2018 Winter Conference, January, 2018, Palmer House Hilton, Chicago, IL
Scope: International
Description: A global forum providing technology transfer, best practices, education and excellent networking opportunities for those who insist upon using the latest innovative solutions to enhance operations and maximize the efficiency and productivity of their buildings.
Contact Information: www.ashrae.org/chicago
Publications:
• ASHRAE [American Society of Heating, Refrigerating & Air Conditioning Engineers] Journal
Type: Journal; *Frequency:* Monthly

British Columbia Chapter
#111, 3790 Canada Way, Burnaby BC V5C 4S2
ashrae.bc.ca/bc
Chief Officer(s):
Kim Rosval, President
krosval@modern-systems.com

Chapitre de Québec Chapter
CP 8652, Succ. Ste-Foy, Québec QC G1V 4N6
info@ashraequebec.org
www.ashraequebec.org
Chief Officer(s):
Alexis T. Gagnon, Président
atg@evap-techmtc.com

Chapitre Montréal Chapter
CP 81, Boucherville QC J4B 5E6
Tél: 450-449-3667
info@ashrae-mtl.org
www.ashraemontreal.org
Chief Officer(s):
Anthony Jonkov, Président, 514-783-9865 Ext. 2232, *Fax:* 514-783-9614
president@ashrae-mtl.org

Halifax Chapter
Halifax NS
e-mail: ASHRAE.Halifax@gmail.com
sites.google.com/site/ashraehalifax/
Chief Officer(s):
Darrell Amirault, President

Hamilton Chapter
Hamilton ON
www.vaxxine.com/ashrae
Chief Officer(s):
Reaz Usmanali, President
reaz.usmanali@jci.com

London Chapter
London ON
londoncanada.ashraechapters.org
Chief Officer(s):
Jamie Kruspel, President, 519-200-2197
jamie.kruspel@td.com

Manitoba Chapter
MB
e-mail: ashrae.mb@gmail.com
www.ashraemanitoba.ca
Chief Officer(s):
Stephen Norsworthy, President, 204-786-8080
stephen.norsworthy@snclavalin.com

New Brunswick/PEI Chapter
PO Box 1629, Moncton NB E1C 9X4
www.ashraenbpei.org
twitter.com/AshraeNBPEI
Chief Officer(s):
Camille Chevarie, President, 506-857-8708

Northern Alberta Chapter
PO Box 42066, Stn. Milbourne, Edmonton AB T6K 4C4
ashraenac.org
Chief Officer(s):
Tom Jacknisky, President, 780-452-1800
president@ashraenac.org

Ottawa Valley Chapter
PO Box 21088, 1166 Bank St., Ottawa ON K1S 5N1
e-mail: contact@ashrae.ottawa.on.ca
www.ashrae.ottawa.on.ca
Chief Officer(s):
Roderic Potter, President
rod@rodders.com

Regina Chapter
PO Box 3958, 2200 Saskatchewan Dr., Regina SK S4P 0B5
regina.ashraechapters.org
Chief Officer(s):
Alana Yip, President
alana.yip@sasktel.net

Saskatoon Chapter
Saskatoon SK
Tel: 306-477-0678
reply@ashraesaskatoon.ca
www.ashraesaskatoon.ca
www.facebook.com/ashraesaskatoon
Chief Officer(s):
Blake Erb, President, 306-242-3663

Southern Alberta Chapter
PO Box 76006, Calgary AB T2Y 2Z9
e-mail: chapter.administrator@sac-ashrae.com
www.sac-ashrae.com
Chief Officer(s):
Brad Bond, President
president@sac-ashrae.com

Toronto Chapter
#201, 2800 Skymark Ave., Mississauga ON L4W 5A6
Tel: 905-602-4714
www.torontoashrae.com
www.linkedin.com/groups/ASHRAE-Toronto-Chapter-2792724
www.facebook.com/torontoashrae
twitter.com/torontoashrae
Chief Officer(s):
David Benedetti, President
dbenedetti@deltacontrols.com
Sabrina Tai, Contact
stai@hrai.ca

Vancouver Island Chapter
BC
Tel: 250-478-8885; *Fax:* 250-478-8827
www.ashrae.bc.ca/vi
Chief Officer(s):
Mark Stitt, President

Windsor Chapter
Windsor ON
windsor.ashraechapters.org
Chief Officer(s):
Mason Hoppe, President, 519-966-1550
Dan Castellan, Contact, 519-253-3000 Ext. 2164, *Fax:* 519-561-1404
danc@uwindsor.ca

American Society of International Law (ASIL)
2223 Massachussetts Ave. NW, Washington DC 20008 USA
Tel: 202-939-6000; *Fax:* 202-797-7133
services@asil.org
www.asil.org
www.facebook.com/AmericanSocietyofInternationalLaw
twitter.com/asilorg
www.youtube.com/asil1906
Overview: A medium-sized international organization founded in 1906 overseen by American Council of Learned Societies
Mission: To promote the study of international law
Affiliation(s): International Law Students' Association
Finances: *Annual Operating Budget:* $1.5 Million-$3 Million; *Funding Sources:* Membership dues; publications; grants
Staff Member(s): 18
Membership: 4,000 individual; *Fees:* Schedule available; *Member Profile:* Scholars; practitioners; government officials; international civil servants; students; *Committees:* Interest Groups: Africa; Antartic Law; Dispute Resolution; Human Rights; Intellectual Property Law; International Criminal Law; International Economic Law; International Environmental Law; International Health Law; International Law in Domestic Courts; International Legal Theory; International Organizations; International Security; International Space Law; International Tax Law; Law in the Pacific Rim Region; Lieber Society on the Law of Armed Conflict; New Professionals; Private International Law; Rights of Indigenous People; Status of Minorities & Other Communities
Activities: *Rents Mailing List:* Yes; *Library*
Chief Officer(s):
Mark Agrast, Executive Director
magrast@asil.org

American Society of Lubrication Engineers *See* Society of Tribologists & Lubrication Engineers

American Society of Mechanical Engineers (ASME)
2 Park Ave., New York NY 10016-5990 USA
Tel: 973-882-1170
Toll-Free: 800-843-2763
customercare@asme.org
www.asme.org
www.linkedin.com/groups/36972
www.facebook.com/ASME.org
twitter.com/asmedotorg
Overview: A large international organization founded in 1880
Mission: To promote the art, science, & practice of multidisciplinary engineering; To focus on the technical, educational, & research issues of the engineering & technology community; To help the engineering community develop solutions to improve the quality of life
Finances: *Funding Sources:* Publications; Meetings; Standards accreditation
Membership: 130,000+ in 151+ countries; *Fees:* Schedule available; *Member Profile:* Students; Engineers; Technical professionals; Researchers; Project managers; Academic leaders; Corporate executives; *Committees:* Audit; Finance & Investment; Honors; Organization & Rules; Past Presidents; Governance; Executive Director Evaluation & Staff Compensation; Sector Management
Activities: Promoting multidisciplinary engineering & allied science throughout the world; Engaging in research; Liaising with government; Enabling knowledge sharing; Offering continuing education & professional development in mechanical engineering; Maintaining codes & standards; Promoting the technical competency of members; Offering a mentoring program; *Library:* American Society of Mechanical Engineers e-Library; Not open to public
Chief Officer(s):
K. Keith Roe, President
roek2@asme.org
James W. Coaker, Secretary-Treasurer
coakerandco@aol.com
Thomas G. Loughlin, Executive Director
execdirector@asme.org
David Soukup, Managing Director, Governance, 212-591-7397
soukupd@asme.org
Awards:
• Service Awards
• Achievement Awards
• Literature Awards
• Unit Awards
• ASME Fellow
• ASME Scholarships
Meetings/Conferences:
• ASME 2018 Power & Energy Conference Exhibition, June, 2018, Lake Buena Vista, FL
Scope: International
• 2018 26th International Conference on Nuclear Engineering, July, 2018, London
Scope: International
• ASME 2018 International Mechanical Engineering Congress & Exposition, November, 2018, Pittsburgh, PA
Scope: International
• 2019 Pressure Vessels & Piping Conference, July, 2019, San Antonio, TX
Scope: International
Publications:
• Applied Mechanics Reviews
Type: Journal; *Frequency:* Bimonthly; *Editor:* Harry Dankowicz; *ISSN:* 0003-6900
Profile: An international review journal featuring topics such as heat transfer, vibration, & dynamics
• ASME [American Society of Mechanical Engineers] Capitol Update
Type: Newsletter; *Frequency:* Weekly
Profile: Legislative & regulatory news of interest to the engineering community
• ASME News [a publication of the American Society of Mechanical Engineers]
Type: Newsletter
Profile: Information on the Society & its activities

• Journal of Applied Mechanics
Type: Journal; *Frequency:* Bimonthly; *Editor:* Yonggang Huang; *ISSN:* 0021-8936
Profile: Peer-reviewed research papers covering subjects such as wave propagation, turbulence, stress analysis, structures, hydraulics, & flow & fracture
• Journal of Biomechanical Engineering
Type: Journal; *Frequency:* Monthly; *Editor:* Beth Winkelstein; *ISSN:* 0148-0731
Profile: Research papers on topics such as cellular mechanics, the design & control of biological systems, bioheat transfer, biomaterials, & biomechanics
• Journal of Computational & Nonlinear Dynamics
Type: Journal; *Frequency:* Quarterly; *Editor:* Bala Balachandran; *ISSN:* 1555-1415
Profile: Technical briefs & research papers cover bio-mechanical dynamics, design & design optimization dynamical analysis & method, vehicular dynamics,stability, & aerospace applications
• Journal of Computing & Information Science in Engineering
Type: Journal; *Frequency:* Quarterly; *Editor:* Bahram Ravani; *ISSN:* 1530-9827
Profile: Research papers & technical briefs about virtual environments & haptics, tolerance mondeling & computational metrology, reverse engineering,& internet-aided design, manufacturing, & commerce
• Journal of Dynamic Systems, Measurement, & Control
Type: Journal; *Frequency:* Bimonthly; *Editor:* Joseph Beaman; *ISSN:* 0022-0434
Profile: Articles on design innovation, research papers, & technical briefs address aerospace systems, energy systems & control, manufacturing technology,power systems, production systems, signal processing, & transportation
• Journal of Electronic Packaging
Type: Journal; *Frequency:* Quarterly; *Editor:* Y.C. Lee; *ISSN:* 1043-7398
Profile: Papers to address mechanical, materials, & reliability problems encountered in the design, manufacturing, & operation of electronic, optoelectronic, & photonic systems
• Journal of Energy Resources Technology
Type: Journal; *Frequency:* Quarterly; *Editor:* Hameed Metghalchi; *ISSN:* 0195-0738
Profile: Research on topics such as extraction of energy from natural resources, enerty resource recovery from biomass & solid wastes, technology for energygenerations, offshore & deepwater mechanics, petroleum engineering, natural gas technology, & rock & material mechanics for energy resources
• Journal of Engineering for Gas Turbines & Power
Type: Journal; *Frequency:* Monthly; *Editor:* David Wisler; *ISSN:* 0742-4795
Profile: Technical briefs & research examime nuclear engineering, coal, biomass & alternative fuels, energy production & conversion, & oil & gas applications
• Journal of Engineering Materials & Technology
Type: Journal; *Frequency:* Quarterly; *Editor:* Mohammed Zikry; *ISSN:* 0094-4289
Profile: Topics include environmental effects, fatigue, fracture, high temperature creep, & phase transformations in materials
• Journal of Fluids Engineering
Type: Journal; *Frequency:* Monthly; *Editor:* Malcolm J. Andrews; *ISSN:* 0098-2202
Profile: Contents include cavitation erosion, flow in biolgical systems, fluid transients & wave motion, naval hydrodynamics, pumps, pipelines, turbines, propulsion systems,& water hammers
• Journal of Fuel Cell Science & Technology
Type: Journal; *Frequency:* Bimonthly; *Editor:* Wilson K. S. Chiu; *ISSN:* 1550-624X
Profile: Subjects include durability & damage tolerance, aging, system design & manufacturing, & fuel cell applications
• Journal of Heat Transfer
Type: Journal; *Frequency:* Monthly; *Editor:* Portonovo S. Ayyaswamy; *ISSN:* 0022-1481
Profile: Featuring research on environmental issues, low temperature & the Arctic, aircraft, & energy technology & systems
• Journal of Manufacturing Science & Engineering
Type: Journal; *Frequency:* Bimonthly; *Editor:* Y. Lawrence Yao; *ISSN:* 1087-1357
Profile: Subjects include rail transportation, inspection & quality control, material removal by machining, production systems optimization, textileproduction, & sensors
• Journal of Mechanical Design
Type: Journal; *Frequency:* Monthly; *Editor:* Shapour Azarm; *ISSN:* 1050-0472
Profile: Technical briefs & research papers address design theory & methodology, design automation, & design of direct contact systems
• Journal of Mechanisms & Robotics
Type: Journal; *Frequency:* Quarterly; *Editor:* Vijay Kumar; *ISSN:* 1942-4302
Profile: Research covers the theory, algorithms, & applications for robotic & machine systems
• Journal of Medical Devices
Type: Journal; *Frequency:* Quarterly; *Editor:* Rupak Banerjee; William Durfee; *ISSN:* 1932-6181
Profile: Design innovation articles & research papers focus upon new medical devices or instrumentation that improve diagnostic interventional & therapeutictreatments
• Journal of Micro & Nano Manufacturing
Type: Journal; *Editor:* Jian Cao
• Journal of Nanotechnology in Engineering & Medicine
Type: Journal; *Frequency:* Quarterly; *Editor:* Boris Khusid; *ISSN:* 1949-2944
Profile: The impact of nanotechnology upon medicine & the direction of research & development
• Journal of Offshore Mechanics & Arctic Engineering
Type: Journal; *Frequency:* Quarterly; *Editor:* Solomon C. Yim; *ISSN:* 0892-7219
Profile: Articles highlight Arctic exploration & drilling, permafrost engineering & Arctic thermal design, offshore structures, ice structure interaction, &marine geotechnique
• Journal of Pressure Vessel Technology
Type: Journal; *Frequency:* Bimonthly; *Editor:* Young W. Kwon; *ISSN:* 0094-9930
Profile: Technology reviews & research papers cover codes & standards, pressure vessel & piping, fatigue & fracture prediction, elevated temperature analysis & design,lifeline earthquake engineering, & safety & reliability
• Journal of Solar Energy Engineering
Type: Journal; *Frequency:* Quarterly; *Editor:* Robert F. Boehm; *ISSN:* 0199-6231
Profile: Research papers & technical information about solar collectors, solar optics, solar chemistry & bioconversion, solar thermal power, energy storage, conservation,solar buildings, solar space applications, wind energy, emerging technologies, & energy policy
• Journal of Thermal Science & Engineering Applications
Type: Journal; *Frequency:* Quarterly; *Editor:* S.A. Sherif; *ISSN:* 1948-5085
Profile: Subjects addressed include applications in areas such as defense systems, aerospace systems, energy systems, refrigeration & air conditioning,petrochemical processing, combustion systems, & medical systems
• Journal of Tribology
Type: Journal; *Frequency:* Quarterly; *Editor:* Michael Khonsari; *ISSN:* 0742-4787
Profile: Technical information & research cover tribological systems, bearing design & technology, gears, seals, & friction & wear
• Journal of Turbomachinery
Type: Journal; *Frequency:* Quarterly; *Editor:* Kenneth Hall; *ISSN:* 0889-504X
Profile: Research papers examine fluid dynamics & heat transfer phenomena in compressor & turbine components
• Journal of Vibration & Acoustics
Type: Journal; *Frequency:* Bimonthly; *Editor:* I.Y. (Steve) Shen; *ISSN:* 1048-9002
Profile: Subjects include areas such as machinery dynamics & noise, structural acoustics, acoustic emission, noise control, & vibration suppression
• ME Today [a publication of the American Society of Mechanical Engineers]
Type: Newsletter; *Frequency:* Quarterly
Profile: Information of interest to early career engineers
• Mechanical Engineering [a publication of the American Society Of Mechanical Engineers]
Type: Magazine; *Frequency:* Monthly
Profile: Engineering trends & breakthroughs
• Member Savvy [a publication of the American Society of Mechanical Engineers]
Type: Newsletter; *Frequency:* Monthly
Profile: The benefits of membership in the American Society of Mechanical Engineer
• Standards & Certification Update [a publication of the American Society of Mechanical Engineers]
Type: Newsletter; *Frequency:* Quarterly
Profile: Information about American Society of Mechanical Engineers standards & certification activities, including newpublications, professional development, & conformity assessment

American Society of Mining & Reclamation (ASMR)
1305 Weathervane Dr., Champaign IL 61821 USA
www.asmr.us
Overview: A medium-sized international charitable organization founded in 1983
Mission: To encourage any agency, institution, organization, or individual in their efforts to protect, re-establish or enhance the surface resources of land disturbances associated with mineral extraction; To promote, support & assist in research & studies; To encourage communication between the research scientist, regulatory agencies, organizations & others who seek assistance; To promote & support related educational programs
Affiliation(s): International Affiliation of Land Reclamationists
Finances: *Annual Operating Budget:* $50,000-$100,000; *Funding Sources:* Membership dues
Staff Member(s): 1; 1 volunteer(s)
Membership: 400; *Fees:* $100 sustaining; $50 regular; $10-$25 student; *Member Profile:* Sustaining - agency, department, organization, corporation, or individual representation; regular - individual representation; student - full-time students at accredited colleges; *Committees:* Publication Policy & Review Board; Awards; National Meeting; Membership; Memorial Scholarship Fund; National Register of Research & Demonstration
Activities: Small independent professional groups affiliated with the Society have been organized to concentrate on a particular aspect of surface mining or reclamation: International Tailings Reclamation, Landscape Architecture, Soil & Overburden, Ecology, Geotechnical Engineering, Meter Management, Forestry & Wildlife
Chief Officer(s):
Robert Darmody, Executive Secretary
Awards:
• Barnhisel Reclamation Researcher of the Year
Awarded to research scientists who have made substantive contributions to the advancement of reclamation science &/or technology, or contributed meaningful information relating to the economic, social, environmental or ecological effects of surface mining
• William T. Plass Award
Awarded irregularly; recognizes outstanding contributions in the areas of mining, teaching, research, &/or regulating authority as they relate to land reclamation. Those nominated should be recognized nationally & internationally for their contibutions covering a significant portion of their career
• Reclamationist of the Year
Awarded to individuals demonstrating outstanding accomplishments in the practical application or evaluation of reclamation technology

American Society of Neuroradiology (ASNR)
#205, 800 Enterprise Dr., Oak Brook IL 60523 USA
Tel: 630-574-0220; *Fax:* 630-574-0661
www.asnr.org
www.facebook.com/TheASNR
twitter.com/TheASNR
Overview: A medium-sized international organization
Mission: To develop standards for the training & practice of neuroradiologists; To promote understanding of neuroradiology among patients & other professionals & public agencies
Membership: *Member Profile:* Radiologists certified by the Royal College of Physicians & Surgeons of Canada, the American Board of Radiology, the American Osteopathic College of Radiology, or other boards or tribunals; Neuroradiologists, radiologists, or physicians with an interest in neuroradiology; Physicists (PhD) or neuroscientists (MS, PhD) with an interest in or position relevant to neuroradiology or radiology; Member in training; *Committees:* Audit; Computer Science & Informatics; Corporate Partners; Economics; Education; Education Exhibits; Evidence Based Medicine; Executive; Financial Management; Gold Medal; Honorary Member; International Collaboration; Health Policy; Membership; Nominating; Program; Publications; Quality, Safety & Value; Research; Rules; Specialty/Regional Societies; Standards & Guidelines; Technical Exhibits; Website & Social Media; Young Professionals
Activities: Fostering research in neuroradiology; Promoting an exchange of ideas among neuroradiologists; Disseminating knowledge; Cooperating with other branches of medicine & allied sciencs
Chief Officer(s):
Mary Beth Hepp, Executive Director & CEO
Angelo Artemakis, Director, Communications
aartemakis@asnr.org

Ken Cammarata, Director, Specialty Societies & Member Services
kcammarata@asnr.org
Tina Cheng, Director, Finance & Information Systems
Meetings/Conferences:
• American Society of Neuroradiology 2018 56th Annual Meeting, June, 2018, Vancouver Convention Centre, Vancouver, BC
Scope: International
Contact Information: Director, Scientific Meetings: Lora Tannehill, E-mail: ltannehill@asnr.org; Manager, Scientific Meetings: Valerie Geisendorfer, E-mail: vgeisendorfer@asnr.org
• American Society of Neuroradiology 2019 57th Annual Meeting, May, 2019, Hynes Convention Center, Boston, MA
Scope: International
Contact Information: Director, Scientific Meetings: Lora Tannehill, E-mail: ltannehill@asnr.org; Manager, Scientific Meetings: Valerie Geisendorfer, E-mail: vgeisendorfer@asnr.org
• American Society of Neuroradiology 2020 58th Annual Meeting, May, 2020, Caesars Palace, Las Vegas, NV
Scope: International
Contact Information: Director, Scientific Meetings: Lora Tannehill, E-mail: ltannehill@asnr.org; Manager, Scientific Meetings: Valerie Geisendorfer, E-mail: vgeisendorfer@asnr.org
• American Society of Neuroradiology 2021 59th Annual Meeting, May, 2021, San Francisco Marriott Marquis, San Francisco, CA
Scope: International
Contact Information: Director, Scientific Meetings: Lora Tannehill, E-mail: ltannehill@asnr.org; Manager, Scientific Meetings: Valerie Geisendorfer, E-mail: vgeisendorfer@asnr.org
• American Society of Neuroradiology 2022 60th Annual Meeting, May, 2022, Hilton New York Midtown, New York, NY
Scope: International
Contact Information: Director, Scientific Meetings: Lora Tannehill, E-mail: ltannehill@asnr.org; Manager, Scientific Meetings: Valerie Geisendorfer, E-mail: vgeisendorfer@asnr.org
• American Society of Neuroradiology 2023 61st Annual Meeting, April, 2023, Sheraton Grand Chicago, Chicago, IL
Scope: International
Contact Information: Director, Scientific Meetings: Lora Tannehill, E-mail: ltannehill@asnr.org; Manager, Scientific Meetings: Valerie Geisendorfer, E-mail: vgeisendorfer@asnr.org
Publications:
• American Journal of Neuroradiology
Type: Journal; *Frequency:* 10 pa; *Number of Pages:* 200
Profile: Peer-reviewed original research papers, review articles, & technical notes

American Society of Pediatric Hematology / Oncology (ASPHO)
#300, 8735 West Higgins Rd., Chicago IL 60631 USA
Tel: 847-375-4716; *Fax:* 847-375-6483
info@aspho.org
www.aspho.org
www.facebook.com/aspho.org
Overview: A medium-sized international organization founded in 1974
Mission: To promote optimal care of children & adolescents with blood disorders & cancer; To advance research, education, treatment, & professional practice
Staff Member(s): 14
Membership: 1,950; *Fees:* Schedule available; *Committees:* Advocacy; Annual Meeting; Communications; Early Career Council; Education; Membership; Practice; Professional Development; Review Course; Training
Activities: Providing a forum for the exchange of ideas; Offering professional development opportunities
Chief Officer(s):
Amy Billett, President
Sally Weir, Executive Director
Bruce Hammond, Director, Governance & Operations
Judith Greifer, Manager, Marketing & Membership
Publications:
• Pediatric Blood & Cancer
Type: Journal; *Frequency:* Monthly; *Editor:* Peter E. Newburger, MD
Profile: Official journal of the American Society of Pediatric Hematology / Oncology & the International Society of Pediatric Oncology

American Society of Piano Technicians *See* Piano Technicians Guild Inc.

American Society of Plant Biologists (ASPB)
15501 Monona Dr., Rockville MD 20855-2768 USA
Tel: 301-251-0560; *Fax:* 301-279-2996
info@aspb.org
www.aspb.org
Overview: A medium-sized international organization founded in 1924
Mission: To advance the plant sciences; To promote the development & outreach of plant biology as a pure & applied science
Staff Member(s): 24
Membership: 5,000; *Fees:* $140 regular; $70 postdoctoral; $45 graduate student; $35 undergraduate member; *Member Profile:* Plant biology researchers, educators, & students from any nation; Any person concerned with the physiology, molecular biology, environmental biology, cell biology, & biophysics of plants; *Committees:* Awards; Constitution & Bylaws; Education; Executive; International; Membership; Minority Affairs; Nominating; Operations Subcommitee; Program; Publications; Women in Plant Biology
Chief Officer(s):
Crispin Taylor, Executive Director
ctaylor@aspb.org
Publications:
• ASPB [American Society of Plant Biologists] News
Type: Newsletter; *Frequency:* Bimonthly; *Price:* Free for American Society Of Plant Biologists members; $30 non-members
• The Plant Cell
Type: Journal; *Frequency:* Monthly; *Accepts Advertising*; *Editor:* John Long; *ISSN:* 1040-4651
Profile: Primary research in the plant sciences
• Plant Physiology
Type: Journal; *Frequency:* Monthly; *Accepts Advertising*; *Editor:* John Long; *ISSN:* 0032-0889
Profile: Physiology, biochemistry, cellular & molecular biology, genetics, biophysics, & environmental biology of plants

American Society of Plastic Surgeons (ASPS)
444 East Algonquin Rd., Arlington Heights IL 60005 USA
Tel: 847-228-9900
media@plasticsurgery.org
www.plasticsurgery.org
www.facebook.com/PlasticSurgeryASPS
twitter.com/ASPS_News
Overview: A medium-sized international organization founded in 1931
Mission: To advance quality care to plastic surgery patients; To promote high standards of training, professionalism, ethics, physician practice, & research
Affiliation(s): Plastic Surgery Educational Foundation (PSEF)
Finances: *Annual Operating Budget:* Less than $50,000
Membership: 7,000+; *Fees:* Schedule available; *Member Profile:* Plastic surgeons, certified by the Royal College of Physicians & Surgeons of Canada or the American Board of Plastic Surgery, who perform cosmetic & reconstructive surgery
Activities: Advocating for patient safety; Providing public education about plastic surgery; Publishing informational brochures
Chief Officer(s):
Debra Johnson, President
Michael D. Costelloe, Executive Vice-President
Heather Gates, Director, Communications
Publications:
• Plastic & Reconstructive Surgery: Journal of the American Society of Plastic Surgeons
Type: Journal; *Frequency:* Monthly; *Editor:* Rod J. Rohrich, M.D.; *ISSN:* 0032-1052

American Society of Plumbing Engineers (ASPE)
#350, 6400 Shafer Ct., Rosemont IL 60018 USA
Tel: 847-296-0002; *Fax:* 847-296-2963
info@aspe.org
www.aspe.org
Overview: A medium-sized international organization founded in 1964
Mission: To advance the science of plumbing engineering; To assist in the professional growth of members
Membership: 6,300; *Committees:* Bylaws; Convention & Exposition; Credentialing; Design Standards; Education; Finance; Legislative; Long-range Planning; Membership; Nominating; Plumbing Engineering Design Handbook; Technical & Research; Technical Symposium
Chief Officer(s):
Billy Smith, Executive Director, 847-296-0002 Ext. 222
bsmith@aspe.org
British Columbia Chapter
PO Box 2201, Vancouver BC V6B 3W2
sites.google.com/site/aspebcchapter
Chief Officer(s):
Happy Wong, President
hwong@fwdeng.ca
Chapitre de Montréal
CP 20024, 8610, boul St-Laurent, Montréal QC H2P 3A4
Tél: 514-237-6559; *Téléc:* 514-383-8760
montreal.aspe.org
Chief Officer(s):
Patrick Lavoie, Président, 514-735-5651
patricklavoie@snclavallin.com
Québec
PO Box 56071, Stn. Père-Lelièvre, Québec QC G1P 4P7
www.aspequebec.com
Chief Officer(s):
Dave Morin, Président, 418-654-9600
dave.morin@roche.ca

American Society of Regional Anesthesia & Pain Medicine (ASRA)
#401, 4 Penn Center West, Pittsburgh PA 15276 USA
Tel: 412-471-2718
Toll-Free: 855-795-2772
asraassistant@asra.com
www.asra.com
www.linkedin.com/groups?gid=4797719
www.facebook.com/228281927234196
twitter.com/asra_society
Overview: A medium-sized international organization founded in 1923
Mission: To assure excellence in patient care utilizing regional anesthesia & pain medicine; To investigate the scientific basis of the specialty
Membership: 4,000; *Fees:* Schedule available; *Member Profile:* Physicians; Scientists; *Committees:* Continuing Medical Education; Guidelines & Regulatory Advocacy; Industry Relations; Membership; Newsletter; Research; Resident Section; Scientific/Educational Planning; Website & Social Media
Activities: Providing professional development activities
Chief Officer(s):
Oscar De Leon-Casasola, President
Angie Stengel, Executive Director
astengel@asra.com
Publications:
• ASRA [American Society of Regional Anesthesia & Pain Medicine] News
Type: Newsletter; *Frequency:* Quarterly; *Editor:* Colin McCartney, M.B., F.R.C.A.
Profile: Society news, articles, & meeting reviews
• ASRA [American Society of Regional Anesthesia & Pain Medicine] E-News
Type: Newsletter
Profile: Society announcements, including information about meetings, workshops, awards
• Regional Anesthesia & Pain Medicine
Type: Journal; *Frequency:* Bimonthly; *Editor:* Joseph M. Neal, M.D.
Profile: Peer-reviewed scientific & clinical studies

American Society of Safety Engineers (ASSE)
520 N. Northwest Hwy, Park Ridge IL 60068 USA
Tel: 847-699-2929
www.asse.org
linkedin.com/company/american-society-of-safety-engineers
www.facebook.com/ASSESafety
twitter.com/ASSE_Safety
www.instagram.com/asse_safety
Overview: A large international organization founded in 1911
Mission: To promote the advancement of the safety profession & to foster the technical, scientific, managerial & ethical knowledge, skills & competency of safety professionals
Affiliation(s): Canadian Society of Safety Engineering, Inc.
Staff Member(s): 60
Membership: 30,000; *Fees:* Schedule available
Activities: Providing a Professional Development Conference & Exposition; Offering continuing education & training seminars; Presenting technical publications & audio-visual training courses; *Awareness Events:* National Safety Week, June; *Rents Mailing List:* Yes
Chief Officer(s):
Fred J. Fortman, Executive Director, 847-768-3450
Dewey Whitmire, Director, Professional Development, 847-768-3418
Micah D'Orazio, Director, Marketing & Communications, 847-768-3419

Awards:
- Honor of Fellow
- Oustanding Safety Educator Award
- Safety Professional of the Year Award
- Regional Safety Professional of the Year (SPY) Award
- Chapter Safety Professional of the Year (SPY) Award
- CoPS Safety Professional of the Year (SPY) Award
- Individual Practice Specialty and Common Interest Group SPY Awards
- Significant Contributor (Branch) Awards
- Safety Management Innovation Award
- Thomas F. Bresnahan Standards Medal
- President's Award
- Culbertson Award
- Diversity in the OSH Profession Award
- Chapter of the Year Award
- Outstanding Student Section Award

Meetings/Conferences:
- American Society of Safety Engineers Safety 2018 Professional Development Conference & Exposition, June, 2018, Henry B. Gonzalez Convention Center, San Antonio, TX
Scope: International

Publications:
- Professional Safety [a publication of the American Society of Safety Engineers]
Type: Journal; Frequency: Monthly; Editor: Sue Trebswether; ISSN: 2163-6176

American Society of Travel Agents (ASTA)
#490, 675 North Washington, Alexandria VA 22314 USA
Toll-Free: 800-275-2782
askasta@asta.org
www.asta.org
www.facebook.com/AmSocTrvlAgents
twitter.com/ASTAAgents
www.youtube.com/user/ASTAsVideos
Overview: A medium-sized national organization
Mission: To be the leading global advocate for travel agents, the travel industry & the traveling public
Chief Officer(s):
Zane Kerby, MBA, President & CEO
zkerby@asta.org
Eben Peck, Executive Vice-President, Advocacy
epeck@asta.org

American Sociological Association (ASA)
#600, 1430 K St. NW, Washington DC 20005 USA
Tel: 202-383-9005; Fax: 202-638-0882; TTY: 202-638-0981
executive.office@asanet.org
www.asanet.org
www.facebook.com/AmericanSociologicalAssociation
twitter.com/ASANews
Overview: A medium-sized national organization founded in 1905
Mission: To advance sociology as a scientific discipline & profession serving the public good
Member of: American Council of Learned Societies; Consortium of Social Science Associations
Affiliation(s): International Sociological Association
Membership: 13,000; Fees: Schedule available; Member Profile: College & university faculty; researchers; students; practitioners; Committees: Annual Meeting Program; Awards; Committees; Executive Office & Budget; Nominations; Professional Ethics; Publications; Sections; Status of Lesbian, Gay, Bisexual, Transgender, & Queer People in Sociology; Status of Persons with Disabilities in Sociology; Status of Racial & Ethnic Minorities in Sociology; Status of Women in Sociology; Task Force on Community College Faculty in Sociology; Task Force on Contingent Faculty; Task Force on Engaging Sociology; Task Force on Liberal Learning; Task Force on Sociology & Climate Change
Activities: Rents Mailing List: Yes; Library: by appointment
Chief Officer(s):
Nancy Kidd, Executive Director
nkidd@asanet.org
Les Briggs, Director, Finance
business@asanet.org
Mark Fernando, Director, Governance & Administration
mfernando@asanet.org
Karen Gray Edwards, Director, Membership
membership@asanet.org
Carmen Russell, Director, Communications
russell@asanet.org
Awards:
- Jessie Bernard Award
- Cox-Johnson-Frazier Award
- Excellence in the Reporting of Social Issues Award
- Distinguished Career Award for the Practice of Sociology
- Distinguished Contributions to Teaching Award
- Distinguished Scholarly Book Award
- Dissertation Award
- Award for the Public Understanding of Sociology
- W.E.B. DuBois Career of Distinguished Scholarship Award

Meetings/Conferences:
- 2018 American Sociological Association Annual Meeting, August, 2018, Philadelphia, PA
Scope: International
Description: Theme: "Feeling Race: An Invitation to Explore Racialized Emotions"

Publications:
- American Sociological Review
Type: Journal; Frequency: Bimonthly; Accepts Advertising; ISSN: 0003-1224; Price: $40 member; $25 student member;$220 institution
Profile: Original works of interest to the sociology discipline in general, new theoretical developments, results of research, & methodological innovations
- ASA Rose Series in Sociology
Profile: Specific substantive areas in sociology
- City & Community
Type: Journal; Frequency: Quarterly; Accepts Advertising; ISSN: 1535-6841; Price: $41 member; $21 student member; $76 non-member; $301 institution
Profile: Journal of the ASA Section on Community & Urban Sociology with research & theory on topics such as community studies, immigration, rural communities, social networks, social support, suburbia,spatial studies, studies that connect specific places to general forces, urban movements, & urban history
- Contemporary Sociology
Type: Journal; Frequency: Bimonthly; Accepts Advertising; ISSN: 0094-3061; Price: $40 member; $25 student member; $220 institution
Profile: A journal of reviews & critical discussions of recent works in sociology & related disciplines of interest to sociologists
- Contexts
Type: Magazine; Frequency: Quarterly; Accepts Advertising; ISSN: 1536-5042; Price: $40 member; $25 student member; $50 non-member; $176 non-member institution
Profile: Original essays
- Footnotes
Type: Newsletter; Frequency: 5 pa; Accepts Advertising; ISSN: 0749-6931; Price: Free with membership; $40 non-member
Profile: Feature stories, calls for papers, meeting calendar, funding opportunities, obituaries, & the ASA Official Reports and Proceedings
- Journal of Health & Social Behavior
Type: Journal; Frequency: Quarterly; Accepts Advertising; ISSN: 0022-1465; Price: $40 member; $25 student member; $185 institution
Profile: A medical sociology journal with empirical & theoretical articles that apply sociological concepts & methods to the understanding of health and illness & the organization ofmedicine & health care
- Social Psychology Quarterly: The Journal of Microsociologies
Type: Journal; Frequency: Quarterly; Accepts Advertising; ISSN: 0190-2725; Price: $40 member; $25 student member; $185 institution
Profile: Theoretical & empirical papers on the link between the individual & society
- Sociological Methodology
Frequency: Annually; Accepts Advertising; ISSN: 0081-1750; Price: $50 member; $40 student member; $256 institution
Profile: Methodological papers of interest to the field of sociology
- Sociological Theory
Type: Journal; Frequency: Quarterly; Accepts Advertising; ISSN: 0735-2751; Price: $40 member; $25 student member; $262institution
Profile: Articles about social thought, including new theories, history of theory, metatheory, formal theory construction, & syntheses of existing bodies of theory
- Sociology of Education
Type: Journal; Frequency: Quarterly; Accepts Advertising; ISSN: 0038-0407; Price: $40 member; $25 student member; $185 institution
Profile: Studies in the sociology of education & human social development
- Teaching Sociology
Type: Journal; Frequency: Quarterly; Accepts Advertising; ISSN: 0092-055X; Price: $40 member; $25 student member; $185 institution
Profile: Articles, notes, & reviews to assist sociology teachers

American Studies Association (ASA)
#301, 1120 - 19th St. NW, Washington DC 20036 USA
Tel: 202-467-4783; Fax: 202-467-4786
Toll-Free: 800-548-1748
asastaff@theasa.net
www.theasa.net
www.linkedin.com/company/american-studies-association-asa-
www.facebook.com/americanstudiesassoc
Overview: A large international charitable organization founded in 1951
Mission: To enable people of diverse interests to exchange ideas about American life
Member of: American Council of Learned Societies
Affiliation(s): Canadian Association for American Studies
Finances: Annual Operating Budget: $500,000-$1.5 Million
Staff Member(s): 2
Membership: 5,000 individual; Fees: Schedule available; Member Profile: Persons with an interdisciplinary interest in American culture; institutions sympathetic to the aims of the association; Committees: American Studies Programs; Electronic Projects; Publications; Secondary Education; International; Minority Scholars; Regional Chapters; Students; Women's; Prize; Annual Meeting; Local Arrangements
Activities: Supporting & assisting programs for teaching American Studies abroad; Disseminating publications; Rents Mailing List: Yes
Chief Officer(s):
David Roediger, President
John F. Stephens, Executive Director
Molly Thacker, Coordinator, Research
Michael Casiano, Coordinator, Convention
Awards:
- Mary C. Turpie Prize
For outstanding contribution to teaching, advising & program development
- John Hope Franklin Publication Prize
For the best published book in American Studies
- Ralph Henry Gabriel Dissertation Prize
For the best completed dissertation in American Studies
- Carl Bode-Norman Holmes Pearson Prize
For outstanding contribution to American Studies
- Wise-Susman Prize
For the best student paper presented at the annual meeting
- Lora Romero First Book Publication Prize
- Angela Y. Davis Prize
- Constance M. Rourke Prize
- Yasuo Sakakibara Prize

Meetings/Conferences:
- American Studies Association Annual Meeting 2018, November, 2018, Atlanta, GA
Scope: International
Description: Theme: "States of Emergence"
Contact Information: Coordinator, Convention: Michael Casiano, E-mail: convention@theasa.net

Publications:
- American Quarterly [a publication of the American Studies Association]
Type: Journal; Frequency: Quarterly; Accepts Advertising; ISSN: 0003-0678
Profile: Encourages cross-disciplinary work through the publishing of forums, exhibition & book reviews, & short articles
- Encyclopedia of American Studies [a publication of the American Studies Association]
Type: Book
Profile: An online database that covers the history, arts, philosophy, & culture of the United States through searchable articles, bibliographies,illustrations, & supplemental material

American Thyroid Association (ATA)
#550, 6066 Leesburg Pike, Falls Church VA 22041 USA
Tel: 703-998-8890; Fax: 703-998-8893
Toll-Free: 800-849-7643
thyroid@thyroid.org
www.thyroid.org
www.linkedin.com/company/american-thyroid-association
www.facebook.com/ThyroidAssociation
twitter.com/thyroidfriends
www.youtube.com/user/thyroidorg
Overview: A medium-sized international organization founded in 1923
Mission: To promote health & understanding of thyroid biology; To encourage innovation in research on physiology, diseases, & thyroid molecular & cell biology; To guide public policies on the causes, diagnosis, & management of thyroid diseases & related disorders; To advocate for thyroid specialists; To encourage

Foreign Associations / American Vegan Society (AVS)

interaction & collaboration among members; To work with other thyroid societies to address public health & scientific issues
Member of: International Thyroid Congress
Finances: *Annual Operating Budget:* $1.5 Million-$3 Million; *Funding Sources:* Donations; Membership fees; Continuing Medical Education grants; Annual meeting
Staff Member(s): 6; 300 volunteer(s)
Membership: 1,700; *Fees:* $599; *Member Profile:* International scientists & physicians who are engaged in researching & treating thyroid diseases; *Committees:* Awards; Bylaws; Clinical Affairs; Development; Ethics Advisory; Finance & Audit; History & Archives; International Coordinating; Internet Communications; Lab Services; Membership; Nominating; Patient Affairs & Education; Program; Publications; Public Health; Public Relations; Research; Surgical Affairs; Trainees & Career Advancement
Activities: Publishing professional journals; Hosting scientific meetings & clinical & research symposia; Offering research grant programs to young investigators; Supporting professional, public, & patient edcuational programs; Developing guidelines for the clinical management of thyroid disease & cancer; Raising awareness & disseminating thyroid information; Providing clinical resources through website; *Speaker Service:* Yes; *Library:* Sawin Library
Chief Officer(s):
John C. Morris, President
Victor J. Bernet, Chief Operating Officer & Secretary
Barbara (Bobbi) R. Smith, Executive Director
thyroidexec@thyroid.org
Adonia C. Coates, Director, Meetings & Program Services
acoates@thyroid.org
Awards:
• Research Grant
Eligibility: Young investigators *Deadline:* March *Amount:* $28,750
Meetings/Conferences:
• American Thyroid Association 2018 88th Annual Meeting, October, 2018, Marriott Marquis, Washington, DC
Scope: International
Attendance: 1,000+
Description: Held each autumn, the meeting includes platform presentations, lectures, symposia, discussion groups, posters, exhibits, & opportunities for networking
Publications:
• Clinical Thyroidology [a publication of the American Thyroid Association]
Type: Journal; *Frequency:* 3 pa; *Editor:* Jerome M. Hershman; *Price:* Free
Profile: A summary of & expert commentary on recently published clinical & preclinical thyroid literature from around the world
• Signal [a publication of the American Thyroid Association]
Type: Newsletter; *Frequency:* 3 pa; *Editor:* Barbara Smith
Profile: American Thyroid Association happenings, such as policies, leaders, & meetings, as well as thyroid-related issues
• Thyroid [a publication of the American Thyroid Association]
Type: Journal; *Frequency:* Monthly; *Editor:* Peter Kopp; *Price:* Free withmembership in the American thyroid association
Profile: A peer-reviewed journal, covering subjects such as the molecular biology of the thyroid gland & the clinical management of thyroid disorders

American Vegan Society (AVS)
PO Box 369, 56 Dinshah Lane, Malaga NJ 08328-0908 USA
Tel: 856-694-2887; *Fax:* 856-694-2288
www.americanvegan.org
Overview: A small international charitable organization founded in 1960
Mission: To advocate a diet without any animal products (no meat, fish, fowl, no animal broths, fat, or gelatin; no eggs, milk, cheese; no honey) on ethical & healthful grounds, & a lifestyle excluding use of animals products such as fur, leather, wool, or silk
Affiliation(s): North American Vegetarian Society; Vegetarian Union of North America; International Vegetarian Union; The Vegan Society (England)
Membership: *Fees:* USD$20; USD$10 low income/student
Publications:
• American Vegan
Profile: Quarterly magazine

American Vintners Association *See* WineAmerica

American Water Resources Association (AWRA)
PO Box 1626, 4 Federal St. West, Middleburg VA 20118 USA
Tel: 540-687-8390; *Fax:* 540-687-8395
info@awra.org
www.awra.org
www.linkedin.com/groups?gid=769747
www.facebook.com/111474035541444
twitter.com/AWRAHQ
Overview: A large national organization founded in 1964
Mission: To advance research, planning, management, development & education in water resources; provides a focal point for the collection, organization & dissemination of ideas & information in the physical, biological, economic, social, political, legal & engineering aspects of water-related problems; to provide a forum for communication among disciplines with a common interest in water supply, quality, use, development & conservation
Finances: *Annual Operating Budget:* $500,000-$1.5 Million
Staff Member(s): 9
Membership: 3,000 worldwide; *Fees:* Schedule available; *Member Profile:* Regular - persons interested in any aspect of water resources; student - full-time student engaged in study of any aspect of water resources at a college or university; institutional - universities, governmental agencies & institutions; corporate - consulting firms & business concerns
Activities: Technical Committees provide a focus for special interests; *Rents Mailing List:* Yes
Chief Officer(s):
Martha Corrozi Narvaez, President
Rafael Frias, President-Elect
Awards:
• Fellow Member Award
• Honorary Member Award
• Icko Iben Award
• Henry P. Caulfield, Jr., Medal
• Mary H. Marsh Medal
• Sandor C. Csallany Award
• William C. Ackermann Medal
• A. Ivan Johnson Award
• IWRM Award
• Outstanding State Section Award
• Outstanding Student Chapter Award
• Richard A. Herbert Memorial Scholarship
Eligibility: AWRA member; full-time undergraduate student
Deadline: April *Amount:* $2,000
Publications:
• JAWRA [Journal of the American Water Resources Association]
Type: Journal

American Water Works Association (AWWA)
6666 West Quincy Ave., Denver CO 80235 USA
Tel: 303-794-7711; *Fax:* 303-347-0804
Toll-Free: 800-926-7337
service@awwa.org
www.awwa.org
www.linkedin.com/company/american-water-works-association
www.facebook.com/AmericanWaterWorksAssociation
twitter.com/AWWAACE
www.youtube.com/user/AmericanWaterWorks
Overview: A large international organization founded in 1881
Mission: To advance public health & safety through the improvement of water quality & supply throughout North America & beyond; To provide standards for the design, manufacturing, installation, & performance of water industry products; To advance & protect the interests of the water industry
Membership: 60,000+; *Fees:* Schedule available; *Member Profile:* Treatment plant operators & managers; Scientists; Environmentalists; Manufacturers; Academics; Regulators; Others interested in water supply & public health; *Committees:* Audit; Conference; Consumer Outreach; Diversity & Member Inclusion; Executive; Section Communication; Standard Methods; Young Professionals; & others
Activities: Providing information about the water industry; *Library:* American Water Works Association Water Library
Chief Officer(s):
David B. LaFrance, CEO
Paula I. MacIlwaine, Deputy CEO
Kevin Mann, Chief Financial Officer
Joe Thielen, Chief Information Officer
Susan Franceschi, Chief Membership Officer
Greg Kail, Director, Communications
April DeBaker, Director, Conferences & Events
Barb Martin, Director, Engineering & Technical Services
Steven Via, Director, Federal Relations
Ron McDonald, Director, Human Resources
Zsolt Silberer, Director, Publications
JoAnn Spinnato, Director, Sales
Awards:
• American Water Works Association Awards Program
35+ awards that honour outstanding service contributions & excellence in research & projects that further the objectives of the AWWA
Meetings/Conferences:
• American Water Works Association Annual Conference & Exposition 2018, June, 2018, Las Vegas, NV
Scope: International
Description: An international gathering of thousands of water professionals, featuring a technical program, workshops, seminars, & exhibits
• American Water Works Association Annual Conference & Exposition 2019, June, 2019, Denver, CO
Scope: International
Description: An international gathering of thousands of water professionals, featuring a technical program, workshops, seminars, & exhibits
• American Water Works Association Annual Conference & Exposition 2020, June, 2020, Orlando, FL
Scope: International
Description: An international gathering of thousands of water professionals, featuring a technical program, workshops, seminars, & exhibits
• American Water Works Association Annual Conference & Exposition 2021, June, 2021, San Diego, CA
Scope: International
Description: An international gathering of thousands of water professionals, featuring a technical program, workshops, seminars, & exhibits
• American Water Works Association Annual Conference & Exposition 2022, June, 2022, San Antonio, TX
Scope: International
Description: An international gathering of thousands of water professionals, featuring a technical program, workshops, seminars, & exhibits
Publications:
• American Water Works Association Officers & Committee Directory
Type: Directory
Profile: Director, trustee, officer, & staff management information, plus the AWWA strategic plan & statements of policy
• Journal AWWA [American Water Works Association]
Type: Journal; *Frequency:* Monthly; *Editor:* Kenneth Mercer; *ISSN:* 1551-8833; *Price:* Free with individual, utility, & service provider membership in AWWA
Profile: Peer-reviewed information about water quality, resources, & supply, in addition to professional & scholarly articles about themanagement & operation of water utilities
• Opflow [a publication of the American Water Works Association]
Type: Magazine; *Frequency:* Monthly; *Accepts Advertising*; *ISSN:* 1551-8701; *Price:* Free with individual, utility, & service provider membership in AWWA
Profile: Practical publication for water supply operators

American Wire Producers Association (AWPA)
#211, 801 North Fairfax St., Alexandria VA 22314-1757 USA
Tel: 703-299-4434; *Fax:* 703-299-9233
info@awpa.org
www.awpa.org
www.facebook.com/332838850061
Overview: A small international organization founded in 1981
Mission: Leading voice of the ferrous wire & wire products industry in North America
Staff Member(s): 5
Membership: 91; *Member Profile:* Wire producers in the United States, Canada & Mexico; *Committees:* PC Strand; Nail; Stainless; Membership

American Zoo & Aquarium Association *See* Association of Zoos & Aquariums

Amnesty International
International Secretariat, 1 Easton St., London WC1X 0DW United Kingdom
Tel: 44-20-7413-5500; *Fax:* 44-20-7956-1157
contactus@amnesty.org
www.amnesty.org
www.facebook.com/amnestyglobal
www.youtube.com/amnestyinternational
Overview: A large international organization
Mission: To play a role within the overall spectrum of human rights work; To focus on the promotion of the Universal Declaration of Human Rights; To seek the release of men &

women detained anywhere for their beliefs, colour, sex, ethnic origin, language, or religion; To advocate fair & early trials for all political prisoners & work on behalf of such persons detained without charge or without trial; To oppose the death penalty & torture or other cruel, inhuman, or degrading treatment, or punishment of all prisoners without reservation
Affiliation(s): Amnesty International, Canadian Section (English Speaking); Amnistie internationale, Section canadienne (Francophone)
Finances: *Annual Operating Budget:* Greater than $5 Million
Membership: *Committees:* International Executive
Activities: *Library:* Virutal Library; Open to public
Chief Officer(s):
Kumi Naidoo, Secretary General

Antarctic & Southern Ocean Coalition (ASOC)
1320 - 19th St., 5th Fl., Washington DC 20036 USA
Tel: 202-234-2480; *Fax:* 202-387-4823
www.asoc.org
www.facebook.com/antarcticsouthernocean
twitter.com/AntarcticaSouth
www.flickr.com/photos/asoc
Also Known As: Secretariat, The Antarctica Project
Overview: A medium-sized international organization founded in 1977
Mission: To protect the biological diversity & pristine wilderness of Antarctica, including its oceans & marine life; To work for the passage of strong measures which protect the marine ecosystem from the harmful effects of overfishing; To ensure that the integrity of the southern ocean whale sanctuary is maintained & internationally respected
Affiliation(s): World Wildlife Fund Canada; World Society for the Protection of Animals; Friends of the Earth; Greenpeace; Sierra Club
Finances: *Annual Operating Budget:* $250,000-$500,000; *Funding Sources:* Foundation grants; membership dues
Staff Member(s): 9; 2 volunteer(s)
Membership: 235
Activities: Conducting policy research & analysis; Testifying at Congress hearings; Producing educational materials; Working with key users of Antarctica, including scientists, tourists, & governments, to ensure that activities have a minimal environmental impact; Attending Atlantic Treaty Meetings & all CCAMLR meetings; *Library:* by appointment
Chief Officer(s):
Claire Christian, Acting Executive Director

The Antiochan Orthodox Christian Archdiocese of North America
Antiochian Orthodox Christian Archdiocese, PO Box 5238, Englewood NJ 07631-5238 USA
Tel: 201-871-1355; *Fax:* 201-871-7954
archdiocese@antiochian.org
www.antiochian.org
Overview: A small national organization founded in 1875
Mission: The Antiochan Orthodox Community in Canada is under the jurisdiction of the Patriarch of Antioch & all the East, with headquarters in Damascus, Syria. There are five churches in Canada & eight missions. The headquarters of all churches in North America is the Antiochan Orthodox Christian archdiocese, in Englewood, New Jersey, under Archbishop Philip Salica
Affiliation(s): Canadian (Can-Am) Region
Staff Member(s): 4; 6 volunteer(s)
Membership: 275 parishes, 19 in Canada
Chief Officer(s):
Joseph Al-Zehlaoui, Archbishop
Sandra Abdelmessih, Registrar
registrar@antiochian.org

Antique Automobile Club of America (AACA)
PO Box 417, 501 West Governor Rd., Hershey PA 17033 USA
Tel: 717-534-1910; *Fax:* 717-534-9101
aaca1@aaca.org
www.aaca.org
www.facebook.com/AntiqueAutomobileClubOfAmerica
Overview: A medium-sized international organization founded in 1935
Staff Member(s): 3
Membership: 62,000; *Fees:* $35
Activities: *Library*
Chief Officer(s):
Steven L. Moskowitz, Executive Director
aaca1@aaca.org
Meetings/Conferences:
• Antique Automobile Club of America 82nd Annual Meeting 2018, February, 2018, Philadelphia, PA
Scope: International
• Antique Automobile Club of America 2018 Annual Grand National Meet, May, 2018, Greensburg, PA
Scope: International
Publications:
• Antique Automobile [a publication of the Antique Automobile Club of America]
Type: Magazine; *Frequency:* Bimonthly; *Accepts Advertising*
Profile: Information for members of the Antique Automobile Club of America
• Rummage Box [a publication of the Automobile Club of America]
Type: Newsletter; *Frequency:* q.
• Speedster [a publication of the Antique Automobile Club of America]
Type: Newsletter; *Frequency:* m.
Profile: Contains club news, member contributions & stories, & trivia
• Wheels [a publication of the Antique Automobile Club of America]
Type: Newsletter; *Frequency:* q.
Profile: Information for junior members of the AACA (children under 13 years of age)
Lord Selkirk Region
305 Carpathia Rd., Winnipeg MB R3N 1T2
Mission: To futher the interest in and preserving of antique automobiles, and the promotion of sportsmanship and of good fellowship amoung all AACA members.
Chief Officer(s):
James Drummond, President
Ontario Region
c/o Ian Cowie, 1636 Northey's Bay Rd., Woodview ON K0L 3E0
www.aacaontario.ca
Mission: To further the interest in and preserving of antique automobiles and the promotion of sportsmanship and good fellowship among all AACA members.
Member of: Antique Automobile Club of America
Chief Officer(s):
Andrew Sommers, President
andrewsommers@sympatico.ca

Archaeological Institute of America (AIA) / Institut Archéologique d'Amérique
Boston University, 656 Beacon St., 6th Fl, Boston MA 02215-2006 USA
Tel: 617-353-9361
aia@aia.bu.edu
www.archaeological.org
www.facebook.com/Archaeological.Institute
twitter.com/archaeology_aia
www.youtube.com/archaeologytv
Overview: A large international charitable organization founded in 1879
Mission: To encourage & support archaeological research & publication; To encourage protection of world's cultural heritage
Member of: American Council of Learned Societies
Affiliation(s): Fédération internationale des associations d'études classiques
Finances: *Annual Operating Budget:* Greater than $5 Million; *Funding Sources:* Membership dues; donations; subscription income
Staff Member(s): 25
Membership: 9,000; *Fees:* Schedule available; *Committees:* AIA Tours; American Committee on the Corpus Vasorum Antiquorum; Archaeology in Higher Education; Archives; Audit; Conservation & Site Preservation; Corresponding Members; Development; Digital Technology; Education; Executive; Fellowship; Gold Medal; Governance; Lecture Program; Museums and Exhibitions; Nominating; Personnel; Professional Responsibilities; Publication Subvention; Societies
Activities: Providing lectures; Disseminating publications; *Speaker Service:* Yes; *Rents Mailing List:* Yes
Chief Officer(s):
Ann Benbow, Executive Director, 617-353-9362
abenbow@aia.bu.edu
Ben Thomas, Director, Programs, 617-353-8708
bthomas@aia.bu.edu
Laurel Nilsen Sparks, Coordinator, Lecture & Fellowship, 617-358-4184
lsparks@aia.bu.edu
Awards:
• Gold Medal Award for Distinguished Archaeological Achievement
• Pomerance Award for Scientific Contributions to Archaeology
• Martha and Artemis Joukowsky Distinguished Service Award
• James R. Wiseman Book Award
• Felicia A. Holton Book Award
• Excellence in Undergraduate Teaching Award
• Conservation & Heritage Management Award
• Best Practices in Site Preservation Award
• Oustanding Public Service Award
• Outstanding Work in Digital Archaeology Award
• Graduate Student Paper Award
• Poster Awards
• Jane C. Waldbaum Archaeological Field School Scholarship
• Cotsen Excavation Grants
• Site Preservation Grant
• Society Outreach Grant Program
Publications:
• American Journal of Archaeology [a publication of the Archaeological Institute of America]
Type: Journal; *Frequency:* Quarterly; *Editor:* Jane Carter; *ISSN:* 0002-9114; *Price:* $295 institutional (print); $80 individual (print); $50 student(print)
Profile: A peer-reviewed archaeological journal
• Archaeological Institute of America Annual Report
Type: Report; *Frequency:* Annually
• Archaeology [a publication of the Archaeological Institute of America]
Type: Magazine; *Frequency:* Bi-monthly; *Editor:* Claudia Vlentino

ARMA International
#450, 11880 College Blvd., Overland Park KS 66215 USA
Tel: 913-341-3808; *Fax:* 913-341-3742
Toll-Free: 800-422-2762
headquarters@armaintl.org
www.arma.org
www.linkedin.com/company/arma-international
www.facebook.com/12941583847
twitter.com/ARMA_INT
Overview: A large international organization
Staff Member(s): 30
Membership: 5,000-14,999
Chief Officer(s):
Bob Baird, Chief Executive Officer
bob.baird@armaintl.org
Peter Kurilecz, President, 214-368-3908
peterkurilecz.arma@gmail.com
Awards:
• Distinguished Service Award
• Chapter of the Year Award
• Chapter Member of the Year Award
• Chapter Newsletter of the Year Award
• Chapter Website of the Year Award
• Special Project Award
• Christine Zanotti Award for Excellence in Non-Serial Publications
• Chapter Innovation Award
• Chapter Leader of the Year
• Chapter Merit Award
• Chapter Participation Award
• Membership Recruitment Award
• Company of Fellows Award
• Region Website of the Year Award
• The Cobalt Award
Meetings/Conferences:
• ARMA Canada Conference 2018, May, 2018, Hyatt Regency, Vancouver, BC
Contact Information: E-mail: conference@armaintl.org
• ARMA Live! Annual Conference & Expo 2018, October, 2018, Anaheim, CA
Contact Information: E-mail: conference@armaintl.org
Publications:
• ARMA International Buyers Guide
Profile: A directory of vendors & companies that provide products & services that benefit information management professionals
• ARMA International Whitepapers
Type: Report
Profile: A series of valuable information for members of the information management sector
• Glossary of Records & Information Management Terms [a publication of ARMA International]
Type: Book; *Price:* $50 with ARMAInternational membership; $70 without membership
Profile: A directory of vendors & companies that provide products & services that benefit information management professionals

Foreign Associations / Art Libraries Society of North America (ARLIS/NA)

- InfoPro [a publication of ARMA International]
Type: Newsletter; Frequency: Monthly
- Information Management [a publication of ARMA International]
Type: Magazine; Editor: Vicki Wiler; ISSN: 2155-3505

Art Libraries Society of North America (ARLIS/NA)
7044 South 13th St., Oak Creek WI 53154 USA
Tel: 414-908-4954
Toll-Free: 800-817-0621
www.arlisna.org
www.linkedin.com/groups/ARLIS-NA-2590950
www.facebook.com/ARLISNA
twitter.com/ARLIS_NA
Overview: A medium-sized international organization founded in 1972
Mission: To promote & support art librarianship & image management.
Affiliation(s): American Library Association; Arbeitsgemeinschaft der Kunst und Museumsbibliotheken; ARLIS/Australia & New Zealand; ARLIS/Netherlands; ARLIS/Norden; ARLIS/United Kingdom & Ireland; Association of Architecture School Librarians; College Art Association; International Federation of Library Associations and Institutions; Japan Art Documentation Society, Tokyo; Museum Computer Network; Society of American Archivists; Society of Architectural Historians; Sous-section des Bibliothèques d'art, Association des bibliothécaires français; Visual Resources Association
Membership: Fees: US$50 students/unemployed; US$75 retired; US$100 introductory; US$150 individuals; Member Profile: Art information professionals; Committees: Awards; Cataloging Advisory; Development; Diversity; Documentation; Finance; International Relations; Membership; Nominating; Professional Development; Public Policy; Strategic Planning
Activities: Networking; Publishing; Communicating; Presenting scholarships & awards
Chief Officer(s):
Robert J. Kopchinski, Executive Director
r.kopchinski@arlisna.org
Heather Gendron, President
heather.gendron@yale.edu
Jennifer Garland, Canadian Liaison
jennifer.garland@mcgill.ca
Meetings/Conferences:
- Art Libraries Society of North America 46th Annual Conference 2018, February, 2018, New York Hilton Midtown, New York, NY
Description: The conference provides the opportunity for professionals involved in art librarianship to meet, learn and share their knowledge of the field. It also allows them to explore exhibitions & interact with vendors involved with art libraries.
- Art Libraries Society of North America 47th Annual Conference 2019, 2019, Salt Lake City, UT
Description: The conference provides the opportunity for professionals involved in art librarianship to meet, learn and share their knowledge of the field. It also allows them to explore exhibitions & interact with vendors involved with art libraries.
- Art Libraries Society of North America 48th Annual Conference 2020, 2020, Saint Louis, MO
Description: The conference provides the opportunity for professionals involved in art librarianship to meet, learn and share their knowledge of the field. It also allows them to explore exhibitions & interact with vendors involved with art libraries.
Publications:
- Art Documentation [a publication of the Art Libraries Society of North America]
Type: Journal; Frequency: 2 pa; Price: Included with membership
Profile: The official journal of the Art Libraries Society of North America. It features articles that pertain to art librarianship & visualresources curatorship.

Montréal, Ottawa & Québec Chapter (ARLIS/NA MOQ)
c/o Jessica Hébert, ARTEXTE, Montréal, #301, 2 rue Sainte-Catherine est, Montréal QC H2X 2S6
e-mail: arlismoq@gmail.com
www.arlismoq.ca
www.linkedin.com/groups/6508102/profile
www.facebook.com/ARLIS.MOQ.Chapter
Chief Officer(s):
Jessica Hébert, President

Northwest Chapter (ARLIS/NA NW)
c/o Paula Farrar, University of British Columbia, #414, 1961 East Mall, Vancouver BC V6T 1Z1
Tel: 604-822-4474
nw.arlisna@gmail.com
nw.arlisna.org
www.facebook.com/175582815809442
twitter.com/ARLISNA_NW
Chief Officer(s):
Bronwyn Dorhofer, Chair
bronwyn.dorhofer@gmail.com

Ontario Chapter (ARLIS/NA ON)
c/o Effie Patelos, 7 Melville St. South, Cambridge ON N1S 2H4
e-mail: arlisna.ontario@gmail.com
arlison.org
www.linkedin.com/groups/ARLIS-NA-Ontario-Chapter-4846604
www.facebook.com/ARLISNA.Ontario
twitter.com/ARLIS_ON
Chief Officer(s):
Effie Patelos, Chair

Asia-Pacific Centre for Environmental Law (APCEL)
Faculty of Law, Ntl. University of Singapore, Eu Tong Sen Bldg., 469G Bukit Timah Rd., Singapore 259776 Singapore
Tel: 65-6516-6246; Fax: 65-6872-1937
lawapcel@nus.edu.sg
law.nus.edu.sg/apcel/
Overview: A small international organization founded in 1996
Chief Officer(s):
Lye Lin Heng, Director
lawlyelh@nus.edu.sg
Shirley Mak, Secretary
lawmaksy@nus.edu.sg

ASM International
9639 Kinsman Rd., Materials Park OH 44073-0002 USA
Tel: 440-338-5151; Fax: 440-338-4634
Toll-Free: 800-336-5152
memberservicecenter@asminternational.org
www.asminternational.org
www.linkedin.com/company/asm-international
www.facebook.com/asminternational
twitter.com/asminternationa
Also Known As: American Society for Metals
Overview: A medium-sized international organization founded in 1913
Mission: To gather, process & disseminate technical information; to foster understanding & application of engineered materials; to provide career support & education for business & information systems professionals
Finances: Annual Operating Budget: $500,000-$1.5 Million
Staff Member(s): 100
Membership: 36,000 worldwide; Fees: US$113; US$15 Student; Member Profile: Business or systems professional
Activities: Rents Mailing List: Yes
Chief Officer(s):
Jon D. Tirpak, President
Meetings/Conferences:
- ASM International 29th AeroMat Conference & Exposition 2018, May, 2018, Gaylord Palms Resort & Convention Center, Orlando, FL
Scope: International
- ASM International Thermal Spray Conference & Exposition, May, 2018, Gaylord Palms Resort & Convention Center, Orlando, FL
Scope: International
- ASM International Conference on Shape Memory & Superelastic Technologies, May, 2018, Clayton Hotel Galway, Galway
Scope: International
- ASM International Thermal Processing In Motion, June, 2018, Spartanburg Marriott, Spartanburg, SC
Scope: International
- ASM International Advanced Thermal Processing Technology Conference & Expo, September, 2018, Fiesta Americana, Querétaro
Scope: International
- ASM International Symposium for Testing & Failure Analysis, October, 2018, Phoenix, AZ
Scope: International
Publications:
- Advanced Materials & Processes (AM&P) [a publication of ASM International]
Type: Magazine; Frequency: q.; Accepts Advertising; ISSN: 2161-9425; Price: Free with ASM International membership
- Advanced Materials & Processes (AM&P) Buyers Guide [a publication of ASM International]
- Electronic Device Failure Analysis (EDFA) [a publication of ASM International]
Type: Magazine; Editor: Felix Beaudoin
Profile: A resource for Failure Analysis Engineers
- HTPro [a publication of ISM International]
Type: Newsletter; Frequency: q.
Profile: A resource for members of the heat treating community
- International Thermal Spray & Surface Engineering (iTSSe) [a publication of ISM International]
Type: Newsletter; Frequency: q.; Editor: Julie Lucko
Profile: The official newsletter of the ASM Thermal Spray Society

Asociación mexicana de estudios sobre Canadá (AMEC) / Mexican Association of Canadian Studies (MACS)
Av. Tepeyac 4800, col. Prados Tepeyac, Zapopan JA 4800 Mexico
Tel: 52 (33) 3134-0800
www.facebook.com/CANADA.AMEC
twitter.com/amec_canada
Overview: A small international organization founded in 1992
Mission: To foster the study & interest on Canada in Mexico through the promotion of several academic, cultural & scientific activities to increase the knowledge & awareness of that country
Member of: International Council for Canadian Studies
Membership: 233

Asociación Nacional de Ejecutivos de Organismos Empresariales y Profesionales, A.C.
Manuel Maria Contreras 133, Piso 5, Despacho 501, Cuauhtémoc, Mexico Mexico
Tel: 0155-5566-9587
angecai.org.mx/web
www.facebook.com/angecaimx
twitter.com/ANGECAI
Also Known As: ANGECAI
Overview: A medium-sized national organization
Chief Officer(s):
Lucy Chavez, Coordinación General
lucy@angecai.org.mx

Asociación Nacional de la Industria Química, A.C See National Association of the Chemistry Industry

Assemblée mondiale de la jeunesse See World Assembly of Youth

Associaçao Brasileira de Estudos Canadense (ABECAN) / Brazilian Association for Canadian Studies
Centro Universitário la Salle, 2288 Victor Barreto Ave., Canoas RS 92010-000 Brazil
Tel: 55-51-3476-8411
abecan@abecan.org.br
www.abecan.org.br
www.facebook.com/abecan
Overview: A small international charitable organization founded in 1991
Mission: To promote the gathering of researchers interested in culture, science and technology in Canada, and their relation to those of Brazil; to contribute to the excellence and disclosure of Canadian Studies; to serve as a source of intelligence among Brazilian communities interested in studying Canadian topics
Member of: International Council for Canadian Studies
Membership: 198; Fees: $40 students; $75 professors, researchers & institutions
Activities: Organizing conferences, seminars, meetings, conferences, studies and research; promote publications; establish agreements and trade cooperation in the fields of competence; support activities related to the Brazilian stock market analysis while studying in Canada; Internships: Yes; Speaker Service: Yes
Chief Officer(s):
Monique Vandressen, President

Associated Country Women of the World
Mary Sumner House, 24 Tufton St., London SW1P 3RB United Kingdom
Tel: 44-20-7799-3875; Fax: 44-20-7340-9950
www.acww.org.uk
www.facebook.com/133340763410423
twitter.com/acww_news
www.youtube.com/user/ACWWnews
Overview: A large international organization
Mission: To raise the standards of living & education of women & their families all over the world through community development projects & training; To promote international goodwill, friendship & understanding between women everywhere; To work for equal opportunites for women by the

elimination of discrimination because of gender, race, nationality, religion or marital status; To act as a forum on international affairs for rural women, speaking for them with an informed voice in the Councils of the world
Membership: Fees: £20 annual; £50 three-year; *Committees:* Promotion & Publications; United Nations; Projects
Activities: Funding more than 900 projects around the world, including the Water for All Fund, the Women Feed the World Fund, & the Projects Fund
Chief Officer(s):
Ruth Shanks, AM, World President
Tish Collins, Manager, Operations

Association Africane de Literature *See* African Literature Association

Association britanniques d'études canadiennes *See* British Association for Canadian Studies

Association Canado-Américaine (ACA)
55 South Commercial St., Manchester NH 03101 USA
Tél: 603-624-1351; *Téléc:* 603-625-1214
Ligne sans frais: 855-712-7482
info@aca-assurance.org
www.aca-assurance.com
Également appelé: ACA Assurance
Aperçu: Dimension: moyenne; *Envergure:* internationale; Organisme sans but lucratif; fondée en 1896
Mission: Union des personnes d'ascendance ou d'affinité française et catholique en Amérique, leur avancement spirituel, civique, culturel, social et économique et la préservation de la langue et la culture française
Membre de: National Fraternal Congress of America
Membre: Critères d'admissibilite: Franco américain et canadien
Activités: Fraternelles: voyages; sorties; cabane à sucre; *Service de conférenciers:* Oui; *Bibliothèque:* ACA Assurance

Association d'études canadiennes dans les pays de langue allemande *See* Association for Canadian Studies in German-Speaking Countries

Association d'Études Canadiennes en Europe Centrale *See* Central European Association for Canadian Studies

Association d'études canadiennes en Israel *See* Israel Association for Canadian Studies

Association de l'endométriose inc. *See* Endometriosis Association, Inc.

Association des études canadiennes aux Pays-Bas *See* Association for Canadian Studies in the Netherlands

Association des galvanoplastes d'Amérique *See* National Association for Surface Finishing

Association des joueurs de la Ligue majeure de baseball (ind.) *See* Major League Baseball Players' Association (Ind.)

Association for Asian Studies - USA (AAS)
#310, 825 Victors Way, Ann Arbor MI 48108 USA
Tel: 734-665-2490; *Fax:* 734-665-3801
mpaschal@asian-studies.org
www.asian-studies.org
www.facebook.com/104663456241055
Previous Name: Far Eastern Association Inc.
Overview: A small international organization founded in 1941
Member of: American Council of Learned Societies
Finances: Annual Operating Budget: $500,000-$1.5 Million; *Funding Sources:* Membership fees; endowment
Staff Member(s): 10
Membership: 8,500; *Fees:* Schedule available; *Member Profile:* Interest in Asian studies
Chief Officer(s):
Thongchai Winichakul, President
twinicha@wisc.edu
Mrinalini Sinha, Vice-President
sinha@umich.edu
Publications:
• Journal of Asian Studies
 Author: Jeffrey Wasserstrom
Profile: Quarterly academic journal

Association for Canadian Studies in Argentina
Universidad Nacional del Comahue, PO Box 8300, Avenida Argentina 1400, Neuquen, Provincia del Neuquen 4.924175 Argentina
Tel: 0299-4490-305
info@asaec.com
Also Known As: Asociación Argentina de Estudios Canadienses
Overview: A small international organization founded in 1997
Chief Officer(s):
Alicia Garro, Secretariat
asaec@fibertel.com.ar

Association for Canadian Studies in Australia & New Zealand (ACSANZ)
University of Wollongong, PO Box U163, Wollongong, New South Wales 2500 Australia
e-mail: info@acsanz.org.au
www.acsanz.org.au
www.facebook.com/189197111101161
Overview: A small international organization founded in 1982
Mission: To encourage Canadian studies within Australia & New Zealand
Member of: International Council for Canadian Studies
Membership: 200+; *Fees:* AUD$85 individual; AUD$50 student
Chief Officer(s):
Robyn Morris, President
robynm@uow.edu.au
Debra Dudek, Acting Treasurer
debrad@uow.edu.au

Association for Canadian Studies in China (ACSC)
c/o School of History & Culture, Shandong University, 27 Shanda Rd. South, Jinan, Shandong Province 250100 China
Tel: 86-531-8836-4661; *Fax:* 86-531-8836-51697
Overview: A small international charitable organization founded in 1984
Mission: To promote a better understanding of Canada; to offer recommendations on Canadian affairs & policies to the Chinese government; to foster improved business relations between Canada & China.
Finances: Funding Sources: Business donations; government
Activities: Speaker Service: Yes; *Library:* Canadian Studies Library; Open to public

Association for Canadian Studies in German-Speaking Countries (GKS) / Association d'études canadiennes dans les pays de langue allemande
c/o Universität Trier, Fachbereich III - Geschichte, Trier 54286 Germany
Tel: 49-0-651-201-2178
gks@kanada-studien.de
www.kanada-studien.org
Overview: A small international organization founded in 1980
Mission: To promote scholarship in Canadian studies to strengthen the cultural relations & understanding between Canada & German-speaking countries.
Member of: International Council for Canadian Studies
Finances: Funding Sources: Membership fees; donations; grants
Membership: 538; *Fees:* 25 Euros student/unemployed; 70 Euros regular
Activities: Speaker Service: Yes
Chief Officer(s):
Ursula Lehmkuhl, President
lehmkuhl@uni-trier.de
Caroline Rosenthal, Vice-President
caroline.rosenthal@uni-jena.de
Bernhard Metz, Treasurer
bernhard.metz@t-online.de
Awards:
• GKS Awards (3)

Association for Canadian Studies in Ireland (ACSI) / Association irlandaise d'étude canadiennes
c/o School of Languages and Literatures, University College Dublin, Belfield, Dublin 4 Ireland
www.canadianstudiesireland.com
Also Known As: An Cumann Le Léann Ceanadach in Éirinn
Overview: A small international organization founded in 1982
Mission: To promote the knowledge of Canada in Ireland & encourage the creation of new universities & the pursuit of research
Member of: International Council for Canadian Studies
Membership: Member Profile: Academics with an interest in Canada
Activities: Speaker Service: Yes
Chief Officer(s):
Michael Brophy, President
michael.brophy@ucd.ie

Association for Canadian Studies in the Netherlands (ACSN) / Association des études canadiennes aux Pays-Bas
Bosweg 12, Nijmegen 6523 NM Netherlands
Tel: 31-243234525
acsn@upcmail.nl
www.acsn.nl
Overview: A small international charitable organization founded in 1985
Mission: The promotion of teaching & research about Canada in the humanities & social sciences at post-secondary level
Member of: International Council for Canadian Studies; European Network for Canadian Studies
Finances: Annual Operating Budget: Less than $50,000
5 volunteer(s)
Membership: 140; *Fees:* 27 Euro; 13.50 Euro students; 100 Euro companies/associations; *Member Profile:* Academic
Activities: Conferences, seminars, lecture tours, publicizing; *Speaker Service:* Yes; *Library:* Not open to public
Chief Officer(s):
Conny J. Steenman-Marcusse, President
Amanda Helderman, Secretary
acsn@amandahelderman.com

Association for Canadian Studies in the United States (ACSUS)
#350, 2030 - M St. NW, Washington DC 20036 USA
Tel: 202-223-9007; *Fax:* 202-775-0061
info@acsus.org
www.acsus.org
www.linkedin.com/groups/ACSUS-6725757/about
twitter.com/ACSUS
Overview: A medium-sized international charitable organization founded in 1971
Mission: To raise awareness & understanding of Canada
Membership: Fees: Schedule available based on income; *Member Profile:* Scholars, professionals, & institutions dedicated to improving understanding of Canada in the United States; *Committees:* Membership; Development; Rufus Z. Smith Prize; Nominations & Elections; Graduate Student; Distinguished Dissertation Award; Jeanne Kissner Award; Affiliates; Status of Women & Diversity; Outreach
Activities: Supporting the teaching of Canadian studies; Promoting research; Engaging in advocacy activities
Chief Officer(s):
David Archibald, Executive Director
Doug Nord, President
Michael Broadway, Vice-President
Nadine Fabbi, Secretary-Treasurer
Awards:
• ACSUS Distinguished Dissertation Award
Awarded biennially to honour outstanding doctoral research on Canada at United States institutions
• Jeanne Kissner Undergraduate Essay Award
• The Thomas O. Enders Endowment
To encourage advanced scholarship on Canada & Canadian - United States relations on divese bilateral issues
• The Rufus Z. Smith Prize
Awarded for the best article in The American Review of Canadian Studies during the two years prior to the biennial conference at which it is awarded
• The Donner Medal in Canadian Studies
Awarded biennially for distinguished achievement, scholarship, & program innovation in the area of Canadian studies in the United States
Meetings/Conferences:
• Association for Canadian Studies in the United States 25th Biennial Conference, 2019
Scope: International
Description: Speakers & panels presenting research & information about Canada across all disciplines
Publications:
• American Review of Canadian Studies
Type: Journal; *Frequency:* Quarterly; *Editor:* Dr. John L. Purdy & Kathy Reigstad; *ISSN:* 0272-2011
Profile: A refereed, multidisciplinary journal, featuring Canada's art, culture, history, economics & politics from an American perspective
• Think Canada!
Type: Newsletter; *Frequency:* Semiannually
Profile: Covering developments in Canada - United States academic relations, as well as the associated institutions & personalities

Association for Childhood Education International (ACEI)
#300, 1101 - 16 St. NW, Washington DC 20036 USA
Tel: 202-372-9986; *Fax:* 202-372-9989
Toll-Free: 800-423-3563
headquarters@acei.org
www.acei.org
www.facebook.com/ACEIpage
twitter.com/ACEI_info
Previous Name: International Kindergarten Union
Overview: A medium-sized international organization founded in 1892
Mission: To promote & support the optimal education & development of chidren, from infancy through middle childhood, in the global community; to influence the professional growth of educators, & the efforts of others who are committed to the needs of children in a changing society
Member of: Alliance for Curriculum Reform; National Council for Accreditation of Teacher Education (NCATE); United Nations; National Committee on the Rights of the Child
Finances: *Funding Sources:* Membership dues; sales of publications; conferences
Membership: *Fees:* Schedule available; *Member Profile:* Educators & persons interested in children's education, rights & well-being; *Committees:* Nominations; Finance; Awards; Program; Special Advisory
Activities: *Speaker Service:* Yes
Chief Officer(s):
Diane Whitehead, Executive Director
Carrie Whaley, President
cwhaley@uu.edu
Awards:
• Outstanding Member Service Award
• Elizabeth Breathwaite Mini-Grants
Implementation of outstanding educational experiences for children
• Elizabeth Breathwaite Student Leadership Award
Available to college students who are ACEI members
• ACEI Friends of Children Award
• Nancy Bartlett Hitch Student Scholarship Award
• Patty Smith Hill Award
• Roll of Honor
• Best Professional Development Workshop / Conference Award
• Best Use of ACEI Materials Award
• Branch Excellence Award
• Best Publicity Award
• Best Communications Award
• Best Global Focus Award
• Best Mentor Program
• Best Fundraiser Award
• Best New Branch Award
• Best Children's Event / Community Service
• Outstanding Branch Member Service Award
• Branch Development Grant
• Local Conference Grant
• International Development Fund Grant
• Presidents' Council Awards / Grants
Publications:
• ACEI Exchange
Type: Newsletter; *Frequency:* 5 pa
• Childhood Education
Type: Journal; *Frequency:* Bimonthly
• Focus on Elementary
 Frequency: Quarterly; *Price:* US$15 members
 Profile: Ages 7 to 10
• Focus on Inclusive Education
 Frequency: Quarterly; *Price:* US$15 members
 Profile: For teachers of children with special needs
• Focus on Infants & Toddlers
 Frequency: Quarterly; *Price:* US$15 members
 Profile: Ages birth to 3
• Focus on Middle School
 Frequency: Quarterly; *Price:* US$15 members
 Profile: Ages 11 to 13
• Focus on Pre-K & K
 Frequency: Quarterly; *Price:* US$15 members
 Profile: Ages 4 to 6
• Focus on Teacher Education
 Frequency: Quarterly; *Price:* US$15 members
 Profile: For teacher educators
• Journal of Research in Childhood Education
Type: Journal; *Frequency:* Quarterly; *Price:* US$79 members
• Retirees' Review
• Student Connection

Association for Computer Operations Management See AFCOM

Association for Computing Machinery (ACM)
PO Box 30777, Stn. General Post Office, #701, 2 Penn Plaza, New York NY 10121-0701 USA
Tel: 212-869-7440; *Fax:* 212-944-1318
Toll-Free: 800-342-6626
acmhelp@acm.org
www.acm.org
www.linkedin.com/company/785681
www.facebook.com/AssociationForComputingMachinery
twitter.com/theofficialacm
www.instagram.com/theofficialacm
Overview: A medium-sized international organization
Mission: To advance computing as a science & profession
Membership: *Member Profile:* Professionals; Libraries; Institutions; Students
Activities: Providing career resources, including access to online books; Publishing over 40 publications; Presenting over 100 special interest group conferences
Chief Officer(s):
Vicki L. Hanson, President
Publications:
• Communications of the ACM [Association for Computing Machinery]
Type: Magazine; *Frequency:* Monthly

Association for Facilities Engineering (AFE)
#400, 8200 Greensboro Dr., McLean VA 22102 USA
Tel: 571-395-8777; *Fax:* 571-766-2142
info@afe.org
www.afe.org
www.linkedin.com/company/association-for-facilities-engineering
www.facebook.com/AFEsocial
twitter.com/FacilitiesEng
Previous Name: American Institute of Plant Engineers
Overview: A large international organization founded in 1954
Mission: To further professional interests of plant engineers; To aid in the development of this branch of engineering in the West; To cooperate with like-minded organizations around the world
Staff Member(s): 4
Membership: 10,000; *Fees:* Schedule available; *Member Profile:* People employed in plant or facility engineering, managing, operation, education with engineering OREQ degree & 4 years supervisory experience
Activities: *Rents Mailing List:* Yes
Chief Officer(s):
Gabriella C. Rodriguez, Manager, Operations
grodriguez@afe.org
Charles C. Clunk, Manager, Professional Development
cclunk@afe.org
Bridgett Owen, Manager, Membership
bridgett.owen@afe.org
Publications:
• Facilities Engineering Journal [a publication of Association for Facilities Engineering]
Type: Journal
• Weekly Headlines [a publication of Association for Facilities Engineering]
Type: Journal; *Frequency:* Weekly

Association for Financial Professionals (AFP)
#800, 4520 East West Hwy., Bethesda MD 20814 USA
Tel: 301-907-2862; *Fax:* 301-907-2864
afp@afponline.org
www.afponline.org
www.linkedin.com/groups/Association-Financial-Professionals-AFP-81522
www.facebook.com/afpsocial
twitter.com/afponline
www.youtube.com/afponline; www.instagram.com/afp_online
Overview: A large international licensing organization
Mission: To operate as a global resource & advocate for financial professionals; To raise the stature & visibility of members, by offering them products & services
Membership: *Fees:* $495; *Member Profile:* Executives in the financial services industry
Activities: Providing professional development activities & networking opportunities; annual conference; newsletters; research & economic data; administering the Certified Treasury Professional & Certified Corporate FP&A Professional credentials
Chief Officer(s):
Jeff Johnson, CTP, CPA, Chair
Meetings/Conferences:
• Association for Financial Professionals 2018 Annual Conference, November, 2018, Chicago, IL
Scope: National
Publications:
• AFP [Association for Financial Professionals] Payments
Type: Newsletter; *Frequency:* Monthly
• AFP [Association for Financial Professionals] EconWatch
Type: Newsletter; *Frequency:* Weekly
• AFP [Association for Financial Professionals] Exchange
Type: Magazine
• FP&A Newsletter [a publication of the Association for Financial Professionals]
Type: Newsletter; *Frequency:* Monthly
• Futures in Finance [a publication of the Association for Financial Professionals]
Type: Newsletter; *Frequency:* Monthly
• Risk! [a publication of the Association for Financial Professionals]
Type: Newsletter; *Frequency:* Monthly

Association for Healthcare Philanthropy (AHP)
#400, 313 Park Ave., Falls Church VA 22046 USA
Tel: 703-532-6243; *Fax:* 703-532-7170
ahp@ahp.org
www.ahp.org
www.linkedin.com/groups/Association-Healthcare-Philanthropy-1142757
www.facebook.com/AHPIntl
twitter.com/AHPIntl
Overview: A small international organization founded in 1967
Mission: Educational organization and advocacy body for health care fundraising professionals in Canada & the United States.
Member of: Association for Healthcare Philanthropy
Staff Member(s): 13
Membership: 5,000
Activities: Education & accreditation opportunities for members through conferences & roundtables
Chief Officer(s):
David L. Flood, Chair
Steven W. Churchill, President & CEO
Awards:
• Culture of Philanthropy Award
• Best Practices Award
• Mentoring Award
• Leadership Award
• AHP Canada Regional Conference Bursaries
Amount: $1,200 (2)
Meetings/Conferences:
• 2018 Association for Healthcare Philanthropy Convene Canada, May, 2018, Ottawa, ON
Scope: National

Association for Jewish Studies - USA (AJS)
15 West 16th St., New York NY 10011-6301 USA
Tel: 917-606-8249; *Fax:* 917-606-8222
ajs@ajs.cjh.org
www.ajsnet.org
www.facebook.com/119828850063
twitter.com/jewish_studies
Overview: A medium-sized national organization founded in 1969
Mission: Promote, maintain, & improve teaching, research, & related endeavors in Jewish Studies in colleges, universities & other institutions of higher learning
Member of: American Council of Learned Societies
Staff Member(s): 3
Membership: 1,800; *Fees:* Schedule available; *Member Profile:* Individuals whose full-time vocation is devoted to either teaching or research in academic Jewish studies or related endeavors in academic Jewish studies
Chief Officer(s):
Rona Sheramy, Executive Director

Association for Preservation Technology International (APT)
#200, 3085 Stevenson Dr., Springfield IL USA
Tel: 217-529-9039; *Fax:* 888-723-4242
Other Communication: admin@apti.org
info@apti.org
www.apti.org
Overview: A medium-sized international organization founded in 1968
Mission: To promote technology to conserve & maintain historic structures & their sites for future appreciation & use

Membership: *Member Profile:* Conservators; Preservationists; Curators; Historians; Architects; Architects; Engineers; Technicians; *Committees:* Executive; Chapters; Conference; Finance; Membership; Nominating; Outreach; Partnerships; Publications; Student Scholarships; Training & Education; Codes for Historic Resources; Modern Heritage; Preservation Engineering; Sustainable Preservation
Activities: Facilitating the exchange of ideas; Providing training for members
Chief Officer(s):
Anne T. Sullivan, President
Kyle Normandin, Secretary-Treasurer
Nathela Chatara, Administrative Director
Meetings/Conferences:
• Association for Preservation Technology International 2018 Annual Conference, September, 2018, Buffalo, NY
Scope: International
Attendance: 1,000
Description: Training & networking opportunities plus exhibits of interest to an international audience of persons involved in the application of methods & materials to conserve historic structures
Publications:
• APT Bulletin: The Journal of Preservation Technology
Type: Journal; *Frequency:* 3 pa; *Editor:* Diana S. Waite
Profile: Peer-reviewed articles about preservation techniques, including case studies, international debates, & reviews of preservation-related books
• Communiqué [a publication of the Association for Preservation Technology International]
Type: Newsletter; *Frequency:* Quarterly; *Accepts Advertising*; *Editor:* Erin Braselll; *Price:* Free with membership in the Association for Preservation Technology International
Profile: Member news, including preservation experience, resources, chapter information, grants, awards, conference reviews, &forthcoming events
• Preservation Technology Primer
Type: Guide; *Price:* $45 members; $50 non-members
Profile: Articles about preservation practice that have been published in the APT Bulletin

Association for Slavic, East European, & Eurasian Studies (ASEEES)
University of Pittsburgh, #203C Bellefield Hall, Pittsburgh PA 15260-6424 USA
Tel: 412-648-9911; *Fax:* 412-648-9815
aseees@pitt.edu
aseees.org
www.facebook.com/slavic.e.european.eurasian.studies
twitter.com/aseeestudies
Previous Name: American Association for the Advancement of Slavic Studies (AAASS)
Overview: A medium-sized international organization founded in 1948 overseen by American Council of Learned Societies
Mission: To advance knowledge about Russia, Central Eurasia & Eastern/Central Europe
Affiliation(s): Central Slavic Conference; Mid-Atlantic Conference; Midwest Slavic Conference; New England Slavic Association; Rocky Mountain Western Slavic Studies Association; Southern Conference on Slavic Studies; Southwest Slavic Association; Western Slavic Association
Membership: 3,500 individual & 40 institutions; *Fees:* Schedule available
Chief Officer(s):
Lynda Park, Executive Director
lypark@pitt.edu
Padraic Kenney, President
pjkenney@indiana.edu
Awards:
• AAASS Distinguished Contributions Award
Contact: Andrew Wachtel, Chair, Contributions Award, E-mail: awachtel59@gmail.com
• CLIR Distinguished Service Award
• Wayne S. Vucinich Book Prize
• USC Book Prize in Literary and Cultural Studies
• Reginald Zelnik Book Prize in History
• Davis Center Book Prize in Political and Social Studies
• Marshall D. Shulman Book Prize
• Ed A Hewett Book Prize
• Barbara Jelavich Book Prize
Contact: Emily Greble, Chair, Jelavich Book Prize, E-mail: egreble@ccny.cuny.edu
• Kulczycki Book Prize in Polish Studies
• W. Bruce Lincoln Book Prize

• Graduate Student Essay Prize
Contact: Elena Prokhorova, Chair, Student Prize, E-mail: evprok@wm.edu
• Tucker/Cohen Dissertation Prize
Contact: Michael David-Fox, Chair, Dissertation Prize, E-mail: md672@georgetown.edu
• Regional Scholar Travel Grant
• Davis Graduate Student Travel Grant
• ASEEES Convention Opportunity Travel Grant
Meetings/Conferences:
• Association for Slavic, East European, & Eurasian Studies (ASEEES) Annual Convention 2018, December, 2018, Boston Marriott Copley Place, Boston, MA
Scope: International
Contact Information: Manager, Convention: Margaret Manges, E-mail: aseees.convention@pitt.edu, Phone: 412-648-4049
Publications:
• NewsNet [a publication of the Association for Slavic, East European, & Eurasian Studies]
Type: Newsletter; *Frequency:* 5 pa.; *Accepts Advertising*; *ISSN:* 1074-3057; *Price:* $30 within US; $47 outside US
Profile: Association news & updates
• Slavic Review [a publication of the Association for Slavic, East European, & Eurasian Studies]
Type: Journal; *Frequency:* q.; *Accepts Advertising*; *Editor:* Harriet L. Murav; *ISSN:* 0037-6779; *Price:* $252 within US; $302 outside US (print & digital)
Profile: Features peer-reviewed content that spans academic disciplines & geographic areas within Slavic,East European, & Eurasian studies

Association française d'études canadiennes (AFEC) / French Association for Canadian Studies (FACS)
Institut des Amérique, 175, rue du Chevaleret, Paris 75013 France
afec@msha.fr
www.afec33.asso.fr
Aperçu: *Dimension:* petite; *Envergure:* internationale; Organisme sans but lucratif; fondée en 1976
Mission: Promotion des études canadiennes en France: en toutes disciplines; Recherches avec rédaction des thèses par les chercheurs/étudiants
Membre de: International Council for Canadian Studies
Membre(s) du personnel: 1
Membre: 400; *Montant de la cotisation:* 45 euros; 50 euros à l'étranger; *Critères d'admissibilite:* Professeur d'universités, chercheurs, étudiants-chercheurs
Activités: *Service de conférenciers:* Oui; *Bibliothèque:* Not open to public
Membre(s) du bureau directeur:
Jean-Michel Lacroix, Président
Annick Monnerie, Secrétariat, Attachée culturelle

Association France-Québec
94, rue de Courcelles, Paris 75008 France
Tél: 01-45-54-35-37
accueil@francequebec.fr
francequebec.fr
www.facebook.com/AssociationFranceQuebec
twitter.com/AssoFrQc
Aperçu: *Dimension:* petite; *Envergure:* internationale; Organisme sans but lucratif; fondée en 1968
Mission: De regrouper des associations régionales; De coordonner non seulement l'ensemble des actions et des activités qui intéressent les adhérents et les Régionales, mais elle assure également la liaison avec tous les partenaires de la coopération franco-québécoise
Affiliation(s): Association Québec-France
Membre(s) du personnel: 5
Membre: 3500
Activités: Programmes d'échanges intermunicipaux; stages professionnels; pommes; tabac; tournée culturelle; prix littéraire; *Stagiaires:* Oui
Membre(s) du bureau directeur:
Marc Martin, Président
president@francequebec.fr

Association francophone internationale des directeurs d'établissements scolaires (AFIDES)
c/o Anne Macherel Rey, Lycee Jean-Piaget, Ecole Supérieure de commerce, Rue des Beaux-Arts 30, Neuchâtel 2000 Switzerland
Tél: 514-383-7335
www.afides.ch
Aperçu: *Dimension:* moyenne; *Envergure:* internationale; fondée en 1983

Mission: Promouvoir les échanges entre les responsables francophones d'établissements scolaires pour répondre à des besoins de perfectionnement international par la coopération et les échanges
Membre de: UNESCO - Comité de liaison des ONG avec l'Agence de la Francophonie
Membre: 1,000-4,999; *Critères d'admissibilite:* Toute personne qui exerce un rôle de direction dans un ou plusieurs établissements scolaires, sous le titre de directeur, directeur adjoint, principal adjoint, proviseur, censeur ou sous toute autre appellation pour les responsabilités identiques
Membre(s) du bureau directeur:
Anne Macherel Rey, Présidente
Anne.MacherelRey@rpn.ch

Association internationale d'études patristiques *See* International Association of Patristic Studies

Association internationale d'histoire économique *See* International Economic History Association

Association internationale de droit pénal (AIDP) / International Association of Penal Law
12, rue Charles Fourier, Paris 75013 France
Tél: 33(0)1.79.25.45.76; *Téléc:* 33(0)1.55.04.92.89
ridp-irpl@penal.org
www.penal.org
Aperçu: *Dimension:* petite; *Envergure:* internationale; fondée en 1924
Mission: L'A.I.D.P. s'est toujours souciée des problèmes de droit pénal international et de la responsabilité des auteurs de crimes internationaux
Finances: *Budget de fonctionnement annuel:* $50,000-$100,000
Membre(s) du personnel: 1
Membre: 3 000 dans 97 pays; *Montant de la cotisation:* Barème
Membre(s) du bureau directeur:
José Luis de la Cuesta, Président

Association internationale de la critique littéraire (AICL)
Paris France
www.aicl-fr.com
Aperçu: *Dimension:* petite; *Envergure:* internationale; Organisme sans but lucratif; fondée en 1970
Mission: Favoriser le rapprochement entre les cultures; favoriser par des rencontres internationales, les échanges culturels, les traductions, en particulier des littératures en langues de petite diffusion
Affiliation(s): UNESCO
Finances: *Fonds:* Cotisations
Membre: 84; *Critères d'admissibilite:* Écrivains et critiques
Activités: *Colloques;* congrès; *Stagiaires:* Oui; *Listes de destinataires:* Oui
Membre(s) du bureau directeur:
Daniel Leuwers, Président

Association internationale de pédiatrie *See* International Pediatric Association

Association internationale de relations professionnelles *See* International Labour & Employment Relations Association

Association internationale de signalisation maritime *See* International Association of Marine Aids to Navigation & Lighthouse Authorities

Association Internationale de Théâtre Amateur *See* International Amateur Theatre Association

Association internationale des bibliothèques, archives et de documentation musicaux *See* International Association of Music Libraries, Archives & Documentation Centres

Association internationale des débardeurs (FAT-COI/CTC) *See* International Longshoremen's Association (AFL-CIO/CLC)

Association internationale des éducateurs pour la paix du monde *See* International Association of Educators for World Peace - USA

Association internationale des études arméniennes *See* International Association for Armenian Studies

Association internationale des études patristiques (AIEP) / International Association for Patristic Studies (IAPS)
c/o University of Ottawa, Desmarais Bldg., 55 Laurier Ave. East, Ottawa ON K1N 6N5
www.aiep-iaps.org

Aperçu: *Dimension:* moyenne; *Envergure:* internationale; fondée en 1965
Mission: Chercheurs et professeurs qui s'intéressent à l'antiquité chrétienne au général
Finances: *Budget de fonctionnement annuel:* Moins de $50,000
Membre: 740; *Montant de la cotisation:* US$17; *Critères d'admissibilite:* Interessé aux pères de l'Eglise; *Comités:* Executive
Activités: *Listes de destinataires:* Oui
Membre(s) du bureau directeur:
Theodore S. de Bruyen, Président
tdebruyn@uottawa.ca

Association internationale des machinistes et des travailleurs de l'aérospatiale *See* International Association of Machinists & Aerospace Workers

Association internationale des métiers alliés de l'imprimerie *See* International Allied Printing Trades Association

Association internationale des pompiers (FAT-COI/CTC) *See* International Association of Fire Fighters (AFL-CIO/CLC)

Association internationale des sociologues de langue française (AISLF)
5, allée Jacques Berque, Nantes 44021 France CEDEX 1
Tél: 33-253-00-93-09
aislf@aislf.org
www.aislf.org
Aperçu: *Dimension:* moyenne; *Envergure:* internationale; Organisme sans but lucratif; fondée en 1958
Mission: Regroupe des sociologues et d'autres spécialistes en sciences sociales donnant une orientation sociologique à leurs travaux, quelle que soit leur nationalité, à condition qu'ils utilisent le français pour une part notable dans leur activité scientifique
Affiliation(s): UNESCO - Agence de la Francophonie
Finances: *Fonds:* Cotisations et subventions
Membre: 1 500 membres en 60 pays; *Critères d'admissibilite:* Sociologues travaillant majoritairement en français
Activités: Colloques; tables rondes; congrès; publications; comités de recherche et groupes de travail internationaux
Membre(s) du bureau directeur:
Marc-Henry Soulet, Président
Prix, Bourses:
• Prix du Jeune sociologue
Attribué lors de chaque congrès à un premier ouvrage; montant 1000 EURO
Publications:
• SociologieS: Revue de l'Association internationale des sociologues de langue française
Type: Journal; *ISSN:* 1992-2655

Association internationale des travailleurs de ponts, de fer structural et ornemental (FAT-COI) *See* International Association of Bridge, Structural, Ornamental & Reinforcing Iron Workers (AFL-CIO)

Association internationale des travailleurs du métal en feuilles (FAT-COI/FCT) *See* Sheet Metal Workers' International Association (AFL-CIO/CFL)

Association internationale du droit nucléaire *See* International Nuclear Law Association

Association internationale permanente des congrès de navigation (AIPCN) / Permanent International Association of Navigation Congresses (PIANC)
Bâtiment Graaf de Ferraris, 11ième étage, boul du Roi Albert II, 20 - Boîte 3, Bruxelles B-1000 Belgique
Tél: 32-2-553-7161; *Téléc:* 32-2-553-7155
info@pianc-aipcn.org
www.pianc-aipcn.org
be.linkedin.com/pub/pianc-international/61/386/2a
www.facebook.com/175978305876451
twitter.com/PIANC1
Également appelé: The World Association for Waterborne Transport Infrastructure
Aperçu: *Dimension:* petite; *Envergure:* internationale; fondée en 1885
Mission: Pour fournir des informations à ses membres, de fournir un réseau de personnes impliquées dans le transport international par voie d'eau
Membre de: Union des Associations Internationales; Union des Associations Techniques Internationales; Comité Scientifique pour les Recherches Hydrologiques
Membre(s) du personnel: 4
Membre: 2,000 individuels; 450 corporations; *Montant de la cotisation:* 95 E individu; 35 E étudiant; 475-950 E corporatif

Membre(s) du bureau directeur:
Geoffrey Caude, Président
president@painc.org
Louis Van Schel, Secrétaire général
secretary.general@pianc.org
André Châteauvert, Représentant canadien
chateauverta@dfo-mpo.gc.ca

Association irlandaise d'étude canadiennes *See* Association for Canadian Studies in Ireland

Association nordique d'études canadiennes *See* Nordic Association for Canadian Studies

Association of American Geographers (AAG)
1710 - 16 St. NW, Washington DC 20009-3198 USA
Tel: 202-234-1450; *Fax:* 202-234-2744
gaia@aag.org
www.aag.org
Overview: A medium-sized national organization founded in 1904
Mission: To advance professional studies in geography & to encourage the application of geographic research in education, government & business; To promote discussion among its members & with scholars in related fields; To support the publication of scholarly studies
Member of: American Council of Learned Societies
Finances: *Annual Operating Budget:* $1.5 Million-$3 Million
Staff Member(s): 10
Membership: 7,100 individual + 800 institutional; *Fees:* Schedule available; *Member Profile:* Members include students & professionals with backgrounds in a wide variety of geographic subfields such as urban geography, geographic information systems, cartography, remote sensing, historical geography, geomorphology, political geography, planning, environmental studies, & area studies
Activities: Specialty groups (comprised of geographers who share a professional interest in a systematic or topical specialty or in a major region of the world) sponsor sessions at the annual meetings, publish newsletters or other communications, & develop workshops & other projects to advance their professional interests; AAG manages several funded projects; AAG supports special symposia; *Internships:* Yes; *Rents Mailing List:* Yes
Chief Officer(s):
Douglas Richardson, Executive Director
drichardson@aag.org
Publications:
• The Professional Geographer
Type: Journal; *Frequency:* Quarterly
Profile: Annual journal

Association of American Publishers
71 - 5th Ave., 2nd Fl., New York NY 10003-3004 USA
Tel: 212-255-0200; *Fax:* 212-255-7007
www.publishers.org
www.linkedin.com/company/association-of-american-publishers
www.facebook.com/40077107889
twitter.com/AmericanPublish
Overview: A large national organization
Mission: To expand the market for American books & other published works in all media; to promote the status of publishing in the United States & throughout the world; To nurture creativity by protecting intellectual property rights, especially copyright; To promote intellectual freedom & to oppose all forms of censorship, at home & abroad
Membership: 300 companies; *Fees:* Schedule available; *Committees:* Core Committees: Compensation Survey Steering; Publishing Latino Voices for America Task Force; Smaller & Independent Publishers; Paper Issues Working Group; Get Caught Reading Marketing Task Force; Freedom to Read; Educational Programs; Diversity/Recruit & Retain; Statistics; Tax; Trade Publishers Executive; Trade Libraries Joint Committee with ALA/ALCTS; AAP Core Copyright Committees; AAP Core International Committees; AAP Digital Issues Committees; AAP Higher Education Committees; AAP Professional/Scholarly Publishing Division Committees; AAP School Division Committees
Chief Officer(s):
Tom Allen, President & CEO
tallen@publishers.org
Susanna Hinds, Vice-President, Communications, 202-220-4552
shinds@publishers.org
Gail Kump, Director, Membership Marketing, 212-255-1041
gkump@publishers.org

Association of Americans & Canadians in Israel (AACI)
Glassman Family Center, PO Box 53349, 37 Pierre Koenig, Jerusalem 91533 Israel
Tel: 972-2-566-1181; *Fax:* 972-2-566-1186
info@aaci.org.il
www.aaci.org.il
www.facebook.com/aacipage
Overview: A small international charitable organization founded in 1951
Mission: To provide a range of services to its members, whether new immigrants or long-time, English-speaking residents of Israel
Member of: Council of Immigrant Associations in Israel; Volunteer Sector Directorate
Finances: *Annual Operating Budget:* $500,000-$1.5 Million; *Funding Sources:* Jewish Agency for Israel; membership fees; grants; fundraising
Staff Member(s): 18; 1000 volunteer(s)
Membership: 20,000; *Member Profile:* North Americans of all ages, all religious streams, with no political affiliations; *Committees:* Absorption; Development; Finance; Membership; Legal; Loans & Mortgages
Activities: Employment Resource Center; loans; advice on legal, tax, banking, translation matters; senior outreach; library for visually impaired
Chief Officer(s):
Helen Har-Tal, Contact
Awards:
• Knesset Prize for Improving Quality of Life in Israel

Association of Children's Prosthetic-Orthotic Clinics (ACPOC)
#727, 6300, North River Rd., Rosemont IL 60018-4226 USA
Tel: 847-698-1637; *Fax:* 847-823-0536
acpoc@aaos.org
www.acpoc.org
Overview: A small international organization founded in 1978
Mission: To provide prosthetic-orthotic care for children with limb loss or orthopaedic disabilities.
Membership: *Fees:* US$90 corresponsing; US$125 non-physician; US$200 physician; *Member Profile:* Orthopaedic Surgeons; PTs; DO; Prosthetists; Orthotists; OTs; Nurses
Chief Officer(s):
David B. Rotter, President

Association of Christian Schools International (ACSI)
PO Box 65130, 731 Chapel Hills Dr., Colorado Springs CO 80962-5130 USA
Tel: 719-528-6906; *Fax:* 719-531-0631
info@acsi.org
www.acsi.org
www.facebook.com/ACSIUSA
twitter.com/ACSIUS
Overview: A medium-sized international organization founded in 1978
Mission: ACSI is an association of Protestant schools. It strives for school improvement, professional development & a provision of resources to enable Christian educators & schools worldwide to effectively prepare students for life.
Finances: *Funding Sources:* Membership fees
Membership: 5300 schools/colleges in 100 countries; *Fees:* Schedule available; *Member Profile:* Christian school; affirmation of ACSI statement of faith
Activities: Teacher conferences; student leadership conferences; board/administrator conferences; district principals meetings; music events; professional development days;
Speaker Service: Yes
Chief Officer(s):
Brian S. Simmons, President
Eastern Canada Office
1 Wenden Ct., RR#2, Minesing ON L0L 1Y2
Tel: 705-728-7344; *Fax:* 705-728-4401
acsiec@sympatico.ca
www.acsiec.org
www.facebook.com/ACSIEC
Chief Officer(s):
Mark Kennedy, Regional Director
Western Canada Office
PO Box 3460, 44 Willow Brook Dr. NW, Airdrie AB T4B 2J5
Tel: 403-948-2332; *Fax:* 403-948-2395
www.acsiwc.org
www.facebook.com/ACSIWC
twitter.com/HillsPhilip

Chief Officer(s):
Philip Hills, Regional Director
phills@acsiwc.org

Association of College & Research Libraries (ACRL)
c/o American Library Association, 50 East Huron St., Chicago IL 60611-2795 USA
Tel: 312-280-2523; *Fax:* 312-280-2520
Toll-Free: 800-545-2433
acrl@ala.org
www.ala.org/acrl
Overview: A large international organization founded in 1940 overseen by American Library Association
Mission: To develop programs & services to help academic & research librarians succeed within the academic community; To advocate for the profession; To provide continuing education opportunities
Finances: *Funding Sources:* Membership dues
Membership: 11,000; *Fees:* Schedule available; *Member Profile:* Academic & Research Librarians & interested individuals
Activities: Providing professional development opportunities; Organizing & facilitating conferences; Offering consulting services
Chief Officer(s):
Irene M.H. Herold, President
Mary Ellen K. Davis, Executive Director
Awards:
• Achievement & Distinguished Service Awards
A series of awards honouring academic & research librarians for significant past achievements
• Publication Awards
A series of awards given for outstanding articles, catalogues, or bibliographies
• WESS-SEES De Gruyter European Librarianship Study Grant
Supports research in European studies with an emphasis on librarianship *Deadline:* December *Amount:* 2,500 Euro
Meetings/Conferences:
• Association of College & Research Libraries (ACRL) Conference 2019, April, 2019, Cleveland, OH
Scope: National
• Association of College & Research Libraries (ACRL) Conference 2021, April, 2021, Seattle, WA
Scope: National
Publications:
• CHOICE: Current Reviews for Academic Libraries [a publication of the Association of College & Research Libraries]
Type: Magazine; *Frequency:* Monthly; *Accepts Advertising*
Profile: Reviews significant current books & electronic media that is of interest to those in higher education
• College & Research Libraries [a publication of the Association of College & Research Libraries]
Type: Journal; *Frequency:* Bi-monthly; *Editor:* Wendi Arant Kaspar; *ISSN:* 0010-0870
Profile: Features scholarly articles on academic librarianship
• College & Research Libraries News [a publication of the Association of College & Research Libraries]
Type: Magazine; *Frequency:* Monthly; *Accepts Advertising*; *Editor:* David Free
Profile: Provides articles on the latest trends & practices affecting academic/research libraries
• Keeping Up With... [a publication of the Association of College & Research Libraries]
Type: Newsletter; *Frequency:* Monthly; *Editor:* David Free; *Price:* Free for ACRL members
Profile: Features concise briefs on trends in academic librarianship/higher education; each edition focuses on asingle issue & its implications for academic libraries
• RBM [a publication of the Association of College & Research Libraries]
Type: Journal; *Frequency:* Semi-annually; *Accepts Advertising*; *Editor:* Jennifer Sheehan
Profile: A journal covering issues that pertain to special collections libraries & other cultural heritageinstitutions
• Resources for College Libraries [a publication of the Association of College & Research Libraries]
Type: Directory
Profile: An extensive list of core print & electronic resources for academic libraries; contains over 75,000 titles in 117subjects

Western New York/Ontario Chapter
c/o David J. Bertuca, Map Librarian, 116 Lockwood Memorial Library, University at Buffalo, Buffalo NY 14260-2200 USA
Tel: 716-645-1332; *Fax:* 716-645-3859
wnyoacrl.org
Mission: To act as a chapter of the Association of College & Research Libraries; to unify academic/research librarians living in a designated area; To advance the profession through resource sharing & professional development opportunities; To disseminate information among its membership
Chief Officer(s):
Marc Bayer, President, 716-878-6305, Fax: 716-878-3163
bayermd@buffalostate.edu
• ACRL WNY/ONT News [a publication of the Association of College & Research Libraries Western New York/Ontario Chapter]
Type: Newsletter; *Editor:* Ted Sherman
Profile: News & updates for members

Association of Construction Inspectors (ACI)
PO Box 879, Palm Springs CA 92263 USA
Tel: 760-327-5284; *Fax:* 760-327-5631
Toll-Free: 877-815-4174
support@assoc-hdqts.org
www.aci-assoc.org
www.linkedin.com/groups/Association-Construction-Inspectors-4463001
Overview: A medium-sized international organization
Mission: To provide professional designation to construction inspectors; education & marketing information to members
Member of: International Association Managers
Membership: *Fees:* Schedule available; *Member Profile:* Construction inspectors
Activities: *Internships:* Yes; *Speaker Service:* Yes; *Rents Mailing List:* Yes

Association of Environmental Engineering & Science Professors (AEESP)
#600, 1211 Connecticut Ave. NW, Washington D.C. IL 20036 USA
Tel: 202-640-6591; *Fax:* 202-223-5537
www.aeesp.org
Overview: A medium-sized international organization founded in 1963
Mission: To assist members in the development & dissemination of knowledge in environmental engineering & science; to strengthen & advance the environmental field through cooperation amongst academic & other communities
Membership: 700; *Fees:* $15 student; $60 affiliate; $50 assistant professor; $75 associate professor; $100 full professor; *Committees:* Administrative Handbook; Arrangements; Audit; Awards; Conference Selection; Education; Government Affairs; Internet Resources; Lecturers; Liaison; Membership & Demographics; Nominating; Publications; Strategic Planning; Student Services; Sustaining Member Stewardship
Activities: *Rents Mailing List:* Yes
Chief Officer(s):
Jennifer G. Becker, President
jgbecker@mtu.edu
Brian Schorr, Manager, Business Office
bschorr@aeesp.org

Association of Fish & Wildlife Agencies
#725, 444 North Capitol St. NW, Washington DC 20001 USA
Tel: 202-624-7890; *Fax:* 202-624-7891
info@fishwildlife.org
www.fishwildlife.org
www.facebook.com/FishWildlifeAgencies
twitter.com/fishwildlife
Previous Name: International Association of Fish & Wildlife Agencies
Overview: A small international organization founded in 1902
Mission: To guide its members toward long term conservation of renewable natural resources by employing conservation science & research.
Staff Member(s): 26
Membership: 142; *Member Profile:* Conservationists; Governments & government agencies; Regional associations; Organizations with similar objectives or supportive of the Association; Sportsmen; Individuals with varied backgrounds; *Committees:* Agricultural Conservation; Amphibian & Reptile; Annual Meeting/Awards/Nominating; Audit; Bird Conservation; Budget Conservation; Climate Change; Drug Approval Working Group; Education/Outreach/Diversity; Energy and Wildlife Policy; Executive; Federal and Tribal Relations; Fish & Wildlife Health; Fish and Wildlife Trust Funds; Fisheries/Water Resources Policy; Hunting/Shooting Sports Participation; International Relations; Invasive Species; Joint Federal/State Joint Policy Task Force on Federal Assistance Policy; Wildlife Resource Policy; Teaming with wildlife; Sustainable Wildlife Use
Activities: All bird conservation; Agency information database; Automated wildlife data systems; Conservation education; Conservation Leadership Institute; Farm Bill program; Furbearer management; International relations; Legislation; National Fish Habitat Action Plan; Science & Research; Teaming with wildlife; Wildlife conflict
Chief Officer(s):
Ron Regan, Executive Director
rregan@fishwildlife.org
Dan Forster, President

Association of Fundraising Professionals (AFP)
#300, 4300 Wilson Blvd., Arlington VA 22203 USA
Tel: 703-684-0410; *Fax:* 703-684-0540
Toll-Free: 800-666-3863
Other Communication: Canadian Membership:
cdnmembership@afpnet.org
afp@afpnet.org
www.afpnet.org
www.linkedin.com/company/878282
www.facebook.com/AFPFan
twitter.com/afpihq
Previous Name: National Society of Fund Raising Executives
Overview: A large international organization founded in 1960
Mission: To promote stewardship, donor trust & effective & ethical fundraising
Membership: 30,000 in 230+ chapters worldwide; *Fees:* $250 professional & associate; $95 young professional; $75 retired; $35 collegiate; $50 global e-membership; $175-$5,000 corporate; all + dues; *Member Profile:* Fundraising professionals, including development directors, fundraising consultants, grant writers, volunteer fundraisers, foundation executives& others
Activities: Conferences; publications; online resource centre; seminars & networking events; professional development opportunities; *Awareness Events:* National Philanthropy Day, November 15
Chief Officer(s):
Patrick J. Feeley, MBA, CFRE, Chair
Karen Dackiw Mercier, CFRE, Chair, AFP Canadian Council
Jason Lee, Interim President & CEO
jlee@afpnet.org
Awards:
• Changing our World/Simms Awards for Outstanding Youth in Philanthropy
Ages 5-17 & Ages 18-23
• Community Counselling Service (CCS) Award for Outstanding Fundraising Professional
• Freeman Philanthropic Services Award for Outstanding Corporation
• Award for Outstanding Philanthropist
• Award for Outstanding Foundation
• Award for Outstanding Volunteer Fundraiser
• Barbara Marion Award for Outstanding Service to AFP
• Awards for Excellence in Fundraising
• Skystone Ryan Prize for Research on Fundraising & Philanthropy
• Charles R. Stephens Excellence in Diversity Award
Publications:
• Advancing Philanthropy [a publication of the Association of Fundraising Professionals]
Type: Magazine; *Frequency:* Quarterly
• AFP [Association of Fundraising Professionals] eWire
Type: E-Newsletter; *Frequency:* Weekly
• AFP [Association of Fundraising Professionals] Fund Development Series
Type: Books
Profile: Career resource publications
• AFP [Association of Fundraising Professionals] Ready reference Series
Type: Booklets
Profile: Information on topics relevant to the industry
• Kaleidoscope [a publication of the Association of Fundraising Professionals]
Type: Newsletter; *Frequency:* Quarterly
• Te Informa [a publication of the Association of Fundraising Professionals]
Type: E-Newsletter; *Frequency:* Quarterly
Profile: Spanish-language covering issues relevant to Mexico/Latin American countries

Calgary & Area Chapter
4620 Manilla Rd. SE, Calgary AB T2G 4B7
Tel: 403-297-1033; *Fax:* 403-724-0091
afp@telus.net
afpcalgary.afpnet.org
Chief Officer(s):
Karen Filbert, CFRE, President
Catherine Yates, Contact, Marketing & Communications

Canada South Chapter
PO Box 32007, 7980 Menard St., Windsor ON N8S 4T8
Tel: 519-818-6973
afpcanadasouth@gmail.com
afpcanadasouth.wordpress.com
ca.linkedin.com/pub/afp-canada-south-chapter/25/4b7/527
www.facebook.com/AFPCanadaSouth
twitter.com/AFPCanadaSouth
Chief Officer(s):
Christine Colautti, President

Cape Breton Chapter
Cape Breton NS
Chief Officer(s):
Paula Eileen MacNeil, Contact, 902-563-1848
paula_macneil@cbu.ca

Central Alberta Chapter
PO Box 148, Stn. Red Deer, Red Deer AB T4N 5E7
afpcentralab.afpnet.org
www.facebook.com/AFPCentralAlberta
Chief Officer(s):
Ian Warwick, President
Greg Shannon, Contact, 403-314-2430
Greg.Shannon@rdc.ab.ca

Central Ontario Chapter
ON
www.afpcentralontario.org
www.linkedin.com/company/afp-central-ontario
Chief Officer(s):
Deborah Loosemore, MBA, Contact, Membership
dmloosemore@gmail.com

Edmonton & Area Chapter
PO Box 4355, Spruce Grove AB T7X 3B5
Tel: 780-960-4188
info@afpedmonton.ca
www.afpedmonton.ca
www.linkedin.com/groups/AFP-Edmonton-Area-Chapter-3796360
www.facebook.com/AFPEdmonton
twitter.com/AFPEdmonton
Chief Officer(s):
Ryan Drury, President
ryan.drury@stollerykids.com
Sabrina Ali, Director, Marketing & Communications
nabafpcomm@gmail.com
Neil Luipasco, Director, Membership
nluipasco@citadeltheatre.com

Golden Horseshoe Chapter
ON
afpgoldenhorseshoe.org
www.linkedin.com/groups/2781017
www.facebook.com/344066545713
twitter.com/AFPGolden
Chief Officer(s):
Mary McPherson, CFRE, President
mmcpherson@haltonhealthcare.com
Brian Hobbs, Vice-President, Membership
bhobbs@hrca.on.ca
Suzanne Hallsworth, Director, Marketing & Communications
shallsworth@haltonhealthcare.on.ca

Greater Toronto Chapter
#412, 260 King St. East, Toronto ON M5A 4L5
Tel: 416-941-9212; *Fax:* 416-941-9013
Toll-Free: 800-796-7373
info@afptoronto.org
www.afptoronto.org
www.linkedin.com/groups/2160522
twitter.com/afptoronto
www.youtube.com/AFPToronto
Affiliation(s): International Society of Fund Raising Executives
Chief Officer(s):
Krishan Mehta, President
Cynthia Quigley, Director
cquigley@afptoronto.org

Manitoba Chapter
PO Box 644, Stn. Main, Winnipeg MB R3C 2K3
Tel: 204-832-1512; *Fax:* 204-897-8094
afp.manitoba@gmail.com
afpmanitoba.afpnet.org
www.facebook.com/AFPManitoba
twitter.com/afpmanitoba
Chief Officer(s):
Sana Mahboob, President
sana.mahboob@umanitoba.ca

Lise Carbonneau, Administrator

New Brunswick Chapter
Saint John NB
e-mail: afpnbchapter@gmail.com
afpnb.afpnet.org
www.linkedin.com/groups/8326390
Chief Officer(s):
Kenn Mainville, President
Kenn@Mainville.com

Newfoundland & Labrador Chapter
PO Box 39021, 430 Topsail Rd., St. John's NL A1E 4N1
e-mail: afp.nlchapter@gmail.com
www.facebook.com/AFPNewfoundlandAndLabrador
Chief Officer(s):
Sonya Smith, Contact, 709-722-1996
ssmith@kidseatsmart.ca

Nova Scotia Chapter
PO Box 33009, Halifax NS B3L 4T6
e-mail: afpnovascotia@gmail.com
www.afpns.afpnet.org
Chief Officer(s):
Brent Platt, CFRE, President, 902-423-4390
bplatt@liberal.ns.ca

Okanagan Chapter
#718, 101 - 1865 Dilworth Dr., Kelowna BC V1Y 9T1
Tel: 250-979-6652
afpokanagan@gmail.com
afpokanagan.afpnet.org
Chief Officer(s):
Shari Slattery, President
shari.slattery@cmha.bc.ca
Margo Buckley, Contact, Membership
mbuckley@ymcaokanagan.ca

Ottawa Chapter
c/o Virtual Works Inc., #436, 900 Greenbank Rd., Ottawa ON K2J 4P6
Tel: 613-590-1412
secretariat@afpottawa.ca
afpottawa.afpnet.org
www.facebook.com/AFPOttawa
twitter.com/AFPottawa
Chief Officer(s):
Kelly Lachance, CFRE, President, 613-590-1412
secretariat@afpottawa.ca
Monique Archambault, Treasurer
treasurer@afpottawa.ca

Québec Chapter
QC
Tél: 514-918-6572
afpquebec@gmail.com
www.afpquebec.ca
www.linkedin.com/company-beta/10266506
www.facebook.com/AFPQuebec
twitter.com/AFPQuebec
Chief Officer(s):
Luce Moreau, CFRE, Présidente
Julie-Anne Houdayer, Gestionnaire

Regina Chapter
PO Box 613, Regina SK S4P 3A3
Toll-Free: 800-666-3863
afpregina@gmail.com
afpregina.afpnet.org
www.facebook.com/afpregina
twitter.com/AFPRegina
Chief Officer(s):
Sarah Fedirko, President
sarah.fedirko@redcross.ca
Michelle Okere, Director, Membership
mgrunerud@unitedwayregina.ca
Trish Taylor, Director, Communications
trish@regina.ca

Saskatoon Chapter
Saskatoon SK S7K 0C8
Toll-Free: 800-666-3863
afpsaskatooncommunications@gmail.com
afpsaskatoon.afpnet.org
Chief Officer(s):
Stephanie Hughes, CFRE, President
stephanie@dcgsk.com
Megan Cantwell, Membership Chair
megan.cantwell@usask.ca

South Eastern Ontario Chapter
PO Box 1695, Kingston ON K7L 5J6

e-mail: afpseo@gmail.com
afpseo.afpnet.org
www.facebook.com/afpseo.afpnet.org
twitter.com/AFP_SEO
Chief Officer(s):
Shannon Coull, CFRE, President
shannon.coull@uhkf.ca
Jessica Kostuck, Membership Chair
jessica.kostuck@queensu.ca
Melanie Barrett, Contact, Marketing, Communications & Outreach
mbarrett@albertcollege.ca

Southern Alberta Chapter
PO Box 431, Lethbridge AB
e-mail: afp.southernalberta@gmail.com
www.facebook.com/AFPSouthernAlbertaChapter
Chief Officer(s):
Barry Knapp, Contact
barry.knapp@uleth.ca

Vancouver Chapter
#720, 999 West Broadway, Vancouver BC V5Z 1K5
Tel: 604-736-1010; *Fax:* 604-738-4080
info@afpvancouver.org
www.afpvancouver.org
www.facebook.com/afpvancouver
twitter.com/AFPVancouver
Karline Mark-Eng, Contact

Vancouver Island Chapter
1075 Portage Rd., Victoria BC V8Z 1L1
Tel: 250-217-0772
afp.vancouverisland@gmail.com
afpvancouverisland.afpnet.org
www.linkedin.com/groups/7452371
www.facebook.com/afp.vi
twitter.com/AFP_VI
Chief Officer(s):
Diane Lloyd, President
Monica Powell, Administrator
monica@monicapowellevents.ca

Association of Great Lakes Outdoor Writers (AGLOW)
PO Box 35, Benld IL 62009 USA
Toll-Free: 877-472-4569
aglowinfo.org
www.facebook.com/145249282212242
Overview: A small local organization founded in 1954
Mission: Dedicated to communicating the outdoor experience in word & image
Finances: *Annual Operating Budget:* Less than $50,000; *Funding Sources:* Membership dues; fundraising
Staff Member(s): 2
Membership: 330; *Fees:* $45-135
Chief Officer(s):
Josh Lantz, Executive Director
josh@sandcreek-media.com
P.J. Perea, President
pperea@nwtf.net

Association of Holocaust Organizations (AHO)
PO Box 230317, Hollis NY 11423 USA
Tel: 516-582-4571
ahoinfo@att.net
www.ahoinfo.org
Overview: A medium-sized international organization founded in 1985
Mission: To serve as a network of organizations & incividuals for the advancement of Holocaust programs, education, awareness & research
Finances: *Annual Operating Budget:* Less than $50,000; *Funding Sources:* Membership dues
Membership: 209 organizations
Chief Officer(s):
William L. Shulman, President
Susan Myers, Vice-President

Association of Personal Computer Users Groups (APCUG)
PO Box 671294, Dallas TX 75367-1294 USA
Toll-Free: 800-558-6867
apcug2.org
Overview: A medium-sized national organization founded in 1990
Mission: To help user groups offer better services to their members
Membership: 400+ groups; 300,000 individuals; *Fees:* US$50

Chief Officer(s):
Marie Vesta, President

Association of Postconsumer Plastic Recyclers (APR)
#500 West, 1001 - G St. NW, Washington DC 20001 USA
Tel: 202-316-3046
info@plasticsrecycling.org
www.plasticsrecycling.org
www.linkedin.com/groups?home=&gid=3176812&trk=anet_ug_hm
www.facebook.com/694931163886120
Overview: A small national organization founded in 1992
Mission: The Association represents companies who acquire, reprocess & sell post-consumer plastic. It strives to enhance the plastics recycling industry by promoting cooperative testing for the development of new packaging, improving the quality of plastics, encouraging better recycling guidelines, & presenting awards for advancements in the industry.
Finances: *Annual Operating Budget:* $100,000-$250,000; *Funding Sources:* Related associations; membership dues
Staff Member(s): 1
Membership: 103; *Fees:* $800-3,500; *Member Profile:* PCR reclaimers; *Committees:* Market Development; Technical; Executive
Activities: Design for Recyclability Programs; Champions for Change
Chief Officer(s):
Steve Alexander, Executive Director
salexander@cmrgroup4.com

Association of Research Libraries (ARL)
#800, 21 Dupont Circle NW, Washington DC 20036 USA
Tel: 202-296-2296; *Fax:* 202-872-0884
webmgr@arl.org
www.arl.org
www.linkedin.com/company/association-of-research-libraries
www.facebook.com/association.of.research.libraries
twitter.com/ARLnews
www.youtube.com/ARLvideo
Overview: A medium-sized international organization founded in 1932
Mission: To identify & influence forces affecting the future of research libraries in the process of scholarly communication
Member of: American Library Association
Affiliation(s): Coalition for Networked Information; Office of Management Services; Scholarly Publishing & Academic Resources Coalition
Finances: *Funding Sources:* Membership dues
Staff Member(s): 23
Membership: 125 research libraries; *Committees:* Executive; Coalition for Networked Information; Diversity & Leadership; Membership; Nominating; Statistics & Assessment; Influencing Public Policies; Advancing Scholarly Communication; Transforming Research Libraries; AAUP/ARL Working Group on University Press/Research Library Collaboration; Research Library Leadership Fellows (RLLF) Program Sponsors Advisor; Coalition for Networked Information; LibQUAL; Scholarly Publishing & Academic Resources Coalition
Activities: Promotes equitable access to & effective use of recorded knowledge in support of teaching, research, scholarship & community service
Chief Officer(s):
Carol Pitts Diedrichs, President
Elliott Shore, Executive Director
elliott@arl.org

Association of Retail Travel Agents (ARTA)
4320 North Miller Rd., Scottsdale AZ 85251-3606 USA
Fax: 866-743-2087
Toll-Free: 866-369-8969
www.arta.travel
Overview: A medium-sized international organization founded in 1963
Mission: To represent travel agents in North America
Membership: *Fees:* $99 individual; $250 agency; $1000 lifetime; *Member Profile:* Travel agents in the USA & Canada
Chief Officer(s):
Nancy Linares, Chair

Association of Telehealth Service Providers (ATSP)
#400, 4702 SW Scholls Ferry Rd., Portland OR 97225-2008 USA
Tel: 503-922-0988; *Fax:* 315-222-2402
www.atsp.org
Overview: A small international organization founded in 1996
Mission: To improve health care through growth of the telehealth industry
Chief Officer(s):
William Engle, Executive Director

Association of Trial Lawyers of America (ATLA); National Association of Claimants' Compensation Attorneys (NACCA) *See* American Association for Justice

Association of Zoos & Aquariums (AZA)
#710, 8403 Colesville Rd., Silver Spring MD 20910-3314 USA
Tel: 301-562-0777; *Fax:* 301-562-0888
membership@aza.org
www.aza.org
www.facebook.com/zoosaquariums
twitter.com/zoos_aquariums
www.instagram.com/zoos_aquariums
Previous Name: American Zoo & Aquarium Association
Overview: A medium-sized international organization founded in 1924
Mission: To help preserve the world's rare & endangered species; To advance zoological parks & aquariums through conservation, education, scientific studies & recreation; To cooperate with government agencies & international conservation groups in matters dealing with the health & welfare of wildlife in captivity
Affiliation(s): World Wildlife Fund - USA; Species Survival Commission of IUCN - World Conservation Union; Captive Breeding Specialist Group; International Species Information System; Wildlife Conservation International; American Committee for International Conservation; Centre for Marine Conservation; International Union of Directors of Zoological Gardens; International Association of Zoo Educators
Finances: *Annual Operating Budget:* $500,000-$1.5 Million
Staff Member(s): 20
Membership: 5,500; *Fees:* $80 associate; $95 affiliate; $195 fellow; *Member Profile:* Comprises zoological institutions, related organizations, societies, zoological staff employees, commercial concerns that provide products & services to zoological facilities & other interested individuals; open to anyone interested in animal welfare, protection of wildlife & the development of better zoos & aquariums for the good of animals & people; *Committees:* Accreditation; Advancement; Animal Health; Animal Welfare; Annual Conference Program; Aquarium Affairs; Business Operations; Conservation Education; Diversity; Ethics; Field Conservation; Government Affairs; Honors & Awards; Human Resources; Marketing; Membership; Nominating; Professional Development; Public Relations; Research & Technology; Safety; Trends; Volunteer Management; Wildlife Conservation & Management
Activities: Species Survival Plan - a strategy for the long-term survival of certain endangered species; computerized inventory of over 60,000 living animals in order to enable zoos to locate the best individuals for their breeding programs; *Rents Mailing List:* Yes
Chief Officer(s):
Dan Ashe, President & CEO
Kris Vehrs, Executive Director

Association pour l'amélioration des cultures biologiques (international) *See* Organic Crop Improvement Association (International)

Association pour la prévention de la contamination de l'air et du sol *See* Air & Waste Management Association

Associazione Italiana di Studi Canadesi *See* Italian Association for Canadian Studies

Australian Association for Environmental Education (AAEE)
PO Box 996, Cotton Tree 4558 Australia
Tel: 61 7 5479 1424
admin@aaee.org.au
www.aaee.org.au
Overview: A small national organization founded in 1980
Mission: To promote environmental education
Finances: *Annual Operating Budget:* $50,000-$100,000; *Funding Sources:* Fees; grants; sponsorship; subsidies
Staff Member(s): 1; 30 volunteer(s)
Membership: 500; *Fees:* $90-$99 individual; $120 family; $240 corporate; $140 school/NGO; $896-$985 lifetime; *Member Profile:* Professionals; *Committees:* Special interest groups
Chief Officer(s):
Phil Smith, President
rephilled@hotmail.com

Australian Bankers' Association Inc.
56 Pitt St., Level 3, Sydney NSW 2000 Australia
Tel: 61-2-8298-0417; *Fax:* 61-2-8298-0402
www.bankers.asn.au
twitter.com/austbankers
www.youtube.com/user/AustralianBankers
Overview: A medium-sized national organization
Mission: To improve the economic well-being of Australians by fostering a banking system recognized as one of the safest, dynamic & most efficient in the world
Chief Officer(s):
Michael Smith, Chair

Australian Society of Association Executives Ltd. (AuSAE)
PO Box 752, Stones Corner, QLD 4120 Australia
Tel: 61 1 300 5764 6576; *Fax:* 61 7 3319 6056
info@ausae.org.au
www.ausae.org.au
twitter.com/AuSAENews
Overview: A small national organization founded in 1954
Mission: To provide support, networking services, & industry information to association managers in the business, professional, technical, trade, sporting, welfare, religious, educational & finance sectors.
Finances: *Funding Sources:* Membership fees
Staff Member(s): 6
Membership: *Fees:* Schedule available
Activities: Networking functions; seminars; trade fairs
Chief Officer(s):
Tony Steven, President
belinda@ausae.org.au
Belinda Moore, Chief Executive Officer

Austrian-Canadian Society
c/o Wolf Theiss, Schubertring 6, Vienna 1010 Austria
e-mail: info@austria-canada.com
www.austria-canada.com
Overview: A small international organization founded in 2003
Mission: To improve the relationships between Austria & Canada in a sustainable manner; to forge contacts in the fields of traditional diplomacy, business, science, & culture.
Membership: *Fees:* 15 euros student; 50 euros regular; 75 euros family/couple
Chief Officer(s):
Heinz Seitinger, President
president@austria-canada.com

Automatic Identification Manufacturers *See* AIM Global

Badminton World Federation (BWF)
Amoda Bldg., #17.05, 22 Jalan Imbi, L. 17, Kuala Lumpur 55100 Malaysia
Tel: 603-2141 7155; *Fax:* 603-2143 7155
bwf@bwfbadminton.org
www.bwfbadminton.org
www.facebook.com/bwfbadminton
twitter.com/bwfmedia
Previous Name: International Badminton Federation (IBF)
Overview: A medium-sized international organization founded in 1934
Mission: To control the game of badminton, from an international aspect, in all countries; to uphold the Laws of Badminton as at present adopted
Finances: *Funding Sources:* Subscriptions & sponsorships
Membership: 180 nationally organized bodies; *Committees:* Continental Confederations; IOC & International Relations; Administration; Events; Development & Sport for All; Marketing; Finance; Para-Badminton
Chief Officer(s):
Poul-Erik Høyer, President
pe.hoyer@bwfbadminton.org
Awards:
• Hall of Fame
Periodic for exceptional achievements by players/administration
• Herbert Scheele Trophy
Awarded periodically for outstandingly eceptional achievements
• Eddy Choong Player of the Year Award
Annual award for achieving outstanding results
• Certificate of Commendation
Awarded semi-annually for commercial & external organisations who contribute to badminton
• Distinguished Associates Award
Annual awared for major support in the development of badminton

Foreign Associations / Bakery, Confectionery, Tobacco Workers & Grain Millers International Union (AFL-CIO/CLC)

- Distinguished Service Award
Semi-annual award for long or distinguished services to badminton
- Meritorious Sevice Award
Awarded semi-annually for long & meritorious services to badminton

Bakery, Confectionery, Tobacco Workers & Grain Millers International Union (AFL-CIO/CLC)
10401 COnnecticut Ave., Floor 4, Kensington MD 20895 US
Tel: 301-933-8600
bctgmwebmaster@gmail.com
www.bctgm.org
www.facebook.com/BCTGM
twitter.com/BCTGM
www.instagram.com/bctgm
Overview: A large international organization
Mission: To represent members & bring justice in the workplace in all jurisdictions
Membership: 13,756 + 32 locals; *Member Profile:* Individuals in the manufacturing, production, maintenance & sanitation sections of the bakery, confectionery, tobacco &Ægrain milling industries in North America
Chief Officer(s):
David B. Durkee, International President
Steve Bertelli, International Secretary-Treasurer
Ron Piercey, International Vice President, Canadian Region

Barbershop Harmony Society
110 - 7th Ave. North, Nashville TN 37203-3704 USA
Tel: 615-823-9339; *Fax:* 615-313-7620
Toll-Free: 800-876-7464
customerservice@barbershop.org
www.barbershop.org
www.facebook.com/barbershopharmonysociety
twitter.com/barbershopnews
www.youtube.com/user/BarbershopHarmony38
Previous Name: Society for the Preservation & Encouragement of Barber Shop Quartet Singing in America Inc.
Overview: A medium-sized international charitable organization founded in 1938
Mission: To celebrate barbershop quartets; To promote & encourage vocal harmony & good fellowship among its members through the formation of local chapters & districts; To encourage & promote the education of its members & the public in music appreciation
Affiliation(s): British Association of Barbershop Singers; Barbershop Harmony Australia; Barbershop in Germany; Dutch Association of Barbershop Singers; Finnish Association of Barbershop Singers; Irish Association of Barbershop Singers; New Zealand Association of Barbershop Singers; Spanish Association of Barbershop Singers; Society of Nordic Barbershop Singers; Southern Part of Africa Tonsorial Singers
Staff Member(s): 36
Membership: 25,000 in the United States & Canada; *Fees:* $120
Activities: Organizing annual, local, district, state, national & international contests in quartet & chorus singing; *Library:* Old Songs Library
Chief Officer(s):
Marty Monson, CEO & Executive Director
ceo@barbershop.org

Bear Biology Association *See* International Association for Bear Research & Management

Beyond Pesticides
#200, 701 East St. SE, Washington DC 20003 USA
Tel: 202-543-5450; *Fax:* 202-543-4791
info@beyondpesticides.org
www.beyondpesticides.org
www.facebook.com/beyondpesticides
twitter.com/bpncamp
www.youtube.com/bpncamp
Previous Name: National Coalition Against the Misuse of Pesticides
Overview: A medium-sized national organization founded in 1981
Mission: To address the issue of hazards of pesticide use; To provide the public with clearinghouse of information on pesticides & pesticides issues; To promote alternative forms of pest management
Finances: *Annual Operating Budget:* $250,000-$500,000
Staff Member(s): 4; 1 volunteer(s)
Membership: 1,400
Activities: *Speaker Service:* Yes; *Library*

Chief Officer(s):
Jay Feldman, Executive Director
jfeldman@beyondpesticides.org
Nichelle Harriott, Director, Science & Regulatory
nharriott@beyondpesticides.org
Drew Toher, Director, Community Resource & Policy
dtoher@beyondpesticides.org

Bibliographical Society of America (BSA)
PO Box 1537, Stn. Lennox Hill, New York NY 10021 USA
Tel: 212-452-2710; *Fax:* 212-452-2710
bsa@bibsocamer.org
www.bibsocamer.org
Overview: A small international organization founded in 1904
Mission: To study books & manuscripts as physical objects; to promote bibliographical research through meetings, lectures, fellowship programs & the publishing of books & journals
Member of: American Council of Learned Societies
Membership: *Fees:* $20 student; $65 individual; $100 institution/contributing; $250 sustaining; $1250 lifetime; *Member Profile:* Interest in bibliographical projects & problems; *Committees:* Audit; Fellowship; Finance; Program; Publications
Activities: *Rents Mailing List:* Yes
Chief Officer(s):
Martin Antonetti, President
Michèle E. Randall, Executive Director
Awards:
- Mitchell Prize
For bibliography or documentary work on early British periodicals or newspapers *Amount:* $1000 + 1 year's membership
- Schiller Prize
Bibliographical work on pre-20th-Century children's books *Amount:* $2000 + 1 year's membership
- St. Louis Mercantile Library Prize
Bibliographical work on American history and literature; awarded every 3 yrs. *Amount:* $2000 + 1 year's membership
Publications:
- The Papers of the Bibliographical Society of America
Type: journal

Bonn Agreement (BONN)
Victoria House, 37-63 Southampton Row, London WC1B 4DA United Kingdom
Tel: 44-20-7430-5200; *Fax:* 44-20-7430-5225
secretariat@bonnagreement.org
www.bonnagreement.org
Overview: A small international organization founded in 1969
Mission: To provide a cooperation forum for dealing with accidental marine pollution of the North Sea & marine pollution aerial surveillance
Staff Member(s): 3
Membership: 9 European & EU countries; *Fees:* Annual contribution
Chief Officer(s):
M. Michel Aymeric, Chair

Brazilian Association for Canadian Studies *See* Associaçao Brasileira de Estudos Canadense

British Association for Canadian Studies (BACS) / Association britanniques d'études canadiennes
c/o UCL Institute of the Americas, 51 Gordon Sq., London WC1H OPN United Kingdom
www.britishassociationforcanadianstudies.org
www.facebook.com/BACS.UK
twitter.com/Canada_BACS
Overview: A small international charitable organization founded in 1975
Mission: To act as a forum for Canadian studies in the United Kingdom
Member of: International Council for Canadian Studies
Membership: *Fees:* $30 students & unwaged persons; $60 regular members; *Member Profile:* Persons with an interest in the study of Canada
Chief Officer(s):
Tony McCulloch, President
Awards:
- British Association for Canadian Studies Travel Awards
To enable qualified British scholars make academic visits to Canada
Meetings/Conferences:
- British Association for Canadian Studies 43rd Annual Conference, April, 2018, London
Scope: International
Description: Distinguished speakers on a great range of topics

Publications:
- British Association for Canadian Studies Newsletter
Type: Newsletter
Profile: Upcoming events & information from the association
- British Journal of Canadian Studies
Type: Journal; *Frequency:* Semiannually; *Editor:* Dr. Susan Billingham
Profile: Articles & book reviews

The Brontë Society
Brontë Parsonage Museum, Church St., Haworth, West Yorkshire BD22 8DR United Kingdom
Tel: 44-1535-642-323; *Fax:* 44-1535-647-131
bronte@bronte.org.uk
www.bronte.org.uk
Overview: A medium-sized international charitable organization founded in 1893
Mission: To bring closer together all who honour the Brontë sisters; To act as the guardian of such letters, writings & personal belongings as could be acquired for the Museum; To foster interest in the Brontës' writing & lives through education programs, publications & exhibitions
Affiliation(s): Alliance of Literary Societies
Finances: *Annual Operating Budget:* $500,000-$1.5 Million; *Funding Sources:* Museum admissions; society subscriptions
Staff Member(s): 35; 10 volunteer(s)
Membership: 2,500; *Fees:* £25 adult; £18.50 senior; £12.50 student; *Committees:* Finance; Membership; Museum Education
Activities: *Library:* Brontë Parsonage Library; by appointment
Chief Officer(s):
Kitty Wright, Executive Director
Awards:
- Heritage Education Trust - The Sandford Award

Brotherhood of Maintenance of Way Employes (AFL-CIO/CLC) / Fraternité des préposés à l'entretien des voies (FAT-COI/CTC)
41475 Gardenbrook Rd., Novi MI 48375-1328 USA
Tel: 248-662-2660; *Fax:* 248-662-2659
www.bmwe.org
www.facebook.com/290792087644965
twitter.com/BMWEDIBT
Overview: A medium-sized international organization
Membership: 12,110 + 133 locals
Chief Officer(s):
Fred N. Simpson, President
fns@bmwe.org
Clark Ballew, Director, Communications
cballew@bmwe.org
Awards:
- James R. Hoffa Memorial Scholarship
Contact: James R. Hoffa Memorial Scholarship Fund, E-mail: scholarship@teamster.org
Publications:
- BMWED [Brotherhood of Maintenance of Way Employes] Journal
Type: Journal; *Frequency:* q.

Building Materials Reuse Association (BMRA)
PO Box 47776, Chicago IL 60647 USA
Tel: 773-340-2672
contact@bmra.org
www.bmra.org
Previous Name: Used Building Materials Association
Overview: A medium-sized national organization
Mission: To represent companies & organizations in the United States & Canada involved in the acquisition &/or redistribution of used building materials
Membership: *Fees:* $95; *Member Profile:* Companies & organizations involved in the acquisition &/or redistribution of used building materials
Chief Officer(s):
Brad Guy, President

Building Owners & Managers Association International (BOMA)
#800, 1101 - 15th St. NW, Washington DC 20005 USA
Tel: 202-408-2662; *Fax:* 202-326-6377
info@boma.org
www.boma.org
Overview: A medium-sized international organization founded in 1907
Finances: *Annual Operating Budget:* Greater than $5 Million
Staff Member(s): 29
Membership: 16,500 individuals & companies
Chief Officer(s):

Henry Chamberlain, APR, FASAE, CAE, President & COO

Bureau international de la paix See International Peace Bureau

Bureau international des poids et mesures (BIPM)
Pavillon de Breteuil, Sévres F-92312 France
Tél: 33-1-45-07-70-00
webmaster@bipm.org
www.bipm.fr
Aperçu: Dimension: petite; *Envergure:* internationale; fondée en 1875
Mission: Établir les étalons fondamentaux et les échelles des principales grandeurs physiques et conserver les prototypes internationaux; effectuer la comparaison des étalons nationaux et internationaux; assurer la coordination des techniques de mesure correspondantes; to ensure world-wide uniformity of measurements & their traceability to the International System of Units (SI)
Membre: *Comités:* International des Poids et Mesure; Consultatif de l'acoustique, des ultrasons et des vibrations; Consultatif d'électricité et magnétisme; Consultatif des longueurs; Consultatif pour la masse et les grandeurs apparentées; Consultatif pour la quantité de matière - métrologie en chimie; Consultatif des rayonnements ionisants; Consultatif de thermométrie; Consultatif du temps et des fréquences; Consultatif des unités; Commun pour les guides en métrologie; Mixte des organisations régionales de métrologie et du BIPM; Commun pour la traçabilité en médecine de laboratoire
Activités: *Bibliothèque*
Membre(s) du bureau directeur:
Martin Milton, Directeur

Bureau of International Recycling (BIR)
24, av Franklin Roosevelt, Brussels 1050 Belgium
Tel: 32-2-627-5770; Fax: 32-2-627-5773
bir@bir.org
www.bir.org
Overview: A medium-sized international organization founded in 1948
Mission: To promote recycling & a recyclability, thereby conserving natural resources, protecting the environment, & facilitating free trade of recyclables in an environmentally sound manner
Membership: 890+; *Fees:* 2,000 Euro regular; 2,400 Euro gold; 1,000 Euro subsidiaries
Chief Officer(s):
Björn Grufman, President

Business & Institutional Furniture Manufacturer's Association (BIFMA)
#150, 678 Front Ave. NW, Grand Rapids MI 49504-5368 USA
Tel: 616-285-3963; Fax: 616-285-3765
email@bifma.org
www.bifma.org
www.linkedin.com/company/BIFMA
twitter.com/BIFMA
Overview: A medium-sized international organization founded in 1973
Mission: To promote the interests of the commercial furniture industry
Staff Member(s): 6
Membership: 245 companies; *Committees:* Engineering Standards; Government Affairs; Statistical Information; Sustainability
Chief Officer(s):
Tom Reardon, Executive Director
treardon@bifma.org

Campaign Against Arms Trade (CAAT)
#4, 5-7 Weeks Terrace, London N4 3JU UK
Tel: 44-20728-10297
enquiries@caat.org.uk
www.caat.org.uk
www.facebook.com/campaignagainstarmstrade
twitter.com/wwwcaatorguk
www.youtube.com/wwwcaatorguk
Overview: A small international organization founded in 1974
Mission: To end the international arms trade; to pursue security by promoting the idea that funds should be funnelled, not into military interests, but into such causes of insecurity as social inequality & climate change.
Activities: *Speaker Service:* Yes; *Library:* by appointment
Chief Officer(s):
Andrew Smith, Media Coordinator
media@caat.org.uk

Canada - United States Trade Center (CUSTAC)
Dept. of Geography, Univ. of Buffalo, 105 Wilkeson Quadrangle, Buffalo NY 14261-0055 USA
Tel: 716-645-2722; Fax: 716-645-2329
geog@buffalo.edu
www.custac.buffalo.edu
Previous Name: International Center for Canadian-American Trade
Overview: A small international organization
Mission: CUSTAC conducts applied & policy-oriented research on the nature of Canada-US commercial relations with respect to trade, capital investment, border management, & regulatory conditions. Specifically, one of its main functions is to assist in the development of the trade corridor between Western New York & Southern Ontario. It also lobbies governments for equitable environments, suitable for stable, economic transactions between the 2 countries.
Activities: Conducting seminars & workshops; developing university courses; *Library:* Information Library
Chief Officer(s):
McConnell James, Associate Director
geojem@acsu.buffalo.edu

Canada New Zealand Business Council
Auckland New Zealand
www.canada-nz.org.nz
Overview: A medium-sized international organization founded in 1989
Mission: To stimulate & promote trade, investment, communication, services & interaction between New Zealand & Canada
Activities: Offering networking opportunities; Providing trade, import, export, investment advisory & marketing services

Canadian American Law Enforcement Organization (CALEO)
PO Box 5000, Niagara Falls NY 14304 USA
www.caleoinfo.org
Overview: A medium-sized international organization founded in 1978
Mission: To enable networking & intelligence sharing among law enforcement officers, government law enforcement, & regulatory agencies
Membership: *Member Profile:* Law enforcement officers representing federal, state, city, county, provincial, regional, or municipal police or law enforcement agencies
Chief Officer(s):
Mike Powell, Chair

Canadian Australian Chamber of Commerce
19-29 Martin Pl., Sydney NSW 2000 Australia
e-mail: admin@cacc.com.au
www.cacc.com.au
www.linkedin.com/company/canadian-australian-chamber-of-commerce
Overview: A medium-sized international organization
Mission: To enhance the trade & business relationship between Canada & Australia
Membership: *Fees:* $150-$7,500 AUD
Activities: Organizing & sponsoring events, presentations & trade delegations
Chief Officer(s):
John Secker, Executive Director

Canadian Bull Riders Association See Professional Bull Riders Inc

Canadian Compensation Association See World at Work

Canadian Cultural Centre *Voir* Centre culturel canadien

Canadian Norwegian Business Association (CNBA)
PO Box 449, Sandvika N-1302 Norway
Tel: 47-928-68-757
post@cnba.no
www.cnba.no
Overview: A small international organization
Mission: To strengthen the business & cultural ties between Canada & Norway
Membership: *Fees:* $200 student; $500 individual; $2,500 corporate
Chief Officer(s):
Kristian Kristiansen, Administrator

The Canadian Philatelic Society of Great Britain
12 Milchester House, Staveley Rd., Meads Eastbourne BN20 7JX United Kingdom
Tel: 01323-438-964
cpsofgb@hotmail.com
www.canadianpsgb.org.uk
Overview: A small national organization founded in 1946
Mission: The study of the philately of Canada, including provinces which were separate colonies prior to Confederation
Finances: *Annual Operating Budget:* Less than $50,000; *Funding Sources:* Membership fees
Membership: 420; *Fees:* £16 or $39 CAN or US$39; *Member Profile:* Members mostly in UK, Canada & USA
Activities: Two auctions, March & at Sept. convention; *Library:* by appointment
Chief Officer(s):
Derrick Scoot, President
J.M. Wright, Secretary

Can-Am Border Trade Alliance
PO Box 929, Lewiston NY 14092 USA
Tel: 716-754-8824; Fax: 716-754-8824
canambta@aol.com
canambta.org
Overview: A medium-sized international organization
Mission: To maximize global commercial activity and ensure continued growth of two-way cross border trade along the entire common U.S./Canadian border and assure efficient, productive border crossing capabilities; and also to provide unified leadership for border concern, operations and needs and to act as an effective, proactive and focused border issues resource.
Membership: *Fees:* Schedule available
Chief Officer(s):
James D. Phillips, President & CEO

Carrying Capacity Network (CCN)
PO Box 457, San Francisco CA 94104-0457 USA
e-mail: info@carryingcapacity.org
www.carryingcapacity.org
Overview: A large international organization founded in 1989
Mission: To function as a clearinghouse of information for participants, a forum for discussion of controversial issues & as a catalyst for cooperation among diverse groups involved in carrying capacity issues; To facilitate the understanding of the crucial linkages between population & the environment by exchanging information, disseminating news & encouraging cooperation among environmental, resource conservation, growth control & population stabilization organizations & activists
Finances: *Annual Operating Budget:* $500,000-$1.5 Million
Staff Member(s): 8
Membership: *Fees:* $20 senior/student; $25 adult; $40 sustaining; $100 major; $250 sponsor; $500 benefactor; $1,000 patron
Activities: Offering a Speakers/Writers Bureau; Disseminating information; *Speaker Service:* Yes

Cátedra de Estudios sobre Canadá / Chair of Canadian Studies
Universidad de la Habana, Edificio Varona (altos), Flasco Cuba, Havana 10400 Cuba
Overview: A small international organization founded in 1994
Mission: The Chair promotes in Cuba knowledge of the history & current socio-economic reality of Canada, as well as facilitating knowledge in Canada of Cuba. It coordinates & promotes scientific/technical & cultural exchange & the development of joint activities between the University of Havana & Canadian institutions.
Member of: International Council for Canadian Studies (ICCS)
Chief Officer(s):
Beatriz Diaz, President
beatriz@flacso.uh.cu

Catholic Biblical Federation (CBF) / Fédération biblique catholique (FBC)
St. Ottilien 86941 Germany
Tel: 49-8193-716900; Fax: 49-8193-716999
gensec@c-b-f.org
www.c-b-f.org
www.facebook.com/Cathbibfed
twitter.com/@cbf_gensec
plus.google.com/u/0/109432940173395804882
Overview: A small international charitable organization founded in 1969
Affiliation(s): Catholic Biblical Association of Canada
Staff Member(s): 6
Membership: 300+ in 130 countries
Activities: Workshops; Plenary Assembly
Chief Officer(s):
Jan J. Stefanów, svd, General Secretary

Cell Stress Society International (CSSI)
91 North Eagleville Rd., Storrs CT 06269-3125 USA
Tel: 860-486-6304; *Fax:* 860-486-5709
www.cellstressresponses.org
Overview: A medium-sized international organization
Mission: To promote stress response research & the dissemination of information; To encourage clinical & industrial applications of research
Member of: Society of the International Union of Biological Sciences
Membership: 230; *Fees:* US$55 student/member from developing countries; US$240 regular membership; US$1,000 lifetime membership
Activities: Supporting young scientists in the field of stress response; Cooperating with related organizations; Increasing public awareness of advances in stress response research
Chief Officer(s):
M. Gabriella Santoro, President
Helen Neumann, General Secretary
Publications:
- Cell Stress & Chaperones: An Integrative Journal of Stress Biology & Medicine
Type: Journal; *Editor:* Lawrence E. Hightower; *ISSN:* 1355-8145; *Price:* Free with membership in Cell Stress Society International

Center for Health, Environment & Justice (CHEJ)
PO Box 6806, Falls Church VA 22040-6806 USA
Tel: 703-237-2249; *Fax:* 703-237-8389
chej@chej.org
www.chej.org
www.facebook.com/CHEJfans
twitter.com/CHEJ
www.youtube.com/CHEJtv
Previous Name: Citizens Clearinghouse for Hazardous Wastes
Overview: A medium-sized national charitable organization founded in 1981
Mission: To help communities win environmental justice
Finances: *Annual Operating Budget:* $500,000-$1.5 Million; *Funding Sources:* Membership dues; donations
Staff Member(s): 14
Membership: 25,000 individual + 7,500 groups; *Fees:* $30 individual; $100 group
Activities: Provides science, organizing & technical assistance to citizens concerned with dioxin, toxic waste, chemical poisons, etc. in their communities; site visits by staff; 130+ self-help guides & fact packs; campaigns: Stop Dioxin Exposure; childproofing communities; BESAFE; *Awareness Events:* March into Spring, March; *Internships:* Yes; *Speaker Service:* Yes; *Library:* Open to public
Chief Officer(s):
Lois Marie Gibbs, Executive Director/Founder
Sharon Franklin, Finance/Administrative Director

Center for Holocaust & Genocide Studies (CHGS)
Social Sciences Bldg., Univ. of Minnesota, #214, 267 - 19th Ave. South, Minneapolis MN 55455 USA
Tel: 612-624-9007
chgs@umn.edu
www.chgs.umn.edu
www.facebook.com/chgsumn
twitter.com/chgsumn
www.youtube.com/CHGSumn
Overview: A small local organization founded in 1997
Mission: To serve as an independent, academic, resource institution for information & teaching about the Holocaust & contemporary aspects of genocide; to act as consultants to universities, news media, & civic organizations; to support secondary-school classroom educators through workshops & curriculum materials.
Member of: Association of Holocaust Organizations
Affiliation(s): Genocide Watch; Acgis Trust
Finances: *Funding Sources:* Donations
Staff Member(s): 3
Activities: Virtual exhibitions; memorials, testaments; reading & discussion groups; *Internships:* Yes; *Speaker Service:* Yes; *Library:* Open to public
Chief Officer(s):
Alejandro Baer, Director
abaer@umn.edu

Center for Marine Conservation; Center for Environmental Education *See* The Ocean Conservancy

Center for Plant Conservation
PO Box 299, St. Louis MO 63166-0299 USA
Tel: 314-577-9450; *Fax:* 314-577-9465
cpc@mobot.org
www.centerforplantconservation.org
Overview: A medium-sized international organization founded in 1984
Mission: To create a systematic, comprehensive national program of plant conservation, research & education within existing institutions, as a complement to the preservation of genetic diversity through habitat protection; to strengthen its collaborative ties with countries contiguous to the US & its territories - Canada, Mexico & nations of the Greater Antilles; to develop & maintain comprehensive & broadly accessible information systems, national networks & databases concerning the biology, horticulture & conservation status of all nationally endangered native plants of the US
Staff Member(s): 3
Membership: *Fees:* Schedule available
Activities: The National Collection of Endangered Species consists of living plant materials collected from the wild, representing to the greatest extent possible the genetic diversity found in natural populations; Participating Institutions - affiliated botanical gardens & arboreta around the US; Priority Regions - areas facing a major plant extinction crisis; Integrated Conservation; Conservation Research; Information & Data Systems; Economic Plant Research; International Conservation
Chief Officer(s):
Kathryn Kennedy, President & Executive Director

Center for Psychology & Social Change; Center for Psychological Studies in the Nuclear Age *See* John E. Mack Institute

Central European Association for Canadian Studies (CEACS) / Association d'Études Canadiennes en Europe Centrale
Institut de Langues et Littératures Romanes, Université Masaryk, A. Nováka 1, Brno 60200 Czech Republic
Tel: 420-542-128-309; *Fax:* 420-542-128-238
www.cecanstud.cz
www.facebook.com/406209616116606
Overview: A small international organization founded in 2003
Mission: The CEACS brings together university teachers, researchers and students from the Central European region who are doing work related to Canada
Membership: 165; *Member Profile:* Members from Bulgaria, Croatia, the Czech Republic, Hungary, Romania, Serbia & Montenegro, Slovakia & Slovenia
Chief Officer(s):
Diana Yankova, President
yankova@nlcv.net
Rodica Albu, Secretary
rr_albu@yahoo.co.uk

Centre culturel canadien / Canadian Cultural Centre
5, rue de Constantine, Paris 75007 France
Tél: 33-144-432-190; *Téléc:* 33-144-432-199
info@canada-culture.org
www.canada-culture.org
www.facebook.com/centreculturelcanadien
twitter.com/cc_canadien
www.youtube.com/user/CCCanadienParis
Aperçu: *Dimension:* petite; *Envergure:* internationale; fondée en 1970
Mission: Les services culturels de l'Ambassade du Canada appuient et présentent plusieurs aspects de l'activité culturelle canadienne en France; de nombreuses manifestations culturelles sont organisées par les services des arts de la scène, des industries culturelles et des arts visuels conjointement avec des organismes français à Paris et en province, à l'occasion de festivals, de spectacles, de sorties de films, de livres ou de disques
Affiliation(s): Canadian Conference of the Arts
Finances: *Budget de fonctionnement annuel:* $100,000-$250,000
Membre(s) du personnel: 16
Activités: *Service de conférenciers:* Oui; *Bibliothèque:* Bibliothèque publique

Centre d'Études Canadiennes de l'Université Libre de Bruxelles *See* Centre d'Études Nord-Américaines de l'Université Libre de Bruxelles

Centre d'Études Nord-Américaines de l'Université Libre de Bruxelles
Faculté de Philosophie et Lettres, Univ. Libre de Bruxelles, Stn. 175/01, 50, av F.D. Roosevelt, Brussels 1050 Belgium
Tel: 32-2-650-3807; *Fax:* 32-2-650-3919
mlebrun@admin.ulb.ac.be
www.ulb.ac.be//cena
Previous Name: Centre d'Études Canadiennes de l'Université Libre de Bruxelles
Overview: A small international organization founded in 1982
Membership: *Member Profile:* Professors, primarily in the humanities, & experts in fields as varied as literature, sociology, law, history, media & computer science
Activities: Research topics: the coexistence of linguistic communities & its impact on history, politics, sociology & culture; the secularization of society (in particular Québec society); relations between Belgium & Canada since the late nineteenth century; Belgian immigration to Canada; gender studies; anglophone & francophone literatures; the economic & institutional evolution of the two states; comparative analysis of museums; & the status of artists
Chief Officer(s):
Serge Jaumain, Director
sjaumain@ulb.ac.be

Centre du Commerce International *See* International Trade Centre

Centre for Environmental Law & Development *See* Foundation for International Environmental Law & Development

Centre international d'informations de sécurité et de santé au travail *See* International Occupational Safety & Health Information Network

La Chaine bleue mondiale *See* World Blue Chain for the Protection of Animals & Nature

Chair of Canadian Studies *See* Cátedra de Estudios sobre Canadá

Chambre de Commerce Internationale *See* International Chamber of Commerce

Chartered Institute of Public Finance & Accountancy (CIPFA)
3 Robert St., London WC2N 6RL United Kingdom
Tel: 020 7543 5600; *Fax:* 020 7543 5700
customerliaison@cipfa.org
www.cipfa.org.uk
www.linkedin.com/company/cipfa
www.facebook.com/CIPFA.org
twitter.com/cipfa
Overview: A medium-sized international organization
Mission: To promote high performance in public financial services; To advance public finance; To support improved public financial services
Membership: 14,000; *Member Profile:* Persons in public finance
Activities: Providing information & guidance; Offering professional, financial, & management development programs; Providing consultancy services; Collaborating other accountancy bodies, the public sector, & donors
Chief Officer(s):
Jaki Salisbury, President
Rob Whiteman, Chief Executive
Adrian Pulham, Director, Education & Membership
Publications:
- Chartered Institute of Public Finance & Accountancy Annual Report & Accounts
Type: Yearbook; *Frequency:* Annually
- Public Finance Magazine
Type: Magazine; *Frequency:* Weekly

Chartered Professional Accountants of Bermuda
Sofia House, 48 Church St., 1st Fl., Hamilton HM 12 Bermuda
Tel: 441-292-7479; *Fax:* 441-295-3121
Also Known As: CPA Bermuda
Previous Name: The Institute of Chartered Accountants of Bermuda
Overview: A small international organization founded in 1973 overseen by Chartered Professional Accountants Canada
Mission: To build a reputation of reliability on behalf of members among the public
Finances: *Funding Sources:* Membership dues
Membership: 9 firms; *Fees:* Schedule available
Activities: Professional development; *Internships:* Yes

Chevaliers de Colomb *See* Knights of Columbus

Children's Tumor Foundation (CTF)
120 Wall St., 16th Fl., New York NY 10005-3904 USA
Tel: 212-344-6633; *Fax:* 212-747-0004
Toll-Free: 800-323-7938

info@ctf.org
www.ctf.org
www.linkedin.com/company/children's-tumor-foundation
www.facebook.com/childrenstumor
twitter.com/childrenstumor
Previous Name: National NF Foundation
Overview: A medium-sized national charitable organization founded in 1978
Mission: To sponsor research to find the cause of & cure for both types of neurofibromatosis - NF1 & NF2; To promote clinical activities which assure individuals with NF ready access to the highest calibre of medical care; To develop programs to increase public awareness of NF; To provide support services for patients & families, with referrals to qualified healthcare professionals
Member of: International NF Association
Affiliation(s): NF Associations worldwide
Finances: Annual Operating Budget: $3 Million-$5 Million
Staff Member(s): 2; 1000 volunteer(s)
Membership: 50,000+; Fees: $40
Activities: Awareness Events: NF Awareness Month, May; Speaker Service: Yes
Chief Officer(s):
Annette Bakker, President & Chief Scientific Officer
Simon Vukelj, Vice-President, Marketing & Communications
Salvo La Rosa, Vice-President, Research & Development

Christian Peace Conference (CPC)
PO Box 136, Prokopova 4, Praha 3, Praha 13011 Czech Republic
Tel: 420-2-2278-1800; Fax: 420-2-2278-1801
christianpeace@volny.cz
www.volny.cz/christianpeace/cpc
Overview: A small international organization founded in 1958
Finances: Funding Sources: Fundraising; donations; membership fees
Membership: Member Profile: Churches; groups; individuals
Publications:
• CPC [Christian Peace Conference] Information
Type: Magazine; Frequency: Bimonthly

Christian Science / La Première Église du Christ, Scientiste
The First Church of Christ, Scientist, 210 Massachusetts Ave., Boston MA 02115 USA
Tel: 617-450-2000
Toll-Free: 888-424-2535
Other Communication: www.marybakereddylibrary.org
info@churchofchristscientist.org
christianscience.com
www.facebook.com/worldwidechristianscience
twitter.com/cschurches
plus.google.com/104001952392468849471
Also Known As: The Mother Church
Overview: A large international organization founded in 1879
Mission: To believe in one God, the Bible & in Christ Jesus as the Messiah; that the application of the laws of God are practical & provable, hence scientific
Finances: Annual Operating Budget: Greater than $5 Million; Funding Sources: Donations
Staff Member(s): 850
Membership: 2,200 churches in over 70 countries; Member Profile: Individuals who are open to doctrines of the Christian Science textbook: Science & Health with Key to the Scriptures, by Rev. Mary Baker Eddy
Activities: Weekly services and testimonial meetings; Sunday School for children; Worldwide speakers bureau; Retail book stores; Christian Science Reading Rooms; Christian Science programs & Weekly Bible Lessons broadcasted on public media; Internships: Yes; Speaker Service: Yes; Library: Mary Baker Eddy Library for the Betterment of Humanity; Open to public by appointment
Chief Officer(s):
Channing Walker, President
Russ Gerber, Manager, Committee on Publication
Publications:
• The Christian Science Journal
Type: Magazine; Frequency: Monthly
Profile: www.spirituality.com/journal
• The Christian Science Monitor
Type: Newspaper; Frequency: Weekly; Editor: Marshall Ingwerson; Price: Print & digital: $5.99/mth. Digital: $4.99/mth.
Profile: Weekly review of global news & ideas

Citizens Clearinghouse for Hazardous Wastes See Center for Health, Environment & Justice

CIVICUS: World Alliance for Citizen Participation
PO Box 933, 24 Gwigwi Mrwebi St., Johannesburg 2135 South Africa
Tel: +27 11 833 5959; Fax: +27 11 833 7997
Other Communication: membership@civicus.org
info@civicus.org
www.civicus.org
Overview: A small international organization
Mission: To strengthen citizen action & civil society around the globe towards a more just & equitable world; To promote the rights of citizens to organize & act collectively; To foster interaction between civil society & other institutions
Membership: 450+; Member Profile: Citizens from 110 countries, including individuals, youth, business associates, citizen organizations, & nongovernmental grantmaking organizations
Activities: Advocating for citizen participation; Amplifying the opinions of ordinary people; Increasing the effectiveness of civil society organizations
Chief Officer(s):
Ingrid Srinath, Secretary General
Katsuji Imata, Deputy Secretary General, Programs
Sebastian Njagi Runguma, Manager, Planning & Learning
Sandra Pires, Manager, Membership
Devendra Tak, Manager, Communications & Media
Publications:
• Affinity Group of National Associations (AGNA) Newsletter
Type: Newsletter
• Civil Society Index (CSI) Newsletter
Type: Newsletter; Frequency: Quarterly
Profile: Project updates
• Civil Society Watch (CSW) Monthly Bulletin
Type: Newsletter; Frequency: Monthly
• e-CIVICUS [a publication of CIVICUS: World Alliance for Citizen Participation]
Type: Newsletter; Frequency: Weekly
Profile: Developments in civil society organizations around the world

Clean Water Action
#400, 1444 Eye St. NW, Washington DC 20005 USA
Tel: 202-895-0420; Fax: 202-895-0438
cwa@cleanwater.org
www.cleanwateraction.org
www.facebook.com/CleanWaterAction
twitter.com/cleanh2oaction
www.youtube.com/cleanwateraction
Overview: A large international organization founded in 1971
Mission: To protect our environment, health, economic stability, & community quality of life
Membership: 1,200,000
Activities: Organizing grassroots groups & coalitions to elect environmental candidates; Creating environmentally safe jobs & businesses
Chief Officer(s):
Robert Wendelgass, President & CEO
bwendelgass@cleanwater.org
Kathy Aterno, National Managing Director
katerno@cleanwater.org
Lynn Thorp, Director, National Campaigns
lthorp@cleanwater.org
Michael Kelly, Director, Communications
mkelly@cleanwater.org

Climate Institute
900 - 17 St. NW, Washington DC 20006 USA
Tel: 202-552-4723; Fax: 202-737-6410
info@climate.org
www.climate.org
Overview: A medium-sized international charitable organization founded in 1986
Mission: To help maintain the balance between climate & life on earth; To strive to be a source of objective, reliable information & a trustworthy facilitator of dialogue among scientists, policy makers, business executives, & citizens
Finances: Funding Sources: Foundation; US government; Corporations
Staff Member(s): 12
Membership: Member Profile: Scientists & environmentalists of many nationalities
Activities: Internships: Yes; Speaker Service: Yes; Library: by appointment
Chief Officer(s):
John Topping, President
jtopping@climate.org
Crispin Tickell, Chair

Publications:
• Climate Alert
Editor: Corrine Kisner
Profile: Quarterly Newsletter
• Sudden & Disruptive Climate Change: Exploring the Real Risks & How We Can Avoid Them
Type: Book; Editor: Michael C. MacKracken et al.
Profile: An outline of the risks of & solutions to climate change

Club de Madrid / Club of Madrid
Palacio del Marqués de Cañete, Calle Mayor, 69, Planta 1, Madrid 28013 Spain
Tel: 34-911-548-230; Fax: 34-911-548-240
clubmadrid@clubmadrid.org
www.clubmadrid.org
www.facebook.com/ClubMadrid
twitter.com/CLUBdeMADRID
www.youtube.com/clubmadrid
Overview: A small international organization founded in 2001
Mission: To contribute to strengthening democracy in the world
Membership: Member Profile: Former heads of state & government; representatives of constituent foundations
Chief Officer(s):
Carlos Westendrop, Secretary General
Vike-Freiberga Vaira, President

Club of Madrid See Club de Madrid

Coalition for Education in the Outdoors
c/o State University of New York College at Cortland, PO Box 2000, Cortland NY 13045-0900 USA
Tel: 607-753-4968; Fax: 607-753-5982
outdoored@outdooredcoalition.org
www.outdooredcoalition.org
Overview: A medium-sized international organization founded in 1987
Mission: To assist in identifying the networking needs of its affiliates & to seek ways to meet those needs
Membership: Fees: Schedule available; Member Profile: A network of agencies, institutions, associations, centres, businesses & organizations linked & communicating in support of the broad purposes of education in, for, & about the outdoors
Activities: Speaker Service: Yes
Chief Officer(s):
Charles H. Yaple, Executive Director
Publications:
• Taproot
Profile: Quarterly Journal

Coalition for International Criminal Court (CICC)
c/o WFM, #1715, 708 - 3rd Ave., New York NY 10017 USA
Tel: 212-687-2863; Fax: 212-599-1332
cicc@coalitionfortheicc.org
www.iccnow.org
www.facebook.com/CoalitionfortheInternationalCriminalCourt
twitter.com/_CICC
Overview: A large international organization
Mission: To advocate for a fair, effective, & independent international criminal court
Membership: 2,500+ NGOs in 150 countries
Chief Officer(s):
William R. Pace, Convenor
Jelena Pia-Comella, Deputy Executive Director
Publications:
• Africa Update [a publication of the Coalition for International Criminal Court]
Type: Newsletter; Frequency: s-a.
Profile: ICC developments in relation to Africa
• Al Mahkamah [a publication of the Coalition for International Criminal Court]
Type: Newsletter
Profile: ICC developments in the Middle East & North Africa; available in Arabic & English
• Asia Update [a publication of the Coalition for International Criminal Court]
Type: Newsletter; Frequency: bi-m.
Profile: ICC developments in relation to Asia
• The Bulletin [a publication of the Coalition for International Criminal Court]
Frequency: bi-m.
Profile: Featuring timely updates about the work of the ICC and the CICC
• LAC Update [a publication of the Coalition for International Criminal Court]
Type: Newsletter

Profile: ICC developments in relation to Latin America & the Caribbean; available in Spanish
• The Monitor [a publication of the Coalition for International Criminal Court]
Type: Journal; *Frequency:* s-a.
Profile: Available in English, French and Spanish

CODA International Training (CIT)
ADKC Centre, Whitstable House, Silchester Rd., London W10 6SB UK
Tel: 44-208-960-8888
www.coda-international.org.uk
Previous Name: Tecnica England
Overview: A small international charitable organization founded in 1986
Mission: To work in partnership with civil society organisations from Latin America, Southern Africa & the Middle East, enabling skill transfer through volunteers who provide training & consultancy in developing countries, with the aim of promoting economic & social equality, & sustainable change without dependency. It is a registered charity in the U.K.
Affiliation(s): tecNICA Canada; Women and Law in Southern Africa (WLSA); KwaZulu Natal; Guatemala Community Movement (GCM); East Jerusalem YMCA; Confederation of Salvadorean Workers; Nicaraguan Association for Community Integration
Finances: *Funding Sources:* Comic Relief; DFID; MRDF; Big Lottery Fund; Hilden Foundation; UNISON/UIDF; Individual donors
Staff Member(s): 2
Activities: Capacity building; health clinics; literacy projects; women's groups; electronics; traffic engineering; preventive health database development; economic issues; English as a Foreign Language
Chief Officer(s):
Kevin Caulfield, Chair
Samira Yussuf, Executive Director

Coffin-Lowry Syndrome Foundation (CLSF)
675 Kalima Pl. NW, Issaquah WA 98027 USA
Tel: 425-427-0939
coffinlowry@gmail.com
clsf.info
Overview: A small international organization founded in 1991
Mission: To serve as a clearinghouse of information on the syndrome, a support group for parents with CLS children & a general forum for exchanging experiences, advice & information with other CLS families; to seek to become a visible group in the medical, scientific, educational & professional communities in order to facilitate referrals of newly diagnosed individuals, & to encourage medical & behavioural research in order to improve methods of social integration of CLS individuals
Finances: *Funding Sources:* Donations
Chief Officer(s):
Mary C. Hoffman, Chairperson

Colonial Waterbird Society *See* The Waterbird Society

Comité international des Sports des Sourds *See* International Committee of Sports for the Deaf

Comité international pour la documentation du Conseil international des musées *See* International Committee for Documentation of the International Council of Museums

Comité maritime international (CMI) / International Maritime Committee
Ernest Van Dijckkaai 8, Antwerpen B-2000 Belgium
Tel: 32-3-231-1331; *Fax:* 32-3-231-1333
info@comitemaritime.org
www.comitemaritime.org
Overview: A medium-sized international organization founded in 1897
Mission: To contribute by all appropriate means & activities to the unification of maritime law
Affiliation(s): Canadian Maritime Law Association
Membership: 53 associations; *Committees:* Audit; CMI Charitable Trust; CMI Archives; CMI Young Memvers; Collection of Outstanding Contributions; Conferences/Seminars; Constitution; Genera; Average Interest Rates; Interpretation of International Organizations; Jurisprudence Database; National Associations; Nominating; Planning; Promotion of Maritime Conventions; PUblications & Website
Activities: *Library:* CMI-Secretariat; Open to public by appointment
Chief Officer(s):

Stuart Hetherington, President
swh@cbp.com.au
John Hare, Secretary General
john.hare@uct.ac.za

Commission des Grands Lacs *See* Great Lakes Commission

Commission internationale de diplomatique
a/s École nationale des Chartes, 19, rue de la Sorbonne, Paris F-75005 France
Tél: 00-33-1-5542-7500; *Téléc:* 00-33-1-5542-7509
cidipl.org
Également appelé: Internal Commission of the Comité international des sciences historiques
Aperçu: *Dimension:* petite; *Envergure:* internationale; Organisme sans but lucratif; fondée en 1971
Mission: Organiser des réunions de spécialistes dans les sciences auxiliaires de l'histoire, notamment l'analyse de l'authenticité des chartes de l'ancien régime (diplomatique).
Membre: 77; *Critères d'admissibilite:* Historien, spécialisé en diplomatique
Membre(s) du bureau directeur:
Olivier Guyotjeannin, Président
ogj@wanadoo.fr
Thérèse de Hemptinne, Secrétaire générale
Therese.deHemptinne@Gent.be

Commission internationale de l'éclairage *See* International Commission on Illumination

Commission internationale de la santé au travail *See* International Commission on Occupational Health

Commission internationale des irrigations & du drainage *See* International Commission on Irrigation & Drainage

Commission Internationale du Genie Rural *See* International Commission of Agricultural & Biosystems Engineering

Commission on Sustainable Development *See* Division of Sustainable Development

Committee for the National Institutes for the Environment *See* National Council for Science & the Environment

Committee on Nutrition in the Commonwealth *See* Commonwealth Human Ecology Council

Commonwealth Association of Surveying & Land Economy (CASLE)
c/o Faculty of Environment & Technology, Univ. of West England, Coldharbour Lane, Bristol BS16 1QY United Kingdom
Tel: 44-117-328-3036
www.casle.org
Overview: A medium-sized international organization founded in 1969
Mission: To maintain & strengthen professional links between Commonwealth countries, with the aim of assisting each country to achieve the scale, quality & integrity of surveying services that it requires; To foster the establishment of professional societies in countries where none exists & to promote their usefulness for the public advantage
Finances: *Annual Operating Budget:* $50,000-$100,000
Membership: 40 societies; *Member Profile:* Open to leading society in each surveying discipline in each Commonwealth country; *Committees:* Management Board
Activities: Conferences/seminars; research into sustainable development
Chief Officer(s):
Susan M. Spedding, Secretary General
susan.spedding@uwe.ac.uk

Commonwealth Geographical Bureau (CGB)
c/o Dept. of Geography, Universitt of Otago, PO Box 56, Dunedin New Zealand
www.commonwealthgeography.org
Overview: A small international organization founded in 1968
Mission: To promote the study & practice of geography at all levels within the Commonwealth, especially in developing countries
Affiliation(s): International Geographical Union
Finances: *Funding Sources:* Commonwealth Foundation; Trusts
Membership: *Member Profile:* Commonwealth geographers
Activities: Organizing workshops
Chief Officer(s):
Tony Binns, President
j.a.binns@geography.otago.ac.nz
Nigel Walford, Treasurer
nwalford@kingston.ac.uk

Commonwealth Human Ecology Council (CHEC)
Church House, 4 Hurlingham Studios, Ranelagh Gardens, London SW6 3PA United Kingdom
Tel: 44-20-3689-0979
contact@checinternational.org
www.checinternational.org
www.facebook.com/247748745381618
twitter.com/CwHumanEcology
Previous Name: Committee on Nutrition in the Commonwealth
Overview: A medium-sized international charitable organization founded in 1969
Mission: To challenge governments to create policies in support of ecological & sustainable communities
Affiliation(s): In consultative status with UN ECOSOC (Economic & Social Council)
Finances: *Funding Sources:* Commonwealth Foundation; UK Government; UK Lottery; Comic Relief
Membership: *Member Profile:* Government; non-government; professionals; cross section of communities & civil society

Commonwealth Parliamentary Association (CPA)
Secretariat, Westminster House, #700, 7 Millbank, London SW1P 3JA United Kingdom
Tel: 44-20-7799-1460; *Fax:* 44-20-7222-6073
hq.sec@cpahq.org
www.cpahq.org
en-gb.facebook.com/CPAHQ
twitter.com/cpa_secretariat
www.flickr.com/photos/cpa_hq
Previous Name: Empire Parliamentary Association
Overview: A medium-sized international charitable organization founded in 1911
Mission: To promote knowledge & understanding of the constitutional, legislative, economic, social & cultural systems within a parliamentary democratic framework
Membership: 17,000; *Member Profile:* British Commonwealth members of parliament & legislature; *Committees:* Executive
Activities: *Internships:* Yes; *Library:* Parliamentary Information & Reference Centre; by appointment
Chief Officer(s):
William F. Shija, Secretary General
Publications:
• The Parliamentarian
Editor: Andrew Imlach; *Price:* £34 annual subscription; £11 per issue
Profile: Quarterly journal
Canadian Branch (CPA)
Parliament of Canada, 131 Queen St., 5th Fl., Ottawa ON K1A 0A6
Tel: 613-992-2093; *Fax:* 613-995-0212
cpa-apc@parl.gc.ca
www.parl.ca
Chief Officer(s):
Rémi Bourgault, Association Secretary

Commonwealth Pharmaceutical Association *See* Commonwealth Pharmacists Association

Commonwealth Pharmacists Association (CPA)
66 - 68 East Smithfield, London E1W 1A2 United Kingdom
Tel: 44-0-7761-574284
admin@commonwealthpharmacy.org
www.commonwealthpharmacy.org
www.facebook.com/509918019095288
Previous Name: Commonwealth Pharmaceutical Association
Overview: A small international organization founded in 1969
Mission: To facilitate the dissemination of knowledge & information about the professional practice of pharmacy & the pharmaceutical sciences; To foster a high standard of control over the quality & distribution of drugs by professional means, & by encouraging the implementation of appropriate legislation
Affiliation(s): Canadian Pharmaceutical Association
Membership: 34; *Fees:* £15; *Member Profile:* Pharmaceutical societies, associations & boards within the Commonwealth
Activities: Symposiums; *Library:* Information Centre; Not open to public
Chief Officer(s):
Raymond Anderson, President

Compressed Gas Association, Inc. (CGA)
#103, 14501 George Carter Way, Chantilly VA 20151 USA
Tel: 703-788-2700; *Fax:* 703-961-1831
Other Communication: customerservice@cganet.com
cga@cganet.com
www.cganet.com
Overview: A small international organization founded in 1913

Mission: To develop & promote safety standards for the industrial gas industry
Membership: *Member Profile:* Manufacturers, suppliers, distributors, & transporters of gases, cryogenic liquids, & related products in Canada & the United States; *Committees:* Canadian Cylinder Specification; Canadian Medical, Food, & Beverage Gases & Equipment; Canadian Pressure Vessels & Piping Sys.; Canadian Health, Safety, & Environment; Canadian Transportation; Acetylene; Atmospheric Gases & Equipment; Bulk Distribution Equipment & Standards; Carbon Dioxide; Compressed Gas Emergency Action Plan; Cylinder Specifications; Cylinder Valve; Distribution & Fleet Safety; Environmental; Food Gases; Hazard Comm.; Hazardous Materials Codes; Hydrogen Tech.; HYCO; Industrial Gases Apparatus; Liquefied Petroleum Gas; Medical Equipment; Medical Gases; Security; Safety/Health
Activities: Working with governmental agencies to produce standards & regulations; Promoting compliance with regulations in the workplace; Providing access to edcuational publications & videos; Offering networking opportunities
Awards:
• Compressed Gas Association Safety Awards
Meetings/Conferences:
• Compressed Gas Association Canada Annual Meeting 2018, 2018
Scope: National
Publications:
• Compressions [a publication of the Compressed Gas Association]
Type: Newsletter; *Frequency:* Quarterly; *Price:* Free with Compressed Gas Association membership
Profile: Association & industry news

Concerned Educators Allied for a Safe Environment (CEASE)
55 Frost St., Cambridge MA 2140 USA
Tel: 617-661-8347
info@peaceeducators.org
www.peaceeducators.org
www.facebook.com/peace.educators
Overview: A small national organization founded in 1979
Mission: To create safe world for children; to seek to end the violence in society & remove the root causes of violence by advocating for peace, justice & economic opportunity
Member of: Survival Education Fund
Affiliation(s): National Association for the Education of Young Children
Finances: *Annual Operating Budget:* Less than $50,000; *Funding Sources:* Subscriptions; membership dues; donations
6 volunteer(s)
Membership: 1,000; *Fees:* $10; $5 student; *Member Profile:* Early childhood educators & trainers
Activities: Workshops; seminars
Chief Officer(s):
Lucy Stroock
Susan Hopkins
Chris Lamm
Lucy Stroock, Sec.-Treas.

Confédération internationale de sages-femmes *See* International Confederation of Midwives

Confederation of Meningitis Organizations
Newminster House, Baldwin St., Bristol BS1 1LT UK
Tel: 44-333-405-6264
info@comomeningitis.org
www.comomeningitis.org
www.facebook.com/ConfederationOfMeningitisOrganisations
twitter.com/COMOmeningitis
www.youtube.com/user/COMOmeningitis
Overview: A small international organization
Mission: To prevent meningitis & to lessen the impact of the disease worldwide through education & advocacy
Activities: Developing global advocacy campaigns; Lobbying; Providing resources & support to members
Chief Officer(s):
Chris Head, President

Conférence des Nations Unies sur le commerce et le développement *See* United Nations Conference on Trade & Development

Conference of Great Lakes & St. Lawrence Governors & Premiers
#2700, 20 North Wacker Dr., Chicago IL 60606 USA
Tel: 312-407-0177; *Fax:* 312-407-0038
www.gsgp.org
Previous Name: Council of Great Lakes Governors
Overview: A small international organization founded in 1990
Mission: To facilitate economic growth in the Great Lakes region, including Ontario, Québec, & the Great Lakes states of Illinois, Indiana, Michigan, Minnesota, New York, Ohio, Pennsylvania, & Wisconsin
Finances: *Funding Sources:* Donations
Activities: Hosting webinars for Great Lakes companies; Leading multi-sector trade missions
Chief Officer(s):
David Naftzger, Executive Director
dnaftzger@gsgp.org
Lee Anthony McCarrick, Executive Director, Great Lakes USA
tmccarrick@gsgp.org
Peter R. Johnson, Deputy Director
pjohnson@gsgp.org
Zoë Munro, Program Manager
zmunro@gsgp.org
Michael Piskur, Program Manager
mpiskur@gsgp.org
Publications:
• The Compass [a publication of the Conference of Great Lakes & St. Lawrence Governors & Premiers]
Type: Newsletter; *Frequency:* Quarterly
Profile: Information about the ongoing work of the Conference of Great Lakes & St. Lawrence Governors & Premiers, such as trademissions & trade offices

Conseil des bureaux d'éthique commerciale *See* Council of Better Business Bureaus

Conseil international d'études de l'Europe centrale et orientale (Canada) *See* International Council for Central & East European Studies (Canada)

Conseil international de la musique *See* International Music Council

Conseil International des Agences Bénévoles *See* International Council of Voluntary Agencies

Conseil international des Monuments et des Sites *See* International Council on Monuments & Sites

Conseil international des musées *See* International Council of Museums

Conseil international des sciences de l'animal de laboratoire *See* International Council for Laboratory Animal Science

Conseil international du droit de l'environnement *See* International Council of Environmental Law

Conseil Mondial de l'Energie *See* World Energy Council

Conservation International (CI)
#500, 2011 Crystal Dr., Arlington VA 22202 USA
Tel: 703-341-2400
Toll-Free: 800-429-5660
community@conservation.org
www.conservation.org
www.facebook.com/conservation.intl
twitter.com/conservationorg
www.instagram.com/conservationorg
Overview: A large international charitable organization founded in 1987
Mission: To conserve the Earth's living natural heritage, our global biodiversity, & to demonstrate that human societies are able to live harmoniously with nature
Finances: *Annual Operating Budget:* Greater than $5 Million; *Funding Sources:* Private; government; agencies; foundations
Staff Member(s): 1200
Membership: 5,000; *Fees:* $35; *Member Profile:* Scientists; economists; communicators; educators; conservation professionals
Activities: Center for Applied Biodiversity Science; Critical Ecosystem Partnership Fund; Global Conservation Fund; Center for Environmental Leadership in Business; Field Support; Resources & Communications; *Internships:* Yes; *Library:* Not open to public
Chief Officer(s):
Peter Seligmann, Chairman/Chief Executive Officer
Greg Stone, Executive Vice President
Jennifer Morris, Chief Operating Officer

Consortium of Multiple Sclerosis Centers (CMSC)
359 Main St., #A, Hackensack NJ 07601 USA
Tel: 201-487-1050; *Fax:* 201-678-2290
www.mscare.org
www.linkedin.com/company/cmsc
www.facebook.com/CMSCmscare
twitter.com/mscare
Also Known As: Consortium of MS Centers
Overview: A medium-sized international organization founded in 1986
Mission: To maximize the ability of multiple sclerosis healthcare professionals to improve the quality of life for people affected by multiple sclerosis; To provide information about the most current research results, clinical trials, treatments, & patient education programs
Staff Member(s): 11
Membership: *Fees:* $600 full & associate members; $350 liaison; $150 individual physicians; $100 individual health professionals; $25 student health professionals; *Member Profile:* Multiple sclerosis healthcare providers & researchers from North America; *Committees:* Advocacy; By-Laws; Clinical Care; Finance; Research; Consensus Conferences; Continuing Professional Education; Membership; Website
Activities: Improving the quality of care for patients with multiple sclerosis through international, multidisciplinary communication; Offering networking opportunities; *Speaker Service:* Yes
Chief Officer(s):
Robert Lisak, President
June Halper, Chief Executive Officer
Publications:
• Consortium of Multiple Sclerosis Centers Membership Directory
Type: Directory; *Price:* Free with Consortium of Multiple Sclerosis Centers membership
• International Journal of Multiple Sclerosis Care
Type: Journal; *Frequency:* Quarterly; *Accepts Advertising*; *Editor:* Lael A. Stone, MD
Profile: Peer-reviewed clinical & original research articles on topics of interest to multiple sclerosis healthcare providers

Consortium on Peace Research, Education & Development; Peace Studies Association *See* Peace & Justice Studies Association

Consultative Group on International Agricultural Research (CGIAR)
The World Bank, MSN P6-601, 1818 H Street NW, Washington DC 20433 USA
Tel: 202-473-8951; *Fax:* 202-473-8110
cgiar@worldbank.org
www.cgiar.org
www.facebook.com/CGIARConsortium
twitter.com/CGIAR
Overview: A medium-sized international organization founded in 1971
Mission: To achieve sustainable food security and reduce poverty in developing countries through scientific research and research-related activities in the fields of agriculture, forestry, fisheries, policy, and environment.
Staff Member(s): 1000
Activities: *Library:* Information Center; by appointment
Chief Officer(s):
Frank Rijsberman, CEO

Consumers International (CI)
24 Highbury Cres., London N5 1RX United Kingdom
Tel: 44-20-7226-6663; *Fax:* 44-20-7354-0607
consint@consint.org
www.consumersinternational.org
Overview: A medium-sized international organization founded in 1960
Mission: To protect consumer interests worldwide through institution building, education, research & lobbying of international decision making bodies
Finances: *Annual Operating Budget:* $1.5 Million-$3 Million; *Funding Sources:* Membership fees; Project funding
Staff Member(s): 80
Membership: links the activities of more than 220 consumer groups in 115 countries; *Fees:* Schedule available
Activities: Special services available only to IOCU members, volunteers, correspondents, networks & participants of like-minded organizations: Consumer Alert (a hazard notification issued by the Consumer Interpol; Consumer Interpol seeks to protect consumers from hazardous products, technologies & wastes); Consumer Interpol Memo (disseminates news on health & safety issues); Pesticide Monitor (disseminates information on the work of the Pesticide Action Network, a global network which aims to curb indiscriminate use; *Internships:* Yes; *Speaker Service:* Yes
Chief Officer(s):

Helen McCallum, Contact

Controlled Release Society (CRS)
3340 Pilot Knob Rd., St. Paul MN 55121 USA
Tel: 651-454-7250; Fax: 651-454-0766
crs@scisoc.org
www.controlledreleasesociety.org
Overview: A medium-sized international organization
Mission: To advance the science & technology of controlled release throughout the world
Membership: 3,000; *Member Profile:* Individuals from industry, academia, & government, from over 50 countries, who are involved in the field of controlled release; *Committees:* Awards Committees; Bioactive Materials Track Program; Board of Scientific Advisors; Books Advisory Board; Books Subcommittee; Chapter; China Initiative Subcommittee; Consumer & Diversified Products; CRS Foundation; CRS Journal Subcommittee; Marketing; Educational Workshop / Satellite Meeting Reviewe; Meetings; Membership & Development; Newsletter Subcommittee; Nominating; Planning & Finance; Regulatory Ad Hoc; Veterinary; Webcast; Young Scientist; Young Scientist Mentorship / Protege Subcommittee
Activities: Promoting & sponsoring educational opportunities; Advocating in regulatory affairs; Supporting 16 international chapters & 4 student chapters; Offering a peer to peer network; Informing members of breakthroughs in science & technology
Chief Officer(s):
Ruth B. Schmid, President
Amy Hope, Executive Vice-President
ahope@scisoc.org
Laura Boehland, Director, Marketing
lboehland@scisoc.org
Meetings/Conferences:
• Controlled Release Society 2018 45th Annual Meeting & Exposition, July, 2018, New York, NY
Scope: International
Contact Information: Meeting Manager: Anthony Celenza, Email: acelenza@ahint.com
Publications:
• Controlled Release Society Membership Directory
Type: Directory
• Controlled Release Society Newsletter
Type: Newsletter; *Accepts Advertising; Price:* Free with membership in theControlled Release Society
Profile: Featuring a patent watch on fields of controlled release, information on scientific publications, & techical information in the field of drug delivery
• Journal of Controlled Release
Type: Journal; *Editor:* Kinam Park
Profile: Original research about controlled release & the delivery of drugs & other biologically active agents

Canadian Local Chapter (CRS)
Emmanuel A. Ho, University of Manitoba, 750 McDermot Ave., Winnipeg MB R3E 0T5
Tel: 204-474-6589
www.cc-crs.com
Mission: To promote education in the science & technology of controlled drug delivery
Chief Officer(s):
Emmanuel Ho, President
emmanuel_ho@umanitoba.ca

Cordage Institute (CI)
#1019, 994 Old Eagle School Rd., Wayne PA 19087 USA
Tel: 610-971-4854; Fax: 610-971-4859
info@cordageinstitute.com
www.ropecord.com
www.linkedin.com/company/cordage-institute
Overview: A small national organization founded in 1920
Mission: To serve the operating, trade, government, liaison & technical needs of the cordage, rope, twine & netting industry
Finances: *Funding Sources:* Membership dues; Sale of publications
Membership: 1-99; *Fees:* Schedule available; *Member Profile:* Manufacturers, producers, & resellers of cordage, rope, & twine; *Committees:* Technical; Inter-Association Liaison
Chief Officer(s):
Peter M. Lance, Executive Director
Dave Richards, Technical Director
drichards@ropecord.com
Meetings/Conferences:
• Cordage Institute 2018 Annual Conference, May, 2018, Rancho Bernardo Inn, San Diego, CA
Scope: International
Publications:
• Ropecord News

Frequency: Quarterly
Profile: New products & applications; trade & legal issues; markets; technical information

Council for Exceptional Children (CEC)
#100, 2900 Crystal Dr., Arlington VA 22202-3557 USA
Tel: 888-232-7733; TTY: 866-915-5000
service@cec.sped.org
www.cec.sped.org
www.linkedin.com/company/2756373
www.facebook.com/cechq
twitter.com/CECMembership
www.pinterest.com/cechq
Overview: A large international organization
Mission: To improve the educational success of children & youth with disabilities &/or gifts & talents
Membership: 35,000; *Committees:* Canadian; Diversity; Finance & Audit; Honors; Professional Standards & Practice; Representative Assembly; Student; Yes I Can
Chief Officer(s):
Alexander T. Graham, Executive Director
agraham@cec.sped.org

Council of Better Business Bureaus / Conseil des bureaux d'éthique commerciale
#600, 3033 Wilson Blvd., Arlington VA 22201 USA
Tel: 703-276-0100
www.bbb.org
www.linkedin.com/groups/1917928
www.facebook.com/BetterBusinessBureau
twitter.com/bbb_us
pinterest.com/BBBConsumerNews
Overview: A large international organization
Mission: To protect consumers & the vitality of the free enterprise system; To foster the highest standards of responsibility & probity in business practice by advocating truth in advertising, by assuring integrity in performance of business services, & by voluntary regulation & monitoring activities designed to enhance public trust & confidence in business
Membership: 31,000 organizations
Chief Officer(s):
W. David Hubbard, Chair
Ken K. Patel, Vice-Chair

Council of Biology Editors *See* Council of Science Editors

Council of Great Lakes Governors *See* Conference of Great Lakes & St. Lawrence Governors & Premiers

Council of Science Editors
#304, 10200 W. 44th Ave., Wheat Ridge CO 80033 USA
Tel: 720-881-6046; Fax: 303-422-8894
cse@councilscienceeditors.org
www.councilscienceeditors.org
www.linkedin.com/groups?gid=3103324&trk=hb_side_g
www.facebook.com/CouncilofScienceEditors?ref=ts
twitter.com/CScienceEditors
Previous Name: Council of Biology Editors
Overview: A small international organization
Mission: To improve communications in the life sciences; to educate authors, editors & publishers; to promote effective communication practices in primary & secondary publishing in any form
Membership: 1,200; *Fees:* $164; $43 student; *Committees:* Awards and Honors; Editorial Policy; Education; Finance; Marketing; Membership; Nominating; Program; Publications; Research; Science Editor; Scientific Style and Format; Short Courses & Workshops; Social Media; Sponsorship; Web
Chief Officer(s):
David Stumph, Executive Director

Council on Hemispheric Affairs (COHA)
1250 Connecticut Ave. NW. #1C, Washington DC 20036 USA
Tel: 202-223-4975; Fax: 202-223-4979
coha@coha.org
www.coha.org
www.linkedin.com/in/councilonhemisphericaffairs
www.facebook.com/council.on.hemispheric.affairs
twitter.com/cohastaff
pinterest.com/cohadc
Overview: A medium-sized international organization founded in 1975
Mission: To monitor US-Canadian-Latin American relations in the areas of economics, politics, human rights, trade & diplomacy through public statements, critical analyses & media appearances

Finances: *Funding Sources:* Subscription revenue; private donations
Activities: Issue press releases, submit op-eds to national newspapers for publication; publish biweekly Washington Report on the Hemisphere; provide congressional testimony & media resource; representatives frequently appear on radio & tv programs to analyze news stories; *Internships:* Yes; *Speaker Service:* Yes; *Library*
Chief Officer(s):
Larry Birns, Director

The Cousteau Society (TCS) / Société Cousteau
PO Box 20321, 4 East 27th St., New York NY 10001 USA
Tel: 212-532-2588
communication@cousteau.org
www.cousteau.org
www.facebook.com/CousteauUSA
twitter.com/CousteauTCS
www.youtube.com/user/cousteauenglish
Overview: A large international charitable organization founded in 1973
Mission: Dedicated to the protection & wise management of natural resources & the improvement of life for present & future generations; to promote an increased awareness & knowledge of the beauty & fragility of the planet's resources
Finances: *Annual Operating Budget:* Greater than $5 Million; *Funding Sources:* Membership fees; production contracts
Staff Member(s): 32; 5 volunteer(s)
Membership: 50,000 worldwide including sister organization Equipe Cousteau; *Fees:* $30 individual; $40 family
Activities: Producing films, filmstrips & books on important environmental concerns for the general public
Chief Officer(s):
Francine Cousteau, President

Craft & Hobby Association (CHA)
319 54th St. East, Elmwood Park NJ 07407 USA
Tel: 201-835-1200
info@craftandhobby.org
www.craftandhobby.org
Overview: A medium-sized international organization
Mission: To provide a platform that allows creative arts & hobby professionals to connect & learn; To drive the growth of the creative arts & hobby industry; To increase interest in arts & crafts
Membership: *Fees:* Schedule available; *Member Profile:* Designers, suppliers, buyers, crafters, educators & other professionals in the creative arts & hobby industry
Activities: Offering networking & business events
Chief Officer(s):
Mark Hill, President & CEO
mhill@craftandhobby.org

Canada Chapter
c/o Coast to Coast Events, 4442 Mill Cres., RR#1, Ailsa Craig ON N0M 1A0
Tel: 519-232-9047
www.craftandhobby.org
Chief Officer(s):
Audrey deJong, President

Croplife International
PO Box 35, 326 Louise Ave., Brussels 1050 Belgium
Tel: 32-2-542-0410; Fax: 32-2-542-0419
croplife@croplife.org
www.croplife.org
www.facebook.com/CropLifeIntl
twitter.com/croplifeintl
www.youtube.com/croplifeint
Previous Name: Global Crop Protection Federation; International Group of National Associations of Manufacturers of Agrochemical Products
Overview: A medium-sized international charitable organization
Mission: To act as an ambassador for the pan science industry, encouraging understanding & dialogue whilst promoting agricultural technology in the context of sustainable development
Staff Member(s): 21
Membership: 23; *Member Profile:* Regional crop protection associations
Chief Officer(s):
Howard Minigh, President & CEO
howard.minigh@croplife.org

Cruise Lines International Association, Inc. (CLIA)
#250, 1201 F St. NW, Washington DC 20004 USA
Tel: 202-759-9370; Fax: 202-759-9344
info@cruising.org

www.cruising.org
www.facebook.com/CLIAGlobal
twitter.com/CLIAGlobal
Merged from: International Council of Cruise Lines (ICCL)
Overview: A large international organization founded in 1975
Mission: To promote & develop the cruise industry; To serve as a non-governmental consultative organization to the International Maritime Organization, an agency of the United Nations; To foster a safe, secure, & healthy cruise ship environment
Affiliation(s): 16,000 travel agencies
Membership: 60+ cruise lines; 340+ executive members; 15,000 travel agencies; 25,000 travel agents; *Member Profile:* Major cruise lines that serve North America
Activities: Providing education & training to travel agent members
Chief Officer(s):
Cindy D'Aoust, President & CEO
Tom Fischetti, CFO
tfischetti@cruising.org
Meetings/Conferences:
• Cruise360 2018, April, 2018
Scope: International
Description: An annual cruise conference hosted by Cruise Lines International Association, Inc., including educational training & networking opportunities.
Publications:
• Cruise Industry Source Book
Type: Guidebook
Profile: Profiles of CLIA's member cruise lines & general information about CLIA

Cyclic Vomiting Syndrome Association (CVSA)
PO Box 925, Elkhorn WI 53121 USA
Tel: 414-342-7880
cvsa@cvsaonline.org
www.cvsaonline.org
www.facebook.com/CyclicVomitingSyndromeAssociation
Overview: A medium-sized international charitable organization founded in 1983
Mission: To raise awareness & provide support to those affected by cyclic vomiting
Finances: *Annual Operating Budget:* $100,000-$250,000; *Funding Sources:* Membership fees; Grants; Donations; Fundraising
Staff Member(s): 1; 12 volunteer(s)
Membership: 650; *Fees:* US$35-130; *Member Profile:* Families; professionals
Activities: Advocating for & funding research; Providing outreach initiatives; Offering educational & support opportunities; *Speaker Service:* Yes
Chief Officer(s):
Ruth Novak, Program Manager
Kathleen Adams, President
Meetings/Conferences:
• International Cyclic Vomiting Syndrome Association Adult & Family Conference 2018, June, 2018, Sheraton Milwaukee Brookfield Hotel, Milwaukee, WI
Scope: International
Publications:
• Code V [a publication of the Cyclic Vomiting Syndrome Association]
Type: Newsletter; *Frequency:* 3 pa
Profile: Provides scientific research news, personal stories, & updates relating to Cyclic Vomiting Syndrome
• Highlights [a publication of the Cyclic Vomiting Syndrome Association]
Type: Newsletter; *Frequency:* Monthly
Profile: Contains information about CVS, medical news, & CVSA event info

Dangerous Goods Advisory Council
#740, 1100 H St. NW, Washington DC 20005 USA
Tel: 202-289-4550; *Fax:* 202-289-4074
info@dgac.org
www.hmac.org
www.linkedin.com/groups/2474343/profile
www.facebook.com/dangerousgoodsadvisorycouncil
twitter.com/dgac_hmac
Also Known As: Hazardous Materials Advisory Council
Overview: A medium-sized international organization founded in 1978
Mission: To promote improvement in the safe transportation of hazardous materials/dangerous goods globally by providing education, assistance & information to the private & public sectors, through our unique status with regulatory bodies, & the diversity & technical strengths of our membership
Affiliation(s): Canadian Government
Membership: *Fees:* Schedule available; *Member Profile:* Shippers; carriers; container manufacturers & reconditioners; emergency response/waste clean-up companies; trade associations
Chief Officer(s):
Vaughn Arthur, President
Gail Cooley, Office Manager

Data & Marketing Association (DMA)
#301, 1333 Broadway, New York NY 10018 USA
Tel: 212-768-7277
MemberServices@the-dma.org
www.thedma.org
www.linkedin.com/company/dma
www.facebook.com/dmausa
twitter.com/dma_usa
www.instagram.com/dma.usa
Previous Name: Direct Marketing Association
Overview: A large international organization
Finances: *Funding Sources:* Membership dues
Staff Member(s): 120
Membership: 3,600
Activities: *Speaker Service:* Yes; *Rents Mailing List:* Yes; *Library:* by appointment
Chief Officer(s):
Thomas J. Benton, CEO
Meetings/Conferences:
• Data & Marketing Association "&THEN" Conference 2018, October, 2018, MGM Grand Las Vegas, Las Vegas, NV
Scope: International

DES Action USA
PO Box 7296, Jupiter FL 33468 USA
Toll-Free: 800-337-9288
info@desaction.org
www.desaction.org
www.facebook.com/DESActionUSA
Overview: A small national charitable organization founded in 1979
Mission: To provide public & physician education on special health needs of those exposed to the synthetic estrogen diethylstilbestrol (DES)
Finances: *Annual Operating Budget:* $50,000-$100,000
Staff Member(s): 3
Membership: 1,000-4,999; *Fees:* $40
Chief Officer(s):
Fran Howell, Executive Director

Development Innovations and Networks *Voir* Innovations et réseaux pour le développement

Dictionary Society of North America (DSNA)
PO Box 537, Collingswood NJ 08108-0537 USA
e-mail: dsnaadmin@gmail.com
www.dictionarysociety.com
twitter.com/DictionarySocNA
Overview: A small international charitable organization founded in 1975
Member of: American Council of Learned Societies; National Humanities Alliance
Finances: *Annual Operating Budget:* Less than $50,000
Staff Member(s): 1
Membership: 400; *Fees:* US$60 North America; US$70 elsewhere; *Member Profile:* Academics; professional lexicographers; bibliophiles
Activities: Biennial meeting
Chief Officer(s):
Steve Kleinedler, President
Kory Stamper, Executive Secretary
Awards:
• DSNA Award

Direct Marketing Association *See* Data & Marketing Association

Division of Sustainable Development (DSD)
Dept. of Economic & Social Affairs, UN Secretariat Bldg., 405 East 42nd St., New York NY 10017 USA
Tel: 212-963-4260
dsd@un.org
sustainabledevelopment.un.org
www.facebook.com/UNRioplus20
twitter.com/sustdev
Previous Name: Commission on Sustainable Development
Mission: The Division for Sustainable Development (DSD) promotes, coordinates & implements the United Nations' sustainable development agenda. It is the primary UN office responsible for supporting intergovernmental processes in sustainable development, including the General Assembly & ECOSOC, the Commission on Sustainable Development & the High Level Political Forum on Sustainable Development, as well as processes launched at the United Nations Conference on Sustainable Development (Rio+20), which concluded on June 22, 2012. The Division has five core functions: support for UN intergovernmental processes on sustainable development; analysis & policy development; capacity development at the country level; inter-agency coordination; & knowledge management, communication & outreach. The Division also houses the SIDS Unit, which utilizes the five functions above in support of the Mauritius Strategy of Implementation of the Barbados Programme of Action for Small Island Developing States.
Activities: Promoting dialogue & building partnerships for sustainable development with governments, the international community & the major groups who have a role to play in the transition toward sustainable development, including women, youth, indigenous peoples, non-governmental organizations, local authorities, workers & trade unions, business & industry, the scientific community & farmers
Chief Officer(s):
Nikhil Seth, Director

Door & Access Systems Manufacturers Association (DASMA)
1300 Sumner Ave., Cleveland OH 44115-2851 USA
Tel: 216-241-7333; *Fax:* 216-241-0105
www.dasma.org
Overview: A medium-sized international organization
Mission: To represent door & access control products manufacturers in North America; To improve & advance the door & access systems manufacturing industry
Membership: 90+; *Member Profile:* Active members consist of door & access systems manufacturers; Associate members consist of manufacturers or suppliers of raw materials or door & access system components; Professional members consist of testing laboratories or other professional industry experts; *Committees:* Audit; Commercial & Residential Garage Door Technical; Door Operator & Electronics Door Operator; Exective; Gate Operator; Magazine/Marketing; Product Liability & Safety; Task Force on Industry Reputation; Training & Education
Activities: *Rents Mailing List:* Yes
Chief Officer(s):
John H. Addington, Executive Director, 216-241-7333 Ext. 7732
jaddington@thomasamc.com
Joseph R. Hetzel, Director, Technical
jhetzel@thomasamc.com
Jay D. Johnson, Director, Architectural Services
jjohnson@thomasamc.com
Rachel James, Administrator, Client Services
rjames@thomasamc.com
Publications:
• Door + Access Systems Magazine [a publication of the Door & Access Systems Manufacturers Association]
Type: Magazine; *Accepts Advertising; Editor:* Tom Wadsworth

Ducks Unlimited Inc. (DU)
1 Waterfowl Way, Memphis TN 38120 USA
Tel: 901-758-3825
Toll-Free: 800-453-8257
www.ducks.org
www.facebook.com/DucksUnlimited
twitter.com/ducksunlimited
www.youtube.com/ducksunlimitedinc
Overview: A medium-sized international organization founded in 1937
Mission: To fulfill the annual life cycle needs of North American waterfowl by protecting, enhancing, restoring & managing important wetlands & associated uplands
Membership: *Fees:* $35
Chief Officer(s):
Dale Hall, Chief Executive Officer
Publications:
• Ducks Unlimited Magazine
Editor: Tom Fulgham
Profile: Bimonthly magazine

Earth Island Institute (EII)
#460, 2150 Allston Way, Berkeley CA 94704-1375 USA
Tel: 510-859-9100; *Fax:* 510-859-9091
www.earthisland.org

www.facebook.com/EarthIslandInstitute
twitter.com/earthisland
Overview: A large international organization founded in 1982
Mission: To develop innovative projects for the conservation, preservation & restoration of the global environment
Finances: *Annual Operating Budget:* $3 Million-$5 Million; *Funding Sources:* Membership dues; grants; contributions
Staff Member(s): 65; 25 volunteer(s)
Membership: 15,000; *Fees:* US$25 regular; US$15 student/limited income
Activities: Operating more than 40 projects, including: Baikal Watch; Borneo Project; Campaign to Safeguard America's Waters; Centre for Safe Energy; Global Service Corps; International Marine Mammal Project; Women's Earth Alliance; *Library:* by appointment
Chief Officer(s):
Michael Mitrani, President
Dave Phillips, Executive Director, 510-859-9145
davep@earthisland.org
Publications:
• Earth Island Journal
Type: Magazine; *Frequency:* q.; *Accepts Advertising*; *Price:* US $9.95

• IslandWire [a publication of Earth Island Institute]
Type: Newsletter
Profile: Campaign updates

Earthwatch Institute
114 Western Ave., Boston MA 02134 USA
e-mail: info@earthwatch.org.uk
www.earthwatch.org
www.facebook.com/Earthwatch
twitter.com/earthwatch_org
www.youtube.com/user/EarthwatchInstitute
Overview: A large international charitable organization
Mission: To engage people worldwide in scientific field research & education
Finances: *Annual Operating Budget:* Greater than $5 Million
Staff Member(s): 50; 5 volunteer(s)
Membership: 5,000-14,999
Activities: *Internships:* Yes; *Speaker Service:* Yes
Chief Officer(s):
Scott Kania, Chief Executice Officer, International
Awards:
• Earthwatch Research Grants
To engage people worldwide in scientific field research and education to promote the understanding and action necessary for a sustainable environment.

East African Wild Life Society (EAWLS)
PO Box 20110-00200, Nairobi 00200 Kenya
Tel: 254-20-387-4145; *Fax:* 254-20-387-0335
info@eawildlife.org
www.eawildlife.org
www.facebook.com/eawildlife
twitter.com/SwaraMag
Overview: A medium-sized international organization founded in 1956
Mission: To promote the conservation & wise use of wildlife & the environment in East Africa
Member of: World Conservation Union
Finances: *Funding Sources:* Membership fees; shop fund; donations
Membership: *Fees:* Schedule available
Activities: Education & awareness; advocacy; monitoring of species; field projects; *Speaker Service:* Yes; *Library:* by appointment
Chief Officer(s):
Michael Gachanja, Executive Director

Eastern Apicultural Society of North America, Inc. (EAS)
c/o Loretta Surprenant, PO Box 300, Essex NY 12936 USA
Tel: 518-963-7593; *Fax:* 518-963-7593
secretary@easternapiculture.org
www.easternapiculture.org
Overview: A medium-sized international organization founded in 1955
Mission: To educate the beekeeping community in eastern the eastern United States & Canada; To promote honey bee culture; To encourage excellent bee research
Membership: *Fees:* $25 / year individuals & families; $50 / year provincial, state, county, & regional associations; $250 life membership; *Member Profile:* Beginning & advanced beekeepers from the eastern United States & Canada

Activities: Sponsoring awards for graduate students & bee researchers; Offering modest research grants
Chief Officer(s):
Jim Bobb, Chair
chairman@easternapiculture.org
Kim Flottum, President
president2009@easternapiculture.org
Loretta Surprenant, Secretary
secretary@easternapiculture.org
John Tulloch, Treasurer
treasurer@easternapiculture.org
Meetings/Conferences:
• Eastern Apicultural Society 2018 Annual Conference & Short Course, August, 2018, Hampton Roads Convention Center, Hampton, VA
Scope: International
Attendance: 500
Description: Annual business meeting, lectures, workshops, short courses, & vendor displays for beginning & advanced beekeepers
Publications:
• EAS Journal
Type: Journal; *Frequency:* Quarterly; *Accepts Advertising*;
Editor: Kathy Summers-Flottum
Profile: Society news, including executive reports, meetings, & honey shows

Echange Photographique Franco Canadien
55 rue Dammartin, étage 1, Roubaix 59100 France
Aperçu: *Dimension:* petite; *Envergure:* internationale
Mission: Rapprocher les étudiants par la production photographique; échange culturel franco canadien

Ecological Society of America (ESA)
#700, 1990 M St. NW, Washington DC 20036 USA
Tel: 202-833-8773; *Fax:* 202-833-8775
esahq@esa.org
www.esa.org
www.linkedin.com/groups?home=&gid=1233137
www.facebook.com/esa.org
twitter.com/esa_org
www.youtube.com/user/ESAVideos
Overview: A medium-sized international organization founded in 1915
Mission: To stimulate & publish research on the interrelations of organisms & their environment; to facilitate an exchange of ideas among those interested in ecology; to instill ecological principles in the decision-making of society at large; provides Professional Certification which constitutes recognition by the Society that an applicant meets the minimum educational, experience & ethical standards adopted by ESA for professional ecologists
Affiliation(s): American Association for the Advancement of Science; American Institute of Biological Sciences; National Resources Council; National Research Council; Council of Scientific Society Presidents; Renewable Natural Resources Foundation
Staff Member(s): 36
Membership: 10,000; *Fees:* Schedule available; *Member Profile:* Ecologists
Activities: Maintains sections for ecologists with special needs & interests: Paleoecology, Aquatic, Physiological, Statistical, Applied Ecology, Vegetation, Education, Long-Term Studies; Professional Certification (constitutes recognition by the Society that an applicant meets the minimum educational experience & ethical standards adopted by ESA for professional ecologists); *Internships:* Yes; *Rents Mailing List:* Yes
Chief Officer(s):
Katherine S. McCarter, Executive Director
ksm@esa.org
Awards:
• The Mercer Award
Given for outstanding paper published by a young ecologist
• The MacArthur Award
Given for outstanding research contributions by an established ecologist
• The Cooper Award
Given for the best paper in geobotany, physiographic ecology, etc.
• The Whittaker Travel Fellowship
Brings a leading foreign scientist to America
• The E. Lucy Braun Award
• The Murray F. Buell Award
Outstanding paper presented orally at the ESA Annual meeting by an undergraduate
• Eminent Ecologist Award
Given to senior ecologist for distinguished contributions

• Corporate Award
Given to a corporation, business, program or individual of a company for incorporating sound ecological concepts in operating procedures

Education International (EI) / Internationale de l'Education
5, boul du Roi Albert II, 8 étage, Brussels B1210 Belgium
Tel: 32-2-224-0611; *Fax:* 32-2-224-0606
headoffice@ei-ie.org
www.ei-ie.org
www.facebook.com/educationinternational
twitter.com/eduint
Also Known As: Internacional de la Educación
Previous Name: World Confederation of Organizations of the Teaching Profession
Overview: A large international organization founded in 1993
Mission: To further the cause of organizations of teachers & education employees; To promote status, interests & welfare of members & defend their trade union & professional rights; To promote peace, democracy, social justice, equality & the application of the Universal Declaration on Human Rights through the development of education & the collective strength of teachers & education employees; To seek & maintain recognition of the trade rights of workers in general & of teachers & education employees in particular
Member of: NGO in formal associate relations with UNESCO, ILO; contacts with UN, WHO, UNAIDS, OECD, TUAC-OECD, IMF, World Bank, CONGO; associated with ICFTU
Finances: *Funding Sources:* Membership dues
Staff Member(s): 30
Membership: 30,000,000 in 400 national member organizations in 270 countries; *Member Profile:* Education personnel from all sectors of education, from pre-school to university; *Committees:* Experts on Membership; Advisory Bodies; Status of Women; Finance; Constitution & By-laws
Activities: *Awareness Events:* World Teachers' Day, Oct. 5; *Library:* Resource Centre; by appointment
Chief Officer(s):
Susan Hopgood, President
Fred van Leeuwen, General Secretary
David Edwards, Deputy General Secretary
Charlie Lennon, Deputy General Secretary
Haldis Holst, Deputy General Secretary

Electrochemical Society (ECS)
Bldg. D, 65 South Main St., Pennington NJ 08534-2839 USA
Tel: 609-737-1902; *Fax:* 609-737-2743
ecs@electrochem.org
www.electrochem.org
www.linkedin.com/groups/ECS-74067
www.facebook.com/TheElectrochemicalSociety
twitter.com/ECSorg
Overview: A medium-sized international organization
Mission: To provide information about the latest scientific & technical advancements in the electrochemical field
Staff Member(s): 25
Membership: 8,000; *Fees:* $105 individual; $25 student; *Member Profile:* Individuals with a a bachelor's degree in natural science or engineering, or relevant work experience in electrochemistry or allied subjects; Students who are full-time undergraduate or graduates registered for a degree in natural science or engineering; Corporate members; *Committees:* Executive Committee of the Board of Directors; Education; Finance; Honors & Awards; Individual Membership; Nominating; Technical Affairs; Tellers of Election; Ways & Means; Audit; Education; Ethical Standards; Sponsorship
Activities: Offering networking opportunities among scientists & engineers
Chief Officer(s):
Roque J. Calvo, Executive Director
roque.calvo@electrochem.org
Publications:
• ECS Transactions
Type: Journal; *Editor:* John W. Weidner; *ISSN:* 1938-5862
Profile: Proceedings from ECS meetings & ECS-sponsored meetings
• Electrochemical & Solid-State Letters
Type: Journal; *Frequency:* Monthly; *Editor:* Dennis W. Hess; *ISSN:* 1099-0062
Profile: Research & development in the field of solid-state & electrochemical science & technology
• Interface
Type: Magazine; *Frequency:* Quarterly; *Accepts Advertising*; *Editor:* Mary Yess; *ISSN:* 1064-8208; *Price:* Free with membership in The Electrochemical Society

Profile: For individuals in the field of solid-state & electrochemical science and technology
• Journal of The Electrochemical Society
Type: Journal; *Frequency:* Monthly; *Number of Pages:* 450; *Editor:* Daniel A. Scherson; *ISSN:* 0013-4651
Profile: Peer-reviewed journal, with 70 articles each month
• Meeting Abstracts
Type: Journal; *ISSN:* 1091-8213
Profile: Extended abstracts of the technical papers presented at the spring & fall meetings of ECS

Emeric & Ilana Csengeri Institute for Holocaust Studies *See* Rosenthal Institute for Holocaust Studies

Emotions Anonymous
PO Box 4245, St. Paul MN 55104-0245 USA
Tel: 651-647-9712; *Fax:* 651-647-1593
info2gh99jsd@emotionsanonymous.org
www.emotionsanonymous.org
Overview: A small international organization
Mission: To help people overcome emotional difficulties

Empire Parliamentary Association *See* Commonwealth Parliamentary Association

Endometriosis Association, Inc. (EA) / Association de l'endometriose inc.
International Headquarters, 8585 North 76th Pl., Milwaukee WI 53223 USA
Tel: 414-355-2200; *Fax:* 414-355-6065
endo@endometriosisassn.org
www.endometriosisassn.org
www.facebook.com/EndoAssn
Overview: A large international charitable organization founded in 1980
Mission: To establish network for women with endometriosis to share information & mutual support; to educate women, families, friends, & community about endometriosis & about living with this chronic disease; to promote & conduct research on endometriosis; to provide advocacy for women with endometriosis, when necessary, either on an individual or on a group level; to support groups & chapters in Canadian centers
Member of: Society of Obstetricians & Gynacologists of Canada; Canadian Fertility/Andrology Society
Finances: *Annual Operating Budget:* $500,000-$1.5 Million; *Funding Sources:* Membership dues; literature sales; donations; grants
Staff Member(s): 5; 1170 volunteer(s)
Membership: 5,000 worldwide; *Fees:* $35 member; $45 associate; $45 member outside USA; $55 associate outside USA; *Member Profile:* Women & girls who have or had endometriosis; associate membership also available for physicians & families; *Committees:* Millennium Campaign for the Cure Coordinating Committee; Endowment Fund Steering Committee; Asians in North America Outreach Council; Nurses Council; Black Outreach Council; Hispanic Outreach Council; Lesbian Outreach Council; Teen Outreach Council
Activities: Sponsors educational events; provides one-on-one support & crisis call assistance; coordinates international network of women, physicians & self-help groups; awards research grants; publications & books; teen program; *Awareness Events:* Endometriosis Awareness Week, last full week in March; *Internships:* Yes; *Library:* Not open to public
Chief Officer(s):
Mary Lou Ballweg, President/Executive Director
support@EndometriosisAssn.org
Publications:
• The Endometriosis Sourcebook
Type: Book; *Author:* Mary Lou Ballweg; *Price:* $12.95
• Endometriosis: The Complete Reference for Taking Charge of Your Health
Type: Book; *Author:* Mary Lou Ballweg; *Price:* $15.95
• Overcoming Endometriosis
Type: Book

Entertainment Merchants Association - International Head Office (EMA)
#400, 16530 Ventura Blvd., Encino CA 91436-4551 USA
Tel: 818-385-1500; *Fax:* 818-385-0567
info@entmerch.org
www.entmerch.org
www.linkedin.com/company/entertainment-merchants-association
www.facebook.com/EntertainmentMerchantsAssociation
twitter.com/EntMerchAssoc
Previous Name: Video Software Dealers Association
Overview: A small international organization founded in 1981
Mission: To protect, promote & provide a forum for all those engaged in the rental & sale of packaged and digitally delivered home entertainment
Finances: *Annual Operating Budget:* $3 Million-$5 Million
Staff Member(s): 10
Membership: 200 members representing 35,000 retail outlets in the U.S. & 45,000 around the world; *Member Profile:* DVD and online video and video game retailers, distributors & suppliers
Activities: *Awareness Events:* Game Supply for Interactive Entertainment; Digital Media Pipeline; GamePlan Summit
Chief Officer(s):
Mark Fisher, President/CEO
mfisher@entmerch.org
Carrie Dieterich, Vice-President, Strategic Initiatives
cdieterich@entmerch.org
Jennifer Lane, Director, Brand Image
jlane@entmerch.org
Awards:
• EMA Digi Awards
• EMA Home Entertainment Awards
Meetings/Conferences:
• Entertainment Merchants Association Los Angeles Entertainment Summit 2018, July, 2018, Loews Hollywood Hotel, Los Angeles, CA
Scope: International
Description: Brings together key retailers, producers, & ancillary product companies in the video & video gaming industries in a forum setting
Contact Information: Vice-President, Strategic Initiatives: Carrie Dieterich, E-mail: cdieterich@entmerch.org; Phone: 818-385-1500, ext. 227
• Entertainment Merchants Association Digital Media Pipeline 2018, September, 2018, Skirball Cultural Center, Los Angeles, CA
Scope: International
Description: Unites executives, retailers, distributors, content aggregators, & new technology companies to discuss the digital delivery of home entertainment
Contact Information: Vice-President, Strategic Initiatives: Carrie Dieterich, E-mail: cdieterich@entmerch.org; Phone: 818-385-1500, ext. 227
• Entertainment Merchants Association Independent Product Market 2018, 2018
Scope: International
Description: A gathering of retail buying & distributing companies & independent studios that facilitates networking opportunities
Contact Information: Vice-President, Strategic Initiatives: Carrie Dieterich, E-mail: cdieterich@entmerch.org, Phone: 818-385-1500, ext. 227

EnviroLink
PO Box 8102, Pittsburgh PA 15217 USA
e-mail: websupport@envirolink.org
www.envirolink.org
Overview: A medium-sized international organization founded in 1991
Mission: To promote a sustainable society by connecting individuals and organizations through communication technologies.

Environmental Bankers Association (EBA)
#410, 510 King St., Alexandria VA 22314 USA
Tel: 703-549-0977; *Fax:* 703-548-5945
eba@envirobank.org
www.envirobank.org
Overview: A medium-sized international organization founded in 1994
Mission: To assist the financial services industry in developing environmental risk management policies & procedures
Membership: *Fees:* Schedule available based upon asset size of financial institutions; *Member Profile:* Members of the financial services industry, such as bank & non-bank financial institutions, asset management firms, insurers, & those who provide services to them; Environmental consultants, appraisers, environmental attorneys, & environmental information management firms; *Committees:* Policy; Finance & Budget; Communications & Programs; Business Development & Membership; Legal & ASTM; Trust; Risk Management; Global Sustainability Issues; Technical
Activities: Facilitating networking opportunities
Chief Officer(s):
Rick Ferguson, President, Policy
richardr.ferguson@usbank.com
Sharon Valverde, Vice-President, Programs
sharon.s.valverde@chase.com
Tacy Telego, Co-Executive Director
Tacytelego@envirobank.org
D. Jeffrey Telego, Co-Executive Director
jefftelego@envirobank.org

Environmental Defense
Membership & Public Information, #600, 1875 Connecticut Ave., NW, Washington DC 20009 USA
Tel: 212-505-2100; *Fax:* 212-505-2375
Toll-Free: 800-684-3322
www.edf.org
www.linkedin.com/company/environmental-defense
www.facebook.com/EnvDefenseFund
twitter.com/EnvDefenseFund
Previous Name: Environmental Defense Fund
Overview: A large international organization founded in 1967
Mission: To protect environmental rights for all people — clean air, clean water, healthy food, & flourishing ecosystems; To work to create practical solutions, guided by science, that win lasting political, economic & social support
Finances: *Annual Operating Budget:* Greater than $5 Million; *Funding Sources:* Donations; foundations
Staff Member(s): 340
Membership: 750,000+
Chief Officer(s):
Fred Krupp, President
Diane Regas, Executive Director
Liza Henshaw, Chief Development Officer
Publications:
• Environmental Defense Annual Report
Type: Report; *Frequency:* Anually

Environmental Defense Fund *See* Environmental Defense

Environmental Industry Associations *See* National Waste & Recycling Association

Environmental Information Association
#306, 6935 Wisconsin Ave., Chevy Chase MD 20815-6112 USA
Tel: 301-961-4999; *Fax:* 301-961-3094
Toll-Free: 888-343-4342
info@eia-usa.org
www.eia-usa.org
Previous Name: National Asbestos Council
Overview: A small international organization
Mission: To protect public health & safety; To provide information about environmental health hazards to occupants of buildings, industrial sites, & other facility operations
Membership: *Fees:* $1,000 executive; $500 organization; $125 individual; *Committees:* Conference; Membership / Marketing; Publications; Strategic Planning; Training; Asbestos; EMS / ESA; Indoor Air Quality; Lead Paint; Sampling & Analysis
Activities: Offering professional development opportunities; Providing networking events
Chief Officer(s):
Michael W Schrum, President
mwschrum@terracon.com
Brent Kynoch, Managing Director
bkynoch@eia-usa.org
Joy Finch, Secretary
joy.finch@gvltec.edu
Kevin Cannan, Treasurer
ktc@aac-contracting.com
Kim Goodman, Manager, Membership & Marketing
kgoodman@kynoch.com
Kelly Ruttman, Manager, Development & Communications
krutt@kynoch.com
Publications:
• Indoor Environment Connections
Type: Newsletter; *Price:* Free with Environmental Information Association membership
• Inside EIA [Environmental Information Association]
Type: Newsletter; *Accepts Advertising; *Price:* Free with Environmental Information Association membership
• Net News [a publication of the Environmental Information Association]
Type: Newsletter; *Frequency:* Weekly; *Price:* Free with Environmental Information Association membership

Environmental Law Institute
#620, 2000 L St. NW, Washington DC 20036 USA
Tel: 202-939-3800; *Fax:* 202-939-3868
law@eli.org
www.eli.org
www.linkedin.com/company/environmental-law-institute
www.facebook.com/35601332048
twitter.com/ELIORG

Overview: A medium-sized international organization
Mission: To advance environmental protection by improving law, policy & management; to research pressing problems; to educate professionals & citizens about the nature of these issues; to convene all sectors in forging effective solutions; to achieve society's goals for improving the health of the biosphere & its inhabitants
Finances: *Annual Operating Budget:* Greater than $5 Million; *Funding Sources:* Subscriptions; fees; grants
Staff Member(s): 56
Membership: 100-499; *Fees:* Schedule available
Activities: *Internships:* Yes; *Speaker Service:* Yes; *Library*
Chief Officer(s):
John Cruden, President
cruden@eli.org

Epilepsy Foundation of America (EFA)
8301 Professional Place, Landover MD 20785-7223 USA
Tel: 301-459-3700; *Fax:* 301-577-4941
Toll-Free: 800-332-1000
ContactUs@efa.org
www.epilepsyfoundation.org
www.facebook.com/EpilepsyFoundationofAmerica
twitter.com/epilepsyfdn
www.youtube.com/epilepsyfoundation
Overview: A small international charitable organization founded in 1967
Mission: To work for people affected by seizures through research, education, advocacy & service
Affiliation(s): Epilepsy Canada
Finances: *Funding Sources:* Charitable contributions; donations
Staff Member(s): 61
Membership: *Fees:* $25
Activities: *Awareness Events:* Epilepsy Month, Nov.; *Speaker Service:* Yes; *Library:* NEL National Epilepsy Library; by appointment
Chief Officer(s):
Eric R. Hargis, President & CEO

EPS Industry Alliance (EPS-IA)
#201, 1298 Cronson Blvd., Crofton MD 21114 USA
Tel: 410-451-8340; *Fax:* 410-451-8343
info@epsindustry.org
www.epspackaging.org
www.facebook.com/EPSRecycling
twitter.com/EPSRecycle
Previous Name: Alliance of Foam Packaging Recyclers
Overview: A small international organization founded in 2012
Mission: To provide leadership to the EPS foam packaging industry through activities that promote the development of recycling; To maintain a network for the collection, reprocessing, & reuse of foam packaging
Member of: Institute of Packaging Professionals
Finances: *Funding Sources:* Manufacturers of expanded polystyrene packaging
Membership: 45; *Fees:* $1,000-$36,000

Eurographics - European Association for Computer Graphics (EG)
Stn. 2926, Goslar 38629 Germany
Fax: 49-532-1676-2998
secretary@eg.org
www.eg.org
Also Known As: Eurographics
Overview: A small international organization founded in 1979
Mission: To serve the needs of professionals working in computer graphics & such related fields as scientific visualization, human-computer interfaces, windowing systems, computer-aided design & image analysis; to promote the exchange of information & skills on a global scale.
Affiliation(s): Gesellschaft für Informatik; NGI; NORSIGD; ACM SIGGRAPH
Membership: *Fees:* 870 Euro organzations; *Member Profile:* Primarily Europeans, but membership is worldwide; researchers, developers, educators, & those who work in the computer graphics industry, both as users & providers of computer graphics hardware, software, & applications
Activities: Annual conference, workshops, tutorials; *Speaker Service:* Yes
Chief Officer(s):
Werner Purgathofer, Chair
wp@cg.tuwien.ac.at
Werner Hansmann, Treasurer
hansmann@informatik.uni-hamburg.de
David Duce, Secretary
daduce@brookes.ac.uk

Canada Branch
c/o Dept. of Computer Science, Univ. of Victoria, PO Box 3055, Stn. CSC, Victoria BC V8W 3P6
Tel: 250-472-5760; *Fax:* 250-472-5708
ca-chapter@eg.org
Chief Officer(s):
Brian Wyvill, Chair

European Academy of Sciences, Arts & Humanities *Voir* Académie européenne des sciences, des arts et des lettres

European Association of Geoscientists & Engineers (EAGE)
PO Box 59, Houten 3990 DB Netherlands
Tel: 31-88-995-5055; *Fax:* 31-30-634-3524
eage@eage.org
www.eage.org
Overview: A medium-sized international organization founded in 1951
Mission: To promote exploration geophysics; to foster fellowship & cooperation among those working, studying, or being otherwise interested in the field; comprised of EAEG Division (formerly European Association of Exploration Geophysicists) & EAPG Division (formerly European Association of Petroleum Geoscientists & Engineers)
Affiliation(s): Society of Exploration Geophysicists
Membership: 17,000; *Fees:* 50 Euro general; 25 Euro student; *Committees:* Technical Program; Awards; Publications; Research; Membership & Co-operation; Education; Student Affairs; Improved Oil Recovery; ECMOR; PACE
Activities: *Speaker Service:* Yes; *Library:* by appointment
Chief Officer(s):
Gladys Gonzalez, President
board@eage.org

European Direct Marketing Association *See* Federation of European Direct & Interactive Marketing

European Geophysical Union *See* European Geosciences Union

European Geosciences Union (EGS)
Luisenstr. 37, Munich 80333 Germany
Tel: 49-89-2180-6549; *Fax:* 49-87-2180-17855
info@egu.eu
www.egu.eu
www.linkedin.com/company/european-geosciences-union
www.facebook.com/EuropeanGeosciencesUnion
twitter.com/EuroGeosciences
www.youtube.com/user/EuroGeosciencesUnion
Previous Name: European Geophysical Union
Overview: A medium-sized international organization founded in 2002
Mission: To promote geophysics including planetary & space sciences by assisting cooperation among scientists, laboratories, institutes & individual research workers
Affiliation(s): Canadian Geophysical Union
Membership: 12,500; *Fees:* 20 Euro regular; 10 Euro student/retired; 500 Euro life; *Member Profile:* Scientists; *Committees:* Awards; Education; Finance; Nominations; Outreach; Programme; Publications; Topical Events
Activities: Organization of conferences; meetings & workshops; publication of scientific journals & books
Chief Officer(s):
Günter Blöschl, President
president@egu.eu
Philippe Courtial, Executive Secretary
executive-secretary@egu.eu

European Photochemistry Association
c/o A.N. Nesmeyanov Institute of Organoelement, Vavilova str. 28, Moscow 119991 Russia
Tel: 7-499-135-8098; *Fax:* 7-499-135-5085
www.photochemistry.eu
Overview: A medium-sized international organization founded in 1970
Mission: To promote & encourage the international development of photochemistry & related subjects with special reference to European & neighbouring countries
Membership: 439; *Fees:* 30 euros regular; 15 euros student; *Member Profile:* Scientists
Chief Officer(s):
Werner Nau, Chair
w.nau@jacobs-university.de
Publications:
- Photochemical & Photobiological Sciences
Type: Journal; *Frequency:* Monthly; *Editor:* Sarah Ruthven

European Society of Association Executives (ESAE)
63 D'auderghem Ave., Brussels 1040 Belgium
Tel: 32-2-280-4696; *Fax:* 32-2-282-9353
office@esae.org
esae.org
Overview: A medium-sized international organization
Membership: *Fees:* Schedule available

European Society of Gynaecological Oncology (ESGO)
c/o LOCUS Workspace, Stn. Post Office 1, 1307/22 Krakovska, Prague 110 00 Czech Republic
e-mail: adminoffice@esgomail.org
www.esgo.org
Overview: A medium-sized international organization founded in 1983
Mission: To promote international & cultural communications between gynaecologists, pathologists, surgeons, oncologists, radiotherapists, & other specialists of disciplines related & pertaining to gynaecological oncology; to promote clinical & basic research investigations & spreading of knowledge in gynaecological oncology
Member of: European board & College Obstetrics & Gynecology
Affiliation(s): Federation of European Cancer Societies
Finances: *Funding Sources:* Membership fees
Membership: 1 800; *Fees:* Schedule available; *Member Profile:* Interest in the field of gynaecological oncology; *Committees:* Advocacy; Research; Training & Education; Guideline; Meeting; Financial; Education; Membership; Nominating
Chief Officer(s):
Vesna Kesic, President

European Solidarity Towards Equal Participation of People / Solidarité européenne pour une égale participation des peuples
115, rue Stévin, Brussels B-1000 Belgium
Tel: 32-2-231-1659; *Fax:* 32-2-230-3780
admin@eurostep.org
www.eurostep.org
www.facebook.com/Eurostep
Also Known As: EUROSTEP
Overview: A small international organization founded in 1990
Mission: To co-ordinate the policy work of its members at European level & to influence the policy & practice of the European Union; with a focus on the EU's cooperation with other countries, particularly in Africa, Asia, & Latin America, Eurostep uses its membership base in 15 European countries & the secretariat located in Brussels to present common policy approaches to the European Commission, European Parliament & Member States governments
Finances: *Annual Operating Budget:* $250,000-$500,000
Activities: *Internships:* Yes
Chief Officer(s):
Simon Stocker, Director

European Space Agency (ESA) / Agence spatiale européenne
8-10, rue Mario Nikis, Paris 75738 France
Tel: 33-1-5369-7654; *Fax:* 33-1-5369-7560
Other Communication:
www.flickr.com/photos/europeanspaceagency
contactesa@esa.int
www.esa.int
www.facebook.com/EuropeanSpaceAgency
twitter.com/esa
www.youtube.com/esa
Merged from: European Space Research Organization; European Organization for the Development & Construction
Overview: A large international organization founded in 1975
Mission: To provide for & promote cooperation among European States in space research & technology & their space applications, with a view to their being used for scientific purposes & for operational space applications systems
Affiliation(s): Canadian Space Agency
Finances: *Annual Operating Budget:* Greater than $5 Million
Staff Member(s): 2200
Membership: 22 member states
Chief Officer(s):
Johann-Dietrich Wörner, Director General
Publications:
- ESA [European Space Agency] Annual Report
Type: Yearbook
- ESA [European Space Agency] Bulletin
Type: Newsletter

The Facial Pain Association (TNA)
#402, 408 West University Ave., Gainesville FL 32601 USA
Tel: 352-384-3600; *Fax:* 352-384-3606
Toll-Free: 800-923-3608
www.fpa-support.org
www.facebook.com/facialpainassociation
twitter.com/facialpainassoc
Previous Name: Trigeminal Neuralgia Association
Overview: A large international charitable organization founded in 1990
Mission: To bring people with trigeminal neuralgia & related facial pain conditions together to share their experience & reduce their isolation; To serve as resource/pooling centre for information on trigeminal neuralgia; To provide mutual aid, support & encouragement to those afflicted, their families & other caring individuals; To increase public/professional awareness, visibility & better understanding of the disorder
Member of: National Organization for Rare Disorders (NORD)
Affiliation(s): Centre for Non-Profit Corporations
Finances: *Funding Sources:* Individual; foundations
Membership: *Fees:* $50; *Member Profile:* Patients with Trigeminal Neuralgia or related facial pain problems; *Committees:* Young Patients
Activities: Maintaining an international support network through the provision of support groups & telephone support; Organizing regional conferences; Offering educational material & information to patients, healthcare professionals, & others; Promoting medical research on facial pain conditions
Chief Officer(s):
John Koff, CEO
Publications:
• FPA [Facial Pain Association] Quarterly
Type: Journal; *Frequency:* 4 pa; *Editor:* John Koff

Far Eastern Association Inc. *See* Association for Asian Studies - USA

Fédération Américaine du travail et congrès des organisations industrielles (FAT-COI) *See* American Federation of Labor & Congress of Industrial Organizations (AFL-CIO)

Fédération biblique catholique *See* Catholic Biblical Federation

Fédération des musiciens des États-Unis et du Canada (FAT-COI/CTC) *See* American Federation of Musicians of the United States & Canada (AFL-CIO/CLC)

Fédération internationale de bobsleigh et de tobogganing (FIBT)
Maison du Sport, Avenue de Rhodanie 54, Lausanne 1007 Switzerland
Tél: 41-21-601-51-01; *Téléc:* 41-21-601-79-23
office@fibt.com
www.fibt.com
www.linkedin.com/groups/FIBT-Fédération-International-de-Bobsleigh-1892484
www.facebook.com/128374647314728
twitter.com/FIBT
www.youtube.com/user/bobskeletv
Aperçu: *Dimension:* petite; *Envergure:* internationale; fondée en 1923
Affiliation(s): Canadian Amateur Bobsleigh & Tobogganing Association
Membre(s) du bureau directeur:
Ivo Ferriani, Président
Ermanno Gardella, Secrétaire général

Fédération Internationale de Camping, Caravanning et Autocaravaning (FICC) / International Federation of Camping, Caravanning, & Motor Caravanning (IFCC)
20, rue Belliard, Brussels B-1040 Belgium
Tél: 32-2-513-87-82; *Téléc:* 32-2-513-87-83
info@ficc.org
www.ficc.be
www.facebook.com/ficc.aisbl
Aperçu: *Dimension:* grande; *Envergure:* internationale; fondée en 1933
Mission: To promote camping & caravanning worldwide
Membre(s) du personnel: 1
Membre: 1,800,000; *Montant de la cotisation:* Barème; *Comités:* Youth; Asia Pacific; North America; Technical; Environmental
Membre(s) du bureau directeur:
Joao Alves Pereira, President

Fédération internationale de hockey (FIH) / International Hockey Federation
Rue du Valentin 61, Lausanne CH-1004 Switzerland
Tél: 41-21-641-0606; *Téléc:* 41-21-641-0607
info@fih.ch
www.fih.ch
www.facebook.com/fihockey
twitter.com/FIH_Hockey
www.youtube.com/user/fihockey
Aperçu: *Dimension:* moyenne; *Envergure:* internationale; fondée en 1924
Mission: The federation works in co-operation with both the national and continental organisations to ensure consistency and unity in hockey around the world. The FIH not only regulates the sport, but is also responsible for its development and promotion so as to guarantee a secure future for hockey
Affiliation(s): Field Hockey Canada
Membre(s) du personnel: 26
Membre: 5 federations, *Comités:* Appointments; Athletes; Competitions; Risk & Compliance; Rules; Umpiring; Equipment Advisory Panel; High Performance & Coaching Advisory Panel; Judicial Commission; Medical Advisory Panel
Membre(s) du bureau directeur:
Leandro Negre, President

Fédération Internationale de l'Art Photographique (FIAP)
37, rue Chanzy, Paris 75011 France
Tél: 331-43-723-724; *Téléc:* 331-43-723-728
fiap@fiap.net
www.fiap.net
www.facebook.com/315152355167952
Aperçu: *Dimension:* petite; *Envergure:* internationale; Organisme sans but lucratif; fondée en 1950
Mission: Promouvoir la photographie par une collaboration internationale dans tous les domaines photographiques afin de créer des liens d'amitié entre toutes les fédérations affiliées en contribuant ainsi à l'évolution d'un climat de confiance entre les peuples dans le but de consolider la paix dans le monde
Affiliation(s): Canadian Association for Photographic Art
Membre: 85; *Critères d'admissibilite:* Regroupe plus de 85 fédérations nationales dans les cinq continents et représente les intérêts de plus d'un demi million de photographes individuels, amateurs pour la plupart; FIAP compte aussi des membres individuels dans ILFIAP (club local) et IRFIAP (association régionale)
Activités: Salons photographiques; *Bibliothèque:* Bibliothèque publique
Membre(s) du bureau directeur:
Riccardo Busi, Président
busi.fiap@gmail.com

Fédération internationale de Laiterie *See* International Dairy Federation

Fédération Internationale de Luge de Course (FIL) / International Luge Federation
Rathausplatz 9, Berchtesgaden 83471 Germany
Tél: 49-86-526-6960; *Téléc:* 49-86-526-6969
office@fil-luge.org
www.fil-luge.org
Aperçu: *Dimension:* petite; *Envergure:* internationale; fondée en 1957
Mission: Promotion et participation aux compétitions de la luge dans le monde; organise des championnats du monde, des coupes du monde, des championnats régionaux; organise des cours et séminaires pour des arbitres et des entraîneurs
Affiliation(s): Canadian Luge Association
Finances: *Budget de fonctionnement annuel:* $250,000-$500,000
Membre(s) du personnel: 5
Membre: 49
Activités: *Bibliothèque*
Membre(s) du bureau directeur:
Josef Fendt, Président
Svein Romstad, Secrétaire général
Christoph Schweiger, Directeur général

Fédération internationale de natation amateur *See* International Amateur Swimming Federation

Fédération Internationale de Volleyball *See* International Volleyball Association

Fédération internationale des Amis de la Terre *See* Friends of the Earth International

Fédération internationale des architectes paysagistes *See* International Federation of Landscape Architects

Fédération internationale des associations de producteurs de films (FIAPF) / International Federation of Film Producers' Associations
9, rue de l'Échelle, Paris 75001 France
Tél: 33-1-44-77-97-50; *Téléc:* 33-1-44-77-97-55
info@fiapf.org
www.fiapf.org
Aperçu: *Dimension:* petite; *Envergure:* internationale; fondée en 1933
Mission: Pour défendre les droits de propriété des producteurs et d'influencer la mise en ouvre des lois de copyright afin d'éviter le piratage
Affiliation(s): Canadian Film & Television Association
Membre: 32 organisations
Membre(s) du bureau directeur:
Luis Alberto Scalella, President

Fédération Internationale des Associations de Professeurs de Sciences *See* International Council of Associations for Science Education

Fédération internationale des culturisme et de remise en forme *See* International Federation of Bodybuilding & Fitness

Fédération internationale des femmes de carrières libérales et commerciales *See* International Federation of Business & Professional Women

Fédération internationale des géomètres *See* International Federation of Surveyors

Fédération internationale des hôpitaux *See* International Hospital Federation

Fédération internationale des industries textiles *See* International Textile Manufacturers Federation

Fédération internationale des ingénieurs et techniciens (FAT-COI/CTC) *See* International Federation of Professional & Technical Engineers (AFL-CIO/CLC)

Fédération internationale des mouvements d'agriculture biologique *See* International Federation of Organic Agriculture Movements

Fédération internationale des professeurs de français (FIPF)
101, boul Raspail, Paris 75270 France
Tél: 33-1-42-84-91-27
secretariat@fipf.org
www.fipf.org
Aperçu: *Dimension:* moyenne; *Envergure:* internationale; Organisme sans but lucratif; fondée en 1969
Mission: Regrouper toutes les associations de professeurs de français et toutes les personnes chargées de l'enseignement du français dans le monde; favoriser la mise en commun de leurs expériences et de leurs recherches pédagogiques en vue de promouvoir l'enseignement du français et d'améliorer les conditions générales et particulières de cet enseignement; susciter et faciliter entre ses membres les échanges de toute nature
Membre de: UNESCO
Affiliation(s): Association des professeurs de français des universités et collèges du Canada; Alliance ontarienne des professeurs d'immersion; Association québécoise des professeurs de français; Association québécoise des enseignants de français langue seconde
Membre: 90 000
Membre(s) du bureau directeur:
Fabienne Lallement, Secrétaire générale
Jean-Pierre Cuq, Président
Meetings/Conferences:
• Fédération internationale des professeurs de français (FIPF) Congrès Mondiaux 2020, 2020
Scope: International
Publications:
• Dialogues et Cultures [publication of the Fédération internationale des professeurs de français]
• Échanges [publication of Fédération internationale des professeurs de français]
Type: Bulletin
• Le français dans le monde [publication of Fédération internationale des professeurs de français]
• Francophonies du Sud [publication of Fédération internationale des professeurs de français]

Foreign Associations / Fédération internationale des professions immobilières (FIABCI) / International Real Estate Federation

- Le Monde en français [publication of Fédération internationale des professeurs de français]
- Recherches et applications [publication of the Fédération internationale des professeurs de français]

Fédération internationale des professions immobilières (FIABCI) / International Real Estate Federation
17, rue Dumont d'Urville, Paris F-75116 France
Tel: 33-1-73-79-58-30; *Fax:* 33-1-73-79-58-33
info@fiabci.com
www.fiabci.org
Overview: A medium-sized international charitable organization founded in 1951
Mission: Pour aider les membres réparties leur réputation à l'échelle internationale
Membership: 100 associations; *Committees:* Africa Region; Americas Region; Asia-Pacific; Europe & Near East; Membership; Conference; Finance; Nominations; Young Members; International Organisations; Exchanges; Environment & Legislation; Education; Forums; Marketing & Networking
Activities: *Internships:* Yes
Chief Officer(s):
Patricia Delaney, Secrétaire général
delaney@fiabci.com

Fédération Internationale des Sociétés de la Croix-Rouge & du Croissant-Rouge *See* International Federation of Red Cross & Red Crescent Societies

Fédération Internationale des Traducteurs (FIT) / International Federation of Translators (IFT)
REGUS, 57 rue d'Amsterdam, Paris 75008 France
secretariat@fit-ift.org
www.fit-ift.org
Aperçu: *Dimension:* petite; *Envergure:* internationale; Organisme sans but lucratif; fondée en 1953
Mission: De rassembler les organisations de traducteurs existant dans les divers pays, de susciter et de favoriser la constitution de telles organisations dans les pays où il n'en existe pas encore; de fournir aux organisations membres les informations et les conseils susceptibles de leur être utiles; d'établir, entre toutes les organisations membres, la bonne entente favorable aux intérêts des traducteurs et de contribuer à aplanir les différences qui pourraient s'élever entre ces organisations; de défendre les droits moraux et matériels des traducteurs dans le monde
Membre de: UNESCO
Affiliation(s): Canadian Translators, Terminologists & Interpreters Council
Finances: *Budget de fonctionnement annuel:* $50,000-$100,000
Membre(s) du personnel: 1; 50 bénévole(s)
Membre: 120; *Montant de la cotisation:* Barème; *Critères d'admissibilité:* Toute organisation professionnelle de traducteurs ayant un caractère représentatif peut demander son admission comme membre ordinaire; les groupements qui s'intéressent aux activités et à la promotion des objectifs de la FIT, mais ne répondent pas entièrement aux qualités requises pour être membre ou ne souhaitent pas le devenir, peuvent postuler en qualité de membres associés ou membres observateurs
Activités: *Service de conférenciers:* Oui
Membre(s) du bureau directeur:
Izabel Arocha, Secrétaire général
secgen@fit-ift.org

Fédération internationale du personnel des services publics *See* International Federation of Employees in Public Service

Fédération internationale pour l'habitation, l'urbanisme et l'aménagement des territoires *See* International Federation for Housing & Planning

Fédération internationale pour la recherche en histoire des femmes *See* International Federation for Research in Women's History

Fédération mondiale des concours internationaux de musique (FMCIM) / World Federation of International Music Competitions (WFIMC)
104, rue de Carouge, Geneva CH-1205 Switzerland
Tél: 41-22-321-3620; *Télec:* 41-22-781-1418
fmcim@fmcim.org
www.fmcim.org
www.facebook.com/FMCIM.WFIMC
Aperçu: *Dimension:* petite; *Envergure:* internationale; fondée en 1957
Mission: Favoriser la coordination des activités des concours membres; aider les jeunes lauréats de concours membres à se faire connaître; maintenir un lien amical entre les membres de la Fédération
Membre de: Conseil international de la musique (UNESCO)
Affiliation(s): Union Européenne des Concours de Musique pour la Jeunesse; Fédération Française des Festivals Internationaux de Musique; Jeunesses Musicales International; European Broadcasting Union; L'Association Internationale des Agents Artistiques; The International Society for the Performing Arts
Membre(s) du personnel: 2
Membre: 120 compétitions musicales internationales
Membre(s) du bureau directeur:
Glen Kwok, Président
Marianne Granvig, Secrétaire générale

Fédération mondiale des sourds *See* World Federation of the Deaf

Fédération mondiale pour la santé mentale *See* World Federation for Mental Health

Fédération mondiale pour les études sur le future *See* World Futures Studies Federation

Federation of European Direct & Interactive Marketing (FEDMA)
Av. Ariane 5, 4th Fl., Brussels 1200 Belgium
Tel: 32-2-779-4268; *Fax:* 32-2-778-9922
www.fedma.org
Previous Name: European Direct Marketing Association
Overview: A medium-sized international organization founded in 1997
Mission: To promote & defend the interests & to advance the image, status & prestige of direct marketing in Europe; to build the business of cross-border direct marketing by representation within the European Union institutions & through its vast network of contacts & businesses from within & outside Europe
Affiliation(s): Canadian Direct Marketing Association; Canadian Advertising Foundation
Staff Member(s): 10
Membership: 350 in 36+ countries; *Fees:* 1.000 to 29.000 EUR; *Member Profile:* Users & suppliers of direct marketing services; *Committees:* Task Forces & Councils
Activities: Information on the European market, European legislation & legal issues, postal regulations, lists availability; providing networking & business links, organizing conferences & seminars; *Library:* Not open to public
Chief Officer(s):
Ivan Vandermeersch, Secretary General
ivan@fedma.org
Awards:
- Best of Europe DM Awards

Federation of Sewage Works Associations; Federation of Sewage & Industrial Wastes Associations; Water Pollution Control Federation *See* Water Environment Federation

Federation of Swiss Association Executives
Boul. de Pérolles 18 A, Fribourg 1700 Switzerland
Tel: 41-31-390-99-09; *Fax:* 41-31-390-99-03
info@verbandssekretaere.ch
www.verbandssekretaere.ch
Also Known As: Vereinigung Schweizerischer Verbandssekretäre
Overview: A medium-sized national organization
Chief Officer(s):
Barbara Gutzwiller, Chair

Fellowship of Reconciliation (FOR)
PO Box 271, Nyack NY 10960 USA
Tel: 845-358-4601; *Fax:* 845-358-4924
for@forusa.org
forusa.org
www.facebook.com/FORUSA
twitter.com/FORpeace
www.youtube.com/FellowshipUSA
Overview: A medium-sized international organization founded in 1914
Mission: To replace violence, war, racism & economic injustice with nonviolence, peace & justice; committed to active nonviolence as a transforming way of life & as a means of radical change; to educate, train, rebuild coalitions & engage in nonviolent & compassionate actions locally, nationally & globally
Member of: International Fellowship of Reconciliation
Staff Member(s): 23
Membership: *Member Profile:* Clergy; teachers; students; peace activists
Activities: Peacemaker Training for young adults; non-violence training; peacebuilder delegations to Palestine/Israel; Campaign of Conscience for the Iraqi People; The Decade for a Culture of Peace & Nonviolence for the Children of the World; publications; sale of cards, calendars & gifts; *Internships:* Yes; *Speaker Service:* Yes; *Library:* FOR Peace Library; Open to public by appointment
Chief Officer(s):
Kristin Stoneking, Executive Director
kstoneking@forusa.org
Awards:
- Martin Luther King, Jr. Award
- Pfeffer Peace Prize

Financial Planning Association (FPA)
#600, 7535 East Hampden Ave., Denver CO 80231 USA
Tel: 303-759-4900; *Fax:* 303-759-0749
Toll-Free: 800-322-4237
member.services@onefpa.org
www.plannersearch.org
www.facebook.com/FinancialPlanningAssociation
twitter.com/fpassociation
Overview: A medium-sized international organization founded in 1969
Mission: To provide leadership & advocacy for persons who need, support, & deliverprofessional financial planning services; To advance the financial planning profession
Membership: 28,500+; *Member Profile:* Members of the financial planning community
Activities: Offering diverse educational opportunities; Liaising with legislative & regulatory bodies, financial services firms, & consumer interest organizations; *Awareness Events:* Financial Planning Week, October
Chief Officer(s):
Lauren Schadle, Chief Executive Officer
Publications:
- FPA SmartBrief [a publication of the Financial Planning Association]
Type: Newsletter; *Frequency:* Weekly; *Price:* Free for Financial Planning Association members
Profile: Government & industry updates for the financial planning community
- Journal of Financial Planning [a publication of the Financial Planning Association]
Type: Journal; *Frequency:* Monthly; *Accepts Advertising*; *Editor:* Lance Ritchlin; *Price:* Free with membership inthe Financial Planning Association; $119 U.S. non-members
Profile: Articles, interviews, & peer-reviewed technical contributions for financial planners & advisers

Fondation pour la conservation de l'environnement *See* Foundation for Environmental Conservation

Fonds mondial pour la nature *See* World Wildlife Fund - USA

Foodservice & Packaging Institute (FPI)
201 Park Washington Crt., Falls Church VA 22046 USA
Tel: 703-538-3550; *Fax:* 703-241-5603
fpi@fpi.org
www.fpi.org
www.linkedin.com/company/1680721
www.facebook.com/FoodservicePackagingInstitute
twitter.com/fpihq
Overview: A small national organization founded in 1933
Finances: *Annual Operating Budget:* $500,000-$1.5 Million; *Funding Sources:* Membership fees
Staff Member(s): 3
Membership: 25; *Fees:* Varies by sales; *Member Profile:* Serves the single-use foodservice packaging industry; is the material-neutral trade association for manufacturers, suppliers & distributors of single-use foodservice packaging products; *Committees:* Market Development; Marketing & Communiciations; Public Affairs; Safety Management; Technical; Standards Council
Activities: Market development; marketing & communications; member services; public affairs & technical programs
Chief Officer(s):
Lynn Dyer, President
ldyer@fpi.org
Jennifer Goldman, Manager, Membership & Meetings, 703-538-3553
jgoldman@fpi.org
Lynn Rosseth, Director, Market Development & Programs

Foundation for Environmental Conservation (FEC) / Fondation pour la conservation de l'environnement
1148 Moiry, Switzerland

Fax: 41-21-8666-6616
envcons@ncl.ac.uk
www.ncl.ac.uk/icef
Overview: A small international organization founded in 1975
Mission: To undertake, in cooperation with appropriate individuals, organizations & other groups, all possible activities to further environmental conservation & global sustainability
Membership: *Committees:* Awards
Activities: International Conferences on Environmental Future (ICEFs); specialist workshops
Chief Officer(s):
Nicholas V.C. Polunin, Editor

Foundation for International Environmental Law & Development (FIELD)
Cityside House, 40 Adler St, 3rd Fl., London E1 1EE United Kingdom
Tel: 44-20-7096 0277; *Fax:* 44-20-7388-2826
www.field.org.uk
www.facebook.com/474981202565918
twitter.com/FIELDLegal
Previous Name: Centre for Environmental Law & Development
Overview: A small international organization founded in 1989
Mission: To help vulnerable countries, communities, & campaigners negotiate for fairer international environmental laws
Finances: *Annual Operating Budget:* $500,000-$1.5 Million; *Funding Sources:* Foundations; Consultancy work
Staff Member(s): 13; 8 volunteer(s)
Membership: *Member Profile:* Public international lawyers
Activities: *Internships:* Yes; *Library*
Chief Officer(s):
Joy Hyvarinen, Executive Director

Fraternité des préposés à l'entretien des voies (FAT-COI/CTC) *See* Brotherhood of Maintenance of Way Employes (AFL-CIO/CLC)

Fraternité internationale des chaudronniers, constructeurs de navires en fer, forgerons, forgeurs et aides (FAT-COI)
See International Brotherhood of Boilermakers, Iron Ship Builders, Blacksmiths, Forgers & Helpers (AFL-CIO)

Fraternité internationale des ouvriers en électricité (FAT-COI/FCT) *See* International Brotherhood of Electrical Workers (AFL-CIO/CFL)

Fraternité internationale des teamsters (FAT-COI/CTC) *See* International Brotherhood of Teamsters (AFL-CIO/CLC)

Fraternité unie des charpentiers et menuisiers d'Amérique (FAT-COI/CTC) *See* United Brotherhood of Carpenters & Joiners of America (AFL-CIO/CLC)

French Association for Canadian Studies *Voir* Association française d'études canadiennes

French Institute / Institut français
500 Salisbury St., Worchester MA 01609 USA
Tel: 508-767-7415
instfran@assumption.edu
www.assumption.edu/academics/academic-institutes/french-institute
Overview: A small international organization founded in 1979
Mission: To encourage the study of French in North America; To serve as a research center that preserves artifacts & promotes French cultural activities; To raise awareness of francophone North Americans through educational & cultural projects

Friends Historical Association (FHA)
Quaker Collection, Haverford College, 370 Lancaster Ave., Haverford PA 19041-1392 USA
Tel: 610-896-1161; *Fax:* 610-896-1102
fha@haverford.edu
www.haverford.edu/library/fha
Overview: A medium-sized international charitable organization founded in 1873
Mission: To promote the study, preservation & publication of material relating to the history of the Religious Society of Friends
Affiliation(s): Conference of Quaker Historians & Archivists
Finances: *Annual Operating Budget:* Less than $50,000; *Funding Sources:* Membership dues; subscriptions; donations
Staff Member(s): 1; 21 volunteer(s)
Membership: 800; *Fees:* $15; *Member Profile:* Friends & interested historians
Activities: Pilgrimages to historic Friends Meetings; lectures; *Rents Mailing List:* Yes
Chief Officer(s):
Kenneth Carroll, President Emeritus

Publications:
• Quaker History
Type: Journal; *Frequency:* Semiannually; *Editor:* Charles L. Cherry

Friends Historical Society - London (FHS)
c/o Friends House, 173 Euston Rd., London NW1 2BJ United Kingdom
Tel: 44 020 7663 1094; *Fax:* 44 020 7663 1001
www.facebook.com/QuakersinBritain
twitter.com/BritishQuakers
Overview: A small international organization founded in 1903
Mission: To encourage the study of Quaker history
Member of: Association of Denominational Historical Societies & Cognate Libraries
Finances: *Funding Sources:* Membership fees
Membership: 400

Friends of Animals (FoA)
#205, 777 Post Rd., Darien CT 06820 USA
Tel: 203-656-1522; *Fax:* 203-656-0267
friendsofanimals.org
www.facebook.com/FriendsOfAnimalsOrg
twitter.com/foaorg
www.youtube.com/user/FriendsofAnimals
Overview: A large national charitable organization founded in 1957
Mission: To free animals from cruelty & institutionalized exploitation around the world; To cultivate a respectful view of nonhuman animals, free-living & domestic
Finances: *Annual Operating Budget:* $3 Million-$5 Million; *Funding Sources:* Membership dues; bequests; grants; donations
Staff Member(s): 23; 185 volunteer(s)
Membership: 200,000; *Fees:* US$25 regular; US$15 students/seniors
Activities: Offering spay/neuter program; Running anti-fur & anti-ivory campgaigns; Opposing hunting & international animal trade; Supporting marine aninmal protection initiatives; Advocating for vegan, plant-based diets
Chief Officer(s):
Priscilla Feral, President
Publications:
• ActùionLine [a publication of Friends of Animals]
Type: Magazine; *Frequency:* Quarterly

Friends of the Earth International (FoEI) / Fédération internationale des Amis de la Terre
International Secretariat, PO Box 19199, Amsterdam 1000 GD Netherlands
Tel: 31-20-622-1369
foei@foei.org
www.foei.org
twitter.com/FoEint
www.youtube.com/user/FriendsoftheEarthInt
Also Known As: Amigos de la Tierra
Overview: A medium-sized international organization founded in 1971
Mission: To promote that environmental problems do not respect geographical & political boundaries; To cooperate with other organizations; To raise awareness that environmental, social, economic & political issues are interdependent; To encourage positive alternatives to policies & practices which cause ecological degradation
Member of: International Union for the Conservation of Nature
Affiliation(s): International Rivers Network; Rainforest Action Network; Rainforest Information Centre; EcoPeace; Action for Solidarity, Equality Environment & Development Europe
Finances: *Funding Sources:* Fees; Donations; Subsidies
Membership: 74 national groups, comprised of 5,000 local groups with over 2 million members; *Member Profile:* Envrionmental organizations
Activities: Workshops on specific campaigns; Political lobbying; Information distribution
Chief Officer(s):
Jagoda Munic, Chair
Dave Hirsch, International Coordinator
Pauline Vincenten, Office Coordinator

La Fundación Canadá *See* Spanish Association for Canadian Studies

The Galpin Society
37 Townsend Dr., St. Albans, Herts AL3 5RF UK
e-mail: administrator@galpinsociety.org
www.galpinsociety.org

Overview: A medium-sized international charitable organization founded in 1946
Mission: To study the history & construction of musical instruments
Finances: *Funding Sources:* Membership dues
Membership: *Fees:* Schedule available
Activities: Symposia, AGM & meetings abroad
Chief Officer(s):
Graham Wells, Chair
grahamwhwells@aol.com

The Geneva Association
53 Route de Malagnou, Geneva CH-1208 Switzerland
Tel: 41-22-707-6600; *Fax:* 41-22-736-7536
secretariat@genevaassociation.org
www.genevaassociation.org
www.linkedin.com/groups?gid=3792189
twitter.com/TheGenevaAssoc
Also Known As: International Association for the Study of Insurance Economics
Overview: A small international organization founded in 1973
Mission: To research the growing economic importance of world-wide insurance activities in the major sectors of the economy
Membership: 90; *Member Profile:* CEOs of the most important insurance companies in Europe, North America, South America, Asia, Africa & Australia
Chief Officer(s):
Anna Maria D'Hulster, Secretary General & Managing Direct

Geochemical Society
c/o Earth & Planetary Sciences Department, Washington University, #CB 11691, Brookings Dr., St. Louis MO 63130-4899 USA
Tel: 314-935-4131; *Fax:* 314-935-4121
gsoffice@geochemsoc.org
www.geochemsoc.org
Overview: A medium-sized international organization
Mission: To encourage the application of chemistry to the solution of geological & cosmological problems
Affiliation(s): American Association for the Advancement of Science; International Union of Geological Sciences; Council of Scientific Society Presidents; Geological Society of America
Membership: *Member Profile:* An international membership with interests in fields such as high & low-temperature geochemistry, fluid-rock interaction, organic geochemistry, petrology, isotope geochemistry, & meteoritics; *Committees:* Joint Publications; Nominations; Program; V.M. Goldschmidt Award; F.W. Clarke Award; C.C. Patterson Award; Geochemical Fellows; OGD Executive; Alfred Treibs Award; OGD Best Paper Award; AAAS Liaison
Chief Officer(s):
Martin Goldhaber, President
mgold@usgs.gov
Samuel Mukasa, Vice-President
mukasa@umich.edu
Neil Sturchio, Secretary
sturchio@uic.edu
Louise Criscenti, Treasurer
ljcrisc@sandia.gov
Seth Davis, Manager, Business
seth.davis@geochemsoc.org
Meetings/Conferences:
• Goldschmidt Conference 2018, August, 2018, Boston, MA
Scope: International
Attendance: 3,000+
Description: An international conference on geochemistry
Publications:
• Elements Magazine [a publication of the Geochemical Society]
Type: Journal; *Frequency:* Bimonthly; *Price:* Free with membership in the Geochemical Society
Profile: Theme issues with peer-reviewed invited papers related to the mineral & geochemical sciences
• GCA: Geochimica et Cosmochimica Acta
Type: Journal; *Frequency:* Biweekly; *Editor:* Dr. Frank Podosek
Profile: Scientific contributions related to geochemistry & cosmochemistry
• G-Cubed (Geochemistry, Geophysics, Geosystems)
Type: Journal
Profile: Research papers on the chemistry, physics, & biology of earth & planetary processes
• Geochemical News
Type: Newsletter; *Frequency:* Quarterly; *Editor:* Stephen Komor
Profile: News of the Geochemical Society
• Geochemical Society Special Publication Series
Profile: Scientifically significant collections of related, original

Foreign Associations / The G.K. Chesterton Institute for Faith & Culture

papers on topics such as magmatic processes, fluid-mineral interactions, stable isotope geochemistry, mineralspectroscopy, mantle petrology, & volcanic, geothermal, & ore-forming fluids

The G.K. Chesterton Institute for Faith & Culture
Seton Hall University, 400 South Orange Ave., South Orange NJ 07079-2687 USA
Tel: 973-275-2431; *Fax:* 973-275-2594
chestertoninstitute@shu.edu
www.shu.edu/chesterton/index.cfm
www.facebook.com/121042177917463
Overview: A medium-sized international organization founded in 1974
Mission: To promote a critical interest in all aspects of the life & work of G.K. Chesterton
Finances: *Annual Operating Budget:* $50,000-$100,000
Staff Member(s): 4
Membership: 237 institutional; 1,800 individual
Chief Officer(s):
Ian Boyd, President
boydjian@shu.edu
Publications:
• The Chesterton Review
Editor: Ian Boyd; *Price:* $40 print subscription
Profile: Quarterly journal

Glass Packaging Institute (GPI)
#510, 700 North Fairfax St., Alexandria VA 22314 USA
Tel: 703-684-6359; *Fax:* 703-299-1543
info@gpi.org
www.gpi.org
www.facebook.com/chooseglass
twitter.com/chooseglass
Overview: A medium-sized national organization founded in 1919
Mission: The trade association representing the North American glass container industry.
Chief Officer(s):
Lynn M. Bragg, President
Awards:
• Clear Choice Awards, Glass Packaging Institute
Awards for consumer product goods manufacturers who expand the fronteirs of glass packaging design my using glass containers in innovatibe ways *Contact:* Kristen LeKander, kristen@lindberggrp.com; 703/778-7644

Glass, Molders, Pottery, Plastic & Allied Workers International Union (AFL-CIO/CLC) (GMP) / Union internationale des travailleurs du verre, mouleurs, poterie, plastique et autres (FAT-COI/CTC)
PO Box 607, 608 East Baltimore Pike, Media PA 19063-0607 USA
Tel: 610-565-5051; *Fax:* 610-565-0983
gmpiu@gmpiu.org
www.gmpiu.org
Also Known As: GMP International Union
Overview: A medium-sized international organization founded in 1842
Mission: To create relationships that create more resources for its members
Affiliation(s): AFL-CIO; Canadia Labour Congress
Finances: *Funding Sources:* Membership dues
Membership: 250+ unions
Chief Officer(s):
Bruce R. Smith, President
David Doyle, Executive Director, Canada

Global Crop Protection Federation; International Group of National Associations of Manufacturers of Agrochemical Products *See* Croplife International

Government Finance Officers Association (GFOA)
#2700, 203 North LaSalle St., Chicago IL 60601-1210 USA
Tel: 312-977-9700; *Fax:* 312-977-4806
bnquiry@gfoa.org
www.gfoa.org
www.linkedin.com/company/gfoa
www.facebook.com/GFOAofUSandCanada
twitter.com/GFOA
www.youtube.com/user/GovFinOffAssn
Overview: A medium-sized international organization founded in 1906
Mission: To serve the public finance profession in the the United States & Canada
Membership: 18,400; *Fees:* Schedule available, based upon population of city or county; *Member Profile:* State, provincial, & local finance officers, in the United States & Canada, who are involved in the management of government financial resources; *Committees:* Governmental Budgeting & Fiscal Policy; Accounting, Auditing, & Financial Reporting; Canadian Issues; Economic Development & Capital Planning; Retirement & Benefits Administration; Governmental Debt Management; Treasury & Investment Management
Activities: Providing opportunities for continuing education; Conducting research; Providing recommended practices for the government finance profession; Publishing over 75 books about government finance, as well as specialty newsletters on the topics of accounting, auditing, and financial reporting, cash management, & pension & benefit issues; Offering technical inquiry services for members; *Library:* GFOA Reference Library; Not open to public
Chief Officer(s):
Jeffrey Esser, Executive Director & CEO
Heather A. Johnston, President
John Jurkash, Chief Financial Officer
Awards:
• Certificate of Achievement for Excellence in Financial Reporting (CAFR)
Established in 1945, the certificate is designed to recognize & encourage excellence in financial reporting by state & local governments
• Popular Annual Financial Reporting Award (PAFR)
To encourage governments to produce reports that make financial data more accessible to those who need less detailed information than what is traditionally found in CAFRPs
• Awards for Excellence
Recognizes contributions to the practice of government finance that exemplify outstanding financial management; awarded in the following categories: accounting, auditing, & financial reporting, budgeting & financial planning, cash managment & investments, captial finance & debt administration, pensions & benefits, management & service delivery, enterprise financial systems & technology
• Canadian Award for Financial Reporting (CANFR)
• Distinguished Budget Awards
Meetings/Conferences:
• Government Finance Officers Association 2018 112th Annual Conference, May, 2018, America's Center Convention Complex, St. Louis, MO
Scope: International
Attendance: 4,100+
Contact Information: Manager, Communications: Natalie Laudadio, Phone: 312-578-2298
• Government Finance Officers Association 2019 113th Annual Conference, May, 2019, Los Angeles Convention Center, Los Angeles, CA
Scope: International
Contact Information: Manager, Communications: Natalie Laudadio, Phone: 312-578-2298
• Government Finance Officers Association 2020 114th Annual Conference, May, 2020, Ernest N. Morial Convention Center, New Orleans, LA
Scope: International
Contact Information: Manager, Communications: Natalie Laudadio, Phone: 312-578-2298
• Government Finance Officers Association 2021 115th Annual Conference, June, 2021, Hyatt Regency & Swiss Hotel Chicago, Chicago, IL
Scope: International
Contact Information: Manager, Communications: Natalie Laudadio, Phone: 312-578-2298
• Government Finance Officers Association 2022 116th Annual Conference, June, 2022, Neal Kocurek Memorial Austin Convention Center, Austin, TX
Scope: International
Contact Information: Manager, Communications: Natalie Laudadio, Phone: 312-578-2298
Publications:
• Government Finance Officers Association Membership Newsletter
Type: Newsletter; *Frequency:* Semimonthly; *Accepts Advertising*; *Editor:* Marcy Boggs
• Government Finance Officers Association Professional Magazine
Type: Magazine; *Frequency:* Bimonthly

Government Refuse Collection & Disposal Association *See* Solid Waste Association of North America

Grain Elevator & Processing Society (GEAPS)
4248 Park Glen Rd., Minneapolis MN 55416 USA
Tel: 952-928-4640; *Fax:* 952-929-1318
info@geaps.com
www.geaps.com
www.linkedin.com/groups/Grain-Elevator-Processing-Society-GEAPS-3895350
www.facebook.com/GEAPS
twitter.com/GEAPSinfo
Overview: A medium-sized international organization founded in 1937
Mission: To provide a forum for the analysis & exchange of information affecting the industries; to advance educational & professional qualifications of the members; to represent the interests of the members in governmental activities; to foster good business ethics & social responsibility throughout the membership; to communicate with the trade media & general public concerning the issues of interest to the members & the industries; to provide technical information on grain handling & storage
Finances: *Funding Sources:* Membership dues; publications
Staff Member(s): 11
Membership: *Fees:* US$185 regular; $0 student; *Member Profile:* Individuals across the grain operations industry worldwide
Activities: Publications; education & training; trade shows; conferences; *Speaker Service:* Yes; *Rents Mailing List:* Yes
Chief Officer(s):
David Krejci, Executive Vice-President

Graphic Communications International Union *See* International Brotherhood of Teamsters

Great Lakes Commission / Commission des Grands Lacs
Eisenhower Corporate Park, #100, 2805 Industrial Way South, Ann Arbor MI 48104-6791 USA
Tel: 734-971-9135; *Fax:* 734-971-9150
www.glc.org
Mission: The Commission is a binational, public agency dedicated to the use, management & protection of water, land & other natural resources of the Great Lakes-St. Lawrence system. In partnership with 8 Great Lakes states & provinces of Ontario & Québec, the Commission applies sustainable development principles addressing issues of resource management, environmental protection, transportation & sustainable development. The Commission provides information on public policy issues; a forum for developing & coordinating public policy; & a unified, system-wide voice to advocate member interests.
Chief Officer(s):
Kenneth G. Johnson, Chair
Tim A. Eder, Executive Director
teder@glc.org

The Great Lakes Research Consortium (GLRC)
College of Environmental Science & Forestry, SUNY, 253 Baker Lab, 1 Forestry Dr., Syracuse NY 13210 USA
Tel: 315-470-6720
glrc@esf.edu
www.esf.edu/glrc
Overview: A medium-sized international organization founded in 1986
Mission: To facilitate research & scholarship on Great Lakes problems; To provide opportunities for training & education of students; To disseminate important information & research findings
Finances: *Annual Operating Budget:* $100,000-$250,000
Staff Member(s): 2
Membership: 18 institutional; *Fees:* $500-$1,000 per campus; *Member Profile:* New York State colleges & universities + 9 affiliate campuses in Ontario
Activities: Speakers exchange; task forces; small grants program; annual student/faculty conferences; *Speaker Service:* Yes
Chief Officer(s):
Greg Boyer, Director
glboyer@esf.edu

Greenpeace International
Ottho Heldringstraat 5, Amsterdam 1066 AZ Netherlands
Tel: 31-20-718-2000; *Fax:* 31-20-718-2002
Other Communication: pinterest.com/greenpeace
info.int@greenpeace.org
www.greenpeace.org
www.facebook.com/greenpeace.international
twitter.com/Greenpeace
www.youtube.com/greenpeacevideo
Also Known As: Stichting Greenpeace Council
Overview: A large international organization founded in 1971

Mission: To protect the environment from the threats of pollution, global warming, & the depletion of natural resources; To protect endangered species, such as whales, dolphins, & seals
Finances: *Annual Operating Budget:* Greater than $5 Million
Membership: 55 countries
Activities: Campaigning; non-violent direct action; publishing environmental reports
Chief Officer(s):
Ayesha Imam, Chair
Publications:
• Greenpeace Annual Report
Type: Yearbook

Greenpeace USA
#300, 702 H St. NW, Washington DC 20001 USA
Tel: 202-462-1177; *Fax:* 202-462-4507
Toll-Free: 800-722-6995
Other Communication: Phone, from Canada: 202-884-7615
info@wdc.greenpeace.org
www.greenpeaceusa.org
www.facebook.com/greenpeaceusa
twitter.com/greenpeaceusa
www.youtube.com/profile?user=greenpeaceusa
Overview: A large international charitable organization founded in 1971
Mission: To use non-violent confrontation to expose global environmental problems & to promote solutions essential to a green & peaceful future; to protect biodiversity in all its forms; to end the nuclear threat & promote global disarmament
Affiliation(s): Greenpeace International
Finances: *Annual Operating Budget:* Greater than $5 Million
Membership: 4 million; *Fees:* $30
Activities: *Internships:* Yes; *Speaker Service:* Yes; *Rents Mailing List:* Yes
Chief Officer(s):
Mads Christensen, International Executive Director
Annie Leonard, Executive Director
Franklyn Baker, Chief Operating Officer
Awards:
• Diversity Scholarship
Amount: $1,750 (2)

Guilde américaine des artistes de variétés (FAT-COI) *See* American Guild of Variety Artists (AFL-CIO)

La Guilde des journalistes (FAT-COI/CTC) *See* The Newspaper Guild (AFL-CIO/CLC)

Hawk Migration Association of North America (HMANA)
PO Box 721, Plymouth NH 03264 USA
e-mail: info@hmana.org
www.hmana.org
www.facebook.com/278725758995
twitter.com/hmanahawkwatch
Overview: A medium-sized international organization founded in 1974
Mission: To conserve raptor populations through the scientific study, enjoyment & appreciation of hawk migration
Staff Member(s): 2
Membership: 600+; *Fees:* US$25 student; US$35 individual; US$55 family; US$60 organization; US$100 benefactor; corporate US$300; US$700 life supporting; *Committees:* RPI; Development; Data; Conservation; Tour
Activities: *Speaker Service:* Yes
Chief Officer(s):
Carolyn Hoffman, Chair

Healthcare Information & Management Systems Society (HIMSS)
#1700, 33 West Monroe St., Chicago IL 60603-5616 USA
Tel: 312-664-4467; *Fax:* 312-664-6143
www.himss.org
www.linkedin.com/company/himss
www.facebook.com/HIMSSpage
twitter.com/himss
www.youtube.com/himss
Overview: A large international organization
Mission: To provide worldwide leadership in the optimal use of healthcare information technology & management systems in order to improve healthcare
Membership: 20,000+; *Fees:* Individual, $160; Chapter-Only, $30; Student, $30; *Committees:* Public Policy; Ambulatory IS; Annual Conference Education; Career Services; Distance Education; Interoperability; Innovation; Physician; Privacy & Security

Chief Officer(s):
Sebastian Krolop, Chair
H. Stephen Lieber, President & Chief Executive Officer
slieber@himss.org
Blain Newton, Executive Vice-President
blain.newton@himssanalytics.org
Carla Smith, Executive Vice-President
csmith@himss.org
John Whelan, Executive Vice-President, Media
john.whelan@himssmedia.com
Awards:
• HIMSS Nicholas E. Davies Award of Excellence
• Stage 7 Award
• Richard P. Covert, PhD, LFHIMSS Scholarship for Management Systems
Meetings/Conferences:
• Healthcare Information & Management Systems Society 2018 Conference & Exhibition, March, 2018, Las Vegas, NV
Scope: International
Attendance: 45,000+
Contact Information: www.himssconference.org
Publications:
• The Digital Office
Type: Newsletter; *Frequency:* Monthly; *Price:* Free with HIMSS membership
Profile: Information about health information technology & electronic medical records
• Financial Edge
Type: Newsletter; *Frequency:* Monthly; *Price:* Free with HIMSS membership
Profile: HIMSS' financial systems e-newsletter, with current issues & trends related to financial systems & other technologies in healthcare
• Healthcare IT News
Type: Newspaper; *Frequency:* Monthly; *Price:* Free with HIMSS membership
Profile: Features the HIMSS Insider newsletter, plus information about advocacy, education, & HIMSS happenings
• HIMSS [Healthcare Information & Management Systems Society] Weekly Insider
Type: Newsletter; *Frequency:* Weekly; *Price:* Free with HIMSS membership
Profile: Current news from HIMSS, member profiles, & interviews
• HIMSS [Healthcare Information & Management Systems Society] Conference Proceedings
Frequency: Annually
Profile: Proceedings from the annual HIMSS conference & exhibition
• HIMSS [Healthcare Information & Management Systems Society] Clinical Informatics Insights
Type: Newsletter; *Frequency:* Monthly; *Price:* Free with HIMSS membership
Profile: Comprehensive articles about informatics across the continuum of care
• HIMSS [Healthcare Information & Management Systems Society] Pulse on Public Policy
Type: Newsletter; *Frequency:* Monthly; *Price:* Free with HIMSS membership
Profile: Information for HIMSS members, policymakers, regulators, & interested stakeholders
• HIMSS [Healthcare Information & Management Systems Society] HIELights
Type: Newsletter; *Frequency:* Monthly; *Price:* Free with HIMSS membership
Profile: Issues pertaining to health information exchange & regional health information organizations
• Journal of Healthcare Information Management
Type: Journal; *Frequency:* Quarterly; *Accepts Advertising*; *Price:* Free with HIMSS membership
Profile: Peer-reviewed journal for healthcare information & management systems professionals

Hedge Fund Association Canada (HFA)
c/o HFA, #900, 2875 NE 191st St., Aventura FL 33180 USA
Tel: 305-935-7296; *Fax:* 305-405-8858
info@thehfa.org
www.thehfa.org
Overview: A small national organization founded in 1996
Member of: International Hedge Fund Association
Membership: *Fees:* $1000-$2000
Chief Officer(s):
Mitch Ackles, President, 646-657-9230
mitch@hedgefundpr.net
Lara Block, Executive Director & Secretary

Heiser Program for Research in Leprosy & Tuberculosis
c/o The New York Community Trust, 909 - 3rd Ave., New York NY 10022 USA
Tel: 212-686-0010; *Fax:* 212-532-8528
Overview: A small international charitable organization
Mission: To award grants to fund research into leoprosy, tuberculosis & their bacterial agents to find measures for prevention & cure.
Membership: *Committees:* Scientific Advisory
Chief Officer(s):
Gilla Kaplan, Chair, Scientific Advisory Committee
Len McNally, Director
lm@nyct-cfi.org
Awards:
• Postdoctoral Research Fellowships
Eligibility: Applicants should have an M.D., Ph.D., or equivalent degree; Although there is no age limit, candidates should be at an early stage of postdoctoral research training *Deadline:* March 1 *Amount:* $80,000 over 2 years
• Research Grants
Eligibility: Applications should come from laboratories that have experience in leprosy research & have demonstrable, ongoing interactions with corresponding laboratories in endemic regions. *Deadline:* prelim. report, Mar. 25 *Amount:* $50,000 renewable for 2nd year

HelpAge International (HAI)
PO Box 70156, London WC1A 9GB United Kingdom
Tel: 44-20-7278-7778; *Fax:* 44-207-148-7623
info@helpage.org
www.helpage.org
uk.linkedin.com/company/helpage-international
www.facebook.com/HelpAgeInternational
twitter.com/helpage
www.youtube.com/helpage
Overview: A medium-sized international charitable organization founded in 1983
Mission: To campaign on behalf of the world's older population & provide expertise & grants to older people's organizations in 70 developing countries; To assist them to help the most disadvantaged lead independent lives
Affiliation(s): Help the Aged - Canada
Membership: 100+; *Member Profile:* Non-profit organizations working with/for older people
Activities: Working via a network of development, research, community-based & social service organisations that share a common mission to improve the lives of disadvantaged older people; Combining support for partners & members, direct programme implementation, research & advocacy; Participating in the formulation of national & international strategies on aging; Library
Chief Officer(s):
Arun Maira, Chair
Justin Derbyshire, Interim Chief Executive
Awards:
• Leslie Kirkley Award
Given to support a particularly innovative programme or individual activity focusing either on direct service delivery, a policy/advocacy initiative, or work in particularly difficult circumstances

Holocaust Memorial Foundation of Illinois (HMFI)
9603 Woods Dr., Skokie IL 60077 USA
Tel: 847-967-4800
info@ilhmec.org
www.ilholocaustmuseum.org
www.facebook.com/IHMEC
twitter.com/ihmec
pinterest.com/ihmec
Also Known As: Illinois Holocaust Museum & Education Center
Overview: A medium-sized international organization founded in 1981
Mission: To ensure the continuance of an open & free society where human rights are respected & preserved
Member of: Association of Holocaust Organizations
Membership: *Fees:* Schedule available
Activities: Provides teacher training courses for college credits; exhibits; tapes oral histories of survivors/liberators of the Holocaust; provides speakers & programming on an outreach basis to schools & the community; documentary film production; development of curriculum & educational resource material; *Internships:* Yes; *Speaker Service:* Yes; *Library:* Open to public
Chief Officer(s):
Richard S. Hirschhaut, Executive Director, Illinois Holocaust Museum & Education Center

Fritzie Fritzshall, President

Holy Trinity Community - North America (HTCNA)
USA
Tel: 412-519-4367
admin@htcna.org
htcna.org
www.facebook.com/HTCNA
Overview: A large international organization
Mission: To experience the Holy Spirit & bring that experience to others
Affiliation(s): Archdiocese of Toronto
Membership: 300 churches

Hong Kong Trade Development Council
Hong Kong Convention & Exhibition Centre, 1 Expo Dr., Wanchai Hong Kong
Tel: 852-1830-668; *Fax:* 852-2824-0249
hktdc@hktdc.org
www.hktdc.com
Overview: A medium-sized international organization founded in 1966
Mission: To promote external trade in goods & services; to create & facilitate opportunities in international trade for Hong Kong companies; to strengthen Hong Kong as the global trade platform of Asia; to assist manufacturers, traders & service providers through marketing opportunities, trade contacts, market knowledge & competitive skills
Activities: *Library:* Business Information Centre; Open to public
Chief Officer(s):
Fred Lam, Executive Director
Toronto Office
Hong Kong Trade Centre, 1st Fl., 9 Temperance St., Toronto ON M5H 1Y6
Tel: 416-366-3594; *Fax:* 416-366-1569
toronto.office@hktdc.org
Chief Officer(s):
Andrew Yui, Director

Housing Inspection Foundation (HIF)
PO Box 879, Palm Springs CA 92263 USA
Toll-Free: 877-743-6806
support@assoc-hdqts.org
www.hif-assoc.org
Overview: A medium-sized international organization
Member of: International Association Managers
Membership: *Fees:* Schedule available; *Member Profile:* Housing inspectors

Human Anatomy & Physiology Society (HAPS)
PO Box 2945, 251 S.L. White Blvd., LaGrange GA 30241-2945 USA
Tel: 800-448-4277; *Fax:* 706-883-8215
info@hapsconnect.org
www.hapsweb.org
www.linkedin.com/groups/972787
twitter.com/humanaandpsoc
Overview: A medium-sized international organization
Mission: To promote excellence in the teaching of human anatomy & physiology
Membership: *Member Profile:* Any person in Canada, the United States, & the rest of the world, with an interest in anatomy & physiology education; *Committees:* Animal Use; Cadaver Use; Communication; Conference; Curriculum & Instruction; Foundation Oversight; HAPS Educator; Membership; Safety; Testing
Activities: Encouraging research; Providing position statements in areas such as animal & cadaver use; Facilitating communication among teachers of human anatomy & physiology; Providing professional development programs; Communicating with other educational & scientific organizations; Awarding grants & scholarships for anatomy & physiology students & instructors
Chief Officer(s):
Terry Thompson, President
tthompson@hapsconnect.org
Peter English, Executive Director
peter@hapsconnect.org
Brittney Roberts, Coordinator, Membership
Meetings/Conferences:
• Human Anatomy & Physiology Society 32nd Annual Conference 2018, May, 2018, Columbus, OH
Scope: International
Description: An international conference, featuring workshops & networking opportunities
Publications:
• HAPS [Human Anatomy & Physiology Society] EDucator
Frequency: Quarterly
Profile: Teaching tips for anatomy & physiology instructors

Human Life International (HLI) / Vie Humaine Internationale
4 Family Life Lane, Front Royal VA 22630 USA
Toll-Free: 800-549-5433
Other Communication: www.vidahumana.org
www.hli.org
www.linkedin.com/company/1122302
www.facebook.com/HumanLifeInternational
twitter.com/HumanLifeIntnl
www.youtube.com/user/HLICommunications
Overview: A small international organization
Mission: To bring the pro-life & pro-family message to countries throughout the world
Membership: 8,000
Chief Officer(s):
Shenan J. Boquet, President

The Humane Society of the United States (HSUS)
2100 L St. NW, Washington DC 20037 USA
Tel: 202-452-1100
Toll-Free: 866-720-2676
donorcare@humanesociety.org
www.humanesociety.org
www.linkedin.com/company/the-humane-society-of-the-united-states
www.facebook.com/humanesociety
twitter.com/HumaneSociety
www.instagram.com/humanesociety
Overview: A large national organization founded in 1954
Mission: To prevent the abuse of all animals; To promote the protection of endangered species
Affiliation(s): Doris Day Animal League; Humane Society International; Humane Society Legislative Fund; Humane Society University; Humane Society Veterinary Medical Association; Humane Society Wildlife Land Trust; The Fund for Animals
Finances: *Annual Operating Budget:* $3 Million-$5 Million
Staff Member(s): 165
Membership: 1.6 million members & constituents; *Fees:* Donation
Activities: *Library* by appointment
Chief Officer(s):
Wayne Pacelle, President & CEO
Michael Markarian, Chief Operating Officer
Andrew Rowan, CIO/CSO
Meetings/Conferences:
• Animal Care Expo 2018, May, 2018, Kansas City, MO
Scope: National
Description: An educational conference & international trade show
Contact Information: URL: animalsheltering.org/expo
• Taking Action for Animals 2018, July, 2018, Hyatt Regency Crystal City, Arlington, VA
Scope: National
Description: An educational conference meant to inspire people to help animals; topics covered include factory farming & animal fighting
Publications:
• All Animals [a publication of The Humane Society of the United States]
Type: Magazine; *Frequency:* bi-m.; *ISSN:* 1948-3597
Profile: Stories about the HSUS & the humane movement
• Animal Sheltering [a publication of The Humane Society of the United States]
Type: Magazine; *Frequency:* bi-m.; *Price:* US$20; $25 international
Profile: An information resource for animal care workers
• Kind News [a publication of The Humane Society of the United States]
Type: Magazine; *Frequency:* bi-m.; *Number of Pages:* 8
Profile: The magazine teaches kindness & respect for animals & their habitats, & is meant for children from kindergarten to grade six

Hydrographic Society *See* International Federation of Hydrographic Societies

IEEE Microwave Theory & Techniques Society (MTT-S)
5829 Bellanca Dr., Elkridge MD 21075 USA
Tel: 410-796-5866
www.mtt.org
www.linkedin.com/groups/51393
www.facebook.com/IEEEMTT
twitter.com/IEEE_MTTS
Overview: A large international organization
Mission: To promote the advancement of microwave theory & its applications, by focussing on scientific, technical, & industrial activities; To enhance the quality of life for all people, through the development & application of microwave technology
Membership: 10,500+; *Member Profile:* Persons who are members of the IEEE, a technical professional association; Individual members should have competence in the field of engineering, computer science, information technology, the physical sciences, biological & medical sciences, mathematics, technical communications, education, management, law, or policy; *Committees:* Awards; Budget; China Business; Education; Electronic Information; Executive; Future Directions; Inter-Society; Image & Visibility; Magazine Outreach; Memorials; Meetings & Symposia; Member & Geographic Activities; Microwave Review & Tutorial Collection; Microwaves101.com; Nominations & Appointments; Newsletter Working Group; Operations; Personnel Management; Publications; Sight; Standards; Strategic Planning; Technical Coordinating
Activities: Distributing knowledge; Supporting professional development; *Speaker Service:* Yes
Chief Officer(s):
Edward C. Niehenke, Ombuds Officer
e.niehenke@ieee.org
Meetings/Conferences:
• Microwave Theory & Techniques Society International Microwave Symposia 2018, June, 2018, Philadelphia, PA
Scope: International
Description: Technical papers; Workshops; Trade show
• Microwave Theory & Techniques Society International Microwave Symposia 2019, June, 2019, Boston, MA
Scope: International
Description: Technical papers; Workshops; Trade show
• Microwave Theory & Techniques Society International Microwave Symposia 2020, June, 2020, Los Angeles, CA
Scope: International
Description: Technical papers; Workshops; Trade show
• Microwave Theory & Techniques Society International Microwave Symposia 2021, June, 2021, Atlanta, GA
Scope: International
Description: Technical papers; Workshops; Trade show
• Microwave Theory & Techniques Society International Microwave Symposia 2022, 2022, Denver, CO
Scope: International
Description: Technical papers; Workshops; Trade show
• Microwave Theory & Techniques Society International Microwave Symposia 2023, June, 2023, San Diego, CA
Scope: International
Description: Technical papers; Workshops; Trade show
Publications:
• IEEE Microwave & Wirelss Component Letters
Type: Journal; *Frequency:* Monthly
Profile: Articles about microwave/millimeter-wave technology, with an emphasis on devices, components, circuits, guided wave structures, & systems & applications covering the frequencyspectrum
• IEEE Microwave Magazine
Type: Magazine; *Accepts Advertising*; *Price:* Free with IEEE Microwave Theory and Techniques Society membership
Profile: Feature articles, application notes, news of the IEEE Microwave Theory & Techniques Society, a conference calendar, & reviews of interest to professionals in the field of microwave theory &techniques
• Transactions
Type: Journal
Profile: Articles about engineering & theory associated with microwave circuits & guided wave structures

Illuminating Engineering Society of North America (IESNA)
120 Wall St., 17th Fl., New York NY 10005-4001 USA
Tel: 212-248-5000; *Fax:* 212-248-5017
ies@ies.org
www.iesna.org
www.linkedin.com/groups?mostPopular=&gid=3790528
www.facebook.com/140309826005859
twitter.com/IllumEngSoc
Overview: A medium-sized international organization founded in 1906

Mission: To improve the lighted environment by bringing together those with lighting knowledge & by translating that knowledge into artforms that benefit the public
Finances: *Annual Operating Budget:* Greater than $5 Million
Staff Member(s): 19
Membership: 8,000; *Fees:* US$170 associate; US$550 individual subscribing member; US$75 associate EP; US$20 student; *Member Profile:* Designers; engineers; architects; utilities; *Committees:* Knowledge; Membership; Public Relations; Programs; Emerging Professionals; Students; IIDA
Activities: *Rents Mailing List:* Yes
Chief Officer(s):
Paul Mercier, President
Awards:
• International Illuminating Design Awards

Fiddlehead Section
c/o John Randall, 26 Robby St., Douglas NB E3G 8B4
Tel: 506-292-3821; *Fax:* 506-852-9118
Chief Officer(s):
John Randall, President
john.randall@focuselectrical.com

Montréal Section
CP 66012, Succ. Haut-Anjou, Anjou QC H1J 3B8
Tél: 514-277-1438; *Téléc:* 514-277-0494
ies-montreal@videotron.ca
montreal.iesna.net
Chief Officer(s):
Christiane de Cesare, Présidente, 514-825-7501

National Capital Section
c/o Gabriel Mackinnon, #1, 109 Murray St., Ottawa ON K1N 5M5
Tel: 613-241-1822
iesottawa.ca
Chief Officer(s):
Andrew MacKinnon, President
andrew@gabrielmackinnon.com

Northumberland Section
c/o R.E. LeBlanc Consultants, #425, 236 St. George St., Moncton NB E1C 1W1
Tel: 506-858-0950; *Fax:* 506-856-6304
info@viziwiz.com
northumberland.iesna.net
Chief Officer(s):
David Knickle, President
releblanc@releblanc.com

Toronto Section
c/o Cree Canada, #3, 6889 Rexwood Rd., Mississauga ON L4V 1R2
Fax: 800-890-7507
Toll-Free: 800-473-1234
ies@iestoronto.org
www.iestoronto.org
www.linkedin.com/groups?home=&gid=4948047
Chief Officer(s):
Brenda Quies, President

Winnipeg Section
PO Box 33081, Stn. Polo Park, Winnipeg MB R3G 0W4
Tel: 204-694-0000; *Fax:* 204-694-0433
winnipeg.iesna.net
Chief Officer(s):
Greg Macdonald, President
gmacdonald@hi-techsales.ca

IMCS Pax Romana / MIEC Pax Romana (MIEC)
7 Impasse Reille, Paris 75014 France
Tél: +33-01-45-44-70-75; *Téléc:* +33-01-42-84-04-53
office@imcs-miec.org
www.imcs-miec.org
www.facebook.com/imcs.miec
twitter.com/PaxRomanaIMCS
www.instagram.com/PaxRomanaIMCS
Également appelé: International Movement of Catholic Students
Nom précédent: International Movement of Catholic Students; International Catholic Movement for Intellectual & Cultural Affairs
Aperçu: *Dimension:* grande; *Envergure:* internationale; fondée en 1921
Mission: To empower students to be agents of transformation in their communities by providing holistic trainings & international experience; To engage in proactive dialogue between Christian faith & cultures in order to promote evangelization & the inculturation of the Gospel for the realization of the Kingdom of God
Membre de: United Nation Major Group for Children & Youth (UNMGCY); cofounder of ICMYO (International Coordination Meeting of Youth Organizations); International Specialised Catholic Action Movements (ISCAM)
Affiliation(s): Mouvement d'étudiants chrétiens du Québec; Association of Canadian Catholic Students
Finances: *Budget de fonctionnement annuel:* $100,000-$250,000; *Fonds:* Donations; projects based funding
Membre(s) du personnel: 2; 8 bénévoles(s)
Membre: *Critères d'admissibilite:* Students from tertiary institutions
Activités: Advocacy (consultative status with the United Nations Economic & Social Council, UNESCO & the European Council, & has accredited representatives to those organisations in New York, Vienna, Paris, Geneve & Strasbourg); Trainings (summer schools, seminars, capacity buildings); Campaigns
Membre(s) du bureau directeur:
Edouard Pihèwa Karoue, International President
president@imcs-miec.org
Evelina Manola, Secretary General
secgeneral@imcs-miec.org
Magdalena Dourron, Contact, Accountancy
Publications:
• Forums [a publication of IMCS Pax Romana]
Type: Newsletter

Indian Association for Canadian Studies (IACS)
101 Dwarkamai, 25/B Pratapgunj, Vadodara 390 002 India
www.iacs-ind.com
Overview: A small international organization founded in 1985
Mission: The Association promotes & encourages teaching, research & publications related to Canadian & Indo-Canadian Studies, especially with regard to interdisciplinary, multidisciplinary & comparative approaches.
Affiliation(s): International Council for Canadian Studies
Membership: 806
Chief Officer(s):
Jaydipsinh K. Dodia, President

Indonesia Canada Chamber of Commerce (ICCC)
c/o Canadian Education International, Wisma Metropolitan I, 11th Fl., Jl. Jend. Sudirman kav 29-31, Jakarta 12920 Indonesia
Tel: +62 21 527 7890; *Fax:* +62 21 527 7891
secretariat@iccc.or.id
www.iccc.or.id
Overview: A small international organization
Mission: To promote trade & investment between Canada & Indonesia.
Membership: 100-499
Chief Officer(s):
Karina Sherlen, Vice Executive Director

Industrial Fabrics Association International (IFAI)
1801 County Rd. BW, Roseville MN 55113-4061 USA
Tel: 651-222-2508; *Fax:* 651-631-9334
Toll-Free: 800-225-4324
Other Communication: membership@ifai.com
generalinfo@ifai.com
www.ifai.com
Overview: A medium-sized international organization founded in 1912
Mission: To represent the specialty fabrics & technical textiles industry; To contribute to the prosperity of the specialty fabrics industry
Membership: 2,100; *Member Profile:* Companies involved in the specialty fabrics & technical textiles industry from 58 countries, including manufacturers of end products, equipment, & hardware, as well as suppliers of fibre & fabric
Activities: Promoting the specialty fabrics industry; Providing educational opportunities, such as hands-on training workshops; Disseminating research reports & other information to members; Creating networking opportunities
Chief Officer(s):
Stephen M. Warner, President & Chief Executive Officer, 800-486-3978
Mary J. Hennessy, Vice-President, Communications & Publishing, 800-319-3133
Kathy J. Mattson, Vice-President, Member Services, 800-272-1852
Steven C. Rider, Vice-President, Finance & Administration, 800-225-6915
Publications:
• Fabric Architecture
Type: Magazine; *Frequency:* Bimonthly; *Editor:* Bruce N. Wright
Profile: Articles about designing with fabric, for architects, designers, specifiers, contractors, & developers
• Fabric Graphics
Type: Magazine; *Frequency:* Bimonthly; *Editor:* Chris P. Tschida
Profile: Information about the use of textiles as a printing medium, with applications for fabric & the technology
• Geosynthetics
Type: Magazine; *Frequency:* Bimonthly; *Editor:* Ron W. Bygness
Profile: Geosynthetic products, design, & applications
• InTents
Type: Magazine; *Frequency:* Bimonthly; *Editor:* Sigrid A. Tornquist
Profile: Information focussing on tents, fabric structures, & accessories tenters need
• Marine Fabricator
Type: Magazine; *Frequency:* Bimonthly; *Editor:* Kelly R. Frush; Chris P. Tschida
Profile: Techniques of marine craftsmanship & upholstery for marine shop professionals
• Review Buyer's Guide
Type: Yearbook; *Frequency:* Annually
• Specialty Fabrics Review
Type: Magazine; *Frequency:* Monthly; *Editor:* Galynn D. Nordstrom; Janet L. Preus; *Price:* Free with membership in Industrial Fabrics Association International
Profile: Information for specialty fabric professionals
• Upholstery Journal
Type: Journal; *Frequency:* Bimonthly; *Editor:* Kelly R. Frush; Chris P. Tschida
Profile: Educational information about the craft & business of upholstery, for persons involved in the after furniture, marine, automotive, & commercial upholstery markets

Industrial Truck Association (ITA)
#460, 1750 K St. NW, Washington DC 20006 USA
Tel: 202-296-9880; *Fax:* 202-296-9884
www.indtrk.org
www.facebook.com/Indtrk
Overview: A medium-sized international organization
Mission: Represents the manufacturers of lift trucks & their suppliers who do business in Canada, the United States or Mexico
Finances: *Annual Operating Budget:* $1.5 Million-$3 Million
Staff Member(s): 5
Membership: 100; *Fees:* Schedule available; *Member Profile:* Manufacturers of industrial trucks or of major components, attachments or manually powered hand pallet trucks that do business in the United States, Canada or Mexico
Activities: Training programs; Market intelligence; *Awareness Events:* National Forklift Safety Day, June 14
Chief Officer(s):
William Montwieler, Executive Director
Meetings/Conferences:
• 2018 Industrial Truck Association Annual Meeting, September, 2018, Ponte Vedra Inn & Club, Ponte Vedra Beach, FL
Description: Annual meeting for members of the Industrial Truck Association

Infectious Diseases Society of America (IDSA)
#300, 1300 Wilson Blvd., Arlington VA 22209 USA
Tel: 703-299-0200; *Fax:* 703-299-0204
membership@idsociety.org
www.idsociety.org
www.linkedin.com/company/357844
www.facebook.com/IDSociety
twitter.com/idsainfo
www.flickr.com/photos/idsociety
Overview: A large international organization
Mission: To improve the health of individuals, communities, & society; To promote excellence in education, research, public health, prevention, & patient care
Membership: *Member Profile:* Physicians; Scientists; Health care professionals who specialize in infectious diseases
Chief Officer(s):
William G. Powderly, MD, FIDSA, President
Cynthia L. Sears, MD, FIDSA, Vice-President
Larry K. Pickering, MD, FIDSA, Secretary
Helen W. Boucher, MD, FIDSA, Treasurer
Meetings/Conferences:
• IDWeek 2018, October, 2018, San Francisco, CA
Scope: International
• Infectious Diseases Society of America Annual Meeting 2018, 2018
Scope: International
Publications:
• Clinical Infectious Diseases
Type: Journal
Profile: State-of-the-art clinical articles, medical & legal issues, review articles, & studies in infectious disease research

Foreign Associations / Information Systems Security Association (ISSA)

- IDSA [Infectious Diseases Society of America] News
Type: Newsletter
Profile: Society activities, education, research, & prevention & treatment advances
- Journal of Infectious Diseases
Type: Journal
Profile: Original research about the pathogenesis, diagnosis, & treatment of infectious diseases

Information Systems Audit & Control Association See ISACA

Information Systems Security Association (ISSA)
#261, 4008 Louetta Rd., Spring TX 77388 USA
Tel: 703-382-8206; Fax: 703-495-2973
memberservices@issa.org
www.issa.org
www.facebook.com/ISSAIntl
twitter.com/ISSAINTL
www.instagram.com/issaintl
Overview: A medium-sized international organization founded in 1984
Mission: To provide education forums, publications & peer interaction opportunities that enhance the knowledge, skill & professional growth of its members; To be a global voice of information security
Finances: Annual Operating Budget: $500,000-$1.5 Million
17 volunteer(s)
Membership: 11,000; Fees: $95
Activities: Rents Mailing List: Yes
Chief Officer(s):
Dave Tyson, Executive Director
dave.tyson@issa.org

Ottawa Chapter
PO Box 71002, 174 Bank St., Ottawa ON K2P 1W6
e-mail: communications@issa-ottawa.ca
www.issa-ottawa.ca
www.linkedin.com/groups?home=&gid=873227
Chief Officer(s):
Doug Lawrence, ISSA Chapter President

Vancouver Chapter
Vancouver BC
e-mail: info@vancouver-issa.org
www.vancouver-issa.org
Chief Officer(s):
Eva Kuiper, ISSA Chapter President

Innovations et réseaux pour le développement (IRED) / Development Innovations and Networks
CP 116, 3, rue Varembé, Genève 1211-20 Suisse
Tél: 41-22-734-17-16; Téléc: 41-22-740-00-11
info@ired.org
www.ired.org
Aperçu: Dimension: grande; Envergure: internationale; Organisme sans but lucratif; fondée en 1981
Activités: Facilite les échanges d'expériences Sud-Sud, Sud-Nord, Nord-Sud; aide à la création et au développement de réseaux locaux et nationaux, d'unions et de fédérations de groupements; organise, avec ses partenaires, des appuis techniques dans les domaines de la formation, de la gestion et de l'organisation, des technologies appropriées, des négociations, etc., de façon à renforcer les institutions promues à tous les niveaux; Bibliothèque: Centre de documentation; rendez-vous
Membre(s) du bureau directeur:
Philippe Egger, Président
Publications:
- IRED [Innovations et réseaux pour le développement] Newsletter en ligne
Type: Newsletter

Institut africain international See International African Institute

Institut Archéologique d'Amérique See Archaeological Institute of America

Institut de recherche des Nations Unies pour le développement social See United Nations Research Institute for Social Development

L'Institut des vérificateurs internes See The Institute of Internal Auditors

Institut français See French Institute

Institut international de l'ocean See International Ocean Institute

L'Institut International de Statistique See International Statistical Institute

Institut pour une synthèse planétaire See Institute for Planetary Synthesis

Institute for Alternative Agriculture See Wallace Center, Winrock International

Institute for Folklore Studies in Britain & Canada (IFSBAC)
c/o National Centre for English Cultural Tradition, University of Sheffield, Sheffield S10 2TN UK
Tel: 44-114-222-2000
Overview: A small international organization founded in 1986
Mission: To promote the study of folklore in Britain & Canada through teaching, research, archive development & publication; to encourage & engage in research on all aspects of folklore & related disciplines. A cooperative endeavour between the University of Sheffield & Memorial University of Newfoundland
Activities: Heritage interpretation; Internships: Yes; Library: IFSBAC Library; by appointment
Chief Officer(s):
P.S. Smith, Co-Director, Memorial University of Newfoundland
J.C. Beal, Co-Director, University of Sheffield

Institute for Local Self-Reliance (ILSR)
1710 Connecticut Ave. NW, 4th Fl., Washington DC 20009 USA
Tel: 202-898-1610
info@ilsr.org
www.ilsr.org
www.facebook.com/localselfreliance
twitter.com/ilsr
Overview: A medium-sized international organization founded in 1974
Mission: To provide innovative strategies & models to support environmentally sound community development; To work with citizens & policymakers to meet local needs; To provide the tools to increase economic effectiveness, to reduce waste & decrease impacts on the environment, & provide for local ownership of infrastructure & resources
Affiliation(s): Healthy Building Network; Black Environment Justice Network; GrassRoots Recycling Network
Finances: Funding Sources: Foundations; Individuals; Speaking; Technical assistance
1 volunteer(s)
Activities: Internships: Yes; Speaker Service: Yes
Chief Officer(s):
John Bailey, Director, Development
development@ilsr.org
Nick Stumo-Langer, Manager, Communications
stumolanger@ilsr.org

Institute for Planetary Synthesis (IPS) / Institut pour une synthése planétaire
PO Box 171, Chatelaine, Geneva CH-1211 Switzerland
Tel: 41-22-733-88-76; Fax: 41-22-733-88-76
ipsbox@ipsgeneva.com
www.ipsgeneva.com
Overview: A small international organization founded in 1981
Mission: To reawaken an awareness of spiritual values in daily life; to promote planetary awareness, leading to planetary citizenship; to analyze & solve world problems on a basis of spiritual values
Member of: Adult Learning Documentation & Information Network (UNESCO Institute for Education)
Affiliation(s): Canadian Peace Research & Education Association; Center Light; Earth Day International; Earth Concert Project; Expanding Boundaries; International Peace Committee; Peal for Peace; Planetary Initiative; Responsibility International Canada
Activities: Speaker Service: Yes; Rents Mailing List: Yes; Library: Ten Seed-Group Documentation Centre; by appointment
Chief Officer(s):
Alice Boainain-Schneider, IPS UN Representative

The Institute of Chartered Accountants of Bermuda See Chartered Professional Accountants of Bermuda

Institute of Electrical & Electronics Engineers Inc. (IEEE)
3 Park Ave., 2nd Fl., New York NY 10016-5997 USA
Tel: 212-419-7900; Fax: 212-752-4929
contactcenter@ieee.org
www.ieee.org
www.linkedin.com/company/ieee
www.facebook.com/IEEE.org
twitter.com/IEEEorg
www.youtube.com/user/IEEEorg
Overview: A large international organization founded in 1884
Mission: To advance theory & practice of electrical engineering, electronics, radio & allied branches of engineering & related arts & sciences; To publish documents in order to enhance the quality of life for all peoples through improved public awareness of the influences & applications of its technologies; To advance the standing of the engineering profession & its members; To provide leadership in areas ranging from aerospace, computers & communications to biomedical technology, electric power & consumer electronics
Staff Member(s): 800; 30 volunteer(s)
Membership: 365,000 worldwide; 39 technical societies; 4 councils; Fees: Schedule available
Activities: Publishing & disseminating information; Organizing events, lectures, & company visits; Internships: Yes; Library: IEEE Xplore Digital Library
Chief Officer(s):
Barry Shoop, President & CEO
Awards:
- IEEE Recognition Awards
Presented to individuals or corporations for significant contributions to IEEE or advances in technology within the technical fields of interest for IEEE; involve categories for service, honorary memberships, staff recognition, & prize papers
- IEEE Technical Field Awards
Awarded for contributions or leadership in specific fields of interest of the IEEE
- IEEE Medals Award Program
Awarded by the IEEE Board of Directors

Institute of Food Technologists (IFT)
#1000, 525 West Van Buren, Chicago IL 60607 USA
Tel: 312-782-8424; Fax: 312-782-8348
Toll-Free: 800-438-3663
info@ift.org
www.ift.org
www.linkedin.com/groups/Institute-Food-Technologists-IFT-36409
www.facebook.com/events/193978063950994
twitter.com/IFT
www.youtube.com/user/IFTlive
Overview: A large international organization founded in 1939
Mission: To advance food & health through science
Finances: Funding Sources: Membership fees; Sponsorships
Membership: Member Profile: Food science & technology professionals from over 90 countries
Activities: Engaging in advocacy activities; Fostering technology development & supporting innovation in food science; Facilitating the exchange of information & ideas among the food community; Offering professional development activities; Increasing the understanding & application of the science of food; Publishing science reports of interest to members, government officials, scientific constituencies, government officials, the media, & the public; Publishing books through IFT Press, a joint publishing venture with Wiley-Blackwell
Chief Officer(s):
Colin Dennis, President
John Neil Coupland, President-Elect
Christie Tarantino-Dean, Executive Vice-President & CEO
Robert Gravani, Treasurer
Awards:
- IFT Achievement Awards
- Marcel Loncin Research Prize
- Feeding Tomorrow Scholarships
- Congressional Support for Science Award
- IFT Fellows
Meetings/Conferences:
- Institute of Food Technologists 2018 Annual Meeting & Food Expo, July, 2018, McCormick Place, Chicago, IL
Scope: International
Description: An annual gathering of thousands of food professionals from around the world to participate in scientific sessions, poster sessions, the IFT Food Expo, an awards celebration, & networking events
Publications:
- Comprehensive Reviews in Food Science & Food Safety
Type: Journal; Frequency: Bimonthly; Editor: Daryl B. Lund
Profile: A peer-reviewed journal, covering topics such as nutrition, physiology, microbiology, engineering, & regulations
- Eat Your Words
Type: Newsletter; Frequency: Monthly

Profile: Food science & technology stories for new professionals in the industry
• Express Connect
Type: Newsletter; *Frequency:* Monthly
Profile: Happenings at the Institute of Food Technologists, for members only
• Food Technology
Type: Magazine; *Frequency:* Monthly; *Accepts Advertising;* *Editor:* Bob Swientek (bswientek@ift.org)
Profile: Industry news, research developments, consumer product innovations, & professional opportunities
• Institute of Food Technologists Annual Meeting & Food Expo Preview
Type: Newsletter; *Frequency:* Annually
Profile: A preview of the annual educational event, which attracts food scientists, technologists, sellers, & buyers from around the globe
• Institute of Food Technologists Annual Meeting & Food Expo Wrap-up
Type: Newsletter; *Frequency:* Annually
Profile: A review of the annual event, which features over 21,500 attendees, as well as more than 900 exhibitors who present recent products & innovations inthe food industry
• Journal of Food Science
Type: Journal; *Frequency:* 9 pa; *Editor:* Daryl B. Lund (dlund@cals.wisc.edu)
Profile: A peer-reviewed journal, featuring original research, & reviews of all aspects of food science
• Journal of Food Science Education
Type: Journal; *Editor:* Daryl B. Lund (dlund@cals.wisc.edu)
Profile: Information of interest to persons in the field of food science education at all levels, including primary, secondary, undergraduate & graduate,continuing, & workplace education
• Nutraraceutical Newsletter
Type: Newsletter
Profile: News & current research from the nutraceutical & functional foods sector
• The Weekly Newsletter
Type: Newsletter; *Frequency:* Weekly
Profile: Industry news & highlights from the food science, technology, & regulatory sectors
• The World of Food Science
Type: Journal; *Editor:* Ken Buckle (k.buckle@unsw.edu.au)
Profile: A publication of current research on sensors & biosensors & its potential application in the food & technology industry, presented to readers by the Institute ofFood Technologists & the International Union of Food Science & Technology

Institute of Industrial & Systems Engineers (IISE)
#200, 3577 Parkway Lane, Norcross GA 30092 USA
Tel: 770-449-0460; *Fax:* 770-441-3295
cs@iienet.org
www.iienet2.org
www.linkedin.com/groups?mostPopular=&gid=75670
www.facebook.com/iienet
twitter.com/iisenet
www.youtube.com/c/iisechannel
Previous Name: Institute of Industrial Engineers
Overview: A large national licensing organization founded in 1948
Mission: To advance the technical & managerial excellence of industrial engineers, concerned with the design, installation & improvement of integrated systems of people, material, information, equipment & energy
Affiliation(s): Organized into three societies: Society for Health Systems (SHS); Society for Engineering & Management Systems (SEMS); Aerospace & Defense Society (ADS)
Finances: *Annual Operating Budget:* $3 Million-$5 Million
Staff Member(s): 35
Membership: 24,000 internationally in 200 senior & 140 university chapters; *Fees:* $37-$154 USD; *Committees:* Divisions: Energy, Environment & Plant Engineering; Engineering Economy; Ergonomics; Facilities Planning & Design; Financial Services; Industrial & Labour Relations; Operations Research; Quality Control & Reliability; Utilities; Work Measurement & Methods Engineering; Interest Groups; Computer & Information Systems; Consultants; Electronics Industry; Engineering Design; Government; Maintenance; Process Industries; Production & Inventory Control; Retail; Transportation & Distribution
Activities: Provides continuing education opportunities through professional trade books, periodicals, journals, technical publications, conferences, seminars & workshops; *Conferences:* International Industrial Engineering, Industrial Engineering Research & International Maintenance; Material Handling Management Course; Management, Maintenance, Quality & Manufacturing Seminars; *Speaker Service:* Yes; *Rents Mailing List:* Yes; *Library:* by appointment
Chief Officer(s):
Don H. Greene, Chief Executive Officer
Awards:
• Albert G. Holzman Distinguished Educator Award, Educator Awards
Outstanding educators who have contributed to industrial engineering.
• Innovations in Curriculum Award, Educator Awards
Outstanding innovation in the design or presentation of an accredited IE, ISE, IEOR, or similar engineering curriculum
• Dr. Hamed K. Eldin Outstanding Early Career IE in Academia Award, Educator Awards
Individuals in academia who have shown outstanding characteristics.
• Captains of Industry Award, Leadership Awards
Business or government leaders who successfully used industrial engineering in the workplace.
• Fellow Award, Leadership Awards
Leaders who have made significant, nationally recognized contributions to industrial engineering.
• Frank and Lillian Gilbreth Industrial Engineering Award, Leadership Awards
Individuals who distinguished themselves through contributions to mankind.
• Outstanding Middle Career IE Leadership Award for Business/Industry, Leadership Awards
Individuals working in industry who have excelled in their role as a practicing manager/leader within their organization.
• Outstanding Achievement in Management Award, Leadership Awards
Executives contributing to the profession through innovative use of its methods.
• Outstanding Early Career IE in Business/Industry, Leadership Awards
Honoring leadership, professionalism, and potential.
Meetings/Conferences:
• Institute of Industrial & Systems Engineers Annual Conference & Expo 2018, May, 2018, Loews Royal Pacific Resort, Orlando, FL
Scope: International
• Institute of Industrial & Systems Engineers Annual Conference & Expo 2019, May, 2019, Caribe Hilton, San Juan, PR
Scope: International
• Institute of Industrial & Systems Engineers Annual Conference & Expo 2020, May, 2020, Hyatt Regency New Orleans, New Orleans, LA
Scope: International

Institute of Industrial Engineers See Institute of Industrial & Systems Engineers

The Institute of Internal Auditors (IIA) / L'Institut des vérificateurs internes
#401, 1035 Greenwood Blvd., Lake Mary FL 32746 USA
Tel: 407-937-1111; *Fax:* 407-937-1101
customerrelations@theiia.org
www.theiia.org
www.facebook.com/TheInstituteofInternalAuditors
twitter.com/theiia
Overview: A large national organization founded in 1941
Mission: To provide leadership for the global profession of internal auditing; To advocate for the profession's value
Finances: *Funding Sources:* Membership dues; Sale of products & services
Membership: 185,000+ in 160 chapters; *Fees:* Schedule available; *Member Profile:* Regular individual members; Educators; Students; Retired individuals; Government; Groups; *Committees:* Academic Relations; Audit; Research & Education Advisors; Exam Development; Executive; Finance; Financial Services Guidance; Global Advocacy; Global professional Development; Guidance Development; Information Technology Guidance; Institute Relations; Internal Audit Foundation Board of Trustees; International Internal Audit Standards Board; Professional Certifications Board; Professional Responsibilities & Ethics; Public Sector Guidance
Activities: Networking; Training; Professional guidance & certification; Audit Career Center; Compiling & disseminating information; *Awareness Events:* International Internal Audit Awareness Month, May; *Speaker Service:* Yes
Chief Officer(s):
Richard F. Chambers, CIA, QIAL, CGAP, President & CEO
Meetings/Conferences:
• Institute of Internal Auditors 2018 International Conference, May, 2018, Dubai
Scope: International
Contact Information: URL: ic.globaliia.org
Publications:
• CAE Bulletin [a publication of the Institute of Internal Auditors]
Type: Newsletter; *Frequency:* s-m; *Price:* Free to Audit Executive Center members
Profile: News & guidance for chief audit executives.
• Certification Corner [a publication of The Institute of Internal Auditors]
Type: E-Newsletter; *Frequency:* Quarterly; *Price:* Free to public
Profile: Developments in The IIA's certificate programs.
• Global Perspectives & Insights [a publication of The Institute of Internal Auditors]
Type: Report Series; *Price:* Free to public
Profile: Offers insight and direction on key global geopolitical and economic issues
• IIA [The Institute of Internal Auditors] SmartBrief
Type: Newsletter; *Price:* Free to public
Profile: Market news & issues
• IIA [The Institute of Internal Auditors] Connection
Type: E-Newsletter; *Price:* Free to members
Profile: Internal audit news; guidance, research, training, services, events, & certification.
• Internal Auditor [a publication of the Institute of Internal Auditors]
Type: Magazine; *Frequency:* Bimonthly; *Accepts Advertising*
Profile: Information for professionals in internal auditing. Web: iaonline.theiia.org
• Tone at the Top [a publication of The Institute of Internal Auditors]
Type: Newsletter; *Frequency:* Quarterly; *Price:* Free to public
Profile: Information on risk, internal control, governance, ethics, & the changing role of internal auditing for executive management, boards of directors, &audit committees.
• Your Career Compass [a publication of The Institute of Internal Auditors]
Type: Guide; *Frequency:* Quarterly; *Number of Pages:* 52; *Price:* Free to members
Profile: Knowledge, tools, & resources for career growth. Replaced IIA Today & Your Training Compass Resource Guide.

Institute of Packaging Professionals (IoPP)
#800, 1 Parkview Plaza, Oakbrook Terrace IL 60181 USA
Tel: 630-544-5050
info@iopp.org
www.iopp.org
www.linkedin.com/company/789360
www.facebook.com/IoPPonline
twitter.com/IoPP_Pros
Overview: A medium-sized national organization
Mission: To create networking & educational opportunities to help packaging professionals succeed
Finances: *Funding Sources:* Corporate sponsors
Membership: 5,000; *Fees:* $0 affiliate; $175 regular; $249 premium; $399 elite; *Member Profile:* Packaging professionals
Chief Officer(s):
Sarah Washburn, General Manager
swashburn@iopp.org
Jim George, Director, Education
jimg@iopp.org
Barbara Dykes, Manager, Member Services, 630-544-5050 Ext. 114
bdykes@iopp.org
Publications:
• IoPP [Institute of Packaging Professionals] Update
Type: Newsletter; *Frequency:* Biweekly
Profile: Institute information, such as awards competitions, scholarships, publications surveys, & professional development activities
• IoPP [Institute of Packaging Professionals] Spotlight
Type: Newsletter
Profile: Selected months focus on a different product packaging segment important to members
• Who's Who in Packaging [a publication of the Institute of Packaging Professionals]
Type: Guide; *Frequency:* Annually; *Accepts Advertising*

Institute of Scrap Recycling Industries, Inc. (ISRI)
#400, 1250 H St. NW, Washington DC 20005 USA
Tel: 202-662-8500
www.isri.org
www.linkedin.com/groups/3422165
www.facebook.com/isri1987

Foreign Associations / Institute of Transportation Engineers (ITE)

twitter.com/ISRI
www.youtube.com/user/ISRI1987
Overview: A medium-sized international organization
Mission: To provide education, advocacy, compliance training; To promote public awareness of the value & importance of recycling to the production of the world's goods & services
Staff Member(s): 34
Membership: 1,300; *Fees:* Schedule available; *Member Profile:* North American companies that process, broker & consume scrap commodities; associate memberships available for international members outside Canada, Mexico & the US, as well as to equipment & service providers of the scrap recycling industry; *Committees:* Communications; Convention; Education & Training; Government Affairs; Finance; Materials Theft; Membership; Safe Operations; Shredders; Trade
Activities: *Internships:* Yes; *Speaker Service:* Yes
Chief Officer(s):
Robin K. Wiener, President
robinwiener@isri.org

Institute of Transportation Engineers (ITE)
#600, 1627 Eye St. NW, Washington DC 20006 USA
Tel: 202-785-0060; *Fax:* 202-785-0609
ite_staff@ite.org
www.ite.org
www.linkedin.com/groups?gid=166463
www.facebook.com/74169838900
twitter.com/ITEHQ
www.youtube.com/user/ITEHQ
Overview: A large international organization founded in 1930
Mission: To facilitate the application of technology & scientific principles for modes of ground transportation
Staff Member(s): 24
Membership: 13,000; *Fees:* Schedule available; *Member Profile:* Transportation professionals responsible for meeting mobility & safety needs, such as transportation educators, researchers, consultants, planners & engineers
Activities: Promoting professional development; Supporting education; Encouraging research; Increasing public awareness; Exchanging professional information
Chief Officer(s):
Jeffrey Paniati, Executive Director & CEO, 202-785-0060 Ext. 131
jpaniati@ite.org
Awards:
• Daniel B. Fambro Student Paper Award
• Student Chapter Award
• Burton W. Marsh Distinguished Service Award
• Theodore M. Matson Memorial Award
• Wilbur S. Smith Distinguished Transportation Educator Award
• Innovative Intermodal Solutions for Urban Transportation Paper Award in Memory of Daniel W. Hoyt
• Past Presidents' Award for Merit in Transportation
• District and Section Newsletter Award
• Section Activities Award
• Transportation Achievement Award
Meetings/Conferences:
• Institute of Transportation Engineers 2018 Annual Meeting & Exhibit, August, 2018, Hilton Minneapolis, Minneapolis, MN
Scope: International
Publications:
• Context Sensitive Solutions in Designing Major Urban Thoroughfares for Walkable Communities
Profile: An ITE Proposed Recommended Practice
• Parking Generation: An ITE Informational Report
• Traffic Engineering Handbook
• Traffic Signal Timing Manual
• Transportation Impact Analyses for Site Development: An ITE Proposed Recommended Practice
• Transportation Planning Handbook
• Trip Generation: An ITE Informational Report
• Urban Street Geometric Design Handbook

Institution of Mechanical Engineers (IMechE)
1 Birdcage Walk, London SW1H 9JJ United Kingdom
Tel: 44-(0)20-7222-7899; *Fax:* 44-(0)20-7222-4557
enquiries@imeche.org
www.imeche.org
www.linkedin.com/groups/2265081
www.facebook.com/imeche
twitter.com/imeche
Overview: A medium-sized international organization founded in 1847
Mission: To educate, train & promote the professional development of engineers; To act as an international centre for technology transfer in mechanical engineering
Finances: *Annual Operating Budget:* $3 Million-$5 Million; *Funding Sources:* Subscriptions & earnings
Staff Member(s): 180
Membership: 115,000+
Activities: *Speaker Service:* Yes; *Library:* by appointment
Chief Officer(s):
Carolyn Griffiths, President
president@imeche.org

Instrument Society of America *See* The Instrumentation, Systems & Automation Society of America

The Instrumentation, Systems & Automation Society of America (ISA)
PO Box 12277, 67 T.W. Alexander Dr., Research Triangle Park NC 27709 USA
Tel: 919-549-8411; *Fax:* 919-549-8288
info@isa.org
www.isa.org
www.linkedin.com/groups?gid=137598
www.facebook.com/InternationalSocietyOfAutomation
twitter.com/ISA_Interchange
www.flickr.com/photos/isaautomation
Previous Name: Instrument Society of America
Overview: A large international charitable organization founded in 1945
Mission: To be the foremost worldwide society involved with the science & application of measurement & control technologies; To advance members' competence, professionalism & recognition
Affiliation(s): American Association for the Advancement of Science; American Institute of Physics; International Measurement Confederation; National Institute for Certification in Engineering Technologies; National Inventors Hall of Fame; American National Standards Institute; American Society of Mechanical Engineers; Fluid Controls Institute; Institute of Electrical & Electronic Engineers
Finances: *Funding Sources:* Membership dues; Sales of books; Magazine ads; Training courses; Exhibit space; Conference registration
5000 volunteer(s)
Membership: 40,000; *Fees:* $110
Activities: *Speaker Service:* Yes; *Rents Mailing List:* Yes; *Library:* by appointment
Chief Officer(s):
Patrick Gouhin, Executive Director, 919-990-9240
pgouhin@isa.org
Tony Fragnito, Chief Financial Officer, 919-990-9438
tfragnito@isa.org
Jennifer Halsey, Director, Marketing, Communications & Corporate Partnerships, 919-990-9287
Awards:
• Bohdan (Bob) Bahniuk Scholarship (Edmonton)
• J.R. (Bob) Connell Memorial Scholarship
Eligibility: Students enrolled in Engineering Technology-related courses of study at the Northern Alberta Institute of Technology and the University of Alberta.
• Norman E. and Mary-Belle Huston Scholarship
• Bob and Mary Ives Scholarship
• Paros-Digiquartz Endowment
Amount: $2,000
• Daris and Gerald Wilbanks Endowment
• UOP Technology Award
• Kermit M. Fischer Environmental Award
• ISA Analysis Division Luft Award
• E.G. Bailey Award
• Douglas H. Annin Award
• Albert F. Sperry Award
• Arnold O. Beckman Award
• Life Achievement Award
• Honorary Member Award
Meetings/Conferences:
• The Instrumentation, Systems & Automation Society of America (ISA) 2018 Leak Detection & Repair Fugitive Emissions Symposium, March, 2018, Galveston, TX
Scope: International
Description: A series of presentations on fugitive emissions for petroleum refineries, chemical processing plants, & pharmaceutical manufacturers
• The Instrumentation, Systems & Automation Society of America (ISA) 63rd Annual Analysis Division Symposium 2018, April, 2018, Galveston Island Convention Center, Galveston, TX
Scope: International
Description: An event sponsored by the ISA Analysis Division; includes discussion of new & innovative processes, techniques, & applications in the field
Contact Information: URL: www.adsymposium.org
• The Instrumentation, Systems & Automation Society of America (ISA) 61st Power Industry Division Symposium 2018, June, 2018, Knoxville, TX
Scope: International
• The Instrumentation, Systems & Automation Society of America (ISA) 2018 Water / Wastewater & Automatic Controls Symposium, August, 2018, Bethesda, MD
Scope: International
Description: An event presented by the ISA Water / Wastewater Industries Division
• The Instrumentation, Systems & Automation Society of America (ISA) 2018 Food & Pharmaceutical Industries Division Symposium, October, 2018, Montréal, QC
Scope: International
Description: An event presented by the ISA Food & Pharmaceutical Industries Division
• The Instrumentation, Systems & Automation Society of America (ISA) 64th International Instrumentation Symposium 2018, October, 2018, Montréal, QC
Scope: International
Description: An event sponsored jointly by the Aerospace Industries, Test Measurement, and Process Measurement and Controls Divisions of ISA; includes ISA training, short courses, workshops, & tutorials

Interamerican Association of Securities Commissions & Similar Agencies *See* International Organization of Securities Commissions

Intermodal Association of North America (IANA)
#1100, 11785 Beltsville Dr., Calverton MD 20705 USA
Tel: 301-982-3400; *Fax:* 301-982-4815
info@intermodal.org
www.intermodal.org
Overview: A medium-sized international organization founded in 1991
Mission: To represent the combined interests of intermodal freight transportation companies & their suppliers
Staff Member(s): 9
Membership: 700; *Fees:* Schedule available; *Member Profile:* Intermodal freight transportation companies & their suppliers; *Committees:* Maintenance & Repair; Operations
Chief Officer(s):
Joanne F. (Joni) Casey, President & CEO, 301-982-3400 Ext. 349
Stephen Keppler, Senior Vice President, 301-982-3400 Ext. 349
Awards:
• Silver Kingpin Award
• Intermodal Achievement Award
• Chairman's Award
Meetings/Conferences:
• Intermodal Association of North America Intermodal Operations & Maintenance Business Meeting 2018, May, 2018, Lombard, IL
Scope: International
• Intermodal Association of North America Intermodal EXPO 2018, September, 2018, Long Beach, CA
Scope: International
• Intermodal Association of North America Intermodal EXPO 2019, September, 2019, Long Beach, CA
Scope: International

International Academy of Cytology (IAC)
c/o Secretary General, PO Box 1347, Freiburg 79013 Germany
Tel: 49-761-292-3801; *Fax:* 49-761-292-3802
centraloffice@cytology-iac.org
www.cytology-iac.org
Overview: A medium-sized international organization founded in 1957
Mission: To further knowledge in the field of cytopathology
Affiliation(s): European Federation of Cytology Societies; African Society of Cytology - West African; African Society of Cytology - East African; Argentinian Society of Cytology; Australian Society of Cytology; Austrian Society for Applied Cytology; Belgian Society of Clinical Cytology; Bolivian Society of Cytology; Brazilian Society of Cytopathology; British Association für Cytopathology; Canadian Society of Cytology - Société Canadienne de Cytologie; Chilean Society of Cytology; Chinese Academy of Clinical Cytology; Chinese Society of Cytopathology; Colombian Association of Cytology
Finances: *Funding Sources:* Membership dues; international congress
Membership: 1,574; *Fees:* Schedule available; *Committees:* Executive; Membership; Nominating; International Board of Cytopathology; Continuing Education; International

Cytotechnology Award; International Cytopathology Award; Budget & Finance; Constitutuin & Bylaws; Cytotechnology Registration & Renewal; Cytotechnology; Congress Organization; Future Congress Site Selection; Liaison
Activities: International Congresses every 3 years
Chief Officer(s):
Philippe Vielh, President
Fernando Schmitt, Secretary/Treasurer
Awards:
• The George L. Wied Life-Time Achievement in Cytologic Research Award
• The International Cytotechnology of the Year Award
• The James W. Reagan Lecture Award
• The Maurice Goldblatt Cytology Award
• The Kazumasa Masubuchi Life-Time Achievement in Clinical Cytology

International African Institute (IAI) / Institut africain international
School of Oriental & African Studies, Thornhaugh St., Russell Square, London WC1H 0XG United Kingdom
Tel: 44-020-7898-4420; *Fax:* 44-020-7898-4419
iai@soas.ac.uk
www.internationalafricaninstitute.org
Previous Name: International Institute of African Languages & Cultures
Overview: A small international charitable organization founded in 1926
Mission: To facilitate communication between scholars within the continent & Africans throughout the world on issues that are of direct relevance to the peoples of this region
Staff Member(s): 3
Membership: *Committees:* Council; Publications
Activities: Encourages the study of African society; bibliographies of Africa (evaluation of the degree to which the results of African research are included in bibliographies & databases); IAI seminars, held usually in Africa, bringing together small groups of African & non-African scholars to explore innovative themes
Chief Officer(s):
Philip Burnham, Honorary Director
V.Y. Mudimbe, Chairman

International Alliance of Dietary/Food Supplement Associations (IADSA)
50, rue de l'Association, Brussels B-1000 Belgium
Tel: 32-2-209-1155; *Fax:* 32-2-223-3064
secretariat@iadsa.be
www.iadsa.org
Overview: A medium-sized international organization founded in 1998
Mission: To represent the views of the industry in the shaping of global policies & regulations that affect dietary supplements; focus on regional & national regulatory programs, scientific research, & technical program for quality assurance in manufacturing of supplements.
Membership: 54 dietary supplement associations representing 20,000 companies worldwide
Chief Officer(s):
Ric Hobby, Chairman

International Alliance of Theatrical Stage Employees, Moving Picture Technicians, Artists & Allied Crafts of the U.S., Its Territories & Canada (IATSE)
207 W. 25th St., 4th Fl., New York NY 10001 USA
Tel: 212-730-1770; *Fax:* 212-730-7809
www.iatse-intl.org
www.facebook.com/iatse
twitter.com/iatse
www.flickr.com/groups/iatse
Overview: A large international organization founded in 1893
Mission: To represent workers in the entertainment industry
Membership: 113,000; *Member Profile:* Members in live theater, motion picture and television production, trade shows and exhibitions, television broadcasting, & concerts; equipment & construction shops that support these areas of the entertainment industry
Chief Officer(s):
Matthew D. Loeb, International President
James B. Wood, Secretary-Treasurer
John M. Lewis, Director, Canadian Affairs
Awards:
• Richard F. Walsh/Alfred W. Di Tolla/ Harold P. Spivak Foundation Scholarship
Eligibility: The son/daughter of a member of the IATSE; high school senior at the time of application; applying to accredited college/university *Deadline:* December 31 *Amount:* 3 at $2,500 *Contact:* IATSE Scholarship Foundation Office, c/o IATSE, 207 W. 25th St., 4th Fl.
Publications:
• Official Bulletin [a publication of IATSE]
Type: Bulletin; *Frequency:* Quarterly; *Price:* $10
• The Organizer [a publication of IATSE]
Type: Newsletter
Profile: A newsletter for the West Coast bargaining units
Canadian Office (IATSE)
511 Adelaide St. West, Toronto ON M5V 1T4
Tel: 416-364-5565; *Fax:* 416-364-5987
iatse58@iatse58.org
www.iatse58.org
Chief Officer(s):
Justin Antheunis, President
president@iatse58.org
Chuck Theil, Vice President
vicepresident@iatse58.org

International Allied Printing Trades Association / Association internationale des métiers alliés de l'imprimerie
6210 No. Capitol St., NW, Washington DC 20011 USA
Tel: 202-882-3000
Overview: A small international organization founded in 1911
Mission: Member Unions: Graphic Communications International Union; Printing, Publishing & Media Workers Sector of Communications Workers of America
6 volunteer(s)
Membership: 32 local councils
Chief Officer(s):
William J. Boarman, President
Robert Lacey, Sec.-Treas.

International Amateur Swimming Federation (IASF) / Fédération internationale de natation amateur (FINA)
Ch de Bellevue 24a/24b, Lausanne 1005 Switzerland
Tel: 41-21-310-4710; *Fax:* 41-21-312-6610
www.fina.org
www.linkedin.com/company/952149
www.facebook.com/fina1908
twitter.com/fina1908
www.youtube.com/user/fina1908
Overview: A large international organization founded in 1908
Mission: To promote and encourage the development of swimming in all possible manifestations throughout the world
Membership: 171 national federations; *Committees:* Technical Swimming, Diving, Water Polo; Technical Synchronized Swimming; Technical Open Water Swimming; Medical; Masters; Doping Panel; Press Commission
Chief Officer(s):
Paolo Barelli, Hon. Secretary
Julio C. Maglione, President
Cornel Marculescu, Executive Director
Meetings/Conferences:
• 18th FINA World Championships, July, 2019, Gwangju
Scope: International
Publications:
• FINA [International Amateur Swimming Federation] Newsletter
Type: Newsletter

International Amateur Theatre Association (IATA) / Association Internationale de Théâtre Amateur (AITA)
c/o The Questors Theatre, 19, Dorset Ave., Southall, Middlesex, London UB2 4HF United Kingdom
Tel: 372-641-8405; *Fax:* 372-641-8406
secretariat@aitaiata.org
www.aitaiata.org
Overview: A small international organization founded in 1952
Mission: To propagate & protect dramatic art by all theatrical groups of the world devoted, without remuneration, to artistic & cultural aims; to promote those activities common to its members; to coordinate the action of its members in their purpose of enriching human experience & educating people through the medium of theatre; to facilitate international exchanges between all groups belonging to the amateur theatre
Affiliation(s): Theatre Canada
Finances: *Annual Operating Budget:* $50,000-$100,000
Staff Member(s): 1; 1 volunteer(s)
Membership: 100-499
Chief Officer(s):
Paddy O'Dwyer, President
odwyerpaddy@gmail.com

International Archery Federation See World Archery Federation

International Arctic Science Committee (IASC)
Telegrafenberg A43, Postdam DE-14473 Germany
Tel: 49-331-288-2214; *Fax:* 49-331-288-2215
iasc@iasc.info
iasc.info
www.linkedin.com/company/international-arctic-science-committee
Overview: A large international organization founded in 1990
Mission: To encourage & facilitate cooperation in all aspects of arctic research, in all countries engaged in arctic research & in all areas of the arctic region; to provide scientific advice on arctic issues including environmental & technological matters
Affiliation(s): Canadian Polar Commission
Finances: *Annual Operating Budget:* $250,000-$500,000; *Funding Sources:* Government of Norway: the IASC Secretariat
Staff Member(s): 2; 150 volunteer(s)
Membership: 18 countries; *Fees:* $7,000-9,000; *Member Profile:* Significant arctic research for a period of at least 5 years
Activities: Circum-Arctic research planning; 12 project groups; Developing Arctic EIA Guidelines under the Arctic Environmental Protection Strategy & International Arctic Environmental Data Directory; *Awareness Events:* Arctic Science Summit Week; *Internships:* Yes
Chief Officer(s):
Susan Barrr, President
susan.barr@ra.no
Naja Mikkelsen, Vice-President
nm@geus.dk
Volker Rachold, Executive Secretary
Volker.Rachold@iasc.info

International Arthurian Society - North American Branch / Société internationale arthurienne
c/o Evelyn Meywer, Secretary Treasurer, 6637A San Bonita Ave., Clayton MO 63105 USA
www.international-arthurian-society-nab.org
Overview: A medium-sized international organization founded in 1948
Mission: To foster research in all areas of the Arthurian legend
Finances: *Annual Operating Budget:* Less than $50,000; *Funding Sources:* Membership dues
1 volunteer(s)
Membership: 350; *Fees:* $US50 regular; $US60 contributing; $US75 patron; $US30 student; $US40 emeritus; $US500 life
Activities: *Rents Mailing List:* Yes
Chief Officer(s):
Kevin Whetter, President
kevin.whetter@acadiau.ca
Evelyn Meyer, Secretary-Treasurer
emeyer16@slu.edu

International Association for Armenian Studies (IAAS) / Association internationale des études arméniennes (AIEA)
c/o Université de Genève, Centre de Recherches Arménologiques, 5 Candolle Rd., Geneva CH 1211 Switzerland
Tel: 41-22-379-7210; *Fax:* 41-21-802-5543
aiea.fltr.ucl.ac.be/AIEAfr/Accueil.html
Overview: A small international charitable organization founded in 1981
Mission: To promote Armenian studies
Affiliation(s): International Union for Oriental & Asian Studies
Membership: *Fees:* US$32 individual; US$20 associate; US$17 student; *Member Profile:* Armenologues
Activities: *Library:* AIEA Library; Not open to public
Chief Officer(s):
Valentina Calzolari, President
valentina.calzolari@unige.ch

International Association for Bear Research & Management (IBA)
c/o Terry While, USGS-SAFL, University of Tennessee, 274 Ellington Hall, Knoxville TN 37996 USA
Fax: 865-974-3555
www.bearbiology.com
Also Known As: IUCN/SSC Bear Specialist Group
Previous Name: Bear Biology Association
Overview: A small international charitable organization founded in 1968
Mission: To support the scientific management of bears & their habitats, through research & distribution of information
Membership: 550+ from 50+ countries; *Member Profile:* Professional biologists with an interest in bears; Wildlife

managers; Others dedicated to the conservation of all bear species; *Committees:* Conference; Publications; Membership; Website
Activities: Encouraging communication & collaboration across scientific disciplines; Increasing public awareness & understanding of bear ecology; Maintaining high standards of professional ethics; Building an endowment & a future funding base; Sponsoring workshops & conferences on bear ecology, management, & biology
Chief Officer(s):
Frank van Manen, President
vanmanen@utk.edu
Harry Reynolds, Vice-President, Americas
hreynolds@reynoldsalaska.com
Diana Doan-Crider, Secretary
d-crider@tamu.edu
Cecily Costello, Treasurer
ccostello@bresnan.net
Awards:
• Research & Conservation Grants
Contact: Dr. Frederick C. Dean, deansfs@alaska.net
• Experience & Exchange Grants
Contact: Ole Jakob Sorensen, ole.j.sorensen@hint.no
Publications:
• International Bear News
Type: Newsletter; *Frequency:* Quarterly; *Editor:* Tanya Rosen; *ISSN:* 1064-1564; *Price:* Free for members of the International Association forBear Research & Management
Profile: Articles about biology, conservation, & management of the world's eight bear species, plus reviews of books on bears
• Ursus [a publication of the International Association for Bear Research & Management]
Type: Journal; *Frequency:* Semiannually; *Editor:* Richard B. Harris; *Price:* Free for members of theInternational Association for Bear Research & Management
Profile: A peer-reviewed journal with articles on all aspects of bear management & research worldwide

International Association for Cross-Cultural Psychology (IACCP)
Institute for Psychology, Hungarian Academy of Sciences, Victor Hugo utca 18-22, Budapest 1132 Hungary
Tel: 36-70-313-87
www.iaccp.org
twitter.com/iaccp
Overview: A small international organization founded in 1972
Mission: To facilitate communication among persons interested in cross-cultural psychology issues
Affiliation(s): International Union of Psychological Science
Finances: *Funding Sources:* Membership fees; Journal revenues
Membership: 800+; *Fees:* US$20 -$85 based upon income; *Member Profile:* Academic psychologists & social scientists from over 65 countries
Chief Officer(s):
Fons van de Vijver, President
Márta Fülöp, Secretary General
martafulop@yahoo.com
Sharon Glazer, Treasurer
sharon.glazer@usa.net
Awards:
• Harry & Pola Triandis Doctoral Thesis Award
• Witkin-Okonji Memorial Fund Award
Publications:
• Cross-Cultural Psychology Bulletin
Type: Journal; *Editor:* William K. Gabrenya Jr.; *Price:* Free to IACCP members
• Journal of Cross-Cultural Psychology
Type: Journal; *Frequency:* Bimonthly; *Editor:* Deborah Best; *ISSN:* 0022-0221
Profile: Papers focussing on the interrelationships between culture & psychological processes

International Association for Earthquake Engineering (IAEE)
Central Office, Ken chiku-kaikan Bldg., 4th Fl., Minatoku Shiba 5, Chome 26-20, Tokyo 108-0014 Japan
Fax: 81-3-5730-2830
secretary@iaee.or.jp
www.iaee.or.jp
Overview: A medium-sized international organization founded in 1963
Mission: To promote international cooperation among scientists, engineers, & other professionals in the field of earthquake engineering through exchange of knowledge, ideas, results of research, & practical experience

Staff Member(s): 2
Membership: 58 countries
Chief Officer(s):
Koichi Kusunoki, Secretary General

International Association for Ecology (INTECOL)
College of Forest Science, Dept. of Forestry, Environment & Systems, Kookmin University, Seoul 136-702 Korea
www.intecol.net
Overview: A medium-sized international organization founded in 1967
Mission: To promote the development of the science of ecology & the application of ecological principles to global needs; to collect, evaluate & disseminate information about ecology; to promote international actions in ecological research
Member of: Union of Biological Societies
Membership: 1,000
Chief Officer(s):
Shona Myers, President
myers@vodafone.co.nz
Eun-Shik Kim, Secretary General
kimeuns@kookmin.ac.kr

International Association for Environmental Hydrology (IAEH)
2607 Hopeton Dr., San Antonio TX 78230 USA
Tel: 201-984-7583; *Fax:* 201-564-8581
hydroweb@gmail.com
www.hydroweb.com
Overview: A medium-sized international organization founded in 1991
Mission: To provide a place to share technical information & exchange ideas; To provide a source of inexpensive tools for the environmental hydrologist, especially hydrologists & water resource engineers in developing countries
Membership: 450; *Fees:* US$75
Publications:
• Journal of Environmental Hydrology
Type: Journal; *Frequency:* Monthly; *ISSN:* 1058-3912
Profile: Covering the fields of hydrology, environmental hydrology, urban hydrology, groundwater, groundwater pollution, groundwater contamination, & groundwater remediation

International Association for Great Lakes Research (IAGLR)
4840 South State Rd., Ann Arbor MI 48108 USA
Tel: 734-665-5303; *Fax:* 734-741-2055
office@iaglr.org
www.iaglr.org
www.facebook.com/iaglr
twitter.com/iaglr
Overview: A small international organization founded in 1967
Mission: To promote all aspects of Great Lakes research & the dissemination of research information through publications & meetings
Membership: 800; *Fees:* Schedule available; *Committees:* Awards; Conference; Endowment; Membership; Nominations; Outreach; Publications; Website
Activities: Organizing conferences on Great Lakes Research to exchange information on all aspects of research applicable to the understanding of large lakes of the world & to the human societies surrounding them; Publishing Great Lakes research; Offering awards & student scholarships
Chief Officer(s):
Tomas Hook, President
president@iaglr.org
Wendy Foster, Business Manager
Paula McIntyre, Director, Communications
mcintyre@iaglr.org
Awards:
• IAGLR Scholarship
To a M.Sc or PhD student whose proposed research topic is relevant to large lake research *Deadline:* December *Amount:* US$2,000
• Norman S. Baldwin Fishery Science Scholarship
Deadline: December *Amount:* US$3,000
• Chandler-Misener Award
Presented annually to the author(s) of the paper in the current volume of the peer reviewed Journal of Great Lakes Research judged to be "most notable"
• Anderson-Everett Award
Recognizes important & continued contributions to the Association
• Editor's Award
Presented for outstanding support of the Journal's review process

• John R. (Jack) Vallentyne Award
Offered for the best oral & poster presentations given by students at the annual conference; co-sponsored by Hydrolab Inc.
• David M. Dolan Scholarship
Awarded annually to senior undergraduate, masters or doctoral student who wishes to pursue a future in research, conservation, education, communication, management or other knowledge-based activity pertaining to the Great Lakes
Deadline: December *Amount:* US$3,000
• IAGLR Best Student Paper Award
• IAGLR Best Student Poster Award
• IAGLR Certificate of Appreciation
• IAGLR Lifetime Achievement Award
• JGLR/Elsevier Early Career Scientist Award
• JGLR/Elsevier Student Award
Meetings/Conferences:
• International Association for Great Lakes Research 2018 Annual Conference, 2018, University of Toronto Scarborough, Toronto, ON
Scope: International
Publications:
• Journal of Great Lakes Research
Type: Journal; *Frequency:* Quarterly; *Editor:* Robert Hecky; Stephanie Guildford
Profile: Peer-reviewed journal publishing research on the world's large lakes & watersheds from a range of fields

International Association for Human Resource Information Management (IHRIM)
10060 Grandview Sq., Duluth GA 30097 USA
e-mail: information@ihrim.org
www.ihrim.org
www.linkedin.com/company/ihrim-international-association-for-human-resource-information-management-
www.facebook.com/IHRIMAssociation
twitter.com/IHRIM
Overview: A medium-sized international charitable organization founded in 1980
Mission: To operate as a clearinghouse for the HRIM industry; To enable members to achieve strategic objectives through the integration of information technology & human resource management
Finances: *Funding Sources:* Membership fees
Membership: 5,000; *Fees:* US$295; schedule
Activities: Offering educational programs, including webinars, conferences, courses, forums, & resources; *Speaker Service:* Yes
Chief Officer(s):
Laurie Carantit, Director, Operations
lcarantit@ihrim.org
Awards:
• IHRIM Chair's Award
• IHRIM Ambassador Award
• IHRIM Summit Award
• IHRIM Partners Award
• Project of the Year Award
Meetings/Conferences:
• International Association for Human Resource Information Management 2018 Select Event, March, 2018, Marina Village Conference Center, San Diego, CA
Scope: International
Description: Theme: "Selecting the Right System and Implementation Partner for Organization Success"
• International Association for Human Resource Information Management 2018 Talent Event, July, 2018, Huntington Convention Center, Cleveland, OH
Scope: International
Description: Theme: "The Talent Management Revolution: Technology's Role in Organizational Success"
• International Association for Human Resource Information Management 2018 Data Event, November, 2018, Austin, TX
Scope: International
Description: Theme: "Advancing from Data to Knowledge & Intelligence"
Publications:
• Workforce Solutions Review
Type: Journal; *Frequency:* Quarterly; *ISSN:* 2154-6975

International Association for Hydrogen Energy (IAHE)
#303, 5794 - 40th St. SW, Miami FL 33155 USA
e-mail: info@iahe.org
www.iahe.org
Overview: A medium-sized international organization

Mission: To provide information about the role of hydrogen energy
Membership: *Member Profile:* Professional individuals in fields related to hydrogen energy; Laypersons with an interest in hydrogen energy; IAHE Fellows; Emeritus members; Students
Chief Officer(s):
T. Nejat Veziroglu, President
veziroglu@iahe.org
John W. Sheffield, Executive Vice President, North America
davidsanbornscott@gmail.com
Awards:
• Jules Verne Award
Honours superior service to the IAHE
• Rudolph A. Erren Award
Honours leadership & excellence in the thermochemical field
• Sir William Grove Award
Honours leadership & excellence in the electrochemical field
• Akira Mitsui Award
Honours leadership & excellence in the biological field
• Konstantin Tsiolkovsky Award
Honours leadership & excellence in the aerospace field
Meetings/Conferences:
• International Association for Hydrogen Energy (IAHE) 22nd World Hydrogen Energy Conference 2018, June, 2018, Rio De Janerio
Scope: International
Description: A conference of the International Association for Hydrogen Energy, for the hydrogen & fuel cell community, featuring an exhibition with hydrogen & fuel cell applications from research institutions & companies
• International Association for Hydrogen Energy (IAHE) 8th World Hydrogen Technology Convention 2019, June, 2019, Tokyo
Scope: International
Description: A conference of the International Association for Hydrogen Energy, for the hydrogen & fuel cell community, featuring an exhibition with hydrogen & fuel cell applications from research institutions & companies
Publications:
• International Journal of Hydrogen Energy
Type: Journal; *Editor:* T. Nejat Veziroglu; *ISBN:* 0360-3199
Profile: Ideas in the field of hydrogen energy for environmentalists, chemists, energy researchers, energy companies, & engineering students

International Association for Impact Assessment (IAIA)
1330 - 23rd St. South, #C, Fargo ND 58103-3705 USA
Tel: 701-297-7908; *Fax:* 701-297-7917
info@iaia.org
www.iaia.org
www.linkedin.com/company/international-association-for-impact-assessme
www.facebook.com/iaia.impact.assessment
www.youtube.com/iaiachannel
Overview: A small international organization founded in 1980
Mission: To be a forum for advancing innovation, development & communication of best practice in impact assessment; to promote the development of local & global capacity for the application of environmental assessment in which sound science & full public participation provide a foundation for equitable & sustainable development
Affiliation(s): International Society of City & Regional Planners; Environment Institute of Australia & New Zealand; South Asian Regional Environment Assessment Association; Japan Society for Impact Assessment; Chinese Association of Environmental Protection Industry
Finances: *Funding Sources:* Membership fees; meeting registration
Staff Member(s): 6
Membership: 1,600 in more than 120 countries; *Fees:* US$110 individual (base rate); US$55 student; US$1,000 standard corporate; US$5,000 stewardship corporate; *Member Profile:* Corporate planners & managers; public interest advocates; government planners & administrators; private consultants & policy analysts; college teachers; students
Activities: Presentation of papers, posters, plenary sessions, exhibits, technical tours, pre-meeting training courses
Chief Officer(s):
Rita R. Hamm, Chief Executive Officer, 701-297-7912
rita@iaia.org
Greg Radford, President, 613-798-1300
gradford@essa.com
Awards:
• Corporate

• Best Poster
• Global Environment
• Regional
• Institutional
• Individual
• IAPA Best Paper
• Outstanding Service to IAIA
• Rose-Hulman Award

International Association for Neo-Latin Studies (IANLS)
c/o Raija Sarasti-Wilenius, Institutum classicum, PB 24, SF-00014 University of Helsinki, Finland
Tel: 358405457597
www.ianls.org
Overview: A small international organization
Mission: To study & promote Neo-Latin studies
Affiliation(s): Fédération internationale des langues et littératures modernes
Finances: *Funding Sources:* Membership dues
Membership: 100-499; *Fees:* 40 Euro; *Member Profile:* Interest in all branches of Neo-Latin studies
Chief Officer(s):
Craig Kallendorf, President
kalendrf@tamu.edu
Jan Papy, Treasurer
jan.papy@arts.kuleuven.be

International Association for Patristic Studies *Voir* Association internationale des études patristiques

International Association for Public Participation (IAP2)
PO Box 270723, Louisville CO 80027 USA
e-mail: iap2hq@iap2.org
www.iap2.org
www.linkedin.com/company/iap2
Previous Name: International Association of Public Participation Practitioners
Overview: A medium-sized international organization founded in 1990
Mission: To serve the learning needs of members through events, publications, & communication technology; To advocate for public participation throughout the world; to promote research; To provide technical assistance
Membership: 1,100; *Fees:* Schedule available; *Member Profile:* Public participation designers & facilitators; Policymakers; Project managers; Representatives from government agencies; Members of advocacy groups & professional organizations; trainers; Mediators; Citizen activists
Chief Officer(s):
Ellen Ernst, Executive Manager

International Association for the Study of Pain (IASP)
IASP Secretariat, #600, 1510 H St. NW, Washington, DC 20005-1020 USA
Tel: 202-524-5300; *Fax:* 202-524-5301
iaspdesk@iasp-pain.org
www.iasp-pain.org
www.linkedin.com/company/1022844
www.facebook.com/IASP.pain
twitter.com/IASPPAIN
Overview: A medium-sized international charitable organization founded in 1973
Mission: To provide a professional forum for science, practice, & education in the field of pain
Member of: World Federation of Neurology; World Federation of Ageing
Affiliation(s): Canadian Pain Society; World Health Organization
Finances: *Funding Sources:* Membership dues; Meetings; Book sales; Journal royalties; Donations
Staff Member(s): 13
Membership: *Fees:* Schedule available; *Member Profile:* All professionals involved in pain research, diagnosis, or treatment, including scientists, clinicians, health care providers, & policy makers; *Committees:* Audit; Committee on Committees; Finance; Local Arrangements; Membership & Chapters; Nominations; Scientific Program
Activities: Special interest groups include the following: Acute Pain; Pain & Pain Management in Non-Human Species; Pain in Childhood; Pain in Older Persons; Pain Related to Torture, Organized Violence, and War; Pain & the Sympathetic Nervous System; Systematic Reviews in Pain Relief; Clinical-Legal Issues; Systematic Reviews in Pain; Placebo; Sex Gender & Pain; Orofacial Pain; Neuropathic Pain; Urogenital Pain; & Pain & Movement; *Rents Mailing List:* Yes
Chief Officer(s):
Matthew D'Uva, Executive Director
matthew.duva@iasp-pain.org
Rolf-Detlef Treede, President
Srinivasa Raja, Secretary
Michael Rowbotham, Treasurer
Awards:
• Patrick D. Wall Young Investigator Award
• IASP Trainee Research Prize
• John J. Bonica Trainee Fellowship
• IASP Research Symposium Grant
• Collaborative Research Grants
• John J. Bonica Distiguished Lecture
Publications:
• IASP Newsletter
Type: Newsletter; *Frequency:* Quarterly
Profile: Activities of IASP, its chapters, & special interest groups for members
• PAIN
Type: Journal; *Frequency:* 18 pa
Profile: Peer-reviewed, original research on the nature, mechanisms, & treatment of pain
• Pain: Clinical Updates
Type: Newsletter
Profile: Details about pain therapy for clinicians, patients & families

International Association of Administrative Professionals (IAAP)
#100, 10502 North Ambassador Dr., Kansas City MO 64153 USA
Tel: 816-891-6600; *Fax:* 816-891-9118
www.iaap-hq.org
www.linkedin.com/groups/97764
www.facebook.com/iaaphq
twitter.com/iaap
Previous Name: Professional Secretaries International
Overview: A large international organization founded in 1981
Mission: To effect increased productivity, career development & quality of work life within office environments by providing opportunities for educational, personal & professional growth; To be the acknowledged, recognized leader of office professionals & to enhance their individual & collective value, image, competence & influence
Affiliation(s): American Society for Training & Development
Finances: *Annual Operating Budget:* $1.5 Million-$3 Million
Staff Member(s): 20
Membership: 22,000 and over 500 chapters; *Fees:* $25 student; $150 professional; *Member Profile:* Professional - employed secretary or certified professional secretary recipient or employed teacher of business education; student - enrolled student of business education; associate - individual, firm or educational institution which sustains objectives; *Committees:* Bylaws & Standing Rules; Nominations; CPS Service; Education & Program; Student Advisory; Membership; Retirement Centre; Bulletin Award; Public Relations; Executive Advisory Board Ad Hoc Committee
Activities: *Internships:* Yes; *Speaker Service:* Yes; *Rents Mailing List:* Yes; *Library*
Chief Officer(s):
Veronica Cochran, CEO
veronica.cochran@iaap-hq.org
Meetings/Conferences:
• International Association of Administrative Professionals Summit 2018, July, 2018, JW Marriott Austin, Austin, TX
Scope: International
Description: Education workshops
• International Association of Administrative Professionals Summit 2019, July, 2019, Gaylord National, National Harbor, MD
Scope: International
Description: Education workshops
Publications:
• OfficePro [a publication of International Association of Administrative Professionals]
Type: Magazine

International Association of Agricultural Economists (IAAE)
#1100, 555 East Wells St., Milwaukee WI 53202 USA
Tel: 414-918-3199; *Fax:* 414-276-3349
iaae@execinc.com
www.iaae-agecon.org
Overview: A medium-sized international organization founded in 1929

Foreign Associations / International Association of Bridge, Structural, Ornamental & Reinforcing Iron Workers (AFL-CIO) / Association internationale des travailleurs de ponts, de fer structural et ornemental (FAT-COI)

Mission: To foster the application of agricultural economics to improve rural economic & social conditions; to advance knowledge of agriculture's economic organization; to facilitate communication & information exchange among those concerned with rural welfare
Affiliation(s): Canadian Council - International Association of Agricultural Economists
Finances: Annual Operating Budget: $50,000-$100,000
Membership: 1,700; Fees: US$60-US$175; Member Profile: A worldwide confederation of agricultural economists & others concerned with agricultural economic problems
Activities: Rents Mailing List: Yes
Chief Officer(s):
Johan Swinnen, President
jo.swinnen@econ.kuleuven.be
Walter J. Armbruster, Secretary-Treasurer, 630-271-1679, Fax: 630-908-3384
walt@farmfoundation.org

International Association of Assembly Managers, Inc. See International Association of Venue Managers, Inc.

International Association of Bridge, Structural, Ornamental & Reinforcing Iron Workers (AFL-CIO) / Association internationale des travailleurs de ponts, de fer structural et ornemental (FAT-COI)
#400, 1750 New York Ave. NW, Washington DC 20006 USA
Tel: 202-383-4800; Fax: 202-638-4856
iwmagazine@iwintl.org
www.ironworkers.org
www.facebook.com/unionironworkers
twitter.com/TheIronworkers
www.youtube.com/user/UnionIronworkers
Overview: A medium-sized international organization
Mission: To represent ironworkers & advocate for employment opportunities, fair pay, health & welfare benefits, continuing education, & other workers' rights
Membership: 15,300 + 23 locals
Chief Officer(s):
Eric Dean, General President
Ron Piksa, General Secretary
Publications:
• The Ironworker [a publication of the International Association of Bridge, Structural, Ornamental & Reinforcing Iron Workers]
Type: Magazine; ISSN: 0021-163X

International Association of Business Communicators (IABC)
#1210, 155 Montgomery St., San Francisco CA 94104 USA
Tel: 415-544-4700; Fax: 415-544-4747
Toll-Free: 800-776-4222
member_relations@iabc.com
www.iabc.org
www.linkedin.com/company/26095
www.facebook.com/IABCWorld
twitter.com/iabc
www.youtube.com/iabclive
Overview: A large international organization founded in 1970
Mission: To lead in use of information technology; To unite a diverse global network; To provide lifelong learning & research; To share ethical & effective performance standards & global best practices
Finances: Annual Operating Budget: $3 Million-$5 Million
Staff Member(s): 22
Membership: 14,000; Committees: Executive; Accreditation
Activities: Speaker Service: Yes; Rents Mailing List: Yes; Library: by appointment
Chief Officer(s):
Dianne Chase, Chair
Stephanie Doute, Acting Executive Director
sdoute@iabc.com
Awards:
• Gold Quill Awards
• Excellence in Communication Leadership (EXCEL) Award
Awarded to individuals who foster excellence in organizational communication Deadline: February
• Fellow Award
For outstanding leadership, professional accomplishment & service to IABC & the profession Deadline: January
• Chairman's Award
Awarded to one or more individuals who have worked behind the scenes to benefit both the IABC & the profession
Publications:
• Communication World (CW) [a publication of the International Association of Business Communicators]
Type: Magazine; Price: $150 non-member

• CW Bulletin [a publication of the International Association of Business Communicators]
Type: Newsletter; Editor: Natasha Nicholson
Calgary Chapter
#400, 1040 - 7 Ave. SW, Calgary AB T2P 2G9
Tel: 403-270-4222; Fax: 403-244-2340
calgary-info@iabc.com
calgary.iabc.com
www.linkedin.com/groups/IABC-Calgary-4958331
www.facebook.com/IABC.Calgary
twitter.com/IABCyyc
Chief Officer(s):
Jennifer de Vries, President
Calgary-executive@iabc.com
Toronto Chapter
#1, 189 Queen St. East, Toronto ON M5A 1S2
Tel: 416-968-0264; Fax: 416-968-6818
toronto-info@iabc.com
toronto.iabc.com
www.linkedin.com/groups?gid=1878089
www.facebook.com/IABCToronto
twitter.com/IABCtoronto
www.youtube.com/user/IABCToronto
Mission: To help members achieve their personal & career aspirations by providing quality programmes & services that advance the standards & practices of communication, & that enable members to help their organizations realize their goals
Chief Officer(s):
Stephanie Engel, President
toronto-president@iabc.com

International Association of Chiefs of Police (IACP)
#200, 44 Canal Center Plaza, Alexandria VA 22314 United States
Tel: 703-836-6767; Fax: 703-836-4543
www.fncpa.ca
www.facebook.com/TheIACP
twitter.com/TheIACP
www.youtube.com/theiacp
Overview: A medium-sized international organization founded in 1893
Mission: To promote improved police services, & cooperation & exchange of information among police chiefs throughout the world
Membership: Committees: Membership Benefits; Conference; Foundation; Communications; Training; Management Assistance; State & Provincial Services
Chief Officer(s):
Michael Wagers, Contact, State & Provincial Police
wagers@theiacp.org

International Association of Educators for World Peace - USA (IAEWP) / Association internationale des éducateurs pour la paix du monde
PO Box 3282, Stn. Mastin Lake, Huntsville AB 35810-0282 USA
Tel: 256-534-5501; Fax: 256-536-1018
Overview: A medium-sized international organization founded in 1969
Mission: To promote international understanding & world peace through education; to protect the environment from man-made pollution; to safeguard human rights; to encourage disarmament & development
Member of: United Nations (ECOSOC); UNDPI; UNICEF; UNCED; UNESCO
Affiliation(s): International Association of Educators for World Peace - National Office
Finances: Annual Operating Budget: Less than $50,000; Funding Sources: Donations
Staff Member(s): 30
Membership: 35,000 in 92 countries
Activities: Conventions; peace education studies & programs; gives more than 20 awards; Speaker Service: Yes; Rents Mailing List: Yes; Library: Research Centre; by appointment
Chief Officer(s):
Charles Mercieca, President

International Association of Environmental Analytical Chemistry (IAEAC)
c/o Dr. Montserrat Filella, Institut F.- A. Forel, Route de Suisse, Versoix 1290 Switzerland
Tel: 41 22 379 03 00; Fax: 41 22 379 03 29
iaeac@dplanet.ch
www.iaeac.ch
Overview: A small international organization founded in 1977
Mission: To support regular exchange of experiences between experts in the field of analytical chemistry of pollutants & related

areas; To orient its members about recent advances in the field; To address relevant problems of environmental analysis & on questions related to environmental protection & control
Staff Member(s): 1
Membership: 110-130; Fees: SFR 110-300
Chief Officer(s):
Montserrat Filella, Secretary
montserrat.filella@unige.ch
José A.C. Broekaert, President
jose.broekaert@chemie.uni-hamburg.de

International Association of Fire Fighters (AFL-CIO/CLC) (IAFF) / Association internationale des pompiers (FAT-COI/CTC)
#300, 1750 New York Ave. NW, Washington DC 20006-5395 USA
Tel: 202-737-8484; Fax: 202-737-8418
membership@iaff.org
www.iaff.org
www.facebook.com/IAFFonline
twitter.com/iaffnewsdesk
www.pinterest.com/iaffnewsdesk;
www.youtube.com/user/IAFFTV
Overview: A large international organization founded in 1918
Mission: To establish professional standards for the North American fire service with active political & legislative programs, & with experts in the fields of occupational health & safety, fire-based emergency medical services & hazardous materials training; to provide a voice in the development & implementation of new training & equipment; to work to ensure the staffing of fire & EMS departments
Membership: 300,000+ fire fighters & paramedics in the U.S. & Canada + 3,200 affiliates; Member Profile: Full-time professional fire fighters & paramedics
Activities: Library
Chief Officer(s):
Harold A. Schaitberger, General President
Thomas H. Miller, General Secretary-Treasurer
Jim Lee, Chief of Staff
Juliet Mason, Director, Membership
jmason@iaff.org
Awards:
• The International Association of Fire Fighters Media Awards Contest
• W. H. "Howie" McClennan Scholarship
Eligibility: Sons, daughters, or legally adopted children of fire fighters killed in the line of duty Deadline: February 1 Amount: $2,500 / year
• Harvard University Trade Union Program Scholarship
Awarded to IAFF members in good standing with an IAFF local affiliate to attend the Harvard University Trade Union Program Deadline: July 1 Amount: Tuition + $1,000
• Harvard Law School/University of Ottawa Executive Leadership Program
Two scholarships are available for IAFF members to attend the Harvard Law School/University of Ottawa Executive Leadership Program; the scholarship is allocated to offset tuition, accomodation, travel, & allowable expenses Deadline: July 31 Amount: $15,000 per year
Publications:
• Fire Fighter Quarterly [a publication of the International Association of Fire Fighters (AFL-CIO/CLC)]
Type: Magazine; Frequency: Quarterly; Editor: Harold A. Schaitberger; ISSN: 2333-3669
Canadian Office
#403, 350 Sparks St., Ottawa ON K1R 7S8
Tel: 613-567-8988; Fax: 613-567-8986
www.iaff.org/canada
www.facebook.com/IAFFCanada
twitter.com/IAFFCanada
Mission: To represent Canada's professional fire fighters and work towards better working conditions & wages; 4 district Vice Presidents respresent regions of Canada
Chief Officer(s):
Scott Marks, Asst. to President, Canadian Operations
smarks@iaff.org

International Association of Fish & Wildlife Agencies See Association of Fish & Wildlife Agencies

International Association of Hydrogeologists (IAH)
IAH Secretariat, PO Box 4130, Stn. Goring, Reading RG8 6BJKOA 1L0 UK
Tel: +44 870 762 4462; Fax: +44 870 762 8462
info@iah.org
www.iah.org

Overview: A medium-sized international organization founded in 1956
Mission: To advance the science of hydrogeology & exchange hydrogeologic information internationally
Affiliation(s): UNESCO; International Union of Geological Sciences
Membership: 4,000 in 135 countries; 300 in Canada
Chief Officer(s):
John Chilton, Executive Manager, IAH Secretariat
jchilton@iah.org
Meetings/Conferences:
• 45th International Association of Hydrogeologists Congress, September, 2018, Daejeon
Scope: International
Contact Information: www.iah2018.org

International Association of Judges (IAJ) / Union internationale des magistrats (UIM)
Palazzo di Giustizia, Piazza Cavour, Rome 00193 Italy
Tel: 39-066-883-2213; Fax: 39-066-871-1195
secretariat@iaj-uim.org
www.iaj-uim.org
Overview: A small international organization founded in 1953
Mission: To defend the independence of the judiciary; to promote the exchange of cultural relations between judges of different countries; the IAJ has full consultative status with the Council of Europe, the International Labour Office, & the UN Economic & Social Council
Affiliation(s): Council of Europe; International Labour Office; UN Economic & Social Council
Finances: Funding Sources: Membership fees
Membership: 81 national associations of judges; Member Profile: National associations of judges which represent the judiciary of their country; Committees: Presidency Committee
Activities: Meetings & exchanges of information & experiences
Chief Officer(s):
Giacomo Oberto, Secretary General
secretariat@iaj-uim.org
Gerhard Reissner, President
Cristina Crespo, First Vice-President
Awards:
• Justice in the World Award

International Association of Machinists & Aerospace Workers (IAMAW) / Association internationale des machinistes et des travailleurs de l'aérospatiale
Machinists Bldg., 9000 Machinists Pl., Upper Marlboro MD 20772-2687 USA
Tel: 301-967-4500
www.iamaw.ca
www.facebook.com/machinistsunion
twitter.com/machinistsunion
Overview: A small international organization
Mission: To work as the negotiating body for its members
Membership: 720,000 across North America
Chief Officer(s):
R. Thomas Buffenbarger, President
Publications:
• IAM Journal for Fighting Machinists
Type: Journal
Profile: International Association of Machinists news & stories

> **Canadian Office (IAMAW-AIMTA)**
> #707, 15 Gervais Dr., Toronto ON M3C 1Y8
> Tel: 416-386-1789
> Toll-Free: 877-426-1426
> info@iamaw.ca
> www.iamaw.ca
> twitter.com/iamawcanada
> www.youtube.com/user/IAMAWCanada
> **Chief Officer(s):**
> Dave Ritchie, General Vice-President, Canada

International Association of Marine Aids to Navigation & Lighthouse Authorities (IALA) / Association internationale de signalisation maritime (AISM)
10, rue des Gaudines, Saint-Germain-en-Laye 78100 France
Tel: 33-1-3451-7001; Fax: 33-1-3451-8205
contact@iala-aism.org
www.iala-aism.org
Overview: A small international organization founded in 1957
Mission: To ensure that the movements of vessels are safe, fast & economical by developing ways to improve navigation aides & maritime traffic
Finances: Annual Operating Budget: $3 Million-$5 Million; Funding Sources: Membership dues; Publications; Seminars & workshops; IALA Conferences; World Wide Academy
Staff Member(s): 12
Membership: 280; Fees: 14,000 Euros national; 5,700 Euros industrial; 2,730 Euros associate; Member Profile: Services de signalisation maritime; ports maritimes; fabricants d'équipement; consultants; Committees: Aids to Navigation Management; Engineering, Environmental and Preservation; e-Navigation; Vessel Traffic Service
Activities: Radionavigation commissions; Operating engineering services; various seminars - conferences; exhibitions every 4 years; Library: by appointment

International Association of Museums of Arms & Military History See International Committee of Museums & Collections of Arms & Military History

International Association of Music Libraries, Archives & Documentation Centres (IAML) / Association internationale des bibliothèques, archives et de documentation musicaux
c/o Roger Flury, Music Room, National Library of New Zealand, PO Box 1467, Wellington 6001 New Zealand
Tel: +64 4 474 3039; Fax: +64 4 474 3035
www.iaml.info
Overview: A small international organization founded in 1951
Mission: To promote the activities of music libraries, archives, & documentation centres nationally & internationally; To encourage international cooperation; To support projects in music bibliography, music documentation, & music library & information science
Member of: International Federation of Library Associations & Institutions (IFLA); International Council on Archives (ICA); European Bureau of Library, Information & Documentation Associations (EBLIDA); International Music Council (IMC)
Affiliation(s): International Association of Sound Archives (IASA); International Association of Music Information Centres (IAMIC)
Membership: 2,000 individual & institutional members from 45 countries; Member Profile: Music & audio-visual librarians; Music archivists; Documentation specialists; Musicologists; Music publishers; Music dealers; Major music collections; Committees: Constitution; Copyright; Information Technology; Outreach; Programme; Publications
Activities: Supporting members' interests
Chief Officer(s):
Roger Flury, Secretary General
roger.flury@natlib.govt.nz
Kathryn Adamson, Treasurer
Meetings/Conferences:
• 2018 International Association of Music Libraries, Archives & Documentation Centres Congress, July, 2018, Leipzig
Scope: International
Description: Educational sessions, social & cultural programs, & exhibits of interest to international music librarians, archivists, & documentation specialists
• 2019 International Association of Music Libraries, Archives & Documentation Centres Congress, July, 2019, Krakow
Scope: International
Description: Educational sessions, social & cultural programs, & exhibits of interest to international music librarians, archivists, & documentation specialists
Publications:
• Fontes artis musicae
Type: Journal; Frequency: Quarterly; Editor: Maureen Buja, PhD
Profile: Articles related to music librarianship, documentation, bibliography, & musicology, available only to association members
• IAML Newsletter
Type: Newsletter; Accepts Advertising; Editor: Brian McMillan
Profile: Association & country reports, plus articles

International Association of Patristic Studies (IAPS) / Association internationale d'études patristiques
Università Cattolica del Sacro Cuore, Largo Gemelli 1, Milan 20123 Italy
www.aiep-iaps.org
Overview: A small international organization founded in 1965
Mission: To promote the study of Christian antiquity; To connect individuals whose work relates to patristic research; To provide information on published works or works in progress in the Christian antiquity field
Membership: Member Profile: Scholars in patristics who have published at least one article in a high-level, peer-reviewed scientific journal
Activities: Offering scholarships to students
Chief Officer(s):
Theodore S. de Bruyn, President
tdebruyn@uottawa.ca
Marco Rizzi, Secretary
marco.rizzi@unicatt.it
Publications:
• Annuaire
Frequency: Biennially
Profile: Contact information of association members
• Bulletin d'information et de liaison
Frequency: Annually
Profile: Information on research projects, dissertations, publications, resources, initiatives, & events in the patristics field

International Association of Penal Law Voir Association internationale de droit pénal

International Association of Physicians in Audiology
c/o Dept. Audiovestibular Medicine, University College London Hospital, London United Kingdom
www.iapa-audiovestibularmedicine.com
Overview: A small international organization founded in 1980
Mission: To promote & improve clinical, ethical & scientific standards in the field of audiological medicine
Finances: Annual Operating Budget: Less than $50,000
Membership: 200; Fees: 50 Euro; Member Profile: Medically qualified in audiology
Chief Officer(s):
Quiju Wang, President
Chrysa Spyridakou, Honorary Secretary

International Association of Ports & Harbours (IAPH)
7F South Tower, New Pier Takeshiba, 1-16-1 Kaigan, Minato-Ku, Tokyo 105-0022 Japan
Tel: 81-3-5403-2770; Fax: 81-3-5403-7651
info@iaphworldports.org
www.iaphworldports.org
www.facebook.com/iaphworldports
Overview: A large international organization founded in 1955
Mission: To promote the development of the international port & maritime industry by fostering cooperation among members in order to build a more cohesive partnership among the world's ports & harboursd; To ensure that the industry's interests & views are represented before international organizations involved n the regulation of international trade & transportation; Tto collect, analyse, exchange & distribute information on developing trends in international trade, transportation, ports & the regulations of these industries
Affiliation(s): International Maritime Organization; United Nations Conference on Trade & Development; United Nations Economic & Social Council; Permanent International Association of Navigation Congresses; International Cargo Handling Coordination Association; International Maritime Pilots Association; International Association of Independent Tanker Owners; Baltic & International Martime Council
Finances: Annual Operating Budget: $1.5 Million-$3 Million; Funding Sources: Membership fees
Staff Member(s): 7
Membership: 360; Fees: Schedule available; Member Profile: Countries with maritime-based industries; Committees: Executive; Communication & Community Relations; Port Finance & Economics; Port Safety & Security; Port Environment; Legal; Port Planning & Development; Port Operations & Logistics; Trade Facilitation & Port Community System; Conference; Finance; Constitution & By-Laws; Membership; Long Range Planning/Review
Activities: Library: International Association of Ports & Harbours Library; Not open to public
Chief Officer(s):
Susumu Naruse, Secretary General
Publications:
• IAPH [International Association of Ports & Harbors] Annual Report
Type: Report; Frequency: a.; Number of Pages: 28
Profile: Highlights executives, information and events relevant to members of the IAPH

International Association of Professional Congress Organizers (IAPCO)
Brambles House, Colwell Rd., Freshwater PO40 9SL UK
Tel: 44 1983 755546
info@iapco.org
www.iapco.org
twitter.com/IAPCO
Overview: A small international organization founded in 1968

Foreign Associations / International Association of Rebekah Assemblies

Mission: To undertake & promote the study of theoretical & practical aspects of international congresses; To develop a programme of educational courses through its Institute for Congress Management Training; To undertake research work concerning all problems confronting professional organizers of international meetings, & to seek & promote relevant solutions; To further the recognition of the profession of congress organizer
Affiliation(s): IAPCO Training Academy
Staff Member(s): 1
Membership: 6 individual + 67 corporate (includes 5 corporate Canadian); *Fees:* 2,200 euro; *Member Profile:* Professional congress organizing companies; individuals employed by the congress dept. of associations & companies; freelance individuals engaged on a permanent basis in the organization of international meetings; must have been responsible for 10 international meetings attended by representatives of more than 3 different countries, of at least 4 days' duration, & at least 5 of which have been attended by at least 400 delegates
Activities: Responsible for the activities of the Institute for Congress Management Training (ICMT) which offers a comprehensive programme of training seminars
Chief Officer(s):
Sarah Storie-Pugh, Administrator

International Association of Public Participation Practitioners *See* International Association for Public Participation

International Association of Rebekah Assemblies
c/o The Sovereign Grand Lodge IOOF, 422 Trade St., Winston-Salem NC 27101 USA
Tel: 336-725-6037; *Fax:* 336-773-1066
Toll-Free: 800-766-1838
iarasec@aol.com
www.ioof.org
Overview: A medium-sized international organization founded in 1914
Mission: The Rebekah lodges are the female auxiliary of the Independent Order of Odd Fellows, but are open to both women and men.
Finances: *Annual Operating Budget:* $250,000-$500,000; *Funding Sources:* Donations
Staff Member(s): 2
Membership: 97,000
Activities: Arthritis Telethon

International Association of Sedimentologists (IAS)
c/o Ghent University, #8, Krijgslaan 281, Gent 90000 Belgium
www.sedimentologists.org
Overview: A medium-sized international organization founded in 1952
Mission: To promote the study of sedimentology by publication, discussion & comparison of research results; To encourage the interchange of research, particularly where international cooperation is desirable; To promote integration with other disciplines
Member of: International Union of Geological Sciences
Finances: *Annual Operating Budget:* $500,000-$1.5 Million; *Funding Sources:* Membership dues; Sales of books
Staff Member(s): 1
Membership: 1,700; *Fees:* EUR 25 full member; EUR 10 student
Chief Officer(s):
Adrian Immenhauser, President
Awards:
• Travel Grants
• Postgraduate Grant Program
• Institutional IAS Grant Program
• Sorby Medal
• Johannest Walther Award
• Early-Career Scientist Award
• Honorary Member Award
• Richard W. Faas Research Prize
Meetings/Conferences:
• International Association of Sedimentologists (IAS) International Sedimentological Congress 2018, August, 2018, Québec, QC
Scope: International
• International Association of Sedimentologists (IAS) 34th Meeting of Sedimentology 2019, 2019
Scope: International
Publications:
• The Depositional Record [a publication of the International Association of Sedimentologists]
Type: Journal; *Editor:* Peter Swart; *ISSN:* 2055-4877

• Sedimentology [a publication of the International Association of Sedimentologists]
Type: Journal; *Frequency:* 7 pa.; *Editor:* Tracy Frank & Nigel Mountney; *ISSN:* 1365-3091

International Association of Theoretical and Applied Limnology; Societas Internationalis Limnologiae, SIL *See* International Society of Limnology

International Association of University Professors of English (IAUPE)
Fribourg Switzerland
e-mail: iaupe.secretarygeneral@gmail.com
www.iaupe.org
Overview: A small international organization founded in 1951
Mission: To promote the development of English studies at the university level on a worldwide basis
Affiliation(s): Fédération internationale des langues et littératures modernes
Finances: *Funding Sources:* Membership dues
Membership: 500; *Member Profile:* University professors of English Language &/or Literature; other scholars of distinction in these & related fields; *Committees:* Executive; International
Chief Officer(s):
Thomas Austenfeld, Secretary General & Treasurer
Jane Roberts, President
Publications:
• IAUPE Bulletin
Type: Newsletter; *Editor:* A. Breeze

International Association of Venue Managers, Inc. (IAVM)
#100, 635 Fritz Dr., Coppell TX 75019-4442 USA
Tel: 972-906-7441; *Fax:* 972-906-7418
Toll-Free: 800-935-4226
www.iavm.org
www.linkedin.com/company/IAVM
www.facebook.com/IAVMWHQ
twitter.com/IAVMWHQ
Previous Name: International Association of Assembly Managers, Inc.
Overview: A medium-sized international organization founded in 1924
Mission: To provide leadership & to educate; to inform & to cultivate friendships among individuals involved in the management, operation & support of venues
Finances: *Annual Operating Budget:* $3 Million-$5 Million; *Funding Sources:* Membership dues; conferences; trade show; seminars; services; IAVM Foundation
Staff Member(s): 25
Membership: 3,900; *Fees:* $445; *Member Profile:* Managers of arenas & stadiums, performing arts venues, convention & conference centres, fairs, race tracks. Allied companies provide products & services used by venue managers.
Activities: *Awareness Events:* Venue Connect - Annual conference & trade show; *Internships:* Yes; *Rents Mailing List:* Yes
Chief Officer(s):
Brad Mayne, President & CEO
brad.mayne@iavm.org

International Association on Water Quality; International Association on Water Pollution Research & Control *See* International Water Association

International Atomic Energy Agency (IAEA) / Agence internationale de l'énergie atomique
Vienna International Centre, PO Box 100, Wagramer Strasse 5, Vienna A-1400 Austria
Tel: 43-1 2600-0; *Fax:* 43-1 2600-7
official.mail@iaea.org
www.iaea.org
www.linkedin.com/company/iaea
www.facebook.com/iaeaorg
twitter.com/iaeaorg
www.youtube.com/user/IAEAvideo
Overview: A large international organization founded in 1957
Mission: An independent intergovernmental organization within the UN system that aims to accelerate & enlarge the contribution of atomic energy to peace, health & prosperity throughout the world; To ensure that assistance provided is not used to further any military purpose
Affiliation(s): United Nations
Finances: *Annual Operating Budget:* Greater than $5 Million; *Funding Sources:* Member states contributions
Staff Member(s): 2300

Membership: 158 sovereign states; *Fees:* Percentage of share of regular budget is fixed by UN General Assembly; *Member Profile:* Intergovernmental organization; *Committees:* Board of Governors composed of 35 member states
Activities: Verification in framework of Nuclear Non-Proliferation Treaty (NPT) that over 1,000 nuclear facilities in over 60 non-nuclear weapon states are used for peaceful purposes only; *Library:* International Atomic Energy Agency Library; by appointment
Chief Officer(s):
Yukiya Amano, Director General
Janice Dunn Lee, Deputy Director General, Management
Publications:
• Animal Production & Health Newsletter [a publication of the International Atomic Energy Agency]
Type: Newsletter; *Editor:* Gerrit Johannes Viljoen; *ISSN:* 1011-2529
• Education & Training in Radiation, Transport & Waste Safety Newsletter
Type: Newsletter; *Editor:* Andrea Luciani; *ISSN:* 2304-5744
• Food & Environmental Protection Newsletter [a publication of the International Atomic Energy Agency]
Type: Newsletter; *Editor:* David Henry Byron; *ISSN:* 1020-6671
• Fuel Cycle & Waste Newsletter [a publication of the International Atomic Energy Agency]
Type: Newsletter; *Editor:* Hiroko Ratcliffe; *ISSN:* 1816-9287
• IAEA [International Atomic Energy Agency] Bulletin
Type: Magazine
• Insect Pest Control Newsletter [a publication of the International Atomic Energy Agency]
Type: Newsletter; *Editor:* Jorge Hendrichs; *ISSN:* 1011-274X
• Nuclear Data Newsletter [a publication of the International Atomic Energy Agency]
Type: Newsletter; *Editor:* Janet Roberts; *ISSN:* 0257-6376
• Nuclear Fusion [a publication of the International Atomic Energy Agency]
Type: Journal; *Editor:* Sophy Le Masurier
• Nuclear Information & Knowledge [a publication of the International Atomic Energy Agency]
Type: Newsletter; *Editor:* Bruna Lecossois; *ISSN:* 1819-9186
• Nuclear Power Newsletter [a publication of the International Atomic Energy Agency]
Type: Newsletter; *Editor:* Elisabeth Dyck; *ISSN:* 1816-9295
• Water & Environment News [a publication of the International Atomic Energy Agency]
Type: Newsletter; *Editor:* Luis Jesus Araguas Araguas; *ISSN:* 1020-7120
• XRF Newsletter [a publication of the International Atomic Energy Agency]
Type: Newsletter; *ISSN:* 1608-4632

  IAEA Regional Office in Canada
  PO Box 20, #1702, 365 Bloor St. East, Toronto ON M4W 3L4
  Tel: 416-928-9149; *Fax:* 416-928-0046

International Badminton Federation (IBF) *See* Badminton World Federation

International Bar Association (IBA)
10 St. Bride St., 4th Fl., London EC4A 4AD United Kingdom
Tel: 44-20-7842-0090; *Fax:* 44-20-7842-0091
iba@int-bar.org
www.ibanet.org
www.linkedin.com/company/international-bar-association
twitter.com/ibanews
Overview: A large international organization founded in 1947
Mission: To develop international law reform; To shape the future of the legal profession throughout the world
Affiliation(s): Canadian Bar Association
Membership: 45,000 individual lawyers + 200 bar associations & law societies; *Fees:* Schedule available; *Member Profile:* International legal practitioners; Bar associations; Law societies; *Committees:* Academic & Professional Development; Anti-Corruption; Antitrust; Arbitration; Art, Cultural Institutions & Heritage Law; Aviation Law; Banking Law; Business Crime; Client Protection; Closely Held & Growing Business Enterprises; Communications Law; Construction Projects; Consumer Litigation; Corporate & M&A Law; Corporate Social Responsibility; Criminal Law; Discrimination Law; Employment & Industrial Relations Law; Environment, Health & Safety Law; Family Law; Healthcare & Life Sciences Law; Human Rights Law; Immigration & Nationality Law; Indigenous Peoples; Insurance; and others
Activities: Providing members with access to timely information; Establishing & operating IBA institutions such as the Bar Issues Commission, the Human Rights Institute, the Southern Africa Litigation Centre, & the International Legal Assistance

Consortium; Supporting the independence of the judiciary & human rights for lawyers
Chief Officer(s):
Mark Ellis, Executive Director
Meetings/Conferences:
• International Bar Association Annual Conference 2018, October, 2018, Rome
Scope: International
Description: An opportunity to network, generate new business & participate in professional development programs
Publications:
• Business Law International [a publication of the International Bar Association]
Type: Journal; *Frequency:* 3 pa; *ISSN:* 1467 632X
Profile: Issues of interest to the international commercial, legal, & academic community
• Competition Law International [a publication of the International Bar Association]
Type: Journal; *Frequency:* 2 pa; *ISSN:* 1817-5708
Profile: Journal of the Antitrust & Trade Law Section of the IBA
• Construction Law International [a publication of the International Bar Association]
Type: Magazine; *Frequency:* Quarterly
Profile: Magazine of the IBA International Construction Projects Committee
• Dispute Resolution International [a publication of the International Bar Association]
Type: Journal; *Frequency:* Semiannually; *ISSN:* 2075-5333
Profile: Journal of the Dispute Resolution Section of the Legal Practice Division of the IBA
• IBA Global Insight [a publication of the International Bar Association]
Type: Magazine; *Frequency:* Bimonthly; *ISSN:* 2221-5859
Profile: Articles about legal & business issues, IBA initiatives, & activities
• The In-House Perspective [a publication of the International Bar Association-
Type: Magazine; *Frequency:* Quarterly; *ISSN:* 1814 0408
Profile: Magazine of the IBA Corporate Counsel Forum
• Insolvency & Restructuring International [a publication of the International Bar Association]
Type: Journal; *Frequency:* 2 pa
Profile: Issues of interest to the international legal business community
• Journal of Energy & Natural Resources Law [a publication of the International Bar Association]
Type: Journal; *Frequency:* Quarterly; *ISSN:* 0264-6811

International Board on Books for Young People (IBBY) / Union internationale pour les livres de jeunesse
Nonnenweg 12, Postfach, Basel CH-4003 Switzerland
Tel: 41-61-272-29-17; *Fax:* 41-61-272-27-57
ibby@ibby.org
www.ibby.org
Overview: A small international organization founded in 1953
Mission: To promote international understanding through children's books; To strives to give children everywhere access to books with high literary & artistic standards
Member of: UNESCO; UNICEF; International Federation of Library Associations
Affiliation(s): International Board on Books for Young People - Canadian National Section
Finances: *Funding Sources:* Membership dues; Donations; Sponsorships; Fundraising
Membership: 70 national sections; *Fees:* Schedule available; *Member Profile:* Countries with developed book publishing & literacy programs; Countries with few professionals in children's book publishing; Members in national sections include authors, illustrators, publishers, editors, translators, journalists, critics, teachers, university professors, students, librarians, booksellers, social workers, & parents
Activities: Advocating for children's books; Encouraging the publication & distribution of quality children's books; Providing support & training for those involved with children & children's literature; Encouraging research in the field; Establishing the IBBY Documentation Centre of Books for Disabled Young People; *Awareness Events:* International Children's Book Day, April 2
Chief Officer(s):
Liz Page, Executive Director
liz.page@ibby.org
Awards:
• IBBY Honour List Diplomas
A biennial selection of outstanding, recently published books, honouring writers, translators, & illustrators from IBBY member countries
• IBBY-Asahi Reading Promotion Award
Presented every two years to a group or institution which, by its outstanding activities, is judged to be making a lasting contribution to reading programs for children & young people
• Hans Christian Andersen Awards
Awards include the Hans Christian Andersen Author Award & the Hans Christian Andersen Illustrator Award
• Jella Lepman Medal
An award named after the founder of IBBY & presented to those who have made lastin gcontribution to children's literature
Meetings/Conferences:
• International Board on Books for Young People 2018 36th International Congress, September, 2018, Istanbul
Scope: International
Description: A biennial congress, hosted by an IBBY national section, for IBBY members & people involved in children's books & reading development from around the world. This year's theme is "East Meets West Around Children's Books & Fairy Tales."
Contact Information: www.ibbycongress2018.org
• International Board on Books for Young People 2020 37th International Congress, September, 2020, Moscow
Scope: International
Description: Theme: "Great Big World Through Children's Books"
Contact Information: www.ibbycongress2020.org
Publications:
• Bookbird: A Journal of International Children's Literature
Type: Journal; *Frequency:* Quarterly; *Editor:* Sylvia Vardell; Catherine Kurkjian; *ISSN:* 0006 7377
Profile: A refereed journal to communicate ideas to readers interested in international children's literature
• A Bridge of Children's Books
Profile: The autobiography of Jella Lepman, the founder of IBBY
• IBBY Honour List
Type: Catalogue; *Frequency:* Biennially; *Editor:* Liz Page; Forest Zhang
Profile: A presentation of outstanding, recently published books selected by national section in the categories of writing, translating, & illustrating
• IBBY Newsletter
Type: Newsletter
Profile: News from IBBY national sections, the IBBY executive committee, the IBBY World Congress, plus information about IBBY projects, workshops, & awards
• Outstanding Books for Young People with Disabilities
Type: Catalogue
Profile: An international selection of titles recommended by the IBBY Documentation Centre of Books for Disabled Young People

International Bottled Water Association (IBWA)
#650, 1700 Diagonal Rd., Alexandria VA 22314 USA
Tel: 703-683-5213; *Fax:* 703-683-4074
Toll-Free: 800-928-3711
info@bottledwater.org
www.bottledwater.org
www.facebook.com/bottledwatermatters
twitter.com/BottledWaterOrg
www.youtube.com/user/BottledWaterMatters
Overview: A large international organization founded in 1958
Mission: To assure that safe, clean, good-tasting bottled water is produced & marketed to consumers
Membership: 1,200; *Fees:* Schedule available
Activities: IBWA works closely with its member companies & with government officials; takes active role at all levels of local, state & federal governments to assist in the development of regulations for bottled water
Chief Officer(s):
Bryan Shinn, Chair
Joseph Doss, President, 703-647-4605
jdoss@bottledwater.org
Michele Campbell, Director, Conventions, Trade Shows, & Meetings, 703-647-4606
mcampbell@bottledwater.org
Claire Crane, Director, Education, Science, & Technical Relations, 703-647-4612
ccrane@bottledwater.org

International Brotherhood of Boilermakers, Iron Ship Builders, Blacksmiths, Forgers & Helpers (AFL-CIO) (IBB) / Fraternité internationale des chaudronniers, constructeurs de navires en fer, forgerons, forgeurs et aides (FAT-COI)
753 State Ave., Kansas City KS 66101 USA
Tel: 913-371-2640; *Fax:* 913-281-8101
www.boilermakers.org
Also Known As: Boilermakers
Overview: A large international organization founded in 1880
Mission: To represent workers employed in shipbuilding, manufacturing, railroads, cement, mining & related industries
Finances: *Funding Sources:* Membership dues; Investments
Staff Member(s): 85
Membership: *Committees:* Departments: Accounting, Audit, Communications, Education & Training, Government Affairs, Industrial Health & Safety, Industrial Sector Services, Information Technology, Membership, Organizing, Research & Collective Bargaining Services
Activities: Library
Chief Officer(s):
Newton B. Jones, International President

Burlington (Toronto Lodge 128)
1035 Sutton Dr., Burlington ON L7L 5Z8
Tel: 905-332-0128; *Fax:* 905-332-9057
info@ibblocal128.org
128.boilermaker.ca

Burnaby (Vancouver Lodge 359)
4514 Dawson St., Burnaby BC V5C 4C1
Tel: 604-291-7531; *Fax:* 604-291-9265
memberservices@boilermakers359.org
www.boilermakers359.org

Calgary (Lodge 146)
11055 - 48 St. SE, Calgary AB T2C 1G8
Tel: 403-253-6976; *Fax:* 403-252-4187
www.boilermakers.ca

Edmonton (Lodge 146)
15220 - 114 Ave., Edmonton AB T5M 2Z2
Tel: 780-451-5992; *Fax:* 780-451-3927
info@boilermakers.ca
www.boilermakers.ca
Chief Officer(s):
Joseph Maloney, International Vice-President, Western Canada

Holyrood (Lodge 203)
PO Box 250, Holyrood NL A0A 2R0
Tel: 709-229-7958; *Fax:* 709-229-7300
dryan@nf.aibn.com

Montréal (Lodge 271)
1205, boul St-Jean Baptiste, Montréal QC H1B 4A2
Tel: 514-327-6135; *Fax:* 514-327-7294
local271@videotron.ca

Regina (Lodge 555)
214 - 4th Ave. East, Regina SK S4N 4Z6
Tel: 306-949-4452; *Fax:* 306-543-9339
local555@sasktel.net
www.boilermakerslocal555.org

Saint John (Lodge 73)
345 King William Rd., Saint John NB E2M 7C9
Tel: 506-634-7386; *Fax:* 506-634-0411
bm73@nbnet.nb.ca
www.boilermaker73.ca
Chief Officer(s):
Edward Power, International Vice-President, Eastern Canada

Thunder Bay (Lodge 555)
878A Tungsten St., Thunder Bay ON P7B 6J3
Tel: 807-623-8186; *Fax:* 807-623-9294
bmtbay@tbaytel.net
www.boilermakerslocal555.org

Truro (Lodge 73)
124 Parkway Dr., Truro Heighs NS B6L 1N8
Tel: 902-897-7306; *Fax:* 902-897-7305
bm73@ns.aliantzinc.ca
www.boilermaker73.ca

Victoria (Lodge 191)
802 Esquimalt Rd., Victoria BC V9A 3M4
Tel: 250-383-4196; *Fax:* 250-386-4688
lodge191adm@shaw.ca

Winnipeg (Lodge 555)
110 Haarsma Rd., East St Paul MB R2E 0M8
Tel: 204-987-9200; *Fax:* 204-987-9219
local555@escape.ca
www.boilermakerslocal555.org

Foreign Associations / International Brotherhood of Electrical Workers (AFL-CIO/CFL) (IBEW) / Fraternité internationale des ouvriers en électricité (FAT-COI/FCT)

International Brotherhood of Electrical Workers (AFL-CIO/CFL) (IBEW) / Fraternité internationale des ouvriers en électricité (FAT-COI/FCT)
900 Seventh St. NW, Washington DC 20001 USA
Tel: 202-833-7000; *Fax:* 202-728-7676
www.ibew.org
www.facebook.com/IBEWFB
twitter.com/IBEW_IP
www.flickr.com/photos/58797631@N07
Overview: A large international organization founded in 1891
Mission: To represent members from a wide variety of fields, including utilities, construction, telecommunications, broadcasting, manufacturing, railroads & government
Finances: *Annual Operating Budget:* $3 Million-$5 Million; *Funding Sources:* Membership dues
Staff Member(s): 198
Membership: 675,000
Activities: *Library* by appointment
Chief Officer(s):
Chris Erickson, Chair, 718-591-4000
Lonnie R. Stephenson, International President
Salvatore J. Chilia, International Secretary-Treasurer

Canadian Office (IBEW)
First District, #300, 1450 Meyerside Dr., Mississauga ON L5T 2N5
Tel: 905-564-5441; *Fax:* 905-564-8114
ivpd_01@ibew.org
www.ibewcanada.ca

International Brotherhood of Painters & Allied Trades (AFL-CIO/CFL) *See* International Union of Painters & Allied Trades

International Brotherhood of Teamsters (AFL-CIO/CLC) / Fraternité internationale des teamsters (FAT-COI/CTC)
25 Louisiana Ave. NW, Washington DC 20001 USA
Tel: 202-624-6800
www.teamster.org
Overview: A large international organization founded in 1903
Mission: To act as North America's strongest & most diverse labour union
Membership: 1,400,000 + 568 locals
Chief Officer(s):
James P. Hoffa, General President
Ken Hall, General Sec.-Treas.
Publications:
• Teamster [a publication of the International Brotherhood of Teamsters]
Type: Magazine; *Frequency:* Quarterly

Graphic Communications Conference (GCC)
25 Louisianna Ave. NW, Washington DC 20001 USA
Tel: 202-624-6800
teamster.org/divisions/graphic-communications
Mission: To represent the interests of those who print, produce & design numerous publications, including major newspapers, magazines, books, brochures & catalogues
Chief Officer(s):
George Tedeschi, President

International Caterers Association (ICA)
3601 East Joppa Rd., Balitmore MD 21234 USA
Tel: 418-931-8100; *Fax:* 418-931-8111
www.internationalcaterers.org
www.facebook.com/internationalcaterers
twitter.com/icacater
instagram.com/icacater
Merged from: Canadian Association of Caterers; National Caterers Association
Overview: A small international organization founded in 1981
Mission: To support, promote & improve all aspects of the business through publications, education, & demonstrations
Staff Member(s): 3
Membership: *Fees:* US$290 caterer; US$350 vendor; *Member Profile:* Licensed, professional off-premise & on-premise caterers, with liability insurance & food premises regularly inspected by a regional health department
Activities: Seminars, workshops & demonstrations on catering sales & marketing, regional & state of the art cuisine, event management, & legal issues; *Speaker Service:* Yes
Chief Officer(s):
Jennifer Perna, President
Paula Kreuzburg, Executive Director
paulak@internationalcaterers.org

International Center for Canadian-American Trade *See* Canada - United States Trade Center

International Centre for Research in Agroforestry (ICRAF) *See* World Agroforestry Centre

International Chamber of Commerce (ICC) / Chambre de Commerce Internationale
#33, 43, av du Président Wilson, Paris 75116 France
Tel: 33-149-53-28-28; *Fax:* 33-149-53-28-59
icc@iccwbo.org
www.iccwbo.org
www.linkedin.com/company/international-chamber-of-commerce
www.facebook.com/iccwbo
twitter.com/iccwbo
www.youtube.com/user/iccwbo1919
Overview: A medium-sized international organization founded in 1919
Mission: Serving as the voice of world business, the ICC champions the global economy as a force for economic growth, job creation, & prosperity.
Affiliation(s): United Nations; World Trade Organization
Finances: *Funding Sources:* Membership fees; services & publications income
Staff Member(s): 200
Membership: *Member Profile:* Corporations & companies in all sectors of every size in more than 130 countries; National professional & sectoral associations; Business & employers federations; Law firms & consultancies; Chambers of commerce; Individuals involved in international business
Activities: Setting rules & standards; Promoting growth & prosperity; Advocating for international business; Providing practical services to business; Fighting commercial crime
Chief Officer(s):
John Danilovich, Secretary General
Harold McGraw, Chair

International Climbing & Mountaineering Federation *See* Union internationale des associations d'alpinisme

International Coaching Federation (ICF)
#A325, 2365 Harrodsburg Rd., Lexington KY 40504 USA
Tel: 859-219-3580; *Fax:* 859-226-4411
Toll-Free: 888-423-3131
www.coachfederation.org
www.linkedin.com/groups/International-Coach-Federation-87212?home=&gid=87212
www.facebook.com/icfhq
twitter.com/icfhq
www.youtube.com/icfheadquarters
Overview: A medium-sized international organization founded in 1995
Mission: ICF is the support network for these professional coaches. Whether it's Life Coaching, Executive Coaching, Leadership Coaching or any other skilled coaching
Membership: 20,000+; *Fees:* US$245
Chief Officer(s):
Dave Wondra, Chair
Awards:
• Prism Award
Recognizes businesses and organizations that demonstrate how professional coaching.
• President's Award
In recognition of the work he or she is doing to promote coaching in a humanitarian capacity.
Publications:
• Coaching World
Type: Magazine; *Frequency:* Quarterly

Toronto Chapter
#185, 14845-6 Yonge St., Aurora ON L4G 6H8
Tel: 416-960-4791
info@icftoronto.com
www.gtacoaches.com
www.linkedin.com/groups/ICF-Toronto-Charter-Chapter-6507451
twitter.com/ICFToronto
Chief Officer(s):
Mia Eng, President

International Coalition of Fisheries Associations (ICFA)
c/o National Fisheries Institute, #700, 7918 Jones Branch Dr., McLean VA 22102 USA
Tel: 703-752-8880; *Fax:* 703-752-7583
www.icfa.net
Overview: A small international organization founded in 1988
Mission: To provide a unified voice for the world's commercial fishing industries in international forums; to preserve & maintain the oceans as a major source of food for the people of the world
Affiliation(s): Fisheries Council of Canada
Membership: 1,000

International Commission for the Conservation of Atlantic Tunas (ICCAT)
Calle Corazón de María, 8, 6th Fl., Madrid 28002 Spain
Tel: 34-914-165-600; *Fax:* 34-914-152-612
info@iccat.int
www.iccat.int
Overview: A medium-sized international organization
Staff Member(s): 25
Chief Officer(s):
Driss Meski, Executive Secretary
driss.meski@iccat.int
Juan Antonio Moreno, Department Head, Administration & Finance
juan.antonio@iccat.int

International Commission of Agricultural & Biosystems Engineering / Commission Internationale du Genie Rural (CIGR)
c/o Dr. Takaaki Maekawa, School of Life & Environmental Sciences, 1-1-1 Tennodai, University of Tsukuba, Tsukuba, Ibaraki Japan
Tel: +81-29-875-6380; *Fax:* +81-29-875-6381
biopro@sakura.cc.tsukuba.ac.jp
www.cigr.org
Overview: A medium-sized international organization
Mission: To ensure food security & the sustainable use of natural resources, through the application of principles of technology & engineering science
Membership: *Member Profile:* National organizations, such as the Canadian Society for Bioengineering; Regional organizations; Individuals; Corporations
Activities: Providing networking opportunities for regional & national societies of agricultural engineering, as well as for private & public companies & individuals throughout the world
Chief Officer(s):
Soren Pedersen, President
Takaaki Maekawan, Secretary General
biopro@sakura.cc.tsukuba.ac.jp
Yutaka Kitamura, Secretary
kitamura@sakura.cc.tsukuba.ac.jp
Meetings/Conferences:
• International Commission of Agricultural Engineering 2020 5th International Conference, 2020
Scope: International
• International Commission of Agricultural Engineering XIX World Congress 2018, April, 2018, Antalya
Scope: International
Publications:
• Agricultural Engineering International: The CIGR Journal of Scientific Research & Development
Type: Journal; *Editor:* Fedro S. Zazueta Ranahan
• CIGR [Commission Internationale du Genie Rural] Newsletter / Bulletin de la CIGR
Type: Newsletter; *Frequency:* Quarterly
Profile: Available in English, French, Arabic, Chinese, Russian, & Spanish

International Commission on Illumination (ICI) / Commission internationale de l'éclairage (CIE)
Babenbergerstrae 9/9A, Vienna 1010 Austria
Tel: 43-1-714-31 87
ciecb@cie.co.at
www.cie.co.at
Also Known As: Internationale Beleuchtungs Kommission
Overview: A medium-sized international organization founded in 1910
Mission: To promote international cooperation & exchange of information among member countries on all matters relating to the science & art of lighting; to develop basic standards & procedures of metrology in the fields of light & lighting
Membership: 39 national committees + 4 individual
Activities: Technical committees; Publishing technical reports & standards; organizaing symposia
Chief Officer(s):
Yoshihiro Ohno, President
Teresa Goodman, Secretary
Meetings/Conferences:
• International Commission on Illumination 2018 Topical Conference, April, 2018
Scope: International

International Commission on Irrigation & Drainage (ICID) / Commission internationale des irrigations & du drainage
48 Nyaya Marg, Chanakyapuri, New Delhi 110021 India
Tel: 91-11-26116837; *Fax:* 91-11-26115962
icid@icid.org
www.icid.org
Overview: A small international organization founded in 1950
Mission: To stimulate & promote development & application of arts, sciences & techniques of engineering, agriculture, economics, ecology & social science in managing water & land resources for irrigation, drainage, flood control & river training &/or for research in a more comprehensive manner adopting up-to-date techniques; to help produce more food from irrigated agriculture on a global basis to alleviate want & hunger without disturbing the environment adversely
Affiliation(s): International Commission on Irrigation & Drainage - Canadian National Committee
Staff Member(s): 25
Membership: 107 countries
Activities: Library
Chief Officer(s):
Avinash C. Tyagi, Secretary General
tyagi@icid.org
S.A. Kulkarni, Executive Secretary
kulkarni@icid.org

International Commission on Occupational Health (ICOH) / Commission internationale de la santé au travail (CIST)
INAIL, Italian Workers' Compensation Authority, Occupational Medicine, Via Fontana Candida 1, Monteporzio Catone, Rome I-00040 Italy
Tel: 39-06-941-815-06; *Fax:* 39-06-941-815-56
icoh@inail.it
www.icohweb.org
Overview: A small international organization founded in 1906
Mission: To foster scientific progress, knowledge & development of occupational health & safety in all its aspects
Affiliation(s): International Association of Agricultural Medicine & Rural Health; International Federation of Associations of Specialists in Occupational Safety & Industrial Hygiene; International Social Security Association; ISSA International Section on Prevention of Occupational Risks in the Iron & Metal Industry
Finances: *Annual Operating Budget:* $100,000-$250,000
Staff Member(s): 2
Membership: 1,900 individual + 19 sustaining + 31 affiliate (in 93 countries); *Member Profile:* Individual & collective members; sustaining - organization, society, industry, or enterprise; affiliate - professional organization or a scientific society; *Committees:* 36 scientific committees & working groups
Activities: International congresses; special meetings; collaboration with international & national bodies & societies having similar aims
Chief Officer(s):
Kazutaka Kogi, President
k.kogi@isl.or.jp
Sergio Iavicoli, Secretary General
S.Iavicoli@inail.it

International Committee for Documentation of the International Council of Museums (ICOM-CIDOC) / Comité international pour la documentation du Conseil international des musées (CIDOC)
Museum Centre Vapriikki, Alaverstaanraitti 5, Tampere Finland
Tel: 358-40-806-2764; *Fax:* 358-83-565-66808
icom.museum/the-committees/international-committees
Overview: A medium-sized international organization founded in 1956
Mission: To provide better methods & standards for the recording of museum information
Member of: International Council of Museums
Finances: *Funding Sources:* Membership stipend from ICOM
8 volunteer(s)
Membership: 750; *Member Profile:* Professionals working in museums documentation & information; *Committees:* 11 Working Groups - Archaeological Sites; Conceptual Reference Model; Contemporary Art; Digital Preservation; Documentation Standards; Ethno; Iconography; Internet; Multimedia; Museum Information Centres; Services
Activities: *Speaker Service:* Yes; *Library:* Centre de documentation; by appointment
Chief Officer(s):
Monika Hagedorn-Saupe, Interim Chair
Maija Ekosaari, Secretariat

International Committee of Museums & Collections of Arms & Military History (ICOMAM)
c/o Secretary Mathieu Willemsen, Conservateur Armes à feu1, Legermuseum, Korte Geer 1, Delft NL-2611 Netherlands
Tel: 31 (0) 15 21 52 622; *Fax:* 31 (0) 15 21 52 608
secretary@icomam.icom.museum
www.klm-mra.be/icomam
Previous Name: International Association of Museums of Arms & Military History
Overview: A small international organization founded in 1957
Mission: To establish & maintain contact between museums & similar institutions within the range of interest of historical weapons & militaria, & to foster the study of objects within those fields
Affiliation(s): ICOM (International Council of Museums)
Membership: 265; *Member Profile:* Senior managers of collections of arms & militaria open to the public
Chief Officer(s):
Mathieu Willemsen, Secretary
Piet De Gryse, President

International Committee of Sports for the Deaf (ICSD) / Comité international des Sports des Sourds (CISS)
Maison du Sport International, Av. de Rhondanie 54, Lausanne CH-1007 Switzerland
Tel: 41 78 733 35 67; *Fax:* 7 (499) 255 04 36
office@ciss.org
www.ciss.org
Also Known As: International Deaflympics
Overview: A medium-sized international charitable organization founded in 1924
Mission: To organize sporting events for deaf & hard of hearing athletes
Member of: International Olympic Committee; General Assembly of International Sports Federations
Affiliation(s): Canadian Deaf Sports Association
Membership: 109 countries; *Member Profile:* National Deaf Sports Federations
Activities: Deaflympics; World Deaf Championships; *Internships:* Yes
Chief Officer(s):
Valery Rukhledev, President
president@ciss.org

International Committee on Alcohol, Drugs & Traffic Safety
See International Council on Alcohol, Drugs & Traffic Safety

International Computer Games Association (ICGA)
c/o David N.L. Levy, 34 Courthope Rd., Hampstead, London NW3 2LD England
e-mail: info@icga.org
ilk.uvt.nl/icga
Overview: A small international organization founded in 1977
Mission: To promote computer games; To share technical knowledge; To foster developments in the man-machine area
Finances: *Funding Sources:* Membership fees; Sponsorships
Membership: *Fees:* US$50
Activities: Encouraging cooperation between computer game researchers; Supporting computer games tournament organizers & computer games organizations; Holding the World Computer-Chess Championships & the Computer Olympiads
Chief Officer(s):
David N.L. Levy, President
davidlevylondon@yahoo.com
Yngvi Björnsson, Vice-President
yngvi@ru.is
Hiroyuki Iida, Secretary-Treasurer
iida@jaist.ac.jp
Publications:
• ICGA Journal
Type: Journal; *Frequency:* Quarterly; *Price:* Free with membership in the International Computer Games Association
Profile: Featuring reports of computer-computer & man-machine events

International Confederation for Plastic Reconstructive & Aesthetic Surgery (IPRAS)
Zita Congress SA, PO Box 155, 1st km Peanias Markopoulou Ave, Peania Attica 190 02 Greece
Tel: (30) 211 100 1777; *Fax:* (30) 210 664 2216
ipras@iprasmanagement.com
www.ipras.org
www.facebook.com/ipras.org
Overview: A large international organization founded in 1955
Mission: To promote plastic surgery both scientifically & clinically; To further education
Membership: Over 50,000; *Member Profile:* Plastic & aesthetic surgeons; Residents in training; Hand surgeons; Micro surgeons; Burn specialists
Chief Officer(s):
Marita Eisenmann-Klein, President
Publications:
• Globalplast
Type: Newsletter; *Frequency:* Annually
• IPRAS [International Confederation for Plastic, Reconstructive & Aesthetic Surgery] Journal
Type: Journal

International Confederation for Thermal Analysis & Calorimetry (ICTAC)
Tokyo Institute of Technology, 2-12-1, S8-29, Ookayama, Meguro-ku, Tokyo 152-8552 Japan
Tel: 81-3-5734-2497; *Fax:* 81-3-5723-3093
www.ictac.org
Overview: A large international organization founded in 1965
Mission: To promote the use of thermal analysis in science & technology; To strengthen the collaboration between scientists & technicians from different parts of the world
Member of: International Union of Pure & Applied Chemistry
Membership: 500 full + 5,000 affiliate; *Fees:* US$100 individual; US$200 corporate; US$320 affiliate with less than 100 members; US$480 affiliate with more than 100 members; *Member Profile:* Open to scientists & technicians who are involved in thermal analysis; *Committees:* ICTAC Advisory; ICTAC Scientific Awards; ICTAC Congress Organising; Education; Environmental Safety; Geosciences; Kinetics; Lifetime Prediction of Materials; Nomenclature; Pharmaceuticals; Polymers; Sample Controlled Thermal Analysis; Standardization; Temperature Modulated Calorimetry; Thermal Analysis Combined Approach to Food Work; Thermal Reactivity; Thermochemistry
Activities: Scientific congress every four years
Chief Officer(s):
Wim De Klerk, President
wim.deklerk@tno.nl
Junko Morikawa, Membership Secretary
morikawa.j.aa@m.titech.ac.jp
Awards:
• TA Instruments-ICTAC Award, ICTAC Scientific Awards
• SETARAM - ICTAC Award for Calorimetry, ICTAC Scientific Awards
• ICTAC Young Scientist Award, ICTAC Scientific Awards
• ICTAC Honorary Lifetime Membership, ICTAC Service Awards
• Robert Mackenzie Memorial Lectureship
• ICTAC Travel Grants
Meetings/Conferences:
• 2020 ICTAC Conference, 2020, Krakow

International Confederation of Midwives (ICM) / Confédération internationale de sages-femmes
Laan van Meerdervoort 70, The Hague 2517 AN Netherlands
Tel: 31-70-3060-520; *Fax:* 31-70-3555-651
info@internationalmidwives.org
www.internationalmidwives.org
www.linkedin.com/company/international-confederation-of-midwives-icm-
www.facebook.com/InternationalConfederationofMidwives
twitter.com/world_midwives
www.youtube.com/user/WorldMidwives/feed
Previous Name: International Union of Midwives
Overview: A medium-sized international charitable organization founded in 1919
Mission: To advance, worldwide, the aims & aspirations of midwives in the attainment of improved outcomes for women in their childbearing years, their newborn, & their families, wherever they reside
Affiliation(s): Association of Ontario Midwives; Alberta Association of Midwives; Midwives Association of British Columbia
Finances: *Annual Operating Budget:* $250,000-$500,000; *Funding Sources:* Membership dues; Fundraising
Staff Member(s): 6; 2 volunteer(s)
Membership: 121 associations worldwide; *Fees:* Schedule available, based on number of midwives in association; *Member Profile:* Independent associations of midwives, or midwives groups within other organizations, provided that the midwives group is autonomous & responsible for the affairs of midwifery; *Committees:* Council; Executive; Board of Management
Activities: Hosting a triennial congress; *Awareness Events:* International Day of the Midwife, May 5; *Library:* by appointment

Foreign Associations / International Confederation of Principals (ICP)

Chief Officer(s):
Frances Gagnes, Chief Executive Officer
Frances Day-Stirk, President
Meetings/Conferences:
• International Confederation of Midwives 32nd Triennial Congress 2020, June, 2020, Bali
Scope: International
Contact Information: URL: www.midwives2020.org

International Confederation of Principals (ICP)
ICP Secretariat, 68 Martin St., Heidelberg, Victoria 3084
Australia
Tel: + 61 3 9326 8077; *Fax:* + 61 3 9326 8147
www.icponline.org
Overview: A medium-sized international organization
Mission: To support the professional development & work of school leaders from over forty countries; To act as the voice for school education
Membership: 40+ school leadership associations; *Member Profile:* School leadership organizations from five continents, with constitutions in agreement with the ICP constitution
Activities: Enhancing the professionalism of school leaders; Providing professional learning for school leaders; Offering access to current educational research; Encouraging equal opportunities for young people; Developing curricula that promotes international understanding
Chief Officer(s):
Andrew Blair, President
ablair@vassp.org.au
Ted Brierley, Executive Secretary
brierted@optusnet.com.au
Lisa Vincent, Regional Representative, Americas, 613-962-9295 Ext. 2119, Fax: 613-962-1047
lvincent@hpedsb.on.ca
Meetings/Conferences:
• 14th World Convention of the International Confederation of Principals, 2018
Scope: International
Description: A convention of interest to principals, vice-principals, education leaders, academics, researchers, policy makers, & government representatives from around the world
Publications:
• International Confederation of Principals Newsletter
Type: Newsletter
Profile: Executive news & information from around the world

International Continence Society (ICS)
19 Portland Sq., Bristol BS2 8SJ United Kingdom
Tel: +44 117 9444881; *Fax:* +44 117 9444882
info@icsoffice.org
www.icsoffice.org
Overview: A medium-sized international charitable organization
Mission: To further education, clinical practice, & scientific research; To remove the stigma of incontinence
Membership: *Member Profile:* Medical professionals; *Committees:* Children's; Continence Promotion; Education; Ethics; Executive; Fistula; Meetings; Neuro-urology Promotion; Nursing; Physiotherapy; Publications & Communications; Scientific; Standardization
Activities: Providing educational opportunities; *Speaker Service:* Yes
Chief Officer(s):
Daniel Snowdon, Director, Administration
Dominic Turner, Director, Information Technology
Avicia Burchill, Manager, Project & Events
Meetings/Conferences:
• International Continence Society 2018 Annual Meeting, August, 2018, Philadelphia, PA
Scope: International
Description: Educational workshops & a scientific meeting for urological, gynaecological, physiotherapy, & nursing professionals.
Publications:
• ICS [International Continence Society] Newsletter
Type: Newsletter; *Price:* Free with International Continence Society membership
• International Continence Society Membership Directory
Type: Directory
Profile: Continence professionals throughout the world
• Neurourology & Urodynamics
Type: Journal; *Frequency:* Bimonthly; *Price:* Free with International Continence Society membership

International Cooperative Alliance (ICA)
PO Box 2100, 150, Route de Ferney, Geneva 1211 Switzerland
Tel: 41-22-929-8838; *Fax:* 41-22-798-4122
ica@ica.coop
ica.coop
Overview: A medium-sized international organization founded in 1895
Mission: To unite, represent & serve cooperatives worldwide
Membership: 233 national & international cooperative
Chief Officer(s):
Ivano Barberini, President
Meetings/Conferences:
• 2018 International Summit of Cooperatives, 2018
Scope: International
Contact Information: Email: info@intlsummit.coop

International Council for Applied Mineralogy (ICAM)
Federal Institute for Geosciences & Natural Resources, B4.15 Inorganic Geochemistry, Stilleweg 2, Hannover D-30655
Germany
Tel: 49-511-643-2565; *Fax:* 49-511-643-3685
icam2000@bgr.de
www.bgr.de/icam
Overview: A small international organization founded in 1981
Mission: To promote scientific & technical interests of applied mineralogy by providing an international forum for exchange of ideas
Affiliation(s): National Mineralogical Association - USA, Australia, South Africa, Europe, Brazil, South America, Poland; International Mineralogical Association
Finances: *Annual Operating Budget:* Less than $50,000; *Funding Sources:* Meeting registrations; donations
Membership: 20; *Member Profile:* Professionals in the field
Chief Officer(s):
Dieter Rammlmair, Secretary General
rammlmair@bgr.de

International Council for Archaeozoology (ICAZ)
c/o University Of Sheffield, Department of Archaeology, Northgate House, West St., Sheffield S1 4ET England
e-mail: icaz@alexandriaarchive.org
www.alexandriaarchive.org/icaz/
Overview: A small international charitable organization founded in 1976
Mission: To develop & stimulate archaeozoological research; To strengthen cooperation among archaeozoologists; To foster cooperation with archaeologists & scientists working in related fields; To promote high ethical & scientific standards for archaeozoological work
Affiliation(s): International Union of Prehistoric & Protohistoric Sciences
Finances: *Annual Operating Budget:* Less than $50,000; *Funding Sources:* Membership fees
Membership: 383; *Fees:* US$15; *Member Profile:* University staff; museums; freelance; *Committees:* Working Groups; Fish Remains; Bird Remains; Archaeozoology of Southwestern Asia & Adjacent Areas; Camelid; Animal Pathology; Worked Bone; North Atlantic Bioarchaeological Organization
Chief Officer(s):
László Bartosiewicz, President
h10459bar@ella.hu
Umberto Albarella, Secretary
u.albarella@sheffield.ac.uk

International Council for Central & East European Studies (Canada) (ICCEES) / Conseil international d'études de l'Europe centrale et orientale (Canada)
c/o Gabriele Freitag, General Secretary, Schaperstrase 30
D-10719, Berlin Germany
Tel: +49 (0)30/214 784 14; *Fax:* +49 (0)30/214 784 12
www.iccees.org
www.facebook.com/ICCEES.org
twitter.com/icceesorg
Overview: A small international organization founded in 1974
Mission: To foster study of East European affairs & to encourage dissemination of this knowledge among specialists; To create an international community of scholars.
Affiliation(s): Assn for Slavic, East European & Eurasian Studies; Assn Italiana degli Slavisti; Australian Assn for Communist & Post-Communist States; Australian & New Zealand Slavists' Assn; British Assn for Slavonic & East European Studies; Centre Belge d'Etudes Slaves; Canadian Assn of Slavists; Chinese Assn for Russian, East European & Central Asian Studies; Deutsche Gesellschaft fur Osteuropakunde; Finnish Assn for Russian & East European Studies; Japan Council of Russian & East European Studies; Korea Assn of Slavic & Eurasian Studies; Sudosteuropa-Gesellschaft
Finances: *Annual Operating Budget:* Less than $50,000
Membership: 8,000 in 18 national associations; *Fees:* US$1; *Member Profile:* Professor; researcher
Activities: *Speaker Service:* Yes
Chief Officer(s):
Georges Mink, President
mink@u-paris10.fr
Andrii Krawchuk, Vice-President & Canadian Contact
akrawchuk@usudbury.ca
Gabriele Freitag, General Secretary
freitag@dgo-online.org

International Council for Laboratory Animal Science (ICLAS) / Conseil international des sciences de l'animal de laboratoire
40 Washington St., Brussels 1050 Belgium
e-mail: info@iclas.org
www.iclas.org
Overview: A small international organization founded in 1956
Mission: To promote the humane use of animals in research through recognition of ethical principles & scientific responsibilities; to be an advocate for the advancement of laboratory animal science & biological research resources throughout the world; to promote international collaboration as a worldwide resource of knowledge in laboratory animal science; to promote the production & monitoring of high-quality laboratory animals by establishing standards & providing support resources
Affiliation(s): Canadian Association for Laboratory Animal Science
Membership: 30 national; 33 scientific; 5 union; 21 associate; 2 institutional; *Fees:* Schedule available; *Committees:* Communications; Education & Training; Finance; Europe Regional; Africa Regional; Americas Regional; Asia Regional; Australia & New Zealand Regional; Harmonization; Membership; Ethics & Animal Welfare
Activities: Scientific meetings; reference & monitoring centres; training courses; publications
Chief Officer(s):
Patri Vergara, President
Cynthia Pekow, Acting Secretary General
Meetings/Conferences:
• International Council for Laboratory Animal Science General Assembly & Annual Symposium, 2018
Scope: International

International Council for Local Environmental Initiatives (ICLEI)
World Secretariat, Kaiser-Friedrich-Str. 7, Bonn 53113 Germany
Tel: 49-228-97-62-99-00; *Fax:* 49-228-97-62-99-01
iclei@iclei.org
www.iclei.org
Overview: A small international organization founded in 1990
Mission: To build & serve a worldwide movement of local governments to achieve tangible improvements in global environmental & sustainable development conditions through cumulative local actions
Affiliation(s): International Union of Local Authorities
Finances: *Funding Sources:* Membership dues; project funding
Membership: *Fees:* Schedule available; *Committees:* Executive; Regional Executive; Management
Activities: *Library* by appointment
Chief Officer(s):
Gino Van Begin, Secretary General
Monika Zimmermann, Deputy Secretary General

International Council for the Exploration of the Sea (ICES)
H.C. Andersens Blvd. 44-46, Copenhagen VDK-1553 Denmark
Tel: 45-3338-6700; *Fax:* 45-3393-4215
info@ices.dk
www.ices.dk
Overview: A medium-sized international organization
Mission: To coordinate research & monitor activities to understand the marine environment & resources & man's impact upon them, including the identification of priority marine contaminants, their distribution, transport & effects; To provide advice regarding marine resources & pollution to member governments & international regulatory commissions; To publish & disseminate the results of research
Membership: 5,000+ scientists from 20 countries
Chief Officer(s):
Alain Vezina, ICES Delegate, Canada
alain.vezina@dfo-mpo.gc.ca
Arran McPherson, ICES Delegate, Canada
arran.mcpherson@dfo-mpo.gc.ca

International Council of Associations for Science Education (ICASE) / Fédération Internationale des Associations de Professeurs de Sciences (FIAPS)
e-mail: info@icaseonline.net
www.icaseonline.net
Overview: A small international organization founded in 1973
Mission: To improve science education worldwide by assisting member organizations
Affiliation(s): Canadian Association for Science Education
Finances: *Annual Operating Budget:* Less than $50,000; *Funding Sources:* Membership fees
Staff Member(s): 1; 14 volunteer(s)
Membership: 155 organizations; *Fees:* Schedule available; *Member Profile:* Organization involved in science education
Activities: Project 2000+, providing appropriate science & technology education for all; exchange of teaching resources; science education research & its application in teaching; exchanges of science teaching personnel
Chief Officer(s):
Beverley Cooper, Secretary
bcooper@waikato.ac.nz
Teresa J. Kennedy, President
tkennedy@uttyler.edu
Dennis Chisman, Treasurer

International Council of Ballroom Dancing *See* World Dance Council Ltd.

International Council of Environmental Law (ICEL) / Conseil international du droit de l'environnement (CIDE)
Godesberger Allee 108-112, Bonn D-53175 Germany
Tel: 49-228-2692-240; *Fax:* 49-228-2692-251
icel@intlawpol.org
www.i-c-e-l.org
Overview: A small international organization founded in 1969
Mission: Promoting the exchange of information on the legal, administrative and policy aspects of environmental conservation and sustainable development, to support new initiatives in this field, and to encourage advice and assistance through its network.
Member of: The World Conservation Union
Finances: *Funding Sources:* Donations
Membership: 340
Activities: ICEL Reference to Environmental Policy & Law Literature; Bulletin online; *Library:* by appointment
Chief Officer(s):
Wolfgang E. Burhenne, Executive Governor

International Council of Museums (ICOM) / Conseil international des musées
Maison de l'UNESCO, 1, rue Miollis, Cedex 15, Paris 75732 France
Tel: 33-1-47-34-05-00; *Fax:* 33-1-43-06-78-62
www.icom.museum
www.facebook.com/IcomOfficiel
twitter.com/IcomOfficiel
Overview: A medium-sized international organization founded in 1946
Mission: To communicate to society the conservation & continuation of the world's natural & cultural heritage
Affiliation(s): International Association of Agricultural Museums; Association of Museums of the Indian Ocean; Commonwealth Association of Museums; International Association of Arms & Military History Museums; International Association of Transport & Communications Museums; International Confederation of Architectural Museums; International Congress of Maritime Museums; Museums Association of the Caribbean; International Movement for a New Museology; Association of European Open-Air Museums; Southern Africa Development Community Association of Museums & Monuments; International Society of Libraries & Museums
Membership: 37,000+; *Member Profile:* Museum professionals; museums; *Committees:* 119 national committees; 30 international committees
Activities: Reinforcing regional cooperative networks; Providing professional training & exchange; Promoting professional ethics; Fighting against illicit traffic of cultural property; Protecting world heritage; Increasing public awareness of museums; Training personnel; *Awareness Events:* International Museums Day, May 18; *Library:* by appointment
Chief Officer(s):
Peter Keller, Director General
Publications:
• ICOM [International Council of Museums] E-Newsletter
Type: Newsletter; *Frequency:* 10 pa

International Council of Ophthalmology (ICO)
#445, 711 Van Ness Ave., San Francisco CA 94102 USA
Tel: 415-521-1651; *Fax:* 415-521-1649
info@icoph.org
www.icoph.org
www.linkedin.com/company/713250
www.facebook.com/InternationalCouncilOphthalmology
twitter.com/intlcounciloph
Overview: A small international charitable organization founded in 1857
Mission: To advocate the prevention & treatment of preventable blindness in developing nations; To support the International Agency for the Prevention of Blindness & Vision 2020: Right to Sight with WHO; To support educational competency in ophthalmologic education worldwide; To evaluate & coordinate standardization in ophthalmology; To support ophthalmologic interchange through supranational organizations & international congresses
Member of: International Federation of Ophthalmological Societies
Affiliation(s): Canadian Ophthalmological Society
Finances: *Funding Sources:* Membership dues
Staff Member(s): 12
Membership: 120 national ophthalmological societies; *Fees:* Sliding scale based on national members; *Member Profile:* Recognized world ophthalmic leaders; *Committees:* Accreditation & Certification; Advocacy; Continuing Professional Development; Curricula & Expectations for Training Programs; Diabetic Eye Care; Education Coordinating; Ethics; Eye Care Delivery; Examinations; Fellowship; Guidelines; Nominations; Society & Leadership Development; Strategic Planning; Teaching for Teachers; Technologies for Teaching & Learning; Training Teams to Meet Public Needs
Activities: Overseeing educational, professional & scientific interchange worldwide in ophthalmology
Chief Officer(s):
Hugh Taylor, AC, MD, President
Kathleen Miller, Executive Director
kmiller@icoph.org
Awards:
• Gonin Medal
• International Duke Elder Medal
• Jules Francois Golden Medal
• Ophthalmic Pathology Award

International Council of Voluntary Agencies (ICVA) / Conseil International des Agences Bénévoles
26-28, av Guiseppe Motta, Geneva CH-1202 Switzerland
Tel: 41-22-950-9600; *Fax:* 41-22-950-9609
secretariat@icva.ch
www.icvanetwork.org
www.linkedin.com/company/international-council-of-voluntary-agencies-icva-
twitter.com/ICVAnetwork
Overview: A large international organization founded in 1962
Mission: To promote & advocate for human rights & a humanitarian perspective in global debates & responses
Affiliation(s): Standing invitee of UN's Inter-Agency Standing Committee (IASC)
Finances: *Annual Operating Budget:* $3 Million-$5 Million; *Funding Sources:* Membership dues; governments; foundations
Staff Member(s): 15
Membership: 90 agencies; *Fees:* Schedule available; *Member Profile:* International & regional voluntary agencies, national umbrella groups, major national non-government organizations
Activities: Mobilizing of voluntary agencies on humanitarian assistance, human rights; facilitation of voluntary agency action on these concerns; representation of collective voluntary agency views on these matters
Chief Officer(s):
Ahmad Faizal Perdaus, Chair
Melissa Pitotti, Interim Executive Director
melissa.pitotti@icvanetwork.org

International Council on Alcohol, Drugs & Traffic Safety (ICADTS)
c/o Joris C. Verster, Secretary, Utrecht Institute for Pharmaceutical Sciences, Universiteitsweg 99, Utrecht 3584CG The Netherlands
Tel: +31-30-253-6909
www.icadts.org
twitter.com/ICADTS
Previous Name: International Committee on Alcohol, Drugs & Traffic Safety
Overview: A small international organization founded in 1963
Mission: To reduce traffic related deaths & injuries by designing, promoting & implementing effective programs & policies, based on sound research
Finances: *Funding Sources:* Charitable donations; Memberships; Project grants; Contracts
Membership: *Fees:* $85 (USD)
Chief Officer(s):
Kathryn Stewart, President
stewart@pire.org
Awards:
• Widmark Award
Honours individuals or institutions that have made an outstanding contribution to the field of the pharmacology of alcohol
• Haddon Award
Recognizes distinguished service by non-governmental organizations
Publications:
• ICADTS [International Council on Alcohol, Drugs & Traffic Safety] Reporter
Type: Newsletter; *Frequency:* Quarterly; *Editor:* Kathryn Stewart; *ISSN:* 1016-0477

International Council on Monuments & Sites (ICOMOS) / Conseil international des Monuments et des Sites
11, rue du Séminaire de Conflans, Charenton-le-Pont 94220 France
Tel: 33-1-41-94-17-59; *Fax:* 33-1-48-93-19-16
secretariat@icomos.org
www.icomos.org
www.linkedin.com/groups/1623567/profile
www.facebook.com/155868924479460
twitter.com/icomos
Overview: A medium-sized international organization founded in 1965
Mission: To work towards the conservation & protection of cultural heritage places, with a focus on the application of theory, methodology & scientific techniques for conservation
Staff Member(s): 9; 2 volunteer(s)
Membership: 9,500 worldwide; *Member Profile:* Architects & specialists in the conservation & renovation of built heritage
Activities: *Library:* UNESCO-ICOMOS Documentation Centre; Open to public
Chief Officer(s):
M. Gustavo Araoz, President
Marie-Laure Lavenir, Director
Meetings/Conferences:
• International Council on Monuments & Sites General Assembly 2018, 2018
Scope: International

International Curling Federation *See* World Curling Federation

International Dairy Federation (IDF) / Fédération internationale de Laiterie (FIL)
70B Auguste Reyers Blvd., Brussels 1030 Belgium
Tel: 32-2-325-6740; *Fax:* 32-2-325-6741
info@fil-idf.org
www.fil-idf.org
www.linkedin.com/company/2265490
twitter.com/FIL_IDF
Overview: A small international organization founded in 1903
Mission: To promote through international cooperation & consultation, the solution of scientific, technical & economic problems in the international dairy field
Member of: International Council of Scientific Unions
Staff Member(s): 11
Membership: 48 national committees; *Committees:* Science & Programming Coordination
Activities: Scientific & technical cooperation within dairy sector; *Library:* by appointment
Chief Officer(s):
Nico van Belzen, Director General
nvanbelzen@fil-idf.org
Pierre Doyle, Executive Director, IDF Canada
pierre.doyle@agr.gc.ca

International Dyslexia Association (IDA)
40 York Rd., 4th Fl/, Baltimore MD 21204 USA
Tel: 410-296-0232; *Fax:* 410-321-5069
info@interdys.org
eida.org
www.linkedin.com/company/international-dyslexia-association
www.facebook.com/interdys

twitter.com/IntlDyslexia
www.youtube.com/user/idachannel
Overview: A medium-sized international organization
Mission: The IDA actively promotes effective teaching approaches and related clinical educational intervention strategies for dyslexics.
Membership: *Fees:* Schedule available

Ontario Branch (ONBIDA)
1785 Foleyet Cres., Pickering ON L1V 2X8
Tel: 416-716-9296
idaontario.com
www.facebook.com/group.php?gid=12300009993
twitter.com/onbida
www.flickr.com/photos/onbida/

International Economic History Association / Association internationale d'histoire économique
c/o University of Tuebingen, Department of Economic History, Mohlstrasse 36, Tuebingen 72074 Germany
Tel: 49 7071 29 72985; *Fax:* 49 7071 29 5119
ieha@uni-tuebingen.de
www.uni-tuebingen.de/ieha/
Overview: A small international organization
Mission: To unite economic historians from countries in Africa, America, Asia, Europe and Oceania.
Affiliation(s): Comité international des sciences historiques
Membership: 45; *Member Profile:* Associations involved with economic history; *Committees:* Local Organizing; Executive
Chief Officer(s):
Jan Luiten van Zanden, President

International Emissions Trading Association (IETA)
24, rue Merle d'Aubigné, Genève CH-1207 Switzerland
Tel: +41 22 737 05 00; *Fax:* +41 22 737 05 08
secretariat@ieta.org
www.ieta.org
www.linkedin.com/company/international-emissions-trading-association
twitter.com/IETA
Overview: A medium-sized international organization founded in 1999
Mission: A nonprofit business organization created to establish a functional international framework for trading in greenhouse gas emission reductions.
Membership: 150 international companies
Chief Officer(s):
Bruce Braine, Chair

Toronto Branch
350 Adelaide St. West, 3rd Fl., Toronto ON M5V 1R8
Tel: 416-913-0135
Chief Officer(s):
Katie Sullivan, Director, North American Policy & International Climate Finance

International Ergonomics Association
Department of Industrial Engineering, National Tsing Hua University, 101, Sec. 2 Guang Fu Rd., Hsinchu 30013 Taiwan
Tel: 886-3-574-2649; *Fax:* 886-3-572-6153
www.iea.cc
Overview: A small international organization
Mission: To elaborate & advance ergonomics science & practice & to improve the quality of life by expanding its scope of application & contribution to society
Membership: *Committees:* Policy & Planning; Professional Standards & Education; Science, Technology & Practice; Communications & Public Relations; Industrially Developing Countries; Awards
Chief Officer(s):
Eric Min-yang Wang, Secretary General
mywang@ie.nthu.edu.tw
Awards:
• K.U. Smith Student Paper Award
• IEA/Liberty Mutual Prize in Occupational Safety & Ergonomics
• IEA Fellow Award
• Distinguished Service Award
• Outstanding Educators Award
• Award for Promotion of Ergonomics in Industrially Developing Countries
• Ergonomics Development Award
• President's Award

International Erosion Control Association (IECA)
#3500, 3401 Quebec St., Denver CO 80207 USA
Tel: 1-303-640-7554; *Fax:* 866-308-3087
Toll-Free: 800-455-4322
ecinfo@ieca.org
www.ieca.org
www.facebook.com/InternationalErosionControlAssociation
twitter.com/IECARegion1
Overview: A medium-sized international organization founded in 1972
Mission: To serve as a global resource for environmental education & exchange of information; To represent, lead & unify a diverse group of people worldwide who share a common responsibility for the causes, prevention & control of erosion
Finances: *Annual Operating Budget:* $500,000-$1.5 Million; *Funding Sources:* Membership dues; conferences; courses; publications
Staff Member(s): 10
Membership: 2,500+; *Fees:* Schedule available; *Member Profile:* 17 Professional Fields of Practice: Academic, Consultant, Contractor, Developer, Engineer, Government Agency, Landscape Architect, Library, Mining, Non-Profit, Publisher, Ski Industry, Supplier, Utility Company, & Other; *Committees:* Awards; Educational Tracks; Ethics; Executive; Finance; Professional Development; Standards & Practices
Activities: Professional development courses; field trips & tours throughout the world; training bureau; scholarship program; research grant program & an erosion control material standards program; *Speaker Service:* Yes
Chief Officer(s):
Thomas W. Schneider, President

International Facility Management Association (IFMA)
#900, 800 Gessner Rd., Houston TX 77024-4257 USA
Tel: 713-623-4362; *Fax:* 713-623-6124
ifma@ifma.org
www.ifma.org
www.linkedin.com/groups?gid=38141
www.facebook.com/InternationalFacilityManagementAssociation
twitter.com/IFMA
www.youtube.com/ifmaglobal
Overview: A small international charitable organization founded in 1980
Mission: To lead & sustain progress of the facility management profession
Affiliation(s): Facility Management Nederland; Health Care Institute; Bulgarian Facility Management Association; British Institute of Facilities Management; Facilities Management Association of Australia; American Society for Healthcare Engineering; ASHRAE; Building & Construction Authority; European Facility Management Network; German Facility Management Association; Japan Facility Management Association; Society of American Military Engineers; South African Facilities Management Association; U.S. Environmental Protection Agency; U.S. Green Building Council
Finances: *Funding Sources:* Dues; educational programs; publications
Staff Member(s): 11
Membership: 23,000+; *Fees:* US$179 professional; US$179 associate; US$10 student; US$100 retired; US$99 young professional; *Member Profile:* Facility management executives, consultants & suppliers; real estate executives; security experts; designers
Activities: Certification, education, research, trade shows, publications, lobbying; *Speaker Service:* Yes; *Rents Mailing List:* Yes
Chief Officer(s):
Tony Keane, President & CEO
tony.keane@ifma.org
Andrea E. Sanchez, Director, Communications
andrea.sanchez@ifma.org

International Federation for Cell Biology (IFCB)
www.ifcbiol.org
Overview: A medium-sized international organization founded in 1972
Mission: To promote cooperation & to contribute to the advancement of cell biology in all its branches
Affiliation(s): International Union of Biological Sciences; International Cell Research Organization
Membership: *Fees:* US$200
Chief Officer(s):
Nobutaka Hirokawa, President, Japan
hirokawa@m.u-tokyo.ac.jp
Hernandez F. Carvalho, Secretary General, Brazil
hern@unicamp.br

International Federation for Home Economics (IFHE)
Kaiser - Friedrich - Strasse 13, Bonn D - 53113 Germany
Tel: 49-0-228-921-2590; *Fax:* 49-0-228-921-2591
office@ifhe.org
www.ifhe.org
Overview: A small international charitable organization founded in 1908
Mission: To provide an international forum for home economists; To develop & express the home economics concerns for individuals, families, & households at the United Nations & among other international non-governmental organizations, whose interests parallel those of home economics
Affiliation(s): Canadian Home Economics Association
Membership: *Fees:* 50 Euro individual; 25 Euro individuals in developing countries; 20 Euro students; 250 Euro organization; *Member Profile:* Individuals & students participating in practise, education or research of home economics or who are interested in these topics; Professional associations, universities, schools, & other organizations involved in home economics; Businesses & industries concerned with home economics; *Committees:* Executive; United Nations; Finance; Membership; IFHE Congress; Young Professionals Network; Publication & Communication; Think Tank; Research; Project Assessment; Senior Advisory; Acccredition/Certification; Partnerships; Consumers & Sustainable Development; Family (and Gender); Food Security & Nutrition & Nutritional Health; Home Economics Policies in Education and Training; Household Technology & Sustainability; IFHE International Business Group; Institutional & Hospitality Management; Outreach to Central & East European Countries; Textiles & Design
Activities: Promoting continuing education; Providing opportunities for global networking; *Library:* National Archives; Open to public
Chief Officer(s):
Carol Warren, President
Elisabeth Leicht-Eckardt, Treasurer General
Publications:
• Home Economics News [a publication of the International Federation for Home Economics]
Type: Newsletter; *Frequency:* Quarterly

International Federation for Housing & Planning (IFHP) / Fédération internationale pour l'habitation, l'urbanisme et l'aménagement des territoires (FIHUAT)
Frederiksholms Kanal 30, Copenhagen 1220 Denmark
Tel: 45-30-56-96-86
info@ifhp.org
www.ifhp.org
www.linkedin.com/company/international-federation-for-housing-and-planning
www.facebook.com/ifhp.official
twitter.com/IFHP
www.instagram.com/instaifhp
Previous Name: International Garden Cities & Town Planning Association
Overview: A medium-sized international organization founded in 1913
Mission: To plan & organize activities; To create opportunities for an exchange of professional knowledge & experience
Membership: 500-999; *Member Profile:* Organizations or individuals who support the aims & objectives of IFHP, & who wish to participate in a worldwide network
Activities: Offering conferences, seminars, symposia, & study tours; Organizing student & film & video competitions
Chief Officer(s):
Anette Galskjot, Chief Executive Officer
a.galskjot@ifhp.org
Regitze Marianne Hess, Chief Operating Officer
r.hess@ifhp.org
Publications:
• IFHP [International Federation for Housing & Planning] Membership List & Directory
Type: Directory; *Number of Pages:* 77; *Price:* Free for members only

International Federation for Medical & Biological Engineering (IFMBE)
www.ifmbe.org
Overview: A medium-sized international organization founded in 1959
Mission: To reflect the interests & initiatives of national affiliated organizations; to generate & disseminate information of interest to the medical & biological engineering community & international organizations; to provide an international forum for the exchange of ideas & concepts; to encourage & foster research & application of medical & biological engineering knowledge & techniques in support of life quality & cost-effective

health care; to stimulate international cooperation & collaboration on medical & biological engineering matters; to encourage educational programs that develop scientific & technical expertise in medical & biological engineering. IFMBE Secretariat currently located in Stockholm, Sweden.
Affiliation(s): International Union of Physical & Engineering Sciences in Medicine; International Organization for Medical Physics
Membership: *Committees:* Finance; Constitution & Bylaws; Women in MBE; International Liaisons; Nominating; Publications; Publicity; Federation Journal; Awards; Bioethics; Conference; Education & Accreditation; Membership; Strategic Planning
Chief Officer(s):
Ratko Magjarevic, President, University of Zagreb, Croatia
ratko.magjarevic@fer.hr
James Cho Hong, Vice President, National University of Singapore, Singapore
dosgohj@nus.edu.sg
Meetings/Conferences:
• World Congress on Medical Physics and Biomedical Engineering 2018, 2018
Scope: International
Description: The Congresses are scheduled on a three-year basis and aligned with Federation's General Assembly meeting at which elections are held.

International Federation for Research in Women's History (IFRWH) / Fédération internationale pour la recherche en histoire des femmes (FIRHF)
Dept. of Philosophy & Social Sciences, St. Kliment Ohridski University of Sofia, 15 Tsar Osvoboditel Blvd., Sofia 1504 Bulgaria
e-mail: krasi@sclg.uni-sofia.bg
www.ifrwh.com
Overview: A small international organization founded in 1990
Mission: To promote women's history around the world
Member of: International Committee for Historical Sciences
Finances: *Annual Operating Budget:* Less than $50,000
Membership: 36; *Fees:* 20 pounds/$30; *Member Profile:* National committees on women's history
Activities: Conferences; publications
Chief Officer(s):
Clare Midgley, President
c.c.midgley@shu.ac.uk

International Federation of Accountants (IFAC)
545 Fifth Ave., 14th Fl., New York NY 10017 USA
Tel: 212-286-9344; *Fax:* 212-286-9570
Communications@ifac.org
www.ifac.org
www.linkedin.com/company/ifac
www.facebook.com/InternationalFederationOfAccountants
twitter.com/IFAC_Update
www.youtube.com/user/IFACMultimedia
Overview: A medium-sized international organization founded in 1977
Mission: Worldwide development & enhancement of an accountancy profession with harmonized standards, able to provide services of consistently high quality in the public interest
Affiliation(s): Canadian Institute of Chartered Accountants; Certified General Accountants Association of Canada; Society of Management Accountants of Canada
Staff Member(s): 12
Membership: 179; *Member Profile:* National accountancy bodies; *Committees:* Compliance Advisory Panel; Developing Nations; Nominating; Professional Accountancy Organization Development; Professional Accountants in Business; Small & Medium Practices; Transnational Auditors
Chief Officer(s):
Warren Allan, President
Laura Wilker, Director, Communications
LauraWilker@ifac.org

International Federation of Aircraft Technology & Engineering *See* International Federation of Airworthiness

International Federation of Airworthiness (IFA)
59 Hurst Farm Rd. East, Sussex RH19 4DQ United Kingdom
www.ifairworthy.com
www.linkedin.com/company/international-federation-of-airworthiness
Previous Name: International Federation of Aircraft Technology & Engineering
Overview: A medium-sized international charitable organization founded in 1975
Mission: To improve aviation safety by increasing international communications, awareness & cooperation on all aspects of airworthiness particularly continuing airworthiness
Member of: Flight Safety Foundation; Aeronautical Repair Station Association
Finances: *Annual Operating Budget:* $50,000-$100,000; *Funding Sources:* Membership fees
10 volunteer(s)
Membership: 115 corporate; *Fees:* Schedule available; *Member Profile:* Corporate bodies; *Committees:* Technical; Execstive Council; Scholarship
Activities: Organizing Technical Conferences on Air Safety; Updating members on proposed changes to airworthiness requirements & procedures; Providing forum for discussion of airworthiness problems; Establishing opinion on outstanding airworthiness problems
Chief Officer(s):
John W. Saull, Executive Director
Awards:
• IFA Whittle Safety Award
• IFA Scholarship
Meetings/Conferences:
• International Federation of Airworthiness Forum 2018, 2018
Scope: International
Publications:
• Airworthiness Matters [a publication of the International Federation of Airworthiness]
Type: Magazine; *Frequency:* a.

International Federation of Beekeepers' Associations
Corso Vittorio Emanuele 101, Rome I-00186 Italy
Tel: 39-06-685-2286; *Fax:* 39-06-685-2287
apimondia@mclink.it
www.apimondia.org
Also Known As: APIMONDIA
Overview: A medium-sized international organization founded in 1897
Mission: To promotes apicultural development in all countries, scientifically, ecologically, socially & economically
Affiliation(s): Canadian Honey Council
Chief Officer(s):
Philip McCabe, President
philipmccabe17@gmail.com
Meetings/Conferences:
• International Federation of Beekeepers' Associations (APIMONDIA) 46th International Apicultural Congress 2018, 2018
Scope: International

International Federation of Bodybuilding & Fitness (IFBB) / Fédération internationale des culturisme et de remise en forme
c/ Dublin, no. 39. I, 28232 Europolis, Las Rozas, Madrid Spain
Tel: 34 91 53528 19
headquarters@ifbb.com
www.ifbb.com
www.facebook.com/International.Federation.Body.Building.Fitness
twitter.com/IFBB_OFFICIAL
www.youtube.com/user/ifbbinternational
Overview: A large international charitable organization founded in 1946
Mission: To promote fitness & a healthy lifestyle through the sport of bodybuilding
Member of: SportAccord
Staff Member(s): 3
Membership: 182 countries affiliated; *Fees:* $300 (national federations only); *Committees:* Judges; Research Development; Technical; Women's
Activities: Professional & amateur championships held worldwide; *Speaker Service:* Yes
Chief Officer(s):
Rafael Santonja, President
William Tierney, General Secretary
Publications:
• International Federation of Bodybuilding & Fitness Newsletter
Type: Newsletter

International Federation of Business & Professional Women (IFBPW) / Fédération internationale des femmes de carrières libérales et commerciales
Rue de Carouge 36bis, Geneva 1205 Switzerland
Other Communication: Membership e-mail:
member.services@bpw-international.org
presidents.office@bpw-international.org
www.bpw-international.org
www.facebook.com/bpw.international
twitter.com/bpwi
Also Known As: BPW International
Overview: A large international organization founded in 1930
Mission: To organize business & professional women in all parts of the world to use their combined abilities & strengths for the attainment of the following objectives: To work for equal opportunities & status for women in the economic, civil & political life of all countries & the removal of discrimination; To encourage women & girls to acquire eduction, occupational training & advanced education & use their occupational capacities & intelligence for the advantage of others as well as themselves; To improve the position of women in business, trade & the professions, & in the economic life of their countries; To stimulate & encourage in women a realization & acceptance of their responsibilites to the community - locally, nationally & internationally; To work for high standards of service in business & the professions; To promote worldwide friendship, cooperation & understanding between business & professional women
Affiliation(s): Canadian Federation of Business & Professional Women's Clubs
Finances: *Funding Sources:* Membership dues
Membership: *Member Profile:* Women employed in business, professions or entrepreneurial; *Committees:* Arts & Culture; Agriculture; Business, Trade & Technology; Development, Training & Employment; Environment & Sustainable Development; Finance; Health; Legislation; Membership; Projects; Public Relations; UN Status of Woman; Young BPW
Activities: Involved in the INSTRAW Women's Training Centre, UNIFEM, Project 5-O International, ILO Training Centre, Women's World Banking & over 50 other on-going projects around the world; *Speaker Service:* Yes; *Library:* IFBPW Archive Centre; by appointment
Chief Officer(s):
Amany Asfour, President
Awards:
• Badge of Honour
• Gertrude Mongella Award
• Jennifer Cox Trophy
Publications:
• International Federation of Business & Professional Women E-News
Type: Newsletter
• International Federation of Business & Professional Women Annual Report
Type: Yearbook

International Federation of Camping, Caravanning, & Motor Caravanning *Voir* Fédération Internationale de Camping, Caravanning et Autocaravaning

International Federation of Clinical Chemistry & Laboratory Medicine (IFCC)
Via Carlo Farini 81, Milan 20159 Italy
Tel: +39 0266809912; *Fax:* +39 0260781846
ifcc@ifcc.org
www.ifcc.org
Overview: A small international organization
Mission: To enhance the scientific level & the quality of diagnosis & therapy for patients throughout the world
Chief Officer(s):
Maurizio Ferrari, President
president@ifcc.org
Graham Beastall, Past President
Sergio Bernardini, Secretary
bernardini@med.uniroma2.it

International Federation of Employees in Public Service (INFEDOP) / Fédération internationale du personnel des services publics
Montoyerstraat 39 bus 20, Rue Montoyer 39 boîte 20, Brussels 1000 Belgium
Tel: 32-2-2303-865; *Fax:* 32-2-2311-472
infedop@infedop.org
www.infedop.org
Overview: A medium-sized international licensing organization
Finances: *Annual Operating Budget:* $250,000-$500,000
Staff Member(s): 6; 3 volunteer(s)
Membership: *Member Profile:* Trade Unions
Chief Officer(s):
Bert Van Caelenberg, Secretary General

International Federation of Film Producers' Associations
Voir Fédération internationale des associations de producteurs de films

International Federation of Hardware & Housewares Association (IHA)
c/o North American Retail Hardware Association, #300, 6325 Digital Way, Indianapolis IN 46278 USA
Tel: 317-275-9400; *Fax:* 317-375-9403
Toll-Free: 800-772-4424
iha@nrha.org
www.nrha.org
Overview: A small international organization founded in 1909
Mission: To inform, educate & influence
Finances: *Funding Sources:* Subscriptions
Staff Member(s): 2
Membership: 35; *Member Profile:* National hardware retail organizations
Activities: *Internships:* Yes; *Speaker Service:* Yes; *Rents Mailing List:* Yes
Chief Officer(s):
Bill Lee, Secretary General
blee@nrha.org

International Federation of Health Information Management Associations (IFHIMA)
c/o University of Erlangen-Nuremberg, DRG Controlling, Quality Mngmnt, Schwabachanlage 6, Erlangen D 91054 Germany
www.ifhima.org
Previous Name: International Federation of Health Records Organizations
Overview: A medium-sized international organization
Mission: To improve health/medical record practices in member countries; to be a forum for the exchange of information relating to health records & information technology
Member of: World Health Organization
Affiliation(s): Canadian Health Record Association
Chief Officer(s):
Angelika Haendel, President
angelika.haendel@uk-erlangen.de

International Federation of Health Records Organizations
See International Federation of Health Information Management Associations

International Federation of Human Genetics Societies (IFHGS)
c/o Vienna Medical Academy, Alserstrasse 4, Vienna 1090 Austria
Tel: +43 1 405 13 83 22; *Fax:* +43 1 407 82 74
ifhgs@medacad.org
www.ifhgs.org
Overview: A small international organization founded in 1996
Mission: To facilitate communication throughout the international community of human geneticists
Membership: 58 societies; *Member Profile:* International professional human genetics societies
Activities: Sharing information about research, education, & clinical services; Encouraging interaction between workers in genetics fields & in related scientific fields
Chief Officer(s):
Stephen Lam, President
ts_lam@dh.gov.hk

International Federation of Hydrographic Societies
PO Box 103, Plymouth PL4 7YP United Kingdom
Tel: 44-175-222-3512; *Fax:* 44-175-222-3512
helen@hydrographicsociety.org
www.hydrographicsociety.org
Previous Name: Hydrographic Society
Overview: A small international charitable organization founded in 1972
Mission: To promote the science of surveying afloat & related sciences; to promote better education & training of persons engaged or intending to engage in the study of hydrography & related sciences; to accumulate, extend & disseminate information, knowledge & expertise
Finances: *Annual Operating Budget:* $100,000-$250,000
Staff Member(s): 1; 10 volunteer(s)
Membership: From over 70 countries; *Fees:* Available on application; *Member Profile:* Individuals & organizations with an interest in any aspect of surveying afloat; *Committees:* Educational Award Scheme
Activities: Publications, conferences, seminars, workshops

International Federation of Landscape Architects (IFLA) / Fédération internationale des architectes paysagistes
c/o Christine Bavassa, Tour Louise - Ave Louise 149/24, Brussels 1050 Belgium
Tel: 32-495-568-285
admin@iflaonline.org
www.iflaonline.org
www.linkedin.com/groups/4216963/profile
www.facebook.com/140052269363180
twitter.com/intfedlandarch
Also Known As: IFLA
Overview: A small international charitable organization founded in 1948
Mission: To develop the profession of landscape architecture; To assist in identifying & preserving the intricate balance of ecological systems; To promote education & encourage scientific research in landscape architecture; To assist all levels of government in establishing & improving legislation connected with the profession of landscape architecture
Membership: 25,000 architects + 71 national associations; *Member Profile:* National associations of professional landscape architects, individuals & corporations; *Committees:* Communications & External Relations; Education & Academic Affairs; Professional Practice & Policy; Finance & Business Planning
Activities: Offering world congresses, regional conferences, symposia & seminars; Organizing an international student design competition & educational programs; *Awareness Events:* World Landscape Architecture Month, April
Chief Officer(s):
Ben Roberts, Executive Director
director@iflaonline.org
Awards:
• Sir Joffrey Gellicoe Award
Awarded to honour the outstanding lifetime achievements & contributions of a landscape architect *Deadline:* October
Contact: Darwina Neal, Chair, Nomination Committee, E-mail: darwina_neal@verizon.net; Phone: 202-295-4021
Publications:
• Guide to International Opportunities in Landscape Architecture, Education & Internships
Profile: Listing of international opportunities sorted by country

International Federation of Library Associations & Institutions (IFLA)
PO Box 95312, The Hague 2509 CH Netherlands
Tel: 31-70-314-0884; *Fax:* 31-70-383-4827
ifla@ifla.org
www.ifla.org
www.facebook.com/115229368506017
twitter.com/IFLA
www.youtube.com/user/iflahq; www.flickr.com/photos/ifla
Overview: A medium-sized international organization founded in 1927
Mission: To promote international cooperation, research, & development in all fields of library activity & information service
Affiliation(s): Gold partners: Australian Science; Elsevier; Emerald; De Gruyter Saur; Intech; nbd/biblion; OCLC; Sage; SirsiDynix. Silver partners: BRILL; Cambridge U. Press; Gale Cengage Learning. Bronze partners: AXIELL Library Group; Annual Reviews; ebrary; Harrassowitz Booksellers & Subscription Agents; Ingressus; Innovative Interfaces Inc.; ProQuest; Schulz Bibliothekstechnik GmbH; Springer
Finances: *Funding Sources:* Membership fees; Sponsorship contributions; Revenues from sales of publications; Foundation grants
Membership: 1,500+; *Fees:* Schedule available; *Member Profile:* Library associations, libraries, information centres, library schools, school libraries, bibliographical & research institutes, students, & information professionals; *Committees:* Executive; Professional
Activities: Providing a forum for information specialists throughout the world to exchange ideas; *Library:* IFLA Library
Chief Officer(s):
Donna Scheeder, President
donna_scheeder@comcast.net
Gerald Leitner, Secretary General
Awards:
• IFLA BibLibre International Library Marketing Award
• IFLA / Brill Open Access Award
Awarded to honour initiatives that promote Open Access Scholarly Monographs in the social sciences or humanities
• De Gruyter Saur / IFLA Research Paper Award
Awarded to the best research paper on a topic of importance to publishing or access to information
• IFLA Professional Unit Communication Award
Awarded to honour excellence in communication activities of IFLA professional units
• Best IFLA Poster
Awarded to the best poster from those displayed during the World Library & Information Congress
• IFLA Certificate of Service
Awarded to individuals retiring from IFLA activities who have served eight years or more as an IFLA Officer
• IFLA Medal
Awarded to an individual who has made a distinguished contribution to IFLA or international librarianship
• IFLA Scroll of Appreciation
Awarded to an individual who has provided distinguished service to IFLA
Meetings/Conferences:
• International Federation of Library Associations & Institutions World Library & Information Congress 2018, August, 2018, Kuala Lumpur
Scope: International
Contact Information: 2018.ifla.org; Congress Secretariat: wlic2018@kit-group.org
Publications:
• IFLA Journal [a publication of the International Federation of Library Associations & Institutions]
Type: Journal; *Frequency:* Quarterly; *Editor:* Steven W. Witt; *ISSN:* 0340-0352
Profile: Feastures peer-reviewed articles on library & information services
• International Federation of Library Associations & Institutions Annual Report
Type: Yearbook; *Frequency:* Annually
Profile: Resolutions, projects, meetings, summaries from the annual conference, finances, membership objectives, & reports on professional activities

International Federation of Medical Students' Associations (IFMSA)
c/o Academic Medical Center, Meibergdreef 15, J0-208, Amsterdam 1105 AZ The Netherlands
e-mail: gs@ifmsa.org
www.ifmsa.org
www.linkedin.com/company/international-federation-of-medical-students
www.facebook.com/ifmsa
twitter.com/@ifmsa
www.instagram.com/youifmsa
Overview: A large international organization founded in 1951
Mission: To represent & serve medical students worldwide; To offer future physicians an understanding of current global health challenges
Membership: 97 national member organizations; *Member Profile:* Medical students' associations from around the world; *Committees:* Public Health; Professional Exchanges; Medical Education; Reproductive Health including AIDS; Research Exchange; Human Rights & Peace
Activities: Providing a forum for discussion for medical students
Chief Officer(s):
Omar Cherkaoui, President
president@ifmsa.org
Marie Hauerslev, Vice President, External Affairs
vpe@ifmsa.org
Joakim Bergman, Vice President, Finance
vpf@ifmsa.org
Publications:
• IFMSA Bulletin

IFMSA-Quebec
QC
Tel: 438-838-0594
www.ifmsa.qc.ca
www.facebook.com/ifmsaquebec
twitter.com/ifmsa_quebec
www.youtube.com/ifmsaquebec
Chief Officer(s):
Claudel P. Desrosiers, President
president@ifmsa.qc.ca

International Federation of Multiple Sclerosis Societies *See* Multiple Sclerosis International Federation

International Federation of Organic Agriculture Movements (IFOAM) / Fédération internationale des mouvements d'agriculture biologique
Charles-de-Gaulle-Str.5, Bonn 53113 Germany
Tel: 49-228-926-5010; *Fax:* 49-228-926-5099
headoffice@ifoam.org
www.ifoam.org
Overview: A small international charitable organization founded in 1972

Foreign Associations / International Genetics Federation (IGF)

Mission: To lead, assist, & unite the organic movement in its full diversity; To promote the worldwide adoption of ecologically, socially, & economically sound systems that are based on the principles of organic agriculture
Member of: Consumers Choice Council
Affiliation(s): Association interprofessionnelle pour le développement agrobiologique; Canadian Organic Growers; International Development Research Center; Ecological Agriculture Projects; Université écologique internationale; Mouvement pour l'agriculture biologique au Québec
Finances: *Annual Operating Budget:* $500,000-$1.5 Million
Staff Member(s): 10
Membership: 750 member organizations & corporate associates in 105 countries; *Fees:* Schedule available; *Committees:* Standards; Third World; Accreditation; Criteria Revision
Activities: *Internships:* Yes; *Speaker Service:* Yes; *Library:* by appointment

International Federation of Physical Medicine & Rehabilitation *See* International Society of Physical & Rehabilitation Medicine

International Federation of Professional & Technical Engineers (AFL-CIO/CLC) (IFPTE) / Fédération internationale des ingénieurs et techniciens (FAT-COI/CTC)
#701, 501 3rd St. NW, Washington DC 20001 USA
Tel: 202-239-4880; *Fax:* 202-239-4881
Other Communication: communication@ifpte.org
generalinfo@ifpte.org
www.ifpte.org
www.facebook.com/IFPTE
twitter.com/IFPTE
Overview: A large international organization founded in 1918
Mission: To represent employees in a wide variety of occupations in the technical, administrative & professional fields
Affiliation(s): AFL-CIO; Canadian Labour Congress; IMF; UNI; PSI
Finances: *Annual Operating Budget:* $3 Million-$5 Million; *Funding Sources:* Per capita tax from local unions
Staff Member(s): 15
Membership: 80,000; *Member Profile:* Professional, technical & administrative employees
Chief Officer(s):
Gregory J. Junemann, President
Paul Shearon, Secretary-Treasurer
Meetings/Conferences:
• International Federation of Professional & Technical Engineers (IFPTE) 2018 59th Convention, June, 2018, Atlantic City, NJ
Scope: International
   Canadian Office - Local 160
   2239 Yonge St., Toronto ON M4S 2B5
   Tel: 416-979-2709; *Fax:* 416-979-5794
   Toll-Free: 866-288-1788
   society@thesociety.ca
   www.thesociety.ca
   Member of: Canadian Council of Professionals; Professional Employees' Network
   Chief Officer(s):
   Adam Chaleff-Freudenthaler, Officer, Communications, 647-500-2394
   adam@thesociety.ca

International Federation of Red Cross & Red Crescent Societies / Fédération Internationale des Sociétés de la Croix-Rouge & du Croissant-Rouge
PO Box 303, Geneva CH-1211 19 Switzerland
Tel: 41-22-730-42-22; *Fax:* 41-730-4200
www.ifrc.org
www.facebook.com/IFRC
twitter.com/Federation
www.youtube.com/user/ifrc
Overview: A small international organization founded in 1919
Mission: To provide assistance & relief operations without discrimination
Affiliation(s): Canadian Red Cross Society
Membership: 190 member Red Cross & Red Crescent societies; *Committees:* Compliance & Mediation; Election; Finance; Youth
Chief Officer(s):
Tadateru Konoé, President
Elhadj As Sy, Secretary General

International Federation of Surveyors (IFS) / Fédération internationale des géomètres (FIG)
Kalvebod Brygge 31-33, Copenhagen 1780 Denmark
Tel: 45 3886 1081; *Fax:* 45 3886 0252
FIG@fig.net
www.fig.net
www.linkedin.com/company/fig---international-federation-of-surveyors
www.facebook.com/internationalfederationofsurveyors
twitter.com/FIG_NEWS
Overview: A medium-sized international organization founded in 1878
Mission: To ensure that the disciplines of surveying and all who practise them meet the needs of the markets and communities that they serve
Affiliation(s): Canadian Institute of Surveying and Mapping
Staff Member(s): 1; 7 volunteer(s)
Membership: 200,000
Chief Officer(s):
Chryssy Potsiou, President
Awards:
• FIG Foundation Academic Research Grants
• FIG Foundation PhD Scholarships

International Federation of Translators *Voir* Fédération Internationale des Traducteurs

International Flying Farmers (IFF)
PO Box 309, Mansfield IL 61854 USA
Tel: 217-489-9300; *Fax:* 217-489-9280
iff1944@hotmail.com
www.internationalflyingfarmers.org
Overview: A medium-sized international organization founded in 1944
Mission: To provide a personalized, unique & economical opportunity to experience agriculture & aviation in a family environment in Canada & the United States
Staff Member(s): 1
Membership: 1,100; *Fees:* US$85 per family
Chief Officer(s):
Alex Knox, President

International Foster Care Organisation (IFCO)
26 Red Lion Square, London WC1R 4AG UK
Tel: +44 (0)208 144 7571
ifco@ifco.info
www.ifco.info
www.facebook.com/IFCO.info
twitter.com/IFCOinfo
Overview: A medium-sized international charitable organization
Mission: To promote family-based solutions for out-of-home children; To support family foster care throughout the world; To provide advice to governmental & non-governmental organizations about the development & improvement of family-based substitute care
Member of: Eurochild; NGO Group for the United Nations Convention Rights of the Child
Membership: *Fees:* Schedule available
Activities: Advising foster care associations; Sharing news & developments from around the globe; Training trainers in aspects of foster care; Establishing regional networks for the sharing of ideas
Chief Officer(s):
Volodymyr Kuzmynskyi, President
Jean Kennedy, Vice-President
Lacy Kendrick Burk, Secretary
Colin Chatten, Treasurer
Meetings/Conferences:
• International Foster Care Organisation 2019 World Conference, 2019
Scope: International
Description: A biennial conference, featuring a youth program, workshops, & plenary sessions about quality care solutions for children & youth living in out-of-home care
Publications:
• IFCO Magazine
Type: Magazine; *Frequency:* Quarterly
Profile: Foster care news from around the world, including projects, research, insights, & upcoming events
• Stakeholders in Foster Care
Type: Study; *Editor:* Shanti George & Nico van Oudenhoven
Profile: An examination of fost care, in the context of family, social networks, non-governmental organizations, & the state
• The Unfolding of The Wings of Foster Care
Type: Book

Profile: A collection of contributions from the 2003 International Foster Care Organisation conference

International Foundation of Employee Benefit Plans
PO Box 69, 18700 West Bluemound Rd., Brookfield WI 53008-0069 USA
Toll-Free: 888-334-3327
membership@ifebp.org
www.ifebp.org
www.linkedin.com/company/international-foundation-of-employee-benefit-plans
www.facebook.com/IFEBP
twitter.com/IFEBP
www.youtube.com/user/IFEBP
Overview: A large international organization founded in 1954
Mission: Dedicated exclusively to employee benefits & compensation education
Finances: *Annual Operating Budget:* Greater than $5 Million; *Funding Sources:* Membership dues; Fees for services
Staff Member(s): 140
Membership: 34,000; *Fees:* Schedule available; *Member Profile:* Trust fund representations & corporate benefits professionals
Activities: *Awareness Events:* National Employee Benefits Day, April 2; *Internships:* Yes; *Library:* Not open to public
Chief Officer(s):
Regina C. Reardon, President
Michael Wilson, CEO
Publications:
• Benefits Magazine [a publication of the International Foundation of Employee Benefit Plans]
Type: Magazine; *Frequency:* Monthly; *ISSN:* 2157-6157
Profile: Features articles by experienced benefits professionals on topics concerning multiemployer, public employer, singleemployer and corporate benefit plans
• Benefits Quarterly [a publication of the International Foundation of Employee Benefit Plans]
Type: Magazine; *Frequency:* Quarterly; *ISSN:* 2168-3336
Profile: Offers comprehensive benefits coverage from a corporate perspective
• Plans & Trust [a publication of the International Foundation of Employee Benefit Plans]
Type: Magazine; *Frequency:* Bimonthly; *ISSN:* 2164-3857
Profile: Provides an in-depth look at benefits issues, and reviews federal and provincial legal decisions and legislativedevelopments

International Game Developers Association (IGDA)
19 Mantua Rd., Mount Royal NJ 08061 USA
Tel: 856-423-2990; *Fax:* 856-423-3420
contact@igda.org
www.igda.org
www.linkedin.com/in/baldwinjames
www.facebook.com/IGDA.org
twitter.com/twistededge
youtube.com/theigda
Overview: A small international organization
Mission: To strengthen & bring together the international game development community while effecting change to benefit that community.
Affiliation(s): Canadian Chapters: Calgary www.igda.org/calgary; Montréal www.igda.org/montreal; Ottawa www.igda.org/ottawa; Toronto www.igda.org/toronto, Jason MacIsaac, Contact; Vancouver www.igda.org/vancouver, James Everett, Contact
Chief Officer(s):
Jon Grande, Chair
Kate Edwards, Executive Director
   Toronto Chapter
   Toronto ON
   www.igda.org/group/Toronto
   www.facebook.com/IGDAToronto
   www.twitter.com/IGDAToronto
   Chief Officer(s):
   Lesley Phord-Toy, Chair

International Garden Cities & Town Planning Association *See* International Federation for Housing & Planning

International Genetics Federation (IGF)
Dept. of Evolution & Ecology, University of California - Davis, 1 Shields Ave., Davis CA 95616-8554 USA
Tel: 530-752-4085; *Fax:* 530-752-1449
info@meiosis.org
www.internationalgeneticsfederation.org
Overview: A small international organization founded in 1968

Foreign Associations / International Geographic Union (IGU) / Union géographique internationale

Mission: To promote the advancement of the science of genetics
Member of: International Union of Biological Sciences
Affiliation(s): Genetics Society of Canada
Membership: 63 national genetics societies
Chief Officer(s):
Alfred Nordheim, President
alred.nordheim@uni-tuebingen.de
Charles H. Langley, Secretary-General
chlangley@ucdavis.edu

International Geographic Union (IGU) / Union géographique internationale
2246N Pollard St., Arlington VA 22207-3805 USA
Fax: 703-527-3227
www.igu-online.org
Overview: A small international organization founded in 1922
Mission: The IGU has the following objectives: to promote the study of geographical problems; to initiate & coordinate geographical research; to provide for the participation of geographers in the work of international organizations; to facilitate the collection & diffusion of geographical data & documentation; & to promote international standardization or compatibility of methods, nomenclature & symbols employed in geography.
Member of: International Social Science Council
Affiliation(s): International Council of Science
Membership: 1-99
Activities: Library: Archives, Royal Geographical Society in London
Chief Officer(s):
Michael Meadows, Secretary-General
mmeadows@mweb.co.za
Adalberto Vallega, President
Awards:
• Planet & Humanity Medal
• Laureat d'Honneur of the IGU
Publications:
• IGU [International Geographic Union] Newsletter
Type: Newsletter; Frequency: Quarterly; Editor: Ronald F. Abler
Profile: Announcements, information, calls for participation in scientific events, programs, & projects

International Geosynthetics Society (IGS)
IGS Secretariat, #4, 1934 Commerce Lane, Jupiter FL 33458 USA
Tel: 561-768-9489; Fax: 561-828-7618
igssec@geosyntheticssociety.org
www.geosyntheticssociety.org
Overview: A medium-sized international organization founded in 1984
Mission: To be dedicated to the scientific & engineering development of geotextiles, geomembranes, related products & associated technologies
Finances: Funding Sources: Membership dues
Staff Member(s): 1; 10 volunteer(s)
Membership: 41 chapters; 3,000+ individuals; 161 corporate members; Fees: Schedule available; Member Profile: Geosynthetics professionals; Committees: Awards; Chapters; Corporate; Education; Technical
Activities: Library Not open to public
Chief Officer(s):
Diana Davis, Secretariat
igssec@geosyntheticssociety.org
Jorge G. Zornberg, President
zornberg@mail.utexas.edu
Russell Jones, Vice-President
Fumio Tatsuoka, Past President
Elizabeth Peggs, Secretary
Peter Legg, Treasurer
Publications:
• IGS (International Geosynthetics Society) News
Type: Newsletter; Editor: Gerhard Bräu
Profile: General information for IGS members, news from IGS chapters, conference reports, & a calendar of events

International Heavy Haul Association (IHHA)
2808 Forest Hills Crt., Virginia Beach VA 23454-1236 USA
Tel: 757-496-8288; Fax: 757-496-2622
scottlovelace@verizon.net
www.ihha.net
Overview: A large international organization
Mission: To pursue excellence in heavy haul railway operations, engineering, technology & maintenance
Finances: Funding Sources: Membership fees; Sponsorships
Membership: Member Profile: Railway organizations; National & state organizations; Private railway systems; Advocates for the world's heavy haul rail operations; Committees: Finance; Strategic Planning
Activities: Organizing specialist seminars & specialist technical sessions; Offering networking opportunities
Chief Officer(s):
Stephen Cathcart, Chairman
W. Scott Lovelace, CEO
scottlovelace@verizon.net
Awards:
• Heavy Haul of Fame Award
• Best Paper Award
Meetings/Conferences:
• International Heavy Haul Association 2018 International Conference, 2018
Scope: International
Description: An international conference, scheduled every four years, featuring meetings covering the complete spectrum of heavy haul subjects, as well as technical tours
Publications:
• Guidelines To Best Practices For Heavy Haul Railway Operations - Infrastructure Construction & Maintenance Issues
Price: $125
• Guidelines To Best Practices For Heavy Haul Railway Operations - Wheel & Rail Interface Issues
Price: $80
• International Heavy Haul Association Conference Proceedings

International Hockey Federation Voir Fédération internationale de hockey

International Hospital Federation (IHF) / Fédération internationale des hôpitaux
P.A. Hôpital de Loëx, Route de Loëx 151, Bernex 1233 Switzerland
Tel: 41-22-850-94-20; Fax: 41-22-757-10-16
info@ihf-fih.org
www.ihf-fih.org
Overview: A medium-sized international charitable organization founded in 1947
Mission: To provide the opportunity for exchange of information, education, experience relevant to the provision of high-quality health services in member countries; to promote modern management techniques to improve efficiency; to participate in & encourage research & experimentation in hospital & health service planning & management; to collect & disseminate international health service data; to serve as advocate for hospital & related health service organizations in world health affairs
Affiliation(s): World Health Organization
Membership: Member Profile: Hospital organizations; ministries of health; individuals in any health care profession; companies engaged in supplying goods & services to the health care industry
Activities: Publications, meetings; networking; Rents Mailing List: Yes
Chief Officer(s):
Eric de Roodenbeke, CEO

International Hotel & Restaurant Association (IH&RA)
42 Ave. General Guisan, Lausanne 1009 Switzerland
Tel: 41-21-711-4283; Fax: 41-21-711-4285
admin@ih-ra.com
www.ih-ra.com
www.facebook.com/260181355823
Overview: A large international charitable organization founded in 1946
Mission: To promote & defend the interests of the hotel & restaurant industry worldwide
Finances: Annual Operating Budget: $500,000-$1.5 Million
Staff Member(s): 5; 50 volunteer(s)
Membership: Over 50,000; Member Profile: National hotel & restaurant associations; international & national hotel & restaurant chains
Activities: Speaker Service: Yes
Chief Officer(s):
Jordi Busquets, President
j.busquets@ih-ra.com
Meetings/Conferences:
• International Hotel & Restaurant Association 55th Annual Congress 2018, 2018
Scope: International

International Humanist & Ethical Union (IHEU) / Union internationale humanite et laique
39 Moreland St., London EC1V 8BB United Kingdom
Tel: 44-20-7490-8468
www.iheu.org
www.facebook.com/iheunion
twitter.com/iheu
Overview: A medium-sized international organization founded in 1952
Mission: To bring into active association groups & individuals throughout the world interested in promoting ethical & scientific humanism, understood as a dedication to responsibility for human life by maintenance, furtherance, & development of human values, cultivation of science, loyalty to democratic principles in all social relations, & practice of good faith, without reliance upon authority or dogma; To work with international agencies & outstanding personalities engaged in promoting human well-being, especially through education & cultural programs
Affiliation(s): Humanist Association of Canada
Finances: Annual Operating Budget: $100,000-$250,000
Staff Member(s): 2; 15 volunteer(s)
Membership: 100 organizations; Member Profile: Rationalists; humanists; secularists; humanist organizations
Activities: Holding a general assembly; Awareness Events: World Humanist Day, June; International Human Rights Day, December 10; Internships: Yes; Speaker Service: Yes
Chief Officer(s):
Andrew Copson, President
Carl Blackburn, Chief Executive Officer
Awards:
• International Humanist Award
• Distinguished Service to Humanism Award
Meetings/Conferences:
• International Humanist & Ethical Union General Assembly 2018, August, 2018, Auckland
Scope: International
Publications:
• The Freedom of Though Report [a publication of the International Humanist & Ethical Union]
Type: Report; Frequency: a.; Price: Free
Profile: An annual survey on discrimination & persecution against non-religious people in every country around the world; published each year on December 10th (International Human Rights Day)

International Husserl & Phenomenological Research Society
1 Ivy Pointe Way, Hanover NH 3755 USA
Tel: 802-295-3487; Fax: 802-295-5963
Overview: A small international organization founded in 1968
Mission: To pursue interdisciplinary research along the lines of phenomenological philosopy; to unfold a philosophy/phenomenology of life answering the needs of our times
Member of: The World Institute for Advanced Phenomenological Research & Learning (USA)
Finances: Annual Operating Budget: $50,000-$100,000; Funding Sources: Membership fees; publications
5 volunteer(s)
Membership: 700 in 25 countries; Fees: $65
Activities: Library by appointment
Chief Officer(s):
Anna-Teresa Tymieniecka, President
Thomas Ryba, Vice-President

International Ice Hockey Federation (IIHF)
Brandschenkestrasse 50, Zurich CH-8027 Switzerland
Tel: 41-44-562-22-00; Fax: 41-44-562-22-29
office@iihf.com
www.iihf.com
www.facebook.com/iihfhockey
twitter.com/IIHFHockey
Overview: A large international organization founded in 1908
Mission: To govern, develop, & promote ice & in-line hockey throughout the world; To develop & control international ice & in-line hockey; To promote friendly relations among the member national associations; To operate in an organized manner for the good order of the sport
Member of: Association of International Olympic Winter Sports Federations
Affiliation(s): Hockey Canada
Staff Member(s): 32
Membership: 76 national associations; Member Profile: National ice hockey associations & in-line hockey associations; Committees: Asian; Athletes; Competition & Coordination;

Coaching; Disciplinary; Environmental & Social Activities; Ethics & Integrity; Event & Evaluation; Facilities Working Group; Finance; Historical; IIHF Governance Reform Group; Legal; Medical; Officiating; Player Safety; TV/New Media/Marketing; Women's; Youth & Junior Development
Activities: *Internships:* Yes; *Speaker Service:* Yes; *Library:* Hockey Hall of Fame, Toronto Canada; Open to public
Chief Officer(s):
Horst Lichtner, General Secretary
Gion Veraguth, Director, Administration & Finance

International Industrial Relations Association *See* International Labour & Employment Relations Association

International Industry Working Group (IIWG)
International Air Transport Association, PO Box 416, Route de l'Aéroport 33 1215, 15 Airport, Geneva Switzerland
Tel: +41-22-770-2525; *Fax:* +41-22-798-3553
www.iata.org/whatwedo/workgroups/Pages/iiwg.aspx
Overview: A small international organization founded in 1970
Mission: To promote & develop an open exchange of information to minimize interface problems through well-informed design, development & operation of both aircraft & airports; To study possible solutions to major problems that impede the development of the air transport system; To share information to establish a unified industry position on matters of common interest; To assist in developing and keeping up to date standard formats for documents specifying aircraft and airport characteristsics & future trends in their designs
Membership: 50; *Member Profile:* Aircraft & aeroengine manufacturers; Airlines & airport authorities; Sometimes addtional members from the International Civil Aviation Organization (ICAO), U.S. Federal Aviation Administration (FAA) & European Civil Aviation Conference (ECAC)
Chief Officer(s):
Koos Noordeloos, Chair
Colin Spear, Secretariat
spearc@iata.org

International Institute for Applied Systems Analysis (IIASA)
Schlossplatz 1, Laxenburg A-2361 Austria
Tel: 43-2236-807-0; *Fax:* 43-2236-71-313
inf@iiasa.ac.at
www.iiasa.ac.at
www.linkedin.com/company/iiasa-vienna
www.facebook.com/IIASA
twitter.com/IIASAVienna
www.youtube.com/user/IIASALive
Overview: A medium-sized international organization founded in 1972
Mission: To initiate & support individual & collaborative research on problems associated with social, economic, technological & environmental change, & thereby assist scientific, industrial & policy communities throughout the world in tackling such problems; current principal focus: scientific study of sustainability & the human dimensions of global change; to bring together scientists from various countries & disciplines to conduct research in a setting that is non-political & scientifically rigorous; to provide policy-oriented research results that deal with issues transcending national boundaries; to coordinate research projects, working in collaboration with worldwide networks of researchers, policy makers & research organizations
Member of: International Council for Science; International Federation of Institutes for Advanced Study
Affiliation(s): Canadian Committee for IIASA
Finances: *Annual Operating Budget:* Greater than $5 Million
Staff Member(s): 180
Membership: 16; *Member Profile:* International & national research & policy institutes, organizations, & universities; *Committees:* Executive; Finance; Program; Membership; Advisory; Science; Steering
Activities: Policy-relevant research carried out by international, interdisciplinary teams, based on the following related themes: 1. Energy & Technology, including studies of environmentally compatible energy strategies, economic transition & integration, decision analysis & support, dynamic systems, & risk, modeling & policy; 2. Natural Resources & the Environment, including modeling land-use & land-cover changes in Europe & Northern Asia, sustainable boreal forest resources, transboundary air pollution, & adaptive dynamics; *Library:* by appointment
Chief Officer(s):
Pavel Kabat, Director General & Chief Executive Officer
kabat@iiasa.ac.at
Awards:
• Young Scientists Summer Program
• Young Postdoctoral Fellows Program
• Luis Donaldo Colosio Fellowship
Publications:
• International Institute for Applied Systems Analysis Annual Report
Type: Yearbook; *Frequency:* a.
• Options [a publication of the International Institute for Applied Systems Analysis]
Type: Magazine
Profile: Presents IIASA activities & research for a non-specialist audience

International Institute for Audio-Visual Communication & Cultural Development *See* International Research Institute for Media, Communication & Cultural Development

International Institute for Conservation of Historic & Artistic Works (IIC)
3 Birdcage Walk, Westminster, London SW1H 9JJ UK
Tel: +44 (0)20 7799 5500; *Fax:* +44 (0)20 7799 4961
iic@iiconservation.org
www.iiconservation.org
Overview: A medium-sized international organization founded in 1950
Mission: To coordinate & improve the knowledge, methods, & working standards needed to protect, preserve & maintain the condition & integrity of historic & artistic works
Membership: *Fees:* £70 individual; £25 student; £100 fellow; £360 institution; *Member Profile:* Restorers; Conservators; Conservation scientists; Educators; Students; Architects; Collection managers; Curators; Art historians; Cultural heritage professionals
Chief Officer(s):
Graham Voce, Executive Secretary
iic@iiconservation.org
Tina Churcher, Membership Secretary
membership@iiconservation.org
Mary Breading, Finance Secretary

International Institute for Energy Conservation (IIEC)
#105, 1850 Centennial Park Dr., Reston VA 20191-1517 USA
Tel: 443-934-2279
iiecdc@iiec.org
www.iiec.org
www.linkedin.com/company/international-institute-for-energy-conservation
twitter.com/iiecasia
Overview: A medium-sized international organization founded in 1984
Mission: To apply global knowledge and experience to customize local sustainability solutions that are replicable & adaptable; To make a global mainstreamm impact toward sustainable development & greenhouse gas emissions
Chief Officer(s):
Felix Gooneratne, Chief Executive Officer

International Institute of African Languages & Cultures *See* International African Institute

International Institute of Fisheries Economics & Trade (IIFET)
Agricultural & Resource Economics, Oregon State University, 220 Ballard Hall, Corvallis OR 97331-3601 USA
Tel: 541-737-1416; *Fax:* 541-737-2563
iifet@oregonstate.edu
www.oregonstate.edu/Dept/IIFET/
Overview: A small international charitable organization founded in 1982
Mission: To promote discussion of factors which affect international trade in seafoods & fisheries policy questions
Staff Member(s): 2
Membership: 100-499; *Fees:* $75 regular; $25 student; $500 corporate/institutional; *Member Profile:* International Fisheries Economists; *Committees:* Executive
Activities: *Rents Mailing List:* Yes
Chief Officer(s):
Dan Holland, President
dholland@gmri.org
Ann L. Shriver, Executive Director
ann.l.shriver@oregonstate.edu

International ISBN Agency
c/o EDItEUR, 39-41 North Rd., London N7 9DP United Kingdom
Tel: +44(0)20 7503 6418
info@isbn-international.org
www.isbn-international.org
Overview: A medium-sized international organization founded in 1972
Mission: To promote, coordinate and supervise the worlwide use of the ISBN (International Standard Book Number) system; To act in an advisory role to group agencies
Affiliation(s): Canadian ISBN Agency
Finances: *Annual Operating Budget:* Less than $50,000
Staff Member(s): 3
Membership: 156 countries
Activities: *Library* Open to public
Chief Officer(s):
Stella Griffiths, Executive Director
Nick Woods, Manager, Operations

International Judo Federation (IJF)
Avenue de La Harpe 49, Lausanne 1007 Switzerland
www.ijf.org
www.facebook.com/ijudo
twitter.com/IntJudoFed
www.youtube.com/judo
Overview: A large international charitable organization
Membership: 200 Federations + 5 Continental Unions
Activities: World Championships; World Judo Tour; World Ranking List
Chief Officer(s):
Marius Vizer, President
president@ijf.org
Jean Luc, General Secretary
gs@ijf.org

International Kindergarten Union *See* Association for Childhood Education International

International Labour & Employment Relations Association (ILERA) / Association internationale de relations professionnelles (AIRP)
c/o DIALOGUE, International Labour Office, 22, Geneva CH-1211 Switzerland
Tel: 41-22-799-73-71; *Fax:* 41-22-799-87-49
ilera@ilo.org
www.ilo.org/public/english/iira
Previous Name: International Industrial Relations Association
Overview: A large international organization founded in 1966
Mission: To promote the study of industrial relations throughout the world by encouraging the establishment of national associations of IR (Industrial Relations) specialists; To facilitate the spread of information in the field of IR; To organize regional & worldwide congresses & to publish their proceedings; To promote international research by organizing study groups on IR topics
Affiliation(s): Association canadienne de relations industrielles
Finances: *Funding Sources:* Membership dues
Staff Member(s): 1
Membership: 1,000+; *Fees:* US$25 individual; US$60 institutional; US$40-$100 full; *Member Profile:* Full members - national or regional (a group of countries in the same geographical area) industrial relations associations whose primary purpose is research in the industrial relations field, or committees where such associations do not exist; Institutional associate members - universities & colleges or departments thereof & other research institutes concerned with the study of industrial relations; Individual associate members - persons engaged in industrial relations research or teaching, as well as practitioners in the industrial relations field; *Committees:* Executive
Activities: World Congress convened every 3 years; IIRA members can take part in any of the following study groups - Industrial Relations as a field & industrial relations theory; Technological change & industrial relations; Equality in pay & employment; Worker's participation; Public policy & industrial relations; Urban labour markets in developing countries; The rights of employees & industrial justice; Pay systems; Flexible work patterns; Trade unions in the future; Theory & practice of negotiations; Human resource management
Chief Officer(s):
Dong-One Kim, President
Moussa Oumarou, Secretary-General
oumarou@ilo.org
Awards:
• Luis Aparicio Prize
To recognize the contribution of emerging scholars in the fields of work, employment, labour & employment relations
Meetings/Conferences:
• 18th International Labour & Employment Relations Association World Congress, July, 2018, Seoul
Scope: International

Foreign Associations / International Labour Organization (ILO)

Publications:
- ILERA [International Labour & Employment Relations Association] Newsletter
Type: Newsletter

International Labour Organization (ILO)
4, route des Morillons, Geneva CH-1211 Switzerland
Tel: 41-22-799-6111; *Fax:* 41-22-798-8685
ilo@ilo.org
www.ilo.org
www.linkedin.com/company/international-labour-organization-ilo
www.facebook.com/ILO.ORG
twitter.com/ilo
www.youtube.com/ilotv
Overview: A large international organization founded in 1919
Mission: To bring governments, employers & trade unions together for united action in the cause of social justice & better living conditions everywhere; To support efforts by the international community & by individual nations to achieve full employment, raise living standards, share the fruits of progress fairly, protect the life & health of workers, & to promote cooperation between workers & employers in order to improve production & working conditions; To employ a tripartite structure (dialogue among governments, workers' & employers' organizations) in order to interpret the aims & aspirations of each country, reflect its preoccupations & reach realistic decisions based on the social & economic situations of the countries concerned; To cooperate with other organizations of the international community
Finances: *Annual Operating Budget:* Greater than $5 Million
Activities: Setting international labour standards; technical cooperation; publications & research; OSH information services through the Collaboration Network; *Internships:* Yes; *Speaker Service:* Yes; *Library:* Open to public
Chief Officer(s):
Guy Ryder, Director General
Meetings/Conferences:
- XXII Congress on Safety & Health at Work, 2020
Scope: International
Description: The World Congress is a forum for the exchange of knowledge, practices & experiences for anyone involved with or interested in health & safety in the workplace.
Publications:
- World Employment & Social Outlook [a publication of the International Labour Organization]
Type: Report

International Ladies' Garment Workers' Union (AFL-CIO/CLC); Union of Needletrades, Industrial & Textile Employees *See* UNITE HERE

International Law Association (ILA)
Charles Clore House, 17 Russell Sq., London WC1B 5JD United Kingdom
Tel: 44-20-7323-2978; *Fax:* 44-20-7323-3580
www.ila-hq.org
www.facebook.com/InternationalLawAssociation
twitter.com/ILA_official
Overview: A medium-sized international organization founded in 1873
Mission: To engage in the study, clarification & development of international law, both public & private; To further an international understanding & respect for international law
Finances: *Funding Sources:* Membership fees; Grants; Appeals
Staff Member(s): 1
Membership: 3,700; *Committees:* Space Law; International Monetary Law; International Human Rights Law & Practice; Water Resources Law; International Commercial Arbitration; Legal Aspects of Sustainable Development; Refugee Procedures; Legal Aspects of Inter-Country Adoption & Protection of the Family; Extraterritorial Jurisdiction; International Securities Regulation; Cultural Heritage Law; International Law in Municipal Courts; Regional Economic Development Law; Arms Control & Disarmament Law; Feminism & International Law; Extradition & Human Rights; International Civil & Commercial Litigation; International Trade Law
Chief Officer(s):
Antonios Tzanakopoulos, Secretary General
Meetings/Conferences:
- International Law Association 78th Biennial International Conference 2018, 2018
Scope: International

International League of Dermatological Societies (ILDS)
Wilan House, 4 Fitzroy Sq., London W1T 5HQ United Kingdom
Tel: 44-20-7388-6515; *Fax:* 44-20-7388-3123
admin@ilds.org
web.ilds.org
Overview: A medium-sized international organization founded in 1888
Mission: To stimulate the cooperation of societies of dermatology and societies interested in all fields of cutaneous medicine and biology throughout the world; encourage the worldwide advancement of dermatological education, care, and sciences; promote personal and professional relations among the dermatologists of the world; represent dermatology in commisions and international health organizations; and organize a World Congress of Dermatology every five years and to sponsor additional international educational and scientific activities.
Membership: *Fees:* Schedule available; *Member Profile:* Members of national & international societies of dermatology; *Committees:* Executive; International Foundation for Dermatology; Finance; Membership & Communications; World Congress of Dermatology Programme; Awards; Commissions & International Health Organization
Activities: *Speaker Service:* Yes
Chief Officer(s):
Joanna Groves, Executive Director
Publications:
- International League of Dermatological Societies Newsletter
Type: Newsletter

International Leisure Information Network (LINK) *See* World Leisure & Recreation Association

International Lilac Society
c/o Karen McCauley, Treasurer, 325 West 82nd St., Chaska MN 55318
Tel: 952-443-3703
ILSExecVP@gmail.com
www.internationallilacsociety.org
Overview: A small international organization
Mission: To promote & stimulate interest in the genus Syringa
Chief Officer(s):
Nicole Jordan, President
njordan236@aol.com
Brad Bittorf, Executive Vice-President
ilsexecvp@gmail.com
Karen McCauley, Treasurer & Membership Secretary
mccauleytk@aol.com

International Literacy Association (ILA)
PO Box 8139, Newark DE 19714-8139 USA
Tel: 302-731-1600
Toll-Free: 800-336-7323
customerservice@reading.org
www.literacyworldwide.org
www.linkedin.com/company/international-literacy-association
www.facebook.com/InternationalLiteracyAssociation
twitter.com/ILAToday
www.instagram.com/ilatoday; www.pinterest.com/ilatoday
Previous Name: International Reading Association
Overview: A large international organization founded in 1956
Mission: To promote high levels of literacy for all; To improve the quality of reading instruction through study; To encourage a lifetime reading habit; To advocate for policy, curriculum, & education reform that supports both teachers & learners; To foster & encourage collaboration among professionals on an international scale
Finances: *Annual Operating Budget:* Greater than $5 Million
Staff Member(s): 6
Membership: 300,000; *Fees:* US$54 basic; $44 online; $39 student; free for residents of countries with developing economies; *Member Profile:* Educators, administrators, reading teachers/specialists, researchers, students
Activities: Developing, managing, & facilitating global literacy & communication programs; Disseminating information; Offering professional development opportunities; Advocating before legislative & regulatory bodies on behalf of its membership; *Awareness Events:* International Literacy Day - Sept. 8; *Library:* Ralph C. Staiger Library; by appointment
Chief Officer(s):
Marcie Craig Post, Executive Director
mpost@reading.org
Awards:
- Advocacy Award
- Award of Excellence
- Celebrate Literacy Award
- Certificate of Distinction for the Reading Preparation of Elementary and Secondary Teachers
- Children's and Young Adults' Book Award
- Constance McCullough Award
- Council Achievement Awards
- Dina Feitelson Research Award
- Elva Knight Research Grant
- Erwin Zolt Digital Literacy Game Changer Award
- Exemplary Reading Program Award
- Grants for Literacy Projects in Countries With Developing Economies
- Helen M. Robinson Grant
- Honor Council Program Award
- Jeanne S. Chall Research Fellowship
- Jerry Johns Outstanding Teacher Educator in Reading Award
- Lee Bennett Hopkins Promising Poet Award
- Local Community Service Award
- Maryann Manning Special Service Award
- National Affiliate Conference Grants
- Nila Banton Smith Teacher as Researcher Grant
- Regie Routman Teacher Recognition Grant
- Steven A. Stahl Research Grant
- Timothy & Cynthia Shanahan Outstanding Dissertation Award
- Travel Grants for Educators
- William S. Gray Citation of Merit
Meetings/Conferences:
- International Literacy Association 2018 Conference, July, 2018, Austin, TX
Scope: International
Contact Information: www.ilaconference.org
Publications:
- ILA E-ssentials [a publication of the International Literacy Association]
Type: Report
Profile: A series of articles by literacy experts tailored to educators; includes practical, evidence-based strategies on a wide range of topics for gradesK-12
- Journal of Adolescent & Adult Literacy [a publication of the International Literacy Association]
Type: Journal; *Frequency:* 8 pa; *Editor:* Kathleen Hinchman et al.; *ISSN:* 1936-2706
Profile: Literacy journal published exclusively for teachers of older learners
- Literacy Today [a publication of the International Literacy Association]
Type: Magazine; *Frequency:* Bimonthly; *ISSN:* 2411-7862
Profile: Highlights members' accomplishments & topics of interest in the field
- Reading Research Quarterly [a publication of the International Literacy Association]
Type: Journal; *Editor:* Linda B. Gambrell et al.; *ISSN:* 1936-2722
Profile: Reports of important studies, multidisciplinary research, & various modes of investigation; diverseviewpoints on literacy practices, teaching, & learning
- The Reading Teacher [a publication of the International Literacy Association]
Type: Journal; *Frequency:* 8 pa; *Editor:* Robin Griffith & Jan Lacina; *ISSN:* 0034-0561
Profile: Journal for educators of literacy learners up to age 12
- Research-Based Standards [a publication of the International Literacy Association]
Type: Report
Profile: A series of research-based standards for preparing & certifying literacy professionals
- Spring Resource Catalog [a publication of the International Literacy Association]
Type: Book
Profile: A compilation of classroom & curriculum resources for educators

International Liver Cancer Association (ILCA)
300, av de Tervueren, Brussels B-1150 Belgium
Tel: +32 (0)2 789 2345; *Fax:* +32 (0)2 743 1550
info@ilca-online.org
www.ilca-online.org
www.linkedin.com/groups/International-Liver-Cancer-Association-ILCA-4642388
www.facebook.com/InternationalLiverCancerAssociation
twitter.com/ILCAnews
Overview: A small international organization
Mission: To advance research in the pathogenesis, prevention, & treatment of liver cancer
Staff Member(s): 7
Membership: *Fees:* Schedule available; *Member Profile:* International researchers, physicians, & allied professionals involved in liver cancer; *Committees:* Executive; Membership; Web Site; Counsensus Guidelines

Activities: Educating healthcare professionals & the general public; Increasing understanding of liver cancer
Chief Officer(s):
Géraldine Damar, Executive Officer
Peter Galle, President

International Longshore & Warehouse Union (CLC) / Syndicat international des débardeurs et magasiniers (CTC)
1188 Franklin St., 4th Fl., San Francisco CA 94109 USA
Tel: 415-775-0533; *Fax:* 415-775-1302
www.ilwu.org
Overview: A small international charitable organization
Mission: To represent the rights of their members, who work in the warehouse industry
Chief Officer(s):
Robert McEllrath, President
Canadian Office (ILWU Canada)
#180, 111 Victoria Ave., Vancouver BC V5L 4C4
Tel: 604-254-8141; *Fax:* 604-254-8183
www.ilwu.ca
www.youtube.com/TheILWUCanada
Affiliation(s): Retail Wholesale Union of BC; Retail Wholesale Department Store Union of SK; Grain Services Union of SK
Chief Officer(s):
Mark Gordienko, President
president@ilwu.ca

International Longshoremen's Association (AFL-CIO/CLC) (ILA) / Association internationale des débardeurs (FAT-COI/CTC)
5000 West Side Ave., North Bergen NJ 07047 USA
Tel: 212-425-1200; *Fax:* 212-425-2928
ilaunion.org
www.facebook.com/ILAUnion
twitter.com/ILAUnion
Overview: A large international organization founded in 1892
Membership: 65,000+; *Member Profile:* Maritime workers in North America
Chief Officer(s):
Harold Daggett, President
hdaggett@ilaunion.org
Stephen Knott, Secretary-Treasurer
Canadian Division
#180, 111 Victoria Dr., Vancouver BC V5L 4C4
Tel: 604-254-8141; *Fax:* 604-254-8183
ilwu.ca
Chief Officer(s):
Rob Ashton, President
president@ilwu.ca

International Luge Federation *Voir* Fédération Internationale de Luge de Course

International Maritime Committee *See* Comité maritime international

International Maritime Organization (IMO) / Organisation maritime internationale
4 Albert Embankment, London SE1 7SR United Kingdom
Tel: 44-20-7735-7611; *Fax:* 44-20-7587-3210
info@imo.org
www.imo.org
www.facebook.com/IMOHQ
twitter.com/imohq
www.youtube.com/user/IMOHQ; www.flickr.com/photos/imo-un
Overview: A large international organization founded in 1948
Mission: To encourage the adoption of high standards in matters concerning maritime safety, security, efficiency of navigation & control of marine pollution from ships
Finances: *Annual Operating Budget:* Greater than $5 Million; *Funding Sources:* Government
Staff Member(s): 300
Membership: 172 member states + 3 associate; *Fees:* Schedule available, based upon shipping fleet tonnage; *Committees:* Maritime Safety; Marine Environment Protection; Legal; Technical Cooperation; Facilitation
Activities: *Awareness Events:* Day of the Seafarer, June; *Library:* International Maritime Organization Library; by appointment
Chief Officer(s):
Kitack Lim, Secretary General

International Masters Games Association (IMGA)
Maison du Sport International, Avenue de Rhodanie 54, Lausanne 1007 Switzerland
Tel: 41-216018171; *Fax:* 41-216017173
info@imga.ch
www.imga.ch
www.facebook.com/IMGAmastersgames
twitter.com/IMGALausanne
www.youtube.com/user/TheIMGA
Overview: A large international organization founded in 1995
Mission: To govern the World Masters Games
Membership: *Member Profile:* International Sports Federations participating in the World Masters Games
Activities: World Masters Games; European Masters Games
Chief Officer(s):
Kai Holm, President, Board of Governors
Jens V. Holm, CEO

International Medical Informatics Association (IMIA)
c/o Health On the Net, Chemin du Petit-Bel-Air 2, Chêne-Bourg, Geneva CH-1225 Switzerland
Tel: 41-22-3727249
imia@imia-services.org
www.imia-medinfo.org
www.facebook.com/191053744240749
Overview: A small international organization founded in 1989
Mission: To promote informatics in health care & biomedical research; To advance international cooperation; To stimulate research, development & education; To disseminate & exchange information
Staff Member(s): 2
Chief Officer(s):
Elaine Huesing, Chief Executive Officer
elaine.huesing@shaw.ca

International Migration Service *See* International Social Service

International Movement of Catholic Students; International Catholic Movement for Intellectual & Cultural Affairs *Voir* IMCS Pax Romana

International Music Council (IMC) / Conseil international de la musique
1, rue Miollis, Paris 75732 CEDEX 15 France
Tel: 33-145-684-850; *Fax:* 33-145-684-866
www.imc-cim.org
Overview: A medium-sized international organization founded in 1949
Mission: To monitor the availability of access to music for all; To support endeavours which assure & secure this right; To inform widely about music & the right to it; To exercise advocacy when & where needed; To aim at contributing to the development & strengthening of friendly working relations between all the musical cultures of the world, on the basis of their absolute equality, mutual respect, & appreciation; To concern itself with musical creativity, education, performance, broadcasting & promotion, research & documentation, the status of musicians, & various other aspects of musical life
Finances: *Funding Sources:* UNESCO; Membership fees; A number of governments & broadcasting organizations provide most of the funds required for the Rostra & recordings
Membership: 65 national music councils + 50 international & regional music organizations; *Fees:* Schedule available
Activities: Working on the effects of globlization upon music mainly through a new action & reflection program entitled "May Musics"; Promoting international & regional Rostra, which are designed to promote local cultures, bring recognition to living composers, promote the career of young performers, & offer performance interchange opportunities for musicians & musics from all regions of the world; *Library:* by appointment
Chief Officer(s):
Paul Dujardin, President
Silja Fischer, Secretary General
Awards:
• IMC/UNESCO International Music Prize
Awarded by competition to eminent personalities in all fields of music & to important national or international institutions for their exceptional contribution to musical life

International Network for Environmental Management (INEM)
Osterstrasse 58, Hamburg 20259 Germany
Tel: 49-89-18935-200; *Fax:* 49-89-18935-199
www.inem.org
Overview: A small international organization founded in 1991
Mission: To be committed to the implementation of environmental management in businesses worldwide, including small- & medium-sized enterprises; To promote clean technologies
Membership: *Member Profile:* Autonomous & non-profit business associations concerned with environmental management
Chief Officer(s):
Ludwig Karg, Chair
L.Karg@INEM.org

International Network for Social Network Analysis (INSNA)
c/o JulNet Solutions, LLC, 3327B US Rte. 60 East, Huntington WV 25705 USA
Tel: 304-523-9700; *Fax:* 304-523-9701
www.insna.org
www.facebook.com/INSNA
twitter.com/SocNetAnalysts
Overview: A small international organization founded in 1978
Membership: *Member Profile:* Researchers interested in social network analysis
Chief Officer(s):
John Skvoretz, President

International Nuclear Law Association (INLA) / Association internationale du droit nucléaire
Square de Meeûs 29, Brussels B-1000 Belgium
Tel: 32-2-547-5841; *Fax:* 32-2-503-0440
info@aidn-inla.be
www.aidn-inla.be
Overview: A small international organization founded in 1970
Mission: To promote international studies of legal problems related to the peaceful use of nuclear energy
Staff Member(s): 2
Membership: 500; *Committees:* Safety and Regulation; Nuclear Liability and Inurance; International Nuclear Trade; Radiological Protection; Waste Management; Radioisotopes
Chief Officer(s):
Rafael Manovil, President
Patrick Reyners, Secretary General

International Occupational Safety & Health Information Network / Centre international d'informations de sécurité et de santé au travail
International Labour Office/CIS, 4 route des Morillons, Geneva CH-1211 Switzerland
Tel: 41-22-799-61-11; *Fax:* 41-22-798-86-85
www.ilo.org/cis/
Also Known As: Centro Internacional de Informacion sobre Seguridad y Salud en el Trabajo
Overview: A small international organization founded in 1959
Mission: To collect & disseminate world information that can contribute to the prevention of occupational accidents & diseases
Affiliation(s): Canadian Centre for Occupational Health & Safety; Canada Safety Council; Institut de recherche en santé et en sécurité de travail - Québec
Membership: 104 national centres; 2 regional centres; 44 collaborating centres
Activities: CIS Information Service (personalized searches on any OSH topic); CIS factual microcomputer databases (covering important OSH topics); CIS Information Sheets (chemical, medical, technical, ergonomic); CIS microfiche service (reproduction of abstracted documents no longer obtainable from original sources); Directory of OSH Institutions (complete international OSH contact information); CIS Glossary of OSH Terms (OSH words & expressions: English, French, Spanish, German, Russian); CIS Bibliographies; *Library:* Open to public

International Ocean Institute (IOI) / Institut international de l'ocean
PO Box 3, Gzira GZR 1000 Malta
Tel: 356-21-346-529; *Fax:* 356-21-346-502
ioihq@ioihq.org.mt
www.ioinst.org
Overview: A small international organization founded in 1972
Mission: To promote education, training & research to enhance the peaceful uses of ocean space & its resources, their management & regulation as well as the protection & conservation of the marine environment, guided by the principle of the common heritage of mankind
Finances: *Annual Operating Budget:* $1.5 Million-$3 Million; *Funding Sources:* Donations; UN & government funding agencies; private foundations; endowment fund
Staff Member(s): 35; 200 volunteer(s)
Membership: 25 operational centres worldwide; *Committees:* Directors; Governing Board
Activities: Policy research; training; advisory services; *Speaker Service:* Yes; *Library:* IOI, Malta HQ Library; Not open to public

Foreign Associations / International Ombudsman Institute

Chief Officer(s):
Awni Behnam, President
awni.behnam@ioihq.org.mt

International Ombudsman Institute
c/o Austrian Ombudsman Board, PO Box 20, Singerstrasse 17, Vienna A-1015 Austria
Tel: 43/1/512 93 88; Fax: 43/1/512 93 88-200
ioi@volksanw.gv.at
www.theioi.org
Overview: A small international organization
Mission: To make an objective investigation into complaints from the public about the administration of government
Chief Officer(s):
Beverley A. Wakem, DNZM, CBE, President
Peter Kostelka, Secretary General

International Order of the King's Daughters & Sons
PO Box 1017, 34 Vincent Ave., Chautauqua NY 14722-1017 USA
Tel: 716-357-4951; Fax: 716-357-3762
iokds5@windstream.net
www.iokds.org
www.facebook.com/IOKDS
Overview: A large international organization founded in 1886
Mission: Interdenominational organization of Christians
Finances: Funding Sources: Donations; Membership dues
Membership: 4,000; Fees: $30 ages 18 & up; $2 under age 18; Committees: By-laws; Chautauqua Building; Editorial; Headquarters; Long Range Development & Planning; Membership Extension; New Horizons; Special Projects; Nominating
Activities: Offering a scholarship program; Supporting mission work
Chief Officer(s):
Christine Dawson, President
Awards:
• Around the World Scholarships
  Deadline: March 1
• Health Career Scholarships
  Deadline: March 1
• North American Indian Scholarships
  Deadline: March 1
• Student Ministry Scholarships
  Deadline: March 1

   Ontario Branch
   c/o David Peale, 2118 Monson Cres., Gloucester ON K1J 6A8
   www.thekingsdaughtersandsons.ca
   Chief Officer(s):
   David Peale, Treasurer

International Organic Inspectors Association (IOIA)
PO Box 6, Broadus MT 59317 USA
Tel: 406-436-2031; Fax: 406-436-2031
ioia@ioia.net
www.ioia.net
www.facebook.com/margaret.scoles.3
Also Known As: Independent Organic Inspectors Association
Overview: A small international organization founded in 1991
Mission: To address issues & concerns relevant to organic inspectors, to provide quality inspector training & to promote integrity & consistency in the orgnic certification process
Staff Member(s): 6
Membership: 250 from 41 countries; Member Profile: Organic farm, livestock & process inspectors dedicated to verification of organic production practices
Chief Officer(s):
Margaret Scoles, Executive Director

International Organisation of La Francophonie Voir
Organisation internationale de la Francophonie

International Organization for Standardization (ISO) / Organisation internationale de normalisation
PO Box 56, 1, ch. de la Voie-Creuse, Geneva 20 1211 Switzerland
Tel: 41-22-749-01-11; Fax: 41-22-733-34-30
central@iso.org
www.iso.org
www.linkedin.com/company/iso-international-organization-for-standardization
www.facebook.com/isostandards
twitter.com/isostandards
plus.google.com/+iso#+iso/posts
Overview: A small international organization founded in 1947
Mission: To promote the development of standardization & related activities in the world with a view to facilitating the international exchange of goods & services; developing cooperation in the spheres of intellectual, scientific, technological & economic activity; the results of ISO's technical work are published as "International Standards"
Affiliation(s): Standards Council of Canada
Finances: Funding Sources: 62% member bodies + 38% subscriptions + publications income + other services
Staff Member(s): 154
Membership: 162; Member Profile: National body, representative of standardization in its country; Committees: 192 technical committees which develop international standards in a wide range of technological areas; the secretariat for a number of committees is held by the ISO member body for Canada (Standards Council of Canada, Ottawa)
Activities: Library: Reference Library; Open to public
Chief Officer(s):
Terry Hill, President
Sadao Takeda, Vice-President, Policy

International Organization of Scenographers, Theatre Architects & Technicians
Center for Innovation Taipei, No.1, Yumen St., #L, Taipei 10452 Taiwan
Tel: 886(0)2 25962294; Fax: 886(0)2 25981647
headquarters@oistat.org
www.oistat.org
Overview: A medium-sized international organization
Mission: To bring together & represent those who work as Scenographers, Theatre Architects & Technicians
Affiliation(s): Canadian Institute for Theatre Technology
Chief Officer(s):
Wan-Jung Wei, Executive Director

International Organization of Securities Commissions (IOSCO) / Organisation internationale des commissions de valeurs (OICV)
General Secretariat, C/ Oquendo 12, Madrid 28006 Spain
Tel: 34-91-417-55-49; Fax: 34-91-555-93-68
Other Communication: Press/Media Enquiries e-mail: press@iosco.org
info@iosco.org
www.iosco.org
www.linkedin.com/groups/4849117
twitter.com/IOSCOPress
Previous Name: Interamerican Association of Securities Commissions & Similar Agencies
Overview: A large international organization founded in 1983
Mission: To cooperate together to ensure a better regulation of the markets, on both the domestic & international level, in order to maintain just & efficient securities markets; To exchange information in order to promote development of domestic markets; To unite efforts to establish standards & effective surveillance of international securities transactions; To provide mutual assistance to ensure the integrity of the markets by rigorous application of standards & by effective enforcement against offences
Finances: Annual Operating Budget: $500,000-$1.5 Million; Funding Sources: Membership dues
Staff Member(s): 25
Membership: 125 ordinary; 25 associate; 64 affiliate; Fees: Schedule available; Member Profile: Ordinary - securities commission or similar governmental agency, self-regulatory organization when there is no governmental regulatory agency; Associate - association that assembles the public regulatory bodies having jurisdiction in subdivisions of a country, when the national regulatory body is already a member or any other regulatory body, with exception of a self-regulatory body, recommended by the Executive Committee; Affiliate - international organization with universal or regional scope or organization recommended by the Executive Committee & recommended self-regulatory organizations; Committees: Presidents; Growth and Emerging Markets Committee; Africa/Middle-East; Asia-Pacific; European; Inter-American; Affiliate Members Consulative
Activities: On-the-job training program; IOSCO Educational Program; Library: Open to public
Chief Officer(s):
Paul P. Andrews, Secretary General
Tajinder Singh, Deputy Secretary General
Meetings/Conferences:
• International Organization of Securities Commissions 43rd Annual Conference 2018, May, 2018, Budapest
Scope: International

Publications:
• International Organization of Securities Commissions Annual Report
Type: Yearbook; Frequency: Annual

International Orienteering Federation (IOF)
Radiokatu 20, Slu FIN-00093 Finland
Tel: 358-9-3481-3112; Fax: 358-9-3481-3113
iof@orienteering.org
www.orienteering.org
www.facebook.com/IOFarena
Overview: A small international organization founded in 1961
Mission: To promote & develop the outdoor sport of orienteering
Affiliation(s): Canadian Orienteering Federation
Staff Member(s): 2
Membership: 70 member countries; Committees: Discipline: Foot Orienteering; Ski Orienteering; Mountain Bike Orienteering; Trail Orienteering; Specialist: Rules; Map; IT; Environment; Medical
Chief Officer(s):
Barbro Rönnberg, Secretary General
barbro.ronnberg.iof@orienteering.org
Anna Jacobson, Assistant to the Secretary General
anna.jacobson@orienteering.org

International Orthoptic Association (IOA)
c/o RPG Crouch Chapman LLP, 62 Wilson St., London EC2A 2BU United Kingdom
e-mail: webmaster@internationalorthoptics.org
www.internationalorthoptics.org
twitter.com/followioa
Overview: A large international organization founded in 1967
Mission: To promote the science of orthoptics throughout the world; To maintain & improve standards of education, training, & orthoptic practice
Membership: 15 full member countries + 5 associate member countries (20,000 orthoptists); Member Profile: National professional orthoptic associations; Individual orthoptists; Ophthalmologists; Affiliate members; Committees: Finance; International Relations; Membership; Public Relations; Scientific; Terminology; Website
Activities: Providing information to national orthoptic bodies & individual orthoptists; Engaging in advocacy activities regarding issues of importance to the orthoptic profession; Offering networking opportunities
Chief Officer(s):
Karen McMain, President
president@internationalorthoptics.org
Jan Roelof Polling, Deputy President
netherlands@internationalorthoptics.org
Katherine J. Fray, Secretary
secretary@internationalorthoptics.org
Jane Tapley, Treasurer
treasurer@internationalorthoptics.org
Meetings/Conferences:
• International Orthoptic Congress 2018, 2018
Scope: International
Description: Plenary sessions, exhibitions, & educational activities

International Pacific Halibut Commission (IPHC)
#300, 2320 West Commodore Way, Seattle WA 98199-1287 USA
Tel: 206-634-1838; Fax: 206-632-2983
www.iphc.int
www.facebook.com/InternationalPacificHalibutCommission
twitter.com/iphcinfo
www.youtube.com/user/IPHCStaff
Overview: A medium-sized international organization founded in 1923
Mission: Mandated to research and manage Pacific halibut stocks, within the Convention waters of the U.S. and Canada.
Staff Member(s): 29
Chief Officer(s):
Bruce M. Leaman, Executive Director

International Papillomavirus Society (IPVS)
c/o Institut Català d'Oncologia, Av. Gran Via de l'Hospitalet 199-203, L'Hospitalet de Llobregat 08908 Spain
Tel: 34-93-2607812; Fax: 34-93-2607787
www.ipvsoc.org
Overview: A medium-sized international organization
Mission: To facilitate research on human & animal papillomaviruses & their associated diseases; To promote the translation of research into applications & policies

Membership: *Member Profile:* Biomedical scientists & physicians engaged in papillomavirus research
Activities: Providing professional communication; Offering public education; Presenting training opportunities
Chief Officer(s):
Silvia de Sanjose, President
s.sanjose@iconcologia.net
Margaret Stanley, Vice-President
mas@mole.bio.cam.ac.uk
W. Martin Kast, Treasurer
martin.kast@med.usc.edu
Robert Burk, Secretary
robert.burk@einstein.yu.edu
Publications:
• International Papillomavirus Society Membership Directory
Type: Directory

International Peace Bureau (IPB) / Bureau international de la paix
41 Zurich Rd., Geneva 1201 Switzerland
Tel: 41-22-731-64-29; *Fax:* 41-22-738-94-19
mailbox@ipb.org
www.ipb.org
www.facebook.com/ipb1910
twitter.com/IntlPeaceBureau
www.youtube.com/user/ipb1910
Overview: A small international organization founded in 1892
Mission: To serve the cause of peace by the promotion of international cooperation & the non-violent & peaceful solution of international conflicts
Affiliation(s): Voice of Women; Act for Disarmament Coalition
Staff Member(s): 3
Membership: *Fees:* Schedule available; *Member Profile:* Full - non-aligned & independent peace organizations; associate (non-voting) - other organizations working for peace as one of their aims (ie. labour unions, churches, cultural organizations); individual - persons who support the work of the IPB; *Committees:* Steering
Activities: Peace education; nuclear weapons; landmines; arms trade; European security; conflicts/human rights; international law; environment; women; Geneva connections; *Library:* Open to public
Chief Officer(s):
Colin Archer, Secretary General
Reiner Braun, Co-President
Ingeborg Breines, Co-President

International Peat Society (IPS)
Kauppakatu 19 D 31, Jyväskylä FIN-40100 Finland
Tel: 358-40-418-4075; *Fax:* 358-14-3385-410
ips@peatsociety.org
www.peatsociety.org
Overview: A small international organization founded in 1968
Mission: IPS works toward the advancement & communication of scientific, technical, & social knowledge for the wise use of peatlands & peat.
Affiliation(s): UNESCO
Membership: 1,450 from 36 countries; *Fees:* Schedule available; *Member Profile:* Scientific, industrial, commercial, & other organizations; Individuals interested in the study, conservation, & utilization of peat & peatlands
Activities: Organizing congresses, symposia & workshops; Publishing scientific publications; *Library*
Chief Officer(s):
Jaakko Silpola, Secretary General
Markku Mäkelä, President
markku.makela@gsf.fi
Awards:
• Wim Tonnis Peat Award
Meetings/Conferences:
• International Peatland Society Annual Convention 2018, 2018
Scope: International
Publications:
• Mires & Peat
Type: Journal; *Editor:* Dr. Olivia Bragg; Prof. Jack Rieley
Profile: A joint scientific journal of the International Peat Society & the International Mire Conservation Group, featuring peer-reviewed academic papers on research related tomires, peatlands, & peat throughout the world
• Peat News
Type: Newsletter; *Frequency:* Monthly; *Editor:* Susann Warnecke
• Peatlands International
Type: Magazine; *Frequency:* Semiannually; *Accepts Advertising*; *Number of Pages:* 60; *Price:* Free for members
Profile: Background reports on peat & peatlands, reviews of conferences & books, research findings, business reports, & internal information about the IPS
• Proceedings
Profile: Proceedings of IPS conferences, symposia, & workshops

International Pediatric Association (IPA) / Association internationale de pédiatrie
418 Webster Forest Dr., Webster Groves MO 63119 USA
Tel: 847-434-7507
adminoffice@ipa-world.org
www.ipa-world.org
www.facebook.com/InternationalPediatricAssociation
twitter.com/ipaworldorg
Overview: A large international organization founded in 1910
Mission: To promote the physical, mental, & social health of all children; To realize high standards of health for newborns, children, & adolescents in all countries of the world
Membership: *Member Profile:* Regional pediatric societies; International pediatric specialty societies; National pediatric societies; *Committees:* Advocacy & Public Affairs; Communications; Education & Training; Ethics; Strategic Planning
Chief Officer(s):
Zulfiqar Bhutta, President
William J. Keenan, Executive Director
Meetings/Conferences:
• 29th International Pediatric Association Congress of Pediatrics 2019, March, 2019, Panama City
Scope: International
Publications:
• IPA [International Pediatric Association] Quarterly Newsletter
Type: Newsletter; *Frequency:* Quarterly

International Permafrost Association (IPA)
c/o H. Lantuit, Alfred Wegener Institute for Polar & Marine Research, Telefrafenberg A43, Potsdam 14473 Germany
Tel: +49-331-288-2162; *Fax:* +49-331-288-2188
contact@ipa-permafrost.org
ipa.arcticportal.org
twitter.com/ipapermafrost
Overview: A medium-sized international organization founded in 1983
Mission: To disseminate knowledge concerning permafrost; To promote cooperation among persons & national or international organizations engaged in scientific investigation & enginering work on permafrost
Affiliation(s): International Union of Geological Science
Membership: *Committees:* Standing Committee on Data, Information & Communications; International Advisory Committee for ICOP
Activities: Assembling the following working groups: Antarctic Permafrost & Periglacial Environments; Coastal & Offshore Permafrost Dynamics; Cryosol; Glaciers & Permafrost Hazards in High Mountain Slopes; Isotopes & Geochemistry of Permafrost; Periglacial Landforms, Processes & Climate; Permafrost & Climate; Planetary Permafrost & Astrobiology; Permafrost Engineering
Chief Officer(s):
Hugues Lantuit, International Secretariat
Hugues.Lantuit@awi.de
Hans-W. Hubberten, President
hans-wolfgang.hubberten@awi.de
Hanne H. Christiansen, Vice-President
hanne.christiansen@unis.no
Antoni G. Lewkowicz, Vice-President
alewkowi@uottawa.ca
Meetings/Conferences:
• International Permafrost Association 12th International Conference on Permafrost 2020, 2020
Scope: International
Publications:
• Frozen Ground: The News Bulletin of the International Permafrost Association
Type: Yearbook; *Frequency:* Annually; *ISSN:* 2076-7463
Profile: Member news, current events, working group & task force reports, calendar, & publications
• Permafrost & Periglacial Processes
Type: Journal; *Frequency:* Semiannually
Profile: Reports from the International Permafrost Association
• Proceedings of the International Conferences on Permafrost
Type: Yearbook; *Frequency:* Annually
Profile: Peer-reviewed conference proceedings

International Plant Nutrition Institute (IPNI)
#550, 3500 Parkway Lane, Peachtree Corners GA 30092-2844 USA
Tel: 770-447-0335; *Fax:* 770-448-0439
info@ipni.net
www.ipni.net
www.facebook.com/InternationalPlantNutritionInstitute
twitter.com/PlantNutrition
www.youtube.com/user/PlantNutritionInst/videos
Previous Name: Potash & Phosphate Institute/Potash & Phosphate Institute of Canada
Overview: A medium-sized international organization founded in 1935
Mission: To assist in the design & implementation of agronomic research; to obtain scientific facts & education programs to tell those facts about balanced fertilization, particularly in relation to agricultural production systems; to conduct & provide on-site support of field experiments worldwide
Finances: *Annual Operating Budget:* Greater than $5 Million; *Funding Sources:* North American potash & phosphate producers; Government of Saskatchewan
Staff Member(s): 6
Membership: 20 corporate + 6 affiliate; *Member Profile:* Companies that are dedicated to the efficient & responsible use of fertilizers in plan nutrition
Activities: *Library* Open to public
Chief Officer(s):
Terry L. Roberts, President
Awards:
• International Plant Nutrition Scholar Awards
Deadline: April 29 *Amount:* $2,000
• Science Award
Deadline: September 30 *Amount:* $5,000
Publications:
• Better Crops China [a publication of the International Plant Nutrition Institute]
Type: Magazine; *Frequency:* s-a.
• Better Crops South Asia [a publication of the International Plant Nutrition Institute]
Type: Magazine; *Frequency:* q.
• IPNI [International Plant Nutrition Institute] Insights
Type: Newsletter
• Plant Food [a publication of the International Plant Nutrition Institute]
Type: Magazine; *Frequency:* q.
• Plant Nutrition Today [a publication of the International Plant Nutrition Institute]
Type: Newsletter

International Plant Propagators Society, Inc. (IPPS)
174 Crestview Dr., Bellefonte PA 16823-8516 USA
Tel: 61-7-3829-9454
secretary@ipps.org
www.ipps.org
www.linkedin.com/groups/3260989/profile
Overview: A medium-sized international organization founded in 1951
Mission: To seek & share information about the art & science of plant propagation
Finances: *Annual Operating Budget:* $100,000-$250,000; *Funding Sources:* Membership dues
Membership: 3,200 individual; *Fees:* Schedule available, based upon region; *Member Profile:* Open to individuals for commercial purposes or to those involved in research, teaching or extension activities
Chief Officer(s):
Alan Jones, Chair, 410-598-2118
ajones@manorview.com

International Primary Care Respiratory Group (IPCRG)
c/o Samantha Louw, PO Box 11961, Westhill AB32 9AE Scotland
Tel: 44-1224-743-753; *Fax:* 44-1224-743-753
businessmanager@theipcrg.org
www.theipcrg.org
Overview: A medium-sized international organization
Mission: To represent international primary care perspectives in respiratory medicine; To raise standards of care worldwide
Activities: Engaging in collaborative research; Disseminating best practice information; Providing educational opportunities
Chief Officer(s):
Siân Williams, Executive Officer
execofficer@theipcrg.org
Publications:
• Primary Care Respiratory Journal

Type: Journal
Profile: Original research papers, review, & discussion papers on respiratory conditions commonly found in primary & community settings in countries around the world

International Primate Protection League (IPPL)
PO Box 766, Summerville SC 29484 USA
Tel: 843-871-2280; *Fax:* 843-871-7988
info@ippl.org
www.ippl.org
www.facebook.com/InternationalPrimateProtectionLeague
www.youtube.com/user/PrimateProtection
Overview: A medium-sized international charitable organization founded in 1973
Mission: To encourage & contribute to a better understanding of matters relating to the conservation of non-human primates & their habitats; To promote relevant training & educational activities with reference to non-human primates; To promote & enhance the welfare of non-human primates; To support primate protection projects; to investigate smuggling of primates
Member of: Monitor Consortium; Summit for the Animals; International Union for Conservation of Nature; Civicus
Finances: *Annual Operating Budget:* $500,000-$1.5 Million; *Funding Sources:* Membership dues; Foundation grants; Bequests; Donations
Staff Member(s): 7; 4 volunteer(s)
Membership: 15,000 in over 60 countries
Chief Officer(s):
Shirley McGreal, OBE, Executive Director

International Reading Association *See* International Literacy Association

International Real Estate Federation *See* Fédération internationale des professions immobilières

International Real Estate Institute (IREI)
PO Box 879, 810 North Farrell Dr., Palm Springs CA 92263 USA
Tel: 760-327-5284; *Fax:* 760-327-5631
Toll-Free: 877-743-6799
support@assoc-hdqts.org
www.irei-assoc.org
Overview: A medium-sized international organization founded in 1967
Mission: To advance the real estate profession around the world
Member of: International Association Managers
Staff Member(s): 14; 4 volunteer(s)
Membership: 2,800; *Fees:* Schedule available; *Member Profile:* International real estate professionals

International Reference Centre for Community Water Supply & Sanitation *See* IRC International Water & Sanitation Centre

International Research Group on Wood Protection (IRG)
PO Box 5609, Stn. Drottning Kristinas väg 67, Stockholm SE-114 86 Sweden
Tel: 46-8-101-453; *Fax:* 46-8-108-081
irg@sp.se
www.irg-wp.com
www.linkedin.com/groups/International-Research-Group-on-Wood-4161596
www.facebook.com/142224589156224
Overview: A small international organization founded in 1969
Mission: To promote research throughout the world on the subject of wood protection; to facilitate collaborative research projects; to promote the exchange of technical information on wood protection
Finances: *Funding Sources:* Membership & conference fees; sponsorships
Membership: *Fees:* 900 SEK (Swedish Kroner) - regular; 450 SEK - student; *Member Profile:* Open to all persons with appropriate qualifications or research experience who are active or interested in wood protection research; *Committees:* Executive; Finance; Scientific Program; Ron Cockcroft Award; IRG Travel Awards; Communications
Activities: 4-day conference; workshops; plenary meetings; *Rents Mailing List:* Yes; *Library:* by appointment
Chief Officer(s):
Jöran Jermer, Secretariat
joran.jermer@sp.se
Awards:
• IRG Travel Awards
• Ron Cockcroft Award
Travel grant for younger scientists, PhD students to attend annual meeting

International Research Institute for Media, Communication & Cultural Development
Marxergasse 48/8, Vienna A-1030 Austria
Tel: 431-236-29-23; *Fax:* 431-236-39-2399
office@mediacult.at
www.mediacult.at
Also Known As: Mediacult
Previous Name: International Institute for Audio-Visual Communication & Cultural Development
Overview: A small international licensing organization founded in 1969
Mission: To observe & to document the influence of new media technologies on cultural development; to produce research findings to serve as decision-making aids to cultural & media policy makers
Finances: *Annual Operating Budget:* $100,000-$250,000; *Funding Sources:* State subsidies
Staff Member(s): 3
Membership: 64
Activities: Research in music & new communication technologies in the arts; consultancy; *Library:* by appointment
Chief Officer(s):
Alfred Smudits, Honorary Secretary General
smudits@mediacult.at

International Right of Way Association (IRWA)
#100, 19210 South Vermont Ave., Gardena CA 90248 USA
Tel: 310-538-0233; *Fax:* 310-538-1471
Toll-Free: 888-340-4792
info@irwaonline.org
www.irwaonline.org
www.linkedin.com/groups?mostPopular=&gid=3270492
www.facebook.com/88967538052
twitter.com/IRWA_Network
Overview: A small international organization founded in 1934
Mission: The IRWA is the central authority of the right of way profession, serving members, the users of our services and the general public.
Membership: 10,000; *Committees:* International Executive; International Service; International Industry; International Discipline
Activities: Educational programs; Professional services
Chief Officer(s):
Lee Hamre, President, 303-623-6112 Ext. 201
lhamre@hcpeck.com
Mark Rieck, Executive Vice President, 303-623-6112 Ext. 140
rieck@irwaonline.org
Publications:
• Right of Way Magazine
Type: Magazine; *Frequency:* Bimonthly

International Sanitary Supply Association, Inc. (ISSA)
3300 Dundee Rd., Northbrook IL 60062 USA
Tel: 847-982-0800; *Fax:* 847-982-1012
Toll-Free: 800-225-4772
info@issa.com
www.issa.com
www.facebook.com/issaworldwide
twitter.com/issaworldwide
Previous Name: National Sanitary Supply Association
Overview: A large international organization founded in 1923
Mission: To link resources & expertise of everyone in the cleaning & maintenance products industry through an ongoing program of training & education, regional & national conferences, publications & the industry's largest annual trade show; to act as one voice before government agencies; to increase product quality, service & value to the customer; to promote the highest standards of public health & sanitation
Finances: *Annual Operating Budget:* Greater than $5 Million; *Funding Sources:* Convention revenue; membership dues; educational materials
Staff Member(s): 24; 15 volunteer(s)
Membership: 5,700 companies in 83 countries; *Fees:* Schedule available; *Member Profile:* Firms which have been continuously engaged in the manufacture &/or distribution of cleaning & maintenance supplies & related products & services; classes of membership are distributor, wholesaler, manufacturer, associate, manufacturer representative, publisher; *Committees:* ISSA/INTERCLEAN; YES Coordinators
Activities: *Awareness Events:* Operation Clean Sweep; *Library*
Chief Officer(s):
David E. Sikes, President
John Barrett, Executive Director
Meetings/Conferences:
• International Sanitary Supply Association INTERCLEAN Amsterdam 2018, May, 2018, Amsterdam
Scope: International
Description: An international exhibition for cleaning professionals which unites leading global brands & manufacturers
• International Sanitary Supply Association INTERCLEAN Dallas 2018, October, 2018, Kay Bailey Hutchinson Convention Center, Dallas, TX
Scope: International
Description: An international exhibition for cleaning professionals which unites leading global brands & manufacturers
Publications:
• Clean Scene [a publication of the International Sanitary Supply Association, Inc.]
Type: Newsletter; *Frequency:* Monthly
Profile: Features articles covering the latest trends in the cleaning industry
• ISSA [International Sanitary Supply Association, Inc.] Formulator News
Type: Newsletter; *Author:* William C. Balek
Profile: Provides updates on legislative, regulatory, & environmental issues that are of interest to ISSA members
• ISSA [International Sanitary Supply Association, Inc.] Times
Type: Magazine
Profile: Features articles covering the latest industry trends, news, & events
• ISSA [International Sanitary Supply Association, Inc.] Today
Type: Newsletter; *Frequency:* Bimonthly
Profile: Features articles by top business & industry experts on a wide range of topics relevant to the industry, including trends, technologies, & legislation
• Sanitation Canada [a publication of the International Sanitary Supply Association, Inc.]
Type: Newsletter
Profile: An information resource for ISSA's Canadian members

International Seed Federation (ISF)
ISF Secretariat, ch du Reposoir 7, 1260, Nyon Switzerland
Tel: +41 22 365 44 20; *Fax:* +41 22 365 44 21
isf@worldseed.org
www.worldseed.org
www.facebook.com/153497914694532?ref=ts&fref=ts
twitter.com/IntSeedFed
www.youtube.com/user/isfprochannel
Overview: A medium-sized international organization
Mission: To represent the interests of the international seed industry; To serve as an international forum for the world seed trade & plant breeders' community
Membership: *Member Profile:* National seed associations & seed companies from more than seventy developed & developing countries
Activities: Interacting with public & private institutions related to the international seed trade; Providing procedural rules for dispute settlement & trade rules; Publishing seed trade statistics
Chief Officer(s):
Marcel Bruins, Secretary General
Radha Ranganathan, Director, Technical Affairs
Piero Sismondohan, Director, Seed Technology & Trade
Publications:
• International Seed Federation Newsletter
Type: Newsletter; *Frequency:* Quarterly
• International Seed Federation World Seed Congress Report
Type: Report; *Frequency:* Annually

International Skating Union (ISU) / Union Internationale de Patinage
Avenue Juste-Olivier 17, Lausanne 1006 Switzerland
Tel: 41-21-612-6666; *Fax:* 41-21-612-6677
info@isu.ch
www.isu.org
www.facebook.com/isuofficial
www.youtube.com/user/SkatingISU/featured
Overview: A small international organization founded in 1892
Mission: To regulate, control & promote the sports of figure & speed skating & their organized development on the basis of friendship & mutual understanding between sportsmen & women & to broaden interest in figure & speed skating sports by increasing their popularity, improving their quality & increasing the number of participants throughout the world
Finances: *Annual Operating Budget:* Greater than $5 Million
Staff Member(s): 11; 60 volunteer(s)
Membership: 73; *Fees:* 300 Swiss francs; *Member Profile:* National skating associations
Activities: Administration of figure skating & speed skating sports throughout the world
Chief Officer(s):
Fredi Schmid, Director General

International Snowmobile Manufacturers Association (ISMA)
#170, 1640 Haslett Rd., Haslett MI 48840 USA
Tel: 517-339-7788; Fax: 517-339-7798
ismasue@aol.com
www.snowmobile.org
Overview: A medium-sized international organization founded in 1995
Mission: To educate the public on safe snowmobiling benefits
Finances: Annual Operating Budget: $250,000-$500,000
Staff Member(s): 2
Activities: Library Open to public
Chief Officer(s):
Edward J. Klim, President

International Social Service (ISS) / Service social international
32 Quai du Seujet, Geneva 1201 Switzerland
Tel: 41-22-906-77-00; Fax: 41-22-906-77-01
info@iss-ssi.org
www.iss-ssi.org
Previous Name: International Migration Service
Overview: A small international organization founded in 1924
Mission: To assist individuals who, as a consequence of voluntary or forced migration or other social problems of an international character have to overcome personal or family difficulties, the solution of which requires coordinated action in several countries or in some cases only in the country of residence of the person concerned; to study from an international standpoint, the conditions & consequences of migration in relation to individual & family life, & as a result of these studies make appropriate recommendations
Member of: NGO Committee on UNICEF; ICSW
Affiliation(s): International Social Service Canada
Finances: Funding Sources: Membership fees; project grants
Membership: 4 associations/affiliated bureaus; 140 correspondants
Activities: Library: International Reference Centre for the Rights of Children Deprive; by appointment
Chief Officer(s):
Jean Ayoub, Secretary General
Doug Lewis, President

International Society for Affective Disorders (ISAD)
c/o Caroline Holebrook, Institute of Psychiatry, King's College London, PO72 De Crespigny Park, Denmark Hill, London SE5 8AF UK
Tel: +44 (0) 20 7848 0295; Fax: +44 (0) 20 7848 0298
Other Communication: help@isad.org.uk
enquiry@isad.org.uk
www.isad.org.uk
twitter.com/ISADTweet
Overview: A large international charitable organization founded in 2001
Mission: To advance research into affective disorders through all relevant scientific disciplines
Finances: Funding Sources: Sponsorships
Membership: Member Profile: Researchers; Clinicians; Members of recognized advocacy groups; Committees: Executive; Membership; Education; External Affairs; Programme
Activities: Engaging in advocacy activities; Promoting networking & the exchange of ideas
Chief Officer(s):
Allan Young, President
Anthony Cleare, Treasurer
John Rush, Regional Representative, North America (Canada & the United States)
Caroline Holebrook, Administrator
caroline.loveland@kcl.ac.uk
Meetings/Conferences:
• International Society for Affective Disorders Conference 2018, 2018
Scope: International
Publications:
• Journal of Affective Disorders
Type: Journal; Editor: Jair Soares; Paolo Brambilla

International Society for Burn Injuries (ISBI)
c/o Administrator, 2172 Hwy. 181 South, Floresville TX 781114 USA
Fax: 830-216-4101
lizals@tgti.net
www.worldburn.org
Overview: A small international organization founded in 1965
Mission: To disseminate knowledge; to stimulate burn prevention
Membership: Member Profile: Specialists in burn care; Committees: Executive; Burn Care; Research; Industry; Disaster Planning; Lab Services; Rehabilitation; Prevention; Nursing
Activities: Collaborating with WHO; Assisting the organization of educational courses
Chief Officer(s):
Elisabeth Greenfield McManus, Administrator, Fax: 830-947-3142
lizals@tgti.net
Richard L. Gamelli, President
rgamell@luc.edu
Nicole S. Gibran, Regional Representative, North America
burnadmn@u.washington.edu
Publications:
• Burns
Type: Journal; Price: Free with ISBI membership

International Society for Business Education (ISBE) / Société internationale pour l'enseignement commercial (SIEC)
#100, 6302 Mineral Point Rd., Madison WI 53705 USA
Tel: 608-273-8467
secretary@siec-isbe.org
www.siec-isbe.org
Overview: A small international organization founded in 1901
Mission: To bridge the gap between business education & the world of business on an international scale
Finances: Annual Operating Budget: Less than $50,000; Funding Sources: Membership dues
Staff Member(s): 1
Membership: 2,000; Fees: Schedule available; Member Profile: Business educators; individuals interested in business education; Committees: Network; Pedagogical
Chief Officer(s):
Judith Olson-Sutton, General Secretary
secretary@siec-isbe.org
Awards:
• Annual Research Award

International Society for Ecological Economics (ISEE)
c/o Secretariat, PO Box 44194, West Allis WI 53214 USA
Tel: 1-414-453-0030; Fax: 1-973-273-2178
secretariat@isecoeco.org
www.isecoeco.org
www.facebook.com/iseeorg
twitter.com/ISEEORG
Overview: A medium-sized international organization founded in 1989
Mission: To extend & integrate the study & management of ecology & economics
Finances: Annual Operating Budget: $100,000-$250,000; Funding Sources: Membership fees; grants
Membership: 2,008; Fees: $15-$130; Committees: Executive
Chief Officer(s):
Marina Fischer-Kowalski, President
Anne Carter Aitken, Treasurer/Secretariat

International Society for Ecological Modelling (ISEM)
PMB 255, 550 M Ritchie Hwy., Severna Park MD 21146 USA
www.isemna.org
Overview: A small international organization founded in 1975
Mission: To promote the international exchange of ideas, scientific results, & general knowledge in the area of the application of systems analysis & simulation in ecology & natural resource management
Membership: Fees: $10 student; $20 individual; $100 institution
Chief Officer(s):
Sven E. Jorgensen, President
msijapan@hotmail.com

International Society for Environmental Epidemiology (ISEE)
c/o ISEE Secretariat, JSI Research & Training Institute, 44 Farnsworth St., Boston MA 2210 USA
Tel: 617-482-9485; Fax: 617-482-0617
www.iseepi.org
Overview: A small international organization founded in 1989
Mission: To provide a forum for the discussion of problems unique to the study of health & the environment, such as environmental exposures, health effects, methodology, environment-gene interactions, & ethics & law
Member of: International Society of Exposure Analysis
Membership: 500-999; Fees: US$220 full member; US$145 basic; US$55 developing country & student; Member Profile: Members include epidemiologists, toxicologists, exposure analysts & others with an interest in environmental epidemiology, from academia, local, state & federal government, industry, & community organizations.; Committees: Nominations; Annual Conference; Awards; Membership; Communications; Ethics & Philosophy; Capacity Building in Developing Countries
Activities: Rents Mailing List: Yes
Chief Officer(s):
Verónica Vieira, Secretary-Treasurer
vvieira@uci.edu
Francine Laden, President
francine.laden@channing.harvard.edu
Francine Laden, Sec.-Treas.
francine.laden@channing.harvard.edu
Awards:
• The ISEE Research Integrity Award
Recognizes those who have remained true to the core values of the profession by maintaining objectivity in protecting the public health interest above any other interest Contact: Daniel Wartenberg, Chair, Awards Committee, dew@eohsi.rutgers.edu
• Rebecca James Baker Memorial Prize
Eligibility: Graduate level students & new investigators who are within three years of completing their degree Contact: Irva Hertz-Picciotto, Co-Chair, ihp@ucdavis.edu
• John Goldsmith Award for Outstanding Conributions to Environmental Epidemiology
Recognizes environmental epidemiologist who seve as models of excellence in research, unwavering promotion of environmental health, & integrity Deadline: March Contact: Daniel Wartenberg, Chair, Awards Committee, dew@eohsi.rutgers.edu
Publications:
• Epidemiology
Type: Journal; Frequency: Bimonthly; Editor: Allen J. Wilcox; ISSN: 1044-3983
Profile: A peer-reviewed scientific journal featuring original research on the full spectrum of epidemiologic topics
• International Society for Environmental Epidemiology Directory of Members
Type: Directory
Profile: Includes all ISEE members

International Society for Environmental Ethics (ISEE)
c/o Allen Thompson, Dept. of Philosophy, Oregon State University, 102C Hovland Hall, Corvallis OR 97331-3902 USA
e-mail: enviroethics@hotmail.com
enviroethics.org
www.facebook.com/EnvironmentalEthics
twitter.com/EnviroEthics
plus.google.com/u/0/105320470303657467396?prsrc=3
Overview: A small international organization founded in 1990
Membership: Fees: $25 regular membership (US); $15 students (US); $25 regular international member
Activities: Providing information about environmental ethics; Maintaining a bibliography on environmental ethics; Offering educational events
Chief Officer(s):
Phil Cafaro, President, 970-491-2061, Fax: 970-491-4900
philip.cafaro@colostate.edu
Ben Hale, Vice-President, 303-735-3624, Fax: 303-735-1576
bhale@colorado.edu
William Grove-Fanning, Secretary
Allen Thompson, Treasurer, 541-737-5654, Fax: 541-737-2571
allen.thompson@oregonstate.edu
Publications:
• Environmental Ethics Syllabus Project
Editor: Robert Hood; ISSN: 1564-001
Profile: Information about courses in environmental philosophy & environmental ethics
• International Society for Environmental Ethics Newsletter
Frequency: 3 pa; Editor: Mark Woods; Price: Free with International Society for Environmental Ethics membership
Profile: Society activities & announcements, plus articles

International Society for Eye Research
655 Beach St., San Francisco CA 94109 USA
Tel: 415-561-8569; Fax: 415-561-8531
mail@iser.org
www.iser.org
www.facebook.com/ISERPage
twitter.com/iserworld
Overview: A medium-sized international organization founded in 1968
Mission: To support & sustain excellent eye & vision research around the globe

Membership: 356; *Fees:* Schedule available; *Member Profile:* Vision research scientists from over 34 countries; *Committees:* Membership
Activities: Engaging in international collaboration; Offering networking opportunities
Chief Officer(s):
John S. Penn, President
Publications:
• Experimental Eye Research
Type: Journal
Profile: Original research papers in the following sections: Aqueous Humor & Blood Flow; Cornea & Ocular Surface; Lens & Retina; & Choroid

International Society for Human & Animal Mycology (ISHAM)
Dept. of Haematology, Radboud University Nijmegen Medical Centre, Geert Grootplein Zuid 8, Nijmegen 6525 GA Netherlands
Tel: 31-24-361-9987; *Fax:* 31-24-354-2080
www.isham.org
Overview: A small international organization founded in 1960
Mission: To be devoted to all aspects of the field of medical mycology (fungal diseases of man & animals)
Membership: 1000+
Chief Officer(s):
Peter Donnelly, General Secretary

International Society for Human Rights (ISHR)
Borsigallee 9, Frankfurt am Main 60388 Germany
Tel: 49-(0)69-420 108-0; *Fax:* 49-(0)69-420 108-33
info@ishr.org
www.ishr.org
Overview: A medium-sized international organization founded in 1972
Mission: To assist isolated individuals or groups striving for human rights; to help divided families & those persecuted for religious beliefs
Member of: Liaison Committee of NGOs enjoying consultative status with eh Council of Europe
Affiliation(s): United Nations, Dept. of Public Information; African Commission on Human Peoples' Rights
Finances: *Funding Sources:* Membership dues; donations; projects
Membership: 30,000 people in 38 countries
Activities: *Internships:* Yes
Chief Officer(s):
Marat Zakhidov, President

International Society for Magnetic Resonance in Medicine (ISMRM)
#620, 2300 Clayton Rd., Concord CA 94520 USA
Tel: 510-841-1899; *Fax:* 510-841-2340
info@ismrm.org
www.ismrm.org
www.linkedin.com/company/ismrm
www.facebook.com/ISMRM
twitter.com/ismrm
Previous Name: Society of Magnetic Resonance
Merged from: Society of Magnetic Resonance in Medicine; Society of Magnetic Resonance Imaging
Overview: A medium-sized international organization founded in 1994
Mission: To further the development & application of magnetic resonance techniques in medicine & biology; To promote research, development, & applications in the field
Membership: 6,000+; *Member Profile:* Clinicians; Physicists; Engineers; Biochemists; Technologists; *Committees:* Executive; Board of Trustees; Committee for Affiliated Sections - SMRT; Annual Meeting Program; Awards; Education; Finance; Governance; Historical Archives; Nominating; Publications; Safety; Workshop & Study Group Review; Ad Hoc Committee on Standards for Quantitative MR; Ad Hoc Committee on Sustainability; Ad Hoc Committee on Web-Based Services
Activities: Promoting communication; Developing continuing education
Chief Officer(s):
Roberta A. Kravitz, Executive Director
roberta@ismrm.org
Kerry Crockett, Associate Executive Director
kerry@ismrm.org
Candace Spradley, Director, Education
candace@ismrm.org
Stephanie M. Haaf, Director, Membership & Study Groups
stephanie@ismrm.org
Mariam Barzin, Director, Finance
mariam@ismrm.org

Mary Keydash, Director, Marketing
mary@ismrm.org
Anne-Marie Kahrovic, Director, Meetings
anne-marie@ismrm.org
Kristina King, Registrar & Coordinator, Accounting
kristina@ismrm.org
Meetings/Conferences:
• International Society for Magnetic Resonance in Medicine 2018 26th Scientific Meeting & Exhibition, June, 2018, Paris
Scope: International
Description: Featuring the 26th Annual Meeting of the Section for Magnetic Resonance Technologists
Contact Information: Director, Meetings: Anne-Marie Kahrovic, E-mail: anne-marie@ismrm.org
• International Society for Magnetic Resonance in Medicine 2019 27th Scientific Meeting & Exhibition, May, 2019, Montréal, QC
Scope: International
Description: Featuring the 26th Annual Meeting of the Section for Magnetic Resonance Technologists
Contact Information: Director, Meetings: Anne-Marie Kahrovic, E-mail: anne-marie@ismrm.org
• International Society for Magnetic Resonance in Medicine 2020 28th Scientific Meeting & Exhibition, April, 2020, Sydney
Scope: International
Description: Featuring the 29th Annual Meeting of the Section for Magnetic Resonance Technologists
• International Society for Magnetic Resonance in Medicine 2021 29th Scientific Meeting & Exhibition, May, 2021, Vancouver, BC
Scope: International
Description: Featuring the 29th Annual Meeting of the Section for Magnetic Resonance Technologists
• International Society for Magnetic Resonance in Medicine 2022 30th Scientific Meeting & Exhibition, May, 2022, London
Scope: International
Description: Featuring the 29th Annual Meeting of the Section for Magnetic Resonance Technologists
• International Society for Magnetic Resonance in Medicine 2023 31st Scientific Meeting & Exhibition, June, 2023, Toronto, ON
Scope: International
Description: Featuring the 29th Annual Meeting of the Section for Magnetic Resonance Technologists
Publications:
• Journal of Magnetic Resonance Imaging
Type: Journal; *Editor:* Mark E. Schweitzer, MD
Profile: Basic & clinical research, plus educational & review articles related to the diagnostic applications of magnetic resonance
• Magnetic Resonance in Medicine
Type: Journal; *Editor:* Matt A. Bernstein
Profile: Original investigations concerned with the development & use of nuclear magnetic resonance & electron paramagnetic resonance techniques for medical applications
• MR Pulse
Type: Newsletter
Profile: Society updates & announcements

International Society for Music Education (ISME)
#148, 45 Glenferrie Rd., Malvern VA 3144 Australia
Tel: 61-8-9386-2654; *Fax:* 61-8-9386-2658
isme@isme.org
www.isme.org
www.facebook.com/136976192999210
twitter.com/official_isme
www.youtube.com/user/isme1953
Overview: A medium-sized international charitable organization founded in 1953
Mission: To serve as a network for the music educators, music researchers & students, & music therapists of the world; to build & maintain a worldwide community of music educators characterized by mutual respect & support
Member of: International Music Council
Affiliation(s): UNESCO
Finances: *Annual Operating Budget:* $50,000-$100,000; *Funding Sources:* Membership dues; conference revenue; sponsorship
Staff Member(s): 1
Membership: 1,330; *Fees:* Based on the Human Development Index determined by the United Nations; *Member Profile:* Individuals, institutions, organizations; *Committees:* Research; Education of the Professional Musician; Music in Schools & Teacher Education; Music in Special Education, Music Therapy & Music Medicine; Community Music Activity; Music in Cultural, Educational & Mass Media Policies; Early Childhood Music Education; Instrumental/Studio Pedagogy
Chief Officer(s):

Margaret Barrett, President
Liane Hentschke, Chair of ISME 2014
Meetings/Conferences:
• 33rd World Conference of the International Society for Music Education, July, 2018, Baku
Scope: International
• 34th World Conference of the International Society for Music Education, August, 2020, Helsinki
Scope: International

International Society for Neurochemistry (ISN)
c/o Kenes International, PO Box 6053, #7, rue François-Versonnex, Geneva 1211 Switzerland
Tel: 41-22-906-9151; *Fax:* 41-22-732-2607
www.neurochemistry.org
www.facebook.com/205062269527045
twitter.com/ISN_secretariat
Overview: A medium-sized international organization founded in 1965
Mission: To facilitate the worldwide advance of neurochemistry & related neuroscience disciplines; To foster the education & development of neurochemists, particularly of young & emerging investigators
Membership: *Fees:* $60 full; $25 student; *Member Profile:* Ordinary - past & present record of neurochemical research; associate - interest in neurochemical aspects of subjects; junior - under the age of 30 with a less than four years' postdoctoral experience; *Committees:* Advanced School; Aid & Education in Neurochemistry; Biennial Program; Conference; Finance; Publication; Schools Initiative; Standing Rules; Travel Grant; Young Scientist Steering
Activities: Organizing biennial international meetings
Chief Officer(s):
Monica Carson, President
monica.carson@ucr.edu
Ralf Dringen, Secretary
Kazuhiro Ikenaka, Treasurer
ikenaka@nips.ac.jp
Meetings/Conferences:
• International Society for Neurochemistry 2019 Biennial Meeting, 2019
Scope: International

International Society for Pediatric & Adolescent Diabetes (ISPAD)
c/o KIT Group GmbH, Kurfürstendamm 71, Berlin 10709 Germany
Tel: +49 30 24603210; *Fax:* +49 30 24603200
secretariat@ispad.org
www.ispad.org
Overview: A medium-sized international organization
Mission: To promote research, science, education, & advocacy in childhood & adolescent diabetes
Membership: *Fees:* $50 emeritus membership; $100 regular members; *Member Profile:* Persons with scientific & clinical expertise in childhood & adolescent diabetes
Chief Officer(s):
Joseph Wolfsdorf, President
David M. Maahs, Secretary General
Andrea Scaramuzza, Treasurer
Meetings/Conferences:
• International Society for Pediatric & Adolescent Diabetes 2018 44th Annual Conference, October, 2018, Hyderabad
Scope: International
Description: A scientific meeting featuring paper, poster, & plenary sessions, workshops, & symposia
Contact Information: 2018.ispad.org
Publications:
• International Society for Pediatric & Adolescent Diabetes Membership Directory
Type: Directory
Profile: A listing of society members with contact information
• ISPAD [International Society for Pediatric & Adolescent Diabetes] Newsletter
Type: Newsletter
Profile: Society activities, including meeting reviews, educational opportunities, forthcoming events
• Pediatric Diabetes
Type: Journal; *Price:* Free with International Society for Pediatric & Adolescent Diabetes memberships

International Society for Performance Improvement (ISPI)
PO Box 13035, Silver Spring MD 20910-2753 USA
Tel: 301-587-8570; *Fax:* 301-587-8573
info@ispi.org

www.ispi.org
www.linkedin.com/ISPIGlobal
www.facebook.com/ISPI1962
twitter.com/ISPI1962
www.youtube.com/user/ISPITube
Overview: A medium-sized international organization founded in 1962
Mission: To improve the performance of individuals & organizations through the application of human performance technology
Finances: *Annual Operating Budget:* $500,000-$1.5 Million
Staff Member(s): 4
Membership: 50 institutional + 200 student + 6,000 individual; *Fees:* Schedule available; *Member Profile:* Performance technologists, training directors, human resources managers, instructional technologists, human factors practitioners, project managers, & organizational consultants
Activities: *Rents Mailing List:* Yes
Chief Officer(s):
April Davis, Executive Director
april@ispi.org

    Vancouver Chapter
    #1000, 35 Burrard St., Vancouver BC V6C 2G8
    Tel: 778-230-9315
    www.ispivancouver.com
    www.linkedin.com/groups/ISPI-Vancouver-Chapter-2264830/about
    www.facebook.com/ISPIVancouver
    twitter.com/ispivancouver
    Chief Officer(s):
    Dan McFaull, President
    president@ispivancouver.com

International Society for Plant Pathology
c/o Secretary General, PO Box 412, Jamison ACT 2612 Australia
Tel: 61-2-62515658
www.isppweb.org
twitter.com/Food_Security
Overview: A small international charitable organization founded in 1968
Mission: To promote the worldwide development of plant pathology & the dissemination of knowledge about plant diseases & plant health management
Member of: International Union of Biological Sciences; International Union of Microbiological Sciences
Membership: *Member Profile:* Open to persons interested in or involved in plant pathology
Chief Officer(s):
M. Lodovica Gullino, President
issp.president@isppweb.org
Thomas Evans, Treasurer
ispp.treasurer@isppweb.org

International Society for Rock Mechanics (ISRM)
c/o Laboratório Nacional de Engenharia Civil, 101 Av. do Brasil, Lisbon 1700-066 Portugal
Tel: 351-21-844-3419; *Fax:* 351-21-844-3021
secretariat@isrm.net
www.isrm.net
www.linkedin.com/company/international-society-for-rock-mechanics
twitter.com/IntSocRockMec
Overview: A medium-sized international organization founded in 1962
Mission: To encourage & coordinate international cooperation in the area of rock mechanics; To maintain liaison with other organizations dealing with fields of science related to rock mechanics, such as geology, geophysics, soil mechanics, mining engineering, petroleum engineering & civil engineering
Member of: International Union of Geological Sciences
Affiliation(s): Canadian Rock Mechanics Association; Canadian Geotechnical Society
Finances: *Funding Sources:* Membership fees; Grants that do not impair the Society's free action
Membership: 5,000 members + 46 national groups; *Member Profile:* Rock mechanics practitioners & corporations; *Committees:* Joint Technical Committee on Landslides & Engineered Slopes; Joint Technical Committee on Representation of Geo-engineering Data in Electronic Form; Joint Technical Committee on Education & Training; Joint Technical Committee on Professional Practice; Joint Technical Committee on Sustainable Use of Underground Space; Joint Technical Committee on Ancient Monuments & Historical Sites; Joint Technical Committee on Soft Rocks & Indurated Soils
Activities: Encouraging teaching, research, & advancement of knowledge in rock mechanics; Operating commissions for studying scientific & technical matters; Sponsoring international & regional symposia; *Library:* by appointment
Chief Officer(s):
Luís Lamas, Secretary General
Eda Freitas de Quadros, President
Awards:
• Rocha Medal
For an outstanding doctoral thesis
• Müller Award
For distinguished contributions to the profession of rock mechanics and rock engineering
• The ISRM Franklin Lecture
Recognizes a mid-career ISRM member who has made a significant contribution to a specific area of rock mechanics or engineering
• ISRM Fellows
Recognizes outstanding achievements in the field of rock mechanics or engineering
Meetings/Conferences:
• International Society for Rock Mechanics 14th International Congress on Rock Mechanics, September, 2019, Foz do Iguacu
Scope: International
Publications:
• ISRM [International Society for Rock Mechanics] News Journal
Type: Journal
Profile: Information about technology related to rock mechanics & news on activities in the rock mechanics community
• ISRM [International Society for Rock Mechanics] Newsletter
Type: Newsletter
• ISRM [International Society for Rock Mechanics] Glossary
Profile: A list of approximately 1000 Rock Mechanics terms; available in over ten languages
• ISRM [International Society for Rock Mechanics] Suggested Methods

International Society for Sexually Transmitted Diseases Research (ISSTDR)
c/o Basil Donovan, The Kirby Institute, University of New South Wales, Sidney Australia
www.isstdr.org
Overview: A medium-sized international organization founded in 1977
Mission: To promote research on sexually transmitted diseases
Activities: Facilitating the timely exhange of information among researchers; Hosting a biennial, interdisciplinary scientific meeting to address the breadth of research on sexually transimitte diesease
Chief Officer(s):
Michel Alary, Chair & President
michel.alary@uresp.ulaval.ca
Meetings/Conferences:
• STI & HIV World Congress 2019, July, 2019, Vancouver, BC
Scope: International

International Society for Soil Mechanics & Foundation Engineering See International Society for Soil Mechanics & Geotechnical Engineering

International Society for Soil Mechanics & Geotechnical Engineering (ISSMGE) / Société Internationale de Mécanique des Sols et de la Géotechnique (SIMSG)
City University, Northampton Square, London EC1V 0HB United Kingdom
Tel: 44-20-7040-8154; *Fax:* 44-20-7040-8832
secretariat@issmge.org
www.issmge.org
Previous Name: International Society for Soil Mechanics & Foundation Engineering
Overview: A medium-sized international organization
Affiliation(s): International Society for Soil Mechanics & Geotechnical Engineering - Canadian Section; Canadian Geotechnical Society
Finances: *Annual Operating Budget:* $250,000-$500,000
Membership: 15,000-49,999; *Committees:* 25 active international Technical Committees working in various specialist areas of geotechnics
Chief Officer(s):
R. N. (Neil) Taylor, Secretary General
Roger Frank, President

International Society for Telemedicine & eHealth
c/o AMTS Luzern, Luzerner Kantonsspital, Luzern 16 CH - 6000 Switzerland
e-mail: telemedicine@skynet.be
www.isft.net
Overview: A small international organization
Mission: To facilitate the international dissemination of knowledge & experience in telemedicine & e-health & to provide access to recognized experts in the field worldwide
Membership: *Fees:* $100
Chief Officer(s):
Andy Fischer, President
president@isfteh.org

International Society for the Sociology of Religion *Voir* Société internationale de sociologie des religions

International Society for the Study of Medieval Philosophy *Voir* Société internationale pour l'étude de la philosophie médiévale

International Society for the Study of the Lumbar Spine (ISSLS)
c/o Institute for Clinical Sciences, Sahlgrenska Academy, PO Box 426, #MG301, 2075 Bayview Ave., Gothenburg SE-405 30 Sweden
Tel: 46-31-786-44-36
www.issls.org
www.facebook.com/1396088907323562
twitter.com/ISSLS_Society
www.youtube.com/user/ISSLSSociety
Overview: A small international organization founded in 1974
Staff Member(s): 1
Membership: 230
Chief Officer(s):
Keith Luk, President
Katarina Olinder Eriksson, Administrator
katarina.olinder@gu.se
Awards:
• ISSLS Wiltse Lifetime Achievement Award
• ISSLS Prize for Lumbar Spine Research
Sponsored by European Spine Journal to encourage lumbar spine research *Amount:* 3 at $20,000 (USD)
• ISSLS Clinical Travelling Fellowship
Sponsored by Seoul Chuk Hospital *Eligibility:* Junior faculty members (in practice less than 10 years) from any part of the world *Amount:* 3 at $20,000 (USD)

International Society for the Study of Trauma & Dissociation (ISSTD)
USA
Tel: 703-610-9037; *Fax:* 703-610-0234
info@isst-d.org
www.isst-d.org
www.facebook.com/people/Isstd-Headquarters/100000004676158
twitter.com/isstd
Overview: A medium-sized international organization
Mission: Promotes research and training in the identification and treatment of dissociative disorders and their relationship to developmental, relational, and other traumas.
Membership: *Fees:* $215 regular/full; $105 student; $97 retired; *Member Profile:* Individuals interested in the study of chronic/complex trauma and the dissociative disorders.; *Committees:* Awards; Certificate Program; Child and Adolescent; ISSTD Core Conference; David Caul Award; Finance; Fund-Raising; Governance; Marketing; Membership; Nominating; Newsletter; Professional Training; Scientific; Student and Emerging Professionals; Volunteer; Webinar; Website
Chief Officer(s):
Lynette S. Danylchuk, President, 650-773-4476
l.danylchuk@usa.net
Awards:
• Audio-Visual Media Achievement Award
• Cornelia B. Wilbur Award
• David Caul Award
• Distinguished Achievement Award
• Lifetime Achievement Award
• Morton Prince Award
• Pierre Janet Writing Award
• Presidents Award
• Student Award
• David Caul Graduate Research Grants
Amount: up to $1500
Publications:
• Journal of Trauma & Dissociation
Type: Journal; *Editor:* Jennifer J. Freyd

International Society for Vascular Behavioural & Cognitive Disorders
c/o Newcastle University Campus for Ageing & Vitality, NIHR Biomedical Research Building, 1st Fl., Newcastle upon Tyne NE4 5PL United Kingdom
Tel: 44-191-248-1352; *Fax:* 44-191-248-1301
vascogsoc@gmail.com
www.vas-cog.org
Also Known As: The Vas-Cog Society
Overview: A medium-sized international organization founded in 2001
Mission: To study the vascular causes of various brain disorders by bringing together diverse basic sciences & clinical research interests
Finances: *Funding Sources:* Sponsorships
Membership: 193; *Fees:* £60 regular; £40 student; *Committees:* By-law; Program; Executive; Scientific; Nominating
Activities: Training researchers; Disseminating information; Raising awareness of various brain disorders & other behavioural disorders & their prevention & treatment; Advocating for patients
Chief Officer(s):
Christopher Chen, Chair
Raj Kalaria, Secretariat
Meetings/Conferences:
• International Society for Vascular Behavioural & Cognitive Disorders Congress 2018, November, 2018, Hong Kong
Scope: International

International Society of Arboriculture
PO Box 3129, Champaign IL 61826-3129 USA
Tel: 217-355-9411; *Fax:* 217-355-9516
Toll-Free: 888-472-8733
isa@isa-arbor.com
www.isa-arbor.com
www.linkedin.com/groups?mostPopular=&gid=1953660
www.facebook.com/InternationalSocietyofArboriculture
twitter.com/ISArboriculture
www.youtube.com/user/ISAAdmin
Overview: A medium-sized international organization founded in 1924
Mission: To foster research & education that promotes the care & the benefits of trees
Staff Member(s): 44
Membership: *Fees:* $0 student; $65 senior; $130 professional; $500 patron; *Committees:* Annual Conference Program; Awards; Best Management Practices; Development; Educational Goods & Services; Finance/Audit; Goverenance & Bylaws; Hispanic; International Safety; International Tree Climbing Championship; Membership; Nominating & Elections; Plant Appraisal & Valuation; Public Relations & Marketing; Science & Research
Chief Officer(s):
Terrence Flanagan, President
terry@teragan.com
Jim Skiera, Executive Director
jskiera@isa-arbor.com

International Society of Biometeorology (ISB) / Société internationale de biométéorolgy
c/o Dept. of Geography, Univ. of Wisconsin-Milwaukee, PO Box 413, Milwaukee WI 53201-0413 USA
Tel: 414-229-6611; *Fax:* 414-229-3981
www.biometeorology.org
Overview: A small international organization founded in 1956
Mission: To promote international collaboration of physicists, biologists, meteorologists & other scientists & the development of the field of meteorology in relation to humans, animals & plants
Finances: *Funding Sources:* Membership fees
Membership: *Fees:* US$85 regular; US$60 retired/student
Activities: *Library:* ISB Archive
Chief Officer(s):
Glenn McGregor, President
g.mcgregor@auckland.ac.nz
Jonathan M. Hanes, Secretary
jmhanes@uwm.edu

International Society of Chemotherapy for Infection & Cancer (ISC)
c/o Dept. of Medical Microbiology, Aberdeen Royal Infirmary, Aberdeen AB25 2ZN United Kingdom
Tel: 44 (0) 1224 554 954
www.ischemo.org
Overview: A medium-sized international organization founded in 1961
Mission: To advance the education & science of chemotherapy
Membership: 94 member societies worldwide; *Committees:* Hamao Umezawa Memorial Award; Tom Bergan Memorial Award; John David Williams Memorial Award; Masaaki Ohkoshi Award; Young Investigator Travel Awards; IASC Awards; Publication/Communication: IJAA; Publication/Communication: Website; Disease Management Series
Activities: Conferences; research & special projects
Chief Officer(s):
Ian Gould, President
i.m.gould@abdn.ac.uk
Po-Ren Hsueh, Secretary General
hsporen@ntu.edu.tw

International Society of Citriculture (ISC)
Dept. of Botany & Plant Sciences, University of California, Riverside CA 92521-0124 USA
Tel: 951-827-4663; *Fax:* 951-827-4437
iscucr@ucr.edu
www.internationalsocietyofcitriculture.org
Overview: A large international organization founded in 1976
Mission: To promote & encourage research, exchange of information & education, in all aspects of citrus production, harvesting, handling, & distribution of both fresh fruit & products
Affiliation(s): International Society for Horticultural Science
Finances: *Funding Sources:* Membership dues; Sales of congress proceedings
Membership: 1,000-4,999; *Fees:* US$30/4 years; *Member Profile:* Any individual, corporation, unincorporated association, or organization interested in an aspect of citrus culture, handling, marketing, processing, transportation, research, or education
Chief Officer(s):
Mikeal L. Roose, Secretary-Treasurer
mikeal.roose@ucr.edu
Publications:
• ISC [International Society of Citriculture] Proceedings
Profile: Papers presented at previous meetings
• ISC [International Society of Citriculture] Newsletter
Type: Newsletter
Profile: Archived newsletters from 1995-2003

International Society of City & Regional Planners
PO Box 983, The Hague 2501 CZ Netherlands
Tel: 31-70-346-2654; *Fax:* 31-70-361-7909
isocarp@isocarp.org
www.isocarp.org
Also Known As: ISOCARP
Overview: A small international licensing organization founded in 1965
Mission: To improve cities & territories through planning practice, training, education, & research
Affiliation(s): UNESCO; Council of Europe; UN/ECOSOC; UNCHS/Habitat
Finances: *Funding Sources:* Membership fees
Membership: 100-499; *Fees:* Schedule available; *Member Profile:* Professional planners; Stakeholders involved in the development & maintenance of the built environment
Activities: Promoting the planning profession; Facilitating exchange between planners from different countries; Providing information on major planning issues; Evaluating developments & trends in planning practice
Chief Officer(s):
Milica Bajic Brkovic, President
Alex Macgregor, Secretary General
Manfred Schrenk, Treasurer
Awards:
• Gerd Albert Award
• Routledge Prize
Poster congress prize
Meetings/Conferences:
• 54th ISOCARP Congress, October, 2018, Bodø
Scope: International
Description: Theme: "Cool Planning: Changing Climate & Our Urban Future"
Publications:
• International Manual of Planning Practice (IMPP)
Editor: Judith Ryser; Teresa Franchini
Profile: Reference guide to the key features of the spatial planning systems
• International Society of City & Regional Planners Annual Congress Report
Type: Yearbook; *Frequency:* Annually
Profile: Final report of each congress
• ISOCARP [International Society of City & Regional Planners] NET
Type: Newsletter; *Editor:* Judy van Hemert
• ISOCARP [International Society of City & Regional Planners] Review
Profile: Complement to the research efforts prepared for the annual ISOCARP Congresses

International Society of Friendship & Good Will (ISFGW) / Société internationale d'amitié et de bonne volonté
3119 Lassiter St., Durham NC 27707-3888 USA
www.friendshipandgoodwill.org
Overview: A small international organization founded in 1978
Mission: To encourage & foster advancement of international understanding, better human relations, friendship, goodwill & peace through world fellowship of men & women; to promote the teaching & learning of Esperanto & to collaborate with national & international Esperanto associations
Finances: *Annual Operating Budget:* Less than $50,000; *Funding Sources:* Membership dues; donations
Staff Member(s): 2
Membership: 46 Canadian; *Fees:* Members pay whatever they can afford
Activities: *Speaker Service:* Yes; *Rents Mailing List:* Yes
Chief Officer(s):
D. Gary Grady, President
dgary@mindspring.com

International Society of Hypertension (ISH)
ISH Secretariat, The Conference Collective Ltd., 8 Waldegrave Rd., Teddington TW11 8GT United Kingdom
Tel: +44 (0) 20 8977 7997
secretariat@ish-world.com
www.ish-world.com
www.facebook.com/ISHNIN
twitter.com/ISHNIN
Overview: A medium-sized international charitable organization
Mission: To advance scientific knowledge in all aspects of research; To promote application of research to the prevention & management of heart disease & stroke in hypertension & related cardiovascular diseases
Affiliation(s): Canadian Hypertension Society; World Hypertension League; American Society of Hypertension; Council for High Blood Pressure Research of the AHA; Cuban National Committee for the Study of Hypertension; Hypertension societies throughout Africa, The Middle East, Asia, Australasia, Europe, & South America
Membership: 800; *Member Profile:* Clinicians, academic scientists, & researchers in hypertension & cardiovascular disease from around the globe; *Committees:* Awards; Communications; Corporate Liaison; Membership; New Investigator; Research, Science & Education; Women in Hypertension Research
Chief Officer(s):
Neil Poulter, President
Alta Schutte, Vice-President
Maciej Tomaszewski, Secretary
Masatsugu Horiuchi, Treasurer
Meetings/Conferences:
• International Society of Hypertension 27th Scientific Meeting, September, 2018, Beijing
Scope: International
Description: Scientific program & exhibition
Publications:
• Hypertension News
Type: Newsletter; *Frequency:* Quarterly; *Price:* Free with International Society of Hypertension membership
• Journal of Hypertension
Type: Journal; *Frequency:* Monthly; *Price:* Free with International Society of Hypertension membership
Profile: Primary papers from experts, authoritative reviews, recent developments, special reports, & time-sensitive information

International Society of Indoor Air Quality & Climate (ISIAQ)
c/o Gina Bendy, 2548 Empire Grade, Santa Cruz CA 95060 USA
Tel: 831-426-0148; *Fax:* 831-426-6522
info@isiaq.org
www.isiaq.org
Overview: A medium-sized international organization founded in 1992
Mission: To support the establishment of healthy, productivity-encouraging indoor environments
Finances: *Funding Sources:* Membership fees; Donations; Sponsorships

Membership: *Fees:* US $15 - $30 /year students; US $135 / year individuals; US $700 / year corporate members; *Member Profile:* Individuals, such as scientist involved in indoor air quality research, occupational health professionals, government & regulatory professionals, & architects; Corporations; Students; *Committees:* Task force on the control of moisture & mould problems in cold climate; Task force on the vocabulary of the indoor air sciences; Task force on the IAQ & climate in cultural & heritage collections; Task force on the criteria for cleaning of air handling systems; Task force on the performance of portable air cleaners; Task force on the education for healthier buildings; Task force on the effect of the indoor environment on productivity in offices; Task force on indoor air research & building practice
Activities: Facilitating international & interdisciplinary communication; Liaising with governments & other agencies with interests in indoor environment
Chief Officer(s):
Richard Shaughnessy, President
rjstulsau@aol.com
Anne Hyvärinen, Secretary
anne.hyvarinen@thl.fi
Carl-Gustaf Bornehag, Treasurer
carl-gustaf.bornehag@kau.se
Meetings/Conferences:
• International Society of Indoor Air Quality & Climate 2018 Indoor Air Conference, July, 2018, Pennsylvania Convention Center, Philadelphia, PA
Scope: International
Contact Information: www.indoorair2018.org
Publications:
• Indoor Air: The International Journal of Indoor Environment & Health
Type: Journal; *Frequency:* Bimonthly; *Accepts Advertising*; *Editor:* Jan Sundell; William Nazaroff; *Price:* Free with International Society of Indoor Air Quality & Climate membership
Profile: Original research about indoor environments
• International Society of Indoor Air Quality & Climate Conference Proceedings
Profile: Proceedings of Healthy Buildings & Indoor Air conferences
• International Society of Indoor Air Quality & Climate Task Force Reports
• International Society of Indoor Air Quality & Climate Newsletter
Type: Newsletter; *Accepts Advertising*; *Price:* Free with International Society of Indoor Air Quality & Climate membership
Profile: Society activities
• Vocabulary of the Indoor Air Sciences

International Society of Limnology / Societas Internationalis Limnologiae (SIL)
c/o Denise L. Johnson, 5020 Swepsonville-Saxapahaw Road, Graham NC 27253 USA
Tel: 336-376-9362; *Fax:* 336-376-8825
www.limnology.org
Previous Name: International Association of Theoretical and Applied Limnology; Societas Internationalis Limnologiae, SIL
Overview: A medium-sized international organization founded in 1922
Mission: To promote communication between limnologists of all countries & all disciplines to increase understanding of inland aquatic ecosystems & their management.
Affiliation(s): Canadian Society of Limnology
Membership: *Fees:* Schedule available; *Member Profile:* Open to those with an interest in limnology, the study of inland water ecosystems (rivers, lakes, streams, reservoirs, fish ponds, aquifers, & bogs); Members have varied interests which include physics of water movements, water chemistry, plankton & water plants, invertebrate ecology, fish & fisheries, watershed & reservoir management, pollution of inland waters, & modelling of aquatic ecosystems; *Committees:* Baldi Memorial; International; Kilham Memorial; Naumann-Thienemann Medal; Nominating; Publication Advisory; Awards; Executive; Regions & Meetings Countries
Chief Officer(s):
Yves Prairie, President, (Canada)
prairie.yves@uqam.ca
Tamar Zohary, General Secretary-Treasurer, (Israel)
tamarz@ocean.org.il

International Society of Physical & Rehabilitation Medicine (ISPRM)
7, rue François-Versonnex, Geneva 1207 Switzerland
Tel: 41-22-908-04-83; *Fax:* 41-22-732-26-07
www.isprm.org
twitter.com/ISPRM
Previous Name: International Federation of Physical Medicine & Rehabilitation
Overview: A medium-sized international organization founded in 1999
Mission: To work with practitioners to improve the quality of life of people with impairments & disabilities
Member of: World Health Organization
Membership: *Fees:* 35 Euros; *Member Profile:* Practitioners of physical & rehabilitation medicine; *Committees:* Audit & Finance; Awards; Congress; Education; International Exchange; Publication; Rehabilitation Disaster Relief; ISPRM - WHO Liaison; Nominating; Sponsorship; Statutes; International Education and Development Fund; Clinical Sciences; Assembly of Individual Members Election
Activities: Improving the knowledge, skills, & attitudes of physicians in understanding impairments & disabilities; Facilitating rehabilitation medicine input to international health organizations; Influencing rehabilitation policies & activities; Facilitating research activities
Chief Officer(s):
Lorraine de Montmollin, Executive Director
isprmoffice@kenes.com
Jianan Li, President
presidentjiananli@isprm.org
Francesca Gimigliano, Secretary
secretary@isprm.org
John Olver, Treasurer
treasurer@isprm.org
Publications:
• International Society of Physical & Rehabilitation Medicine Congress Abstracts
• The Journal of Rehabilitation Medicine
Type: Journal; *Frequency:* 8 pa; *Editor:* Professor Gunnar Grimby
Profile: International peer-review scientific journal of original articles, reviews, case reports, brief communications, special reports, letters to the editor, &editorials
• News & Views [a publication of the International Society of Physical & Rehabilitation Medicine]
Type: Newsletter; *Frequency:* Monthly; *Editor:* Nicholas Christodoulou

International Society of Radiographers & Radiological Technologists (ISRRT)
143 Bryn Pinwydden, Cardiff CF23 7DG Wales
Tel: 44-(0)-29-20735038; *Fax:* 44-(0)-29-540551
www.isrrt.org
Overview: A large international charitable organization founded in 1959
Mission: To advance radiation medicine technology through international communication & sponsorship of professional activities
Affiliation(s): World Health Organization; United Nations
Finances: *Annual Operating Budget:* $100,000-$250,000; *Funding Sources:* Membership fees; donations; conferences
Staff Member(s): 5; 30 volunteer(s)
Membership: 75 countries; 350,000 radiographers; *Fees:* Schedule available; *Member Profile:* National radiation medicine technology societies; associate - individuals who support objectives
Activities: *Awareness Events:* World Radiography Day, Nov.
Meetings/Conferences:
• 20th [International Society of Radiographers & Radiological Technologists] ISRRT World Congress, 2018
Scope: International

International Society of Soil Science *See* International Union of Soil Sciences

International Society of Surgery (ISS) / La Société internationale de Chirurgie (SIC)
c/o Allveco AG, Seltisbergerstrasse 16, Lupsingen CH-4419 Switzerland
Tel: 41-61-815-9666; *Fax:* 41-61-811-4775
surgery@iss-sic.ch
www.iss-sic.ch
www.facebook.com/iss.sic
Overview: A medium-sized international organization founded in 1902
Mission: To contribute to the advancement of the science & art of surgery by researching & discussing surgical problems, through congresses, courses, & publications
Finances: *Funding Sources:* Membership dues; Congress
Membership: 1,000-4,999; *Fees:* 145 Euro regular; 72.50 Euro members 40 or younger or in surgical training; *Member Profile:* Medical doctors who have received training in a field of surgery & are or have been engaged in a career involving a recognized field of surgery; Non-medical scientists involved in medical research related to surgery; *Committees:* Executive; Nominating; Program
Activities: *Awareness Events:* International Surgical Week, Sept.
Chief Officer(s):
Jean-Claude Givel, Secretary General
givel@cabchirvisc.ch
Victor Bertschi, Administrative Director
victor.bertschi@iss-sic.ch
Awards:
• ISS/SIC Prize
• Robert Danis Prize
• René Leriche Prize
• ISS/SIC Honorary Membership
Publications:
• International Society of Surgery Newsletter
Type: Newsletter; *Frequency:* Semiannually
• World Journal of Surgery: The Official Journal of the International Society of Surgery/Société Internationale de Chirurgie
Type: Journal; *Editor:* John G. Hunter, M.D.; *ISSN:* 0364-2313
Profile: Authoritative scientific reports in the fields of clinical &experimental surgery, surgical education, & socioeconomic aspects of surgical care

International Sociological Association (ISA)
Faculty of Political Science & Sociology, University Complutense, Madrid 28223 Spain
Tel: 34-913-527-650; *Fax:* 34-913-524-945
isa@isa-sociology.org
www.isa-sociology.org
www.facebook.com/180226035354843
twitter.com/isa_sociology
www.youtube.com/user/isasociotube
Overview: A small international organization founded in 1949
Mission: To represent sociologists; to advance sociological knowledge
Member of: International Social Science Council
Membership: 5,000; *Fees:* Schedule available; *Committees:* Executive; Research Coordinating; National Associations Liaison; Programme; Publications; Finance & Membership; Research
Chief Officer(s):
Michel Burawoy, President
Izabela Barlinska, Executive Secretary

International Soil Reference & Information Centre (ISRIC)
PO Box 353, #101, Droevendaalsesteeg 3, Wageningen 6700 AJ Netherlands
Tel: 31-317-483-735
soil.isric@wur.nl
www.isric.org
Overview: A small international organization founded in 1966
Mission: To contribute to the challenge of providing sufficient food for the growing world populations while preserving the biophysical potential of natural resources & minimizing environmental degradation
Member of: World Data Centres of International Council of Sciences; World Data Centre for Soils
Affiliation(s): Wageningen University & Research Centre
Finances: *Annual Operating Budget:* $500,000-$1.5 Million; *Funding Sources:* Dutch government, international/bilateral project donor organizations
Staff Member(s): 25
Membership: 1-99
Activities: *Library* Open to public by appointment
Chief Officer(s):
Ir P.S. Bindraban, Director
Prem.Bindraban@wur.nl

International Solar Energy Society (ISES)
International Headquarters, Villa Tannheim, Wiesentalstrasse 50, Freiburg 79115 Germany
Tel: 49-761-459-06-0; *Fax:* 49-761-459-06-99
hq@ises.org
www.ises.org
www.linkedin.com/company/international-solar-energy-society
www.facebook.com/InternationalSolarEnergySociety
twitter.com/ISES_Solar
www.instagram.com/ises_solar
Overview: A medium-sized international charitable organization founded in 1954

Foreign Associations / International Solid Waste Association (ISWA)

Mission: To promote sustainable development, research & the use of renewable energy, with solar energy being the primary focus
Member of: International Renewable Energy Alliance
Staff Member(s): 8
Membership: 4,000; *Fees:* Schedule available; *Member Profile:* Individuals engaged in the research, development & utilisation of solar energy
Activities: International congresses on solar energy
Chief Officer(s):
David Renné, President
Awards:
• Achievement through Action Award
Monetary, biennial; awarded to an individual, a group, or corporate body that has made an important contribution to the harnessing of solar energy for practical use or is proposing a new concept, development or product for the same purpose
• Farrington Daniels Award
Recognition for outstanding intellectual leadership in the field of solar energy
• Special Service Award
• Global Leadership Award
• Karl W. Böer Solar Energy Award
• Solar Energy Journal Best Paper Award
Meetings/Conferences:
• International Solar Energy Society (ISES) EuroSun 2018, September, 2018, Rapperswil
Scope: International
• International Solar Energy Society (ISES) Solar World Congress 2019, 2019
Scope: International
Publications:
• International Solar Energy Society Newsletter
Type: Newsletter; *Frequency:* Monthly; *Price:* Free with ISES membership
Profile: Current association news
• Renewable Energy Focus [a publication of the International Solar Energy Society]
Type: Magazine; *Price:* Free with ISES membership
Profile: Editorials & news updates on all areas of renewable energy
• Solar Energy [a publication of the International Solar Energy Society]
Type: Journal; *Frequency:* Monthly; *Editor:* David Hopwood
Profile: Information on research & development in the utilization of solar energy

International Solid Waste Association (ISWA)
Auerspergstrasse 15, Top 41, Vienna 1080 Austria
Tel: +43 1 253 6001; *Fax:* +43 1 523 6001 99
iswa@iswa.org
www.iswa.org
www.linkedin.com/company/iswa-international-solid-waste-association
www.facebook.com/ISWA.org
twitter.com/ISWA_org
Overview: A medium-sized international organization founded in 1931
Mission: To promote & develop sustainable & professional waste management worldwide
Finances: *Funding Sources:* Sponsorships
Membership: *Member Profile:* Non-profit waste management associations representing the waste management industry in a particular country; Organizations or companies associated with or working in the field of waste management
Activities: Promoting professionalism; Supporting developing countries
Chief Officer(s):
Antonis Mavropoulos, President, Greece
Carlos Silva Filho, Vice President, Brazil
Weine Wiqvist, Treasurer, Sweden
Bettina Kamuk, Scientific & Technical Committee Chair, Denmark
Derek Greedy, Landfill Expert, United Kingdom
Awards:
• Communication Award
• Publication Award
• Video Award
Publications:
• Global News [a publication of the International Solid Waste Association]
Type: Newsletter
Profile: Contents include news from the association president, conference information, awards, news from around the world, & forthcoming events

• International Solid Waste Association Conference Proceedings
Type: Yearbook; *Frequency:* Annually
Profile: Information from the International Solid Waste Association Annual Congress, the Beacon Conference, & other conferences organized by the association
• International Solid Waste Association Annual Report
Type: Yearbook; *Frequency:* Annually
• Waste Management & Research
Type: Journal; *Frequency:* Monthly; *Editor:* Jens Aage Hansen
Profile: The theory & practice of waste management & research
• Waste Management World
Type: Magazine; *Frequency:* Bimonthly; *Accepts Advertising*; *Editor:* Tom Freyberg
Profile: Incorporates the International Directory of Solid Waste Management, with a listing of ISWA members & waste management companies

International Statistical Institute (ISI) / L'Institut International de Statistique
PO Box 24070, The Hague 2490 AB Netherlands
Tel: 31-70-337-5737; *Fax:* 31-70-3860025
isi-web.org
www.facebook.com/435104499838038
twitter.com/IntStat
Overview: A medium-sized international licensing charitable organization founded in 1885
Mission: Seeks to develop & improve statistical methods & their application through the promotion of international activity & co-operation
Affiliation(s): International Association of Survey Statisticians; Bernoulli Society; International Association for Statistical Computing; International Association for Official Statistics; International Association for Statistical Education; International Society for Business & Industrial Statistics; The International Environmetrics Society
Finances: *Annual Operating Budget:* $500,000-$1.5 Million; *Funding Sources:* Membership fees
Staff Member(s): 9; 2 volunteer(s)
Membership: 2,000 ISI; 3,000 in specialised sections; *Fees:* Schedule available; *Member Profile:* Honorary - elected from the ranks of ordinary members in recognition of their contributions to statistics merit special honour; Elected - elected by virtue of their distinguished contributions to the development or application of statistical methods; ex officio - occupants of certain positions in official national statistical agencies & international organizations designated by the Council or are the representatives of organizations affiliated with the Institute; corporate - national & international statistical agencies to certain cultural, educational, & scientific institutions, & to commercial, industrial & business enterprises which share or support the aims of the Institute; *Committees:* Numerous
Activities: Project implementation; cooperation with the UN; technical advice & assistance; project funding; training; conferences; publications; *Rents Mailing List:* Yes; *Library:* by appointment
Chief Officer(s):
Vijayan N. Nair, President
Ada van Krimpen, Director

International Student Pugwash (ISP)
c/o Student Pugwash USA, USA
e-mail: spusa@spusa.org
www.spusa.org
www.facebook.com/StudentPugwash
twitter.com/StudentPugwash
www.youtube.com/StudentPugwashUSA
Overview: A medium-sized international organization founded in 1979
Mission: To build a committment among young people to integrate social concerns into their academic, professional & personal lives; To educate young people on the relevance of science & technology to their own lives & its ability to shape the future of the global community
Affiliation(s): Science for Peace International
Finances: *Annual Operating Budget:* $100,000-$250,000
Staff Member(s): 5; 3 volunteer(s)
Membership: 50 chapters in the US; 15 chapters abroad
Activities: International & National Conferences; Chapter Program (at over 120 colleges, universities & high schools); New Careers Program; PUGWASHinton Seminars; *Internships:* Yes; *Rents Mailing List:* Yes
Chief Officer(s):
Rachel Svetanoff, Vice-President

International Telecommunications Society (ITS)
c/o Bohdan (Don) Romaniuk, ITS Secretariat, 416 Wilverside Way SE, Calgary AB T2J 1Z7
e-mail: secretariat@itsworld.org
www.itsworld.org
Overview: A medium-sized international organization
Mission: To research & analyze issues related to the emergence of a global information society
Membership: 400; *Fees:* US$125 individual; US$6,000 corporate global; US$3,000 corporate international; US$1,500 corporate societal; US$500-1,000 government/not-for-profit; *Member Profile:* Professionals from the communications, technology & information sectors; *Committees:* Strategic Planning; Conference & Seminars; Publications; Membership & Nominations; Finance; Marketing & Promotions; Web Development
Activities: Organizing courses, seminars & workshops; Disseminating research results & news to members & the public
Chief Officer(s):
Bohdan (Don) Romaniuk, ITS Secretariat
secretariat@itsworld.org
Publications:
• Interconnect [a publication of the International Telecommunications Society]
Type: Newsletter; *Editor:* Don Romaniuk
Profile: Member profiles, conference information, committee reports, & society news

International Tennis Federation (ITF)
Bank Lane, Roehampton, London SW15 5XZ United Kingdom
Tel: 44-20-8878-6464; *Fax:* 44-20-8878-7799
www.itftennis.com
www.facebook.com/InternationalTennisFederation
twitter.com/ITF_Tennis
www.youtube.com/OfficialITFTennis
Overview: A medium-sized international organization founded in 1913
Affiliation(s): Tennis Canada
Staff Member(s): 53
Membership: 205 nations; *Fees:* Schedule available
Activities: Grand Slam tennis events; Davis Cup; Grand Slam Cup
Chief Officer(s):
Francesco Ricci Bitti, President
Juan Margets, Executive Vice-President

International Textile Manufacturers Federation (ITMF) / Fédération internationale des industries textiles
Wiedingstrasse 9, Zurich CH-8055 Switzerland
Tel: 41-44-283-6380; *Fax:* 41-44-283-6389
secretariat@itmf.org
www.itmf.org
Overview: A medium-sized international organization founded in 1904
Mission: To provide a neutral forum for the textile industries of the world; to act as clearinghouse of ideas, information & experience; to act as the spokesman for the industry in matters relating to raw materials (cotton & man-made fibres); to provide a safeguard for the interests of the textile industry in world affairs; to maintain official liaison status with various intergovernmental organizations; also enjoys consultative status with the Economic & Social Council of the United Nations; maintains permanent liaison with private national & international textile & fibre organizations
Affiliation(s): Food & Agriculture Organization; WTO; International Cotton Advisory Committee; International Labour Organization; the Organization for Economic Cooperation & Development; United Nations Industrial Development Organization; the World Bank
Finances: *Funding Sources:* Membership fees
Staff Member(s): 1
Membership: 17 members; 14 associates; 35 corporate; *Member Profile:* Full - associations & other trade organizations of manufacturers of textiles; Associate - organizations allied to textile industry; the Federation's members are not the individual textile enterprises, but the trade associations in the countries concerned; corporate membership possible since 2000; *Committees:* Joint Cotton; Management; Spinners; Statistical; Home Textile Producers; Cotton Testing Methods; Man-Made Fibres
Chief Officer(s):
Christian P. Schindler, Director General
Josué C. Gomes da Silva, President

International Titanium Association (ITA)
#100, 11674 Huron St., Northglenn CO 80234 USA
Tel: 303-404-2221; Fax: 303-404-9111
ita@titanium.org
www.titanium.org
Overview: A large international organization founded in 1984
Mission: To connect the public with titanium specialists throughout the world, who can offer technical & sales assistance
Staff Member(s): 4
Membership: 200 companies; 1,500 individuals; Fees: Schedule available based on previous year's shipments (producers), receipts (users & consumers); $500-$4,500 non-voting; Committees: Education; Safety; Conference Planning; Trade Show; Achievement Award; Grant; Applications
Activities: Offering titanium literature; Sponsoring educational workshops & seminars
Chief Officer(s):
Jennifer Simpson, Executive Director
jsimpson@titanium.org
Chris Slager, Representative, Titanium Resource Center, 727-329-4416
Awards:
• Titanium Achievement Award
• Ti Applications Development Award
Meetings/Conferences:
• Titanium Asia 2018, February, 2018, Grand Hyatt Singapore, Singapore
Scope: International
• Titanium USA 2018, October, 2018, Bellagio Las Vegas, Las Vegas, NV
Scope: International
Publications:
• Titanium Update Newsletter
Type: Newsletter; Price: Free
Profile: Titanium news, awards, & membership information

International Touring Alliance See Alliance internationale de tourisme

International Trade Centre (ITC) / Centre du Commerce International (CCI)
Palais des Nations, 54-56 Rue de Montbrillant, Geneva CH-1211 Switzerland
Tel: 41-22-730-0111; Fax: 41-22-733-4439
itcreg@intracen.org
www.intracen.org
Overview: A small international organization founded in 1964
Mission: Trade promotion for developing countries
Affiliation(s): Joint subsidiary organ of WTO & the United Nations
Finances: Funding Sources: United Nations organization
Staff Member(s): 30
Activities: Institutional infrastructure for trade promotion & export development; product & market research, development & promotion; import operations & techniques; human resource development for trade promotion
Chief Officer(s):
Patricia Francis, Executive Director

International Trade Union Confederation (ITUC)
5 Boul du Roi Albert II, Bte 1, Brussels B-1210 Belgium
Tel: 32 (0)2 224 0211; Fax: 32 (0)2 201 5815
info@ituc-csi.org
www.ituc-csi.org
www.facebook.com/ituccsi/
twitter.com/ituc
www.youtube.com/ituccsi
Previous Name: World Confederation of Labour
Overview: A large international organization founded in 1920
Mission: To promote & defend workers' rights & interests, through international cooperation between trade unions, global campaigning & advocacy within the major global institutions
Member of: International Labour Organization
Staff Member(s): 40
Membership: Affiliates in 155 countries & territories; Fees: Schedule available
Activities: Speaker Service: Yes; Library: Documentation Service; by appointment
Chief Officer(s):
Sharan Burrow, General Secretary
Joao Antonio Felicio, President

International Trademark Association (INTA)
655 Third Ave., 10th Fl., New York NY 10017-5617 USA
Tel: 212-642-1700; Fax: 212-768-7796
memberservices@inta.org
www.inta.org
www.linkedin.com/company/international-trademark-association-inta-
www.facebook.com/GoINTA
twitter.com/INTA
Previous Name: U.S. Trademark Association
Overview: A large international organization founded in 1878
Mission: To represent trademark owners & professionals that support trademarks & intellectual property; To protect consumers & promote fair commerce
Finances: Annual Operating Budget: $3 Million-$5 Million; Funding Sources: Membership dues; publications; seminars, forums & other meetings
Staff Member(s): 28
Membership: 3,500; Fees: Schedule available; Member Profile: Trademark owner or supplier; Committees: Brief Amicus; Trademark Management; Education; Communications; Finance; Forums; International: Management; Membership; Nominating; Planning; Publications; US Legislation; Information Resources ADR; Industry Advisory Council; Public Relations
Activities: Advocating on behalf of its membership; Speaker Service: Yes; Library: Open to public by appointment
Chief Officer(s):
Etienne Sanz de Acedo, Chief Executive Officer
Ronald van Tuijl, President
Randi Mustello, Chief Governance Officer
Lisa Paulen, Chief Operations Officer
Meetings/Conferences:
• The International Trademark Association 140th Annual Meeting 2018, May, 2018, Seattle, WA
Scope: International
Attendance: 9,500+
Contact Information: E-mail: meetings@inta.org

International Union Against Cancer (IUAC) / Union internationale contre le cancer (UICC)
62, rte de Frontenex, Geneva 1207 Switzerland
Tel: 41-22-809-1811; Fax: 41-22-809-1810
info@uicc.org
www.uicc.org
Overview: A small international organization founded in 1933
Mission: To advance scientific & medical knowledge in research, diagnosis, treatment & prevention of cancer; To promote all other aspects of the campaign against cancer throughout the world, with emphasis on professional & public education
Affiliation(s): Canadian Cancer Society
Finances: Annual Operating Budget: $3 Million-$5 Million; Funding Sources: Membership dues; national subscription; foundations; corporations; individuals
Staff Member(s): 20
Membership: 300+; Fees: Schedule available; Member Profile: Voluntary organizations; cancer leagues & societies, cancer research &/or treatment centres & institutes; cancer patient associations &, in some countries Ministries of Health
Activities: Extensive fellowships programme; international symposia; training courses; advisory visits; capacity building; tobacco control; prevention & early detection; knowledge transfer; Awareness Events: UICC International No Smoking Days; World Cancer Day (February 4th); Library
Chief Officer(s):
Sanchia Aranda, President
Cary Adams, Chief Executive Officer
Awards:
• Reach to Recovery International Theresa Lasser Award
• Reach to Recovery International Medal

International Union for Conservation of Nature (IUCN)
28, rue Mauverney, Gland 1196 Switzerland
Tel: 41-22-999-0000; Fax: 41-22-999-0002
Other Communication: www.flickr.com/photos/iucnweb
mail@iucn.org
www.iucn.org
www.facebook.com/iucn.org
twitter.com/IUCN
www.youtube.com/user/IUCN
Previous Name: The World Conservation Union; International Union for Conservation of Nature & Natural Resources
Overview: A large international organization founded in 1948
Mission: To find solutions to environment & development challenges; To conserve the integrity & diversity of nature; To ensure the use of natural resources is equitable & ecologically sustainable
Finances: Funding Sources: Member organizations; Governments; Foundations; Bilateral & multilateral agencies; Corporations
Staff Member(s): 1000
Membership: 1,300+ government organizations & NGOs + 11,000 volunteer scientist from over 160 countries; Member Profile: Government organizations; NGOs; Volunteer scientists
Activities: Supporting scientific research; Managing field projects; Coordinatingpersons & organization to develop & implement policies, laws, & best practices; Publishing over 100 books, reports, documents, & guidelines each year
Chief Officer(s):
Zhang Xinsheng, President
president@iucn.org
Patrick de Henry, Treasurer
Inger Andersen, Director General
Awards:
• John C. Phillips Memorial Medal
To recognize outstanding service in international conservation
• Harold Jefferson Coolidge Memorial Medal
To recognize the outstanding conservation contributions of one conservation professional
• Honorary membership of IUCN
To recognize the outstanding contributions of two or three individuals to furthering the goals of the IUCN
Publications:
• Arborvitae [a publication of the International Union for Conservation of Nature]
Type: Newsletter; Frequency: 3 pa
Profile: Issues affecting how forest resources are used & governed
• Building Bridges [a publication of the International Union for Conservation of Nature]
Type: Newsletter; Frequency: Quarterly
Profile: Newsletter on conservation & the private sector from the Global Business & Biodiversity Programme.
• CEC Newsletter [a publication of the International Union for Conservation of Nature]
Type: Newsletter; Frequency: Monthly
Profile: Newsletter from the Commission on Education & Communication
• European Newsletter [a publication of the International Union for Conservation of Nature]
Type: Newsletter; Frequency: q.
Profile: Provides updates on IUCN's work in Europe
• Off the Shelf [a publication of the International Union for Conservation of Nature]
Type: Newsletter; Frequency: Monthly
Profile: International Union for Conservation of Nature's latest & most notable publications

International Union of Academies Voir Union académique internationale

International Union of Anthropological & Ethnological Sciences (IUAES) / Union internationale des sciences anthropologiques et ethnologiques
1-2 Yamadaoka, Suita, Osaka 565-0871 Japan
Tel: 81-06-6879-8085
iuaes@glocol.osaka-u.ac.jp
www.iuaes.org
Overview: A small international organization founded in 1948
Mission: To develop international scientific & professional cooperation in the fields of anthropology & ethnology; to foster the development of scientific & professional institutions internationally & regionally; to stimulate scientific & professional cooperation among institutions devoted to the relevant fields of knowledge; to develop appropriate roles for anthropology & ethnology in international inter-disciplinary scientific endeavours
Affiliation(s): International Council for Philosophy & Humanistic Studies; International Social Science Council; International Council of Scientific Unions; International Council of Museums
Finances: Funding Sources: Membership fees; ISSC subvention
Membership: 200; Fees: US$50 institutes (first time); US$35 institutes (continuing)
Chief Officer(s):
Peter J.M. Nas, President
Junji Koizumi, Secretary General

International Union of Architects Voir Union internationale des architectes

International Union of Basic & Clinical Pharmacology (IUPHAR)
c/o Dr. S.J. Enna, University of Kansas Medical Center, PO Box 4016, 3901 Rainbow Blvd., Kansas City KS 66160 USA
Tel: 913-588-7533; Fax: 913-588-7373
admin@iuphar.org
www.iuphar.org
Previous Name: International Union of Pharmacology
Overview: A large international organization founded in 1959
Mission: To foster international cooperation in pharmacology by promoting cooperation between societies representing pharmacology & related disciplines throughout the world; To sponsor international & regional congresses & meetings; To encourage international cooperation & free exchange of scientists & of ideas in research; To act as a body through which pharmacologists can participate with scientists from other disciplines; To promote programmes of public awareness on pharmacological issues
Finances: Funding Sources: National Pharmacological Societies; benefactors
Membership: Member Profile: Academic & industrial pharmacologists; Committees: Executive; Nominating; Membership; Past Executives
Chief Officer(s):
S.J. Enna, President
Michael Spedding, Secretary-General
Awards:
• Young Investigator Awards
Publications:
• Pharmacology International
Type: Newsletter; Frequency: Biannually

International Union of Biological Sciences (IUBS) / Union internationale des sciences biologiques
Secretariat, Bat 442 Université Paris-Sud 11, Orsay cedex, Paris 91405 France
Tel: 33-1-69-15-50-27; Fax: 33-1-69-15-79-47
secretariat@iubs.org
www.iubs.org
twitter.com/IUBS_bio
Overview: A medium-sized international charitable organization founded in 1919
Mission: To promote the study of biological sciences; To initiate, facilitate & coordinate research & other scientific activities that require international cooperation; To ensure the discussion & dissemination of the results of cooperative research; To promote the organization of international conferences & to assist in the publication of their reports
Staff Member(s): 2
Membership: 31 ordinary + 96 scientific (associations, societies or commissions); Fees: Schedule available; Member Profile: National science academies; International scientific organizations
Activities: Speaker Service: Yes
Chief Officer(s):
Nathalie Fomproix, Executive Director
Publications:
• Biology International [a publication of the International Union of Biological Sciences]
Type: Journal; Frequency: Quarterly

International Union of Bricklayers & Allied Craftworkers (AFL-CIO/CFL) (BAC) / Union internationale des briqueteurs et métiers connexes (FAT-COI/FCT)
620 F St. NW, Washington DC 20004 USA
Tel: 202-783-3788
Toll-Free: 888-880-8222
askbac@bacweb.org
www.bacweb.org
www.facebook.com/IUBAC
twitter.com/IUBAC
www.youtube.com/user/BACInternational
Overview: A small international organization founded in 1865
Mission: To improve the quality of life of their members
Chief Officer(s):
James Boland, President

Canadian Office (BAC Canada)
141 Laurier Ave. West, #A, Ottawa ON K1P 5J3
Tel: 613-233-7920
Toll-Free: 877-276-7771
www.bacweb.org/canada/index.php
Mission: To improve their members' quality of life- on and off the job- through access to fair wages, good benefits, safe working conditions, and solidarity among members.
Chief Officer(s):
Oliver Swan, Co-Chair, Canadian Congress
James Boland, Co-Chair, Canadian Congress

International Union of Crystallography (ICUr)
c/o Executive Secretariat, 2 Abbey Sq., Chester CH1 2HU United Kingdom
Tel: 44 1244 345431; Fax: 44 1244 344843
execsec@iucr.org
www.iucr.org
Overview: A small international organization founded in 1947
Mission: To promote international cooperation in crystallography; To contribute to all aspects of crystallography; To standardize methods, symbols, nomenclatures, & units
Membership: Member Profile: Adhering bodies, such as the Canadian National Committee for Crystallography; Regional associates, such as the American Crystallographic Association; Scientific associates such as the International Organization of Crystal Growth; Other bodies whose interests overlap with the aims & activities of the union, such as the International Council for Science; Committees: Aperiodic Crystals; Biological Macromolecules; Charge, Spin & Momentum Densities; Crystal Growth & Characterization of Materials; Crystallographic Computing; Crystallographic Nomenclature; Crystallographic Teaching; Crystallography in Art & Cultural Heritage; Electron Crystallography; High Pressure; Inorganic & Mineral Structures; International Tables; Journals; Mathematical & Theoretical Crystallography; Neutron Scattering; Powder Diffraction; Small-Angle Scattering; Structural Chemistry; Synchrotron Radiation; XAFS
Activities: Encouraging publication of crystallographic research throughout the world
Meetings/Conferences:
• International Union of Crystallography 25th Triennial Congress & General Assembly, August, 2020, Prague Congress Centre, Prague
Scope: International
Publications:
• Biological Crystallography
Type: Journal
Profile: Research papers & short communications
• Crystal Structure Communications
Type: Journal
Profile: Organic, inorganic, & metal-organic compounds
• Foundations of Crystallography
Type: Journal
Profile: Research papers & book reviews
• Journal of Applied Crystallography
Type: Journal
Profile: Research papers, computer programs, laboratory notes, & meetings
• Journal of Synchrotron Radiation
Type: Journal
Profile: Facility information, research papers, short communications, current events & meetings
• Structural Biology & Crystallization Communications
Type: Journal
Profile: Structural communications
• Structural Science
Type: Journal
Profile: Research papers
• Structure Reports
Type: Journal
Profile: Organic, inorganic, & metal-organic compounds
• World Directory of Crystallographers
Type: Directory
Profile: Contact information & research interests

International Union of Elevator Constructors (IUEC) / Union internationale des constructeurs d'ascenseurs
7154 Columbia Gateway Dr., Columbia MD 21046 USA
Tel: 410-953-6150; Fax: 410-953-6169
iuechdq@aol.com
www.iuec.org
Overview: A medium-sized international organization founded in 1901
Finances: Funding Sources: Membership dues
Staff Member(s): 17
Membership: 25,000 members in the U.S. & Canada
Chief Officer(s):
Frank J. Christensen, General President
Larry McGann, General Secretary-Treasurer

Local 50 - Toronto (IUEC)
400 Westney Rd. South, Ajax ON L1S 6M6
Tel: 416-754-2424; Fax: 905-686-7355
www.iuec50.org
Chief Officer(s):
Terry Shannon, President

International Union of Forest Research Organizations (IUFRO) / Union internationale des instituts de recherches forestières
IUFRO Secretariat, Marxergasse 2, Vienna A-1140 Austria
Tel: 43-1-877-01-510; Fax: 43-1-877-01-5150
office@iufro.org
www.iufro.org
twitter.com/iufro
www.youtube.com/user/IUFRO
Overview: A medium-sized international organization founded in 1892
Mission: To promote international cooperation in scientific studies embracing the whole field of research related to forestry & forest products by facilitating exchanges of ideas, methods, data & results among researchers throughout the world
Membership: 15,000 scientists in 700 member organizations in 110 countries worldwide; Fees: Schedule available; Member Profile: Open to organizations conducting research related to forestry, including government agencies, universities, private institutions, natural resource associations; associate - individuals
Activities: Environmental change; forests in sustainable mountain development; internet resources; sustainable forest management; management & conservation of forest gene resources; water & forests; on-line reference library; Library: Open to public
Chief Officer(s):
Alexander Buck, Executive Director
buck@iufro.org
Niels Elers Koch, President, (Denmark)
nek@life.ku.dk
Awards:
• Student Award for Excellence in Forest Service
• Distinguished Service Award
• Honorary Membership
• Scientific Achievement Award
• Outstanding Doctoral Research Award

International Union of Geodesy & Geophysics (IUGG) / Union géodésique et géophysique internationale
Helmholtz Centre Potsdam, GFZ German Research Centre for Geosciences, Telegrafenberg, A17, Potsdam 14473 Germany
Fax: 49-331-288-1759
secretariat@iugg.org
www.iugg.org
www.facebook.com/InternationalUnionGeodesyGeophysics
Overview: A medium-sized international organization founded in 1919
Mission: To promote & coordinate studies of the Earth & its environment in space
Membership: 70 member countries; Member Profile: 8 member associations: International Assn of Cryospheric Sciences; International Assn of Geodesy; International Assn of Geomagnetism & Aeronomy; International Assn of Hydrological Sciences; International Assn of Meteorology & Atmospheric Sciences; International Assn of the Physical Sciences of the Ocean; International Assn of Seismology & Physics of the Earth's Interior; and International Assn of Volcanology & Chemistry of the Earth's Interior; Committees: Capacity Building & Education; Membership Issues; Honours & Recognition; Visioning; Nominating; Site Evaluation; Statutes & ByLaws; Resolution
Chief Officer(s):
Franz G. Kuglitsch, Secretariat
secretariat@iugg.org

International Union of Microbiological Societies
CBS Fungal Biodiversity Centre, PO Box 85167, Utrecht 3508AD Netherlands
Tel: 31-30-21-22-600; Fax: 31-30-251-2097
www.iums.org
Overview: A small international organization
Mission: To promote & support the international study of microbiological sciences
Affiliation(s): International Council of Scientific Unions
Membership: Member Profile: National & international societies & other organizations having a common interest in microbiological sciences
Chief Officer(s):
Robert A. Samson, Secretary General
r.samson@cbs.knaw.nl

Meetings/Conferences:
• International Union of Microbiological Societies 16th Congress, 2020, Daejon
Scope: International
Description: Meetings of the three divisions of the International Union of Microbiological Societies
• International Union of Microbiological Societies 17th Congress, 2023
Scope: International
Description: Meetings of the three divisions of the International Union of Microbiological Societies

International Union of Midwives *See* International Confederation of Midwives

International Union of Nutritional Sciences
c/o The Nutrition Society, 210 Shepherd's Bush Rd., London W6 7NJ London United Kingdom
e-mail: office@IUNS.org
www.iuns.org
Overview: A medium-sized international organization founded in 1946
Mission: To accomplish extensive international cooperation among scientists in nutrition-related research & education
Finances: *Funding Sources:* International Council of Scientific Unions; UNESCO; membership
Staff Member(s): 1; 5 volunteer(s)
Chief Officer(s):
Anna Lartey, President
aalartey@ug.edu.gh

International Union of Operating Engineers (AFL-CIO/CFL) / Union internationale des opérateurs de machines lourdes (FAT-COI/FCT)
1125 - 17 St. NW, Washington DC 20036 USA
Tel: 202-429-9100; *Fax:* 202-778-2613
www.iuoe.org
Overview: A small international organization
Membership: 400,000 + 138 locals
Chief Officer(s):
James T. Callahan, President

Local 772
Mount James Square, #401, 1030 Upper James St., Hamilton ON L9C 6X6
Tel: 905-527-5250; *Fax:* 905-527-6336
Toll-Free: 800-286-0422
iuoe772hamilton@shaw.ca
www.iuoe772.org
Mission: To serve members in Hamilton & Ottawa

International Union of Painters & Allied Trades (IUPAT) / Syndicat international des peintres et métiers connexes
7234 Parkway Dr., Hanover MD 21076 USA
Tel: 410-564-5900
mail@iupat.org
www.iupat.org
www.facebook.com/iupat
twitter.com/goiupat
www.youtube.com/GoIUPAT
Previous Name: International Brotherhood of Painters & Allied Trades (AFL-CIO/CFL)
Overview: A small international organization founded in 1887
Membership: 160,000; *Member Profile:* Active & retired members of the finishing trades industry
Chief Officer(s):
Kenneth E. Rigmaiden, President
Robert Kucheran, Vice-President

District Council 28 - British Columbia
7621 Kingsway, Burnaby BC V3N 3C7
Tel: 604-524-8334; *Fax:* 604-524-8011
Toll-Free: 800-866-1527
www.dc38.ca
www.facebook.com/IUPATdc38
twitter.com/DC38Trades
www.flickr.com/photos/dc38
Mission: District Council 38 includes the Painters' Union Local 138, the Glaziers' Union Local 1527, the Drywall Finishers' Union Local 2009, and the Lathers and Allied Trades Local 163. Offices in Burnaby, Victoria and Prince George
Chief Officer(s):
David Holmes, Business Manager & Secretary-Treasurer

International Union of Pharmacology *See* International Union of Basic & Clinical Pharmacology

International Union of Pure & Applied Chemistry (IUPAC)
IUPAC Secretariat, Bldg. 19, PO Box 13757, Research Triangle Park NC 27709-3757 USA
Fax: 919-485-8706
www.iupac.org
Overview: A small international organization founded in 1919
Mission: To advance the worldwide aspects of the chemical sciences & to contribute to the application of chemistry in the service of mankind
Member of: International Council of Scientific Unions
Affiliation(s): World Health Organization; UN Food & Agricultural Organization; United Nations Education, Scientific & Cultural Organization; International Organization for Standardization; Organization internationale de métrologie légale
Finances: *Annual Operating Budget:* $1.5 Million-$3 Million
Staff Member(s): 5; 1000 volunteer(s)
Membership: 49 National Adhering Organizations which represent the chemists of different member countries; *Fees:* Schedule available; *Member Profile:* Adhering organizations are the members of the Union & they may be a national chemical council, a national society representing chemistry, a national academy of science, or any institution or association of institutions representative of national chemical interests; *Committees:* Bureau; Chemical Research Applied to World Needs (CHEMRAWN); Chemistry & Industry; Chemistry Education; Publications & Cheminformatics Data Standards; Evaluation; Executive; Finance; Terminology, Nomenclature & Symbols; Project; Pure & Applied Chemistry Editorial Advisory
Chief Officer(s):
Lynn Soby, Executive Director, 919-485-8700
lsoby@iupac.org
Enid M. Weatherwax, Administrative Assistant, 919-485-8701
eweatherwax@iupac.org
Meetings/Conferences:
• International Union of Pure & Applied Chemistry 8th Annual Conference on Green Chemistry 2018, September, 2018, Bangkok
Scope: International
• International Union of Pure & Applied Chemistry 22nd Annual Conference on Organic Synthesis, September, 2018, Florence
Scope: International
• International Union of Pure & Applied Chemistry 47th World Chemistry Congress 2019, July, 2019, Palais des Congrès de Paris, Paris
Scope: International
Publications:
• Chemistry International [a publication of the International Union of Pure & Applied Chemistry]
Type: Magazine; *Frequency:* bi-m.; *Accepts Advertising*; *Editor:* Fabienne Meyers; *ISSN:* 1365-2192; *Price:* $110 USD fororganizations; $50 USD for individuals; free for IUPAC members
Profile: Contains news about IUPAC members, publications, & ongoing work
• Pure & Applied Chemistry [a publication of the International Union of Pure & Applied Chemistry]
Type: Journal; *Frequency:* Monthly; *ISSN:* 1365-3075; *Price:* $2279 USD for organizations; $374 for individuals
Profile: Publishes works arising from international scientific events & projects that are sponsored or undertakenby IUPAC

International Union of Societies for Biomaterials Science & Engineering (IUSBSE)
c/o Prof. Nicholas A. Peppas, The University of Texas at Austin, 1 University Station, #C-0400, Austin TX 78712-0231 USA
Tel: 512-471-6644; *Fax:* 512-471-8227
www.worldbiomaterials.org
Overview: A medium-sized international organization
Mission: To advance biomaterials, surgical implants, prosthetics, artificial organs, tissue engineering, & regenerative medicine
Membership: *Member Profile:* National & multi-national groups from Canada, the United States, the European Union, China, Japan, Korea, India, & Australia
Chief Officer(s):
Nicholas A. Peppas, President
peppas@che.utexas.edu
Meetings/Conferences:
• 11th World Biomaterials Congress, May, 2020, Glasgow
Scope: International

International Union of Soil Sciences (IUSS) / Union internationale de la science du sol
c/o University of Wisconsin, Department of Soil Science, 1525 Observatory Dr., Madison WI 53706-1299 USA
www.iuss.org
www.facebook.com/unionsoilsciences
Previous Name: International Society of Soil Science
Overview: A medium-sized international charitable organization founded in 1924
Mission: To promote soil science & give support to soil scientists
Member of: International Council of Scientific Unions
Affiliation(s): Canadian Society of Soil Science
Finances: *Funding Sources:* Membership fees
Membership: *Member Profile:* National soil science societies; *Committees:* Awards & Prizes; Budget & Finances; Statutues & Bylaws
Activities: *Rents Mailing List:* Yes; *Library*
Chief Officer(s):
Jae Yang, President, (Korea)
yangjay@kangwon.ac.kr
Aldred Hartemink, Secretary General
hartemink@wisc.edu

International Union of Theoretical & Applied Mechanics (IUTAM)
Institute of Fundamental Technological Research, Pawinskiego 5B, Warsaw 02-106 Poland
Tel: 48-22-826-9834
www.iutam.org
Overview: A large international organization founded in 1947
Mission: To carry out & promote scientific work in mechanics & related sciences
Finances: *Annual Operating Budget:* $250,000-$500,000; *Funding Sources:* Membership fees; grants
Membership: 450 members in 55 nations; *Member Profile:* National Committees of Mechanics; *Committees:* Congress; 2 Symposia - Panels
Activities: *Internships:* Yes; *Library:* Open to public
Chief Officer(s):
Nadine Aubry, President
Henryk Petryk, Secretary General
Publications:
• International Union of Theoretical & Applied Mechanics Newsletter
Type: Newsletter
• International Union of Theoretical & Applied Mechanics Annual Report
Type: Yearbook
• IUTAMM [International Union of Theoretical & Applied Mechanics] - A Short History
Type: Book; *Editor:* S. Juhasz; *ISBN:* 3-540-50043-X
• Mechanics at the Turn of the Century [a publication of the International Union of Theoretical & Applied Mechanics]
Type: Report; *Editor:* W. Schiehlen & L. van Wijngaarden; *ISBN:* 3-8265-7714-0

International Union, United Automobile, Aerospace & Agricultural Implement Workers of America (UAW) / Syndicat international des travailleurs unis de l'automobile, de l'aérospatiale et de l'outillage agricole d'Amérique
8000 East Jefferson Ave., Detroit MI 48214 USA
Tel: 313-926-5000
Toll-Free: 800-243-8829
www.uaw.org
www.facebook.com/uaw.union
twitter.com/uaw
www.youtube.com/uaw
Overview: A small international organization founded in 1935
Mission: To act as the collective bargaining body for its members, negotiating for wages & benefits.
Membership: 390,000 active members; 600,000 retired members; 750 locals
Chief Officer(s):
Dennis Williams, President
Gary Casteel, Sec.-Treas.

UAW Local 251 - Wallaceburg, ON
88 Elm Dr. South, Wallaceburg ON N8A 5E7
Tel: 519-627-1629; *Fax:* 519-627-2055
Toll-Free: 800-646-5437
local251@uaw.ca
www.canadianuaw.ca
Chief Officer(s):
Bill Pollock, President

International Vegetarian Union (IVU) / Union internationale végéterienne
Shropshire United Kingdom

e-mail: manager@ivu.org
www.ivu.org
www.facebook.com/InternationalVegUnion
Overview: A small international organization founded in 1908
Mission: To further vegetarianism worldwide by promoting knowledge of vegetarianism as a means of advancing the spiritual, moral, mental, physical & economic well-being of mankind; to promote research into all aspects of vegetarianism; to encourage the formation of vegetarian organizations & cooperation amongst them
Affiliation(s): Toronto Vegetarian Association
Membership: *Member Profile:* Vegetarian societies subscribing to the vegetarian ethic whose executive authority is vested exclusively in vegetarians; Associate - organization which is in sympathy with animal welfare, humanitarian, health or similar relevant objectives
Activities: *Speaker Service:* Yes
Chief Officer(s):
Dilip Barman, Regional Representative, North America

International Virtual Assistants Association
#400, 2360 Corporate Circle, Henderson NV 89074 USA
Toll-Free: 877-440-2750
www.ivaa.org
www.linkedin.com/groups?gid=695327&trk=myg_ugrp_ovr
www.facebook.com/IVAA.org
twitter.com/ivaa_org
www.youtube.com/user/IVAAVirtualAssistant
Overview: A small international organization
Mission: Dedicated to the professional education & development of members, & to educating the public on the role & function of the Virtual Assistant
Membership: *Member Profile:* Independent entrepreneur providing administrative, creative &/or technical services, utilizing advanced technological modes of communication & data delivery
Activities: Offers IVAA Certified Virtual Assistant (CVA) exam
Chief Officer(s):
Kathy Colaiacovo, President, 877-440-2750 Ext. 712
president@ivaa.org

International Volleyball Association / Fédération Internationale de Volleyball (FIVB)
Château Les Tourelles, Edouard-Sandoz 2-4, Lausanne 1006 Switzerland
Tel: 41-21-345-3535; *Fax:* 41-21-345-3545
info@fivb.org
www.fivb.ch
www.facebook.com/FIVB.InternationalVolleyballFederation
twitter.com/fivbvolleyball
www.youtube.com/videofivb; instagram.com/fivbvolleyball
Overview: A small international organization founded in 1947
Affiliation(s): Canadian Volleyball Association
Staff Member(s): 20
Membership: 211
Chief Officer(s):
Ary S. Graça Filho, President
president.office.sec@fivb.org
Fabio Azevedo, General Director

International Warehouse Logistics Association (IWLA)
#260, 2800 South River Rd., Des Plaines IL 60018 USA
Tel: 847-813-4699; *Fax:* 847-813-0175
email@iwla.com
www.iwla.com
Overview: A medium-sized international organization founded in 1997
Mission: To encourage, promote, & further the use of public warehousing & distribution services among potential existing users; to establish & enforce adherence to appropriate industry operating standards; to provide forum for members to meet, study & discuss problems & opportunities of common interest; to encourage a spirit of cooperation in the implementation of solutions & the pursuit of those opportunities; to make representations to governments at all levels & their regulatory agencies for benefit of the industry, members & their clients; to provide vehicle for industry-related educational services. The Canadian Council represents the interests of Canadian member companies & provides a forum to share resources & information about the Canadian warehousing & 3PL industry.
Finances: *Funding Sources:* Membership dues; interest; programs
Staff Member(s): 9
Membership: *Committees:* Canadian Council; Education Advisory; Executive; Government Affairs; Insurance & Legal Affairs; IWLA Convention & Expo Planning; Nominating; Partner Member; Political Action; Warehouse Membership
Activities: *Speaker Service:* Yes
Chief Officer(s):
Paul Verst, Chair
Steve DeHaan, President & CEO
sdehaan@IWLA.com
John Levi, Executive Director, Canadian Council
jlevi@primus.ca

International Water Association (IWA)
Alliance House, 12 Caxton St., London SW1H 0QS United Kingdom
Tel: 44-20-7654-5500; *Fax:* 44-20-7654-5555
water@iwahq.org
www.iwa-network.org
www.linkedin.com/company/international-water-association
www.facebook.com/InternationalWaterAssociation
twitter.com/IWAwaternews
vimeo.com/iwahq
Previous Name: International Association on Water Quality; International Association on Water Pollution Research & Control
Overview: A large international organization founded in 1999
Mission: To advance the science & practice of water management internationally
Finances: *Annual Operating Budget:* $250,000-$500,000
Staff Member(s): 20
Membership: 9,000; *Committees:* Executive; Finance & Investment; Renumeration; Program; Publications; Young Professionals
Activities: Wastewater treatment processes; hazardous wastes & source control; impacts of pollutants on receiving waters; environmental restoration
Chief Officer(s):
Diane D'Arras, President
Ger Bergkamp, Executive Director
ger.bergkamp@iwahq.org
Meetings/Conferences:
• International Water Association World Water Congress & Exhibition 2018, September, 2018, Tokyo
Scope: International
Description: Provides international water experts the change to explore the science & practice of water management
Publications:
• Hydrology Research [a publication of the International Water Association]
Type: Journal; *Editor:* Nevil Quinn & Chong-Yu Xu; *ISSN:* 0029-1277
Profile: Official journal of the Nordic Association for Hydrology, British Hydrological Society, German HydrologicalSociety, & Italian Hydrological Society
• Journal of Hydroinformatics [a publication of the International Water Association]
Type: Journal; *Editor:* Orazio Giustolisi; *ISSN:* 1464-7141
Profile: Devoted to the application of information technology to problems of the aquatic environment
• Journal of Water & Climate Change [a publication of the International Water Association]
Type: Journal; *Editor:* Fransje L. Hooimeijer
• Journal of Water & Health [a publication of the International Water Association]
Type: Journal; *Editor:* Paul R. Hunter; *ISSN:* 1477-8920
Profile: Promotes research into the challenges of harnessing water for health in developing & developed countries
• Journal of Water Reuse & Desalination [a publication of the International Water Association]
Type: Journal; *Frequency:* q.; *Editor:* Blanca Jiménez Cisneros; *ISSN:* 2220-1319
• Journal of Water Supply: Research & Technology - Aqua [a publication of the International Water Association]
Type: Journal; *Editor:* Rita Henderson; *ISSN:* 0003-7214
Profile: Research & development in water supply technology & management
• Journal of Water, Sanitation & Hygiene for Development [a publication of the International Water Association]
Type: Journal; *Editor:* Jamie Bartram; *ISSN:* 2043-9083
Profile: Science, policy & practice of drinking-water supply, sanitation & hygiene
• The Source [a publication of the International Water Association]
Type: Magazine; *Frequency:* 6 pa.; *Editor:* James Workman
Profile: Formerly Water21; official magazine of the International Water Association
• Water Asset Management International [a publication of the International Water Association]
Type: Newsletter; *ISSN:* 1814-5434
Profile: Asset management in water & wastewater utilities
• Water Policy [a publication of the International Water Association]
Type: Journal; *Editor:* Dr. Jerome Delli Priscoli
Profile: Official journal of the World Water Council
• Water Practice & Technology [a publication of the International Water Association]
Type: Journal; *Editor:* Wolfgang Rauch; *ISSN:* 1751-231X
Profile: Online journal under the control of the Water Science & Technology Editorial Board
• Water Quality Research Journal of Canada [a publication of the International Water Association]
Type: Journal; *Editor:* R. Droste & P. Vanrolleghem
• Water Science & Technology [a publication of the International Water Association]
Type: Journal; *Editor:* Wolfgang Rauch
• Water Science & Technology: Water Supply [a publication of the International Water Association]
Type: Journal; *Editor:* Wolfgang Rauch

International Whaling Commission (IWC)
The Red House, 135 Station Rd., Impington, Cambridge CB24 9NP United Kingdom
Tel: 44-1223-233-971; *Fax:* 44-1223-232-876
secretariat@iwcoffice.org
iwc.int
Overview: A medium-sized international organization founded in 1946
Mission: To keep under review & revise as necessary those measures which provide for the complete protection of certain species of whales; to designate specified areas as whale sanctuaries; to set limits on the maximum numbers of whales which may be taken in one season; to prescribe open & closed seasons & areas for whaling; to set limits on the size of whales that may be killed; to prohibit the capture of suckling calves & female whales accompanied by calves; to encourage, coordinate & fund whale research; to publish results of research & other scientific research; to promote studies into related matters. Canada is not currently a member.
Membership: 89 whaling governments; *Member Profile:* Open to any country in the world that formally adheres to the 1946 Convention; *Committees:* Scientific; Finance & Administration; Conservation; Aboriginal Subsistence Whaling; Infractions; Working Group on Whale Killing Methods & Associated Welfare Issues
Activities: *Speaker Service:* Yes; *Library:* Open to public by appointment
Chief Officer(s):
Simon Brockington, Secretariat
secretariat@iwc.int

International Wildlife Rehabilitation Council (IWRC)
PO Box 3197, Eugene OR 97403 USA
Tel: 866-871-1869
Toll-Free: 866-871-1869
info@iwrc-online.org
www.iwrc-online.org
www.linkedin.com/companies/the-international-wildlife-rehabilitation-council-iwrc
www.facebook.com/theiwrc
twitter.com/theiwrc
Overview: A small international charitable organization founded in 1972
Mission: To further knowledge & experience in the field of wildlife rehabilitation, through education, networking, & professional standards of review; to preserve our wildlife & its habitat
Finances: *Annual Operating Budget:* $250,000-$500,000; *Funding Sources:* Membership dues; course fees; private donations; sales of literature; annual conference
Staff Member(s): 3; 12 volunteer(s)
Membership: 1,850; *Fees:* $49 individual; $59 family; $75 organization; $32 library; *Member Profile:* Individual - persons actively working in the field of wildlife rehabilitation in administration, conservation, management, education, research, humane work, or veterinary or allied professional residing in practice; Family - two or more active rehabilitators residing at the same address; Organizational/Institutional - non-profit corporations or public agencies affiliated with a branch of local, state, or federal government actively supporting or operating wildlife rehabilitation programs; Affiliate/Corporate - small & large businesses or foundations that are not actively involved in wildlife rehabilitation but wish to provide financial support for IWRC programs; Library/Agency: Accredited library or government, state, provincial agency

Activities: Nationwide certification program which includes a series of hands-on training seminars in state-of-the-art wildlife rehabilitation techniques, from beginner through advanced levels
Chief Officer(s):
Kai Williams, Executive Director
director@theiwrc.org

International Wine & Food Society (IWFS)
The Naval & Military Club, 4 St James's Square, London SW1J 4JU United Kingdom
Tel: 44-20-7827-5732; *Fax:* 44-20-7827-5733
sec@iwfs.org
www.iwfs.org
Overview: A medium-sized international organization founded in 1933
Mission: To bring together & serve all who believe that a right understanding of good food & wine is an essential part of personal contentment & health, & that an intelligent approach to the pleasures & problems of the table offers far greater rewards than the mere satisfaction of appetite
Membership: 6,000+ members in 130 branches; *Committees:* Wines; European & African; Asian Pacific Zone; Board of Governors of the Americas
Activities: *Library:* Guildhall Library; Open to public by appointment
Chief Officer(s):
David R. Felton, Chair
  Edmonton Branch
  Edmonton AB
  www.iwfs.org/americas/edmonton
  Chief Officer(s):
  Bruce Ambrose, President
  Kitchener-Waterloo Branch
  Waterloo ON
  www.rjengineering.com/iwfs
  Montréal Branch
  Montréal QC
  www.iwfs.org/americas/montreal
  Chief Officer(s):
  Mark Lazar, President
  Niagara Branch
  St Catharines ON
  Oakville Branch
  Oakville ON
  Chief Officer(s):
  Christian Frayssignes, President
  Toronto Branch
  Toronto ON
  Tel: 416-725-0425
  info@iwfstoronto.org
  www.iwfstoronto.org
  Chief Officer(s):
  Chris Tierney, President
  ctiern@yahoo.ca
  Vancouver Branch
  #1201, 1169 Cordova St. West, Vancouver BC V6C 3T1
  Tel: 604-620-9008
  info@iwfsvancouver.com
  www.iwfsvancouver.com
  www.facebook.com/128978526019
  Chief Officer(s):
  James Robertson, President
  Victoria Branch
  Victoria BC

International Women's Forum (IWF)
#460, 2120 L St. NW, Washington DC 20037 USA
Tel: 202-387-1010; *Fax:* 202-387-1009
iwf@iwforum.org
www.iwforum.org
Overview: A small international organization founded in 1982
Mission: To advance women's leadership across careers, cultures & continents
Membership: 5,500; *Member Profile:* Female leaders
Chief Officer(s):
Ludmila Shvetsova, President

International WWOOF Association
PO Box 2675, Lewes BN7 1RB United Kingdom
www.wwoof.org
Also Known As: World-Wide Opportunities on Organic Farms
Overview: A small international organization
Mission: To help those who would like to volunteer on organic farms internationally
Chief Officer(s):
Amanda Pearson, Administrator
amanda@wwoof.net

Internationale de l'Education *See* Education International

Internationale des services publics *See* Public Services International

Inter-Parliamentary Union (IPU) / Union interparlementaire
PO Box 330, 5, ch du Pommier, Geneva CH-1218 Switzerland
Tel: 41-22-919-41-50; *Fax:* 41-22-919-41-60
postbox@ipu.org
www.ipu.org
www.facebook.com/InterParliamentaryUnion
twitter.com/IPUparliament
www.youtube.com/user/iparliamentaryunion
Overview: A large international organization founded in 1889
Mission: To foster contacts, coordination, & exchange of experience among parliaments & parliamentarians of all countries; To consider questions of international interest & concern; To contribute to the defence & promotion of human rights; To contribute to the better knowledge of the working of representative institutions & to the strengthening & development of their means of action
Affiliation(s): Canadian Inter-Parliamentary Group
Finances: *Funding Sources:* Assessed contributions from National Groups
Membership: *Member Profile:* Parliaments of sovereign states (National Groups of parliamentarians); *Committees:* Peace & International Security; Democracy & Human Rights; Sustainable Development, Finance & Trade; Human Rights of Parliamentarians; Middle East Questions; Facilitators for Cyprus; Promote Respect for International Humanitarian Law; Advisory Group on HIV/AIDS & Maternal, Newborn & Child Health; Women Parliamentarians; Gender Partnership Group; United Nations Affairs
Activities: *Library* Open to public
Chief Officer(s):
Gabriela Cuevas Barron, President
Martin Chungong, Secretary General

IRC International Water & Sanitation Centre
PO Box 82327, The Hague 2508 EH Netherlands
Tel: 31-70-304-4000; *Fax:* 31-70-304-4044
www.irc.nl
Previous Name: International Reference Centre for Community Water Supply & Sanitation
Overview: A small international organization founded in 1968
Mission: The IRC helps people in developing countries to get the best water & sanitation services they can afford
Finances: *Annual Operating Budget:* $1.5 Million-$3 Million
Staff Member(s): 38
Activities: *Internships:* Yes; *Library:* by appointment
Chief Officer(s):
L. de Waal, Chairman, Supervisory Board
Michel van der Leest, Office Coordinator, Services Section

Ireland Canada University Foundation
c/o The Canadian Embassy, 7-8 Wilton Terrace, Dublin 2 Ireland
www.icuf.ie
Overview: A medium-sized international organization
Mission: To strengthen the scholarly relationship between Canada & Ireland; To provide scholarships to scholars & academics whose research relates to Irish & Canadian matters
Chief Officer(s):
Mark Dobbin, Chair

ISACA
#1010, 3701 Algonquin Rd., Rolling Meadows IL 60008 USA
Tel: 847-253-1545; *Fax:* 847-253-1443
news@isaca.org
www.isaca.org
www.linkedin.com/groups/ISACA-Official-3839870
www.facebook.com/ISACAHQ
twitter.com/ISACANews
Previous Name: Information Systems Audit & Control Association
Overview: A large international organization founded in 1967
Mission: To be the recognized global leader in IT governance, control, & assurance
Finances: *Annual Operating Budget:* $50,000-$100,000; *Funding Sources:* Membership dues; Education; Certification exam
Membership: 86,000 worldwide in 175 chapters
Activities: *Speaker Service:* Yes; *Rents Mailing List:* Yes
Chief Officer(s):
Michele Luckman, Coordinator, Certification, 847-660-5574
Awards:
• Michael Cangemi Best Book/Article Award
• Eugene M. Frank Award for Meritorious Performance
• John Kuyers Best Speaker/Conference Contributor Award
• John Lainhart Common Body of Knowledge Award
• Harold Weiss Award for Oustanding Achievement
• Paul Williams Award for Inspirational Leadership
Meetings/Conferences:
• ISACA North America CACS Conference 2018, April, 2018, Chicago, IL
Scope: International
Description: An industry event for ISACA members, IS Audit, Assurance, Security & Risk Management Professionals worldwide; includes expert-led workshops & professional development opportunities
Contact Information: ISACA Training & Education, Phone: 847-660-5670, Fax: 847-253-1443
• EuroCACS Conference 2018, May, 2018, Edinburgh
Scope: International
Description: An industry event for ISACA members, IS Audit, Assurance, Security & Risk Management Professionals worldwide; includes expert-led workshops & professional development opportunities
Contact Information: ISACA Training & Education, Phone: 847-660-5670, Fax: 847-253-1443
• Latin America CACS Conference 2018, August, 2018, Lima
Scope: International
Description: An industry event for ISACA members, IS Audit, Assurance, Security & Risk Management Professionals worldwide; includes expert-led workshops & professional development opportunities
Contact Information: ISACA Training & Education, Phone: 847-660-5670, Fax: 847-253-1443
• CSX North America 2018, October, 2018, Las Vegas, NV
Scope: International
Description: A cybersecurity conference involving relevant professional development opportunities & information sessions
Contact Information: ISACA Training & Education, Phone: 847-660-5670, Fax: 847-253-1443
Publications:
• @ISACA Newsletter
Type: Newsletter; *Frequency:* bi-weekly
Profile: News & updates for members
• CGEIT Exam Resources [publications of ISACA]
Type: Book
Profile: A series of review manuals for the Certified in the Governance of Enterprise IT (CGEIT) designation exam
• CISA Exam Resources [publications of ISACA]
Type: Book
Profile: A series of review manuals for the Certified Information Systems Auditor (CISA) certification exam
• CISM Exam Resources [publications of ISACA]
Type: Book
Profile: A series of review manuals for the Certified Information Systems Manager (CISM) certification exam
• CRISC Exam Resources [publications of ISACA]
Type: Book
Profile: A series of review manuals for the Certified in Risk and Information Systems Control (CRISC) designation exam
• CSX Exam Resources [publications of ISACA]
Type: Book
Profile: A series of review manuals for the Cybersecurity Nexus (CSX) certification exam
• ISACA Annual Report
Type: Report; *Frequency:* a.
• ISACA Journal
Type: Journal; *Frequency:* Bimonthly; *Editor:* Jen Hajigeorgiou; *ISSN:* 1944-1967
Profile: Contains information on industry advancements & professional development to individuals & groups involved in the IS audit, information security & governancecommunities

Israel Association for Canadian Studies (IACS) / Association d'études canadiennes en Israel
c/o Halbert Centre for Canadian Studies, Faculty of Social Sciences, Hebrew University of Jerusalem, Jerusalem 91905 Israel
Tel: 972-2-588-1344; *Fax:* 972-2-582-6267
mscanada@mscc.huji.ac.il
Overview: A small international organization founded in 1985
Mission: To promote, develop, & expand Canadian Studies in Israel; to encourage the teaching of courses with Canadian content & engage in research on Canada & Canadian issues within Israeli universities

Member of: International Council for Canadian Studies
Affiliation(s): Association of Canadian Studies
Finances: *Annual Operating Budget:* $50,000-$100,000
Staff Member(s): 2
Membership: 370; *Member Profile:* University faculty; students; civil servants; journalists; general public; *Committees:* Executive
Activities: Biennial international conference, public lecture series, research grants, publications, library facilities, resource & information; *Speaker Service:* Yes; *Library*
Chief Officer(s):
Daniel Ben-Natan, President

Italian Association for Canadian Studies / Associazione Italiana di Studi Canadesi
c/o Oriana Palusci, Vis Duomo, 219, Università di Napoli 'L'Orientale', Napoli 80138 Italy
Tel: 0039-816909840; *Fax:* 0039-81-204639
Also Known As: AISC
Overview: A small international organization founded in 1979
Mission: To promote Canadian Studies in Italy, encouraging collaboration & scholarly publishing, promoting & maintaining academic & cultural links with Canada & sponsoring conferences, seminars & courses related to the study of Canada
Affiliation(s): International Council for Canadian Studies
Finances: *Annual Operating Budget:* $50,000-$100,000; *Funding Sources:* Canadian government; charities
Staff Member(s): 9; 2 volunteer
Membership: 206; *Fees:* 22 euros
Activities: Organizes seminars, conferences & conventions; sponsors Canadianist cultural activities in Italy
Chief Officer(s):
Oriana Palusci, President
opalusci@unior.it
Awards:
• Italian Association of Canadian Studies Award

The Jane Goodall Institute for Wildlife Research, Education & Conservation (JGI)
#550, 1595 Spring Hill Rd., Vienna VA 22182 USA
Tel: 703-682-9220; *Fax:* 703-682-9312
www.janegoodall.org
www.facebook.com/janegoodallinst
twitter.com/JaneGoodallInst
www.youtube.com/user/JaneGoodallInstitute
Overview: A small international organization founded in 1977
Mission: To increase primate habitat conservation; to increase awareness of, support for & training in issues related to our relationship with each other, the environment & other animals (leading to behaviour change); to expand non-invasive research program on chimpanzees & other primates; to promote activities that ensure the well-being of chimpanzees, other primates & animal welfare activities in general
Activities: Gombe Stream Research Centre; ChimpanZoo Project; reforestation projects; conservation centres; educational & communcation resources
Chief Officer(s):
Mary Humphrey, Chief Executive Officer
Chris Fanning, Vice President, Finance

Japanese Association for Canadian Studies
c/o Meiji University, 1-1 Kanda-Surugadia, Chiyoda, Tokyo 101-8301 Japan
Tel: 81-3-3219-5822; *Fax:* 81-3-3219-5822
jacsmeiji@jacs.jp
www.jacs.jp
Overview: A small international organization founded in 1979
Mission: To promote Canadian studies research, teaching & publishing in Japan
Member of: International Council for Canadian Studies
Membership: 265; *Fees:* 7,000 yen; *Member Profile:* University teachers, research fellows of institutes, graduate students, government officials, journalists & business people
Chief Officer(s):
Naoharu Fujita, President

John E. Mack Institute
PO Box 7046, Boulder CO 80306 USA
e-mail: info@johnemackinstitute.org
www.johnemackinstitute.org
Previous Name: Center for Psychology & Social Change; Center for Psychological Studies in the Nuclear Age
Overview: A medium-sized international charitable organization founded in 1982
Mission: To explore the frontiers of human experience; to serve the transformation of individual consciousness; to further the evolution of the paradigms by which we understand human identity.
Affiliation(s): Consultative status with the Economic & Social Council at the UN
Finances: *Funding Sources:* Membership dues; donations; grants
Activities: Integrative Healing Research Program; Ecopsychology Institute; Marine Advocacy Program; United Nations Program; Balkans Trauma Project; Program for Extraordinary Experience Research; Psychospiritual Institute; *Speaker Service:* Yes; *Rents Mailing List:* Yes
Chief Officer(s):
Will Bueché, Contact, 303-875-5394

Joubert Syndrome & Related Disoarders Foundation (JSRDF)
c/o Pete Asman, Treasurer, 1415 West Ave., Cincinnati OH 45215 USA
Tel: 614-864-1362
president@jsrdf.org
www.jsrdf.org
www.facebook.com/180691234440
twitter.com/jsrdf
Overview: A small international charitable organization founded in 1992
Mission: To serve as an international network of parents who share knowledge, experience & emotional support; to educate physicians & their support teams; to increase awareness & understanding of Joubert Syndrome; to provide support to families who have loved ones diagnosed with Joubert Syndrome
Finances: *Annual Operating Budget:* Less than $50,000
8 volunteer(s)
Membership: 350; *Fees:* US$35; $40 international; *Member Profile:* Interested professionals & affected persons & their families
Activities: Networking list of affected families; biennial conference; development & maintenance of database
Chief Officer(s):
Karen Tompkins, President
president@jsrdf.org

Junior Chamber International (JCI)
15645 Olive Blvd., Chesterfield MO 63017 USA
Tel: 636-449-3100; *Fax:* 636-449-3107
Other Communication: www.flickr.com/groups/1513948@N23
info@jci.cc
www.jci.cc
www.facebook.com/jciwhq
twitter.com/jcinews
Merged from: Lions Clubs International
Overview: A large international organization founded in 1944
Mission: To contribute to the advancement of the community through service & volunteer projects, encouraging the development of leadership skills among youth for the benefit of the community
Affiliation(s): United Nations; UN Global Compact; International Chamber of Commerce-World Chambers Federation; UN Foundation; United Nations Educational, Scientific & Cultural Organization; Pan American Health Organization
Membership: 100+ countries + 5,000 communities + 200,000 individuals; *Member Profile:* Young professionals & entrepreneurs between ages 18 & 40
Activities: *Speaker Service:* Yes
Chief Officer(s):
Marc Brian Lim, President
Publications:
• Be Better [a publication of Junior Chamber International]
Type: Newsletter
• JCI [Junior Chamber International] World Congress Report
Type: Report
• JCI [Junior Chamber International] Impact Update
Type: Newsletter

Kitchen Cabinet Manufacturers Association (KCMA)
1899 Preston White Dr., Reston VA 20191-5435 USA
Tel: 703-264-1690; *Fax:* 703-620-6530
www.kcma.org
twitter.com/KCMAorg
Overview: A small international organization founded in 1955
Mission: To serve & represent kitchen, bath & other residential cabinet manufacturers & suppliers in the US & Canada
Membership: 360 in US & Canada; *Member Profile:* Manufacturers of kitchen cabinets, bath vanities; countertop fabricators; goods & services suppliers; *Committees:* Government & Regulatory Affairs; Standards; Environmental Stewardship Program; Marketing; Associates; Entrepreneurs Council
Chief Officer(s):
C. Richard Titus, Executive Vice-President
dtitus@kcma.org

Knights of Columbus / Chevaliers de Colomb
1 Columbus Plaza, New Haven CT 06510 USA
Tel: 203-752-4000
www.kofc.org
www.facebook.com/KnightsofColumbus
twitter.com/kofc
www.youtube.com/knightsofcolumbus
Also Known As: K of C
Overview: A large international charitable organization founded in 1882
Mission: To render financial aid to members & their families; To render mutual aid & assistance to sick, disabled & needy members; To promote social & intellectual intercourse among members; To promote & conduct educational, charitable, religious, social welfare, war relief & welfare, & public relief work
Member of: Canadian Life & Health Insurance Association; Canadian Fraternal Association
Finances: *Annual Operating Budget:* Greater than $5 Million
Staff Member(s): 650
Membership: 228,812 individuals + 1,873 groups in Canada; 1,678,205 individuals + 12,522 groups worldwide; *Fees:* Schedule available, based on province or state; *Member Profile:* Male aged 18+ & practicing Catholics in Union with the Holy See
Activities: *Library:* Archives; by appointment
Chief Officer(s):
Carl A. Anderson, Supreme Knight
Charles E. Maurer, Supreme Secretary
Awards:
• Percy J. Johnson Endowed Scholarships
Eligibility: Young men who demonstrate financial need.
• Matthews and Swift Educational Trust Scholarships
• Vocations Scholarships
• Mexico, Philippines and Puerto Rico Scholarships
• Anthony J. LaBella Endowed Scholarships
• Frank L. Goularte Endowed Scholarships
Meetings/Conferences:
• Knights of Columbus 136th Supreme Convention 2018, 2018
Scope: International
Contact Information: Phone: 203-752-4000
Publications:
• Knightline [a publication of the Knights of Columbus]
Type: Newsletter; *Frequency:* Monthly
Profile: Features news from the Supreme Council office & other important information for members
• Knights of Columbus Annual Report of the Supreme Knight
Type: Report; *Frequency:* Annual

Laborers' International Union of North America (AFL-CIO/CLC) (LiUNA) / Union internationale des journaliers d'Amérique (FAT-COI/CTC)
905 - 16 St. NW, Washington DC 20006 USA
Tel: 202-737-8320
communications@liuna.org
www.liuna.org
www.facebook.com/LaborersInternationalUnionofNorthAmerica
twitter.com/LIUNA
www.youtube.com/user/liunavideo
Overview: A large international organization founded in 1903
Mission: To represent construction workers & other public service employees
Affiliation(s): American Federation of Labour & Congress of Industrial Organizations; Canadian Labour Congress
Membership: 500,000 + 629 locals
Activities: Collective bargaining
Chief Officer(s):
Terry O'Sullivan, President
Greg Davis, Director, Construction, 202-942-2335
constmail@liuna.org
Eric Hutson, Director, Corporate Affairs, 202-369-4149
John R. Billi, Inspector General, 614-895-6970
oigliuna@outlook.com

Canada - Central & Eastern Office (LIUNA)
44 Hughson St. South, Hamilton ON L8N 2A7
Tel: 905-522-7177; *Fax:* 905-522-9310
www.liuna.ca
www.facebook.com/LiunaCanada
twitter.com/liunacanada
www.youtube.com/channel/UCPBf4i-7euKD47I5IHzsFdw
Mission: To represent construction workers & other public service employees in Central & Eastern Canada
Chief Officer(s):

Joseph S. Mancinelli, Vice President & Regional Manager, Central & Eastern Canada Region
joseph@liuna.ca
Joe Missori, International Representative
joemissori@uijan.org
Leo D'Agostini, International Representative
leo@liuna.ca
Anthony Primerano, Government Liaison
a.prime@rogers.com

Ladies' Golf Union (LGU)
The Scores, St. Andrews, Fife KY16 9AT United Kingdom
Tel: 44-13-34-475811; *Fax:* 44-13-34-472818
www.lgu.org
www.facebook.com/ladiesgolfunion
twitter.com/LadiesGolfUnion
youtube.com/ladiesgolfunion1893; pinterest.com/ladiesgolfunion
Overview: A small international organization founded in 1893
Mission: To uphold the rules of golf; to advance & safeguard the interests of ladies' golf & to decide all doubtful & disputed points in connection therewith; to maintain LGU Scratch Score System; to employ the funds of the LGU in such a manner as shall be deemed best for the interests of ladies' golf, with power to borrow or raise money for the same purpose; to promote, maintain & regulate international events, championships & competitions held under the LGU regulations & to promote the interests of Great Britain & Ireland in ladies' international golf; to promulgate, maintain, enforce & publish such regulations as may be considered necessary
Affiliation(s): Canadian Ladies' Golf Association
Staff Member(s): 8
Membership: 2,750 clubs; *Committees:* Finance & General Purposes; International Selection; Rules & Regulations; Scratch Score; Training
Activities: *Library* by appointment
Chief Officer(s):
Diane Bailey, President
Susan Simpson, Head, Golf Operations

Land Trust Alliance (LTA)
#1100, 1660 L St. NW, Washington DC 20036 USA
Tel: 202-638-4725; *Fax:* 202-638-4730
info@lta.org
www.landtrustalliance.org
www.linkedin.com/company/land-trust-alliance
www.facebook.com/landtrustalliance
twitter.com/ltalliance
Overview: A large international organization founded in 1982
Mission: To strengthen the land trust movement & ensure that land trusts have the information, skills & resources they use to save land
Finances: *Annual Operating Budget:* $3 Million-$5 Million
Staff Member(s): 32
Membership: 1,000
Activities: *Awareness Events:* National Land Trust Rally; *Internships:* Yes
Chief Officer(s):
Rand Wentworth, President, 202-800-2249
rwentworth@lta.org
Marilyn Ayres, Chief Operating, 202-800-2235
mayres@lta.org

Latin American Studies Association (LASA)
416 Bellefield Hall, University of Pittsburgh, Pittsburgh PA 15260 USA
Tel: 412-648-7929; *Fax:* 412-624-7145
lasa@pitt.edu
lasa.international.pitt.edu
Overview: A medium-sized international organization founded in 1966
Mission: To foster the concerns of all scholars interested in Latin American studies; to encourage more effective training, teaching & research in connection with such studies; to provide a forum for dealing with matters of common interest to scholars & individuals concerned with Latin American studies
Member of: American Council of Learned Societies; National Council of Area Studies Associations
Finances: *Funding Sources:* Membership dues; congresses; donations from members
Staff Member(s): 6
Membership: 7,000+ worldwide; *Fees:* Schedule available; *Member Profile:* Interest in Latin American studies
Chief Officer(s):
Milagros Pereyra-Rojas, Executive Director
Awards:
• Bryce Wood Book
• Diskin Award
• Kalman Silbert Memorial Award
• Media Award
• Premio Iberoamericano Book Award

Lawson Wilkins Pediatric Endocrine Society *See* Pediatric Endocrine Society

La Leche League International (LLLI)
957 North Plum Grove Rd., Schaumburg IL 60173 USA
Tel: 847-519-7730; *Fax:* 847-696-0460
Toll-Free: 800-525-3243
www.llli.org
Overview: A medium-sized international organization founded in 1956
Mission: To help mothers worldwide to breastfeed through mother-to-mother support, encouragement, information & education; to promote a better understanding of breastfeeding as an important element in the healthy development of the baby & mother.
Affiliation(s): United Nations Children's Fund (UNICEF); World Health Organization (WHO); World Alliance for Breastfeeding Action (WABA)
Membership: *Fees:* $25; *Member Profile:* Breastfeeding mothers or parents; *Committees:* Health Advisory; Legal Advisory; Management Advisory
Activities: Annual Seminar For Physicians; Workshops for Lactation Consultants; Biennial International Conference; Annual World Walk for Breastfeeding; *Library:* Center for Breastfeeding Information
Chief Officer(s):
Cynthia Garrison, Co-Chair
Lydia de Raad, Co-Chair

Linguistic Society of America (LSA)
#120, 522 - 21st St. NW, Washington DC 20006-5012 USA
Tel: 202-835-1714; *Fax:* 202-835-1717
lsa@lsadc.org
www.linguisticsociety.org
www.facebook.com/LingSocAm
twitter.com/LingSocAm
www.flickr.com/photos/lingsocam
Overview: A large international organization founded in 1924
Mission: To advance the scientific study of language
Member of: American Council of Learned Societies
Affiliation(s): Permanent International Committee of Linguists
Finances: *Annual Operating Budget:* $500,000-$1.5 Million
Staff Member(s): 3
Membership: 4,593 individual + 2,060 institutional; *Fees:* Schedule available; *Member Profile:* Interest in the advancement of the scientific study of language
Activities: *Internships:* Yes
Chief Officer(s):
Alyson Reed, Executive Director
areed@lsadc.org
David Robinson, Director, Membership & Meetings
drobinson@lsadc.org

Lions Clubs International
300 - 22nd St. West, Oak Brook IL 60523-8842 USA
Tel: 630-571-5466
Other Communication: flickr.com/photos/lionsclubsorg
pr@lionsclubs.org
www.lionsclubs.org
www.linkedin.com/company/lions-clubs-international
www.facebook.com/lionsclubs
twitter.com/lionsclub
www.youtube.com/user/lionsclubsorg;
www.instagram.com/lionsclubs
Overview: A large international organization
Mission: To act as the world's largest service club organization; To organize, charter, & supervise Lions clubs; To promote the principles of good government & good citizenship
Chief Officer(s):
Jitsuhiro Yamada, International President
Publications:
• Lion [a publication of Lions Clubs International]
Type: Magazine; *Frequency:* Quarterly; *ISSN:* 0024-4163

Major League Baseball Players' Association (Ind.) / Association des joueurs de la Ligue majeure de baseball (ind.)
12 East 49th St., 24th Fl., New York NY 10017 USA
Tel: 212-826-0808; *Fax:* 212-752-4378
feedback@mlbpa.org
www.mlb.com/pa
twitter.com/MLB_PLAYERS
Overview: A medium-sized international organization
Mission: To represent and protect the interests of professional baseball players in the United States.
Membership: 80 + 2 locals (in Canada)
Activities: Baseball Card Clubhouse; Baseball Tomorrow Fund; Rookie Career Development; *Awareness Events:* Players Choice Awards
Chief Officer(s):
Tony Clark, Executive Director
Martha Child, CAO
Marietta DiCamillo, Chief Financial Officer

Master Brewers Association of The Americas (MBAA)
3340 Pilot Knob Rd., St. Paul MN 55121-2097 USA
Tel: 651-454-7250; *Fax:* 651-454-0766
mbaa@mbaa.com
www.mbaa.com
www.facebook.com/MasterBrewers
twitter.com/masterbrewers
Overview: A large international organization founded in 1887
Mission: To advance brewing, fermentation, & allied industries
Membership: 1,000-4,999; *Fees:* Schedule available; *Member Profile:* Professionals in the fermentation & brewing industry; *Committees:* ASBC/MBAA Steering; Beer Specialist Certification Program; Board of Governor Representatives; Bylaws; Committee Chairs; Communicator; Education; Executive; Finance; Heritage; International Brewers Symposium Planning; MBAA Global Emerging Issues; Membership; Nominating; Publications; Technical; Technical Quarterly Editorial Board; Website
Activities: Developing continuing education programs; Advocating knowledge exchange; Disseminating information; *Speaker Service:* Yes
Chief Officer(s):
Amy Hope, Executive Vice-President, 651-994-3827
Awards:
• Brewery Award of Excellence
• Award of Honor
• Award of Merit
• Distinguished Life Service Award
• Honorary Life Member Award
• Inge Russell Best Paper Award
• Best Oral Presentation Award
Presented at the MBAA Annual Conference
• Best Poster Award
Presented at the MBAA Annual Conference
• MBAA Scholarship
• North American Brewers Association Scholarship
Provides support to an MBAA member to cover full tuition to the MBAA Brewing & Malting Science course
• Walt Powell Scholarship
Provides support to an MBAA member to cover full tuition to the MBAA Brewing & Malting Science course *Amount:* $1,000
Meetings/Conferences:
• Master Brewers Association of the Americas 2018 Brewing Summit, August, 2018, San Diego, CA
Scope: International
Publications:
• Beer Packaging [a publication of the Master Brewers Association of The Americas]
Type: Book; *Number of Pages:* 60; *Author:* Ray Klimovitz & Karl Ockert; *ISBN:* 978-0-9787726-7-3; *Price:* $119.95
• Beer Steward Handbook [a publication of the Master Brewers Association of The Americas]
Type: Book; *Number of Pages:* 248; *Editor:* Stephen R. Holle et al.; *ISBN:* 987-0-9877726-3-5; *Price:* $29.95
• Beer Tasting Journal [a publication of the Master Brewers Association of The Americas]
Type: Book; *Number of Pages:* 100; *ISBN:* 978-0-9787726-2-8; *Price:* $11.95
• Brewing, Engineering, & Plant Operations [a publication of the Master Brewers Association of The Americas]
Type: Book; *Number of Pages:* 198; *Editor:* Karl Ockert; *ISBN:* 978-0-9770519-3-9; *Price:* $49.95
Profile: The third volume in a series of practical handbooks for specialty brewers
• Fermentation, Cellaring, & Packaging Operations [a publication of the Master Brewers Association of The Americas]
Type: Book; *Number of Pages:* 263; *Editor:* Karl Ockert; *ISBN:* 978-0-9770519-2-2; *Price:* $49.95
Profile: The second volume in a series of practical handbooks for specialty brewers
• A Handbook of Basic Brewing Calculations [a publication of the Master Brewers Association of The Americas]

Type: Book; *Number of Pages:* 96; *Author:* Stephen R. Holle; *ISBN:* 978-0-9718255-1-2; *Price:* $49
• Master Brewers Association of The Americas Technical Quarterly
Type: Journal; *Frequency:* Quarterly; *Accepts Advertising*; *ISSN:* 0542-9811
Profile: Papers covering technical aspects of brewing ingredients, the brewing process, brewing by-products, brewery ecological matters, beer packaging, beerflavor, & physical stability
• The MBAA [Master Brewers Association of The Americas] Communicator
Type: Newsletter; *Frequency:* Quarterly; *Accepts Advertising*
Profile: Features MBAA news & updates exclusive to members
• Raw Materials & Brewhouse Operations [a publication of the Master Brewers Association of The Americas]
Type: Book; *Number of Pages:* 189; *Editor:* Karl Ockert; *ISBN:* 978-0-9770519-1-5; *Price:* $49.95
Profile: The first volume in a series of practical handbooks for specialty brewers

District Eastern Canada
c/o Labatt Brewery, 50, av Labatt, La Salle QC H8R 3E7
Tel: 514-364-5050
www.mbaa.com/Districts/EasternCanada
Chief Officer(s):
Thibaut X. Huchet, District President
Marilène Dumouchel, District Secretary
Marie Lajeunesse, District Treasurer

District Western Canada
c/o Canadian Malting Barley Technical Centre, #1365, 303 Main St., Winnipeg MB R3C 3G7
Tel: 204-983-1981
www.mbaa.com/Districts/WesternCanada
Chief Officer(s):
Peter Watts, District President
pwatts@cmbtc.com
Douglas R. Wilkie, District Vice-President & Treasurer
dwilkie@mts.net

Ontario District
c/o Molson Coors Canada, 33 Carlingview Dr., Toronto ON M9W 5E4
Tel: 416-679-7549
www.mbaa.com/Districts/Ontario
Chief Officer(s):
Paddy Finnegan, District President
paddy.finnegan@burkert.com
Jonathan C. Morse, District Secretary
jonathan.morse@molsoncoors.com
Debbie Mowat, District Treasurer

Medical Library Association (MLA)
#1900, 65 East Wacker Pl., Chicago IL 60601-7246 USA
Tel: 312-419-9094; *Fax:* 312-419-8950
websupport@mail.mlahq.org
www.mlanet.org
www.linkedin.com/company/medical-library-association
www.facebook.com/MedicalLibraryAssn
twitter.com/MedLibAssn
www.youtube.com/user/MedLibrAssoc
Overview: A large international organization founded in 1898
Mission: To provide lifelong educational opportunities, support a knowledgebase of health information research, & work with partners worldwide to promote the importance of quality information for improved health to the health care community & the public
Finances: *Annual Operating Budget:* $3 Million-$5 Million
Staff Member(s): 14; 4000 volunteer(s)
Membership: 4,000+; *Fees:* $195 regular; $130 introductory & international; $120 annual salary under $40,000 & affiliate; $50 student; *Member Profile:* Health sciences information professionals & institutions; *Committees:* Awards; Board & Administrative; Books Panel; Bylaws; Continuing Education/Education Annual Programming; Credentialing; Education Steering; Governmental Relations; Grants & Scholarships; Joseph Leiter NLM/MLA Lectureship; Leadership Curriculum; Librarians Without Borders; Membership; National Program; Nominating; Oral History; Professional Recruitment & Retention; Rising Stars; Scholarly Communications
Activities: *Awareness Events:* Medical Information Week, Apr.; National Medical Librarians Month, Oct.
Chief Officer(s):
Teresa Knott, AHIP, President
Kevin Baliozian, Executive Director
baliozian@mail.mlahq.org
Kate E. Corcoran, Director, Membership, Research & Information Systems
corcoran@mail.mlahq.org
Barry Grant, Director, Education
grant@mail.mlahq.org
Awards:
• Virginia L. & William K. Beatty Volunteer Service Award
• Estelle Brodman Award for the Academic Medical Librarian of the Year
• Lois Ann Colaianni Award for Excellence & Achievement in Hospital Librarianship
• Louise Darling Medal for Distinguished Achievement in Collection Development in the Health Sciences
• Janet Doe Lectureship
• Ida & George Eliot Prize
• Fellowship & Honorary Membership
• Carla J. Funk Governmental Relations Award
• Erich Meyerhoff Prize
• T. Mark Hodges International Service Award
• Joseph Leiter NLM/MLA Lectureship
• Majors/MLA Chapter Project of the Year
• Lucretia W. McClure Excellence in Education Award
• John P. McGovern Award Lectureship
• Marcia C. Noyes Award
• Michael E. DeBakey Library Services Outreach Award
• MLA Award for Distinguished Public Service
• President's Award
• Rittenhouse Award
• Section Project of the Year Award
• Thomson Reuters/Frank Bradway Rogers Information Advancement Award
Meetings/Conferences:
• Medical Library Association 2018 Annual Meeting & Exhibition, May, 2018, Atlanta, GA
Scope: International
• Medical Library Association 2019 Annual Meeting & Exhibition, May, 2019, Chicago, IL
Scope: International
• Medical Library Association 2020 Annual Meeting & Exhibition, 2020
Scope: International
Publications:
• Journal of the Medical Library Association (JMLA)
Type: Journal; *Frequency:* Quarterly; *ISSN:* 1536-5050
• MLA [Medical Library Association] FOCUS
Type: Newsletter; *Frequency:* s-m.
• MLA [Medical Library Association] News
Type: Newsletter; *Frequency:* 10 pa

Medieval Academy of America
#202, 17 Dunster St., Cambridge MA 02138 USA
Tel: 617-491-1622; *Fax:* 617-492-3303
info@medievalacademy.org
www.medievalacademy.org
www.facebook.com/359124130807175
twitter.com/MedievalAcademy
Overview: A large international organization founded in 1925
Mission: To promote and support research, publication, & teaching in all aspects of medieval studies
Member of: American Council of Learned Societies
Affiliation(s): Fédération internationale des instituts d'études médiévales
Membership: 5,000-14,999; *Fees:* Schedule available; *Member Profile:* Individuals & institutions with interests in the Middle Ages; *Committees:* Centers & Regional Associations; Electronic Resources; AHA Program; Professional Development; Committees: Finance; Graduate Student; Kalamazoo Program; Mart Advisory Board; Nominating; Publications Advisory Board; Haskins Medal; John Nicholas Brown Prize; Van Courtlandt Elliott Prize
Activities: *Rents Mailing List:* Yes
Chief Officer(s):
Barbara Newman, President
bjnewman@northwestern.edu
Lisa Fagin Davis, Executive Director
lfd@themedievalacademy.org
Awards:
• Schallek Fellowship & Awards Program
• Medieval Academy Dissertation Grants
• Leyerle-CARA Prize
• Olivia Remie Constable Award
• CARA Tuition Scholarships
• Service Awards
• Teaching Awards
• Book & Article Awards Program
Meetings/Conferences:
• Medieval Academy of America Annual Meeting 2018, March, 2018, Emory University, Atlanta, GA
Scope: International
Contact Information: Coordinator, Communications & Memberships: Christopher Cole, E-mail:
ccole@themedievalacademy.org
Publications:
• Medieval Academy of America Member Directory
Type: Directory
• Speculum [a publication of the Medieval Academy of America]
Type: Journal; *Frequency:* Quarterly; *Accepts Advertising*;
Editor: Sarah Spence; *ISSN:* 0038-7134
Profile: Features contributions in all fields studying the Western Middle Ages

Meeting Planners International *See* Meeting Professionals International

Meeting Professionals International (MPI)
#1700, 3030 Lyndon B. Johnson Freeway, Dallas TX 75234-2759 USA
Tel: 972-702-3053; *Fax:* 972-702-3065
Toll-Free: 866-318-2743
feedback@mpiweb.org
www.mpiweb.org
www.linkedin.com/company/165050
www.facebook.com/MPIfans
twitter.com/mpi
www.instagram.com/meetingprofessionalsintl
Previous Name: Meeting Planners International
Overview: A large international organization founded in 1972
Mission: To position meetings as a primary communications vehicle & a critical component of an organization's success; To lead the industry by serving the diverse needs of all people with a direct interest in the outcome of meetings; To educate & prepare members for their changing roles in the greater business world; To validate relevant knowledge & skills while simultaneously demonstrating a commitment to meeting excellence.
Member of: American Society of Association Executives; Convention Liaison Council; Unity Team
Finances: *Annual Operating Budget:* Greater than $5 Million
Staff Member(s): 66
Membership: 17,000; 90 chapters in 19 countries; *Fees:* $279-$449 planner; $399-$569 supplier; $40-$199 student & faculty; *Member Profile:* Planners, suppliers & students of the meetings industry
Activities: *Speaker Service:* Yes; *Library:* Resource Centre; Open to public
Chief Officer(s):
Amanda Armstrong, CMP, Chair
Paul Van Deventer, President & CEO
Publications:
• The Meeting Professional [a publication of Meeting Professionals International]
Type: Magazine; *Frequency:* monthly; *Editor:* Rich Luna
• Meetings Outlook [a publication of Meeting Professionals International]
Type: Report; *Frequency:* q.
• Plan Your Meetings [a publication of Meeting Professionals International]
Type: Magazine; *Frequency:* bi-annual; *Editor:* Michael Pinchera

Atlantic Canada Chapter
PO Box 8441, Halifax NS B3K 5M2
e-mail: info@mpiatlantic.com
mpiatlantic.com
www.facebook.com/MPIatlantic
Chief Officer(s):
Moira Pellerine, President

British Columbia Chapter
PO Box 2343, Stn. Main Terminal, #300 - 1275 West 6th Ave., Vancouver BC V6H 1A6
Tel: 604-731-5262
admin@mpibcchapter.com
www.mpibc.org
www.linkedin.com/groups/139718
www.facebook.com/MPIBC
twitter.com/mpibcchapter
www.instagram.com/mpibcchapter
Chief Officer(s):
Patricia Tait, Chapter Administrator

Toronto Chapter
#100, 6700 Century Ave., Mississauga ON L5N 6A4

Tel: 905-567-9591; Fax: 866-768-8168
office@mpitoronto.org
www.mpitoronto.org
www.linkedin.com/groups/1888685
www.facebook.com/MPIToronto
twitter.com/MPIToronto
www.instagram.com/mpitoronto
Chief Officer(s):
Leslie Wright, Executive Director
lwright@mpitoronto.org
Greater Calgary Chapter
Calgary AB
e-mail: info@mpi-gcc.org
mpi-gcc.org
www.linkedin.com/company/10783557
www.facebook.com/MPICalgary
twitter.com/MPIGCC
www.instagram.com/mpiyyc
Chief Officer(s):
Jade Marage, President
president@mpi-gcc.org
Greater Edmonton Chapter
#93, 11007 Jasper Ave. NW, Edmonton AB T5K 0K6
www.mpiedmonton.org
www.linkedin.com/in/mpi-greater-edmonton-chapter-527b774b
twitter.com/mpiedmonton
instagram.com/mpiedmonton
Chief Officer(s):
Andrea Cliff, President, 780-248-2003
andrea.cliff@ualberta.ca
Montréal/Québec
#1700, 2001, boul Robert-Bourassa, Montréal QC H3A 1T9
info@mpimontrealquebec.com
mpimontrealquebec.com
www.facebook.com/MPIMontrealQuebec
twitter.com/MPI_MTLQC
Chief Officer(s):
Thierry Marlier, Président

Métallurgistes unis d'Amérique (FAT-COI/CTC) See United Steelworkers of America (AFL-CIO/CLC)

Mexican Association of Canadian Studies See Asociación mexicana de estudios sobre Canadá

Middle East Studies Association of North America (MESA)
3542 N. Geronimo Ave., Tucson AZ 85705 USA
Tel: 520-333-2577
secretariat@mesana.org
www.mesana.org
Overview: A medium-sized international charitable organization founded in 1966
Mission: To promote high standards of scholarship & instruction; To facilitate communication among scholars through meetings & publications; To promote cooperation among persons & organizations concerned with the scholarly study of the Middle East
Member of: American Council of Learned Societies; National Humanities Alliance
Finances: Annual Operating Budget: $250,000-$500,000; Funding Sources: Membership dues; contributions
Staff Member(s): 5
Membership: 3,000 individual + 70 institutional; Fees: US$75-$300 individual (based on income); $65 student; $80 retired; Member Profile: Scholars & others interested in the study of the Middle East; Committees: Academic Freedom; Annual Meeting Program; Canadian Members; Conflict of Interest Statement; Nominating; Publications; Task Force on Civil & Human Rights; Undergraduate Middle East Studies
Activities: Academic conferences; publications; Rents Mailing List: Yes
Chief Officer(s):
Amy W. Newhall, Executive Director/Treasurer
amy@mesana.org
Sara L. Palmer, Manager, External Relations
sara@mesana.org
Rose Veneklasen, Program Coordinator
rose@mesana.org
Publications:
• International Journal of Middle East Studies
Type: Journal; Frequency: Quarterly
Profile: Academic journal

MIEC Pax Romana Voir IMCS Pax Romana

Mineurs unis d'Amérique (CTC) See United Mine Workers of America (CLC)

Modern Language Association of America (MLA)
26 Broadway, 3rd Fl., New York NY 10004-1789 USA
Tel: 646-576-5000; Fax: 646-458-0030
www.mla.org
Also Known As: Modern Language Association
Overview: A medium-sized international organization founded in 1883 overseen by American Council of Learned Societies
Mission: To share the results of scholarly activity & teaching experiences with colleagues; To discuss trends in the study & teaching of language & literature
Affiliation(s): Fédération internationale des langues et littératures modernes
Membership: 30,000 individual; Fees: Schedule available; Member Profile: Persons professionally interested in modern languages & literature
Activities: Publishing books & journals; Rents Mailing List: Yes
Chief Officer(s):
Marianne Hirsch, President
Rosemary G. Feal, Executive Director
rfeal@mla.org
Meetings/Conferences:
• Modern Language Association 2018 Convention, January, 2018, New York, NY
Scope: Provincial
Publications:
• ADE Bulletin
Type: Journal
• ADFL Bulletin
Type: Journal
• MLA International Bibliography
Type: Bibliography
Profile: Print & online
• Profession
Type: Journal; Frequency: Annually

Monte Cassino Society
c/o White Horses, Meadway, East Looe, Cornwall PL13 1JT
United Kingdom
www.montecassinosociety.org
Overview: A small international organization
Mission: To further an interest in the experiences of those who took part in the battles of Monte Cassino & in the Italian Campaign
Membership: Fees: Free for veterans & spouses; £12 in the UK for children of veterans or others interested in the society
Chief Officer(s):
Judith Coote, Contact, England
jude@whlooe.eclipse.co.uk

Mouvement féderalist mondial See World Federalist Movement

Multinational Association for Supportive Care in Cancer (MASCC)
Herredsvejen 2, Hiller³d DK-3400 Denmark
Tel: 45-4820-7022; Fax: 45-4821-7022
www.mascc.org
www.linkedin.com/groups/MASCC-ISOO-Supportive-Care-in-5128277
www.facebook.com/589292597781443
twitter.com/CancerCareMASCC
www.youtube.com/user/MASCCorg
Overview: A medium-sized international organization founded in 1990
Mission: To promote research & education in all aspects of supportive care for patients with cancer
Membership: Fees: Schedule available; Member Profile: Physicians; Nurses; Dentists; Pharmacists; Psychologists; Social workers; Dieticians; Infectious disease specialists; Educators; Representatives from industry and non-profit sectors; Committees: Awards; Finance; Governance; Guidelines; Membership; Publications; Nominations; Communications
Activities: Providing recent scientific & social information on medical, surgical, nursing, & psycho-social supportive care for cancer patients in all stages of their disease; Organizing research & education through study groups; Encouraging networking among disciplines
Chief Officer(s):
Åge Schultz, Executive Director
aschultz@mascc.org
Publications:
• MASCC E-News
Type: Newsletter; Frequency: Quarterly
Profile: Recent information about organizational changes, deadlines, surveys, & study groups for Multinational Association for Supportive Care in Cancer members
• MASCC Society News
Type: Newsletter; Frequency: Monthly; Editor: Lisa Schulmeister; Snezana Bosnjak
Profile: Published on the web & in the back of the SCC journal
• Supportive Care in Cancer: The Journal of MASCC
Type: Journal; Frequency: Monthly; Editor: Fred Ashbury; Price: Free with MASCC / ISOO membership
Profile: Original work, reviews, consensus papers, guidelines, & short communications

Multiple Sclerosis International Federation (MSIF)
Skyline House, 200 Union St., London SE1 0LX UK
Tel: 44-20-7620-1911
www.msif.org
www.facebook.com/110033075774139
twitter.com/MSIntFederation
www.youtube.com/user/MSIFmedia
Previous Name: International Federation of Multiple Sclerosis Societies
Overview: A medium-sized international charitable organization founded in 1967
Mission: To link the work of national MS societies worldwide; to eliminate MS & its devastating effects; to promote global research, exchange of information, advocacy & development of new & existing MS societies
Affiliation(s): Multiple Sclerosis Society of Canada
Finances: Funding Sources: Member societies; subscriptions; corporate, foundation & individual donations
Membership: 33 full; 11 associate; 50 corresponding; Fees: Schedule available based on organizations income; Member Profile: MS Organizations; Committees: Finance & Audit; Fundraising; Nominating; CEO Advisory Group; People with MS advisory
Activities: MS Global Dinner Party
Chief Officer(s):
Weyman Johnson, President & Chair

NACE International (NACE)
15835 Park Ten Pl., Houston TX 77084 USA
Tel: 281-228-6200; Fax: 281-228-6300
firstservice@nace.org
www.nace.org
www.linkedin.com/company/nace-international
www.facebook.com/NACEinternational
twitter.com/NACEtweet
Previous Name: The National Association of Corrosion Engineers
Overview: A large international licensing charitable organization founded in 1943
Mission: To protect people, assets & the environment from the effects of corrosion; Northern Area sections include: Atlantic Canada, B.C., Calgary, Canadian National Capital Section, Edmonton, Montreal, Saskatchewan & Toronto
Finances: Annual Operating Budget: Greater than $5 Million; Funding Sources: Membership dues; Registration fees; Publication sales
Staff Member(s): 65
Membership: 19,000 members in 100 countries; Fees: US$130 individual; US$20 student; Schedule (based upon number of representatives) for corporate memberships; Member Profile: Engineers & others involved in corrosion prevention & control
Activities: Providing technical training & certification; Organizing technical conferences; Speaker Service: Yes; Rents Mailing List: Yes; Library: Open to public
Chief Officer(s):
Bob Chalker, Executive Director, 281-228-6250
Awards:
• R.A. Brannon Award
Awarded to recognize outstanding service that promotes NACE objectives Amount: $1,000
• A.B. Campbell Award
Awarded to recognize an outstanding paper published in MP Magazine or CORROSION journal by an author aged 35 or younger Amount: $1,000
• CORROSION Best Paper Award
Awarded to honour the best paper published in a journal
• T.J. Hull Award
Awarded to honour contributions in publications Amount: $1,000
• Frank Newman Speller Award
Honours contributions in corrosion engineering Amount: $1,000
• H.H. Uhlig Award
Honours contributions in corrosion education Amount: $1,000

- Willis Rodney Whitney Award
Honours contributions in corrosion science *Amount:* $1,000
- Distinguished Organization Award
Awarded to an organization to recognize contributions to corrosion science and/or engineering
- Distinguished Service Award
Awarded to recognize outstanding service to NACE
- Technical Achievement Award
Recognizes technical contributions in corrosion engineering
- Fellow Honor
Recognizes distinguished contributions in corrosion prevention
- Founders Award
Awarded to honour meritorious work by an individual on behalf of the NACE Foundation
- Outstanding Student Award
Awarded to honour exceptional service to NACE International/NACE Foundation, a NACE student chapter, or the ACC Student Sub-committee

Meetings/Conferences:
- NACE International CORROSION 2018, April, 2018, Phoenix Convention Center, Phoenix, AZ
Scope: International
Description: A corrosion conference & exposition
- NACE International CORROSION 2019, March, 2019, Nashville, TN
Scope: International
Description: A corrosion conference & exposition
- NACE International CORROSION 2020, March, 2020, Houston, TX
Scope: International
Description: A corrosion conference & exposition
- NACE International CORROSION 2021, April, 2021, Salt Lake City, UT
Scope: International
Description: A corrosion conference & exposition

Publications:
- Coatings Pro [a publication of NACE International]
Type: Magazine; *Frequency:* Monthly; *Editor:* Eliina Lizarraga
Profile: An information resource for the high-performance coating industry
- CorrDefense [a publication of NACE International]
Type: Magazine; *Frequency:* 3 pa.; *Editor:* Cynthia Greenwood
Profile: Covers Department of Defense efforts & programs aimed at preventing corrosion on military infrastructure
- CORROSION [a publication of NACE International]
Type: Journal; *Frequency:* Monthly; *Editor:* Marlene Walters; *ISSN:* 0010-9312
Profile: An information resource containing the latest progress in corrosion control science & technology
- EAPA News [a publication of NACE International]
Type: Newsletter
Profile: Industry news for the East Acia & Pacific Area
- InspectThis! [a publication of NACE International]
Type: Newsletter; *Frequency:* 3 pa
Profile: An information resource for coating inspectors who are certified by the NACE Coating Inspector Program
- LatinCorr [a publication of NACE International]
Type: Magazine; *ISSN:* 2165-9524
Profile: Published in Spanish & Portuguese; dedicated to corrosion control & mechanical integrity of assets
- MP Buyers Guide [a publication of NACE International]
Frequency: Annually
Profile: A directory of manufacturers, suppliers, & constultants worldwide that provide products for corrosion prevention & control
- NACE Corrosion Press [a publication of NACE International]
Type: Newsletter; *Frequency:* Weekly
Profile: Contains weekly briefings on industry news
- Section Officer News [a publication of NACE International]
Type: Newsletter
Profile: News for Section Officers
- Stay Current [a publication of NACE International]
Type: Newsletter; *Frequency:* s-a.
Profile: An information resource for cathodic protection professionals who are certified by NACE
- TCC e-News [a publication of NACE International]
Type: Newsletter
Profile: News for the Technical Coordination Committee

Canadian Region - Atlantic Canada Section
c/o AMC Atlantic Met Consulting Ltd., #106, 11 Morris Dr., Dartmouth NS B3B 1M2
Tel: 902-405-3600
Chief Officer(s):
Scott MacIntyre, Section Trustee
scott.amc@ns.aliantzinc.ca

Canadian Region - British Columbia Section
c/o FortisBC Energy Inc., 1111 West Georgia St., Vancouver BC V6E 4M3
Tel: 604-443-6500
Chief Officer(s):
Scott Bowing, Section Trustee
scott.bowing@fortisbc.com

Canadian Region - Calgary Section
c/o Pipetech Corporation Inc., 3311 - 114 Ave. SE, Calgary AB T2Z 3X2
Tel: 403-287-3558
Chief Officer(s):
Jana Johnson, Section Chair, 403-237-1221
chair@nacecalgary.ca

Canadian Region - Edmonton Section
c/o Enbridge Inc., 10201 Jasper Ave. NW, Edmonton AB T5J 3N7
Tel: 780-420-8465
Chief Officer(s):
Haralampos Tsaprailis, Section Vice Chair
harry.tsaprailis@enbridge.com

Canadian Region - Quebéc Section
c/o The Sherwin-Williams Company, QC
Tél: 514-754-8008
Chief Officer(s):
Yanick Croteau, Section Chair
yanick.croteau@sherwin.com

Canadian Region - National Capital Section
c/o CANMET Materials Technology Laboratory, 183 Longwood South, Hamilton ON L8P 0A5
Tel: 905-645-0688
Chief Officer(s):
Sankara Papavinasam, Section Chair
spapavin@nrcan.gc.ca

Canadian Region - Toronto Section
c/o Kinectrics Inc., #215, 800 Kipling Ave., Toronto ON M8Z 6C4
Tel: 416-207-6000
Chief Officer(s):
Joseph Beutler, Section Chair

NAFSA: Association of International Educators
1307 New York Ave. NW, 8th Fl., Washington DC 20005-4701 USA
Tel: 202-737-3699; *Fax:* 202-737-3657
inbox@nafsa.org
www.nafsa.org
www.linkedin.com/groups/71923
www.facebook.com/nafsa
twitter.com/nafsa
Overview: A large international organization founded in 1948
Mission: To promote international education; To offer professional development opportunities
Membership: 10,000
Activities: Providing networking opportunities; Building government & public awareness of the role of international education
Chief Officer(s):
Esther Brimmer, Executive Director & CEO

Meetings/Conferences:
- NAFSA: Association of International Educators 2018 Annual Conference & Expo, May, 2018, Philadelphia, PA
Scope: International

Publications:
- International Educator Magazine
Type: Magazine; *Frequency:* Bimonthly; *Accepts Advertising*
- Journal of Studies in International Education
Type: Journal; *Editor:* Hans de Wit; *Price:* $15/yr. members
Profile: Peer-reviewed historical, analytical, & experimental research in the field of international education
- NAFSA: Association of International Educators Membership Directory
Type: Directory
- NAFSA.news
Type: Newsletter; *Frequency:* Weekly
Profile: Developments in international education, resources, policy developments, & conferences for NAFSA members only

National Alopecia Areata Foundation (NAAF)
#200B, 65 Mitchel Blvd., San Rafael CA 94903 USA
Tel: 415-472-3780; *Fax:* 415-480-1800
info@naaf.org
www.naaf.org
www.facebook.com/NAAFUSA
twitter.com/NAAF_Org
www.youtube.com/user/naaforg
Overview: A medium-sized international charitable organization founded in 1981
Mission: To support research to find a cure or acceptable treatment for aropecia areata; to support those with the disease & educate the public about aropecia areata
Member of: National Health Council; National Organization of Rare Disorders; BBB Wise Giving Alliance Accredited Charities; Dermatology Nurses' Association; Coalition of Skin Diseases; Research America
Affiliation(s): Society for Investigative Dermatology; American Academy of Dermatology; National Institute for Arthritis & Musculoskeletal & Skin Diseases
Activities: *Awareness Events:* Alopecia Areata Awareness Month, Sept.
Chief Officer(s):
Dory Kranz, President/CEO

National Asbestos Council *See* Environmental Information Association

National Association for Environmental Education (UK) (NAEE)
United Kingdom
Tel: 0747-928-7183
info@naee.org.uk
www.naee.org.uk
www.linkedin.com/company/3666656
www.facebook.com/NAEEUK
twitter.com/NAEE_UK
Overview: A medium-sized international charitable organization founded in 1965
Mission: To promote environmental education for sustainability in the formal education sector by teachers for teachers
Member of: Council for Environmental Education
Finances: *Annual Operating Budget:* Less than $50,000; *Funding Sources:* Dept. of Environment grant; membership dues; publication sales
Staff Member(s): 2
Membership: 1,000; *Fees:* £20 individual; £30 schools; £40 universities; £40 organizations (Europe); £50 organizations (worldwide); *Member Profile:* Educationalists
Activities: Conferences & courses which attempt to further environmental education in both its natural & human setting; seminars on current topics; publications; *Speaker Service:* Yes; *Library:* Not open to public
Chief Officer(s):
Justin Dillon, President

National Association for Environmental Management (NAEM)
#1002, 1612 K St. NW, Washington DC 20006 USA
Tel: 202-986-6616; *Fax:* 202-530-4408
Toll-Free: 800-391-6236
programs@naem.org
www.naem.org
www.linkedin.com/groups?home=&gid=151419
www.facebook.com/NAEM.org
twitter.com/thegreentie
www.youtube.com/user/NAEMorgTV
Overview: A large international organization founded in 1990
Mission: To promote global sustainability; To advance environmental stewardship; To establish safe & healthy workplaces
Staff Member(s): 7
Membership: *Fees:* $1,500-$7,500; *Member Profile:* Corporate environmental, health & safety, & sustainability decision-makers
Activities: Conducting research; Creating a knowledge sharing network; Offering educational webinars
Chief Officer(s):
Carol Singer Neuvelt, Executive Director
csinger@naem.org
Virginia Hoekenga, Deputy Director
Virginia@naem.org
Mike Mahanna, Manager, Programs
mike@naem.org
Elizabeth Ryan, Director, Communications
elizabeth@naem.org

Meetings/Conferences:
- National Association for Environmental Management 2018 EHS & Sustainability Management Forum, October, 2018, Louisville Marriott Downtown, Louisville, KY
Scope: International
Attendance: 500+

Publications:
• Affiliates Council Guide [a publication of the National Association for Environmental Management]
Type: Guide
Profile: A guide to finding a service provider or consultant
• Green TIPS Guide
Type: Guide
Profile: A resource to engage others about a company's sustainability goals
• NAEM [National Association for Environmental Management] Network E-News
Type: Newsletter; *Frequency:* Biweekly
Profile: Relevant news for environmental, health & safety, & sustainability professionals

National Association for Information Destruction (NAID)
#350, 1951 W Camelback Rd., Phoenix AZ 85015 USA
Tel: 602-788-6243; *Fax:* 602-788-4144
info@naidonline.org
www.naidonline.org
www.linkedin.com/groups?gid=3957595
www.facebook.com/NAIDHQ
twitter.com/NAIDinc
www.youtube.com/user/NAIDTV
Overview: A small international organization
Mission: NAID is the international, non-profit trade association of the information destruction industry. Its members are companies and individuals involved in providing information destruction services. NAID's mission is to educate business, industry and government of the importance of destroying discarded information and the value of contract destruction services
Membership: *Fees:* Schedule available; *Member Profile:* Includes 50+ Canadian companies
Chief Officer(s):
Robert Johnson, Executive Director
rjohnson@naidonline.org

National Association for PET Container Resources (NAPCOR)
PO Box 1327, Sonoma CA 95476 USA
Tel: 707-996-4207; *Fax:* 707-935-1998
Toll-Free: 800-762-7267
information@napcor.com
www.napcor.com
www.facebook.com/173626632687722?sk=wall
Overview: A small national organization founded in 1987
Mission: To promote the usage of PET packaging & to facilitate the collection of PET plastic containers
Finances: *Funding Sources:* Membership dues
Membership: 13; *Member Profile:* PET bottle manufacturers & suppliers to the PET industry
Chief Officer(s):
Rick Moore, Executive Director
rmoore@napcor.com

National Association for Surface Finishing (AESF) / Association des galvanoplastes d'Amérique
#500, 1155 - 15th St. NW, Washington DC 20005 USA
Tel: 202-457-8404; *Fax:* 202-530-0659
info@nasfmembership.com
www.nasf.org
www.linkedin.com/company/nasf-the-national-association-for-surface-finishing
www.facebook.com/SurfaceFinishers
Previous Name: American Electroplaters & Surface Finishers Society
Overview: A medium-sized international organization founded in 1909
Mission: To advance the science of electroplating & surface finishing
Finances: *Annual Operating Budget:* $500,000-$1.5 Million; *Funding Sources:* Membership dues; publications; education events
Staff Member(s): 6
Membership: 3,500 individual; *Fees:* Schedule available; *Member Profile:* Technical; professional; doctorate; managers; owners; job shop personnel; *Committees:* Over 25 technical/membership/social
Activities: *Library* Open to public
Chief Officer(s):
Fred Mueller, President, 908-862-6200, Fax: 908-862-6110
fmueller@magnaplate.com
Fred Assante, Contact, Membership
passante@nasf.org

Awards:
• NASF Scholarships Program
Eligibility: Undergraduate & graduate students interested in studying chemical engineering, material science or engineering, mechanical engineering, metallurgical engineering, environmental engineering or chemistry *Amount:* $1,500 each
Meetings/Conferences:
• National Association for Surface Finishing (NASF) Leadership Conference 2018, February, 2018, Koloa, HI
Scope: International
• National Association for Surface Finishing (NASF) Washington Forum, April, 2018, Ritz-Carlton Pentagon City, Washington, DC
Scope: International
Contact Information: Contact, Washington Forum: Jeff Hannapel, E-mail: jhannapel@thepolicygroup.com
• National Association for Surface Finishing (NASF) SUR/FIN Manufacturing & Technology Trade Show & Conference, June, 2018, Cleveland, OH
Scope: International
Contact Information: Contact, Event Director: Cheryl Clark, E-mail: cclark@NASF.org

National Association of Addiction Treatment Providers
#1303, 1120 Lincoln St., Denver CO 80203 USA
Toll-Free: 888-574-1008
info@naatp.org
www.naatp.org
Overview: A small international organization founded in 1978
Mission: To promote, assist & enhance the delivery of ethical, effective, research-based treatment for alcoholism & other drug addictions; To provide its members & the public with accurate, responsible information & other resources related to the treatment of these diseases; To advocate for increased access to & availability of quality treatment for those who suffer from alcoholism & other drug addictions; To work in partnership with other organizations & individuals that share NAATP's mission & goals
Affiliation(s): Fifteen treatment centres in Canada
Membership: 250
Chief Officer(s):
Carlton Kester, Chair
Marvin Ventrell, Executive Director
Katie Strand, Director, Operations
Jessica Swan, Manager, Outcomes & Surveys
Tiffany Rode, Coordinator, Programs

National Association of College Auxiliary Services (NACAS)
PO Box 5546, 7 Boar's Head Lane, Charlottesville VA 22905-5546 USA
Tel: 434-245-8425; *Fax:* 434-245-8453
info@nacas.org
www.nacas.org
Overview: A medium-sized international organization founded in 1969
Mission: To provide information & opportunity for auxiliary service professionals
Membership: 835 USA institutions + 69 Canadian institutions + 5 overseas institutions; *Member Profile:* International college auxiliary service professionals; Non-academic campus support services such as bookstores, food services, housing, recreation services, & security
Activities: Offering professional development opportunities
Chief Officer(s):
Bob Hassmiller, Chief Executive Officer, 434-245-8425 Ext. 222
bob@nacas.org
Jeff Perdue, Deputy Executive Director, 434-245-8425 Ext. 223
jeff@nacas.org
Abby Tammen, Associate Executive Director, 434-245-8425 Ext. 238
abby@nacas.org
Heather W. Brown, Director, Business Partner Services, 434-245-8425 Ext. 228
heather@nacas.org
Anne P. Munson, Director, Education & Membership Services, 434-245-8425 Ext. 235
anne@nacas.org
Meetings/Conferences:
• 2018 National Association of College Auxiliary Services Annual Conference, October, 2018, Rosen Shingle Creek, Orlando, FL
Scope: International
Publications:
• College Services
Type: Magazine; *Frequency:* Quarterly; *Accepts Advertising*

• NACAS Quarterly
Type: Newsletter; *Frequency:* Quarterly
Profile: Current events, member news, professional development activities, & brief articles of interest to college auxiliary services professionals

National Association of Collegiate Directors of Athletics (NACDA)
24651 Detroit Rd., Westlake OH 44145 USA
Tel: 440-892-4000; *Fax:* 440-892-4007
www.nacda.com
www.facebook.com/nacda
twitter.com/nacda
Overview: A small international organization founded in 1965
Mission: To serve as the professional association for those in the field of intercollegiate athletics administration; To serves as a vehicle for networking, the exchange of information, & advocacy on behalf of the profession
Membership: 6,100 individuals; 1,600 institutions; *Fees:* Schedule available; *Member Profile:* Collegiate athletics administrators in the United States, Canada, & Mexico
Activities: Providing educational opportunities
Chief Officer(s):
Bob Vecchione, Executive Director
bvecchione@nacda.com

The National Association of Corrosion Engineers *See* NACE International

National Association of Environmental Professionals (NAEP)
PO Box 460, Collingswood NJ 08108 USA
Tel: 856-283-7816; *Fax:* 856-210-1619
naep@bowermanagementservices.com
www.naep.org
www.linkedin.com/groups/National-Association-Environmental-Professionals-NAEP-3834863
www.facebook.com/267926723515
Overview: A medium-sized national organization founded in 1975
Mission: To promote a code of ethics & standard of practice among environmental professionals
Finances: *Annual Operating Budget:* $100,000-$250,000
Staff Member(s): 2; 30 volunteer(s)
Membership: 2,000; *Fees:* US$150 general membership; *Committees:* Education; Membership; Awards; Conference; NAEP Operations; Chapters; Environmental Policy; Communications
Activities: *Rents Mailing List:* Yes
Chief Officer(s):
Harold Draper, President
Ron Deverman, President
deverman415@comcast.net
Tim Bower, Managing Director, 856-283-7816
Awards:
• NAEP Presidential Award For Excellence

National Association of Railroad Passengers (NARP)
#240, 1200 G St. NW, Washington DC 20005 USA
Tel: 202-408-8362; *Fax:* 202-408-8287
narp@narprail.org
www.narprail.org
www.facebook.com/narprail
twitter.com/narprail
plus.google.com/110252908993287069826
Also Known As: Rail Passengers Association
Overview: A medium-sized national charitable organization founded in 1967
Mission: To encourage & promote a more balanced North American transporation system including promotion of federal & state/provincial policies beneficial to all forms of rail service, urban rail transit, rural public transporation & intermodal terminals
Affiliation(s): Transport 2000 Ltd.
Finances: *Funding Sources:* Membership dues
Staff Member(s): 6
Membership: *Fees:* Schedule available; *Member Profile:* Rail passengers
Activities: *Rents Mailing List:* Yes; *Library:* National Association of Railroad Passengers Library; Not open to public
Chief Officer(s):
Jim Mathews, President & CEO
Awards:
• Golden Spike Award

Presented to individuals who have made important contributions to passenger rail service
• John R. Martin Passenger Train Advocacy Award
Presented to individuals who have given many years of exceptional service to the organization
• Youth Passenger Citizenship Award
Presented to students and young people who demonstrate exceptional leadership, initiative or passion in making meaningful improvements to passenger train travel
• NARP Academic Award
Presented to university & college professors who have an excellent record in developing and promoting knowledge about and the progress of passenger train transportation
• Dr. Gary Burch Memorial Safety Award
Presented to a railroad worker who has made a significant contribution to the improvement of the safety of railroad passengers
• Tracks to the Future Leadership Award
Presented to individuals and organizations that have demonstrated outstanding leadership in their commitment to improving and expanding passenger rail-based transportation
Meetings/Conferences:
• Rail Passengers Association 2018 Spring Advocacy Summit & Meeting, April, 2018, Hilton Alexandria Old Town, Alexandria, VA

National Association of Real Estate Appraisers (NAREA)
PO Box 879, Palm Springs CA 92263 USA
Fax: 760-327-5631
Toll-Free: 877-815-4172
support@assoc-hdqts.org
www.narea-assoc.org
Overview: A medium-sized international organization founded in 1966
Member of: International Association Managers
Membership: 10,000 (includes Canadian); *Fees:* US$155-295
Activities: *Library:* National Association of Real Estate Appraiser's Library
Publications:
• The Appraisal Times
Type: Newsletter; *Frequency:* q.

National Association of Review Appraisers & Mortgage Underwriters (NARAMU)
PO Box 879, 810 Farrell Dr. North, Palm Springs CA 92263 USA
Tel: 760-327-5284; *Fax:* 760-327-5631
Toll-Free: 877-743-6805
Other Communication: Alt. E-mail: support@assoc-hdqts.org
info@naramu.org
www.naramu.org
Overview: A medium-sized international organization founded in 1975
Member of: International Association Managers
Affiliation(s): National Association of Real Estate Appraisers
Membership: 4,200; *Fees:* US$245; US$205 associate;
Member Profile: Review Appraisers
Chief Officer(s):
Bill Merrell, Member, Advisory Council

National Association of Sanitarians *See* National Environmental Health Association

National Association of Secondary School Principals (NASSP)
1904 Association Dr., Reston VA 20191-1537 USA
Tel: 703-860-0200; *Fax:* 703-860-3422
Toll-Free: 800-253-7746
www.nassp.org
www.linkedin.com/company/4816413
www.facebook.com/principals
twitter.com/NASSP
www.youtube.com/user/NASSPtv
Overview: A medium-sized international organization founded in 1916
Mission: To lead school principals, assistant principals, & other school leaders across the United States & internationally
Affiliation(s): Canadian Association of Principals
Membership: *Member Profile:* Middle level & high school principals; assistant principals; aspiring school leaders from across the United States & more than 45 countries around the world
Chief Officer(s):
JoAnn D. Bartoletti, Executive Director

National Association of Teachers of Singing (NATS)
#401, 9957 Moorings Dr., Jacksonville FL 32257 USA
Tel: 904-992-9101; *Fax:* 904-262-2587
info@nats.org
www.nats.org
www.linkedin.com/company/nat%27l-assoc.-of-teachers-of-singing-nats-
www.facebook.com/OfficialNATS
twitter.com/OfficialNATS
www.youtube.com/user/OfficialNATS
Overview: A small international organization founded in 1944
Mission: To encourage the highest standards of the vocal art & of ethical principles in the teaching of singing; to promote vocal education & research at all levels, both for the enrichment of the general public & for the professional advancement of the talented
Member of: National Music Council
Finances: *Annual Operating Budget:* $500,000-$1.5 Million
Staff Member(s): 6; 22 volunteer(s)
Membership: 14 regions in United States & Canada; *Fees:* US$100-110; *Member Profile:* Teachers of singing
Activities: *Internships:* Yes; *Rents Mailing List:* Yes
Chief Officer(s):
Allen Henderson, Executive Director
allen@nats.org
Deborah L. Guess, Director of Operations
deborah@nats.org
Kathryn Protor Duax, President
president@nats.org
Norman Spivey, President Elect
presidentelect@nats.org
Carole Blankenship, Vice-President
vpnatsaa@nats.org

National Association of Television Program Executives (NATPE)
5757 Wilshire Blvd., Penthouse 10, Los Angeles CA 90036-3681 USA
Tel: 310-453-4440
www.natpe.com
www.facebook.com/NATPE
twitter.com/NATPE
Overview: A medium-sized international organization
Mission: To create, develop, & distribute televised programming in all forms, across all platforms; To develop & nurture opportunities for buying, selling, & sharing of content & ideas
Chief Officer(s):
JP Bommel, President & CEO, 310-857-1655
jpbommel@natpe.org

National Association of the Chemistry Industry / Asociación Nacional de la Industria Química, A.C (ANIQ)
Angel Urraza No. 505, Col del Valle, Mexico 03100 DF Mexico
Tel: 52-55-5230-5100; *Fax:* 52-55-5230-5107
anavarrete@aniq.org.mx
www.aniq.org.mx
Overview: A medium-sized national organization
Mission: To promote the sustainable development of the chemical sector, in harmony with the environment that surrounds it, as well as to look for joint solutions to common problems by dialogue & agreement, under strict rules of ethics & supported by specialized services, consulting, information, negotiation & diffusion
Finances: *Annual Operating Budget:* $500,000-$1.5 Million;
Funding Sources: Membership fees & services
Staff Member(s): 50
Membership: 223; *Member Profile:* Chemical producers & distributors; *Committees:* International Trade; Human Resources; Logistics & Transportation; Environment; Safety & Health; Communication & Information
Activities: National Forum of the Chemical Industry; *Internships:* Yes; *Speaker Service:* Yes; *Rents Mailing List:* Yes; *Library:* ANIQ's Information Centre; Open to public
Chief Officer(s):
Miguel Benedetto Alexanderson, President

National Association of Towns & Townships (NATaT)
#300, 1130 Connecticut Ave., Washington DC 20036 USA
Tel: 202-454-3950; *Fax:* 202-331-1598
www.natat.org
www.facebook.com/168130923318590
Overview: A large national organization founded in 1976
Mission: To help improve the quality of life for suburban and non-metro communities
Finances: *Annual Operating Budget:* $500,000-$1.5 Million
Staff Member(s): 6
Membership: 13,000 towns; *Member Profile:* Small, generally rural, communities
Activities: Offering technical assistance, educational services, & public policy support to local government officials from small communities across the USA; Conducting research & developing public policy recommendations through the National Center for Small Communities; *Awareness Events:* America's Town Meeting, 1st week Sept.
Chief Officer(s):
Jennifer Imo, Federal Director
jimo@tfgnet.com
Publications:
• Washington Report [a publication of the National Association of Towns & Townships]
Type: Newsletter; *Frequency:* Weekly
Profile: A resource focusing on legislative issues of importance to small governments

National Association of Watch & Clock Collectors, Inc. (NAWCC)
514 Poplar St., Columbia PA 17512-2130 USA
Tel: 717-684-8261; *Fax:* 717-684-0878
Toll-Free: 877-255-1849
info@nawcc.org
www.nawcc.org
www.linkedin.com/company/556039
www.facebook.com/nawcc
twitter.com/museumoftime
Also Known As: National Watch & Clock Museum
Overview: A large international organization founded in 1943
Mission: To stimulate interest in timepieces; To collect & preserve horological materials & information; To work with others in exhibiting timepieces; To encourage timepiece collection; To disseminate information on timepieces; To facilitate timepiece markets
Member of: American Alliance of Museums; Association of Science-Technology Centers
Finances: *Annual Operating Budget:* $1.5 Million-$3 Million;
Funding Sources: Membership dues; Donations; Advertising; Educational programs; Admissions
Staff Member(s): 30; 40 volunteer(s)
Membership: 13,500; *Fees:* $90 (USD) individual; $175 (USD) business
Activities: Operating National Watch & Clock Museum, as well as a Library & Research Centre; Offering publishing programs; Sponsoring conventions & symposia; Hosting meetings; *Internships:* Yes; *Speaker Service:* Yes; *Library:* NAWCC Library & Research Center
Chief Officer(s):
J. Steven Humphrey, Executive Director
shumphrey@nawcc.org
Charles Auman, Controller
cauman@nawcc.org
Awards:
• Pritchard Award
Deadline: January *Amount:* $1,500
Meetings/Conferences:
• National Association of Watch & Clock Collectors 2018 National Convention, July, 2018, Wyndham Garden Hotel, York, PA
Scope: International
Publications:
• Watch & Clock Bulletin [a publication of the National Association of Watch & Clock Collectors]
Type: Journal; *Frequency:* bi-m.; *Editor:* Therese Umerlik; *ISSN:* 2152-4858
Profile: Contains member research articles, answers to questions about timekeeping, &association news

British Columbia Chapter
Heritage Hall, 3102 Main St., Vancouver BC V5T 3G7
net.nawcc.org/Chapter121BritishColumbia
Chief Officer(s):
Delores Fox, Treasurer

Calgary Chapter
Calgary AB
Tel: 403-238-2808
www.cawcca.com
Chief Officer(s):
Jim Johnson, President
jim40@shaw.ca

Quinte Timekeepers
Belleville ON
www.quintetimekeepers.com
Chief Officer(s):
Jim Hartog, President

Montréal Association of Watch & Clock Collectors
Montréal QC
nawcc.org
Chief Officer(s):
Andre Gagnon, Contact
Ottawa Valley Chapter
Ottawa ON
e-mail: secretary.chapter111@yahoo.com
www.ottawaclocksandwatches.ca
Chief Officer(s):
Don Purchase, President
• Bytown Times [a publication of the National Association of Watch & Clock Collectors, Ottawa Valley Chapter]
Type: Newsletter; Frequency: 5 pa
Southwestern Ontario
Royal Canadian Legion, Branch 251, 33 Veterans Dr., Mount Brydges ON N0L 1W0
Tel: 519-264-1580
www.nawcc92.mysite.com
Chief Officer(s):
Janet Clarke, Executive Member, 705-645-9938
Toronto Chapter
Crowne Plaza Hotel, 33 Carlson Ct., Toronto ON M9W 6H5
Tel: 416-675-1234
chapter33toronto@gmail.com
www.torontochapter33.ca
Chief Officer(s):
Ben Orszulak, President

National Association of Women in Construction (NAWIC)
327 South Adams St., Fort Worth TX 76104 USA
Tel: 817-877-5551; Fax: 817-877-0324
Toll-Free: 800-552-3506
nawic@nawic.org
www.nawic.org
www.linkedin.com/company/national-association-of-women-in-construction
www.facebook.com/nawicnational
Overview: A large international organization founded in 1955
Mission: To promote & support the advancement & employment of women in the construction industry
Finances: Annual Operating Budget: $500,000-$1.5 Million; Funding Sources: Membership dues; Sponsorship
Staff Member(s): 5
Membership: 6,000; Fees: $42 student-at-large; $52 student chapter; $201 international; $225 active and member-at-large; $346 corporate; Member Profile: Women employed in construction & construction-related fields
Activities: Speaker Service: Yes; Library: Not open to public
Chief Officer(s):
Dede Hughes, Executive Vice President
dedeh@nawic.org
Awards:
• Lifetime Achievement Award
• Member of the Year Award
• Future Leader of the Year Award
• National Association of Women in Construction Founders' Scholarship Program
Amount: $500-$2,500 Contact: Judy DeWeese, Fund Administrator, Scholarship, E-mail: JuDeNAWIC@aol.com; nfsfscholarship@gmail.com
Publications:
• The NAWIC Image [a publication of the National Association of Women in Construction]
Type: Magazine

National Audubon Society, Inc. (NAS)
225 Varick St., New York NY 10014 USA
Tel: 212-979-3000
Toll-Free: 844-428-3826
audubon@emailcustomerservice.com
www.audubon.org
www.facebook.com/NationalAudubonSociety
twitter.com/AudubonSociety
www.youtube.com/user/NationalAudubon
Also Known As: Audubon
Overview: A large national charitable organization founded in 1905
Mission: To conserve & restore natural ecosystems, focusing on birds, other wildlife & their habitats for the benefit of humanity & the earth's biological diversity
Membership: 500,000; Fees: $20 USA; $45 Canada; $50 international
Activities: Seminars, educational events & workshops on various conservation topics
Chief Officer(s):
David Yarnold, President & CEO
Anne Lieberman, Chief Development Officer
Susan Lunden, Chief Operations Officer
Publications:
• Audubon Magazine [a publication of the National Audubon Society, Inc.]
Type: Magazine; Frequency: bi-m.; ISSN: 0097-7136
• National Audubon Society, Inc. Annual Report
Type: Yearbook; Frequency: Annual

National Bison Association (NBA)
#200, 8690 Wolff Ct., Westminster CO 80031 USA
Tel: 303-292-2833; Fax: 303-845-9081
info@bisoncentral.com
www.bisoncentral.com
www.facebook.com/125262637531750
Overview: A medium-sized international organization founded in 1975
Mission: To promote the production, marketing & preservation of bison
Affiliation(s): Canadian Bison Association
Finances: Funding Sources: Membership dues; sales; donations
Staff Member(s): 4
Membership: 1,000+; Fees: Schedule available; Member Profile: Active - actively involved in production, management &/or marketing of bison; associate - non-owner of bison, interested in bison; Committees: Bison Registry; Commercial Marketers; Conservation; Finance; GTSS Consignors; Government Relations; Grass-Fed Bison; Heritage; Membership; Promotions; State & Regional; Winter Conference; Youth/Education
Activities: Gold Trophy Show & Sale; Internships: Yes
Chief Officer(s):
Dave Carter, Executive Director
david@bisoncentral.com
Peter Cook, President
pcookbuffaloman@aol.com
Publications:
• Bison World Magazine
Type: Journal; Frequency: Quarterly

National Coalition Against the Misuse of Pesticides See Beyond Pesticides

National Conferences of Firemen & Oilers (SEIU)
1023 - 15th St. NW, 10th Fl., Washington DC 20005 USA
Tel: 202-962-0981; Fax: 202-872-1222
mail@ncfo.org
www.ncfo.org
Overview: A small international organization founded in 1898
Chief Officer(s):
John R. Thacker, President
Dean Devits, Secretary-Treasurer

National Council for Science & the Environment (NCSE)
#250, 1101 17th St. NW, Washington DC 20036 USA
Tel: 202-530-5810; Fax: 202-628-4311
info@ncseonline.org
www.ncseonline.org
www.linkedin.com/company/national-council-for-science-and-the-environment
www.facebook.com/167494469941852
twitter.com/NCSEonline
www.youtube.com/user/NCSEonline
Previous Name: Committee for the National Institutes for the Environment
Overview: A medium-sized national organization founded in 1990
Mission: Improving the scientific basis for environmental decision making
Affiliation(s): Council of Environmental Deans & Directors; National Commission on Science for Sustainable Forestry
Finances: Annual Operating Budget: $500,000-$1.5 Million
Staff Member(s): 12; 10 volunteer(s)
Membership: Member Profile: Open to any concerned individual or organization
Activities: National Conference on Science Policy & the Environment; education & outreach programs; Library: National Library for the Environment
Chief Officer(s):
Peter D. Saundry, Executive Director
peter@ncseonline.org

National Council of Philippine American Canadian Accountants (NCPACA)
c/o Ed Ortiz, #2-N, 333 South Des Plaines St., Chicago IL 60661 USA
Tel: 312-876-1900; Fax: 312-876-1911
NCPACAWebmaster@ncpaca.org
www.ncpaca.org
Overview: A medium-sized international organization founded in 1984
Mission: To promote the continuing education of Filipino Canadian accountants; To promote high professional standards; To liaise with other international organizations
Affiliation(s): Philippine Certified Public Accountants of Greater Chicago; Philippine American Society of CPAs; Filipino American Accountants of Texas; Association of Filipino American Accountants; Philippine Institute of Certified Public Accountants, USA; Filipino American Association of CPAs; Filipino American Institute of Accountants; Association of Filipino Canadian Accountants; Association of Filipino Canadian Accountants
Membership: 10 organizations; Member Profile: Filipino professional accounting organizations
Activities: Annual convention; professional development
Chief Officer(s):
Chris Banagan, President
chris.banagan@verizon.net
Leonora Galleros, Executive VP & President-Elect
Marlo Mallari, Secretary
Lucy Macabenta, Treasurer
Imelda Bautista, Public Relations Officer
Awards:
• NCPACA College Scholarship Grant

National Court Reporters Association (NCRA)
#400, 12030 Sunrise Valley Dr., Reston VA 20191 USA
Tel: 703-556-6272; Fax: 703-391-0629
Toll-Free: 800-272-6272
msic@ncra.org
www.ncra.org
www.facebook.com/NCRAfb
twitter.com/NCRA
www.youtube.com/user/NCRAonline
Overview: A large international organization founded in 1899
Mission: To promote excellence in the reporting & captioning professions; To support those who capture & convert the spoken word to text to achieve professional expertise
Finances: Funding Sources: Membership fees; NCRA store
Membership: Member Profile: Participating members, such as freelance, official, hearing, legislative, & caption reporters; Associate members, such as instructors, retired reporters, proofreaders, attorneys, & transcriptionists; Students enrolled in a stenographic court reporting program or a scoping program; Committees: Broadcast & CART Captioning; CLVS WKT Item Writing; Certified Realtime Captioner (CRC) Certification; Committee on Professional Ethics; Constitution & Bylaws; Contests; Distinguished Service Award; Education Content; National Committee of State Associations Governing; New Professionals Advisory; Nominating; Realtime & Technology Resource; Skills Test Writing; Student/Teacher; Test Advisory; Written Knowledge Test
Activities: Offering educational opportunities
Chief Officer(s):
Marcia Ferranto, Executive Director & CEO
Kevin Kelly, Chief Financial Officer
Awards:
• Fellows of the Academy of Professional Reporters
To honour extraordinary qualifications & experiences in shorthand reporting
• Distinguished Service Award
To recognize work by individual members for the benefit of the reporting profession
• CASE Award of Excellence
To recognize dedication to students & extraordinary contributions to reporter education
Publications:
• Certification News [a publication of the National Court Reporters Association]
Type: Newsletter
• Court Reporter Sourcebook [a publication of the National Court Reporters Association]
Type: Yearbook; Frequency: Annually; Accepts Advertising
Profile: A listing of court reporters, with their credentials & specialties

Foreign Associations / National Education Association

- EventFlash [a publication of the National Court Reporters Association]
Type: Newsletter
- Journal of Court Reporting [a publication of the National Court Reporters Association]
Type: Journal; *Frequency:* Monthly; *Accepts Advertising*; *Price:* Free with membership in the National Court Reporters Association
Profile: Activities of the National Court Reporters Association & information related to court reporting & captioning sent to associationmembers & other reporting & captioning professionals
- NCRA [National Court Reporters Association] News
Type: Newsletter
Profile: Current events of the National Court Reporters Association
- NewsFlash [a publication of the National Court Reporters Association]
Type: Newsletter
- TechTracker [a publication of the National Court Reporters Association]
Type: Newsletter
Profile: Articles about the effects of technology on the reporting & captioning profession, as well as technology in the news

National Education Association
1201 - 16th St. NW, Washington DC 20036-3290 USA
Tel: 202-833-4000; *Fax:* 202-822-7974
www.nea.org
www.facebook.com/neatoday
twitter.com/NEAToday
www.flickr.com/photos/nea-hq; www.instagram.com/neatoday
Overview: A large national organization founded in 1857
Mission: To promote the cause of quality public education & advance the profession of education; To expand the rights & further the interest of educational employees & advocate human, civil & economic rights for all
Membership: 3.2 million; *Fees:* Schedule available;
Committees: Executive
Chief Officer(s):
Lily Eskelsen García, President
John C. Stocks, Executive Director
Awards:
- NEA Foundation Grants
- NEA Student Program Annual Awards
Meetings/Conferences:
- National Education Association Annual Meeting & Representative Assembly 2018, June, 2018, Minneapolis Convention Center, Minneapolis, MN
Scope: National
Attendance: 8,000+
Description: A meeting of delegates representing state & local affiliates; duties include adopting the strategic plan & budget, forming resolutions, debating & taking action on new business items for the NEA; & voting by secret ballot on proposed amendments to the Constituion & By-Laws
Publications:
- Higher Education Advocate [a publication of the National Education Association]
Type: Newsletter; *Frequency:* Bi-monthly; *ISSN:* 1522-5682
Profile: Post-secondary education trends, legislation, resource material & news
- NEA [National Education Association] Today Magazine for NEA-Retired Members
Type: Magazine; *Frequency:* Quarterly
Profile: Features a blend of info from NEA Today & news specifically targeted toward retired educators
- NEA [National Education Association] Today Magazine
Type: Magazine; *Frequency:* Quarterly; *ISSN:* 0734-7219
Profile: Features articles on today's relevant teaching challenges & situations
- The NEA [National Education Association] Almanac of Higher Education
Type: Directory; *Frequency:* Annually; *ISSN:* 0743-670X
Profile: Up-to-date information on the entire scope of American higher education
- Thought & Action [a publication of the National Education Association]
Type: Journal; *Frequency:* Annually; *ISSN:* 0748-8475
Profile: Theoretical & practical information on issues in higher education
- Tomorrow's Teachers [a publication of the National Education Association]
Type: Magazine; *Frequency:* Annually; *ISSN:* 1074-2794

Profile: Intended for student members & those new to the teaching profession

National Environmental Health Association (NEHA)
#1000N, 720 South Colorado Blvd., Denver CO 80246 USA
Tel: 303-756-9090; *Fax:* 303-691-9490
Toll-Free: 866-956-2258
staff@neha.org
www.neha.org
www.facebook.com/NEHA.org
twitter.com/nehaorg
Previous Name: National Association of Sanitarians
Overview: A medium-sized national charitable organization founded in 1937
Mission: To advance the environmental health & protection professional, in order to improve the environment throughout the world & provide a more healthful quality of life for all
Staff Member(s): 26
Membership: 4,500+; *Member Profile:* Environmental health practitioners in both the public & private sectors; Academia; Uniformed services, employed mainly by health departments
Activities: Providing national credential programs; Advocating for the profession; Offering networking opportunities; Working cooperatively with other national professional societies & government agencies
Chief Officer(s):
Nelson Fabian, Executive Director
nfabian@neha.org
Mel Knight, President
melknight@sbcglobal.net
Brian Collins, President Elect
brianc@plano.gov
Meetings/Conferences:
- National Environmental Health Association 2018 Annual Educational Conference & Exhibition, June, 2018, Anaheim Marriott Hotel, Anaheim, CA
Scope: International
Publications:
- Journal of Environmental Health
Type: Journal; *Frequency:* 10 pa; *Accepts Advertising*; *Editor:* Nelson Fabian
Profile: Current issues, peer-reviewed research, products, & services in the area or environmental health

National Ground Water Association (NGWA)
601 Dempsey Rd., Westerville OH 43081 USA
Tel: 614-898-7791; *Fax:* 614-898-7786
Toll-Free: 800-551-7379
ngwa@ngwa.org
www.ngwa.org
www.linkedin.com/groups?home=&gid=4204578
www.facebook.com/NGWAFB
twitter.com/ngwatweets
www.youtube.com/user/NGWATUBE
Overview: A medium-sized international organization founded in 1948
Mission: To advance the expertise of all groundwater professionals & advocate for the responsible development, management & use of water
Member of: Advisory Committee on Water Information; American National Standards Institute; Coalition for National Science Funding; Geological Society of America; Global Water Partnership; Groundwater Foundation; International Union of Geological Sciences; Source Water Collaborative; U.S. Water Alliance
Finances: *Annual Operating Budget:* Greater than $5 Million
Membership: *Fees:* Schedule available; *Member Profile:* Ground water scientists & engineers; water well drillers; pump installers; suppliers & manufacturers; *Committees:* Geothermal Heat Pump Technical; Government Affairs; Membership Standing; Professional Development; Public Awareness; Publishing and Information Products; Standard Development Oversight; Water Systems Technical
Activities: *Speaker Service:* Yes; *Library:* National Ground Water Information Centre
Chief Officer(s):
Kevin McCray, Chief Executive Officer
kmmcray@ngwa.org
Awards:
- Awards of Excellence
Includes: Ross L. Oliver Award, M. King Hubbert Award, Robert Storm Award, Life Member Award, Honorary Member Award, Technology Award, Individual Safety Advocate Award, Equipment Design Award, Special Recognition Award, Groundwater Protector Award, Standard Bearer Award & Industry Champion Award

- Outstanding Groundwater Project Awards
Includes: Groundwater Supply Award, Groundwater Protection Award. Groundwater Remediation Award & Groundwater Awareness Award
- Sectional Awards
Includes: John Hem Award, Keith E. Anderson Award, Manufacturers Section Special Recognition Award & Supplier of the Year Award

National Institute of Governmental Purchasing, Inc. (NIGP)
151 Spring St., Herndon VA 20170-5223 USA
Tel: 703-736-8900; *Fax:* 703-635-2326
Toll-Free: 800-367-6447
customercare@nigp.org
www.nigp.org
www.linkedin.com/groups?home=&gid=1800364
www.facebook.com/OfficialNIGP
twitter.com/OfficialNIGP
Overview: A medium-sized national organization founded in 1944
Mission: To develop, support & promote the public procurement profession through premier educational & research programs, professional support & advocacy initiatives
Member of: International Federation of Purchasing & Supply Management
Affiliation(s): National Association of Purchasing Card Professionals; National Council for Public Procurement and Contracting; National Purchasing Institute
Finances: *Funding Sources:* Membership dues; services (education & technical/audit services)
Staff Member(s): 32
Membership: 2,600 member agencies, representing 16,000 individuals in the U.S., Canada & elsewhere; *Fees:* Schedule available; *Member Profile:* Organizational or Agency membership provides the operational & administrative framework for the Institute, but individual, affiliate & associate memberships are available
Activities: *Speaker Service:* Yes; *Rents Mailing List:* Yes; *Library:* Procurement Information Exchanges; Not open to public
Chief Officer(s):
Rick Grimm, Chief Executive Officer
rgrimm@nigp.org
Awards:
- Lewis E. Spangler Education & Professional Development Foundation
Provides scholarships, grants & loans to students & the public purchasing professionals of the NIGP

National Marine Manufacturers Association (NMMA)
#2050, 231 South LaSalle St., Chicago IL 60604 USA
Tel: 312-946-6200
www.nmma.org
Overview: A medium-sized international organization
Mission: To create, promote & protect an environment where members can achieve financial success through excellence in manufacturing, in selling, and in servicing their customers.
Affiliation(s): National Association of Boat Manufacturers; National Association of Marine Products & Services; Association of Marine Engine Manufacturers
Finances: *Funding Sources:* Membership fees & shows
Membership: *Fees:* Schedule available; *Member Profile:* Canadian/American manufacturer, distributor, or retailer of boating-related products
Activities: *Internships:* Yes
Chief Officer(s):
Thomas Dammrich, President, 312-946-6220
tdammrich@nmma.org
Sara Anghel, Vice President, Government Relations and Public Affairs (Canada), 905-951-4048
sanghel@nmma.org

National NF Foundation *See* Children's Tumor Foundation

National Oil Recyclers Association *See* NORA, An Association of Responsible Recyclers

National Organization for Rare Disorders, Inc. (NORD)
55 Kenosia Ave., Danbury CT 06810 USA
Tel: 203-744-0100; *Fax:* 203-263-9938
www.rarediseases.org
www.linkedin.com/company/national-organization-for-rare-disorders
www.facebook.com/NationalOrganizationforRareDisorders

twitter.com/rarediseases
www.youtube.com/rarediseases
Overview: A large international organization founded in 1983
Mission: To identify, treat & cure rare diseases through programs of education, services & research
Affiliation(s): 127 national voluntary agencies for rare disorders
Finances: *Funding Sources:* Public donations; grants
Membership: *Committees:* Medical Advisory
Activities: Education; patient advocacy and mentorship programs; *Library:* Open to public
Chief Officer(s):
Peter L. Saltonstall, President & CEO

National Parks Conservation Association (NPCA)
#700, 777 6th St. NW, Washington DC 20001-3723 USA
Tel: 202-223-6722; *Fax:* 202-659-0650
Toll-Free: 800-628-7275
npca@npca.org
www.npca.org
www.facebook.com/NationalParks
twitter.com/npca
www.instagram.com/npcapics; www.pinterest.com/npca
Overview: A large national organization founded in 1919
Mission: To protect, preserve, & enhance the National Park system; To protect & improve the quality of parks & to promote an appreciation & sense of responsibility towards the wellbeing of parklands
Finances: *Annual Operating Budget:* Greater than $5 Million
Membership: 460,000; *Fees:* Schedule available
Chief Officer(s):
Theresa Pierno, President & CEO
Mark Wenzler, Senior Vice-President, Conservation Programs

National Psoriasis Foundation - USA
#300, 6600 SW 92nd Ave., Portland OR 97223-7195 USA
Tel: 503-244-7404; *Fax:* 503-245-0626
Toll-Free: 800-723-9166
getinfo@psoriasis.org
www.psoriasis.org
www.facebook.com/National.Psoriasis.Foundation
twitter.com/NPF
www.youtube.com/user/PsoriasisFoundation
Overview: A medium-sized international charitable organization founded in 1968
Mission: To improve the quality of life of people who have psoriasis & psoriatic arthritis; To promote & ensure access to treatment; To support research that will lead to effective management & ultimately a cure
Member of: International Federation of Psoriasis Associations
Affiliation(s): Canadian Psoriasis Foundation
Finances: *Annual Operating Budget:* Greater than $5 Million; *Funding Sources:* Donations
Activities: *Awareness Events:* Psoriasis Awareness Month, Aug.; *Internships:* Yes; *Library:* Not open to public
Chief Officer(s):
Randy Beranek, President & CEO

National Recycling Coalition, Inc. (NRC)
1220 L St. NW, Washington DC 20005 USA
Tel: 202-618-2107
info@nrcrecycles.org
nrcrecycles.org
Overview: A small national organization founded in 1978
Mission: To advance & improve recycling, source reduction, composting & reuse by providing technical information, education, training, outreach & advocacy services to its members in order to conserve resources & benefit the environment
Affiliation(s): California Resource Recovery Association; Northern California Recycling Association; Recycling Council of Alberta; Indiana Recycling Coalition; North Carolina Recycling Association; Oklahoma Recycling Association; Association of Oregon Recyclers; Pennsylvania Resources Council; Arizona Recycling Coalition; Arkansas Recycling Coalition; RECARIBE; Colorado Association for Recycling; Connecticut Recyclers Coalition; Recycle Florida Today; Illinois Recycling Association; Iowa Recycling Association; Kansas Recyclers Association; Louisiana Recycling Association
Staff Member(s): 7
Membership: 5,000+
Activities: *Internships:* Yes
Chief Officer(s):
Mark Lichtenstein, Executive Director
MarkL@nrcrecycles.org
Margretta Morris, Vice-President/Treasurer
Meg@nrcrecycles.org

National Sanitary Supply Association *See* International Sanitary Supply Association, Inc.

National Society of Fund Raising Executives *See* Association of Fundraising Professionals

National Space Society (NSS)
PO Box 98106, Washington DC 20090-8106 USA
Tel: 202-429-1600; *Fax:* 703-435-4390
Other Communication: Membership E-mail: members@nss.org
nsshq@nss.org
www.nss.org
www.linkedin.com/company/national-space-society
www.facebook.com/NSS
twitter.com/nss
www.youtube.com/user/NationalSpaceSociety
Overview: A large international organization
Mission: To promote social, economic, technological & political change; To advance the day when humans will live & work in space
Affiliation(s): Calgary Space Frontier Society; Niagara Peninsula Space Frontier Society
Membership: 22,000; *Fees:* Schedule available; *Committees:* Executive
Activities: *Speaker Service:* Yes; *Rents Mailing List:* Yes
Chief Officer(s):
Hugh Downs, Chair
Ken Money, President
Meetings/Conferences:
• National Space Society's International Space Development Conference 2018, May, 2018, Sheraton Gateway Hotel, Los Angeles, CA
Scope: International
Description: Discussions of the future of space exploration
Publications:
• Ad Astra [a publication of the National Space Society]
Type: Magazine; *Frequency:* q.; *ISSN:* 1041-102X
Profile: News & photography related to space exploration
• To the Stars International Quarterly [a publication of the National Space Society]
Type: Magazine; *Frequency:* q.
Profile: An information resource dedicated to students & teachers interested in space

National Waste & Recycling Association (NWRA)
#804, 1550 Crystal Dr., Arlington VA 22202 USA
Tel: 202-244-4700; *Fax:* 202-966-4824
Toll-Free: 800-424-2869
info@wasterecycling.org
wasterecycling.org
www.linkedin.com/company/national-waste-&-recycling-association
www.facebook.com/wasterecycling
twitter.com/wasterecycling
www.youtube.com/user/envasns
Previous Name: Environmental Industry Associations
Overview: A medium-sized international organization founded in 1962
Mission: To promote the environmentally responsible, efficient, profitable & ethical management of waste
Membership: *Member Profile:* Companies in North America that provide solid, hazardous & medical waste collection, recycling & disposal services; Companies that provide professional & consulting services to the waste services industry
Activities: Offering educational & training opportunities; Engaging in research; Facilitating networking
Chief Officer(s):
Bret Biggers, Director, Standards & Statistics, 202-364-3710
bbiggers@wasterecycling.org
Anne Germain, Director, Waste & Recycling Technology, 202-364-3724
agermain@wasterecycling.org
Anthony Hargis, Director, National Safety, 202-364-3750
ahargis@wasterecycling.org
Megan Passinger, Director, Education, 202-364-3702
mpassinger@wasterecycling.org
Chaz Miller, Director, Policy & Advocacy, 202-364-3742
cmiller@wasterecycling.org
Meetings/Conferences:
• WasteEXPO 50, April, 2018, Las Vegas Convention Center, Las Vegas, NV
Publications:
• NSWMA [National Solid Wastes Management Association] e-News
Type: Newsletter
Profile: Timely information to help businesses make decisions

National Wildlife Federation (NWF)
PO Box 1583, Merrifield VA 22116-1583 USA
Toll-Free: 800-822-9919
www.nwf.org
www.linkedin.com/company/national-wildlife-federation
www.facebook.com/NationalWildlife
twitter.com/nwf
www.youtube.com/user/NationalWildlife
Overview: A large national organization founded in 1936
Mission: To advance conservation policies through advocacy, education & litigation in concert with affiliate groups & other like-minded organizations across the country & around the world; To focus on the conservation of wildlife & the health of the environment, with special emphasis on wetlands, water quality, endangered habitats, land stewardship & sustainable communities
Finances: *Annual Operating Budget:* Greater than $5 Million; *Funding Sources:* Memberships; donations; bequests; magazine subscriptions; sales of nature education materials
Staff Member(s): 600
Membership: Over 4 million members & supporters + 46 affiliated organizations + 11 field office locations; *Fees:* $15+
Activities: *Awareness Events:* National Wildlife Week; *Internships:* Yes; *Rents Mailing List:* Yes; *Library*
Chief Officer(s):
Collin O'Mara, President & CEO
Bruce Wallace, Chair
Awards:
• National Conservation Achievement Awards Program
Program that recognizes outstanding individual & group achievements in conservation
Meetings/Conferences:
• National Wildlife Federation 81st Annual Meeting 2018, 2018
Scope: International
Contact Information: Phone: 1-800-822-9919

New Music USA
#1902, 90 Broad St., New York NY 10004 USA
Tel: 212-645-6949
info@newmusicusa.org
www.newmusicusa.org
www.facebook.com/NewMusicUSA
twitter.com/NewMusicUSA
Merged from: American Music Centre; Meet The Composer
Overview: A medium-sized national organization founded in 2011
Mission: To promote the creation, performance & appreciation of American contemporary music
Chief Officer(s):
Ed Harsh, President & CEO, 212-645-6949 Ext. 109
eharsh@newmusicusa.org
Awards:
• New Music USA Project Grants
• New Music Impact Fund
Publications:
• NewMusicBox [a publication of New Music USA]
Type: Magazine; *Editor:* Molly Sheridan

Newsletter Publishers Association *See* Specialized Information Publishers Association

The Newspaper Guild (AFL-CIO/CLC) (TNG) / La Guilde des journalistes (FAT-COI/CTC)
501 Third St. NW, 6th Fl., Washington DC 20001-2797 USA
Tel: 202-434-7177; *Fax:* 202-434-1472
guild@cwa-union.org
www.newsguild.org
twitter.com/news_guild
Previous Name: American Newspaper Guild
Overview: A large international organization founded in 1933
Mission: To act as a media union
Affiliation(s): International Federation of Journalists
Finances: *Annual Operating Budget:* $3 Million-$5 Million; *Funding Sources:* Membership dues
Staff Member(s): 32
Membership: 34,000; *Member Profile:* Journalists, sales & media workers, designers, reporters, commercial artists, circulation & distribution staff
Activities: *Library* by appointment
Chief Officer(s):
Bernard J. Lunzer, President
Melissa Nelson, Director, Collective Bargaining
Martin O'Hanlon, Director, Canada Office
Awards:
• David S. Barr Award for Student Journalism
Amount: $1,500 college winner; $1,000 high school winner

Foreign Associations / The Ninety-Nines Inc.

- Heywood Broun Award
Amount: One at $5,000 + two at $1,000

The Ninety-Nines Inc.
4300 Amelia Earhart Rd., #A, Oklahoma City OK 73159 USA
Tel: 405-685-7969*Tel:* 33-1-405-685-7969; *Fax:* 405-685-7985;
Fax: 33-1-405-685-7985
Toll-Free: 800-994-1929
PR@ninety-nines.org
www.ninety-nines.org
www.facebook.com/100905045593
twitter.com/TheNinetyNines
www.instagram.com/theninetyninesinc
Also Known As: International Organization of Women Pilots
Overview: A medium-sized international charitable organization founded in 1929
Mission: To promote world fellowship through flight; To provide networking & scholarship opportunities for women & aviation education in the community; To preserve the unique history of women in aviation
Membership: *Fees:* Ninety-nine members - US$65 US; US$57 Canada; US$44 international; Student Pilots - US$35 US/Canadian; US$30 international; *Member Profile:* Women pilots
Activities: Museums & historical archives; Endowment Fund; Aviation & space education; *Speaker Service:* Yes; *Library:* 99s Museum of Women Pilots
Chief Officer(s):
Jan McKenzie, President
president@ninety-nines.org
Corbi Bulluck, Vice President
vicepresident@ninety-nines.org
Barbara Crooker, Treasurer
treasurer@ninety-nines.org
Lisa Cotham, Secretary
secretary@ninety-nines.org
Awards:
- Award of Achievement for Contributions to The Ninety-Nines, Ninety-Nines Awards
- Award of Achievement for Contributions to Aviation
- Humanitarian Award
- Award of Merit
- Award of Inspiration
- President's Award
- George Palmer Putnam Award
- Amelia Earhart Memorial Scholarship for Women Pilots
Include: Flight Training Scholarship, Academic Scholarship, Technical Training Scholarship, Emergency Maneuver Training Scholarship & the Kitty Houghton Memorial Scholarship
Deadline: December
- Fly Now Award
Semiannual award granted on completion of specific training milestones *Eligibility:* Student Pilot members of the 99s who hold a student pilot certificate & show financial need *Deadline:* March 15; September 15 *Amount:* $6,000
Meetings/Conferences:
- Ninety-Nines International Conference 2018, July, 2018, Philadelphia, PA
Description: Meet & network with international members; Learn about flight safety, new tools & opportunities, leadership skills & charitable opportunities
Publications:
- 99 News: The Official Magazine of the International Organization of Women Pilots
Type: Magazine; *Frequency:* bi-m.; *Number of Pages:* 28; *Price:* Free download
Profile: News, events and information about the Ninety-Nines

NORA, An Association of Responsible Recyclers (NORA)
#201, 7250 Heritage Village Plaza, Gainesville VA 20155 USA
Tel: 703-753-4277; *Fax:* 703-733-2445
www.noranews.org
www.linkedin.com/groups?gid=1675687
Previous Name: National Oil Recyclers Association
Overview: A medium-sized national licensing organization founded in 1985
Member of: American Society of Association Executives
Finances: *Annual Operating Budget:* $250,000-$500,000
Staff Member(s): 4
Membership: 200 companies; *Fees:* Based on company type; *Member Profile:* Liquid recyclers & vendors; *Committees:* Membership; Marketing; Conference; Governmental Affairs; Parts cleanin; Chemical Recycling; Used Oil Recycling; Ethics/Standards; Strategic Planning; Associate Advisory
Activities: *Rents Mailing List:* Yes

Chief Officer(s):
Scott D. Parker, Executive Director
sparker@noranews.org

Nordic Association for Canadian Studies (NACS) / Association nordique d'études canadiennes
Department of English, Turku University, Turku 20014 Finland
Fax: 385-2-333-5630
www.hum.au.dk/nacs
Overview: A small international organization founded in 1984
Mission: To promote Canadian studies in the five Nordic countries: Denmark, Finland, Iceland, Norway & Sweden
Member of: International Council for Canadian Studies
Staff Member(s): 3; 2 volunteer(s)
Membership: 320; *Fees:* 17 euros
Activities: *Library:* Canadian Collection
Chief Officer(s):
Janne Korkka, Contact
jkorkka@utu.fi

North American Association for Environmental Education (NAAEE)
#540, 2000 P St. NW, Washington DC 20036 USA
Tel: 202-419-0412; *Fax:* 202-419-0415
bredy@naaee.org
www.naaee.org
www.facebook.com/126762430689361
twitter.com/NAAEEStaff
Overview: A medium-sized international organization founded in 1971
Mission: To promote education about environmental issues
Finances: *Funding Sources:* Donations
Membership: *Member Profile:* Practitioners in the fields of environmental education, outdoor education, & conservation education; Students in the field of environmental education
Activities: Providing professional development events; Offering networking opportunities
Chief Officer(s):
Judy Braus, Executive Director, 202-419-0414
jbraus@naaee.org
Publications:
- Conservation Education & Outreach Techniques
Number of Pages: 496; *Author:* S. Jacobson; M. McDuff; M.C. Monroe; *ISBN:* 0-19-856772-3
Profile: Case sudies & application exercises
- EE News [a publication of the North American Association for Environmental Education]
Type: Newsletter
- Elementary School Teachers' Beliefs About Teaching Environmental Education
Number of Pages: 48; *Author:* S. Middlestadt; R. Ledsky; *ISBN:* 1-884008-76-3
- Environmental Education at the Early Childhood Level
Number of Pages: 126; *Editor:* R. Wilson; *ISBN:* 1-884008-14-3
- Environmental Education in the Schools: Creating a Program That Works!
Number of Pages: 500; *Author:* J. Braus; D. Wood; *ISBN:* 1-884008-08-9
- Environmental Education Research, Special Issue on Significant Life Experiences
Number of Pages: 114; *Editor:* T. Tanner; *ISBN:* 1350-4622
- Environmental Education Undergraduate & Graduate Programs & Faculty in the United States
Author: Michaela Zint; Aimee Giles; *ISBN:* 1-884008-79-B
- Environmental Education: Academia's Response
Number of Pages: 96; *Author:* E. Kormondy; P.B. Corcoran; *ISBN:* 1-884008-51-8
- Environmental Literacy in the United States: What Should Be...What Is...Getting from Here to There
Number of Pages: 80; *Editor:* T. Volk; W. McBeth; *ISBN:* 1-884008-73-9
- Evaluating Your Environmental Education Programs: A Workbook for Practitioners
Author: J.A. Ernst; M.C. Monroe; B. Simmons
Profile: Case sudies & application exercises
- A Field Guide to Environmental Literacy: Making Strategic Investments in Environmental Education
Number of Pages: 110; *Author:* J.L. Elder; *ISBN:* 1-884008-87-9
- NAAEE [North American Association for Environmental Education] Communicator
Type: Newsletter
- North American Association for Environmental Education Conference Proceedings
- Preparing Effective Environmental Educators
Type: Monograph; *Number of Pages:* 89; *Editor:* Dr. Bora Simmons; *ISBN:* 1-884008-88-7

- Using a Logic Model to Review & Analyze an Environmental Education Program
Type: Monograph; *Number of Pages:* 72; *Editor:* Thomas C. Marcinkowski; *ISBN:* 1-884008-86-0
- What's Fair Got To Do With It: Diversity Cases from Environmental Educators
Number of Pages: 119; *Editor:* Tania J. Madfes; *ISBN:* 0-914409-20-4

North American Association of Central Cancer Registries, Inc. (NAACCR, Inc.)
2050 West Iles, #A, Springfield IL 62704-7412 USA
Tel: 217-698-0800; *Fax:* 217-698-0188
www.naaccr.org
Overview: A small international organization
Mission: To develop & promote data standards for cancer registration; To provide certification for population-based registries; To promote the use of cancer surveillance data & systems for cancer control
Membership: *Committees:* Bylaws; Nominating; Communications; Program; Data Evaluation & Certification; Registry Operations; Data Use & Research; Education; Uniform Data Standards; Information & Technology; GIS; Interoperability; Cancer Registration; Scientific Editorial Board; Institutional Review Board
Activities: Promoting epidemiologic research; Providing educational & training opportunities; Publishing data from central cancer registries; Promoting public health programs to reduce the burden of cancer
Chief Officer(s):
Betsy Kohler, Executive Director
bkohler@naaccr.org
Charlie Blackburn, Chief Operating Officer
cblackburn@naaccr.org
Recinda Sherman, Manager, Data Use & Research
rsherman@naaccr.org
Meetings/Conferences:
- North American Association of Central Cancer Registries 2018 Annual Conference, June, 2018, Pittsburgh, PA
Scope: International
Attendance: 450
- North American Association of Central Cancer Registries 2019 Annual Conference, June, 2019, Vancouver, BC
Scope: International
Attendance: 450
Publications:
- NAACCR [North American Association of Central Cancer Registries] Narrative
Type: Newsletter; *Frequency:* Quarterly
Profile: NAACCR updates, reports, & education & training calendar

North American Butterfly Association (NABA)
4 Delaware Rd., Morristown NJ 7960 USA
e-mail: naba@naba.org
www.naba.org
www.facebook.com/153175048034815
Overview: A small international organization
Mission: To increase public enjoyment & conservation of butterflies; To work to save butterfly species throughout North America
Membership: *Fees:* $US30 regular; $US40 family; *Member Profile:* The largest group of people in North America (Canada, United States & Mexico) interested in butterflies
Chief Officer(s):
Jeffrey Glassberg, President

North American Conference on British Studies (NACBS)
c/o University of Colorado Denver, PO Box 173364, Stn. 182, Denver CO 80217 USA
Tel: 303-556-2896; *Fax:* 303-556-6037
www.nacbs.org
Overview: A medium-sized international organization founded in 1950
Mission: To pursue the study of British civilization
Affiliation(s): American Historical Association
Membership: *Fees:* Schedule available; *Member Profile:* Interest in British studies; *Committees:* Executive; Nominating
Chief Officer(s):
Marjorie Levine-Clark, Executive Secretary
marjorie.levine-clark@ucdenver.edu
Awards:
- Huntington Library Fellowship
Annual, for at least one month of study in the collections of the Huntington Library in San Marino, California *Amount:* $1,800

- John Ben Snow Foundation Book Prize
Annual, for the best book in any field of British Studies before 1800 *Amount:* $1,000
- British Council Book Prize
Annual, for the best book in any field of British Studies after 1800 *Amount:* $1,000
- Walter D. Love Article Prize
Annual, for the best article or article-length study in any field of British Studies *Amount:* $150
- Dissertation-Year Fellowship
Annual, for study in British archives & collections *Amount:* $5,000

Publications:
- Journal of British Studies
Editor: Anna Clark
Profile: Quarterly academic journal

North American Die Casting Association (NADCA)
#101, 3250 Arlington Heights Rd., Arlington Heights IL 60004 USA
Tel: 847-279-0001; *Fax:* 847-279-0002
nadca@diecasting.org
www.diecasting.org
www.linkedin.com/company/north-american-die-casting-association
www.facebook.com/84385559055
www.youtube.com/user/NADCAvideos
Previous Name: Society of Die Casting Engineers
Overview: A small international organization founded in 1954
Mission: To promote the industry & its members
Membership: *Fees:* US$85 individual; $25 student; corporate fee by sales volume; *Member Profile:* Custom die casters; Captive die casters; Suppliers to the industry
Chief Officer(s):
Daniel Twarog, President
twarog@diecasting.org

Ontario Chapter
ON
Chief Officer(s):
Eric V. Klaassen, Chair
Boris Lukezic, Secretary
lukezic@yahoo.com

North American Farmers' Direct Marketing Association, Inc. (NAFDMA)
62 White Loaf Rd., Southampton MA 01073 USA
Tel: 413-244-5374
www.farmersinspired.com
Overview: A small international organization
Mission: To promote the farm direct marketing & agritourism industry
Membership: *Fees:* Schedule available
Chief Officer(s):
Charlie Touchette, Executive Director
charlie@farmersinspired.com
Meetings/Conferences:
- North American Farmers' Direct Marketing Association 2018 Farmers Inspired Convention, February, 2018
Scope: International

North American Insulation Manufacturers Association (NAIMA)
#103, 11 Canal Center Plaza, Alexandria VA 22314 USA
Tel: 703-684-0084; *Fax:* 703-684-0427
www.insulationinstitute.org
www.linkedin.com/company/insulation-institute
www.facebook.com/insulationinstitute
twitter.com/knowinsulation
www.youtube.com/user/NAIMAVideo
Overview: A medium-sized national organization founded in 1933
Mission: To serve as the voice of fiberglass & mineral wool insulation manufacturers in North America
Affiliation(s): NAIMA Canada
Finances: *Annual Operating Budget:* $3 Million-$5 Million
Staff Member(s): 10
Membership: 1-99
Chief Officer(s):
Curt Rich, President & CEO

North American Lincoln Red Association
c/o Sarah Pedelty, 9724 County Rd. 138 SE, Chatfield MN 55923 USA
Tel: 507-867-9041; *Fax:* 507-867-4852
www.lincolnred.org
Also Known As: Lincoln Red Association of North America
Overview: A small international organization founded in 2004
Mission: To develop & regulate the breeding of Lincoln Red cattle in Canada & the United States; To carry out a system of registration for Lincoln Red cattle
Affiliation(s): Canadian Livestock Records Corporation
Membership: 1-99; *Fees:* $80 / year; $15 junior membership (up to 18 years of age); $800 life membership; *Member Profile:* Breeders & ownders of Lincoln Red cattle in Canada & the United States; *Committees:* Executive; Pedigree; Breed Improvement; *Special Committees:*
Activities: Compiling statistics related to the Lincoln Red cattle industry; Publishing data related to Lincoln Red cattle; Assisting & supervising persons engaged in the breeding of Lincoln Red cattle; Inspecting herds or private breeding records of breeders
Chief Officer(s):
Scott McClinchey, President, 519-928-3106
hlm.dvm@sympatico.ca
Sarah Pedelty, Secretary, 507-867-9041
sarahpedelty@yahoo.com
Publications:
- The Lincoln Letter
Type: Newsletter; *Frequency:* Y
Profile: Association announcements, president's report, & meeting information

North American Piedmontese Association (NAPA)
1740 Co. Rd 185, Ramah CO 80832 USA
Tel: 306-329-8600
NAPA@yourlink.ca
www.piedmontese.org
Overview: A small international organization founded in 2000
Mission: To offer registry services to Piedmontese breeders throughout Canada & the United States; to develop & improve the Piedmontese breed; to promote & preserve fullblood Piedmontese cattle
Affiliation(s): Canadian Livestock Records Corporation
Membership: *Fees:* $90; *Member Profile:* Canadian & American Piedmontese breeders
Chief Officer(s):
Vicki Johnson, NAPA Executive Director

North American Riding for the Handicapped Association *See* Professional Association of Therapeutic Horsemanship International

North American Society for Oceanic History (NASOH)
Texas Christian University, Department Of History, PO Box 297260, Fort Worth TX 76129 USA
www.nasoh.org
Overview: A small international organization founded in 1974
Mission: To provide a forum for maritime history; To study & promote naval & maritime history; To promote exchange of information among its members & others interested in history of seas, lakes & inland waterways; To call attention to books, articles, other publications & documents pertinent to naval & maritime history; to work with local, regional, national & international organizations as well as appropriate government agencies towards goal of fostering a more general awareness & appreciation for North America's naval & maritime heritage
Finances: *Annual Operating Budget:* Less than $50,000
Membership: 220; *Fees:* $65 US individual/corporate; $18 US student
Chief Officer(s):
Warren Reiss, President
Awards:
- John Lyman Book Awards
- Jack Bauer Award

North American Society of Adlerian Psychology (NASAP)
#276, 429 East Dupont Rd., Fort Wayne IN 46825 USA
Tel: 260-267-8807; *Fax:* 260-818-2098
info@alfredadler.org
www.alfredadler.org
www.linkedin.com/company/nasap-north-american-society-of-adlerian-psychology
Overview: A medium-sized international organization
Mission: To promote the teaching, understanding, & application of the core concepts of Adlerian (Individual) Psychology; To maintain the principles of Adlerian Psychology; To foster research, knowledge, & training; To operate according to the Codes of Ethics of the American Psychological Association, the International Coach Federation, & the National Board of Certified Counselors
Affiliation(s): Adler Graduate School of Minesota; Adler International Learning Inc.; Adler School of Professional Psychology; Aderian Psychology Association of British Columbia; Adlerian Society of Arizona; Adlerian Student Affiliate; Alfred Adler Institute of New York; ALFREDS - Adler Learning Federation for Research, Education & Delivery of Services; Central PA Society of Adlerian Psychology; Georgia Society of Adlerian Psychology; McAbee Adlerian Psychology Society (MAPS); Parent Encouragement Program (PEP); South Carolina Society of Adlerian Psychology; The Individual Psychology Society - Chicago (TIPS)
Membership: *Fees:* $25 students; $35 associates; $45 retired persons; $55 family members; $135 individuals & affiliate organizations; *Member Profile:* Psychologists; Psychiatrists; Cousellors; Educators; Community organizations; Parents
Activities: Encouraging scientific inquiry & the growth of Adlerian Psychology; Developing & supporting training centres & educational opportunities; Providing a home study course; Awarding the NASAP Certificate of Adlerian Studies; Expanding the availability of counselling & family enrichment programs, based on Adlerian Psychology; Networking with other organizations in the fields of psychology & education; *Speaker Service:* Yes
Chief Officer(s):
Susan Belangee, Vice-President
Michele Frey, Secretary
Susan Brokaw, Treasurer
Meetings/Conferences:
- North American Society of Adlerian Psychology 2018 Annual Conference, June, 2018, Toronto, ON
Scope: International
Description: Theme: "Community, Connections & Social Interest in Challenging Times"
Publications:
- Journal of Individual Psychology
Type: Journal; *Frequency:* Quarterly; *Editor:* Bill Curlette; Roy Kern
- NASAP [North American Society of Adlerian Psychology] Newsletter
Type: Newsletter; *Frequency:* Bimonthly

North Atlantic Salmon Conservation Organization (NASCO)
11 Rutland Sq., Edinburgh EH1 2AS United Kingdom
Tel: 44-131-228-2551; *Fax:* 44-131-228-4384
hq@nasco.int
www.nasco.int
Overview: A medium-sized international organization
Mission: To promote the conservation, restoration, enhancement & rational management of salmon stocks in North Atlantic
Staff Member(s): 3
Membership: 6; *Member Profile:* National & multi-national governments; *Committees:* Finance & Administration
Chief Officer(s):
Mary Collingan, President
Peter Hutchinson, Secretary

Northeast Council for Québec Studies *See* American Council for Québec Studies

Northeast Modern Language Association (NeMLA)
c/o Dr. Elizabeth Abele, Dept. of English, Nassau Community College, One Education Dr., Garden City NY 11530-6793 USA
e-mail: nemlasupport@gmail.com
www.nemla.org
Overview: A small international organization founded in 1967
Finances: *Funding Sources:* Membership fees
Membership: *Fees:* $167 full-time faculty, registration & membership; $106 independent scholars; *Member Profile:* Professionals in English, French, German, Italian, Spanish, & other modern languages, such as professors & students at colleges & universities in eastern Canada & the northeast United States
Activities: Supporting research in modern languages through fellowship programs
Chief Officer(s):
Elizabeth Abele, Executive Director
northeast.mla@gmail.com
Simona Wright, President
simona@tcnj.edu
William Waddell, First Vice-President
bwaddell@sjfc.edu
Meetings/Conferences:
- 49th Annual Northeast Modern Language Association Convention, April, 2018, University of Pittsburgh, Pittsburgh, PA
Scope: International

Foreign Associations / Northeast Organic Farming Association (NOFA)

Description: Theme: "Global Spaces, Local Landscapes & Imagined Worlds"
Publications:
• Modern Language Studies
Type: Newsletter; *Frequency:* Semiannually; *Editor:* Laurence Roth (roth@susqu.edu); *Price:* $15members; $20 individuals; $30 institutions
Profile: Articles, essays, & reviews, plus information from the Northeast Modern Language Association, including conference highlights & previews, awards, & board news
• NeMLA Italian Studies
Type: Journal; *Frequency:* Annually; *Editor:* Simona Wright; *Price:* $15
Profile: Critical studies on Italian language pedagogy, literature, linguistics, culture, & cinema

Northeast Organic Farming Association (NOFA)
Massachusetts Chapter, 411 Sheldon Rd., Barre MA 01005 USA
Tel: 978-355-2853; *Fax:* 978-355-4046
info@nofamass.org
www.nofamass.org
www.facebook.com/NOFAMass
twitter.com/nofamass
www.flickr.com/photos/46485133@N08
Overview: A small local charitable organization founded in 1982
Mission: To educate members & the general public about the benefits of local organic systems based on complete cycles, natural materials & minimal waste for the health of individual beings, communities & the living planet
Finances: *Annual Operating Budget:* $500,000-$1.5 Million; *Funding Sources:* Private donations; membership dues; conference fees
Staff Member(s): 15
Membership: 1,200; *Fees:* US$40 individual; US$25 low income; US$50 family/institution/small farm; US$75 large farm/business; US$125 premier business; US$250 supporting
Activities: Educational conferences & workshops; videos on organic growing; information about apprenticeship programs matching farms seeking workers with people wanting to learn organic methods; Organic Food Guide map listing organic farmers in Massachusetts; bulk order of soil amendments; genetic engineering awareness; *Speaker Service:* Yes
Chief Officer(s):
Julie Rawson, Executive & Education Director
julie@nofamass.org

Northwest Coalition for Alternatives to Pesticides (NCAP)
PO Box 1393, Eugene OR 97440-1393 USA
Tel: 541-344-5044; *Fax:* 541-344-6923
info@pesticide.org
www.pesticide.org
www.facebook.com/pesticide.free
twitter.com/_ncap
www.youtube.com/user/NCAPVids
Overview: A medium-sized local charitable organization founded in 1977
Mission: To protect the health of people & the environment by advancing alternatives to pesticides
Finances: *Annual Operating Budget:* $250,000-$500,000; *Funding Sources:* Grants; donations
Staff Member(s): 9; 10 volunteer(s)
Membership: 2,300; *Fees:* $25; $15 limited income; $50 associate
Activities: Clean water for salmon; public education; sustainable agriculture; pesticide free parks; inert ingredient disclosure; *Internships:* Yes; *Library:* Open to public
Chief Officer(s):
Kim Leval, Executive Director
kleval@pesticide.org
Edward Winter, Chief Operating & Financial Officer
ewinter@pesticide.org

Northwest Wall & Ceiling Bureau (NWCB)
1032A NE 65th St., Seattle WA 98115 USA
Tel: 206-524-4243; *Fax:* 206-524-4136
info@nwcb.org
www.nwcb.org
www.facebook.com/nwcb1
Overview: A medium-sized international organization founded in 1946
Mission: To serve professionals in the wall & ceiling industry from northwestern United States & western Canada
Membership: *Member Profile:* Manufacturers; Suppliers & distributors; Subcontractors; Labour organizations
Activities: Providing information, such as technical information & advice, to help members operate their businesses effectively; Offering continuing education, through workshops & seminars; Facilitating networking opportunities, for the exchange of experiences & ideas; Providing promotion & marketing to help members market their products & services
Chief Officer(s):
Jim Dunham, President
jim@vanderlipco.com
Robert Drury, Executive Director
bob@nwcb.org
Tiina Freeman, Director, Communications & Events
tiina@nwcb.org
Karen Morales, Manager, Office
karen@nwcb.org
Terry Kastner, Technical Consultant
terry@nwcb.org
Meetings/Conferences:
• Northwest Wall & Ceiling Bureau 2018 Annual Convention & Trade Show, May, 2018, Westin La Paloma Resort & Spa, Tucson, AZ
Scope: International
Description: Informative seminars & exhibits, plus networking opportunities, for persons in the northwestern wall & ceiling industry
Contact Information: Director, Communications & Events: Tiina Freeman, E-mail: tiina@nwcb.org; Exhibitor & Sponsorship Information, Phone: 206-524-4243
Publications:
• Change Order
Type: Newsletter; *Frequency:* Quarterly; *Accepts Advertising*; *Editor:* Tiina Freeman (tiina@nwcb.org)
Profile: Organization activities, regional unpdates, convention & trade show highlights, technical information, new products, & awards
• Impacts to Labor Productivity in Steel Framing & the Installation & Finishing of Gypsum Wallboard
Price: $199 members; $299non-members
Profile: A study testing variables generated by industry experts against labour productivity in over 200 sample projects
• Northwest Wall & Ceiling Bureau Membership Directory
Type: Directory
• Stucco Resource Guide & CD-ROM
Type: Manual; *Price:* $65 members; $85 non-members
Profile: A comprehensive, updated manual for designing & building with stucco, produced with industry experts
• Walls & Ceilings
Type: Magazine

Nuclear Information & Resource Service (NIRS)
#340, 6930 Carroll Ave., Tacoma Park MD 20912 USA
Tel: 301-270-6477; *Fax:* 301-270-4291
nirsnet@nirs.org
www.nirs.org
www.facebook.com/26490791479
twitter.com/nirsnet
www.youtube.com/user/nirsnet
Overview: A small international organization founded in 1978
Mission: To raise awareness about the effects of nuclear power
Affiliation(s): Nuclear Awareness Project
Staff Member(s): 6
Activities: *Internships:* Yes; *Speaker Service:* Yes; *Library:* by appointment
Chief Officer(s):
Tim Judson, Executive Director

The Ocean Conservancy
1300 19th St. NW, 8th Fl., Washington DC 20036 USA
Tel: 202-429-5609; *Fax:* 202-872-0619
Toll-Free: 800-519-1541
membership@oceanconservancy.org
www.oceanconservancy.org
www.facebook.com/oceanconservancy
twitter.com/OurOcean
www.instagram.com/oceanconservancy
Previous Name: Center for Marine Conservation; Center for Environmental Education
Overview: A large international organization founded in 1972
Mission: To protect ocean ecosystems & conserve the global abundance & diversity of marine wildlife
Finances: *Annual Operating Budget:* $3 Million-$5 Million; *Funding Sources:* Bequests; contributions; grants
Staff Member(s): 40
Membership: 110,000; *Fees:* Schedule available
Activities: Promoting public awareness through education; Conducting research; *Internships:* Yes
Chief Officer(s):
Andreas Merkl, Chief Executive Officer
amerkl@oceanconservancy.org
Janis Searles Jones, President
jjones@oceanconservancy.org
Larry Amon, Chief Financial Officer
lamon@oceanconservancy.org
Chris Dorsett, Vice-President, Conservation Policy & Programs
cdorsett@oceanconservancy.org

The Oceanography Society
PO Box 1931, Rockville MD 20849-1931 USA
Tel: 301-251-7708; *Fax:* 301-251-7709
info@tos.org
www.tos.org
www.linkedin.com/company/the-oceanography-society
www.facebook.com/274812976299?v=wall
twitter.com/TOSOceanography
Overview: A small international organization founded in 1988
Chief Officer(s):
Jennifer Ramarui, Executive Director
Publications:
• Oceanography
Editor: Dr. Ellen Kappel; *ISSN:* 1042-8275
Profile: Monthly magazine; peer reviewed

Office & Professional Employees International Union (AFL-CIO/CLC) / Union internationale des employés professionnels et de bureau (FAT-COI/CTC)
80 - 8 Ave., 20th Fl., New York NY 10011 USA
Tel: 800-346-7348
www.opeiu.org
Overview: A small international organization
Membership: 125,000
Chief Officer(s):
Michael Goodwin, President

Opera America Inc.
330 Seventh Ave., New York NY 10001 USA
Tel: 212-796-8620; *Fax:* 212-796-8621
info@operaamerica.org
www.operaamerica.org
www.facebook.com/operaamerica
twitter.com/operaamerica
Overview: A medium-sized international organization founded in 1970
Mission: To support professional opera companies in North America; To promote opera as an exciting & accessible art form to all segments of society; To develop a national climate conducive to increased public & private support
Affiliation(s): Canadian Conference of the Arts
Finances: *Annual Operating Budget:* $500,000-$1.5 Million
Staff Member(s): 20
Membership: 2,000 individual; 200 company; 300 affiliate & business; *Fees:* Schedule available; *Member Profile:* Professional opera companies; affiliate companies; individuals; the media & funding communities; government agencies, representing Australia, Asia, Europe & South America; *Committees:* Affirmative Action; Annual Conference; Development; Education; Executive; Fellowship; Information Service; Opera for a New America
Activities: *Speaker Service:* Yes; *Rents Mailing List:* Yes; *Library*
Chief Officer(s):
Marc A. Scorca, President & CEO
mscorca@operaamerica.org

Optimist International
4494 Lindell Blvd., St. Louis MO 63108 USA
Tel: 314-371-6000; *Fax:* 314-371-6006
Toll-Free: 800-500-8130
www.optimist.org
www.linkedin.com/groups/117333
www.facebook.com/optimistintl
twitter.com/optimistorg
www.youtube.com/user/OptimistIntl
Overview: A medium-sized international organization
Mission: To bring out the best in youth, their communities & themselves
Membership: 2,500 clubs; *Fees:* Schedule available

Organic Crop Improvement Association (International) (OCIA) / Association pour l'amélioration des cultures biologiques (international)
1340 North Cotner Blvd., Lincoln NE 68505 USA

Tel: 402-477-2323; Fax: 402-477-4325
info@ocia.org
www.ocia.org
Also Known As: OCIA International
Overview: A medium-sized international licensing organization founded in 1988
Mission: To support all farmers with the technical knowledge, skills & organizational aids they need to develop workable crop management systems capable of supplying the growing market demand for organic foods; To provide third party certification of organic foods
Member of: Organic Trade Association
Affiliation(s): International Federation of Organic Agriculture Movements; Japan Agriculture Standards; US National Organic Program; Conseil des Appelations Agroalimentaires du Québec; Costa Rica Ministry of Agriculture & Livestock; ISO Guide 65
Finances: *Annual Operating Budget:* $1.5 Million-$3 Million; *Funding Sources:* Member-owned & funded
Staff Member(s): 30
Membership: 3,000+; *Fees:* US$75 corporate & chapter level; individual chapter membership fees vary; *Member Profile:* Farmers, processors & merchants who are committed to seeking alternatives to conventional chemical & energy-intensive food system; *Committees:* By-Laws; Crop Improvement; Finance; Inspector Accreditation; Internal Review; Certification Analysis; International Certification; International Standards; Chapter Licensing; Promotions; AGMM; Canadian Organic Regulatory Committee; Research & Education
Activities: *Speaker Service:* Yes
Chief Officer(s):
Jeff Kienast, President

Organic Food Production Association of North America *See* Organic Trade Association

Organic Trade Association (OTA)
#45A, 444 North Capital St., Washington DC 20001 USA
Tel: 202-403-8520
www.ota.com
www.linkedin.com/company/organic-trade-association
www.facebook.com/OrganicTrade
twitter.com/organictrade
Previous Name: Organic Food Production Association of North America
Overview: A medium-sized international organization founded in 1985
Mission: To encourage global sustainability through promoting & protecting the growth of diverse organic trade
Member of: International Federation of Organic Agriculture Movements
Finances: *Annual Operating Budget:* $500,000-$1.5 Million; *Funding Sources:* Membership fees; merchandise sales; fundraising
Staff Member(s): 22; 20 volunteer(s)
Membership: 1,500; *Fees:* Schedule available, based upon revenues; *Member Profile:* Organic food processors; certifiers; distributors; organic farm organizations; consultants; farmers; retail outlets; restaurants; *Committees:* Legislative; Quality Assurance; Marketing; International Relations; Organic Certifiers Council; Organic Fiber Council; Organic Suppliers Advisory Council; Canadian Council
Activities: *Awareness Events:* Organic Harvest Month, Sept.; *Speaker Service:* Yes
Chief Officer(s):
Melissa Hughes, President
Laura Batcha, Executive Director/CEO, 202-403-8512
lbatcha@ota.com
Amy Bovaird, Director, Development, 802-275-3812
abovaird@ota.com
Sonja Favaloro, Coordinator, Communications, 802-275-3825
sfavaloro@ota.com
Awards:
• OTA Leadership Awards
• Member of the Year Award
Meetings/Conferences:
• Organic Trade Association (OTA) Expo West 2018, March, 2018, Anaheim Convention Center, Anaheim, CA
Scope: International
Description: Hosted in conjunction with Natural Products Expo West
• Organic Trade Association (OTA) Annual Membership Meeting 2018, September, 2018, Baltimore, MD
Scope: International
• Organic Trade Association (OTA) Expo East 2018, September, 2018, Baltimore Convention Center, Baltimore, MD
Scope: International

• Organic Trade Association (OTA) All Things Organic Conference, September, 2018, Baltimore Convention Center, Baltimore, MD
Scope: International
Description: Hosted in conjunction with Natural Products Expo East
Publications:
• Organic Trade Association Organic Industry Survey
Type: Report; *Frequency:* a.
Profile: A resource for information on the U.S. organic market; features charts, graphs, & sales data statistics

Organisation de coopération et de développement économique *See* Organization for Economic Co-operation & Development

Organisation internationale de la Francophonie (OIF) / International Organisation of La Francophonie (IOF)
19-21, av Bosquet, Paris 75007 France
Tél: (33) 1 44 37 33 00; Téléc: (33) 1 45 79 14 98
www.francophonie.org
twitter.com/OIFfrancophonie
Aperçu: *Dimension:* grande; *Envergure:* internationale; fondée en 1970
Mission: L'OIF a pour objectif de contribuer à améliorer le niveau de vie de ses populations en les aidant à devenir les acteurs de leur propre développement. Elle apporte à ses États membres un appui dans l'élaboration ou la consolidation de leurs politiques et mène des actions de politique internationale et de coopération multilatérale, conformément aux 4 grandes missions tracées par le Sommet de la Francophonie.
Finances: *Budget de fonctionnement annuel:* Plus de $5 Million
Membre: 77 États et gouvernements membres
Membre(s) du bureau directeur:
Michaëlle Jean, Secrétaire générale

Organisation internationale de normalisation *See* International Organization for Standardization

Organisation internationale des commissions de valeurs *See* International Organization of Securities Commissions

Organisation maritime internationale *See* International Maritime Organization

Organisation météorologique mondiale *See* World Meteorological Organization

Organisation mondiale de la santé *See* World Health Organization

Organisation mondiale du mouvement scout *See* World Organization of the Scout Movement

Organisation Mondiale pour la Systémique et la Cybernétique *Voir* World Organisation of Systems & Cybernetics

Organization for Economic Co-operation & Development (OECD) / Organisation de coopération et de développement économique (OCDE)
2, rue André-Pascal, Paris 75775 Cedex 16 France
Tel: 33-1-45-24-82-00; Fax: 33-1-45-24-85-00
www.oecd.org
www.linkedin.com/company-beta/165285
www.facebook.com/theOECD
twitter.com/oecd
www.youtube.com/oecd; www.flickr.com/photos/oecd
Overview: A large international organization founded in 1961
Mission: To achieve the highest sustainable economic growth & employment; To promote economic & social welfare throughout the OECD area by coordinating the policies of its member countries; To stimulate & harmonize its members' efforts in favour of developing countries
Member of: International Organization of Securities Commissions - Canada
Affiliation(s): International Energy Agency (IEA); Nuclear Energy Agency
Finances: *Annual Operating Budget:* Greater than $5 Million
Staff Member(s): 2500
Membership: 36 member countries
Activities: Provides a forum for monitoring economic trends & coordinating economic policies among its member countries: the free-market democracies of North America, Western Europe & the Pacific; provides the largest source of comparative data on the industrial economies in the world; produces a wide range of publications, economic surveys, statistics, analyses & policy recommendations

Chief Officer(s):
Angel Gurría, Secretary General
Publications:
• OECD [Organization for Economic Co-operation & Development] Observer
Type: Magazine
Profile: Magazine & online service providing analysis of global economic & social issues. Web: www.oecdobserver.org

Organization of American Historians (OAH)
Indiana University, 112 North Bryan Ave., Bloomington IN 47408-4141 USA
Tel: 812-855-7311; Fax: 812-855-0696
oah@oah.org
www.oah.org
www.linkedin.com/company/444102
www.facebook.com/TheOAH
twitter.com/The_OAH
Overview: A medium-sized international charitable organization founded in 1907
Mission: To promote teaching & scholarship about the history of the United States, both before & after its formation as a nation-state
Member of: American Council of Learned Societies
Finances: *Annual Operating Budget:* $1.5 Million-$3 Million
Staff Member(s): 27
Membership: 11,000; *Fees:* Schedule available; *Member Profile:* Interest in promotion of historical study & research in American history; *Committees:* Academic Freedom; Committees; Community Colleges; Disability & Disability History; Executive; Finance; International; Marketing & Communications; Membership; National Park Service Collaboration; Nominating Board; Part-Time, Adjunct, & Contingent Employment; Public History; Research & Government; Status of African American, Latino/a, Asian American, & Native American Historians & ALANA Histories; Status of Lesbian, Gay, Bisexual, Transgender, & Queer Historians & Histories; Status of Women in the Historical Profession; Teaching
Activities: *Internships:* Yes; *Speaker Service:* Yes; *Rents Mailing List:* Yes
Chief Officer(s):
Katherine Finley, Executive Director
kmfinley@oah.org
Awards:
• Louis Pelzer Memorial Award
Best essay in American history by a graduate student *Deadline:* November *Amount:* $500
• Tachau Teacher of the Year Award
Deadline: December *Amount:* $1,000
• Frederick Jackson Turner Award
Deadline: October *Amount:* $1,000
• Willi Paul Adams Award
Best article (annual) and best book (biennial) on American history published in languages other than English *Deadline:* May 1 *Amount:* $1,000
• ABC-CLIO America: History And Life Award (biennial)
Deadline: December *Amount:* $750
• Binkley-Stephenson Award
For the best article in the JAH from the previous year *Amount:* $500
• Avery O. Craven Award
Most original book on the Civil War or Era of Reconstruction
Deadline: October *Amount:* $500
• Merle Curti Award
Deadline: October *Amount:* $2,000
• Huggins-Quarles Awards
Deadline: December *Amount:* $1,000
• Ray Allen Billington Prize (biennial)
Best book on American frontier history *Deadline:* October *Amount:* $1,000
• Ellis W. Hawley Prize
Best book-length historical study of U.S. politics from the Civil War to the present *Deadline:* October *Amount:* $500
• Richard W. Leopold Prize (biennial)
Deadline: October *Amount:* $1,500
• Lerner-Scott Prize
Best doctoral dissertation in U.S. women's history *Deadline:* December *Amount:* $1,000
• James A. Rawley Prize
Best book dealing with the history of race relations in the U.S.
Deadline: October *Amount:* $1,000
• Erik Barnouw Award
Deadline: December *Amount:* $1,000
• John Higham Research Fellowship
Amount: $1,000

Foreign Associations / OSPAR Commission (OSPAR)

- Liberty Legacy Fdn. Award
Amount: $2,000
Publications:
- Journal of American History
Type: Journal; *Frequency:* Quarterly
Profile: Scholarly journal

Oslo & Paris Commissions See OSPAR Commission

OSPAR Commission (OSPAR)
#37, 63 Southampton Row, London WC1B 4DA United Kingdom
Tel: 44-207-430-5200; *Fax:* 44-207-242-3737
secretariat@ospar.org
www.ospar.org
www.linkedin.com/company/ospar
twitter.com/osparcomm
Previous Name: Oslo & Paris Commissions
Overview: A small international organization founded in 1998
Mission: To control pollution of the marine environment of the North-East Atlantic
Finances: *Funding Sources:* Membership
Staff Member(s): 12
Membership: 15 European countries & EU
Chief Officer(s):
Darius Campbell, Executive Secretary
Publications:
- OSPAR Commission Annual Report
Type: Yearbook; *Frequency:* Annually

Pacific NorthWest Economic Region (PNWER)
World Trade Center West, #460, 2200 Alaskan Way, Seattle WA 98121 USA
Tel: 206-443-7723; *Fax:* 206-443-7703
www.pnwer.org
www.facebook.com/147636495253612
twitter.com/PNWER
Previous Name: Pacific Northwest Legislative Leadership
Overview: A medium-sized local organization founded in 1989
Mission: To promote greater collaboration among the seven state & provincial members in order to enhance the economic competitiveness of the region in international & domestic markets
Staff Member(s): 8
Membership: *Member Profile:* Consists of the Pacific Northwestern states of Alaska, Idaho, Montana, Oregon & Washington & the provinces of Alberta, British Columbia & the Yukon Territory; includes Legislators, Governors/Premiers & private sector individuals
Activities: 9 Working Groups; *Internships:* Yes
Chief Officer(s):
Matt Morrison, Chief Executive Officer
matt.morrison@pnwer.org

Pacific Northwest Legislative Leadership See Pacific NorthWest Economic Region

Paint & Decorating Retailers Association (PDRA)
1401 Triad Center Dr., St. Peters MO 63376 USA
Toll-Free: 800-737-0107
info@pdra.org
www.pdra.org
www.linkedin.com/groups/4087345
www.facebook.com/PaintandDecoratingRetailersAssociation
twitter.com/PaintDecoRetail
Overview: A large national organization founded in 1949
Mission: To educate, promote & represent the interests of decorating products dealers
Affiliation(s): National Decorating Products Association
Membership: 100 associate + 450 retail; *Fees:* Schedule available; *Member Profile:* Independent retailers selling paint, wallcoverings, window treatments &/or floor coverings, operating from a storefront or showroom & selling into a local market
Activities: Organizing trade shows; Providing educational information to membership; *Library:* Open to public
Chief Officer(s):
LeAnn Day, CEO
leann@pdra.org
Meetings/Conferences:
- Paint & Decorating Retailers Association Trade Show at the National Hardware Show 2018, May, 2018
Scope: National
Publications:
- Paint & Decorating Retailer [a publication of Paint & Decorating Retailers Association]
Type: Magazine; *Frequency:* Monthly; *Accepts Advertising*;
ISSN: 1096-6927

Pan American Sports Organization (PASO)
Valentin Gomez Farías #51, San Rafael 06470 Mexico
Tel: 52 55 57054657; *Fax:* 52 55 57052275
www.paso-odepa.org
Overview: A large international organization founded in 1948
Mission: Its principal objectives are the celebration and conduct of the Pan American Games and the development and protection of Sports, as well as the Olympic Movement in the Americas through its member National Olympic Committees.
Membership: *Committees:* Technical; Pan American Olympic Solidarity; Marketing & Financial Sources; Image; Sports Venues; Olympic Academies; Legislative; Women & Sport; Medical; Olympic Education; Sport & Environment; Evaluation Commission of Candidate Cities to Host the Pan American Games; Athletes; Coordination Commission of the XVII Pan American Games "Toronto 2015"; Presentation of Awards
Activities: Pan American Games
Chief Officer(s):
Julio Cesar Maglione, President

Paperboard Packaging Council
#1508, 1350 Main St., Springfield MA 01103-1670 USA
Tel: 413-686-9191; *Fax:* 413-747-7777
www.ppcnet.org
www.linkedin.com/groups/1134757
www.facebook.com/paperboard.packaging.3
twitter.com/ppcnet
www.youtube.com/user/PaperBoxChannel
Overview: A large national organization
Mission: To represent paperboard packaging converters & industry suppliers
Finances: *Funding Sources:* Membership fees
Membership: *Committees:* Executive; Associate Members; Financial Executives; Government Affairs; Human Resources; Industry Benchmarking; Marketing & Sustainability; Membership; New Generation Leaders; Rigid Box; Technical & Production; Canadian Committee; Women's Leadership
Activities: *Speaker Service:* Yes
Chief Officer(s):
Ben Markens, President
ben@paperbox.org
Lou Kornet, Chief of Staff & Vice-President, 413-686-9180
lou@paperbox.org
Nicole Miller, Director, Marketing & Communications, 413-686-9193
nicole@paperbox.org
Jennie Markens, Director, Next Generation Leaders, 413-686-9191
jen@paperbox.org
Brian Westerlind, Manager, Communications, 413-686-9178
bwesterlind@paperbox.org
Susan Martins, Controller, 413-686-9192
susan@paperbox.org
Awards:
- The Volunteer Leader Award
- Robert T. Gair Award
- The Safety Boxscore Award
- The National Paperboard Packaging Competition Awards

Parents Without Partners Inc. (PWP)
1100-H Brandywine Blvd., Zanesville OH 43701-7303 USA
Toll-Free: 800-637-7974
www.parentswithoutpartners.org
www.facebook.com/parentswithoutpartnersinternational
Overview: A large international organization founded in 1957
Mission: To provide single parents & their children with an opportunity for enhancing personal growth, self-confidence & sensitivity towards others by offering an environment for support, friendship & the exchange of parenting techniques
Membership: *Member Profile:* A person must be the parent of one or more living sons or daughters, & be single by reason of death, divorce, separation or never married, or other reason which may be deemed acceptable by PWP
Activities: Various activities for parent & family at each chapter; Spring conference
Chief Officer(s):
Janet Gallinati, President
intl.pres@parentswithoutpartners.org
Awards:
- Distinguished Service to Children Award
Awarded annually to a person or group that has made a great contribution to children's welfare
- Family Individual Talent Awards Program
Presented annually in all arts-related categories to member children & teens
- PWP Scholarships
Cash awards presented to member teens to help with college expenses *Amount:* $750
- Single Parent of the Year Award
Awarded annually to an outstanding member parent
Meetings/Conferences:
- Parents Without Partners 2018 International Convention, 2018
Scope: International

Coquitlam Chapter
Surrey BC V3N 5B7
Tel: 604-616-6315
pwp722@gmail.com
www.pwpcanada.com

Mississauga Valley Chapter
PO Box 29623, RPO Central Parkway, Mississauga ON L5A 4H2
Tel: 905-278-0111; *Crisis Hot-Line:* 416-463-9355
pwpmississauga@yahoo.com
www.pwpcanada.com

New Dawn Chapter
PO Box 69011, RPO Rosedale, Hamilton ON L8K 5R4
Tel: 905-544-4444
general@pwphamilton.com
www.pwpcanada.com

Royal City Chapter
c/o Florence Boys, 73 Knightwood Blvd., Guelph ON N1E 3W5
Tel: 519-823-0227
guelphpwp@hotmail.com
www.pwpcanada.com

Stepping Stone (Winnipeg) Chapter
PO Box 1756, Winnipeg MB R3C 2Z9
Tel: 204-957-7172
pwp.winnipeg@gmail.com
www.pwpcanada.com

Toronto Chapter
Toronto ON
Tel: 416-489-2221; *Crisis Hot-Line:* 416-463-9355
info@pwptoronto.com
www.pwpcanada.com

Parents, Families & Friends of Lesbians & Gays (PFLAG)
#660, 1828 L St. NW, Washington DC 20036-5112 USA
Tel: 202-467-8180; *Fax:* 202-467-8194
info@pflag.org
www.pflag.org
www.linkedin.com/company/pflag---parents-families-and-friends-of-lesbians-and-gays
www.facebook.com/PFLAG
twitter.com/PFLAG
www.instagram.com/pflagnational
Overview: A medium-sized national organization founded in 1981
Mission: To promote the health & well-being of gay, lesbian, bisexual & transgendered persons, their families & friends, through: support, to cope with an adverse society; education, to enlighten an ill-informed public; & advocacy, to end discrimination & to secure equal civil rights; provides opportunity for dialogue about sexual orientation & gender identity, & acts to create a society that is healthy & respectful of human diversity
Finances: *Annual Operating Budget:* $1.5 Million-$3 Million
Staff Member(s): 17
Membership: 200,000 +; *Fees:* $25
Activities: *Internships:* Yes; *Speaker Service:* Yes
Chief Officer(s):
Jean Hodges, President
Dale Bernstein, Vice-President
Jody M. Huckaby, Executive Director, 202-467-8180 Ext. 216
jhuckaby@pflag.org
Diego Sanchez, Director, Policy, 202-467-8180 Ext. 221
dsanchez@pflag.org
Liz Owen, Director, Communications, 202-467-8180 Ext. 214
lowen@pflag.org
Jean-Marie Navetta, Director, Equality & Diversity Partnerships, 202-467-8180 Ext. 213
jnavetta@pflag.org

Parliamentarians for Global Action (PGA) / Action Mondiale des Parlementaires
#1604, 211 East 43 St., New York NY 10017 USA
Tel: 212-687-7755; *Fax:* 212-687-8409
info@pgaction.org
www.pgaction.org
Previous Name: Parliamentarians for World Order

Overview: A medium-sized international organization founded in 1979
Mission: To service parliamentarians, informing them on issues of global security, including but not confined to disarmament, peacekeeping, economic development & the environment, & assisting them in cooperative efforts to resolve such problems; to approach governments with suggested courses of action
Affiliation(s): Parliamentarians for Global Action - Canadian Section
Finances: Annual Operating Budget: $500,000-$1.5 Million; Funding Sources: Individual donors; foundations; institutes; governments
Staff Member(s): 14; 5 volunteer(s)
Membership: 1,400 individuals from 100 parliaments; Fees: US$50; Committees: Executive
Activities: Nuclear test ban & non-proliferation; United Nations peacekeeping & collective security; sustainable development (including environmental security & international economic reform); international law & global institutions (focussing on the creation of an International Criminal Court); a parliamentary initiative for democracy; special programme on Africa
Chief Officer(s):
Shazia Z. Rafi, Secretary-General
sg@pgaction.org
Awards:
• Defender of Democracy Award
Presented to individuals who have made significant progress in strengthening democracy and democratic principles

Parliamentarians for World Order See Parliamentarians for Global Action

Peace & Justice Studies Association (PJSA)
Poulton Hall, Georgetown University, #130, 1421 - 37th St. NW, Washington DC 20057 USA
www.peacejusticestudies.org
Previous Name: Consortium on Peace Research, Education & Development; Peace Studies Association
Overview: A medium-sized national organization founded in 2001
Mission: To bring together researchers, educators & activists working for the peaceful resolution of conflict
Affiliation(s): International Peace Research Association; Canadian Peace Research & Education Association; Center for UN Reform; Council on Peace Research in History; Consejo Latinoamericano de Investigadores para la Pax; National Peace Institute Foundation; National Conference on Peacemaking & Conflict Resolution; International Studies Association; American Association for the Advancement of Science; Pan-American Council on Peace Research
2 volunteer(s)
Membership: 650 individual + 150 institutional; Fees: Schedule available; Member Profile: Individual - includes students, K-12 educators, conflict resolution practitioners, peace activists, university professors, clergy; institutional - includes peace studies programs at colleges & universities, religious organizations, community centres, professional associations, institutes & foundations, activist organizations; Committees: Arts & Media; Conference; Conflict Resolution; Cross-Cultural; Feminisms & Gender Issues; Finance; LesBiGay Friends & Allies; Nonviolence; Peace Action; Peace Education; Peace & Justice Resource Centers; Peace Research; Religion & Ethics; Student Peace Network; University Peace Studies
Activities: Internships: Yes; Speaker Service: Yes; Rents Mailing List: Yes

Pediatric Endocrine Society (PES)
6728 Old McLean Village Dr., McLean VA 22101 USA
Tel: 703-556-9222; Fax: 703-556-8729
info@pedsendo.org
www.pedsendo.org
www.facebook.com/410788862293625
twitter.com/PedsEndoSociety
Previous Name: Lawson Wilkins Pediatric Endocrine Society
Overview: A medium-sized international organization
Mission: To promote the acquisition of knowledge about endocrine & metabolic disorders, from conception through adolescence
Membership: 900+; Member Profile: Persons who represent the disciplines of pediatric endocrinology; Committees: Awards; Drug & Therapeutics; Education Council; Ethics; History; Honors & Lectures; International Relations Council; Membership; MOC & QI; Nominating; Obesity; Practice Management Council; Program; Public Policy; Publications; Research Affairs Council; Training Council; Website

Activities: Promoting research into endocrine disorders; Disseminating information about endocrine & metabolic disorders; Encouraging continuing education
Chief Officer(s):
Stephen M. Rosenthal, President
Maureen Thompson, Executive Director
Janice Wilkins, Association Manager
John Fuqua, Secretary
Peter A. Lee, Treasurer
Meetings/Conferences:
• 11th International Meeting of Pediatric Endocrinology, 2018
Scope: International
• Pediatric Endocrine Society 2018 Annual Meeting, May, 2018, Toronto, ON
Scope: International
Description: An annual gathering of persons from the disciplines of pediatric endocrinology, including business meetings, lectures, topic symposia, poster sessions, workshops, exhibits, & social activities
Contact Information: E-mail: info@pedsendo.org
• Pediatric Endocrine Society 2019 Annual Meeting, April, 2019, Baltimore, MD
Scope: International
Description: An annual opportunity for medical education for those engaged in the disciplines of pediatric endocrinology
Contact Information: E-mail: info@pedsendo.org
• Pediatric Endocrine Society 2020 Annual Meeting, May, 2020, Philadelphia, PA
Scope: International
Description: An annual continuing education event, featuring speaker presentations, a scientific program, poster sessions, exhibits, & networking occasions for persons who represent the field of pediatric endocrinology
Contact Information: E-mail: info@pedsendo.org
• Pediatric Endocrine Society 2021 Annual Meeting, 2021
Scope: International
Publications:
• Pediatric Endocrine Society Membership Directory
Type: Directory
• PES [Pediatric Endocrine Society] Newsletter
Type: Newsletter
Profile: Pediatric Endocrine Society news, including award winners, meeting reviews, forthcoming meetings, & workshops

PEN International
Koops Mill Mews, #A, 162-164 Abbey St., London SE1 2AN United Kingdom
Tel: +44(0) 20 7405 0338; Fax: +44(0) 20 7405 0339
info@pen-international.org
www.pen-international.org
www.linkedin.com/company/international-pen
www.facebook.com/peninternational
twitter.com/pen_int
Overview: A medium-sized international charitable organization founded in 1921
Mission: To promote friendship & goodwill among writers everywhere, regardless of their political or other views; To fight for freedom of expression & to defend vigorously writers suffering from oppressive regimes whether of the extreme right or the extreme left
Affiliation(s): Canadian PEN Centre; Centre québécois du PEN international
Finances: Annual Operating Budget: $100,000-$250,000; Funding Sources: Membership dues
Staff Member(s): 4
Membership: 14,000; 144 Centres in 102 countries worldwide; Fees: Schedule available; Member Profile: All qualified writers regardless of nationality, race, colour, or religion; each centre, being autonomous, sets its own membership qualifications
Activities: Library: PEN Global Library (at Slovak PEN); Open to public
Chief Officer(s):
Carles Torner, Executive Director
carles.torner@pen-international.org
Jennifer Clement, International President
Awards:
• Oxfam Novib/PEN Award for Freedom of Expression
• PEN International/New Voices Award
Meetings/Conferences:
• PEN International Annual Congress 2018, 2018
Scope: International
Contact Information: Coordinator, Congress: Jena Patel, E-mail: jena.patel@pen-international.org

People for the Ethical Treatment of Animals (PETA)
501 Front St., Norfolk VA 23510 USA

Tel: 757-622-7382; Fax: 757-628-0457
Other Communication: pinterest.com/officialpeta
www.peta.org
www.linkedin.com/in/ingridnewkirk
www.facebook.com/officialpeta
twitter.com/peta
www.youtube.com/profile?user=officialpeta
Overview: A large international charitable organization founded in 1980
Mission: To protect animals from exploitation & cruelty; To bring positive changes in the ways humans regard other species; To expose animal abuse so it will not be perpetuated; To promote a world in which animals are respected & people are aware of & concerned with how their daily decisions affect the lives of other sentient beings
Finances: Annual Operating Budget: Greater than $5 Million; Funding Sources: Contributions
Staff Member(s): 180; 40 volunteer(s)
Membership: 5,000,000+; Fees: US$16; $25 Cdn.
Activities: International campaigns on vegetarianism, against animal testing, against fur & dissection, against animal abuse in the entertainment industry; Internships: Yes; Rents Mailing List: Yes; Library: PETA Library; Open to public
Chief Officer(s):
Ingrid E. Newkirk, President
Lisa Lange, Senior Vice-President, Communications

Permanent International Association of Navigation Congresses Voir Association internationale permanente des congrès de navigation

Pesticide Action Network North America (PANNA)
#1200, 1611 Telegraph Ave., Oakland CA 94612 USA
Tel: 510-788-9020; Fax: 415-981-1991
panna@panna.org
www.panna.org
www.facebook.com/pesticideactionnetwork
twitter.com/pesticideaction
www.youtube.com/user/pannavideo
Overview: A medium-sized international charitable organization founded in 1984
Mission: Works to replace pesticide use with ecologically sound & socially just alternatives; links local & international consumer, labor, health, environment & agriculture groups into an international citizens' action network; network challenges the global proliferation of pesticides, defends basic rights to health & environmental quality & works to insure the transition to a just & viable society
Finances: Annual Operating Budget: $1.5 Million-$3 Million; Funding Sources: Grants & individual donors
Staff Member(s): 21; 5 volunteer(s)
Membership: 225 affiliate organizations; Fees: US$35 organizations with paid staff; US$20 all volunteer organizations
Activities: Campaign to stop pesticide drift; documenting pesticide body burden; holding corporations accountable for the use & promotion of pesticides & genetically engineered crops; campaign to transform agricultural development through the International Assessment of Agricultural Science & Technology for Development; California & Midwest pesticide use reduction; public education; farmworkers' rights campaign; promotion of alternatives to pesticides; Internships: Yes; Library: by appointment
Chief Officer(s):
Jennifer Sokolove, President
Monica Moore, Founding Executive Director
Steve Scholl-Buckwald, CFO & Managing Director

Piano Technicians Guild Inc. (PTG)
4444 Forest Ave., Kansas City KS 66106 USA
Tel: 913-432-9975; Fax: 913-432-9986
ptg@ptg.org
www.ptg.org
www.facebook.com/pianotechniciansguild
twitter.com/pianotechguild
www.youtube.com/user/PTGHomeOffice
Previous Name: American Society of Piano Technicians
Merged from: National Association of Piano Tuners
Overview: A medium-sized international organization founded in 1957
Mission: To promote the highest possible standards of piano service by providing members with opportunities for professional development, by recognizing technical competence through examinations & by advancing the interests of its members
Member of: International Association of Piano Builders & Technicians (IAPBT)
Staff Member(s): 7

Foreign Associations / The Planetary Society (TPS)

Membership: 4,000; *Member Profile:* Individuals with a professional or vocational interest in piano technology
Activities: *Library:* The Stephen S. Jellen Library; by appointment
Chief Officer(s):
Barbara Cassaday, Executive Director
barbara@ptg.org
   Calgary Chapter
   Calgary AB

The Planetary Society (TPS)
60 South Robles Ave., Pasadena CA 91101 USA
Tel: 626-793-5100; *Fax:* 626-793-5528
Other Communication: www.flickr.com/photos/77417785@N05
tps@planetary.org
www.planetary.org
www.linkedin.com/company/the-planetary-society
www.facebook.com/planetarysociety
twitter.com/exploreplanets
www.youtube.com/planetarysociety
Overview: A large international organization founded in 1980
Mission: To educate & inform the general public about planetary exploration & the search for extraterrestrial life
Member of: Coalition for Space Exploration; Space Exploration Alliance; International Astronautical Federation; American Association for the Advancement of Science; International Year of Astronomy; United Nations
Finances: *Annual Operating Budget:* $1.5 Million-$3 Million; *Funding Sources:* Membership dues; Donations
Staff Member(s): 20
Membership: 100,000; *Fees:* $37 US; $45 Canada; $57 international
Activities: *Internships:* Yes; *Rents Mailing List:* Yes; *Library:* Resource Library
Chief Officer(s):
Bill Nye, CEO
Richard Chute, Director, Development
richard.chute@planetary.org
Erin Greeson, Director, Communications
erin.greeson@planetary.org
Publications:
• The Planetary Report [a publication of The Planetary Society]
Type: Magazine; *ISSN:* 0736-3680
Profile: Coverage of discoveries on Earth & other planets

Plastic Loose Fill Council (PLFC)
#201, 1298 Cronson Blvd., Crofton MD 21114 USA
Crisis Hot-Line: 800-828-2214
www.loosefillpackaging.com
Overview: A small national organization founded in 1991
Mission: Promoted the reuse of plastic packing peanuts through its national collection program the Peanut Hotline, with over 240 drop-off sites.
Membership: 4; *Member Profile:* Manufacturers of expanded polystyrene loose fill packaging
Activities: Operates the Peanut Hotline, the consumer reuse program in US for plastic packaging peanuts
Chief Officer(s):
John D. Mellott

Plastics Foodservice Packaging Group (PFPG)
1300 Wilson Blvd., 8th Fl., Arlington VA 22209 USA
Tel: 703-741-5649; *Fax:* 703-741-5651
pspc@plastics.org
www.polystyrene.org
Previous Name: Polystyrene Packaging Council
Overview: A small international organization overseen by American Chemistry Council
Mission: To promote & defend the polystyrene industry by providing a forum for issues of importance to the polystyrene industry; keeping markets free by eliminating or amending anti-polystyrene legislation & regulation & avoiding future burdensome polystyrene legislation/regulation; & serving as the polystyrene industry communications voice to selected audiences & the general public
Finances: *Annual Operating Budget:* $500,000-$1.5 Million
Staff Member(s): 2
Membership: 16; *Fees:* Schedule available; *Member Profile:* Major suppliers & manufacturers of polystyrene products
Chief Officer(s):
Michael H. Levy, Director, 202-249-6614
Mike_Levy@americanchemistry.com

Polish Association for Canadian Studies (PACS)
c/o Dr. Marcin Gabrys, Institute of American Studies & Polish Diaspora, Jagiellonian University, Rynek Główny 34, Cracow 31-010 Poland
Tel: 48 12 4325060
ptbk@uj.edu.pl
www.ptbk.org.pl
Overview: A small international organization founded in 1998
Mission: To promote activities in favour of the development of Canadian studies in all scholarly areas; to spread knowledge about Canada & to develop contacts with scholars & academics researching into Canadian studies & all people interested in any form of expanding knowledge about Canada
Activities: Four Canadian Studies Centres in Poland
Chief Officer(s):
Marcin Gabrys, President
Tomasz Soroka, Secretary

Polystyrene Packaging Council *See* Plastics Foodservice Packaging Group

Polyurethane Manufacturers Association (PMA)
#1300, 6737 West Washington St., Milwaukee WI 53214 USA
Tel: 414-431-3094; *Fax:* 414-276-7704
info@pmahome.org
www.pmahome.org
www.linkedin.com/company/pma---polyurethane-manufacturers-association
www.facebook.com/PMAhome
twitter.com/PMA_home
Mission: To represent polyurethane manufacturers; To disseminate information among its membership regarding improvements to the industry as a whole; To foster & encourage communication & networking within its membership; To promote polyurethane's advantages over rubber, plastic, & metal by expanding business opportunities in various markets
Finances: *Funding Sources:* Membership dues
Membership: 75+; *Fees:* Schedule available, based upon annual urethane-related sales; *Member Profile:* Polyurethane manufacturing companies, suppliers; *Committees:* Environmental, Health, Safety & Regulatory; Technical; Awards; Membership Growth; Member Services
Activities: Offering professional development & certification resources for members; Holding an annual meeting; *Awareness Events:* John Jarvis Memorial Golf Tournament, annually; *Library:* Virtual Technical Library; Open to public
Chief Officer(s):
Phil Green, President
phil.green@anddev.com
Linda Katz, Vice-President/Secretary/Treasurer
lkatz@moldeddimensions.com
Geoff McIsaac, Liaison, Canadian Communications
Geoffrey.McIsaac@chemtura.com
Awards:
• Lifetime Achievement Award
• Distinguished Service Award
• President's Special Award
• Best Paper Awards
Meetings/Conferences:
• Polyurethane Manufacturers Association 2018 Annual Meeting, May, 2018, Naples Beach Hotel & Golf Club, Naples, FL
Scope: International
Description: Events also include a supplier showcase & a processing technique seminar
Contact Information: E-mail: info@pmahome.org
Publications:
• Polyurethane Manufacturers Association Technical Papers
Price: $50
Profile: A series of technical papers on practical matters relating to the polyurethane manufacturing industry
• Polyurethane Manufacturers Association Glossary
Profile: A glossary of terms relative to the industry
• Regulatory Ramblings [a publication of the Polyurethane Manufacturers Association]
Type: Newsletter; *Frequency:* q.
Profile: Information on regulations & legislative updates, compiled by the Regulatory Committee

Population Connection (PC)
#500, 2120 L St. NW, Washington DC 20037 USA
Tel: 202-332-2200; *Fax:* 202-332-2302
Toll-Free: 800-767-1956
info@populationconnection.org
www.populationconnection.org
www.facebook.com/PopConnectAction
twitter.com/popconnect
Previous Name: Zero Population Growth
Overview: A large international organization founded in 1968
Mission: To advocate progressive action to stabilize world population at a level that can be sustained by Earth's resources
Finances: *Annual Operating Budget:* $3 Million-$5 Million; *Funding Sources:* Memberships; foundations; private donations
Staff Member(s): 40; 20 volunteer(s)
Membership: 30,000; *Fees:* $25
Activities: Encouraging media coverage of population issues; Defending family planning programs; Supporting the United Nations Population Fund; Defending comprehensive sex education for teens; *Speaker Service:* Yes
Chief Officer(s):
John Seager, President & CEO
john@popconnect.org
Brian Dixon, Senior Vice-President, Media & Government Relations
bdixon@popconnect.org
Maria Orozco-Marquez, Director, Administration & Membership Services
morozco@popconnect.org
Publications:
• Population Connection Magazine
Type: Magazine; *Frequency:* Quarterly; *Price:* US$25
Profile: Covers environmental, social & health-related topics

Potash & Phosphate Institute/Potash & Phosphate Institute of Canada *See* International Plant Nutrition Institute

POWERtalk International
PO Box 13260, Tauranga New Zealand
Tel: 64 7 579 9972; *Fax:* 64 7 579 9976
info@powertalkinternational.com
powertalkinternational.com
Also Known As: International Training in Communication
Overview: A medium-sized international organization founded in 1938
Mission: International Training in Communication & POWERtalk International developed from the International Toastmistress Clubs in the U.S. It's mission is to be a world leader in the promotion of opportunities for quality training in communication & leadership skills
Membership: Clubs in 15 countries
Activities: *Speaker Service:* Yes
Chief Officer(s):
Margaret Sutherland, International President
Mary Flentge, Secretary, (Netherlands)
   Atlantic Canada
   Fredericton NB
   Tel: 506-453-8643
   dennis.m@corknb.ca
   itc-northeast.tripod.com/fredericton
   Chief Officer(s):
   Shelley Petley, Contact
   shelley.petley@unb.ca
   Québec/Ontario
   North Bay ON
   Tel: 705-474-8660
   itc-northeast.tripod.com/northbay
   Chief Officer(s):
   Karen Sherry, President
   Geraldine Lightfoot, Contact
   gerryvl@thot.net
   Western Canada
   Winnipeg MB
   e-mail: sbgeorge@mts.net

La Première Église du Christ, Scientiste *See* Christian Science

Professional Association of Therapeutic Horsemanship International (PATH)
PO Box 33150, Denver CO 80233 USA
Tel: 303-452-1212; *Fax:* 303-252-4610
Toll-Free: 800-369-7433
www.pathintl.org
Previous Name: North American Riding for the Handicapped Association
Overview: A medium-sized international charitable organization founded in 1969
Mission: Promotes the benefit of the horse riding for individuals with physical, emotional & learning disabilities
Membership: 1,000-4,999; *Fees:* $355-$2000
Chief Officer(s):
Kathy Alm, Chief Executive Officer
kalm@pathintl.org

Professional Bull Riders Inc
101 West Riverwalk, Pueblo CO 81003 USA
Tel: 719-242-2800; *Fax:* 719-242-2855
admin@pbrnow.com
pbrnow.com
www.facebook.com/PBR
twitter.com/PBR
www.youtube.com/user/PBRNow
Previous Name: Canadian Bull Riders Association
Overview: A small international organization founded in 1992
Chief Officer(s):
Randy Bernard, CEO
Ty Murray, President
Publications:
• Pro Bull Rider Magazine
Profile: Bi-monthly magazine

Professional Secretaries International See International Association of Administrative Professionals

Programme des nations unies pour l'environnement See United Nations Environment Programme

Project Management Institute (PMI)
14 Campus Blvd., Newtown Square PA 19073-3299 USA
Tel: 610-356-4600; *Fax:* 610-356-4647
Toll-Free: 855-746-4849
customercare@pmi.org
www.pmi.org
www.linkedin.com/groups?gid=2784738
www.facebook.com/PMInstitute
twitter.com/pminstitute
www.youtube.com/PMInstitute
Overview: A medium-sized international organization founded in 1969
Mission: To advance the state-of-the-art of the practice of managing projects & programs; To advocate acceptance of project management as a profession & discipline
Finances: *Annual Operating Budget:* Greater than $5 Million
Staff Member(s): 90
Membership: 265,000 worldwide; *Fees:* US$129 individual; US$60 retiree; US$40 student
Chief Officer(s):
Gregory Balestrero, President/CEO
Meetings/Conferences:
• Project Management Institute Global Congress 2018, May, 2018, Berlin
Scope: International

  Durham Highlands
  #1021, 4-1550 Kingston Rd., Pickering ON L1V 6W9
  e-mail: websupport@pmi-dhc.ca
  www.pmi-dhc.ca
  www.linkedin.com/groups/2228530
  Chief Officer(s):
  Madeleine Sanders, President
  president@pmi-dhc.ca

  Canada's Technology Triangle
  PO Box 24041, Stn. Highland West, Kitchener ON N2M 5P1
  www.pmi-ctt.ca
  Chief Officer(s):
  Dale Van Looyen, CEO

  Lakeshore
  #361, 6-2400 Dundas St. West, Mississauga ON L5K 2R8
  e-mail: info@pmiloc.org
  www.pmiloc.org
  www.linkedin.com/company/24784748
  www.facebook.com/PMILakeshoreChapter
  twitter.com/pmilakeshoresm
  Chief Officer(s):
  Michael Ghobros, President

  Lévis-Québec
  Québec QC
  Tel: 418-780-5383
  secretariat@pmiquebec.qc.ca
  www.pmiquebec.qc.ca
  www.linkedin.com/groups/1385577
  www.facebook.com/pmiquebec
  Chief Officer(s):
  Jean Gariépy, Président

  Manitoba
  #333, Unit 3 - 363 Broadway Ave., Winnipeg MB R3C 3N9
  e-mail: communications@pmimanitoba.org
  www.pmimanitoba.org
  www.linkedin.com/groups/2961710
  twitter.com/pmiManitoba

  Mission: To serve as Manitoba's organization for project management professionals
  Chief Officer(s):
  Christa Ferreira, President
  president@pmimanitoba.org
  Juan Saldivar, Director, Information Technology & Communications
  communications@pmimanitoba.org

  Montréal
  #520, 630, rue Sherbrooke ouest, Montréal QC H3A 1E4
  Tel: 514-861-8788
  www.pmimontreal.org
  www.linkedin.com/in/pmimontreal
  www.facebook.com/pmimontreal
  twitter.com/pmimontreal
  Chief Officer(s):
  Louise Fournier, Executive Director

  New Brunswick
  145 Highmeadow Dr., Moncton NB E1G 2B8
  e-mail: communications@pminb.ca
  www.pminb.ca
  www.linkedin.com/groups/7445835
  www.facebook.com/PMINewBrunswick
  twitter.com/pminb
  Chief Officer(s):
  Reg Wilson, President
  president@pminb.ca

  Newfoundland & Labrador
  #358, 38 Pearson St., St. John's NL A1A 3R1
  e-mail: info@pminl.ca
  www.pminl.ca
  www.linkedin.com/groups/3702248
  Chief Officer(s):
  Mark Fahey, President

  North Saskatchewan
  PO Box 278, #8B, 3110 - 8th St. East, Saskatoon SK S7H 0W2
  e-mail: info@pminorthsask.com
  www.pminorthsask.com
  Chief Officer(s):
  Jonathan Moore-Wright, President
  president@pminorthsask.com

  Northern Alberta
  PO Box 11868, Stn. Main, Edmonton AB T5J 3K9
  e-mail: info@pminac.com
  www.pminac.com
  Chief Officer(s):
  Phil Beck, President
  president@pminac.com

  Nova Scotia
  PO Box 34054, Halifax NS B3J 3S1
  Tel: 902-423-1764; *Fax:* 902-484-6697
  www.pmins.ca
  Chief Officer(s):
  Dylan Boudreau, President

  Ottawa Valley Outaouais
  #256, 1568 Merivale Rd., Ottawa ON K2G 5Y7
  Tel: 613-569-6236
  www.pmiovoc.org
  Chief Officer(s):
  Darlene McTavish, Secretariat

  Regina/South Saskatchewan
  PO Box 3181, Regina SK S4P 3G7
  www.pmisouthsask.org
  Chief Officer(s):
  Bob Berthiaume, President

  South Western Ontario
  PO Box 583, Stn. B, London ON N6A 4W8
  Tel: 226-377-0012
  president@pmiswoc.org
  www.pmiswoc.org
  www.linkedin.com/groups/2425554
  www.facebook.com/pmiswoc
  twitter.com/pmiswoc
  Chief Officer(s):
  Kamran Khan, President
  kamran.khan@pmiswoc.org

  Southern Alberta
  #600, 900 - 6 Ave. SW, Calgary AB T2P 3K2
  Tel: 403-244-4487; *Fax:* 403-244-2340
  news@pmisac.com
  www.pmisac.com
  www.linkedin.com/groups/79052

  www.facebook.com/PMISAC
  twitter.com/pmi_sac
  Chief Officer(s):
  Randy George, President

  Toronto
  #300, 1370 Don Mills Rd., Toronto ON M3B 3N7
  Tel: 416-381-4058; *Fax:* 416-441-0591
  info@soc.pmi.on.ca
  www.pmitoronto.ca
  www.linkedin.com/groups/48405
  www.youtube.com/PMInstitute
  Chief Officer(s):
  Marc Blanchette, President

  Vancouver Island
  PO Box 8208, Stn. Main Post Office, 709 Yates St., Victoria BC V8W 3R8
  e-mail: membership@pmivi.org
  www.pmivi.org
  twitter.com/pmivi
  Chief Officer(s):
  Manji Sekhon, President
  president@pmivi.org

  West Coast
  e-mail: membership@pmi.bc.ca
  www.pmi.bc.ca
  Chief Officer(s):
  Qudsia Ahmed, President

Public Services International (PSI) / Internationale des services publics
Centre d'Aumard, PO Box 9, 45, av Voltaire, Ferney-Voltaire Cedex F-01211 France
Tel: 330-450-406-464; *Fax:* 330-450-407-320
Other Communication: www.flickr.com/photos/psi_isp_iska
psi@world-psi.org
www.world-psi.org
www.facebook.com/PSIglobalunion
twitter.com/PSIglobalunion
www.youtube.com/user/PSIglobalunion
Overview: A large international organization founded in 1907
Mission: To represent public sector trade unions in countries around the world; has consultative status with ECOSOC & observer status with other UN bodies such as UNCTAD & UNESCO
Finances: *Annual Operating Budget:* Greater than $5 Million
Membership: Represents over 20 million workers from 700 unions in 154 countries worldwide; *Committees:* 4 regions within each of which are Regional, Regional Conference, & Woman's committees
Activities: National reports; conferences
Chief Officer(s):
Dave Prentis, President
Rosa Pavanelli, General Secretary
rosa.pavanelli@world-psi.org
Publications:
• Privatization Watch [a publication of Public Services International]
Type: Newsletter
• Right to Health [a publication of Public Services International]
Type: Newsletter

The Publishers Association (PA)
50 Southwark St., London SE1 1UN United Kingdom
Tel: 44-20-7378-0504
mail@publishers.org.uk
www.publishers.org.uk
www.linkedin.com/company/894890
twitter.com/PublishersAssoc
Overview: A medium-sized national organization founded in 1896
Mission: To represent the British book publishing industry; To negotiate & liaise with the government of the UK, the Commission of the EEC & other bodies in the book trade in the UK & in other countries; To collect essential data about the British publishing industry & its markets
Member of: International Publishers Association; Federation of European Publishers; National Book Committee; British Copyright Council
Finances: *Annual Operating Budget:* $500,000-$1.5 Million
Staff Member(s): 10
Membership: 200; *Fees:* Schedule available; *Committees:* Academic, Professional & Learning Publishers Council; Accessibility Action Group; Consumer Publishers Council; Digital Piracy Working Group; Educational Publishers Council; International Board; Policy Group; Publishing Law Group

Chief Officer(s):
Stephen Lotinga, Chief Executive
Emma House, Deputy Chief Executive
Mark Wharton, Director, Operations
Chloe Smith, Manager, Communications & Policy

Rainforest Action Network (RAN)
#300, 425 Bush St., San Francisco CA 94108 USA
Tel: 415-398-4404; Fax: 415-398-2732
answers@ran.org
www.ran.org
www.facebook.com/rainforestactionnetwork
twitter.com/ran
www.youtube.com/user/ranvideo
Overview: A medium-sized international organization founded in 1985
Mission: To protect the Earth's rainforests & support the rights of their inhabitants through campaigns that work to bring corporate & government policies into alignment with popular support for rainforest conservation
Member of: Friends of the Earth International
Affiliation(s): 150 Rainforest Action Groups (RAGs) in the US & Europe; the RAGs are informally affiliated with RAN, receiving support materials, but no funding; RAGs organize local community actions
Finances: Funding Sources: 45% membership; 55% grants & donations
Staff Member(s): 35
Activities: Oil Exploration Campaign; Old Growth Wood Consumption Campaign; Traditional Forest Peoples Campaign; Education Campaign; Grass Roots Team; Zero Emissions Campaign; Global Finance Campaign; Awareness Events: World Rainforest Week; Internships: Yes; Library
Chief Officer(s):
James D. Gollin, President
Lindsey Allen, Executive Director

Rainforest Alliance (RA)
233 Broadway, 28th Fl., New York NY 10279 USA
Tel: 212-677-1900; Fax: 212-677-2187
info@ra.org
www.rainforest-alliance.org
www.facebook.com/8895898655
twitter.com/RnfrstAlliance
www.youtube.com/user/rainforestalliance
Overview: A medium-sized international charitable organization founded in 1987
Mission: To protect ecosystems & the people & wildlife that depend on them by transforming land-use practices, business practices & consumer behavior
Finances: Annual Operating Budget: Greater than $5 Million
Staff Member(s): 300
Membership: 35,000; Fees: $35+ donation
Activities: Internships: Yes; Rents Mailing List: Yes
Chief Officer(s):
Tensie Whelan, President

Red Hat Society Inc.
431 South Acacia Ave., Fullerton CA 92831 USA
Tel: 714-738-0001
Toll-Free: 866-386-2850
info@redhatsociety.com
www.redhatsociety.com
www.linkedin.com/company/1175774
www.facebook.com/RedHatSocietyPage
twitter.com/redhatsociety
Overview: A medium-sized international organization
Mission: To offer women an opportunity to have fun with kindred spirits
Affiliation(s): 32 chapters across Canada (www.redhatchapters.com)
Membership: Fees: US$39 Queen; $US20 regular; Member Profile: Pink Hatters (pink hats & lavender clothing) - women younger than 50; Red Hatters - women 50 & older

Religions for Peace (RFP)
777 United Nations Plaza, 4th Fl., New York NY 10017 USA
Tel: 212-687-2163
info@rfp.org
www.religionsforpeace.org
www.facebook.com/591924330856540
twitter.com/religions4peace
Overview: A large international organization founded in 1975
Mission: To establish peace & justice at the local, national & international levels; To encourage members to work together with like-minded organizations on issues of social & economic justice, human rights, ecological harmony, arms limitation & nuclear disarmament; To aim for world peace through interfaith dialogue & applied ethics
20 volunteer(s)
Membership: 100-499; Fees: $100 institutional; $10 student; $25 individual; $15 senior; Member Profile: Distinguished religious leaders who are dedicated to building peace
Activities: Meetings; Occasional conferences; Newsletter
Chief Officer(s):
Pascale Frémond, President
pascale.fremond@videotron.ca

Renaissance Society of America (RSA)
Graduate School & University Center, City University of New York, #5400, 365 Fifth Ave., New York NY 10016-4309 USA
Tel: 212-817-2130; Fax: 212-817-1544
rsa@rsa.org
www.rsa.org
Overview: A medium-sized international organization founded in 1954
Mission: To promote the study of the era 1300-1700
Member of: American Council of Learned Societies
Affiliation(s): International Federation of Renaissance Societies & Institutes
Finances: Annual Operating Budget: $50,000-$100,000
Staff Member(s): 4
Membership: 3,000 individual + 1,200 institutional; Fees: Schedule available; Member Profile: Interest in the Renaissance Period
Chief Officer(s):
Carla Zecher, Executive Director
czecher@rsa.org
Awards:
• William Nelson Prize
Recognizes the best manuscript submitted to Renaissance Quarterly Amount: $600
• Phyllis Goodhart Gordan Book Prize
Awards an author of the best book in Renaissance studies Amount: $1,000
• Paul Oskar Kristeller Lifetime Achievement Award
Honours a scholar for lifetime achievement
• RSA Research Grants

Renewable Natural Resources Foundation (RNRF)
5430 Grosvenor Lane, Bethesda MD 20814-2142 USA
Tel: 301-493-9101; Fax: 301-493-6148
info@rnrf.org
www.rnrf.org
Overview: A small national charitable organization founded in 1972
Mission: To advance sciences & public education in renewable natural resources; to promote the application of sound, scientific practices in managing & conserving renewable natural resources; to foster coordination & cooperation among professional, scientific & educational organizations having leadership responsibilities for renewable natural resources; to develop a Renewable Natural Resources Center
Staff Member(s): 5
Membership: 12; Member Profile: Professional & scientific societies with interest in natural resources
Activities: Public policy roundtables, national congresses, annual awards, quarterly journal, internship program; Internships: Yes
Chief Officer(s):
Robert D. Day, Executive Director
Awards:
• Outstanding Achievement Award
• Excellence in Journalism Award

Resource Recycling Inc.
PO Box 42270, Portland OR 97242-0270 USA
Tel: 503-233-1305; Fax: 503-233-1356
info@resource-recycling.com
www.resource-recycling.com
www.facebook.com/ResourceRecycling
twitter.com/rrecycling
Overview: A medium-sized international organization founded in 1982
Finances: Annual Operating Budget: $500,000-$1.5 Million
Staff Member(s): 8
Activities: Rents Mailing List: Yes
Chief Officer(s):
Cara Bergeson, Publisher
cara@resource-recycling.com
Publications:
• Resource Recycling
Editor: Jerry Powell; Price: $52 annual subscription
Profile: Monthly magazine

Retail, Wholesale & Department Store Union (AFL-CIO/CLC) (RWDSU) / Union des employés de gros, de détail et de magasins à rayons (FAT-COI/CTC)
#501, 370 - 7th Ave., New York NY 10001 USA
Tel: 212-684-5300
admin@rwdsu.org
www.rwdsu.org
www.facebook.com/RWDSU.UFCW
twitter.com/RWDSU
www.youtube.com/RetailUnion
Overview: A large international organization founded in 1937
Mission: To represent workers throughout much of the United States and Canada
Membership: 7,000 individuals + 12 locals + 1 joint council in Canada
Activities: Internships: Yes
Chief Officer(s):
Stuart Appelbaum, President
Jack Wurm, Secretary-Treasurer
Gemma de Leon, Executive Vice-President
Awards:
• Alvin E. Heaps Memorial Scholarship

Road Scholar
11 Ave. de Lafayette, Boston MA 02111 USA
Fax: 613-530-2096
Toll-Free: 866-745-1690
registration@roadscholar.org
www.roadscholar.org
www.facebook.com/rsadventures
twitter.com/roadscholarorg
www.youtube.com/user/roadscholarorg
Previous Name: Routes to Learning
Overview: A large national charitable organization founded in 1980
Mission: To develop, manage & facilitate educational experiences for older adults through cooperative partnership with educational agents; To balance education & travel in an environment of comradeship & respect; To continue to experiment with pilot projects to reach broader populations of older adults; To be a "learner-centered" organization that responds to the learning needs of older adults; To work towards a better understanding of our relationship with our current populations; To use new methods of reaching out to an ever more diverse multicultural Canada; to promote cost-effective educational opportunities to an ever widening group of older adults
Finances: Annual Operating Budget: $500,000-$1.5 Million
Staff Member(s): 15; 175 volunteer(s)
Membership: 300,000; Member Profile: Open to people in their retirement years, 55 & over
Activities: Offering programs to interested adults (55+) through a variety of educational institutions; Speaker Service: Yes
Chief Officer(s):
Victoria Pearson, President/CEO

Rocky Mountain Elk Foundation Canada
5705 Grant Creek, Missoula MT 59808 USA
Tel: 406-523-4500
Toll-Free: 800-225-5355
www.rmef.org
facebook.com/RMEF1
twitter.com/RMEF
youtube.com/elkfoundation
Overview: A small local organization founded in 1984
Mission: To ensure the future of elk, other wildlife & their habitat

The Rocky Mountain Institute (RMI)
22830 Two Rivers Rd., Basalt CO 81621 USA
Tel: 970-927-3851; Fax: 970-927-3420
media@rmi.org
www.rmi.org
www.linkedin.com/company/rocky-mountain-institute
www.facebook.com/RockyMtnInst
twitter.com/RockyMtnInst
www.youtube.com/user/RockyMtnInstitute
Overview: A medium-sized international organization founded in 1982
Mission: To foster the efficient & sustainable use of resources as a path to global security; To focus on five program areas - energy, water, agriculture, economic renewal, security; To stress the importance of understanding the interconnections between

resource issues, honoring people's integrity, seeking ideas that transcend ideology & harnessing the problem-solving power of free-market economics
Finances: *Annual Operating Budget:* Greater than $5 Million; *Funding Sources:* Personal donations; grants
Staff Member(s): 45
Membership: 23,000; *Fees:* $10
Activities: *Internships:* Yes; *Speaker Service:* Yes; *Library:* by appointment
Chief Officer(s):
Jules Kortenhorst, CEO

Rosenthal Institute for Holocaust Studies
c/o Graduate Center of the City Univ. of New York, #5301, 365 - 5th Ave., New York NY 10016 USA
Tel: 212-817-1949
web.gc.cuny.edu/dept/cjstu/pages/Holocaust.html
Previous Name: Emeric & Ilana Csengeri Institute for Holocaust Studies
Overview: A small international organization founded in 1979
Mission: To conduct research revolving Holocaust
Member of: Centre for Jewish Studies
Activities: *Library* by appointment
Chief Officer(s):
Randolph L. Braham, Director
rbraham@gc.cuny.edu

Rotary International
One Rotary Center, 1560 Sherman Ave., Evanston IL 60201-3698 USA
Toll-Free: 866-976-8279
www.rotary.org
www.linkedin.com/groups/858557
www.facebook.com/rotary
twitter.com/rotary
www.youtube.com/user/RotaryInternational
Overview: A large international organization
Mission: To support its member clubs in fulfilling the Object of Rotary by fostering unity among member clubs, strengthening & expanding rotary around the world, communicating worldwide the work of Rotary & providing a system of international administration
Membership: 1.2 million belonging to 35,000 clubs
Chief Officer(s):
Ian H.S. Riseley, President
Awards:
• Rotary Youth Leadership Awards (RYLA)
Meetings/Conferences:
• Rotary International Convention 2018, June, 2018, Toronto, ON
Scope: International
Contact Information: www.riconvention.org

Routes to Learning *See* Road Scholar

The Royal Commonwealth Society
7 Lion Yard, Tremadoc Road, London SW4 7NQ United Kingdom
Tel: 44-0-20-7766-9200
info@thercs.org
thercs.org
www.linkedin.com/company/royal-commonwealth-society
www.facebook.com/thercs
twitter.com/TheRCSLondon
www.youtube.com/user/TheRCSociety
Previous Name: Royal Empire Society
Overview: A small international organization founded in 1868
Mission: To promote an understanding of the nature & working of the Commonwealth & of the factors which shape the lives of its peoples & the policies of its governments
Staff Member(s): 8
Chief Officer(s):
Michael Lake, Director
michael.lake@thercs.org

Royal Empire Society *See* The Royal Commonwealth Society

The Royal Scottish Country Dance Society (RSCDS)
12 Coates Cres., Edinburgh EH15 1EY UK
Tel: 44-0131-225-3854; *Fax:* 44-0131-225-7783
info@rscds.org
www.rscds.org
www.facebook.com/RSCDS
twitter.com/rscdsdancescot
www.youtube.com/user/TheRSCDS
Overview: A medium-sized international charitable organization founded in 1923
Mission: To preserve & further the practice of traditional Scottish Country Dancing; to provide or assist in providing special education or instruction in the practice of Scottish Country Dances
Finances: *Annual Operating Budget:* $1.5 Million-$3 Million
Staff Member(s): 6; 60 volunteer(s)
Membership: 13,000; *Fees:* Schedule available; *Committees:* Education & Training; Membership Services; Youth Services; Schools
Activities: *Library* by appointment
Chief Officer(s):
Gillian Wilson, Executive Officer
gillian.wilson@rscds.org
Publications:
• Scottish Country Dancer [a publication of the Royal Scottish Country Dance Society]
Type: Magazine; *Frequency:* s-a.; *Accepts Advertising; Editor:* Marilyn Healy; *Price:* Free with RSCDS membership
Profile: A resource that aims to inform, enterain, & inspire Scottish Country Dancers; includes news andarticle contributions from RSCDS members

Burlington Branch
2266 Glenwood School Dr., Burlington ON L7R 3R7
Tel: 905-639-8782
Chief Officer(s):
Gillian Young, Secretary

Calgary Branch
PO Box 1471, Stn. M, Calgary AB T2P 2L6
Tel: 403-862-6114
secretary@rscdscalgary.org
www.rscdscalgary.org
www.facebook.com/rscdscalgary
Debby Henderson, President
president@rscdscalgary.org
Nancy Laing, Secretary

Hamilton Branch
405 Caithness St. East, Caledonia ON N3W 1C8
Tel: 519-621-8274
www.rscdshamilton.org
Chief Officer(s):
Heather Pate, Chair

Kingston Branch
40 Murray Pl., Kingston ON K7N 1P6
Tel: 613-384-2597
www.rscdskingston.org
Chief Officer(s):
Mary Clipperton, Secretary
maryclipperton@yahoo.ca

Kitchener-Waterloo Branch
Waterloo Town Square, PO Box 40029, 75 King St. South, Waterloo ON N2J 4V1
Tel: 519-894-6995
secretaryws@rscds.kitchener.on.ca
www.rscds.kitchener.on.ca
Chief Officer(s):
Lynn Dramnitzki, Secretary

London Branch
14 Hyatt Ave., London ON N5Z 1Y5
Tel: 519-679-9366
www.rscdslondoncanada.org
Chief Officer(s):
Margaret Allan, Secretary

Medicine Hat Branch
PO Box 447, Stn. Main, Medicine Hat AB T1A 7G2
Tel: 403-526-3140
rscdsmh@gmail.com
nonprofit.memlane.com/scottish
Chief Officer(s):
Stewart Kennedy, President
Jennifer Sissons, Secretary

Montréal Branch
3690, rue Sainte Famille, Montréal QC H2X 2L4
Tel: 514-288-0992
info@scdmontreal.org
www.scdmontreal.org
Chief Officer(s):
Holly Boyd, Secretary
secretary@scdmontreal.org

Ottawa Branch
19 Morenz Terrace, Kanata ON K2K 3H1
Tel: 613-270-9787
www.rscdsottawa.ca
Chief Officer(s):
Michael Hamilton, Secretary
secretary@rscdsottawa.ca

St. John's Branch
PO Box 23097, Stn. Churchill Square, St. John's NL A1B 4J9
Tel: 709-754-1703
www.rscdsstjohns.ca
Chief Officer(s):
Catherine Wright, Chair
catherinewright@hotmail.com

Saskatchewan Branch
#106, 65 Woodlily Dr., Moose Jaw SK S6H 3V2
Tel: 306-692-9851
info@rscdssask.org
www.rscdssask.org
Chief Officer(s):
Mike Blanchard, Secretary

Toronto Branch
#113, 942 Yonge St., Toronto ON M4W 3S8
Tel: 416-923-4392
www.dancescottish.ca
Chief Officer(s):
Nancy White, Secretary
nawhite15@gmail.com

Vancouver Branch
8886 Hudson St., Vancouver BC V6P 4N2
e-mail: secretary@rscdsvancouver.org
www.rscdsvancouver.org
Chief Officer(s):
Gillian Beattie, Secretary

Vancouver Island Branch
PO Box 30123, Stn. Reynolds, 3943C Quadra St., Victoria BC V8X 1J5
Tel: 250-598-0207
viscds@shaw.ca
viscds.ca
Dora Dempster, President
doradempster@shaw.ca
Susannah Andersen, Secretary

Windsor Branch
Windsor ON
www.rscdswindsor.org
Miriam Wright, Secretary

Winnipeg Branch
821 Parkhill St., Winnipeg MB R2Y 0V4
Tel: 204-488-7386; *Fax:* 204-837-7346
info@rscdswinnipeg.ca
www.rscdswinnipeg.ca
Chief Officer(s):
Agnes Brydon, Secretary

The Royal Society for the Encouragement of Arts, Manufactures & Commerce (RSA)
8 John Adam St., London WC2N 6EZ United Kingdom
Tel: 44-020-7930-5115; *Fax:* 44-020-7839-5805
general@rsa.org.uk
www.rsa.org.uk
www.linkedin.com/company/royal-society-for-the-encouragement-of-arts-manufactures-and-commerce-the-rsa-S
www.facebook.com/theRSAorg
twitter.com/theRSAorg
www.youtube.com/user/theRSAorg
Overview: A medium-sized international charitable organization founded in 1754
Mission: To encourage the development of a principled, prosperous society & the release of human potential
Finances: *Annual Operating Budget:* $3 Million-$5 Million; *Funding Sources:* Membership fees; sponsorship for projects; conference facilities
Staff Member(s): 50
Membership: 27,000 fellows worldwide; *Committees:* Audit, Risk & Governance; Environment; Arts Advisory Group; Marketing Panel; History, Records & Collections Panel; Finance & General Purpose
Activities: *Library* by appointment
Chief Officer(s):
Vikki Heywood, CBE, Chair
Amanda Kanojia, Administrator
amanda.kanojia@rsa.org.uk

Rubber Manufacturers Association (RMA)
#900, 1400 K St. NW, Washington DC 20005 USA
Tel: 202-682-4800
info@rma.org
www.rma.org
Previous Name: The Scrap Tire Management Council

Foreign Associations / Russian Association of Canadian Studies

Overview: A small national organization founded in 1990
Mission: To advocate on behalf of the rubber products industry
Membership: *Member Profile:* Tire group companies include tire manufacturers & retread & repair material suppliers; Elastomer Products Group companies include manufacturers of non-tire elastomer products & suppliers of raw materials & machinery
Activities: Producing publications on consumer tire information, the market, industry standards, government affairs, safety, scrap tire activities, & tire service professionals; *Awareness Events:* National Tire Safety Week, June
Chief Officer(s):
Charles A. Cannon, President/CEO
Publications:
• Rubber Manufacturers Association Member Directory
Type: Directory
Profile: RMA member company contact & product information

Russian Association of Canadian Studies
Russian Academy of Sciences, 2/3 Khlebny Pereulok, Moscow 121814 Russia
Tel: 7-095-202-3084; *Fax:* 7-095-202-3016
racs@yandex.ru
Overview: A small international organization
Mission: Promotes study, research, teaching & publication about Canada in all academic disciplines
Member of: International Council for Canadian Studies
Membership: 160
Chief Officer(s):
Tatiana Shchukina, Executive Director
Sergei Rogov, President

Salt Institute
Fairfax Plaza, #600, 700 North Fairfax St., Alexandria VA 22314-2040 USA
Tel: 703-549-4648; *Fax:* 703-548-2194
info@saltinstitute.org
www.saltinstitute.org
www.facebook.com/ALittleSalt
twitter.com/WithALittleSalt
www.youtube.com/user/SaltGuru
Overview: A medium-sized national organization founded in 1914
Mission: To advocate fpr responsible salt use, enabling improved quality of water, healthy nutrition, & safe roadways.
Affiliation(s): Transportation Association of Canada
Finances: *Funding Sources:* Membership dues
Staff Member(s): 4
Membership: 37; *Fees:* Based on salt sales by company; *Member Profile:* Manufacturers, producers & sellers of sodium chloride
Activities: *Speaker Service:* Yes; *Library:* Not open to public
Chief Officer(s):
Lori Roman, President
lori@saltinstitute.org
Jorge Amselle, Director, Communications
Awards:
• Excellence in Storage Award

SCOPE for People with Cerebral Palsy
6 Market Rd., London N7 9PW United Kingdom
Tel: 0-20-7619-7100
response@scope.org.uk
www.scope.org.uk
www.linkedin.com/companies/165883
www.facebook.com/scope
twitter.com/scope
www.youtube.com/user/scopestories
Previous Name: The Spastics Society
Overview: A small international organization founded in 1952
Mission: To enable men, women & children with cerebral palsy & associated disabilities to claim their rights, lead fulfilling & rewarding lives & play a full part in society; to provide activities & services which respond to individuals' needs, choices & rights
Affiliation(s): Canadian Cerebral Palsy Association
Finances: *Funding Sources:* Individual; corporate; events
Membership: *Committees:* Resources; Development; Audit
Activities: Creates housing, education & employment opportunities; provides expert & loving care; supports families, carers & self-help groups; *Speaker Service:* Yes; *Library:* Open to public by appointment
Chief Officer(s):
Richard Hawkes, Chief Executive

The Scrap Tire Management Council *See* Rubber Manufacturers Association

Screen Actors Guild - American Federation of Television & Radio Artists (SAG-AFTRA)
5757 Wilshire Blvd., 7th Fl., Los Angeles CA 90036-3600 USA
Tel: 323-954-1600
Toll-Free: 855-724-2387
sagaftrainfo@sagaftra.org
www.sagaftra.org
www.facebook.com/SAGAFTRA
twitter.com/SAGAFTRA
www.youtube.com/user/SAGAFTRATV
Merged from: Screen Actors Guild; American Federation of Television & Radio Artists
Overview: A small international organization founded in 2012
Mission: To ensure that its members receive fair wages, health benefits & work in safe conditions; to work to protect their members from exploitation
Member of: AFL-CIO
Membership: 165,000; *Fees:* $198 + 1.575% of earnings under SAG-AFTRA from $1 to $500,000; *Member Profile:* Actors; announcers; broadcast journalists; DJs; news writers; news editors; program hosts; puppeteers; recording artists; singers; stunt performers; voiceover artists
Chief Officer(s):
David White, National Executive Director
Mathis Dunn, Associate National Executive Director
New York Office
1900 Broadway, 5th Fl., New York NY 10023 USA
Tel: 212-944-1030

Screenprinting & Graphic Imaging Association International *See* Specialty Graphic Imaging Association

Sea Shepherd Conservation Society - USA (SSCS)
#45, 2226 Eastlake Ave. East, Seattle WA 98102-3419 USA
Tel: 212-220-2302; *Fax:* 360-370-5651
info@seashepherd.org
www.seashepherd.org
www.linkedin.com/company/sea-shepherd-conservation-society
www.facebook.com/seashepherdconservationsociety
twitter.com/SeaShepherdSSCS
www.youtube.com/seashepherd;
www.instagram.com/seashepherdsscs
Overview: A large international charitable organization founded in 1977
Mission: A direct action organization to protect dolphins, whales, seals & other marine life
Finances: *Annual Operating Budget:* $500,000-$1.5 Million; *Funding Sources:* Grants, public contributions
Staff Member(s): 5; 40 volunteer(s)
Membership: 30,000 worldwide; *Fees:* $25
Activities: Research, documentation & enforcement of international marine conservation law; *Rents Mailing List:* Yes; *Library:* Sea Shepherd Media Library
Chief Officer(s):
Paul Watson, Founder & President

SEDS - USA
USA
www.seds.org
www.linkedin.com/groups/51612
www.facebook.com/sedsusa
twitter.com/sedsusa
www.youtube.com/user/sedsusa
Also Known As: Students for the Exploration & Development of Space
Overview: A medium-sized international organization founded in 1980
Mission: To operate as an international student-run space interest group, with chapters in Canada, the United States, South America, Europe, & Asia; To educate students & the public about space & space-related issues
Finances: *Funding Sources:* Chapter dues; corporate donations
Membership: 85 chapters
Activities: Hosts an international conference; offers a space information e-mail network (SEDSNEWS) & a communications e-mail link for members internationally (SEDSLINK)
Chief Officer(s):
Sam Albert, Chair, Council of Chapters
sam.albert@seds.org

Service Employees International Union (AFL-CIO/CLC) / Union internationale des employés des services (FAT-COI/CTC)
1800 Massachusetts Ave. NW, Washington DC 20036 USA
Tel: 202-730-7000
Toll-Free: 800-424-8592; *TTY:* 202-730-7481
www.seiu.org
www.facebook.com/SEIU
twitter.com/SEIU
www.youtube.com/user/SEIU; www.flickr.com/photos/seiu
Overview: A large international organization
Mission: To unite workers in 3 sectors: healthcare, property services, & public services; To improve the lives of its members, their families, & the services they provide
Membership: 2 million members in 150 local unions
Activities: *Internships:* Yes; *Speaker Service:* Yes; *Library:* by appointment
Chief Officer(s):
Mary Kay Henry, President
SEIU Healthcare
125 Mural St., Richmond Hill ON L4B 1M4
Tel: 905-695-1767; *Fax:* 905-695-1768
Toll-Free: 800-267-7348
info@seiuhealthcare.ca
www.seiu.ca
www.facebook.com/SEIUHealthcareCanada
twitter.com/seiucanada
www.youtube.com/user/seiulocal1canada
Chief Officer(s):
Sharleen Stewart, President

Service social international *See* International Social Service

Seva Foundation
1786 - 5th St., Berkeley CA 94710 USA
Tel: 510-845-7382; *Fax:* 510-845-7410
Toll-Free: 877-764-7382
www.seva.org
www.facebook.com/seva.foundation
twitter.com/Seva_Foundation
Overview: A small international charitable organization founded in 1979
Mission: To prevent & relieve suffering; to generate hope through compassionate action
Staff Member(s): 30
Chief Officer(s):
Jack Blanks, Executive Director

Sheet Metal & Air Conditioning Contractors' National Association (SMACNA)
PO Box 221230, 4201 Lafayette Center Dr., Chantilly VA 20153-1230 USA
Tel: 703-803-2980; *Fax:* 703-803-3732
info@smacna.org
www.smacna.org
www.facebook.com/SMACNA
Overview: A large international organization founded in 1943
Finances: *Funding Sources:* Membership dues; Industry fund
Staff Member(s): 34
Membership: 1,834 firms in 103 chapters; *Member Profile:* Firms performing work in industrial, commercial, institutional, & residential markets, specializing in the following: heating, ventilation, & air conditioning; architectural sheet metal; industrial sheet metal; kitchen equipment; specialty stainless steel work; manufacturing; siding & decking; testing & balancing; service & retrofit; energy management & maintenance
Chief Officer(s):
Vincent R. Sandusky, Chief Executive Officer
vsandusky@smacna.org
Meetings/Conferences:
• 2018 Sheet Metal and Air Conditioning Contractors' National Association (SMACNA) Annual Convention, October, 2018, San Diego Marriott Marquis & Marina, San Diego, CA
Scope: National
Contact Information: www.smacna.org/annualconvention

Sheet Metal Workers' International Association (AFL-CIO/CFL) (SMWIA) / Association internationale des travailleurs du métal en feuilles (FAT-COI/FCT)
1750 New York Ave. NW, 6th Fl., Washington DC 20006 USA
Toll-Free: 800-457-7694
www.smwia.org
www.facebook.com/smartunion
twitter.com/smwia
Overview: A small international organization
Mission: To establish & maintain desirable working conditions for its members, & is their collective bargaining agent.
Affiliation(s): American Federation of Labor & Congress of Industrial Organizations; Canadian Labour Congress
Membership: 150,000; *Member Profile:* Men & women employed in the United States, Canada & Puerto Rico, working

in the construction, manufacturing, service, railroad & shipyard industries
Chief Officer(s):
Joseph J. Nigro, General President
Canadian Office
190 Thames Rd. East, Exeter ON N0M 1S3

Sierra Club
85 Second St., 2nd Fl., San Francisco CA 94105-3441 USA
Tel: 415-977-5500; *Fax:* 415-977-5797
information@sierraclub.org
www.sierraclub.org
www.linkedin.com/company/sierra-club
www.facebook.com/SierraClub
twitter.com/sierra_club
www.instagram.com/sierraclub;
www.youtube.com/user/NationalSierraClub
Overview: A large international organization founded in 1892
Mission: To promote conservation of the natural environment by influencing public policy decisions - legislative, administrative, legal & electoral; To explore, enjoy & protect the wild places of the earth; To practice & promote the responsible use of the earth's ecosystems & resources; To educate & enlist humanity to protect & restore the quality of the natural & human environment; To use all lawful means to carry out these objectives at the federal, state & local levels
Finances: *Annual Operating Budget:* $3 Million-$5 Million
Membership: 1,300,000; *Fees:* $15-$100
Activities: *Awareness Events:* John Muir Day, April 21; *Library:* Not open to public
Chief Officer(s):
Michael Brune, Executive Director
Aaron Mair, President
Publications:
• Sierra [a publication of the Sierra Club]
Type: Magazine; *Frequency:* bi-m.; *ISSN:* 0161-7362

Sjogren's Syndrome Foundation Inc. (SSF)
#325, 6707 Democracy Blvd., Bethesda MD 20817 USA
Tel: 301-530-4420; *Fax:* 301-530-4415
Toll-Free: 800-475-6473
tms@sjogrens.org
www.sjogrens.org
www.facebook.com/SjogrensSyndromeFoundation
twitter.com/MoistureSeekers
Also Known As: The Moisture Seekers
Overview: A medium-sized international charitable organization founded in 1983
Mission: To educate patients & their families about Sjogren's syndrome; to increase public & professional awareness of Sjogren's syndrome; to encourage research into new treatments & a cure; provides patients practical information & coping strategies that minimize the effects of Sjogren's syndrome; Foundation is clearing house for medication information & is the recognized national advocate for Sjogren's syndrome
Finances: *Funding Sources:* Membership dues; contributions
Staff Member(s): 10
Membership: *Fees:* US$36 US; US$43 Canada; US$49 Overseas
Activities: *Library* by appointment
Chief Officer(s):
Steven Taylor, CEO
staylor@sjogrens.org

Slow Food
Piazza XX Settembre, 5, Bra 12042 Italy
Tel: 39-0172-419-611; *Fax:* 39-0172-421-293
international@slowfood.com
www.slowfood.com
www.facebook.com/slowfoodinternational
twitter.com/SlowFoodHQ
www.instagram.com/slowfood_international
Overview: A medium-sized international organization founded in 1986
Mission: To protect the pleasures of the table from the homogenization of modern fast food & life; To promote gastronomic culture; To develop taste education; To conserve agricultural biodiversity & to protect traditional foods at risk of extinction
Membership: 100,000
Chief Officer(s):
Carlo Petrini, President

Small Publishers Association of North America (SPAN)
PO Box 9725, Colorado Springs CO 80932-0725 USA
Tel: 719-924-5534; *Fax:* 719-213-2602
info@spannet.org
www.spannet.org
Overview: A medium-sized international organization founded in 1996
Mission: To advance the image & profits of independent publishers & authors, through education & marketing opportunities
Membership: *Member Profile:* Independent publishers, self publishers, & authors in Canada & the USA
Chief Officer(s):
Brian Jud, Executive Director

Snack Food Association
1600 Wilson Blvd., Arlington VA 22209 USA
Tel: 703-836-4500; *Fax:* 703-836-8262
Toll-Free: 800-628-1334
www.snacintl.org
Also Known As: SNAC International
Overview: A medium-sized international organization founded in 1937
Mission: To provide value for members by offering services & relationship building that strengthen the performance of member companies & support industry growth
Membership: 800+ companies worldwide
Chief Officer(s):
Elizabeth Avery, President & CEO
eavery@snacintl.org

Societas Internationalis Limnologiae *See* International Society of Limnology

Société Cousteau *See* The Cousteau Society

Société des tribologistes et ingénieurs en lubrification *See* Society of Tribologists & Lubrication Engineers

Société internationale arthurienne *See* International Arthurian Society - North American Branch

Société internationale d'amitié et de bonne volonté *See* International Society of Friendship & Good Will

Société internationale de biométéorolgy *See* International Society of Biometeorology

La Société internationale de Chirurgie *See* International Society of Surgery

Société Internationale de Mécanique des Sols et de la Géotechnique *See* International Society for Soil Mechanics & Geotechnical Engineering

Société internationale de sociologie des religions (SISR) / International Society for the Sociology of Religion (ISSR)
c/o Giuseppe Giordan, General Secretary, Università di Padova, Dipartimento di Sociologia, Via cesarotti, 10, Padova 35123 Italy
Tél: +39.049.8274325; *Téléc:* +39.049.657508
www.sisr.org
Aperçu: *Dimension:* petite; *Envergure:* internationale; fondée en 1948
Finances: *Budget de fonctionnement annuel:* Moins de $50,000; *Fonds:* Cotisations des membres
2 bénévole(s)
Membre: 300; *Montant de la cotisation:* 106 E; *Critères d'admissibilite:* En sciences sociales des religions
Membre(s) du bureau directeur:
Giuseppe Giordan, Secrétaire générale
generalsecretary.issr@unipd.it

Société internationale pour l'enseignement commercial *See* International Society for Business Education

Société internationale pour l'étude de la philosophie médiévale (SIEPM) / International Society for the Study of Medieval Philosophy
CP 3200, Kardinaal Mercierplein 2, Leuven B-3000 Belgium
www.siepm.uni-freiburg.de
Aperçu: *Dimension:* moyenne; *Envergure:* internationale; fondée en 1958
Mission: A pour but la coordination des recherches scientifiques sur la pensée médiévale
Membre: 800; *Montant de la cotisation:* 35 Euro
Activités: *Bibliothèque* Not open to public
Membre(s) du bureau directeur:
Pieter De Leemans, Secrétaire général

Society for Adolescent Health & Medicine (SAHM)
#800, 1 Parkview Plaza, Oakbrook Terrace IL 60181 USA
Tel: 847-686-2246; *Fax:* 847-686-2251
info@adolescenthealth.org
www.adolescenthealth.org
www.facebook.com/adolescenthealth.medicine
twitter.com/SAHMtweets
www.youtube.com/SAHMAdolescentHealth
Overview: A medium-sized international organization founded in 1968
Mission: To advance the physical & psychosocial health & well-being of adolescents & young adults; To improve the delivery of health services for adolescents; To promote the field of adolescent medicine & health
Staff Member(s): 9
Membership: *Fees:* Schedule available; *Member Profile:* Healthcare professionals from a wide range of disciplines from thirty countries who want to learn more about adolescent health; *Committees:* Advocacy; Awards; Communications & Media Relations; Development; Diversity; Education; FSAHM Review; Health Services; Multidisciplinary Membership; Research
Activities: Engaging in advocacy activities; Promoting optimal health; Providing professional development activities; Researching
Chief Officer(s):
Ryan Norton, Executive Director
Caitlyn Gibson, Director, Administration
Justin Dreyfuss, Manager, Marketing Communications
Publications:
• Journal of Adolescent Health
Type: Journal; *Frequency:* Monthly; *Editor:* Charles E. Irwin, Jr., M.D., FSAM; *Price:* Free with Society forAdolescent Medicine membership dues
Profile: Peer-reviewed articles on clinical medicine, public health policy, youth development, international health, & behavioral science
• SAHM [Society for Adolescent Health & Medicine] Newsletter
Type: Newsletter; *Frequency:* Quarterly
Profile: News from programs & members, presidential messages, announcements, committee reports, special interest group reports, professional development opportunities,& chapter activities

Society for Classical Studies (APA)
University of Pennsylvania, #201E, 220 South 40th St., Philadelphia PA 19104-3512 USA
Tel: 215-898-4975; *Fax:* 215-573-7874
info@classicalstudies.org
classicalstudies.org
www.facebook.com/SocietyforClassicalStudies
twitter.com/scsclassics
Previous Name: American Philological Association
Overview: A large international organization founded in 1869
Mission: To ensure an adequate number of well-trained, inspirational Classics teachers at all levels, kindergarten through graduate school; To give Classics scholars & teachers the tools they need to preserve & extend our knowledge of classical civilization & to communicate that knowledge as widely as possible; To develop the necessary infrastructure to achieve these goals & to make the APA a model for other societies confronting similar challenges
Member of: American Council of Learned Societies; International Federation of Classical Studies
Affiliation(s): International Federation of Classical Studies
Finances: *Annual Operating Budget:* $500,000-$1.5 Million
Staff Member(s): 3; 300 volunteer(s)
Membership: 3,000; *Fees:* Schedule available; *Member Profile:* Open
Activities: *Speaker Service:* Yes
Chief Officer(s):
Adam D. Blistein, Executive Director
John Marincola, President
Awards:
• The President's Award of the Society for Classical Studies
• The Charles J. Goodwin Award of Merit
• Distinguished Service Awards
• SCS Awards for Excellence in Teaching at the College Level
• SCS Awards for Excellence in Teaching at the Precollegiate Level
• SCS Outreach Prize
Meetings/Conferences:
• Society for Classical Studies 149th Annual Meeting, January, 2018, Boston, MA
Scope: International
• Society for Classical Studies 150th Annual Meeting, January, 2019, San Diego, CA
Scope: International

Foreign Associations / Society for Conservation Biology (SCB)

Publications:
- Amphora [a publication of the Society for Classical Studies]
Frequency: a.; *ISSN:* 1542-2380
Profile: Offers accessible articles written by professional scholars & experts on topics of classical interest
- TAPA [a publication of the Society for Classical Studies]
Editor: Craig Gibson; *ISSN:* 1533-0699
Profile: The official research publication of the APA; reflects the wide range and high quality of research currently undertaken byclassicists.

Society for Conservation Biology (SCB)
1017 O St. NW, Washington DC 20001-4229 USA
Tel: 202-234-4133; *Fax:* 703-995-4633
info@conbio.org
www.conbio.org
www.facebook.com//227557507333973
twitter.com/Society4ConBio
www.youtube.com/user/society4conbio
Overview: A medium-sized international organization founded in 1985
Mission: To advance the scientific study of the phenomena that affect the maintenance, loss, & restoration of biological diversity; To promote the practice of conserving biological diversity
Membership: 10,000+; *Member Profile:* Persons from around the world, who are interested in the study & conservation of biological diversity, such as conservation workers, educators, government workers, resource managers, & students
Activities: Providing recommendations about policies to advance the conservation of biological diversity; Developing educational programs; Providing mentorship opportunities in the field of conservation; Facilitating networking with the professional community
Chief Officer(s):
Geri Unger, Executive Director, 202-234-4133 Ext. 102
gunger@conbio.org
Publications:
- Conservation
Type: Magazine; *Frequency:* Quarterly; *Accepts Advertising*;
Editor: Kathryn A. Kohm
Profile: Conservation articles for members of the Society for Conservation Biology
- Conservation Biology
Type: Journal; *Frequency:* Bimonthly; *Editor:* Erica Fleishman; *ISSN:* 0888-8892
Profile: Information about conservation science for members of the Society for Conservation Biology
- Conservation Letters, A Journal of the Society for Conservation Biology
Type: Journal; *Editor:* Corey Bradshaw
Profile: Empirical, theoretical, & interdisciplinary research about the conservation of biological diversity worldwide
- SCB [Society for Conservation Biology] Newsletter
Type: Newsletter; *Frequency:* Quarterly; *Editor:* Sharon Collinge;
Price: Free with membership in the Society for Conservation Biology

Society for Ecological Restoration International (SER)
1017 O St. NW, Washington DC 20001 USA
Tel: 202-299-9518; *Fax:* 270-626-5485
info@ser.org
www.ser.org
www.linkedin.com/groups/Society-Ecological-Restoration-4076378
www.facebook.com/SocietyforEcologicalRestoration
twitter.com/SERestoration
Overview: A medium-sized international organization founded in 1988
Mission: To promote ecological restoration as a means of sustaining the diversity of life; To reestablish an ecologically healthy relationship between nature & culture
Staff Member(s): 5
Membership: *Fees:* Schedule available; *Member Profile:* Individuals & organizations involved in ecologically-sensitive repair & the management of ecosystems, such as scientists, ecological consultants, planners, engineers, teachers, growers, & natural areas managers; *Committees:* Executive; Assessment; Board Development; Finance; Science & Policy
Activities: Raising public awareness of restoration; Facilitating communication among restorationists; Encouraging research; Providing input to discussions of public policy
Chief Officer(s):
Steve Bosak, Executive Director
steve@ser.org

Levi Wickwire, Manager, Program
levi@ser.org
Leah Bregman, Manager, Membership & Communications
leah@ser.org
Awards:
- John Rieger Award
Awarded to those that have dedicated their time & skills to the advancement of ecological restoration &/or to the devleopment of the Society
- Model Project Award
Recognizes those restoration projects that have truly advanced with craft of ecosystem restoration & upon which future projects may well be modeled
- Full Circle Award
Awarded to those indigenous people whose projects have brought ecosystems full circle, returning them to their condition prior to the impacts caused by non-indigenous peoples
- Project Facilitation Award
Awarded in recognition of well-conceived & properly initiated ecosystem restoration projects that may require or significantly benefit from supplemental funding
- Theodore M. Sperry Award
Recognizes achievement in those elements & approaches that improve restoration programs
- Communication Award
Acknowledges the importance of all forms of communication that advance the goals of the Society
Publications:
- Ecological Restoration
Type: Journal; *Frequency:* Quarterly; *Price:* Included with Society for Ecological Restoration International membership
Profile: Philosophical essays & summaries of current projects & techniques
- Restoration Ecology
Type: Journal; *Frequency:* Quarterly
Profile: Peer-reviewed scientific & technical research articles on topics of restoration & ecological principles
- Restore [a publication of the Society for Ecological Restoration International]
Type: Newsletter; *Frequency:* Weekly
Profile: Annotated links to news stories from around the globe
- Society for Ecological Restoration International Newsletter
Type: Newsletter; *Frequency:* Quarterly
Profile: Up-to-date information for members about the Society & it chapters

Ontario Branch
ON
e-mail: info@serontario.org
chapter.ser.org/ontario/
Affiliation(s): Carolinian Canada; Forest Gene Conservation Association; Ontario Environmental Network; Tallgrass Ontario
Chief Officer(s):
Sal Spitale, Chair
salspitale@hotmail.com

Western Canada Chapter
BC
e-mail: restorewc@gmail.com
chapter.ser.org/westerncanada/
www.facebook.com/ser.westerncanada
twitter.com/ser_wc
Chief Officer(s):
Michael Keefer, Chair

Society for Environmental Graphic Design (SEGD)
#400, 1000 Vermont Ave. NW, Washington DC 20005 USA
Tel: 202-638-5555; *Fax:* 202-478-2286
segd@segd.org
www.segd.org
www.linkedin.com/groups?gid=1806064
www.facebook.com/SEGDcommunity
twitter.com/segd
Overview: A medium-sized international organization
Mission: To promote graphic design & educate the public about the graphic design community
Staff Member(s): 10
Membership: *Fees:* Schedule available; *Member Profile:* Individuals who work in the planning, design, fabrication, & implementation of communications in the built environment
Activities: Fostering research; Providing educational resources; Refining standards of practice; Collaborating across various design disciplines; Offering referrals to fabricators or designers; Providing networking opportunities
Chief Officer(s):

Clive Roux, Chief Executive Officer, 202-638-5555
clive@segd.org
Ann Makowski, Chief Operating Officer, 202-638-5555
ann@segd.org
Jill Ayers, President
Publications:
- segdDESIGN: The International Journal of Environmental Graphic Design
Type: Journal; *Frequency:* Quarterly; *Accepts Advertising*;
Editor: Pat Matson Knapp
Profile: Information about the people, research, technologies, materials, & resources that influence communications in the built environment
- Society for Environmental Graphic Design Membership Directory
Type: Directory

Society for Ethnomusicology (SEM)
Indiana University, 800 East 3rd St., Bloomington IN 47405-3700 USA
Tel: 812-855-6672; *Fax:* 812-855-6673
sem@indiana.edu
www.ethnomusicology.org
Overview: A medium-sized international organization founded in 1955
Mission: To promote the study & performance of all forms of music
Member of: American Council of Learned Societies
Membership: 1,800; *Fees:* $60-$105 individual; $40 student;
Member Profile: Interest in the field of ethnomusicology;
Committees: Academic Labor; Board Nominating; Council Nominating; Diversity Action; Ethics; Investment Advisory; Local Arrangements; Program; Publications; Strategic Planning
Chief Officer(s):
Stephen Stuempfle, Executive Director
semexec@indiana.edu

Society for Information Management (SIM)
#200, 1120 route 73, Mount Laurel NJ 08054 USA
Tel: 856-380-6807
sim@simnet.org
www.simnet.org
www.linkedin.com/company/society-for-information-management
www.facebook.com/societyforinformationmanagement
twitter.com/SIMInt
www.youtube.com/user/societyofIM
Overview: A medium-sized international organization founded in 1968
Mission: To support IT leaders by increasing the knowledge base of SIM members & associates; To act as the voice of the IT community on critical issues; To develop the next generation of effective IT leaders
Membership: 3,500; *Fees:* Schedule available
Chief Officer(s):
Kevin More, Chair
Steve Hufford, Chief Executive
Veronica Sullivan, Director, Operations, 856-380-6859
vsullivan@simnet.org
Meetings/Conferences:
- Society for Information Management (SIM) SIMposium 2018, 2018
Scope: International

Society for Research in Child Development (SRCD)
#401, 2950 South State St., Ann Arbor MI 48104 USA
Tel: 734-926-0600; *Fax:* 734-926-0601
info@srcd.org
www.srcd.org
www.linkedin.com/company/society-for-research-in-child-development
www.facebook.com/143127176115
twitter.com/SRCDtweets
Overview: A medium-sized international organization founded in 1933
Mission: To promote multidisciplinary research in the field of human development; To encourage applications of research findings
Staff Member(s): 17
Membership: 5,400+; *Fees:* Schedule available; *Member Profile:* Multidisciplinary professionals, such as practitioners, researchers, & human development professionals, from more than 50 countries; *Committees:* Ethnic & Racial Issues; History; International Affairs; Policy & Communications; Programs; Publications; Audit; Awards; Equity & Justice; Finance; Interdisciplinary; Nominations; Student & Early Career Council; Teaching

Activities: Facilitating the exchange of information among scientists & other professionals
Chief Officer(s):
Lonnie Sherrod, Executive Director, 734-926-0611, Fax: 734-926-0601
sherrod@srcd.org
Susan Lennon, Deputy Executive Director, 734-926-0619, Fax: 734-926-0601
slennon@srcd.org
Meetings/Conferences:
• 2019 Society for Research in Child Development Biennial Meeting, March, 2019, Baltimore, MD
Scope: International
• 2021 Society for Research in Child Development Biennial Meeting, April, 2021, Minneapolis, MN
Scope: International
Publications:
• Child Development
Type: Journal; *Accepts Advertising; Editor:* Detra Davis
Profile: Topics in child development from the fetal period through adolescence
• Child Development Perspectives
Type: Journal; *Editor:* Detra Davis
Profile: Emerging trends or conclusions within domains of developmental research
• Developments
Type: Newsletter; *Frequency:* Quarterly; *Accepts Advertising*
• Monographs of Society for Research in Child Development
Frequency: 3-4 pa; *Editor:* Detra Davis
Profile: In-depth research studies in child development & related disciplines
• Social Policy Report
Editor: Amy D. Glaspie

Society for Research on Nicotine & Tobacco (SNRT)
2424 American Lane, Madison WI 53704 USA
Tel: 608-443-2462; *Fax:* 608-443-2474
info@srnt.org
www.srnt.org
Overview: A small international organization
Mission: To generate new knowledge about nicotine
Membership: *Member Profile:* Full members possess training beyond the undergraduate level, plus at least one peer-reviewed publication on nicotine, tobacco-control, or a related topic; Affiliate members possess a documented interest in some aspect of research on nicotine or tobacco-control; Retired full members; Students; *Committees:* Awards; Development; Finance; Membership; Nominations; Program; Publications; Training; Website
Activities: Encouraging scientific research on on public health efforts for the prevention & treatment of cigarette & tobacco use; Sponsoring publications & scientific meetings on the effects of nicotine; Engaging in advocacy activities
Chief Officer(s):
Bruce Wheeler, Executive Director, 608-443-2462 Ext. 143
Dianne Benson, Financial Contact, 608-443-2462 Ext. 147
Meetings/Conferences:
• 2018 Society for Research on Nicotine and Tobacco 24th Annual Meeting, February, 2018, Hilton Baltimore, Baltimore, MD
Scope: International
Publications:
• Nicotine & Tobacco Research: The Journal of SRNT [Society for Research on Nicotine & Tobacco]
Type: Journal; *Frequency:* Monthly; *ISSN:* 1462-2203
Profile: Peer reviewed articles about the study of nicotine & tobacco
• Society for Research on Nicotine & Tobacco Annual Meeting Abstracts
Type: Yearbook; *Frequency:* Annually
• SRNT [Society for Research on Nicotine & Tobacco] Newsletter
Type: Newsletter; *Editor:* Karen Cropsey
Profile: Current society information for members, featuring reviews, meetings, publications, position openings, & funding news
• SRNT [Society for Research on Nicotine & Tobacco] Membership Directory
Type: Directory

Society for Technical Communication (STC)
#300, 9401 Lee Hwy., Fairfax VA 22031 USA
Tel: 703-522-4114; *Fax:* 703-522-2075
www.stc.org
www.linkedin.com/company/society-for-technical-communication
www.facebook.com/stc.org
twitter.com/stc_org
www.youtube.com/user/society4techcomm
Overview: A medium-sized international licensing organization founded in 1953
Mission: To work together in a spirit of community to promote & develop professional technical communication
Finances: *Annual Operating Budget:* $1.5 Million-$3 Million
Staff Member(s): 11; 100 volunteer(s)
Membership: 16,000 worldwide; *Fees:* Schedule available;
Member Profile: Technical writers; editors; graphic designers; multimedia artists; web & intranet page information designers; translators; others that make technical information understandable & available to those who need it
Activities: Facilitating an annual conference; Providing webinars & online classes; Organizing professional chapters & special interest groups, Offering professional certification
Chief Officer(s):
Liz Pohland, Director, Communications
liz.pohland@stc.org
Awards:
• STC President's Award
Awarded at the discretion of the President to recognize members who have made distinguished contributions to the technical communication profession
• STC Intercom Awards
Awarded to select the outstanding magazine article & the outstanding guest-edited issue from the previous year's Intercom magazine *Deadline:* February *Contact:* Liz Pohland, Editor, Intercom, E-mail: liz.pohland@stc.org, Phone: 571-366-1910
• STC Frank R. Smith Award
Awarded to recognize the authors of exceptional articles appearing iin STC journal Technical Communication
• STC Distinguished Community Service Awards
Awarded to recognize the hard work and dedication of STC's community members; involves distinctions for Chapter Service, SIG Service, and Student Service *Deadline:* October *Contact:* Adam Evans, Chair, Community Service Awards, aevansb@gmail.com
• STC Jay R. Gould Award for Excellence in Teaching Technical Communication
Honours commitment, innovation, and excellence in the teaching of technical communication *Eligibility:* STC members belonging to the Society for over ten years & who have been involved in post-secondary education for 15 years, teaching technical communication *Deadline:* November *Contact:* Elaine Gilliam, Manager, Communities, E-mail: elaine.gilliam@stc.org, Phone: 571-366-1902
• STC Ken Rainey Award
Honours research that has made positive & significant contributions to technical communication practice *Eligibility:* STC members belonging to the Society for at least one year *Deadline:* November *Contact:* Elaine Gilliam, Manager, Communities, E-mail: elaine.gilliam@stc.org, Phone: 571-366-1902
• STC Community Achievement Award
Recognizes outstanding community accomplishments in achieving the Society's goals *Eligibility:* STC Professional Chapter, Special Interest Group (SIG), or Student Chapter *Deadline:* January *Contact:* MaryKay Grueneberg, Chair, Community Award, E-mail: marykay.stc@gmail.com
• STC Community Pacesetter Award
Recognizes the successful implementation of a single beneficial innovation that can be used by other STC communities *Eligibility:* STC Professional Chapter, Special Interest Group (SIG), or Student Chapter *Deadline:* March *Contact:* Tricia Spayer, Chair, Pacesetter Award, E-mail: stc.caa@gmail.com
Meetings/Conferences:
• Society for Technical Communication Annual Summit 2018, May, 2018, Hyatt Regency Orlando, Orlando, FL
Scope: International
Publications:
• Intercom [a publication of the Society for Technical Communication]
Type: Magazine; *Frequency:* 10 pa; *Accepts Advertising; Editor:* Liz Pohland; *ISSN:* 0164-6206; *Price:* Free with STCmembership; $160-$215 without membership
Profile: A resource that publishes articles about issues & topics relating to technical communication
• Society for Technical Communication Salary Database
Type: Report; *Frequency:* a.; *Price:* Free with STC membership; $149 without membership
• TechComm Today [a publication of the Society for Technical Communication]
Type: Newsletter; *Frequency:* bi-m.; *Accepts Advertising; Price:* Free with STC membership
Profile: Industry news and Society information
• Technical Communication [a publication of the Society for Technical Communication]
Type: Journal; *Frequency:* q.; *Accepts Advertising; ISSN:* 0049-3155; *Price:* Free with STC membership
Profile: A resource that includes research from the field's most notable writers & book reviews

Alberta Chapter
#494, 3553 - 31 St. NW, Calgary AB T2L 2K7
e-mail: secretary@stc-alberta.org
www.stc-alberta.org/wp
www.linkedin.com/groups/STC-Alberta-3904559?trk=myg_ugrp_ovr
twitter.com/#STCAlberta
Mission: Represents technical communicators within Alberta, Saskatchewan, and the Northwest Territories.
Chief Officer(s):
Jessie Channey, President
president@stc-alberta.org

Canada West Coast Chapter (STC-CWC)
#415, 2416 Main St., Vancouver BC V5T 3E2
e-mail: secretary@stc-alberta.org
stcwestcoast.ca
www.linkedin.com/groups/STC-Canada-West-Coast-122291/about
www.facebook.com/stccwc
twitter.com/stccwc
Mission: To provide knowledge and to build connection between peers in order to strengthen the role of technical communication in industry.
Chief Officer(s):
Aaron Fultz, President, 604-347-6521
president@stcwestcoast.ca

Manitoba Chapter
MB
www.stcmanitoba.org
Chief Officer(s):
Andrew Quarry, Secretary
andrewquarry@shaw.ca

Southwestern Ontario Chapter
ON
www.stc-soc.org
www.linkedin.com/company/southwestern-ontario-chapter-stc
www.facebook.com/279888462067083
twitter.com/STC_SOC
www.youtube.com/watch?v=ARkkVuxwz-c
Chief Officer(s):
Rob Cundari, President
rcundari@technicallywrite.ca

Society for the History of Technology (SHOT)
c/o Dept. of History, Auburn University, #310, Thach Hall, Auburn AL 36849-5207 USA
Tel: 334-844-6770; *Fax:* 334-844-6673
www.historyoftechnology.org
twitter.com/SocHistTech
Overview: A large national organization founded in 1958
Mission: To promote the historical study of technology & its relation to politics, economics, labor, business, the environment, public policy, science, & the arts
Member of: American Council of Learned Societies
Affiliation(s): American Association for the Advancement of Science; American Historical Association
Finances: *Annual Operating Budget:* Less than $50,000
Membership: 1,500 individual + 1,000 institutional; *Fees:* $64 individual; $34 student; *Member Profile:* Persons with an interest in the development of technology & its relations with society & culture; *Committees:* Nominating; Editorial; Awards; Finance; Sites; Program; International Scholars
Chief Officer(s):
Francesca Bray, President
francesca.bray@ed.ac.uk
David Lucsko, Secretary
shotsec@auburn.edu
Awards:
• Leonardo da Vinci Medal
For outstanding contribution to the history of technology, through research, teaching, publications, and other activities
• Sidney Edelstein Prize
Recognizing outstanding scholarly work in the history of technology.
• Sally Hacker Prize
Established in 1999 to honor exceptional scholarship that reaches beyond the academy toward a broad audience.

Foreign Associations / Society for the Prevention of Cruelty to Animals International (SPCA)

- Abbot Payson Usher Prize
Awarded annually to honor the best scholarly work published under the auspices of SHOT.
- Joan Cahalin Robinson Prize
Awarded for the best-presented paper at the SHOT annual meeting by a scholar of any age presenting for the first time.
- Samuel Eleazar and Rose Tartakow Levinson Prize
For an original essay in the history of technology that examines technology within the framework of social or intellectual history.
- IEEE Life Members' Prize in Electrical History
For the best article in the history of electrotechnology-power, electronics, telecommunications, and computer science.
- Dibner Award for Excellence in Museum Exhibits
Recognizing museums and exhibits that interpret the history of technology, industry, and engineering to the general public.
- Eugene S. Ferguson Prize
For original reference works that support future scholarship in the history of technology.
Meetings/Conferences:
- Society for the History of Technology Annual Meeting 2018, October, 2018, St. Louis, MO
Scope: International
Contact Information: Secretary: Jan Korsten, E-mail: j.w.a.korsten@tue.nl
Publications:
- SHOT [Society for the History of Technology] Newsletter
Type: Newsletter; *Frequency:* Annually; *Accepts Advertising*; *Price:* $15
- Technology and Culture [a publication of the Society for the History of Technology]
Type: Journal; *Frequency:* Quarterly; *Editor:* Suzanne Moon; *ISSN:* 1097-3729

Society for the Preservation & Encouragement of Barber Shop Quartet Singing in America Inc. *See* Barbershop Harmony Society

Society for the Prevention of Cruelty to Animals International (SPCA)
PO Box 8682, New York NY 10001 USA
www.spcai.org
www.facebook.com/spcai
twitter.com/SPCAINT
www.youtube.com/user/SPCAI
Also Known As: SPCA International
Overview: A large international charitable organization founded in 2006
Mission: To advocate for humane laws; To promote humane education & public awareness of the humane treatment of animals; To assist animals in areas of conflict & disaster
Finances: *Funding Sources:* Fundraising; Public donations

Society for the Study of Pathophysiology of Pregnancy
www.gestosis.ge
Also Known As: Organisation Gestosis
Overview: A medium-sized international organization founded in 1969
Mission: To spread knowledge about EPH-Gestosis, training, exchange of information amongst scientists; To standartize nomenclature, classification & definition of EPH - Gestosis
Affiliation(s): International Federation of Social Workers; International Federation for Medical & Biological Engineering; Canadian Public Health Association; Society of Obstetricians & Gynaecologists of Canada
Finances: *Annual Operating Budget:* Less than $50,000
Membership: 4,500; *Fees:* US$50; *Member Profile:* MDs, RNs, midwives, social workers; *Committees:* O.G. Press; Consulting; Steering
Activities: Annual meetings; discussion groups; congresses; exchange of scientists; postgraduate training; *Internships:* Yes; *Speaker Service:* Yes; *Library:* by appointment
Chief Officer(s):
Sanjay Gupte, Secretary General
guptehospital@gmail.com

Society of Actuaries (SOA)
#600, 475 North Martingale Rd., Schaumburg IL 60173 USA
Tel: 847-706-3500; Fax: 847-706-3599
customerservice@soa.org
www.soa.org
twitter.com/soasupport
Overview: A medium-sized international organization
Mission: To advance actuarial knowledge & improve decision making to benefit society

Membership: 24,000 worldwide; *Member Profile:* Actuaries in the United States, Canada & worldwide; *Committees:* Admissions; Audit; Employers; Finance; International; Issues Advisory; Leadership Development; Leadership Team; Learning Strategy Task Force; Marketing Executive; Nominating; Policy; Research Executive; Risk
Activities: Professional development; education; research
Chief Officer(s):
Errol Cramer, President
Greg Heidrich, Executive Director
gheidrich@soa.org
Publications:
- The Actuary Magazine [a publication of the Society of Actuaries]
Type: Magazine; *Frequency:* bi-m.
- The Future Actuary [a publication of the Society of Actuaries]
Type: Newsletter; *Frequency:* q.
- In Touch: Your Canadian Connection [a publication of the Society of Actuaries]
Type: Newsletter; *Frequency:* q.
- The North American Actuarial Journal [a publication of the Society of Actuaries]
Type: Journal
- SOA [Society of Actuaries] Candidate Connect
Type: E-Newsletter
- SOA [Society of Actuaries] News Weekly
Type: E-Newsletter

Society of Architectural Historians (SAH)
1365 North Astor St., Chicago IL 60610-2144 USA
Tel: 312-573-1365
info@sah.org
www.sah.org
www.linkedin.com/company/society-of-architectural-historians
www.facebook.com/SAH1365/
twitter.com/sah1365
www.instagram.com/sah1365
Overview: A large international organization founded in 1940
Mission: To advance knowledge & understanding of the history of architecture, design, landscape & urbanism worldwide
Member of: American Council of Learned Societies
Staff Member(s): 5
Membership: 3,500; *Fees:* Schedule available; *Member Profile:* Interest in past, present & future architecture
Activities: *Internships:* Yes
Chief Officer(s):
Kenneth Breisch, President
breisch@usc.edu
Ken Tadashi Oshima, 1st Vice-President
koshima@uw.edu
Pauline Saliga, Executive Director
psaliga@sah.org
Awards:
- SAH Awards for Architectural Excellence
- SAH Publication Awards
- SAH Award for Film & Video
- Fellows of the Society of Architectural Historians Awards Program
- SAH Membership Grants for Emerging Scholars
- H. Allen Brooks Travelling Fellowship
- Research Fellowships
- Annual Conference Fellowships
Meetings/Conferences:
- Society of Architectural Historians Annual International Conference 2018, April, 2018, Saint Paul, MN
Scope: International
- Society of Architectural Historians Annual International Conference 2019, April, 2019, Providence, RI
Scope: International
Publications:
- Buildings of the United States [publications of the Society of Architectural Historians]
Type: Book
Profile: An illustrated series documenting architecture in America
- Journal of the Society of Architectural Historians
Type: Journal; *Frequency:* Quarterly; *Editor:* Patricia Morton; *ISSN:* 2150-5926
Profile: Features scholarly articles, book reviews, exhibitions, & editorials relating to all periods of history
- SAH [Society of Architectural Historians] Newsletter
Type: Newsletter; *Frequency:* Monthly; *Accepts Advertising*
- SAH Archipedia [a publication of the Society of Architectural Historians]
Profile: An interactive online encyclopedia of American architecture

Society of Bead Researchers (SBR)
PO Box 13719, Portland OR 97213 USA
www.beadresearch.org
Overview: A small international organization founded in 1981
Mission: To foster serious research on beads of all materials & periods; To expedite dissemination of resultant knowledge
Finances: *Annual Operating Budget:* Less than $50,000; *Funding Sources:* Membership dues
9 volunteer(s)
Membership: 3 senior/lifetime + 275 individuals; *Fees:* US$20; US$30 overseas; *Member Profile:* Anyone conducting research on beads, or interested in subject
Activities: *Rents Mailing List:* Yes
Chief Officer(s):
J. Mark Kenoyer, President
jkenoyer@wisc.edu
Alice Scherer, Secretary-Treasurer
sec-treas@beadresearch.org
Karlis Karklins, Editor, Journal
karlis4444@gmail.com

Society of Cardiovascular Anesthesiologists (SCA)
#300, 8735 West Higgins Rd., Chicago IL 60631 USA
Fax: 847-375-6323
Toll-Free: 855-658-2828
info@scahq.org
www.scahq.org
www.facebook.com/210665095719456
Overview: A large international organization
Mission: To promote excellence in clinical care & research in perioperative care for patients undergoing cardiothoracic & vascular procedures
Membership: 6,000+; *Fees:* Fellow, $40; Resident, $40; Membership, $210; Active/Associate/Career Scientist, $175; *Member Profile:* International cardiac, thoracic, & vascular anesthesiologists; *Committees:* ACTA Fellowship Certification Task Force; Annual Scientific Program; Atrial Fibrillation Working Group; Blood Conservation Working Group; Bylaws; Cerebral Protection Working Group; Clinical Practice Improvement Project; CME; Echo Week Program; Economics & Governmental Affairs; Ethics; Fellowship Program Directors Council; Fellowship Web Education Task Force; Guidelines & Standards; International; Member Engagement; Newsletter; Nominating; Perioperative Ultrasound Course Planning; Quality & Safety Leadership; Research; SCA/STS Database Task Force; Website Redesign Task Force
Activities: Providing continuing medical education for physicians, through accreditation from the Accreditation Council for Continuing Medical Education; Offering networking opportunities with the leading physicians & practitioners in the field of cardiovascular anesthesiology; Publishing monographs
Chief Officer(s):
Colleen Lawler, Executive Director
clawler@scahq.org
Andrea King, Manager, Operations
aking@scahq.org
Meetings/Conferences:
- Society of Cardiovascular Anesthesiologists 21st Annual Echo Week, February, 2018, Loews Atlanta Hotel, Atlanta, GA
Scope: International
- Society of Cardiovascular Anesthesiologists 7th Annual Thoracic Anesthesia Symposium 2018, April, 2018
Scope: International
- Society of Cardiovascular Anesthesiologists 40th Annual Meeting, April, 2018
Scope: International
- Society of Cardiovascular Anesthesiologists 21st Annual Comprehensive Review & Update of Perioperative Echo 2018, 2018
Scope: International
Publications:
- Annual Update of Cardiopulmonary Bypass
Type: Yearbook; *Frequency:* Annually
- SCA [Society of Cardiovascular Anesthesiologists] Bulletin
Type: Newsletter; *Frequency:* Bimonthly
- Society of Cardiovascular Anesthesiologists Annual Meeting Syllabi
Type: Yearbook; *Frequency:* Annually
- TEE Review Courses [a publication of the Society of Cardiovascular Anesthesiologists]

Society of Die Casting Engineers *See* North American Die Casting Association

Society of Environmental Toxicology & Chemistry (SETAC)

SETAC Asia / Pacific, SETAC Latin America, & SETAC North America, 1010 - 12th Ave. North, Pensacola FL 32501-3370 USA
Tel: 850-469-1500; Fax: 850-469-9778
setac@setac.org
www.setac.org
Overview: A small international organization founded in 1979
Mission: To develop principles & practices for the protection, enhancement, & management of sustainable environmental quality
Membership: *Member Profile:* Individuals & institutions involved in environmental research, development, & education, as well as the management & regulation of natural resources; *Committees:* Awards & Fellowships; Development; Education; Endowment Fund; Finance; Long-range Planning; Meetings; Membership; Mentoring; Nominations; Regional Chapters; Short Courses; Student Activities; Student Council; Technical
Chief Officer(s):
Mike Mozur, Executive Director
mike.mozur@setac.org
Linda Fenner, Manager, Finance
linda.fenner@setac.org
Mimi Meredith, Manager, Publications
mimi.meredith@setac.org
Bruce Vigon, Manager, Scientific Affairs
bruce.vigon@setac.org
Awards:
• SETAC/ABC Laboratories Environmental Education Award
Given to an individual, group, organization, or coporation for significant contributions to environmental education
• SETAC Government Service Award
Recognizes exemplary dedication & service by a scientist or scientific organization toward promoting the collective application of environmental toxicology & chemistry to risk assessment in a goverment function
• Environmental Toxicology & Chemistry Best Student Paper Award
Recognizes the best paper published by a student in ET&C during the last year
• SETAC/Battelle Best Student Platform & Poster Presentation Awards
Given to the best student platform & poster presentations at the SETAC annual meetings *Eligibility:* Must be a member of SETAC
• Rachel Carson Award
Given to an individual who has substantially increased public awareness & understanding of an issue concerning contaminants in the environment *Eligibility:* Recipient's action must result in a redefintion of environmental policies & practices
• Herb Ward Exceptional Service Award
Given to SETAC mambers who have performed long-term, exceptionally high-quality service for SETAC
• SETAC Founders Awards
Given to a person with an outstanding career who has made clearly identifiable contributions in the environmental sciences that are consistent with the goals of SETAC
• SETAC Student Travel Awards Program
Provides travel support assistance for graduate students to attend the SETAC annual meeting
• SETAC Program for North American Minority Students & Mentors
Program introduces North American minority students &/or their faculty mentors to the Society & the professional opportunities offered in the fields of environmental toxicoloy, environmental chemistry & risk assessment *Amount:* Selected individuals receive 1 year membership to the Society & funds to support their travel
• SETAC/Taylor & Francis Advanced Training Fellowship
To provide pre-doctoral or post-doctoral scholars the opportunity to expand their research skills & grantsmanship through specialized training not available at their institution
• SETAC/Roy F. Weston Environmental Chemistry Award
Given to a scientist under the age of 40 for contributions made to the field of environmental chemistry
• SETAC/EA Engineering Jeff Black Award
Eligibility: SETAC members & masters students who have been accepted to or are participating in an environmental science or engineering award *Amount:* US$2,000 & certificate
Meetings/Conferences:
• Society of Environmental Toxicology & Chemistry North America 2018 39th Annual Meeting, November, 2018, Sacramento Convention Center, Sacramento, CA

Scope: International
Attendance: 2,300
Publications:
• Environmental Toxicology & Chemistry
Type: Journal; *Editor:* C.H. Ward; *ISSN:* 0730-7268
• Integrated Environmental Assessment & Management
Type: Journal; *Editor:* Richard J. Wenning; *ISSN:* 1551-3777
• Society of Environmental Toxicology & Chemistry Annual Report
Type: Yearbook; *Frequency:* Annually

Society of Fire Protection Engineers (SFPE)

#380, 9711 Washingtonian Blvd., Gaithersburg MD 20878 USA
Tel: 301-718-2910; Fax: 240-328-6225
info@sfpe.org
www.sfpe.org
www.linkedin.com/groups/96627
www.facebook.com/sfpe.org
twitter.com/SFPE_Inc
www.youtube.com/user/SFPEorg
Overview: A medium-sized international organization founded in 1950
Mission: To advance the practice & science of fire protection engineering & its allied fields; To maintain a high ethical standard among its members; To foster fire protection engineering education
Finances: *Annual Operating Budget:* $500,000-$1.5 Million
Staff Member(s): 9
Membership: 4,200; *Fees:* Schedule available; *Committees:* Continuing Professional Development; Membership & Chapter Relations; Nominations; Outreach & Advocacy; Professional Qualifications; Research, Tools & Methods
Activities: *Rents Mailing List:* Yes
Chief Officer(s):
Nicole Testa Boston, CEO, 301-915-9723
ntboston@sfpe.org
Melissa Franco, Manager, Marketing, 301-915-9724
mfranco@sfpe.org
Jani Zhu, Manager, Accounting & Administrative, 301-915-9726
jzhu@sfpe.org
  British Columbia Chapter
  BC
  www.sfpe.bc.ca
  Chief Officer(s):
  John Ivison, President, 778-989-1909
  executive@sfpe.bc.ca
  Conseil St-Laurent
  Montréal QC
  www.sfpe-st-lawrence-quebec.com
  Chief Officer(s):
  Gilles Carrier, President
  g.carrier@pgaexperts.com
  National Capital Region (SFPE-NCR)
  c/o Mark Ramlochan, #200, 440 Laurier Ave. West, Ottawa ON K1R 7X6
  eng.sfpe.org/Chapters/CanadaNCR
  www.linkedin.com/groups?home=&gid=4783650
  Chief Officer(s):
  Robert Salvador, President
  robert.salvador@labour-travail.gc.ca
  Southern Ontario Chapter
  Toronto ON
  e-mail: info@sfpesoc.com
  www.sfpesoc.com
  Chief Officer(s):
  Ed Koe, President
  president@sfpesoc.com

Society of Magnetic Resonance *See* International Society for Magnetic Resonance in Medicine

Society of Motion Picture & Television Engineers (SMPTE)

3 Barker Ave, 5th Fl., White Plains NY 10601 USA
Tel: 914-761-1100; Fax: 914-761-3115
membership@smpte.org
www.smpte.org
www.linkedin.com/groups?mostPopular=&gid=71716
www.facebook.com/smpteconnect
twitter.com/smpteconnect
www.youtube.com/user/smpteconnect;
www.flickr.com/photos/smpte
Overview: A medium-sized international organization founded in 1916
Finances: *Annual Operating Budget:* $1.5 Million-$3 Million; *Funding Sources:* Membership dues; educational programs

Staff Member(s): 20; 200 volunteer(s)
Membership: 10,000 worldwide (800 in Canada); *Fees:* $135
Chief Officer(s):
Aylsworth Wendy, President
Robert P. Seidel, Executive Vice-President
Jean-Claude Krelic, Chair, Montréal/Québec Section
Paul Roeser, Chair, Toronto Section
Barbara Lange, Executive Director
  SMPTE Toronto
  Toronto ON
  Tel: 416-642-4304
  www.smptetoronto.org
  Chief Officer(s):
  Paul Briscoe, Chair
  Tony Meerakker, Secretary-Treasurer

Society of Petroleum Engineers (SPE)

PO Box 833836, 222 Palisades Creek Dr., Richardson TX 75083-3868 USA
Tel: 972-952-9393; Fax: 972-952-9435
Toll-Free: 800-456-6863
service@spe.org
www.spe.org
www.linkedin.com/groups?about=&gid=57660
www.facebook.com/spemembers
twitter.com/SPE_Events
www.youtube.com/user/2012SPE
Overview: A large international organization founded in 1957
Mission: To collect, disseminate & exchange technical knowledge concerning the exploration, development & production of oil & gas resources & related technologies for the benefit of the public; To provide opportunities for professionals to enhance their technical & professional competence
Finances: *Annual Operating Budget:* $3 Million-$5 Million
Staff Member(s): 87
Membership: 79,000+ (active operations in some 50 countries); *Member Profile:* Managers, engineers, operating personnel & scientists engaged in the exploration, drilling & production sectors of the global oil & gas industry; *Committees:* Student Development; Global Training; Distinguished Lecturer; Membership; Forum Series Coordinating; DAA For PE Faculty; Education & Accreditation; Oil & Gas Reserves; Editorial Review; Twenty Five Year Club; TIG Coordinating; Research & Development; Young Professional Coordinating; SPE Energy Information; Sustainability; Robert Earll McConnell; Online Communities Advisory; Awards
Activities: *Speaker Service:* Yes; *Library:* Society of Petroleum Engineers Library
Chief Officer(s):
Janeen Judah Chevron, President
president@spe.org
Awards:
• Health Safety Social Resp. & Environ. Award
• Reservoir Description & Dynamics Award
• Drilling Engineering Award
• Production & Operations Award
• Management & Information Award
• Carll, Lucas & Uren Award
• DeGolyer & Distinguished Service Award
• Completions Optimization & Technology Award
• Charles F. Rand Memorial Gold Medal
Publications:
• JPT [Journal of Petroleum Technology]
Type: Journal
• Oil Gas Facilities
Type: Magazine
• TWA [The Way Ahead]
Type: Magazine

Society of Plastics Engineers (SPE)

#306, 6 Berkshire Blvd., Bethel CT 06801 USA
Tel: 203-775-0471; Fax: 203-775-8490
www.4spe.org
www.linkedin.com/company/society-of-plastics-engineers
www.facebook.com/SocietyofPlasticsEngineers
twitter.com/4SPE_Plastics
Overview: A large international organization founded in 1942
Mission: To promote the scientific & engineering knowledge related to plastics
Membership: 20,000 in 70+ countries; *Fees:* US$31 student; US$90 young professional (under 35 years of age); US$144 professional; *Member Profile:* Engineers, scientists, & other plastics professionals, including technicians, salespeople, marketers, retailers, & representatives from tertiary industries
Activities: *Library:* Online Technical Library; by appointment
Chief Officer(s):

Foreign Associations / Society of the Sacred Heart

Dick Cameron, President, 412-860-6696
dcameron@4spe.org
Willem De Vos, Chief Executive Officer, 203-775-0471
wdevos@4spe.org
Awards:
- The SPE Foundation General Scholarships
- The SPE Foundation Special Scholarships
- The SPE Foundation General Grants
- Thermoforming Equipment Grants

Meetings/Conferences:
- Society of Plastics Engineers Thermoset 2018, February, 2018, Indianapolis, IN
Scope: International
- Society of Plastics Engineers 2018 International Polyolefins Conference, February, 2018, Hilton Houston North Hotel, Houston, TX
Scope: International
Attendance: 600+
Contact Information: Chair, Texas Conference: Robert Portnoy, Phone: 713-529-2272
- Society of Plastics Engineers 2018 Shanghai TPO Conference, March, 2018, Shanghai
Scope: International
Contact Information: Chair, China Conference: Sassan Tarahomi, E-mail: starahomi@auto-tpo.com
- Society of Plastics Engineers Additives & Colors Conference Middle East 2018, April, 2018, Westin Bahrain City Centre, Manama
Scope: International
Contact Information: Contact: Carine Roos, Phone: +32-498-85-07-32
- Society of Plastics Engineers 2018 AUTO EPCON, April, 2018, Troy Marriott, Troy, MI
Scope: International
Contact Information: Scott Marko, Phone: 203-740-5442
- Society of Plastics Engineers ANTEC 2018, May, 2018, Orange County Convention Center, Orlando, FL
Scope: International
Contact Information: Manager, Events: Scott Marko, Phone: 203-740-5442
- Society of Plastics Engineers Rotational Molding Conference 2018, June, 2018, Cleveland, OH
Scope: International
- Society of Plastics Engineers Automotive Composites Conference & Exhibition 2018, September, 2018, Novi, MI
Scope: International
- Society of Plastics Engineers 16th Conference on Advances in Foam Materials & Technology 2018, September, 2018, Montréal, QC
Scope: International
- Society of Plastics Engineers CAD RETEC 2018, September, 2018, North Charleston, SC
Scope: International
- Society of Plastics Engineers Automotive TPO Conference 2018, October, 2018, Troy Marriott, Troy, MI
Scope: International
- Society of Plastics Engineers Blow Molding Conference 2018, October, 2018, Pittsburgh, PA
Scope: International
- Society of Plastics Engineers Vinyltec 2019 Conference, October, 2019, Akron, OH
Scope: International

Publications:
- Journal of Vinyl & Additive Technology [a publication of the Society of Plastics Engineers]
Type: Journal; *Frequency:* Quarterly; *ISSN:* 1083-5601
- Plastics Engineering [a publication of the Society of Plastics Engineers]
Type: Magazine; *Frequency:* 10 pa; *Accepts Advertising*
Profile: Industry news & perspectives, developments in machinery, processing, & materials technology
- Polymer Composites [a publication of the Society of Plastics Engineers]
Type: Journal; *Frequency:* Bimonthly; *ISSN:* 0272-8397
- Polymer Engineering & Science [a publication of the Society of Plastics Engineers]
Type: Journal; *Frequency:* Monthly; *ISSN:* 0032-3888

Ontario Section
Chief Officer(s):
Renee Morin, President
Bruce Howie, Secretary

Québec Section
PO Box 632, 131, rue Jacques Ménard, Boucherville QC J4B 6Y3
Tel: 450-573-1004; *Fax:* 450-573-1004
info@spequebec.org
www.spequebec.org
Chief Officer(s):
Michel Vinette, President

Society of the Plastics Industry, Inc. See SPI: The Plastics Industry Trade Association

Society of the Sacred Heart
4120 Forest Park Ave., St. Louis MO 63108 USA
Tel: 314-652-1500; *Fax:* 314-534-6800
rscj.org
www.facebook.com/SocietyoftheSacredHeart
twitter.com/RSCJUSC
www.instagram.com/_societyofthesacredheart_
Overview: A medium-sized international charitable organization founded in 1800
Mission: To make known the love of Jesus in the world, through educaton & social justice activities
Staff Member(s): 35
Membership: 1-99; *Member Profile:* Women in the Catholic church
Activities: *Library:* Society of the Sacred Heart Provincial Archives; by appointment Not open to public
Chief Officer(s):
Barbara Dawson, Provincial Superior

Society of Toxicology (SOT)
#300, 1821 Michael Faraday Dr., Reston VA 20190 USA
Tel: 703-438-3115; *Fax:* 703-438-3113
sothq@toxicology.org
www.toxicology.org
www.facebook.com/societyoftoxicology
twitter.com/SOToxicology
Overview: A large international organization founded in 1961
Mission: To advance the science of toxicology; To promote the acquisition & utilization of knowledge in toxicology; To protect public health
Membership: 7,800; *Member Profile:* Scientists from academic institutions, government, & industry who practice toxicology
Chief Officer(s):
John B. Morris, President
Patricia E. Ganey, Vice President
Leigh Ann Burns Naas, Vice-President Elect
Ruth A. Roberts, Secretary
Meetings/Conferences:
- Society of Toxicology 57th Annual Meeting & ToxExpo, 2018
Scope: International
Contact Information: Phone: 703-438-3115; Fax: 703-438-3113; E-mail: sothq@toxicology.org
Publications:
- Communiqué [a publication of the Society of Toxicology]
Type: Newsletter; *Frequency:* Quarterly; *Accepts Advertising*
Profile: Society of Toxicology news; Member spotlight; Regional chapters, specialty sections, & special interest groups; Annual meeting; Science news
- Preliminary Program [a publication of the Society of Toxicology]
Accepts Advertising
Profile: Information about the annual meeting program, a registration form, & housing information
- Society of Toxicology Membership Directory
Accepts Advertising
Profile: Names, addresses, & e-mail addresses for more than 6,000 SOT members
- ToxExpo Directory
Accepts Advertising
- ToxSci Journal
Type: Journal

Society of Tribologists & Lubrication Engineers / Société des tribologistes et ingénieurs en lubrification
840 Busse Hwy., Park Ridge IL 60068-2302 USA
Tel: 847-825-5536; *Fax:* 847-825-1456
www.stle.org
www.facebook.com/stle.org
twitter.com/@stle_tribology
www.youtube.com/user/STLEMedia
Previous Name: American Society of Lubrication Engineers
Overview: A large international organization founded in 1987
Mission: To promote study of tribology, friction, wear & lubrication; To function as resource for distribution of new information & techniques
Membership: *Committees:* Nominations; Rules; Finance; Technical; Operations; Annual Meeting Program; Fellows; Young Tribologists; Wear Technical; Tribotesting Technical; Organization & Operations
Activities: *Speaker Service:* Yes; *Rents Mailing List:* Yes
Chief Officer(s):
Tom Astrene, Associate Executive Director
tastrene@stle.org
Robert Gresham, Director, Professional Development
rgresham@stle.org
Myrna Scott-Perez, Director, Operations
mscott@stle.org
Awards:
- STLE International Award
- Edmond E. Bisson Award
- Frank B. Bussick
- Walter D. Hodson Award
- Wilbur Deutsch Memorial Award
- Captain Alfred E. Hunt Memorial Award
- Al Sonntag Award

Meetings/Conferences:
- Society of Tribologists & Lubrication Engineers 73rd Annual Meeting & Exhibition 2018, May, 2018, Minneapolis Convention Center, Minneapolis, MN
Scope: International
Contact Information: Contact, STLE Conference Office: Merle Hedland, E-mail: mhedland@bacon-hedland.com, Phone: 630-428-2133
- Society of Tribologists & Lubrication Engineers Tribology Frontiers Conference 2018, October, 2018, Drake Hotel Chicago, Chicago, IL
Scope: International

Publications:
- Tribology & Lubrication Technology [a publication of the Society of Tribologists & Lubrication Engineers]
Type: Magazine; *Frequency:* Monthly
Profile: Features articles, best practice analyses, industry surveys & interviews with individuals in theindustry
- Tribology Transactions [a publication of the Society of Tribologists & Lubrication Engineers]
Type: Journal; *Frequency:* Bi-monthly; *ISSN:* 1040-2004
Profile: Features peer-reviewed experimental and theoretical technical papers on lubrication, friction, & wear of materials

Alberta Section
AB
Tel: 780-591-5339
Chief Officer(s):
Terrence Lee Veenstra, Chair
tveenstra@suncor.com

Hamilton Section
PO Box 47623, 1183 Bartin St. East, Hamilton ON L8H 7S7
Tel: 905-671-2355
Chief Officer(s):
Mike Deckert, Chair
mdeckert@flocomponents.com

Manitoba/North-West Ontario Section
MB

Toronto Section
c/o Lorne Brock, 421 Wallace St., Wallaceburg ON N8A 1L5
Tel: 705-321-1192; *Fax:* 519-628-5688
www.torontostle.com
Chief Officer(s):
Wayne Mackwood, Chair
wayne.mackwood@chemtura.com

Society of Women Engineers
#3500, 130 East Randolph St., Chicago IL 60601 USA
Toll-Free: 877-793-4636
societyofwomenengineers.swe.org
www.linkedin.com/company/society-of-women-engineers
www.facebook.com/SWEorg
twitter.com/SWETalk
www.instagram.com/swetalk
Overview: A medium-sized international organization founded in 1950
Membership: *Fees:* Schedule available
Chief Officer(s):
Karen Horting, Executive Director & CEO

Soil & Water Conservation Society (SWCS)
945 SW Ankeny Rd., Ankeny IA 50023-9723 USA
Tel: 515-289-2331; *Fax:* 515-289-1227
www.swcs.org
www.linkedin.com/company/soil-and-water-conservation-society
www.facebook.com/soilandwaterconservation
twitter.com/swcsnews
Overview: A large international organization founded in 1945

Mission: To promote the conservation of soil, water, & related resources; To promote an ethic that recognizes the interdependence of people & the environment
Membership: 5,000-14,999; *Fees:* $220 Presidents Club; $145 leader; $90 conservationist; $30 student; $110 conservation district; $36 developing country conservationist; *Member Profile:* Researchers; Administrators; Educators; Planners; Technicians; Legislators; Farmers & ranchers; Local conservation officials; Consultants; Students
Chief Officer(s):
Jim Gulliford, Executive Director, 515-289-2331 Ext. 113, Fax: 515-289-1227
jim.gulliford@swcs.org
Kim Johnson-Smith, Director, Professional Development, 515-289-2331 Ext. 112, Fax: 515-289-1227
kim.johnson-smith@swcs.org
Awards:
• Donald A. Williams Soil Conservation Scholarship
Offered to members wanting to improve their professional competency *Amount:* $1,000
• Kenneth E. Grant Research Scholarship
For graduate level research *Amount:* $300-$500
• Melville H. Cohee Student Leader Conservation Scholarship
For graduate level research *Amount:* $500
• Commendation Award
For graduate level research
• Conservation Research Award
For graduate level research
• Fellow Award
For graduate level research
• The Harold & Kay Scholl Excellence in Conservation Award
For graduate level research
• The Honor Award
For graduate level research
• The Hugh Hammond Bennett Award
For graduate level research
• Outstanding Service Award
For graduate level research
• Merit Award
For graduate level research
Meetings/Conferences:
• Soil & Water Conservation Society 73rd Annual International Conference, July, 2018, Albuquerque, NM
Scope: International
Contact Information: Director, Professional Development: Kim Johnson-Smith, E-mail: kim.johnson-smith@swcs.org, Phone: 515-289-2331, ext. 112
Publications:
• The Journal of Soil and Water Conservation (JSWC)
Type: Journal; *Frequency:* Bimonthly; *Editor:* Annie Binder; *ISSN:* 0022-4561
Profile: A multidisciplinary journal of natural resource conservation research, practice, policy, and perspectives
Ontario Chapter
School of Environmental Sciences, University of Guelph, 50 Stone Rd. East, Guelph ON N1G 2W1
swcs-canada.org
Chief Officer(s):
Chris Duke, Secretary-Treasurer

Solid Waste Association of North America (SWANA)
#650, 1100 Wayne Ave., Silver Spring MD 20910 USA
Fax: 301-589-7068
Toll-Free: 800-467-9262
info@swana.org
www.swana.org
www.linkedin.com/groups?home=&gid=45037
www.facebook.com/MySWANA
twitter.com/SWANA
Previous Name: Government Refuse Collection & Disposal Association
Overview: A large international organization founded in 1961
Mission: To serve individuals & organizations responsible for the operation & management of solid waste management systems; To advance professional standards in the field through training programs, technical assistance & education
Member of: International Solid Waste Association; Federation of Canadian Municipalities
Finances: *Annual Operating Budget:* $3 Million-$5 Million; *Funding Sources:* Membership dues; Publications
Staff Member(s): 22
Membership: 8,000; *Fees:* US$78 retired; US$212 public sector; US$281 small business; US$398 private sector; US$100 young professional; free for students; *Committees:* Technical; Recycling & Special Waste Management; Communication, Education & Marketing; Collection & Transfer; Landfill; Landfill Gas; Planning & Management; Waste-to-Energy
Activities: Technical divisions: collection & transfer, waste-to-energy, landfill gas management, landfill management, planning & management, special waste management; Waste reduction, recycling & composting; Communication, education & marketing; Publications; Trade shows & conferences;
Internships: Yes; *Library:* Solid Waste Association of North America Library; Open to public
Chief Officer(s):
David Biderman, Executive Director & CEO, 301-585-2898
Awards:
• Excellence Awards
SWANA's Excellence Awards Program recognizes outstanding solid waste programs and facilities that advance the practice of environmentally and economically sound solid waste management through their commitment to utilizing effective technologies and processes in system design and operations, advancing worker and community health and safety, and implementing successful public education and outreach programs.
Atlantic Canada Chapter
#100, 137 Chainlake Dr., Halifax NS B3S 1V3
Fax: 902-450-2008
info@atcanswana.org
www.atcanswana.org
Chief Officer(s):
Nicole Haverkort, President, 902-232-2563, Fax: 902-533-4909
nicole@erswm.ca
Gerry Isenor, Executive Director, 902-404-7723, Fax: 902-444-6348
gisenor@eastlink.ca
Christopher Shortall, Treasurer, 902-450-4000
cshortall@dillon.ca
Northern Lights Chapter
PO Box 3317, Sherwood Park AB T8H 2T2
Tel: 780-496-5614; *Fax:* 866-698-8203
info@swananorthernlights.org
www.swananorthernlights.org
Mission: To serve commmunities & individuals responsible for the operation of municipal solid waste management systems
Chief Officer(s):
Sheri Praski, Executive Director
sheri.praski@swananorthernlights.org
Dick Ellis, President
dick.ellis@swananorthernlights.org
Sheila Reithmayer, Administrator, 780-496-5614
sheila.reithmayer@swananorthernlights.org
Bud Latta, Treasurer
bud.latta@swananorthernlights.org
Ontario Chapter
c/o Debbie Conrad, PO Box 20757, Guelph ON N1G 4T4
Tel: 226-203-0906
office@swanaontario.org
www.swanaontario.com
Chief Officer(s):
Debbie Conrad, Executive Director
Pacific Chapter - BC & Yukon
PO Box 47007, #15, 555 West 12th Ave., Vancouver BC V5Z 3X0
Tel: 250-538-0110; *Fax:* 250-538-0120
Toll-Free: 800-648-2560
info@swanabc.org
www.swanabc.org
twitter.com/SWANAPacific
Chief Officer(s):
Ralph Bischoff, Executive Director

Solidarité européenne pour une égale participation des peuples *See* European Solidarity Towards Equal Participation of People

Soroptimist International of the Americas (SIA)
1709 Spruce St., Philadelphia PA 19103-6103 USA
Tel: 215-893-9000; *Fax:* 215-893-5200
siahq@soroptimist.org
www.soroptimist.org
www.facebook.com/69575569890
twitter.com/soroptimist
www.youtube.com/siahq
Overview: A large international charitable organization founded in 1921
Mission: To maintain high ethical standards in business & professional life; To strive for human rights for all people & in particular, to advance the status of women; To develop a spirit of friendship & unity among Soroptimists of all countries; To develop interest in community, national & international affairs; To contribute to international understanding & universal friendship
Member of: Soroptimist International
Staff Member: 20
Membership: 38,000+; *Fees:* Schedule available; *Member Profile:* Business & professional women
Activities: *Library:* Soroptimist Archives
Chief Officer(s):
Elizabeth Lucas, Executive Director
Nancy Montvydas, Senior Director, Development, 215-893-9000 Ext. 125
Iesha Brown, Senior Director, Membership, 215-893-9000 Ext. 115
Lori Blair, Senior Director, Programs, 215-893-9000 Ext. 114
Awards:
• Live Your Dream Award
Improve the lives of women by giving them the resources they need to improve their education, skills, & employment prospects
• Violet Richardson Award
Honor girls who donate their time & energy to causes that make the community & world a better place
• Soroptimist Club Grants for Women & Girls
Intended to help clubs meet community need by improving their financial resources
Meetings/Conferences:
• Soroptimist 45th Biennial Convention 2018, July, 2018, Pacifico Yokohama, Yokohama
Scope: International
Publications:
• Best for Women [a publication of Soroptimist International of the Americas]
Type: Newsletter

Southeast Asian Ministers of Education Organization (SEAMEO)
Mom Luang Pin Malakul Centenary Bldg., 920 Sukhumvit Rd., Bangkok 10110 Thailand
Tel: 66-2-391-0144; *Fax:* 66-2-381-2587
secretariat@seameo.org
www.seameo.org
www.facebook.com/143394040311
Overview: A medium-sized international organization founded in 1965
Mission: To enhance a regional understanding, cooperation & unity of purpose among member countries & achieve a better quality of life through the establishment of networks & partnerships, the provision of an intellectual forum for policy makers & experts, & the development of regional centres of excellence for the promotion of sustainable human resource development
Affiliation(s): International Council for Open & Distance Education
Finances: *Annual Operating Budget:* $500,000-$1.5 Million
Staff Member(s): 32
Membership: 11 states + 8 associate member countries
Activities: *Internships:* Yes; *Library:* Open to public
Chief Officer(s):
Gatot Hari Priowirjanto, Secretariat Director
Awards:
• Jasper Fellowship

Spanish Association for Canadian Studies / La Fundación Canadá
Espronceda 40, Madrid 28003 Spain
Tel: 34-91-441-1895; *Fax:* 34-91-399-2378
secretaria@estudioscanadienses.org
www.estudioscanadienses.org
Overview: A small international organization founded in 1988
Mission: To promote interdisciplinary research in Canadian Studies; to encourage the exchange of knowledge between members; to establish international relations with other Canadian Studies associations; to develop linkages between Canadian & Spanish universities; to cultivate an interest in Canada among students of Spanish universities; & to promote Canadian activities in Spanish society

The Spastics Society *See* SCOPE for People with Cerebral Palsy

Special Libraries Association (SLA)
#300, 7918 Jones Branch Dr., McLean VA 22102 USA

Foreign Associations / Special Olympics International

Tel: 703-647-4900; *Fax:* 703-506-3266
www.sla.org
www.linkedin.com/company/sla
www.facebook.com/slahq
twitter.com/slahq
www.youtube.com/user/SLAVideos
Overview: A medium-sized international organization founded in 1909
Mission: To promote & strengthen information professionals from around the globe
Finances: *Funding Sources:* Membership dues; Sponsorship
Staff Member(s): 16
Membership: *Fees:* $750 organizational; $50 student; Schedule, based upon salary, for individuals; *Member Profile:* Persons in the information profession from around the world; Library & information science students; *Committees:* Annual Conference Advisory Council; Awards & Honours; Emergency Preparedness & Recovery Advisory Council; Finance; Governance & Bylaws; Information Outlook Advisory Council; Membership Advisory Council; Nominating; Online Content Advisory Council; Professional Development Advisory Council; Public Relations Advisory Council; Students & New Professionals Advisory Council; Technology Advisory Council
Activities: Providing professional development opportunities, including online education programs; Offering networking opportunities; Engaging in advocacy activities
Chief Officer(s):
Amy Lestition Burke, Executive Director
aburke@sla.org
Kristen Hewlett, Chief Financial Officer
khewlett@sla.org
Kate O'Donnell, Vice-President, Brand & Content Strategy
kodonnell@sla.org
Kathy Bradley, Vice-President, Fundraising & Partnerships
kbradley@sla.org
Colleen Eubanks, Vice-President, Governance & Special Projects
ceubanks@sla.org
Mary Katherine Bilowus, Director, Events
mkbilowus@sla.org
Andrea Bomar, Manager, Media & Communications
abomar@sla.org
Awards:
• Fellow of the Special Libraries Association
• John Cotton Dana Award
• Special Libraries Association Presidential Citations
• Rose L. Vormelker Award
• Special Libraries Association Rising Star Award
• Special Libraries Association Hall of Fame
Meetings/Conferences:
• Special Libraries Association 2018 Annual Conference & INFO-EXPO, June, 2018, Baltimore, MD
Scope: International
Description: A gathering of information professionals, providing informative educational sessions, keynote speakers, & exhibitors
Contact Information: Senior Manager, Exhibits & Events: Sarah Driver, E-mail: sdriver@sla.org
Publications:
• Information Outlook [a publication of the Special Libraries Association]
Type: Magazine; *Frequency:* Bimonthly; *Accepts Advertising*; *ISSN:* 1091-0808; *Price:* Free with SLA membership; $240 without membership
Profile: News & information on trends & practices in the information profession
• SLA [Special Library Association] Member Directory
Type: Directory
Profile: Organization of members by name, organization, city, country, & chapter
• SLA [Special Library Associations] Newsletter
Type: Newsletter; *Frequency:* Weekly
Profile: News & information from the Special Libraries Association, including executive updates, learning center information, public policy issues, & conferences

Eastern Canada
PO Box 549, Stn. B, 800, boul René-Lévesque ouest, Montréal QC H3B 3K3
ecanada.sla.org
www.linkedin.com/groups/SLA-Section-de-lest-du-4587961/about
twitter.com/SLAsec
Mission: To represent the interests of information professionals in Eastern Canada.
Chief Officer(s):
Emanuelle René de Cotret, President

Toronto
Toronto ON
toronto.sla.org
www.linkedin.com/groups/1961919/profile
www.facebook.com/slatoronto
twitter.com/slatoronto
www.youtube.com/user/SLAVideos
Mission: To represent the interests of information professionals from Toronto & the surrounding region
Chief Officer(s):
Christine DeLuca, President
cdelucac@gmail.com
Kathryn Kingston, Director, Membership
kathryn.e.kingston@pwc.com
• The Courier [a publication of Special Libraries Association - Toronto]
Type: Newsletter; *Frequency:* Quarterly; *Accepts Advertising*
Profile: Chapter reports plus information about continuing education & networking opportunities

Western Canada
Vancouver BC
wcanada.sla.org
www.linkedin.com/groups?home=&gid=2200726
twitter.com/SLAWCC
www.flickr.com/groups/slawcc
Mission: To represent the interests of information professionals in Western Canada.
Chief Officer(s):
Bronwyn Guiton, President
president@wcanada.sla.org

Special Olympics International
1133 - 19th St. NW, Washington DC 20036-3604 USA
Tel: 202-628-3630; *Fax:* 202-824-0200
Toll-Free: 800-700-8585
info@specialolympics.org
www.specialolympics.org
www.facebook.com/SpecialOlympics
twitter.com/SpecialOlympics
www.youtube.com/SpecialOlympicsHQ
Overview: A large international organization
Mission: To offer year-round training & athletic competition for more than one million athletes in nearly 150 countries
Affiliation(s): Canadian Special Olympics Inc.
Activities: *Awareness Events:* Eunice Kennedy Shriver Day
Chief Officer(s):
Mary Davis, CEO

Specialized Information Publishers Association (SIPA)
1090 Vermont Ave. NW, 6th Fl., Washington DC 20005-4905 USA
Tel: 202-289-7442; *Fax:* 202-289-7097
www.sipaonline.com
www.linkedin.com/company/specialized-information-publishers-association
twitter.com/sipaonline
Previous Name: Newsletter Publishers Association
Overview: A medium-sized international organization founded in 1977
Mission: To advance the interests of for-profit subscription newsletter publishers & specialized information services; to provide information & services that enhance the ability of members to build & manage profitable newsletter publishing ventures
Finances: *Annual Operating Budget:* $500,000-$1.5 Million
Staff Member(s): 5
Membership: 600; *Fees:* Schedule available, based upon company revenue
Activities: Providing resources & networking opportunities to publishers & media companies; *Internships:* Yes; *Speaker Service:* Yes; *Rents Mailing List:* Yes; *Library:* by appointment
Chief Officer(s):
Nancy Brand, Managing Director
nbrand@siia.net
Ronn Levine, Editorial Director
rlevine@siia.net
Awards:
• SIPA Awards Program
Meetings/Conferences:
• Specialized Information Publishers Association (SIPA) Annual Conference 2018, June, 2018, The Capital Hilton, Washington, DC
Scope: International

Specialty Graphic Imaging Association (SGIA)
10015 Main St., Fairfax VA 22031-3489 USA
Toll-Free: 888-385-3588
sgia@sgia.org
www.sgia.org
www.linkedin.com/groups/101519
www.facebook.com/SGIAORG
twitter.com/SGIAGraphic
Previous Name: Screenprinting & Graphic Imaging Association International
Overview: A large international organization founded in 1948
Mission: To provide the tools & information needed so that imaging professionals can make the best possible business decisions
Affiliation(s): Screen Printing Association of Korea; Screenprinting & Graphic Imaging Association of Japan; South Africa Screen Printing Association; China Screenprinting & Graphic Imaging Association; Screenprinting & Graphic Imaging Association of Australia; Screenprinting & Graphic Imaging Association of the Philippines
Finances: *Funding Sources:* Membership fees; seminar, conferences & expositions
Membership: *Fees:* $200+; *Member Profile:* Printers; Suppliers to screen printers
Activities: SGIA Information Network; *Speaker Service:* Yes; *Library*
Chief Officer(s):
Edward Cook, Chair
Christopher Bernat, Treasurer
Awards:
• Dave Swormstedt Sr. Memorial Award
For the best published article or technical paper written for any aspect of the screen printing industry
• Safety Recognition Award
• Sustainable Business Recognition
Meetings/Conferences:
• Specialty Graphic Imaging Association 2018 Expo, October, 2018, Las Vegas Convention Center, Las Vegas, NV
Scope: International
Publications:
• Buyer's Guide [a publication of the Specialty Graphic Imaging Association]
Profile: SGIA member suppliers who provide screen printers & graphic imagers
• SGIA [Specialty Graphic Imaging Association] News
Type: Newsletter; *Frequency:* Monthly
• SGIA [Specialty Graphic Imaging Association] Journal
Type: Journal; *Frequency:* Quarterly

SPI: The Plastics Industry Trade Association (SPI)
#500, 1425 K St. NW, Washington DC 20005 USA
Tel: 202-974-5200; *Fax:* 202-296-7005
www.plasticsindustry.org
www.linkedin.com/company/spi-the-plastics-industry-trade-association
www.facebook.com/SPIplasticsindustry
twitter.com/SPI_4_Plastics
Previous Name: Society of the Plastics Industry, Inc.
Overview: A large international organization founded in 1937
Mission: To be a world class trade association representing the entire plastics industry; To promote the development of the plastics industry & enhance the public's understanding of its contributions
Finances: *Annual Operating Budget:* Greater than $5 Million
Staff Member(s): 65
Membership: 1,100; *Member Profile:* Members represent the entire plastics supply chain; *Committees:* Finance, Administration & Membership; Communications & Marketing Advisory; Equipment Statistics; Nominating; NPE Executive; Special Committees
Activities: Advocating on behalf of its membership; Conducting market research; Promiting the plastic industry; Fostering business relationships; *Library:* Plastics Data Source
Chief Officer(s):
William R. Carteaux, President & CEO
Meetings/Conferences:
• SPI: The Plastics Industry Trade Association 2018 Spring National Board Meeting, March, 2018, Gaylord National Resort & Convention Center, Oxon Hill, MD
Scope: National
• SPI: The Plastics Industry Trade Association 6th Annual Global Plastics Summit 2018, October, 2018, Radisson Blu Aqua, Chicago, IL
Scope: National

Steel Can Recycling Institute *See* Steel Recycling Institute

Steel Recycling Institute (SRI)
680 Andersen Dr., Pittsburgh PA 15220 USA
Tel: 412-922-2772
www.recycle-steel.org
www.facebook.com/envirometal
twitter.com/envirometal
www.youtube.com/envirometal
Previous Name: Steel Can Recycling Institute
Overview: A medium-sized international organization founded in 1988
Mission: To promote the recycling of steel products
Chief Officer(s):
Gregory Crawford, Executive Director

Stockholm Environment Institute (SEI)
Kräftriket 2B, Stockholm SE-106 91 Sweden
Tel: 46-8-674-7070
info@sei-international.org
www.sei-international.org
Overview: A medium-sized international organization founded in 1988
Mission: International research institute focusing on local, regional & global environmental issues
Finances: *Annual Operating Budget:* Greater than $5 Million; *Funding Sources:* Government; other sources in Sweden, UK, USA
Staff Member(s): 60; 2 volunteer(s)
Activities: *Internships:* Yes; *Speaker Service:* Yes; *Library:* by appointment
Chief Officer(s):
Johan Kuylenstierna, Executive Director
executive.director@sei-international.org

Sustainable Forestry Initiative Inc.
#750, 2121 K St. NW, Washington DC 20037 USA
Tel: 202-596-3450; *Fax:* 202-596-3451
info@sfiprogram.org
www.sfiprogram.org
www.linkedin.com/company/sustainable-forestry-initiative-inc-
www.facebook.com/SustainableForestryInitiative
twitter.com/sfiprogram
www.youtube.com/user/SFIProgram
Overview: A large international charitable organization founded in 1994
Mission: To promote sustainable forest management; To maintain & improve the sustainable forestry certification program
Staff Member(s): 18
Activities: Promoting research to improve forestry practices
Chief Officer(s):
Kathy Abusow, President & CEO, 613-722-8734
kathy.abusow@sfiprogram.org
Nadine Block, COO & Senior Vice-President, Public Affairs, 202-596-3456
nadine.block@sfiprogram.org
Daniel Pellegrom, Senior Director, Communications, 202-596-3452
daniel.pellegrom@sfiprogram.org
Meetings/Conferences:
- Sustainable Forestry Initiative 2018 Annual Conference, October, 2018
Scope: International
Publications:
- Sustainable Forestry Initiative In Brief
Type: Newsletter
Profile: Recent information about the SFI program, including conservation grants updates, new certifications, & program statistics

Syndicat international des débardeurs et magasiniers (CTC) See International Longshore & Warehouse Union (CLC)

Syndicat international des peintres et métiers connexes See International Union of Painters & Allied Trades

Syndicat international des travailleurs unis de l'automobile, de l'aérospatiale et de l'outillage agricole d'Amérique See International Union, United Automobile, Aerospace & Agricultural Implement Workers of America

Syndicat uni du transport (FAT-COI/CTC) See Amalgamated Transit Union (AFL-CIO/CLC)

Teachers of English to Speakers of Other Languages, Inc. (TESOL)
#500, 1925 Ballenger Ave., Alexandria VA 22314-6820 USA
Tel: 703-836-0774; *Fax:* 703-836-7864
info@tesol.org
www.tesol.org
www.linkedin.com/company/tesol-international-association
www.facebook.com/tesol.assn
twitter.com/TESOL_Assn
www.instagram.com/tesol_assn
Overview: A medium-sized national organization founded in 1966
Mission: To ensure excellence in English language teaching to speakers of other languages
Affiliation(s): 42 organizations in the US; 51 outside the US
Finances: *Annual Operating Budget:* $3 Million-$5 Million
Staff Member(s): 23
Membership: 13,000 teachers, teachers-in-training, administrators, researchers, materials writers, curriculum developers; *Fees:* $75; *Committees:* Awards; Nominations; Professional Development; Publications; Rules & Resolutions; Sociopolitical Concerns; Serial Publications; Standards
Activities: Members choose a primary interest section: ESL in Adult, Bilingual, Elementary Education or Higher Education; ESL in Secondary Schools; Applied Linguistics; Computer-Assisted Language Learning; English as a Foreign Language; Intensive English Programs; Materials Writers; Program Administration; Refugee Concerns; Research; Teacher Education; Video; International Teaching Assistants
Chief Officer(s):
Rosa Aronson, Executive Director
raronson@tesol.org
Andy Curtis, President
andycurtiswork@gmail.com
Awards:
- TESOL Awards for Excellence & Service
- Convention Grants & Scholarships Program
- TESOL President's Award
- TESOL Outstanding Advocate Honor
- Teaching Materials Grant
Meetings/Conferences:
- Teachers of English to Speakers of Other Languages, Inc. (TESOL) International Convention & English Language Expo, March, 2018, Chicago, IL
Scope: International
Contact Information: Director, Conference Services: Lisa Dyson, Phone: 703-836-0774, ext. 515, E-mail: conventions@tesol.org
- Teachers of English to Speakers of Other Languages, Inc. (TESOL) International Convention & English Language Expo, March, 2019, Atlanta, GA
Scope: International
Contact Information: Director, Conference Services: Lisa Dyson, Phone: 703-836-0774, ext. 515, E-mail: conventions@tesol.org
- Teachers of English to Speakers of Other Languages, Inc. (TESOL) International Convention & English Language Expo, March, 2020, Denver, CO
Scope: International
Contact Information: Director, Conference Services: Lisa Dyson, Phone: 703-836-0774, ext. 515, E-mail: conventions@tesol.org
- Teachers of English to Speakers of Other Languages, Inc. (TESOL) International Convention & English Language Expo, March, 2021, Houston, TX
Scope: International
Contact Information: Director, Conference Services: Lisa Dyson, Phone: 703-836-0774, ext. 515, E-mail: conventions@tesol.org
Publications:
- TESOL [Teachers of English to Speakers of Other Languages, Inc.] English Language Bulletin
Type: Newsletter; *Frequency:* weekly
Profile: Features important news affecting English language teachers worldwide
- TESOL [Teachers of English to Speakers of Other Languages, Inc.] Professional Papers
Type: Report
Profile: A series of professional papers that are valuable resources in the field of English language teaching & learning; topics include policy & issue briefs
- TESOL [Teachers of English to Speakers of Other Languages, Inc.] Annual Report
Type: Yearbook; *Frequency:* a.
Profile: A summary of the activities & highlights of the previous year
- TESOL Connections [a publication of Teachers of English to Speakers of Other Languages, Inc.]
Type: Newsletter; *Frequency:* m.
Profile: Features practical articles & useful resources for English language teachers; also features Association news
- TESOL Journal (TJ) [a publication of Teachers of English to Speakers of Other Languages, Inc.]
Type: Journal; *Editor:* Joy Egbert; *ISSN:* 1949-3533
Profile: A practitioner-centric journal based on current theory & research in the field of TESOL; includes articles that foster dialogue about research- & theory-based practices
- TESOL Quarterly (TQ) [a publication of Teachers of English to Speakers of Other Languages, Inc.]
Type: Journal; *Frequency:* q.; *Editor:* Meaghan McDonnell; *ISSN:* 0039-8322
Profile: A professional journal that fosters inquiry into English language teaching; reaches an audience of ESOL teacher educators, student teachers, researchers, linguists, & ESOL instructors

Teachers Without Borders
PO Box 25067, Seattle WA 98165 USA
Tel: 206-623-0394; *Fax:* 425-491-7070
info@twb.org
www.teacherswithoutborders.org
www.linkedin.com/groups?home=&gid=1713607
www.facebook.com/teacherswithoutborders
twitter.com/teachersnetwork
www.youtube.com/user/TeachersWB
Overview: A medium-sized international organization founded in 2000
Mission: To invite, gather, distill, synthesize, & disseminate the best collective wisdom from teacher leaders from every culture to make all teachers even more effective in contributing to the creation of a world that works for all
Staff Member(s): 7
Activities: Nine offices around the world
Chief Officer(s):
Fred Mednick, Founder
mednick@teacherswithoutborders.org

Technology Services Industry Association (TSIA)
#200, 17065 Camino San Bernardo, San Diego CA 92127 USA
Tel: 858-674-5491
www.tsia.com
www.linkedin.com/company/technology-services-industry-association-tsia-
twitter.com/TSIACommunity
www.youtube.com/user/tsiavideos
Overview: A large international organization
Mission: To further the knowledge, understanding, & career development of executives, managers, & professionals from around the globe in the high-tech & other emerging services & support industries
Chief Officer(s):
J.B. Wood, President & CEO
Thomas Lah, Executive Director
Awards:
- Vision Awards
- Star Awards
- TechBEST Awards
Publications:
- TSIA [Technology Services Industry Association] News
Type: Newsletter; *Frequency:* Monthly

Tecnica England See CODA International Training

TelecomPioneers
#225, 1801 California St., Denver CO 80202 USA
Tel: 303-571-1200; *Fax:* 303-572-0520
Toll-Free: 800-872-5995
info@pioneersvolunteer.org
www.telecompioneers.org
www.facebook.com/111882325524028
twitter.com/TelecomPioneers
Also Known As: Pioneers
Previous Name: Telephone Pioneers of America
Overview: A large international organization founded in 1911
Mission: To act as an industry-related volunteer organization; To effect immediate & tangible change in local communities
Membership: 620,000; *Member Profile:* Current & retired telecommunications employees
Chief Officer(s):
Charlene Hill, Executive Director
chill@pioneersvolunteer.org

Telephone Pioneers of America See TelecomPioneers

Tellus Institute
2 Garden St., Cambridge MA 02138 USA
Tel: 617-266-5400; *Fax:* 617-266-8303
info@tellus.org
www.tellus.org
www.linkedin.com/company/tellus-institute
www.facebook.com/TellusInstitute
twitter.com/TellusInstitute

Overview: A medium-sized international charitable organization founded in 1976
Mission: To conduct a diverse program of research, consulting, & communications; To address policy & planning issues in such areas as energy, water, waste, & land use for a sustainable world for future generations
Member of: Stockholm Environment Institute
Finances: *Funding Sources:* Government agencies; Foundations; Non-governmental organizations
2 volunteer(s)
Activities: Conducting research; Analyzing problems & evaluating options for technological & institutional change
Chief Officer(s):
Paul Raskin, President
praskin@tellus.org
Kathy Nguyen, Manager, Operations

TOPS Club, Inc.
PO Box 070360, 4575 South Fifth St., Milwaukee WI 53207-0360 United States
Tel: 414-482-4620
wondering@tops.org
www.tops.org
Also Known As: Take Off Pounds Sensibly
Overview: A small provincial organization
Mission: To help overweight persons attain & maintain their goal weight
Activities: Numerous chapters in Canada
Chief Officer(s):
Sandra Seidlitz, Area Coordinator, AB, BC, MB, NT, NU, ON, SK, YT
Debra-Ann MacLean, Area Coordinator, NB, NL, NS, PE, QC

Travailleurs unis des transports (FAT-CIO/CTC) *See* United Transportation Union (AFL-CIO/CLC)

Trigeminal Neuralgia Association *See* The Facial Pain Association

UFI - The Global Association of the Exhibition Industry (UFI)
17, rue Louise Michel, Levallois-Perret F-92300 France
Tél: 33-1-46-39-75-00; *Téléc:* 33-1-46-39-75-01
info@ufi.org
www.ufi.org
twitter.com/ufilive
Nom précédent: Union des foires internationales
Aperçu: *Dimension:* moyenne; *Envergure:* internationale; Organisme sans but lucratif; fondée en 1925
Finances: *Budget de fonctionnement annuel:* $500,000-$1.5 Million
Membre(s) du personnel: 10
Membre: 298 institutionnels; 395 associations; 18 partenaires; *Critères d'admissibilite:* Organisations et associations de foires/salons; gestionnaires de parcs; partenaires de l'Industrie des Foires/Salons
Activités: *Stagiaires:* Oui
Membre(s) du bureau directeur:
Kai Hattendorf, Directeur
kh@ufi.org

UNEP - World Conservation Monitoring Centre (UNEP-WCMC)
219 Huntingdon Rd., Cambridge CB3 0DL United Kingdom
Tel: 44-1223-277-314; *Fax:* 44-1223-277-136
info@unep-wcmc.org
www.unep-wcmc.org
Previous Name: World Conservation Monitoring Centre
Overview: A small international charitable organization founded in 1988
Mission: To provide information services on conservation & sustainable use of the world's living resources; to help others to develop information system on their own
Affiliation(s): United Nations Environment Programme
Staff Member(s): 50; 10 volunteer(s)
Activities: *Library* by appointment
Chief Officer(s):
Jonathan Hutton, Director

Union académique internationale (UAI) / International Union of Academies
Palais des Académies, 1, rue Ducale, Brussels B-1000 Belgium
Tél: 32-2-550-2200; *Téléc:* 32-2-550-2205
info@uai-iua.org
www.uai-iua.org
Aperçu: *Dimension:* grande; *Envergure:* internationale; Organisme sans but lucratif; fondée en 1919
Membre de: Conseil international de la philosophie et des sciences humaines; UNESCO
Affiliation(s): Société Royale du Canada
Finances: *Budget de fonctionnement annuel:* $50,000-$100,000
Membre: 50 pays; *Montant de la cotisation:* Schedule available; *Comités:* Comités des candidatures
Activités: 60 entreprises scientifiques internationales; *Bibliothèque:* Not open to public
Membre(s) du bureau directeur:
Hervé Hasquin, Secrétaire général
Meetings/Conferences:
• Union académique internationale Assemblée générale 2018, 2018
Scope: International

Union des employés de gros, de détail et de magasins à rayons (FAT-COI/CTC) *See* Retail, Wholesale & Department Store Union (AFL-CIO/CLC)

Union des foires internationales *Voir* UFI - The Global Association of the Exhibition Industry

Union géodésique et géophysique internationale *See* International Union of Geodesy & Geophysics

Union géographique internationale *See* International Geographic Union

Union internationale contre le cancer *See* International Union Against Cancer

Union internationale de la presse francophone (UPF)
3, Cité Bergère, Paris 75009 France
Tél: 33-1-47-70-02-80; *Téléc:* 33-1-48-24-26-32
fr-fr.facebook.com/114481718630592
Nom précédent: Union internationale des journalistes et de la presse de langue française
Aperçu: *Dimension:* petite; *Envergure:* internationale; Organisme sans but lucratif; Organisme de réglementation; fondée en 1950
Mission: Défendre et rapprocher les journalistes, les éditeurs de la presse francophone; entreprendre toutes actions d'entraide et de solidarité
Membre de: Organisation internationale de la Francophonie; UNESCO; Parlement européen de Strasbourg
Finances: *Budget de fonctionnement annuel:* $500,000-$1.5 Million
Membre(s) du personnel: 7; 5 bénévole(s)
Membre: 3 000; *Montant de la cotisation:* 50$; *Critères d'admissibilite:* Journaliste
Activités: Expositions sur la Presse; *Stagiaires:* Oui; *Service de conférenciers:* Oui; *Bibliothèque:* La Pressothèque; Bibliothèque publique
Membre(s) du bureau directeur:
Georges Gros, Secrétaire général
Prix, Bourses:
• Prix de la Libre Expression
Est décerné à un journaliste qui a "dans un environnement difficile, maintenu son indépendance malgré les atteintes à sa personne"

Union internationale de la science du sol *See* International Union of Soil Sciences

Union Internationale de Patinage *See* International Skating Union

Union internationale des architectes (UIA) / International Union of Architects (IUA)
33, av du Maine, Paris 75755 France
Tél: 33-1-45-24-36-88; *Téléc:* 33-1-45-24-02-78
uia@uia-architectes.org
www.uia-architectes.org/
www.facebook.com/161916773874971
Aperçu: *Dimension:* moyenne; *Envergure:* internationale; fondée en 1948
Mission: Unir les architectes de tous les pays du monde
Finances: *Budget de fonctionnement annuel:* $500,000-$1.5 Million
Membre(s) du personnel: 7
Membre: 124 pays; *Critères d'admissibilite:* Organisations nationales d'architectes
Activités: *Listes de destinataires:* Oui
Prix, Bourses:
• UIA Gold Medal
Awarded to a living architect in recognition of his/her life's work & contribution to mankind, to society & to the promotion of the art of architecture; awarded every three years
• Auguste Perret Prize
Awarded every three years for technology applied to architecture
• Jean Tschumi Prize
Awarded every three years for architectural criticism &/or education
• Sir Robert Matthew Prize
Awarded every three years for improvement in the quality of human settlements
• Sir Patrick Abercrombie Prize
Awarded every three years for town Planning & territorial development

Union internationale des associations d'alpinisme (UIAA) / International Climbing & Mountaineering Federation
PO Box 23, Monbijoustrasse 61, Bern CH-3000 Switzerland
Tel: 41-(0)31-370-18-28; *Fax:* 41-(0)31-370-18-38
office@uiaa.ch
www.theuiaa.org
www.facebook.com/theuiaa
twitter.com/UIAAmountains
www.youtube.com/uiaabern
Overview: A medium-sized international organization founded in 1932
Mission: To study & solve all problems in connection with mountaineering in general & particularly those of an international nature; To contribute to the development & promotion of mountaineering on an international level
Affiliation(s): Alpine Club of Canada; Fédération québecoise de la montagne
Membership: 80 institutional from 50 countries; *Member Profile:* National alpine associations from all over the world; *Committees:* Management; Mountaineering; Sports; Access; Anti-Doping; Ice Climbing; Medical; Mountain Protection; Safety; Youth
Chief Officer(s):
Vrijlandt Frits, President

Union internationale des briqueteurs et métiers connexes (FAT-COI/FCT) *See* International Union of Bricklayers & Allied Craftworkers (AFL-CIO/CFL)

Union internationale des constructeurs d'ascenseurs *See* International Union of Elevator Constructors

Union internationale des employés des services (FAT-COI/CTC) *See* Service Employees International Union (AFL-CIO/CLC)

Union internationale des employés professionnels et de bureau (FAT-COI/CTC) *See* Office & Professional Employees International Union (AFL-CIO/CLC)

Union internationale des instituts de recherches forestières *See* International Union of Forest Research Organizations

Union internationale des journaliers d'Amérique (FAT-COI/CTC) *See* Laborers' International Union of North America (AFL-CIO/CLC)

Union internationale des journalistes et de la presse de langue française *Voir* Union internationale de la presse francophone

Union internationale des magistrats *See* International Association of Judges

Union internationale des opérateurs de machines lourdes (FAT-COI/FCT) *See* International Union of Operating Engineers (AFL-CIO/CFL)

Union internationale des sciences anthropologiques et ethnologiques *See* International Union of Anthropological & Ethnological Sciences

Union internationale des sciences biologiques *See* International Union of Biological Sciences

Union internationale des travailleurs du verre, mouleurs, poterie, plastique et autres (FAT-COI/CTC) *See* Glass, Molders, Pottery, Plastic & Allied Workers International Union (AFL-CIO/CLC)

Union internationale des travailleurs et travailleuses unis de l'alimentation et du commerce *See* United Food & Commercial Workers' International Union

Union internationale humanite et laique *See* International Humanist & Ethical Union

Union internationale pour les livres de jeunesse *See* International Board on Books for Young People

Union internationale végéterienne See International Vegetarian Union

Union interparlementaire See Inter-Parliamentary Union

Union mondiale des organisations féminines catholiques (UMOFC) / World Union of Catholic Women's Organizations (WUCWO)
1, via della Conciliazione, Rome 00193 Italy
Tél: +39-0688805260
wucwoparis@gmail.com
www.wucwo.org
Aperçu: Dimension: grande; *Envergure:* internationale; fondée en 1910
Mission: De promouvoir la présence, la participation et la co-responsabilité des femmes catholiques dans la société et l'Eglise, afin de leur permettre de remplir leur mission d'évangélisation et de travailler pour le développement humain
Membre de: Conférence des Organisations Internationales Catholiques (OIC)
Affiliation(s): Catholic Women's League of Canada; Ukrainian Catholic Women's League of Canada; Association féminine d'éducation d'action sociale; Mouvement des femmes chrétiennes - Inter-Montréal
Membre(s) du personnel: 3
Membre: 100 organisations + 8,000,000 femmes; *Critères d'admissibilite:* Organisation féminine catholique ayant 3 ans d'existance; *Comités:* Commissions Permanentes - Droits Humains; Développement et Coopération; Femmes et Église; Famille; Oecuménisme; Comités permanents - Finances; Statuts et Procédures; Communication, Information et Publications; International
Activités: Groupe de travail sur la violence contre les femmes, santé et prises de décisions; Éducation; Droits humains
Membre(s) du bureau directeur:
Maria Giovanna Ruggieri, Présidente générale
wucwopregen@gmail.com
Liliane Stevenson, Secrétaire générale
wucwosecgen@gmail.com
Publications:
• Voix de Femmes [a publication of Union mondiale des organisations féminines catholiques]
Type: Newsletter

Union mondiale ORT See World ORT Union

Union of International Associations (UAI)
Rue Washington 40, Brussels B-1050 Belgium
Tel: 32-2-640-1808; *Fax:* 32-2-643-6199
uia@uia.org
www.uia.org
www.linkedin.com/company/union-of-international-associations—-uia
www.facebook.com/uiabrussels
twitter.com/uia_org
Overview: A large international organization founded in 1910
Mission: To act as a research institute & documentation centre; To monitor international organizations, associations, & their global challenges
Staff Member(s): 20
Membership: Fees: Schedule available; *Member Profile:* National, regional, & local offices of tourism & convention bureaus, congress centres, hotels, airlines, congress organizers, industry representatives, consultants, other associations
Chief Officer(s):
Anne-Marie Boutin, President
Publications:
• International Congress Calendar [a publication of the Union of International Associations]
; *ISSN:* 0538-6349
Profile: A comprehensive directory of over 428,000 meetings, organized by international associations
• World of Associations News [a publication of the Union of International Associations]
Type: Newsletter; *Frequency:* Monthly
• Yearbook of International Organizations [a publication of the Union of International Associations]
Editor: Carol Williams; *ISSN:* 0084-3814
Profile: A comprehensive directory of over 68,000 international non-profit organizations & associations worldwide

UNITE HERE
275 - 7th Ave., New York NY 10001-6708 USA
Tel: 212-265-7000
www.uniteunion.org
www.facebook.com/UniteHere
twitter.com/unitehere
Previous Name: International Ladies' Garment Workers' Union (AFL-CIO/CLC); Union of Needletrades, Industrial & Textile Employees
Overview: A large international organization founded in 1995
Mission: To represent workers in the following major sectors: apparel & textile manufacturing, apparel distribution centers, apparel retail, industrial laundries, hotels, casinos, foodservice, airport concessions, & restaurants
Membership: 450,000 active members & 400,000 + retirees throughout North America
Activities: Internships: Yes
Chief Officer(s):
D. Taylor, President
Jo Marie Agriesti, General Vice-President
Sherri Chiesa, Scretary-Treasurer

United Association of Journeymen & Apprentices of the Plumbing & Pipe Fitting Industry of the United States & Canada (UA)
3 Park Place, Annapolis MD 21401 USA
Tel: 410-269-2000; *Fax:* 410-267-0262
ua.org
www.facebook.com/UnitedAssociation
twitter.com/uapipetrades
www.youtube.com/uaweb901
Also Known As: United Association
Overview: A large international organization founded in 1889
Mission: The union for plumbers, fitters, welders & HVAC Service Techs
Membership: 300 unions with 340,000 members
Chief Officer(s):
Mark McManus, General President
Patrick H. Kellett, General Secretary-Treasurer
Michael Pleasant, Assistant General President
Canadian Office
442 Gilmour St., Ottawa ON K2P 0R8
Tel: 613-565-1100; *Fax:* 613-562-1200
www.uacanada.ca
www.facebook.com/uacanadamembers
twitter.com/UACanada
www.youtube.com/user/theuacanada
Chief Officer(s):
John Telford, Canadian Affairs Director
john.telford@uacanada.ca

United Brotherhood of Carpenters & Joiners of America (AFL-CIO/CLC) / Fraternité unie des charpentiers et menuisiers d'Amérique (FAT-COI/CTC)
101 Constitution Ave. NW, Washington DC 20001 USA
Tel: 202-546-6206; *Fax:* 202-543-5724
www.carpenters.org
www.facebook.com/905962876138436
twitter.com/UBCJA_Official
Overview: A large international organization
Membership: 56,000 + 121 locals
Chief Officer(s):
Douglas J. McCarron, General President
Publications:
• Carpenter Magazine [a publication of the United Brotherhood of Carpenters & Joiners of America]
Type: Magazine; *Editor:* Andris J. Silins

United Food & Commercial Workers' International Union (UFCW) / Union internationale des travailleurs et travailleuses unis de l'alimentation et du commerce
1775 K St. NW, Washington DC 20006 USA
Tel: 202-223-3111; *Fax:* 202-466-1562
ufcw@ufcw.ca
www.ufcw.org
www.facebook.com/ufcwinternational
twitter.com/UFCW
youtube.com/UFCWInternational;
flickr.com/photos/ufcwinternational
Overview: A large international organization founded in 1979
Mission: To empower workers to unite & find their voice
Membership: 1,300,000; *Member Profile:* People working primarily in grocery & retail stores, & in the food processing & meat packing industries.
Chief Officer(s):
Anthony Perrone, International President
Esther López, International Secretary-Treasurer

United Mine Workers of America (CLC) / Mineurs unis d'Amérique (CTC)
#200, 18354 Quantico Gateway Dr., Triangle VA 22172-1179 USA
Tel: 703-291-2400
www.umwa.org
Overview: A small international organization
Chief Officer(s):
Cecil Roberts, President
Canada
PO Box 129, Glace Bay NS B1A 5V2
Tel: 902-849-8692; *Fax:* 902-849-0652
umwa@ns.sympatico.ca
www.umwa.org
Mission: To represent U.S. & Canadian coal miners, clean coal technicians, health care workers, truck drivers, manufacturing workers & public employees
District 26
33 Gallant St., Glace Bay NS B1A 1T2
Tel: 902-849-8692
umwa@ns.sympatico.ca
www.umwa.org

United Mitochondrial Disease Foundation (UMDF)
#201, 8085 Saltsburg Rd., Pittsburgh PA 15239 USA
Tel: 412-793-8077; *Fax:* 412-793-6477
Toll-Free: 888-317-8633
info@umdf.org
www.umdf.org
Overview: A small international organization founded in 1995
Mission: To promote research & education for the diagnosis, treatment & cure of mitochondrial disorders & to provide support to affected individuals & families
Staff Member(s): 10; 100 volunteer(s)
Membership: 1,045; *Fees:* US$50; *Member Profile:* Unification of the COX Foundation, PALS (People Affected by Leigh's Syndrome), & the National Leigh's Disease Foundation; *Committees:* Scientific Advisory; Executive; Governence; Symposium
Activities: Research grants; *Library:* Open to public
Chief Officer(s):
Charles A. Mohan, CEO/Executive Director
chuckm@umdf.org
Charles A. Mohan, Jr., CEO

United Nations Centre for Human Settlements (Habitat) See United Nations Human Settlements Programme (Habitat)

United Nations Conference on Trade & Development (UNCTAD) / Conférence des Nations Unies sur le commerce et le développement (CNUCED)
Palais des Nations, 8-14, av de la Paix, Geneva 10 1211 Switzerland
Tel: 41-22-917-1234; *Fax:* 41-22-917-0057
Other Communication: www.flickr.com/photos/53390373@N06
sgo@unctad.org
www.unctad.org
www.linkedin.com/company/unctad
www.facebook.com/UNCTAD
twitter.com/unctad
www.youtube.com/user/UNCTADOnline
Overview: A large international organization founded in 1964
Mission: To foster sustainable growth & development in developing countries & countries in transition through analytical & operational activities in the areas of trade & related development issues, such as finance, technology, investment, enterprise development, & environment
Finances: Annual Operating Budget: Greater than $5 Million
Membership: 194 countries
Activities: Promotes & examines the participation of developing countries in international trade & investment; monitors the implementation of the UN Programme of Action for the Least Developed Countries (LDCs); analyzes trends in foreign direct investment & their impact on development; strengthens the service sector capacity in developing countries; promotes the integration of trade, environment & development; reduces commodity dependence through diversification & risk management; faciliates trade; *Internships:* Yes; *Speaker Service:* Yes; *Library:* Not open to public
Chief Officer(s):
Mukhisa Kituyi, Secretary General
sgo@unctad.org

United Nations Development Programme (UNDP)
One United Nations Plaza, New York NY 10017 USA

Foreign Associations / United Nations Environment Programme (UNEP) / Programme des nations unies pour l'environnement

Tel: 212-906-5000
UNDP-newsroom@undp.org
www.undp.org
www.linkedin.com/company/UNDP
www.facebook.com/UNDP
twitter.com/undp
www.youtube.com/user/undp
Overview: A medium-sized international organization
Mission: To help the United Nations become a powerful & cohesive force for sustainable human development; To focus its own resources on a series of objectives central to sustainable human development: democratic governance, poverty reduction, crisis prevention & recovery, energy & environment, information & communications technology & HIV/AIDS; To help developing countries attract & use aid effectively; To promote the protection of human rights & the empowerment of women
Chief Officer(s):
Achim Steiner, Administrator

United Nations Environment Programme (UNEP) / Programme des nations unies pour l'environnement
Regional Office for North America (RONA), #506, 900 - 17th St. NW, Washington DC 20006 USA
Tel: 202-785-0465; *Fax:* 202-785-2096
www.facebook.com/unep.org
twitter.com/unep
www.youtube.com/unepandyou
Overview: A large international organization founded in 1972
Mission: To provide leadership & encourage partnership in caring for the environment by inspiring, informing & enabling nations & peoples to improve their quality of life without compromising that of future generations
Affiliation(s): Canadian Committee for UNEP
Finances: *Annual Operating Budget:* Greater than $5 Million; *Funding Sources:* UN member countries; private sector
Staff Member(s): 20
Activities: Developing environmental law; Collecting & disseminating environmental data; Assisting to developing countries; *Awareness Events:* World Environment Day, June 5; *Internships:* Yes; *Speaker Service:* Yes
Chief Officer(s):
Achim Steiner, Executive Director
Chenje Munyaradzi, Director, Regional Support Office
Elizabeth Mrema, Director, Environmental Law & Conventions
Ligia Noronha, Director, Technology, Industry & Economics
Publications:
• Our Planet [a publication of the United Nations Environment Programme]
Type: Magazine
Profile: Topics regarding environmentally sustainable development
• Tunza [a publication of the United Nations Environment Programme]
Type: Magazine
Profile: Magazine aimed at youth
• The UNEP [United Nations Environment Program] Year Book
Type: Yearbook
• UNEP [United Nations Environment Program] Annual Report
Type: Report

United Nations Human Settlements Programme (Habitat)
PO Box 30030, Nairobi 00100 Kenya
Tel: 254-20-7621234
Other Communication: Bookstore:
www.scribd.com/UN-HABITAT
infohabitat@unhabitat.org
www.unhabitat.org
www.linkedin.com/company/un-habitat-united-nation-human-settlements-programme
www.facebook.com/UNHABITAT
twitter.com/UNHABITAT
www.youtube.com/user/unhabitatglobal
Also Known As: UN-HABITAT
Previous Name: United Nations Centre for Human Settlements (Habitat)
Overview: A large international organization
Mission: To act as the United Nations agency for human settlement; To promote socially and environmentally sustainable towns and cities with the goal of providing adequate shelter for all, under the mandate of the UN General Assembly
Chief Officer(s):
Joan Clos, Executive Director

United Nations Industrial Development Organization (UNIDO)
Vienna International Centre, PO Box 300, Wagramerstr. 5, Vienna A-1400 Austria
Tel: 43-1-26026-0; *Fax:* 43-1-269-2669
unido@unido.org
www.unido.org
www.linkedin.com/company/unido
www.facebook.com/UNIDO.HQ
twitter.com/UNIDO
www.youtube.com/user/UNIDObeta
Overview: A large international organization founded in 1966
Mission: To relieve poverty by fostering productivity growth; To help developing countries & countries in transition in their fight against marginalization in the globalized world; To mobilize knowledge, skills, information & technology to promote productive employment, a competitive economy & a sound environment
Finances: *Annual Operating Budget:* Greater than $5 Million; *Funding Sources:* Regular & operational budgets; special contributions for technical cooperation activities
Staff Member(s): 700
Membership: *Member Profile:* States ratifying the UNIDO Constitution
Activities: Business Plan is to strengthen industrial capacities; cleaner & sustainable industrial development; focused on least developed countries, in particular Africa, on agro-based & industries & small & medium enterprises; *Awareness Events:* Africa Industrialization Day; *Internships:* Yes
Chief Officer(s):
Li Yong, Director General

United Nations Research Institute for Social Development (UNRISD) / Institut de recherche des Nations Unies pour le développement social
Palais des Nations, Geneva CH-1211 Switzerland
Tel: 41-22-917-3020; *Fax:* 41-22-917-0650
info@unrisd.org
www.unrisd.org
www.linkedin.com/company/unrisd
www.facebook.com/UNRISD
twitter.com/unrisd
www.youtube.com/unrisd
Overview: A small international organization founded in 1963
Mission: Engages in multi-disciplinary research on the social dimensions of contemporary problems affecting development; attempts to provide governments, development agencies, grassroots organizations & scholars with a better understanding of how development policies & processes of economic, social & environmental change affect different social groups; works in affiliation with a wide range of international, national & regional organizations
Finances: *Annual Operating Budget:* $3 Million-$5 Million; *Funding Sources:* Voluntary grants from governments, & a variety of national & international grant-giving bodies
Staff Member(s): 20; 10 volunteer(s)
Membership: 1-99
Activities: Cross-country, multidisciplinary research on six themes: Civil Society & Social Movements; Identities, Conflict & Cohesion; Social Policy & Development; Gender & Development; Democracy, Governance & Well-Being; Markets, Business & Regulation; *Internships:* Yes
Chief Officer(s):
Sarah Cook, Director
Peter Utting, Deputy Director

United Steelworkers of America (AFL-CIO/CLC) / Métallurgistes unis d'Amérique (FAT-COI/CTC)
5 Gateway Center, Pittsburgh PA 15222 USA
Tel: 412-562-2400
webmaster@uswa.org
www.usw.org
www.facebook.com/steelworkers
twitter.com/steelworkers
www.youtube.com/steelworkers
Also Known As: Steelworkers
Overview: A large international organization
Affiliation(s): AFL-CIO; Alliance for American Manufacturing; Blue Green Alliance; National College Players Association; Sierra Club; Steelworkers Organization of Active Retirees; Transortation Trades Department; Union Sportsmen Alliance; Union Veterans Council; United Students Against Sweatshops; We Can Solve It
Membership: 1.2 million active & retired; *Member Profile:* Members from the following industries: Metals; Manufacturing; Paper & Forestry Products; Chemical Industry; Pharmacies & Pharmaceuticals; Public Employee Council; Mining; Energy & Utilities
Chief Officer(s):
Leo W. Gerard, President
Stan Johnson, Secretary-Treasurer
Publications:
• FrontLines [a publication of United Steelworkers of America (AFL-CIO/CLC)]
Type: Newsletter
• The Oilworker [a publication of United Steelworkers of America (AFL-CIO/CLC)]
Type: Newsletter
• SOAR in Action [a publication of United Steelworkers of America (AFL-CIO/CLC)]
Type: Newsletter
• USW@Work [a publication of United Steelworkers of America (AFL-CIO/CLC)]
Type: Magazine
USWA Canadian National Office
234 Eglinton Ave. East, 8th Fl., Toronto ON M4P 1K7
Tel: 416-487-1571; *Fax:* 416-482-5548
Toll-Free: 877-669-8792
info@usw.ca
www.usw.ca
www.facebook.com/uswmetallos
twitter.com/SteelworkersCA
www.flickr.com/photos/usw-metallos
www.youtube.com/user/uswmetallos
Mission: To enhance members' economic security & human well-being by negotiating strong collective agreements by playing progressive role in Canada's social & political affairs
Affiliation(s): Alliance of Canadian Cinema, Television & Radio Artists (ACTRA); Broadbent Institute; Canadian Labour of Congress; Communications Workers of America; Environmental Defence & Blue Green Canada; IndustriALL; iTaxiworkers; National Union of Mine & Metal Workers of the Mexican Republic; Workers Uniting
Chief Officer(s):
Ken Neumann, National Director, Canada

United Transportation Union (AFL-CIO/CLC) (UTU) / Travailleurs unis des transports (FAT-CIO/CTC)
#340, 24950 Country Club Blvd., North Olmsted OH 44070-5333 USA
Tel: 216-228-9400; *Fax:* 216-228-5755
www.utu.org
Overview: A medium-sized international organization founded in 1969
Chief Officer(s):
John Previsich, International President
president_td@smart-union.org

United Way of America See United Way Worldwide

United Way Worldwide
701 North Fairfax St., Alexandria VA 22314 USA
Tel: 703-836-7112
www.unitedway.org
www.facebook.com/UnitedWay
twitter.com/UnitedWay
www.youtube.com/user/UnitedWayPSAs
Previous Name: United Way of America
Overview: A large international organization
Mission: To create solutions for communities & improve lives around the world
Chief Officer(s):
Brian A. Gallagher, President & CEO
Awards:
• Student United Way Awards

Universal Esperanto Association See Universala Esperanto-Asocio

Universala Esperanto-Asocio (UEA) / Universal Esperanto Association
Nieuwe Binnenweg 176, Rotterdam 3015 BJ Netherlands
Tel: 31-10-436-1044; *Fax:* 31-10-436-1751
info@uea.org
www.uea.org
www.linkedin.com/company/universal-esperanto-association
www.facebook.com/Universala.Esperanto.Asocio
Overview: A medium-sized international organization founded in 1908
Mission: To promote the use of Esperanto as a solution of the language problem in international relations; To improve the spiritual & material relations between the peoples of the world
Affiliation(s): Canadian Esperanto Association

Finances: *Annual Operating Budget:* $250,000-$500,000; *Funding Sources:* Membership fees
Staff Member(s): 9; 2 volunteer(s)
Membership: 6,050 individual + 12,200 in 65 national affiliates + 50 national youth organizations + 77 interest groups; *Fees:* 9 euros; *Member Profile:* People with a working knowledge of Esperanto
Activities: World Esperanto Congress; *Library:* Hector Hodler Library; Open to public
Chief Officer(s):
Mark Fettes, President
mfettes@sfu.ca
Martin Schaffer, Secretary General
esperantst@gmail.com

The Uranium Institute *See* World Nuclear Association

Urban & Regional Information Systems Association (URISA)
#680, 701 Lee St., Des Plaines IL 60016 USA
Tel: 847-824-6300; *Fax:* 847-824-6363
www.urisa.org
Overview: A small international organization founded in 1963
Mission: To support the effective application of information technology; to provide a means for the exchange of information among members & others; to develop members' skills & knowledge relating to information management technology & systems; provides ongoing educational programs about Geographic Information Systems (GIS) & automated information management within all levels of government & a wide cross-section of the private sector (GIS - computer based technology that captures, stores, analyzes & displays information about places on the earth's surface; more than 80 percent of all information used by local governments is geographically referenced; with GIS any location, any point on the map can become an index to cultural, economic, environmental, demographic & political information about that location)
Finances: *Annual Operating Budget:* $1.5 Million-$3 Million
Staff Member(s): 9
Membership: 3,500; *Fees:* US$20 student; US$125 young professional; US$175 individual; *Member Profile:* IT professionals in all levels of government
Chief Officer(s):
Teresa Townsend, President

British Columbia Chapter
PO Box 608, #101, 1001 West Broadway, Vancouver BC V6H 4E4
e-mail: info@urisabc.org
www.urisabc.org
Mission: To promote the use of spatial information technologies
Chief Officer(s):
Robert Schultz, Treasurer
treasurer@urisabc.org
• Urban & Regional Information Systems Association British Columbia Chapter Newsletter
Type: Newsletter

URISA Alberta
PO Box 76137, 468 Southgate Shopping Centre NW, Edmonton AB T6H 4M0
www.urisab.org
Chief Officer(s):
Sylvia Leong, President
president@urisab.org

URISA Ontario
15 Thornlea Rd., Thornhill ON L3T 1X2
e-mail: info@urisaontario.ca
www.urisaontario.ca
www.linkedin.com/groups/2314556
twitter.com/URISAOntario
Chief Officer(s):
Sandra Crutcher, Executive Director

URISA Québec
CP 32255, Succ. Waverly, Montréal QC H3L 3X1
Tél: 514-382-3873; *Téléc:* 514-382-9534
www.agmq.qc.ca
Chief Officer(s):
Gilles Boislard, Direction générale
Jasmine Ratté, Service aux membres
jasmine.ratte@agmq.qc.ca

U.S. Committee for Refugees & Immigrants (USCRI)
#350, 2231 Crystal Dr., Arlington VA 22202-3711 USA
Tel: 703-310-1130; *Fax:* 703-769-4241
uscri@uscridc.org
www.refugees.org
www.facebook.com/USCRI
twitter.com/uscridc
Overview: A large international organization founded in 1958
Mission: To defend the basic human rights of refugees, most fundamentally, the principle of nonrefoulement - no forced return of a person with a well-founded fear of persecution to his or her homeland; To defend the rights of asylum seekers to a fair & impartial determination of their status; To defend the right to decent & humane treatment for all internally displaced persons
Member of: Immigration & Refugee Services of America
Finances: *Annual Operating Budget:* $500,000-$1.5 Million; *Funding Sources:* Foundations; individuals & corporations
Staff Member(s): 12; 12 volunteer(s)
Activities: Refugee resettling; *Internships:* Yes; *Speaker Service:* Yes; *Rents Mailing List:* Yes; *Library*
Chief Officer(s):
Lavinia Limón, President & CEO
Saba Berhane, Director, Programs
Stacie Blake, Director, Government & Community Relations

U.S. Green Building Council (USGBC)
#500, 2101 L Street NW, Washington DC 20037 USA
Tel: 202-742-3792
Toll-Free: 800-795-1747
leedinfo@usgbc.org
new.usgbc.org
www.linkedin.com/company/u-s—green-building-council
www.facebook.com/USGBC
twitter.com/usgbc
www.youtube.com/usgbc; instagram.com/usgbc
Overview: A medium-sized national organization founded in 1993
Mission: To promote buildings that are environmentally responsible, profitable & healthy places to live & work
Staff Member(s): 15
Membership: 15,000+; *Fees:* Schedule available; *Committees:* Executive; Finance & Audit; Governance; Nominating Working Group
Activities: Promotes LEED, Leadership in Energy & Environmental Design, green building rating system, a voluntary consensus-based national standard for developing high-performance, sustainable buildings
Chief Officer(s):
Mahesh Ramanujam, President & CEO
Taryn Holowka, Senior Vice-President, Marketing, Communications & Advocacy
Meetings/Conferences:
• Greenbuild International Conference & Expo 2018 (Europe), April, 2018, Radisson Blu Hotel & Meeting Center, Berlin
Scope: International
Contact Information: URL: greenbuild.usgbc.org
• Greenbuild International Conference & Expo 2018 (Chicago), November, 2018, McCormick Place (West Building), Chicago, IL
Scope: International
Contact Information: URL: greenbuild.usgbc.org

U.S. Trademark Association *See* International Trademark Association

Used Building Materials Association *See* Building Materials Reuse Association

Video Software Dealers Association *See* Entertainment Merchants Association - International Head Office

Vie Humaine Internationale *See* Human Life International

The Vinyl Institute (VI)
#390, 1737 King St., Alexandria VA 22314 USA
Tel: 571-970-3400; *Fax:* 571-970-3271
www.vinylinfo.org
twitter.com/VinylinDesign
www.youtube.com/user/vinylinstitute
Overview: A small local organization founded in 1982
Mission: Clearinghouse for information about vinyl's environmental performance
Chief Officer(s):
Richard M. Doyle, President, 571-970-3372
ddoyle@vinylinfo.org

VZW Belgium-Canada
Bloemestraat, 62, Maldegem 9990 Belgium
e-mail: vzw@belgiumcanada.net
www.belgiumcanada.net
Overview: A small international organization founded in 1995
Mission: To strengthen the relations between Belgium & Canada
Membership: *Fees:* 15 Euros
Chief Officer(s):
Rik Debal De Baere, Contact

Wallace Center, Winrock International
#500, 2121 Crystal Dr., Arlington VA 22202 USA
Tel: 703-302-6500; *Fax:* 703-302-6512
wallace@winrock.org
www.wallacecenter.org
Previous Name: Institute for Alternative Agriculture
Overview: A small national charitable organization founded in 1983
Mission: To serve as publisher of reliable scientific information on alternative agriculture; to sponsor research & education outreach programs; to be a voice for alternative agriculture; to act as a contact for farmers & others who seek information on diversified, sustainable farming systems; to encourage & facilitate the adoption of low-cost, resource-conserving & environmentally sound farming methods
Finances: *Annual Operating Budget:* $500,000-$1.5 Million
Staff Member(s): 10
Membership: 995; *Fees:* US$16 individual; *Member Profile:* Farmers, researchers, Extension personnel, policy makers & consumers
Activities: Research; policy analysis & development; education & outreach; scientific & general audience publications; symposia
Chief Officer(s):
Erin Caricofe, Program Assistant
John Fisk, Director

Water Environment Federation (WEF)
601 Wythe St., Alexandria VA 22314-1994 USA
Tel: 703-684-2400
Toll-Free: 800-666-0206
csc@wef.org
www.wef.org
www.linkedin.com/company/water-environment-federation
www.facebook.com/WaterEnvironmentFederation
twitter.com/WEForg
Previous Name: Federation of Sewage Works Associations; Federation of Sewage & Industrial Wastes Associations; Water Pollution Control Federation
Overview: A large international organization founded in 1928
Mission: To ensure clean water for the protection of public health; To advance the water profession
Staff Member(s): 100
Membership: 36,000 individuals + 75 affiliated associations; *Member Profile:* Water quality professionals from around the globe; *Committees:* Air Quality & Odor Control; Audit; Automation & Info Tech; Awards & Recognitions; Collection Systems; Constitution & Bylaws; Disinfection & Public Health; Government Affairs; Industrial Wastewater; Laboratory Practices; Literature Review; Manufacturers & Representatives; Membership; Municipal Resource Recovery Design; Operations Challenge; Plant Operations & Maintenance; Program; Public Communication & Outreach; Research & Innovation; Residuals & Biosolids; & others...
Activities: Providing water quality information; offering networking opportunities; & Knowledge Center for members; *Library:* WEF Knowledge Center; Not open to public
Chief Officer(s):
Eileen O'Neill, Executive Director, 703-684-2430
eoneill@wef.org
Awards:
• Camp Applied Research Award, WEF Individual Service & Contribution Awards
• Emerson Distinguished Service Award, WEF Individual Service & Contribution Awards
• Outstanding Young Water Environment Professional Award, WEF Individual Service & Contribution Awards
• Ralph Fuhrman Medal for Outstanding Water Quality Academic-Practice Collaboration, WEF Individual Service & Contribution Awards
• W. Wesley Eckenfelder Industrial Water Quality Lifetime Achievement Award, WEF Individual Service & Contribution Awards
• Water Heroes Award, WEF Individual Service & Contribution Awards
• WEF Canham Graduate Studies Scholarship, WEF Education Awards
Eligibility: A post-baccalaureate student in the water environment field *Amount:* $25,000
• Fair Distinguished Engineering Educator, WEF Education Awards
• Media & Public Education Award, WEF Education Awards

Foreign Associations / The Waterbird Society

- Public Communication & Outreach Program Award, WEF Education Awards
- Bedell Award, WEF Organization & Association Recognition Awards
- Burke Award, WEF Organization & Association Recognition Awards
- Hatfield Award, WEF Organization & Association Recognition Awards
- Laboratory Analyst Award, WEF Organization & Association Recognition Awards
- Collection Systems Award, WEF Operational & Design Excellence Awards
- Innovative Technology Award, WEF Operational & Design Excellence Awards
- Morgan Operational Solutions Award, WEF Operational & Design Excellence Awards
- Schroepfer Innovative Facility Design Award, WEF Operational & Design Excellence Awards
- Water Quality Improvement Award, WEF Operational & Design Excellence Awards
- Water Environment Federation Project Excellence Award, WEF Operational & Design Excellence Awards
- Water Environment Federation Safety Award, WEF Operational & Design Excellence Awards
- Eddy Wastewater Principles/Processes Award, WEF Published Papers Awards
- Gascoigne Wastewater Treatment Plant Operational Improvement Award, WEF Published Papers Awards
- McKee Groundwater Protection, Restoration, or Sustainable Use Award, WEF Published Papers Awards
- Rudolfs Industrial Waste Management Award, WEF Published Papers Awards

Meetings/Conferences:
- AWWA/WEF The Utility Management Conference 2018, February, 2018, San Antonio, TX
Scope: International
- Membrane Technology Conference 2018, March, 2018, Palm Beach Convention Center, West Palm Beach, FL
Scope: International
Description: A conference on developments in membrane technology
- WEFTEC 2018: 91st Annual Water Environment Federation Technical Exhibition & Conference, September, 2018, New Orleans Morial Convention Center, New Orleans, LA
Scope: International
Attendance: 18,000
Description: An annual educational & networking event drawing water quality experts from around the world
Contact Information: Manager, WEFTEC Registration & Housing: Tangela Williams, E-mail: registration@wef.org
- Collection Systems 2018, 2018
Scope: International

Publications:
- The Stormwater Report [a publication of the Water Environment Federation]
Type: Newsletter; *Frequency:* Monthly
Profile: Highlights the latest events in stormwater sector news
- This Week in Washington [a publication of the Water Environment Federation]
Type: Newsletter; *Frequency:* weekly
Profile: Provides updates on legislative & regulatory developments that affect the water & wastewater industries
- Water Environment & Technology [a publication of the Water Environment Federation]
Type: Magazine; *Frequency:* Monthly; *Accepts Advertising*; *Editor:* Steve Spicer; *ISSN:* 1044-9493; *Price:* Free with WEF membership; $215-$245 without WEF membership
Profile: Information for water professionals such as regulatory & legislative impacts, technologies, solutions, & professional development activities
- Water Environment Laboratory Solutions [a publication of the Water Environment Federation]
Type: Newsletter
Profile: Contents include equipment use, sample tracking, quality control, analytical methods, & certification
- Water Environment Regulation Watch [a publication of the Water Environment Federation]
Type: Newsletter; *Frequency:* Monthly; *ISSN:* 1945-4961; *Price:* $50 with WEF membership; $116 without WEF membership
Profile: Reports of federal government actions related to water quality
- Water Environment Research [a publication of the Water Environment Federation]
Type: Journal; *Frequency:* Monthly; *Editor:* Anthony Krizel; *ISSN:* 1554-7531; *Price:* $160 (print) or $100 (online) with WEF membership; $380-835 without WEF membership
Profile: Peer-reviewed research papers related to pollution control, water quality, & management
- WEF [Water Environment Federation] Highlights
Type: Newsletter; *ISSN:* 1938-1948
Profile: Water Environment Federation activities & information for members
- World Water [a publication of the Water Environment Federation]
Type: Magazine
Profile: An international magazine focussing on water issues, such as groundwater, wastewater, sludge, desalination, & treatment
- World Water: Stormwater Management [a publication of the Water Environment Federation]
Type: Magazine; *Frequency:* q.; *Price:* $75 with WEF membership; $270 without WEF membership
Profile: Technical, scientific, policy, public health & financial aspects to water reuse & desalination
- World Water: Water Reuse & Desalination [a publication of the Water Environment Federation]
Type: Magazine; *Frequency:* q.; *Price:* $55 with WEF membership; $145 without WEF membership
Profile: Technical, scientific, policy, public health & financial aspects to water reuse & desalination

The Waterbird Society
c/o ONSA, #680, 5400 Bosque Blvd., Waco TX 76710-4446 USA
www.waterbirds.org
Previous Name: Colonial Waterbird Society
Overview: A small international organization founded in 1976
Mission: To study & conserve all aquatic birds
Affiliation(s): Ornithological Council; American Bird Conservancy
Finances: *Funding Sources:* Membership dues
Membership: *Fees:* $45 students; $55 regular members; $60 families; $1000 lifetimes members (Fees include copies of the paper journal); *Member Profile:* Persons interested in studying & monitoring aquatic birds; *Committees:* Archives; Membership; Nominations; Bylaws; Finance & Investment; Research Awards; Conservation; Publications; Future Meetings; Outreach & Communications; Recognition Awards; Research Awards; Students Activities
Activities: Facilitating communication among persons who study waterbirds
Chief Officer(s):
Katharine Parsons, President
kparsons@massaudubon.org
Susan Elbin, Vice-President & President-Elect
selbin@nycaudubon.org
Clay Green, Secretary
claygreen@txstate.edu
Christine Custer, Treasurer
christine_custer@usgs.gov
Publications:
- Waterbirds
Type: Journal; *Frequency:* 3 pa; *Editor:* Dr. Robert W. Elner
Profile: Papers about biology, conservation, & techniques for study of the world's waterbirds, such as wading birds, seabirds, waterfowl, & shorebirds

Weed Science Society of America (WSSA)
PO Box 7050, Lawrence KS 66044-8897 USA
Fax: 785-843-1274
Toll-Free: 800-627-0629
wssa@allenpress.com
www.wssa.net
www.linkedin.com/groups?gid=5020473
www.facebook.com/189815314505652
twitter.com/WorldOfWeeds
Overview: A small national organization
Mission: To protect the environment through the use of safe & efficient weed control practices; to facilitate the exchange of information about weeds & their control; to enhance professionalism among scientists in teaching, extension & research
Chief Officer(s):
Joyce Lancaster, Executive Secretary
jlancaster@allenpress.com

Western Finance Association (WFA)
c/o Bryan Routledge, Tepper School of Business, Carnegie Mellon Univ., 5000 Forbes Ave., Pittsburgh PA 15213 USA
Tel: 412-268-7588
admin@westernfinance.org
www.westernfinance.org
Overview: A medium-sized international organization
Mission: To improve teaching & scholarship; To enable communication among members
Membership: *Fees:* $150 lifetime membership; $50 three year membership; *Member Profile:* Academicians & practitioners with an interest in the development & application of research in finance
Activities: Disseminating information
Chief Officer(s):
Bryan Routledge, Secretary-Treasurer
Meetings/Conferences:
- Western Finance Association 2018 Annual Meeting, June, 2018, Hotel Del Coronado, Coronado, CA
Scope: International

WineAmerica
#500, 1015 - 18 St. NW, Washington DC 20036 USA
Tel: 202-783-2756
www.wineamerica.org
www.facebook.com/102925946431027
Also Known As: The National Association of American Wineries
Previous Name: American Vintners Association
Overview: A medium-sized international organization founded in 1978
Mission: To encourage the dynamic growth & development of American wineries & winegrowing through the advancement & advocacy of sound public policy
Staff Member(s): 3
Membership: 600+; *Fees:* Schedule available
Chief Officer(s):
Edward O'Keefe, Chair
Mark Chandler, Executive Director
mchandler@wineamerica.org

Women's Environment & Development Organization (WEDO)
9 East 37th St., 5th Fl., New York NY 10016 USA
Tel: 212-973-0325
www.wedo.org
www.facebook.com/WEDOworldwide
twitter.com/wedo_worldwide
www.youtube.com/wedoworldwide;
www.flickr.com/photos/wedoworldwide
Overview: A medium-sized international organization founded in 1989
Mission: To empower women to be equal & active decision makers in environment & development matters
Activities: Monitor Implementation (focuses on specific recommendations for women); Outreach & Leadership (to help women become policy makers as well as policy monitors); Education & Communications; *Internships:* Yes
Chief Officer(s):
Eleanor Blomstrom, Co-Director
Bridget Burns, Co-Director

World Agroforestry Centre
PO Box 30677, United Nations Ave., Gigiri, Nairobi 00100 Kenya
Tel: 254 20 7224000; Fax: 254 20 7224001
Other Communication: www.flickr.com/photos/icraf
worldagroforestry@cgiar.org
www.worldagroforestry.org
www.facebook.com/worldagroforestry
twitter.com/ICRAF
www.youtube.com/user/WorldAgroforestry
Previous Name: International Centre for Research in Agroforestry (ICRAF)
Overview: A large international organization founded in 1977
Mission: To improve human welfare by alleviating poverty, increasing cash income, improving food & nutritional security, & enhancing environmental resilience in the tropics; To conduct strategic & applied research, in partnership with national agricultural systems, for more sustainable & productive land use. Programmes in Africa, India, Sri Lanka, Bangladesh, Indonesia, the Philippines, Vietnam, China, Brazil & Peru.
Member of: Consultative Group on International Agricultural Research
Finances: *Annual Operating Budget:* Greater than $5 Million; *Funding Sources:* Donations; foundations
Activities: *Awareness Events:* Field Days; *Rents Mailing List:* Yes; *Library:* ICRAF Library; by appointment
Chief Officer(s):
Tony Simons, Director General

World Aquaculture Society (WAS)
143 J.M. Parker Coliseum, LSU, Baton Rouge LA 70803-0001 USA
Tel: 225-578-3137; *Fax:* 225-578-3493
www.was.org
www.linkedin.com/company/world-aquaculture-society
www.facebook.com/WorldAquacultureSociety
twitter.com/wrldaquaculture
Previous Name: World Mariculture Society
Overview: A medium-sized international organization founded in 1970
Mission: To secure, evaluate, promote & distribute educational, scientific & technological advancement of aquaculture & mariculture throughout the world
Affiliation(s): Aquaculture Association of Canada; European Acquaculture Association; Asian Fisheries Society; KOSFAS; Aquaculture Association of South Africa; Sociedad Brasileira de Acicultura; Indonesian Aquaculture Society; Society of Aquaculture Professionals (India); Malaysian Fisheries Society; Egyptian Aquaculture Society; Spanish Aquaculture Association; Aquaculture Without Frontiers; IAFI
Staff Member(s): 2
Membership: 3,000+ direct & affiliated; *Fees:* $65 individual; $255 corporate; $45 student; sustaining $105
Chief Officer(s):
Francisco Gomes, President
Carol Mendoza, Director, Home Office
carolm@was.org
Meetings/Conferences:
• World Aquaculture Society Aquaculture America Conference 2018, February, 2018, Paris Hotel, Las Vegas, NV
Scope: International
Contact Information: Conference Manager, Phone: 760-751-5005
Publications:
• Journal of the World Aquaculture Society (JWAS)
Type: Journal; *ISSN:* 1749-7345

World Arabian Horse Organization (WAHO)
Newbarn Farmhouse, Forthampton, Gloucestershire GL19 4QD United Kingdom
Tel: 44-1684-274-455; *Fax:* 44-1684-274-422
waho@btconnect.com
www.waho.org
Overview: A medium-sized international charitable organization founded in 1972
Mission: To acquire, promote & facilitate the acquisition & dissemination of knowledge or information in all or any countries directly or indirectly concerning horses of the Arabian breed
Affiliation(s): Canadian Arabian Horse Registry
Finances: *Annual Operating Budget:* $50,000-$100,000; *Funding Sources:* Membership fees; Donations
Staff Member(s): 1
Membership: 64 countries; *Fees:* Schedule available; *Member Profile:* Big M - Registering Authorities; associate - affiliates; individual associate - individual supporters
Activities: Holding a biennial general assembly; *Library:* Arabian Horse Stud Books of the World; by appointment
Chief Officer(s):
Katrina Murray, Executive Secretary
Peter Pond, President
Awards:
• WAHO Trophy

World Archery Federation
Maison du Sport International, Avenue de Rhodanie 54, Lausanne 1007 Switzerland
Tel: 41-21-614-3050; *Fax:* 41-21-614-3055
info@archery.org
www.worldarchery.org
www.facebook.com/WorldArcheryPage
twitter.com/worldarchery
www.youtube.com/archerytv; instagram.com/worldarchery
Previous Name: International Archery Federation
Overview: A small international organization founded in 1931
Mission: To promote & encourage archery throughout the world in conformity with the Olympic principles; to frame & interpret FITA rules & regulations; to arrange for the organization of World Championships; to confirm & maintain world record scores & Olympic Games record scores; to maintain complete lists of scores from FITA Championships & Olympic Games
Member of: International Olympic Committee
Affiliation(s): Federation of Canadian Archers Inc.
Finances: *Annual Operating Budget:* $500,000-$1.5 Million
Staff Member(s): 8; 70 volunteer(s)
Membership: 141 countries; *Member Profile:* National federations; *Committees:* Athletes; Elections Procedure; Coaches; Manuals; Information from Judges & Coaches; Constitution & Rules; Field Archery; Judges; Medical & Sport Sciences; Para-Archery; Target Archery; Technical
Chief Officer(s):
Ugur Erdener, President
Tom Dielen, Secretary General & Executive Director

World Armwrestling Federation (WAF)
Sofia Park Trading Zone, Bldg. 16V, Fl.1, Office 1-2, Sofia 1166 Bulgaria
www.waf-armwrestling.com
Overview: A medium-sized international organization founded in 1977

World Assembly of Youth (WAY) / Assemblée mondiale de la jeunesse
World Youth Complex, Jalan Lebuh Raya, Melaka 75450 Malaysia
Tel: 603-232-1871; *Fax:* 603-232-7271
office@way.org.my
www.way.org.my
www.facebook.com/WAYHQ
Overview: A small international organization founded in 1950
Mission: An international coordinating body of national youth councils & organizations throughout the world; seeks to increase interracial respect & to foster international understanding & cooperation; to facilitate the collection of information about the needs & problems of youth; to disseminate information about the methods, techniques, activities of youth organizations; to support & encourage the national youth movement of self-governing countries in their struggle for attainment of self-government
Affiliation(s): Canada World Youth
Membership: 90 countries
Activities: *Rents Mailing List:* Yes
Chief Officer(s):
Datuk Ir. Idris Haron, President

World Association for World Federation *See* World Federalist Movement

World Association of Industrial & Technological Research Organizations (WAITRO)
c/o SIRIM Berhad, PO Box 7035, 1 Persiaran Dato'Menteri, Section 2, Shah Alam 40700 Malaysia
Tel: 603-544-6635; *Fax:* 603-544-6735
info@waitro.sirim.my
www.waitro.org
Overview: A small international organization founded in 1970
Mission: To be the leading global network of research & technological organizations through collaboration & knowledge sharing for sustainable development; encourage & facilitate transfer of research results & technical know-how; promote exchange of experience in research & technology management; enhance capabilities in management of research & technological organizations; identify & promote fields of research suitable for international collaboration, new opportunities & markets; promote technological research & capability building in developing countries
Affiliation(s): Research & Productivity Council; Centre de recherche industrielle du Québec; International Development Research Centre; Canadian International Development Agency; BC Research
Membership: 157; *Member Profile:* Technical membership - laboratories & other organizations actively engaged in industrial & technological research & development; sustaining membership - bodies active in encouraging & promoting technological research & assisting the Association with financial support or by otherwise advancing its aims
Chief Officer(s):
R.K. Khandal, President
Charles Kwesiga, 1st Vice-President
Eckhart Bierdümpel, 2nd Vice-President

World Association of Sleep Medicine (WASM)
#109, 3270 19th St. NW, Rochester MN 55901 USA
Tel: 507-316-0084; *Fax:* 877-659-0760
info@wasmonline.org
www.wasmonline.org
www.facebook.com/wasmf
Overview: A medium-sized international organization
Mission: To advance knowledge about sleep health throughout the world; To improve sleep health; To encourage prevention of sleep disorders; To act as a bridge between different sleep societies & cultures; To encourage standards of practice for sleep medicine
Membership: *Fees:* $55; *Member Profile:* Healthcare professionals, active in the field of sleep medicine, from around the world; *Committees:* Awards; Bylaws; Education; Examination; Executive Council; Governing Council; Membership; Nominating; Publication; Scientific Affairs; World Sleep Day
Activities: Encouraging education & research in sleep medicine around the world; Facilitating the exchange of clinical information & scientific studies; Advancing knowledge of sleep & its disorders among the public
Chief Officer(s):
Luigi Ferini-Strambi, President
Publications:
• Sleep Medicine Worldwide: Sleep Health around the World
Type: Newsletter; *Editor:* Liborio Parrino; Robert Thomas

World Association of Veteran Athletes *See* World Masters Athletics

World at Work
14041 Northside Blvd. North, Scottsdale AZ 85260 USA
Toll-Free: 877-951-9191
customerrelations@worldatwork.com
www.worldatwork.org
www.linkedin.com/groups?about=&gid=84761
www.facebook.com/WorldatWorkAssociation
twitter.com/worldatwork
www.youtube.com/worldatworktv
Previous Name: Canadian Compensation Association
Overview: A medium-sized international organization founded in 1985
Mission: To promote the education for, compensation of & benefits to professionals
Member of: Canadian Council of Human Resource Associations
Finances: *Annual Operating Budget:* $500,000-$1.5 Million
Membership: 1,625 individual; *Fees:* Schedule available; *Member Profile:* Human resource professionals; *Committees:* Conference; Education; Communications
Activities: *Rents Mailing List:* Yes; *Library*
Chief Officer(s):
Anne Ruddy, President
Marcia Rhodes, Contact, Media Relations
marcia.rhodes@worldatwork.org

World Blue Chain for the Protection of Animals & Nature / La Chaine bleue mondiale
Avenue de Visé 39, Brussels B-1170 Belgium
Tel: 32-2-673-5230; *Fax:* 32-2-672-0947
contact@bwk-cbm.be
www.bwk-cbm.be
Also Known As: Blauwe Wereldketen
Overview: A medium-sized international organization founded in 1962
Mission: Protection of animals by inspections, propaganda & cultural education
Member of: World Society for Protection of Animals
Finances: *Annual Operating Budget:* $250,000-$500,000
Staff Member(s): 9; 250 volunteer(s)
Membership: 35,000 individual; *Fees:* 7.50, 12.50, 30.00 euros
Activities: *Library* Open to public by appointment

World Business Council for Sustainable Development (WBCSD)
4, ch de Conches, Geneva 1231 Switzerland
Tel: 41-22-839-3100; *Fax:* 41-22-839-3131
info@wbcsd.org
www.wbcsd.ch
twitter.com/wbcsd
Overview: A small international organization
Mission: To provide business leadership as a catalyst for change toward sustainable development; to promote the role of eco-efficiency, innovation & corporate social responsibility
Affiliation(s): The EXCEL Partnership (Canada)
Membership: 170 companies in 35 countries
Chief Officer(s):
Peter Bakker, President & CEO
Bakker@wbcsd.org
Peter White, COO
white@wbcsd.org

World Chambers Federation (WCF)
33-43, av du Président Wilson, Paris 75116 France
Tel: 33-1-4953-2967
wcf@iccwbo.org
iccwbo.org/about-icc/organization/world-chambers-federation
www.linkedin.com/company/international-chamber-of-commerce
www.facebook.com/ICCWCF

twitter.com/WorldChambers
www.youtube.com/user/03WCF
Overview: A large international organization founded in 1951
Affiliation(s): Specialized div. of International Chamber of Commerce
Staff Member(s): 160
Membership: *Member Profile:* Chambers of commerce worldwide
Chief Officer(s):
Peter Mihok, Chair
Stephen Cartwright, Chief Executive Officer

World Citizen Foundation (WCF)
#905, 211 East 43rd St., New York NY 10017 USA
www.worldcitizen.org
Previous Name: World Citizens Assembly
Overview: A large international organization founded in 1975
Mission: To raise awareness in the general public around the world to the need for world citizenship & the global rule of law as the foundation of a future World Democracy
Finances: *Annual Operating Budget:* Less than $50,000; *Funding Sources:* Fundraising
Chief Officer(s):
Troy Davis, President

World Citizens Assembly *See* World Citizen Foundation

World Coal Institute (WCI)
Heddon House, 5th Fl., #149, 151 Regent St., London W1B 4JD United Kingdom
Tel: 44 (0) 20 7851 0052; *Fax:* 44 (0) 20 7851 0061
info@worldcoal.org
www.worldcoal.org
twitter.com/WorldCoal
www.youtube.com/worldcoal
Overview: A small international organization founded in 1985
Mission: To promote the use of coal as an economic & environmentally sound energy source; to provide a voice for coal in international debates on energy & the environment; to improve public awareness of the merits & importance of coal as the single largest source of fuel for the generation of electricity; to ensure that decision makers, & public opinion generally, are fully informed on the advances in modern clean coal technology; to widen understanding of the vital role that metallurgical coal fulfills in the worldwide production of steel; to support other sectors of the worldwide coal industry
Finances: *Annual Operating Budget:* $500,000-$1.5 Million
Staff Member(s): 4
Membership: 20; *Committees:* Executive; Standing
Activities: *Library*
Chief Officer(s):
Milton Catelin, Chief Executive
Christine Copley, Senior Manager
Zhang Xiwu, Chair

World Confederation for Physical Therapy (WCPT)
Victoria Charity Centre, 11 Belgrave Rd., London SW1V 1RB United Kingdom
Tel: 44-20-7931-6465; *Fax:* 44-20-7931-6494
info@wcpt.org
www.wcpt.org
www.linkedin.com/company/world-confederation-for-physical-therapy-wcpt-
www.facebook.com/116826698351147
twitter.com/WCPT1951
www.youtube.com/user/theWCPT
Overview: A small international charitable organization founded in 1951
Mission: To better global health by encouraging high standards of physical therapy research, education & practice, by supporting communication & by collaborating with national & international organizations
Affiliation(s): Canadian Physiotherapy Association
Finances: *Funding Sources:* Membership fees
Membership: 112 member organizations
Activities: Establishing new standards & networks; Collecting data; Sharing expertise; Supporting investigation of workforce & migration issues; *Awareness Events:* International Physical Therapy Day, Sept.
Chief Officer(s):
Jonathon Kruger, Chief Executive Officer
Tracy Bury, Director, Professional Policy
Mia Lockner, Manager, Communications & Office
Publications:
• WCPT [World Confederation for Physical Therapy] News
Type: Newsletter; *Frequency:* Quarterly

Profile: News from member organizations, regions & subgroups, reports on WCPT initiatives, executive committee & general meeting decisions, & opinion articles on international issues relevant to the profession

World Confederation of Labour *See* International Trade Union Confederation

World Confederation of Organizations of the Teaching Profession *See* Education International

World Conservation Monitoring Centre *See* UNEP - World Conservation Monitoring Centre

The World Conservation Union; International Union for Conservation of Nature & Natural Resources *See* International Union for Conservation of Nature

World Council of Churches
PO Box 2100, 150, rte de Ferney, Geneva CH-1211 Switzerland
Tel: 41-22-791-6111; *Fax:* 41-22-791-0361
oikoumene.org
Overview: A medium-sized international organization
Mission: To be a community of churches on the way to visible unity in one faith & one eucharistic fellowship
Affiliation(s): International Council of World Religions & Cultures
Chief Officer(s):
Olav Fykse Tveit, General Secretary

World Council of Credit Unions, Inc. (WOCCU)
PO Box 2982, 5710 Mineral Point Rd., Madison WI 53705-4493 USA
Tel: 608-395-2000; *Fax:* 608-395-2001
mail@woccu.org
www.woccu.org
www.linkedin.com/company/world-council-of-credit-unions
www.facebook.com/woccu
twitter.com/woccu
www.youtube.com/user/WOCCU/featured
Overview: A large international organization founded in 1971
Mission: To promote the sustainable growth & expansion of credit unions & financial cooperatives worldwide; to provide technical assistance & trade association services to members
Affiliation(s): Canadian Credit Union Association; Assoc. of British Credit Unions Ltd.; Assoc. of Asian Confederation of Credit Unions; Caribbean Confederation of Credit Unions; Confederacion Latinoamericana de Cooperativas de Ahorro y Credito; Credit Union National Association; CUNA Caribbean Insurance Society Ltd; CUNA Mutual Group; Credit Union Services Corp. (Australia) Ltd.; ECCU Assurance Company Ltd.; Irish League of Credit Unions; International Raiffeisen Union; National Credit Union Federation of Korea; and others
Finances: *Annual Operating Budget:* Greater than $5 Million; *Funding Sources:* Membership dues; grants
Staff Member(s): 59
Membership: Over 50,000; *Fees:* Schedule available; *Member Profile:* Represents the largest credit union cooperative network in the world: over 60,000 credit unions in 109 countries, with over 222 million members.
Activities: Information; education; advocacy; leadership & technical services; Global Credit Union Network, an international clearinghouse for credit unions, offers affiliated credit unions access to resources produced by other members, electronically links credit union movements & leaders together from across the globe; *Awareness Events:* International Credit Union Day, 3rd Thursday in Oct.; *Internships:* Yes; *Library:* Information Resource Centre; Open to public
Chief Officer(s):
Daniel Burns, Chair
Manfred Alfonso Dasenbrock, Secretary
Brian Branch, President & CEO
Awards:
• Distinguished Service Award
Meetings/Conferences:
• World Credit Union Conference 2018, July, 2018, Singapore
Scope: International
Contact Information: www.wcuc.org
Publications:
• Credit Union World [a publication of the World Council of Credit Unions, Inc.]
Type: Magazine; *Frequency:* Annually
Profile: Highlights credit union developments, & provides information & WOCCU members, products & services

World Curling Federation (WCF)
74 Tay St., Perth PH2 8NP Scotland

Tel: 44-173-845-1630; *Fax:* 44-173-845-1641
info@worldcurling.org
www.worldcurling.org
www.linkedin.com/company/world-curling-federation
www.facebook.com/WorldCurlingFederation
twitter.com/worldcurling
www.youtube.com/user/WorldCurlingTV
Previous Name: International Curling Federation
Overview: A medium-sized international organization founded in 1966
Mission: To represent curling internationally & to facilitate the growth of the sport through a network of member nations
Member of: General Association of International Sports Federations (GAISF)
Staff Member(s): 11
Membership: 53 member associations; *Member Profile:* National associations
Activities: World & World Junior & World Senior Curling Championships, Men & Women; World Wheelchair Curling Championship, Mixed teams
Chief Officer(s):
Kate Caithness, President
Bent Ånund Ramsfjell, Vice-President
Colin Grahamslaw, Secretary General

World Dance Council Ltd. (WDC)
63-67 Kingston Rd., New Malden, Surrey KT3 3PB England
Tel: 43-664-8720145
gensec@wdcdance.com
www.wdcdance.com
Previous Name: International Council of Ballroom Dancing
Overview: A small international organization founded in 1950
Affiliation(s): International Dance Organization
Staff Member(s): 3
Membership: 50; *Committees:* Dance Sport; Social Dance
Chief Officer(s):
Hannes Emrich, Company & General Secretary
gensec@wdcdance.com

World Darts Federation (WDF)
4 Byron Plavce, Croespenmaen, Crumlin, Newport NP11 3BP Wales
Tel: 44 1495 247732; *Fax:* 44-774-704-8025
www.dartswdf.com
www.facebook.com/159256067495664?sk=wall
twitter.com/wdfdarts
Overview: A small international organization founded in 1976
Mission: The WDF is a non-political, non-racial and non-profit making organization dedicated toward achieving and maintaining the highest possible standard of presentation and organization, around the world
Affiliation(s): National Darts Federation of Canada
Membership: 250,000 players representing 60 nations
Chief Officer(s):
Roy Price, President
president@dartswdf.com
Kelvin James, Vice-President
kelvindjames@optusnet.com.au
Dave Alderman, Secretary General
daveralderman@dartswdf.com

World Energy Council (WEC) / Conseil Mondial de l'Energie (CME)
62-64 Cornhill St., London EC3V 3NH United Kingdom
Tel: 44-20-7734-5996; *Fax:* 44-20-7734-5926
www.worldenergy.org
www.linkedin.com/company/world-energy-council
twitter.com/WECouncil
Overview: A large international organization founded in 1923
Mission: To promote the sustainable supply & use of energy for the greatest benefit
Finances: *Annual Operating Budget:* $3 Million-$5 Million
Staff Member(s): 14
Membership: 92 member countries; *Fees:* Schedule available; *Member Profile:* Energy leaders & practitioners from around the world; *Committees:* Communications & Strategy; Programme; Studies; Finance
Activities: Energy; energy conservation; *Library:* World Energu Council Information Services; by appointment
Chief Officer(s):
Younghoon David Kim, Chair
Meetings/Conferences:
• World Energy Council Executive Assembly 2018, October, 2018, Milan
Scope: International

- World Energy Council World Energy Congress 2019, September, 2019, Abu Dhabi
Scope: International

World Federalist Movement (WFM) / Mouvement féderalist mondial
708 - 3rd Ave., 24th Fl., New York NY 10017 USA
Tel: 212-599-1320; *Fax:* 212-599-1332
info@wfm-igp.org
www.wfm-igp.org
www.facebook.com/worldfederalist
twitter.com/worldfederalist
Previous Name: World Association for World Federation
Overview: A medium-sized international organization founded in 1947
Mission: To work for justice, peace & sustainable prosperity; to promote an end to the rule of force through a world governed by law, based on strengthened & democratized world institutions
Affiliation(s): World Federalists of Canada
Membership: 31 organizations
Activities: Conferences, seminars; policy research; publishing of papers & monographs; lobbying; *Library*
Chief Officer(s):
William Pace, Executive Director

World Federation for Mental Health (WFMH) / Fédération mondiale pour la santé mentale
PO Box 807, Occoquan VA 22125 USA
e-mail: info@wfmh.com
www.wfmh.global
www.facebook.com/WFMH1
Overview: A large international charitable organization founded in 1948
Mission: To promote mental health through advocacy, transfer of knowledge, & consultation; To prevent or reduce the incidence & disabling consequences of mental illness throughout the world
Affiliation(s): World Health Organization
Finances: *Funding Sources:* Membership dues; grants
Membership: *Fees:* Schedule available based on operating budget; *Member Profile:* Psychiatrists; psychologists; mental health consultants; lay people; *Committees:* Public Impact; Prevention & Promotion; World Mental Health Day; Constituency Development; Education & Mental Health Information; Financial Policy & Sustainability; Ethics & Human Rights; By-laws; Meetings; Scientific Activities
Activities: *Awareness Events:* World Mental Health Day, Oct. 10
Chief Officer(s):
Alberto Trimboli, President
Yoram Cohen, Corporate Secretary

World Federation of International Music Competitions *Voir* Fédération mondiale des concours internationaux de musique

World Federation of Occupational Therapists (WFOT)
PO Box 30, Forrestfield 6058 Australia
Fax: 61-8-9453-9746
admin@wfot.org.au
www.wfot.org.au
Overview: A small international organization founded in 1952
Mission: To promote occupational therapy & international cooperation; To maintain the ethics of the profession & to advance the practice & standards; To promote internationally recognized standards for the education of the profession; to facilitate international exchange & placement of therapists & students; To facilitate the exchange of information & publications; To promote research
Affiliation(s): Council of Occupational Therapists of the European Community
Finances: *Annual Operating Budget:* Less than $50,000; *Funding Sources:* Membership fees
Membership: 55 national associations; *Fees:* Schedule available; *Member Profile:* Occupational therapists; *Committees:* Education & Research; Promotion & Development; Executive Programes; International Cooperation; Standards & Quality
Activities: *Speaker Service:* Yes; *Library*
Chief Officer(s):
E. Sharon Brintnell, President
Susan Baptiste, Vice-President
Samantha Shann, Vice-President, Finance
Marilyn Pattison, Executive Director

World Federation of the Deaf (WFD) / Fédération mondiale des sourds
PO Box 65, Ilkantie 4, Helsinki FIN-00401 Finland
e-mail: info@wfd.fi
www.wfdeaf.org
www.facebook.com/Wfdeaf.org
Overview: A medium-sized international licensing charitable organization founded in 1951
Mission: To work for the realization of the human rights of deaf individuals in partnership with the United Nations & its agencies, national organizations of deaf people, & relevant stakeholders; To promote the unification of national associations, federations & other organizations of & for deaf people at both regional & international levels; To ensure that the government in each country observe all international declarations & recommendations on human rights & the rights of deaf persons & other persons with disabilities; To promote the creation & development of national organizations of deaf people & organizations providing services to deaf people where such organizations do not exist; To disseminate scientific & legal materials about deafness & the current needs of deaf people; To promote the coordination & conduct of research & studies in all fields of deafness, including other categories of hearing loss; To facilitate the efforts of deaf people to make contributions to cultural enrichment in every country
Member of: International Disability Alliance (IDA)
Affiliation(s): World Association of Sign Language Interpreters (WASLI); International Disability Alliance (IDA); International Federation of the Hard of Hearing (IFHOH); International Committee of Sports for the Deaf (ICSD); United Nations; World Health Organization; International Labor Organization; UN Educational, Scientific & Cultural Organization (UNESCO); International Deaf Emergency (IDE); Council of Europe
Finances: *Annual Operating Budget:* $100,000-$250,000; *Funding Sources:* Regular membership fees; contributions, donations & government or foundation grants
Staff Member(s): 5
Membership: *Member Profile:* Ordinary; Associate; International; Individual
Activities: Promoting human rights & access to sign language; Working with deaf leaders & policymakers to implement human rights mechanisms such as the CRPD & 2030 Agenda; Offering human rights training; Representing deaf people's interests on a global scale; *Awareness Events:* International Week of the Deaf, 4th week of Sept.; *Internships:* Yes; *Speaker Service:* Yes
Chief Officer(s):
Colin Allen, President
wfdpresident@gmail.com
Phillipa Sandholm, Administrative Secretary
info@wfd.fi

World Fellowship of Orthodox Youth
Syndesmos General Secretariat, 91 rue Olivier de Serres, Paris 75015 France
Tel: 32-2-640-15-96
syndesmos@syndesmos.org
www.syndesmos.org
Also Known As: Syndesmos
Overview: A small international organization founded in 1953
Mission: To serve as a bond of unity among Orthodox youth movements, organisations & theological schools around the world, promoting a consciousness of the catholicity of the Orthodox faith; to foster relations, coordination & mutal aid among them; to promote among young people a full understanding of the Orthodox faith & the mission of the Church in the contemporary world & an active participation of youth in ecclesial life; to promote a way of life founded in eucharistic communion, in the Gospel & in patristic teaching, for witness & service to the world; to assist & promote Orthodox effocrts for visible Christian unity & for positive relations with people of other faiths; to encourage reflection & action on issues affecting the lives of Orthodox Christians & the local churches; to be an instrument for furthering cooperation & deeper communion between the Orthodox Church & the Oriental Orthodox Churches
Finances: *Annual Operating Budget:* $50,000-$100,000; *Funding Sources:* Orthodox churches; Orthodox church organisations; council of Eurpoe; European Christina Diakonia age
Staff Member(s): 2; 4 volunteer(s)
Membership: 121 organizations in 42 countries; *Fees:* $500 affiliated; *Member Profile:* Christian Orthodox youth organizations & theological schools; *Committees:* Publications
Activities: Orthodox youth camps, festivals, encounters, seminars, consultations, conferences, training courses, workshops; *Internships:* Yes; *Library:* Not open to public
Chief Officer(s):
Jean Rehbinder, President
Georges El Hage, Vice-President

World Future Society (WFS)
#161, 3220 N St. NW, Washington DC 20007 USA
Tel: 301-656-8274
Toll-Free: 800-989-8274
info@wfs.org
www.wfs.org
www.facebook.com/146987498680054
twitter.com/WorldFutureSoc
Overview: A medium-sized international organization founded in 1966
Mission: To serve as a clearinghouse for ideas about the future, including forecasts, recommendations, & alternative scenarios
Finances: *Funding Sources:* Membership fees
Membership: 25,000 in over 80 countries; *Fees:* Schedule available; *Member Profile:* Persons who would like to know more about what the future will hold, including sociologists, scientists, corporate planners, educators, students, & retirees
Activities: *Speaker Service:* Yes
Chief Officer(s):
Amy Zalman, President & CEO
Meetings/Conferences:
- World Future Society Annual Conference 2018, 2018
Scope: International
Publications:
- The Futurist [a publication of the World Future Society]
Type: Magazine; *Editor:* Patrick Tucker; *ISSN:* 0016-3317
Profile: Feature articles, news briefs, & book reviews
- Futurist Update [a publication of the World Future Society]
Type: Newsletter; *Frequency:* Monthly; *Editor:* Cindy Wagner
Profile: News & previews from the Society
- Outlook [a publication of the World Future Society]
Type: Yearbook; *Frequency:* a.
Profile: A compilation of the most thought-provoking ideas & forecasts appearing in the year's editions of The Futurist magazine
- World Future Review [a publication of the World Future Society]
Type: Journal; *Editor:* James Allen Dator; *ISSN:* 1946-7567; *Price:* US $112 individual; US $401institutional
Profile: Encourages & facilitates communication among researchers & practitioners in all related fields

World Futures Studies Federation (WFSF) / Fédération mondiale pour les études sur le future
c/o Evelyne Koenig, 35, bis rue du Château, Lauw 68290 France
e-mail: secretariat@wfsf.org
www.wfsf.org
www.linkedin.com/company/1590066
www.facebook.com/109772375809270
Overview: A small international organization founded in 1973
Mission: To promote & encourage futures studies in different disciplines & areas; to provide a forum for generating ideas concerning the future; to stimulate awareness of the need for future studies in governments & international organizations, as well as other decision making & educational groups & institutions; to resolve problems at local, national & global levels; to assist with national & global futures research activities; to encourage the democratization of future-oriented thinking & acting
Finances: *Funding Sources:* Membership fees; UNESCO
Membership: *Fees:* Schedule available; *Member Profile:* Members are institutes & individuals from more than 70 countries from all regions, sectors & ideological perspectives of the world; they come from many disciplines & include scholars, policy makers & other people seriously involved in futures studies; membership is open to students
Activities: Coordinates research in the following: education towards the future; cultural aspects of the futures of peace; futures of political institutions; futures of communication & information; changing structures of social support; futures of development; methods of social forecasting & design
Chief Officer(s):
Jennifer Gidley, President
Annie Ferguson, Secretariat Director

World Health Organization (WHO) / Organisation mondiale de la santé (OMS)
20 Appia Ave., Geneva 1202 Switzerland
Tel: 41-22-791-21-11; *Fax:* 41-22-791-31-11
www.who.int
www.linkedin.com/company/world-health-organization
www.facebook.com/WorldHealthOrganization
twitter.com/WHO
www.youtube.com/who
Overview: A large international organization founded in 1948

Mission: To attain for all peoples the highest possible level of health
Membership: 194 member states
Activities: Global strategy to achieve optimal health for all peoples of the world is based on the primary health care approach, involving the following components: education concerning prevailing health problems, proper food supply & nutrition, safe water & sanitation, maternal & child health, immunization against major infectious diseases, prevention & control of local diseases, appropriate treatment of common diseases & injuries, provision of essential drugs; *Awareness Events:* World Health Day, April 7; World No-Tobacco Day, May 31; World AIDS Day, Dec. 1; World TB (Tuberculosis) Day, March
Chief Officer(s):
Tedros Adhanom Ghebreyesus, Director General
Awards:
• The Léon Bernard Foundation Prize
• Dr. A.T. Shousha Foundation Prize & Fellowship
• Jacques Parisot Foundation Fellowship
• Ihsan Dogramaci Family Health Foundation Prize
• The Sasakawa Health Prize
• Dr. Comlan A.A. Quenum Prize for Public Health
• Francesco Pocchiari Fellowship
• United Arab Emirates Health Foundation Prize
• Down Syndrome Research Prize in the Eastern Mediterranean Region
• The State of Kuwait Prize for Research in Health Promotion
• The Dr. LEE Jong-wook Memorial Prize for Public Health
Publications:
• International Classification of Diseases [a publication of the World Health Organization]
Profile: A diagnostic tool for epidemiology, health management & clinical purposes
• International Health Regulations [a publication of the World Health Organization]
Profile: Rules to enhance national, regional & global public health security
• The International Pharmacopoeia [a publication of the World Health Organization]
Profile: To harmonize global quality specifications for selected pharmaceutical products, excipients & dosage forms
• International Travel & Health [a publication of the World Health Organization]
Type: Report
Profile: Information on health risks for travellers
• The World Health Report [a publication of the World Health Organization]
Type: Report
Profile: An expert assessment of global health
• World Health Statistics [a publication of the World Health Organization]
Type: Report
Profile: Recent health statistics for member states

World Health Organization Health in Prisons Programme; International Council of Prison Medical Services *See* World Health Organization Partnership for Health in the Criminal Justice Sytem

World Health Organization Partnership for Health in the Criminal Justice Sytem
c/o WHO Regional Office for Europe, Marmorvej 51, Copenhagen DK-2100 Denmark
Tel: 45-45-33-70-00; *Fax:* 45-45-33-70-01
hpp@euro.who.int
www.euro.who.int
Previous Name: World Health Organization Health in Prisons Programme; International Council of Prison Medical Services
Overview: A small international organization founded in 1995
Chief Officer(s):
Lars Moller, Programme Manager, Alcohol & Illicit Drugs
lmo@euro.who.int

World Leisure & Recreation Association (WLRA)
Institute of Leisure Studies, University of Duesto, Bilbao 48007 Spain
Tel: 34-94-413-90-86
secretariat@worldleisure.org
www.worldleisure.org
www.facebook.com/159197134114790
twitter.com/WorldLeisureOrg
www.youtube.com/user/WorldLeisureOrg
Previous Name: International Leisure Information Network (LINK)

Overview: A medium-sized international charitable organization founded in 1956
Mission: To discover & foster conditions best permitting leisure to serve as a force to optimize individual & collective well-being
Affiliation(s): UNESCO & other UN agencies
Finances: *Annual Operating Budget:* $100,000-$250,000; *Funding Sources:* Donations; membership fees; projects; grants; subsidies
Membership: 1,000; *Fees:* Schedule available
Activities: Education; Management; Research; Tourism; Centre of Excellence; Professional Services; Women & Gender; Access & Inclusion; Voluntarism; Low; Older Persons; Children & Youth; World Congress; *Speaker Service:* Yes
Chief Officer(s):
Cristina Ortega-Nuere, Chief Operating Officer
Meetings/Conferences:
• World Leisure & Recreation Association World Leisure Congress 2018, August, 2018, Sao Paulo
Scope: International
Contact Information: E-mail: communication@worldleisure.org

World Lottery Association (WLA)
c/o Interkantonale Landeslotterie, Swisslos, Lange Gasse 20, PO Box CH-4002, Basel Switzerland
Tel: +41 61 284 1502; *Fax:* +41 61 284 1350
info@world-lotteries.org
www.world-lotteries.org
Overview: A medium-sized international organization founded in 1999
Mission: To control runaway gambling; To protect territorial integrity & promote the role of state-licensed lotteries as generators of funds for good causes
Membership: 138 regular + 61 associate; *Fees:* US$5,000-10,000 based on sales level of the lottery; *Member Profile:* Restricted to state lotteries & suppliers of goods or services to lotteries; *Committees:* Strategic Development; Corporate Social Responsibility; Audit; Nominating; New Media/Cross-Border; Security & Risk Management; RFP Standardization; GRADE Sub-Committee; Training Program; Supplier Relations; WLA Conventions; Bylaws
Activities: *Library*: Centre de documentation de Loto-Québec; Open to public by appointment
Chief Officer(s):
Jean-Luc Moner-Banet, President
moner-banet@loro.ch
Rebecca Paul Paul Hargrove, Senior Vice-President,
615-324-6501, Fax: 615-324-6537
rebecca.p.hargrove@tnlottery.com
Awards:
• The WLA Advertising Awards
• The Guy Simonis Lifetime Achievement Award

World Mariculture Society *See* World Aquaculture Society

World Masters Athletics
c/o Stan Perkins, 4 Lawnton St., Daisy Hill QLD 4127 Australia
Tel: 61 7 3209 1131; *Fax:* 61 7 3209 1131
info@world-masters-athletics.org
www.world-masters-athletics.org
twitter.com/wmaforlife
Previous Name: World Association of Veteran Athletes
Overview: A small international organization founded in 1977
Mission: To organize, regulate and administer athletics for masters (women and men of not less than thirty-five years of age); To sanction World Masters' Athletic Championships and other international masters athletic competitions; To ratify and register world masters five-year age-group records and maintain data on other outstanding athletic performances by masters; To foster international friendship, understanding and co-operation through masters athletics
Member of: International Association of Athletic Federations
Finances: *Annual Operating Budget:* $100,000-$250,000
Membership: 140; *Member Profile:* National Athletic Federations; *Committees:* Stadia; Non-Stadia; Medical & Anti-doping; Women's; Law & Legislation
Activities: Athletics/track & field for veterans & masters
Chief Officer(s):
Stan Perkins, President
stanperkins@me.com

World Meteorological Organization (WMO) / Organisation météorologique mondiale (OMM)
Information & Public Affairs, PO Box 2300, 7 bis, av de la Paix, Geneva 2, Geneva CH-1211 Switzerland
Tel: 41-22-730-8111; *Fax:* 41-22-730-8181
cpa@wmo.int

www.wmo.int
www.facebook.com/71741701887
twitter.com/WMOnews
www.youtube.com/wmovideomaster
Overview: A medium-sized international organization founded in 1950
Mission: Coordinates global scientific activity to allow prompt & accurate weather information & other services for public, private & commercial use; contributes to the safety of life & property, the socio-economic development of nations & the protection of the environment; disaster mitigation & reduction
Finances: *Annual Operating Budget:* Greater than $5 Million; *Funding Sources:* Member governments
Staff Member(s): 246
Membership: 191 governments; *Fees:* Assessed contributions; *Committees:* WMO Congress; Executive Council; Regional Associations; Technical
Activities: World Weather Watch; World Climate; Atmospheric Research & Environment; Applications of Meteorology; Hydrology & Water Resources; Education & Training; Technical Cooperation; Regional; *Library:* WMO Technical Library; Open to public
Chief Officer(s):
David Grimes, President, (Canada)
Antonio Divino Moura, 1st Vice-President, (Brazil)
Mieczyslaw S. Ostojski, Ph.D., 2nd Vice-President, (Poland)
Abdalah Mokssit, 3rd Vice-President, (Morocco)

World Nuclear Association (WNA)
Carlton House, 22A St. James's Sq., London SW1Y 4JH United Kingdom
Tel: 44-20-7451-1520; *Fax:* 44-20-7839-1501
wna@world-nuclear.org
www.world-nuclear.org
www.linkedin.com/company/world-nuclear-association
www.facebook.com/worldnuclearassociation
twitter.com/WorldNuclear
www.youtube.com/user/WorldNuclear
Previous Name: The Uranium Institute
Overview: A medium-sized international charitable organization founded in 2001
Mission: To promote the use of nuclear energy for peaceful purposes; to provide a forum for research & debate on economic & political issues affecting the nuclear industry; to play a central role in the collection, analysis & communication of information on all aspects of the industry & related subjects
Finances: *Annual Operating Budget:* $1.5 Million-$3 Million
Staff Member(s): 17
Membership: 165; *Fees:* Schedule available; *Member Profile:* Uranium producers, electrical utilities, fuel processing, handling & trading companies, government organizations
Activities: *Library*: Information Library; Open to public
Chief Officer(s):
John B. Ritch, Director General
Tim Gitzel, Chair
Jean-Jacques Gautrot, Vice-Chair

World Organisation of Systems & Cybernetics (WOSC) / Organisation Mondiale pour la Systémique et la Cybernétique (OMSC)
North Place, #3, 30 Nettleham Rd., Lincoln LN2 1RE United Kingdom
Tél: 44-1522-589-252
wosc.co
www.facebook.com/WOSC.org
twitter.com/WOSC_
Aperçu: *Dimension:* petite; *Envergure:* internationale; fondée en 1969
Membre: 24 institutions; *Critères d'admissibilite:* Federation of national associations & institutions devoted to systems or cybernetics, with English, French & Russian as official languages
Activités: Operates Norbert Wiener Institute
Membre(s) du bureau directeur:
Raul Espejo, Director General
r.espejo@syncho.org
Robert Vallée, President
r.vallee@afscet.asso.fr

World Organization of the Scout Movement (WOSM) / Organisation mondiale du mouvement scout
World Scout Bureau, Menara Sentral Vista, #3, 150 Jalan Sultan Abdul Samad, Kuala Lumpur 50470 Malaysia
Tel: 60-3-2276-9000; *Fax:* 60-3-2276-9089
worldbureau@scout.org
www.scout.org

www.facebook.com/WOSM.OMMS?v=wall
twitter.com/worldscouting
www.youtube.com/worldscouting
www.instagram.com/worldscouting
Overview: A large international organization
Mission: To contribute positively to the education of young people, through a value system based on the Scout Promise & Law; To promote Scouting as the world's leading educational youth movement; To enable young people to enact positive change in their communities and as a global community
Affiliation(s): Scouts Canada; Association des Scouts du Canada
Membership: 28 million; *Member Profile:* Young people & adults in 217 countries & territories
Chief Officer(s):
Scott A. Teare, Secretary General
Goran Hagerdal, Global Director, Scouting Development
ghagerdale@scout.org
Lin Lin Yeoh, Global Director, Communications & External Relations
linlinyeoh@scout.org
Stephen Peck, Director, World Events
stephen.peck@scout.org
Awards:
• The Bronze World Award
To recognize outstanding service by an individual to the World Scout Movement

World ORT Union (ORT) / Union mondiale ORT
ORT House, 126 Albert St., London NW1 7NE United Kingdom
Tel: 44-20-7446-8500; *Fax:* 44-20-7446-8650
wo@ort.org
www.ort.org
www.linkedin.com/company/world-ort
www.facebook.com/WorldORT
twitter.com/worldort
Overview: A medium-sized international charitable organization founded in 1921
Mission: To work for the advancement of Jewish people to cope with the complexities & uncertainties of their environment; foster self-sufficiency, mobility, & a sense of identity
Affiliation(s): Canadian ORT Federation; Women's Canadian ORT
Finances: *Funding Sources:* Donations
Activities: Providing vocational training & technical assistance; Supporting non-sectarian economic & social development in under-developed regions of the world
Chief Officer(s):
Shmuel Sisso, Director General
Mauricio Merikanskas, President

World Packaging Organization (WPO)
#123, 1833 Centre Point Circle, Naperville IL 60563 USA
Tel: 630-596-9007; *Fax:* 630-544-5055
info@worldpackaging.org
www.worldpackaging.org
www.linkedin.com/groups?gid=2602547
twitter.com/WorldPackOrg
www.flickr.com/photos/worldpackorg/
Overview: A medium-sized international organization founded in 1968
Membership: 2,614
Chief Officer(s):
Carl Olsmats, General Secretary
carl.olsmats@stfi.se

World Petroleum Council (WPC)
#1, 1 Duchess St., 4th Fl., London W1W 6AN United Kingdom
Tel: +44 (0)20 7637 4995
info@world-petroleum.org
www.world-petroleum.org
Overview: A medium-sized international organization founded in 1933
Mission: To promote sustainable management and use of the world's petroleum resources
Affiliation(s): IEA; OPEN; United Nations
Finances: *Funding Sources:* Membership dues; royalties; levy on registration
Staff Member(s): 4
Membership: 57 countries; *Fees:* Schedule available; *Member Profile:* Major oil producing & consuming nations of the world. Each country has a National Committee made up of representatives of the oil industry, academic & research institutions & government departments; *Committees:* Permanent Council; Executive Board; Scientific Program; Congress Arrangements; Environmental Affairs; Development
Chief Officer(s):
Pierce Riemer, Director General
pierce@world-petroleum.org
Randy Gossen, President

World Pheasant Association (WPA)
Biology Field Station, Newcastle University, Close House Estate, Heddon-on-the-Wall NE15 0HT United Kingdom
Tel: 44(0)1661 853397
office@pheasant.org.uk
www.pheasant.org.uk
Overview: A small international charitable organization founded in 1975
Mission: To develop & promote the conservation of all species in the order galliformes, which are, broadly speaking the game birds of the world
Finances: *Annual Operating Budget:* $50,000-$100,000; *Funding Sources:* Donations
Staff Member(s): 2
Membership: 2,000
Activities: Habitat Survey & Protection; Education; Aviculture; Species Studies; International Symposia; Reintroduction Programs; Conservation Strategy
Chief Officer(s):
Zheng Guangmei, President
Richard Carden, Chairman

World Ploughing Organization (WPO)
Grolweg2, Hall 6964 BL Netherlands
Tel: 31-313-619-634; *Fax:* 31-313-619-735
www.worldploughing.org
twitter.com/worldploughing
Overview: A small international charitable organization founded in 1952
Mission: To foster & preserve the art & improve the skill of ploughing the land; To urge the development & adoption of improved techniques & aids for all branches of agriculture
Affiliation(s): Canadian Plowing Organization
Finances: *Annual Operating Budget:* $50,000-$100,000
Staff Member(s): 1
Membership: 30; *Fees:* CHF 3,000; *Member Profile:* National ploughing championships organizations
Activities: World Championship Ploughing Contests; Tillage Clinics
Chief Officer(s):
Hans Spieker, General Secretary
hans.spieker@worldploughing.org

World Presidents' Organization
c/o Young Presidents' Organization, #1000, 600 East Las Colinas Blvd., Irving TX 75039 USA
Tel: 972-587-1500; *Fax:* 972-587-1611
Toll-Free: 800-773-7976
info@wpo.org
www.wpo.org
Overview: A small international organization founded in 1970
Mission: To create an environment where the power of idea exchange enhances lives, enriches families & improves communities
Membership: 9,000
Chief Officer(s):
Paul N. Summers, International Chair & CEO

World Resources Institute (WRI)
#800, 10 G St. NE, Washington DC 20002 USA
Tel: 202-729-7600; *Fax:* 202-729-7610
www.wri.org
www.linkedin.com/groups?gid=69154
www.facebook.com/worldresources
twitter.com/worldresources
www.youtube.com/WorldResourcesInst
Overview: A small international organization founded in 1982
Mission: To generate accurate information about global resources & environmental conditions, analyze emerging issues & develop creative responses to both problems & opportunities; to bring the insights of scientific research, economic analysis & practical experience to political, business & other leaders around the world by publishing books, reports & papers
Staff Member(s): 200
Activities: Policy studies to present accurate infromation about global resources & environmental conditions, analysis of emerging issues & development of creative yet workable policy responses; in developing countries, provides field services & technical support for governments & nongovernmental organizations that are working to ensure the sustainability of natural resources; *Internships:* Yes; *Library:* Open to public by appointment
Chief Officer(s):
Andrew Steer, President & CEO
asteer@wri.org
Manish Bapna, Exec. Vice-President & Managing Dir
mbapna@wri.org
Steve Barker, CFO & Vice-President, Finance & Administration
sbarker@wri.org

World Safety Organization (WSO)
WSO World Management Centre, PO Box 518, Warrensburg MO 64093 USA
Tel: 660-747-3132; *Fax:* 660-747-2647
info@worldsafety.org
www.worldsafety.org
www.facebook.com/WorldSafetyOrganization
twitter.com/WorldSafetyOrg
Overview: A medium-sized international organization founded in 1875
Mission: To protect people, property, resources & the environment; To internationalize occupational & environmental safety through exchange of knowledge, programs, etc.
Member of: Consultative Status Category II (non-governmental) with Economic & Social Council of the United Nations
Membership: *Fees:* $55 associate; $80 affiliate; $35 student; $185 institution; $1,000 corporate; *Member Profile:* Open to all individuals & entities involved in the safety & accident prevention field; *Committees:* Aviation Transportation; Construction; Maritime Transportation; Highway Transportation; Rail Transportation; Transportation of Dangerous Goods
Activities: World Safety & Accident Prevention Congress (every 2-6 years); World Safety & Accident Prevention Educational Conference (annually); Professional development courses & seminars; *Library*
Chief Officer(s):
Vlado Senkovich, President & Director General
Edward E. Hogue, Vice-President & Deputy Director General
Lon S. McDaniel, Chief Executive Officer
Charles H. Baker, Chief Operations Officer
Awards:
• WSO Concerned Company/Corporation Honorable Mention Certificate
• WSO Educational Award
• WSO Concerned Organization Award
• WSO Safety Person of the Year
• WSO James K. Williams Award
• WSO Concerned Citizen Award
• WSO Concerned Professional Award
• WSO Concerned Company/Corporation Award

World Society for Ekistics (WSE)
24, Strat. Syndesmou St., Athens 106 73 Greece
Tel: 30-210-3623-216; *Fax:* 30-210-3629-337
ekistics@otenet.gr
www.ekistics.org
Overview: A small international organization founded in 1965
Mission: To advance the science of ekistics (human settlements) by drawing on the research & experience of professionals in such fields as architecture, engineering, ekistics, regional & city planning & sociology
Finances: *Annual Operating Budget:* Less than $50,000; *Funding Sources:* Membership dues; grants
5 volunteer(s)
Membership: 200; *Fees:* $40
Activities: Human settlements
Chief Officer(s):
Suzanne Keller, President
Panayis Psomopoulos, Secretary General/Treasurer

World Tourism Organization (UNWTO)
Calle Capitán Haya, 42, Madrid 28020 Spain
Tel: 34-91-567-8100; *Fax:* 34-91-571-3733
omt@unwto.org
www.unwto.org
www.facebook.com/WorldTourismOrganization
twitter.com/unwto
vimeo.com/unwto
Overview: A medium-sized international organization founded in 1975
Mission: To promote responsibile & accessible world tourism
Membership: 400 affiliate members; 156 member countries; 6 associate members; *Member Profile:* Executive Council comprised of 22 full members, one for every five in WTO plus host State Spain (as ex officio member), one Associate member, & one Affiliate member

Foreign Associations / World Trade Centres Association (WTCA)

Chief Officer(s):
Taleb D. Rifai, Secretary General

World Trade Centres Association (WTCA)
#518, 420 Lexington Ave., New York NY 10170 USA
Tel: 212-432-2626; Fax: 212-488-0064
wtca@wtca.org
www.wtca.org
twitter.com/WTCAonline
Overview: A small international organization founded in 1968
Mission: To encourage expansion of world trade, promote international business relations & increase participation in world trade by less developed countries
Membership: Member Profile: Regular - organizations substantially involved in development or operation of World Trade Centre; Committees: Clubs & Associations; Industrializing Nations; Research & Development; Trade Policy; Legal; Facilities; Information & Communications
Chief Officer(s):
Eric Dahl, CEO
edahl@wtca.org

World Union of Catholic Women's Organizations Voir Union mondiale des organisations féminines catholiques

World University Roundtable (WUR)
Desert Sanctuary Campus, PO Box 2470, Benson AZ 85602 USA
Tel: 520-586-2985; Fax: 520-586-4764
info@worlduniversity.org
www.worlduniversity.org
Overview: A small international licensing organization founded in 1946
Mission: To set before the student a broad overview of man's extant learning & to suggest areas of research & study which will advance his comprehension of what lies within his immediate future
Member of: American Library Association
Affiliation(s): World University Association of Schools
Finances: Funding Sources: Membership dues
Membership: Member Profile: All professional in science, education & culture
Activities: International promotion of national offices & affiliated schools; Library: World University Library; by appointment

World Veterinary Poultry Association (WVPA)
Merial, Lyon Gerland Laboratory, 254, rue Marcel Mérieux, BP 391, Lyon 69007 France
www.wvpa.net
Overview: A medium-sized international organization founded in 1959
Mission: To organize meetings for studying diseases & conditions relating to the avian species; To promote research & the exchange of information; To establish & maintain liaison with other bodies with related interests
Membership: 1,000-4,999; Member Profile: Ordinary members are veterinarians interested in avian science & related subjects, or non-veterinarians engaged in research, advisory work or teaching concerned with avian science.
Chief Officer(s):
Francois-Xavier Le Gros, Secretary-Treasurer
francois-xavier.le-gros@merial.com
Awards:
• Avian Pathology Lecture Award
• Bart Rispens Research Award
• WVPA-Zoetis Young Poultry Veterinarian Award
• WVPA-Boehringer Ingelheim Innovation in Vaccination Award
Publications:
• Aerosols
Type: Newsletter; Frequency: Annually
• Avian Pathology
Type: Journal; Frequency: Bimonthly

Profile: Original research papers & occasional reviews related to infectious & non-infectious diseases of poultry & all other birds

World Wildlife Fund - USA (WWF-USA) / Fonds mondial pour la nature
PO Box 97180, 1250 - 24 St. NW, Washington DC 20037 USA
Tel: 202-293-4800
membership@wwfus.org
www.worldwildlife.org
www.facebook.com/worldwildlifefund
twitter.com/world_wildlife
www.youtube.com/wwfus; www.instagram.com/World_Wildlife
Overview: A large international organization founded in 1961
Mission: To preserve the diversity & abundance of life on Earth & the health of ecological systems by protecting natural areas & wild populations of plants & animals, including endangered species; To promote sustainable approaches to the use of renewable natural resources; To promote more efficient use of resources & energy & the maximum reduction of pollution; To reverse the degradation of natural environment & build a future in which human needs are met in harmony with nature; To determine how best to manage individual species & habitats & to obtain critical data for setting conservation priorities
Affiliation(s): WWF has national organizations, national associates & representatives in nearly 40 countries across five continents; affiliation with international WWF network headquarters in Gland, Switzerland
Finances: Funding Sources: Contributions from members; grants from foundations, corporations & government agencies
Membership: 1,000,000+; Fees: $25-$500
Activities: Library Open to public
Chief Officer(s):
Carter S. Roberts, President
Marcia Marsh, Chief Operating Officer
Michael Bauer, Chief Financial Officer

World Wildlife Fund for Nature See WWF International

World's Poultry Science Association
PO Box 31, Beekbergen 7360AA Netherlands
Tel: 31-6-515-19584; Fax: 31-207-508-941
www.wpsa.com
Overview: A medium-sized international organization founded in 1912
Mission: Strives to advance knowledge and understanding of all aspects of poultry science and the poultry industry. Its major role is to encourage, and help facilitate, liaison among research scientists and educators, and between those in research and education and those working in the many diverse sectors of the industry.
Affiliation(s): World's Poultry Science Association - Canadian Branch
Membership: 7,000 in 60 countries; Fees: Schedule available
Chief Officer(s):
E.N. Silva, President
edit@fea.unicamp.br
F.A. Bradley, Treasurer

Worldwatch Institute
#430, 1400 16th St. NW, Washington DC 20036 USA
Tel: 202-745-8092; Fax: 202-478-2534
worldwatch@worldwatch.org
www.worldwatch.org
www.linkedin.com/company/worldwatch-institute
www.facebook.com/WorldwatchInst
twitter.com/Worldwatch
www.youtube.com/user/WorldwatchInst;
flickr.com/photos/worldwatchinst
Overview: A medium-sized international charitable organization founded in 1974
Mission: To work towards an environmentally sustainable & socially just society; To provide compelling, accessible fact-based analysis of critical global issues; To inform people about the interaction between nature, people & economies; To focus on the underlying causes & practical solutions to the world's problems
Finances: Annual Operating Budget: $3 Million-$5 Million
Staff Member(s): 30
Activities: Internships: Yes; Rents Mailing List: Yes; Library: Not open to public
Chief Officer(s):
Barbara Fallin, Director, Finance & Administration

WWF International (WWF)
Avenue du Mont-Blanc, Gland CH-1196 Switzerland
Tel: 41-22-364-9111; Fax: 41-22-364-8836
wwf.panda.org
www.linkedin.com/groups/WWF-44458
www.facebook.com/WWF
twitter.com/wwf
www.youtube.com/wwf
Also Known As: World Wide Fund for Nature
Previous Name: World Wildlife Fund for Nature
Overview: A large international charitable organization founded in 1961
Mission: To stop the degradation of the planet's natural environment & to build a future in which humans live in harmony with nature by conserving the world's biological diversity, ensuring that the use of renewable & natural resources is sustainable, promoting the reduction of pollution & wasteful consumption
Affiliation(s): The World Conservation Union; International Council for Bird Protection; International Waterfowl Research Bureau; Charles Darwin Foundation
Finances: Annual Operating Budget: Greater than $5 Million; Funding Sources: Individuals & general donations; legacies & bequests; corporate subscriptions & donations
Staff Member(s): 3800
Membership: 4.7 million; Fees: Schedule available
Activities: Six international environmental issues: Climate Change, Endangered Seas, Forests, Fresh Water Programmes, Species, Toxics; sponsors educational & training programs for park & wildlife managers, ecologists & teachers; Internships: Yes
Chief Officer(s):
Yolanda Kakabadse, President
Marco Lambertini, Director General
Awards:
• WWF Prince Bernhard Scholarships for Nature Conservation
To help build conservation expertise and leadership in the developing world. Amount: Up to CHF 10,000
• The Kathryn Fuller Science for Nature Fund
• The e8 Sustainable Energy Development Scholarship Programme

Young Presidents' Organization (YPO)
#1000, 600 East Las Colinas Blvd., Irving TX 75039 USA
Tel: 972-587-1500; Fax: 972-587-1611
Toll-Free: 800-773-7976
askypo@ypo.org
www.ypo.org
www.linkedin.com/company/young-presidents%27-organization
www.facebook.com/youngpresorg
twitter.com/YPO
www.youtube.com/YPOvideo
Overview: A small international organization founded in 1950
Mission: To create better leaders through idea exchange
Affiliation(s): 10 Chapters in Canada
Membership: 22,000 in 125 countries; Member Profile: Young global business leaders

Zero Population Growth See Population Connection

Indexes

Acronym Index

A

A&WMA - Air & Waste Management Association, 1486
A5-PBA - Alberta 5 Pin Bowlers' Association, 21
AA - Alcoholics Anonymous (GTA Intergroup), 52
AAA - Alberta Assessors' Association, 22
AAA - Alberta Association of Architects, 23
AAA - American Anthropological Association, 1488
AAAC - Association of Accrediting Agencies of Canada, 138
AAADFQ - Association des avocats et avovates en droit familial du Québec, 107
AAAE - Atlantic Association of Applied Economists, 182
AAAF - Association of Alberta Agricultural Fieldmen, 139
AAAL - Alberta Association of Academic Libraries, 23
AAAPNB - Association acadienne des artistes professionnel.le.s du Nouveau-Brunswick inc., 89
AAARBRIP - Association des avocats et avocates représentant les bénéficiaires des régimes d'indemnisation publics, 107
AAAS - Alberta Association of Agricultural Societies, 23
AAAS - American Association for the Advancement of Science, 1489
AAAV - Association des artistes en arts visuels de Saint-Jérôme, 106
AAB - L'Association des artistes Baltes à Montréal, 106
AABC - Alberta Associations for Bright Children, 25
AABC - Archives Association of British Columbia, 80
AABC - Alberta Amateur Baseball Council, 22
AABP - American Association of Bovine Practitioners, 1489
AAC - Abbotsford Arts Council, 1
AAC - Algonquin Arts Council, 53
AAC - Animal Alliance of Canada, 70
AAC - Alberta Assessment Consortium, 22
AAC - Auditing Association of Canada, 187
AAC - Agricultural Adaptation Council, 14
AAC - Aquaculture Association of Canada, 75
AAC - Aluminium Association of Canada, 61
AACA - Antique Automobile Club of America, 1505
AACC - Avicultural Advancement Council of Canada, 191
AACI - Association of Americans & Canadians in Israel, 1510
AACL - Inclusion Alberta, 831
AACM - Alberta Association of Clinic Managers, 23
AACPDM - American Academy for Cerebral Palsy & Developmental Medicine, 1487
AAD - Alberta Association of Optometrists, 24
AAD - Alberta Association of the Deaf, 25
AADM - Association des avocats de la défense de Montréal, 106
AAEA - Alberta Agricultural Economics Association, 21
AAEE - Australian Association for Environmental Education, 1513
AAESBC - Aboriginal Agricultural Education Society of British Columbia, 2
AAESQ - Association of Administrators of English Schools of Québec, 139
AAFA - Algoma Arts Festival Association, 53
AAFA - Alberta Amateur Football Association, 22

AAFRE - Alberta Association of Fund Raising Executives, 23
AAFSLW - Alberta Association of Family School Liaison Workers, 23
AAG - Alberta Association on Gerontology, 25
AAG - Association of American Geographers, 1510
AAHP - Association of Allied Health Professionals: Newfoundland & Labrador (Ind.), 139
AAIA - Allergy/Asthma Information Association, 54
AAIDD - American Association on Intellectual & Developmental Disabilities, 1490
AAIRP - Alberta Association of Insolvency & Restructuring Professionals, 23
AAJ - American Association for Justice, 1488
AALA - Alberta Association of Landscape Architects, 23
AALT - Alberta Association of Library Technicians, 23
AAM - Alberta Association of Midwives, 24
AAMAC - Aplastic Anemia & Myelodysplasia Association of Canada, 73
AAMDC - Alberta Association of Municipal Districts & Counties, 24
AAMFT - Alberta Association of Marriage & Family Therapy, 24
AAN - American Academy of Neurology, 1487
AANB - Agricultural Alliance of New Brunswick, 14
AANB - Architects' Association of New Brunswick, 78
AANB - Archery Association of New Brunswick, 78
AANEM - American Association of Neuromuscular & Electrodiagnostic Medicine, 1490
AANP - American Association of Naturopathic Physicians, 1489
AANS - Aquaculture Association of Nova Scotia, 75
AANS - Archers Association of Nova Scotia, 78
AAO - Archives Association of Ontario, 80
AAO - Acoustical Association Ontario, 5
AAOF - Association des auteures et des auteurs de l'Ontario français, 106
AAP - Association of Administrative Professionals, 139
AAP - Association des avocats et avocates de province, 106
AAPARS - Association des artistes peintres affiliés de la Rive-Sud, 106
AAPEI - Architects Association of Prince Edward Island, 78
AAPG - The American Association of Petroleum Geologists, 1490
AAPG - Alberta Association of Police Governance, 24
AAPP - Alberta Association of Professional Paralegals, 24
AAPPQ - Association des Architectes en pratique privée du Québec, 105
AAPQ - Association des architectes paysagistes du Québec, 105
AAPQ - Association des agences de publicité du Québec, 105
AAPS-UBC - Association of Administrative & Professional Staff - University of British Columbia, 138
AAQ - Association des archivistes du Québec, 105
AAQ - Association des archéologues du Québec, 105
AAR - American Academy of Religion, 1488
AARC - Alberta Association of Rehabilitation Centres, 24

AARDA - Alberta Automotive Recyclers & Dismantlers Association, 25
AARQ - Association des Aménagistes Régionaux du Québec, 105
AARS - American Association for Thoracic Surgery, 1489
AAS - American Antiquarian Society, 1488
AAS - Association for Asian Studies - USA, 1507
AAS - The American Astronautical Society, 1490
AASA - Alberta Amateur Softball Association, 22
AASA - Alberta Alpine Ski Association, 22
AASMM - Association des alternatives en santé mentale de la Montérégie, 105
AASRA - Alberta Amputee Sports & Recreation Association, 22
AASSA - Alberta Amateur Speed Skating Association, 22
AASSC - Association for the Advancement of Scandinavian Studies in Canada, 134
AAS-UA - Association of Academic Staff - University of Alberta, 138
AATHP - Alberta Association of Travel Health Professionals, 25
AATO - Association of Architectural Technologists of Ontario, 139
AATQ - Association des arts thérapeutes du Québec, 106
AAU - Association of Atlantic Universities, 139
AAU - Amateur Athletic Union, 1487
AAW - Advertising Association of Winnipeg Inc., 10
AAWA - Alberta Amateur Wrestling Association, 22
ABA - Alberta Bicycle Association, 26
ABA - Allied Beauty Association, 58
ABA - Alberta Band Association, 25
ABA - Alberta Broomball Association, 26
ABA - Alberta Bowhunters Association, 26
ABA - American Birding Association, Inc., 1490
ABA - Alberta Bobsleigh Association, 26
ABA - American Bankers Association, 1490
ABAC - Antiquarian Booksellers' Association of Canada, 72
ABAC - Ayrshire Breeders Association of Canada, 191
ABAM - Archers & Bowhunters Association of Manitoba, 78
ABAQC - Association des Boulangers Artisans du Québec, 107
ABBA - Alberta Bodybuilding Association, 26
ABC - Apparel BC, 73
ABC Ontario - Association for Bright Children (Ontario), 132
ABCDE - Association of BC Drama Educators, 140
ABCFP - Association of British Columbia Forest Professionals, 140
ABCLS - Association of British Columbia Land Surveyors, 140
ABDA - Alberta Bottle Depot Association, 26
ABDM - Association des bibliothèques de droit de Montréal, 107
ABDS - Association des bénévoles du don de sang, 107
ABE - Au bas de l'échelle, 187
ABEABC - Adult Basic Education Association of British Columbia, 9
ABEC - Alberta Building Envelope Council (South), 26
ABECAN - Associaçao Brasileira de Estudos Canadense, 1506
ABIPE - Association des bibliothèques publiques de l'Estrie, 107

ABJHLLL - Association de balle des jeunes handicapés de Laval-Laurentides-Lanaudière, 99
ABMB - Alberta Conference of Mennonite Brethren Churches, 30
ABMRF - Alcoholic Beverage Medical Research Foundation, 1486
ABP - Alberta Beef Producers, 25
ABPBC - Association of Book Publishers of British Columbia, 140
ABPNB - Association des bibliothécaires professionnel(le)s du Nouveau-Brunswick, 107
ABPPUM - Association des bibliothécaires, des professeures et professeurs de l'Université de Moncton, 107
ABPQ - Association des bibliothèques publiques du Québec, 107
ABQ - Association des brasseurs du Québec, 108
ABQ - Association Béton Québec, 90
ABQA - Artisan Bakers' Quality Alliance, 85
ABQSJ - Associés bénévoles qualifiés au service des jeunes, 179
ABS - Association for Bahá'í Studies, 132
ABSA - Alberta Boilers Safety Association, 26
ABSAUM - Association des bibliothèques de la santé affiliées à l'Université de Montréal, 107
ABSDA - Atlantic Building Supply Dealers Association, 182
ABSW - Nova Scotia Association of Black Social Workers, 1040
ABTA - Alberta Baton Twirling Association, 25
ABTAM - Architectural & Building Technologists Association of Manitoba Inc., 78
ABVTA - Alberta Veterinary Technologist Association, 50
ACA - Alberta Chess Association, 28
ACA - Adult Children of Alcoholics, 9
ACA - Association of Canadian Advertisers Inc., 140
ACA - Association of Canadian Archivists, 141
ACA - Alberta Construction Association, 31
ACA - Atlantic Concrete Association, 183
ACA - Alberta Camping Association, 27
ACA - Cricket Alberta, 642
ACA - Archives du Centre acadien, 80
ACA - Association Canado-Américaine, 1507
ACA - Alberta Conservation Association, 31
ACA - Alberta Cheerleading Association, 28
ACA Canada - AirCrew Association - Western Canada Region, 29
ACAA - HIV Community Link, 816
ACAA - Atlantic Collegiate Athletic Association, 183
ACAAP - Arab Canadian Association of the Atlantic Provinces, 75
ACAC - Alberta College & Association of Chiropractors, 28
ACAC - Alberta Colleges Athletic Conference, 30
ACAF - Association canadienne des ataxies familiales, 92
ACAS - Asian Community AIDS Services, 87
ACAT - Action des Chrétiens pour l'abolition de la torture, 6
ACAT - Alberta Council on Admissions & Transfer, 31
ACATCM - Alberta College of Acupuncture & Traditional Chinese Medicine, 28
ACBO - Assembly of Catholic Bishops of Ontario, 88
ACC - The Anglican Church of Canada, 69
ACC - Alberta Chambers of Commerce, 28
ACC - Assiniboia Chamber of Commerce (MB), 88
ACC - Alpine Club of Canada, 59

Acronym Index

ACC - Atlantic Council of Canada, 183
ACC - Atlantic Chamber of Commerce, 183
ACC - Alberta Craft Council, 32
ACC - American Chemistry Council, 1491
ACC - Adoption Council of Canada, 8
ACCA - Alberta Continuing Care Association, 31
ACCA - American Cave Conservation Association, 1491
ACCA - Alberta Community & Co-operative Association, 30
ACCA - Afro-Canadian Caribbean Association of Hamilton & District Inc., 13
ACCA - Atlantic Canada Cruise Association, 182
ACCB - AIDS Coalition of Cape Breton, 15
ACCC - Association of Canadian Choral Communities, 141
ACCD - Alberta Committee of Citizens with Disabilities, 30
ACCEM - Association des chercheurs et chercheures étudiants en médecine, 108
ACCES - African Canadian Continuing Education Society, 12
ACCES - Atlantic Canada Centre for Environmental Science, 12
ACCÉSSS - Alliance des communautés culturelles pour l'égalité dans la santé et les services sociaux, 55
ACCHO - African & Caribbean Council on HIV/AIDS in Ontario, 12
ACCI - Adventive Cross Cultural Initiatives, 10
ACCKWA - AIDS Committee of Cambridge, Kitchener/Waterloo & Area, 16
ACCLXT - Alberta College of Combined Laboratory & X-Ray Technologists, 29
ACCM - Association of Christian Churches in Manitoba, 145
ACCP - American College of Chest Physicians, 1491
ACCPA - The Alberta Community Crime Prevention Association, 30
ACCPE - Association des cadres des centres de la petite enfance, 108
ACCS - British Columbia Aboriginal Child Care Society, 229
ACCT - Academy of Canadian Cinema & Television, 3
ACCTI - Association of Canadian Corporations in Translation & Interpretation, 141
ACCUTE - Association of Canadian College & University Teachers of English, 141
ACD - Association of Canadian Distillers, 142
ACDA - Alberta Carriage Driving Association, 27
ACDE - Association of Canadian Deans of Education, 141
ACDQ - Association des chirurgiens dentistes du Québec, 109
ACDR - AIDS Committee of Durham Region, 16
ACDRO - Australian Cattle Dog Rescue of Ontario, 188
ACE - Advocacy Centre for the Elderly, 10
ACE - Association des collections d'entreprises, 109
ACE - Association of Canadian Ergonomists, 142
ACEC - Association of Consulting Engineering Companies - Canada, 145
ACEC - Alberta Council for Exceptional Children, 31
ACEC-BC - Association of Consulting Engineering Companies - British Columbia, 145
ACEC-MB - Association of Consulting Engineering Companies - Manitoba, 146
ACEC-NB - Association of Consulting Engineering Companies - New Brunswick, 146
ACEC-PEI - Association of Consulting Engineering Companies - Prince Edward Island, 146
ACEC-SK - Association of Consulting Engineering Companies - Saskatchewan, 146

ACEE - Alberta Council for Environmental Education, 31
ACEEE - American Council for an Energy-Efficient Economy, 1492
ACEF - Association coopérative d'économie familiale Rimouski-Neigette et Mitis, 98
ACEF - Association coopérative d'économie familliale de Québec, 98
ACEF - Association coopérative d'économie familliale de l'Outaouais, 98
ACEI - Association for Childhood Education International, 1508
ACELF - Association canadienne d'éducation de langue française, 90
ACEN - Academy of Canadian Executive Nurses, 4
ACER - Association for Canadian Educational Resources, 132
ACES - Air Currency Enhancement Society, 19
ACESC - Alliance of Credential Evaluation Services of Canada, 58
ACF - Alberta Curling Federation, 32
ACF - Assemblée communautaire fransaskoise, 87
ACF - Choir Alberta, 566
ACF - Alberta Cancer Foundation, 27
ACFA - Association canadienne-française de l'Alberta, 96
ACFA - Alberta Cattle Feeders' Association, 27
ACFAS - Association francophone pour le savoir, 135
ACFD - Association of Canadian Faculties of Dentistry, 142
ACFFA - Atlantic Canada Fish Farmers Association, 182
ACFI - Association of Certified Forensic Investigators of Canada, 145
ACFM - Association Carrefour Famille Montcalm, 96
ACFO - Association of Canadian Financial Officers, 142
ACFOMI - Association canadienne-française de l'Ontario, Mille-Îles, 96
ACFR - Association canadienne-française de Régina, 96
ACFSJ - L'Association communautaire francophone de St-Jean, 97
ACG - Association for Corporate Growth, Toronto Chapter, 133
ACGL - Association des conseils en gestion linguistique Inc., 109
ACHA - African Canadian Heritage Association, 12
ACHC - Covenant Health, 637
ACI - American Concrete Institute, 1491
ACI - Association of Construction Inspectors, 1511
ACID - Association of Canadian Industrial Designers, 142
ACIDO - Association of Chartered Industrial Designers of Ontario, 145
ACIPBC - Association of Complementary & Integrative Physicians of BC, 145
ACIS - Atlantic Conference of Independent Schools, 183
ACJ - A coeur joie Nouveau-Brunswick Inc., 580
ACJA - Alberta Criminal Justice Association, 32
ACJQ - Association des centres jeunesse du Québec, 108
ACJS - Association for Canadian Jewish Studies, 132
ACJT - Association canadienne des juristes-traducteurs, 93
ACLC - Army Cadet League of Canada, 83
ACLE - Association des consultants et laboratoires experts, 110
ACLRC - Alberta Civil Liberties Research Centre, 28
ACM - Association for Computing Machinery, 1508
ACMAO - Armenian Canadian Medical Association of Ontario, 82

ACMDP - Association des conseils des médecins, dentistes et pharmaciens du Québec, 109
ACMG - Association of Canadian Mountain Guides, 142
ACMLA - Association of Canadian Map Libraries & Archives, 142
ACMM - Association des cadres municipaux de Montréal, 108
ACMO - Association of Condominium Managers of Ontario, 145
ACNBA - AIDS Committee of North Bay & Area, 16
ACNL - AIDS Committee of Newfoundland & Labrador, 16
ACNMP - Alliance for Canadian New Music Projects, 56
ACNO - Arts Council of the North Okanagan, 85
ACNS - AIDS Coalition of Nova Scotia, 15
ACO - The Architectural Conservancy of Ontario, 78
ACO - AIDS Committee of Ottawa, 16
ACO - Alberta College of Optometrists, 29
ACO - Adoption Council of Ontario, 8
ACOC - Abbotsford Chamber of Commerce, 1
ACOP - Apostolic Church of Pentecost of Canada Inc., 73
ACORN - Atlantic Canadian Organic Regional Network, 183
ACOT - Alberta College of Occupational Therapists, 29
ACP - Association of Canadian Publishers, 143
ACP - Alberta College of Pharmacists, 30
ACP - Alberta College of Paramedics, 29
ACPA - Alberta Cowboy Poetry Association, 32
ACPA - Association of Canadian Port Authorities, 143
ACPA - Association of the Chemical Profession of Alberta, 162
ACPA - Air Canada Pilots Association, 19
ACPBA - Atlantic Canada Pipe Band Association, 182
ACPC - Alberta Canola Producers Commission, 27
ACPG - Association des capitaines propriétaires de Gaspésie inc, 108
ACPI - Association canadienne des professeurs d'immersion, 94
ACPI - Association of Career Professionals Internatinal, 144
ACPI - Association coopérative des pêcheurs de l'Île Itée, 98
ACPM - Association of Canadian Pension Management, 143
ACPO - Association of the Chemical Profession of Ontario, 163
ACPOC - Association of Children's Prosthetic-Orthotic Clinics, 1510
ACPOL - L'Alliance des Caisses populaires de l'Ontario limitée, 55
ACPQ - Association des cinémas parallèles du Québec, 109
ACPQ - Association des collèges privés du Québec, 109
ACPSA - Alberta Cerebral Palsy Sport Association, 27
ACQ - Association de la construction du Québec, 100
ACQ - Association du camionnage du Québec inc., 130
ACQ - Alliance des chorales du Québec, 55
ACQ - Association des camps du Québec inc., 108
ACQ - Association des cardiologues du Québec, 108
ACQL - Association for Canadian & Québec Literatures, 132
ACQS - American Council for Québec Studies, 1492
ACRA - Association of Catholic Retired Administrators, 144
ACREF - Alliance canadienne des responsables et enseignants en français (langue maternelle), 55

ACRGTQ - Association des constructeurs de routes et grands travaux du Québec, 110
ACRI - Association canadienne des relations industrielles, 94
ACRL - Association of College & Research Libraries, 1511
ACRY - Association de la Construction Richelieu Yamaska, 101
ACS - Ancaster Community Services, 68
ACS - Amalgamated Conservation Society, 66
ACS - Association for Canadian Studies, 133
ACSA - Agincourt Community Services Association, 14
ACSA - Alberta Construction Safety Association, 31
ACSA - Agincourt Community Services Association, 14
ACSA - Atlantic Convenience Store Association, 183
ACSANZ - Association for Canadian Studies in Australia & New Zealand, 1507
ACSC - Association for Canadian Studies in China, 1507
ACSC - AIDS Committee of Simcoe County, 16
ACSD - Alberta Cultural Society of the Deaf, 32
ACSDC - African Canadian Social Development Council, 12
ACSESS - Association of Canadian Search, Employment & Staffing Services, 143
ACSI - Association of Christian Schools International, 1510
ACSI - Association for Canadian Studies in Ireland, 1507
ACSIQ - Association des chefs en sécurité incendie du Québec, 108
ACSLPA - Alberta College of Speech-Language Pathologists & Audiologists, 30
ACSN - Association for Canadian Studies in the Netherlands, 1507
ACSR - Association canadienne des sciences régionales, 95
ACSSSS - Association des cadres supérieurs de la santé et des services sociaux du Québec, 108
ACSTA - Alberta Catholic School Trustees Association, 27
ACSUS - Association for Canadian Studies in the United States, 1507
ACSW - Alberta College of Social Workers, 30
ACT - AIDS Committee of Toronto, 16
ACT - Association canadienne de traductologie, 92
ACT - Association des compagnies de théâtre, 109
ACTA - Alberta Construction Trucking Association, 31
ACTA - Association of Canadian Travel Agencies, 143
ACTE - Association des accidentés cérébro-vasculaires et traumatisés crâniens de l'Estrie, 104
ACTLA - Alberta Civil Trial Lawyers' Association, 28
ACTRA - Alliance of Canadian Cinema, Television & Radio Artists, 58
ACTRA - Atlantic Canada Trail Riding Association, 182
ACTS - Alberta Conservation Tillage Society II, 31
ACUNS - Association of Canadian Universities for Northern Studies, 144
ACUP - Association of Canadian University Presses, 144
ACUUS - Associated Research Centres for the Urban Underground Space, 89
ACVA - Alberta Country Vacations Association, 32
ACVA-TCC du BSL - Association des personnes accidentées cérébro-vasculaires, aphasiques et traumatisées crânio-cérébrales du Bas-Saint-Laurent, 122
ACVRQ - Association des commerçants de véhicules récréatifs du Québec, 109
ACW - AIDS Committee of Windsor, 16

Acronym Index

ACWC - Association of Canadian Women Composers, 144
ACWR - Arts Council Windsor & Region, 85
ACWWA - Atlantic Canada Water & Wastewater Association, 182
ADA - Association des détaillants en alimentation du Québec, 110
ADA - Alberta Dance Alliance, 32
ADA - Alberta Dressage Association, 33
ADAC - Alberta Dental Association & College, 32
ADAC - Art Dealers Association of Canada Inc., 84
ADAC - Anxiety Disorders Association of Canada, 72
ADAM - Anxiety Disorders Association of Manitoba, 72
ADAO - Anxiety Disorders Association of Ontario, 72
ADAV - Animal Defence & Anti-Vivisection Society of BC, 70
ADBOT - Annapolis District Board of Trade, 71
ADC - Atlantic Dairy Council, 183
ADC - Associated Designers of Canada, 89
ADCC - The Advertising & Design Club of Canada, 10
ADCKC - Atlantic Division, CanoeKayak Canada, 183
ADCO - Association of Day Care Operators of Ontario, 146
ADCofC - Athabasca & District Chamber of Commerce, 180
ADELF - Association des distributeurs exclusifs de livres en langue française inc., 111
ADGSSSQ - Association des directeurs généraux des services de santé et des services sociaux du Québec, 111
ADHIS - Association pour le développement de la personne handicapée intellectuelle du Saguenay, 167
ADICIM - Association des diffuseurs culturels de l'Ile de Montréal, 110
ADIGECS - Association des directeurs généraux des commissions scolaires du Québec, 111
ADIQ - Association des designers industriels du Québec, 110
ADIRS - Association de la déficience intellectuelle de la région de Sorel, 101
ADISQ - Association québécoise de l'industrie du disque, du spectacle et de la vidéo, 170
ADLA - Algoma District Law Association, 53
ADLC - Animal Defence League of Canada, 70
ADMQ - Association des directeurs municipaux du Québec, 111
ADOA - Alberta Development Officers Association, 32
ADOQ - L'Association des orthopédagogues du Québec inc., 121
ADQ - Diabète Québec, 655
ADQ - Association des dermatologistes du Québec, 110
ADQ - Association des denturologistes du Québec, 110
ADQ - Association des démographes du Québec, 110
ADQDA - Association de Dards du Québec inc., 100
ADRA - Adventist Development & Relief Agency Canada, 10
ADRIC - ADR Institute of Canada, 9
ADRIQ - Association de la recherche industrielle du Québec, 102
ADS - American Dialect Society, 1492
ADSA - Alberta Debate & Speech Association, 32
ADSA - Alberta Deaf Sports Association, 32
ADTO - Association of Dental Technologists of Ontario, 146
AE - African Enterprise (Canada), 13
AEA - American Economic Association, 1492
AEA - Atlantic Episcopal Assembly, 183
AEAQ - Association des expositions agricoles du Québec, 113

AEAQ - Association des entomologistes amateurs du Québec inc., 112
AEC - Acadia Entrepreneurship Centre, 4
AECEA - Association of Early Childhood Educators of Alberta, 147
AECENL - Association of Early Childhood Educators of Newfoundland & Labrador, 147
AECEO - Association of Early Childhood Educators Ontario, 147
AECEQ - Association of Early Childhood Educators of Quebec, 147
AECQ - Association des entrepreneurs en construction du Québec, 112
AEEQ - Association des embouteilleurs d'eau du Québec, 111
AEESP - Association of Environmental Engineering & Science Professors, 1511
AEF - Alberta Equestrian Federation, 34
AEFAA - Alberta Educational Facilities Administrators Association, 33
AEFMQ - Association des Églises des frères mennonites du Québec, 111
AEFNB - Association des enseignantes et des enseignants francophones du Nouveau-Brunswick, 112
AEFO - Association des enseignantes et des enseignants franco-ontariens, 112
AEG - Association of Applied Geochemists, 139
AEGQ - Association des employées et employés du gouvernement du Québec, 112
AEIQ - Association des enseignants en infographie et en imprimerie du Québec, 112
AEL - Alberta Electrical League, 33
AELAQ - Association of English Language Publishers of Québec, 148
AEM-Canada - Association of Equipment Manufacturers - Canada, 148
AEMQ - Association de l'exploration minière du Québec, 100
AEMQ - Association des entrepreneurs en maçonnerie du Québec, 112
AEN - Alberta Environmental Network, 33
AEPC - Association des établissements privés conventionnés - santé services sociaux, 113
AÉPQ - Association d'éducation préscolaire du Québec, 99
AEPSA - Adult Educators' Provincial Specialist Association, 9
AEQ - Assemblée des évêques catholiques du Québec, 88
AERO - Association of Educational Researchers of Ontario, 147
AES - The Acadian Entomological Society, 4
AES - Audio Engineering Society, 187
AESAC - Associated Environmental Site Assessors of Canada Inc., 89
AESAL - Académie européenne des sciences, des arts et des lettres, 1485
AESES - Association of Employees Supporting Education Services, 147
AESF - National Association for Surface Finishing, 1573
AESIQ - Association des experts en sinistre indépendants du Québec inc, 113
AESS - Aerospace & Electronic Systems Society, 1485
AESTQ - Association pour l'enseignement de la science et de la technologie au Québec, 165
AETC - Association of Electromyography Technologists of Canada, 147
AETTNL - Association of Engineering Technicians & Technologists of Newfoundland & Labrador, 147
AEUM - Association des employés de l'Université de Moncton, 112
AF - Alliance Française, 57
AF & AM - Ancient, Free & Accepted Masons of Canada, 68
AF&PA - American Forest & Paper Association, 1493
AFA - Alberta Foundation for the Arts, 35
AFA - Alberta Fencing Association, 35
AFA - Atlantic Floor Covering Association, 184
AFAC - Air Force Association of Canada, 19

AFAC - Aboriginal Firefighters Association of Canada, 2
AFAM - Association des femmes d'assurance de Montréal, 114
AFB - Abbotsford Food Bank & Christmas Bureau, 1
AFB - Airdrie Food Bank, 20
AFC - Aquatic Federation of Canada, 75
AFC - Alliance Française de Calgary, 57
AFC - Alliance for Chiropractic, 57
AFCA - Alberta Floor Covering Association, 35
AFCA - Association of Filipino Canadian Accountants, 148
AFCA - Alberta Fire Chiefs Association, 35
AFCA-BC - Association of Filipino Canadian Accountants in British Columbia, 148
AFCCA - Alberta Family Child Care Association, 34
AFCOOP - Atlantic Filmmakers Cooperative, 184
AFCY - Association franco-culturelle de Yellowknife, 135
AFDICQ - Association des fabricants et détaillants de l'industrie de la cuisine du Québec, 113
AFDM - Association des francophones du delta du Mackenzie, 114
AFE - Association for Facilities Engineering, 1508
AFEAS - Association féminine d'éducation et d'action sociale, 132
AFEC - Association française d'études canadiennes, 1509
AFÉSAQ - Association des fondations d'établissements de santé du Québec, 114
AFÉSEO - Association francophone à l'éducation des services à l'enfance de l'Ontario, 135
AFFA - The Atlantic Film Festival Association, 184
AFFC - Alliance des femmes de la francophonie canadienne, 55
AFFPA - Alberta Farm Fresh Producers Association, 34
AFFS - Association des francophones de Fort Smith, 114
AFG - Association des firmes de génie-conseil - Québec, 114
AFGA - Alberta Fish & Game Association, 35
AFH - Alliance Française Halifax, 57
AFHA - Abbotsford Female Hockey Association, 1
AFHS - Alberta Family History Society, 34
AFHTO - Association of Family Health Teams of Ontario, 148
AFICC - Association des fonctionnaires issus des communautés culturelles, 114
AFIDES - Association francophone internationale des directeurs d'établissements scolaires, 1509
AFL - Alberta Federation of Labour, 34
AFLCA - Provincial Fitness Unit of Alberta, 1191
AFL-CIO - American Federation of Labor & Congress of Industrial Organizations (AFL-CIO), 1493
AFLO - Australian Football League Ontario, 188
AFM - American Federation of Musicians of the United States & Canada (AFL-CIO/CLC), 1493
AFM - Addictions Foundation of Manitoba, 8
AFM, Local 571 - Atlantic Federation of Musicians, Local 571, 184
AFMA - Alberta Farmers' Market Association, 34
AFMC - Association of Faculties of Medicine of Canada, 148
AFMNB - Association francophone des municipalités du Nouveau-Brunswick Inc., 135
AFMQ - Association des fabricants de meubles du Québec inc., 113
AFMRO - Association des familles monoparentales et recomposées de l'Outaouais, 113

AFMS - Alberta Family Mediation Society, 34
AFN - Alouette Field Naturalists, 59
AFN - Assembly of First Nations, 88
AFN - Association des francophones du Nunavut, 114
AFNOO - Association des francophones du nord-ouest de l'Ontario, 114
AFNS - Easter Seals Nova Scotia, 669
AFO - Association des fermières de l'Ontario, 114
AFO - Assemblée de la francophonie de l'Ontario, 87
AFO - Asparagus Farmers of Ontario, 87
AFP - Association for Financial Professionals, 1508
AFP - Association of Fundraising Professionals, 1511
AFP/AAC - Armed Forces Pensioners'/Annuitants' Association of Canada, 82
AFPA - Alberta Federation of Police Associations, 34
AFPA - Alberta Forest Products Association, 35
AFPA - Alberta Food Processors Association, 35
AFPA - Alberta Foster Parent Association, 35
AFPC - Association of Faculties of Pharmacy of Canada, 148
AFPC - Association for Financial Professionals - Calgary, 133
AFPH - Affected Families of Police Homicide, 11
AFPNB - Association francophone des parents du Nouveau-Brunswick, 135
AFRA - Association des familles Rioux d'Amérique inc., 113
AFRC - Alberta Federation of Rock Clubs, 35
AFS - American Foundry Society, 1493
AFS - American Fisheries Society, 1493
AFSA - Alberta Funeral Service Association, 36
AFSA - African Students Association - Univeristy of Alberta, 13
AFSA - Alberta Freestyle Ski Association, 36
AFSAS - Centre de soutien entr'Aidants, 530
AFSIC - AFS Interculture Canada, 13
AFSPC - L'association québécoise des fournisseurs de services pétroliers et gaziers du Québec, 172
AFSRB - Alberta Funeral Services Regulatory Board, 35
AFSS - Alberta Federation of Shooting Sports, 35
AFT - American Farmland Trust, 1492
AFY - Association franco-yukonnaise, 136
AGA - American Galvanizers Association, 1493
AGA - Alberta Golf Association, 37
AGBA - American Galloway Breeders Association, 66
AGBU - Armenian General Benevolent Union, 83
AGC - Associated Gospel Churches, 89
AGEC - Association for German Education in Calgary, 133
AGEQ - Association des gastro-entérologues du Québec, 114
AGESSS - Association des gestionnaires des établissements de santé et des services sociaux, 115
AGF - Alberta Gymnastics Federation, 37
AGGA - Alberta Greenhouse Growers Association, 37
AGIDD-SMQ - Association des groupes d'intervention en défense de droits en santé mentale du Québec, 116
AGIR - Association générale des insuffisants rénaux, 136
AGISQ - Association des Gestionnaires de l'information de la santé du Québec, 115
AGLLL Inc. - Alliance des gais et lesbiennes Laval-Laurentides, 56
AGLOW - Association of Great Lakes Outdoor Writers, 1512
AGLS - Association des Gais et Lesbiennes Sourds, 114

Acronym Index

AGMCA - Architectural Glass & Metal Contractors Association, 78
AGNA - Alberta Gerontological Nurses Association, 37
AGP - Association des golfeurs professionnels du Québec, 115
AGPQ - Association des garderies privées du Québec, 114
AGRBQ - Association des gestionnaires de ressources bénévoles du Québec, 115
AGS - Alberta Genealogical Society, 36
AGTQ - Association des guides touristiques de Québec, 116
AGVA - American Guild of Variety Artists (AFL-CIO), 1493
AHA - Alberta Hereford Association, 37
AHA - American Historical Association, 1494
AHA - American Humane Association, 1494
AHA - Alberta Handball Association, 37
AHAC - Armenian Holy Apostolic Church - Canadian Diocese, 83
AHAEC - Arabian Horse Association of Eastern Canada, 76
AHAM - Association of Home Appliance Manufacturers Canada Council, 149
AHAM - Association des handicapés adultes de la Mauricie, 116
AHC - Action for Healthy Communities, 6
AHCDC - Association of Hemophilia Clinic Directors of Canada, 149
AHEA - Alberta Home Education Association, 37
AHFC - Aerospace Heritage Foundation of Canada, 11
AHHA - Atlantic Halfway House Association, 184
AHIP - Association of Hearing Instrument Practitioners of Ontario, 148
AHLA - American Hotel & Lodging Association, 1494
AHM - Artists in Healthcare Manitoba, 85
AHO - Association of Holocaust Organizations, 1512
AHP - Association for Healthcare Philanthropy, 1508
AHPA - Arthritis Health Professions Association, 84
AHPA - Alberta Horseshoe Pitchers Association, 38
AHPCA - Alberta Hospice Palliative Care Association, 38
AHPRC - Atlantic Health Promotion Research Centre, 184
AHQ - Association Hôtellerie Québec, 136
AHQ - Avocats Hors Québec, 191
AHRC - Apparel Human Resources Council, 74
AHRF - Alberta Historical Resources Foundation, 37
AHS - American Hiking Society, 1494
AHS - Antigonish Highland Society, 72
AHSABC - Aboriginal Head Start Association of British Columbia, 2
AHSS - Architectural Heritage Society of Saskatchewan, 79
AHTA - Alberta Horse Trials Association, 37
AHVEI - Association des personnes handicapés visuels de l'Estrie, inc, 123
AIA - Archaeological Institute of America, 1505
AIABC - Aerospace Industry Association of British Columbia, 11
AIAC - Aerospace Industries Association of Canada, 11
AIAC - Automotive Industries Association of Canada, 189
AIAS - Abbotsford International Air Show Society, 1
AIBC - Architectural Institute of British Columbia, 79
AIC - Association of Independent Consultants, 149
AIC - Agricultural Institute of Canada, 14
AIC - Appraisal Institute of Canada, 74
AIC - Alberta Insurance Council, 38
AIC-AB - The Appraisal Institute of Canada - Alberta, 74

AIC-BC - The Appraisal Institute of Canada - British Columbia, 74
AICF - Agricultural Institute of Canada Foundation, 15
AICI Canada - Association of Image Consultants International Canada, 149
AICL - Association internationale de la critique littéraire, 1509
AIC-MB - The Appraisal Institute of Canada - Manitoba, 75
AIC-NL - The Appraisal Institute of Canada - Newfoundland & Labrador, 75
AIC-ON - The Appraisal Institute of Canada - Ontario, 75
AICP - Association of Islamic Charitable Projects, 149
AIC-PEI - The Appraisal Institute of Canada - Prince Edward Island, 75
AICQ - Association des implantés cochléaires du Québec, 116
AIC-SK - The Appraisal Institute of Canada - Saskatchewan, 75
AICW - Association of Italian Canadian Writers, 150
AIDI - Action Intégration en Déficience Intellectuelle, 6
AIDP - Association internationale de droit pénal, 1509
AIDQ - Association des intervenants en dépendance du Québec, 117
AIEP - Association internationale des études patristiques, 1509
AIEQ - Association de l'industrie électrique du Québec, 100
AIESTC - Alliance internationale des employé(e)s de scène, de théâtre et de cinéma, 57
AIHA - American Industrial Hygiene Association, 1494
AIIC Canada - Association canadienne des interprètes de conférence, 90
AIIM Canada - Association for Image & Information Management International - 1st Canadian Chapter, 133
AIIQ - Association des Illustrateurs et Illustratrices du Québec, 116
AIISSQ - Association des intervenantes et des intervenants en soins spirituels du Québec, 117
AILA - American Immigration Lawyers Association - Canadian Chapter, 66
AILIA - Association d'informations en logements et immeubles adaptés, 99
AILIA - Language Industry Association, 899
AIM - Africa Inland Mission International (Canada), 12
AIM - AIM Global, 1486
AIMF - Association internationale des maires francophones - Bureau à Québec, 136
AIMQ - Association des ingénieurs municipaux du Québec, 116
AIMS - Association of Internet Marketing & Sales, 149
AIMS - Atlantic Institute for Market Studies, 184
AINA - Arctic Institute of North America, 81
AIPA - Alberta Irrigation Projects Association, 38
AIPCN - Association internationale permanente des congrès de navigation, 1510
AIPSA - Association des ingénieurs-professeurs des sciences appliquées, 116
AIPSO - Association of International Physicians & Surgeons of Ontario, 149
AIQ - Association d'isolation du Québec, 99
AIS - Association pour l'intégration sociale (Rouyn-Noranda) inc., 166
AISCA - Association of Independent Schools & Colleges in Alberta, 149
AISG - Artists in Stained Glass, 85
AISI - American Iron & Steel Institute, 1494
AISLF - Association internationale des sociologues de langue française, 1510
AISO - Association pour l'intégration sociale d'Ottawa, 166

AISQ - Association pour l'intégration sociale (Région de Québec), 166
AITQ - Association des intervenants en toxicomanie du Québec inc., 117
AJAC - Automobile Journalists Association of Canada, 189
AJAVA - Association des juristes pour l'avancement de la vie artistique, 118
AJBM - Association du jeune barreau de Montréal, 130
AJBQ - Association des jeunes Barreaux du Québec, 117
AJBQ - Association des jeunes bègues de Québec, 117
AJDS - Association of Jewish Day Schools, 150
AJEFM - Association des juristes d'expression française du Manitoba inc., 118
AJEFNB - Association des juristes d'expression française du Nouveau-Brunswick, 118
AJEFO - Association des juristes d'expression française de l'Ontario, 117
AJEFS - Association des juristes d'expression française de la Saskatchewan, 118
AJF - Association jeunesse fransaskoise, 137
AJIQ - Association des journalistes indépendants du Québec, 117
AJIS - Association Jeannoise pour l'intégration sociale inc., 136
AJL - Montréal - Association of Jewish Libraries (Montréal), 150
AJL - Toronto - Association of Jewish Libraries (Toronto), 150
AJRQ - Association des jeunes ruraux du Québec, 117
AJS - Association of Jewish Seniors, 150
AJS - Association for Jewish Studies - USA, 1508
AKBA - Aurora King Baseball Association, 188
AKBLG - Association of Kootenay & Boundary Local Governments, 150
AKCSE - Association of Korean Canadian Scientists & Engineers, 150
AKFC - Aga Khan Foundation Canada, 14
AKTA - Algoma Kinniwabi Travel Association, 53
ALA - African Literature Association, 1486
ALA - American Lung Association, 1495
ALA - American Library Association, 1494
ALA - Alberta Luge Association, 39
ALA - Alberta Lacrosse Association, 38
ALC - Adult Literacy Council of Greater Fort Erie, 9
ALC - The Arts & Letters Club, 85
ALCIT - Association of Legal Court Interpreters & Translators, 150
ALCOA - Active Living Coalition for Older Adults, 7
ALDA - Adult Learning Development Association, 9
ALDI - Association de Laval pour la déficience intellectuelle, 102
ALECC - Association for Literature, Environment, & Culture in Canada, 133
ALF - Alberta Law Foundation, 39
ALGI - Association des lesbiennes et des gais sur Internet, 118
ALIS/NITA - Association des locataires de l'Ile-des-Soeurs, 118
ALLPPVQ - Alliance des professionels et des professionnelles de la Ville de Québec, 56
ALMS - Alberta Lake Management Society, 39
ALPA - Air Line Pilots Association, International - Canada, 19
ALPA - Association longueuilloise des photographes amateurs, 137
ALPACA - Alpaca Livestock Producers & Cooperators Association, 59
ALPHA - Association of Local Public Health Agencies, 150
ALPHPL - Association de loisirs pour personnes handicapées psychiques de Laval, 102
ALQ - Association des libraires du Québec, 118
ALRI - Alberta Law Reform Institute, 39
ALS - ALS Society of Canada, 60

ALSA - Alberta Land Surveyors' Association, 39
ALSO - Assisted Living Southwestern Ontario, 89
ALST - Aboriginal Legal Services of Toronto, 2
ALTA - Alberta Library Trustees Association, 39
AMA - Association for Manitoba Archives, 133
AMA - Alberta Motor Association, 40
AMA - Alberta Medical Association, 40
AMA - American Management Association, 1495
AMA - American Marketing Association, 1495
AMAC - The Association of Maritime Arbitrators of Canada, 151
AMAF - Associated Manitoba Arts Festivals, Inc., 89
AMANB - Association of Municipal Administrators of New Brunswick, 152
AMANS - Association of Municipal Administrators, Nova Scotia, 152
AMAPCEO - Association of Management, Administrative & Professional Crown Employees of Ontario, 151
AMBA - Association of MBAs in Canada, 151
AMBAQ - Association des MBA du Québec, 119
AMBP - Association of Manitoba Book Publishers, 151
AMBQ - Association des médecins biochimistes du Québec, 119
AMC - Agricultural Manufacturers of Canada, 15
AMC - Association of Mature Canadians, 151
AMCA - Alberta Municipal Clerks Association, 40
AMCEL - Association des médecins cliniciens enseignants de Laval, 119
AMCEM - Association des médecins cliniciens enseignants de Montréal, 119
AMCEQ - Association des maisons de commerce extérieur du Québec, 118
AMCM - Antique Motorcycle Club of Manitoba Inc., 72
AMCO - Airport Management Council of Ontario, 20
AMCO - Association of Millwrighting Contractors of Ontario Inc., 152
AMCQ - Association des maîtres couvreurs du Québec, 118
AMCTO - Association of Municipal Managers, Clerks & Treasurers of Ontario, 152
AMDEQ - Association des marchands dépanneurs et épiciers du Québec, 119
AMDES - Association montréalaise des directions d'établissement scolaire, 137
AMDI - Association de Montréal pour la déficience intellectuelle, 102
AMDT - Moroccan Association of Toronto, 974
AMEA - Algoma Manitoulin Environmental Awareness, 53
AMEBC - Association for Mineral Exploration British Columbia, 134
AMEC - Asociación mexicana de estudios sobre Canadá, 1506
AMECQ - Association des médias écrits communautaires du Québec, 120
AMEIPH - Association multi-ethnique pour l'intégration des personnes handicapées, 137
AMEN - Antisemitism Must End Now, 72
AMF - Autorité des marchés financiers, 190
AMFQ - Association de médiation familiale du Québec, 102
AMGQ - Association des motocyclistes gais du Québec, 120
AMHOQ - Association des médecins hématologistes-oncologistes du Québec, 119
AMHSSE - Association of Manitoba Hydro Staff & Supervisory Employees, 151
AMI - Accessible Media Inc., 5
AMIA - Alberta Music Industry Association, 41
AMIQ - Apparel Quebec, 74
AMJ - Youth Media Alliance, 1476
AML - Association for Media Literacy, 134
AMM - Association of Manitoba Museums, 151
AMM - Association of Manitoba Municipalities, 151

Acronym Index

AMMAQ - Association des marchands de machines aratoires de la province de Québec, 119
AMMI Canada - Association of Medical Microbiology & Infectious Disease Canada, 151
AMMIQ - Association des médecins microbiologistes-infectiologues du Québec, 119
AMMSA - Aboriginal Multi-Media Society, 2
AMNB - Association Museums New Brunswick, 138
AMNL - Association of Midwives of Newfoundland & Labrador, 152
AMO - Association of Municipalities of Ontario, 152
AMOM - Association des médecins omnipraticiens de Montréal, 119
AMOQ - Association des médecins ophtalmologistes du Québec, 120
AMPA - Alberta Magazine Publishers Association, 39
AMPCO - Association of Major Power Consumers in Ontario, 151
AMPIA - Alberta Media Production Industries Association, 39
AMPPE - Association for Mountain Parks Protection & Enjoyment, 134
AMPQ - Association des médecins-psychiatres du Québec, 120
AMQ - Association médicale du Québec, 137
AMQ - Association des microbiologistes du Québec, 120
AMQ - Association minière du Québec, 137
AMQ - Académie de musique du Québec, 3
AMQ - Association mathématique du Québec, 137
AMQ - Association des malentendants Québécois, 118
AMQ - Association maritime du Québec, 137
AMQ - Alliance des massothérapeutes du Québec, 56
AMREF Canada - African Medical & Research Foundation Canada, 13
AMRQ - Association des médecins rhumatologues du Québec, 120
AMS - American Musicological Society, 1495
AMS - Association montérégienne de la surdité inc., 137
AMS - Associated Medical Services Inc., 89
AMS - Atlantic Mission Society, 184
AMSMNQ - Association des médecins spécialistes en médecine nucléaire du Québec, 120
AMSSA - Affiliation of Multicultural Societies & Service Agencies of BC, 11
AMSSCQ - Association des médecins spécialistes en santé communautaire du Québec, 120
AMTA - Alberta Motor Transport Association, 40
AMVPQ - Association des médecins vétérinaires praticiens du Québec, 120
ANAC - Acoustic Neuroma Association of Canada, 5
ANAC - Animal Nutrition Association of Canada, 70
ANAVETS - Army, Navy & Air Force Veterans in Canada, 83
ANB - Athletics New Brunswick, 181
ANBLPN - Association of New Brunswick Licensed Practical Nurses, 153
ANBLS - Association of New Brunswick Land Surveyors, 153
ANBMT - Association of New Brunswick Massage Therapists, 154
ANBPE - Association of New Brunswick Professional Educators, 154
ANC - Association for New Canadians, 134
ANCAI - Association nationale des camionneurs artisans inc., 138
ANCQ - Association de neurochirurgie du Québec, 103

ANDPSA - Association nationale des distributeurs aux petites surfaces alimentaires, 138
ANDPVA - Association for Native Development in the Performing & Visual Arts, 134
ANEL - Association nationale des éditeurs de livres, 138
ANFC - Atikokan Native Friendship Centre, 181
ANFCA - Alberta Native Friendship Centres Association, 41
ANFQ - L'Association de la Neurofibromatose du Québec, 101
ANH - Association of Neighbourhood Houses BC, 153
ANLA - Association of Newfoundland & Labrador Archives, 154
ANNS - Association of Nigerians in Nova Scotia, 154
ANO - Association des neurotraumatisés de l'Outaouais, 121
ANPC - Alberta Native Plant Council, 41
ANPQ - Association des naturopathes professionnels du Québec, 120
ANQ - Association des neurologues du Québec, 120
ANS - Autism Nova Scotia, 188
ANS - American Numismatic Society, 1496
ANSLS - Association of Nova Scotia Land Surveyors, 154
ANSM - Association of Nova Scotia Museums, 154
ANSMA - African Nova Scotian Music Association, 13
ANTSLPA - Association of Northwest Territories Speech Language Pathologists & Audiologists, 154
ANZA - Australia-New Zealand Association, 188
AOA - Alpine Ontario Alpin, 59
AOA - Alberta Orienteering Association, 41
AOA - American Optometric Association, 1496
AOE - Arts Ottawa East-Est, 86
AOGQ - Association des obstétriciens et gynécologues du Québec, 121
AOHC - Association of Ontario Health Centres, 154
AOHNA - Alberta Occupational Health Nurses Association, 41
AOHNNL - Association of Occupational Health Nurses of Newfoundland & Labrador, 154
AOJM - Association des orchestres de jeunes de la Montérégie, 121
AOJQ - Association des orchestres de jeunes du Québec inc., 121
AOLS - Association of Ontario Land Surveyors, 155
AOM - Association of Ontario Midwives, 155
AOM - Academy of Management, 1485
AOPA - Alberta Organic Producers Association, 41
AOPQ - Association des orthésistes et prothésistes du Québec, 121
AOQ - Association des optométristes du Québec, 121
AORS - Association of Ontario Road Supervisors, 155
AOS - American Ornithological Society, 1496
AOS - Association of Ontario Snowboarders, 155
AOSF - Association ontarienne des Sourd(e)s francophones, 164
APA - Automobile Protection Association, 189
APA - Association du Patrimoine d'Aylmer, 131
APA - Society for Classical Studies, 1589
APA - American Psychological Association, 1497
APA - American Planning Association, 1496
APA - Academic Pediatric Association, 1485
APA - Alberta Pinzgauer Association, 42
APA - Alberta Psychiatric Association, 43
APAA - Association of Professional Archaeologists, 156
APAA - Africans in Partnership Against AIDS, 13

APABC - Adlerian Psychology Association of British Columbia, 8
APADY - Association des parents ayant droit de Yellowknife, 121
APAGA - Atlantic Provinces Art Gallery Association, 184
APALA - Atlantic Provinces Association of Landscape Architects, 185
APAMM-RS - Association des parents et amis de la personne atteinte de maladie mentale Rive-Sud, 122
APAPUM - Association du personnel administratif et professionnel de l'Université de Moncton, 131
APAQ - Association de parents pour l'adoption québécoise, 103
APARL - Association pour aînés résidant à Laval, 165
APASQ - Association des professionnels des arts de la scène du Québec, 125
APATA - Atlantic Provinces Athletic Therapists Association, 185
APATC - The Association of Professional Accounting & Tax Consultants Inc., 156
APB - Association of Professional Biology, 156
APBOT - Ajax-Pickering Board of Trade, 20
APBQ - Association des Aviateurs et Pilotes de Brousse du Québec, 106
APBU - Association of Professors of Bishop's University, 160
APC - Associaça Portuguesa Do Canadà, 89
APC - Association des professionnels du chauffage, 125
APCAS - Association pour la prévention de la contamination de l'air et du sol, 166
APCC - Association of Professional Computer Consultants - Canada, 157
APCEL - Asia-Pacific Centre for Environmental Law, 1506
APCHQ - Association provinciale des constructeurs d'habitations du Québec inc., 168
APCM - Association des professionnels de la chanson et de la musique, 125
APCMQ - Association des procureurs de cours municipales du Québec, 124
APCP - Association des propriétaires canins de Prévost, 126
APCQ - Association des parents catholiques du Québec, 121
APCQ - Association de paralysie cérébrale du Québec, 103
APCQ - Association des propriétaires de cinémas du Québec, 126
APCUG - Association of Personal Computer Users Groups, 1512
APDEQ - Association des professionnels en développement économique du Québec, 126
APDIQ - Association professionnelle des designers d'intérieur du Québec, 167
APEBC - Association of Professional Economists of British Columbia, 157
APEC - Atlantic Provinces Economic Council, 185
APEC - Association professionnelle des enseignantes et enseignants en commerce, 167
APECQ - Association patronale des entreprises en construction du Québec, 165
APEGA - Association of Professional Engineers & Geoscientists of Alberta, 157
APEGM - Association of Professional Engineers & Geoscientists of Manitoba, 158
APEGNB - Association of Professional Engineers & Geoscientists of New Brunswick, 158
APEGS - Association of Professional Engineers & Geoscientists of Saskatchewan, 158
APEIL - Association of Prince Edward Island Libraries, 156
APEILS - Association of Prince Edward Island Land Surveyors, 156
APELL - Association professionnelle des entreprises en logiciels libres, 167

APEP - Association des professeurs de l'École Polytechnique de Montréal, 124
APEPEI - Association of Professional Engineers of Prince Edward Island, 159
APEQ - Association des professionnels en exposition du Québec, 126
APEQ - Association provinciale des enseignantes et enseignants du Québec, 168
APERSSS - APER Santé et services sociaux, 73
APES - Association des pharmaciens des établissements de santé du Québec, 123
APES - Association professionnelle des écrivains de la Sagamie-Côte-Nord, 167
APEX - Association of Professional Executives of the Public Service of Canada, 159
APEY - Association of Professional Engineers of Yukon, 159
APF - Association des parents fransaskois, 122
APF - Assemblée parlementaire de la Francophonie (Section canadienne), 88
APF - Assemblée parlementaire de la Francophonie, 88
APF - The Avian Preservation Foundation, 190
APF - Association de la presse francophone, 101
APFC - Asia Pacific Foundation of Canada, 86
APFF - Association de planification fiscale et financière, 103
APFUCC - Association des professeurs de français des universités et collèges canadiens, 124
APGA - American Public Gardens Association, 1497
APGM - Association des pères gais de Montréal inc., 122
APGNS - Association of Professional Geoscientists of Nova Scotia, 159
APGO - Association of Professional Geoscientists of Ontario, 159
APGP - Association des professionnels en gestion philanthropique, 126
APGQ - Association pétrolière et gazière du Québec, 165
APHA - Alberta Public Health Association, 43
APHAA - Alberta Public Housing Administrators' Association, 43
APHC - Association des personnes handicapées de Charlevoix inc., 122
ApHCC - Appaloosa Horse Club of Canada, 73
APHIS - Alberta Professional Home Inspectors Society, 43
APHPSSJ - Association des personnes handicapées physiques et sensorielles du secteur Joliette, 123
APHRSM - Association des parents et des handicapés de la Rive-Sud métropolitaine, 122
APHRSO - Association des personnes handicapées de la Rive-Sud Ouest, 122
APHVR - Association des personnes handicapées de la Vallée du Richelieu, 123
API - Atlantic Planners Institute, 184
APIA - Association des personnes intéressées à l'aphasie et à l'accident vasculaire cérébral, 123
APIBQ - Association des physiciens et ingénieurs biomédicaux du Québec, 123
APICO - Association pour l'intégration communautaire de l'Outaouais, 165
APICS - Association for Operations Management, 134
APIGQ - Association professionnelle des ingénieurs du gouvernement du Québec (ind.), 167
APJTM - Association de Parents de Jumeaux et de Triplés de la région de Montréal, 103
APLA - Atlantic Provinces Library Association, 185
APLA - Atlantic Provinces Linguistic Association, 185
APLIC - Association of Parliamentary Libraries in Canada, 155
APLNB - Association of Professional Librarians of New Brunswick, 159

Acronym Index

APM - Association des professionnels de la communication et du marketing, 125
APM - Association des Pompiers de Montréal inc., 124
APMA - Atlantic Publishers Marketing Association, 186
APMA - Automotive Parts Manufacturers' Association, 190
APMAQ - Amis et propriétaires de maisons anciennes du Québec, 68
APMLQ - Association des propriétaires de machinerie lourde du Québec inc., 126
APMO - Atlantic Pest Management Association, 184
APMQ - Association des producteurs maraîchers du Québec, 124
APN - Alberta Playwrights' Network, 42
APNA - Atlantic Provinces Numismatic Association, 185
APNL - Association of Psychology Newfoundland & Labrador, 160
APNS - Association of Psychologists of Nova Scotia, 160
APOM - Association des professionnels à l'outillage municipal, 125
APOP - Association pour les applications pédagogiques de l'ordinateur au postsecondaire, 167
APOS - Alberta Professional Outfitters Society, 43
APPAVL - Alliance du personnel professionel et administratif de Ville de Laval, 56
APPC - Association des psychothérapeutes pastoraux du Canada, 126
APPFMUS - Association des professeures et professeurs de la Faculté de médecine de l'Université de Sherbrooke, 124
APPI - Alberta Professional Planners Institute, 43
APPIPF - Association Provinciale des Professeurs d'Immersion et du Programme Francophone, 168
APPLE - A Post Psychiatric Leisure Experience, 1167
APPM - Alliance des professeures et professeurs de Montréal, 56
APPQ - Association des pneumologues de la province de Québec, 123
APPQ - Association des policières et policiers provinciaux du Québec, 123
APPrO - Association of Power Producers of Ontario, 156
APPSQ - Association professionnelle des pharmaciens salariés du Québec, 167
APQ - Association des propriétaires du Québec inc., 126
APQ - Association des pathologistes du Québec, 122
APQ - Association des physiatres du Québec, 123
APQ - Association des Physiques Québécois, 123
APQI - Association des Perfusionnistes du Québec Inc., 122
APR - Association of Postconsumer Plastic Recyclers, 1513
APRA - Alberta Pioneer Railway Association, 42
APRA - Alberta Plastics Recycling Association, 42
APS SRC - Association des professionnels et superviseurs de Radio-Canada, 126
APSA - American Political Science Association, 1496
APSA - Administrative & Professional Staff Association, 8
APSAM - Association paritaire pour la santé et la sécurité du travail - Secteur Affaires municipales, 165
APSDS - Association pour la promotion des services documentaires scolaires, 166
APSGO - Association of Parent Support Groups in Ontario Inc., 155
APSS - AIDS Programs South Saskatchewan, 17

APST - Association des professionnels en santé du travail, 126
APT - Association for Preservation Technology International, 1508
APTA - Atlantic Provinces Trucking Association, 185
APTDQ - Association professionnelle des techniciennes et techniciens en documentation du Québec, 167
APTLA - Atlantic Provinces Trial Lawyers Association, 185
APTPUO - Association des professeur(e)s à temps partiel de l'Université d'Ottawa, 124
APTS - Alliance du personnel professionnel et technique de la santé et des services sociaux, 56
APU - Alberta Powerlifting Union, 42
APUO - Association des professeurs de l'université d'Ottawa, 125
APWA - American Public Works Association, 1497
AQA - Aviron Québec, 191
AQAA - Association québécoise des allergies alimentaires, 171
AQAAD - Association québécoise des avocats et avocates de la défense, 171
AQAADI - Association québécoise des avocats et avocates en droit de l'immigration, 171
AQAD - Association québécoise des auteurs dramatiques, 171
AQAIRS - Association québécoise des arénas et des installations récréatives et sportives, 171
AQCC - Association québécoise des critiques de cinéma, 172
AQCKV - Association québécoise de canoë-kayak de vitesse, 169
AQCM - Association québécoise du chauffage au mazout, 175
AQCMER - Association québécoise de commercialisation de poissons et de fruits de mer, 169
AQCPE - L'Association québécoise des centres de la petite enfance, 172
AQCS - Association québécoise des cadres scolaires, 171
AQDA - Association Québécoise des dépanneurs en alimentation, 172
AQDC - Association québécoise de doit comparé, 169
AQDC - Association québécoise de doit constitutionel, 169
AQDFL - Association professionnelle de la distribution de fruits et légumes, 170
AQDR - Association québécoise de défense des droits des personnes retraitées et préretraitées, 169
AQEFLE - Association québécoise des écoles de français langue étrangère, 172
AQEFLS - Association québécoise des enseignants de français langue seconde, 172
AQEI - Association québécoise pour l'évaluation d'impacts, 176
AQEM - Association québécoise des éditeurs de magazines, 172
AQEP - Association québécoise des enseignantes et des enseignants du primaire, 172
AQEPA - Association du Québec pour enfants avec problèmes auditifs, 131
AQÉSAP - Association québécoise des éducatrices et éducateurs spécialisés en arts plastiques, 172
AQETA - Association québécoise des troubles d'apprentissage, 175
AQF - Association québécoise de la fibromyalgie, 170
AQG - Association québécoise de gérontologie, 169
AQGP - Association québécoise de la gestion parasitaire, 170
AQHSST - Association québécoise pour l'hygiène, la santé et la sécurité du travail, 176

AQI - Anglophones for Québec Independence, 70
AQICE - L'Association du Québec de l'Institut canadien des évaluateurs, 131
AQIII - Association québécoise des informaticiennes et informaticiens indépendants, 173
AQIIRC - Association québécoise des infirmières et intervenants en recherche clinique, 173
AQINAC - Association québécoise des industries de nutrition animale et céréalière, 173
AQIP - Association québécoise de l'industrie de la pêche, 170
AQIP - Association québécoise des interprètes du patrimoine, 173
AQIP - Association québécoise de l'industrie de la peinture, 170
AQISEP - Association québécoise d'information scolaire et professionnelle, 168
AQIS-IQDI - Association du Québec pour l'intégration sociale / Institut québécois de la déficience intellectuelle, 131
AQJD - Association québécoise des joueurs de dames, 173
AQJEHV - Association québécoise de joueurs d'échechs handicapeés visuels, 169
AQL - Association Québécoise du Lymphoedème, 176
AQLF - Association Québécoise des Loisirs Folkloriques, 173
AQLM - Association québécoise du loisir municipal, 175
AQLPA - Association québécoise de lutte contre la pollution atmosphérique, 170
AQLPH - Association québécoise pour le loisir des personnes handicapées, 176
AQM - Association québécoise des marionnettistes, 173
AQMAT - Association québécoise de la quincaillerie et des matériaux de construction, 170
AQME - Association québécoise pour la maîtrise de l'énergie, 176
AQOA - Association québécoise des orthophonistes et des audiologistes, 173
AQOCI - Association québécoise des organismes de coopération internationale, 173
AQP - Association québécoise des phytothérapeutes, 174
AQPC - Association québécoise de pédagogie collégiale, 170
AQPDE - Association québécoise du personnel de direction des écoles, 176
AQPEHV - Association québécoise des parents d'enfants handicapés visuels, 173
AQPER - Association québécoise de la production d'énergie renouvelable, 170
AQPF - Association québécoise des professeurs de français, 174
AQPM - Association québécoise de la production médiatique, 170
AQPP - Association québécoise des pharmaciens propriétaires, 174
AQPPT - Association québécoise des personnes de petite taille, 174
AQPS - Association québécoise de prévention du suicide, 171
AQPTSC - Association québécoise de promotion du tourisme socioculturel, 171
AQPV - Association québécoise Plaidoyer-Victimes, 176
AQR - Association québécoise de racquetball, 171
AQS - Association Québec Snowboard, 168
AQSA - Association of Quantity Surveyors of Alberta, 160
AQSL - Association québécoise des salons du livre, 174
AQSMN - Association Québécoise pour la Santé Mentale des Nourrisson, 176
AQSPC - Association québécoise de sports pour paralytiques cérébraux, 171

AQT - Association québécoise des technologies, 174
AQTA - Association québécoise du transport aérien, 176
AQTC - Association québécoise des traumatisés craniens, 175
AQTC - Association québécoise des traumatisés crâniens, 175
AQTIS - Alliance québécoise des techniciens de l'image et du son, 58
AQTr - Association québécoise des transports, 175
AQU - Association québécoise d'urbanisme, 168
AQUOPS - Association québécoise des utilisateurs de l'ordinateur au primaire-secondaire, 175
AQVL - Association québécoise de Vol Libre, 171
ARA - Alberta Rowing Association, 45
ARA - Alberta Racquetball Association, 43
ARAAC - Automotive Recyclers Association of Atlantic Canada, 190
ARAS - Alberta Reappraising AIDS Society, 43
ARBC - Association of Regular Baptist Churches (Canada), 161
ARBI - Association for the Rehabilitation of the Brain Injured, 135
ARC - Automotive Recyclers of Canada, 190
ARC - Association pour la recherche au collégial, 166
ARC - Alberta Research Council Inc., 44
ARCA - Alberta Roofing Contractors Association, 44
ARCAC - Annapolis Region Community Arts Council, 71
ARCC - Alfa Romeo Club of Canada, 53
ARCf - Association régionale de la communauté francophone de Saint-Jean inc., 177
ARCH - HIV/AIDS Resources and Community Health, 817
ARCHA - Alberta Reined Cow Horse Association, 44
ARCQ - Association des radiodiffuseurs communautaires du Québec, 127
AREA - Alberta Real Estate Association, 43
ARECA - Agricultural Research & Extension Council of Alberta, 15
ARFLL - Association régionale de football Laurentides Lanaudière, 177
ARHCA - Alberta Roadbuilders & Heavy Construction Association, 44
ARIDNB - Association of Registered Interior Designers of New Brunswick, 161
ARIDO - Association of Registered Interior Designers of Ontario, 161
ARJA - Alberta Restorative Justice Association, 44
ARL - Association of Research Libraries, 1513
ARLIS/NA - Art Libraries Society of North America, 1506
ARM - Automotive Recyclers Association of Manitoba, 190
ARM - Programme Action Réfugiés Montréal, 1187
ARMCA - Alberta Ready Mixed Concrete Association, 43
ARMTA - Alberta Registered Music Teachers' Association, 44
ARNPEI - Association of Registered Nurses of Prince Edward Island, 161
AROQ - Association des radio-oncologues du Québec, 127
ARPA - Alberta Recreation & Parks Association, 44
ARPAC - Association des recyclers de pièces d'autos et de camions, 127
ARPFNB - Association of Registered Professional Foresters of New Brunswick, 161
ARPTC - Association renaissance des personnes traumatisées crâniennes du Saguenay-Lac-Saint-Jean, 178

Acronym Index

ARQ - Association des restaurateurs du Québec, 127
ARR - Adoption Roots & Rights, 9
ARRQ - Association des réalisateurs et réalisatrices du Québec, 127
ARRTQ - Association des réalisateurs et réalisatrices de Télé-Québec, 127
ARS - American Rhododendron Society, 1497
ARS Canada - Armenian Relief Society of Canada, Inc., 83
ARSM - Association de la Rivière Ste-Marguerite Inc., 102
ARTA - Association of Retail Travel Agents, 1513
ARUCC - Association of Registrars of the Universities & Colleges of Canada, 161
ASA - Alberta Snowmobile Association, 47
ASA - Alberta Soccer Association, 47
ASA - Autism Society Alberta, 188
ASA - Alberta Simmental Association, 46
ASA - Archives Society of Alberta, 80
ASA - American Sociological Association, 1503
ASA - American Studies Association, 1503
ASA - Archaeological Society of Alberta, 76
ASA - Ability Society of Alberta, 2
ASA - Alberta Society of Artists, 47
ASA - Alberta Sailing Association, 45
ASA - Alberta Snowboard Association, 47
ASAA - Alberta Schools' Athletic Association, 46
ASAAP - Alliance for South Asian AIDS Prevention, 57
ASAC - Administrative Sciences Association of Canada, 8
ASAC - African Students Association of Concordia, 13
ASAE - American Society of Association Executives, 1499
ASAM - Association des sports pour aveugles de Montréal, 128
ASAP - Active Support Against Poverty, 7
ASAPS - American Society for Aesthetic Plastic Surgery, 1497
ASAQ - Association sportive des aveugles du Québec inc., 178
ASBA - Alberta School Boards Association, 45
ASBA - Alberta Sheep Breeders Association, 46
ASBA - Atlantic Standardbred Breeders Association, 186
ASBC - Archaeological Society of British Columbia, 76
ASBHQ - L'Association de spina-bifida et d'hydrocéphalie du Québec, 104
ASBMR - American Society for Bone & Mineral Research, 1497
ASBOA - Association of School Business Officials of Alberta, 161
ASC - Alzheimer Society Canada, 61
ASC - Anthroposophical Society in Canada, 72
ASC - Asthma Society of Canada, 179
ASC - Advertising Standards Canada, 10
ASC - Alberta Securities Commission, 46
ASCA - Alberta School Councils' Association, 45
ASCCS - Association sportive et communautaire du Centre-Sud, 178
ASCHA - Alberta Senior Citizens' Housing Association, 46
ASCPEQ - Association des spécialistes en chirurgie plastique et esthétique du Québec, 128
ASCQ - Association des syndicats de copropriété du Québec, 129
ASCSRA - Alberta Senior Citizens Sport & Recreation Association, 46
ASDE - Association du syndrome de Down de L'Estrie, 131
ASDÉQ - Association des économistes québécois, 111
ASDI - Association de Sherbrooke pour la déficience intellectuelle, 104
ASDR - Alzheimer Society of Durham Region, 62

ASE - Associated Senior Executives of Canada Ltd., 89
ASE - Association des Sourds de l'Estrie Inc., 128
ASE - American Society of Echocardiography, 1499
ASEEES - Association for Slavic, East European, & Eurasian Studies, 1509
ASEH - American Society for Environmental History, 1498
ASEPS - Association syndicale des employées de production et de service, 178
ASEQ - Association pour la santé environnementale du Québec, 166
ASET - Association of Science & Engineering Technology Professionals of Alberta, 162
ASF - Atlantic Salmon Federation, 186
ASFC - Avocats sans frontières Canada, 191
ASFETM - Association sectorielle: Fabrication d'équipement de transport et de machines, 178
ASFP - Association of Saskatchewan Forestry Professionals, 161
ASFQ - Association forestières du sud du Québec, 135
ASGQ - Association des surintendants de golf du Québec, 129
ASH - Action on Smoking & Health, 6
ASHA AB - American Saddlebred Horse Association of Alberta, 66
ASHA of BC - American Saddlebred Horse Association of British Columbia, 66
ASHAC - American Saddlebred Horse Association of Canada, 66
ASHE - Association of Saskatchewan Home Economists, 161
ASHFM - Alberta Sports Hall of Fame & Museum, 48
ASHRAE - American Society of Heating, Refrigerating & Air Conditioning Engineers, 1499
ASI - The Association for the Soldiers of Israel, 135
ASIL - American Society of International Law, 1500
ASIQ - Association de la sécurité de l'information du Québec, 102
ASIS&T - American Society for Information Science & Technology, 1498
ASJ - AIDS Saint John, 17
ASJNC - Alberta Ski Jumping & Nordic Combined, 46
ASL - Armateurs du Saint-Laurent, 82
ASLC - Alberta School Learning Commons Council, 45
ASLH - American Society for Legal History, 1498
ASLIA - Association of Sign Language Interpreters of Alberta, 162
ASLM - Alzheimer Society London & Middlesex, 61
ASME - American Society of Mechanical Engineers, 1500
ASMR - American Society of Mining & Reclamation, 1501
ASN - Association for the Study of Nationalities, 135
ASNL - Autism Society Newfoundland & Labrador, 189
ASNR - American Society of Neuroradiology, 1501
ASO - Alzheimer Society of Oxford, 64
ASOC - Antarctic & Southern Ocean Coalition, 1505
ASOS - Alzheimer Society of Saskatchewan Inc., 64
ASPA - Alberta Sport Parachuting Association, 48
ASPA - Administrative & Supervisory Personnel Association, 8
ASPB - Alberta Society of Professional Biologists, 47
ASPB - American Society of Plant Biologists, 1502

ASPE - American Society of Plumbing Engineers, 1502
ASPECT - Association of Service Providers for Employability & Career Training, 162
ASPEN - American Society for Parenteral & Enteral Nutrition, 1498
ASPHO - American Society of Pediatric Hematology / Oncology, 1502
ASPKLNH - Alzheimer Society Peterborough, Kawartha Lakes, Northumberland, & Haliburton, 65
ASPMQ - Association des spécialistes du pneus et Mécanique du Québec, 128
ASPQ - Association pour la santé publique du Québec, 166
ASPRS - Association Sclérose en Plaques Rive-Sud, 178
ASPS - American Society of Plastic Surgeons, 1502
ASQ - Association des sexologues du Québec, 128
ASQ - American Society for Quality, 1498
ASQ - Auto Sport Québec, 189
ASQ - Amicale des Sommeliers du Québec, 67
ASR - Association of Saskatchewan Realtors, 161
ASR - Alberta Society of Radiologists, 47
ASR - Association for Science & Reason, 134
ASRA - Alberta Shorthand Reporters Association, 46
ASRA - American Society of Regional Anesthesia & Pain Medicine, 1502
ASRAB - Alberta Sports & Recreation Association for the Blind, 48
ASRL - Alberta Sulphur Research Ltd., 48
ASRSQ - Association des services de réhabilitation sociale du Québec inc., 128
ASS - Alberta Speleological Society, 48
ASSA - Alberta Summer Swimming Association, 48
ASSE - American Society of Safety Engineers, 1502
ASSIFQ-ASSPPQ - Association de la santé et de la sécurité des pâtes et papiers et des industries de la forêt du Québec, 102
ASSMT - Alberta Society of Surveying & Mapping Technologies, 48
ASSOM - Association de soccer du Sud-Ouest de Montréal, 104
ASSQ - Association sportive des sourds du Québec inc., 178
ASSQ - Association des statisticiennes et statisticiens du Québec, 128
ASSQ - Association des stations de ski du Québec, 128
ASTA - American Society of Travel Agents, 1503
ASTB - Alzheimer Society of Thunder Bay, 65
ASTED - Association pour l'avancement des sciences et des techniques de la documentation, 165
ASTR - American Society for Theatre Research, 1499
ASTRO - Ontario Summer Theatre Association, 1109
ASTSBC - The Association of School Transportation Services of British Columbia, 162
ASTTBC - Applied Science Technologists & Technicians of British Columbia, 74
ASWCO - Aboriginal Sport & Wellness Council of Ontario, 2
ASWNC - The Association of Social Workers of Northern Canada, 162
ATA - Association des technologues en agroalimentaire, 129
ATA - Alberta Tennis Association, 49
ATA - Alberta Teachers' Association, 49
ATA - American Thyroid Association, 1503
ATA - Alberta Triathlon Association, 50
ATA - Appalachian Teachers' Association, 73
ATA - Alberta Taekwondo Association, 49
ATAA - Alberta Target Archers Association, 49
ATABC - Athletic Therapy Association of British Columbia, 180

ATAC - Air Transport Association of Canada, 19
ATAQ - Association Trot & Amble du Québec, 179
ATASO - Aboriginal Tourism Association of Southern Ontario, 2
ATB - Elevate NWO, 684
ATCA - Tourisme Chaudière-Appalaches, 1392
ATCC - Association des traumatisés cranio-cérébraux Mauricie-Centre-du-Québec, 130
ATCCM - Association des Traumatisés cranio-cérébraux de la Montérégie, 129
ATDA - Atlantic Tire Dealers Association, 186
ATEQ - Association of Teachers of English in Quebec, 162
ATESL - Alberta Teachers of English as a Second Language, 49
ATFC - Association des théâtres francophones du Canada, 129
ATHAQ - Association/Troubles de l'Humeur et d'Anxiété au Québec, 179
ATHF - Alberta Team Handball Federation, 49
ATIA - Association of Translators & Interpreters of Alberta, 163
ATIM - Association of Translators, Terminologists & Interpreters of Manitoba, 163
ATINS - Association of Translators & Interpreters of Nova Scotia, 163
ATIO - Association of Translators & Interpreters of Ontario, 163
ATIS - Association of Translators & Interpreters of Saskatchewan, 163
ATLA - Alberta Texas Longhorn Association, 50
ATMIA - ATM Industry Association Canada Region, 187
ATQ - Les AmiEs de la Terre de Québec, 67
ATRA - Alberta Therapeutic Recreation Association, 50
ATRAQ - Associations touristiques régionales associées du Québec, 179
ATRC - Atlantic Turfgrass Research Foundation, 186
ATSAQ - Association des techniciens en santé animale du Québec, 129
ATSP - Association of Telehealth Service Providers, 1513
ATTA - Alberta Table Tennis Association, 48
ATTN - Atlantic Therapeutic Touch Network, 186
ATU - Amalgamated Transit Union (AFL-CIO/CLC), 1487
ATUQ - Association du transport urbain du Québec, 132
ATVANS - All Terrain Vehicle Association of Nova Scotia, 54
AUC - Alberta Underwater Council, 50
AUCC - Universities Canada, 1418
AUF - Agence universitaire de la Francophonie, 14
AUFA - Acadia University Faculty Association, 4
AUFA - Athabasca University Faculty Association, 180
AUFC - Association des universités de la francophonie canadienne, 130
AUFSC - Association of University Forestry Schools of Canada, 163
AUMA - Alberta Urban Municipalities Association, 50
AUNBT - Association of University of New Brunswick Teachers, 163
AUQ - Association des urologues du Québec, 130
AUS - Atlantic University Sport Association, 186
AuSAE - Australian Society of Association Executives Ltd., 1513
AUSU - Athabasca University Students' Union, 180
AUTAL - Association des usagers du transport adapté de Longueuil, 130
AV - AIDS Vancouver, 17
AVA - Action Volunteers for Animals, 7
AVA - Aviation Alberta, 190

Acronym Index

AVFQ - Association de vitrerie et fenestrations du Québec, 104
AVHS - Annapolis Valley Historical Society, 71
AVI - AIDS Vancouver Island, 17
AVICC - Association of Vancouver Island Coastal Communities, 163
AVLIC - Association of Visual Language Interpreters of Canada, 164
AVLI-NB - Association of Visual Language Interpreters of New Brunswick, 164
AVMA - Alberta Veterinary Medical Association, 50
AVRBC - Administrators of Volunteer Resources BC, 8
AVRDI - Association de la Vallée-du-Richelieu pour la déficience intellectuelle, 102
AVS - Association des vietnamiens de Sherbrooke, 130
AVS - American Vegan Society, 1504
AWA - Alberta Wilderness Association, 52
AWA - Alberta Whitewater Association, 52
AWCA - Alberta Wall & Ceiling Association, 51
AWCBC - Association of Workers' Compensation Boards of Canada, 164
AWCS - Alexandra Writers' Centre Society, 53
AWF - Animal Welfare Foundation of Canada, 71
AWF - African Wildlife Foundation, 1486
AWF - Association of Women in Finance, 164
AWGIC - Arctic Winter Games International Committee, 81
AWH - Assaulted Women's Helpline, 87
AWHA - Alberta Walking Horse Association, 51
AWI - Alberta Women's Institutes, 52
AWIC - AWIC Community & Social Services, 191
AWMA-BC - Architectural Woodwork Manufacturers Association of British Columbia, 79
AWMAC - Architectural Woodwork Manufacturers Association of Canada, 79
AWMAC-ON - Architectural Woodwork Manufacturers Association of Canada - Ontario Chapter, 79
AWNA - Alberta Weekly Newspapers Association, 51
AWPA - Alberta Water Polo Association, 51
AWPA - American Wire Producers Association, 1504
AWR - Alliance for the Wild Rockies, 1487
AWRA - American Water Resources Association, 1504
AWS - Australian Wine Society of Toronto, 188
AWWA - American Water Works Association, 1504
AWWDA - Alberta Water Well Drilling Association, 51
AWWOA - Alberta Water & Wastewater Operators Association, 51
AYC - Association of Yukon Communities, 164
AZA - Association of Zoos & Aquariums, 1513
AZQ - L'Association Zoroastrianne du Québec, 179

B

BA - Baseball Alberta, 198
BAC - Burnaby Arts Council, 265
BAC - Brampton Arts Council, 225
BAC - International Union of Bricklayers & Allied Craftworkers (AFL-CIO/CFL), 1564
BAC - Baking Association of Canada, 194
BACC - Bridgetown & Area Chamber of Commerce, 229
BACC - Bridgewater & Area Chamber of Commerce, 229
BACC - Bonavista Area Chamber of Commerce, 217
BACI - Burnaby Association for Community Inclusion, 265
BACL - Barrhead Association for Community Living, 197
BACS - British Association for Canadian Studies, 1514
BAMQ - Balle au mur Québec, 194

BANA - Bulimia Anorexia Nervosa Association, 264
BAND - Burlington Association for Nuclear Disarmament, 265
BANNS - Black Artists Network of Nova Scotia, 212
BAO - Bereavement Authority of Ontario, 205
BARS - Barrhead Animal Rescue Society, 197
BAS - Battlefords Agricultural Society, 200
BAS - Binbrook Agricultural Society, 211
BASF - Black Academic Scholarship Fund, 212
BB&DSFA - Barrow Bay & District Sports Fishing Association, 197
BBAC - Blind Bowls Association of Canada, 214
BBAY - Bed & Breakfast Association of the Yukon, 203
BBB of SK - Better Business Bureau of Saskatchewan, 206
BBBSC - Big Brothers Big Sisters of Canada, 209
BBC - B'nai Brith Canada, 192
BBC - Best Buddies Canada, 206
BBCF - The Barnard-Boecker Centre Foundation, 196
BBEMA - Bedeque Bay Environmental Management Association, 203
BBFF - Brian Bronfman Family Foundation, 228
BBI - Black Business Initiative, 213
BBNC - Birchmount Bluffs Neighbourhood Centre, 212
BBO - Beaverhill Bird Observatory, 203
BBOT - Burnaby Board of Trade, 265
BBOT - The Brampton Board of Trade, 225
BBPA - Black Business & Professional Association, 213
BBSG - Base Borden Soaring, 197
BBSRDA - Border Boosters Square & Round Dance Association, 218
BBYO - B'nai Brith Youth Organization, 192
BC - BeautyCouncil, 203
BC CCA - British Columbia Contact Centre Association, 237
BC TEAL - Association of British Columbia Teachers of English as an Additional Language, 140
BCA - Breast Cancer Action, 227
BCAA - CAA British Columbia, 267
BCAA - British Columbia Archery Association, 230
BCAAFC - British Columbia Association of Aboriginal Friendship Centres, 231
BCAAFE - British Columbia Association of Agricultural Fairs & Exhibitions, 231
BCAB - British Columbia Association of Broadcasters, 231
BC-ABA - British Columbia Association for Behaviour Analysis, 231
BCABBA - British Columbia Amateur Bodybuilding Association, 230
BCAC - British Columbia Aviation Council, 233
BCACC - British Columbia Association of Clinical Counsellors, 231
BCACS - BC Assocation for Crane Safety, 201
BCAEA - British Columbia Alternate Education Association, 230
BCAHA - British Columbia Amateur Hockey Association, 230
BCAIRP - British Columbia Association of Insolvency & Restructuring Professionals, 232
BCAK - British Columbia Association of Kinesiologists, 232
BCALM - British Columbia Aboriginal Lands Managers, 229
BCALP - British Columbia Association of Laboratory Physicians, 232
BCAMFT - British Columbia Association for Marriage & Family Therapy, 231
BCAMRT - British Columbia Association of Medical Radiation Technologists, 232
BCAMT - British Columbia Association of Mathematics Teachers, 232
BCANDS - British Columbia Aboriginal Network on Disability Society, 229

BCANS - Breast Cancer Action Nova Scotia, 227
BCAOMA - British Columbia Apartment Owners & Managers Association, 230
BCAPS - British Columbia Association of People Who Stutter, 232
BCARA - British Columbia Association for Regenerative Agriculture, 231
BCAS - BC Adaptive Snowsports, 200
BCASA - British Columbia Amateur Softball Association, 230
BCASBO - British Columbia Association of School Business Officials, 232
BCASLPA - British Columbia Association of Speech-Language Pathologists & Audiologists, 233
BCASP - British Columbia Association of School Psychologists, 232
BCASW - British Columbia Association of Social Workers, 232
BCATA - British Columbia Art Teachers' Association, 230
BCATA - British Columbia Art Therapy Association, 230
BCATML - British Columbia Association of Teachers of Modern Languages, 233
BCB - Bowls Canada Boulingrin, 220
BCBA - British Columbia Bailiffs Association, 233
BCBA - British Columbia Broadband Association, 234
BCBBA - British Columbia Bee Breeders' Association, 233
BCBC - Belgian Canadian Business Chamber, 204
BCBEA - British Columbia Business Educators Association, 234
BCBHA - British Columbia Ball Hockey Association, 233
BCBHEC - British Columbia Broiler Hatching Egg Producers' Association, 234
BCBIA - British Columbia Brain Injury Association, 234
BCBPS - Block Watch Society of British Columbia, 215
BCBRDA - British Columbia Bottle & Recycling Depot Association, 234
BCBS - British Columbia Broomball Society, 234
BCBSRA - British Columbia Blind Sports & Recreation Association, 234
BCC - Belleville & District Chamber of Commerce, 204
BCC - Breakfast Cereals Canada, 227
BCC - Bladder Cancer Canada, 214
BCC - Brain Care Centre, 225
BCC - Barley Council of Canada, 196
BCCA - British Columbia Chiropractic Association, 236
BCCA - British Columbia Construction Association, 237
BCCA - British Columbia Cattlemen's Association, 235
BCCA - British Columbia Co-operative Association, 237
BCCA - BC Cheerleading Association, 201
BCCCA - British Columbia Career College Association, 235
BCCCA - British Columbia Contract Cleaner's Association, 237
BCCDA - British Columbia Career Development Association, 235
BCCEAS - British Columbia Coalition to Eliminate Abuse of Seniors, 236
BCCEC - British Columbia Council for Exceptional Children, 237
BCCEWH - British Columbia Centre of Excellence for Women's Health, 235
BCCF - British Columbia Council for Families, 237
BCCF - British Columbia Cancer Foundation, 234
BCCF - British Columbia Choral Federation, 236

BCCF - British Columbia Conservation Foundation, 237
BCCFA - British Columbia Centre for Ability Association, 235
BCCGA - British Columbia Chicken Growers' Association, 236
BCCHF - British Columbia's Children's Hospital Foundation, 259
BCCJA - British Columbia Criminal Justice Association, 238
BCCL - Brampton Caledon Community Living, 226
BCCLA - British Columbia Civil Liberties Association, 236
BCCMA - BC Chinese Music Association, 201
BCCMC - British Columbia Cranberry Marketing Commission, 238
BCCPA - British Columbia Crime Prevention Association, 238
BCCPA - British Columbia Care Providers Association, 234
BCCPAC - British Columbia Confederation of Parent Advisory Councils, 236
BCCSA - BC Construction Safety Alliance, 201
BCCSF - BC Chinese Soccer Federation, 201
BCCT - British Columbia Teacher Regulation Branch, 255
BCCTRA - British Columbia Competitive Trail Riders Association, 236
BCDEA - British Columbia Dance Educators' Association, 238
BCDHA - British Columbia Dental Hygienists' Association, 238
BCDO - British Columbia Doctors of Optometry, 239
BCDSF - British Columbia Deaf Sports Federation, 238
BCDSS - British Columbia Disc Sports, 238
BCEA - British Columbia Electrical Association, 239
BCEDA - British Columbia Economic Development Association, 239
BCEIA - British Columbia Environment Industry Association, 239
BCEN - British Columbia Environmental Network, 240
BCES - British Columbia Epilepsy Society, 240
BCFA - British Columbia Funeral Association, 242
BCFA - British Columbia Fencing Association, 241
BCFCA - British Columbia Floor Covering Association, 241
BCFCCA - British Columbia Family Child Care Association, 240
BCFF - British Columbia Floorball Federation, 241
BCFFPA - British Columbia Federation of Foster Parent Associations, 240
BCFFPA - British Columbia Federation of Foster Parent Associations, 240
BCFIRB - British Columbia Farm Industry Review Board, 240
BCFL - British Columbia Federation of Labour, 240
BCFMWU - British Columbia Ferry & Marine Workers' Union (CLC), 241
BCFROA - British Columbia Fishing Resorts & Outfitters Association, 241
BCFS - British Columbia Folklore Society, 241
BCGA - British Columbia Grapegrowers' Association, 242
BCGA - British Columbia Golf Association, 242
BCGEU - British Columbia Government & Service Employees' Union, 242
BCGS - British Columbia Genealogical Society, 242
BCGSA - British Columbia Golf Superintendents Association, 242
BCGWA - British Columbia Ground Water Association, 242
BCHA - British Columbia Hereford Association, 243
BCHA - British Columbia Hotel Association, 243

Acronym Index

BCHBC - Back Country Horsemen of British Columbia, 192
BCHF - British Columbia Historical Federation, 243
BCHGA - British Columbia Herb Growers Association, 243
BCHPA - British Columbia Hang Gliding & Paragliding Association, 243
BCHPA - British Columbia Honey Producers Association, 243
BCHPCA - British Columbia Hospice Palliative Care Association, 243
BCHS - Brome County Historical Society, 260
BCI - Blissymbolics Communication International, 214
BCIA - British Columbia Institute of Agrologists, 244
BCICAC - British Columbia International Commercial Arbitration Centre, 244
BCID - British Columbia Industrial Designer Association, 244
BCIT FSA - British Columbia Institute of Technology Faculty & Staff Association, 244
BCITS - BC Association for Individualized Technology and Supports, 201
BCLA - British Columbia Library Association, 244
BCLA - British Columbia Lung Association, 245
BCLA - BC Lymphedema Association, 201
BCLA - BC Lacrosse Association, 201
BCLCA - British Columbia Lodging & Campgrounds Association, 245
BCLCIRA - British Columbia Literacy Council, 245
BCLI - British Columbia Law Institute, 244
BCLNA - British Columbia Landscape & Nursery Association, 244
BCLP - British Columbia Libertarian Party, 244
BCLS - British Columbia Lions Society for Children with Disabilities, 245
BCLS - British Columbia Lupus Society, 245
BCLTA - British Columbia Library Trustees' Association, 245
BCMA - British Columbia Museums Association, 246
BCMA - British Columbia Muslim Association, 246
BCMB - British Columbia Conference of MB Churches, 237
BCMCL - British Columbia Mainland Cricket League, 246
BCMEA - British Columbia Music Educators' Association, 246
BCMEA - British Columbia Maritime Employers Association, 246
BCMHC - British Columbia Miniature Horse Club, 246
BCMSA - British Columbia Municipal Safety Association, 246
BCNA - British Columbia Naturopathic Association, 247
BCNF - British Columbia Neurofibromatosis Foundation, 247
BCNPA - British Columbia Nurse Practitioner Association, 248
BCNPHA - British Columbia Non-Profit Housing Association, 247
BCNU - British Columbia Nurses' Union, 248
BCPA - British Columbia Paralegal Association, 248
BCPA - British Columbia Powerlifting Association, 249
BCPA - British Columbia Paleontological Alliance, 248
BCPA - Spinal Cord Injury British Columbia, 1343
BCPA - British Columbia Psychological Association, 249
BCPGA - British Columbia Psychogeriatric Association, 249
BCPhA - British Columbia Pharmacy Association, 248
BCPIA - British Columbia Printing & Imaging Association, 249

BCPIAC - British Columbia Public Interest Advocacy Centre, 250
BCPMA - British Columbia Paint Manufacturers' Association, 248
BCPMA - British Columbia Podiatric Medical Association, 249
BCPRA - British Columbia Provincial Renal Agency, 249
BCPSBA - British Columbia Purebred Sheep Breeders' Association, 250
BCPTA - British Columbia Primary Teachers Association, 249
BCPTA - British Columbia Play Therapy Association, 249
BCPVPA - British Columbia Principals & Vice-Principals Association, 249
BCPWSA - British Columbia Prader-Willi Syndrome Association, 249
BCRA - British Columbia Ringette Association, 251
BCRA - British Columbia Rifle Association, 251
BCRA - British Columbia Racquetball Association, 202
BCRA - Bosnian Canadian Relief Association, 218
BCRB&HCA - British Columbia Road Builders & Heavy Construction Association, 251
BCRC - Beef Cattle Research Council, 203
BCRC - Black Community Resource Centre, 213
BCREA - British Columbia Real Estate Association, 250
BCRFA - British Columbia Restaurant & Foodservices Association, 251
BCRHA - British Columbia Railway Historical Association, 250
BCRMCA - Concrete B.C., 610
BCRMTA - BC Rural & Multigrade Teachers' Association, 202
BCRMTA - British Columbia Registered Music Teachers' Association, 250
BCRPA - British Columbia Recreation & Parks Association, 250
BCRSGF - British Columbia Rhythmic Sportive Gymnastics Federation, 251
BCRSP - Board of Canadian Registered Safety Professionals, 216
BCSA - British Columbia Seafood Alliance, 253
BCSB - British Columbia Snowboard Association, 253
BCSC - British Columbia Securities Commission, 253
BCSC - Breast Cancer Society of Canada, 228
BCSCC - British Columbia Scientific Cryptozoology Club, 252
BCScTA - British Columbia Science Teachers' Association, 252
BCSEA - British Columbia Sustainable Energy Association, 255
BCSET - British Columbia Society of Electroneurophysiology Technologists, 254
BCSF - British Columbia Snowmobile Federation, 253
BCSFA - British Columbia Salmon Farmers Association, 252
BCSFA - British Columbia Saw Filers Association, 252
BCSGA - British Columbia Shellfish Growers Association, 253
BCSLA - British Columbia Society of Landscape Architects, 254
BCSLA - British Columbia Seniors Living Association, 253
BCSLS - British Columbia Society of Laboratory Science, 254
BCSMSSA - British Columbia Society for Male Survivors of Sexual Abuse, 254
BCSP - British Columbia Society of Prosthodontists, 254
BCSRA - British Columbia Shorthand Reporters Association, 253
BCSRT - British Columbia Society of Respiratory Therapists, 254
BCSS - British Columbia Surgical Society, 255
BCSS - BC School Sports, 202

BCSSA - British Columbia School Superintendents Association, 252
BCSSA - British Columbia Summer Swimming Association, 255
BCSSGA - British Columbia Stone, Sand & Gravel Association, 255
BCSSTA - British Columbia Social Studies Teachers Association, 253
BCSTA - British Columbia School Trustees Association, 252
BCSTH - BC Society of Transition Houses, 202
BCTA - British Columbia Trucking Association, 257
BCTA - BC Trappers' Association, 202
BCTF - British Columbia Teachers' Federation, 256
BCTF - British Columbia Food Technolgists, 241
BCTHF - British Columbia Team Handball Federation, 256
BCTIA - British Columbia Technology Industries Association, 256
BCTLA - British Columbia Teacher-Librarians' Association, 255
BCTRA - British Columbia Therapeutic Recreation Association, 256
BCTRA - British Columbia Therapeutic Riding Association, 257
BCTS - British Columbia Transplant Society, 257
BCTTA - British Columbia Table Tennis Association, 255
BCUS - British Columbia Ultrasonographers' Society, 257
BCVMC - British Columbia Vegetable Marketing Commission, 257
BCVTA - British Columbia Veterinary Technologists Association, 257
BCWA - British Columbia Wrestling Association, 258
BCWA - British Columbia Weightlifting Association, 258
BCWCA - British Columbia Wall & Ceiling Association, 257
BCWI - British Columbia Women's Institutes, 258
BCWI - British Columbia Wine Institute, 258
BCWSA - British Columbia Wheelchair Sports Association, 258
BCWWA - British Columbia Water & Waste Association, 257
BCYCNA - British Columbia & Yukon Community Newspapers Association, 229
BCYHHA - British Columbia-Yukon Halfway House Association, 259
BDAC - Boundary District Arts Council, 219
BDACI - Brockville & District Association for Community Involvement, 260
BDKK - German-Canadian Mardi Gras Association Inc., 772
BDSRA - Batten Disease Support & Research Association - Canadian Chapter, 199
BEA - Black Educators Association of Nova Scotia, 213
BEAC - Broadcast Educators Association of Canada, 259
BECOR - Building Envelope Council of Ottawa Region, 262
BEMM - Building Energy Management Manitoba, 261
BES - Broadcast Executives Society, 259
BFES - Building Futures Employment Society, 262
BFL - Breakfast for Learning, 227
BFM - Bibles for Missions Foundation, 208
BFN - Brereton Field Naturalists' Club Inc., 228
BFO - Beef Farmers of Ontario, 204
BFO - Bereaved Families of Ontario, 205
BGCC - Baptist General Conference of Canada, 196
BGCC - Boys & Girls Clubs of Canada, 222
BGCFS - Bruce Grey Child & Family Services, 260
BGEAC - Billy Graham Evangelistic Association of Canada, 211

BHA - Bus History Association, Inc., 266
BHS - Brant Historical Society, 226
BHS - Burlington Historical Society, 265
BHS - Bertie Historical Society, 206
BHTF - Bonavista Historic Townscape Foundation, 217
BIAA - Brain Injury Association of Alberta, 225
BIAC - Bowen Island Arts Council, 219
BIAC - Brain Injury Association of Canada, 225
BIAGH - Bosnian Islamic Association, 218
BIANS - Brain Injury Association of Nova Scotia, 225
BIC - Brethren in Christ, 228
BICPEI - Brain Injury Coalition of Prince Edward Island, 225
BIFHSGO - British Isles Family History Society of Greater Ottawa, 259
BIFMA - Business & Institutional Furniture Manufacturer's Association, 1515
BILD - Building Industry & Land Development Association, 262
BIMA - Buy-Side Investment Management Association, 267
BIO - Beef Improvement Ontario, 204
BIPM - Bureau international des poids et mesures, 1515
BIR - Bureau of International Recycling, 1515
BIS - Benevolent Irish Society of Prince Edward Island, 205
BISQC - Banff International String Quartet Competition, 195
BIWF - British Israel World Federation (Canada) Inc., 259
BJM - Les Ballets Jazz de Montréal, 195
BLC - Braille Literacy Canada, 224
BLF - Bibles & Literature in French Canada, 208
BLHS - Black Loyalist Heritage Society, 213
BLITS - Bureau local d'intervention traitant du SIDA, 264
BLMS - Brantford Lapidary & Mineral Society Inc., 227
BLSA - Black Law Students' Association of Canada, 213
BMA - Brantford Musicians' Association, 227
BMAC - Bluegrass Music Association of Canada, 215
BMBRI - Brewing & Malting Barley Research Institute, 228
BMDLC - Peel Regional Labour Council, 1148
BME - The British Methodist Episcopal Church of Canada, 259
BMFA - Blue Mountain Foundation for the Arts, 215
BMRA - Building Materials Reuse Association, 1514
BMS - Burnaby Multicultural Society, 266
BMWCC - BMW Clubs Canada, 216
BNAPS - British North America Philatelic Society Ltd., 259
BNB - Baseball New Brunswick, 198
BNB - Baton New Brunswick, 199
BNB - Basketball New Brunswick, 198
BNFC - Barrie Native Friendship Centre, 197
BNL - Badminton Newfoundland & Labrador Inc., 193
BNNB - Badminton New Nouveau Brunswick, 193
BNS - Bicycle Nova Scotia, 208
BNS - Baseball Nova Scotia, 198
BNS - Blomidon Naturalists Society, 215
BOABC - Building Officials' Association of British Columbia, 262
BOMA - Building Owners & Managers Association International, 1514
BON - Badminton Ontario, 193
BON - Bereavement Ontario Network, 205
BONN - Bonn Agreement, 1514
BOPA - Boundary Organic Producers Association, 219
BOTPMA - Break Open Ticket Program Management Alliance, 227
BPA - Brandon Police Association, 226
BPA - Brantford Police Association, 227

Acronym Index

BPA Canada - Business Professional Association of Canada, 267
BPAA - Book Publishers Association of Alberta, 218
BPAC - Bowling Proprietors' Association of Canada, 219
BPAO - Bowling Proprietors' Association of Ontario, 219
BPC - Book & Periodical Council, 218
BPEG - Bruce Peninsula Environment Group, 261
BPOC - Beaver Party of Canada, 203
BPPCI - Block Parent Program of Canada, 214
BQ - Bloc québécois, 214
BQDS - Bay of Quinte Dental Society, 200
BRA - Bluewater Recycling Association, 215
BRAS - Bureau régional d'action sida (Outaouais), 264
BRAVO - Bureau des regroupements des artistes visuels de l'Ontario, 264
BRC - Broadcast Research Council of Canada, 259
BRCC - Chamber of Commerce of Brantford & Brant, 539
BRCC - Blind River Chamber of Commerce, 214
BRCC - Baffin Regional Chamber of Commerce, 194
BRCD - The Bob Rumball Centre for the Deaf, 216
BREB - Brandon Real Estate Board, 226
BREB - Brampton Real Estate Board, 226
BRLA - Big Rideau Lake Association, 210
BRREA - Brantford Regional Real Estate Association Inc., 227
BRRG - Battle River Research Group, 199
BRS - Bytown Railway Society, 267
BSA - Bibliographical Society of America, 1514
BSAC - Blind Sailing Association of Canada, 214
BSC - Bird Studies Canada, 212
BSC - Bibliographical Society of Canada, 208
BSC - Biophysical Society of Canada, 211
BSC - Black Studies Centre, 213
BSCC - The Barbra Schlifer Commemorative Clinic, 196
BSI - Basketball Saskatchewan, 199
BSIA of BC - Building Supply Industry Association of British Columbia, 263
BSL - Fort Erie Business Success & Loan Centre, 752
BTABC - Baton Twirling Association of British Columbia, 199
BTAC - Burrows Trail Arts Council, 266
BTFC - Brain Tumour Foundation of Canada, 225
BTW - Black Theatre Workshop, 213
BTWBC - Bike to Work BC Society, 211
BUFA - Brock University Faculty Association, 259
BUFA - Brandon University Faculty Association, 226
BUM - Bi Unité Montréal, 207
BUW - Brant United Way, 226
BVC - Bathurst Volunteer Centre de Bénévolat Inc., 199
BVN - Bulkley Valley Naturalists, 264
BWB - Bikes Without Borders, 211
BWF - Badminton World Federation, 1513
BWNA - Business Women's Networking Association, 267

C

C&FS Western - Child & Family Services of Western Manitoba, 558
C&MA - The Christian & Missionary Alliance in Canada, 566
C5PBA - Canadian 5 Pin Bowlers' Association, 285
CA - Southern Ontario Cocaine Anonymous, 1338
CAA - Canadian Automobile Association, 339
CAA - Canadian Acoustical Association, 287
CAA - Canadian Authors Association, 338
CAA - Canadian Angus Association, 293
CAA - Canadian Academy of Audiology, 285
CAA - Canadian Archaeological Association, 294
CAA - Canadian Avalanche Association, 340
CAA - Canadian Albacore Association, 291
CAA - Canadian Acquirer's Association, 287
CAAA - Canadian Academic Accounting Association, 285
CAAA - Canadian Aviation Artists Assocation, 340
CAAA - Canadian Aerial Applicators Association, 288
CAAAS - Calgary Aboriginal Arts Awareness Society, 270
CAABC - Canadian Associated Air Balance Council, 297
CAAC - Canadian Association of Ambulatory Care, 308
CAACTM - Canadian Association of Acupuncture & Traditional Chinese Medicine, 307
CAAE - Canadian Association for Astrological Education, 297
CAALL - Canadian Association of Administrators of Labour Legislation, 307
CAAM - Canadian Association of Aesthetic Medicine, 308
CAAMA - Canadian Association for the Advancement of Music & the Arts, 305
CAAN - Canadian Aboriginal AIDS Network, 285
CAAN - Canadian Association of Apheresis Nurses, 308
CAANCB - Canadian Association for Anatomy, Neurobiology, & Cell Biology, 297
CAANS - Central Alberta AIDS Network Society, 523
CAANS - Canadian Association for the Advancement of Netherlandic Studies, 305
CAAQ - Centre d'amitié autochtone du Québec, 527
CAAR - Canadian Association of Agri-Retailers, 308
CAAS - Canadian Association for American Studies, 297
CAAT - Campaign Against Arms Trade, 1515
CAAWS - Canadian Association for the Advancement of Women & Sport & Physical Activity, 305
CAB - Canadian Association of Broadcasters, 309
CABA - Canadian Amateur Boxing Association, 292
CABA - Continental Automated Buildings Association, 626
CABA - Charlottetown Area Baseball Association, 552
CABC - Canadian Armenian Business Council Inc., 295
CABC - Convention of Atlantic Baptist Churches, 627
CABC - Canadian Association of Broadcast Consultants, 309
CABC - Canada-Arab Business Council, 283
CABC - Canada - Albania Business Council, 277
CABCP - Canadian Association of Blue Cross Plans, 309
CABE - Canadian Association for Business Economics, 297
CABI - Canadian Association of Business Incubation, 309
CABL - Canadian Association of Black Lawyers, 308
CABM - Centre d'action bénévole de Montréal, 527
CABP - Canadian Alliance of British Pensioners, 291
CABPS - Canadian Association of Bariatric Physicians & Surgeons, 308
CAC - Coffee Association of Canada, 580
CAC - Coaching Association of Canada, 577
CAC - Cement Association of Canada, 521
CAC - Consumers' Association of Canada, 626
CAC - Canadian Association for Conservation of Cultural Property, 298
CAC - Classical Association of Canada, 572
CAC - Canadian Airports Council, 291
CAC - Coal Association of Canada, 577
CACAP - Canadian Academy of Child & Adolescent Psychiatry, 285
CACB - Canadian Architectural Certification Board, 295
CACC - Canadian Association of Crown Counsel, 312
CACC - Cancer Advocacy Coalition of Canada, 507
CACCF - Canadian Addiction Counsellors Certification Federation, 288
CACCN - Canadian Association of Critical Care Nurses, 311
CACCS - Canadian Association of Credit Counselling Services, 311
CACD - Canadian Association of Chemical Distributors, 310
CACE - Canadian Association of Communicators in Education, 310
CACEE - Canadian Association of Career Educators & Employers, 309
CACGV - Community Arts Council of Greater Victoria, 595
CACH - Canadian Adult Congenital Heart Network, 288
CACHC - Canadian Association of Community Health Centres, 311
CACL - Canadian Association for Community Living, 298
CACL - Cheticamp Association for Community Living, 557
CACLALS - Canadian Association for Commonwealth Literature & Language Studies, 298
CACLALS - Canadian Association for Commonwealth Literature & Language Studies, 298
CACMID - Canadian Association for Clinical Microbiology & Infectious Diseases, 297
CACN - Canadian Association of Child Neurology, 310
CACN - Canadian Anti-Counterfeiting Network, 293
CACP - Canadian Association of Chiefs of Police, 310
CACPR - Canadian Association of Cardiovascular Prevention & Rehabilitation, 309
CACPT - Canadian Association of Cardio-Pulmonary Technologists, 309
CACPT - Canadian Association of Certified Planning Technicians, 310
CACQ - Coalition des associations de consommateurs du Québec, 577
CACR - Community Arts Council of Richmond, 595
CACS - Canadian Association for Curriculum Studies, 299
CACSMA - Canadian Association for Composite Structures & Materials, 298
CACTS - Canadian Air Cushion Technology Society, 290
CACTUS - Canadian Association of Community Television Users & Stations, 311
CACUSS - Canadian Association of College & University Student Services, 310
CAD - Canadian Association of the Deaf, 334
CAD - College of Alberta Denturists, 582
CADA - Canadian Automobile Dealers' Association, 339
CADA ON - Canadian Alliance of Dance Artists, 291
CADD - Corporations des assureurs directs de dommage, 631
CADDAC - Centre for ADHD Awareness, Canada, 531
CADDRA - Canadian ADHD Resource Alliance, 288
CADE - Canadian Association of Drilling Engineers, 312
CADÉUL - Confédération des associations d'étudiants et étudiantes de l'Université Laval, 610
CADR - Canadian Association for Dental Research, 299
CADRÉ - Centre d'animation de développement et de recherche en éducation, 528
CADRI - Canadian Association of Direct Response Insurers, 312
CADS - Canadian Association for Disabled Skiing, 299
CADS Alberta - Canadian Association for Disabled Skiing - Alberta, 299
CADSI - Canadian Association of Defence & Security Industries, 312
CADS-NCD - Canadian Association for Disabled Skiing - National Capital Division, 299
CADTH - Canadian Agency for Drugs & Technologies in Health, 289
CAE - The Canadian Academy of Engineering, 286
CAE - W. Maurice Young Centre for Applied Ethics, 1439
CAE - Canadian Epilepsy Alliance, 382
CAEA - Canadian Actors' Equity Association (CLC), 287
CAEF - Chartered Accountants' Education Foundation of Alberta, 552
CAEFS - Canadian Association of Elizabeth Fry Societies, 312
CAELS - Canadian Association of Environmental Law Societies, 313
CAEM - Canadian Association of Exposition Management, 313
CAEP - Canadian Association for Educational Psychology, 300
CAES - Canadian Agricultural Economics Society, 289
CAET - Canadian Association of Electroneurophysiology Technologists Inc., 312
CAET - Canadian Association for Enterostomal Therapy, 300
CAF - Canadian Apparel Federation, 294
CAF - Canadian Arab Federation, 294
CAF - Canadian Apprenticeship Forum, 294
CAFA - Confederation of Alberta Faculty Associations, 611
CAFA - Canadian Association of Farm Advisors, 314
CAFA - Canadian Association of Freediving & Apnea, 316
CAFC - Canadian Association of Fire Chiefs, 315
CAFCL - Camrose Association for Community Living, 277
CAFCN - Canadian Association of Foot Care Nurses, 315
CAFDE - Canadian Association of Film Distributors & Exporters, 314
CAFE - Canadian Association for Free Expression, 300
CAFE - Canadian Association of Fairs & Exhibitions, 314
CAFE - Canadian Association of Foundations of Education, 315
CAFII - Canadian Association of Financial Institutions in Insurance, 314
CAFIP - Canadian Association for Israel Philately, 301
CAFP - Canadian Association of Foodservice Professionals, 315
CAFP - Canadian Association of Former Parliamentarians, 315
CAFPRS - Canadian Academy of Facial Plastic & Reconstructive Surgery, 286
CAFS - Canadian Association for Food Studies, 300
CAG - Canadian Association of Geographers, 316
CAG - Canadian Association on Gerontology, 337
CAG - Canadian Apheresis Group, 294

Acronym Index

CAGA - Canadian Amputee Golf Association, 292
CaGBC - Canada Green Building Council, 279
CAGC - Canadian Association of Geophysical Contractors, 317
CAGC - Canadian Association of Genetic Counsellors, 316
CAGP - Canadian Academy of Geriatric Psychiatry, 286
CAGP - Canadian Association of Gift Planners, 317
CAGS - Canadian Association for Graduate Studies, 300
CAGS - Canadian Association of General Surgeons, 316
CAGT - Credit Association of Greater Toronto, 639
CAH - Conseil des arts de Hearst, 617
CAHF - Canada's Aviation Hall of Fame, 282
CAHI - Canadian Animal Health Institute, 293
CAHN - Canadian Association for the History of Nursing, 305
CAHN - Canadian Association of Hepatology Nurses, 317
CAHP - Canadian Academy of the History of Pharmacy, 287
CAHPI - Canadian Association of Home & Property Inspectors, 317
CAHR - Canadian Arabian Horse Registry, 294
CAHR - Council for Automotive Human Resources, 632
CAHR - The Canadian Association for HIV Research, 301
CAHRC - Canadian Agricultural Human Resource Council, 289
CAHS - Canadian Aviation Historical Society, 340
CAHSPR - Canadian Association for Health Services & Policy Research, 300
CAHT - Canadian Association for Humane Trapping, 301
CAIA - Canadian Aquaculture Industry Alliance, 294
CAIC - Canadian Association of Interventional Cardiology, 319
CAICCA - Canadian Association of Independent Credit Counselling Agencies, 318
CAIET - Canadian Association for Integrative & Energy Therapies, 301
CAIFC - CanAm Indian Friendship Centre of Windsor, 507
CAILBA - Canadian Association of Independent Life Brokerage Agencies, 318
CAIMS - Canadian Applied & Industrial Mathematics Society, 294
CAIRP - Canadian Association of Insolvency & Restructuring Professionals, 318
CAIS - Canadian Association for Information Science, 301
CAIS - Canadian Accredited Independent Schools, 287
CAIS - Canadian Association for Irish Studies, 301
CAITI - Canadian Association of Income Trusts Investors, 318
CAIW - Canadian Association of Insurance Women, 318
CAJ - Canadian Association of Journalists, 319
CAJLE - Canadian Association for Japanese Language Education, 301
CAL - Coalition for Active Living, 578
CALA - Canadian Association for Laboratory Accreditation Inc., 301
CALACS - Canadian Association for Latin American & Caribbean Studies, 302
CALAS - Canadian Association for Laboratory Animal Science, 302
CALEO - Canadian American Law Enforcement Organization, 1515
CALJ - Canadian Association of Learned Journals, 319
CALL - Canadian Association of Law Libraries, 319

CALM - Canadian Association of Labour Media, 319
CALS - Canadian Association for Leisure Studies, 302
CALTC - Canadian Alliance for Long Term Care, 291
CAM - Commonwealth Association of Museums, 593
CAM - Canadian Association of Movers, 321
CAM - Conseil des arts de Montréal, 617
CAM - Canadian Association of Midwives, 321
CAMA - Canadian Automatic Merchandising Association, 338
CAMA - Canadian Association of Municipal Administrators, 321
CAMA - Canadian Agri-Marketing Association (Alberta), 290
CAMA - Canadian Agri-Marketing Association, 290
CAMA - Canadian Aboriginal Minerals Association, 285
CAMAP - Canadian Association of MAiD Assessors & Providers, 320
CAMAQ - Centre d'adaptation de la main-d'oeuvre aérospatiale du Québec, 527
CAMB - Canadian Association of Medical Biochemists, 320
CAMCD - Canadian Association of Medical Cannabis Dispensaries, 320
CAMDR - Canadian Association of Medical Device Reprocessing, 320
CAME - Canadian Association for Medical Education, 302
CAMEO - Canadian Association for Mine & Explosive Ordnance Security, 302
CAMET - Council of Atlantic Ministers of Education & Training, 632
CAMH - Centre for Addiction & Mental Health, 531
CAMIC - Canadian Association of Mutual Insurance Companies, 322
CAMIMH - Canadian Alliance on Mental Illness & Mental Health, 291
CAMIRO - Canadian Mining Industry Research Organization, 437
CAML - Canadian Association of Music Libraries, Archives & Documentation Centres, 321
CAMLI - Canadian Anti-Money Laundering Institute, 293
CAMM - Canadian Association of Moldmakers, 321
CAMMAC - Canadian Amateur Musicians, 292
CAMO - Canadian Association of Medical Oncologists, 320
CAMPUT - CAMPUT, 277
CAMRT - Canadian Association of Medical Radiation Technologists, 320
CAMSC - Canadian Aboriginal & Minority Supplier Council, 285
CAMT - Canadian Association of Music Therapists, 321
CAMT - Canadian Association of Montessori Teachers, 321
CAMTA - Canadian Association of Medical Teams Abroad, 321
CAM-X - Canadian Call Management Association, 348
CAN - Canadian Arthritis Network, 295
CAN - Canadian Association for Neuroscience, 302
CANA - Canadian Assembly of Narcotics Anonymous, 296
CANAAF - Canadian Alopecia Areata Foundation, 292
CANAC - Canadian Association of Nurses in HIV/AIDS Care, 323
CANARIE - Canada's Advanced Internet Development Organization, 281
CANASA - Canadian Security Association, 469
CANB - Council of Archives New Brunswick, 632
CANB - Construction Association of New Brunswick, 623

CanBPA - Canadian Book Professionals Association, 346
CANCID - Canadian National Committee for Irrigation & Drainage, 439
CAND - Canadian Association of Numismatic Dealers, 323
CAND - The Canadian Association of Naturopathic Doctors, 322
CANDO - Council for Advancement of Native Development Officers, 632
CANFAR - Canadian Foundation for AIDS Research, 392
CaNIOS - Canadian Network for Improved Outcomes in Systemic Lupus Erythematosus, 440
CANM - Canadian Association of Nuclear Medicine, 323
CANN - Canadian Association of Neuroscience Nurses, 322
CANNT - Canadian Association of Nephrology Nurses & Technologists, 322
CANO - Canadian Association of Nurses in Oncology, 323
CANP - Canadian Association of Neuropathologists, 322
CANR - Canadian Association for Nursing Research, 302
CANS - Cosmetology Association of Nova Scotia, 631
CANS - Mechanical Contractors Association of Nova Scotia, 957
CANSCAIP - Canadian Society of Children's Authors, Illustrators & Performers, 481
CANSI - Canadian Association of Nordic Ski Instructors, 322
CANSPEI - Camping Association of Nova Scotia & PEI, 277
CanSPEP - Canadian Society of Professional Event Planners, 487
CANSTAT - Canadian Society of Teachers of the Alexander Technique, 488
CanTYD - Canadian Tamil Youth Development Centre, 492
CanWEA - Canadian Wind Energy Association, 504
CAO - Canadian Association of Optometrists, 324
CAO - Canadian Association of Orthodontists, 324
CAO - Canadian Association of Paralegals, 325
CAO - Coaches Association of Ontario, 576
CAOAC - Canadian Association of Aquarium Clubs, 308
CAODC - Canadian Association of Oilwell Drilling Contractors, 324
CAOMS - Canadian Association of Oral & Maxillofacial Surgeons, 324
CAOT - Canadian Association of Occupational Therapists, 323
CAOT-BC - Canadian Association of Occupational Therapists - British Columbia, 324
CAP - Canadian Association of Pathologists, 325
CAP - Canadian Association of Physicists, 327
CAP - Canadian Academy of Periodontology, 286
CAP - Canadian Association of Principals, 328
CAP - Congress of Aboriginal Peoples, 613
CAP - Council of Atlantic Premiers, 633
CAP - Canadian Association of Palynologists, 325
CAPA - Canadian Association for Photographic Art, 303
CAPA - Calgary & Area Medical Staff Society, 270
CAPA - Canadian Association of Professional Apiculturists, 328
CAPA - Canadian Association of Physician Assistants, 327
CAPACOA - Canadian Arts Presenting Association, 296
CAPACS - Point d'appui, centre d'aide et de prévention des agressions à caractère sexuel de Rouyn-Noranda, 1163

CAPAL - Canadian Association of Professional Academic Librarians, 328
CAPAM - Commonwealth Association for Public Administration & Management, 593
CAPC - Canadian Association of Professional Conservators, 328
CAPCA - Canadian Association of Provincial Cancer Agencies, 329
CAPCJ - Canadian Association of Provincial Court Judges, 329
CAPDHHE - Canadian Association for the Prevention of Discrimination & Harassment in Higher Education, 305
CAPDM - Canadian Association for Pharmacy Distribution Management, 303
CAPE - Canadian Association of Professional Employees, 328
CAPE - Canadian Association of Physicians for the Environment, 327
CAPE - Canadian Association of Police Educators, 327
CAPE - Comité d'action Parc Extension, 591
CAPEI - Construction Association of Prince Edward Island, 623
CAPEI - Coaches Association of PEI, 576
CAPER - Canadian Post-MD Education Registry, 458
CAPG - Canadian Association of Police Governance, 327
CAPHC - Canadian Association of Paediatric Health Centres, 325
CAPHC - Canadian Association of Heritage Professionals, 317
CAPHD - Canadian Association of Public Health Dentistry, 330
CAPhO - Canadian Association of Pharmacy in Oncology, 326
CAPIC - Canadian Association of Professional Image Creators, 328
CAPIC - Canadian Association of Professional Immigration Consultants, 329
CAPIH - Canadian Association of Physicians of Indian Heritage, 327
CAPL - Canadian Association of Petroleum Landmen, 326
CAPL - Canadian Academy of Psychiatry & the Law, 286
CAPLA - Canadian Association for Prior Learning Assesment, 303
CAPLA - Canadian Association of Petroleum Land Administration, 325
CAPLS - Canadian Association of Private Language Schools, 328
CAPM&R - Canadian Association of Physical Medicine & Rehabilitation, 327
CAPMA - Canadian Agencies Practicing Marketing Activation, 289
CAPO - Canadian Association of Psychosocial Oncology, 330
CAPP - Canadian Association of Petroleum Producers, 326
CAPP - Canadian Association of Prawn Producers, 328
CAPPA - Canadian Association of Personal Property Appraisers, 325
CAPPA - Canadian Positive Psychology Association, 458
CAPPA - Canadian Association of Programs in Public Administration, 329
CAPPDT - Canadian Association of Professional Pet Dog Trainers, 329
CAPRA - Canadian Association of Professional Regulatory Affairs, 329
CAPS - Canadian Association of Professional Speakers, 329
CAPS - Canadian Association of Paediatric Surgeons, 325
CAPS - Canadian Antique Phonograph Society, 293
CAPSA - Canadian Association of Pension Supervisory Authorities, 325
CAPSI - Canadian Association of Pharmacy Students & Interns, 326
CAPSLE - Canadian Association for the Practical Study of Law in Education, 305

Acronym Index

CAPT - Canadian Association of Pharmacy Technicians, 326
CAPT - Canadian Association for Population Therapeutics, 303
CAPTCHPL - Centre d'aide personnes traumatisées crâniennes et handicapées physiques Laurentides, 527
CAPWHN - Canadian Association of Perinatal & Women's Health Nurses, 325
CAQ - Corporation des approvisionneurs du Québec, 629
CAR - Canadian Association of Radiologists, 330
CARA - Canadian Association of Research Administrators, 331
CARA - Chinook Applied Research Association, 565
CARAS - Canadian Academy of Recording Arts & Sciences, 286
CARC - Community Action Resource Centre, 595
CARC - Community Action Resource Centre, 595
CARD - Community Association for Riding for the Disabled, 596
CARE - Canadian Association for Renewable Energies, 303
CARFAC - Canadian Artists Representation, 295
CARFLEO - Catholic Association of Religious & Family Life Educators of Ontario, 517
CARHA - Canadian Adult Recreational Hockey Association, 288
CARI - Canadian Association of Recycling Industries, 330
CARI - Canadian Association of Regulated Importers, 331
CARL - Canadian Association of Research Libraries, 331
CARM - Construction Association of Rural Manitoba Inc., 623
CARMA - Canadian Rock Mechanics Association, 467
CARMS - Canadian Resident Matching Service, 467
CARNA - The College & Association of Registered Nurses of Alberta, 581
CARO - Canadian Association of Radiation Oncology, 330
CAROP - Canadian Association of Rent to Own Professionals, 331
CARP - Canadian Alliance of Physiotherapy Regulators, 291
CARP - Clean Annapolis River Project, 573
CARR - Canadian Automobile Insurance Rate Regulators Association, 339
CARS - Canadian Association of Railway Suppliers, 330
CARS - Canadian Association of Rhodes Scholars, 331
CARSP - Canadian Association of Road Safety Professionals, 331
CART - Canadian Association of Retired Teachers, 332
CARTA - College & Association of Respiratory Therapists of Alberta, 581
CAS - Canadian Aerophilatelic Society, 289
CAS - Canadian AIDS Society, 290
CAS - Canadian Association of Slavists, 333
CAS - Chiropractors' Association of Saskatchewan, 565
CAS - Canadian Anesthesiologists' Society, 292
CAS - Children's Aid Society of the Districts of Sudbury & Manitoulin, 561
CASA - Canadian Amputee Sports Association, 292
CASA - Canadian Asian Studies Association, 296
CASA - Canadian Automatic Sprinkler Association, 338
CASA - Canadian Agricultural Safety Association, 289
CASA - Central Alberta Soccer Association, 523
CASA - Clean Air Strategic Alliance, 572

CASA - Canadian Alliance of Student Associations, 291
CASA - Canadian Association for Size Acceptance, 304
CASA - Canadian Association of Smallmouth Anglers, 333
CASAC - Canadian Association of Sexual Assault Centres, 333
CASAE - Canadian Association for the Study of Adult Education, 306
CASARA - Civil Air Search & Rescue Association, 571
CASC - Canadian Association for Spiritual Care, 304
CASC - Canadian Association of Science Centres, 332
CASC - Canadian Association for Studies in Co-operation, 304
CASCA - Canadian Astronomical Society, 337
CASCA - Canadian Anthropology Society, 293
CASC-OR - Canadian Automobile Sport Clubs - Ontario Region Inc., 339
CASDW - Canadian Association for the Study of Discourse & Writing, 306
CASE - Canadian Association for Supported Employment, 304
CASEA - Canadian Association for the Study of Educational Administration, 306
CASFAA - Canadian Association of Student Financial Aid Administrators, 334
CASH - Canadian Association for School Health, 303
CASHRA - Canadian Association of Statutory Human Rights Agencies, 333
CASI - Canadian Aeronautics & Space Institute, 288
CASI - Canadian Association of Snowboard Instructors, 333
CASID - Canadian Association for the Study of International Development, 306
CASIE - Canadian Association for the Study of Indigenous Education, 306
CASIS - Canadian Association for Security & Intelligence Studies, 303
CASL - Canadian Association for the Study of the Liver, 306
CASLE - Commonwealth Association of Surveying & Land Economy, 1518
CASLPM - College of Audiologists and Speech-Language Pathologists of Manitoba, 582
CASLPO - College of Audiologists & Speech-Language Pathologists of Ontario, 582
CASLT - Canadian Association of Second Language Teachers, 332
CASM - Canadian Academy of Sport Medicine, 287
CASMF - Centre d'action sida Montréal (Femmes), 527
CASMP - The Child Abuse Survivor Monument Project, 558
CASN - Canadian Association of Schools of Nursing, 332
CASO - Children's Aid Society of Ottawa, 561
CASP - Canadian Association for Suicide Prevention, 304
CASPR - Canadian Association of Staff Physician Recruiters, 333
CASS - Canadian Association for Scottish Studies, 303
CASS - Canadian Angelman Syndrome Society, 293
CASSA - Canadian Association of School System Administrators, 332
CASSA - Council of Agencies Serving South Asians, 632
CASSOC - Clans & Scottish Societies of Canada, 572
CASSWAC - Canadian Association of School Social Workers & Attendance Counsellors, 332
CAST - Canadian Association for Sandplay Therapy, 303

CASU - Canadian Association of SAS Users, 331
CASV - Canadian Association of Swine Veterinarians, 334
CASW - Canadian Association of Social Workers, 333
CASWE - Canadian Association for the Study of Women & Education, 306
CASWE - Canadian Association for Social Work Education, 304
CATA - Canadian Art Therapy Association, 295
CATA - Canadian Athletic Therapists Association, 337
CATA Alliance - Canadian Advanced Technology Alliance, 288
CATC - Canadian Association of Token Collectors, 334
CATCA - Canadian Air Traffic Control Association, 291
CATE - Canadian Association for Teacher Education, 304
CATIE - Canadian AIDS Treatment Information Exchange, 290
CATO - Canadian Association of Tour Operators, 334
CATR - Canadian Association for Theatre Research, 306
CATS - Canadian Association of Thoracic Surgeons, 334
CAUBO - Canadian Association of University Business Officers, 334
CAUCE - Canadian Association for University Continuing Education, 306
CAUT - Canadian Association of University Teachers, 335
CAUTG - Canadian Association of University Teachers of German, 335
CAV - Canadian Vocational Association, 501
CAV - Canadian Aboriginal Veterans & Serving Members Association, 285
CAVEWAS - Canadian Assessment, Vocational Evaluation & Work Adjustment Society, 297
CAVUNP - Canadian Association of Veterans in United Nations Peacekeeping, 335
CAWA - Canadian Amateur Wrestling Association, 292
CAWC - Canadian Association of Wound Care, 337
CAWEE - Canadian Association of Women Executives & Entrepreneurs, 336
CAWF - Canadian Arm Wrestling Federation, 295
CAWMC - Canadian Association of Wooden Money Collectors, 336
CAWOS - Central Alberta Women's Outreach Society, 524
CAWQ - Canadian Association on Water Quality, 337
CAWS - Canadian Association of Wholesale Sales Representatives, 336
CAWS - Canadian Association for Williams Syndrome, 307
CAYC - Canadian Association for Young Children, 307
CAZA - Canada's Accredited Zoos & Aquariums, 281
CBA - Canadian Bankers Association, 341
CBA - Canadian Botanical Association, 346
CBA - Chinese Benevolent Association of Vancouver, 564
CBA - Canadian Bar Association, 341
CBA - Canadian Bison Association, 344
CBA - Canadian Band Association, 340
CBA - Canadian Booksellers Association, 346
CBA - Central Beekeepers' Alliance, 524
CBAA - Canadian Business Aviation Association, 347
CBAC - Catholic Biblical Association of Canada, 517
CBAM - Canadian Bureau for the Advancement of Music, 347
CBBA - Canadian Belgian Blue Association, 342
CBBAG - Canadian Bookbinders & Book Artists Guild, 346

CBBC - Canadian Beef Breeds Council, 342
CBBF - Canadian Bodybuilding Federation, 345
CBC - Cycling British Columbia, 647
CBCMHA - Cape Breton County Minor Hockey Association, 509
CBCN - Canadian Breast Cancer Network, 347
CBCN - Canadian Botanical Conservation Network, 346
CBCVO - Cape Breton Chamber of Voluntary Organizations, 509
CBDC - Canadian Board Diversity Council, 345
CBEPS - Canadian Board of Examiners for Professional Surveyors, 345
CBF - Catholic Biblical Federation, 1515
CBHA - Canadian Ball Hockey Association, 340
CBIA - Canadian Bar Insurance Association, 342
CBIA - Canadian Bond Investors' Association, 345
CBIE - Canadian Bureau for International Education, 347
CBIWA - Cape Breton Injured Workers' Association, 509
CBM - Canadian Baptist Ministries, 341
CBMI - Christian Blind Mission International, 566
CBMTG - Canadian Blood & Marrow Transplant Group, 344
CBMU - Canadian Board of Marine Underwriters, 345
CBOQ - Canadian Baptists of Ontario & Quebec, 341
CBP - Canadian Business Press, 348
CBPA - Centre de Bénévolat de la Péninsule Acadienne Inc., 528
CBPQ - Corporation des bibliothécaires professionnels du Québec, 629
CBQ - Corporation des bijoutiers du Québec, 629
CBRC - Canadian Board for Respiratory Care Inc., 345
CBRET - Canadian Board of Registration of Electroencephalograph Technologists Inc., 345
CBS - Canadian Bible Society, 343
CBS - Canadian Blood Services, 344
CBS - Canadian Bioethics Society, 343
CBSA - Canadian Billiards & Snooker Association, 343
CBSA - Canadian Blind Sports Association Inc., 344
CBSC - Canadian Burn Survivors Community, 347
CBSC - Canadian Broadcast Standards Council, 347
CBSO - Cathedral Bluffs Symphony Orchestra, 517
CBSR - Canadian Business for Social Responsibility, 348
CBTC - Canadian Brain Tumour Consortium, 346
CBTF - Canadian Baton Twirling Federation, 342
CBWA - Canadian Bottled Water Association, 346
CBWC - Canadian Baptists of Western Canada, 341
CCA - Canadian Centre for Architecture, 353
CCA - Canadian Council for the Americas, 367
CCA - Canadian Conference of the Arts, 363
CCA - Canadian Curling Association, 374
CCA - Canadian Carwash Association, 350
CCA - Canadian Cartographic Association, 350
CCA - Canadian Celiac Association, 352
CCA - Canadian Chiropractic Association, 356
CCA - Canadian Construction Association, 363
CCA - Canadian Co-operative Association, 364
CCA - Canadian Council of Archives, 367
CCA - Canadian Cattlemen's Association, 351
CCA - Canadian Charolais Association, 355
CCA - Canadian Camping Association, 348
CCA - Canadian Communication Association, 361
CCA - Canadian Cowboys' Association, 372
CCA - Cross Country Alberta, 643

Acronym Index

CCA - Canadian Cat Association, 351
CCA - Canadian Contractors Association, 364
CCAA - Canadian Collegiate Athletic Association, 360
CCAA - Canadian Council for Aviation & Aerospace, 366
CCAAC - Child Care Advocacy Association of Canada, 558
CCAB - Canadian Council for Aboriginal Business, 366
CCAB - Canadian Circulations Audit Board Inc., 357
CCA-BC - Canadian Council for the Americas - British Columbia, 367
CCAC - Canadian Council on Animal Care, 370
CCAC - Centre canadien d'arbitrage commercial, 526
CCAC - Cabbagetown Community Arts Centre, 268
CCAC - Colorectal Cancer Association of Canada, 591
CCADP - Canadian Coalition Against the Death Penalty, 357
CCAE - Canadian Council for the Advancement of Education, 367
CCAFT - Citizens Concerned About Free Trade, 570
CCAGA - Canadian Caribbean Amateur Golfers Association, 350
CCANE - Conseil coopératif acadien de la Nouvelle-Écosse, 614
CCANS - Continuing Care Association of Nova Scotia, 626
CCANS - Civil Constables Association of Nova Scotia, 571
CCAO - Chambre de commerce et d'industrie d'Abitibi-Ouest, 545
CCAPEI - Chinese Canadian Association of Prince Edward Island, 564
CCAPP - The Canadian Council for Accreditation of Pharmacy Programs, 366
CCAQ - Corporation des concessionnaires d'automobiles du Québec inc., 630
CCAS - Catholic Children's Aid Society of Toronto, 518
CCAS - Catholic Children's Aid Society of Hamilton, 518
CCASJ - Chinese Cultural Association of Saint John, 564
C-CAVE - Canadians Concerned About Violence in Entertainment, 506
CCB - The Canadian Council of the Blind, 370
CCBA - Canadian Cattle Breeders' Association, 351
CCBC - Canada China Business Council, 278
CCBC - Craft Council of British Columbia, 638
CCBC - Canadian Children's Book Centre, 355
CCBC - College of Chiropractors of British Columbia, 583
CCBC - Cross Country British Columbia, 643
CCBCA - Canada-China Bilateral Cooperation Association, 283
CCBDA - Canadian Copper & Brass Development Association, 364
CCBE - Central Canada Broadcast Engineers, 524
CCBF - Canadian Christian Business Federation, 356
CCC - The Canadian Council of Churches, 368
CCC - Cross Country Canada, 643
CCC - Chinese Cultural Centre of Greater Toronto, 564
CCC - Chinese Cultural Centre, 564
CCC - Consumers Council of Canada, 626
CCC - Credit Counselling Canada, 639
CCCA - Canadian Cosmetics Careers Association Inc., 640
CCCA - Canadian Correspondence Chess Association, 366
CCCA - Canada Chinese Computer Association, 278
CCCA - Canadian Corporate Counsel Association, 365
CCCB - Canadian Conference of Catholic Bishops, 362

CCCC - Congregational Christian Churches in Canada, 613
CCCC - Canadian Council of Christian Charities, 368
CCCC - Central Coast Chamber of Commerce, 524
CCC-CCAN - Canadian Caregiver Coalition, 350
CCCEP - The Canadian Council on Continuing Education in Pharmacy, 371
CCCF - Canadian Child Care Federation, 355
CCCFA - Calgary Canada-China Friendship Association, 271
CCCM - Culture Mauricie, 645
CCCM - Chambre de commerce au Coeur de la Montérégie, 539
CCCM - Canadian Catholic Campus Ministry, 351
CCCM - Conseil canadien de la coopération et de la mutualité, 613
CCCN - Canadian Council of Cardiovascular Nurses, 367
CCCNS - Child Care Connection Nova Scotia, 558
CCCS - Canadian Critical Care Society, 373
CCCS - Chinese Canadian Chiropractic Society, 564
CCCS - Calgary Chinese Cultural Society, 271
CCCS - Central Coast Communications Society, 524
CCCS - Canadian Council of Conservative Synagogues, 368
CCCT - Chambre de commerce Canado-Tunisienne, 540
CCD - Council of Canadians with Disabilities, 633
CCDF - Canadian Career Development Foundation, 350
CCDS - Canadian Centre on Disability Studies, 354
CCDT - Canadian Contemporary Dance Theatre, 364
CCE - Club des collectionneurs d'épinglettes Inc., 575
CCEA - Canadian Council on Ecological Areas, 371
CCEB - Canadian Chiropractic Examining Board, 356
CCECENS - Certification Council of Early Childhood Educators of Nova Scotia, 538
CCECP - Canadian Centre for Ethics & Corporate Policy, 353
CCEMS - Canadian College of Emergency Medical Services, 358
CCES - Chambre de commerce et d'entrepreneuriat des Sources, 544
CCES - Canadian Centre for Ethics in Sport, 353
CCF - Canadian Crafts Federation, 372
CCF - Conseil culturel fransaskois, 614
CCF - Canadian Communications Foundation, 361
CCFA - Camosun College Faculty Association, 276
CCFA - Canadian-Cuban Friendship Association Toronto, 506
CCFA - Canadian Coalition for Farm Animals, 357
CCFC - Chambre de commerce francophone de Vancouver, 548
CCFC - Christian Children's Fund of Canada, 567
CCFCC - Canadian Culinary Federation, 373
CCFDA - Canadian Coalition for Fair Digital Access, 357
CCFI - Canadian Centre for Fisheries Innovation, 353
CCFM - Centre culturel franco-manitobain, 526
CCFM - Canadian Council of Forest Ministers, 368
CCFMFC - Council of Canadian Fire Marshals & Fire Commissioners, 633
CCFMS - Central Canadian Federation of Mineralogical Societies, 524

CCFSB - Chambre de commerce francophone de Saint-Boniface, 548
CCFS-O - Federation of Canada-China Friendship Associations - Ottawa Chapter, 722
CCFV - Le Centre culturel francophone de Vancouver, 526
CCG - Conseil de la culture de la Gaspésie, 615
CCGA - Canadian Canola Growers Association, 349
CCGF - Canadian Coalition for Genetic Fairness, 357
CCGG - Canadian Coalition for Good Governance, 357
CCGLM - Centre communautaire des gais et lesbiennes de Montréal, 526
CCGS - Cumberland County Genealogical Society, 645
CCGSE - Canadian Committee of Graduate Students in Education, 361
CCHA - Canadian Cutting Horse Association, 375
CCHA - Canadian Catholic Historical Association - English Section, 351
CCHA - Canadian Crop Hail Association, 373
CCHL - Canadian College of Health Leaders, 358
CCHM - Commission canadienne d'histoire militaire, 592
CCHMS - Compton County Historical Museum Society, 609
CCHS - Carleton County Historical Society, Inc., 513
CCHYR - Chambre de commerce Haute-Yamaska et Région, 548
CCI - Canadian Condominium Institute, 362
CCI - Canadian Copyright Institute, 365
CCI - Canadian Crossroads International, 373
CCI - Canadian Conservation Institute, 363
CCI - Canadian Circumpolar Institute, 357
CCI2M - Chambre de commerce et d'industrie MRC de Deux-Montagne, 547
CCIA - Canadian Captive Insurance Association, 349
CCIA - China Canada Investment Association, 564
CCIB - Chambre de commerce et d'industrie du bassin de Chambly, 547
CCIC - Canadian Council for International Co-operation, 366
CCID - Chambre de commerce et d'industrie de Drummond, 545
CCIEF - Canadian Credit Institute Educational Foundation, 372
CCIFC - Chambre de commerce et d'industrie française au canada, 547
CCIL - Canadian Council on International Law, 371
CCIL - Chambre de commerce et d'industrie de Laval, 545
CCIL - Canadian Council of Independent Laboratories, 368
CCIM - Chambre de commerce des Îles-de-la-Madeleine, 544
CCIM - Chambre de commerce et d'industrie de Malartic, 545
CCIM - Chambre de commerce et d'industrie de Maniwaki & Vallée de la Gatineau, 546
CCINB - Chambre de commerce et d'industrie Nouvelle-Beauce, 547
CCIO - Chambre de commerce de l'Ile d'Orléans, 541
CCIR - Canadian Council of Insurance Regulators, 368
CCIRC - Chambre de commerce et d'Industrie de la région de Coaticook, 545
CCIRN - Chambre de commerce et d'industrie de Rouyn-Noranda, 546
CCIS - Calgary Catholic Immigration Society, 271
CCISJ - Chambre de commerce et d'industrie St-Jérôme, 548
CCITB - Chambre de commerce et d'industrie Thérèse-De Blainville, 548

CCITM - Chambre de commerce et d'industrie de Thetford Mines, 546
CCIV - Chambre de commerce et d'industrie de Varennes, 546
CCJA - Canadian Criminal Justice Association, 373
CCJC - Church Council on Justice & Corrections, 569
CCKL - Chambre de commerce Kamouraska-L'Islet, 548
CCL - Conseil de la culture des Laurentides, 616
CCL&D - Centre for Community Learning & Development, 531
CCL&D - Toronto Centre for Community Learning & Development, 1383
CCLA - Canadian Civil Liberties Association, 357
CCLA - Canadian Comparative Literature Association, 361
CCLA - Carleton County Law Association, 513
CCLA - Canadian Courier & Logistics Association, 372
CCLAQ - Chambre de commerce Latino-américaine du Québec, 549
CCLB - Centre for Canadian Language Benchmarks, 531
CCLD - Council of Canadian Law Deans, 633
CCLGBTQ - Chambre de commerce LGBT du Québec, 549
CCLH - Canadian Committee on Labour History, 361
CCLS - Calgary Community Living Society, 271
CCMA - Canadian Country Music Association, 372
CCMA - Canadian Council of Montessori Administrators, 369
CCMA - Canadian Capital Markets Association, 349
CCMB - CancerCare Manitoba, 508
CCMBC - Canadian Conference of Mennonite Brethren Churches, 363
CCME - Canadian Council of Ministers of the Environment, 368
CCMG - Canadian College of Medical Geneticists, 359
CCMM-CSN - Conseil central du Montréal métropolitain, 614
CCMPA - Canadian Concrete Masonry Producers Association, 362
CCMS - Calgary Co-operative Memorial Society, 271
CCMSB - Chambre de commerce Mont-Saint-Bruno, 549
CCMT - Canadian Council of Muslim Theologians, 369
CCMTA - Canadian Council of Motor Transport Administrators, 369
CCMW - Canadian Council of Muslim Women, 369
CCN - Carrying Capacity Network, 1515
CCN - Chebucto Community Net, 555
CCNA - Canadian Community Newspapers Association, 361
CCNB - Conservation Council of New Brunswick, 621
CCNC - Chinese Canadian National Council, 564
CCNM - The Canadian College of Naturopathic Medicine, 360
CCNP - Canadian College of Neuropsychopharmacology, 360
CCNR - Canadian Coalition for Nuclear Responsibility, 357
CCO - Conseil de coopération de l'Ontario, 615
CCO - Conservation Council of Ontario, 622
CCO - Cricket Council of Ontario, 642
CCO - Career Colleges Ontario, 511
CCO - Cancer Care Ontario, 507
CCOA - Corridor Community Options for Adults, 631
CCOC - Canadian Children's Opera Company, 356
CCOF - Canadian Children's Optimist Foundation, 356

Acronym Index

CCOHS - Canadian Centre for Occupational Health & Safety, 353
CCP - Canadian Church Press, 356
CCP - Canadians' Choice Party, 507
CCPA - Canadian Columbian Professional Association, 360
CCPA - Canadian Counselling & Psychotherapy Association, 371
CCPA - Canadian Centre for Policy Alternatives, 354
CCPA - Canadian Colombian Professional Association, 360
CCPA - Canadian Concrete Pipe Association, 362
CCPC - Canadian Clean Power Coalition, 357
CCPC - Canadian Council of Professional Certification, 369
CCPCP - Canadian College of Professional Counsellors & Psychotherapists, 360
CCPE - Council for Continuing Pharmaceutical Education, 632
CCPFH - Canadian Council of Professional Fish Harvesters, 369
CCPG - Canadian Council of Professional Geoscientists, 370
CCPIT - China Council for the Promotion of International Trade - Canadian Office, 564
CCPM - Canadian College of Physicists in Medicine, 360
CCPNR - Canadian Council of Practical Nurse Regulators, 361
CCPPP - The Canadian Council for Public-Private Partnerships, 366
CCPS - Canadian Connemara Pony Society, 363
CCPSA - Canadian Cerebral Palsy Sports Association, 354
CCQ - Conseil québécois de la coopération et de la mutualité, 620
CCQTA - Canadian Crude Quality Technical Association, 373
CCRA - Canadian Carbonization Research Association, 350
CCRC - Catholic Charismatic Renewal Council, Toronto, 517
CCRC - Canadian Coalition for the Rights of Children, 358
CCRC - Community Counselling & Resource Centre, 596
CCRC - Canadian Community Reinvestment Coalition, 361
CCRCC - Christian Catholic Church Canada, 566
CCRDA - Canadian Christian Relief & Development Association, 356
CCRF - Canadian Chiropractic Research Foundation, 356
CCRJ - Canadian Council for Reform Judaism, 367
CCRL - Catholic Civil Rights League, 518
CCRN - Credit Counselling of Regional Niagara, 639
CCRSR - Chambre de commerce régionale de St-Raymond, 549
CCRT - Canadian Chihuahua Rescue & Transport, 355
CCRW - Canadian Council on Rehabilitation & Work, 371
CCS - Caledon Community Services, 270
CCS - Canadian Cancer Society, 348
CCS - Canadian Cardiovascular Society, 350
CCS - Catholic Cross Cultural Services, 518
CCS - Conseil communauté en santé du Manitoba, 614
CCS - Conseil de la Coopération de la Saskatchewan, 615
CCS - Cross Country Saskatchewan, 643
CCS - Canadian Cue Sport Association, 373
CCS&CF - Canada-Cuba Sports & Cultural Festivals, 283
CCSA - Canadian Centre on Substance Use & Addiction, 354
CCSA - Canadian Cable Systems Alliance, 348
CCSA - Canadian Convenience Stores Association, 364

CCSAC - Credit Counselling Services of Atlantic Canada, Inc., 639
CCSAM - Cross Country Ski Association of Manitoba, 644
CCSBE - Canadian Council for Small Business & Entrepreneurship, 367
CCSCL - Chambre de commerce de St-Côme-Linière, 543
CCSD - Canadian Council on Social Development, 371
CCSD - Canadian Cultural Society of The Deaf, Inc., 374
CCSMH - Canadian Coalition for Seniors Mental Health, 358
CCSMM - Centre de la Communauté sourde du Montréal métropolitain, 529
CCSN - Canadian Cancer Survivor Network, 349
CCSNE - Conseil central de l'Estrie (CSN), 614
CCSNS - Cross Country Nova Scotia, 643
CCSO - Canadian Council of Snowmobile Organizations, 370
CCSP - Canadian Centre for Studies in Publishing, 354
CCSPA - Canadian Consumer Specialty Products Association, 363
CCSSA - Council of Catholic School Superintendents of Alberta, 633
CCSTA - Canadian Catholic School Trustees' Association, 351
CCSU - Concordia Caribbean Students' Union, 609
CCTC - Canadian Council for Tobacco Control, 367
CCTELA - Canadian Council of Teachers of English Language Arts, 370
CCTFA - Canadian Cosmetic, Toiletry & Fragrance Association, 366
CCTK - Chambre de commerce Témiscaming-Kipawa, 550
CCToMM - Commission canadienne pour la théorie des machines et des mécanismes, 593
CCTT - Canadian Council of Technicians & Technologists, 370
CCUA - Canadian Credit Union Association, 372
CCUA - Canada Cricket Umpires Association Inc., 278
CCUFSA - Canadian College & University Food Service Association, 358
CCUNESCO - Canadian Commission for UNESCO, 360
CCUPEKA - Canadian Council of University Physical Education & Kinesiology Administrators, 370
CCVD - Chambre de commerce de Val-d'Or, 543
CCVO - Calgary Chamber of Voluntary Organizations, 271
CCVT - Canadian Centre for Victims of Torture, 354
CCW - Canadian Construction Women, 363
CCWC - Castle-Crown Wilderness Coalition, 516
CCWG - Canadian Co-operative Wool Growers Ltd., 364
CCY - Cross Country Yukon, 644
CDA - Canadian Dermatology Association, 377
CDA - Canadian Dove Association, 378
CDA - Diabetes Canada, 655
CDA - Conference of Defence Associations, 612
CDA - Canadian Dental Association, 376
CDA - Canadian Dyslexia Association, 379
CDA - Canadian Dam Association, 375
CDAA - Canadian Dental Assistants Association, 376
CDAA/AADQ - Association des assistant(e)s-dentaires du Québec, 106
CDAAC - Communicative Disorders Assistant Association of Canada, 594
CDABC - Certified Dental Assistants of BC, 538
CDAC - Cranbrook & District Arts Council, 638

CDBA - Canadian Deafblind Association (National), 376
CDBC - College of Dietitians of British Columbia, 584
CDBC - College of Denturists of British Columbia, 583
CDC - Cariboo Chilcotin Child Development Centre Association, 512
CDC - Canadian Dairy Commission, 375
CDC - Casting Directors Society of Canada, 516
CDCA - Canadian Dexter Cattle Association, 377
CDCA - Canadian Die Casters Association, 378
CDCA - Canadian Deals & Coupons Association, 376
CDCA - Canadian Deaf Curling Association, 375
CDCC - Canadian Disaster Child Care Society, 378
CDCD - Community Development Council Durham, 596
CDCoC - Castlegar & District Chamber of Commerce, 517
CDDA - Canadian Diamond Drilling Association, 377
CDEACF - Centre de documentation sur l'éducation des adultes et la condition féminine, 529
CDECA - Canadian Decorators' Association, 376
CDEC-CSPMR - Corporation de développement économique communautaire Centre-Sud/Plateau Mont-Royal, 629
CDEM - Conseil de développement économique des municipalités bilingues du Manitoba, 615
CDGA - Canadian Depression Glass Association, 377
CDGA - Canadian Deaf Golf Association, 376
CDH - Community Development Halton, 596
CDHA - Canadian Dental Hygienists Association, 377
CDHBC - College of Dental Hygienists of British Columbia, 583
CDHF - Canadian Digestive Health Foundation, 378
CDHMS - Creston & District Historical & Museum Society, 641
CDHNS - College of Dental Hygienists of Nova Scotia, 583
CDHS - Cobourg & District Historical Society, 579
CDI - Child Development Institute, 559
CDI - Canadian Door Institute of Dealers, Manufacturers & Distributors, 378
CDIC - Community Connection, 596
CDIHF - Canadian Deaf Ice Hockey Federation, 376
CDLC - Calgary & District Labour Council, 270
CDMA - Canadian Donkey & Mule Association, 378
CDMQ - Conseil des directeurs médias du Québec, 617
CDO - College of Denturists of Ontario, 583
CDO - College of Dietitians of Ontario, 584
CDOA - Canadian Dental Protective Association, 377
CDPC - Canadian Drug Policy Coalition, 379
CDRA - Charlottetown Downtown Residents Association, 552
CDRG - Canadian Disaster Restoration Group, 378
CDRIN - Canadian Depression Research & Intervention Network, 377
CDS - The Canadian Doukhobor Society, 378
CDS - Canada DanceSport, 278
CDSA - Canadian Deaf Sports Association, 376
CDSBC - College of Dental Surgeons of British Columbia, 583
CDSS - Canadian Down Syndrome Society, 378
CDT - College of Dental Technicians of British Columbia, 583

CDTA - Canadian Dance Teachers' Association, 375
CDTA - Canadian Dental Therapists Association, 375
CDTA - College of Dental Technologists of Alberta, 583
CDTSA - Calgary & District Target Shooters Association, 276
CEA - Canadian Economics Association, 379
CEA - Canadian Education Association, 379
CEA - Citizens' Environment Alliance, 570
CEA - Consulting Engineers of Alberta, 625
CEA - Canadian Electricity Association, 380
CEA - Community Energy Association, 597
CEA - Conseil des entrepreneurs agricoles, 617
CEACS - Central European Association for Canadian Studies, 1516
CEAD - Centre des auteurs dramatiques, 530
CEAEC - Canadian Explosives Industry Association, 383
CÉAF - Centre d'éducation et d'action des femmes de Montréal, 528
CEAPA - Canadian Employee Assistance Program Association, 380
CEASE - Concerned Educators Allied for a Safe Environment, 1519
CEBC - Clean Energy British Columbia, 573
CEBQ - Conseil de l'enveloppe du bâtiment du Québec, 615
CEC - Council for Exceptional Children, 1520
CEC - Canadian Ethnocultural Council, 382
CEC - Commission for Environmental Cooperation, 593
CECA - Canadian Electrical Contractors Association, 380
CECAB - Canadian Environmental Certification Approvals Board, 381
CECC - The Christian Episcopal Church of Canada, 567
CECCO - Construction Employers Coordinating Council of Ontario, 624
CECI - Centre canadien d'étude et de coopération internationale, 526
CEDHS - Caledon East & District Historical Society, 270
CEDI - Carrefour d'entraide de Drummond, 515
CEEA - Canadian Energy Efficiency Alliance, 381
CEEA - Canadian Engineering Education Association, 381
CEED - Centre for Entrepreneurship Education & Development Inc., 532
CEEDA - Canada East Equipment Dealers' Association, 278
CEEDS - Community Enhancement & Economic Development Society, 597
CEEF - Canadian Education Exchange Foundation, 380
CEEP - Centre for Excellence in Emergency Preparedness, 532
CEFI - Children's Education Funds Inc., 561
CEFO - Catholic Education Foundation of Ontario, 518
CEFRIO - Centre francophone d'informatisation des organisations, 534
CEGN - Canadian Environmental Grantmakers' Network, 382
CEGQ - Corporation des entrepreneurs généraux du Québec, 630
CEIA - Canadian Environment Industry Association, 381
CEIU - Canada Employment & Immigration Union, 278
CELA - Canadian Environmental Law Association, 382
CELF - Canadian Energy Law Foundation, 381
CEMA - Canadian Ethnic Media Association, 382
CEMA - Cumulative Environmental Management Association, 646
CEMC - Consumer Electronics Marketers of Canada: A Division of Electro-Federation Canada, 625
CEMRA - Canadian Electrical Manufacturers Representatives Association, 380

Acronym Index

CÉNB - Conseil économique du Nouveau-Brunswick inc., 618
CENL - Consulting Engineers of Newfoundland & Labrador, 625
CENS - Consulting Engineers of Nova Scotia, 625
CENT - Consulting Engineers of the Northwest Territories, 625
CEO - Consulting Engineers of Ontario, 625
CEO - Canadian Examiners in Optometry, 383
CEPA - Canadian Energy Pipeline Association, 381
CEPME - Centre d'entrepreneuriat et PME, 528
CERA - Centre for Equality Rights in Accommodation, 532
CERA - Canadian Educational Researchers' Association, 380
CERBA - Canada Eurasia Russia Business Association, 279
CERC - Canadian Educational Resources Council, 380
CERC - Canadian Employee Relocation Council, 380
CERD - Cumberland Equal Rights for the Disabled, 645
CERF - Centre d'entraide et de ralliement familial, 528
CERI - Canadian Energy Research Institute, 381
CERLAC - Centre for Research on Latin America & The Caribbean, 533
CES - Canadian Evaluation Society, 383
CESA - Canadian Ethnic Studies Association, 382
CESB - Canadian Society for Epidemiology & Biostatistics, 474
CESGM - Corporation des entrepreneurs spécialisés du Grand Montréal inc., 630
CESO - Canadian Executive Service Organization, 383
CETA - Canadian Explosive Technicians' Association, 383
CETAC - Canadian Education & Training Accreditation Commission, 379
CETAC - Canadian Environmental Technology Advancement Corporation - West, 382
CETAF - Corporation des entreprises de traitement de l'air et du froid, 630
CETFA - Canadian ETF Association, 382
CETFA - Canadians for Ethical Treatment of Food Animals, 507
CEU - Compensation Employees' Union (Ind.), 608
CEW - Citizens' Environment Watch, 570
CEWA - Canadian Energy Workers' Association, 381
CEWHA - Canadian Electric Wheelchair Hockey Association, 380
CEWIL - Co-operative Education & Work-Integrated Learning Canada, 627
CEY - Consulting Engineers of Yukon, 625
CFA - Canadian Fraternal Association, 394
CFA - Canadian Federation of Agriculture, 384
CFA - Canadian Franchise Association, 394
CFA - Canadian Ferry Association, 389
CFA - Canadian Flag Association, 391
CFA - Canadian Forestry Association, 392
CFA - Canadian Foundry Association, 394
CFA - Capilano University Faculty Association, 510
CFA - Commonwealth Forestry Association - Canadian Chapter, 593
CFAA - Canadian Fire Alarm Association, 390
CFAA - Canadian Federation of Apartment Associations, 385
CFAB - Canadian Forestry Accreditation Board, 392
CFAC - Community Folk Art Council of Toronto, 597
CFAMEA - Canadian Federation of Aircraft Maintenance Engineers Associations, 384
CFANB - Canadian Forestry Association of New Brunswick, 392
CFAO - Concrete Forming Association of Ontario, 610

CFAS - Canadian Fertility & Andrology Society, 389
CFASC - CFA Society Calgary, 538
CFAVM - Canadian Faculties of Agriculture & Veterinary Medicine, 383
CFAY - Canadian-Filipino Association of Yukon, 506
CFB - Canadian Bridge Federation, 347
CFBA - Canadian Farm Builders Association, 384
CFBC - Community Futures Development Association of British Columbia, 598
CFBIU - Canadian Friends of Bar-Ilan University, 394
CFBPWC - The Canadian Federation of Business & Professional Women's Clubs, 385
CFBSD - Canadian Federation of Business School Deans, 386
CFC - Canadian Film Centre, 390
CFC - Couples For Christ, 636
CFC - Chicken Farmers of Canada, 557
CFC - Conseil francophone de la chanson, 618
CFC - Child Find Canada Inc., 559
CFC - Canine Federation of Canada, 508
CFC - Couples for Christ Canada, 636
CFCA - Change for Children Association, 551
CFCAS - Canadian Foundation for Climate & Atmospheric Sciences, 393
CFCFFL - Couples For Christ Foundation for Family & Life, 636
CFCI - Centre de formation à la coopération interculturelle du Québec, 529
CFCN - Canadian Families & Corrections Network, 383
CFCREAB - Canadian Federation of Chiropractic Regulatory & Educational Accrediting Boards, 386
CFCS - Community Financial Counselling Services, 597
CFDF - Canadian Foundation for Dietetic Research, 393
CFEA - Canadian Food Exporters Association, 391
CFEE - Canadian Foundation for Economic Education, 393
CFES - Canadian Federation of Earth Sciences, 386
CFES - Canadian Federation of Engineering Students, 386
CFF - Canadian Fencing Federation, 389
CFFAR - Canadian Foundation on Fetal Alcohol Research, 394
CFFB - Centre for Family Business, 532
CFFBTS - Calgary Firefighters Burn Treatment Society, 272
CFFC - Canadian Food for Children, 391
CFFM - Canadian Federation of Friends of Museums, 386
CFFO - Christian Farmers Federation of Ontario, 567
CFGA - Canadian Forage & Grassland Association, 392
CFGB - Canadian Foodgrains Bank, 391
CFHI - Canadian Foundation for Healthcare Improvement, 393
CFHS - Canadian Federation of Humane Societies, 386
CFHSS - Canadian Federation for the Humanities & Social Sciences, 384
CFHU - Canadian Friends of the Hebrew University, 395
CFI - Canadian Film Institute, 390
CFI - Canada Foundation for Innovation, 279
CFIA - Canadian Fence Industry Association, 389
CFIB - Canadian Federation of Independent Business, 386
CFIG - Canadian Federation of Independent Grocers, 387
CFIQ - Collectif des femmes immigrantes du Québec, 581
CFIS - Centre for Indigenous Sovereignty, 532
CFJL - Canadian Federation of Junior Leagues, 387

CFL - Canadian Football League, 392
CFLA - Canadian Federation of Library Associations, 387
CFLA - Canadian Finance & Leasing Association, 390
CFLAA - Canadian Football League Alumni Association, 392
CFLPA - Canadian Football League Players' Association, 392
CFLRI - Canadian Fitness & Lifestyle Research Institute, 390
CFM - Community Futures Manitoba Inc., 598
CFMDC - Canadian Filmmakers Distribution Centre, 390
CFMHN - Canadian Federation of Mental Health Nurses, 388
CFMJ - Canadian Foundation for Masorti Judaism, 393
CFMS - Canadian Federation of Medical Students, 388
CFMTA - Canadian Federation of Music Teachers' Associations, 388
CFN - Centre for Newcomers Society of Calgary, 533
CFNA - Community Futures Network Society of Alberta, 598
CFNS - Calgary Field Naturalists' Society, 272
CFNU - Canadian Federation of Nurses Unions, 388
CFO - Community Foundation of Ottawa, 597
CFO - Canadian Federation of Orthotherapists, 388
CFOA - Canadian Football Officials Association, 392
CFOB - Canadian Friends of Burma, 395
CFOCCF - Concerned Friends of Ontario Citizens in Care Facilities, 609
CFOF - Centre franco-ontarien de folklore, 534
CFORP - Centre franco-ontarien de ressources pédagogiques, 534
CFP - Canadian Foundation for Pharmacy, 393
CFP - Canadian Federation of Pensioners, 388
CFPA - Canadian Fluid Power Association, 391
CFPA - Canadian Federal Pilots Association, 384
CFPA - Coast Forest Products Association, 579
CFPC - College of Family Physicians of Canada, 584
CFPDP - Canadian Foundation for Physically Disabled Persons, 394
CFPM - Canadian Federation of Podiatric Medicine, 388
CFPN - Canadian Friends of Peace Now (Shalom Achshav), 395
CFQ - Cercles de fermières du Québec, 537
CFS - Coast Foundation Society, 579
CFS - Canadian Federation of Students, 388
CFS - Catholic Family Services of Hamilton, 518
CFS - Chicken Farmers of Saskatchewan, 557
CFS - Catholic Family Services of Saskatoon, 519
CFS Ottawa - Catholic Family Service of Ottawa, 518
CFS Toronto - Catholic Family Services of Toronto, 519
CFSA - Canadian Fire Safety Association, 390
CFSC - Canadian Friends Service Committee, 395
CFSC - Clan Fraser Society of Canada, 571
CFSPD - Catholic Family Services of Peel Dufferin, 519
CFSSC - Catholic Family Services of Simcoe County, 519
CFT - Centre francophone de Toronto, 535
CFTC - Canadian Feed The Children, 389
CFTO - Christmas Tree Farmers of Ontario, 568
CFU - Canadian Friends of Ukraine, 395
CFUS - Canadian Foundation for Ukrainian Studies, 394
CFUW - Canadian Federation of University Women, 388
CFWF - Canadian Farm Writers' Federation, 384

CFYU - Canadian Friends of Yeshiva University, 395
CGA - Compressed Gas Association, Inc., 1518
CGA - Canadian Gas Association, 396
CGA - Canadian Gemmological Association, 396
CGA - Canadian Galloway Association, 396
CGA - Canadian Gelbvieh Association, 396
CGA - Canadian Gaming Association, 396
CGB - Commonwealth Geographical Bureau, 1518
CGC - Canada Grains Council, 279
CGC - Canadian GeoExchange Coalition, 397
CGC - Canada Games Council, 279
CGC - Commonwealth Games Canada, 593
CGCIC - Canadian German Chamber of Industry & Commerce Inc., 397
CGDB - Canadian Guide Dogs for the Blind, 399
CGDN - Canadian Genetic Diseases Network, 397
CGHF - Canadian Golf Hall of Fame & Museum, 398
CGIAR - Consultative Group on International Agricultural Research, 1519
CGMFA - Canadian Grand Masters Fiddling Association, 398
CGNA - Canadian Gerontological Nursing Association, 397
CGPA - Canadian Generic Pharmaceutical Association, 397
CGPA - Canadian Group Psychotherapy Association, 399
CGRA - Canadian Grandparents' Rights Association, 399
CGS - Canadian Goat Society, 398
CGS - Canadian Geriatrics Society, 397
CGS - Canadian Geotechnical Society, 397
CGSA - Canadian Golf Superintendents Association, 398
CGSB - Canadian General Standards Board, 396
CGU - Canadian Geophysical Union, 397
CgyAD - Calgary Association of the Deaf, 271
CHA - Craft & Hobby Association, 1520
CHA - Canadian Handball Association, 400
CHA - Canadian Historical Association, 405
CHA - Canadian Hydrographic Association, 409
CHA - Canadian Hereford Association, 404
CHA - Canadian Haflinger Association, 400
CHA - Canadian Hydropower Association, 410
CHA - Canadian Hypnosis Association, 410
CHAA - Christian Health Association of Alberta, 567
CHAA - Canadian Harvard Aircraft Association, 401
CHABC - Catholic Health Association of British Columbia, 519
CHACI - Cypress Hills Ability Centres, Inc., 647
CHAD - Chambre de l'assurance de dommages, 550
CHAM - Catholic Health Association of Manitoba, 519
CHANB - Catholic Health Association of New Brunswick, 520
CHAPA - College of Hearing Aid Practitioners of Alberta, 585
CHAS - Catholic Health Association of Saskatchewan, 520
CHASE - Children's Heart Association for Support & Education, 561
CHBA - Canadian Home Builders' Association, 406
CHBA - Canadian Horse Breeders' Association, 408
CHBA BC - Canadian Home Builders' Association - British Columbia, 406
CHBA-EN - Canadian Home Builders' Association - Newfoundland Labrador, 407
CHBA-PEI - Canadian Home Builders' Association - Prince Edward Island, 407
CHC - Canadian Horticultural Council, 408
CHC - Canadian Health Coalition, 401
CHCA - Canadian Home Care Association, 408
CHCS - Canadian Highland Cattle Society, 405

Acronym Index

CHEA - Canadian History of Education Association, 405
CHEC - Commonwealth Human Ecology Council, 1518
CHEJ - Center for Health, Environment & Justice, 1516
CHEP - Canadian Hatching Egg Producers, 401
CHES - Canadian Healthcare Engineering Society, 402
CHF Canada - Cooperative Housing Federation of Canada, 628
CHFA - Canadian Home Furnishings Alliance, 408
CHFA - Canadian Health Food Association, 401
CHFBC - Cooperative Housing Federation of British Columbia, 628
CHFCA - Canadian Hydrogen & Fuel Cell Association, 409
CHFT - Co-operative Housing Federation of Toronto, 628
CHGG - Colchester Highland Games & Gathering Society, 580
CHGS - Center for Holocaust & Genocide Studies, 1516
CHHA - Canadian Hard of Hearing Association, 400
CHHAPS - Canadian Horse Heritage & Preservation Society, 408
CHHMA - Canadian Hardware & Housewares Manufacturers' Association, 401
CHILD - CHILD Foundation, 560
CHIMA - Canadian Health Information Management Association, 402
CHIN - Canadian Heritage Information Network, 405
CHIPS - Canadian Hearing Instrument Practitioners Society, 403
CHJQ - Chambre des huissiers de justice du Québec, 550
CHLA - Canadian Health Libraries Association, 402
CHMSE - Canadian Hotel Marketing & Sales Executives, 409
CHNA - Canadian Holistic Nurses Association, 406
CHNC - Community Health Nurses of Canada, 599
CHO - Community Heritage Ontario, 599
CHOA - Canadian Heavy Oil Association, 403
CHOA - Condominium Home Owners' Association of British Columbia, 610
CHOC - Consumer Health Organization of Canada, 625
CHP - Christian Heritage Party of Canada, 567
CHPCA - Canadian Hospice Palliative Care Association, 409
CHPVA - Canadian Hardwood Plywood & Veneer Association, 401
CHR - Canadians for Health Research, 507
CHRA - Canadian Housing & Renewal Association, 409
CHRA - Cole Harbour Ringette Association, 581
CHRC - Cultural Human Resources Council, 645
CHRHS - Cole Harbour Rural Heritage Society, 581
CHS - Cardston Historical Society, 511
CHS - Canadian Hearing Society, 403
CHS - Canadian Hemophilia Society, 404
CHS - Canadian Hematology Society, 404
CHS - Calgary Horticultural Society, 272
CHS - Canadian Hemochromatosis Society, 404
CHSF - Canadian Home & School Federation, 406
CHTA - Canadian Horticultural Therapy Association, 408
CHW - Canadian Hadassah WIZO, 399
CI - The Canadian Institute, 412
CI - Cordage Institute, 1520
CI - Consumers International, 1519
CI - Conservation International, 1519
CIA - Canadian Institute of Actuaries, 414
CIAA - Canadian Insurance Accountants Association, 420

CIAA - Canadian Independent Adjusters' Association, 410
CIAC - Chemistry Industry Association of Canada, 556
CIAFT - Conseil d'intervention pour l'accès des femmes au travail, 615
CIAJ - Canadian Institute for the Administration of Justice, 413
CIAS - Canadian International Air Show, 421
CIAS - Immigrant Services Calgary, 830
CIAT - Chambre immobilière de l'Abitibi-Témiscamingue Inc., 550
CIB - Canadian Institute of Bookkeeping, 414
C-IBC - Canada-India Business Council, 283
CIBPA - Canadian Italian Business & Professional Association of Ottawa, 423
CIBPA - Canadian Italian Business & Professional Association, 423
CIBRA - Canadian Independent Bicycle Retailers Association, 410
CIBS - Centre for International Business Studies, 533
CIC - Community Information Centre of Ottawa, 599
CIC - Credit Institute of Canada, 640
CIC - Canadian International Council, 421
CIC - Chemical Institute of Canada, 556
CIC - Canadian Innovation Centre, 411
CICan - Colleges and Institutes Canada, 590
CICAPP - Canadian Institute for Child & Adolescent Psychoanalytic Psychotherapy, 412
CICBP - Canadian Institute of Chartered Business Planners, 414
CICBV - Canadian Institute of Chartered Business Valuators, 414
CICC - Centre international de criminologie comparée, 535
CICC - Coalition for International Criminal Court, 1517
CICD - Centre d'information communautaire et de dépannage Ste-Marie, 528
CICF - Canada-Israel Cultural Foundation, 283
CICH - Canadian Institute of Child Health, 414
CICIC - Canadian Information Centre for International Credentials, 411
CICMA - Canadian Insurance Claims Managers Association, 420
CICR - Canadian Institute for Conflict Resolution, 412
CICS - Centre for Immigrant & Community Services, 532
CICS - Canadian Intergovernmental Conference Secretariat, 420
CID - Community Involvement of the Disabled, 599
CIDBFS - Canadian International Dragon Boat Festival Society, 421
CIDEF - Centre international de documentation et d'échanges de la francophonie, 535
CIDX - Canadian International DX Club, 421
CIE - Canadian Institute of Energy (British Columbia), 415
CIE - Canadian Institute of Entrepreneurship, 415
CIEC - Canada Israel Experience Centre, 280
CIEL - Centre intégré d'employabilité locale des Collines-de-l'Outaouais, 535
CIER - Centre for Indigenous Environmental Resources, Inc., 532
CIESC - The Comparative & International Education Society of Canada, 608
CIET - Canadian Institute for Energy Training, 412
CIF - Community Information Fairview, 599
CIF - Canadian Institute of Forestry, 416
CIFAR - Canadian Institute for Advanced Research, 412
CIFFA - Canadian International Freight Forwarders Association, 421
CIF-NL - Canadian Institute of Forestry, Newfoundland & Labrador, 416
CIFPs - Canadian Institute of Financial Planners, 415

CIFQ - Conseil de l'industrie forestière du Québec, 615
CIFST - Canadian Institute of Food Science & Technology, 415
CIG - Canadian Institute of Gemmology, 416
CIG - Canadian Institute of Geomatics, 416
CIG - Canadian Institute in Greece, 414
CIH - Community Information Hamilton, 599
CIHF - Canadian Icelandic Horse Federation, 410
CIHF - Canadian Italian Heritage Foundation, 423
CIHI - Canadian Institute for Health Information, 412
CIHY - Chambre immobilière de la Haute Yamaska Inc., 550
CII - Coady International Institute, 577
CIIAN - Canadian International Institute of Applied Negotiation, 421
CIISOQ - Corporation des infirmières et infirmiers de salle d'opération du Québec, 630
CIJA - The Centre for Israel & Jewish Affairs, 533
CIJR - Canadian Institute for Jewish Research, 412
CIL - Chambre immobilière des Laurentides, 551
CIL - Club informatique de Longueuil, 575
CILQ - Conseil des industriels laitiers du Québec inc., 617
CILT - The Chartered Institute of Logistics & Transport in North America, 552
CILT - Centre for Independent Living in Toronto, 532
CIM - Canadian Institute of Management, 416
CIM - Canadian Institute of Mining, Metallurgy & Petroleum, 417
CIMA - Canadian Independent Music Association, 410
CIMS - Canadian Institute for Mediterranean Studies, 412
CINA - Canadian Indigenous Nurses Association, 411
CINDE - Canadian Institute for Research in Nondestructive Examination, 413
CINDEA - Canadian Integrative Network for Death Education & Alternatives, 420
CINS - Canadian Institute for Neutron Scattering, 413
CIOCAN - CIO Association of Canada, 570
CION - Cultural Industries Ontario North, 645
CIP - Canadian Institute of Planners, 418
CIPA - Couchiching Institute on Public Affairs, 632
CIPC - Centre international pour la prévention de la criminalité, 535
CIPF - Canadian Investor Protection Fund, 422
CIPFA - Chartered Institute of Public Finance & Accountancy, 1516
CIPH - Canadian Institute of Plumbing & Heating, 418
CIPHI - Canadian Institute of Public Health Inspectors, 419
CIPP - Civic Institute of Professional Personnel, 571
CIPPRS - Canadian Image Processing & Pattern Recognition Society, 410
CIPS - Canadian Information Processing Society, 411
CIPTO - Centre d'intervention et de prévention en toxicomanie de l'Outaouais, 528
CIQ - Conseil interprofessionnel du Québec, 618
CIQS - Canadian Institute of Quantity Surveyors, 419
CIRA - Canadian Internet Registration Authority, 422
CIRAC - Central Interior Regional Arts Council, 524
CIRAL - Centre interdisciplinaire de recherches sur les activités langagières, 535
CIRCCO - Centre d'information et de recherche en consommation de Charlevoix-Ouest, 528

CIREQ - Centre interuniversitaire de recherche en économie quantitative, 535
CIRI - Canadian Investor Relations Institute, 422
CIRID - Centre for Immunization & Respiratory Infectious Diseases, 532
CIRL - Canadian Institute of Resources Law, 419
CIRPA - Canadian Institutional Research & Planning Association, 420
CIRPD - Canadian Institute for the Relief of Pain & Disability, 413
CIS - Cape Breton University Centre for International Studies, 510
CIS - Canadian Institute of Stress, 419
CIS - Canadian Interuniversity Sport, 422
CIS - Conference of Independent Schools (Ontario), 612
CIS - Canadian Iris Society, 422
CISC - Canadian Institute of Steel Construction, 419
CISL - Chambre immobilière du Saguenay-Lac St-Jean Inc., 551
CISO - Centre international de solidarité ouvrière, 535
CISS - Community Integration Services Society, 599
CISV - Children's International Summer Villages (Canada) Inc., 562
CIT - CODA International Training, 1518
CITA - Canadian Independent Telephone Association, 411
CITA - Canadian Imaging Trade Association, 410
CITE - Canadian Institute of Transportation Engineers, 420
CITIG - Canadian Interoperability Technology Interest Group, 422
CITT - Canadian Institute of Traffic & Transportation, 419
CITT - Canadian Institute for Theatre Technology, 413
CIU - Customs & Immigration Union, 646
CIU - Canadian Institute of Underwriters, 420
CIUS - Canadian Institute of Ukrainian Studies, 420
CIVA - Canada India Village Aid Association, 280
CIWA - Canadian Injured Workers Alliance, 411
CIWA - Calgary Immigrant Women's Association, 272
CJA - Canadian Jewellers Association, 423
CJAO - Ontario Criminal Justice Association, 1076
CJBS - Coastal Jazz & Blues Society, 579
CJCA - Calgary Japanese Community Association, 273
CJE - Centre for Jewish Education, 533
CJEO - Carrefour jeunesse emploi de l'Outaouais, 515
CJEP - Carrefour jeunesse emploi du Pontiac, 515
CJEP - Carrefour jeunesse-emploi Papineau, 516
CJEVG - Carrefour Jeunesse Emploi Vallée-de-la-Gatineau, 516
CJF - Canadian Journalism Foundation, 423
CJFCB - Conseil jeunesse francophone de la Colombie-Britannique, 618
CJFE - Canadian Journalists for Free Expression, 423
CJFL - Canadian Junior Football League, 423
CJG - Creative Jewellers Guild of BC, 639
CJGA - Canadian Junior Golf Association, 423
CJI - Canadian Jesuits International, 423
CJMIU - Centre de protection de l'enfance et de la jeunesse, 529
CJN - Cercles des jeunes naturalistes, 537
CJO - Les Centres jeunesse de l'Outaouais, 537
CJP - Conseil jeunesse provincial (Manitoba), 619
CJQ - Le centre jeunesse de Québec, 536
CKBA - Canada Korea Business Association, 280

Acronym Index

CKC - CanoeKayak Canada, 509
CKC - Canadian Kennel Club, 424
CKCA - Canadian Kitchen Cabinet Association, 424
CKCF - Canadian Kennel Club Foundation, 424
CKF - Canadian Kendo Federation, 424
CKNB - Canoe Kayak New Brunswick, 508
CKNS - Canoe Kayak Nova Scotia, 508
CKS - Canoe Kayak Saskatchewan, 509
CKSA - Canadian Katahdin Sheep Association Inc., 423
CLA - Community Living Atikokan, 600
CLA - Canadian Lacrosse Association, 425
CLA - Canadian Linguistic Association, 427
CLA - Canadian Lung Association, 428
CLA - Criminal Lawyers' Association, 642
CLA - Canadian Limousin Association, 427
CLA (LC) - Community Living Association (Lanark County), 600
CLAA - Canadian Llama & Alpaca Association, 428
CLABC - Church Library Association of British Columbia, 569
CLAC - Christian Labour Association of Canada, 567
CLAE - Canadian League Against Epilepsy, 426
CLAIHR - Canadian Lawyers Association for International Human Rights, 426
CLAO - Church Library Association of Ontario, 569
CLAQ - Confrérie de la librairie ancienne du Québec, 612
CLAS - Community Living Alternatives Society, 600
CLASS - Community Living Association for South Simcoe, 600
CLASS - The Canadian Laser and Aesthetic Specialists Society, 425
CLB - The Church Lads' Brigade, 569
CLC - Campaign Life Coalition, 276
CLC - Canadian Labour Congress, 424
CLC - Shipyard General Workers' Federation of British Columbia, 1296
CLCA - Canadian Lowline Cattle Association, 428
CLCA - Canadian Lactation Consultant Association, 425
CLCB - Community Living Campbellford/Brighton, 601
CLD R-N - Centre local de développement Rouyn-Noranda, 536
CLDC - Community Living Dundas County, 601
CLDSL - Community Living Dryden-Sioux Lookout, 601
CLE - Community Living Elgin, 601
CLÉ - Centre canadien de leadership en éducation, 526
CLEA - Community Legal Education Association (Manitoba) Inc., 600
CLEO - Community Legal Education Ontario, 600
CLF - Canadian Liver Foundation, 427
CLF - Canadian Lymphedema Framework, 429
CLFE - Community Living Fort Erie, 602
CLFFD - Community Living Fort Frances & District, 602
CLG - Community Living Glengarry, 602
CLGA - Canadian Lesbian & Gay Archives, 426
CLGS - Community Living Greater Sudbury, 602
CLH - Community Living Huntsville, 602
CLH - Community Living Huronia, 602
CLHIA - Canadian Life & Health Insurance Association Inc., 426
CLIA - Canadian Lawyers Insurance Association, 426
CLIA - Cruise Lines International Association, Inc., 1520
CLIA PEI - Community Legal Information Association of Prince Edward Island, 600
CLiFF - Canadian Labour International Film Festival, 425
CLIMOA - Canadian Life Insurance Medical Officers Association, 426

CLKL - Community Living Kawartha Lakes, 603
CLL - Community Living London, 603
CLLG - Calgary Law Library Group, 273
CLLN - Canadian Literacy & Learning Network, 427
CLM - Community Living Mississauga, 603
CLNAD - Community Living Newmarket/Aurora District, 603
CLNH - Community Living North Halton, 603
CLO - Community Living Oakville, 604
CLO - Community Living Ontario, 604
CLP - Community Living Peterborough, 604
CLPNA - College of Licensed Practical Nurses of Alberta, 585
CLPNBC - College of Licensed Practical Nurses of BC, 585
CLPNM - College of Licensed Practical Nurses of Manitoba, 585
CLPNNL - College of Licensed Practical Nurses of Newfoundland & Labrador, 585
CLPNNS - College of Licensed Practical Nurses of Nova Scotia, 585
CLPS - Community Living Parry Sound, 604
CLQ - Communauté Laotienne du Québec, 594
CLQW - Community Living Quinte West, 604
CLRA - Canadian Land Reclamation Association, 425
CLRA - Construction Labour Relations Association of Newfoundland & Labrador, 624
CLRA - Construction Labour Relations - An Alberta Association, 624
CLRC - Canadian Livestock Records Corporation, 428
CLRC - Canadian Piedmontese Association, 455
CLS - Community Living Society, 605
CLSA - Canadian Laboratory Suppliers Association, 424
CLSA - Canadian Law & Society Association, 425
CLSAB - Canadian Lumber Standards Accreditation Board, 428
CLSC - Community Living Stormont County, 605
CLSF - Coffin-Lowry Syndrome Foundation, 1518
CLSL - Community Living Sarnia-Lambton, 605
CLTB - Community Living Thunder Bay, 605
CLW - Community Living Wallaceburg, 606
CLW - Community Living Windsor, 606
CLWD - Community Living Walkerton & District, 606
CLWN - Community Living West Nipissing, 606
CLWR - Canadian Lutheran World Relief, 428
CLYS - Community Living York South, 606
CMA - Canadian Marketing Association, 430
CMA - Canadian Motorcycle Association, 437
CMA - Canadian Museums Association, 437
CMA - Canadian Medical Association, 433
CMA - Canadian Marfan Association, 430
CMA - Conseil des métiers d'art du Québec (ind.), 617
CMA - Canadian Mineral Analysts, 436
CMA - Chess'n Math Association, 556
CMA NWT&NU - CMA Canada - Northwest Territories & Nunavut, 576
CMAA - Canadian Maine-Anjou Association, 429
CMAA - Canadian Masters Athletic Association, 431
CMAAC - Chinese Medicine & Acupuncture Association of Canada, 565
CMAF - Canadian Mountain Arts Foundation, 437
CMAW - Construction Maintenance & Allied Workers Canada, 624
CMBC - College of Midwives of British Columbia, 586
CMBC - Contagious Mountain Bike Club, 626
CMBES - Canadian Medical & Biological Engineering Society, 433
CMC - Circulation Management Association of Canada, 570
CMC - Canadian Meat Council, 432

CMC - Chamber of Marine Commerce, 539
CMC - Canadian Music Centre, 438
CMC - Concours de musique du Canada inc., 610
CMC - Co-operatives & Mutuals Canada, 628
CMCA - Canadian Masonry Contractors' Association, 431
CMC-Alberta - Institute of Certified Management Consultants of Alberta, 845
CMC-BC - Institute of Certified Management Consultants of British Columbia, 845
CMCC - Conseil montérégien de la culture et des communications, 619
CMCC - Canadian Memorial Chiropractic College, 434
CMC-Canada - Canadian Association of Management Consultants, 320
CMCFA - Canadian Military Colleges Faculty Association, 436
CMC-Manitoba - Institute of Certified Management Consultants of Manitoba, 845
CMCSA - Canadian Masters Cross-Country Ski Association, 431
CMDA - Canadian Magen David Adom for Israel, 429
CMDA - Calgary Motor Dealers Association, 273
CMDC - Canadian Media Directors' Council, 432
CMDS - Christian Medical & Dental Society of Canada, 568
CME - Canadian Manufacturers & Exporters, 429
CME - Coalition for Music Education in British Columbia, 578
CMEA - Canadian Music Educators' Association, 438
CMEC - Coalition for Music Education in Canada, 578
CMEC - Council of Ministers of Education, Canada, 834
CMEQ - Corporation des maîtres électriciens du Québec, 630
CMF - Canadian Medical Foundation, 434
CMF - Canadian Melanoma Foundation, 434
CMF - Canada Media Fund, 280
CMFAA - Canadian Music Festival Adjudicators' Association, 438
CMG - Computer Modelling Group, 609
CMG - Canadian Media Guild, 432
CMGA - Mushrooms Canada, 983
CMGA - Canadian Murray Grey Association, 437
CMGA - Canadian Meat Goat Association, 432
CMHA - Canadian Mental Health Association, 434
CMHA - Canadian Morgan Horse Association, 437
CMHI - Canadian Manufactured Housing Institute, 429
CMHO - Children's Mental Health Ontario, 562
CMHS - Chester Municipal Heritage Society, 557
CMI - Comité maritime international, 1518
CMIC - Catholic Missions in Canada, 520
CMISA - The Canadian Marine Industries and Shipbuilding Association, 430
CMLTA - College of Medical Laboratory Technologists of Alberta, 586
CMM - Confederacy of Mainland Mi'kmaq, 610
CMMA - Canadian MedTech Manufacturers' Alliance, 434
CMMTQ - Corporation des maîtres mécaniciens en tuyauterie du Québec, 630
CMNS - Classical & Medieval Numismatic Society, 572
CMNVA - Canadian Merchant Navy Veterans Association Inc., 435
CMOS - Canadian Meteorological & Oceanographic Society, 435
CMP - Canadian Mineral Processors Society, 437
CMPA - Canadian Media Production Association, 432

CMPA - Canadian Marine Pilots' Association, 430
CMPS - Canadian Militaria Preservation Society, 436
CMQ - Collège des médecins du Québec, 582
CMQ - Centre multiethnique de Québec, 536
CMR - Centre Montérégien de réadaptation, 536
CMRC - Canadian Midwifery Regulators Consortium, 436
CMRRA - Canadian Musical Reproduction Rights Agency, 438
CMRT - Cranbrook Archives, Museum & Landmark Foundation, 638
CMS - Canadian Mathematical Society, 431
CMSA - Canadian Meat Science Association, 432
CMSC - Clan MacLeod Societies of Canada, 572
CMSC - Consortium of Multiple Sclerosis Centers, 1519
CMSG - Canadian Merchant Service Guild, 435
CMSS - Canadian Milking Shorthorn Society, 436
CMTA - Canadian Massage Therapist Alliance, 431
CMTBC - College of Massage Therapists of British Columbia, 585
CMTO - College of Massage Therapists of Ontario, 585
CMVA - Canadian Machinery Vibration Association, 429
CMW - Canadian Music Week Inc., 438
CNA - Newspapers Canada, 1024
CNA - Canadian Nuclear Association, 442
CNA - Canadian Nurses Association, 442
CNAF - Canadian National Autism Foundation, 438
CNANW - Canadian Network to Abolish Nuclear Weapons, 441
CNAREA - Canadian National Association of Real Estate Appraisers, 438
CNB - Cricket New Brunswick, 642
CNBA - Cities of New Brunswick Association, 570
CNBA - Canadian Norwegian Business Association, 1515
CNBH - Canada's National Bible Hour, 282
CNBPA - Canadian Netherlands Business & Professional Association Inc., 440
CNBSL - Club de Numismates du Bas St-Laurent, 575
CNBTA - Canadian National Baton Twirling Association, 438
CNC/IEC - International Electrotechnical Commission - Canadian National Committee, 857
CNCA - Canadian Nurse Continence Advisors Association, 442
CNDA - College of Naturopathic Doctors of Alberta, 586
CNEA - Canadian National Exhibition Association, 439
CNEA - Canadian National Energy Alliance, 439
CNF - Canadian Nurses Foundation, 443
CNFC - Canadian Native Friendship Centre, 440
CNFIU - Canadian National Federation of Independent Unions, 439
CNFIU - Independent Canadian Extrusion Workers Union, 832
CNHA - Canadian Natural Health Association, 440
CNIA - Canadian Nursing Informatics Association, 443
CNIB - Canadian National Institute for the Blind, 439
CNIE - Canadian Network for Innovation in Education, 440
CNLA - Canadian Nursery Landscape Association, 442
C-NLOPB - Canada - Newfoundland & Labrador Offshore Petroleum Board, 277

Acronym Index

CNMA - Canadian National Millers Association, 440
CNMAA - The Crow's Nest Military Artifacts Association, 644
CNMN - Canadian New Music Network, 441
CNNAR - Canadian Network of National Associations of Regulators, 441
CNO - College of Nurses of Ontario, 586
CNP - Campaign for Nuclear Phaseout, 276
CNPBC - College of Naturopathic Physicians of British Columbia, 586
CNPF - Commission nationale des parents francophones, 593
CNPS - Canadian Nurses Protective Society, 443
CNRC - Canadian Network for Respiratory Care, 441
CNRPA - Canadian National Railways Police Association (Ind.), 440
CNRS - Canadian Nautical Research Society, 440
CNRS - Canadian Numismatic Research Society, 442
CNS - Canadian Nuclear Society, 442
CNS - Clean Nova Scotia Foundation, 573
CNS - Canadian Neurological Society, 441
CNS - Canadian Northern Society, 441
CNS - Canadian Navigation Society, 440
CNS - Calgary Numismatic Society, 273
CNS - Canadian Nutrition Society, 443
CNS - Clinical Nurse Specialist Association of Ontario, 574
CNS - Caregivers Nova Scotia, 512
CNSA - Council of Nova Scotia Archives, 634
CNSA - Canadian Nursing Students' Association, 443
CNSF - Canadian Neurological Sciences Federation, 441
CNSOPB - Canada - Nova Scotia Offshore Petroleum Board, 278
CNTA - Central Nova Tourist Association, 524
CNTC - Canadian Network of Toxicology Centres, 441
COA - Council on Aging, Windsor - Essex County, 636
COA - The Council on Aging of Ottawa, 635
COA - College of Opticians of Alberta, 587
COA - Canadian Orthopaedic Association, 448
COAA - Construction Owners Association of Alberta, 624
COABC - Certified Organic Associations of British Columbia, 538
COANS - Campground Owners Association of Nova Scotia, 277
COAT - Coalition to Oppose the Arms Trade, 579
COBC - College of Opticians of British Columbia, 587
COBCB - Coalition of BC Businesses, 578
COC - The Council of Canadians, 633
COC - Canadian Opera Company, 446
COC - Canadian Olympic Committee, 445
COC - Carl Orff Canada Music for Children, 513
COCA - Council of Ontario Construction Associations, 634
COCA - Canadian Organization of Campus Activities, 447
COCLA - Corporation culturelle Latino-Américaine de l'Amitié, 629
COCOO - College of Chiropodists of Ontario, 583
COCQ-SIDA - Coalition des organismes communautaires québécois de lutte contre le sida, 578
CODA - Council on Drug Abuse, 636
CODACNB - Conseil pour le développement de l'alphabétisme et des compétences des adultes du Nouveau-Brunswick, 619
CODE - Canadian Organization for Development through Education, 447
CODE - Council of Ontario Drama & Dance Educators, 634
CODEM - Les Conseillers en développement de l'employabilité, 621
CODEV - CoDevelopment Canada, 580

CODRP - Central Ontario Developmental Riding Program, 525
COEO - Council of Outdoor Educators of Ontario, 635
COF - Canadian Orienteering Federation, 447
COF - Canadian Orthopaedic Foundation, 448
COF - Central Okanagan Foundation, 525
COF - Childhood Obesity Foundation, 560
COFAQ - Confédération des organismes familiaux du Québec, 611
COFI - Council of Forest Industries, 633
COFRD - Conseil des organismes francophones de la région de Durham, 617
COG - Canadian Organic Growers Inc., 446
COG - CANDU Owners Group Inc., 508
CoGS - Church of the Good Shepherd, 569
COHA - Canadian Oral History Association, 446
COHA - Canadian Oil Heat Association, 445
COHA - Council on Hemispheric Affairs, 1520
COHNA - Canadian Occupational Health Nurses Association, 444
COIRI - Central Ontario Industrial Relations Institute, 525
COL - The Commonwealth of Learning, 594
COMA - Central Ontario Musicians' Association, 525
COMAQ - Corporation des officiers municipaux agréés du Québec, 630
COMB - Canadian Out-of-Home Measurement Bureau, 448
COMIR - Club d'ornithologie de Mirabel, 574
COMP - Canadian Organization of Medical Physicists, 447
COMSEP - Centre d'organisation mauricien de services et d'éducation populaire, 528
CON - Canadian Obesity Network, 444
CONA - Canadian Orthopaedic Nurses Association, 448
CONC - Central Okanagan Naturalists Club, 525
CONC - Christie-Ossington Neighbourhood Centre, 568
CONE - Coalition on the Niagara Escarpment, 578
COO - College of Opticians of Ontario, 587
COOL - Club d'observateurs d'oiseaux de Laval, 574
COOP SORE - La coopérative de Solidarité de Répit et d'Etraide, 627
COOS - Central Ontario Orchid Society, 525
COPA - Canadian Oilseed Processors Association, 445
COPA - Canadian Owners & Pilots Association, 448
COPA - Canadian Office Products Association, 445
COPE - Citizens Opposed to Paving the Escarpment, 570
COPEU - Canadian Office & Professional Employees Union, 444
COPF - Canadian Ornamental Plant Foundation, 448
COPHAN - Confédération des Organismes de Personnes Handicapées du Québec, 611
COPOM - College of Podiatrists of Manitoba, 589
COPPUL - Council of Prairie & Pacific University Libraries, 635
COQ - Club des ornithologues de Québec inc., 575
CORA - Canadian Orthopaedic Residents Association, 448
CORD - Canadian Organization for Rare Disorders, 447
CORFA - College of the Rockies Faculty Association, 590
CORIM - Conseil des relations internationales de Montréal, 617
CORPIQ - Corporation des propriétaires immobiliers du Québec, 630
CORRA - Confederation of Resident & Ratepayer Associations, 611
CORS - Canadian Operational Research Society, 446
COS - Canadian Oncology Societies, 446

COS - Canadian Ophthalmological Society, 446
COSA - Central Ontario Standardbred Association, 525
COSCO - The Council of Senior Citizens Organization of British Columbia, 635
COSIA - Canada's Oil Sands Innovation Alliance, 282
COSUM - Centre d'orientation sexuelle de l'université McGill, 528
COTA - Canada Organic Trade Association, 280
COTBC - College of Occupational Therapists of British Columbia, 586
COTF - Canadian Occupational Therapy Foundation, 444
COTM - College of Occupational Therapists of Manitoba, 586
COTNS - College of Occupational Therapists of Nova Scotia, 587
COTO - College of Occupational Therapists of Ontario, 587
COU - Council of Ontario Universities, 635
COUSA - Confederation of Ontario University Staff Associations & Unions, 611
COVA - Comité des orphelins victimes d'abus, 592
CP - The Canadian Press, 459
CPA - Commonwealth Pharmacists Association, 1518
CPA - Chartered Professional Accountants Canada, 552
CPA - Canadian Polo Association, 457
CPA - Canadian Payments Association, 452
CPA - Canadian Payroll Association, 452
CPA - Canadian Peace Alliance, 452
CPA - Canadian Philosophical Association, 454
CPA - Canadian Poetry Association, 456
CPA - Canadian Police Association, 456
CPA - Canadian Psychological Association, 462
CPA - Commonwealth Parliamentary Association, 1518
CPA - Canadian Physiotherapy Association, 454
CPA - Canadian Psychiatric Association, 461
CPA - Canadian Propane Association, 461
CPA - Cornwall Police Association, 629
CPA - Cabbagetown Preservation Association, 268
CPA - Canadian Parking Association, 450
CPA - Concrete Precasters Association of Ontario, 610
CPA - Canadian Poolplayers Association, 458
CPA - Canadian Pinzgauer Association, 455
CPA - Calgary Police Association, 274
CPA NL - Chartered Professional Accountants of Newfoundland & Labrador, 553
CPA PEI - Chartered Professional Accountants of Prince Edward Island, 553
CPA SK - Chartered Professional Accountants of Saskatchewan, 553
CPAA - Cerebral Palsy Association in Alberta, 537
CPAA - Canadian Postmasters & Assistants Association, 458
CPAA - Community Planning Association of Alberta, 607
CPAB - Canadian Public Accountability Board, 462
CPABC - Cerebral Palsy Association of British Columbia, 537
CPABC - Chartered Professional Accountants of British Columbia, 553
CPAC - Chronic Pain Association of Canada, 568
CPAC - Chinese Professionals Association of Canada, 565
CPAM - Cerebral Palsy Association of Manitoba Inc., 538
CPAMB - Chartered Professional Accountants of Manitoba, 553
CPAN - Renfrew County Child Poverty Action Network, 1217
CPANB - Chartered Professional Accountants of New Brunswick, 553

CPA-NCR - Canada-Pakistan Association of the National Capital Region, 283
CPAQ - Confederation des peuples autochtones du Québec, 611
CPAR - Canadian Physicians for Aid & Relief, 454
CPATH - Canadian Professional Association for Transgender Health, 460
CPAVIH - Comité des personnes atteintes du VIH du Québec, 592
CPAWS - Canadian Parks & Wilderness Society, 450
CPAYT - Chartered Professional Accountants of the Yukon, 554
CPBC - College of Psychologists of British Columbia, 589
CPBC - Canadian Professional Boxing Council, 460
CPBI - Canadian Pension & Benefits Institute, 453
CPC - Christian Peace Conference, 1517
CPC - Canadian Paralympic Committee, 449
CPC - Canadian Pony Club, 457
CPC - Canadian Publishers' Council, 464
CPC - Canadian Polish Congress, 456
CPC - Canadian Pork Council, 458
CPC - Communist Party of Canada, 594
CPC(ML) - Communist Party of Canada (Marxist-Leninist), 595
CPCA - Canadian Paint & Coatings Association, 449
CPCA - Canadian Process Control Association, 460
CPC-A - Communist Party of Canada (Alberta), 594
CPCBC - Communist Party of BC, 594
CPCC - Canadian Private Copying Collective, 460
CPCF - Canadian Progress Charitable Foundation, 460
CPCG - Canadian Pastry Chefs Guild Inc., 451
CPCHE - Canadian Partnership for Children's Health & Environment, 451
CPCI - Canadian Precast / Prestressed Concrete Institute, 459
CPC-M - Communist Party of Canada (Manitoba), 594
CPCO - The Catholic Principals' Council of Ontario, 520
CPCO - Communist Party of Canada (Ontario), 595
CPDJA - Canadian Professional DJ Association Inc., 460
CPEG - Canadian Pediatric Endocrine Group, 452
CPEI - Cycling PEI, 647
CPEIA - Canadian Printable Electronics Industry Association, 459
CPEN - Canada - Cancer Patient Education Network Canada, 507
CPEPC - Canadian Poultry & Egg Processors Council, 458
CPEQ - Conseil patronal de l'environnement du Québec, 619
CPES - Canadian Philosophy of Education Society, 454
CPF - Canadian Parents for French, 450
CPF - Canadian Pediatric Foundation, 452
CPF - Canadian Porphyria Foundation Inc., 458
CPF - Canadian Powerlifting Federation, 459
CPF - Canadian Peregrine Foundation, 453
CPHA - Canadian Public Health Association, 462
CPHA - Canadian Palomino Horse Association, 449
CPhA - Canadian Pharmacists Association, 453
CPHR - Chartered Professionals in Human Resources, 554
CPI - Consumer Policy Institute, 626
CPI - Canada Pork International, 280
CPIA - Canadian Printing Industries Association, 459
CPIA - Canadian Plastics Industry Association, 455

Acronym Index

CPIC - Canadian Photonic Industry Consortium, 454
CPIMA - Canadian Printing Ink Manufacturers' Association, 460
CPIO - Council of Private Investigators - Ontario, 635
CPIQ - Conseil pédagogique interdisciplinaire du Québec, 619
CPJ - CPJ Corp., 638
CPLA - Canadian Payday Loan Association, 452
CPM - College of Physiotherapists of Manitoba, 588
CPM - Chosen People Ministries (Canada), 566
CPMA - Canadian Produce Marketing Association, 460
CPMA - Canadian Pest Management Association, 453
CPMA - Canadian Pasta Manufacturers Association, 451
CPMA - Canadian Podiatric Medical Association, 456
CPMDQ - Corporation des praticiens en médecine douce du Canada, 630
CPMS - Canadian Paper Money Society, 449
CPNB - College of Psychologists of New Brunswick, 589
CPNL - Cerebral Palsy Association of Newfoundland & Labrador, 538
CPO - Calgary Philharmonic Society, 273
CPO - The College of Psychologists of Ontario, 589
CPO - College of Physiotherapists of Ontario, 589
CPP - Canadian Picture Pioneers, 455
CPPA - College of Podiatric Physicians of Alberta, 589
CPPE - Comité du patrimoine paysager estrien, 592
CPPPBC - Council of Parent Participation Preschools in British Columbia, 635
CPQ - Conseil du patronat du Québec, 618
CPQ - Conseil de presse du Québec, 616
CPRA - Canadian Parks & Recreation Association, 450
CPRI - Child & Parent Resource Institute, 558
CPRMV - Centre de prévention de la radicalisation menant à la violence, 529
CPRS - Canadian Public Relations Society Inc., 462
CPS - Canadian Phytopathological Society, 455
CPS - Canadian Power & Sail Squadrons (Canadian Headquarters), 459
CPS - Canadian Physiological Society, 454
CPS - Canadian Paediatric Society, 449
CPS - Canadian Psychoanalytic Society, 461
CPS - Calgary Philatelic Society, 273
CPSA - Canadian Political Science Association, 457
CPSA - College of Physicians & Surgeons of Alberta, 588
CPSA - Canadian Professional Sales Association, 460
CPSBC - College of Physicians & Surgeons of British Columbia, 588
CPSI - Canadian Patient Safety Institute, 452
CPSLD - Council of Post Secondary Library Directors, British Columbia, 635
CPSM - College of Physicians & Surgeons of Manitoba, 588
CPSNS - College of Physicians & Surgeons of Nova Scotia, 588
CPSO - College of Physicians & Surgeons of Ontario, 588
CPSS - College of Physicians & Surgeons of Saskatchewan, 588
CPSSA - Canadian Political Science Students' Association, 457
CPSSTQ - Centre patronal de santé et sécurité du travail du Québec, 536
CPTA - Canadian Property Tax Association, Inc., 461
CPTBC - College of Physical Therapists of British Columbia, 587
CPTN - Certified Professional Trainers Network, 538
CPU - Canadian Powerlifting Union, 459
CPVA - Canadian Peacekeeping Veterans Association, 452
CPWA - Canadian Public Works Association, 464
CQA - Canadian Quilters' Association, 464
CQAM - Conseil québécois des arts médiatiques, 620
CQCD - Conseil québécois du commerce de détail, 620
CQCH - Confédération québécoise des coopératives d'habitation, 611
CQCT - Coalition québécoise pour le contrôle du tabac, 578
CQDE - Centre québécois du droit de l'environnement, 536
CQF - Conseil québécois de la franchise, 620
CQFD - Comité québécois femmes et développement, 592
CQGL - Conseil québécois des gais et lesbiennes du Québec, 620
CQHA - Canadian Quarter Horse Association, 464
CQM - Conseil québécois de la musique, 620
CQT - Conseil québécois du théâtre, 620
CRA - Canadian Rheumatology Association, 467
CRA - Canadian Rental Association, 467
CRA - Canadian Reiki Association, 466
CRADI - Comité régional des associations pour la déficience intellectuelle, 592
CRARR - Center for Research-Action on Race Relations, 522
CRBC - Creative BC, 639
CRC - Canadian Retransmission Collective, 467
CRC - Conseil régional de la culture Saguenay-Lac-Saint-Jean, 621
CRC - Cavalier Riding Club Ltd., 521
CRC - Canadian Red Cross, 465
CRC - Community Resource Centre (Killaloe) Inc., 607
CRCA - Canadian Roofing Contractors' Association, 468
CRCA - Canadian Race Communications Association, 464
CRCAT - Conseil de la culture de L'Abitibi-Témiscamingue, 615
CRCBSL - Conseil de la culture du Bas-Saint-Laurent, 616
CRCCCN - Conseil régional de la culture et des communications de la Côte-Nord, 621
CRCL - Centre de réadaptation Constance-Lethbridge, 529
CRCNA - Christian Reformed Church in North America, 568
CRDA - Canadian Resort Development Association, 467
CRDHA - College of Registered Dental Hygienists of Alberta, 589
CREA - The Canadian Real Estate Association, 465
CREB - Calgary Real Estate Board Cooperative Limited, 274
CRÉDIL - Comité régional d'éducation pour le développement international de Lanaudière, 592
CREGIM - Conseil régional de l'environnement de la Gaspésie et des Îles-de-la-Madeleine, 620
CREPA - Chinese Real Estate Professionals Association of British Columbia, 565
CREPUQ - Conférence des recteurs et des principaux des universités du Québec, 612
CRFTQSLSJ - Conseil régional FTQ Saguenay-Lac-St-Jean-Chibougamau-Chapais, 621
CRHA - Ordre des conseillers en ressources humaines agréés, 592
CRHA - Canadian Railroad Historical Association, 465
CRHF - Chinook Regional Hospital Foundation, 565
CRHP - Canadian Respiratory Health Professionals, 467
CRHSP - Canadian Register of Health Service Psychologists, 466
CRI - Construction Resource Initiatives Council, 624
CRIA - Carleton Road Industries Association, 513
CRIAW - Canadian Research Institute for the Advancement of Women, 467
CRIC - Carrefour de ressources en interculturel, 515
CRIEVAT - Centre de recherche et d'intervention interuniversitaire sur l'éducation et la vie au travail, 530
CRIMN - Chambre de commerce et d'industrie de Montréal-Nord, 546
CRIPHASE - Centre de ressources et d'intervention pour hommes abusés sexuellement dans leur enfance, 530
CRI-VIFF - Centre de recherche interdisciplinaire sur la violence familiale et la violence faite aux femmes, 530
CRMCA - Canadian Ready Mixed Concrete Association, 465
CRNBC - College of Registered Nurses of British Columbia, 589
CRNM - College of Registered Nurses of Manitoba, 589
CRNNS - College of Registered Nurses of Nova Scotia, 589
CRNO - Cardiac Rehabilitation Network of Ontario, 510
CRNV - Centre des ressources sur la non-violence inc, 530
CRPA - Canadian Radiation Protection Association, 464
CRPNBC - College of Registered Psychiatric Nurses of B.C., 590
CRPNM - College of Registered Psychiatric Nurses of Manitoba, 590
CRPO - College of Registered Psychotherapists of Ontario, 590
CRQCA - Conseil régional FTQ Québec et Chaudière-Appalaches, 621
CRRA - Calgary Residential Rental Association, 274
CRRF - Canadian Race Relations Foundation, 464
CRS - Coalition of Rail Shippers, 578
CRS - Canadian Rose Society, 468
CRS - Controlled Release Society, 1520
CRSF - Canadian Rope Skipping Federation, 468
CRSS - Canadian Remote Sensing Society, 466
CRTA - Cowichan Therapeutic Riding Association, 637
CRTO - College of Respiratory Therapists of Ontario, 590
CRTWH - Canadian Registry of Tennessee Walking Horse, 466
CRUB - Calgary Round-Up Band Association, 274
CRVA - Canadian Recreational Vehicle Association, 465
CRWRC - World Renew, 1467
CSA - Canadian Stuttering Association, 491
CSA - Canadian Snowsports Association, 472
CSA - Canadian Soccer Association, 472
CSA - Canadian Society for Aesthetics, 473
CSA - Canadian Spice Association, 489
CSA - Canadian Sociological Association, 488
CSA - Centre sida amitié, 536
CSA - Canadian Snowbird Association, 472
CSA - Canadian Standards Association, 490
CSA - Canadian Securities Administrators, 469
CSA - Canadian Sablefish Association, 468
CSAAC - Commercial Seed Analysts Association of Canada Inc., 592
CSACI - Canadian Society of Allergy & Clinical Immunology, 479
CSAE - Canadian Society of Association Executives, 480
CSAM - Construction Safety Association of Manitoba, 624
CSAM - Canadian Society of Addiction Medicine, 479
CSAPS - Canadian Society for Aesthetic Plastic Surgery, 472
CSAS - Canadian Society of Animal Science, 480
CSASI - Canadian Society of Air Safety Investigators, 479
CSATVB - Canadian Society of Atherosclerosis, Thrombosis & Vascular Biology, 480
CSB - Congregation of St. Basil, 613
CSB - Canadian Biomaterials Society, 344
CSBA - Canadian School Boards Association, 468
CSBA - Canadian Sheep Breeders' Association, 470
CSBA - Canadian Swine Breeders' Association, 491
CSBBCS - Canadian Society for Brain, Behaviour & Cognitive Science, 473
CSBC - Canadian Safe Boating Council, 468
CSBD - Counselling Services of Belleville & District, 636
CSBE - Canadian Society for Bioengineering, 473
CSBM - Canadian Society for Molecular Biosciences, 476
CSBS - Canadian Society of Biblical Studies, 481
CSC - Canadian Society of Cinematographers, 481
CSC - Canada Safety Council, 280
CSC - Canadian Ski Council, 471
CSC - Construction Specifications Canada, 624
CSC - Cryonics Society of Canada, 645
CSC - Canadian Society of Cytology, 482
CSC - Curriculum Services Canada, 646
CSC - Canadian Society for Chemistry, 473
CSC NL - Community Sector Council, Newfoundland & Labrador, 607
CSCA - Canadian Special Crops Association, 489
CSCA - Canadian Swiss Cultural Association, 491
CSCB - Canadian Society of Customs Brokers, 482
CSCC - Canadian Slovenian Chamber of Commerce, 472
CSCC - Canadian Steel Construction Council, 490
CSCC - Canadian Society of Clinical Chemists, 481
CSCE - Canadian Society for Civil Engineering, 473
CSCH - Canadian Society of Church History, 481
CSChE - Canadian Society for Chemical Engineering, 473
CSCHN - Community Support Centre Haldimand-Norfolk, 607
CSCI - Canadian Society for Clinical Investigation, 474
CSCL - Cranbrook Society for Community Living, 638
CSCL - Chilliwack Society for Community Living, 563
CSCM - Canadian Society of Club Managers, 482
CSCMA - Canadian Society of Chinese Medicine & Acupuncture, 481
CSCN - Canadian Society of Clinical Neurophysiologists, 482
CSCP - Canadian Society of Clinical Perfusion, 482
CSCP - Canadian Society for Continental Philosophy, 474
CSCP - Canadian Society of Consultant Pharmacists, 482
CSCS - Comité Social Centre-Sud, 592
CSCS - Canadian Safe Cannabis Society, 468
CSCT - Canadian Society of Cardiology Technologists Inc., 481

Acronym Index

CSCT - Canadian Society for Chemical Technology, 473
CSD - Centrale des syndicats démocratiques, 525
CSDA - Canadian Stamp Dealers' Association, 490
CSDA - Canadian South Devon Association, 489
CSDA - Canadian Search Dog Association, 469
CSDMA - Canadian Steel Door Manufacturers Association, 491
CSE - Citizens for a Safe Environment, 570
CSEA - Canadian Society for Education through Art, 474
CSEA - Canadian Swine Exporters Association, 491
CSEB - Canadian Society of Environmental Biologists, 482
CSECS - Canadian Society for Eighteenth-Century Studies, 474
CSEG - Canadian Society of Exploration Geophysicists, 483
CSEM - Canadian Society of Endocrinology & Metabolism, 482
CSEM - Canadian Society for Engineering Management, 474
CSEP - Canadian Society for Exercise Physiology, 475
CSF - Canadian-Scandinavian Foundation, 507
CSF - Chambre de la sécurité financière, 550
CSFA - Canadian Snack Food Association, 472
CSFS - Canadian Society of Forensic Science, 483
CSGA - Canadian Seed Growers' Association, 469
CSGA - Canadian Sporting Goods Association, 490
CSGNA - Canadian Society of Gastroenterology Nurses & Associates, 483
CSHA - Canadian Sport Horse Association, 489
CSHA - Canadian Shire Horse Association, 470
CSHM - Canadian Society for the History of Medicine, 477
CSHP - Canadian Society of Hospital Pharmacists, 483
CSHPS - Canadian Society for the History & Philosophy of Science, 477
CSHS - Canadian Society for Horticultural Science, 475
CSHT - Canadian Society of Hand Therapists, 483
CSI - Collaboration Santé Internationale, 581
CSI - Canadian Securities Institute, 469
CSI - Canadian Sugar Institute, 491
CSI - Canadian Society for Immunology, 475
CSIA - Canadian Ski Instructors' Alliance, 471
CSIF - Calgary Society of Independent Filmmakers, 274
CSIH - Canadian Society for International Health, 475
CSIM - Canadian Society of Internal Medicine, 484
CSIO - Centre for Study of Insurance Operations, 534
CSIS - Canadian Society for Italian Studies, 476
CSJ - Sisters of Saint Joseph of Pembroke, 1301
CSJ - Sisters of Saint Joseph of Peterborough, 1301
CSJS - Canadian Society for Jewish Studies, 476
CSL - Canadian School Libraries, 468
CSLA - Canadian Society of Landscape Architects, 484
CSLA - Canadian Student Leadership Association, 491
CSLBC - Canada-Sri Lanka Business Council, 284
CSLP - Centre for the Study of Learning & Performance, 534
CSLS - Centre for the Study of Living Standards, 534
CSM - Canadian Society of Microbiologists, 485
CSM - Canadian Ski Marathon, 471
CSM - Canadian Society of Medievalists, 484

CSMA - Calgary Minor Soccer Association, 273
CSME - Canadian Society of Medical Evaluators, 484
CSME - Canadian Society for Mechanical Engineering, 476
CSMLS - Canadian Society for Medical Laboratory Science, 476
CSMS - The Canadian Society for Mesopotamian Studies, 476
CSMTA - Canadian Sport Massage Therapists Association, 490
CSN - Canadian Society of Nephrology, 485
CSN - Confédération des syndicats nationaux, 611
CSN - Canadian Syringomyelia Network, 491
CSO - Costume Society of Ontario, 632
CSO - Chilliwack Symphony Orchestra & Chorus, 563
CSO-HNS - Canadian Society of Otolaryngology - Head & Neck Surgery, 485
CSORN - Canadian Society of Ophthalmic Registered Nurses, 485
CSOT - Canadian Society of Orthopaedic Technologists, 485
CSP - Canadian Ski Patrol, 471
CSP - Centre for Suicide Prevention, 534
CSPA - Canadian Sport Parachuting Association, 490
CSPA - Canadian Steel Producers Association, 491
CSPA - Canadian Skin Patient Alliance, 471
CSPA - Canadian Speckle Park Association, 489
CSPCC - Canadian Society for the Prevention of Cruelty to Children, 477
CSPCP - Canadian Society of Palliative Care Physicians, 486
CSPDM - Canadian Society of Professionals in Disability Management, 487
CSPE - Canadian Society of Physician Executives, 486
CSPG - Canadian Society of Petroleum Geologists, 486
CSPHQ - Commission de Ski pour Personnes Handicapées du Québec, 593
CSPI - Corrugated Steel Pipe Institute, 631
CSPLSP - Canadian Society for Psychomotor Learning & Sport Psychology, 477
CSPMA - Canadian Sphagnum Peat Moss Association, 489
CSPN - Customer Service Professionals Network, 646
CSPP - Canadian Society of Plant Biologists, 486
CSPRA - Canadian Senior Pro Rodeo Association, 470
CSPS - Canadian Society of Plastic Surgeons, 487
CSPS - Canadian Society for Pharmaceutical Sciences, 477
CSPS - Canadian Society of Patristic Studies, 486
CSPT - Canadian Society of Pharmacology & Therapeutics, 486
CSPWC - Canadian Society of Painters in Water Colour, 486
CSQ - Centrale des syndicats du Québec, 525
CSQ - Conseil de la souveraineté du Québec, 616
CSQ - Canadian Society for Quality, 477
CSRAO - Chartered Shorthand Reporters' Association of Ontario, 554
CSRDS - Canadian Square & Round Dance Society, 490
CSRO - Canadian Spinal Research Organization, 489
CSRT - Canadian Society of Respiratory Therapists, 487
CSS - Christian Stewardship Services, 568
CSS - Canadian Sleep Society, 472
CSS - Canadian Space Society, 489
CSSA - Canadian Shooting Sports Association, 470
CSSA - Canadian Self Storage Association, 470
CSSA - Canadian Society of Sugar Artistry, 488

CSSAM - Canadian Society for the Study of the Aging Male, 478
CSSB - Calgary Stetson Show Band, 274
CSSBC - Canadian Shiatsu Society of British Columbia, 470
CSSBI - Canadian Sheet Steel Building Institute, 470
CSSE - Canadian Society of Safety Engineering, Inc., 487
CSSE - Canadian Society for the Study of Education, 478
CSSEA - Community Social Services Employers' Association, 607
CSSHE - Canadian Society for the Study of Higher Education, 478
CSSI - Creation Science of Saskatchewan Inc., 639
CSSI - Cell Stress Society International, 1516
CSSM-M - Le Centre de soutien en santé mentale - Montérégie, 530
CSSN - Canadian Society for the Study of Names, 478
CSSN - Canadian Safe School Network, 468
CSSO - Canadian Society for Surgical Oncology, 477
CSSPE - Canadian Society for the Study of Practical Ethics, 478
CSSQ - Coalition sida des sourds du Québec, 578
CSSR - Canadian Society for the Study of Religion, 478
CSSS - Canadian Society of Soil Science, 488
CST - Canadian Scholarship Trust Foundation, 468
CST - Canadian Society of Transplantation, 488
CSTA - Canadian Seed Trade Association, 470
CSTA - Canadian Society of Technical Analysts, 488
CSTA - Canadian Security Traders Association, Inc., 469
CSTA - Canadian Sport Tourism Alliance, 490
CSTHA - Canadian Science & Technology Historical Association, 468
CSTM - Canadian Society for Transfusion Medicine, 479
CSTM - Canadian Society for Traditional Music, 479
CSUQ - Communauté sépharade unifiée du Québec, 594
CSVS - Canadian Society for Vascular Surgery, 479
CSWF - Canadian Social Work Foundation, 472
CSWIS - The Canadian Society for the Weizmann Institute of Science, 478
CSYO - Canadian Sinfonietta Youth Orchestra, 470
CSZ - Canadian Society of Zoologists, 488
CTA - Canadian Toy Association / Canadian Toy & Hobby Fair, 496
CTA - Canadian Trucking Alliance, 497
CTA - Canadian Tarentaise Association, 492
CTA - Canadian Textile Association, 494
CTA - Canadian Trapshooting Association, 497
CTA - Canadian Transplant Association, 496
CTAA - Canadian Technical Asphalt Association, 493
CTABC - Cardiology Technologists' Association of British Columbia, 511
CTAC - Conseil de la transformation agroalimentaire et des produits de consommation, 616
CTAO - Canadian Tibetan Association of Ontario, 495
CTC - Canadian Test Centre Inc., 494
CTC - Canada Tibet Committee, 280
CTCA - Canadian Theatre Critics Association, 494
CTCA - Construction Technology Centre Atlantic, 625
CTCCC - Canadian Tire Coupon Collectors Club, 495
CTCMABC - College of Traditional Chinese Medicine Practitioners & Acupuncturists of British Columbia, 590

CTCS - Canadian Toy Collectors' Society Inc., 496
CTEA - Canadian Transportation Equipment Association, 497
C-TEP - Centre for Transportation Engineering & Planning, 534
CTF - Canadian Tenpin Federation, Inc., 493
CTF - Canadian Teachers' Federation, 493
CTF - Canadian Tax Foundation, 492
CTF - Children's Tumor Foundation, 1516
CTF - Canadian Taxpayers Federation, 492
CTHF - Canadian Team Handball Federation, 493
CTHR - Canadian Tribute to Human Rights, 497
CTHRB - Canadian Technology Human Resources Board, 493
CTHRC - Canadian Tourism Human Resource Council, 495
CTHS - Canadian Thoroughbred Horse Society, 494
CTHS - Canadian Trakehner Horse Society, 496
CTI - Canadian Training Institute, 496
CTINB - Corporation des traducteurs, traductrices, terminologues et interprètes du Nouveau-Brunswick, 631
CTLA - Canadian Transport Lawyers Association, 497
CTM - Carrefour Tiers-Monde, 516
CTMA - Canadian Tooling & Machining Association, 495
CTMA - Canadian Transverse Myelitis Association, 497
CTMA - Canadian Tamil Medical Association, 492
CTMRA - Canadian Trail & Mountain Running Association, 496
CTN - Canadian HIV Trials Network, 405
CTQ - Corporation des thanatologues du Québec, 630
CTQ - Club de trafic de Québec, 575
CTRF - Canadian Transportation Research Forum, 497
CTS - Canadian Thoracic Society, 494
CTS - Canadian Theological Society, 494
CTS - Canadian Titanic Society, 495
CTSQ - Corporation des thérapeutes du sport du Québec, 631
CTTA - Canada Taiwan Trade Association, 280
CTTAM - Certified Technicians & Technologists Association of Manitoba, 538
CTTC - Canadian Toy Testing Council, 496
CTTIC - Canadian Translators, Terminologists & Interpreters Council, 496
CUA - Canadian Urological Association, 500
CUASA - Carleton University Academic Staff Association, 513
CUC - Canadian Unitarian Council, 499
CUCCA - Canadian University & College Counselling Association, 499
CUCCOA - Canadian University & College Conference Organizers Association, 499
CUCM - Credit Union Central of Manitoba, 641
CUFA - Concordia University Faculty Association, 609
CUFA BC - Confederation of University Faculty Associations of British Columbia, 611
CUFCA - Canadian Urethane Foam Contractors Association, 500
CUFCA - Canadian University Football Coaches Association, 499
CUGA - Canadian Underwater Games Association, 498
CUI - Canadian Urban Institute, 499
CUIAS - Canadian Ukrainian Immigrant Aid Society, 498
CUJS - Canadian Unitarians for Social Justice, 499
CULC - Canadian Urban Libraries Council, 500
CUMS - Canadian University Music Society, 499
CUOG - Canadian Urologic Oncology Group, 500
CUP - Canadian University Press, 499

Acronym Index

CUPE - Canadian Union of Public Employees, 498
CUPFA - Concordia University Part-time Faculty Association, 610
CUPS - Calgary Urban Project Society, 275
CUPW - Canadian Union of Postal Workers, 498
CURAC - College & University Retiree Associations of Canada, 581
CURC - Congress of Union Retirees Canada, 613
CUSTAC - Canada - United States Trade Center, 1515
CUTA - Canadian Urban Transit Association, 500
CVA - Canadian Vintners Association, 501
CVAA - Canadian Vascular Access Association, 501
CVAC - Carleton-Victoria Arts Council, 513
CVBC - College of Veterinarians of British Columbia, 590
CVCA - Canada's Venture Capital & Private Equity Association, 283
CVCAC - Comox Valley Community Arts Council, 607
CVCC - Comox Valley Chamber of Commerce, 607
CVCC - Columbia Valley Chamber of Commerce, 591
CVF - Canadian Volkssport Federation, 501
CVIMS - Central Vancouver Island Multicultural Society, 525
CVMA - Canadian Vehicle Manufacturers' Association, 501
CVMA - Canadian Veterinary Medical Association, 501
CVMG - Canadian Vintage Motorcycle Group, 501
CVNS - Cowichan Valley Naturalists' Society, 637
CVO - College of Veterinarians of Ontario, 590
CVPV - Centre de valorisation du patrimoine vivant, 530
CVSA - Cyclic Vomiting Syndrome Association, 1521
CVTRS - Comox Valley Therapeutic Riding Society, 608
CWA - Canadian Western Agribition Association, 503
CWA - Cecebe Waterways Association, 521
CWB - Canadian Welding Bureau, 503
CWB - Centre for Women in Business, 534
CWBA - Canadian Wheelchair Basketball Association, 503
CWBCS - Canadian Welsh Black Cattle Society, 503
CWC - Canadian Wood Council, 505
CWC - The Crime Writers of Canada, 642
CWC - Canadian Women in Communications, 505
CWC - Canadian Croatian Congress, 373
CWCF - Canadian Worker Co-operative Federation, 505
CWEDA - Canada West Equipment Dealers Association, 283
CWES - Calgary Women's Emergency Shelter Association, 275
CWF - Canada West Foundation, 281
CWF - Canadian Wildlife Federation, 504
CWF - The Canadian Woodlands Forum, 505
CWF - Canadian Writers' Foundation Inc., 506
CWGC - Commonwealth War Graves Commission - Canadian Agency, 594
CWH - Canadian Warplane Heritage, 502
CWHBA - Canadian Warmblood Horse Breeders Association, 502
CWILL BC - Children's Writers & Illustrators of British Columbia Society, 563
CWL - Catholic Women's League of Canada, 520
CWLC - Child Welfare League of Canada, 560
CWLS - Canadian Well Logging Society, 503
CWM - Community of Christ - Canada West Mission, 607

CWMA - Coast Waste Management Association, 579
CWN - Canadian Water Network, 502
CWPCA - Canadian Wood Pallet & Container Association, 505
CWQA - Canadian Water Quality Association, 502
CWRA - Canadian Water Resources Association, 503
CWRS - Calgary Wildlife Rehabilitation Society, 275
CWSA - Canadian Wheelchair Sports Association, 503
CWSA - Calgary Women's Soccer Association, 275
CWTA - Canadian Wireless Telecommunications Association, 504
CWTA - Canadian Wood Truss Association, 505
CWTF - Canadian Wild Turkey Federation, 504
CWWA - Canadian Water & Wastewater Association, 502
CWY - Canada World Youth, 281
CYAC - Boost Child & Youth Advocacy Centre, 218
CYC - Ukrainian Self-Reliance League of Canada, 1403
CYCAA - Child & Youth Care Association of Alberta, 558
CYCANL - Child & Youth Care Association of Newfoundland & Labrador, 558
CYCC - Children and Youth in Challenging Contexts Network, 560
CYFN - Council of Yukon First Nations, 635
CZCA - The Canadian Zionist Cultural Association, 506
CZCA - Coastal Zone Canada Association, 579
CZF - Canadian Zionist Federation, 506

D

DAA - DanceSport Atlantic, 650
DAANS - Deafness Advocacy Association Nova Scotia, 652
DABC - Disability Alliance British Columbia, 658
DABT - Digby & Area Board of Trade, 656
DAC - Delta Arts Council, 653
DAC - Denturist Association of Canada, 653
DAC - Diman Association Canada (Lebanese), 657
DAC - Disability Awareness Consultants, 658
DAC - Dufferin Arts Council, 664
DAO - Denturist Association of Ontario, 654
DAPEI - Dental Association of Prince Edward Island, 653
DAS - Durham Avicultural Society of Ontario, 664
DASC - Dartmouth Adult Services Centre, 650
DASMA - Door & Access Systems Manufacturers Association, 1521
DBA - Downtown Business Association of Edmonton, 661
DBC - Dragon Boat Canada, 662
DBCA - Darts British Columbia Association, 651
DC - Dietitians of Canada, 656
DCBC - Dutch Canadian Business Club of Calgary, 665
DCCC - Duncan-Cowichan Chamber of Commerce, 664
DCCC - Danish Canadian Chamber of Commerce, 650
DCD - Distress Centre of Durham Region, 659
DCFA - Douglas College Faculty Association, 661
DCLS - Delta Community Living Society, 653
DCNMS - Danish Canadian National Museum Society, 650
DCO - Distress Centres Ontario, 659
DCOR - Distress Centre of Ottawa & Region, 659
DCRA - Dominion of Canada Rifle Association, 660
DCS - Deaf Children's Society of B.C., 652
DDAAC - Dauphin & District Allied Arts Council Inc., 651

DDCC - Drumheller & District Chamber of Commerce, 663
DDCC - Dryden District Chamber of Commerce, 663
DDRC - Developmental Disabilities Resource Centre of Calgary, 655
DDS - Durham Deaf Services, 665
DEANS - Destination Eastern & Northumberland Shores, 654
DFC - Dairy Farmers of Canada, 648
DFC - Dauphin Friendship Centre, 651
DFM - Dairy Farmers of Manitoba, 648
DFNB - Dairy Farmers of New Brunswick, 648
DFNL - Dairy Farmers of Newfoundland & Labrador, 648
DFNS - Dairy Farmers of Nova Scotia, 648
DFO - Dairy Farmers of Ontario, 648
DGC - Directors Guild of Canada, 657
DIA - Digital Imaging Association, 656
DIAL - Disabled Individuals Alliance, 658
DISCAN - Christian Church (Disciples of Christ) in Canada, 567
DLS - Downtown Legal Services, 661
DMA - Data & Marketing Association, 1521
DNFC - Dryden Native Friendship Centre, 663
DOC - Documentary Organization of Canada, 660
DOD - Dance Oremus Danse, 649
DPC - Diving Plongeon Canada, 659
DPCUC - Durham Personal Computer Users' Club, 665
DPERWA - Dufferin Peel Educational Resource Workers' Association, 664
DPI - Disabled Peoples' International, 658
DPIC - British Columbia Drug & Poison Information Centre, 239
DPNC - Drug Prevention Network of Canada, 663
DPNCHC - Davenport-Perth Neighbourhood & Community Health Centre, 651
DPOM - Durham Parents of Multiples, 665
DR&CBA - Dominion Rabbit & Cavy Breeders Association, 661
DRAR - Durham Region Association of REALTORS, 665
DRIC - Disaster Recovery Institute Canada, 658
DRLA - Durham Region Law Association, 665
DRLC - Durham Regional Labour Council, 665
DRMA - Distance Riders of Manitoba Association, 658
DRSO - Deep River Symphony Orchestra, 652
DSA - Direct Sellers Association of Canada, 657
DSA - Disabled Sailing Association of B.C., 658
DSAB - DanceSport Alberta, 650
DSAO - Down Syndrome Association of Ontario, 661
DSAO - Drainage Superintendents Association of Ontario, 662
DSAO - Driving School Association of Ontario, 663
DSAT - Down Syndrome Association of Toronto, 661
DSC - The Donkey Sanctuary of Canada, 661
DSD - Division of Sustainable Development, 1521
DSF - David Suzuki Foundation, 651
DSNA - Dictionary Society of North America, 1521
DSQ - DanceSport Québec, 650
DSRF - Down Syndrome Research Foundation, 661
DTP - Downtown Truro Partnership, 662
DTRC - Dancer Transition Resource Centre, 649
DU - Ducks Unlimited Inc., 1521
DUC - Ducks Unlimited Canada, 663
DUO - Dance Umbrella of Ontario, 649
DVA - Downtown Vancouver Association, 662
DVDCC - Drayton Valley & District Chamber of Commerce, 662
DWD - Dying with Dignity, 665
DX - Design Exchange, 654
DYO - Durham Youth Orchestra, 665

E

E3 - E3 Community Services, 666
EA - Endometriosis Association, Inc., 1523
EAA - Education Assistants Association of the Waterloo Region District School Board, 680
EAC - Elora Arts Council, 685
EAC - Ecology Action Centre, 672
EAC - Editors' Association of Canada, 674
EAC - Embroiderers' Association of Canada, Inc., 685
EAC - Edmonton Arts Council, 675
EAC - EFILE Association of Canada, 681
EACO - Environmental Abatement Council of Ontario, 691
EAD - Edmonton Association of the Deaf, 675
EADM - Eucharistic Apostles of the Divine Mercy, 698
EAGE - European Association of Geoscientists & Engineers, 1524
EAM - Electrical Association of Manitoba Inc., 682
EANPA - Edmonton (Alberta) Nerve Pain Association, 675
EANS - Epilepsy Association of Nova Scotia, 693
EANS - Exhibitions Association of Nova Scotia, 699
EAP - Ecological Agriculture Projects, 672
EAS - Eastern Apicultural Society of North America, Inc., 1522
EAWLS - East African Wild Life Society, 1522
EAY - Equine Association of Yukon, 694
EBA - Environmental Bankers Association, 1523
EBBC - Eye Bank of BC, 700
EBTC - Edmonton Bicycle & Touring Club, 675
EC - Equestrian Canada, 694
EC - Epilepsy Canada, 693
EC - Engineers Canada, 689
ECA Hamilton - Electrical Construction Association of Hamilton, 682
ECAA - Electrical Contractors Association of Alberta, 682
ECABC - Electrical Contractors Association of BC, 682
ECAL - Electrical Contractors Association of London, 682
ECANB - Electrical Contractors Association of New Brunswick, Inc., 682
ECAO - Electrical Contractors Association of Ontario, 682
ECAS - Electrical Contractors Association of Saskatchewan, 683
ECAS - East Coast Aquarium Society, 668
ECATB - Electrical Contractors Association of Thunder Bay, 683
ECCC - Evangelical Covenant Church of Canada, 698
ECCC - Eastern Charlotte Chamber of Commerce, 670
ECCC - Eritrean Canadian Community Centre of Metropolitan Toronto, 695
ECCENB - Early Childhood Care & Education New Brunswick, 668
ECCS - Edmonton Composers' Concert Society, 676
ECDA - Early Childhood Development Association of Prince Edward Island, 666
ECEBC - Early Childhood Educators of British Columbia, 666
ECFB - Eden Community Food Bank, 674
ECLC - Edmonton Community Legal Centre, 676
ECM+ - Ensemble contemporain de Montréal, 690
ECMA - East Coast Music Association, 668
ECN - Edmonton Community Networks, 676
ECOO - Educational Computing Organization of Ontario, 680
ECO-PEI - Environmental Coalition of Prince Edward Island, 691
ECOS - Eastern Canada Orchid Society, 670
ECS - Essex Community Services, 696
ECS - Electrochemical Society, 1522

Acronym Index

ECSC - Edmonton Combative Sports Commission, 676
ECUADFA - Emily Carr University of Art & Design Faculty Association, 686
EDA - Electricity Distributors Association, 683
EDA - Economic Developers Alberta, 672
EDAA - Edmonton Dental Assistants Association, 676
EDAC - Economic Developers Association of Canada, 672
EDAC - Enderby & District Arts Council, 687
EDAC - Eating Disorder Association of Canada, 671
EDAM - EDAM Performing Arts Society, 674
EDAM - Economic Developers Association of Manitoba, 673
EDB - Economic Development Brandon, 673
EDC - Earth Day Canada, 667
EDCC - Edmonton & District Council of Churches, 675
EDCO - Economic Developers Council of Ontario Inc., 673
EDHS - Municipality of Port Hope Historical Society, 982
EDLC - Edmonton & District Labour Council, 675
EDLPSA - Educators for Distributed Learning PSA (British Columbia), 680
EDN - Entrepreneurs with Disabilities Network, 691
EDSA - Edmonton District Soccer Association, 677
EDT - Evangelical Tract Distributors, 699
EDW - Economic Development Winnipeg Inc., 673
EEA - Edmonton Epilepsy Association, 677
EEAY - Environmental Education Association of the Yukon, 691
EEC - Employment & Education Centre, 687
EECOM - Canadian Network for Environmental Education & Communication, 440
EEDC - Edmonton Economic Development Corporation, 677
EEGS - East European Genealogical Society, Inc., 668
EELC - Estonian Evangelical Lutheran Church Consistory, 697
EEON - Environmental Education Ontario, 691
EEPSA - Environmental Educators' Provincial Specialist Association, 691
EEQ - Éco Entreprises Québec, 671
EESC - Earth Energy Society of Canada, 667
EFA - Alberta Egg Producers' Board, 33
EFA - Epilepsy Foundation of America, 1524
EFC - Evangelical Fellowship of Canada, 698
EFC - Electro-Federation Canada, 683
EFC - Electronic Frontier Canada Inc., 683
EFC - Egg Farmers of Canada, 681
EFCL - Edmonton Federation of Community Leagues, 677
EFO - Ecological Farmers of Ontario, 672
EFWC - Eskasoni Fish & Wildlife Commission, 695
EG - Eurographics - European Association for Computer Graphics, 1524
EGBC - Association of Professional Engineers & Geoscientists of British Columbia, 157
EGCOC - East Gwillimbury Chamber of Commerce, 668
EGS - European Geosciences Union, 1524
EHA Ontario - Environmental Health Association of Ontario, 692
EHABC - Environmental Health Association of British Columbia, 691
EHANS - Environmental Health Association of Nova Scotia, 692
EHDCC - East Hants & District Chamber of Commerce, 668
EHFA - Edmonton Heritage Festival Association, 677
EHFC - Environmental Health Foundation of Canada, 692
EHM - Evangel Hall Mission, 698
EHRC - Electricity Human Resources Canada, 683

EHS - Etobicoke Humane Society, 697
EHSPCA - Edmonton Humane Society for the Prevention of Cruelty to Animals, 677
EI - Education International, 1522
EIA - Edmonton Insurance Association, 678
EIBF - Edmonton International Baseball Foundation, 678
EIC - Emmanuel International Canada, 686
EIC - The Engineering Institute of Canada, 688
EIC - Electronics Import Committee, 683
EICHS - Edmonton Inner City Housing Society, 677
EIF - École internationale de français, 672
EIFFS - Edmonton International Film Festival Society, 678
EII - Earth Island Institute, 1521
EIS - Ecoforestry Institute Society, 671
EISA - Edmonton Immigrant Services Association, 677
EIYSA - Edmonton Interdistrict Youth Soccer Association, 678
EJS - Edmonton Jazz Society, 678
EKCC - Annapolis Valley Chamber of Commerce, 71
EKN - Estonian Central Council in Canada, 697
ELAN - English-Language Arts Network, 689
ELC - The Environmental Law Centre (Alberta) Society, 692
ELCIC - Evangelical Lutheran Church in Canada, 698
ELLA - Edmonton Law Libraries Association, 678
ELP - End Legislated Poverty, 687
EMA - Edmonton Musicians' Association, 678
EMA - Entertainment Merchants Association - International Head Office, 1523
EMABC - Environmental Managers Association of British Columbia, 692
EMAS - Evangelical Medical Aid Society Canada, 698
EMC - Evangelical Mennonite Conference, 699
EMC - Electric Mobility Canada, 681
EMC - Elder Mediation Canada, 681
EMDA - Edmonton Motor Dealers' Association, 678
EMEA - Electrical & Mechanical Engineering Association, 682
EMSA - Edmonton Minor Soccer Association, 678
EMV - Early Music Vancouver, 667
EnerACT - Energy Action Council of Toronto, 688
EOBA - Eastern Ontario Beekeepers' Association, 670
EOCPCA - Evangelical Order of Certified Pastoral Counsellors of America, 699
EPA - Edmonton Police Association, 678
EPAC - Explorers & Producers Association of Canada, 700
EPAC - Ethics Practitioners' Association of Canada, 697
EPO - Etobicoke Philharmonic Orchestra, 697
EPRF - Energy Probe Research Foundation, 688
EPSC - Electronics Product Stewardship Canada, 684
EPS-IA - EPS Industry Alliance, 1524
EPTC - Society for Existential & Phenomenological Theory & Culture, 1326
EPYDC - East Prince Youth Development Centre, 668
ERA - Endurance Riders of Alberta, 687
ERA - Elder Active Recreation Association, 681
ERA - Electronic Recycling Association, 683
ERABC - Endurance Riders Association of British Columbia, 687
ERAS - Edmonton Reptile & Amphibian Society, 679
ERO - Esperanto Rondo de Otavo, 695
ERQ - L'Église Réformée du Québec, 681
ERRS - Edmonton Radial Railway Society, 679
ERS - ERS Training & Development Corporation, 695
ESA - European Space Agency, 1524
ESA - Ecological Society of America, 1522

ESA - Entomological Society of Alberta, 690
ESAA - Environmental Services Association of Alberta, 692
ESAC - Environmental Studies Association of Canada, 692
ESAC - Entertainment Software Association of Canada, 690
ESAE - European Society of Association Executives, 1524
ESANS - Environmental Services Association of Nova Scotia, 692
ESBC - Entomological Society of British Columbia, 690
ESC - Edmonton Soaring Club, 679
ESC - Earthsave Canada, 667
ESC - Edmonton Stamp Club, 679
ESC - Entomological Society of Canada, 690
ESCC - English Speaking Catholic Council, 689
ESGO - European Society of Gynaecological Oncology, 1524
ESIASP - Eastern Shores Independent Association for Support Personnel, 671
ESM - Entomological Society of Manitoba Inc., 690
ESNA - Economics Society of Northern Alberta, 673
ESNB - Easter Seals New Brunswick, 669
ESO - Edmonton Symphony Orchestra, 679
ESO - Entomological Society of Ontario, 690
ESOP - ESOP Association Canada, 679
ESPC - Edmonton Social Planning Council, 679
ESRA - Eastern Shore Ringette Association, 671
ESS - Entomological Society of Saskatchewan, 690
ESS/OSSTF - Education Support Staff of the Ontario Secondary School Teachers' Federation - District 24 - Waterloo, 680
ESSF - Edmonton Space & Science Foundation, 679
ETFO - Elementary Teachers' Federation of Ontario, 684
ETLC - Edmonton Tumblewood Lapidary Club, 679
ETRA - Errington Therapeutic Riding Association, 695
ETRC - Eastern Townships Resource Centre, 671
ETTC - Edmonton Twin & Triplet Club, 679
EUCOCIT - European Union Chamber of Commerce in Toronto, 698
EVA BC - Ending Violence Association of British Columbia, 687
EVAC - Eagle Valley Arts Council, 666
EVCO - Electric Vehicle Council of Ottawa, 682
EVS - Electric Vehicle Society, 682
EVSCL - Elk Valley Society for Community Living, 685
EVTA - Eastern Veterinary Technician Association, 671
EWB - Engineers Without Borders, 689
EWC - EcoWatch Canada, 673
EWCS - East Wellington Community Services, 669
EWG - Edmonton Weavers' Guild, 679
EYA - Environmental Youth Alliance, 692
EYHS - East York Historical Society, 669
EYLE - East York Learning Experience, 669
EYO - Edmonton Youth Orchestra Association, 679
EZMSA - Edmonton Zone Medical Staff Association, 680

F

F&CS - Family & Children's Services of Guelph & Wellington County, 702
F4S-CSQ - Fédération des syndicats de la santé et des services sociaux, 719
FAAFC - Fédération des aînées et aînés francophones du Canada, 711
FAAFNB - Fédération des agriculteurs et agricultrices francophones du Nouveau-Brunswick, 711

FAC - Fédération autonome du collégial (ind.), 707
FACNC - Faculty Association of the College of New Caledonia, 701
FACS - Family & Children's Services Niagara, 701
FACS - Family & Children's Services of the District of Rainy River, 702
FACTOR - Foundation Assisting Canadian Talent on Recordings, 755
FAÉCUM - Fédération des associations étudiantes du campus de l'université de Montréal, 712
FAF - Fédération des aînés fransaskois, 711
FAFA - Fédération des aînés Franco-Albertains, 711
FAFIA - Feminist Alliance for International Action, 731
FAFM - Fédération des aînés franco-manitobains inc., 711
FAFM - Foundation for Advancing Family Medicine of the College of Family Physicians of Canada, 755
FAFMRQ - Fédération des associations de familles monoparentales et recomposées du Québec, 711
FAFP - Federation of Aboriginal Foster Parents, 722
FAFQ - Fédération des associations de familles du Québec, 711
FAJEF - Fédération des associations de juristes d'expression française de common law, 712
FAMÉQ - Fédération des Associations de Musiciens-Éducateurs du Québec, 712
FAMOM - Fredericton Area Moms of Multiples, 758
FAMS - Funeral Advisory & Memorial Society, 764
FAMSS - Funeral Advisory & Memorial Society of Saskatchewan, 764
FANE - Fédération acadienne de la Nouvelle-Écosse, 707
FANS - Filipino Association of Nova Scotia, 735
FANS - Fencing Association of Nova Scotia, 732
FAPO - Fredericton Anti-Poverty Association, 758
FAQ - Fédération des agricultrices du Québec, 711
FAQ - Femmes autochtones du Québec inc., 731
FAQ - Fondation des aveugles du Québec, 744
FARDC - Faculty Association of Red Deer College, 700
FARFO - Fédération des aînés et des retraités francophones de l'Ontario, 711
FARMS - Foreign Agricultural Resource Management Services, 751
FARSHA - Farm & Ranch Safety & Health Association, 705
FASO - Federal Association of Security Officials, 706
FATA - Fondation pour l'aide aux travailleuses et travailleurs accidentés, 747
FAUST - Faculty Association of University of Saint Thomas, 701
FAVA - Film & Video Arts Society Alberta, 735
FBBC - Food Banks British Columbia, 749
FBBQ - Fédération de basketball du Québec, 708
FBC - Food Beverage Canada, 749
FBC - Fraser Basin Council, 757
FBCN - British Columbia Nature (Federation of British Columbia Naturalists), 247
FBCW - Federation of British Columbia Writers, 722
FBCYICN - Federation of B.C. Youth in Care Networks, 722
FBD - Fur-Bearer Defenders, 765
FBO - Field Botanists of Ontario, 733
FBWR - Food Bank of Waterloo Region, 749
FC - Flowers Canada, 741
FCA - Federation of Canadian Artists, 722
FCA - Freight Carriers Association of Canada, 759

Acronym Index

FCA - Flowers Canada Growers, 741
FCAA - Financial & Consumer Affairs Authority of Saskatchewan, 736
FCABQ - Fédération des centres d'action bénévole du Québec, 712
FCALD - Filipino Canadian Association of London & District, 735
FCAV - Filipino Canadian Association of Vaughan, 735
FCB - Friends of Canadian Broadcasting, 760
FCC - Federation of Calgary Communities, 722
FCC - Flamborough Chamber of Commerce, 740
FCC - Fisheries Council of Canada, 739
FCC - The Fur Council of Canada, 765
FCCCPC - Filipino Canadian Catholic Charismatic Prayer Communities, 735
FCCF - Fédération culturelle canadienne-française, 708
FCCFA - Federation of Canada-China Friendship Associations, 722
FCCP - Federation of Chinese Canadian Professionals (Ontario), 723
FCCP Québec - Federation of Chinese Canadian Professionals (Québec), 723
FCCQ - Fédération des chambres de commerce du Québec, 713
FCCQ - Fédération des clubs de croquet du Québec, 713
FCCQ - Fédération des chambres de commerce du Québec, 713
FCCS - Foundation of Catholic Community Services Inc., 756
FCEA - Federation of Canadian Electrolysis Associations, 723
FCEF - Friends of the Central Experimental Farm, 762
FCFAC - Fédération des communautés francophones et acadienne du Canada, 713
FCG-Q - Fondation communautaire du Grand-Québec, 743
FCHE - Fédération des coopératives d'habitation de l'Estrie, 714
FCI - Folklore Canada International, 742
FCIPE - Fédération culturelle de L'Ile-du-Prince-Édouard inc., 708
FCIQ - Fédération des Chambres immobilières du Québec, 713
FCM - Federation of Canadian Municipalities, 723
FCMF - Federation of Canadian Music Festivals, 723
FCMQ - Fédération des clubs de motoneigistes du Québec, 713
FCN - Federation of Canadian Naturists, 723
FCNB - Financial & Consumer Services Commission, 736
FCPC - Food & Consumer Products of Canada, 749
FCPQ - Fédération des comités de parents du Québec inc., 713
FCQ - Fédération de crosse du Québec, 708
FCQ - Fédération de cheerleading du Québec, 708
FCQGED - Front commun québécois pour une gestion écologique des déchets, 763
FCSA - Frequency Co-ordination System Association, 760
FCSCS - Funeral & Cremation Services Council of Saskatchewan, 764
FCSQ - La Fédération des commissions scolaires du Québec, 713
FCSS - Family Counselling & Support Services for Guelph-Wellington, 702
FCSSAA - Family & Community Support Services Association of Alberta, 702
FCTA - Federation of Canadian Turkish Associations, 723
FCTPAM - Filipino Canadian Technical Professionals Association of Manitoba, Inc., 735
FCWM - Friends of The Canadian War Museum, 762
FDAC - Fernie & District Arts Council, 732

FDCNB - Federation of Dance Clubs of New Brunswick, 723
FDFA - Frontier Duty Free Association, 763
FDSDQ - Fédération de soccer du Québec, 710
FDSQ - Fédération des dentistes spécialistes du Québec, 714
FEC - Foundation for Environmental Conservation, 1526
FECANE - Fédération culturelle acadienne de la Nouvelle-Écosse, 708
FÉCHAM - Fédération des coopératives d'habitation Montérégiennes, 714
FECHAQC - Fédération des coopératives de Québec, Chaudière-Appalaches, 714
FECHIMM - Fédération des coopératives d'habitation intermunicipale du Montréal métropolitain, 714
FECHMACQ - Fédération des coopératives d'habitation de la Mauricie et du Centre-du-Québec, 714
FEDMA - Federation of European Direct & Interactive Marketing, 1526
FEEP - Fédération des établissements d'enseignement privés, 714
FEEPEQ - Fédération des éducateurs et éducatrices physiques enseignants du Québec, 714
FEESP - Fédération des employées et employés de services publics inc. (CSN), 714
FEIC - Financial Executives International Canada, 736
FENB - Fencing - Escrime New Brunswick, 732
FEN-BC - Fenestration Association of BC, 732
FEO - Festivals & Events Ontario, 733
FEQ - Festivals et Événements Québec, 733
FEQ - Fédération équestre du Québec inc., 720
FER - Friends of Ecological Reserves, 761
FESFO - Fédération de la jeunesse franco-ontarienne, 709
FEUQ - Fédération étudiante universitaire du Québec, 720
FEW - Focus for Ethnic Women, 741
FEX - Family Enterprise Xchange, 703
FF/OB - Frontiers Foundation, 763
FFA-CNC - Forum francophone des affaires, 754
FFAFNB - Fédération des femmes acadiennes et francophones du Nouveau-Brunswick, 715
FFANE - La Fédération des femmes acadiennes de la Nouvelle-Écosse, 715
FFAPAMM - Fédération des familles et amis de la personne atteinte de maladie mentale, 715
FFAQ - Football Québec, 750
FFAW - Fish, Food & Allied Workers, 739
FFB - The Foundation Fighting Blindness, 755
FFBF - Firefighters Burn Fund Inc., 738
FFCA - Falher Friendship Corner Association, 701
FFCB - La Fédération des francophones de la Colombie-Britannique, 715
FFCC - Fort Frances Chamber of Commerce, 752
FFFH - Friends of the Forestry Farm House Inc., 762
FFFNS - Federation of Foster Families of Nova Scotia, 724
FFGA - Fredericton Fish & Game Association, 759
FFGA - Foothills Forage & Grazing Association, 750
FFO - Fondation franco-ontarienne, 746
FFQ - Fédération des femmes du Québec, 715
FFQ - Fondation de la faune du Québec, 744
FFSBC - Freshwater Fisheries Society of British Columbia, 760
FFT - Fédération franco-ténoise, 721
FFTNL - La Fédération des francophones de Terre-Neuve et du Labrador, 715
FGBMFI - Full Gospel Business Men's Fellowship in Canada, 764
FGICR - Zane Cohen Centre for Digestive Diseases Familial Gastrointestinal Cancer Registry, 1482

FGMOEQ - Fondation de la greffe de moelle osseuse de l'Est du Québec, 744
FGQ - Fédération de gymnastique du Québec, 708
FGTA - From Grief To Action, 763
FHA - Field Hockey Alberta, 734
FHA - Friends Historical Association, 1527
FHBC - Field Hockey BC, 734
FHC - Field Hockey Canada, 734
FHCLM - Fondation Hôpital Charles-LeMoyne, 746
FHM - Field Hockey Manitoba, 734
FHO - Field Hockey Ontario, 734
FHOSQ - Fédération des harmonies et des orchestres symphoniques du Québec, 715
FHRCO - Federation of Health Regulatory Colleges of Ontario, 724
FHS - Friends Historical Society - London, 1527
FIAA - University of Toronto, Faculty of Information Alumni Association, 1421
FIABCI - Fédération internationale des professions immobilières, 1526
FIAP - Fédération Internationale de l'Art Photographique, 1525
FIAPF - Fédération internationale des associations de producteurs de films, 1525
FIBT - Fédération internationale de bobsleigh et de tobogganing, 1525
FIC - Fur Institute of Canada, 765
FICC - Fédération Internationale de Camping, Caravanning et Autocaravaning, 1525
FICS - Flamborough Information & Community Services, 740
FIELD - Foundation for International Environmental Law & Development, 1527
FIFCO - International Federation of Corporate Football, 857
FIH - Fédération internationale de hockey, 1525
FIHOQ - Fédération interdisciplinaire de l'horticulture ornementale du Québec, 721
FIL - Fédération Internationale de Luge de Course, 1525
FIPA-BC - British Columbia Freedom of Information & Privacy Association, 241
FIPEQ - Fédération des intervenantes en petite enfance du Québec, 715
FIPF - Fédération internationale des professeurs de français, 1525
FIPOE - Fraternité interprovinciale des ouvriers en électricité (CTC), 758
FIQ - Fédération interprofessionnelle de la santé du Québec, 721
FISA - Federation of Independent School Associations of BC, 724
FISA - Fédération indépendante des syndicats autonomes, 721
FIT - Fédération Internationale des Traducteurs, 1526
FIT - Foundation for International Training, 755
FITT - Forum for International Trade Training, 754
FJA - Francophonie jeunesse de l'Alberta, 757
FJCF - Fédération de la jeunesse canadienne-française inc., 709
FJFNB - Fédération des jeunes francophones du Nouveau-Brunswick Inc., 715
FJTNL - Franco-Jeunes de Terre-Neuve et du Labrador, 757
FKQ - Fibrose kystique Québec, 733
FLA - Foothills Library Association, 750
FLDQ - Fédération des loisirs-danse du Québec, 715
FLG - Fondation Lionel-Groulx, 747
FLK - Fung Loy Kok Institute of Taoism, 764
FLL - Fountain of Love & Life, 756
FLR - Foundation for Legal Research, 755
FLSC - Federation of Law Societies of Canada, 724
FMA - Freight Management Association of Canada, 759
FMAC - Flavour Manufacturers Association of Canada, 740
FMAC - Financial Markets Association of Canada, 737

FMACL - Fort McMurray Association for Community Living, 752
FMAS - Fibromyalgia Association of Saskatchewan, 733
FMC - Family Mediation Canada, 703
FMCBC - Federation of Mountain Clubs of British Columbia, 725
FMCIC - Free Methodist Church in Canada, 759
FMCIM - Fédération mondiale des concours internationaux de musique, 1526
FMCQ - Fondation des maladies du coeur du Québec, 745
FMFD - Federation of Mutual Fund Dealers, 725
FMHF - Fédération des maisons d'hébergement pour femmes, 715
FMI - Financial Management Institute of Canada, 737
FMM - Family Mediation Manitoba, 704
FMNS - Farmers' Markets of Nova Scotia Cooperative Ltd., 706
FMO - Farmers' Markets Ontario, 706
FMOQ - Fédération des médecins omnipraticiens du Québec, 716
FMQ - Fédération motocycliste du Québec, 721
FMRAC - Federation of Medical Regulatory Authorities of Canada, 724
FMRAC - Federation of Medical Regulatory Authorities of Canada, 724
FMRQ - Fédération des médecins résidents du Québec inc. (ind.), 716
FMSQ - Fédération des médecins spécialistes du Québec, 716
FMTA - Federation of Metro Tenants' Associations, 725
FMWC - Federation of Medical Women of Canada, 724
FMYSA - Fort McMurray Youth Soccer Association, 753
FNA - Farmers of North America, 705
FNALA - First Nations Agricultural Lending Association, 738
FNA-SAG - Farmers of North America Strategic Agriculture Institute, 705
FNBFA - Federation of New Brunswick Faculty Associations, 725
FNC - Fédération nationale des communications (CSN), 721
FNCPA - First Nations Chiefs of Police Association, 738
FNE - Federation of North American Explorers, 725
FNEC - First Nations Education Council, 738
FNEEQ - Fédération nationale des enseignants et des enseignantes du Québec, 715
FNFC - First Nations Friendship Centre, 738
FNLMAQ&L - First Nation Lands Managers Association of Québec & Labrador, 738
FNQ - Fédération de natation du Québec, 710
FNS - Feed Nova Scotia, 731
FNS - First Nations SchoolNet, 738
FNSPM - Fédération nationale des services de préparation au mariage, 722
FoA - Friends of Animals, 1527
FOBBA - Federation of Ontario Bed & Breakfast Accommodation, 725
FOCA - Federation of Ontario Cottagers' Associations, 725
FOCAM - Fondation Cardio-Montérégienne, 743
FOCS - Friends of Clayoquot Sound, 760
FoE - Friends of the Earth Canada, 762
FoEI - Friends of the Earth International, 1527
FOF - Fresh Outlook Foundation, 760
FOLA - Federation of Ontario Law Associations, 725
FOLRAC - Federation of Law Reform Agencies of Canada, 724
FONOM - Federation of Northern Ontario Municipalities, 725
FOOMS-FCA - Federation of Ontario Memorial Societies - Funeral Consumers Alliance, 726
FOPL - Federation of Ontario Public Libraries, 726
FOR - Friends of the Oldman River, 763
FOR - Fellowship of Reconciliation, 1526

Acronym Index

FOTCSI - Friends of the Coves Subwatershed Inc., 762
4K - 4Korners Family Resource Center, 756
FPA - Financial Planning Association, 1526
FPAC - Forest Products Association of Canada, 751
FPAMQ - Fédération des producteurs d'agneaux et moutons du Québec, 717
FPANE - Fédération des parents acadiens de la Nouvelle-Écosse, 716
FPAQ - Fédération du plongeon amateur du Québec, 720
FPAQ - Fédération des procuteurs acéricoles du Québec, 717
FPBQ - Fédération des producteurs de bovins du Québec, 717
FPC - Food Processors of Canada, 750
FPC - Fire Prevention Canada, 738
FPCBP - Federation of Portuguese Canadian Business & Professionals Inc., 726
FPCCQ - Fédération des producteurs de cultures commerciales du Québec, 717
FPCP - Fédération des parents du Manitoba, 716
FPCSN - Fédération des professionnèles, 717
FPEIM - Federation of Prince Edward Island Municipalities Inc., 726
FPEP - Fédération du personnel de l'enseignement privé, 720
FPFA - Fédération des parents francophones de l'Alberta, 717
FPFCB - Fédération des parents francophones de Colombie-Britannique, 716
FPFTNL - Fédération des parents francophones de Terre-Neuve et du Labrador, 717
FPHQ - Fédération des employés du préhospitaliers du Québec, 714
FPI - Foodservice & Packaging Institute, 1526
FPIPE - Fédération des parents de l'Ile-du-Prince-Édouard, 716
FPJQ - Fédération professionnelle des journalistes du Québec, 726
FPM - Family Prayer Mission (Ontario), 704
FPMQ - Fédération des policiers et policières municipaux du Québec (ind.), 717
FPO - Freedom Party of Ontario, 759
FPOCQ - Fédération des producteurs d'oeufs de consommation du Québec, 717
FPPAC - Further Poultry Processors Association of Canada, 765
FPPC - Fédération du personnel professionnel des collèges, 720
FPPE - Fédération des professionnelles et professionnels de l'éducation du Québec, 718
FPPTQ - Fédération des producteurs de pommes de terre du Québec, 717
FPPU - Fédération du personnel professionnel des universités et de la recherche, 720
FPPVQ - Fraternité des Policiers et Policières de la Ville de Québec, 758
FPSC - Financial Planning Standards Council, 737
FPSS - Fédération du personnel de soutien scolaire (CSQ), 720
FPSS - Foster Parent Support Services Society, 755
FPWR Canada - Foundation for Prader-Willi Research in Canada, 756
FQA - Fédération québécoise d'athlétisme, 727
FQA - Fédération québécoise de l'autisme, 727
FQAS - Fédération québécoise des activités subaquatiques, 728
FQBO - Fédération Québécoise de Boxe Olympique, 727
FQCC - Fédération québécoise de camping et de caravaning inc., 727
FQCCL - Fédération québécoise des centres communautaires de loisir inc., 728
FQCF - Fédération québécoise des coopératives forestières, 728
FQCK - Fédération québécoise du canot et du kayak, 730
FQCMS - Fédération québécoise des coopératives en milieu scolaire, 728

FQD - Fédération Québécoise de Dynamophilie, 727
FQDE - Fédération québécoise des directions d'établissements d'enseignement, 728
FQDI - Fondation québécoise de la déficience intellectuelle, 747
FQE - Fédération québécoise des échecs, 728
FQHG - Hockey Québec, 818
FQHO - Fédération québécoise de handball olympique, 727
FQISI - Fédération Québécoise des Intervenants en Sécurité Incendie, 728
FQJR - Fédération québécoise des jeux récréatifs, 729
FQLL - Fédération québécoise du loisir littéraire, 731
FQM - Fédération Québécoise des Municipalités, 729
FQM - Fédération québécoise des massothérapeutes, 729
FQMC - Fondation québécoise de la maladie coeliaque, 747
FQME - Fédération québécoise de la montagne et de l'escalade, 727
FQN - Fédération québécoise de naturisme, 727
FQOCF - La Fédération québécoise des organismes communautaires Famille, 729
FQP - Fédération québécoise de philatélie, 728
FQPN - Fédération du Québec pour le planning des naissances, 720
FQPPU - Fédération québécoise des professeures et professeurs d'université, 729
FQRS - Fédération québécoise des revêtements de sol, 729
FQRS - Fédération québécoise des revêtements de sol, 729
FQSA - Fédération québécoise des sociétés Alzheimer, 729
FQSA - Fédération québécoise pour le saumon atlantique, 731
FQSC - Fédération québécoise des sports cyclistes, 730
FQSG - Fédération québécoise des sociétés de généalogie, 730
FQT - Fédération québécoise de tir, 728
FQTA - Fédération québécoise du théâtre amateur, 731
FRAQ - Fédération de la relève agricole du Québec, 709
FRC - Fish Harvesters Resource Centres, 739
FREB - Real Estate Board of the Fredericton Area Inc., 1205
FRI - Fondation Richelieu International, 748
FRJ - Fondation Ressources-Jeunesse, 748
FRPO - The Fair Rental Policy Organization of Ontario, 701
FRQ - Fédération de rugby du Québec, 710
FSAC - Fédération des syndicats de l'action collective, 719
FSAC - Funeral Service Association of Canada, 764
FSAC - Folklore Studies Association of Canada, 742
FSAC/ACÉC - Film Studies Association of Canada, 735
FSACC - Fredericton Sexual Assault Crisis Centre, 759
FSAT - Filipino Students' Association of Toronto, 735
FSC - Family Service Canada, 704
FSCNS - Federation for Scottish Culture in Nova Scotia, 726
FSCO - Financial Services Commission of Ontario, 737
FSCPNS - Federation of Senior Citizens & Pensioners of Nova Scotia, 726
FSE - Fédération des Syndicats de l'Enseignement, 719
FSGV - Family Services of Greater Vancouver, 704
FSHÉQ - Fédération des sociétés d'horticulture et d'écologie du Québec, 719
FSJACL - Fort St. John Association for Community Living, 753

FSMSA - Fort Saskatchewan Minor Sports Association, 754
FSNA - National Association of Federal Retirees, 990
FSNS - Freestyle Ski Nova Scotia, 759
FSO - Freestyle Skiing Ontario, 759
FSPH - Family Services Perth-Huron, 705
FSPQ - Fédération des secrétaires professionnelles du Québec, 718
FSQ-CSQ - Fédération de la santé du Québec - CSQ, 709
FSRS - Fishermen & Scientists Research Society, 740
FSSC - Fertilizer Safety & Security Council, 733
FSSRA - Federation of Saskatchewan Surface Rights Association, 726
FSSS - Fédération de la santé et des services sociaux, 710
FST - Family Service Toronto, 704
FSTV - Family Service Thames Valley, 704
FTAQ - Fédération de tir à l'arc du Québec, 710
FTGQ - Fédération des trappeurs gestionnaires du Québec, 719
FTJS - Federation of Teachers of Jewish Schools, 726
FTQ - Fédération des travailleurs et travailleuses du Québec, 719
FTTQ - Fédération de tennis de table du Québec, 710
FVBQ - Fédération de volleyball du Québec, 710
FVC - Fair Vote Canada, 701
FVS - Fraser Valley Symphony Society, 758
FVTS - First Vancouver Theatre Space Society, 739
FWHLCC - Falcon, West Hawk & Caddy Lakes Chamber of Commerce, 701
FWIC - Federated Women's Institutes of Canada, 706
FWIO - Federated Women's Institutes of Ontario, 706
FWKP - The Friends of West Kootenay Parks Society, 763
FWPQ - Fédération de Water-Polo du Québec, 711
FXRFC - Fragile X Research Foundation of Canada, 757
FYFB - Fort York Food Bank, 754
FYSS - Forever Young Seniors Society, 752

G

GAA - Groupement des assureurs automobiles, 792
GAA/BC - Gelbvieh Association of Alberta/BC, 768
GAAC - Glass Art Association of Canada, 774
GAC - Guelph Arts Council, 792
GAC - Global Automakers of Canada, 774
GAC - Geological Association of Canada, 769
GACC - Gander & Area Chamber of Commerce, 766
GACC - Greater Arnprior Chamber of Commerce, 782
GAIHST - Groupe d'aide et d'information sur le harcèlement sexuel au travail de la province de Québec, 791
GAMA - Glass & Architectural Metals Association, 774
GANS - Genealogical Association of Nova Scotia, 768
GAO - Golf Association of Ontario, 777
GAP-VIES - Groupe d'action pour la prévention de la transmission du VIH et l'éradication du Sida, 791
GBC - Gymnastics B.C., 795
GBC - Georgian Bay Country Tourism Association, 771
GBCM - Les Grands Ballets Canadiens de Montréal, 781
GBFS - Georgian Bay Folk Society, 771
GBNFC - Georgian Bay Native Friendship Centre, 771
GBS - Georgian Bay Symphony, 771
GBSA - George Bray Sports Association, 770

GBSFCI - Guillain-Barré Syndrome Foundation of Canada, 794
GBTA - Global Business Travel Association (Canada), 774
GCA - Geneva Centre for Autism, 769
GCAA - German-Canadian Association of Alberta, 772
GCAA - Guelph Creative Arts Association, 793
GCAM - Guyana Cultural Association of Montréal, 794
GCBBT - Greater Corner Brook Board of Trade, 783
GCC - Guelph Chamber of Commerce, 793
GCC - German-Canadian Congress (Ontario), 772
GCC - Green Communities Canada, 788
GCCA - Greek-Canadian Cultural Centre, 788
GCCABC - Guyanese Canadian Cultural Association of BC, 794
GCFL - GATEWAY Centre For Learning, 767
GCG - Gymnastics Canada Gymnastique, 795
GCHA - Guysborough Historical Society, 795
GCHA - German-Canadian Historical Association Inc., 772
GCHS - Grenville County Historical Society, 789
GCIA - Global Commercial Insurers' Association, 774
GCIC - General Church of the New Jerusalem in Canada, 768
GCIFA - Guysborough County Inshore Fishermen's Association, 795
GCO - The Garden Clubs of Ontario, 766
GDBA - Glendon & District Business Alliance, 774
GDC - Society of Graphic Designers of Canada, 1329
GDTA - Great Divide Trails Association, 782
GEAC - Groundfish Enterprise Allocation Council, 790
GEAPS - Grain Elevator & Processing Society, 1528
GEAQC - Groupe export agroalimentaire Québec - Canada, 792
GEIPSI - Groupe d'entraide à l'intention des personnes séropositives, itinérantes et toxicomanes, 791
GELA - Greater Edmonton Library Association, 783
GEOEC - Global, Environmental & Outdoor Education Council, 775
GFD - Guaranteed Funeral Deposits of Canada, 792
GFGS - Association des Grands Frères et Grandes Soeurs du Québec, 115
GFOA - Government Finance Officers Association, 1528
GFOABC - Government Finance Officers Association of British Columbia, 778
GGC - Girl Guides of Canada, 773
GGC - Gatineau Gliding Club, 768
GGC - Grain Growers of Canada, 779
GGPAAF - Governor General's Performing Arts Awards Foundation, 778
GGUL - Groupe gai de l'Université Laval, 792
GHCHF - Golden Horseshoe Co-operative Housing Federation, 776
GHS - Guelph Historical Society, 793
GHTA - Ganaraska Hiking Trail Association, 766
GHTC - Guelph Hiking Trail Club, 793
GIAC - Geomatics Industry Association of Canada, 770
GICC - Greater Innisfil Chamber of Commerce, 783
GIM - Genealogical Institute of The Maritimes, 768
GIO - General Insurance OmbudService, 769
GIRC - Guelph International Resource Centre, 793
GIV - Groupe intervention vidéo, 792
GKCC - Greater Kingston Chamber of Commerce, 783
GKS - Association for Canadian Studies in German-Speaking Countries, 1507
GLGC - Great Lakes Gliding Club, 782

Acronym Index

GLIER - Great Lakes Institute for Environmental Research, 782
GLQ - Grand Lodge of Québec - Ancient, Free & Accepted Masons, 779
GLRC - The Great Lakes Research Consortium, 1528
GMAA - Greater Montreal Athletic Association, 784
GMCC - Greater Moncton Chamber of Commerce, 784
GMCCA - Greater Moncton Chinese Cultural Association, 784
GMCFA - Grant MacEwan College Faculty Association, 782
GMCS - Gem & Mineral Club of Scarborough, 768
GMFA - Grand Manan Fishermen's Association, 779
GMFC - Gem & Mineral Federation of Canada, 768
GMMQ - La Guilde des Musiciens/Musiciennes du Québec, 794
GMP - Glass, Molders, Pottery, Plastic & Allied Workers International Union (AFL-CIO/CLC), 1528
GMSPCA - Greater Moncton Society for the Prevention of Cruelty to Animals, 784
GMWSRS - Grand Manan Whale & Seabird Research Station, 780
GN - Grasslands Naturalists, 782
GNABC - Gerontological Nursing Association of British Columbia, 772
GNAO - Gerontological Nursing Association of Ontario, 772
GNCC - Greater Niagara Chamber of Commerce, 784
GNDI - Global Network of Director Institutes, 775
GNL - Gymnastics Newfoundland & Labrador Inc., 795
GNL - Golf Newfoundland & Labrador, 777
GNS - Gymnastics Nova Scotia, 795
GOABC - Guide Outfitters Association of British Columbia, 793
GOC - Society of Gynecologic Oncologists of Canada, 1329
GOCA - Guyana Ottawa Cultural Association, 794
GPAAR - Grande Prairie & Area Association of Realtors, 781
GPAC - Golden Prairie Arts Council, 776
GPAC - Gas Processing Association Canada, 767
GPACS - Greyhound Pets of Atlantic Canada Society, 790
GPBC - Green Party Political Association of British Columbia, 789
GPC - Green Party of Canada, 788
GPC - Governance Professionals of Canada, 778
GPCC - Greater Peterborough Chamber of Commerce, 784
GPDAPDD - Grande Prairie & District Association for Persons with Developmental Disabilities, 781
GPI - Glass Packaging Institute, 1528
GPO - The Green Party of Ontario, 789
GPPA - General Practice Psychotherapy Association, 769
GPRC - Grande Prairie Regional College Academic Staff Association, 781
GPSPCA - Grande Prairie Society for the Prevention of Cruelty to Animals, 781
GRAME - Groupe de recherche appliquée en macroécologie, 791
GRAPE - Groupe de recherche en animation et planification économique, 791
GRCF - Grand River Conservation Foundation, 780
GRESOC - Groupe de recherche en écologie sociale, 791
GRHC - Green Roofs for Healthy Cities, 789
GRIS-Montréal - Groupe de recherche et d'intervention sociale, 791

GRIS-Québec - Groupe régional d'intervention social - Québec, 792
GRO - Gateway Research Organization, 767
GSCC - Greater Summerside Chamber of Commerce, 785
GSCC - Greater Sackville Chamber of Commerce, 785
GSE - Geotechnical Society of Edmonton, 771
GSML Ministry - God, Sex, & the Meaning of Life Ministry, 776
GSO - Guelph Symphony Orchestra, 793
GSU - Grain Services Union (CLC), 779
GSU - Government Services Union, 778
GTAA - Greater Toronto Apartment Association, 785
GTAIS - Greater Toronto Al-Anon Information Services, 785
GTHA - Greater Toronto Hotel Association, 786
GTMA - Greater Toronto Marketing Alliance, 786
GTO - Gitxsan Treaty Office, 774
GTWGHS - Greater Toronto Water Garden & Horticultural Society, 786
GVAD - Greater Vancouver Association of the Deaf, 786
GVCC - Greater Vernon Chamber of Commerce, 787
GVCC - Greater Victoria Chamber of Commerce, 787
GVCSS - Greater Vancouver Community Services Society, 786
GVFBS - Greater Vancouver Food Bank Society, 786
GVHBA - Greater Vancouver Home Builders' Association, 786
GVHS - Gatineau Valley Historical Society, 768
GVJCAA - Greater Vancouver Japanese Canadian Citizens' Association, 787
GVN - Global Village Nanaimo, 775
GVPS - Greater Victoria Philatelic Society, 787
GVPTA - Greater Vancouver Professional Theatre Alliance, 787
GVRDEU - Greater Vancouver Regional District Employees' Union, 787
GVTA - Grand Valley Trails Association, 780
GVYO - Greater Victoria Youth Orchestra, 787
GWFA - Grey Wooded Forage Association, 790
GWNFA - Great White North Franchisee Association, 782
GWRCS - Golden Women's Resource Centre Society, 776
GWU - Grain Workers' Union, Local 333, 779
GYVN - Global Youth Volunteer Network, 775

H

HAAC - Health Association of African Canadians, 806
HAAO - Hospital Auxiliaries Association of Ontario, 823
HAC - Hotel Association of Canada Inc., 823
HAC - Helicopter Association of Canada, 811
HAC - Heatherton Activity Centre, 810
HACC - Hampton Area Chamber of Commerce, 802
HAI - HelpAge International, 1529
HAN - Hamilton AIDS Network, 800
HANS - Health Action Network Society, 805
HANS - Hotel Association of Nova Scotia, 824
HANS - Handball Association of Nova Scotia, 802
HAPEI - Health Association of PEI, 806
HAPS - Human Anatomy & Physiology Society, 1530
HARC - Halifax Amateur Radio Club, 798
HARS - HIV/AIDS Regional Services, 817
HASC - Historical Automobile Society of Canada, Inc., 816
HASTe - Hub for Active School Travel, 824
HAT - Habitat Acquisition Trust, 795
HAV - Hotel Association of Vancouver, 824
HAV - Halifax Association of Vegetarians, 798
HBDREB - Hamilton-Burlington & District Real Estate Board, 802

HBUA - Hamilton Baseball Umpires' Association, 801
HC - Humanist Canada, 826
HCACA - Hispanic Canadian Arts & Culture Association, 815
HCANL - Heavy Civil Association of Newfoundland & Labrador, Inc., 810
HCBC - Horse Council British Columbia, 822
HCBT - Hellenic Canadian Board of Trade, 811
HCC - Hamilton Chamber of Commerce, 801
HCC - Homeopathic College of Canada, 819
HCC - Harbourfront Community Centre, 803
HCC(BC) - Hellenic Canadian Congress of BC, 811
HCCAO - Home Child Care Association of Ontario, 819
HCCC - Health Charities Coalition of Canada, 806
HCEA - Hungarian Canadian Engineers' Association, 827
HCF - National Trust for Canada, 996
HCF - Hamilton Community Foundation, 801
HCHC - Hispanic Canadian Heritage Council, 815
HCI - Human Concern International, 824
HCLA - Hastings County Law Association, 804
HCPRA - Health Care Public Relations Association, 806
HCQ - L'Héritage canadien du Québec, 813
HCRA - Halifax Citadel Regimental Association, 799
HDADA - Halifax-Dartmouth Automobile Dealers' Association, 800
HDBA - Huronia & District Beekeepers' Association, 828
HDC - Hispanic Development Council, 815
HDCO - Hockey Development Centre for Ontario, 817
HDEAA - Halton District Educational Assistants Association, 800
HDSDC - Hamilton District Society for Disabled Children, 801
HEA - Halifax Employers Association, 799
HEABC - Health Employers Association of British Columbia, 806
HEAT - Heavy Equipment & Aggregate Truckers Association of Manitoba, 810
HEIRS - Harrow Early Immigrant Research Society, 804
HEO - Hockey Eastern Ontario, 817
HepNS - Hepatitis Outreach Society of Nova Scotia, 812
HEU - Hospital Employees' Union, 823
HFA - Hedge Fund Association Canada, 1529
HFH - Help for Headaches, 812
HFHC - Habitat for Humanity Canada, 796
HFMHA - Hong Fook Mental Health Association, 820
HFN - Halifax Field Naturalists, 799
HFNL - Heritage Foundation of Newfoundland & Labrador, 813
HFP - Council of the Haida Nation - Haida Fisheries Program, 635
HFS - Halton Family Services, 800
HHCofC - Haliburton Highlands Chamber of Commerce, 798
HHGFA - Haliburton Highlands Guild of Fine Arts, 798
HIAA - Horse Industry Association of Alberta, 822
HIABC - Home Inspectors Association BC, 819
HI-C - Hostelling International - Canada, 823
HIEA - Hamilton Industrial Environmental Association, 801
HIF - Housing Inspection Foundation, 1530
HIMSS - Healthcare Information & Management Systems Society, 1529
HIP - Healthy Indoors Partnership, 807
HIT - Hamilton Technology Centre, 802
HKCBA - Hong Kong-Canada Business Association, 820
HLA - Hamilton Law Association, 801
HLABC - Health Libraries Association of British Columbia, 806
HLI - Human Life International, 1530

HLI - Health Law Institute, 806
HLL - Houston Link to Learning, 824
HM - Héritage Montréal, 813
HMAC - Homeopathic Medical Association Of Canada, 820
HMANA - Hawk Migration Association of North America, 1529
HMC - Halton Multicultural Council, 800
HMFI - Holocaust Memorial Foundation of Illinois, 1529
HMYO - Halton Mississauga Youth Orchestra, 800
HNA - Helios Nudist Association, 811
HNB - Hockey New Brunswick, 818
HNC - Hamilton Naturalists' Club, 801
HNC - Headache Network Canada, 805
HNHB CCAC - Hamilton Niagara Haldimand Brant Community Care Access Centre, 801
HNIC - Haldimand-Norfolk Information Centre, 798
HNL - Hospitality Newfoundland & Labrador, 823
HNLC - Haldimand-Norfolk Literacy Council, 798
HNO - Hockey Northwestern Ontario, 818
HNWTA - Halifax North West Trails Association, 799
HOF - Horizons of Friendship, 821
HON - Healing Our Nations, 805
HOPE - Helping Other Parents Everywhere Inc., 812
HORT NS - Horticulture Nova Scotia, 822
HPA - Hamilton Police Association, 802
HPAAC - Hang Gliding & Paragliding Association of Atlantic Canada, 803
HPAC - Hang Gliding & Paragliding Association of Canada, 803
HPBAC - Hearth, Patio & Barbecue Association of Canada, 809
HPCM - Palliative Manitoba, 1137
HPCO - Hospice Palliative Care Ontario, 823
HPS - Hamilton Program for Schizophrenia, 802
HPYO - Hamilton Philharmonic Youth Orchestra, 801
HRABC - Health Record Association of British Columbia, 807
HRAI - Heating, Refrigeration & Air Conditioning Institute of Canada, 810
HRANB - Human Resources Association of New Brunswick, 825
HRC@P - Halifax Regional CAP Association, 799
HRI - Human Rights Internet, 826
HRMSC - H.R. MacMillan Space Centre Society, 824
HRMSP - HRMS Professionals Association, 824
HRPA - Human Resources Professionals Association, 825
HRPA - Halifax Regional Police Association, 799
HRPA - Halton Regional Police Association, 800
HRPAD - Human Resources Professionals of Durham, 826
HRPNL - Human Resources Professionals of Newfoundland & Labrador, 826
HRREC - Human Rights Research & Education Centre, 826
HRS - Historic Restoration Society of Annapolis County, 815
HSA - Historical Society of Alberta, 816
HSAA - Health Sciences Association of Alberta, 807
HSABC - Health Sciences Association of British Columbia, 807
HSAC - Hungarian Studies Association of Canada, 827
HSANL - Historic Sites Association of Newfoundland & Labrador, 815
HSAS - Health Sciences Association of Saskatchewan, 807
HSC - Huntington Society of Canada, 827
HSC - Hamilton Stamp Club, 802
HSCF - Hospital for Sick Children Foundation, 823

Acronym Index

HSCF - Health Sciences Centre Foundation, 807
HSCSA - Health & Safety Conference Society of Alberta, 805
HSFA - Heart & Stroke Foundation of Alberta, NWT & Nunavut, 808
HSFBCY - Heart & Stroke Foundation of British Columbia & Yukon, 808
HSFC - Heart & Stroke Foundation of Canada, 808
HSFM - Heart & Stroke Foundation of Manitoba, 808
HSFNS - Heart & Stroke Foundation of Nova Scotia, 809
HSFO - Heart & Stroke Foundation of Ontario, 809
HSFS - Heart & Stroke Foundation of Saskatchewan, 809
HSI Canada - Humane Society International/Canada, 826
HSLDA - Home School Legal Defence Association of Canada, 819
HSLS - Helping Spirit Lodge Society, 812
HSO - Huronia Symphony Orchestra, 828
HSSC - Historical Society of St. Catharines, 816
HSSC - Halifax Sport & Social Club, 799
HSUS - The Humane Society of the United States, 1530
HTCNA - Holy Trinity Community - North America, 1530
HTNS - Heritage Trust of Nova Scotia, 813
HTNS - Horse Trials Nova Scotia, 822
HUGG - Helping Unite Grandparents & Grandchildren, 812
HVSO - Historic Vehicle Society of Ontario, 815
HW - Heritage Winnipeg Corp., 813

I

IAAC - Infertility Awareness Association of Canada, 836
IAAC - International Association of Art Critics - Canada, 853
IAAE - International Association of Agricultural Economists, 1537
IAAP - International Association of Administrative Professionals, 1537
IAAS - International Association for Armenian Studies, 1535
IAAW - Institute for the Advancement of Aboriginal Women, 844
IABC - International Association of Business Communicators, 1538
IAC - International Academy of Cytology, 1534
IACAC - Inter-American Commercial Arbitration Commission, 851
IACCP - International Association for Cross-Cultural Psychology, 1536
IACP - International Association of Chiefs of Police, 1538
IACS - Indian Association for Canadian Studies, 1531
IACS - Israel Association for Canadian Studies, 1567
IADQ - L'Institut d'assurance de dommages du Québec, 841
IADSA - International Alliance of Dietary/Food Supplement Associations, 1535
IAEA - International Atomic Energy Agency, 1540
IAEAC - International Association of Environmental Analytical Chemistry, 1538
IAEE - International Association for Earthquake Engineering, 1536
IAEH - International Association for Environmental Hydrology, 1536
IAEMM - International Academy of Energy, Minerals & Materials, 852
IAESTE - IAESTE Canada (International Association for the Exchange of Students for Technical Experience), 829
IAEVG - International Association for Educational & Vocational Guidance, 853
IAEWP - International Association of Educators for World Peace - USA, 1538

IAF - Inuit Art Foundation, 862
IAF - British Columbia Investment Agriculture Foundation, 244
IAFF - International Association of Fire Fighters (AFL-CIO/CLC), 1538
IAGLR - International Association for Great Lakes Research, 1536
IAGSA - International Airborne Geophysics Safety Association, 853
IAH - International Association of Hydrogeologists, 1538
IAH-CNC - International Association of Hydrogeologists - Canadian National Chapter, 854
IAHE - International Association for Hydrogen Energy, 1536
IAI - International African Institute, 1535
IAIA - International Association for Impact Assessment, 1537
IAJ - International Association of Judges, 1539
IALA - International Association of Marine Aids to Navigation & Lighthouse Authorities, 1539
IALJS - International Association for Literary Journalism Studies, 853
IALMH - International Academy of Law & Mental Health, 853
IAMAT - International Association for Medical Assistance to Travellers, 853
IAMAW - International Association of Machinists & Aerospace Workers, 1539
IAML - International Association of Music Libraries, Archives & Documentation Centres, 1539
IANA - Intermodal Association of North America, 1534
IANE - Inter-Provincial Association on Native Employment, 861
IANLS - International Association for Neo-Latin Studies, 1537
IANS - Islamic Association of Nova Scotia, 864
IAOGI - Independent Assemblies of God International - Canada, 832
IAP2 - International Association for Public Participation, 1537
IAP2 - International Association for Public Participation Canada, 853
IAPCO - International Association of Professional Congress Organizers, 1539
IAPH - International Association of Ports & Harbours, 1539
IAPO - Indian Agricultural Program of Ontario, 834
IAPS - International Association of Patristic Studies, 1539
IAR - Institute of Asian Research, 844
IAS - International Association of Sedimentologists, 1540
IASC - International Arctic Science Committee, 1535
IASF - International Amateur Swimming Federation, 1535
IASL - Institute of Air & Space Law, 844
IASP - International Association for the Study of Pain, 1537
IASS - Independent Association of Support Staff, 832
IASTED - International Association of Science & Technology for Development, 854
IATA - International Air Transport Association, 853
IATA - International Amateur Theatre Association, 1535
IATSE - International Alliance of Theatrical Stage Employees, Moving Picture Technicians, Artists & Allied Crafts of the U.S., Its Territories & Canada, 1535
IAUPE - International Association of University Professors of English, 1540
IAVGO - Industrial Accident Victims Group of Ontario, 835
IAVM - International Association of Venue Managers, Inc., 1540
IBA - International Bar Association, 1540
IBA - International Association for Bear Research & Management, 1535

IBAC - Insurance Brokers Association of Canada, 848
IBB - International Brotherhood of Boilermakers, Iron Ship Builders, Blacksmiths, Forgers & Helpers (AFL-CIO), 1541
IBBY - International Board on Books for Young People, 1541
IBBY - Canada - International Board on Books for Young People - Canadian Section, 854
IBC - Insurance Bureau of Canada, 848
IBEW - International Brotherhood of Electrical Workers (AFL-CIO/CFL), 1542
IBWA - International Bottled Water Association, 1541
IC - Interpretation Canada - A Professional Association for Heritage Interpretation, 861
ICA - Institute of Communication Agencies, 845
ICA - Inner City Angels, 838
ICA - International Cooperative Alliance, 1544
ICA - Inter-Cultural Association of Greater Victoria, 851
ICA - International Caterers Association, 1542
ICAA - International Council on Active Aging, 856
ICADTS - International Council on Alcohol, Drugs & Traffic Safety, 1545
ICAI - Institute of Cultural Affairs International, 846
ICAM - International Council for Applied Mineralogy, 1544
ICAM - Ileostomy & Colostomy Association of Montréal, 829
ICANTNU - Institute of Chartered Accountants of the Northwest Territories & Nunavut, 845
ICAS - International Credential Assessment Service of Canada, 856
ICASE - International Council of Associations for Science Education, 1545
ICASO - International Council of AIDS Service Organizations, 855
ICAZ - International Council for Archaeozoology, 1544
ICBA - Independent Contractors & Businesses Association of British Columbia, 832
ICC - International Chamber of Commerce, 1542
ICC - Islamic Care Centre, 864
ICCA - Inverness County Centre for the Arts, 862
ICCA NB - Irish Canadian Cultural Association of New Brunswick, 864
ICCA NS - Italian Canadian Cultural Association of Nova Scotia, 866
ICCAT - International Commission for the Conservation of Atlantic Tunas, 1542
ICCC - Ireland-Canada Chamber of Commerce, 863
ICCC - Indonesia Canada Chamber of Commerce, 1531
ICCC - International Cheese Council of Canada, 855
ICCC - Indo-Canada Chamber of Commerce, 835
ICCC - Italian Chamber of Commerce in Canada, 866
ICCEES - International Council for Central & East European Studies (Canada), 1544
ICCLR - International Centre for Criminal Law Reform & Criminal Justice Policy, 854
ICCO - Italian Chamber of Commerce of Ontario, 866
ICCS - International Council for Canadian Studies, 855
ICD - Institute of Corporate Directors, 845
ICDA - International Catholic Deaf Association, 854
ICEA - Institut de coopération pour l'éducation des adultes, 841
ICEL - International Council of Environmental Law, 1545
ICES - International Council for the Exploration of the Sea, 1544
ICES - Institute for Clinical Evaluative Sciences, 843

ICF - InformCanada, 838
ICF - International Coaching Federation, 1542
ICFA - International Coalition of Fisheries Associations, 1542
ICGA - International Computer Games Association, 1543
ICHOS - Inner City Home of Sudbury, 839
ICI - International Commission on Illumination, 1542
ICID - International Commission on Irrigation & Drainage, 1543
ICING - International Curling Information Network Group, 856
ICJ - International Commission of Jurists (Canadian Section), 855
ICLAS - International Council for Laboratory Animal Science, 1544
ICLEI - International Council for Local Environmental Initiatives, 1544
ICLR - Institute for Catastrophic Loss Reduction, 843
ICM - International Confederation of Midwives, 1543
ICM - Institut de cardiologie de Montréal, 841
ICM - Institut du cancer de Montréal, 842
ICM - Insurance Council of Manitoba, 849
ICO - International Council of Ophthalmology, 1545
ICOH - International Commission on Occupational Health, 1543
ICOM - International Council of Museums, 1545
ICOMAM - International Committee of Museums & Collections of Arms & Military History, 1543
ICOM-CIDOC - International Committee for Documentation of the International Council of Museums, 1543
ICOMOS - International Council on Monuments & Sites, 1545
ICP - International Confederation of Principals, 1544
ICQ - L'Institut canadien de Québec, 840
ICRF - Israel Cancer Research Fund, 866
ICROSS - International Community for Relief of Suffering & Starvation Canada, 855
ICRP - International Commission on Radiological Protection, 855
ICS - Insurance Councils of Saskatchewan, 849
ICS - International Continence Society, 1544
ICSA Canada - Institute of Chartered Secretaries & Administrators - Canadian Division, 845
ICSC - International Centre for Sustainable Cities, 855
ICSD - International Committee of Sports for the Deaf, 1543
ICSDP - International Centre for Science in Drug Policy, 854
ICTAC - International Confederation for Thermal Analysis & Calorimetry, 1543
ICTAM - Information & Communication Technologies Association of Manitoba, 836
ICTC - Information & Communications Technology Council of Canada, 836
ICTCMV - International College of Traditional Chinese Medicine of Vancouver, 855
ICUr - International Union of Crystallography, 1564
ICURR - Muniscope, 982
ICVA - International Council of Voluntary Agencies, 1545
ICW - Inverness Cottage Workshop, 862
ICWF - InScribe Christian Writers' Fellowship, 839
IDA - International Dyslexia Association, 1545
IDA - Interior Designers of Alberta, 852
IDAS - Interior Designers Association of Saskatchewan, 852
IDAS - Indefinite Arts Society, 832
IDC - Interior Designers of Canada, 852
IDF - International Dairy Federation, 1545
IDHHC - Island Deaf & Hard of Hearing Centre, 865
IDIBC - Interior Designers Institute of British Columbia, 852

Acronym Index

IDNL - Interior Designers of Newfoundland & Labrador, 852
IDNS - Association of Interior Designers of Nova Scotia, 149
IDP - L'Institut de développement de produits, 841
IDRC - International Development Research Centre, 856
IDRF - International Development & Relief Foundation, 856
IDSA - Infectious Diseases Society of America, 1531
IECA - International Erosion Control Association, 1546
IEEE - Institute of Electrical & Electronics Engineers Inc., 1532
IESNA - Illuminating Engineering Society of North America, 1530
IETA - International Emissions Trading Association, 1546
IFA - International Federation of Airworthiness, 1547
IFA - International Federation on Aging, 857
IFAC - International Federation of Accountants, 1547
IFAI - Industrial Fabrics Association International, 1531
IFAI Canada - Industrial Fabrics Association International Canada, 835
IFAW - International Fund for Animal Welfare Canada, 857
IFB - Independent Financial Brokers of Canada, 832
IFBA - International Federation of Broomball Associations, 857
IFBB - International Federation of Bodybuilding & Fitness, 1547
IFBPW - International Federation of Business & Professional Women, 1547
IFC - International Financial Centre of Montréal, 857
IFCB - International Federation for Cell Biology, 1546
IFCC - International Federation of Clinical Chemistry & Laboratory Medicine, 1547
IFCO - Independent Filmmakers' Co-operative of Ottawa, 832
IFCO - International Foster Care Organisation, 1549
IFDD - Institut de la Francophonie pour le développement durable, 841
IFF - International Flying Farmers, 1549
IFHE - International Federation for Home Economics, 1546
IFHGS - International Federation of Human Genetics Societies, 1548
IFHIMA - International Federation of Health Information Management Associations, 1548
IFHP - International Federation for Housing & Planning, 1546
IFIC - Investment Funds Institute of Canada, 862
IFLA - International Federation of Landscape Architects, 1548
IFLA - International Federation of Library Associations & Institutions, 1548
IFMA - International Facility Management Association, 1546
IFMBE - International Federation for Medical & Biological Engineering, 1546
IFMSA - International Federation of Medical Students' Associations, 1548
IFNA - Independent First Nations' Alliance, 832
IFOAM - International Federation of Organic Agriculture Movements, 1548
IFPTE - International Federation of Professional & Technical Engineers (AFL-CIO/CLC), 1549
IFRWH - International Federation for Research in Women's History, 1547
IFS - International Federation of Surveyors, 1549
IFSBAC - Institute for Folklore Studies in Britain & Canada, 1532
IFT - Islamic Foundation of Toronto, 864
IFT - Institute of Food Technologists, 1532

IGA - The International Grenfell Association, 857
IGC - Interactive Gaming Council, 851
IGDA - International Game Developers Association, 1549
IGF - International Genetics Federation, 1549
IGNS - Innkeepers Guild of Nova Scotia, 839
IGS - International Geosynthetics Society, 1550
IGU - International Geographic Union, 1550
IGUA - Industrial Gas Users Association, 835
IH&RA - International Hotel & Restaurant Association, 1550
IHA - International Federation of Hardware & Housewares Association, 1548
IHAF - Institut d'histoire de l'Amérique française, 841
IHC - Island Horse Council, 865
IHE - Institute of Health Economics, 846
IHEU - International Humanist & Ethical Union, 1550
IHF - International Hospital Federation, 1550
IHHA - International Heavy Haul Association, 1550
IHM - Institute of Housing Management, 846
IHRIM - International Association for Human Resource Information Management, 1536
IHSA - Infrastructure Health & Safety Association, 838
IIA - The Institute of Internal Auditors, 1533
IIAC - Investment Industry Association of Canada, 863
IIASA - International Institute for Applied Systems Analysis, 1551
IIBC - Insurance Institute of British Columbia, 849
IIC - Insurance Institute of Canada, 849
IIC - International Institute for Conservation of Historic & Artistic Works, 1551
IICPH - International Institute of Concern for Public Health, 858
IIEC - International Institute for Energy Conservation, 1551
IIF - Islamic Information Foundation, 864
IIFET - International Institute of Fisheries Economics & Trade, 1551
IIHF - International Ice Hockey Federation, 1550
IIHS - International Institute of Integral Human Sciences, 858
IIM - Insurance Institute of Manitoba, 849
IINA - Insurance Institute of Northern Alberta, 849
IINB - Insurance Institute of New Brunswick, 849
IINL - Insurance Institute of Newfoundland & Labrador Inc., 849
IINS - Insurance Institute of Nova Scotia, 849
IIO - Insurance Institute of Ontario, 849
IIPEI - Insurance Institute of Prince Edward Island, 850
IIROC - Investment Industry Regulatory Organization of Canada, 863
IIS - Insurance Institute of Saskatchewan, 850
IISA - Insurance Institute of Southern Alberta, 850
IISD - International Institute for Sustainable Development, 858
IISE - Institute of Industrial & Systems Engineers, 1533
IIWG - International Industry Working Group, 1551
IJF - International Judo Federation, 1551
ILA - International Literacy Association, 1552
ILA - International Law Association, 1552
ILA - International Longshoremen's Association (AFL-CIO/CLC), 1553
ILC - Independent Living Canada, 833
ILCA - International Liver Cancer Association, 1552
ILCO - Institute of Law Clerks of Ontario, 846
ILDC - Independent Lumber Dealers Co-operative, 833
ILDS - International League of Dermatological Societies, 1552
ILEA - International Live Events Association Canada, 858

ILERA - International Labour & Employment Relations Association, 1551
ILNS - Independent Living Nova Scotia, 833
ILO - International Labour Organization, 1552
ILPA - Institutional Limited Partners Association, 848
ILSA - Indigenous Literary Studies Association, 835
ILSR - Institute for Local Self-Reliance, 1532
IMA - Institute of Municipal Assessors, 846
IMA - Israel Medical Association-Canadian Chapter, 866
IMAA - Independent Media Arts Alliance, 833
IMAC - Island Media Arts Co-op, 865
IMAQ - Institut de médiation et d'arbitrage du Québec, 841
IMC - International Music Council, 1553
IMCF - Indian Métis Christian Fellowship, 834
IMCRSC - International Machine Cancel Research Society of Canada, 858
IMechE - Institution of Mechanical Engineers, 1534
IMFC - Indian & Metis Friendship Centre of Winnipeg Inc., 834
IMFCPA - Indian & Metis Friendship Centre of Prince Albert, 834
IMGA - International Masters Games Association, 1553
IMHA - International Mennonite Health Association Inc., 858
IMIA - International Medical Informatics Association, 1553
IMO - International Maritime Organization, 1553
IMR - Installation, Maintenance & Repair Sector Council & Trade Association, 840
IMSS - Immigrant & Multicultural Services Society, 830
INEM - International Network for Environmental Management, 1553
INFEDOP - International Federation of Employees in Public Service, 1547
INLA - International Nuclear Law Association, 1553
INLB - Institut Nazareth et Louis-Braille, 843
INLNA - Icelandic National League of North America, 829
INO - Institut national d'optique, 843
INS - International Napoleonic Society, 858
INSNA - International Network for Social Network Analysis, 1553
INT - Island Nature Trust, 865
INTA - International Trademark Association, 1563
INTECOL - International Association for Ecology, 1536
IO - InformOntario, 838
IO - Interactive Ontario, 851
IOA - International Orthoptic Association, 1554
IODE - IODE Canada, 863
IOF - International Orienteering Federation, 1554
IOG - Institute On Governance, 848
IOI - International Ocean Institute, 1553
IOIA - International Organic Inspectors Association, 1554
IOIC - International Oceans Institute of Canada, 858
IOPA - Islands Organic Producers Association, 866
IoPP - Institute of Packaging Professionals, 1533
IOSCO - International Organization of Securities Commissions, 1554
IPA - International Permafrost Association, 1555
IPA - International Pediatric Association, 1555
IPA Canada - International Police Association - Canada, 859
IPAC - Institute of Public Administration of Canada, 847
IPAC - Indigenous Physicians Association of Canada, 835
IPAM - Incident Prevention Association of Manitoba, 831
IPB - International Peace Bureau, 1555

IPBC - Institute of Professional Bookkeepers of Canada, 847
IPC - Islamic Propagation Centre of Ontario, 865
IPCRG - International Primary Care Respiratory Group, 1555
IPE - Institute of Power Engineers, 846
IPEBLA - International Pension & Employee Benefits Lawyers Association, 859
IPF - Independent Production Fund, 833
IPHC - International Pacific Halibut Commission, 1554
IPIC - Intellectual Property Institute of Canada, 850
IPM - Institute of Professional Management, 847
IPMA-Canada - International Personnel Management Association - Canada, 859
IPNI - International Plant Nutrition Institute, 1555
IPNIG - Independent Practice Nurses Interest Group, 833
IPOACB - Investment Property Owners Association of Cape Breton, 863
IPOANS - Investment Property Owners Association of Nova Scotia Ltd., 863
IPPL - International Primate Protection League, 1556
IPPS - International Plant Propagators Society, Inc., 1555
IPPSA - Independent Power Producers Society of Alberta, 833
IPRAS - International Confederation for Plastic Reconstructive & Aesthetic Surgery, 1543
IPS - International Peat Society, 1555
IPS - Institute for Planetary Synthesis, 1532
IPSA - International Political Science Association, 859
IPU - Inter-Parliamentary Union, 1567
IPVS - International Papillomavirus Society, 1554
IQHEI - Hautes études internationales, 804
IQPF - Institut québécois de planification financière, 843
IRA - International Relief Agency Inc., 859
IRBV - Institut de recherche en biologie végétale, 842
IRCM - Institut de recherches cliniques de Montréal, 842
IRCS - India Rainbow Community Services of Peel, 834
IRDPQ - Institut de réadaptation en déficience physique de Québec, 841
IRED - Innovations et réseaux pour le développement, 1532
IREI - International Real Estate Institute, 1556
IRG - International Research Group on Wood Protection, 1556
IRMAC - Information Resource Management Association of Canada, 837
IRR - Institute for Risk Research, 844
IRSST - Institut de recherche Robert-Sauvé en santé et en sécurité du travail, 842
IRWA - International Right of Way Association, 1556
ISA - The Instrumentation, Systems & Automation Society of America, 1534
ISA - International Sociological Association, 1561
ISAAC - International Society for Augmentative & Alternative Communication, 860
ISAD - International Society for Affective Disorders, 1557
ISANS - Immigrant Services Association of Nova Scotia, 830
ISAPC - Canadian Accredited Independent Schools Advancement Professionals, 287
ISAS - Institute of Space & Atmospheric Studies, 847
ISB - International Society of Biometeorology, 1560
ISBE - International Society for Business Education, 1557
ISBI - International Society for Burn Injuries, 1557

Acronym Index

ISBN - Canadian ISBN Agency, 422
ISC - International Society of Citriculture, 1560
ISC - Indexing Society of Canada, 834
ISC - International Society of Chemotherapy for Infection & Cancer, 1560
ISCA - Interior Systems Contractors Association of Ontario, 852
ISCT - International Society for Cellular Therapy, 860
ISDA - Interprovincial School Development Association, 861
ISEE - International Society for Ecological Economics, 1557
ISEE - International Society for Environmental Ethics, 1557
ISEE - International Society for Environmental Epidemiology, 1557
ISEFT - International Society for Emotion Focused Therapy, 860
ISEM - International Society for Ecological Modelling, 1557
ISEP - International Society for Evolutionary Protistology, 860
ISES - International Solar Energy Society, 1561
ISF - International Schizophrenia Foundation, 860
ISF - International Seed Federation, 1556
ISFGW - International Society of Friendship & Good Will, 1560
ISFQ - Ingénieurs Sans Frontières Québec, 838
ISH - International Society of Hypertension, 1560
ISHAM - International Society for Human & Animal Mycology, 1558
ISHM - International Society for the History of Medicine - Canadian Section, 860
ISHR - International Society for Human Rights, 1558
ISI - International Statistical Institute, 1562
ISIAQ - International Society of Indoor Air Quality & Climate, 1560
ISKCON - Toronto's Hare Krishna Centre, 1388
ISL - Information Sarnia Lambton, 837
ISLSSL - International Society for Labour & Social Security Law - Canadian Chapter, 860
ISMA - International Snowmobile Manufacturers Association, 1557
ISME - International Society for Music Education, 1558
ISMP Canada - Institute for Safe Medication Practices Canada, 844
ISMRM - International Society for Magnetic Resonance in Medicine, 1558
ISN - International Society for Neurochemistry, 1558
ISNL - Interpreting Services of Newfoundland & Labrador Inc., 861
ISO - International Organization for Standardization, 1554
ISP - International Student Pugwash, 1562
ISPAD - International Society for Pediatric & Adolescent Diabetes, 1558
ISPI - International Society for Performance Improvement, 1558
ISPRM - International Society of Physical & Rehabilitation Medicine, 1561
ISPX - Institut Séculier Pie X, 843
ISRI - Institute of Scrap Recycling Industries, Inc., 1533
ISRIC - International Soil Reference & Information Centre, 1561
ISRM - International Society for Rock Mechanics, 1559
ISRRT - International Society of Radiographers & Radiological Technologists, 1561
ISS - International Social Service, 1557
ISS - International Society of Surgery, 1561
ISSA - International Sanitary Supply Association, Inc., 1556
ISSA - Information Systems Security Association, 1532
ISSC - International Social Service Canada, 860
ISSLS - International Society for the Study of the Lumbar Spine, 1559

ISSMGE - International Society for Soil Mechanics & Geotechnical Engineering, 1559
ISSofBC - Immigrant Services Society of BC, 830
ISSTD - International Society for the Study of Trauma & Dissociation, 1559
ISSTDR - International Society for Sexually Transmitted Diseases Research, 1559
ISTAR, CIP - Institute for Stuttering Treatment & Research & the Communication Improvement Program, 844
ISTOP - Institute for the Study & Treatment of Pain, 844
ISU - International Skating Union, 1556
ISWA - International Solid Waste Association, 1562
ITA - Industrial Truck Association, 1531
ITA - Industry Training Authority, 835
ITA - International Titanium Association, 1563
ITAC - Inland Terminal Association of Canada, 838
ITAC - Information Technology Association of Canada, 837
ITANS - Digital Nova Scotia, 656
ITAP - Innovation & Technology Association of Ontario, 839
ITC - International Trade Centre, 1563
ITE - Institute of Transportation Engineers, 1534
ITF - International Tennis Federation, 1562
ITHQ - Institut de tourisme et d'hôtellerie du Québec, 842
ITK - Inuit Tapiriit Kanatami, 862
ITMF - International Textile Manufacturers Federation, 1562
ITP - Island Technology Professionals, 865
ITPA - Independent Telecommunications Providers Association, 833
ITS - Institute of Textile Science, 847
ITS - International Telecommunications Society, 1562
ITSA - Infant & Toddler Safety Association, 836
ITUC - International Trade Union Confederation, 1563
IUAC - International Union Against Cancer, 1563
IUAES - International Union of Anthropological & Ethnological Sciences, 1563
IUBS - International Union of Biological Sciences, 1564
IUCN - International Union for Conservation of Nature, 1563
IUEC - International Union of Elevator Constructors, 1564
IUFoST - International Union of Food Science & Technology, 861
IUFRO - International Union of Forest Research Organizations, 1564
IUGG - International Union of Geodesy & Geophysics, 1564
IUPAC - International Union of Pure & Applied Chemistry, 1565
IUPAT - International Union of Painters & Allied Trades, 1565
IUPHAR - International Union of Basic & Clinical Pharmacology, 1564
IUS - Institute of Urban Studies, 847
IUSBSE - International Union of Societies for Biomaterials Science & Engineering, 1565
IUSS - International Union of Soil Sciences, 1565
IUTAM - International Union of Theoretical & Applied Mechanics, 1565
IVCF - Inter-Varsity Christian Fellowship, 862
IVMA of BC - Integrated Vegetation Management Association of British Columbia, 850
IVU - International Vegetarian Union, 1565
IWA - International Water Association, 1566
IWAM - Injured Workers Association of Manitoba Inc., 838
IWC - International Whaling Commission, 1566
IWF - International Women's Forum, 1567
IWFS - International Wine & Food Society, 1567

IWH - Institute for Work & Health, 844
IWHC - Immigrant Women's Health Centre, 831
IWKF - IWK Health Centre Foundation, 867
IWLA - International Warehouse Logistics Association, 1566
IWRC - International Wildlife Rehabilitation Council, 1566
IWSO - Immigrant Women Services Ottawa, 831

J

JACAN - Junior Achievement Canada, 877
JAFLIPE - Jeunesse Acadienne et Francophone de l'Île-du-prince-Édouard, 870
JASNA - Jane Austen Society of North America, 868
JBAC - Jockeys Benefit Association of Canada, 873
JC - Jersey Canada, 869
JCA - Jamaican Canadian Association, 867
JCAM - Japanese Cultural Association of Manitoba, 869
JCAY - Japanese Canadian Association of Yukon, 869
JCCC - Japanese Canadian Cultural Centre, 869
JCCF - Justice Centre for Constitutional Freedoms, 878
JCCM - Jeune chambre de commerce de Montréal, 870
JCFS - Jewish Child & Family Services, 871
JCI - Junior Chamber International, 1568
JDO - Jesuit Development Office, 870
JDRF - Juvenile Diabetes Research Foundation Canada, 878
JEA - Jasper Environmental Association, 869
JESC - Jewish Family Services - Calgary, 871
JETRO - Japan External Trade Organization (Toronto), 868
JFAO - Junior Farmers' Association of Ontario, 878
JFAS - Vancouver Jewish Film Centre Society, 1427
JFCS - Jewish Family & Child, 871
JFC-UIA - Jewish Federations of Canada - UIA, 872
JFCY - Justice for Children & Youth, 878
JFGV - Jewish Federation of Greater Vancouver, 872
JFLT - Jewish Free Loan Toronto, 872
JFM - Jewish Foundation of Manitoba, 872
JFSOC - Jewish Family Services of Ottawa-Carleton, 872
JGHF - Jewish General Hospital Foundation, 872
JGI - The Jane Goodall Institute for Wildlife Research, Education & Conservation, 1568
JGST - Jewish Genealogical Society of Toronto, 872
JHC - Jewish Heritage Centre of Western Canada Inc., 872
JHS - Jewish Historical Society of BC, 872
JHSMB - The John Howard Society of Manitoba, 874
JHSNL - The John Howard Society of Newfoundland & Labrador, 874
JHSSA - Jewish Historical Society of Southern Alberta, 872
JIAS - Jewish Immigrant Aid Services of Canada, 873
JIBC - Justice Institute of British Columbia, 878
JIRS - Jewish Information Referral Service Montréal, 873
JIST - Jewish Information Service of Greater Toronto, 873
JLC - Junior League of Calgary, 878
JLE - Junior League of Edmonton, 878
JLHB - Junior League of Hamilton-Burlington, Inc., 878
JMC - Jeunesses Musicales du Canada, 871
JOCA - Jamaican Ottawa Community Association, 867
JSH - Jamaican Self-Help Organization, 867

JSRDF - Joubert Syndrome & Related Disoarders Foundation, 1568
JTC - Jean Tweed Treatment Centre, 869
JVC - Jewellers Vigilance Canada Inc., 871

K

KAA - Karate Alberta Association, 881
KAC - Kingston Arts Council, 888
KACL - Kenora Association for Community Living, 883
KADREA - Kamloops & District Real Estate Association, 880
KAM - Kingston Association of Museums, Art Galleries & Historic Sites, 889
KAO - Karate Ontario, 882
KAP - Keystone Agricultural Producers, 884
KBC - Karate BC, 881
KBCABC - Korean Businessmen's Cooperative Association of British Columbia, 893
KBSCC - Kimberley & District Chamber of Commerce, 887
KBUA - Kawartha Baseball Umpires Association, 882
KCA - Kingston Construction Association, 889
KCAO - Korean Canadian Association of Ottawa, 893
KCC - Kashmiri Canadian Council, 882
KCCA - Korean Canadian Cultural Association of the Greater Toronto Area, 893
KCFA - Keyano College Faculty Association, 884
KCMA - Kitchen Cabinet Manufacturers Association, 1568
KCWA - Korean Canadian Women's Association, 893
KCWA - Kings County Wildlife Association, 888
KDCC - Kenora & District Chamber of Commerce, 883
KDLC - Kamloops & District Labour Council, 880
KEA - Esperanto Association of Canada, 695
KEDCO - Kingston Economic Development Corporation, 889
KFA - Kwantlen Faculty Association, 894
KFC - Kapuskasing Friendship Centre, 881
KFN - Kingston Field Naturalists, 889
KFOC - Kidney Foundation of Canada, 885
KFS - Ki-Low-Na Friendship Society, 887
KGSO - Korean-Canadian Symphony Orchestra, 894
KHCCC - Kicking Horse Country Chamber of Commerce, 884
KHP - Kids Help Phone, 886
KHS - Kingston Historical Society, 889
KINWU - Kingston Independent Nylon Workers Union, 889
KIS - Kamloops Immigrant Services, 880
KLCC - Kirkland Lake District Chamber of Commerce, 890
KMS - Kamloops Multicultural Society, 880
KNC - Kamloops Naturalist Club, 880
KNL - Karate Newfoundland & Labrador, 882
KNS - Karate Nova Scotia, 882
KORLCC - Kanien'kehaka Onkwawen'na Raotitiohkwa Language & Cultural Centre, 881
KOS - Kingston Orchid Society, 889
KRBT - Kitikmeot Regional Board of Trade, 891
KREB - Kootenay Real Estate Board, 892
KRF - Kinsmen Foundation of British Columbia & Yukon, 890
KSA - Kitchener Sports Association, 890
KSA - Kingston Symphony Association, 889
KSA - Klondike Snowmobile Association, 892
KSAC - Korean Students' Association of Canada, 893
KSCL - Kootenay Society for Community Living, 892
KSCL - Kamloops Society for Community Living, 880
KSCST - Korean Senior Citizens Society of Toronto, 893
KSM - Catholic Youth Studio - KSM Inc., 521
KSN - Kabuki Syndrome Network Inc., 879

Acronym Index

KSO - Kamloops Symphony, 880
KTC - Keewatin Tribal Council, 883
KTPS - Kaleidoscope Theatre Productions Society, 880
KVA - Korea Veterans Association of Canada Inc., Heritage Unit, 893
KVA - Klondike Visitors Association, 892
KWCF - The Kitchener & Waterloo Community Foundation, 890
KWCMS - Kitchener-Waterloo Chamber Music Society, 890
KWCO - Kitchener-Waterloo Chamber Orchestra, 890
KWIC - Kawartha World Issues Centre, 882
KWPS - Kitchener-Waterloo Philatelic Society, 891
KWSOA - Kitchener-Waterloo Symphony Orchestra Association Inc., 891
KWSYO - Kitchener-Waterloo Symphony Youth Orchestra, 891

L

L'AAQ - Association des Acupuncteurs du Québec, 105
LAA - Library Association of Alberta, 910
LAA - Legal Aid Society of Alberta, 906
LAC - Langley Arts Council, 899
LACL - Langley Association for Community Living, 899
LACL - Lethbridge Association for Community Living, 907
LADPEI - Learning Disabilities Association of Prince Edward Island, 905
LAEA - Lloydminster Agricultural Exhibition Association, 916
LAHMS - Lennoxville-Ascot Historical & Museum Society, 907
LAMP - Latin American Mission Program, 899
LAMP - Lutheran Association of Missionaries & Pilots, 922
LAMP - Lakeshore Area Multi-Service Project, 896
LANS - The Lung Association of Nova Scotia, 921
LAO - Lymphovenous Association of Ontario, 923
LAO - Legal Aid Ontario, 906
LARA - Lakeland Agricultural Research Association, 896
LASA - Latin American Studies Association, 1569
LASA - Legal Archives Society of Alberta, 906
LATA - Learning Assistance Teachers' Association, 903
LBANS - Library Boards Association of Nova Scotia, 910
LBE - Living Bible Explorers, 915
LBMAO - Lumber & Building Materials Association of Ontario, 920
LBTC - Lutheran Bible Translators of Canada Inc., 922
LCBA - Lanark County Beekeepers' Association, 897
LCC - The Lithuanian Canadian Community, 914
LCC - Lutheran Church - Canada, 922
LCCA - Latino Canadian Cultural Association, 900
LCCC - Latvian Canadian Cultural Centre, 900
LCCFA - Lethbridge Community College Faculty Association, 908
LCDR - Literacy Council of Durham Region, 913
LCDS - Lambton County Developmental Services, 897
LCF - Lithuanian-Canadian Foundation, 915
LCF - London Community Foundation, 918
LCFA - Lakeland College Faculty Association, 896
LCG - Learning Centre for Georgina, 903
LCHS - Lunenburg County Historical Society, 921
LCHS - Lambton County Historical Society, 897

LCMN - The Lanark County Museums Network, 897
LCNB - Literacy Coalition of New Brunswick, 913
LCO - London Community Orchestra, 918
LCP - The League of Canadian Poets, 903
LCS - Lakeshore Community Services, 897
LCTRP - Lanark County Therapeutic Riding Program, 897
LCYS - Literacy Council York-Simcoe, 913
LDAA - Learning Disabilities Association of Alberta, 903
LDAC - Learning Disabilities Association of Canada, 904
LDAM - Learning Disabilities Association of Manitoba, 904
LDANB - Learning Disabilities Association of New Brunswick, 904
LDANL - Learning Disabilities Association of Newfoundland & Labrador Inc., 904
LDA-NWT - Learning Disabilities Association of The Northwest Territories, 905
LDAO - Learning Disabilities Association of Ontario, 904
LDAS - Learning Disabilities Association of Saskatchewan, 905
LDAV - Learning Disabilities Association of British Columbia, 904
LDAY - Learning Disabilities Association of Yukon Territory, 905
LDFGA - Lloydminster & District Fish & Game Association, 915
LDSA - Lakeland District Soccer Association, 896
LEAF - Women's Legal Education & Action Fund, 1462
LEF - Learning Enrichment Foundation, 905
LESA - Legal Education Society of Alberta, 906
LESA - Lupus Society of Alberta, 922
LFGA - Lethbridge Fish & Game Association, 908
LFN - Langley Field Naturalists Society, 899
LFO - Lupus Foundation of Ontario, 921
LFO - Law Foundation of Ontario, 901
LGANT - Local Government Administrators of the Northwest Territories, 916
LGMA BC - Local Government Management Association of British Columbia, 916
LGU - Ladies' Golf Union, 1569
LHC - Lethbridge HIV Connection, 908
LHS - Langley Heritage Society, 899
LHSF - London Health Sciences Foundation, 918
LHSQ - Literary & Historical Society of Québec, 914
LICA - Lakeland Industry & Community Association, 896
LIFT - Liaison of Independent Filmmakers of Toronto, 909
LIMM - LaHave Islands Marine Museum Society, 895
LISAA - University of Alberta Library & Information Studies Alumni Association, 1419
LISNS - Legal Information Society of Nova Scotia, 906
LiUNA - Laborers' International Union of North America (AFL-CIO/CLC), 1568
LJCA - Lakehead Japanese Cultural Association, 896
LJYO - La Jeunesse Youth Orchestra, 870
LLAC - Logan Lake Arts Council, 917
LLHA - Luggage, Leathergoods, Handbags & Accessories Association of Canada, 920
LLHS - Lundy's Lane Historical Society, 920
LLL-C - Lutheran Laymen's League of Canada, 922
LLLC - La Leche League Canada, 905
LLLI - La Leche League International, 1569
LLSC - The Leukemia & Lymphoma Society of Canada, 914
LLSC - Literacy Link South Central, 914
LMBA - London Multiple Births Association, 918
LMC - Lay Missionaries of Charity - Canada, 902

LMHS - London & Middlesex Historical Society, 917
LMISSAA - Lower Mainland Independent Secondary School Athletic Association, 920
LMLGA - Lower Mainland Local Government Association, 920
LMMC - Ladies' Morning Musical Club, 895
LMMI - L.M. Montgomery Institute, 916
LNAK - Latvian National Federation in Canada, 900
LNBHTA - Landscape New Brunswick Horticultural Trades Association, 898
LNBW - Lutte NB Wrestling, 922
LNCC - Labrador North Chamber of Commerce, 894
LNFC - Lloydminster Native Friendship Centre, 916
LNHS - Lu'ma Native Housing Society, 920
LNL - Landscape Newfoundland & Labrador, 898
LNS - Literacy Nova Scotia, 914
LOBA - Ladies' Orange Benevolent Association of Canada, 895
LOCS - Literacy Ontario Central South, 914
LOFT - LOFT Community Services, 917
LOHTA - Landscape Ontario Horticultural Trades Association, 898
LORDA - Lansdowne Outdoor Recreational Development Association, 899
LOSA - Lethbridge Oldtimers Sports Association, 908
LOVE - Leave Out Violence Everywhere, 905
LPA - London Police Association, 919
LPA - Licensed Paralegals Association (Ontario), 910
LPC - The Liberal Party of Canada, 909
LPC(A) - Liberal Party of Canada in Alberta, 909
LPC(O) - Liberal Party of Canada (Ontario), 909
LPCBC - The Liberal Party of Canada (British Columbia), 909
LPF - Last Post Fund, 899
LPG - The Literary Press Group of Canada, 914
LPM - Little People of Manitoba, 915
LPNABC - Licensed Practical Nurses Association of British Columbia, 910
LPO - Little People of Ontario, 915
LPRC - Living Positive Resource Centre, Okanagan, 915
LRHF - Lloydminster Region Health Foundation, 916
LSA - Linguistic Society of America, 1569
LSA - Law Society of Alberta, 901
LSAM - Life Science Association of Manitoba, 910
LSF - Learning for a Sustainable Future, 905
LSHT - La Société d'histoire de Toronto, 1311
LSLIRC - Lesser Slave Lake Indian Regional Council, 907
LSM - Law Society of Manitoba, 901
LSNU - Law Society of Nunavut, 901
LSO - Lethbridge Symphony Orchestra, 908
LSO - Life Sciences Ontario, 911
LSPC - Lakehead Social Planning Council, 896
LSS - Legal Services Society, 906
LSY - Law Society of Yukon, 902
LTA - Land Trust Alliance, 1569
LTAC - Literary Translators' Association of Canada, 914
LTCAM - Long Term & Continuing Care Association of Manitoba, 919
LTDJ - La Troupe du Jour, 1399
LTRA - Lethbridge Therapeutic Riding Association, 908
LTU - Laurier Teachers Union, 900
LUCW - League of Ukrainian Canadian Women, 903
LUFA - Laurentian University Faculty Association, 900
LUFA - Lakehead University Faculty Association, 896
LUSU - Laurentian University Staff Union, 900
LUYC - Lace Up Your Cleats, 895
LVQ - Literacy Volunteers of Quebec, 914
LWB - Librarians Without Borders, 910

LWI - Lambton Wildlife Inc., 897
LYS - London Youth Symphony, 919

M

M2/W2 - M2/W2 Association - Restorative Christian Ministries, 923
M4C - Men for Change, 960
M5PBA - Manitoba 5 Pin Bowlers' Association, 928
MAA - Manitoba Association of Architects, 929
MAA - Maritime Aberdeen Angus Association, 950
MAA - Manitoba Antique Association, 928
MAAC - Model Aeronautics Association of Canada Inc., 970
MAAE - Manitoba Association for Art Education, 929
MAAP - Manitoba Association of Asian Physicians, 929
MAB - Montréal Association for the Blind, 972
MABA - Manitoba Amateur Broomball Association, 928
MABA - Manitoba Association for Behaviour Analysis, 929
MABBA - Manitoba Amateur Bodybuilding Association, 928
MABC - Mining Association of British Columbia, 967
MABE - Manitoba Association for Business Economics, 929
MAC - Mississauga Arts Council, 969
MAC - Mineralogical Association of Canada, 966
MAC - Mining Association of Canada, 967
MAC - Manitoba Association of Friendship Centres, 929
MAC - Manitoba Arts Council, 929
MAC - Muslim Association of Canada, 985
MAC - Muskoka Arts & Crafts Inc., 985
MAC - Manitoba Association of Cheerleading, 929
MAC - Media Access Canada, 957
MACHS - Manitoba Association of Christian Home Schools, 929
MACL - Mission Association for Community Living, 968
MACS - Mi'kmaq Association for Cultural Studies, 964
MAFA - Mount Allison Faculty Association, 976
MAFC - Mission Aviation Fellowship of Canada, 969
MAFC - Manitoba Association of Fire Chiefs, 929
MAFRP - Metro (Toronto) Association of Family Resource Programs, 963
MAGC - The Metal Arts Guild of Canada, 962
MAGMA - Multicultural Association of the Greater Moncton Area, 979
MAHCP - Manitoba Association of Health Care Professionals, 929
MAHE - Manitoba Association of Home Economists, 930
MAHIP - Manitoba Association of Health Information Providers, 930
MAHTA - Manitoba Animal Health Technologists Association, 928
MAIP - Manitoba Association of Insurance Professionals, 930
MAIRP - Manitoba Association of Insolvency & Restructuring Professionals, 930
MALA - Manitoba Association of Landscape Architects, 930
MALA - Moncton Area Lawyers' Association, 972
MALT - Manitoba Association of Library Technicians, 930
MAMI - Mining Association of Manitoba Inc., 967
MAMLS - Manitoba Association for Medical Laboratory Science, 929
MAMRT - Manitoba Association of Medical Radiation Technologists, 930
MANB - Muslim Association of New Brunswick, 985

Acronym Index

MANL - Museum Association of Newfoundland & Labrador, 982
MANS - Mining Association of Nova Scotia, 967
MANS - Multicultural Association of Nova Scotia, 979
MANTE - Manitoba Association of Non-Teaching Employees, 930
MANWO - Multicultural Association of Northwestern Ontario, 979
MAO - Manitoba Association of Optometrists, 930
MAOC - Model "A" Owners of Canada Inc., 970
MAP - Mères avec pouvoir, 961
MAP - Manitoba Association of Playwrights, 931
MAPC - Manitoba Association of Parent Councils, 930
MAPC - Maritime Aboriginal Peoples Council, 950
MAPCHSW - Manitoba Association of Personal Care Home Social Workers, 931
MAPSLI - Maritime Association of Professional Sign Language Interpreters, 950
MARA - Mackenzie Applied Research Assciation, 924
MARRT - Manitoba Association of Registered Respiratory Therapists, Inc., 931
MAS - Multifaith Action Society, 979
MAS - Museums Association of Saskatchewan, 983
MAS - Midwives Association of Saskatchewan, 965
MASBO - Manitoba Association of School Business Officials, 931
MASCC - Multinational Association for Supportive Care in Cancer, 1571
MASMAHC - Manitoba Association of Sheet Metal & Air Handling Contractors Inc., 931
MASS - Manitoba Association of School Superintendents, 931
MATA - Manitoba Athletic Therapists Association Inc., 931
MAVA - Manitoba Association for Volunteer Administration, 929
MAVLI - Manitoba Association of Visual Language Interpreters, 931
MAWA - Manitoba Amateur Wrestling Association, 928
MAWA - Manitoba Arm Wrestling Association, 928
MAWS - Manitoba Association of Women's Shelters, 931
MBA - Manitoba Badminton Association, 931
MBA - Manitoba Bar Association, 932
MBA - Manitoba Beekeepers' Association, 932
MBA - Manitoba Bison Association, 932
MBA - Maritime Breeders Association, 950
MBAA - Master Brewers Association of The Americas, 1569
MBAM - Master Bowlers' Association of Manitoba, 953
MBAO - Master Bowlers' Association of Ontario, 953
MBC - Multiple Births Canada, 979
MBCM - Mennonite Brethren Church of Manitoba, 960
MBCPA - Manitoba Beef Cattle Performance Association, 932
MBCTC - Manitoba Building & Construction Trades Council, 933
MBEC - Manitoba Building Envelope Council, 933
MBFA - Multiple Birth Families Association, 979
MBFC - Marguerite Bourgeoys Family Centre Fertility Care Programme, 949
MBHA - Manitoba Ball Hockey Association, 931
MBMSI - MB Mission, 954
MBOT - Mississauga Board of Trade, 969
MBP - Manitoba Beef Producers, 932
MBS - Manitoba Blues Society Inc., 932
MBSA - Manitoba Blind Sports Association, 932
MBT - Markham Board of Trade, 951
MBTSA - Manitoba Baton Twirling Sportive Association, 932
MC - La Maison de la culture inc., 926
MC Canada - Mennonite Church Canada, 961

MCA - Manitoba Choral Association, 934
MCA - Manitoba Chiropractors' Association, 933
MCA - Manitoba Camping Association, 933
MCA - Manitoba Cricket Association, 935
MCA - Manitoba Cycling Association, 935
MCA AB - Mechanical Contractors Association of Alberta, 956
MCABC - Mechanical Contractors Association of British Columbia, 956
MCAC - Mechanical Contractors Association of Canada, 956
MCAF - Multicultural Association of Fredericton, 978
MCAM - Mechanical Contractors Association of Manitoba, 957
MCAO - Mechanical Contractors Association of Ontario, 957
MCAS - Mechanical Contractors Association of Saskatchewan Inc., 957
MCC - Manitoba Crafts Council, 934
MCC - Miramichi Chamber of Commerce, 968
MCC - Medical Council of Canada, 958
MCC - Multicultural Council of Windsor & Essex County, 979
MCC - Motor Coach Canada, 975
MCC of Canada - Military Collectors Club of Canada, 965
MCCA - Manitoba Child Care Association, 933
MCCA - Manitoba Customer Contact Association, Inc., 935
MCCC - Mennonite Central Committee Canada, 960
MCDA - Manitoba Conservation Districts Association, 934
MCEC - Manitoba Council for Exceptional Children, 934
MCF - Manitoba Cheer Federation Inc., 933
MCFS - Métis Child & Family Services Society (Edmonton), 962
MCIC - Manitoba Council for International Cooperation, 934
MCJA - Manitoba Criminal Justice Association, 935
MCM - Muslim Council of Montréal, 985
MCNA - Manitoba Community Newspapers Association, 934
MCO - Motorsport Club of Ottawa, 976
MCO - Manitoba Chamber Orchestra, 933
MCP - Manitoba Chicken Producers, 933
MCPCC - Motor Carrier Passenger Council of Canada, 975
MCPEI - Meetings & Conventions Prince Edward Island, 959
MCPSA - Manitoba Cerebral Palsy Sports Association, 933
MCQ - Muslim Community of Québec, 985
MCS - McCreary Centre Society, 955
MCS - Mississauga Choral Society, 970
MCSA - Metro Toronto Chinese & Southeast Asian Legal Clinic, 963
MCSC - Manitoba Combative Sports Commission, 934
MCSC - Missing Children Society of Canada, 968
MCSD - Manitoba Cultural Society of the Deaf, 935
MCSS - Mission Community Services Food Centre, 969
MCST - Maltese-Canadian Society of Toronto, Inc., 928
MCTGA - Manitoba Christmas Tree Growers Association, 934
MCVI - Mouvement contre le viol et l'inceste, 976
MCW - Montréal Council of Women, 972
MDA - Motor Dealers' Association of Alberta, 975
MDA - Manitoba Dental Association, 935
MDA - Mood Disorders Association of British Columbia, 973
MDAI - Manitoba Darts Association Inc., 935
MDAM - Mood Disorders Association of Manitoba, 973

MDAO - Mood Disorders Association of Ontario, 973
MDC - Muscular Dystrophy Canada, 982
MDCC - Meaford Chamber of Commerce, 956
MDHA - Manitoba Dental Hygienists Association, 935
MDHS - Millet & District Historical Society, 966
MDRAO - Medical Device Reprocessing Association of Ontario, 958
MDSA - Manitoba Deaf Sports Association Inc., 935
MDSC - Mood Disorders Society of Canada, 973
MDSS - Manitoba Down Syndrome Society, 935
MEA - Municipal Engineers Association, 980
MEAO - Myalgic Encephalomyelitis Association of Ontario, 986
MECSCC - Mississauga-Etobicoke Coin Stamp & Collectibles Club, 970
MÉDAC - Mouvement d'éducation et de défense des actionnaires, 977
MEIA - Manitoba Environmental Industries Association Inc., 936
MEN - Manitoba Eco-Network Inc., 936
MEOA - Manitoba Environment Officers Association Inc., 936
MÉPACQ - Mouvement d'éducation populaire et d'action communautaire du Québec, 977
MER - Maintenance, Engineering & Reliability (MER) Society, 926
MESA - Middle East Studies Association of North America, 1571
METRAC - Metropolitan Action Committee on Violence Against Women & Children, 964
MetSoc - Metallurgy & Materials Society of the Canadian Institute of Mining, Metallurgy & Petroleum, 962
MFA - Manitoba Fencing Association, 936
MFA - Middlesex Federation of Agriculture, 965
MFC - Mouvement des femmes Chrétiennes, 977
MFCA - Maritime Fire Chiefs' Association, 950
MFDA - Mutual Fund Dealers Association of Canada, 986
MFGA - Manitoba Forage & Grassland Association, 937
MFIS - Manitoba Federation of Independent Schools Inc., 936
MFNL - Model Forest of Newfoundland & Labrador, 971
MFOA - Municipal Finance Officers' Association of Ontario, 981
MFPA - Manitoba Food Processors Association, 936
MFPBF - Manitoba Five Pin Bowling Federation, Inc., 936
MFSA - Manitoba Funeral Service Association, 937
MFU - Maritime Fishermen's Union (CLC), 950
MGA - Manitoba Gymnastics Association, 937
MGABC - Myasthenia Gravis Association of British Columbia, 986
MGEU - Manitoba Government & General Employees' Union, 937
MGI - Murray Grey International, Incorporated, 982
MGMC - Montréal Gem & Mineral Club, 972
MGNA - Manitoba Gerontological Nurses' Association, 937
MGS - Manitoba Genealogical Society Inc., 937
MH - Maison D'Haiti, 926
MHA - Mission Heritage Association, 969
MHA - Markland Homes Association, 952
MHA - Manitoba Hotel Association, 938
MHANS - Miniature Horse Association of Nova Scotia, 966
MHAR - Lakelands Association of Realtors, 896
MHBA - Manitoba Home Builders' Association, 938
MHCA - Manitoba Heavy Construction Association, 937
MHCO - Miniature Horse Club of Ontario, 966
MHF - Mississauga Heritage Foundation Inc., 970

MHGA - Manitoba Hang Gliding Association, 937
MHLA - Maritimes Health Libraries Association, 951
MHMC - The Montréal Holocaust Memorial Centre, 972
MHRMI - Macedonian Human Rights Movement International, 923
MHS - Manitoba Historical Society, 938
MHS - Milton Historical Society, 966
MHSAA - Manitoba High Schools Athletic Association, 938
MHSC - Mennonite Historical Society of Canada, 961
MHSO - Multicultural History Society of Ontario, 979
MHSPCA - Medicine Hat Society for the Prevention of Cruelty to Animals, 959
M.I. - Militia of the Immaculata Canada, 965
MIA - Manitoba Islamic Association, 939
MIA - Manitoba Institute of Agrologists, 939
MIABC - Marine Insurance Association of British Columbia, 949
MIABC - Mortgage Investment Association of British Columbia, 975
MICCC - Mayne Island Community Chamber of Commerce, 954
MICEC - Manitoba Indian Cultural Education Centre, 939
MIECO - Masonry Industry Employers Council of Ontario, 952
MIENS - Mouvement d'information, d'éducation et d'entraide dans la lutte contre le sida, 977
MIFC - Mission Indian Friendship Centre, 969
MIHR - Mining Industry Human Resources Council, 967
MIRS - Maison internationale de la Rive-Sud, 927
MIRSW - Manitoba College of Registered Social Workers, 934
MISA - Municipal Information Systems Association of Canada, 981
MISA - Immigrant Welcome Centre, 831
MISC - McGill Institute for the Study of Canada, 955
MITACS - Mathematics of Information Technology & Complex Systems, 954
MIW - Manitoba Indian Education Association Inc., 939
MJMC - Moose Jaw Multicultural Council, 974
MLA - Manitoba Library Association, 939
MLA - Modern Language Association of America, 1571
MLA - Middlesex Law Association, 965
MLA - Medical Library Association, 1570
MLAR - Multilingual Association of Regina, Inc., 979
MLB - Maritime Lumber Bureau, 951
MLC - Monarchist League of Canada, 971
MLCI - Manitoba Library Consortium Inc., 940
MLDAO - Municipal Law Departments Association of Ontario, 981
MLEOA - Municipal Law Enforcement Officers' Association, 981
MLP - Manitoba Liberal Party, 939
MLPD - Manitoba League of Persons with Disabilities, 939
MLSAY - Medical Laboratory Science Association of Yukon, 958
MLTA - Manitoba Library Trustees Association, 940
MLTC - Meadow Lake Tribal Council, 956
MMDA - Manitoba Motor Dealers Association, 940
MME - Movement for Marriage Enrichment, 978
MMHA - Modular Housing Association Prairie Provinces, 971
MMHC&SA - Maritime Model Horse Collectors & Showers Association, 951
MMHS - Manitoba Mennonite Historical Society, 940
MMIC - Motorcycle & Moped Industry Council, 975
MMM - Margaret Morris Method (Canada), 949

MMPA - Manitoba Magazine Publishers Association, 940
MMSA - Manitoba Medical Students' Association, 940
MMSF - Manitoba Medical Service Foundation Inc., 940
MNA - Manitoba Naturopathic Association, 941
MNC - Métis National Council, 963
MNCW - Métis National Council of Women, 963
MNDA - Messagères de Notre-Dame de l'Assomption, 962
MNECA - Mechanical Contractors Association of New Brunswick, 957
MNL - Municipalities Newfoundland & Labrador, 982
MNPHA - Manitoba Non-Profit Housing Association, 941
MNQ - Mouvement national des québécoises et québécois, 977
MNU - Manitoba Nurses' Union, 941
MOA - Manitoba Orienteering Association Inc., 941
MOCCA - Museum of Contemporary Canadian Art, 983
MODC - March of Dimes Canada, 949
MODS - Manitoba Organization of Disc Sports, 941
MONA - Museums of Niagara Association, 983
MOPIA - Manitoba Ozone Protection Industry Association, 941
MORN - Mother of Red Nations Women's Council of Manitoba, 975
MORNA - Manitoba Operating Room Nurses Association, 941
MOS - Manitoba Orchid Society, 941
MOSAIC - Multilingual Orientation Service Association for Immigrant Communities, 979
MPA - Manitoba Powerlifting Association, 942
MPA - Manitoba Paddling Association Inc., 942
MPA - Manitoba Physiotherapy Association, 942
MPDA - Master Painters & Decorators Association, 954
MPH&CS - Mossley Post Heritage & Citizenship Society, 975
MPHA - Manitoba Public Health Association, 942
MPHA - Manitoba Provincial Handgun Association, 942
MPI - Meeting Professionals International, 1570
MPMA - Manitoba Pest Management Association, 942
MPPAC - Mounted Police Professional Association of Canada, 976
MPPCA - Manitoba Professional Painting Contractors Association, 942
MPPI - Manitoba Professional Planners Institute, 942
MPRA - Manitoba Provincial Rifle Association Inc., 942
MPRA - Municipal Pension Retirees Association, 981
MPS - Malaspina Printmakers Society, 927
MQQ - Mouvement québécois de la qualité, 978
MQVF - Mouvement québécois des vacances familiales inc., 978
MRA - Manitoba Ringette Association, 943
MRA - Muskoka Ratepayers' Association, 985
MRA - Manitoba Runners' Association, 943
MRAS - Millarville Racing & Agricultural Society, 965
MRDA - Manitoba Riding for the Disabled Association Inc., 943
MREA - Manitoba Real Estate Association, 943
MRFA - Manitoba Restaurant & Food Services Association, 943
MRIA - Marketing Research & Intelligence Association, 951
MRMCA - Concrete Manitoba, 610
MRSA - Mount Royal Staff Association, 976
MRT - Mulgrave Road Theatre Foundation, 978
MRTA - Manitoba Rural Tourism Association Inc., 943
MS - Multiple Sclerosis Society of Canada, 980
MSA - Manitoba Society of Artists, 944

MSA - Manitoba Simmental Association, 944
MSA - MacEwan Staff Association, 924
MSBC - Memorial Society of British Columbia, 960
MSC - Montréal Soaring Council, 973
MSC - Microscopical Society of Canada, 964
MSC - Manitoba Securities Commission, 944
MSCA - Manitoba School Counsellors' Association, 944
MSCC - Mechanical Service Contractors of Canada, 957
MSCCA - Mining Suppliers, Contractors & Consultants Association of BC, 967
MSCCC - Morgan Sports Car Club of Canada, 974
MSCL - Mill Woods Society for Community Living, 965
MSED - Memorial Society of Edmonton & District, 960
MSF - Doctors without Borders Canada, 660
MSFHR - Michael Smith Foundation for Health Research, 964
MSHF&M - Manitoba Sports Hall of Fame & Museum, 945
MSHS - Mainland South Heritage Society, 926
MSIF - Multiple Sclerosis International Federation, 1571
MSLA - Manitoba School Library Association, 944
MSM - Mineral Society of Manitoba, 966
MSNO - Memorial Society of Northern Ontario, 960
MSOC - Mazda Sportscar Owners Club, 954
MSOT - Manitoba Society of Occupational Therapists, 945
MSP - Manitoba Society of Pharmacists Inc., 945
MSPA - Manitoba Sport Parachute Association, 945
MSPDA - Manitoba-Saskatchewan Prospectors & Developers Association, 948
MSPEI - Medical Society of Prince Edward Island, 958
MSS - Maritime Sikh Society, 951
MSS - Manitoba Schizophrenia Society, Inc., 943
MST - Mycological Society of Toronto, 986
MSTA - Mining Suppliers Trade Association Canada, 967
MSVUFA - Mount Saint Vincent University Faculty Association, 976
MTA - Manitoba Trucking Association, 946
MTA - The Maitland Trail Association, 927
MTAA - Massage Therapist Association of Alberta, 953
MTAM - Massage Therapy Association of Manitoba Inc., 953
MTANS - Massage Therapists' Association of Nova Scotia, 953
MTAS - Massage Therapist Association of Saskatchewan, 953
MTC - Royal Manitoba Theatre Centre, 1242
MTCS - Mid-Toronto Community Services, 965
MTEC - The Manitoba Tourism Education Council, 946
MTML - Metro Toronto Movement for Literacy, 963
MTRC - Manitoba Trail Riding Club Inc., 946
MTS - Manitoba Teachers' Society, 946
MTTA - Manitoba Table Tennis Association, 945
MTT-S - IEEE Microwave Theory & Techniques Society, 1530
MUC - Manitoba Underwater Council, 946
MUCDA - Manitoba Used Car Dealers Association, 946
MUFA - McMaster University Faculty Association, 956
MUNACA - McGill University Non Academic Certified Association, 955
MURA - McMaster University Retirees Association, 956
MUSA - McMaster University Staff Association, 956
MUUG - Manitoba UNIX User Group, 946

MVA - Manitoba Volleyball Association, 946
MVA - Meewasin Valley Authority, 959
MVMA - Manitoba Veterinary Medical Association, 946
MVSRA - Mount View Special Riding Association, 976
MWA - Municipal Waste Association, 981
MWANB - The Metal Working Association of New Brunswick, 962
MWCA - Manitoba Wall & Ceiling Association, 947
MWF - Manitoba Wildlife Federation, 947
MWG - Manitoba Writers' Guild Inc., 947
MWI - Manitoba Women's Institutes, 947
MWIA - Medical Women's International Association, 958
MWWA - Manitoba Water Well Association, 947
MWWA - Manitoba Water & Wastewater Association, 947
MYC - Music for Young Children, 983

N

N&LFA - Newfoundland & Labrador Fencing Association, 1019
N&LORNA - Newfoundland & Labrador Operating Room Nurses Association, 1020
NAAAP - North American Association of Asian Professionals Vancouver, 1029
NAABA - Northeastern Alberta Aboriginal Business Association, 1034
NAACCR, Inc. - North American Association of Central Cancer Registries, Inc., 1578
NAAEE - North American Association for Environmental Education, 1578
NAAF - National Alopecia Areata Foundation, 1572
NABA - North American Broadcasters Association, 1029
NABA - North American Butterfly Association, 1578
NABCI - North American Bird Conservation Initiative Canada, 1029
NABS - National Advertising Benevolent Society, 989
NAC - National Action Committee on the Status of Women, 989
NACA - Northern Alberta Curling Association, 1034
NACA - Nunavut Arts & Crafts Association, 1051
NACAS - National Association of College Auxiliary Services, 1573
NACBS - North American Conference on British Studies, 1578
NACC - National Association of Career Colleges, 990
NACCA - National Aboriginal Capital Corporations Association, 988
NACDA - National Association of Collegiate Directors of Athletics, 1573
NACE - NACE International, 1571
NACL - Nanaimo Association for Community Living, 987
NACL - Norfolk Association for Community Living, 1028
NACM - Native Addictions Council of Manitoba, 997
NACO - National Arts Centre Orchestra of Canada, 989
NACO - National Angel Capital Organization, 989
NACOI - National Association of Canadians of Origins in India, 990
NACOR - National Association of Canadian Optician Regulators, 989
NACS - Nordic Association for Canadian Studies, 1578
NACS - The Northern AIDS Connection Society, 1034
NACY - National Alliance for Children & Youth, 989
NADA - National Aboriginal Diabetes Association Inc., 988

NADCA - North American Die Casting Association, 1579
NAEE - National Association for Environmental Education (UK), 1572
NAEM - National Association for Environmental Management, 1572
NAEP - National Association of Environmental Professionals, 1573
NAFA - National Aboriginal Forestry Association, 988
NAfA - Niagara Action for Animals, 1024
NAFC - National Association of Friendship Centres, 990
NAFDMA - North American Farmers' Direct Marketing Association, Inc., 1579
NAFO - Northwest Atlantic Fisheries Organization, 1036
NAIA - Newfoundland Aquaculture Industry Association, 1022
NAID - National Association for Information Destruction, 1573
NAIFA - National African Integration & Families of Ontario, 989
NAIMA - North American Insulation Manufacturers Association, 1579
NAJC - National Association of Japanese Canadians, 990
NALC - North Algoma Literacy Coalition, 1028
NALMA - National Aboriginal Lands Managers Association, 989
NALVMA - Newfoundland & Labrador Veterinary Medical Association, 1022
NAMMU - National Association of Major Mail Users, Inc., 990
NANB - Nurses Association of New Brunswick, 1052
NANPS - North American Native Plant Society, 1029
NAO - The Nile Association of Ontario, 1027
NAO - National Academy Orchestra, 989
NAPA - North American Piedmontese Association, 1579
NAPAH - National Association of Physical Activity & Health, 990
NAPCOR - National Association for PET Container Resources, 1573
NAPE - Newfoundland & Labrador Association of Public & Private Employees, 1016
NAPEG - Northwest Territories & Nunavut Association of Professional Engineers & Geoscientists, 1036
NAPRA - National Association of Pharmacy Regulatory Authorities, 990
NAR - Niagara Association of REALTORS, 1024
NARAMU - National Association of Review Appraisers & Mortgage Underwriters, 1574
NAREA - National Association of Real Estate Appraisers, 1574
NARHF - North America Railway Hall of Fame, 1029
NARP - National Association of Railroad Passengers, 1573
NARRA - North American Recycled Rubber Association, 1029
NAS - National Audubon Society, Inc., 1575
NASA - Northern Alberta Institute of Technology Academic Staff Association, 1034
NASA - Nakiska Alpine Ski Association, 987
NASAP - North American Society of Adlerian Psychology, 1579
NASCO - North Atlantic Salmon Conservation Organization, 1579
NASOH - North American Society for Oceanic History, 1579
NASSP - National Association of Secondary School Principals, 1574
NATA - Northern Air Transport Association, 1034
NATaT - National Association of Towns & Townships, 1574
NATI - Newfoundland & Labrador Association of Technology Industries, 1016

Acronym Index

NATOA - National Aboriginal Trust Officers Association, 989
NATPE - National Association of Television Program Executives, 1574
NATS - National Association of Teachers of Singing, 1574
NAVLI - Newfoundland Association of Visual Language Interpreters, 1022
NAWCC - National Association of Watch & Clock Collectors, Inc., 1574
NAWIC - National Association of Women in Construction, 1575
NAWL - National Association of Women & the Law, 990
NAWMP - North American Waterfowl Management Plan, 1029
NB Sigs - New Brunswick Signallers Association, 1012
NBA - National Bison Association, 1575
NBACL - New Brunswick Association for Community Living, 1004
NBAD - New Brunswick Association of Dietitians, 1005
NBADA - New Brunswick Aerospace & Defence Association, 1004
NBAFB - New Brunswick Association of Food Banks, 1005
NBAFRC - New Brunswick Association of Family Resource Centres, 1005
NBAIRP - New Brunswick Association of Insolvency & Restructuring Professionals, 1005
NBAMRT - New Brunswick Association of Medical Radiation Technologists, 1005
NBAND - New Brunswick Association of Naturopathic Doctors, 1005
NBANH - New Brunswick Association of Nursing Homes, Inc., 1005
NBAO - New Brunswick Association of Optometrists, 1005
NBAOT - New Brunswick Association of Occupational Therapists, 1005
NBAPC - New Brunswick Aboriginal Peoples Council, 1004
NBAREA - New Brunswick Association of Real Estate Appraisers, 1005
NBART - The New Brunswick Association of Respiratory Therapists Inc., 1005
NBASLPA - New Brunswick Association of Speech-Language Pathologists & Audiologists, 1006
NBASW - New Brunswick Association of Social Workers, 1006
NBBC - Native Brotherhood of British Columbia, 997
NBBOA - New Brunswick Building Officials Association, 1006
NBCA - New Brunswick Curling Association, 1007
NBCA - New Brunswick Chiropractors' Association, 1006
NBCA - New Brunswick Camping Association, 1006
NBCC - Nickel Belt Coin Club, 1026
NBCC - New Brunswick Chamber of Commerce, 1006
NBCF - New Brunswick Choral Federation, 1006
NBCFAL - Fitness New Brunswick, 740
NBCP - New Brunswick Cattle Producers, 1006
NBCSA - New Brunswick Construction Safety Association, 1007
NBCTA - Northern British Columbia Tourism Association, 1034
NBCTGC - New Brunswick Christmas Tree Growers Co-op Ltd., 1006
NBDA - New Brunswick Dart Association, 1007
NBDAA - New Brunswick Dental Assistants Association, 1007
NBEA - New Brunswick Equestrian Association, 1008
NBEC - National Building Envelope Council, 991
NBEMB - New Brunswick Egg Marketing Board, 1007

NBEN - New Brunswick Environmental Network, 1007
NBFDEA - New Brunswick Funeral Directors & Embalmers Association, 1008
NBFHSA - New Brunswick Federation of Home & School Associations, Inc., 1008
NBFL - New Brunswick Federation of Labour, 1008
NBFMF - New Brunswick Federation of Music Festivals Inc., 1008
NBFPA - New Brunswick Forest Products Association Inc., 1008
NBFY - New Beginnings for Youth, 1004
NBGA - New Brunswick Gymnastics Association, 1009
NBGA - New Brunswick Golf Association, 1009
NBGS, Inc. - New Brunswick Genealogical Society Inc., 1008
NBGSARA - New Brunswick Ground Search & Rescue Association, 1009
NBIA - New Brunswick Institute of Agrologists, 1009
NBIAA - New Brunswick Interscholastic Athletic Association, 1009
NBIFC - North Bay Indian Friendship Centre, 1030
NBLTA - New Brunswick Library Trustees' Association, 1010
NBMA - New Brunswick Massotherapy Association, 1010
NBMC - New Brunswick Multicultural Council, 1010
NBMS - New Brunswick Medical Society, 1010
NBMSA - New Brunswick Maple Syrup Association, 1010
NBNU - New Brunswick Nurses Union, 1010
NBOA Inc. - New Brunswick Outfitters Association Inc., 1011
NBORN - New Brunswick Operating Room Nurses, 1010
NBPA - North Bay Police Association, 1030
NBPA - New Brunswick Pharmacists' Association, 1011
NBPA - New Brunswick Physiotherapy Association, 1011
NBPFA - New Brunswick Physique & Figure Association, 1011
NBPhS - New Brunswick Pharmaceutical Society, 1011
NBRA - New Brunswick Racquetball Association, 1011
NBRCA - New Brunswick Roofing Contractors Association, Inc., 1011
NBREA - New Brunswick Real Estate Association, 1011
NBRU - New Brunswick Rugby Union, 1011
NBSA - New Brunswick Sailing Association, 1011
NBSC - New Brunswick Salmon Council, 1011
NBSCA - New Brunswick Scottish Cultural Association Inc., 1012
NBSCETT - New Brunswick Society of Certified Engineering Technicians & Technologists, 1012
NBSCF - New Brunswick Senior Citizens Federation Inc., 1012
NBSCIA - New Brunswick Soil & Crop Improvement Association, 1012
NBSCT - New Brunswick Society of Cardiology Techologists, 1012
NBSFA - New Brunswick Sportfishing Association, 1013
NBSHF - New Brunswick Sports Hall of Fame, 1013
NBSMLT - New Brunswick Society of Medical Laboratory Technologists, 1012
NBSWA - New Brunswick Solid Waste Association, 1012
NBTA - New Brunswick Teachers' Association, 1013
NBU - New Brunswick Union, 1013
NBVMA - New Brunswick Veterinary Medical Association, 1013
NBWF - New Brunswick Wildlife Federation, 1013

NBWI - New Brunswick Women's Institute, 1013
NBWSWBA - Waterski & Wakeboard New Brunswick, 1442
NCA - Nunavut Curling Association, 1051
NCAA - New College Alumni Association, 1014
NCAP - Northwest Coalition for Alternatives to Pesticides, 1580
NCBAC - National Council of Barbadian Associations in Canada, 991
NCBC - National Chinchilla Breeders of Canada, 991
NCC - The Nature Conservancy of Canada, 999
NCC - New Canadians Centre Peterborough Immigrant Services, 1013
NCCABC - Native Courtworker & Counselling Association of BC, 997
NCCAR - National Council on Canada-Arab Relations, 992
NCCM - National Council of Canadian Muslims, 991
NCCT - Native Canadian Centre of Toronto, 997
NCEP - Nepali Children's Education Project, 1003
NCF - National Capital FreeNet, 991
NCFA - National Crowdfunding Association of Canada, 992
NCFST - Native Child & Family Services of Toronto, 997
NCHS - The North Cumberland Historical Society, 1030
NCIC - National Congress of Italian-Canadians, 991
NCJWC - National Council of Jewish Women of Canada, 992
NCLF - North Central Library Federation, 1030
NCLGA - North Central Local Government Association, 1030
NCNS - Native Council of Nova Scotia, 997
NCO - Native Clan Organization Inc., 997
NCP - Les normes canadiennes de la publicité, 1028
NCPACA - National Council of Philippine American Canadian Accountants, 1575
NCPEI - Native Council of Prince Edward Island, 997
NCRA - National Court Reporters Association, 1575
NCRA - National Campus & Community Radio Association, 991
NCS - Native Communications Society of the Northwest Territories, 997
NCSA - Native Counselling Services of Alberta, 997
NCSC - Nordic Combined Ski Canada, 1028
NCSE - National Council for Science & the Environment, 1575
NCTRF - Newfoundland Cancer Treatment & Research Foundation, 1023
NCTTOC - National Council of Trinidad & Tobago Organizations in Canada, 992
NCVA - National Council of Veteran Associations, 992
NCWC - The National Council of Women of Canada, 992
NDAC - Nelson & District Arts Council, 1003
NDAEB - National Dental Assisting Examining Board, 992
NDDLC - Nanaimo, Duncan & District Labour Council, 988
NDFC - National Darts Federation of Canada, 992
NDM - Nanaimo District Museum, 987
NDMS - Nunavummi Disabilities Makinnasuaqtiit Society, 1051
NDP - New Democratic Party, 1014
NEA - Newfoundland Equestrian Association, 1023
NEADS - National Educational Association of Disabled Students, 993
NED - Niagara Economic Development, 1025
NEDA - Nunavut Economic Developers Association, 1051

NEDIC - National Eating Disorder Information Centre, 992
NEEA - National Elevator & Escalator Association, 993
NEHA - National Environmental Health Association, 1576
NEIA - Newfoundland & Labrador Environmental Industry Association, 1018
NeMLA - Northeast Modern Language Association, 1579
NENA - National Emergency Nurses Association, 993
NEPA - Native Earth Performing Arts Inc., 998
NER - National Electricity Roundtable, 993
NEU - Nunavut Employees Union, 1051
NEW - Newcomer Women's Services Toronto, 1015
NEW - Nipissing Environmental Watch, 1027
NFA - Canada's National Firearms Association, 282
NFA - Native Fishing Association, 998
NFA - Northern Finance Association, 1035
NFCA - National Floor Covering Association, 993
NFCM - Native Friendship Centre of Montréal Inc., 998
NFLA - Nanaimo Family Life Association, 988
NFN - Norfolk Field Naturalists, 1028
NFNC - Niagara Falls Nature Club, 1025
NFSO - Neurofibromatosis Society of Ontario, 1003
NFT - Niagara Falls Tourism, 1025
NFU - National Farmers Union, 993
NFVA - Northern Frontier Visitors Association, 1035
NFVIA - Northern Film & Video Industry Association, 1034
NGCOA - National Golf Course Owners Association Canada, 993
NGEA - Natural Gas Employees' Association, 998
NGHS - North Grenville Historical Society, 1031
NGWA - National Ground Water Association, 1576
NHA - Nunavut Harvesters Association, 1051
NHC - Norfolk Historical Society, 1028
NHCC - Neurological Health Charities Canada, 1004
NHCIA - North Hastings Community Integration Association, 1031
NHLA - National Hockey League Alumni Association, 994
NHLPA - National Hockey League Players' Association, 994
NHP - Natural Health Practitioners of Canada, 998
NHPCA - Natural Health Practitioners of Canada Association, 999
NHS - Newfoundland Historical Society, 1023
NHS - Nanaimo Historical Society, 988
NHU - National Health Union, 994
NIAC - Nuclear Insurance Association of Canada, 1050
NICE - National Initiative for the Care of the Elderly, 994
NICFA - North Island College Faculty Association, 1031
NICHE - National Institute for Cannabis Health & Education, 994
NIDMAR - National Institute of Disability Management & Research, 994
NIGP - National Institute of Governmental Purchasing, Inc., 1576
NIP - Neighbourhood Information Post, 1002
NIPA - National Information Program on Antibiotics, 994
NIRS - Nuclear Information & Resource Service, 1580
NITA - Native Investment & Trade Association, 998
NIYC - National Inuit Youth Council, 994
NJI - National Judicial Institute, 994
NLA - Nunavut Library Association, 1051
NLAA - Newfoundland & Labrador Athletics Association, 1017

Acronym Index

NLABBA - Newfoundland & Labrador Amateur Bodybuilding Association, 1015
NLAC - Newfoundland & Labrador Arts Council, 1015
NLACL - Newfoundland & Labrador Association for Community Living, 1015
NLAD - Newfoundland & Labrador Association of the Deaf, 1016
NLAMRT - Newfoundland & Labrador Association of Medical Radiation Technologists, 1016
NLAO - Newfoundland & Labrador Association of Optometrists, 1016
NLAOT - Newfoundland & Labrador Association of Occupational Therapists, 1016
NLAR - Newfoundland & Labrador Association of Realtors, 1016
NLART - Newfoundland & Labrador Association of Respiratory Therapists, 1016
NLASLPA - Newfoundland & Labrador Association of Speech-Language Pathologists & Audiologists, 1016
NLASW - Newfoundland & Labrador Association of Social Workers, 1016
NLAWA - Newfoundland & Labrador Amateur Wrestling Association, 1015
NLBHA - Newfoundland & Labrador Ball Hockey Association, 1017
NLBIA - Newfoundland & Labrador Brain Injury Association, 1017
NLCA - Newfoundland & Labrador Construction Association, 1017
NLCA - Newfoundland & Labrador Cheerleading Athletics, 1017
NLCD - Newfoundland & Labrador College of Dietitians, 1017
NLCP - Newfoundland & Labrador College of Physiotherapists, 1017
NLCSA - Newfoundland & Labrador Construction Safety Association, 1017
NLDAA - Newfoundland Dental Assistants Association, 1023
NLDS - Newfoundland & Labrador Drama Society, 1018
NLDSA - Newfoundland & Labrador Deaf Sports Association, 1018
NLEN - Newfoundland & Labrador Environment Network, 1018
NLFAS - Newfoundland & Labrador Folk Arts Society, 1019
NLFBA - Newfoundland & Labrador Fur Breeders Association, 1019
NLFC - Newfoundland-Labrador Federation of Cooperatives, 1024
NLFL - Newfoundland & Labrador Federation of Labour, 1018
NLFSA - Newfoundland & Labrador Funeral Services Association, 1019
NLFSC - Newfoundland & Labrador Federation of School Councils, 1019
NLHA - Hockey Newfoundland & Labrador, 818
NLHLA - Newfoundland & Labrador Health Libraries Association, 1019
NLHP - National Literacy & Health Program, 994
NLIA - Newfoundland & Labrador Institute of Agrologists, 1019
NLLA - Newfoundland & Labrador Lung Association, 1020
NLLA - Newfoundland & Labrador Library Association, 1019
NLLA - Newfoundland & Labrador Lacrosse Association, 1019
NLLLC - Newfoundland & Labrador Laubach Literacy Council, 1019
NLMA - Newfoundland & Labrador Medical Association, 1020
NLMC - Newfoundland & Labrador Multicultural Council Inc., 1020
NLMTA - Newfoundland & Labrador Massage Therapists' Association, 1020
NLNPA - Newfoundland & Labrador Nurse Practitioner Association, 1020
NLNU - Newfoundland & Labrador Nurses' Union, 1020

NLOA - Newfoundland & Labrador Outfitters Association, 1020
NLOTB - Newfoundland & Labrador Occupational Therapy Board, 1020
NLOWE - Newfoundland & Labrador Organization of Women Entrepreneurs, 1020
NLPA - Newfoundland & Labrador Prospectors Association, 1021
NLPA - Newfoundland & Labrador Physiotherapy Association, 1021
NLPB - Newfoundland & Labrador Pharmacy Board, 1021
NLPCA - Newfoundland & Labrador Palliative Care Association, 1020
NLPHA - Newfoundland & Labrador Public Health Association, 1021
NLSACPC - Newfoundland & Labrador Sexual Assault Crisis & Prevention Centre Inc., 1021
NLSBA - Newfoundland & Labrador School Boards Association, 1021
NLSHC - Planned Parenthood - Newfoundland & Labrador Sexual Health Centre, 1161
NLSMLS - Newfoundland & Labrador Society for Medical Laboratory Science, 1021
NLSSA - Newfoundland & Labrador Speed Skating Association, 1022
NLTA - Newfoundland & Labrador Teachers' Association, 1022
NLTTA - Newfoundland & Labrador Table Tennis Association, 1022
NLVA - Newfoundland & Labrador Volleyball Association, 1022
NMAF - National Magazine Awards Foundation, 994
NMAS - Naval Museum of Alberta Society, 1001
NMMA - National Marine Manufacturers Association, 1576
NMMA - National Marine Manufacturers Association Canada, 995
NNAPF - National Native Addictions Partnership Foundation, 995
NNC - National NewsMedia Council, 995
NNCA - Northwest Territories & Nunavut Construction Association, 1037
NNFC - Northern Native Fishing Corporation, 1035
NNMH - National Network for Mental Health, 995
NOAC - The Naval Officers' Association of Canada, 1001
NOACC - Northwestern Ontario Associated Chambers of Commerce, 1039
NOASARA - Northwestern Ontario Air Search & Rescue Association, 1039
NOC - Northumberland Orchestra Society, 1036
NODA - Northern Ontario Darts Association, 1035
NOFA - Northeast Organic Farming Association, 1580
NOHA - Northern Ontario Hockey Association, 1035
NOIVMWC - National Organization of Immigrant & Visible Minority Women of Canada, 995
NOMA - Northwestern Ontario Municipal Association, 1039
NONA - North Okanagan Neurological Association, 1031
NONC - North Okanagan Naturalists Club, 1031
NONTA - Northern Ontario Native Tourism Association, 1035
NOOA - North Okanagan Organic Association, 1031
NORA - NORA, An Association of Responsible Recyclers, 1578
NORD - National Organization for Rare Disorders, Inc., 1576
NOSFA - North of Superior Film Association, 1031
NOSTA - North of Superior Tourism Association, 1031
NOTA - Northwestern Ontario Technology Association, 1040
NPA - Northern Prospectors Association, 1035

NPAA - Nurse Practitioners Association of Alberta, 1052
NPAC - Nurse Practitioner Association of Canada, 1051
NPAC - News Photographers Association of Canada, 1024
NPAFC - North Pacific Anadromous Fish Commission, 1031
NPANS - Nurse Practitioners' Association of Nova Scotia, 1052
NPAO - Nurse Practitioners' Association of Ontario, 1052
NPARA - North Peace Applied Research Association, 1032
NPCA - National Parks Conservation Association, 1577
NPCA - Niagara Peninsula Conservation Authority, 1025
NPCC - North Peace Cultural Society, 1032
NPECA - Niagara Peninsula Electrical Contractors Association, 1025
NPF - National Pensioners Federation, 995
NPGS - Niagara Peninsula Geological Society, 1025
NPHC - March of Dimes Non-Profit Housing Corporation, 949
NPOS - Nurse Practitioners of Saskatchewan, 1052
NRAHTA - Northern Rockies Alaska Highway Tourism Association, 1035
NRC - National Recycling Coalition, Inc., 1577
NRCC - Northern Ramblers Car Club Inc., 1035
NRFS - North Renfrew Family Services Inc., 1032
NRG - Naut'sa mawt Resource Group, 1001
NRNC - Niagara Regional Native Centre, 1026
NRPA - Niagara Region Police Association, 1025
NRU - Natural Resources Union, 999
NS SPCA - Nova Scotia Society for the Prevention of Cruelty to Animals, 1049
NSA - Nepisiguit Salmon Association, 1003
NSA - University of Toronto Native Students Association, 1421
NSAA - Nova Scotia Association of Architects, 1040
NSABBA - Nova Scotia Amateur Bodybuilding Association, 1040
NSAC - National Sunflower Association of Canada, 996
NSACL - Nova Scotia Association for Community Living, 1040
NSADA - Nova Scotia Automobile Dealers' Association, 1041
NSAIRP - Nova Scotia Association of Insolvency & Restructuring Professionals, 1041
NSAMRT - Nova Scotia Association of Medical Radiation Technologists, 1041
NSAND - Nova Scotia Association of Naturopathic Doctors, 1041
NSAO - Nova Scotia Association of Optometrists, 1041
NSAR - Nova Scotia Association of REALTORS, 1041
NSAS - Nova Scotia Archaeology Society, 1040
NSASW - Nova Scotia Association of Social Workers, 1041
NSAWA - Nova Scotia Arm Wrestling Association, 1040
NSBA - Nova Scotia Boxing Authority, 1042
NSBA - Nova Scotia Beekeepers' Association, 1042
NSBHA - Nova Scotia Ball Hockey Association, 1041
NSBS - Nova Scotia Barristers' Society, 1042
NSC - Edmonton Aboriginal Senior Centre, 675
NSCA - Nova Scotia Curling Association, 1043
NSCA - Nova Scotia Cricket Association, 1043
NSCC - Nova Scotia College of Chiropractors, 1042
NSCF - Nova Scotia Choral Federation, 1042
NSCF - Nova Scotia Council for the Family, 1043

NSCJA - Nova Scotia Criminal Justice Association, 1043
NSCLRA - Nova Scotia Construction Labour Relations Association Limited, 1043
NSCMLT - Nova Scotia College of Medical Laboratory Technologists, 1042
NSCP - Nova Scotia Cattle Producers, 1042
NSCP - Nova Scotia College of Pharmacists, 1042
NSCP - Nova Scotia College of Physiotherapists, 1042
NSCRT - Nova Scotia College of Respiratory Therapists, 1043
NSCSA - Nova Scotia Construction Safety Association, 1043
NSCSC-ICI - Nova Scotia Construction Sector Council - Industrial-Commercial-Institutional, 1043
NSDA - Nova Scotia Dietetic Association, 1044
NSDA - Nova Scotia Dental Association, 1044
NSDAA - Nova Scotia Dental Assistants' Association, 1044
NSDCC - Nova Scotia Designer Crafts Council, 1044
NSDRC - North Shore Disability Resource Centre Association, 1032
NSDSA - Nova Scotia Deaf Sports Association, 1043
NSEF - Nova Scotia Equestrian Federation, 1044
NSEP - Nova Scotia Egg Producers, 1044
NSERC - Natural Sciences & Engineering Research Council of Canada, 999
NSF - The Neil Squire Foundation, 1002
NSFA - Nova Scotia Federation of Agriculture, 1044
NSFA - Nova Scotia Forestry Association, 1045
NSFAH - Nova Scotia Federation of Anglers & Hunters, 1044
NSFGA - Nova Scotia Fruit Growers' Association, 1045
NSFHSA - Nova Scotia Federation of Home & School Associations, 1044
NSFPA - Nova Scotia Fish Packers Association, 1044
NSFTA - Nova Scotia Forest Technicians Association, 1045
NSGA - Nova Scotia Golf Association, 1045
NSGEU - Nova Scotia Government & General Employees Union, 1045
NSGLC - Nova Scotia Government Libraries Council, 1045
NSGNA - The Nova Scotia Genealogy Network Association, 1045
NSGNA - Nova Scotia Gerontological Nurses Association, 1045
NSGWA - Nova Scotia Ground Water Association, 1045
NSHBA - Nova Scotia Home Builders' Association, 1045
NSHPA - Nova Scotia Horseshoe Players Association, 1046
NSHPCA - Nova Scotia Hospice Palliative Care Association, 1046
NSI - National Screen Institute - Canada, 996
NSI - The North-South Institute, 1036
NSIA - Nova Scotia Institute of Agrologists, 1046
NSIS - Nova Scotian Institute of Science, 1050
NSIWA - Nova Scotia Insurance Women's Association, 1046
NSLA - Nova Scotia Library Association, 1046
NSLEO - Nova Scotia League for Equal Opportunities, 1046
NSLPS - Nova Scotia Lighthouse Preservation Society, 1047
NSMEA - Nova Scotia Music Educators' Association, 1047
NSMGS - The Nova Scotia Mineral & Gem Society, 1047
NSMS - North Shore Multicultural Society, 1033
NSNS - North Shore Numismatic Society, 1033
NSNT - Nova Scotia Nature Trust, 1047
NSNU - Nova Scotia Nurses' Union, 1047

Acronym Index

NSNWA - Nova Scotia Native Women's Society, 1047
NSO - Newfoundland Symphony Orchestra Association, 1023
NSPA - Northumberland Salmon Protection Association, 1036
NSPA - Nova Scotia Prospectors Association, 1047
NSPA - Nova Scotia Physiotherapy Association, 1047
NSPIRG - Nova Scotia Public Interest Research Group, 1047
NSRA - Nova Scotia Rifle Association, 1048
NSRA - Non-Smokers' Rights Association, 1028
NSREAA - Nova Scotia Real Estate Appraisers Association, 1048
NSREC - Nova Scotia Real Estate Commission, 1048
NSRPH - Nova Scotia Recreation Professionals in Health, 1048
NSS - Niagara Support Services, 1026
NSS - National Space Society, 1577
NSSA - Nova Scotia Salmon Association, 1048
NSSAF - Nova Scotia School Athletic Federation, 1048
NSSBA - Nova Scotia School Boards Association, 1048
NSSC - Nova Scotia Stamp Club, 1049
NSSC - National Seafood Sector Council, 996
NSSC - Nova Scotia Securities Commission, 1048
NSSCA - Nova Scotia School Counsellor Association, 1048
NSSHF - Nova Scotia Sports Hall of Fame, 1050
NSSOT - Nova Scotia Society of Occupational Therapists, 1049
NSTALL - Nova Scotia Teachers Association of Literacy & Learning, 1049
NSTF - Nova Scotia Trails Federation, 1050
NSTTA - Nova Scotia Table Tennis Association, 1049
NSTU - Nova Scotia Teachers Union, 1049
NSUPE - Nova Scotia Union of Public & Private Employees (CCU), 1050
NSYO - Newfoundland Symphony Youth Orchestra, 1023
NTA - Nunavut Teachers' Association, 1051
NTBA - National Transportation Brokers Association, 996
NTCCC - National Trade Contractors Coalition of Canada, 996
NTF - National Taekwon-Do Federation, 996
NTNB - Nature Trust of New Brunswick, 1001
NTNUPHA - Canadian Public Health Association - NWT/Nunavut Branch, 462
NuALA - Nunavut Association of Landscape Architects, 1051
NUPATH - National United Professional Association of Trained Homeopaths, 996
NUPGE - National Union of Public & General Employees, 996
NVCAC - North Vancouver Community Arts Council, 1033
NVCC - North Vancouver Chamber of Commerce, 1033
NVICS - Nanaimo Volunteer and Information Centre Society, 988
NW - Northwatch, 1036
NWAC - Native Women's Association of Canada, 998
NWCB - Northwest Wall & Ceiling Bureau, 1580
NWCTA - North West Commercial Travellers' Association, 1033
NWDLC - New Westminster & District Labour Council, 1015
NWELRC - Niagara West Employment & Learning Resource Centres, 1026
NWF - National Wildlife Federation, 1577
NWHS - New Westminster Historical Society, 1015
NWHS - Norman Wells Historical Society, 1028
NWLF - Newfoundland & Labrador Wildlife Federation, 1022
NWLF - North West Library Federation, 1033

NWOPA - Northwestern Ontario Prospectors Association, 1039
NWPS - Northwest Wildlife Preservation Society, 1039
NWPSA - Northwest Peace Soccer Association, 1036
NWRA - National Waste & Recycling Association, 1577
NWRCT - Native Women's Resource Centre of Toronto, 998
NWSA - National Winter Sports Association, 997
NWT5PBA - Northwest Territories 5 Pin Bowlers' Association, 1037
NWTAA - Northwest Territories Association of Architects, 1037
NWTAC - Northwest Territories Archives Council, 1037
NWTAC - Northwest Territories Association of Communities, 1037
NWTALA - Northwest Territories Association of Landscape Architects, 1037
NWTASSA - Northwest Territories Amateur Speed Skating Association, 1037
NWTCFA - Northwest Territories Community Futures Association, 1038
NWTCPD - NWT Disabilities Council, 1052
NWTLA - Northwest Territories Library Association, 1038
NWTMA - Northwest Territories Medical Association, 1038
NWTNC - Northwest Territories & Nunavut Council of the Canadian Physiotherapy Association, 1037
NWTRPA - Northwest Territories Recreation & Parks Association, 1038
NWTSA - Northwest Territories Soccer Association, 1038
NWTSAF - NWT School Athletic Federation, 1052
NWTSPCA - Northwest Territories Society for the Prevention of Cruelty to Animals, 1038
NWTSS - NWT Seniors' Society, 1052
NWTT - Northwest Territories Tourism, 1039
NWTTA - Northwest Territories Teachers' Association, 1038
NWTVA - Northwest Territories Volleyball Association, 1039
NYAP - Northern Youth Abroad Program, 1035
NYCC - North York Coin Club, 1033
NYOC - National Youth Orchestra Canada, 997

O

O5PBA - Ontario 5 Pin Bowlers' Association, 1058
OA - Opéra Atelier, 1114
OAA - Ontario Association of Architects, 1061
OAA - Ontario Angus Association, 1059
OAA - Ontario Association of Archers Inc., 1061
OAAG - Ontario Association of Art Galleries, 1062
OAAQ - Ordre des administrateurs agréés du Québec, 1119
OAAS - Ontario Association of Agricultural Societies, 1061
OAATCM - Ontario Association of Acupuncture & Traditional Chinese Medicine, 1061
OAB - Ontario Association of Broadcasters, 1062
OABA - Ontario Agri Business Association, 1059
OABA - Ontario Artist Blacksmith Association, 1060
OABC - Orienteering Association of British Columbia, 1126
OAC - Oakville Arts Council, 1053
OAC - Ottawa Arts Council, 1129
OAC - Ontario Arts Council, 1060
OAC - Opticians Association of Canada, 1116
OAC - Ontario Aerospace Council, 1058
OACA - Ontario Association of Committees of Adjustment & Consent Authorities, 1063
OACA - Ontario Arms Collectors' Association, 1060

OACAO - Older Adult Centres' Association of Ontario, 1056
OACAS - Ontario Association of Children's Aid Societies, 1062
OACCAC - Ontario Association of Community Care Access Centres, 1063
OACCPP - Ontario Association of Consultants, Counsellors, Psychometrists & Psychotherapists, 1063
OACCS - Ontario Association of Credit Counselling Services, 1063
OACETT - Ontario Association of Certified Engineering Technicians & Technologists, 1062
OACFDC - Ontario Association of Community Futures Development Corporations, 1063
OACFP - Ontario Association of Cemetery & Funeral Professionals, 1062
OACIQ - Organisme d'autoréglementation du courtage immobilier du Québec, 1125
OACP - Ontario Association of Chiefs of Police, 1062
OACRS - Ontario Association of Children's Rehabilitation Services, 1062
OACS - Ontario Alliance of Christian Schools, 1059
OACYC - Ontario Association of Child & Youth Care, 1062
OADD - Ontario Association on Developmental Disabilities, 1067
OADE - Ontario Association of Deans of Education, 1063
OADS - Ontario Association of Dental Specialists, 1063
OAEA - Ontario Art Education Association, 1060
OAEM - Ontario Association of Emergency Managers, 1063
OAEP - Ontario Association of Equine Practitioners, 1063
OAFB - Ontario Association of Food Banks, 1064
OAFC - Ontario Association of Fire Chiefs, 1063
OAFE - Ontario Agri-Food Education Inc., 1059
OAFM - Ontario Association for Family Mediation, 1061
OAFT - Ontario Agri-Food Technologies, 1059
OAG - Ontario Association of Gastroenterology, 1064
OAGEE - Ontario Association for Geographic & Environmental Education, 1061
OAGQ - Ordre des arpenteurs-géomètres du Québec, 1120
OAH - Organization of American Historians, 1581
OAIA - Ontario Association for Impact Assessment, 1061
OAIRP - Ontario Association of Insolvency & Restructuring Professionals, 1064
OAITH - Ontario Association of Interval & Transition Houses, 1064
OALA - Ontario Association of Landscape Architects, 1064
OALA - Ontario Aboriginal Lands Association, 1058
OALASA - Ontario Amputee & Les Autres Sports Association, 1059
OALT - Ontario Association of Library Technicians, 1064
OAMFT - Ontario Association for Marriage & Family Therapy, 1061
OAML - Ontario Association of Medical Laboratories, 1064
OAMRS - Ontario Association of Medical Radiation Sciences, 1064
OAND - Ontario Association of Naturopathic Doctors, 1065
OANS - Orienteering Association of Nova Scotia, 1126
OAO - Ontario Association of Optometrists, 1065
OAO - Ontario Association of Orthodontists, 1065
OAP - Ontario Association of Pathologists, 1065

OAPC - Ontario Asphalt Pavement Council, 1060
OAPO - Ontario Association of Prosthetists & Orthotists, 1065
OAPSB - Ontario Association of Police Services Boards, 1065
OAPT - Ontario Association of Physics Teachers, 1065
OAPWS - Ottawa Association of People Who Stutter, 1129
OAQ - Ordre des agronomes du Québec, 1120
OAQ - Ordre des architectes du Québec, 1120
OAQ - Ordre des acupuncteurs de Québec, 1119
OAQ - Ordre des audioprothésistes du Québec, 1120
OAQP - Ontario Association of Quick Printers, 1065
OARA - Ontario Automotive Recyclers Association, 1067
OARC - Ontario Association of Residents' Councils, 1066
OARM - Ontario Association of Radiology Managers, 1065
OARTY - Ontario Association of Residences Treating Youth, 1065
OASA - Ontario Amateur Softball Association, 1059
OASAR - Ontario Association For Students At Risk, 1061
OASBO - Ontario Association of School Business Officials, 1066
OASFAA - Ontario Association of Student Financial Aid Administrators, 1066
OASIS - Ontario Agencies Supporting Individuals with Special Needs, 1059
OASLI - Ontario Association of Sign Language Interpreters, 1066
OASW - Ontario Association of Social Workers, 1066
OAT - Ontario Association of Triathletes, 1066
OATA - Ontario Art Therapy Association, 1060
OATA - Ontario Athletic Therapists Association, 1067
OATH - Ontario Association of Trading Houses, 1066
OAVT - Ontario Association of Veterinary Technicians, 1066
OAWA - Ontario Amateur Wrestling Association, 1059
OBA - Ontario Beekeepers' Association, 1067
OBA - Ottawa Baptist Association, 1129
OBA - Ontario Bailiff Association, 1067
OBAD - The Organization for Bipolar Affective Disorder, 1125
OBEC - Ontario Building Envelope Council, 1069
OBEP - Ontario Business Education Partnership, 1070
OBG - Ontario Bean Growers Association, 1067
OBGA - Ontario Berry Growers' Association, 1068
OBHA - Ontario Ball Hockey Association, 1067
OBHECC - Ontario Broiler Hatching Egg & Chick Commission, 1069
OBHS - Ontario Black History Society, 1068
OBIA - Ontario Brain Injury Association, 1068
OBOA - Ontario Building Officials Association Inc., 1070
OBPO - Ontario Book Publishers Organization, 1068
OBSA - Ontario Blind Sports Association, 1068
OBSA - Ontario Brown Swiss Association, 1069
OBSA - Ontario Bobsleigh Skeleton Association, 1068
OBSI - Ombudsman for Banking Services & Investments, 1057
OBTA - Ontario Baton Twirling Association, 1067
OC - Orchestras Canada, 1117
OCA - Ontario Curling Association, 1076
OCA - Ontario Chiropractic Association, 1071
OCA - Ottawa Construction Association, 1130
OCA - Ontario Camps Association, 1070
OCA - Ontario Cycling Association, 1076

Acronym Index

OCA - Ontario Camelids Association, 1070
OCA ADOC - Orthodox Church in America Archdiocese of Canada, 1127
OCAA - Ontario Crown Attorneys Association, 1076
OCAA - Ontario Colleges Athletic Association, 1073
OCAA - Ontario Clean Air Alliance, 1071
OCAB - Ontario Council of Alternative Businesses, 1075
OCAC - Oceanside Community Arts Council, 1054
OCAC - Oliver Community Arts Council, 1057
OCAC - Ontario Coalition for Abortion Clinics, 1071
OCAP - Ontario Coalition of Aboriginal Peoples, 1071
OCAP - Ontario Coalition Against Poverty, 1071
OCASA - Ontario College Administrative Staff Associations, 1072
OCASI - Ontario Council of Agencies Serving Immigrants, 1075
OCB - Ontario Craft Brewers, 1075
OCBCC - Ontario Coalition for Better Child Care, 1071
OCC - Ontario Chamber of Commerce, 1071
OCC - Ontario Crafts Council, 1075
OCC - Ottawa Chamber of Commerce, 1129
OCC - Ontario Cavy Club, 1070
OCC - Ovarian Cancer Canada, 1133
OCCOQ - Ordre des conseillers et conseillères d'orientation du Québec, 1121
OCCQ - L'Office de Certification Commerciale du Québec Inc., 1054
OCCSC - Ottawa Chinese Community Services Centre, 1129
OCDS - Discalced Carmelite Secular Order - Canada, 658
OCE - Ontario Centres of Excellence, 1070
OCEA - Ontario Cooperative Education Association, 1074
OCEC - Ontario Council for Exceptional Children, 1075
OCF - Ontario Cheerleading Federation, 1071
OCFA - Olds College Faculty Association, 1057
OCFA - Ontario Commercial Fisheries' Association, 1073
OCGS - Ontario Council on Graduate Studies, 1075
OCIA - Organic Crop Improvement Association (International), 1580
OCIA-NB - Organic Crop Improvement Association - New Brunswick, 1125
OCIC - Ontario Council for International Cooperation, 1075
OCISO - Ottawa Community Immigrant Services Organization, 1130
OCJA - Ontario Community Justice Association, 1073
OCM - Orchestre de chambre de Montréal, 1117
OCMBC - Ontario Conference of Mennonite Brethren Churches, 1074
OCNA - Ontario Community Newspapers Association, 1073
OCNI - Organization of Canadian Nuclear Industries, 1125
OCO - Ottawa Chamber Orchestra, 1129
OCP - Ontario College of Pharmacists, 1072
OCPA - Ontario Concrete Pipe Association, 1074
OCPSA - Ontario Cerebral Palsy Sports Association, 1071
OCQ - Ordre des chimistes du Québec, 1120
OCR - Ontario College of Reflexology, 1072
OCRCC - Ontario Coalition of Rape Crisis Centres, 1072
OCRT - Ontario Consultants on Religious Tolerance, 1074
OCS - Ontario Construction Secretariat, 1074
OCSA - Ontario Community Support Association, 1073
OCSA - Ontario Convenience Store Association, 1074

OCSOA - Ontario Catholic Supervisory Officers' Association, 1070
OCSRA - Ontario Canoe Kayak Sprint Racing Affiliation, 1070
OCSTA - Ontario Catholic School Trustees' Association, 1070
OCSWSSW - Ontario College of Social Workers & Social Service Workers, 1072
OCT - Ontario College of Teachers, 1072
OCTRA - Ontario Competitive Trail Riding Association Inc., 1073
OCUA - Ottawa Carleton Ultimate Association, 1129
OCUFA - Ontario Confederation of University Faculty Associations, 1074
OCUL - Ontario Council of University Libraries, 1075
OCULA - Ontario College & University Library Association, 1072
OCYC - Oxford Child & Youth Centre, 1134
ODA - Ontario Dental Association, 1077
ODAA - Ontario Dental Assistants Association, 1077
ODACE - Organisme de développement d'affaires commerciales et économiques, 1125
ODC - Ontario Dairy Council, 1076
ODC - Ottawa Duck Club, 1130
ODHA - Ontario Dental Hygienists' Association, 1077
ODLC - Ottawa & District Labour Council, 1129
ODM - L'Opéra de Montréal, 1114
ODMHA - Ottawa District Minor Hockey Association, 1130
ODQ - Ordre des denturologistes du Québec, 1121
ODQ - Ordre des dentistes du Québec, 1121
ODRCC - Oshawa-Durham Rape Crisis Centre, 1128
ODREB - Orangeville & District Real Estate Board, 1117
ODS - Osoyoos Desert Society, 1128
ODS - Ontario Daylily Society, 1076
ODS - Ontario DanceSport, 1076
ODSA - Ontario Deaf Sports Association, 1076
ODSA - Ontario Disc Sports Association, 1077
ODUM - Ukrainian Democratic Youth Association, 1403
OEA - Ottawa Economics Association, 1130
OEA - Ontario Energy Association, 1077
OEAQ - Ordre des évaluateurs agréés du Québec, 1121
OECD - Organization for Economic Co-operation & Development, 1581
OECTA - Ontario English Catholic Teachers' Association (CLC), 1077
OEF - Ontario Equestrian Federation, 1078
OEL - Ontario Electrical League, 1077
OEMAC - Occupational & Environmental Medical Association of Canada, 1054
OEN - Ontario Environmental Network, 1078
OEQ - Ordre des ergothérapeutes du Québec, 1121
OERA - Offshore Energy Research Association of Nova Scotia, 1055
OETA - Ontario East Tourism Association, 1077
OFA - Ontario Federation of Agriculture, 1079
OFA - Ontario Fencing Association, 1080
OFA - Ottawa Flute Association, 1130
OFA - Ontario Formwork Association, 1081
OFA - Opportunity For Advancement, 1116
OFAAA - Occupational First Aid Attendants Association of British Columbia, 1054
OFAH - Ontario Federation of Anglers & Hunters, 1079
OFBA - Ontario Fire Buff Associates, 1080
OFC - One Full Circle, 1058
OFCA - Ontario Farm & Country Accommodations Association, 1078
OFCP - Ontario Federation for Cerebral Palsy, 1079
OFCRC - The Olde Forge Community Resource Centre, 1056
OFCTGMB - Ontario Flue-Cured Tobacco Growers' Marketing Board, 1080

OFDA - Ontario Folk Dance Association, 1080
OFE - Ontario Fashion Exhibitors, 1078
OFFMA - Ontario Farm Fresh Marketing Association, 1078
OFHSA - Ontario Federation of Home & School Associations Inc., 1079
OFIA - Ontario Forest Industries Association, 1081
OFIFC - Ontario Federation of Indian Friendship Centres, 1079
OFIS - Ontario Federation of Independent Schools, 1079
OFL - Ontario Federation of Labour, 1079
OFNC - Ottawa Field-Naturalists' Club, 1130
OFO - Ontario Field Ornithologists, 1080
OFPA - Ontario Food Protection Association, 1080
OFSA - Ontario Funeral Service Association, 1081
OFSAA - Ontario Federation of School Athletic Associations, 1079
OFSC - Ontario Federation of Snowmobile Clubs, 1080
OFT - Ontario Farmland Trust, 1078
OFTP - Ontario Federation of Teaching Parents, 1080
OFVGA - Ontario Fruit & Vegetable Growers' Association, 1081
OFVIC - Ontario Foundation for Visually Impaired Children Inc., 1081
OGA - Ontario Gerontology Association, 1082
OGA - Ontario Geothermal Association, 1082
OGBA - Ontario Goat Breeders Association, 1083
OGCA - Ontario General Contractors Association, 1082
OGF - Ontario Gymnastic Federation, 1083
OGRA - Ontario Good Roads Association, 1083
OGS - Ontario Genealogical Society, 1081
OGSA - Ontario Golf Superintendents' Association, 1083
OGVG - Ontario Greenhouse Vegetable Growers, 1083
OGWA - Ontario Ground Water Association, 1083
OHA - Ontario Herbalists Association, 1084
OHA - Ontario Hospital Association, 1086
OHA - Ontario Horticultural Association, 1086
OHA - Ontario Homeopathic Association, 1086
OHA - Ontario Handball Association, 1083
OHAO - Occupational Hygiene Association of Ontario, 1054
OHBA - Ontario Home Builders' Association, 1085
OHCA - Ontario Home Care Association, 1086
OHCC - Ontario Healthy Communities Coalition, 1084
OHCOW - Occupational Health Clinics for Ontario Workers, 1054
OHDQ - Ordre des hygiénistes dentaires du Québec, 1121
OHEA - Ontario Home Economics Association, 1086
OHF - Ontario Hockey Federation, 1084
OHHA - Ontario Halfway House Association, 1083
OHHA - Ontario Healthcare Housekeepers' Association Inc., 1084
OHLA - Ontario Health Libraries Association, 1084
OHRA - Open Harbour Refugee Association, 1114
OHRIA - Ontario Horse Racing Industry Association, 1086
OHRSA - Ontario Home Respiratory Services Association, 1086
OHS - Ottawa Humane Society, 1130
OHS - Ontario Historical Society, 1084
OHS - Okanagan Historical Society, 1055
OHT - Ontario Heritage Trust, 1084
OHTA - Ontario Horse Trials Association, 1086
OHTN - Ontario HIV Treatment Network, 1084
OIA - Ontario Institute of Agrologists, 1087
OIAA - Ontario Insurance Adjusters Association, 1088

OIC - Optimist International Canada, 1116
OIF - Organisation internationale de la Francophonie, 1581
OIFPA - Ontario Industrial Fire Protection Association, 1087
OIFQ - Ordre des ingénieurs forestiers du Québec, 1123
OIIAQ - Ordre des infirmières et infirmiers auxiliaires du Québec, 1121
OIIQ - Ordre des infirmières et infirmiers du Québec, 1121
OIMP - Ontario Independent Meat Processors, 1087
OIQ - Ordre des ingénieurs du Québec, 1122
OIRCA - Ontario Industrial Roofing Contractors' Association, 1087
OIW - Ottawa Independent Writers, 1130
OJA - Ontario Jiu-Jitsu Association, 1088
OJCA - Ottawa Japanese Community Association Inc., 1131
OJOA - Ontario Jaguar Owners Association, 1088
OKA - Ontario Kinesiology Association, 1088
OKSA - Ontario Katahdin Sheep Association Inc., 1088
OL - Operation Lifesaver, 1115
OLA - Ontario Luge Association, 1089
OLA - Ontario Library Association, 1088
OLA - Ontario Lung Association, 1089
OLBA - Ontario Library Boards' Association, 1089
OLC - Essential Skills Ontario, 696
OLGH - Our Lady of Good Health Tamil Parish, 1133
OLHI - OmbudService for Life & Health Insurance, 1057
OLITA - Ontario Library & Information Technology Association, 1088
OLMA - Ontario Lumber Manufacturers' Association, 1089
OLMAA - Ontario Labour-Management Arbitrators Association, 1088
OLOA - Ontario Limousine Owners Association, 1089
OLP - Ontario Liberal Party, 1088
OLTCA - Ontario Long Term Care Association, 1089
OM - Operation Mobilization Canada, 1116
OMA - Ontario Medical Association, 1090
OMA - Ontario Mining Association, 1091
OMA - Ontario Museum Association, 1092
OMA - Ottawa Muslim Association, 1131
OMA - Ontario Masters Athletics, 1090
OMAAA - Ontario Municipal Administrators' Association, 1092
OMAC - Out-of-Home Marketing Association of Canada, 1133
OMBA - Ontario Monument Builders Association, 1091
OMCA - Ontario Motor Coach Association, 1091
OMCA - Ontario Masonry Contractors' Association, 1090
OMCC - Oro-Medonte Chamber of Commerce, 1127
OMCKRA - Ontario Marathon Canoe & Kayak Racing Association, 1090
OMEA - Ontario Music Educators' Association, 1093
OMF - OMF International - Canada, 1057
OMFA - Ontario Music Festivals Association, 1093
OMHA - Ontario Minor Hockey Association, 1091
OMHC - Okanagan Miniature Horse Club, 1055
OMHL - Office municipal d'habitation de Longueuil, 1055
OMHRA - Ontario Municipal Human Resources Association, 1092
OMIA - Ontario Mutual Insurance Association, 1093
OMLA - Ontario Muzzle Loading Association, 1093
OMLTA - Ontario Modern Language Teachers Association, 1091

Acronym Index

OMMC - Organization of Military Museums of Canada, 1125
OMMI - Ontario Municipal Management Institute, 1092
OMMI - Les Oblates Missionnaires de Marie Immaculée, 1054
OMPAC - Organisation multiressources pour les personnes atteintes de cancer, 1125
OMREB - Okanagan Mainline Real Estate Board, 1055
OMSA - Ontario Medical Students Association, 1090
OMSPA - Ontario Maple Syrup Producers' Association, 1090
OMSSA - Ontario Municipal Social Services Association, 1092
OMTA - Ontario Milk Transport Association, 1091
OMTRA - Ontario Municipal Tax & Revenue Association, 1092
OMVA - Ontario Military Vehicle Association, 1091
OMVIC - Ontario Motor Vehicle Industry Council, 1091
OMVQ - Ordre des médecins vétérinaires du Québec, 1123
OMWA - Ontario Municipal Water Association, 1092
ONA - Ontario Nurses' Association, 1094
ONA - Ontario Numismatic Association, 1094
ONB - Orienteering New Brunswick, 1126
ONCAT - Ontario Council on Articulation and Transfer, 1075
ONECA - Ontario Native Education Counselling Association, 1093
ONEIA - Ontario Environment Industry Association, 1078
ONF - Ontario Neurotrauma Foundation, 1093
ONGIA - Ontario Gang Investigators Association, 1081
ONPHA - Ontario Non-Profit Housing Association, 1093
ONSA BC - Occupational Nurses' Specialty Association of British Columbia, 1054
ONTABA - Ontario Association for Behaviour Analysis, 1061
OnTRA - Ontario Therapeutic Riding Association, 1110
ONWA - Ontario Native Women's Association, 1093
OOA - Ontario Opticians Association, 1094
OOAQ - Ordre des orthophonistes et audiologistes du Québec, 1123
OOHNA - Ontario Occupational Health Nurses Association, 1094
OOM - Opticians of Manitoba, 1116
OOOQ - Ordre des opticiens d'ordonnances du Québec, 1123
OP - Ontario Philharmonic, 1095
OPA - Ottawa Police Association, 1131
OPA - Ontario Plowmen's Association, 1096
OPA - Ontario Psychological Association, 1098
OPA - Ontario Parks Association, 1095
OPA - Ontario Pharmacists' Association, 1095
OPA - Ontario Psychiatric Association, 1098
OPA - Ontario Physiotherapy Association, 1096
OPA - Ontario Paramedic Association, 1094
OPA - Ontario Powerlifting Association, 1097
OPA - Ontario Prospectors Association, 1098
OPA - Ontario Physique Association, 1096
OPAM - Organic Producers Association of Manitoba Co-operative Inc., 1125
OPB - Ontario Potato Board, 1097
OPBA - Ontario Public Buyers Association, 1098
OPBA - Ontario Pinzgauer Breeders Association, 1096
OPC - Ontario Principals' Council, 1097
OPC - Orthotics Prosthetics Canada, 1127
OPCA - Ontario Painting Contractors Association, 1094
OPCEA - Ontario Pollution Control Equipment Association, 1096
OPFA - Ontario Professional Foresters Association, 1097

OPFFA - Ontario Professional Fire Fighters Association, 1097
OPHA - Ontario Public Health Association, 1098
OPHA - Ontario Percheron Horse Association Inc., 1095
OPHEA - Ontario Physical & Health Education Association, 1095
OPI - Ontario Petroleum Institute Inc., 1095
OPIA - Ontario Plumbing Inspectors Association, 1096
OPIA - Ontario Printing & Imaging Association, 1097
OPIQ - Ordre professionnel des inhalothérapeutes du Québec, 1124
OPIRG - Ontario Public Interest Research Group, 1099
OPLA - Ontario Public Library Association, 1099
OPMA - Ontario Podiatric Medical Association, 1096
OPP - Ordre des psychoéducateurs et psychoéducatrices du Québec, 1123
OPPA - Ontario Provincial Police Association, 1098
OPPI - Ontario Professional Planners Institute, 1098
OPPMB - Ontario Pork Producers' Marketing Board, 1097
OPPQ - Ordre professionnel de la physiothérapie du Québec, 1124
OPQ - Ordre des pharmaciens du Québec, 1123
OPQ - L'Ordre des psychologues du Québec, 1123
OPS - Ottawa Philatelic Society, 1131
OPSBA - Ontario Public School Boards Association, 1099
OPSEU - Ontario Public Service Employees Union, 1099
OPSOA - Ontario Public Supervisory Officers' Association, 1100
OPSQ - Ordre professionnel des sexologues du Québec, 1124
OPSWA - Ontario Personal Support Worker Association, 1095
OPT - Options for Sexual Health, 1117
OPTA - Ontario Public Transit Association, 1100
OPTA - Ontario Provincial Trapshooting Association, 1098
OPTA - Ojibway Power Toboggan Association, 1055
OPTMQ - Ordre professionnel des technologistes médicaux du Québec, 1124
OPTSQ - Ordre professionnel des travailleurs sociaux du Québec, 1125
OPWA - Ontario Public Works Association, 1100
OPWSA - Ontario Prader-Willi Syndrome Association, 1097
OQ - Orienteering Québec, 1126
OQPAC - Organisation québécoise des personnes atteintes de cancer, 1125
ORA - Ontario Ringette Association, 1102
ORA - Ontario Rowing Association, 1102
ORA - Ontario Rodeo Association, 1102
ORA - Ontario Rifle Association, 1102
ORA - Ontario Rheumatology Association, 1102
ORAC - Ontario Refrigeration & Air Conditioning Contractors Association, 1101
ORAD - Ontario Rainbow Alliance of the Deaf, 1100
ORBA - Ontario Road Builders' Association, 1102
ORC - Outdoor Recreation Council of British Columbia, 1133
ORCA - Ontario Retirement Communities Association, 1102
ORCC - Ottawa Rape Crisis Centre, 1131
ORCGA - Ontario Regional Common Ground Alliance, 1101
ORCKA - Ontario Recreational Canoeing & Kayaking Association, 1101

ORCOL - Ontario Research Council on Leisure, 1101
ORCS - Ontario Respiratory Care Society, 1101
ORE - Olds Regional Exhibition, 1057
OREA - Ontario Real Estate Association, 1100
OREB - Ottawa Real Estate Board, 1131
ORFA - Ontario Recreation Facilities Association, 1100
ORG - Ontario Recovery Group Inc., 1100
ORHMA - Ontario Restaurant, Hotel & Motel Association, 1101
ORMF - Oak Ridges Moraine Foundation, 1053
ORMTA - Ontario Registered Music Teachers' Association, 1101
ORNAA - Operating Room Nurses of Alberta Association, 1115
ORNAC - Operating Room Nurses Association of Canada, 1115
ORNANS - Operating Room Nurses Association of Nova Scotia, 1115
ORNAO - Operating Room Nurses Association of Ontario, 1115
ORPIC - Ontario Regional Poison Information Centre, 1101
ORSA - Ontario Rett Syndrome Association, 1102
ORSA - Ontario Rural Softball Association, 1103
ORT - World ORT Union, 1607
ORTA - Oak Ridges Trail Association, 1053
OS - Open Space Arts Society, 1114
OSA - Ontario Shuffleboard Association, 1104
OSA - Ontario Soccer Association, 1105
OSA - Ontario Shorthorn Association, 1104
OSA - Ontario Simmental Association, 1104
OSA - Ontario Spondylitis Association, 1108
OSA - Ontario Society of Artists, 1107
OSAC - Organization of Saskatchewan Arts Councils, 1126
OSAPA - Ontario Steam & Antique Preservers Association, 1109
OSAS - Ontario Standardbred Adoption Society, 1109
OSB - Sisters of St. Benedict, 1301
OSBA - Ontario School Bus Association, 1103
OSC - Ottawa Safety Council, 1131
OSC - Ontario Society of Chiropodists, 1107
OSC - Ontario Securities Commission, 1104
OSCA - Ontario School Counsellors' Association, 1103
OSCA - Ottawa South Community Association, 1131
OSCIA - Ontario Soil & Crop Improvement Association, 1108
OSEA - Ontario Sustainable Energy Association, 1109
OSEE - Ontario Society for Environmental Education, 1105
OSEM - Ontario Society for Environmental Management, 1105
OSF - Old Strathcona Foundation, 1056
OSGA - Ontario Senior Games Association, 1104
OSGA - Ontario Sportfishing Guides' Association, 1108
OSGA - Ontario Seed Growers Association, 1104
OSGC - Ontario Sikh & Gurudwara Council, 1104
OSHA - Ontario Sledge Hockey Association, 1105
OSHOF - Ottawa Sports Hall of Fame Inc., 1131
OSJ - Knights Hospitallers, Sovereign Order of St. John of Jerusalem, Knights of Malta, Grand Priory of Canada, 892
OSJM - Orchestre symphonique des jeunes de Montréal, 1118
OSJWI - Orchestre symphonique des jeunes du West Island, 1118
OSL - Ontario Safety League, 1103
OSLA - Ontario Association of Speech-Language Pathologists & Audiologists, 1066

OSLA - Ontario School Library Association, 1103
OSM - Ontario Sheet Metal Contractors Association, 1104
OSMA - Ontario Sheep Marketing Agency, 1104
OSMT - Ontario Society of Medical Technologists, 1107
OSNPPH - Ontario Society of Nutrition Professionals in Public Health, 1107
OSO - Ottawa Symphony Orchestra Inc., 1132
OSO - Oakville Symphony Orchestra, 1053
OSOT - Ontario Society of Occupational Therapists, 1107
OSP - Ontario Society of Psychotherapists, 1108
OSP - Ontario Society of Periodontists, 1107
OSPAR - OSPAR Commission, 1582
OSPCA - Ontario Society for the Prevention of Cruelty to Animals, 1105
OSPE - Ontario Society of Professional Engineers, 1107
OSPS - Okanagan Similkameen Parks Society, 1056
OSQ - Jeux Olympiques Spéciaux du Québec Inc., 871
OSRDF - Ontario Square & Round Dance Federation, 1108
OSS - Orchestre symphonique de Sherbrooke, 1118
OSSA - Ontario Speed Skating Association, 1108
OSSA - Ontario Skeet Shooting Association, 1104
OSSCO - Ontario Society of Senior Citizens' Organizations, 1108
OSSGA - Ontario Stone, Sand & Gravel Association, 1109
OSSLSJ - Orchestre symphonique du Saguenay-Lac-St-Jean, 1119
OSSTF - Ontario Secondary School Teachers' Federation, 1103
OSTR - Orchestre symphonique de Trois-Rivières, 1118
OSUM - Ontario Small Urban Municipalities, 1105
OSWCA - Ontario Sewer & Watermain Construction Association, 1104
OT - Orchestra Toronto, 1117
OTA - Ontario Tennis Association, 1110
OTA - Ontario Trucking Association, 1111
OTA - Organic Trade Association, 1581
OTC - Ontario Trails Council, 1111
OTC - Ontario Traffic Council, 1110
OTC - Ogemawahj Tribal Council, 1055
OTCQ - Office du tourisme et des congrès de Québec, 1055
OTF - Ontario Teachers' Federation, 1110
OTLA - Ontario Trial Lawyers Association, 1111
OTPQ - Ordre des technologues professionnels du Québec, 1124
OTRA - Ontario Trail Riders Association, 1111
OTRP - Office de Tourisme du Rocher-Percé, 1055
OTS - Ontario Thoracic Society, 1110
OTSA - Ottawa Tamil Seniors Association, 1132
OTTA - Ontario Table Tennis Association, 1109
OTTDQ - Ordre des techniciens et techniciennes dentaires du Québec, 1124
OTTIAQ - Ordre des traducteurs, terminologues et interprètes agréés du Québec, 1124
OUA - Ontario University Athletics, 1112
OUC - Ontario Underwater Council, 1112
OUFC - Ontario Urban Forest Council, 1112
OUQ - Ordre des urbanistes du Québec, 1124
OUSA - Ontario Undergraduate Student Alliance, 1111
OUSA - Ontario University Registrars' Association, 1112
OVA - Ontario Volleyball Association, 1112
OVCA - Ottawa Valley Curling Association, 1132
OVHLA - Ottawa Valley Health Libraries Association, 1132

Acronym Index

OVHS - Ottawa Valley Historical Society, 1132
OVMA - Ontario Veterinary Medical Association, 1112
OVMA - Ontario Vegetation Management Association, 1112
OVRA - Ontario Vintage Radio Association, 1112
OVTA - Ottawa Valley Tourist Association, 1132
OWA - Ontario Weightlifting Association, 1113
OWA - One World Arts, 1058
OWA - Ontario Waterpower Association, 1113
OWA - Orphan Well Association, 1127
OWHA - Ontario Women's Hockey Association, 1113
OWHN - Ontario Women's Health Network, 1113
OWJN - Ontario Women's Justice Network, 1113
OWMA - Ontario Waste Management Association, 1112
OWN - The Older Women's Network, 1056
OWP - Ontario Water Polo Association Incorporated, 1113
OWSA - Ontario Water Ski Association, 1113
OWSA - Ontario Wheelchair Sports Association, 1113
OWWA - Ontario Water Works Association, 1113
OXDA - Ontario DX Association, 1077
OYO - Ottawa Youth Orchestra Academy, 1132
OYSO - Orillia Youth Symphony Orchestra, 1126
OZCF - Ontario Zoroastrian Community Foundation, 1114

P

P10 - Projet 10, 1188
P4E - People for Education, 1151
PA - The Publishers Association, 1585
PAA - Psychologists Association of Alberta, 1192
PAA - Protected Areas Association of Newfoundland & Labrador, 1190
PAAC - The Public Affairs Association of Canada, 1192
PAACL - Port Alberni Association for Community Living, 1165
PABC - Physiotherapy Association of British Columbia, 1158
PAC - Packaging Association of Canada, 1136
PAC - Polish Alliance of Canada, 1163
PAC - Parrot Association of Canada, 1143
PACC - Placentia Area Chamber of Commerce, 1161
PACE - Planetary Association for Clean Energy, Inc., 1161
PACE - Pacific Corridor Enterprise Council, 1135
PACS - Polish Association for Canadian Studies, 1584
PACT - Professional Association of Canadian Theatres, 1181
PACT - Pickering & Ajax Citizens Together for the Environment, 1159
PACWEST - Pacific Western Athletic Association, 1136
PAD - Parent Action on Drugs, 1139
PADLC - Port Alberni & District Labour Council, 1165
PAEX - Prince Albert Exhibition Association, 1171
PAFE - Parents as First Educators, 1140
PAFN - Pembroke Area Field Naturalists, 1149
PAFSO - Professional Association of Foreign Service Officers, 1182
PAG&SC - Prince Albert Gliding & Soaring Club, 1171
PAGE - British Columbia Teachers for Peace & Global Education, 256
PAHF - Pan American Hockey Federation, 1138
PAIRN - Professional Association of Internes & Residents of Newfoundland, 1182
PALS - Project Adult Literacy Society, 1187

PAM - Psychological Association of Manitoba, 1191
PAM - Paramedic Association of Manitoba, 1138
PAM - Philippine Association of Manitoba, Inc., 1157
PAMBA - Programme d'aide aux membres du barreau, 1187
PAMF - Prince Albert Model Forest Association Inc., 1171
PAMI - Prairie Agricultural Machinery Institute, 1169
PANB - Paramedic Association of New Brunswick, 1138
PANL - Pharmacists' Association of Newfoundland & Labrador, 1156
PANL - Paramedic Association of Newfoundland & Labrador, 1138
PANNA - Pesticide Action Network North America, 1583
PANS - Pharmacy Association of Nova Scotia, 1157
PANS - Police Association of Nova Scotia, 1163
PAO - Police Association of Ontario, 1163
PAOC - Pentecostal Assemblies of Canada, 1150
PAONL - The Pentecostal Assemblies of Newfoundland & Labrador, 1150
PAPEI - Psychological Association of Prince Edward Island, 1192
PAPTAC - Pulp & Paper Technical Association of Canada, 1194
PARA - Professional Association of Residents of Alberta, 1182
PARC - Promoting Awareness of RSD & CRPS in Canada, 1188
PARCS - Provincial Association of Resort Communities of Saskatchewan, 1190
PARD - PARD Therapeutic Riding, 1139
PARDS - Peace Area Riding for the Disabled, 1146
PARIM - Professional Association of Residents & Interns of Manitoba, 1182
PARI-MP - Professional Association of Residents in the Maritime Provinces, 1182
PARN - PARN Your Community AIDS Resource Network, 1143
PARO - Professional Association of Residents of Ontario, 1182
PAS - Pharmacists' Association of Saskatchewan, Inc., 1156
PAS - Parkinson Alberta Society, 1141
PASAN - Prisoners' HIV/AIDS Support Action Network, 1180
PASC - Petroleum Accountants Society of Canada, 1154
PASO - Pan American Sports Organization, 1582
PATA - Pacific Asia Travel Association (Eastern Canada Chapter), 1134
PATH - Professional Association of Therapeutic Horsemanship International, 1584
PAVRO - Professional Association of Volunteer Leaders Ontario, 1183
PAY - Physiotherapy Association of Yukon, 1159
PBBA - Provincial Black Basketball Association, 1190
PBHS - Pacific Bluegrass Heritage Society, 1135
PBI - Peace Brigades International (Canada), 1146
PBLO - Pro Bono Law Ontario, 1180
PC - Paddle Canada, 1137
PC - Population Connection, 1584
PC SPCA - Pincher Creek Humane Society, 1160
PCA - Peace Curling Association, 1147
PCAE - Pakistan Canada Association of Edmonton, 1137
PCAWA - Peel Committee Against Woman Abuse, 1147
PCC - Presbyterian Church in Canada, 1170
PCC - Poplar Council of Canada, 1165
PCC - Prostate Cancer Canada, 1189

PCCA-BC - Pakistani Canadian Cultural Association of British Columbia, 1137
PCGFA - Peace Country Beef & Forage Association, 1147
PCHF - Prince County Hospital Foundation, 1171
PCIC - Parkdale Community Information Centre, 1140
PCMA - Professional Convention Management Association - Canada West Chapter, 1183
PCMA - Private Capital Markets Association of Canada, 1180
PCMH - Parents for Children's Mental Health, 1140
PCP - Pacific Cinémathèque Pacifique, 1135
PCPI - Parent Cooperative Preschools International, 1139
PCQ - Parti communiste du Québec, 1143
PCR - Parti communiste révolutionnaire, 1144
PCS - Partenariat communauté en santé, 1143
PCWF - Phoenix Community Works Foundation, 1157
PCWM - Provincial Council of Women of Manitoba Inc., 1190
PDAC - Portage & District Arts Council, 1166
PDAC - Prospectors & Developers Association of Canada, 1189
PDACL - Parksville & District Association for Community Living, 1142
PDCA - Pembroke District Construction Association, 1149
PDCAC - Penticton & District Community Arts Council, 1150
PDCRS - Penticton & District Community Resources Society, 1150
PDRA - Paint & Decorating Retailers Association, 1582
PDSCL - Penticton & District Society for Community Living, 1150
PEA - Professional Employees Association (Ind.), 1183
PEAC - Physiotherapy Education Accreditation Canada, 1159
PE-BC - Physical Education in British Columbia, 1158
PEBC - The Pharmacy Examining Board of Canada, 1157
PECAC - Prince Edward County Arts Council, 1171
PECCTAC - Prince Edward County Chamber of Tourism & Commerce, 1171
PEDVAC - PEDVAC Foundation, 1147
PEGNL - Professional Engineers & Geoscientists Newfoundland & Labrador, 1183
PEI ANC - Prince Edward Island Association for Newcomers to Canada, 1172
PEI CPA - Prince Edward Island Physiotherapy Association, 1176
PEIAA - Prince Edward Island Aquaculture Alliance, 1171
PEIACL - Prince Edward Island Association for Community Living, 1172
PEIAE - Prince Edward Island Association of Exhibitions, 1172
PEIAMRT - Prince Edward Island Association of Medical Radiation Technologists, 1172
PEIAO - Prince Edward Island Association of Optometrists, 1172
PEIASW - Prince Edward Island Association of Social Workers, 1172
PEIBUA - Prince Edward Island Baseball Umpires Association, 1172
PEIBWA - Prince Edward Island Business Women's Association, 1172
PEICA - Prince Edward Island Chiropractic Association, 1173
PEICA - Prince Edward Island Curling Association, 1173
PEI-CA - PEI Cricket Association, 1148
PEICC - Prince Edward Island Crafts Council, 1173
PEICOD - Prince Edward Island Council of People with Disabilities, 1173

PEICP - Prince Edward Island Cattle Producers, 1173
PEICP - Prince Edward Island College of Physiotherapists, 1173
PEIDA - Prince Edward Island Dietetic Association, 1173
PEIDHA - Prince Edward Island Draft Horse Association, 1173
PEIEN - Prince Edward Island Eco-Net, 1173
PEIFA - Prince Edward Island Fencing Association, 1174
PEIFA - Prince Edward Island Federation of Agriculture, 1174
PEIFA - Prince Edward Island Fishermen's Association Ltd., 1174
PEIFIA - Prince Edward Island Forest Improvement Association, 1174
PEIGA - Prince Edward Island Golf Association, 1174
PEIGNA - Prince Edward Island Gerontological Nurses Association, 1174
PEIGS - Prince Edward Island Genealogical Society Inc., 1174
PEIHRIA - Prince Edward Island Harness Racing Industry Association, 1174
PEIHS - Prince Edward Island Humane Society, 1175
PEIHSF - Prince Edward Island Home & School Federation Inc., 1175
PEIIA - Prince Edward Island Institute of Agrologists, 1175
PEIKA - Prince Edward Island Karate Association, 1175
PEIMHF - Prince Edward Island Museum & Heritage Foundation, 1175
PEIMLS - Prince Edward Island Society for Medical Laboratory Science, 1177
PEINU - Prince Edward Island Nurses' Union, 1176
PEIOTS - Prince Edward Island Occupational Therapy Society, 1176
PEIPA - Prince Edward Island Police Association, 1176
PEIPB - Prince Edward Island Pharmacy Board, 1176
PEIPLA - PEI Powerlifting Association, 1148
PEIPRA - Prince Edward Island Rifle Association, 1176
PEIREA - Prince Edward Island Real Estate Association, 1176
PEIRSAC - Prince Edward Island Rape & Sexual Assault Centre, 1176
PEIRU - Prince Edward Island Rugby Union, 1177
PEISA - Prince Edward Island Soccer Association, 1177
PEISA - PEI Sailing Association, 1149
PEISAA - Prince Edward Island School Athletic Association, 1177
PEISCF - Prince Edward Island Senior Citizens Federation Inc., 1177
PEISHA - Prince Edward Island Speech & Hearing Association, 1177
PEISO - Prince Edward Island Symphony Society, 1178
PEITF - Prince Edward Island Teachers' Federation, 1178
PEITLA - PEI Teacher-Librarians' Association, 1149
PEITSC - Prince Edward Island Trucking Sector Council, 1178
PEITTA - Prince Edward Island Table Tennis Association, 1178
PEIVMA - Prince Edward Island Veterinary Medical Association, 1178
PEIWI - Prince Edward Island Women's Institute, 1178
PEMAC - Plant Engineering & Maintenance Association of Canada, 1162
PEN - The Canadian Centre/International P.E.N., 354
PEO - Professional Engineers Ontario, 1183
PEPSA - Professional Engineers for Public Safety Association, 1183
PES - Pediatric Endocrine Society, 1583

ASSOCIATIONS CANADA 2018

Acronym Index

PESDA - Printing Equipment & Supply Dealers' Association of Canada, 1180
PETA - People for the Ethical Treatment of Animals, 1583
PFAC - Pet Food Association of Canada, 1153
PFC - People First of Canada, 1151
PFC - Portage Friendship Centre Inc., 1166
PFC - Philanthropic Foundations Canada, 1157
PFGA - Prairie Fruit Growers Association, 1169
PFI - Pagan Federation International - Canada, 1137
PFLA - Private Forest Landowners Association, 1180
PFLAG - Parents, Families & Friends of Lesbians & Gays, 1582
PFN - Peninsula Field Naturalists, 1149
PFN - Peterborough Field Naturalists, 1153
PFPG - Plastics Foodservice Packaging Group, 1584
PFSRB - Partners FOR the Saskatchewan River Basin, 1144
PGA - Parliamentarians for Global Action, 1582
PGA - Potato Growers of Alberta, 1168
PGA of BC - Professional Golfers' Assocation of British Columbia, 1185
PGBIG - Prince George Brain Injured Group, 1179
PGBRS - Prince George Backcountry Recreation Society, 1179
PGC - Playwrights Guild of Canada, 1162
PGCA - Prince George Construction Association, 1179
PGCOC - Prince George Chamber of Commerce, 1179
PGIA - Printing & Graphics Industries Association of Alberta, 1180
PGNC - Prince George Naturalists Club, 1179
PGOSA - Parksville Golden Oldies Sports Association, 1142
PGPOTTA - Prince George Parents of Twins & Triplets Association, 1179
PGS - Physicians for Global Survival (Canada), 1158
PGSO - Prince George Symphony Orchestra Society, 1179
PHABC - Public Health Association of British Columbia, 1192
PHAC - Peruvian Horse Association of Canada, 1152
PHANS - Public Health Association of Nova Scotia, 1192
PHPA - Professional Hockey Players' Association, 1185
PHS - Peterborough Historical Society, 1153
PHSC - Photographic Historical Society of Canada, 1157
PHSC - Postal History Society of Canada, 1168
PHSC - Grey, Bruce, Dufferin, & Simcoe Postal History Study Group, 790
PHTCC - Pool & Hot Tub Council of Canada, 1164
PI - Probe International, 1181
PIA - Parkdale Intercultural Association, 1140
PIAC - The Public Interest Advocacy Centre, 1192
PIAC - Pension Investment Association of Canada, 1150
PIAMP - Projet d'Intervention auprès des mineurs-res prostitués-ées, 1188
PIBC - Planning Institute of British Columbia, 1162
PIC - Pitch-In Canada, 1160
PIC - Poultry Industry Council, 1168
PICES - North Pacific Marine Science Organization, 1032
PIFN - Pender Island Field Naturalists, 1149
PIJAC - Pet Industry Joint Advisory Council, 1153
PIMS - Pacific Institute for the Mathematical Sciences, 1135
PIN - Portuguese Interagency Network, 1167
PIPSC - The Professional Institute of the Public Service of Canada, 1185
PIR - Partners in Research, 1144

PIRS - Pacific Immigrant Resources Society, 1135
PISE - Pacific Institute for Sport Excellence, 1135
PJSA - Peace & Justice Studies Association, 1583
PKAR - Peterborough & the Kawarthas Association of Realtors Inc., 1153
PLA - Peel Law Association, 1148
PLAA - Professional Locksmith Association of Alberta, 1186
PLAN - Planned Lifetime Advocacy Network, 1161
PLAN - Planning & Land Administrators of Nunavut, 1162
PLCAC - Pipe Line Contractors Association of Canada, 1160
PLEA - PLEA Community Services Society of BC, 1162
PLEA Sask. - Public Legal Education Association of Saskatchewan, Inc., 1192
PLEAC - Public Legal Education Association of Canada, 1192
PLFC - Plastic Loose Fill Council, 1584
PLIAN - Public Legal Information Association of Newfoundland, 1192
PLN - Positive Living North: No kheyoh t'sih'en t'sehena Society, 1168
PLQ - Les producteurs de lait du Québec, 1181
PLQ - Parti libéral du Québec, 1144
PLRAC - Peace-Laird Regional Arts Council, 1147
PLRCC - Pigeon Lake Regional Chamber of Commerce, 1159
PMA - Polyurethane Manufacturers Association, 1584
PMAA - Police Martial Arts Association Inc., 1163
PMAA - Pest Management Association of Alberta, 1152
PMAC - Portfolio Management Association of Canada, 1167
PMAI - Photo Marketing Association International - Canada, 1157
PMC - Peel Multicultural Council, 1148
PMC - Periodical Marketers of Canada, 1152
PMI - Project Management Institute, 1585
PMIA - Music BC Industry Association, 983
PMLQ - Parti marxiste-léniniste du Québec, 1144
PMTC - Private Motor Truck Council of Canada, 1180
PNEIG - Provincial Nurse Educator Interest Group, 1191
PNLA - Pacific Northwest Library Association, 1135
PNWER - Pacific NorthWest Economic Region, 1582
POABC - Plumbing Officials' Association of British Columbia, 1163
POABC - Prosthetics & Orthotics Association of British Columbia, 1190
POAO - Probation Officers Association of Ontario, 1181
POC - Professional Organizers in Canada, 1186
POV - Pacific Opera Victoria, 1135
PPA - Peterborough Police Association, 1154
PPASS/BC - Post-Polio Awareness & Support Society of BC, 1168
PPDAM - Postpartum Depression Association of Manitoba, 1168
PPDM - Professional Petroleum Data Management Association, 1186
PPE - Parents partenaires en éducation, 1140
PPEC - Paper & Paperboard Packaging Environmental Council, 1138
PPF - The Pollution Probe Foundation, 1164
PPMA - Professional Property Managers Association Inc., 1186
PPN-MB - Post-Polio Network Manitoba Inc., 1168
PPOC - Professional Photographers of Canada, 1186
PPOC - Planned Parenthood Ottawa, 1161
PPP - Pacific Peoples' Partnership, 1135

PPPC - Pulp & Paper Products Council, 1194
PPPSS - Pacific Post Partum Support Society, 1136
PPSC - Sexual Health Centre Saskatoon, 1293
PPT - Planned Parenthood of Toronto, 1161
PPWC - Pulp, Paper & Woodworkers of Canada, 1194
PPWR - Planned Parenthood Waterloo Region, 1162
PQ - Parti québécois, 1144
PQRA - Province of Québec Rifle Association, 1190
PRDA - Pacific Riding for Developing Abilities, 1136
PRDCC - Prince Rupert & District Chamber of Commerce, 1179
PRGS - Prairie Rock & Gem Society, 1169
PRHHA - Prairie Region Halfway House Association, 1169
PRIS - Peace Region Internet Society, 1147
PRLN - Project READ Literacy Network Waterloo-Wellington, 1188
PRNABC - Perioperative Registered Nurses Association of British Columbia, 1152
PRO - Parks & Recreation Ontario, 1142
PRPA - Peel Regional Police Association, 1148
PSA - Paralympic Sports Association (Alberta), 1138
PSA - Pain Society of Alberta, 1137
PSAC - Petroleum Services Association of Canada, 1154
PSAC - Public Service Alliance of Canada, 1193
PSBAA - Public School Boards' Association of Alberta, 1193
PSBC - Parkinson Society British Columbia, 1141
PSC - Police Sector Council, 1163
PSF - Pacific Salmon Foundation, 1136
PSHSA - Public Services Health & Safety Association, 1193
PSI - Public Services International, 1585
PSMR - Parkinson Society Maritime Region, 1141
PSNM - Pacific Society of Nutrition Management, 1136
PSO - Peterborough Symphony Orchestra, 1154
PSPC - Peterborough Social Planning Council, 1154
PSQI - Parents-secours du Québec inc., 1140
PSS - Parkinson Society Saskatchewan, 1141
PSSP - Professional Student Services Personnel, 1186
PSSS - Parent Support Services Society of BC, 1139
PTAC - Petroleum Technology Alliance Canada, 1154
PTAO - Provincial Towing Association (Ontario), 1191
PTE - Prairie Theatre Exchange, 1170
PTG - Piano Technicians Guild Inc., 1583
PTMAA - Petroleum Tank Management Association of Alberta, 1154
PTPLC - Provincial & Territorial Public Library Council, 1190
PTSA - Pharmacy Technician Society of Alberta, 1157
PUHA - Pacific Urchin Harvesters Association, 1136
PVEA - Peace Valley Environment Association, 1147
PVQ - Parti Vert du Québec, 1144
PWABC - Public Works Association of British Columbia, 1193
PWAC - Professional Writers Association of Canada, 1187
PWC - People, Words & Change, 1152
PWM - Playwrights' Workshop Montréal, 1162
PWN - Positive Women's Network, 1168
PWNHC - Prince of Wales Northern Heritage Centre, 1179
PWP - Parents Without Partners Inc., 1582
PWRDF - The Primate's World Relief & Development Fund, 1170

PWSAO - Provincial Women's Softball Association of Ontario, 1191
PWU - Power Workers' Union, 1169
PYO - Positive Youth Outreach, 1168

Q

QAAC - Quaker Aboriginal Affairs Committee, 1195
QAC - Quinte Arts Council, 1201
QAHN - Québec Anglophone Heritage Network, 1195
QAIRP - Quebec Association of Insolvency & Restructuring Professionals, 1196
QAIS - Québec Association of Independent Schools, 1196
QAMFT - Québec Association of Marriage & Family Therapy, 1196
QANM - Québec Association of Naturopathic Medicine, 1196
QAS - Quickdraw Animation Society, 1201
QASL - Queens Association for Supported Living, 1200
QBA - Quinte Beekeepers' Association, 1201
QBBE - Québec Board of Black Educators, 1196
QBHA - Québec Ball Hockey Association, 1196
QCA - Quinte Construction Association, 1201
QCLA - Quesnel Community Living Association, 1200
QCNA - Québec Community Newspaper Association, 1196
QCSS - Quad County Support Services, 1195
QDCAC - Quesnel & District Arts Council, 1200
QDCDCA - Quesnel & District Child Development Centre Association, 1200
QDF - The Québec Drama Federation, 1197
QDLC - Quesnel & District Labour Council, 1200
QELA - Quebec English Literacy Alliance, 1197
QESBA - Québec English School Boards Association, 1197
QFA - Québec Farmers' Association, 1197
QFB - Québec Federation of the Blind Inc., 1197
QFHS - Québec Family History Society, 1197
QFHSA - Québec Federation of Home & School Associations Inc., 1197
QFJ - Quakers Fostering Justice, 1195
QIA - Qikiqtani Inuit Association, 1194
QLA - Québec Library Association, 1198
QLA - Québec Lung Association, 1198
QLF (Canada) - Québec-Labrador Foundation (Canada) Inc., 1199
QSA - Québec Simmental Association, 1198
QSLNM - Québec Society of Lipidology, Nutrition & Metabolism Inc., 1199
QUFA - Queen's University Faculty Association, 1199
QUIC - Queen's University International Centre, 1200
QUILL - Quality in Lifelong Learning Network, 1195
QUINTRA - Quinte Therapeutic Riding Association, 1202
QVFC - Qu'Appelle Valley Friendship Centre, 1195
QVRRDF - Quidi Vidi Rennie's River Development Foundation, 1201
QWCC - Quinte West Chamber of Commerce, 1202
QWF - Québec Writers' Federation, 1199
QWI - Québec Women's Institutes, 1199

R

RA - Rainforest Alliance, 1586
RAA - Recreational Aircraft Association, 1208
RAAMM - Regroupement des aveugles et amblyopes du Montréal métropolitain, 1215
RAANM - Regroupement des Aidantes et Aidants Naturel(le)s de Montréal, 1214
RAAV - Regroupement des artistes en arts visuels du Québec (ind.), 1214
RABC - Radio Advisory Board of Canada, 1202
RAC - Revelstoke Arts Council, 1228

Acronym Index

RAC - Retail Advertising & Marketing Club of Canada, 1228
RAC - Radio Amateurs of Canada Inc., 1202
RAC - Railway Association of Canada, 1203
RAC - Reflexology Association of Canada, 1210
RACQ - Regroupement des assureurs de personnes à charte du Québec, 1215
RADO - Atelier RADO Inc., 180
RAGBOS - REALTORS Association of Grey Bruce Owen Sound, 1206
RAIC - Royal Architectural Institute of Canada, 1237
RAN - Rainforest Action Network, 1586
RAPSIM - Réseau d'aide aux personnes seiles et itinérantes de Montréal, 1218
RAPTCCQ - Regroupement des associations de personnes traumatisées craniocérébrales du Québec, 1214
RAQ - Réseau des services d'archives du Québec, 1222
RAQI - Radio Amateur Québec inc., 1202
RAS - Ringette Association of Saskatchewan, 1232
RASC - Royal Astronomical Society of Canada, 1238
RASCA - Realtors Association of South Central Alberta, 1206
RAUSI - Royal Alberta United Services Institute, 1237
RAWF - Royal Agricultural Winter Fair Association, 1237
RAY - Resource Assistance for Youth, 1226
RBC - Rare Breeds Canada, 1204
RBG - Royal Botanical Gardens, 1239
RBO - Regroupement de Bouches à Oreilles, 1214
RBSLSJ - Réseau BIBLIO du Saguenay-Lac-Saint-Jean, 1218
RC - Ringette Canada, 1232
RCA - Royal Canadian Academy of Arts, 1239
RCA - Rowing Canada Aviron, 1237
RCA - Recycling Council of Alberta, 1208
RCAA - Royal Canadian Artillery Association, 1239
RCAAQ - Regroupement des centres d'amitié autochtone du Québec, 1215
RCABC - Roofing Contractors Association of British Columbia, 1236
RCABC - Recreational Canoeing Association BC, 1208
RCAM - Roofing Contractors Association of Manitoba Inc., 1236
RCANS - Roofing Contractors Association of Nova Scotia, 1236
RCASC Atlantic - Royal Canadian Army Service Corps Association-(Atlantic Region), 1239
RCBC - Recycling Council of British Columbia, 1208
RCC - Retail Council of Canada, 1228
RCC - Regina Coin Club, 1211
RCCFC - Réseau des cégeps et des collèges francophones du Canada, 1219
RCCO - Royal Canadian College of Organists, 1239
RCD - Richmond County Disabled Association, 1230
RCDC - Royal College of Dentists of Canada, 1241
RCEA - Research Council Employees' Association (Ind.), 1218
RCEN - Canadian Environmental Network, 382
RCGS - The Royal Canadian Geographical Society, 1239
RCHS - Richmond County Historical Society, 1230
RCI - Royal Canadian Institute, 1240
RCL - The Royal Canadian Legion, 1240
RCLC - Rexdale Community Legal Services, 1229
RCM - Green Action Centre, 788
RCMI - Royal Canadian Military Institute, 1240
RCNA - Royal Canadian Numismatic Association, 1241

RCNBF - Royal Canadian Naval Benevolent Fund, 1240
RCO - Recycling Council of Ontario, 1208
RCPS - Richmond Caring Place Society, 1230
RCPSC - The Royal College of Physicians & Surgeons of Canada, 1241
RCR - The Royal Canadian Regiment Association, 1241
RCREB - Renfrew County Real Estate Board, 1217
RCS - The Royal Commonwealth Society of Canada, 1241
RCVAA - Restigouche County Volunteer Action Association Inc., 1228
RDBA - Registered Deposit Brokers Association, 1213
RDDCC - Red Deer Danish Canadian Club, 1209
RDDCF - Red Deer & District Community Foundation, 1209
RDLC - Regina & District Labour Council, 1211
RDoC - Resident Doctors of Canada, 1226
RDOC - Responsible Dog Owners of Canada, 1227
RDRN - Red Deer River Naturalists, 1209
REAL - Regina Exhibition Association Ltd., 1211
REAL - Rideau Environmental Action League, 1231
REAP Canada - Resource Efficient Agricultural Production, 1227
REAPS - Prince George Recycling & Environmental Action Planning Society, 1179
RECA - Real Estate Council of Alberta, 1205
RECBC - Real Estate Council of British Columbia, 1205
RECF - Regroupement des éditeurs canadiens-français, 1215
RECLAIM - Reading Council for Literacy Advance in Montréal, 1205
RECO - Real Estate Council of Ontario, 1205
RECWCAN - The Reformed Episcopal Church of Canada - Diocese of Western Canada & Alaska, 1210
REFAD - Le Réseau d'enseignement francophone à distance du Canada, 1219
REIC - Real Estate Institute of Canada, 1205
ReQIS - Réseau québécois pour l'inclusion social des personnnes sourdes et malentendantes, 1225
RES - Richard Eaton Singers, 1229
RESCON - Residential Construction Council of Ontario, 1226
RESDAC - Réseau pour le développement de l'alphabétisme et des compétences, 1225
RFA - Ryerson Faculty Association, 1244
RFABC - Recreation Facilities Association of British Columbia, 1207
RFAQ - Réseau des femmes d'affaires du Québec inc., 1219
RFB - Richmond Food Bank Society, 1230
RFCAO - Resilient Flooring Contractors Association of Ontario, 1226
RFP - Religions for Peace, 1586
RFQ - Réseau Femmes Québec, 1224
RFSSO - Réseau franco-santé du Sud de l'Ontario, 1224
RGA - Rhythmic Gymnastics Alberta, 1229
RGC(O) - Responsible Gambling Council (Ontario), 1227
RGM - Rhythmic Gymnastics Manitoba Inc., 1229
RHAM - The Regional Health Authorities of Manitoba, 1212
RHCOC - Richmond Hill Chamber of Commerce, 1230
RHGNS - Rug Hooking Guild of Nova Scotia, 1243
RHHA - Regional Halfway House Association, 1212
RHN - Richmond Hill Naturalists, 1230
RHQ - Réseau Hommes Québec, 1224
RI - Richelieu International, 1229
RIA - Responsible Investment Association, 1227

RIAC - Receivables Insurance Association of Canada, 1206
RIB - Club informatique de Brossard, 575
RIBO - Registered Insurance Brokers of Ontario, 1213
RIDC - Raspberry Industry Development Council, 1204
RIDEAU - Réseau indépendant des diffuseurs d'événements artistiques unis, 1224
RIIB - Rotman Institute for International Business, 1236
RIMS - Risk & Insurance Management Society Inc., 1233
RISA - Resource Industry Suppliers Association, 1227
RISC - Regroupement pour l'intégration sociale de Charlevoix, 1216
RIWC - Riverdale Immigrant Women's Centre, 1234
RIWC - Regina Immigrant Women Centre, 1211
RJCC - Rose & Max Rady Jewish Community Centre, 1236
RJCCQ - Regroupement des jeunes chambres de commerce du Québec, 1215
RLIFC - Red Lake Indian Friendship Centre, 1210
RLQ - Réseau des lesbiennes du Québec, 1219
RMA - Rubber Manufacturers Association, 1587
RMAA - Rural Municipal Administrators' Association of Saskatchewan, 1244
RMACL - Ridge Meadows Association of Community Living, 1232
RMC - Regina Multicultural Council, 1212
RMC - Regroupement des Marocains au Canada, 1215
RMCAO - Concrete Ontario, 610
RMCS - Richmond Multicultural Community Services, 1231
RMHC - Ronald McDonald House Charities of Canada, 1235
RMI - The Rocky Mountain Institute, 1586
RMRA - Roncesvalles Macdonell Residents' Association, 1235
RMTAO - Registered Massage Therapists' Association of Ontario, 1213
RMTBC - Registered Massage Therapists' Association of British Columbia, 1213
RNANT/NU - The Registered Nurses Association of the Northwest Territories & Nunavut, 1213
RNAO - Registered Nurses' Association of Ontario, 1213
RNB - Ringette New Brunswick, 1233
RNBA - Rowing New Brunswick Aviron, 1237
RNBRA - Royal New Brunswick Rifle Association Inc., 1242
RNCA - Royal Newfoundland Constabulary Association, 1242
RNRF - Renewable Natural Resources Foundation, 1586
RNS - Recreation Nova Scotia, 1207
RNSHS - The Royal Nova Scotia Historical Society, 1242
RO - Racquetball Ontario, 1202
ROBVQ - Regroupement des organismes de bassins versants du Québec, 1215
ROHQ - Regroupement des offices d'habitation du Québec, 1215
ROMA - Rural Ontario Municipal Association, 1244
ROS - Regina Orchid Society, 1212
RPAC - Retirement Planning Association of Canada, 1228
RPAY - Recreation & Parks Association of the Yukon, 1207
RPEI - Ringette PEI, 1233
RPFANS - Registered Professional Foresters Association of Nova Scotia, 1214
RPFO - Réseau du patrimoine franco-ontarien, 1222
RPNAO - Registered Practical Nurses Association of Ontario, 1213
RPNAS - Registered Psychiatric Nurses Association of Saskatchewan, 1214

RPSC - The Royal Philatelic Society of Canada, 1242
RQAM - Réseau québécois de l'asthme et de la MPOC, 1225
RQD - Regroupement québécois de la danse, 1216
RQGE - Réseau québécois des groupes écologistes, 1225
RQMO - Regroupement québécois des maladies orphelines, 1216
RQOH - Réseau québécois des OSBL d'habitation, 1225
RQuODE - Regroupement québécois des organismes pour le développement de l'employabilité, 1216
RRAA - Red River Apiarists' Association, 1210
RRC - Reinsurance Research Council, 1217
RRDMA - Rainy River District Municipal Association, 1204
RRHAN - Red Road HIV/AIDS Network, 1210
RRN - Refugee Research Network, 1211
RROC - Regina Regional Opportunities Commission, 1212
RSA - The Royal Society for the Encouragement of Arts, Manufactures & Commerce, 1587
RSA - Renaissance Society of America, 1586
RSBA - Robson Street Business Association, 1235
RSC - The Royal Society of Canada, 1242
RSCA - Regroupement des Sourds de Chaudière-Appalaches, 1215
RSCB - Réso Santé Colombie Britannique, 1226
RSCDS - The Royal Scottish Country Dance Society, 1587
RSCL - Richmond Society for Community Living, 1231
RSEQ - Réseau du sport étudiant du Québec, 1222
RSEQAT - Réseau du sport étudiant du Québec Abitibi-Témiscamingue, 1222
RSEQ-QCA - Réseau du sport étudiant du Québec Chaudière-Appalaches, 1222
RSES Canada - Refrigeration Service Engineers Society (Canada), 1211
RSFS - Réseau Santé en français de la Saskatchewan, 1225
RSIO - Reinforcing Steel Institute of Ontario, 1217
RSO - Regina Symphony Orchestra, 1212
RT21 - Regroupement pour la Trisomie 21, 1216
RTA - Rideau Trail Association, 1231
RTDNA Canada - Radio Television Digital News Association (Canada), 1203
RTDSC - The Right to Die Society of Canada, 1232
RTO - The Retired Teachers of Ontario, 1228
RTRA - Regina Therapeutic Riding Association, 1212
RTRA - Regina Therapeutic Recreation Association, 1212
RTSO - Respiratory Therapy Society of Ontario, 1227
RUFDA - Rushnychok Ukrainian Folk Dancing Association, 1244
RUHF - Royal University Hospital Foundation, 1243
RUSI - Royal United Services Institute - Vancouver Society, 1243
RUSIR - Royal United Services Institute of Regina, 1243
RUSI-VI - Royal United Services Institute of Vancouver Island, 1243
RVCA - Rideau Valley Conservation Authority, 1231
RVDA - Recreation Vehicle Dealers Association of Canada, 1208
RVFN - Rideau Valley Field Naturalists, 1231
RVLT - Ruiter Valley Land Trust, 1244
RVTTC - Registered Veterinary Technologists & Technicians of Canada, 1214
RWB - Royal Winnipeg Ballet, 1243
RWC - Rexdale Women's Centre, 1229

Acronym Index

RWDSU - Retail, Wholesale & Department Store Union (AFL-CIO/CLC), 1586

S

S5PBA - Saskatchewan 5 Pin Bowlers' Association, 1254
SA - Squash Alberta, 1347
SAA - Saskatchewan Association of Architects, 1256
SAA - Saskatchewan Archery Association, 1256
SAA - Sculptors' Association of Alberta, 1287
SAASE - Saskatchewan Association of Agricultural Societies & Exhibitions, 1256
SAB - Saskatchewan Arts Board, 1256
SABBA - Saskatchewan Bodybuilding Association, 1260
SABIS - Southern Alberta Brain Injury Society, 1337
SABNES - Salmon Arm Bay Nature Enhancement Society, 1252
SAC - Scarborough Arts Council, 1282
SAC - Sudbury Arts Council, 1353
SAC - Steinbach Arts Council, 1349
SAC - Soaring Association of Canada, 1305
SAC - Speech-Language & Audiology Canada, 1341
SAC - Salers Association of Canada, 1251
SAC - Songwriters Association of Canada, 1333
SAC - Sign Association of Canada, 1298
SAC - Surety Association of Canada, 1357
SAC - Saskatchewan Association of Chiropractors, 1257
SAC - Sholem Aleichem Community Inc., 1297
SACA - Southern Alberta Curling Association, 1337
SACC - Salmon Arm & District Chamber of Commerce, 1252
SACC - Sexual Assault Crisis Centre of Essex County Inc., 1293
SACC - Sydney & Area Chamber of Commerce, 1359
SACC-CSN - Syndicat des Agents Correctionnels du Canaca (CSN), 1362
SACCK - Sexual Assault Centre Kingston Inc., 1292
SACE - Sexual Assault Centre of Edmonton, 1292
SACL - Shuswap Association for Community Living, 1297
SACL - Surrey Association for Community Living, 1357
SACL - Saskatchewan Association for Community Living, 1256
SACL - Sexual Assault Centre London, 1292
SACLA - Southern Alberta Community Living Association, 1337
SACQ - Syndicat des agricultrices du Centre du Québec, 1362
SADA - Saskatchewan Automobile Dealers Association, 1259
SADC - Réseau des SADC et CAE, 1219
SAEN - Salmonid Association of Eastern Newfoundland, 1252
SAFA - SAIT Academic Faculty Association, 1251
SAFE - Shuswap Area Family Emergency Society, 1297
SAFP - Save a Family Plan, 1281
SAFRAN - Réseau de Santé en Français au Nunavut, 1219
SAGA - Saskatchewan Agricultural Graduates' Association Inc., 1255
SAG-AFTRA - Screen Actors Guild - American Federation of Television & Radio Artists, 1588
SAGE - Seniors Association of Greater Edmonton, 1290
SAH - Society of Architectural Historians, 1592
SAHF - Saskatchewan Agricultural Hall of Fame, 1255
SAHLA - Southern Alberta Health Libraries Association, 1337

SAHM - Society for Adolescent Health & Medicine, 1589
SAHO - Saskatchewan Association of Health Organizations, 1257
SAHRA - Société des archives historiques de la région de l'Amiante, 1317
SAIF - Stop Abuse in Families Society, 1350
SAIRP - Saskatchewan Association of Insolvency & Restructuring Professionals, 1257
SAJAC - Southern African Jewish Association of Canada, 1337
SALA - Saskatchewan Association of Landscape Architects, 1257
SALPN - Saskatchewan Association of Licensed Practical Nurses, 1257
SALT - Saskatchewan Association of Library Technicians, Inc., 1257
SALT - Saskatchewan Aboriginal Land Technicians, 1255
SALTS - S.A.L.T.S. Sail & Life Training Society, 1252
SAM - Suicide Action Montréal, 1353
SAM - Strome & District Historical Society, 1352
SAME - Saskatchewan Association for Multicultural Education, 1256
SAMHA - Summerside & Area Minor Hockey Association, 1354
SAMRT - Saskatchewan Association of Medical Radiation Technologists, 1257
SAMT - Syndicat des agents de maîtrise de TELUS (ind.), 1362
SANB - Société de l'Acadie du Nouveau-Brunswick, 1316
SANP - Saskatchewan Association of Naturopathic Practitioners, 1257
SANS - Snowmobilers Association of Nova Scotia, 1305
SAO - Saskatchewan Association of Optometrists, 1257
SAP - South Asia Partnership Canada, 1334
SAPO - Saskatchewan Association of Prosthetists & Orthotists, 1257
SAPPSS - Southern Alberta Post Polio Support Society, 1337
SAPSCQ - Syndicat des agents de la paix en services correctionnels du Québec, 1362
SARC - Saskatchewan Association of Rehabilitation Centres, 1258
SARDA - Smoky Applied Research & Demonstration Association, 1304
SARM - Saskatchewan Association of Rural Municipalities, 1258
SARP - Saskatchewan Association of Recreation Professionals, 1258
SARTEC - Société des Auteurs de Radio, Télévision et Cinéma, 1317
SARVAC - Search & Rescue Volunteer Association of Canada, 1288
SAS - Saskatchewan Archaeological Society, 1256
SASA - St. Albert Soccer Association, 1248
SASC - Sexual Assault Support Centre Ottawa, 1293
SASC - Saskatchewan Association of School Councils, 1258
SASI - Shelburne Association Supporting Inclusion, 1295
SASKFEAT - Saskatchewan Families for Effective Autism Treatment, 1265
SASKI - Saskatchewan Ski Association - Skiing for Disabled, 1274
SASLPA - Saskatchewan Association of Speech-Language Pathologists & Audiologists, 1258
SASM - St. Andrew's Society of Montréal, 1248
SASSA - Saskatchewan Amateur Speed Skating Association, 1255
SASSM - Société Alzheimer Society Sudbury-Manitoulin, 1307
SASTT - Saskatchewan Applied Science Technologists & Technicians, 1255
SASW - Saskatchewan Association of Social Workers, 1258

SATA - Saskatchewan Athletic Therapists Association, 1258
SATQ - Société des attractions touristiques du Québec, 1317
SAVT - Saskatchewan Association of Veterinary Technologists, Inc., 1258
SAWA - Saskatchewan Amateur Wrestling Association, 1255
SAWC - South Asian Women's Centre, 1334
SAWDAC - Siding & Window Dealers Association of Canada, 1298
SB&H - Spina Bifida & Hydrocephalus Association of Ontario, 1342
SBA - Saskatchewan Baseball Association, 1259
SBA - Saskatchewan Beekeepers Association, 1259
SBA - Saskatchewan Badminton Association, 1259
SBA - Saskatchewan Band Association, 1259
SBA - Saskatchewan Broomball Association, 1260
SBA - Small Business Association, 1304
SBA - Saskatchewan Bison Association, 1259
SBAM - Spina Bifida Association of Manitoba, 1342
SBBA - Saskatchewan Bed & Breakfast Association, 1259
SBC - Service budgétaire et communautaire de Chicoutimi inc, 1291
SBC - Sustainable Buildings Canada, 1357
SBC - Small Business Centre, 1304
SBHABC - Spina Bifida & Hydrocephalus Association of British Columbia, 1341
SBHAC - Spina Bifida & Hydrocephalus Association of Canada, 1341
SBHANA - Spina Bifida & Hydrocephalus Association of Northern Alberta, 1342
SBHANS - Spina Bifida & Hydrocephalus Association of Nova Scotia, 1342
SBHASA - Spina Bifida & Hydrocephalus Association of Southern Alberta, 1342
SBIA - Saskatchewan Brain Injury Association, 1260
SBOA - Saskatchewan Building Officials Association Inc., 1260
SBOA - Standardbred Breeders of Ontario Association, 1347
SBOT - Surrey Board of Trade, 1357
SBPA - Saskatchewan Black Powder Association, 1259
SBR - Society of Bead Researchers, 1592
SBS - Sargeant Bay Society, 1253
SBSA - Saskatchewan Blind Sports Association Inc., 1259
SBTA - Saskatchewan Baton Twirling Association, 1259
SC - Standardbred Canada, 1347
SC - Sisters of Charity of Halifax, 1300
SCA - Saskatchewan Construction Association, 1261
SCA - Society of Canadian Artists, 1327
SCA - Saskatchewan Curling Association, 1263
SCA - Saskatchewan Camping Association, 1260
SCA - Saskatchewan Co-operative Association, 1262
SCA - Strathcona Christian Academy Society, 1351
SCA - Sarnia Concert Association, 1254
SCA - Society of Cardiovascular Anesthesiologists, 1592
SCA - Scarborough Cricket Association, 1282
SCA - Saskatchewan Cheerleading Association, 1261
SCA - Saskatchewan Cricket Association, 1262
SCAA - Saskatchewan Council for Archives & Archivists, 1262
SCAC - Summerland Community Arts Council, 1354
SCAC - Sunshine Coast Arts Council, 1355
SCAC - Sheep Creek Arts Council, 1295
SCAO - Sickle Cell Association of Ontario, 1297
SCAW - Sleeping Children Around the World, 1303

SCB - Society for Conservation Biology, 1590
SCBC - Société culturelle de la Baie des Chaleurs, 1309
SCC - Save the Children Canada, 1281
SCC - Sierra Club of Canada, 1298
SCC - Saskatchewan Craft Council, 1262
SCC - Syrian Canadian Council, 1365
SCCA - Society of Canadian Cine Amateurs, 1327
SCCBC - Sports Car Club of British Columbia, 1345
SCCC - Swiss Canadian Chamber of Commerce (Ontario) Inc., 1359
SCCC - South Cowichan Chamber of Commerce, 1334
SCCC - The Swedish-Canadian Chamber of Commerce, 1358
SCCC - Soil Conservation Council of Canada, 1332
SCCC - Scadding Court Community Centre, 1282
SCCCQ - Chambre de commerce Canado-Suisse (Québec) Inc., 540
SCC-CSQ - Syndicat des conseillères et conseillers de la CSQ, 1362
SCCFV - South Central Committee on Family Violence, Inc., 1334
SCCPQ - Société des chefs, cuisiniers et pâtissiers du Québec, 1317
SCCSS - Sunshine Coast Community Services Society, 1355
SCCWS - Swift Current Creek Watershed Stewards, 1358
SCDLC - Shuswap Columbia District Labour Council, 1297
SCEC - Saskatchewan Council for Exceptional Children, 1262
SCEM - Société des collectionneurs d'estampes de Montréal, 1317
SCENES - Saskatchewan Council for Educators of Non-English Speakers, 1262
SCES - Saskatchewan Cultural Exchange Society, 1262
SCF - Saskatchewan Choral Federation, 1261
SCFR - Société canadienne-française de radiologie, 1309
SCGC - Screen Composers Guild of Canada, 1287
SCHA - Simcoe County Historical Association, 1299
SCHC - Scarborough Centre for Healthy Communities, 1282
SCHEC - Société canadienne d'histoire de l'Église Catholique - Section française, 1307
SCHS - Stoney Creek Historical Society, 1350
SCI NL - Spinal Cord Injury Newfoundland & Labrador, 1343
SCIC - Saskatchewan Council for International Co-operation, 1262
SCI-PEI - Spinal Cord Injury (Prince Edward Island), 1342
SCLA - Simcoe County Law Association, 1299
SCM - Student Christian Movement of Canada, 1352
SCMA - Supply Chain Management Association, 1355
SCMAAB - Supply Chain Management Association - Alberta, 1355
SCMABC - Supply Chain Management Association - British Columbia, 1355
SCMAMB - Supply Chain Management Association - Manitoba, 1356
SCMANB - Supply Chain Management Association - New Brunswick, 1356
SCMANL - Supply Chain Management Association - Newfoundland & Labrador, 1356
SCMANS - Supply Chain Management Association - Nova Scotia, 1356
SCMANWT - Supply Chain Management Association - Northwest Territories, 1356
SCMAO - Supply Chain Management Association - Ontario, 1356
SCMASK - Supply Chain Management Association - Saskatchewan, 1356

Acronym Index

SCMMA - Saskatoon Civic Middle Management Association, 1279
SCN - Stem Cell Network, 1349
SCNHS - Sunshine Coast Natural History Society, 1355
SCO - Society of Canadian Ornithologists, 1327
SCOP - Saskatchewan College of Podiatrists, 1261
SCoP - Saskatchewan College of Paramedics, 1261
SCOPE - Supporting Choices of People Edson, 1356
SCP - Saskatchewan College of Pharmacists, 1261
SCP - Saskatchewan College of Psychologists, 1261
SCPA - Saskatoon City Police Association, 1279
SCPA - Saskatchewan Cerebral Palsy Association, 1260
SCPT - Saskatchewan College of Physical Therapists, 1261
SCQ - Société de criminologie du Québec, 1314
SCRLC - Société culturelle régionale Les Chutes, 1309
SCRS - Salmo Community Resource Society, 1251
SCSA - Smithers Community Services Association, 1304
SCSA - Société culturelle Sud-Acadie, 1309
SCSA - Saskatchewan Construction Safety Association Inc., 1262
SCSBC - Society of Christian Schools in British Columbia, 1304
SCSP - Société canadienne de la sclérose en plaques (Division du Québec), 1308
SCTR - Saskatchewan Coalition for Tobacco Reduction, 1261
SCWA - Spruce City Wildlife Association, 1346
SCWIST - Society for Canadian Women in Science & Technology, 1325
SDA - Saskatchewan Dietitians Association, 1263
SDA - Saskatchewan Darts Association, 1263
SDAA - Saskatchewan Dental Assistants' Association, 1263
SDACC - Seventh-day Adventist Church in Canada, 1292
SDBA - Sudbury & District Beekeepers' Association, 1353
SDCC - Slocan District Chamber of Commerce, 1303
SDGQ - Société des designers graphiques du Québec, 1317
SDHA - Saskatchewan Dental Hygienists' Association, 1263
SDHHNS - Society of Deaf & Hard of Hearing Nova Scotians, 1328
SDHHS - Saskatchewan Deaf & Hard of Hearing Services Inc., 1263
SDLC - Sarnia & District Labour Council, 1254
SDLC - Saskatoon & District Labour Council, 1279
SDLC - Squamish & District Labour Committee, 1346
SDRCC - Sport Dispute Resolution Centre of Canada, 1344
SDSA - Saskatchewan Deaf Sports Association, 1263
SDTA - Saskatchewan Dental Therapists Association, 1263
SDTC - Sustainable Development Technology Canada, 1357
SEA - Southeast Environmental Association, 1337
SEA - Saskatchewan Economics Association, 1264
SEAMEO - Southeast Asian Ministers of Education Organization, 1595
SEAS - Support Enhance Access Service Centre, 1356
SEASA - University of Alberta South East Asian Students' Association, 1419
SEBIQ - Société des écoles du monde du BI du Québec et de la francophonie, 1317

SECA - Saskatchewan Early Childhood Association, 1263
SECC - South Essex Community Centre, 1334
SECLS - South Etobicoke Community Legal Services, 1334
SEDA - Saskatchewan Elocution & Debate Association, 1264
SEDA - Saskatchewan Economic Development Association, 1264
SEESOCQ - Syndicat des employés et employées des syndicats et des organismes collectifs du Québec, 1363
SEESUS - Syndicat des employées de soutien de l'Université de Sherbrooke, 1362
SEGD - Society for Environmental Graphic Design, 1590
SEGSS - South-East Grey Support Services, 1337
SEHC - Saint Elizabeth Health Care, 1246
SEHQ - Société pour les enfants handicapés du Québec, 1322
SEI - Stockholm Environment Institute, 1597
SEIMA - Saskatchewan Environmental Industry & Managers' Association, 1264
SEJ - Sisters of the Child Jesus, 1301
SEM - Society for Ethnomusicology, 1590
SEMB SAQ - Syndicat des employé(e)s de magasins et de bureau de la Société des alcools du Québec (ind.), 1362
SEMSA - Saskatchewan Emergency Medical Services Association, 1264
SEN - Saskatchewan Eco-Network, 1264
SEPAQ - Société des établissements de plein air du Québec, 1318
SEQ - Société d'entomologie du Québec, 1309
SER - Society for Ecological Restoration International, 1590
SERC - Sexuality Education Resource Centre Manitoba, 1293
SES - Saskatchewan Environmental Society, 1264
SETAC - Society of Environmental Toxicology & Chemistry, 1593
SFA - Saskatchewan Forestry Association, 1265
SFA - Saskatchewan Fencing Association, 1265
SFC - Shooting Federation of Canada, 1297
SfC - Skills for Change, 1302
SFC - Selkirk Friendship Centre, 1289
SFL - Saskatchewan Federation of Labour, 1265
SFM - Scarboro Foreign Mission Society, 1282
SFM - Société de la francophonie manitobaine, 1316
SFM - Saskatoon Farmers' Markets, 1279
SFN - Sydenham Field Naturalists, 1359
SFNC - Southern First Nations Secretariat, 1337
SFNC - Shibogama First Nations Council, 1296
SFNCC - Seniors for Nature Canoe Club, 1290
SFNS - Shooting Federation of Nova Scotia, 1297
SfP - Science for Peace, 1285
SFPA - Saskatchewan Food Processors Association, 1265
SFPE - Society of Fire Protection Engineers, 1593
SFPIRG - Simon Fraser Public Interest Research Group, 1300
SFPO - Saskatchewan Federation of Police Officers, 1265
SFPQ - Syndicat de la fonction publique du Québec inc. (ind.), 1361
SFS - Service familial de Sudbury, 1291
SFUFA - Simon Fraser University Faculty Association, 1300
SFV - Société francophone de Victoria, 1319
SGACL - Superior Greenstone Association for Community Living, 1355
SGAIA - Saskatchewan Graphic Arts Industries Association, 1266
SGAR - Société de généalogie et d'archives de Rimouski, 1316

SGC - Saskatchewan German Council Inc., 1266
SGCE - Société de généalogie des Cantons de l'Est, 1315
SGCF - Société généalogique canadienne-française, 1319
SGEU - Saskatchewan Government & General Employees' Union, 1266
SGIA - Specialty Graphic Imaging Association, 1596
SGL - Société de généalogie des Laurentides, 1316
SGLJ - Société de généalogie de la Jemmerais, 1315
SGQ - Société de généalogie de Québec, 1315
SGS - Saskatchewan Genealogical Society, 1265
SGS - Société de généalogie du Saguenay, inc., 1316
SGWA - Saskatchewan Ground Water Association, 1266
SHA - Saskatchewan Hockey Association, 1267
SHA - Saskatchewan Hereford Association, 1267
SHA - Saskatchewan Handball Association, 1267
SHAD - Société historique Alphonse-Desjardins, 1319
SHAID - Shelter for Helpless Animals in Distress, 1295
SHAS - Saanich Historical Artifacts Society, 1245
SHBE - Saskatchewan Home Based Educators, 1267
SHBMSH - Société d'histoire de Beloeil - Mont-Saint-Hilaire, 1310
SHCA - Saskatchewan Heavy Construction Association, 1267
SHCDN - Société d'histoire de la Côte-des-Neiges, 1310
SHCN - Société historique de la Côte-Nord, 1320
SHCR - La Société historique du Cap-Rouge, 1320
SHEB - Société d'Horticulture et d'Écologie de Brossard, 1314
SHELI - Société d'Horticulture et d'Écologie de Longueuil, 1314
SHEP - Société d'Horticulture et d'Écologie de Prévost, 1314
SHETA - Saskatchewan Home Economics Teachers Association, 1267
SHF - Saskatchewan Horse Federation, 1267
SHFS - Saskatchewan History & Folklore Society Inc., 1267
SHGG - Société d'histoire et généalogie du granit, 1313
SHGIJ - Société d'histoire et de généalogie de l'Ile Jésus, 1312
SHGM - Société d'histoire et de généalogie de Matane, 1312
SHGRDL - Société d'histoire et de généalogie de Rivière-du-Loup, 1312
SHGS - Société d'histoire et de généalogie de Salaberry, 1313
SHGSS - Société d'histoire et de généalogie de Shawinigan-sud, 1313
SHGTP - Société d'histoire et généalogique de Trois-Pistoles, inc., 1321
SHGVD - Société d'histoire et de généalogie de Val-d'Or, 1313
SHHA - Saskatchewan Hotel & Hospitality Association, 1267
SHHR - Société d'histoire du Haut-Richelieu, 1312
SHHY - Société d'histoire de la Haute-Yamaska, 1310
SHIP - Société d'histoire des Iles-Percées, 1312
SHL - Société d'histoire du Lac-St-Jean/Maison des Bâtisseurs, 1312
SHL - Société d'histoire de Longueuil, 1311
SHLA - Saskatchewan Health Libraries Association, 1267
SHLM - Société d'histoire de La Prairie-de-la-Magdeleine, 1310

SHM - Société d'histoire de Montarville, 1311
SHM - Société d'histoire de Magog, 1311
SHNB - La Société historique de Nouvelle-Beauce, 1320
SHO - Société d'histoire de l'Outaouais inc., 1310
SHO - Ski Hawks Ottawa, 1302
SHOC - Sledge Hockey of Canada, 1303
SHOT - Society for the History of Technology, 1591
SHPS - Société historique Pierre-de-Saurel inc., 1321
SHQ - Société Huntington du Québec, 1321
SHRC - Self-Help Resource Centre, 1289
SHRC - Société d'histoire régionale de Chibougamau, 1313
SHRDM - Société d'histoire régionale Deux-Montagnes, 1313
SHRMCLASS - Société d'histoire de la MRC de l'Assomption, 1310
SHRML - Société historique de la région de Mont-Laurier, 1320
SHS - Semiahmoo House Society, 1289
SHS - Société historique du Saguenay, 1321
SHS - Streetsville Historical Society, 1352
SHS - Stanstead Historical Society, 1348
SHS - Société d'histoire de Sherbrooke, 1311
SHS - Société d'histoire de Sillery, 1311
SHSA - Saskatchewan Herb & Spice Association, 1267
SHSAA - Saskatchewan High Schools Athletic Association, 1267
SHSB - Société historique de Saint-Boniface, 1320
SHSC - Société d'histoire de la Seigneurie de Chambly, 1311
SHSM - Société d'histoire de la Seigneurie de Monnoir, 1311
SHSR - Société historique de Saint-Romuald, 1320
SIA - Saskatchewan Institute of Agrologists, 1268
SIA - Soroptimist International of the Americas, 1595
SIA - Saskatchewan Intercultural Association Inc., 1268
SICA - Southern Interior Construction Association, 1338
SIDIIEF - Secrétariat international des infirmières et infirmiers de l'espace francophone, 1288
SIECCAN - Sex Information & Education Council of Canada, 1292
SIEPM - Société internationale pour l'étude de la philosophie médiévale, 1589
SIJ - Société d'investissement jeunesse, 1314
SIJHL - Superior International Junior Hockey League, 1355
SILGA - Southern Interior Local Government Association, 1338
SIM - Society for Information Management, 1590
SIM - The Secular Institute of Missionaries of the Kingship of Christ, 1288
SIP - Society of Internet Professionals, 1329
SIPA - Specialized Information Publishers Association, 1596
SIPA - Small Investor Protection Association, 1304
SIRE - Société internationale du réseau ÉCONOMUSÉE et Société ÉCONOMUSÉE du Québec, 1321
SISR - Société internationale de sociologie des religions, 1589
SITO - Service Intégration Travail Outaouais, 1291
SIWA - Somali Immigrant Women's Association, 1332
SJA - Société des Jeux de l'Acadie inc., 1318
SJBRWDSU - Saskatchewan Joint Board Retail, Wholesale & Department Store Union, 1268
SJC - Ski Jumping Canada, 1302
SJCAB - St. John's Clean & Beautiful, 1249
SJCC - Saint John Coin Club, 1246

Acronym Index

SJDHHS - Saint John Deaf & Hard of Hearing Services, Inc, 1246
SJDLC - Saint John & District Labour Council, 1246
SJIWFF - St. John's International Women's Film Festival, 1249
SKA - Saskatchewan Karate Association, 1268
SKAC - Southern Kings Arts Council, 1338
SKILLS - Skills Unlimited, 1302
SKMB - Saskatchewan Conference of Mennonite Brethren Churches, 1261
SKSA - Saskatchewan Katahdin Sheep Association Inc., 1268
SLA - Saskatchewan Library Association, 1269
SLA - Special Libraries Association, 1595
SLA - Saskatchewan Livestock Association, 1269
SLC - Secours aux lépreux (Canada) inc., 1288
SLCFDC - South Lake Community Futures Development Corporation, 1335
SLEA - Sarnia-Lambton Environmental Association, 1254
SLF - Strategic Leadership Forum, 1351
SLINC - Sign Language Interpreters of the National Capital, 1299
SLND - Société Louis-Napoléon Dugal/Société Grande-Rivière, 1321
SLREB - Sarnia-Lambton Real Estate Board, 1254
SLSA - Saskatchewan Land Surveyors' Association, 1268
SLSC - St. Leonard's Society of Canada, 1250
SLTA - Saskatchewan Library Trustees' Association, 1269
SLVNHS - St. Lawrence Valley Natural History Society, 1250
SMA - Saskatoon Musicians' Association, 1279
SMA - Saskatchewan Medical Association, 1270
SMA - Saskatchewan Mining Association, 1270
SMA - Scarborough Muslim Association, 1282
SMAA - Sarnia Minor Athletic Association, 1254
SMAA - Saskatchewan Martial Arts Association, 1269
SMAC - Shoe Manufacturers' Association of Canada, 1296
SMACNA - Sheet Metal & Air Conditioning Contractors' National Association, 1588
SMACNA-BC - British Columbia Sheet Metal Association, 253
SMCA - Sport Medicine Council of Alberta, 1344
SMCAA - Sheet Metal Contractors Association of Alberta, 1295
SMD - Society for Manitobans with Disabilities Inc., 1326
SMDI - Society for Muscular Dystrophy Information International, 1326
SME - Society of Manufacturing Engineers - Canada Office, 1330
SMEA - Saskatchewan Music Educators Association, 1270
SMEV - Sales & Marketing Executives of Vancouver, 1251
SMFNL - School Milk Foundation of Newfoundland & Labrador, 1284
SMHI - Saskatchewan Municipal Hail Insurance Association, 1270
SMLN - Simcoe/Muskoka Literacy Network, 1300
SMPA - Saskatchewan Meat Processors' Association, 1270
SMPIA - Saskatchewan Motion Picture Industry Association, 1270
SMPTE - Society of Motion Picture & Television Engineers, 1593
SMQ - Société des musées québécois, 1318
SMRA - St Mary's River Association, 1250
SMUFU - Saint Mary's University Faculty Union, 1247
SMWIA - Sheet Metal Workers' International Association (AFL-CIO/CFL), 1588
SNA - Société nationale de l'Acadie, 1322
SNB - Softball NB Inc., 1331

SNLA - Saskatchewan Nursery Landscape Association, 1270
SNM - Swim-Natation Manitoba, 1359
SNRT - Society for Research on Nicotine & Tobacco, 1591
SNS - Soccer Nova Scotia, 1305
SNS - Sport Nova Scotia, 1345
SNS - Symphony Nova Scotia, 1360
SNS - Swim Nova Scotia, 1358
SOA - Special Olympics Alberta, 1339
SOA - Saskatchewan Orchestral Association, Inc., 1270
SOA - Saskatchewan Outfitters Association, 1271
SOA - Society of Actuaries, 1592
SOAR - Society of Ontario Adjudicators & Regulators, 1330
SOAR - Steelworkers Organization of Active Retirees, 1349
SOAR - Survivors of Abuse Recovering, 1357
SOBC - Special Olympics BC, 1339
SOBLC - South Okanagan Boundary Labour Council, 1335
SOC - Special Olympics Canada, 1339
SOCABI - Société catholique de la Bible, 1309
SOCAM - Société de communication Atikamekw-Montagnais, 1314
SOCAN - Society of Composers, Authors & Music Publishers of Canada, 1328
SOCHEB - Société d'horticulture et d'écologie de Boucherville, 1314
SOCODEVI - Société de coopération pour le développement international, 1314
SOCOM - Société des communicateurs du Québec, 1317
SoDC - Seeds of Diversity Canada, 1289
SODEC - Société de développement des entreprises culturelles, 1314
SODEP - Société de développement des périodiques culturels québécois, 1314
SODES - Société de développement économique du Saint-Laurent, 1315
SODRAC - Société du droit de reproduction des auteurs, compositeurs et éditeurs au Canada (SODRAC 2003) inc., 1318
SODS - Saskatoon Open Door Society Inc., 1279
SOEA - Schneider Office Employees' Association, 1284
SOEEA - Saskatchewan Outdoor & Environmental Education Association, 1271
SOGA - Southwestern Ontario Gliding Association, 1338
SOGC - Society of Obstetricians & Gynaecologists of Canada, 1330
SOHL - Saskatchewan Organization for Heritage Languages Inc., 1270
SOHLIN - Southwestern Ontario Health Libraries & Information Network, 1338
SOHO - Save Our Heritage Organization, 1281
SOHO - SOHO Business Group, 1332
SOICS - South Okanagan Immigrant & Community Services, 1335
SOM - Special Olympics Manitoba, 1339
SONG - Society of Ontario Nut Growers, 1330
SONG - Unifor87-M, 1405
SONS - Special Olympics Nova Scotia, 1340
SONWT - Special Olympics Northwest Territories, 1340
SOO - Special Olympics Ontario, 1340
SOOPA - Similkameen Okanagan Organic Producers Association, 1300
SOPEI - Special Olympics Prince Edward Island, 1340
SOPFIM - Société de protection des forêts contre les insectes et maladies, 1317
SoQAD - Société québécoise des auteurs dramatiques, 1324
SOREB - South Okanagan Real Estate Board, 1335
SORNG - Saskatchewan PeriOperative Registered Nurses' Group, 1271
SOS - Save Ontario Shipwrecks, 1281
SOS - Saskatchewan Orchid Society, 1270

SOSBIS - South Okanagan Similkameen Brain Injury Society, 1335
SOSN - Southern Ontario Seismic Network, 1338
SOT - Society of Toxicology, 1594
SOUL - Society for Organic Urban Land Care, 1326
SOWINS - South Okanagan Women in Need Society, 1335
SOY - Special Olympics Yukon, 1340
SPA - Saskatchewan Powerlifting Association, 1272
SPA - Saskatchewan Physiotherapy Association, 1272
SPA - Sheridan Park Association, 1296
SPAC - The Society of Professional Accountants of Canada, 1330
SPACQ - Société professionnelle des auteurs et des compositeurs du Québec, 1322
SPAN - St. Paul Abilities Network, 1251
SPAN - Single Parent Association of Newfoundland, 1300
SPAN - Small Publishers Association of North America, 1589
SPARC BC - Social Planning & Research Council of BC, 1306
SPAWN - Salmon Preservation Association for the Waters of Newfoundland, 1252
SPC - Samaritan's Purse Canada, 1253
SPC - Sport Physiotherapy Canada, 1345
SPC - Socialist Party of Canada, 1307
SPC - Social Planning Council of Sudbury Region, 1306
SPC - Saskatchewan Playwrights Centre, 1272
SPCA - Society for the Prevention of Cruelty to Animals International, 1592
SPCNO - Social Planning Council for the North Okanagan, 1306
SPCO - Social Planning Council of Ottawa, 1306
SPCOC - Saanich Peninsula Chamber of Commerce, 1245
SPCQ - Syndicat des producteurs de chèvres du Québec, 1363
SPCRS - South Peace Community Resources Society, 1335
SPDAC - Société de Promotion et de Diffusion des Arts et de la Culture, 1316
SPE - Society of Petroleum Engineers, 1593
SPE - Society of Plastics Engineers, 1593
SPEA - Society of Professional Engineers & Associates, 1330
SPEA - Saskatchewan Physical Education Association, 1271
SPEAQ - Society for the Promotion of the Teaching of English as a Second Language in Quebec, 1326
SPEC - Society Promoting Environmental Conservation, 1331
SPEI - Softball Prince Edward Island, 1332
SPEIAC - Scented Products Education & Information Association of Canada, 1283
SPEQ - Syndicat des professeurs de l'État du Québec (ind.), 1363
SPES - Stanley Park Ecology Society, 1348
SPG - Saskatchewan Publishers Group, 1272
SPG - Saskatchewan Pulse Growers, 1273
SPGQ - Syndicat de professionnelles et professionnels du gouvernement du Québec, 1362
SPHNC - Société Provancher d'histoire naturelle du Canada, 1322
SPHQ - Société des professeurs d'histoire du Québec inc., 1318
SPHQ - Syndicat professionnel des homéopathes du Québec, 1365
SPI - Saskatchewan Prevention Institute, 1272
SPI - SPI: The Plastics Industry Trade Association, 1596
SPIAO - Society of Public Insurance Administrators of Ontario, 1330
SPIC - Service de protection et d'information du consommateur, 1291
SPIHQ - Syndicat professionnel des ingénieurs d'Hydro-Québec, 1365

SPK - Polish Combatants Association, 1164
SPLA - Saskatchewan Pro Life Association, 1272
SPMABC - Structural Pest Management Association of British Columbia, 1352
SPMAO - Structural Pest Management Association of Ontario, 1352
SPMGQ - Syndicat professionnel des médecins du gouvernement du Québec (ind.), 1365
SPNC - South Peel Naturalists' Club, 1336
SPO - Slo-Pitch Ontario Association, 1303
SPOOM - Society for the Preservation of Old Mills - Canadian Chapter, 1326
SPOTTO - Saskatoon Parents of Twins & Triplets Organization, 1280
SPPI - Saskatchewan Professional Planners Institute, 1272
SPPMM - Syndicat des professionnelles et professionnels municipaux de Montréal, 1364
SPPUQAC - Syndicat des professeures et professeurs de l'Université du Québec à Chicoutimi, 1363
SPPUQAR - Syndicat des professeures et professeurs de l'Université du Québec à Rimouski, 1363
SPPUS - Syndicat des professeures et professeurs de l'Université de Sherbrooke, 1363
SPQ - Syndicat des pompiers et pompières du Québec (CTC), 1363
SPQ - Société Philatélique de Québec, 1322
SPQ - Société de philosophie du Québec, 1316
SPRA - Saskatchewan Parks & Recreation Association, 1271
SPRA - Saskatchewan Provincial Rifle Association Inc., 1272
SPSEA - Senate Protective Service Employees Association, 1290
SPSI - Syndicat professionnel des scientifiques de l'IREQ, 1365
SPSPEM - Syndicat professionnel des scientifiques à pratique exclusive de Montréal, 1365
SPSQ - Syndicat des producteurs en serre du Québec, 1363
SPT - Social Planning Toronto, 1306
SPTP-SAQ - Syndicat du personnel technique et professionnel de la Société des alcools du Québec (ind.), 1364
SPTSQ - Syndicat des professeurs et des techniciens de la santé du Québec, 1364
SPUQ - Syndicat des professeurs et professeures de l'Université du Québec à Montréal, 1364
SPUQO - Syndicat des professeures et professeurs de l'Université du Québec en Outaouais, 1364
SQA - Ski Québec alpin, 1302
SQC - Syndicat québécois de la construction, 1365
SQDA - Société québécoise pour la défense des animaux, 1324
SQDI - Société Québécoise de droit international, 1323
SQE - Société québécoise d'espéranto, 1323
SQE - Society for Quality Education, 1326
SQE - Société québécoise d'ethnologie, 1323
SQÉR - Société québécoise pour l'étude de la religion, 1324
SQG - Société québécoise de gériatrie, 1323
SQHH - Société québécoise des hostas et des hémérocalles, 1324
SQP - Société Québécoise de Psilogie inc, 1323
SQPP - Société québécoise des psychothérapeutes professionnels, 1324
SQPTO - Société québécoise de psychologie du travail, 1323
SQRP - Société québécoise de la rédaction professionnelle, 1323
SQS - Société québécoise de spéléologie, 1324
SQS - Société québécoise de la schizophrénie, 1323
SQSP - Société québécoise de science politique, 1324

Acronym Index

SRA - Saskatchewan Rowing Association, 1274
SRA - Sackville Rivers Association, 1245
SRA - Saskatchewan Racquetball Association, 1273
SRABC - Stroke Recovery Association of BC, 1352
SRAR - Saskatoon Region Association of REALTORS, 1280
SRC NL - Seniors Resource Centre Association of Newfoundland & Labrador Inc., 1290
SRCD - Society for Research in Child Development, 1590
SRHIA - Saskatchewan Rental Housing Industry Association, 1274
SRI - Steel Recycling Institute, 1597
SRIA - Saskatchewan Recording Industry Association, 1273
SRLS - Sudbury Rock & Lapidary Society, 1353
SRMCA - Concrete Sask, 610
SRMTA - Saskatchewan Registered Music Teachers' Association, 1273
SRNA - Saskatchewan Registered Nurses' Association, 1273
SRPC - Society of Rural Physicians of Canada, 1330
SRU - Saskatchewan Rugby Union, 1274
SSA - Schizophrenia Society of Alberta, 1283
SSA - Saskatchewan Soccer Association Inc., 1275
SSA - Saskatchewan Snowmobile Association, 1275
SSA - Saskatchewan Snowboard Association, 1275
SSAC - Society for the Study of Architecture in Canada, 1327
SSBA - Saskatchewan School Boards Association, 1274
SSBRY - Société St-Jean-Baptiste Richelieu-Yamaska, 1325
SSC - Sculptors Society of Canada, 1287
SSC - Speed Skating Canada, 1341
SSC - Schizophrenia Society of Canada, 1283
SSC - Statistical Society of Canada, 1348
SSC - School Sport Canada, 1284
SSCA - Saskatchewan Soil Conservation Association, 1275
SSCA - Saskatchewan Sailing Clubs Association, 1274
SSCS - Sea Shepherd Conservation Society, 1287
SSCS - Sea Shepherd Conservation Society - USA, 1588
SSEA - Society for the Study of Egyptian Antiquities, 1327
SSEA - Saskatchewan Society for Education through Art, 1275
SSEA - Severn Sound Environmental Association, 1292
SSF - Sjogren's Syndrome Foundation Inc., 1589
SSF - Société Santé en français, 1325
SSFHM - Saskatchewan Sports Hall of Fame & Museum, 1275
SSF-IIIHS - Spiritual Science Fellowship/International Institute of Integral Human Sciences, 1344
SSGA - Saskatchewan Stock Growers Association, 1276
SSHS - Scottish Settlers Historical Society, 1286
SSI Chamber - Salt Spring Island Chamber of Commerce, 1252
SSJ - Congregation des Soeurs de Saint-Joseph de Saint-Vallier, 612
SSJBM - Société Saint-Jean-Baptiste de Montréal, 1324
SSLA - Saskatchewan School Library Association, 1274
SSM - Safety Services Manitoba, 1245
SSMCOC - Sault Ste Marie Chamber of Commerce, 1281
SSMEDC - Sault Ste Marie Economic Development Corporation, 1281
SSMEFFNB - Société Santé et Mieux-être en français du Nouveau-Brunswick, 1325

SSMLT - Saskatchewan Society of Medical Laboratory Technologists, 1275
SSMREB - Sault Ste Marie Real Estate Board, 1281
SSNB - Schizophrenia Society of New Brunswick, 1283
SSNB - Safety Services New Brunswick, 1245
SSNL - School Sports Newfoundland & Labrador, 1284
SSNS - Schizophrenia Society of Nova Scotia, 1284
SSNS - Safety Services Nova Scotia, 1245
SSO - The Scleroderma Society of Ontario, 1285
SSO - Schizophrenia Society of Ontario, 1284
SSO - Saskatoon Symphony Society, 1280
SSO - Sudbury Symphony Orchestra Association Inc., 1353
SSO - Solo Swims of Ontario Inc., 1332
SSOCC - Sunbeam Sportscar Owners Club of Canada, 1354
SSOT - Saskatchewan Society of Occupational Therapists, 1275
SSPEI - Schizophrenia Society of Prince Edward Island, 1284
SSRC - South Shore Reading Council, 1336
SSS - Schizophrenia Society of Saskatchewan, 1284
SSS - Surrey Symphony Society, 1357
SSS - Society for Socialist Studies, 1326
SSTA - Société Saint-Thomas-d'Aquin, 1325
SSVP - Conseil national Société de Saint-Vincent de Paul, 619
SSYO - South Saskatchewan Youth Orchestra, 1336
STA - Saskatchewan Trucking Association, 1276
STA - Stratford Tourism Alliance, 1351
STAC - Saskatchewan Triathlon Association Corporation, 1276
STAO - Shiatsu Therapy Association of Ontario, 1296
STAO - Science Teachers' Association of Ontario, 1285
STAQ - Société touristique des Autochtones du Québec, 1325
STARF - Syndicat des technicien(ne)s et artisan(e)s du réseau français de Radio-Canada (ind.), 1364
STARS - Shock Trauma Air Rescue Society, 1296
STC - Society of Toxicology of Canada, 1331
STC - Society for Technical Communication, 1591
STEEN - Syndicat des travailleurs énergie électrique nord, 1364
STEP - Saskatchewan Trade & Export Partnership, 1276
STEP - Society of Trust & Estate Practitioners, 1331
STF - Saskatchewan Teachers' Federation, 1276
STIBC - Society of Translators & Interpreters of British Columbia, 1331
STIQ - Sous-Traitance Industrielle Québec, 1334
STLEO - St. Leonard's Youth & Family Services Society, 1250
STN - Société des technologues en nutrition, 1318
STPMB - Saskatchewan Turkey Producers' Marketing Board, 1276
STQ - Société des traversiers du Québec, 1318
STRQ - Syndicat des technologues en radiologie du Québec, 1364
STTA - Saskatchewan Table Tennis Association Inc., 1276
SUCO - Service universitaire canadien outre-mer, 1291
SUDA - Sustainable Urban Development Association, 1358
SUMA - Saskatchewan Urban Municipalities Association, 1277
SUN - Saskatchewan Union of Nurses, 1277

SUSO - Society of Urologic Surgeons of Ontario, 1331
SVGAM - St. Vincent & the Grenadines Association of Montreal Inc., 1251
SVMA - Saskatchewan Veterinary Medical Association, 1277
SVOPD - Saskatchewan Voice of People with Disabilities, Inc., 1277
SWA - Sealant & Waterproofing Association, 1288
SWANA - Solid Waste Association of North America, 1595
SWATCA - South Western Alberta Teachers' Convention Association, 1336
SWC - Scarborough Women's Centre, 1283
SWC - Status of Women Council of the Northwest Territories, 1349
SWCS - Soil & Water Conservation Society, 1594
SWCS - South Wellington Coin Society, 1336
SWF - Saskatchewan Wildlife Federation, 1278
SWG - Saskatchewan Writers Guild, 1278
SWI - Saskatchewan Women's Institute, 1278
SWNA - Saskatchewan Weekly Newspapers Association, 1278
SWNFC - Syme-Woolner Neighbourhood & Family Centre, 1360
SWRC - Saskatchewan Waste Reduction Council, 1277
SWSA - Saskatchewan Wheelchair Sports Association, 1278
SWWA - Saskatchewan Water & Wastewater Association, 1277
SYC - Sierra Youth Coalition, 1298
SYICCN - Saskatchewan Youth in Care & Custody Network, 1279

T

TA - Townshippers' Association, 1393
TA - Théâtre Action, 1373
TAAS - Toronto Association of Acting Studios, 1382
TABE - Toronto Association for Business Economics Inc., 1382
TAC - Toronto Autosport Club, 1382
TAC - Transportation Association of Canada, 1395
TAC - Tunnelling Association of Canada, 1400
TAC - Trauma Association of Canada, 1396
TAC - Tea Association of Canada, 1367
TAC - Toronto Arts Council, 1381
TADA - Trillium Automobile Dealers' Association, 1398
TADC - Toronto Association for Democracy in China, 1382
TAF - Toronto Arts Foundation, 1381
TAGL - Toronto Area Gays & Lesbians Phoneline & Crisis Counselling, 1381
TAI - Théâtres associés inc., 1375
TAIS - Toronto Animated Image Society, 1381
TALK - Telephone Aid Line Kingston, 1369
TALL - Toronto Association of Law Libraries, 1382
TALSAA - Treaty & Aboriginal Land Stewards Association of Alberta, 1396
TAMAC - Talent Agents & Managers Association of Canada, 1366
TANS - Truckers Association of Nova Scotia, 1399
TAO - Tel-Aide Outaouais, 1369
TAOL - The Association of Ontario Locksmiths, 155
TAPA - Toronto Alliance for the Performing Arts, 1381
TAS - Travellers' Aid Society of Toronto, 1396
TASSQ - Toronto Association of Systems & Software Quality, 1382
TATI - Toronto Art Therapy Institute, 1381
TAWBAS - Thebacha & Wood Buffalo Astronomical Society, 1375
TAWC - Timmins & Area Women in Crisis Support & Information Centre on Violence Against Women, 1379
TBC - Tennis BC, 1370

TBCC - Thunder Bay Chamber of Commerce, 1377
TBDML - Thunder Bay District Municipal League, 1377
TBFN - Thunder Bay Field Naturalists, 1377
TBHMS - Thunder Bay Historical Museum Society, 1378
TBIFC - Thunder Bay Indian Friendship Centre, 1378
TBJ - Tourisme Baie-James, 1392
TBLA - Thunder Bay Law Association, 1378
TBMA - Thunder Bay Multicultural Association, 1378
TBMFA - Thunder Bay Minor Football Association, 1378
TBMHA - Thunder Bay Minor Hockey Association, 1378
TBPA - Thunder Bay Police Association, 1378
TBRAC - Thunder Bay Regional Arts Council, 1378
TBS - Toronto Blues Society, 1382
TBSF - The Belinda Stronach Foundation, 204
TBSO - Thunder Bay Symphony Orchestra Association, 1378
TC - Teamsters Canada (CLC), 1368
TCA - Toronto Curling Association, 1383
TCA - Temiskaming Cattlemen's Association, 1370
T-CAAN - Trans-Canada Advertising Agency Network, 1395
TCC - Toronto Coin Club, 1383
TCCFA - Toronto Canada-China Friendship Association, 1383
TCCS - Taiwanese Canadian Cultural Society, 1366
TCCSA - The Cross-Cultural Community Services Association, 644
TCF - Toronto Community Foundation, 1383
TCHHC - Turkish Community Heritage Centre of Canada, 1400
TCMHA - Township of Clarence Minor Hockey Association, 1393
TCRC - Teamsters Canada Rail Conference, 1368
TCS - The Cousteau Society, 1520
TCTF - Trans Canada Trail Foundation, 1394
TCU&SA - Toronto Cricket Umpires' & Scorers' Association, 1383
TCVA - Tourism Toronto, 1391
TCYHA - Trans Canada Yellowhead Highway Association, 1394
TDBA - Toronto District Beekeepers' Association, 1384
TDC - The Dance Centre, 649
TDCSS - Terrace & District Community Services Society, 1371
TDES - The Duke Ellington Society - Toronto Chapter #40, 664
TDMSC - Tillsonburg & District Multi-Service Centre, 1379
TDT - Toronto Dance Theatre, 1383
TEA - Toronto Entomologists Association, 1384
TEA - Toronto Environmental Alliance, 1384
TEAC - Temiskaming Environmental Action Committee, 1370
TEAM - TEAM of Canada Inc., 1368
TEAM - Telecommunications Employees Association of Manitoba, 1369
TECA - Thermal Environmental Comfort Association, 1375
TEDRA - Toronto Entertainment District Residental Association, 1384
TEOSC - Tamil Eelam Society of Canada, 1366
TESL Canada - TESL Canada Federation, 1372
TESL NL - TESL Newfoundland & Labrador, 1372
TESL PEI - TESL Prince Edward Island, 1373
TESLNS - TESL Nova Scotia, 1372
TESOL - Teachers of English to Speakers of Other Languages, Inc., 1597
TESS - Easter Seals Ontario, 669
TFC - Turkey Farmers of Canada, 1400
TFI - Toronto Fashion Incubator, 1384
TFN - Toronto Field Naturalists, 1384

Acronym Index

TFN - Toronto Free-Net, 1384
TFO - Touch Football Ontario, 1388
TFS - Toronto Film Society, 1384
TFSA - Toronto Financial Services Alliance, 1384
THAA - Tiger Hills Arts Association Inc., 1379
THANS - Transition House Association of Nova Scotia, 1395
THC - Telephone Historical Centre, 1369
THESA - Teachers of Home Economics Specialist Association, 1367
THIA - Travel Health Insurance Association of Canada, 1396
THLA - Toronto Health Libraries Association, 1385
THO - Team Handball Ontario, 1368
THRC - Trucking Human Resources Canada, 1399
TIABC - Tourism Industry Association of British Columbia, 1389
TIAC - Tourism Industry Association of Canada, 1389
TIAC - Thermal Insulation Association of Canada, 1376
TIANB - Tourism Industry Association of New Brunswick Inc., 1390
TIANS - Tourism Industry Association of Nova Scotia, 1390
TIAPEI - Tourism Industry Association of PEI, 1390
TIC - Toronto Insurance Conference, 1385
TICO - Travel Industry Council of Ontario, 1396
TIE-BC - Teachers of Inclusive Education - British Columbia, 1367
TIFF - Toronto International Film Festival Inc., 1385
TIIAC - Title Insurance Industry Association of Canada, 1380
TIRF - Traffic Injury Research Foundation, 1394
TIWA - Toronto Insurance Women's Association, 1385
TIWLT - Thousand Islands Watershed Land Trust, 1376
TJFS - Toronto Jewish Film Society, 1385
TKCC - Kurdish Community & Information Centre of Toronto, 894
TLA - Toronto Lawyers Association, 1385
TLA - Truck Loggers Association, 1399
TLABC - Trial Lawyers Association of British Columbia, 1397
TLK - Toronto Latvian Concert Association, 1385
TLOMA - Toronto Law Office Management Association, 1385
TLSARL - The Lord Selkirk Association of Rupert's Land, 919
TMA - Toronto Musicians' Association, 1386
TMAC - Travel Media Association of Canada, 1396
TMI - Toronto Montessori Institute, 1386
TMJSC - Temporomandibular Joint Society of Canada, 1370
TNA - The Facial Pain Association, 1525
TNB - Theatre New Brunswick, 1374
TNG - The Newspaper Guild (AFL-CIO/CLC), 1577
TNO - Théâtre du Nouvel-Ontario, 1374
TNS - Theatre Nova Scotia, 1374
TOC - Toronto Ornithological Club, 1386
TOGA - The Ontario Greenhouse Alliance, 1083
TOPS - The Ontario Poetry Society, 1096
TOTA - Thompson Okanagan Tourism Association, 1376
TP&aP - Two Planks & a Passion Theatre Company, 1401
TPA - Toronto Police Association, 1386
TPA - Théâtre populaire d'Acadie, 1375
TPAC - Toronto Police Accountability Coalition, 1386
TPFN - 2-Spirited People of the First Nations, 1401
TPOMBA - Toronto Parents of Multiple Births Association, 1386
TPS - The Planetary Society, 1584

TPSI - Toronto Public Spaces Initiative, 1386
TPWAF - Toronto PWA Foundation, 1386
TQ - Tennis Québec, 1371
TRAC - Tire and Rubber Association of Canada, 1380
TRAC - Trail Riding Alberta Conference, 1394
TRAS - Trans-Himalayan Aid Society, 1395
TRD - Tourism Red Deer, 1390
TREA - Thames Region Ecological Association, 1373
TRÉAQFP - Table des responsables de l'éducation des adultes et de la formation professionnelle des commissions scolaires du Québec, 1366
TREB - Toronto Real Estate Board, 1386
TREC - Toronto Renewable Energy Co-operative, 1387
TRHA - Toronto Railway Historical Association, 1386
TRRC - Toronto Renaissance & Reformation Colloquium, 1387
TRUFA - Thompson Rivers University Faculty Association, 1376
TRUFOLA - Thompson Rivers University Open Learning Faculty Association, 1376
TRU-OL - Open Learning at Thompson Rivers University, 1114
TSA - Toronto Sportsmen's Association, 1387
TSACC - Temiskaming Shores & Area Chamber of Commerce, 1370
TSBC - Tire Stewardship BC Association, 1380
TSCST - Tuberous Sclerosis Canada Sclérose Tubéreuse, 1400
TSF - Terre sans frontières, 1372
TSFC - Tourette Syndrome Foundation of Canada, 1388
TSIA - Technology Services Industry Association, 1597
TSL - Tourism Sarnia Lambton, 1391
TSMCA - Toronto Sheet Metal Contractors Association, 1387
TSME - Toronto Society of Model Engineers, 1387
TSO - Toronto Symphony Orchestra, 1387
TSS - Turner's Syndrome Society, 1400
TSSU - Teaching Support Staff Union, 1367
TSYO - Toronto Symphony Youth Orchestra, 1387
TTMAC - Terrazzo Tile & Marble Association of Canada, 1371
TTMAC - Twins, Triplets & More Association of Calgary, 1400
TTMGO - Terrazzo, Tile & Marble Guild of Ontario, Inc., 1372
TTNO - The Therapeutic Touch Network of Ontario, 1375
TTRA - Travel and Tourism Research Association (Canada Chapter), 1396
TTS - Toronto Transportation Society, 1388
TTS - The Transplantation Society, 1395
TTSAO - Truck Training Schools Association of Ontario Inc., 1399
TUC - Trout Unlimited Canada, 1399
TUEJ - Théâtres unis enfance jeunesse, 1375
TUFA - Trent University Faculty Association, 1397
TURAY - Trail & Ultra Running Association Of The Yukon, 1394
TVA - Toronto Vegetarian Association, 1388
TVAC - Thalidomide Victims Association of Canada, 1373
TVB - Television Bureau of Canada, Inc., 1370
TVTA - Thames Valley Trail Association Inc., 1373
TWBCA - The West Bend Community Association, 1444
TWHAWC - Tennessee Walking Horse Association of Western Canada, 1370
TWIG - Toronto Workforce Innovation Group, 1388
TWS - Toxics Watch Society of Alberta, 1394
TWUC - The Writers' Union of Canada, 1469
TYHS - Town of York Historical Society, 1393

U

UA - United Association of Journeymen & Apprentices of the Plumbing & Pipe Fitting Industry of the United States & Canada, 1599
UAAC - Universities Art Association of Canada, 1418
UAI - Union académique internationale, 1598
UAI - Union of International Associations, 1599
UARR - Urban Alliance on Race Relations, 1422
UASBC - Underwater Archaeological Society of British Columbia, 1404
UAW - International Union, United Automobile, Aerospace & Agricultural Implement Workers of America, 1565
UBCFA - University of British Columbia Faculty Association, 1419
UBCM - Union of British Columbia Municipalities, 1407
UCA - Utility Contractors Association of Ontario, Inc., 1423
UCBC - Underwater Council of British Columbia, 1404
UCC - United Church of Canada, 1409
UCC - Ukrainian Canadian Congress, 1402
UCCE - Union of Calgary Co-op Employees, 1407
UCCLA - Ukrainian Canadian Civil Liberties Association, 1402
UCD - Upper Canada District Canadian Horse Breeders, 1421
UCDA - Used Car Dealers Association of Ontario, 1423
UCFO - L'Union culturelle des Franco-Ontariennes, 1406
UCFO - Union des cultivateurs franco-ontariens, 1406
UCOC - Ucluelet Chamber of Commerce, 1402
UCRDC - Ukrainian Canadian Research & Documentation Centre, 1402
UCT - The Order of United Commercial Travelers of America, 1119
UCTE - Union of Canadian Transportation Employees, 1407
UDA - Union des artistes, 1406
UDA - Union des Artistes (FIA) - Bureau de Québec, 1406
UDA - Union des Artistes (FIA) - Bureau de Toronto, 1406
UDI - Urban Development Institute of Canada, 1422
UEA - Universala Esperanto-Asocio, 1600
UELAC - United Empire Loyalists' Association of Canada, 1410
UEW - Union of Environment Workers, 1407
UFCW - United Food & Commercial Workers' International Union, 1599
UFCW CANADA - United Food & Commercial Workers Canada, 1410
UFI - UFI - The Global Association of the Exhibition Industry, 1598
UFSC - Ukrainian Fraternal Society of Canada, 1403
UF FSA - University of the Fraser Valley Faculty & Staff Association, 1420
UGFSEA - University of Guelph Food Service Employees Association, 1419
UGHSC - Ukrainian Genealogical & Historical Society of Canada, 1403
UGO - United Generations Ontario, 1411
UHC - Unemployed Help Centre, 1404
UIA - Union internationale des architectes, 1598
UIAA - Union internationale des associations d'alpinisme, 1598
UJPO - United Jewish Peoples' Order, 1411
ULC - Underwriters' Laboratories of Canada, 1404
ULCC - Uniform Law Conference of Canada, 1405
ULFA - University of Lethbridge Faculty Association, 1419
UMAAS - Urban Municipal Administrators' Association of Saskatchewan, 1422

UMAC - Urban Music Association of Canada, 1422
UMDF - United Mitochondrial Disease Foundation, 1599
UMFA - University of Manitoba Faculty Association, 1419
UMNB - Union of Municipalities of New Brunswick, 1407
UMOC - United Macedonians Organization of Canada, 1411
UMOFC - Union mondiale des organisations féminines catholiques, 1599
UMQ - Union des municipalités du Québec, 1406
UNA - United Nurses of Alberta, 1412
UNAC - United Nations Association in Canada, 1411
UNCTAD - United Nations Conference on Trade & Development, 1599
UNDE - Union of National Defence Employees, 1407
UNDP - United Nations Development Programme, 1599
UNE - Union of National Employees, 1407
UNEP - United Nations Environment Programme, 1600
UNEP-WCMC - UNEP - World Conservation Monitoring Centre, 1598
UNEQ - Union des écrivaines et écrivains québécois, 1406
UNF - Ukrainian National Federation of Canada, 1403
UNFC - United Native Friendship Centre, 1412
UNIA - Universal Negro Improvement Association of Montreal, 1418
UNIDO - United Nations Industrial Development Organization, 1600
UNRISD - United Nations Research Institute for Social Development, 1600
UNSI - Union of Nova Scotia Indians, 1407
UNSM - Union of Nova Scotia Municipalities, 1407
UNWTO - World Tourism Organization, 1607
UOCC - Ukrainian Orthodox Church of Canada, 1403
UOI - Union of Ontario Indians, 1408
UPA - Union des producteurs agricoles, 1406
UPAA Toronto - University of the Philippines Alumni Association of Toronto, 1420
UPAC - Ultralight Pilots Association of Canada, 1404
UPCE - Union of Postal Communications Employees, 1408
UPEIFA - University of Prince Edward Island Faculty Association, 1420
UPF - Union internationale de la presse francophone, 1598
UQROP - Union québécoise de réhabilitation des oiseaux de proie, 1408
URFA - University of Regina Faculty Association, 1420
URISA - Urban & Regional Information Systems Association, 1601
USAC - University of Saskatchewan Arts Council, 1420
USCC - Union of Spiritual Communities of Christ, 1408
USCJ - United Synagogue of Conservative Judaism, Canadian Region, 1412
USCO - United Senior Citizens of Ontario Inc., 1412
USCRI - U.S. Committee for Refugees & Immigrants, 1601
USFA - University of Saskatchewan Faculty Association, 1420
USGBC - U.S. Green Building Council, 1601
USGE - Union of Solicitor General Employees, 1408
USRC - University Settlement, 1421
USY - United Synagogue Youth, 1412
UTBQ - Union des tenanciers de bars du Québec, 1406
UTE - Union of Taxation Employees, 1408
UTFA - University of Toronto Faculty Association, 1420

Acronym Index

UTU - United Transportation Union (AFL-CIO/CLC), 1600
UUWA - United Utility Workers' Association, 1412
UVAE - Union of Veterans' Affairs Employees, 1408
UW/CO - United Way/Centraide Ottawa, 1418
UWAC - Ukrainian Women's Association of Canada, 1403
UWFA - University of Winnipeg Faculty Association, 1421
UWFV - United Way of the Fraser Valley, 1417
UWGMSENB - United Way of Greater Moncton & Southeastern New Brunswick, 1414
UWO - United Way of Oakville, 1415
UWOSA - University of Western Ontario Staff Association, 1421
UWOSO - University of Western Ontario Symphony Orchestra, 1421
UWSA - University of Waterloo Staff Association, 1421
UWSN - United Way South Niagara, 1417
UWVA - Ukrainian War Veterans Association of Canada, 1403
UWVC - United Way for the City of Kawartha Lakes, 1413

V

VA - Vues d'Afriques - Les Journées du cinéma africain et créole, 1439
VAA - Volkssport Association of Alberta, 1437
VABC - Volkssport Association of British Columbia, 1437
VACC - Valemount & Area Chamber of Commerce, 1423
VAFCS - Vancouver Aboriginal Friendship Centre Society, 1424
VAG - Vancouver Art Gallery Association, 1424
VALID - VALID Association, 1424
VALL - Vancouver Association of Law Libraries, 1425
VanCHI - Special Interest Group on Computer Human Interaction, 1339
VANL-CARFAC - Visual Artists Newfoundland & Labrador, 1436
VanPS - Vancouver Paleontological Society, 1428
VANS - Visual Arts Nova Scotia, 1436
VAQ - Voitures anciennes du Québec inc., 1437
VAST - Vancouver Association for the Survivors of Torture, 1425
VAT - Vietnamese Association, Toronto, 1434
VBDS - Vulcan Business Development Society, 1439
VBGA - VanDusen Botanical Garden Association, 1429
VC - Volleyball Canada, 1437
VCBIA - Vancouver Chinatown Business Improvement Area Society, 1425
VCC - Viscount Cultural Council Inc., 1435
VCC - Vaughan Chamber of Commerce, 1430
VCCFA - Vancouver Community College Faculty Association, 1425
VCCFA - Victoria Canada-China Friendship Association, 1432
VCF - Vietnamese Canadian Federation, 1434
VCN - Vancouver Community Network, 1425
VDLC - Vancouver & District Labour Council, 1424
VEDC - Viking Economic Development Committee, 1434
VEQ - Voice of English-speaking Québec, 1437
VESTA - Vancouver Elementary School Teachers' Association, 1425
VEVA - Vancouver Electric Vehicle Association, 1425
VGAM - Vegetable Growers' Association of Manitoba, 1430
VHEC - Vancouver Holocaust Centre Society - A Museum for Education & Remembrance, 1425
VHF - Victoria Hospitals Foundation, 1432
VHS - Vancouver Humane Society, 1426
VI - The Vinyl Institute, 1601

VIATeC - Vancouver Island Advanced Technology Centre, 1426
VIC - Vision Institute of Canada, 1435
VIC FAN - Vancouver Island Community Forest Action Network, 1426
VICA - Vancouver Island Construction Association, 1426
VIDEA - Victoria International Development Education Association, 1432
VIDO - Vaccine & Infectious Disease Organization, 1423
VIF - Vanier Institute of The Family, 1429
VIFF - Greater Vancouver International Film Festival Society, 786
VIMHC - Vancouver Island Miniature Horse Club, 1426
VIP - Volunteer Grandparents, 1438
VIPIRG - Vancouver Island Public Interest Research Group, 1426
VIRAGS - Vancouver Island Rock & Alpine Garden Society, 1427
VIREB - Vancouver Island Real Estate Board, 1426
VIS - Village International Sudbury, 1435
VIUFA - Vancouver Island University Faculty Association, 1427
VIVA - Vancouver Island Vegan Association, 1427
VJCS - Vernon Japanese Cultural Society, 1431
VLC - Victoria Labour Council, 1433
VLMS - Victoria Lapidary & Mineral Society, 1433
VMA - Vancouver Musicians' Association, 1427
VMPC - Volunteer Management Professionals of Canada, 1439
VMS - Vancouver Multicultural Society, 1427
VMS - Victoria Medical Society, 1433
VMT - Vancouver Moving Theatre, 1427
VNFC - Victoria Native Friendship Centre, 1433
VNM - Vancouver New Music, 1427
VNS - Vancouver Numismatic Society, 1428
VOA - Vancouver Opera, 1428
VOA - Vegetarians of Alberta Association, 1430
VON Canada - Victorian Order of Nurses for Canada, 1434
VoSNL - Visions of Science Network for Learning, 1436
VOV - Victims of Violence, 1432
VPC - Victoria Peace Coalition, 1433
VPO - Vancouver Philharmonic Orchestra, 1428
VQA - Vintners Quality Alliance, 1435
VRA Canada - Vocational Rehabilitation Association of Canada, 1436
VRAN - Vaccination Risk Awareness Network Inc., 1423
VREB - Victoria Real Estate Board, 1433
VRRA - Vintage Road Racing Association, 1435
VRS - Vancouver Recital Society, 1428
VSHJ - Victoria Society for Humanistic Judaism, 1433
VSIVMW - Vancouver Society of Immigrant & Visible Minority Women, 1428
VSO - Vancouver Symphony Society, 1429
VSW - Vancouver Status of Women, 1428
VTA - Voyageur Trail Association, 1439
VTRA - Victoria Therapeutic Riding Association, 1434
VTSL - Vancouver TheatreSports League, 1429
VWS - Valhalla Wilderness Society, 1424
VYSO - Vancouver Youth Symphony Orchestra Society, 1429

W

WAAC - Women's Art Association of Canada, 1461
WAB - Western Association of Broadcasters, 1447
WABC - Worldwide Association of Business Coaches, 1468
WABE - Western Association of Broadcast Engineers, 1447
WACC - World Association for Christian Communication, 1465

WAD - Windsor Association for the Deaf, 1456
WAF - World Armwrestling Federation, 1603
WAHO - World Arabian Horse Organization, 1603
WAITRO - World Association of Industrial & Technological Research Organizations, 1603
WAMTAC - World Amateur Muay Thai Association of Canada, 1465
WANL - Writers' Alliance of Newfoundland & Labrador, 1468
WANTE - Winnipeg Association of Non-Teaching Employees, 1458
WAPSO - Winnipeg Association of Public Service Officers, 1458
WAS - World Aquaculture Society, 1603
WASM - World Association of Sleep Medicine, 1603
WASPaLM - World Association of Societies of Pathology and Laboratory Medicine, 1465
WAVLI - Westcoast Association of Visual Language Interpreters, 1447
WAY - World Assembly of Youth, 1603
WBANA - Wild Blueberry Association of North America, 1453
WBCC - Wild Bird Care Centre, 1453
WBCSD - World Business Council for Sustainable Development, 1603
WBEA - Wood Buffalo Environmental Association, 1463
WBFN - Willow Beach Field Naturalists, 1455
WBGA - Western Barley Growers Association, 1447
WBN - Women's Business Network of Ottawa, 1462
WBOM - Women Business Owners of Manitoba, 1460
WBPANS - Wild Blueberry Producers Association of Nova Scotia, 1454
WBTC - Wycliffe Bible Translators of Canada, Inc., 1470
WCA - Wilderness Canoe Association, 1454
WCAMS - West Coast Amateur Musicians' Society, 1444
WCC - Wetaskiwin Chamber of Commerce, 1451
WCC - Winnipeg Chamber of Commerce, 1458
WCC - Whitby Chamber of Commerce, 1452
WCC - Whitehorse Chamber of Commerce, 1452
WCC - Woodland Cultural Centre, 1464
WCCD - World Council on City Data, 1465
WCCWM - Western Canada Children's Wear Markets, 1447
WCDWA - West Coast Domestic Workers' Association, 1444
WCEA - Winnipeg Clinic Employees Association, 1458
WCEL - West Coast Environmental Law, 1444
WCF - World Curling Federation, 1604
WCF - World Citizen Foundation, 1604
WCF - World Chambers Federation, 1603
WCFA - West Central Forage Association, 1444
WCGCE - The Western Canada Group of Chartered Engineers, 1448
WCHS - Wellington County Historical Society, 1443
WCI - World Coal Institute, 1604
WCIDTA - Western Canada Irish Dancing Teachers Association, 1448
WCM - Women in Capital Markets, 1460
WCMA - Western Canadian Music Alliance, 1449
WCMHC - Western Canadian Miniature Horse Club, 1448
WCPT - World Confederation for Physical Therapy, 1464
WCRA - West Coast Railway Association, 1445
WCS - Woolwich Community Services, 1464
WCS - Waterloo Coin Society, 1442
WCSA - Western Convenience Store Association, 1449
WCSC - Western Canadian Shippers' Coalition, 1449
WCT - Western Canada Theatre Company Society, 1448

WCTD - Western Canada Tire Dealers Association, 1448
WCW - Western Canada Water, 1448
WCWC - Wilderness Committee, 1454
WDACS - Wetaskiwin & District Association for Community Service, 1451
WDBUA - Windsor & District Baseball Umpires Association, 1456
WDC - World Dance Council Ltd., 1604
WDDS - Woodstock & District Developmental Services, 1464
WDF - World Darts Federation, 1604
WE - Women Entrepreneurs of Saskatchewan Inc., 1460
WEA - Winnipeg Executives Association, 1458
WEAO - Water Environment Association of Ontario, 1441
WEC - World Energy Council, 1604
WECAS - Windsor-Essex Children's Aid Society, 1457
WEDO - Women's Environment & Development Organization, 1602
WEF - Water Environment Federation, 1601
WEST - Women Educating in Self-Defense Training, 1460
WESTAC - Western Transportation Advisory Council, 1450
WETRA - Windsor-Essex Therapeutic Riding Association, 1457
WETT - Wood Energy Technology Transfer Inc., 1463
WFA - Welcome Friend Association, 1443
WFA - Western Fair Association, 1449
WFA - Western Finance Association, 1602
WFC - World Federation of Chiropractic, 1466
WFCA - Western Forestry Contractors Association, 1449
WFD - World Federation of the Deaf, 1605
WFG - Winnipeg Film Group, 1458
WFH - World Federation of Hemophilia, 1466
WFIM - Women in Food Industry Management, 1461
WFM - World Federalist Movement, 1605
WFMC - World Federalist Movement - Canada, 1465
WFMH - World Federation for Mental Health, 1605
WFNB - Writers' Federation of New Brunswick, 1468
WFNS - Writers' Federation of Nova Scotia, 1468
WFOT - World Federation of Occupational Therapists, 1605
WFS - World Future Society, 1605
WFSF - World Futures Studies Federation, 1605
WFUES - World Federation of Ukrainian Engineering Societies, 1466
WFUWO - World Federation of Ukrainian Women's Organizations, 1466
WGA - The Writers' Guild of Alberta, 1469
WGC - Winnipeg Gliding Club, 1459
WGC - Writers Guild of Canada, 1468
WGRF - Western Grains Research Foundation, 1449
WGSG - Vasculitis Foundation Canada, 1430
WGSRF - Women's & Gender Studies et Recherches Féminstes, 1461
WHA - Westmount Historical Association, 1451
WHC - Wildlife Habitat Canada, 1454
WHEN - Women's Healthy Environments Network, 1462
WHHS - West Hants Historical Society, 1445
WHL - World Hypertension League, 1466
WHL - Western Hockey League, 1449
WHO - World Health Organization, 1605
WHS - Westmorland Historical Society, 1451
WHS - Winnipeg Humane Society, 1459
WHS - Waterloo Historical Society, 1442
WIA - Windsor Islamic Association, 1456
WIBCA - West Island Black Community Association, 1445
WIC - Women In Crisis (Algoma) Inc., 1460
WICC - Women's Inter-Church Council of Canada, 1462

Acronym Index

WIDHH - Western Institute for the Deaf & Hard of Hearing, 1450
WIFTA - Women in Film & Television Alberta, 1461
WIFTV - Women in Film & Television Vancouver, 1461
WILPF - Women's International League for Peace & Freedom, 1462
WINS - Women's Institutes of Nova Scotia, 1462
WIPSK - Western Independence Party of Saskatchewan, 1450
WJFB - The World Job & Food Bank Inc., 1466
WKRAC - West Kootenay Regional Arts Council, 1445
WLA - World Lottery Association, 1606
WLC - World Literacy of Canada, 1466
WLHS - West Lincoln Historical Society & Archives, 1446
WLRA - World Leisure & Recreation Association, 1606
WLUFA - Wilfrid Laurier University Faculty Association, 1455
WMAF - Western Magazine Awards Foundation, 1450
WMC - Walker Mineralogical Club, 1439
WMC - Wood Manufacturing Council, 1463
WMCT - Women's Musical Club of Toronto, 1463
WMHA - Whitehorse Minor Hockey Association, 1453
WMO - World Meteorological Organization, 1606
WMS - Whitehorse Minor Soccer Association, 1453
WMS - Women's Missionary Society, 1463
WMSC - William Morris Society of Canada, 1455
WNA - World Nuclear Association, 1606
WNHA - Waterton Natural History Association, 1442
WOA - Winnipeg Ostomy Association, 1459
WOBO - World Organization of Building Officials, 1466
WOCCU - World Council of Credit Unions, Inc., 1604
WOD - CanoeKayak Canada Western Ontario Division, 509
WOSC - World Organisation of Systems & Cybernetics, 1606
WOSM - World Organization of the Scout Movement, 1606
WOW - Women of the Word - Toronto, 1461
WPA - Windsor Police Association, 1457
WPA - Winnipeg Police Association, 1459
WPA - World Pheasant Association, 1607
WPABP - Western Canadian Association of Bovine Practitioners, 1448
WPAC - Wood Pellet Association of Canada, 1463
WPC - Water Polo Canada, 1441
WPC - Wood Preservation Canada, 1463
WPC - World Petroleum Council, 1607
WPC - Wildlife Preservation Canada, 1455
WPCAO - Welsh Pony & Cob Association of Ontario, 1444
WPCSC - Welsh Pony & Cob Society of Canada, 1444
WPNB - Water Polo New Brunswick, 1441
WPNL - Water Polo Newfoundland, 1441
WPO - World Ploughing Organization, 1607
WPO - World Packaging Organization, 1607
WPS - Water Polo Saskatchewan Inc., 1441
WPS - Winnipeg Philatelic Society, 1459
WQLC - Western Québec Literacy Council, 1450
WRA - Whistler Resort Association, 1452
WRA - Wildlife Rescue Association of British Columbia, 1455
WRAGS - Western Regional Advocacy Group Society, 1450
WRCLA - Western Red Cedar Lumber Association, 1450
WRDHA - Wild Rose Draft Horse Association, 1454
WREB - Winnipeg Real Estate Board, 1459
WRHF - Waterloo Regional Heritage Foundation, 1442
WRI - World Resources Institute, 1607
WRIB - Women for Recreation, Information & Business, 1460
WRLA - Western Retail Lumber Association, 1450
WRLC - Waterloo Regional Labour Council, 1442
WSAC - West Shore Arts Council, 1446
WSAH - Women's Support Network of York Region, 1463
WSAL - Women's Soccer Assocation of Lethbridge, 1463
WSANL - Wheelchair Sports Association of Newfoundland & Labrador, 1452
WSAVA - World Small Animal Veterinary Association, 1467
WSCA - Western Silvicultural Contractors' Association, 1450
WSE - World Society for Ekistics, 1607
WSGA - The Western Stock Growers' Association, 1450
WSO - World Safety Organization, 1607
WSO - Windsor Symphony Orchestra, 1457
WSO - Winnipeg Symphony Orchestra Inc., 1459
WSO - World Sikh Organization of Canada, 1467
WSPA - World Animal Protection, 1465
WSPS - Workplace Safety & Prevention Services, 1464
WSSA - Weed Science Society of America, 1602
WSWA - Water Ski & Wakeboard Alberta, 1441
WSWBC - Water Ski & Wakeboard British Columbia, 1441
WSWC - Water Ski & Wakeboard Canada, 1441
WSWM - Water Ski - Wakeboard Manitoba, 1441
WSWS - Water Ski & Wakeboard Saskatchewan, 1442
WTA - Wilderness Tourism Association, 1454
WTAY - Wilderness Tourism Association of the Yukon, 1454
WTCA - World Trade Centres Association, 1608
WTCAC - World Trade Centre Atlantic Canada, 1467
WTCM - World Trade Centre Montréal, 1467
WTJHS - West Toronto Junction Historical Society, 1446
WUFA - Windsor University Faculty Association, 1457
WUR - World University Roundtable, 1608
WUSC - World University Service of Canada, 1467
WVA - Winnipeg Vegetarian Association, 1459
WVC - World Vision Canada, 1467
WVMEA - West Vancouver Municipal Employees Association, 1447
WVPA - World Veterinary Poultry Association, 1608
WWCC - Working Women Community Centre, 1464
WWDGBCTC - Waterloo, Wellington, Dufferin & Grey Building & Construction Trades Council, 1442
WWDHLN - Wellington Waterloo Dufferin Health Library Network, 1444
WWE - Women Who Excel Inc., 1461
WWF - WWF International, 1608
WWF-Canada - World Wildlife Fund - Canada, 1468
WWF-USA - World Wildlife Fund - USA, 1608
WWHA - Whitehorse Women's Hockey Association, 1453
WWOOF Canada - WWOOF Canada, 1469
WWWWIW - Windsor Women Working with Immigrant Women, 1457
WXN - Women's Executive Network, 1462

Y

YAA - Yoga Association of Alberta, 1473
YABS - Young Alberta Book Society, 1474
YAC - Yukon Arts Centre, 1477
YACL - Yukon Association for Community Living, 1477
YARA - Yukon Amateur Radio Association, 1477
YAS - Yukon Art Society, 1477
YASC - Yukon Aboriginal Sport Circle, 1476
YAY - Youth Assisting Youth, 1475
YBA - Yukon Broomball Association, 1477
YBC - Youth Bowling Canada, 1475
YBCS - Youth Ballet & Contemporary Dance of Saskatchewan Inc., 1475
YCA - Yukon Council of Archives, 1478
YCA - Yukon Curling Association, 1478
YCA - Yukon Contractors Association, 1478
YCC - Yukon Chamber of Commerce, 1477
YCC - Yarmouth & Area Chamber of Commerce, 1470
YCCA - Yukon Child Care Association, 1477
YCHS - Yukon Church Heritage Society, 1477
YCI - Youth Challenge International, 1475
YCM - Yukon Chamber of Mines, 1477
YCOA - Yukon Council on Aging, 1478
YCS - Yukon Conservation Society, 1477
YDLC - Yorkton & District Labour Council, 1474
YESS - Youth Empowerment & Support Services, 1475
YEU - Yukon Employees Union, 1478
YFC - Youth Flight Canada, 1475
YFF - Yorkton Film Festival, 1474
YFGA - Yukon Fish & Game Association, 1478
YFL - Yukon Federation of Labour, 1478
YFNCT - Yukon First Nations Culture & Tourism Association, 1478
YFS - Yukon Film Society, 1478
YHMA - Yukon Historical & Museums Association, 1478
YHRA - Yukon Horse & Rider Association, 1479
YICC - Youth in Care Canada, 1475
YIHA - Yukon Indian Hockey Association, 1479
YKACL - Yellowknife Association for Community Living, 1470
YKSC - Yellowknife Shooting Club, 1471
YLC - Your Life Counts, 1475
YLC - Yamaska Literacy Council, 1470
YLS - Yukon Learn Society, 1479
YMTA - Yukon Mine Training Association, 1479
YNOT - Youth Now on Track Program, 1476
YOA - Yukon Outfitters' Association, 1479
YOA - Yukon Orienteering Association, 1479
YOC - Yukon Outdoors Club, 1479
YOOP - Yukon Order of Pioneers, 1479
YPA - Yukon Prospectors' Association, 1479
YPLEA - Yukon Public Legal Education Association, 1479
YPO - Young Presidents' Organization, 1608
YPP - Your Political Party of BC, 1475
YPT - Young People's Theatre, 1474
YRAA - York Region Athletic Association, 1473
YREA - Yorkton Real Estate Association Inc., 1474
YRNA - Yukon Registered Nurses Association, 1480
YRPA - York Regional Police Association, 1473
YSAA - Yukon Schools' Athletic Association, 1480
YSC - Youth Singers of Calgary, 1476
YSC - Youth Science Canada, 1476
YSLPAA - Yukon Speech-Language Pathology & Audiology Association, 1480
YSM - Yonge Street Mission, 1473
YTA - Yukon Teachers' Association, 1480
YTEC - Yukon Tourism Education Council, 1480
YUDA - Yukon Underwater Diving Association, 1480
YUFA - York University Faculty Association, 1474
YWS - Youth Without Shelter, 1476

Z

ZSO - Zoroastrian Society of Ontario, 1482

Budget Index

- Canadian and foreign associations listed by annual budget size in eight ranges (less than $50,000; $50,000 - $100,000; $100,000 - $250,000; $250,000 - $500,000; $500,000 - $1,500,000; $1,500,000 - $3,000,000; $3,000,000 - $5,000,000; greater than $5 million)
- Each entry is accompanied by a page number which points you to the corresponding listing in the alphabetical listings of Canadian and foreign associations

Less than $50,000

Aboriginal Women's Association of Prince Edward Island, 3
Académie de musique du Québec, 3
The Acadian Entomological Society, 4
Accelerated Christian Education Canada, 4
ACT for the Earth, 5
Adoption Roots & Rights, 9
Adventive Cross Cultural Initiatives, 10
Aerospace Heritage Foundation of Canada, 11
Affirm United, 11
African Literature Association, 1486
Agricultural Institute of Canada Foundation, 15
Aguasabon Chamber of Commerce, 15
Alberta Agricultural Economics Association, 21
Alberta Associations for Bright Children, 25
Alberta Cerebral Palsy Sport Association, 27
Alberta Criminal Justice Association, 32
Alberta Family History Society, 34
Alberta Horse Trials Association, 37
Alberta Lake Management Society, 39
Alberta Metallic Silhouette Association, 40
Alberta Municipal Clerks Association, 40
Alberta Reappraising AIDS Society, 43
Alberta Reined Cow Horse Association, 44
Alberta Salers Association, 45
Alberta Sheep Breeders Association, 46
Alberta Shorthorn Association, 46
Alberta Society of Surveying & Mapping Technologies, 48
The Alcuin Society, 53
Alexandra Writers' Centre Society, 53
Alfa Romeo Club of Canada, 53
Algoma District Law Association, 53
Algonquin Arts Council, 53
Alix Chamber of Commerce, 54
Alliance des massothérapeutes du Québec, 56
Alliance for Sustainability, 1487
Amalgamated Conservation Society, 66
American Rhododendron Society, 1497
American Saddlebred Horse Association of Alberta, 66
American Society of Plastic Surgeons, 1502
Amici dell'Enotria Toronto, 67
Les AmiEs de la Terre de Québec, 67
Ancient, Free & Accepted Masons of Canada - Grand Lodge of Prince Edward Island, 69
Antiquarian Booksellers' Association of Canada, 72
Arborfield Board of Trade, 76
ARC - Aînés et retraités de la communauté, 76
Archaeological Society of Alberta, 76
Archelaus Smith Historical Society, 78
Archers Association of Nova Scotia, 78
Architectural Woodwork Manufacturers Association of Canada - Atlantic, 79
Architectural Woodwork Manufacturers Association of Canada - Manitoba, 79
Architectural Woodwork Manufacturers Association of Canada - Ontario Chapter, 79
Architectural Woodwork Manufacturers Association of Canada - Québec, 80
Armenian General Benevolent Union, 83
Arrow Lakes Historical Society, 84
Arrowsmith Naturalists, 84
Arthur & District Chamber of Commerce, 84
Arts Council of Sault Ste Marie & District, 85
Arts Richmond Hill, 86
Artscape, 86
Assemblée parlementaire de la Francophonie, 88
Assiniboia & District Arts Council, 88
Associated Research Centres for the Urban Underground Space, 89
Association canadienne des relations industrielles, 94

Association canadienne des sciences régionales, 95
Association coopérative d'économie familiale du Grand-Portage, 98
Association de la sécurité de l'information du Québec, 102
L'Association des artistes Baltes à Montréal, 106
Association des artistes en arts visuels de Saint-Jérôme, 106
Association des bibliothèques de la santé affiliées à l'Université de Montréal, 107
Association des éleveurs de chevaux Belge du Québec, 111
Association des enseignants en infographie et en imprimerie du Québec, 112
Association des entrepreneurs en maçonnerie du Québec, 112
Association des familles Rioux d'Amérique inc., 113
Association des ingénieurs-professeurs des sciences appliquées, 116
Association des médecins cliniciens enseignants de Laval, 119
Association des personnes handicapés visuels de l'Estrie, inc, 123
Association des professeurs de Campus Notre-Dame-de-Foy, 124
Association des véhicules électriques du Québec, 130
Association des vietnamiens de Sherbrooke, 130
Association du syndrome de Down de L'Estrie, 131
Association for Canadian Educational Resources, 132
Association for Canadian Jewish Studies, 132
Association for Canadian Studies in the Netherlands, 1507
Association for Corporate Growth, Toronto Chapter, 133
Association for the Advancement of Scandinavian Studies in Canada, 134
Association internationale des études patristiques, 1509
Association montérégienne de la surdité inc., 137
Association of Administrative Professionals, 139
Association of Alberta Agricultural Fieldmen, 139
Association of Canadian Choral Communities, 141
Association of Canadian Industrial Designers, 142
Association of Canadian University Presses, 144
Association of Chartered Industrial Designers of Ontario, 145
Association of Christian Churches in Manitoba, 145
Association of Great Lakes Outdoor Writers, 1512
Association of Holocaust Organizations, 1512
The Association of Maritime Arbitrators of Canada, 151
Association of Municipal Administrators of New Brunswick, 152
Association of Registrars of the Universities & Colleges of Canada, 161
Association of Saskatchewan Forestry Professionals, 161
Association of the Chemical Profession of Ontario, 163
Association pour la prévention de la contamination de l'air et du sol, 166
Association pour les applications pédagogiques de l'ordinateur au postsecondaire, 167

Association québécoise d'urbanisme, 168
Association québécoise de soins palliatifs, 171
Association québécoise de Vol Libre, 171
Association québécoise des écoles de français langue étrangère, 172
Association québécoise des infirmières et intervenants en recherche clinique, 173
Association québécoise des interprètes du patrimoine, 173
Association québécoise des orthophonistes et des audiologistes, 173
Association syndicale des employées de production et de service, 178
Athabasca University Faculty Association, 180
Atikokan Chamber of Commerce, 181
Atlantic Canada Pipe Band Association, 182
Atlantic Episcopal Assembly, 183
Atlantic Provinces Linguistic Association, 185
Atlin Board of Trade, 187
Ausable Bayfield Conservation Foundation, 188
The Avian Preservation Foundation, 190
Avicultural Advancement Council of Canada, 191
Barrhead & District Chamber of Commerce, 197
Barriere & District Chamber of Commerce, 197
Baseball PEI, 198
Batten Disease Support & Research Association - Canadian Chapter, 199
Baycrest Foundation, 200
BC Rural & Multigrade Teachers' Association, 202
Beausejour & District Chamber of Commerce, 203
Benevolent Irish Society of Prince Edward Island, 205
The Bible Holiness Movement, 208
Biggar & District Chamber of Commerce, 211
Bikes Without Borders, 211
Binbrook Agricultural Society, 211
Blaine Lake & District Chamber of Commerce, 214
Blankets for Canada Society Inc., 214
Blenheim & District Chamber of Commerce, 214
Bonavista Area Chamber of Commerce, 217
Bonavista Historic Townscape Foundation, 217
Boot'n Bonnet British Car Club, 218
Bothwell-Zone & District Historical Society, 218
Boundary Organic Producers Association, 219
Brantford Musicians' Association, 227
Brereton Field Naturalists' Club Inc., 228
British Columbia Farm Machinery & Agriculture Museum Association, 240
British Columbia Fuchsia & Begonia Society, 242
British Columbia Genealogical Society, 242
British Columbia Grapegrowers' Association, 242
British Columbia Historical Federation, 243
British Columbia Veterinary Technologists Association, 257
British Isles Family History Society of Greater Ottawa, 259
Bruce Peninsula Environment Group, 261
Buckskinners Muzzleloading Association, Limited, 261
Building Envelope Council of Ottawa Region, 262
Bully B'Ware, 264
BullyingCanada Inc., 264
Burlington Association for Nuclear Disarmament, 265
Cabbagetown Preservation Association, 268
Caledon East & District Historical Society, 270
Calgary & District Target Shooters Association, 270
Calgary Field Naturalists' Society, 272
Calgary Numismatic Society, 273

Campbellford/Seymour Heritage Society, 276
Canadian Agri-Marketing Association (Manitoba), 290
Canadian Association for Commonwealth Literature & Language Studies, 298
Canadian Association for Renewable Energies, 303
Canadian Association for Teacher Education, 304
Canadian Association of Foundations of Education, 315
Canadian Association of Pharmacy Students & Interns, 326
Canadian Association of Physicians of Indian Heritage, 327
Canadian Association of Physicians with Disabilities, 327
Canadian Association of School Social Workers & Attendance Counsellors, 332
Canadian Aviation Artists Assocation, 340
Canadian Band Association, 340
Canadian Battlefields Foundation, 342
Canadian Carwash Association, 350
Canadian Catholic Historical Association - English Section, 351
Canadian Committee of Byzantinists, 360
Canadian Concrete Pipe Association, 362
Canadian Council of Muslim Women, 369
Canadian Council of Teachers of English Language Arts, 370
Canadian Crafts Federation, 372
Canadian Dance Teachers' Association, 375
Canadian Dexter Cattle Association, 377
Canadian Farm Builders Association, 384
Canadian Federation of Apartment Associations, 385
Canadian Fluid Power Association, 391
Canadian Galloway Association, 396
Canadian Geophysical Union, 397
Canadian Haflinger Association, 400
Canadian Institute of Quantity Surveyors - British Columbia, 419
Canadian Institute of Quantity Surveyors - Maritimes, 419
Canadian Lesbian & Gay Archives, 426
Canadian Nautical Research Society, 440
Canadian Nursing Informatics Association, 443
Canadian Occupational Health Nurses Association, 444
Canadian Orthopaedic Nurses Association, 448
The Canadian Philatelic Society of Great Britain, 1515
Canadian Plowing Organization, 456
Canadian Pony Society, 458
Canadian Psychological Association, 462
Canadian Quilters' Association, 464
Canadian Red Poll Cattle Association, 466
Canadian Rose Society, 468
Canadian Science & Technology Historical Association, 468
Canadian Snack Food Association, 472
Canadian Society for Chemical Technology, 473
Canadian Society for Education through Art, 474
Canadian Society for Engineering Management, 474
The Canadian Society for Mesopotamian Studies, 476
Canadian Society for the Prevention of Cruelty to Children, 477
Canadian Society for Traditional Music, 479
Canadian Society for Transfusion Medicine, 479
Canadian Society of Consultant Pharmacists, 482
Canadian Society of Environmental Biologists, 482

Budget Index / Less than $50,000

Canadian Sport Massage Therapists Association, 490
Canadian Theosophical Association, 494
Canadian Tire Coupon Collectors Club, 495
Canadian Toy Collectors' Society Inc., 496
Canadian Trapshooting Association, 497
Canadian Tribute to Human Rights, 497
Canadian Unitarians for Social Justice, 499
Canadian University Music Society, 499
Canadian Volkssport Federation, 501
Canadian Well Logging Society, 503
Canadian Women's Foundation, 505
Canadian Wood Truss Association, 505
Canadian-Cuban Friendship Association Toronto, 506
CANGRANDS Kinship Support, 508
Cape Breton University Faculty Association, 510
Carleton Literacy Council, 513
Carleton Place & District Chamber of Commerce & Visitor Centre, 513
Carman & Community Chamber of Commerce, 514
Central Ontario Orchid Society, 525
Centre de recherche et d'intervention interuniversitaire sur l'éducation et la vie au travail, 530
Certification Council of Early Childhood Educators of Nova Scotia, 538
Chambre de commerce au Coeur de la Montérégie, 539
Chambre de commerce de Brandon, 540
Chambre de commerce de Chibougamau, 540
Chambre de commerce de Ferme-Neuve, 541
Chambre de commerce de Mont-Tremblant, 542
Chambre de commerce et d'industrie de Dolbeau-Mistassini, 545
Chambre de commerce et d'Industrie de la région de Coaticook, 545
Chambre de commerce et d'industrie de Roberval, 546
Chambre de commerce et d'industrie de Shawinigan, 546
Chambre de commerce et d'industrie du bassin de Chambly, 547
Chambre de commerce Mont-Saint-Bruno, 549
Child & Family Services of Western Manitoba, 558
Child & Youth Care Association of Alberta, 558
Children's Heart Association for Support & Education, 561
Christian Catholic Church Canada, 566
Clan Fraser Society of Canada, 571
Clan Gunn Society of North America - Eastern Canada Branch, 571
Clan Lamont Society of Canada, 571
Clan Mackenzie Society of Canada, 571
Clans & Scottish Societies of Canada, 572
Club des collectionneurs d'épinglettes Inc., 575
Club des ornithologues de Québec inc., 575
Coaldale & District Chamber of Commerce, 577
A coeur joie Nouveau-Brunswick Inc., 580
College of Dental Hygienists of Nova Scotia, 583
Comité culturel "La Chaussée", 591
Comité de bénévolat de Rogersville, 591
Commission canadienne d'histoire militaire, 592
Commission de la Médiathèque Père-Louis-Lamontagne, 593
Commonwealth Forestry Association - Canadian Chapter, 593
The Comparative & International Education Society of Canada, 608
Compton Historical Society, 609
Concerned Educators Allied for a Safe Environment, 1519
Concrete Forming Association of Ontario, 610
Confederation of Resident & Ratepayer Associations, 611
Congregation of St. Basil, 613
Connexions Information Sharing Services, 613
Conseil de l'enveloppe du bâtiment du Québec, 615
Cornwall Township Historical Society, 629

Coronach Community Chamber of Commerce, 629
Coronation Chamber of Commerce, 629
Corporation des thérapeutes du sport du Québec, 631
Corporation des traducteurs, traductrices, terminologues et interprètes du Nouveau-Brunswick, 631
Corsa Ontario, 631
Council of Canadian Law Deans, 633
Council of Outdoor Educators of Ontario, 635
Cowichan Lake District Chamber of Commerce, 637
The CPR Stockholder's Society, 638
Creation Science Association of British Columbia, 639
Creation Science of Saskatchewan Inc., 639
Crystal City & District Chamber of Commerce, 645
Cumberland Chamber of Commerce, 645
Customer Service Professionals Network, 646
Dads Can, 648
Danish Canadian Chamber of Commerce, 650
Dartmouth Historical Association, 651
Dartmouth N.S. Family History Centre, 651
DeBolt & District Pioneer Museum Society, 652
Deloraine & District Chamber of Commerce, 653
Devon & District Chamber of Commerce, 655
Diamond Valley Chamber of Commerce, 656
Dictionary Society of North America, 1521
Digital Imaging Association, 656
Dignity Toronto Dignité, 657
Dignity Vancouver Dignité, 657
Dignity Winnipeg Dignité, 657
Disability Awareness Consultants, 658
Dundalk Historical Society, 664
Dutch-Canadian Association Ottawa Valley/Outaouais, 665
East European Genealogical Society, Inc., 668
East Georgian Bay Historical Foundation, 668
East York Historical Society, 669
Edmonton & District Council of Churches, 675
Edmonton Composers' Concert Society, 676
Edmonton Stamp Club, 679
Edmonton Weavers' Guild, 679
Enderby & District Museum Society, 687
The Endometriosis Network, 687
Endurance Riders Association of British Columbia, 687
Entomological Society of Alberta, 690
Entomological Society of Manitoba Inc., 690
Entomological Society of Ontario, 690
Entomological Society of Saskatchewan, 690
Environmental Abatement Council of Ontario, 691
Errington Therapeutic Riding Association, 695
Esperanto Association of Canada, 695
Esperanto Rondo de Otavo, 695
Esperanto-Toronto, 695
Essex County Stamp Club (Windsor), 696
Essex-Kent Cage Bird Society, 696
Eston Arts Council, 697
Ex Libris Association, 699
Explorer's Club (Canadian Chapter), 700
Falcon, West Hawk & Caddy Lakes Chamber of Commerce, 701
Federation of Canadian Music Festivals, 723
Federation of Ontario Bed & Breakfast Accommodation, 725
Federation of Ontario Memorial Societies - Funeral Consumers Alliance, 726
Fédération québécoise de naturisme, 727
Fédération québécoise de philatélie, 728
Fédération québécoise du loisir littéraire, 731
Fibromyalgia Support Group of Winnipeg, Inc., 733
Finnish Canadian Cultural Federation, 737
Fire Fighters Historical Society of Winnipeg, Inc., 738
FloraQuebeca, 741
Folklore Studies Association of Canada, 742
Fondation Caritas-Sherbrooke inc., 743
Fort St. James Chamber of Commerce, 753
Fort Simpson Chamber of Commerce, 754

Foundation for Prader-Willi Research in Canada, 756
Fredericton Fish & Game Association, 759
Frères de Notre-Dame de la Miséricorde, 760
Friends Historical Association, 1527
Friends of Nature Conservation Society, 761
Friends of the Forestry Farm House Inc., 762
Friends of the Greater Sudbury Public Library, 762
Friends of the Oldman River, 763
Funeral Consumers Advocacy of London & Windsor, 764
Funeral Information & Memorial Society of Guelph, 764
Galiano Island Chamber of Commerce, 766
Gander & Area Society for the Prevention of Cruelty to Animals, 766
Gay Fathers of Toronto, 768
Georgian Bay Steam & Antique Association, 771
German-Canadian Congress (Manitoba) Inc., 772
Global Village Nanaimo, 775
Grand Chapter, R.A.M. of Nova Scotia, 779
Grand Manan Museum Inc., 780
Grand Manan Tourism Association & Chamber of Commerce, 780
Grand Orange Lodge of Canada, 780
Grand River Conservation Foundation, 780
Grande Cache Chamber of Commerce, 780
Grandview & District Chamber of Commerce, 781
Gravelbourg Chamber of Commerce, 782
The Great Herd of Bisons of the Fertile Plains, 782
Great Slave Snowmobile Association, 782
Grey Highlands Chamber of Commerce, 790
Grimshaw & District Chamber of Commerce, 790
Groupe de recherche en écologie sociale, 791
Guelph Hiking Trail Club, 793
Guelph Historical Society, 793
Guelph Musicfest, 793
Guid'amies franco-manitobaines, 793
Guillain-Barré Syndrome Foundation of Canada, 794
Guitar Society of Toronto, 794
Guysborough Historical Society, 795
Halifax Field Naturalists, 799
Halifax Regional Cerebral Palsy Association, 799
Hamilton Naturalists' Club, 801
Hamilton Stamp Club, 802
Hampton Food Basket & Clothing Centre Inc., 802
Hanna Museum & Pioneer Village, 803
Hantsport & Area Historical Society, 803
Harry A. Newman Memorial Foundation, 804
Hawkesbury & Region Chamber of Commerce, 805
Hearst, Mattice - Val Côté & Area Chamber of Commerce, 808
Help for Headaches, 812
Heritage Winnipeg Corp., 813
Historical Automobile Society of Canada, Inc., 816
Historical Society of St. Catharines, 816
Horse Trials New Brunswick, 822
Horse Trials Nova Scotia, 822
Horseshoe Saskatchewan Inc., 822
Hudson's Hope Museum, 824
Human Rights & Race Relations Centre, 826
Humanist Canada, 826
Hungarian Canadian Engineers' Association, 827
Icelandic National League of North America, 829
ICOMOS Canada, 829
Infant & Toddler Safety Association, 836
Ingersoll District Nature Club, 838
Injured Workers Association of Manitoba Inc., 838
Innisfail & District Chamber of Commerce, 839
Innkeepers Guild of Nova Scotia, 839
InScribe Christian Writers' Fellowship, 839

Insitut canadien des économistes en construction - Québec, 840
Institute of Certified Management Consultants of British Columbia, 845
Institute of Certified Management Consultants of Manitoba, 845
Institute of Textile Science, 847
Insurance Women's Association of Western Manitoba, 850
Integrity Toronto, 850
International Arthurian Society - North American Branch, 1535
International Association of Educators for World Peace - USA, 1538
International Association of Hydrogeologists - Canadian National Chapter, 854
International Association of Physicians in Audiology, 1539
International Catholic Deaf Association, 854
International Commission of Jurists (Canadian Section), 855
International Council for Applied Mineralogy, 1544
International Council for Archaeozoology, 1544
International Council for Central & East European Studies (Canada), 1544
International Council of Associations for Science Education, 1545
International Federation for Research in Women's History, 1547
International ISBN Agency, 1551
International Law Association - Canadian Branch, 858
International Peat Society - Canadian National Committee, 859
International PhotoTherapy Association, 859
International Society for Business Education, 1557
International Society of Friendship & Good Will, 1560
International Symphony Orchestra Youth String Ensemble, 861
Irma Fish & Game Association, 864
Iroquois Falls & District Chamber of Commerce, 864
Jeunes canadiens pour une civilisation chrétienne, 870
Jewish Genealogical Society of Toronto, 872
Joubert Syndrome & Related Disoarders Foundation, 1568
Judo Yukon, 876
Junior League of Halifax, 878
Kabuki Syndrome Network Inc., 879
Kamloops Naturalist Club, 880
Kamsack & District Arts Council, 881
Kensington & Area Chamber of Commerce, 883
Kent Centre Chamber of Commerce, 883
Killam & District Chamber of Commerce, 887
Kindersley Chamber of Commerce, 888
Kingston Field Naturalists, 889
Kingston Historical Society, 889
Kingston Stamp Club, 889
Kirkland Lake District Chamber of Commerce, 890
Kitchener-Waterloo Field Naturalists, 890
Kitimat Community Services Society, 891
LaHave Islands Marine Museum Society, 895
Lakeland United Way, 896
Lambton County Historical Society, 897
Lambton Wildlife Inc., 897
Land Improvement Contractors of Ontario, 897
Langley Field Naturalists Society, 899
Leaf Rapids Chamber of Commerce, 903
Legislative Recording & Broadcast Association, 906
Lethbridge & District Humane Society, 907
Lethbridge Fish & Game Association, 908
Lighthouse Food Bank Society, 912
Likely & District Chamber of Commerce, 912
The Lithuanian Society of Edmonton, 915
Little People of Manitoba, 915
Little People of Ontario, 915
London Philatelic Society, 918
The Lord's Flock Charismatic Community, 919
Lumby Chamber of Commerce, 920

Budget Index / Less than $50,000

Lundy's Lane Historical Society, 920
Lunenburg County Historical Society, 921
Lunenburg Heritage Society, 921
Lymphovenous Association of Ontario, 923
Lytton & District Chamber of Commerce, 923
MacGregor Chamber of Commerce, 924
Mackenzie & District Museum Society, 924
Mackenzie Community Arts Council, 924
Macklin Chamber of Commerce, 924
Mactaquac Country Chamber of Commerce, 924
The Magic of Christmas, 925
Mahatma Gandhi Canadian Foundation for World Peace, 925
La Maison de la culture inc., 926
Maltese-Canadian Society of Toronto, Inc., 928
Manitoba Antique Association, 928
Manitoba Association of Landscape Architects, 930
Manitoba Association of Parent Councils, 930
Manitoba Association of Sheet Metal & Air Handling Contractors Inc., 931
Manitoba Blind Sports Association, 932
Manitoba Cultural Society of the Deaf, 935
Manitoba Underwater Council, 946
Manitoba UNIX User Group, 946
Mannville & District Chamber of Commerce, 948
Maple Creek Chamber of Commerce, 948
Marathon & District Chamber of Commerce, 949
Margaret M. Allemang Centre for the History of Nursing, 949
Margaret Morris Method (Canada), 949
Maritime Aberdeen Angus Association, 950
Maritime Sikh Society, 951
Marwayne & District Chamber of Commerce, 952
Mazda Sportscar Owners Club, 954
McBride & District Chamber of Commerce, 955
Meadow Lake & District Chamber of Commerce, 956
Medicine Hat Fish & Game Association, 958
Melville & District Chamber of Commerce, 959
Memorial Society of Edmonton & District, 960
Memorial Society of Northern Ontario, 960
Merit Canada, 961
Merit Contractors Association of Manitoba, 962
Metro (Toronto) Association of Family Resource Programs, 963
Metropolitan Community Church of Toronto, 964
Middle River & Area Historical Society, 964
Miniature Horse Association of Nova Scotia, 966
Minnedosa Chamber of Commerce, 968
Mission Bon Accueil, 969
Mission Community Services Food Centre, 969
Moosomin Chamber of Commerce, 974
Morgan Sports Car Club of Canada, 974
Morris & District Chamber of Commerce, 974
Mount View Special Riding Association, 976
Mouvement des femmes Chrétiennes, 977
Multiple Births Canada, 979
Municipal Information Systems Association of Canada, 981
Muskoka Lakes Chamber of Commerce, 985
Muslim Council of Montréal, 985
Nakusp & District Chamber of Commerce, 987
Nanton & District Chamber of Commerce, 988
National Association for Environmental Education (UK), 1572
National ME/FM Action Network, 995
National Pensioners Federation, 995
Natural History Society of Newfoundland & Labrador, 999
Nelson & District Arts Council, 1003
Netball Alberta, 1003
New Brunswick Arts Board, 1004
New Brunswick Association of Dietitians, 1005
New Brunswick Association of Food Banks, 1005
The New Brunswick Association of Respiratory Therapists Inc., 1005

New Brunswick Association of Speech-Language Pathologists & Audiologists, 1006
New Brunswick Federation of Home & School Associations, Inc., 1008
New Brunswick Federation of Music Festivals Inc., 1008
New Brunswick Filmmakers' Co-op, 1008
New Brunswick Ground Water Association, 1009
New Brunswick Multicultural Council, 1010
New Denmark Historical Society, 1014
Newfoundland & Labrador College of Dietitians, 1017
Newfoundland & Labrador Institute of Agrologists, 1019
Newfoundland & Labrador Occupational Therapy Board, 1020
Newfoundland Horticultural Society, 1023
Nicola Valley Community Arts Council, 1026
Nipawin & District Chamber of Commerce, 1027
Norfolk Field Naturalists, 1028
North American Society for Oceanic History, 1579
North Durham Social Development Council, 1030
North Grenville Historical Society, 1031
North Lanark Historical Society, 1031
North Okanagan Naturalists Club, 1031
North Okanagan Organic Association, 1031
North Sydney Historical Society, 1033
North York Coin Club, 1033
North York General Foundation, 1033
Northern Ramblers Car Club Inc., 1035
Northwatch, 1036
Northwest Territories Amateur Speed Skating Association, 1037
Northwestern Ontario Associated Chambers of Commerce, 1039
Northwestern Ontario Technology Association, 1040
Nova Scotia Ball Hockey Association, 1041
Nova Scotia Dental Assistants' Association, 1044
Nova Scotia Dietetic Association, 1044
Nova Scotia Federation of Home & School Associations, 1044
Nova Scotia Forest Technicians Association, 1045
The Nova Scotia Genealogy Network Association, 1045
Nova Scotia Hereford Club, 1045
Nova Scotia Horseshoe Players Association, 1046
Nova Scotia Institute of Agrologists, 1046
Nova Scotia Lighthouse Preservation Society, 1047
Nova Scotia Music Educators' Association, 1047
Nova Scotia Public Interest Research Group, 1047
Nova Scotia Rifle Association, 1048
Nova Scotia School Counsellor Association, 1048
Nova Scotia Society of Occupational Therapists, 1049
Nova Scotia Stamp Club, 1049
Nova Scotia Wild Flora Society, 1050
NSERC Chair for Women in Science & Engineering, 1050
Oak Ridges Trail Association, 1053
Okanagan Similkameen Parks Society, 1056
Olds College Faculty Association, 1057
Oliver Community Arts Council, 1057
Oliver-Osoyoos Naturalists, 1057
100 Mile & District Arts Council, 1058
Ontario Amputee & Les Autres Sports Association, 1059
Ontario Art Therapy Association, 1060
Ontario Association of Pathologists, 1065
Ontario Association of Quick Printers, 1065
Ontario Association of Student Financial Aid Administrators, 1066
Ontario Cavy Club, 1070
Ontario CGIT Association, 1071

Ontario Coalition of Rape Crisis Centres, 1072
Ontario Community Justice Association, 1073
Ontario Consultants on Religious Tolerance, 1074
Ontario Farm Fresh Marketing Association, 1078
Ontario Fire Buff Associates, 1080
Ontario Goat Breeders Association, 1083
Ontario Horse Trials Association, 1086
Ontario Horticultural Association, 1086
Ontario Provincial Trapshooting Association, 1098
Ontario Recovery Group Inc., 1100
Ontario Rock Garden Society, 1102
Ontario Shorthorn Association, 1104
Ontario Skeet Shooting Association, 1104
Ontario Society for Environmental Education, 1105
Ontario Therapeutic Riding Association, 1110
Ontario Trails Council, 1111
Ontario Urban Forest Council, 1112
Operation Springboard, 1116
Organization of Canadian Nuclear Industries, 1125
Orienteering New Brunswick, 1126
Orillia & District Construction Association, 1126
Orléans Chamber of Commerce, 1126
Ottawa Economics Association, 1130
Ottawa Independent Writers, 1130
Ottawa Valley Curling Association, 1132
Our Lady of Good Health Tamil Parish, 1133
Pakistan Canada Association of Calgary, 1137
Parent Cooperative Preschools International, 1139
Parent Finders Ottawa, 1139
Parkland Food Bank, 1142
Parrot Association of Canada, 1143
Parrsborough Shore Historical Society, 1143
Parti communiste révolutionnaire, 1144
The Pas Arts Council Inc., 1144
Peace Curling Association, 1147
Peace Parkland Naturalists, 1147
Peel Regional Labour Council, 1148
Pemberton & District Chamber of Commerce, 1149
Pembroke Area Field Naturalists, 1149
Pembroke Kiwanis Music Festival, 1149
Pender Harbour & District Chamber of Commerce, 1149
The Pennsylvania German Folklore Society of Ontario, 1149
Personal Computer Club of Toronto, 1152
Pesticide Education Network, 1153
Peterborough Numismatic Club, 1153
Picton United Church County Food Bank, 1159
Pigeon Lake Regional Chamber of Commerce, 1159
Pilot Mound & District Chamber of Commerce, 1160
Pincher Creek Humane Society, 1160
Pittsburgh Historical Society, 1160
Plum Coulee & District Chamber of Commerce, 1163
Police Martial Arts Association Inc., 1163
Port Clements Historical Society, 1165
Port McNeill & District Chamber of Commerce, 1166
Portage Plains United Way, 1167
Portuguese Interagency Network, 1167
Postal History Society of Canada, 1168
Pouce Coupe & District Museum & Historical Society, 1168
Prince Edward Island Dietetic Association, 1173
Prince Edward Island Eco-Net, 1173
Prince Edward Island Forest Improvement Association, 1174
Prince Edward Island Karate Association, 1175
Prince Edward Island Rifle Association, 1176
Prince Edward Island Senior Citizens Federation Inc., 1177
Prince Edward Island Table Tennis Association, 1178
Prince Rupert Fire Museum Society, 1179
Princess Patricia's Canadian Light Infantry Association, 1180

Project Peacemakers, 1187
Provincial Association of Resort Communities of Saskatchewan, 1190
Provincial Council of Women of Manitoba Inc., 1190
Psychosocial Rehabilitation Canada, 1192
Québec Family History Society, 1197
Québec Simmental Association, 1198
Québec Thistle Council Inc., 1199
Québec Women's Institutes, 1199
Quesnel & District Arts Council, 1200
RA Stamp Club, 1202
Rainy River District Municipal Association, 1204
Rare Breeds Canada, 1204
Recreational Canoeing Association BC, 1208
Red Deer Action Group, 1209
Red Deer River Naturalists, 1209
Red River Apiarists' Association, 1210
The Reformed Episcopal Church of Canada - Diocese of Western Canada & Alaska, 1210
Regina Coin Club, 1211
Regroupement des personnes vivant avec le VIH-sida de Québec et la région, 1215
Regroupement des Sourds de Chaudière-Appalaches, 1215
Regroupement pour l'intégration sociale de Charlevoix, 1216
Réseau des SADC et CAE, 1219
Réseau Tara Canada (Québec), 1226
Resilient Flooring Contractors Association of Ontario, 1226
Rideau Valley Field Naturalists, 1231
Right to Quiet Society, 1232
Rimbey Fish & Game Association, 1232
Ringette Nova Scotia, 1233
Rivers & District Chamber of Commerce, 1234
Roblin & District Chamber of Commerce, 1235
Romanian Children's Relief, 1235
La Ronge & District Chamber of Commerce, 1236
Rosetown & District Chamber of Commerce, 1236
Rossburn & District Chamber of Commerce, 1236
Royal Alberta United Services Institute, 1237
Royal Canadian Artillery Association, 1239
The Royal Nova Scotia Historical Society, 1242
Rushnychok Ukrainian Folk Dancing Association, 1244
Russell & District Chamber of Commerce, 1244
St. Andrew's Society of Toronto, 1248
St Anthony & Area Chamber of Commerce, 1248
St. John's Philatelic Society, 1249
St. Stephen Area Chamber of Commerce, 1251
St. Walburg Chamber of Commerce, 1251
Sar-El Canada, 1253
Saskatchewan Agricultural Graduates' Association Inc., 1255
Saskatchewan Agricultural Hall of Fame, 1255
Saskatchewan Deaf Sports Association, 1263
Saskatchewan Library Trustees' Association, 1269
Saskatoon Heritage Society, 1279
Saskatoon Musicians' Association, 1279
Sauble Beach Chamber of Commerce, 1280
Sault Naturalists, 1281
Sault Ste Marie Musicians' Association, 1281
Save Ontario Shipwrecks, 1281
Scarborough Historical Society, 1282
The Scots Society of Colchester, 1286
Scugog Chamber of Commerce, 1287
Seagull Foundation, 1288
Sealant & Waterproofing Association, 1288
Selkirk & District Chamber of Commerce, 1289
Seniors for Nature Canoe Club, 1290
Service budgétaire Lac-Saint-Jean-Est, 1291
Shaarei Tefillah, 1293
Shaunavon Arts Council, 1294
Shaunavon Chamber of Commerce, 1294
Sheet Harbour & Area Chamber of Commerce & Civic Affairs, 1295
Shiatsu Therapy Association of Ontario, 1296
Shooting Federation of Nova Scotia, 1297
Sidaction Mauricie, 1298

Silver Trail Chamber of Commerce, 1299
Similkameen Okanagan Organic Producers Association, 1300
Ski Hawks Ottawa, 1302
Small Business Association, 1304
Socialist Party of Canada, 1307
Société canadienne d'histoire de l'Église Catholique - Section française, 1307
Société canadienne-française de radiologie, 1309
Société culturelle régionale Les Chutes, 1309
Société d'entomologie du Québec, 1309
Société d'histoire d'Amos, 1310
Société d'histoire de l'Outaouais inc., 1310
Société d'histoire de la MRC de l'Assomption, 1310
Société d'histoire de la Rivière du Nord inc., 1310
Société d'histoire de la Seigneurie de Chambly, 1311
Société d'histoire de Sainte-Foy, 1311
Société d'histoire de Sillery, 1311
La Société d'histoire de Toronto, 1311
Société d'histoire de Warwick, 1312
Société d'histoire des Six Cantons, 1312
Société d'histoire du Haut-Richelieu, 1312
Société d'histoire du Témiscamingue, 1312
Société d'histoire et de généalogie de Matane, 1312
Société d'histoire et de généalogie de Saint-Casimir, 1312
Société d'histoire et généalogie du granit, 1313
Société d'histoire régionale de Lévis, 1313
Société de généalogie de la Beauce, 1315
Société de généalogie de la Mauricie et des Bois-Francs, 1315
Société de généalogie des Cantons de l'Est, 1315
Société de généalogie du Saguenay, inc., 1316
Société de généalogie et d'archives de Rimouski, 1316
Société de généalogie Gaspésie-Les Îles, 1316
Société de généalogie Saint-Hubert, 1316
Société de philosophie du Québec, 1316
Société historique acadienne de la Baie Sainte-Marie, 1319
Société historique de Charlesbourg, 1319
Société historique de Joliette-De Lanaudière, 1319
Société historique de la Côte-du-Sud, 1320
La Société historique de Nouvelle-Beauce, 1320
Société historique de Saint-Romuald, 1320
Société historique et généalogique de Trois-Pistoles, inc., 1321
Société internationale de sociologie des religions, 1589
Société québécoise d'ethnologie, 1323
Société québécoise de gériatrie, 1323
Société québécoise de Psilogie inc, 1323
Société québécoise du dahlia, 1324
Society for the History of Technology, 1591
Society for the Preservation of Old Mills - Canadian Chapter, 1326
Society for the Study of Pathophysiology of Pregnancy, 1592
Society of Bead Researchers, 1592
Society of Canadian Artists, 1327
Society of Canadian Ciné Amateurs, 1327
Society of Graphic Designers of Canada, 1329
Society of Ontario Nut Growers, 1330
Sooke Chamber of Commerce, 1333
South Asia Partnership Canada, 1334
South Cariboo Chamber of Commerce, 1334
South Cowichan Chamber of Commerce, 1334
South Lake Simcoe Naturalists, 1335
South Peel Naturalists' Club, 1336
South Shore Genealogical Society, 1336
South Shuswap Chamber of Commerce, 1336
Southern Kings Arts Council, 1338
Southern Ontario Thunderbird Club, 1338
Squash Nova Scotia, 1347
Ste Rose & District Chamber of Commerce, 1349
Steinbach Chamber of Commerce, 1349

Stewart-Hyder International Chamber of Commerce, 1350
Stonewall & District Chamber of Commerce, 1350
Stratford Coin Club, 1351
Stratford Musicians' Association, Local 418 of the American Federation of Musicians, 1351
Streetsville Historical Society, 1352
Strome & District Historical Society, 1352
Sunbeam Sportscar Owners Club of Canada, 1354
Support Organization for Trisomy 18, 13 & Related Disorders, 1356
Surrey Symphony Society, 1357
Sussex & District Chamber of Commerce, 1357
Swan Hills Chamber of Commerce, 1358
Swimming Prince Edward Island, 1359
Syndicat des agricultrices de la Côte-du-Sud, 1362
Syndicat des agricultrices du Centre du Québec, 1362
Tahsis Chamber of Commerce, 1366
Taras H. Shevchenko Museum & Memorial Park Foundation, 1367
TESL Nova Scotia, 1372
Thames Region Ecological Association, 1373
Theresians International - Canada, 1375
Thompson Chamber of Commerce, 1376
Thunder Bay Musicians' Association, 1378
Thunder Bay Regional Arts Council, 1378
Tilbury Chamber of Commerce, 1379
Tillicum Centre - Hope Association for Community Living, 1379
Tillsonburg District Chamber of Commerce, 1379
Tobermory & District Chamber of Commerce, 1380
Toronto Area Gays & Lesbians Phoneline & Crisis Counselling, 1381
Toronto Association of Synagogue & Temple Administrators, 1382
Toronto Autosport Club, 1382
Toronto Entomologists Association, 1384
Toronto Latvian Concert Association, 1385
Toronto Ornithological Club, 1386
Toronto Renaissance & Reformation Colloquium, 1387
T.P.U.G., 1394
Trager Canada, 1394
Trans-Canada Advertising Agency Network, 1395
The Trident Mediation Counselling & Support Foundation, 1398
Tuberous Sclerosis Canada Sclérose Tubéreuse, 1400
Twins, Triplets & More Association of Calgary, 1400
Two/Ten Charity Trust of Canada Inc., 1401
Ukrainian Canadian Civil Liberties Association, 1402
Ukrainian Genealogical & Historical Society of Canada, 1403
Ultralight Pilots Association of Canada, 1404
United Macedonians Organization of Canada, 1411
United Way of East Kootenay, 1414
United Way of Halton Hills, 1414
United Way of Morden & District Inc., 1415
Universities Art Association of Canada, 1418
University of Prince Edward Island Faculty Association, 1420
University of Saskatchewan Arts Council, 1420
University of Toronto Symphony Orchestra, 1421
University of Western Ontario Symphony Orchestra, 1421
Urban Alliance on Race Relations, 1422
Urban Municipal Administrators' Association of Saskatchewan, 1422
Valley Chamber of Commerce, 1424
The Van Horne Institute for International Transportation & Regulatory Affairs, 1424
Vancouver Island Community Forest Action Network, 1426
Vancouver Island Danish-Canadian Club, 1426

Vancouver Numismatic Society, 1428
Vancouver Paleontological Society, 1428
Vancouver Philharmonic Orchestra, 1428
Vancouver Pro Musica Society, 1428
Vegetarians of Alberta Association, 1430
Victims of Violence, 1432
Victoria Peace Coalition, 1433
Virden Community Chamber of Commerce, 1435
Voice for Animals Humane Society, 1436
Volkssport Association of Alberta, 1437
Volunteer Grandparents, 1438
Vulcan & District Chamber of Commerce, 1439
Wallaceburg Arts Council, 1440
Wasagaming Community Arts Inc., 1440
Waterloo Coin Club, 1442
Waterloo Historical Society, 1442
Watrous Area Arts Council, 1442
Wellington County Historical Society, 1443
West Grey Chamber of Commerce, 1445
West Kootenay Regional Arts Council, 1445
West Shore Arts Council, 1446
West Toronto Junction Historical Society, 1446
West Vancouver Community Arts Council, 1446
Westlock & District Chamber of Commerce, 1451
Westport & Rideau Lakes Chamber of Commerce, 1451
Weyburn & District United Way, 1451
White River District Historical Society, 1452
White Rock & Surrey Naturalists, 1452
Whitecourt Fish & Game Association, 1452
Wilderness Canoe Association, 1454
William Morris Society of Canada, 1455
Willow Beach Field Naturalists, 1455
Windermere District Historical Society, 1456
Winnipeg Clinic Employees Association, 1458
Winnipeg Vegetarian Association, 1459
Women Educating in Self-Defense Training, 1460
Women of the Word - Toronto, 1461
Women's Business Network of Ottawa, 1462
World Citizen Foundation, 1604
World Federation of Occupational Therapists, 1605
World Federation of Ukrainian Engineering Societies, 1466
World Federation of Ukrainian Women's Organizations, 1466
World Society for Ekistics, 1607
WWOOF Canada, 1469
Yarmouth Food Bank Society, 1470
York Pioneer & Historical Society, 1473
York-Grand River Historical Society, 1474
Yorkton & District United Way Inc., 1474
Yorkton Real Estate Association Inc., 1474
Youth Flight Canada, 1475
Yukon Amateur Radio Association, 1477
Zeballos Board of Trade, 1482

$50,000-$100,000

Abbotsford Arts Council, 1
Action des Chrétiens pour l'abolition de la torture, 6
Action Volunteers for Animals, 7
Administrative & Supervisory Personnel Association, 8
Alberta Angus Association, 22
Alberta Camping Association, 27
Alberta Dance Alliance, 32
Alberta Funeral Service Association, 36
Alberta Music Festival Association, 41
Alberta Music Industry Association, 41
Alberta Registered Music Teachers' Association, 44
Alberta Sailing Association, 45
Alberta School Councils' Association, 45
Alberta Shorthand Reporters Association, 46
Alberta Society of Artists, 47
Alberta Sport Parachuting Association, 48
Alberta Whitewater Association, 52
Altona & District Chamber of Commerce, 61
American Society for Theatre Research, 1499

American Society of Mining & Reclamation, 1501
Anthroposophical Society in Canada, 72
Appalachian Teachers' Association, 73
The Appraisal Institute of Canada - Manitoba, 75
Architectural Heritage Society of Saskatchewan, 79
Arts Council of Surrey, 85
Associated Designers of Canada, 89
Association canadienne des professeurs d'immersion, 94
Association cooopérative d'économie familiale Rimouski-Neigette et Mitis, 98
Association des Illustrateurs et Illustratrices du Québec, 116
Association des intervenantes et des intervenants en soins spirituels du Québec, 117
Association des jeunes bègues de Québec, 117
Association des juristes d'expression française de l'Ontario, 117
Association des juristes d'expression française du Manitoba inc., 118
Association des juristes d'expression française du Nouveau-Brunswick, 118
Association des malentendants Québécois, 118
L'Association des orthopédagogues du Québec inc., 121
Association des parents catholiques du Québec, 121
Association des personnes handicapées de Charlevoix inc., 122
Association des professeures et professeurs de la Faculté de médecine de l'Université de Sherbrooke, 124
Association des professionnels en électrolyse et soins esthétiques du Québec, 126
Association des professionnels en exposition du Québec, 126
Association des propriétaires de cinémas du Québec, 126
Association des sports pour aveugles de Montréal, 128
Association des surintendants de golf du Québec, 129
Association francophone des municipalités du Nouveau-Brunswick Inc., 135
Association internationale de droit pénal, 1509
Association of Applied Geochemists, 139
Association of Battlefords Realtors, 139
Association of Canadian Faculties of Dentistry, 142
Association of Canadian Travel Agents - Manitoba & Nunavut, 144
Association of Consulting Engineering Companies - Manitoba, 146
Association of Consulting Engineering Companies - Saskatchewan, 146
Association of Unity Churches Canada, 163
Association pour la protection des intérêts des consommateurs de la Côte-Nord, 166
Association québécoise de canoë-kayak de vitesse, 169
Association québécoise de racquetball, 171
Association québécoise des professeurs de français, 174
Atelier d'histoire Hochelaga-Maisonneuve, 179
Audition Québec, 187
Australian Association for Environmental Education, 1513
Badminton Newfoundland & Labrador Inc., 193
Badminton Ontario, 193
Balle au mur Québec, 194
Bamfield Chamber of Commerce, 195
Les banques alimentaires du Québec, 196
Barrow Bay & District Sports Fishing Association, 197
Black Creek Conservation Project, 213
Bladder Cancer Canada, 214
Blomidon Naturalists Society, 215
Boating BC Association, 216
Boundary Country Regional Chamber of Commerce, 218
Bowls Saskatchewan Inc., 220

Budget Index / $50,000-$100,000

Brant Skills Centre, 226
Brighton-Cramahe Chamber of Commerce, 229
British Columbia Economic Development Association, 239
British Columbia Snowmobile Federation, 253
British Columbia Women's Institutes, 258
Brockville & District Chamber of Commerce, 260
Brome County Historical Society, 260
Burnaby Arts Council, 265
Calgary Aboriginal Arts Awareness Society, 270
Canadian Association for Disabled Skiing - Alberta, 299
Canadian Association of Communicators in Education, 310
Canadian Association of School System Administrators, 332
Canadian Call Management Association, 348
Canadian Cattle Breeders' Association, 351
Canadian Centre for Ethics & Corporate Policy, 353
Canadian Committee on Labour History, 361
Canadian Council on International Law, 371
Canadian Diamond Drilling Association, 377
Canadian Farm Animal Care Trust, 384
Canadian Friends of Peace Now (Shalom Achshav), 395
Canadian Gerontological Nursing Association, 397
Canadian Honey Council, 408
Canadian Hotel Marketing & Sales Executives, 409
Canadian Imaging Trade Association, 410
Canadian Music Educators' Association, 438
Canadian Occupational Therapy Foundation, 444
Canadian Podiatric Medical Association, 456
Canadian Porphyria Foundation Inc., 458
Canadian Process Control Association, 460
Canadian Society of Orthopaedic Technologists, 485
Canadian Sociological Association, 488
Canadian Translators, Terminologists & Interpreters Council, 496
Canadian University & College Conference Organizers Association, 499
Canadian Writers' Foundation Inc., 506
Canadian Zionist Federation, 506
Caribbean Community Council of Calgary, 512
Carl Orff Canada Music for Children, 513
Centraide Gatineau-Labelle-Hautes-Laurentides, 522
Centraide sud-ouest du Québec, 523
Central British Columbia Railway & Forest Industry Museum Society, 524
Centre d'entrepreneuriat et PME, 528
Centre des ressources sur la non-violence inc, 530
Cercles des jeunes naturalistes, 537
Chambre de commerce de St-Donat, 543
Chambre de commerce du Haut-Saint-François, 544
Chambre de commerce et d'industrie Berthier-D'Autray, 545
Chambre de commerce et d'industrie de Montréal-Nord, 546
Chambre de commerce et d'industrie Nouvelle-Beauce, 547
Chambre de commerce et d'industrie secteur Saint-Félicien inc., 547
Chambre de commerce Vallée de la Missisquoi, 550
The Champlain Society, 551
Chemainus Harvest House Society Food Bank, 555
Christian Health Association of Alberta, 567
The Church Lads' Brigade, 569
Citizens' Environment Alliance, 570
Classical Accordion Society of Canada, 572
Clean North, 573
Coastal Ecosystems Research Foundation, 579
Cochrane & District Chamber of Commerce, 579
Colchester Highland Games & Gathering Society, 580

Cold Lake Native Friendship Centre, 580
Collectif féministe Rouyn-Noranda/Centre de femmes "Entre-Femmes", 581
College of the Rockies Faculty Association, 590
Commonwealth Association of Surveying & Land Economy, 1518
Community Folk Art Council of Toronto, 597
Community One Foundation, 607
Community Support Centre Haldimand-Norfolk, 607
Conseil régional de l'environnement de la Gaspésie et des Îles-de-la-Madeleine, 620
Conseil régional FTQ Saguenay-Lac-St-Jean-Chibougamau-Chapais, 621
Council of Private Investigators - Ontario, 635
La Crete & Area Chamber of Commerce, 642
Cricket Alberta, 642
Crowsnest Pass Chamber of Commerce, 644
Cu Nim Gliding Club, 645
Cumberland Museum Society, 645
DES Action USA, 1521
District of Mission Arts Council, 659
Downtown Vancouver Association, 662
Dress for Success, 662
Durham Regional Labour Council, 665
Dying with Dignity, 665
Echo-Edson Cultural Heritage Organization, 671
The Eckhardt-Gramatté Foundation, 671
Ecoforestry Institute Society, 671
École internationale de français, 672
Ecology North, 672
Edith Lando Charitable Foundation, 674
Edmonton Bicycle & Touring Club, 675
Edmonton Combative Sports Commission, 676
Edmonton Motor Dealers' Association, 678
Electrical Contractors Association of New Brunswick, Inc., 682
Elora Environment Centre, 685
Estevan Arts Council, 697
Etobicoke Humane Society, 697
Fairview & District Chamber of Commerce, 701
Fédération des agriculteurs et agricultrices francophones du Nouveau-Brunswick, 711
Fédération des parents acadiens de la Nouvelle-Écosse, 716
Fédération des sociétés d'horticulture et d'écologie du Québec, 719
Fédération des syndicats de l'action collective, 719
Fédération Internationale des Traducteurs, 1526
Federation of Broomball Associations of Ontario, 722
Federation of Canadian Naturists, 723
Fédération québécoise des sociétés de généalogie, 730
Fondation de la banque d'yeux du Québec inc., 744
Fondation roumaine de Montréal, 748
Food Depot Alimentaire, Inc., 749
Francofonds inc., 757
Franco-Jeunes de Terre-Neuve et du Labrador, 757
Freedom Party of Ontario, 759
Friends of Devonian Botanic Garden, 761
Friends of the Haileybury Heritage Museum, 762
The Gairdner Foundation, 766
The Garden Clubs of Ontario, 766
The G.K. Chesterton Institute for Faith & Culture, 1528
Golden Women's Resource Centre Society, 776
Grand Manan Whale & Seabird Research Station, 780
Grande Prairie Regional College Academic Staff Association, 781
Green Party of Canada, 788
Grey County Law Association, 790
Haliburton Highlands Chamber of Commerce, 798
Hamilton District Society for Disabled Children, 801
Hamilton Right to Life, 802

Hang Gliding & Paragliding Association of Canada, 803
HIV West Yellowhead Society, 817
Infertility Network, 836
Information Burlington, 836
Information Durham, 837
Information Oakville, 837
Institute of Power Engineers, 846
Inter-American Commercial Arbitration Commission, 851
International Amateur Theatre Association, 1535
International Association of Agricultural Economists, 1537
International Federation of Airworthiness, 1547
International Husserl & Phenomenological Research Society, 1550
International Society for Music Education, 1558
Interpreting Services of Newfoundland & Labrador Inc., 861
Investment Property Owners Association of Nova Scotia Ltd., 863
Iranian Community Association of Ontario, 863
ISACA, 1567
Islamic Care Centre, 864
Islamic Propagation Centre of Ontario, 865
Israel Association for Canadian Studies, 1567
Italian Association for Canadian Studies, 1568
Jake Thomas Learning Centre, 867
Jeunesse Acadienne et Francophone de l'Île-du-prince-Édouard, 870
The Joe Brain Foundation, 873
Junior League of Calgary, 878
Junior League of Edmonton, 878
Kawartha Chamber of Commerce & Tourism, 882
Kimberley Arts Council - Centre 64 Society, 887
Kings Historical Society, 888
Kingston Arts Council, 888
Labrador North Chamber of Commerce, 894
Lanark County Therapeutic Riding Program, 897
Langham Cultural Society, 898
Lansdowne Outdoor Recreational Development Association, 899
Latin American Mission Program, 899
Learning for Living South Muskoka, 905
Legal Aid Society of Alberta, 906
Lethbridge Chamber of Commerce, 907
Life Sciences Ontario, 911
The Literacy Council of Burlington, 913
Literacy Council of Durham Region, 913
London Building & Construction Trades Council, 918
Macedonian Human Rights Movement International, 923
Manitoba Athletic Therapists Association Inc., 931
Manitoba Band Association, 932
Manitoba Cricket Association, 935
Manitoba Paraplegia Foundation Inc., 942
Manitoba School Counsellors' Association, 944
McIlwraith Field Naturalists, 955
Melfort & District Chamber of Commerce, 959
Melville & District Agri-Park Association Inc., 959
Melville Arts Council, 959
Messagères de Notre-Dame de l'Assomption, 962
Middlesex Federation of Agriculture, 965
Moncton Area Lawyers' Association, 972
Morden & District Chamber of Commerce, 974
Motorsport Club of Ottawa, 976
Mount Pearl-Paradise Chamber of Commerce, 976
Mount Royal Staff Association, 976
Municipal Law Enforcement Officers' Association, 981
Musicians' Association of Victoria & the Islands, Local 247, AFM, 984
National Association of Canadians of Origins in India, 990
National Association of Computer Consulting Business (Canada), 990
National Darts Federation of Canada, 992

National Floor Covering Association, 993
National Inuit Youth Council, 994
Nature Vancouver, 1001
Naval Museum of Alberta Society, 1001
Newfoundland Baseball, 1022
Nipawin Exhibition Association Inc., 1027
North Peace Historical Society, 1032
North Saskatchewan Watershed Alliance, 1032
Northwest Territories Recreation & Parks Association, 1038
Nova Scotia Fish Packers Association, 1044
Nova Scotia Real Estate Appraisers Association, 1048
Occupational Hygiene Association of Ontario, 1054
Old Chrysler Corporation Auto Club, 1056
Ontario Association of Agricultural Societies, 1061
Ontario Beekeepers' Association, 1067
Ontario Business Education Partnership, 1070
Ontario DX Association, 1077
Ontario Plumbing Inspectors Association, 1096
Ontario Public Interest Research Group, 1099
Ontario Rett Syndrome Association, 1102
Osoyoos & District Arts Council, 1128
Ottawa Arts Council, 1129
Oxford County Law Association, 1134
Pacific Corridor Enterprise Council, 1135
Peace-Laird Regional Arts Council, 1147
Perth & District Chamber of Commerce, 1152
Petroleum Accountants Society of Canada, 1154
Photographic Historical Society of Canada, 1157
Pillar Nonprofit Network, 1160
Pilot Parents, 1160
Pincher Creek Allied Arts Council, 1160
Point d'appui, centre d'aide et de prévention des agressions à caractère sexuel de Rouyn-Noranda, 1163
Polio Québec, 1163
Ponoka & District Chamber of Commerce, 1164
Port Moody Heritage Society, 1166
Portage Industrial Exhibition Association, 1166
Portuguese Club of London, 1167
Post-Polio Awareness & Support Society of BC, 1168
Prince Edward Island Kiwanis Music Festival Association, 1175
Prince Edward Island Marketing Council, 1175
Prince Edward Island Road Builders & Heavy Construction Association, 1177
Printing & Graphics Industries Association of Alberta, 1180
Printing Equipment & Supply Dealers' Association of Canada, 1180
Probe International, 1181
Professional Association of Volunteer Leaders Ontario, 1183
Professional Locksmith Association of Alberta, 1186
Projet 10, 1188
Provincial Towing Association (Ontario), 1191
Psychological Association of Manitoba, 1191
Quality in Lifelong Learning Network, 1195
Québec Anglophone Heritage Network, 1195
The Québec Drama Federation, 1197
Québec Society of Lipidology, Nutrition & Metabolism Inc., 1199
REAL Women of Canada, 1206
Refrigeration Service Engineers Society (Canada), 1211
Regina Musicians' Association, 1212
Regroupement des femmes de la Côte-de-Gaspé, 1215
Renaissance Society of America, 1586
Le Réseau d'enseignement francophone à distance du Canada, 1219
Royal Canadian Mounted Police Veterans' Association, 1240
The Royal Philatelic Society of Canada, 1242
Saint Mary's University Faculty Union, 1247
St. Andrews Chamber of Commerce, 1248
St Mary's River Association, 1250
St Paul & District Chamber of Commerce, 1250

Budget Index / $100,000-$250,000

Salmon Preservation Association for the Waters of Newfoundland, 1252
Saskatchewan Archery Association, 1256
Saskatchewan Bed & Breakfast Association, 1259
Saskatchewan Lions Eye Bank, 1269
Saskatchewan Society of Occupational Therapists, 1275
Schneider Office Employees' Association, 1284
The Scleroderma Society of Ontario, 1285
Scottish Studies Foundation Inc., 1286
Sex Information & Education Council of Canada, 1292
Shuswap District Arts Council, 1297
Sicamous & District Chamber of Commerce, 1297
Social Justice Committee, 1305
Société culturelle Sud-Acadie, 1309
Société d'histoire et de généalogie de Val-d'Or, 1313
Société de criminologie du Québec, 1314
Société de généalogie de Québec, 1315
Société des archives historiques de la région de l'Amiante, 1317
Société historique de Pubnico-Ouest, 1320
Société historique du Saguenay, 1321
Société historique et culturelle du Marigot inc., 1321
Society for the Study of Architecture in Canada, 1327
The Society of Professional Accountants of Canada, 1330
Softball NB Inc., 1331
Soroptimist Foundation of Canada, 1333
South Saskatchewan Community Foundation Inc., 1336
South Shore Chamber of Commerce, 1336
Spina Bifida & Hydrocephalus Association of British Columbia, 1341
Squash Québec, 1347
Stoney Creek Chamber of Commerce, 1350
Student Christian Movement of Canada, 1352
Summerland Community Arts Council, 1354
Swim Nova Scotia, 1358
Syndicat des conseillères et conseillers de la CSQ, 1362
Syndicat des professeures et professeurs de l'Université du Québec en Outaouais, 1363
Telephone Historical Centre, 1369
Thunder Bay Field Naturalists, 1377
Tofino-Long Beach Chamber of Commerce, 1381
Toronto Blues Society, 1382
Toronto Curling Association, 1383
Tourism Prince Albert, 1390
Transport Action Canada, 1395
Travel Media Association of Canada, 1396
Travellers' Aid Society of Toronto, 1396
Trent Hills & District Chamber of Commerce, 1397
Truro & Colchester Chamber of Commerce, 1399
Tweed & Area Historical Society, 1400
Ucluelet Chamber of Commerce, 1402
Ultimate Canada, 1404
Uniform Law Conference of Canada, 1405
Union académique internationale, 1598
Union of Municipalities of New Brunswick, 1407
The United Brethren Church in Canada, 1409
United Way of Stormont, Dundas & Glengarry, 1417
Uxbridge Historical Centre, 1423
Vancouver Society of Immigrant & Visible Minority Women, 1428
Viscount Cultural Council Inc., 1435
Voitures anciennes du Québec inc., 1437
Volunteer Circle of the National Gallery of Canada, 1438
W. Maurice Young Centre for Applied Ethics, 1439
Waterton Natural History Association, 1442
Welcome Friend Association, 1443
Welfare Committee for the Assyrian Community in Canada, 1443
Wellington Law Association, 1443

West Coast Amateur Musicians' Society, 1444
West Kootenay Women's Association, 1445
Western Québec Literacy Council, 1450
Western Silvicultural Contractors' Association, 1450
Weyburn Agricultural Society, 1451
Whitchurch-Stouffville Chamber of Commerce, 1452
Wildlife Haven Rehabilitation Centre, 1454
Windsor Women Working with Immigrant Women, 1457
Women's Musical Club of Toronto, 1463
World Arabian Horse Organization, 1603
World Fellowship of Orthodox Youth, 1605
World Organization of Building Officials, 1466
World Pheasant Association, 1607
World Ploughing Organization, 1607
Yamaska Literacy Council, 1470
York Symphony Orchestra Inc., 1474
Yukon Art Society, 1477
Yukon Church Heritage Society, 1477
Yukon Outfitters' Association, 1479
Yukon Public Legal Education Association, 1479

$100,000-$250,000

Abbotsford Food Bank & Christmas Bureau, 1
Action Life (Ottawa) Inc., 6
Active Living Coalition for Older Adults, 7
Administrative Sciences Association of Canada, 8
Adoption Council of Canada, 8
Adoption Council of Ontario, 8
Advanced Card Technology Association of Canada, 9
Agricultural Alliance of New Brunswick, 14
Agricultural Institute of Canada, 14
Ajax-Pickering Board of Trade, 20
Alberta Amateur Wrestling Association, 22
Alberta Bobsleigh Association, 26
Alberta Chambers of Commerce, 28
Alberta Council on Aging, 31
Alberta Equestrian Federation, 34
Alberta Hospice Palliative Care Association, 38
Alberta Law Foundation, 39
Alberta Luge Association, 39
Alberta Media Production Industries Association, 39
Alberta Public Health Association, 43
Alberta Ready Mixed Concrete Association, 43
Alberta Senior Citizens Sport & Recreation Association, 46
Alberta Table Tennis Association, 48
Alberta Triathlon Association, 50
Alberta Veterinary Technologist Association, 50
Algoma Arts Festival Association, 54
Alliance des chorales du Québec, 55
Alliance for Chiropractic, 57
Alzheimer Society of Hamilton Halton, 62
Alzheimer Society of Thunder Bay, 65
Ancaster Community Services, 68
Animal Welfare Foundation of Canada, 71
Annapolis Region Community Arts Council, 71
Antigonish Highland Society, 72
The Appraisal Institute of Canada - British Columbia, 74
Archives du Centre acadien, 80
Arctic Winter Games International Committee, 81
Armateurs du Saint-Laurent, 82
Armed Forces Communications & Electronics Association (Canada), 82
Army, Navy & Air Force Veterans in Canada, 83
Arts Council Windsor & Region, 85
Arts Mosaic, 85
Arts Ottawa East-Est, 86
ArtsConnect - Tri-Cities Regional Arts Council, 86
Assiniboia Chamber of Commerce (MB), 88
Associated Manitoba Arts Festivals, Inc., 89
Association canadienne des ataxies familiales, 92
Association coopérative d'économie familiale - Lanaudière, 97

Association coopérative d'économie familiale - Rive-Sud de Québec, 97
Association coopérative d'économie familiale du Nord de Montréal, 98
Association de chasse et pêche nordique, inc., 100
Association de l'exploration minière de Québec, 100
Association de la Construction Richelieu Yamaska, 101
Association de la Rivière Ste-Marguerite Inc., 102
Association des employées et employés du gouvernement du Québec, 112
Association des ingénieurs municipaux du Québec, 116
Association des médias écrits communautaires du Québec, 120
Association des neurotraumatisés de l'Outaouais, 121
Association des professionnels en gestion philanthropique, 126
Association des Sourds de l'Estrie Inc., 128
Association des universités de la francophonie canadienne, 130
Association for Bahá'í Studies, 132
Association for Manitoba Archives, 133
Association Museums New Brunswick, 138
Association of Book Publishers of British Columbia, 140
Association of Canadian Ergonomists, 142
Association of Canadian Travel Agents - Québec, 144
Association of Day Care Operators of Ontario, 146
Association of Independent Schools & Colleges in Alberta, 149
Association of Manitoba Museums, 151
Association of Postconsumer Plastic Recyclers, 1513
Association pour l'intégration sociale (Région de Québec), 166
Association pour la promotion des droits des personnes handicapées, 166
Association professionnelle des designers d'intérieur du Québec, 167
Association québécoise des personnes de petite taille, 174
Association québécoise pour l'hygiène, la santé et la sécurité du travail, 176
Au bas de l'échelle, 187
Autism Canada, 188
BC Adaptive Snowsports, 200
Beaton Institute, 203
Biathlon Alberta, 207
The Bible Holiness Movement, 208
Block Parent Program of Canada, 214
BMW Clubs Canada, 216
Book Publishers Association of Alberta, 218
Boxing BC Association, 220
Bracebridge Chamber of Commerce, 224
Breast Cancer Action Nova Scotia, 227
British Columbia Association of Family Resource Programs, 231
British Columbia Association of Social Workers, 232
British Columbia Association of Speech-Language Pathologists & Audiologists, 233
British Columbia Civil Liberties Association, 236
British Columbia Deaf Sports Federation, 238
British Columbia Fishing Resorts & Outfitters Association, 241
British Columbia Primary Teachers Association, 249
British Columbia Shellfish Growers Association, 253
British Columbia Waterfowl Society, 258
Calgary Musicians Association, 273
Calgary Zoological Society, 275
Canadian Architectural Certification Board, 295
Canadian Association for Medical Education, 302
Canadian Association for the Study of International Development, 306

Canadian Association of Community Health Centres, 311
Canadian Association of Home & Property Inspectors, 317
Canadian Association of Independent Credit Counselling Agencies, 318
Canadian Concrete Masonry Producers Association, 362
Canadian Crossroads International, 373
Canadian Employee Relocation Council, 380
Canadian Evaluation Society, 383
Canadian Fallen Firefighters Foundation, 383
Canadian Federation of Chiropractic Regulatory & Educational Accrediting Boards, 386
Canadian Federation of Earth Sciences, 386
Canadian Football Hall of Fame & Museum, 391
Canadian Friends of Boys Town Jerusalem, 395
Canadian Historical Association, 405
Canadian Injured Workers Alliance, 411
Canadian Institute for NDE, 413
Canadian Institute for the Administration of Justice, 413
Canadian Institute of Geomatics, 416
Canadian Machinery Vibration Association, 429
Canadian National Federation of Independent Unions, 439
Canadian Partnership for Consumer Food Safety Education, 451
Canadian Ready Mixed Concrete Association, 465
Canadian Rental Association, 467
Canadian Safe Boating Council, 468
Canadian Shorthorn Association, 470
Canadian Society for Bioengineering, 473
Canadian Society for the Study of Education, 478
Canadian Society of Landscape Architects, 484
Canadian Society of Plastic Surgeons, 487
Canadian Society of Professional Event Planners, 487
Canadian Swine Breeders' Association, 491
Canadian Thoroughbred Horse Society, 494
Canadian Tooling & Machining Association, 495
Canadian Tourism Human Resource Council, 495
Canadian Toy Testing Council, 496
Canadian University Press, 499
Canadian Water Resources Association, 503
Canmore Folk & Blues Club, 508
Carrefour d'entraide de Drummond, 515
Carrefour Tiers-Monde, 516
Casa dos Acores do Ontário, 516
Catholic Biblical Association of Canada, 517
Central Okanagan Foundation, 525
Centre culturel canadien, 1516
Centre d'aide et de lutte contre les agressions à caractère sexuel de Granby, 527
Centre de la Communauté sourde du Montréal métropolitain, 529
Centre de ressources et d'intervention pour hommes abusés sexuellement dans leur enfance, 530
Centre québécois du droit de l'environnement, 536
Cercles de fermières du Québec, 537
Cerebral Palsy Association of British Columbia, 537
Ceta-Research Inc., 538
Chambre de commerce de l'Ile d'Orléans, 541
Chambre de commerce de la MRC de L'Assomption, 541
Chambre de commerce des Îles-de-la-Madeleine, 544
Chambre de commerce et d'industrie de Maniwaki & Vallée de la Gatineau, 546
Chambre de commerce et d'industrie de Rouyn-Noranda, 546
Chambre de commerce et d'industrie de Thetford Mines, 546
Chambre de commerce Kamouraska-L'Islet, 548
Chambre immobilière du Saguenay-Lac St-Jean Inc., 551
Chartered Professionals in Human Resources Manitoba, 554

Budget Index / $100,000-$250,000

Child Find British Columbia, 559
Child Find Saskatchewan Inc., 559
Children's Cottage Society, 561
Christian Church (Disciples of Christ) in Canada, 567
The Christian Episcopal Church of Canada, 567
Church of God of Prophecy in Canada, 569
Club canadien de Toronto, 574
Club de trafic de Québec, 575
Clubs 4-H du Québec, 576
Columbia Valley Chamber of Commerce, 591
Commonwealth Games Canada, 593
Community Arts Council of Greater Victoria, 595
Community Foundation for Kingston & Area, 597
Community Information Centre of Ottawa, 599
Community Information Hamilton, 599
Community Legal Information Association of Prince Edward Island, 600
Community Planning Association of Alberta, 607
Conference of Independent Schools (Ontario), 612
Congrégation des Soeurs de Sainte-Anne, 612
Congregational Christian Churches in Canada, 613
Conseil des organismes francophones de la région de Durham, 617
Conseil national Société de Saint-Vincent de Paul, 619
Conseil régional de la culture Saguenay-Lac-Saint-Jean, 621
Conservation Halton Foundation, 622
Construction Association of Rural Manitoba Inc., 623
Couchiching Institute on Public Affairs, 632
The Council on Aging of Ottawa, 635
Cross Country Saskatchewan, 643
Cross Country Yukon, 644
Culture Mauricie, 645
Cyclic Vomiting Syndrome Association, 1521
Dance Nova Scotia, 649
Dance Oremus Danse, 649
Danish Canadian National Museum Society, 650
DisAbled Women's Network of Canada, 658
Distress Centre of Durham Region, 659
Dominion of Canada Rifle Association, 660
Drayton Valley & District Chamber of Commerce, 662
Earthsave Canada, 667
East York Learning Experience, 669
Ecological Agriculture Projects, 672
Economic Developers Alberta, 672
Edmonton & District Labour Council, 675
Edmonton Federation of Community Leagues, 677
Edmonton Radial Railway Society, 679
The Engineering Institute of Canada, 688
Environmental Services Association of Nova Scotia, 692
Environmental Youth Alliance, 692
Eye Bank of BC, 700
Faculty Association of the College of New Caledonia, 701
FarmFolk CityFolk, 706
Fédération de crosse du Québec, 708
Fédération de l'industrie manufacturière (FIM-CSN), 708
Fédération de l'UPA de la Montérégie, 709
Fédération des aînées et aînés francophones du Canada, 711
Fédération des apiculteurs du Québec, 711
Fédération des coopératives d'habitation du Royaume Saguenay Lac-Saint-Jean, 714
Fédération des éducateurs et éducatrices physiques enseignants du Québec, 714
Fédération des maisons d'hébergement pour femmes, 715
Federation of Calgary Communities, 722
Federation of Independent School Associations of BC, 724
Federation of Prince Edward Island Municipalities Inc., 726

Fédération québécoise de la montagne et de l'escalade, 727
Fédération québécoise des échecs, 728
Fernie & District Arts Council, 732
Field Hockey Ontario, 734
Firefighters Burn Fund Inc., 738
Fondation québécoise de la maladie coeliaque, 747
Fort Edmonton Foundation, 752
Fort Erie Business Success & Loan Centre, 752
Fort Macleod Historical Association, 752
Fort Saskatchewan Chamber of Commerce, 753
Forum for Intercultural Leadership & Learning, 754
Foundation for Legal Research, 755
Freight Management Association of Canada, 759
The Friends of Bon Echo Park, 760
Friends of Chamber Music, 760
Friends of Clayoquot Sound, 760
Front commun des personnes assistées sociales du Québec, 763
Full Gospel Business Men's Fellowship in Canada, 764
Gai Écoute inc., 766
Gander & Area Chamber of Commerce, 766
GATEWAY Centre For Learning, 767
General Conference of the Canadian Assemblies of God, 768
Governance Professionals of Canada, 778
Grant MacEwan College Faculty Association, 782
The Great Lakes Research Consortium, 1528
Green Action Centre, 788
Groupe d'aide et d'information sur le harcèlement sexuel au travail de la province de Québec, 791
Groupe de recherche en animation et planification économique, 791
Groupe intervention vidéo, 792
Groupe régional d'intervention social - Québec, 792
Guelph International Resource Centre, 793
Halton Hills Chamber of Commerce, 800
Hamilton Arts Council, 800
Heart & Stroke Foundation of Alberta, NWT & Nunavut, 808
Hearth, Patio & Barbecue Association of Canada, 809
Heritage Foundation of Newfoundland & Labrador, 813
Humboldt & District Chamber of Commerce, 827
IAESTE Canada (International Association for the Exchange of Students for Technical Experience), 829
IMCS Pax Romana, 1531
Independent Assemblies of God International - Canada, 832
Independent Media Arts Alliance, 833
Indian Métis Christian Fellowship, 834
Industrial Accident Victims Group of Ontario, 835
Inland Refugee Society of BC, 838
Institut Séculier Pie X, 843
Institut Voluntas Dei, 843
Interior Designers Institute of British Columbia, 852
International Association for Educational & Vocational Guidance, 853
International Commission on Occupational Health, 1543
International Federation of Hydrographic Societies, 1548
International Humanist & Ethical Union, 1550
International Institute of Integral Human Sciences, 858
International Napoleonic Society, 858
International Personnel Management Association - Canada, 859
International Plant Propagators Society, Inc., 1555

International Research Institute for Media, Communication & Cultural Development, 1556
International Social Service Canada, 860
International Society for Ecological Economics, 1557
International Society of Radiographers & Radiological Technologists, 1561
International Student Pugwash, 1562
Islamic Information Foundation, 864
Jodo Shinshu Buddhist Temples of Canada, 873
The John Howard Society of Prince Edward Island, 875
Judo Alberta, 875
Judo BC, 876
Judo Manitoba, 876
Judo Saskatchewan, 876
Junior League of Hamilton-Burlington, Inc., 878
Kashmiri Canadian Council, 882
Kimberley & District Chamber of Commerce, 887
Kind Space, 888
Kitchener-Waterloo Chamber Music Society, 890
Kitimat Chamber of Commerce, 891
Kosher Check, 894
Lacombe & District Chamber of Commerce, 895
Ladies' Morning Musical Club, 895
Ladysmith Chamber of Commerce, 895
Lakehead University Faculty Association, 896
Language Industry Association, 899
Laurentian University Faculty Association, 900
Learning Disabilities Association of Alberta, 903
Learning Disabilities Association of British Columbia, 904
Lethbridge Association for Community Living, 907
Lethbridge Therapeutic Riding Association, 908
Literacy Link South Central, 914
Lloydminster Society for the Prevention of Cruelty to Animals, 916
London Food Bank, 918
LUE-42 Enterprises, 920
Mackenzie Chamber of Commerce, 924
The Mackenzie Institute, 924
Macleod Institute, 924
Madawaska Forest Products Marketing Board, 924
Mainland Nova Scotia Building & Construction Trades Council, 926
Maison de Campagne & d'Entraide Communautaire du Lac, 926
Maison du Tourisme, 927
Manitoba Choral Association, 934
Manitoba Federation of Independent Schools Inc., 936
Manitoba League of Persons with Disabilities, 939
Manitoba Table Tennis Association, 945
Mariners' House of Montréal, 950
The Marquis Project, Inc., 952
Mechanical Contractors Association of New Brunswick, 957
Melfort Agricultural Society, 959
Métis National Council of Women, 963
Metro Toronto Movement for Literacy, 963
Mining Suppliers, Contractors & Consultants Association of BC, 967
Les Missions des Soeurs Missionnaires du Christ-Roi, 969
Missisquoi Historical Society, 969
Mississauga Choral Society, 970
Modular Housing Association Prairie Provinces, 971
Montréal Soaring Council, 973
Moose Jaw & District Chamber of Commerce, 973
Multicultural Council of Windsor & Essex County, 979
National Association of Environmental Professionals, 1573
The National Council of Women of Canada, 992
National Eating Disorder Information Centre, 992

Native North American Traveling College, 998
Nelson & District Chamber of Commerce, 1003
New Brunswick Crafts Council, 1007
New Brunswick Society of Certified Engineering Technicians & Technologists, 1012
Newfoundland & Labrador Sexual Assault Crisis & Prevention Centre Inc., 1021
Newmarket Chamber of Commerce, 1024
Niagara Peninsula Conservation Authority, 1025
Niagara-on-the-Lake Chamber of Commerce, 1026
Nordic Walking Nova Scotia, 1028
North Bay & District Stamp Club, 1030
North Bay Food Bank, 1030
North Pacific Cannery - National Historic Site, 1032
Northeast Avalon ACAP, Inc., 1034
Northwest Territories & Nunavut Chamber of Mines, 1037
Northwest Wildlife Preservation Society, 1039
Northwestern Ontario Sports Hall of Fame & Museum, 1039
Nova Scotia Choral Federation, 1042
Nova Scotia Fruit Growers' Association, 1045
Nova Scotia Road Builders Association, 1048
Office de Tourisme du Rocher-Percé, 1055
The Olde Forge Community Resource Centre, 1056
Ontario Amateur Wrestling Association, 1059
Ontario Association for Marriage & Family Therapy, 1061
Ontario Association of Credit Counselling Services, 1063
Ontario Association of Food Banks, 1064
Ontario Association of Residents' Councils, 1066
Ontario Blind Sports Association, 1068
Ontario Council for International Cooperation, 1075
Ontario Environment Industry Association, 1078
Ontario Home Respiratory Services Association, 1086
Ontario Professional Foresters Association, 1097
Ontario Public Buyers Association, 1098
Ontario Recreational Canoeing & Kayaking Association, 1101
Ontario Water Polo Association Incorporated, 1113
Open Space Arts Society, 1114
Order of Malta - Canadian Association, 1119
Organization of Military Museums of Canada, 1125
Pacific Opera Victoria, 1135
Pacific Peoples' Partnership, 1135
Pacific Post Partum Support Society, 1136
Pan American Hockey Federation, 1138
Parents-Unis Lanaudière, 1140
Parkdale Community Information Centre, 1140
Parrainage civique Montréal, 1143
PEDVAC Foundation, 1147
PEN International, 1583
People, Words & Change, 1152
Persons Living with AIDS Network of Saskatchewan Inc., 1152
Planetary Association for Clean Energy, Inc., 1161
Planned Parenthood Waterloo Region, 1162
Port Dover Board of Trade, 1165
Port Renfrew Chamber of Commerce, 1166
Powell River & District United Way, 1168
Prairie Fruit Growers Association, 1169
Prince Albert & District Chamber of Commerce, 1171
Prince Edward Island Aquaculture Alliance, 1171
Prince Edward Island Federation of Agriculture, 1174
Prince George Recycling & Environmental Action Planning Society, 1179
Prince Rupert & District Chamber of Commerce, 1179
Programme Action Réfugiés Montréal, 1187
Project READ Literacy Network Waterloo-Wellington, 1188

Budget Index / $250,000-$500,000

Protected Areas Association of Newfoundland & Labrador, 1190
Public Legal Information Association of Newfoundland, 1192
Québec dans le monde, 1196
Quest Centre Community Initiatives, 1200
Quetico Foundation, 1201
Quickdraw Animation Society, 1201
Quinte Arts Council, 1201
Quinte Immigrant Services, 1201
Radio Television Digital News Association (Canada), 1203
Rainbow Resource Centre, 1203
Raspberry Industry Development Council, 1204
Reception House Waterloo Region, 1206
Recreation New Brunswick, 1207
Recreational Aircraft Association, 1208
Red Deer Food Bank Society, 1209
Red Deer Symphony Orchestra, 1209
Regroupement québécois des organismes pour le développement de l'employabilité, 1216
Regroupement QuébecOiseaux, 1216
Retail Advertising & Marketing Club of Canada, 1228
Rhythmic Gymnastics Alberta, 1229
Richmond Food Bank Society, 1230
Robson Street Business Association, 1235
Rocky Mountain House & District Chamber of Commerce, 1235
Rotman Institute for International Business, 1236
Royal Canadian Academy of Arts, 1239
Saint Francis Xavier Association of University Teachers, 1246
St. John's Cathedral Polish Catholic Church, 1249
St. Leonard's Society of Canada, 1250
Salmon Arm & District Chamber of Commerce, 1252
Salt Spring Island Chamber of Commerce, 1252
Saskatchewan 5 Pin Bowlers' Association, 1254
Saskatchewan Amateur Speed Skating Association, 1255
Saskatchewan Blind Sports Association Inc., 1259
Saskatchewan Choral Federation, 1261
Saskatchewan Fencing Association, 1265
Saskatchewan Filmpool Co-operative, 1265
Saskatchewan History & Folklore Society Inc., 1267
Saskatchewan Orchestral Association, Inc., 1270
Saskatchewan Physical Education Association, 1271
Saskatchewan Pro Life Association, 1272
Saskatchewan Rugby Union, 1274
Saskatchewan Voice of People with Disabilities, Inc., 1277
Sault Ste Marie & 49th Field Regt. RCA Historical Society, 1281
Sault Ste Marie Chamber of Commerce, 1281
Schizophrenia Society of Nova Scotia, 1284
Science Atlantic, 1285
Self-Help Connection Clearinghouse Association, 1289
Shelburne Historical Society, 1295
Simon Fraser Public Interest Research Group, 1300
Smithers District Chamber of Commerce, 1304
Société catholique de la Bible, 1309
Société d'histoire de la Haute-Yamaska, 1310
Société d'histoire et d'archéologie du Témiscouata, 1312
Société de développement économique du Saint-Laurent, 1315
Société généalogique canadienne-française, 1319
Société historique Pierre-de-Saurel inc., 1321
Société Provancher d'histoire naturelle du Canada, 1322
La Société Saint-Pierre, 1325
Société Saint-Thomas-d'Aquin, 1325
Society for the Promotion of the Teaching of English as a Second Language in Quebec, 1326

Society of Gynecologic Oncologists of Canada, 1329
Society of Translators & Interpreters of British Columbia, 1331
South Okanagan Chamber Of Commerce, 1335
SPCA of Western Québec, 1339
Special Olympics Newfoundland & Labrador, 1340
Special Olympics Prince Edward Island, 1340
Spina Bifida & Hydrocephalus Association of Northern Alberta, 1342
Sport PEI Inc., 1345
SportMedBC, 1345
Spruce Grove & District Chamber of Commerce, 1346
Station Arts Centre Cooperative, 1348
Steinbach Arts Council, 1349
Stephan G. Stephansson Icelandic Society, 1349
Stony Plain & District Chamber of Commerce, 1350
Stormont, Dundas & Glengarry Historical Society, 1350
Strategic Leadership Forum, 1351
Summerland Chamber of Commerce, 1354
Swift Current & District Chamber of Commerce, 1358
Synchro Saskatchewan, 1361
Syndicat des agents de maîtrise de TELUS (ind.), 1362
Syndicat des employés en radio-télédiffusion de Télé-Québec (CSQ), 1363
Syndicat des producteurs en serre du Québec, 1363
Syndicat des professeures et professeurs de l'Université du Québec à Chicoutimi, 1363
Syndicat des professeures et des professeures de l'Université du Québec à Trois-Rivières, 1364
Syndicat du personnel technique et professionnel de la Société des alcools du Québec (ind.), 1364
Taber & District Chamber of Commerce, 1365
Tel-Aide Outaouais, 1369
Terrace & District Chamber of Commerce, 1371
TESL Ontario, 1373
Tetra Society of North America, 1373
Tiger Hills Arts Association Inc., 1379
Timmins & Area Women in Crisis Support & Information Centre on Violence Against Women, 1379
Timmins, Cochrane & Timiskaming District Association of REALTORS, 1380
Toronto Vegetarian Association, 1388
Tourism Vernon, 1391
Trail & District Chamber of Commerce, 1394
Trans Canada Yellowhead Highway Association, 1394
Trent University Faculty Association, 1397
Tri-Cities Chamber of Commerce Serving Coquitlam, Port Coquitlam & Port Moody, 1398
Truck Training Schools Association of Ontario Inc., 1399
Union des cultivateurs franco-ontariens, 1406
Union of Injured Workers of Ontario, 1407
United Way of Greater Moncton & Southeastern New Brunswick, 1414
United Way of Greater Saint John Inc., 1414
United Way of Haldimand-Norfolk, 1414
United Way of Kingston, Frontenac, Lennox & Addington, 1414
United Way of Lethbridge & South Western Alberta, 1415
United Way of Trail & District, 1417
The Vancouver Art Therapy Institute, 1425
Vancouver Association for the Survivors of Torture, 1425
Vancouver Humane Society, 1426
Vancouver Status of Women, 1428
Vancouver Youth Symphony Orchestra Society, 1429
Vaughan Chamber of Commerce, 1430
Vermilion & District Chamber of Commerce, 1431

Victoria International Development Education Association, 1432
Village International Sudbury, 1435
Wallaceburg & District Historical Society, Inc., 1440
Waterloo Regional Heritage Foundation, 1442
The Welland/Pelham Chamber of Commerce, 1443
Wetaskiwin Chamber of Commerce, 1451
Whitehorse Chamber of Commerce, 1452
Whole Village, 1453
Windsor-Essex Children's Aid Society, 1457
Windsor-Essex Therapeutic Riding Association, 1457
Winkler & District Chamber of Commerce, 1458
Winnipeg Executives Association, 1458
Women in Film & Television Vancouver, 1461
Women's Network PEI, 1463
Wood Buffalo Food Bank, 1463
Wood Energy Technology Transfer Inc., 1463
The Workers' Educational Association of Canada, 1464
World Federalist Movement - Canada, 1465
World Federation of the Deaf, 1605
World Leisure & Recreation Association, 1606
World Masters Athletics, 1606
Yarmouth County Historical Society, 1470
Yukon Law Foundation, 1479
Yukon Learn Society, 1479
Yukon Trappers Association, 1480
Zoroastrian Society of Ontario, 1482

$250,000-$500,000

Abbotsford Chamber of Commerce, 1
Ability Online Support Network, 2
Advanced Coronary Treatment (ACT) Foundation of Canada, 10
Agricultural Manufacturers of Canada, 15
AIDS Coalition of Nova Scotia, 15
AIDS New Brunswick, 17
Air Cadet League of Canada, 19
Alberta Association of Architects, 23
Alberta Craft Council, 32
Alberta Fencing Association, 35
Alberta Roofing Contractors Association, 44
Alberta Sports Hall of Fame & Museum, 48
Alberta Turkey Producers, 50
Alberta Wilderness Association, 52
ALIGN Association of Community Services, 54
Alliance for the Wild Rockies, 1487
Alliance internationale des employé(e)s de scène, de théâtre et de cinéma, 57
Amelia Rising Sexual Assault Centre of Nipissing, 66
American Public Gardens Association, 1497
Antarctic & Southern Ocean Coalition, 1505
Apparel BC, 73
The Appraisal Institute of Canada - Ontario, 75
Architectural Woodwork Manufacturers Association of British Columbia, 79
Armenian Holy Apostolic Church - Canadian Diocese, 83
Arusha Centre Society, 86
Associated Gospel Churches, 89
Association de la presse francophone, 101
Association des accidentés cérébro-vasculaires et traumatisés crâniens de l'Estrie, 104
Association des camps du Québec inc., 108
Association des collèges privés du Québec, 109
Association des expositions agricoles du Québec, 113
Association des parents fransaskois, 122
Association for Mineral Exploration British Columbia, 134
Association francophone des parents du Nouveau-Brunswick, 135
Association Hôtellerie Québec, 136
Association jeunesse fransaskoise, 137
Association maritime du Québec, 137
Association multi-ethnique pour l'intégration des personnes handicapées, 137
Association nationale des éditeurs de livres, 138

Association of Condominium Managers of Ontario, 145
Association of Ontario Midwives, 155
Association of Ontario Road Supervisors, 155
Association of Professional Executives of the Public Service of Canada, 159
Association pour l'enseignement de la science et de la technologie au Québec, 165
Association québécoise de défense des droits des personnes retraitées et préretraitées, 169
Association québécoise de l'industrie de la pêche, 170
Association québécoise de pédagogie collégiale, 170
Association québécoise du personnel de direction des écoles, 176
Atelier RADO Inc., 180
Atlantic Publishers Marketing Association, 186
Basketball Nova Scotia, 199
Better Business Bureau of Manitoba & Northwest Ontario, 206
Better Business Bureau of Vancouver Island, 206
Better Business Bureau of Western Ontario, 207
Better Business Bureau Serving the Atlantic Provinces, 207
Beyond Pesticides, 1514
Black Coalition for AIDS Prevention, 213
Board of Canadian Registered Safety Professionals, 216
Bowls Canada Boulingrin, 220
Boxing Ontario, 220
Brandon Chamber of Commerce, 226
Breast Cancer Society of Canada, 228
British Columbia & Yukon Community Newspapers Association, 229
British Columbia Association of Agricultural Fairs & Exhibitions, 231
British Columbia Epilepsy Society, 240
British Columbia Federation of Foster Parent Associations, 240
British Columbia Hospice Palliative Care Association, 243
British Columbia Institute of Agrologists, 244
British Columbia Lodging & Campgrounds Association, 245
British Columbia Society for Male Survivors of Sexual Abuse, 254
Canada Games Council, 279
Canadian Arts Presenting Association, 296
Canadian Association for Disabled Skiing - Nova Scotia, 299
Canadian Association for Graduate Studies, 300
Canadian Association of Fairs & Exhibitions, 314
Canadian Association of Medical Teams Abroad, 321
Canadian Association of Movers, 321
Canadian Association of Nephrology Nurses & Technologists, 322
Canadian Association of Second Language Teachers, 332
Canadian Association of Wireless Internet Service Providers, 336
Canadian Blind Sports Association Inc., 344
Canadian Booksellers Association, 346
Canadian Copper & Brass Development Association, 364
Canadian Corporate Counsel Association, 365
Canadian Council for Aviation & Aerospace, 366
The Canadian Council for Public-Private Partnerships, 366
The Canadian Council on Continuing Education in Pharmacy, 371
Canadian Criminal Justice Association, 373
Canadian Croatian Congress, 373
Canadian Energy Efficiency Alliance, 381
Canadian Environmental Certification Approvals Board, 381
Canadian Federation of University Women, 388
Canadian Guild of Crafts, 399

Budget Index / $250,000-$500,000

Canadian Hard of Hearing Association, 400
Canadian Housing & Renewal Association, 409
Canadian Institute for the Relief of Pain & Disability, 413
Canadian Journalism Foundation, 423
Canadian Lacrosse Association, 425
Canadian Limousin Association, 427
Canadian Magen David Adom for Israel, 429
Canadian National Millers Association, 440
Canadian Printing Industries Association, 459
Canadian Race Relations Foundation, 464
Canadian Research Institute for the Advancement of Women, 467
Canadian School Boards Association, 468
Canadian Ski Marathon, 471
Canadian Society of Club Managers, 482
Canadian Society of Petroleum Geologists, 486
Canadian Society of Safety Engineering, Inc., 487
Canadian Sphagnum Peat Moss Association, 489
Canadian Technology Human Resources Board, 493
Canadian Unitarian Council, 499
Canadian Urological Association, 500
Carefree Society, 511
Caregivers Nova Scotia, 512
Carrefour 50+ du Québec, 515
Catholic Charities of The Archdiocese of Toronto, 518
Catholic Family Services of Simcoe County, 519
Centraide Gaspésie Îles-de-la-Madeleine, 522
Centre canadien d'arbitrage commercial, 526
Centre d'action bénévole de Montréal, 527
Centre d'aide et de lutte contre les agressions à caractère sexuel de Châteauguay, 527
Centre de services Guigues, 530
Centre multiethnique de Québec, 536
Cerebral Palsy Association in Alberta, 537
Chicken Farmers of Newfoundland & Labrador, 557
Child Welfare League of Canada, 560
Choir Alberta, 566
Christian Heritage Party of Canada, 567
Church Council on Justice & Corrections, 569
Circle of Eagles Lodge, 570
Citizens' Environment Watch, 570
Clean Annapolis River Project, 573
Community Development Council Durham, 596
The Community Foundation of Durham Region, 597
Community Foundation of Ottawa, 597
Community Futures Development Association of British Columbia, 598
Concours de musique du Canada inc., 610
Confédération québécoise des coopératives d'habitation en Outaouais, 611
Conseil de la culture des Laurentides, 616
Conseil des arts de Hearst, 617
Conseil québécois de la musique, 620
Conseil québécois sur le tabac et la santé, 620
Conservation Foundation of Greater Toronto, 622
Consulting Engineers of Ontario, 625
Corporation des bijoutiers du Québec, 629
Cosmetology Association of Nova Scotia, 631
Council of Prairie & Pacific University Libraries, 635
Craft Council of British Columbia, 638
Crossroads for Women Inc., 644
Cycle Toronto, 647
Dance Centre, 648
Disaster Recovery Institute Canada, 658
The Dream Factory, 662
Earthroots, 667
Economic Development Brandon, 673
Edmonton Heritage Festival Association, 677
Edmonton Social Planning Council, 679
Edson Friendship Centre, 680
Eli Bay Relaxation Response Institute, 684
Enfant-Retour Québec, 688
Epilepsy Association of Calgary, 693
ERS Training & Development Corporation, 695
Essa & District Agricultural Society, 696
Essential Skills Ontario, 696

European Solidarity Towards Equal Participation of People, 1524
Farm Radio International, 705
Federated Women's Institutes of Ontario, 706
Fédération des aînés et des retraités francophones de l'Ontario, 711
Fédération des coopératives d'habitation Montérégiennes, 714
Fédération des parents du Manitoba, 716
Fédération des parents francophones de Colombie-Britannique, 716
Fédération des producteurs d'agneaux et moutons du Québec, 717
Fédération du personnel professionnel des collèges, 720
Fédération du personnel professionnel des universités et de la recherche, 720
Fédération du plongeon amateur du Québec, 720
Fédération Internationale de Luge de Course, 1525
Federation of Ontario Cottagers' Associations, 725
Federation of Ontario Law Associations, 725
Fédération québécoise de la marche, 727
Fédération québécoise de tir, 728
Fédération québécoise des activités subaquatiques, 728
Fédération québécoise des centres communautaires de loisir inc., 728
Film & Video Arts Society Alberta, 735
First Unitarian Congregation of Toronto, 739
Fondation de l'Ordre des infirmières et infirmiers du Québec, 744
Fondation Lionel-Groulx, 747
Football Canada, 750
Football Québec, 750
Forests Ontario, 751
Foundation for Education Perth Huron, 755
4Korners Family Resource Center, 756
Foursquare Gospel Church of Canada, 756
Francophonie jeunesse de l'Alberta, 757
Friends of the Earth Canada, 762
Funeral & Cremation Services Council of Saskatchewan, 764
GAMA International Canada, 766
Greater Barrie Chamber of Commerce, 782
Greater Charlottetown & Area Chamber of Commerce, 783
Greater Kamloops Chamber of Commerce, 783
Greater Montreal Athletic Association, 784
Greater Oshawa Chamber of Commerce, 784
Greater Vernon Chamber of Commerce, 787
Green Calgary, 788
Gymnastics Saskatchewan, 795
Habitat Acquisition Trust, 795
Hebdos Québec, 810
L'Héritage canadien du Québec, 813
Héritage Montréal, 813
Historic Vehicle Society of Ontario, 815
Hockey PEI, 818
Holy Face Association, 819
Hope Air, 821
Independent Lumber Dealers Co-operative, 833
Inner City Angels, 838
Institute of Chartered Secretaries & Administrators - Canadian Division, 845
Institute of Law Clerks of Ontario, 846
Institute of Municipal Assessors, 846
Intellectual Property Institute of Canada, 850
International Arctic Science Committee, 1535
International Association of Rebekah Assemblies, 1540
International Commission on Radiological Protection, 855
International Confederation of Midwives, 1543
International Federation of Employees in Public Service, 1547
International Political Science Association, 859
International Snowmobile Manufacturers Association, 1557
International Society for Soil Mechanics & Geotechnical Engineering, 1559
International Union of Theoretical & Applied Mechanics, 1565

International Water Association, 1566
International Wildlife Rehabilitation Council, 1566
Jamaican Self-Help Organization, 867
James Bay Association for Community Living, 868
The Jane Goodall Institute of Canada, 868
John Gordon Home, 873
The John Howard Society of Canada, 874
Judo Ontario, 876
Junior League of Toronto, 878
Justice for Children & Youth, 878
Kaleidoscope Theatre Productions Society, 880
Karate BC, 881
Kéroul, Tourisme pour personnes à capacité physique restreinte, 884
Latvian Canadian Cultural Centre, 900
Laurier Teachers Union, 900
The League of Canadian Poets, 903
Legal Archives Society of Alberta, 906
Lethbridge Handicraft Guild, 908
Lethbridge Symphony Orchestra, 908
The Literacy Group of Waterloo Region, 914
The Literary Press Group of Canada, 914
Living Bible Explorers, 915
Lutheran Bible Translators of Canada Inc., 922
M2/W2 Association - Restorative Christian Ministries, 923
Maison Amaryllis, 926
Maison des femmes de Québec inc., 926
Manitoba Customer Contact Association, Inc., 935
Manitoba Tobacco Reduction Alliance, 946
Massage Therapist Association of Saskatchewan, 953
Master Painters & Decorators Association, 954
McCreary Centre Society, 955
McMaster University Faculty Association, 956
Memorial Society of British Columbia, 960
Metropolitan Action Committee on Violence Against Women & Children, 964
Middle East Studies Association of North America, 1571
Mill Woods Society for Community Living, 965
Millarville Racing & Agricultural Society, 965
Moisson Laurentides, 971
Moisson Mauricie/Centre-du-Québec, 971
Monarchist League of Canada, 971
Mood Disorders Association of Ontario, 973
Mouvement québécois de la qualité, 978
Multicultural History Society of Ontario, 979
Musée minéralogique et minier de Thetford Mines, 982
Muskoka Community Futures Development Corporation, 985
Nanaimo District Museum, 987
National Association of Women & the Law, 990
National Campus & Community Radio Association, 991
Natural Resources Union, 999
New Westminster Chamber of Commerce, 1015
Newfoundland & Labrador Basketball Association, 1017
Newfoundland & Labrador Environmental Industry Association, 1018
Newfoundland & Labrador School Boards Association, 1021
NORA, An Association of Responsible Recyclers, 1578
North Bay & District Humane Society, 1030
North Vancouver Community Arts Council, 1033
North West Commercial Travellers' Association, 1033
Northern Alberta Institute of Technology Academic Staff Association, 1034
Northern Youth Abroad Program, 1035
Northwest Coalition for Alternatives to Pesticides, 1580
Northwest Territories Society for the Prevention of Cruelty to Animals, 1038
Nova Scotia College of Respiratory Therapists, 1043
Nova Scotia Egg Producers, 1044
Nova Scotia Progressive Conservative Association, 1047

Nunavut Economic Developers Association, 1051
Oakville Arts Council, 1053
Occupational First Aid Attendants Association of British Columbia, 1054
Ontario Association of Community Futures Development Corporations, 1063
Ontario Association of Interval & Transition Houses, 1064
Ontario Association of School Business Officials, 1066
Ontario Coalition for Better Child Care, 1071
Ontario Concrete Pipe Association, 1074
Ontario Equestrian Federation, 1078
Ontario Formwork Association, 1081
Ontario Funeral Service Association, 1081
Ontario Museum Association, 1092
Ontario Painting Contractors Association, 1094
Ontario Plowmen's Association, 1096
Ontario Public Supervisory Officers' Association, 1100
Ontario Society of Occupational Therapists, 1107
Ontario Stone, Sand & Gravel Association, 1109
Ontario University Athletics, 1112
Operation Come Home, 1115
Operation Lifesaver, 1115
Orchestre de chambre de Montréal, 1117
The Order of United Commercial Travelers of America, 1119
Organisation multiressources pour les personnes atteintes de cancer, 1125
ORT Canada, 1127
Oshawa-Durham Rape Crisis Centre, 1128
Ottawa Riverkeeper, 1131
Palliative Manitoba, 1137
Parasports Québec, 1139
Parents partenaires en éducation, 1140
Parlimage CCF, 1143
Partners FOR the Saskatchewan River Basin, 1144
Patronato INAS (Canada), 1145
Pauktuutit Inuit Women of Canada, 1146
PAVED Arts, 1146
Peel Multicultural Council, 1148
Pension Investment Association of Canada, 1150
Pioneer Clubs Canada Inc., 1160
Playwrights Guild of Canada, 1162
The Pollution Probe Foundation, 1164
Pork Nova Scotia, 1165
Positive Women's Network, 1168
Prince Albert Model Forest Association Inc., 1171
Prince Edward Island Association of Exhibitions, 1172
Prince Edward Island Humane Society, 1175
Prince Edward Island Real Estate Association, 1176
Prince Edward Island Soccer Association, 1177
Prince George Chamber of Commerce, 1179
Private Motor Truck Council of Canada, 1180
Pro Coro Canada, 1181
Professional Organizers in Canada, 1186
Project Share, 1188
Provincial Building & Construction Trades Council of Ontario, 1190
Public School Boards' Association of Alberta, 1193
Pumphouse Theatres Society, 1194
Québec Community Newspaper Association, 1196
Queen's University International Centre, 1200
Quidi Vidi Rennie's River Development Foundation, 1201
Quinte West Chamber of Commerce, 1202
Reading Council for Literacy Advance in Montréal, 1205
Real Estate Board of the Fredericton Area Inc., 1205
Real Estate Institute of British Columbia, 1205
Recreation Vehicle Dealers Association of Canada, 1208
Regina Multicultural Council, 1212

Budget Index / $500,000-$1.5 Million

Regroupement des artistes en arts visuels du Québec (ind.), 1214
Regroupement provincial des maisons d'hébergement et de transition pour femmes victimes de violence conjugale, 1216
Regroupement québécois de la danse, 1216
Réseau des femmes d'affaires du Québec inc., 1219
Réseau du sport étudiant du Québec Est-du-Québec, 1223
Réseau Québec-France, 1225
Revivre - Association Québécoise de soutien aux personnes souffrant de troubles anxieux, dépressifs ou bipolaires, 1228
Richelieu International, 1229
Richmond Agricultural Society, 1229
The Rotary Club of Toronto, 1236
Royal Newfoundland Constabulary Association, 1242
Safety Services New Brunswick, 1245
SalvAide, 1252
Sarnia & District Humane Society, 1254
Saskatchewan Amateur Wrestling Association, 1255
Saskatchewan Archaeological Society, 1256
Saskatchewan Association of Medical Radiation Technologists, 1257
Saskatchewan Baseball Association, 1259
Saskatchewan Brain Injury Association, 1260
Saskatchewan Cultural Exchange Society, 1262
Saskatchewan Genealogical Society, 1265
Saskatchewan Lacrosse Association, 1268
Saskatchewan Motion Picture Industry Association, 1270
Saskatchewan Prevention Institute, 1272
Saskatchewan Publishers Group, 1272
Saskatchewan Sports Hall of Fame & Museum, 1275
Saskatchewan Turkey Producers' Marketing Board, 1276
Saskatoon Food Bank & Learning Centre, 1279
Savoy Foundation Inc., 1282
Scarborough Women's Centre, 1283
Scottish Rite Charitable Foundation of Canada, 1286
Scouts Canada, 1286
Seasons Centre for Grieving Children, 1288
SEEDS Foundation, 1289
Sherwood Park & District Chamber of Commerce, 1296
SkyWorks Charitable Foundation, 1303
Social Planning Council of Kitchener-Waterloo, 1306
Société d'histoire de Sherbrooke, 1311
Société des Jeux de l'Acadie inc., 1318
Société Logique, 1321
Société professionnelle des auteurs et des compositeurs du Québec, 1322
Société québécoise de la schizophrénie, 1323
Soeurs de Sainte-Marie de Namur, 1331
South Okanagan Immigrant & Community Services, 1335
Spina Bifida & Hydrocephalus Association of Ontario, 1342
Sport New Brunswick, 1344
SportAbility BC, 1345
Squamish Chamber of Commerce, 1346
Squash Alberta, 1347
Stanstead Historical Society, 1348
Status of Women Council of the Northwest Territories, 1349
Student Legal Services of Edmonton, 1352
Sun Ergos, A Company of Theatre & Dance, 1354
Sunrise Therapeutic Riding & Learning Centre, 1354
Supporting Choices of People Edson, 1356
Surrey Food Bank, 1357
Swim-Natation Manitoba, 1359
Symphony New Brunswick, 1360
Syndicat des employées de soutien de l'Université de Sherbrooke, 1362
Syndicat des professeures et professeurs de l'Université de Sherbrooke, 1363

Tecumseh Community Development Corporation, 1369
The Teresa Group, 1371
Theatre Ontario, 1374
Thunder Bay Historical Museum Society, 1378
Tire and Rubber Association of Canada, 1380
Toronto Arts Foundation, 1381
The Toronto Consort, 1383
Toronto Environmental Alliance, 1384
Toronto Sheet Metal Contractors Association, 1387
Tourism Burlington, 1389
Tourisme Baie-James, 1392
Tourisme Côte-Nord, 1392
Townshippers' Association, 1393
Trans Canada Trail Foundation, 1394
Triathlon Québec, 1398
True Sport Foundation, 1399
Ukrainian Canadian Foundation of Taras Shevchenko, 1402
Ukrainian Fraternal Society of Canada, 1403
Union of Nova Scotia Municipalities, 1407
United Way Central & Northern Vancouver Island, 1413
United Way for the City of Kawartha Lakes, 1413
United Way of Cochrane-Timiskaming, 1413
United Way of Perth-Huron, 1416
United Way of Sarnia-Lambton, 1416
Universala Esperanto-Asocio, 1600
Vancouver Chinatown Business Improvement Area Society, 1425
Vancouver Holocaust Centre Society - A Museum for Education & Remembrance, 1425
Vancouver Island Construction Association, 1426
Vancouver New Music, 1427
Vancouver Rape Relief & Women's Shelter, 1428
Victoria Epilepsy & Parkinson's Centre Society, 1432
Vietnamese Association, Toronto, 1434
Vintage Locomotive Society Inc., 1435
Vintners Quality Alliance, 1435
VOICE for Hearing Impaired Children, 1437
West Scarborough Neighbourhood Community Centre, 1446
West Vancouver Chamber of Commerce, 1446
Western Front Society, 1449
Whitby Chamber of Commerce, 1452
The White Ribbon Campaign, 1452
Women in Film & Television - Toronto, 1461
Women's Support Network of York Region, 1463
World Blue Chain for the Protection of Animals & Nature, 1603
Writers' Federation of Nova Scotia, 1468
The Writers' Guild of Alberta, 1469
Yellowknife Chamber of Commerce, 1471
Yoga Association of Alberta, 1473
York Soaring Association, 1473
Young Alberta Book Society, 1474
Youth Media Alliance, 1476

$500,000-$1.5 Million

A.C.C.E.S. Employment, 4
Active Healthy Kids Canada, 7
Active Support Against Poverty, 7
The Actors' Fund of Canada, 7
Acupuncture Canada, 7
Aerospace & Electronic Systems Society, 1485
AFCOM, 1485
Affiliation of Multicultural Societies & Service Agencies of BC, 11
AFOA Canada, 12
AIESEC, 18
Air Force Association of Canada, 19
Alberta Association of Municipal Districts & Counties, 24
Alberta Association of Optometrists, 24
Alberta Association of Recreation Facility Personnel, 24
Alberta Canola Producers Commission, 27
Alberta College of Medical Diagnostic & Therapeutic Technologists, 29
Alberta Committee of Citizens with Disabilities, 30
Alberta Community & Co-operative Association, 30
Alberta Conservation Tillage Society II, 31
Alberta Professional Outfitters Society, 43
Alberta Roadbuilders & Heavy Construction Association, 44
The Alberta Seventh Step Society, 46
Alberta Society for the Prevention of Cruelty to Animals, 47
Alberta Sulphur Research Ltd., 48
Allied Beauty Association, 58
ALS Society of Québec, 60
Alzheimer Society of Alberta & Northwest Territories, 61
Alzheimer Society of Calgary, 62
Alzheimer Society of Nova Scotia, 64
Alzheimer Society of Perth County, 64
Alzheimer Society Peterborough, Kawartha Lakes, Northumberland, & Haliburton, 65
The American Astronautical Society, 1490
American Birding Association, Inc., 1490
American Galvanizers Association, 1493
American Hiking Society, 1494
American Numismatic Society, 1496
American Studies Association, 1503
American Water Resources Association, 1504
The Apostolic Church in Canada, 73
Applegrove Community Complex, 74
Arctic Institute of North America, 81
ASM International, 1506
Assemblée de la francophonie de l'Ontario, 87
Assemblée des évêques catholiques du Québec, 88
Association canadienne d'éducation de langue française, 90
Association de l'industrie électrique du Québec, 100
Association de Montréal pour la déficience intellectuelle, 102
Association des cinémas parallèles du Québec, 109
Association des clubs d'entrepreneurs étudiants du Québec, 109
Association des commerçants de véhicules récréatifs du Québec, 109
Association des enseignantes et des enseignants francophones du Nouveau-Brunswick, 112
Association des entrepreneurs en construction du Québec, 112
Association des jeunes travailleurs et travailleuses de Montréal inc, 117
Association du camionnage du Québec inc., 130
Association du Québec pour l'intégration sociale / Institut québécois de la déficience intellectuelle, 131
Association for Asian Studies - USA, 1507
Association for Canadian Studies, 133
Association francophone pour le savoir, 135
Association minière du Québec, 137
Association nationale des distributeurs aux petites surfaces alimentaires, 138
Association of Americans & Canadians in Israel, 1510
Association of British Columbia Forest Professionals, 140
Association of British Columbia Land Surveyors, 140
Association of Manitoba Municipalities, 151
Association of Professional Engineers & Geoscientists of Manitoba, 158
Association of Regina Realtors, 160
Association of Registered Nurses of Prince Edward Island, 161
Association of Zoos & Aquariums, 1513
Association paritaire pour la santé et la sécurité du travail - Imprimerie et activités connexes, 164
Association paritaire pour la santé et la sécurité du travail - Secteur Affaires municipales, 165

Association québécoise de la distribution de fruits et légumes, 170
Association québécoise des organismes de coopération internationale, 173
Association québécoise des technologies, 174
Association québécoise des transports, 175
Association sectorielle: Fabrication d'équipement de transport et de machines, 178
Asthma Society of Canada, 179
Athabasca University Students' Union, 180
Automobile Protection Association, 189
Ayrshire Breeders Association of Canada, 191
B'nai Brith Youth Organization, 192
Banff & Lake Louise Tourism, 195
Barreau de Montréal, 197
Baseball Ontario, 198
Basketball New Brunswick, 198
BC School Sports, 202
Better Business Bureau of Mainland BC, 206
Better Business Bureau of Saskatchewan, 206
Better Business Bureau Serving Southern Alberta & East Kootenay, 207
Bloc québécois, 214
Boîte à science - Conseil du loisir scientifique du Québec, 217
Brethren in Christ, 228
Brewery, Winery & Distillery Workers Union - Local 300, 228
British Columbia Amateur Hockey Association, 230
British Columbia Confederation of Parent Advisory Councils, 236
British Columbia Co-operative Association, 237
British Columbia Council for Families, 237
British Columbia Institute of Technology Faculty & Staff Association, 244
British Columbia's Children's Hospital Foundation, 259
The Brontë Society, 1514
The Brothers of the Good Shepherd, 260
Building Owners & Managers Association of Ottawa, 263
Bulimia Anorexia Nervosa Association, 264
Canada's National Firearms Association, 282
Canadian Alliance of Physiotherapy Regulators, 291
The Canadian Art Foundation, 295
Canadian Association of Chiefs of Police, 310
Canadian Association of Professional Employees, 328
Canadian Association of Schools of Nursing, 332
Canadian Beverage Association, 342
Canadian Broadcast Standards Council, 347
Canadian Cerebral Palsy Sports Association, 354
Canadian Charolais Association, 355
Canadian Children's Opera Company, 356
Canadian Conference of the Arts, 363
Canadian Cosmetic, Toiletry & Fragrance Association, 366
Canadian Council for the Advancement of Education, 367
Canadian Council of Christian Charities, 368
Canadian Federation of Agriculture, 384
Canadian Federation of Humane Societies, 386
Canadian Fencing Federation, 389
Canadian Finance & Leasing Association, 390
Canadian Fire Alarm Association, 390
Canadian Foundation for AIDS Research, 392
Canadian Freestyle Ski Association, 394
Canadian Friends Service Committee, 395
Canadian Hemophilia Society, 404
Canadian HIV/AIDS Legal Network, 405
Canadian Horticultural Council, 408
Canadian Independent Bicycle Retailers Association, 410
Canadian International Freight Forwarders Association, 421
Canadian Livestock Records Corporation, 428
Canadian Mathematical Society, 431
Canadian Meteorological & Oceanographic Society, 435
Canadian Motorcycle Association, 437

Budget Index / $500,000-$1.5 Million

Canadian Music Centre, 438
Canadian Nursery Landscape Association, 442
Canadian Nurses Association, 442
Canadian Nurses Foundation, 443
Canadian Ophthalmological Society, 446
Canadian Orthopaedic Association, 448
Canadian Owners & Pilots Association, 448
Canadian Paint & Coatings Association, 449
Canadian Precast / Prestressed Concrete Institute, 459
Canadian Snowbird Association, 472
The Canadian Society for the Weizmann Institute of Science, 478
Canadian Society of Respiratory Therapists, 487
Canadian Solar Industries Association, 489
Canadian Steel Producers Association, 491
Canadian Sugar Institute, 491
Canadian Team Handball Federation, 493
Canadian Test Centre Inc., 494
Canadian Toy Association / Canadian Toy & Hobby Fair, 496
Canadian Water & Wastewater Association, 502
Canadian Women in Communications, 505
Canadian Wood Pallet & Container Association, 505
CanLearn Society for Persons with Learning Difficulties, 508
Carrying Capacity Network, 1515
Catholic Family Services of Peel Dufferin, 519
Catholic Family Services of Saskatoon, 519
CAUSE Canada, 521
Center for Health, Environment & Justice, 1516
Centraide Bas St-Laurent, 522
Centraide Estrie, 522
Centraide Mauricie, 522
Centraide Saguenay-Lac St-Jean, 523
Central Alberta AIDS Network Society, 523
Centre Communautaire Bon Courage De Place Benoît, 526
Le Centre culturel francophone de Vancouver, 526
Centre d'amitié autochtone du Québec, 527
Centre d'animation de développement et de recherche en éducation, 528
Centre de caractérisation microscopique des matériaux, 528
Centre de documentation sur l'éducation des adultes et la condition féminine, 529
Centre de formation à la coopération interculturelle du Québec, 529
Centre for International Business Studies, 533
Centre francophone de Toronto, 535
Centre international de solidarité ouvrière, 535
Chambre des huissiers de justice du Québec, 550
Change for Children Association, 551
Chartered Professional Accountants of Nova Scotia, 553
Chicken Farmers of Canada, 557
Child Evangelism Fellowship of Canada, 559
Chilliwack Community Arts Council, 563
Chiropractors' Association of Saskatchewan, 565
Chosen People Ministries (Canada), 566
Christian Farmers Federation of Ontario, 567
La Clé d'la Baie en Huronie - Association culturelle francophone, 572
Les Clubs 4-H du Québec, 576
Coaches Association of Ontario, 576
Collaboration Santé Internationale, 581
Collectif des femmes immigrantes du Québec, 581
College of Dietitians of British Columbia, 584
College of Licensed Practical Nurses of Newfoundland & Labrador, 585
College of Midwives of British Columbia, 586
College of Occupational Therapists of British Columbia, 586
Comité de solidarité/Trois-Rivières, 592
Communauté sépharade unifiée du Québec, 594
Community Development Halton, 596
Community Living St. Marys & Area Association, 604

Community Sector Council, Newfoundland & Labrador, 607
Compensation Employees' Union (Ind.), 608
Confédération québécoise des coopératives d'habitation, 611
Conseil de la transformation agroalimentaire et des produits de consommation, 616
Conseil de presse du Québec, 616
Conseil du patronat du Québec, 618
Conseil interprofessionnel du Québec, 618
Conseil québécois du commerce de détail, 620
Construction Maintenance & Allied Workers Canada, 624
Construction Specifications Canada, 624
Consumer Health Products Canada, 626
Copian, 628
Corporation des maîtres mécaniciens en tuyauterie du Québec, 630
Corporation des thanatologues du Québec, 630
Cowichan Intercultural Society, 637
Craft Council of Newfoundland & Labrador, 638
Cross Country Canada, 643
Cypress Hills Ability Centres, Inc., 647
Destination Halifax, 654
Direction Chrétienne, 657
Disabled Peoples' International, 658
The Donkey Sanctuary of Canada, 661
Doorsteps Neighbourhood Services, 661
Durham Region Association of REALTORS, 665
Early Music Vancouver, 667
Easter Seals New Brunswick, 669
Edmonton Inner City Housing Society, 677
Edmonton Police Association, 678
Elder Abuse Ontario, 681
Endometriosis Association, Inc., 1523
Environmental Defence, 691
The Environmental Law Centre (Alberta) Society, 692
Evangelical Medical Aid Society Canada, 698
Evangelical Order of Certified Pastoral Counsellors of America, 699
Family Enterprise Xchange, 703
Family Service Moncton Inc., 704
Fédération culturelle canadienne-française, 708
Fédération de l'UPA - Abitibi-Témiscamingue, 709
Fédération de volleyball du Québec, 710
Fédération des jeunes francophones du Nouveau-Brunswick Inc., 715
Fédération des producteurs forestiers du Québec, 717
Fédération étudiante universitaire du Québec, 720
Fédération nationale des communications (CSN), 721
Fédération québécoise de camping et de caravaning inc., 727
Fédération québécoise des coopératives forestières, 728
Fédération québécoise des directions d'établissements d'enseignement, 728
Fédération québécoise des sports cyclistes, 730
Festivals et Événements Québec, 733
Field Hockey BC, 734
Flemingdon Neighbourhood Services, 740
Folk Arts Council of St Catharines, 742
Fondation québécoise en environnement, 748
Foodservice & Packaging Institute, 1526
Foundation for International Environmental Law & Development, 1527
The Friends of Algonquin Park, 760
German Canadian Cultural Association, 772
Goethe-Institut (Toronto), 776
Greater Nanaimo Chamber of Commerce, 784
Greater Niagara Chamber of Commerce, 784
Green Thumb Theatre for Young People, 789
Guelph Chamber of Commerce, 793
Guide Outfitters Association of British Columbia, 793
Healing Our Spirit BC Aboriginal HIV/AIDS Society, 805
Healthy Minds Canada, 807
HelpAge Canada, 812
Heritage Toronto, 813

HIV North Society, 817
HIV/AIDS Resources and Community Health, 817
Hockey Development Centre for Ontario, 817
Horizons of Friendship, 821
Hotel Association of Canada Inc., 823
Humanity First Canada, 827
Immigrant & Multicultural Services Society, 830
Immigrant Services - Guelph Wellington, 830
Independent Contractors & Businesses Association of British Columbia, 832
Independent Financial Brokers of Canada, 832
India Rainbow Community Services of Peel, 834
Industrial Gas Users Association, 835
Information Services Vancouver, 837
Information Systems Security Association, 1532
Inside Education, 839
Institut Tshakapesh, 843
Institute for Performance & Learning, 844
Institute of Corporate Directors, 845
Institute of Cultural Affairs International, 846
Insurance Institute of Northern Alberta, 849
Intercede International, 851
Interior Indian Friendship Society, 852
International Association of Sedimentologists, 1540
International Council for Canadian Studies, 855
International Development & Relief Foundation, 856
International Erosion Control Association, 1546
International Federation of Organic Agriculture Movements, 1548
International Fund for Animal Welfare Canada, 857
International Hotel & Restaurant Association, 1550
International Organization of Securities Commissions, 1554
International Primate Protection League, 1556
International Society for Performance Improvement, 1558
International Soil Reference & Information Centre, 1561
International Statistical Institute, 1562
Intrepid Theatre Co. Society, 862
Island Deaf & Hard of Hearing Centre, 865
Jessie's - The June Callwood Centre for Young Women, 870
Jeunesse du Monde, 870
Jeunesses Musicales du Canada, 871
Jewish Family Services - Calgary, 871
The John Howard Society of Newfoundland & Labrador, 874
The John Howard Society of Ontario, 874
Judo-Québec inc, 876
Junior Achievement Canada, 877
Kamloops Foodbank & Outreach Society, 880
Kamloops Immigrant Services, 880
Kamloops Wildlife Park Society, 881
Khalsa Diwan Society, 884
Kidney Cancer Canada Association, 884
Ki-Low-Na Friendship Society, 887
Kin Canada, 887
Kitimat Child Development Centre, 891
Learning Disabilities Association of Saskatchewan, 905
Liaison of Independent Filmmakers of Toronto, 909
Lifesaving Society, 911
Linguistic Society of America, 1569
Lunenburg Marine Museum Society, 921
Lutheran Association of Missionaries & Pilots, 922
Lutheran Laymen's League of Canada, 922
Lymphoma Canada, 923
Maison Plein Coeur, 927
Manitoba Chamber Orchestra, 933
Manitoba Child Care Association, 933
Manitoba Chiropractors' Association, 933
Manitoba Federation of Labour, 936
Maple Ridge Pitt Meadows Arts Council, 948
March of Dimes Non-Profit Housing Corporation, 949
Markham Board of Trade, 951

MATCH International Women's Fund, 954
The McLean Foundation, 955
Mechanical Contractors Association of Alberta, 956
Medicine Hat & District Chamber of Commerce, 958
Mining Suppliers Trade Association Canada, 967
Miramichi Salmon Association, 968
Mississauga Arts Council, 969
Moisson Québec, 971
MultiPrévention, 980
Muslim Community of Québec, 985
The Muttart Foundation, 986
National Action Committee on the Status of Women, 989
National Association for Surface Finishing, 1573
National Association of Teachers of Singing, 1574
National Association of the Chemistry Industry, 1574
National Association of Towns & Townships, 1574
National Association of Women in Construction, 1575
National Council for Science & the Environment, 1575
National Farmers Union, 993
National Magazine Awards Foundation, 994
National Organization of Immigrant & Visible Minority Women of Canada, 995
National Press Club of Canada Foundation, 995
National Trust for Canada, 996
Nature Québec, 1000
Nature Saskatchewan, 1000
Nature Trust of New Brunswick, 1001
Nellie's Shelter, 1003
Newfoundland & Labrador Arts Council, 1015
Newfoundland Symphony Orchestra Association, 1023
Niagara Association of REALTORS, 1024
Niagara Region Police Association, 1025
Noia, 1027
North Pacific Anadromous Fish Commission, 1031
North Peace Cultural Society, 1032
North Shore Multicultural Society, 1033
Northeast Organic Farming Association, 1580
Northern Ontario Native Tourism Association, 1035
Northumberland United Way, 1036
Northwest Atlantic Fisheries Organization, 1036
Northwest Territories Teachers' Association, 1038
Northwood Neighbourhood Services, 1040
Nova Scotia Advisory Council on the Status of Women, 1040
Nova Scotia Home Builders' Association, 1045
Nova Scotia Society for the Prevention of Cruelty to Animals, 1049
O Vertigo Danse, 1052
Oakville & Milton Humane Society, 1053
Ontario Alliance of Christian Schools, 1059
Ontario Building Officials Association Inc., 1070
Ontario Chamber of Commerce, 1071
Ontario Commercial Fisheries' Association, 1073
Ontario Dairy Council, 1076
Ontario East Tourism Association, 1077
Ontario Fruit & Vegetable Growers' Association, 1081
Ontario Historical Society, 1084
Ontario Network of Employment Skills Training Projects, 1093
Ontario Sailing, 1103
Ontario Society of Medical Technologists, 1107
Opera America Inc., 1580
Opéra Atelier, 1114
Opération Nez rouge, 1116
Orchestras Canada, 1117
Ordre des chimistes du Québec, 1120
Ordre des denturologistes du Québec, 1121
Ordre des ergothérapeutes du Québec, 1121
Ordre des ingénieurs forestiers du Québec, 1123

Budget Index / $1.5 Million-$3 Million

Ordre des médecins vétérinaires du Québec, 1123
Ordre des technologues professionnels du Québec, 1124
Ordre des traducteurs, terminologues et interprètes agréés du Québec, 1124
Ordre professionnel de la physiothérapie du Québec, 1124
Organic Trade Association, 1581
Orillia & District Chamber of Commerce, 1126
Ottawa Symphony Orchestra Inc., 1132
Pacific Cinémathèque Pacifique, 1135
Parkdale Community Legal Services, 1140
Parkdale Intercultural Association, 1140
Parks & Recreation Ontario, 1142
Parliamentarians for Global Action, 1582
Parliamentary Centre, 1142
Pet Industry Joint Advisory Council, 1153
PIJAC Canada, 1159
Plastics Foodservice Packaging Group, 1584
Police Association of Ontario, 1163
Pool & Hot Tub Council of Canada, 1164
Port Colborne Community Association for Research Extension, 1165
Potato Growers of Alberta, 1168
Prairie Theatre Exchange, 1170
Prince Edward Island Museum & Heritage Foundation, 1175
Professional Employees Association (Ind.), 1183
Professional Golfers' Association of Canada, 1185
Project Ploughshares, 1188
The Publishers Association, 1585
Quad County Support Services, 1195
Québec English School Boards Association, 1197
Québec-Labrador Foundation (Canada) Inc., 1199
Quesnel & District Child Development Centre Association, 1200
Ralph Thornton Centre, 1204
Real Estate Institute of Canada, 1205
Real Property Association of Canada, 1206
Recreation Nova Scotia, 1207
Red River Exhibition Association, 1210
Réseau Technoscience, 1226
Resource Recycling Inc., 1586
Rexdale Community Legal Services, 1229
Road Scholar, 1586
Ronald McDonald House Toronto, 1235
Saint John Region Chamber of Commerce, 1247
St. Lawrence Valley Natural History Society, 1250
S.A.L.T.S. Sail & Life Training Society, 1252
Sask Sport Inc., 1254
Saskatchewan Heavy Construction Association, 1267
Saskatchewan Institute of Agrologists, 1268
Saskatchewan Volleyball Association, 1277
Saskatchewan Writers Guild, 1278
Saskatoon Region Association of REALTORS, 1280
Saskatoon Society for the Prevention of Cruelty to Animals Inc., 1280
School Sports Newfoundland & Labrador, 1284
Sea Shepherd Conservation Society - USA, 1588
Secours aux lépreux (Canada) inc., 1288
Seniors Resource Centre Association of Newfoundland & Labrador Inc., 1290
Serbian Orthodox Church - Orthodox Diocese of Canada, 1290
Seva Canada Society, 1292
Sexual Assault Centre Kingston Inc., 1292
Shad Valley International, 1293
SHARE Agriculture Foundation, 1294
ShareLife, 1294
Sierra Club of Canada, 1298
Silent Voice Canada Inc., 1299
Smart Commute, 1304
Snowmobilers of Manitoba Inc., 1305
Soccer New Brunswick, 1305

Société d'histoire du Lac-St-Jean/Maison des Bâtisseurs, 1312
Société de l'Acadie du Nouveau-Brunswick, 1316
Société des Auteurs de Radio, Télévision et Cinéma, 1317
Société des écoles du monde du BI du Québec et de la francophonie, 1317
Société des musées québécois, 1318
Société historique Alphonse-Desjardins, 1319
Société internationale du réseau ÉCONOMUSÉE et Société ÉCONOMUSÉE du Québec, 1321
Société Saint-Jean-Baptiste du Centre du Québec, 1324
Society for Classical Studies, 1589
Society of Fire Protection Engineers, 1593
Sons of Scotland Benevolent Association, 1333
Southeast Asian Ministers of Education Organization, 1595
Special Olympics Alberta, 1339
Specialized Information Publishers Association, 1596
Squash Canada, 1347
Suicide Action Montréal, 1353
Swift Current Agricultural & Exhibition Association, 1358
Swim BC, 1358
Syndicat des technologues en radiologie du Québec, 1364
Syndicat professionnel des ingénieurs d'Hydro-Québec, 1365
Table Tennis Canada, 1366
Tennis Québec, 1371
Théâtre français de Toronto, 1374
Thompson Okanagan Tourism Association, 1376
Thompson, Nicola, Cariboo United Way, 1376
Thunder Bay Chamber of Commerce, 1377
Tides Canada Foundation, 1379
Toronto Cat Rescue, 1383
Toronto Lawyers Association, 1385
Toronto Montessori Institute, 1386
Toronto PWA Foundation, 1386
Toronto Zoo, 1388
Tourism Industry Association of New Brunswick Inc., 1390
Tourism Sarnia Lambton, 1391
Tourism Saskatoon, 1391
Tourism Thunder Bay, 1391
Tourisme Bas-Saint-Laurent, 1392
Tourisme Chaudière-Appalaches, 1392
Tourisme Gaspésie, 1392
Tourisme Lanaudière, 1392
Traffic Injury Research Foundation, 1394
Trout Unlimited Canada, 1399
Truck Loggers Association, 1399
UBC Alumni Association, 1401
UFI - The Global Association of the Exhibition Industry, 1598
Union internationale de la presse francophone, 1598
Union internationale des architectes, 1598
Union of British Columbia Municipalities, 1407
United Nations Association in Canada, 1411
United Way of Greater Simcoe County, 1414
United Way of Leeds & Grenville, 1415
United Way of Oxford, 1415
United Way of Prince Edward Island, 1416
United Way of St Catharines & District, 1416
United Way of Sault Ste Marie & District, 1417
United Way of the Fraser Valley, 1417
Urban Development Institute of Canada, 1422
U.S. Committee for Refugees & Immigrants, 1601
Vancouver International Children's Festival, 1426
VanDusen Botanical Garden Association, 1429
Vanier Institute of The Family, 1429
Variety - The Children's Charity of Manitoba, Tent 58 Inc., 1430
Victoria READ Society, 1433
Vidéographe, 1434
Vues d'Afriques - Les Journées du cinéma africain et créole, 1439

Wallace Center, Winrock International, 1601
Water Ski & Wakeboard Canada, 1441
WaterCan, 1442
West Coast Railway Association, 1445
The Wesleyan Church of Canada - Central Canada District, 1447
Western Transportation Advisory Council, 1450
Wildlife Preservation Canada, 1455
Windsor Symphony Orchestra, 1457
Wine Country Ontario, 1457
Winnipeg Harvest Inc., 1459
Women In Crisis (Algoma) Inc., 1460
Woodland Cultural Centre, 1464
World Accord, 1465
World Archery Federation, 1603
World at Work, 1603
World Coal Institute, 1604
Yasodhara Ashram Society, 1470
Youth Assisting Youth, 1475
Youth Challenge International, 1475
YWCA Canada, 1481

$1.5 Million-$3 Million

ABC Life Literacy Canada, 1
Adventist Development & Relief Agency Canada, 10
The Advocates' Society, 11
Africa Inland Mission International (Canada), 12
AIDS Vancouver, 17
Aish Thornhill Community Shul & Learning Centre, 20
Alberta Diabetes Foundation, 32
Alberta Museums Association, 40
Alliance des professeures et professeurs de Montréal, 56
Alzheimer Manitoba, 61
Alzheimer Society of Niagara Region, 63
Alzheimer Society of Ottawa & Renfrew County, 64
Alzheimer Society of Saskatchewan Inc., 64
Alzheimer Society of Windsor/Essex County, 65
Alzheimer Society of York Region, 65
American Economic Association, 1492
American Fisheries Society, 1493
American Rivers, 1497
American Society of International Law, 1500
American Thyroid Association, 1503
APCHQ - Montréal Métropolitain, 73
Apostolic Church of Pentecost of Canada Inc., 73
L'Arche Foundation, 77
Architectural Institute of British Columbia, 79
Asia Pacific Foundation of Canada, 86
Assaulted Women's Helpline, 87
Assiniboine Park Conservancy, 88
Association des gestionnaires des établissements de santé et des services sociaux, 115
Association des policières et policiers provinciaux du Québec, 123
Association des Pompiers de Montréal inc., 124
Association des Scouts du Canada, 127
Association of American Geographers, 1510
Association of Canadian Travel Agencies, 143
Association of Neighbourhood Houses BC, 153
Association régionale de la communauté francophone de Saint-Jean inc., 177
Association touristique régionale de Charlevoix, 178
Association touristique régionale du Saguenay-Lac-Saint-Jean, 179
B'nai Brith Canada, 192
Les Ballets Jazz de Montréal, 195
Banff World Television Festival Foundation, 196
The Barbra Schlifer Commemorative Clinic, 196
Benevolent & Protective Order of Elks of Canada, 204
Birchmount Bluffs Neighbourhood Centre, 212
Bird Studies Canada, 212
Boys & Girls Clubs of Canada Foundation, 222
British Columbia Ferry & Marine Workers' Union (CLC), 241
British Columbia Landscape & Nursery Association, 244

British Columbia Wood Specialities Group Association, 258
Calgary Immigrant Women's Association, 272
Canada West Foundation, 281
Canada's History, 282
Canadian Agricultural Safety Association, 289
The Canadian Association of Fitness Professionals, 315
Canadian Association of Management Consultants, 320
Canadian Association of Petroleum Landmen, 326
Canadian Centre for Victims of Torture, 354
Canadian Council of Ministers of the Environment, 368
Canadian Franchise Association, 394
Canadian Generic Pharmaceutical Association, 397
Canadian German Chamber of Industry & Commerce Inc., 397
Canadian Marketing Association, 430
Canadian Medical Foundation, 434
Canadian Network of Toxicology Centres, 441
Canadian Physicians for Aid & Relief, 454
Canadian Plywood Association, 456
Canadian Political Science Association, 457
Canadian Power & Sail Squadrons (Canadian Headquarters), 459
Canadian Produce Marketing Association, 460
Canadian Propane Association, 461
Canadian Psychiatric Association, 461
Canadian Railroad Historical Association, 465
Canadian Veterinary Medical Association, 501
Cariboo Chilcotin Child Development Centre Association, 512
Catholic Family Service of Ottawa, 518
Catholic Family Services of Toronto, 519
Catholic Health Alliance of Canada, 519
The Catholic Principals' Council of Ontario, 520
Centraide Laurentides, 522
Centraide Outaouais, 523
Centre for Spanish Speaking Peoples, 533
Chambre de commerce et d'industrie de Laval, 545
Chambre de l'assurance de dommages, 550
Chess'n Math Association, 556
Childhood Cancer Canada Foundation, 560
Children's Aid Society of Oxford County, 561
Children's Mental Health Ontario, 562
Chinese Family Services of Ontario, 565
La cinémathèque québécoise, 569
Coady International Institute, 577
CODE, 580
College of Physical Therapists of British Columbia, 587
Community Legal Assistance Society, 599
Community Living Association (Lanark County), 600
Community Living Renfrew County South, 604
Consumers International, 1519
Convention of Atlantic Baptist Churches, 627
Corporation des propriétaires immobiliers du Québec, 630
Diabète Québec, 655
Down Syndrome Research Foundation, 661
Ecojustice Canada Society, 672
Edmonton Folk Music Festival, 677
Emmanuel International Canada, 686
Energy Probe Research Foundation, 688
Evangelical Fellowship of Canada, 698
Evangelical Lutheran Church in Canada, 698
Evangelical Mennonite Conference, 699
Excellence Canada, 699
Farm Management Canada, 705
Fédération des chambres de commerce du Québec, 713
Fédération des producteurs de bovins du Québec, 717
Fédération nationale des enseignants et des enseignantes du Québec, 721
Financial Executives International Canada, 736
FOCUS, 741
Folklorama, 742
Fondation de l'entrepreneurship, 743
Fondation des étoiles, 744

Fondation Père-Ménard, 747
Fort Calgary Society, 752
Foundation of Catholic Community Services Inc., 756
Free Methodist Church in Canada, 759
Freight Carriers Association of Canada, 759
Friends of Canadian Broadcasting, 760
Greater Vancouver Food Bank Society, 786
Greater Vancouver International Film Festival Society, 786
Greenpeace Canada, 789
Groupement des assureurs automobiles, 792
Gymnastics B.C., 795
Hamilton Chamber of Commerce, 801
Hamilton Program for Schizophrenia, 802
HealthCareCAN, 807
Heating, Refrigeration & Air Conditioning Institute of Canada, 810
Historic Sites Association of Newfoundland & Labrador, 815
Hospice Niagara, 822
H.R. MacMillan Space Centre Society, 824
Human Rights Research & Education Centre, 826
Immigrant Centre Manitoba Inc., 830
Industrial Truck Association, 1531
Institut de coopération pour l'éducation des adultes, 841
Institut de recherche en biologie végétale, 842
Institut québécois de planification financière, 843
Insurance Council of British Columbia, 849
International Association of Administrative Professionals, 1537
International Association of Ports & Harbours, 1539
International Ocean Institute, 1553
International Union of Pure & Applied Chemistry, 1565
IRC International Water & Sanitation Centre, 1567
Jewish Family Services Edmonton, 871
KAIROS: Canadian Ecumenical Justice Initiatives, 880
Kingston Economic Development Corporation, 889
Learning Disabilities Association of Ontario, 904
Lloydminster Agricultural Exhibition Association, 916
Local Government Management Association of British Columbia, 916
Maison D'Haiti, 926
Manitoba Interfaith Welcome Place, 939
Many Rivers Counselling & Support Services, 948
Mennonite Economic Development Associates Canada, 961
Mining Association of Canada, 967
Mission Aviation Fellowship of Canada, 969
Moose Jaw Exhibition Company Ltd., 974
National Aboriginal Capital Corporations Association, 988
National Association of Federal Retirees, 990
National Association of Pharmacy Regulatory Authorities, 990
National Association of Watch & Clock Collectors, Inc., 1574
The National Citizens Coalition, 991
National Screen Institute - Canada, 996
Native Courtworker & Counselling Association of BC, 997
Newfoundland & Labrador Association of Technology Industries, 1016
Les normes canadiennes de la publicité, 1028
The North-South Institute, 1036
Nova Scotia Association of REALTORS, 1041
Ontario Basketball, 1067
Ontario Coalition of Aboriginal Peoples, 1071
Ontario Council of Agencies Serving Immigrants, 1075
Ontario Genealogical Society, 1081
Ontario Nature, 1093
Ontario Neurotrauma Foundation, 1093
Ontario Professional Planners Institute, 1098
Ontario Safety League, 1103

Ontario Teachers' Federation, 1110
Operation Mobilization Canada, 1116
Ordre des administrateurs agréés du Québec, 1119
Organic Crop Improvement Association (International), 1580
Organization of American Historians, 1581
Ottawa Community Immigrant Services Organization, 1130
Ottawa Safety Council, 1131
Outward Bound Canada, 1133
Parents, Families & Friends of Lesbians & Gays, 1582
The Pentecostal Assemblies of Newfoundland & Labrador, 1150
Pesticide Action Network North America, 1583
Physicians Services Inc. Foundation, 1158
Physiotherapy Alberta - College + Association, 1158
The Planetary Society, 1584
Planned Parenthood of Toronto, 1161
Prologue to the Performing Arts, 1188
Prostate Cancer Canada, 1189
Public Accountants Council for the Province of Ontario, 1192
Public Services Health & Safety Association, 1193
Réseau des cégeps et des collèges francophones du Canada, 1219
Réseau HEC Montréal, 1224
Ringette Canada, 1232
Roofing Contractors Association of British Columbia, 1236
Rose & Max Rady Jewish Community Centre, 1236
Royal Academy of Dance Canada, 1237
The Royal Scottish Country Dance Society, 1587
Rugby Ontario, 1244
Sail Canada, 1245
The Salvation Army START Program, 1253
Saskatchewan Hockey Association, 1267
SeCan Association, 1288
Seniors Association of Greater Edmonton, 1290
Sexuality Education Resource Centre Manitoba, 1293
Smithers Community Services Association, 1304
Société du droit de reproduction des auteurs, compositeurs et éditeurs au Canada (SODRAC 2003) inc., 1318
Société pour les enfants handicapés du Québec, 1322
Society for Technical Communication, 1591
Society of Motion Picture & Television Engineers, 1593
Speech-Language & Audiology Canada, 1341
Sport BC, 1344
Sport Nova Scotia, 1345
Sunshine Coast Community Services Society, 1355
Tafelmusik Baroque Orchestra & Chamber Choir, 1366
TEAM of Canada Inc., 1368
Threshold Ministries, 1377
Tourism Industry Association of Canada, 1389
Tourism Industry Association of PEI, 1390
Tourisme Laurentides, 1392
Tourisme Montérégie, 1393
Tourisme Outaouais, 1393
Unemployed Help Centre, 1404
Union of Nova Scotia Indians, 1407
Union of Postal Communications Employees, 1408
United Way of Cambridge & North Dumfries, 1413
United Way of Peterborough & District, 1416
United Way of Quinte, 1416
United Way of Regina, 1416
Urban & Regional Information Systems Association, 1601
Used Car Dealers Association of Ontario, 1423
Vancouver Island Real Estate Board, 1426
Vancouver Museum Society, 1427

Vancouver, Coast & Mountains Tourism Region, 1429
Victoria Real Estate Board, 1433
Victoria Youth Empowerment Society, 1434
Victorian Order of Nurses for Canada, 1434
Wilderness Committee, 1454
Wildlife Habitat Canada, 1454
World Animal Protection, 1465
World Nuclear Association, 1606
YOUTHLINK, 1476

$3 Million-$5 Million

Access Copyright, 4
AFS Interculture Canada, 13
Alberta Ballet, 25
Alberta Historical Resources Foundation, 37
Alberta Teachers' Association, 49
Alliance of Canadian Cinema, Television & Radio Artists, 58
ALS Society of Canada, 60
American Anthropological Association, 1488
American Historical Association, 1494
American Humane Association, 1494
American Marketing Association, 1495
American Planning Association, 1496
Association internationale des maires francophones - Bureau à Québec, 136
Association pour l'intégration sociale d'Ottawa, 166
Bamfield Marine Sciences Centre, 195
The Bible League of Canada, 208
The Bob Rumball Centre for the Deaf, 216
The Calgary Foundation, 272
Canada's Public Policy Forum, 282
Canadian AIDS Treatment Information Exchange, 290
Canadian Association for Laboratory Accreditation Inc., 301
Canadian Association of University Business Officers, 334
Canadian Baptists of Ontario & Quebec, 341
Canadian General Standards Board, 396
Canadian HIV Trials Network, 405
Canadian Mental Health Association, 434
Canadian Pension & Benefits Institute, 453
Canadian Teachers' Federation, 493
Canadian Warplane Heritage, 502
Canadian Water Network, 502
CanoeKayak Canada, 509
Carizon Family & Community Services, 513
Catholic Cross Cultural Services, 518
Catholic Missions in Canada, 520
C.D. Howe Institute, 521
Central Neighbourhood House, 524
Centre for Canadian Language Benchmarks, 531
Centre for Immigrant & Community Services, 532
Centre franco-ontarien de ressources pédagogiques, 534
Centre international de criminologie comparée, 535
Centre patronal de santé et sécurité du travail du Québec, 536
Chambre de commerce du Montréal métropolitain, 544
Children's Arts Umbrella Association, 561
Children's Tumor Foundation, 1516
Coastal Jazz & Blues Society, 579
College of Licensed Practical Nurses of BC, 585
College of Occupational Therapists of Ontario, 587
College of Registered Dental Hygienists of Alberta, 589
Community Living Durham North, 601
Community Living Grimsby, Lincoln & West Lincoln, 602
Community Living Oshawa / Clarington, 604
Community Social Services Employers' Association, 607
Congress of Aboriginal Peoples, 613
Daily Bread Food Bank, 648
DIVERSEcity Community Resources Society, 659

Dog Guides Canada, 660
Earth Island Institute, 1521
EastGen, 671
Edmonton Space & Science Foundation, 679
Electro-Federation Canada, 683
Entertainment Merchants Association - International Head Office, 1523
Family Service Centre of Ottawa-Carleton, 704
Fédération des clubs de motoneigistes du Québec, 713
La Fédération des commissions scolaires du Québec, 713
Fédération des professionnelles et professionnels de l'éducation du Québec, 718
Fédération québécoise des sociétés Alzheimer, 729
Fédérations de l'UPA de Lévis Bellechasse, Rive Nord, Lotbinière-Mégantic, 731
Fibrose kystique Québec, 733
Fife House, 734
The 519 Church St. Community Centre, 740
Fondation de la faune du Québec, 744
Fondation Hôpital Charles-LeMoyne, 746
Foothills Research Institute, 751
Foundation Assisting Canadian Talent on Recordings, 755
Friends of Animals, 1527
Friends of the Greenbelt Foundation, 762
Garth Homer Society, 767
Geneva Centre for Autism, 769
Girl Guides of Canada, 773
Groupe CTT Group, 791
Habitat for Humanity Canada, 796
The Harold Greenberg Fund, 804
Hong Fook Mental Health Association, 820
The Humane Society of the United States, 1530
Huntington Society of Canada, 827
Institut de la Francophonie pour le développement durable, 841
Institute for Work & Health, 844
Institute of Industrial & Systems Engineers, 1533
Institution of Mechanical Engineers, 1534
Inter Pares, 851
International Association of Business Communicators, 1538
International Association of Marine Aids to Navigation & Lighthouse Authorities, 1539
International Association of Venue Managers, Inc., 1540
International Brotherhood of Electrical Workers (AFL-CIO/CFL), 1542
International Council of Voluntary Agencies, 1545
International Federation of Professional & Technical Engineers (AFL-CIO/CLC), 1549
International Trademark Association, 1563
International Union Against Cancer, 1563
Inuit Community Centre, 862
Islamic Foundation of Toronto, 864
Jean Tweed Treatment Centre, 869
K3C Community Counselling Centres, 879
Kenora Association for Community Living, 883
Kerby Centre for the 55 Plus, 884
Laidlaw Foundation, 895
Land Trust Alliance, 1569
Law Society of Upper Canada, 902
Lions Foundation of Canada, 913
Livres Canada Books, 915
Lu'ma Native Housing Society, 920
Massey Centre for Women, 953
Medical Library Association, 1570
Mining Industry Human Resources Council, 967
Mission Association for Community Living, 968
Museum London, 983
NEC Native Education College Society, 1002
The Newspaper Guild (AFL-CIO/CLC), 1577
Niagara Support Services, 1026
Nisga'a Lisims Government, 1027
North American Insulation Manufacturers Association, 1579
The Ocean Conservancy, 1580
Ontario Association of Landscape Architects, 1064

Budget Index / Greater than $5 Million

Ontario Federation of Labour, 1079
Ontario Library Association, 1088
Ontario Principals' Council, 1097
Ordre des dentistes du Québec, 1121
Penticton & District Community Resources Society, 1150
Penticton & District Society for Community Living, 1150
Population Connection, 1584
Positive Living BC, 1167
Prince of Wales Northern Heritage Centre, 1179
Regina & District Food Bank Inc., 1211
The Renascent Centres for Alcoholism & Drug Addiction, 1217
The Royal Society for the Encouragement of Arts, Manufactures & Commerce, 1587
The Salvation Army in Canada, 1252
Saskatchewan Arts Board, 1256
Save a Family Plan, 1281
Seventh-day Adventist Church in Canada, 1292
Sierra Club, 1589
SIM Canada, 1299
Skills for Change, 1302
Society of Petroleum Engineers, 1593
Solid Waste Association of North America, 1595
South Peace Community Resources Society, 1335
Spinal Cord Injury Alberta, 1342
Standardbred Canada, 1347
Strathcona Christian Academy Society, 1351
Surrey Association for Community Living, 1357
Syndicat de la fonction publique du Québec inc. (ind.), 1361
Teachers of English to Speakers of Other Languages, Inc., 1597
Toronto's Hare Krishna Centre, 1388
Tourism Calgary, 1389
Tourism Victoria/Greater Victoria Visitors & Convention Bureau, 1391
Tourisme Cantons-de-l'Est, 1392
Union des artistes, 1406
Union des municipalités du Québec, 1406
Union of Ontario Indians, 1408
United Church of Canada Foundation, 1409
United Nations Research Institute for Social Development, 1600
United Way of Canada - Centraide Canada, 1413
United Way of Kitchener-Waterloo & Area, 1415
United Way of London & Middlesex, 1415
United Way of Oakville, 1415
University Settlement, 1421
Victoria Symphony Society, 1433
World Association for Christian Communication, 1465
World Energy Council, 1604
Worldwatch Institute, 1608
Youth Empowerment & Support Services, 1475

Greater than $5 Million

Abbotsford Community Services, 1
Addictions Foundation of Manitoba, 8
Agence universitaire de la Francophonie, 14
Ahmadiyya Muslim Jama'at Canada, 15
AiMHi, Prince George Association for Community Living, 18
Alberta Foundation for the Arts, 35
Alberta Innovates, 38
Alberta Research Council Inc., 44
Alberta School Boards Association, 45
Alberta Sport Connection, 48
Alzheimer Society Canada, 61
Alzheimer Society of British Columbia, 62
Alzheimer Society of Peel, 64
Alzheimer Society of PEI, 64
Alzheimer Society Ontario, 65
American Antiquarian Society, 1488
American Concrete Institute, 1491
American Psychological Association, 1497
American Public Works Association, 1497
American Society for Quality, 1498
American Society of Association Executives, 1499
Amnesty International, 1504

Amnesty International - Canadian Section (English Speaking), 68
Archaeological Institute of America, 1505
Atlantic Salmon Federation, 186
AUTO21 Network of Centres of Excellence, 189
The Bahá'í Community of Canada, 194
Beaver Party of Canada, 203
Billy Graham Evangelistic Association of Canada, 211
The Bloom Group, 215
Bluewater Recycling Association, 215
Brant Family & Children's Services, 226
British Columbia Cancer Foundation, 234
British Columbia Centre for Ability Association, 235
British Columbia Egg Marketing Board, 239
British Columbia Government & Service Employees' Union, 242
British Columbia Provincial Renal Agency, 249
British Columbia Securities Commission, 253
Building Owners & Managers Association International, 1514
CAA British Columbia, 267
Calgary Exhibition & Stampede, 271
Calgary Philharmonic Society, 273
Calgary Urban Project Society, 275
Camrose Association for Community Living, 277
Canada World Youth, 281
Canadian Baptist Ministries, 341
Canadian Bar Association, 341
Canadian Centre for Architecture, 353
Canadian Centre for Occupational Health & Safety, 353
Canadian Centre on Substance Use & Addiction, 354
The Canadian Chamber of Commerce, 355
The Canadian Corps of Commissionaires, 365
Canadian Federal Pilots Association, 384
Canadian Feed The Children, 389
Canadian Foundation for Climate & Atmospheric Sciences, 393
Canadian Foundation for Healthcare Improvement, 393
Canadian Hearing Society, 403
Canadian Kennel Club, 424
Canadian Museums Association, 437
Canadian Olympic Committee, 445
Canadian Opera Company, 446
Canadian Organization for Development through Education, 447
Canadian Physiotherapy Association, 454
Canadian Red Cross, 465
Canadian Society for Medical Laboratory Science, 476
Cancer Research Society, 507
CARE Canada, 511
Carefirst Seniors & Community Services Association, 511
Carnaval de Québec, 514
Catholic Children's Aid Society of Hamilton, 518
Centrale des syndicats du Québec, 525
Centre de réadaptation et dépendance le virage, 529
Centre for Addiction & Mental Health, 531
Centre for Newcomers Society of Calgary, 533
Chambre de la sécurité financière, 550
Chartered Professional Accountants of Ontario, 553
Children's Aid Society of Algoma, 560
Children's Aid Society of Toronto, 561
Children's Hospital Foundation of Manitoba, 562
Children's Wish Foundation of Canada, 562
The Christian & Missionary Alliance in Canada, 566
Christian Blind Mission International, 566
Christian Reformed Church in North America, 568
Christian Science, 1517
Clean Nova Scotia Foundation, 573
College of Family Physicians of Canada, 584
College of Massage Therapists of Ontario, 585
College of Physicians & Surgeons of Nova Scotia, 588
College of Physiotherapists of Ontario, 589
Colleges and Institutes Canada, 590

The Commonwealth of Learning, 594
Communitas Supportive Care Society, 595
Community Living Brantford, 600
Community Living Campbellford/Brighton, 601
Community Living Fort Frances & District, 602
Community Living Guelph Wellington, 602
Community Living London, 603
Community Living Sarnia-Lambton, 605
Community Microskills Development Centre, 606
Confédération des syndicats nationaux, 611
Conseil des arts de Montréal, 617
Conservation International, 1519
La Coop Fédérée, 627
Council of Ontario Universities, 635
The Cousteau Society, 1520
Covenant House Toronto, 637
CUSO International, 646
Davenport-Perth Neighbourhood & Community Health Centre, 651
Doctors without Borders Canada, 660
Ducks Unlimited Canada, 663
Earthwatch Institute, 1522
Easter Seals Ontario, 669
effect:hope, 680
Electricity Distributors Association, 683
Elementary Teachers' Federation of Ontario, 684
Éleveurs de volailles du Québec, 684
Environmental Defense, 1523
Environmental Law Institute, 1523
European Space Agency, 1524
Experiences Canada, 699
Family & Children's Services Niagara, 701
Family & Children's Services of Guelph & Wellington County, 702
Family Day Care Services (Toronto), 703
Fédération des médecins omnipraticiens du Québec, 716
Fédération des producteurs d'oeufs de consommation du Québec, 717
Fédération interprofessionnelle de la santé du Québec, 721
Fellowship of Evangelical Baptist Churches, 731
Fondation de l'Hôpital de Montréal pour enfants, 744
Fondation des maladies du coeur du Québec, 745
Fondation québécoise du cancer, 748
Foodshare Toronto, 750
Fred Victor Centre, 758
Gideons International in Canada, 773
Good Shepherd Refuge Social Ministries, 777
Goodwill Industries Essex Kent Lambton, 777
Goodwill, The Amity Group, 778
Greater Toronto Marketing Alliance, 786
Greenpeace International, 1528
Greenpeace USA, 1529
Groupe export agroalimentaire Québec - Canada, 792
Hamilton Community Foundation, 801
Health Sciences Association of British Columbia, 807
Health Sciences Centre Foundation, 807
Heart & Stroke Foundation of British Columbia & Yukon, 808
Heritage Park Society, 813
Hincks-Dellcrest Treatment Centre & Foundation, 815
HOPE International Development Agency, 821
Illuminating Engineering Society of North America, 1530
Immigrant Services Association of Nova Scotia, 830
Immigrant Services Society of BC, 830
Indspire, 835
Information & Communications Technology Council of Canada, 836
L'Institut canadien de Québec, 840
Institut de réadaptation en déficience physique de Québec, 841
Institut de recherche Robert-Sauvé en santé et en sécurité du travail, 842
Institut de tourisme et d'hôtellerie du Québec, 842

Institut national d'optique, 843
Institute for Clinical Evaluative Sciences, 843
Insurance Institute of Canada, 849
International Atomic Energy Agency, 1540
International Development Research Centre, 856
International Foundation of Employee Benefit Plans, 1549
International Institute for Applied Systems Analysis, 1551
International Institute for Sustainable Development, 858
International Labour Organization, 1552
International Literacy Association, 1552
International Maritime Organization, 1553
International Plant Nutrition Institute, 1555
International Sanitary Supply Association, Inc., 1556
International Skating Union, 1556
Islamic Relief Canada, 865
IWK Health Centre Foundation, 867
Jewish Federation of Greater Vancouver, 872
Jewish General Hospital Foundation, 872
Jewish Information Referral Service Montréal, 873
Kawartha-Haliburton Children's Aid Society, 882
Kensington Foundation, 883
Kerry's Place Autism Services, 884
Kidney Foundation of Canada, 885
Kids Cancer Care Foundation of Alberta, 886
Kinsight, 890
Knights of Columbus, 1568
Lakeshore Area Multi-Service Project, 896
LAMP Community Health Centre, 897
Law Society of British Columbia, 901
Legal Services Society, 906
Leucan - Association pour les enfants atteints de cancer, 908
The Liberal Party of Canada, 909
Lions Gate Hospital Foundation, 913
LOFT Community Services, 917
Lookout Emergency Aid Society, 919
Make-A-Wish Canada, 927
Makivik Corporation, 927
Manitoba Arts Council, 929
Manitoba Teachers' Society, 946
March of Dimes Canada, 949
Masonic Foundation of Ontario, 952
McCord Museum of Canadian History, 955
McMan Youth, Family & Community Services Association, 955
Meeting Professionals International, 1570
Muscular Dystrophy Canada, 982
Musicaction, 984
NACE International, 1571
National Ground Water Association, 1576
National Judicial Institute, 994
National Parks Conservation Association, 1577
National Psoriasis Foundation - USA, 1577
National Wildlife Federation, 1577
Native Child & Family Services of Toronto, 997
Natural Sciences & Engineering Research Council of Canada, 999
The Neil Squire Foundation, 1002
Nickel Institute, 1026
North Shore Forest Products Marketing Board, 1032
North York Community House, 1033
Office du tourisme et des congrès de Québec, 1055
Ontario Arts Council, 1060
Ontario College of Teachers, 1072
Ontario Society for the Prevention of Cruelty to Animals, 1105
Organisation internationale de la Francophonie, 1581
Organization for Economic Co-operation & Development, 1581
Ottawa Humane Society, 1130
Ottawa Tourism, 1132
Parachute, 1138
Parkinson Canada, 1141
Parkinson Society Central & Northern Ontario, 1141
Pentecostal Assemblies of Canada, 1150

Budget Index / Greater than $5 Million

People for the Ethical Treatment of Animals, 1583
PLEA Community Services Society of BC, 1162
posAbilities Association of BC, 1167
The Primate's World Relief & Development Fund, 1170
Prince Edward Island Vegetable Growers Co-op Association, 1178
Les producteurs de lait du Québec, 1181
Project Management Institute, 1585
Public Service Alliance of Canada, 1193
Public Services International, 1585
Railway Association of Canada, 1203
Rainforest Alliance, 1586
Real Estate Council of Alberta, 1205
Real Estate Council of British Columbia, 1205
The Recreation Association, 1207
Regina Exhibition Association Ltd., 1211
Registered Nurses' Association of Ontario, 1213
REHOBOTH Christian Ministries, 1216
Réseau du sport étudiant du Québec, 1222
Rick Hansen Foundation, 1231
Rideau Valley Conservation Authority, 1231
The Rocky Mountain Institute, 1586
Royal Botanical Gardens, 1239
The Royal Canadian Legion, 1240
Royal College of Dental Surgeons of Ontario, 1241
Royal Manitoba Theatre Centre, 1242
St. Joseph's Healthcare Foundation, 1249
Samaritan's Purse Canada, 1253

Saskatchewan Government & General Employees' Union, 1266
Saskatchewan Municipal Hail Insurance Association, 1270
Saskatchewan Pulse Growers, 1273
Saskatchewan School Boards Association, 1274
Saskatoon Open Door Society Inc., 1279
SaskCulture Inc., 1280
Sault Ste Marie Economic Development Corporation, 1281
Save the Children Canada, 1281
The Scott Mission, 1286
Semiahmoo House Society, 1289
Senior Link, 1290
Share Family & Community Services Society, 1294
The Shepherds' Trust, 1295
Simcoe Muskoka Family Connexions, 1300
Société de coopération pour le développement international, 1314
Société de développement des entreprises culturelles, 1314
Société des traversiers du Québec, 1318
Société québécoise de récupération et de recyclage, 1323
Society of Composers, Authors & Music Publishers of Canada, 1328
Special Olympics Ontario, 1340
SPI: The Plastics Industry Trade Association, 1596

Stockholm Environment Institute, 1597
Syndicat de professionnelles et professionnels du gouvernement du Québec, 1362
Syndicat des producteurs de bois du Saguenay-Lac-Saint-Jean, 1363
Teamsters Canada (CLC), 1368
Terre sans frontières, 1372
The Terry Fox Foundation, 1372
Tikinagan Child & Family Services, 1379
Toronto Arts Council, 1381
Toronto Community Care Access Centre, 1383
Toronto Community Foundation, 1383
Toronto International Film Festival Inc., 1385
Toronto Region Board of Trade, 1387
Toronto Symphony Orchestra, 1387
Tourism Toronto, 1391
Tourism Vancouver/Greater Vancouver Convention & Visitors Bureau, 1391
Transportation Association of Canada, 1395
Travel Manitoba, 1396
UNICEF Canada, 1404
Unison Health & Community Services, 1408
United Church of Canada, 1409
United Nations Conference on Trade & Development, 1599
United Nations Environment Programme, 1600
United Nations Industrial Development Organization, 1600
United Way of Calgary & Area, 1413
United Way Toronto & York Region, 1417
Universities Canada, 1418

USC Canada, 1423
Vancouver Art Gallery Association, 1424
Vancouver Opera, 1428
Vancouver Symphony Society, 1429
Variety - The Children's Charity (Ontario), 1429
VHA Home HealthCare, 1431
Victoria Cool Aid Society, 1432
WE Charity, 1443
Western Fair Association, 1449
Westgen, 1450
Whistler Resort Association, 1452
Winnipeg Symphony Orchestra Inc., 1459
Woodgreen Community Centre, 1463
Woodstock & District Developmental Services, 1464
Woodview Mental Health & Autism Services, 1464
World Agroforestry Centre, 1602
World Council of Credit Unions, Inc., 1604
World Federation of Hemophilia, 1466
World Meteorological Organization, 1606
World University Service of Canada, 1467
World Vision Canada, 1467
World Wildlife Fund - Canada, 1468
WWF International, 1608
Wycliffe Bible Translators of Canada, Inc., 1470
YMCA Canada, 1471
Yonge Street Mission, 1473

Conferences & Conventions

- Conferences and conventions of both Canadian and foreign associations scheduled to take place in 2018, 2019, and several beyond 2020
- Canadian and foreign associations listed here together by year and month
- Name of conference, date, place, host organization or sponsor, scope, contact information, and an overview are included when available
- Conferences and conventions for which only the year is known are listed at the end of the respective year, sorted by conference name
- Since plans can change and the list of conferences is not comprehensive, please check with associations of interest to you, which are listed in alphabetical order under Canadian Associations and Foreign Associations

2018

January

- **2018 Guelph Organic Conference & Trade Show**
Date: January 25-28, 2018
Location: Guelph, ON
Sponsor/Contact: Ecological Agriculture Projects
Macdonald Campus of McGill University
Sainte-Anne-de-Bellevue, QC H9X 3V9
514-398-7771; *Fax:* 514-398-7621
E-mail: ecological.agriculture@mcgill.ca
URL: eap.mcgill.ca
Scope: Local
Anticipated Attendance: 1800-2000
Contact Information:
www.guelphorganicconf.ca

- **2018 ROMA Annual Conference**
Date: January 21-23, 2018
Location: Sheraton Centre Hotel
Toronto, ON
Sponsor/Contact: Rural Ontario Municipal Association
#801, 200 University Ave.
Toronto, ON M5H 3C6
416-971-9856; *Fax:* 416-971-6191
Toll-Free: 877-426-6527
URL: www.roma.on.ca
Scope: Provincial

- **2018 Rowing Canada Aviron National Conference & Semi-Annual Meeting**
Date: January 25-27, 2018
Location: Chelsea Hotel
Toronto, ON
Sponsor/Contact: Rowing Canada Aviron
#321, 4371 Interurban Rd.
Victoria, BC V9E 2C5
877-722-4769; *Fax:* 250-220-2503
E-mail: rca@rowingcanada.org
URL: www.rowingcanada.org

- **2018 Western Canadian Association of Bovine Practitioners Conference**
Date: January 18-20, 2018
Location: Calgary, AB
Sponsor/Contact: Western Canadian Association of Bovine Practitioners
226E Wheeler St., 2nd Fl.
Saskatoon, SK S7P 0A9
Fax: 306-956-0607
Toll-Free: 866-269-8387
E-mail: info@wcabp.com
URL: www.wcabp.com
Scope: National

- **30th Annual Conference of the Saskatchewan Soil Conservation Association**
Date: January 8, 2018
Location: Western Development Museum
Saskatoon, SK
Sponsor/Contact: Saskatchewan Soil Conservation Association
P.O. Box 1360
Indian Head, SK S0G 2K0
306-695-4233; *Fax:* 306-695-4236
Toll-Free: 800-213-4287
E-mail: info@ssca.ca
URL: www.ssca.ca
Scope: Provincial
Purpose: Theme: "Soil Health In a New Climate"

- **ALIGN Association of Community Services 2018 Annual Conference**
Date: January 25-26, 2018
Location: Fantasyland Hotel, West Edmonton Mall
Edmonton, AB
Sponsor/Contact: ALIGN Association of Community Services
Bonnie Doon Mall
#255, 8330 - 82nd Ave.
Edmonton, AB T6C 4E3
780-428-3660; *Fax:* 780-428-3844
E-mail: info@alignab.ca
URL: www.alignab.ca
Scope: Provincial
Purpose: Theme: "Strengthening Today, Building Tomorrow"

- **American Society of Heating, Refrigerating and Air-Conditioning Engineers 2018 Winter Conference**
Date: January 20-24, 2018
Location: Palmer House Hilton
Chicago, IL
Sponsor/Contact: American Society of Heating, Refrigerating & Air Conditioning Engineers
1791 Tullie Circle NE
Atlanta, GA 30329
404-636-8400; *Fax:* 404-321-5478
Toll-Free: 800-527-4723
E-mail: ashrae@ashrae.org
URL: www.ashrae.org
Scope: International
Purpose: A global forum providing technology transfer, best practices, education and excellent networking opportunities for those who insist upon using the latest innovative solutions to enhance operations and maximize the efficiency and productivity of their buildings.
Contact Information:
www.ashrae.org/chicago

- **Association for Mineral Exploration British Columbia 2018 Mineral Exploration Roundup**
Date: January 22-25, 2018
Location: Vancouver Convention Centre
Vancouver, BC
Sponsor/Contact: Association for Mineral Exploration British Columbia
#800, 889 West Pender St.
Vancouver, BC V6C 3B2
604-689-5271; *Fax:* 604-681-2363
E-mail: info@amebc.ca
URL: www.amebc.ca
Scope: Provincial
Contact Information: Phone: 604-630-3930, Email: roundup@amebc.ca

- **Association of Canadian Publishers 2018 Mid-Winter Meeting**
Date: January 30-31, 2018
Sponsor/Contact: Association of Canadian Publishers
#306, 174 Spadina Ave.
Toronto, ON M5T 2C2
416-487-6116; *Fax:* 416-487-8815
E-mail: admin@canbook.org
URL: www.publishers.ca
Scope: National

- **BC Camps Conference & Trade Show 2018**
Date: January 28 - February 1, 2018
Location: Stillwood Camp and Conference Centre
Lindell Beach, BC
Sponsor/Contact: British Columbia Camping Association
E-mail: info@bccamping.org
URL: bccamping.org
Scope: Provincial

- **British Columbia Association of Mathematics Teachers 2018 New Teachers' Conference**
Date: January 27, 2018
Location: Surrey, BC
Sponsor/Contact: British Columbia Association of Mathematics Teachers
c/o British Columbia Teachers' Federation
#100, 550 West 6th Ave.
Vancouver, BC V5Z 4P2
604-871-2283
Toll-Free: 800-663-9163
URL: www.bcamt.ca
Scope: Provincial

- **CFA Society Calgary 41st Annual Forecast Dinner**
Date: January 18, 2018
Location: Calgary, AB
Sponsor/Contact: CFA Society Calgary
P.O. Box 118
#100, 111 - 5th Ave. SW
Calgary, AB T2P 3Y6
403-249-2009; *Fax:* 403-206-0650
E-mail: membership@cfacalgary.com
URL: www.cfacalgary.com
Scope: Local

- **CFA Society Winnipeg 53rd Annual Forecast Dinner**
Date: January 22, 2018
Location: RBC Convention Centre
Winnipeg, MB
Sponsor/Contact: CFA Society Winnipeg
P.O. Box 2684
Winnipeg, MB R3C 4B3
204-471-3640
E-mail: info@cfawinnipeg.ca
URL: www.cfasociety.org/winnipeg/
Scope: Local

- **Canadian Association for Pharmacy Distribution Management 2018 Executive Conference**
Date: January 15-16, 2018
Sponsor/Contact: Canadian Association for Pharmacy Distribution Management
#301A, 3800 Steeles Ave. West
Woodbridge, ON L4L 4G9
905-265-1706; *Fax:* 905-265-9372
URL: www.capdm.ca
Scope: National

- **Canadian Association of Numismatic Dealers 2018 Annual Convention**
Date: January 27-28, 2018
Location: Sheraton Hamilton Hotel
Hamilton, ON
Sponsor/Contact: Canadian Association of Numismatic Dealers
c/o Jo-Anne Simpson, Executive Secretary
P.O. Box 10272 Stn. Winona
Stoney Creek, ON L8E 5R1
905-643-4988; *Fax:* 905-643-6329
E-mail: email@cand.org
URL: www.cand.org
Scope: National
Contact Information: Tom Kennedy, E-mail: cand@cogeco.ca, Phone: 519-271-8825

- **Canadian Association of University Teachers Forum for Presidents 2018**
Date: January 19-20, 2018
Location: Ottawa, ON
Sponsor/Contact: Canadian Association of University Teachers
2705 Queensview Dr.
Ottawa, ON K2B 8K2
613-820-2270; *Fax:* 613-820-7244
E-mail: acppu@caut.ca
URL: www.caut.ca
Scope: National
Purpose: Information for academic staff association presidents

- **Canadian Dairy Commission Annual Public Meeting 2018**
Date: January 17, 2018
Location: Delta City Centre Hotel
Ottawa, ON
Sponsor/Contact: Canadian Dairy Commission
NCC Driveway, Bldg. 55
960 Carling Ave.
Ottawa, ON K1A 0Z2
613-792-2000; *Fax:* 613-792-2009
E-mail: carole.cyr@cdc-ccl.gc.ca
URL: www.cdc-ccl.gc.ca
Scope: National

- **Canadian Law & Society Association Annual Mid-Winter Meeting 2018**
Date: January 27, 2018
Sponsor/Contact: Canadian Law & Society Association
E-mail: info@acds-clsa.org
URL: www.acds-clsa.org
Scope: National

- **Canadian Media Producers Association's Prime Time in Ottawa 2018**
Date: January 31 - February 2, 2018
Location: Ottawa, ON

Conferences & Conventions Index

Sponsor/Contact: Canadian Media Production Association
601 Bank St., 2nd Fl.
Ottawa, ON K1S 3T4
613-233-1444; Fax: 613-233-0073
Toll-Free: 800-656-7440
E-mail: ottawa@cmpa.ca
URL: www.cmpa.ca
Scope: National
Contact Information:
www.primetimeinottawa.ca

- **Canadian Mineral Processors 50th Annual Conference 2018**
Date: January 23-25, 2018
Location: Westin Hotel
Ottawa, ON
Sponsor/Contact: Canadian Mineral Processors Society
555 Booth St.
Ottawa, ON K1A 0G1
URL: www.cmpsoc.ca
Scope: National
Purpose: Theme: "Past, Present & Future: Celebrating 50 Years of Innovation"

- **Canadian Museums Association 2018 Museum Enterprises Conference**
Date: January 25-27, 2018
Location: Toronto, ON
Sponsor/Contact: Canadian Museums Association
#400, 280 Metcalfe St.
Ottawa, ON K2P 1R7
613-567-0099; Fax: 613-233-5438
Toll-Free: 888-822-2907
E-mail: info@museums.ca
URL: www.museums.ca
Scope: National
Purpose: Keynote sessions, educational presentations, workshops, & networking opportunities for museum professionals involved in operations, admissions, retail, & food services

- **Canadian Nursing Students' Association 2018 National Conference**
Date: January 24-27, 2018
Location: Nanaimo, BC
Sponsor/Contact: Canadian Nursing Students' Association
#450, 1145 Hunt Club Rd.
Ottawa, ON K1V 0Y3
613-235-3150
E-mail: communications@cnsa.ca
URL: www.cnsa.ca
Scope: Provincial
Purpose: A conference to promote professional & personal development & discussion in the field of nursing

- **Canadian Quarter Horse Association 2018 Annual General Meeting**
Date: January 13, 2018
Location: Sheraton Conference Centre
Red Deer, AB
Sponsor/Contact: Canadian Quarter Horse Association
c/o Sherry Clemens, Secretary
P.O. Box 2132
Moose Jaw, SK S6H 7T2
306-692-8393
E-mail: admin@huntseahorses.com
URL: www.cqha.ca
Scope: National

- **Council of Outdoor Educators of Ontario Make Peace With Winter 2018**
Date: January 19-21, 2018
Location: Ontario

Sponsor/Contact: Council of Outdoor Educators of Ontario
c/o Sport Alliance Ontario
3 Concorde Gate
Toronto, ON M3C 3N7
E-mail: info@coeo.org
URL: www.coeo.org
Scope: National

- **Glass & Architectural Metals Association 2018 General Meeting**
Date: January 11, 2018
Sponsor/Contact: Glass & Architectural Metals Association
c/o Calgary Construction Association
2725 - 12 St. NE
Calgary, AB T2E 7J2
URL: www.pgaa.ca/gama
Scope: Provincial
Purpose: The yearly business meeting of the association

- **Human Resources Professionals Association 2018 Annual Conference & Trade Show**
Date: January 31 - February 2, 2018
Location: Metro Toronto Convention Centre
Toronto, ON
Sponsor/Contact: Human Resources Professionals Association
#200, 150 Bloor St. West
Toronto, ON M5S 2X9
416-923-2324; Fax: 416-923-7264
Toll-Free: 800-387-1311
E-mail: info@hrpa.ca
URL: www.hrpa.ca
Scope: Provincial

- **Keystone Agricultural Producers 2018 Annual Meeting**
Date: January 24-25, 2018
Location: Delta Hotel
Winnipeg, MB
Sponsor/Contact: Keystone Agricultural Producers
#203, 1700 Ellice Ave.
Winnipeg, MB R3H 0B1
204-697-1140; Fax: 204-697-1109
E-mail: kap@kap.mb.ca
URL: www.kap.mb.ca
Scope: National

- **Manitoba Bar Association 2018 Mid-Winter Conference**
Date: January 18-20, 2018
Location: Fairmont Hotel
Winnipeg, MB
Sponsor/Contact: Manitoba Bar Association
#1020, 444 St. Mary Ave.
Winnipeg, MB R3C 3T1
204-927-1210; Fax: 204-927-1212
E-mail: admin@cba-mb.ca
URL: cba-mb.ca
Scope: Provincial

- **Manitoba Dental Association's 2018 Annual Convention**
Date: January 26-27, 2018
Location: RBC Convention Centre
Winnipeg, MB
Sponsor/Contact: Manitoba Dental Association
#202, 1735 Corydon Ave.
Winnipeg, MB R3N 0K4
204-988-5300; Fax: 204-988-5310
E-mail: office@manitobadentist.ca
URL: www.manitobadentist.ca
Scope: Provincial
Purpose: A conference & trade show, with

business meetings, educational presentations, & networking opportunities, for dentists, dental hygienists, the oral health team, lab personnel, practice consultants, & dental students

- **Modern Language Association 2018 Convention**
Date: January 4-7, 2018
Location: New York, NY USA
Sponsor/Contact: Modern Language Association of America
26 Broadway, 3rd Fl.
New York, NY 10004-1789
646-576-5000; Fax: 646-458-0030
URL: www.mla.org
Scope: Provincial

- **Nova Scotia Fruit Growers' Association Annual Convention 2018**
Date: January 23-24, 2018
Location: Old Orchard Inn
Greenwich, NS
Sponsor/Contact: Nova Scotia Fruit Growers' Association
Kentville Agricultural Centre
32 Main St.
Kentville, NS B4N 1J5
902-678-1093; Fax: 902-678-1567
E-mail: contact@nsapples.com
URL: www.nsfga.com
Scope: Provincial

- **Ontario Golf Superintendents' Association 2018 Conference**
Date: January 16-18, 2018
Location: Fallsview Casino Resort Conference Centre
Niagara Falls, ON
Sponsor/Contact: Ontario Golf Superintendents' Association
328 Victoria Rd. South
Guelph, ON N1L 0H2
519-767-3341; Fax: 519-766-1704
Toll-Free: 877-824-6472
E-mail: admin@ogsa.ca
URL: www.ogsa.ca
Scope: National

- **Ontario Insurance Adjusters Association 2018 Claims Conference**
Date: January 30, 2018
Sponsor/Contact: Ontario Insurance Adjusters Association
29 De Jong Dr.
Mississauga, ON L5M 1B9
905-542-0576; Fax: 905-542-1301
Toll-Free: 888-259-1555
E-mail: manager@oiaa.com
URL: www.oiaa.com
Scope: Provincial

- **Ontario Library Association 2018 Super Conference**
Date: January 31 - February 3, 2018
Location: Metro Toronto Convention Centre
Toronto, ON
Sponsor/Contact: Ontario Library Association
2 Toronto St., 3rd Fl.
Toronto, ON M5C 2B6
416-363-3388; Fax: 416-941-9581
Toll-Free: 866-873-9867
E-mail: info@accessola.com
URL: www.accessola.org
Scope: Provincial
Purpose: An annual gathering of delegates, speakers, & exhibitors for a continuing education event in librarianship
Anticipated Attendance: 4,500+

Contact Information:
superconference@accessola.com

- **Ontario Public School Boards Association Public Education Symposium 2018**
Date: January 25-27, 2018
Location: Sheraton Centre Hotel
Toronto, ON
Sponsor/Contact: Ontario Public School Boards Association
#1850, 439 University Ave.
Toronto, ON M5G 1Y8
416-340-2540; Fax: 416-340-7571
E-mail: webmaster@opsba.org
URL: www.opsba.org
Scope: Provincial
Contact Information: Contact, Conference & Event Planning: Susan Weinberg, Phone: 416-340-2540, ext. 128

- **Professional Locksmiths Association of Alberta Annual General Meeting 2018**
Date: January 13, 2018
Location: Baymont Inn & Suites
Red Deer, AB
Sponsor/Contact: Professional Locksmith Association of Alberta
36 Sunridge Close
Airdrie, AB T4B 2G6
403-948-9997; Fax: 403-948-9997
Toll-Free: 877-765-7522
URL: www.plaa.org
Scope: Provincial

- **Public Health Association of British Columbia 2018 Early Years Conference**
Date: January 25-27, 2018
Location: Vancouver, BC
Sponsor/Contact: Public Health Association of British Columbia
#210, 1027 Pandora Ave.
Victoria, BC V8V 3P6
250-595-8422; Fax: 250-595-8622
E-mail: staff@phabc.org
URL: www.phabc.org
Scope: Provincial
Purpose: Theme: "Strengthening Resilience in Today's World: Leading with Kindness & Understanding"

- **Safety Services Manitoba Occupational Health & Safety Conference 2018**
Date: January 24-25, 2018
Location: Victoria Inn Hotel & Convention Centre
Winnipeg, MB
Sponsor/Contact: Safety Services Manitoba
#3, 1680 Notre Dame Ave.
Winnipeg, MB R3H 1H6
204-949-1085; Fax: 204-949-2897
Toll-Free: 800-661-3321
E-mail: registrar@safetyservicesmanitoba.ca
URL: www.safetyservicesmanitoba.ca
Scope: Provincial

- **Saskatchewan Beef Industry Conference 2018**
Date: January 24-25, 2018
Location: Saskatoon Inn
Saskatoon, SK
Sponsor/Contact: Saskatchewan Livestock Association
Canada Center Building, Evraz Place
P.O. Box 3771
Regina, SK S4P 3N8

306-757-6133; *Fax:* 306-525-5852
E-mail: sla@accesscomm.ca
URL: www.sasklivestock.com
Scope: Provincial
Purpose: An event organized by the Saskatchewan Livestock Association, Saskatchewan Cattlemen's Association, Saskatchewan Cattle Feeders Association, Saskatchewan Beef & Forage Symposium Committee, & the Saskatchewan Stock Growers Association
Contact Information: Shannon McArton, Conference Coordinator; Email: shannon.mcarton@sasktel.net; Phone: 306-731-7610, www.saskbeefconference.com

- **Society for Classical Studies 149th Annual Meeting**
Date: January 4-7, 2018
Location: Boston, MA USA
Sponsor/Contact: Society for Classical Studies
University of Pennsylvania
#201E, 220 South 40th St.
Philadelphia, PA 19104-3512
215-898-4975; *Fax:* 215-573-7874
E-mail: info@classicalstudies.org
URL: classicalstudies.org
Scope: International

- **The Maritimes Energy Association Annual General Meeting & Dinner 2018**
Date: January 17, 2018
Location: Westin Nova Scotian
Halifax, NS
Sponsor/Contact: The Maritimes Energy Association
Cambridge Tower 1
#420, 202 Brownlow Ave.
Dartmouth, NS B3B 1T5
902-425-4774; *Fax:* 902-422-2332
E-mail: communications@maritimesenergy.com
URL: www.maritimesenergy.com
Scope: Provincial
Purpose: A gathering of interest to decision makers in the offshore & onshore & renewable & non-renewable energy sectors to participate in roundtable discussions & networking events

- **Toronto Gift Fair Spring**
Date: January 28 - February 1, 2018
Location: The International Centre & Congress Centre
Toronto, ON
Sponsor/Contact: Canadian Gift Association
42 Voyager Ct. South
Toronto, ON M9W 5M7
416-679-0170; *Fax:* 416-679-0175
Toll-Free: 800-611-6100
E-mail: info@cangift.org
URL: www.cangift.org
Scope: Local
Purpose: The Toronto Gift Fair is Canada's largest temporary trade gift fair.
Anticipated Attendance: 24,600

- **Western Retail Lumber Association 2018 Buying Show**
Date: January 17-19, 2018
Location: Calgary, AB
Sponsor/Contact: Western Retail Lumber Association
Western Retail Lumber Association Inc.
#1004, 213 Notre Dame Ave.
Winnipeg, MB R3B 1N3
204-957-1077; *Fax:* 204-947-5195
Toll-Free: 800-661-0253
E-mail: wrla@wrla.org
URL: www.wrla.org
Scope: Provincial

- **World of Conrete**
Date: January 22-26, 2018
Location: Las Vegas, NV USA
Sponsor/Contact: Canadian Ready Mixed Concrete Association
#3, 365 Brunel Rd.
Mississauga, ON L4Z 1Z5
905-507-1122; *Fax:* 905-890-8122
E-mail: info@concretealberta.ca
URL: www.crmca.ca
Purpose: Annual event dedicated to conrete & masonry professionls
Anticipated Attendance: 55,000

February

- **2018 Canadian Golf Course Management Conference**
Date: February 26 - March 1, 2018
Location: Québec, QC
Sponsor/Contact: Ontario Golf Superintendents' Association
328 Victoria Rd. South
Guelph, ON N1L 0H2
519-767-3341; *Fax:* 519-766-1704
Toll-Free: 877-824-6472
E-mail: admin@ogsa.ca
URL: www.ogsa.ca
Scope: National

- **2018 Canadian Pediatric Endocrine Group Annual Scientific Meeting**
Date: February 22-24, 2018
Location: Sheraton Vancouver Wall Centre
Vancouver, BC
Sponsor/Contact: Canadian Pediatric Endocrine Group
c/o Robert Barnes, M.D., Montreal Children's Hospital
#316E, 2300, rue Tupper
Montréal, QC H3H 1P3
514-412-4315; *Fax:* 514-412-4264
URL: www.cpeg-gcep.net
Scope: National

- **2018 Canadian Rheumatology Association Annual Scientific Meeting**
Date: February 21-24, 2018
Location: Vancouver, BC
Sponsor/Contact: Canadian Rheumatology Association
#244, 12 - 16715 Yonge St.
Newmarket, ON L3X 1X4
905-952-0698; *Fax:* 905-952-0708
E-mail: info@rheum.ca
URL: rheum.ca
Scope: National

- **2018 Saskatoon & District Labour Council Annual General Meeting**
Date: February 9-10, 2018
Location: Heritage Inn
Saskatoon, SK
Sponsor/Contact: Saskatoon & District Labour Council
#110B, 2103 Airport Dr.
Saskatoon, SK S7L 6W2
306-384-0303
E-mail: sdlc@sasktel.net
URL: www.saskatoondlc.ca
Scope: Local

- **2018 Society for Research on Nicotine and Tobacco 24th Annual Meeting**
Date: February 21-24, 2018
Location: Hilton Baltimore
Baltimore, MD USA
Sponsor/Contact: Society for Research on Nicotine & Tobacco
2424 American Lane
Madison, WI 53704
608-443-2462; *Fax:* 608-443-2474
E-mail: info@srnt.org
URL: www.srnt.org
Scope: International

- **27th Annual Police Employment Conference**
Date: February 26-27, 2018
Location: Sheraton Parkway
Richmond Hill, ON
Sponsor/Contact: Police Association of Ontario
#302, 1650 Yonge St.
Toronto, ON M4T 2A2
E-mail: pao@pao.ca
URL: www.pao.ca
Scope: Provincial
Purpose: Labour relations

- **27th Annual Saskatchewan Home Based Educators Convention**
Date: February 23-24, 2018
Location: Queensbury Convention Center
Regina, SK
Sponsor/Contact: Saskatchewan Home Based Educators
P.O. Box 8541
Saskatoon, SK S7K 6K6
E-mail: help_desk@shbe.info
URL: www.shbe.info
Scope: Provincial

- **28th Annual Conference of the Centre for Comparative Literature**
Date: February 23-24, 2018
Location: University of Toronto
Toronto, ON
Sponsor/Contact: Centre for Comparative Literature
c/o Isabel Bader Theatre
93 Charles St. West, 3rd Fl.
Toronto, ON M5S 1K9
416-813-4041; *Fax:* 416-813-4040
URL: www.complit.utoronto.ca
Scope: National
Purpose: Theme: "The Ocean & the Seas"

- **AWWA/WEF The Utility Management Conference 2018**
Date: February 20-23, 2018
Location: San Antonio, TX USA
Sponsor/Contact: Water Environment Federation
601 Wythe St.
Alexandria, VA 22314-1994
703-684-2400
Toll-Free: 800-666-0206
E-mail: csc@wef.org
URL: www.wef.org
Scope: International

- **Alberta Chicken Producers 2018 Annual General Meeting**
Date: February 26, 2018
Location: Sheraton Red Deer
Red Deer, AB
Sponsor/Contact: Alberta Chicken Producers
2518 Ellwood Dr. SW
Edmonton, AB T6X 0A9
780-488-2125; *Fax:* 780-488-3570
Toll-Free: 877-822-4425
URL: www.chicken.ab.ca
Scope: Provincial
Purpose: An interactive educational event focussing upon biosecurity & emergency preparedness, plus a business meeting, & a keynote speaker

- **Alberta Gift Fair Spring**
Date: February 25-28, 2018
Location: Edmonton Expo Centre
Edmonton, AB
Sponsor/Contact: Canadian Gift Association
42 Voyager Ct. South
Toronto, ON M9W 5M7
416-679-0170; *Fax:* 416-679-0175
Toll-Free: 800-611-6100
E-mail: info@cangift.org
URL: www.cangift.org
Scope: Local
Purpose: The Alberta Gift Fair contains Western Canada's most comprehensive collection of products and services, catering to the specialized needs of retailers, sales representatives and manufacturers.
Anticipated Attendance: 16,000

- **Alberta Percheron Club 2018 AGM**
Date: February 3, 2018
Location: Westerner Park
Red Deer, AB
Sponsor/Contact: Alberta Percheron Club
c/o Julie Roy
RR#1
Markerville, AB T0M 1M0
403-728-3127
E-mail: sanlan@platinum.ca
URL: www.albertapercherons.com
Scope: Provincial
Contact Information: Lisa Evans, E-mail: albertapercheronclub@yahoo.ca, Phone: 403-809-4630

- **Alzheimer Society Manitoba: A Night in Tuscany Gala 2018**
Date: February 8, 2018
Location: RBC Convention Centre
Winnipeg, MB
Sponsor/Contact: Alzheimer Manitoba
#10, 120 Donald St.
Winnipeg, MB R3C 4G2
204-943-6622; *Fax:* 204-942-5408
Toll-Free: 800-378-6699
E-mail: alzmb@alzheimer.mb.ca
URL: www.alzheimer.mb.ca
Scope: Provincial

- **American Association for Justice 2018 Winter Convention**
Date: February 3-7, 2018
Location: Grand Wailea
Maui, HI USA
Sponsor/Contact: American Association for Justice
#200, 777 - 6th St. NW
Washington, DC 20001
202-965-3500
Toll-Free: 800-424-2725
E-mail: membership@justice.org
URL: www.justice.org
Scope: International

- **American Association for the Advancement of Science 2018 Annual Meeting**
Date: February 15-19, 2018
Location: Austin, TX USA
Sponsor/Contact: American Association for the Advancement of Science
1200 New York Ave. NW
Washington, DC 20005
202-326-6440
E-mail: membership@aaas.org
URL: www.aaas.org

Conferences & Conventions Index

Scope: International
Purpose: Information for scientists, engineers, educators, & policy-makers
Contact Information: Phone: 202-326-6450; *Fax:* 202-289-4021; *E-mail:* meetings@aaas.org; Director, Meetings: Andrew Black, E-mail: ablack@aaas.org

- **American Library Association 2018 Midwinter Meeting & Exhibits**
Date: February 9-13, 2018
Location: Denver, CO USA
Sponsor/Contact: American Library Association
50 East Huron St.
Chicago, IL 60611-2795
312-944-6780; *Fax:* 312-440-9374
Toll-Free: 800-545-2433
E-mail: ala@ala.org
URL: www.ala.org
Scope: International
Purpose: A library & information service meeting presenting speakers, discussion groups, exhibits, & committee meetings

- **Antique Automobile Club of America 82nd Annual Meeting 2018**
Date: February 8-10, 2018
Location: Philadelphia, PA USA
Sponsor/Contact: Antique Automobile Club of America
P.O. Box 417
501 West Governor Rd.
Hershey, PA 17033
717-534-1910; *Fax:* 717-534-9101
E-mail: aaca1@aaca.org
URL: www.aaca.org
Scope: International

- **Art Libraries Society of North America 46th Annual Conference 2018**
Date: February 25 - March 1, 2018
Location: New York Hilton Midtown
New York, NY USA
Sponsor/Contact: Art Libraries Society of North America
7044 South 13th St.
Oak Creek, WI 53154
414-908-4954
Toll-Free: 800-817-0621
URL: www.arlisna.org
Purpose: The conference provides the opportunity for professionals involved in art librarianship to meet, learn and share their knowledge of the field. It also allows them to explore exhibitions & interact with vendors involved with art libraries.

- **Association of Ontario Land Surveyors 2018 Annual General Meeting**
Date: February 28 - March 2, 2018
Location: Sheraton On The Falls Hotel
Niagara Falls, ON
Sponsor/Contact: Association of Ontario Land Surveyors
1043 McNicoll Ave.
Toronto, ON M1W 3W6
416-491-9020; *Fax:* 416-491-2576
Toll-Free: 800-268-0718
E-mail: info@aols.org
URL: www.aols.org
Scope: Provincial
Contact Information: Lena Kassabian; Email: lena@aols.org; Phone: 416-491-9020 ext. 25

- **Atlantic Concrete Association 2018 General Meeting**
Date: February 25 - March 4, 2018
Location: Play Del Carmen, Mexico

Sponsor/Contact: Atlantic Concrete Association
#301, 3845 Joseph Howe Dr.
Halifax, NS B3L 4H9
902-443-4456; *Fax:* 902-404-8074
E-mail: info@atlanticconcrete.ca
URL: www.atlanticconcrete.ca

- **BC Pension Leadership Forum 2018**
Date: February 21-22, 2018
Sponsor/Contact: British Columbia Federation of Labour
#200, 5118 Joyce St.
Vancouver, BC V5R 4H1
604-430-1421; *Fax:* 604-430-5917
E-mail: bcfed@bcfed.ca
URL: www.bcfed.com
Scope: Provincial
Purpose: Hosted by the British Columbia Federation of Labour & SHARE
Contact Information: E-mail: bcfed@bcfed.ca

- **Black Law Students Association of Canada 27th Annual National Conference**
Date: February 15-18, 2018
Location: Hotel Omni Mont-Royal
Montréal, QC
Sponsor/Contact: Black Law Students' Association of Canada
E-mail: Admin@blsacanada.com
URL: www.blsacanada.com
Scope: National
Purpose: Theme: "Advancing the Vision: Continuing in the Spirit of Excellence"
Contact Information: E-mail: conference@blsacanada.com

- **British Columbia Lung Association 15th Annual Air Quality & Health Workshop 2018**
Date: February 5, 2018
Location: Vancouver, BC
Sponsor/Contact: British Columbia Lung Association
2675 Oak St.
Vancouver, BC V6H 2K2
604-731-5864; *Fax:* 604-731-5810
Toll-Free: 800-665-5864
E-mail: info@bc.lung.ca
URL: www.bc.lung.ca
Scope: Provincial

- **British Columbia Recreation & Parks Association 2018 41st Annual ProvincialParks & Grounds Spring Training**
Date: February 28 - March 1, 2018
Location: Coast Hotel & Convention Centre
Langley, BC
Sponsor/Contact: British Columbia Recreation & Parks Association
#301, 470 Granville St.
Vancouver, BC V6C 1V5
604-629-0965; *Fax:* 604-629-2651
Toll-Free: 866-929-0965
E-mail: bcrpa@bcrpa.bc.ca
URL: www.bcrpa.bc.ca
Scope: Provincial
Purpose: Continuing education sessions that cover a wide range of interests for parks & grounds professionals

- **Calgary City Teachers Convention 2018**
Date: February 15-16, 2018
Location: Telus Convention Centre
Calgary, AB

Sponsor/Contact: Alberta Teachers' Association
Barnett House
11010 - 142 St. NW
Edmonton, AB T5N 2R1
780-447-9400; *Fax:* 780-455-6481
Toll-Free: 800-232-7208
E-mail: postmaster@ata.ab.ca
URL: www.teachers.ab.ca
Scope: Provincial
Contact Information: Executive Staff Officer, Dan Grassick, E-mail: dan.grassick@ata.ab.ca, Phone: 780-447-9487

- **Canadian Association of Agri-Retailers Conference 2018**
Date: February 13-15, 2018
Location: Saskatoon, SK
Sponsor/Contact: Canadian Association of Agri-Retailers
#628, 70 Arthur St.
Winnipeg, MB R3B 1G7
204-989-9300; *Fax:* 204-989-9306
Toll-Free: 800-463-9323
E-mail: info@caar.org
URL: www.caar.org
Scope: National
Purpose: A conference & exhibition featuring the annual general meeting, educational workshops, guest speaker sessions, the presentation of awards, & networking events

- **Canadian Association of Hepatology Nurses 2018 Annual General Meeting**
Date: February 11, 2018
Location: InterContinental Hotel
Toronto, ON
Sponsor/Contact: Canadian Association of Hepatology Nurses
c/o Lori Lee Walston
506 Fader St.
New Westminster, BC V3L 3T5
URL: www.cahn.ca
Scope: National

- **Canadian Aviation Regulation Advisory Council (CARAC) 17th Plenary Meeting**
Date: February 22, 2018
Sponsor/Contact: Canadian Federation of Aircraft Maintenance Engineers Associations
c/o AME Association of Ontario
P.O. Box 160 Stn. Toronto AMF
Mississauga, ON L5P 1B1
905-673-5681; *Fax:* 905-673-6328
URL: www.cfamea.com
Scope: National

- **Canadian Bar Association Annual General Meeting 2018**
Date: February 15, 2018
Location: Delta Hotels Ottawa City Centre
Ottawa, ON
Sponsor/Contact: Canadian Bar Association
#500, 865 Carling Ave.
Ottawa, ON K1S 5S8
613-237-2925; *Fax:* 613-237-0185
Toll-Free: 800-267-8860
E-mail: info@cba.org
URL: www.cba.org
Scope: National

- **Canadian Council for Refugees Winter Working Group Meetings 2018**
Date: February 23-24, 2018
Location: Toronto, ON

Sponsor/Contact: Canadian Council for Refugees
#302, 6839, rue Drolet
Montréal, QC H2S 2T1
514-277-7223; *Fax:* 514-277-1447
E-mail: info@ccrweb.ca
URL: www.ccrweb.ca
Scope: National
Purpose: Meetings of the Overseas Protection & Sponsorship Working Group, the Immigration & Settlement Working Group, & the Inland Protection Working Group, for all Canadian Council for Refugees members, plus anyone who is interested in participating

- **Canadian Critical Care Conference 2018**
Date: February 5-8, 2018
Location: Four Seasons Resort
Whistler, BC
Sponsor/Contact: Canadian Critical Care Society
#6, 20 Crown Steel Dr.
Toronto, ON L3R 9X9
905-415-3917; *Fax:* 905-415-0071
Toll-Free: 855-415-3917
E-mail: cccs@secretariatcentral.com
URL: www.canadiancriticalcare.org
Scope: National
Contact Information: www.canadiancriticalcare.ca

- **Canadian Digestive Diseases Week: Canadian Association of Gastroenterology Annual Scientific Conference 2018**
Date: February 4-14, 2018
Location: Toronto, ON
Sponsor/Contact: Canadian Association of Gastroenterology
#224, 1540 Cornwall Rd.
Oakville, ON L6J 7W5
905-829-2504; *Fax:* 905-829-0242
Toll-Free: 888-780-0007
E-mail: general@cag-acg.org
URL: www.cag-acg.org
Scope: National

- **Canadian Health Food Association (CHFA) West 2018**
Date: February 22-25, 2018
Location: Vancouver Convention Centre, West Building
Vancouver, BC
Sponsor/Contact: Canadian Health Food Association
#302, 235 Yorkland Blvd.
Toronto, ON M2J 4Y8
416-497-6939; *Fax:* 416-497-3214
Toll-Free: 800-661-4510
E-mail: info@chfa.ca
URL: www.chfa.ca
Scope: Provincial
Purpose: A conference & trade show attended by owners, managers, employees, & nutrition & health care practitioners from pharmacies, health stores, grocery stores, specialty stores, & online retailers
Contact Information: Phone: 416-497-6939, Toll-Free Phone: 1-800-661-4510, E-mail: info@chfa.ca

- **Canadian Liver Meeting 2018**
Date: February 9-11, 2018
Location: Intercontinental Toronto Hotel Center
Toronto, ON
Sponsor/Contact: Canadian Association for the Study of the Liver

c/o BUKSA Strategic Conference Services
#307, 10328 - 81st Ave.
Edmonton, AB T6C 3T5
780-436-0983
E-mail: casl@hepatology.ca
URL: www.hepatology.ca
Scope: National
Purpose: Meeting of the Canadian Association for the Study of the Liver (CASL), the Canadian Network on Hepatitis C (CANHEPC), & the Canadian Association of Hepatology Nurses (CAHN)

- **Canadian Marketing Association CMAideas**
Date: February 27, 2018
Sponsor/Contact: Canadian Marketing Association
#603, 55 University Ave.
Toronto, ON M5J 2H7
416-391-2362; Fax: 416-441-4062
Toll-Free: 800-267-8805
E-mail: info@thecma.ca
URL: www.the-cma.org
Scope: National
Purpose: Brings together a unique conference of creators, innovators and leaders with insights from unlikely places and undiscovered territories.

- **Canadian Marketing Association CMAinsights**
Date: February 13, 2018
Sponsor/Contact: Canadian Marketing Association
#603, 55 University Ave.
Toronto, ON M5J 2H7
416-391-2362; Fax: 416-441-4062
Toll-Free: 800-267-8805
E-mail: info@thecma.ca
URL: www.the-cma.org
Scope: National
Purpose: CMAinsights will feature multiple content streams; focusing on both the marketer and the data practitioner.

- **Canadian Society of Hospital Pharmacists 49th Professional Practice Conference 2018**
Date: February 3-7, 2018
Location: Beanfield Centre
Toronto, ON
Sponsor/Contact: Canadian Society of Hospital Pharmacists
#3, 30 Concourse Gate
Ottawa, ON K2E 7V7
613-736-9733; Fax: 613-736-5660
E-mail: info@cshp.ca
URL: www.cshp.ca
Scope: National
Purpose: Informative sessions to educate & motivate participants

- **Cargo Logistics Canada Expo & Conference 2018**
Date: February 6-8, 2018
Location: Vancouver Convention Centre
Vancouver, BC
Sponsor/Contact: Freight Management Association of Canada
#405, 580 Terry Fox Dr.
Ottawa, ON K2L 4B9
613-599-3283; Fax: 613-599-1295
E-mail: info@fma-agf.ca
URL: www.fma-agf.ca
Scope: National
Contact Information: cargologisticscanada.com

- **Central Alberta Teachers Convention 2018**
Date: February 22-23, 2018
Location: Red Deer College
Red Deer, AB
Sponsor/Contact: Alberta Teachers' Association
Barnett House
11010 - 142 St. NW
Edmonton, AB T5N 2R1
780-447-9400; Fax: 780-455-6481
Toll-Free: 800-232-7208
E-mail: postmaster@ata.ab.ca
URL: www.teachers.ab.ca
Scope: Provincial
Contact Information: Executive Staff Officer: Dan Grassick, E-mail: dan.grassick@ata.ab.ca, Phone: 780-447-9487

- **Club des ornithologues de Québec 2018 Assemblée générale annuelle**
Date: February 23, 2018
Sponsor/Contact: Club des ornithologues de Québec inc.
Domaine de Maizerets
2000, boul Montmorency
Québec, QC G1J 5E7
418-661-3544
E-mail: coq@coq.qc.ca
URL: www.coq.qc.ca
Scope: Provincial

- **Construction Safety Association of Manitoba - The Safety Conference 2018**
Date: February 6-7, 2018
Location: RBC Convention Centre
Winnipeg, MB
Sponsor/Contact: Construction Safety Association of Manitoba
1447 Waverly St.
Winnipeg, MB R3T 0P7
204-775-3171; Fax: 204-779-3505
E-mail: safety@constructionsafety.ca
URL: www.constructionsafety.ca
Scope: Provincial
Purpose: A safety & health conference for construction owners, supervisors, foremen, safety committees, workers, & students, featuring workshops & a trade show with more than 100 exhibitors

- **Economic Developers Council of Ontario 61st Annual Conference & Showcase 2018**
Date: February 5-7, 2018
Location: Sheraton Centre Toronto Hotel
Toronto, ON
Sponsor/Contact: Economic Developers Council of Ontario Inc.
6506 Marlene Ave.
Cornwall, ON K6H 7H9
613-931-9827; Fax: 613-931-9828
E-mail: edco@edco.on.ca
URL: www.edco.on.ca
Scope: Provincial
Purpose: Theme: "Mission Possible: Agents of Change"
Contact Information: www.edcoconference.com

- **Elementary Teachers' Federation of Ontario 2018...And Still We Rise**
Date: February 21-23, 2018
Location: Fairmont Royal York Hotel
Toronto, ON
Sponsor/Contact: Elementary Teachers' Federation of Ontario
136 Isabella St.
Toronto, ON M4Y 1P6
416-962-3836; Fax: 416-642-2424
Toll-Free: 888-838-3836
URL: www.etfo.ca
Scope: Provincial
Purpose: Annual women's leadership conference
Contact Information: Conference Contact: Kelly Hayes, E-mail: khayes@etfo.org

- **Engineers Yukon 2018 Annual General Meeting**
Date: February 15, 2018
Sponsor/Contact: Association of Professional Engineers of Yukon
312B Hanson St.
Whitehorse, YT Y1A 1Y6
867-667-6727; Fax: 867-668-2142
E-mail: staff@apey.yk.ca
URL: www.apey.yk.ca

- **Fenestration Association of BC Technical Conference 2018**
Date: February 28, 2018
Location: Surrey, BC
Sponsor/Contact: Fenestration Association of BC
#101, 20351 Duncan Way
Langley, BC V3A 7N3
778-571-0245; Fax: 866-253-9979
E-mail: info@fen-bc.org
URL: www.fen-bc.org
Scope: Provincial

- **Festivals & Events Ontario 2018 Conference**
Date: February 28 - March 2, 2018
Location: Hamilton Convention Centre
Hamilton, ON
Sponsor/Contact: Festivals & Events Ontario
#301, 5 Graham St.
Woodstock, ON N4S 6J5
519-537-2226; Fax: 519-537-2226
E-mail: info@festivalsandeventsontario.ca
URL: www.festivalsandeventsontario.ca
Scope: Provincial
Contact Information: www.feo2018.com

- **GlobalChem Conference & Exhibition 2018**
Date: February 28 - March 2, 2018
Location: Washington, DC USA
Sponsor/Contact: American Chemistry Council
700 Second St. NE
Washington, DC 20002
202-249-7000; Fax: 202-249-6100
URL: www.americanchemistry.com
Scope: International

- **Hotel Association of Canada 2018 Annual National Conference**
Date: February 7-8, 2018
Location: Toronto, ON
Sponsor/Contact: Hotel Association of Canada Inc.
#1206, 130 Albert St.
Ottawa, ON K1P 5G4
613-237-7149; Fax: 613-237-8928
E-mail: info@hotelassociation.ca
URL: www.hotelassociation.ca
Scope: National
Contact Information: Executive Assistant: Linda Crouch, E-mail: crouch@hotelassociation.ca; Phone: 613-237-7149, ext. 101

- **Institute of Public Administration of Canada National Leadership Conference & Awards Gala 2018**
Date: February 5-6, 2018
Location: Chelsea Hotel
Toronto, ON
Sponsor/Contact: Institute of Public Administration of Canada
#401, 1075 Bay St.
Toronto, ON M5S 2B1
416-924-8787; Fax: 416-924-4992
URL: www.ipac.ca
Scope: National
Purpose: Conference for IPAC members featuring leadership seminars & professional development opportunities; theme is "Facing New Frontiers: Leadership Without Borders"
Contact Information: URL: leadership.ipac.ca

- **Languages Canada 2018 Conference**
Date: February 19-22, 2018
Location: Toronto Marriott Downtown Eaton Centre Hotel
Toronto, ON
Sponsor/Contact: Languages Canada
c/o Member Services
27282 - 12B Ave.
Aldergrove, BC V4W 2P6
604-574-1532; Fax: 888-277-0522
E-mail: info@languagescanada.ca
URL: www.languagescanada.ca
Scope: National
Anticipated Attendance: 200+
Contact Information: conference@languagescanada.ca

- **Manitoba Water & Wastewater Association Annual Conference & Trade Show 2018**
Date: February 25-28, 2018
Location: Keystone Centre
Brandon, MB
Sponsor/Contact: Manitoba Water & Wastewater Association
P.O. Box 1600
#215, 9 Saskatchewan Ave. West
Portage la Prairie, MB R1N 3P1
204-239-6868; Fax: 204-239-6872
Toll-Free: 866-396-2549
E-mail: mwwaoffice@shaw.ca
URL: www.mwwa.net
Scope: Provincial
Purpose: The presentation of technical papers plus the opportunity to view industry products & services
Contact Information: Executive Director: Iva Last, Phone: 204-239-6868, Toll-Free Phone: 1-866-396-2549, Fax: 204-239-6872, E-mail: mwwaoffice@shaw.ca

- **METROSHOW Vancouver Fall 2018**
Date: February 3-7, 2018
Location: Vancouver, BC
Sponsor/Contact: METROSHOW Vancouver
#103, 1951 Glen Dr.
Vancouver, BC V6A 4J6
604-929-8995; Fax: 604-357-1995
E-mail: info@metroshow.ca
URL: www.metroshow.ca
Scope: Provincial
Purpose: A one-of-a-kind fashion industry buying show held at various venues around Vancouver; contains 130+ apparel, footwear & giftware agencies selling in showrooms

- **National Association for Surface Finishing (NASF) Leadership Conference 2018**
Date: February 25 - March 1, 2018
Location: Koloa, HI USA
Sponsor/Contact: National Association for Surface Finishing
#500, 1155 - 15th St. NW
Washington, DC 20005

Conferences & Conventions Index

202-457-8404; *Fax:* 202-530-0659
E-mail: info@nasfmembership.com
URL: www.nasf.org
Scope: International

- **North American Farmers' Direct Marketing Association 2018 Farmers Inspired Convention**
Date: February 1-7, 2018
Sponsor/Contact: North American Farmers' Direct Marketing Association, Inc.
62 White Loaf Rd.
Southampton, MA 01073
413-244-5374
URL: www.farmersinspired.com
Scope: International

- **North Central Teachers Convention 2018**
Date: February 8-9, 2018
Location: Edmonton, AB
Sponsor/Contact: Alberta Teachers' Association
Barnett House
11010 - 142 St. NW
Edmonton, AB T5N 2R1
780-447-9400; *Fax:* 780-455-6481
Toll-Free: 800-232-7208
E-mail: postmaster@ata.ab.ca
URL: www.teachers.ab.ca
Scope: Provincial
Contact Information: Executive Staff Officer: Dan Grassick, E-mail: dan.grassick@ata.ab.ca, Phone: 780-447-9487

- **North East Teachers Convention 2018**
Date: February 15-16, 2018
Location: Doubletree by Hilton Hotel Edmonton, AB
Sponsor/Contact: Alberta Teachers' Association
Barnett House
11010 - 142 St. NW
Edmonton, AB T5N 2R1
780-447-9400; *Fax:* 780-455-6481
Toll-Free: 800-232-7208
E-mail: postmaster@ata.ab.ca
URL: www.teachers.ab.ca
Scope: Provincial
Contact Information: Executive Staff Officer: Dan Grassick, E-mail: dan.grassick@ata.ab.ca, Phone: 780-447-9487

- **Ontario Conference of Mennonite Brethren Churches 87th Annual Convention 2018**
Date: February 23-24, 2018
Location: Behta Darya Community Church Mississauga, ON
Sponsor/Contact: Ontario Conference of Mennonite Brethren Churches
3970 Glendale Ave.
Vineland, ON L0R 2C0
905-562-7391
E-mail: info@onmb.org
URL: www.onmb.org
Scope: Provincial

- **Ontario Fruit & Vegetable Convention 2018**
Date: February 21-22, 2018
Sponsor/Contact: Ontario Fruit & Vegetable Growers' Association
#105, 355 Elmira Rd. North
Guelph, ON N1K 1S5
519-763-6160; *Fax:* 519-763-6604
E-mail: info@ofvga.org
URL: www.ofvga.org
Scope: Provincial
Purpose: An annual gathering of horticultural crop enthusiasts involved in producing fruits and vegetables.
Contact Information: www.ofvc.ca

- **Ontario Geothermal Association 2018 Conference**
Date: February 27-28, 2018
Location: Westin Toronto Airport Toronto, ON
Sponsor/Contact: Ontario Geothermal Association
905-602-4700
Toll-Free: 800-267-2231
URL: www.ontariogeothermal.ca
Scope: Provincial
Purpose: Theme: "From the Ground Up"

- **Ontario Good Roads Association 2018 Conference**
Date: February 25-28, 2018
Location: Fairmont Royal York Toronto, ON
Sponsor/Contact: Ontario Good Roads Association
#22, 1525 Cornwall Rd.
Oakville, ON L6J 0B2
289-291-6472; *Fax:* 289-291-6477
E-mail: info@ogra.org
URL: www.ogra.org
Scope: Provincial
Purpose: Workshops, information about current municipal issues, a trade show, & social events
Anticipated Attendance: 2,200
Contact Information: www.ograconference.ca

- **Ontario Soil & Crop Improvement Association 2018 AGM**
Date: February 2018
Location: Ontario
Sponsor/Contact: Ontario Soil & Crop Improvement Association
1 Stone Rd. West
Guelph, ON N1G 4Y2
519-826-4214; *Fax:* 519-826-4224
Toll-Free: 800-265-9751
E-mail: oscia@ontariosoilcrop.org
URL: www.ontariosoilcrop.org
Scope: Provincial
Purpose: An opportunity for farmers & persons involved in agriculture in Ontario to bring local views to give direction to the association

- **Ontario Trial Lawyers Association 2018 Medical Malpractice Conference**
Date: February 15-16, 2018
Sponsor/Contact: Ontario Trial Lawyers Association
1190 Blair Rd.
Burlington, ON L7M 1K9
905-639-6852; *Fax:* 905-639-3100
URL: www.otla.com
Scope: Provincial
Purpose: Theme: "New Frontiers in Technology"

- **Ontario University Registrars' Association 2018 Conference**
Date: February 14-16, 2018
Location: Marriott Eaton Centre Hotel Toronto, ON
Sponsor/Contact: Ontario University Registrars' Association
900 McGill Rd.
Kamloops, BC V2C 0C8
250-828-5019
URL: www.oura.ca
Scope: Provincial
Purpose: Theme: "Collaborating in Changing Times"

- **Price Edward Island Road Builders & Heavy Construction Association 2018 56th Annual General Meeting**
Date: February 1-2, 2018
Location: Prince Edward Island
Sponsor/Contact: Prince Edward Island Road Builders & Heavy Construction Association
P.O. Box 1901
#223, 40 Enman Cres.
Charlottetown, PE C1A 7N5
902-894-9514; *Fax:* 902-894-9512
E-mail: info@peirb.ca
URL: www.peirb.ca
Scope: Provincial

- **Promotional Product Professionals of Canada 2018 National Convention**
Date: February 9-13, 2018
Location: The International Centre Mississauga, ON
Sponsor/Contact: Promotional Product Professionals of Canada Inc.
#202, 455, boul Fénelon
Montréal, QC H9S 5T8
514-489-5359; *Fax:* 800-489-8741
Toll-Free: 866-450-7722
E-mail: info@promocan.com
URL: www.promocan.com
Scope: National
Purpose: Educational seminars, business meetings, roundtable discussions, networking events, plus a trade show with over 600 exhibitors

- **Restaurants Canada Show 2018**
Date: February 25-27, 2018
Location: Enercare Centre Toronto, ON
Sponsor/Contact: Restaurants Canada
1155 Queen St. West
Toronto, ON M6J 1J4
416-923-8416; *Fax:* 416-923-1450
Toll-Free: 800-387-5649
E-mail: info@restaurantscanada.org
URL: www.restaurantscanada.org
Scope: National
Purpose: An event featuring culinary demonstrations, seminars, workshops, presentations, more than 700 exhibitors, & numerous networking opportunities for members of Canada's foodservice sector
Anticipated Attendance: 13,000+

- **Sail Nova Scotia Annual General Meeting 2018**
Date: February 10, 2018
Location: Halifax, NS
Sponsor/Contact: Sail Nova Scotia
5516 Spring Garden Rd., 4th Fl.
Halifax, NS B3J 1G6
902-425-5450
E-mail: office@sailnovascotia.ca
URL: www.sailnovascotia.ca
Scope: Provincial

- **Saskatchewan Urban Municipalities Association 113th Annual Convention and Tradeshow 2018**
Date: February 4-7, 2018
Location: Regina, SK
Sponsor/Contact: Saskatchewan Urban Municipalities Association
#200, 2222 - 13th Ave.
Regina, SK S4P 3M7
306-525-3727; *Fax:* 306-525-4373
E-mail: suma@suma.org
URL: www.suma.org
Scope: Provincial

- **Saskatchewan Wildlife Federation 89th Annual Convention 2018**
Date: February 8-10, 2018
Location: Prince Albert, SK
Sponsor/Contact: Saskatchewan Wildlife Federation
9 Lancaster Rd.
Moose Jaw, SK S6J 1M8
306-692-8812; *Fax:* 306-692-4370
Toll-Free: 877-793-9453
E-mail: sask.wildlife@sasktel.net
URL: www.swf.sk.ca
Scope: Provincial
Purpose: A yearly gathering of members, featuring the presentation of awards

- **Society of Cardiovascular Anesthesiologists 21st Annual Echo Week**
Date: February 25 - March 2, 2018
Location: Loews Atlanta Hotel Atlanta, GA USA
Sponsor/Contact: Society of Cardiovascular Anesthesiologists
#300, 8735 West Higgins Rd.
Chicago, IL 60631
Fax: 847-375-6323
Toll-Free: 855-658-2828
E-mail: info@scahq.org
URL: www.scahq.org
Scope: International

- **Society of Plastics Engineers 2018 International Polyolefins Conference**
Date: February 25-28, 2018
Location: Hilton Houston North Hotel Houston, TX USA
Sponsor/Contact: Society of Plastics Engineers
#306, 6 Berkshire Blvd.
Bethel, CT 06801
203-775-0471; *Fax:* 203-775-8490
URL: www.4spe.org
Scope: International
Anticipated Attendance: 600+
Contact Information: Chair, Texas Conference: Robert Portnoy, Phone: 713-529-2272

- **Society of Plastics Engineers Thermoset 2018**
Date: February 20-21, 2018
Location: Indianapolis, IN USA
Sponsor/Contact: Society of Plastics Engineers
#306, 6 Berkshire Blvd.
Bethel, CT 06801
203-775-0471; *Fax:* 203-775-8490
URL: www.4spe.org
Scope: International

- **Teachers of Inclusive Education - British Columbia 2018 Crosscurrents Conference**
Date: February 22-23, 2018
Location: Sheraton Vancouver Airport Hotel
Richmond, BC
Sponsor/Contact: Teachers of Inclusive Education - British Columbia
w/o British Columbia Teachers' Federation
#100, 550 West 6th Ave.
Vancouver, BC V5Z 4P2
E-mail: tiebcwebmanager@gmail.com
URL: www.tiebc.com

Scope: Provincial
Purpose: Sessions for regular & special education teachers, as well as administrators, teacher assistants, & parents

- **Thunder Bay Chamber of Commerce Annual General Meeting & Chair's Reception 2018**
Date: February 8, 2018
Location: Thunder Bay, ON
Sponsor/Contact: Thunder Bay Chamber of Commerce
#102, 200 Syndicate Ave. South
Thunder Bay, ON P7E 1C9
807-624-2626; *Fax:* 807-622-7752
E-mail: chamber@tbchamber.ca
URL: www.tbchamber.ca
Scope: Local

- **Titanium Asia 2018**
Date: February 4-6, 2018
Location: Grand Hyatt Singapore
Singapore
Sponsor/Contact: International Titanium Association
#100, 11674 Huron St.
Northglenn, CO 80234
303-404-2221; *Fax:* 303-404-9111
E-mail: ita@titanium.org
URL: www.titanium.org
Scope: International

- **Trauma 2018**
Date: February 22-23, 2018
Location: Hilton Toronto
Toronto, ON
Sponsor/Contact: Trauma Association of Canada
P.O. Box 8862
Halifax, NS B3K 5M5
Fax: 902-850-2289
Toll-Free: 855-403-5463
E-mail: info@traumacanada.org
URL: www.traumacanada.org
Scope: National

- **World Aquaculture Society Aquaculture America Conference 2018**
Date: February 19-22, 2018
Location: Paris Hotel
Las Vegas, NV USA
Sponsor/Contact: World Aquaculture Society
143 J.M. Parker Coliseum, LSU
Baton Rouge, LA 70803-0001
225-578-3137; *Fax:* 225-578-3493
URL: www.was.org
Scope: International
Contact Information: Conference Manager, Phone: 760-751-5005

March

- **2018 SP Conference & Annual General Meeting**
Date: March 26-29, 2018
Location: Ottawa, ON
Sponsor/Contact: Canadian Association of Wireless Internet Service Providers
#300, 162 Metcalfe St.
Ottawa, ON K2P 1P2
Toll-Free: 844-370-0404
E-mail: info@canwisp.ca
URL: www.canwisp.ca

- **20th National Metropolis Conference**
Date: March 22-24, 2018
Location: Westin Calgary
Calgary, AB
Sponsor/Contact: Association for Canadian Studies
1822A, rue Sherbooke ouest
Montréal, QC H3H 1E4
514-925-3097; *Fax:* 514-925-3095
E-mail: general@acs-aec.ca
URL: acs-aec.ca
Scope: National
Purpose: Theme: "Immigration Futures: Marking 20 Years of the National Metropolis Conference"

- **52nd Annual General Meeting & 25th Annual Convention**
Date: March 23-24, 2018
Location: Delta Grand Okanagan
Kelowna, BC
Sponsor/Contact: Guide Outfitters Association of British Columbia
#103, 19140 - 28th Ave.
Surrey, BC V3S 6M3
604-541-6332; *Fax:* 604-541-6339
E-mail: info@goabc.org
URL: www.goabc.org

- **AFCOM Data Center World Global Conference 2018**
Date: March 12-15, 2018
Location: San Antonio, TX USA
Sponsor/Contact: AFCOM
910 West Chester Towne Centre Rd.
West Chester, OH 45069
714-997-9743; *Fax:* 714-997-9743
E-mail: membership@AFCOM.com
URL: www.afcom.com
Scope: International
Contact Information: URL: global.datacenterworld.com

- **Aboriginal Youth 2018 16th Annual Gathering Our Voices Conference**
Date: March 2018
Location: Richmond, BC
Sponsor/Contact: British Columbia Association of Aboriginal Friendship Centres
551 Chatham St.
Victoria, BC V8T 1E1
250-388-5522; *Fax:* 250-388-5502
Toll-Free: 800-990-2432
E-mail: frontdesk@bcaafc.com
URL: www.bcaafc.com
Scope: Provincial
Purpose: Hosted by the British Columbia Association of Aboriginal Friendship Centres & their Provincial Aboriginal Youth Council
Contact Information: Manager, Events: Nadine Collison, E-mail: ncollison@bcaafc.com, Phone: 250-388-5522, ext. 210

- **Alberta Association of Municipal Districts & Counties Spring 2018 Convention**
Date: March 19-21, 2018
Location: Shaw Conference Centre
Edmonton, AB
Sponsor/Contact: Alberta Association of Municipal Districts & Counties
2510 Sparrow Dr.
Nisku, AB T9E 8N5
780-955-3639; *Fax:* 780-955-3615
Toll-Free: 855-548-7233
E-mail: aamdc@aamdc.com
URL: www.aamdc.com

- **Alberta Camping Association Annual Conference 2018**
Date: March 19-21, 2018
Location: Camp Kindle
Water Valley, AB
Sponsor/Contact: Alberta Camping Association
Percy Page Centre
11759 Groat Rd.
Edmonton, AB T5M 3K6
403-477-5443
E-mail: info@albertacamping.com
URL: www.albertacamping.com
Scope: Provincial

- **Alberta Magazines Conference 2018**
Date: March 8-9, 2018
Location: Calgary, AB
Sponsor/Contact: Alberta Magazine Publishers Association
#304, 1240 Kensington Rd. NW
Calgary, AB T2N 3P7
403-262-0081; *Fax:* 403-670-0492
E-mail: ampa@albertamagazines.com
URL: www.albertamagazines.com
Scope: Provincial

- **Alberta Pharmacists' Association 2018 Spring Professional Development Conference**
Date: March 2-3, 2018
Location: DoubleTree by Hilton Hotel West Edmonton
Edmonton, AB
Sponsor/Contact: Alberta Pharmacists' Association (RxA)
Canadian Western Bank Building
#1725, 10303 Jasper Ave.
Edmonton, AB T5J 3N6
780-990-0326; *Fax:* 780-990-1236
E-mail: rxa@rxa.ca
URL: www.rxa.ca
Scope: Provincial

- **Alberta Psychiatric Association Scientific Conference and AGM 2018**
Date: March 22-25, 2018
Location: Rimrock Resort Hotel
Banff, AB
Sponsor/Contact: Alberta Psychiatric Association
#400, 1040 - 7 Ave. SW
Calgary, AB T2P 3G9
403-244-4487; *Fax:* 403-244-2340
E-mail: info@albertapsych.org
URL: www.albertapsych.org
Scope: Provincial
Anticipated Attendance: 300+

- **Alberta Recreation & Parks Association 2018 Youth Development Through Recreation Services Symposium**
Date: March 7-8, 2018
Location: Radisson Hotel
Red Deer, AB
Sponsor/Contact: Alberta Recreation & Parks Association
11759 Groat Rd.
Edmonton, AB T5M 3K6
780-415-1745; *Fax:* 780-451-7915
Toll-Free: 877-544-1747
E-mail: arpa@arpaonline.ca
URL: arpaonline.ca
Scope: Provincial
Contact Information: Coordinator, Administration: Lori Simmonds, E-mail: lsimmonds@arpaonline.ca, Phone: 780-415-1745

- **Alberta Society of Professional Biologists 2018 Conference**
Date: March 13-14, 2018
Location: Calgary Zoo
Calgary, AB
Sponsor/Contact: Alberta Society of Professional Biologists
#370, 105 - 12 Ave. East
Calgary, AB T2G 1A1
403-264-1273
E-mail: pbiol@aspb.ab.ca
URL: www.aspb.ab.ca
Scope: Provincial
Purpose: Theme: "Keeping Pace with a Changing Landscape: Technology, Regulations & Policy Navigation"
Anticipated Attendance: 200+

- **Allied Beauty Association Trade Show - Montréal 2018**
Date: March 19, 2018
Location: Montréal, QC
Sponsor/Contact: Allied Beauty Association
#26-27, 145 Traders Blvd. East
Mississauga, ON L4Z 3L3
905-568-0158; *Fax:* 905-568-1581
E-mail: abashows@abacanada.com
URL: www.abacanada.com
Scope: National
Purpose: A trade show for beauty professionals to learn about new happenings in the beauty industry

- **Allied Beauty Association Trade Show - Toronto 2018**
Date: March 25-26, 2018
Location: Metro Toronto Convention Centre
Toronto, ON
Sponsor/Contact: Allied Beauty Association
#26-27, 145 Traders Blvd. East
Mississauga, ON L4Z 3L3
905-568-0158; *Fax:* 905-568-1581
E-mail: abashows@abacanada.com
URL: www.abacanada.com
Scope: National
Purpose: A trade show for beauty professionals to learn about new happenings in the beauty industry

- **American Astronautical Society 2018 56th Robert H. Goddard Memorial Symposium**
Date: March 13-15, 2018
Location: Greenbelt, MD USA
Sponsor/Contact: The American Astronautical Society
#102, 6352 Rolling Mill Pl.
Springfield, VA 22152-2370
703-866-0020; *Fax:* 703-866-3526
E-mail: aas@astronautical.org
URL: www.astronautical.org
Scope: International

- **American Concrete Institute Spring 2018 Concrete Conference & Exhibition**
Date: March 25-29, 2018
Location: Grand America & Little America
Salt Lake City, UT USA
Sponsor/Contact: American Concrete Institute
38800 Country Club Dr.
Farmington Hills, MI 48331-3439
248-848-3700; *Fax:* 248-848-3701
URL: www.concrete.org
Scope: International
Purpose: Theme: "Concrete Elevated"
Contact Information: Event Planner: Alexandria R. Prokic, E-mail: alex.prokic@concrete.org

- **Association of Canada Lands Surveyors 2018 National**

Conferences & Conventions Index

Surveyors'/Canadian Hydrographic Conference
Date: March 26-29, 2018
Location: Empress Hotel & Victoria Conference Center
Victoria, BC
Sponsor/Contact: Association of Canada Lands Surveyors
100E, 900 Dynes Rd.
Ottawa, ON K2C 3L6
613-723-9200; Fax: 613-723-5558
URL: www.acls-aatc.ca
Scope: National

• Association québécoise des utilisateurs de l'ordinateur au primaire-secondaire (AQUOPS) Colloque 2018
Date: March 27-29, 2018
Location: Québec, QC
Sponsor/Contact: Association québécoise des utilisateurs de l'ordinateur au primaire-secondaire
#1, 6818, rue Saint-Denis
Montréal, QC H2S 2S2
514-948-1234; Fax: 514-948-1231
E-mail: accueil@aquops.qc.ca
URL: www.aquops.qc.ca
Scope: Provincial

• BC Career Development Association Conference 2018
Date: March 5-6, 2018
Location: Pinnacle Hotel Harbourfront
Vancouver, BC
Sponsor/Contact: British Columbia Career Development Association
#728, 510 West Hastings St.
Vancouver, BC V6B 1L8
604-684-3638
E-mail: info@bccda.org
URL: www.bccda.org
Scope: Provincial

• BC Honey Producers Association 2018 Semi-Annual AGM
Date: March 9-10, 2018
Location: Kamloops, BC
Sponsor/Contact: British Columbia Honey Producers Association
P.O. Box 1650
Comox, BC V9M 8A2
URL: www.bcbeekeepers.com
Scope: Provincial

• British Columbia Teachers' Federation 103rd Annual General Meeting 2018
Date: March 17-20, 2018
Location: Hyatt Regency Hotel
Vancouver, BC
Sponsor/Contact: British Columbia Teachers' Federation
#100, 550 Wsst 6th Ave.
Vancouver, BC V5Z 4P2
604-871-2283
Toll-Free: 800-663-9163
E-mail: webinfo@bctf.ca
URL: www.bctf.ca
Scope: Provincial

• CANM [Canadian Association of Nuclear Medicine] 2018 Annual Scientific Meeting
Date: March 22-25, 2018
Location: Marriott Vancouver Pinnacle Downtown
Vancouver, BC
Sponsor/Contact: Canadian Association of Nuclear Medicine
P.O. Box 4383 Stn. E
Ottawa, ON K1S 5B4
613-882-5097
E-mail: canm@canm-acmn.ca
URL: www.canm-acmn.ca
Scope: National

• Canada Grains Council Canadian Global Crops Symposium 2018
Date: March 26-28, 2018
Location: Westin Harbour Castle
Toronto, ON
Sponsor/Contact: Canada Grains Council
#476, 167 Lombard Ave.
Winnipeg, MB R3B 0T6
204-925-2130; Fax: 204-956-9506
E-mail: office@canadagrainscouncil.ca
URL: www.canadagrainscouncil.ca
Scope: National

• Canadian Academy of Psychiatry & the Law Annual Conference
Date: March 4-7, 2018
Location: Fairmont Empress
Victoria, BC
Sponsor/Contact: Canadian Academy of Psychiatry & the Law
c/o Katie Hardy, Canadian Psychiatric Association
#701, 141 Laurier Ave. West
Ottawa, ON K1P 5J3
613-234-2815; Fax: 613-234-9857
E-mail: capl@cpa-apc.org
URL: www.capl-acpd.org
Scope: National
Purpose: Information for psychiatrists working in law & psychiatry, & for any physicians interested in furthering their knowledge of this field

• Canadian Association for Dental Research 42nd Annual Meeting
Date: March 21-24, 2018
Location: Fort Lauderdale, FL USA
Sponsor/Contact: Canadian Association for Dental Research
c/o Western University
1151 Richmond St.
London, ON N6A 5B8
519-661-2111
URL: www.cadr-acrd.ca
Scope: International
Purpose: In conjunction with the 47th Annual Meeting of the American Association of Dental Research & the 96th General Session & Exhibition of the International Association for Dental Research

• Canadian Carwash Association Annual General Meeting 2018
Date: March 7, 2018
Location: Toronto Congress Centre
Toronto, ON
Sponsor/Contact: Canadian Carwash Association
#340, 4195 Dundas St. West
Toronto, ON M8X 1Y4
416-239-0339; Fax: 416-239-1076
E-mail: office@canadiancarwash.ca
URL: www.canadiancarwash.ca
Scope: National

• Canadian Cattlemen's Association 2018 Annual General Meeting
Date: March 21-23, 2018
Location: Ottawa Marriott Hotel
Ottawa, ON
Sponsor/Contact: Canadian Cattlemen's Association
#180, 6815 - 8 St. NE
Calgary, AB T2E 7H7
403-275-8558; Fax: 403-274-5686
E-mail: feedback@cattle.ca
URL: www.cattle.ca
Scope: National
Purpose: An opportunity for members to address industry issues & to elect officers

• Canadian Construction Association 100th Annual Conference 2018
Date: March 12-15, 2018
Location: Banff, AB
Sponsor/Contact: Canadian Construction Association
#1900, 275 Slater St.
Ottawa, ON K1P 5H9
613-236-9455; Fax: 613-236-9526
E-mail: cca@cca-acc.ca
URL: www.cca-acc.com
Scope: National
Purpose: Theme: "Building to New Heights"
Contact Information: Director, Meetings & Conferences: Chantal Montpetit, Phone: 613-236-9455 ext. 406; E-mail: infoconference@cca-acc.com; conference.cca-acc.com

• Canadian Foundry Association 2018 Issues Meeting
Date: March 22, 2018
Location: Waterfront Banquet & Conference Centre
Hamilton, ON
Sponsor/Contact: Canadian Foundry Association
#1500, 1 Nicholas St.
Ottawa, ON K1N 7B7
613-789-4894; Fax: 613-789-5957
E-mail: info@foundryassociation.ca
URL: www.foundryassociation.ca
Scope: National
Purpose: Technical committees work on issues to represent members' interests

• Canadian Gas Association 2018 Regulatory Course
Date: March 5-7, 2018
Location: Ottawa, ON
Sponsor/Contact: Canadian Gas Association
#1220, 350 Albert St.
Ottawa, ON K1R 1A4
613-748-0057; Fax: 613-748-9078
E-mail: info@cga.ca
URL: www.cga.ca
Scope: National
Contact Information: E-mail: help@canavents.com

• Canadian Home Builders' Association 2018 75th National Conference
Date: March 21-23, 2018
Location: Fairmont Empress
Victoria, BC
Sponsor/Contact: Canadian Home Builders' Association
#500, 150 Laurier Ave. West
Ottawa, ON K1P 5J4
613-230-3060; Fax: 613-232-8214
E-mail: chba@chba.ca
URL: www.chba.ca
Scope: National
Purpose: Featuring the Canadian Home Builders' Association Annual Meeting of Members, provincial caucus meetings, guest speakers, the association's annual economic session, presentation of the National SAM Awards, social events, & networking opportunities
Contact Information: Director, Conferences & Special Events: Lynda Barrett, E-mail: conference@chba.ca

• Canadian Horticultural Council Annual General Meeting 2018
Date: March 2018
Sponsor/Contact: Canadian Horticultural Council
#102, 2200 Prince of Wales Dr.
Ottawa, ON K2E 6Z9
613-226-4880; Fax: 613-226-4497
E-mail: admin@hortcouncil.ca
URL: www.hortcouncil.ca
Scope: National
Purpose: Members come together to deal with the challenges and opportunities facing Canada's horticultural industry.

• Canadian Morgan Horse Association 2018 AGM
Date: March 23-25, 2018
Location: Marriott Airport
Toronto, ON
Sponsor/Contact: Canadian Morgan Horse Association
P.O. Box 286
Port Perry, ON L9L 1A3
905-982-0060; Fax: 905-982-0097
E-mail: info@morganhorse.ca
URL: www.morganhorse.ca
Scope: National

• Canadian Retina Society 2018 6th Annual Meeting
Date: March 1-3, 2018
Location: Fairmont Tremblant
Mont-Tremblant, QC
Sponsor/Contact: Canadian Retina Society
c/o Canadian Ophthalmological Society
110 - 2733 Lancaster Rd.
Ottawa, ON K1B 0A9
Toll-Free: 800-267-5763
URL: www.cos-sco.ca/cpd/canadian-retina-society-meeting
Scope: National

• Canadian Union of Public Employees (CUPE) Saskatchewan 2018 Annual Convention
Date: March 7-9, 2018
Location: Radisson Hotel
Saskatoon, SK
Sponsor/Contact: Canadian Union of Public Employees
Saskatchewan Regional Office
3275 East Eastgate Dr.
Regina, SK S4Z 1A5
306-757-1009; Fax: 306-757-0102
E-mail: cupesask@sasktel.net
URL: www.sk.cupe.ca
Scope: Provincial
Purpose: A meeting to debate & pass resolutions
Contact Information: E-mail: cupesask@sasktel.net

• Canola Council of Canada 2018 Convention
Date: March 6-8, 2018
Location: Hyatt Regency Indian Wells
Palm Springs, CA USA
Sponsor/Contact: Canola Council of Canada
#400, 167 Lombard Ave.
Winnipeg, MB R3B 0T6
204-982-2100; Fax: 204-942-1841
Toll-Free: 866-834-4378
E-mail: admin@canolacouncil.org
URL: www.canolacouncil.org

Conferences & Conventions Index

Scope: National
Contact Information:
convention.canolacouncil.org

- **Catholic Association of Religious and Family Life Educators of Ontario Conference & Annual General Meeting**
Date: March 22-23, 2018
Location: Queen of Apostles
Mississauga, ON
Sponsor/Contact: Catholic Association of Religious & Family Life Educators of Ontario
E-mail: contact@carfleo.org
URL: www.carfleo.org
Scope: Provincial

- **Central East Alberta Teachers Convention 2018**
Date: March 8-9, 2018
Location: Shaw Conference Centre
Edmonton, AB
Sponsor/Contact: Alberta Teachers' Association
Barnett House
11010 - 142 St. NW
Edmonton, AB T5N 2R1
780-447-9400; *Fax:* 780-455-6481
Toll-Free: 800-232-7208
E-mail: postmaster@ata.ab.ca
URL: www.teachers.ab.ca
Scope: Provincial
Contact Information: Executive Staff Officer: Dan Grassick, E-mail: dan.grassick@ata.ab.ca, Phone: 780-447-9487

- **Economic Developers Alberta 2018 Annual Professional Conference & AGM**
Date: March 21-23, 2018
Location: Banff Centre
Banff, AB
Sponsor/Contact: Economic Developers Alberta
Suite 127
#406, 917 - 85 St. SW
Calgary, AB T3H 5Z9
403-214-0224; *Fax:* 403-214-0224
Toll-Free: 866-671-8182
URL: www.edaalberta.ca
Scope: Provincial
Purpose: Theme: "Diverse. Determined. Driven."

- **GLOBE Forum 2018**
Date: March 14-16, 2018
Location: Vancouver, BC
Sponsor/Contact: GLOBE Foundation
World Trade Centre
#578, 999 Canada Pl.
Vancouver, BC V6C 3E1
604-695-5001; *Fax:* 604-695-5019
Toll-Free: 800-274-6097
E-mail: info@globe.ca
URL: www.globe.ca
Scope: International
Contact Information: General Information: Phone: 604-695-5000, Toll-Free Phone: 1-800-274-6097, E-mail: info@globeseries.com; URL: www.globeseries.com

- **Grain Farmers of Ontario 2018 March Classic**
Date: March 2018
Location: Ontario
Sponsor/Contact: Grain Farmers of Ontario
679 Southgate Dr.
Guelph, ON N1G 4S2

519-767-6537; *Fax:* 519-767-9713
Toll-Free: 800-265-0550
E-mail: info@gfo.ca
URL: www.gfo.ca
Scope: Provincial
Purpose: A gathering of representatives from government, industry, & farms throughout Ontario to attend presentations about trade, world markets, & new oppotunities
Anticipated Attendance: 700+
Contact Information: E-mail: info@gfo.ca

- **Healthcare Information & Management Systems Society 2018 Conference & Exhibition**
Date: March 5-9, 2018
Location: Las Vegas, NV USA
Sponsor/Contact: Healthcare Information & Management Systems Society
#1700, 33 West Monroe St.
Chicago, IL 60603-5616
312-664-4467; *Fax:* 312-664-6143
URL: www.himss.org
Scope: International
Anticipated Attendance: 45,000+
Contact Information:
www.himssconference.org

- **Heating, Refrigeration & Air Conditioning Institute of Canada Canadian Mechanical & Plumbing Exposition (CMPX) 2018**
Date: March 21-23, 2018
Location: Metro Toronto Convention Centre
Toronto, ON
Sponsor/Contact: Heating, Refrigeration & Air Conditioning Institute of Canada
Bldg. 1
#201, 2800 Skymark Ave.
Mississauga, ON L4W 5A6
905-602-4700; *Fax:* 905-602-1197
Toll-Free: 800-267-2231
E-mail: hraimail@hrai.ca
URL: www.hrai.ca
Scope: National
Contact Information: Phone: 416-444-5225, E-mail: cmpx@salshow.com, www.cmpxshow.com

- **International Association for Human Resource Information Management 2018 Select Event**
Date: March 1-2, 2018
Location: Marina Village Conference Center
San Diego, CA USA
Sponsor/Contact: International Association for Human Resource Information Management
10060 Grandview Sq.
Duluth, GA 30097
E-mail: information@ihrim.org
URL: www.ihrim.org
Scope: International
Purpose: Theme: "Selecting the Right System and Implementation Partner for Organization Success"

- **International Association for Public Participation Canada 2018 Skills Symposium**
Date: March 19-23, 2018
Location: Four Points Sheraton
Ottawa, ON
Sponsor/Contact: International Association for Public Participation Canada
E-mail: info@iap2canada.ca
URL: www.iap2canada.ca

- **Jack Summit 2018 6th Annual Conference**
Date: March 2-4, 2018
Location: Toronto, ON
Sponsor/Contact: Jack.org
#505, 192 Spadina Ave.
Toronto, ON M5T 2C2
416-425-2494
URL: www.jack.org
Scope: National

- **Manitoba School Boards Association Convention 2018**
Date: March 15-16, 2018
Location: Delta Winnipeg
Winnipeg, MB
Sponsor/Contact: Manitoba School Boards Association
191 Provencher Blvd.
Winnipeg, MB R2H 0G4
204-233-1595; *Fax:* 204-231-1356
Toll-Free: 800-262-8836
E-mail: webmaster@mbschoolboards.ca
URL: www.mbschoolboards.ca
Scope: Provincial
Purpose: Theme: "Leadership, Service & Advocacy"

- **Manitoba Society of Artists 2018 86th Annual Open Juried Art Exhibition**
Date: March 1-29, 2018
Location: Warehouse Artworks Gallery
Winnipeg, MB
Sponsor/Contact: Manitoba Society of Artists
c/o Luba Olesky
2018 Henderson Hwy.
Winnipeg, MB R2G 1P2
URL: www.mbsa.ca
Scope: Provincial
Purpose: A major exhibition & the presentation of awards for both professional & amateur artists

- **Medieval Academy of America Annual Meeting 2018**
Date: March 1-3, 2018
Location: Emory University
Atlanta, GA USA
Sponsor/Contact: Medieval Academy of America
#202, 17 Dunster St.
Cambridge, MA 02138
617-491-1622; *Fax:* 617-492-3303
E-mail: info@medievalacademy.org
URL: www.medievalacademy.org
Scope: International
Contact Information: Coordinator, Communications & Memberships: Christopher Cole, E-mail: ccole@themedievalacademy.org

- **Membrane Technology Conference 2018**
Date: March 12-16, 2018
Location: Palm Beach Convention Center
West Palm Beach, FL USA
Sponsor/Contact: Water Environment Federation
601 Wythe St.
Alexandria, VA 22314-1994
703-684-2400
Toll-Free: 800-666-0206
E-mail: csc@wef.org
URL: www.wef.org
Scope: International
Purpose: A conference on developments in membrane technology

- **METROSHOW Vancouver Fall 2018**
Date: March 11-16, 2018

Location: Vancouver, BC
Sponsor/Contact: METROSHOW Vancouver
#103, 1951 Glen Dr.
Vancouver, BC V6A 4J6
604-929-8995; *Fax:* 604-357-1995
E-mail: info@metroshow.ca
URL: www.metroshow.ca
Scope: Provincial
Purpose: A one-of-a-kind fashion industry buying show held at various venues around Vancouver; contains 130+ apparel, footwear & giftware agencies selling in showrooms

- **Ontario Association of Veterinary Technicians 2018 Conference**
Date: March 1-3, 2018
Location: Scotiabank Convention Centre
Niagara Falls, ON
Sponsor/Contact: Ontario Association of Veterinary Technicians
#104, 100 Stone Rd. West
Guelph, ON N1G 5L3
519-836-4910; *Fax:* 519-836-3638
Toll-Free: 800-675-1859
E-mail: oavt@oavt.org
URL: www.oavt.org
Scope: Provincial

- **Ontario Automotive Recyclers Association 2018 Convention & Trade Show**
Date: March 22-24, 2018
Location: Hilton Toronto/Markham Suites Conference Centre
Markham, ON
Sponsor/Contact: Ontario Automotive Recyclers Association
#1, 1447 Upper Ottawa St.
Hamilton, ON L8W 3J6
905-383-9788; *Fax:* 905-383-1904
Toll-Free: 800-390-8743
E-mail: admin@oara.com
URL: www.oara.com
Scope: Provincial
Contact Information: Program & Exhibitors/Sponsors: Steve, Phone: 519-858-8761; Registration/Invoicing: Sherry, Phone: 1-800-390-8743

- **Ontario Construction Secretariat State of the Industry & Outlook Conference 2018**
Date: March 8, 2018
Location: Metro Toronto Convention Centre
Toronto, ON
Sponsor/Contact: Ontario Construction Secretariat
#360, 180 Attwell Dr.
Toronto, ON M9W 6A9
416-620-5210; *Fax:* 416-620-5310
Toll-Free: 888-878-8868
E-mail: info@iciconstruction.com
URL: www.iciconstruction.com
Scope: Provincial
Contact Information: Administrator: Gianluca Cipriani, E-mail: gcipriani@iciconstruction.com

- **Ontario Ground Water Association 2018 66th Convention & Annual General Meeting**
Date: March 23-24, 2018
Location: Brookstreet Hotel
Ottawa, ON
Sponsor/Contact: Ontario Ground Water Association
48 Front St. East
Strathroy, ON N7G 1Y6

519-245-7194; *Fax:* 519-245-7196
URL: www.ogwa.ca
Scope: National

• **Ontario Modern Language Teachers Association Spring Conference 2018**
Date: March 23-24, 2018
Location: Toronto, ON
Sponsor/Contact: Ontario Modern Language Teachers Association
P.O. Box 268
71 George St.
Lanark, ON K0G 1K0
E-mail: omlta@omlta.org
URL: www.omlta.org
Scope: Provincial
Purpose: Professional development & networking opportunities for members; 2018 theme is "Many Voices, Many Stories"

• **Ontario Parks Association 62nd Annual Education Forum**
Date: March 1, 2018
Location: Ontario
Sponsor/Contact: Ontario Parks Association
7856 - 5th Line South, RR#4
Milton, ON L9T 2X8
905-864-6182; *Fax:* 905-864-6184
Toll-Free: 866-560-7783
E-mail: opa@ontarioparksassociation.ca
URL: www.ontarioparksassociation.ca
Scope: Provincial
Purpose: Description Educational presentations of interest to park & green space managers

• **Ontario Secondary School Teachers' Federation Annual Meeting of the Provincial Assembly (AMPA) 2018**
Date: March 9-12, 2018
Location: Sheraton Centre Toronto
Toronto, ON
Sponsor/Contact: Ontario Secondary School Teachers' Federation
60 Mobile Dr.
Toronto, ON M4A 2P3
416-751-8300
Toll-Free: 800-267-7867
URL: www.osstf.on.ca
Scope: Provincial
Anticipated Attendance: 500+

• **Organic Trade Association (OTA) Expo West 2018**
Date: March 9-11, 2018
Location: Anaheim Convention Center
Anaheim, CA USA
Sponsor/Contact: Organic Trade Association
#45A, 444 North Capital St.
Washington, DC 20001
202-403-8520
URL: www.ota.com
Scope: International
Purpose: Hosted in conjunction with Natural Products Expo West

• **Pacific Dental Conference 2018**
Date: March 8-10, 2018
Location: Vancouver, BC
Sponsor/Contact: British Columbia Dental Association
#400, 1765 - 8th Ave. West
Vancouver, BC V6J 5C6
604-736-7202; *Fax:* 604-736-7588
Toll-Free: 888-396-9888
E-mail: info@yourdentalhealth.ca
URL: www.bcdental.org
Scope: Provincial

Contact Information: Address: Pacific Dental Conference, #305, 1505 West 2nd Ave., Vancouver, BC V6H 3Y4; Phone: 604-736-3781; E-mail: info@pdconf.com; URL: www.pdconf.com

• **Pest Management Canada 2018**
Date: March 6-8, 2018
Sponsor/Contact: Canadian Pest Management Association
#360, 13 - 3120 Rutherford Rd.
Vaughan, ON L4K 0B2
Fax: 866-957-7378
Toll-Free: 866-630-2762
E-mail: cpma@pestworld.org
URL: pestworldcanada.net
Scope: National
Purpose: Educational sessions, networking opportunities, & exhibits of products, services & techniques

• **Prospectors & Developers Association of Canada (PDAC) 2018 Convention**
Date: March 4-7, 2018
Location: Metro Toronto Convention Centre
Toronto, ON
Sponsor/Contact: Prospectors & Developers Association of Canada
135 King St. East
Toronto, ON M5C 1G6
416-362-1969; *Fax:* 416-362-0101
E-mail: info@pdac.ca
URL: www.pdac.ca
Scope: International
Purpose: A four-day event that attracts more than 900 exhibitors & 22,000 attendees from 125 countries to participate in short courses, technical sessions, & networking opportunities
Anticipated Attendance: 23,000+
Contact Information: Director, Convention: Nicole Sampson, Phone: 416-362-1969, ext. 226, E-mail: nsampson@pdac.ca

• **Provincial Exhibition of Manitoba Royal Manitoba Winter Fair & Tradeshow 2018**
Date: March 26-31, 2018
Location: Keystone Centre
Brandon, MB
Sponsor/Contact: Provincial Exhibition of Manitoba
115 - 10th St.
Brandon, MB R7A 4E7
204-726-3590; *Fax:* 204-725-0202
Toll-Free: 877-729-0001
E-mail: info@provincialexhibition.com
URL: www.provincialexhibition.com
Scope: Provincial

• **Saskatchewan Association of Rural Municipalities 2018 Annual Convention**
Date: March 13-16, 2018
Location: Evraz Place
Regina, SK
Sponsor/Contact: Saskatchewan Association of Rural Municipalities
2075 Hamilton St.
Regina, SK S4P 2E1
306-757-3577; *Fax:* 306-565-2141
Toll-Free: 800-667-3604
E-mail: sarm@sarm.ca
URL: www.sarm.ca
Scope: Provincial
Anticipated Attendance: 2,000

• **Society of Christian Schools in BC Business & Development Conference**
Date: March 6-7, 2018

Sponsor/Contact: Society of Christian Schools in British Columbia
Fosmark Centre, Trinity Western University
7600 Glover Rd.
Langley, BC V2Y 1Y1
604-888-6366; *Fax:* 604-888-2791
E-mail: contact@scsbc.ca
URL: www.scsbc.ca
Scope: Provincial
Purpose: Offers workshops & networking opportunities for staff members of Christian schools
Contact Information: busdev2018.scsbc.net

• **Society of Plastics Engineers 2018 Shanghai TPO Conference**
Date: March 27-29, 2018
Location: Shanghai, China
Sponsor/Contact: Society of Plastics Engineers
#306, 6 Berkshire Blvd.
Bethel, CT 06801
203-775-0471; *Fax:* 203-775-8490
URL: www.4spe.org
Scope: International
Contact Information: Chair, China Conference: Sassan Tarahomi, E-mail: starahomi@auto-tpo.com

• **SPI: The Plastics Industry Trade Association 2018 Spring National Board Meeting**
Date: March 8-9, 2018
Location: Gaylord National Resort & Convention Center
Oxon Hill, MD USA
Sponsor/Contact: SPI: The Plastics Industry Trade Association
#500, 1425 K St. NW
Washington, DC 20005
202-974-5200; *Fax:* 202-296-7005
URL: www.plasticsindustry.org
Scope: National

• **TRENDS: The Apparel Show 2018 (sponsored by the Alberta Men's Wear Agents Association)**
Date: March 4-7, 2018
Location: Edmonton Expo Centre
Edmonton, AB
Sponsor/Contact: Alberta Men's Wear Agents Association
P.O. Box 66037 Stn. Heritage
Edmonton, AB T6J 6T4
780-455-1881
E-mail: amwa@shaw.ca
URL: www.trendsapparel.com
Scope: Provincial
Purpose: A semiannual show involving the participation of wholesale sales representatives showing clothing & shoes
Contact Information: E-mail: amwa@shaw.ca

• **Teachers of English to Speakers of Other Languages, Inc. (TESOL) International Convention & English Language Expo**
Date: March 27-30, 2018
Location: Chicago, IL USA
Sponsor/Contact: Teachers of English to Speakers of Other Languages, Inc.
#500, 1925 Ballenger Ave.
Alexandria, VA 22314-6820
703-836-0774; *Fax:* 703-836-7864
E-mail: info@tesol.org
URL: www.tesol.org
Scope: International
Contact Information: Director, Conference Services: Lisa Dyson, Phone:

703-836-0774, ext. 515, E-mail: conventions@tesol.org

• **The Instrumentation, Systems & Automation Society of America (ISA) 2018 Leak Detection & Repair Fugitive Emissions Symposium**
Date: March 6-7, 2018
Location: Galveston, TX USA
Sponsor/Contact: The Instrumentation, Systems & Automation Society of America
P.O. Box 12277
67 T.W. Alexander Dr.
Research Triangle Park, NC 27709
919-549-8411; *Fax:* 919-549-8288
E-mail: info@isa.org
URL: www.isa.org
Scope: International
Purpose: A series of presentations on fugitive emissions for petroleum refineries, chemical processing plants, & pharmaceutical manufacturers

• **The Profile Show Spring 2018**
Date: March 4-7, 2018
Location: Ontario
Sponsor/Contact: Ontario Fashion Exhibitors
P.O. Box 218
#2219, 160 Tycos Dr.
Toronto, ON M6B 1W8
416-596-2401; *Fax:* 416-596-1808
Toll-Free: 800-765-7508
E-mail: info@profileshow.ca
URL: www.profileshow.ca
Scope: Provincial

• **Western Barley Growers Association 40th Annual Convention**
Date: March 7-8, 2018
Location: Deerfoot Inn & Casino
Calgary, AB
Sponsor/Contact: Western Barley Growers Association
Agriculture Centre
97 East Lake Ramp NE
Airdrie, AB T4A 0C3
403-912-3998; *Fax:* 403-948-2069
E-mail: wbga@wbga.org
URL: www.wbga.org
Scope: Provincial
Purpose: Theme: "A New Era in Agriculture"

April

• **10th Annual Electric Vehicles Conference & Trade Show 2018**
Date: April 24-27, 2018
Location: Westin Ottawa
Ottawa, ON
Sponsor/Contact: Electric Mobility Canada
#11-530, 38, Place du Commerce
Iles de Soeurs, QC H3E 1T8
Fax: 514-769-1286
E-mail: info@emc-mec.ca
URL: www.emc-mec.ca
Scope: National

• **14th Annual Saskatchewan Nurse Practitioners Conference & AGM**
Date: April 20-21, 2018
Location: Regina, SK
Sponsor/Contact: Nurse Practitioners of Saskatchewan
1301 Central Ave.
Prince Albert, SK S6V 4W1
306-765-3876
E-mail: info@npos.ca
URL: www.npos.ca
Scope: Provincial

Conferences & Conventions Index

- **2018 Annual Ontario Cooperative Education Association Spring Conference**
Date: April 22-24, 2018
Location: The Westin Prince
Toronto, ON
Sponsor/Contact: Ontario Cooperative Education Association
35 Reynar Dr.
Quispamsis, NB E2G 1J9
Fax: 506-849-8375
E-mail: ocea@rogers.com
URL: www.ocea.on.ca
Scope: Provincial

- **2018 CCSPA Annual Government Interface**
Date: April 23-25, 2018
Location: Marriott Hotel
Ottawa, ON
Sponsor/Contact: Canadian Consumer Specialty Products Association
#800, 130 Albert St.
Ottawa, ON K1P 5G4
613-232-6616; Fax: 613-233-6350
E-mail: assoc@ccspa.org
URL: www.ccspa.org
Scope: National

- **2018 Canadian Agency for Drugs & Technologies in Health Symposium**
Date: April 15-17, 2018
Location: Halifax, NS
Sponsor/Contact: Canadian Agency for Drugs & Technologies in Health
#600, 865 Carling Ave.
Ottawa, ON K1S 5S8
613-226-2553; Fax: 613-226-5392
Toll-Free: 866-988-1444
E-mail: requests@cadth.ca
URL: www.cadth.ca
Scope: National
Purpose: Theme: "Managing Health Technologies: Supporting Appropriate, Affordable, & Accessible Care"

- **2018 Canadian Association of Pregnancy Support Services Conference**
Date: April 17-20, 2018
Location: Niagara Falls, ON
Sponsor/Contact: Canadian Association of Pregnancy Support Services
#304 - 4820 Gaetz Ave.
Red Deer, AB T4N 4A4
403-347-2827; Fax: 403-343-2847
Toll-Free: 866-845-2151
URL: www.capss.com
Scope: National

- **2018 Canadian Federation of Humane Societies National Animal Welfare Conference**
Date: April 22-23, 2018
Location: Hyatt Regency Calgary
Calgary, AB
Sponsor/Contact: Canadian Federation of Humane Societies
#102, 30 Concourse Gate
Ottawa, ON K2E 7V7
613-224-8072; Fax: 613-723-0252
Toll-Free: 888-678-2347
E-mail: info@cfhs.ca
URL: www.cfhs.ca
Scope: National

- **2018 Canadian Society of Landscape Architects Congress**
Date: April 5-7, 2018
Location: Westin Harbour Castle
Toronto, ON
Sponsor/Contact: Canadian Society of Landscape Architects
12 Forillon Cres.
Ottawa, ON K2M 2S5
866-781-9799; Fax: 866-871-1419
E-mail: info@csla.ca
URL: www.csla.ca
Scope: National
Anticipated Attendance: 4,500+

- **2018 Community Planning Association of Alberta Annual Planning Conference**
Date: April 30 - May 2, 2018
Location: Black Knight Inn
Red Deer, AB
Sponsor/Contact: Community Planning Association of Alberta
#205, 10940 - 166A St.
Edmonton, AB T5P 3V5
780-432-6387; Fax: 780-452-7718
E-mail: cpaa@cpaa.biz
URL: www.cpaa.biz
Scope: Provincial

- **2018 Equestrian Canada Convention**
Date: April 5-8, 2018
Location: Ottawa, ON
Sponsor/Contact: Equestrian Canada
#100, 308 Legget Dr.
Ottawa, ON K2K 1Y6
613-287-1515; Fax: 613-248-3484
Toll-Free: 866-282-8395
E-mail: inquiries@equestrian.ca
URL: www.equestrian.ca
Scope: National

- **2018 Health Sciences Association Convention**
Date: April 26-28, 2018
Location: Hyatt Regency
Vancouver, BC
Sponsor/Contact: Health Sciences Association of British Columbia
180 East Columbia St.
New Westminster, BC V3L 0G7
604-517-0994; Fax: 604-515-8889
Toll-Free: 800-663-2017
URL: www.hsabc.org
Scope: Provincial
Purpose: A gathering of health care & social services professionals

- **2018 Ontario Coaches Conference**
Date: April 20-22, 2018
Location: London, ON
Sponsor/Contact: Coaches Association of Ontario
#200A, 1 Concorde Gate
Toronto, ON M3C 3N6
416-426-7086; Fax: 416-426-7331
URL: www.coachesontario.ca
Scope: Provincial

- **2018 Ontario Rett Syndrome Association Conference**
Date: April 13-15, 2018
Location: Holiday Inn
Toronto, ON
Sponsor/Contact: Ontario Rett Syndrome Association
P.O. Box 50030
London, ON N6A 6H8
519-474-6877; Fax: 519-850-1272
URL: www.rett.ca
Scope: Provincial

- **2018 Pharmacists Manitoba Conference**
Date: April 13-15, 2018
Location: RBC Convention Centre
Winnipeg, MB
Sponsor/Contact: Manitoba Society of Pharmacists Inc.
#202, 90 Garry St.
Winnipeg, MB R3C 4H1
204-956-6680; Fax: 204-956-6686
Toll-Free: 800-677-7170
URL: www.pharmacistsmb.ca
Scope: Provincial

- **2018 Royal Winnipeg Ballet Ball**
Date: April 28, 2018
Location: Winnipeg, MB
Sponsor/Contact: Royal Winnipeg Ballet
380 Graham Ave.
Winnipeg, MB R3C 4K2
204-956-0183; Fax: 204-943-1994
Toll-Free: 800-667-4792
E-mail: customerservice@rwb.org
URL: www.rwb.org
Scope: Local

- **25th Annual Canadian Association of Gift Planners 2018 National Conference**
Date: April 11-13, 2018
Location: Winnipeg, MB
Sponsor/Contact: Canadian Association of Gift Planners
#201, 1188 Wellington St. West
Ottawa, ON K1Y 2Z5
613-232-7991; Fax: 613-232-7286
Toll-Free: 888-430-9494
E-mail: communications@cagp-acpdp.org
URL: www.cagp-acpdp.org
Scope: National
Purpose: An annual spring meeting, featuring educational workshops, experienced speakers, & exhibits
Contact Information:
www.cagpconference.org

- **27th Annual Canadian Conference on HIV/AIDS Research**
Date: April 26-29, 2018
Location: Vancouver, BC
Sponsor/Contact: The Canadian Association for HIV Research
#744, 1 Rideau St.
Ottawa, ON K1N 8S7
613-241-5785; Fax: 613-670-5701
E-mail: info@cahr-acrv.ca
URL: www.cahr-acrv.ca
Scope: National

- **38th Annual Luggage, Leathergoods, Handbags & Accessories Show 2018**
Date: April 29-30, 2018
Location: International Centre
Toronto, ON
Sponsor/Contact: Luggage, Leathergoods, Handbags & Accessories Association of Canada
P.O. Box 144 Stn. A
Toronto, ON M9C 4V2
Fax: 519-624-6408
Toll-Free: 866-872-2420
E-mail: info@llha.ca
URL: www.llha.ca
Scope: National

- **49th Annual Northeast Modern Language Association Convention**
Date: April 12-15, 2018
Location: University of Pittsburgh
Pittsburgh, PA USA
Sponsor/Contact: Northeast Modern Language Association
c/o Dr. Elizabeth Abele, Dept. of English, Nassau Community College
One Education Dr.
Garden City, NY 11530-6793
E-mail: nemlasupport@gmail.com
URL: www.nemla.org
Scope: International
Purpose: Theme: "Global Spaces, Local Landscapes & Imagined Worlds"

- **53e Congrès et Salon des transports: l'innovation, ça nous transporte!**
Date: April 9-11, 2018
Location: Centre des congrès de Québec
Québec, QC
Sponsor/Contact: Association québécoise des transports
Bureau de Montréal
#200, 1255, boul Robert-Bourassa
Montréal, QC H3B 3B2
514-523-6444; Fax: 514-523-2666
URL: aqtr.com
Scope: National

- **73rd BC Trappers Association AGM & Convention**
Date: April 20-22, 2018
Location: Coast Kamloops Hotel & Conference Centre
Kamloops, BC
Sponsor/Contact: BC Trappers' Association
c/o Alana Leclerc
P.O. Box 1063
Prince George, BC V2L 4V2
250-962-5452; Fax: 250-962-5462
E-mail: info@bctrappers.bc.ca
URL: bctrappers.bc.ca
Scope: Provincial

- **Adult Basic Education Association of British Columbia Conference 2018**
Date: April 26-27, 2018
Location: Harrison Hot Springs Resort and Spa
Harrison Hot Springs, BC
Sponsor/Contact: Adult Basic Education Association of British Columbia
5476 - 45th Ave.
Delta, BC V4K 1L4
604-296-6901
URL: www.abeabc.ca
Scope: Provincial
Contact Information:
abeabcnews@gmail.com

- **AdvantAge Ontario 2018 Annual General Meeting & Convention**
Date: April 16-18, 2018
Location: Westin Harbour Castle
Toronto, ON
Sponsor/Contact: AdvantAge Ontario
#700, 7050 Weston Rd.
Woodbridge, ON L4L 8G7
905-851-8821; Fax: 905-851-0744
URL: www.advantageontario.ca
Scope: Provincial
Purpose: A professional development event & trade show, featuring expert speakers, for senior staff from the long term care, seniors' housing, & community services sectors

- **Agricultural Institute of Canada 2018 Conference**
Date: April 23-24, 2018
Location: Guelph, ON
Sponsor/Contact: Agricultural Institute of Canada
#320, 176 Gloucester St.
Ottawa, ON K2P 0A6
613-232-9459; Fax: 613-594-5190
E-mail: office@aic.ca
URL: www.aic.ca

Conferences & Conventions Index

Scope: National
Purpose: Theme: "Education in Agricultural Sciences & Technology - Ready for the Future?"

- **Alberta Assessors' Association 2018 Conference**
Date: April 25-27, 2018
Location: Sheraton Cavalier Calgary
Calgary, AB
Sponsor/Contact: Alberta Assessors' Association
10555 - 172 St.
Edmonton, AB T5S 1P1
780-483-4222
E-mail: membership@assessor.ab.ca
URL: www.assessor.ab.ca
Scope: Provincial

- **Alberta Association of Academic Libraries Spring Meeting 2018**
Date: April 12, 2018
Location: Calgary, AB
Sponsor/Contact: Alberta Association of Academic Libraries
c/o Genevieve Luthy, SAIT
1301 - 16 Ave. NW
Calgary, AB T2M 0L4
URL: aaal.ca
Scope: Provincial

- **Alberta Association of Police Governance 2018 Conference and Annual General Meeting**
Date: April 27-28, 2018
Location: Best Western Plus Lacombe Inn & Suites
Lacombe, AB
Sponsor/Contact: Alberta Association of Police Governance
P.O. Box 36098 Stn. Lakeview Post Office
Calgary, AB T3E 7C6
587-892-7874
E-mail: admin@aapg.ca
URL: www.aapg.ca
Scope: Provincial

- **Alberta Association of Recreation Facility Personnel 2018 Conference**
Date: April 15-18, 2018
Location: Banff, AB
Sponsor/Contact: Alberta Association of Recreation Facility Personnel
P.O. Box 100
312 - 3rd St. West, #B
Cochrane, AB T4C 1A4
403-851-7626; Fax: 403-851-9181
Toll-Free: 888-253-7544
E-mail: office@aarfp.com
URL: www.aarfp.com
Scope: Provincial

- **Alberta Home Education Association Convention 2018**
Date: April 12-14, 2018
Location: Red Deer, AB
Sponsor/Contact: Alberta Home Education Association
URL: www.aheaonline.com
Scope: Provincial

- **Alberta Hotel and Lodging Association 98th Annual Convention and Trade Show 2018**
Date: April 15-17, 2018
Location: Fairmont Jasper Park Lodge
Jasper, AB
Sponsor/Contact: Alberta Hotel & Lodging Association
2707 Ellwood Dr. SW
Edmonton, AB T6X 0P7
780-436-6112; Fax: 780-436-5404
Toll-Free: 888-436-6112
URL: www.ahla.ca
Scope: Provincial
Contact Information: Administrator: Gayle Day, E-mail: gday@ahla.ca, Phone: 780-436-6112, ext. 220

- **Alberta Institute of Agrologists 14th Annual Banff Conference 2018**
Date: April 3-5, 2018
Location: Banff, AB
Sponsor/Contact: Alberta Institute of Agrologists
#1430, 5555 Calgary Trail NW
Edmonton, AB T6H 5P9
780-435-0606; Fax: 780-464-2155
Toll-Free: 855-435-0606
URL: www.albertaagrologists.ca
Scope: Provincial
Purpose: Theme: "Governments & People"

- **Alberta Motor Transport Association 2018 Leadership Conference & AGM**
Date: April 20-21, 2018
Location: Rimrock Resort Hotel
Banff, AB
Sponsor/Contact: Alberta Motor Transport Association
#1, 285005 Wrangler Way
Rocky View, AB T1X 0K3
Fax: 403-243-4610
Toll-Free: 800-267-1003
E-mail: amtamsc@amta.ca
URL: www.amta.ca
Scope: Provincial
Purpose: An event for transportation leaders to learn about the latest issues facing the industry & to set the direction for the association for the upcoming year

- **Alberta Municipal Clerks Association 2018 30th Annual Conference**
Date: April 18-20, 2018
Location: Canmore, AB
Sponsor/Contact: Alberta Municipal Clerks Association
c/o Town of Canmore
902 7th Ave.
Canmore, AB T1W 3K1
403-678-1500
URL: www.albertamunicipalclerks.com
Scope: Provincial
Purpose: A conference providing professional development & discussion opportunities for municipal clerks, returning officers, & election officers

- **Alberta School Councils' Association School Councils Conference & Annual General Meeting 2018**
Date: April 20-22, 2018
Location: Delta Edmonton South
Edmonton, AB
Sponsor/Contact: Alberta School Councils' Association
#1200, 9925 - 109 St.
Edmonton, AB T5K 2J8
780-454-9867; Fax: 780-455-0167
Toll-Free: 800-661-3470
URL: www.albertaschoolcouncils.ca
Scope: Provincial
Purpose: Features school council delegates & a discussion of issues concerning Alberta school councils

- **Alberta Seniors Communities & Housing Association 2018 Convention & Tradeshow**
Date: April 11-13, 2018
Location: Sheraton Red Deer
Red Deer, AB
Sponsor/Contact: Alberta Senior Citizens' Housing Association
9711 - 47 Ave.
Edmonton, AB T6E 5M7
780-439-6473; Fax: 780-433-3717
E-mail: ascha@ascha.com
URL: www.ascha.com
Scope: Provincial

- **Alberta Society of Radiologists 19th Annual Continuing Medical Education Conference**
Date: April 20-22, 2018
Location: Banff Springs Hotel
Banff, AB
Sponsor/Contact: Alberta Society of Radiologists
#220, 10339 - 124th St.
Edmonton, AB T5N 3W1
780-443-2615
URL: www.radiologists.ab.ca
Scope: Provincial
Purpose: Theme: "Grey is the New Black"

- **American Academy of Neurology 2018 70th Annual Meeting**
Date: April 21-27, 2018
Location: Los Angeles, CA USA
Sponsor/Contact: American Academy of Neurology
201 Chicago Ave.
Minneapolis, MN 55415
612-928-6000; Fax: 612-454-2746
Toll-Free: 800-879-1960
E-mail: memberservices@aan.com
URL: www.aan.com
Scope: International
Purpose: Education, science, & practice programs & exhibits
Anticipated Attendance: 12,000+

- **American Association for Thoracic Surgery 98th Annual Meeting**
Date: April 28 - May 1, 2018
Location: San Diego Convention Center
San Diego, CA USA
Sponsor/Contact: American Association for Thoracic Surgery
#4550, 500 Cummings Center
Beverly, MA 01915
978-927-8330; Fax: 978-524-0498
URL: www.aats.org
Scope: International
Purpose: Education in the field of thoracic & cardiovascular surgery, for cardiothoracic surgeons, physicians in related specialties, allied health professionals, fellows & residents in cardiothoracic & general surgical training programs, as well as medical students with an interest in cardiothoracic surgery

- **American Council of Learned Societies Annual Meeting 2018**
Date: April 26-28, 2018
Location: Sheraton Society Hill Hotel
Philadelphia, PA USA
Sponsor/Contact: American Council of Learned Societies
633 Third Ave.
New York, NY 10017-6795
212-697-1505; Fax: 212-949-8058
URL: www.acls.org
Scope: International
Contact Information: Director, Member Relations: Sandra Bradley, E-mail: sbradley@acls.org, Phone: 212-697-1505, ext. 123

- **American Galvanizers Association 2018 Annual Conference**
Date: April 7-11, 2018
Location: Westin LaPaloma
Tucson, AZ USA
Sponsor/Contact: American Galvanizers Association
#108, 6881 South Holly Circle
Centennial, CO 80112
720-554-0900; Fax: 720-554-0909
Toll-Free: 800-468-7732
E-mail: aga@galvanizeit.org
URL: www.galvanizeit.org
Scope: National

- **American Psychological Association 2018 Conference**
Date: April 5-7, 2018
Location: Washington, DC USA
Sponsor/Contact: American Psychological Association
750 - 1st St. NE
Washington, DC 20002-4242
202-336-5500
Toll-Free: 800-374-2721
E-mail: executiveoffice@apa.org
URL: www.apa.org
Scope: International
Purpose: Theme: "Technology, Mind, & Society"

- **American Society for Quality 2018 World Conference on Quality & Improvement**
Date: April 30 - May 2, 2018
Location: Seattle, WA USA
Sponsor/Contact: American Society for Quality
P.O. Box 3005
600 Plankinton Ave. North
Milwaukee, WI 53203
414-272-8575; Fax: 414-272-1734
Toll-Free: 800-248-1946
E-mail: help@asq.org
URL: www.asq.org
Scope: International

- **Annual Canadian Association for Spiritual Care Conference: Exploring Spiritual Landscapres through the Arts**
Date: April 25-28, 2018
Location: Deerhurst, ON
Sponsor/Contact: Canadian Association for Spiritual Care
#27, 1267 Dorval Dr.
Oakville, ON L6M 3Z4
289-837-2272; Fax: 289-837-4800
Toll-Free: 866-442-2773
URL: www.spiritualcare.ca
Scope: National

- **Association of Kootenay & Boundary Local Governments AGM 2018**
Date: April 18-20, 2018
Location: Fernie, BC
Sponsor/Contact: Association of Kootenay & Boundary Local Governments
c/o Arlene Parkinson
790 Shakespeare St.
Trail, BC V1R 2B4
250-368-8650
E-mail: akblg@shaw.ca
URL: www.akblg.ca
Scope: Local

- **Association of Professional Biology 2018 Conference & Annual General Meeting**
Date: April 5-7, 2018
Location: Westin Wall Conference Centre
Richmond, BC

Conferences & Conventions Index

Sponsor/Contact: Association of Professional Biology
#300, 1095 McKenzie Ave.
Victoria, BC V8P 2L5
250-483-4283; *Fax:* 250-483-3439
E-mail: info@professionalbiology.com
URL: professionalbiology.com
Scope: Provincial
Contact Information: Director, Operations: Isabelle Houde, E-mail: registrar@professionalbiology.com

- **Association of Vancouver Island Coastal Communities 2018 Annual General Meeting & Convention**
Date: April 13-15, 2018
Location: Fairmont Empress & Victoria Conference Centre
Victoria, BC
Sponsor/Contact: Association of Vancouver Island Coastal Communities
Local Government House
525 Government St.
Victoria, BC V8W 0A8
250-356-5122; *Fax:* 250-356-5119
URL: www.avicc.ca
Scope: Local

- **BC Career Colleges Association Conference 2018**
Date: April 4-6, 2018
Location: British Columbia
Sponsor/Contact: British Columbia Career College Association
10040 King George Ave.
Surrey, BC V3T 2W4
778-869-2605
E-mail: membership@bccca.com
URL: www.bccca.com
Scope: Provincial

- **BC School Superintendents Association Spring Forum 2018**
Date: April 6, 2018
Location: Westin Bayshore
Vancouver, BC
Sponsor/Contact: British Columbia School Superintendents Association
#208, 1118 Homer St.
Vancouver, BC V6B 6L5
604-687-0590; *Fax:* 604-687-8118
E-mail: information@bcssa.org
URL: www.bcssa.org
Scope: Provincial
Purpose: Topics related to the British Columbia School Superintendents Association's Dimensions of Practice, featuring innovative & successful models of leadership

- **BILD Alberta 2018 Spring Conference**
Date: April 19-20, 2018
Location: Fairmont Banff Springs Hotel
Banff, AB
Sponsor/Contact: Building Industry & Land Development Alberta
#328, 9707 - 110 St.
Edmonton, AB T5K 2L9
780-424-5890
Toll-Free: 800-661-3348
E-mail: info@bildalberta.ca
URL: www.bildalberta.ca
Scope: Provincial
Contact Information: Email: conference@bildalberta.ca

- **Bakery Showcase 2018**
Date: April 29-30, 2018
Location: The International Centre
Mississauga, ON

Sponsor/Contact: Baking Association of Canada
#202, 7895 Tranmere Dr.
Mississauga, ON L5S 1V9
905-405-0288; *Fax:* 905-405-0993
Toll-Free: 888-674-2253
E-mail: info@baking.ca
URL: www.baking.ca
Scope: National
Contact Information: Ahmed Mutaher, E-mail: amutaher@baking.ca

- **British Association for Canadian Studies 43rd Annual Conference**
Date: April 19-21, 2018
Location: London, United Kingdom
Sponsor/Contact: British Association for Canadian Studies
c/o UCL Institute of the Americas
51 Gordon Sq.
London, WC1H OPN
URL: www.britishassociationforcanadianstudies.org
Scope: International
Purpose: Distinguished speakers on a great range of topics

- **British Columbia Recreation & Parks Association Symposium 2018**
Date: April 30 - May 2, 2018
Location: The Westin Bayshore
Vancouver, BC
Sponsor/Contact: British Columbia Recreation & Parks Association
#301, 470 Granville St.
Vancouver, BC V6C 1V5
604-629-0965; *Fax:* 604-629-2651
Toll-Free: 866-929-0965
E-mail: bcrpa@bcrpa.bc.ca
URL: www.bcrpa.bc.ca
Scope: Provincial
Purpose: An annual meeting of interest to parks & recreation professionals & volunteers, as well as elected officials from across British Columbia

- **British Columbia School Trustees Association 114th Annual General Meeting 2018**
Date: April 26-29, 2018
Location: British Columbia
Sponsor/Contact: British Columbia School Trustees Association
1580 West Broadway, 4th Fl.
Vancouver, BC V6J 5K9
604-734-2721; *Fax:* 604-732-4559
E-mail: bcsta@bcsta.org
URL: www.bcsta.org
Scope: Provincial

- **Canadian Association of Montessori Teachers 2018 Mini-Conference**
Date: April 21, 2018
Location: Woodland Cultural Centre
Brantford, ON
Sponsor/Contact: Canadian Association of Montessori Teachers
312 Oakwood Crt.
Newmarket, ON L3Y 3C8
416-755-7184; *Fax:* 866-328-7974
E-mail: info@camt100.ca
URL: www.camt100.ca
Scope: National
Purpose: Theme: "Walking the Path to Reconciliation"

- **Canadian Association of Nurses in HIV/AIDS Care 26th Annual Conference 2018**
Date: April 5-7, 2018

Location: Coast Coal Harbour Hotel
Vancouver, BC
Sponsor/Contact: Canadian Association of Nurses in HIV/AIDS Care
St. Paul's Hospital
#B552, 1081 Burrard St.
Vancouver, BC V6Z 1Y6
E-mail: admin@canac.org
URL: www.canac.org
Scope: National
Purpose: Theme: "Acting Up, Reducing Harm: Clinical Practice & Advocacy in the Context of Crisis"

- **Canadian Association of Petroleum Producers (CAPP) Scotiabank Energy Symposium 2018**
Date: April 10-11, 2018
Sponsor/Contact: Canadian Association of Petroleum Producers
#2100, 350 - 7 Ave. SW
Calgary, AB T2P 3N9
403-267-1100; *Fax:* 403-261-4622
E-mail: communication@capp.ca
URL: www.capp.ca
Scope: National
Purpose: High-profile speakers on energy and industry discussion panels.
Contact Information: Email: communication@capp.ca, Phone: 403-267-1100

- **Canadian Association of Radiologists 81st Annual Scientific Meeting**
Date: April 26-29, 2018
Location: Le Centre Sheraton
Montréal, QC
Sponsor/Contact: Canadian Association of Radiologists
#600, 294 Albert St.
Ottawa, ON K1P 6E6
613-860-3111; *Fax:* 613-860-3112
E-mail: info@car.ca
URL: www.car.ca
Scope: National
Purpose: Theme: "Artificial Intelligence in Radiology: Present & Future"

- **Canadian Association of Research Libraries Spring General Meeting 2018**
Date: April 30 - May 1, 2018
Location: Regina, SK
Sponsor/Contact: Canadian Association of Research Libraries
#203, 309 Cooper St.
Ottawa, ON K2P 0G5
613-482-9344
E-mail: info@carl-abrc.ca
URL: www.carl-abrc.ca
Scope: National

- **Canadian Association of Staff Physician Recruiters 2018 Conference**
Date: April 29 - May 1, 2018
Location: Fredericton, NB
Sponsor/Contact: Canadian Association of Staff Physician Recruiters
E-mail: info@caspr.ca
URL: caspr.ca
Scope: National

- **Canadian Conference on Medical Education 2018**
Date: April 28 - May 1, 2018
Location: Halifax Convention Centre
Halifax, NS
Sponsor/Contact: Canadian Association for Medical Education
#100, 2733 Lancaster Rd.
Ottawa, ON K1B 0A9

613-730-0687; *Fax:* 613-730-1196
E-mail: came@afmc.ca
URL: www.came-acem.ca
Scope: National
Contact Information: www.mededconference.ca

- **Canadian Corporate Counsel Association 2018 National Conference**
Date: April 29 - May 1, 2018
Location: Fairmont Royal York Hotel
Toronto, ON
Sponsor/Contact: Canadian Corporate Counsel Association
#1210, 20 Toronto St.
Toronto, ON M5C 2B8
416-869-0522; *Fax:* 416-869-0946
E-mail: ccca@ccca-cba.org
URL: www.ccca-accje.org
Scope: National
Purpose: Theme: "Beyond Borders: Business & Law in the Global Village"

- **Canadian Credit Union Association 2018 National Conference for Canada's Credit Unions**
Date: April 29 - May 1, 2018
Location: Toronto, ON
Sponsor/Contact: Canadian Credit Union Association
Corporate Office
#1000, 151 Yonge St.
Toronto, ON M5C 2W7
416-232-1262
Toll-Free: 800-649-0222
E-mail: inquiries@ccua.com
URL: www.ccua.com
Scope: National
Contact Information: Conference Registrar, E-mail: conferences@ccua.com

- **Canadian Federation of Independent Grocers Grocery & Specialty Food West 2018**
Date: April 23-24, 2018
Location: Vancouver Convention Centre
Vancouver, BC
Sponsor/Contact: Canadian Federation of Independent Grocers
#401, 105 Gordon Baker Rd.
Toronto, ON M2H 3P8
416-492-2311; *Fax:* 416-492-2347
Toll-Free: 800-661-2344
E-mail: info@cfig.ca
URL: www.cfig.ca
Scope: National
Purpose: An annual two day event for grocery industry professionals & over 350 exhibitors, featuring innovative products & ideas
Contact Information: Director, Sales: Rolster Taylor, E-mail: rtaylor@cfig.ca, Phone: 416-492-2311, ext. 223

- **Canadian Franchise Association 2018 National Convention**
Date: April 22-24, 2018
Location: Ottawa, ON
Sponsor/Contact: Canadian Franchise Association
#116, 5399 Eglinton Ave. West
Toronto, ON M9C 5K6
416-695-2896; *Fax:* 416-695-1950
Toll-Free: 800-665-4232
E-mail: info@cfa.ca
URL: www.cfa.ca
Scope: National

- **Canadian Gas Association 2018 Operations, Engineering & Integrity Conference**

Conferences & Conventions Index

Date: April 8-13, 2018
Location: Winnipeg, MB
Sponsor/Contact: Canadian Gas Association
#1220, 350 Albert St.
Ottawa, ON K1R 1A4
613-748-0057; *Fax:* 613-748-9078
E-mail: info@cga.ca
URL: www.cga.ca
Scope: National
Contact Information: E-mail: help@canavents.com

- **Canadian Geriatrics Society 38th Annual Scientific Meeting**
Date: April 19-21, 2018
Location: Montréal, QC
Sponsor/Contact: Canadian Geriatrics Society
#6, 20 Crown Steel Dr.
Markham, ON L3R 9X9
905-415-3917; *Fax:* 905-415-0071
Toll-Free: 855-415-3917
URL: www.canadiangeriatrics.ca
Scope: National

- **Canadian Heavy Oil Association 2018 Slugging it Out Conference**
Date: April 17, 2018
Location: BMO Centre Stampede Park
Calgary, AB
Sponsor/Contact: Canadian Heavy Oil Association
#2310, 144 - 4th Ave. SW
Calgary, AB T2P 3N4
403-269-1755; *Fax:* 403-453-0179
E-mail: e-suggestions@choa.ab.ca
URL: www.choa.ab.ca
Scope: National

- **Canadian Home Builders' Association - Newfoundland Labrador 35th Annual Home Show 2018**
Date: April 27-29, 2018
Location: The Glacier
Mount Pearl, NL
Sponsor/Contact: Canadian Home Builders' Association - Newfoundland Labrador
435 Blackmarsh Rd.
St. John's, NL A1E 1T7
709-753-2000; *Fax:* 709-753-7469
Toll-Free: 800-265-2800
E-mail: admin@chbanl.ca
URL: chbanl.ca
Scope: Provincial
Purpose: An event showcasing residential construction products & services; allows visitors to network with suppliers & consumers alike
Contact Information: Manager, Office Administration: Kelly Rogers, E-mail: admin@chbanl.ca

- **Canadian Museums Association 71st National Conference 2018**
Date: April 11-12, 2018
Location: Sheraton Vancouver Wall Centre
Vancouver, BC
Sponsor/Contact: Canadian Museums Association
#400, 280 Metcalfe St.
Ottawa, ON K2P 1R7
613-567-0099; *Fax:* 613-233-5438
Toll-Free: 888-822-2907
E-mail: info@museums.ca
URL: www.museums.ca
Scope: National
Purpose: A conference & tradeshow for Canadian museum professionals, such as directors, administrators, & curators

- **Canadian Produce Marketing Association 93rd Annual Convention & Trade Show**
Date: April 24-26, 2018
Location: Vancouver Convention Centre
Vancouver, BC
Sponsor/Contact: Canadian Produce Marketing Association
162 Cleopatra Dr.
Ottawa, ON K2G 5X2
613-226-4187; *Fax:* 613-226-2984
E-mail: question@cpma.ca
URL: www.cpma.ca
Scope: International
Purpose: Featuring business sessions, a trade show, a keynote speaker, & awards
Contact Information:
www.convention.cpma.ca

- **Canadian Respiratory Conference 2018**
Date: April 12-14, 2018
Location: Vancouver, BC
Sponsor/Contact: Canadian Lung Association
National Office
#502, 885 Meadowlands Dr.
Ottawa, ON K2C 3N2
613-569-6411
Toll-Free: 888-566-5864
E-mail: info@lung.ca
URL: www.lung.ca
Scope: National
Purpose: Jointly organized by the Canadian Lung Association, the Canadian Thoracic Society, & the Canadian Respiratory Health Professionals
Anticipated Attendance: 650

- **Canadian Society of Hand Therapists Annual Conference 2018**
Date: April 27-28, 2018
Location: Westin Ottawa
Ottawa, ON
Sponsor/Contact: Canadian Society of Hand Therapists
#101, 10277 154 St.
Surrey, BC V3R 4J7
E-mail: secretary@csht.org
URL: www.csht.org
Scope: National

- **Canadian Union of Public Employees (CUPE) British Columbia Division 2018 55th Annual Convention**
Date: April 18-21, 2018
Location: Westin Bayshore
Vancouver, BC
Sponsor/Contact: Canadian Union of Public Employees
British Columbia Regional Office
#500, 4940 Canada Way
Burnaby, BC V5G 4T3
604-291-9119; *Fax:* 604-291-9043
E-mail: info@cupe.bc.ca
URL: www.cupe.bc.ca
Scope: Provincial

- **Canadian Union of Public Employees New Brunswick 2018 Convention**
Date: April 24-27, 2018
Location: Fredericton Inn
Fredericton, NB
Sponsor/Contact: Canadian Union of Public Employees
Maritime Regional Office
91 Woodside Lane
Fredericton, NB E3C 0C5
506-458-8059; *Fax:* 506-452-1702
URL: www.nb.cupe.ca
Scope: Provincial

- **Carl Orff Canada Music for Children 25th National Conference**
Date: April 19-22, 2018
Location: Sheraton on the Falls
Niagara Falls, ON
Sponsor/Contact: Carl Orff Canada Music for Children
P.O. Box 1
Grp 23 RR#1
East Selkirk, MB R0E 0M0
URL: www.orffcanada.ca
Scope: National

- **Chartered Professionals in Human Resources of Alberta 2018 Conference**
Date: April 11-12, 2018
Location: Telus Convention Centre
Calgary, AB
Sponsor/Contact: Chartered Professionals in Human Resources of Alberta
#990, 105 - 12 Ave. SE
Calgary, AB T2G 1A1
403-209-2420; *Fax:* 403-209-2401
Toll-Free: 800-668-6125
E-mail: info@cphrab.ca
URL: www.cphrab.ca
Scope: Provincial
Purpose: Theme: "HR Undefined"

- **CHHMA [Canadian Hardware & Housewares Manufacturers Association] Spring Conference & AGM 2018**
Date: April 3, 2018
Location: Mississauga Convention Centre
Mississauga, ON
Sponsor/Contact: Canadian Hardware & Housewares Manufacturers' Association
#101, 1335 Morningside Ave.
Toronto, ON M1B 5M4
416-282-0022
URL: www.chhma.ca
Scope: National

- **CIO Peer Forum 2018**
Date: April 10-11, 2018
Location: Vancouver Marriott Pinnacle Downtown
Vancouver, BC
Sponsor/Contact: CIO Association of Canada
National Office
#305, 7270 Woodbine Ave.
Markham, ON L3R 4B9
905-752-1899; *Fax:* 905-513-1248
Toll-Free: 877-865-9009
URL: www.ciocan.ca
Scope: National

- **Colleges and Institutes Canada 2018 Conference**
Date: April 29 - May 1, 2018
Location: Victoria, BC
Sponsor/Contact: Colleges and Institutes Canada
#701, 1 Rideau St.
Ottawa, ON K1N 8S7
613-746-2222; *Fax:* 613-746-6721
E-mail: info@collegesinstitutes.ca
URL: www.collegesinstitutes.ca
Scope: National
Anticipated Attendance: 800

- **Computer Human Interaction 2018 Conference: Human Factors in Computing Systems**
Date: April 21-26, 2018
Location: Montréal, QC
Sponsor/Contact: Special Interest Group on Computer Human Interaction
P.O. Box 93672 Stn. Nelson Park
Vancouver, BC V6E 4L7
604-876-8985
E-mail: chi-VanCHI@acm.org
URL: www.sigchi.org
Scope: International

- **Corporation des thérapeutes du sport du Québec Annual Athletic Therapy Conference 2018**
Date: April 27-28, 2018
Location: Montréal, QC
Sponsor/Contact: Corporation des thérapeutes du sport du Québec
7141, rue Sherbrooke ouest, #SP165
Montréal, QC H4B 1R6
514-848-2424
E-mail: admin@ctsq.qc.ca
URL: www.ctsq.qc.ca
Scope: Provincial

- **Council of Forest Industries 2018 Annual Convention**
Date: April 10-12, 2018
Location: Kelowna, BC
Sponsor/Contact: Council of Forest Industries
Pender Place I Business Building
#1501, 700 Pender St. West
Vancouver, BC V6C 1G8
604-684-0211; *Fax:* 604-687-4930
E-mail: info@cofi.org
URL: www.cofi.org
Scope: National
Purpose: A meeting about issues affecting the forestry industries of British Columbia.
Anticipated Attendance: 500-900
Contact Information: Phone: 604-684-0211; Fax: 604-687-4930

- **Cruise360 2018**
Date: April 17-23, 2018
Sponsor/Contact: Cruise Lines International Association, Inc.
#250, 1201 F St. NW
Washington, DC 20004
202-759-9370; *Fax:* 202-759-9344
E-mail: info@cruising.org
URL: www.cruising.org
Scope: International
Purpose: An annual cruise conference hosted by Cruise Lines International Association, Inc., including educational training & networking opportunities.

- **Environmental Services Association of Alberta EnviroTech 2018**
Date: April 3-5, 2018
Location: Hyatt Regency Calgary
Calgary, AB
Sponsor/Contact: Environmental Services Association of Alberta
#102, 2528 Ellwood Dr. SW
Edmonton, AB T6X 0A9
780-429-6363; *Fax:* 780-429-4249
Toll-Free: 800-661-9278
E-mail: info@esaa.org
URL: www.esaa.org
Scope: Provincial
Contact Information: Director, Program & Event Development: Joe Chowaniec, Phone: 780-429-6363, ext. 223, E-mail: chowaniec@esaa.org

- **Federation of Ontario Bed & Breakfast Accommodation 2018 Conference & Annual General Meeting**
Date: April 9-10, 2018
Location: Deerhurst Resort
Huntsville, ON

Conferences & Conventions Index

Sponsor/Contact: Federation of Ontario Bed & Breakfast Accommodation
29 Albert St.
Orillia, ON L3V 5J9
705-329-3242
E-mail: talk2us@fobba.com
URL: www.fobba.com
Scope: Provincial

- **Gerontological Nurses Association of British Columbia 2018 Conference & AGM**
Date: April 12-14, 2018
Location: Coast Bastion Hotel
Nanaimo, BC
Sponsor/Contact: Gerontological Nursing Association of British Columbia
c/o 328 Nootka St.
New Westminster, BC V3L 4X4
604-484-5698; *Fax:* 604-874-4378
E-mail: gnabc@shaw.ca
URL: gnabc.com
Scope: Provincial
Purpose: Theme: "What Really Matters"

- **Gerontological Nursing Association of Ontario Conference & AGM 2018**
Date: April 12-13, 2018
Location: Embassy Suites
Niagara Falls, ON
Sponsor/Contact: Gerontological Nursing Association of Ontario
P.O. Box 368 Stn. K
Toronto, ON M4P 2E0
E-mail: info@gnaontario.org
URL: www.gnaontario.org
Scope: Provincial
Purpose: Theme: "It Takes a Village"

- **Global Business Travel Association Canada Conference 2018**
Date: April 16-18, 2018
Location: Metro Toronto Convention Centre
Toronto, ON
Sponsor/Contact: Global Business Travel Association (Canada)
#301, 1235 Fairview St.
Burlington, ON L7S 2K9
416-840-6128
E-mail: info@gbta.org
URL: www.gbta.org/canada
Scope: National
Purpose: Featuring exhibitors, education sessions & general session featured speakers
Anticipated Attendance: 550+
Contact Information:
canadaconference.gbta.org

- **Greenbuild International Conference & Expo 2018 (Europe)**
Date: April 17-18, 2018
Location: Radisson Blu Hotel & Meeting Center
Berlin, Germany
Sponsor/Contact: U.S. Green Building Council
#500, 2101 L Street NW
Washington, DC 20037
202-742-3792
Toll-Free: 800-795-1747
E-mail: leedinfo@usgbc.org
URL: new.usgbc.org
Scope: International
Contact Information: URL: greenbuild.usgbc.org

- **Holstein Canada National Holstein Convention 2018**
Date: April 11-14, 2018
Location: Québec, QC
Sponsor/Contact: Holstein Canada
P.O. Box 610
20 Corporate Pl.
Brantford, ON N3T 5R4
519-756-8300; *Fax:* 519-756-3502
Toll-Free: 855-756-8300
URL: www.holstein.ca
Scope: National

- **Hospice Palliative Care Ontario Annual Conference 2018**
Date: April 22-24, 2018
Location: Sheraton Parkway Toronto North Hotel & Suites
Richmond Hill, ON
Sponsor/Contact: Hospice Palliative Care Ontario
#707, 2 Carlton St.
Toronto, ON M5B 1J3
416-304-1477; *Fax:* 416-304-1479
Toll-Free: 800-349-3111
E-mail: info@hpco.ca
URL: www.hpco.ca
Scope: Provincial
Purpose: Theme: "Striving for Equity in Hospice Palliative Care"

- **ISACA North America CACS Conference 2018**
Date: April 30 - May 2, 2018
Location: Chicago, IL USA
Sponsor/Contact: ISACA
#1010, 3701 Algonquin Rd.
Rolling Meadows, IL 60008
847-253-1545; *Fax:* 847-253-1443
E-mail: news@isaca.org
URL: www.isaca.org
Scope: International
Purpose: An industry event for ISACA members, IS Audit, Assurance, Security & Risk Management Professionals worldwide; includes expert-led workshops & professional development opportunities
Contact Information: ISACA Training & Education, Phone: 847-660-5670, Fax: 847-253-1443

- **Icelandic National League of North America 2018 Annual Convention**
Date: April 26-28, 2018
Location: Edmonton, AB
Sponsor/Contact: Icelandic National League of North America
#103, 94 - 1st Ave.
Gimli, MB R0C 1B1
204-642-5897; *Fax:* 204-642-9382
URL: www.inlofna.org
Scope: National

- **InterACTION 2018: Ontario Physiotherapy Association Annual Conference**
Date: April 13-14, 2018
Location: Marriott Toronto Airport Hotel
Toronto, ON
Sponsor/Contact: Ontario Physiotherapy Association
#210, 55 Eglinton Ave. East
Toronto, ON M4P 1G8
416-322-6866; *Fax:* 416-322-6705
Toll-Free: 800-672-9668
E-mail: physiomail@opa.on.ca
URL: www.opa.on.ca
Scope: Provincial

- **International Commission of Agricultural Engineering XIX World Congress 2018**
Date: April 22-26, 2018
Location: Antalya, Turkey
Sponsor/Contact: International Commission of Agricultural & Biosystems Engineering
c/o Dr. Takaaki Maekawa, School of Life & Environmental Sciences
1-1-1 Tennodai, University of Tsukuba
Tsukuba, Ibaraki
E-mail: biopro@sakura.cc.tsukuba.ac.jp
URL: www.cigr.org
Scope: International

- **International Commission on Illumination 2018 Topical Conference**
Date: April 24-28, 2018
Sponsor/Contact: International Commission on Illumination
Babenbergerstrae 9/9A
Vienna, 1010
E-mail: ciecb@cie.co.at
URL: www.cie.co.at
Scope: International

- **Library Association of Alberta Annual Conference 2018**
Date: April 26-29, 2018
Location: Alberta
Sponsor/Contact: Library Association of Alberta
80 Baker Cres. NW
Calgary, AB T2L 1R4
403-284-5818
Toll-Free: 877-522-5550
E-mail: info@laa.ca
URL: www.laa.ca
Scope: Provincial
Purpose: A conference held each spring for members of the Alberta library community, featuring association annual general meetings, session presentations, networking opportunities, & a trade show. Beginning this year, the conference is no longer held jointly with the Alberta Library Trustees Association (ALTA).
Contact Information: Library Association of Alberta, Phone: 403-284-5818, Toll-Free Phone: 1-877-522-5550, Fax: 403-282-6646, E-mail: info@laa.ca, info@albertalibraryconference.com

- **Manitoba Trucking Association Annual General Meeting 2018**
Date: April 6, 2018
Location: RBC Convention Center
Winnipeg, MB
Sponsor/Contact: Manitoba Trucking Association
25 Bunting St.
Winnipeg, MB R2X 2P5
204-632-6600; *Fax:* 204-694-7134
E-mail: info@trucking.mb.ca
URL: www.trucking.mb.ca
Scope: Provincial
Contact Information: E-mail: info@trucking.mb.ca

- **NACE International CORROSION 2018**
Date: April 15-19, 2018
Location: Phoenix Convention Center
Phoenix, AZ USA
Sponsor/Contact: NACE International
15835 Park Ten Pl.
Houston, TX 77084
281-228-6200; *Fax:* 281-228-6300
E-mail: firstservice@nace.org
URL: www.nace.org
Scope: International
Purpose: A corrosion conference & exposition

- **National Association for Surface Finishing (NASF) Washington Forum**
Date: April 16-18, 2018
Location: Ritz-Carlton Pentagon City
Washington, DC USA
Sponsor/Contact: National Association for Surface Finishing
#500, 1155 - 15th St. NW
Washington, DC 20005
202-457-8404; *Fax:* 202-530-0659
E-mail: info@nasfmembership.com
URL: www.nasf.org
Scope: International
Contact Information: Contact, Washington Forum: Jeff Hannapel, E-mail: jhannapel@thepolicygroup.com

- **National Emergency Nurses Association 2018 Conference**
Date: April 19-22, 2018
Location: Kelowna, BC
Sponsor/Contact: National Emergency Nurses Association
144 - 8485 Young Rd.
Chilliwack, BC V2P 7Y7
URL: www.nena.ca
Scope: National

- **New Brunswick Real Estate Association 2018 Annual General Meeting**
Date: April 23-25, 2018
Sponsor/Contact: New Brunswick Real Estate Association
#1, 22 Durelle St.
Fredericton, NB E3C 1N8
506-459-8055; *Fax:* 506-459-8057
Toll-Free: 800-762-1677
E-mail: info@nbrea.ca
URL: nbrea.ca

- **Northern Air Transport Association 42nd Annual Conference & Tradeshow**
Date: April 23-25, 2018
Location: Whitehorse, YT
Sponsor/Contact: Northern Air Transport Association
c/o Colin Dempsey
P.O. Box 20102
Yellowknife, NT X1A 3X8
867-446-6282; *Fax:* 866-977-6282
E-mail: admin@nata-yzf.ca
URL: www.nata-yzf.ca
Purpose: Conference presentations & exhibitors
Contact Information: admin@nata-yzf.ca

- **Ontario Art Education Association Conference 2018**
Date: April 2018
Location: Hamilton, ON
Sponsor/Contact: Ontario Art Education Association
E-mail: membership@OAEA.ca
URL: www.oaea.ca
Scope: Provincial
Purpose: Theme: "Moving Forward with Visual & Media Arts Education"

- **Ontario Association on Developmental Disabilities Annual Conference 2018**
Date: April 10-13, 2018
Location: Ambassador Hotel & Conference Centre
Kingston, ON
Sponsor/Contact: Ontario Association on Developmental Disabilities
2 Surrey Pl.
Toronto, ON M5S 2C2
416-429-3720; *Fax:* 647-260-2016
E-mail: oadd@oadd.org
URL: www.oadd.org

Conferences & Conventions Index

Scope: Provincial
Purpose: Theme: "Working Together: Innovative Ideas for Complex Care"

• **Ontario Construction Secretariat Future Building 2018**
Date: April 10-12, 2018
Location: International Centre
Toronto, ON
Sponsor/Contact: Ontario Construction Secretariat
#360, 180 Attwell Dr.
Toronto, ON M9W 6A9
416-620-5210; *Fax:* 416-620-5310
Toll-Free: 888-878-8868
E-mail: info@iciconstruction.com
URL: www.iciconstruction.com
Scope: Provincial
Purpose: An interactive three-day exhibition that provides young career seekers with the opportunity to experience hands-on activities in all areas of the construction sector; event is targeted towards youth 14-26, Aboriginal youth, youth at risk, & individuals in career transition
Anticipated Attendance: 7,000+
Contact Information: Administrator: Gianluca Cipriani, E-mail: gcipriani@iciconstruction.com

• **Ontario Council on Articulation & Transfer 2018 Student Pathways in Higher Education Conference**
Date: April 16-17, 2018
Location: Toronto Marriott Downtown Eaton Centre
Toronto, ON
Sponsor/Contact: Ontario Council on Articulation and Transfer
#1902, 180 Dundas St. West
Toronto, ON M5G 1Z8
416-640-6951; *Fax:* 416-640-6959
E-mail: info@oncat.ca
URL: www.oncat.ca
Scope: Provincial

• **Ontario Dental Association Annual Spring Meeting 2018**
Date: April 26-28, 2018
Location: Metro Toronto Convention Centre
Toronto, ON
Sponsor/Contact: Ontario Dental Association
4 New St.
Toronto, ON M5R 1P6
416-922-3900; *Fax:* 416-922-9005
Toll-Free: 800-387-1393
E-mail: info@oda.ca
URL: www.oda.ca
Scope: Provincial
Anticipated Attendance: 12,000

• **Ontario Food Protection Association Spring Technical Meeting**
Date: April 2018
Location: Ontario
Sponsor/Contact: Ontario Food Protection Association
P.O. Box 51575
2140A Queen St. East
Toronto, ON M4E 1C0
519-265-4119; *Fax:* 416-981-3368
E-mail: info@ofpa.on.ca
URL: www.ofpa.on.ca
Scope: Provincial

• **Ontario Lawn Bowls Association Spring General Meeting 2018**
Date: April 21, 2018
Location: Holiday Inn Oakville
Oakville, ON
Sponsor/Contact: Ontario Lawn Bowls Association
c/o Edith Pedden
471 Silvery Lane
Marberly, ON K0H 2B0
E-mail: olba@olba.ca
URL: www.olba.ca
Scope: Provincial

• **Ontario Municipal Human Resources Association 2018 Spring Conference**
Date: April 11-13, 2018
Location: Hilton Hotel
Niagara Falls, ON
Sponsor/Contact: Ontario Municipal Human Resources Association
#307, 1235 Fairview St.
Burlington, ON L7S 2K9
905-631-7171; *Fax:* 905-631-2376
E-mail: customerservice@omhra.on.ca
URL: www.omhra.ca
Scope: Provincial

• **Ontario Numismatic Association's 56th Annual Convention 2018**
Date: April 20-22, 2018
Location: Kitchener Holiday Inn
Kitchener, ON
Sponsor/Contact: Ontario Numismatic Association
c/o Bruce Raszmann
P.O. Box 40033 Stn. Waterloo Square
75 King St. South
Waterloo, ON N2J 4V1
URL: the-ona.ca
Scope: Provincial
Purpose: Education program, dealer participation, business meetings, & networking events

• **Ontario Refrigeration & Air Conditioning Contractors Association 2018 AGM**
Date: April 26-29, 2018
Location: The Blue Mountains, ON
Sponsor/Contact: Ontario Refrigeration & Air Conditioning Contractors Association
#43, 6770 Davand Dr.
Mississauga, ON L5T 2G3
905-670-0010; *Fax:* 905-670-0474
E-mail: contact@oraca.ca
URL: www.oraca.ca
Scope: Provincial

• **Ontario Retirement Communities Association "Together We Care" Convention & Trade Show**
Date: April 9-11, 2018
Location: Toronto Congress Centre
Toronto, ON
Sponsor/Contact: Ontario Retirement Communities Association
#202, 2401 Bristol Circle
Oakville, ON L6H 6P1
905-403-0500; *Fax:* 905-829-1594
Toll-Free: 888-263-5559
E-mail: info@orcaretirement.com
URL: www.orcaretirement.com
Scope: Provincial
Purpose: A gathering of retirement and long term care professionals.
Contact Information: www.together-we-care.com

• **Ontario Transportation Expo Conference & Trade Show 2018**
Date: April 22-25, 2018

Location: International Plaza Hotel; International Centre, Hall 5
Toronto, ON
Sponsor/Contact: Ontario Public Transit Association
#200, 5063 North Service Rd.
Burlington, ON L7L 5H6
416-229-6222; *Fax:* 416-969-8916
E-mail: info@ontariopublictransit.ca
URL: www.ontariopublictransit.ca
Scope: Provincial
Purpose: Conference and trade show organized by three partnering associations: the Ontario Motor Coach Association (OMCA), the Ontario Public Transit Association (OPTA) and the Ontario School Bus Assocation (OSBA)
Contact Information: 416-229-6622; info@ote.ca

• **Ontario's Water Conference & Trade Show 2018**
Date: April 29 - May 2, 2018
Location: Niagara Falls, ON
Sponsor/Contact: Ontario Water Works Association
#100, 922 The East Mall Dr.
Toronto, ON M9B 6K1
416-231-1555; *Fax:* 416-231-1556
Toll-Free: 866-975-0575
E-mail: waterinfo@owwa.ca
URL: www.owwa.com
Scope: Provincial
Purpose: This annual industry highlight features a full slate of plenary and technical sessions focusing on the latest in technology and research affecting drinking water from source to tap. The Trade Show consistently has more than 100 exhibitors representing the manufacturers and suppliers of products and services for the water industry.
Anticipated Attendance: 1,400+

• **Pet Industry Joint Advisory Council Western Canadian Pet Industry Trade Show 2018**
Date: April 15-16, 2018
Location: Richmond Olympic Oval
Richmond, BC
Sponsor/Contact: Pet Industry Joint Advisory Council
#14, 1010 Polytek St.
Ottawa, ON K1J 9H9
613-730-8111; *Fax:* 613-730-9111
Toll-Free: 800-667-7452
E-mail: info@pijaccanada.com
URL: www.pijaccanada.com
Scope: Provincial
Purpose: A trade show providing visitors with the opportunity to explore the BC pet market

• **Provincial Intermediate Teachers' Association Annual Whistler Conference**
Date: April 27, 2018
Location: Whistler Hilton Resort
Whistler, BC
Sponsor/Contact: Provincial Intermediate Teachers' Association
URL: www.pita.ca
Scope: Provincial

• **RIMS (Risk & Insurance Management Society Inc.) 2018 Annual Conference & Exhibition**
Date: April 15-18, 2018
Location: San Antonio, TX
Sponsor/Contact: Risk & Insurance Management Society Inc.
c/o Darius Delon, RIMS Canada Council,
Mount Royal University
4825 Mount Royal Gate SW
Calgary, AB T3E 6K6
E-mail: rcc@rimscanada.ca
URL: www.rimscanada.ca
Scope: International
Purpose: A gathering of risk professionals from around the world to share experiences

• **Rail Passengers Association 2018 Spring Advocacy Summit & Meeting**
Date: April 15-18, 2018
Location: Hilton Alexandria Old Town
Alexandria, VA USA
Sponsor/Contact: National Association of Railroad Passengers
#240, 1200 G St. NW
Washington, DC 20005
202-408-8362; *Fax:* 202-408-8287
E-mail: narp@narprail.org
URL: www.narprail.org

• **Recreation Facilities Association of BC 2018 Annual Conference**
Date: April 24-26, 2018
Location: Delta Grand Okanagan Resort & Conference Centre
Kelowna, BC
Sponsor/Contact: Recreation Facilities Association of British Columbia
P.O. Box 112
Powell River, BC V8A 4Z5
Toll-Free: 877-285-3421
E-mail: info@rfabc.com
URL: www.rfabc.com
Scope: Provincial
Purpose: Theme: "70 Years, Building for the Future"

• **Saskatchewan School Boards Association Spring 2018 General Assembly**
Date: April 12-13, 2018
Location: Hilton DoubleTree
Regina, SK
Sponsor/Contact: Saskatchewan School Boards Association
#400, 2222 - 13th Ave.
Regina, SK S4P 3M7
306-569-0750; *Fax:* 306-352-9633
E-mail: admin@saskschoolboards.ca
URL: www.saskschoolboards.ca
Scope: Provincial
Contact Information: Director, Communications: Jill Welke, E-mail: jwelke@saskschoolboards.ca, Phone: 306-569-0750, ext. 142

• **Science Writers & Communicators of Canada 2018 Conference**
Date: April 12-14, 2018
Location: Vancouver, BC
Sponsor/Contact: Science Writers & Communicators of Canada
P.O. Box 75 Stn. A
Toronto, ON M5W 1A2
Toll-Free: 800-796-8595
URL: www.sciencewriters.ca
Scope: National

• **Society of Architectural Historians Annual International Conference 2018**
Date: April 18-22, 2018
Location: Saint Paul, MN USA
Sponsor/Contact: Society of Architectural Historians
1365 North Astor St.
Chicago, IL 60610-2144

312-573-1365
E-mail: info@sah.org
URL: www.sah.org
Scope: International

- **Society of Cardiovascular Anesthesiologists 40th Annual Meeting**
Date: April 28 - May 2, 2018
Sponsor/Contact: Society of Cardiovascular Anesthesiologists
#300, 8735 West Higgins Rd.
Chicago, IL 60631
Fax: 847-375-6323
Toll-Free: 855-658-2828
E-mail: info@scahq.org
URL: www.scahq.org
Scope: International

- **Society of Cardiovascular Anesthesiologists 7th Annual Thoracic Anesthesia Symposium 2018**
Date: April 27, 2018
Sponsor/Contact: Society of Cardiovascular Anesthesiologists
#300, 8735 West Higgins Rd.
Chicago, IL 60631
Fax: 847-375-6323
Toll-Free: 855-658-2828
E-mail: info@scahq.org
URL: www.scahq.org
Scope: International

- **Society of Plastics Engineers 2018 AUTO EPCON**
Date: April 30 - May 1, 2018
Location: Troy Marriott
Troy, MI USA
Sponsor/Contact: Society of Plastics Engineers
#306, 6 Berkshire Blvd.
Bethel, CT 06801
203-775-0471; *Fax:* 203-775-8490
URL: www.4spe.org
Scope: International
Contact Information: Scott Marko, Phone: 203-740-5442

- **Society of Plastics Engineers Additives & Colors Conference Middle East 2018**
Date: April 18-19, 2018
Location: Westin Bahrain City Centre
Manama, Bahrain
Sponsor/Contact: Society of Plastics Engineers
#306, 6 Berkshire Blvd.
Bethel, CT 06801
203-775-0471; *Fax:* 203-775-8490
URL: www.4spe.org
Scope: International
Contact Information: Contact: Carine Roos, Phone: +32-498-85-07-32

- **Society of Rural Physicians of Canada Rural and Remote 2018**
Date: April 12-14, 2018
Location: St. John's, NL
Sponsor/Contact: Society of Rural Physicians of Canada
P.O. Box 893
269, rue Main
Shawville, QC J0X 2Y0
Fax: 819-647-2485
Toll-Free: 877-276-1949
E-mail: info@srpc.ca
URL: www.srpc.ca
Scope: National

- **The Instrumentation, Systems & Automation Society of America (ISA) 63rd Annual Analysis Division Symposium 2018**
Date: April 22-26, 2018
Location: Galveston Island Convention Center
Galveston, TX USA
Sponsor/Contact: The Instrumentation, Systems & Automation Society of America
P.O. Box 12277
67 T.W. Alexander Dr.
Research Triangle Park, NC 27709
919-549-8411; *Fax:* 919-549-8288
E-mail: info@isa.org
URL: www.isa.org
Scope: International
Purpose: An event sponsored by the ISA Analysis Division; includes discussion of new & innovative processes, techniques, & applications in the field
Contact Information: URL: www.adsymposium.org

- **The Society of Gynecologic Oncology of Canada 18th Annual Continuing Professional Development Meeting**
Date: April 26-28, 2018
Location: Sheraton Centre Toronto Hotel
Toronto, ON
Sponsor/Contact: Society of Gynecologic Oncologists of Canada
780 Echo Dr.
Ottawa, ON K1S 5R7
613-730-4192; *Fax:* 613-730-4314
Toll-Free: 800-561-2416
URL: www.g-o-c.org
Scope: National

- **Truck World 2018**
Date: April 19-21, 2018
Location: International Centre
Mississauga, ON
Sponsor/Contact: Ontario Trucking Association
555 Dixon Rd.
Toronto, ON M9W 1H8
416-249-7401; *Fax:* 866-713-4188
URL: www.ontruck.org
Scope: Provincial
Purpose: An event fully endorsed by the OTA; features new equipment, technology, & career opportunities for both carriers & suppliers

- **WasteEXPO 50**
Date: April 23-26, 2018
Location: Las Vegas Convention Center
Las Vegas, NV USA
Sponsor/Contact: National Waste & Recycling Association
#804, 1550 Crystal Dr.
Arlington, VA 22202
202-244-4700; *Fax:* 202-966-4824
Toll-Free: 800-424-2869
E-mail: info@wasterecycling.org
URL: wasterecycling.org

- **Water Environment Association of Ontario 2018 Annual Conference**
Date: April 15-17, 2018
Location: London, ON
Sponsor/Contact: Water Environment Association of Ontario
P.O. Box 176
Milton, ON L9T 4N9
416-410-6933; *Fax:* 416-410-1626
E-mail: weao@weao.org
URL: www.weao.org
Scope: Provincial
Purpose: A conference featuring technical sessions, a keynote speaker, a student program, an awards presentation, & networking opportunities

May

- **101st Canadian Chemistry Conference & Exhibition**
Date: May 27-31, 2018
Location: Edmonton, AB
Sponsor/Contact: Chemical Institute of Canada
#400, 222 Queen St.
Ottawa, ON K1P 5V9
613-232-6252; *Fax:* 613-232-5862
Toll-Free: 888-542-2242
E-mail: info@cheminst.ca
URL: www.cheminst.ca
Scope: National

- **14th Annual Advanced Learning in Palliative Medicine Conference**
Date: May 31 - June 2, 2018
Location: Toronto, ON
Sponsor/Contact: Canadian Society of Palliative Care Physicians
c/o Fraser Health Authority
#400, 13450 - 102 Ave.
Surrey, BC V3T 0H1
604-341-3174; *Fax:* 604-587-4644
E-mail: office@cspcp.ca
URL: www.cspcp.ca
Scope: National

- **14th Annual BC Broadband Conference**
Date: May 1-2, 2018
Location: Radisson Hotel
Richmond, BC
Sponsor/Contact: British Columbia Broadband Association
248 Reid St.
Quesnel, BC V2J 2M2
250-992-1230
E-mail: info@bcba.ca
URL: www.bcba.ca
Scope: Provincial

- **2018 12th Annual Canadian Neuroscience Meeting**
Date: May 13-16, 2018
Location: Vancouver, BC
Sponsor/Contact: Canadian Association for Neuroscience
c/o DeArmond Management
2661 Queenswood Dr.
Victoria, BC V8N 1X6
250-472-7644
E-mail: info@can-acn.org
URL: can-acn.org
Scope: National
Purpose: Neuroscientists meet to discuss neuroscience research in Canada.

- **2018 Association for Healthcare Philanthropy Convene Canada**
Date: May 16-18, 2018
Location: Ottawa, ON
Sponsor/Contact: Association for Healthcare Philanthropy
#400, 313 Park Ave.
Falls Church, VA 22046
703-532-6243; *Fax:* 703-532-7170
E-mail: ahp@ahp.org
URL: www.ahp.org
Scope: National

- **2018 BC Association of School Business Officials Annual General Meeting**
Date: May 23-25, 2018
Location: Penticton, BC
Sponsor/Contact: British Columbia Association of School Business Officials
#208, 1118 Homer St.
Vancouver, BC V6B 6L5
604-687-0595; *Fax:* 604-687-8118
E-mail: executivedirector@bcasbo.ca
URL: www.bcasbo.ca
Scope: Provincial

- **2018 BC Funeral Association Annual Conference & General Meeting**
Date: May 1-3, 2018
Location: River Rock Resort
Richmond, BC
Sponsor/Contact: British Columbia Funeral Association
#211, 2187 Oak Bay Ave.
Victoria, BC V8R 1G1
250-592-3213; *Fax:* 250-592-4362
Toll-Free: 800-665-3899
E-mail: info@bcfunerals.com
URL: www.bcfunerals.com
Scope: Provincial

- **2018 BC Surgical Society Annual Spring Meeting**
Date: May 3-5, 2018
Location: Fairmont Chateau Whistler
Whistler, BC
Sponsor/Contact: British Columbia Surgical Society
#115, 1665 West Broadway
Vancouver, BC V6J 5A4
604-638-2843; *Fax:* 604-638-2938
URL: www.bcss.ca
Scope: Provincial

- **2018 CAMPUT Annual Conference**
Date: May 8-11, 2018
Location: Royal York Hotel
Toronto, ON
Sponsor/Contact: CAMPUT
#646, 200 North Service Rd. West
Oakville, ON L6M 2Y1
905-827-5139; *Fax:* 905-827-3260
E-mail: info@camput.org
URL: www.camput.org
Scope: National
Purpose: An annual event to address current regulatory issues & energy related subjects

- **2018 Canadian Association of Career Educators & Employers National Conference**
Date: May 27-30, 2018
Location: Waterloo, ON
Sponsor/Contact: Canadian Association of Career Educators & Employers
#200, 411 Richmond St. East
Toronto, ON M5A 3S5
Fax: 416-929-5256
Toll-Free: 866-922-3303
URL: www.cacee.com
Scope: National
Anticipated Attendance: 250-350

- **2018 Canadian Association of Foodservice Professionals National Conference**
Date: May 30 - June 2, 2018
Location: Pacific Gateway Hotel
Vancouver, BC
Sponsor/Contact: Canadian Association of Foodservice Professionals
CAFP National Office
#130, 10691 Shellbridge Way
Richmond, BC V6X 2W8
604-248-0215; *Fax:* 604-270-3644
Toll-Free: 877-599-2237
E-mail: national@cafp.ca
URL: www.cafp.ca
Scope: National

- **2018 Canadian Bioethics Society Conference**

Conferences & Conventions Index

Date: May 23-25, 2018
Location: Dalhousie University
Halifax, NS
Sponsor/Contact: Canadian Bioethics Society
c/o Amy Middleton, Administrator
P.O. Box 33
Hubbards, NS B0J 1T0
E-mail: info@bioethics.ca
URL: www.bioethics.ca
Scope: National

• **2018 Canadian Board of Marine Underwriters Spring Conference**
Date: May 23-24, 2018
Location: Queen's Landing Hotel
Niagara-on-the-Lake, ON
Sponsor/Contact: Canadian Board of Marine Underwriters
#100, 2233 Argentia Rd.
Mississauga, ON L5N 2X7
905-826-4768; *Fax:* 905-826-4873
E-mail: cbmu@cbmu.com
URL: www.cbmu.com
Scope: National

• **2018 Canadian Nutrition Society Annual Conference**
Date: May 3-5, 2018
Location: Halifax Convention Centre
Halifax, NS
Sponsor/Contact: Canadian Nutrition Society
1867 La Chapelle St.
Ottawa, ON K1C 6A8
Toll-Free: 888-414-7188
E-mail: info@cns-scn.ca
URL: www.cns-scn.ca
Scope: National

• **2018 Canadian Paint and Coatings Association Annual Conference & AGM**
Date: May 2018
Location: Toronto, ON
Sponsor/Contact: Canadian Paint & Coatings Association
#608, 170 Laurier Ave. West
Ottawa, ON K1P 5V5
613-231-3604; *Fax:* 613-231-4908
E-mail: cpca@canpaint.com
URL: www.canpaint.com
Scope: National
Purpose: Paint & coatings professionals gather to discuss the state of the Canadian paint & coatings industries.

• **2018 Canadian Population Society Annual Meeting**
Date: May 30 - June 1, 2018
Location: University of Regina
Regina, SK
Sponsor/Contact: Canadian Population Society
520-17 Aberdeen St.
Ottawa, ON K1S 3J3
E-mail: admin@canpopsoc.ca
URL: www.canpopsoc.ca
Scope: National

• **2018 Conference of the Hungarian Studies Association of Canada**
Date: May 26-28, 2018
Location: University of Regina
Regina, SK
Sponsor/Contact: Hungarian Studies Association of Canada
c/o Margit Lovrics
#1804, 75 Graydon Hall Dr.
Toronto, ON M3A 3M5
URL: www.hungarianstudies.org

Purpose: Held in conjunction with the Congress of the Humanities & Social Sciences

• **2018 Manitoba Association of Fire Chiefs Annual Conference & Trade Show**
Date: May 31 - June 2, 2018
Location: Selkirk, MB
Sponsor/Contact: Manitoba Association of Fire Chiefs
P.O. Box 1208
Portage la Prairie, MB R1N 3J9
204-857-6249
E-mail: mb.firechiefs@mymts.net
URL: mafc.ca
Scope: Provincial

• **2018 Manitoba Association of Parent Councils AGM & Conference**
Date: May 5, 2018
Location: Victoria Inn Hotel & Convention Centre
Winnipeg, MB
Sponsor/Contact: Manitoba Association of Parent Councils
#1005, 401 York Ave.
Winnipeg, MB R3C 0P8
204-956-1770; *Fax:* 204-948-2855
Toll-Free: 877-290-4702
E-mail: info@mapc.mb.ca
URL: www.mapc.mb.ca
Scope: Provincial

• **2018 Ontario Association of Architects Conference**
Date: May 23-25, 2018
Location: Metro Toronto Convention Centre & Delta Toronto
Toronto, ON
Sponsor/Contact: Ontario Association of Architects
111 Moatfield Dr.
Toronto, ON M3B 3L6
416-449-6898; *Fax:* 416-449-5756
Toll-Free: 800-565-2724
E-mail: oaamail@oaa.on.ca
URL: www.oaa.on.ca
Scope: Provincial

• **2018 Orchestras Canada National Conference**
Date: May 30 - June 1, 2018
Location: Calgary, AB
Sponsor/Contact: Orchestras Canada
P.O. Box 2386
Peterborough, ON K9J 2Y8
416-366-8834
Toll-Free: 877-809-7288
E-mail: info@oc.ca
URL: www.orchestrascanada.org
Scope: National
Contact Information: Executive Director: Katherine Carlton, *E-mail:* katherine@oc.ca

• **2018 Volunteer Management Professionals of Canada National Conference**
Date: May 30 - June 1, 2018
Location: Winnipeg, MB
Sponsor/Contact: Volunteer Management Professionals of Canada
#1101, 60 Richmond St. East
Toronto, ON M5C 1N8
URL: www.vmpc.ca
Scope: National

• **22nd Vision Quest Conference & Trade Show 2018**
Date: May 15-17, 2018

Location: RBC Convention Centre
Winnipeg, MB
Sponsor/Contact: Community Futures Manitoba Inc.
#559, 167 Lombard Ave.
Winnipeg, MB R3B 0V3
204-943-2905; *Fax:* 204-956-9363
E-mail: info@cfmanitoba.ca
URL: www.cfmanitoba.ca
Scope: Provincial
Purpose: An annual event for business leaders, innovators, & entrepreneurs, from Manitoba, Saskatchewan, Alberta, northern Ontario, Nunavut, Northwest Territories, & the United States, to discuss & promote Aboriginal business & community development, featuring interactive workshops, motivational keynote presentations from business leaders, a trade show with more than 80 booths, & social & networking events
Anticipated Attendance: 1,000+
Contact Information: www.vqconference.com

• **31st Canadian Down Syndrome Conference**
Date: May 18-20, 2018
Location: Hamilton, ON
Sponsor/Contact: Canadian Down Syndrome Society
#103, 2003 - 14 St. NW
Calgary, AB T2M 3N4
403-270-8500; *Fax:* 403-270-8291
Toll-Free: 800-883-5608
URL: www.cdss.ca
Scope: National

• **34th Annual Meeting of the Canadian Biomaterials Society 2018**
Date: May 16-19, 2018
Location: Victoria, BC
Sponsor/Contact: Canadian Biomaterials Society
URL: www.biomaterials.ca

• **41st Annual BC Care Providers Association Conference**
Date: May 27-29, 2018
Location: Whistler, BC
Sponsor/Contact: British Columbia Care Providers Association
Metrotower I
#738, 4710 Kingsway
Burnaby, BC V5H 4M2
604-736-4233; *Fax:* 604-736-4266
E-mail: info@bccare.ca
URL: www.bccare.ca
Scope: Provincial

• **43rd Canadian Cartographic Association Conference 2018**
Date: May 30 - June 2, 2018
Location: Nova Scotia Community College
Lawrencetown, NS
Sponsor/Contact: Canadian Cartographic Association
c/o Paul Heersink
39 Wales Ave.
Markham, ON L3P 2C4
Fax: 416-446-1639
E-mail: treasurer@cca-acc.org
URL: www.cca-acc.org
Scope: National
Purpose: Theme: "Community Mapping: Place-Making Through Maps"

• **4th Canadian Conference on Positive Psychology**
Date: May 23-25, 2018

Location: University of Toronto
Toronto, ON
Sponsor/Contact: Canadian Positive Psychology Association
#703, 1 Eglinton Ave. East
Toronto, ON M4P 3A1
416-481-8930
E-mail: info@positivepsychologycanada.com
URL: www.positivepsychologycanada.com
Scope: National

• **95th Canadian Paediatric Society Annual Conference 2018**
Date: May 30 - June 2, 2018
Location: Québec City Convention Centre
Québec, QC
Sponsor/Contact: Canadian Paediatric Society
#100, 2305 St. Laurent Blvd.
Ottawa, ON K1G 4J8
613-526-9397; *Fax:* 613-526-3332
URL: www.cps.ca
Scope: National
Contact Information: Phone: 613-526-9397 ext. 248, Email: meetings@cps.ca, www.annualconference.cps.ca

• **AMCO Workshop 2018**
Date: May 31, 2018
Location: Niagara District Airport
Niagara-on-the-Lake, ON
Sponsor/Contact: Airport Management Council of Ontario
#5, 50 Terminal St.
North Bay, ON P1B 8G2
705-474-1080; *Fax:* 705-474-4073
Toll-Free: 877-636-2626
E-mail: amco@amco.on.ca
URL: www.amco.on.ca
Purpose: Informative speakers, round table discussions, tours, demonstrations & a half-day live emergency exercise

• **ARMA Canada Conference 2018**
Date: May 28-30, 2018
Location: Hyatt Regency
Vancouver, BC
Sponsor/Contact: ARMA International
#450, 11880 College Blvd.
Overland Park, KS 66215
913-341-3808; *Fax:* 913-341-3742
Toll-Free: 800-422-2762
E-mail: headquarters@armaintl.org
URL: www.arma.org
Contact Information: E-mail: conference@armaintl.org

• **ASM International 29th AeroMat Conference & Exposition 2018**
Date: May 7-9, 2018
Location: Gaylord Palms Resort & Convention Center
Orlando, FL USA
Sponsor/Contact: ASM International
9639 Kinsman Rd.
Materials Park, OH 44073-0002
440-338-5151; *Fax:* 440-338-4634
Toll-Free: 800-336-5152
E-mail: memberservicecenter@asminternational.org
URL: www.asminternational.org
Scope: International

• **ASM International Conference on Shape Memory & Superelastic Technologies**
Date: May 17, 2018
Location: Clayton Hotel Galway
Galway, Ireland

Conferences & Conventions Index

Sponsor/Contact: ASM International
9639 Kinsman Rd.
Materials Park, OH 44073-0002
440-338-5151; Fax: 440-338-4634
Toll-Free: 800-336-5152
E-mail: memberservicecenter@asminternational.org
URL: www.asminternational.org
Scope: International

- **ASM International Thermal Spray Conference & Exposition**
Date: May 7-10, 2018
Location: Gaylord Palms Resort & Convention Center
Orlando, FL USA
Sponsor/Contact: ASM International
9639 Kinsman Rd.
Materials Park, OH 44073-0002
440-338-5151; Fax: 440-338-4634
Toll-Free: 800-336-5152
E-mail: memberservicecenter@asminternational.org
URL: www.asminternational.org
Scope: International

- **Academic Pediatric Association 2018 Quality Improvement & Implementation Science Conference**
Date: May 4, 2018
Sponsor/Contact: Academic Pediatric Association
6728 Old McLean Village Dr.
McLean, VA 22101
703-556-9222; Fax: 703-556-8729
E-mail: info@academicpeds.org
URL: www.academicpeds.org
Scope: International

- **Administrative Sciences Association of Canada 2018 Conference**
Date: May 27-29, 2018
Location: Ryerson University
Toronto, ON
Sponsor/Contact: Administrative Sciences Association of Canada
c/o Thompson Rivers University
900 McGill Rd.
Kamloops, BC V2C 0C8
250-828-5000
URL: www.asac.ca
Scope: National

- **African Literature Association 2018 Conference**
Date: May 23-26, 2018
Location: Marriott Wardman Park
Washington, DC USA
Sponsor/Contact: African Literature Association
c/o Hobart & William Smith Colleges
300 Pulteney St.
Geneva, NY 14456
315-781-3491; Fax: 315-781-3822
URL: www.africanlit.org
Scope: International
Purpose: Theme: "The Environments of African Literature"

- **Alberta Chambers of Commerce 2018 AGM & Policy Plenary Session**
Date: May 24-26, 2018
Location: Grande Prairie, AB
Sponsor/Contact: Alberta Chambers of Commerce
#1808, 10025 - 102A Ave.
Edmonton, AB T5J 2Z2
780-425-4180; Fax: 780-429-1061
Toll-Free: 800-272-8854
E-mail: tacom@abchamber.ca
URL: www.abchamber.ca
Scope: Provincial

- **Alberta Fire Chiefs Association 71st Annual Conference & Trade Show 2018**
Date: May 27-30, 2018
Location: Edmonton EXPO Centre
Edmonton, AB
Sponsor/Contact: Alberta Fire Chiefs Association
780-719-7939; Fax: 780-892-3333
URL: www.afca.ab.ca
Scope: Provincial

- **Alberta Occupational Health Nurses Association 2018 Annual Professional Development Conference**
Date: May 30 - June 1, 2018
Location: Banff Centre for Arts & Creativity
Banff, AB
Sponsor/Contact: Alberta Occupational Health Nurses Association
c/o College & Association of Registered Nurses of Alberta (CARNA)
11620 - 168 St.
Edmonton, AB T5M 4A6
Fax: 866-877-0228
Toll-Free: 888-566-3343
E-mail: info@aohna.org
URL: aohna.org
Scope: National
Contact Information: E-mail: info@aohna.org

- **Alberta Public Housing Administrators' Association Spring AGM & Education Sessions 2018**
Date: May 2-3, 2018
Sponsor/Contact: Alberta Public Housing Administrators' Association
14220 - 109 Ave. NW
Edmonton, AB T5N 4B3
780-498-1971; Fax: 780-464-7039
URL: www.aphaa.org
Scope: Provincial

- **American Industrial Hygiene Conference & Exposition 2018**
Date: May 19-24, 2018
Location: Philadelphia, PA USA
Sponsor/Contact: American Industrial Hygiene Association
#777, 3141 Fairview Park Dr.
Falls Church, VA 22042
703-849-8888; Fax: 703-207-3561
URL: www.aiha.org
Scope: International

- **American Society of Colon & Rectal Surgeons 2018 Annual Scientific Meeting**
Date: May 19-23, 2018
Location: Omni Nashville Hotel
Nashville, TN USA
Sponsor/Contact: American Society of Colon & Rectal Surgeons
#550, 85 West Algonquin Rd.
Arlington Heights, IL 60005
847-290-9184; Fax: 847-427-9656
E-mail: ascrs@fascrs.org
URL: www.fascrs.org
Scope: International
Purpose: Courses, workshops, symposia, lectures, & scientific sessions for surgeons
Anticipated Attendance: 1,500+

- **Animal Care Expo 2018**
Date: May 14-17, 2018
Location: Kansas City, MO USA
Sponsor/Contact: The Humane Society of the United States
2100 L St. NW
Washington, DC 20037
202-452-1100
Toll-Free: 866-720-2676
E-mail: donorcare@humanesociety.org
URL: www.humanesociety.org
Scope: National
Purpose: An educational conference & international trade show
Contact Information: URL: animalsheltering.org/expo

- **Animal Nutrition Association of Canada 2018 Animal Nutrition Conference of Canada**
Date: May 2-3, 2018
Location: Chateau Lacombe Hotel
Edmonton, AB
Sponsor/Contact: Animal Nutrition Association of Canada
#1301, 150 Metcalfe St.
Ottawa, ON K2P 1P1
613-241-6421; Fax: 613-241-7970
E-mail: info@anacan.org
URL: www.anacan.org
Scope: National

- **Antique Automobile Club of America 2018 Annual Grand National Meet**
Date: May 31 - June 2, 2018
Location: Greensburg, PA USA
Sponsor/Contact: Antique Automobile Club of America
P.O. Box 417
501 West Governor Rd.
Hershey, PA 17033
717-534-1910; Fax: 717-534-9101
E-mail: aaca1@aaca.org
URL: www.aaca.org
Scope: International

- **Architectural Institute of British Columbia Annual Conference 2018**
Date: May 7-9, 2018
Location: Vancouver Convention Centre West
Vancouver, BC
Sponsor/Contact: Architectural Institute of British Columbia
#100, 440 Cambie St.
Vancouver, BC V6B 2N5
604-683-8588; Fax: 604-683-8568
Toll-Free: 800-667-0753
E-mail: info@aibc.ca
URL: www.aibc.ca
Scope: Provincial
Purpose: Theme: "Spaces Between"
Contact Information: www.conference.aibc.ca

- **Architectural Woodwork Manufacturers Association of Canada 2018 Convention & Annual General Meeting**
Date: May 31 - June 2, 2018
Location: Fairmont Hotel Macdonald
Edmonton, AB
Sponsor/Contact: Architectural Woodwork Manufacturers Association of Canada
P.O. Box 36525 Stn. MacTaggart
Edmonton, AB T6R 0T4
403-981-7300
E-mail: info@awmac.com
URL: www.awmac.com
Scope: National

- **Association du camionnage du Québec inc. 67e congrès annuel 2018**
Date: May 3-5, 2018
Location: Fairmont Le Manoir Richelieu
La Malbaie, QC
Sponsor/Contact: Association du camionnage du Québec inc.
#200, 6450, rue Notre-Dame ouest
Montréal, QC H4C 1V4
514-932-0377; Fax: 514-932-1358
E-mail: info@carrefour-acq.org
URL: www.carrefour-acq.org
Scope: Provincial
Contact Information: Coordonatrice, événements: Brigitte Laguë, Courriel: blague@carrefour-acq.org

- **Association for Canadian Jewish Studies Annual Conference 2018**
Date: May 13-15, 2018
Location: Montréal, QC
Sponsor/Contact: Association for Canadian Jewish Studies
c/o Institute for Canadian Jewish Studies, Concordia University
1455, boul de Maisonneuve ouest, #SB215
Montréal, QC H3G 1M8
514-848-2424; Fax: 514-848-4541
URL: acjs-aejc.ca
Scope: National
Purpose: Allows members to share scholarly research on Canadian Jewish life, culture, & history

- **Association of Canadian Search, Employment & Staffing Services Conference 2018**
Date: May 15-17, 2018
Location: Fallsview Casino Resort
Niagara Falls, ON
Sponsor/Contact: Association of Canadian Search, Employment & Staffing Services
#100, 2233 Argentia Rd.
Mississauga, ON L5N 2X7
905-826-6869; Fax: 905-826-4873
Toll-Free: 888-232-4962
E-mail: acsess@acsess.org
URL: www.acsess.org
Scope: National
Purpose: Theme: "Leading Canada to Work"

- **Association of Medical Microbiology & Infectious Disease Canada 2018 Annual Conference**
Date: May 2-5, 2018
Location: Sheraton Vancouver Wall Centre
Vancouver, BC
Sponsor/Contact: Association of Medical Microbiology & Infectious Disease Canada
192 Bank St.
Ottawa, ON K2P 1W8
613-260-3233; Fax: 613-260-3235
E-mail: communications@ammi.ca
URL: www.ammi.ca
Scope: National
Purpose: A yearly professional development event for AMMI members; features workshops on a variety of topics
Contact Information: Coordinator, Meetings: Paul Glover, E-mail: paul@ammi.ca

- **Association of School Business Officials of Alberta Conference 2018**
Date: May 6-9, 2018
Location: Alberta
Sponsor/Contact: Association of School Business Officials of Alberta
#1200, 9925 - 109 St.
Edmonton, AB T5K 2J8
780-451-7103; Fax: 780-482-5659
URL: www.asboa.ab.ca
Scope: Provincial

Conferences & Conventions Index

- **Association québécoise des infirmières et intervenants en recherche clinique Congrès 2018**
Date: May 2-4, 2018
Sponsor/Contact: Association québécoise des infirmières et intervenants en recherche clinique
4200, rue Molson
Montréal, QC H1Y 4V4
514-935-2501; *Fax:* 514-935-1799
E-mail: info@aqiirc.qc.ca
URL: aqiirc.qc.ca
Scope: Provincial

- **Automotive Recyclers Association of Atlantic Canada 2018 Annual Meeting & Trade Show**
Date: May 25-26, 2018
Location: Atlantica Hotel Halifax
Halifax, NS
Sponsor/Contact: Automotive Recyclers Association of Atlantic Canada
519-858-8761
E-mail: araac@execulink.com
URL: araac.ca
Scope: Provincial

- **BC Association of Broadcasters 71st Annual Conference**
Date: May 15-17, 2018
Location: Manteo Resort
Kelowna, BC
Sponsor/Contact: British Columbia Association of Broadcasters
URL: www.bcab.ca
Scope: Provincial

- **BC Pharmacy Association Annual Conference 2018**
Date: May 24-26, 2018
Location: Fairmont Empress
Victoria, BC
Sponsor/Contact: British Columbia Pharmacy Association
#1530, 1200 West 73rd Ave.
Vancouver, BC V6P 6G5
604-261-2092; *Fax:* 604-261-2097
Toll-Free: 800-663-2840
E-mail: info@bcpharmacy.ca
URL: www.bcpharmacy.ca
Scope: National
Anticipated Attendance: 300+

- **Boys and Girls Clubs of Canada 2018 National Conference**
Date: May 1-4, 2018
Location: Delta Prince Edward
Charlottetown, PE
Sponsor/Contact: Boys & Girls Clubs of Canada
National Office
#400, 2005 Sheppard Ave. East
Toronto, ON M2J 5B4
905-477-7272; *Fax:* 416-640-5331
E-mail: info@bgccan.com
URL: www.bgccan.com
Scope: National

- **British Columbia Historical Federation 2018 Conference & Annual General Meeting**
Date: May 24-27, 2018
Location: Nakusp, BC
Sponsor/Contact: British Columbia Historical Federation
P.O. Box 5254 Stn. B
Victoria, BC V8R 6N4
E-mail: info@bchistory.ca
URL: www.bchistory.ca
Scope: Provincial
Contact Information: E-mail: info@bchistory.ca

- **British Columbia Hospice Palliative Care Association 2018 Conference**
Date: May 25-26, 2018
Location: British Columbia
Sponsor/Contact: British Columbia Hospice Palliative Care Association
#1100, 1200 West 73rd Ave.
Vancouver, BC V6P 6G5
604-267-7024; *Fax:* 604-267-7026
Toll-Free: 877-410-6297
E-mail: office@bchpca.org
URL: www.bchpca.org
Scope: Provincial
Purpose: An annual meeting of members, with guest speakers, exhibits, regional meetings, the presentation of awards, & networking sessions
Contact Information: Assistant, Administration: Bonnie Atwood, E-mail: office@bchpca.org

- **British Columbia Nurses' Union Convention 2018**
Date: May 1-3, 2018
Location: Hyatt Regency Vancouver
Vancouver, BC
Sponsor/Contact: British Columbia Nurses' Union
4060 Regent St.
Burnaby, BC V5C 6P5
604-433-2268; *Fax:* 604-433-7945
Toll-Free: 800-663-9991
URL: www.bcnu.org
Scope: Provincial

- **CAILBA 2018 National Conference & AGM**
Date: May 28-30, 2018
Location: Fairmont le Château Frontenac
Québec, QC
Sponsor/Contact: Canadian Association of Independent Life Brokerage Agencies
#1300, 60 Adelaide St. East
Toronto, ON M5C 3E4
416-548-4223
E-mail: info@cailba.com
URL: www.cailba.com
Scope: National

- **CAUCE 2018: The 65th Annual Conference & General Meeting of the Canadian Association for University Continuing Education**
Date: May 29-31, 2018
Location: Dalhousie University
Halifax, NS
Sponsor/Contact: Canadian Association for University Continuing Education
c/o Centre for Continuing & Distance Education, U. of Saskatchewan
#464, 221 Cumberland Ave. North
Saskatoon, SK S7N 1M3
306-966-5604; *Fax:* 306-966-5590
E-mail: cauce.secratariat@usask.ca
URL: www.cauce-aepuc.ca
Scope: National
Purpose: Theme: "Over the Horizon: The Future of Work & Learning Opportunities for Continuing Education"

- **CURAC/ARUCC 2018**
Date: May 23-25, 2018
Location: Dalhousie University
Halifax, NS
Sponsor/Contact: College & University Retiree Associations of Canada
255 Morrison Rd.
Kitchener, ON N2A 2W6
E-mail: curac@curac.ca
URL: www.curac.ca
Scope: National
Purpose: Hosted by the Association of Dalhousie Retirees & Pensioners
Contact Information: E-mail: adrp@dal.ca

- **Canadian Aeronautics & Space Institute ASTRO 2018 Conference**
Date: May 15-17, 2018
Location: Delta Québec
Québec, QC
Sponsor/Contact: Canadian Aeronautics & Space Institute
#104, 350 Terry Fox Dr.
Ottawa, ON K2K 2W5
613-591-8787; *Fax:* 613-591-7291
E-mail: casi@casi.ca
URL: www.casi.ca
Scope: International
Contact Information: Phone: 613-591-8787; E-mail: astro@casi.ca

- **Canadian Association for Clinical Microbiology and Infectious Diseases Annual Conference 2018**
Date: May 2-5, 2018
Location: Vancouver, BC
Sponsor/Contact: Canadian Association for Clinical Microbiology & Infectious Diseases
c/o National Microbiology Laboratory
1015 Arlington St.
Winnipeg, MB R3E 3R2
Fax: 204-789-2097
URL: www.cacmid.ca
Scope: National

- **Canadian Association for Commonwealth Literature & Language Studies Conference 2018**
Date: May 26-28, 2018
Location: University of Regina
Regina, SK
Sponsor/Contact: Canadian Association for Commonwealth Literature & Language Studies
c/o Kristina Fagan, Department of English, University of Saskatchewan
9 Campus Dr.
Saskatoon, SK S7N 5A5
URL: www.caclals.ca
Scope: National
Purpose: Keynote speakers, roundtables, sessions, & readings

- **Canadian Association for Conservation 2018 44th Annual Conference**
Date: May 8-12, 2018
Location: Kingston, ON
Sponsor/Contact: Canadian Association for Conservation of Cultural Property
c/o Danielle Allard
#419, 207 Bank St.
Ottawa, ON K2P 2N2
613-231-3977; *Fax:* 613-231-4406
E-mail: coordinator@cac-accr.com
URL: www.cac-accr.ca
Scope: National
Purpose: Educational sessions & a tradeshow

- **Canadian Association for Enterostomal Therapy National Conference 2018**
Date: May 3-6, 2018
Location: Victoria, BC
Sponsor/Contact: Canadian Association for Enterostomal Therapy
66 Leopolds Dr.
Ottawa, ON K1V 7E3
Fax: 613-834-6351
Toll-Free: 888-739-5072
E-mail: office@caet.ca
URL: www.caet.ca
Scope: National
Purpose: Theme: "Turn Knowledge into Action: Education in Specialized Wound, Ostomy & Continence Care"

- **Canadian Association for Health Services and Policy Research 2018 Conference**
Date: May 29-31, 2018
Location: Hotel Bonaventure
Montréal, QC
Sponsor/Contact: Canadian Association for Health Services & Policy Research
292 Somerset St. West
Ottawa, ON K2P 0J6
613-288-9239; *Fax:* 613-599-7805
E-mail: info@cahspr.ca
URL: www.cahspr.ca
Scope: National
Purpose: Theme: "Shaping the Future of Canada's Health Systems"

- **Canadian Association for Latin American & Caribbean Studies 2018 Congress**
Date: May 16-18, 2018
Location: Université du Québec à Montréal
Montréal, QC
Sponsor/Contact: Canadian Association for Latin American & Caribbean Studies
c/o Juan Pablo Crespo Vasquez, York Research Tower, York University
#8-17, 4700 Keele St.
Toronto, ON M3J 1P3
416-736-2100; *Fax:* 519-971-3610
E-mail: calacs@yorku.ca
URL: www.can-latam.org
Scope: National

- **Canadian Association for Pharmacy Distribution Management 2018 Annual Conference**
Date: May 5-9, 2018
Location: The Diplomat Beach Resort
Hollywood, FL USA
Sponsor/Contact: Canadian Association for Pharmacy Distribution Management
#301A, 3800 Steeles Ave. West
Woodbridge, ON L4L 4G9
905-265-1706; *Fax:* 905-265-9372
URL: www.capdm.ca
Scope: National

- **Canadian Association for Social Work Education Conference 2018**
Date: May 28-31, 2018
Location: University of Regina
Regina, SK
Sponsor/Contact: Canadian Association for Social Work Education
#410, 383 Parkdale Ave.
Ottawa, ON K1Y 4R4
613-792-1953
Toll-Free: 888-342-6522
E-mail: admin@caswe-acfts.ca
URL: caswe-acfts.ca
Scope: National
Purpose: Theme: "Honouring Reconciliation & Respecting our Differences"

- **Canadian Association for Teacher Education 2018 Annual Conference**
Date: May 2018

Location: University of Regina
Regina, SK
Sponsor/Contact: Canadian Association for Teacher Education
c/o Canadian Society for the Study of Education
#204, 260 Dalhousie St.
Ottawa, ON K1N 7E4
613-241-0018; *Fax:* 613-241-0019
URL: cate-acfe.ca
Scope: National

- **Canadian Association for Theatre Research 2018 Conference**
Date: May 29 - June 1, 2018
Location: Kingston, ON
Sponsor/Contact: Canadian Association for Theatre Research
E-mail: catr.membership@gmail.com
URL: www.catracrt.ca
Scope: National

- **Canadian Association for the Study of Adult Education 2018 Conference**
Date: May 27-31, 2018
Location: University of Regina
Regina, SK
Sponsor/Contact: Canadian Association for the Study of Adult Education
#204, 260 Dalhousie St.
Ottawa, ON K1N 7E4
613-241-0018; *Fax:* 613-241-0019
E-mail: casae.aceea@csse.ca
URL: www.casae-aceea.ca
Scope: National

- **Canadian Association for the Study of Discourse & Writing Annual Conference 2018**
Date: May 26-28, 2018
Location: University of Regina
Regina, SK
Sponsor/Contact: Canadian Association for the Study of Discourse & Writing
c/o W. Brock MacDonald, Woodsworth College, University of Toronto
119 St. George St.
Toronto, ON M5S 1A9
URL: casdwacr.wordpress.com
Scope: National
Purpose: Held during the Congress of the Social Sciences & Humanities; involves opportunities for speakers to hold lengthy discussions & forge networking relationships

- **Canadian Association of Journalists 2018 Annual Conference**
Date: May 4-5, 2018
Location: Hyatt Regency Toronto
Toronto, ON
Sponsor/Contact: Canadian Association of Journalists
P.O. Box 117 Stn. F
Toronto, ON MRY 2L4
647-968-2393
URL: www.caj.ca
Scope: National

- **Canadian Association of Labour Media Conference 2018**
Date: May 10-12, 2018
Location: Lord Nelson Hotel
Halifax, NS
Sponsor/Contact: Canadian Association of Labour Media
P.O. Box 10624 Stn. Bloorcourt
Toronto, ON M6H 4H9
581-983-4397; *Fax:* 581-983-4397
E-mail: editor@calm.ca
URL: www.calm.ca

- **Canadian Association of MAiD Assessors & Providers 2018 Medical Assistance in Dying Conference**
Date: May 4-5, 2018
Location: Shaw Centre
Ottawa, ON
Sponsor/Contact: Canadian Association of MAiD Assessors & Providers
326 - 1964 Fort St.
Victoria, BC V8R 6R3
E-mail: camap.web@gmail.com
URL: www.camapcanada.ca
Scope: National
Contact Information:
www.maidconference.ca

- **Canadian Association of Municipal Administrators 2018 47th Annual Conference & Annual General Meeting**
Date: May 28-30, 2018
Location: Fredericton Convention Centre
Fredericton, NB
Sponsor/Contact: Canadian Association of Municipal Administrators
P.O. Box 128 Stn. A
Fredericton, NB E3B 4Y2
Toll-Free: 866-771-2262
URL: www.camacam.ca
Scope: National
Purpose: Information & a trade show for senior managers from Canadian municipalities throughout Canada

- **Canadian Association of Music Libraries, Archives & Documentation Centres 2018 Conference**
Date: May 26 - June 1, 2018
Location: University of Regina
Regina, SK
Sponsor/Contact: Canadian Association of Music Libraries, Archives & Documentation Centres
Edward Johnson Bldg., University of Toronto
80 Queen's Park Cres.
Toronto, ON M5S 2C5
URL: caml-acbm.org
Scope: National
Purpose: A national meeting covering issues & information of interest to music librarians, archivists, & researchers

- **Canadian Association of Music Therapists 2018 Conference**
Date: May 24-26, 2018
Location: Sheraton Hotel Newfoundland
St. John's, NL
Sponsor/Contact: Canadian Association of Music Therapists
#5, 1124 Gainsborough Rd.
London, ON N6H 5N1
Fax: 519-641-0431
Toll-Free: 800-996-2268
E-mail: info@musictherapy.ca
URL: www.musictherapy.ca
Scope: National
Purpose: Theme: "Keeping Us Anchored: Music Therapy, Connection & Culture"

- **Canadian Association of Pharmacy Technicians 2018 Professional Development Conference**
Date: May 4-6, 2018
Location: Whistler, BC
Sponsor/Contact: Canadian Association of Pharmacy Technicians
#164, 9-6975 Meadowvale Town Centre Circle
Mississauga, ON L5N 2V7
416-410-1142; *Fax:* 416-410-1142
URL: www.capt.ca

Scope: National

- **Canadian Association of Pharmacy in Oncology Conference 2018**
Date: May 3-6, 2018
Location: Hilton Lac-Leamy
Gatineau, QC
Sponsor/Contact: Canadian Association of Pharmacy in Oncology
c/o Sea to Sky Meeting Management Inc.
#206, 201 Bewicke Ave.
Winnipeg, MB V7M 3M7
778-338-4142; *Fax:* 704-984-6434
E-mail: info@capho.org
URL: www.capho.ca
Scope: National

- **Canadian Association of Physical Medicine & Rehabilitation 66th Annual Scientific Meeting**
Date: May 30 - June 3, 2018
Location: Whitehorse, YT
Sponsor/Contact: Canadian Association of Physical Medicine & Rehabilitation
#310, 4 Cataraqui St.
Kingston, ON K7K 1Z7
613-507-0480; *Fax:* 866-531-0626
E-mail: info@capmr.ca
URL: www.capmr.ca
Scope: National

- **Canadian Association of Psychosocial Oncology 2018 Conference**
Date: May 30 - June 1, 2018
Location: Toronto, ON
Sponsor/Contact: Canadian Association of Psychosocial Oncology
#1, 189 Queen St. East
Toronto, ON M5A 1S2
416-968-0207; *Fax:* 416-968-6818
E-mail: capo@funnel.ca
URL: www.capo.ca
Scope: National
Purpose: Theme: "Tailored & Targeted Interventions: The New Psychosocial Frontier"

- **Canadian Association of Research Administrators 2018 Annual Conference**
Date: May 27-30, 2018
Location: Westin Ottawa
Ottawa, ON
Sponsor/Contact: Canadian Association of Research Administrators
#1710, 350 Albert St.
Ottawa, ON K1R 1B1
289-244-3744
E-mail: webinars@cara-acaar.ca
URL: cara-acaar.ca
Scope: National
Purpose: Theme: "Research Administration: Resilience in a Time of Change"
Contact Information: Manager, Professional Development & Membership Services: Nina Darkeff, *E-mail:* conference@cara-acaar.ca, *Phone:* 289-244-3744

- **Canadian Association of Slavists 2018 Annual Conference**
Date: May 26-28, 2018
Location: University of Regina
Regina, SK
Sponsor/Contact: Canadian Association of Slavists
Alumni Hall, Dept. of History & Classics, University of Alberta
#2, 28 Tory Bldg.
Edmonton, AB T6G 2H4

780-492-2566; *Fax:* 780-492-9125
E-mail: csp@ulberta.ca
URL: www.ualberta.ca/~csp/cas/contact.html
Scope: National
Purpose: Annual conference held in conjunction with yearly congress of the Canadian Federation for the Humanities and Social Sciences.

- **Canadian Association of Student Financial Aid Administrators 2018 Annual Conference**
Date: May 28-30, 2018
Sponsor/Contact: Canadian Association of Student Financial Aid Administrators
c/o Treasurer, University of Manitoba
422 University Centre
Winnipeg, MB R3T 2N2
204-474-9532
E-mail: info@casfaa.ca
URL: www.casfaa.ca
Scope: National

- **Canadian Association of Wound Care 2018 Spring Conference**
Date: May 11-12, 2018
Location: RBC Convention Centre
Winnipeg, MB
Sponsor/Contact: Canadian Association of Wound Care
#608, 920 Yonge St.
Toronto, ON M4W 3C7
416-485-2292; *Fax:* 416-485-2291
Toll-Free: 866-474-0125
E-mail: info@cawc.net
URL: www.cawc.net
Scope: National

- **Canadian Athletic Therapists Association 52nd National Conference**
Date: May 31 - June 2, 2018
Location: Québec, QC
Sponsor/Contact: Canadian Athletic Therapists Association
#300, 400 - 5th Ave. SW
Calgary, AB T2P 0L6
403-509-2282; *Fax:* 403-509-2280
Toll-Free: 888-509-2282
E-mail: info@athletictherapy.org
URL: www.athletictherapy.org
Scope: National

- **Canadian Aviation Historical Society (CAHS) National Convention and Annual General Meeting**
Date: May 30 - June 3, 2018
Location: Sheraton Cavalier Hotel
Calgary, AB
Sponsor/Contact: Canadian Aviation Historical Society
P.O. Box 2700 Stn. D
Ottawa, ON K1P 5W7
URL: www.cahs.ca
Purpose: Featuring speaker sessions, meet & greets, and a field trip to participate in CHAA's Fly Day

- **Canadian Church Press/Association of Roman Catholic Communicators of Canada Convention 2018**
Date: May 2-4, 2018
Location: Sheraton Hamilton
Hamilton, ON
Sponsor/Contact: Canadian Church Press
8 MacDonald Ave.
Hamilton, ON L8P 4N5
905-521-2240
E-mail: cdnchurchpress@hotmail.com
URL: www.canadianchurchpress.com

Conferences & Conventions Index

- **Canadian Comparative Literature Association 2018 Congress**
Date: May 26 - June 1, 2018
Location: Regina, SK
Sponsor/Contact: Canadian Comparative Literature Association
c/o Markus Reisenleitner, Department of Humanities, York University
217 Vanier College
Toronto, ON M3H 1P3
URL: complit.ca
Scope: National
Purpose: Theme: "Gathering Diversities"

- **Canadian Council for Small Business & Entrepreneurship 2018 Conference**
Date: May 3-5, 2018
Location: Dalhousie University
Halifax, NS
Sponsor/Contact: Canadian Council for Small Business & Entrepreneurship
c/o Pat Sargeant, Women's Enterprise Centre of Manitoba
#100, 207 Donald St.
Winnipeg, MB R3C 1M5
204-988-1873; Fax: 902-988-1871
E-mail: ccsbesecretariat@wecm.ca
URL: www.ccsbe.org
Scope: National

- **Canadian Council of Cardiovascular Nurses 2018 Spring Nursing Conference & Annual General Meeting**
Date: May 25-26, 2018
Location: DoubleTree Fallsview Resort & Spa
Niagara Falls, ON
Sponsor/Contact: Canadian Council of Cardiovascular Nurses
#202, 300 March Rd.
Ottawa, ON K2K 2E2
613-599-9210; Fax: 613-595-1155
E-mail: info@cccn.ca
URL: www.cccn.ca
Scope: National

- **Canadian Counselling and Psychotherapy Association 2018 Conference**
Date: May 10-13, 2018
Location: Delta Hotel
Winnipeg, MB
Sponsor/Contact: Canadian Counselling & Psychotherapy Association
#6, 203 Colonnade Rd. South
Ottawa, ON K2E 7K3
613-237-1099; Fax: 613-237-9786
Toll-Free: 877-765-5565
URL: www.ccpa-accp.ca
Scope: National
Anticipated Attendance: 5000+
Contact Information:
www.ccpa-accp.ca/continuing-education/annual-conference

- **Canadian Environmental Grantmakers' Network 2018 Conference**
Date: May 15-17, 2018
Location: The Banff Centre
Banff, AB
Sponsor/Contact: Canadian Environmental Grantmakers' Network
c/o Foundation House
2 St. Clair Ave. East
Toronto, ON M4T 2T5
647-288-8891
E-mail: info@cegn.org
URL: www.cegn.org
Scope: National

Contact Information: Executive Director: Pegi Dover; Email: pegi_dover@cegn.org; Phone: 647-288-8891

- **Canadian Evaluation Society 2018 National Conference**
Date: May 26-29, 2018
Location: Hyatt Regency Calgary
Calgary, AB
Sponsor/Contact: Canadian Evaluation Society
#3, 247 Barr St.
Renfrew, ON K7V 1J6
Fax: 613-432-6840
Toll-Free: 855-251-5721
E-mail: secretariat@evaluationcanada.ca
URL: www.evaluationcanada.ca
Scope: National
Purpose: Theme: "Co-creation"
Contact Information: Conference website: c2018.evaluationcanada.ca

- **Canadian Federation of Apartment Associations Rental Housing Conference 2018**
Date: May 14-16, 2018
Location: Coast Coal Harbour Hotel
Vancouver, BC
Sponsor/Contact: Canadian Federation of Apartment Associations
#640, 1600 Carling Ave.
Ottawa, ON K1Z 1G3
613-235-0101; Fax: 613-238-0101
E-mail: admin@cfaa-fcapi.org
URL: www.cfaa-fcapi.org
Scope: National

- **Canadian Historical Association 2018 Annual Meeting**
Date: May 28-30, 2018
Location: University of Regina
Regina, SK
Sponsor/Contact: Canadian Historical Association
#1912, 130 Albert St.
Ottawa, ON K1P 5G4
613-233-7885; Fax: 613-565-5445
E-mail: cha-shc@cha-shc.ca
URL: www.cha-shc.ca
Scope: National
Purpose: An event for historians to showcase their research & to discuss issues related to the discipline

- **Canadian Industrial Relations Association 2018 Conference**
Date: May 2-4, 2018
Location: Montréal, QC
Sponsor/Contact: Association canadienne des relations industrielles
Département des relations industrielles, Université Laval
#3129, 1025, av des Sciences-Humaines
Québec, QC G1V 0A6
E-mail: acri-cira@rlt.ulaval.ca
URL: www.cira-acri.ca
Scope: National

- **Canadian Linguistic Association 2018 Conference**
Date: May 30 - June 1, 2018
Location: University of Regina
Regina, SK
Sponsor/Contact: Canadian Linguistic Association
c/o University of Toronto Press, Journals Division
5201 Dufferin Ave.
Toronto, ON M3H 5T8
URL: www.cla-acl.ca

Scope: National
Purpose: Information from all areas of linguistics

- **Canadian Medical & Biological Engineering Society 2018 41st Annual National Conference**
Date: May 8-11, 2018
Location: Delta Prince Edward Island
Charlottetown, PE
Sponsor/Contact: Canadian Medical & Biological Engineering Society
1485 Laperriere Ave.
Ottawa, ON K1Z 7S8
613-728-1759
E-mail: secretariat@cmbes.ca
URL: www.cmbes.ca
Scope: National

- **Canadian Nursing Education Conference 2018**
Date: May 28-29, 2018
Location: Montréal, QC
Sponsor/Contact: Canadian Association of Schools of Nursing
#450, 1145 Hunt Club Rd.
Ottawa, ON K1V 0Y3
613-235-3150; Fax: 613-235-4476
E-mail: inquire@casn.ca
URL: www.casn.ca
Scope: National
Purpose: Theme: "Canadian Nursing Education: Responding to a Changing World"

- **Canadian Ophthalmological Society 2018 Annual Meeting & Exhibition**
Date: May 31 - June 3, 2018
Location: Metro Toronto Convention Centre
Toronto, ON
Sponsor/Contact: Canadian Ophthalmological Society
#110, 2733 Lancaster Rd.
Ottawa, ON K1B 0A9
613-729-6779; Fax: 613-729-7209
E-mail: cos@cos-sco.ca
URL: www.cos-sco.ca
Scope: National

- **Canadian Orthopaedic Nurses Association 2018 Annual National Conference**
Date: May 27-30, 2018
Location: Regina, SK
Sponsor/Contact: Canadian Orthopaedic Nurses Association
7714 - 80 Ave.
Edmonton, AB T6C 0S4
URL: www.cona-nurse.org
Scope: National

- **Canadian Pain Society 2018 39th Annual Scientific Meeting**
Date: May 22-25, 2018
Location: Hotel Bonaventure Montréal
Montréal, QC
Sponsor/Contact: Canadian Pain Society
#301, 250 Consumers Rd.
Toronto, ON M2J 4V6
416-642-6379; Fax: 416-495-8723
E-mail: office@canadianpainsociety.ca
URL: www.canadianpainsociety.ca
Scope: National
Purpose: The exchange of current information about pain assessment, pain mechanisms, & pain management for healthcare professionals, scientists, & trainees from clinical, research, industry, & policy settings

- **Canadian Pediatric Society 95th Annual Conference**
Date: May 30 - June 2, 2018
Location: Québec City Convention Centre
Québec, QC
Sponsor/Contact: Canadian Pediatric Foundation
#100, 2305 St. Laurent Blvd.
Ottawa, ON K1G 4J8
613-526-9397; Fax: 613-526-3332
URL: www.cps.ca
Scope: National
Contact Information:
www.annualconference.cps.ca

- **Canadian Political Science Association 2018 Annual Conference (within the Congress of the Humanities & Social Sciences)**
Date: May 26 - June 1, 2018
Location: University of Regina
Regina, SK
Sponsor/Contact: Canadian Political Science Association
#204, 260 Dalhousie St.
Ottawa, ON K1N 7E4
613-562-1202; Fax: 613-241-0019
E-mail: cpsa-acsp@cpsa-acsp.ca
URL: www.cpsa-acsp.ca
Scope: National
Purpose: A conference including the association's business & committee meetings, special presentations, workshops, & exhibits
Contact Information: Administrator: Michelle Hopkins, E-mail: cpsa-acsp@cpsa-acsp.ca

- **Canadian Public Health Association 2018 Conference**
Date: May 28-31, 2018
Location: Montréal, QC
Sponsor/Contact: Canadian Public Health Association
#404, 1525 Carling Ave.
Ottawa, ON K1Z 8R9
613-725-3769; Fax: 613-725-9826
E-mail: info@cpha.ca
URL: www.cpha.ca
Scope: National
Purpose: A conference for policy-makers, researchers, environmental health professionals, academics, & students from across Canada
Contact Information: Conference Manager: Sarah Pettenuzzo, Phone: 613-725-3769, ext. 153

- **Canadian Public Relations Society 2018 National Conference**
Date: May 27-29, 2018
Location: Charlottetown, PE
Sponsor/Contact: Canadian Public Relations Society Inc.
#346, 4195 Dundas St. West
Toronto, ON M8X 1Y4
416-239-7034; Fax: 416-239-1076
E-mail: admin@cprs.ca
URL: www.cprs.ca
Scope: National
Purpose: An education conference, with networking opportunities with public relations professionals from across Canada

- **Canadian Society for Italian Studies 2018 Annual Conference**
Date: May 11-13, 2018
Location: University of Ottawa
Ottawa, ON

Conferences & Conventions Index

Sponsor/Contact: Canadian Society for Italian Studies
c/o Sandra Parmegiani, School of Languages & Literatures, U of Guelph
50 Stone Rd. East
Guelph, ON N1G 2W1
519-824-4120; *Fax:* 519-763-9572
E-mail: sparmegi@uoguelph.ca
URL: www.canadiansocietyforitalianstudies.camp7.org
Scope: International

• **Canadian Society for Mechanical Engineering International Congress 2018**
Date: May 27-30, 2018
Location: York University
Toronto, ON
Sponsor/Contact: Canadian Society for Mechanical Engineering
1295 Hwy. 2 East
Kingston, ON K7L 4V1
613-547-5989; *Fax:* 613-547-0195
E-mail: csme@cogeco.ca
URL: www.csme-scgm.ca
Scope: International

• **Canadian Society for Medical Laboratory Science LABCON2018**
Date: May 25-27, 2018
Location: Caesars Windsor
Windsor, ON
Sponsor/Contact: Canadian Society for Medical Laboratory Science
33 Wellington St. North
Hamilton, ON L8R 1M7
905-528-8642; *Fax:* 905-528-4968
Toll-Free: 800-263-8277
E-mail: info@csmls.org
URL: www.csmls.org
Scope: National

• **Canadian Society for Pharmaceutical Sciences 2018 Annual Symposium**
Date: May 22-25, 2018
Location: Chelsea Hotel
Toronto, ON
Sponsor/Contact: Canadian Society for Pharmaceutical Sciences
Katz Group Centre, University of Alberta
#2-020L, 11361 - 87 Ave.
Edmonton, AB T6G 2E1
780-492-0950; *Fax:* 780-492-0951
URL: www.cspscanada.org
Scope: National
Purpose: Educational sessions, networking opportunities, & the presentation of awards

• **Canadian Society for the History of Medicine 2018 Annual Conference**
Date: May 26-28, 2018
Location: University of Regina
Regina, SK
Sponsor/Contact: Canadian Society for the History of Medicine
c/o University of Ottawa
#14022, 120 University
Ottawa, ON K1N 6N5
613-562-5700
URL: www.cshm-schm.ca
Scope: National
Purpose: Theme: "Gathering Diversities"

• **Canadian Society for the Study of Education 2018 Annual Conference**
Date: May 26-30, 2018
Location: University of Regina
Regina, SK
Sponsor/Contact: Canadian Society for the Study of Education

#204, 260 Dalhousie St.
Ottawa, ON K1N 7E4
613-241-0018; *Fax:* 613-241-0019
E-mail: csse-scee@csse.ca
URL: www.csse-scee.ca
Scope: National
Purpose: Held in conjunction with the Congress of the Humanities & Social Sciences

• **Canadian Society for the Study of Religion 2018 Annual Meeting**
Date: May 26-29, 2018
Location: University of Regina
Regina, SK
Sponsor/Contact: Canadian Society for the Study of Religion
c/o Richard Mann, 2A51 Paterson Hall, Dept. of Religion, Carleton U.
1125 Colonel By Dr.
Ottawa, ON K1S 5B6
URL: www.cssrscer.ca
Scope: Provincial

• **Canadian Society of Biblical Studies 2018 Annual Meeting (in conjunction with the 2018 Congress of the Humanities & Social Sciences)**
Date: May 26-28, 2018
Location: University of Regina
Regina, SK
Sponsor/Contact: Canadian Society of Biblical Studies
c/o Prof. Robert A. Derrenbacker, Jr., Regent College
5800 University Blvd.
Vancouver, BC V6T 2E4
URL: www.ccsr.ca
Scope: National

• **Canadian Society of Church History 2018 Annual Meeting**
Date: May 30 - June 1, 2018
Location: Regina, SK
Sponsor/Contact: Canadian Society of Church History
c/o Robynne R. Healey, Dept. of History, Trinity Western University
7600 Glover Rd.
Langley, BC V2Y 1Y1
URL: csch-sche.ca
Scope: National

• **Canadian Society of Medievalists 2018 Annual Meeting Congress**
Date: May 28-30, 2018
Location: Regina, SK
Sponsor/Contact: Canadian Society of Medievalists
104 Mount Aubrun St., 5th Fl.
Cambridge, MA 02138
617-491-1622; *Fax:* 617-492-3303
E-mail: csmtreasurer@gmail.com
URL: www.canadianmedievalists.ca
Scope: National

• **Canadian Society of Nephrology 50th Annual General Meeting 2018**
Date: May 3-4, 2018
Location: Vancouver Convention Center
Vancouver, BC
Sponsor/Contact: Canadian Society of Nephrology
P.O. Box 25255 Stn. RDP
Montréal, QC H1E 7P9
514-643-4985
E-mail: info@csnscn.ca
URL: www.csnscn.ca
Scope: National

• **Canadian Society of Patristic Studies 2018 Annual Meeting**

Date: May 27-29, 2018
Location: University of Regina
Regina, SK
Sponsor/Contact: Canadian Society of Patristic Studies
c/o Dr. S. Muir, Religious Studies, Concordia University College of AB
7128 Ada Blvd.
Edmonton, AB T5B 4E4
URL: www.ccsr.ca/csps
Scope: National

• **Canadian Society of Respiratory Therapists 2018 Annual Education Conference**
Date: May 24-26, 2018
Location: Vancouver, BC
Sponsor/Contact: Canadian Society of Respiratory Therapists
#201, 2460 Lancaster Rd.
Ottawa, ON K1B 4S5
613-731-3164; *Fax:* 613-521-4314
Toll-Free: 800-267-3422
URL: www.csrt.com
Scope: National
Purpose: Featuring internationally renowned speakers, workshops, & presentations for respiratory therapists
Anticipated Attendance: 400+
Contact Information: conference.csrt.com

• **Canadian Society of Zoologists 2018 57th Annual Meeting**
Date: May 7-11, 2018
Location: Memorial University
St. John's, NL
Sponsor/Contact: Canadian Society of Zoologists
c/o Département de biologie, Université Laval
Québec, QC G1V 0A6
902-820-2979
URL: www.csz-scz.ca
Scope: National

• **Canadian Union of Public Employees (CUPE) Ontario 2018 55th Convention**
Date: May 30 - June 2, 2018
Location: Toronto Sheraton Centre
Toronto, ON
Sponsor/Contact: Canadian Union of Public Employees
Ontario Regional Office
#1, 80 Commerce Valley Dr. East
Markham, ON L3T 0B2
905-739-9739; *Fax:* 905-739-9740
E-mail: info@cupe.on.ca
URL: www.cupe.on.ca
Scope: Provincial
Purpose: A gathering where convention delegates debate & vote on resolutions
Contact Information: CUPE Ontario,
E-mail: info@cupe.on.ca

• **Canadian Union of Public Employees Nova Scotia Annual Convention 2018**
Date: May 27-30, 2018
Location: Delta Halifax
Halifax, NS
Sponsor/Contact: Canadian Union of Public Employees
c/o President, Nan McFadgen
P.O. Box 1794
Pictou, NS B0K 1H0
902-759-3231
URL: www.novascotia.cupe.ca
Scope: Provincial

• **Canadian Unitarian Council National Conference & AGM 2018**
Date: May 18-20, 2018

Location: McMaster University
Hamilton, ON
Sponsor/Contact: Canadian Unitarian Council
#400, 215 Spadina Ave.
Toronto, ON M5T 2C7
416-489-4121
Toll-Free: 888-568-5723
E-mail: info@cuc.ca
URL: www.cuc.ca
Scope: National

• **Canadian University Music Society Annual Conference 2018**
Date: May 23-25, 2018
Location: MacEwan University
Edmonton, AB
Sponsor/Contact: Canadian University Music Society
#202, 10 Morrow Ave.
Toronto, ON M6R 2J1
416-538-1650; *Fax:* 416-489-1713
E-mail: office@muscan.org
URL: www.muscan.org
Scope: National
Purpose: Theme: "MusEcologies"

• **Canadian Water Resources Association 2018 Conference**
Date: May 28 - June 1, 2018
Location: Victoria, BC
Sponsor/Contact: Canadian Water Resources Association
1401 - 14th St. North
Lethbridge, AB T1H 2W6
403-317-0017
E-mail: services@aic.ca
URL: www.cwra.org
Scope: National
Purpose: Theme: "Our Common Water Future: Building Resilience Through Innovation"
Contact Information: URL: conference.cwra.org

• **Career Colleges Ontario Annual Conference 2018**
Date: May 30-31, 2018
Location: Niagara Falls, ON
Sponsor/Contact: Career Colleges Ontario
#2, 155 Lynden Rd.
Brantford, ON N3R 8A7
519-752-2124; *Fax:* 519-752-3649
URL: www.careercollegesontario.ca
Scope: Provincial
Contact Information: Assistant, Administration: April Chato, E-mail: aprilchato@careercollegesontario.ca, Phone: 519-752-2124, ext. 113; Assistant, Administration: Dena Stuart, E-mail: denastuart@careercollegesontario.ca, Phone: 519-752-2124, ext. 200

• **Catholic Health Alliance of Canada 2018 Annual Conference**
Date: May 9-11, 2018
Location: Marriott Gateway on the Falls
Niagara Falls, ON
Sponsor/Contact: Catholic Health Alliance of Canada
Annex C, Saint-Vincent Hospital
60 Cambridge St. North
Ottawa, ON K1R 7A5
613-562-6262; *Fax:* 613-782-2857
URL: www.chac.ca
Scope: National

• **Chartered Professional Accountants of British Columbia Spring Pacific Summit 2018**
Date: May 30 - June 1, 2018

Conferences & Conventions Index

Location: Vancouver Convention Centre West
Vancouver, BC
Sponsor/Contact: Chartered Professional Accountants of British Columbia
#800, 555 West Hastings St.
Vancouver, BC V6B 4N6
604-872-7222
Toll-Free: 800-663-2677
URL: www.bccpa.ca
Scope: Provincial

- **Chartered Professionals in Human Resources of British Columbia & Yukon 2018 Conference & Tradeshow**
Date: May 1-2, 2018
Location: Vancouver, BC
Sponsor/Contact: Chartered Professionals in Human Resources of British Columbia & Yukon
#1101, 1111 West Hastings St.
Vancouver, BC V6E 2J3
604-684-7228; *Fax:* 604-684-3225
Toll-Free: 800-665-1961
E-mail: info@cphrbc.ca
URL: www.cphrbc.ca
Scope: Provincial
Purpose: A human resources professional development event, with guest speakers, educational sessions, exhibits, the presentation of awards, & networking events

- **Chemical Institute of Canada 101st Canadian Chemistry Conference & Exhibition 2018**
Date: May 27-31, 2018
Location: Edmonton, AB
Sponsor/Contact: Canadian Society for Chemistry
#550, 130 Slater St.
Ottawa, ON K1P 6E2
613-232-6252; *Fax:* 613-232-5862
Toll-Free: 888-542-2242
E-mail: info@cheminst.ca
URL: www.cheminst.ca
Scope: National
Contact Information: www.csc2018.ca

- **Classical Association of Canada Annual Conference 2018**
Date: May 8-10, 2018
Location: University of Calgary
Calgary, AB
Sponsor/Contact: Classical Association of Canada
c/o Guy Chamberland, Thornloe College at Laurentian University
Laurentian University
Sudbury, ON P3E 2C6
URL: www.cac-scec.ca
Scope: National
Contact Information: URL: cacscec2018.wordpress.com

- **College of Audiologists and Speech-Language Pathologists of Manitoba AGM 2018**
Date: May 23, 2018
Sponsor/Contact: College of Audiologists and Speech-Language Pathologists of Manitoba
#1, 333 Vaughan St.
Winnipeg, MB R3B 3J9
204-453-4539; *Fax:* 204-477-1881
E-mail: office@caslpm.ca
URL: www.caslpm.ca
Scope: Provincial

- **Commercial Seed Analysts Association of Canada Annual Convention 2018**
Date: May 28-30, 2018
Location: Saskatoon, SK
Sponsor/Contact: Commercial Seed Analysts Association of Canada Inc.
5788 L&A Rd.
Vernon, BC V1B 3PG
204-720-0052
URL: www.seedanalysts.ca

- **Construction Owners Association of Alberta Best Practices Conference 2018**
Date: May 8-9, 20187
Location: Shaw Conference Centre
Edmonton, AB
Sponsor/Contact: Construction Owners Association of Alberta
Sun Life Place
#800, 10123 - 99 St. NW
Edmonton, AB T5J 3H1
780-420-1145; *Fax:* 780-425-4623
E-mail: coaa.admin@coaa.ab.ca
URL: www.coaa.ab.ca
Scope: Provincial

- **Construction Specifications Canada 2018 Conference**
Date: May 23-27, 2018
Sponsor/Contact: Construction Specifications Canada
#312, 120 Carlton St.
Toronto, ON M5A 4K2
416-777-2198; *Fax:* 416-777-2197
URL: www.csc-dcc.ca
Scope: National
Contact Information: Executive Director: Nick Franjic, E-mail: nfranjic@csc-dcc.ca

- **Cordage Institute 2018 Annual Conference**
Date: May 21-23, 2018
Location: Rancho Bernardo Inn
San Diego, CA USA
Sponsor/Contact: Cordage Institute
#1019, 994 Old Eagle School Rd.
Wayne, PA 19087
610-971-4854; *Fax:* 610-971-4859
E-mail: info@cordageinstitute.com
URL: www.ropecord.com
Scope: International

- **Council of Post Secondary Library Directors, British Columbia Spring 2018 Meeting**
Date: May 9, 2018
Location: Emily Carr University of Art & Design
Vancouver, BC
Sponsor/Contact: Council of Post Secondary Library Directors, British Columbia
c/o Patricia Cia, Langara College
100 West 49th Ave.
Vancouver, BC V5Y 2Z6
604-323-5243
URL: www.cpsld.ca
Scope: Provincial
Purpose: A meeting held with a program of interest to library directors & chief librarians from not-for-profit post secondary education institutions in British Columbia

- **e-Health 2018**
Date: May 27-30, 2018
Location: Vancouver, BC
Sponsor/Contact: Digital Health Canada
#110, 151 Yonge St.
Toronto, ON M5C 2W7
647-775-8555
E-mail: info@digitalhealthcanada.com
URL: digitalhealthcanada.com
Scope: National
Anticipated Attendance: 1,500+

- **Editors' Association of Canada Conference 2018**
Date: May 25-27, 2018
Location: Radisson Hotel Saskatoon
Saskatoon, SK
Sponsor/Contact: Editors' Association of Canada
#505, 27 Carlton St.
Toronto, ON M5B 1L2
416-975-1379; *Fax:* 416-975-1637
Toll-Free: 866-226-3348
E-mail: info@editors.ca
URL: www.editors.ca
Scope: National

- **Engineers Canada Board, Annual & Executive Committee Meetings 2018**
Date: May 23-26, 2018
Location: Saskatoon, SK
Sponsor/Contact: Engineers Canada
#300, Metcalfe St.
Ottawa, ON K1P 6L5
613-232-2474; *Fax:* 613-230-5759
Toll-Free: 877-408-9273
E-mail: info@engineerscanada.ca
URL: www.engineerscanada.ca
Scope: National

- **Environmental Studies Association of Canada 2018 Annual Conference & AGM**
Date: May 28-30, 2018
Sponsor/Contact: Environmental Studies Association of Canada
c/o Dean's Office, Faculty of Environmental Studies, Univ. of Waterloo
Waterloo, ON N2L 3G1
519-888-4442; *Fax:* 519-746-0292
Toll-Free: 866-437-2587
URL: www.esac.ca
Scope: National
Anticipated Attendance: 8,000+

- **EuroCACS Conference 2018**
Date: May 28-30, 2018
Location: Edinburgh, Scotland
Sponsor/Contact: ISACA
#1010, 3701 Algonquin Rd.
Rolling Meadows, IL 60008
847-253-1545; *Fax:* 847-253-1443
E-mail: news@isaca.org
URL: www.isaca.org
Scope: International
Purpose: An industry event for ISACA members, IS Audit, Assurance, Security & Risk Management Professionals worldwide; includes expert-led workshops & professional development opportunities
Contact Information: ISACA Training & Education, Phone: 847-660-5670, Fax: 847-253-1443

- **Existential & Phenomenological Theory & Culture Conference 2018**
Date: May 28-30, 2018
Location: University of Regina
Regina, SK
Sponsor/Contact: Society for Existential & Phenomenological Theory & Culture
URL: www.eptc-tcep.net

- **Federation of Canadian Municipalities 2018 Annual Conference & Trade Show**
Date: May 31 - June 3, 2018
Location: Halifax, NS
Sponsor/Contact: Federation of Canadian Municipalities
24 Clarence St.
Ottawa, ON K1N 5P3
613-241-5221; *Fax:* 613-241-7440
E-mail: info@fcm.ca
URL: www.fcm.ca
Scope: National

- **Federation of Danish Associations in Canada 2018 Danish Canadian Conference**
Date: May 24-27, 2018
Location: Halifax, NS
Sponsor/Contact: Federation of Danish Associations in Canada
679 Eastvale Ct.
Gloucester, ON K1J 6Z7
E-mail: secretary@danishfederation.ca
URL: www.danishfederation.ca
Scope: National

- **Federation of Northern Ontario Municipalities 2018 58th Annual Conference**
Date: May 9-11, 2018
Location: Parry Sound, ON
Sponsor/Contact: Federation of Northern Ontario Municipalities
88 Riverside Dr.
Kapuskasing, ON P5N 1B3
705-337-4454; *Fax:* 705-337-1741
E-mail: fonom.info@gmail.com
URL: www.fonom.org
Scope: Local
Purpose: A meeting for northern Ontario's municipal decision makers, featuring exhibits by suppliers, vendors, & professionals who provide services to municipalities

- **Film Studies Association of Canada 2018 Annual Conference**
Date: May 29-31, 2018
Location: University of Regina
Regina, SK
Sponsor/Contact: Film Studies Association of Canada
c/o Peter Lester, Brock University
500 Glenridge Ave.
St Catharines, ON L2S 3A1
E-mail: fsac@filmstudies.ca
URL: www.filmstudies.ca
Scope: National

- **Government Finance Officers Association 2018 112th Annual Conference**
Date: May 6-9, 2018
Location: America's Center Convention Complex
St. Louis, MO USA
Sponsor/Contact: Government Finance Officers Association
#2700, 203 North LaSalle St.
Chicago, IL 60601-1210
312-977-9700; *Fax:* 312-977-4806
E-mail: bnquiry@gfoa.org
URL: www.gfoa.org
Scope: International
Anticipated Attendance: 4,100+
Contact Information: Manager, Communications: Natalie Laudadio, Phone: 312-578-2298

- **Government Finance Officers Association of BC Annual Conference 2018**
Date: May 30 - June 1, 2018
Location: Kelowna, BC

Conferences & Conventions Index

Sponsor/Contact: Government Finance Officers Association of British Columbia
#408, 612 View St.
Victoria, BC V8W 1J5
250-382-6871
E-mail: office@gfoabc.ca
URL: www.gfoabc.ca
Scope: Provincial

- **Greater Vancouver Home Builders' Association Members Expo 2018**
Date: May 2, 2018
Location: Molson Canadian Theatre
Coquitlam, BC
Sponsor/Contact: Greater Vancouver Home Builders' Association
#1003, 7495 - 132 St.
Surrey, BC V3W 1J8
778-565-4288; Fax: 778-565-4289
E-mail: info@gvhba.org
URL: www.gvhba.org
Scope: Provincial
Purpose: A networking & showcase event at which members can exchange information about products & services, as well as communicate directly with suppliers

- **Human Anatomy & Physiology Society 32nd Annual Conference 2018**
Date: May 26-30, 2018
Location: Columbus, OH USA
Sponsor/Contact: Human Anatomy & Physiology Society
P.O. Box 2945
251 S.L. White Blvd.
LaGrange, GA 30241-2945
E-mail: info@hapsconnect.org
URL: www.hapsweb.org
Scope: International
Purpose: An international conference, featuring workshops & networking opportunities

- **IPAC Canada 2018 National Education Conference**
Date: May 27-30, 2018
Location: Banff Centre
Banff, AB
Sponsor/Contact: Infection & Prevention Control Canada
P.O. Box 46125 Stn. Westdale
Winnipeg, MB R3R 3S3
204-897-5990; Fax: 204-895-9595
Toll-Free: 866-999-7111
E-mail: info@ipac-canada.org
URL: www.ipac-canada.org
Scope: National

- **Institute of Industrial & Systems Engineers Annual Conference & Expo 2018**
Date: May 19-22, 2018
Location: Loews Royal Pacific Resort
Orlando, FL USA
Sponsor/Contact: Institute of Industrial & Systems Engineers
#200, 3577 Parkway Lane
Norcross, GA 30092
770-449-0460; Fax: 770-441-3295
E-mail: cs@iienet.org
URL: www.iienet2.org
Scope: International

- **Institute of Internal Auditors 2018 International Conference**
Date: May 6-9, 2018
Location: Dubai, United Arab Emirates
Sponsor/Contact: The Institute of Internal Auditors
#401, 1035 Greenwood Blvd.
Lake Mary, FL 32746
407-937-1111; Fax: 407-937-1101
E-mail: customerrelations@theiia.org
URL: www.theiia.org
Scope: International
Contact Information: URL: ic.globaliia.org

- **Institute of Law Clerks of Ontario 28th Annual Conference 2018**
Date: May 2-5, 2018
Location: Delta Ottawa City Centre
Ottawa, ON
Sponsor/Contact: Institute of Law Clerks of Ontario
P.O. Box 44
#502, 20 Adelaide St. East
Toronto, ON M5C 2T6
416-214-6252; Fax: 416-214-6255
E-mail: reception@ilco.on.ca
URL: www.ilco.on.ca
Scope: Provincial

- **Insurance Brokers Association of British Columbia 70th Annual Conference & Trade Show**
Date: May 30 - June 1, 2018
Location: Vancouver, BC
Sponsor/Contact: Insurance Brokers Association of Canada
#1600, 543 Granville St.
Vancouver, BC V6C 1X6
604-606-8000; Fax: 604-683-7831
URL: www.ibabc.org
Scope: Provincial
Contact Information: Coordinator, Membership & Events: Jennifer Reddicopp, Phone: 604-606-8002

- **Intermodal Association of North America Intermodal Operations & Maintenance Business Meeting 2018**
Date: May 1-3, 2018
Location: Lombard, IL USA
Sponsor/Contact: Intermodal Association of North America
#1100, 11785 Beltsville Dr.
Calverton, MD 20705
301-982-3400; Fax: 301-982-4815
E-mail: info@intermodal.org
URL: www.intermodal.org
Scope: International

- **International Organization of Securities Commissions 43rd Annual Conference 2018**
Date: May 7-11, 2018
Location: Budapest, Hungary
Sponsor/Contact: International Organization of Securities Commissions General Secretariat
C/ Oquendo 12
Madrid, 28006
E-mail: info@iosco.org
URL: www.iosco.org
Scope: International

- **International Sanitary Supply Association INTERCLEAN Amsterdam 2018**
Date: May 15-18, 2018
Location: Amsterdam, Netherlands
Sponsor/Contact: International Sanitary Supply Association, Inc.
3300 Dundee Rd.
Northbrook, IL 60062
847-982-0800; Fax: 847-982-1012
Toll-Free: 800-225-4772
E-mail: info@issa.com
URL: www.issa.com
Scope: International
Purpose: An international exhibition for cleaning professionals which unites leading global brands & manufacturers

- **Jasper Dental Congress 2018**
Date: May 24-27, 2018
Location: Fairmont Jasper Park Lodge
Jasper, AB
Sponsor/Contact: Alberta Dental Association & College
#402, 7609 - 109 St.
Edmonton, AB T6G 1C3
780-432-1012; Fax: 780-433-4864
Toll-Free: 800-843-3848
E-mail: reception@adaandc.com
URL: www.dentalhealthalberta.ca
Scope: Provincial

- **Journées dentaires internationales du Québec (JDIQ) 2018**
Date: May 25-29, 2018
Location: Quebec
Sponsor/Contact: Ordre des dentistes du Québec
#1640, 800, boul René-Lévesque ouest
Montréal, QC H3B 1X9
514-875-8511; Fax: 514-393-9248
Toll-Free: 800-361-4887
URL: www.odq.qc.ca
Scope: Provincial
Contact Information: Président, Comité d'organisation des JDIQ: Pierre Boudrias, Courriel: congres@odq.qc.ca

- **Local Government Management Association of British Columbia 2018 Annual Conference & AGM**
Date: May 15-17, 2018
Location: Victoria Conference Centre
Victoria, BC
Sponsor/Contact: Local Government Management Association of British Columbia
710 - 880 Douglas St.
Victoria, BC V8W 1B7
250-383-7032; Fax: 250-384-4879
E-mail: office@lgma.ca
URL: www.lgma.ca
Scope: Provincial
Contact Information: Program Manager: Ana Fuller, Phone: 250-383-7032, ext. 227, E-mail: afuller@lgma.ca

- **Lower Mainland Local Government Association 2018 Annual General Meeting & Conference**
Date: May 9-11, 2018
Location: Whistler, BC
Sponsor/Contact: Lower Mainland Local Government Association
#60, 10551 Shellbridge Way
Richmond, BC V6X 2W9
250-356-5122; Fax: 604-270-9116
URL: www.lmlga.ca
Scope: Local
Purpose: Tradeshow, workshops, & seminars for persons involved in local government

- **Manitoba Child Care Association 2018 Annual Conference**
Date: May 24-26, 2018
Location: Victoria Inn
Winnipeg, MB
Sponsor/Contact: Manitoba Child Care Association
2350 McPhillips St., 2nd Fl.
Winnipeg, MB R2V 4J6
204-586-8587; Fax: 204-589-5613
Toll-Free: 888-323-4676
E-mail: info@mccahouse.org
URL: www.mccahouse.org
Scope: Provincial
Purpose: Keynote speakers, a trade show, & an awards banquet

- **Manitoba Federation of Labour 2018 Convention**
Date: May 24-27, 2018
Location: Winnipeg, MB
Sponsor/Contact: Manitoba Federation of Labour
#303, 275 Broadway
Winnipeg, MB R3C 4M6
204-947-1400; Fax: 204-943-4276
E-mail: admin@mfl.mb.ca
URL: www.mfl.mb.ca
Scope: Provincial
Contact Information: Coordinator, Communications: Andrew Tod; E-mail: atod@mfl.mb.ca

- **Medical Library Association 2018 Annual Meeting & Exhibition**
Date: May 18-23, 2018
Location: Atlanta, GA USA
Sponsor/Contact: Medical Library Association
#1900, 65 East Wacker Pl.
Chicago, IL 60601-7246
312-419-9094; Fax: 312-419-8950
E-mail: websupport@mail.mlahq.org
URL: www.mlanet.org
Scope: International

- **NAFSA: Association of International Educators 2018 Annual Conference & Expo**
Date: May 27 - June 1, 2018
Location: Philadelphia, PA USA
Sponsor/Contact: NAFSA: Association of International Educators
1307 New York Ave. NW, 8th Fl.
Washington, DC 20005-4701
202-737-3699; Fax: 202-737-3657
E-mail: inbox@nafsa.org
URL: www.nafsa.org
Scope: International

- **National Space Society's International Space Development Conference 2018**
Date: May 24-27, 2018
Location: Sheraton Gateway Hotel
Los Angeles, CA USA
Sponsor/Contact: National Space Society
P.O. Box 98106
Washington, DC 20090-8106
202-429-1600; Fax: 703-435-4390
E-mail: nsshq@nss.org
URL: www.nss.org
Scope: International
Purpose: Discussions of the future of space exploration

- **North Pacific Anadromous Fish Commission Annual Meeting 2018**
Date: May 21-25, 2018
Location: Khabarovsk, Russia
Sponsor/Contact: North Pacific Anadromous Fish Commission
#502, 889 West Pender St.
Vancouver, BC V6C 3B2
604-775-5550; Fax: 604-775-5577
E-mail: secretariat@npafc.org
URL: www.npafc.org

- **Northwest Wall & Ceiling Bureau 2018 Annual Convention & Trade Show**
Date: May 3-5, 2018
Location: Westin La Paloma Resort & Spa
Tucson, AZ USA
Sponsor/Contact: Northwest Wall & Ceiling Bureau

1032A NE 65th St.
Seattle, WA 98115
E-mail: info@nwcb.org
URL: www.nwcb.org
Scope: International
Purpose: Informative seminars & exhibits, plus networking opportunities, for persons in the northwestern wall & ceiling industry
Contact Information: Director, Communications & Events: Tiina Freeman, E-mail: tiina@nwcb.org; Exhibitor & Sponsorship Information, Phone: 206-524-4243

- **Ontario Association of Fire Chiefs 2018 Conference & Trade Show**
Date: May 4-5, 2018
Location: The International Centre Mississauga, ON
Sponsor/Contact: Ontario Association of Fire Chiefs
#22, 520 Westney Rd. South
Ajax, ON L1S 6W6
905-426-9865; Fax: 905-426-3032
Toll-Free: 800-774-6651
E-mail: info@oafc.on.ca
URL: www.oafc.on.ca
Scope: Provincial
Anticipated Attendance: 600+

- **Ontario Association of Police Services Boards 2018 Spring Conference & AGM**
Date: May 23-26, 2018
Location: Blue Mountain Resort The Blue Mountains, ON
Sponsor/Contact: Ontario Association of Police Services Boards
Suite A, 10 Peel Centre Dr.
Brampton, ON L6T 4B9
905-458-1488; Fax: 905-458-2260
Toll-Free: 800-831-7727
E-mail: admin@oapsb.ca
URL: www.oapsb.ca
Scope: Provincial

- **Ontario Association of School Business Officials 75th Annual Conference & Education Industry Show**
Date: May 9-11, 2018
Location: Ottawa, ON
Sponsor/Contact: Ontario Association of School Business Officials
#207, 144 Main St.
Markham, ON L3P 5T3
905-209-9704; Fax: 905-209-9705
E-mail: office@oasbo.org
URL: www.oasbo.org
Scope: Provincial

- **Ontario College of Teachers Conference 2018**
Date: May 31 - June 1, 2018
Location: Toronto Marriott Downtown Eaton Centre Hotel
Toronto, ON
Sponsor/Contact: Ontario College of Teachers
101 Bloor St. West
Toronto, ON M5S 0A1
416-961-8800; Fax: 416-961-8822
Toll-Free: 888-534-2222
E-mail: info@oct.ca
URL: www.oct.ca
Scope: Provincial
Purpose: Presentations of interest to teachers

- **Ontario Native Education Counselling Association Annual Conference**
Date: May 28-30, 2018
Location: Thunder Bay, ON
Sponsor/Contact: Ontario Native Education Counselling Association
P.O. Box 220
37A Reserve Rd.
Naughton, ON P0M 2M0
705-692-2999; Fax: 705-692-9988
E-mail: oneca@oneca.com
URL: www.oneca.com
Scope: Provincial

- **Ontario Public School Boards' Association Annual General Meeting 2018**
Date: May 31 - June 3, 2018
Location: Marriott on the Falls Niagara Falls, ON
Sponsor/Contact: Ontario Public School Boards Association
#1850, 439 University Ave.
Toronto, ON M5G 1Y8
416-340-2540; Fax: 416-340-7571
E-mail: webmaster@opsba.org
URL: www.opsba.org
Scope: Provincial
Contact Information: Contact, Conference & Event Planning: Susan Weinberg, Phone: 416-340-2540, ext. 128

- **Ontario Rheumatology Association 2018 Annual Meeting**
Date: May 25-27, 2018
Location: Ontario
Sponsor/Contact: Ontario Rheumatology Association
#244, 12 - 16715 Yonge St.
Newmarket, ON L3X 1X4
905-952-0698; Fax: 905-952-0708
E-mail: admin@ontariorheum.ca
URL: ontariorheum.ca
Scope: Provincial

- **Ontario Small Urban Municipalities 2018 65th Annual Conference & Trade Show**
Date: May 2-4, 2018
Location: Niagara Falls, ON
Sponsor/Contact: Ontario Small Urban Municipalities
c/o Association of Municipalities of Ontario
#801, 200 University Ave.
Toronto, ON M5H 3C6
416-971-9856; Fax: 416-971-6191
Toll-Free: 877-426-6527
E-mail: amo@amo.on.ca
URL: www.osum.ca
Scope: Provincial
Anticipated Attendance: 200+
Contact Information: Coordinator, Conference & Trade Show: Jim Collard, Phone: 905-468-3266, E-mail: collard@niagara.com

- **Ontario Society for Environmental Education EcoLinks Conference 2018**
Date: May 11, 2018
Location: High Park
Toronto, ON
Sponsor/Contact: Ontario Society for Environmental Education
P.O. Box 587
Lakefield, ON K0L 2H0
705-652-0923
URL: home.osee.ca
Scope: Provincial

- **Ordre des technologues en imagerie médicale, en radio-oncologie et en élétrophysiologie médicale du Québec 44e Congrès 2018**
Date: May 24-26, 2018
Location: Hilton Lac-Leamy
Gatineau, QC
Sponsor/Contact: Ordre des technologues en imagerie médicale, en radio-oncologie et en élétrophysiologie médicale du Québec
#401, 6455, rue Jean-Talon
Saint-Léonard, QC H1S 3E8
514-351-0052
Toll-Free: 800-361-8759
URL: www.otimroepmq.ca
Scope: Provincial

- **Paint & Decorating Retailers Association Trade Show at the National Hardware Show 2018**
Date: May 8-10, 2018
Sponsor/Contact: Paint & Decorating Retailers Association
1401 Triad Center Dr.
St. Peters, MO 63376
Toll-Free: 800-737-0107
E-mail: info@pdra.org
URL: www.pdra.org
Scope: National

- **Partners in Prevention 2018 Health & Safety Conference & Trade Show**
Date: May 1-2, 2018
Sponsor/Contact: Workplace Safety & Prevention Services
Centre for Health & Safety Innovation
5110 Creekbank Rd.
Mississauga, ON L4W 0A1
905-614-1400; Fax: 905-614-1414
Toll-Free: 877-494-9777
E-mail: customercare@wsps.ca
URL: www.wsps.ca
Scope: National
Purpose: Theme: "Shifting Landscapes in Health & Safety"

- **Pediatric Academic Societies' 2018 Annual Meeting**
Date: May 5-8, 2018
Location: Toronto, ON
Sponsor/Contact: Academic Pediatric Association
6728 Old McLean Village Dr.
McLean, VA 22101
703-556-9222; Fax: 703-556-8729
E-mail: info@academicpeds.org
URL: www.academicpeds.org
Scope: International
Purpose: An international meeting focussing on research in child health
Contact Information: Address: #7B, 3400 Research Forest Dr., The Woodlands, TX, 77381, USA; Phone: 346-980-9717

- **Pediatric Endocrine Society 2018 Annual Meeting**
Date: May 5-8, 2018
Location: Toronto, ON
Sponsor/Contact: Pediatric Endocrine Society
6728 Old McLean Village Dr.
McLean, VA 22101
E-mail: info@pedsendo.org
URL: www.pedsendo.org
Scope: International
Purpose: An annual gathering of persons from the disciplines of pediatric endocrinology, including business meetings, lectures, topic symposia, poster sessions, workshops, exhibits, & social activities
Contact Information: E-mail: info@pedsendo.org

- **Petroleum Safety Conference 2018**
Date: May 1-3, 2018
Location: Fairmont Banff Springs
Banff, AB
Sponsor/Contact: Enform
Head Office
5055 - 11th St. NE
Calgary, AB T2E 8N4
403-516-8000; Fax: 403-516-8166
Toll-Free: 800-667-5557
E-mail: customerservice@enform.ca
URL: www.enform.ca
Scope: National

- **Physical & Health Education Canada 2018 National Conference**
Date: May 17-19, 2018
Location: Whistler, BC
Sponsor/Contact: Physical & Health Education Canada
#301, 2197 Riverside Dr.
Ottawa, ON K1H 7X3
613-523-1348; Fax: 613-523-1206
Toll-Free: 800-663-8708
E-mail: info@phecanada.ca
URL: www.phecanada.ca
Scope: National

- **Planning Institute of British Columbia 2018 Annual Conference**
Date: May 29 - June 1, 2018
Location: Victoria Conference Centre
Victoria, BC
Sponsor/Contact: Planning Institute of British Columbia
#1750, 355 Burrard St.
Vancouver, BC V6C 2G8
604-696-5031; Fax: 604-696-5032
Toll-Free: 866-696-5031
E-mail: info@pibc.bc.ca
URL: www.pibc.bc.ca
Scope: Provincial

- **Polyurethane Manufacturers Association 2018 Annual Meeting**
Date: May 5-8, 2018
Location: Naples Beach Hotel & Golf Club
Naples, FL USA
Sponsor/Contact: Polyurethane Manufacturers Association
#1300, 6737 West Washington St.
Milwaukee, WI 53214
414-431-3094; Fax: 414-276-7704
E-mail: info@pmahome.org
URL: www.pmahome.org
Scope: International
Purpose: Events also include a supplier showcase & a processing technique seminar
Contact Information: E-mail: info@pmahome.org

- **Professional Photographers of Canada 2018 Canadian Imaging Conference & Expo**
Date: May 4-9, 2018
Sponsor/Contact: Professional Photographers of Canada
209 Light St.
Woodstock, ON N4S 6H6
519-537-2555; Fax: 519-537-5573
Toll-Free: 888-643-7762
URL: www.ppoc.ca
Scope: National
Purpose: An opportunity for the exchange of professional ideas

- **Project Management Institute Global Congress 2018**
Date: May 7-9, 2018
Location: Berlin, Germany

Sponsor/Contact: Project Management Institute
14 Campus Blvd.
Newtown Square, PA 19073-3299
610-356-4600; *Fax:* 610-356-4647
Toll-Free: 855-746-4849
E-mail: customercare@pmi.org
URL: www.pmi.org
Scope: International

• **Quilt Canada 2018**
Date: May 31 - June 2, 2018
Location: Vancouver Convention Centre
Vancouver, BC
Sponsor/Contact: Canadian Quilters' Association
6 Spruce St.
Pasadena, NL A0L 1K0
E-mail: administration@canadianquilter.com
URL: www.canadianquilter.com
Scope: National
Contact Information: E-mail: confcoordinator@canadianquilter.com

• **Real Estate Institute of Canada 2018 Annual Conference & Annual General Meeting**
Date: May 29-31, 2018
Location: Montréal, QC
Sponsor/Contact: Real Estate Institute of Canada
#208, 5407 Eglinton Ave. West
Toronto, ON M9C 5K6
416-695-9000; *Fax:* 416-695-7230
Toll-Free: 800-542-7342
E-mail: infocentral@reic.com
URL: www.reic.ca
Scope: National
Purpose: A gathering of real estate professionals to participate in professional development programs, listen to guest speakers, & to network with industry experts, colleages, & suppliers
Contact Information: Coordinator, Events: Natalie Wallace, E-mail: natalie.wallace@reic.com, Phone: 416-695-9000, ext. 270

• **Recycling Council of British Columbia 44th Annual Zero Waste Conference 2018**
Date: May 30 - June 1, 2018
Location: Whistler, BC
Sponsor/Contact: Recycling Council of British Columbia
#10, 119 West Pender St.
Vancouver, BC V6B 1S5
604-683-6009; *Fax:* 604-683-7255
Toll-Free: 800-667-4321
E-mail: rcbc@rcbc.ca
URL: www.rcbc.ca
Scope: Provincial
Contact Information: Manager, Member Services: Ben Ramos, Phone: 604-683-6009, ext. 314,Email: conference@rcbc.ca

• **Royal Canadian Mounted Police Veterans Association 2018 Annual General Meeting**
Date: May 25, 2018
Location: Best Western Plus Winnipeg Airport Hotel
Winnipeg, MB
Sponsor/Contact: Royal Canadian Mounted Police Veterans' Association
1200 Vanier Pkwy.
Ottawa, ON K1A 0R2
613-993-8633; *Fax:* 613-993-4353
Toll-Free: 877-251-1771
E-mail: rcmp.vets@rcmp-grc.gc.ca
URL: www.rcmpvetsnational.ca
Scope: National

• **Saskatchewan Physical Education Association Conference 2018**
Date: May 9-11, 2018
Location: Saskatchewan
Sponsor/Contact: Saskatchewan Physical Education Association
P.O. Box 193
Harris, SK S0L 1K0
306-656-4423; *Fax:* 306-656-4405
E-mail: spea@xplornet.com
URL: www.speaonline.ca
Scope: Provincial
Purpose: Theme: "Moving Together: Embracing Possibilities"

• **Society for Technical Communication Annual Summit 2018**
Date: May 20-23, 2018
Location: Hyatt Regency Orlando
Orlando, FL USA
Sponsor/Contact: Society for Technical Communication
#300, 9401 Lee Hwy.
Fairfax, VA 22031
703-522-4114; *Fax:* 703-522-2075
URL: www.stc.org
Scope: International

• **Society of Plastics Engineers ANTEC 2018**
Date: May 7-10, 2018
Location: Orange County Convention Center
Orlando, FL USA
Sponsor/Contact: Society of Plastics Engineers
#306, 6 Berkshire Blvd.
Bethel, CT 06801
203-775-0471; *Fax:* 203-775-8490
URL: www.4spe.org
Scope: International
Contact Information: Manager, Events: Scott Marko, Phone: 203-740-5442

• **Society of Tribologists & Lubrication Engineers 73rd Annual Meeting & Exhibition 2018**
Date: May 20-24, 2018
Location: Minneapolis Convention Center
Minneapolis, MN USA
Sponsor/Contact: Society of Tribologists & Lubrication Engineers
840 Busse Hwy.
Park Ridge, IL 60068-2302
847-825-5536; *Fax:* 847-825-1456
URL: www.stle.org
Scope: International
Contact Information: Contact, STLE Conference Office: Merle Hedland, E-mail: mhedland@bacon-hedland.com, Phone: 630-428-2133

• **Sonography Canada 2018 National Conference & Annual General Meeting**
Date: May 25-27, 2018
Location: St. John's, NL
Sponsor/Contact: Sonography Canada
P.O. Box 119
Kemptville, ON K0G 1J0
Fax: 613-258-0899
Toll-Free: 877-488-0788
E-mail: info@sonographycanada.ca
URL: www.sonographycanada.ca
Scope: National

• **Speech-Language & Audiology Canada 2018 Annual General Meeting & Conference**
Date: May 2-5, 2018
Location: Edmonton, AB
Sponsor/Contact: Speech-Language & Audiology Canada
#1000, 1 Nicholas St.
Ottawa, ON K1N 7B7
613-567-9968; *Fax:* 613-567-2859
Toll-Free: 800-259-8519
E-mail: info@sac-oac.ca
URL: www.sac-oac.ca
Scope: National

• **The 9th Canadian Association of Foot Care Nurses AGM & Conference 2018**
Date: May 25-27, 2018
Location: DoubleTree by Hilton Hotel & Conference Centre
Regina, SK
Sponsor/Contact: Canadian Association of Foot Care Nurses
c/o Pat MacDonald, President
110 Linden Park Bay
Winnipeg, MB R2R 1Y3
E-mail: secretary@cafcn.ca
URL: www.cafcn.ca

• **The Comparative & International Education Society of Canada 2018 Conference**
Date: May 26-30, 2018
Location: University of Regina
Regina, SK
Sponsor/Contact: The Comparative & International Education Society of Canada
c/o Canadian Society for the Study of Education
#204, 260 Dalhousie St.
Ottawa, ON K1N 7E4
613-241-0018; *Fax:* 613-241-0019
URL: ciescanada.ca
Scope: National

• **The International Trademark Association 140th Annual Meeting 2018**
Date: May 19-23, 2018
Location: Seattle, WA USA
Sponsor/Contact: International Trademark Association
655 Third Ave., 10th Fl.
New York, NY 10017-5617
212-642-1700; *Fax:* 212-768-7796
E-mail: memberservices@inta.org
URL: www.inta.org
Scope: International
Anticipated Attendance: 9,500+
Contact Information: E-mail: meetings@inta.org

• **Total Health '18 Convention & Exhibition**
Date: May 11-13, 2018
Location: Metro Toronto Convention Centre
Toronto, ON
Sponsor/Contact: Consumer Health Organization of Canada
#1901, 355 St. Clair Ave. West
Toronto, ON M5P 1N5
416-924-9800; *Fax:* 416-924-6404
E-mail: info@consumerhealth.org
URL: www.consumerhealth.org
Scope: International
Purpose: Speakers will focus on creating good health and preventing disease using natural methods: energy medicine, organic gardening, traditional farming, agricultural biodiversity, healthy homes, ecologically based communities, renewable energy source and preserving a healthy environment for our children. We as consumers must choose foods and medicines which do no harm to people, animals or our planet.

• **Vocational Rehabilitation Association of Canada 2018 National Conference**
Date: May 31 - June 1, 2018
Location: Four Points Hotel
Kingston, ON
Sponsor/Contact: Vocational Rehabilitation Association of Canada
P.O. Box 370
#3, 247 Barr St.
Renfrew, ON K7V 1J6
Fax: 613-432-6840
Toll-Free: 888-876-9992
URL: www.vracanada.com
Scope: National

• **Western Canada's Transportation Forum Spring 2018**
Date: May 3-4, 2018
Location: Fairmont Hotel
Winnipeg, MB
Sponsor/Contact: Western Transportation Advisory Council
#401, 899 Pender St. West
Vancouver, BC V6C 3B2
604-687-8691; *Fax:* 604-687-8751
E-mail: infoservices@westac.com
URL: www.westac.com
Purpose: Members representing the shipper and service provider communities wil be encouraged to share information and insight to improve capacity and service

June

• **13th Annual BC Nurse Practitioner Association Conference 2018**
Date: June 7-9, 2018
Location: Vancouver Island Conference Centre
Nanaimo, BC
Sponsor/Contact: British Columbia Nurse Practitioner Association
27656 - 110th Ave.
Maple Ridge, BC V2W 1P6
E-mail: info@bcnpa.org
URL: www.bcnpa.org
Scope: Provincial

• **142nd American Association on Intellectual & Developmental Disabilities Annual Meeting**
Date: June 25-28, 2018
Location: St. Louis, MO USA
Sponsor/Contact: American Association on Intellectual & Developmental Disabilities
#200, 501 - 3rd St. NW
Washington, DC 20001
E-mail: admin@aaidd.org
URL: aaidd.org
Scope: International

• **2018 Association of Municipal Managers, Clerks & Treasurers of Ontario Annual Conference**
Date: June 10-13, 2018
Location: Blue Mountain Resort
The Blue Mountains, ON
Sponsor/Contact: Association of Municipal Managers, Clerks & Treasurers of Ontario
#610, 2680 Skymark Ave.
Mississauga, ON L4W 5L6
905-602-4294; *Fax:* 905-602-4295
E-mail: amcto@amcto.com
URL: www.amcto.com
Scope: Provincial

• **2018 BC Economic Summit**
Date: June 10-12, 2018

Conferences & Conventions Index

Location: Delta Grand Okanagan Resort
Kelowna, BC
Sponsor/Contact: British Columbia
Economic Development Association
#102, 9300 Nowell St.
Chilliwack, BC V2P 4V7
604-858-7199; *Fax:* 604-795-7118
E-mail: info@bceda.ca
URL: www.bceda.ca
Scope: Provincial

• **2018 Canadian Academic Accounting Association Annual Conference**
Date: June 14-16, 2018
Location: Calgary, AB
Sponsor/Contact: Canadian Academic Accounting Association
245 Fairview Mall Dr.
Toronto, ON M2J 4T1
416-486-5361; *Fax:* 416-486-6158
E-mail: admin@caaa.ca
URL: www.caaa.ca
Scope: National
Purpose: Theme: "Accounting & Public Trust"

• **2018 Canadian Association of Ambulatory Care Conference**
Date: June 7-8, 2018
Location: Ottawa, ON
Sponsor/Contact: Canadian Association of Ambulatory Care
#200, 100 Consilium Pl.
Toronto, ON M1H 3E3
E-mail: canadianambulatorycare@gmail.com
URL: www.canadianambulatorycare.com
Scope: National
Purpose: Theme: "Strategies for Improving the Patient Experience in Ambulatory Care"

• **2018 Canadian Mathematical Society Summer Meeting**
Date: June 1-4, 2018
Location: Fredericton, NB
Sponsor/Contact: Canadian Mathematical Society
#209, 1725 St Laurent Blvd.
Ottawa, ON K1G 3V4
613-733-2662
E-mail: office@cms.math.ca
URL: www.cms.math.ca
Scope: National

• **2018 Canadian Orthopaedic Residents Association Annual Meeting**
Date: June 20-23, 2018
Location: Victoria, BC
Sponsor/Contact: Canadian Orthopaedic Residents Association
#450, 4150, rue Sainte-Catherine ouest
Montréal, QC H3Z 2Y5
514-874-9003; *Fax:* 514-874-0464
E-mail: coraweb@canorth.org
URL: www.coraweb.org
Scope: National

• **2018 Canadian Phytopathological Society Annual Meeting**
Date: June 17-20, 2018
Location: Québec, QC
Sponsor/Contact: Canadian Phytopathological Society
c/o Vikram Bisht
P.O. Box 1149
65 - 3 Ave. NE
Carman, MB R0G 0J0
204-745-0260; *Fax:* 204-745-5690
URL: phytopath.ca

Scope: National
Purpose: The objectives of CPS are to encourage research, education, and the dissemination of knowledge on the nature, cause, and control of plant diseases.

• **2018 Canadian Society of Soil Science Annual Meeting**
Date: June 10-14, 2018
Location: Niagara Falls, ON
Sponsor/Contact: Canadian Society of Soil Science
Business Office
P.O. Box 637
Pinawa, MB R0E 1L0
204-282-9486; *Fax:* 204-753-8478
E-mail: sheppards@ecomatters.com
URL: www.csss.ca
Purpose: Joint meeting with Canadian Geophysical Union (CGU) & Computational Infrastructure in Geodynamics (CIG)

• **2018 International Conference of Control, Dynamic Systems & Robotics**
Date: June 7-9, 2018
Location: Niagara Falls, ON
Sponsor/Contact: International Academy of Science, Engineering & Technology
#414, 1376 Bank St.
Ottawa, ON K1H 7Y3
613-695-3040
E-mail: info@international-aset.com
URL: www.international-aset.com
Scope: National
Purpose: Annual conference in fields related to traditional & modern control and dynamic systems.
Contact Information: cdsr.net

• **2018 National Health Leadership Conference**
Date: June 4-5, 2018
Location: St. John's, NL
Sponsor/Contact: HealthCareCAN
#100, 17 York St.
Ottawa, ON K1N 5S7
613-241-8005; *Fax:* 613-241-5055
Toll-Free: 855-236-0213
E-mail: info@healthcarecan.ca
URL: www.healthcarecan.ca
Scope: National

• **2018 Ontario Minor Hockey Association AGM**
Date: June 2018
Location: Ontario
Sponsor/Contact: Ontario Minor Hockey Association
#3, 25 Brodie Dr.
Richmond Hill, ON L4B 3K7
905-780-6642; *Fax:* 905-780-0344
E-mail: omha@omha.net
URL: www.omha.net
Scope: Provincial
Purpose: Addressing the business of the association, plus revisions to regulations, policies, & procedures for the upcoming season

• **25th World Mining Congress & Expo**
Date: June 19-22, 2018
Location: Astana, Kazakhstan
Sponsor/Contact: Canadian Institute of Mining, Metallurgy & Petroleum
CIM National Office
#1250, 3500, boul de Maisonneuve ouest
Westmount, QC H3Z 3C1
514-939-2710; *Fax:* 514-939-2714
E-mail: cim@cim.org
URL: www.cim.org

Scope: International
Anticipated Attendance: 1,500

• **31st Annual Canadian Society for Immunology Meeting**
Date: June 1-4, 2018
Location: Western University
London, ON
Sponsor/Contact: Canadian Society for Immunology
c/o Dept. of Veterinary Microbiology, Univ. of Saskatchewan
52 Campus Dr.
Saskatoon, SK S7N 5B4
306-966-7214; *Fax:* 306-966-7244
E-mail: info@csi-sci.ca
URL: www.csi-sci.ca
Scope: National

• **50th Annual International Snowmobile Congress 2018**
Date: June 13-16, 2018
Location: Halifax, NS
Sponsor/Contact: Canadian Council of Snowmobile Organizations
P.O. Box 21059
Thunder Bay, ON P7A 8A7
807-345-5299
E-mail: ccso.ccom@tbaytel.net
URL: www.ccso-ccom.ca
Scope: International

• **52nd Canadian Meteorological & Oceanographic Society Congress**
Date: June 10-14, 2018
Location: Halifax Convention Centre
Halifax, NS
Sponsor/Contact: Canadian Meteorological & Oceanographic Society
P.O. Box 3211 Stn. D
Ottawa, ON K1P 6H7
613-990-0300
E-mail: cmos@cmos.ca
URL: www.cmos.ca
Scope: National
Purpose: Theme: "Marine & Environmental Risks & Impacts"

• **55th Annual Canadian Culinary Federation 2018 National Convention**
Date: June 10-15, 2018
Location: Charlottetown, PE
Sponsor/Contact: Canadian Culinary Federation
30 Hamilton Ct.
Riverview, NB E1B 3C3
506-387-4882; *Fax:* 506-387-4884
E-mail: admin@ccfcc.ca
URL: www.ccfcc.ca
Scope: National

• **84th Annual Western Association of Broadcasters Conference 2018**
Date: June 6-7, 2018
Location: Banff, AB
Sponsor/Contact: Western Association of Broadcasters
#507, 918 - 16th Ave. NW
Calgary, AB T2M 0K3
Toll-Free: 877-814-2719
E-mail: info@wab.ca
URL: www.wab.ca
Scope: Provincial

• **8th International Conference on Ocean Energy 2018**
Date: June 2018
Location: Normandy, France
Sponsor/Contact: Marine Renewables Canada

P.O. Box 34066
1690 Hollis St., 10th Fl.
Halifax, NS B3J 3S1
URL: www.marinerenewables.ca
Scope: International
Purpose: Global marine renewable energy event focused on the industrial development of marine renewable energy.
Contact Information: www.icoe-conference.com

• **Air & Waste Management Association 111th Annual Conference & Exhibition 2018**
Date: June 25-28, 2018
Location: Hartford, CT USA
Sponsor/Contact: Air & Waste Management Association
One Gateway Center
420 Fort Duquesne Blvd., 3rd Fl.
Pittsburgh, PA 15222-1435
412-232-3444; *Fax:* 412-232-3450
Toll-Free: 800-270-3444
E-mail: info@awma.org
URL: www.awma.org
Scope: International
Purpose: Theme: "Charting the Future: Environment, Energy & Health"

• **Alberta Association of Clinic Managers 2018 Conference**
Date: June 11-14, 2018
Location: Coast Hotel
Canmore, AB
Sponsor/Contact: Alberta Association of Clinic Managers
c/o Jennifer Hendricks, Treasurer
30 Prestwick Row SE
Calgary, AB T2Z 3L7
E-mail: info@aacm.ca
URL: aacm.ca
Scope: Provincial
Purpose: Joint conference with the Medical Group Management Association of Canada (MGMAC)

• **Alberta Association of Travel Health Professionals 2018 Conference**
Date: June 1-2, 2018
Location: Coast Canmore Hotel
Canmore, AB
Sponsor/Contact: Alberta Association of Travel Health Professionals
North Tower
#440, 10030-107 St.
Edmonton, AB T5J 3E4
URL: www.aathp.com
Scope: Provincial

• **American Chemistry Council 2018 Annual Meeting**
Date: June 4-6, 2018
Location: Colorado Springs, CO USA
Sponsor/Contact: American Chemistry Council
700 Second St. NE
Washington, DC 20002
202-249-7000; *Fax:* 202-249-6100
URL: www.americanchemistry.com
Scope: International

• **American Library Association 2018 Annual Conference**
Date: June 21-26, 2018
Location: New Orleans, LA USA
Sponsor/Contact: American Library Association
50 East Huron St.
Chicago, IL 60611-2795
312-944-6780; *Fax:* 312-440-9374
Toll-Free: 800-545-2433

E-mail: ala@ala.org
URL: www.ala.org
Scope: International
Purpose: A conference providing speakers, educational programs, committee meetings, & exhibits related to library & information services

• **American Society of Neuroradiology 2018 56th Annual Meeting**
Date: June 2-7, 2018
Location: Vancouver Convention Centre
Vancouver, BC
Sponsor/Contact: American Society of Neuroradiology
#205, 800 Enterprise Dr.
Oak Brook, IL 60523
630-574-0220; Fax: 630-574-0661
URL: www.asnr.org
Scope: International
Contact Information: Director, Scientific Meetings: Lora Tannehill, E-mail: ltannehill@asnr.org; Manager, Scientific Meetings: Valerie Geisendorfer, E-mail: vgeisendorfer@asnr.org

• **American Society of Safety Engineers Safety 2018 Professional Development Conference & Exposition**
Date: June 3-6, 2018
Location: Henry B. Gonzalez Convention Center
San Antonio, TX USA
Sponsor/Contact: American Society of Safety Engineers
520 N. Northwest Hwy
Park Ridge, IL 60068
847-699-2929
URL: www.asse.org
Scope: International

• **American Water Works Association Annual Conference & Exposition 2018**
Date: June 10-13, 2018
Location: Las Vegas, NV USA
Sponsor/Contact: American Water Works Association
6666 West Quincy Ave.
Denver, CO 80235
303-794-7711; Fax: 303-347-0804
Toll-Free: 800-926-7337
E-mail: service@awwa.org
URL: www.awwa.org
Scope: International
Purpose: An international gathering of thousands of water professionals, featuring a technical program, workshops, seminars, & exhibits

• **Ancient, Free & Accepted Masons of the Grand Lodge of Alberta 2018 Annual Communication**
Date: June 6-10, 2018
Location: Grande Prairie, AB
Sponsor/Contact: Ancient, Free & Accepted Masons of Canada - Grand Lodge of Alberta
330 - 12 Ave. SW
Calgary, AB T2R 0H2
403-262-1149; Fax: 403-290-0671
E-mail: grandsecretary@freemasons.ab.ca
URL: www.freemasons.ab.ca
Scope: Provincial

• **Appraisal Institute of Canada / Institut canadien des évaluateurs 2018 Conference**
Date: June 13-16, 2018
Location: Québec, QC
Sponsor/Contact: Appraisal Institute of Canada
#403, 200 Catherine St.
Ottawa, ON K2P 2K9
613-234-6533; Fax: 613-234-7197
Toll-Free: 888-551-5521
E-mail: info@aicanada.ca
URL: www.aicanada.ca
Scope: National

• **ASM International Thermal Processing In Motion**
Date: June 5-7, 2018
Location: Spartanburg Marriott
Spartanburg, SC USA
Sponsor/Contact: ASM International
9639 Kinsman Rd.
Materials Park, OH 44073-0002
440-338-5151; Fax: 440-338-4634
Toll-Free: 800-336-5152
E-mail: memberservicecenter@asminternational.org
URL: www.asminternational.org
Scope: International

• **ASME 2018 Power & Energy Conference Exhibition**
Date: June 25-28, 2018
Location: Lake Buena Vista, FL USA
Sponsor/Contact: American Society of Mechanical Engineers
2 Park Ave.
New York, NY 10016-5990
Toll-Free: 800-843-2763
E-mail: customercare@asme.org
URL: www.asme.org
Scope: International

• **Association des professionnels à l'outillage municipal rencontre annuelle 2018**
Date: June 7-9, 2018
Location: Victoriaville, QC
Sponsor/Contact: Association des professionnels à l'outillage municipal
11, av du Ruisseau
Montréal, QC H4K 2C8
Fax: 866-334-1264
Toll-Free: 866-337-5136
E-mail: info@apom-quebec.ca
URL: www.apom-quebec.ca
Scope: Local

• **Association minière du Québec congrès annuel 2018**
Date: June 6-7, 2018
Location: Fairmont Tremblant
Mont-Tremblant, QC
Sponsor/Contact: Association minière du Québec
Place de la Cité - Tour Belle Cour
#720, 2590, boul Laurier
Québec, QC G1V 4M6
418-657-2016; Fax: 418-657-2154
E-mail: amq@amq-inc.com
URL: www.amq-inc.com
Scope: Provincial

• **Association of Canadian Archivists 2018 43rd Annual Conference**
Date: June 7-9, 2018
Location: Chateau Lacombe Hotel
Edmonton, AB
Sponsor/Contact: Association of Canadian Archivists
P.O. Box 2596 Stn. D
#911, 75 Albert St.
Ottawa, ON K1P 5W6
613-234-6977; Fax: 613-234-8500
URL: www.archivists.ca
Scope: National
Purpose: A meeting occurring in May or June each year, for archivists from across Canada, featuring educational presentations, trade show exhibits, networking opportunities, as well as workshops immediately prior or following conference sessions

• **Association of Canadian Publishers 2018 Annual General Meeting**
Date: June 4-6, 2018
Sponsor/Contact: Association of Canadian Publishers
#306, 174 Spadina Ave.
Toronto, ON M5T 2C2
416-487-6116; Fax: 416-487-8815
E-mail: admin@canbook.org
URL: www.publishers.ca
Scope: National
Purpose: An event featuring plenary sessions, professional development seminars, presentations, as well as committee meetings & reports

• **Association of Local Public Health Agencies 2018 Annual General Meeting & Conference**
Date: June 10-12, 2018
Location: Toronto, ON
Sponsor/Contact: Association of Local Public Health Agencies
#1306, 2 Carlton St.
Toronto, ON M5B 1J3
416-595-0006; Fax: 416-595-0030
E-mail: info@alphaweb.org
URL: www.alphaweb.org
Scope: Provincial

• **Association of Municipal Administrators of New Brunswick 2018 Annual Conference**
Date: June 6-8, 2018
Location: K.C. Irving Regional Centre
Bathurst, NB
Sponsor/Contact: Association of Municipal Administrators of New Brunswick
20 Courtney St.
Douglas, NB E3G 8A1
506-453-4229; Fax: 506-444-5452
E-mail: amanb@nb.aibn.com
URL: www.amanb-aamnb.ca
Scope: Provincial

• **Association of Ontario Health Centres 2018 Annual Conference & General Meeting**
Date: June 13-14, 2018
Location: Sheraton Parkway Toronto North
Richmond Hill, ON
Sponsor/Contact: Association of Ontario Health Centres
#500, 970 Lawrence Ave. West
Toronto, ON M6A 3B6
416-236-2539; Fax: 416-236-0431
E-mail: mail@aohc.org
URL: www.aohc.org
Scope: Provincial
Purpose: Theme: "Health Equity Action & Transformation"

• **Association of Registrars of the Universities and Colleges of Canada 2018 Conference**
Date: June 2018
Sponsor/Contact: Association of Registrars of the Universities & Colleges of Canada
c/o Angelique Saweczko, Thompson Rivers University
900 McGill Rd.
Kamloops, BC V2C 0C8
250-828-5019
URL: www.arucc.ca
Scope: National

• **Association québécoise de pédagogie collégiale 38e colloque annuel**
Date: June 6-8, 2018
Location: Saint-Hyacinthe, QC
Sponsor/Contact: Association québécoise de pédagogie collégiale
Cégep marie-victorin
7000, rue Marie-Victorin
Montréal, QC H2G 1J6
514-328-3805; Fax: 514-328-3824
E-mail: info@aqpc.qc.ca
URL: www.aqpc.qc.ca
Scope: National

• **Banff World Media Festival 2018**
Date: June 10-13, 2018
Location: Fairmont Banff Springs
Banff, AB
Sponsor/Contact: Banff World Television Festival Foundation
c/o Achilles Media Ltd.
#202, 102 Boulder Cres.
Canmore, AB T1W 1L2
403-678-1216; Fax: 403-678-3357
E-mail: info@achillesmedia.com
URL: www.btvf.com
Scope: National

• **Book Summit 18**
Date: June 14, 2018
Location: Harbourfront Centre
Toronto, ON
Sponsor/Contact: Book & Periodical Council
#107, 192 Spadina Ave.
Toronto, ON M5T 2C2
416-975-9366; Fax: 416-975-1839
E-mail: info@thebpc.ca
URL: www.thebpc.ca
Scope: National
Contact Information: www.booksummit.ca

• **Business & Professional Women's Clubs of Ontario 72nd Provincial Conference**
Date: June 1-3, 2018
Location: Toronto, ON
Sponsor/Contact: Canadian Federation of Business & Professional Women's Clubs
#201, Bramalea Rd.
Brampton, ON L6T 2W4
URL: www.bpwontario.org
Scope: Provincial
Purpose: Theme: "Empowered Women - Empower Women"

• **Canadian Anesthesiologists' Society 2018 74th Annual Meeting**
Date: June 15-18, 2018
Location: Palais de Congrès
Montréal, QC
Sponsor/Contact: Canadian Anesthesiologists' Society
#208, 1 Eglinton Ave. East
Toronto, ON M4P 3A1
416-480-0602; Fax: 416-480-0320
E-mail: anesthesia@cas.ca
URL: www.cas.ca
Scope: National
Purpose: A convention, with an exhibition pharmaceutical companies & equipment manufacturers

• **Canadian Animal Health Institute Annual Meeting 2018**
Date: June 4-6, 2018
Location: Pillar & Post
Niagara-on-the-Lake, ON
Sponsor/Contact: Canadian Animal Health Institute

Conferences & Conventions Index

#102, 160 Research Lane
Guelph, ON N1G 5B2
519-763-7777; *Fax:* 519-763-7407
E-mail: cahi@cahi-icsa.ca
URL: www.cahi-icsa.ca
Scope: National

• **Canadian Association for Supported Employment 2018 Conference**
Date: June 19-21, 2018
Location: Halifax Convention Centre
Halifax, NS
Sponsor/Contact: Canadian Association for Supported Employment
c/o AiMHi
950 Kerry St.
Prince George, BC V2M 5A3
250-564-6408; *Fax:* 250-564-6801
URL: www.supportedemployment.ca
Scope: National

• **Canadian Association for the History of Nursing 2018 Annual Conference**
Date: June 15-17, 2018
Sponsor/Contact: Canadian Association for the History of Nursing
College of Nursing, University of Saskatchewan
4440 - 4th Ave.
Regina, SK S4T 0H8
URL: www.cahn-achn.ca
Purpose: Theme: "Tracing Nurses' Footsteps: Nursing & the Tides of Change"

• **Canadian Association of College & University Student Services 2018 Conference**
Date: June 17-20, 2018
Location: PEI Convention Centre
Charlottetown, PE
Sponsor/Contact: Canadian Association of College & University Student Services
#202, 720 Spadina Ave.
Toronto, ON M5S 2T9
647-345-1116
E-mail: contact@cacuss.ca
URL: www.cacuss.ca
Scope: National

• **Canadian Association of Neuroscience Nurses 2018 49th Annual General Meeting**
Date: June 24-27, 2018
Location: Atlantica Hotel Halifax
Halifax, NS
Sponsor/Contact: Canadian Association of Neuroscience Nurses
c/o Janet White
#212, 324 Larry Uteck Blvd.
Halifax, NS B3M 0E7
URL: www.cann.ca
Scope: National
Purpose: Scientific sessions offering professional development for neuroscience nurses

• **Canadian Association of Occupational Therapists Conference 2018**
Date: June 20-23, 2018
Location: Sheraton Vancouver Wall Centre
Vancouver, BC
Sponsor/Contact: Canadian Association of Occupational Therapists
#100, 34 Colonnade Rd.
Ottawa, ON K2E 7J6
613-523-2268; *Fax:* 613-523-2552
Toll-Free: 800-434-2268
E-mail: membership@caot.ca
URL: www.caot.ca
Scope: National

• **Canadian Association of Physicists Congress 2018**
Date: June 11-15, 2018
Location: Dalhousie University
Halifax, NS
Sponsor/Contact: Canadian Association of Physicists
555 King Edward Ave., 3rd Fl.
Ottawa, ON K1N 7N5
613-562-5614; *Fax:* 613-562-5615
E-mail: cap@uottawa.ca
URL: www.cap.ca
Scope: National

• **Canadian Association of Police Educators 2018 Conference**
Date: June 25-29, 2018
Location: Pacific Region Training Centre
Chilliwack, BC
Sponsor/Contact: Canadian Association of Police Educators
c/o Wayne Jacobsen
1430 Victoria Ave. East
Brandon, MB R7A 2A9
204-725-8700
E-mail: cape.educators@gmail.com
URL: cape-educators.ca
Scope: National

• **Canadian Association of Recycling Industries (CARI) 2018 Annual Convention**
Date: June 7-9, 2018
Location: Hilton Hotels & Suites
Niagara Falls, ON
Sponsor/Contact: Canadian Association of Recycling Industries
#1906, 130 Albert St.
Ottawa, ON K1P 5G4
613-728-6946; *Fax:* 705-835-6196
E-mail: info@cari-acir.org
URL: www.cari-acir.org
Scope: National

• **Canadian Association of University Business Officers 2018 Annual Conference**
Date: June 10-12, 2018
Location: Simon Fraser University
Vancouver, BC
Sponsor/Contact: Canadian Association of University Business Officers
#315, 350 Albert St.
Ottawa, ON K1R 1B1
613-230-6760; *Fax:* 613-563-7739
E-mail: info@caubo.ca
URL: www.caubo.ca
Scope: National

• **Canadian Blood & Marrow Transplant Group 2018 Annual Conference**
Date: June 7-9, 2018
Location: Delta Hotel
Ottawa, ON
Sponsor/Contact: Canadian Blood & Marrow Transplant Group
#400, 570 West 7th Ave.
Vancouver, BC V5Z 1B3
604-874-4944; *Fax:* 604-874-4378
E-mail: cbmtg@malachite-mgmt.com
URL: www.cbmtg.org
Scope: National

• **Canadian Business Aviation Association's 2018 Convention and Exhibition**
Date: June 12-14, 2018
Location: Waterloo, ON
Sponsor/Contact: Canadian Business Aviation Association
#700, 1 Rideau St.
Ottawa, ON K1N 8S7
613-236-5611; *Fax:* 613-236-2361
URL: www.cbaa-acaa.ca
Purpose: Exhibitions & static displays; educational & information sessions

• **Canadian Catholic School Trustees' Association 2018 AGM**
Date: June 7-9, 2018
Location: Delta Hotels Grand Okanagan Resort
Kelowna, BC
Sponsor/Contact: Canadian Catholic School Trustees' Association
Catholic Education Centre
570 West Hunt Club Rd.
Nepean, ON K2G 3R4
613-224-4455; *Fax:* 613-224-3187
E-mail: ccsta@ocsb.ca
URL: www.ccsta.ca
Contact Information: ccsta@ocsb.ca

• **Canadian College & University Food Service Association Conference 2018**
Date: June 27 - July 1, 2018
Location: Blue Mountain Resort
Collingwood, ON
Sponsor/Contact: Canadian College & University Food Service Association
c/o Drew Hall, University of Guelph
Gordon St.
Guelph, ON N1G 2W1
519-824-4120; *Fax:* 519-837-9302
E-mail: mcollins@hrs.uoguelph.ca
URL: www.ccufsa.on.ca
Scope: National

• **Canadian College of Medical Geneticists 2018 Annual Meeting**
Date: June 10-13, 2018
Sponsor/Contact: Canadian College of Medical Geneticists
#310, 4 Cataraqui St.
Kingston, ON K7K 1Z7
613-507-8345; *Fax:* 866-303-0626
E-mail: info@ccmg-ccgm.org
URL: www.ccmg-ccgm.org
Scope: National
Purpose: Theme: "The Future is Now"

• **Canadian College of Neuropsychopharmacology 41st Annual Meeting 2018**
Date: June 28-30, 2018
Location: UBC Robson Square
Vancouver, BC
Sponsor/Contact: Canadian College of Neuropsychopharmacology
c/o Rachelle Anderson, Dept. of Psychiatry, University of Alberta
#IE7.19, 8440 - 112 St., Walter MacKenzie Centre
Edmonton, AB T6G 2B7
780-407-6543; *Fax:* 780-407-6672
E-mail: Rachelle@ccnp.ca
URL: www.ccnp.ca
Scope: National

• **Canadian Council for Refugees 2018 International Refugee Rights Conference**
Date: June 7-9, 2018
Location: Toronto, ON
Sponsor/Contact: Canadian Council for Refugees
#302, 6839, rue Drolet
Montréal, QC H2S 2T1
514-277-7223; *Fax:* 514-277-1447
E-mail: info@ccrweb.ca
URL: www.ccrweb.ca
Scope: National

• **Canadian Council for the Advancement of Education National Conference 2018**
Date: June 5-7, 2018
Location: Westin Nova Scotian Hotel
Halifax, NS
Sponsor/Contact: Canadian Council for the Advancement of Education
#310, 4 Cataraqui St.
Kingston, ON K7K 1Z7
613-531-9213; *Fax:* 613-531-0626
E-mail: admin@ccaecanada.org
URL: www.ccaecanada.org
Scope: National
Purpose: An annual national gathering, with keynote speakers, plenary sessions, roundtables, & the presentation of awards

• **Canadian Council of Motor Transport Administrators 2018 Annual Meeting**
Date: June 3-6, 2018
Location: Quebec City, QC
Sponsor/Contact: Canadian Council of Motor Transport Administrators
#404, 1111 Prince of Wales
Ottawa, ON K2C 3T2
613-736-1003; *Fax:* 613-736-1395
E-mail: info@ccmta.ca
URL: www.ccmta.ca
Scope: National
Purpose: Educational events, an exhibition, a working forum where important decisions are made, & an excellent networking opportunity for government decision-makers & members of the private sector
Contact Information: Phone: 613-736-1003 Fax: 613-736-1395, E-mail: ccmta-secretariat@ccmta.ca

• **Canadian Dermatology Association 2018 93rd Annual Conference**
Date: June 20-23, 2018
Location: Montréal, QC
Sponsor/Contact: Canadian Dermatology Association
#425, 1385 Bank St.
Ottawa, ON K1H 8N4
613-738-1748; *Fax:* 613-738-4695
Toll-Free: 800-267-3376
E-mail: info@dermatology.ca
URL: www.dermatology.ca
Scope: National
Purpose: Oral & poster presentations on subjects relevant to practicing dermatologists

• **Canadian Economics Association 52nd Annual Conference 2018**
Date: June 1-3, 2018
Location: McGill University
Montreal, QC
Sponsor/Contact: Canadian Economics Association
Department of Economics, Brock Univ.
500 Glenridge Ave.
St Catharines, ON L2S 3A1
905-688-5550
URL: www.economics.ca
Scope: National
Purpose: An annual conference held during the last week of May or the first week of June

• **Canadian Energy Research Institute 2018 Petrochemical Conference**
Date: June 10-12, 2018
Location: Kananaskis, AB

Sponsor/Contact: Canadian Energy Research Institute
#150, 3512 - 33 St. NW
Calgary, AB T2L 2A6
403-282-1231; *Fax:* 403-284-4181
E-mail: info@ceri.ca
URL: www.ceri.ca
Scope: National

- **Canadian Engineering Education Association 2018 Conference**
Date: June 3-6, 2018
Location: University of British Columbia
Vancouver, BC
Sponsor/Contact: Canadian Engineering Education Association
c/o Design Engineering, University of Manitoba
E2-262 EITC, 75 Chancellors Circle
Winnipeg, MB R3T 5V6
204-474-7113; *Fax:* 204-474-7676
E-mail: ceea@umanitoba.ca
URL: ceea.ca
Scope: National

- **Canadian Gaming Summit 2018**
Date: June 18-20, 2018
Location: Niagara Falls, ON
Sponsor/Contact: Canadian Gaming Association
#503, 131 Bloor St. West
Toronto, ON M5S 1P7
416-304-7800; *Fax:* 416-304-7805
E-mail: info@canadiangaming.ca
URL: www.canadiangaming.ca
Scope: International
Purpose: A conference & trade show for representatives from gaming & regulatory agencies, First Nations gaming, provincial lotteries, casinos, race tracks, & charitable gaming organizations
Contact Information:
www.canadiangamingsummit.com

- **Canadian Gas Association Gas Measurement & Regulation School 2018**
Date: June 4-7, 2018
Location: Edmonton, AB
Sponsor/Contact: Canadian Gas Association
#1220, 350 Albert St.
Ottawa, ON K1R 1A4
613-748-0057; *Fax:* 613-748-9078
E-mail: info@cga.ca
URL: www.cga.ca
Scope: National
Contact Information: E-mail: help@canavents.com

- **Canadian Geophysical Union 2018 Joint Annual Meeting**
Date: June 10-14, 2018
Location: Niagara Falls, ON
Sponsor/Contact: Canadian Geophysical Union
c/o Dept. of Geology & Geophysics, University of Calgary
ES #278, 2500 University Dr. NW
Calgary, AB T2N 1N4
403-220-5596; *Fax:* 403-284-0074
E-mail: cgu@ucalgary.ca
URL: www.cgu-ugc.ca
Scope: National

- **Canadian Institute of Actuaries 2018 Annual Meeting**
Date: June 21-22, 2018
Location: Toronto, ON
Sponsor/Contact: Canadian Institute of Actuaries

Secretariat
#1740, 360 Albert St.
Ottawa, ON K1R 7X7
613-236-8196; *Fax:* 613-233-4552
E-mail: head.office@cia-ica.ca
URL: www.cia-ica.ca
Scope: National

- **Canadian Institute of Financial Planners 16th Annual National Conference 2018**
Date: June 10-13, 2018
Location: Halifax Marriott Harbourfront
Halifax, NS
Sponsor/Contact: Canadian Institute of Financial Planners
#600, 3660 Hurontario St.
Mississauga, ON L5B 3C4
647-723-6450; *Fax:* 647-723-6457
Toll-Free: 866-933-0233
E-mail: cifps@cifps.ca
URL: www.cifps.ca
Scope: National

- **Canadian Institute of Plumbing & Heating 2018 Annual Business Conference**
Date: June 17-19, 2018
Location: Fairmont Chateau Whistler
Whistler, BC
Sponsor/Contact: Canadian Institute of Plumbing & Heating
#504, 295 The West Mall
Toronto, ON M9C 4Z4
416-695-0447
Toll-Free: 800-639-2474
E-mail: info@ciph.com
URL: www.ciph.com
Scope: National

- **Canadian Institute of Transportation Engineers 2018 Conference**
Date: June 2-6, 2018
Location: Shaw Conference Centre
Edmonton, AB
Sponsor/Contact: Canadian Institute of Transportation Engineers
P.O. Box 25118
1221 Weber St. East
kitchener, ON N2A 4A5
202-785-0060; *Fax:* 202-785-0609
E-mail: webmaster@cite7.org
URL: www.cite7.org
Scope: National

- **Canadian Institute of Underwriters Annual General Meeting 2018**
Date: June 3-5, 2018
Location: Marriott Bloor-Yorkville
Toronto, ON
Sponsor/Contact: Canadian Institute of Underwriters
c/o Marian Kingsmill, DKCI Events (David Kingsmill Consultants Inc.)
P.O. Box 91516 Stn. Roseland Plaza
3023 New St.
Burlington, ON L7R 4L6
URL: www.ciu.ca
Scope: National

- **Canadian Investor Relations Institute 31st Annual Conference**
Date: June 3-5, 2018
Location: Toronto Marriott Downtown
Toronto, ON
Sponsor/Contact: Canadian Investor Relations Institute
#601, 67 Yonge St.
Toronto, ON M5E 1J8

416-364-8200; *Fax:* 416-364-2805
E-mail: enquiries@ciri.org
URL: www.ciri.org
Scope: National

- **Canadian Law & Society Association Annual Meeting 2018**
Date: June 7-10, 2018
Sponsor/Contact: Canadian Law & Society Association
E-mail: info@acds-clsa.org
URL: www.acds-clsa.org
Scope: National

- **Canadian Manufacturers & Exporters 2018 LEAN Conference**
Date: June 4-7, 2018
Location: RBC Convention Center
Winnipeg, MB
Sponsor/Contact: Canadian Manufacturers & Exporters
#620, 55 Standish Ct.
Mississauga, ON L5R 4B2
905-672-3466; *Fax:* 905-672-1764
URL: www.cme-mec.ca
Scope: National
Contact Information:
www.embracingexcellence.ca

- **Canadian Marketing Association CMAdigital**
Date: June 6, 2018
Sponsor/Contact: Canadian Marketing Association
#603, 55 University Ave.
Toronto, ON M5J 2H7
416-391-2362; *Fax:* 416-441-4062
Toll-Free: 800-267-8805
E-mail: info@thecma.ca
URL: www.the-cma.org
Scope: National

- **Canadian Nautical Research Society 2018 Conference & Annual General Meeting**
Date: June 21-23, 2018
Location: Toronto, ON
Sponsor/Contact: Canadian Nautical Research Society
P.O. Box 34029
Ottawa, ON K2J 4B0
613-476-1177
URL: www.cnrs-scrn.org
Scope: National
Purpose: Theme: "Lower Lakes, Upper Lakes: Connecting Maritime Heritage"

- **Canadian Neurological Sciences Federation 2018 53rd Congress**
Date: June 24-27, 2018
Location: Halifax, NS
Sponsor/Contact: Canadian Neurological Sciences Federation
143N - 8500 Macleod Trail SE
Calgary, AB T2H 2N1
403-229-9544; *Fax:* 403-229-1661
URL: www.cnsfederation.org
Scope: National
Purpose: Courses, lectures, oral & digital poster presentations, plus exhibits & social events

- **Canadian Nuclear Society 38th Annual Conference**
Date: June 3-6, 2018
Location: Sheraton Cavalier Saskatoon Hotel
Saskatoon, SK
Sponsor/Contact: Canadian Nuclear Society
655 Bay St., 17th Fl.
Toronto, ON M5G 2K4

416-977-7620; *Fax:* 416-977-8131
E-mail: cns-snc@on.aibn.com
URL: www.cns-snc.ca
Scope: National

- **Canadian Nurses Association 2018 Annual Meeting & Biennial Convention**
Date: June 18-20, 2018
Location: Shaw Centre
Ottawa, ON
Sponsor/Contact: Canadian Nurses Association
50 Driveway
Ottawa, ON K2P 1E2
613-237-2133; *Fax:* 613-237-3520
Toll-Free: 800-361-8404
E-mail: cna@cna-aiic.ca
URL: www.cna-aiic.ca
Scope: National
Purpose: One of Canada's largest nursing conferences, featuring presentations, speakers, workshops, & the opportunity to view new products in the health-care marketplace
Anticipated Attendance: 1,000+
Contact Information: E-mail: conferences@cna-aiic.ca

- **Canadian Organization of Campus Activities 2018 National Conference**
Date: June 12-16, 2018
Location: Fredericton, NB
Sponsor/Contact: Canadian Organization of Campus Activities
#202, 509 Commissioners Rd. West
London, ON N6J 1Y5
519-690-0207; *Fax:* 519-681-4328
E-mail: cocaoffice@coca.org
URL: www.coca.org
Scope: National
Purpose: Educational sessions, plus showcases featuring music, films, & comedy, plus the Campus Activities Biz Hall trade show

- **Canadian Orthopaedic Association 2018 Annual Meeting**
Date: June 20-23, 2018
Location: Victoria, BC
Sponsor/Contact: Canadian Orthopaedic Association
#620, 4060, rue Sainte-Catherine ouest
Westmount, QC H3Z 2Z3
514-874-9003; *Fax:* 514-874-0464
URL: www.coa-aco.org
Scope: National

- **Canadian Owners and Pilots Association Convention & Trade Show 2018**
Date: June 21-23, 2018
Location: Saint John, NB
Sponsor/Contact: Canadian Owners & Pilots Association
#903, 75 Albert St.
Ottawa, ON K1P 5E7
613-236-4901; *Fax:* 613-236-8646
E-mail: copa@copanational.org
URL: www.copanational.org

- **Canadian Payroll Association 36th Annual Conference & Trade Show**
Date: June 27-29, 2018
Location: Ottawa, ON
Sponsor/Contact: Canadian Payroll Association
#1600, 250 Bloor St. East
Toronto, ON M4W 1E6
416-487-3380; *Fax:* 416-487-3384
Toll-Free: 800-387-4693

Conferences & Conventions Index

E-mail: infoline@payroll.ca
URL: www.payroll.ca
Scope: National
Purpose: Theme: "Full Steam Ahead: 40 Years of Payroll Compliance"

- **Canadian Pension & Benefits Institute Forum 2018**
Date: June 4-6, 2018
Location: Fairmont Le Château Frontenac Québec, QC
Sponsor/Contact: Canadian Pension & Benefits Institute
CPBI National Office
1175, av Union
Montréal, QC H3B 3C3
514-288-1222; Fax: 514-288-1225
E-mail: info@cpbi-icra.ca
URL: www.cpbi-icra.ca
Scope: International

- **Canadian Pharmacists Association 2018 Canadian Pharmacists Conference**
Date: June 2-5, 2018
Location: Fredericton, NB
Sponsor/Contact: Canadian Pharmacists Association
1785 Alta Vista Dr.
Ottawa, ON K1G 3Y6
613-523-7877; Fax: 613-523-0445
Toll-Free: 800-917-9489
E-mail: info@pharmacists.ca
URL: www.pharmacists.ca
Scope: National
Purpose: A yearly event for Canadian pharmacists, featuring educational workshops, a trade show, awards, & social events
Contact Information: E-mail: info@pharmacists.ca

- **Canadian Philosophical Association Annual Congress 2018**
Date: June 4-7, 2018
Location: Université du Québec Montréal, QC
Sponsor/Contact: Canadian Philosophical Association
P.O. Box 47077
Gloucester, ON K1B 5P9
613-236-1393; Fax: 613-782-3005
E-mail: administration@acpcpa.ca
URL: www.acpcpa.ca

- **Canadian Poultry and Egg Processors Council 2018 Convention**
Date: June 3-5, 2018
Location: Montréal, QC
Sponsor/Contact: Canadian Poultry & Egg Processors Council
#400, 1545 Carling Ave.
Ottawa, ON K1Z 8P9
613-724-6605; Fax: 613-724-4577
URL: www.cpepc.ca
Scope: National

- **Canadian Psychological Association 2018 29th International Congress on Applied Psychology**
Date: June 26-30, 2018
Location: Montréal, QC
Sponsor/Contact: Canadian Psychological Association
#702, 141 Laurier Ave. West
Ottawa, ON K1P 5J3
613-237-2144; Fax: 613-237-1674
Toll-Free: 888-472-0657
E-mail: cpa@cpa.ca
URL: www.cpa.ca
Scope: National
Anticipated Attendance: 1,800

Contact Information: URL: www.icap2018.com, E-mail: icap2018@cpa.ca

- **Canadian Society for Transfusion Medicine Conference 2018**
Date: June 2-7, 2018
Location: Toronto, ON
Sponsor/Contact: Canadian Society for Transfusion Medicine
#6, 20 Crown Steel Dr.
Markham, ON L3R 9X9
905-415-3917; Fax: 905-415-0071
Toll-Free: 855-415-3917
E-mail: office@transfusion.ca
URL: www.transfusion.ca
Scope: National
Purpose: In conjunction with the 35th International Congress of the ISBT

- **Canadian Society of Microbiologists 68th Annual Conference**
Date: June 18-21, 2018
Location: University of Manitoba Winnipeg, MB
Sponsor/Contact: Canadian Society of Microbiologists
CSM-SCM Secretariat
17 Dossetter Way
Ottawa, ON K1G 4S3
613-421-7229; Fax: 613-421-9811
E-mail: info@csm-scm.org
URL: www.csm-scm.org
Scope: National
Contact Information: Conference Organizer: Wafaa H. Antonious, E-mail: info@csm-scm.org

- **Canadian Society of Otolaryngology - Head & Neck Surgery 2018 72nd Annual Meeting**
Date: June 16-19, 2018
Location: Centre des Congrès de Québec Québec, QC
Sponsor/Contact: Canadian Society of Otolaryngology - Head & Neck Surgery Administrative Office
68 Gilkison Rd.
Elora, ON N0B 1S0
519-846-0630; Fax: 519-846-9529
Toll-Free: 800-655-9533
URL: www.entcanada.org
Scope: National
Purpose: Scientific information for those who specialize in head & neck surgery

- **Canadian Society of Plastic Surgeons 2018 72nd Annual Meeting**
Date: June 18-23, 2018
Location: Jasper, AB
Sponsor/Contact: Canadian Society of Plastic Surgeons
P.O. Box 60192 Stn. Saint-Denis
Montréal, QC H2J 4E1
514-843-5415; Fax: 514-843-7005
E-mail: csps_sccp@bellnet.ca
URL: www.plasticsurgery.ca
Scope: National
Purpose: An opportunity for participants to learn during the scientific program & to view exhibits

- **Canadian Solar Industries Association 2018 Solar Canada Annual Conference & Exposition**
Date: June 20-21, 2018
Location: BMO Centre
Calgary, AB
Sponsor/Contact: Canadian Solar Industries Association
#605, 150 Isabella St.
Ottawa, ON K1S 1V7
Fax: 613-736-8939
Toll-Free: 866-522-6742
E-mail: info@cansia.ca
URL: www.cansia.ca
Scope: National
Purpose: The presentation of timely topics for solar industry professionals from across Canada, featuring more than 60 speakers & 225 exhibitors
Anticipated Attendance: 4000+
Contact Information: www.solarcanadaconference.ca

- **Canadian Standards Association 2018 Annual Conference & Committee Week**
Date: June 18-22, 2018
Location: Shaw Conference Centre Edmonton, AB
Sponsor/Contact: Canadian Standards Association
178 Rexdale Blvd.
Toronto, ON M9W 1R3
416-747-4000; Fax: 416-747-2473
Toll-Free: 800-463-6727
E-mail: member@csagroup.org
URL: www.csagroup.org
Scope: National
Purpose: Educational presentations & committee meetings
Anticipated Attendance: 700+

- **Canadian Urological Association 2018 73rd Annual Meeting**
Date: June 23-26, 2018
Location: Halifax Convention Centre Halifax, NS
Sponsor/Contact: Canadian Urological Association
#401, 185, av Dorval
Dorval, QC H9S 5J9
514-395-0376; Fax: 514-395-1664
E-mail: cua@cua.org
URL: www.cua.org
Scope: National
Anticipated Attendance: 600

- **Community Health Nurses of Canada 2018 National Community Health Nursing Conference**
Date: June 26-28, 2018
Location: The Double Tree Hotel & Conference Centre
Regina, SK
Sponsor/Contact: Community Health Nurses of Canada
632 Hugel Ave.
Midland, ON L4R 1W7
705-527-1014
E-mail: info@chnc.ca
URL: www.chnc.ca
Scope: National
Purpose: Theme: "Caring, Connecting & Leading for a Healthy Canada"

- **Community Heritage Ontario 2018 Ontario Heritage Conference**
Date: June 7-9, 2018
Location: Sault Ste Marie, ON
Sponsor/Contact: Community Heritage Ontario
24 Conlins Rd.
Toronto, ON M1C 1C3
416-282-2710; Fax: 416-282-9482
E-mail: info@communityheritageontario.ca
URL: www.communityheritageontario.ca
Scope: Provincial

- **Crane Rental Association of Canada 2018 Conference**
Date: June 6-9, 2018
Location: Fort Garry Hotel Winnipeg, MB
Sponsor/Contact: Crane Rental Association of Canada
P.O. Box 26
Regina, SK S4P 2Z5
306-585-2722; Fax: 306-584-3566
Toll-Free: 855-680-2722
E-mail: info@crac-canada.com
URL: www.crac-canada.com
Scope: National

- **Dietitians of Canada National Conference 2018**
Date: June 6-9, 2018
Location: Westin Bayshore Vancouver, BC
Sponsor/Contact: Dietitians of Canada
#604, 480 University Ave.
Toronto, ON M5G 1V2
416-596-0857; Fax: 416-596-0603
E-mail: contactus@dietitians.ca
URL: www.dietitians.ca
Scope: National
Purpose: Theme: "Elevate Influence Inspire"

- **Doctors Nova Scotia 2018 Annual Conference**
Date: June 8-9, 2018
Location: Membertou Convention Centre Sydney, NS
Sponsor/Contact: Doctors Nova Scotia
25 Spectacle Lake Dr.
Dartmouth, NS B3B 1X7
902-468-1866; Fax: 902-468-6578
Toll-Free: 800-563-3427
E-mail: info@doctorsns.com
URL: www.doctorsns.com
Scope: Provincial

- **Federation of Medical Regulatory Authorities of Canada 2018 Annual Meeting & Conference**
Date: June 9-11, 2018
Location: Charlottetown, PE
Sponsor/Contact: Federation of Medical Regulatory Authorities of Canada
1021 Thomas Spratt Pl.
Ottawa, ON K1G 5L5
613-738-0372; Fax: 613-738-9169
E-mail: info@fmrac.ca
URL: www.fmrac.ca
Scope: National

- **Financial Executives International Canada Annual Conference 2018**
Date: June 13-15, 2018
Location: Halifax Conference Centre Halifax, NS
Sponsor/Contact: Financial Executives International Canada
#300, 116 Simcoe St.
Toronto, ON M5H 4E2
416-366-3007
Toll-Free: 866-677-3007
E-mail: membership@feicanada.org
URL: www.feicanada.org
Scope: National
Contact Information: Rita Plaskett, Director of Events, 416-366-3007 x5116

- **Funeral Service Association of Canada 2018 Convention & Trade Show**
Date: June 18-22, 2018
Location: Ottawa, ON
Sponsor/Contact: Funeral Service Association of Canada
#304, 555 Legget Dr.
Ottawa, ON K2K 2K3

613-271-2107; *Fax:* 613-271-3737
Toll-Free: 866-841-7779
E-mail: info@fsac.ca
URL: www.fsac.ca
Scope: National

• **Fédération des transporteurs par autobus congrès annuel**
Date: June 28-30, 2018
Location: Hilton Québec
Québec, QC
Sponsor/Contact: Fédération des transporteurs par autobus
#250, 5700, boul des Galeries
Québec, QC G2K 0H5
418-476-8181; *Fax:* 418-476-8177
Toll-Free: 844-476-8181
URL: www.federationautobus.com
Purpose: Panel de discussion, atelier

• **Geological Association of Canada - Mineralogical Association of Canada Annual Meeting 2018**
Date: June 16-21, 2018
Location: Vancouver, BC
Sponsor/Contact: Geological Association of Canada
c/o Heather Rafuse, Department of Natural Resources, Geological Survey
P.O. Box 8700
St. John's, NL A1B 4J6
URL: gac.esd.mun.ca/nl/nfsection.htm
Scope: Provincial

• **Geological Association of Canada 2018 Annual Meeting**
Date: June 17-21, 2018
Location: Vancouver, BC
Sponsor/Contact: Geological Association of Canada
c/o Department of Earth Sciences, Memorial University of Newfoundland
#ER4063, Alexander Murray Bldg.
St. John's, NL A1B 3X5
709-864-7660; *Fax:* 709-864-2532
E-mail: gac@mun.ca
URL: www.gac.ca
Scope: National

• **Indexing Society of Canada Annual Conference 2018**
Date: June 8-9, 2018
Location: Winnipeg, MB
Sponsor/Contact: Indexing Society of Canada
133 Major St.
Toronto, ON M5S 2K9
URL: www.indexers.ca
Scope: National

• **Institute of Municipal Assessors 62nd Annual Conference 2018**
Date: June 17-19, 2018
Location: Caesars Windsor Hotel
Windsor, ON
Sponsor/Contact: Institute of Municipal Assessors
#206, 10720 Yonge St.
Richmond Hill, ON L4C 3C9
905-884-1959; *Fax:* 905-884-9263
Toll-Free: 877-877-8703
E-mail: info@theima.ca
URL: www.assessorsinstitute.ca
Scope: National

• **International Ait Transport Association 74th Annual General Meeting & World Air Transport Summit**
Date: June 3-5, 2018
Location: Sydney, Australia
Sponsor/Contact: International Air Transport Association

P.O. Box 113
800, Place Victoria
Montréal, QC H4Z 1M1
514-874-0202; *Fax:* 514-874-9632
URL: www.iata.org
Purpose: Annual meeting of aviation leaders and media representatives; Presentations, debates & panel discussions

• **International Association for Hydrogen Energy (IAHE) 22nd World Hydrogen Energy Conference 2018**
Date: June 17-22, 2018
Location: Rio De Janerio, Brazil
Sponsor/Contact: International Association for Hydrogen Energy
#303, 5794 - 40th St. SW
Miami, FL 33155
E-mail: info@iahe.org
URL: www.iahe.org
Scope: International
Purpose: A conference of the International Association for Hydrogen Energy, for the hydrogen & fuel cell community, featuring an exhibition with hydrogen & fuel cell applications from research institutions & companies

• **International Cyclic Vomiting Syndrome Association Adult & Family Conference 2018**
Date: June 29 - July 1, 2018
Location: Sheraton Milwaukee Brookfield Hotel
Milwaukee, WI USA
Sponsor/Contact: Cyclic Vomiting Syndrome Association
P.O. Box 925
Elkhorn, WI 53121
414-342-7880
E-mail: cvsa@cvsaonline.org
URL: www.cvsaonline.org
Scope: International

• **International Federation of Professional & Technical Engineers (IFPTE) 2018 59th Convention**
Date: June 25-28, 2018
Location: Atlantic City, NJ USA
Sponsor/Contact: International Federation of Professional & Technical Engineers (AFL-CIO/CLC)
#701, 501 3rd St. NW
Washington, DC 20001
202-239-4880; *Fax:* 202-239-4881
E-mail: generalinfo@ifpte.org
URL: www.ifpte.org
Scope: International

• **International Society for Magnetic Resonance in Medicine 2018 26th Scientific Meeting & Exhibition**
Date: June 16-22, 2018
Location: Paris, France
Sponsor/Contact: International Society for Magnetic Resonance in Medicine
#620, 2300 Clayton Rd.
Concord, CA 94520
510-841-1899; *Fax:* 510-841-2340
E-mail: info@ismrm.org
URL: www.ismrm.org
Scope: International
Purpose: Featuring the 26th Annual Meeting of the Section for Magnetic Resonance Technologists
Contact Information: Director, Meetings: Anne-Marie Kahrovic, E-mail: anne-marie@ismrm.org

• **Invest Canada 2018: Canada's Private Equity & Venture Capital Conference**
Date: June 5-7, 2018
Location: Calgary, AB
Sponsor/Contact: Canada's Venture Capital & Private Equity Association
#1201, 372 Bay St.
Toronto, ON M5H 2W9
416-487-0519
E-mail: cvca@cvca.ca
URL: www.cvca.ca
Purpose: Hosted by the Canadian Venture Capital & Private Equity Association and Réseau Capital

• **Microwave Theory & Techniques Society International Microwave Symposia 2018**
Date: June 11-15, 2018
Location: Philadelphia, PA USA
Sponsor/Contact: IEEE Microwave Theory & Techniques Society
5829 Bellanca Dr.
Elkridge, MD 21075
410-796-5866
URL: www.mtt.org
Scope: International
Purpose: Technical papers; Workshops; Trade show

• **National Association for Surface Finishing (NASF) SUR/FIN Manufacturing & Technology Trade Show & Conference**
Date: June 4-6, 2018
Location: Cleveland, OH USA
Sponsor/Contact: National Association for Surface Finishing
#500, 1155 - 15th St. NW
Washington, DC 20005
202-457-8404; *Fax:* 202-530-0659
E-mail: info@nasfmembership.com
URL: www.nasf.org
Scope: International
Contact Information: Contact, Event Director: Cheryl Clark, E-mail: cclark@NASF.org

• **National Campus & Community Radio Association 2018 Conference**
Date: June 6-10, 2018
Location: Fredericton, NB
Sponsor/Contact: National Campus & Community Radio Association
#608, 180 Metcalfe St.
Ottawa, ON K2P 1P5
613-321-1440
Toll-Free: 866-859-8086
URL: www.ncra.ca
Scope: National

• **National Education Association Annual Meeting & Representative Assembly 2018**
Date: June 30 - July 5, 2018
Location: Minneapolis Convention Center
Minneapolis, MN USA
Sponsor/Contact: National Education Association
1201 - 16th St. NW
Washington, DC 20036-3290
202-833-4000; *Fax:* 202-822-7974
URL: www.nea.org
Scope: National
Purpose: A meeting of delegates representing state & local affiliates; duties include adopting the strategic plan & budget, forming resolutions, debating & taking action on new business items for the NEA; & voting by secret ballot on proposed amendments to the Constituion & By-Laws
Anticipated Attendance: 8,000+

• **National Environmental Health Association 2018 Annual Educational Conference & Exhibition**
Date: June 25-28, 2018
Location: Anaheim Marriott Hotel
Anaheim, CA USA
Sponsor/Contact: National Environmental Health Association
#1000N, 720 South Colorado Blvd.
Denver, CO 80246
303-756-9090; *Fax:* 303-691-9490
Toll-Free: 866-956-2258
E-mail: staff@neha.org
URL: www.neha.org
Scope: International

• **National Health Leadership Conference 2018**
Date: June 4-5, 2018
Location: St. John's, NL
Sponsor/Contact: Canadian College of Health Leaders
292 Somerset St. West
Ottawa, ON K2P 0J6
613-235-7218; *Fax:* 613-235-5451
Toll-Free: 800-363-9056
E-mail: info@cchl-ccls.ca
URL: www.cchl-ccls.ca
Scope: National
Purpose: Theme: "Creating the Winning Conditions for Change"

• **Noia Conference 2018**
Date: June 18, 2018
Location: St. John's Convention Centre
St. John's, NL
Sponsor/Contact: Noia
Atlantic Pl.
P.O. Box 44
#602, 215 Water St.
St. John's, NL A1C 6C9
709-758-6610; *Fax:* 709-758-6611
E-mail: noia@noia.ca
URL: www.noia.ca
Scope: National
Purpose: The Annual Noia Conference is a key service that provides members and the general public with information on trends and business opportunities in the East Coast Canada oil & gas industry.
Contact Information: noiaconference.com

• **North American Association of Central Cancer Registries 2018 Annual Conference**
Date: June 9-16, 2018
Location: Pittsburgh, PA USA
Sponsor/Contact: North American Association of Central Cancer Registries, Inc.
2050 West Iles, #A
Springfield, IL 62704-7412
217-698-0800; *Fax:* 217-698-0188
URL: www.naaccr.org
Scope: International
Anticipated Attendance: 450

• **North American Society of Adlerian Psychology 2018 Annual Conference**
Date: June 7-10, 2018
Location: Toronto, ON
Sponsor/Contact: North American Society of Adlerian Psychology
#276, 429 East Dupont Rd.
Fort Wayne, IN 46825
260-267-8807; *Fax:* 260-818-2098
E-mail: info@alfredadler.org
URL: www.alfredadler.org

Conferences & Conventions Index

Scope: International
Purpose: Theme: "Community, Connections & Social Interest in Challenging Times"

- **Ontario Association of Chiefs of Police 2018 Annual Meeting**
Date: June 10-13, 2018
Location: Deerhurst Resort
Huntsville, ON
Sponsor/Contact: Ontario Association of Chiefs of Police
#605, 40 College St.
Toronto, ON M5G 2J3
416-926-0424; *Fax:* 416-926-0436
Toll-Free: 800-816-1767
E-mail: oacpadmin@oacp.ca
URL: www.oacp.on.ca
Scope: Provincial
Contact Information:
www.oacpconference.on.ca

- **Ontario Genealogical Society 2018 Annual Conference**
Date: June 1-3, 2018
Location: University of Guelph
Guelph, ON
Sponsor/Contact: Ontario Genealogical Society
#202, 2100 Steeles Ave. West
Concord, ON L4K 2V1
416-489-0734; *Fax:* 855-695-8080
Toll-Free: 855-697-6687
E-mail: info@ogs.on.ca
URL: www.ogs.on.ca
Scope: International
Purpose: Theme: "Upper Canada to Ontario - The Birth of a Nation"

- **Ontario Pharmacists Association Conference 2018**
Date: June 7-9, 2018
Location: Deerhurst Resort
Huntsville, ON
Sponsor/Contact: Ontario Pharmacists' Association
#600, 155 University Ave.
Toronto, ON M5H 3B7
416-441-0788; *Fax:* 416-441-0791
Toll-Free: 877-341-0788
E-mail: mail@opatoday.com
URL: www.opatoday.com
Scope: Provincial
Anticipated Attendance: 600

- **Ontario Plumbing Inspectors Association 2018 Annual Meeting**
Date: June 10-12, 2018
Location: Ontario
Sponsor/Contact: Ontario Plumbing Inspectors Association
c/o Ursula Wengler
22 Dalegrove Cres.
Toronto, ON M9B 6A7
URL: www.opia.info
Scope: Provincial

- **Operating Room Nurses Association of Nova Scotia Annual General Meeting 2018**
Date: June 2018
Location: St. Francis Xavier University
Antigonish, NS
Sponsor/Contact: Operating Room Nurses Association of Nova Scotia
URL: www.ornans.ca
Scope: Provincial

- **Private Motor Truck Council of Canada 2018 Annual Conference**
Date: June 14-15, 2018
Location: Crowne Plaza Fallsview
Niagara Falls, ON
Sponsor/Contact: Private Motor Truck Council of Canada
#5, 225 Main St. East
Milton, ON L9T 1N9
905-827-0587; *Fax:* 905-827-8212
Toll-Free: 877-501-7682
E-mail: info@pmtc.ca
URL: www.pmtc.ca
Scope: National

- **Provincial Exhibition of Manitoba Royal Manitoba Summer Fair 2018**
Date: June 6-10, 2018
Location: Manitoba
Sponsor/Contact: Provincial Exhibition of Manitoba
115 - 10th St.
Brandon, MB R7A 4E7
204-726-3590; *Fax:* 204-725-0202
Toll-Free: 877-729-0001
E-mail: info@provincialexhibition.com
URL: www.provincialexhibition.com
Scope: Provincial

- **Registered Nurses' Association of Ontario 7th Annual Nurse Executive Leadership Academy**
Date: June 12-15, 2018
Location: Old Mill Toronto
Toronto, ON
Sponsor/Contact: Registered Nurses' Association of Ontario
158 Pearl St.
Toronto, ON M5H 1L3
416-599-1925; *Fax:* 416-599-1926
Toll-Free: 800-268-7199
URL: www.rnao.ca
Scope: Provincial
Purpose: The program features expert faculty from policy, practice and academic settings, providing up-to-date insights for knowledge and competence in governance, policy formulation, evidence-based accountability and leadership.

- **Responsible Investment Association 2018 Conference**
Date: June 4-5, 2018
Location: Hyatt Regency Toronto
Toronto, ON
Sponsor/Contact: Responsible Investment Association
#300, 215 Spadina Ave.
Toronto, ON M5T 2C7
416-461-6042
E-mail: staff@riacanada.ca
URL: riacanada.ca
Scope: National

- **Rotary International Convention 2018**
Date: June 23-27, 2018
Location: Toronto, ON
Sponsor/Contact: Rotary International
One Rotary Center
1560 Sherman Ave.
Evanston, IL 60201-3698
Toll-Free: 866-976-8279
URL: www.rotary.org
Scope: International
Contact Information: www.riconvention.org

- **Saskatchewan Publishers Group 2018 Annual Conference**
Date: June 2018
Location: Regina, SK
Sponsor/Contact: Saskatchewan Publishers Group
#324, 1831 College Ave.
Regina, SK S4P 4V5
306-780-9808; *Fax:* 306-780-9811
E-mail: info@skbooks.com
URL: www.skbooks.com
Scope: Provincial

- **Secrétariat international des infirmières et infirmiers de l'espace francophone 7e Congrès mondial**
Date: June 3-6, 2018
Location: Bordeaux, France
Sponsor/Contact: Secrétariat international des infirmières et infirmiers de l'espace francophone
#142, 4200, rue Molson
Montréal, QC H1Y 4V4
514-849-6060; *Fax:* 514-849-7870
E-mail: info@sidiief.org
URL: www.sidiief.org
Scope: International
Contact Information:
www.congres-sidiief.org

- **Society of Plastics Engineers Rotational Molding Conference 2018**
Date: June 3-6, 2018
Location: Cleveland, OH USA
Sponsor/Contact: Society of Plastics Engineers
#306, 6 Berkshire Blvd.
Bethel, CT 06801
203-775-0471; *Fax:* 203-775-8490
URL: www.4spe.org
Scope: International

- **Special Libraries Association 2018 Annual Conference & INFO-EXPO**
Date: June 11-13, 2018
Location: Baltimore, MD USA
Sponsor/Contact: Special Libraries Association
#300, 7918 Jones Branch Dr.
McLean, VA 22102
703-647-4900; *Fax:* 703-506-3266
URL: www.sla.org
Scope: International
Purpose: A gathering of information professionals, providing informative educational sessions, keynote speakers, & exhibitors
Contact Information: Senior Manager, Exhibits & Events: Sarah Driver, E-mail: sdriver@sla.org

- **Specialized Information Publishers Association (SIPA) Annual Conference 2018**
Date: June 5-7, 2018
Location: The Capital Hilton
Washington, DC USA
Sponsor/Contact: Specialized Information Publishers Association
1090 Vermont Ave. NW, 6th Fl.
Washington, DC 20005-4905
202-289-7442; *Fax:* 202-289-7097
URL: www.sipaonline.com
Scope: International

- **Statistical Society of Canada 2018 Annual Meeting**
Date: June 3-6, 2018
Location: McGill University
Montréal, QC
Sponsor/Contact: Statistical Society of Canada
#209, 1725 St. Laurent Blvd.
Ottawa, ON K1G 3V4
613-733-2662; *Fax:* 613-733-1386
E-mail: info@ssc.ca
URL: www.ssc.ca
Scope: National

- **TechnoCentre éolien/ Wind Energy TechnoCentre 12th Colloque de l'industrie éolienne québécoise 2018**
Date: June 11-13, 2018
Location: Carleton-sur-Mer, QC
Sponsor/Contact: TechnoCentre éolien
70, rue Bolduc
Gaspé, QC G4X 1G2
418-368-6162; *Fax:* 418-368-4315
E-mail: info@eolien.qc.ca
URL: www.eolien.qc.ca
Scope: Provincial
Anticipated Attendance: 200

- **The Instrumentation, Systems & Automation Society of America (ISA) 61st Power Industry Division Symposium 2018**
Date: June 26-28, 2018
Location: Knoxville, TX USA
Sponsor/Contact: The Instrumentation, Systems & Automation Society of America
P.O. Box 12277
67 T.W. Alexander Dr.
Research Triangle Park, NC 27709
919-549-8411; *Fax:* 919-549-8288
E-mail: info@isa.org
URL: www.isa.org
Scope: International

- **The L.M. Montgomery Institute's 13th Biennial Conference**
Date: June 21-24, 2018
Location: University of Prince Edward Island
Charlottetown, PE
Sponsor/Contact: L.M. Montgomery Institute
University of Prince Edward Island
550 University Ave.
Charlottetown, PE C1A 4P3
902-628-4346; *Fax:* 902-628-4305
E-mail: lmmi@upei.ca
URL: www.lmmontgomery.ca

- **The League of Canadian Poets 2018 Annual Conference & AGM**
Date: June 14-17, 2018
Location: Toronto, ON
Sponsor/Contact: The League of Canadian Poets
#312, 192 Spadina Ave.
Toronto, ON M5T 2C2
416-504-1657; *Fax:* 416-504-0096
E-mail: info@poets.ca
URL: www.poets.ca
Scope: National

- **The Society of Gynecologic Oncology of Canada 39th Annual General Meeting**
Date: June 28-30, 2018
Location: Victoria, BC
Sponsor/Contact: Society of Gynecologic Oncologists of Canada
780 Echo Dr.
Ottawa, ON K1S 5R7
613-730-4192; *Fax:* 613-730-4314
Toll-Free: 800-561-2416
URL: www.g-o-c.org
Scope: National

- **Western Finance Association 2018 Annual Meeting**
Date: June 17-20, 2018
Location: Hotel Del Coronado
Coronado, CA USA
Sponsor/Contact: Western Finance Association
c/o Bryan Routledge, Tepper School of Business, Carnegie Mellon Univ.

5000 Forbes Ave.
Pittsburgh, PA 15213
412-268-7588
E-mail: admin@westernfinance.org
URL: www.westernfinance.org
Scope: International

July

• **104th Maritime Fire Chiefs Association Annual Conference**
Date: July 13-16, 2018
Location: Moncton, NB
Sponsor/Contact: Maritime Fire Chiefs' Association
P.O. Box 6
Dartmouth, NS B2Y 3Y2
URL: www.mfca.ca
Scope: Provincial
Purpose: Information about the latest trends & innovations within the fire service

• **18th International Labour & Employment Relations Association World Congress**
Date: July 23-27, 2018
Location: Seoul, South Korea
Sponsor/Contact: International Labour & Employment Relations Association
c/o DIALOGUE
International Labour Office, 22
Geneva, CH-1211
E-mail: ilera@ilo.org
URL: www.ilo.org/public/english/iira
Scope: International

• **2018 26th International Conference on Nuclear Engineering**
Date: July 22-26, 2018
Location: London, UK
Sponsor/Contact: American Society of Mechanical Engineers
2 Park Ave.
New York, NY 10016-5990
Toll-Free: 800-843-2763
E-mail: customercare@asme.org
URL: www.asme.org
Scope: International

• **2018 American Society of Animal Science & Canadian Society of Animal Science Annual Meeting & Trade Show**
Date: July 2018
Sponsor/Contact: Canadian Society of Animal Science
c/o Eveline Ibeagha-Awemu, Agriculture & Agri-Food Canada
2000, rue College
Sherbrooke, QC J1M 0C8
819-780-7249; Fax: 819-564-5507
URL: www.asas.org/CSAS
Scope: National

• **2018 Canadian Veterinary Medical Association Convention**
Date: July 5-8, 2018
Location: Vancouver, BC
Sponsor/Contact: Canadian Veterinary Medical Association
339 Booth St.
Ottawa, ON K1R 7K1
613-236-1162; Fax: 613-236-9681
Toll-Free: 800-567-2862
E-mail: admin@cvma-acmv.org
URL: www.canadianveterinarians.net
Scope: National

• **2018 International Association of Music Libraries, Archives & Documentation Centres Congress**
Date: July 22-27, 2018
Location: Leipzig, Germany
Sponsor/Contact: International Association of Music Libraries, Archives & Documentation Centres
c/o Roger Flury, Music Room, National Library of New Zealand
P.O. Box 1467
Wellington, 6001
URL: www.iaml.info
Scope: International
Purpose: Educational sessions, social & cultural programs, & exhibits of interest to international music librarians, archivists, & documentation specialists

• **2018 Utility Contractors Association of Ontario Convention**
Date: July 29-31, 2018
Location: JW Marriott The Rosseau Muskoka Resort & Spa
Minett, ON
Sponsor/Contact: Utility Contractors Association of Ontario, Inc.
P.O. Box 762
Oakville, ON L6K 0A9
905-847-7305; Fax: 905-412-0339
E-mail: bbrown@uca.on.ca
URL: www.uca.on.ca
Scope: Provincial
Purpose: An event with guest speakers & networking activities for association members & their guests

• **33rd World Conference of the International Society for Music Education**
Date: July 15-20, 2018
Location: Baku, Azerbaijan
Sponsor/Contact: International Society for Music Education
#148, 45 Glenferrie Rd.
Malvern, VA 3144
E-mail: isme@isme.org
URL: www.isme.org
Scope: International

• **Ahmadiyya Muslim Jama'at Canada 2018 42nd Annual Convention**
Date: July 6-8, 2018
Location: International Center
Mississauga, ON
Sponsor/Contact: Ahmadiyya Muslim Jama'at Canada
10610 Jane St.
Maple, ON L6A 3A2
905-303-4000; Fax: 905-832-3220
E-mail: info@ahmadiyya.ca
URL: www.ahmadiyya.ca
Scope: National
Purpose: A Muslim convention, featuring religious addresses & the presentation of awards

• **Amalgamated Transit Union Canada Conference 2018**
Date: July 25-28, 2018
Location: St. John's, NL
Sponsor/Contact:
#210, 61 International Blvd.
Toronto, ON M9W 6K4
416-679-8846; Fax: 416-679-9195
E-mail: office@atucanada.ca
URL: www.atucanada.ca
Scope: National

• **American Association for Justice 2018 Annual Convention**
Date: July 7-10, 2018
Location: Denver Convention Center
Denver, CO USA
Sponsor/Contact: American Association for Justice
#200, 777 - 6th St. NW
Washington, DC 20001
202-965-3500
Toll-Free: 800-424-2725
E-mail: membership@justice.org
URL: www.justice.org
Scope: International

• **American Association of Naturopathic Physicians 2018 Annual Conference**
Date: July 12-14, 2018
Location: Town & Country Resort
San Diego, CA USA
Sponsor/Contact: American Association of Naturopathic Physicians
#250, 818 - 18th St. NW
Washington, DC 20006
202-237-8150; Fax: 202-237-8152
Toll-Free: 866-538-2267
E-mail: member.services@naturopathic.org
URL: www.naturopathic.org
Scope: International

• **Association of Visual Language Interpreters of Canada Summer 2018 Biennial Conference**
Date: July 9-14, 2018
Location: Niagara Falls, ON
Sponsor/Contact: Association of Visual Language Interpreters of Canada
#562, 125-A - 1030 Denman St.
Vancouver, BC V6G 2M6
778-874-3165
E-mail: avlic@avlic.ca
URL: www.avlic.ca
Scope: National

• **Canadian Association of School System Administrators Annual Conference 2018**
Date: July 4-6, 2018
Location: Ottawa Westin Hotel
Ottawa, ON
Sponsor/Contact: Canadian Association of School System Administrators
1123 Glenashton Dr.
Oakville, ON L6H 5M1
905-845-2345; Fax: 905-845-2044
URL: www.cassa-acgcs.ca
Scope: National

• **Canadian Institute of Planners 2018 Conference**
Date: July 19-22, 2018
Location: Winnipeg, MB
Sponsor/Contact: Canadian Institute of Planners
#1112, 141 Laurier Ave. West
Ottawa, ON K1P 5J3
613-237-7526; Fax: 613-237-7045
Toll-Free: 800-207-2138
E-mail: general@cip-icu.ca
URL: www.cip-icu.ca
Scope: National

• **Canadian School Boards Association / Association canadienne des commissions/conseils scolaires 2018 Congress**
Date: July 4-8, 2018
Location: Halifax, NS
Sponsor/Contact: Canadian School Boards Association
#400, 3 Place Ville Marie
Montréal, QC H3B 2E3
514-289-2988; Fax: 514-788-3334
E-mail: info@cdnsba.org
URL: www.cdnsba.org
Scope: National

• **Canadian Seed Growers' Association Annual General Meeting 2018**
Date: July 9-12, 2018
Location: Montréal, QC
Sponsor/Contact: Canadian Seed Growers' Association
P.O. Box 8455
#202, 240 Catherine St.
Ottawa, ON K1G 3T1
613-236-0497; Fax: 613-563-7855
E-mail: seeds@seedgrowers.ca
URL: www.seedgrowers.ca
Scope: National

• **Canadian Society for Brain, Behaviour & Cognitive Science 2018 Annual Meeting**
Date: July 4-8, 2018
Location: Memorial University
St. John's, NL
Sponsor/Contact: Canadian Society for Brain, Behaviour & Cognitive Science
c/o Dept. of Psychology, University of British Columbia
Vancouver, BC V6T 1Z4
E-mail: secretary@csbbcs.org
URL: www.csbbcs.org

• **Canadian Society of Plant Biologists/Société canadienne de biologie végétale Annual General Meeting 2018**
Date: July 14-18, 2018
Location: Montréal, QC
Sponsor/Contact: Canadian Society of Plant Biologists
c/o Barry Micallef, Crop Science Building, University of Guelph
117 Reynolds Walk
Guelph, ON N1G 1Y4
E-mail: secretary@cspb-scbv.ca
URL: www.cspb-scbv.ca
Scope: National
Purpose: Held in conjunction with the American Society of Plant Biologists & the International Society of Photosynthesis Research
Contact Information: URL: plantbiology.aspb.org

• **Co-operative Education & Work-Integrated Learning Canada 2018 National Conference**
Date: July 29 - August 1, 2018
Location: Concordia University
Montréal, QC
Sponsor/Contact: Co-operative Education & Work-Integrated Learning Canada
#200, 411 Richmond St. East
Toronto, ON M5A 3S5
Fax: 416-929-5256
E-mail: cewil@cewilcanada.ca
URL: www.cewilcanada.ca
Scope: National

• **Controlled Release Society 2018 45th Annual Meeting & Exposition**
Date: July 22-24, 2018
Location: New York, NY USA
Sponsor/Contact: Controlled Release Society
3340 Pilot Knob Rd.
St. Paul, MN 55121
651-454-7250; Fax: 651-454-0766
E-mail: crs@scisoc.org
URL: www.controlledreleasesociety.org
Scope: International
Contact Information: Meeting Manager: Anthony Celenza, Email: acelenza@ahint.com

Conferences & Conventions Index

- **CSBE/SCGAB 2018 AGM & Technical Conference**
Date: July 2018
Location: Guelph, ON
Sponsor/Contact: Canadian Society for Bioengineering
2028 Calico Crescent
Orléans, ON K4A 4L7
613-590-0975
E-mail: bioeng@csbe-scgab.ca
URL: csbe-scgab.ca
Scope: National

- **Entertainment Merchants Association Los Angeles Entertainment Summit 2018**
Date: July 16-18, 2018
Location: Loews Hollywood Hotel
Los Angeles, CA USA
Sponsor/Contact: Entertainment Merchants Association - International Head Office
#400, 16530 Ventura Blvd.
Encino, CA 91436-4551
818-385-1500; Fax: 818-385-0567
E-mail: info@entmerch.org
URL: www.entmerch.org
Scope: International
Purpose: Brings together key retailers, producers, & ancillary product companies in the video & video gaming industries in a forum setting
Contact Information: Vice-President, Strategic Initiatives: Carrie Dieterich, E-mail: cdieterich@entmerch.org; Phone: 818-385-1500, ext. 227

- **Institute of Food Technologists 2018 Annual Meeting & Food Expo**
Date: July 15-18, 2018
Location: McCormick Place
Chicago, IL USA
Sponsor/Contact: Institute of Food Technologists
#1000, 525 West Van Buren
Chicago, IL 60607
312-782-8424; Fax: 312-782-8348
Toll-Free: 800-438-3663
E-mail: info@ift.org
URL: www.ift.org
Scope: International
Purpose: An annual gathering of thousands of food professionals from around the world to participate in scientific sessions, poster sessions, the IFT Food Expo, an awards celebration, & networking events

- **International Association for Human Resource Information Management 2018 Talent Event**
Date: July 9-10, 2018
Location: Huntington Convention Center
Cleveland, OH USA
Sponsor/Contact: International Association for Human Resource Information Management
10060 Grandview Sq.
Duluth, GA 30097
E-mail: information@ihrim.org
URL: www.ihrim.org
Scope: International
Purpose: Theme: "The Talent Management Revolution: Technology's Role in Organizational Success"

- **International Association of Administrative Professionals Summit 2018**
Date: July 28-31, 2018
Location: JW Marriott Austin
Austin, TX USA
Sponsor/Contact: International Association of Administrative Professionals
#100, 10502 North Ambassador Dr.
Kansas City, MO 64153
816-891-6600; Fax: 816-891-9118
URL: www.iaap-hq.org
Scope: International
Purpose: Education workshops

- **International Literacy Association 2018 Conference**
Date: July 20-23, 2018
Location: Austin, TX USA
Sponsor/Contact: International Literacy Association
P.O. Box 8139
Newark, DE 19714-8139
302-731-1600
Toll-Free: 800-336-7323
E-mail: customerservice@reading.org
URL: www.literacyworldwide.org
Scope: International
Contact Information:
www.ilaconference.org

- **International Society for Augmentative & Alternative Communication (ISAAC) Biennial Conference 2018**
Date: July 21-26, 2018
Location: Gold Coast Convention and Exhibition Centre
Gold Coast, Australia
Sponsor/Contact: International Society for Augmentative & Alternative Communication
#216, 312 Dolomite St.
Toronto, ON M3J 2N2
905-850-6848; Fax: 905-850-6852
E-mail: isaac@isaac-online.org
URL: www.isaac-online.org
Scope: International

- **International Society of Indoor Air Quality & Climate 2018 Indoor Air Conference**
Date: July 22-27, 2018
Location: Pennsylvania Convention Center
Philadelphia, PA USA
Sponsor/Contact: International Society of Indoor Air Quality & Climate
c/o Gina Bendy
2548 Empire Grade
Santa Cruz, CA 95060
831-426-0148; Fax: 831-426-6522
E-mail: info@isiaq.org
URL: www.isiaq.org
Scope: International
Contact Information:
www.indoorair2018.org

- **Joint Statistical Meetings 2018**
Date: July 28 - August 2, 2018
Location: Vancouver, BC
Sponsor/Contact: Statistical Society of Canada
#209, 1725 St. Laurent Blvd.
Ottawa, ON K1G 3V4
613-733-2662; Fax: 613-733-1386
E-mail: info@ssc.ca
URL: www.ssc.ca
Scope: International
Purpose: Held jointly with the Statistical Society of Canada, American Statistical Association, the International Biometric Society (ENAR & WNAR), the International Chinese Statistical Association, the Institute of Mathematical Statistics, & the International Indian Statistical Association

- **National Association of Watch & Clock Collectors 2018 National Convention**
Date: July 18-22, 2018
Location: Wyndham Garden Hotel
York, PA USA
Sponsor/Contact: National Association of Watch & Clock Collectors, Inc.
514 Poplar St.
Columbia, PA 17512-2130
717-684-8261; Fax: 717-684-0878
Toll-Free: 877-255-1849
E-mail: info@nawcc.org
URL: www.nawcc.org
Scope: International

- **Ninety-Nines International Conference 2018**
Date: July 3-8, 2018
Location: Philadelphia, PA United States
Sponsor/Contact: The Ninety-Nines Inc.
4300 Amelia Earhart Rd., #A
Oklahoma City, OK 73159
405-685-7969; Fax: 405-685-7985
Toll-Free: 800-994-1929
E-mail: PR@ninety-nines.org
URL: www.ninety-nines.org
Purpose: Meet & network with international members; Learn about flight safety, new tools & opportunities, leadership skills & charitable opportunities

- **Ontario Horticultural Association 112th Convention**
Date: July 27-29, 2018
Location: Ambassador Hotel & Conference Centre
Kingston, ON
Sponsor/Contact: Ontario Horticultural Association
448 Paterson Ave.
London, ON N5W 5C7
E-mail: secretary@gardenontario.org
URL: www.gardenontario.org
Scope: Provincial

- **Ontario Registered Music Teachers' Association 2018 Convention**
Date: July 28-29, 2018
Location: Infinity Convention Centre
Ottawa, ON
Sponsor/Contact: Ontario Registered Music Teachers' Association
P.O. Box 635
Timmins, ON P4N 7G2
705-267-1224; Fax: 705-264-0978
E-mail: ormta@ntl.sympatico.ca
URL: www.ormta.org
Scope: Provincial

- **Recreational Aircraft Association 86th Annual Fly-In**
Date: July 14, 2018
Location: Midland, ON
Sponsor/Contact: Recreational Aircraft Association
22 - 4881 Fountain St. North
Breslau, ON N0B 1M0
519-648-3030
Toll-Free: 800-387-1028
E-mail: raa@raa.ca
URL: www.raa.ca
Purpose: Pancake breakfast; BBQ lunch; Camping; Aircraft displays

- **Soil & Water Conservation Society 73rd Annual International Conference**
Date: July 29 - August 1, 2018
Location: Albuquerque, NM USA
Sponsor/Contact: Soil & Water Conservation Society
945 SW Ankeny Rd.
Ankeny, IA 50023-9723
515-289-2331; Fax: 515-289-1227
URL: www.swcs.org
Scope: International
Contact Information: Director, Professional Development: Kim Johnson-Smith, E-mail: kim.johnson-smith@swcs.org, Phone: 515-289-2331, ext. 112

- **Soroptimist 45th Biennial Convention 2018**
Date: July 30 - August 2, 2018
Location: Pacifico Yokohama
Yokohama, Japan
Sponsor/Contact: Soroptimist International of the Americas
1709 Spruce St.
Philadelphia, PA 19103-6103
215-893-9000; Fax: 215-893-5200
E-mail: siahq@soroptimist.org
URL: www.soroptimist.org
Scope: International

- **Storytellers of Canada Conference 2018**
Date: July 4-8, 2018
Location: Peterborough, ON
Sponsor/Contact: Storytellers of Canada
#201, 192 Spadina Ave.
Toronto, ON M5T 2C2
E-mail: admin@storytellers-conteurs.ca
URL: www.storytellers-conteurs.ca
Scope: National
Purpose: Theme: "The Honour of One is the Honour of All"

- **Taking Action for Animals 2018**
Date: July 20-23, 2018
Location: Hyatt Regency Crystal City
Arlington, VA USA
Sponsor/Contact: The Humane Society of the United States
2100 L St. NW
Washington, DC 20037
202-452-1100
Toll-Free: 866-720-2676
E-mail: donorcare@humanesociety.org
URL: www.humanesociety.org
Scope: National
Purpose: An educational conference meant to inspire people to help animals; topics covered include factory farming & animal fighting

- **The Canadian Society of Professional Event Planners Annual Conference 2018**
Date: July 26-28, 2018
Location: Sudbury, ON
Sponsor/Contact: Canadian Society of Professional Event Planners
19270 Conc. #4
Alexandria, ON K0C 1A0
613-288-4539
Toll-Free: 866-467-2299
E-mail: infoc@canspep.ca
URL: www.canspep.ca
Scope: National

- **Victorian Studies Association of Western Canada 2018 Conference**
Date: July 26-28, 2018
Location: University of Victoria
Victoria, BC
Sponsor/Contact: Victorian Studies Association of Western Canada
LLPA Department, Douglas College, University of Victoria
#2635, 700 Royal Ave.
New Westminster, BC V3M 5Z5

URL: web.uvic.ca/vsawc
Scope: National
Purpose: Theme: "The Body & the Page in Victorian Culture"

• **World Credit Union Conference 2018**
Date: July 15-18, 2018
Location: Singapore
Sponsor/Contact: World Council of Credit Unions, Inc.
P.O. Box 2982
5710 Mineral Point Rd.
Madison, WI 53705-4493
608-395-2000; Fax: 608-395-2001
E-mail: mail@woccu.org
URL: www.woccu.org
Scope: International
Contact Information: www.wcuc.org

August

• **2018 Aerospace, Defence & Security Expo**
Date: August 9-10, 2018
Location: Abbotsford, BC
Sponsor/Contact: Aerospace Industries Association of Canada
#703, 255 Albert St.
Ottawa, ON K1P 6A9
613-232-4297; Fax: 613-232-1142
E-mail: info@aiac.ca
URL: www.aiac.ca
Scope: National
Purpose: Promotes the Western Canadian aerospace industry; takes place at the same time as the Abbotsford International Airshow

• **2018 American Sociological Association Annual Meeting**
Date: August 11-14, 2018
Location: Philadelphia, PA USA
Sponsor/Contact: American Sociological Association
#600, 1430 K St. NW
Washington, DC 20005
202-383-9005; Fax: 202-638-0882
E-mail: executive.office@asanet.org
URL: www.asanet.org
Scope: International
Purpose: Theme: "Feeling Race: An Invitation to Explore Racialized Emotions"

• **2018 Association of Municipalities of Ontario AGM & Annual Conference**
Date: August 19-22, 2018
Location: Shaw Centre
Ottawa, ON
Sponsor/Contact: Association of Municipalities of Ontario
#801, 200 University Ave.
Toronto, ON M5H 3C6
416-971-9856; Fax: 416-971-6191
Toll-Free: 877-426-6527
E-mail: amo@amo.on.ca
URL: www.amo.on.ca
Scope: Provincial
Purpose: A yearly gathering of municipal government officials to discuss current issues.

• **2018 Canadian Association of Insolvency & Restructuring Professionals Annual Conference**
Date: August 16-18, 2018
Location: Charlottetown, PE
Sponsor/Contact: Canadian Association of Insolvency & Restructuring Professionals
277 Wellington St. West
Toronto, ON M5V 3H2
416-204-3242; Fax: 416-204-3410
E-mail: info@cairp.ca
URL: www.cairp.ca
Scope: National
Purpose: Technical sessions plus networking opportunities & social events

• **43rd Annual International Institute of Integral Human Sciences International Conference 2018**
Date: August 10-19, 2018
Location: Montréal, QC
Sponsor/Contact: International Institute of Integral Human Sciences
P.O. Box 1387 Stn. H
Montréal, QC H3G 2N3
514-937-8359; Fax: 514-937-5380
Toll-Free: 877-937-8359
E-mail: iiihs@iiihs.org
URL: www.iiihs.org
Scope: International

• **70th Annual Institute of Public Administration of Canada Conference 2018**
Date: August 19-22, 2018
Location: Hilton Québec
Québec, QC
Sponsor/Contact: Institute of Public Administration of Canada
#401, 1075 Bay St.
Toronto, ON M5S 2B1
416-924-8787; Fax: 416-924-4992
URL: www.ipac.ca
Scope: National
Contact Information: URL: 2018.ipac.ca

• **7th International Conference on Mechanics & Industrial Engineering 2018**
Date: August 16-18, 2018
Location: Madrid, Spain
Sponsor/Contact: International Academy of Science, Engineering & Technology
#414, 1376 Bank St.
Ottawa, ON K1H 7Y3
613-695-3040
E-mail: info@international-aset.com
URL: www.international-aset.com
Scope: International
Contact Information: icmie.net

• **8th International Conference on Environmental Pollution & Remediation 2018**
Date: August 19-21, 2018
Location: Madrid, Spain
Sponsor/Contact: International Academy of Science, Engineering & Technology
#414, 1376 Bank St.
Ottawa, ON K1H 7Y3
613-695-3040
E-mail: info@international-aset.com
URL: www.international-aset.com
Scope: International
Contact Information: icepr.org

• **9th International Conference on Nanotechnology: Fundamentals and Applications 2018**
Date: August 19-21, 2018
Location: Madrid, Spain
Sponsor/Contact: International Academy of Science, Engineering & Technology
#414, 1376 Bank St.
Ottawa, ON K1H 7Y3
613-695-3040
E-mail: info@international-aset.com
URL: www.international-aset.com
Scope: International
Contact Information: icnfa.com

• **Academy of Management 2018 Annual Meeting**
Date: August 10-14, 2018
Location: Chicago, IL USA
Sponsor/Contact: Academy of Management
P.O. Box 3020
Briarcliff Manor, NY 10510-8020
914-326-1800; Fax: 914-326-1900
E-mail: membership@aom.org
URL: www.aom.org
Scope: International
Purpose: Sharing of research and expertise in all management disciplines through distinguished speakers, competitive paper sessions, symposia, panels, workshops, & special programs for doctoral students
Anticipated Attendance: 10,000+
Contact Information: Director, Meetings & Conferences: Taryn Fiore, E-mail: tfiore@aom.org

• **American Fisheries Society 148th Annual Meeting 2018**
Date: August 19-23, 2018
Location: Atlantic City Convention Center
Atlantic City, NJ USA
Sponsor/Contact: American Fisheries Society
#110, 5410 Grosvenor Lane
Bethesda, MD 20814-2199
301-897-8616; Fax: 301-897-8096
URL: www.fisheries.org
Scope: International

• **American Political Science Association 114th Annual Meeting 2018**
Date: August 31-September 2, 2018
Location: Boston, MA USA
Sponsor/Contact: American Political Science Association
1527 New Hampshire Ave. NW
Washington, DC 20036-1206
202-483-2512; Fax: 202-483-2657
E-mail: apsa@apsanet.org
URL: www.apsanet.org
Scope: International

• **Association for Baha'i Studies 2018 42nd Annual Conference**
Date: August 9-12, 2018
Location: Sheraton Atlanta Hotel
Atlanta, GA USA
Sponsor/Contact: Association for Bahá'í Studies
34 Copernicus St.
Ottawa, ON K1N 7K4
613-233-1903; Fax: 613-233-3644
E-mail: abs-na@bahai-studies.ca
URL: www.bahai-studies.ca

• **BC School Superintendents Association Summer Leadership Academy 2018**
Date: August 16-17, 2018
Location: British Columbia
Sponsor/Contact: British Columbia School Superintendents Association
#208, 1118 Homer St.
Vancouver, BC V6B 6L5
604-687-0590; Fax: 604-687-8118
E-mail: information@bcssa.org
URL: www.bcssa.org
Scope: Provincial

• **Business & Professional Women of Canada National Convention 2018**
Date: August 10-12, 2018
Sponsor/Contact: The Canadian Federation of Business & Professional Women's Clubs
2913 Centre St. North
Calgary, ON T2E 2V9
URL: www.bpwcanada.com
Scope: National
Purpose: An opportunity to educate & empower Canadian women to improve economic, political, employment, & social conditions

• **Canadian Association for Japanese Language Education Annual Conference 2018**
Date: August 21-22, 2018
Location: Huron University College
London, ON
Sponsor/Contact: Canadian Association for Japanese Language Education
P.O. Box 75133
20 Bloor St. East
Toronto, ON M4W 3T3
E-mail: cajle.pr@gmail.com
URL: www.cajle.info
Scope: National
Purpose: Theme: "Diversity & Assessment: Exploring the Significance of Assessment in a Diversifying Society"

• **Canadian Association of Chiefs of Police 2018 113th Annual Conference**
Date: August 12-15, 2018
Location: Halifax Convention Centre
Halifax, NS
Sponsor/Contact: Canadian Association of Chiefs of Police
#100, 300 Terry Fox Dr.
Kanata, ON K2K 0E3
613-595-1101; Fax: 613-383-0372
E-mail: cacp@cacp.ca
URL: www.cacp.ca
Scope: National
Purpose: Conference sessions & exhibits

• **Canadian Association of Geographers 2018 Annual Meeting**
Date: August 6-10, 2018
Location: Québec City Convention Centre
Québec, QC
Sponsor/Contact: Canadian Association of Geographers
Department of Geography, McGill University
#425, 805, rue Sherbrooke ouest
Montréal, QC H3A 2K6
514-398-4946; Fax: 514-398-7437
E-mail: valerie.shoffey@cag-acg.ca
URL: www.cag-acg.ca
Scope: National

• **Canadian Association of Police Governance Conference 2018**
Date: August 8-12, 2018
Location: Fort Gary Hotel
Winnipeg, MB
Sponsor/Contact: Canadian Association of Police Governance
#204, 78 George St.
Ottawa, ON K1N 5W1
613-344-2384; Fax: 613-344-2385
E-mail: communications@capg.ca
URL: capg.ca
Scope: National
Contact Information: capgconference.ca

• **Canadian Institute for Theatre Technology Rendez-vous 2018 Annual Conference & Trade Show**
Date: August 15-18, 2018
Location: St Catharines, ON

Conferences & Conventions Index

Sponsor/Contact: Canadian Institute for Theatre Technology
#404, 4529, rue Clark
Montréal, QC H2T 2T3
514-504-9998; Fax: 514-504-9997
Toll-Free: 888-271-3383
E-mail: info@citt.org
URL: www.citt.org
Scope: National

- **Canadian Medical Association 2018 151st Annual Meeting**
Date: August 19-22, 2018
Location: Winnipeg, MB
Sponsor/Contact: Canadian Medical Association
1209 Michael St.
Ottawa, ON K1J 7T2
613-731-8610; Fax: 613-236-8864
Toll-Free: 888-855-2555
E-mail: cmamsc@cma.ca
URL: www.cma.ca
Scope: National
Purpose: A meeting, featuring a business session to consider business & matters referred by the General Council

- **Canadian National Exhibition 2018**
Date: August 17 - September 3, 2018
Location: Canadian National Exhibition Place
Toronto, ON
Sponsor/Contact: Canadian National Exhibition Association
Exhibition Place
Toronto, ON M6K 3C3
416-263-3800; Fax: 416-263-3838
E-mail: info@theex.com
URL: www.theex.com
Scope: National

- **Canadian Quaternary Association 2018 Conference**
Date: August 2018
Sponsor/Contact: Canadian Quaternary Association
c/o Kathryn Hargan, Department of Biology, Queen's University
116 Barrie St.
Kingston, ON K7L 3N6
613-533-6000
URL: www.canqua.com
Scope: National
Purpose: Joint meeting with the American Quaternary Association (AMQUA)

- **Canadian Security Traders Association 25th Annual Conference**
Date: August 16-19, 2018
Location: Hilton Québec City
Québec, QC
Sponsor/Contact: Canadian Security Traders Association, Inc.
P.O. Box 3
31 Adelaide St. East
Toronto, ON M5C 2J6
E-mail: janice.cooper@canadiansta.org
URL: www.canadiansta.org
Scope: National

- **Catholic Women's League of Canada 2018 National Convention**
Date: August 11-14, 2018
Location: Winnipeg, MB
Sponsor/Contact: Catholic Women's League of Canada
702C Scotland Ave.
Winnipeg, MB R3M 1X5
204-927-2310; Fax: 888-831-9507
Toll-Free: 888-656-4040

E-mail: info@cwl.ca
URL: www.cwl.ca
Scope: National

- **Eastern Apicultural Society 2018 Annual Conference & Short Course**
Date: August 13-17, 2018
Location: Hampton Roads Convention Center
Hampton, VA USA
Sponsor/Contact: Eastern Apicultural Society of North America, Inc.
c/o Loretta Surprenant
P.O. Box 300
Essex, NY 12936
518-963-7593; Fax: 518-963-7593
E-mail: secretary@easternapiculture.org
URL: www.easternapiculture.org
Scope: International
Purpose: Annual business meeting, lectures, workshops, short courses, & vendor displays for beginning & advanced beekeepers
Anticipated Attendance: 500

- **Elementary Teachers' Federation of Ontario 2018 Annual Meeting**
Date: August 13-16, 2018
Location: Sheraton Centre Toronto Hotel
Toronto, ON
Sponsor/Contact: Elementary Teachers' Federation of Ontario
136 Isabella St.
Toronto, ON M4Y 1P6
416-962-3836; Fax: 416-642-2424
Toll-Free: 888-838-3836
URL: www.etfo.ca
Scope: Provincial

- **Fertilizer Canada 2018 Annual Conference**
Date: August 20-22, 2018
Location: Fairmont Le Château Frontenac
Québec, QC
Sponsor/Contact: Fertilizer Canada
#907, 350 Sparks St.
Ottawa, ON K1R 7S8
613-230-2600; Fax: 613-230-5142
E-mail: info@fertilizercanada.ca
URL: www.fertilizercanada.ca
Scope: National

- **Goldschmidt Conference 2018**
Date: August 11-17, 2018
Location: Boston, MA USA
Sponsor/Contact: Geochemical Society
c/o Earth & Planetary Sciences Department, Washington University
#CB 11691, Brookings Dr.
St. Louis, MO 63130-4899
314-935-4131; Fax: 314-935-4121
E-mail: gsoffice@geochemsoc.org
URL: www.geochemsoc.org
Scope: International
Purpose: An international conference on geochemistry
Anticipated Attendance: 3,000+

- **Institute of Transportation Engineers 2018 Annual Meeting & Exhibit**
Date: August 20-23, 2018
Location: Hilton Minneapolis
Minneapolis, MN USA
Sponsor/Contact: Institute of Transportation Engineers
#600, 1627 Eye St. NW
Washington, DC 20006
202-785-0060; Fax: 202-785-0609
E-mail: ite_staff@ite.org
URL: www.ite.org
Scope: International

- **International Academy of Energy, Minerals & Materials 2018 International Conference & Exhibition on Advanced and Nano Materials**
Date: August 6-8, 2018
Location: Québec, QC
Sponsor/Contact: International Academy of Energy, Minerals & Materials
P.O. Box 62047 Stn. Convent Glen
Orléans, ON K1C 7H8
613-830-1760
E-mail: info@iaemm.com
URL: iaemm.com
Scope: International
Contact Information: icanm2018.iaemm.com

- **International Academy of Energy, Minerals & Materials 2018 International Conference & Exhibition on Clean Energy**
Date: August 20-22, 2018
Location: Québec, QC
Sponsor/Contact: International Academy of Energy, Minerals & Materials
P.O. Box 62047 Stn. Convent Glen
Orléans, ON K1C 7H8
613-830-1760
E-mail: info@iaemm.com
URL: iaemm.com
Scope: International
Purpose: Conference topics include the following: Biomass energy, materials & technologies; Hydro energy, materials & technologies; Wind energy resources & technologies; Solar cells energy, materials & technologies; Fuel cells materials & hydrogen energy; Battery materials & technologies; Energy storage techniques; Nanotechnology & energy; Green buildings; Energy process & system simulation, modelling & optimization; & more
Contact Information: icce2018.iaemm.com

- **International Association of Sedimentologists (IAS) International Sedimentological Congress 2018**
Date: August 13-17, 2018
Location: Québec, QC
Sponsor/Contact: International Association of Sedimentologists
c/o Ghent University
#8, Krijgslaan 281
Gent, 90000
URL: www.sedimentologists.org
Scope: International

- **International Continence Society 2018 Annual Meeting**
Date: August 28-31, 2018
Location: Philadelphia, PA USA
Sponsor/Contact: International Continence Society
19 Portland Sq.
Bristol, BS2 8SJ
E-mail: info@icsoffice.org
URL: www.icsoffice.org
Scope: International
Purpose: Educational workshops & a scientific meeting for urological, gynaecological, physiotherapy, & nursing professionals.

- **International Federation of Library Associations & Institutions World Library & Information Congress 2018**
Date: August 24-30, 2018
Location: Kuala Lumpur, Malaysia
Sponsor/Contact: International Federation of Library Associations & Institutions

P.O. Box 95312
The Hague, 2509 CH
E-mail: ifla@ifla.org
URL: www.ifla.org
Scope: International
Contact Information: 2018.ifla.org;
Congress Secretariat: wlic2018@kit-group.org

- **International Humanist & Ethical Union General Assembly 2018**
Date: August 3-6, 2018
Location: Auckland, New Zealand
Sponsor/Contact: International Humanist & Ethical Union
39 Moreland St.
London, EC1V 8BB
URL: www.iheu.org
Scope: International

- **International Ornithological Congress 2018**
Date: August 19-26, 2018
Location: Vancouver, BC
Sponsor/Contact: Society of Canadian Ornithologists
C/O Lance Laviolette, Membership Secretary
22350 County Rd. 10, RR #1
Glen Robertson, ON K0B 1H0
URL: www.sco-soc.ca
Scope: International

- **Latin America CACS Conference 2018**
Date: August 27-28, 2018
Location: Lima, Peru
Sponsor/Contact: ISACA
#1010, 3701 Algonquin Rd.
Rolling Meadows, IL 60008
847-253-1545; Fax: 847-253-1443
E-mail: news@isaca.org
URL: www.isaca.org
Scope: International
Purpose: An industry event for ISACA members, IS Audit, Assurance, Security & Risk Management Professionals worldwide; includes expert-led workshops & professional development opportunities
Contact Information: ISACA Training & Education, Phone: 847-660-5670, Fax: 847-253-1443

- **Master Brewers Association of the Americas 2018 Brewing Summit**
Date: August 13-15, 2018
Location: San Diego, CA USA
Sponsor/Contact: Master Brewers Association of The Americas
3340 Pilot Knob Rd.
St. Paul, MN 55121-2097
651-454-7250; Fax: 651-454-0766
E-mail: mbaa@mbaa.com
URL: www.mbaa.com
Scope: International

- **METROSHOW Vancouver Spring 2018**
Date: August 8-12, 2018
Location: Vancouver, BC
Sponsor/Contact: METROSHOW Vancouver
#103, 1951 Glen Dr.
Vancouver, BC V6A 4J6
604-929-8995; Fax: 604-357-1995
E-mail: info@metroshow.ca
URL: www.metroshow.ca
Scope: Provincial
Purpose: A one-of-a-kind fashion industry buying show held at various venues around Vancouver; contains 130+ apparel, footwear & giftware agencies selling in showrooms

- **Oasis 2018**
Date: August 23-26, 2018
Location: Acadia University
Wolfville, NS
Sponsor/Contact: Convention of Atlantic Baptist Churches
1655 Manawagonish Rd.
Saint John, NB E2M 3Y2
506-635-1922; *Fax:* 506-635-0366
E-mail: cabc@baptist-atlantic.ca
URL: www.baptist-atlantic.ca
Scope: Provincial

- **Orthotics Prosthetics Canada 2018 National Conference**
Date: August 8-11, 2018
Location: The Westin Hotel
Ottawa, ON
Sponsor/Contact: Orthotics Prosthetics Canada
National Office
#202, 300 March Rd.
Ottawa, ON K2K 2E2
613-595-1919; *Fax:* 613-595-1155
E-mail: info@opcanada.ca
URL: www.opcanada.ca
Scope: National

- **Pacific Northwest Library Association 2018 Conference**
Date: August 1-3, 2018
Location: Kalispell, MT USA
Sponsor/Contact: Pacific Northwest Library Association
c/o Candice Stenstrom, Public Library InterLINK
#158, 5489 Byrne Rd.
Burnaby, BC V5J 3J1
604-437-8441; *Fax:* 604-437-8410
URL: www.pnla.org
Scope: Provincial

- **Pet Industry Joint Advisory Council ExpoZoo 2018**
Date: August 26-27, 2018
Location: Centrexpo Drummondville
Drummondville, QC
Sponsor/Contact: Pet Industry Joint Advisory Council
#14, 1010 Polytek St.
Ottawa, ON K1J 9H9
613-730-8111; *Fax:* 613-730-9111
Toll-Free: 800-667-7452
E-mail: info@pijaccanada.com
URL: www.pijaccanada.com
Scope: Provincial
Purpose: A trade show providing visitors with the opportunity to explore the Québec pet market

- **Royal Canadian Numismatic Association 2018 Convention**
Date: August 7-11, 2018
Location: Hilton Mississauga
Mississauga, ON
Sponsor/Contact: Royal Canadian Numismatic Association
#432, 5694 Hwy. 7 East
Markham, ON L3P 1B4
647-401-4014; *Fax:* 905-472-9645
E-mail: info@rcna.ca
URL: www.rcna.ca
Scope: National
Purpose: An annual event, presenting an education symposium, a bourse & display, business meetings, award presentations, plus social & networking activities
Contact Information: E-mail: info@rcna.ca

- **The Canadian Medical Protective Association 2018 Annual Meeting**
Date: August 22, 2018
Location: Winnipeg, MB
Sponsor/Contact: The Canadian Medical Protective Association
P.O. Box 8225 Stn. T
Ottawa, ON K1G 3H7
613-725-2000; *Fax:* 613-725-1300
Toll-Free: 800-267-6522
E-mail: inquiries@cmpa.ca
URL: www.cmpa-acpm.ca

- **The Instrumentation, Systems & Automation Society of America (ISA) 2018 Water / Wastewater & Automatic Controls Symposium**
Date: August 8-9, 2018
Location: Bethesda, MD USA
Sponsor/Contact: The Instrumentation, Systems & Automation Society of America
P.O. Box 12277
67 T.W. Alexander Dr.
Research Triangle Park, NC 27709
919-549-8411; *Fax:* 919-549-8288
E-mail: info@isa.org
URL: www.isa.org
Scope: International
Purpose: An event presented by the ISA Water / Wastewater Industries Division

- **The Royal Canadian Legion 47th Dominion Convention 2018**
Date: August 25-29, 2018
Location: Winnipeg, MB
Sponsor/Contact: The Royal Canadian Legion
Dominion Command
86 Aird Place
Ottawa, ON K2L 0A1
613-591-3335; *Fax:* 613-591-9335
Toll-Free: 888-556-6222
E-mail: info@legion.ca
URL: www.legion.ca
Scope: International
Contact Information: Phone: 888-556-6222

- **Uniform Law Conference of Canada 2018 Conference**
Date: August 12-16, 2018
Location: Delta Hotel
Québec, QC
Sponsor/Contact: Uniform Law Conference of Canada
c/o 622 Hochelaga St.
Ottawa, ON K1K 2E9
613-747-1695; *Fax:* 613-941-9310
E-mail: conference@ulcc.ca
URL: www.ulcc.ca
Scope: National

- **World Leisure & Recreation Association World Leisure Congress 2018**
Date: August 28 - September 1, 2018
Location: Sao Paulo, Brazil
Sponsor/Contact: World Leisure & Recreation Association
Institute of Leisure Studies, University of Duesto
Bilbao, 48007
E-mail: secretariat@worldleisure.org
URL: www.worldleisure.org
Scope: International
Contact Information: E-mail: communication@worldleisure.org

September

- **10th Canadian Society for Quality Congress**
Date: September 24-25, 2018
Location: Vancouver, BC
Sponsor/Contact: Canadian Society for Quality
c/o Dr. Madhav Sinha
Winnipeg, MB
204-261-6606
E-mail: csq@shaw.ca
URL: canadianqualitycongress.com
Scope: National
Purpose: Theme: "Innovation & Transformation to Embrace Change"

- **2018 Association of Canadian Pension Management National Conference**
Date: September 11-13, 2018
Location: Fairmont Le Château Frontenac
Québec, QC
Sponsor/Contact: Association of Canadian Pension Management
#304, 1255 Bay St.
Toronto, ON M5R 2A9
416-964-1260; *Fax:* 416-964-0567
E-mail: info@acpm.com
URL: www.acpm.com
Scope: National

- **2018 Canadian Association of Thoracic Surgeons Annual Meeting**
Date: September 13-16, 2018
Location: St. John's, NL
Sponsor/Contact: Canadian Association of Thoracic Surgeons
#300, 421 Gilmour St.
Ottawa, ON K2P 0R5
E-mail: cats@canadianthoracicsurgeons.ca
URL: www.canadianthoracicsurgeons.ca
Scope: National

- **2018 Canadian Society for Aesthetic Plastic Surgery 45th Annual Meeting**
Date: September 21-22, 2018
Location: Westin Montréal
Montréal, QC
Sponsor/Contact: Canadian Society for Aesthetic Plastic Surgery
70 Carson Ave.
Whitby, ON L1M 1J5
905-665-9889; *Fax:* 905-665-7319
E-mail: info@csaps.ca
URL: www.csaps.ca
Scope: National

- **2018 Canadian Surgery Forum**
Date: September 13-15, 2018
Location: Delta Hotel St. John's & The St. John's Convention Centre
St. John's, NL
Sponsor/Contact: Canadian Association of General Surgeons
P.O. Box 1428 Stn. B
Ottawa, ON K1P 5R4
613-882-6510
E-mail: cags@cags-accg.ca
URL: www.cags-accg.ca
Scope: National
Contact Information: URL: www.canadiansurgeryforum.com

- **2018 Industrial Truck Association Annual Meeting**
Date: September 26-29, 2018
Location: Ponte Vedra Inn & Club
Ponte Vedra Beach, FL USA
Sponsor/Contact: Industrial Truck Association
#460, 1750 K St. NW
Washington, DC 20006
202-296-9880; *Fax:* 202-296-9884
URL: www.indtrk.org
Purpose: Annual meeting for members of the Industrial Truck Association

- **26th Supply Chain Management Association BC Education Conference**
Date: September 26-28, 2018
Location: British Columbia
Sponsor/Contact: Supply Chain Management Association - British Columbia
#300, 435 Columbia St.
New Westminster, BC V3L 5N8
604-540-4494; *Fax:* 604-540-4023
Toll-Free: 800-411-7622
E-mail: info@scmabc.ca
URL: www.scmabc.ca
Scope: Provincial

- **38th Annual Conference of the Canadian Healthcare Engineering Society**
Date: September 16-18, 2018
Location: St. John's Convention Centre
St. John's, NL
Sponsor/Contact: Canadian Healthcare Engineering Society
#310, 4 Cataraqui St.
Kingston, ON K7K 1Z7
613-531-2661; *Fax:* 613-531-0626
E-mail: ches@eventsmgt.com
URL: www.ches.org
Scope: National
Purpose: Theme: "Smarter Infrastructure for Enhanced Patient Outcomes"

- **39th Annual Canadian Association of Petroleum Landmen Conference 2018**
Date: September 2018
Location: Regina, SK
Sponsor/Contact: Canadian Association of Petroleum Landmen
#1600, 520 - 5 Ave. SW
Calgary, AB T2P 3R7
403-237-6635; *Fax:* 403-263-1620
E-mail: reception@landman.ca
URL: www.landman.ca
Scope: National

- **45th International Association of Hydrogeologists Congress**
Date: September 9-14, 2018
Location: Daejeon, Korea
Sponsor/Contact: International Association of Hydrogeologists
IAH Secretariat
P.O. Box 4130 Stn. Goring
Reading, KOA 1L0 RG8 6BJ
E-mail: info@iah.org
URL: www.iah.org
Scope: International
Contact Information: www.iah2018.org

- **60th Association of Canadian Port Authorities Annual Conference & General Meeting**
Date: September 10-13, 2018
Location: Saint John, NB
Sponsor/Contact: Association of Canadian Port Authorities
#1006, 75 Albert St.
Ottawa, ON K1P 5E7
613-232-2036; *Fax:* 613-232-9554
E-mail: info@acpa-ports.net
URL: www.acpa-ports.net
Purpose: Brings together Canadian professionals and key decision makers to discuss port trade topics and issues; speaker series

- **71st Canadian Geotechnical Conference**
Date: September 23-26, 2018

Conferences & Conventions Index

Location: Edmonton, AB
Sponsor/Contact: Canadian Geotechnical Society
8828 Pigott Rd.
Richmond, BC V7A 2C4
604-277-7527; Fax: 604-277-7529
Toll-Free: 800-710-9867
URL: www.cgs.ca
Scope: National
Purpose: Theme: "Transportation Geotechnique - Moving Forward"
Contact Information:
www.geoedmonton2018.ca

- **Alberta Automotive Recyclers & Dismantlers Association AGM & Conference 2018**
Date: September 22-23, 2018
Location: Drumheller, AB
Sponsor/Contact: Alberta Automotive Recyclers & Dismantlers Association
20 Oakmount Dr.
St. Albert, AB T8N 6K6
780-478-5820; Fax: 780-628-6463
E-mail: admin@aarda.com
URL: www.aarda.com
Scope: Provincial

- **Alberta Professional Planners Institute 2018 Conference**
Date: September 30 - October 2, 2018
Location: Kananaskis Lodge
Kananaskis, AB
Sponsor/Contact: Alberta Professional Planners Institute
P.O. Box 596
Edmonton, AB T5J 2K8
780-435-8716; Fax: 780-452-7718
Toll-Free: 888-286-8716
E-mail: admin@albertaplanners.com
URL: www.albertaplanners.com
Scope: National

- **American Planning Association Policy & Advocacy Conference 2018**
Date: September 23-25, 2018
Location: Washington, DC USA
Sponsor/Contact: American Planning Association
#750 West, 1030 15th St. NW
Washington, DC 20005-1503
202-872-0611; Fax: 202-872-0643
E-mail: customerservice@planning.org
URL: www.planning.org
Scope: International

- **American Society for Bone & Mineral Research 2018 Annual Meeting**
Date: September 28 - October 1, 2018
Location: Palais des Congrès de Montréal
Montréal, QC
Sponsor/Contact: American Society for Bone & Mineral Research
#800, 2025 M St. NW
Washington, DC 20036-3309
E-mail: asbmr@asbmr.org
URL: www.asbmr.org
Scope: International
Purpose: Plenary & poster sessions, panel discussions, & networking events

- **ASM International Advanced Thermal Processing Technology Conference & Expo**
Date: September 25-28, 2018
Location: Fiesta Americana
Querétaro, Mexico
Sponsor/Contact: ASM International
9639 Kinsman Rd.
Materials Park, OH 44073-0002
440-338-5151; Fax: 440-338-4634
Toll-Free: 800-336-5152
E-mail: memberservicecenter@asminternational.org
URL: www.asminternational.org
Scope: International

- **Association canadienne d'éducation de langue française 2018 Congrès pancanadien**
Date: September 27-29, 2018
Location: Moncton, NB
Sponsor/Contact: Association canadienne d'éducation de langue française
#303, 265, rue de la Couronne
Québec, QC G1K 6E1
418-681-4661; Fax: 418-681-3389
E-mail: info@acelf.ca
URL: www.acelf.ca
Scope: National

- **Association for Preservation Technology International 2018 Annual Conference**
Date: September 22-26, 2018
Location: Buffalo, NY USA
Sponsor/Contact: Association for Preservation Technology International
#200, 3085 Stevenson Dr.
Springfield, IL
E-mail: info@apti.org
URL: www.apti.org
Scope: International
Purpose: Training & networking opportunities plus exhibits of interest to an international audience of persons involved in the application of methods & materials to conserve historic structures
Anticipated Attendance: 1,000

- **Atlantic Canada Water & Wastewater Association 2018 71st Annual Conference**
Date: September 16-19, 2018
Location: Sydney, NS
Sponsor/Contact: Atlantic Canada Water & Wastewater Association
131 Shrewsbury Rd.
Dartmouth, NS B2V 2R6
902-434-6002; Fax: 902-435-7796
E-mail: contact@acwwa.ca
URL: www.acwwa.ca
Scope: Provincial
Purpose: A trade show, plus educational sessions & networking opportunities for Atlantic Canada's water professionals

- **Atlantic Insurance Brokers Convention 2018**
Date: September 19-20, 2018
Location: St. John's, NL
Sponsor/Contact: Insurance Brokers Association of Canada
380 Bedford Hwy
Halifax, NS B3M 2L4
902-876-0526; Fax: 902-876-0527
E-mail: info@ibans.com
URL: www.ibans.com
Scope: Provincial
Contact Information: URL: www.brokersconvention.ca

- **BC Road Builders Fall Conference**
Date: September 16, 2018
Location: British Columbia
Sponsor/Contact: British Columbia Road Builders & Heavy Construction Association
#307, 8678 Greenall Ave.
Burnaby, BC V5J 3M6
604-436-0220; Fax: 604-436-2627
E-mail: info@roadbuilders.bc.ca
URL: www.roadbuilders.bc.ca
Scope: Provincial

- **Canadian Academy of Child and Adolescent Psychiatry 38th Annual Conference**
Date: September 16-18, 2018
Location: Halifax, NS
Sponsor/Contact: Canadian Academy of Child & Adolescent Psychiatry
#701, 141 Laurier Ave. West
Ottawa, ON K1P 5J3
613-288-0408; Fax: 613-234-9857
E-mail: info@cacap-acpea.org
URL: www.cacap-acpea.org
Scope: National

- **Canadian Association for Pharmacy Distribution Management 2018 September Member Forum**
Date: September 18, 2018
Location: Angus Glen Golf Club
Markham, ON
Sponsor/Contact: Canadian Association for Pharmacy Distribution Management
#301A, 3800 Steeles Ave. West
Woodbridge, ON L4L 4G9
905-265-1706; Fax: 905-265-9372
URL: www.capdm.ca
Scope: National
Contact Information: Allison Chan, Phone: 905-265-1706, ext. 223, Email: allison@capdm.ca

- **Canadian Association of Fire Chiefs Fire-Rescue Canada 2018**
Date: September 16-19, 2018
Location: Ottawa, ON
Sponsor/Contact: Canadian Association of Fire Chiefs
#702, 280 Albert St.
Ottawa, ON K1P 5G8
613-270-9138
Toll-Free: 800-775-5189
URL: www.cafc.ca
Scope: National
Purpose: Speaker presentations, seminars, & workshops for the fire & emergency services community from across Canada & the United States
Contact Information: Director, Events & Operations: Vicky Constantineau, E-mail: vconstantineau@cafc.ca

- **Canadian Association of Orthodontists 2018 70th Annual Scientific Session**
Date: September 6-8, 2018
Location: Westin Bayshore Hotel
Vancouver, BC
Sponsor/Contact: Canadian Association of Orthodontists
#210, 2800 - 14th Ave.
Toronto, ON L3R 0E4
416-491-3186; Fax: 416-491-1670
Toll-Free: 877-226-8800
E-mail: cao@associationconcepts.ca
URL: www.cao-aco.org
Scope: National
Purpose: A scientific session with exhibits

- **Canadian Association of Radiation Oncology 2018 Annual Scientific Meeting**
Date: September 12-15, 2018
Location: Le Centre Sheraton Montréal Hôtel
Montréal, QC
Sponsor/Contact: Canadian Association of Radiation Oncology
#6, 20 Crown Steel Dr.
Markham, ON L3R 9X9
905-415-3917; Fax: 905-415-0071
Toll-Free: 855-415-3917
E-mail: caro-acro@secretariatcentral.com
URL: www.caro-acro.ca
Scope: National
Purpose: Joint meeting held in partnership with the Canadian Organization of Medical Physicists (COMP) & the Canadian Association of Medical Radiation Technologists (CAMRT)

- **Canadian Chamber of Commerce 2018 AGM and Convention**
Date: September 22-24, 2018
Location: Thunder Bay, ON
Sponsor/Contact: The Canadian Chamber of Commerce
#420, 360 Albert St.
Ottawa, ON K1R 7X7
613-238-4000; Fax: 613-238-7643
E-mail: info@chamber.ca
URL: www.chamber.ca
Scope: National

- **Canadian Council for Refugees Summer Working Group Meetings 2018**
Date: September 7-8, 2018
Location: Montréal, QC
Sponsor/Contact: Canadian Council for Refugees
#302, 6839, rue Drolet
Montréal, QC H2S 2T1
514-277-7223; Fax: 514-277-1447
E-mail: info@ccrweb.ca
URL: www.ccrweb.ca
Scope: National

- **Canadian Ferry Association's Conference**
Date: September 30 - October 2, 2018
Location: Whistler, BC
Sponsor/Contact: Canadian Ferry Association
c/o Mr. Serge Buy
70 George St., 3rd Fl.
Ottawa, ON K1N 5V9
613-686-3838; Fax: 866-851-5689
E-mail: info@canadianferry.ca
URL: www.canadianferry.ca
Purpose: Provides industry-specific workshops, networking, exhibitors & a speaker series

- **Canadian Fertility & Andrology Society 2018 64th Annual Meeting**
Date: September 13-15, 2018
Location: Le Westin Montreal
Montréal, QC
Sponsor/Contact: Canadian Fertility & Andrology Society
#301, 1719, rue Grand Trunk
Montréal, QC H3K 1M1
514-524-9009; Fax: 514-524-2163
E-mail: info@cfas.ca
URL: www.cfas.ca
Scope: National
Purpose: Educational presentations, a trade show, & networking opportunities for persons involved in the field of reproductive medicine

- **Canadian Health Food Association (CHFA) East 2018**
Date: September 13-16, 2018
Location: Metro Toronto Convention Centre, South Building
Toronto, ON

Sponsor/Contact: Canadian Health Food Association
#302, 235 Yorkland Blvd.
Toronto, ON M2J 4Y8
416-497-6939; *Fax:* 416-497-3214
Toll-Free: 800-661-4510
E-mail: info@chfa.ca
URL: www.chfa.ca
Scope: Provincial
Purpose: A trade event, featuring exhibits from leading suppliers, manufacturers, distributors, & brokers of natural health products & organics
Anticipated Attendance: 2,900
Contact Information: Phone: 416-497-6939, Toll-Free Phone: 1-800-661-4510, E-mail: info@chfa.ca

- **Canadian Institute of Forestry 110th AGM 2018**
Date: September 16-21, 2018
Location: Grande Prairie, AB
Sponsor/Contact: Canadian Institute of Forestry
P.O. Box 99
6905 Hwy. 17 West
Mattawa, ON P0H 1V0
705-744-1715; *Fax:* 705-744-1716
E-mail: admin@cif-ifc.org
URL: www.cif-ifc.org
Scope: National

- **Canadian Insurance Accountants Association 2018 54th Annual Conference**
Date: September 23-26, 2018
Location: Fairmont Montebello
Montebello, QC
Sponsor/Contact: Canadian Insurance Accountants Association
#301, 250 Consumers Rd.
Toronto, ON M2J 4V6
416-494-1440
E-mail: ciaa@ciaa.org
URL: www.ciaa.org
Scope: National

- **Canadian Marketing Association CMAideas**
Date: September 19, 2018
Sponsor/Contact: Canadian Marketing Association
#603, 55 University Ave.
Toronto, ON M5J 2H7
416-391-2362; *Fax:* 416-441-4062
Toll-Free: 800-267-8805
E-mail: info@thecma.ca
URL: www.the-cma.org
Scope: National
Purpose: Brings together a unique conference of creators, innovators and leaders with insights from unlikely places and undiscovered territories.

- **Canadian Mineral Analysts Annual Conference & Exhibition 2018**
Date: September 9-13, 2018
Location: Prestige Mountain Resort & Conference Centre
Rossland, BC
Sponsor/Contact: Canadian Mineral Analysts
c/o John Gregorchuk
444 Harold Ave. West
Winnipeg, MB R2C 2E2
204-224-1443
URL: www.canadianmineralanalysts.com
Scope: National
Contact Information: www.2018cma.com

- **Canadian Parking Association 2018 Conference & Trade Show**
Date: September 16-20, 2018
Location: Sheraton Centre Toronto
Toronto, ON
Sponsor/Contact: Canadian Parking Association
#350, 2255 St. Laurent Blvd.
Ottawa, ON K1G 4K3
613-727-0700; *Fax:* 613-727-3183
E-mail: info@canadianparking.ca
URL: www.canadianparking.ca
Scope: National

- **Canadian Psychiatric Association 68th Annual Conference / 68e Conférence annuelle de l'Association des psychiatres du Canada**
Date: September 27-29, 2018
Location: The Westin Harbour Castle
Toronto, ON
Sponsor/Contact: Canadian Psychiatric Association
#701, 141 Laurier Ave. West
Ottawa, ON K1P 5J3
613-234-2815; *Fax:* 613-234-9857
Toll-Free: 800-267-1555
E-mail: cpa@cpa-apc.org
URL: www.cpa-apc.org
Scope: National
Anticipated Attendance: 1,100
Contact Information: E-mail: conference@cpa-apc.org

- **Canadian Society for Vascular Surgery 2018 40th Annual Meeting**
Date: September 28-29, 2018
Location: Montréal, QC
Sponsor/Contact: Canadian Society for Vascular Surgery
P.O. Box 58062
Ottawa, ON K1C 7H4
613-286-7583
E-mail: info@canadianvascular.ca
URL: canadianvascular.ca
Scope: National
Purpose: The annual general meeting of the society, plus continuing education sessions, lectures, exhibits, & social events

- **Canadian Society of Safety Engineering 2018 Professional Development Conference**
Date: September 16-19, 2018
Location: Niagara Falls, ON
Sponsor/Contact: Canadian Society of Safety Engineering, Inc.
468 Queen St. East, LL-02
Toronto, ON M5A 1T7
416-646-1600; *Fax:* 416-646-9460
Toll-Free: 877-446-2674
URL: www.csse.org
Scope: National
Purpose: Theme: "People, Purpose & Passion: The Pathway to OHS Success"

- **Canadian Student Leadership Conference 2018**
Date: September 25, 2018
Location: Edmonton, AB
Sponsor/Contact: Canadian Student Leadership Association
2460 Tanner Rd.
Victoria, BC V8Z 5R1
URL: studentleadership.ca
Scope: National

- **Coal Association of Canada 2018 Conference**
Date: September 12-14, 2018
Location: Westin Bayshore
Vancouver, BC
Sponsor/Contact: Coal Association of Canada
#150, 205 - 9th Ave. SE
Calgary, AB T2G 0R3
403-262-1544; *Fax:* 403-265-7604
Toll-Free: 800-910-2625
E-mail: info@coal.ca
URL: www.coal.ca
Scope: National

- **Dynamics 2018: The Annual National Convention & Product Exhibition of the Canadian Association of Critical Care Nurses**
Date: September 24-26, 2018
Location: Calgary, AB
Sponsor/Contact: Canadian Association of Critical Care Nurses
P.O. Box 25322
London, ON N6B 6B1
519-649-5284; *Fax:* 519-649-1458
Toll-Free: 866-477-9077
E-mail: caccn@caccn.ca
URL: www.caccn.ca
Scope: National
Purpose: Featuring programming to enhance education, clinical practice, research, & leadership.
Contact Information: Toll-Free Phone: 1-866-477-9077; E-mail: caccn@caccn.ca

- **Economic Developers Association of Canada 50th Annual Conference**
Date: September 8-11, 2018
Location: Fredericton, NB
Sponsor/Contact: Economic Developers Association of Canada
#200, 7 Innovation Dr.
Hamilton, ON L9H 7H9
905-689-8771
E-mail: info@edac.ca
URL: www.edac.ca
Scope: National

- **Entertainment Merchants Association Digital Media Pipeline 2018**
Date: September 26, 2018
Location: Skirball Cultural Center
Los Angeles, CA USA
Sponsor/Contact: Entertainment Merchants Association - International Head Office
#400, 16530 Ventura Blvd.
Encino, CA 91436-4551
818-385-1500; *Fax:* 818-385-0567
E-mail: info@entmerch.org
URL: www.entmerch.org
Scope: International
Purpose: Unites executives, retailers, distributors, content aggregators, & new technology companies to discuss the digital delivery of home entertainment
Contact Information: Vice-President, Strategic Initiatives: Carrie Dieterich, E-mail: cdieterich@entmerch.org; Phone: 818-385-1500, ext. 227

- **Family Enterprise Xchange 2018 Symposium**
Date: September 24-26, 2018
Location: Niagara-on-the-Lake, ON
Sponsor/Contact: Family Enterprise Xchange
#135, 690 Dorval Dr.
Oakville, ON L6K 3W7
905-337-8375; *Fax:* 905-337-0572
Toll-Free: 866-849-0099
URL: www.family-enterprise-xchange.com

- **Highland Games & Gathering 2018**
Date: September 8-9, 2018
Location: Bible Hill, NS
Sponsor/Contact: Colchester Highland Games & Gathering Society
60 Eastmount Ct.
East Mountain, NS B6L 2E8
902-897-4712
E-mail: events@colchesterhighlandgames.com
URL: www.colchesterhighlandgames.com
Scope: Local

- **Intermodal Association of North America Intermodal EXPO 2018**
Date: September 16-18, 2018
Location: Long Beach, CA USA
Sponsor/Contact: Intermodal Association of North America
#1100, 11785 Beltsville Dr.
Calverton, MD 20705
301-982-3400; *Fax:* 301-982-4815
E-mail: info@intermodal.org
URL: www.intermodal.org
Scope: International

- **International Board on Books for Young People 2018 36th International Congress**
Date: September 1-4, 2018
Location: Istanbul, Turkey
Sponsor/Contact: International Board on Books for Young People
Nonnenweg 12, Postfach
Basel, CH-4003
E-mail: ibby@ibby.org
URL: www.ibby.org
Scope: International
Purpose: A biennial congress, hosted by an IBBY national section, for IBBY members & people involved in children's books & reading development from around the world. This year's theme is "East Meets West Around Children's Books & Fairy Tales."
Contact Information: www.ibbycongress2018.org

- **International Society of Hypertension 27th Scientific Meeting**
Date: September 19-23, 2018
Location: Beijing, China
Sponsor/Contact: International Society of Hypertension
ISH Secretariat, The Conference Collective Ltd.
8 Waldegrave Rd.
Teddington, TW11 8GT
E-mail: secretariat@ish-world.com
URL: www.ish-world.com
Scope: International
Purpose: Scientific program & exhibition

- **International Solar Energy Society (ISES) EuroSun 2018**
Date: September 10-13, 2018
Location: Rapperswil, Switzerland
Sponsor/Contact: International Solar Energy Society
International Headquarters, Villa Tannheim
Wiesentalstrasse 50
Freiburg, 79115
E-mail: hq@ises.org
URL: www.ises.org
Scope: International

- **International Union of Pure & Applied Chemistry 22nd Annual Conference on Organic Synthesis**
Date: September 16-21, 2018
Location: Florence, Italy

Conferences & Conventions Index

Sponsor/Contact: International Union of Pure & Applied Chemistry
IUPAC Secretariat, Bldg. 19
P.O. Box 13757
Research Triangle Park, NC 27709-3757
Fax: 919-485-8706
URL: www.iupac.org
Scope: International

- **International Union of Pure & Applied Chemistry 8th Annual Conference on Green Chemistry 2018**
Date: September 9-14, 2018
Location: Bangkok, Thailand
Sponsor/Contact: International Union of Pure & Applied Chemistry
IUPAC Secretariat, Bldg. 19
P.O. Box 13757
Research Triangle Park, NC 27709-3757
Fax: 919-485-8706
URL: www.iupac.org
Scope: International

- **International Water Association World Water Congress & Exhibition 2018**
Date: September 16-21, 2018
Location: Tokyo, Japan
Sponsor/Contact: International Water Association
Alliance House
12 Caxton St.
London, SW1H 0QS
E-mail: water@iwahq.org
URL: www.iwa-network.org
Scope: International
Purpose: Provides international water experts the change to explore the science & practice of water management

- **Investment Funds Institute of Canada (IFIC) Annual Leadership Conference 2018**
Date: September 27, 2018
Location: The Carlu
Toronto, ON
Sponsor/Contact: Investment Funds Institute of Canada
11 King St. West, 4th Fl.
Toronto, ON M5H 4C7
416-363-2150
Toll-Free: 866-347-1961
E-mail: member-services@ific.ca
URL: www.ific.ca
Scope: National

- **LOMA 2018 Annual Conference**
Date: September 5-7, 2018
Sponsor/Contact: LOMA Canada
East Tower
675 Cochrane Dr., 6th Floor
Markham, ON L3R 0B8
905-530-2309; *Fax:* 905-530-2001
E-mail: lomacanada@loma.org
URL: www.loma.org/canada
Scope: National
Contact Information: E-mail: meetings@loma.org

- **METROSHOW Vancouver Spring 2018**
Date: September 13-18, 2018
Location: Vancouver, BC
Sponsor/Contact: METROSHOW Vancouver
#103, 1951 Glen Dr.
Vancouver, BC V6A 4J6
604-929-8995; *Fax:* 604-357-1995
E-mail: info@metroshow.ca
URL: www.metroshow.ca
Scope: Provincial
Purpose: A one-of-a-kind fashion industry buying show held at various venues around Vancouver; contains 130+ apparel, footwear & giftware agencies selling in showrooms

- **Mechanical Contractors Association of Canada 77th Annual National Conference**
Date: September 19-22, 2018
Location: Whistler, BC
Sponsor/Contact: Mechanical Contractors Association of Canada
#701, 280 Albert St.
Ottawa, ON K1P 5G8
613-232-0492
E-mail: mcac@mcac.ca
URL: www.mcac.ca
Scope: National

- **Municipal Finance Officers' Association of Ontario 2018 Annual Conference**
Date: September 19-21, 2018
Location: Niagara Falls, ON
Sponsor/Contact: Municipal Finance Officers' Association of Ontario
2169 Queen St. East, 2nd Fl.
Toronto, ON M4L 1J1
416-362-9001; *Fax:* 416-362-9226
E-mail: office@mfoa.on.ca
URL: www.mfoa.on.ca
Scope: Provincial

- **National Insurance Conference of Canada 2018**
Date: September 30 - October 2, 2018
Location: Hilton Lac Leamy
Gatineau, QC
Sponsor/Contact: Insurance Bureau of Canada
Head Office / Ontario Office
P.O. Box 121
#2400, 777 Bay St.
Toronto, ON M5G 2C8
416-362-2031; *Fax:* 416-361-5952
Toll-Free: 844-227-5422
URL: www.ibc.ca
Scope: National
Purpose: Sponsored by the Insurance Bureau of Canada, among other companies & organizations
Contact Information: Web Site: www.niccanada.com; Phone: 416-368-0777; Fax: 416-363-7454

- **Northern Finance Association 2018 Conference**
Date: September 21-23, 2018
Location: Charlevoix, QC
Sponsor/Contact: Northern Finance Association
c/o Rotman School of Management
105 St. George St.
Toronto, ON M5S 3E6
URL: www.northernfinance.org
Scope: Local

- **Ontario Association for Family Mediation Conference & AGM 2018**
Date: September 20-21, 2018
Location: Novotel Toronto Centre
Toronto, ON
Sponsor/Contact: Ontario Association for Family Mediation
#204, 2167 Victoria Park Ave.
Toronto, ON M1R 1V5
416-740-6236
Toll-Free: 844-989-3026
URL: www.oafm.on.ca
Scope: Provincial

- **Ontario Association of Pathologists 2018 Annual Meeting**
Date: September 28-29, 2018
Location: Mont-Tremblant, QC
Sponsor/Contact: Ontario Association of Pathologists
#310, 4 Cataraqui St.
Kingston, ON K7K 1Z7
613-507-7663
E-mail: oap@eventsmgt.com
URL: www.ontariopathologists.org
Scope: Provincial

- **Ontario Association of Radiology Managers 2018 Annual Fall Conference**
Date: September 2018
Location: Ontario
Sponsor/Contact: Ontario Association of Radiology Managers
26 Gateway Crt.
Whitby, ON L1R 3M9
905-655-5645
E-mail: headoffice@oarm.org
URL: www.oarm.org
Scope: Provincial

- **Ontario Energy Association Energy Conference 2018**
Date: September 24, 2018
Location: Toronto, ON
Sponsor/Contact: Ontario Energy Association
#202, 121 Richmond St. West
Toronto, ON M5H 2K1
416-961-2339; *Fax:* 416-961-1173
E-mail: oea@energyontario.ca
URL: www.energyontario.ca
Scope: Provincial
Purpose: Examples of programming includes panel sessions, the presentation of awards, information sharing opportunities, & social events

- **Ontario Funeral Service Association Annual Convention 2018**
Date: September 24-26, 2018
Location: Blue Mountain Resort
The Blue Mountains, ON
Sponsor/Contact: Ontario Funeral Service Association
#103, 3228 South Service Rd.
Burlington, ON L7N 3N1
905-637-3371; *Fax:* 905-637-3583
Toll-Free: 800-268-2727
E-mail: info@ofsa.org
URL: www.ofsa.org
Scope: Provincial

- **Organic Trade Association (OTA) All Things Organic Conference**
Date: September 13-14, 2018
Location: Baltimore Convention Center
Baltimore, MD USA
Sponsor/Contact: Organic Trade Association
#45A, 444 North Capital St.
Washington, DC 20001
202-403-8520
URL: www.ota.com
Scope: International
Purpose: Hosted in conjunction with Natural Products Expo East

- **Organic Trade Association (OTA) Annual Membership Meeting 2018**
Date: September 12, 2018
Location: Baltimore, MD USA
Sponsor/Contact: Organic Trade Association
#45A, 444 North Capital St.
Washington, DC 20001
202-403-8520
URL: www.ota.com
Scope: International

- **Organic Trade Association (OTA) Expo East 2018**
Date: September 12-15, 2018
Location: Baltimore Convention Center
Baltimore, MD USA
Sponsor/Contact: Organic Trade Association
#45A, 444 North Capital St.
Washington, DC 20001
202-403-8520
URL: www.ota.com
Scope: International

- **OSMT 2018 Annual General Meeting**
Date: September 22, 2018
Sponsor/Contact: Ontario Society of Medical Technologists
#402, 234 Eglinton Ave. East
Toronto, ON M4P 1K5
416-485-6768; *Fax:* 416-485-7660
Toll-Free: 800-461-6768
E-mail: osmt@osmt.org
URL: www.osmt.org
Scope: National

- **Packaging Association of Canada Conference 2018**
Date: September 25-27, 2018
Location: Montréal, QC
Sponsor/Contact: Packaging Association of Canada
#607, 1 Concorde Gate
Toronto, ON M3C 3N6
416-490-7860
E-mail: pacinfo@pac.ca
URL: www.pac.ca
Scope: National
Contact Information: Director, National Events & Member Services: Lisa Abraham, E-mail: labraham@pac.ca, Phone: 416-646-4640

- **Palliative Manitoba 27th Annual Provincial Conference**
Date: September 13-14, 2018
Location: Victoria Inn & Conference Centre
Winnipeg, MB
Sponsor/Contact: Palliative Manitoba
2109 Portage Ave.
Winnipeg, MB R3J 0L3
204-889-8525; *Fax:* 204-888-8874
Toll-Free: 800-539-0295
E-mail: info@manitobahospice.mb.ca
URL: palliativemanitoba.ca
Scope: Provincial
Purpose: Theme: "Keep It Simple"
Anticipated Attendance: 400+

- **Pet Industry Joint Advisory Council National Pet Industry Trade Show 2018**
Date: September 16-17, 2018
Location: International Center
Mississauga, ON
Sponsor/Contact: Pet Industry Joint Advisory Council
#14, 1010 Polytek St.
Ottawa, ON K1J 9H9
613-730-8111; *Fax:* 613-730-9111
Toll-Free: 800-667-7452
E-mail: info@pijaccanada.com
URL: www.pijaccanada.com
Scope: National
Purpose: A trade show providing exhibitors with the opportunity to meet new clients & explore the Canadian pet industry

- **Prince Edward Island Tennis Association Annual General Meeting 2018**
Date: September 2018

Location: Prince Edward Island
Sponsor/Contact: Prince Edward Island Tennis Association
P.O. Box 302
40 Enman Cres.
Charlottetown, PE C1A 7K7
902-368-4985; *Fax:* 902-368-4548
E-mail: tennisprinceedwardisland@gmail.com
URL: www.tennispei.ca
Scope: Provincial

- **RIMS (Risk & Insurance Management Society Inc.) Canada 2018 Conference**
Date: September 23-26, 2018
Location: St. John's, NL
Sponsor/Contact: Risk & Insurance Management Society Inc.
c/o Darius Delon, RIMS Canada Council, Mount Royal University
4825 Mount Royal Gate SW
Calgary, AB T3E 6K6
E-mail: rcc@rimscanada.ca
URL: www.rimscanada.ca
Scope: National
Purpose: An annual risk management conference & exhibition held in the autumn for risk managers & the vendor community

- **Recycling Council of Alberta 2018 Waste Reduction Conference**
Date: September 19-21, 2018
Location: The Banff Centre for Arts and Creativity
Banff, AB
Sponsor/Contact: Recycling Council of Alberta
P.O. Box 23
Bluffton, AB T0C 0M0
403-843-6563; *Fax:* 403-843-4156
E-mail: info@recycle.ab.ca
URL: www.recycle.ab.ca
Scope: Provincial
Purpose: Presentations, exhibits, & networking opportunities. Held jointly with the Conference on Canadian Stewardship.
Contact Information: info@recycle.ab.ca

- **Society of Plastics Engineers 16th Conference on Advances in Foam Materials & Technology 2018**
Date: September 11-14, 2018
Location: Montréal, QC
Sponsor/Contact: Society of Plastics Engineers
#306, 6 Berkshire Blvd.
Bethel, CT 06801
203-775-0471; *Fax:* 203-775-8490
URL: www.4spe.org
Scope: International

- **Society of Plastics Engineers Automotive Composites Conference & Exhibition 2018**
Date: September 5-7, 2018
Location: Novi, MI USA
Sponsor/Contact: Society of Plastics Engineers
#306, 6 Berkshire Blvd.
Bethel, CT 06801
203-775-0471; *Fax:* 203-775-8490
URL: www.4spe.org
Scope: International

- **Society of Plastics Engineers CAD RETEC 2018**
Date: September 23-25, 2018
Location: North Charleston, SC USA
Sponsor/Contact: Society of Plastics Engineers

#306, 6 Berkshire Blvd.
Bethel, CT 06801
203-775-0471; *Fax:* 203-775-8490
URL: www.4spe.org
Scope: International

- **TRENDS: The Apparel Show 2018 (sponsored by the Alberta Men's Wear Agents Association)**
Date: September 6-9, 2018
Location: Edmonton Expo Centre
Edmonton, AB
Sponsor/Contact: Alberta Men's Wear Agents Association
P.O. Box 66037 Stn. Heritage
Edmonton, AB T6J 6T4
780-455-1881
E-mail: amwa@shaw.ca
URL: www.trendsapparel.com
Scope: Provincial
Purpose: A semiannual show involving the participation of wholesale sales representatives showing clothing & shoes
Contact Information: E-mail: amwa@shaw.ca

- **The American Association of Bovine Practitioners 2018 Annual Conference**
Date: September 13-15, 2018
Location: Phoenix, AZ USA
Sponsor/Contact: American Association of Bovine Practitioners
P.O. Box 3610
#802, 3320 Skyway Dr.
Auburn, AL 36831-3610
334-821-0442; *Fax:* 334-821-9532
E-mail: aabphq@aabp.org
URL: www.aabp.org
Scope: International

- **The Profile Show Fall 2018**
Date: September 8-11, 2018
Location: Ontario
Sponsor/Contact: Ontario Fashion Exhibitors
P.O. Box 218
#2219, 160 Tycos Dr.
Toronto, ON M6B 1W8
416-596-2401; *Fax:* 416-596-1808
Toll-Free: 800-765-7508
E-mail: info@profileshow.ca
URL: www.profileshow.ca
Scope: Provincial

- **Thermal Insulation Association of Canada 2018 Annual Conference**
Date: September 7-10, 2018
Location: Fairmont Banff Springs
Banff, AB
Sponsor/Contact: Thermal Insulation Association of Canada
1485 Laperriere Ave.
Ottawa, ON K1Z 7S8
613-724-4834; *Fax:* 613-729-6206
E-mail: info@tiac.ca
URL: www.tiac.ca
Scope: National

- **Transportation Association of Canada 2018 Conference & Exhibition**
Date: September 30 - October 3, 2018
Location: Saskatoon, SK
Sponsor/Contact: Transportation Association of Canada
#401, 1111 Prince of Wales Dr.
Ottawa, ON K2C 3T2
613-736-1350; *Fax:* 613-736-1395
E-mail: secretariat@tac-atc.ca
URL: www.tac-atc.ca

Scope: National
Purpose: Theme: "Innovation & Technology: Evolving Transportation"

- **Travel and Tourism Research Association Canada Conference 2018**
Date: September 26-28, 2018
Location: Halifax, NS
Sponsor/Contact: Travel and Tourism Research Association (Canada Chapter)
#600, 116 Lisgar St.
Ottawa, ON K2P 0C2
613-238-6378
E-mail: info@ttracanada.ca
URL: www.ttracanada.ca
Scope: National

- **Union of British Columbia Municipalities 2018 Annual Convention**
Date: September 10-14, 2018
Location: Whistler Conference Centre
Whistler, BC
Sponsor/Contact: Union of British Columbia Municipalities
#60, 10551 Shellbridge Way
Richmond, BC V6X 2W9
604-270-8226; *Fax:* 604-270-9116
URL: www.ubcm.ca
Scope: Provincial

- **WEFTEC 2018: 91st Annual Water Environment Federation Technical Exhibition & Conference**
Date: September 29 - October 3, 2018
Location: New Orleans Morial Convention Center
New Orleans, LA USA
Sponsor/Contact: Water Environment Federation
601 Wythe St.
Alexandria, VA 22314-1994
703-684-2400
Toll-Free: 800-666-0206
E-mail: csc@wef.org
URL: www.wef.org
Scope: International
Purpose: An annual educational & networking event drawing water quality experts from around the world
Anticipated Attendance: 18,000
Contact Information: Manager, WEFTEC Registration & Housing: Tangela Williams, E-mail: registration@wef.org

- **Western Canada Water 2018 70th Annual Conference & Exhibition**
Date: September 18-21, 2018
Location: Winnipeg Convention Centre
Winnipeg, MB
Sponsor/Contact: Western Canada Water
P.O. Box 1708
240 River Ave.
Cochrane, AB T4C 1B6
403-709-0064; *Fax:* 403-709-0068
Toll-Free: 877-283-2003
E-mail: member@wcwwa.ca
URL: www.wcwwa.ca
Scope: Provincial
Purpose: A technical program, a keynote speaker, & a trade show for delegates from Western Canada Water
Anticipated Attendance: 500+
Contact Information: Western Canada Water, Toll-Free Phone: 1-877-283-2003, Toll-Free Fax: 1-877-283-2007, E-mail: info@wcwwa.ca

- **World Small Animal Veterinary Association Annual Congress 2018**
Date: September 25-28, 2018
Location: Singapore

Sponsor/Contact: World Small Animal Veterinary Association
72 Melville St.
Dundas, ON L9H 2A1
905-627-8540
E-mail: wsavasecretariat@gmail.com
URL: www.wsava.org
Scope: International
Contact Information: URL: www.wsava2018.com

October

- **108th BC Fairs Conference**
Date: October 18-20, 2018
Location: Hotel Grand Pacific
Victoria, BC
Sponsor/Contact: British Columbia Association of Agricultural Fairs & Exhibitions
#20, 16655 - 64th Ave.
Surrey, BC V3S 3V1
778-574-4082
URL: www.bcfairs.ca
Scope: Provincial

- **18th Annual Power of Water Canada Conference 2018**
Date: October 29-31, 2018
Location: White Oaks Conference Resort
Niagara-on-the-Lake, ON
Sponsor/Contact: Ontario Waterpower Association
#264, 380 Armour Rd.
Peterborough, ON K9H 7L7
Toll-Free: 866-743-1500
E-mail: info@owa.ca
URL: www.owa.ca
Scope: Provincial
Purpose: The largest gathering of the hydroelectric sector in Canada; will feature a tradeshow with more than 60 exhibitors.
Anticipated Attendance: 400+
Contact Information: Manager, Conference & Events: Janelle Bates, E-mail: jbates@owa.ca, Phone: 1-866-743-1500, ext. 23

- **2018 AFOA Canada National Conference**
Date: October 2-4, 2018
Location: Shaw Centre
Ottawa, ON
Sponsor/Contact: AFOA Canada
#301, 1066 Somerset St. West
Ottawa, ON K1Y 4T3
613-722-5543; *Fax:* 613-722-3467
Toll-Free: 866-722-2362
E-mail: info@afoa.ca
URL: www.afoa.ca
Scope: National

- **2018 Canadian Association of Perinatal & Women's Health Nurses National Conference**
Date: October 11-13, 2018
Location: Ottawa, ON
Sponsor/Contact: Canadian Association of Perinatal & Women's Health Nurses
2781 Lancaster Rd.
Ottawa, ON K1B 1A7
613-730-4192; *Fax:* 613-730-4314
Toll-Free: 800-561-2416
E-mail: admin@capwhn.ca
URL: www.capwhn.ca
Scope: National

- **2018 Canadian Association of Physician Assistants Annual Conference**
Date: October 18-21, 2018

Conferences & Conventions Index

Location: Fairmont Empress
Victoria, BC
Sponsor/Contact: Canadian Association of Physician Assistants
#704, 265 Carling Ave.
Ottawa, ON K1S 2E1
613-248-2272; Fax: 613-521-2226
Toll-Free: 877-744-2272
E-mail: admin@capa-acam.ca
URL: capa-acam.ca
Scope: National

- **2018 Canadian Cardiovascular Congress**
Date: October 20-23, 2018
Location: Toronto, ON
Sponsor/Contact: Canadian Cardiovascular Society
#1403, 222 Queen St.
Ottawa, ON K1P 5V9
613-569-3407; Fax: 613-569-6574
Toll-Free: 877-569-3407
E-mail: info@ccs.ca
URL: www.ccs.ca
Scope: National

- **2018 National Association of Career Colleges Conference**
Date: October 24-26, 2018
Location: Ottawa, ON
Sponsor/Contact: National Association of Career Colleges
#270, 44 Byward Market Sq.
Ottawa, ON K1N 7A2
613-800-0340; Fax: 613-789-9669
URL: www.nacc.ca
Scope: National

- **2018 National Association of College Auxiliary Services Annual Conference**
Date: October 14-17, 2018
Location: Rosen Shingle Creek
Orlando, FL USA
Sponsor/Contact: National Association of College Auxiliary Services
P.O. Box 5546
7 Boar's Head Lane
Charlottesville, VA 22905-5546
434-245-8425; Fax: 434-245-8453
E-mail: info@nacas.org
URL: www.nacas.org
Scope: International

- **2018 Ontario Museum Association Annual Conference**
Date: October 24-26, 2018
Location: Kingston, ON
Sponsor/Contact: Ontario Museum Association
George Brown House
50 Baldwin St.
Toronto, ON M5T 1L4
416-348-8672; Fax: 416-348-0438
Toll-Free: 866-662-8672
URL: www.museumsontario.ca
Scope: National

- **2018 Sheet Metal and Air Conditioning Contractors' National Association (SMACNA) Annual Convention**
Date: October 14-17, 2018
Location: San Diego Marriott Marquis & Marina
San Diego, CA USA
Sponsor/Contact: Sheet Metal & Air Conditioning Contractors' National Association
P.O. Box 221230
4201 Lafayette Center Dr.
Chantilly, VA 20153-1230
703-803-2980; Fax: 703-803-3732
E-mail: info@smacna.org
URL: www.smacna.org
Scope: National
Contact Information: www.smacna.org/annualconvention

- **2018 Universities Art Association of Canada Conference**
Date: October 25-27, 2018
Location: University of Waterloo
Waterloo, ON
Sponsor/Contact: Universities Art Association of Canada
189 Mill Ridge Rd.
Arnprior, ON K7S 3G8
613-622-5570; Fax: 613-622-0671
E-mail: uaac@gozoom.ca
URL: www.uaac-aauc.com
Scope: National

- **54th CAM-X Annual Convention & Trade Show**
Date: October 25-28, 2018
Sponsor/Contact: Canadian Call Management Association
#10, 24 Olive St.
Grimsby, ON L3M 2B6
905-309-0224; Fax: 905-309-0225
Toll-Free: 800-896-1054
E-mail: info@camx.ca
URL: www.camx.ca
Scope: National

- **54th ISOCARP Congress**
Date: October 1-5, 2018
Location: Bodø, Norway
Sponsor/Contact: International Society of City & Regional Planners
P.O. Box 983
The Hague, 2501 CZ
E-mail: isocarp@isocarp.org
URL: www.isocarp.org
Scope: International
Purpose: Theme: "Cool Planning: Changing Climate & Our Urban Future"

- **68th Canadian Chemical Engineering Conference**
Date: October 28-31, 2018
Location: Toronto, ON
Sponsor/Contact: Chemical Institute of Canada
#400, 222 Queen St.
Ottawa, ON K1P 5V9
613-232-6252; Fax: 613-232-5862
Toll-Free: 888-542-2242
E-mail: info@cheminst.ca
URL: www.cheminst.ca
Scope: National
Contact Information: www.csche2018.ca

- **Alberta Association of Optometrists 2018 Conference**
Date: October 18-21, 2018
Location: Sheraton
Red Deer, AB
Sponsor/Contact: Alberta Association of Optometrists
#100, 8407 Argyll Rd.
Edmonton, AB T6C 4B2
780-451-6824; Fax: 780-452-9918
Toll-Free: 800-272-8843
URL: www.optometrists.ab.ca
Scope: Provincial

- **AMCO's 33rd Annual Convention & Trade Show**
Date: October 1-3, 2018
Location: Kenora, ON
Sponsor/Contact: Airport Management Council of Ontario
#5, 50 Terminal St.
North Bay, ON P1B 8G2
705-474-1080; Fax: 705-474-4073
Toll-Free: 877-636-2626
E-mail: amco@amco.on.ca
URL: www.amco.on.ca
Purpose: Informative speakers & exhibitors

- **American Academy for Cerebral Palsy & Developmental Medicine 72nd Annual Meeting**
Date: October 9-13, 2018
Location: Duke Energy Convention Center
Cincinnati, OH
Sponsor/Contact: American Academy for Cerebral Palsy & Developmental Medicine
#1100, 555 East Wells St.
Milwaukee, WI 53202
414-918-3014; Fax: 414-276-2146
E-mail: info@aacpdm.org
URL: www.aacpdm.org
Scope: International

- **American Association of Neuromuscular & Electrodiagnostic Medicine 2018 65th Annual Meeting**
Date: October 10-13, 2018
Location: Gaylord National
Washington, DC USA
Sponsor/Contact: American Association of Neuromuscular & Electrodiagnostic Medicine
2621 Superior Dr. NW
Rochester, MN 55901
507-288-0100; Fax: 507-288-1225
E-mail: aanem@aanem.org
URL: www.aanem.org
Scope: International

- **American College of Chest Physicians Conference: CHEST 2018**
Date: October 6-10, 2018
Location: San Antonio, TX USA
Sponsor/Contact: American College of Chest Physicians
2595 Patriot Blvd.
Glenview, IL 60062-2348
Toll-Free: 800-343-2227
URL: www.chestnet.org
Scope: International
Purpose: Educational sessions, CME credits, clinical instruction, & networking opportunities for health professionals

- **American Concrete Institute Fall 2018 Concrete Conference & Exhibition**
Date: October 14-18, 2018
Location: Rio All-Suites Hotel & Casino
Las Vegas, NV USA
Sponsor/Contact: American Concrete Institute
38800 Country Club Dr.
Farmington Hills, MI 48331-3439
248-848-3700; Fax: 248-848-3701
URL: www.concrete.org
Scope: International
Contact Information: Event Planner: Alexandria R. Prokic, E-mail: alex.prokic@concrete.org

- **American Numismatic Society Annual Meeting 2018**
Date: October 20, 2018
Sponsor/Contact: American Numismatic Society
75 Varick St., 11th Fl.
New York, NY 10013
212-571-4470; Fax: 212-571-4479
E-mail: info@numismatics.org
URL: www.numismatics.org
Scope: International
Contact Information: Director, Development: Eshel Kreiter, E-mail: ekreiter@numismatics.org, Phone: 212-571-4470, ext. 130

- **American Thyroid Association 2018 88th Annual Meeting**
Date: October 3-7, 2018
Location: Marriott Marquis
Washington, DC USA
Sponsor/Contact: American Thyroid Association
#550, 6066 Leesburg Pike
Falls Church, VA 22041
703-998-8890; Fax: 703-998-8893
Toll-Free: 800-849-7643
E-mail: thyroid@thyroid.org
URL: www.thyroid.org
Scope: International
Purpose: Held each autumn, the meeting includes platform presentations, lectures, symposia, discussion groups, posters, exhibits, & opportunities for networking
Anticipated Attendance: 1,000+

- **APRA Canada Conference 2018**
Date: October 17-19, 2018
Location: DoubleTree by Hilton
Toronto, ON
Sponsor/Contact: Association of Professional Researchers for Advancement - Canada
c/o Sheila Larin, Trillium Health Partners Foundation
#800, 89 Queensway West
Mississauga, ON L5B 2V2
URL: www.apracanada.ca
Scope: National
Contact Information: Co-Chair: Katherine Scott, E-mail: katherine.scott@redcross.ca; Co-Chair: Crystal Leochko Johnston, E-mail: crystal@eclipseresearchgroup.com

- **ARMA Live! Annual Conference & Expo 2018**
Date: October 22-24, 2018
Location: Anaheim, CA USA
Sponsor/Contact: ARMA International
#450, 11880 College Blvd.
Overland Park, KS 66215
913-341-3808; Fax: 913-341-3742
Toll-Free: 800-422-2762
E-mail: headquarters@armaintl.org
URL: www.arma.org
Contact Information: E-mail: conference@armaintl.org

- **ASM International Symposium for Testing & Failure Analysis**
Date: October 28 - November 1, 2018
Location: Phoenix, AZ USA
Sponsor/Contact: ASM International
9639 Kinsman Rd.
Materials Park, OH 44073-0002
440-338-5151; Fax: 440-338-4634
Toll-Free: 800-336-5152
E-mail: memberservicecenter@asminternational.org
URL: www.asminternational.org
Scope: International

- **Association of Canadian Ergonomists Conference 2018**
Date: October 15-18, 2018
Location: Sudbury, ON
Sponsor/Contact: Association of Canadian Ergonomists
#200, 411 Richmond St. East
Toronto, ON M5A 3S5

Conferences & Conventions Index

416-477-0914; *Fax:* 416-929-5256
Toll-Free: 888-432-2223
E-mail: info@ace-ergocanada.ca
URL: www.ace-ergocanada.ca
Scope: National

• **Association of Consulting Engineering Companies Leadership Conference 2018**
Date: October 21-23, 2018
Location: Ottawa, ON
Sponsor/Contact: Association of Consulting Engineering Companies - Canada
#420, 130 Albert St.
Ottawa, ON K1P 5G4
613-236-0569; *Fax:* 613-236-6193
Toll-Free: 800-565-0569
E-mail: info@acec.ca
URL: www.acec.ca
Scope: National

• **Association of Family Health Teams of Ontario 2018 Conference**
Date: October 24-25, 2018
Sponsor/Contact: Association of Family Health Teams of Ontario
#800, 60 St. Clair Ave. East
Toronto, ON M4T 1N5
647-234-8605
E-mail: info@afhto.ca
URL: www.afhto.ca
Scope: Provincial

• **Association of Professional Engineers & Geoscientists of British Columbia 2018 Conference & 99th Annual General Meeting**
Date: October 18-20, 2018
Location: Vancouver, BC
Sponsor/Contact: Association of Professional Engineers & Geoscientists of British Columbia
#200, 4010 Regent St.
Burnaby, BC V5C 6N2
604-430-8035; *Fax:* 604-430-8085
Toll-Free: 888-430-8035
E-mail: info@egbc.ca
URL: www.egbc.ca
Scope: Provincial
Purpose: A chance to learn & network with colleagues & suppliers during business & technical sessions, a trade exhibition, & social events
Anticipated Attendance: 750+
Contact Information: Director, Member Services: Deesh Olychick, E-mail: dolychick@apeg.bc.ca

• **Atlantic Planners Institute Conference 2018**
Date: October 24-26, 2018
Location: Moncton, NB
Sponsor/Contact: Atlantic Planners Institute
35 Ascot Ct.
Fredericton, NB E3B 6C4
506-455-7203; *Fax:* 506-455-1113
E-mail: apiexecutivedirector@gmail.com
URL: www.atlanticplanners.org
Scope: Provincial
Purpose: Theme: "Planning in a New Environment"

• **BC Music Educators' Association 2018 Annual Conference**
Date: October 18-20, 2018
Location: River Rock Casino Resort Richmond, BC
Sponsor/Contact: British Columbia Music Educators' Association
c/o British Columbia Teachers' Federation
#100, 550 West 6th Ave.
Vancouver, BC V5Z 4P2
E-mail: bcmusiced@gmail.com
URL: www.bcmusiced.ca
Scope: Provincial
Purpose: Professional development activities & exhibits for British Columbia teachers
Contact Information: www.bcmeaconference.com

• **BC Science Teachers' Association Catalyst Conference 2018**
Date: October 19, 2018
Location: Kelowna, BC
Sponsor/Contact: British Columbia Science Teachers' Association
c/o Ashcroft Secondary School
P.O. Box 669
Ashcroft, BC V0K 1A0
250-453-9144; *Fax:* 250-453-2368
E-mail: bcscta@gmail.com
URL: www.bcscta.ca
Scope: Provincial

• **Brain Injury Canada Annual Conference 2018**
Date: October 18-19, 2018
Location: Ottawa, ON
Sponsor/Contact: Brain Injury Association of Canada
#200, 440 Laurier Ave. West
Ottawa, ON K1R 7X6
613-762-1012; *Fax:* 613-782-2228
Toll-Free: 866-977-2492
E-mail: info@braininjurycanada.ca
URL: www.braininjurycanada.ca
Scope: National

• **British Columbia Teacher-Librarians' Association 2018 Provincial Conference**
Date: October 19, 2018
Location: British Columbia
Sponsor/Contact: British Columbia Teacher-Librarians' Association
c/o Grahame Rainey, Treasurer
#1607 - 511 Rochester Ave.
Coquitlam, BC V3K 0A2
URL: www.bctf.ca/bctla
Scope: Provincial
Purpose: A gathering of British Columbia's teacher-librarians for workshops, keynote presentations, & social events
Contact Information: bctlaconference.ca

• **CSX North America 2018**
Date: October 15-17, 2018
Location: Las Vegas, NV USA
Sponsor/Contact: ISACA
#1010, 3701 Algonquin Rd.
Rolling Meadows, IL 60008
847-253-1545; *Fax:* 847-253-1443
E-mail: news@isaca.org
URL: www.isaca.org
Scope: International
Purpose: A cybersecurity conference involving relevant professional development opportunities & information sessions
Contact Information: ISACA Training & Education, Phone: 847-660-5670, Fax: 847-253-1443

• **Canada Logistics Conference 2018**
Date: October 24-26, 2018
Location: Vancouver, BC
Sponsor/Contact: Canadian Institute of Traffic & Transportation
#400, 10 King St. East
Toronto, ON M5C 1C3
416-363-5696; *Fax:* 416-363-5698
E-mail: info@citt.ca
URL: www.citt.ca
Purpose: Annual leadership conference for supply chain logistics professionals

• **Canadian Academy of Audiology 21st Annual Conference & Exhibition 2018**
Date: October 17-20, 2018
Location: Sheraton on the Falls Niagara Falls, ON
Sponsor/Contact: Canadian Academy of Audiology
P.O. Box 22531
300 Coxwell Ave.
Toronto, ON M4L 3B6
647-794-7305
Toll-Free: 800-264-5106
E-mail: contact@canadianaudiology.ca
URL: www.canadianaudiology.ca
Scope: National
Purpose: Annual general meeting, educational sessions, speaker presentations, exhibits, & networking opportunities

• **Canadian Association of Aesthetic Medicine 15th Annual Conference**
Date: October 26-27, 2018
Location: Hilton Toronto/Markham Suites Conference Centre
Toronto, ON
Sponsor/Contact: Canadian Association of Aesthetic Medicine
#220, 445 Mountain Hwy.
North Vancouver, BC V7J 2L1
604-988-0450; *Fax:* 604-929-0871
E-mail: info@caam.ca
URL: www.caam.ca
Scope: National

• **Canadian Association of Medical Device Reprocessing 2018 Conference**
Date: October 11-13, 2018
Location: Halifax, NS
Sponsor/Contact: Canadian Association of Medical Device Reprocessing
147 Parkside Dr.
Oak Bluff, MB R4G 0A6
E-mail: info@camdr.ca
URL: www.camdr.ca
Scope: National

• **Canadian Association of Midwives Annual Conference & Exhibit 2018**
Date: October 17-19, 2018
Location: Hilton Lac-Leamy Gatineau, QC
Sponsor/Contact: Canadian Association of Midwives
59, av Riverview
Montréal, QC H8R 3R9
514-807-3668; *Fax:* 514-738-0370
E-mail: admin@canadianmidwives.org
URL: www.canadianmidwives.org
Scope: National

• **Canadian Association of Nurses in Oncology Annual Conference 2018**
Date: October 26-29, 2018
Location: Charlottetown, PE
Sponsor/Contact: Canadian Association of Nurses in Oncology
#301, 750 West Pender St.
Vancouver, BC V6C 2T7
604-874-4322; *Fax:* 604-874-4378
E-mail: cano@malachite-mgmt.com
URL: www.cano-acio.ca
Scope: National
Purpose: Theme: "Excellence in Oncology: Our Patients, Our Passion"

• **Canadian Association of Paediatric Health Centres Annual Conference 2018**
Date: October 14-16, 2018
Location: Saskatoon, SK
Sponsor/Contact: Canadian Association of Paediatric Health Centres
c/o Canadian Association of Paediatric Health Centres
#104, 2141 Thurston Dr.
Ottawa, ON K1G 6C9
613-738-4164; *Fax:* 613-738-3247
E-mail: info@caphc.org
URL: www.caphc.org
Scope: National

• **Canadian Association on Gerontology 2018 47th Annual Scientific & Educational Meeting**
Date: October 18-20, 2018
Location: Vancouver, BC
Sponsor/Contact: Canadian Association on Gerontology
c/o University of Toronto
#160, 500 University Ave.
Toronto, ON M5G 1V7
Toll-Free: 855-224-2240
URL: www.cagacg.ca
Scope: National
Purpose: A multi-discplinary conference for persons interested in individual & population aging

• **Canadian Crafts Federation 2018 13th Annual National Craft Conference**
Date: October 2018
Sponsor/Contact: Canadian Crafts Federation
P.O. Box 1231
Fredericton, NB E3B 5C8
506-462-9560
E-mail: info@canadiancraftsfederation.ca
URL: www.canadiancraftsfederation.ca
Scope: National

• **Canadian Dam Association 2018 Annual Conference**
Date: October 22-24, 2018
Location: Québec City Convention Centre Québec, QC
Sponsor/Contact: Canadian Dam Association
P.O. Box 2281
Moose Jaw, SK S6TH 7W6
URL: www.cda.ca
Scope: National
Purpose: Featuring technical paper presentations, workshops, tours, exhibitor presentations, & a social program

• **Canadian Diabetes Association Professional Conference 2018**
Date: October 10-13, 2018
Location: Halifax Convention Centre Halifax, NS
Sponsor/Contact: Diabetes Canada
#1400, 522 University Ave.
Toronto, ON M5G 2R5
416-363-3373; *Fax:* 416-363-7465
Toll-Free: 800-226-8464
E-mail: info@diabetes.ca
URL: www.diabetes.ca
Scope: National
Contact Information: professional.conference@diabetes.ca

• **Canadian Energy Psychology Conference 2018**
Date: October 19-21, 2018
Location: Toronto, ON
Sponsor/Contact: Canadian Association for Integrative & Energy Therapies

Conferences & Conventions Index

416-221-5639; *Fax:* 416-221-7126
URL: www.caiet.org
Scope: National
Contact Information: www.epccanada.ca

• **Canadian Federation of Independent Grocers Grocery Innovations Canada 2018**
Date: October 23-24, 2018
Location: Toronto Congress Centre
Toronto, ON
Sponsor/Contact: Canadian Federation of Independent Grocers
#401, 105 Gordon Baker Rd.
Toronto, ON M2H 3P8
416-492-2311; *Fax:* 416-492-2347
Toll-Free: 800-661-2344
E-mail: info@cfig.ca
URL: www.cfig.ca
Scope: National
Purpose: An annual event, featuring the Canadian Federation of Independent Grocers' annual general meeting, keynote presentations, panel presentations, informative conference sessions, over 500 grocery exhibits, the presentation of industry awards, & networking opportunities
Contact Information: Director, Conference & Events: Diana Stevenson, E-mail: dstevenson@cfig.ca, Phone: 416-492-2311, ext. 242

• **Canadian Greenhouse Conference 2018**
Date: October 3-4, 2018
Location: Scotiabank Convention Centre
Niagara Falls, ON
Sponsor/Contact: Ontario Institute of Agrologists
Ontario AgriCentre
#108, 100 Stone Rd. West
Guelph, ON N1G 5L3
519-826-4226; *Fax:* 519-826-4228
Toll-Free: 866-339-7619
URL: www.oia.on.ca
Scope: National
Purpose: Held annually since 1979 the CGC is committed to providing a high quality conference experience for the extension of information through speakers, workshops, demonstration and exhibits.

• **Canadian Institute for the Administration of Justice 2018 Annual Conference**
Date: October 17-19, 2018
Location: Westin Ottawa
Ottawa, ON
Sponsor/Contact: Canadian Institute for the Administration of Justice
Faculté de droit, Univ. de Montréal
P.O. Box 6128 Stn. Centre-Ville
#A3421, 3101, chemin de la Tour
Montréal, QC H3C 3J7
514-343-6157; *Fax:* 514-343-6296
E-mail: ciaj@ciaj-icaj.ca
URL: www.ciaj-icaj.ca
Scope: National
Purpose: Theme: "Justice & Mental Health"

• **Canadian Marketing Association CMAmedia**
Date: October 10, 2018
Sponsor/Contact: Canadian Marketing Association
#603, 55 University Ave.
Toronto, ON M5J 2H7
416-391-2362; *Fax:* 416-441-4062
Toll-Free: 800-267-8805
E-mail: info@thecma.ca
URL: www.the-cma.org
Scope: National

• **Canadian Mental Health Association 2018 National Conference**
Date: October 22-24, 2018
Location: Montréal, QC
Sponsor/Contact: Canadian Mental Health Association
#1110, 151 Slater St.
Ottawa, ON K1P 5H3
613-745-7750
E-mail: info@cmha.ca
URL: www.cmha.ca
Scope: National

• **Canadian Network of Agencies for Regulation 2018 Conference**
Date: October 16-18, 2018
Location: Fairmont Banff Springs
Banff, AB
Sponsor/Contact: Canadian Network of National Associations of Regulators
528 River Rd.
Ottawa, ON K1V 1E9
613-739-4376
URL: www.cnnar.ca
Scope: National
Anticipated Attendance: 400+

• **Canadian Power and Sail Squadrons National Conference 2018**
Date: October 16-21, 2018
Location: Ottawa, ON
Sponsor/Contact: Canadian Power & Sail Squadrons (Canadian Headquarters)
26 Golden Gate Ct.
Toronto, ON M1P 3A5
416-293-2438; *Fax:* 416-293-2445
Toll-Free: 888-277-2628
E-mail: hqg@cps-ecp.ca
URL: www.cps-ecp.ca
Scope: National

• **Canadian Society for Eighteenth-Century Studies 2018 Conference**
Date: October 10-14, 2018
Location: Niagara Falls, ON
Sponsor/Contact: Canadian Society for Eighteenth-Century Studies
c/o Department of French, University of Manitoba
427 Fletcher Argue Bldg.
Winnipeg, MB R3T 2N2
204-474-9206
URL: www.csecs.ca

• **Canadian Society for Exercise Physiology 2018 AGM**
Date: October 31 - November 3, 2018
Location: Brock University
Niagara Falls, ON
Sponsor/Contact: Canadian Society for Exercise Physiology
#370, 18 Louisa St.
Ottawa, ON K1R 6Y6
613-234-3755; *Fax:* 613-234-3565
Toll-Free: 877-651-3755
E-mail: info@csep.ca
URL: www.csep.ca
Scope: National

• **Canadian Society of Association Executives / Société canadienne d'association 2018 Conference & Showcase**
Date: October 24-26, 2018
Location: Ottawa, ON
Sponsor/Contact: Canadian Society of Association Executives
#1100, 10 King St. East
Toronto, ON M5C 1C3
416-363-3555; *Fax:* 416-363-3630
Toll-Free: 800-461-3608
URL: www.csae.com
Scope: National

• **Canadian Society of Endocrinology & Metabolism & Diabetes Canada Professional Conference & Annual Meetings**
Date: October 10-13, 2018
Location: Halifax Convention Centre
Halifax, NS
Sponsor/Contact: Canadian Society of Endocrinology & Metabolism
#1403, 222 Queen St.
Ottawa, ON K1P 5V9
613-594-0005; *Fax:* 613-569-6574
E-mail: info@endo-metab.ca
URL: www.endo-metab.ca
Scope: National
Purpose: Interactive workshops, oral abstract sessions, poster presentations, speakers addressing current diagnosis & treatment issues, a trade show, social activities, & networking opportunities

• **Canadian Society of Hospital Pharmacists 2018 Annual General Meeting**
Date: October 19-20, 2018
Location: Winnipeg, MB
Sponsor/Contact: Canadian Society of Hospital Pharmacists
#3, 30 Concourse Gate
Ottawa, ON K2E 7V7
613-736-9733; *Fax:* 613-736-5660
E-mail: info@cshp.ca
URL: www.cshp.ca
Scope: National
Purpose: The annual general meeting of the society & educational workshops held each year in partnership with one of the society's branches

• **Canadian Transplant Summit 2018**
Date: October 16-20, 2018
Location: The Westin Ottawa
Ottawa, ON
Sponsor/Contact: Canadian Society of Transplantation
114 Cheyenne Way
Ottawa, ON K2J 0E9
Toll-Free: 877-968-9449
E-mail: admin@cst-transplant.ca
URL: www.cst-transplant.ca
Scope: National
Purpose: Hosted by the Canadian Society of Transplantation (CST), Canadian Blood Services (CBS), Canadian Blood & Marrow Transplant Group (CBMTG), & Canadian National Transplant Research Program (CNTRP)

• **Canadian Transportation Equipment Association 55th Annual Conference**
Date: October 22-24, 2018
Location: Westin Prince
Toronto, ON
Sponsor/Contact: Canadian Transportation Equipment Association
#505, 4510 Rhodes Dr.
Windsor, ON N8W 5K5
226-620-0779; *Fax:* 519-944-4912
E-mail: don.moore@atminc.on.ca
URL: www.ctea.ca

• **Canadian Wind Energy Association (CanWEA) 34th Annual Conference and Exhibition**
Date: October 23-25, 2018
Location: BMO Centre
Calgary, AB
Sponsor/Contact: Canadian Wind Energy Association
#710, 1600 Carling Ave.
Ottawa, ON K1Z 1G3
613-234-8716; *Fax:* 613-234-5642
Toll-Free: 800-922-6932
E-mail: info@canwea.ca
URL: www.canwea.ca
Scope: National
Purpose: To discuss the opportunities and latest developments in the wind energy industry.
Contact Information: www.windenergyevent.ca

• **Chartered Professional Accountants Canada 2018 ONE National Conference**
Date: October 1-2, 2018
Location: Halifax, NS
Sponsor/Contact: Chartered Professional Accountants Canada
277 Wellington St. West
Toronto, ON M5V 3H2
416-977-3222; *Fax:* 416-977-8585
Toll-Free: 800-268-3793
E-mail: member.services@cpacanada.ca
URL: www.cpacanada.ca
Scope: National

• **Chartered Professionals in Human Resources Manitoba Human Resources & Leadership Conference 2018**
Date: October 23-24, 2018
Location: RBC Convention Centre Winnipeg
Winnipeg, MB
Sponsor/Contact: Chartered Professionals in Human Resources Manitoba
#1810, 275 Portage Ave.
Winnipeg, MB R3B 2B3
204-943-2836; *Fax:* 204-943-1109
E-mail: hrmam@hrmam.org
URL: www.hrmam.org
Scope: Provincial

• **Data & Marketing Association "&THEN" Conference 2018**
Date: October 8-10, 2018
Location: MGM Grand Las Vegas
Las Vegas, NV USA
Sponsor/Contact: Data & Marketing Association
#301, 1333 Broadway
New York, NY 10018
212-768-7277
E-mail: MemberServices@the-dma.org
URL: www.thedma.org
Scope: International

• **Environmental Services Association of Alberta RemTech 2018**
Date: October 10-12, 2018
Location: Fairmont Banff Springs
Banff, AB
Sponsor/Contact: Environmental Services Association of Alberta
#102, 2528 Ellwood Dr. SW
Edmonton, AB T6X 0A9
780-429-6363; *Fax:* 780-429-4249
Toll-Free: 800-661-9278
E-mail: info@esaa.org
URL: www.esaa.org
Scope: Provincial
Purpose: Remediation technology information for environmental professionals, such as engineering firms, pipeline companies, drill companies, energy marketers, natural gas producers,

oil & gase services companies, environmental consulting firms, & mining companies
Contact Information: Director, Program & Event Development: Joe Chowaniec, Phone: 780-429-6363, ext. 223, E-mail: chowaniec@esaa.org

- **Harmony, Inc. 2018 International Convention & Contests**
Date: October 31 - November 4, 2018
Location: Lake Buena Vista, FL
Sponsor/Contact: Harmony, Inc.
Toll-Free: 855-750-3341
E-mail: info@harmonyinc.org
URL: www.harmonyinc.org
Anticipated Attendance: 1,000

- **IDWeek 2018**
Date: October 3-7, 2018
Location: San Francisco, CA USA
Sponsor/Contact: Infectious Diseases Society of America
#300, 1300 Wilson Blvd.
Arlington, VA 22209
703-299-0200; Fax: 703-299-0204
E-mail: membership@idsociety.org
URL: www.idsociety.org
Scope: International

- **Industrial Fabrics Association International 2018 Expo**
Date: October 15-18, 2018
Location: Kay Bailey Hutchison Convention Center
Dallas, TX USA
Sponsor/Contact: Industrial Fabrics Association International Canada
1485 Laperriere Ave.
Ottawa, ON K1Z 7S8
613-792-1218; Fax: 613-729-6206
Toll-Free: 800-225-4324
E-mail: ifaicanada@ifai.com
URL: www.ifaicanada.com
Scope: International

- **International Bar Association Annual Conference 2018**
Date: October 7-12, 2018
Location: Rome, Italy
Sponsor/Contact: International Bar Association
10 St. Bride St., 4th Fl.
London, EC4A 4AD
E-mail: iba@int-bar.org
URL: www.ibanet.org
Scope: International
Purpose: An opportunity to network, generate new business & participate in professional development programs

- **International Forum on Disability Management**
Date: October 2018
Location: Vancouver, BC
Sponsor/Contact: National Institute of Disability Management & Research
c/o Pacific Coast University for Workplace Health Sciences
4755 Cherry Creek Rd.
Port Alberni, BC V9Y 0A7
778-421-0821; Fax: 778-421-0823
E-mail: nidmar@nidmar.ca
URL: www.nidmar.ca
Scope: International

- **International Sanitary Supply Association INTERCLEAN Dallas 2018**
Date: October 29 - November 1, 2018
Location: Kay Bailey Hutchinson Convention Center
Dallas, TX USA
Sponsor/Contact: International Sanitary Supply Association, Inc.
3300 Dundee Rd.
Northbrook, IL 60062
847-982-0800; Fax: 847-982-1012
Toll-Free: 800-225-4772
E-mail: info@issa.com
URL: www.issa.com
Scope: International
Purpose: An international exhibition for cleaning professionals which unites leading global brands & manufacturers

- **International Society for Pediatric & Adolescent Diabetes 2018 44th Annual Conference**
Date: October 11-14, 2018
Location: Hyderabad, India
Sponsor/Contact: International Society for Pediatric & Adolescent Diabetes
c/o KIT Group GmbH
Kurfürstendamm 71
Berlin, 10709
E-mail: secretariat@ispad.org
URL: www.ispad.org
Scope: International
Purpose: A scientific meeting featuring paper, poster, & plenary sessions, workshops, & symposia
Contact Information: 2018.ispad.org

- **Manitoba Non-Profit Housing Association 2018 Building Partnerships Conference**
Date: October 15-16, 2018
Location: Manitoba
Sponsor/Contact: Manitoba Non-Profit Housing Association
#200A, 1215 Henderson Hwy.
Winnipeg, MB R2G 1L8
204-797-6746; Fax: 204-336-3809
E-mail: info@mnpha.com
URL: mnpha.com
Scope: Provincial
Anticipated Attendance: 150+

- **Metallurgy & Materials Society 2018 57th Annual Conference of Metallurgists**
Date: October 14-18, 2018
Location: Hyatt Regency Columbus
Columbus, OH USA
Sponsor/Contact: Metallurgy & Materials Society of the Canadian Institute of Mining, Metallurgy & Petroleum
#1250, 3500, boul de Maisonneuve ouest
Montréal, QC H3Z 3C1
514-939-2710; Fax: 514-939-2714
E-mail: metsoc@cim.org
URL: www.metsoc.org
Scope: International
Purpose: A technical program, with short courses & industrial tours, plus a metals trade show, the poster session, plenary sessions, & student activities

- **National Association for Environmental Management 2018 EHS & Sustainability Management Forum**
Date: October 23-26, 2018
Location: Louisville Marriott Downtown
Louisville, KY USA
Sponsor/Contact: National Association for Environmental Management
#1002, 1612 K St. NW
Washington, DC 20006
202-986-6616; Fax: 202-530-4408
Toll-Free: 800-391-6236
E-mail: programs@naem.org
URL: www.naem.org
Scope: International
Anticipated Attendance: 500+

- **National Trust for Canada National Heritage Conference 2018**
Date: October 17-20, 2018
Location: Fredericton, NB
Sponsor/Contact: National Trust for Canada
190 Bronson Ave.
Ottawa, ON K1R 6H4
613-237-4262; Fax: 613-237-5987
Toll-Free: 866-964-1066
E-mail: nationaltrust@nationaltrustcanada.ca
URL: www.nationaltrustcanada.ca
Scope: National

- **Nova Scotia Pharmacy Conference 2018**
Date: October 19-21, 2018
Location: Holiday Inn
Truro, NS
Sponsor/Contact: Pharmacy Association of Nova Scotia
#225, 170 Cromarty Dr.
Dartmouth, NS B3B 0G1
902-422-9583; Fax: 902-422-2619
E-mail: pans@pans.ns.ca
URL: pans.ns.ca
Scope: Provincial
Purpose: Educational sessions on topics of interest to pharmacists in Nova Scotia

- **Ontario Association of Emergency Managers 2018 Ontario Disaster & Emergency Management Conference**
Date: October 3-4, 2018
Location: Toronto, ON
Sponsor/Contact: Ontario Association of Emergency Managers
c/o McCauley Nichols
14 Caledonia Terrace
Goderich, ON N7A 2M8
519-524-5992; Fax: 519-612-1992
E-mail: secretary@oaem.ca
URL: www.oaem.ca
Scope: Provincial

- **Ontario Non-Profit Housing Association 2018 Annual Conference, General Meeting & Trade Show**
Date: October 26-28, 2018
Location: Sheraton Centre
Toronto, ON
Sponsor/Contact: Ontario Non-Profit Housing Association
#400, 489 College St.
Toronto, ON M6G 1A5
416-927-9144; Fax: 416-927-8401
Toll-Free: 800-297-6660
E-mail: mail@onpha.org
URL: www.onpha.on.ca
Scope: Provincial
Purpose: Featuring speakers, workshops, & company exhibitors
Contact Information: Coordinator, Conference & Events: Sunny Chen, E-mail: Sunny.Chen@onpha.org, Phone: 416-927-9144, ext. 126

- **Ontario Professional Planners Institute 2018 Symposium**
Date: October 11-12, 2018
Location: Laurentian University
Sudbury, ON
Sponsor/Contact: Ontario Professional Planners Institute
#201, 234 Eglinton Ave. East
Toronto, ON M4P 1K5
416-483-1873; Fax: 416-483-7830
Toll-Free: 800-668-1448
E-mail: info@ontarioplanners.ca
URL: www.ontarioplanners.ca
Scope: Provincial

- **Ontario Society of Occupational Therapists Conference 2018**
Date: October 19-20, 2018
Location: Sheraton Parkway Toronto North
Richmond Hill, ON
Sponsor/Contact: Ontario Society of Occupational Therapists
#210, 55 Eglinton Ave. East
Toronto, ON M4P 1G8
416-322-3011; Fax: 416-322-6705
Toll-Free: 877-676-6768
E-mail: osot@osot.on.ca
URL: www.osot.on.ca
Scope: Provincial

- **Organization of Saskatchewan Arts Councils Showcase 2018**
Date: October 2018
Location: Saskatchewan
Sponsor/Contact: Organization of Saskatchewan Arts Councils
1102 - 8th Ave.
Regina, SK S4R 1C9
306-586-1250; Fax: 306-586-1550
E-mail: info@osac.ca
URL: www.osac.ca
Scope: Provincial

- **Pain Society of Alberta 12th Annual Conference**
Date: October 18-21, 2018
Location: Banff, AB
Sponsor/Contact: Pain Society of Alberta
132 Warwick Rd.
Edmonton, AB T5X 4P8
780-457-5225; Fax: 780-475-7968
E-mail: info@painsocietyofalberta.org
URL: painsocietyofalberta.org
Scope: Provincial

- **Physical & Health Educators of Manitoba 2018 Manitoba Teachers Society Professional Development Day**
Date: October 19, 2018
Location: Manitoba
Sponsor/Contact: Physical & Health Educators of Manitoba
#319, 145 Pacific Ave.
Winnipeg, MB R3B 2Z6
204-925-5786
E-mail: phemb@sportmanitoba.ca
URL: www.phemanitoba.ca
Scope: Provincial

- **Provincial Exhibition of Manitoba Agricultural Exhibition (Ag Ex) 2018**
Date: October 2018
Sponsor/Contact: Provincial Exhibition of Manitoba
115 - 10th St.
Brandon, MB R7A 4E7
204-726-3590; Fax: 204-725-0202
Toll-Free: 877-729-0001
E-mail: info@provincialexhibition.com
URL: www.provincialexhibition.com
Scope: Provincial

- **Saskatchewan Parks & Recreation Association 2018 Conference & AGM**
Date: October 18-20, 2018
Location: Saskatchewan
Sponsor/Contact: Saskatchewan Parks & Recreation Association
#100, 1445 Park St.
Regina, SK S4N 4C5

Conferences & Conventions Index

306-780-9231; *Fax:* 306-780-9257
Toll-Free: 800-563-2555
E-mail: office@spra.sk.ca
URL: www.spra.sk.ca
Scope: Provincial

- **Saskatchewan Writers' Guild Annual General Meeting & Fall Conference 2018**
Date: October 2018
Location: Saskatoon, SK
Sponsor/Contact: Saskatchewan Writers Guild
P.O. Box 3986
Regina, SK S4P 3R9
306-757-6310; *Fax:* 306-565-8554
Toll-Free: 800-667-6788
E-mail: info@skwriter.com
URL: www.skwriter.com
Scope: Provincial

- **SCAPPS [Canadian Society for Psychomotor Learning & Sport Psychology] Conference 2018**
Date: October 18-20, 2018
Location: Toronto, ON
Sponsor/Contact: Canadian Society for Psychomotor Learning & Sport Psychology
#360, 125 University Private
Ottawa, ON K1N 6N5
URL: www.scapps.org
Scope: National

- **Society for the History of Technology Annual Meeting 2018**
Date: October 10-14, 2018
Location: St. Louis, MO USA
Sponsor/Contact: Society for the History of Technology
c/o Dept. of History, Auburn University
#310, Thach Hall
Auburn, AL 36849-5207
334-844-6770; *Fax:* 334-844-6673
URL: www.historyoftechnology.org
Scope: International
Contact Information: Secretary: Jan Korsten, E-mail: j.w.a.korsten@tue.nl

- **Society of Plastics Engineers Automotive TPO Conference 2018**
Date: October 7-10, 2018
Location: Troy Marriott
Troy, MI USA
Sponsor/Contact: Society of Plastics Engineers
#306, 6 Berkshire Blvd.
Bethel, CT 06801
203-775-0471; *Fax:* 203-775-8490
URL: www.4spe.org
Scope: International

- **Society of Plastics Engineers Blow Molding Conference 2018**
Date: October 8-10, 2018
Location: Pittsburgh, PA USA
Sponsor/Contact: Society of Plastics Engineers
#306, 6 Berkshire Blvd.
Bethel, CT 06801
203-775-0471; *Fax:* 203-775-8490
URL: www.4spe.org
Scope: International

- **Society of Tribologists & Lubrication Engineers Tribology Frontiers Conference 2018**
Date: October 28-31, 2018
Location: Drake Hotel Chicago
Chicago, IL USA
Sponsor/Contact: Society of Tribologists & Lubrication Engineers
840 Busse Hwy.
Park Ridge, IL 60068-2302

847-825-5536; *Fax:* 847-825-1456
URL: www.stle.org
Scope: International

- **Specialty Graphic Imaging Association 2018 Expo**
Date: October 18-20, 2018
Location: Las Vegas Convention Center
Las Vegas, NV USA
Sponsor/Contact: Specialty Graphic Imaging Association
10015 Main St.
Fairfax, VA 22031-3489
Toll-Free: 888-385-3588
E-mail: sgia@sgia.org
URL: www.sgia.org
Scope: International

- **SPI: The Plastics Industry Trade Association 6th Annual Global Plastics Summit 2018**
Date: October 30 - November 1, 2018
Location: Radisson Blu Aqua
Chicago, IL USA
Sponsor/Contact: SPI: The Plastics Industry Trade Association
#500, 1425 K St. NW
Washington, DC 20005
202-974-5200; *Fax:* 202-296-7005
URL: www.plasticsindustry.org
Scope: National

- **Sustainable Forestry Initiative 2018 Annual Conference**
Date: October 16-18, 2018
Sponsor/Contact: Sustainable Forestry Initiative Inc.
#750, 2121 K St. NW
Washington, DC 20037
E-mail: info@sfiprogram.org
URL: www.sfiprogram.org
Scope: International

- **The Canadian Society of Clinical Perfusion 2018 National Meeting**
Date: October 20-23, 2018
Location: Toronto, ON
Sponsor/Contact: Canadian Society of Clinical Perfusion
914 Adirondack Rd.
London, ON N6K 4W7
Fax: 866-648-2763
Toll-Free: 888-496-2727
URL: www.cscp.ca
Scope: National
Purpose: Continuing education sessions on product development involving the society's corporate members, a business meeting, Canadian Society of Clinical Perfusion cerification examinations held off site from the convention centre, the presentation of awards, & networking opportunities

- **The Instrumentation, Systems & Automation Society of America (ISA) 2018 Food & Pharmaceutical Industries Division Symposium**
Date: October 16-17, 2018
Location: Montréal, QC
Sponsor/Contact: The Instrumentation, Systems & Automation Society of America
P.O. Box 12277
67 T.W. Alexander Dr.
Research Triangle Park, NC 27709
919-549-8411; *Fax:* 919-549-8288
E-mail: info@isa.org
URL: www.isa.org
Scope: International
Purpose: An event presented by the ISA Food & Pharmaceutical Industries Division

- **The Instrumentation, Systems & Automation Society of America (ISA) 64th International Instrumentation Symposium 2018**
Date: October 16-17, 2018
Location: Montréal, QC
Sponsor/Contact: The Instrumentation, Systems & Automation Society of America
P.O. Box 12277
67 T.W. Alexander Dr.
Research Triangle Park, NC 27709
919-549-8411; *Fax:* 919-549-8288
E-mail: info@isa.org
URL: www.isa.org
Scope: International
Purpose: An event sponsored jointly by the Aerospace Industries, Test Measurement, and Process Measurement and Controls Divisions of ISA; includes ISA training, short courses, workshops, & tutorials

- **Titanium USA 2018**
Date: October 7-10, 2018
Location: Bellagio Las Vegas
Las Vegas, NV USA
Sponsor/Contact: International Titanium Association
#100, 11674 Huron St.
Northglenn, CO 80234
303-404-2221; *Fax:* 303-404-9111
E-mail: ita@titanium.org
URL: www.titanium.org
Scope: International

- **Western Canadian Music Alliance BOW [Break Out West] Conference 2018**
Date: October 10-14, 2018
Location: Kelowna, BC
Sponsor/Contact: Western Canadian Music Alliance
#1, 118 Sherbrook St.
Winnipeg, MB R3C 2B4
204-943-8485; *Fax:* 204-453-1594
E-mail: info@breakoutwest.ca
URL: breakoutwest.ca
Scope: Provincial

- **World Energy Council Executive Assembly 2018**
Date: October 8-11, 2018
Location: Milan, Italy
Sponsor/Contact: World Energy Council
62-64 Cornhill St.
London, EC3V 3NH
URL: www.worldenergy.org
Scope: International

November

- **2018 Canadian Aerospace Summit**
Date: November 13-14, 2018
Sponsor/Contact: Aerospace Industries Association of Canada
#703, 255 Albert St.
Ottawa, ON K1P 6A9
613-232-4297; *Fax:* 613-232-1142
E-mail: info@aiac.ca
URL: www.aiac.ca
Scope: National
Purpose: Visionaries and practitioners will speak on the new evolution and expectations in aerospace, meet leading industry decision-makers, and gain first-hand intelligence on key business opportunities.

- **2018 Entomological Society of Canada Annual Meeting**
Date: November 11-14, 2018
Location: Vancouver, BC

Sponsor/Contact: Entomological Society of Canada
393 Winston Ave.
Ottawa, ON K2A 1Y8
613-725-2619
E-mail: entsoc.can@bellnet.ca
URL: www.esc-sec.ca
Scope: National
Purpose: Joint meeting with Entomological Society of America (ESA) & Entomological Society of British Columbia (ESBC)

- **Alberta Association of Academic Libraries Fall Meeting 2018**
Date: November 15, 2018
Location: Edmonton, AB
Sponsor/Contact: Alberta Association of Academic Libraries
c/o Genevieve Luthy, SAIT
1301 - 16 Ave. NW
Calgary, AB T2M 0L4
URL: aaal.ca
Scope: Provincial

- **Alberta Association of Municipal Districts & Counties Fall 2018 Convention**
Date: November 20-22, 2018
Location: Shaw Conference Centre
Edmonton, AB
Sponsor/Contact: Alberta Association of Municipal Districts & Counties
2510 Sparrow Dr.
Nisku, AB T9E 8N5
780-955-3639; *Fax:* 780-955-3615
Toll-Free: 855-548-7233
E-mail: aamdc@aamdc.com
URL: www.aamdc.com

- **American Anthropological Association 2018 Annual Meeting**
Date: November 14-18, 2018
Location: San Jose Convention Center
San Jose, CA USA
Sponsor/Contact: American Anthropological Association
#1301, 2300 Clarendon Blvd.
Arlington, VA 22201
703-528-1902; *Fax:* 703-528-3546
URL: www.americananthro.org
Scope: International
Contact Information: Director, Meetings & Conferences: Ushma Suvarnakar, Phone: 703-528-1902 ext. 1172

- **American Studies Association Annual Meeting 2018**
Date: November 8-11, 2018
Location: Atlanta, GA USA
Sponsor/Contact: American Studies Association
#301, 1120 - 19th St. NW
Washington, DC 20036
202-467-4783; *Fax:* 202-467-4786
Toll-Free: 800-548-1748
E-mail: asastaff@theasa.net
URL: www.theasa.net
Scope: International
Purpose: Theme: "States of Emergence"
Contact Information: Coordinator, Convention: Michael Casiano, E-mail: convention@theasa.net

- **ASME 2018 International Mechanical Engineering Congress & Exposition**
Date: November 9-15, 2018
Location: Pittsburgh, PA USA
Sponsor/Contact: American Society of Mechanical Engineers
2 Park Ave.
New York, NY 10016-5990

Conferences & Conventions Index

Toll-Free: 800-843-2763
E-mail: customercare@asme.org
URL: www.asme.org
Scope: International

- **Association for Financial Professionals 2018 Annual Conference**
Date: November 4-7, 2018
Location: Chicago, IL USA
Sponsor/Contact: Association for Financial Professionals
#800, 4520 East West Hwy.
Bethesda, MD 20814
301-907-2862; Fax: 301-907-2864
E-mail: afp@afponline.org
URL: www.afponline.org
Scope: National

- **Association of Manitoba Municipalities 20th Annual Convention**
Date: November 26-28, 2018
Location: RBC Convention Centre
Winnipeg, MB
Sponsor/Contact: Association of Manitoba Municipalities
1910 Saskatchewan Ave. West
Portage la Prairie, MB R1N 0P1
204-857-8666; Fax: 204-856-2370
E-mail: amm@amm.mb.ca
URL: www.amm.mb.ca

- **Association of Power Producers of Ontario 2018: 30th Annual Canadian Power Conference & Networking Centre**
Date: November 12-13, 2018
Location: Ontario
Sponsor/Contact: Association of Power Producers of Ontario
#1602, 25 Adelaide St. East
Toronto, ON M5C 3A1
416-322-6549; Fax: 416-481-5785
E-mail: appro@appro.org
URL: www.appro.org
Scope: Provincial

- **Association provinciale des enseignantes et enseignants du Québec/Québec Provincial Association of Teachers Convention 2018**
Date: November 23-24, 2018
Sponsor/Contact: Association provinciale des enseignantes et enseignants du Québec
#1, 17035, boul Brunswick
Kirkland, QC H9H 5G6
514-694-9777; Fax: 514-694-0189
Toll-Free: 800-361-9870
URL: www.qpat-apeq.qc.ca
Scope: Provincial

- **ATAC 84th Canadian Aviation Conference & Tradeshow**
Date: November 13-15, 2018
Location: Westin Bayshore Hotel
Vancouver, BC
Sponsor/Contact: Air Transport Association of Canada
#700, 255 Albert St.
Ottawa, ON K1P 6A9
613-233-7727; Fax: 613-230-8648
E-mail: atac@atac.ca
URL: www.atac.ca
Scope: National
Purpose: National gathering for operators, suppliers to the industry & government stakeholders involved in commerical aviation and flight training in Canada
Contact Information: Debbie Simpson; dsimpson@atac.ca; 613-233-7727 ext. 312

- **Atlantic Provinces Trial Lawyers Association Annual Plaintiff Practice Conference**
Date: November 23, 2018
Location: Delta Halifax
Halifax, NS
Sponsor/Contact: Atlantic Provinces Trial Lawyers Association
PO Box 2618, Central RPO
Halifax, NS B3J 3N5
902-446-4446; Fax: 902-425-9552
Toll-Free: 866-314-4446
URL: www.aptla.ca
Scope: Provincial

- **BC Kidney Days 2018**
Date: November 1-2, 2018
Location: JW Marriott Parq Vancouver
Vancouver, BC
Sponsor/Contact: British Columbia Provincial Renal Agency
#700, 1380 Burrard St.
Vancouver, BC V6Z 2H3
604-875-7340
E-mail: bcpra@bcpra.ca
URL: www.bcrenalagency.ca
Scope: Provincial
Purpose: Unites clinicians & administrators from BC, Canada, & the United States to discuss current research, trends, clinical treatment & surgical breakthroughs in renal patient care.
Contact Information: URL: www.bcrenalagency.ca/bc-kidney-days

- **BC School Superintendents Association Fall Conference & AGM 2018**
Date: November 8-9, 2018
Location: Westin Bayshore
Vancouver, BC
Sponsor/Contact: British Columbia School Superintendents Association
#208, 1118 Homer St.
Vancouver, BC V6B 6L5
604-687-0590; Fax: 604-687-8118
E-mail: information@bcssa.org
URL: www.bcssa.org
Scope: Provincial
Purpose: Themes include leadership, school effectiveness, & improvement

- **British Columbia Federation of Labour 2018 Convention**
Date: November 26-30, 2018
Sponsor/Contact: British Columbia Federation of Labour
#200, 5118 Joyce St.
Vancouver, BC V5R 4H1
604-430-1421; Fax: 604-430-5917
E-mail: bcfed@bcfed.ca
URL: www.bcfed.com
Scope: Provincial
Purpose: A meeting held every two years to set the direction of the labour movement in British Columbia, attended by rank & file trade union members
Contact Information: E-mail: bcfed@bcfed.ca

- **Canadian ADHD Resource Alliance 14th Annual Conference**
Date: November 9-11, 2018
Location: Hyatt Regency Calgary
Calgary, AB
Sponsor/Contact: Canadian ADHD Resource Alliance
#604, 3950 - 14th Ave.
Markham, ON L3R 0A9
416-637-8583; Fax: 416-385-3232
E-mail: info@caddra.ca
URL: www.caddra.ca
Scope: National

- **Canadian Acoustical Association "Acoustics Week in Canada" Conference**
Date: November 5-9, 2018
Location: Victoria, BC
Sponsor/Contact: Canadian Acoustical Association
c/o C. Laroche, Faculty of Health Sciences, University of Ottawa
#3062, 451 Smyth Rd.
Ottawa, ON K1H 8M5
613-562-5800; Fax: 613-562-5248
URL: www.caa-aca.ca
Scope: National

- **Canadian Association for Graduate Studies 56th Annual Conference**
Date: November 6-8, 2018
Location: Fort Garry Hotel
Winnipeg, MB
Sponsor/Contact: Canadian Association for Graduate Studies
#301, 260 St. Patrick St.
Ottawa, ON K1N 5K5
613-562-0949; Fax: 613-562-9009
E-mail: info@cags.ca
URL: www.cags.ca
Scope: National
Purpose: A yearly conference held at the end of October or the beginning of November, including plenary & breakout sessions, workshops, the presentation of awards, & the Killam Lecture related to graduate studies

- **Canadian Association of Fairs & Exhibitions Annual Convention 2018**
Date: November 21-23, 2018
Location: Banff, AB
Sponsor/Contact: Canadian Association of Fairs & Exhibitions
P.O. Box 21053 Stn. WEPO
Brandon, MB R7B 3W8
Toll-Free: 800-663-1714
E-mail: info@canadian-fairs.ca
URL: www.canadian-fairs.ca
Scope: National

- **Canadian Association of Movers 2018 Annual Conference & Trade Show**
Date: November 18-20, 2018
Location: Crowne Plaza
Niagara Falls, ON
Sponsor/Contact: Canadian Association of Movers
P.O. Box 26004 Stn. Churchill
Mississauga, ON L5L 5W7
905-848-6579; Fax: 866-601-8499
Toll-Free: 866-860-0065
E-mail: admin@mover.net
URL: www.mover.net
Scope: National

- **Canadian Marketing Association CMAfuture**
Date: November 6, 2018
Sponsor/Contact: Canadian Marketing Association
#603, 55 University Ave.
Toronto, ON M5J 2H7
416-391-2362; Fax: 416-441-4062
Toll-Free: 800-267-8805
E-mail: info@thecma.ca
URL: www.the-cma.org

Scope: National
Purpose: A look at the newest methods, strategies and technology on the horizon

- **Canadian Society for International Health 24th Canadian Conference on Global Health 2018**
Date: November 19-21, 2018
Location: Toronto, ON
Sponsor/Contact: Canadian Society for International Health
#726, 1 Nicholas St.
Ottawa, ON K1N 7B7
613-241-5785
E-mail: csih@csih.org
URL: www.csih.org
Scope: National
Purpose: The conference is the largest meeting of researchers, academics, decision makers, NGOs, policy makers, students & health care providers involved with global health in Canada.

- **Canadian Tax Foundation 70th Annual Tax Conference**
Date: November 25-27, 2018
Location: Vancouver, BC
Sponsor/Contact: Canadian Tax Foundation
#1200, 595 Bay St.
Toronto, ON M5G 2N5
416-599-0283; Fax: 416-599-9283
Toll-Free: 877-733-0283
URL: www.ctf.ca
Scope: National

- **Canadian Urban Transit Association 2018 Fall Conference & Transit Show**
Date: November 18-21, 2018
Location: Metro Toronto Convention Centre
Toronto, ON
Sponsor/Contact: Canadian Urban Transit Association
#1401, 55 York St.
Toronto, ON M5J 1R7
416-365-9800; Fax: 416-365-1295
URL: www.cutaactu.ca
Scope: National
Purpose: A yearly technical conference, which also includes the presentation of Employee Awards based on accomplishments in areas such as attendance, safety, & acts of heroism

- **Coaching Association of Canada 2018 Petro-Canada Sport Leadership sportif Conference**
Date: November 8-10, 2018
Location: Westin Ottawa
Ottawa, ON
Sponsor/Contact: Coaching Association of Canada
2451 Riverside Dr.
Ottawa, ON K1H 7X7
613-235-5000; Fax: 613-235-9500
URL: www.coach.ca
Scope: National
Purpose: An inpiring event for coaches, featuring guest speakers & the presentation of sport leadership awards

- **Financial Management Institute of Canada Professional Development Week 2018**
Date: November 2018
Sponsor/Contact: Financial Management Institute of Canada
#601, 200 Elgin St.
Ottawa, ON K2P 1L5

Conferences & Conventions Index

613-569-1158; *Fax:* 613-569-4532
E-mail: national@fmi.ca
URL: www.fmi.ca
Scope: National

- **Green Industry Show & Conference 2018**
Date: November 15-16, 2018
Location: Edmonton Expo Centre at Northlands
Edmonton, AB
Sponsor/Contact: Landscape Alberta Nursery Trades Association
#200, 10331 - 178 St. NW
Edmonton, AB T5S 1R5
780-489-1991; *Fax:* 780-444-2152
Toll-Free: 800-378-3198
E-mail: admin@landscape-alberta.com
URL: www.landscape-alberta.com
Scope: National
Purpose: An opportunity for members of the landscape, greenhouse, nursery, garden centre, tree care, & turf industries to network

- **Greenbuild International Conference & Expo 2018 (Chicago)**
Date: November 14-16, 2018
Location: McCormick Place (West Building)
Chicago, IL USA
Sponsor/Contact: U.S. Green Building Council
#500, 2101 L Street NW
Washington, DC 20037
202-742-3792
Toll-Free: 800-795-1747
E-mail: leedinfo@usgbc.org
URL: new.usgbc.org
Scope: International
Contact Information: URL: greenbuild.usgbc.org

- **Helicopter Association of Canada 2018 23rd Annual Convention & Trade Show**
Date: November 1-3, 2018
Location: Vancouver, BC
Sponsor/Contact: Helicopter Association of Canada
#500, 130 Albert St.
Ottawa, ON K1P 5G4
613-231-1110; *Fax:* 613-369-5097
URL: www.h-a-c.ca
Scope: National
Purpose: Professional development programs & information sessions to help Helicopter Association of Canada members achieve in the present economic & regulatory climate
Anticipated Attendance: 800+
Contact Information: Office Manager & Contact, Member Services: Barb Priestley, Phone: 613-231-1110, ext. 237, Fax: 613-369-5097, E-mail: barb.priestley@h-a-c.ca

- **International Association for Human Resource Information Management 2018 Data Event**
Date: November 5-6, 2018
Location: Austin, TX USA
Sponsor/Contact: International Association for Human Resource Information Management
10060 Grandview Sq.
Duluth, GA 30097
E-mail: information@ihrim.org
URL: www.ihrim.org

Scope: International
Purpose: Theme: "Advancing from Data to Knowledge & Intelligence"

- **International Society for Vascular Behavioural & Cognitive Disorders Congress 2018**
Date: November 14-18, 2018
Location: Hong Kong
Sponsor/Contact: International Society for Vascular Behavioural & Cognitive Disorders
c/o Newcastle University Campus for Ageing & Vitality
NIHR Biomedical Research Building, 1st Fl.
Newcastle upon Tyne, NE4 5PL
E-mail: vascogsoc@gmail.com
URL: www.vas-cog.org
Scope: International

- **Municipal Engineers Association 2018 Annual General Meeting**
Date: November 2018
Sponsor/Contact: Municipal Engineers Association
#22, 1525 Cornwall Rd.
Oakville, ON L6J 0B2
289-291-6472; *Fax:* 289-291-6477
URL: www.municipalengineers.on.ca
Scope: Provincial

- **National Railway Day Conference 2018**
Date: November 7, 2018
Location: Westin Hotel
Ottawa, ON
Sponsor/Contact: Canadian Association of Railway Suppliers
#901, 99 Bank St.
Ottawa, ON K1P 6B9
613-237-3888; *Fax:* 613-237-4888
E-mail: info@railwaysuppliers.ca
URL: www.railwaysuppliers.ca
Purpose: The event will bring suppliers, railways and government bodies together to celebrate the railway industry

- **Ontario Association of Social Workers 2018 Provincial Conference**
Date: November 2-3, 2018
Location: Ontario
Sponsor/Contact: Ontario Association of Social Workers
410 Jarvis St.
Toronto, ON M4Y 2G6
416-923-4848; *Fax:* 416-923-5279
E-mail: info@oasw.org
URL: www.oasw.org
Scope: Provincial
Purpose: Theme: "Mental Health Across the Lifespan: Social Workers on the Front Line of Real Issues"

- **Ontario Food Protection Association 60th Meeting & Fall Symposium**
Date: November 2018
Location: Ontario
Sponsor/Contact: Ontario Food Protection Association
P.O. Box 51575
2140A Queen St. East
Toronto, ON M4E 1C0
519-265-4119; *Fax:* 416-981-3368
E-mail: info@ofpa.on.ca
URL: www.ofpa.on.ca
Scope: Provincial

- **Ontario Music Educators' Association Counterpoint 2018**
Date: November 1-3, 2018
Location: Hamilton, ON

Sponsor/Contact: Ontario Music Educators' Association
URL: www.omea.on.ca
Scope: Provincial

- **Saskatchewan Water and Wastewater Association 2018 Tradeshow and Conference**
Date: November 6-9, 2018
Sponsor/Contact: Saskatchewan Water & Wastewater Association
P.O. Box 7831 Stn. Mn
Saskatoon, SK S7K 4R5
306-761-1278
Toll-Free: 888-668-1278
E-mail: office@swwa.ca
URL: www.swwa.ca
Scope: National

- **Snowmobilers of Manitoba Inc. 2018 8th Annual Snoman Congress**
Date: November 2-3, 2018
Location: Canad Inns Destination Centre
Winnipeg, MB
Sponsor/Contact: Snowmobilers of Manitoba Inc.
2121 Henderson Hwy.
Winnipeg, MB R2G 1P8
204-940-7533; *Fax:* 204-940-7531
E-mail: info@snoman.mb.ca
URL: www.snoman.mb.ca
Scope: Provincial

- **Society of Environmental Toxicology & Chemistry North America 2018 39th Annual Meeting**
Date: November 4-8, 2018
Location: Sacramento Convention Center
Sacramento, CA USA
Sponsor/Contact: Society of Environmental Toxicology & Chemistry
SETAC Asia / Pacific, SETAC Latin America, & SETAC North America
1010 - 12th Ave. North
Pensacola, FL 32501-3370
850-469-1500; *Fax:* 850-469-9778
E-mail: setac@setac.org
URL: www.setac.org
Scope: International
Anticipated Attendance: 2,300

- **The Canadian Council for Public-Private Partnerships 2018 26th Annual Conference**
Date: November 2018
Sponsor/Contact: The Canadian Council for Public-Private Partnerships
#608, 55 University Ave.
Toronto, ON M5J 2H7
416-861-0500
E-mail: partners@pppcouncil.ca
URL: www.pppcouncil.ca
Scope: National

- **The Royal Agricultural Winter Fair 2018**
Date: November 2-11, 2018
Location: Exhibition Place
Toronto, ON
Sponsor/Contact: Royal Agricultural Winter Fair Association
The Ricoh Coliseum
100 Prince's Blvd.
Toronto, ON M6K 3C3
416-263-3400
E-mail: info@royalfair.org
URL: www.royalfair.org
Scope: International
Purpose: The Royal is the largest combined indoor agricultural fair and international equestrian competition in the world.
Contact Information: www.royalfair.org

December

- **Association for Slavic, East European, & Eurasian Studies (ASEEES) Annual Convention 2018**
Date: December 6-9, 2018
Location: Boston Marriott Copley Place
Boston, MA USA
Sponsor/Contact: Association for Slavic, East European, & Eurasian Studies
University of Pittsburgh
#203C Bellefield Hall
Pittsburgh, PA 15260-6424
412-648-9911; *Fax:* 412-648-9815
E-mail: aseees@pitt.edu
URL: aseees.org
Scope: International
Contact Information: Manager, Convention: Margaret Manges, E-mail: aseees.convention@pitt.edu, Phone: 412-648-4049

- **BC Road Builders AGM**
Date: December 6, 2018
Location: British Columbia
Sponsor/Contact: British Columbia Road Builders & Heavy Construction Association
#307, 8678 Greenall Ave.
Burnaby, BC V5J 3M6
604-436-0220; *Fax:* 604-436-2627
E-mail: info@roadbuilders.bc.ca
URL: www.roadbuilders.bc.ca
Scope: Provincial

- **Win-Door North America 2018 (an event owned & produced by Fenestration Canada)**
Date: December 3-5, 2018
Location: Québec City Convention Centre
Québec, QC
Sponsor/Contact: Fenestration Canada
#1208, 130 Albert St.
Ottawa, ON K1P 5G4
613-235-5511; *Fax:* 613-235-4664
E-mail: info@fenestrationcanada.ca
URL: www.fenestrationcanada.ca
Scope: International
Purpose: Meetings, demonstrations, & seminars, plus an opportunity for suppliers to show their products & services to manufacturers & fabricators from across Canada, the United States, & international destinations

Other Conferences in 2018

- **10th Annual Quebec Oil and Gas Association Conference 2018**
Location: Quebec
Sponsor/Contact: Association pétrolière et gazière du Québec
#200, 140, Grande Allée est
Québec, QC G1R 5P7
418-261-2941
E-mail: info@apgq-qoga.com
URL: www.apgq-qoga.com
Scope: Provincial

- **11th International Meeting of Pediatric Endocrinology**
Sponsor/Contact: Pediatric Endocrine Society
6728 Old McLean Village Dr.
McLean, VA 22101
E-mail: info@pedsendo.org
URL: www.pedsendo.org
Scope: International

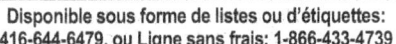

Conferences & Conventions Index

- **13th Annual Manitoba Association for Behaviour Analysis Conference 2018**
Location: Manitoba
Sponsor/Contact: Manitoba Association for Behaviour Analysis
P.O. Box 53017 Stn. South St. Vital
Winnipeg, MB R2N 3X2
E-mail: president@maba.ca
URL: www.maba.ca
Scope: Provincial

- **13th Annual National Initiative for the Care of the Elderly Knowledge Exchange 2018**
Sponsor/Contact: National Initiative for the Care of the Elderly
#234, 246 Bloor St. West
Toronto, ON M5S 1V4
416-978-7037
E-mail: nicenetadmin@utoronto.ca
URL: www.nicenet.ca
Scope: National

- **14e Congrès annuel de l'Association québécoise du lymphoedème**
Location: Quebec
Sponsor/Contact: Association Québécoise du Lymphoedème
6565, rue St-Hubert
Montréal, QC H2S 2M5
514-979-2463
E-mail: aql@infolympho.ca
URL: www.infolympho.ca
Scope: Provincial

- **14th World Convention of the International Confederation of Principals**
Sponsor/Contact: International Confederation of Principals
ICP Secretariat
68 Martin St.
Heidelberg, Victoria, 3084
URL: www.icponline.org
Scope: International
Purpose: A convention of interest to principals, vice-principals, education leaders, academics, researchers, policy makers, & government representatives from around the world

- **16th Ostomy Canada Society National Conference**
Sponsor/Contact: Ostomy Canada Society
#210, 5800 Ambler Dr.
Mississauga, ON L4W 4J4
905-212-7111; Fax: 905-212-9002
Toll-Free: 888-969-9698
E-mail: info1@ostomycanada.ca
URL: www.ostomycanada.ca
Scope: National

- **17th Annual Gang & Organized Crime Professional Development Conference**
Location: Ontario
Sponsor/Contact: Ontario Gang Investigators Association
P.O. Box 57085 Stn. Jackson Square
Hamilton, ON L8P 4W9
URL: ongia.org
Scope: Provincial

- **18th Annual Hydropower Forum 2018**
Sponsor/Contact: Canadian Hydropower Association
#1402 - 150 Metcalfe St.
Ottawa, ON K2P 1P1
613-751-6655; Fax: 613-751-4465
E-mail: info@canadahydro.ca
URL: canadahydro.ca
Scope: National

- **18th Annual National Scleroderma Conference 2018**
Location: Calgary, AB
Sponsor/Contact: Scleroderma Canada
#202, 41 King William St.
Hamilton, ON L8R 1A2
Toll-Free: 866-279-0632
E-mail: info@scleroderma.ca
URL: www.scleroderma.ca

- **2018 Alberta Foster Parent Association It's All About Kids Annual Conference**
Sponsor/Contact: Alberta Foster Parent Association
9750 - 35th Ave.
Edmonton, AB T6E 6J6
780-429-9923; Fax: 780-426-7151
Toll-Free: 800-667-2372
E-mail: reception@afpaonline.com
URL: www.afpaonline.com
Scope: Provincial

- **2018 Alberta Water Council Symposium**
Sponsor/Contact: Alberta Water Council
Petroleum Plaza, South Tower
#1400, 9915 - 108 St.
Edmonton, AB T5K 2G8
780-644-7380
E-mail: info@awchome.ca
URL: www.albertawatercouncil.ca
Scope: Provincial

- **2018 Annual General Meeting & Symposium of the Federation of Foster Families of Nova Scotia**
Location: Nova Scotia
Sponsor/Contact: Federation of Foster Families of Nova Scotia
#350, 99 Wyse Rd.
Dartmouth, NS B3A 4S5
902-424-3071; Fax: 902-424-5199
Toll-Free: 888-845-1555
URL: www.fosterfamilies.ns.ca
Scope: Provincial

- **2018 Annual General Meeting of Canada's National Firearms Association**
Sponsor/Contact: Canada's National Firearms Association
P.O. Box 49090
Edmonton, AB T6E 6H4
780-439-1394; Fax: 780-439-4091
Toll-Free: 877-818-0393
E-mail: info@nfa.ca
URL: nfa.ca
Scope: National

- **2018 Annual Meeting of the BC Society of Respiratory Therapists**
Location: British Columbia
Sponsor/Contact: British Columbia Society of Respiratory Therapists
P.O. Box 4760
Vancouver, BC V6B 4A4
604-623-2227
URL: www.bcsrt.ca
Scope: Provincial

- **2018 Annual Ontario Podiatric Medical Association Conference**
Location: Ontario
Sponsor/Contact: Ontario Podiatric Medical Association
#900, 45 Sheppard Ave. East
Toronto, ON M2N 5W9
416-927-9111; Fax: 416-927-9111
Toll-Free: 866-424-6762
E-mail: contact@opma.ca
URL: www.opma.ca
Scope: Provincial

- **2018 Association des recycleurs de pièces d'autos et de camions Congrès**
Sponsor/Contact: Association des recycleurs de pièces d'autos et de camions
#101, 37, rue de la Gare
Saint-Jérôme, QC J7Z 2B7
450-504-8315; Fax: 450-504-8313
Toll-Free: 855-504-8315
E-mail: info@arpac.org
URL: arpac.org
Scope: Provincial

- **2018 Association of Professional Engineers & Geoscientists of New Brunswick Annual Meeting**
Location: New Brunswick
Sponsor/Contact: Association of Professional Engineers & Geoscientists of New Brunswick
183 Hanwell Rd.
Fredericton, NB E3B 2R2
506-458-8083; Fax: 506-451-9629
Toll-Free: 888-458-8083
E-mail: info@apegnb.com
URL: www.apegnb.com
Scope: Provincial

- **2018 Auditing Association of Canada Annual Conference**
Sponsor/Contact: Auditing Association of Canada
9 Forest Rd.
Whitby, ON L1N 3N7
905-404-9511
E-mail: admin@auditingcanada.com
URL: www.auditingcanada.com
Scope: National

- **2018 BC Crime Prevention Association Training Symposium**
Location: British Columbia
Sponsor/Contact: British Columbia Crime Prevention Association
#120, 12414 - 82nd Ave.
Surrey, BC V3W 3E9
604-501-9222; Fax: 604-501-2261
Toll-Free: 888-405-2288
E-mail: info@bccpa.org
URL: www.bccpa.org
Scope: Provincial

- **2018 BC Municipal OH&S Conference**
Location: British Columbia
Sponsor/Contact: British Columbia Municipal Safety Association
20430 Fraser Hwy.
Langley, BC V3A 4G2
Fax: 778-278-0029
URL: www.bcmsa.ca

- **2018 BC Psychogeriatric Association Conference**
Location: British Columbia
Sponsor/Contact: British Columbia Psychogeriatric Association
P.O. Box 47028
1030 Denman St.
Vancouver, BC V6G 3E1
Fax: 888-835-2451
URL: www.bcpga.com
Scope: Provincial

- **2018 BC Saw Filers Association Annual General Meeting & Trade Show**
Location: British Columbia
Sponsor/Contact: British Columbia Saw Filers Association
6521 Orchard Hill Rd.
Vernon, BC V1H 1B6
250-546-2234; Fax: 604-585-4014
E-mail: info@bcsawfilers.com
URL: www.bcsawfilers.com
Scope: Provincial

- **2018 Biennial Canadian Police Association Conference**
Sponsor/Contact: Canadian Police Association
#100, 141 Catherine St.
Ottawa, ON K2P 1C3
613-231-4168; Fax: 613-231-3254
E-mail: cpa-acp@cpa-acp.ca
URL: www.cpa-acp.ca
Scope: National

- **2018 Biennial Conference of the Pentecostal Assemblies of Canada**
Sponsor/Contact: Pentecostal Assemblies of Canada
2450 Milltower Ct.
Mississauga, ON L5N 5Z6
905-542-7400; Fax: 905-542-7313
Toll-Free: 800-779-7262
E-mail: info@paoc.org
URL: www.paoc.org
Scope: National

- **2018 CNIB National Braille Conference**
Sponsor/Contact: Canadian National Institute for the Blind
1929 Bayview Ave.
Toronto, ON M4G 3E8
Toll-Free: 800-563-2642
E-mail: info@cnib.ca
URL: www.cnib.ca
Scope: National

- **2018 Calgary Chamber of Voluntary Organizations Connections Conference**
Location: Calgary, AB
Sponsor/Contact: Calgary Chamber of Voluntary Organizations
#1175, 105 - 12 Ave. SE
Calgary, AB T2G 1A1
403-261-6655; Fax: 403-261-6602
E-mail: info@calgarycvo.org
URL: www.calgarycvo.org
Scope: Local

- **2018 Canadian Association for Studies in Co-operation Conference**
Sponsor/Contact: Canadian Association for Studies in Co-operation
c/o Centre for the Study of Co-operatives, University of Saskatchewan
101 Diefenbaker Pl.
Saskatoon, SK S7N 5B8
E-mail: casc.acec@usask.ca
URL: www.coopresearch.coop
Scope: National

- **2018 Canadian Association of Aquarium Clubs Convention**
Sponsor/Contact: Canadian Association of Aquarium Clubs
#223, 1717 60th St. SE
Calgary, AB T2A 7Y7
E-mail: amtowell@shaw.ca
URL: www.caoac.ca
Scope: National

- **2018 Canadian Association of Orthodontists Annual Conference**
Sponsor/Contact: Canadian Association of Orthodontists
#210, 2800 - 14th Ave.
Toronto, ON L3R 0E4
416-491-3186; Fax: 416-491-1670
Toll-Free: 877-226-8800
E-mail: cao@associationconcepts.ca
URL: www.cao-aco.org

Conferences & Conventions Index

Scope: National
Purpose: A scientific session with exhibits

• 2018 Canadian Association of Statutory Human Rights Agencies Annual Conference
Sponsor/Contact: Canadian Association of Statutory Human Rights Agencies
#170, 99 - 5th Ave.
Ottawa, ON K1P 5P5
URL: www.cashra.ca
Scope: National

• 2018 Canadian Celiac Association National Conference
Sponsor/Contact: Canadian Celiac Association
Bldg. 1
#400, 5025 Orbitor Dr.
Mississauga, ON L4W 4Y5
905-507-6208; *Fax:* 905-507-4673
Toll-Free: 800-363-7296
E-mail: info@celiac.ca
URL: www.celiac.ca
Scope: National

• 2018 Canadian Farm Writers Federation Conference
Sponsor/Contact: Canadian Farm Writers' Federation
P.O. Box 250
Ormstown, QC J0S 1K0
Fax: 450-829-2226
Toll-Free: 877-782-6456
E-mail: secretariat@cfwf.ca
URL: cfwf.wildapricot.org
Scope: National

• 2018 Canadian Group Psychotherapy Association Conference
Sponsor/Contact: Canadian Group Psychotherapy Association
c/o First Stage Enterprises
#109, 1 Corcorde Gate
Toronto, ON M3C 3N6
416-426-7229; *Fax:* 416-726-7280
Toll-Free: 866-433-9695
E-mail: admin@cgpa.ca
URL: www.cgpa.ca
Scope: National

• 2018 Canadian Health Libraries Association (CHLA) / Association des bibliothèques de la santé du Canada (ABSC) 42nd Annual Conference
Sponsor/Contact: Canadian Health Libraries Association
468 Queen St. East, #LL02
Toronto, ON M5A 1T7
416-646-1600; *Fax:* 416-646-9460
E-mail: info@chla-absc.ca
URL: www.chla-absc.ca
Scope: National
Purpose: An annual May or June gathering of health science librarians to participate in continuing education courses & lectures, & to view products & services related to their work

• 2018 Canadian Hypertension Congress
Sponsor/Contact: Hypertension Canada
#211, 3780 - 14th Ave.
Markham, ON L3R 9Y5
905-943-9400; *Fax:* 905-943-9401
URL: www.hypertension.ca
Scope: National

• 2018 Canadian Institute of Food Science & Technology National Conference
Sponsor/Contact: Canadian Institute of Food Science & Technology
#1311, 3-1750 The Queensway
Toronto, ON M9C 5H5
905-271-8338; *Fax:* 905-271-8344
E-mail: cifst@cifst.ca
URL: www.cifst.ca
Scope: International

• 2018 Canadian Pool & Spa Conference & Expo
Sponsor/Contact: Pool & Hot Tub Council of Canada
5 MacDougall Dr.
Brampton, ON L6S 3P3
905-458-7242; *Fax:* 905-458-7037
Toll-Free: 800-879-7066
E-mail: office@poolcouncil.ca
URL: www.poolcouncil.ca
Purpose: The conference features seminars & courses, as well as the expo
Contact Information: www.poolcouncil.ca

• 2018 Canadian Propane Association Leadership Summit
Sponsor/Contact: Canadian Propane Association
#300, 100 Gloucester St.
Ottawa, ON K2P 0A2
613-683-2270
E-mail: info@propane.ca
URL: www.propane.ca
Scope: National
Purpose: The summit provides the opportunity for leaders in the propane industy to share ideas & knowledge among each other

• 2018 Canadian Society for Civil Engineering Annual Conference & Annual General Meeting
Sponsor/Contact: Canadian Society for Civil Engineering
4877, rue Sherbrooke ouest
Montréal, QC H3Z 1G9
514-933-2634; *Fax:* 514-933-3504
E-mail: info@csce.ca
URL: www.csce.ca
Scope: National

• 2018 Canadian Society of Clinical Chemists Conference
Sponsor/Contact: Canadian Society of Clinical Chemists
P.O. Box 1570
#310, 4 Cataraqui St.
Kingston, ON K7K 1Z7
613-531-8899; *Fax:* 866-303-0626
E-mail: office@cscc.ca
URL: www.cscc.ca
Scope: National

• 2018 Canadian Society of Pharmacology & Therapeutics Meeting
Sponsor/Contact: Canadian Society of Pharmacology & Therapeutics
E-mail: info@pharmacologycanada.org
URL: www.pharmacologycanada.org
Scope: National

• 2018 Centre for Transportation Engineering & Planning Annual General Meeting
Sponsor/Contact: Centre for Transportation Engineering & Planning
c/o Stantec, Transportation
#200, 325 - 25 St. SE
Calgary, AB T2A 7H8
403-607-4482; *Fax:* 403-716-8129
URL: www.c-tep.com

• 2018 College of Dental Surgeons of British Columbia Annual General Meeting
Location: British Columbia
Sponsor/Contact: College of Dental Surgeons of British Columbia
#500, 1765 West 8th Ave.
Vancouver, BC V6J 5C6
604-736-3621; *Fax:* 604-734-9448
Toll-Free: 800-663-9169
E-mail: info@cdsbc.org
URL: www.cdsbc.org
Scope: Provincial

• 2018 Down Syndrome Association of Ontario Conference
Location: Ontario
Sponsor/Contact: Down Syndrome Association of Ontario
300 Sunset Blvd.
Peterborough, ON K9H 5L3
905-439-6644
Toll-Free: 855-921-3726
URL: www.dsao.ca
Scope: Provincial

• 2018 Engineers PEI Annual General Meeting
Sponsor/Contact: Association of Professional Engineers of Prince Edward Island
135 Water St.
Charlottetown, PE C1A 1A8
902-566-1268; *Fax:* 902-566-5551
E-mail: info@engineerspei.com
URL: www.engineerspei.com

• 2018 Environmental Managers Association of British Columbia Workshop
Location: British Columbia
Sponsor/Contact: Environmental Managers Association of British Columbia
P.O. Box 3741
Vancouver, BC V6B 3Z8
604-998-2226; *Fax:* 604-998-2226
E-mail: info@emaofbc.com
URL: www.emaofbc.com
Scope: Provincial

• 2018 Fisheries Council of Canada Annual Conference
Location: Ottawa, ON
Sponsor/Contact: Fisheries Council of Canada
#610, 170 Laurier Ave. West
Ottawa, ON K1P 5V5
613-727-7450; *Fax:* 613-727-7453
E-mail: info@fisheriescouncil.org
URL: www.fisheriescouncil.ca
Scope: National
Purpose: Educational sessions, opportunities to network, & social programs

• 2018 Golf Business Canada Conference & Trade Show
Sponsor/Contact: National Golf Course Owners Association Canada
#810, 515 Legget Dr.
Ottawa, ON K2K 3G4
613-226-3616; *Fax:* 613-226-4148
Toll-Free: 866-626-4262
E-mail: ngcoa@ngcoa.ca
URL: www.ngcoa.ca
Scope: National

• 2018 Industrial Gas Users Association Spring Seminar
Sponsor/Contact: Industrial Gas Users Association
#202, 260 Centrum Blvd.
Orleans, ON K1E 3P4
613-236-8021; *Fax:* 613-830-7196
E-mail: info@igua.ca
URL: www.igua.ca
Scope: National

• 2018 Insurance Brokers Association of Manitoba Convention
Sponsor/Contact: Insurance Brokers Association of Canada
#600, 1445 Portage Ave.
Winnipeg, MB R3G 3P4
204-488-1857; *Fax:* 204-489-0316
Toll-Free: 800-204-5649
E-mail: info@ibam.mb.ca
URL: www.ibam.mb.ca
Scope: Provincial

• 2018 International Summit of Cooperatives
Sponsor/Contact: International Cooperative Alliance
P.O. Box 2100
150, Route de Ferney
Geneva, 1211
E-mail: ica@ica.coop
URL: ica.coop
Scope: International
Contact Information: Email: info@intlsummit.coop

• 2018 Leaders & Innovators Conference
Sponsor/Contact: Ontario College Administrative Staff Associations
P.O. Box 263
#201-202, 120 Centre St. North
Napanee, ON K7R 3M4
Fax: 866-742-5430
Toll-Free: 866-742-5429
E-mail: info@ocasa.on.ca
URL: www.ocpinfo.com
Scope: Provincial

• 2018 Ontario Association of Child & Youth Care Conference
Location: Ontario
Sponsor/Contact: Ontario Association of Child & Youth Care
c/o The School of Child & Youth Care, Ryerson University
350 Victoria St.
Toronto, ON M5B 2K3
416-621-4340; *Fax:* 866-403-5961
E-mail: office@oacyc.org
URL: www.oacyc.org
Scope: Provincial

• 2018 Ontario Kinesiology Association Conference & AGM
Location: Ontario
Sponsor/Contact: Ontario Kinesiology Association
#100, 6700 Century Ave.
Mississauga, ON L5N 6A4
905-567-7194; *Fax:* 905-567-7191
E-mail: info@oka.on.ca
URL: www.oka.on.ca
Scope: Provincial

• 2018 Ontario Waste Management Association Annual General Meeting
Location: Ontario
Sponsor/Contact: Ontario Waste Management Association
#3, 2005 Clark Blvd.
Brampton, ON L6T 5P8
905-791-9500; *Fax:* 905-791-9514
E-mail: info@owma.org
URL: www.owma.org
Scope: Provincial

Conferences & Conventions Index

- **2018 Pharmacists' Association of Newfoundland & Labrador Annual Conference**
Sponsor/Contact: Pharmacists' Association of Newfoundland & Labrador
#203, 85 Thorburn Rd.
St. John's, NL A1B 3M2
709-753-7881; Fax: 709-753-8882
Toll-Free: 866-753-7881
E-mail: email@panl.net
URL: www.panl.net
Scope: Provincial
Purpose: Educational sessions & networking opportunities

- **2018 Prince Edward Island Veterinary Medical Association AGM**
Location: Rodd Charlottetown Hotel Charlottetown, PE
Sponsor/Contact: Prince Edward Island Veterinary Medical Association
P.O. Box 21097 Stn. 465 University Ave.
Charlottetown, PE C1A 9h6
902-367-3757; Fax: 902-367-3176
E-mail: admin.peivma@gmail.com
URL: www.peivma.com
Scope: Provincial

- **2018 Rowing New Brunswuck Aviron Annual General Meeting**
Sponsor/Contact: Rowing New Brunswick Aviron
P.O. Box 30047 Stn. Prospect Plaza
Fredericton, NB E3B 0H8
E-mail: president@rowingnb.ca
URL: www.rowingnb.ca

- **2018 Saskatchewan Emergency Medical Services Association Convention & Trade Show**
Location: Saskatchewan
Sponsor/Contact: Saskatchewan Emergency Medical Services Association
#105, 111 Research Dr.
Saskatoon, SK S7N 3R2
306-382-2147; Fax: 306-955-5353
E-mail: semsa@semsa.org
URL: www.semsa.org
Scope: Provincial
Purpose: An informative convention with a trade show that provides the opportunitiy for those working in emergency medicl services to meet with suppliers to discuss products & services
Contact Information: semsa@semsa.org

- **2018 Saskatchewan Home Economics Teachers Association Conference**
Location: Saskatchewan
Sponsor/Contact: Saskatchewan Home Economics Teachers Association
Saskatoon, SK
URL: www.sheta.ca
Scope: Provincial

- **2018 Saskatchewan Professional Planners Institute Annual Conference**
Sponsor/Contact: Saskatchewan Professional Planners Institute
2424 College Ave.
Regina, SK S4P 1C8
306-584-3879; Fax: 306-352-6913
E-mail: msteranka@sasktel.net
URL: sppi.ca
Scope: Provincial
Purpose: A meeting of planners & related professionals to share new ideas, enhance professional practice, network & socialize

- **2018 Yukon Geoscience Forum & Trade Show**
Sponsor/Contact: Yukon Chamber of Mines
3151B - 3rd Ave.
Whitehorse, YT Y1A 1G1
867-667-2090; Fax: 867-668-7127
E-mail: info@yukonminers.ca
URL: www.yukonminers.ca
Scope: Provincial
Purpose: A conference for the mining & exploration industry, featuring technical events, short courses, & exhibits

- **20th [International Society of Radiographers & Radiological Technologists] ISRRT World Congress**
Sponsor/Contact: International Society of Radiographers & Radiological Technologists
143 Bryn Pinwydden
Cardiff, CF23 7DG
URL: www.isrrt.org
Scope: International

- **21st Annual Brain Injury Conference 2018**
Sponsor/Contact: Ontario Brain Injury Association
201 King St.
London, ON N6A 1C9
519-642-4539; Fax: 519-642-4124
E-mail: info@braininjurylondon.on.ca
URL: www.braininjurylondon.on.ca
Scope: Local
Purpose: A conference for professionals & survivors

- **21st Supply Chain Management Association Ontario Annual Conference**
Location: Ontario
Sponsor/Contact: Supply Chain Management Association - Ontario
P.O. Box 64
#2704, 1 Dundas St. West
Toronto, ON M5G 1Z3
416-977-7566; Fax: 416-977-4135
Toll-Free: 877-726-6968
E-mail: info@scmao.ca
URL: www.scmao.ca
Scope: Provincial
Anticipated Attendance: 400+

- **25th Convention of the Ukrainian Fraternal Society of Canada**
Sponsor/Contact: Ukrainian Fraternal Society of Canada
235 McGregor St.
Winnipeg, MB R2W 4W5
204-568-4482; Fax: 204-589-6411
Toll-Free: 800-988-8372
E-mail: info@ufsc.ca
URL: www.ufsc.ca
Scope: National

- **27th Alberta Association of Family School Liaison Workers 2018 Conference**
Sponsor/Contact: Alberta Association of Family School Liaison Workers
c/o Tonia Koversky, St. Albert Family & Community Support Services
#10, 50 Bellerose Dr.
St. Albert, AB T8N 3L5
780-459-1749; Fax: 780-458-1260
URL: www.aafslw.ca
Scope: Provincial

- **27th International Congress of The Transplantation Society 2018**
Location: Madrid, Spain
Sponsor/Contact: The Transplantation Society
International Headquarters
#1401, 505, boul René-Lévesque ouest
Montréal, QC H2Z 1Y7
514-874-1717; Fax: 514-874-1716
E-mail: info@tts.org
URL: www.tts.org
Scope: International

- **28e congrès annuel d'Association québecoise de soins palliatifs**
Sponsor/Contact: Association québecoise de soins palliatifs
P.O. Box 321 Stn. Chef
Granby, QC J2G 8E5
514-826-9400; Fax: 438-238-1336
E-mail: info@aqsp.org
URL: www.aqsp.org
Purpose: La réunion accueille des médecins, des professionnels et des bénévoles qui sont intéressés par les soins palliatifs. Le but de la conférence est de partager les expériences et de connaissances entre ceux dans le milieu des soins palliatifs.

- **30th Annual Canadian Bottled Water Association Convention & Trade Show**
Sponsor/Contact: Canadian Bottled Water Association
#617, 7357 Woodbine Ave.
Markham, ON L3R 6R3
416-618-1763; Fax: 877-354-2788
URL: www.cbwa.ca
Scope: National

- **39th Canadian Remote Sensing Society Conference 2018**
Sponsor/Contact: Canadian Remote Sensing Society
c/o Canadian Aeronautics & Space Institute
#104, 350 Terry Fox Dr.
Kanata, ON K2K 2W5
613-591-8787; Fax: 613-591-7291
E-mail: casi@casi.ca
URL: www.crss-sct.ca
Scope: National

- **4-H Ontario 2018 Conference & Annual Meeting**
Location: Ontario
Sponsor/Contact: Canadian 4-H Council
P.O. Box 212
111 Main St. North
Rockwood, ON N0B 2K0
519-856-0992; Fax: 519-856-0515
Toll-Free: 877-410-6748
E-mail: inquiries@4-hontario.ca
URL: www.4-hontario.ca
Scope: Provincial

- **42nd Anniversary Modular Housing Association Prairie Provinces Annual General Meeting**
Sponsor/Contact: Modular Housing Association Prairie Provinces
P.O. Box 3538 Stn. Main
Sherwood Park, AB T8H 2T4
780-429-1798; Fax: 780-429-1871
Toll-Free: 866-866-8106
URL: www.mhaprairies.ca
Scope: Provincial

- **43rd Manitoba Conservation Districts Association Conference**
Location: Manitoba
Sponsor/Contact: Manitoba Conservation Districts Association
#4, 940 Princess Ave.
Brandon, MB R7A 0P6
204-570-0164
E-mail: info@mcda.ca
URL: www.mcda.ca
Scope: Provincial

- **46th Annual Newspapers Atlantic Conference 2018**
Sponsor/Contact: Newspapers Atlantic
#216, 7075 Bayers Rd.
Halifax, NS B3L 2C2
902-832-4480; Fax: 902-832-4484
Toll-Free: 877-842-4480
E-mail: info@newspapersatlantic.ca
URL: newspapersatlantic.ca
Scope: Provincial
Purpose: A Maritime meeting with speakers, educational seminars, an awards banquet, networking opportunities with colleagues, & social events

- **47e Congrès de l'Association des archivistes du Québec**
Location: Quebec
Sponsor/Contact: Association des archivistes du Québec
P.O. Box 9768 Stn. Sainte-Foy
Québec, QC G1V 4C3
418-652-2357; Fax: 418-646-0868
E-mail: infoaaq@archivistes.qc.ca
URL: www.archivistes.qc.ca
Scope: Provincial

- **47th Ontario Occupational Health Nurses Association Annual Conference**
Location: Ontario
Sponsor/Contact: Ontario Occupational Health Nurses Association
#605, 302 The East Mall
Toronto, ON M9B 6C7
416-239-6462; Fax: 416-239-5462
Toll-Free: 866-664-6276
E-mail: administration@oohna.on.ca
URL: www.oohna.on.ca
Scope: Provincial
Purpose: Theme: "Keeping Workers Well"

- **48th Annual Agricultural Manufacturers of Canada Convention & Trade Show**
Sponsor/Contact: Agricultural Manufacturers of Canada
Evraz Place, Stockman's Arena
P.O. Box 636 Stn. Main
Regina, SK S4P 3A3
306-522-2710; Fax: 306-781-7293
E-mail: admin@a-m-c.ca
URL: www.a-m-c.ca

- **48th Annual Saskatchewan Reading Conference 2018**
Location: Saskatchewan
Sponsor/Contact: Saskatchewan Reading Council
c/o Good Spirit School Div., Fairview Education Centre
63 King St. East
Yorkton, SK S3N 0T7
306-786-5500; Fax: 306-783-0355
Toll-Free: 866-390-0773
URL: saskreading.com
Scope: Provincial

- **53rd Annual Association of School Transportation Services of British Columbia Convention and Trade Show**
Location: British Columbia
Sponsor/Contact: The Association of School Transportation Services of British Columbia
250-804-7892; Fax: 250-832-2584
E-mail: info@astsbc.org
URL: www.astsbc.org

Conferences & Conventions Index

Scope: Provincial
Contact Information: info@astsbc.org

- **67th Newfoundland & Labrador Association of Medical Radiation Technologists Annual General Meeting 2018**
Location: Newfoundland & Labrador
Sponsor/Contact: Newfoundland & Labrador Association of Medical Radiation Technologists
P.O. Box 29141 Stn. Torbay Rd. Post Office
St. John's, NL A1A 5B5
709-777-6036
URL: www.nlamrt.ca
Scope: Provincial

- **75th Truck Loggers Association Convention & Trade Show**
Sponsor/Contact: Truck Loggers Association
#725, 815 Hastings St. West
Vancouver, BC V6C 1B4
604-684-4291; *Fax:* 604-684-7134
E-mail: contact@tla.ca
URL: www.tla.ca
Scope: National

- **86e Congrès annuel de l'Association des bibliothécaires du Québec 2018**
Location: Quebec
Sponsor/Contact: Québec Library Association
P.O. Box 26717 Stn. Beaconsfield
50, boul St-Charles
Montréal, QC H9W 6G7
514-697-0146; *Fax:* 514-697-0146
URL: www.abqla.qc.ca
Scope: Provincial

- **90th Ontario Federation of Anglers & Hunters AGM and Fish & Wildlife Conference**
Location: Ontario
Sponsor/Contact: Ontario Federation of Anglers & Hunters
P.O. Box 2800
4601 Guthrie Dr.
Peterborough, ON K9J 8L5
705-748-6324; *Fax:* 705-748-9577
E-mail: ofah@ofah.org
URL: www.ofah.org
Scope: Provincial

- **91st Ontario Road Builders' Association 2018 Convention & Annual General Meeting**
Location: Ontario
Sponsor/Contact: Ontario Road Builders' Association
#1, 365 Brunel Rd.
Mississauga, ON L4Z 1Z5
905-507-1107; *Fax:* 905-890-8122
E-mail: info@orba.org
URL: www.orba.org
Scope: Provincial
Purpose: Informative sessions of interest to members of the road building industry

- **92nd Annual Ontario Trucking Association Convention & Executive Conference 2018**
Location: Ontario
Sponsor/Contact: Ontario Trucking Association
555 Dixon Rd.
Toronto, ON M9W 1H8
416-249-7401; *Fax:* 866-713-4188
URL: www.ontruck.org
Scope: Provincial

- **98th Annual Canadian Meat Council Conference 2018**
Sponsor/Contact: Canadian Meat Council
#930, 220 Laurier Ave. West
Ottawa, ON K1P 5Z9
613-729-3911; *Fax:* 613-729-4997
E-mail: info@cmc-cvc.com
URL: www.cmc-cvc.com
Scope: National
Purpose: A meeting with a technical symposium & exhibits, a general session, as well as the announcement of scholarship recipients

- **ANNISSA Organization of Canada Women's Health Conference**
Sponsor/Contact: ANNISAA Organization of Canada
#111, 7 St. Dennis Dr.
Toronto, ON M3C 1E4
647-761-0745
E-mail: info@annisaa.org
URL: annisaa.org

- **Aboriginal Financial Officers Association of BC Fall Conference 2018**
Location: British Columbia
Sponsor/Contact: AFOA Canada
#1010, 100 Park Royal
West Vancouver, BC V7T 1A2
604-925-6370; *Fax:* 604-925-6390
E-mail: exec@afoabc.org
URL: www.afoabc.org
Scope: Provincial

- **Aboriginal Financial Officers Association of BC Spring Conference 2018**
Location: British Columbia
Sponsor/Contact: AFOA Canada
#1010, 100 Park Royal
West Vancouver, BC V7T 1A2
604-925-6370; *Fax:* 604-925-6390
E-mail: exec@afoabc.org
URL: www.afoabc.org
Scope: Provincial

- **Accreditation Canada Quality Conference 2018**
Sponsor/Contact: Accreditation Canada
1150 Cyrville Rd.
Ottawa, ON K1J 7S9
613-738-3800; *Fax:* 613-738-7755
Toll-Free: 800-814-7769
URL: www.accreditation.ca
Scope: National

- **Airports Canada Conference & Exhibition**
Sponsor/Contact: Canadian Airports Council
#600, 116 Lisgar St.
Ottawa, ON K2P 0C2
613-560-9302; *Fax:* 613-560-6599
URL: www.cacairports.ca
Purpose: A targeted opportunity for key decision-makers to share ideas & gain the latest information on the best strategic & operational tools & practices concerning airports across Canada & internationally

- **Alberta Association of Agricultural Societies 2018 Annual Meeting & Convention**
Location: Alberta
Sponsor/Contact: Alberta Association of Agricultural Societies
J.G. O'Donoghue Building
#200, 7000 - 113 St.
Edmonton, AB T6H 5T6

780-427-2174; *Fax:* 780-422-7755
E-mail: aaas@gov.ab.ca
URL: www.albertaagsocieties.ca
Scope: Provincial
Purpose: An event attended by members of the Alberta Association of Agricultural Societies, where agricultural societies can submit resolutions to the annual general meeting & vote
Contact Information: E-mail: aaas@gov.ab.ca

- **Alberta Association of Landscape Architects 2018 Annual General Meeting**
Location: Alberta
Sponsor/Contact: Alberta Association of Landscape Architects
P.O. Box 21052
Edmonton, AB T6R 2V4
780-435-9902; *Fax:* 780-413-0076
E-mail: aala@aala.ab.ca
URL: www.aala.ab.ca
Scope: Provincial

- **Alberta Beef Industry Conference**
Location: Alberta
Sponsor/Contact: Alberta Beef Producers
#165, 6815 - 8th St. NE
Calgary, AB T2E 7H7
403-275-4400; *Fax:* 403-274-0007
E-mail: abpfeedback@albertabeef.org
URL: www.albertabeef.org
Scope: Provincial
Contact Information: www.abiconference.ca

- **Alberta Broomball Association Annual General Meeting 2018**
Location: Alberta
Sponsor/Contact: Alberta Broomball Association
11759 Groat Rd.
Edmonton, AB T5M 3K6
URL: www.albertabroomball.ca
Scope: Provincial

- **Alberta College of Medical Diagnostic & Therapeutic Technologists 2018 Annual General Conference**
Location: Alberta
Sponsor/Contact: Alberta College of Medical Diagnostic & Therapeutic Technologists
#800, 4445 Calgary Trail NW
Edmonton, AB T6H 5R7
780-487-6130; *Fax:* 780-432-9106
Toll-Free: 800-282-2165
E-mail: info@acmdtt.com
URL: acmdtt.com
Scope: Provincial

- **Alberta College of Medical Diagnostic & Therapeutic Technologists 2018 Annual General Meeting**
Location: Alberta
Sponsor/Contact: Alberta College of Medical Diagnostic & Therapeutic Technologists
#800, 4445 Calgary Trail NW
Edmonton, AB T6H 5R7
780-487-6130; *Fax:* 780-432-9106
Toll-Free: 800-282-2165
E-mail: info@acmdtt.com
URL: acmdtt.com
Scope: Provincial

- **Alberta Conference of Mennonite Brethren Churches Annual Convention 2018**
Location: Alberta

Sponsor/Contact: Alberta Conference of Mennonite Brethren Churches
MB Ministry Centre
#60, 340 Midpark Way SE
Calgary, AB T2X 1P1
403-256-3211; *Fax:* 403-256-3788
Toll-Free: 855-256-3211
URL: www.abmb.ca
Scope: Provincial
Contact Information: Administrator: Ruthie Kopp, Phone: 403-256-3211

- **Alberta Development Officers Association 2018 Conference**
Location: Alberta
Sponsor/Contact: Alberta Development Officers Association
c/o Diane Burtnick
P.O. Box 164
Sangudo, AB T0E 2A0
780-913-4214; *Fax:* 780-963-9762
E-mail: admin@adoa.net
URL: www.adoa.net
Scope: Provincial

- **Alberta Educational Facilities Administrators Association 2018 Conference**
Location: Alberta
Sponsor/Contact: Alberta Educational Facilities Administrators Association
7 White Pelican Way
Lake Newell Resort, AB T1R 0X5
403-376-0461
URL: www.aefaa.ca
Scope: Provincial

- **Alberta Equestrian Federation Annual General Meeting 2018**
Sponsor/Contact: Alberta Equestrian Federation
#100, 251 Midpark Blvd. SE
Calgary, AB T2X 1S3
403-253-4411; *Fax:* 403-252-5260
Toll-Free: 877-463-6233
E-mail: info@albertaequestrian.com
URL: www.albertaequestrian.com
Scope: Provincial

- **Alberta Family Mediation Society Conference 2018**
Sponsor/Contact: Alberta Family Mediation Society
#1650, 246 Stewart Green SW
Calgary, AB T3H 3C8
403-233-0143
Toll-Free: 877-233-0143
E-mail: info@afms.ca
URL: www.afms.ca
Scope: Provincial

- **Alberta Fish & Game Association 2018 Annual Conference**
Location: Alberta
Sponsor/Contact: Alberta Fish & Game Association
6924 - 104 St.
Edmonton, AB T6H 2L7
780-437-2342; *Fax:* 780-438-6872
E-mail: office@afga.org
URL: www.afga.org
Scope: Provincial

- **Alberta Forest Products Association 76th Annual General Meeting & Conference 2018**
Location: Alberta
Sponsor/Contact: Alberta Forest Products Association
#900, 10707 - 100 Ave.
Edmonton, AB T5J 3M1

780-452-2841; *Fax:* 780-455-0505
URL: www.albertaforestproducts.ca
Scope: Provincial
Purpose: A business meeting, sessions on topics relevant to the industry, networking opportunities, & a recognition dinner

• **Alberta Gerontological Nurses Association 37th AGM & Conference 2018**
Location: Alberta
Sponsor/Contact: Alberta Gerontological Nurses Association
P.O. Box 67040 Stn. Meadowlark
Edmonton, AB T5R 5Y3
E-mail: info@agna.ca
URL: www.agna.ca
Scope: Provincial

• **Alberta Horse Trials Association Annual General Meeting & Awards Banquet**
Location: Alberta
Sponsor/Contact: Alberta Horse Trials Association
c/o Aislyn Havell, Membership Secretary
#23, 38440 Range Rd. 284
Red Deer County, AB T4S 2E2
E-mail: albertahorsetrials@gmail.com
URL: www.albertahorsetrials.com
Scope: Provincial
Contact Information: Coordinator, Special Events: Carly Moore, E-mail: ahtaspecialevents@gmail.com

• **Alberta Hospice Palliative Care Association 2018 Imagine Conference**
Location: Alberta
Sponsor/Contact: Alberta Hospice Palliative Care Association
#1245, 70 Ave. SE
Calgary, AB T2H 2X8
403-206-9938; *Fax:* 403-206-9958
E-mail: director@ahpca.ca
URL: www.ahpca.ca
Scope: Provincial

• **Alberta Institute of Agrologists Annual General Meeting 2018**
Location: Alberta
Sponsor/Contact: Alberta Institute of Agrologists
#1430, 5555 Calgary Trail NW
Edmonton, AB T6H 5P9
780-435-0606; *Fax:* 780-464-2155
Toll-Free: 855-435-0606
URL: www.albertaagrologists.ca
Scope: Provincial

• **Alberta Land Surveyors' Association 2018 Annual General Meeting**
Location: Alberta
Sponsor/Contact: Alberta Land Surveyors' Association
#1000, 10020 - 101A Ave.
Edmonton, AB T5J 3G2
780-429-8805; *Fax:* 888-459-1664
Toll-Free: 800-665-2572
E-mail: info@alsa.ab.ca
URL: www.alsa.ab.ca
Scope: Provincial

• **Alberta Library Trustees Association 2018 Alberta Library Conference**
Location: Alberta
Sponsor/Contact: Alberta Library Trustees Association
4024 - 37A Ave.
Edmonton, AB T6L 7A1
780-761-2582; *Fax:* 866-419-1451
URL: www.librarytrustees.ab.ca

Scope: Provincial
Purpose: Hosted annually in conjunction with the Library Association of Alberta (LAA); Provides attendees with professional development & networking opportunities

• **Alberta Library Trustees Association 2018 Annual General Meeting**
Location: Alberta
Sponsor/Contact: Alberta Library Trustees Association
4024 - 37A Ave.
Edmonton, AB T6L 7A1
780-761-2582; *Fax:* 866-419-1451
URL: www.librarytrustees.ab.ca
Scope: Provincial
Purpose: Financial statements, a proposed budget, nominations report, & special resolutions

• **Alberta Museums Association 2018 Annual Conference**
Location: Alberta
Sponsor/Contact: Alberta Museums Association
#404, 10408 - 124 St.
Edmonton, AB T5N 1R5
780-424-2626; *Fax:* 780-425-1679
E-mail: info@museums.ab.ca
URL: www.museums.ab.ca
Scope: Provincial
Purpose: Theme: "Cultivating Connections: Museums & the Environment"

• **Alberta Music Festival Association Annual General Meeting 2018**
Location: Alberta
Sponsor/Contact: Alberta Music Festival Association
E-mail: info@albertamusicfestival.org
URL: www.albertamusicfestival.org
Scope: Provincial

• **Alberta Public Housing Administrators' Association Fall Conference 2018**
Sponsor/Contact: Alberta Public Housing Administrators' Association
14220 - 109 Ave. NW
Edmonton, AB T5N 4B3
780-498-1971; *Fax:* 780-464-7039
URL: www.aphaa.org
Scope: Provincial

• **Alberta Ready Mixed Concrete Association 2018 Annual General Meeting & Convention**
Location: Alberta
Sponsor/Contact: Alberta Ready Mixed Concrete Association
4944 Roped Rd. NW
Edmonton, AB T6B 3T7
780-436-5645; *Fax:* 780-436-6503
E-mail: info@concretealberta.ca
URL: www.concretealberta.ca
Scope: Provincial
Purpose: Featuring speakers, meetings, & networking opportunities

• **Alberta Rural Municipal Administrators' Association 2018 Conference**
Sponsor/Contact: Alberta Rural Municipal Administrators Association
6027 - 4th St. NE
Calgary, AB T2K 4Z5
403-275-0622; *Fax:* 403-275-8179
URL: www.armaa.ca
Scope: Provincial

• **Alberta School Boards Association 2018 Fall General Meeting**
Location: Alberta
Sponsor/Contact: Alberta School Boards Association
#1200, 9925 - 109 St.
Edmonton, AB T5K 2J8
780-482-7311
E-mail: reception@asba.ab.ca
URL: www.asba.ab.ca
Scope: Provincial
Purpose: An Alberta School Boards Association professional development event
Contact Information: Contact, Meetings: Noreen Pownall, E-mail: npownall@asba.ab.ca

• **Alberta School Boards Association 2018 Spring General Meeting**
Location: Alberta
Sponsor/Contact: Alberta School Boards Association
#1200, 9925 - 109 St.
Edmonton, AB T5K 2J8
780-482-7311
E-mail: reception@asba.ab.ca
URL: www.asba.ab.ca
Scope: Provincial
Purpose: An Alberta School Boards Association professional development event
Contact Information: Contact, Meetings: Noreen Pownall, E-mail: npownall@asba.ab.ca

• **Alberta School Learning Commons Council Annual General Meeting 2018**
Location: Alberta
Sponsor/Contact: Alberta School Learning Commons Council
c/o Alberta Teachers' Association, Barnett House
11010 - 142 St. NW
Edmonton, AB T5N 2R1
URL: www.aslc.ca
Scope: Provincial

• **Alberta Snowmobile & Powersports Show 2018**
Location: Alberta
Sponsor/Contact: Alberta Snowmobile Association
11759 Groat Rd.
Edmonton, AB T5M 3K6
780-427-2695; *Fax:* 780-415-1779
URL: www.altasnowmobile.ab.ca
Scope: Provincial
Contact Information: www.albertasnowmobileshow.com

• **Alberta Society for the Prevention of Cruelty to Animals 2018 Annual General Meeting**
Location: Alberta
Sponsor/Contact: Alberta Society for the Prevention of Cruelty to Animals
17904 - 118 Ave. NW
Edmonton, AB T5S 2W3
780-447-3600; *Fax:* 780-447-4748
E-mail: info@albertaspca.org
URL: www.albertaspca.org
Scope: Provincial

• **Alberta Speleological Society 2018 Annual General Meeting**
Location: Alberta
Sponsor/Contact: Alberta Speleological Society

c/o Andrea Corlett
#1606 924 - 14 Ave. SW
Calgary, AB T2R 0N7
E-mail: info@caving.ab.ca
URL: www.caving.ab.ca
Scope: Provincial
Purpose: A meeting of cavers, featuring the election of executive members, the presentation of awards
Contact Information: info@caving.ab.ca

• **Alberta Teachers' Association Annual Representative Assembly 2018**
Sponsor/Contact: Alberta Teachers' Association
Barnett House
11010 - 142 St. NW
Edmonton, AB T5N 2R1
780-447-9400; *Fax:* 780-455-6481
Toll-Free: 800-232-7208
E-mail: postmaster@ata.ab.ca
URL: www.teachers.ab.ca
Scope: Provincial

• **Alberta Teachers' Association Summer Conference 2018**
Sponsor/Contact: Alberta Teachers' Association
Barnett House
11010 - 142 St. NW
Edmonton, AB T5N 2R1
780-447-9400; *Fax:* 780-455-6481
Toll-Free: 800-232-7208
E-mail: postmaster@ata.ab.ca
URL: www.teachers.ab.ca
Scope: Provincial

• **Alberta Urban Municipalities Association Convention & AMSC Trade Show 2018**
Location: Alberta
Sponsor/Contact: Alberta Urban Municipalities Association
#300, 8616 51 Ave.
Edmonton, AB T6E 6E6
780-433-4431; *Fax:* 780-433-4454
Toll-Free: 877-421-6644
E-mail: main@auma.ca
URL: www.auma.ca
Scope: Provincial

• **Alberta Water & Wastewater Operators Association 2018 43rd Annual Operators Seminar**
Location: Alberta
Sponsor/Contact: Alberta Water & Wastewater Operators Association
10806 - 119 St.
Edmonton, AB T5H 3P2
780-454-7745; *Fax:* 780-454-7748
Toll-Free: 877-454-7745
URL: www.awwoa.ab.ca
Scope: Provincial
Purpose: Speakers, including operators, supervisors, technical industry representatives, & other experts in their fields, bring operators up-to-date on numerous topics in the water & wastewater field

• **Alberta Weekly Newspapers Association 97th Annual General Meeting & Convention 2018**
Location: Alberta
Sponsor/Contact: Alberta Weekly Newspapers Association
3228 Parsons Rd.
Edmonton, AB T6H 5R7
780-434-8746; *Fax:* 780-438-8356
Toll-Free: 800-282-6903

Conferences & Conventions Index

E-mail: info@awna.com
URL: www.awna.com
Scope: Provincial

- **AllerGen 2018 Research Conference**
Sponsor/Contact: AllerGen NCE Inc.
Michael DeGroote Centre for Learning & Discovery, McMaster University
#3120, 1280 Main St. West
Hamilton, ON L8S 4K1
905-525-9140; Fax: 905-524-0611
E-mail: info@allergen-nce.ca
URL: www.allergen-nce.ca
Scope: National

- **Allied Beauty Association 2018 Annual General Meeting**
Sponsor/Contact: Allied Beauty Association
#26-27, 145 Traders Blvd. East
Mississauga, ON L4Z 3L3
905-568-0158; Fax: 905-568-1581
E-mail: abashows@abacanada.com
URL: www.abacanada.com
Scope: National

- **American Academy of Religion 2018 Annual Meeting**
Sponsor/Contact: American Academy of Religion
#300, 825 Houston Mill Rd. NE
Atlanta, GA 30329-4205
404-727-3049; Fax: 404-727-7959
E-mail: info@aarweb.org
URL: www.aarweb.org
Purpose: Meeting bringing together thousands of professors & students, authors & publishers, religious leaders & interested laypersons for academic sessions, meetings & workshops in the fields of religious studies & theology

- **American Council for Québec Studies Biennial Conference**
Location: , USA
Sponsor/Contact: American Council for Québec Studies
c/o University of Maine
213 Litle Hall
Orono, ME 04469
E-mail: acqs2@maine.edu
URL: www.southalabama.edu/acqs

- **American Musicological Society Annual Meeting 2018**
Sponsor/Contact: American Musicological Society
20 Cooper Sq., 2nd Fl.
New York, NY 10003
212-992-6340; Fax: 212-995-4022
Toll-Free: 877-679-7648
E-mail: ams@ams-net.org
URL: www.ams-net.org
Scope: International

- **American Society for Aesthetic Plastic Surgery 2018 Annual Meeting**
Sponsor/Contact: American Society for Aesthetic Plastic Surgery
c/o Renato Saltz, M.D., FACS
5445 South Highland Dr.
Salt Lake City, UT 84117
801-274-9500; Fax: 801-274-9515
Toll-Free: 888-272-7711
E-mail: findasurgeon@surgery.org
URL: www.surgery.org
Scope: International

- **Ancient, Free & Accepted Masons of the Grand Lodge of British Columbia & Yukon 2018 Masonic Leadership & Ladies Conference**
Sponsor/Contact: Ancient, Free & Accepted Masons of Canada - Grand Lodge of British Columbia & Yukon
1495 West 8th Ave.
Vancouver, BC V6H 1C9
604-736-8941; Fax: 604-736-5097
E-mail: grand_secretary@freemasonry.bcy.ca
URL: freemasonry.bcy.ca
Scope: Provincial
Purpose: Discussions of leadership skills, best practices in lodge leadership, & information about the Grand Lodge

- **Aquaculture Canada 2018**
Sponsor/Contact: Aquaculture Association of Canada
16 Lobster Lane
St Andrews, NB E5B 3T6
506-529-4766; Fax: 506-529-4609
E-mail: aac@dfo-mpo.gc.ca
URL: www.aquacultureassociation.ca
Scope: National
Purpose: Featuring presentations, special sessions, workshops, & posters

- **Archives Association of British Columbia 2018 Annual General Meeting**
Sponsor/Contact: Archives Association of British Columbia
#249, 34A-2755 Lougheed Hwy.
Port Coquitlam, BC V3B 5Y9
E-mail: info@aabc.ca
URL: www.aabc.ca
Scope: Provincial

- **Archives Association of British Columbia 2018 Conference**
Sponsor/Contact: Archives Association of British Columbia
#249, 34A-2755 Lougheed Hwy.
Port Coquitlam, BC V3B 5Y9
E-mail: info@aabc.ca
URL: www.aabc.ca
Scope: Provincial

- **Archives Association of Ontario Conference 2018**
Location: Waterloo, ON
Sponsor/Contact: Archives Association of Ontario
#200, 411 Richmond St. East
Toronto, ON M5A 3S5
647-343-3334
E-mail: aao@aao-archivists.ca
URL: aao-archivists.ca
Scope: Provincial

- **Archives Society of Alberta 2018 Annual General Meeting**
Location: Alberta
Sponsor/Contact: Archives Society of Alberta
#407, 10408 - 124 St. NW
Edmonton, AB T5N 1R5
780-424-2697; Fax: 780-425-1679
E-mail: info@archivesalberta.org
URL: www.archivesalberta.org
Scope: Provincial

- **Archives Society of Alberta 2018 Biennial Conference**
Location: Alberta
Sponsor/Contact: Archives Society of Alberta
#407, 10408 - 124 St. NW
Edmonton, AB T5N 1R5
780-424-2697; Fax: 780-425-1679
E-mail: info@archivesalberta.org
URL: www.archivesalberta.org
Scope: Provincial

- **ArcticNet Annual Scientific Meeting 2018**
Sponsor/Contact: ArcticNet Inc.
Pavillon Alexandre-Vachon, Université Laval
#4081, 1045, av de la Médecine
Québec, QC G1V 0A6
418-656-5830; Fax: 418-656-2334
E-mail: arcticnet@arcticnet.ulaval.ca
URL: www.arcticnet.ulaval.ca
Scope: National

- **Assemblée générale annuelle d'Aéro Montréal 2018**
Location: Quebec
Sponsor/Contact: Aéro Montréal
#8000, 380, rue Saint-Antoine ouest
Montréal, QC H2Y 3X7
514-987-9330; Fax: 514-987-1948
E-mail: info@aeromontreal.ca
URL: www.aeromontreal.ca
Scope: Local

- **Association de la construction du Québec 2018 congrès annuel**
Location: Quebec
Sponsor/Contact: Association de la construction du Québec
9200, boul Métropolitain est
Anjou, QC H1K 4L2
514-354-0609; Fax: 514-354-8292
Toll-Free: 888-868-3424
E-mail: info@prov.acq.org
URL: www.acq.org
Scope: Provincial

- **Association de la presse francophone Congrès annuel**
Sponsor/Contact: Association de la presse francophone
267, rue Dalhousie
Ottawa, ON K1N 7E3
613-241-1017; Fax: 613-241-6313
E-mail: admin@apf.ca
URL: www.apf.ca
Scope: National
Purpose: Les éditeurs de journaux de langue française du Canada se réunissent pour discuter de nouvelles de l'industrie et de participer à des occasions de perfectionnement professionnel

- **Association des bibliothèques publiques du Quebec Rendez-vous des bibliotheques publiques du Quebec**
Location: Quebec
Sponsor/Contact: Association des bibliothèques publiques du Québec
#215, 1453, rue Beaubien est
Montréal, QC H2G 3C6
514-279-0550; Fax: 514-845-1618
E-mail: info@abpq.ca
URL: www.abpq.ca
Scope: Provincial

- **Association des bibliothèques de l'Ontario-Franco (ABO-Franco) Assemblée générale annuelle 2018**
Location: Quebec
Sponsor/Contact: Association des bibliothèques de l'Ontario-Franco a/s Association des bibliothèques de l'Ontario
2, rue Toronto, 3e étage
Toronto, ON M5C 2B6
416-363-3388; Fax: 416-941-9581
Toll-Free: 866-873-9867
URL: www.accessola.org
Scope: Provincial

- **Association des cadres des centres de la petite enfance Conference 2018**
Sponsor/Contact: Association des cadres des centres de la petite enfance
P.O. Box 4042 Stn. D
Montréal, QC
514-933-3954
E-mail: info@associationdescadres.ca
URL: www.associationdescadres.ca
Scope: Provincial

- **Association des conseils des médecins, dentistes et pharmaciens du Québec Colloque 2018**
Sponsor/Contact: Association des conseils des médecins, dentistes et pharmaciens du Québec
#212, 560, boul Henri-Bourassa ouest
Montréal, QC H3L 1P4
514-858-5885; Fax: 514-858-6767
E-mail: acmdp@acmdp.qc.ca
URL: www.acmdp.qc.ca
Scope: Provincial

- **Association for Bright Children Ontario 2018 Annual Conference**
Location: Ontario
Sponsor/Contact: Association for Bright Children (Ontario)
c/o 135 Brant St.
Oakville, ON L6K 2Z8
416-925-6136
E-mail: abcinfo@abcontario.ca
URL: www.abcontario.ca
Scope: Provincial
Contact Information: E-mail: president@abcontario.ca

- **Association for Information Management Professionals Canada Conference 2018**
Sponsor/Contact: ARMA Canada
6, rue Viateur Gauvreau
Chambly, QC J3L 6V3
URL: www.armacanada.org
Scope: National
Purpose: Brings together delegates & exhibitors & provides professional development opportunities
Contact Information: Director, Conference Program: Christy Walters, Email: armacanadaprogramdirector@gmail.com; Phone: 604-926-9903

- **Association for Literature, Environment, & Culture in Canada 2018 Biennial Conference**
Sponsor/Contact: Association for Literature, Environment, & Culture in Canada
c/o Department of English, University of Calgary
2500 University Dr. NW, 11th Fl.
Calgary, AB T2N 1N4
E-mail: contactus@alecc.ca
URL: www.alecc.ca
Scope: National

- **Association of BC Drama Educators 2018 Fall Conference**
Location: British Columbia
Sponsor/Contact: Association of BC Drama Educators
c/o BC Teachers' Federation
#100, #550 West 6 Ave.
Vancouver, BC V5Z 4P2
604-871-2283; Fax: 604-871-2286
Toll-Free: 800-663-9163
URL: www.bcdramateachers.com
Scope: Provincial

- **Association of BC Forest Professionals 70th Annual Forestry**

Conference and Annual General Meeting 2018
Location: British Columbia
Sponsor/Contact: Association of British Columbia Forest Professionals
#602 - 1281 West Georgia St.
Vancouver, BC V6E 3J7
604-687-8027; Fax: 604-687-3264
E-mail: info@abcfp.ca
URL: www.abcfp.ca
Scope: Provincial

• **Association of British Columbia Land Surveyors 2018 113th Annual General Meeting**
Location: British Columbia
Sponsor/Contact: Association of British Columbia Land Surveyors
#301, 2400 Bevan Ave.
Sidney, BC V8L 1W1
250-655-7222; Fax: 250-655-7223
Toll-Free: 800-332-1193
E-mail: office@abcls.ca
URL: www.abcls.ca
Scope: Provincial
Contact Information: Board & Administrative Coordinator: Bev Renny, E-mail: office@abcls.ca

• **Association of Canadian Map Libraries & Archives 2018 Annual Conference**
Sponsor/Contact: Association of Canadian Map Libraries & Archives
c/o Deena Yanofsky, Humanities & Social Sciences Library, McGill U
3459, rue McTavish
Montréal, QC H3A 0C9
514-398-1087
URL: www.acmla-acacc.ca
Scope: National
Purpose: A yearly gathering of map librarians & archivists & other individuals with an interest in maps & geographic data who support the objectives of the association

• **Association of Consulting Engineering Companies British Columbia 2018 AGM**
Location: British Columbia
Sponsor/Contact: Association of Consulting Engineering Companies - British Columbia
#1258, 409 Granville St.
Vancouver, BC V6C 1T2
604-687-2811; Fax: 604-688-7110
E-mail: info@acec-bc.ca
URL: www.acec-bc.ca
Scope: Provincial

• **Association of Consulting Engineering Companies British Columbia 2018 Annual Transportation Conference**
Location: British Columbia
Sponsor/Contact: Association of Consulting Engineering Companies - British Columbia
#1258, 409 Granville St.
Vancouver, BC V6C 1T2
604-687-2811; Fax: 604-688-7110
E-mail: info@acec-bc.ca
URL: www.acec-bc.ca
Scope: Provincial

• **Association of Consulting Engineering Companies British Columbia 2018 Awards Gala**
Location: British Columbia
Sponsor/Contact: Association of Consulting Engineering Companies - British Columbia
#1258, 409 Granville St.
Vancouver, BC V6C 1T2
604-687-2811; Fax: 604-688-7110
E-mail: info@acec-bc.ca
URL: www.acec-bc.ca
Scope: Provincial
Purpose: The presentation of the Awards for Engineering Excellence in categories such as buildings, municipal, transportation, natural resources, energy & industry, & soft engineering

• **Association of Early Childhood Educators Ontario 2018 68th Annual Provincial Conference**
Location: Ontario
Sponsor/Contact: Association of Early Childhood Educators Ontario
#211, 40 Orchard View Blvd.
Toronto, ON M4R 1B9
416-487-3157; Fax: 416-487-3758
Toll-Free: 866-932-3236
E-mail: info@aeceo.ca
URL: www.aeceo.ca
Scope: Provincial
Purpose: A conference & exhibits for delegates from across Ontario

• **Association of Manitoba Museums Annual Conference 2018**
Location: Manitoba
Sponsor/Contact: Association of Manitoba Museums
#1040, 555 Main St.
Winnipeg, MB R3B 1C3
204-947-1782; Fax: 204-942-3749
URL: www.museumsmanitoba.com
Scope: Provincial

• **Association of New Brunswick Land Surveyors 2018 Annual General Meeting**
Location: New Brunswick
Sponsor/Contact: Association of New Brunswick Land Surveyors
#312, 212, Queen St.
Fredericton, NB E3B 1A8
506-458-8266; Fax: 506-458-8267
E-mail: anbls@nb.aibn.com
URL: www.anbls.nb.ca
Scope: Provincial

• **Association of New Brunswick Licensed Practical Nurses 2018 Annual General Meeting**
Sponsor/Contact: Association of New Brunswick Licensed Practical Nurses
384 Smythe St.
Fredericton, NB E3B 3E4
506-453-0747; Fax: 506-459-0503
Toll-Free: 800-942-0222
URL: www.anblpn.ca
Scope: Provincial

• **Association of Newfoundland & Labrador Archives Annual General Meeting 2018**
Location: Newfoundland & Labrador
Sponsor/Contact: Association of Newfoundland & Labrador Archives
P.O. Box 23155
St. John's, NL A1B 4J9
709-726-2867; Fax: 709-722-9035
E-mail: anla@nf.aibn.com
URL: www.anla.nf.ca
Scope: Provincial

• **Association of Ontario Midwives 2018 Annual General Meeting & Conference**
Sponsor/Contact: Association of Ontario Midwives
#301, 365 Bloor St. E.
Toronto, ON M3W 3L4
416-425-9974; Fax: 416-425-6905
Toll-Free: 866-418-3773
E-mail: admin@aom.on.ca
URL: www.aom.on.ca
Scope: Provincial

• **Association of Professional Engineers, Geologists & Geophysicists of Alberta 2018 Annual Conference & Annual General Meeting**
Location: Alberta
Sponsor/Contact: Association of Professional Engineers & Geoscientists of Alberta
Scotia One
#1500, 10060 Jasper Ave. NW
Edmonton, AB T5J 4A2
780-426-3990; Fax: 780-426-1877
Toll-Free: 800-661-7020
E-mail: email@apega.ca
URL: www.apega.ca
Scope: Provincial
Purpose: An annual gathering in Calgary or Edmonton, featuring professional development activities & other conference events

• **Association of Registered Nurses of British Columbia 2018 Annual General Meeting**
Location: British Columbia
Sponsor/Contact: College of Registered Nurses of British Columbia
2855 Arbutus St.
Vancouver, BC V6J 3Y8
604-736-7331; Fax: 604-738-2272
Toll-Free: 800-565-6505
E-mail: info@crnbc.ca
URL: www.crnbc.ca
Scope: Provincial

• **Association of Registered Professional Foresters of New Brunswick Annual General Meeting 2018**
Location: New Brunswick
Sponsor/Contact: Association of Registered Professional Foresters of New Brunswick
#221, 1350 Regent St.
Fredericton, NB E3C 2G6
506-452-6933; Fax: 506-450-3128
E-mail: info@arpfnb.ca
URL: www.arpfnb.ca
Scope: Provincial

• **Association of the Chemical Profession of Alberta 2018 Annual General Meeting**
Sponsor/Contact: Association of the Chemical Profession of Alberta
P.O. Box 21017
Edmonton, AB T6R 2V4
780-413-0004; Fax: 780-413-0076
URL: www.pchem.ca
Scope: Provincial

• **Association paritaire pour la santé et la sécurité du travail du secteur affaires sociales (ASSTSAS) colloque régionale 2018**
Location: Quebec
Sponsor/Contact: Association paritaire pour la santé et la sécurité du travail du secteur affaires sociales
#950, 5100, rue Sherbrooke est
Montréal, QC H1V 3R9
514-253-6871; Fax: 514-253-1443
Toll-Free: 800-361-4528
URL: www.asstsas.qc.ca
Scope: Local

• **Association pour l'avancement des sciences et des techniques de la documentation (ASTED) Congrès des professionnels de l'information 2018**
Location: Quebec
Sponsor/Contact: Association pour l'avancement des sciences et des techniques de la documentation
#387, 2065, rue Parthenais
Montréal, QC H2K 3T1
514-281-5012; Fax: 514-281-8219
E-mail: info@asted.org
URL: asted.org
Scope: Provincial
Contact Information: Courriel: info@congrescpi.com; site Internet: congrescpi.com

• **Association professionnelle des techniciennes et techniciens en documentation du Québec 16e congrès 2018**
Sponsor/Contact: Association professionnelle des techniciennes et techniciens en documentation du Québec
594, rue des Érables
Neuville, QC G0A 2R0
418-909-0608; Fax: 418-909-0608
E-mail: info@aptdq.org
URL: www.aptdq.org
Scope: Provincial

• **Association québécoise de lutte contre la pollution atmosphérique Coquetel bénéfice 2018**
Sponsor/Contact: Association québécoise de lutte contre la pollution atmosphérique
473, rue Principale
Saint-Léon-de-Standon, QC G0R 4L0
418-642-1322
Toll-Free: 855-702-7572
E-mail: info@aqlpa.com
URL: www.aqlpa.com
Scope: Provincial

• **Association québécoise des professeurs de français Congrès 2018**
Location: Quebec
Sponsor/Contact: Association québécoise des professeurs de français
1151, André-Charpentier
LeMoyne, QC J4R 1S9
450-923-9422
E-mail: info@aqpf.qc.ca
URL: www.aqpf.qc.ca
Scope: National

• **Athletic Therapists Association of BC 13th Annual Member's Meeting**
Sponsor/Contact: Athletic Therapy Association of British Columbia
#200, 4170 Still Creek Dr.
Burnaby, BC V5C 6C6
604-918-5077
E-mail: info@athletictherapybc.ca
URL: www.athletictherapybc.ca
Scope: Provincial

• **Atlantic Provinces Library Association 2018 Annual Conference**
Sponsor/Contact: Atlantic Provinces Library Association
c/o Kenneth C. Rowe Management Bldg., Dalhousie University
Stn. 15000
#4010, 6100 University Ave.
Halifax, NS B3H 4R2

Conferences & Conventions Index

E-mail: contact@apla.ca
URL: www.apla.ca
Scope: Provincial
Purpose: An educational program to support the interests & concerns of the library community in the Atlantic provinces

- **Atlantic Publishers Marketing Association 2018 Annual General Meeting**
Sponsor/Contact: Atlantic Publishers Marketing Association
1484 Carlton St.
Halifax, NS B3H 3B7
902-420-0711; Fax: 902-423-4302
URL: www.atlanticpublishers.ca
Scope: Provincial

- **Atlantic Universities Physics & Astronomy Conference (AUPAC) 2018**
Sponsor/Contact: Science Atlantic
Dept. of Psychology & Neuroscience, Dalhousie University
P.O. Box 15000
Halifax, NS B3H 4R2
902-494-3421
E-mail: admin@scienceatlantic.ca
URL: www.scienceatlantic.ca
Scope: Provincial

- **Automotive Parts Manufacturers' Association 22nd Annual Automotive Outlook Conference 2018**
Sponsor/Contact: Automotive Parts Manufacturers' Association
#801, 10 Four Seasons Pl.
Toronto, ON M9B 6H7
416-620-4220; Fax: 416-620-9730
URL: www.apma.ca
Scope: National

- **Avicultural Advancement Council of Canada 80th Canadian National Cage Bird Show & Expo**
Sponsor/Contact: Avicultural Advancement Council of Canada
77 Long Island Cres.
Unionville, ON L3P 7M1
URL: www.aacc.ca
Scope: National
Contact Information: URL: www.national-birdshow.com

- **Badminton BC Annual General Meeting & Congress 2018**
Location: British Columbia
Sponsor/Contact: Badminton BC
#110, 12761 - 16 Ave.
Surrey, BC V4A 1N2
604-385-3595
E-mail: info@badmintonbc.com
URL: www.badmintonbc.com
Scope: Provincial

- **Bakery Congress 2018 Trade Show & Conference**
Location: Montréal, QC
Sponsor/Contact: Baking Association of Canada
#202, 7895 Tranmere Dr.
Mississauga, ON L5S 1V9
905-405-0288; Fax: 905-405-0993
Toll-Free: 888-674-2253
E-mail: info@baking.ca
URL: www.baking.ca
Scope: National
Contact Information: Ahmed Mutaher, E-mail: amutaher@baking.ca

- **BC Association for Charitable Gaming 2018 Symposium**
Location: British Columbia
Sponsor/Contact: British Columbia Association for Charitable Gaming
#401, 151 - 10090 152nd St.
Surrey, BC V2R 8X8
604-568-8649
Toll-Free: 888-672-2224
URL: www.bcacg.com
Scope: Provincial

- **BC Association of Medical Radiation Technologists 2018 Annual General Conference**
Sponsor/Contact: British Columbia Association of Medical Radiation Technologists
Central Office
#102, 211 Columbia St.
Vancouver, BC V6A 2R5
604-682-8171; Fax: 604-305-0424
Toll-Free: 800-990-7090
E-mail: office@bcamrt.bc.ca
URL: www.bcamrt.bc.ca
Scope: Provincial
Purpose: Speakers present on a variety of educational topics as well as tips for the workplace and health and wellness.

- **BC Association of School Psychologists Conference 2018**
Location: British Columbia
Sponsor/Contact: British Columbia Association of School Psychologists
c/o Barbara Nichols
7715 Loedel Cres.
Prince George, BC V2N 0A5
E-mail: executives@bcasp.ca
URL: www.bcasp.ca
Scope: Provincial

- **BC Association of Social Workers Annual General Meeting 2018**
Location: British Columbia
Sponsor/Contact: British Columbia Association of Social Workers
#402, 1755 West Broadway
Vancouver, BC V6J 4S5
604-730-9111; Fax: 604-730-9112
Toll-Free: 800-665-4747
E-mail: bcasw@bcasw.org
URL: www.bcasw.org
Scope: Provincial

- **BC Association of Speech/Language Pathologists & Audiologists 2018 Conference**
Location: British Columbia
Sponsor/Contact: British Columbia Association of Speech-Language Pathologists & Audiologists
#402, 1755 Broadway West
Vancouver, BC V6J 4S5
604-420-2222; Fax: 604-736-5606
Toll-Free: 877-222-7572
E-mail: contact@bcaslpa.ca
URL: www.bcaslpa.ca
Scope: Provincial

- **BC Association of Teachers of Modern Languages 2018 Conference**
Location: British Columbia
Sponsor/Contact: British Columbia Association of Teachers of Modern Languages
c/o BC Teachers' Federation
#100, 550 West 6th Ave.
Vancouver, BC V5Z 4P2
604-871-2283; Fax: 604-871-2286
E-mail: psac51@bctf.ca
URL: www.bcatml.org
Scope: Provincial

- **BC Cattlemen's Association 90th Annual General Meeting**
Location: British Columbia
Sponsor/Contact: British Columbia Cattlemen's Association
#4, 10145 Dallas Dr.
Kamloops, BC V2C 6T4
250-573-3611; Fax: 250-573-5155
E-mail: info@cattlemen.bc.ca
URL: www.cattlemen.bc.ca
Scope: Provincial

- **BC Chiropractic Association 2018 Annual General Meeting**
Location: British Columbia
Sponsor/Contact: College of Chiropractors of British Columbia
#125, 3751 Shell Rd.
Richmond, BC V6X 2W2
604-270-1332; Fax: 604-278-0093
Toll-Free: 866-256-1474
URL: www.chirobc.com
Scope: Provincial

- **BC Dance Educators' Association Conference 2018**
Location: British Columbia
Sponsor/Contact: British Columbia Dance Educators' Association
c/o BC Teachers' Federation
#100, 550 West 6th Ave.
Vancouver, BC V5Z 4P2
604-871-2283
Toll-Free: 800-663-9163
E-mail: psac73@bctf.ca
URL: www.bcdea.ca
Scope: Provincial

- **BC Federation of Foster Parent Associations 2018 AGM**
Location: British Columbia
Sponsor/Contact: British Columbia Federation of Foster Parent Associations
#207, 22561 Dewdney Truck Rd.
Burnaby, BC V2X 3K1
604-466-7487; Fax: 604-466-7490
Toll-Free: 800-663-9999
E-mail: office@bcfosterparents.ca
URL: www.bcfosterparents.ca
Scope: Provincial
Purpose: Workshops & a business meeting of the federation for members from all regions of British Columbia

- **BC Fruit Growers' Association 129th Annual General Meeting 2018**
Location: British Columbia
Sponsor/Contact: British Columbia Fruit Growers' Association
880 Vaughan Ave.
Kelowna, BC V1Y 7E4
250-762-5226; Fax: 250-861-9089
E-mail: info@bcfga.com
URL: www.bcfga.com
Scope: Provincial
Contact Information: Email: info@bcfga.com

- **BC Honey Producers Association 2018 Annual General Meeting, Convention & Trade Show**
Sponsor/Contact: British Columbia Honey Producers Association
P.O. Box 1650
Comox, BC V9M 8A2
URL: www.bcbeekeepers.com
Scope: Provincial

- **BC Lacrosse Association Annual General Meeting 2018**
Location: British Columbia
Sponsor/Contact: BC Lacrosse Association
#101, 7382 Winston St.
Burnaby, BC V5A 2G9
604-421-9755; Fax: 604-421-9775
E-mail: info@bclacrosse.com
URL: www.bclacrosse.com
Scope: Provincial

- **BC Nature 2018 Annual General Meeting**
Sponsor/Contact: British Columbia Nature (Federation of British Columbia Naturalists)
c/o Parks Heritage Centre
1620 Mount Seymour Rd.
North Vancouver, BC V7G 2R9
URL: www.bcnature.ca
Scope: Provincial
Purpose: An annual meeting of naturalists, environmentalists, biologists, & academics who are members of British Columbia Nature

- **BC Play Therapy Association 2018 Conference**
Location: British Columbia
Sponsor/Contact: British Columbia Play Therapy Association
#335, 2818 Main St.
Vancouver, BC V5T 0C1
778-710-7529
URL: bcplaytherapy.ca
Scope: Provincial

- **BC Primary Teachers' Association Spring Event 2018**
Location: British Columbia
Sponsor/Contact: British Columbia Primary Teachers Association
c/o BC Teachers' Federation
#100, 550 West 6th Ave.
Vancouver, BC V5Z 4P2
604-871-2283; Fax: 604-871-2286
Toll-Free: 800-663-9163
URL: www.bcpta.ca
Scope: Provincial

- **BC School Superintendents Association Winter Conference 2018**
Location: British Columbia
Sponsor/Contact: British Columbia School Superintendents Association
#208, 1118 Homer St.
Vancouver, BC V6B 6L5
604-687-0590; Fax: 604-687-8118
E-mail: information@bcssa.org
URL: www.bcssa.org
Scope: Provincial

- **BC Seniors Living Association 2018 Conference**
Location: British Columbia
Sponsor/Contact: British Columbia Seniors Living Association
#300, 3665 Kingsway
Vancouver, BC V5R 5W2
604-689-5949; Fax: 604-689-5946
Toll-Free: 888-402-2722
E-mail: info@bcsla.ca
URL: www.bcsla.ca
Scope: Provincial

- **BC Soccer Referees Association AGM 2018**
Sponsor/Contact: BC Soccer Referees Association
8130 Selkirk St.
Vancouver, BC V6P 4H7
E-mail: bcreferees@gmail.com
URL: www.bcsra.com
Scope: Provincial

Conferences & Conventions Index

- **BC Social Studies Teachers' Association Conference 2018**
Location: British Columbia
Sponsor/Contact: British Columbia Social Studies Teachers Association
c/o BC Teachers' Federation
#100, 550 West 6th Ave.
Vancouver, BC V5Z 4P2
604-871-2283; Fax: 604-871-2286
Toll-Free: 800-663-9163
E-mail: bcssta@gmail.com
URL: bcssta.wordpress.com
Scope: Provincial

- **BC Veterinary Technologists Association 2018 Conference**
Location: British Columbia
Sponsor/Contact: British Columbia Veterinary Technologists Association
101 Todd Rd.
Kamloops, BC V5C 5A9
250-319-0027; Fax: 866-319-1929
URL: bcvta.com
Scope: Provincial

- **BC Welsh Pony & Cob Association 2018 Annual General Meeting**
Location: British Columbia
Sponsor/Contact: British Columbia Welsh Pony & Cob Association
c/o Debbie Miyashita
P.O. Box 192
Canoe, BC V0E 1K0
Scope: Provincial

- **Beef Farmers of Ontario 2018 Annual General Meeting**
Location: Ontario
Sponsor/Contact: Beef Farmers of Ontario
130 Malcolm Rd.
Guelph, ON N1K 1B1
519-824-0334; Fax: 519-824-9101
E-mail: info@ontariobeef.com
URL: www.ontariobeef.com
Scope: Provincial
Purpose: An opportunity for Ontario's beef farmers to help set policy direction on cattle industry issues

- **Bereavement Ontario Network 28th Annual Fall Conference 2018**
Location: Ontario
Sponsor/Contact: Bereavement Ontario Network
174 Oxford St.
Woodstock, ON N4S 6B1
519-290-0219
E-mail: info@bereavementontarionetwork.ca
URL: www.bereavementontarionetwork.ca
Scope: Provincial

- **Bibliographical Society of Canada 2018 Annual Meeting**
Sponsor/Contact: Bibliographical Society of Canada
P.O. Box 19035 Stn. Walmer
360 Bloor St. West
Toronto, ON M5S 3C9
E-mail: secretary@bsc-sbc.ca
URL: www.bsc-sbc.ca
Scope: National

- **Brain Care Centre 2018 Defying Limitations Gala**
Sponsor/Contact: Brain Care Centre
#305, 11010 - 101 St. NW
Edmonton, AB T5H 4B9
780-477-7575; Fax: 780-474-4415
Toll-Free: 800-425-5552
URL: www.braincarecentre.com
Scope: Provincial

- **Brain Injury Canada Semi-Annual Conference 2018**
Sponsor/Contact: Brain Injury Association of Canada
#200, 440 Laurier Ave. West
Ottawa, ON K1R 7X6
613-762-1012; Fax: 613-782-2228
Toll-Free: 866-977-2492
E-mail: info@braininjurycanada.ca
URL: www.braininjurycanada.ca
Scope: National

- **Breast Cancer Action Nova Scotia 2018 Annual General Meeting**
Location: Nova Scotia
Sponsor/Contact: Breast Cancer Action Nova Scotia
Mill Cove Plaza
#205, 967 Bedford Hwy.
Bedford, NS B4A 1A9
902-465-2685; Fax: 902-484-6436
E-mail: bcans@bcans.ca
URL: www.bcans.ca
Scope: Provincial
Purpose: A business meeting for members, featuring reports from committee chairs

- **British Columbia & Yukon Community Newspapers Association 2018 Annual General Meeting**
Sponsor/Contact: British Columbia & Yukon Community Newspapers Association
9 West Broadway
Vancouver, BC V5Y 1P1
604-669-9222; Fax: 604-684-4713
Toll-Free: 866-669-9222
E-mail: info@bccommunitynews.com
URL: www.bccommunitynews.com
Scope: Provincial

- **British Columbia Blind Sports & Recreation Association Annual General Meeting 2018**
Sponsor/Contact: British Columbia Blind Sports & Recreation Association
#170, 5055 Joyce St.
Vancouver, BC V5R 6B2
604-325-8638; Fax: 604-325-1638
Toll-Free: 877-604-8638
E-mail: info@bcblindsports.bc.ca
URL: www.bcblindsports.bc.ca
Scope: Provincial

- **British Columbia College of Social Workers 2018 Annual Meeting**
Sponsor/Contact: British Columbia College of Social Workers
#302, 1765 West 8th Ave.
Vancouver, BC V6J 5C6
604-737-4916; Fax: 604-737-6809
E-mail: info@bccsw.bc.ca
URL: www.bccollegeofsocialworkers.ca
Scope: Provincial
Purpose: A business meeting featuring an election of social workers to the board

- **British Columbia Competitive Trail Riders Association Annual General Meeting 2018**
Sponsor/Contact: British Columbia Competitive Trail Riders Association
c/o Christine Pacukiewicz
14 Amber Pl.
Victoria, BC V9A 7A2
250-881-8153
E-mail: bcctra@shaw.ca
URL: www.bcctra.ca
Scope: Provincial

- **British Columbia Conference of MB Churches Annual Convention 2018**
Location: British Columbia
Sponsor/Contact: British Columbia Conference of MB Churches
#101, 32310 South Fraser Way
Abbotsford, BC V2T 1X1
604-853-6959; Fax: 604-853-6990
Toll-Free: 888-653-9933
E-mail: office@bcmb.org
URL: www.bcmb.org
Scope: Provincial
Contact Information: Assistant, Administration & Communications: Tamara Okoti, E-mail: tamara@bcmb.org

- **British Columbia Fencing Association Annual General Meeting 2018**
Location: British Columbia
Sponsor/Contact: British Columbia Fencing Association
#15, 12900 Jack Bell Dr.
Richmond, BC V6V 2V8
URL: www.fencing.bc.ca
Scope: Provincial

- **British Columbia Food Technologists Suppliers' Night 2018**
Location: British Columbia
Sponsor/Contact: British Columbia Food Technolgists
c/o Nilmini Wijewickreme, SGS Canada
50-655 West Kent Ave. North
Vancouver, BC V6P 6T7
E-mail: info@bcft.ca
URL: www.bcft.ca
Scope: Provincial
Purpose: A learning event featuring over 100 supplier exhibits of interest to food scientists, research & development technologists, & senior managers & purchasers from food & beverage companies

- **British Columbia Institute of Agrologists 71st Annual General Meeting & Conference 2018**
Location: British Columbia
Sponsor/Contact: British Columbia Institute of Agrologists
2777 Claude Rd.
Victoria, BC V9B 3T7
250-380-9292; Fax: 250-380-9233
Toll-Free: 877-855-9291
E-mail: admin@bcia.com
URL: www.bcia.com
Scope: Provincial

- **British Columbia Library Association (BCLA) Library Conference 2018**
Location: British Columbia
Sponsor/Contact: British Columbia Library Association
#150, 900 Howe St.
Vancouver, BC V6Z 2M4
604-683-5354; Fax: 604-609-0707
Toll-Free: 888-683-5354
E-mail: bclaoffice@bcla.bc.ca
URL: www.bclaconnect.ca
Scope: Provincial

- **British Columbia Library Trustees' Association 2018 Annual General Meeting**
Sponsor/Contact: British Columbia Library Trustees' Association
#108, 9865 - 140th St.
Surrey, BC V3T 4M4
604-913-1424
Toll-Free: 888-206-1245

E-mail: office@bclta.ca
URL: www.bclta.ca
Scope: Provincial

- **British Columbia Museums Association 2018 Annual Conference**
Sponsor/Contact: British Columbia Museums Association
675 Belleville St.
Victoria, BC V8W 9W2
250-356-5700
E-mail: bcma@museumsassn.bc.ca
URL: www.museumsassn.bc.ca
Scope: Provincial

- **British Columbia Recreation & Parks Association Provincial Ripple Effects: Aquatics Workshop 2018**
Sponsor/Contact: British Columbia Recreation & Parks Association
#301, 470 Granville St.
Vancouver, BC V6C 1V5
604-629-0965; Fax: 604-629-2651
Toll-Free: 866-929-0965
E-mail: bcrpa@bcrpa.bc.ca
URL: www.bcrpa.bc.ca
Scope: Provincial
Purpose: A two-day conference which occurs every two years, presenting operations, programming, & best practices for aquatics professionals

- **British Columbia Salmon Farmers Association Annual General Meeting 2018**
Sponsor/Contact: British Columbia Salmon Farmers Association
#201, 911 Island Hwy.
Campbell River, BC V9W 2C2
250-286-1636; Fax: 800-849-9430
Toll-Free: 800-661-7256
E-mail: info@bcsalmonfarmers.ca
URL: www.bcsalmonfarmers.ca
Scope: Provincial

- **British Columbia Speed Skating Association Annual General Meeting 2018**
Location: British Columbia
Sponsor/Contact: British Columbia Speed Skating Association
P.O. Box 2023 Stn. A
Abbotsford, BC V2T 3T8
604-746-4349; Fax: 604-746-4549
URL: www.speed-skating.bc.ca
Scope: Provincial

- **British Columbia Teachers' Federation Summer Leadership Conference 2018**
Sponsor/Contact: British Columbia Teachers' Federation
#100, 550 Wsst 6th Ave.
Vancouver, BC V5Z 4P2
604-871-2283
Toll-Free: 800-663-9163
E-mail: webinfo@bctf.ca
URL: www.bctf.ca
Scope: Provincial

- **British Columbia Trucking Association 2018 105th Annual General Meeting & Management Conference**
Location: British Columbia
Sponsor/Contact: British Columbia Trucking Association
#100, 20111 - 93A Ave.
Langley, BC V1M 4A9
604-888-5319; Fax: 604-888-2941
E-mail: bcta@bctrucking.com
URL: www.bctrucking.com

Conferences & Conventions Index

Scope: Provincial
Purpose: A meeting of members of the British Columbia motor carrier association

- **British Columbia Water & Waste Association 2018 46th Annual Conference & Trade Show**
Location: British Columbia
Sponsor/Contact: British Columbia Water & Waste Association
#620, 1090 West Pender St.
Vancouver, BC V6E 2N7
604-433-4389; *Fax:* 604-433-9859
Toll-Free: 877-433-4389
E-mail: contact@bcwwa.org
URL: www.bcwwa.org
Scope: Provincial
Purpose: A four day conference, including technical sessions & the chance to view current products at the trade show

- **British Columbia Weightlifting Association Annual General Meeting 2018**
Sponsor/Contact: British Columbia Weightlifting Association
5249 Laurel Dr.
Delta, BC V4K 4S4
E-mail: info@bcweightlifting.ca
URL: www.bcweightlifting.ca
Scope: Provincial

- **Building Energy Management Manitoba 2018 Better Buildings Conference**
Sponsor/Contact: Building Energy Management Manitoba
#309, 23 - 845 Dakota St.
Winnipeg, MB R2M 5M3
204-452-2098
E-mail: info@bemm.ca
URL: www.bemm.ca
Scope: Provincial

- **Building Industry & Land Development Association Annual General Meeting 2018**
Sponsor/Contact: Building Industry & Land Development Association
#100, 20 Upjohn Rd.
Toronto, ON M3B 2V9
416-391-3445; *Fax:* 416-391-2118
E-mail: info@bildgta.ca
URL: www.bildgta.ca
Scope: Local

- **Building Owners & Managers Association 2018 Conference**
Sponsor/Contact: Building Owners & Managers Association - Canada
P.O. Box 61
#1801, 1 Dundas St. West
Toronto, ON M5G 1Z3
416-214-1912; *Fax:* 416-214-1284
E-mail: info@bomacanada.ca
URL: www.bomacanada.ca
Scope: National

- **Bus History Association 2018 Convention**
Sponsor/Contact: Bus History Association, Inc.
c/o Bernie Drouillard
965 McEwan Ave.
Windsor, ON N9B 2G1
URL: www.bus-history.org
Scope: National

- **Calgary Law Library Group 2018 Annual General Meeting**
Location: Calgary, AB
Sponsor/Contact: Calgary Law Library Group
c/o Osler, Hoskin & Harcourt LLP
#2500, 450 - 1st St. SW
Calgary, AB T2P 5H1
E-mail: calgarylawlibrarygroup@gmail.com
URL: www.cllg.wildapricot.org
Scope: Local
Purpose: An annual meeting of legal information professionals & law librarians from Calgary & the surrounding area

- **Calgary Zoological Society 2018 AGM**
Location: Alberta
Sponsor/Contact: Calgary Zoological Society
1300 Zoo Rd. NE
Calgary, AB T2E 7V6
403-232-9300; *Fax:* 403-237-7582
Toll-Free: 800-588-9993
URL: www.calgaryzoo.org
Scope: Provincial
Purpose: Members of the society receive voting rights at the annual meeting

- **Canada East Equipment Dealers' Association 2018 Annual Meeting & Convention**
Sponsor/Contact: Canada East Equipment Dealers' Association
580 Bryne Dr, #C1
Barrie, ON L4N 9P6
705-726-2100; *Fax:* 705-726-2187
URL: www.ceeda.ca
Scope: Provincial

- **Canada Green Building Council 2018 National Conference**
Sponsor/Contact: Canada Green Building Council
#202, 47 Clarence St.
Ottawa, ON K1N 9K1
613-241-1184; *Fax:* 613-241-4782
Toll-Free: 866-941-1184
E-mail: info@cagbc.org
URL: www.cagbc.org
Scope: National

- **Canada's Accredited Zoos & Aquariums Annual Conference 2018**
Sponsor/Contact: Canada's Accredited Zoos & Aquariums
#400, 280 Metcalfe St.
Ottawa, ON K2P 1R7
613-567-0099; *Fax:* 613-233-5438
Toll-Free: 888-822-2907
E-mail: info@caza.ca
URL: www.caza.ca
Scope: National
Purpose: A meeting of members to vote on the business of the association

- **CanadaGAP Annual General Meeting 2018**
Sponsor/Contact: CanadaGAP
#312, 245 Menten Pl.
Ottawa, ON K2H 9E8
613-829-4711; *Fax:* 613-829-9379
E-mail: info@canadagap.ca
URL: www.canadagap.ca
Scope: National
Purpose: Includes a presentation of the year's financial statements & an annual report

- **Canadian AIDS Treatment Information Exchange 2018 Forum**
Sponsor/Contact: Canadian AIDS Treatment Information Exchange
P.O. Box 1104
#505, 555 Richmond St. West
Toronto, ON M5V 3B1
416-203-7122; *Fax:* 416-203-8284
Toll-Free: 800-263-1638
E-mail: info@catie.ca
URL: www.catie.ca
Scope: National

- **Canadian Acceleration and Business Incubation Leadership Summit 2018**
Sponsor/Contact: Canadian Association of Business Incubation
#2002A, 1 Yonge St.
Toronto, ON M5E 1E5
416-345-9937; *Fax:* 416-345-9044
E-mail: info@cabi.ca
URL: www.cabi.ca
Scope: National

- **Canadian Agricultural Safety Association Conference 2018**
Sponsor/Contact: Canadian Agricultural Safety Association
3325-C Pembina Hwy.
Winnipeg, MB R3V 0A2
204-452-2272; *Fax:* 204-261-5004
Toll-Free: 877-452-2272
E-mail: info@casa-acsa.ca
URL: www.casa-acsa.ca
Scope: National
Purpose: A forum for members, supporters, researchers and innovators to network, share, and learn about important trends and developments in agricultural safety.

- **Canadian Amateur Wrestling Association / Association canadienne de lutte amateur 2018 Annual General Meeting**
Sponsor/Contact: Canadian Amateur Wrestling Association
#7, 5370 Canotek Rd.
Gloucester, ON K1J 9E6
613-748-5686; *Fax:* 613-748-5756
E-mail: info@wrestling.ca
URL: www.wrestling.ca
Scope: National

- **Canadian Anti-Money Laundering Institute 2018 Conference**
Sponsor/Contact: Canadian Anti-Money Laundering Institute
P.O. Box 427
Merrickville, ON K0G 1N0
613-283-9659; *Fax:* 613-526-9384
E-mail: contactus@camli.org
URL: www.camli.org
Scope: National

- **Canadian Archaeological Association Annual Meeting 2018**
Location: Winnipeg, MB
Sponsor/Contact: Canadian Archaeological Association
URL: www.canadianarchaeology.com
Scope: National

- **Canadian Arts Presenting Association / Association canadienne des organismes artistiques 2018 30th Annual Conference**
Sponsor/Contact: Canadian Arts Presenting Association
#200, 17 York St.
Ottawa, ON K1N 5S7
613-562-3515; *Fax:* 613-562-4005
E-mail: mail@capacoa.ca
URL: www.capacoa.ca
Scope: National

- **Canadian Association for American Studies 2018 Conference**
Sponsor/Contact: Canadian Association for American Studies
c/o Bryce Traister, Prof. & Chair, Dept. of English, Western Univ.
2G02, 1151 Richmond St.
London, ON N6A 3K7
E-mail: webmaster@american-studies.ca
URL: www.american-studies.ca
Scope: National

- **Canadian Association for Food Studies 13th Annual Assembly**
Sponsor/Contact: Canadian Association for Food Studies
c/o Centre for Studies in Food Security, Ryerson University
350 Victoria St.
Toronto, ON M5B 2K3
416-979-5000; *Fax:* 416-979-5362
E-mail: cafsadmin@foodstudies.ca
URL: cafs.landfood.ubc.ca
Scope: National

- **Canadian Association for Laboratory Accreditation 2018 Annual General Meeting**
Sponsor/Contact: Canadian Association for Laboratory Accreditation Inc.
#102, 2934 Baseline Rd.
Ottawa, ON K2H 1B2
613-233-5300; *Fax:* 613-233-5501
E-mail: webmaster@cala.ca
URL: www.cala.ca
Scope: National

- **Canadian Association for Population Therapeutics Conference 2018**
Sponsor/Contact: Canadian Association for Population Therapeutics
c/o Peggy Kee, Sunnybrook Health Sciences Centre
2075 Bayview Ave., #E240
Toronto, ON M4N 3M5
416-480-6100; *Fax:* 416-480-6025
URL: www.capt-actp.com
Scope: National

- **Canadian Association for Suicide Prevention 2018 Annual Conference**
Sponsor/Contact: Canadian Association for Suicide Prevention
285 Benjamin Rd.
Waterloo, ON N2J 3Z4
519-884-1470
E-mail: casp@suicideprevention.ca
URL: www.suicideprevention.ca
Scope: National

- **Canadian Association for the Prevention of Discrimination and Harassment in Higher Education 2018 Conference**
Sponsor/Contact: Canadian Association for the Prevention of Discrimination & Harassment in Higher Education
c/o University of British Columbia
Vancouver, BC V6T 1Z2
604-822-4859; *Fax:* 604-822-3260
E-mail: amlong@ubc.ca
URL: www.capdhhe.org
Scope: National

- **Canadian Association of Chemical Distributors 32nd Annual General Meeting**
Sponsor/Contact: Canadian Association of Chemical Distributors
#1, 1160 Blair Rd.
Burlington, ON L7M 1K9
905-332-8777; *Fax:* 905-332-0777
URL: www.cacd.ca

Conferences & Conventions Index

Scope: National
Purpose: An event featuring keynote speakers

- **Canadian Association of Communicators in Education 2018 Annual General Meeting**
Sponsor/Contact: Canadian Association of Communicators in Education
#310, 1390 Prince of Wales Dr.
Ottawa, ON K2C 3N6
URL: www.cace-acace.org
Scope: National

- **Canadian Association of Electroneurophysiology Technologists 2018 Annual General Meeting**
Sponsor/Contact: Canadian Association of Electroneurophysiology Technologists Inc.
c/o St. Boniface Hospital
409 Taché Ave.
Winnipeg, MB R2H 2A6
204-233-8563
URL: www.caet.org
Scope: National

- **Canadian Association of Environmental Law Societies 2018 Conference**
Sponsor/Contact: Canadian Association of Environmental Law Societies
Scope: National

- **Canadian Association of Farm Advisors 2018 Conference**
Sponsor/Contact: Canadian Association of Farm Advisors
P.O. Box 270
Seven Sisters Falls, MB R0E 1Y0
204-348-3578
Toll-Free: 877-474-2871
E-mail: info@cafanet.com
URL: www.cafanet.com
Scope: National

- **Canadian Association of Genetic Counsellors 2018 Annual Education Conference**
Sponsor/Contact: Canadian Association of Genetic Counsellors
P.O. Box 52083
Oakville, ON L6J 7N5
905-847-1363; *Fax:* 905-847-3855
E-mail: CAGCOffice@cagc-accg.ca
URL: www.cagc-accg.ca
Scope: National

- **Canadian Association of Home & Property Inspectors 2018 National Conference**
Sponsor/Contact: Canadian Association of Home & Property Inspectors
P.O. Box 76065 Stn. Morgan's Grant
832 March Rd.
Ottawa, ON K2W 0E1
613-832-3536
Toll-Free: 888-748-2244
E-mail: info@cahpi.ca
URL: www.cahpi.ca
Scope: National

- **Canadian Association of Importers & Exporters 2018 Annual Conference**
Sponsor/Contact: Canadian Association of Importers & Exporters
P.O. Box 149
777 Bay St.
Toronto, ON M5G 2C8
416-595-5333
E-mail: info@iecanada.com
URL: www.iecanada.com
Scope: National

- **Canadian Association of Law Libraries 2018 Conference**
Sponsor/Contact: Canadian Association of Law Libraries
#200, 411 Richmond St. East
Toronto, ON M5A 3S5
647-346-8723
E-mail: office@callacbd.ca
URL: www.callacbd.ca
Scope: National
Contact Information:
www.callacbd.ca/Conference

- **Canadian Association of Law Libraries Annual General Meeting 2018**
Sponsor/Contact: Canadian Association of Law Libraries
#200, 411 Richmond St. East
Toronto, ON M5A 3S5
647-346-8723
E-mail: office@callacbd.ca
URL: www.callacbd.ca
Scope: National

- **Canadian Association of Medical Radiation Technologists 76th Annual General Conference**
Location: Vancouver, BC
Sponsor/Contact: Canadian Association of Medical Radiation Technologists
#1300, 180 Elgin St.
Ottawa, ON K2P 2K3
613-234-0012; *Fax:* 613-234-1097
Toll-Free: 800-463-9729
E-mail: info@camrt.ca
URL: www.camrt.ca
Scope: National
Purpose: Joint conference with The Canadian Association of Nuclear Medicine (CANM)

- **Canadian Association of Professional Academic Librarians 2018 Annual Conference**
Sponsor/Contact: Canadian Association of Professional Academic Librarians
P.O. Box 19543
Toronto, ON M4W 3T9
E-mail: capalibrarians@gmail.com
URL: capalibrarians.org
Scope: National

- **Canadian Association of Provincial Court Judges 2018 Annual Conference**
Sponsor/Contact: Canadian Association of Provincial Court Judges
150 Bond St. East
Oshawa, ON L1G 0A2
905-743-2820
URL: www.judges-juges.ca
Scope: National

- **Canadian Association of Science Centres 2018 Annual Conference**
Sponsor/Contact: Canadian Association of Science Centres
100 Ramsey Lake Rd.
Sudbury, ON P3E 5S9
705-522-6825
E-mail: info@casc-accs.com
URL: www.canadiansciencecentres.ca
Scope: National

- **Canadian Association of Wound Care 2018 Fall Conference**
Sponsor/Contact: Canadian Association of Wound Care
#608, 920 Yonge St.
Toronto, ON M4W 3C7
416-485-2292; *Fax:* 416-485-2291
Toll-Free: 866-474-0125

E-mail: info@cawc.net
URL: www.cawc.net
Scope: National
Purpose: Educational components of the conference include basic clinical, advanced clinical, research, & public policy & education

- **Canadian Association on Water Quality 53rd CENTRAL Canadian Symposium on Water Quality Research 2018**
Sponsor/Contact: Canadian Association on Water Quality
P.O. Box 5050
Burlington, ON L7R 4A6
289-780-0378
URL: www.cawq.ca
Scope: National
Purpose: A gathering of people in diverse fields of water quality research to present innovations in engineering, science, & policy.

- **Canadian Astronomical Society 2018 Annual Meeting**
Sponsor/Contact: Canadian Astronomical Society
c/o R. Hanes, Dept. of Physics, Engineering, Physics & Astronomy
64 Bader Lane, Stirling Hall, Queen's University
Kingston, ON K7L 3N6
613-533-6000; *Fax:* 613-533-6463
E-mail: casca@astro.queensu.ca
URL: www.casca.ca
Scope: National
Purpose: Annual meetings are open to all interested persons, but the presentation of scientific papers is restricted to members or applicants for membership & speakers invited by the Local Organizing Committee

- **Canadian Authors Association 2018 Conference**
Sponsor/Contact: Canadian Authors Association
#203, 6 West St. North
Orillia, ON L3V 5B8
705-325-3926
E-mail: admin@canadianauthors.org
URL: canadianauthors.org
Scope: National
Purpose: Educational seminars, awards, readings, & networking opportunities

- **Canadian Avalanche Association 2018 Annual General Meeting & Spring Conference**
Sponsor/Contact: Canadian Avalanche Association
P.O. Box 2759
110 MacKenzie Ave.
Revelstoke, BC V0E 2S0
250-837-2435; *Fax:* 866-366-2094
URL: www.avalancheassociation.ca
Scope: National
Purpose: An introduction for technicians & supervisors from transportation & utility & resource sectors, such as forestry, mining, & railways, who manage winter operations & avalanche hazard programs

- **Canadian Bureau for International Education 2018 Annual Conference**
Sponsor/Contact: Canadian Bureau for International Education
#1550, 220 Laurier Ave. West
Ottawa, ON K1P 5Z9

613-237-4820; *Fax:* 613-237-1073
E-mail: communications@cbie.ca
URL: www.cbie-bcei.ca
Scope: National
Purpose: The Conference features professional development workshops, concurrent sessions and networking opportunities.

- **Canadian Centre for Occupational Health & Safety Forum**
Sponsor/Contact: Canadian Centre for Occupational Health & Safety
135 Hunter St. East
Hamilton, ON L8N 1M5
905-572-2981; *Fax:* 905-572-2206
Toll-Free: 800-668-4284
E-mail: clientservices@ccohs.ca
URL: www.ccohs.ca
Scope: National

- **Canadian Child Care Federation 2018 Annual General Meeting**
Sponsor/Contact: Canadian Child Care Federation
#600, 700 Industrial Ave.
Ottawa, ON K1G 0Y9
613-729-5289; *Fax:* 613-729-3159
Toll-Free: 800-858-1412
E-mail: info@cccf-fcsge.ca
URL: www.cccf-fcsge.ca
Scope: National

- **Canadian Chiropractic Association National Convention & Tradeshow 2018**
Sponsor/Contact: Canadian Chiropractic Association
#6, 186 Spadina Ave.
Toronto, ON M5T 3B2
416-585-7902; *Fax:* 416-585-2970
Toll-Free: 877-222-9303
E-mail: info@chiropractic.ca
URL: www.chiropractic.ca
Scope: National

- **Canadian Commission for UNESCO 58th Annual General Meeting, 2018**
Sponsor/Contact: Canadian Commission for UNESCO
P.O. Box 1047
150 Elgin St.
Ottawa, ON K1P 5V8
613-566-4414; *Fax:* 613-566-4405
Toll-Free: 800-263-5588
E-mail: ccunesco@unesco.ca
URL: www.unesco.ca

- **Canadian Conference on Building Science and Technology 2018**
Sponsor/Contact: National Building Envelope Council
c/o 5041 Regent St.
Burnaby, BC V5C 4H4
604-473-9587
E-mail: nbec@cebq.org
URL: www.nbec.net
Scope: National
Purpose: Provides a forum for the presentation, discussion and sharing of practical building science research, knowledge and field experience

- **Canadian Council of Cardiovascular Nurses 2018 Fall Conference**
Sponsor/Contact: Canadian Council of Cardiovascular Nurses
#202, 300 March Rd.
Ottawa, ON K2K 2E2
613-599-9210; *Fax:* 613-595-1155
E-mail: info@cccn.ca
URL: www.cccn.ca

Scope: National
Purpose: Held during the Canadian Cardiovascular Congress; includes sessions showcasing the wide range of clinical & research work in the cardiovascular research field

- **Canadian Council of Technicians & Technologists (CTTT) 2018 National Technology Conference**
Sponsor/Contact: Canadian Council of Technicians & Technologists
#405, 2197 Riverside Dr.
Ottawa, ON K1H 7X3
613-238-8123; *Fax:* 613-238-8822
E-mail: cctt@cctt.ca
URL: www.cctt.ca
Scope: National

- **Canadian Council on International Law 47th Annual Conference**
Sponsor/Contact: Canadian Council on International Law
275 Bay St.
Ottawa, ON K1R 5Z5
613-235-0442; *Fax:* 613-232-8228
E-mail: manager@ccil-ccdi.ca
URL: www.ccil-ccdi.ca
Scope: International

- **Canadian Depression Research & Intervention Network Conference 2018**
Sponsor/Contact: Canadian Depression Research & Intervention Network
c/o CDRIN Secretariat, Mood Disorders Society of Canada
#736, 304 Stone Rd. West
Guelph, ON N1G 4W4
E-mail: info@cdrin.org
URL: www.cdrin.org
Scope: National

- **Canadian Employee Relocation Council 2018 Conference**
Sponsor/Contact: Canadian Employee Relocation Council
#1010, 180 Dundas St. W.
Toronto, ON M5G 1Z8
416-593-9812; *Fax:* 416-593-1139
Toll-Free: 866-357-2372
E-mail: info@cerc.ca
URL: www.cerc.ca
Scope: National

- **Canadian Federation of Agriculture 2018 Annual Meeting**
Sponsor/Contact: Canadian Federation of Agriculture
21 Florence St.
Ottawa, ON K2P 0W6
613-236-3633; *Fax:* 613-236-5749
E-mail: info@canadian-farmers.ca
URL: www.cfa-fca.ca
Scope: National

- **Canadian Federation of Library Associations 2018 Annual General Meeting**
Sponsor/Contact: Canadian Federation of Library Associations
c/o Canadian Association of Research Libraries
#203, 309 Cooper St.
Ottawa, ON K2P 0G5
613-482-9344
E-mail: info@cfla-fcab.ca
URL: www.cfla-fcab.ca
Scope: National

- **Canadian Federation of Music Teachers' Associations 2018 National Conference**
Sponsor/Contact: Canadian Federation of Music Teachers' Associations
#7, 6179 No. 1 Rd.
Richmond, BC V7C 1T4
604-354-6776
E-mail: admin@cfmta.org
URL: www.cfmta.org
Scope: National

- **Canadian Federation of University Women 2018 AGM & Conference**
Sponsor/Contact: Canadian Federation of University Women
National Office
#502, 331 Cooper St.
Ottawa, ON K2P 0G5
613-234-8252; *Fax:* 613-234-8221
Toll-Free: 888-220-9606
E-mail: cfuwgen@rogers.com
URL: www.cfuw.org
Scope: National

- **Canadian Fencing Federation 2018 Annual General Meeting**
Sponsor/Contact: Canadian Fencing Federation
44 - 1554 Carling Ave.
Ottawa, ON K1Z 7M4
613-323-5605; *Fax:* 647-476-2402
E-mail: cff@fencing.ca
URL: www.fencing.ca
Scope: National

- **Canadian Finance & Leasing Association 2018 Conference**
Sponsor/Contact: Canadian Finance & Leasing Association
#301, 15 Toronto St.
Toronto, ON M5C 2E3
416-860-1133; *Fax:* 416-860-1140
Toll-Free: 877-213-7373
E-mail: info@cfla-acfl.ca
URL: www.cfla-acfl.ca
Scope: National

- **Canadian Fluid Power Association Annual General Meeting 2018**
Sponsor/Contact: Canadian Fluid Power Association
#25, 1250 Marlborough Ct.
Oakville, ON L6H 2W7
905-844-6822
E-mail: info@cfpa.ca
URL: www.cfpa.ca
Scope: National

- **Canadian Foundry Association Annual Meeting 2018**
Sponsor/Contact: Canadian Foundry Association
#1500, 1 Nicholas St.
Ottawa, ON K1N 7B7
613-789-4894; *Fax:* 613-789-5957
E-mail: info@foundryassociation.ca
URL: www.foundryassociation.ca
Scope: National
Purpose: A gathering of members to address issues facing the Canadian foundry industry

- **Canadian Golf Course Management Conference & Trade Show 2018**
Sponsor/Contact: Canadian Golf Superintendents Association
#201, 5399 Eglinton Ave. West
Toronto, ON M9C 5K6
416-626-8873
Toll-Free: 800-387-1056
E-mail: cgsa@golfsupers.com
URL: www.golfsupers.com

Scope: International
Purpose: An international conference & trade show featuring over 100 exhibitors
Contact Information: Director, Professional Development & Meetings: Kathryn Wood, Phone: 519-589-9282, Email: kwood@golfsupers.com

- **Canadian Hard of Hearing Association 2018 National Conference**
Sponsor/Contact: Canadian Hard of Hearing Association
#205, 2415 Holly Lane
Ottawa, ON K1V 7P2
613-526-1584; *Fax:* 613-526-4718
Toll-Free: 800-263-8068
E-mail: chhanational@chha.ca
URL: www.chha.ca
Scope: National

- **Canadian Health Information Management Association National Conference 2018**
Sponsor/Contact: Canadian Health Information Management Association
99 Enterprise Dr. South
London, ON N6N 1B9
519-438-6700; *Fax:* 519-438-7001
Toll-Free: 877-332-4462
URL: www.echima.ca
Scope: National
Contact Information: Director, Professional Development: Paula Weisflock, Phone: 519-438-6700, ext. 222, E-mail: paula.weisflock@echima.ca

- **Canadian Healthcare Association 2018 Annual General Meeting**
Sponsor/Contact: HealthCareCAN
#100, 17 York St.
Ottawa, ON K1N 5S7
613-241-8005; *Fax:* 613-241-5055
Toll-Free: 855-236-0213
E-mail: info@healthcarecan.ca
URL: www.healthcarecan.ca
Scope: National
Purpose: The association's business meeting, including the presentation of the Marion Stephenson Award & the CHA Award for Distinguished Service by the Board of Directors

- **Canadian History of Education Association 20th Biennial Conference**
Sponsor/Contact: Canadian History of Education Association
University of Saskatchewan, College of Education
28 Campus Dr.
Saskatoon, SK S7N 0X1
URL: www.ache-chea.ca
Scope: National

- **Canadian Home Builders' Association of British Columbia Annual General Meeting 2018**
Location: British Columbia
Sponsor/Contact: Canadian Home Builders' Association - British Columbia
c/o Bldg. NW5, British Columbia Institute of Technology Campus
3700 Willingdon Ave.
Burnaby, BC V5G 3H2
604-432-7112; *Fax:* 604-432-9038
Toll-Free: 800-933-6777
E-mail: info@chbabc.org
URL: www.chbabc.org
Scope: Provincial

- **Canadian Home Care Association 2018 International Home Care Summit**

Sponsor/Contact: Canadian Home Care Association
#302, 2000 Argentia Rd.
Mississauga, ON L5N 1W1
905-567-7373
E-mail: chca@cdnhomecare.ca
URL: www.cdnhomecare.ca
Scope: National

- **Canadian Horse Heritage & Preservation Society 2018 Annual General Meeting**
Sponsor/Contact: Canadian Horse Heritage & Preservation Society
c/o Judi Hayward, Five Winds Farm
1745 Lockyer Rd.
Roberts Creek, BC V0N 2W1
URL: chhaps.ca
Scope: National

- **Canadian Indigenous Nurses Association 2018 Annual General Meeting**
Sponsor/Contact: Canadian Indigenous Nurses Association
50 Driveway
Ottawa, ON K2P 1E2
613-724-4677
E-mail: info@anac.on.ca
URL: www.indigenousnurses.ca
Scope: National

- **Canadian Institute of Food Science & Technology, Manitoba Section Annual General Meeting 2018**
Location: Manitoba
Sponsor/Contact: Canadian Institute of Food Science & Technology
c/o M. Samelo, Manitoba Harvest Hemp Foods
#1108, 40 Dalhousie Dr.
Winnipeg, MB R3T 2Y7
E-mail: manitobasection@cifst.ca
URL: www.cifst.ca
Scope: Provincial

- **Canadian Institute of Mining, Metallurgy & Petroleum 2018 Convention**
Sponsor/Contact: Canadian Institute of Mining, Metallurgy & Petroleum
CIM National Office
#1250, 3500, boul de Maisonneuve ouest
Westmount, QC H3Z 3C1
514-939-2710; *Fax:* 514-939-2714
E-mail: cim@cim.org
URL: www.cim.org
Purpose: A mining event, featuring a technical program, workshops, field trips, a student program, & a social program
Contact Information: convention.cim.org

- **Canadian Institute of Public Health Inspectors 84th National Educational Conference 2018**
Sponsor/Contact: Canadian Institute of Public Health Inspectors
#720, 999 West Broadway Ave.
Vancouver, BC V5Z 1K5
604-739-8180; *Fax:* 604-738-4080
Toll-Free: 888-245-8180
E-mail: questions@ciphi.ca
URL: www.ciphi.ca
Scope: National
Purpose: Featuring the presentation of Institute awards

- **Canadian Katahdin Sheep Association 2018 Annual General Meeting**
Sponsor/Contact: Canadian Katahdin Sheep Association Inc.

c/o Canadian Livestock Records
Corporation
2417 Holly Lane
Ottawa, ON K1V 0M7
613-731-7110; *Fax:* 613-731-0704
E-mail: katahdin@clrc.ca
URL: www.katahdinsheep.com
Scope: National

• **Canadian Labour Congress 2018 National Convention**
Sponsor/Contact: Canadian Labour Congress
National Headquarters
2841 Riverside Dr.
Ottawa, ON K1V 8X7
613-521-3400; *Fax:* 613-521-4655
URL: www.canadianlabour.ca
Scope: National
Purpose: A convention for members of the labour movement to develop an Action Plan, based on committee reports, resolutions, & the discussion of policies

• **Canadian Land Reclamation Association / Association canadienne de réhabilitation des sites dégradés 2018 43rd Annual General Meeting**
Sponsor/Contact: Canadian Land Reclamation Association
c/o ManageWise, Inc.
P.O. Box 21085
Edmonton, AB T6R 2V4
780-437-0044
URL: www.clra.ca
Scope: National
Purpose: Business affairs of the association

• **Canadian Land Reclamation Association National 2018 Annual General Meeting and Conference**
Sponsor/Contact: Canadian Land Reclamation Association
URL: www.clra.ca
Scope: Provincial

• **Canadian Marine Pilots' Association 6th Congress**
Sponsor/Contact: Canadian Marine Pilots' Association
c/o Tristan Laflamme
#901, 50 O'Connor St.
Ottawa, ON K1P 6L2
613-220-8954
E-mail: apmc-cmpa@apmc-cmpa.ca
URL: www.marinepilots.ca
Scope: National

• **Canadian Media Directors' Council 2018 Annual Conference**
Sponsor/Contact: Canadian Media Directors' Council
#1097, 1930 Yonge St.
Toronto, ON M4S 1Z4
416-967-7282
URL: www.cmdc.ca
Scope: National

• **Canadian Nuclear Association Conference & Trade Show 2018**
Sponsor/Contact: Canadian Nuclear Association
#1610, 130 Albert St.
Ottawa, ON K1P 5G4
613-237-4262; *Fax:* 613-237-0989
E-mail: info@cna.ca
URL: www.cna.ca
Scope: National
Contact Information: Email: conference@cna.ca

• **Canadian Parks & Wilderness Society Calgary - Southern Alberta Chapter Annual General Meeting 2018**
Sponsor/Contact: Canadian Parks & Wilderness Society
c/o Bob Niven Training Centre, Canada Olympic Park
88 Canada Olympic Rd. SW
Calgary, AB T3B 5R5
403-232-6686; *Fax:* 403-232-6988
E-mail: infosab@cpaws.org
URL: www.cpaws-southernalberta.org
Scope: Provincial

• **Canadian Physiotherapy Association 2018 Congress**
Sponsor/Contact: Canadian Physiotherapy Association
#270, 955 Green Valley Cres.
Ottawa, ON K2C 3V4
613-564-5454; *Fax:* 613-564-1577
Toll-Free: 800-387-8679
E-mail: information@physiotherapy.ca
URL: www.physiotherapy.ca
Scope: National
Purpose: Educational courses, workshops, the presentation of scientific research, private practice leadership information, & networking opportunities for physiotherapists from across Canada

• **Canadian Plastics Industry Association Annual General Meeting 2018**
Sponsor/Contact: Canadian Plastics Industry Association
#125, 5955 Airport Rd.
Mississauga, ON L4V 1R9
905-678-7748; *Fax:* 905-678-0774
URL: www.plastics.ca
Contact Information: Coordinator, Projects & Administration: Shannon Laszlo, Phone: 905-678-7748, ext. 231

• **Canadian Process Control Association 2018 Annual General Meeting**
Sponsor/Contact: Canadian Process Control Association
146 Delarmbro Dr
Erin, ON N0B 1T0
519-833-7414
E-mail: cpca@cpca-assoc.com
URL: www.cpca-assoc.com
Scope: National

• **Canadian Public Relations Society 2018 Annual General Meeting**
Sponsor/Contact: Canadian Public Relations Society Inc.
c/o Lois Marsh, CPRS Toronto Secretariat
#1801, 1 Yonge St.
Toronto, ON M5E 1W7
416-360-1988; *Fax:* 416-369-0515
URL: www.cprstoronto.com
Scope: Local

• **Canadian School Boards Association 2018 Annual Meeting**
Sponsor/Contact: Canadian School Boards Association
#400, 3 Place Ville Marie
Montréal, QC H3B 2E3
514-289-2988; *Fax:* 514-788-3334
E-mail: info@cdnsba.org
URL: www.cdnsba.org
Scope: National

• **Canadian Snack Food Association 2018 62nd Annual Conference**
Sponsor/Contact: Canadian Snack Food Association
c/o Ileana Lima
P.O. Box 42252
128 Queen St. South
Mississauga, ON L5M 4Z0
289-997-1379
URL: www.canadiansnack.com
Scope: National

• **Canadian Society for Jewish Studies 14th Annual Conference 2018**
Sponsor/Contact: Canadian Society for Jewish Studies
c/o Dr. Ira Robinson, Department of Religion, Concordia University
1455, boul de Maisonneuve ouest
Montréal, QC H3G 1M8
URL: www.csjs.ca
Scope: National

• **Canadian Society for the Study of Practical Ethics 2018 Annual Conference**
Sponsor/Contact: Canadian Society for the Study of Practical Ethics
c/o Dept. of Philosophy, #618, Jorgenson Hall, Ryerson Univ.
350 Victoria St.
Toronto, ON M5B 2K3
416-979-5000; *Fax:* 416-979-5362
URL: www.csspe.ca
Scope: National

• **Canadian Society of Questers Fall Conference 2018**
Sponsor/Contact: Canadian Society of Questers
P.O. Box 1465
Salmon Arm, BC V1E 4P6
E-mail: pinkrose4233@gmail.com
URL: www.questers.ca
Scope: National

• **Canadian Society of Questers Spring Conference 2018**
Sponsor/Contact: Canadian Society of Questers
P.O. Box 1465
Salmon Arm, BC V1E 4P6
E-mail: pinkrose4233@gmail.com
URL: www.questers.ca
Scope: National

• **Canadian Sport Massage Therapists Association 2018 Conference & AGM**
Sponsor/Contact: Canadian Sport Massage Therapists Association
#236, 229 St. Clair St.
Chatham, ON N7L 3J4
519-800-7134
E-mail: natoffice@csmta.ca
URL: www.csmta.ca
Scope: National

• **Canadian Stuttering Association 2018 Annual General Meeting**
Sponsor/Contact: Canadian Stuttering Association
P.O. Box 69001 Stn. St. Clair Centre
Toronto, ON M4T 3A1
416-840-5169
Toll-Free: 866-840-5169
E-mail: csa-info@stutter.ca
URL: www.stutter.ca
Scope: National

• **Canadian Teachers' Federation 2018 Annual General Meeting**
Sponsor/Contact: Canadian Teachers' Federation
2490 Don Reid Dr.
Ottawa, ON K1H 1E1
613-232-1505; *Fax:* 613-232-1886
Toll-Free: 866-283-1505
E-mail: info@ctf-fce.ca
URL: www.ctf-fce.ca
Scope: National
Purpose: Approval of a budget for the upcoming year, a discussion & determination of policy priorities, & an election of directors

• **Canadian Technical Asphalt Association 63rd Annual Conference 2018**
Sponsor/Contact: Canadian Technical Asphalt Association
#300, 895 Fort St.
Victoria, BC V8W 1H7
250-361-9187; *Fax:* 250-361-9187
E-mail: admin@ctaa.ca
URL: www.ctaa.ca
Scope: National

• **Canadian Tenpin Federation 2018 AGM**
Sponsor/Contact: Canadian Tenpin Federation, Inc.
152 Cowichan Ct. West
Lethbridge, AB T1K 7T7
Toll-Free: 833-381-2830
E-mail: ctf@gotenpinbowling.ca
URL: www.gotenpinbowling.ca
Scope: National

• **Canadian Transportation Research Forum 53rd Annual Conference**
Sponsor/Contact: Canadian Transportation Research Forum
P.O. Box 23033
Woodstock, ON N4T 1R9
519-421-9701; *Fax:* 519-421-9319
URL: www.ctrf.ca
Scope: National

• **Canadian Union of Postal Workers National Convention 2018**
Sponsor/Contact: Canadian Union of Postal Workers
377 Bank St.
Ottawa, ON K2P 1Y3
613-236-7238; *Fax:* 613-563-7861
E-mail: feedback@cupw-sttp.org
URL: www.cupw-sttp.org
Scope: National

• **Canadian Union of Public Employees (CUPE) Manitoba 2018 55th Annual Convention**
Location: Manitoba
Sponsor/Contact: Canadian Union of Public Employees
Manitoba Regional Office
#703, 275 Broadway
Winnipeg, MB R3C 4M6
204-942-0343; *Fax:* 204-956-7071
E-mail: cupemb@cupe.mb.ca
URL: www.cupe.mb.ca
Scope: Provincial
Contact Information: E-mail: cupemb@cupe.mb.ca

• **Canadian Union of Public Employees 2018 National Convention**
Sponsor/Contact: Canadian Union of Public Employees
1375 St. Laurent Blvd.
Ottawa, ON K1G 0Z7
613-237-1590; *Fax:* 613-237-5508
Toll-Free: 844-237-1590
URL: www.cupe.ca
Scope: National

Conferences & Conventions Index

- **Canadian Urban Transit Association 2018 Annual Conference**
Sponsor/Contact: Canadian Urban Transit Association
#1401, 55 York St.
Toronto, ON M5J 1R7
416-365-9800; Fax: 416-365-1295
URL: www.cutaactu.ca
Scope: National
Purpose: Professional development sessions & the presentation of Corporate Awards, held in May or June each year

- **Canadian Water & Wastewater Association 2018 National Conference**
Sponsor/Contact: Canadian Water & Wastewater Association
#11, 1010 Polytek St.
Ottawa, ON K1J 9H9
613-747-0524; Fax: 613-747-0523
E-mail: admin@cwwa.ca
URL: www.cwwa.ca
Scope: National
Purpose: An exchange of news & views from Canadian utility conservation specialists

- **Canadian Water Quality Association 2018 Annual General Meeting**
Sponsor/Contact: Canadian Water Quality Association
#504, 295 The West Mall
Toronto, ON M9C 4Z4
416-695-3068; Fax: 416-695-2945
Toll-Free: 866-383-7617
E-mail: info@cwqa.com
URL: www.cwqa.com
Scope: National

- **Catholic Health Association of BC 78th Annual General Meeting and Conference**
Location: British Columbia
Sponsor/Contact: Catholic Health Association of British Columbia
9387 Holmes St.
Burnaby, BC V3N 4C3
604-524-3427; Fax: 604-524-3428
E-mail: smhouse@shawlink.ca
URL: chabc.bc.ca
Scope: Provincial

- **Certified Organic Associations of BC Conference 2018**
Location: British Columbia
Sponsor/Contact: Certified Organic Associations of British Columbia
#202, 3002 - 32nd Ave.
Vernon, BC V1T 2L7
250-260-4429; Fax: 250-260-4436
E-mail: office@certifiedorganic.bc.ca
URL: www.certifiedorganic.bc.ca
Scope: Provincial

- **Chambre de Commerce du Grand Joliette Assemblée générale annuelle 2018**
Location: Quebec
Sponsor/Contact: Chambre de commerce du Grand Joliette
500, boul Dollard
Joliette, QC J6E 4M4
450-759-6363; Fax: 450-759-5012
E-mail: info@ccgj.qc.ca
URL: www.ccgj.qc.ca
Scope: Local

- **Chartered Professional Accountants of New Brunswick Spring CPD Conference 2018**
Location: New Brunswick
Sponsor/Contact: Chartered Professional Accountants of New Brunswick
#602, 860 Main St.
Moncton, NB E1C 1G2
506-830-3300; Fax: 506-830-3310
E-mail: info@cpanewbrunswick.ca
URL: www.cpanewbrunswick.ca
Scope: Provincial

- **Chartered Professional Accountants of Newfoundland & Labrador 2018 Fall Professional Development Conference**
Location: Newfoundland & Labrador
Sponsor/Contact: Chartered Professional Accountants of Newfoundland & Labrador
#500, 95 Bonaventure Ave.
St. John's, NL A1B 2X5
709-753-3090; Fax: 709-753-3609
URL: www.cpanl.ca
Scope: Provincial

- **Chartered Professional Accountants of Saskatchewan Conference 2018**
Location: Saskatchewan
Sponsor/Contact: Chartered Professional Accountants of Saskatchewan
#101, 4581 Parliament Ave.
Regina, SK S4W 0G3
306-359-0272; Fax: 306-347-8580
Toll-Free: 800-667-3535
E-mail: info@cpask.ca
URL: www.cpask.ca
Scope: Provincial

- **Chartered Professionals in Human Resources Saskatchewan 2018 Conference**
Location: Saskatchewan
Sponsor/Contact: Chartered Professionals in Human Resources Saskatchewan
2106 Lorne St.
Regina, SK S4P 2M5
306-522-0184; Fax: 306-522-1783
E-mail: info@cphrsk.ca
URL: www.cphrsk.ca

- **Children's Mental Health Ontario Annual Conference 2018**
Location: Ontario
Sponsor/Contact: Children's Mental Health Ontario
#309, 40 St. Clair Ave. East
Toronto, ON M4T 1M9
416-921-2109; Fax: 416-921-7600
E-mail: info@cmho.org
URL: www.cmho.org
Scope: National

- **Church Library Association of British Columbia (CLABC) Conference 2018**
Location: British Columbia
Sponsor/Contact: Church Library Association of British Columbia
c/o Membership Secretary
1732 - 10 St. East
Courtenay, BC V9N 7H7
E-mail: clabc.ca@gmail.com
URL: www.clabc.ca
Scope: Provincial

- **Church Library Association of Ontario 2018 Spring Conference**
Location: Ontario
Sponsor/Contact: Church Library Association of Ontario
c/o Alice Meems, Treasurer
112 Bristol St.
Guelph, ON N1H 3L6
E-mail: treasurer@clao.ca
URL: www.clao.ca
Scope: Provincial
Purpose: Workshops, speakers, exhibitors, vendors & a book swap.
Contact Information: conference@clao.ca

- **CIAA's 34th Annual General Meeting & Conference**
Sponsor/Contact: Canadian Independent Adjusters' Association
Centennial Centre
#100, 5401 Eglinton Ave. West
Toronto, ON M9C 5K6
416-621-6222; Fax: 416-621-7776
Toll-Free: 877-255-5589
E-mail: info@ciaa-adjusters.ca
URL: www.ciaa-adjusters.ca
Scope: National

- **CIFFA Annual General Meeting**
Sponsor/Contact: Canadian International Freight Forwarders Association
#480, 170 Attwell Dr.
Toronto, ON M9W 5Z5
416-234-5100; Fax: 416-234-5152
Toll-Free: 866-282-4332
E-mail: secretariat@ciffa.com
URL: www.ciffa.com

- **Clean Energy BC 28th AGM & Industry Outlook**
Location: British Columbia
Sponsor/Contact: Clean Energy British Columbia
#354, 409 Granville St.
Vancouver, BC V6C 1T2
604-568-4778; Fax: 604-568-4724
Toll-Free: 855-568-4778
URL: www.cleanenergybc.org
Scope: Provincial

- **Coastal Zone Canada 2018**
Sponsor/Contact: Coastal Zone Canada Association
c/o Jennifer Barr, Dalhousie University
P.O. Box 15000
6414 Coburg Rd.
Halifax, NS B3H 4R2
902-494-4650; Fax: 902-494-1334
E-mail: czcadmin@dal.ca
URL: www.czca-azcc.org
Scope: National
Contact Information: Peter Zuzek; Email: pzuzek@baird.com

- **Collection Systems 2018**
Sponsor/Contact: Water Environment Federation
601 Wythe St.
Alexandria, VA 22314-1994
703-684-2400
Toll-Free: 800-666-0206
E-mail: csc@wef.org
URL: www.wef.org
Scope: International

- **College of Audiologists and Speech-Language Pathologists of Manitoba Annual Educational Conference 2018**
Sponsor/Contact: College of Audiologists and Speech-Language Pathologists of Manitoba
#1, 333 Vaughan St.
Winnipeg, MB R3B 3J9
204-453-4539; Fax: 204-477-1881
E-mail: office@caslpm.ca
URL: www.caslpm.ca
Scope: Provincial

- **College of Family Physicians of Canada / Collège des médecins de famille du Canada 2018 Annual General Meeting**
Sponsor/Contact: College of Family Physicians of Canada
2630 Skymark Ave.
Mississauga, ON L4W 5A4
905-629-0900; Fax: 888-843-2372
Toll-Free: 800-387-6197
E-mail: info@cfpc.ca
URL: www.cfpc.ca
Scope: Provincial

- **College of Optometrists of BC 2018 Annual General Meeting**
Location: British Columbia
Sponsor/Contact: College of Optometrists of BC
#906, 938 Howe St.
Vancouver, BC V6Z 1N9
604-623-3464; Fax: 604-623-3465
Toll-Free: 866-910-3464
E-mail: college@optometrybc.ca
URL: www.optometrybc.com
Scope: Provincial
Purpose: The presentation of financial statements, as well as reports from the chair, the registrar, the deputy registrar, & college board members

- **Colloque annuel de l'Association du transport urbain du Québec 2018**
Sponsor/Contact: Association du transport urbain du Québec
#8090, 800, rue de la Gauchetière
Montréal, QC H5A 1J6
514-280-4640; Fax: 514-280-7053
E-mail: info@atuq.com
URL: www.atuq.com

- **Collège des médecins du Québec Colloque et assemblée générale annuelle 2018**
Sponsor/Contact: Collège des médecins du Québec
2170, boul René-Lévesque ouest
Montréal, QC H3H 2T8
514-933-4441; Fax: 514-933-3112
Toll-Free: 888-633-3246
E-mail: info@cmq.org
URL: www.cmq.org
Scope: Provincial

- **Community Futures Manitoba 2018 Annual Provincial Conference**
Location: Manitoba
Sponsor/Contact: Community Futures Manitoba Inc.
#559, 167 Lombard Ave.
Winnipeg, MB R3B 0V3
204-943-2905; Fax: 204-956-9363
E-mail: info@cfmanitoba.ca
URL: www.cfmanitoba.ca
Scope: Provincial
Purpose: A yearly event to explore economic development issues in Manitoba, featuring keynote addresses
Anticipated Attendance: 150
Contact Information: info@cfmanitoba.ca

- **Community Living Grimsby, Lincoln & West Lincoln 53rd Annual General Meeting**
Sponsor/Contact: Community Living Grimsby, Lincoln & West Lincoln
P.O. Box 220
Beamsville, ON L0R 1B0
905-563-4115; Fax: 905-563-8887
E-mail: info@cl-grimsbylincoln.ca
URL: www.cl-grimsbylincoln.ca
Scope: Local

- **Community Living Oshawa / Clarington 2018 Annual General Meeting**
Location: Ontario
Sponsor/Contact: Community Living Oshawa / Clarington
39 Wellington St. East
Oshawa, ON L1H 3Y1
905-576-3011; Fax: 905-576-9754
URL: www.communitylivingoc.ca
Scope: Local

- **Compost Council of Canada 2018 28th Annual National Compost Conference**
Sponsor/Contact: Compost Council of Canada
16 Northumberland St.
Toronto, ON M6H 1P7
416-535-0240; Fax: 416-536-9892
Toll-Free: 877-571-4769
E-mail: info@compost.org
URL: www.compost.org
Scope: National
Purpose: Current developments in the composting industry, such as research, processing improvements, & community developments

- **Compressed Gas Association Canada Annual Meeting 2018**
Sponsor/Contact: Compressed Gas Association, Inc.
#103, 14501 George Carter Way
Chantilly, VA 20151
703-788-2700; Fax: 703-961-1831
E-mail: cga@cganet.com
URL: www.cganet.com
Scope: National

- **Confédération des organismes familiaux du Québec Assemblée générale 2018**
Location: Quebec
Sponsor/Contact: Confédération des organismes familiaux du Québec
4657, rue Papineau
Montréal, QC H2H 1V4
514-521-4777; Fax: 514-521-6272
URL: www.cofaq.qc.ca
Scope: Provincial

- **Congregational Christian Churches in Canada National Conference 2018**
Sponsor/Contact: Congregational Christian Churches in Canada
442 Grey St.
Brantford, ON N3S 7N3
519-751-0606
E-mail: 4cnational@gmail.com
URL: www.cccc.ca

- **Congrés Association des médecins vétérinaires praticiens du Québec 2018**
Location: Quebec
Sponsor/Contact: Association des médecins vétérinaires praticiens du Québec
#4500, 2336, ch Ste-Foy
Québec, QC G1V 1S5
418-651-0477; Fax: 450-261-9435
E-mail: amvpq@amvpq.org
URL: www.amvpq.org
Scope: Provincial

- **Congrès 2018 de l'Association des professeurs de français des universités et collèges canadiens**
Sponsor/Contact: Association des professeurs de français des universités et collèges canadiens
Département de Françaises, Université de Simon Fraser

8888 University Dr.
Burnaby, BC V5A 1S6
URL: www.apfucc.net

- **Congrès OUQ 2018**
Location: Quebec
Sponsor/Contact: Ordre des urbanistes du Québec
#410, 85, rue St-Paul ouest
Montréal, QC H2Y 3V4
514-849-1177; Fax: 514-849-7176
E-mail: info@ouq.qc.ca
URL: www.ouq.qc.ca
Scope: Provincial

- **Congrès annuel de l'Association québécoise pour l'hygiène, la santé et la sécurité du travail 2018**
Location: Quebec
Sponsor/Contact: Association québécoise pour l'hygiène, la santé et la sécurité du travail
P.O. Box 52
89, boul de Bromont
Bromont, QC J2L 1A9
450-776-2169
Toll-Free: 888-355-3830
E-mail: info@aqhsst.qc.ca
URL: www.aqhsst.qc.ca
Scope: Provincial

- **Congrès annuel de l'Opération Nez rouge 2018**
Sponsor/Contact: Opération Nez rouge
Maison Couillard, Université Laval
2539, rue Marie-Fitzbach
Québec, QC G1V 0A6
418-653-1492; Fax: 418-653-3315
Toll-Free: 800-463-7222
E-mail: info@operationnezrouge.com
URL: www.operationnezrouge.com
Scope: National

- **Congrès de l'association des économistes québécois 2018**
Location: Quebec
Sponsor/Contact: Association des économistes québécois
#7118, 385, rue Sherbrooke est
Montréal, QC H2X 1E3
514-342-7537; Fax: 514-342-3967
Toll-Free: 866-342-7537
E-mail: info@economistesquebecois.com
URL: www.economistesquebecois.com
Scope: Provincial

- **Connect 2018**
Sponsor/Contact: Canadian Cable Systems Alliance
447 Gondola Point Rd.
Quispamsis, NB E2E 1E1
506-849-1334; Fax: 506-849-1338
E-mail: info@ccsa.cable.ca
URL: www.ccsa.cable.ca
Scope: National

- **Consulting Engineers of Alberta 40th Annual General Meeting**
Location: Alberta
Sponsor/Contact: Consulting Engineers of Alberta
Phipps-McKinnon Building
#870, 10020 - 101A Ave.
Edmonton, AB T5J 3G2
780-421-1852; Fax: 780-424-5225
E-mail: info@cea.ca
URL: www.cea.ca
Scope: Provincial
Anticipated Attendance: 700+

- **Consulting Engineers of Nova Scotia 2018 Annual General Meeting**

Location: Nova Scotia
Sponsor/Contact: Consulting Engineers of Nova Scotia
P.O. Box 613 Stn. M
Halifax, NS B3J 2R7
902-461-1325; Fax: 902-461-1321
E-mail: cens@eastlink.ca
URL: www.cens.org
Scope: Provincial

- **Consulting Engineers of Ontario 2018 Annual General Meeting**
Location: Ontario
Sponsor/Contact: Consulting Engineers of Ontario
#405, 10 Four Seasons Pl.
Toronto, ON M9B 6H7
416-620-1400; Fax: 416-620-5803
URL: www.ceo.on.ca
Scope: Provincial

- **Continuing Care Association of Nova Scotia 2018 AGM**
Sponsor/Contact: Continuing Care Association of Nova Scotia
c/o Sunshine Personal Home Care
38A Withrod Dr.
Halifax, NS B3N 1B1
902-446-3140
E-mail: ccans@eastlink.ca
URL: www.ccans.info
Scope: Provincial

- **Council of Archives New Brunswick Annual General Meeting 2018**
Location: New Brunswick
Sponsor/Contact: Council of Archives New Brunswick
P.O. Box 1204 Stn. A
Fredericton, NB E3B 5C8
506-453-4327; Fax: 506-453-3288
E-mail: archives.advisor@gnb.ca
URL: www.canbarchives.ca
Scope: Provincial

- **Council of Nova Scotia Archives Annual General Meeting 2018**
Location: Nova Scotia
Sponsor/Contact: Council of Nova Scotia Archives
6016 University Ave.
Halifax, NS B3H 1W4
902-424-7093
E-mail: advisor@councilofnsarchives.ca
URL: www.councilofnsarchives.ca
Scope: Provincial

- **Council of Ontario Construction Associations Annual General Meeting 2018**
Location: Ontario
Sponsor/Contact: Council of Ontario Construction Associations
#2001, 180 Dundas St. West
Toronto, ON M5G 1Z8
416-968-7200; Fax: 416-968-0362
E-mail: info@coca.on.ca
URL: www.coca.on.ca
Scope: Provincial
Contact Information: Manager, Operations & Member Services: Martin Benson, E-mail: mbenson@coca.on.ca; Phone: 416-968-7200, ext. 222

- **CPA Manitoba Annual General Meeting 2018**
Location: Manitoba
Sponsor/Contact: Chartered Professional Accountants of Manitoba
#1675, 1 Lombard Place
Winnipeg, MB R3B 0X3

204-943-1538; Fax: 204-943-7119
Toll-Free: 800-841-7148
E-mail: cpamb@cpamb.ca
URL: www.cpamb.ca
Scope: Provincial

- **Cross Country Ski Ontario 2018 Annual General Meeting**
Location: Ontario
Sponsor/Contact: Cross Country Ski Ontario
c/o Liz Inkila
738 River St.
Thunder Bay, ON P7A 3S8
807-768-4617
E-mail: admin@xco.org
URL: www.xco.org
Scope: Provincial
Purpose: Board meetings are held each month by telephone, & the annual general meeting takes place each May

- **Dairy Farmers of Ontario Annual Meeting 2018**
Location: Ontario
Sponsor/Contact: Dairy Farmers of Ontario
6780 Campobello Rd.
Mississauga, ON L5N 2L8
905-821-8970; Fax: 905-821-3160
E-mail: questions@milk.org
URL: www.milk.org
Scope: Provincial

- **Doctors Manitoba 2018 Annual General Meeting**
Sponsor/Contact: Doctors Manitoba
20 Desjardins Dr.
Winnipeg, MB R3X 0E8
204-985-5888; Fax: 204-985-5844
Toll-Free: 888-322-4242
E-mail: general@docsmb.org
URL: www.docsmb.org
Scope: Provincial

- **Eating Disorder Association of Canada 6th Biennial Conference**
Sponsor/Contact: Eating Disorder Association of Canada
E-mail: edacatac@gmail.com
URL: www.edac-atac.ca
Scope: National

- **Edmonton Law Libraries Association Annual General Meeting 2018**
Sponsor/Contact: Edmonton Law Libraries Association
P.O. Box 47093
62 Edmonton City Centre
Edmonton, AB T5J 4N1
E-mail: secretary@edmontonlawlibraries.ca
URL: www.edmontonlawlibraries.ca
Scope: Provincial

- **Electric Mobility Canada 2018 Annual General Meeting**
Sponsor/Contact: Electric Mobility Canada
#11-530, 38, Place du Commerce
Iles de Soeurs, QC H3E 1T8
Fax: 514-769-1286
E-mail: info@emc-mec.ca
URL: www.emc-mec.ca
Scope: National

- **Electrical Contractors Association of Ontario Annual Industry Conference 2018**
Location: Ontario
Sponsor/Contact: Electrical Contractors Association of Ontario
#702, 10 Carlson Court
Toronto, ON M9W 6L2

Conferences & Conventions Index

416-675-3226; *Fax:* 416-675-7736
Toll-Free: 800-387-3226
E-mail: ecao@ecao.org
URL: www.ecao.org
Scope: Provincial

- **Electricity Distributors Association 2018 Annual General Meeting**
Sponsor/Contact: Electricity Distributors Association
#1100, 3700 Steeles Ave. West
Vaughan, ON L4L 8K8
905-265-5300; *Fax:* 905-265-5301
Toll-Free: 800-668-9979
E-mail: email@eda-on.ca
URL: www.eda-on.ca
Scope: Provincial

- **Electro-Federation Canada Conference 2018**
Sponsor/Contact: Electro-Federation Canada
#300, 180 Attwell Dr.
Toronto, ON M9W 6A9
905-602-8877; *Fax:* 416-679-9234
Toll-Free: 866-602-8877
E-mail: info@electrofed.com
URL: www.electrofed.com
Scope: National

- **Energy Council of Canada 2018 Canadian Energy Industry: Updates & Insights**
Sponsor/Contact: Energy Council of Canada
#608, 350 Sparks St.
Ottawa, ON K1R 7S8
613-232-8239; *Fax:* 613-232-1079
URL: www.energy.ca
Scope: National

- **Engineers Nova Scotia Conference & AGM 2018**
Location: Nova Scotia
Sponsor/Contact: Engineers Nova Scotia
1355 Barrington St.
Halifax, NS B3J 1Y9
902-429-2250; *Fax:* 902-423-9769
Toll-Free: 888-802-7367
E-mail: info@engineersnovascotia.ca
URL: www.engineersnovascotia.ca
Scope: Provincial
Purpose: A business meeting with guest speakers for professional engineers & engineers-in-training in Nova Scotia

- **Entertainment Merchants Association Independent Product Market 2018**
Sponsor/Contact: Entertainment Merchants Association - International Head Office
#400, 16530 Ventura Blvd.
Encino, CA 91436-4551
818-385-1500; *Fax:* 818-385-0567
E-mail: info@entmerch.org
URL: www.entmerch.org
Scope: International
Purpose: A gathering of retail buying & distributing companies & independent studios that facilitates networking opportunities
Contact Information: Vice-President, Strategic Initiatives: Carrie Dieterich, E-mail: cdieterich@entmerch.org, Phone: 818-385-1500, ext. 227

- **Entomological Society of British Columbia Annual General Meeting & Symposium 2018**
Location: British Columbia
Sponsor/Contact: Entomological Society of British Columbia
c/o Bob Lalonde, UBC Okanagan, Science Bldg.
1177 Research Rd.
Kelowna, BC V1V 1V7
URL: entsocbc.ca
Scope: Provincial

- **Entomological Society of Ontario 155th Annual General Meeting 2018**
Sponsor/Contact: Entomological Society of Ontario
c/o Vista Centre
P.O. Box 83025
1830 Bank St.
Ottawa, ON K1V 1A3
603-736-3393
URL: www.entsocont.ca
Scope: Provincial
Purpose: A gathering of entomologists of all disciplines

- **Environmental Education Ontario AGM 2018**
Location: Ontario
Sponsor/Contact: Environmental Education Ontario
32 Springdale Dr.
Kitchener, ON N2K 1P9
519-579-3097
E-mail: admin@eeon.org
URL: www.eeon.org
Scope: Provincial

- **Essential Skills Ontario Annual General Meeting 2018**
Location: Ontario
Sponsor/Contact: Essential Skills Ontario
#503, 65 Wellesley St. East
Toronto, ON M4Y 1G7
416-963-5787; *Fax:* 416-963-8102
E-mail: info@essentialskillsontario.ca
URL: www.essentialskillsontario.ca
Scope: Provincial
Contact Information: Director, Finance & Administration: Susanne Smith, E-mail: susanne@essentialskillsontario.ca

- **Excellence Canada 2018 Performance Excellence Summit & Canada Awards for Excellence**
Sponsor/Contact: Excellence Canada
#402, 154 University Ave.
Toronto, ON M5H 3Y9
416-251-7600; *Fax:* 416-251-9131
Toll-Free: 800-263-9648
E-mail: info@excellence.ca
URL: www.excellence.ca
Scope: National

- **Expo Hightex 2018**
Sponsor/Contact: Groupe CTT Group
3000, rue Boullé
Saint-Hyacinthe, QC J2S 1H9
450-778-1870; *Fax:* 450-778-3901
Toll-Free: 877-288-8378
E-mail: info@gcttg.com
URL: www.gcttg.com
Scope: National
Contact Information: URL: www.expohightex.com

- **Federated Women's Institutes of Ontario Annual General Meeting 2018**
Location: Ontario
Sponsor/Contact: Federated Women's Institutes of Ontario
552 Ridge Rd.
Stoney Creek, ON L8J 2Y6
905-662-2691; *Fax:* 905-930-8631
URL: www.fwio.on.ca
Scope: Provincial

Contact Information: Administrator: Kim Sauder, E-mail: kim@fwio.on.ca

- **Federation of Prince Edward Island Municipalities Inc. Annual General Meeting 2018**
Sponsor/Contact: Federation of Prince Edward Island Municipalities Inc.
1 Kirkdale Rd.
Charlottetown, PE C1E 1R3
902-566-1493; *Fax:* 902-566-2880
E-mail: info@fpeim.ca
URL: www.fpeim.ca
Scope: Provincial
Contact Information: Assistant, Administrative: Julie McMurrer, E-mail: jmcmurrer@fpeim.ca

- **Fenestration Canada 2018 Annual General Meeting**
Sponsor/Contact: Fenestration Canada
#1208, 130 Albert St.
Ottawa, ON K1P 5G4
613-235-5511; *Fax:* 613-235-4664
E-mail: info@fenestrationcanada.ca
URL: www.fenestrationcanada.ca
Scope: National
Purpose: A business meeting to keep current with industry trends & opportunities

- **Field Botanists of Ontario Annual General Meeting**
Location: Ontario
Sponsor/Contact: Field Botanists of Ontario
c/o W.D. McIlveen
RR#1
Acton, ON L7J 2L7
URL: www.trentu.ca/fbo
Scope: Provincial

- **Fitness New Brunswick Annual General Meeting 2018**
Sponsor/Contact: Fitness New Brunswick
Lady Beaverbrook Gym, University of New Brunswick
P.O. Box 4400
#A112A, 2 Peter Kelly Dr.
Fredericton, NB E3B 5A3
506-453-1094; *Fax:* 506-453-1099
Toll-Free: 888-790-1411
E-mail: membershipservices@fitnessnb.ca
URL: www.fitnessnb.ca
Scope: Provincial

- **Fitness New Brunswick Annual Summit 2018**
Sponsor/Contact: Fitness New Brunswick
Lady Beaverbrook Gym, University of New Brunswick
P.O. Box 4400
#A112A, 2 Peter Kelly Dr.
Fredericton, NB E3B 5A3
506-453-1094; *Fax:* 506-453-1099
Toll-Free: 888-790-1411
E-mail: membershipservices@fitnessnb.ca
URL: www.fitnessnb.ca
Scope: Provincial

- **Food & Consumer Products of Canada Annual Supply Chain Symposium 2018**
Sponsor/Contact: Food & Consumer Products of Canada
#600, 100 Sheppard Ave. East
Toronto, ON M2N 6N5
416-510-8024; *Fax:* 416-510-8043
E-mail: info@fcpc.ca
URL: www.fcpc.ca
Scope: National

- **Food & Consumer Products of Canada National Sales Symposium 2018**
Sponsor/Contact: Food & Consumer Products of Canada
#600, 100 Sheppard Ave. East
Toronto, ON M2N 6N5
416-510-8024; *Fax:* 416-510-8043
E-mail: info@fcpc.ca
URL: www.fcpc.ca
Scope: National

- **Forest Nova Scotia 2018 84th Annual Meeting**
Location: Nova Scotia
Sponsor/Contact: Forest Nova Scotia
P.O. Box 696
Truro, NS B2N 5E5
902-895-1179; *Fax:* 902-893-1197
URL: forestns.ca
Scope: Provincial
Purpose: A yearly gathering of association members
Contact Information: Phone: 902-895-1179

- **Forests Ontario Conference 2018**
Location: Ontario
Sponsor/Contact: Forests Ontario
#700, 144 Front St. West
Toronto, ON M5J 2L7
416-646-1193; *Fax:* 416-493-4608
Toll-Free: 877-646-1193
E-mail: info@treesontario.ca
URL: www.forestsontario.ca
Scope: Provincial

- **Fraser Valley Labour Council 2018 Annual General Meeting**
Location: British Columbia
Sponsor/Contact: Fraser Valley Labour Council
#202, 9292 - 200th St.
Langley, BC V1M 3A6
604-314-9867; *Fax:* 604-430-6762
E-mail: bharder@usw.ca
URL: www.fvlc.ca
Scope: Local

- **Freestyle Ski Nova Scotia Annual General Meeting 2018**
Sponsor/Contact: Freestyle Ski Nova Scotia
5516 Spring Garden Rd., 4th Fl.
Halifax, NS B3J 1G6
902-425-5450; *Fax:* 902-425-5606
E-mail: alpinens@sportnovascotia.ca
URL: freestylenovascotia.ca
Scope: Provincial

- **Fédération de golf du Québec Assemblée générale annuelle 2018**
Sponsor/Contact: Fédération de golf du Québec
4545, av Pierre-de Coubertin
Montréal, QC H1V 0B2
514-252-3345; *Fax:* 514-252-3346
E-mail: golfquebec@golfquebec.org
URL: www.golfquebec.org
Scope: Provincial

- **Fédération des associations de familles du Québec Congrès & assemblée générale 2018**
Location: Quebec
Sponsor/Contact: Fédération des associations de familles du Québec
650, rue Graham-Bell
Québec, QC G1N 4H5
418-653-2137; *Fax:* 418-653-6387
E-mail: info@fafq.org
URL: fafq.org
Scope: Provincial

Contact Information: Directeur: Yves Boisvert, Courriel: yboisvert@fafq.org

- **Fédération du plongeon amateur du Québec assemblée générale annuelle 2018**
Location: Quebec
Sponsor/Contact: Fédération du plongeon amateur du Québec
4545, av Pierre-de Coubertin
Montréal, QC H1V 0b2
514-252-3096; *Fax:* 514-252-3094
E-mail: info@plongeon.qc.ca
URL: www.plongeon.qc.ca
Scope: Provincial

- **Garrod Association 2018 Garrod Symposium**
Sponsor/Contact: Garrod Association
11797 rue Poincaré
Montréal, QC H3L 3L6
URL: www.garrod.ca
Scope: National

- **German-Canadian Congress (Manitoba) Inc. Annual General Meeting 2018**
Location: Manitoba
Sponsor/Contact: German-Canadian Congress (Manitoba) Inc.
#58, 81 Garry St.
Winnipeg, MB R3C 4J9
204-989-8300; *Fax:* 204-989-8304
E-mail: info@gccmb.ca
URL: www.gccmb.ca
Scope: Provincial

- **Global Environmental & Outdoor Education Council 2018 Annual Conference**
Sponsor/Contact: Global, Environmental & Outdoor Education Council
c/o Barnett House, Alberta Teachers' Association
11010 - 142 St. NW
Edmonton, AB T5N 2R1
780-987-7315; *Fax:* 780-455-6481
Toll-Free: 800-232-7208
E-mail: info@geoec.org
URL: www.geoec.org
Scope: Provincial
Purpose: Features information sessions, resources, & a keynote speaker

- **GPAC/PJVA 25th Annual Joint Conference**
Sponsor/Contact: Gas Processing Association Canada
#600, 900 - 6th Ave. SW
Calgary, AB T2P 3K2
403-244-4487; *Fax:* 403-244-2340
E-mail: info@gpacanada.com
URL: www.gpacanada.com
Scope: National

- **Greater Summerside Chamber of Commerce Annual General Meeting 2018**
Location: Prince Edward Island
Sponsor/Contact: Greater Summerside Chamber of Commerce
#10, 263 Heather Moyse Dr.
Summerside, PE C1N 5P1
902-436-9651; *Fax:* 902-436-8320
E-mail: info@summersidechamber.com
URL: www.summersidechamber.com
Scope: Local

- **Greater Vancouver Home Builders' Association 2018 Annual General Meeting**
Location: British Columbia

Sponsor/Contact: Greater Vancouver Home Builders' Association
#1003, 7495 - 132 St.
Surrey, BC V3W 1J8
778-565-4288; *Fax:* 778-565-4289
E-mail: info@gvhba.org
URL: www.gvhba.org
Scope: Local

- **GrowCanada 2018**
Sponsor/Contact: CropLife Canada
#612, 350 Sparks St.
Ottawa, ON K1R 7S8
613-230-9881
URL: www.croplife.ca
Scope: National

- **Gymnastics Nova Scotia 2018 Annual General Meeting**
Location: Nova Scotia
Sponsor/Contact: Gymnastics Nova Scotia
5516 Spring Garden Rd., 4th Fl.
Halifax, NS B3J 1G6
902-425-5450; *Fax:* 902-425-5606
E-mail: gns@sportnovascotia.ca
URL: www.gymns.ca
Scope: Provincial
Purpose: A yearly gathering to establish the general policy & direction of the association, consider committee reports, & elect the new executive committee

- **Gymnastics Ontario AGM & Conference**
Location: Ontario
Sponsor/Contact: Ontario Gymnastic Federation
#214, 3 Concorde Gate
Toronto, ON M3C 3N7
416-426-7100; *Fax:* 416-426-7377
Toll-Free: 866-565-0650
E-mail: info@ogf.com
URL: www.ogf.com
Scope: Provincial

- **Health Libraries Association of British Columbia (HLABC) Annual General Meeting 2018**
Location: British Columbia
Sponsor/Contact: Health Libraries Association of British Columbia
c/o Antje Helmuth, Ministry of Health, Health & Human Services Library
P.O. Box 9637 Stn. Prov Govt
1515 Blanshard St.
Victoria, BC V8W 9P1
250-952-1478; *Fax:* 250-952-2180
URL: hlabc.chla-absc.ca
Scope: Provincial

- **Human Resources Association of Nova Scotia 2018 Conference**
Location: Nova Scotia
Sponsor/Contact: Human Resources Association of Nova Scotia
#103, 84 Chain Lake Dr.
Halifax, NS B3S 1A2
902-446-3660; *Fax:* 902-446-3677
URL: www.cphrns.ca
Scope: Provincial

- **Hydrogen + Fuel Cells 2018 International Conference**
Sponsor/Contact: Canadian Hydrogen & Fuel Cell Association
#900, 1188 West Georgia St.
Vancouver, BC V6E 4A2
604-283-1040; *Fax:* 604-283-1043
E-mail: info@chfca.ca
URL: www.chfca.ca
Scope: International

- **ICOMOS Canada 2018 Annual Meeting**
Sponsor/Contact: ICOMOS Canada
P.O. Box 737 Stn. B
Ottawa, ON K1P 5P8
613-749-0971; *Fax:* 613-749-0971
E-mail: secretariat@canada.icomos.org
URL: canada.icomos.org
Scope: National

- **Incident Prevention Association of Manitoba 2018 Safety Saves Conference & Tradeshow**
Location: Manitoba
Sponsor/Contact: Incident Prevention Association of Manitoba
#51, 162 - 2025 Corydon Ave.
Winnipeg, MB R3P 0N5
204-275-3727
E-mail: office@ipam-manitoba.com
URL: ipam-manitoba.com
Scope: Provincial

- **Inclusion Alberta Annual Family Conference 2018**
Location: Alberta
Sponsor/Contact: Inclusion Alberta
11724 Kingsway Ave.
Edmonton, AB T5G 0X5
780-451-3055; *Fax:* 780-453-5779
Toll-Free: 800-252-7556
E-mail: mail@inclusionalberta.org
URL: inclusionalberta.org
Scope: Provincial

- **Inclusion BC 2018 Conference & AGM**
Sponsor/Contact: Inclusion BC
227 - 6th St.
New Westminster, BC V3L 3A5
604-777-9100; *Fax:* 604-777-9394
Toll-Free: 800-618-1119
E-mail: info@inclusionbc.org
URL: www.inclusionbc.org
Scope: Provincial

- **Independent Power Producers Society of Alberta Annual Conference 2018**
Location: Alberta
Sponsor/Contact: Independent Power Producers Society of Alberta
#2600, 144 - 4th Ave. SW
Calgary, AB T2P 3N4
Fax: 403-256-8342
URL: www.ippsa.com
Scope: Provincial
Purpose: An event featuring guest speakers, panel discussions, debates, a trade show, social events, & networking opportunities
Anticipated Attendance: 500+
Contact Information: Executive Director: Evan Bahry, Phone: 403-282-8811, E-mail: Evan.Bahry@ippsa.com

- **Independent Telecommunications Providers Association 53rd Annual Convention 2018**
Sponsor/Contact: Independent Telecommunications Providers Association
29 Peevers Cres.
Newmarket, ON L3Y 7T5
519-595-3975; *Fax:* 519-595-3976
URL: www.ota.on.ca
Scope: Provincial
Purpose: An event featuring guest speakers, informative seminars, the annual general meeting, social events, & opportunities to meet with telecommunications industry representatives

- **Indigenous Bar Association 30th Annual Fall Conference 2018**
Sponsor/Contact: Indigenous Bar Association
c/o Anne Chalmers
70 Pineglen Cres.
Ottawa, ON K2G 0G8
URL: www.indigenousbar.ca
Scope: National
Contact Information: Assistant, Administration: Anne Chalmers, E-mail: achalmers@indigenousbar.ca

- **Indigenous Literary Studies Association 2018 4th Annual Gathering**
Sponsor/Contact: Indigenous Literary Studies Association
E-mail: indigenouslsa@gmail.com
URL: www.indigenousliterarystudies.org
Scope: National

- **Infectious Diseases Society of America Annual Meeting 2018**
Sponsor/Contact: Infectious Diseases Society of America
#300, 1300 Wilson Blvd.
Arlington, VA 22209
703-299-0200; *Fax:* 703-299-0204
E-mail: membership@idsociety.org
URL: www.idsociety.org
Scope: International

- **Infrastructure Health & Safety Association 2018 Annual General Meeting**
Sponsor/Contact: Infrastructure Health & Safety Association
Centre for Health & Safety Innovation
#400, 5110 Creekbank Rd.
Mississauga, ON L4W 0A1
905-625-0100; *Fax:* 905-625-8998
Toll-Free: 800-263-5024
E-mail: info@ihsa.ca
URL: www.ihsa.ca
Scope: Provincial
Purpose: A business meeting featuring a guest speaker & the presentation of awards

- **Institute for Performance & Learning 2018 Conference**
Sponsor/Contact: Institute for Performance & Learning
#315, 720 Spadina Ave.
Toronto, ON M5S 2T9
416-367-5900
Toll-Free: 866-257-4275
E-mail: hello@performanceandlearning.ca
URL: www.performanceandlearning.ca
Scope: National

- **Institute of Textile Science 117th Scientific Session 2018**
Sponsor/Contact: Institute of Textile Science
c/o CTT Group
3000, av Boullé
Saint-Hyacinthe, ON J2S 1H9
450-778-1870
E-mail: info@textilescience.ca
URL: www.textilescience.ca
Scope: National

- **Insurance Brokers Association of Ontario Convention 2018**
Location: Ontario
Sponsor/Contact: Insurance Brokers Association of Canada
#700, 1 Eglinton Ave. East
Toronto, ON M4P 3A1

Conferences & Conventions Index

416-488-7422; *Fax:* 416-488-7526
Toll-Free: 800-268-8845
URL: www.ibao.org
Scope: Provincial

- **Insurance Brokers Association of Ontario Young Brokers Conference**
Sponsor/Contact: Insurance Brokers Association of Canada
#700, 1 Eglinton Ave. East
Toronto, ON M4P 3A1
416-488-7422; *Fax:* 416-488-7526
Toll-Free: 800-268-8845
URL: www.ibao.org
Scope: Provincial

- **International Academy of Energy, Minerals & Materials 2018 International Conference and Exhibition on Mining, Material and Metallurgical Education**
Sponsor/Contact: International Academy of Energy, Minerals & Materials
P.O. Box 62047 Stn. Convent Glen
Orléans, ON K1C 7H8
613-830-1760
E-mail: info@iaemm.com
URL: iaemm.com
Scope: International

- **International Association for Great Lakes Research 2018 Annual Conference**
Location: University of Toronto Scarborough
Toronto, ON
Sponsor/Contact: International Association for Great Lakes Research
4840 South State Rd.
Ann Arbor, MI 48108
734-665-5303; *Fax:* 734-741-2055
E-mail: office@iaglr.org
URL: www.iaglr.org
Scope: International

- **International Council for Laboratory Animal Science General Assembly & Annual Symposium**
Sponsor/Contact: International Council for Laboratory Animal Science
40 Washington St.
Brussels, 1050
E-mail: info@iclas.org
URL: www.iclas.org
Scope: International

- **International Council on Monuments & Sites General Assembly 2018**
Sponsor/Contact: International Council on Monuments & Sites
11, rue du Séminaire de Conflans
Charenton-le-Pont, 94220
E-mail: secretariat@icomos.org
URL: www.icomos.org
Scope: International

- **International Federation of Airworthiness Forum 2018**
Sponsor/Contact: International Federation of Airworthiness
59 Hurst Farm Rd. East
Sussex, RH19 4DQ
URL: www.ifairworthy.com
Scope: International

- **International Federation of Beekeepers' Associations (APIMONDIA) 46th International Apicultural Congress 2018**
Sponsor/Contact: International Federation of Beekeepers' Associations
Corso Vittorio Emanuele 101
Rome, I-00186

E-mail: apimondia@mclink.it
URL: www.apimondia.org
Scope: International

- **International Heavy Haul Association 2018 International Conference**
Sponsor/Contact: International Heavy Haul Association
2808 Forest Hills Crt.
Virginia Beach, VA 23454-1236
E-mail: scottlovelace@verizon.net
URL: www.ihha.net
Scope: International
Purpose: An international conference, scheduled every four years, featuring meetings covering the complete spectrum of heavy haul subjects, as well as technical tours

- **International Hotel & Restaurant Association 55th Annual Congress 2018**
Sponsor/Contact: International Hotel & Restaurant Association
42 Ave. General Guisan
Lausanne, 1009
E-mail: admin@ih-ra.com
URL: www.ih-ra.com
Scope: International

- **International Law Association 78th Biennial International Conference 2018**
Sponsor/Contact: International Law Association
Charles Clore House
17 Russell Sq.
London, WC1B 5JD
URL: www.ila-hq.org
Scope: International

- **International Orthoptic Congress 2018**
Sponsor/Contact: International Orthoptic Association
c/o RPG Crouch Chapman LLP
62 Wilson St.
London, EC2A 2BU
E-mail: webmaster@internationalorthoptics.org
URL: www.internationalorthoptics.org
Scope: International
Purpose: Plenary sessions, exhibitions, & educational activities

- **International Peatland Society Annual Convention 2018**
Sponsor/Contact: International Peat Society
Kauppakatu 19 D 31
Jyväskylä, FIN-40100
E-mail: ips@peatsociety.org
URL: www.peatsociety.org
Scope: International

- **International Society for Affective Disorders Conference 2018**
Sponsor/Contact: International Society for Affective Disorders
c/o Caroline Holebrook, Institute of Psychiatry, King's College London
PO72 De Crespigny Park, Denmark Hill
London, SE5 8AF
E-mail: enquiry@isad.org.uk
URL: www.isad.org.uk
Scope: International

- **Jewish Federation of Edmonton Annual General Meeting 2018**
Location: Edmonton, AB
Sponsor/Contact: The Centre for Israel & Jewish Affairs
#200, 10220 - 156 St.
Edmonton, AB T5P 2R1

780-487-0585
E-mail: info@edjfed.org
URL: www.jewishedmonton.org
Scope: Local
Contact Information: Director, Communications: Tal Toubiana, E-mail: talt@edjfed.org, Phone: 780-487-0585, ext. 204

- **Jewish Federation of Winnipeg Annual General Meeting 2018**
Location: Winnipeg, MB
Sponsor/Contact: The Centre for Israel & Jewish Affairs
#300C, 123 Doncaster St.
Winnipeg, MB R3N 2B2
204-477-7400
E-mail: info@jewishwinnipeg.org
URL: www.jewishwinnipeg.org
Scope: Local
Contact Information: Coordinator, Events: Jessica Kraut, E-mail: jkraut@jewishwinnipeg.org, Phone: 204-478-8593

- **Karate BC Annual General Meeting 2018**
Location: British Columbia
Sponsor/Contact: Karate BC
Fortius Athlete Development Centre, Sydney Landing
#2002A, 3713 Kensington Ave.
Burnaby, BC V5B 0A7
604-333-3610; *Fax:* 604-333-3612
Toll-Free: 855-806-8126
URL: www.karatebc.org
Scope: Provincial

- **Kidney Cancer Canada 2018 Patient & Caregiver Forum**
Sponsor/Contact: Kidney Cancer Canada Association
#226, 4936 Yonge St.
Toronto, ON M2N 6S3
416-603-0277; *Fax:* 416-603-0277
Toll-Free: 866-598-7166
E-mail: info@kidneycancercanada.ca
URL: www.kidneycancercanada.ca
Scope: National

- **Kidney Foundation of Canada 2018 Kidney Care Conference**
Sponsor/Contact: Kidney Foundation of Canada
#310, 5160, boul Decarie
Montréal, QC H3X 2H9
514-369-4806; *Fax:* 514-369-2472
Toll-Free: 800-361-7494
E-mail: info@kidney.ca
URL: www.kidney.ca
Scope: National

- **Kin Canada 2018 National Convention**
Location: Sarnia, ON
Sponsor/Contact: Kin Canada
P.O. Box 3460
1920 Rogers Dr.
Cambridge, ON N3H 5C6
519-653-1920; *Fax:* 519-650-1091
Toll-Free: 800-742-5546
E-mail: kinhq@kincanada.ca
URL: www.kincanada.ca
Scope: National

- **Kitchener-Waterloo Chamber Music Society 2018 Annual General Meeting**
Location: The Music Room
Waterloo, ON
Sponsor/Contact: Kitchener-Waterloo Chamber Music Society
57 Young St. West
Waterloo, ON N2L 2Z4

519-886-1673
E-mail: kwcms@yahoo.ca
URL: www.k-wcms.com

- **Knights of Columbus 136th Supreme Convention 2018**
Sponsor/Contact: Knights of Columbus
1 Columbus Plaza
New Haven, CT 06510
203-752-4000
URL: www.kofc.org
Scope: International
Contact Information: Phone: 203-752-4000

- **Landscape NL Annual General Meeting 2018**
Sponsor/Contact: Landscape Newfoundland & Labrador
P.O. Box 8062
St. John's, NL A1B 3M9
Fax: 866-833-8603
Toll-Free: 855-872-8722
E-mail: lnl@landscapenl.com
URL: members.landscapenl.com
Scope: Provincial

- **Law Union of Ontario 2018 Annual Conference**
Location: Ontario
Sponsor/Contact: Law Union of Ontario
31 Prince Arthur Ave.
Toronto, ON M5R 1B2
416-927-9662; *Fax:* 416-960-5456
E-mail: law.union.of.ontario@gmail.com
URL: www.lawunion.ca
Scope: Provincial

- **Lethbridge Symphony Orchestra 2018 Annual General Meeting**
Sponsor/Contact: Lethbridge Symphony Orchestra
P.O. Box 1101
Lethbridge, AB T1J 4A2
403-328-6808; *Fax:* 403-380-4418
Toll-Free: 855-328-6808
E-mail: info@lethbridgesymphony.org
URL: www.lethbridgesymphony.org
Scope: Local

- **Leucan - Association pour les enfants atteints de cancer Assemblée générale annuelle 2018**
Sponsor/Contact: Leucan - Association pour les enfants atteints de cancer
#300, 550, av Beaumont
Montréal, QC H3N 1V1
514-731-3696; *Fax:* 514-731-2667
Toll-Free: 800-361-9643
URL: www.leucan.qc.ca
Scope: Provincial

- **Library Boards Association of Nova Scotia Annual Conference 2018**
Sponsor/Contact: Library Boards Association of Nova Scotia
135 North Park St.
Bridgewater, NS B4V 9B3
902-543-2548
URL: www.standupforlibraries.ca
Scope: Provincial

- **Licensed Practical Nurses Association of BC AGM 2018**
Location: British Columbia
Sponsor/Contact: Licensed Practical Nurses Association of British Columbia
#211, 3030 Lincoln Ave.
Coquitlam, BC V3B 6B4
604-434-1972
E-mail: info@lpnabc.ca
URL: www.lpnabc.ca
Scope: Provincial

- **Local Government Administrators of the Northwest Territories Conference & Annual General Meeting**
Sponsor/Contact: Local Government Administrators of the Northwest Territories
P.O. Box 2083
5018 - 52nd St., 2nd Fl.
Yellowknife, NT X1A 2P6
867-765-5630; Fax: 867-765-5635
E-mail: information@lgant.com
URL: www.lgant.com
Scope: Provincial

- **Manitoba Association of Health Information Providers Annual General Meeting 2018**
Location: Manitoba
Sponsor/Contact: Manitoba Association of Health Information Providers
c/o Neil John Maclean Health Sciences Library, University of Manitoba
727 McDermott Ave.
Winnipeg, MB R3E 3P5
Fax: 204-789-3922
E-mail: contact.mahip@gmail.com
URL: mahip.chla-absc.ca
Scope: Provincial

- **Manitoba Association of Library Technicians 2018 Annual General Meeting**
Location: Manitoba
Sponsor/Contact: Manitoba Association of Library Technicians
P.O. Box 1872
Winnipeg, MB R3C 3R1
E-mail: malt.mb.ca@gmail.com
URL: www.malt.mb.ca
Scope: Provincial

- **Manitoba Association of Medical Radiation Technologists 2018 Annual General Conference**
Sponsor/Contact: Manitoba Association of Medical Radiation Technologists
Sargent Professional Centre
#202, 819 Sargent Ave.
Winnipeg, MB R3E 0B9
204-774-5346
E-mail: admin@mamrt.ca
URL: www.mamrt.ca
Scope: Provincial
Purpose: A conference providing educational sessions, held each spring

- **Manitoba Beef Producers 2018 39th Annual General Meeting**
Location: Manitoba
Sponsor/Contact: Manitoba Beef Producers
#220, 530 Century St.
Winnipeg, MB R3H 0Y4
204-772-4542; Fax: 204-774-3264
Toll-Free: 800-772-0458
URL: www.mbbeef.ca
Scope: Provincial

- **Manitoba Dental Assistants Association 2018 Annual General Meeting**
Location: Manitoba
Sponsor/Contact: Manitoba Dental Assistants Association
#142, 99 Scurfield Blvd.
Winnipeg, MB R3Y 1Y1
204-586-7378; Fax: 204-489-8033
Toll-Free: 877-475-6322
E-mail: mdaa@mdaa.ca
URL: www.mdaa.ca
Scope: Provincial

- **Manitoba Environmental Industries Association 2018 Annual General Meeting**
Location: Manitoba
Sponsor/Contact: Manitoba Environmental Industries Association Inc.
#100, 62 Albert St.
Winnipeg, MB R3B 1E9
204-783-7090; Fax: 204-783-6501
E-mail: admin@meia.mb.ca
URL: www.meia.mb.ca
Scope: Provincial
Purpose: A gathering of members to address the business of the association & to provide networking opportunities

- **Manitoba Freestyle Ski Association Annual General Meeting 2018**
Sponsor/Contact: Manitoba Freestyle Ski Association
145 Pacific Ave.
Winnipeg, MB R3B 2Z6
204-795-9754
E-mail: info@mbfreestyle.com
URL: www.mbfreestyle.com
Scope: Provincial

- **Manitoba Heavy Construction Association 2018 Expo**
Location: Manitoba
Sponsor/Contact: Manitoba Heavy Construction Association
#3, 1680 Ellice Ave.
Winnipeg, MB R3G 0Z2
204-947-1379; Fax: 204-943-2279
E-mail: info@mhca.mb.ca
URL: www.mhca.mb.ca
Scope: Provincial
Purpose: An educational event to help train & educate workers in the heavy construction industry
Contact Information: Manager, Operations: Christine Miller, Phone: 204-947-1379

- **Manitoba Hotel Association & Manitoba Restaurant & Foodservices Association 2018 Tradeshow**
Location: Manitoba
Sponsor/Contact: Manitoba Restaurant & Food Services Association
103-D Scurfield Blvd.
Winnipeg, MB R3Y 1M6
204-783-9955; Fax: 204-783-9909
Toll-Free: 877-296-2909
E-mail: info@mrfa.mb.ca
URL: www.mrfa.mb.ca
Scope: Provincial

- **Manitoba Hotel Association Convention & Tradeshow 2018**
Location: Manitoba
Sponsor/Contact: Manitoba Hotel Association
#200, 1534 Gamble Pl.
Winnipeg, MB
204-942-0671; Fax: 204-942-6719
Toll-Free: 888-859-9976
URL: www.manitobahotelassociation.ca
Scope: Provincial
Purpose: Presentations from government ministers, educational speakers, & others from the hospitality industry

- **Manitoba Institute of Agrologists 2018 68th Annual General Meeting & Professional Development Event**
Location: Manitoba
Sponsor/Contact: Manitoba Institute of Agrologists
#201, 38 Dafoe Ave.
Winnipeg, MB R3T 2N2
204-275-3721; Fax: 888-315-6661
E-mail: agrologist@mia.mb.ca
URL: www.mia.mb.ca
Scope: Provincial
Purpose: The business meeting of the institute, plus presentations & networking opportunities

- **Manitoba Magazine Publishers Association 2018 Annual General Meeting**
Sponsor/Contact: Manitoba Magazine Publishers Association
#606 - 100 Arthur St.
Winnipeg, MB R3B 1H3
204-942-0189; Fax: 204-257-2467
E-mail: exedir@manitobamagazines.ca
URL: manitobamagazines.ca
Scope: Provincial

- **Manitoba Operating Room Nurses Association Annual Meeting 2018**
Sponsor/Contact: Manitoba Operating Room Nurses Association
URL: www.ornac.ca/en/morna
Scope: Provincial

- **Manitoba Percheron & Belgian Club 2018 Annual Meeting**
Location: Manitoba
Sponsor/Contact: Manitoba Percheron & Belgian Club
c/o Brenda Hunter
P.O. Box 159
Kenton, MB R0M 0Z0
204-764-3789
E-mail: bhunterphoto@gmail.com
URL: www.manpercheronbelgianclub.com
Scope: Provincial

- **Manitoba Planning Conference 2018**
Sponsor/Contact: Manitoba Professional Planners Institute
137 Bannatyne Ave., 2nd Fl.
Winnipeg, MB R3B 0R3
204-943-3637; Fax: 204-925-4624
E-mail: mppiadmin@shaw.ca
URL: www.mppi.mb.ca
Scope: Provincial

- **Manitoba Provincial Handgun Association Annual General Meeting 2018**
Sponsor/Contact: Manitoba Provincial Handgun Association
P.O. Box 314 Stn. Corydon Ave.
Winnipeg, MB R3M 3S7
URL: www.handgunmb.ca
Scope: Provincial

- **Manitoba School Library Association 2018 Annual General Meeting**
Location: Manitoba
Sponsor/Contact: Manitoba School Library Association
307 Shaftesbury Blvd.
Winnipeg, MB R3P 0L9
URL: www.manitobaschoollibraries.ca
Scope: Provincial

- **Manitoba Teachers' Society 2018 Annual General Meeting**
Location: Manitoba
Sponsor/Contact: Manitoba Teachers' Society
McMaster House
191 Harcourt St.
Winnipeg, MB R3J 3H2
204-888-7961; Fax: 204-831-0877
Toll-Free: 800-262-8803
URL: www.mbteach.org
Scope: Provincial

- **Manitoba's Credit Unions Conference and AGM 2018**
Sponsor/Contact: Credit Union Central of Manitoba
#400, 317 Donald St.
Winnipeg, MB R3B 2H6
204-985-4700; Fax: 204-949-0217
E-mail: cuinfo@cucm.org
URL: www.creditunion.mb.ca
Scope: Provincial

- **Marine Renewables Canada 2018 Annual Conference**
Sponsor/Contact: Marine Renewables Canada
P.O. Box 34066
1690 Hollis St., 10th Fl.
Halifax, NS B3J 3S1
URL: www.marinerenewables.ca
Scope: National
Purpose: Multiple networking opportunities to meet leaders and experts from business, government, and academia that will help build connections and support emerging industry needs.

- **Maritime Angus Field Day and Junior Show 2018**
Sponsor/Contact: Maritime Aberdeen Angus Association
c/o Betty Lou Scott
840 Mount Thom Rd.
Upper Mount Thom, NS B0K 1P0
902-925-2057; Fax: 902-925-2265
URL: maritimeangus.blogspot.ca
Scope: Provincial

- **Massage Therapist Association of Saskatchewan 5th Annual Research Symposium 2018**
Location: Saskatchewan
Sponsor/Contact: Massage Therapist Association of Saskatchewan
#16, 1724 Quebec Ave.
Saskatoon, SK S7K 1V9
306-384-7077; Fax: 306-384-7175
E-mail: mtas@sasktel.net
URL: www.saskmassagetherapy.com
Scope: Provincial
Purpose: Includes information & research on massage therapy from keynote presenters

- **Medical Council of Canada 2018 Annual Meeting**
Sponsor/Contact: Medical Council of Canada
1021 Thomas Spratt Pl.
Ottawa, ON K1G 5L5
613-521-6012; Fax: 613-248-5234
E-mail: service@mcc.ca
URL: www.mcc.ca
Scope: National

- **Microscopical Society of Canada 45th Annual Meeting**
Sponsor/Contact: Microscopical Society of Canada
c/o Line Mongeon, McGill University, Strathcona Bldg., #1-48
Montréal, QC H3A 2B2
514-398-2878; Fax: 514-398-5047
URL: www.msc-smc.org
Scope: National

- **Mining Society of Nova Scotia 131st Annual Meeting 2018**
Location: Nova Scotia
Sponsor/Contact: Mining Society of Nova Scotia
88 Leeside Dr.
Sydney, NS B1R 1S6

Conferences & Conventions Index

902-567-2147; *Fax:* 902-567-2147
URL: www.miningsocietyns.ca
Scope: Provincial

• **Model Aeronautics Association of Canada 2018 Annual Meeting**
Sponsor/Contact: Model Aeronautics Association of Canada Inc.
#9, 5100 South Service Rd.
Burlington, ON L7L 6A5
905-632-9808; *Fax:* 905-632-3304
Toll-Free: 855-359-6222
URL: www.maac.ca
Scope: National

• **Motion Picture Theatre Association of Central Canada 2018 Annual General Meeting**
Sponsor/Contact: Motion Picture Theatre Association of Central Canada
URL: www.mptaccentral.ca
Scope: Provincial

• **Municipal Equipment & Operations Association (Ontario) 2018 Annual Municipal & Contractor Fall Equipment Show**
Sponsor/Contact: Municipal Equipment & Operations Association (Ontario) Inc.
38 Summit Ave.
Kitchener, ON N2M 4W2
519-741-2600; *Fax:* 519-741-2750
E-mail: admin@meoa.org
URL: www.meoa.org
Scope: Provincial
Purpose: An opportunity for suppliers to promote & demonstrate their products & services

• **Municipal Equipment & Operations Association (Ontario) Inc. 2018 Annual Professional Development Day**
Sponsor/Contact: Municipal Equipment & Operations Association (Ontario) Inc.
38 Summit Ave.
Kitchener, ON N2M 4W2
519-741-2600; *Fax:* 519-741-2750
E-mail: admin@meoa.org
URL: www.meoa.org
Scope: Provincial
Purpose: A learning opportunity for members of the association

• **Municipal Equipment & Operations Association (Ontario) Inc. 2018 Annual Spring Meeting**
Sponsor/Contact: Municipal Equipment & Operations Association (Ontario) Inc.
38 Summit Ave.
Kitchener, ON N2M 4W2
519-741-2600; *Fax:* 519-741-2750
E-mail: admin@meoa.org
URL: www.meoa.org
Scope: Provincial
Purpose: An event to elect the new executive, to address the business of the association, to participate in a plant tour, to hear guest speakers, & to attend educational presentations

• **Municipal Waste Association 2018 Annual General Meeting**
Location: Ontario
Sponsor/Contact: Municipal Waste Association
P.O. Box 1894
Guelph, ON N1H 7A1
519-823-1990; *Fax:* 519-823-0084
URL: www.municipalwaste.ca
Scope: Provincial
Purpose: A yearly event featuring a business meeting, trade show, & networking opportunities

• **Municipalities Newfoundland & Labrador Municipal Symposium**
Location: Gander, NL
Sponsor/Contact: Municipalities Newfoundland & Labrador
460 Torbay Rd.
St. John's, NL A1A 5J3
709-753-6820; *Fax:* 709-738-0071
Toll-Free: 800-440-6536
E-mail: info@municipalnl.ca
URL: www.municipalitiesnl.com
Scope: Provincial
Purpose: Held each spring in Gander, NL.
Contact Information: Contact, Christine Carter, E-mail: ccarter@municipalnl.ca.

• **National United Professional Association of Trained Homeopaths Conference**
Sponsor/Contact: National United Professional Association of Trained Homeopaths
#102, 2680 Matheson Blvd.
Mississauga, ON L4W 0A5
905-267-8539; *Fax:* 905-267-3401
E-mail: info@nupath.org
URL: www.nupath.org
Scope: National

• **National Wildlife Federation 81st Annual Meeting 2018**
Location: , USA
Sponsor/Contact: National Wildlife Federation
P.O. Box 1583
Merrifield, VA 22116-1583
Toll-Free: 800-822-9919
URL: www.nwf.org
Scope: International
Contact Information: Phone: 1-800-822-9919

• **Nature Canada 2018 Annual General Meeting**
Sponsor/Contact: Nature Canada
#300, 75 Albert St.
Ottawa, ON K1P 5E7
613-562-3447
Toll-Free: 800-267-4088
E-mail: info@naturecanada.ca
URL: www.naturecanada.ca
Scope: National
Purpose: The annual meeting usually features the election of the Board of Directors, the presentation of Nature Canada awards, & the adoption of resolutions
Contact Information: Executive Assistant & Manager, Office Operations: Marie du Plessis, Phone: 800-267-4088, ext. 298, E-mail: mduplessis@naturecanada.ca

• **Nature Manitoba 2018 Annual General Meeting**
Sponsor/Contact: Nature Manitoba
Hammond Building
#401, 63 Albert St.
Winnipeg, MB R3B 1G4
204-943-9029; *Fax:* 204-943-9029
E-mail: info@naturemanitoba.ca
URL: www.naturemanitoba.ca
Scope: Provincial
Purpose: An opportunity for Nature Manitoba members to discuss & advance policy positions about nature in Manitoba

• **Nature Nova Scotia 2018 Annual General Meeting & Conference**
Location: Nova Scotia
Sponsor/Contact: Nature Nova Scotia (Federation of Nova Scotia Naturalists)
c/o Nova Scotia Museum of Natural History
1747 Summer St.
Halifax, NS B3H 3A6
902-582-7176
E-mail: doug@fundymud.com
URL: www.naturens.ca
Scope: Provincial
Purpose: A weekend event, with an annual meeting featuring reports on the past year's activities to the membership, plus educational talks & field trips

• **New Brunswick Environmental Network 2018 Annual General Meeting**
Location: New Brunswick
Sponsor/Contact: New Brunswick Environmental Network
167 Creek Rd.
Waterford, NB E4E 4L7
506-433-6101; *Fax:* 506-433-6111
E-mail: nben@nben.ca
URL: www.nben.ca
Scope: Provincial
Purpose: Featuring the election of a Steering Committee by member groups

• **New Brunswick Institute of Agrologists 2018 Annual Meeting**
Location: New Brunswick
Sponsor/Contact: New Brunswick Institute of Agrologists
P.O. Box 3479 Stn. B
Fredericton, NB E3B 5H2
506-459-5536; *Fax:* 506-454-7837
URL: www.ianbia.com
Scope: Provincial

• **New Brunswick Potato Conference & Trade Show 2018**
Location: New Brunswick
Sponsor/Contact: Potatoes New Brunswick
P.O. Box 7878
Grand Falls, NB E3Z 3E8
506-473-3036; *Fax:* 506-473-4647
E-mail: gfpotato@potatoesnb.com
URL: www.potatoesnb.com
Scope: Provincial
Purpose: An event for New Brunswick potato growers & interested stakeholders to present happening in the industry
Contact Information: E-mail: gfpotato@potatoesnb.com

• **Newfoundland & Labrador Construction Association 2018 Annual Awards Gala**
Location: Newfoundland & Labrador
Sponsor/Contact: Newfoundland & Labrador Construction Association
#202, 397 Stavanger Dr.
St. John's, NL A1A 0A1
709-753-8920; *Fax:* 709-754-3968
E-mail: info@nfld.com
URL: www.nlca.ca
Scope: Provincial
Purpose: An awards presentation to honour industry professionals, featuring a keynote address to delegates

• **Newfoundland & Labrador Construction Association 2018 Annual Conference & General Meeting**
Location: Newfoundland & Labrador
Sponsor/Contact: Newfoundland & Labrador Construction Association
#202, 397 Stavanger Dr.
St. John's, NL A1A 0A1
709-753-8920; *Fax:* 709-754-3968
E-mail: info@nfld.com
URL: www.nlca.ca
Scope: Provincial
Purpose: Sessions & keynote addresses of interest to persons such as general, electrical, & mechanical contractors, manufacturers, suppliers, safety professionals, engineers, training providers, LEED accredited professionals, & municipalities

• **Newfoundland & Labrador Federation of Labour Annual Conference 2018**
Location: Newfoundland & Labrador
Sponsor/Contact: Newfoundland & Labrador Federation of Labour
NAPE Bldg.
P.O. Box 8597 Stn. A
330 Portugal Cove Pl., 2nd Fl.
St. John's, NL A1B 3P2
709-754-1660; *Fax:* 709-754-1220
E-mail: fed@nlfl.nf.ca
URL: www.nlfl.nf.ca
Scope: Provincial
Contact Information: Executive Secretary: Jennifer Rideout, E-mail: jrideout@nlfl.nf.ca

• **Newfoundland & Labrador Health Libraries Association (NLHLA) Annual Conference & Annual General Meeting 2018**
Location: Newfoundland & Labrador
Sponsor/Contact: Newfoundland & Labrador Health Libraries Association
c/o Health Sciences Library, Memorial University of Newfoundland
St. John's, NL A1B 3V6
E-mail: nlhla@chla-absc.ca
URL: nlhla.chla-absc.ca
Scope: Provincial

• **Newfoundland & Labrador Library Association Annual Conference & Annual General Meeting 2018**
Location: Newfoundland & Labrador
Sponsor/Contact: Newfoundland & Labrador Library Association
P.O. Box 23192 Stn. Churchill Square
St. John's, NL A1B 4J9
URL: www.nlla.ca
Scope: Provincial
Purpose: An annual spring meeting, presenting opportunities to learn about new services, current issues, & research in Newfoundland & Labrador libraries

• **Newfoundland Equestrian Association Annual General Meeting 2018**
Sponsor/Contact: Newfoundland Equestrian Association
P.O. Box 372 Stn. C
St. John's, NL A1C 5J9
URL: equestriannl.ca
Scope: Provincial

• **Niagara Support Services 2018 65th Annual General Meeting**
Location: Ontario
Sponsor/Contact: Niagara Support Services
P.O. Box 190
120 Canby St.
Port Robinson, ON L0S 1K0
905-384-1172; *Fax:* 905-384-2691
E-mail: nssinfo@ntc-nss.com
URL: www.ntc-nss.com
Scope: Local

Conferences & Conventions Index

- **North American Broadcasters Association 2018 Annual General Meeting & Conference**
Sponsor/Contact: North American Broadcasters Association
P.O. Box 500 Stn. A
#6C300, 25 John St.
Toronto, ON M5V 3G7
416-598-9877
E-mail: contact@nabanet.com
URL: www.nabanet.com
Scope: International

- **North Central Local Government Association 2018 Convention**
Sponsor/Contact: North Central Local Government Association
c/o Maxine Koppe
#206, 155 George St.
Prince George, BC V2L 1P8
250-564-6585; Fax: 250-564-6514
URL: www.nclga.ca
Scope: Local

- **Northern Alberta Health Libraries Association Annual General Meeting 2018**
Location: Alberta
Sponsor/Contact: Northern Alberta Health Libraries Association
c/o J.W. Scott Health Sciences Library, University of Alberta
2K3.28 Walter MacKenzie Ctr.
Edmonton, AB T6G 2R7
E-mail: contact.nahla@gmail.com
URL: nahla.chla-absc.ca
Scope: Provincial

- **Northern Alberta Health Libraries Association Research Exposition**
Location: Alberta
Sponsor/Contact: Northern Alberta Health Libraries Association
c/o J.W. Scott Health Sciences Library, University of Alberta
2K3.28 Walter MacKenzie Ctr.
Edmonton, AB T6G 2R7
E-mail: contact.nahla@gmail.com
URL: nahla.chla-absc.ca
Scope: Provincial
Purpose: An annual event that showcases recent & in-progress research by members through a series of brief presentations on a wide range of topics

- **Northern Alberta Health Libraries Association TRENDS Mini Conference 2018**
Location: Alberta
Sponsor/Contact: Northern Alberta Health Libraries Association
c/o J.W. Scott Health Sciences Library, University of Alberta
2K3.28 Walter MacKenzie Ctr.
Edmonton, AB T6G 2R7
E-mail: contact.nahla@gmail.com
URL: nahla.chla-absc.ca
Scope: Provincial
Purpose: An annual, half-day conference that features keynote speakers

- **Northern Ontario Hockey Association Annual General Meeting 2018**
Location: Ontario
Sponsor/Contact: Northern Ontario Hockey Association
110 Lakeshore Dr.
North Bay, ON P1A 2A8
705-474-8851; Fax: 705-474-6019
E-mail: noha@noha.on.ca
URL: www.noha.on.ca

Scope: Local
Contact Information: Executive Director: Jason Marchand, E-mail: jmarchand@noha.on.ca

- **Northwestern Ontario Associated Chambers of Commerce 83rd AGM**
Sponsor/Contact: Northwestern Ontario Associated Chambers of Commerce
#102, 200 Syndicate Ave. South
Thunder Bay, ON P7E 1C9
807-624-2626; Fax: 807-622-7752
URL: www.noacc.ca
Scope: Local

- **Northwestern Ontario Municipal Association 2018 Annual Conference & AGM**
Location: Ontario
Sponsor/Contact: Northwestern Ontario Municipal Association
P.O. Box 10308
Thunder Bay, ON P7B 6T8
807-683-6662
E-mail: admin@noma.on.ca
URL: www.noma.on.ca
Scope: Local
Contact Information: Phone: 807-683-6662, E-mail: admin@noma.on.ca

- **Nova Scotia Association of Medical Radiation Technologists 2018 Annual Fall Education Seminar**
Location: Nova Scotia
Sponsor/Contact: Nova Scotia Association of Medical Radiation Technologists
Park Lane Terraces
P.O. Box 142
#502, 5657 Spring Garden Rd.
Halifax, NS B3J 3R4
902-434-6525; Fax: 902-832-8676
Toll-Free: 866-788-6525
E-mail: info@nsamrt.ca
URL: www.nsamrt.ca
Scope: Provincial
Purpose: Held the weekend before Medical Radiation Technologists Week, the annual continuing education meeting consists of talks related to the disciplines of radiation therapy, nuclear medicine, & radiological technology, as well as a keynote address related to all medical radiation technology disciplines

- **Nova Scotia Association of Medical Radiation Technologists 78th Annual General Conference 2018**
Sponsor/Contact: Nova Scotia Association of Medical Radiation Technologists
Park Lane Terraces
P.O. Box 142
#502, 5657 Spring Garden Rd.
Halifax, NS B3J 3R4
902-434-6525; Fax: 902-832-8676
Toll-Free: 866-788-6525
E-mail: info@nsamrt.ca
URL: www.nsamrt.ca
Scope: Provincial

- **Nova Scotia Automobile Dealers' Association AGM 2018**
Location: Nova Scotia
Sponsor/Contact: Nova Scotia Automobile Dealers' Association
#700, 6009 Quinpool Rd.
Halifax, NS B3K 5S3
902-425-2445; Fax: 902-425-2441
E-mail: info@nsada.ca
URL: www.nsada.ca

Scope: Provincial
Purpose: An event for association members from across Nova Scotia

- **Nova Scotia Federation of Home & School Associations 2018 Annual General Meeting**
Sponsor/Contact: Nova Scotia Federation of Home & School Associations
P.O. Box 28123 Stn. Tacoma Dr.
Dartmouth, NS B2W 6E2
902-266-9507
Toll-Free: 800-214-9507
E-mail: nsfhsapresident@gmail.com
URL: www.nsfhsa.org
Scope: Provincial

- **Nova Scotia Ground Water Association 2018 Annual General Meeting**
Location: Nova Scotia
Sponsor/Contact: Nova Scotia Ground Water Association
#417, 3 - 644 Portland St.
Dartmouth, NS B2W 2M3
Fax: 902-435-0089
Toll-Free: 888-242-4440
E-mail: nsgwa@ns.aliantzinc.ca
URL: www.nsgwa.ca
Scope: Provincial
Purpose: A yearly gathering featuring divisional meetings, presentations, & association business

- **Nova Scotia Library Association 2018 Annual Conference**
Sponsor/Contact: Nova Scotia Library Association
c/o Nova Scotia Provincial Library
6016 University Ave., 5th Fl.
Halifax, NS B3H 1W4
URL: www.nsla.ns.ca
Scope: Provincial
Purpose: Hosted by Cumberland Regional Library in the autumn
Contact Information: E-mail: conference@nsla.ns.ca

- **Nunavut Economic Developers Association 2018 Annual Conference**
Sponsor/Contact: Nunavut Economic Developers Association
P.O. Box 1990
1104B Inuksugait Plaza, Phase II
Iqaluit, NU X0A 0H0
867-979-4620; Fax: 867-979-4622
URL: www.nunavuteda.com
Scope: Provincial

- **Nurse Practitioners' Association of Ontario Annual Conference 2018**
Location: Ontario
Sponsor/Contact: Nurse Practitioners' Association of Ontario
#1801, 1 Yonge St.
Toronto, ON M5E 1W7
416-593-9779; Fax: 416-369-0515
E-mail: admin@npao.org
URL: www.npao.org
Scope: Provincial

- **Older Adult Centres' Association of Ontario Annual Conference 2018**
Location: Ontario
Sponsor/Contact: Older Adult Centres' Association of Ontario
P.O. Box 65
Caledon East, ON L7C 3L8
905-584-8125; Fax: 905-584-8126
Toll-Free: 866-835-7693
E-mail: admin@oacao.org
URL: www.oacao.org

Scope: Provincial

- **Ontario Association for Behaviour Analysis Annual Conference 2018**
Location: Ontario
Sponsor/Contact: Ontario Association for Behaviour Analysis
#413, 283 Danforth Ave.
Toronto, ON M4K 1N2
E-mail: contact@ontaba.org
URL: www.ontaba.org
Scope: Provincial

- **Ontario Association for Marriage & Family Therapy 2018 Annual General Meeting**
Sponsor/Contact: Ontario Association for Marriage & Family Therapy
P.O. Box 693
Tottenham, ON L0G 1W0
905-936-3338; Fax: 905-936-9192
Toll-Free: 800-267-2638
E-mail: admin@oamft.com
URL: rmft.oamft.com
Scope: Provincial

- **Ontario Association of Broadcasters' 2018 Conference & AGM**
Location: Ontario
Sponsor/Contact: Ontario Association of Broadcasters
P.O. Box 54040
5762 Hwy. 7 East
Markham, ON L3P 7Y4
905-554-2730; Fax: 905-554-2731
URL: www.oab.ca
Scope: Provincial
Anticipated Attendance: 300+

- **Ontario Association of Consultants, Counsellors, Psychometrists & Psychotherapists 40th Annual Conference & AGM**
Sponsor/Contact: Ontario Association of Consultants, Counsellors, Psychometrists & Psychotherapists
#410, 586 Eglinton Ave. East
Toronto, ON M4P 1P2
416-298-7333; Fax: 416-298-9593
Toll-Free: 888-622-2779
E-mail: oaccpp@oaccpp.ca
URL: www.oaccpp.ca
Scope: Provincial

- **Ontario Association of Geographic & Environmental Educators 2018 Fall Conference**
Sponsor/Contact: Ontario Association for Geographic & Environmental Education
#202, 10 Morrow Ave.
Toronto, ON M6R 2J1
416-538-1650; Fax: 416-489-1713
URL: www.oagee.org
Scope: Provincial

- **Ontario Association of Geographic & Environmental Educators 2018 Spring Conference**
Sponsor/Contact: Ontario Association for Geographic & Environmental Education
#202, 10 Morrow Ave.
Toronto, ON M6R 2J1
416-538-1650; Fax: 416-489-1713
URL: www.oagee.org
Scope: Provincial

- **Ontario Association of Library Technicians / Association des bibliotechniciens de l'Ontario 2018 45th Annual Conference**
Sponsor/Contact: Ontario Association of Library Technicians

Conferences & Conventions Index

Abbey Market
P.O. Box 76010
1500 Upper Middle Rd. West
Oakville, ON L6M 3H5
E-mail: info@oaltabo.on.ca
URL: oaltabo.on.ca
Scope: Provincial
Purpose: Featuring educational sessions, speeches, the annual business meeting, & award presentations

- **Ontario Association of Medical Radiation Sciences 2018 Annual General Conference**
Location: Ontario
Sponsor/Contact: Ontario Association of Medical Radiation Sciences
#415A, 175 Longwood Rd. South
Hamilton, ON L8P 0A1
289-674-0034; Fax: 289-674-0037
Toll-Free: 800-387-4674
URL: www.oamrs.org
Scope: Provincial

- **Ontario Association of Naturopathic Doctors 2018 Convention & Tradeshow**
Sponsor/Contact: Ontario Association of Naturopathic Doctors
#603, 789 Don Mills Rd.
Toronto, ON M3C 1T5
416-233-2001; Fax: 416-233-2924
Toll-Free: 877-628-7284
E-mail: info@oand.org
URL: www.oand.org
Scope: Provincial

- **Ontario Branch International Dyslexia Association Annual Conference**
Location: Ontario
Sponsor/Contact: International Dyslexia Association
1785 Foleyet Cres.
Pickering, ON L1V 2X8
416-716-9296
URL: idaontario.com
Scope: Provincial

- **Ontario Camps Association 2018 Annual Conference**
Location: Ontario
Sponsor/Contact: Ontario Camps Association
70 Martin Ross Ave.
Toronto, ON M3J 2L4
416-485-0425; Fax: 416-485-0422
E-mail: info@ontariocamps.ca
URL: www.ontariocamps.ca
Scope: Provincial

- **Ontario College & University Library Association Annual General Meeting 2018**
Location: Ontario
Sponsor/Contact: Ontario College & University Library Association
c/o Ontario Library Association
2 Toronto St., 3rd Fl.
Toronto, ON M5C 2B6
416-363-3388; Fax: 416-941-9581
Toll-Free: 866-873-9867
E-mail: info@accessola.com
URL: www.accessola.org
Scope: Provincial

- **Ontario College of Teachers 2018 Annual Meeting of Members**
Sponsor/Contact: Ontario College of Teachers
101 Bloor St. West
Toronto, ON M5S 0A1
416-961-8800; Fax: 416-961-8822
Toll-Free: 888-534-2222
E-mail: info@oct.ca
URL: www.oct.ca
Scope: Provincial
Purpose: Presentations of interest to teachers

- **Ontario Community Justice Association 38th Annual Conference 2018**
Sponsor/Contact: Ontario Community Justice Association
416-304-1974
Scope: Provincial

- **Ontario Community Support Association 2018 Annual Conference**
Location: Ontario
Sponsor/Contact: Ontario Community Support Association
#104, 970 Lawrence Ave. West
Toronto, ON M6A 3B6
416-256-3010; Fax: 416-256-3021
Toll-Free: 800-267-6272
E-mail: reception@ocsa.on.ca
URL: www.ocsa.on.ca
Scope: Provincial

- **Ontario Cycling Association Annual General Meeting 2018**
Sponsor/Contact: Ontario Cycling Association
#2, 2015 Pan Am Blvd.
Milton, ON L9T 8Y9
416-855-1717
URL: www.ontariocycling.org
Scope: Provincial

- **Ontario English Catholic Teachers' Association 2018 Annual General Meeting**
Location: Ontario
Sponsor/Contact: Ontario English Catholic Teachers' Association (CLC)
#400, 65 St. Clair Ave. East
Toronto, ON M4T 2Y8
416-925-2493; Fax: 416-925-7764
Toll-Free: 800-268-7230
E-mail: contact@oecta.on.ca
URL: www.oecta.on.ca
Scope: Provincial
Purpose: Delegates attend to the business of the association, elect Provincial Executive members, & listen to presentations by guest speakers

- **Ontario Environment Network AGM 2018**
Sponsor/Contact: Ontario Environmental Network
P.O. Box 192
Georgetown, ON L7G 4T1
E-mail: oen@oen.ca
URL: www.oen.ca
Scope: Provincial

- **Ontario Equestrian Federation Annual General Meeting 2018**
Sponsor/Contact: Ontario Equestrian Federation
#201, 1 West Pearce St.
Richmond Hill, ON L4B 3K3
905-709-6545; Fax: 905-709-1867
Toll-Free: 877-441-7112
E-mail: horse@horse.on.ca
URL: www.horse.on.ca
Scope: Provincial

- **Ontario Federation of Agriculture 2018 Annual General Meeting**
Sponsor/Contact: Ontario Federation of Agriculture
Ontario AgriCentre
#206, 100 Stone Rd. West
Guelph, ON N1G 5L3
519-821-8883; Fax: 519-821-8810
Toll-Free: 800-668-3276
URL: www.ofa.on.ca
Scope: Provincial

- **Ontario Field Ornithologists 2018 Annual Convention**
Location: Ontario
Sponsor/Contact: Ontario Field Ornithologists
P.O. Box 116 Stn. F
Toronto, ON M4Y 2L4
E-mail: membership@ofo.ca
URL: www.ofo.ca
Scope: Provincial
Purpose: Activities include guest speakers, birding displays, field trips, & a social event

- **Ontario Health Libraries Association Annual General Meeting 2018**
Location: Ontario
Sponsor/Contact: Ontario Health Libraries Association
c/o Ontario Library Association
2 Toronto St., 3rd Fl.
Toronto, ON M5C 2B6
416-363-3388; Fax: 416-941-9581
Toll-Free: 866-873-9867
URL: www.ohla.on.ca
Scope: Provincial
Purpose: Held during OLA's annual Super Conference

- **Ontario Home Builders' Association Annual Conference 2018**
Location: Ontario
Sponsor/Contact: Ontario Home Builders' Association
#101, 20 Upjohn Rd.
Toronto, ON M3B 2V9
416-443-1545; Fax: 416-443-9982
Toll-Free: 800-387-0109
URL: www.ohba.ca
Scope: Provincial
Contact Information: Manager, Business: Sajida Jiwani, E-mail: sjiwani@ohba.ca

- **Ontario Home Economics Association 2018 Conference & AGM**
Location: Ontario
Sponsor/Contact: Ontario Home Economics Association
c/o Registrar/Office Administrator
1225 Meadowview Rd., RR#2
Omemee, ON K0L 2W0
705-799-2081; Fax: 705-799-0605
E-mail: info@ohea.on.ca
URL: www.ohea.on.ca
Scope: Provincial

- **Ontario Independent Meat Processors Meat Industry Expo 2018**
Location: Ontario
Sponsor/Contact: Ontario Independent Meat Processors
52 Royal Rd., #B-1
Guelph, ON N1H 1G3
519-763-4558; Fax: 519-763-4164
E-mail: info@oimp.ca
URL: www.oimp.ca
Scope: Provincial
Contact Information:
www.meatindustryexpo.ca

- **Ontario Lacrosse Association 2018 Annual General Meeting**
Location: Ontario
Sponsor/Contact: Ontario Lacrosse Association
#306, 3 Concorde Gate
Toronto, ON M3C 3N7
416-426-7066; Fax: 416-426-7382
URL: www.ontariolacrosse.com
Scope: Provincial

- **Ontario Library & Information Technology Association Annual General Meeting 2018**
Sponsor/Contact: Ontario Library & Information Technology Association
c/o Ontario Library Association
2 Toronto St., 3rd Fl.
Toronto, ON M5C 2B6
416-363-3388; Fax: 416-941-9581
Toll-Free: 866-873-9867
URL: www.accessola.com/olita
Scope: Provincial

- **Ontario Library Boards' Association 2018 Annual General Meeting**
Location: Ontario
Sponsor/Contact: Ontario Library Boards' Association
c/o Ontario Library Association
2 Toronto St., 3rd Fl.
Toronto, ON M5C 2B6
416-363-3388; Fax: 416-941-9581
Toll-Free: 866-873-9867
E-mail: info@accessola.com
URL: www.accessola.org
Scope: Provincial
Purpose: AGM reports from executive members, the business of the association, statement of expenses, & the introduction of the new council

- **Ontario Municipal Social Services Association Annual General Meeting 2018**
Sponsor/Contact: Ontario Municipal Social Services Association
#2500, 1 Dundas St West
Toronto, ON M5G 1Z3
416-646-0513; Fax: 416-979-4627
E-mail: info@omssa.com
URL: www.omssa.com
Scope: Provincial

- **Ontario Municipal Tax & Revenue Association 2018 Fall Conference**
Location: Ontario
Sponsor/Contact: Ontario Municipal Tax & Revenue Association
#119, 14845 - 6 Yonge St.
Aurora, ON L4G 6H8
E-mail: webmaster@omtra.ca
URL: www.omtra.ca
Scope: Provincial

- **Ontario Municipal Tax & Revenue Association 2018 Spring Seminar**
Location: Ontario
Sponsor/Contact: Ontario Municipal Tax & Revenue Association
#119, 14845 - 6 Yonge St.
Aurora, ON L4G 6H8
E-mail: webmaster@omtra.ca
URL: www.omtra.ca
Scope: Provincial

- **Ontario Percheron Horse Association 2018 AGM**
Location: Ontario
Sponsor/Contact: Ontario Percheron Horse Association Inc.
c/o Michelle Campbell
2321 Cockshutt Rd.
Waterford, ON N0E 1Y0
519-443-6399
E-mail: Secretary@ontariopercherons.ca
URL: www.ontariopercherons.ca

Conferences & Conventions Index

- **Ontario Petroleum Institute 2018 57th Annual Conference & Trade Show**
Sponsor/Contact: Ontario Petroleum Institute Inc.
#104, 555 Southdale Rd. East
London, ON N6E 1A2
519-680-1620; Fax: 519-680-1621
E-mail: opi@ontariopetroleuminstitute.com
URL: ontariopetroleuminstitute.com
Scope: Provincial
Purpose: Presentation of papers about oil & natural gas exploration, production, & storage

- **Ontario Petroleum Institute 2018 AGM**
Sponsor/Contact: Ontario Petroleum Institute Inc.
#104, 555 Southdale Rd. East
London, ON N6E 1A2
519-680-1620; Fax: 519-680-1621
E-mail: opi@ontariopetroleuminstitute.com
URL: ontariopetroleuminstitute.com
Scope: Provincial

- **Ontario Processing Vegetable Industry Conference 2018**
Location: Ontario
Sponsor/Contact: Ontario Processing Vegetable Growers
435 Consortium Ct.
London, ON N6E 2S8
519-681-1875; Fax: 519-685-5719
E-mail: opvg@opvg.org
URL: www.opvg.org
Scope: Provincial

- **Ontario Professional Fire Fighters Association 2018 Annual Legislative Conference**
Location: Ontario
Sponsor/Contact: Ontario Professional Fire Fighters Association
292 Plains Rd. East
Burlington, ON L7T 2C6
905-681-7111; Fax: 905-681-1489
URL: www.opffa.org
Scope: Provincial
Purpose: An opportunity for representatives from across Ontario to meet with MPPs to advocate on issues of concern

- **Ontario Professional Fire Fighters Association 20th Annual Convention 2018**
Sponsor/Contact: Ontario Professional Fire Fighters Association
292 Plains Rd. East
Burlington, ON L7T 2C6
905-681-7111; Fax: 905-681-1489
URL: www.opffa.org
Scope: Provincial

- **Ontario Professional Foresters Association 2018 61st Annual Conference**
Location: Ontario
Sponsor/Contact: Ontario Professional Foresters Association
#201, 5 Wesleyan St.
Georgetown, ON L7G 2E2
905-877-3679; Fax: 905-877-6766
E-mail: opfa@opfa.ca
URL: www.opfa.ca
Scope: Provincial

- **Ontario Psychological Association 2018 Annual Conference**
Sponsor/Contact: Ontario Psychological Association
#403, 21 St. Clair Ave. East
Toronto, ON M4T 1L8
416-961-5552; Fax: 416-961-5516
E-mail: opa@psych.on.ca
URL: www.psych.on.ca
Scope: Provincial

- **Ontario Public Health Association 2018 Annual Conference & General Meeting**
Sponsor/Contact: Ontario Public Health Association
#502, 44 Victoria St.
Toronto, ON M5C 1Y2
416-367-3313; Fax: 416-367-2844
E-mail: admin@opha.on.ca
URL: www.opha.on.ca
Scope: Provincial
Purpose: A review of association bylaws, presentation of the annual report, & the appointment of the Board of Directors

- **Ontario Public Library Association 2018 39th Annual General Meeting**
Location: Ontario
Sponsor/Contact: Ontario Public Library Association
c/o Ontario Library Association
2 Toronto St., 3rd Fl.
Toronto, ON M5C 2B6
416-363-3388; Fax: 416-941-9581
Toll-Free: 866-873-9867
E-mail: info@accessola.com
URL: www.accessola.org
Scope: Provincial
Purpose: Featuring the introduction of the new council, as well as reports from the association's president, treasurer, & committees

- **Ontario Public Supervisory Officers' Association Annual Conference 2018**
Location: Ontario
Sponsor/Contact: Ontario Public Supervisory Officers' Association
1123 Glenashton Dr.
Oakville, ON L6H 5M1
905-845-7003; Fax: 905-845-2044
URL: www.opsoa.org
Scope: Provincial

- **Ontario Real Estate Association 2018 Conference**
Location: Ontario
Sponsor/Contact: Ontario Real Estate Association
99 Duncan Mill Rd.
Toronto, ON M3B 1Z2
416-445-9910; Fax: 416-445-2644
Toll-Free: 800-265-6732
E-mail: info@orea.com
URL: www.orea.com
Scope: Provincial
Purpose: Educational & networking opportunities for current & future leaders in the real estate industry, plus the Ontario Real Estate Association Annual Assembly Meeting & elections

- **Ontario School Counsellors' Association Conference 2018**
Sponsor/Contact: Ontario School Counsellors' Association
P.O. Box 60
Hillsburgh, ON N0B 1Z0
519-800-0872; Fax: 519-800-0874
URL: www.osca.ca
Scope: Provincial

- **Ontario School Library Association 2018 Annual General Meeting**
Location: Ontario
Sponsor/Contact: Ontario School Library Association
c/o Ontario Library Association
2 Toronto St., 3rd Fl.
Toronto, ON M5C 2B6
416-363-3388; Fax: 416-941-9581
Toll-Free: 866-873-9867
E-mail: info@accessola.com
URL: www.accessola.org
Scope: Provincial

- **Ontario Stone, Sand & Gravel Association 2018 Conference & Annual General Meeting**
Location: Ontario
Sponsor/Contact: Ontario Stone, Sand & Gravel Association
#103, 5720 Timberlea Blvd.
Mississauga, ON L4W 4W2
905-507-0711; Fax: 905-507-0717
URL: www.ossga.com
Scope: Provincial

- **Ontario Teachers' Federation Annual General Meeting 2018**
Location: Ontario
Sponsor/Contact: Ontario Teachers' Federation
#200, 1300 Yonge St.
Toronto, ON M4T 1X3
416-966-3424; Fax: 416-966-5450
Toll-Free: 800-268-7061
URL: www.otffeo.on.ca
Scope: Provincial
Contact Information: Administrator: Lavinia George, E-mail: lavinia.george@otffeo.on.ca

- **Ontario Tire Dealers Association 2018 Winter Conference**
Sponsor/Contact: Ontario Tire Dealers Association
P.O. Box 516
22 John St.
Drayton, ON N0G 1P0
888-207-9059; Fax: 866-375-6832
URL: www.otda.com
Scope: Provincial

- **Ontario Trail Council Trailhead Ontario 2018**
Location: Ontario
Sponsor/Contact: Ontario Trails Council
P.O. Box 500
Deseronto, ON K0K 1X0
URL: www.ontariotrails.on.ca
Scope: Provincial

- **Operating Room Nurses of Alberta Association AGM 2018**
Location: Alberta
Sponsor/Contact: Operating Room Nurses of Alberta Association
E-mail: info@ornaa.org
URL: www.ornaa.org
Scope: Provincial

- **Ordre des administrateurs agréés du Québec Congrès 2018**
Location: Quebec
Sponsor/Contact: Ordre des administrateurs agréés du Québec
#360, 1050, côte du Beaver Hall
Montréal, QC H2Z 0A5
514-499-0880; Fax: 514-499-0892
Toll-Free: 800-465-0880
E-mail: info@adma.qc.ca
URL: www.adma.qc.ca
Scope: Provincial

- **Ordre des arpenteurs-géomètres du Québec 50e Congrès**
Location: Quebec
Sponsor/Contact: Ordre des arpenteurs-géomètres du Québec
Iberville Quatre
#350, 2954 boul Laurier
Québec, QC G1V 4T2
418-656-0730; Fax: 418-656-6352
Toll-Free: 800-243-6490
E-mail: oagq@oagq.qc.ca
URL: www.oagq.qc.ca
Scope: Provincial

- **Ordre des ingénieurs du Québec Assemblée générale annuelle 2018**
Location: Quebec
Sponsor/Contact: Ordre des ingénieurs du Québec
Gare Windsor
#350, 1100, av des Canadiens-de-Montréal
Montréal, QC H3B 2S2
514-845-6141; Fax: 514-845-1833
Toll-Free: 800-461-6141
E-mail: info@oiq.qc.ca
URL: www.oiq.qc.ca
Scope: Provincial

- **Ottawa Valley Health Libraries Association Annual General Meeting 2018**
Sponsor/Contact: Ottawa Valley Health Libraries Association
c/o Canadian Agency for Drugs and Technologies in Health (CADTH)
#600, 865 Carling Ave.
Ottawa, ON K1S 5S8
613-226-2553
URL: ovhla.chla-absc.ca
Scope: Provincial

- **Outdoor Writers of Canada 2018 National Conference**
Sponsor/Contact: Outdoor Writers of Canada
P.O. Box 934
Cochrane, AB T4C 1B1
403-932-3585; Fax: 403-851-0618
E-mail: outdoorwritersofcanada@shaw.ca
URL: www.outdoorwritersofcanada.com
Scope: National
Purpose: Craft improvement sessions for communicators with expertise in the outdoor field

- **Parents Without Partners 2018 International Convention**
Sponsor/Contact: Parents Without Partners Inc.
1100-H Brandywine Blvd.
Zanesville, OH 43701-7303
Toll-Free: 800-637-7974
URL: www.parentswithoutpartners.org
Scope: International

- **Parents partenaires en éducation congrès et assemblée générale annuelle 2018**
Location: Ontario
Sponsor/Contact: Parents partenaires en éducation
435 rue Donald, #B-204
Ottawa, ON K1K 4X5
613-741-8846; Fax: 613-741-7322
Toll-Free: 800-342-0663
URL: www.ppeontario.ca
Scope: Provincial
Contact Information: Directrice générale: Sylvie Ross, Courriel: dg@ppeontario.ca

- **Parkinson Canada 2018 Annual General Meeting**
Sponsor/Contact: Parkinson Canada

Conferences & Conventions Index

#316, 4211 Yonge St.
Toronto, ON M2P 2A9
416-227-9700; *Fax:* 844-440-8963
Toll-Free: 800-565-3000
E-mail: info@parkinson.ca
URL: www.parkinson.ca
Scope: National

• **Parks & Recreation Ontario Educational Forum & Trade Show 2018**
Location: Ontario
Sponsor/Contact: Parks & Recreation Ontario
#302, 1 Concorde Gate
Toronto, ON M3C 3N6
416-426-7142; *Fax:* 416-426-7371
E-mail: pro@prontario.org
URL: www.prontario.org
Scope: Provincial

• **Pathways Abilities Society Annual General Meeting 2018**
Sponsor/Contact: Pathways Abilities Society
123 Franklyn Rd.
Kelowna, BC V1X 6A9
250-763-4387; *Fax:* 250-763-4488
E-mail: ed@pathwayskelowna.ca
URL: www.pathwayskelowna.ca
Scope: Local

• **PEI Association of Medical Radiation Technologists 2018 AGM & Education Day**
Location: Prince Edward Island
Sponsor/Contact: Prince Edward Island Association of Medical Radiation Technologists
60 Riverside Dr.
Charlottetown, PE C1A 8T5
E-mail: peiamrt@gmail.com
URL: www.peiamrt.com
Scope: Provincial

• **PEN International Annual Congress 2018**
Sponsor/Contact: PEN International
Koops Mill Mews, #A
162-164 Abbey St.
London, SE1 2AN
E-mail: info@pen-international.org
URL: www.pen-international.org
Scope: International
Contact Information: Coordinator, Congress: Jena Patel, E-mail: jena.patel@pen-international.org

• **People First Nova Scotia Annual General Meeting & Conference 2018**
Location: Nova Scotia
Sponsor/Contact: People First Nova Scotia
568A Prince St.
Truro, NS B2N 1G3
902-893-3033
Toll-Free: 877-454-3860
E-mail: pfns2014@gmail.com
URL: www.peoplefirstns.ca
Scope: Provincial

• **People First Society of Yukon Annual General Meeting 2018**
Location: Yukon Territory
Sponsor/Contact: People First Society of Yukon
P.O. Box 31478
Whitehorse, YT Y1A 6K8
867-667-4606; *Fax:* 867-668-8169
E-mail: peoplefirstyukon@hotmail.com
Scope: Provincial

• **People First of Canada 2018 27th Annual General Meeting & Conference**
Sponsor/Contact: People First of Canada
#20, 226 Osborne St. North
Winnipeg, MB R3C 1V4
204-784-7362; *Fax:* 204-784-7364
E-mail: info@peoplefirstofcanada.ca
URL: www.peoplefirstofcanada.ca
Scope: National
Purpose: A meeting for People First representatives from across Canada, featuring the presentation of awards

• **People First of Ontario Annual General Meeting 2018**
Location: Ontario
Sponsor/Contact: People First of Ontario
#4, 2495 Parkedale Ave.
Brockville, ON
613-213-3214; *Fax:* 613-345-4092
E-mail: info@peoplefirstontario.ca
URL: www.peoplefirstontario.com
Scope: Provincial

• **People for Education Annual Conference 2018**
Sponsor/Contact: People for Education
641 Bloor St. West
Toronto, ON M6G 1L1
416-534-0100; *Fax:* 416-536-0100
E-mail: info@peopleforeducation.ca
URL: www.peopleforeducation.ca
Scope: International

• **Petroleum Services Association of Canada 2018 Annual General Meeting**
Sponsor/Contact: Petroleum Services Association of Canada
#1150, 734 - 7 Ave. SW
Calgary, AB T2P 3P8
403-264-4195; *Fax:* 403-263-7174
Toll-Free: 800-818-7722
E-mail: info@psac.ca
URL: www.psac.ca
Scope: National
Purpose: At the end of October each year, the Petroleum Services Association of Canada Annual Report is released, in conjunction with the Annual General Meeting & the Canadian Drilling Activity Forecast

• **Pipe Line Contractors Association of Canada 2018 64th Annual Convention**
Sponsor/Contact: Pipe Line Contractors Association of Canada
#201, 1075 North Service Rd. West
Oakville, ON L6M 2G2
905-847-9383; *Fax:* 905-847-7824
E-mail: plcac@pipeline.ca
URL: www.pipeline.ca
Scope: National
Purpose: A program about the special pipeline construction industry, including various speakers & the association's annual general meeting
Contact Information: Contact: Neil Lane, Phone: 905-847-9383

• **Professional Engineers Ontario 96th Annual General Meeting 2018**
Sponsor/Contact: Professional Engineers Ontario
#101, 40 Sheppard Ave. West
Toronto, ON M2N 6K9
416-224-1100; *Fax:* 416-224-9527
Toll-Free: 800-339-3716
URL: www.peo.on.ca

• **Provincial Intermediate Teachers' Association Fall Conference**
Sponsor/Contact: Provincial Intermediate Teachers' Association
URL: www.pita.ca
Scope: Provincial

• **Public Works Association of BC 2018 Technical Conference & Trade Show**
Location: British Columbia
Sponsor/Contact: Public Works Association of British Columbia
#102, 211 Columbia St.
Vancouver, BC V6A 2R5
Toll-Free: 877-356-0699
E-mail: info@pwabc.ca
URL: www.pwabc.ca
Scope: Provincial

• **Quebec Mineral Exploration Association Explo Abitibi 2018**
Sponsor/Contact: Association de l'exploration minière de Québec
#203, 132, av du Lac
Rouyn-Noranda, QC J9X 4N5
819-762-1599; *Fax:* 819-762-1522
E-mail: info@aemq.org
URL: www.aemq.org

• **Quebec Urological Association 2018 Congress**
Location: Quebec
Sponsor/Contact: Association des urologues du Québec
Tour de l'est
2, Complexe Desjardins, 32e étage
Montréal, QC H5B 1G8
514-350-5131; *Fax:* 514-350-5181
E-mail: info@auq.org
URL: www.auq.org
Scope: Provincial

• **Radio Television Digital News Association (Canada) National Conference 2018**
Location: Sheraton Centre Toronto Hotel
Toronto, ON
Sponsor/Contact: Radio Television Digital News Association (Canada)
#300, 1201 West Pender St.
Vancouver, BC V6E 2V2
604-681-2153
E-mail: admin@rtdnacanada.com
URL: www.rtdnacanada.com
Scope: National

• **Recycling Council of Ontario 2018 Annual General Meeting & Policy Forum**
Location: Ontario
Sponsor/Contact: Recycling Council of Ontario
#225, 215 Spadina Ave.
Toronto, ON M5T 2C7
416-657-2797
Toll-Free: 888-501-9637
E-mail: rco@rco.on.ca
URL: www.rco.on.ca
Scope: Provincial
Contact Information: Manager, Events: Diane Blackburn, E-mail: events@rco.on.ca, Phone: 416-657-2797, ext. 4

• **Registered Massage Therapists' Association of Ontario (RMTAO) Education Conference 2018**
Location: Ontario
Sponsor/Contact: Registered Massage Therapists' Association of Ontario
#704, 1243 Islington Ave.
Toronto, ON M8X 1Y9
416-979-2010; *Fax:* 416-979-1144
Toll-Free: 800-668-2022
E-mail: info@rmtao.com
URL: www.rmtao.com
Scope: Provincial

• **Registered Nurses Association of the Northwest Territories & Nunavut Annual General Meeting 2018**
Sponsor/Contact: The Registered Nurses Association of the Northwest Territories & Nunavut
P.O. Box 2757
Yellowknife, NT X1A 2R1
867-873-2745; *Fax:* 867-873-2336
E-mail: info@rnantnu.ca
URL: www.rnantnu.ca
Scope: Provincial

• **Registered Nurses' Association of Ontario Annual General Meeting 2018**
Sponsor/Contact: Registered Nurses' Association of Ontario
158 Pearl St.
Toronto, ON M5H 1L3
416-599-1925; *Fax:* 416-599-1926
Toll-Free: 800-268-7199
URL: www.rnao.ca
Scope: Provincial

• **Registered Professional Foresters Association of Nova Scotia 2018 Annual General Meeting**
Sponsor/Contact: Registered Professional Foresters Association of Nova Scotia
P.O. Box 1031
Truro, NS B2N 5G9
902-893-0099
E-mail: contact@rpfans.ca
URL: www.rpfans.ca
Scope: Provincial
Purpose: A business meeting for Nova Scotia's professional foresters

• **Registered Veterinary Technologists & Technicians of Canada 2018 Annual General Meeting**
Sponsor/Contact: Registered Veterinary Technologists & Technicians of Canada
P.O. Box 961
Kemptville, ON K0G 1J0
613-215-0619
Toll-Free: 844-626-0796
URL: beta.rvttcanada.ca
Scope: National

• **Rhythmic Gymnastics Manitoba 2018 AGM**
Location: Manitoba
Sponsor/Contact: Rhythmic Gymnastics Manitoba Inc.
145 Pacific Ave.
Winnipeg, MB R3B 2Z6
201-925-5738
E-mail: rhythmic@sportmanitoba.ca
URL: www.rgmanitoba.com
Scope: Provincial

• **Richmond Gem & Mineral Society 57th Annual Show & Sale 2018**
Location: Richmond, BC
Sponsor/Contact: Richmond Gem & Mineral Society
c/o Richmond Cultural Centre
7700 Minoru Gate
Richmond, BC V6Y 1R9
604-278-5141
URL: www.richmondbclapidary.wordpress.com
Scope: Local
Purpose: Features vendors selling gems, minerals & related items

• **RMCAO [Ready Mixed Concrete Association of Ontario] 58th Annual General Meeting & Convention**
Location: Ontario
Sponsor/Contact: Concrete Ontario

#102B, 1 Prologis Blvd.
Mississauga, ON L5w 0G2
905-564-2726; *Fax:* 905-564-5680
URL: www.rmcao.org
Scope: Provincial

- **Rowing British Columbia Annual General Meeting 2018**
Sponsor/Contact: Rowing British Columbia
#155, 3820 Cessna Dr.
Richmond, BC V7B 0A2
604-273-4769; *Fax:* 888-398-5818
Toll-Free: 877-330-3638
E-mail: admin@rowingbc.ca
URL: www.rowingbc.ca
Scope: Provincial

- **Royal Canadian Academy of Arts 2018 138th Annual General Assembly**
Sponsor/Contact: Royal Canadian Academy of Arts
#375, 401 Richmond St. West
Toronto, ON M5V 3A8
416-408-2718; *Fax:* 416-408-2286
E-mail: rcaarts@interlog.com
URL: www.rca-arc.ca
Scope: National

- **Royal College of Dentists of Canada 2018 Annual General Meeting**
Sponsor/Contact: Royal College of Dentists of Canada
#2404, 180 Dundas St. West
Toronto, ON M5G 1Z8
416-512-6571; *Fax:* 416-512-6468
E-mail: office@rcdc.ca
URL: www.rcdc.ca
Scope: National

- **Royal College of Physicians & Surgeons of Canada 2018 Annual General Meeting**
Sponsor/Contact: The Royal College of Physicians & Surgeons of Canada
774 Echo Dr.
Ottawa, ON K1S 5N8
613-730-8177; *Fax:* 613-730-8830
Toll-Free: 800-668-3740
E-mail: feedback@royalcollege.ca
URL: www.royalcollege.ca
Scope: National

- **Royal Society of Canada Annual General Meeting 2018**
Sponsor/Contact: The Royal Society of Canada
Walter House
282 Somerset West
Ottawa, ON K2P 0J6
613-991-6990; *Fax:* 613-991-6996
URL: www.rsc.ca
Scope: National

- **Réseau des services d'archives du Québec (RAQ) Assemblée générale annuelle 2018**
Location: Quebec
Sponsor/Contact: Réseau des services d'archives du Québec
a/s Archives nationales du Québec à Montréal
#5.27.1, 535, av Viger est
Montréal, QC H2L 2P3
514-864-9213
E-mail: archiviste.conseil.raq@gmail.com
URL: archiviteraq.com
Scope: Provincial

- **Réseau québécois des OSBL d'habitation 2018 Congrès national sur le logement et l'itinérance**
Location: Quebec

Sponsor/Contact: Réseau québécois des OSBL d'habitation
#102, rue Fullum
Montréal, QC H2K 0B5
514-846-0163; *Fax:* 514-846-3402
Toll-Free: 866-846-0163
E-mail: info@rqoh.com
URL: www.rqoh.com
Scope: Provincial

- **Safety Services New Brunswick Health & Safety Conference 2018**
Location: New Brunswick
Sponsor/Contact: Safety Services New Brunswick
#204, 440 Wilsey Rd.
Fredericton, NB E3B 7G5
506-458-8034; *Fax:* 506-444-0177
Toll-Free: 877-762-7233
E-mail: info@safetyservicesnb.ca
URL: www.safetyservicesnb.ca
Scope: Provincial

- **SaskCentral 2018 Annual General Meeting**
Sponsor/Contact: SaskCentral
P.O. Box 3030
2055 Albert St.
Regina, SK S4P 3G8
306-566-1200
Toll-Free: 866-403-7499
E-mail: info@saskcentral.com
URL: www.saskcentral.com
Scope: Provincial

- **SaskOutdoors Annual General Meeting 2018**
Location: Saskatchewan
Sponsor/Contact: Saskatchewan Outdoor & Environmental Education Association
P.O. Box 398
Craven, SK S0G 0W0
URL: www.saskoutdoors.org
Scope: Provincial

- **Saskatchewan Association of Library Technicians 2018 Annual General Meeting & Fall Workshops**
Location: Saskatchewan
Sponsor/Contact: Saskatchewan Association of Library Technicians, Inc.
P.O. Box 24019
Saskatoon, SK S7K 8B4
E-mail: sasksalt@gmail.com
URL: www.sasksalt.ca
Scope: Provincial
Purpose: A business meeting, speakers, & networking opportunities for library technicians from Saskatchewan
Contact Information: E-mail: sasksalt@gmail.com

- **Saskatchewan Association of Social Workers 2018 Annual General Meeting & Provincial Conference**
Location: Saskatchewan
Sponsor/Contact: Saskatchewan Association of Social Workers
Edna Osborne House
2110 Lorne St.
Regina, SK S4P 2M5
306-545-1922; *Fax:* 306-545-1895
Toll-Free: 877-517-7279
E-mail: sasw@accesscomm.ca
URL: www.sasw.ca
Scope: Provincial
Purpose: A conference usually held each April at one of the association's branch locations

- **Saskatchewan Beekeepers Association 2018 Annual Convention**

Location: Saskatchewan
Sponsor/Contact: Saskatchewan Beekeepers Association
P.O. Box 55
RR#3
Yorkton, SK S3N 2X5
306-743-5469; *Fax:* 306-743-5528
E-mail: whowland@accesscomm.ca
URL: www.saskbeekeepers.com
Scope: Provincial
Purpose: Featuring speakers & research results

- **Saskatchewan Camping Association 2018 Annual General Meeting**
Location: Saskatchewan
Sponsor/Contact: Saskatchewan Camping Association
3950 Castle Rd.
Regina, SK S4S 6A4
306-586-4026; *Fax:* 306-790-8634
Scope: Provincial
Purpose: Featuring the election of the board of directors of the association

- **Saskatchewan Conference of Mennonite Brethren Churches 72nd Annual Conference 2018**
Sponsor/Contact: Saskatchewan Conference of Mennonite Brethren Churches
#201, 401 - 3rd St. E
Saskatoon, SK S7K 8B7
306-652-2752
URL: www.skmb.ca
Scope: Provincial

- **Saskatchewan Council for Archives & Archivists Annual General Meeting 2018**
Location: Saskatchewan
Sponsor/Contact: Saskatchewan Council for Archives & Archivists
#202, 1275 Broad St.
Regina, SK S4R 1Y2
306-780-9414; *Fax:* 306-585-1765
E-mail: scaa@sasktel.net
URL: www.scaa.sk.ca
Scope: Provincial

- **Saskatchewan Early Childhood Association 2018 Annual General Meeting**
Location: Saskatchewan
Sponsor/Contact: Saskatchewan Early Childhood Association
1015 Railway Ave.
Weyburn, SK S4H 2V5
306-842-1209; *Fax:* 306-842-1206
Toll-Free: 888-658-4408
URL: www.seca-sk.ca
Scope: Provincial

- **Saskatchewan Early Childhood Association 2018 Excellence in Early Learning Conference**
Location: Saskatchewan
Sponsor/Contact: Saskatchewan Early Childhood Association
1015 Railway Ave.
Weyburn, SK S4H 2V5
306-842-1209; *Fax:* 306-842-1206
Toll-Free: 888-658-4408
URL: www.seca-sk.ca
Scope: Provincial
Purpose: A conference offering demonstration classrooms, peer to peer learning, & hands-on activities

- **Saskatchewan Federation of Labour 2018 62nd Annual Convention**
Location: Saskatchewan

Sponsor/Contact: Saskatchewan Federation of Labour
#220, 2445 - 13th Ave.
Regina, SK S4P 0W1
306-525-0197; *Fax:* 306-525-8960
URL: www.sfl.sk.ca
Scope: Provincial
Contact Information: Office Administration
Contact: Kathy Abel, E-mail: k.abel@sfl.sk.ca

- **Saskatchewan Federation of Police Officers 2018 Annual Meeting**
Location: Saskatchewan
Sponsor/Contact: Saskatchewan Federation of Police Officers
306-539-0960
URL: www.saskpolice.com
Scope: Provincial
Purpose: The Executive Board reports on matters dealt with for & on behalf of members of the Federation at a meeting held each year between April 1st & May 31st

- **Saskatchewan Library Association 2018 Annual Conference & Annual General Meeting**
Location: Saskatchewan
Sponsor/Contact: Saskatchewan Library Association
#15, 2010 - 7th Ave.
Regina, SK S4R 1C2
Fax: 306-780-9447
URL: www.saskla.ca
Scope: Provincial
Contact Information: Saskatchewan Library Association, Phone: 306-780-9413, Fax: 306-780-9447, E-mail: slaprograms@sasktel.net

- **Saskatchewan Library Trustees' Association Annual General Meeting 2018**
Sponsor/Contact: Saskatchewan Library Trustees' Association
c/o Nancy Kennedy
79 Mayfair Cres.
Regina, SK S4S 5T9
306-584-2495; *Fax:* 306-585-1473
URL: www.slta.ca
Scope: Provincial

- **Saskatchewan Literacy Network Annual General Meeting 2018**
Location: Saskatchewan
Sponsor/Contact: Saskatchewan Literacy Network
#11, 2155 Airport Dr.
Saskatoon, SK S7L 6M5
306-651-7288; *Fax:* 306-651-7287
Toll-Free: 888-511-2111
E-mail: saskliteracy@saskliteracy.ca
URL: saskliteracy.ca
Scope: Provincial

- **Saskatchewan Mining Association 52nd Annual General Meeting 2018**
Location: Saskatchewan
Sponsor/Contact: Saskatchewan Mining Association
#1500, 2002 Victoria Ave.
Regina, SK S4P 0R7
306-757-9505; *Fax:* 306-569-1085
E-mail: info@saskmining.ca
URL: www.saskmining.ca
Scope: Provincial

- **Saskatchewan School Library Association Annual General Meeting 2018**

Conferences & Conventions Index

Sponsor/Contact: Saskatchewan School Library Association
c/o Saskatchewan Teachers' Federation
2317 Arlington Ave.
Saskatoon, SK S7J 2H8
E-mail: sasksla@gmail.com
URL: www.ssla.ca
Scope: Provincial
Purpose: An annual event for members with a new facilitator each year

- **Saskatchewan Snowmobile Association 2018 AGM**
Location: Saskatchewan
Sponsor/Contact: Saskatchewan Snowmobile Association
P.O. Box 533
221 Centre St.
Regina Beach, SK S0G 4C0
306-729-3500
Toll-Free: 800-499-7533
E-mail: sasksnow@sasktel.net
URL: www.sasksnow.com
Scope: Provincial
Purpose: Reports from the chairman, president & chief executive officer, & discussions about finances & association issues

- **Saskatchewan Trucking Association Annual General Meeting 2018**
Location: Saskatchewan
Sponsor/Contact: Saskatchewan Trucking Association
103 Hodsman Rd.
Regina, SK S4N 5W5
306-569-9696; Fax: 306-569-1008
Toll-Free: 800-563-7623
E-mail: info@sasktrucking.com
URL: www.sasktrucking.com
Scope: Provincial
Contact Information: Executive Assistant: Cecilia Taylor, E-mail: ctaylor@sasktrucking.com

- **Saskatchewan Waste Reduction Council Waste ReForum 2018**
Sponsor/Contact: Saskatchewan Waste Reduction Council
The Two-Twenty
#208, 220 - 20th St. West
Saskatoon, SK S7M 0W9
306-931-3242; Fax: 306-955-5852
E-mail: info@saskwastereduction.ca
URL: www.saskwastereduction.ca
Scope: Provincial
Purpose: Workshops & sessions on environmental issues

- **Scandinavian Society of Nova Scotia 2018 Annual General Meeting**
Location: Nova Scotia
Sponsor/Contact: Scandinavian Society of Nova Scotia
Box 31241, Gladstone RPO
Halifax, NS B3K 5Y1
E-mail: scansons@gmail.com
URL: www.scandinaviansociety.ca
Scope: Provincial
Purpose: The presentation of society reports, a summary of events from the previous year, & an award ceremony

- **School Sports Newfoundland & Labrador Annual General Meeting**
Sponsor/Contact: School Sports Newfoundland & Labrador
P.O. Box 8700
1296A Kenmount Rd.
St. John's, NL A1B 4J6
709-729-2795; Fax: 709-729-2705
URL: www.schoolsportsnl.ca

- **Science Teachers' Association of Ontario 2018 Conference**
Sponsor/Contact: Science Teachers' Association of Ontario
P.O. Box 771
Dresden, ON N0P 1M0
Fax: 800-754-1654
Toll-Free: 800-461-2264
E-mail: info@stao.org
URL: www.stao.org
Scope: Provincial

- **Scotia Horticultural Congress 2018**
Location: Nova Scotia
Sponsor/Contact: Horticulture Nova Scotia
Kentville Agricultural Centre
32 Main St.
Kentville, NS B4N 1J5
902-678-9335; Fax: 902-678-1280
E-mail: info@horticulturens.ca
URL: www.horticulturens.ca
Scope: Provincial

- **Shevchenko Scientific Society of Canada Annual Conference 2018**
Sponsor/Contact: Shevchenko Scientific Society of Canada
516 The Kingsway
Toronto, ON M9A 3W6
E-mail: ntsh.ca@gmail.com
URL: www.ntsh.ca
Scope: National

- **Society Promoting Environmental Conservation AGM 2018**
Sponsor/Contact: Society Promoting Environmental Conservation
2060 Pine St.
Vancouver, BC V6J 4P8
604-736-7732; Fax: 604-736-7115
E-mail: admin@spec.bc.ca
URL: www.spec.bc.ca
Scope: Provincial

- **Society for Information Management (SIM) SIMposium 2018**
Sponsor/Contact: Society for Information Management
#200, 1120 route 73
Mount Laurel, NJ 08054
856-380-6807
E-mail: sim@simnet.org
URL: www.simnet.org
Scope: International

- **Society for the Promotion of the Teaching of English as a Second Language in Quebec 2018 46th Annual Convention**
Location: Quebec
Sponsor/Contact: Society for the Promotion of the Teaching of English as a Second Language in Quebec
6662, rue Saint-Denis, #C
Montréal, QC H2S 2R9
514-271-3700; Fax: 514-271-4587
E-mail: speaq@speaq.qc.ca
URL: www.speaq.qc.ca
Scope: Provincial
Purpose: Featuring presentations on language, award ceremonies, workshops & exhibits

- **Society of Cardiovascular Anesthesiologists 21st Annual Comprehensive Review & Update of Perioperative Echo 2018**
Sponsor/Contact: Society of Cardiovascular Anesthesiologists
#300, 8735 West Higgins Rd.
Chicago, IL 60631
Fax: 847-375-6323
Toll-Free: 855-658-2828
E-mail: info@scahq.org
URL: www.scahq.org
Scope: International

- **Society of Christian Schools in BC Leadership Conference & AGM**
Sponsor/Contact: Society of Christian Schools in British Columbia
Fosmark Centre, Trinity Western University
7600 Glover Rd.
Langley, BC V2Y 1Y1
604-888-6366; Fax: 604-888-2791
E-mail: contact@scsbc.ca
URL: www.scsbc.ca
Scope: Provincial

- **Society of Toxicology 57th Annual Meeting & ToxExpo**
Sponsor/Contact: Society of Toxicology
#300, 1821 Michael Faraday Dr.
Reston, VA 20190
703-438-3115; Fax: 703-438-3113
E-mail: sothq@toxicology.org
URL: www.toxicology.org
Scope: International
Contact Information: Phone: 703-438-3115; Fax: 703-438-3113; E-mail: sothq@toxicology.org

- **Société québécoise de la schizophrénie 2018 Conférences mensuelles**
Location: Montréal, QC
Sponsor/Contact: Société québécoise de la schizophrénie
7401, rue Hochelaga
Montréal, QC H1N 3M5
514-251-4125; Fax: 514-251-6347
Toll-Free: 866-888-2323
E-mail: info@schizophrenie.qc.ca
URL: www.schizophrenie.qc.ca
Scope: Provincial

- **Softball Saskatchewan Annual General Meeting 2018**
Sponsor/Contact: Softball Saskatchewan
2205 Victoria Ave.
Regina, SK S4P 0S4
306-780-9235; Fax: 306-780-9483
E-mail: info@softball.sk.ca
URL: www.softball.sk.ca
Scope: Provincial

- **Southern Alberta Health Libraries Association Annual General Meeting 2018**
Location: Alberta
Sponsor/Contact: Southern Alberta Health Libraries Association
c/o Health Sciences Library, University of Calgary
3330 University Dr. NW
Calgary, AB T2N 4N1
URL: sahla.chla-absc.ca
Scope: Provincial

- **Southern Interior Local Government Association 2018 Annual General Meeting & Convention**
Sponsor/Contact: Southern Interior Local Government Association
c/o Alison Slater
1996 Sheffield Way
Kamloops, BC V2E 2M2
250-374-3678; Fax: 250-374-3678
URL: www.silga.ca
Scope: Local

- **Southwestern Ontario Health Libraries & Information Network Fall General Meeting 2018**
Location: Ontario
Sponsor/Contact: Southwestern Ontario Health Libraries & Information Network
c/o Carolynne Gabriel, Library, Middlesex London Health Unit
50 King St.
London, ON N6A 5L7
URL: sohlin.chla-absc.ca
Scope: Provincial

- **Southwestern Ontario Health Libraries & Information Network Spring General Meeting 2018**
Location: Ontario
Sponsor/Contact: Southwestern Ontario Health Libraries & Information Network
c/o Carolynne Gabriel, Library, Middlesex London Health Unit
50 King St.
London, ON N6A 5L7
URL: sohlin.chla-absc.ca
Scope: Provincial

- **Speed Skate Nova Scotia Annual General Meeting 2018**
Sponsor/Contact: Speed Skate Nova Scotia
5516 Spring Garden Rd.
Halifax, NS B3J 1G6
902-425-5450
E-mail: info@speedskatens.ca
URL: www.speedskatens.ca
Scope: Provincial

- **Speed Skating Canada 2018 Annual General Meeting**
Sponsor/Contact: Speed Skating Canada
House of Sport, RA Centre
2451 Riverside Dr.
Ottawa, ON K1H 7X7
613-260-3669
Toll-Free: 877-572-4772
E-mail: ssc@speedskating.ca
URL: www.speedskating.ca
Scope: National
Purpose: A gathering of the organization's Board of Directors, branches, & committees

- **Spina Bifida & Hydrocephalus Association of BC 2018 Annual General Meeting**
Location: British Columbia
Sponsor/Contact: Spina Bifida & Hydrocephalus Association of British Columbia
4480 Oak St.
Vancouver, BC V6H 3V4
604-878-7000; Fax: 604-677-6608
URL: www.sbhabc.org
Scope: Provincial

- **Teachers of Home Economics Specialist Association (THESA) Conference 2018**
Location: Prince George, BC
Sponsor/Contact: Teachers of Home Economics Specialist Association
c/o G.W. Graham Middle-Secondary School
45955 Thomas Rd.
Chilliwack, BC V2R 0B5
604-847-0772; Fax: 604-824-0711
E-mail: membership@thesa.ca
URL: www.bctf.ca/thesa
Scope: Provincial

- **TEAL Manitoba 2018 Conference**
Location: Manitoba

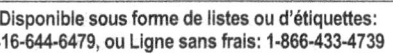

Sponsor/Contact: TEAL Manitoba
c/o Manitoba Teachers' Society
191 Harcourt St.
Winnipeg, MB R3J 3H2
204-888-7961
E-mail: manitoba.teal@gmail.com
URL: www.tealmanitoba.ca
Scope: Provincial
Purpose: Featuring presentations on EAL issues & professional development for EAL educators

- **Tennis BC Annual General Meeting 2018**
Location: British Columbia
Sponsor/Contact: Tennis BC
#204, 210 West Broadway
Vancouver, BC V5Y 3W2
604-737-3086; *Fax:* 604-737-3124
E-mail: tbc@tennisbc.org
URL: www.tennisbc.org
Scope: Provincial

- **Terrazzo Tile & Marble Association of Canada 2018 Convention**
Sponsor/Contact: Terrazzo Tile & Marble Association of Canada
#8, 163 Buttermill Ave.
Concord, ON L4K 3X8
905-660-9640; *Fax:* 905-660-0513
Toll-Free: 800-201-8599
E-mail: association@ttmac.com
URL: www.ttmac.com
Scope: National

- **TESL Ontario 2018 46th Annual Conference**
Location: Ontario
Sponsor/Contact: TESL Ontario
#405, 27 Carlton St.
Toronto, ON M5B 1L2
416-593-4243; *Fax:* 416-593-0164
Toll-Free: 800-327-4827
E-mail: administration@teslontario.org
URL: www.teslontario.net
Scope: Provincial

- **The Acadian Entomological Society 77th Annual Meeting**
Sponsor/Contact: The Acadian Entomological Society
P.O. Box 4000
Atlantic Forestry Centre, 1350 Regent St.
Fredericton, NB E3B 597
E-mail: Drew.Carleton@gnb.ca
URL: www.acadianes.org

- **The Annual General Meeting of the Law Society of Upper Canada**
Sponsor/Contact: Law Society of Upper Canada
Osgoode Hall
130 Queen St. West
Toronto, ON M5H 2N6
416-947-3300; *Fax:* 416-947-3924
Toll-Free: 800-668-7380
E-mail: lawsociety@lsuc.on.ca
URL: www.lsuc.on.ca
Scope: Provincial

- **The Canadian Addison Society Annual General Meeting 2018**
Sponsor/Contact: The Canadian Addison Society
1 Palace Arch Dr.
Toronto, ON M9A 2S1
Toll-Free: 888-550-5582
E-mail: info@addisonsociety.ca
URL: www.addisonsociety.ca
Scope: National

- **The National Pro-Life Conference 2018**
Sponsor/Contact: LifeCanada
P.O. Box 138
Carleton Place, ON K7C 3P3
613-722-1552; *Fax:* 613-482-4937
Toll-Free: 866-780-5433
E-mail: info@lifecanada.org
URL: www.lifecanada.org
Scope: National
Purpose: A 3-day national gathering of experts and pro-life professionals from across the country and abroad.

- **The Navy League of Canada 2018 Annual General Meeting**
Sponsor/Contact: Navy League of Canada
#201, 1505 Laperriere Ave.
Ottawa, ON K1Z 7T1
Toll-Free: 800-375-6289
E-mail: info@navyleague.ca
URL: www.navyleague.ca
Scope: National

- **The Professional Institute of the Public Service of Canada 99th Annual General Meeting 2018**
Sponsor/Contact: The Professional Institute of the Public Service of Canada
250 Tremblay Rd.
Ottawa, ON K1G 3J8
613-228-6310; *Fax:* 613-228-9048
Toll-Free: 800-267-0446
URL: www.pipsc.ca
Scope: International
Contact Information: Manager, Membership & Administration: Linda Martel, E-mail: lmartel@pipsc.ca; Phone: 613-228-6310, ext. 4854

- **The Provincial Towing Association 20th Annual Tow Show**
Sponsor/Contact: Provincial Towing Association (Ontario)
65 Keith Rd.
Bracebridge, ON P1L 0A1
705-646-0536; *Fax:* 705-645-0017
Toll-Free: 866-582-0855
URL: www.ptao.org
Purpose: The Trade & Tow Show features training sessions, the PTAO general meeting, competitions & the awards banquet

- **The Royal Canadian Geographical Society College of Fellows Annual Dinner 2018**
Sponsor/Contact: The Royal Canadian Geographical Society
#200, 1155 Lola St.
Ottawa, ON K1K 4C1
613-745-4629; *Fax:* 613-744-0947
E-mail: rcgs@rcgs.org
URL: www.rcgs.org
Scope: National
Purpose: A gathering of Society members, featuring the approval of the audited financial statement, a guest speaker, & the presentation of awards

- **The Saskatchewan Hotel & Hospitality Association Hotel & Hospitality Conference**
Location: Saskatchewan
Sponsor/Contact: Saskatchewan Hotel & Hospitality Association
#302, 2080 Broad St.
Regina, SK S4P 1Y3
306-522-1664
Toll-Free: 800-667-1118

E-mail: info@skhha.com
URL: www.skhha.com
Scope: Provincial

- **The Society of Toxicology of Canada 50th Annual Symposium 2018**
Sponsor/Contact: Society of Toxicology of Canada
P.O. Box 55094
Montréal, QC H3G 2W5
E-mail: stcsecretariat@mcgill.ca
URL: www.stcweb.ca
Scope: National

- **The United Church of Canada 45th General Council 2018**
Sponsor/Contact: United Church of Canada
#200, 3250 Bloor St. West
Toronto, ON M8X 2Y4
416-231-5931; *Fax:* 416-231-3103
Toll-Free: 800-268-3781
E-mail: info@united-church.ca
URL: www.united-church.ca
Scope: National
Contact Information: Secretary: Nora Sanders, E-mail: nsanders@united-church.ca

- **Thermal Insulation Association of Alberta 2018 Annual General Meeting**
Location: Alberta
Sponsor/Contact: Thermal Insulation Association of Alberta
#400, 1040 - 7 Ave. SW
Calgary, AB T2P 3G9
403-244-4487; *Fax:* 403-244-2340
E-mail: info@tiaa.cc
URL: www.tiaa.cc
Scope: Provincial

- **Toronto Health Libraries Association 2018 Annual General Meeting**
Location: Toronto, ON
Sponsor/Contact: Toronto Health Libraries Association
c/o Raluca Serban, UHN - Toronto Rehabilitation Institute
550 University Ave.
Toronto, ON M5G 2A2
E-mail: secretary@thla.ca
URL: thla.chla-absc.ca
Scope: Local

- **Tourette Syndrome Foundation of Canada 2018 National Conference**
Sponsor/Contact: Tourette Syndrome Foundation of Canada
#245, 5955 Airport Rd.
Mississauga, ON L4V 1R9
905-673-2255; *Fax:* 905-673-2638
Toll-Free: 800-361-3120
URL: www.tourette.ca
Scope: National

- **Tourism Industry Association of PEI 2018 Annual General Meeting**
Sponsor/Contact: Tourism Industry Association of PEI
P.O. Box 2050
25 Queen St., 3rd Fl.
Charlottetown, PE C1A 7N7
902-566-5008; *Fax:* 902-368-3605
Toll-Free: 866-566-5008
E-mail: webmaster@tiapei.pe.ca
URL: www.tiapei.pe.ca

- **Trans-Canada Advertising Agency Network 56th Annual Conference**
Sponsor/Contact: Trans-Canada Advertising Agency Network

#300, 25 Sheppard Ave. West
Toronto, ON M2N 6S6
416-221-6984; *Fax:* 416-221-8260
E-mail: bill@waginc.ca
URL: www.tcaan.ca
Scope: National

- **Transport Action Canada 2018 Annual General Meeting**
Sponsor/Contact: Transport Action Canada
P.O. Box 858 Stn. B
#303, 211 Bronson Ave.
Ottawa, ON K1P 5P9
613-594-3290; *Fax:* 613-594-3271
E-mail: info@transport-action.ca
URL: www.transport-action.ca

- **Trappers Association of Nova Scotia 2018 Annual Workshop & Convention**
Sponsor/Contact: Trappers Association of Nova Scotia
355 Meister Rd., RR#2
New Ross, NS B0J 2M0
E-mail: info@trappersassociationofnovascotia.ca
URL: www.trappersassociationofnovascotia.ca
Scope: Provincial

- **Travel Media Association of Canada 2018 Conference & AGM**
Sponsor/Contact: Travel Media Association of Canada
#602, 319 Merton St.
Toronto, ON M4S 1A5
416-934-0599
E-mail: info@travelmedia.ca
URL: www.travelmedia.ca
Scope: National

- **Tunnelling Association of Canada 2018 Annual Conference**
Location: Ontario
Sponsor/Contact: Tunnelling Association of Canada
8828 Pigott Rd.
Richmond, ON V7A 2C4
604-241-1297; *Fax:* 604-241-1399
E-mail: admin@tunnelcanada.ca
URL: www.tunnelcanada.ca
Scope: National

- **Union académique internationale Assemblée générale 2018**
Sponsor/Contact: Union académique internationale
Palais des Académies
1, rue Ducale
Brussels, B-1000
E-mail: info@uai-iua.org
URL: www.uai-iua.org
Scope: International

- **United Church of Canada Manitoba & Northwestern Ontario Conference 93rd Annual Meeting**
Sponsor/Contact: United Church of Canada
#1622-B, St. Mary's Rd.
Winnipeg, MB R2M 3W7
204-233-8911; *Fax:* 204-233-3289
Toll-Free: 866-860-9662
E-mail: office@confmnwo.mb.ca
URL: www.mnwo.united-church.ca
Scope: Provincial

- **United Church of Canada Saskatchewan Conference 2018 Annual Meeting**
Location: Saskatchewan
Sponsor/Contact: United Church of Canada

Conferences & Conventions Index

418A McDonald St.
Regina, SK S4N 6E1
306-721-3311; *Fax:* 306-721-3171
E-mail: ucskco@sasktel.net
URL: www.sk.united-church.ca
Scope: Provincial

- **United Steelworkers of America 55th National Policy Conference 2018**
Sponsor/Contact: United Steelworkers of America (AFL-CIO/CLC)
234 Eglinton Ave. East, 8th Fl.
Toronto, ON M4P 1K7
416-487-1571; *Fax:* 416-482-5548
Toll-Free: 877-669-8792
E-mail: info@usw.ca
URL: www.usw.ca
Scope: National

- **University of Alberta African Students' Association 2018 Conference**
Sponsor/Contact: African Students Association - Univeristy of Alberta
c/o Student Group Services Office,
Students' Union Bldg., Univ. of Alb
#040A, 8900 - 114 St. NW
Edmonton, AB
780-915-8151
E-mail: Afsa09@ualberta.ca
URL: sites.ualberta.ca/~afsu
Scope: Local

- **University of the Fraser Valley Faculty & Staff Association 2018 Annual General Meeting**
Location: British Columbia
Sponsor/Contact: University of the Fraser Valley Faculty & Staff Association
33844 King Rd.
Abbotsford, BC V2S 7M8
604-854-4530; *Fax:* 604-853-9540
E-mail: FSA.Info@ufv.ca
URL: www.ufv-fsa.ca
Scope: Local
Contact Information: Administrator: Tanja Rourke, E-mail: tanja.rourke@ufv.ca, Phone: 604-854-4530, ext. 4530

- **Vision Institute of Canada 2018 Conference**
Sponsor/Contact: Vision Institute of Canada
#205, 4025 Yonge St.
Toronto, ON M2P 2E3
416-224-2273; *Fax:* 416-224-9234
URL: www.visioninstitutecanada.com
Scope: National

- **West Coast Environmental Law 2018 Annual General Meeting**
Sponsor/Contact: West Coast Environmental Law
#200, 2006 West 10th Ave.
Vancouver, BC V6J 2B3
604-684-7378; *Fax:* 604-684-1312
Toll-Free: 800-330-9235
E-mail: admin@wcel.org
URL: www.wcel.org
Scope: Provincial
Purpose: The appointment of board members takes place each year

- **Westcoast Building & Hardware Show 2018**
Location: British Columbia
Sponsor/Contact: Building Supply Industry Association of British Columbia
#2, 19299 - 94th Ave.
Surrey, BC V4N 4E6
604-513-2205; *Fax:* 604-513-2206
Toll-Free: 888-711-5656
URL: www.bsiabc.ca

Scope: Provincial
Purpose: A trade show for members of the building supply industry, presenting educational opportunities & new & innovative products & services
Contact Information: Phone: 604-513-2205, E-mail: info@bsiabc.ca

- **Western Canada's Transportation Forum Fall 2018**
Sponsor/Contact: Western Transportation Advisory Council
#401, 899 Pender St. West
Vancouver, BC V6C 3B2
604-687-8691; *Fax:* 604-687-8751
E-mail: infoservices@westac.com
URL: www.westac.com

- **Western Retail Lumber Association 2018 Prairie Showcase Buying Show & Convention**
Sponsor/Contact: Western Retail Lumber Association
Western Retail Lumber Association Inc.
#1004, 213 Notre Dame Ave.
Winnipeg, MB R3B 1N3
204-957-1077; *Fax:* 204-947-5195
Toll-Free: 800-661-0253
E-mail: wrla@wrla.org
URL: www.wrla.org
Scope: Provincial

- **Western Stock Growers' Association Annual General Meeting 2018**
Sponsor/Contact: The Western Stock Growers' Association
P.O. Box 179
#14, 900 Village Lane
Okotoks, AB T1S 1Z6
403-250-9121
E-mail: office@wsga.ca
URL: www.wsga.ca
Scope: Provincial

- **Wilderness Tourism Association BC 2018 Annual General Meeting**
Sponsor/Contact: Wilderness Tourism Association
P.O. Box 423
Cumberland, BC V0R 1S0
250-336-2862; *Fax:* 250-336-2861
E-mail: admin@wilderness-tourism.bc.ca
URL: www.wilderness-tourism.bc.ca
Scope: Provincial
Purpose: Informative sessions & workshops about nature based tourism

- **Windfall Ecology Festival 2018**
Sponsor/Contact: Windfall Ecology Centre
93A Industrial Pkwy. South
Aurora, ON L4G 3V5
905-727-0491; *Fax:* 905-727-0491
Toll-Free: 866-280-4431
E-mail: info@windfallcentre.ca
URL: www.windfallcentre.ca
Scope: Local
Purpose: Electric vehicles, infrastructure development and practical information on how to incorporate electric mobility into your organization and strategy planning.
Contact Information: Email: festival@windfallcentre.ca

- **Women's Inter-Church Council of Canada 2018 Annual General Meeting**
Sponsor/Contact: Women's Inter-Church Council of Canada
47 Queen's Park Cres. East
Toronto, ON M5S 2C3
416-929-5184; *Fax:* 416-929-4064
E-mail: wicc@wicc.org
URL: www.wicc.org

Scope: National

- **World Congress on Medical Physics and Biomedical Engineering 2018**
Sponsor/Contact: International Federation for Medical & Biological Engineering
URL: www.ifmbe.org
Scope: International
Purpose: The Congresses are scheduled on a three-year basis and aligned with Federation's General Assembly meeting at which elections are held.

- **World Federation of Ukrainian Women's Organizations Annual General Meeting 2018**
Sponsor/Contact: World Federation of Ukrainian Women's Organizations
#206, 145 Evans Ave.
Toronto, ON M8Z 5X8
416-546-2491
E-mail: info@wfuwo.org
URL: www.wfuwo.org
Scope: International

- **World Future Society Annual Conference 2018**
Sponsor/Contact: World Future Society
#161, 3220 N St. NW
Washington, DC 20007
301-656-8274
Toll-Free: 800-989-8274
E-mail: info@wfs.org
URL: www.wfs.org
Scope: International

- **YouthCAN's 12th Annual Conference**
Sponsor/Contact: Youth in Care in Ontario
E-mail: youthcan@oacas.org
URL: ontarioyouthcan.org
Purpose: So youth can enhance communication, teamwork & leadership skills; develop connections; expand educational & professional options & participate in speaker events, workshops & other activities

- **Yukon Conservation Society 2018 Annual General Meeting**
Location: Yukon Territory
Sponsor/Contact: Yukon Conservation Society
302 Hawkins St.
Whitehorse, YT Y1A 1X6
867-668-5678; *Fax:* 867-668-6637
E-mail: ycs@ycs.yk.ca
URL: www.yukonconservation.org
Scope: Provincial

- **Yukon Horse & Rider Association AGM 2018**
Sponsor/Contact: Yukon Horse & Rider Association
P.O. Box 31482
Whitehorse, YT Y1A 6K8
E-mail: yukonhorseandriderassociation@gmail.com
URL: yukonhorseandrider.wordpress.com
Scope: Provincial

- **ZAP Montérégie assemblée générale annuelle**
Location: Quebec
Sponsor/Contact: ZAP Montérégie
3205, boul Rome
Brossard, QC J4Y 1R2
514-800-0935
E-mail: info@zapmonteregie.org
URL: www.zapmonteregie.org
Scope: Local

2019

January

- **2019 ROMA Annual Conference**
Date: January 26-29, 2019
Location: Sheraton Centre Hotel
Toronto, ON
Sponsor/Contact: Rural Ontario Municipal Association
#801, 200 University Ave.
Toronto, ON M5H 3C6
416-971-9856; *Fax:* 416-971-6191
Toll-Free: 877-426-6527
URL: www.roma.on.ca
Scope: Provincial

- **American Library Association 2019 Midwinter Meeting & Exhibits**
Date: January 25-29, 2019
Location: Seattle, WA USA
Sponsor/Contact: American Library Association
50 East Huron St.
Chicago, IL 60611-2795
312-944-6780; *Fax:* 312-440-9374
Toll-Free: 800-545-2433
E-mail: ala@ala.org
URL: www.ala.org
Scope: International
Purpose: A library & information service meeting presenting speakers, discussion groups, exhibits, & committee meetings

- **Society for Classical Studies 150th Annual Meeting**
Date: January 3-6, 2019
Location: San Diego, CA USA
Sponsor/Contact: Society for Classical Studies
University of Pennsylvania
#201E, 220 South 40th St.
Philadelphia, PA 19104-3512
215-898-4975; *Fax:* 215-573-7874
E-mail: info@classicalstudies.org
URL: classicalstudies.org
Scope: International

February

- **17th Annual Health & Safety Conference & Trade Fair**
Date: February 21-22, 2019
Location: Shaw Conference Center
Edmonton, AB
Sponsor/Contact: Health & Safety Conference Society of Alberta
P.O. Box 38009
Calgary, AB T3K 5G9
403-236-2225; *Fax:* 780-455-1120
E-mail: info@hsconference.com
URL: www.hsconference.com
Scope: Provincial
Purpose: Theme: "Facing Forward"

- **American Association for Justice 2019 Winter Convention**
Date: February 2-6, 2019
Location: Loews Miami Beach
Miami Beach, FL USA
Sponsor/Contact: American Association for Justice
#200, 777 - 6th St. NW
Washington, DC 20001
202-965-3500
Toll-Free: 800-424-2725
E-mail: membership@justice.org
URL: www.justice.org
Scope: International

- **American Association for the Advancement of Science 2019 Annual Meeting**
Date: February 14-18, 2019
Location: Washington, DC USA
Sponsor/Contact: American Association for the Advancement of Science
1200 New York Ave. NW
Washington, DC 20005
202-326-6440
E-mail: membership@aaas.org
URL: www.aaas.org
Scope: International
Purpose: Information for scientists, engineers, educators, & policy-makers

- **Canadian Digestive Diseases Week: Canadian Association of Gastroenterology Annual Scientific Conference 2019**
Date: February 24 - March 6, 2019
Location: Banff, AB
Sponsor/Contact: Canadian Association of Gastroenterology
#224, 1540 Cornwall Rd.
Oakville, ON L6J 7W5
905-829-2504; *Fax:* 905-829-0242
Toll-Free: 888-780-0007
E-mail: general@cag-acg.org
URL: www.cag-acg.org
Scope: National

- **Manitoba Water & Wastewater Association Annual Conference & Trade Show 2019**
Date: February 3-6, 2019
Location: Victoria Inn Airport
Winnipeg, MB
Sponsor/Contact: Manitoba Water & Wastewater Association
P.O. Box 1600
#215, 9 Saskatchewan Ave. West
Portage la Prairie, MB R1N 3P1
204-239-6868; *Fax:* 204-239-6872
Toll-Free: 866-396-2549
E-mail: mwwaoffice@shaw.ca
URL: www.mwwa.net
Scope: Provincial
Purpose: The presentation of technical papers plus the opportunity to view industry products & services
Contact Information: Executive Director: Iva Last, Phone: 204-239-6868, Toll-Free Phone: 1-866-396-2549, Fax: 204-239-6872, E-mail: mwwaoffice@shaw.ca

- **The Profile Show Spring 2019**
Date: February 22-25, 2019
Location: Ontario
Sponsor/Contact: Ontario Fashion Exhibitors
P.O. Box 218
#2219, 160 Tycos Dr.
Toronto, ON M6B 1W8
416-596-2401; *Fax:* 416-596-1808
Toll-Free: 800-765-7508
E-mail: info@profileshow.ca
URL: www.profileshow.ca
Scope: Provincial

March

- **2019 Society for Research in Child Development Biennial Meeting**
Date: March 21-23, 2019
Location: Baltimore, MD USA
Sponsor/Contact: Society for Research in Child Development
#401, 2950 South State St.
Ann Arbor, MI 48104
734-926-0600; *Fax:* 734-926-0601
E-mail: info@srcd.org
URL: www.srcd.org
Scope: International

- **29th International Pediatric Association Congress of Pediatrics 2019**
Date: March 17-21, 2019
Location: Panama City, Panama
Sponsor/Contact: International Pediatric Association
418 Webster Forest Dr.
Webster Groves, MO 63119
847-434-7507
E-mail: adminoffice@ipa-world.org
URL: www.ipa-world.org
Scope: International

- **American Concrete Institute Spring 2019 Concrete Conference & Exhibition**
Date: March 24-28, 2019
Location: Quebec City Convention Centre & Hilton Quebec
Québec, QC
Sponsor/Contact: American Concrete Institute
38800 Country Club Dr.
Farmington Hills, MI 48331-3439
248-848-3700; *Fax:* 248-848-3701
URL: www.concrete.org
Scope: International
Contact Information: Event Planner: Alexandria R. Prokic, E-mail: alex.prokic@concrete.org

- **Canadian Gas Association 2019 Engineering Conference**
Date: March 25-26, 2019
Location: Calgary, AB
Sponsor/Contact: Canadian Gas Association
#1220, 350 Albert St.
Ottawa, ON K1R 1A4
613-748-0057; *Fax:* 613-748-9078
E-mail: info@cga.ca
URL: www.cga.ca
Scope: National
Contact Information: E-mail: help@canavents.com

- **Canadian Gas Association 2019 Regulatory Course**
Date: March 4-6, 2019
Location: Calgary, AB
Sponsor/Contact: Canadian Gas Association
#1220, 350 Albert St.
Ottawa, ON K1R 1A4
613-748-0057; *Fax:* 613-748-9078
E-mail: info@cga.ca
URL: www.cga.ca
Scope: National
Contact Information: E-mail: help@canavents.com

- **NACE International CORROSION 2019**
Date: March 24-28, 2019
Location: Nashville, TN USA
Sponsor/Contact: NACE International
15835 Park Ten Pl.
Houston, TX 77084
281-228-6200; *Fax:* 281-228-6300
E-mail: firstservice@nace.org
URL: www.nace.org
Scope: International
Purpose: A corrosion conference & exposition

- **Teachers of English to Speakers of Other Languages, Inc. (TESOL) International Convention & English Language Expo**
Date: March 12-15, 2019
Location: Atlanta, GA USA
Sponsor/Contact: Teachers of English to Speakers of Other Languages, Inc.
#500, 1925 Ballenger Ave.
Alexandria, VA 22314-6820
703-836-0774; *Fax:* 703-836-7864
E-mail: info@tesol.org
URL: www.tesol.org
Scope: International
Contact Information: Director, Conference Services: Lisa Dyson, Phone: 703-836-0774, ext. 515, E-mail: conventions@tesol.org

April

- **26th Operating Room Nurses Association of Canada National Conference 2019**
Date: April 26-30, 2019
Location: Halifax Convention Centre
Halifax, NS
Sponsor/Contact: Operating Room Nurses Association of Canada
Toll-Free: 844-594-0052
E-mail: info@ornac.ca
URL: www.ornac.ca
Scope: National
Purpose: Theme: "Tides of Change, Oceans of Perioperative Excellence"

- **American Council of Learned Societies Annual Meeting 2019**
Date: April 25-27, 2019
Location: New York Marriott Downtown Hotel
New York, NY USA
Sponsor/Contact: American Council of Learned Societies
633 Third Ave.
New York, NY 10017-6795
212-697-1505; *Fax:* 212-949-8058
URL: www.acls.org
Scope: International
Contact Information: Director, Member Relations: Sandra Bradley, E-mail: sbradley@acls.org, Phone: 212-697-1505, ext. 123

- **Association of College & Research Libraries (ACRL) Conference 2019**
Date: April 10-13, 2019
Location: Cleveland, OH USA
Sponsor/Contact: Association of College & Research Libraries
c/o American Library Association
50 East Huron St.
Chicago, IL 60611-2795
312-280-2523; *Fax:* 312-280-2520
Toll-Free: 800-545-2433
E-mail: acrl@ala.org
URL: www.ala.org/acrl
Scope: National

- **Association of Medical Microbiology & Infectious Disease Canada 2019 Annual Conference**
Date: April 3-6, 2019
Location: The Westin Ottawa
Ottawa, ON
Sponsor/Contact: Association of Medical Microbiology & Infectious Disease Canada
192 Bank St.
Ottawa, ON K2P 1W8
613-260-3233; *Fax:* 613-260-3235
E-mail: communications@ammi.ca
URL: www.ammi.ca
Scope: National
Purpose: A yearly professional development event for AMMI members; features workshops on a variety of topics
Contact Information: Coordinator, Meetings: Paul Glover, E-mail: paul@ammi.ca

- **Canadian Gas Association 2019 Operations Conference**
Date: April 8-9, 2019
Location: London, ON
Sponsor/Contact: Canadian Gas Association
#1220, 350 Albert St.
Ottawa, ON K1R 1A4
613-748-0057; *Fax:* 613-748-9078
E-mail: info@cga.ca
URL: www.cga.ca
Scope: National
Contact Information: E-mail: help@canavents.com

- **Council of Forest Industries 2019 Annual Convention**
Date: April 2-4, 2019
Location: Prince George, BC
Sponsor/Contact: Council of Forest Industries
Pender Place I Business Building
#1501, 700 Pender St. West
Vancouver, BC V6C 1G8
604-684-0211; *Fax:* 604-687-4930
E-mail: info@cofi.org
URL: www.cofi.org
Scope: National
Purpose: A meeting about issues affecting the forestry industries of British Columbia.
Anticipated Attendance: 500-900
Contact Information: Phone: 604-684-0211; Fax: 604-687-4930

- **Library Association of Alberta Annual Conference 2019**
Date: April 25-28, 2019
Location: Alberta
Sponsor/Contact: Library Association of Alberta
80 Baker Cres. NW
Calgary, AB T2L 1R4
403-284-5818
Toll-Free: 877-522-5550
E-mail: info@laa.ca
URL: www.laa.ca
Scope: Provincial
Purpose: A conference held each spring for members of the Alberta library community, featuring association annual general meetings, session presentations, networking opportunities, & a trade show. Beginning this year, the conference is no longer held jointly with the Alberta Library Trustees Association (ALTA).
Contact Information: Library Association of Alberta, Phone: 403-284-5818, Toll-Free Phone: 1-877-522-5550, Fax: 403-282-6646, E-mail: info@laa.ca, info@albertalibraryconference.com

- **Manitoba Reading Association 5th Adolescent Literacy Summit**
Date: April 11-12, 2019
Location: Winnipeg, MB
Sponsor/Contact: Manitoba Reading Association
c/o Child Guidance Clinic, Winnipeg School Division
700 Elgin Ave.
Winnipeg, MB R2E 1B2
204-786-7841
URL: www.readingmanitoba.org

Conferences & Conventions Index

Scope: Provincial
Contact Information:
mrasummit.weebly.com

- **Pediatric Academic Societies' 2019 Annual Meeting**
Date: April 27-30, 2019
Location: Baltimore, MD USA
Sponsor/Contact: Academic Pediatric Association
6728 Old McLean Village Dr.
McLean, VA 22101
703-556-9222; *Fax:* 703-556-8729
E-mail: info@academicpeds.org
URL: www.academicpeds.org
Scope: International
Purpose: An international meeting focussing on research in child health
Contact Information: Address: #7B, 3400 Research Forest Dr., The Woodlands, TX, 77381, USA; Phone: 346-980-9717

- **Pediatric Endocrine Society 2019 Annual Meeting**
Date: April 27-30, 2019
Location: Baltimore, MD USA
Sponsor/Contact: Pediatric Endocrine Society
6728 Old McLean Village Dr.
McLean, VA 22101
E-mail: info@pedsendo.org
URL: www.pedsendo.org
Scope: International
Purpose: An annual opportunity for medical education for those engaged in the disciplines of pediatric endocrinology
Contact Information: E-mail: info@pedsendo.org

- **Society of Architectural Historians Annual International Conference 2019**
Date: April 24-28, 2019
Location: Providence, RI USA
Sponsor/Contact: Society of Architectural Historians
1365 North Astor St.
Chicago, IL 60610-2144
312-573-1365
E-mail: info@sah.org
URL: www.sah.org
Scope: International

May

- **2019 Ontario Association of Architects Conference**
Date: May 22-24, 2019
Location: Quebec City Convention Centre & Fairmont Le Chateau Frontenac Québec, QC
Sponsor/Contact: Ontario Association of Architects
111 Moatfield Dr.
Toronto, ON M3B 3L6
416-449-6898; *Fax:* 416-449-5756
Toll-Free: 800-565-2724
E-mail: oaamail@oaa.on.ca
URL: www.oaa.on.ca
Scope: Provincial

- **Alberta Federation of Labour Convention 2019**
Date: May 2-6, 2019
Location: Calgary Telus Convention Centre Calgary, AB
Sponsor/Contact: Alberta Federation of Labour
#300, 10408 - 124 St.
Edmonton, AB T5N 1R5
780-483-3021; *Fax:* 780-484-5928
Toll-Free: 800-661-3995

E-mail: afl@afl.org
URL: www.afl.org
Scope: Provincial
Contact Information: Administrator: Maureen Werlin, E-mail: afl@afl.org

- **American Society of Neuroradiology 2019 57th Annual Meeting**
Date: May 18-23, 2019
Location: Hynes Convention Center Boston, MA USA
Sponsor/Contact: American Society of Neuroradiology
#205, 800 Enterprise Dr.
Oak Brook, IL 60523
630-574-0220; *Fax:* 630-574-0661
URL: www.asnr.org
Scope: International
Contact Information: Director, Scientific Meetings: Lora Tannehill, E-mail: ltannehill@asnr.org; Manager, Scientific Meetings: Valerie Geisendorfer, E-mail: vgeisendorfer@asnr.org

- **Canadian Catholic School Trustees' Association 2019 AGM**
Date: May 30 - June 1, 2019
Location: Canmore, AB
Sponsor/Contact: Canadian Catholic School Trustees' Association
Catholic Education Centre
570 West Hunt Club Rd.
Nepean, ON K2G 3R4
613-224-4455; *Fax:* 613-224-3187
E-mail: ccsta@ocsb.ca
URL: www.ccsta.ca
Contact Information: ccsta@ocsb.ca

- **Canadian Gerontological Nursing Association 2019 20th Biennial Conference**
Date: May 2-4, 2019
Location: Calgary, AB
Sponsor/Contact: Canadian Gerontological Nursing Association
URL: www.cgna.net
Scope: National
Contact Information: cgna2019.ca

- **Canadian Health Food Association (CHFA) Québec 2019**
Date: May 3-4, 2019
Location: Palais des congrès de Montréal Montréal, QC
Sponsor/Contact: Canadian Health Food Association
#302, 235 Yorkland Blvd.
Toronto, ON M2J 4Y8
416-497-6939; *Fax:* 416-497-3214
Toll-Free: 800-661-4510
E-mail: info@chfa.ca
URL: www.chfa.ca
Scope: Provincial
Purpose: A conference & trade show designed for owners & decision makers from both small & large establishments, such as natural & health food retail stores, specialty stores, food chains, & pharmacies
Contact Information: Phone: 416-497-6939, Toll-Free Phone: 1-800-661-4510, E-mail: info@chfa.ca

- **Canadian Psychological Association 2019 National Convention & Annual Meeting**
Date: May 31 - June 2, 2019
Location: Halifax Marriott Harbourfront Halifax, NS
Sponsor/Contact: Canadian Psychological Association

#702, 141 Laurier Ave. West
Ottawa, ON K1P 5J3
613-237-2144; *Fax:* 613-237-1674
Toll-Free: 888-472-0657
E-mail: cpa@cpa.ca
URL: www.cpa.ca
Scope: National
Purpose: Co-convention with NACCJPC
Anticipated Attendance: 1,800

- **Commercial Seed Analysts Association of Canada Annual Convention 2019**
Date: May 27-29, 2019
Location: London, ON
Sponsor/Contact: Commercial Seed Analysts Association of Canada Inc.
5788 L&A Rd.
Vernon, BC V1B 3PG
204-720-0052
URL: www.seedanalysts.ca

- **Computer Human Interaction 2019 Conference: Human Factors in Computing Systems**
Date: May 4-9, 2019
Location: Glasgow, UK
Sponsor/Contact: Special Interest Group on Computer Human Interaction
P.O. Box 93672 Stn. Nelson Park
Vancouver, BC V6E 4L7
604-876-8985
E-mail: chi-VanCHI@acm.org
URL: www.sigchi.org
Scope: International

- **Federation of Northern Ontario Municipalities 2019 59th Annual Conference**
Date: May 8-10, 2019
Location: Sudbury, ON
Sponsor/Contact: Federation of Northern Ontario Municipalities
88 Riverside Dr.
Kapuskasing, ON P5N 1B3
705-337-4454; *Fax:* 705-337-1741
E-mail: fonom.info@gmail.com
URL: www.fonom.ca
Scope: Local
Purpose: A meeting for northern Ontario's municipal decision makers, featuring exhibits by suppliers, vendors, & professionals who provide services to municipalities

- **Government Finance Officers Association 2019 113th Annual Conference**
Date: May 19-22, 2019
Location: Los Angeles Convention Center Los Angeles, CA USA
Sponsor/Contact: Government Finance Officers Association
#2700, 203 North LaSalle St.
Chicago, IL 60601-1210
312-977-9700; *Fax:* 312-977-4806
E-mail: bnquiry@gfoa.org
URL: www.gfoa.org
Scope: International
Contact Information: Manager, Communications: Natalie Laudadio, Phone: 312-578-2298

- **Institute of Industrial & Systems Engineers Annual Conference & Expo 2019**
Date: May 18-21, 2019
Location: Caribe Hilton San Juan, PR USA
Sponsor/Contact: Institute of Industrial & Systems Engineers

#200, 3577 Parkway Lane
Norcross, GA 30092
770-449-0460; *Fax:* 770-441-3295
E-mail: cs@iienet.org
URL: www.iienet2.org
Scope: International

- **International Society for Magnetic Resonance in Medicine 2019 27th Scientific Meeting & Exhibition**
Date: May 11-17, 2019
Location: Montréal, QC
Sponsor/Contact: International Society for Magnetic Resonance in Medicine
#620, 2300 Clayton Rd.
Concord, CA 94520
510-841-1899; *Fax:* 510-841-2340
E-mail: info@ismrm.org
URL: www.ismrm.org
Scope: International
Purpose: Featuring the 26th Annual Meeting of the Section for Magnetic Resonance Technologists
Contact Information: Director, Meetings: Anne-Marie Kahrovic, E-mail: anne-marie@ismrm.org

- **Journées dentaires internationales du Québec (JDIQ) 2019**
Date: May 24-28, 2019
Location: Quebec
Sponsor/Contact: Ordre des dentistes du Québec
#1640, 800, boul René-Lévesque ouest
Montréal, QC H3B 1X9
514-875-8511; *Fax:* 514-393-9248
Toll-Free: 800-361-4887
URL: www.odq.qc.ca
Scope: Provincial
Contact Information: Président, Comité d'organisation des JDIQ: Pierre Boudrias, Courriel: congres@odq.qc.ca

- **Language Without Borders 2019 Conference**
Date: May 2-4, 2019
Location: Fredericton, NB
Sponsor/Contact: Canadian Association of Second Language Teachers
2490 Don Reid Dr.
Ottawa, ON K1H 1E1
613-727-0994
Toll-Free: 877-727-0994
E-mail: admin@caslt.org
URL: www.caslt.org

- **Medical Library Association 2019 Annual Meeting & Exhibition**
Date: May 3-8, 2019
Location: Chicago, IL USA
Sponsor/Contact: Medical Library Association
#1900, 65 East Wacker Pl.
Chicago, IL 60601-7246
312-419-9094; *Fax:* 312-419-8950
E-mail: websupport@mail.mlahq.org
URL: www.mlanet.org
Scope: International

- **Ontario's Water Conference & Trade Show 2019**
Date: May 5-8, 2019
Location: Ottawa, ON
Sponsor/Contact: Ontario Water Works Association
#100, 922 The East Mall Dr.
Toronto, ON M9B 6K1
416-231-1555; *Fax:* 416-231-1556
Toll-Free: 866-975-0575
E-mail: waterinfo@owwa.ca
URL: www.owwa.com

Scope: Provincial
Purpose: This annual industry highlight features a full slate of plenary and technical sessions focusing on the latest in technology and research affecting drinking water from source to tap. The Trade Show consistently has more than 100 exhibitors representing the manufacturers and suppliers of products and services for the water industry.
Anticipated Attendance: 1,400+

June

• **102nd Canadian Chemistry Conference & Exhibition**
Date: June 3-7, 2019
Location: Québec, QC
Sponsor/Contact: Chemical Institute of Canada
#400, 222 Queen St.
Ottawa, ON K1P 5V9
613-232-6252; *Fax:* 613-232-5862
Toll-Free: 888-542-2242
E-mail: info@cheminst.ca
URL: www.cheminst.ca
Scope: National

• **American Library Association 2019 Annual Conference**
Date: June 20-25, 2019
Location: Washington, DC USA
Sponsor/Contact: American Library Association
50 East Huron St.
Chicago, IL 60611-2795
312-944-6780; *Fax:* 312-440-9374
Toll-Free: 800-545-2433
E-mail: ala@ala.org
URL: www.ala.org
Scope: International
Purpose: A conference providing speakers, educational programs, committee meetings, & exhibits related to library & information services

• **American Water Works Association Annual Conference & Exposition 2019**
Date: June 9-12, 2019
Location: Denver, CO USA
Sponsor/Contact: American Water Works Association
6666 West Quincy Ave.
Denver, CO 80235
303-794-7711; *Fax:* 303-347-0804
Toll-Free: 800-926-7337
E-mail: service@awwa.org
URL: www.awwa.org
Scope: International
Purpose: An international gathering of thousands of water professionals, featuring a technical program, workshops, seminars, & exhibits

• **Canadian Anesthesiologists' Society 2019 75th Annual Meeting**
Date: June 21-24, 2019
Location: Telus Convention Centre
Calgary, AB
Sponsor/Contact: Canadian Anesthesiologists' Society
#208, 1 Eglinton Ave. East
Toronto, ON M4P 3A1
416-480-0602; *Fax:* 416-480-0320
E-mail: anesthesia@cas.ca
URL: www.cas.ca
Scope: National
Purpose: A convention, with an exhibition pharmaceutical companies & equipment manufacturers

• **Canadian Association for Dental Research 43rd Annual Meeting**
Date: June 19-22, 2019
Location: Vancouver, BC
Sponsor/Contact: Canadian Association for Dental Research
c/o Western University
1151 Richmond St.
London, ON N6A 5B8
519-661-2111
URL: www.cadr-acrd.ca
Scope: International
Purpose: In conjunction with the 48th Annual Meeting of the American Association of Dental Research & the 97th General Session & Exhibition of the International Association for Dental Research

• **Canadian Council of Motor Transport Administrators 2019 Annual Meeting**
Date: June 2-5, 2019
Location: Ottawa, ON
Sponsor/Contact: Canadian Council of Motor Transport Administrators
#404, 1111 Prince of Wales
Ottawa, ON K2C 3T2
613-736-1003; *Fax:* 613-736-1395
E-mail: info@ccmta.ca
URL: www.ccmta.ca
Scope: National
Purpose: Educational events, an exhibition, a working forum where important decisions are made, & an excellent networking opportunity for government decision-makers & members of the private sector
Contact Information: Phone: 613-736-1003
Fax: 613-736-1395, E-mail: ccmta-secretariat@ccmta.ca

• **Canadian Dermatology Association 2019 94th Annual Conference**
Date: June 26-29, 2019
Location: Calgary, AB
Sponsor/Contact: Canadian Dermatology Association
#425, 1385 Bank St.
Ottawa, ON K1H 8N4
613-738-1748; *Fax:* 613-738-4695
Toll-Free: 800-267-3376
E-mail: info@dermatology.ca
URL: www.dermatology.ca
Scope: National
Purpose: Oral & poster presentations on subjects relevant to practicing dermatologists

• **Canadian Gas Association Gas Measurement & Regulation School 2019**
Date: June 8-9, 2019
Location: Quebec City, QC
Sponsor/Contact: Canadian Gas Association
#1220, 350 Albert St.
Ottawa, ON K1R 1A4
613-748-0057; *Fax:* 613-748-9078
E-mail: info@cga.ca
URL: www.cga.ca
Scope: National
Contact Information: E-mail: help@canavents.com

• **Canadian Political Science Association 2019 Annual Conference (within the Congress of the Humanities & Social Sciences)**
Date: June 1-7, 2019
Location: University of British Columbia
Vancouver, BC
Sponsor/Contact: Canadian Political Science Association
#204, 260 Dalhousie St.
Ottawa, ON K1N 7E4
613-562-1202; *Fax:* 613-241-0019
E-mail: cpsa-acsp@cpsa-acsp.ca
URL: www.cpsa-acsp.ca
Scope: National
Purpose: A conference including the association's business & committee meetings, special presentations, workshops, & exhibits
Contact Information: Administrator: Michelle Hopkins, E-mail: cpsa-acsp@cpsa-acsp.ca

• **Canadian Sociological Association 2019 Annual Conference**
Date: June 2019
Location: University of British Columbia
Vancouver, BC
Sponsor/Contact: Canadian Sociological Association
P.O. Box 98014
2126 Burnhamthorpe Rd. West
Mississauga, ON L5L 5V4
416-660-4378
E-mail: office@csa-scs.ca
URL: www.csa-scs.ca
Scope: National

• **Federation of Medical Regulatory Authorities of Canada 2019 Annual Meeting & Conference**
Date: June 8-10, 2019
Location: Whistler, BC
Sponsor/Contact: Federation of Medical Regulatory Authorities of Canada
1021 Thomas Spratt Pl.
Ottawa, ON K1G 5L5
613-738-0372; *Fax:* 613-738-9169
E-mail: info@fmrac.ca
URL: www.fmrac.ca
Scope: National

• **International Association for Hydrogen Energy (IAHE) 8th World Hydrogen Technology Convention 2019**
Date: June 2-7, 2019
Location: Tokyo, Japan
Sponsor/Contact: International Association for Hydrogen Energy
#303, 5794 - 40th St. SW
Miami, FL 33155
E-mail: info@iahe.org
URL: www.iahe.org
Scope: International
Purpose: A conference of the International Association for Hydrogen Energy, for the hydrogen & fuel cell community, featuring an exhibition with hydrogen & fuel cell applications from research institutions & companies

• **Local Government Management Association of British Columbia 2019 Annual Conference & AGM**
Date: June 9-13, 2019
Location: Westin Bayshore
Vancouver, BC
Sponsor/Contact: Local Government Management Association of British Columbia
710 - 880 Douglas St.
Victoria, BC V8W 1B7
250-383-7032; *Fax:* 250-384-4879
E-mail: office@lgma.ca
URL: www.lgma.ca
Scope: Provincial
Contact Information: Program Manager: Ana Fuller, Phone: 250-383-7032, ext. 227, E-mail: afuller@lgma.ca

• **Microwave Theory & Techniques Society International Microwave Symposia 2019**
Date: June 3-7, 2019
Location: Boston, MA USA
Sponsor/Contact: IEEE Microwave Theory & Techniques Society
5829 Bellanca Dr.
Elkridge, MD 21075
410-796-5866
URL: www.mtt.org
Scope: International
Purpose: Technical papers; Workshops; Trade show

• **North American Association of Central Cancer Registries 2019 Annual Conference**
Date: June 8-15, 2019
Location: Vancouver, BC
Sponsor/Contact: North American Association of Central Cancer Registries, Inc.
2050 West Iles, #A
Springfield, IL 62704-7412
217-698-0800; *Fax:* 217-698-0188
URL: www.naaccr.org
Scope: International
Anticipated Attendance: 450

July

• **18th FINA World Championships**
Date: July 12-28, 2019
Location: Gwangju, Korea
Sponsor/Contact: International Amateur Swimming Federation
Ch de Bellevue 24a/24b
Lausanne, 1005
URL: www.fina.org
Scope: International

• **2019 International Association of Music Libraries, Archives & Documentation Centres Congress**
Date: July 14-19, 2019
Location: Krakow, Poland
Sponsor/Contact: International Association of Music Libraries, Archives & Documentation Centres
c/o Roger Flury, Music Room, National Library of New Zealand
P.O. Box 1467
Wellington, 6001
URL: www.iaml.info
Scope: International
Purpose: Educational sessions, social & cultural programs, & exhibits of interest to international music librarians, archivists, & documentation specialists

• **2019 Pressure Vessels & Piping Conference**
Date: July 14, 2019
Location: San Antonio, TX USA
Sponsor/Contact: American Society of Mechanical Engineers
2 Park Ave.
New York, NY 10016-5990
Toll-Free: 800-843-2763
E-mail: customercare@asme.org
URL: www.asme.org
Scope: International

• **American Association for Justice 2019 Annual Convention**
Date: July 27-30, 2019

Conferences & Conventions Index

Location: San Diego Convention Center
San Diego, CA USA
Sponsor/Contact: American Association for Justice
#200, 777 - 6th St. NW
Washington, DC 20001
202-965-3500
Toll-Free: 800-424-2725
E-mail: membership@justice.org
URL: www.justice.org
Scope: International

- **Canadian Association of Optometrists 2019 36th Biennial Congress**
Date: July 11-13, 2019
Location: Victoria, BC
Sponsor/Contact: Canadian Association of Optometrists
234 Argyle Ave.
Ottawa, ON K2P 1B9
613-235-7924; Fax: 613-235-2098
Toll-Free: 888-263-4676
E-mail: info@opto.ca
URL: www.opto.ca
Scope: National
Anticipated Attendance: 600

- **Canadian Institute of Planners 2019 Conference**
Date: July 3-6, 2019
Location: Ottawa, ON
Sponsor/Contact: Canadian Institute of Planners
#1112, 141 Laurier Ave. West
Ottawa, ON K1P 5J3
613-237-7526; Fax: 613-237-7045
Toll-Free: 800-207-2138
E-mail: general@cip-icu.ca
URL: www.cip-icu.ca
Scope: National

- **International Association of Administrative Professionals Summit 2019**
Date: July 18-21, 2019
Location: Gaylord National
National Harbor, MD USA
Sponsor/Contact: International Association of Administrative Professionals
#100, 10502 North Ambassador Dr.
Kansas City, MO 64153
816-891-6600; Fax: 816-891-9118
URL: www.iaap-hq.org
Scope: International
Purpose: Education workshops

- **International Union of Pure & Applied Chemistry 47th World Chemistry Congress 2019**
Date: July 7-12, 2019
Location: Palais des Congrès de Paris
Paris, France
Sponsor/Contact: International Union of Pure & Applied Chemistry
IUPAC Secretariat, Bldg. 19
P.O. Box 13757
Research Triangle Park, NC 27709-3757
Fax: 919-485-8706
URL: www.iupac.org
Scope: International

- **STI & HIV World Congress 2019**
Date: July 14-17, 2019
Location: Vancouver, BC
Sponsor/Contact: International Society for Sexually Transmitted Diseases Research
c/o Basil Donovan, The Kirby Institute, University of New South Wales
Sidney
URL: www.isstdr.org
Scope: International

August

- **2019 Association of Municipalities of Ontario AGM & Annual Conference**
Date: August 18-21, 2019
Location: Shaw Centre
Ottawa, ON
Sponsor/Contact: Association of Municipalities of Ontario
#801, 200 University Ave.
Toronto, ON M5H 3C6
416-971-9856; Fax: 416-971-6191
Toll-Free: 877-426-6527
E-mail: amo@amo.on.ca
URL: www.amo.on.ca
Scope: Provincial
Purpose: A yearly gathering of municipal government officials to discuss current issues.

- **American Political Science Association 115th Annual Meeting 2019**
Date: August 29-September 1, 2019
Location: Washington, DC USA
Sponsor/Contact: American Political Science Association
1527 New Hampshire Ave. NW
Washington, DC 20036-1206
202-483-2512; Fax: 202-483-2657
E-mail: apsa@apsanet.org
URL: www.apsanet.org
Scope: International

- **Catholic Women's League of Canada 2019 National Convention**
Date: August 18-21, 2019
Location: Calgary, AB
Sponsor/Contact: Catholic Women's League of Canada
702C Scotland Ave.
Winnipeg, MB R3M 1X5
204-927-2310; Fax: 888-831-9507
Toll-Free: 888-656-4040
E-mail: info@cwl.ca
URL: www.cwl.ca
Scope: National

- **Thermal Insulation Association of Canada 2019 Annual Conference**
Date: August 24-27, 2019
Location: Le Centre Sheraton Montréal
Montréal, QC
Sponsor/Contact: Thermal Insulation Association of Canada
1485 Laperriere Ave.
Ottawa, ON K1Z 7S8
613-724-4834; Fax: 613-729-6206
E-mail: info@tiac.ca
URL: www.tiac.ca
Scope: National

September

- **American Fisheries Society 149th Annual Meeting 2019**
Date: September 29 - October 3, 2019
Location: Reno, NV USA
Sponsor/Contact: American Fisheries Society
#110, 5410 Grosvenor Lane
Bethesda, MD 20814-2199
301-897-8616; Fax: 301-897-8096
URL: www.fisheries.org
Scope: International

- **Canadian Association of Orthodontists 2019 71st Annual Scientific Session**
Date: September 19-21, 2019
Location: Delta Fredericton Hotel & Fredericton Convention Centre
Fredericton, NB
Sponsor/Contact: Canadian Association of Orthodontists
#210, 2800 - 14th Ave.
Toronto, ON L3R 0E4
416-491-3186; Fax: 416-491-1670
Toll-Free: 877-226-8800
E-mail: cao@associationconcepts.ca
URL: www.cao-aco.org
Scope: National
Purpose: A scientific session with exhibits

- **Canadian Fertility & Andrology Society 2019 65th Annual Meeting**
Date: September 19-21, 2019
Location: The Westin Ottawa
Ottawa, ON
Sponsor/Contact: Canadian Fertility & Andrology Society
#301, 1719, rue Grand Trunk
Montréal, QC H3K 1M1
514-524-9009; Fax: 514-524-2163
E-mail: info@cfas.ca
URL: www.cfas.ca
Scope: National
Purpose: Educational presentations, a trade show, & networking opportunities for persons involved in the field of reproductive medicine

- **Intermodal Association of North America Intermodal EXPO 2019**
Date: September 15-17, 2019
Location: Long Beach, CA USA
Sponsor/Contact: Intermodal Association of North America
#1100, 11785 Beltsville Dr.
Calverton, MD 20705
301-982-3400; Fax: 301-982-4815
E-mail: info@intermodal.org
URL: www.intermodal.org
Scope: International

- **International Society for Rock Mechanics 14th International Congress on Rock Mechanics**
Date: September 20-27, 2019
Location: Foz do Iguacu, Brazil
Sponsor/Contact: International Society for Rock Mechanics
c/o Laboratório Nacional de Engenharia Civil
101 Av. do Brasil
Lisbon, 1700-066
E-mail: secretariat@isrm.net
URL: www.isrm.net
Scope: International

- **The American Association of Bovine Practitioners 2019 Annual Conference**
Date: September 12-14, 2019
Location: St. Louis, MO USA
Sponsor/Contact: American Association of Bovine Practitioners
P.O. Box 3610
#802, 3320 Skyway Dr.
Auburn, AL 36831-3610
334-821-0442; Fax: 334-821-9532
E-mail: aabphq@aabp.org
URL: www.aabp.org
Scope: International

- **The Profile Show Fall 2019**
Date: September 7-10, 2019
Location: Ontario
Sponsor/Contact: Ontario Fashion Exhibitors
P.O. Box 218
#2219, 160 Tycos Dr.
Toronto, ON M6B 1W8
416-596-2401; Fax: 416-596-1808
Toll-Free: 800-765-7508
E-mail: info@profileshow.ca
URL: www.profileshow.ca
Scope: Provincial

- **Union of British Columbia Municipalities 2019 Annual Convention**
Date: September 23-27, 2019
Location: Vancouver Convention & Exhibition Centre
Vancouver, BC
Sponsor/Contact: Union of British Columbia Municipalities
#60, 10551 Shellbridge Way
Richmond, BC V6X 2W9
604-270-8226; Fax: 604-270-9116
URL: www.ubcm.ca
Scope: Provincial

- **Western Canada Water 2019 71st Annual Conference & Exhibition**
Date: September 17-20, 2019
Location: Shaw Conference Center
Edmonton, AB
Sponsor/Contact: Western Canada Water
P.O. Box 1708
240 River Ave.
Cochrane, AB T4C 1B6
403-709-0064; Fax: 403-709-0068
Toll-Free: 877-283-2003
E-mail: member@wcwwa.ca
URL: www.wcwwa.ca
Scope: Provincial
Purpose: A technical program, a keynote speaker, & a trade show for delegates from Western Canada Water
Anticipated Attendance: 500+
Contact Information: Western Canada Water, Toll-Free Phone: 1-877-283-2003, Toll-Free Fax: 1-877-283-2007, E-mail: info@wcwwa.ca

- **World Energy Council World Energy Congress 2019**
Date: September 8-12, 2019
Location: Abu Dhabi, United Arab Emirates
Sponsor/Contact: World Energy Council
62-64 Cornhill St.
London, EC3V 3NH
URL: www.worldenergy.org
Scope: International

October

- **American Concrete Institute Fall 2019 Concrete Conference & Exhibition**
Date: October 20-24, 2019
Location: Duke Energy Convention Center & Hyatt Regency Cincinnati
Cincinnati, OH USA
Sponsor/Contact: American Concrete Institute
38800 Country Club Dr.
Farmington Hills, MI 48331-3439
248-848-3700; Fax: 248-848-3701
URL: www.concrete.org
Scope: International
Contact Information: Event Planner: Alexandria R. Prokic, E-mail: alex.prokic@concrete.org

- **Association of Family Health Teams of Ontario 2019 Conference**
Date: October 23-24, 2019
Sponsor/Contact: Association of Family Health Teams of Ontario
#800, 60 St. Clair Ave. East
Toronto, ON M4T 1N5
647-234-8605
E-mail: info@afhto.ca
URL: www.afhto.ca
Scope: Provincial

Conferences & Conventions Index

- **Canadian Society for Exercise Physiology 2019 AGM**
Date: October 2019
Sponsor/Contact: Canadian Society for Exercise Physiology
#370, 18 Louisa St.
Ottawa, ON K1R 6Y6
613-234-3755; Fax: 613-234-3565
Toll-Free: 877-651-3755
E-mail: info@csep.ca
URL: www.csep.ca
Scope: National

- **Canadian Society of Association Executives / Société canadienne d'association 2019 Conference & Showcase**
Date: October 23-25, 2019
Location: Vancouver, BC
Sponsor/Contact: Canadian Society of Association Executives
#1100, 10 King St. East
Toronto, ON M5C 1C3
416-363-3555; Fax: 416-363-3630
Toll-Free: 800-461-3608
URL: www.csae.com
Scope: National

- **Society of Plastics Engineers Vinyltec 2019 Conference**
Date: October 1-3, 2019
Location: Akron, OH USA
Sponsor/Contact: Society of Plastics Engineers
#306, 6 Berkshire Blvd.
Bethel, CT 06801
203-775-0471; Fax: 203-775-8490
URL: www.4spe.org
Scope: International

November

- **American Anthropological Association 2019 Annual Meeting**
Date: November 20-24, 2019
Location: Vancouver Convention Center Vancouver, BC
Sponsor/Contact: American Anthropological Association
#1301, 2300 Clarendon Blvd.
Arlington, VA 22201
703-528-1902; Fax: 703-528-3546
URL: www.americananthro.org
Scope: International
Contact Information: Director, Meetings & Conferences: Ushma Suvarnakar, Phone: 703-528-1902 ext. 1172

- **Association of Manitoba Municipalities 21st Annual Convention**
Date: November 25-27, 2019
Location: Keystone Centre
Brandon, MB
Sponsor/Contact: Association of Manitoba Municipalities
1910 Saskatchewan Ave. West
Portage la Prairie, MB R1N 0P1
204-857-8666; Fax: 204-856-2370
E-mail: amm@amm.mb.ca
URL: www.amm.mb.ca

- **ATAC 85th Canadian Aviation Conference & Tradeshow**
Date: November 18-20, 2019
Location: Fairmont Queen Elizabeth Hotel Montreal, QC
Sponsor/Contact: Air Transport Association of Canada
#700, 255 Albert St.
Ottawa, ON K1P 6A9
613-233-7727; Fax: 613-230-8648
E-mail: atac@atac.ca
URL: www.atac.ca
Scope: National
Purpose: National gathering for operators, suppliers to the industry & government stakeholders involved in commerical aviation and flight training in Canada
Contact Information: Debbie Simpson; dsimpson@atac.ca; 613-233-7727 ext. 312

- **International Commission on Radiological Protection 5th International Symposium**
Date: November 19-21, 2019
Location: Adelaide, Australia
Sponsor/Contact: International Commission on Radiological Protection
280 Slater St.
Ottawa, ON K1P 5S9
613-947-9750; Fax: 613-944-1920
E-mail: admin@icrp.org
URL: www.icrp.org
Scope: International

- **Saskatchewan Water and Wastewater Association 2019 Tradeshow and Conference**
Date: November 5-8, 2019
Sponsor/Contact: Saskatchewan Water & Wastewater Association
P.O. Box 7831 Stn. Mn
Saskatoon, SK S7K 4R5
306-761-1278
Toll-Free: 888-668-1278
E-mail: office@swwa.ca
URL: www.swwa.ca
Scope: National

Other Conferences in 2019

- **27th Canadian Congress of Applied Mechanics 2019**
Sponsor/Contact: Canadian Society for Mechanical Engineering
1295 Hwy. 2 East
Kingston, ON K7L 4V1
613-547-5989; Fax: 613-547-0195
E-mail: csme@cogeco.ca
URL: www.csme-scgm.ca
Scope: National
Purpose: Tech tracks at past conferences have included civil engineering, computational mechanics, dynamics & vibration, education in applied mechanics, fluid mechanics, manufacturing, mechatronics, micro-electro-mechanical systems, solid mechanics & materials, & thermodynamics & heat transfer

- **3rd National Construction & Maintenance Industry Strategy Summit 2019**
Sponsor/Contact: BuildForce Canada
#1150, 220 Laurier Ave. West
Ottawa, ON K1P 5Z9
613-569-5552
E-mail: info@buildforce.ca
URL: www.buildforce.ca
Scope: National
Purpose: Biennial conference

- **8th International Conference on Fog, Fog Collection and Dew**
Location: Taipei, Taiwan
Sponsor/Contact: FogQuest
448 Monarch Pl.
Kamloops, BC V2E 2B2
250-374-1745; Fax: 250-374-1746
E-mail: info@fogquest.org
URL: www.fogquest.org
Scope: International

- **Annual Alberta Horse Conference 2019**
Sponsor/Contact: Horse Industry Association of Alberta
97 East Lake Ramp NE
Airdrie, AB T4A 0C3
403-420-5949; Fax: 403-948-2069
URL: www.albertahorseindustry.ca
Scope: Provincial
Purpose: Internationally recognized speakers of interest to horse breeders, owners, & professionals

- **Art Libraries Society of North America 47th Annual Conference 2019**
Location: Salt Lake City, UT USA
Sponsor/Contact: Art Libraries Society of North America
7044 South 13th St.
Oak Creek, WI 53154
414-908-4954
Toll-Free: 800-817-0621
URL: www.arlisna.org
Purpose: The conference provides the opportunity for professionals involved in art librarianship to meet, learn and share their knowledge of the field. It also allows them to explore exhibitions & interact with vendors involved with art libraries.

- **Association for Canadian Studies in the United States 25th Biennial Conference**
Sponsor/Contact: Association for Canadian Studies in the United States
#350, 2030 - M St. NW
Washington, DC 20036
E-mail: info@acsus.org
URL: www.acsus.org
Scope: International
Purpose: Speakers & panels presenting research & information about Canada across all disciplines

- **Association of Canadian Archivists 2019 44th Annual Conference**
Sponsor/Contact: Association of Canadian Archivists
P.O. Box 2596 Stn. D
#911, 75 Albert St.
Ottawa, ON K1P 5W6
613-234-6977; Fax: 613-234-8500
URL: www.archivists.ca
Scope: National
Purpose: A meeting occurring in May or June each year, for archivists from across Canada, featuring educational presentations, trade show exhibits, networking opportunities, as well as workshops immediately prior or following conference sessions

- **Canadian Accredited Independent Schools Advancement Professionals Biennial National Conference 2019**
Sponsor/Contact: Canadian Accredited Independent Schools Advancement Professionals
E-mail: isapcanada@gmail.com
URL: www.isapc.ca
Scope: National

- **Canadian Air Traffic Control Association 2019 Convention**
Location: Calgary Tower, Springbank Tower & Edmonton ACC
Calgary, AB
Sponsor/Contact: Canadian Air Traffic Control Association
#304, 265 Carling Ave.
Ottawa, ON K1S 2E1
613-225-3553; Fax: 613-225-8448
E-mail: catca@catca.ca
URL: www.catca.ca
Scope: National
Purpose: A biennial convention attended by delegates from regions across Canada

- **Canadian Archaeological Association Annual Meeting 2019**
Location: Québec, QC
Sponsor/Contact: Canadian Archaeological Association
URL: www.canadianarchaeology.com
Scope: National

- **Canadian Economics Association 52nd Annual Conference 2019**
Location: Banff Centre for Arts & Creativity Banff, AB
Sponsor/Contact: Canadian Economics Association
Department of Economics, Brock Univ.
500 Glenridge Ave.
St Catharines, ON L2S 3A1
905-688-5550
URL: www.economics.ca
Scope: National
Purpose: An annual conference held during the last week of May or the first week of June

- **Canadian Federation of Mental Health Nurses 2019 National Conference**
Sponsor/Contact: Canadian Federation of Mental Health Nurses
#109, 1 Concorde Gate
Toronto, ON M3C 3N6
416-426-7029; Fax: 416-426-7280
URL: www.cfmhn.ca
Scope: National

- **Canadian Federation of Nurses Unions 2019 Biennial Convention**
Sponsor/Contact: Canadian Federation of Nurses Unions
2841 Riverside Dr.
Ottawa, ON K1V 8X7
613-526-4661; Fax: 613-526-1023
Toll-Free: 800-321-9821
URL: www.nursesunions.ca
Scope: National

- **Canadian Historical Association 2019 Annual Meeting**
Location: University of British Columbia Vancouver, BC
Sponsor/Contact: Canadian Historical Association
#1912, 130 Albert St.
Ottawa, ON K1P 5G4
613-233-7885; Fax: 613-565-5445
E-mail: cha-shc@cha-shc.ca
URL: www.cha-shc.ca
Scope: National
Purpose: An event for historians to showcase their research & to discuss issues related to the discipline

- **Canadian Network for Respiratory Care National Respiratory Education Conference 2019**
Sponsor/Contact: Canadian Network for Respiratory Care
16851 Mount Wolfe Rd.
Caledon, ON L7E 3P6
905-880-1092; Fax: 905-880-9733
Toll-Free: 855-355-4672
E-mail: info@cnrchome.net
URL: www.cnrchome.net

Conferences & Conventions Index

- **Canadian Obesity Summit 2019**
Sponsor/Contact: Canadian Obesity Network
Li Ka Shing Centre for Health Research & Innovation, Univ. of Alberta
#1-116, 8602 - 112 St.
Edmonton, AB T6G 2E1
780-492-8361; Fax: 780-492-9414
E-mail: info@obesitynetwork.ca
URL: www.obesitynetwork.ca
Scope: National

- **Canadian Pharmacists Association 2019 Canadian Pharmacists Conference**
Sponsor/Contact: Canadian Pharmacists Association
1785 Alta Vista Dr.
Ottawa, ON K1G 3Y6
613-523-7877; Fax: 613-523-0445
Toll-Free: 800-917-9489
E-mail: info@pharmacists.ca
URL: www.pharmacists.ca
Scope: National
Purpose: Professional development activities, workshops, & a trade show for pharmacists from across Canada

- **Canadian Professional Association for Transgender Health Conference**
Sponsor/Contact: Canadian Professional Association for Transgender Health
#201, 1770 Fort St.
Ottawa, ON V8R 1J5
250-592-6183; Fax: 250-592-6123
E-mail: info@cpath.ca
URL: www.cpath.ca
Scope: National

- **Canadian Society for Epidemiology & Biostatistics 2019 Biennial Conference**
Sponsor/Contact: Canadian Society for Epidemiology & Biostatistics
c/o Pamela Wilson, The Willow Group
1485 Laperriere Ave.
Ottawa, ON K1Z 7S8
613-722-8796; Fax: 613-729-6206
E-mail: secretariat@cseb.ca
URL: cseb.ca
Scope: National

- **Family Resource Program Conference 2019**
Sponsor/Contact: Canadian Association of Family Resource Programs
#149, 150 Isabella St.
Ottawa, ON K1S 1V7
613-237-7667; Fax: 613-237-8515
Toll-Free: 866-637-7226
E-mail: info@frp.ca
URL: www.frp.ca
Scope: National
Purpose: A biennial conference, presenting a keynote speaker, a panel discussion, workshops, & exhibits

- **Federation of Ontario Law Associations 2019 Bi-Annual Plenary**
Location: Ontario
Sponsor/Contact: Federation of Ontario Law Associations
731 - 9th St. West
Owen Sound, ON N4K 3P5
519-270-4283
E-mail: info@fola.ca
URL: www.fola.ca
Scope: Provincial

- **Geological Association of Canada 2019 Annual Meeting**
Location: Québec, QC
Sponsor/Contact: Geological Association of Canada
c/o Department of Earth Sciences, Memorial University of Newfoundland
#ER4063, Alexander Murray Bldg.
St. John's, NL A1B 3X5
709-864-7660; Fax: 709-864-2532
E-mail: gac@mun.ca
URL: www.gac.ca
Scope: National

- **International Academy of Law & Mental Health 2019 International Congress on Law and Mental Health**
Sponsor/Contact: International Academy of Law & Mental Health
c/o Philippe Pinel, Faculty of Medicine, University of Montreal
P.O. Box 6128 Stn. Centre-Ville
Montréal, QC H3C 3J7
514-343-5938; Fax: 514-343-2452
E-mail: admin@ialmh.org
URL: www.ialmh.org
Scope: International

- **International Association of Sedimentologists (IAS) 34th Meeting of Sedimentology 2019**
Sponsor/Contact: International Association of Sedimentologists
c/o Ghent University
#8, Krijgslaan 281
Gent, 90000
URL: www.sedimentologists.org
Scope: International

- **International Foster Care Organisation 2019 World Conference**
Sponsor/Contact: International Foster Care Organisation
26 Red Lion Square
London, WC1R 4AG
E-mail: ifco@ifco.info
URL: www.ifco.info
Scope: International
Purpose: A biennial conference, featuring a youth program, workshops, & plenary sessions about quality care solutions for children & youth living in out-of-home care

- **International Society for Neurochemistry 2019 Biennial Meeting**
Sponsor/Contact: International Society for Neurochemistry
c/o Kenes International
P.O. Box 6053
#7, rue François-Versonnex
Geneva, 1211
URL: www.neurochemistry.org
Scope: International

- **International Solar Energy Society (ISES) Solar World Congress 2019**
Sponsor/Contact: International Solar Energy Society
International Headquarters, Villa Tannheim
Wiesentalstrasse 50
Freiburg, 79115
E-mail: hq@ises.org
URL: www.ises.org
Scope: International

- **New Brunswick Federation of Labour 54th Biennial Convention 2019**
Location: New Brunswick
Sponsor/Contact: New Brunswick Federation of Labour
#314, 96 Norwood Ave.
Moncton, NB E1C 6L9
506-857-2125; Fax: 506-383-1597
E-mail: info@fednb.ca
URL: www.nbfl-fttnb.ca
Scope: Provincial
Purpose: A biennial gathering where approximately sixty resolutions are normally submitted & handled

- **Ontario Federation of Labour 15th Biennial Convention 2019**
Location: Ontario
Sponsor/Contact: Ontario Federation of Labour
#202, 15 Gervais Dr.
Toronto, ON M3C 1Y8
416-441-2731; Fax: 416-441-0722
Toll-Free: 800-668-9138
E-mail: info@ofl.ca
URL: www.ofl.ca
Scope: Provincial

- **Pacific Dental Conference 2019**
Location: British Columbia
Sponsor/Contact: British Columbia Dental Association
#400, 1765 - 8th Ave. West
Vancouver, BC V6J 5C6
604-736-7202; Fax: 604-736-7588
Toll-Free: 888-396-9888
E-mail: info@yourdentalhealth.ca
URL: www.bcdental.org
Scope: Provincial
Contact Information: Address: Pacific Dental Conference, #305, 1505 West 2nd Ave., Vancouver, BC V6H 3Y4; Phone: 604-736-3781; E-mail: info@pdconf.com; URL: www.pdconf.com

- **Ukrainian Canadian Congress Triennal Congress 2019**
Sponsor/Contact: Ukrainian Canadian Congress
#203, 952 Main St.
Winnipeg, MB R2W 3P4
204-942-4627; Fax: 204-947-3882
Toll-Free: 866-942-4627
E-mail: ucc@ucc.ca
URL: www.ucc.ca
Scope: National

- **Ukrainian Self-Reliance League of Canada Biennial National Convention 2019**
Sponsor/Contact: Ukrainian Self-Reliance League of Canada
1027 North Service Rd.
Stoney Creek, ON L8E 5C8
905-643-3250
URL: www.usrl-cyc.org
Scope: National

- **UNIFOR 3rd Biennial Pride Conference**
Sponsor/Contact: UNIFOR
205 Placer Ct.
Toronto, ON M2H 3H9
416-497-4110
Toll-Free: 800-268-5763
E-mail: communications@unifor.org
URL: www.unifor.org
Scope: National
Contact Information: E-mail: communications@unifor.org, Phone: 416-497-4110

2020

January

- **2020 ROMA Annual Conference**
Date: January 18-21, 2020
Location: Sheraton Centre Hotel Toronto, ON
Sponsor/Contact: Rural Ontario Municipal Association
#801, 200 University Ave.
Toronto, ON M5H 3C6
416-971-9856; Fax: 416-971-6191
Toll-Free: 877-426-6527
URL: www.roma.on.ca
Scope: Provincial

- **American Library Association 2020 Midwinter Meeting & Exhibits**
Date: January 24-28, 2020
Location: Philadelphia, PA USA
Sponsor/Contact: American Library Association
50 East Huron St.
Chicago, IL 60611-2795
312-944-6780; Fax: 312-440-9374
Toll-Free: 800-545-2433
E-mail: ala@ala.org
URL: www.ala.org
Scope: International
Purpose: A library & information service meeting presenting speakers, discussion groups, exhibits, & committee meetings

February

- **American Association for the Advancement of Science 2020 Annual Meeting**
Date: February 13-17, 2020
Location: Seattle, WA USA
Sponsor/Contact: American Association for the Advancement of Science
1200 New York Ave. NW
Washington, DC 20005
202-326-6440
E-mail: membership@aaas.org
URL: www.aaas.org
Scope: International
Purpose: Information for scientists, engineers, educators, & policy-makers

- **Canadian Digestive Diseases Week: Canadian Association of Gastroenterology Annual Scientific Conference 2020**
Date: February 23 - March 4, 2020
Location: Montréal, QC
Sponsor/Contact: Canadian Association of Gastroenterology
#224, 1540 Cornwall Rd.
Oakville, ON L6J 7W5
905-829-2504; Fax: 905-829-0242
Toll-Free: 888-780-0007
E-mail: general@cag-acg.org
URL: www.cag-acg.org
Scope: National

March

- **American Concrete Institute Spring 2020 Concrete Conference & Exhibition**
Date: March 29 - April 2, 2020
Location: Hyatt Regency O'Hare Rosemont, IL USA
Sponsor/Contact: American Concrete Institute
38800 Country Club Dr.
Farmington Hills, MI 48331-3439
248-848-3700; Fax: 248-848-3701
URL: www.concrete.org
Scope: International
Contact Information: Event Planner: Alexandria R. Prokic, E-mail: alex.prokic@concrete.org

- **Canadian Association for Dental Research 44th Annual Meeting**
Date: March 18-21, 2020
Location: Washington, DC USA
Sponsor/Contact: Canadian Association for Dental Research

c/o Western University
1151 Richmond St.
London, ON N6A 5B8
519-661-2111
URL: www.cadr-acrd.ca
Scope: International
Purpose: In conjunction with the 49th Annual Meeting of the American Association of Dental Research & the 98th General Session & Exhibition of the International Association for Dental Research

- **CONEXPO-CON/AGG**
Date: March 10-14, 2020
Location: Las Vegas, NV USA
Sponsor/Contact: Canadian Ready Mixed Concrete Association
#3, 365 Brunel Rd.
Mississauga, ON L4Z 1Z5
905-507-1122; Fax: 905-890-8122
E-mail: info@concretealberta.ca
URL: www.crmca.ca
Purpose: North American's largest construction trade show representing asphalt, aggregates, concrete, earthmoving, lifting, mining, and other utilities
Anticipated Attendance: 130,000
Contact Information: Phone: 800-867-6060

- **NACE International CORROSION 2020**
Date: March 15-19, 2020
Location: Houston, TX USA
Sponsor/Contact: NACE International
15835 Park Ten Pl.
Houston, TX 77084
281-228-6200; Fax: 281-228-6300
E-mail: firstservice@nace.org
URL: www.nace.org
Scope: International
Purpose: A corrosion conference & exposition

- **Teachers of English to Speakers of Other Languages, Inc. (TESOL) International Convention & English Language Expo**
Date: March 31 - April 3, 2020
Location: Denver, CO USA
Sponsor/Contact: Teachers of English to Speakers of Other Languages, Inc.
#500, 1925 Ballenger Ave.
Alexandria, VA 22314-6820
703-836-0774; Fax: 703-836-7864
E-mail: info@tesol.org
URL: www.tesol.org
Scope: International
Contact Information: Director, Conference Services: Lisa Dyson, Phone: 703-836-0774, ext. 515, E-mail: conventions@tesol.org

April

- **Association of Medical Microbiology & Infectious Disease Canada 2020 Annual Conference**
Date: April 29 - May 2, 2020
Location: Sheraton Vancouver Wall Centre Vancouver, BC
Sponsor/Contact: Association of Medical Microbiology & Infectious Disease Canada
192 Bank St.
Ottawa, ON K2P 1W8
613-260-3233; Fax: 613-260-3235
E-mail: communications@ammi.ca
URL: www.ammi.ca
Scope: National
Purpose: A yearly professional development event for AMMI members; features workshops on a variety of topics
Contact Information: Coordinator, Meetings: Paul Glover, E-mail: paul@ammi.ca

- **International Society for Magnetic Resonance in Medicine 2020 28th Scientific Meeting & Exhibition**
Date: April 18-24, 2020
Location: Sydney, Australia
Sponsor/Contact: International Society for Magnetic Resonance in Medicine
#620, 2300 Clayton Rd.
Concord, CA 94520
510-841-1899; Fax: 510-841-2340
E-mail: info@ismrm.org
URL: www.ismrm.org
Scope: International
Purpose: Featuring the 29th Annual Meeting of the Section for Magnetic Resonance Technologists

- **Library Association of Alberta Annual Conference 2020**
Date: April 30-May 3, 2020
Location: Alberta
Sponsor/Contact: Library Association of Alberta
80 Baker Cres. NW
Calgary, AB T2L 1R4
403-284-5818
Toll-Free: 877-522-5550
E-mail: info@laa.ca
URL: www.laa.ca
Scope: Provincial
Purpose: A conference held each spring for members of the Alberta library community, featuring association annual general meetings, session presentations, networking opportunities, & a trade show. Beginning this year, the conference is no longer held jointly with the Alberta Library Trustees Association (ALTA).
Contact Information: Library Association of Alberta, Phone: 403-284-5818, Toll-Free Phone: 1-877-522-5550, Fax: 403-282-6646, E-mail: info@laa.ca, info@albertalibraryconference.com

May

- **103rd Canadian Chemistry Conference & Exhibition**
Date: May 24-28, 2020
Location: Winnipeg, MB
Sponsor/Contact: Chemical Institute of Canada
#400, 222 Queen St.
Ottawa, ON K1P 5V9
613-232-6252; Fax: 613-232-5862
Toll-Free: 888-542-2242
E-mail: info@cheminst.ca
URL: www.cheminst.ca
Scope: National

- **11th World Biomaterials Congress**
Date: May 19-24, 2020
Location: Glasgow, Scotland
Sponsor/Contact: International Union of Societies for Biomaterials Science & Engineering
c/o Prof. Nicholas A. Peppas, The University of Texas at Austin
1 University Station, #C-0400
Austin, TX 78712-0231
512-471-6644; Fax: 512-471-8227
URL: www.worldbiomaterials.org
Scope: International

- **American Society of Neuroradiology 2020 58th Annual Meeting**
Date: May 30 - June 4, 2020
Location: Caesars Palace
Las Vegas, NV USA
Sponsor/Contact: American Society of Neuroradiology
#205, 800 Enterprise Dr.
Oak Brook, IL 60523
630-574-0220; Fax: 630-574-0661
URL: www.asnr.org
Scope: International
Contact Information: Director, Scientific Meetings: Lora Tannehill, E-mail: ltannehill@asnr.org; Manager, Scientific Meetings: Valerie Geisendorfer, E-mail: vgeisendorfer@asnr.org

- **Canadian Council of Motor Transport Administrators 2020 Annual Meeting**
Date: May 31-June 3, 2020
Location: Charlottetown, PE
Sponsor/Contact: Canadian Council of Motor Transport Administrators
#404, 1111 Prince of Wales
Ottawa, ON K2C 3T2
613-736-1003; Fax: 613-736-1395
E-mail: info@ccmta.ca
URL: www.ccmta.ca
Scope: National
Purpose: Educational events, an exhibition, a working forum where important decisions are made, & an excellent networking opportunity for government decision-makers & members of the private sector
Contact Information: Phone: 613-736-1003 Fax: 613-736-1395, E-mail: ccmta-secretariat@ccmta.ca

- **Government Finance Officers Association 2020 114th Annual Conference**
Date: May 17-20, 2020
Location: Ernest N. Morial Convention Center
New Orleans, LA USA
Sponsor/Contact: Government Finance Officers Association
#2700, 203 North LaSalle St.
Chicago, IL 60601-1210
312-977-9700; Fax: 312-977-4806
E-mail: bnquiry@gfoa.org
URL: www.gfoa.org
Scope: International
Contact Information: Manager, Communications: Natalie Laudadio, Phone: 312-578-2298

- **Institute of Industrial & Systems Engineers Annual Conference & Expo 2020**
Date: May 30 - June 2, 2020
Location: Hyatt Regency New Orleans
New Orleans, LA USA
Sponsor/Contact: Institute of Industrial & Systems Engineers
#200, 3577 Parkway Lane
Norcross, GA 30092
770-449-0460; Fax: 770-441-3295
E-mail: cs@iienet.org
URL: www.iienet2.org
Scope: International

- **Journées dentaires internationales du Québec (JDIQ) 2020**
Date: May 22-26, 2020
Location: Quebec
Sponsor/Contact: Ordre des dentistes du Québec
#1640, 800, boul René-Lévesque ouest Montréal, QC H3B 1X9
514-875-8511; Fax: 514-393-9248
Toll-Free: 800-361-4887
URL: www.odq.qc.ca
Scope: Provincial
Contact Information: Président, Comité d'organisation des JDIQ: Pierre Boudrias, Courriel: congres@odq.qc.ca

- **Pediatric Academic Societies' 2020 Annual Meeting**
Date: May 2-5, 2020
Location: Philadelphia, PA USA
Sponsor/Contact: Academic Pediatric Association
6728 Old McLean Village Dr.
McLean, VA 22101
703-556-9222; Fax: 703-556-8729
E-mail: info@academicpeds.org
URL: www.academicpeds.org
Scope: International
Purpose: An international meeting focussing on research in child health
Contact Information: Address: #7B, 3400 Research Forest Dr., The Woodlands, TX, 77381, USA; Phone: 346-980-9717

- **Pediatric Endocrine Society 2020 Annual Meeting**
Date: May 2-5, 2020
Location: Philadelphia, PA USA
Sponsor/Contact: Pediatric Endocrine Society
6728 Old McLean Village Dr.
McLean, VA 22101
E-mail: info@pedsendo.org
URL: www.pedsendo.org
Scope: International
Purpose: An annual continuing education event, featuring speaker presentations, a scientific program, poster sessions, exhibits, & networking occasions for persons who represent the field of pediatric endocrinology
Contact Information: E-mail: info@pedsendo.org

June

- **American Library Association 2020 Annual Conference**
Date: June 23-28, 2020
Location: Chicago, IL USA
Sponsor/Contact: American Library Association
50 East Huron St.
Chicago, IL 60611-2795
312-944-6780; Fax: 312-440-9374
Toll-Free: 800-545-2433
E-mail: ala@ala.org
URL: www.ala.org
Scope: International
Purpose: A conference providing speakers, educational programs, committee meetings, & exhibits related to library & information services

- **American Water Works Association Annual Conference & Exposition 2020**
Date: June 14-17, 2020
Location: Orlando, FL USA
Sponsor/Contact: American Water Works Association
6666 West Quincy Ave.
Denver, CO 80235
303-794-7711; Fax: 303-347-0804
Toll-Free: 800-926-7337
E-mail: service@awwa.org
URL: www.awwa.org
Scope: International
Purpose: An international gathering of thousands of water professionals, featuring

Conferences & Conventions Index

a technical program, workshops, seminars, & exhibits

- **Canadian Psychological Association 2020 National Convention & Annual Meeting**
Date: June 5-7, 2020
Location: Hyatt Regency Calgary
Calgary, AB
Sponsor/Contact: Canadian Psychological Association
#702, 141 Laurier Ave. West
Ottawa, ON K1P 5J3
613-237-2144; Fax: 613-237-1674
Toll-Free: 888-472-0657
E-mail: cpa@cpa.ca
URL: www.cpa.ca
Scope: National
Anticipated Attendance: 1,800

- **International Confederation of Midwives 32nd Triennial Congress 2020**
Date: June 21-25, 2020
Location: Bali, Indonesia
Sponsor/Contact: International Confederation of Midwives
Laan van Meerdervoort 70
The Hague, 2517 AN
E-mail: info@internationalmidwives.org
URL: www.internationalmidwives.org
Scope: International
Contact Information: URL: www.midwives2020.org

- **Microwave Theory & Techniques Society International Microwave Symposia 2020**
Date: June 14-19, 2020
Location: Los Angeles, CA USA
Sponsor/Contact: IEEE Microwave Theory & Techniques Society
5829 Bellanca Dr.
Elkridge, MD 21075
410-796-5866
URL: www.mtt.org
Scope: International
Purpose: Technical papers; Workshops; Trade show

July

- **Canadian Institute of Planners 2020 Conference**
Date: July 7-10, 2020
Location: Whistler, BC
Sponsor/Contact: Canadian Institute of Planners
#1112, 141 Laurier Ave. West
Ottawa, ON K1P 5J3
613-237-7526; Fax: 613-237-7045
Toll-Free: 800-207-2138
E-mail: general@cip-icu.ca
URL: www.cip-icu.ca
Scope: National

August

- **2020 Association of Municipalities of Ontario AGM & Annual Conference**
Date: August 16-19, 2020
Location: Shaw Centre
Ottawa, ON
Sponsor/Contact: Association of Municipalities of Ontario
#801, 200 University Ave.
Toronto, ON M5H 3C6
416-971-9856; Fax: 416-971-6191
Toll-Free: 877-426-6527
E-mail: amo@amo.on.ca
URL: www.amo.on.ca
Scope: Provincial
Purpose: A yearly gathering of municipal government officials to discuss current issues.

- **34th World Conference of the International Society for Music Education**
Date: August 9-14, 2020
Location: Helsinki, Finland
Sponsor/Contact: International Society for Music Education
#148, 45 Glenferrie Rd.
Malvern, VA 3144
E-mail: isme@isme.org
URL: www.isme.org
Scope: International

- **American Fisheries Society 150th Annual Meeting 2020**
Date: August 30 - September 3, 2020
Location: Columbus, OH USA
Sponsor/Contact: American Fisheries Society
#110, 5410 Grosvenor Lane
Bethesda, MD 20814-2199
301-897-8616; Fax: 301-897-8096
URL: www.fisheries.org
Scope: International

- **Catholic Women's League of Canada 2020 National Convention**
Date: August 9-12, 2020
Location: Montréal, QC
Sponsor/Contact: Catholic Women's League of Canada
702C Scotland Ave.
Winnipeg, MB R3M 1X5
204-927-2310; Fax: 888-831-9507
Toll-Free: 888-656-4040
E-mail: info@cwl.ca
URL: www.cwl.ca
Scope: National

- **International Union of Crystallography 25th Triennial Congress & General Assembly**
Date: August 22-30, 2020
Location: Prague Congress Centre
Prague, Czech Republic
Sponsor/Contact: International Union of Crystallography
c/o Executive Secretariat
2 Abbey Sq.
Chester, CH1 2HU
E-mail: execsec@iucr.org
URL: www.iucr.org
Scope: International

September

- **American Political Science Association 116th Annual Meeting 2020**
Date: September 3-6, 2020
Location: San Francisco, CA USA
Sponsor/Contact: American Political Science Association
1527 New Hampshire Ave. NW
Washington, DC 20036-1206
202-483-2512; Fax: 202-483-2657
E-mail: apsa@apsanet.org
URL: www.apsanet.org
Scope: International

- **International Board on Books for Young People 2020 37th International Congress**
Date: September 5-7, 2020
Location: Moscow, Russia
Sponsor/Contact: International Board on Books for Young People
Nonnenweg 12, Postfach
Basel, CH-4003
E-mail: ibby@ibby.org
URL: www.ibby.org
Scope: International
Purpose: Theme: "Great Big World Through Children's Books"
Contact Information: www.ibbycongress2020.org

- **The American Association of Bovine Practitioners 2020 Annual Conference**
Date: September 24-26, 2020
Location: Louisville, KY USA
Sponsor/Contact: American Association of Bovine Practitioners
P.O. Box 3610
#802, 3320 Skyway Dr.
Auburn, AL 36831-3610
334-821-0442; Fax: 334-821-9532
E-mail: aabphq@aabp.org
URL: www.aabp.org
Scope: International

- **Western Canada Water 2020 72nd Annual Conference & Exhibition**
Date: September 22-25, 2020
Location: Regina, SK
Sponsor/Contact: Western Canada Water
P.O. Box 1708
240 River Ave.
Cochrane, AB T4C 1B6
403-709-0064; Fax: 403-709-0068
Toll-Free: 877-283-2003
E-mail: member@wcwwa.ca
URL: www.wcwwa.ca
Scope: Provincial
Purpose: A technical program, a keynote speaker, & a trade show for delegates from Western Canada Water
Anticipated Attendance: 500+
Contact Information: Western Canada Water, Toll-Free Phone: 1-877-283-2003, Toll-Free Fax: 1-877-283-2007, E-mail: info@wcwwa.ca

October

- **American Concrete Institute Fall 2020 Concrete Conference & Exhibition**
Date: October 25-29, 2020
Location: Raleigh Marriott
Raleigh, NC USA
Sponsor/Contact: American Concrete Institute
38800 Country Club Dr.
Farmington Hills, MI 48331-3439
248-848-3700; Fax: 248-848-3701
URL: www.concrete.org
Scope: International
Contact Information: Event Planner: Alexandria R. Prokic, E-mail: alex.prokic@concrete.org

November

- **American Anthropological Association 2020 Annual Meeting**
Date: November 17-22, 2020
Location: Cervantes Convention Center at America's Center
St. Louis, MO USA
Sponsor/Contact: American Anthropological Association
#1301, 2300 Clarendon Blvd.
Arlington, VA 22201
703-528-1902; Fax: 703-528-3546
URL: www.americananthro.org
Scope: International
Contact Information: Director, Meetings & Conferences: Ushma Suvarnakar, Phone: 703-528-1902 ext. 1172

- **ATAC 86th Canadian Aviation Conference & Tradeshow**
Date: November 17-19, 2020
Location: Westin Bayshore Hotel
Vancouver, BC
Sponsor/Contact: Air Transport Association of Canada
#700, 255 Albert St.
Ottawa, ON K1P 6A9
613-233-7727; Fax: 613-230-8648
E-mail: atac@atac.ca
URL: www.atac.ca
Scope: National
Purpose: National gathering for operators, suppliers to the industry & government stakeholders involved in commerical aviation and flight training in Canada
Contact Information: Debbie Simpson; dsimpson@atac.ca; 613-233-7727 ext. 312

- **Canadian Society of Association Executives / Société canadienne d'association 2020 Conference & Showcase**
Date: November 4-6, 2020
Location: Halifax, NS
Sponsor/Contact: Canadian Society of Association Executives
#1100, 10 King St. East
Toronto, ON M5C 1C3
416-363-3555; Fax: 416-363-3630
Toll-Free: 800-461-3608
URL: www.csae.com
Scope: National

- **Saskatchewan Water and Wastewater Association 2020 Tradeshow and Conference**
Date: November 3-5, 2020
Sponsor/Contact: Saskatchewan Water & Wastewater Association
P.O. Box 7831 Stn. Mn
Saskatoon, SK S7K 4R5
306-761-1278
Toll-Free: 888-668-1278
E-mail: office@swwa.ca
URL: www.swwa.ca
Scope: National

Other Conferences in 2020

- **13th International Energy Agency Heat Pump Conference**
Sponsor/Contact: Canadian GeoExchange Coalition
#109, 7240 rue Waverly
Montréal, QC H2R 2Y8
514-807-7559; Fax: 514-807-8221
E-mail: info@geoexchange.ca
URL: www.geo-exchange.ca
Scope: International
Purpose: Promotes heat pumping technologies through discussions, networking, and information exchange.

- **2020 ICTAC Conference**
Location: Krakow, Poland
Sponsor/Contact: International Confederation for Thermal Analysis & Calorimetry
Tokyo Institute of Technology
2-12-1, S8-29, Ookayama, Meguro-ku
Tokyo, 152-8552
URL: www.ictac.org

- **Art Libraries Society of North America 48th Annual Conference 2020**
Location: Saint Louis, MO USA
Sponsor/Contact: Art Libraries Society of North America

7044 South 13th St.
Oak Creek, WI 53154
414-908-4954
Toll-Free: 800-817-0621
URL: www.arlisna.org
Purpose: The conference provides the opportunity for professionals involved in art librarianship to meet, learn and share their knowledge of the field. It also allows them to explore exhibitions & interact with vendors involved with art libraries.

- **Canadian Archaeological Association Annual Meeting 2020**
Location: Edmonton, AB
Sponsor/Contact: Canadian Archaeological Association
URL: www.canadianarchaeology.com
Scope: National

- **Canadian Association for Leisure Studies Canadian Congress on Leisure 2020**
Sponsor/Contact: Canadian Association for Leisure Studies
c/o Recreation & Leisure Studies, Faculty of Applied Health Sciences
University of Waterloo
Waterloo, ON N2L 3G1
URL: www.cals.uwaterloo.ca
Scope: National
Purpose: A triennial meeting at the Canadian Congress on Leisure Research.

- **Canadian Economics Association 52nd Annual Conference 2020**
Location: University of Toronto
Toronto, ON
Sponsor/Contact: Canadian Economics Association
Department of Economics, Brock Univ.
500 Glenridge Ave.
St Catharines, ON L2S 3A1
905-688-5550
URL: www.economics.ca
Scope: National
Purpose: An annual conference held during the last week of May or the first week of June

- **Fédération internationale des professeurs de français (FIPF) Congrès Mondiaux 2020**
Sponsor/Contact: Fédération internationale des professeurs de français
101, boul Raspail
Paris, 75270
E-mail: secretariat@fipf.org
URL: www.fipf.org
Scope: International

- **Geological Association of Canada 2020 Annual Meeting**
Location: Calgary, AB
Sponsor/Contact: Geological Association of Canada
c/o Department of Earth Sciences, Memorial University of Newfoundland
#ER4063, Alexander Murray Bldg.
St. John's, NL A1B 3X5
709-864-7660; Fax: 709-864-2532
E-mail: gac@mun.ca
URL: www.gac.ca
Scope: National

- **International Commission of Agricultural Engineering 2020 5th International Conference**
Sponsor/Contact: International Commission of Agricultural & Biosystems Engineering
c/o Dr. Takaaki Maekawa, School of Life & Environmental Sciences
1-1-1 Tennodai, University of Tsukuba
Tsukuba, Ibaraki
E-mail: biopro@sakura.cc.tsukuba.ac.jp
URL: www.cigr.org
Scope: International

- **International Permafrost Association 12th International Conference on Permafrost 2020**
Sponsor/Contact: International Permafrost Association
c/o H. Lantuit, Alfred Wegener Institute for Polar & Marine Research
Telefrafenberg A43
Potsdam, 14473
E-mail: contact@ipa-permafrost.org
URL: ipa.arcticportal.org
Scope: International

- **International Union of Microbiological Societies 16th Congress**
Location: Daejon, South Korea
Sponsor/Contact: International Union of Microbiological Societies
CBS Fungal Biodiversity Centre
P.O. Box 85167
Utrecht, 3508AD
URL: www.iums.org
Scope: International
Purpose: Meetings of the three divisions of the International Union of Microbiological Societies

- **Medical Library Association 2020 Annual Meeting & Exhibition**
Sponsor/Contact: Medical Library Association
#1900, 65 East Wacker Pl.
Chicago, IL 60601-7246
312-419-9094; Fax: 312-419-8950
E-mail: websupport@mail.mlahq.org
URL: www.mlanet.org
Scope: International

- **Thermal Insulation Association of Canada 2020 Annual Conference**
Location: Whitehorse, YT
Sponsor/Contact: Thermal Insulation Association of Canada
1485 Laperriere Ave.
Ottawa, ON K1Z 7S8
613-724-4834; Fax: 613-729-6206
E-mail: info@tiac.ca
URL: www.tiac.ca
Scope: National

- **Union of Canadian Transportation Employees 18th Triennial Convention**
Sponsor/Contact: Union of Canadian Transportation Employees
#702, 233 Gilmour St.
Ottawa, ON K2P 0P2
613-238-4003; Fax: 613-236-0379
URL: www.ucte.com

- **XXII Congress on Safety & Health at Work**
Sponsor/Contact: International Labour Organization
4, route des Morillons
Geneva, CH-1211
E-mail: ilo@ilo.org
URL: www.ilo.org
Scope: International
Purpose: The World Congress is a forum for the exchange of knowledge, practices & experiences for anyone involved with or interested in health & safety in the workplace.

2021

January

- **2021 ROMA Annual Conference**
Date: January 23-26, 2021
Location: Sheraton Centre Hotel
Toronto, ON
Sponsor/Contact: Rural Ontario Municipal Association
#801, 200 University Ave.
Toronto, ON M5H 3C6
416-971-9856; Fax: 416-971-6191
Toll-Free: 877-426-6527
URL: www.roma.on.ca
Scope: Provincial

- **American Library Association 2021 Midwinter Meeting & Exhibits**
Date: January 22-26, 2021
Location: Indianapolis, IN USA
Sponsor/Contact: American Library Association
50 East Huron St.
Chicago, IL 60611-2795
312-944-6780; Fax: 312-440-9374
Toll-Free: 800-545-2433
E-mail: ala@ala.org
URL: www.ala.org
Scope: International
Purpose: A library & information service meeting presenting speakers, discussion groups, exhibits, & committee meetings

February

- **Canadian Digestive Diseases Week: Canadian Association of Gastroenterology Annual Scientific Conference 2021**
Date: February 28 - March 10, 2021
Location: Banff, AB
Sponsor/Contact: Canadian Association of Gastroenterology
#224, 1540 Cornwall Rd.
Oakville, ON L6J 7W5
905-829-2504; Fax: 905-829-0242
Toll-Free: 888-780-0007
E-mail: general@cag-acg.org
URL: www.cag-acg.org
Scope: National

March

- **American Concrete Institute Spring 2021 Concrete Conference & Exhibition**
Date: March 28 - April 1, 2021
Location: Hilton & Marriott Baltimore
Baltimore, MD USA
Sponsor/Contact: American Concrete Institute
38800 Country Club Dr.
Farmington Hills, MI 48331-3439
248-848-3700; Fax: 248-848-3701
URL: www.concrete.org
Scope: International
Contact Information: Event Planner: Alexandria R. Prokic, E-mail: alex.prokic@concrete.org

- **Teachers of English to Speakers of Other Languages, Inc. (TESOL) International Convention & English Language Expo**
Date: March 23-26, 2021
Location: Houston, TX USA
Sponsor/Contact: Teachers of English to Speakers of Other Languages, Inc.
#500, 1925 Ballenger Ave.
Alexandria, VA 22314-6820
703-836-0774; Fax: 703-836-7864
E-mail: info@tesol.org
URL: www.tesol.org
Scope: International
Contact Information: Director, Conference Services: Lisa Dyson, Phone: 703-836-0774, ext. 515, E-mail: conventions@tesol.org

April

- **2021 Society for Research in Child Development Biennial Meeting**
Date: April 8-10, 2021
Location: Minneapolis, MN USA
Sponsor/Contact: Society for Research in Child Development
#401, 2950 South State St.
Ann Arbor, MI 48104
734-926-0600; Fax: 734-926-0601
E-mail: info@srcd.org
URL: www.srcd.org
Scope: International

- **Association of College & Research Libraries (ACRL) Conference 2021**
Date: April 14-17, 2021
Location: Seattle, WA USA
Sponsor/Contact: Association of College & Research Libraries
c/o American Library Association
50 East Huron St.
Chicago, IL 60611-2795
312-280-2523; Fax: 312-280-2520
Toll-Free: 800-545-2433
E-mail: acrl@ala.org
URL: www.ala.org/acrl
Scope: National

- **NACE International CORROSION 2021**
Date: April 18-22, 2021
Location: Salt Lake City, UT USA
Sponsor/Contact: NACE International
15835 Park Ten Pl.
Houston, TX 77084
281-228-6200; Fax: 281-228-6300
E-mail: firstservice@nace.org
URL: www.nace.org
Scope: International
Purpose: A corrosion conference & exposition

- **Pediatric Academic Societies' 2021 Annual Meeting**
Date: April 30-May 4, 2021
Location: Vancouver, BC
Sponsor/Contact: Academic Pediatric Association
6728 Old McLean Village Dr.
McLean, VA 22101
703-556-9222; Fax: 703-556-8729
E-mail: info@academicpeds.org
URL: www.academicpeds.org
Scope: International
Purpose: An international meeting focussing on research in child health
Contact Information: Address: #7B, 3400 Research Forest Dr., The Woodlands, TX, 77381, USA; Phone: 346-980-9717

May

- **American Society of Neuroradiology 2021 59th Annual Meeting**
Date: May 22-27, 2021
Location: San Francisco Marriott Marquis
San Francisco, CA USA
Sponsor/Contact: American Society of Neuroradiology
#205, 800 Enterprise Dr.
Oak Brook, IL 60523

630-574-0220; *Fax:* 630-574-0661
URL: www.asnr.org
Scope: International
Contact Information: Director, Scientific Meetings: Lora Tannehill, E-mail: ltannehill@asnr.org; Manager, Scientific Meetings: Valerie Geisendorfer, E-mail: vgeisendorfer@asnr.org

• **International Society for Magnetic Resonance in Medicine 2021 29th Scientific Meeting & Exhibition**
Date: May 15-21, 2021
Location: Vancouver, BC
Sponsor/Contact: International Society for Magnetic Resonance in Medicine
#620, 2300 Clayton Rd.
Concord, CA 94520
510-841-1899; *Fax:* 510-841-2340
E-mail: info@ismrm.org
URL: www.ismrm.org
Scope: International
Purpose: Featuring the 29th Annual Meeting of the Section for Magnetic Resonance Technologists

June

• **American Library Association 2021 Annual Conference**
Date: June 24-29, 2021
Location: Chicago, IL USA
Sponsor/Contact: American Library Association
50 East Huron St.
Chicago, IL 60611-2795
312-944-6780; *Fax:* 312-440-9374
Toll-Free: 800-545-2433
E-mail: ala@ala.org
URL: www.ala.org
Scope: International
Purpose: A conference providing speakers, educational programs, committee meetings, & exhibits related to library & information services

• **American Water Works Association Annual Conference & Exposition 2021**
Date: June 13-16, 2021
Location: San Diego, CA USA
Sponsor/Contact: American Water Works Association
6666 West Quincy Ave.
Denver, CO 80235
303-794-7711; *Fax:* 303-347-0804
Toll-Free: 800-926-7337
E-mail: service@awwa.org
URL: www.awwa.org
Scope: International
Purpose: An international gathering of thousands of water professionals, featuring a technical program, workshops, seminars, & exhibits

• **Canadian Psychological Association 2021 National Convention & Annual Meeting**
Date: June 4-6, 2021
Location: Westin Ottawa Hotel
Ottawa, ON
Sponsor/Contact: Canadian Psychological Association
#702, 141 Laurier Ave. West
Ottawa, ON K1P 5J3
613-237-2144; *Fax:* 613-237-1674
Toll-Free: 888-472-0657
E-mail: cpa@cpa.ca
URL: www.cpa.ca
Scope: National
Anticipated Attendance: 1,800

• **Government Finance Officers Association 2021 115th Annual Conference**
Date: June 27-30, 2021
Location: Hyatt Regency & Swiss Hotel Chicago
Chicago, IL USA
Sponsor/Contact: Government Finance Officers Association
#2700, 203 North LaSalle St.
Chicago, IL 60601-1210
312-977-9700; *Fax:* 312-977-4806
E-mail: bnquiry@gfoa.org
URL: www.gfoa.org
Scope: International
Contact Information: Manager, Communications: Natalie Laudadio, Phone: 312-578-2298

• **Microwave Theory & Techniques Society International Microwave Symposia 2021**
Date: June 21-25, 2021
Location: Atlanta, GA USA
Sponsor/Contact: IEEE Microwave Theory & Techniques Society
5829 Bellanca Dr.
Elkridge, MD 21075
410-796-5866
URL: www.mtt.org
Scope: International
Purpose: Technical papers; Workshops; Trade show

August

• **Catholic Women's League of Canada 2021 National Convention**
Date: August 8-11, 2021
Location: Toronto, ON
Sponsor/Contact: Catholic Women's League of Canada
702C Scotland Ave.
Winnipeg, MB R3M 1X5
204-927-2310; *Fax:* 888-831-9507
Toll-Free: 888-656-4040
E-mail: info@cwl.ca
URL: www.cwl.ca
Scope: National

September

• **The American Association of Bovine Practitioners 2021 Annual Conference**
Date: September 23-25, 2021
Location: Minneapolis, MN USA
Sponsor/Contact: American Association of Bovine Practitioners
P.O. Box 3610
#802, 3320 Skyway Dr.
Auburn, AL 36831-3610
334-821-0442; *Fax:* 334-821-9532
E-mail: aabphq@aabp.org
URL: www.aabp.org
Scope: International

October

• **American Concrete Institute Fall 2021 Concrete Conference & Exhibition**
Date: October 17-21, 2021
Location: Hilton Atlanta Downtown
Atlanta, GA USA
Sponsor/Contact: American Concrete Institute
38800 Country Club Dr.
Farmington Hills, MI 48331-3439
248-848-3700; *Fax:* 248-848-3701
URL: www.concrete.org
Scope: International
Contact Information: Event Planner: Alexandria R. Prokic, E-mail: alex.prokic@concrete.org

November

• **ATAC 87th Canadian Aviation Conference & Tradeshow**
Date: November 16-18, 2021
Location: Fairmont Queen Elizabeth Hotel
Montreal, QC
Sponsor/Contact: Air Transport Association of Canada
#700, 255 Albert St.
Ottawa, ON K1P 6A9
613-233-7727; *Fax:* 613-230-8648
E-mail: atac@atac.ca
URL: www.atac.ca
Scope: National
Purpose: National gathering for operators, suppliers to the industry & government stakeholders involved in commerical aviation and flight training in Canada
Contact Information: Debbie Simpson; dsimpson@atac.ca; 613-233-7727 ext. 312

• **American Anthropological Association 2021 Annual Meeting**
Date: November 15-21, 2021
Location: Baltimore Convention Center
Baltimore, MD USA
Sponsor/Contact: American Anthropological Association
#1301, 2300 Clarendon Blvd.
Arlington, VA 22201
703-528-1902; *Fax:* 703-528-3546
URL: www.americananthro.org
Scope: International
Contact Information: Director, Meetings & Conferences: Ushma Suvarnakar, Phone: 703-528-1902 ext. 1172

Other Conferences in 2021

• **Pediatric Endocrine Society 2021 Annual Meeting**
Sponsor/Contact: Pediatric Endocrine Society
6728 Old McLean Village Dr.
McLean, VA 22101
E-mail: info@pedsendo.org
URL: www.pedsendo.org
Scope: International

• **Western Canada Water 2021 73rd Annual Conference & Exhibition**
Location: Winnipeg, MB
Sponsor/Contact: Western Canada Water
P.O. Box 1708
240 River Ave.
Cochrane, AB T4C 1B6
403-709-0064; *Fax:* 403-709-0068
Toll-Free: 877-283-2003
E-mail: member@wcwwa.ca
URL: www.wcwwa.ca
Scope: Provincial
Purpose: A technical program, a keynote speaker, & a trade show for delegates from Western Canada Water
Anticipated Attendance: 500+
Contact Information: Western Canada Water, Toll-Free Phone: 1-877-283-2003, Toll-Free Fax: 1-877-283-2007, E-mail: info@wcwwa.ca

2022

April

• **Pediatric Academic Societies' 2022 Annual Meeting**
Date: April 22-28, 2022
Location: Denver, CO
Sponsor/Contact: Academic Pediatric Association
6728 Old McLean Village Dr.
McLean, VA 22101
703-556-9222; *Fax:* 703-556-8729
E-mail: info@academicpeds.org
URL: www.academicpeds.org
Scope: International
Purpose: An international meeting focussing on research in child health
Contact Information: Address: #7B, 3400 Research Forest Dr., The Woodlands, TX, 77381, USA; Phone: 346-980-9717

May

• **American Society of Neuroradiology 2022 60th Annual Meeting**
Date: May 13-19, 2022
Location: Hilton New York Midtown
New York, NY USA
Sponsor/Contact: American Society of Neuroradiology
#205, 800 Enterprise Dr.
Oak Brook, IL 60523
630-574-0220; *Fax:* 630-574-0661
URL: www.asnr.org
Scope: International
Contact Information: Director, Scientific Meetings: Lora Tannehill, E-mail: ltannehill@asnr.org; Manager, Scientific Meetings: Valerie Geisendorfer, E-mail: vgeisendorfer@asnr.org

• **International Society for Magnetic Resonance in Medicine 2022 30th Scientific Meeting & Exhibition**
Date: May 7-13, 2022
Location: London, United Kingdom
Sponsor/Contact: International Society for Magnetic Resonance in Medicine
#620, 2300 Clayton Rd.
Concord, CA 94520
510-841-1899; *Fax:* 510-841-2340
E-mail: info@ismrm.org
URL: www.ismrm.org
Scope: International
Purpose: Featuring the 29th Annual Meeting of the Section for Magnetic Resonance Technologists

June

• **American Water Works Association Annual Conference & Exposition 2022**
Date: June 12-15, 2022
Location: San Antonio, TX USA
Sponsor/Contact: American Water Works Association
6666 West Quincy Ave.
Denver, CO 80235
303-794-7711; *Fax:* 303-347-0804
Toll-Free: 800-926-7337
E-mail: service@awwa.org
URL: www.awwa.org
Scope: International
Purpose: An international gathering of thousands of water professionals, featuring a technical program, workshops, seminars, & exhibits

• **Government Finance Officers Association 2022 116th Annual Conference**
Date: June 5-8, 2022
Location: Neal Kocurek Memorial Austin Convention Center
Austin, TX USA

Sponsor/Contact: Government Finance Officers Association
#2700, 203 North LaSalle St.
Chicago, IL 60601-1210
312-977-9700; *Fax:* 312-977-4806
E-mail: bnquiry@gfoa.org
URL: www.gfoa.org
Scope: International
Contact Information: Manager, Communications: Natalie Laudadio, Phone: 312-578-2298

September

- **The American Association of Bovine Practitioners 2022 Annual Conference**
Date: September 14-16, 2022
Location: Long Beach, CA USA
Sponsor/Contact: American Association of Bovine Practitioners
P.O. Box 3610
#802, 3320 Skyway Dr.
Auburn, AL 36831-3610
334-821-0442; *Fax:* 334-821-9532
E-mail: aabphq@aabp.org
URL: www.aabp.org
Scope: International

- **Western Canada Water 2022 74th Annual Conference & Exhibition**
Date: September 20-23, 2022
Location: Calgary, AB
Sponsor/Contact: Western Canada Water
P.O. Box 1708
240 River Ave.
Cochrane, AB T4C 1B6
403-709-0064; *Fax:* 403-709-0068
Toll-Free: 877-283-2003
E-mail: member@wcwwa.ca
URL: www.wcwwa.ca
Scope: Provincial
Purpose: A technical program, a keynote speaker, & a trade show for delegates from Western Canada Water
Anticipated Attendance: 500+
Contact Information: Western Canada Water, Toll-Free Phone: 1-877-283-2003, Toll-Free Fax: 1-877-283-2007, E-mail: info@wcwwa.ca

November

- **ATAC 88th Canadian Aviation Conference & Tradeshow**
Date: November 15-17, 2022
Location: Westin Bayshore Hotel
Vancouver, BC
Sponsor/Contact: Air Transport Association of Canada
#700, 255 Albert St.
Ottawa, ON K1P 6A9
613-233-7727; *Fax:* 613-230-8648
E-mail: atac@atac.ca
URL: www.atac.ca
Scope: National
Purpose: National gathering for operators, suppliers to the industry & government stakeholders involved in commerical aviation and flight training in Canada
Contact Information: Debbie Simpson; dsimpson@atac.ca; 613-233-7727 ext. 312

Other Conferences in 2022

- **Microwave Theory & Techniques Society International Microwave Symposia 2022**
Location: Denver, CO USA
Sponsor/Contact: IEEE Microwave Theory & Techniques Society
5829 Bellanca Dr.
Elkridge, MD 21075
410-796-5866
URL: www.mtt.org
Scope: International
Purpose: Technical papers; Workshops; Trade show

2023

April

- **American Society of Neuroradiology 2023 61st Annual Meeting**
Date: April 29 - May 4, 2023
Location: Sheraton Grand Chicago
Chicago, IL USA
Sponsor/Contact: American Society of Neuroradiology
#205, 800 Enterprise Dr.
Oak Brook, IL 60523
630-574-0220; *Fax:* 630-574-0661
URL: www.asnr.org
Scope: International
Contact Information: Director, Scientific Meetings: Lora Tannehill, E-mail: ltannehill@asnr.org; Manager, Scientific Meetings: Valerie Geisendorfer, E-mail: vgeisendorfer@asnr.org

- **Pediatric Academic Societies' 2023 Annual Meeting**
Date: April 28-May 3, 2023
Location: Washington, DC
Sponsor/Contact: Academic Pediatric Association
6728 Old McLean Village Dr.
McLean, VA 22101
703-556-9222; *Fax:* 703-556-8729
E-mail: info@academicpeds.org
URL: www.academicpeds.org
Scope: International
Purpose: An international meeting focussing on research in child health
Contact Information: Address: #7B, 3400 Research Forest Dr., The Woodlands, TX, 77381, USA; Phone: 346-980-9717

June

- **International Society for Magnetic Resonance in Medicine 2023 31st Scientific Meeting & Exhibition**
Date: June 3-9, 2023
Location: Toronto, ON
Sponsor/Contact: International Society for Magnetic Resonance in Medicine
#620, 2300 Clayton Rd.
Concord, CA 94520
510-841-1899; *Fax:* 510-841-2340
E-mail: info@ismrm.org
URL: www.ismrm.org
Scope: International
Purpose: Featuring the 29th Annual Meeting of the Section for Magnetic Resonance Technologists

- **Microwave Theory & Techniques Society International Microwave Symposia 2023**
Date: June 11-16, 2023
Location: San Diego, CA USA
Sponsor/Contact: IEEE Microwave Theory & Techniques Society
5829 Bellanca Dr.
Elkridge, MD 21075
410-796-5866
URL: www.mtt.org
Scope: International
Purpose: Technical papers; Workshops; Trade show

November

- **ATAC 89th Canadian Aviation Conference & Tradeshow**
Date: November 14-15, 2023
Location: Fairmont Queen Elizabeth Hotel
Montreal, QC
Sponsor/Contact: Air Transport Association of Canada
#700, 255 Albert St.
Ottawa, ON K1P 6A9
613-233-7727; *Fax:* 613-230-8648
E-mail: atac@atac.ca
URL: www.atac.ca
Scope: National
Purpose: National gathering for operators, suppliers to the industry & government stakeholders involved in commerical aviation and flight training in Canada
Contact Information: Debbie Simpson; dsimpson@atac.ca; 613-233-7727 ext. 312

Other Conferences in 2023

- **International Union of Microbiological Societies 17th Congress**
Sponsor/Contact: International Union of Microbiological Societies
CBS Fungal Biodiversity Centre
P.O. Box 85167
Utrecht, 3508AD
URL: www.iums.org
Scope: International
Purpose: Meetings of the three divisions of the International Union of Microbiological Societies

Executive Name Index

- Names of key contacts for Canadian and foreign associations, listed alphabetically by surname
- An executive name may appear more than once in cases where an individual is involved in more than one association
- Included are both volunteer and paid staff
- Each entry is accompanied by a page number which points you to the corresponding listing in the alphabetical listings of Canadian and foreign associations

A

Aalders, Les, *Air Transport Association of Canada*, 19
Aalders, Michelle, *Saskatchewan Registered Music Teachers' Association*, 1273
Aarup, Carolyn, *Miniature Horse Club of Ontario*, 967
Aasgard, Michele, *Alberta Community & Co-operative Association*, 30
Ababou, Rachid, *Association québécoise pour le loisir des personnes handicapées*, 177
Abai, Mulugeta, *Canadian Centre for Victims of Torture*, 354
Abar, Daniel, *Chisholm Services for Children*, 566
Abara, Emmanuel, *Arts Richmond Hill*, 86
Abatzoglou, Nicolas, *Canadian Society for Chemical Engineering*, 473
Abbey, Deb, *Responsible Investment Association*, 1227
Abbot, Sue, *Nature Nova Scotia (Federation of Nova Scotia Naturalists)*, 1000
Abbot, Mary Jane, *CanoeKayak BC*, 509
Abbott, Jamie, *Business Professional Association of Canada*, 267
Abbott, David, *Canadian Council for Aboriginal Business*, 366
Abbott, Frank, *Canadian Society for Pharmaceutical Sciences*, 477
Abbott, Jim, *Burgess Shale Geoscience Foundation*, 265
Abbott, Kelsey, *Bikes Without Borders*, 211
Abdallah, Angela, *Direct Sellers Association of Canada*, 657
Abdelmessih, Sandra, *The Antiochan Orthodox Christian Archdiocese of North America*, 1505
Abdi, Garnayl, *Human Concern International*, 825
Abdool, Paul, *Xplor Canada Association*, 1470
Abdulrahman, Fayez, *Corporation des thérapeutes du sport du Québec*, 631
Abecia, Manny, *Huntington Society of Canada*, 827
Abel, Terry, *Canadian Association of Petroleum Producers*, 326
Abel, Scott, *Canadian Bar Association*, 342
Abel, Matt, *Nova Scotia Prospectors Association*, 1047
Abele, Elizabeth, *Northeast Modern Language Association*, 1579
Abid, Masood, *Magazines Canada*, 925
Ablett, Marie, *Canadian Celiac Association*, 352
Ablett, Jackie, *Canadian Pension & Benefits Institute*, 453
Ablog-Morrant, Kelly, *British Columbia Lung Association*, 245
Aboud, Manuel, *Canadian Well Logging Society*, 503
Abouelenein, Ibby, *AIESEC*, 18
Aboumansour, Nahid, *Petites-Mains*, 1154
Abrahamson, Ruth, *Canadian Association of Direct Response Insurers*, 312
Abram, Stephen, *Federation of Ontario Public Libraries*, 726
Abram, Joanne, *Alberta Insurance Council*, 38
Abrami, Phil, *BMW Clubs Canada*, 216
Abrami, Philip C., *Centre for the Study of Learning & Performance*, 534
Abrams, Ilana, *Jewish Heritage Centre of Western Canada Inc.*, 872
Abramsen, Karen, *North Okanagan Labour Council*, 1031

Abramson, Ralph, *Treaty & Aboriginal Rights Research Centre of Manitoba Inc.*, 1397
Abramson, Thea, *Southern African Jewish Association of Canada*, 1337
Abreu, Catherine, *Climate Action Network - Canada*, 573
Abu-Ghazaleh, Lara, *Saskatchewan Construction Safety Association Inc.*, 1262
Abugov, Alma, *MindFuel*, 966
Abusow, Kathy, *Sustainable Forestry Initiative Inc.*, 1597
Abutan, Evelyn, *Filipino Canadian Catholic Charismatic Prayer Communities*, 735
Accolas, Claude, *Association des professionnels des arts de la scène du Québec*, 125
Aceja-Uy, Marilyn, *Association of Filipino Canadian Accountants in British Columbia*, 148
Aceto-Guerin, Anna, *Human Resources Professionals Association*, 825
Achermann, Thomas, *Alberta Bison Association*, 26
Achtelstetter, Karin, *World Association for Christian Communication*, 1465
Achter, David, *Childhood Cancer Canada Foundation*, 560
Achter, Tangy, *Childhood Cancer Canada Foundation*, 560
Ackerman, Andy, *Child Development Centre Society of Fort St. John & District*, 559
Ackert Ferguson, Sarah, *Professional Engineers Ontario*, 1184
Ackland, Shirley, *North Island College Faculty Association*, 1031
Ackles, Kathy, *Canadian Percheron Association*, 453
Ackles, Mitch, *Hedge Fund Association Canada*, 1529
Acoba, Rodel, *Association of Filipino Canadian Accountants*, 148
Acorn, Dayle, *Canadian Foundation for Pharmacy*, 393
Acosta, Julien, *Conseil de presse du Québec*, 616
Acosta, Pilar, *The Lord's Flock Charismatic Community*, 919
Acott-Smith, Angela, *Carleton Literacy Council*, 513
Acres, Steven J., *Ontario Blonde d'Aquitaine Association*, 1068
Actemichuk, Cheryl, *Okotoks & District Chamber of Commerce*, 1056
Adair, Bill, *Spinal Cord Injury Canada*, 1343
Adair, Gerald, *Saskatchewan Genealogical Society*, 1266
Adair, Gerald, *United Empire Loyalists' Association of Canada*, 1410
Adair, Gertie, *Alberta Beekeepers Commission*, 26
Adam, Steve, *Chambre de commerce St-Jean-de-Matha*, 549
Adam, Louis, *Multiple Sclerosis Society of Canada*, 980
Adam, Louis, *Société canadienne de la sclérose en plaques (Division du Québec)*, 1308
Adam, Barry, *Ontario HIV Treatment Network*, 1084
Adamakos, Peter, *Fire Prevention Canada*, 738
Adams, Ron, *OMF International - Canada*, 1057
Adams, Angela, *Cardston & District Chamber of Commerce*, 511
Adams, Patricia, *Probe International*, 1181

Adams, David C., *Global Automakers of Canada*, 774
Adams, Sean, *Catholic Teachers Guild*, 520
Adams, Patricia, *Energy Probe Research Foundation*, 688
Adams, William A., *Insurance Bureau of Canada*, 849
Adams, John, *Investment Funds Institute of Canada*, 863
Adams, William, *United Empire Loyalists' Association of Canada*, 1410
Adams, Cary, *International Union Against Cancer*, 1563
Adams, Jane, *Health Care Public Relations Association*, 806
Adams, Amanda, *Nipissing Law Association*, 1027
Adams, Bill, *North Grenville Historical Society*, 1031
Adams, John, *Canadian Organization for Rare Disorders*, 447
Adams, Kathleen, *Cyclic Vomiting Syndrome Association*, 1521
Adams, John, *Canadian PKU and Allied Disorders Inc.*, 455
Adams, Lisa, *Tennessee Walking Horse Association of Western Canada*, 1370
Adams, Aimee, *Standardbred Breeders of Ontario Association*, 1347
Adamson, Margaret, *Funeral Advisory & Memorial Society*, 764
Adamson, Kathryn, *International Association of Music Libraries, Archives & Documentation Centres*, 1539
Adamson, Barb, *Sport Medicine Council of Alberta*, 1344
Adamson, Arthur, *Canadian Association of Veterans in United Nations Peacekeeping*, 336
Adamson, President, *The Michener Institute for Applied Health Sciences*, 964
Adamson, Dan, *McGregor Model Forest*, 955
Addario, Susan, *College of Massage Therapists of British Columbia*, 585
Addington, John H., *Door & Access Systems Manufacturers Association*, 1521
Addison, John, *Kaslo & Area Chamber of Commerce*, 882
Addison, Martin, *Mood Disorders Association of British Columbia*, 973
Adekat, Barb, *High Level Native Friendship Centre*, 814
Adelakoun, Corinne, *Foundation of Greater Montreal*, 756
Adelberg, Ellen, *Canadian Parks & Wilderness Society*, 450
Adem, Alejandro, *Pacific Institute for the Mathematical Sciences*, 1135
Adhami, Ayesha, *Immigrant Women's Health Centre*, 831
Adhanom Ghebreyesus, Tedros, *World Health Organization*, 1606
Adkins, Shirlyn A., *American Association of Neuromuscular & Electrodiagnostic Medicine*, 1490
Adlard, Cheryl, *Racquetball Canada*, 1202
Adler, Susan, *Electro-Federation Canada*, 683
Adnams, Ian, *Canadian Church Press*, 356
Adriaans, Eric, *Centre for Inquiry Canada*, 533
Adrian, Nancy, *Canadian Celiac Association*, 353
Adsett, Dave, *Ontario Community Newspapers Association*, 1073
Adunuri, Vivender, *Professional Engineers Ontario*, 1184

Aebi, Renata, *St. Leonard's Youth & Family Services Society*, 1250
Aerts, Louise, *College of Midwives of British Columbia*, 586
Affleck, George, *British Columbia & Yukon Community Newspapers Association*, 229
Afkari, Afsaneh, *Information Resource Management Association of Canada*, 837
Afzal, Mariya, *British Council - Canada*, 259
Agar, Douglas, *British Columbia Association of School Psychologists*, 232
Agatiello, Sandy, *Canadian Pony Club*, 457
Aggarwal, Aditya, *Cricket New Brunswick*, 642
Aggas, Roger, *Registered Professional Foresters Association of Nova Scotia*, 1214
Aggus, Heather, *Alberta Continuing Care Association*, 31
Agnew, Wilma, *Sheet Metal Contractors Association of Alberta*, 1295
Agnew, Theresa, *Nurse Practitioners' Association of Ontario*, 1052
Agombar, Lisa, *4Korners Family Resource Center*, 756
Agostino, Garry, *Thunder Bay Musicians' Association*, 1378
Agostino, Ray, *Physical & Health Educators of Manitoba*, 1158
Agrast, Mark, *American Society of International Law*, 1500
Agrey, Noreen, *Saskatchewan Prevention Institute*, 1272
Agriesti, Jo Marie, *UNITE HERE*, 1599
Aguilar-Zeleny, Patricia E., *Vancouver Status of Women*, 1429
Agwa, Peter, *Evangelical Medical Aid Society Canada*, 698
Ahad, Edward, *Promotional Product Professionals of Canada Inc.*, 1189
Ahearn, Brian, *Canadian Fuels Association*, 396
Ahearn, Peggy, *Canadian Association of Wound Care*, 337
Ahee, Jonathan, *NABET 700 CEP*, 987
Ahern, Stephen, *Acadia University Faculty Association*, 4
Ahern, Shirley, *Blind Bowls Association of Canada*, 214
Ahmad, Arif, *Re:Sound Music Licensing Company*, 1204
Ahmadzai, Haris, *Professional Engineers Ontario*, 1184
Ahmed, Faris, *USC Canada*, 1423
Ahmed, Qudsia, *Project Management Institute*, 1585
Ahmed, Faiyaz, *Islamic Association of Saskatchewan*, 864
Ahmed, Khalil, *Smoky Applied Research & Demonstration Association*, 1305
Ahntholz, Ivan, *Manitoba Beef Cattle Performance Association*, 932
Ahrendt, Lu, *Osoyoos Food Bank*, 1128
Ahron, Reuven, *Iraqi Jewish Association of Ontario*, 863
Ahuja, Ashley, *Canadian Nursing Students' Association*, 443
Aiello, Albert, *Boys & Girls Clubs of Ontario*, 223
Ainsworth, Tara, *Atlantic Association of Applied Economists*, 182
Ainsworth, Jon, *Freight Carriers Association of Canada*, 759
Ainsworth-Vincze, Cameron, *Prospectors & Developers Association of Canada*, 1189
Aird, Brian, *Entrepreneurs with Disabilities Network*, 691

Executive Name Index

Airhart, Chuck, *Napanee Sports Association*, 988
Airiants, Vadim, *Association of Professional Engineers & Geoscientists of British Columbia*, 158
Aitchison, Chrissy, *Canadian Institute of Traffic & Transportation*, 420
Aitken, Cindy, *Applied Science Technologists & Technicians of British Columbia*, 74
Aitken, Avril, *Canadian Association for Curriculum Studies*, 299
Aitken, Jim, *Bowls British Columbia*, 220
Aitken, Ian, *Enactus Canada*, 687
Aitken, Lois J., *Canadian Porphyria Foundation Inc.*, 458
Aitken, Murray, *Quintiles IMS Canada*, 1202
Aitken, Julie, *Electricity Human Resources Canada*, 683
Aitken, Iain, *Canadian Luing Cattle Association*, 428
Aitken, Paul D., *American Association on Intellectual & Developmental Disabilities*, 1490
Aitken, Peter, *Canadian Frailty Network*, 394
Akhtar, Kaleem, *Human Concern International*, 825
Akhtar, Nabeek, *British Columbia Muslim Association*, 247
Akhter, Shakil, *Islamic Foundation of Toronto*, 864
Akroyd Bombino, Sally, *Canadian Farm Builders Association*, 384
Al, Baswick, *Employees Association of Milltronics - CNFIU Local 3005*, 686
Al-Hamdani, Mohammed, *The Lung Association of Nova Scotia*, 921
Al-Saedy, Huda, *Ecojustice Canada Society*, 672
Al-Ubaidi, Halah, *Conseil communautaire Notre-Dame-de-Grâce*, 614
Al-Zehlaoui, Joseph, *The Antiochan Orthodox Christian Archdiocese of North America*, 1505
Alabi, Kayode (Kay), *African Canadian Social Development Council*, 13
Alahmad, Samir, *Association des garderies privées du Québec*, 114
Alain, Louiselle, *Société d'histoire et de généalogie de Val-d'Or*, 1313
Alain, Joey, *Open Door Group*, 1114
Alanko, MaryJane, *Alberta Professional Planners Institute*, 43
Alarie, Deborah, *Employment & Education Centre*, 687
Alary, Mireille, *Pontiac Chamber of Commerce*, 1164
Alary, Michel, *International Society for Sexually Transmitted Diseases Research*, 1559
Alashi, Basel, *Canadian Bureau for International Education*, 347
Albanese, Robert, *Vancouver Jewish Film Centre Society*, 1427
Albarella, Umberto, *International Council for Archaeozoology*, 1544
Albert, Sam, *SEDS - USA*, 1588
Albert, Darrell, *Orchid Soceity of Alberta*, 1119
Albert, Mario, *International Financial Centre of Montréal*, 857
Albert, Paul, *Canadian College of Neuropsychopharmacology*, 360
Alberti, Mary, *Schizophrenia Society of Ontario*, 1284
Albisser, Shannon, *Yukon Gymnastics Association*, 1478
Albrecht, Tina, *British Columbia Council for Families*, 238
Albrecht, Brian, *Canada's National Bible Hour*, 282, 775
Albright, Kevin, *Manning & District Chamber of Commerce*, 948
Albright, Calvin, *Kermode Friendship Society*, 884
Albu, Rodica, *Central European Association for Canadian Studies*, 1516

Alcock, Lindsay, *Canadian Health Libraries Association*, 402
Alcock, Tim, *Ontario Lung Association*, 1090
Alcorn, Emmy, *Mulgrave Road Theatre Foundation*, 978
Aldcorn, Jamison, *Canadian Academic Accounting Association*, 285
Alder, Martina, *Battle River Research Group*, 200
Alderman, Dave, *World Darts Federation*, 1604
Alderman, Art, *Canadian Pony Society*, 458
Alderton, Lillian, *Canadian Snowsports Association*, 472
Aldrich, Elizabeth, *Sexual Assault Support Centre Ottawa*, 1293
Aldrich, Patrick, *American Association of Neuromuscular & Electrodiagnostic Medicine*, 1490
Aldworth, Rebecca, *Humane Society International/Canada*, 826
Aleman, Dionne, *Canadian Operational Research Society*, 446
Alex, Rozen, *Canadian Psychological Association*, 462
Alex, Osei, *Pontifical Mission Societies*, 1164
Alexander, Aruna, *United Nations Association in Canada*, 1411
Alexander, Dana, *Battlefords Agricultural Society*, 200
Alexander, Jane, *The Anglican Church of Canada*, 69
Alexander, Stephen, *AIDS New Brunswick*, 17
Alexander, Craig, *The Conference Board of Canada*, 612
Alexander, Carl, *The Bruce Trail Conservancy*, 261
Alexander, Sandra, *Weyburn & District United Way*, 1451
Alexander, Amanda, *YMCA Canada*, 1472
Alexander, Paul, *Canada - Newfoundland & Labrador Offshore Petroleum Board*, 277
Alexander, Steve, *Association of Postconsumer Plastic Recyclers*, 1513
Alexander, Lisa, *Skate Ontario*, 1302
Alexander, Bob, *The Alberta Seventh Step Society*, 46
Alexander, Denny, *Canadian Foundation for Climate & Atmospheric Sciences*, 393
Alexander, Charlene, *Yukon First Nations Culture & Tourism Association*, 1478
Alexander, Duncan, *Chawkers Foundation*, 555
Alexanderson, Miguel Benedetto, *National Association of the Chemistry Industry*, 1574
Aleyaseen, Val, *Society of Professional Engineers & Associates*, 1330
Alford, Johanna, *Canadian Quilters' Association*, 464
Alfred, Christopher, *Canadian Football Hall of Fame & Museum*, 392
Alho, Joann, *Brantford Symphony Orchestra Association Inc.*, 227
Ali, Shabna, *BC Society of Transition Houses*, 202
Ali, Mary, *Inner City Home of Sudbury*, 839
Ali, Safiatou, *Regroupement des éditeurs canadiens-français*, 1215
Ali, Nazreen, *Ontario Motor Vehicle Industry Council*, 1091
Ali, Saiyad, *British Columbia Muslim Association*, 247
Ali, Tazul, *British Columbia Muslim Association*, 247
Ali, Sabrina, *Association of Fundraising Professionals*, 1512
Aliweiwi, Jehad, *Thorncliffe Neighbourhood Office*, 1376
Aliweiwi, Jehad, *Laidlaw Foundation*, 895
Aliyarzadeh, Golnaz, *Canadian Translators, Terminologists & Interpreters Council*, 496
Alkema, J.D., *Christian Labour Association of Canada*, 568
Alkenbrack, Peggy, *Alberta Floor Covering Association*, 35

Alkrunz, Abdallah, *Canadian Arab Federation*, 294
Allaby, Jennifer, *Canadian Association of Exposition Management*, 313
Allain, Louis, *Conseil de développement économique des municipalités bilingues du Manitoba*, 615
Allan, Mark, *Regina Exhibition Association Ltd.*, 1211
Allan, Warren, *International Federation of Accountants*, 1547
Allan, Reid, *Canadian Association of Slavists*, 333
Allan, John, *Council of Forest Industries*, 633
Allan, James, *Grand Orange Lodge of Canada*, 780
Allan, Judy, *Etobicoke Philharmonic Orchestra*, 698
Allan, David, *Ontario Public Buyers Association*, 1098
Allan, Steve, *Alberta Recreation & Parks Association*, 44
Allan, Dennis, *Alberta Sports Hall of Fame & Museum*, 48
Allan, Margaret, *The Royal Scottish Country Dance Society*, 1587
Allan, Tom, *Bonnyville & District Chamber of Commerce*, 217
Allan, Elaine, *Skills/Compétences Canada*, 1303
Allan, Sheila, *Megantic County Historical Society*, 959
Allanson, Nancy, *Trent Hills & District Chamber of Commerce*, 1397
Allard, Pierre, *Garrod Association*, 767
Allard, Alexandre, *Association des Gestionnaires de l'information de la santé du Québec*, 115
Allard, Eric, *Association régionale de ringuette Laval*, 177
Allard, Louis-Paul, *Fondation québécoise en environnement*, 748
Allard, Jean-Marie, *Association canadienne-française de Régina*, 96
Allard, Paul, *British Columbia Stone, Sand & Gravel Association*, 255
Allen, Nathalie, *Jeunesses Musicales du Canada*, 871
Allen, Maureen, *Vancouver Ballet Society*, 1425
Allen, David, *United Church of Canada*, 1409
Allen, Lindsey, *Rainforest Action Network*, 1586
Allen, Colin, *World Federation of the Deaf*, 1605
Allen, Susan, *Building Owners & Managers Association Toronto*, 263
Allen, Kim, *Sexual Assault Centre Kingston Inc.*, 1292
Allen, Donna L., *Canadian College of Health Leaders*, 359
Allen, Lorraine, *Holstein Canada*, 819
Allen, Chrystal, *New Brunswick Society of Medical Laboratory Technologists*, 1012
Allen, William, *New Brunswick Society of Medical Laboratory Technologists*, 1012
Allen, Pam, *Ontario Music Festivals Association*, 1093
Allen, Pam, *Kiwanis Music Festival Association of Greater Toronto*, 892
Allen, Leona, *Tourism Sarnia Lambton*, 1391
Allen, David, *YMCA Canada*, 1471, 1472
Allen, Kim, *Engineers Canada*, 689
Allen, Michael, *United Way/Centraide Ottawa*, 1418
Allen, Heather, *Goodwill Industries Essex Kent Lambton*, 777
Allen, Diana, *International Association of Hydrogeologists - Canadian National Chapter*, 854
Allen, Tom, *King Chamber of Commerce*, 888
Allen, Tom, *Association of American Publishers*, 1510
Allen, Robert, *Ontario Brain Injury Association*, 1069

Allen, Carolle, *Bowls British Columbia*, 220
Allen, Deanna, *Laubach Literacy New Brunswick*, 900
Allen, Nyree, *Canadian Pastry Chefs Guild Inc.*, 451
Allen, Gloria, *AFOA Canada*, 12
Allen, Diane, *Infertility Network*, 836
Allen, Rory, *PFLAG Canada Inc.*, 1156
Allen, Marg, *Manitoba Welsh Pony & Cob Association*, 947
Allen, Jon, *Alberta Association of Prosthetists & Orthotists*, 24
Allen, Kait, *Manitoba Cheer Federation Inc.*, 933
Allen, Bob, *British Columbia Broadband Association*, 234
Allen, Serge, *Agence municipale de financement et de développement des centres d'urgence 9-1-1 du Québec*, 14
Allenby, Christine, *Ontario Construction Secretariat*, 1074
Alley, Sean, *PFLAG Canada Inc.*, 1155
Alleyne, Johwanna, *Alberta Farmers' Market Association*, 34
Alleyne-Martin, Natasha, *TD Friends of the Environment Foundation*, 1367
Alling, Elizabeth, *Québec-Labrador Foundation (Canada) Inc.*, 1199
Allingham, Ted, *New Brunswick Lung Association*, 1010
Allison, Gwendoline C., *Continuing Legal Education Society of BC*, 627
Allison, Sheree A., *Big Brothers Big Sisters of New Brunswick*, 209, 222
Allison, Luna, *Canadian Federation of Humane Societies*, 386
Allison, Paul, *Association of Canadian Faculties of Dentistry*, 142
Allman, Grant, *Fenelon Falls & District Chamber of Commerce*, 732
Allmark, Phil, *Western Transportation Advisory Council*, 1450
Alm, Kathy, *Professional Association of Therapeutic Horsemanship International*, 1584
Alma, Nahanni, *YMCA Canada*, 1473
Almadi, Karen, *Pumphouse Theatres Society*, 1194
Almedia, José E., *AdvaMed*, 1485
Almeida, Fernanda, *Canadian Association for Dental Research*, 299
Almond, Margo, *The Canadian Federation of Business & Professional Women's Clubs*, 386
Almond, Nicole, *Enactus Canada*, 687
Alofs, Paul, *Princess Margaret Cancer Foundation*, 1180
Alongi, Deene, *American Planning Association*, 1496
Aloni, Yariv, *Greater Victoria Youth Orchestra*, 787
Alovisi, Franceen, *APER Santé et services sociaux*, 73
Alsop, John, *Collingwood Chamber of Commerce*, 591
Alsop, Ken, *Beaverton Thorah Eldon Historical Society*, 203
Altenbeck, Ashley, *Canadian Association of Critical Care Nurses*, 312
Alter, Doris, *Toronto Association of Synagogue & Temple Administrators*, 1382
Altner, Sandra, *Women's Enterprise Centre of Manitoba*, 1462
Altner, Sandra, *Canadian Council for Small Business & Entrepreneurship*, 367
Alvarez, Jacqueline, *Crohn's & Colitis Canada*, 643
Alves, Natasha, *Canada's Medical Technology Companies*, 282
Alves, Natasha, *Canadian MedTech Manufacturers' Alliance*, 434
Alwazani, Sandra, *Risk & Insurance Management Society Inc.*, 1234
Am Rhyn, Jost, *Canadian Veterinary Medical Association*, 501

Executive Name Index

Amanda, Caravan, *YMCA Canada*, 1472
Amanda, Macrae, *Age & Opportunity Inc.*, 14
Amano, Yukiya, *International Atomic Energy Agency*, 1540
Amar, Eric, *Arthritis Society*, 84
Amarook, Tani, *Rocky Native Friendship Society*, 1235
Amarshi, Hussain, *Canadian Association of Film Distributors & Exporters*, 314
Amarshi, Fatima, *Coastal Jazz & Blues Society*, 579
Amato, Lindy, *Ontario Teachers' Federation*, 1110
Amato, Raphael, *L'Arche Ontario*, 77
Amato, Myriam, *Almas Jiwani Foundation*, 59
Amber, Arnold, *Canadian Journalists for Free Expression*, 423
Amberman, Shawn, *Association of Professional Engineers & Geoscientists of New Brunswick*, 158
Ambidge, Chris, *Integrity Toronto*, 850
Ambrose, Bruce, *International Wine & Food Society*, 1567
Ambrosie, Randy, *Canadian Football League*, 392
Ames, Tim, *Planned Lifetime Advocacy Network*, 1161
Ames, Doris, *Native Orchid Conservation Inc.*, 998
Amir, Muradali, *Association of MBAs in Canada*, 151
Amirault, Darrell, *American Society of Heating, Refrigerating & Air Conditioning Engineers*, 1500
Amirzadeh, Haidah, *Saskatoon Open Door Society Inc.*, 1279
Amit, Uri Ron, *Hashomer Hatzair Canada*, 804
Ammar, Ed, *United Conservative Association*, 1410
Ammendolea, Cathy, *Canadian Breast Cancer Network*, 347
Amminson, Wayne, *Handball Association of Newfoundland & Labrador*, 802
Amon, Larry, *The Ocean Conservancy*, 1580
Amort, Joe, *IntegrityLink*, 850
Amos, Paula, *Aboriginal Tourism Association of British Columbia*, 2
Amselle, Jorge, *Salt Institute*, 1588
Amygdalidis, Christine, *Cypriot Federation of Canada*, 647
Amyot, Denise, *Colleges and Institutes Canada*, 590
Amyot, Claude, *Société historique de Joliette-De Lanaudière*, 1320
Amyot, Guy, *Conseil de presse du Québec*, 616
Amyotte, Judy, *Professional Association of Volunteer Leaders Ontario*, 1183
Amzallag, Nicole, *Société pour les enfants handicapés du Québec*, 1322
An, Jeannie, *University of Toronto, Faculty of Information Alumni Association*, 1421
Anand, Havelin, *Canadian Association of Occupational Therapists*, 323
Anang, Charles, *Kolbe Eucharistic Apostolate*, 892
Anani, Namir, *Information & Communications Technology Council of Canada*, 836
Anas, Dimitrios, *Greek Orthodox Metropolis of Toronto (Canada)*, 788
Anbolt, Susan, *Kenaston & District Chamber of Commerce*, 883
Anckle, Danny, *Scouts Canada*, 1286
Anctil, Pierre, *Institut de cardiologie de Montréal*, 841
Andersen, Inger, *International Union for Conservation of Nature*, 1563
Andersen, Connie, *Saskatchewan Association for Community Living*, 1256
Andersen, Gert, *Federation of Danish Associations in Canada*, 723
Andersen, Erica, *Transportation Association of Canada*, 1395
Andersen, Finn, *Saskatchewan History & Folklore Society Inc.*, 1267

Andersen, Susannah, *The Royal Scottish Country Dance Society*, 1587
Andersen, Vi, *Women's Association of the Mining Industry of Canada*, 1461
Andersen, Megan, *CADORA British Columbia*, 268
Anderson, Fortner, *Vidéographe*, 1434
Anderson, Patricia E., *The John Howard Society of Ontario*, 875
Anderson, William, *The Anglican Church of Canada*, 69
Anderson, Gay, *Children's Wish Foundation of Canada*, 563
Anderson, Katherine, *North Central Library Federation*, 1030
Anderson, Farel, *E3 Community Services*, 666
Anderson, Debbie, *Toronto Art Therapy Institute*, 1381
Anderson, Brad, *Alberta Chamber of Resources*, 28
Anderson, Diana, *Red Deer & District Allied Arts Council*, 1209
Anderson, Sharon, *Camrose Chamber of Commerce*, 277
Anderson, Sacha, *Crowsnest Pass Chamber of Commerce*, 644
Anderson, Gwen, *Aylsham & District Board of Trade*, 191
Anderson, Andy, *Morris & District Chamber of Commerce*, 974
Anderson, Linda, *Iroquois Falls & District Chamber of Commerce*, 864
Anderson, Raymond, *Commonwealth Pharmacists Association*, 1518
Anderson, Alex, *Canadian Public Relations Society Inc.*, 463
Anderson, Dean, *Ontario Institute of Agrologists*, 1087
Anderson, Carol, *Alberta Genealogical Society*, 36
Anderson, Colin, *Association of Major Power Consumers in Ontario*, 151
Anderson, Derek, *Canadian Boating Federation*, 345
Anderson, Sylvia, *Special Olympics Yukon*, 1340
Anderson, Andy, *Canadian Aviation Historical Society*, 340
Anderson, Janice, *Canadian Bridge Federation*, 347
Anderson, Kari, *Association of Professional Engineers & Geoscientists of Alberta*, 157
Anderson, Bruce, *Canadian Hydrographic Association*, 409
Anderson, G., *Canadian Society of Forensic Science*, 483
Anderson, Nichole, *Business for the Arts*, 267
Anderson, Scott, *Geological Association of Canada*, 770
Anderson, Holly, *Insurance Institute of Manitoba*, 849
Anderson, Carl A., *Knights of Columbus*, 1568
Anderson, Ashley, *Alberta Simmental Association*, 46
Anderson, Alexandra, *Camping in Ontario*, 277
Anderson, Elliott, *Alliance of Canadian Cinema, Television & Radio Artists*, 58
Anderson, Leslie, *Professional Association of Residents & Interns of Manitoba*, 1182
Anderson, Neil, *Association for Media Literacy*, 134
Anderson, Dean, *Canadian Agricultural Safety Association*, 290
Anderson, Mollie, *Canadians for Clean Prosperity*, 507
Anderson, Shelley, *Antigonish Ceilidh Association*, 72
Anderson, Kelly, *Nishnawbe - Gamik Friendship Centre*, 1027
Anderson, Traci, *Boys & Girls Clubs of British Columbia*, 222
Anderson, Shirley, *Sisters of Saint Joseph of Sault Ste Marie*, 1301

Anderson, Garry W., *Cranbrook Archives, Museum & Landmark Foundation*, 638
Anderson, Gail, *Ontario Public School Boards Association*, 1099
Anderson, Jeff, *Evangelical Covenant Church of Canada*, 698
Anderson, Don, *North Eastern Ontario Family & Children's Services*, 1031
Anderson, Mary K., *The Municipal Chapter of Toronto IODE*, 980
Anderson, Jay, *Supply Chain Management Association - Manitoba*, 1356
Anderson, Etta, *Scottish Settlers Historical Society*, 1286
Anderson, Val, *British Columbia Registered Music Teachers' Association*, 251
Anderson, John, *Interactive Gaming Council*, 851
Anderson, Nicole Laflèche, *L'Association du Québec de l'Institut canadien des évaluateurs*, 131
Anderson, Richard, *Smart Serve Ontario*, 1304
Anderson, Jamie, *Canadian Capital Markets Association*, 349
Anderson, Scott, *British Columbia Conservative Party*, 237
Anderson, Terry, *Murray Grey International, Incorporated*, 982
Anderson, Kenneth, *Manitoba Deaf Sports Association Inc.*, 935
Anderson, Carl, *Canadian Safe Cannabis Society*, 468
Anderson-Kellett, Lisa, *British Columbia Video Relay Services Committee*, 257
Andersson, Roland, *Chemical Institute of Canada*, 556
Andersson, Roland, *Canadian Society for Chemical Engineering*, 473
Andersson, Roland, *Canadian Society for Chemical Technology*, 473
Andersson, K. David, *Pacific Corridor Enterprise Council*, 1135
Andersson, Roland, *Canadian Society for Chemistry*, 473
Andersson-Charest, Petra, *Parliamentary Centre*, 1142
Andison, Thomas K., *International Symphony Orchestra of Sarnia, Ontario & Port Huron, Michigan*, 861
Andrais, Brian, *Alberta Teachers' Association*, 49
André, Deschênes, *Learning Disabilities Association of New Brunswick*, 904
André-Guimont, Catherine, *Association des Perfusionnistes du Québec Inc.*, 122
Andrea, Shelley, *Alberta Construction Association*, 31
Andrea, Trish, *Chartered Professionals in Human Resources of British Columbia & Yukon*, 554
Andree-Anne, Dionne, *Canadian Amateur Boxing Association*, 292
Andreiuk, Gordon, *Alberta Family Mediation Society*, 34
Andrejas, Rozi, *Huntington Society of Canada*, 827
Andreozzi, Peter, *4Korners Family Resource Center*, 756
Andres, Francis, *Canadian Beef*, 342
Andres, Gerd, *Alberta Milk*, 40
Andrew, Evan, *Sport Manitoba*, 1344
Andrew, Gail, *Voyageur Trail Association*, 1439
Andrew, Murray, *Saskatchewan Livestock Association*, 1269
Andrews, Paul P., *International Organization of Securities Commissions*, 1554
Andrews, Stephen, *The Anglican Church of Canada*, 69
Andrews, Barbara, *Community Living Ajax-Pickering & Whitby*, 600
Andrews, Keith, *Prince Albert Gliding & Soaring Club*, 1171

Andrews, Carrie, *The Brampton Board of Trade*, 226
Andrews, Alex, *Alberta Association of Midwives*, 24
Andrews, David, *Canadian Corrugated Containerboard Association*, 366
Andrews, Mary Jane, *Canadian Institute of Chartered Business Valuators*, 414
Andrews, Peter, *Epilepsy Ontario*, 694
Andrews, Stephen, *The Public Affairs Association of Canada*, 1192
Andrews, Sharon, *Karate Manitoba*, 881
Andrews, Suzanne, *Quinte West Chamber of Commerce*, 1202
Andrews, Gilbert G., *Keewatin Tribal Council*, 883
Andrews, Robert, *AFOA Canada*, 12
Andrews, Dave, *Visual Artists Newfoundland & Labrador*, 1436
Andrews-Clay, Kathryn, *Canadian Skin Patient Alliance*, 472
Andrey, Jean, *International Geographical Union - Canadian Committee*, 857
Andreychuk, Brittaney, *Federation of B.C. Youth in Care Networks*, 722
Andricciola, Salvatore, *Chambre de commerce de St-Léonard*, 543
Andringa, Calvin, *Tofield & District Chamber of Commerce*, 1380
Andruschak, Maureen, *SPEC Association for Children & Families*, 1339
Andy, Louise, *Ordre des ingénieurs du Québec*, 1122
Angeconeb, Rick, *First Nations Chiefs of Police Association*, 738
Angela, Leatherland, *Risk & Insurance Management Society Inc.*, 1234
Angeli, Marco, *Canada Employment & Immigration Union*, 279
Angevine, Pansy, *Alberta Hospice Palliative Care Association*, 38
Anghel, Sara, *National Marine Manufacturers Association*, 1576
Anghel, Sara, *National Marine Manufacturers Association Canada*, 995
Angus, Scot, *York Region Athletic Association*, 1473
Angus, Dave, *Winnipeg Chamber of Commerce*, 1458
Angus, Iain, *Northwestern Ontario Municipal Association*, 1039
Angus, Sasha, *Tourism Nanaimo*, 1390
Angus, Garry, *Community Futures Development Association of British Columbia*, 598
Anholt, Susan, *Saskatchewan Dental Assistants' Association*, 1263
Ania, Idoia, *Homeopathic College of Canada*, 820
Anis, Aslam, *Canadian HIV Trials Network*, 405
Anisman, Stephen, *Chartered Professional Accountants Canada*, 552
Anisman, Sharon E., *Canadian Friends of Boys Town Jerusalem*, 395
Annable, Cliff, *South Surrey & White Rock Chamber of Commerce*, 1336
Annett, Carol, *VHA Home HealthCare*, 1431
Annis, Susan, *Cultural Human Resources Council*, 645
Annis, Robert, *Community Futures Development Association of British Columbia*, 598
Ansell, Wendy, *Canadian Association for Laboratory Animal Science*, 302
Anson, Emily, *The Ontario Archaeological Society*, 1060
Anstey, Christopher, *American Society for Quality*, 1499
Anstey, Jessica, *Newfoundland Equestrian Association*, 1023
Antal, Mordechai, *Federation of Teachers of Jewish Schools*, 726
Antaya, G.A. (Gail), *Chatham-Kent Chamber of Commerce*, 555

Executive Name Index

Antheunis, Justin, *International Alliance of Theatrical Stage Employees, Moving Picture Technicians, Artists & Allied Crafts of the U.S., Its Territories & Canada*, 1535

Anthonette Tecson, Mary, *Association of Filipino Canadian Accountants in British Columbia*, 148

Anthony, Clarke, *Ontario Council on Graduate Studies*, 1075

Anthony, Julie, *Ontario Brain Injury Association*, 1068

Anthony-Malone, Kristin, *Canadian Avalanche Association*, 340

Antle, Al, *Credit Counselling Services of Newfoundland & Labrador*, 640

Antler, Susan, *Compost Council of Canada*, 609

Antolick, Haida, *Confederation of University Faculty Associations of British Columbia*, 611

Anton, Gordon, *E3 Community Services*, 666

Antonel, Robert, *Architectural Woodwork Manufacturers Association of Canada - Ontario Chapter*, 79

Antonello, Sean, *CADORA Ontario Association Inc.*, 269

Antonetti, Martin, *Bibliographical Society of America*, 1514

Antonio, Francine, *Federation of Portuguese Canadian Business & Professionals Inc.*, 726

Antonio, Tina, *Marine Insurance Association of British Columbia*, 950

Antoniow, Barry, *Canadian Powerlifting Union*, 459

Anvari, Mehran, *Canadian Association of Bariatric Physicians & Surgeons*, 308

Anwar, Fahima, *Social Planning Council of Kitchener-Waterloo*, 1306

Anwender, Paul, *Sunny South District Soccer Association*, 1354

Aoki, Jodi, *Archives Association of Ontario*, 80

Aoki, Tatsuya, *Jodo Shinshu Buddhist Temples of Canada*, 873

Appelbaum, Stuart, *Retail, Wholesale & Department Store Union (AFL-CIO/CLC)*, 1586

Appels, Rachel, *Alberta Soccer Association*, 47

Applebaum, Heath, *Canadian Public Relations Society Inc.*, 463

Applebaum, Laurence, *Golf Canada*, 777

Applebaum, Neil, *Ontario Association of Dental Specialists*, 1063

Appleby, Tom, *Epilepsy Ontario*, 694

Appleby, Lianne, *Beef Farmers of Ontario*, 204

Appleby, Lianne, *Pipe Line Contractors Association of Canada*, 1160

Appleby-Goosen, Jennifer, *Prosserman Jewish Community Centre*, 1189

Appleton, Jodi, *Federation of Mountain Clubs of British Columbia*, 725

Appleton, Tom, *Canada's Aviation Hall of Fame*, 282

Apps, Stephen, *Canadian Institute of Plumbing & Heating*, 418

Apramian, Tavis, *Canadian Federation of Medical Students*, 388

April, Alain, *Carnaval de Québec*, 514

Apruzzese, Antonio, *Società Unita*, 1307

Aqeel, Maliha, *Institute of Corporate Directors*, 845

Aquash, Mark, *Canadian Association for the Study of Indigenous Education*, 306

Aquilina-Bock, Marlene, *Better Business Bureau of Western Ontario*, 207

Aquin, Elizabeth, *Petroleum Services Association of Canada*, 1154

Aquino, Angie, *Mount Pleasant Group*, 976

Aquino, Paula, *Teachers of Home Economics Specialist Association*, 1367

Araia, Makda, *Canadian Fitness & Lifestyle Research Institute*, 390

Aranda, Sanchia, *International Union Against Cancer*, 1563

Araneda, Cecilia, *Winnipeg Film Group*, 1459

Araoz, M. Gustavo, *International Council on Monuments & Sites*, 1545

Arata, Martin, *Association des conseils des médecins, dentistes et pharmaciens du Québec*, 109

Araujo, George, *Norfolk County Agricultural Society*, 1028

Arbeid, Esther, *Toronto Jewish Film Society*, 1385

Arbez, Madeleine, *Francofonds inc.*, 757

Arbic, Jacques, *Epilepsy Ontario*, 694

Arbour, Marianne, *Big Brothers Big Sisters of Ontario*, 210

Arbour, Christine, *Centre d'information et de recherche en consommation de Charlevoix-Ouest*, 528

Arbour, Jean-François, *Association de la construction du Québec*, 100

Arbour, Judith, *Canadian Foundry Association*, 394

Arbuckle, Michelle, *Ontario Library Association*, 1089

Arcamone, Pina, *Enfant-Retour Québec*, 688

Arcand, Nancy, *District of Mission Arts Council*, 659

Arcand, George, *Softball Yukon*, 1332

Arcand, Christian, *Association québécoise des interprètes du patrimoine*, 173

Archambault, Sandrine, *Jeune chambre de commerce de Montréal*, 871

Archambault, Jacques, *L'Héritage canadien du Québec*, 813

Archambault, Rachel, *Association des réalisateurs et réalisatrices de Télé-Québec*, 127

Archambault, Sylvain, *Canada Employment & Immigration Union*, 279

Archambault, Georges, *Research & Development Institute for the Agri-Environment*, 1218

Archambault, Monique, *Association of Fundraising Professionals*, 1512

Archer, Walter, *Canadian Society for the Study of Higher Education*, 478

Archer, Colin, *International Peace Bureau*, 1555

Archibald, Esther, *Canadian Association of Foodservice Professionals*, 315

Archibald, Susan, *BALANCE for Blind Adults*, 194

Archibald, David, *Association for Canadian Studies in the United States*, 1507

Archibald, Karen, *Fraser Valley Rock & Gem Club*, 758

Archibald, Gord, *Association of Regina Realtors*, 160

Archibald, Terry, *North Central Labour Council of British Columbia*, 1030

Archibald-Barber, Jesse, *Indigenous Literary Studies Association*, 835

Arcot, Chitra, *Pulp & Paper Centre*, 1194

Arcuri, Joseph, *Villa Charities Inc. (Toronto District)*, 1434

Ardon, Jennifer, *Canadian Lutheran World Relief*, 428

Arel, Priscille, *Association des personnes handicapées de la Rive-Sud Ouest*, 122

Arens, Raphael, *L'Arche Ontario*, 77

Arès, Denise, *Association de paralysie cérébrale du Québec*, 103

Argue, Shawna, *Association of Professional Engineers & Geoscientists of Saskatchewan*, 159

Argue, Allan, *Cannington & Area Historical Society*, 508

Argue, Bob, *EcoPerth*, 673

Argue, Charlotte, *Fraser Basin Council*, 757

Arguin, Nathalie, *Fédération des employées et employés de services publics inc. (CSN)*, 714

Arguin, Chantal, *GEOIDE Network*, 769

Argyle, Ray, *Periodical Marketers of Canada*, 1152

Ariganello, Anthony, *Chartered Professionals in Human Resources of British Columbia & Yukon*, 554

Ariganello, Anthony, *Chartered Professionals in Human Resources*, 554

Arisman, Audrey, *Western Canada Water*, 1448

Arita, Yukio, *Toronto Japanese Association of Commerce & Industry*, 1385

Arkeveld, Patrick, *Canadian Ski Council*, 471

Armbruster, Walter J., *International Association of Agricultural Economists*, 1538

Armbruster, Susan, *Shorthorn Breeders of Manitoba Inc.*, 1297

Armorer, Quincy, *Black Theatre Workshop*, 214

Armour, Stuart, *Canadian Security Association*, 469

Armour, David, *United Church of Canada Foundation*, 1410

Armstrong, Stafanie, *Dryden District Chamber of Commerce*, 663

Armstrong, Mary, *Guysborough Historical Society*, 795

Armstrong, Suzanne, *Christian Farmers Federation of Ontario*, 567

Armstrong, Debra, *Skate Canada*, 1301

Armstrong, Mike, *Canadian Powerlifting Union*, 459

Armstrong, Jay, *Association of Professional Engineers & Geoscientists of British Columbia*, 158

Armstrong, Paul, *Ontario Seaplane Association*, 1103

Armstrong, Amanda, *Meeting Professionals International*, 1570

Armstrong, Andrea, *Symphony on the Bay*, 1360

Armstrong, Richard, *Printing Equipment & Supply Dealers' Association of Canada*, 1180

Armstrong, John, *United Way of Oakville*, 1415

Armstrong, Rob, *YMCA Canada*, 1471

Armstrong, Bob, *The Chartered Institute of Logistics & Transport in North America*, 552

Armstrong, Mike, *Canadian Merchant Service Guild*, 435

Armstrong, Sharon, *Saskatchewan Library Trustees' Association*, 1269

Armstrong, Steve, *Swim-Natation Manitoba*, 1359

Armstrong, Thom, *Cooperative Housing Federation of British Columbia*, 628

Armstrong, Greg, *Stoney Creek Historical Society*, 1350

Armstrong, Angus, *Pembroke Symphony Orchestra*, 1149

Armstrong, Hugh, *Grasslands Naturalists*, 782

Armstrong, Kate, *Western Front Society*, 1449

Armstrong, Gail Paul, *Saskatchewan Arts Board*, 1256

Armstrong, Robin, *Canadian Arthritis Network*, 295

Armstrong, Ruth, *Law Society of Saskatchewan*, 902

Armstrong, Steven, *Genome Canada*, 769

Armstrong, Andrew, *Triathlon British Columbia*, 1397

Armstrong, Cailey, *Hub for Active School Travel*, 824

Arnaquq-Baril, Alethea, *Ajjiit Nunavut Media Association*, 21

Arnaud, Patricia, *Association des parents et amis de la personne atteinte de maladie mentale Rive-Sud*, 122

Arndt, Mark, *Tennis Manitoba*, 1371

Arndt, Lyndsay, *Alberta College of Combined Laboratory & X-Ray Technologists*, 29

Arnett, John, *Psychological Association of Manitoba*, 1192

Arney, Kathy, *Canadian Council for the Advancement of Education*, 367

Arngaq, Charlie, *Avataq Cultural Institute*, 190

Arnold, Tom, *Food & Consumer Products of Canada*, 749

Arnold, Lorna, *Nature Saskatchewan*, 1001

Arnold, Sharon, *Credit Unions Atlantic Canada*, 641

Arnold, Julie, *Netball Alberta*, 1003

Arnold, Tracey, *Canadian Arm Wrestling Federation*, 295

Arnold Cormier, Cathy, *Canadian Society of Gastroenterology Nurses & Associates*, 483

Arnott, G.N. (Arnie), *Canadian Association of Blue Cross Plans*, 309

Arnott, Anne, *Thames Region Ecological Association*, 1373

Arocha, Izabel, *Fédération Internationale des Traducteurs*, 1526

Aronson, Rosa, *Teachers of English to Speakers of Other Languages, Inc.*, 1597

Arora, Paul, *Canadian Society for Epidemiology & Biostatistics*, 474

Arrano, Carla, *Step-By-Step Child Development Society*, 1349

Arrowsmith, Emily, *Jane Austen Society of North America*, 868

Arrowsmith, Jamie, *Sudbury Youth Orchestra Inc.*, 1353

Arruda, Joan, *Family Day Care Services (Toronto)*, 703

Arsenault, Roger, *Association des constructeurs de routes et grands travaux du Québec*, 110

Arsenault, Mélanie, *Sign Association of Canada*, 1299

Arsenault, Max, *Energy Council of Canada*, 688

Arsenault, Michel, *Fédération des travailleurs et travailleuses du Québec*, 719

Arsenault, Kelly, *Prince County Hospital Foundation*, 1171

Arsenault, Jim, *Safety Services New Brunswick*, 1245

Arsenault, Marc, *Aéroclub des cantons de l'est*, 11

Arsenault, Élise, *Réseau Santé en français I.-P.-É.*, 1226

Arsenault, Vaughn, *Longlac Chamber of Commerce*, 919

Arsenault, Marc, *Commission canadienne pour la théorie des machines et des mécanismes*, 593

Arsenault, Jean-Yves, *Société de protection des forêts contre les insectes et maladies*, 1317

Arsenault, Nathalie, *Société Saint-Thomas-d'Aquin*, 1325

Arsenault, Monique, *Société Saint-Thomas-d'Aquin*, 1325

Arsenault, Nick, *Société Saint-Thomas-d'Aquin*, 1325

Arsenault, Maurice, *Théâtre populaire d'Acadie*, 1375

Arsenault, Raymond, *Chambre de commerce acadienne et francophone de l'Ile-du-Prince-Édouard*, 539

Arsenault, Althea, *Triathlon New Brunswick*, 1398

Arsenault, Chris, *Northern Ontario Darts Association*, 1035

Arsenault, Kenneth, *PEI Shellfish Association*, 1149

Arsenault, Margot, *Boston Terrier Rescue Canada*, 218

Arseneau, Catherine, *Beaton Institute*, 203

Arseneau, Nicole, *Agricultural Alliance of New Brunswick*, 14

Arseneau, Marc, *Association des enseignantes et des enseignants francophones du Nouveau-Brunswick*, 112

Arseneau, Martin, *Société nationale de l'Acadie*, 1322

Arseneau, Martin, *Fondation franco-ontarienne*, 746

Arseneau, Jacynthe, *Association des personnes handicapées physiques et sensorielles du secteur Joliette*, 123

Arseneau, Bernard, *Alliance québécoise des techniciens de l'image et du son*, 58

Executive Name Index

Arseneault, Betty, Association of Applied Geochemists, 139
Arseneault, Marius, Chambre de commerce des Îles-de-la-Madeleine, 544
Arseneault, Daniel, Prince Edward Island Tennis Association, 1178
Arseneault, Guy, New Brunswick Teachers' Association, 1013
Arseneault, Harold, Conseil régional FTQ Estrie, 621
Arseneault, Isabelle, New Brunswick Senior Citizens Federation Inc., 1012
Arseneault, Yvan, New Brunswick Interscholastic Athletic Association, 1010
Arseniuk, Stephen, Canadian Heavy Oil Association, 404
Arsiradam, Prema, Learning Disabilities Association of Saskatchewan, 905
Artemakis, Andonis, Greek Community of Toronto, 787
Artemakis, Angelo, American Society of Neuroradiology, 1501
Arthur, Kevin, Roblin & District Chamber of Commerce, 1235
Arthur, Vaughn, Dangerous Goods Advisory Council, 1521
Artok, Nur, Ontario Council of University Libraries, 1075
Arturi, Paul, Grand Chapter, Royal Arch Masons of Québec, 779
Arzani, B. Maggie, Association of Hearing Instrument Practitioners of Ontario, 149
Asabea Blair, Ekua, Massey Centre for Women, 953
Asano, Craig, National Crowdfunding Association of Canada, 992
Asaph, Allan, Abbotsford Chamber of Commerce, 1
Asari, Mohammad, Iranian Community Association of Ontario, 863
Asaro, Pino, National Congress of Italian-Canadians, 991
Aschemeier, Barb, Okanagan Miniature Horse Club, 1056
Ascher, Nancy L., The Transplantation Society, 1395
Asfour, Amany, International Federation of Business & Professional Women, 1547
Asgarpour, Soheil, Petroleum Technology Alliance Canada, 1155
Asgill, Sandra, Barbados Ottawa Association, 196
Ash, Brian, Table Tennis Canada, 1366
Ash, Maria, Canadian National Institute for the Blind, 439
Ash, Don, Newfoundland & Labrador Teachers' Association, 1022
Ash, Stacey, Ontario Pork Producers' Marketing Board, 1097
Ash, Kathy, The Canadian Association of Fitness Professionals, 315
Ashby, Zoë, Ottawa Arts Council, 1129
Ashby, Jamie, Ontario Puppetry Association, 1100
Ashby, David, The Royal Commonwealth Society of Canada, 1242
Ashcroft, Bob, Community Living Elgin, 601
Ashcroft, Audrey, Sask Taekwondo, 1254
Ashdown, David, The Anglican Church of Canada, 69
Ashe, Linda, Special Olympics Ontario, 1340
Ashe, Dan, Association of Zoos & Aquariums, 1513
Ashekian, Ferida, Armenian Relief Society of Canada, Inc., 83
Ashfield, Kelly, New Brunswick Aerospace & Defence Association, 1004
Ashford, Malcolm, British Columbia Society of Laboratory Science, 254
Ashkenazi, Yaron, Canadian Society for Yad Vashem, 479
Ashley, Kevin, Canadian Electrical Contractors Association, 380
Ashmore, Debby, Alberta Rugby Football Union, 45

Ashton, Richard, MSA Society for Community Living, 978
Ashton, Rob, International Longshoremen's Association (AFL-CIO/CLC), 1553
Ashton, Brian, Canadian National Exhibition Association, 439
Ashton, Stacy, Volunteer BC, 1438
Ashworth, Kelly, Canadian Simmental Association, 470
Ashworth, Alexis, Habitat for Humanity Canada, 797
Ashworth, Hilary, Association of Registered Graphic Designers of Ontario, 161
Asif Khan, Sardar, Professional Engineers Ontario, 1185
Asikainen, Lauri, Canada-Finland Chamber of Commerce, 283
Askerow, Gasan, Chinese Medicine & Acupuncture Association of Canada, 565
Askew, Kim, Geotechnical Society of Edmonton, 771
Askin, Jessica, Canadian Association of School Social Workers & Attendance Counsellors, 332
Aslanowicz, Kelly, Chartered Professionals in Human Resources of British Columbia & Yukon, 554
Asp, P. Jerry, Yukon Mine Training Association, 1479
Asper, David, Asper Foundation, 87
Asper, Gail, Asper Foundation, 87
Aspiotis, Jim, Ontario Gang Investigators Association, 1081
Aspirot, Gilles, Association québécoise de l'épilepsie, 169
Assabgui, Rita, Canadian Association of Perinatal & Women's Health Nurses, 325
Assante, Fred, National Association for Surface Finishing, 1573
Asselin, Denise, Syndicat des professeurs et des professeures de l'Université du Québec à Trois-Rivières, 1364
Asselin, Susan, Association camadienne des interprètes de conférence, 90
Asselin, Michèle, Association québécoise des organismes de coopération internationale, 173
Asselin, Micheline, Fédération de l'industrie manufacturière (FIM-CSN), 709
Asselin, Marie-Andrée, Fédération des parents francophones de Colombie-Britannique, 717
Asselin, Marie-Claude, Sport Dispute Resolution Centre of Canada, 1344
Asselin, Mario, Club Lions de Chibougamau, 575
Assels, Jonathan, Association of Professional Engineers & Geoscientists of Alberta, 157
Astle, Josh, Special Olympics New Brunswick, 1340
Astle, Rick, Didsbury & District Historical Society, 656
Astle, Laura, New Brunswick Operating Room Nurses, 1011
Astleford, James, Adventist Development & Relief Agency Canada, 10
Astofooroff, Cathy, British Columbia Snowboard Association, 253
Aston, Tim, Canadian Foundation for Climate & Atmospheric Sciences, 393
Aston, Mark, Fred Victor Centre, 758
Astrene, Tom, Society of Tribologists & Lubrication Engineers, 1594
Atamanenko, Boris, Northwest Territories Arts Council, 1037
Atangana, Daniel, United Nations Association in Canada, 1411
Atchison, Chris, British Columbia Construction Association, 237
Atchison, Connor, Canadian College of Health Leaders, 359
Atebe, James, Lower Mainland Local Government Association, 920
Atehortua, Veronica, Society of Toxicology of Canada, 1331
Ater, Joshua, AFCOM, 1486

Aterno, Kathy, Clean Water Action, 1517
Athoe, Shirley, Ontario Brain Injury Association, 1068
Athwal, Ayden, Dress for Success, 663
Atkey, Jill, British Columbia Non-Profit Housing Association, 248
Atkinson, John, Swimming Canada, 1359
Atkinson, Blaine, Institute of Certified Management Consultants of Atlantic Canada, 845
Atkinson, Lauren, The Leukemia & Lymphoma Society of Canada, 909
Atkinson, Howard, Canadian ETF Association, 382
Atkinson, Roy, Federation of Canada-China Friendship Associations - Ottawa Chapter, 722
Atkinson, Daren, CFA Society Vancouver, 539
Atkinson, Rick, Central Beekeepers' Alliance, 524
Atlas, Adam, Canadian Acquirer's Association, 287
Attara, Gail, GI (Gastrointestinal) Society, 773
Attia, Audrey, Association des bibliothèques de la santé affiliées à l'Université de Montréal, 107
Attley, Mark, Receivables Insurance Association of Canada, 1206
Attwood, Randy, Royal Astronomical Society of Canada, 1238
Atwood, Chris, Yarmouth & Area Chamber of Commerce, 1470
Atwood, Corinne, British Columbia Bottle & Recycling Depot Association, 234
Atwood, Michelle, Canadian Senior Pro Rodeo Association, 470
Au, Patrick, Chinese Family Services of Ontario, 565
Au Bui, Hai, Canadian Association of Professional Image Creators, 329
Au Bui, Hai, Canadian Association of Professional Image Creators, 329
Au-Yeung, Stephen, Hope & District Chamber of Commerce, 821
Aubé, Cédric, Association/Troubles de l'Humeur et d'Anxiété au Québec, 179
Aubin, Gaétan, Club de Numismates du Bas St-Laurent, 575
Aubin, Michel, Réseau des SADC et CAE, 1219
Aubin, Lise, World Trade Centre Montréal, 1467
Aubin-Robert, Janik, Centre franco-ontarien de folklore, 534
Aubrey, Jacques, Navy League of Canada, 1002
Aubrey, Marie-Christine, Association des francophones de Fort Smith, 114
Aubrey, Marie-Christine, Fédération des aînées et aînés francophones du Canada, 711
Aubry, Dominic, Vintage Road Racing Association, 1435
Aubry, Pierre, Ligue des propriétaires de Montréal, 912
Aubry, Nadine, International Union of Theoretical & Applied Mechanics, 1565
Aubry-Abel, Caroline, Confédération des associations d'étudiants et étudiantes de l'Université Laval, 611
Aubut, Dorima, Syndicat interprovincial des ferblantiers et couvreurs, la section locale 2016 à la FTQ-Construction, 1364
Aubut, Alain, Chambre de commerce et d'industrie de Québec, 546
Aubut, Sandra, Chambre de commerce de Saint-Quentin Inc., 543
Aubut, Michel, La fédération des mouvements personne d'abord du Québec, 716
Auch, Susan, Speed Skating Canada, 1341
Auclair, Sylvano, Société québécoise d'espéranto, 1323
AuCoin, Nicole, Save Ontario Shipwrecks, 1281

Aucoin, Rene, Nova Scotia Salmon Association, 1048
Aucoin-Bourgeois, Lisette, Fédération acadienne de la Nouvelle-Écosse, 707
Aucoin-Bourgeois, Lisette, La Société Saint-Pierre, 1325
Audet, Karen, Greater Fort Erie Chamber of Commerce, 783
Audet, Louis, Société d'histoire et de généalogie de Matane, 1312
Audet, Mona, Centre de documentation sur l'éducation des adultes et la condition féminine, 529
Audouin, Anne-Raphaëlle, Canadian Hydropower Association, 410
Audy, Justine, Jeune chambre de commerce de Québec, 870
Auffrey-Arsenault, Lise, Skate Canada, 1301
Augaitis, Sylvia, Wine Country Ontario, 1458
Auger, Gerald, Impact Society, 831
Auger, Louise, Federation of Medical Regulatory Authorities of Canada, 724
August, Linda, Canadian College of Health Leaders, 359
Augusta-Scott, Tod, Bridges, 228
Augustin, John V., International Civil Aviation Organization: Legal Affairs & External Relations Bureau, 855
Augustin, Agnes, Shaw Rocket Fund, 1295
Augustine, Terresa, People's Law School, 1152
Augustyn, Nicole, American College of Chest Physicians, 1491
Aujala, Harvinder, Recycling Council of British Columbia, 1208
Auman, Charles, National Association of Watch & Clock Collectors, Inc., 1574
Aunger, Pauline, The Canadian Real Estate Association, 465
Auriat, Anne, Recycling Council of Alberta, 1208
Aurilio, Vince, Ontario Asphalt Pavement Council, 1061
Aurilio, Vince, Ontario Road Builders' Association, 1102
Aussant, Carole, Canadian Hardwood Plywood & Veneer Association, 401
Austen, Douglas J., American Fisheries Society, 1493
Austenfeld, Thomas, International Association of University Professors of English, 1540
Austin, Rick, Lethbridge Therapeutic Riding Association, 908
Austin, Elaine, The Literacy Council of Burlington, 913
Austin, Janet, YWCA Canada, 1482
Austin, Todd, Grain Farmers of Ontario, 779
Austin, Arthur, Cross Country New Brunswick, 643
Austin, Kris, People's Alliance of New Brunswick, 1151
Auston, Geraldine, British Columbia Hog Marketing Commission, 243
Auty, Stuart, Canadian Safe School Network, 468
Auyeung, Alan, Storytellers of Canada, 1350
Avaria, Carolina, Les Clefs d'Or Canada, 573
Avery, Ben, The Logistics Institute, 917
Avery, Julie, Nova Scotia Association of Medical Radiation Technologists, 1041
Avery, Granger, Canadian Medical Association, 433
Avery, Craig, Prince Edward Island Fishermen's Association Ltd., 1174
Avery, Randy, Newfoundland & Labrador Association of Public & Private Employees, 1016
Avery, Val, Health Sciences Association of British Columbia, 807
Avery, Sharon, UNICEF Canada, 1404
Avery, Elizabeth, Snack Food Association, 1589
Avery, Jeff, Nunavut Teachers' Association, 1051

Executive Name Index

Avila, Yvonne, *YWCA December 6 Fund of Toronto*, 1482
Awan, Mahmood, *British Columbia Muslim Association*, 247
Axford, Dan, *London Police Association*, 919
Ayad, Farid, *Canadian Arab Federation*, 294
Ayala, Mario, *Inland Refugee Society of BC*, 838
Ayer, George, *Professional Engineers Ontario*, 1184
Ayers, John, *Socialist Party of Canada*, 1307
Ayers, Jill, *Society for Environmental Graphic Design*, 1590
Aylott, Jenna, *Kitchener-Waterloo Parents of Multiple Births Association*, 891
Aylward, Chris, *Public Service Alliance of Canada*, 1193
Aylward, James, *Progressive Conservative Association of Prince Edward Island*, 1187
Aymeric, M. Michel, *Bonn Agreement*, 1514
Ayotte, Chantal, *Kirkland Lake District Chamber of Commerce*, 890
Ayoub, Jean, *International Social Service*, 1557
Ayranto, Mark, *Yukon Chamber of Mines*, 1477
Ayres, Marilyn, *Land Trust Alliance*, 1569
Aysola, Aruna, *Canadian Physicians for Aid & Relief*, 454
Ayyash, Matt, *Nova Scotia Deaf Sports Association*, 1043
Azevedo, Fabio, *International Volleyball Association*, 1566
Aziz, Jameel, *Canadian Association of Principals*, 328
Aziz, Andrew, *The Pembina Institute*, 1149
Aziz, Donna, *Ontario Katahdin Sheep Association Inc.*, 1088
Aziz Khalifa, Abdul, *Ahmadiyya Muslim Jama'at Canada*, 15
Azizi, Rosa, *Automotive Industries Association of Canada*, 190
Azrieli, Naomi, *Azrieli Foundation*, 192
Azzano, Becky, *Grey County Kiwanis Festival of Music*, 790
Azzopardi, Jonathon, *Canadian Association of Moldmakers*, 321

B

Baar, Michael, *Canadian Council on Animal Care*, 371
Baatz, Ernest, *Spectrum Society for Community Living*, 1340
Baba, Jim, *Baseball Canada*, 198
Baba-Khelil, Amina, *Fédération des producteurs d'agneaux et moutons du Québec*, 717
Babb, Marcia, *Lachine Black Community Association*, 895
Babb, Angela, *American Academy of Neurology*, 1488
Babbitt, Dave, *Wallaceburg Arts Council*, 1440
Babbitt, Adeena, *American Society for Aesthetic Plastic Surgery*, 1497
Babcock, Glenys, *Pragmora*, 1169
Babiak, Eric, *Resilient Flooring Contractors Association of Ontario*, 1226
Babiak, Barb, *Olds & District Chamber of Commerce*, 1057
Babiak, Todd, *Alliance Française d'Edmonton*, 57
Babich, Brenda, *Jane Austen Society of North America*, 868
Babin, Bernard, *Fédération québécoise des sociétés Alzheimer*, 730
Babineau, Mary Lou, *Faculty Association of University of Saint Thomas*, 701
Babineau, Rodney Lance, *Edmonton CFA Society*, 675
Babineau, Giselle, *Société Saint-Thomas-d'Aquin*, 1325
Babineau, Marcia, *Théâtre l'Escaouette*, 1374
Babu, Mohan, *Canadian Society of Microbiologists*, 485
Baby, Victoria, *Canadian Hearing Society*, 403

Baca, Fito Zamudio, *West Central Forage Association*, 1444
Bach, Michael, *Canadian Association for Community Living*, 298
Bach, Heather, *Medicine Hat Soccer Association*, 959
Bachand, Gilles, *Société d'histoire et de généalogie des Quatre Lieux*, 1313
Bacher, Chris, *Canadian Pony Society*, 458
Bachiu, Leonard, *Canadian Bible Society*, 343
Bachman, Brent, *Tennessee Walking Horse Association of Western Canada*, 1370
Bachmann, Karen, *Canadian Museums Association*, 437
Bachynsky, John, *Canadian Academy of the History of Pharmacy*, 287
Bacic, Jadranka, *Canadian Psychiatric Association*, 461
Back, Margaret, *Historical Society of Ottawa*, 816
Backer, Wayne, *DanceSport Alberta*, 650
Backman, Charles, *Grande Prairie Regional College Academic Staff Association*, 781
Backman, Clare, *Canadian Aquaculture Industry Alliance*, 294
Bacon, Corey, *Saskatchewan Beekeepers Association*, 1259
Bacon, Joy, *Canadian Association for Community Living*, 298
Bacon, Patricia, *Blood Ties Four Directions Centre*, 215
Bacon, Jean, *Ontario HIV Treatment Network*, 1084
Badali, Sal, *Association of Canadian Deans of Education*, 142
Badawi, Jamal, *Islamic Information Foundation*, 864
Badder, Joy, *Ontario Public Supervisory Officers' Association*, 1100
Badgley, Kerry, *Ontario Library Boards' Association*, 1089
Badiere, Cathia, *Alliance of Canadian Cinema, Television & Radio Artists*, 58
Badwi, Abby, *Canada - Albania Business Council*, 277
Baek, Eunyoung, *Korean Canadian Women's Association*, 893
Baenziger, John E., *Biophysical Society of Canada*, 211
Baer, Marvin, *Queen's University Faculty Association*, 1200
Baer, Doug, *University of Victoria Faculty Association*, 1421
Baer, Alejandro, *Center for Holocaust & Genocide Studies*, 1516
Baerg, Kim, *Canadian Donkey & Mule Association*, 378
Baëta, Amesika, *International Cheese Council of Canada*, 855
Baetz, Kristin, *Canadian Society for Molecular Biosciences*, 477
Baezner, Regina, *Ontario Percheron Horse Association Inc.*, 1095
Bagatto, Marlene, *Canadian Academy of Audiology*, 285
Baggs, Paula, *Association of Newfoundland Land Surveyors*, 154
Baghdadi, Azzeddine, *Association de soccer du Sud-Ouest de Montréal*, 104
Bagnall, Rhonda-Lynn, *Television Bureau of Canada, Inc.*, 1370
Bagnell, Jean, *Sydney & Louisburg Railway Historical Society*, 1360
Bagnell, Carolyn, *Mechanical Contractors Association of Saskatchewan Inc.*, 957
Bagnell, Alexa, *Canadian Academy of Child & Adolescent Psychiatry*, 285
Bagshaw, Ken, *Bladder Cancer Canada*, 214
Bagshaw, Elina, *Business Women's Networking Association*, 267
Baher Formuli, Mahmood, *Afghan Association of Ontario*, 12
Bahnfleth, William, *American Society of Heating, Refrigerating & Air Conditioning Engineers*, 1500

Bahr-Gedalia, Ulrike, *Digital Nova Scotia*, 656
Bahry, Evan, *Independent Power Producers Society of Alberta*, 833
Bahuaud, Lucienne, *Congress of Union Retirees Canada*, 613
Baig, Kathy, *Ordre des ingénieurs du Québec*, 1122
Baig, Iftikhar, *Islamic Association of Nova Scotia*, 864
Baig, Mirza, *Windsor Islamic Association*, 1456
Bailey, Gail, *Learning Assistance Teachers' Association*, 903
Bailey, Tracey, *Lakeshore Community Services*, 897
Bailey, Barry, *St. Albert & District Chamber of Commerce*, 1247
Bailey, Devin, *Yukon Liberal Party*, 1479
Bailey, Peter, *Canadian Federation of Library Associations*, 388
Bailey, Cathy, *Canadian College of Health Leaders*, 359
Bailey, Clayton, *Navy League of Canada*, 1002
Bailey, John, *YMCA Canada*, 1472
Bailey, Diane, *Ladies' Golf Union*, 1569
Bailey, Raymond, *Funeral & Cremation Services Council of Saskatchewan*, 764
Bailey, John, *Institute for Local Self-Reliance*, 1532
Bailey, Tina, *Community Foundation for Kingston & Area*, 597
Bailey, David, *Genome Canada*, 769
Baillargeon, Pierre, *Syndicat des professeurs et des professeures de l'Université du Québec à Trois-Rivières*, 1364
Baillargeon, Amélie, *Canadian Health Coalition*, 401
Baillargeon, Chantale, *Association des jeunes bègues du Québec*, 117
Baillie, Rossie, *Beaverton District Chamber of Commerce*, 203
Baillie, Andrea, *The Canadian Press*, 459
Baillie, Cory, *Canadian Rheumatology Association*, 467
Baillie, Jamie, *Nova Scotia Progressive Conservative Association*, 1047
Bain, Ron, *Ontario Association of Chiefs of Police*, 1062
Bain, Ken, *Canadian Association of School System Administrators*, 332
Bain, Allison, *Heritage Toronto*, 813
Bain, Martin, *Ontario Provincial Police Association*, 1098
Bainas, Zandra, *Ottawa Valley Rock Garden & Horticultural Society*, 1132
Bainbridge, Melissa, *Ontario Society for the Prevention of Cruelty to Animals*, 1105
Baines, Debbie, *Credit Institute of Canada*, 641
Baines, Robert, *Canada - Albania Business Council*, 277
Bains, Rav, *Children's Aid Society of the Region of Peel*, 561
Bains, Jatinder, *Canadian Association of Ambulatory Care*, 308
Baird, Kim, *Boys & Girls Clubs of Ontario*, 223
Baird, Vicki, *Northern Alberta Curling Association*, 1034
Baird, Don, *Canadian Aviation Historical Society*, 340
Baird, Sheila, *Exploits Valley Society for the Prevention of Cruelty to Animals*, 700
Baird, Mitch, *Niagara Regional Native Centre*, 1026
Baird, Alastair, *Ottawa Valley Tourist Association*, 1132
Baird, Bob, *ARMA International*, 1505
Baisi, Patricia, *British Columbia Teacher-Librarians' Association*, 255
Baissi, Lahcen, *Regroupement des Marocains au Canada*, 1215
Bajic Brkovic, Milica, *International Society of City & Regional Planners*, 1560
Bajwa, Jeginger Singh, *Maritime Sikh Society*, 951
Bajwa, Caite, *Semiahmoo Foundation*, 1289

Bakalovski, Mendo, *United Macedonians Organization of Canada*, 1411
Baker, Sara, *West Vancouver Community Arts Council*, 1447
Baker, William, *Gibsons & District Chamber of Commerce*, 773
Baker, Craig, *CurlManitoba Inc.*, 646
Baker, Charles H., *World Safety Organization*, 1607
Baker, Jeffrey, *Alberta Sprint Racing Canoe Association*, 48
Baker, Rick, *CARP*, 515
Baker, Len, *Canadian National Institute for the Blind*, 439
Baker, Brian, *Directors Guild of Canada*, 657
Baker, Cynthia, *Canadian Association of Schools of Nursing*, 332
Baker, Danalee, *Thompson, Nicola, Cariboo United Way*, 1376
Baker, Mike, *Canada - Newfoundland & Labrador Offshore Petroleum Board*, 277
Baker, Dave, *Niagara Peninsula Geological Society*, 1025
Baker, Franklyn, *Greenpeace USA*, 1529
Baker, Bob, *Nepisiguit Salmon Association*, 1003
Baker, James, *Fur Institute of Canada*, 765
Baker, Michael, *Institute for Clinical Evaluative Sciences*, 843
Baker, Scott, *WE Charity*, 1443
Baker, Jim, *Manitoba Hotel Association*, 938
Baker, Mike, *Calgary Police Association*, 274
Baker, Marcia, *Orphan Well Association*, 1127
Bakker, Sarah, *National Farmers Union*, 993
Bakker, Adrienne, *Heart & Stroke Foundation of British Columbia & Yukon*, 808
Bakker, Linda, *Wildlife Rescue Association of British Columbia*, 1455
Bakker, Annette, *Children's Tumor Foundation*, 1517
Bakker, Peter, *World Business Council for Sustainable Development*, 1603
Bala, Vandhana, *Mercy for Animals Canada*, 961
Balabanov, Tom, *British Columbia Philatelic Society*, 248
Balabanova, Katherine, *Canada Eurasia Russia Business Association*, 279
Balaburski, Oliver, *Huronia Symphony Orchestra*, 828
Balak, Darcy, *Ontario Rett Syndrome Association*, 1102
Balanóa, Joao, *Filarmónica Portuguesa de Montreal*, 735
Balay, Cheryl, *Cosmopolitan Music Society*, 631
Balberman, Penny, *The Gairdner Foundation*, 766
Balderston, Callie, *Beaverlodge Chamber of Commerce*, 203
Baldridge, William H., *Canadian Association for Anatomy, Neurobiology, & Cell Biology*, 297
Baldry, Marcy, *Seasons Centre for Grieving Children*, 1288
Baldwin, Christa, *Canadian Mental Health Association*, 435
Baldwin, Jeff, *Saskatchewan Archaeological Society*, 1256
Baldwin, Jeannie, *Public Service Alliance of Canada*, 1193
Baldwin, Neal, *Administrative & Professional Staff Association*, 8
Baldwin, Michelle, *Pillar Nonprofit Network*, 1160
Baldwin, Linda, *Treasury Management Association of Canada - Toronto*, 1396
Balestrero, Gregory, *Project Management Institute*, 1585
Balfour, Leanne, *Alberta Genealogical Society*, 37
Balicki, Kevin, *Architectural Woodwork Manufacturers Association of Canada - Northern Alberta*, 79
Balinov, Ivo, *Parliamentary Centre*, 1143

Executive Name Index

Baliozian, Kevin, *Medical Library Association*, 1570
Balisch, Karl, *Gymnastics Canada Gymnastique*, 795
Ball, Bruan, *Parksville Golden Oldies Sports Association*, 1142
Ball, Dale, *Canadian Manufactured Housing Institute*, 429
Ball, Christine A., *Ontario Municipal Human Resources Association*, 1092
Ball, Dwight, *Liberal Party of Newfoundland & Labrador*, 909
Ball, Mark, *Receivables Management Assocation of Canada Inc.*, 1206
Ball, Russell, *Courtenay Gem & Mineral Club*, 637
Ball, Mike, *School Sports Newfoundland & Labrador*, 1284
Ball, James, *Ontario Association of Physics Teachers*, 1065
Ballachey, Peter, *Financial Executives International Canada*, 736
Ballam, Debbie, *Sherwood Park District Soccer Association*, 1296
Ballance, Don, *Churchill Park Family Care Society*, 569
Ballantyne, Robert H., *Coalition of Rail Shippers*, 578
Ballantyne, Linda, *Association camadienne des interprètes de conférence*, 90
Ballantyne, Robert, *Freight Management Association of Canada*, 760
Ballantyne, Robert, *British Columbia Spaces for Nature*, 254
Ballard, Joe, *Colchester Historical Society*, 580
Ballard, Sean, *Alberta Chambers of Commerce*, 28
Balleine, Lorraine, *McGill University Health Centre Foundation*, 955
Ballermann, Elisabeth, *Health Sciences Association of Alberta*, 807
Ballew, Clark, *Brotherhood of Maintenance of Way Employes (AFL-CIO/CLC)*, 1514
Ballinger, Julie, *Ontario Association of Equine Practitioners*, 1063
Ballweg, Mary Lou, *Endometriosis Association, Inc.*, 1523
Bally-Brown, Jlonka, *Bowen Nature Club*, 219
Balme, Olivier, *Western Ayrshire Club*, 1447
Balmer, David, *Treasury Management Association of Canada - Toronto*, 1396
Balon-Smith, Linda, *Saskatchewan Council for Exceptional Children*, 1262
Baloo, Moe, *Canadian College of Health Leaders*, 359
Balsille, John, *Canadian Band Association*, 341
Balsillie, John, *Manitoba Band Association*, 932
Balsillie, Jim, *Sustainable Development Technology Canada*, 1357
Balsom, Elaine, *Single Parent Association of Newfoundland*, 1300
Balsom, Mishka, *Greater Niagara Chamber of Commerce*, 784
Balson, Iris, *Beiseker & District Chamber of Commerce*, 204
Baltaz, Carolyn, *Bereaved Families of Ontario*, 205
Baltgailis, Karen, *Yukon Conservation Society*, 1478
Baltz, Jay, *Canadian Fertility & Andrology Society*, 389
Bamberger, Kiki, *Education Assistants Association of the Waterloo Region District School Board*, 680
Bambrick, Rick, *Grande Cache Chamber of Commerce*, 781
Bambrick, Sean, *Kingston Police Association*, 889
Bamford De Gante, Lisa, *Multicultural Association of Fredericton*, 978
Banagan, Chris, *National Council of Philippine American Canadian Accountants*, 1575

Bancescu, Brenda, *Youth Ballet & Contemporary Dance of Saskatchewan Inc.*, 1475
Bancroft, Bob, *Nature Nova Scotia (Federation of Nova Scotia Naturalists)*, 1000
Bancroft, Juliet, *Eastern Ontario Beekeepers' Association*, 670
Bander, Elaine, *Jane Austen Society of North America*, 868
Bando, Christine, *Guelph Hiking Trail Club*, 793
Bandow, Carl, *Canadian Association for Humane Trapping*, 301
Bandow, Donna, *Canadian Association for Humane Trapping*, 301
Banfield, David, *Learning Disabilities Association of Newfoundland & Labrador Inc.*, 904
Bangar, Priya, *British Columbia Psychological Association*, 250
Banh, Duy Cuong, *Association of Dental Technologists of Ontario*, 146
Banham, Tyler, *Liberal Party of Canada (Ontario)*, 909
Banka, John, *Sustainable Urban Development Association*, 1358
Banks, Warren, *Community Legal Information Association of Prince Edward Island*, 600
Banks, Sandra G., *Royal Agricultural Winter Fair Association*, 1237
Banks, Todd, *Sherwood Park & District Chamber of Commerce*, 1296
Banks, Susannah, *New Brunswick Soil & Crop Improvement Association*, 1012
Banks, Kathy, *GATEWAY Centre For Learning*, 767
Banks, Melany, *Canadian Society for the Study of Practical Ethics*, 478
Banks, Phillip, *Peel HIV/AIDS Network*, 1148
Banman, Yvan, *Fenestration Canada*, 732
Banmen, Stephen, *Local Government Management Association of British Columbia*, 917
Banner, Holly, *Sexuality Education Resource Centre Manitoba*, 1293
Banner, Sandra, *Canadian Resident Matching Service*, 467
Bannister, Dirk, *Kiwanis International (Western Canada District)*, 892
Banting, Arnold, *Essa Historical Society*, 696
Bantle, Murray, *Canadian Crop Hail Association*, 373
Banville, Patrick, *Editors' Association of Canada*, 674
Banville, Rick, *Young People's Theatre*, 1475
Bapna, Manish, *World Resources Institute*, 1607
Baptiste, Susan, *World Federation of Occupational Therapists*, 1605
Baptiste, Eric, *Society of Composers, Authors & Music Publishers of Canada*, 1328
Bapty, Eric, *Ontario Association of Prosthetists & Orthotists*, 1065
Baqi, Anowara, *Sierra Club of Canada*, 1298
Baraban, Elena, *Canadian Association of Slavists*, 333
Baratta, Lisa, *Western Transportation Advisory Council*, 1450
Barbe, Nathalie, *Réseau du patrimoine de Gatineau et de l'Outaouais*, 1222
Barbeau, Louis, *Fédération québécoise des sports cyclistes*, 730
Barbeau, Denis, *Sign Association of Canada*, 1299
Barbeau, Shirley, *The Pas & District Chamber of Commerce*, 1144
Barbeau, Gilles, *Société d'histoire de Saint-Tite*, 1311
Barber, Ernie M., *Association of Professional Engineers & Geoscientists of Saskatchewan*, 159
Barber, Valerie, *Risk & Insurance Management Society Inc.*, 1234
Barber, Kyle, *YMCA Canada*, 1472

Barber, Alan, *Municipal Law Departments Association of Ontario*, 981
Barber, Barb, *Central Alberta Women's Outreach Society*, 524
Barber, David, *Ontario Agencies Supporting Individuals with Special Needs*, 1059
Barber, Scott, *Richmond Club of Toronto*, 1230
Barber, Kristy, *CADORA Ontario Association Inc.*, 269
Barberini, Ivano, *International Cooperative Alliance*, 1544
Barberstock, Susan, *Hamilton Regional Indian Centre*, 802
Barbosa, Sandro, *Polanie-Polish Song & Dance Association*, 1163
Barbour, Sharon, *Canada Employment & Immigration Union*, 279
Barclay, Monica, *Hong Kong-Canada Business Association*, 820
Barclay, Marion, *Parksville & District Rock & Gem Club*, 1142
Barclay, Robert, *Truck Training Schools Association of Ontario Inc.*, 1399
Barclay, Helen, *Saskatchewan Registered Music Teachers' Association*, 1273
Barclay, Barb, *Alberta Restorative Justice Association*, 44
Bard, Shalom, *Toronto Symphony Youth Orchestra*, 1387
Bardell, Lorenda, *Society of Kabalarians of Canada*, 1329
Barden, Nancy, *Canadian Institute of Plumbing & Heating*, 418
Bardes, Todd, *The Bruce Trail Conservancy*, 261
Barelli, Paolo, *International Amateur Swimming Federation*, 1535
Barfoot-O'Neill, Shelley, *Real Estate Institute of Canada*, 1205
Barg, Stephen, *Friends of the Earth Canada*, 762
Barham, Jeremy, *St. Stephen Area Chamber of Commerce*, 1251
Barham, Mark, *The Royal Canadian Legion*, 1240
Baril, Daniel, *Institut de coopération pour l'éducation des adultes*, 841
Baril, Louise-Andrée, *Société Pro Musica Inc.*, 1322
Baril, Daniel, *Centre de documentation sur l'éducation des adultes et la condition féminine*, 529
Baril, Marc, *American Concrete Institute*, 1492
Barker, Cassie, *Women's Healthy Environments Network*, 1462
Barker, Stella, *Norfolk Association for Community Living*, 1028
Barker, E.T., *Canadian Society for the Prevention of Cruelty to Children*, 477
Barker, Steve, *World Resources Institute*, 1607
Barker, Steve, *Georgian Bay Association*, 769
Barker, Nina, *CADORA Ontario Association Inc.*, 269
Barlee, Gwen, *Wilderness Committee*, 1454
Barley, Lara, *Family Services of Greater Vancouver*, 705
Barlinska, Izabela, *International Sociological Association*, 1561
Barlow, Melanie, *Ancaster Community Services*, 68
Barlow, Thomas A., *Canadian Federation of Independent Grocers*, 387
Barlow, Maude, *The Council of Canadians*, 633
Barlow, Reni, *Youth Science Canada*, 1476
Barlow, James, *Habitat for Humanity Canada*, 796
Barlow, Deanna, *Nurse Practitioners of Saskatchewan*, 1052
Barman, Dilip, *International Vegetarian Union*, 1566
Barnabé, Mairin, *University of Regina Faculty Association*, 1420
Barnable, Shirley, *Canadian 4-H Council*, 284
Barnard, Chris, *Lions Eye Bank of Manitoba & Northwest Ontario, Incorporated*, 913

Barnard, Kathy, *Save Your Skin Foundation*, 1282
Barndt, Joshua, *Parkdale Neighbourhood Land Trust*, 1141
Barnes, Shannon Howe, *Canadian Children's Book Centre*, 355
Barnes, Lorne, *Ingersoll Coin Club*, 838
Barnes, Robert, *Canadian Pediatric Endocrine Group*, 452
Barnes, Donald J., *Canadian Dressage Owners & Riders Association*, 379
Barnes, Don, *CADORA Ontario Association Inc.*, 269
Barnes, Amanda, *Manitoba Cheer Federation Inc.*, 933
Barnet, Barry, *All Terrain Vehicle Association of Nova Scotia*, 54
Barnet, Bill, *Cheticamp Association for Community Living*, 557
Barnett, Liz, *North Shore Disability Resource Centre Association*, 1032
Barnett, John, *Ontario Council of University Libraries*, 1075
Barnett-Cowan, Alyson, *The Canadian Council of Churches*, 368
Barnhill, Jo Anne, *British Columbia Miniature Horse Club*, 246
Barns, Lawrence, *Learning Disabilities Association of Ontario*, 905
Barnuevo Mackenzie, Alma, *Filipino Association of Nova Scotia*, 735
Baron, Cheryl, *Canadian Friends of the Hebrew University*, 395
Baron, Christian, *Canadian Society for Molecular Biosciences*, 477
Baron, Arlene, *Caregivers Alberta*, 512
Barr, Janice, *Richmond Society for Community Living*, 1231
Barr, Alanna J., *Community Living Fort Frances & District*, 602
Barr, Jack, *Powell River Chamber of Commerce*, 1169
Barr, Judy, *National Farmers Union*, 993
Barr, Cathy, *Imagine Canada*, 830
Barr, James, *Association of Professional Engineers & Geoscientists of British Columbia*, 158
Barr, Robert, *Okanagan Symphony Society*, 1056
Barr, Bill, *Manitoba Environment Officers Association Inc.*, 936
Barraball, Lesley, *Carizon Family & Community Services*, 513
Barrack, Andrea Cohen, *The Ontario Trillium Foundation*, 1111
Barraclough, Rhonda, *ALIGN Association of Community Services*, 54
Barraclough, Joe, *Environmental Services Association of Alberta*, 692
Barratt, Jane, *International Federation on Aging*, 857
Barre, Greg, *Architectural Woodwork Manufacturers Association of Canada - Manitoba*, 79
Barrett, Jeff, *West Hants Historical Society*, 1445
Barrett, Maureen, *Brandon University Faculty Association*, 226
Barrett, Scott, *Alpine Ontario Alpin*, 59
Barrett, Terry, *Uxbridge Chamber of Commerce*, 1423
Barrett, Margaret, *International Society for Music Education*, 1558
Barrett, Deborah, *Autism Society Alberta*, 188
Barrett, Debbie, *Canadian Celiac Association*, 352
Barrett, John, *Canadian Nuclear Association*, 442
Barrett, Brian, *Dental Association of Prince Edward Island*, 653
Barrett, Vern, *Huntington Society of Canada*, 827
Barrett, Nancy, *Institute of Chartered Secretaries & Administrators - Canadian Division*, 845

Executive Name Index

Barrett, Ryan, *Canadian Milking Shorthorn Society*, 436
Barrett, Nancy, *Canadian College of Physicists in Medicine*, 360
Barrett, Debra, *Navy League of Canada*, 1002
Barrett, Derrick, *Canadian Union of Public Employees*, 498
Barrett, John, *International Sanitary Supply Association, Inc.*, 1556
Barrett, Michael, *Ontario Public School Boards Association*, 1099
Barrett, Jeffrey, *Avon Chamber of Commerce*, 191
Barrett, Nancy, *Canadian Organization of Medical Physicists*, 447
Barrett, Melanie, *Association of Fundraising Professionals*, 1512
Barrette, Gilles, *Valoris for Children & Adults of Prescott-Russell*, 1424
Barrette, Chantal, *Directors Guild of Canada*, 657
Barrette, Denis, *Association des personnes handicapés visuels de l'Estrie, inc*, 123
Barrette, Nathalie, *Centre d'écoute Montérégie*, 528
Barriault, Crystal, *Société Saint-Thomas-d'Aquin*, 1325
Barrick, Cathy, *Alzheimer Society of Toronto*, 65
Barrie, Carol, *Canadian Frailty Network*, 394
Barrieau, Jolene, *The Canadian Federation of Business & Professional Women's Clubs*, 385
Barrière, Flore, *Fédération québécoise des sociétés Alzheimer*, 730
Barriffe, Nigel, *Urban Alliance on Race Relations*, 1422
Barrington, Hannah, *Junior League of Edmonton*, 878
Barron, John, *Canadian Image Processing & Pattern Recognition Society*, 410
Barron, Andrew, *Jews for Jesus*, 873
Barron, Carole, *Foundation for Prader-Willi Research in Canada*, 756
Barron, Dan, *Ontario Percheron Horse Association Inc.*, 1095
Barrow, Marsha, *The Garden Clubs of Ontario*, 767
Barrr, Susan, *International Arctic Science Committee*, 1535
Barrucco, Bernard, *Association des économistes québécois*, 111
Barry, Pat, *Alberta Genealogical Society*, 36
Barry, Christopher, *Restaurants Canada*, 1227
Barry, Mireille, *Canadian Amateur Musicians*, 292
Barry, Holly, *College of Hearing Aid Practitioners of Alberta*, 585
Barry, Chris, *The Greater Vancouver Board of Trade*, 786
Barry, Bob, *Canadian Association of Veterans in United Nations Peacekeeping*, 336
Barry, Robert, *Newfoundland Aquaculture Industry Association*, 1022
Barry-Keith, Tina, *Deer Lake Chamber of Commerce*, 652
Barsalou, Geneviève, *Canadian Literary & Artistic Association*, 427
Barsoum, Jad-Patrick, *Jeune Barreau de Québec*, 870
Barss, Bob, *Alberta Association of Municipal Districts & Counties*, 24
Bart, John, *ShareOwner Education Inc.*, 1294
Bartels, Kathleen, *Vancouver Art Gallery Association*, 1424
Barter, Sandra, *Ontario Municipal Management Institute*, 1092
Bartfai, Sarah, *Vancouver Island Construction Association*, 1426
Barth, Gillian, *CARE Canada*, 511
Barth, David, *World Accord*, 1465
Bartholomew, Jim, *Compassion Canada*, 608
Bartlett, James, *Alberta Powerlifting Union*, 42
Bartlett, Ed, *Corsa Ontario*, 631

Bartlett, Wanda, *Weyburn & District Labour Council*, 1451
Bartlett, Eric, *St. Martins & District Chamber of Commerce*, 1250
Bartlett, Jackie, *St. Martins & District Chamber of Commerce*, 1250
Bartlett-Bitar, Jennifer, *Prince Edward Island Speech & Hearing Association*, 1177
Bartlette, Deborah, *Yukon Arts Centre*, 1477
Bartley, Nikki, *Carman & Community Chamber of Commerce*, 514
Bartman, Monica, *Lacombe & District Chamber of Commerce*, 895
Bartoletti, JoAnn D., *National Association of Secondary School Principals*, 1574
Barton, Ted, *Skate Canada*, 1301
Barton, Helene T., *Home Inspectors Association BC*, 819
Barton, Jill, *Arabian Horse Association of Eastern Canada*, 76
Barton Dyke, Penny, *United Way for the City of Kawartha Lakes*, 1413
Bartosiewicz, László, *International Council for Archaeozoology*, 1544
Barua, Sumana, *TESL Canada Federation*, 1372
Baruth, Mary E., *Jack Miner Migratory Bird Foundation, Inc.*, 867
Barycki, Jerzy, *Canadian Polish Congress*, 457
Barzin, Mariam, *International Society for Magnetic Resonance in Medicine*, 1558
Bas, Mojca, *Association of Early Childhood Educators of Newfoundland & Labrador*, 147
Basch, Debbie, *Canadian Friends of Boys Town Jerusalem*, 395
Baschuk, Corey, *Manitoba Association of Medical Radiation Technologists*, 930
Bashir, Khalid, *British Columbia Muslim Association*, 247
Basil, Cory, *Canadian Wind Energy Association*, 504
Basile, Paola, *Canadian Society for Italian Studies*, 476
Basilio, Hubie, *Ontario Recreation Facilities Association*, 1100
Basiukiewicz, Slawomir, *Association of Polish Engineers in Canada*, 156
Baskin, Russel, *Family Enterprise Xchange*, 703
Baskind, Colin, *Southern African Jewish Association of Canada*, 1337
Basnayaka, Nimesha, *Association for Canadian Educational Resources*, 132
Basnett, Steve, *Canadian Security Association*, 469
Basov, Jenny, *Toronto Region Board of Trade*, 1387
Baspaly, Dave, *Burnaby Volunteer Centre Society*, 266
Basque, Christine, *Arthritis Society*, 84
Bass, Michele, *Maccabi Canada*, 923
Bass, Nicholas, *Alpine Canada Alpin*, 59
Bassarear, Elizabeth, *Madonna House Apostolate*, 925
Basser, Tuvia, *Kashruth Council of Canada*, 882
Bassett, Ken, *Seva Canada Society*, 1292
Bassett-Spiers, Kent, *Ontario Neurotrauma Foundation*, 1093
Bassett-Spiers, Kent, *Canadian Spinal Research Organization*, 489
Bassi, Amarjett, *Canadian Society for Chemical Engineering*, 473
Bassi, Bally, *Ending Violence Association of British Columbia*, 687
Bassingthwaighte, Tasha, *West Kootenay Women's Association*, 1445
Basskin, David A., *Canadian Musical Reproduction Rights Agency*, 438
Bastarache, William, *The John Howard Society of New Brunswick, Inc.*, 874
Bastedo, Marilyn, *Canadian Motorcycle Association*, 437
Bastidas, Carlos, *Hispanic Canadian Arts & Culture Association*, 815

Bastien, Lisa, *Canadian Labour Congress*, 425
Bastien, Lise, *First Nations Education Council*, 738
Bastien, Lise, *First Nations SchoolNet*, 739
Bastien, Deborah, *Golden Age Society*, 776
Bastille, Solange, *Association des services de réhabilitation sociale du Québec inc.*, 128
Batani, Philippe, *Association des brasseurs du Québec*, 108
Batcha, Laura, *Organic Trade Association*, 1581
Bateman, Lisa, *CIO Association of Canada*, 570
Bateman, Robert, *Harmony Foundation of Canada*, 803
Bateman, Bill, *Indian Agricultural Program of Ontario*, 834
Bateman, Jordan, *Canadian Taxpayers Federation*, 493
Bateman, Lisa, *Clean Energy British Columbia*, 573
Bates, Margo, *Canadian Authors Association*, 338
Bates, Barbara, *Magazines Canada*, 925
Bates, Judy, *Ontario Confederation of University Faculty Associations*, 1074
Bates, Hudson, *Nickel Institute*, 1026
Bates, Jack, *British Columbia Waterfowl Society*, 258
Bates, Janelle, *Ontario Waterpower Association*, 1113
Bates, Jack, *British Columbia Blueberry Council*, 234
Bates, Ken, *British Columbia Investment Agriculture Foundation*, 244
Bathurst, Barbara, *Bereaved Families of Ontario*, 205
Batstone, Kathleen, *Credit Counselling of Regional Niagara*, 639
Batstone, Tashia, *Chartered Professional Accountants Canada*, 552
Batt, Deborah, *PFLAG Canada Inc.*, 1155
Battagliotti, A., *Independent Lumber Dealers Co-operative*, 833
Battcock, Lois, *Canadian Association of Pharmacy Technicians*, 326
Batten, Justin Richard, *Prince Edward Island Canoe Kayak Association*, 1173
Battersby, Cali, *Yukon Soccer Association*, 1480
Battersby, Cali, *Whitehorse Minor Soccer Association*, 1453
Battershill, James, *Keystone Agricultural Producers*, 884
Battista, Anthony, *Children's Aid Society of Toronto*, 561
Battiston, Italica, *Rexdale Community Legal Services*, 1229
Battiston, Grace, *Architectural Institute of British Columbia*, 79
Battiston, Mariah, *Parent Cooperative Preschools International*, 1139
Battle, Patricia M., *Canadian Independent Adjusters' Association*, 410
Battle, Susan, *Alberta College of Combined Laboratory & X-Ray Technologists*, 29
Batty, Graham, *Canadian Aviation Historical Society*, 340
Batycki, Deborah, *British Columbia Registered Music Teachers' Association*, 251
Bauch, Sandahl, *Grahamdale Community Development Corporation*, 779
Baudais, Suedelle, *Edmonton's Food Bank*, 680
Baudemont, Frédérique, *Réseau Santé en français de la Saskatchewan*, 1225
Baudry, Lise Marie, *Centre francophone de Toronto*, 535
Bauer, Lorraine, *Family Enterprise Xchange*, 703
Bauer, Cindy, *Risk & Insurance Management Society Inc.*, 1234
Bauer, Michael, *World Wildlife Fund - USA*, 1608

Bauer, Nancy, *Urology Nurses of Canada*, 1423
Bauer, R.A., *Pax Natura Society for Rehabilitation of the Deaf*, 1146
Bauermann, Jenn, *CADORA Ontario Association Inc.*, 270
Baugh, Elisabeth, *Ovarian Cancer Canada*, 1133
Baum, Sherry, *Community Living Dryden-Sioux Lookout*, 601
Bauman, Vicki, *Chartered Professionals in Human Resources of British Columbia & Yukon*, 554
Baumann, Alain, *World Federation of Hemophilia*, 1466
Baumbusch, Jennifer, *British Columbia Centre for Ability Association*, 235
Bautista, Fulgencio (Sonny), *Couples For Christ*, 636
Bautista, Imelda, *Association of Filipino Canadian Accountants*, 148
Bautista, Imelda, *National Council of Philippine American Canadian Accountants*, 1575
Bawden, Geoff, *Radio Amateurs of Canada Inc.*, 1202
Bax, Janet, *Council of Canadian Academies*, 633
Baxendale, Dean, *Ontario Association of Quick Printers*, 1065
Baxter, Dan, *British Columbia Chamber of Commerce*, 235
Baxter, Bryonie, *Canadian Association of Elizabeth Fry Societies*, 313
Baxter, Bryonie, *Canadian Association of Elizabeth Fry Societies*, 312
Baxter, Rob, *Society Promoting Environmental Conservation*, 1331
Baxter, Sharon, *Canadian Hospice Palliative Care Association*, 409
Baxter, James, *National Press Club of Canada Foundation*, 995
Baxter, Gerry, *Calgary Residential Rental Association*, 274
Baxter, Jill, *Conway Workshop Association*, 627
Bay, Eli, *Eli Bay Relaxation Response Institute*, 685
Baydack, Lorraine, *Manitoba Down Syndrome Society*, 936
Bayens, E. Eddy, *Edmonton Musicians' Association*, 678
Bayer, Marc, *Association of College & Research Libraries*, 1511
Bayes, Heather, *British Columbia Federation of Foster Parent Associations*, 240
Bayes, Shawn, *Canadian Association of Elizabeth Fry Societies*, 313
Bayes, Heather, *British Columbia Federation of Foster Parent Associations*, 240
Bayko, John, *Canadian Association of Oilwell Drilling Contractors*, 324
Bayne, Clarence, *Québec Board of Black Educators*, 1196
Bayne, Clarence S., *Black Studies Centre*, 213
Baz, Migues, *Avocats sans frontières Canada*, 191
Bazdarick, Janet, *Ontario Genealogical Society*, 1082
Bazinet, Carmen, *Easter Seals Ontario*, 670
Bazinet, Bruno, *Association de la Construction Richelieu Yamaska*, 101
Bazylewski, Brenda, *Manitoba Egg Farmers*, 936
Beach, Charles, *Canadian Economics Association*, 379
Beach, Heather, *British Columbia Prader-Willi Syndrome Association*, 249
Beacham, Derek, *Shuswap Naturalists*, 1297
Beacon, Nancy, *Ontario Competitive Trail Riding Association Inc.*, 1074
Beal, Deryk, *Institute for Stuttering Treatment & Research & the Communication Improvement Program*, 844
Beal, Gord, *Chartered Professional Accountants Canada*, 552

Executive Name Index

Beal, J.C., *Institute for Folklore Studies in Britain & Canada*, 1532
Beal, Todd, *Halifax North West Trails Association*, 799
Beale, Elizabeth, *Atlantic Provinces Economic Council*, 185
Bealing, Rod, *Private Forest Landowners Association*, 1180
Beamish, Gary, *Bereaved Families of Ontario*, 205
Beamish, Peter, *Ceta-Research Inc.*, 538
Beamish, Edward, *Manitoba Square & Round Dance Federation*, 945
Beamish, Rosalie, *Manitoba Square & Round Dance Federation*, 945
Beamish, Anne, *Association of Teachers of English in Quebec*, 162
Bean, Garth, *Fraser Valley Egg Producers' Association*, 757
Bean, Tupper, *Centre for Effective Practice Inc.*, 532
Beanlands, Sara, *Nova Scotia Archaeology Society*, 1040
Bear, Tim, *St. Paul Abilities Network*, 1251
Bear, Jeff, *Registered Insurance Brokers of Ontario*, 1213
Bear, Gwen, *Aboriginal Friendship Centres of Saskatchewan*, 2
Bear, Austin, *National Native Addictions Partnership Foundation*, 995
Beard, Carol, *Ontario Society for the Prevention of Cruelty to Animals*, 1106
Beardsley, Gisele, *Potatoes New Brunswick*, 1168
Beardsworth, Adam, *Canadian Association for American Studies*, 297
Beardsworth, Derrick, *Boys & Girls Clubs of New Brunswick*, 222
Bearman, Barbara, *Thompson Rivers University Faculty Association*, 1376
Bears, David, *Building Industry & Land Development Calgary Region*, 262
Beasley, Bob, *Back to the Bible Canada*, 193
Beastall, Graham, *International Federation of Clinical Chemistry & Laboratory Medicine*, 1547
Beaton, Michael, *Ontario Ringette Association*, 1102
Beaton, Nancy, *Canadian Paraplegic Association (Nova Scotia)*, 450
Beaton, John, *Durham Youth Orchestra*, 665
Beatson, Joel, *Landscape Alberta Nursery Trades Association*, 898
Beattie, Liz, *South Simcoe Community Information Centre*, 1336
Beattie, Mike, *Municipal Equipment & Operations Association (Ontario) Inc.*, 981
Beattie, Joseph, *Hamilton-Brantford Building & Construction Trades Council*, 802
Beattie, Gillian, *The Royal Scottish Country Dance Society*, 1587
Beattie, Alan, *Sanctuary*, 1253
Beattie, Richard, *Foundation for International Training*, 755
Beatty, Perrin, *The Canadian Chamber of Commerce*, 355
Beatty, Brad, *Stratford & District Chamber of Commerce*, 1351
Beatty, Lisa, *Ontario Soccer Association*, 1105
Beatty, Lawrence, *Door & Hardware Institute in Canada*, 661
Beaubier, Karen, *Greater Westside Board of Trade*, 787
Beauchamp, Nicole, *Association des enseignantes et des enseignants franco-ontariens*, 112
Beauchamp, Denis, *Ordre des technologues professionnels du Québec*, 1124
Beauchamp, Luc, *Canadian Rock Mechanics Association*, 467
Beauchamp, Denis, *Association des technologues en agroalimentaire*, 129
Beauchamp, Audrey, *Association sportive des sourds du Québec inc.*, 178
Beauchamp, Jerome, *Swim BC*, 1358

Beauchemin, Mario, *Fédération des enseignants de cégeps*, 714
Beauchemin, Eric, *Association des camps du Québec inc.*, 108
Beauchemin, Patrick, *Association de Ringuette de Vallée-du-Richelieu*, 104
Beauchemin, Michel, *Association des professionnels des arts de la scène du Québec*, 125
Beauchemin, Esther, *Théâtre de la Vieille 17*, 1374
Beauchesne, Yves J., *Enfant-Retour Québec*, 688
Beauchesne, Lise, *Family Services of Greater Vancouver*, 705
Beaudet, Normand, *Centre des ressources sur la non-violence inc*, 531
Beaudette, Neil, *Fibrose kystique Québec*, 733
Beaudette, Paul, *Catholic Association of Religious & Family Life Educators of Ontario*, 517
Beaudin, René, *Société d'histoire de la Haute-Yamaska*, 1310
Beaudin, Joanne, *Réseau des SADC et CAE*, 1221
Beaudin, Yves E., *Alliance of Credential Evaluation Services of Canada*, 58
Beaudoin, Michel, *Canadian National Association of Real Estate Appraisers*, 438
Beaudoin, Manon, *Association québécoise des traumatisés crâniens*, 175
Beaudry, Lee, *Community Arts Council of Richmond*, 595
Beaudry, Maureen, *Canadian Hearing Society*, 403
Beaudry, Christall, *Canadian National Institute for the Blind*, 439
Beaudry, Myriam, *Canadian Pension & Benefits Institute*, 453
Beaudry, Diane, *Chambre de l'assurance de dommages*, 550
Beaudry, Sue, *Vernon Jubilee Hospital Foundation*, 1431
Beaudry, Rene, *Utility Contractors Association of Ontario, Inc.*, 1423
Beaukaboom, Mike, *Sundre Chamber of Commerce*, 1354
Beaulac, Michel, *L'Opéra de Montréal*, 1115
Beaulieu, Christian, *Institut Séculier Pie X*, 843
Beaulieu, Rico, *Ontario Shuffleboard Association*, 1104
Beaulieu, Jean-Pierre, *Fédération de golf du Québec*, 708
Beaulieu, Pail-Alain, *The Canadian Society for Mesopotamian Studies*, 476
Beaulieu, Dave G., *Nova Scotia Rifle Association*, 1048
Beaulieu, Manon, *Alliance des femmes de la francophonie canadienne*, 56
Beaulieu, Alain, *Institut d'histoire de l'Amérique française*, 841
Beaulieu, Omer, *Frères de Notre-Dame de la Miséricorde*, 760
Beaulieu, Isabelle, *Ordre professionnel des sexologues du Québec*, 1124
Beaulieu, Kathy, *Fédération de l'industrie manufacturière (FIM-CSN)*, 709
Beaulieu, Guy, *Réseau des SADC et CAE*, 1221
Beaulieu, Mario, *Bloc québécois*, 214
Beaulieu, Pierre, *Club de vol à voile de Québec*, 575
Beaulieu, Anne, *Mouvement national des québécoises et québécois*, 977
Beaulieu, Mario, *Mouvement national des québécoises et québécois*, 978
Beaulieu, Maryse, *Association des professionnels en gestion philanthropique*, 126
Beaulieu, Hélène L., *Law Society of New Brunswick*, 901
Beaulieu, Troy, *Planning & Land Administrators of Nunavut*, 1162

Beaulne, Trudy, *Social Planning Council of Kitchener-Waterloo*, 1306
Beaumier, Alain, *Club de curling Mont-Bruno*, 574
Beaumont, Martha, *Cystic Fibrosis Canada*, 647
Beaumont, Martin, *Canadian College of Health Leaders*, 359
Beaumont, André, *Association Hereford du Québec*, 136
Beaumont, Joanie, *Les AmiEs de la Terre de Québec*, 67
Beaumont, Bob, *Greater Vancouver Regional District Employees' Union*, 787
Beaupré, Patrick, *Association québécoise des utilisateurs de l'ordinateur au primaire-secondaire*, 175
Beaupré, Danielle, *Chambre de commerce de Port-Cartier*, 542
Beaupré-Lazure, Monique, *Ovarian Cancer Canada*, 1134
Beauregard, Lynn, *Governance Professionals of Canada*, 776
Beauregard, Ronald, *Fondation des aveugles du Québec*, 744
Beauregard, Roni, *Golden Women's Resource Centre Society*, 777
Beauvais, Nicole, *Randonnées plein air du Québec*, 1204
Beauvilliers, Johanne, *Fondation Dufresne et Gauthier*, 746
Beauvois, Christiane, *Secours aux lépreux (Canada) inc.*, 1288
Beaver, Chantal, *Boys & Girls Clubs of Alberta*, 221
Beaver, Tracy, *Atlantic Chamber of Commerce*, 183
Beazley, Amanda, *Boys & Girls Clubs of Prince Edward Island*, 224
Beazley, Christy, *Paramedic Association of Manitoba*, 1138
Beca, Kaitlin, *Canadian Investor Relations Institute*, 422
Béchard, Jacques, *Corporation des concessionnaires d'automobiles du Québec inc.*, 630
Beck, Kumari, *The Comparative & International Education Society of Canada*, 608
Beck, Thomas, *Canadian German Chamber of Industry & Commerce Inc.*, 397
Beck, Stewart, *Asia Pacific Foundation of Canada*, 87
Beck, Jaime, *Mahatma Gandhi Canadian Foundation for World Peace*, 926
Beck, Jason, *British Columbia Sports Hall of Fame & Museum*, 255
Beck, Phil, *Project Management Institute*, 1585
Beck, Terry, *Pork Nova Scotia*, 1165
Beck, Dale, *Saskatchewan Provincial Mediation Board*, 1272
Beck, Erica, *National Golf Course Owners Association Canada*, 993
Beck, Thomas, *European Union Chamber of Commerce in Toronto*, 698
Becker, Paul, *Architectural Institute of British Columbia*, 79
Becker, Lucy, *Investment Industry Regulatory Organization of Canada*, 863
Becker, Dana, *AIDS Vancouver Island*, 17
Becker, Jennifer G., *Association of Environmental Engineering & Science Professors*, 1511
Becker, Christina, *Ontario Society of Psychotherapists*, 1108
Becker, Chris, *American Academy of Neurology*, 1488
Beckett, John, *British Columbia Maritime Employers Association*, 246
Beckett, Chris, *Royal Astronomical Society of Canada*, 1238
Beckett, Greg, *Richmond Club of Toronto*, 1230
Beckett, Jean, *National Network for Mental Health*, 995

Beckmann, Toni, *Durham Region Beekeepers' Association*, 665
Beckwith, Gaye, *Kingston Field Naturalists*, 889
Bédard, Raymond, *Société des professeurs d'histoire du Québec inc.*, 1318
Bédard, Luc, *Association Béton Québec*, 90
Bédard, Stéphanie, *Chambre de commerce et d'industrie d'Abitibi-Ouest*, 545
Bédard, Sylvie, *Association paritaire pour la santé et la sécurité du travail - Administration provinciale*, 164
Bédard, Gaston, *Conseil québécois de la coopération et de la mutualité*, 620
Bedard, Linda, *Standardbred Canada*, 1348
Bédard, Gabriel, *Syndicat de la fonction publique du Québec inc. (ind.)*, 1361
Bédard, Sylvie, *Fédération québécoise des massothérapeutes*, 729
Bédard, Gilles, *Fédération québécoise de tir*, 728
Bedard, Laurette G., *Canadian Association of Veterans in United Nations Peacekeeping*, 335
Bédard, Annie, *Conseil communauté en santé du Manitoba*, 614
Bédard, Louise, *Louise Bédard Danse*, 920
Bédard, Christian, *Regroupement des artistes en arts visuels du Québec (ind.)*, 1214
Bédard, Éric, *American Concrete Institute*, 1492
Bédard, Greta, *Société des traversiers du Québec*, 1318
Bédard, Alex, *Association de la sécurité de l'information du Québec*, 169
Bédard, Claude, *Club de karaté Shotokan Chibougamau*, 574
Beddis, Eric, *TB Vets*, 1367
Beddis, Marg, *Health Sciences Association of British Columbia*, 807
Beddome, James R., *The Green Party of Manitoba*, 788
Beddows, Joël, *Théâtre français de Toronto*, 1374
Bedesky, Birgit, *Credit Counselling of Regional Niagara*, 639
Bedford, Jessica, *Speech-Language & Audiology Canada*, 1341
Bedford, Karen, *Appaloosa Horse Club of Canada*, 73
Bedford, Judy, *Peachland Food Bank*, 1147
Bedford-Clooney, Heather, *Edmonton Kiwanis Music Festival*, 678
Bednarz, Frédéric, *Académie de musique du Québec*, 3
Beed, Richard, *Central 1 Credit Union*, 523
Beekhuis, Hank, *Christian Labour Association of Canada*, 567
Beeler, Karin, *Canadian Comparative Literature Association*, 361
Beer, Martin, *Morgan Sports Car Club of Canada*, 974
Beerling, Russ, *United Way of Northern BC*, 1415
Beesley, Chris, *Community Living Ontario*, 604
Beganovic, Dino, *PFLAG Canada Inc.*, 1155, 1156
Begg, Sheila, *British Columbia College of Social Workers*, 236
Begin, Francois, *Junior Chamber International Canada*, 878
Bégin, Florent, *Société de communication Atikamekw-Montagnais*, 1314
Bégin, Richard M., *Fédération des sociétés d'histoire du Québec*, 719
Begley, Jeff, *Fédération de la santé et des services sociaux*, 710
Bègue, Sophie, *Association de la presse francophone*, 102
Behairy, Hossam, *Windsor Islamic Association*, 1456
Behan, Rita, *Alberta Dressage Association*, 33
Behardien, Tanya, *Penticton & District Community Resources Society*, 1150

Executive Name Index

Behman, Fadel, *International Institute of Integral Human Sciences*, 858
Behnam, Awni, *International Ocean Institute*, 1554
Behrns, Ray, *Rocanville & District Museum Society Inc.*, 1235
Beiser, Roberta, *Edith Lando Charitable Foundation*, 674
Belair, Danielle, *Community Care Peterborough*, 596
Belair, Kate, *Federated Women's Institutes of Canada*, 706
Belair, Dennis, *Boxing Alberta*, 220
Belangee, Susan, *North American Society of Adlerian Psychology*, 1579
Bélanger, Chantale, *Conseil québécois du commerce de détail*, 620
Bélanger, Anne, *Moisson Laurentides*, 971
Bélanger, Mario, *Association québécoise des joueurs de dames*, 173
Bélanger, Marie-France, *Fédération des cégeps*, 712
Bélanger, Nicole, *Association québécoise de l'épilepsie*, 169
Bélanger, Claude, *Association minière du Québec*, 137
Bélanger, Nicolas, *Orchestre symphonique de Sherbrooke*, 1118
Bélanger, Johanne R., *Tourism Toronto*, 1391
Bélanger, Diane, *Fédération des professionnelles et professionnels de l'éducation du Québec*, 718
Bélanger, Pierre, *Fédération des professionnelles et professionnels de l'éducation du Québec*, 718
Bélanger, Mireille, *Corporation des infirmières et infirmiers de salle d'opération du Québec*, 630
Bélanger, Louis, *Hautes études internationales*, 805
Bélanger, Dominique Caron, *Confédération des associations d'étudiants et étudiantes de l'Université Laval*, 611
Belanger, Neil, *British Columbia Aboriginal Network on Disability Society*, 229
Bélanger, Daniel, *Association des médecins hématologistes-oncologistes du Québec*, 119
Belanger, Alain, *American Concrete Institute*, 1492
Bélanger, Micheline, *Association des diffuseurs culturels de l'Ile de Montréal*, 110
Bélanger, Gervais, *Asthme et allergies Québec*, 179
Bélanger, Bev, *PFLAG Canada Inc.*, 1155
Bélanger, Luc, *Association provinciale des constructeurs d'habitations du Québec inc.*, 168
Bélanger, Diane, *Fondation communautaire du Grand-Québec*, 743
Bélanger, Joline, *Club de patinage artistique Les lames givrées inc.*, 575
Belbin, Victoria, *Canadian Home Builders' Association - Newfoundland Labrador*, 407
Belcastro, Angela, *Canadian Council of University Physical Education & Kinesiology Administrators*, 370
Belcher, Wendy, *Canadian Gelbvieh Association*, 396
Belcourt, Susan, *HIV North Society*, 817
Belcourt, Annie, *Réseau FADOQ*, 1224
Bélec, Éliane, *Association québécoise des interprètes du patrimoine*, 173
Belgrade, Pam, *Tourism Burlington*, 1389
Belhadjsalah, Abdel, *Jobs Unlimited*, 873
Belhocine, Noureddine, *Maison internationale de la Rive-Sud*, 927
Belhumeur, Diane, *Association des Poneys Welsh & Cob au Québec*, 124
Bélisle, France, *Tourisme Outaouais*, 1393
Belisle, Chloe, *Dystonia Medical Research Foundation Canada*, 666
Bélisle, Jean-Pascal, *Syndicat des agents de la paix en services correctionnels du Québec*, 1362

Bélisle, Johanne, *Women's Centre of Montréal*, 1462
Bélisle, André, *Association québécoise de lutte contre la pollution atmosphérique*, 170
Bélisle, Fernand, *Ombudsman for Banking Services & Investments*, 1057
Bélisle, Marie-Marthe, *Centre d'Histoire de Saint-Hyacinthe*, 528
Bélisle, François, *Centre for Canadian Language Benchmarks*, 531
Bélisle, Johanne, *Centre des femmes de Montréal*, 530
Béliveau, Gary, *Fondation Jules et Paul-Émile Léger*, 747
Belkie, Mark, *Canadian Institute for Theatre Technology*, 414
Bell, Michele, *Bruce Peninsula Association for Community Living*, 261
Bell, Shirley, *Deloraine & District Chamber of Commerce*, 653
Bell, Jeff, *Badminton Alberta*, 193
Bell, Mike, *Canadian Masters Cross-Country Ski Association*, 431
Bell, Jim, *Canadian Aviation Historical Society*, 340
Bell, James A., *Canadian Aviation Historical Society*, 340
Bell, Jeff, *Manitoba Water Well Association*, 947
Bell, Laurie, *Dystonia Medical Research Foundation Canada*, 666
Bell, Penny, *Centre franco-ontarien de ressources pédagogiques*, 534
Bell, Rosalind, *Canadian Amateur Musicians*, 292
Bell, Regina, *London-Middlesex Children's Aid Society*, 919
Bell, Adam, *Ontario Traffic Council*, 1111
Bell, Charlotte, *Tourism Industry Association of Canada*, 1389
Bell, Geoffrey G., *J. Douglas Ferguson Historical Research Foundation*, 867
Bell, Jillian, *Saskatchewan Publishers Group*, 1273
Bell, Margaret, *Elgin Baptist Association*, 684
Bell, Delaina, *West Vancouver Community Foundation*, 1447
Bell, Linda, *Carleton-Victoria Forest Products Marketing Board & Wood Producers Association*, 514
Bell, Pat, *Association of Unity Churches Canada*, 163
Bell, Shannon, *Melville Dance Association*, 960
Bell, Cindy, *Genome Canada*, 769
Bell, Mike, *National Golf Course Owners Association Canada*, 993
Bell, Patricia, *Community Energy Association*, 597
Bell, Hannah, *Prince Edward Island Business Women's Association*, 1173
Bell-Webster, Josh, *Ontario Colleges Athletic Association*, 1073
Bellaire, Allan, *Friends of the Haileybury Heritage Museum*, 763
Bellavance, Erin, *Canadian Association of Elizabeth Fry Societies*, 313
Bellavance, Pascale, *Chambre de commerce de Saint-Quentin Inc.*, 543
Belle-Isle, Lynne, *Canadian AIDS Society*, 290
Belleau, Francine, *Syndicat de professionnelles et professionnels du gouvernement du Québec*, 1362
Belleau, Fabien, *Patrouille de ski St-Jean*, 1146
Bellefeuille, Susan, *Canadian Office & Professional Employees Union*, 1073
Bellegarde, Perry, *Assembly of First Nations*, 88
Bellemare, Dominique, *World Animal Protection*, 1465
Bellini, Paul, *Rainbow Association of Canadian Artists (Spectra Talent Contest)*, 1203
Bellissimo, Lucy, *Ontario University Registrars' Association*, 1112

Belliveau, Juliette, *Association du personnel administratif et professionnel de l'Université de Moncton*, 131
Bellows, Theresa, *Alberta Hospice Palliative Care Association*, 38
Bellows, Reilly, *Alberta Hospice Palliative Care Association*, 38
Bellrose, Cecil, *Métis Nation of Alberta*, 963
Belluk, Brent, *Westgen*, 1451
Belof, Chris, *Athletics Manitoba*, 181
Belshaw, Juniper, *Head & Hands*, 805
Belsten, Norm, *Canadian Association of Wooden Money Collectors*, 337
Belter, Karen, *Alberta School Learning Commons Council*, 45
Belton, Mark, *Canadian Construction Association*, 363
Beltzner, Klaus, *Transport Action Canada*, 1395
Belzberg, Brent S., *Mount Sinai Hospital Foundation*, 976
Belzile, Charles, *Canadian Battlefields Foundation*, 342
Bembridge, Suzanne, *United Way of London & Middlesex*, 1415
Bemis, Brenda, *Whitby Chamber of Commerce*, 1452
Ben, Eden, *Couples For Christ Foundation for Family & Life*, 636
Ben, Vuoleen, *Couples For Christ Foundation for Family & Life*, 636
Ben-Natan, Daniel, *Israel Association for Canadian Studies*, 1568
Benabdelkader, Djamila, *Comité régional des associations pour la déficience intellectuelle*, 592
Benaissa, Becky, *Canadian Urban Transit Association*, 500
Bénard, Angèle, *Huntington Society of Canada*, 828
Bénard, Mireille, *Conseil central du Montréal métropolitain*, 614
Benarroch, Al, *Jewish Child & Family Services*, 871
BenAvram, Debra, *American Society for Parenteral & Enteral Nutrition*, 1498
Benbow, Ann, *Archaeological Institute of America*, 1505
Bence, Jim, *Saskatchewan Hotel & Hospitality Association*, 1268
Benchaouche, Dalila, *Social Justice Committee*, 1305
Benchley, Christie, *Ontario Society of Occupational Therapists*, 1107
Bencz, Marjorie, *Edmonton's Food Bank*, 680
Bendana, Lola, *Language Industry Association*, 899
Bender, Tim, *New Hamburg Board of Trade*, 1014
Bender, Dave, *Ontario Agri Business Association*, 1059
Benedetti, David, *American Society of Heating, Refrigerating & Air Conditioning Engineers*, 1500
Benegbi, Mercedes, *Thalidomide Victims Association of Canada*, 1373
Benes, David, *Canadian Federation of Apartment Associations*, 385
Benesa, Mina, *Filipino Canadian Association of Vaughan*, 735
Beneteau, Kim, *Kiwanis Music Festival of Windsor/Essex County*, 892
Benevides, Sylvia, *Concrete Ontario*, 610
Beney, William, *Charlotte Seafood Employees Association*, 552
Benhoff, Maryse M., *Association of Canadian Corporations in Translation & Interpretation*, 141
Benizri, Sidney, *Canadian Magen David Adom for Israel*, 429
Benjamin, Stacey, *Stettler Regional Board of Trade & Community Development*, 1350
Benjamin, Anjula, *Dawson Creek & District Chamber of Commerce*, 652

Benjamin, Chris, *Atlantic Publishers Marketing Association*, 186
Benlolo, Avi, *Friends of Simon Wiesenthal Centre for Holocaust Studies - Canada*, 762
Benn, Mary, *Christian Stewardship Services*, 568
Benn-Frenette, Rob, *BullyingCanada Inc.*, 264
Benn-John, Jacqueline, *Ontario Coalition of Rape Crisis Centres*, 1072
Benner, Judy, *Vancouver Island University Faculty Association*, 1427
Benner, Shannon, *Canadian 4-H Council*, 284
Bennett, Tim, *Big Brothers Big Sisters of British Columbia*, 209
Bennett, Robert F., *The Anglican Church of Canada*, 69
Bennett, Patricia, *Kensington & Area Chamber of Commerce*, 883
Bennett, Nancy, *Daily Bread Food Bank*, 648
Bennett, Carla, *Manitoba School Counsellors' Association*, 944
Bennett, Andrew, *Kitchener-Waterloo Symphony Orchestra Association Inc.*, 891
Bennett, John, *Sierra Club of Canada*, 1298
Bennett, Greg, *The Appraisal Institute of Canada - Newfoundland & Labrador*, 75
Bennett, Ben, *Municipal Waste Association*, 981
Bennett, Sherry, *Alberta Assessment Consortium*, 22
Bennett, Rob, *Vancouver Island Advanced Technology Centre*, 1426
Bennett, Julie, *Northwest Territories Tennis Association*, 1039
Bennett, Pat, *Seacoast Trail Arts Association*, 1287
Bennett, Bob, *DIRECTIONS Council for Vocational Services Society*, 657
Bennett, Bob, *Summer Street*, 1354
Bennett Olczak, Sally, *Alzheimer Society of Windsor/Essex County*, 65
Benning, Kirby, *Saskatchewan Professional Fire Fighters Burn Unit Fund*, 1272
Benoist, Gilles, *Canadian Institute for Theatre Technology*, 414
Benoit, Denis, *Fédération du personnel de l'enseignement privé*, 720
Benoit, Bill, *Vancouver Island Real Estate Board*, 1427
Benoit, Janine, *Canadian Society of Cytology*, 482
Benoit, Michel, *British Columbia Turkey Farms*, 257
Benoit, Gil, *Sudbury Rock & Lapidary Society*, 1353
Benoît, Liliane, *Canadian Toy Testing Council*, 496
Benoit, Aimee, *Alberta Historical Resources Foundation*, 37
Benoit, Mildred, *Québec Thistle Council Inc.*, 1199
Benoit, Trevor, *Cold Lake Regional Chamber of Commerce*, 581
Benoît, Éric, *Réseau du sport étudiant du Québec Saguenay-Lac St-Jean*, 1223
Benoît, Suzanne M., *Aéro Montréal*, 11
Benoit, Adele, *Black Theatre Workshop*, 214
Bensimon, Eric, *Canadian Society for Aesthetic Plastic Surgery*, 472
Bensimon, Simon, *Canadian Friends of the Hebrew University*, 395
Bensimon, Éric, *Association des spécialistes en chirurgie plastique et esthétique du Québec*, 128
Benson, Martin, *Council of Ontario Construction Associations*, 634
Benson, Allen, *Native Counselling Services of Alberta*, 997
Benson, Rick, *British Columbia Amateur Softball Association*, 230
Benson, Robyn, *Public Service Alliance of Canada*, 1193
Benson, Margaret, *Canadian Transplant Association*, 497

Executive Name Index

Benson, Dianne, *Society for Research on Nicotine & Tobacco*, 1591
Benson-Mandl, Claire, *Vocational Rehabilitation Association of Canada*, 1436
Bent, Kim, *New Brunswick Crafts Council*, 1007
Bentham, Rebecca, *Hamilton Law Association*, 801
Benthin, Janice, *Science Writers & Communicators of Canada*, 1285
Bentley, Sam, *Geological Association of Canada*, 770
Bentley, Bob, *Biathlon Prince Edward Island*, 208
Bentley, Monte, *Peace Region Internet Society*, 1147
Bentley, Bradford, *Canadian Deaf Curling Association*, 376
Bento Martins, Isabel Christina, *Federation of Portuguese Canadian Business & Professionals Inc.*, 726
Benton, Thomas J., *Data & Marketing Association*, 1521
Benton, Mark, *Legal Services Society*, 906
Benton, Al, *Ontario Home Respiratory Services Association*, 1086
Benty, Christina, *Association of Kootenay & Boundary Local Governments*, 150
Bentz, Lloyd, *Alberta Sport Connection*, 48
Benzaquen, Jack, *Association des directeurs généraux des municipalités du Québec*, 111
Beranek, Randy, *National Psoriasis Foundation - USA*, 1577
Bérard-Chagnon, Julien, *Association des démographes du Québec*, 110
Bercov, Arnold, *Pulp, Paper & Woodworkers of Canada*, 1194
Berdowski, Max, *Saskatchewan Motion Picture Industry Association*, 1270
Berekoff, Bev, *Canadian Society for Pharmaceutical Sciences*, 477
Berg, Frank, *Music for Young Children*, 984
Berg, Steven, *Canadian Association of Oilwell Drilling Contractors*, 324
Berg, Wayne, *Hong Kong-Canada Business Association*, 820
Berg, Joanne, *Saskatchewan Genealogical Society*, 1266
Berg, Angelique, *Hypertension Canada*, 829
Bergamini, Massimo, *Canada's Accredited Zoos & Aquariums*, 281
Bergdahl, Heather, *Moose Jaw & District Chamber of Commerce*, 973
Berge, Kathi, *American Association for Justice*, 1488
Bergen, Cameron, *Steinbach Chamber of Commerce*, 1349
Bergen, Jeremy, *Canadian Theological Society*, 494
Bergen, Reynold, *Beef Cattle Research Council*, 204
Bergen, Annamarie, *Calgary Law Library Group*, 273
Berger, Iris, *Canadian Association for Young Children*, 307
Berger, Howard, *Jewish Immigrant Aid Services of Canada*, 873
Berger, Monica E., *Jerusalem Foundation of Canada Inc*, 870
Bergerman, Roy, *Little League Canada*, 915
Bergeron, Lorraine, *Association des artistes en arts visuels de Saint-Jérôme*, 106
Bergeron, André, *Corporation des maîtres mécaniciens en tuyauterie du Québec*, 630
Bergeron, Sophie, *Association Provinciale des Professeurs d'Immersion et du Programme Francophone*, 168
Bergeron, Hélène, *Chambre de commerce et d'industrie de la Rive-Sud*, 545
Bergeron, Pascal, *Chambre de commerce St-Martin de Beauce*, 549
Bergeron, Francine, *Société de développement des périodiques culturels québécois*, 1315

Bergeron, Diane, *Canadian National Institute for the Blind*, 439
Bergeron, Joël, *Ordre des médecins vétérinaires du Québec*, 1123
Bergeron, Sylvie, *Association des gastro-entérologues du Québec*, 115
Bergeron, Karoline, *St. John Ambulance*, 1249
Bergeron, François, *CDC Centre-Sud*, 521
Bergeron, Gabrielle, *Bureau local d'intervention traitant du SIDA*, 264
Bergeron, Paul, *Fondation de l'Hôpital du Sacré-Coeur de Montréal*, 744
Bergeron, Mélissa, *Réseau des SADC et CAE*, 1220
Bergeron, Brigitte, *Regroupement des éditeurs canadiens-français*, 1215
Bergeron, Lison, *Syndicat des professeures et professeurs de l'Université du Québec à Chicoutimi*, 1363
Bergeron, Lynda, *Chartered Professionals in Human Resources of Alberta*, 554
Bergeron, Colombe, *Cercle des Fermières - Chibougamau*, 537
Bergeson, Cara, *Resource Recycling Inc.*, 1586
Bergevin, Alexandre, *Association des avocats de la défense de Montréal*, 106
Bergin, Michelle, *Catholic Family Services of Simcoe County*, 519
Bergin, Patrick J., *African Wildlife Foundation*, 1486
Bergkamp, Ger, *International Water Association*, 1566
Berglund, Chris, *Volleyball BC*, 1437
Bergman, Charmaine, *Canadian Warmblood Horse Breeders Association*, 502
Bergman, Joakim, *International Federation of Medical Students' Associations*, 1548
Berhane, Saba, *U.S. Committee for Refugees & Immigrants*, 1601
Beriau, Tania, *Sierra Club of Canada*, 1298
Beriault, Susanne, *Canadian Deaf Curling Association*, 376
Berk, Len, *Sar-El Canada*, 1253
Berk, Maureen, *Salmo Community Resource Society*, 1252
Berkeley, Vivian, *Blind Bowls Association of Canada*, 214
Berkin, Deniz, *Independent Filmmakers' Co-operative of Ottawa*, 832
Berlin-Romalis, Deborah, *Sheena's Place*, 1295
Berman, Elaine, *Queen's University Faculty Association*, 1200
Berman, Deanne, *Seva Canada Society*, 1292
Bermudez, Rebecca, *British Columbia Miniature Horse Club*, 246
Bermundo, Gerald, *Filipino Association of Nova Scotia*, 735
Bernard, Gary, *Professional Golfers' Association of Canada*, 1185
Bernard, Serge, *Association of Prince Edward Island Land Surveyors*, 156
Bernard, Charles, *Collège des médecins du Québec*, 582
Bernard, Joanne, *Parkinson Society Southwestern Ontario*, 1142
Bernard, Louise, *Société historique de Rivière-des-Prairies*, 1320
Bernard, Shirley, *Portage Friendship Centre Inc.*, 1166
Bernard, Jeannita, *Société Saint-Thomas-d'Aquin*, 1325
Bernard, Randy, *Professional Bull Riders Inc*, 1585
Bernard, Claude, *Apprenp'tits Numismates*, 75
Bernard, Terry, *KidSport PEI*, 887
Bernardin, Louis, *Fédération des aînées et aînés francophones du Canada*, 711
Bernardini, Sergio, *International Federation of Clinical Chemistry & Laboratory Medicine*, 1547
Bernat, Christopher, *Specialty Graphic Imaging Association*, 1596

Berndt, Lindsay, *Canadian Business Aviation Association*, 347
Berner, David, *Drug Prevention Network of Canada*, 663
Bernet, Victor J., *American Thyroid Association*, 1504
Berney, Mary, *Birthright International*, 212
Bernhard, Jorge, *Equestrian Canada*, 694
Bernhardt, Kevin, *St Paul & District Chamber of Commerce*, 1250
Bernhardt, Heidi, *Centre for ADHD Awareness, Canada*, 531
Bernier, Guy, *Société de généalogie et d'archives de Rimouski*, 1316
Bernier, Alain, *Association des technologues en agroalimentaire*, 129
Bernier, Tanya, *Brewers Association of Canada*, 228
Bernier, Michèle, *Canadian Pension & Benefits Institute*, 453
Bernier, Monique, *Association of Canadian Universities for Northern Studies*, 144
Bernier, Ginette, *Ordre des infirmières et infirmiers du Québec*, 1122
Bernier, Monique, *Canadian Remote Sensing Society*, 466
Bernier, Denis, *Destination Sherbrooke*, 654
Bernier, Alain, *Association provinciale des constructeurs d'habitations du Québec inc.*, 168
Bernstein, Dale, *Parents, Families & Friends of Lesbians & Gays*, 1582
Bernstein, Alan, *Canadian Institute for Advanced Research*, 412
Berrette, Wanda, *International Catholic Deaf Association*, 854
Berridge, Alma, *Alberta Genealogical Society*, 36
Berrigan, Douglas, *LaHave Islands Marine Museum Society*, 895
Berrill, Donald A., *Air Cadet League of Canada*, 19
Berringer, Gladys, *Big Brothers Big Sisters of Ontario*, 210
Berry, Tim, *Crohn's & Colitis Canada*, 642
Berry, Jennifer, *Carizon Family & Community Services*, 513
Berry, Pauline, *Barrie Post Polio Association*, 197
Berry, Brian, *Québec Association of Baptist Churches*, 1196
Berry, Robert, *Manitoba Percheron & Belgian Club*, 942
Berry, Scott, *SPEC Association for Children & Families*, 1339
Berry Merriam, Dawn, *Peterborough Social Planning Council*, 1154
Berryman, Martin, *Architectural Woodwork Manufacturers Association of British Columbia*, 79
Bertamini, Karen, *Realtors Association of South Central Alberta*, 1206
Bertelli, Steve, *Bakery, Confectionery, Tobacco Workers & Grain Millers International Union (AFL-CIO/CLC)*, 1514
Berthelot, Marco, *Curling Québec*, 646
Berthiaume, Pierre-Luc, *Children's Wish Foundation of Canada*, 563
Berthiaume, Sandra, *Jersey Canada*, 869
Berthiaume, Bob, *Project Management Institute*, 1585
Berthiaume, Yves, *Institut de recherches cliniques de Montréal*, 842
Berthoff, Andrew, *Society of Composers, Authors & Music Publishers of Canada*, 1328
Bertholet-Schweizer, Catherine, *Association of Translators & Interpreters of Ontario*, 163
Berting, Terry, *British Columbia Confederation of Parent Advisory Councils*, 237
Bertoia, Rose, *Ontario East Tourism Association*, 1077
Bertrand, Michèle, *United Nations Association in Canada*, 1411
Bertrand, Jacques, *HelpAge Canada*, 812

Bertrand, Jennifer, *Association of Science & Engineering Technology Professionals of Alberta*, 162
Bertrand, Robert, *Alliance autochtone du Québec*, 54
Bertrand, Francois, *Canadian Society for Chemical Engineering*, 473
Bertrand, Lisa, *Société généalogique canadienne-française*, 1319
Bertrand, Lilianne, *Association pour la santé publique du Québec*, 167
Bertrand, Joanne, *Canadian Society of Gastroenterology Nurses & Associates*, 483
Bertrand, Anthony, *Alliance Française d'Edmonton*, 57
Bertrand, Diane, *Foundation of Greater Montreal*, 756
Bertschi, Victor, *International Society of Surgery*, 1561
Bertucci, Vince, *Canadian Dermatology Association*, 377
Bérubé, Jonatan, *Fédération des comités de parents du Québec inc.*, 713
Berube, Evangeline, *Alberta & Northwest Territories Lung Association*, 21
Bérubé, Richard, *Fédération québécoise des échecs*, 728
Bérubé, Louiselle, *Fondation des maladies du coeur du Québec*, 745
Bérubé, Bernard, *Fédération du personnel professionnel des collèges*, 720
Besenski, Maria, *Canadian Employee Assistance Program Association*, 380
Besner, JC, *Water Polo New Brunswick*, 1441
Besner, Diane, *Fédération acadienne de la Nouvelle-Écosse*, 707
Besner, Jacques, *Associated Research Centres for the Urban Underground Space*, 89
Bespalko, Jenny, *Ashmont & District Agricultural Society*, 86
Besse, Randy, *Risk & Insurance Management Society Inc.*, 1234
Bessell, Jennifer, *Boys & Girls Clubs of Canada*, 222
Bessette, Suzie, *Association de la construction du Québec*, 101
Best, Doug, *Canadian Air Traffic Control Association*, 291
Best, Dave, *Ottawa Sports Hall of Fame Inc.*, 1132
Best, Jennifer, *Ontario Association of Sign Language Interpreters*, 1066
Best, Stephen, *Animal Protection Party of Canada*, 71
Best, Dwight, *African & Caribbean Students' Network of Montréal*, 12
Best, Dorothy, *Miniature Horse Association of Nova Scotia*, 966
Beswick, Jodi, *Association of Electromyography Technologists of Canada*, 147
Betcher, Peter, *Navy League of Canada*, 1002
Bethany, McLeod, *Prince Edward Island Teachers' Federation*, 1178
Bethlenfalvy, Peter, *Canadian Scholarship Trust Foundation*, 468
Bethune, Craig, *Nova Scotia Tennis Association*, 1049
Bethune, Drew, *Canadian Association of Thoracic Surgeons*, 334
Betito, Laurie, *Sexual Health Network of Québec Inc.*, 1293
Bettauer, Robert, *Pacific Institute for Sport Excellence*, 1135
Betteridge, Lisa, *Ontario College of Social Workers & Social Service Workers*, 1072
Betti, Mirko, *Canadian Institute of Food Science & Technology*, 415
Betts, John, *Western Silvicultural Contractors' Association*, 1450
Betts, John, *Western Forestry Contractors Association*, 1449
Betts, Ted, *Family Service Toronto*, 704

Executive Name Index

Betts, Adrian, *AIDS Committee of Durham Region*, 16
Betz, Sonya, *Alberta Association of Academic Libraries*, 23
Beunder, Kristi, *Jump Alberta*, 877
Beusekom, Andrew, *Fort Macleod & District Chamber of Commerce*, 752
Beutler, Joseph, *NACE International*, 1572
Bevan, Sian, *Canadian Cancer Society Research Institute*, 349
Bevan-Baker, Peter, *Green Party of Prince Edward Island*, 789
Bevand, Larry, *Chess'n Math Association*, 556
Bevelander, Kirsten, *British Columbia Aboriginal Child Care Society*, 229
Beveridge, Navarana, *Qikiqtani Inuit Association*, 1194
Bevilacqua, Frank, *Ontario Dental Association*, 1077
Bevilacqua, Dan, *Top of Lake Superior Chamber of Commerce*, 1381
Bew, Mairi, *Victoria County Historical Society*, 1432
Bewick, Dave, *North American Wild Fur Shippers Council*, 1030
Bews, Kerry, *Canadian Federation of Aircraft Maintenance Engineers Associations*, 385
Bewzak, Dianne, *Community Living Welland Pelham*, 606
Bezanson, Gerry, *Bridgetown & Area Chamber of Commerce*, 229
Bezanson, Lynne, *Canadian Career Development Foundation*, 350
Bezanson, Jessica, *Maritime Association of Professional Sign Language Interpreters*, 950
Bezeau, Brian, *Association coopérative des pêcheurs de l'Île Itée*, 98
Bezzubetz, Joanne, *Canadian College of Health Leaders*, 359
Bhagnari, Ria, *Association of Professional Engineers & Geoscientists of British Columbia*, 158
Bhandal, Gogi, *Canadian Labour Congress*, 425
Bhandari, Renu, *Focus for Ethnic Women*, 741
Bhardwaj, Ajay, *Canadian College of Health Leaders*, 359
Bhardwaj, Jyoti, *Canadian Association of Nurses in Oncology*, 323
Bharmal, Aleem, *Community Legal Assistance Society*, 599
Bhat, Rama B., *Canadian Society for Mechanical Engineering*, 476
Bhatt, Jay, *Heart & Stroke Foundation of Ontario*, 809
Bhattacharya, Eugene, *Peel Law Association*, 1148
Bhavishi, Devansh, *Cricket New Brunswick*, 642
Bhayat, Nafis, *Islamic Propagation Centre of Ontario*, 865
Bhimji, Omar, *Hub for Active School Travel*, 824
Bhullar, Kirandeep, *Regina Immigrant Women Centre*, 1212
Bhutta, Zulfiqar, *International Pediatric Association*, 1555
Bialek, Murray, *Naval Museum of Alberta Society*, 1001
Bianchi, Ed, *KAIROS: Canadian Ecumenical Justice Initiatives*, 880
Bianchi, Douglas, *International Symphony Orchestra of Sarnia, Ontario & Port Huron, Michigan*, 861
Bibaud, Lise, *Association québécoise des troubles d'apprentissage*, 175
Bibby, David, *The Chartered Institute of Logistics & Transport in North America*, 552
Bibeau, Alain, *Ordre des ergothérapeutes du Québec*, 1121
Bibeau, François, *Centre de formation et de consultation en métiers d'art*, 529
Bibeault, Michel, *Canadian Union of Public Employees*, 499

Bick, Myer, *Jewish General Hospital Foundation*, 872
Bickerton, Sean, *Canadian Music Centre*, 438
Bickerton, Bob, *Wasagaming Chamber of Commerce*, 1440
Bickerton, Jaime, *Bereaved Families of Ontario*, 205
Bickford, Deanna, *Inside Out Toronto LGBT Film & Video Festival*, 840
Biddell, Dale, *United Way of Greater Simcoe County*, 1414
Biddle, Peter, *Scouts Canada*, 1287
Biderman, David, *Solid Waste Association of North America*, 1595
Bidzinski, Heather, *Association for Manitoba Archives*, 133
Biel, Krystyna, *Immigrant Services Calgary*, 830
Bienvenu, Alain, *Chambre de commerce de la MRC de L'Assomption*, 541
Bienvenu, Claudyne, *Investment Industry Regulatory Organization of Canada*, 863
Bier, Charlene, *Western Canadian Miniature Horse Club*, 1448
Bierdimpel, Eckhart, *World Association of Industrial & Technological Research Organizations*, 1603
Bierlmeier, Richelle, *Whitehorse Minor Hockey Association*, 1453
Bierman, Barbara, *Ontario Federation of Independent Schools*, 1079
Biese, Alison, *International Personnel Management Association - Canada*, 859
Bieser, Jillian, *Ontario Association for Impact Assessment*, 1061
Bigalky, Gloria, *Canadian South Devon Association*, 489
Bigeau, Kurt, *Timmins Chamber of Commerce*, 1380
Bigelow, Barb, *Child Care Connection Nova Scotia*, 558
Biggar, Anthony, *Athletics Ontario*, 181
Biggers, Bret, *National Waste & Recycling Association*, 1577
Biggin, Philip, *Union of Injured Workers of Ontario*, 1407
Biggs, Sylvia, *Canadian Association of Management Consultants*, 320
Biggs Brock, Heidi, *The Aluminum Association*, 1487
Bignell, Bob, *Canadian Fence Industry Association*, 389
Bignell, Robert, *Ontario Tire Dealers Association*, 1110
Bignell, Michelle, *Ontario Competitive Trail Riding Association Inc.*, 1074
Bigras, Suzanne, *Société de généalogie de l'Outaouais*, 1315
Bigwin, Elizabeth, *Ogemawahj Tribal Council*, 1055
Bijl, Janetta, *Stem Cell Network*, 1349
Bilawchuk, Erin, *KidSport Alberta*, 886
Biletski, Burgundy, *Field Hockey Alberta*, 734
Bilinski, Lech, *Association of Polish Engineers in Canada*, 156
Bilinski, Lech, *Association of Polish Engineers in Canada*, 156
Billesberger, Denece, *Sisters of the Child Jesus*, 1301
Billett, Amy, *American Society of Pediatric Hematology / Oncology*, 1502
Billi, John R., *Laborers' International Union of North America (AFL-CIO/CLC)*, 1568
Billingham, Jackie, *Québec Family History Society*, 1197
Billings, Laurie, *Alberta Safety Council*, 45
Billings, Daryl, *Grimshaw & District Chamber of Commerce*, 790
Billings, Joan, *Grimshaw & District Chamber of Commerce*, 790
Billingsley, Ron, *Yukon Schools' Athletic Association*, 1480
Biln, Norma K., *BioTalent Canada*, 212
Bilodeau, Nicole, *Chambre de commerce et d'industrie du secteur Normandin*, 547

Bilodeau, Ghislain, *Réseau FADOQ*, 1224
Bilodeau, Denis, *Canadian Agricultural Safety Association*, 290
Bilodeau, Marc, *Canadian Association for the Study of the Liver*, 306
Bilodeau, Marc, *Association de vitrerie et fenestrations du Québec*, 104
Bilodeau, Valérie, *Technoscience Estrie*, 1369
Bilodeau, Rémi, *A Coeur d'Homme*, 580
Bilowus, Mary Katherine, *Special Libraries Association*, 1596
Bilsky, Tracey, *Sport Yukon*, 1345
Bilton, Corey, *Arthur & District Chamber of Commerce*, 85
Binbrek, Salim, *Pragmora*, 1169
Bindraban, Ir P.S., *International Soil Reference & Information Centre*, 1561
Binet, Pascal, *Société de généalogie et d'histoire de la région de Thetford-Mines*, 1316
Binette, Marie, *Canadian Association of Recycling Industries*, 330
Bing, Peter, *Canadian Business Aviation Association*, 348
Bing, Richard, *BC Association for Individualized Technology and Supports*, 201
Bingeman, Shannon, *Alberta Society of Artists*, 47
Bingham, Peter, *EDAM Performing Arts Society*, 674
Bingham, Quinn, *Pathways to Education Canada*, 1145
Bingham, Andrea, *CADORA Ontario Association Inc.*, 270
Bink, Marc, *Edmonton Numismatic Society*, 678
Binkley, Adam, *Boys & Girls Clubs of Prince Edward Island*, 224
Binning, Lou Ann, *Niagara Regional Labour Council*, 1026
Binns, Curt, *ATM Industry Association Canada Region*, 187
Binns, Tony, *Commonwealth Geographical Bureau*, 1518
Binns, Sandra, *Ontario Federation of Home & School Associations Inc.*, 1079
Binns, Lisa, *Kerry's Place Autism Services*, 884
Binsfeld, Gwen, *Canadian Association for Disabled Skiing - Ontario*, 300
Birch, Gary, *The Neil Squire Foundation*, 1002
Bird, Michael A., *The Anglican Church of Canada*, 70
Bird, Ian, *Community Foundations of Canada*, 598
Birjandian, Fariborz, *Calgary Catholic Immigration Society*, 271
Birley, Dale, *Saskatchewan Deaf & Hard of Hearing Services Inc.*, 1263
Birnie, Brad, *Saskatchewan Squash*, 1276
Birnie, Lyle, *Alberta Snowmobile Association*, 47
Birns, Larry, *Council on Hemispheric Affairs*, 1520
Biro, Dave, *Calgary Faceter's Guild*, 272
Biro, Melissa, *Theatre Saskatchewan*, 1375
Biros, Jim, *Toronto Musicians' Association*, 1386
Birthistle, Anne, *Animal Defence & Anti-Vivisection Society of BC*, 70
Bisaillon, Michel, *Pentecostal Assemblies of Canada*, 1150
Bisaillon, Sylvain, *Alliance internationale des employé(e)s de scène, de théâtre et de cinéma*, 57
Bischof, Harvey, *Ontario Secondary School Teachers' Federation*, 1103
Bischoff, Ralph, *Solid Waste Association of North America*, 1595
Bischoff, Angela, *Ontario Clean Air Alliance*, 1071
Bishop, Hazel, *Gander & Area Chamber of Commerce*, 766
Bishop, Angela, *Aquaculture Association of Nova Scotia*, 75

Bishop, Cindy, *Cerebral Palsy Association of Newfoundland & Labrador*, 538
Bishop, Nicole Arsenault, *New Brunswick Association of Dietitians*, 1005
Bishop, John R., *Korea Veterans Association of Canada Inc., Heritage Unit*, 893
Bishop, Hayley, *Society of Incentive & Travel Executives of Canada*, 1329
Bishop, Laurence, *Ontario Fencing Association*, 1080
Bishop, Gary, *Newfoundland & Labrador Institute of Agrologists*, 1019
Bishop, Wayne, *Amherst & Area Chamber of Commerce*, 67
Bishop, Toby, *Association of Certified Fraud Examiners - Toronto Chapter*, 145
Bishop, Gart, *Kennebecasis Naturalists' Society*, 883
Bishop, Ron, *Canadian Association of Aquarium Clubs*, 308
Bishop, Angela, *Community Foundation of Nova Scotia*, 597
Bishop, Lynn, *Alternative Land Use Services Canada*, 61
Bishop-Spencer, Lisa, *Chicken Farmers of Canada*, 557
Bissell, Shawna, *Boys & Girls Clubs of Alberta*, 221
Bissell, Eric, *B'nai Brith Canada Institute for International Affairs*, 192
Bissett, Winnie, *Boys & Girls Clubs of Alberta*, 221
Bissett, Gerald, *Royal Astronomical Society of Canada*, 1238
Bissig, Thomas, *Geological Association of Canada*, 770
Bissig, Hans, *British Columbia Katahdin Sheep Association*, 244
Bisson, Barry, *Shad Valley International*, 1294
Bisson, Émilie, *Fédération québécoise du canot et du kayak*, 730
Bisson, Nathalie, *Chambre immobilière Centre du Québec Inc.*, 550
Bisson, Donald A., *Ontario College of Reflexology*, 1072
Bisson, Luce, *Fédérations de l'UPA de Lévis Bellechasse, Rive Nord, Lotbinière-Mégantic*, 731
Bisson, Rebecca, *Northern Youth Abroad Program*, 1035
Bisson, Robert, *Building Energy Management Manitoba*, 262
Bisson-Girard, Suzanne, *Oxygène*, 1134
Bissonnette, Sylvie, *Canadian Association of Broadcasters*, 309
Bissonnette, Randy, *The Catholic Principals' Council of Ontario*, 520
Bittner, Alex, *Travel Health Insurance Association of Canada*, 1396
Bitton, Albert S., *Canadian Deals & Coupons Association*, 376
Bittorf, Brad, *International Lilac Society*, 1552
Bitz, Heather, *Drumheller & District Chamber of Commerce*, 663
Bizier, André, *Chambre des huissiers de justice du Québec*, 550
Bizzarri, Aoura, *Collectif des femmes immigrantes du Québec*, 581
Bjergso, Eric, *Canadian Co-operative Wool Growers Ltd.*, 364
Bjerland, Karen, *Canadian Fraternal Association*, 394
Bjornson, Tyler, *Canada Grains Council*, 279
Björnsson, Yngvi, *International Computer Games Association*, 1543
Blache, Caroline, *Association des avocats et avocates de province*, 107
Blacher, John, *Manitoba Volleyball Association*, 947
Black, Paul, *Peel Regional Police Association*, 1148
Black, Claudia, *Centre canadien d'étude et de coopération internationale*, 526
Black, Maegen, *Canadian Crafts Federation*, 372

Executive Name Index

Black, Ron, *Canadian Galloway Association*, 396
Black, Ron, *Canadian Red Poll Cattle Association*, 466
Black, Amanda, *The Ontario Archaeological Society*, 1060
Black, Dean, *Air Force Association of Canada*, 19
Black, Iain, *The Greater Vancouver Board of Trade*, 786
Black, Lorna, *Saskatchewan Library Trustees' Association*, 1269
Black, David, *Canadian Office & Professional Employees Union*, 445
Black, Gail, *Canadian Feed The Children*, 389
Black, David, *Independence Plus Inc.*, 832
Black, Mark, *Canadian Transplant Association*, 497
Black, Karen, *Canine Federation of Canada*, 508
Black, Ron, *Canadian Piedmontese Association*, 455
Black, Ron, *Canadian Katahdin Sheep Association Inc.*, 424
Black, Scott, *The Metal Working Association of New Brunswick*, 962
Black, Kathleen, *Association of Canadian Compliance Professionals*, 141
Black-Schrubb, Sherry, *Haldimand-Norfolk Literacy Council*, 798
Blackall, Diane, *SARI Therapeutic Riding*, 1254
Blackburn, Jacquie, *Durham Avicultural Society of Ontario*, 665
Blackburn, Carl, *International Humanist & Ethical Union*, 1550
Blackburn, John, *Association of Ontario Land Economists*, 155
Blackburn, John, *Canadian Electric Wheelchair Hockey Association*, 380
Blackburn, Lynn, *Canadian Institute of Actuaries*, 414
Blackburn, Diane, *Recycling Council of Ontario*, 1209
Blackburn, Pat, *United Empire Loyalists' Association of Canada*, 1410
Blackburn, Charlie, *North American Association of Central Cancer Registries, Inc.*, 1578
Blackie, Bill, *Ontario Association of School Business Officials*, 1066
Blacklock, Steve, *The Appraisal Institute of Canada - British Columbia*, 74
Blackman, Lori, *Recreation Facilities Association of British Columbia*, 1207
Blackman, Joan, *Vetta Chamber Music Society*, 1431
Blackmore, Ashleigh, *Family Enterprise Xchange*, 703
Blackmore, Marva, *Storytellers of Canada*, 1350
Blackstock, Cindy, *First Nations Child & Family Caring Society of Canada*, 738
Blackwell, Jessica, *Archives Association of Ontario*, 80
Blacquiere, Jason, *Prince Edward Island Police Association*, 1176
Blade, Linda, *Athletics Alberta*, 181
Blaikie-Birkigt, Kurtis, *Archaeological Society of Alberta*, 76
Blain, Kathryn, *Meningitis Research Foundation of Canada*, 960
Blain, Chris, *Alberta Snowboard Association*, 47
Blaine, Jane D., *Canadian Blind Sports Association Inc.*, 344
Blaine, Brent, *Manitoba Hereford Association*, 938
Blair, Claudia, *Williams Lake & District Chamber of Commerce*, 1455
Blair, Charles, *Canadian Association of Nordic Ski Instructors*, 323
Blair, Mary, *Canadian Association of Management Consultants*, 320

Blair, Kay, *Community Microskills Development Centre*, 606
Blair, Allan, *Canadian Lacrosse Hall of Fame*, 425
Blair, Lori, *Soroptimist International of the Americas*, 1595
Blair, Margaret, *Friends of the Orphans, Canada*, 763
Blair, John, *Ontario Masonry Contractors' Association*, 1090
Blair, Andrew, *International Confederation of Principals*, 1544
Blair, Anne, *Lymphovenous Association of Ontario*, 923
Blais, Chris, *Scouts Canada*, 1286
Blais, Marie-Camille, *Canadian National Institute for the Blind*, 439
Blais, Jana, *Battlefords United Way Inc.*, 200
Blais, Élise, *Association québécoise pour le loisir des personnes handicapées*, 176
Blais, Myriam, *Canadian Architectural Certification Board*, 271
Blais, Ingrid, *L'Arche Atlantic Region*, 77
Blais, Marcel, *La fédération des mouvements personne d'abord du Québec*, 716
Blake, Jennifer, *Society of Obstetricians & Gynaecologists of Canada*, 1330
Blake, Laurie, *Canadian Pony Club*, 457
Blake, Bill, *Benevolent & Protective Order of Elks of Canada*, 205
Blake, Marie, *Eastern Canadian Galloway Association*, 670
Blake, Stacie, *U.S. Committee for Refugees & Immigrants*, 1601
Blake, Ann, *Kingston Association of Museums, Art Galleries & Historic Sites*, 889
Blake, Jean, *Parkinson Society British Columbia*, 1141
Blakeborough, Johnny, *Vancouver Island University Faculty Association*, 1427
Blakely, Robert, *Operative Plasterers' & Cement Masons' International Association of the US & Canada (AFL-CIO/CFL) - Canadian Office*, 1116
Blakemore, Dave, *Ontario Brain Injury Association*, 1069
Blakey, Janet, *Archaeological Society of Alberta*, 76
Blakley, Carla, *Canadian Lutheran World Relief*, 428
Blanc, Marie-Hélène, *Association québécoise Plaidoyer-Victimes*, 176
Blanchard, Jeannette, *Canadian Health Information Management Association*, 402
Blanchard, Adam, *Manitoba Association of Friendship Centres*, 929
Blanchard, Lyn, *Institute of Certified Management Consultants of British Columbia*, 845
Blanchard, Mike, *The Royal Scottish Country Dance Society*, 1587
Blanchard, Paul, *New Brunswick Pharmacists' Association*, 1011
Blanchard, Michelle, *Fédération culturelle de L'Ile-du-Prince-Édouard inc.*, 708
Blanchard, Ed, *Boxing New Brunswick Boxe*, 220
Blanchet, Yvon, *Mouvement national des québécoises et québécois*, 977
Blanchet, Bernard, *Chambre de commerce et d'industrie du Sud-Ouest de Montréal*, 547
Blanchet Legendre, Marie, *Ordre des infirmières et infirmiers du Québec*, 1122
Blanchett, Katie, *Petroleum Technology Alliance Canada*, 1155
Blanchette, Serge, *Abbotsford Community Services*, 1
Blanchette, Angela, *Edam & District Board of Trade*, 674
Blanchette, Marc, *Project Management Institute*, 1585
Blane, Don, *Autism Canada*, 188
Blaney, Paul, *Kingston Lapidary & Mineral Club*, 889

Blankenship, Carole, *National Association of Teachers of Singing*, 1574
Blanks, Jack, *Seva Foundation*, 1588
Blanshay, Anita, *Na'amat Canada Inc.*, 987
Blaquière, Suzanne, *New Brunswick Genealogical Society Inc.*, 1009
Blasetti, Cecilia, *Edmonton Inner City Housing Society*, 678
Blashko, Denise, *South Okanagan Chamber Of Commerce*, 1335
Blasutig, Ivan, *Canadian Society of Clinical Chemists*, 481
Blaufarb, Rafe, *International Napoleonic Society*, 858
Blegen, Harley, *American Galloway Breeders Association*, 66
Blenkhorn, Diana L., *Maritime Lumber Bureau*, 951
Blenkiron, Jamie, *Ontario Shorthorn Association*, 1104
Blevins, Sandra, *Canadian College of Health Leaders*, 359
Blickstead, Rick, *Diabetes Canada*, 655
Bliid, David, *Alberta Construction Trucking Association*, 31
Blin, Anne-Lise, *Conseil pour le développement de l'alphabétisme et des compétences des adultes du Nouveau-Brunswick*, 619
Blinn, William, *The Nova Scotia Mineral & Gem Society*, 1047
Bliss, Kathryn, *Church Council on Justice & Corrections*, 569
Blistein, Adam D., *Society for Classical Studies*, 1589
Blixt, Gail, *Alberta Family Child Care Association*, 34
Blize, Gord, *Fort Saskatchewan Fish & Game Association*, 754
Block, Kim, *British Columbia Association of People Who Stutter*, 232
Block, Yvonne, *Addictions Foundation of Manitoba*, 8
Block, Matthew, *Lutheran Church - Canada*, 922
Block, Nadine, *Sustainable Forestry Initiative Inc.*, 1597
Block, Lara, *Hedge Fund Association Canada*, 1529
Block, Len, *Mennonite Central Committee Canada*, 960
Blom, David, *Ducks Unlimited Canada*, 663
Blomstrom, Eleanor, *Women's Environment & Development Organization*, 1602
Blood, Ryan, *Brain Injury Association of Nova Scotia*, 225
Bloodworth, Margaret, *Council of Canadian Academies*, 633
Bloom, Anita, *The Olde Forge Community Resource Centre*, 1056
Bloom, Michael, *The Conference Board of Canada*, 612
Bloom, Shauna, *Ecological Farmers of Ontario*, 672
Bloom, Steven, *Pride of Israel*, 1170
Bloomer, Chris, *Canadian Energy Pipeline Association*, 381
Bloomfield, Michael, *Harmony Foundation of Canada*, 803
Bloomfield, Harry J.F., *Eldee Foundation*, 681
Blöschl, Günter, *European Geosciences Union*, 1524
Blossier, Benoît, *Association des professionnels en santé du travail*, 126
Blottner, Dave, *Yukon Sourdough Rendezvous Society*, 1480
Blouet, Chantal, *Fédération québécoise des laryngectomisés*, 729
Blouin, Gilles, *Société d'histoire et généalogie du granit*, 1313
Blouin, Anick, *Fédération des secrétaires professionnelles du Québec*, 719
Bloxom, Cecilia, *Canadian Patient Safety Institute*, 452
Blue, Dan, *Central 1 Credit Union*, 523

Bluesky, Gord, *Manitoba Uske*, 946
Blugerman, Michael, *Children's Resource & Consultation Centre of Ontario*, 562
Blum, Teresa, *Ontario Federation of Home & School Associations Inc.*, 1079
Blum, Jennifer, *VHA Home HealthCare*, 1431
Blumenschein, Mike, *Yukon Agricultural Association*, 1477
Blumenthal, Henry, *Corporations des assureurs directs de dommage*, 631
Blumer, Lorie, *The Canadian Society for the Weizmann Institute of Science*, 478
Blumer, Kira, *B'nai Brith Youth Organization*, 192
Blundell, Doug, *Port Hope & District Chamber of Commerce*, 1166
Blundon, Bert, *Newfoundland & Labrador Association of Public & Private Employees*, 1016
Blyskal, Stephanie, *Academic Pediatric Association*, 1485
Blyth, Tracy, *CIO Association of Canada*, 570
Blyth, Tracy, *Canadian Society of Association Executives*, 480
Blyth, Charles, *Northwest Territories Federal Liberal Association*, 1038
Blythe, Robin, *Ontario Institute of Agrologists*, 1088
Blythe, Don, *Tire Stewardship BC Association*, 1380
Boa, Heather, *Huron Chamber of Commerce - Goderich, Central & North Huron*, 828
Boag, Peter, *Canadian Fuels Association*, 396
Boainain-Schneider, Alice, *Institute for Planetary Synthesis*, 1532
Boal, David, *Lupus Ontario*, 922
Boardman, Debbie, *Community Living Dundas County*, 601
Boardman, Andrew, *Society of Graphic Designers of Canada*, 1329
Boarman, William J., *International Allied Printing Trades Association*, 1535
Boaventura, Rogerio, *American Society for Quality*, 1499
Boback-Lane, Brynn, *Children's Hospital Foundation of Saskatchewan*, 562
Bobb, Geoff, *Epilepsy Ontario*, 694
Bobb, Jim, *Eastern Apicultural Society of North America, Inc.*, 1522
Bobbett, Angela, *Neurofibromatosis Society of Ontario*, 1004
Bobin, Jérôme, *Handicap International Canada*, 803
Bobinski, Pat, *Northwest Territories Biathlon Association*, 1037
Bobkowicz, Andrea, *Foundation of Catholic Community Services Inc.*, 756
Bobowski, Ron, *North Okanagan Labour Council*, 1031
Bobyk, Valerie, *Family Service Association of Halifax*, 704
Bocchini, Sherri, *Children's Health Foundations*, 561
Bochatay, Lydie, *La Biennale de Montréal*, 209
Bocking, Alan, *Genesis Research Foundation*, 769
Bodden, Heather, *Professional Golfers' Association of Canada*, 1185
Boddez, Brian, *Alberta Building Officials Association, Inc.*, 27
Bode, Cameron, *Canada West Equipment Dealers Association*, 281
Bode, Ray, *Darts British Columbia Association*, 651
Bodei, Natasha, *Southern Alberta Brain Injury Society*, 1337
Bodeven, Dominique, *Société d'histoire et de généalogie de l'Ile Jésus*, 1312
Bodle, Cathy, *Information Barrie*, 836
Bodley, Steven, *College of Physicians & Surgeons of Ontario*, 588
Bodnar, Faith, *Inclusion BC*, 832
Bodnar, Allison, *Pharmacy Association of Nova Scotia*, 1157

Executive Name Index

Bodnar, Dana, *Waldorf School Association of Kelowna*, 1439
Bodnarchuk, Rhonda, *Pharmacy Technician Society of Alberta*, 1157
Bodnarchuk, Mike, *Alberta Ski Jumping & Nordic Combined*, 47
Bodnaruk-Wide, Tamara, *Family Mediation Canada*, 704
Boeckh, Ian, *Graham Boeckh Foundation*, 779
Boeckner, David, *Canadian College & University Food Service Association*, 358
Boehland, Laura, *Controlled Release Society*, 1520
Boehm, Carol, *Canadian Fjord Horse Association*, 391
Boehm, David, *Risk & Insurance Management Society Inc.*, 1234
Boehm, Marilynn, *Alberta Food Processors Association*, 35
Boer, Richard, *Canadian Aviation Historical Society*, 340
Boersma, Simon, *Morinville & District Chamber of Commerce*, 974
Boersma, Deb, *Windsor Orchid Society*, 1457
Boettcher, Herbert, *Canadian Trakehner Horse Society*, 496
Bogart, Ronald J., *Ontario Underwater Council*, 1112
Bogdanowicz, Harriet, *American Planning Association*, 1496
Bogie, Don, *Kamloops Wildlife Park Society*, 881
Bogosyan, Avedis, *Armenian Canadian Medical Association of Ontario*, 82
Bogzaran, Faramarz, *Environmental Careers Organization of Canada*, 691
Bohach, Adrian, *Ability Society of Alberta*, 2
Bohachewski, Chad, *Saskatchewan Institute of Agrologists*, 1268
Bohme, Sherri, *Cold Lake Regional Chamber of Commerce*, 581
Bohn, Dianne, *British Columbia Registered Music Teachers' Association*, 251
Boice, Janine, *Mustard Seed Food Bank*, 986
Boies, Sébastien, *Conseil régional FTQ Québec et Chaudière-Appalaches*, 621
Boilard, Madeleine, *Réseau du patrimoine franco-ontarien*, 1222
Boileau, Sophie, *Carrefour pour Elle*, 516
Boileau, Tina, *DEBRA Canada*, 652
Boilon, Annie, *Place Vermeil*, 1161
Boily, Sylvain, *Office municipal d'habitation de Longueuil*, 1055
Boily, André, *Réseau des SADC et CAE*, 1221
Bois, Francine, *Association québécoise des salons du livre*, 174
Bois, Charles, *Canadian Institute of Energy (British Columbia)*, 415
Boisjoly, Christiane, *Mediation Yukon Society*, 958
Boisjoly, Martin, *Chants Libres, compagnie lyrique de création*, 552
Boislard, Gilles, *Urban & Regional Information Systems Association*, 1601
Boissonnault, Anne-Marie, *Société des communicateurs du Québec*, 1317
Boissonneault, Estelle, *Post-Polio Network Manitoba Inc.*, 1168
Boissonneault, Bernard, *Canadian Marine Pilots' Association*, 430
Boissonneault, David, *Éleveurs de porcs du Québec*, 684
Boissonneault, Marie, *Société historique Alphonse-Desjardins*, 1319
Boissonneault, Réal, *Motor Coach Canada*, 975
Boisvert, Yves, *Fédération des associations de familles du Québec*, 711
Boisvert, Christine, *Théâtres associés inc.*, 1375
Boisvert, Josée, *Association des Grands Frères et Grandes Soeurs du Québec*, 115
Boisvert, Claude, *Association sectorielle: Fabrication d'équipement de transport et de machines*, 178

Boivin, Susan, *Alberta Easter Seals Society*, 33
Boivin, Diane, *Canadian College of Health Leaders*, 359
Boivin, Robert, *Réseau québécois des OSBL d'habitation*, 1225
Bokalo, Mike, *Western Boreal Growth & Yield Association*, 1447
Boksman, Laura, *Radiation Safety Institute of Canada*, 1202
Boland, Michael W., *Newfoundland & Labrador Credit Union*, 1018
Boland, James, *International Union of Bricklayers & Allied Craftworkers (AFL-CIO/CFL)*, 1564
Boland, James, *International Union of Bricklayers & Allied Craftworkers (AFL-CIO/CFL)*, 1564
Boland, Leo, *Pembroke Area Field Naturalists*, 1149
Boland, Corey, *American Concrete Institute*, 1492
Boland, Todd, *Newfoundland Rock Garden Society*, 1023
Boldon, Ryley, *Volleyball New Brunswick*, 1438
Boldt, Jamie, *The John Howard Society of Saskatchewan*, 875
Boldt, Stephanie, *Brain Care Centre*, 225
Bolduc, Danielle, *Insurance Institute of British Columbia*, 849
Bolduc, Bertrand, *Ordre des pharmaciens du Québec*, 1123
Bolduc, Patrice, *Conseil des métiers d'art du Québec (ind.)*, 617
Bolduc, Sophie, *Réseau BIBLIO du Saguenay-Lac-Saint-Jean*, 1218
Bolduc, Sylvie, *Réseau des SADC et CAE*, 1221
Bolduc, Alice, *Société Canada-Japon de Montréal*, 1307
Bolduc, Dennis, *Fédération des coopératives d'habitation du Royaume Saguenay Lac-Saint-Jean*, 714
Bolduc, Yves, *Association des gestionnaires des établissements de santé et des services sociaux*, 115
Bole, Mary, *Manitoba Genealogical Society Inc.*, 937
Boles, Derek, *Toronto Railway Historical Association*, 1386
Boles, George, *Kneehill Historical Society*, 892
Boles, Stephen, *South Huron Chamber of Commerce*, 1335
Bolger, Glenn, *Newfoundland & Labrador Credit Union*, 1018
Bolger, Phil, *Speech-Language & Audiology Canada*, 1341
Bolger, Phil, *Canadian Psychological Association*, 462
Bolger, Jim, *Ontario Geothermal Association*, 1082
Bolibruck, Kevin, *Your Life Counts*, 1475
Bollenbach, Sharon, *Special Olympics Canada*, 1339
Bolton, Bruce, *Canadian Federation of Friends of Museums*, 386
Bomar, Andrea, *Special Libraries Association*, 1596
Bombardier, Isabelle, *Centre d'intervention budgétaire et sociale de la Mauricie*, 528
Bombardier, Claire, *Canadian Arthritis Network*, 295
Bommel, JP, *National Association of Television Program Executives*, 1574
Bonaise, Douglas, *Rocky Native Friendship Society*, 1235
Bonaldo, Édouard, *Réseau des SADC et CAE*, 1219
Bonato, Michel, *Tourisme Îles-de-la-Madeleine*, 1393
Bond, Roxanne, *Brantford & District Labour Council*, 227
Bond, Denis, *Fédération québécoise des sociétés Alzheimer*, 729

Bond, Brad, *American Society of Heating, Refrigerating & Air Conditioning Engineers*, 1500
Bond, Marianne, *Kootenay Real Estate Board*, 892
Bond, Bonnie, *Seagull Foundation*, 1288
Bondar, Dominique, *Canadian Media Guild*, 432
Bondon, Sylvie, *Bureau local d'intervention traitant du SIDA*, 264
Bondrup-Neilsen, Soren, *Blomidon Naturalists Society*, 215
Bone, Scott, *British Columbia Construction Association*, 237
Bone, William (Bill), *Canadian Mental Health Association*, 434
Bone, Mary, *Habitat for Humanity Canada*, 797
Bonetti, Adele, *Interior Designers of Alberta*, 852
Bonetto, Estelle, *Association of Translators & Interpreters of Saskatchewan*, 163
Bonga, Mike, *Nature Trust of New Brunswick*, 1001
Bongain, Valérie, *Ordre des ingénieurs du Québec*, 1122
Bongiovanni, Esteban, *Fondation Jules et Paul-Émile Léger*, 747
Bonham, Oliver, *Canadian Council of Professional Geoscientists*, 370
Bonhomme, P., *Independent Lumber Dealers Co-operative*, 833
Bonhomme, Léanne, *Ingénieurs Sans Frontières Québec*, 838
Boniface, Giovanna, *Canadian Association of Occupational Therapists - British Columbia*, 324
Bonilla-Rodriguez, Maikel, *Association of Professional Engineers & Geoscientists of New Brunswick*, 158
Bonin, Jessica, *British Columbia Teacher-Librarians' Association*, 255
Bonin, Mark, *Canadian Association of Neuroscience Nurses*, 322
Bonish, Peter, *Human Resources Professionals Association*, 826
Bonn, Kris, *Ontario Brain Injury Association*, 1068
Bonneau, Pierre, *Chambre de commerce de Valcourt et Région*, 543
Bonnell, Carey, *National Seafood Sector Council*, 996
Bonnell-Eisnor, Christine, *Canada - Nova Scotia Offshore Petroleum Board*, 278
Bonner, Richard, *The Coaster Enthusiasts of Canada*, 579
Bonnet, Olivier, *Ethiopiaid*, 697
Bonnett, Ron, *Canadian Federation of Agriculture*, 384
Bonneville, Claude, *Association de Laval pour la déficience intellectuelle*, 102
Bonraisin, Guy, *Association des Boulangers Artisans du Québec*, 108
Bonser, John, *Ontario East Tourism Association*, 1077
Bookbinder, Sharona, *Canadian Art Therapy Association*, 295
Boon, Kevin, *British Columbia Cattlemen's Association*, 235
Boone-Watt, Wendy, *Ontario Healthcare Housekeepers' Association Inc.*, 1084
Boos, Greg, *Pacific Corridor Enterprise Council*, 1135
Booth, Tracy, *Canadian Association of Elizabeth Fry Societies*, 313
Booth, Brad, *Canadian Academy of Psychiatry & the Law*, 286
Booth, Alice, *Community Futures Wild Rose*, 599
Booth, Joanne, *Edmonton Federation of Community Leagues*, 677
Boothman, Brendon, *Battlefords United Way Inc.*, 200
Bootman, Brendon, *Battlefords Chamber of Commerce*, 200

Boquet, Shenan J., *Human Life International*, 1530
Bordan, Jack, *Sar-El Canada*, 1253
Bordeleau, Marie, *Uniform Law Conference of Canada*, 1405
Borden, Chester, *Boys & Girls Clubs of Nova Scotia*, 223
Borduas, Greg, *Economic Developers Association of Canada*, 673
Borer, Murray, *Upper Ottawa Valley Beekeepers' Association*, 1422
Borkwood, Brad, *Ontario Brain Injury Association*, 1068
Borlace, Pat, *Montréal Field Naturalists Club*, 972
Borland, Heather, *Autism Society of British Columbia*, 189
Borland, Barbara, *College of Midwives of Ontario*, 586
Bornehag, Carl-Gustaf, *International Society of Indoor Air Quality & Climate*, 1561
Bornstein, Joe, *Elder Abuse Ontario*, 681
Boro, Jeffrey, *Association d'entraide des avocats de Montréal*, 99
Borque, Kaitlin, *Ontario Society for the Prevention of Cruelty to Animals*, 1107
Borrett, Paul, *Alberta & Northwest Territories Lung Association*, 21
Borshuk, Chris, *Windsor Federation of Musicians*, 1456
Borski, Ric, *Better Business Bureau of Mid-Western & Central Ontario*, 206
Bortolotti, Julie, *Ontario Lung Association*, 1090
Bos, Clayton, *Association of Professional Engineers & Geoscientists of Alberta*, 157
Bos, Ron, *REHOBOTH Christian Ministries*, 1216
Bosak, Steve, *Society for Ecological Restoration International*, 1590
Bosak, Olga, *Société d'horticulture et d'écologie de Boucherville*, 1314
Boscariol, Celso, *Italian Chamber of Commerce in Canada - West*, 866
Boscariol, Celso A. A., *posAbilities Association of BC*, 1167
Boscart, Veronique, *Canadian Gerontological Nursing Association*, 397
Bosch, Landon, *Drumheller & District Chamber of Commerce*, 663
Boschman, Robert, *Association for Literature, Environment, & Culture in Canada*, 133
Bosco, Mary Lou, *AIM Global*, 1486
Boshard, Greg, *Master Painters & Decorators Association*, 954
Bosomworth, Virginia, *World Literacy of Canada*, 1466
Bossé, Suzanne, *Fédération des communautés francophones et acadienne du Canada*, 713
Bossenberry, Lorna, *Saskatchewan Genealogical Society*, 1266
Bossert, Elisabeth, *Société Provancher d'histoire naturelle du Canada*, 1323
Boston, Nicole Testa, *Society of Fire Protection Engineers*, 1593
Boswell, Phillip W., *Canadian Assessment, Vocational Evaluation & Work Adjustment Society*, 297
Bota, Jean, *The Alberta Community Crime Prevention Association*, 30
Botchar, Dwayne, *Canadian Association of Foodservice Professionals*, 315
Bott, Shannon, *Digital Health Canada*, 656
Bott, Shannon, *Couchiching Institute on Public Affairs*, 632
Bottin, Isha, *Association canadienne des ataxies familiales*, 92
Botting, Kelsey, *Canadian Home Builders' Association - British Columbia*, 407
Bottner, Michelle, *Canadian Hadassah WIZO*, 399
Boucha, Bonnie, *Lake of the Woods Adult Learning Line*, 896

Executive Name Index

Bouchard, Pascale, *Leucan - Association pour les enfants atteints de cancer*, 908
Bouchard, Louis, *L'Opéra de Montréal*, 1115
Bouchard, Josée, *La Fédération des commissions scolaires du Québec*, 713
Bouchard, Maryse, *Association coopérative d'économie familiale de l'est de Montréal*, 97
Bouchard, Jean-François, *Association nationale des éditeurs de livres*, 138
Bouchard, Monique, *Ordre des denturologistes du Québec*, 1121
Bouchard, Louis, *Société des écoles du monde du BI du Québec et de la francophonie*, 1318
Bouchard, Nicole, *Association québécoise de l'épilepsie*, 170
Bouchard, Raymond, *Association nationale des distributeurs aux petites surfaces alimentaires*, 138
Bouchard, Nancy, *Ordre des infirmières et infirmiers du Québec*, 1122
Bouchard, Natasha, *Camping Québec*, 277
Bouchard, Johanne, *Centraide Saguenay-Lac St-Jean*, 523
Bouchard, Marie-Noël, *Association du jeune barreau de Montréal*, 131
Bouchard, Gérard, *Table de développement de la production biologique*, 1365
Bouchard, Sydney, *Canadian Association of Veterans in United Nations Peacekeeping*, 335
Bouchard, Julie, *Chambre de commerce et d'industrie de Rouyn-Noranda*, 546
Bouchard, Jonathan, *Fédération étudiante universitaire du Québec*, 720
Bouchard, Carole, *National Association of Pharmacy Regulatory Authorities*, 990
Bouchard, Manuel, *Réseau indépendant des diffuseurs d'événements artistiques unis*, 1225
Bouchard, Gabrielle, *Saskatchewan Intercultural Association Inc.*, 1268
Bouchard, Sue, *Partners FOR the Saskatchewan River Basin*, 1144
Bouchard, Isabelle, *Recherches amérindiennes au Québec*, 1207
Bouchard, Claire, *Mouvement national des québécoises et québécois*, 977
Bouchard, Marie-Josée, *Association provinciale des constructeurs d'habitations du Québec inc.*, 168
Bouchard, Danny, *Les Chevaliers de Colomb du Québec, District No 37, Conseil 5198*, 557
Bouchard, Simon, *Association des fabricants et détaillants de l'industrie de la cuisine du Québec*, 113
Bouchard-Vincent, Thierry, *Confédération des associations d'étudiants et étudiantes de l'Université Laval*, 611
Bouchart d'Orval, Marie, *Partage Humanitaire*, 1143
Boucher, Allison, *Frontier Duty Free Association*, 763
Boucher, Mathieu, *Cycling Canada Cyclisme*, 647
Boucher, Johanne, *Ordre des traducteurs, terminologues et interprètes agréés du Québec*, 1124
Boucher, Marie, *Fédération québécoise des directions d'établissements d'enseignement*, 728
Boucher, Daniel, *Société de la francophonie manitobaine*, 1316
Boucher, Lorraine, *Working Women Community Centre*, 1464
Boucher, André G., *Ontario Lumber Manufacturers' Association*, 1089
Boucher, France, *Canadian Society of Hospital Pharmacists*, 484
Boucher, Huguette, *Centraide Abitibi Témiscamingue et Nord-du-Québec*, 522
Boucher, Shilo, *YMCA Canada*, 1471
Boucher, Jocelyn, *Association des policières et policiers provinciaux du Québec*, 123

Boucher, Nicole, *Club de photo de Boucherville*, 575
Boucher, Mark, *Canadian Merchant Service Guild*, 435
Boucher, Stéphan, *Centraide Gaspésie Îles-de-la-Madeleine*, 522
Boucher, Danielle, *Association québécoise du personnel de direction des écoles*, 176
Boucher, France, *Association des pharmaciens des établissements de santé du Québec*, 123
Boucher, Emily, *Digital Nova Scotia*, 656
Boucher, Rozanne, *Société québécoise de la rédaction professionnelle*, 1323
Boucher, Jo-Anne, *Maintenance, Engineering & Reliability (MER) Society*, 926
Boucher, Helen W., *Infectious Diseases Society of America*, 1531
Boucher, Nathalie, *Association québécoise des traumatisés crâniens*, 175
Boucher, Hélène, *Réseau du sport étudiant du Québec Outaouais*, 1223
Bouck, Thayer, *Canadian Tire Coupon Collectors Club*, 495
Boudreau, Brian, *Canadian Association of Police Governance*, 328
Boudreau, Nadine, *Association of Consulting Engineering Companies - New Brunswick*, 146
Boudreau, Claudette, *New Brunswick Denturists Society*, 1007
Boudreau, Justin, *Sign Association of Canada*, 1299
Boudreau, Alanna, *Water Ski - Wakeboard Manitoba*, 1441
Boudreau, Dylan, *Project Management Institute*, 1585
Boudreau, Marc, *Réseau du sport étudiant du Québec Est-du-Québec*, 1223
Boudreau, Ginette, *Syndicat des employés et employées des syndicats et des organismes collectifs du Québec*, 1363
Boudreau, David, *Association provinciale des constructeurs d'habitations du Québec inc.*, 168
Boudreau, Virginia, *Guysborough County Inshore Fishermen's Association*, 795
Boudreau, Roger, *Centre de Bénévolat de la Péninsule Acadienne Inc.*, 528
Boudreault, Félix, *Ordre des ingénieurs du Québec*, 1123
Boudreault, Jean-Sébastien, *Association québécoise des avocats et avocates en droit de l'immigration*, 171
Boudreault, Laurence, *Canadian Society of Atherosclerosis, Thrombosis & Vascular Biology*, 481
Boudreault, Carole, *Association des propriétaires de cinémas du Québec*, 126
Boué, Danielle, *Ordre des technologues en imagerie médicale, en radio-oncologie et en élétrophysiologie médicale du Québec*, 1124
Bouffard, Jacques, *Association québécoise de l'épilepsie*, 169
Bouffioux, Bill, *British Columbia Bison Association*, 234
Bouganin, Lioz, *Saskatchewan Motion Picture Industry Association*, 1270
Bougie, André, *L'Association de spina-bifida et d'hydrocéphalie du Québec*, 104
Bougie, Martin, *Association des radiodiffuseurs communautaires du Québec*, 127
Bougie, Michel, *Association des Poneys Welsh & Cob au Québec*, 124
Bouida, Younes, *Soccer New Brunswick*, 1305
Boulanger, Guy, *Chambre de commerce du Haut-Saint-François*, 544
Boulanger, Lauren, *Association of Professional Engineers & Geoscientists of New Brunswick*, 158
Boulanger, André, *Institut du cancer de Montréal*, 842
Boulanger, Guy, *Canada Employment & Immigration Union*, 279

Boulanger, Linda, *Centre de Femmes Les Elles du Nord*, 529
Boulanger-Bonnelly, Jérémy, *New Democratic Party*, 1014
Boulanger-Lemieux, Marie, *Association pour l'intégration sociale (Région de Québec)*, 166
Boulay, Pat, *Shooting Federation of Canada*, 1297
Boulay, Carmen, *Regroupement des femmes de la Côte-de-Gaspé*, 1215
Boulding, Jamie, *Strathcona Park Lodge & Outdoor Education Centre*, 1351
Boulet, Hubert, *Concrete Manitoba*, 610
Boulet, Gilles, *Réseau des SADC et CAE*, 1220
Boulet, Jacques, *Société de Conservation du Patrimoine de Saint-François-de-la-Rivière-du-Sud inc.*, 1314
Bouliane, Denis, *Alliance autochtone du Québec*, 55
Boulos-Winton, Marina, *Chez Doris*, 557
Boulton, Bob, *Canadian Institute of Chartered Business Valuators*, 414
Bouman, Mary Lynn, *Goodwill Industries Essex Kent Lambton*, 778
Bouman, Sheila, *ViaSport*, 1432
Bourassa, Jack, *Public Service Alliance of Canada*, 1193
Bourassa, Jack, *Public Service Alliance of Canada*, 1193
Bourassa, Armand, *Saskatchewan Pattern Dance Association*, 1271
Bourbeau, Alain, *Les producteurs de lait du Québec*, 1181
Bourbeau, Jean, *Réseau québécois de l'asthme et de la MPOC*, 1225
Bourbeau, Doris Levasseur, *Ordre professionnel des technologistes médicaux du Québec*, 1125
Bourbonnais, Chantal, *Association canadienne des professeurs d'immersion*, 94
Bourbonniere, Stephane, *ARMA Canada*, 82
Bourdages, Hélène, *Association montréalaise des directions d'établissement scolaire*, 137
Bourdeau, Francine, *Juvenile Diabetes Research Foundation Canada*, 879
Bourdeault, Michel, *Ayrshire Breeders Association of Canada*, 191
Bourdon, Ron, *Association of Architectural Technologists of Ontario*, 139
Boureaud, Natalia, *Orchestre de chambre de Montréal*, 1118
Bourgaize, Hélène, *Canadian Hemophilia Society*, 404
Bourgault, Louise, *Chambre de commerce de Sherbrooke*, 543
Bourgault, Rémi, *Commonwealth Parliamentary Association*, 1518
Bourgault, Denis, *Conseil national du meuble*, 619
Bourgeois, Michel, *Chambre de Commerce Bois-des-Filion - Lorraine*, 540
Bourgeois, Euclide, *New Brunswick Fruit Growers Association Inc.*, 1008
Bourgeois, Marc, *Engineers Canada*, 689
Bourgeois, Jacques, *Mineral Society of Manitoba*, 966
Bourgeois, Jackie, *Southeast Environmental Association*, 1337
Bourgeois, Aurele, *Canadian Deaf Golf Association*, 376
Bourgeois, Zoe, *New Brunswick Youth in Care Network*, 1013
Bourget, Ann, *Fédération Québécoise des Municipalités*, 729
Bourget, Shadie, *Conseil jeunesse francophone de la Colombie-Britannique*, 618
Bourgie, Nicole, *Chambre de commerce de Ste-Julienne*, 543
Bourgoin, Stéphane, *New Brunswick Association of Food Banks*, 1005
Bourguignon, Chantal, *Association des Traumatisés cranio-cérébraux de la Montérégie*, 129

Bourinot, Sue, *Mahone Bay & Area Chamber of Commerce*, 926
Bourk, Jean-Francois, *Canadian Ski Patrol*, 471
Bournival, Simon, *Fédération nationale des services de préparation au mariage*, 722
Bourns, Elizabeth, *Ontario Municipal Human Resources Association*, 1092
Bourque, Conrad, *Société culturelle de la Baie des Chaleurs*, 1309
Bourque, Ron, *Canadian Grand Masters Fiddling Association*, 398
Bourque, Gisèle, *Association des constructeurs de routes et grands travaux du Québec*, 110
Bourque, Paul C., *Investment Funds Institute of Canada*, 863
Bourque, Michael, *Railway Association of Canada*, 1203
Bourque, Caroline, *St. Lawrence Valley Natural History Society*, 1250
Bourque-Bearskin, Lisa, *Canadian Indigenous Nurses Association*, 411
Bourree, Frank, *Greater Victoria Chamber of Commerce*, 787
Bourret, Raymond, *Ordre des acupuncteurs de Québec*, 1119
Bourrie, Andrea, *Ontario Professional Planners Institute*, 1098
Bousquet, Francine, *Fédération nationale des communications (CSN)*, 721
Boutilier, Roger, *Nova Scotia Association of REALTORS*, 1041
Boutilier, Brian, *Nunavut Employees Union*, 1051
Boutilier, Robert, *Port Morien Wildlife Association*, 1166
Boutin, Conia, *Association de la construction du Québec*, 101
Boutin, Anne-Marie, *Union of International Associations*, 1599
Boutiyeb, Soukaïna, *Réseau du patrimoine franco-ontarien*, 1222
Bouvet, Sylvie, *Association des obstétriciens et gynécologues du Québec*, 121
Bouzan, Rick, *Newfoundland & Labrador Wildlife Federation*, 1022
Bovaird, Amy, *Organic Trade Association*, 1581
Bovenizer, Cindy, *Biathlon Nouveau-New Brunswick*, 207
Bovyer, Debbie, *Prince Edward Island Union of Public Sector Employees*, 1178
Bowell, Liz, *Financial Executives International Canada*, 736
Bowen, Ian, *Canadian Ski Patrol*, 471
Bowen, Chantal, *Youth Media Alliance*, 1476
Bowen, Fiona, *Association of Canadian Travel Agents - Ontario*, 144
Bowen, David, *Haldimand-Norfolk District Beekeepers' Association*, 798
Bowen, Caroline, *Edmonton Construction Association*, 676
Bower, Marietjie, *Financial Executives International Canada*, 736
Bower, Tim, *National Association of Environmental Professionals*, 1573
Bower, Bill, *Ottawa Duck Club*, 1130
Bowering, Ian, *Stormont, Dundas & Glengarry Historical Society*, 1350
Bowes, Dan, *Financial Executives International Canada*, 736
Bowie, Glenn, *Water Ski & Wakeboard Canada*, 1442
Bowie, Peggy, *Canadian Security Traders Association, Inc.*, 469
Bowing, Scott, *NACE International*, 1572
Bowland, Jim, *Canadian Association for Disabled Skiing - New Brunswick*, 299
Bowles, Bob, *Ganaraska Hiking Trail Association*, 766
Bowles, Ron, *Local Government Management Association of British Columbia*, 917
Bowles, Paul, *Canadian Railroad Historical Association*, 465

Executive Name Index

Bowman, Trish, *Inclusion Alberta*, 831
Bowman, Paul, *Canadian Conference of Catholic Bishops*, 363
Bowman, Nicole, *Woodstock-Ingersoll & District Real Estate Board*, 1464
Bowman, Karen, *Traffic Injury Research Foundation*, 1394
Bowman, John, *Canadian Association for Disabled Skiing - Alberta*, 299
Bowman, Dan, *Alberta Freestyle Ski Association*, 36
Bowman, Debi, *DanceSport Alberta*, 650
Bowmer, Ian, *Medical Council of Canada*, 958
Bowser, Kerry, *Boys & Girls Clubs of Ontario*, 224
Bowser, Dara, *Heating, Refrigeration & Air Conditioning Institute of Canada*, 810
Bowser, Kerry, *Eastview Neighbourhood Community Centre*, 671
Bowser, Judy, *Embroiderers' Association of Canada, Inc.*, 686
Box, Corinne, *The Bahá'í Community of Canada*, 194
Boxall, James, *Canadian Association of Geographers*, 316
Boxshall, James, *AIDS Vancouver Island*, 17
Boyce, Lyle, *British Columbia Association of School Business Officials*, 232
Boyce, James N., *Ontario Tennis Association*, 1110
Boyce, Brad, *Hamilton Police Association*, 802
Boyce, Jane, *Upper Thames River Conservation Authority*, 1422
Boyce-Found, Sherry, *Kawartha Chamber of Commerce & Tourism*, 882
Boychuk, Robin, *Responsible Gambling Council (Ontario)*, 1227
Boyd, Roger, *Woodstock Field Naturalists*, 1464
Boyd, Jacquie, *Big Brothers Big Sisters of Alberta*, 209
Boyd, Jacquie, *Boys & Girls Clubs of Alberta*, 221
Boyd, Jeana, *British Columbia Amateur Softball Association*, 230
Boyd, Holly, *The Royal Scottish Country Dance Society*, 1587
Boyd, Marie, *Sickle Cell Association of Ontario*, 1298
Boyd, Terry, *Ontario Rett Syndrome Association*, 1102
Boyd, Lindsay, *Canadian Alliance of Student Associations*, 291
Boyd, Ian, *The G.K. Chesterton Institute for Faith & Culture*, 1528
Boyd, Bruce, *Canadian Life Insurance Medical Officers Association*, 427
Boyd Landry, Jane, *Nova Scotia Council for the Family*, 1043
Boyer, Lisa, *Canadian Security Association*, 469
Boyer, Greg, *The Great Lakes Research Consortium*, 1528
Boyer, Chris, *Waterloo Coin Society*, 1442
Boyes, Richard, *Ontario Association of Fire Chiefs*, 1063
Boyko, Bill, *Canadian Welding Bureau*, 503
Boyko, Carmen, *Alberta Association of Fund Raising Executives*, 23
Boyko, Susan, *Cancer Patient Education Network Canada*, 507
Boylan, John, *Canadian Association of Student Financial Aid Administrators*, 334
Boyle, Megan, *Canadian Beverage Association*, 343
Boynton, Bruce, *Canadian Ski Patrol*, 471
Boynton, Bryce, *Canadian Nursing Students' Association*, 443
Boys, Beverley, *British Columbia Diving*, 239
Bozard, John, *Children's Miracle Network*, 562
Bozzer, Stephanie, *Edmonton Japanese Community Association*, 678
Bozzo, Pietro, *Boys & Girls Clubs of Québec*, 224

Braaksma, Betty, *Manitoba Library Consortium Inc.*, 940
Braaten, Joanne, *Canadian Archaeological Association*, 294
Braaten, Justin, *Saskatchewan Independent Insurance Adjusters' Association*, 1268
Brace, Ian, *Saskatchewan Genealogical Society*, 1266
Brace, Sarah, *Pacific States-British Columbia Oil Spill Task Force*, 1136
Brachaniec, Jacek, *Acupuncture Canada*, 7
Brachi, Nigel, *University of Alberta Students' Union*, 1419
Bracken, Joanne, *Alzheimer Society of Saskatchewan Inc.*, 64
Bracken, Joe, *Canadian Heartland Training Railway*, 403
Bracken, Amber, *News Photographers Association of Canada*, 1024
Bracklow, Wende, *Big Brothers Big Sisters of British Columbia*, 209
Bradbury, Mark, *Easter Seals Newfoundland & Labrador*, 669
Braden, Esther, *Canadian Hard of Hearing Association*, 400
Braden, Bill, *Great Slave Snowmobile Association*, 782
Bradfield, Philip, *Health Association Nova Scotia*, 806
Bradford, Erin, *Canadian University & College Counselling Association*, 499
Bradley, F.A., *World's Poultry Science Association*, 1608
Bradley, Monica, *Alberta Association of Agricultural Societies*, 23
Bradley, Penny, *Association of Neighbourhood Houses BC*, 153
Bradley, Tammie, *Alberta Amateur Wrestling Association*, 22
Bradley, Tracy, *Canadian Orienteering Federation*, 447
Bradley, Jillian, *Inclusion BC*, 832
Bradley, Josie, *British Columbia Lupus Society*, 246
Bradley, Adam, *Canadian Society of Orthopaedic Technologists*, 485
Bradley, Michael, *Royal Astronomical Society of Canada*, 1239
Bradley, Jamie, *Alliance of Canadian Cinema, Television & Radio Artists*, 58
Bradley, Sandra, *American Council of Learned Societies*, 1492
Bradley, Kathy, *Special Libraries Association*, 1596
Bradley, Rinnie, *Prince Edward Island Cattle Producers*, 1173
Bradley, Nancy, *Jean Tweed Treatment Centre*, 869
Bradley, Francis, *Canadian Electricity Association*, 380
Bradley, Roger, *Saskatoon Civic Middle Management Association*, 1279
Bradley, David, *Bonavista Historic Townscape Foundation*, 217
Bradshaw, Janet, *Professional Engineers & Geoscientists Newfoundland & Labrador*, 1183
Bradshaw, Jim, *Sarnia Building Trades Council*, 1254
Bradshaw, Mike, *Northwest Territories Chamber of Commerce*, 1038
Bradstock, Christine, *Squash British Columbia*, 1347
Bradstreet, Michael, *The Nature Conservancy of Canada*, 999
Brady, Patrick, *National Pensioners Federation*, 995
Brady, Nancy, *Royal Canadian Naval Benevolent Fund*, 1241
Brady, Allyson, *Saskatchewan Environmental Society*, 1265
Brady, Tim, *Basketball Yukon*, 199
Brady, Mike, *Consulting Engineers of Newfoundland & Labrador*, 625

Brady Fields, Donna, *United Way of East Kootenay*, 1414
Braeuer, Frank, *Industrial Fabrics Association International Canada*, 835
Bragg, Lynn M., *Glass Packaging Institute*, 1528
Braham, Randolph L., *Rosenthal Institute for Holocaust Studies*, 1587
Braid, G.W. Wayne, *The Society of Notaries Public of British Columbia*, 1330
Braid, Virginia, *Manitoba Genealogical Society Inc.*, 937
Braid, Peter, *Insurance Brokers Association of Canada*, 848
Braid, Marianne, *Southeast Georgian Bay Chamber of Commerce*, 1337
Brain, Martin, *Ontario Podiatric Medical Association*, 1096
Braine, Bruce, *International Emissions Trading Association*, 1546
Braithwaite, Howard, *The Retired Teachers of Ontario*, 1228
Braithwaite, Tannis, *British Columbia Public Interest Advocacy Centre*, 250
Braithwaite, Tony, *PFLAG Canada Inc.*, 1156
Brake, Virginia, *Canadian Hard of Hearing Association*, 400
Brake, Angie, *Planned Parenthood - Newfoundland & Labrador Sexual Health Centre*, 1161
Braley, Scott, *Curl BC*, 646
Branch, Shawn C., *Threshold Ministries*, 1377
Branch, Mark, *Boys & Girls Clubs of Québec*, 224
Branch, Brian, *World Council of Credit Unions, Inc.*, 1604
Branch, Kate, *British Columbia Environment Industry Association*, 239
Branch, David E., *Canadian Hockey League*, 406
Branchaud, Alain, *Canadian Parks & Wilderness Society*, 451
Brand, Nancy, *Specialized Information Publishers Association*, 1596
Brandell, Curtis, *Canadian Hemophilia Society*, 404
Brandes, Linda, *Alberta Sheep Breeders Association*, 46
Brandly, Ken, *Kugluktuk Chamber of Commerce*, 894
Brandon, Stuart, *Professional Engineers Ontario*, 1184
Brandon, Josh, *Canadian Environmental Network*, 382
Brandsma, Bryan, *British Columbia Broiler Hatching Egg Producers' Association*, 234
Brandson, Grant, *Canadian Authors Association*, 338
Brandt, Christine, *Walkerton Business Improvement Area*, 1440
Brandt, Monique, *Association of Manitoba Museums*, 151
Brandt, Todd, *Tourism Saskatoon*, 1391
Brandt, Perry, *Nova Scotia Beekeepers' Association*, 1042
Branfireun, Brian, *Canadian Geophysical Union*, 397
Branigan, Michelle, *Electricity Human Resources Canada*, 683
Branton, Cathy, *Boys & Girls Clubs of Alberta*, 221
Brar, Ramandeep, *Field Hockey Ontario*, 734
Brascoupé, Simon, *AFOA Canada*, 12
Brasier, Steven, *Canadian Institute of Planners*, 418
Brassard, Pierre, *Fédération CSN - Construction (CSN)*, 708
Brassard, Matt, *Consulting Engineers of Alberta*, 625
Brasset, Andrea, *Canadian Centre on Substance Use & Addiction*, 354
Bratt, Alan, *Alliance of Canadian Cinema, Television & Radio Artists*, 58
Brattinga, Denise, *Alberta Milk*, 40
Brault, Paul, *Manitoba Liberal Party*, 939

Braun, Reiner, *International Peace Bureau*, 1555
Braun-Jackson, Jeff, *Ontario Professional Fire Fighters Association*, 1097
Braun-Janzen, Rick, *Abundance Canada*, 3
Braun-Pollon, Marilyn, *Canadian Federation of Independent Business*, 387
Braus, Judy, *North American Association for Environmental Education*, 1578
Brautigam, Karla, *Mount View Special Riding Association*, 976
Bray, Randeen, *Medicine Hat Real Estate Board Co-operative Ltd.*, 958
Bray, Tricia, *Canadian Association of Critical Care Nurses*, 312
Bray, Patrick, *Syndicat du personnel technique et professionnel de la Société des alcools du Québec (ind.)*, 1364
Bray, Francesca, *Society for the History of Technology*, 1591
Bray, Heather, *Dance Centre*, 649
Bray, Evan, *Saskatchewan Federation of Police Officers*, 1265
Brayton, Bonnie, *DisAbled Women's Network of Canada*, 658
Brazeau, Daniel, *Association des chefs en sécurité incendie du Québec*, 108
Brazill, James L., *Royal Canadian Artillery Association*, 1239
Breading, Mary, *International Institute for Conservation of Historic & Artistic Works*, 1551
Breadner, Mark, *FIRST Robotics Canada*, 739
Brealey, Chad, *Pacific Salmon Foundation*, 1136
Brears, Trent, *Canadian Culinary Federation*, 374
Breau, Barry, *Devon & District Chamber of Commerce*, 655
Breau, Samuel, *Théâtre la Catapulte*, 1374
Brebner, Lois-Anne, *Opimian Society*, 1116
Brebner, Judy, *Association of Teachers of English in Quebec*, 162
Breckles, Brian, *Junior Achievement Canada*, 877
Breda, Cathy, *Canadian Soccer Association*, 472
Breden, Erin, *Chartered Professionals in Human Resources of British Columbia & Yukon*, 554
Breen, David, *Canadian Association of Foodservice Professionals*, 315
Breen, Ed, *Newfoundland & Labrador Association of Optometrists*, 1016
Bregman, Leah, *Society for Ecological Restoration International*, 1590
Breher, Don, *Saskatchewan Graphic Arts Industries Association*, 1266
Breines, Ingeborg, *International Peace Bureau*, 1555
Breisch, Kenneth, *Society of Architectural Historians*, 1592
Brekke, Kris, *Canadian Parks & Wilderness Society*, 451
Bremault, Gerard, *Centre for Child Development*, 531
Bremner, Janet, *Lambton Wildlife Inc.*, 897
Bremner, Terry, *Chronic Pain Association of Canada*, 568
Brenda, Flaherty, *YMCA Canada*, 1471
Brenholen, Michael, *St. John Ambulance*, 1249
Brennan, Peter, *College of Family Physicians of Canada*, 585
Brennan, Michael, *AIDS Committee of Windsor*, 16
Brennan, Shirley, *Christmas Tree Farmers of Ontario*, 568
Brennan, Brian, *Food Allergy Canada*, 749
Brennan, Vince, *Ontario Association of Agricultural Societies*, 1061
Brennan, Bob, *Palliative Manitoba*, 1137
Brennan, Joe, *Potatoes New Brunswick*, 1168
Brennan, Anne, *LAMP Community Health Centre*, 897

Executive Name Index

Brennan, Jon, *Northwest Territories Tennis Association*, 1039
Brenneman, Anna, *Probation Officers Association of Ontario*, 1181
Brenneman, Laura-Lee, *CADORA Ontario Association Inc.*, 269
Brenton, Tammy, *Pharmacists' Association of Newfoundland & Labrador*, 1156
Brereton, Dave, *Youth for Christ Canada*, 1475
Brescia, Vince, *The Fair Rental Policy Organization of Ontario*, 701
Brescia, Vince, *Ontario Energy Association*, 1077
Bresky, Luke, *Canadian Association for American Studies*, 297
Bresolin, Stephen, *Foundation for Legal Research*, 756
Bretherick, Michelle, *Canadian Baton Twirling Federation*, 342
Breton, Joanne, *Chambre de Commerce et d'Industrie du Centre-Abitibi*, 547
Breton, Kathy, *Chambre de commerce et d'entrepreneuriat des Sources*, 545
Breton, Sylvie, *Association des personnes handicapées de Charlevoix inc.*, 122
Breton, Josée, *Ordre des infirmières et infirmiers du Québec*, 1122
Breton, Jennifer, *College of Licensed Practical Nurses of Manitoba*, 585
Breton, Jean, *Société historique de Charlesbourg*, 1319
Breton, Loïc, *Canadian Office & Professional Employees Union*, 444
Breton, Bruno-Gil, *Association des professionnels en santé du travail*, 126
Brett, Lori, *Skate Canada*, 1301
Brewer, Monica, *New Brunswick Lung Association*, 1010
Brewer, Nicole, *The League of Canadian Poets*, 903
Brewer, Angelia, *Acclaim Health*, 5
Brewin, Dave, *Volleyball BC*, 1437
Brewster, John, *Statistical Society of Canada*, 1348
Brewster, Cara, *Saskatchewan Association of Licensed Practical Nurses*, 1257
Brewster, Pepper, *British Columbia Aboriginal Child Care Society*, 229
Brezeanu, Olivia, *Windsor Women Working with Immigrant Women*, 1457
Briand, Jennifer, *Caregivers Nova Scotia*, 512
Briard, Ernie, *Financial Executives International Canada*, 736
Bricks, Shari, *Association for Operations Management*, 134
Bricks, Shari, *Ontario Society of Periodontists*, 1107
Brideau, Chantal, *Association Museums New Brunswick*, 138
Bridges, Kerri, *YMCA Canada*, 1471
Bridges, Trevor, *Prince Edward Island School Athletic Association*, 1177
Brien, Guillaume, *Confédération québécoise des coopératives d'habitation*, 611
Brien, Danielle, *Fondation pour enfants diabétiques*, 747
Brière, Robert, *Chambre immobilière de l'Abitibi-Témiscamingue Inc.*, 550
Brierley, Ted, *International Confederation of Principals*, 1544
Briggs, Fred, *Society of Canadian Cine Amateurs*, 1327
Briggs, Don, *Canadian Celiac Association*, 352
Briggs, Darby, *Saskatchewan Wildlife Federation*, 1278
Briggs, Helen, *Canadian Society of Hospital Pharmacists*, 484
Briggs, Les, *American Sociological Association*, 1503
Briggs, Gary, *Osgoode Twp. Historical Society*, 1127
Briggs, David, *Albert County Chamber of Commerce*, 21
Briggs, Darrell, *Canadian Race Communications Association*, 464

Briggs, Jim, *Canadian Vintage Motorcycle Group*, 501
Bright, Buck, *Kipling Chamber of Commerce*, 890
Brigitzer, Kim, *Alberta Amateur Baseball Council*, 22
Briglio, Grace, *Ontario Lung Association*, 1090
Brillant, Sean, *Fencing Association of Nova Scotia*, 732
Brillant, Madeleine, *Co-operatives & Mutuals Canada*, 628
Brimacombe, Glenn, *Canadian Psychiatric Association*, 461
Brimicombe, Elaine, *Ottawa Valley Curling Association*, 1132
Brimley, C. Charlie, *Canadian Association for Laboratory Accreditation Inc.*, 301
Brimmer, Esther, *NAFSA: Association of International Educators*, 1572
Brimner, Kim, *Historic Vehicle Society of Ontario*, 815
Brinch, Jens, *Arctic Winter Games International Committee*, 81
Brinckman, Nicholas, *reBOOT Canada*, 1206
Brinder, Joni, *Canadian Celiac Association*, 353
Bringolf, Brian J.H., *Starlight Children's Foundation Canada*, 1348
Bringolf, Brian J.H., *Starlight Children's Foundation Canada*, 1348
Brink, Johann, *Canadian Academy of Psychiatry & the Law*, 286
Brinker, Bonnie, *Alberta Baton Twirling Association*, 25
Brinkman, Anne, *Kidney Foundation of Canada*, 886
Brinston Levandier, Tara, *Canadian Association for Community Living*, 298
Brinston-Kurschat, Gillian, *Parkland Music Festival*, 1142
Brintnell, E. Sharon, *World Federation of Occupational Therapists*, 1605
Brinton, Jeff, *Alberta Foundation for the Arts*, 36
Brisbin, Dan, *Cross Country Saskatchewan*, 644
Briscoe, Paul, *Society of Motion Picture & Television Engineers*, 1593
Brisebois, Diane J., *Retail Council of Canada*, 1228
Brisebois, Andre, *Children's Safety Association of Canada*, 562
Briskin, David, *National Ballet of Canada*, 991
Brissett, Tannis, *Canadian Mortgage Brokers Association*, 437
Brisson, Anne, *Canadian Liver Foundation*, 427
Brisson, Richard, *Fédération des professionnelles et professionnels de l'éducation du Québec*, 715
Brisson, Monique, *Office municipal d'habitation de Longueuil*, 1055
Brisson, Marie-France, *Association des denturologistes du Québec*, 110
Brisson, Nancy, *Réseau québécois des OSBL d'habitation*, 1225
Bristow, Ryan, *Canadian Institute of Plumbing & Heating*, 418
Brittain, Sandy, *Canada DanceSport*, 278
Brittain, Gord, *Ontario DanceSport*, 1076
Brittin, Andrea, *Ranch Ehrlo Society*, 1204
Britton, Gordon, *Association de Ringuette Repentigny*, 104
Brizi, Rosy, *Thunder Bay Community Foundation*, 1377
Briño, Karina, *Mining Association of British Columbia*, 967
Broad, Michael, *Shipping Federation of Canada*, 1296
Broad, Stefanie, *Wildlife Rescue Association of British Columbia*, 1455
Broad, Robert, *Edmonton Zone Medical Staff Association*, 680
Broadfield, Larry, *Cancer Advocacy Coalition of Canada*, 507

Broadhurst, Debora, *British Columbia Art Therapy Association*, 230
Broadway, Brett, *Insurance Brokers Association of Canada*, 848
Broadway, Michael, *Association for Canadian Studies in the United States*, 1507
Brobyn, Arlette, *Brampton Caledon Community Living*, 226
Brochu, Rose, *Alzheimer Society London & Middlesex*, 61
Brochu, Isabelle, *Réseau des SADC et CAE*, 1219
Brock, Mark, *Canada Grains Council*, 279
Brock, Kathy, *Canadian Association of Programs in Public Administration*, 329
Brockhoff, Joan, *Strome & District Historical Society*, 1352
Brockington, Simon, *International Whaling Commission*, 1566
Brocklebank, John, *College of Veterinarians of British Columbia*, 590
Brocklebank, Andrea, *Beef Cattle Research Council*, 204
Brockway, Ken, *Windsor Association for the Deaf*, 1456
Broda, Yuri, *Ukrainian Youth Association of Canada*, 1404
Broddy, Kenzie, *Princess Margaret Cancer Foundation*, 1180
Broderick, Bill, *Canadian Council of Professional Fish Harvesters*, 369
Brodeur, Stéphanie, *Chambre de commerce et d'industrie de la Rive-Sud*, 545
Brodeur, Karen, *Cooperative Housing Federation of Canada*, 628
Brodeur, Micheline, *Editors' Association of Canada*, 674
Brodeur, Patrice, *Société québécoise pour l'étude de la religion*, 1324
Brodeur, Pascal, *Association québécoise des traumatisés craniens*, 175
Brodeur, Pascal, *Regroupement des associations de personnes traumatisées craniocérébrales du Québec*, 1214
Brodhead, Mary, *Institute for Performance & Learning*, 844
Brodie, Brian, *Canadian Medical Association*, 433
Broekaert, José A.C., *International Association of Environmental Analytical Chemistry*, 1538
Broerse, Nancy, *The Canadian Federation of Business & Professional Women's Clubs*, 385
Brogly, John, *Canada's Oil Sands Innovation Alliance*, 282
Brokaw, Susan, *North American Society of Adlerian Psychology*, 1579
Bromberg, Anita, *Canadian Race Relations Foundation*, 464
Bromley, Ralph, *Hope for the Nations*, 821
Bronfman, Brian, *Brian Bronfman Family Foundation*, 228
Brong, Sandra, *Saskatchewan Abilities Council*, 1255
Bronk, Bob, *Sign Association of Canada*, 1298
Brook, Andrew, *Canadian Psychoanalytic Society*, 461
Brooker, Vicki, *Elk Point Chamber of Commerce*, 685
Brooks, Paul, *Delta Community Living Society*, 653
Brooks, Karen, *Canadian Celiac Association*, 352
Brooks, Michael, *Real Property Association of Canada*, 1206
Brooks, Joan, *GRAND Society*, 780
Brooks, Perry, *Sign Association of Canada*, 1298
Brooks, Yolanda, *Wildlife Rescue Association of British Columbia*, 1455
Brooks, Jake, *Association of Power Producers of Ontario*, 156
Brooks, David, *Canadian Friends of Peace Now (Shalom Achshav)*, 395
Brooks, Donna, *YWCA Canada*, 1481

Brooks, Dan, *Habitat for Humanity Canada*, 796
Brooks Kirkland, Anita, *Canadian School Libraries*, 468
Brooks-Joiner, Carrie, *Tourism Hamilton*, 1389
Broome, Barb, *East Prince Youth Development Centre*, 668
Brophey, Brian, *Ontario Professional Planners Institute*, 1098
Brophy, Wendy, *AiMHi, Prince George Association for Community Living*, 19
Brophy, Michael, *Brewing & Malting Barley Research Institute*, 228
Brophy, Michael, *Association for Canadian Studies in Ireland*, 1507
Brophy, Tracey, *Start2Finish*, 1348
Bross, Audrey, *Human Resources Professionals Association*, 825
Brossard, Helen, *Fédération de gymnastique du Québec*, 708
Brossard-Ménard, Xavier, *Société chorale de Saint-Lambert*, 1309
Brossart, Bonnie, *Saskatchewan Medical Association*, 1270
Brosseau, Julie, *Association québécoise des salons du livre*, 174
Brosseau, Julie, *Association québécoise des salons du livre*, 174
Brosseau, Ghislaine, *Ordre professionnel des travailleurs sociaux du Québec*, 1125
Brosseau, Nancy, *Fédération des établissements d'enseignement privés*, 715
Brosseau, Denise, *Ordre des infirmières et infirmiers du Québec*, 1122
Brosseau, Pascale, *Centre d'aide et de lutte contre les agressions à caractère sexuel de la Rive-Sud*, 527
Broten, Cam, *Saskatchewan Egg Producers*, 1264
Brothers, George, *Peace River & District Chamber of Commerce*, 1147
Brothers, Hal, *Association of Consulting Engineering Companies - Prince Edward Island*, 146
Brothwell, Annie, *Victoria Therapeutic Riding Association*, 1434
Brotman, Yael, *Canadian Artists Representation*, 295
Brott, Boris, *McGill Chamber Orchestra*, 955
Brott, Boris, *National Academy Orchestra*, 989
Broué, Gilles, *Mouvement national des québécoises et québécois*, 977
Broughton, Jean, *Canadian Media Guild*, 432
Brouillard, Chantal, *Badminton Québec*, 194
Brouillette, Ghislaine, *Société d'histoire St-Stanislas inc.*, 1314
Brouillette, Lynn, *Association des universités de la francophonie canadienne*, 130
Brouillette, Carl, *Association des professionnels en santé du travail*, 126
Brousseau, Sylvie, *Union des artistes*, 1406
Brousseau, Tara, *Mood Disorders Association of Manitoba*, 973
Brousseau, Serge, *Organisme d'autoréglementation du courtage immobilier du Québec*, 1125
Browett, Bill, *Science for Peace*, 1285
Brown, Ron, *Whitecourt Fish & Game Association*, 1452
Brown, George, *Ballon sur glace Broomball Canada*, 195
Brown, Brian E., *Windsor University Faculty Association*, 1457
Brown, Jason, *Thompson Rivers University Faculty Association*, 1376
Brown, Rhonda, *Big Brothers Big Sisters of British Columbia*, 209
Brown, Auna-Marie, *Big Brothers Big Sisters of Manitoba*, 209
Brown, Philip, *Credit Canada Debt Solutions, Inc.*, 639
Brown, Leanne, *Children's Wish Foundation of Canada*, 563

Executive Name Index

Brown, David G., *Vancouver Musicians' Association*, 1427
Brown, Nancy, *Community Living Campbellford/Brighton*, 601
Brown, Maureen, *Community Living Fort Erie*, 602
Brown, Greg, *Burns Lake & District Chamber of Commerce*, 266
Brown, Patricia, *Grand Manan Tourism Association & Chamber of Commerce*, 780
Brown, Doug W., *Burlington Association for Nuclear Disarmament*, 265
Brown, Glenn, *College of Family Physicians of Canada*, 585
Brown, Joanne, *Ontario School Counsellors' Association*, 1103
Brown, Robert, *Artists in Stained Glass*, 85
Brown, Michael, *Rugby Ontario*, 1244
Brown, Dana, *Tennis New Brunswick*, 1371
Brown, Colin, *Engineers Canada*, 689
Brown, Debra, *Canadian 4-H Council*, 284
Brown, Melinda, *Council of Ontario Construction Associations*, 634
Brown, Vicki, *Canadian Association for Young Children*, 307
Brown, Nicolas, *Canadian University Press*, 499
Brown, Barbara, *Ontario Federation of Independent Schools*, 1079
Brown, Peter, *The Fraser Institute*, 757
Brown, Debbie, *Heart & Stroke Foundation of Manitoba*, 808
Brown, Robert, *Hong Kong-Canada Business Association*, 820
Brown, Brian, *Canadian Maine-Anjou Association*, 429
Brown, Alan, *EastGen*, 671
Brown, Anne, *International Symphony Orchestra of Sarnia, Ontario & Port Huron, Michigan*, 861
Brown, Anne, *International Symphony Orchestra Youth String Ensemble*, 861
Brown, Colin T., *The National Citizens Coalition*, 991
Brown, Dennis, *Northwestern Ontario Municipal Association*, 1039
Brown, Danielle, *K3C Community Counselling Centres*, 879
Brown, Jennifer, *Society of Composers, Authors & Music Publishers of Canada*, 1328
Brown, Janiece, *Risk & Insurance Management Society Inc.*, 1234
Brown, Dave, *United Way of Sarnia-Lambton*, 1416
Brown, Jason, *YMCA Canada*, 1472
Brown, Barry, *John Milton Society for the Blind in Canada*, 875
Brown, Julie, *Canadian Board for Respiratory Care Inc.*, 345
Brown, David, *Gymnastics Nova Scotia*, 795
Brown, Sara, *Northwest Territories Association of Communities*, 1037
Brown, Linda, *Alzheimer Society of North Bay & District*, 64
Brown, Barry, *Utility Contractors Association of Ontario, Inc.*, 1423
Brown, Charlene, *Manitoba Arts Council*, 929
Brown, Loraine, *National Advertising Benevolent Society*, 989
Brown, Joanna, *New Brunswick Environmental Network*, 1008
Brown, Dawn, *Prince Edward Island Karate Association*, 1175
Brown, Lloyd O., *Alzheimer Society of Nova Scotia*, 64
Brown, Mary, *Colchester-East Hants Public Library Foundation*, 580
Brown, Karen, *South Shuswap Chamber of Commerce*, 1336
Brown, Iesha, *Soroptimist International of the Americas*, 1595
Brown, Paul J., *Sandbox Project*, 1253
Brown, Lesley, *Essential Skills Ontario*, 696
Brown, Marianne, *Glanbrook Heritage Society*, 774

Brown, Lyn, *Spinal Cord Injury Saskatchewan*, 1344
Brown, Darlene, *Union of Canadian Transportation Employees*, 1407
Brown, Adalsteinn (Steini), *Canadian Association for Health Services & Policy Research*, 301
Brown, Richard, *World Federation of Chiropractic*, 1466
Brown, Aaron, *Habitat for Humanity Canada*, 797
Brown, Joyce, *Ontario Council of Alternative Businesses*, 1075
Brown, Betty, *The North Cumberland Historical Society*, 1030
Brown, Emilie, *Brantwood Foundation*, 227
Brown, Yvonne, *Durham Deaf Services*, 665
Brown, Mike, *Registered Professional Foresters Association of Nova Scotia*, 1214
Brown, David Grainger, *Edmonton Classical Guitar Society*, 676
Brown, Amanda, *Ontario Agencies Supporting Individuals with Special Needs*, 1059
Brown, Catherine, *Ontario Association of Community Care Access Centres*, 1063
Brown, Heather, *Toronto Cat Rescue*, 1383
Brown, Eric, *British Columbia Wall & Ceiling Association*, 257
Brown, Steven, *PFLAG Canada Inc.*, 1155
Brown, Ron, *Boys & Girls Clubs of Manitoba*, 222
Brown, Glen, *Prisoners' HIV/AIDS Support Action Network*, 1180
Brown, Heather W., *National Association of College Auxiliary Services*, 1573
Brown, Suzanne, *English Speaking Catholic Council*, 689
Brown, Stephanie, *Canadian Coalition for Farm Animals*, 357
Brown, Bess, *Coastal First Nations*, 579
Browne, Steve, *Denturist Association of Newfoundland & Labrador*, 654
Browne, Jennifer, *Contact Point*, 626
Brownell, Lynn, *Workplace Safety & Prevention Services*, 1465
Brownell, Norm, *Alberta Foster Parent Association*, 35
Browning, Kate, *Ontario Nonprofit Network*, 1094
Brownlee, Rick, *Manitoba Sports Hall of Fame & Museum*, 945
Brownoff, Larry, *Goodwill Industries of Alberta*, 778
Brownridge, Murray, *SHARE Agriculture Foundation*, 1294
Brownrigg, Helen, *Big Brothers Big Sisters of British Columbia*, 209
Brownrigg, Shannon, *Registered Veterinary Technologists & Technicians of Canada*, 1214
Browton, Chris, *Skills/Compétences Canada*, 1303
Bru, Carrie, *Canadian Association of Medical Radiation Technologists*, 320
Brubacher, Kevin, *Ontario Potato Board*, 1097
Brubaker, Elizabeth, *Energy Probe Research Foundation*, 688
Bruce, Terri, *Information Niagara*, 837
Bruce, Barbara, *Alberta Association of Architects*, 23
Bruce, Harry W., *American Society for Information Science & Technology*, 1498
Bruce, Robert, *Association of Mature Canadians*, 151
Bruce, Leslie, *Banff & Lake Louise Tourism*, 195
Bruce, Shirliana, *Speed Skate PEI*, 1341
Bruce, Katelyn, *Women Entrepreneurs of Saskatchewan Inc.*, 1460
Bruce, James, *Halifax Citadel Regimental Association*, 799
Bruce, Toby, *Grey Bruce Beekeepers' Association*, 790
Bruce-Kavanagh, Kathy, *Alberta Funeral Services Regulatory Board*, 36

Bruckhardt, Marlene, *Historical Society of St. Boniface & Maryhill Community*, 816
Bruder, Kerry, *Diabetes Canada*, 655
Bruderer, Jenna, *Manitoba Association of Medical Radiation Technologists*, 930
Bruehl, Christoph, *Printing & Graphics Industries Association of Alberta*, 1180
Bruins, Marcel, *International Seed Federation*, 1556
Brûlé, Lori, *Chartered Professionals in Human Resources Manitoba*, 554
Brun, Christian, *Maritime Fishermen's Union (CLC)*, 950
Brune, Michael, *Sierra Club*, 1589
Bruneau, Annette, *Alberta 5 Pin Bowlers' Association*, 21
Bruneau, Anne, *Canadian Botanical Association*, 346
Bruneau, Anne, *Institut de recherche en biologie végétale*, 842
Bruneau, Robert, *St. Pierre Chamber of Commerce*, 1251
Bruneau, Annette, *Bowling Federation of Alberta*, 219
Brunelle, Jacques, *Epilepsy Canada*, 693
Brunelle, Denis, *Canadian Federal Pilots Association*, 384
Brunelle, Steve, *Réseau des SADC et CAE*, 1221
Bruner, Lori, *Brant Skills Centre*, 226
Brunet, Bob, *Canadian Roofing Contractors' Association*, 468
Brunet, Louis, *Canadian Psychoanalytic Society*, 461
Brunet, Sylvie, *Association pour aînés résidant à Laval*, 165
Brunet-Colvey, Jennifer, *Canadian Ophthalmological Society*, 446
Brunet-Lusignan, Sylvie, *Association des services de réhabilitation sociale du Québec inc.*, 128
Brunette, Jennifer, *Alberta Cattle Feeders' Association*, 27
Brunnen, Ben, *Canadian Association of Petroleum Producers*, 326
Brushett, Bill, *Family Enterprise Xchange*, 703
Brushey, David, *Muskoka Community Futures Development Corporation*, 985
Brusse, Sara, *West Coast Amateur Musicians' Society*, 1444
Brutesco, Giulia, *Fertilizer Safety & Security Council*, 733
Bruynooghe, Donna, *Saskatchewan Katahdin Sheep Association Inc.*, 1268
Bryan, Mike, *Canadian Antique Phonograph Society*, 294
Bryans, Dave, *Ontario Convenience Store Association*, 1074
Bryant, Deb, *Association of Neighbourhood Houses BC*, 153
Bryant, Michael, *Canadian Civil Liberties Association*, 357
Bryant, Lea Ann, *British Columbia Federation of Foster Parent Associations*, 240
Bryant, Michael, *Public Accountants Council for the Province of Ontario*, 1192
Bryant, Don, *Environmental Managers Association of British Columbia*, 692
Bryant, Joanne, *Ontario Canoe Kayak Sprint Racing Affiliation*, 1070
Bryce, Jessica, *Canadian Federation of Medical Students*, 388
Bryce, Bill, *The Friends of West Kootenay Parks Society*, 763
Bryden, Lea, *Medical Society of Prince Edward Island*, 958
Bryden, J. Douglas, *Muskoka Ratepayers' Association*, 985
Brydon, Agnes, *The Royal Scottish Country Dance Society*, 1587
Bu, Bill, *Hong Kong-Canada Business Association*, 820
Buahene, Abena, *College of Dentursts of Ontario*, 584

Bublitz, Krissy, *British Columbia Library Association Library Technicians' & Assistants' Section*, 245
Bucci, Anna, *Alliance of Canadian Cinema, Television & Radio Artists*, 58
Bucci, Anna, *Canadian Private Copying Collective*, 460
Bucciarelli, Angelo, *Canadian Security Association*, 469
Buchan, Tom, *Slo-Pitch Ontario Association*, 1304
Buchanan, Bev, *CARP*, 514
Buchanan, Jonathan, *Association for Mineral Exploration British Columbia*, 134
Buchanan, Christine, *Open Door Group*, 1114
Buchanan, James, *Tarragon Theatre*, 1367
Buchanan, Martin, *Professional Engineers for Public Safety Association*, 1183
Buchanan, Linda, *Back Country Horsemen of British Columbia*, 193
Buchel, Tamara, *College of Family Physicians of Canada*, 584
Buchert, Lavern, *Wetaskiwin & District Association for Community Service*, 1451
Buck, Alexander, *International Union of Forest Research Organizations*, 1564
Buck, William D., *Association of Ontario Land Surveyors*, 155
Buckingham, Clayton, *CAA British Columbia*, 267
Buckingham, Jackie, *Synchro Canada*, 1360
Buckle, Susan, *Saskatchewan Automobile Dealers Association*, 1259
Buckle, Robert, *ICOMOS Canada*, 829
Buckle, Tim, *Royal Newfoundland Constabulary Association*, 1242
Buckler, Shelley, *Calgary Law Library Group*, 273
Buckley, Joyce, *Miramichi Chamber of Commerce*, 968
Buckley, Kristen, *Tobermory & District Chamber of Commerce*, 1380
Buckley, Jane, *Oromocto & Surrounding Area Food & Clothing Bank*, 1127
Buckley, Valdene, *Manitoba Professional Planners Institute*, 942
Buckley, Noel, *Ottawa Tourism*, 1132
Buckley, Chris, *Ontario Federation of Labour*, 1079
Buckley, Kristen, *InformCanada*, 838
Buckley, Margo, *Association of Fundraising Professionals*, 1512
Bucksbaum, Caroline, *Governance Professionals of Canada*, 778
Buckway, Bev, *Association of Yukon Communities*, 164
Buckway, Bev, *Yukon Agricultural Association*, 1477
Buckwold, Tamara, *Legal Education Society of Alberta*, 906
Budd, Bruce, *Transport Action Canada*, 1395
Budden, Gerald, *Grand Orange Lodge of Canada*, 780
Budden, Florence, *Canadian Federation of Mental Health Nurses*, 388
Budeisky, Alberto, *Pan American Hockey Federation*, 1138
Budero, Peter, *South Lake Community Futures Development Corporation*, 1335
Budhoo, Garvin, *Manitoba Cricket Association*, 935
Budilean, Carmen, *Green Party of New Brunswick*, 789
Budrevics, Aina, *Ontario Association of Landscape Architects*, 1064
Bueché, Will, *John E. Mack Institute*, 1568
Bueckert, Jayson, *Christian Labour Association of Canada*, 568
Buell, Bryan, *College & Association of Respiratory Therapists of Alberta*, 581
Buell, Stan I., *Small Investor Protection Association*, 1304
Buensuceso, Mike, *Canadian-Filipino Association of Yukon*, 506

Buettner, Richard, *University of Regina Faculty Association*, 1420
Buettner, Adam, *Canadian Society of Respiratory Therapists*, 487
Buffenbarger, R. Thomas, *International Association of Machinists & Aerospace Workers*, 1539
Bugayong, Kristine, *Red Deer & District Community Foundation*, 1209
Bugbee, Robert, *Lutheran Church - Canada*, 922
Bugg, Angie, *Saskatchewan Environmental Society*, 1265
Bugg, Grace, *Toronto Curling Association*, 1383
Buhl, Fabienne, *Coalition des femmes de l'Alberta*, 578
Buhler, Diane, *Parent Action on Drugs*, 1139
Buhler, Jackie, *Wycliffe Bible Translators of Canada, Inc.*, 1470
Buijs, Adriaan, *Canadian Nuclear Society*, 442
Buis, Mike, *Kent County Cattlemen's Association*, 884
Buis, Mike, *Beef Improvement Ontario*, 204
Buisson, Isabelle, *Insitut canadien des économistes en construction - Québec*, 840
Bujea, John, *Romanian Orthodox Deanery of Canada*, 1235
Bujold, Christine, *Association de la construction du Québec*, 100
Bujold, Robert, *Les Vieux Brachés de Longueuil*, 1434
Bujold, Mario, *Conseil québécois sur le tabac et la santé*, 620
Bujold, Monette, *Conseil régional de l'environnement de la Gaspésie et des Îles-de-la-Madeleine*, 620
Bukhari, Rukhsana, *Canadian Psychoanalytic Society*, 461
Bukowski, Brent, *Langham Cultural Society*, 898
Buksa, Jewel, *Canadian College of Health Leaders*, 359
Bulik, Jerzy, *Association of Polish Engineers in Canada*, 156
Bulko, Kathryn, *Municipal Information Systems Association of Canada*, 981
Bull, Natalie, *National Trust for Canada*, 996
Bull, Linda, *Nova Scotia Youth Orchestra*, 1050
Bullas, Michelle, *Women's Legal Education & Action Fund*, 1463
Bullock, Greg, *Ontario Ground Water Association*, 1083
Bullock, Dale, *Wilberforce Project*, 1453
Bullock, Carol, *The Change Foundation*, 551
Bullock, Naomi, *Open Door Group*, 1114
Bullock, François, *Association de loisirs pour personnes handicapées psychiques de Laval*, 102
Bullough, Vaughn, *Manitoba Environmental Industries Association Inc.*, 936
Bulluck, Corbi, *The Ninety-Nines Inc.*, 1578
Bultheel, Suzanne, *International Association for Educational & Vocational Guidance*, 853
Bulthuis, Peter, *World Renew*, 1467
Bun-Lebert, Maly, *Centre for Research on Violence Against Women & Children*, 533
Bunch, Michelle, *NAIMA Canada*, 987
Bunde, Monica, *Amherstburg Chamber of Commerce*, 67
Bunge, Steffen, *Pinawa Chamber of Commerce*, 1160
Bunt, Darron, *Alberta Soccer Association*, 47
Bunting, Christopher, *Canadian Foundation for AIDS Research*, 393
Buonpensiere, Rosanna, *Manitoba Cardiac Institute (Reh-Fit) Inc.*, 933
Buott, Kyle, *Nova Scotia Federation of Labour*, 1044
Bur, Justin, *Transport Action Canada*, 1395
Burak, Rob, *Canadian Precast / Prestressed Concrete Institute*, 459
Burak, Kelly, *Canadian Association for the Study of the Liver*, 306

Burawoy, Michel, *International Sociological Association*, 1561
Burbank, Bruce, *Children's Aid Society of Oxford County*, 561
Burbano, Raul, *Centre for Spanish Speaking Peoples*, 534
Burbridge, Erin, *Clean Nova Scotia Foundation*, 573
Burch, Jeff, *Folk Arts Council of St Catharines*, 742
Burch, Lorraine, *Canadian Association for Disabled Skiing - Nova Scotia*, 300
Burch, Lorraine, *Freestyle Ski Nova Scotia*, 759
Burchill, Avicia, *International Continence Society*, 1544
Burd, Robert, *Licensed Paralegals Association (Ontario)*, 910
Burden, Kim, *Parksville & District Chamber of Commerce*, 1142
Bureau, Mélanie, *Canadian Arts Presenting Association*, 296
Bureau, France, *La Mine d'Or, entreprise d'insertion sociale*, 966
Bureau, Pierre, *Club d'astronomie Quasar de Chibougamau*, 574
Bureau, Jean-René, *Association des résidents du Lac Renaud*, 127
Burford, Jay, *Toronto Users Group for Power Systems*, 1388
Burg, Ronald G., *American Concrete Institute*, 1491
Burgaretta, Mary, *British Columbia Aboriginal Child Care Society*, 229
Burger, Mike, *Community Counselling & Resource Centre*, 596
Burgess, Colleen, *Canadian Association of Professional Academic Librarians*, 328
Burgess, Gerry, *West Coast Railway Association*, 1445
Burgess, Mike, *Canadian Marine Pilots' Association*, 430
Burgess, John, *Minto Chamber of Commerce*, 968
Burgess, Nicole, *Supply Chain Management Association - Saskatchewan*, 1356
Burgin, Diane, *Toronto Vegetarian Association*, 1388
Burgsma, Hugh, *Ontario Home Builders' Association*, 1085
Burhenne, Wolfgang E., *International Council of Environmental Law*, 1545
Burhoe, John, *Prince Edward Island Beekeepers' Cooperative Association*, 1172
Burich, Shelly, *Canadian Public Relations Society Inc.*, 463
Burima, Kenna, *Calgary Horticultural Society*, 272
Burk, Allan, *Kent County Stamp Club*, 884
Burk, Robert, *International Papillomavirus Society*, 1555
Burkart, Garry, *Saskatchewan Joint Board Retail, Wholesale & Department Store Union*, 1268
Burke, Carol, *Canadian Condominium Institute*, 362
Burke, Reid, *Canadian Mental Health Association*, 435
Burke, David, *Sarnia-Lambton Real Estate Board*, 1254
Burke, Tony, *British Columbia Professional Fire Fighters' Burn Fund*, 249
Burke, Tracey, *YWCA Canada*, 1481
Burke, Cathy, *Canadian Association of Certified Planning Technicians*, 310
Burke, Sarah, *Habitat for Humanity Canada*, 797
Burke, Jodie, *Newfoundland & Labrador Association of the Deaf*, 1017
Burke, Peter, *Accessible Media Inc.*, 5
Burke, Phylicia, *Québec Board of Black Educators*, 1196
Burke-Perry, Rosemary, *College of Family Physicians of Canada*, 585

Burkey, Leona, *Brain Injury Association of Nova Scotia*, 225
Burkholder, Crystal, *American Foundry Society*, 1493
Burky, Ron, *Canadian Paraplegic Association (Manitoba)*, 450
Burleson, Jessica, *Professional Association of Residents & Interns of Manitoba*, 1182
Burley, Brittany, *United Way of Haldimand-Norfolk*, 1414
Burley, Dave, *Canada - Newfoundland & Labrador Offshore Petroleum Board*, 277
Burman, Lyndsay, *Chemical Institute of Canada*, 556
Burnell, Tom, *British Columbia Career Development Association*, 235
Burnell, Tom, *Open Door Group*, 1114
Burneo, Jorge, *Canadian League Against Epilepsy*, 426
Burnett, Medda, *Church Library Association of Ontario*, 569
Burnett, Matt, *The Green Party of Alberta*, 788
Burnett, Wyatt, *Saskatchewan Institute of Agrologists*, 1268
Burnett, Mary, *Alzheimer Society of Brant*, 62
Burnett, Mary, *Alzheimer Society of Hamilton Halton*, 62
Burnett, Mary, *Alzheimer Society of Haldimand Norfolk*, 62
Burnett, Beryl, *Embroiderers' Association of Canada, Inc.*, 685
Burnett, Heather, *Starlight Children's Foundation Canada*, 1348
Burnham, John, *College of Alberta Denturists*, 582
Burnham, Philip, *International African Institute*, 1535
Burns, Sandra, *Alberta Shorthand Reporters Association*, 46
Burns, Jeremy, *Alberta Speleological Society*, 48
Burns, Maggy, *Ecology Action Centre*, 672
Burns, Andrew, *Tillsonburg District Chamber of Commerce*, 1379
Burns, Daniel, *World Council of Credit Unions, Inc.*, 1604
Burns, Dennis, *Canadian Council of Snowmobile Organizations*, 370
Burns, Ian, *Alberta Real Estate Association*, 43
Burns, Conor, *Canadian Society for the History & Philosophy of Science*, 477
Burns, Paul, *Canadian Gaming Association*, 396
Burns, Bridget, *Women's Environment & Development Organization*, 1602
Burns, Susan, *Mid-Toronto Community Services*, 965
Burns, Sarah, *Canada Green Building Council*, 279
Burns, Lynn, *Pro Bono Law Ontario*, 1181
Burns, Howard, *Calgary Police Association*, 274
Burns Naas, Leigh Ann, *Society of Toxicology*, 1594
Burpee, Jane, *Manitoba Schizophrenia Society, Inc.*, 944
Burpee, Terry, *New Brunswick Ground Water Association*, 1009
Burpee, Rick, *The Canadian Addison Society*, 288
Burr, Tracy, *American Academy for Cerebral Palsy & Developmental Medicine*, 1487
Burrell, Carol Ann, *Canadian Institute of Food Science & Technology*, 415
Burrell, Danny, *Natural Gas Employees' Association*, 998
Burret, Wayne, *Roller Sports Canada*, 1235
Burridge, Christina, *British Columbia Seafood Alliance*, 253
Burrill, Gary, *New Democratic Party*, 1014
Burrill, Adrian, *The Guild Society*, 794
Burrow, Sharan, *International Trade Union Confederation*, 1563
Burrows, Bruce, *Chamber of Marine Commerce*, 539

Burrows, Holly-Ann, *British Columbia Recreation & Parks Association*, 250
Burrows, Will, *Coast Waste Management Association*, 579
Burrows, Colin, *World Small Animal Veterinary Association*, 1467
Burry, Dean, *Canadian Children's Opera Company*, 356
Burry, Michael, *Spinal Cord Injury Newfoundland & Labrador*, 1343
Bursey, Alistair, *Canadian Pharmacists Association*, 454
Bursey, Tom, *Council of Canadian Academies*, 633
Burt, Helene, *Toronto Art Therapy Institute*, 1381
Burt, Bryan, *Island Technology Professionals*, 865
Burt, Murray, *The Royal Commonwealth Society of Canada*, 1242
Burt, Earl, *Ontario Secondary School Teachers' Federation*, 1103
Burton, Craig, *Pentecostal Assemblies of Canada*, 1150
Burton, Gregory, *Halton Mississauga Youth Orchestra*, 800
Burton, Barb, *Seniors Association of Greater Edmonton*, 1290
Burton, Sandi, *Operating Room Nurses of Alberta Association*, 1115
Burton, Ken, *Vancouver Maritime Museum*, 1427
Burton, Odele, *Canadian Institute of Financial Planners*, 415
Burton, Kevin, *First Nations SchoolNet*, 739
Burton, Marion, *Peterborough & District Labour Council*, 1153
Buruma, Bruce, *Canadian Association of Communicators in Education*, 311
Burwash, Jordan, *Physical & Health Education Canada*, 1158
Burwash, Karen, *Family Mediation Manitoba*, 704
Bury, Tracy, *World Confederation for Physical Therapy*, 1604
Bury, Greg, *Gas Processing Association Canada*, 767
Buscemi, Georges, *Association des parents catholiques du Québec*, 122
Busch, Lynda, *Ontario Home Builders' Association*, 1085
Busch, Lennard, *First Nations Chiefs of Police Association*, 738
Busenius, Marvin, *Canadian Bible Society*, 343
Busenius, Marvin, *Canadian Bible Society*, 343
Buset, Alexis, *Young People's Theatre*, 1475
Bush, Karen, *Society of Christian Schools in British Columbia*, 1328
Bush, Geoffrey, *Hong Kong-Canada Business Association*, 820
Bushewsky, Darlene, *Na'amat Canada Inc.*, 987
Bushfield, Janice, *Cerebral Palsy Association in Alberta*, 537
Busi, Riccardo, *Fédération Internationale de l'Art Photographique*, 1525
Buske, Lynda, *Canadian Post-MD Education Registry*, 458
Buskirk, Amy, *Donner Canadian Foundation*, 661
Busniuk, Larry, *Thunder Bay Minor Hockey Association*, 1378
Busquets, Jordi, *International Hotel & Restaurant Association*, 1550
Bussey, William, *Sydney & Louisburg Railway Historical Society*, 1360
Bussière, Simon, *Corporation des maîtres électriciens du Québec*, 630
Bussières, Virginie, *Éco Entreprises Québec*, 671
Bussoli, Adrian, *Apparel Human Resources Council*, 74

Executive Name Index

Bustamante, Stephanie, *Saskatchewan Youth in Care & Custody Network*, 1279
Butany, Jagdish, *World Association of Societies of Pathology and Laboratory Medicine*, 1465
Butcher, Lyndsey, *Planned Parenthood Waterloo Region*, 1162
Buteau, Léo, *Fédération des apiculteurs du Québec*, 711
Buth, Len, *J. Douglas Ferguson Historical Research Foundation*, 867
Buth, JoAnne, *Canadian International Grains Institute*, 421
Butler, Robin, *Canadian Masters Cross-Country Ski Association*, 431
Butler, David, *Rugby Ontario*, 1244
Butler, Mollie, *Canadian College of Health Leaders*, 359
Butler, Michael J.A., *International Oceans Institute of Canada*, 859
Butler, Juanita, *Lupus Ontario*, 922
Butler, Juanita, *Lupus Ontario*, 922
Butler, Jennifer, *Canadian Health Information Management Association*, 402
Butler, David, *Nickel Institute*, 1026
Butler, Scott, *Ontario Good Roads Association*, 1083
Butler, Malcolm, *Youth Science Canada*, 1476
Butler, Joan, *Swimming Newfoundland & Labrador*, 1359
Butler, Kathy, *Canadian Council for the Advancement of Education*, 367
Butler, Colleen, *Canadian Alopecia Areata Foundation*, 292
Butler, Julie, *Association of Early Childhood Educators of Quebec*, 147
Butler, David, *Canadian Clean Power Coalition*, 357
Butler, Derek, *Association of Seafood Producers*, 162
Butler, Sarah, *Projet 10*, 1188
Butler, Barb, *Brain Injury Association of Canada*, 225
Butler, Keltie, *Farmers' Markets of Nova Scotia Cooperative Ltd.*, 706
Butler, Shannon, *Butler Family Foundation*, 267
Butler-McPhee, Janet, *Canadian HIV/AIDS Legal Network*, 406
Butt, Jeff, *Newfoundland & Labrador Powerlifting Association*, 1021
Butt, Andrew, *ADR Institute of Canada*, 9
Butt, Mary Ann, *Heart & Stroke Foundation of Newfoundland & Labrador*, 809
Butt, Asif R., *British Columbia Muslim Association*, 247
Buttenham, Dave, *Animal Nutrition Association of Canada*, 71
Buttenham, Dave, *Ontario Agri Business Association*, 1059
Butters, David, *Association of Power Producers of Ontario*, 156
Butterwick, Shauna, *Canadian Association for the Study of Adult Education*, 306
Butterworth, Roy, *Canadian Culinary Federation*, 374
Butterworth, Cole, *Canadian Hockey League*, 406
Buttler, Terry, *Ontario Genealogical Society*, 1082
Butts, Patrice, *Canadian Association of Elizabeth Fry Societies*, 312
Butz, Stephen, *YMCA Canada*, 1471, 1472
Buxton, Yvonne, *PFLAG Canada Inc.*, 1155
Buy, Serge, *Agricultural Institute of Canada*, 15
Buy, Serge, *Canadian Ferry Association*, 389
Buy, Serge, *National Association of Career Colleges*, 990
Buzan, Larry, *Canadian Association of Petroleum Landmen*, 326
Buzan, Mark, *Association of Consulting Engineering Companies - Canada*, 146
Byard, Malcolm, *Streetsville Historical Society*, 1352

Byberg, Leslie, *Ontario Securities Commission*, 1104
Bychkov, Alexander, *North Pacific Marine Science Organization*, 1032
Byers, Sheila, *Fernie Chamber of Commerce*, 732
Byford, Bruce, *Banff Centre for Arts & Creativity*, 195
Bylsma, Dave, *Christian Heritage Party of Canada*, 567
Bymoen, Bob, *Saskatchewan Government & General Employees' Union*, 1266
Bynum, Laura, *Canadian Public Works Association*, 464
Byrne, Randy, *Baseball PEI*, 198
Byrne, John, *Special Olympics Alberta*, 1339
Byrne, Mary-Louise, *Canadian Association of Geographers*, 316
Byrne, Michael, *Maritime Limousin Association*, 951
Byrne, Charles (Chuck), *Insurance Brokers Association of Canada*, 848
Byrne, Nelson, *Canadian Association of Psychosocial Oncology*, 330
Byrne, Melissa, *Newfoundland & Labrador Outfitters Association*, 1020
Byrne, Joyce, *Alberta Magazine Publishers Association*, 39
Byrne, Joe, *Cooper Institute*, 627
Byrnes, Anne Marie, *Association des fabricants de meubles du Québec inc.*, 113
Byrtus, Lilly, *Allergy/Asthma Information Association*, 54
Bystrzycki, Henryk, *Canadian Polish Congress*, 456

C

Cabado, Fabienne, *Regroupement québécois de la danse*, 1216
Cabana, Hubert, *Canadian Association on Water Quality*, 337
Cabana, Robert, *Ordre des denturologistes du Québec*, 1121
Cabana, Martin, *Association des enseignants en infographie et en imprimerie du Québec*, 112
Cable, Susan, *Child & Family Services of Western Manitoba*, 558
Cabrita, Judith, *Canadian Parks & Wilderness Society*, 451
Caddeo, Caddeo, *Association multi-ethnique pour l'intégration des personnes handicapées*, 138
Cadete, Nelson, *Ontario Traffic Council*, 1111
Cadieux, Luc, *Les Centres jeunesse de l'Outaouais*, 537
Cadieux, Cathy, *Canadian Wheelchair Sports Association*, 504
Cadieux, Marc, *Association du camionnage du Québec inc.*, 130
Cadieux, Normand, *Association québécoise des pharmaciens propriétaires*, 174
Cadieux, Serge, *Canadian Office & Professional Employees Union*, 444
Cadieux, Chantal, *Les Productions DansEncorps Inc.*, 1181
Cadigan, Robert, *Noia*, 1027
Cadogan, Carl, *Reception House Waterloo Region*, 1207
Cadogan, Carl, *Brain Tumour Foundation of Canada*, 225
Cadrin, Paul, *LAUDEM, L'Association des musiciens liturgiques du Canada*, 900
Cadwalader, Rebecca, *Stem Cell Network*, 1349
Cafarelli, Mario, *Congregation of Missionaries of the Precious Blood, Atlantic Province*, 613
Cafaro, Phil, *International Society for Environmental Ethics*, 1557
Cafiso, Jenny, *Canadian Jesuits International*, 423
Cafley, Julie, *Canada's Public Policy Forum*, 282

Cahill, Deborah, *Electrical Contractors Association of BC*, 682
Cahill, Jacqueline, *The Canadian Continence Foundation*, 364
Caignon, Philippe, *Association canadienne de traductologie*, 92
Caillaud, Jeanne-Françoise, *Réseau Santé - Nouvelle-Écosse*, 1225
Cain, Kristyn, *Manitoba Brain Injury Association Inc.*, 932
Caines, Cassandra, *Springdale & Area Chamber of Commerce*, 1346
Caines, Maria, *The Lung Association of Nova Scotia*, 921
Caines, Paul, *Canadian College of Health Leaders*, 359
Caines, Jennifer, *Newfoundland Aquaculture Industry Association*, 1022
Caird, Alison, *Spectra Helpline*, 1340
Cairns, Brian, *Canadian Pain Society*, 449
Cairns, Laurie, *Canadian Paralympic Committee*, 449
Cairns, Bridget, *Prince Edward Island Association for Community Living*, 1172
Cairns, Peter, *The Canadian Marine Industries and Shipbuilding Association*, 430
Cairns, Malcolm, *Canadian Transportation Research Forum*, 497
Cairns, Michael, *Ontario Brain Injury Association*, 1069
Cairns, Pierce, *Grandview & District Chamber of Commerce*, 782
Cairns, Bill, *Dorchester & Westmorland Literacy Council*, 661
Cairns, Scott, *Yellowknife Shooting Club*, 1471
Cairns, Jadine, *Eating Disorder Association of Canada*, 671
Caissie, Morel, *Canadian Social Work Foundation*, 472
Caissie, Amber, *New Brunswick Dental Assistants Association*, 1007
Caithness, Kate, *World Curling Federation*, 1604
Cake, Susan, *Alberta Federation of Labour*, 34
Caldas, Josie, *Federation of Portuguese Canadian Business & Professionals Inc.*, 726
Calder, Iain, *Toronto Free-Net*, 1384
Calder, Maureen, *Alberta Freestyle Ski Association*, 36
Calder, Lyn, *Assisted Living Southwestern Ontario*, 89
Calder, David, *Rowing British Columbia*, 1237
Calderon, Paula, *Canadian Colombian Professional Association*, 360
Calderon, Jorge, *Association des professeurs de français des universités et collèges canadiens*, 124
Calderwood, Jeff, *National Golf Course Owners Association Canada*, 993
Caldwell, Paul, *Carp Agricultural Society*, 515
Caldwell, Peter, *Ontario Arts Council*, 1060
Caldwell, Colin, *Peterborough Numismatic Club*, 1153
Caldwell, Lois, *Ontario Brain Injury Association*, 1069
Caldwell, Fran, *Brampton Horticultural Society*, 226
Caldwell, Sarah, *Saskatchewan Youth in Care & Custody Network*, 1279
Caley, Brenda, *Canadian Sport Massage Therapists Association*, 490
Calhoune, Robert, *Porcupine Prospectors & Developers Association*, 1165
Calihou, Joan, *Quesnel Community Living Association*, 1200
Calla, Andrea, *Association of Ontario Land Economists*, 155
Calla, Mario J., *COSTI Immigrant Services*, 632
Callaghan, Janet, *Canadian Media Directors' Council*, 432
Callaghan, Catherine, *Canadian Society of Ophthalmic Registered Nurses*, 485
Callahan, Sharron, *CARP*, 515

Callahan, James T., *International Union of Operating Engineers (AFL-CIO/CFL)*, 1565
Callahan-Cross, Tim, *Nova Scotia Choral Federation*, 1042
Callard, Linda, *Hospice Palliative Care Association of Prince Edward Island*, 823
Calma, Stephanie, *L'Arche Ontario*, 77
Calvé, Jeanne-Mance, *Ligue des propriétaires de Montréal*, 912
Calvert, Mitch, *Construction Safety Association of Manitoba*, 624
Calvert, Brent, *Capilano University Faculty Association*, 510
Calvin, Linda, *Saskatchewan Genealogical Society*, 1266
Calvo, Roque J., *Electrochemical Society*, 1522
Calzolari, Valentina, *International Association for Armenian Studies*, 1535
Cam, Pixie, *One World Arts*, 1058
Camara, Lucy, *Women Business Owners of Manitoba*, 1460
Camaso-Catalan, Lesley, *Manitoba Association for Volunteer Administration*, 929
Camazzola, Janette, *Kitimat Community Services Society*, 891
Cambise, Lisa, *Canadian Ski Instructors' Alliance*, 471
Camden, Robert, *Syndicat des producteurs de chèvres du Québec*, 1363
Cameletti, David, *Guelph Historical Society*, 793
Camellato, D., *Canadian Society of Forensic Science*, 483
Camenzuli, Vena, *Canadian Association of Critical Care Nurses*, 311
Cameron, Margie, *Sydney & Louisburg Railway Historical Society*, 1360
Cameron, Al, *Canadian Curling Association*, 374
Cameron, Ruth, *AIDS Committee of Cambridge, Kitchener/Waterloo & Area*, 16
Cameron, Patricia, *Saskatoon Society for the Prevention of Cruelty to Animals Inc.*, 1280
Cameron, Christine, *Canadian Fitness & Lifestyle Research Institute*, 390
Cameron, Caroyln, *New Brunswick Real Estate Association*, 1011
Cameron, Andrea, *Risk & Insurance Management Society Inc.*, 1234
Cameron, Mark, *Canadians for Clean Prosperity*, 507
Cameron, Nancy, *Historical Society of St. Catharines*, 816
Cameron, John, *TechConnex*, 1368
Cameron, Dora, *Human Resources Professionals Association*, 826
Cameron, Nancy, *Tourism Kelowna*, 1390
Cameron, Ronald, *Réseau d'action et de communication pour le développement international*, 1218
Cameron, Dick, *Society of Plastics Engineers*, 1594
Cameron, Jane, *Business Women's Networking Association*, 267
Cameron, Matt, *New Brunswick Ground Search & Rescue Association*, 1009
Cameron, Brian, *Dairy Farmers of Nova Scotia*, 648
Cameron Scott, Denise, *Canadian Bar Association*, 342
Cameron-Laninga, Debbie, *Caregivers Alberta*, 512
Camilleri, Ivan Philip, *The Shepherds' Trust*, 1295
Caminiti, Giuseppe, *Canadian Hatching Egg Producers*, 401
Camirand, Marc, *Association Trot & Amble du Québec*, 179
Camman, Rick, *Ontario Undergraduate Student Alliance*, 1112
Cammarata, Ken, *American Society of Neuroradiology*, 1502
Campagna, Lyne, *Ordre des infirmières et infirmiers du Québec*, 1122

Executive Name Index

Campbell, Ian, *Drinks Ontario*, 663
Campbell, Donna, *Foothills Library Association*, 750
Campbell, Candace, *Canadian Billiards & Snooker Association*, 343
Campbell, Scott, *Baptist General Conference of Canada*, 196
Campbell, Bonnie, *Quad County Support Services*, 1195
Campbell, Cathy, *Canadian Association of Chemical Distributors*, 310
Campbell, Ann, *Ingersoll District Chamber of Commerce*, 838
Campbell, Wendi, *Food Bank of Waterloo Region*, 749
Campbell, Les, *Alberta Genealogical Society*, 36
Campbell, Jennifer, *Special Olympics Manitoba*, 1339
Campbell, Duncan, *Canadian Wheelchair Sports Association*, 504
Campbell, Jack, *Canadian Automobile Association North & East Ontario*, 339
Campbell, Neil, *Manitoba Association of Optometrists*, 930
Campbell, Terry, *Canadian Bankers Association*, 341
Campbell, Bruce, *Canadian Centre for Policy Alternatives*, 354
Campbell, Steve, *Prince Edward Island Road Builders & Heavy Construction Association*, 1177
Campbell, Melissa, *Nova Scotia Dietetic Association*, 1044
Campbell, Lyndsay, *Canadian Law & Society Association*, 426
Campbell, Louise, *Canadian Picture Pioneers*, 455
Campbell, Julie, *Canadian College of Health Leaders*, 359
Campbell, Ian, *Investment Industry Regulatory Organization of Canada*, 863
Campbell, Sally, *Canadian Amateur Musicians*, 292
Campbell, Audrey, *Jamaican Canadian Association*, 867
Campbell, Elaine, *Innovative Medicines Canada*, 839
Campbell, Sherry, *Royal Astronomical Society of Canada*, 1238
Campbell, Graham, *Energy Council of Canada*, 688
Campbell, Prisca, *Muskoka Steamship & Historical Society*, 985
Campbell, Jennifer, *Canadian Archaeological Association*, 294
Campbell, Sandy, *Northern Alberta Health Libraries Association*, 1034
Campbell, Alexi, *Canadian Association of Medical Oncologists*, 320
Campbell, Daniel G., *Federation for Scottish Culture in Nova Scotia*, 721
Campbell, Darius, *OSPAR Commission*, 1582
Campbell, Michele, *International Bottled Water Association*, 1541
Campbell, David, *Nova Scotia Golf Association*, 1045
Campbell, Melissa, *Municipal Waste Association*, 981
Campbell, Debra, *The Canadian Art Foundation*, 295
Campbell, Kenneth, *Jaku Konbit*, 867
Campbell, Anita, *Ma-Mow-We-Tak Friendship Centre Inc.*, 928
Campbell, Janna, *Canadian Association of Nurses in HIV/AIDS Care*, 323
Campbell, Jason, *BC Adaptive Snowsports*, 200
Campbell, Steve, *Ringette PEI*, 1233
Campbell, Marcella, *Bragg Creek Chamber of Commerce*, 224
Campbell, Cory, *Manitoba Association of Registered Respiratory Therapists, Inc.*, 931
Campbell, Robert, *Union of Taxation Employees*, 1408

Campbell, Scott, *Ontario Rett Syndrome Association*, 1102
Campbell, Karen, *Elementary Teachers' Federation of Ontario*, 684
Campbell, Allan, *Manitoba Beekeepers' Association*, 932
Campbell, Jim, *Manitoba Beekeepers' Association*, 932
Campbell, Fay, *Alberta Clydesdale & Shire Association*, 28
Campbell, Diane, *Prince Edward Island Kiwanis Music Festival Association*, 1175
Campbell, Brad, *Inside Out Toronto LGBT Film & Video Festival*, 840
Campbell, Carolyn, *Concrete B.C.*, 610
Campbell, Neil R., *Dads Can*, 648
Campbell, Robert, *Contact Centre Canada*, 626
Campbell, Carol Ann, *National Golf Course Owners Association Canada*, 993
Campbell, Stacey, *Prison Fellowship Canada*, 1180
Campbell, Carolyn, *Canadian Association for Social Work Education*, 304
Campbell, Blair, *Prince Edward Island Harness Racing Industry Association*, 1174
Campbell, David, *Canadian Horse Breeders' Association*, 408
Campbell, Michelle, *Ontario Percheron Horse Association Inc.*, 1095
Campbell, Angus, *Caregivers Nova Scotia*, 512
Campbell, Elaine E., *Prince Edward Island Gerontological Nurses Association*, 1174
Campbell, Mike, *Canadian Federation of Pensioners*, 388
Campbell, Pat, *Canadian Supply Chain Sector Council*, 491
Campbell, Sherry, *Gordon Foundation*, 778
Campbell, Gertie, *Eastern Kings Health Foundation Inc.*, 670
Campbell-Chudoba, Roberta, *Dress for Success*, 663
Campbell-Palmer, Shelagh, *Nova Scotia College of Pharmacists*, 1042
Campbell-Yeo, Marsha, *Canadian Pain Society*, 449
Campeau, Guy, *Royal Astronomical Society of Canada*, 1238
Campeau, Nicole, *Centraide Lanaudière*, 522
Campeau, Carole, *Société des traversiers du Québec*, 1318
Campeau, Stephanie, *AUTO21 Network of Centres of Excellence*, 189
Campey, John, *Ralph Thornton Centre*, 1204
Campione, Dominic, *Canadian Ethnocultural Council*, 383
Campkin, Paula, *Enform*, 688
Campos, Alonso, *British Columbia Chess Federation*, 236
Campos, Anna, *Canadian Council for International Co-operation*, 366
Campos, Milton, *Communication & Natural Logic International Society*, 594
Campsall, Mitch, *North Central Local Government Association*, 1030
Canales, Nancy, *Nova Scotia Construction Labour Relations Association Limited*, 1043
Canapini, Jamie M., *Municipal Law Departments Association of Ontario*, 981
Cancade, Carolynn, *Brandon Chamber of Commerce*, 226
Cancelli, Ariana, *Canadian Urban Institute*, 499
Candy, Jean, *Nova Scotia Nurses' Union*, 1047
Canel, Eduardo, *Centre for Research on Latin America & The Caribbean*, 533
Cangemi, Angela, *American Society for Bone & Mineral Research*, 1498
Canlas, Pat, *Bukas Loob sa Diyos Covenant Community*, 264
Cann, Alexander, *Bach Elgar Choir*, 192
Cann, Rick, *Association of Battlefords Realtors*, 140
Cann, Billy, *The Island Party of Prince Edward Island*, 865

Cannan, Kevin, *Environmental Information Association*, 1523
Canniff, Christopher, *Canadian Authors Association*, 338
Canning, Paul, *The International Grenfell Association*, 858
Canning, Glen, *Rehtaeh Parsons Society*, 1217
Cannings, Syd, *Bowden Historical Society*, 219
Cannon, Brian, *HOPE International Development Agency*, 821
Cannon, Elizabeth, *Chatham-Kent Labour Council*, 555
Cannon, Charles A., *Rubber Manufacturers Association*, 1588
Cannon, Sarah, *Parents for Children's Mental Health*, 1140
Canoll, Tim, *Air Line Pilots Association, International - Canada*, 19
Cant Elliott, Dawn, *Insurance Institute of Ontario*, 850
Cantarovich, Marcelo, *The Transplantation Society*, 1395
Cantin, Étienne, *Association canadienne des relations industrielles*, 94
Cantin, Audrey, *Association québécoise des enseignantes et des enseignants du primaire*, 172
Cantin, Steeve, *Société d'histoire et de généalogie Maria-Chapdelaine*, 1313
Cantin, M. Jean, *Société des traversiers du Québec*, 1318
Canton, Maria, *YMCA Canada*, 1471
Cantor, Warren J., *Canadian Association of Interventional Cardiology*, 319
Cantrill, Sarah, *Architectural Woodwork Manufacturers Association of Canada - Southern Alberta*, 80
Cantwell, Jordan, *United Church of Canada*, 1409
Cantwell, Megan, *Association of Fundraising Professionals*, 1512
Canuel, Ron, *Canadian Education Association*, 380
Cape, David J., *The Centre for Israel & Jewish Affairs*, 533
Cape, Geoff, *Evergreen*, 699
Caplan, David, *Ontario Road Builders' Association*, 1102
Capobianco, John, *The Public Affairs Association of Canada*, 1192
Capobianco, Michelle, *Pancreatic Cancer Canada Foundation*, 1138
Caporossi, Terry, *Alzheimer Society of Sault Ste. Marie & District of Algoma*, 64
Capuano, Mike, *Canadian Medical & Biological Engineering Society*, 433
Carabin, Pierre, *Association pour la prévention de la contamination de l'air et du sol*, 166
Caranfil, Gabriela, *ArtsConnect - Tri-Cities Regional Arts Council*, 86
Carantit, Laurie, *International Association for Human Resource Information Management*, 1536
Carbone, Linda, *BOMA Québec*, 217
Carbone, Mark, *Educational Computing Organization of Ontario*, 680
Carbone, Linda, *Ordre des techniciens et techniciennes dentaires du Québec*, 1124
Carbonneau, Lise, *Canadian Institute of Plumbing & Heating*, 418
Carbonneau, Lise, *Association of Fundraising Professionals*, 1512
Card, Malcolm, *Canadian Baptist Ministries*, 341
Card, Lorraine, *Alberta Motor Transport Association*, 40
Carden, Richard, *World Pheasant Association*, 1607
Cardia, Emanuela, *Centre interuniversitaire de recherche en économie quantitative*, 535
Cardillo, Sandra, *LA Centre for Active Living*, 531

Cardin, Michel, *Association des bibliothécaires, des professeures et professeurs de l'Université de Moncton*, 107
Cardin, Stéphane, *Canada Media Fund*, 280
Cardinal, Natalie, *Boys & Girls Clubs of Alberta*, 221
Cardinal, Glenda, *Appraisal Institute of Canada*, 74
Cardoso, Décio, *Banda de nossa Senhora dos Milagres*, 195
Cardozo, L. Robin, *Hospital for Sick Children Foundation*, 823
Careau, Jean, *Chambre de commerce Vallée de la Petite-Nation*, 550
Careau, Madeleine, *Orchestre symphonique de Montréal*, 1118
Carew, Geno, *Nova Scotia Rugby Football Union*, 1048
Carew, Nadine, *Green Thumb Theatre for Young People*, 789
Carew Flemming, Sandi, *Professional Association of Residents in the Maritime Provinces*, 1182
Carey, Bethany, *Ontario Association of Optometrists*, 1065
Carey, Judy, *Reflexology Association of Canada*, 1210
Carey, John, *Flemingdon Neighbourhood Services*, 740
Carfantan-Mclachlan, Melanie, *Mediate BC Society*, 957
Carfoot, Dillon, *Les Clefs d'Or Canada*, 573
Carhart, Juanita, *Canadian Home Builders' Association - New Brunswick*, 407
Caricofe, Erin, *Wallace Center, Winrock International*, 1601
Carignan, Vincent, *Ordre des ingénieurs du Québec*, 1122
Carignan, Suzanne G., *Société d'histoire des Iles-Percées*, 1312
Carignan, Emile, *Multilingual Association of Regina, Inc.*, 979
Caringal, Liza, *Filipino Students' Association of Toronto*, 735
Cariou, Gerry, *Northwest Ontario Sunset Country Travel Association*, 1036
Caris, Patricia, *Orchidophiles de Québec*, 1119
Carkner, Shannon, *Juvenile Diabetes Research Foundation Canada*, 879
Carlaw, Melissa, *Ontario Veterinary Medical Association*, 1112
Carleton, Drew, *The Acadian Entomological Society*, 4
Carleton, Katherine, *Orchestras Canada*, 1117
Carleton, Joyce, *Saskatchewan Genealogical Society*, 1266
Carley, Patty, *Alberta Carriage Driving Association*, 27
Carlos, Marbella, *National Eating Disorder Information Centre*, 993
Carlson, Karin, *Recreation Facilities Association of British Columbia*, 1207
Carlson, Karen, *Ontario Jaguar Owners Association*, 1088
Carlson, Richard, *The Pollution Probe Foundation*, 1164
Carlson, Judy, *Alberni Valley Outdoor Club*, 21
Carlson, Christine, *Boundary Organic Producers Association*, 219
Carlson, Marion, *John Howard Society of Alberta*, 874
Carlton, Elizabeth, *Ontario Hospital Association*, 1087
Carlton, Tanya, *Lupus Canada*, 921
Carlyle, Marianne, *Ontario Society for the Prevention of Cruelty to Animals*, 1106
Carman, Derren J., *British Columbia Philatelic Society*, 249
Carman, Carol J., *Victoria READ Society*, 1433
Carmichael, Barb, *PEI Field Hockey Association*, 1148
Carmichael, Susan, *Simcoe Muskoka Family Connexions*, 1300
Carmichael, Brenda, *Westcoast Association of Visual Language Interpreters*, 1447

Executive Name Index

Carmichael, Kelly, *Fair Vote Canada*, 701
Carmona, Carlos, *Association québécoise des enseignants de français langue seconde*, 172
Carnegie, Rob, *Kingston Economic Development Corporation*, 889
Carnegie, Richard, *Saskatoon Youth Orchestra*, 1280
Carneiro, Renata, *Pan American Hockey Federation*, 1138
Carney, Sean, *Head-of-the-Lake Historical Society*, 805
Carol, Katharine, *Vancouver International Children's Festival*, 1426
Carolan, Chris, *Thunder Bay Beekeepers' Association*, 1377
Carole, Cushnie, *African Canadian Heritage Association*, 12
Carolo, Humberto, *The White Ribbon Campaign*, 1452
Caron, Gisèle, *Au Coup de pouce Centre-Sud inc.*, 187
Caron, Laurier, *Fédération des Syndicats de l'Enseignement*, 719
Caron, Rosanne, *Canadian Out-of-Home Measurement Bureau*, 448
Caron, Rosanne, *Out-of-Home Marketing Association of Canada*, 1133
Caron, Gilles, *Syndicat interprovincial des ferblantiers et couvreurs, la section locale 2016 à la FTQ-Construction*, 1364
Caron, Nancy, *Association Sclérose en Plaques Rive-Sud*, 178
Caron, Christine, *Table de concertation du faubourg Saint-Laurent*, 1365
Caron, Maxime, *Société Louis-Napoléon Dugal/Société Grande-Rivière*, 1321
Caron, Ghislain, *Théâtre français de Toronto*, 1374
Caron, Jean-François, *Société historique de Québec*, 1320
Caron, Steve, *Ringuette de la Capitale*, 1233
Caron, France, *Association mathématique du Québec*, 137
Caron, David, *Fédération des parents francophones de l'Alberta*, 717
Caron, Claude, *Ballet West*, 195
Caron, Donald A., *Association syndicale des employées de production et de service*, 178
Caron, Guillaume, *Association syndicale des employées de production et de service*, 178
Caron, David, *Ontario Book Publishers Organization*, 1068
Carousol, Paul, *Rainy River & District Chamber of Commerce*, 1204
Carparelli, Gianni, *Caritas School of Life Therapeutic Community*, 513
Carpay, John, *Justice Centre for Constitutional Freedoms*, 878
Carpenter, Jackie, *Inclusion BC*, 832
Carpenter, Donna, *Penticton Geology & Lapidary Club*, 1151
Carpenter, Lenny, *Wawatay Native Communications Society*, 1443
Carpenter, Les L., *Native Communications Society of the Northwest Territories*, 997
Carpenter, Denise, *Neighbourhood Pharmacy Association of Canada*, 1002
Carpenter, Corinne, *American Association on Intellectual & Developmental Disabilities*, 1490
Carpenter, Steve, *Manitoba Freestyle Ski Association*, 937
Carpentier, Richard, *National Council on Ethics in Human Research*, 992
Carpentier, Richard, *Association des pompiers de Laval*, 124
Carpentier, Léo-Denis, *Société d'histoire et de généalogie de Saint-Casimir*, 1313
Carr, Sheila, *Bowling Federation of Canada*, 219
Carr, Denis, *Cornwall & Area Chamber of Commerce*, 629
Carr, Patti, *North Bay & District Chamber of Commerce*, 1030

Carr, Sheila, *Canadian 5 Pin Bowlers' Association*, 285
Carr, Jonathan, *Atlantic Salmon Federation*, 186
Carr, Krista, *New Brunswick Association for Community Living*, 1004
Carr, Joe, *Canadian Association of Critical Care Nurses*, 311
Carr, Catherine, *Society of Public Insurance Administrators of Ontario*, 1330
Carr, Bill, *Fort McMurray Youth Soccer Association*, 753
Carr, Susan, *Prince Albert Model Forest Association Inc.*, 1171
Carr, Mark, *Bereaved Families of Ontario*, 205
Carr-Locke, Sarah, *Prince of Wales Northern Heritage Centre*, 1179
Carretero, Juan, *Association of University of New Brunswick Teachers*, 163
Carrie, Jim, *Christian Children's Fund of Canada*, 567
Carrier, Claudette, *Corporation des entreprises de traitement de l'air et du froid*, 630
Carrier, Steven, *Association des optométristes du Québec*, 121
Carrier, Serge, *Association des urologues du Québec*, 130
Carrier, Gilles, *Society of Fire Protection Engineers*, 1593
Carrière, Suzanne, *Suicide Action Montréal*, 1353
Carrière, Marie-Andrée, *Community Information Centre of Ottawa*, 599
Carrière, Jean-Marc, *Association of Consulting Engineering Companies - Canada*, 146
Carrière, Normand, *Les Amis du vitrail*, 68
Carrigan-Weir, Diane, *Denturist Society of Nova Scotia*, 654
Carrington, Kelly, *Massage Therapists' Association of Nova Scotia*, 953
Carroll, Kathy, *Saskatchewan Association of Speech-Language Pathologists & Audiologists*, 1258
Carroll, Cathie W., *College of Family Physicians of Canada*, 585
Carroll, Janine, *Alberta Genealogical Society*, 36
Carroll, Laureen, *Credit Institute of Canada*, 641
Carroll, Tim, *Shaw Festival*, 1295
Carroll, Veronica, *Children's Health Foundation of Vancouver Island*, 561
Carroll, Kenneth, *Friends Historical Association*, 1527
Carroll, Margaret, *High Level & District Chamber of Commerce*, 814
Carroll, Marcia, *Prince Edward Island Council of People with Disabilities*, 1173
Carroll, Ryan, *Irish Dance Teacher's Association of Eastern Canada*, 864
Carron, Julian, *Communion & Liberation Canada*, 594
Carros, Briony, *Visual Arts Nova Scotia*, 1436
Carrothers, Tom, *CARP*, 514
Carrusca, Ken, *Cement Association of Canada*, 521
Carruth, Meg, *Toronto Association of Law Libraries*, 1382
Carruthers, Kathy, *PARD Therapeutic Riding*, 1139
Carruthers, Ivan, *West Lincoln Chamber of Commerce*, 1446
Carruthers, Jim, *The Naval Officers' Association of Canada*, 1001
Carruthers, Harry, *Bowls British Columbia*, 220
Carruthers, Deborah, *Copyright Visual Arts*, 628
Carruthers, Cindy, *People First Nova Scotia*, 1151
Carscallen, John, *Canadian Angelman Syndrome Society*, 293
Carsley, Kathy, *Unity for Autism*, 1418
Carson, George, *Society of Obstetricians & Gynaecologists of Canada*, 1330

Carson, Monica, *International Society for Neurochemistry*, 1558
Carson, Tim, *Alberta Association of Agricultural Societies*, 23
Carson, Dorothy, *Alberta Construction Association*, 31
Carson, Arthur, *New Brunswick Shorthorn Breeders Association*, 1012
Carson, Ann Louise, *Holstein Canada*, 819
Carson, Kimberly, *Breast Cancer Society of Canada*, 228
Carson, Nancy, *Urology Nurses of Canada*, 1422
Carstairs, Bill, *Alberta College of Paramedics*, 30
Carswell, Cam, *Canadian Association of Movers*, 321
Carswell, Anne, *Nova Scotia Society of Occupational Therapists*, 1049
Carswell, Robert, *Lakeshore Stamp Club Inc.*, 897
Carswell, Marcie, *Moose Jaw Music Festival*, 974
Carteaux, William R., *SPI: The Plastics Industry Trade Association*, 1596
Carter, Wendy, *Edmonton Heritage Festival Association*, 677
Carter, Kimberly, *ALS Society of New Brunswick & Nova Scotia*, 60
Carter, Mike, *Alberni Valley Chamber of Commerce*, 21
Carter, Bruce, *Greater Victoria Chamber of Commerce*, 787
Carter, Bill, *Yarmouth Food Bank Society*, 1470
Carter, Jim, *Canadian Marketing Association*, 431
Carter, Bill, *Canadian Automobile Association South Central Ontario*, 339
Carter, Cal, *Canadian Hard of Hearing Association*, 400
Carter, Mallory, *Canadian Home Builders' Association - New Brunswick*, 407
Carter, Mike, *Council of Ontario Construction Associations*, 634
Carter, Lorraine, *Canadian Network for Innovation in Education*, 441
Carter, Pam, *Mariposa Folk Foundation*, 950
Carter, Kelly, *Lifesaving Society*, 911
Carter, Lynda, *Women's Business Network of Ottawa*, 1462
Carter, David C., *Association of Professional Geoscientists of Nova Scotia*, 159
Carter, Dave, *National Bison Association*, 1575
Carter, Jay, *Evergreen*, 699
Carter, Cal, *Saskatchewan Orchid Society*, 1270
Carter, Fran, *British Columbia Fuchsia & Begonia Society*, 242
Carter, Jane, *Bereaved Families of Ontario*, 205
Carter, Nancy E., *Canada's Advanced Internet Development Organization*, 282
Carter, Wayne, *The Atlantic Film Festival Association*, 184
Carter, Jen, *Ontario Undergraduate Student Alliance*, 1111
Carter, Jen, *Ontario Undergraduate Student Alliance*, 1112
Carter, Karen, *CADORA Ontario Association Inc.*, 269
Carter Aitken, Anne, *International Society for Ecological Economics*, 1557
Cartier, Jacques, *Conseil des entrepreneurs agricoles*, 617
Cartwright, John, *Toronto & York Region Labour Council*, 1381
Cartwright, Barbara, *Canadian Federation of Humane Societies*, 386
Cartwright, Stephen, *World Chambers Federation*, 1604
Carty, James, *Canadian National Association of Real Estate Appraisers*, 438
Carty, Johnathan, *Canadian National Association of Real Estate Appraisers*, 438

Carty, Lisa, *Reach for the Rainbow*, 1205
Caruso, Colette, *Ontario Good Roads Association*, 1083
Caruso, Kim, *YMCA Canada*, 1473
Caruso, Rosanne, *Mississauga Choral Society*, 970
Carvajal, Andrew, *Canadian Columbian Professional Association*, 360
Carvalho, Hernandez F., *International Federation for Cell Biology*, 1546
Carvell, Rob, *Construction Association of New Brunswick*, 623
Casara, Danielle, *Conseil régional FTQ Montréal Métropolitain*, 621
Casault, Pierre, *La Clé d'la Baie en Huronie - Association culturelle francophone*, 572
Casavant, Rachelle, *Tisdale & District Chamber of Commerce*, 1380
Casavant, Colette, *Mouvement québécois des vacances familiales inc.*, 978
Casavent, Bernard, *Canadian Culinary Federation*, 319
Cascaden, Lori, *British Columbia Funeral Association*, 242
Case, Cheryl, *Canadian Public Health Association - NWT/Nunavut Branch*, 462
Caseley, Jessica, *Kensington & Area Chamber of Commerce*, 883
Casey, Mike, *Canadian Business Aviation Association*, 348
Casey, Michael, *Canadian Co-operative Association*, 364
Casey, Bea, *Canadian Association of Insolvency & Restructuring Professionals*, 318
Casey, Kathy, *Montréal Danse*, 972
Casey, Joanne F. (Joni), *Intermodal Association of North America*, 1534
Casey, Suze, *Calgary Folk Club*, 272
Casey, Andrew, *BIOTECanada*, 212
Casey, Linda, *Helping Unite Grandparents & Grandchildren*, 812
Casgrain-Robertson, Sommer, *Rideau Valley Conservation Authority*, 1231
Cashman, Paul, *Alberta Roadbuilders & Heavy Construction Association*, 44
Casiano, Michael, *American Studies Association*, 1503
Casper, Cindy, *Canadian Celiac Association*, 352
Casquinha, Peter G., *Canadian Pension & Benefits Institute*, 453
Cass-Toole, Sharon, *Canadian Association for Integrative & Energy Therapies*, 301
Cassaday, Barbara, *Piano Technicians Guild Inc.*, 1584
Cassar Torreggiani, Kim, *Habitat for Humanity Canada*, 796
Cassell, Nancy, *Community Living Dundas County*, 601
Casselman, Mark, *Digital Health Canada*, 656
Casselman, Alice, *Association for Canadian Educational Resources*, 132
Cassels, Jim, *Cypress River Chamber of Commerce*, 647
Cassidy, Tara, *British Columbia Society of Electroneurophysiology Technologists*, 254
Cassidy, Brian, *Canadian Tinnitus Foundation*, 495
Casson, Jane, *International Ringette Federation - Canada*, 859
Casson, Jane, *CADORA Ontario Association Inc.*, 269
Cassone, Céline, *Les Ballets Jazz de Montréal*, 195
Casteel, Gary, *International Union, United Automobile, Aerospace & Agricultural Implement Workers of America*, 1565
Castell, Barb, *Millarville Racing & Agricultural Society*, 965
Castellan, Dan, *American Society of Heating, Refrigerating & Air Conditioning Engineers*, 1500
Castellani, Martine, *HRMS Professionals Association*, 824

Executive Name Index

Castellarin, Jackie, *Oliver-Osoyoos Naturalists*, 1057
Castellarin, Mark, *Yukon Order of Pioneers*, 1479
Castonguay, Roger, *Alliance autochtone du Québec*, 55
Castonguay, Christopher, *Ottawa Carleton Ultimate Association*, 1129
Castro, Diana, *The Counselling Foundation of Canada*, 636
Castro Herrera, Miriam, *Fondation Père-Ménard*, 747
Catania, Thomas, *Building Owners & Managers Association Toronto*, 263
Catchpole, Charlene, *Ontario Association of Interval & Transition Houses*, 1064
Catelin, Milton, *World Coal Institute*, 1604
Cathcart, Bronco, *Association of Neighbourhood Houses BC*, 153
Cathcart, Wendy, *Softball Ontario*, 1332
Cathcart, Stephen, *International Heavy Haul Association*, 1550
Cato, Jacqueline, *Ontario Council of University Libraries*, 1075
Catry, Frank, *Tillsonburg District Real Estate Board*, 1379
Catte, Dan, *Antique Motorcycle Club of Manitoba Inc.*, 72
Cattle, Robert, *Canadian Tooling & Machining Association*, 495
Catto, Vanessa, *CADORA Ontario Association Inc.*, 269
Cattrall, Beverley, *Canadian Volkssport Federation*, 502
Cauchy, Daniel, *Centre international pour la prévention de la criminalité*, 535
Caude, Geoffrey, *Association internationale permanente des congrès de navigation*, 1510
Caughey, Karen, *ALS Society of Alberta*, 60
Cauley, Jane, *American Society for Bone & Mineral Research*, 1498
Caulfield, Kevin, *CODA International Training*, 1518
Caulier, Brigitte, *Institut d'histoire de l'Amérique française*, 841
Causgrove, Judy, *Music for Young Children*, 983
Cautillo, Giovanni, *Ontario Sewer & Watermain Construction Association*, 1104
Cavanagh, J'net, *Native Canadian Centre of Toronto*, 997
Cavanagh, Gary, *Canadian Academy of the History of Pharmacy*, 287
Cavanagh, Christina A., *Mooredale Youth Concert Orchestra*, 973
Cavanaugh, Barry, *Association of Science & Engineering Technology Professionals of Alberta*, 162
Cave, William R., *Ancient, Free & Accepted Masons of Canada - Grand Lodge of British Columbia & Yukon*, 68
Cave, Nigel P., *British Columbia Securities Commission*, 253
Caverley, Natasha, *Canadian Counselling & Psychotherapy Association*, 371
Cavicchia, Lisa, *Canadian Urban Institute*, 499
Cavoukian, Ann, *International Council on Global Privacy & Security, By Design*, 856
Cawley, John, *The J.W. McConnell Family Foundation*, 879
Cawthorne, John, *Canadian Albacore Association*, 291
Caya, Marie-Josée, *Centre québécois du droit de l'environnement*, 536
Cayen, Greg, *Nunasi Corporation*, 1051
Cayer, Brigitte, *Risk & Insurance Management Society Inc.*, 1234
Cayouette, Heather, *Universities Canada*, 1418
Cayouette, Heather, *Association of Canadian Universities for Northern Studies*, 144
Cejalvo, Chi, *College of Dietitians of British Columbia*, 584
Cekerevac, Carrie, *Family Mediation Canada*, 704

Celenza, Felicetta, *Canadian Council on Animal Care*, 371
Celestino, Benoît, *Syndicat des technicien(ne)s et artisan(e)s du réseau français de Radio-Canada (ind.)*, 1364
Cenedese, Roberta, *Association Internationale pour le Développement de l'Apnée Canada*, 136
Cermak, Bob, *Ontario Field Ornithologists*, 1080
Cerquiglini, Bernard, *Agence universitaire de la Francophonie*, 14
Ch'ng, Damien, *Professional Engineers Ontario*, 1184
Chabih, Barbara, *Canadian Agri-Marketing Association (Manitoba)*, 290
Chabot, Diane, *Mount Pleasant Group*, 976
Chabot, Louise, *Centrale des syndicats du Québec*, 526
Chabot, Susan, *People, Words & Change*, 1152
Chabot, Frédérique, *Action Canada for Sexual Health & Rights*, 6
Chabot, Madeleine, *L'Union culturelle des Franco-Ontariennes*, 1406
Chabot, Andy, *Cancer Research Society*, 507
Chabot, Annie, *Association des jeunes ruraux du Québec*, 117
Chabot, Jean-François, *Association de médiation familiale du Québec*, 102
Chabot, Jeff, *Canadian Society of Professional Event Planners*, 487
Chacha, Joel, *Teamwork Children's Services International*, 1368
Chadderton, Ted, *Simcoe County Law Association*, 1299
Chaggan, Zulfikar, *March of Dimes Canada*, 949
Chaggar, Harpreet, *Alberta College of Speech-Language Pathologists & Audiologists*, 30
Chagnon, André, *Fondation Lucie et André Chagnon*, 747
Chahal, Rita, *Manitoba Interfaith Welcome Place*, 939
Chaikelson, Morris, *Lord Reading Law Society*, 919
Chainey, Daniel, *Comité logement de Lacine-Lasalle*, 592
Chaisson, Ali, *Société de l'Acadie du Nouveau-Brunswick*, 1316
Chakrabarty, Biswanath, *Certified General Accountants Association of the Northwest Territories & Nunavut*, 538
Chakraborty, Pranesh, *Garrod Association*, 767
Chaleff-Freudenthaler, Adam, *International Federation of Professional & Technical Engineers (AFL-CIO/CLC)*, 1549
Chalifour, Micheline, *Réseau FADOQ*, 1224
Chalifour, Yvan, *Lifesaving Society*, 911
Chalifour, JoAnne, *Alzheimer Society of Hamilton Halton*, 62
Chalifoux, Pierre, *Parents-secours du Québec inc.*, 1140
Chalifoux, Francine, *Association des traumatisés crâniens de l'Abitibi-Témiscamingue (Le Pilier)*, 129
Chalker, George, *Heritage Foundation of Newfoundland & Labrador*, 813
Chalker, Bob, *NACE International*, 1571
Challand, Shirley, *Canadian Association of Oilwell Drilling Contractors*, 324
Chalmers, John, *Grand Orange Lodge of Canada*, 780
Chalmers, John, *Ladies' Orange Benevolent Association of Canada*, 895
Chalmers, Anne, *Indigenous Bar Association*, 834
Chalmers, Joy, *Pacific Association of First Nations' Women*, 1135
Chalouhi, Mark, *Association des Scouts du Canada*, 127
Chaloux, Véronique, *Association d'éducation préscolaire du Québec*, 99

Chalut, Carine, *Réseau de Santé en Français au Nunavut*, 1219
Chamaillard, Pascal, *Association des distributeurs exclusifs de livres en langue française inc.*, 111
Chamberlain, Nancy, *Thunder Bay Counselling Centre*, 1377
Chamberlain, Henry, *Building Owners & Managers Association International*, 1515
Chamberlain, Marijoel, *Building Supply Industry Association of British Columbia*, 263
Chamberlain, Donna, *Ontario Association for Marriage & Family Therapy*, 1061
Chamberlain, Rae, *Saskatchewan Genealogical Society*, 1266
Chamberlain, Mary, *CADORA Ontario Association Inc.*, 269
Chamberland, Louise, *Ordre des orthophonistes et audiologistes du Québec*, 1123
Chamberland, Guy, *Classical Association of Canada*, 572
Chamberlin, Cindy, *South Saskatchewan Community Foundation Inc.*, 1336
Chambers, Dione, *Fort Saskatchewan Chamber of Commerce*, 754
Chambers, Richard F., *The Institute of Internal Auditors*, 1533
Chambers, Kathy, *Saskatchewan Families for Effective Autism Treatment*, 1265
Chambers, Bill, *Save the Children Canada*, 1282
Chambers, Kelly, *Ontario Association of Archers Inc.*, 1061
Chambers, Albert, *Canadian Supply Chain Food Safety Coalition*, 491
Chambers, Greg, *Association of Canadian Film Craftspeople*, 142
Chambers, Brad, *Manitoba Speed Skating Association*, 945
Chambers, RJ, *Parkland Music Festival*, 1142
Chamois, Léon, *Organization of Military Museums of Canada*, 1126
Champagne, Bernard, *Air Transport Association of Canada*, 19
Champagne, Jean-François, *Automotive Industries Association of Canada*, 190
Champagne, Mario, *Association québécoise des cadres scolaires*, 172
Champagne, Chantal, *Occupational & Environmental Medical Association of Canada*, 1054
Champagne, Carolynne, *United Way of Perth-Huron*, 1416
Champagne, Joan, *Canada Pork International*, 280
Champagne, Agnès, *Alliance Française du Manitoba*, 57
Champagne, Marc, *Société historique de la Côte-Nord*, 1320
Champagne-Bent, Teresa, *Building Owners & Managers Association Toronto*, 263
Chan, Mandart, *British Columbia Music Educators' Association*, 246
Chan, Rosaline, *British Columbia Chamber of Commerce*, 235
Chan, Emily, *Justice for Children & Youth*, 878
Chan, Karen, *Professional Engineers Ontario*, 1184
Chan, Edith, *Chinese Canadian National Council*, 564
Chan, Catherine, *Canadian Physiological Society*, 454
Chan, Denise, *YOUTHLINK*, 1476
Chan, Allison, *Canadian Association for Pharmacy Distribution Management*, 303
Chan, Janice, *Canadian Celtic Arts Association*, 353
Chan, Gordon, *Canada Chinese Computer Association*, 278
Chan, Janice, *Toronto Gaelic Learners Association*, 1385
Chan, Tung, *Pier 21 Society*, 1159
Chan, Janice, *Ovarian Cancer Canada*, 1133

Chan, Karen, *Ontario Society of Professional Engineers*, 1107
Chan, Ming-Ka, *Canadian Association for Medical Education*, 302
Chan, Pius, *Chinese Federation of Commerce of Canada*, 565
Chan, Steve, *Vancouver Second Mile Society*, 1428
Chancey, Glyn, *Canadian Seed Growers' Association*, 469
Chandler, Sheryl, *Community Living Dufferin*, 601
Chandler, Linda, *Peterborough Historical Society*, 1153
Chandler, Philip S., *Essex Law Association*, 696
Chandler, Mark, *WineAmerica*, 1602
Chandrasekere, Sarath, *PEI Cricket Association*, 1148
Chang, Donna, *Association of Neighbourhood Houses BC*, 153
Chang, Minku, *WTF Taekwondo Federation of British Columbia*, 1469
Chang, Dyland, *Korean Students' Association of Canada*, 894
Chang, Gap Soo, *Association of Korean Canadian Scientists & Engineers*, 150
Chang, Ruth R. H., *Taiwan Trade Center, Vancouver*, 1366
Channan, Omkar Nath, *World Organization of Building Officials*, 1466
Channey, Jessie, *Society for Technical Communication*, 1591
Chantal, Claude, *Association des entomologistes amateurs du Québec inc.*, 112
Chantelois, Mathieu, *Boys & Girls Clubs of Canada*, 222
Chapdelaine, France, *Chambre de commerce de la Haute-Matawinie*, 541
Chapin, Paul, *Goodwill, The Amity Group*, 778
Chaplin, Neil, *Construction Labour Relations Association of Newfoundland & Labrador*, 624
Chapman, John H, *The Anglican Church of Canada*, 70
Chapman, Luke, *Brewers Association of Canada*, 228
Chapman, Felicia, *Diabetes Canada*, 656
Chapman, Jennifer, *Ontario Kinesiology Association*, 1088
Chapman, Barry, *Toronto Film Society*, 1384
Chapman, Larry, *Canadian Tax Foundation*, 492
Chapman, Marie, *Pier 21 Society*, 1159
Chapman, Harry, *Dartmouth Historical Association*, 651
Chapman, Audrey, *Association des Perfusionnistes du Québec Inc.*, 122
Chapman, Bruce, *Canadian Association of Prawn Producers*, 328
Chapman, Peter, *Shareholder Association for Research & Education*, 1294
Chappell, Andrew, *Ontario Tennis Association*, 1110
Chappell, Sylvia, *GRAND Society*, 780
Chappell, Heather, *Kidney Cancer Canada Association*, 885
Chaput, Odette, *Association de l'Agricotourism et du Tourisme Gourmand*, 100
Char, Stephanie, *The Logistics Institute*, 917
Charanduk, Brian, *Alberta Association of Landscape Architects*, 23
Charania, Irina, *College & Association of Respiratory Therapists of Alberta*, 581
Charasse, Alice, *Centre de ressources et d'intervention pour hommes abusés sexuellement dans leur enfance*, 530
Charboneau, Renee, *Professional Photographers of Canada*, 1186
Charbonneau, Guillaume, *College of Family Physicians of Canada*, 584
Charbonneau, Janne, *Canadian AIDS Society*, 290

Executive Name Index

Charbonneau, Éric, *Chambre immobilière du Grand Montréal*, 551
Charbonneau, Robert, *Association des néphrologues du Québec*, 120
Charbonneau, Pierre, *Canadian Postmasters & Assistants Association*, 458
Charbonneau, Wendy, *Ontario Brain Injury Association*, 1069
Charbonneau, George, *Canadian Association of Swine Veterinarians*, 334
Charbonneau, Françoise, *La fédération des mouvements personne d'abord du Québec*, 716
Charbonneau, Lise, *Foundation of Greater Montreal*, 756
Chard, Yvonne, *Adult Basic Education Association of British Columbia*, 9
Charest, Sébastien, *Société professionnelle des auteurs et des compositeurs du Québec*, 1322
Charest, Jane, *Castlegar & District Chamber of Commerce*, 517
Charest, Marc, *Chambre de commerce région de Matane*, 549
Charest, Denise, *Réseau FADOQ*, 1224
Charest, Pierre M., *Microscopical Society of Canada*, 964
Charest, Rose-Marie, *L'Ordre des psychologues du Québec*, 1123
Charest, Marie-Pier, *Voitures anciennes du Québec inc.*, 1437
Charest, Crystal, *New Brunswick Association of Naturopathic Doctors*, 1005
Charette, François, *Livres Canada Books*, 915
Charette, Denis, *Iroquois Falls Historical Society*, 864
Charette, Ariane, *Armateurs du Saint-Laurent*, 82
Charette, Ariane, *Société de développement économique du Saint-Laurent*, 1315
Charette, Jacques, *Salon du livre de Toronto et Festival des écrivains*, 1252
Chariyil, Genesh, *Association of Professional Engineers & Geoscientists of Alberta*, 157
Charland, Marc, *Fédération des comités de parents du Québec inc.*, 713
Charland, Chantal, *Association de Sherbrooke pour la déficience intellectuelle*, 104
Charlebois, Joanne, *Speech-Language & Audiology Canada*, 1341
Charlebois, Pascal André, *Development & Peace*, 655
Charlebois, Simon, *Réseau des SADC et CAE*, 1220
Charlebois, Michel G., *Association des syndicats de copropriété du Québec*, 129
Charles, Susan, *Association of Canadian Advertisers Inc.*, 140
Charles, Decroix, *Alliance des chorales du Québec*, 55
Charlton, Natalie, *Hinton & District Chamber of Commerce*, 815
Charlton, Marilyn, *Saskatchewan Hereford Association*, 1267
Charlton, Guy, *Pragmora*, 1169
Charnell, Maya, *Association of Professional Engineers & Geoscientists of British Columbia*, 158
Charpentier, Nicole, *Société Parkinson du Québec*, 1322
Charron, Jean-Benoit, *Canadian Society of Plant Biologists*, 487
Charron, Danielle, *Association of Municipal Administrators of New Brunswick*, 152
Charron, Carmen, *Alberta Soccer Association*, 47
Charron, Denise, *Canadian Home Builders' Association - New Brunswick*, 407
Charron, Denise, *Canadian Mathematical Society*, 432
Charron, J.G. Gilles, *Société d'histoire et de généalogie des Mille-Iles*, 1313
Charron-Matte, Ginette, *Associés bénévoles qualifiés au service des jeunes*, 179

Charter, Claude, *Association des artistes peintres de Longueuil*, 106
Charters, Owen, *Boys & Girls Clubs of Canada*, 222
Charters, Stephanie, *Border Boosters Square & Round Dance Association*, 218
Charters, Sarah, *United Church of Canada Foundation*, 1410
Chartier, Simon, *Centre d'entrepreneuriat et PME*, 528
Chartier, Clément, *Métis National Council*, 963
Chartier, Candace, *Ontario Long Term Care Association*, 1089
Chartier, Annie, *Fédération des professionnelles et professionnels de l'éducation du Québec*, 718
Chartier, Brenda, *Buffalo Narrows Friendship Centre*, 261
Chartier, Claude, *Réseau des SADC et CAE*, 1220
Chartier, Danielle, *Canada's History*, 282
Chartier, Jessica, *Association canadienne-française de Régina*, 96
Chartrand, Anne, *Federal Libraries Coordination Secretariat*, 706
Chartrand, Nathalie, *Association sportive des aveugles du Québec inc.*, 178
Chartrand, David, *Manitoba Métis Federation*, 940
Chartrand, Beth, *Alliance for Canadian New Music Projects*, 56
Chartrand, Jean, *Professional Photographers of Canada*, 1186
Chartrand, Diane, *Groupe de droit collaboratif du Québec*, 791
Chartrand, Mylène, *Association des francophones du Nunavut*, 114
Chartrand, François, *Association des conseils en gestion linguistique Inc.*, 110
Chartrand, Monique, *Ontario Brain Injury Association*, 1068
Chartrand, Nathalie, *Association des sports pour aveugles de Montréal*, 128
Chartrand, Rachelle, *Women in Film & Television Vancouver*, 1461
Chartrand, Jacques-André, *Amis de la Bibliothèque de Brossard Georgette-Lepage*, 67
Chase, Michelle, *Vélo New Brunswick*, 1431
Chase, Kate, *British Columbia Association of Speech-Language Pathologists & Audiologists*, 233
Chase, Christine, *Credit Institute of Canada*, 641
Chase, Dianne, *International Association of Business Communicators*, 1538
Chase, James, *British Columbia Hotel Association*, 243
Chase-Nugent, Christina, *Simcoe County Parents of Multiples*, 1300
Chassé, Brigitte, *Association des parents fransaskois*, 122
Chatara, Nathela, *Association for Preservation Technology International*, 1509
Chataway, Bob, *Northwestern Ontario Prospectors Association*, 1039
Chateau, Ray, *Ontario Colleges Athletic Association*, 1073
Chateauneuf, Tanya, *Winkler & District Chamber of Commerce*, 1458
Châteauvert, André, *Association internationale permanente des congrès de navigation*, 1510
Châtelain, Jean, *Association des golfeurs professionnels du Québec*, 115
Chatenoud, Françoise, *Canadian Association of Nordic Ski Instructors*, 322
Chater, Matthew, *Big Brothers Big Sisters of Canada*, 209
Chatten, Colin, *International Foster Care Organisation*, 1549
Chatterson, Mora, *Community Foundation for Kingston & Area*, 597
Chattopadhyay, Rupak, *Forum of Federations*, 755

Chaudhdry, Naveed, *Peel Multicultural Council*, 1148
Chaudhry, Mohsin, *British Columbia Muslim Association*, 247
Chauveau, Jocelyn, *Association de la Vallée-du-Richelieu pour la déficience intellectuelle*, 102
Chauvet, Gaby, *Association of Early Childhood Educators Ontario*, 147
Chave, John, *Oshawa-Whitby Kiwanis Music & Theatre Festival*, 1128
Chávez, César Rafael, *Commission for Environmental Cooperation*, 593
Chavez, Lucy, *Asociación Nacional de Ejecutivos de Organismos Empresariales y Profesionales, A.C.*, 1506
Chawla, Satish, *Ontario Association of Pathologists*, 1065
Chaykowski, Lloyd, *Thunder Bay Adventure Trails*, 1377
Chaytor-Loveys, Allison, *Newfoundland & Labrador Credit Union*, 1018
Cheasley, C. Stephen, *Canadian Railroad Historical Association*, 465
Cheatle, Andrew, *Prospectors & Developers Association of Canada*, 1189
Cheatle, Andrew, *Association of Professional Geoscientists of Ontario*, 159
Chedore, Bill, *Canadian Injured Workers Alliance*, 411
Chee, Doris, *Ontario Association of Landscape Architects*, 1064
Cheesman, Jane, *Canadian Media Production Association*, 433
Cheesman, Jane, *Canadian Pediatric Foundation*, 452
Cheff, Chantal, *Canadian Association of Foodservice Professionals*, 315
Chen, Benjamin, *Canadian Society of Internal Medicine*, 484
Chen, John, *Federation of Chinese Canadian Professionals (Québec)*, 723
Chen, Christopher, *International Society for Vascular Behavioural & Cognitive Disorders*, 1560
Chenail, Louise, *Musicaction*, 984
Chenard, Thomas, *Association of Professional Engineers & Geoscientists of New Brunswick*, 158
Chenard, Jean-Pierre, *Centre de valorisation du patrimoine vivant*, 530
Chenel, Frederick, *Association CFA Montréal*, 96
Cheney, Ronn, *Grey County Law Association*, 790
Cheng, Alec, *British Columbia Society of Prosthodontists*, 254
Cheng, Alice, *Canadian Society of Endocrinology & Metabolism*, 482
Cheng, Catherine, *Professional Association of Residents of Alberta*, 1182
Cheng, Zhao, *Canadian Society of Chinese Medicine & Acupuncture*, 481
Cheng, Ernest W., *Canadian Test Centre Inc.*, 494
Cheng, Tina, *American Society of Neuroradiology*, 1502
Chenier, Stephen, *Ontario Curling Association*, 1076
Chénier, Pierre, *Parti marxiste-léniniste du Québec*, 1144
Cheperdak, David, *British Columbia Care Providers Association*, 235
Chepesiuk, Ray, *Pharmaceutical Advertising Advisory Board*, 1156
Chera, Satinder, *Canadian Convenience Stores Association*, 364
Chergui, Belkacem, *British Columbia Muslim Association*, 247
Cherkaoui, Omar, *International Federation of Medical Students' Associations*, 1548
Cherney, Lawrence, *Soundstreams Canada*, 1333
Chernousov, Pavel, *Canadian Association of the Deaf*, 334

Cherry-Lemire, Jane, *Camrose Arts Society*, 277
Chervin, Michael, *Project Genesis*, 1187
Chervinsky, Tom, *Canadians for Clean Prosperity*, 507
Chesnais, Servane, *Association des neurotraumatisés de l'Outaouais*, 121
Chessell, Tom, *Power Workers' Union*, 1169
Chester, Terry, *Air Force Association of Canada*, 19
Chetan, Mehta, *Professional Engineers Ontario*, 1183
Cheuk, Aviva, *Canadian Hadassah WIZO*, 399
Cheung, Cedric, *Chinese Medicine & Acupuncture Association of Canada*, 565
Cheung, Jane, *Chinese Medicine & Acupuncture Association of Canada*, 565
Cheung, Kenneth, *Chinese Neighbourhood Society of Montréal*, 565
Cheung, Ming-Tat, *Chinese Cultural Centre of Greater Toronto*, 564
Cheung, Francis, *British Columbia Summer Swimming Association*, 255
Chevalier, Guylaine, *Association paritaire pour la santé et la sécurité du travail - Secteur Affaires municipales*, 165
Chevarie, Camille, *American Society of Heating, Refrigerating & Air Conditioning Engineers*, 1500
Chevrier, François-G., *Associations touristiques régionales associées du Québec*, 179
Chew, Ange, *Tourism Vernon*, 1391
Chezick, Karen, *Medical Group Management Association of Canada*, 958
Chezzi, David, *Occupational Health Clinics for Ontario Workers*, 1054
Chi, Simon, *Alberta Rugby Football Union*, 45
Chiarelli, Catherine, *Vision Institute of Canada*, 1436
Chiarotto, Frank, *Villa Charities Inc. (Toronto District)*, 1434
Chiasson, Eugène, *Chambre de commerce des Iles Lamèque et Miscou inc.*, 544
Chiasson, Marcellin, *Dystonia Medical Research Foundation Canada*, 666
Chiasson, Emilie, *Ovarian Cancer Canada*, 1134
Chief, Ron, *The Pas Friendship Centre Inc.*, 1145
Chieffallo, Giovanni, *Canadian Italian Business & Professional Association*, 423
Chiesa, Sherri, *UNITE HERE*, 1599
Chik, Connie, *Canadian Society of Endocrinology & Metabolism*, 482
Chikermane, Vihaya, *Alliance for South Asian AIDS Prevention*, 57
Child, Martha, *Major League Baseball Players' Association (Ind.)*, 1569
Childs, Scott, *Ontario Crown Attorneys Association*, 1076
Childs, Carol, *United Empire Loyalists' Association of Canada*, 1410
Childs, Winston, *Canadian Association of Veterans in United Nations Peacekeeping*, 336
Chilia, Salvatore J., *International Brotherhood of Electrical Workers (AFL-CIO/CFL)*, 1542
Chilibeck, Phil, *Canadian Society for Exercise Physiology*, 475
Chilton, Ross, *Community Living Society*, 605
Chilton, John, *International Association of Hydrogeologists*, 1539
Chin, Renee, *Federation of Chinese Canadian Professionals (Québec)*, 723
Chirgwin, Juan Carolos, *Physicians for Global Survival (Canada)*, 1158
Chisholm, Danita, *The War Amputations of Canada*, 1440
Chisholm, Brad, *Nova Scotia Real Estate Commission*, 1048
Chisholm, Alison, *First Pacific Theatre Society*, 739
Chisholm, Matthew, *Esperanto-Toronto*, 695

Executive Name Index

Chisholm, George, *Oakville Historical Society*, 1053
Chisman, Dennis, *International Council of Associations for Science Education*, 1545
Chitale, Angeli, *Ontario Association of Naturopathic Doctors*, 1065
Chitaroni, Gino, *Northern Prospectors Association*, 1035
Chittock, Brian, *AIDS Vancouver*, 17
Chiu, Fiona, *Physiotherapy Association of British Columbia*, 1159
Chiv, Susan, *Simon Fraser Public Interest Research Group*, 1300
Chivers, Doug, *University of Saskatchewan Faculty Association*, 1420
Chivilo, Lois, *Salers Association of Canada*, 1251
Chmelicek, John, *College of Family Physicians of Canada*, 584
Chmielewski, Linda, *Alberta Genealogical Society*, 37
Cho, Raymond, *Toronto Zoo*, 1388
Cho, Jennifer, *Association of Professional Engineers & Geoscientists of British Columbia*, 157
Cho, Chung Won, *Korean Association of Newfoundland & Labrador*, 893
Cho, Sun Hee, *Association of Korean Canadian Scientists & Engineers*, 150
Cho Hong, James, *International Federation for Medical & Biological Engineering*, 1547
Choi, June, *Korean-Canadian Symphony Orchestra*, 894
Choi, Haloo, *Association of Korean Canadian Scientists & Engineers*, 150
Choinière, Martin, *Association des Diplômés de Polytechnique*, 111
Chokie, Linton, *North American Association of Asian Professionals Vancouver*, 1029
Cholewa, Natalie, *Literacy Council York-Simcoe*, 914
Chong, Tony, *Association of Professional Engineers & Geoscientists of British Columbia*, 157
Chong, Connie, *College of Opticians of British Columbia*, 587
Chong, Flora, *Toronto Association for Learning & Preserving the History of WWII in Asia*, 1382
Choo, Song, *Chinese Canadian National Council*, 564
Choo-Smith, Lin-P'ing, *Biathlon Manitoba*, 207
Chopyk, Wilmar, *Catholic Health Association of Manitoba*, 519
Choquet, Gilles, *Orchestre symphonique de Longueuil*, 1118
Choquette, Daniel, *Association des détaillants en alimentation du Québec*, 110
Choquette, Lucien, *Chambre immobilière de l'Estrie inc.*, 550
Choquette, Ronald, *Audition Québec*, 187
Choquette, Vicky, *Coalition des femmes de l'Alberta*, 578
Chorney, Harvey, *Prairie Agricultural Machinery Institute*, 1169
Chorney, Robert T., *Farmers' Markets Ontario*, 706
Chorostecki, Jim, *British Columbia Federation of Labour*, 241
Chotai, Vasant, *Edmonton Social Planning Council*, 679
Chothia, Meherab, *Zoroastrian Society of Ontario*, 1482
Chou, Lynn, *The Canadian Club of Toronto*, 357
Choucha, Sam, *Canadian Institute of Food Science & Technology*, 416
Choudhary, Manzoor, *Cricket Alberta*, 642
Chouinard, Sylvain, *Association des neurologues du Québec*, 121
Chouinard, Hélène, *Syndicat de la fonction publique du Québec inc. (ind.)*, 1361
Chouinard, Robert, *Canadian Association of Veterans in United Nations Peacekeeping*, 336

Chouinard, Marie, *Compagnie Marie Chouinard*, 608
Chouinard, Jean-Luc, *Union québécoise du bison*, 1408
Chouinard, Daniel, *Fédération des employés du préhospitaliers du Québec*, 714
Chow, Henry P.H., *Canadian Ethnic Studies Association*, 382
Chow, Marlyn, *British Columbia Epilepsy Society*, 240
Chow, Ivy, *Canadian Society of Hospital Pharmacists*, 484
Chow, Olivia, *Institute for Change Leaders*, 843
Chowaniec, Joe, *Environmental Services Association of Alberta*, 692
Choy, Jeremy, *BMW Clubs Canada*, 216
Choy, Rose, *Canadian Home Builders' Association - British Columbia*, 407
Chretien, Leon, *South Cariboo Chamber of Commerce*, 1334
Chrétien, Stéphane, *Northern Finance Association*, 1035
Chris, Paul, *Vision Institute of Canada*, 1436
Chrisfield, Jeff, *African Wildlife Foundation*, 1486
Chrisiaen, Alysia, *Ontario Brain Injury Association*, 1069
Chrisjohn, Andrea, *Toronto Council Fire Native Cultural Centre*, 1383
Chrisman, Nicholas, *GEOIDE Network*, 769
Christakos, Demetra, *Ontario Association of Art Galleries*, 1062
Christensen, Peter, *Danish Canadian Club of Calgary*, 650
Christensen, Kjeld, *Dania Home Society*, 650
Christensen, Frank J., *International Union of Elevator Constructors*, 1564
Christensen, Rolf Buschardt, *Federation of Danish Associations in Canada*, 723
Christensen, Aase, *Federation of Danish Associations in Canada*, 723
Christensen, Mads, *Greenpeace USA*, 1529
Christensen, Tammy, *Horseshoe Saskatchewan Inc.*, 822
Christensen, Bruce D., *North Central Local Government Association*, 1030
Christensen, Grant, *Chartered Professional Accountants of Manitoba*, 553
Christenson, Jonathan, *Catalyst Theatre Society of Alberta*, 517
Christian, Pauline, *Black Business & Professional Association*, 213
Christian, Claire, *Antarctic & Southern Ocean Coalition*, 1505
Christian, Holly, *Canadian Airports Council*, 291
Christian, Marie, *Voices: Manitoba's Youth in Care Network*, 1437
Christiansen, Hanne H., *International Permafrost Association*, 1555
Christiansen, Heather, *Surrey Symphony Society*, 1357
Christiansen, Jeff, *Saskatchewan Palliative Care Association*, 1271
Christiansen, Kathy, *Calgary Alpha House Society*, 271
Christiansson, Jackie, *Canadian Union of Public Employees*, 499
Christidis, George, *Canadian Nuclear Association*, 442
Christie, Chris, *McMan Youth, Family & Community Services Association*, 956
Christie, Jim, *Ontario Provincial Police Association*, 1098
Christie, Erica, *Government Finance Officers Association of British Columbia*, 778
Christmas, Dayna, *Alberta Water Polo Association*, 51
Christmas, Debbie, *AFOA Canada*, 12
Christo, Kelly, *Woodstock & District Developmental Services*, 1464
Christodoulou, Steven, *Association of Condominium Managers of Ontario*, 145
Christoff, Barry, *Institute On Governance*, 848

Christopherson, Denise, *YWCA Canada*, 1481
Chrumka, Elizabeth, *Canadian Organic Growers Inc.*, 447
Chrysler, Judy, *Skeena Valley Naturalists*, 1302
Chua-Tan, Shirley, *Autism Yukon*, 189
Chuang, Laura, *Toronto Association of Law Libraries*, 1382
Chuang, Ryan, *Poison & Drug Information Service*, 1163
Chubby, Steve, *Big Brothers Big Sisters of British Columbia*, 209
Chud, Gyda, *Pacific Immigrant Resources Society*, 1135
Chui, Monica, *Canadian Liver Foundation*, 427
Chummar, Noble, *Empire Club of Canada*, 686
Chung, Joyce, *Hong Kong-Canada Business Association*, 820
Chung, Shine, *Korean Canadian Women's Association*, 893
Chung, Rudy, *North American Association of Asian Professionals Vancouver*, 1029
Chung, Su Hwan, *Alberta Taekwondo Association*, 49
Chung, Yong Hoo, *Korean Senior Citizens Society of Toronto*, 893
Chungong, Martin, *Inter-Parliamentary Union*, 1567
Chunilall, Andrew, *Community Foundations of Canada*, 598
Church, Georgina, *Canadian Dance Teachers' Association*, 375
Church, Rosemary E., *Lupus Society of Alberta*, 922
Church, André, *Association des francophones du delta du Mackenzie*, 114
Church, David, *Ontario English Catholic Teachers' Association (CLC)*, 1078
Churcher, Tina, *International Institute for Conservation of Historic & Artistic Works*, 1551
Churchill, Lloyd, *North Hastings Community Integration Association*, 1031
Churchill, Steven W., *Association for Healthcare Philanthropy*, 1508
Churchill, Jennifer, *Ontario Association of Children's Rehabilitation Services*, 1063
Churchman, Monty, *Canadian Sport Massage Therapists Association*, 490
Chute, Ron, *Shelburne & Area Chamber of Commerce*, 1295
Chute, Richard, *The Planetary Society*, 1584
Chutter, Stuart, *Canadian Meat Goat Association*, 432
Chychul, Grace, *The Professional Institute of the Public Service of Canada*, 1185
Chychul, Grace, *The Professional Institute of the Public Service of Canada*, 1185
Chyczij, Alexandra, *The Advocates' Society*, 11
Cia, Patricia, *Council of Post Secondary Library Directors, British Columbia*, 635
Ciampini, Gabriella, *Institute of Public Administration of Canada*, 847
Cianflone, Dino, *General Conference of the Canadian Assemblies of God*, 768
Cicchetto, Kim, *Nova Scotia League for Equal Opportunities*, 1046
Cicinelli, Mary, *Pan American Hockey Federation*, 1138
Cicinelli, Mary, *Institute for Work & Health*, 844
Ciecwierz, Roman J, *Order of Malta - Canadian Association*, 1119
Cindy, Reid, *The Cultch*, 645
Cinelli, Marilina, *The Rosary Apostolate, Inc.*, 1236
Cinq-Mars, François, *Musée minéralogique et minier de Thetford Mines*, 982
Ciocan, Mihaela, *Association of Image Consultants International Canada*, 149
Ciona, Andrea, *Calgary Stetson Show Band*, 274
Ciotola, Celia, *GAMA International Canada*, 766

Ciprietti, Ben, *The Japan Society Canada*, 869
Cirillo, Lisa, *Downtown Legal Services*, 662
Ciss, Julius, *Jews for Judaism*, 873
Ciufo, Jody, *Royal Architectural Institute of Canada*, 1237
Civak, Bob, *Ontario Centres of Excellence*, 1071
Cizmic, Phil, *British Columbia Wrestling Association*, 259
Claiman, Barbara, *Ontario Brain Injury Association*, 1068
Clairoux, Jacques, *Fondation Sommeil: Association de personnes atteintes de déficiences reliées au sommeil*, 748
Clamen, Mark, *Toronto Jewish Film Society*, 1385
Clancy, Ann, *Canadian Red Cross*, 466
Clancy, Mary, *Family Service Association of Halifax*, 704
Clancy, James, *National Union of Public & General Employees*, 996
Clare, Sally, *CanoeKayak Canada*, 509
Clare, Sheldon, *Canada's National Firearms Association*, 282
Clare, John, *Canadian Fallen Firefighters Foundation*, 383
Clark, Garnet, *West Hants Historical Society*, 1445
Clark, Greg, *Canadian Society for Bioengineering*, 473
Clark, Andrew, *New Brunswick Federation of Woodlot Owners Inc.*, 1008
Clark, Simone, *Prince Rupert & District Chamber of Commerce*, 1179
Clark, Evelyn, *Qualicum Beach Chamber of Commerce*, 1195
Clark, Colleen, *Sechelt & District Chamber of Commerce*, 1288
Clark, Rob, *Moose Jaw & District Chamber of Commerce*, 973
Clark, Marilyn, *Nova Scotia Fish Packers Association*, 1045
Clark, Ian, *Orienteering Association of Nova Scotia*, 1126
Clark, Rob, *Saskatchewan Weekly Newspapers Association*, 1278
Clark, Bruce, *Alberta Land Surveyors' Association*, 39
Clark, Scott, *Professional Engineers Ontario*, 1183
Clark, Judith, *Aboriginal Women's Association of Prince Edward Island*, 3
Clark, Heather, *Hospital for Sick Children Foundation*, 823
Clark, Tony, *Major League Baseball Players' Association (Ind.)*, 1569
Clark, Cynthia, *Edmonton Dental Assistants Association*, 676
Clark, Mary, *College of Occupational Therapists of British Columbia*, 586
Clark, Trevor, *Alzheimer Society of Hamilton Halton*, 62
Clark, Graham, *Alzheimer Society of Sault Ste. Marie & District of Algoma*, 64
Clark, Kyla, *Alberta Federation of Shooting Sports*, 35
Clark, Shauna, *Supply Chain Management Association - Newfoundland & Labrador*, 1356
Clark, Isaura, *The Dream Factory*, 662
Clark, Anne, *The Québec Drama Federation*, 1197
Clark, Patricia, *Active Living Coalition for Older Adults*, 7
Clark, Garry, *Ontario Prospectors Association*, 1098
Clark, Tom, *Prince Edward Island Harness Racing Industry Association*, 1174
Clark, Glenn, *Canadian Piedmontese Association*, 455
Clark, Bill, *Western Canadian Miniature Horse Club*, 1448
Clark, Shari, *CADORA Ontario Association Inc.*, 269

Executive Name Index

Clark Lafleur, Christine, *Port Colborne Community Association for Research Extension*, 1165
Clark-Stewart, Anne, *Canadian Federation of Pensioners*, 388
Clarke, Deb, *Hussar Fish & Game Association*, 829
Clarke, Kimberlee, *Association des collections d'entreprises*, 109
Clarke, Victoria, *Rideau Chamber of Commerce*, 1231
Clarke, Pat, *Québec Women's Institutes*, 1199
Clarke, Gordon, *Manitoba Historical Society*, 938
Clarke, Colin, *Hamilton Philharmonic Youth Orchestra*, 802
Clarke, Christine, *Strathcona Park Lodge & Outdoor Education Centre*, 1351
Clarke, Beth, *Wilderness Committee*, 1454
Clarke, Jeanine, *United Way of Perth-Huron*, 1416
Clarke, Trina, *YMCA Canada*, 1472
Clarke, Gillian, *Alberta Diabetes Foundation*, 33
Clarke, Janice, *Alzheimer Society of York Region*, 65
Clarke, Rick, *Nova Scotia Federation of Labour*, 1044
Clarke, Janet, *National Association of Watch & Clock Collectors, Inc.*, 1575
Clarke, Ronald V., *Canadian Association of Veterans in United Nations Peacekeeping*, 336
Clarke, Maria-Leena, *Canada Basketball*, 278
Clarke, Graham, *Canadian Association of Home & Property Inspectors*, 317
Clarke, Teren, *Spinal Cord Injury Alberta*, 1342
Clarke, Paul, *Programme Action Réfugiés Montréal*, 1187
Clarke, MacAndrew, *Canadian Alliance of Student Associations*, 291
Clarke, Teri, *The Rainbow Society of Alberta*, 1204
Clarke, Susan, *Parrsborough Shore Historical Society*, 1143
Clarke, Sandra, *Advanced Coronary Treatment (ACT) Foundation of Canada*, 10
Clarke, Kerry, *Folk Festival Society of Calgary*, 742
Clarke, Susan, *Flowers Canada*, 741
Clarke, Shirley, *North Shore ConneXions Society*, 1032
Clarke, Peter, *Egg Farmers of Canada*, 681
Clarkes, Greg, *Canadian College of Emergency Medical Services*, 358
Clary, Selina, *Springboard Dance*, 1346
Clause, Debbie, *Canadian Culinary Federation*, 374
Clausen, Kurt, *Canadian Association of Foundations of Education*, 316
Claveau, Brigitte, *Syndicat de la fonction publique du Québec inc. (ind.)*, 1362
Clavet-Gaumont, Ariane, *Fédération de Water-Polo du Québec*, 711
Clavette, Ken, *Canadian Association of Learned Journals*, 319
Clawson, Kim, *Manitoba Darts Association Inc.*, 935
Claxton, Adelynne, *Saanich Native Heritage Society*, 1245
Claxton, Steve, *Canada Employment & Immigration Union*, 279
Claypool, Shylo, *Canadian Cowboys' Association*, 372
Clayton, Helen, *Equestrian Association for the Disabled*, 694
Clayton, Ben, *Impact Society*, 831
Cleare, Anthony, *International Society for Affective Disorders*, 1557
Cleary, Jana, *Canadian Progress Club*, 461
Cleave, Patricia, *Speech & Hearing Association of Nova Scotia*, 1340
Cleave, Marge, *Saskatchewan Genealogical Society*, 1266

Cleave, Dwayne, *Lutheran Church - Canada*, 922
Cleaveley, Judy, *Saskatchewan Darts Association*, 1263
Cleaves, Sheldon, *ALS Society of British Columbia*, 60
Clelford, Sally, *Alliance of Canadian Cinema, Television & Radio Artists*, 58
Clemenger, Bruce J., *Evangelical Fellowship of Canada*, 698
Clemens, Steve, *Canadian Fire Alarm Association*, 390
Clement, Christopher, *International Commission on Radiological Protection*, 855
Clement, Jennifer, *PEN International*, 1583
Clément, Peter L., *ERS Training & Development Corporation*, 695
Clement, Laurie, *Canadian Association of Optometrists*, 324
Clement, Tom, *Co-operative Housing Federation of Toronto*, 628
Clement, Ken, *Canadian Aboriginal AIDS Network*, 285
Clément, Michel, *Réseau des SADC et CAE*, 1221
Clement, Ken, *Circle of Eagles Lodge*, 570
Clement, Peter L., *T.R.E.E. Foundation for Youth Development*, 1397
Clément, Jacques, *Orchestre symphonique du Saguenay-Lac-St-Jean*, 1119
Clement, Gino, *First Nation Lands Managers Association of Québec & Labrador*, 738
Clements, Tracey, *Sport PEI Inc.*, 1345
Clements, Daniel, *Canadian Culinary Federation*, 374
Clements, Eliana, *Local Government Management Association of British Columbia*, 917
Cleret de Langavant, Ghislaine, *Canadian Bioethics Society*, 343
Cleroux, Jaime, *Canadian College of Health Leaders*, 358
Clibbon, Peter, *Canadian Wind Energy Association*, 504
Cliche, Levi, *Clean Annapolis River Project*, 573
Cliff, William Grant, *The Anglican Church of Canada*, 69
Cliff, Andrea, *Meeting Professionals International*, 1571
Clifford, Linda, *Ontario Gymnastic Federation*, 1083
Clin, Marie-Chantal, *Association du Québec pour enfants avec problèmes auditifs*, 131
Cline, Cliff, *Yonge Street Mission*, 1473
Clinton, John T., *St. Leonard's Society of Canada*, 1250
Clipperton, Tasha, *Canadian Health Information Management Association*, 402
Clipperton, Mary, *The Royal Scottish Country Dance Society*, 1587
Clode, Brent, *Central 1 Credit Union*, 523
Clogg, Jessica, *West Coast Environmental Law*, 1445
Clory, Mike, *Registered Psychiatric Nurses Association of Saskatchewan*, 1214
Clory, Kim, *Registered Psychiatric Nurses Association of Saskatchewan*, 1214
Clos, Joan, *United Nations Human Settlements Programme (Habitat)*, 1600
Close, Jon, *Community Futures Network Society of Alberta*, 598
Closner, Neil, *Cannabis Canada Association*, 508
Clough, Larry, *Swimming Canada*, 1359
Clough, Brian, *The Shepherds' Trust*, 1295
Clouston, Janet, *Salt Spring Island Chamber of Commerce*, 1252
Cloutier, Mélanie, *Syndicat des employées de soutien de l'Université de Sherbrooke*, 1362
Cloutier, Sylvie, *Conseil de la transformation agroalimentaire et des produits de consommation*, 616
Cloutier, Nicole, *College of Family Physicians of Canada*, 584

Cloutier, Kiki, *Canadian Public Relations Society Inc.*, 463
Cloutier, Lise, *Association de la Fibromyalgie des Laurentides*, 101
Cloutier, Louise, *La Société historique du Cap-Rouge*, 1321
Cloutier, Édith, *Centre d'amitié autochtone de Val-d'Or*, 527
Cloutier, Philippe, *Association de l'exploration minière de Québec*, 100
Cloutier, Réal, *Canadian Home Care Association*, 408
Cloutier, Marie-Eve, *Association des journalistes indépendants du Québec*, 117
Cloutier, O'Neil, *Canadian Council of Professional Fish Harvesters*, 369
Cloutier-Dupuis, Christiane, *Société catholique de la Bible*, 1309
Clovechok, Susan E., *Columbia Valley Chamber of Commerce*, 591
Clowater, Roberta, *Canadian Parks & Wilderness Society*, 451
Cluff, Pearl, *Professional Organizers in Canada*, 1186
Clunis, Susette, *ADR Institute of Canada*, 9
Clunis, Andrew, *Power Workers' Union*, 1169
Clunk, Charles C., *Association for Facilities Engineering*, 1508
Clute, Bob, *Habitat for Humanity Canada*, 797
Clutsam, Karen, *Canadian Investor Relations Institute*, 422
Clyne, Guy, *Health & Safety Conference Society of Alberta*, 805
Coakeley, Simon, *National Association of Federal Retirees*, 990
Coaker, James W., *American Society of Mechanical Engineers*, 1500
Coates, Patty, *Ontario Federation of Labour*, 1079
Coates, Rebecca, *Ontario Ginseng Growers Association*, 1082
Coates, Adonia C., *American Thyroid Association*, 1504
Coatsworth, Jamie, *Cross Country Canada*, 643
Cobb-Reeves, Tracy, *Greater Vernon Chamber of Commerce*, 787
Coburn, Craig, *Canadian Association of Geographers*, 316
Coburn, Brian, *Canadian Co-operative Association*, 364
Coburn, Stephanie, *Conservation Council of New Brunswick*, 622
Coburn, Pam, *Ontario Equestrian Federation*, 1078
Cochet, Benoit, *Réseau des SADC et CAE*, 1220
Cochran, Veronica, *International Association of Administrative Professionals*, 1537
Cochran, Bob, *Saskatchewan Cycling Association*, 1263
Cochrane, Teri, *Nova Scotia School Counsellor Association*, 1048
Cochrane, Bridget, *Association of Administrative Professionals*, 139
Cochrane, Penny, *Canadian Institute of Energy (British Columbia)*, 415
Cochrane, Ron, *Professional Association of Foreign Service Officers*, 1182
Cochrane, Cathy, *Atlantic Floor Covering Association*, 184
Cochrane, Doug, *Canadian Patient Safety Institute*, 452
Cochrane, Meredith, *Citizens' Environment Watch*, 571
Cochrane, Ryan, *Alberta Association of Prosthetists & Orthotists*, 24
Cockburn, Tom, *British Columbia Paleontological Alliance*, 248
Cockerill, Kate, *Western Magazine Awards Foundation*, 1450
Cockerton, Stan, *Ontario Lacrosse Association*, 1088
Cocks, Fraser, *Canadian Hoisting & Rigging Safety Council*, 406

Cocks, Malcolm, *Australian Wine Society of Toronto*, 188
Code, Bill, *Association of Complementary & Integrative Physicians of BC*, 145
Code, Kathy, *Ecoforestry Institute Society*, 671
Codjoe, Esi, *Canadian Association of Black Lawyers*, 309
Coe-Kirkham, Linda, *Dance Saskatchewan Inc.*, 649
Coehn, Glenn, *ARZA-Canada: The Zionist Voice of the Canadian Reform Movement*, 86
Coelho, Don, *Master Mariners of Canada*, 954
Coelho, Fernando, *posAbilities Association of BC*, 1167
Coffey, Colleen, *Public Service Alliance of Canada*, 1193
Coffey, Marlene, *Ontario Non-Profit Housing Association*, 1093
Coffin, Percy D., *The Anglican Church of Canada*, 70
Coffin, Scott, *Receivables Management Assocation of Canada Inc.*, 1206
Coffman, Peter, *Society for the Study of Architecture in Canada*, 1327
Coghlan, Anne, *College of Nurses of Ontario*, 586
Cohen, David R., *Association of Applied Geochemists*, 139
Cohen, Matt, *Advertising Association of Winnipeg Inc.*, 10
Cohen, David, *Manitoba Fencing Association*, 936
Cohen, Karen R., *Canadian Psychological Association*, 462
Cohen, Baruch, *Canadian Institute for Jewish Research*, 412
Cohen, Jeffrey I., *The Canadian Society for the Weizmann Institute of Science*, 478
Cohen, Athol, *Model Aeronautics Association of Canada Inc.*, 971
Cohen, Yoram, *World Federation for Mental Health*, 1605
Cohen, Maud, *Fondation CHU Sainte-Justine*, 743
Cohen, James, *Canadian Magen David Adom for Israel*, 429
Cohen, Eric, *Canadian Association of Interventional Cardiology*, 319
Cohen, Cheryl, *Harry & Martha Cohen Foundation*, 804
Cohen Hackett, Lorie, *Association of Canadian Travel Agencies - Atlantic*, 144
Cohn, Carla, *Manitoba Dental Association*, 935
Cohon, Mark, *Canadian Academy of Recording Arts & Sciences*, 286
Coignaud, René, *Association coopérative d'économie familiale de l'Outaouais*, 98
Coke, Tom, *Epilepsy Ontario*, 694
Colaiacovo, Kathy, *International Virtual Assistants Association*, 1566
Colangelo, Anya, *Dying with Dignity*, 665
Colarusso, Robert, *The Transplantation Society*, 1395
Colas, Bernard, *International Law Association - Canadian Branch*, 858
Colautti, Christine, *Association of Fundraising Professionals*, 1512
Colbert, Julie, *Centraide Mauricie*, 523
Colbourne, Sheila, *Vélo New Brunswick*, 1431
Colbourne, Terry, *Barrhead Animal Rescue Society*, 197
Cole, Catherine C., *Commonwealth Association of Museums*, 593
Cole, Andrew B., *Canadian Urethane Foam Contractors Association*, 500
Cole, David, *Toronto Soaring Club*, 1387
Cole, Thomass, *Amalgamated Conservation Society*, 66
Cole, John, *Financial Executives International Canada*, 736
Cole, David, *Jersey Canada*, 869
Cole, Roger, *Vancouver Youth Symphony Orchestra Society*, 1429
Cole, Brian, *St. John Ambulance*, 1249

Executive Name Index

Cole, Michelle, *Shuswap Columbia District Labour Council*, 1297
Cole, Pat, *Human Resources Professionals Association*, 826
Cole, Laura, *Prince Edward Island Crafts Council*, 1173
Cole, Brian M., *Canada-Singapore Business Association*, 284
Cole, Nathan, *KidSport Saskatchewan*, 887
Cole, Barry, *Cole Foundation*, 581
Coleborn, Ron, *British Columbia Association of Mathematics Teachers*, 232
Colello, Darren, *Northwest Wildlife Preservation Society*, 1039
Coleman, Chrystal, *United Nations Association in Canada*, 1411
Coleman, Sandra, *South West Community Care Access Centre*, 1336
Coleman, Todd, *Family Enterprise Xchange*, 703
Coleman, Steve, *Mechanical Contractors Association of Ontario*, 957
Coleman, Peter, *The National Citizens Coalition*, 991
Coleman, Jean, *Nova Scotia Association for Community Living*, 1040
Coleman, Mary Ann, *New Brunswick Environmental Network*, 1008
Coleman, Grant, *Teamsters Canada (CLC)*, 1368
Coleman, Rob, *Triathlon Newfoundland & Labrador*, 1398
Coleman, Brian, *Alberta Percheron Club*, 42
Coleman, Jan, *Kidney Cancer Canada Association*, 885
Coleman-Lawrie, Tamara, *United Way of Niagara Falls & Greater Fort Erie*, 1415
Coleman-Lawrie, Tamara, *United Way South Niagara*, 1417
Coleridge, Peter, *Big Brothers Big Sisters of Canada*, 209
Colero, Michelle, *Hospice Palliative Care Ontario*, 823
Coles, Trent, *Prince Edward Island Sheep Breeders Association*, 1177
Coles, Virginia, *CFA Society Vancouver*, 539
Coles, Ken, *Farming Smarter*, 706
Colford, Cindy, *Canadian Association for Conservation of Cultural Property*, 298
Colford, Patrick, *New Brunswick Federation of Labour*, 1008
Collard, Jim, *Ontario Small Urban Municipalities*, 1105
Colle, Sharon M., *The Foundation Fighting Blindness*, 755
Colledge, Tanya, *Canadian Public Relations Society Inc.*, 463
Colledge, Martin, *College of Podiatrists of Manitoba*, 589
Collenette, David, *The Chartered Institute of Logistics & Transport in North America*, 552
Collet, Anouk, *United Food & Commercial Workers Canada*, 1411
Collett, Michelle, *Chinese Medicine & Acupuncture Council of Canada*, 565
Collette, Wayne, *Canadian Tarentaise Association*, 492
Collette, Alain, *Ordre professionnel des technologistes médicaux du Québec*, 1125
Collette, Don, *Canadian Professional Boxing Council*, 460
Collin, Guy, *Ordre des chimistes du Québec*, 1120
Collin, Yvan, *Réseau des SADC et CAE*, 1220
Collingan, Mary, *North Atlantic Salmon Conservation Organization*, 1579
Collings, Rhonda, *Newfoundland & Labrador Construction Association*, 1017
Collins, Dan, *Langley Association for Community Living*, 899
Collins, Shirley, *Prince Albert Exhibition Association*, 1171
Collins, Linda, *Mining Suppliers Trade Association Canada*, 967

Collins, Ken, *Qualifications Evaluation Council of Ontario*, 1195
Collins, Thomas C., *Catholic Missions in Canada*, 520
Collins, Korinne, *Canadian Credit Union Association*, 372
Collins, Eugene, *Placentia Area Chamber of Commerce*, 1161
Collins, Bob, *Gravenhurst Chamber of Commerce/Visitors Bureau*, 782
Collins, Colleen, *Canada West Foundation*, 281
Collins, Angela, *Canadian Society of Customs Brokers*, 482
Collins, Kevin J., *Easter Seals Ontario*, 670
Collins, Thomas Cardinal, *Catholic Charities of The Archdiocese of Toronto*, 518
Collins, Gary N., *Epilepsy Canada*, 693
Collins, Tina, *Canadian Morgan Horse Association*, 437
Collins, Karen (KC), *Métis Nation of Alberta*, 963
Collins, Thomas, *Assembly of Catholic Bishops of Ontario*, 88
Collins, Lawrence E., *Law Foundation of Newfoundland & Labrador*, 901
Collins, Brian, *National Environmental Health Association*, 1576
Collins, Bev, *Canadian Union of Postal Workers*, 498
Collins, Norval, *Environmental Services Association of Nova Scotia*, 692
Collins, Christine, *Union of Canadian Transportation Employees*, 1407
Collins, Tish, *Associated Country Women of the World*, 1507
Collins, Cass, *Yukon Art Society*, 1477
Collins, A. Bruce, *Nova Scotia Construction Safety Association*, 1043
Collins, Faye, *Ontario Daylily Society*, 1076
Collins, Sandra, *Canada Media Fund*, 280
Collins, Colleen, *Lindsay & District Chamber of Commerce*, 912
Collins, Angie, *Peace Region Internet Society*, 1147
Collins, Maureen, *John Howard Society of Alberta*, 874
Collinson, Melissa, *Calgary Minor Soccer Association*, 273
Colliou, Lynn, *Squash Manitoba*, 1347
Collis, Diane, *Greater Vancouver Food Bank Society*, 786
Collishaw, Barbara, *Association of Translators & Interpreters of Ontario*, 163
Collos, Debra, *British Columbia Shorthand Reporters Association*, 253
Collver, David, *International Machine Cancel Research Society of Canada*, 858
Coloma, Fides, *Eye Bank of Canada - Ontario Division*, 700
Colomb, Chuck, *Lakeshore Stamp Club Inc.*, 897
Colpitts, Dave, *Animal Nutrition Association of Canada*, 71
Colpitts-Waddell, Nathalie, *New Brunswick Gymnastics Association*, 1009
Colpron, Emile, *Canadian Parks & Wilderness Society*, 451
Colquhoun, Lynn, *Early Childhood Intervention Program (ECIP) Sask. Inc.*, 667
Colton, Glenn, *Canadian University Music Society*, 499
Colton, Micky, *CADORA Ontario Association Inc.*, 269
Colvin, Miriam, *Bulkley Valley Community Arts Council*, 264
Colwell, Linda, *Friends of The Canadian War Museum*, 762
Colwell, Gary, *Royal Astronomical Society of Canada*, 1238
Colwell, Bruce, *Canadian Association of Medical Oncologists*, 320
Colwill, Susan, *Prince Edward Island Association of Medical Radiation Technologists*, 1172

Combres, Nicole, *Boys & Girls Clubs of Saskatchewan*, 224
Combs, Brenda, *National Aboriginal Circle Against Family Violence*, 988
Comeau, Tracey, *Villa Charities Inc. (Toronto District)*, 1435
Comeau, Yves, *Canadian Association on Water Quality*, 337
Comeau, Tracey, *Queen Elizabeth Hospital Foundation*, 1199
Comeau, Jean-Marie, *Fédération des professionnelles et professionnels de l'éducation du Québec*, 718
Comeau, Darrell, *PFLAG Canada Inc.*, 1156
Comeau, Phil, *Western Boreal Growth & Yield Association*, 1447
Comer, Cheryl, *The Neil Squire Foundation*, 1002
Comerford, Gary, *Canada-India Business Council*, 283
Comerford, Rob, *Newfoundland & Labrador Soccer Association*, 1021
Commanda, Claudette, *First Nations Confederacy of Cultural Education Centres*, 738
Commerford, Jim, *YMCA Canada*, 1472
Compagne, Suzanne, *Conseil culturel fransaskois*, 614
Compton, Steve, *Regina & District Food Bank Inc.*, 1211
Compton, Carl, *Ontario Motor Vehicle Industry Council*, 1091
Comrie, David, *Educators for Distributed Learning PSA (British Columbia)*, 680
Comrie, Charlotte, *Heart & Stroke Foundation of Prince Edward Island Inc.*, 809
Comte, Brenda, *Manitoba Deaf Sports Association Inc.*, 935
Comte, Joseph, *Manitoba Deaf Sports Association Inc.*, 935
Comtois, Marie Jose (MJ), *Independent Financial Brokers of Canada*, 832
Comtois, Ginette, *Société québécoise de la schizophrénie*, 1323
Conacher, Duff, *Democracy Watch*, 653
Conant, Bernadette, *Canadian Water Network*, 502
Conconi, Bill, *Canadian Student Leadership Association*, 491
Condello, Tony, *Association de balle des jeunes handicapés de Laval-Laurentides-Lanaudière*, 99
Condon, Darryl, *British Columbia Recreation & Parks Association*, 250
Conley, Rob, *Information Services Vancouver*, 837
Conliffe, James, *Geological Association of Canada*, 769
Conliffe, Alex, *Engineers Without Borders*, 689
Conliffe, Alexandra, *Canadian-Palestinian Education Exchange*, 506
Conlin, Ted, *Carizon Family & Community Services*, 513
Conlon, Michael, *Confederation of University Faculty Associations of British Columbia*, 611
Conlon, Debra, *Grain Farmers of Ontario*, 779
Conn, Robert, *Professional Association of Residents of Ontario*, 1182
Connell, Akoulina, *New Brunswick Arts Board*, 1004
Connell, Warren, *Calgary Exhibition & Stampede*, 272
Connell, Akoulina, *Manitoba Arts Council*, 929
Connell, Marlene, *Berwick & District Ringette Association*, 206
Conner, Deborah, *British Columbia Schizophrenia Society*, 252
Conner, Marilyn, *Wetaskiwin & District Association for Community Service*, 1451
Connolly, Kathleen, *Dawson Creek & District Chamber of Commerce*, 652
Connolly, Mike, *Skate Canada*, 1302
Connolly, Kore, *Denturist Association of British Columbia*, 653

Connolly, Michelle, *Canadian Printing Ink Manufacturers' Association*, 460
Connolly, Mike, *Cycling PEI*, 647
Connolly, Michael, *Nova Scotia Independent Adjusters' Association*, 1046
Connolly, Joan, *Literacy Ontario Central South*, 914
Connolly, James, *Association des motocyclistes gais du Québec*, 120
Connor, Patrick, *Ontario Trails Council*, 1111
Connor, Dean, *Canadian Life & Health Insurance Association Inc.*, 426
Connor, Liette, *Urology Nurses of Canada*, 1423
Connor, Frank, *Atlantic Tire Dealers Association*, 186
Connors, Peter, *Eastern Shore Fisherman's Protective Association*, 670
Connors, Cheryl, *Canadian Network for Respiratory Care*, 441
Connors, Paul, *Newfoundland & Labrador Federation of Agriculture*, 1018
Connors, Richie, *Softball Nova Scotia*, 1332
Connoy, Terry, *Canadian Tire Dealers Association*, 495
Conrad, Heather, *Interprovincial School Development Association*, 861
Conrad, Tim, *Canadian Public Relations Society Inc.*, 463
Conrad, Debbie, *Solid Waste Association of North America*, 1595
Conrad, Grace, *Native Council of Nova Scotia*, 997
Conrad, Damon, *Sackville Rivers Association*, 1245
Conradi, Alexa, *Fédération des femmes du Québec*, 715
Conroy, Joe, *Salesian Cooperators, Association of St. Benedict Centre*, 1251
Constable, Janet, *Manitoba Home Builders' Association*, 938
Constantine, David, *Newfoundland & Labrador Basketball Association*, 1017
Constantine, Danny, *New Brunswick Ground Water Association*, 1009
Constantineau, Guy, *Société de généalogie des Laurentides*, 1316
Conway, Marg, *Brantford Musicians' Association*, 227
Conway, Paul, *ADR Institute of Canada*, 9
Conway, Dawn, *Canadian Foundation for Climate & Atmospheric Sciences*, 393
Cook, Susan, *Blue Mountain Foundation for the Arts*, 215
Cook, Mary, *Ontario Association of Speech-Language Pathologists & Audiologists*, 1066
Cook, Claudine, *ALS Society of Québec*, 60
Cook, Chris, *Community Living Ajax-Pickering & Whitby*, 600
Cook, Madge, *Lighthouse Food Bank Society*, 912
Cook, Sarah, *United Nations Research Institute for Social Development*, 1600
Cook, Edward, *Specialty Graphic Imaging Association*, 1596
Cook, Janice, *Aplastic Anemia & Myelodysplasia Association of Canada*, 73
Cook, Graham, *Huntington Society of Canada*, 827
Cook, Misha, *Pitch-In Canada*, 1160
Cook, Elaine, *Terrazzo Tile & Marble Association of Canada*, 1371
Cook, Sheena, *Canadian Society of Professionals in Disability Management*, 487
Cook, Peter, *National Bison Association*, 1575
Cook, Brad, *Literacy Council of Durham Region*, 913
Cook, Angela, *Canadian Paraplegic Association (Nova Scotia)*, 450
Cook, Peter E., *Hamilton Program for Schizophrenia*, 802
Cook, Valerie, *British Columbia Registered Music Teachers' Association*, 251

Executive Name Index

Cook, Mike, Manitoba Criminal Justice Association, 935
Cook, Kathleen, Manitoba Dental Assistants Association, 935
Cook, Doug, College of Dietitians of Alberta, 584
Cook, Dale, Canadian Cable Systems Alliance, 348
Cook, Cathy, British Columbia Municipal Safety Association, 246
Cook, Stan, Newfoundland & Labrador Lacrosse Association, 1019
Cook, Peter D., Seniors in Need, 1290
Cook, Jackie, Shareholder Association for Research & Education, 1294
Cooke, Derek, Yukon Council of Archives, 1478
Cooke, Max, Canadian Education Association, 380
Cooke, Wendy, Canadian Society of Hospital Pharmacists, 484
Cooke, Cherilyn, The Royal Canadian Legion, 1240
Cooke, Terry, Hamilton Community Foundation, 801
Cooke, Bruce, Ontario Respiratory Care Society, 1101
Cooke, Kate, Canadian Frailty Network, 394
Cooke-Landry, Stephanie, Insurance Brokers Association of Canada, 848
Cookson, Martha, Festivals & Events Ontario, 733
Cool, Jacques, Centre d'animation de développement et de recherche en éducation, 528
Cool, Mary, Delta Rockhound Gem & Mineral Club, 653
Cooley, Martha, Atlantic Filmmakers Cooperative, 184
Cooley, Hudson, Directors Guild of Canada, 657
Cooley, Miriam, Canadian Society for Education through Art, 474
Cooley, Gail, Dangerous Goods Advisory Council, 1521
Cools, Romain, World Potato Congress, 1467
Coomber-Bendtsen, Melissa, YWCA Canada, 1481
Coombs, Shannon, Canadian Consumer Specialty Products Association, 364
Coombs, Michelle, Ontario Non-Profit Housing Association, 1093
Coombs, Neil, Human Resources Professionals of Newfoundland & Labrador, 826
Coon, David, Green Party of New Brunswick, 789
Coon Come, Mathew, Grand Council of the Crees, 779
Cooney, Nicole, Alberta Amateur Speed Skating Association, 22
Cooney, Nick, Mercy for Animals Canada, 961
Coopee, Todd, Resident Doctors of Canada, 1226
Cooper, Carol, Canadian Retransmission Collective, 467
Cooper, Mark, Saskatchewan Construction Association, 1261
Cooper, Darlene, Canadian Paraplegic Association (Manitoba), 450
Cooper, Debbie, Boys & Girls Clubs of Nova Scotia, 223
Cooper, Doug, Tillsonburg & District Association for Community Living, 1379
Cooper, Beverley, International Council of Associations for Science Education, 1545
Cooper, Graham, Animal Nutrition Association of Canada, 71
Cooper, Debbie, Boys & Girls Clubs of Canada, 222
Cooper, Karyn, Hamilton AIDS Network, 800
Cooper, Mike, The Canadian Corps of Commissionaires, 365
Cooper, Stacy, Ontario Home Builders' Association, 1085

Cooper, Mark, Canadian Society of Petroleum Geologists, 486
Cooper, Morris, Canadian Council for Reform Judaism, 367
Cooper, Lisa, Native Council of Prince Edward Island, 997
Cooper, Dave, Ottawa Orchid Society, 1131
Cooper, Janet, Association of Faculties of Pharmacy of Canada, 148
Cooper, Kathy, Kootenay Rockies Tourism, 892
Cooper, Cyril, Kingston Economic Development Corporation, 889
Cooper, Delane, The Metal Arts Guild of Canada, 962
Cooper, Conan, Karate BC, 881
Cooper, Josh, Baycrest Foundation, 200
Cooper, Craig, Battle River Soccer Association, 200
Cooper, James, General Church of the New Jerusalem in Canada, 768
Cooper, Meghan, Alberta Pharmacists' Association (RxA), 42
Cooper, Kimberley, Decidedly Jazz Danceworks, 652
Cooper, Audrey, Victoria Therapeutic Riding Association, 1434
Cooper, Cynthia, McCord Museum of Canadian History, 955
Cooper, Brent, Learning for Living South Muskoka, 905
Cooper, Curtis, The Canadian Association for HIV Research, 301
Cooper, Dana, Orthotics Prosthetics Canada, 1127
Cooper, Judy, Corbrook Awakening Abilities, 628
Coote, Judith, Monte Cassino Society, 1571
Copas, Lorraine, Social Planning & Research Council of BC, 1306
Copeland, Michael, Toronto Canada-China Friendship Association, 1383
Copithorne, Sharon, Building Industry & Land Development Alberta, 262
Copley, Darren, Victoria Natural History Society, 1433
Copley, Christine, World Coal Institute, 1604
Copple, Peter, Alberta Criminal Justice Association, 32
Copplestone, Glen, Ontario Confederation of University Faculty Associations, 1074
Copson, Andrew, International Humanist & Ethical Union, 1550
Coran, Johanne, Mineralogical Association of Canada, 966
Corazza, Caroline, Association du personnel administratif et professionnel de l'Université de Moncton, 131
Corbeil, Robert, Canadian Catholic Campus Ministry, 351
Corbeil, Monique, Canadian Institute for Theatre Technology, 413
Corbeil, Monique, Canadian Institute for Theatre Technology, 414
Corbeil, Karine, Association des bibliothèques publiques de l'Estrie, 107
Corbeil, André, Chambre de commerce Saint-Lin-Laurentides, 549
Corber, Deborah, The Centre for Israel & Jewish Affairs, 533
Corber, Deborah, Jewish Information Referral Service Montréal, 873
Corbett, Thomas, Ontario Painting Contractors Association, 1094
Corbett, Kathy, College of Occupational Therapists of British Columbia, 586
Corbett, Jane, LOFT Community Services, 917
Corbett, Chris, Canadian Association of Farm Advisors, 314
Corbett, Liz, Quinte Beekeepers' Association, 1201
Corbitt, Ann, Global Business Travel Association (Canada), 774
Corcoran, Kate E., Medical Library Association, 1570

Corcoran, Hazel, Canadian Worker Co-operative Federation, 506
Cord, Ena, National Council of Jewish Women of Canada, 992
Cordeau, Luc, Centre d'Histoire de Saint-Hyacinthe, 528
Cordeiro, Carlos, Chambre immobilière du Saguenay-Lac St-Jean Inc., 551
Cordeiro, Michelle, Foundation for Prader-Willi Research in Canada, 756
Corey, David, Victoria Real Estate Board, 1433
Corey, Murray, British Columbia Wall & Ceiling Association, 257
Coristine, Ron, Community Living Chatham-Kent, 601
Cork, David, Toronto Renewable Energy Co-operative, 1387
Cork, Mary, Welsh Pony & Cob Society of Canada, 1444
Corke, Sarah Jane, Canadian Association for Security & Intelligence Studies, 303
Corkery, James, Rotary Club of Stratford Charitable Foundation, 1236
Corkum, Diane, Project Share, 1188
Corlett, Al, Forests Ontario, 752
Cormack, Lesley, Canadian Society for the History & Philosophy of Science, 477
Cormie, Joel, Lighthouse Mission, 912
Cormier, Wayne, Early Childhood Intervention Program (ECIP) Sask. Inc., 667
Cormier, Bernard, Greater Bathurst Chamber of Commerce, 783
Cormier, Laverne, Alberta Genealogical Society, 36
Cormier, Martin, Fédération de rugby du Québec, 710
Cormier, Lynn, Automotive Industries Association of Canada, 190
Cormier, Amanda, Canadian Anesthesiologists' Society, 293
Cormier, Jacques, New Brunswick Forest Products Association Inc., 1008
Cormier, Sophie, Stanstead Historical Society, 1348
Cormier, Ronald, Greater Shediac Chamber of Commerce, 785
Cormier, Martin, Association des entrepreneurs en maçonnerie du Québec, 113
Cormier, Jacqueline A., Moncton Area Lawyers' Association, 972
Cormier, Keith, Salmon Preservation Association for the Waters of Newfoundland, 1252
Cormier, Jean-Noël, Conseil national Société de Saint-Vincent de Paul, 619
Cormier, Guy, Fédération des caisses Desjardins du Québec, 712
Cormier, Murielle, Chartered Professional Accountants of New Brunswick, 553
Corn, Earle, Navy League of Canada, 1001
Corn, Earle, Navy League of Canada, 1002
Corneault, Jean-Pierre, Conseil de la culture de Lanaudière, 616
Cornelius, Murray, Pentecostal Assemblies of Canada, 1150
Cornelius, Jim, Canadian Foodgrains Bank, 391
Cornelius, Betty, CANGRANDS Kinship Support, 508
Cornell, Leslie, Saskatchewan Nursery Landscape Association, 1270
Cornell, April, Ontario Foundation for Visually Impaired Children Inc., 1081
Cornell, Lindsay, Boys & Girls Clubs of Yukon, 224
Cornellier, Sylvie, Réseau du sport étudiant du Québec Montérégie, 1223
Cornett, Sarah, Professional Surveyors Canada, 1187
Cornett, Sarah, Athabasca University Students' Union, 180
Cornies, Karen, Mennonite Central Committee Canada, 961

Cornish, Stephen, Doctors without Borders Canada, 660
Cornwell, Melissa, Electrical Contractors Association of BC, 682
Coronado, Palermo, Starlight Children's Foundation Canada, 1348
Corr, Tom, Ontario Centres of Excellence, 1071
Correa, Carolina, Professional Engineers Ontario, 1185
Correa, Jorge, Canadian Meat Council, 432
Correia, Marrianna, Woodstock & District Developmental Services, 1464
Corrigan, Maureen, Alzheimer Society of Hastings - Prince Edward, 63
Corrigan, Chris, Royal Canadian Military Institute, 1240
Corriveau, Nancy, Syndicat des professionnels et des techniciens de la santé du Québec, 1364
Corriveau, Sébastien, Rhinoceros Party, 1229
Corriveau, Robert, Potatoes New Brunswick, 1168
Corriveau, Robert, Canadian Photonic Industry Consortium, 454
Corriveau, Stéphan, Réseau québécois des OSBL d'habitation, 1225
Corrozi Narvaez, Martha, American Water Resources Association, 1504
Corso, Francesca, Association des Grands Frères et Grandes Soeurs du Québec, 115
Corston, Erin, National Association of Friendship Centres, 990
Cortellucci, Mario, Knights Hospitallers, Sovereign Order of St. John of Jerusalem, Knights of Malta, Grand Priory of Canada, 892
Cortellucci, Mario, Universal Youth Foundation, 1418
Cosburn, Marla, Sealant & Waterproofing Association, 1288
Cosco, Frank, Vancouver Community College Faculty Association, 1425
Cosgrove, Mark, Risk & Insurance Management Society Inc., 1234
Cosgrove, Julie, Kawartha World Issues Centre, 882
Cosier, Janet, Canadian Payments Association, 452
Cosma, Flavia, Romanian Children's Relief, 1235
Cosman, Allan, Food Banks Canada, 749
Cosman, Dean, Financial Executives International Canada, 736
Cossar, Darren, Hockey Nova Scotia, 818
Cossette, Stephane, Risk & Insurance Management Society Inc., 1234
Cossette, François, Réseau des SADC et CAE, 1221
Costa, Maria, Radiation Safety Institute of Canada, 1202
Costa, Sandy, Canadian Pest Management Association, 453
Costa, Sherry, Independent Living Nova Scotia, 833
Costache, Florentina, Association des bénévoles du don de sang, 107
Costantini-Powell, Trina, National Congress of Italian-Canadians, 991
Costantino, Gina, Canadian Fabry Association, 383
Costas-Bradstreet, Christa, Coalition for Active Living, 578
Costello, Michael, Canadian Cancer Society, 349
Costello, Denis, Catholic Family Services of Toronto, 519
Costello, Joseph, Risk & Insurance Management Society Inc., 1234
Costello, Cecily, International Association for Bear Research & Management, 1536
Costello, Boyce, The Appraisal Institute of Canada - Prince Edward Island, 75
Costello, Keith, Canadian Institute of Financial Planners, 415

Executive Name Index

Costello, Joey, *Canadian Arm Wrestling Federation*, 295
Costelloe, Michael D., *American Society of Plastic Surgeons*, 1502
Côté, Michel, *Association régionale de la communauté francophone de Saint-Jean inc.*, 177
Côté, Margaret, *Canadian Grand Masters Fiddling Association*, 399
Côté, Louisane, *La Fédération québécoise des organismes communautaires Famille*, 729
Côté, Jacques, *Réseau BIBLIO du Québec*, 1218
Côté, Johanne, *Chambre de commerce de Charlevoix*, 540
Côté, Alain, *Chambre de commerce et d'industrie de Drummond*, 545
Côté, Manon, *Chambre de commerce et d'industrie du Haut St-Maurice*, 547
Côté, Louise, *Chambre de commerce et d'industrie Magog-Orford*, 547
Côté, Véronique, *Chambre de commerce au Coeur de la Montérégie*, 540
Côté, Elaine, *Moisson Québec*, 971
Côté, Denis, *Canadian Police Association*, 456
Côté, Serge, *Canadian Ski Patrol*, 471
Côté, Daniel, *Canadian Ski Patrol*, 471
Côté, Jean, *Canadian Ski Patrol*, 471
Côté, William-Jean, *Canadian College of Health Leaders*, 359
Côté, Geneviève, *Society of Composers, Authors & Music Publishers of Canada*, 1328
Côté, Lois, *Save a Family Plan*, 1281
Côté, Denis, *Fédération des policiers et policières municipaux du Québec (ind.)*, 717
Côté, Joanne, *L'Écrit Tôt de Saint-Hubert*, 674
Côté, Réjean, *Club informatique Mont-Bruno*, 575
Côté, Élisabeth Circé, *Coalition des associations de consommateurs du Québec*, 577
Côté, Larry, *Canadian Institute for Research in Nondestructive Examination*, 413
Côté, Martin, *Fédération des professionnelles et professionnels de l'éducation du Québec*, 718
Côté, Michèle, *Fédération de l'industrie manufacturière (FIM-CSN)*, 709
Côté, Guy, *Réseau des SADC et CAE*, 1221
Côté, Marlène, *Association québecoise de soins palliatifs*, 171
Côté, Marc-André, *Fédération des producteurs forestiers du Québec*, 717
Côté, André, *Association des directeurs généraux des services de santé et des services sociaux du Québec*, 111
Côté, Florence, *Confédération des associations d'étudiants et étudiantes de l'Université Laval*, 611
Côté, Pierre, *Ontario Secondary School Teachers' Federation*, 1103
Côté, Alain, *Société d'histoire de Beloeil - Mont-Saint-Hilaire*, 1310
Côté, Nancy, *Association des personnes handicapées de la Rive-Sud Ouest*, 122
Côté, Martin, *Organisation québécoise des personnes atteintes de cancer*, 1125
Côté, Diane, *Fédération des agriculteurs et agricultrices francophones du Nouveau-Brunswick*, 711
Côté, Josée, *Regroupement des Aidantes et Aidants Naturel(le)s de Montréal*, 1214
Côté, Eric, *Corporation des entrepreneurs généraux du Québec*, 630
Côté, Connie, *Health Charities Coalition of Canada*, 806
Côté, Frédéric, *TechnoCentre éolien*, 1368
Côté, François, *Alliance des radios communautaires du Canada*, 56
Cotham, Lisa, *The Ninety-Nines Inc.*, 1578
Cothran, Tanya, *Canadian Unitarian Council*, 499
Cotroneo, Teresa, *Folklorama*, 742
Cotter, Anita, *Canadian Society of Painters in Water Colour*, 486

Cotter, Adrian, *Grand Orange Lodge of Canada*, 780
Cotter, Matthew, *Ireland-Canada Chamber of Commerce*, 864
Cotter, Richard, *North American Waterfowl Management Plan*, 1030
Cotterill, Peter, *Family Enterprise Xchange*, 703
Cotton, Cassandra, *Fertilizer Canada*, 733
Cotton, Mario, *Réseau des SADC et CAE*, 1220
Cottrell, Tom, *North Saskatchewan Watershed Alliance*, 1032
Cottrell, Justin, *Ontario Medical Students Association*, 1090
Cottrell, Jim, *Ontario Umpires Association*, 1111
Couch, Warren, *Canadian Federation of Aircraft Maintenance Engineers Associations*, 385
Coudé, Colette, *Organisation multiressources pour les personnes atteintes de cancer*, 1125
Coueslan, Sue, *Genome Canada*, 769
Coughlin, Anne Marie, *Canadian Association for Young Children*, 307
Couillard, François, *Canadian Association of Medical Radiation Technologists*, 320
Couillard, Lucie, *Le Centre de soutien en santé mentale - Montérégie*, 530
Couillard, Philippe, *Parti libéral du Québec*, 1144
Couillard, Jean-Pierre, *Association des capitaines propriétaires de Gaspésie inc*, 108
Couilliard, Jamie, *Canadian Cutting Horse Association*, 375
Coulas, Nancy, *Canadian Manufacturers & Exporters*, 429
Coulas, Mike, *Wilno Heritage Society*, 1456
Coulic-Salahub, Marcia, *Saskatchewan Fencing Association*, 1265
Coull, Steven G., *Canadian National Association of Real Estate Appraisers*, 438
Coull, Shannon, *Association of Fundraising Professionals*, 1512
Coulliard, Yvon, *Groupe d'entraide à l'intention des personnes séropositives, itinérantes et toxicomanes*, 791
Coulombe, Caroline, *Canadian Institute of Management*, 417
Coulombe, Isabelle, *Canadian Labour Congress*, 425
Coulombe, Gilles C., *Syndicat des travailleurs de la construction du Québec (CSD)*, 1364
Coulson, Heather, *Alberta Library Trustees Association*, 39
Coulson, Diana, *Tourism Simcoe County*, 1391
Coulson, Joeann, *Naval Club of Toronto*, 1001
Coulter, Melanie, *Ontario Society for the Prevention of Cruelty to Animals*, 1107
Coulter, Laverne, *Heating, Refrigeration & Air Conditioning Institute of Canada*, 810
Coulter, Tom, *McMan Youth, Family & Community Services Association*, 956
Coulthurst, Lori, *Canadian Society for Immunology*, 475
Coumans, Catherine, *MiningWatch Canada*, 968
Countway, Kelly, *Women That Hunt*, 1461
Coupal, Amy, *Curriculum Services Canada*, 646
Coupland, Ian, *Big Brothers Big Sisters of Manitoba*, 209
Coupland, George, *Manitoba School Boards Association*, 944
Coupland, John Neil, *Institute of Food Technologists*, 1532
Courchesne, Chantal, *Canadian Dermatology Association*, 377
Courchesne, Renée, *Réseau des SADC et CAE*, 1220
Court, Carol, *American Saddlebred Horse Association of British Columbia*, 66
Courteau, Gilles, *Canadian Hockey League*, 406

Courtial, Philippe, *European Geosciences Union*, 1524
Courtney, Paul, *Canadian International Freight Forwarders Association*, 421
Courville, Kathleen, *Fédération des intervenantes en petite enfance du Québec*, 715
Cousar, Grant, *Whistler Chamber of Commerce*, 1452
Cousineau, Marie-Marthe, *Centre de recherche interdisciplinaire sur la violence familiale et la violence faite aux femmes*, 530
Cousins, Pauline, *College of Occupational Therapists of Nova Scotia*, 587
Cousins, Joanne, *United Way Alberta Northwest*, 1413
Cousins, Bill, *Stratford Coin Club*, 1351
Cousteau, Francine, *The Cousteau Society*, 1520
Coutellier, Stephanie, *Association des parents et des handicapés de la Rive-Sud métropolitaine*, 122
Couto, Joe, *Ontario Association of Chiefs of Police*, 1062
Couto, Sandra, *British Columbia Recreation & Parks Association*, 250
Coutts, David E., *Clan Farquharson Association of Canada*, 571
Coutts, Petra, *Family Enterprise Xchange*, 703
Coutts, Patricia, *Canadian Association of Wound Care*, 337
Coutts, Dennis, *Habitat for Humanity Canada*, 796
Coutu, Silvy, *Canadian Hearing Society*, 403
Coutu, Louise, *Fédération des professionnelles et professionnels de l'éducation du Québec*, 718
Coutu, André A., *Groupe export agroalimentaire Québec - Canada*, 792
Coutu, Louise, *Society of St. Vincent de Paul - Toronto Central Council*, 1331
Coutu-Poirier, Ginette, *Chambre de commerce et d'industrie de la région de Richmond*, 545
Couture, Hervé, *Insitut canadien des économistes en construction - Québec*, 840
Couture, Doug, *Canadian Ski Patrol*, 471
Couture, Jean-Marc, *Fédération québécoise des revêtements de sol*, 729
Couture, Melanie, *Manitoba Association for Medical Laboratory Science*, 929
Couture, Yvon, *Fondation Caritas-Sherbrooke inc.*, 743
Couture, Vincent, *Société d'histoire régionale de Lévis*, 1313
Couture, Kathleen, *Nova Scotia Child Care Association*, 1042
Couture, Alexis, *Association des juristes d'expression française du Nouveau-Brunswick*, 1243
Couture, Léonie, *La rue des femmes*, 1243
Couturier, David, *Atelier RADO Inc.*, 180
Couturier, Jean-Pierre, *LAUDEM, L'Association des musiciens liturgiques du Canada*, 900
Couturier, Brigitte, *Association des techniciens en santé animale du Québec*, 129
Couturier, Cyr, *Newfoundland Aquaculture Industry Association*, 1022
Couzens, Deb, *Canadian Home & School Federation*, 406
Covington, Siobhan, *Ontario Gymnastic Federation*, 1083
Cowan, Emily, *Prince Edward County Chamber of Tourism & Commerce*, 1171
Cowan, Suzanne, *The Liberal Party of Canada*, 909
Cowan, Marsha, *Jewish Foundation of Manitoba*, 872
Cowan, Robert, *Okanagan Historical Society*, 1055
Cowan, Ruth, *Canada's Sports Hall of Fame*, 283
Cowan, Josh, *Grain Farmers of Ontario*, 779

Cowan, Becky, *Community Foundation for Kingston & Area*, 597
Cowan, John, *Newfoundland & Labrador Rugby Union*, 1021
Cowan, John, *Adult Basic Education Association of British Columbia*, 9
Cowan, Michael, *Society for Organic Urban Land Care*, 1326
Cowen, Diane, *Alzheimer Society of Dufferin County*, 62
Cowie, Helen, *Developmental Disabilities Resource Centre of Calgary*, 655
Cowie, Brian, *British Columbia Blind Sports & Recreation Association*, 234
Cowie, Doug, *The Great Lakes Marine Heritage Foundation*, 782
Cowie Bonne, Jennifer, *Active Healthy Kids Canada*, 7
Cowin, Dan, *Municipal Finance Officers' Association of Ontario*, 981
Cowin, Doreen, *Child Care Providers Resource Network of Ottawa-Carleton*, 558
Cowley, Roisin, *Association of Early Childhood Educators of Newfoundland & Labrador*, 147
Cowman, Geoff, *CARP*, 515
Cox, Susan, *Canadian Association of Foodservice Professionals*, 315
Cox, Jason, *Penticton & Wine Country Chamber of Commerce*, 1151
Cox, Joanne, *The Canadian Federation of Business & Professional Women's Clubs*, 385
Cox, Romacordelia, *Gelbvieh Association of Alberta/BC*, 768
Cox, Bryan, *Mining Association of British Columbia*, 967
Cox, Nora, *The Gairdner Foundation*, 766
Cox, Mojdeh, *Canadian Labour Congress*, 425
Cox, Tim, *Saskatchewan Water & Wastewater Association*, 1277
Cox, Jane, *College of Occupational Therapists of Ontario*, 587
Cox, Dave, *Lawn Bowls Association of Alberta*, 902
Cox, Beverly, *Black Loyalist Heritage Society*, 213
Cox, Bryan, *Youth Challenge International*, 1475
Cox, Pamela, *Greater Arnprior Chamber of Commerce*, 782
Cox, Ron, *Community Futures Wild Rose*, 599
Cox, Carol, *Ontario Association of Consultants, Counsellors, Psychometrists & Psychotherapists*, 1063
Cox-Lloyd, Barb, *Habitat for Humanity Canada*, 798
Cox-Ziegler, Jackie, *Mustard Seed Food Bank*, 986
Coyle, Nancy, *Toronto Montessori Institute*, 1386
Cozza, Claudia, *Epilepsy Ontario*, 694
Crabbe, Darrell, *Saskatchewan Wildlife Federation*, 1278
Crack, Isabel, *Songwriters Association of Canada*, 1333
Cracknell, Gill, *Canadian Parks & Wilderness Society*, 451
Craig, Corinne, *SEEDS Foundation*, 1289
Craig, John, *The Japan Society Canada*, 869
Craig, John, *Athletics Ontario*, 181
Craig, Sarah, *Conference of Independent Schools (Ontario)*, 612
Craig, Jane, *Deep River Symphony Orchestra*, 652
Craig, Rodney, *United Empire Loyalists' Association of Canada*, 1410
Craig, Linda, *Kingston Youth Orchestra*, 890
Craig, Graham, *Boxing Saskatchewan*, 220
Craig, Vanessa, *College of Applied Biology British Columbia*, 582
Craig Post, Marcie, *International Literacy Association*, 1552
Craig-Peddie, Heather, *Association of Canadian Travel Agencies*, 143

Executive Name Index

Craik, Janet, *Canadian Association of Occupational Therapists*, 323
Cram, Robert, *Doctors Manitoba*, 660
Cram, Carol, *Bowen Island Arts Council*, 219
Cramer, Albert, *Alberta Greenhouse Growers Association*, 37
Cramer, Errol, *Society of Actuaries*, 1592
Cramm, Derek George, *Nova Scotia Association of Insolvency & Restructuring Professionals*, 1041
Cran, Bruce, *Consumers' Association of Canada*, 626
Crane, Clyde, *Grand Orange Lodge of Canada*, 780
Crane, Claire, *International Bottled Water Association*, 1541
Crane, Angus, *NAIMA Canada*, 987
Crane-Burt, Daphne, *Newfoundland & Labrador Palliative Care Association*, 1020
Cranfield, Grant, *Saskatchewan Rugby Union*, 1274
Cranford, Mark, *South Peel Naturalists' Club*, 1336
Cranham, Scott, *Diving Plongeon Canada*, 660
Cranston, Lynda, *GI (Gastrointestinal) Society*, 773
Crass, John, *Ontario Traffic Council*, 1111
Craver, Lyle, *British Columbia Chess Federation*, 236
Craw, David, *Washademoak Region Chamber of Commerce*, 1440
Crawford, Jacqueline, *Beehive Support Services Association*, 204
Crawford, Jo-Anne, *Shuswap Association for Community Living*, 1297
Crawford, Kim, *Algonquin Arts Council*, 54
Crawford, Kim, *Canadian Association of Wholesale Sales Representatives*, 336
Crawford, Duncan, *Prince Edward Island Wildlife Federation*, 1178
Crawford, Trish, *Canadian Association of Elizabeth Fry Societies*, 313
Crawford, Marie, *Union of British Columbia Municipalities*, 1407
Crawford, Leonard, *Canadian Union of Public Employees*, 499
Crawford, Bill, *Eden Community Food Bank*, 674
Crawford, Bryan, *Canada Basketball*, 278
Crawford, Helen, *Canadian Skin Patient Alliance*, 472
Crawford, Iris, *Canada's Medical Technology Companies*, 282
Crawford, Iris, *Canadian MedTech Manufacturers' Alliance*, 434
Crawford, Patty, *Registered Insurance Brokers of Ontario*, 1213
Crawford, Gregory, *Steel Recycling Institute*, 1597
Crawford, Cailey, *Ovarian Cancer Canada*, 1134
Crawford, Joan, *Motor Carrier Passenger Council of Canada*, 975
Crawford, Shawn, *Alberta Council for Exceptional Children*, 31
Crawhall, Robert, *Canadian Association for Security & Intelligence Studies*, 303
Crawley, Sandy, *National Reading Campaign, Inc.*, 996
Creary, Anisara, *AFS Interculture Canada*, 13
Creasor, Sharon, *Association of Architectural Technologists of Ontario*, 139
Creber, Ross, *Direct Sellers Association of Canada*, 657
Creeden, Jennifer, *Community Living Renfrew County South*, 604
Creedon, Tim, *Red Deer Chamber of Commerce*, 1209
Creighton, Anne, *PFLAG Canada Inc.*, 1156
Creighton, Valerie, *Canada Media Fund*, 280
Crellin, John, *Homeopathic College of Canada*, 820
Crespi, Mario, *Canadian Institute for Mediterranean Studies*, 413

Crespo, Cristina, *International Association of Judges*, 1539
Cressman, Erin, *Canadian Society for Psychomotor Learning & Sport Psychology*, 477
Cressman, Jan, *Sexual Health Centre Lunenburg County*, 1293
Cressman, Jeff, *Yukon Schools' Athletic Association*, 1480
Cresswell, John, *Ontario 5 Pin Bowlers' Association*, 1058
Cresswell, Marsha, *Human Resources Professionals Association*, 825
Cresswell-Melville, Amanda, *Eczema Society of Canada*, 674
Crête, Denis, *Association de Sherbrooke pour la déficience intellectuelle*, 104
Crewe, Heather, *Ontario Good Roads Association*, 1083
Crews, Frank, *Heritage Foundation of Newfoundland & Labrador*, 813
Crighton, Jessica, *Skate Canada*, 1301
Criminisi, Al, *Canadian Pastry Chefs Guild Inc.*, 451
Cripps, Joanne, *Canadian Cultural Society of The Deaf, Inc.*, 374
Criscenti, Louise, *Geochemical Society*, 1527
Crisp, Ken, *British Columbia Square & Round Dance Federation*, 255
Critch, Jim, *Federation of Newfoundland & Labrador Square Dance*, 725
Critch, Candace, *Newfoundland & Labrador Amateur Bodybuilding Association*, 1015
Critchley, John, *University of Western Ontario Staff Association*, 1421
Crittenden, Joyce, *Lethbridge Soup Kitchen Association*, 908
Crizzle, Renate, *CARP*, 515
Crocker, Scott, *Autism Society Newfoundland & Labrador*, 189
Crocker, Cal, *Canadian Mental Health Association*, 434
Crocker, Shirley, *United Way of Peel Region*, 1416
Crockett, Wayne, *Electrical Contractors Association of London*, 682
Crockett, Kerry, *International Society for Magnetic Resonance in Medicine*, 1558
Crockett, Maureen, *Helicopter Association of Canada*, 811
Crockwell, Lisa, *Newfoundland & Labrador Association of Social Workers*, 1016
Croft, Dene, *Federation of Canadian Artists*, 722
Croft, Troy, *Sport Newfoundland & Labrador*, 1345
Croft, Paul-Henri, *Société de généalogie du Saguenay, inc.*, 1316
Croisier, Caytlynn, *Ontario Society for the Prevention of Cruelty to Animals*, 1106
Croitoru, Nancy, *Food & Consumer Products of Canada*, 749
Crombie, David, *Waterfront Regeneration Trust*, 1442
Crompton, Carolyn, *British Exservicemen's Association*, 259
Cron, Charles, *Nova Scotia Wild Flora Society*, 1050
Crone, Lindsay, *Canadian Wheelchair Basketball Association*, 503
Cronier, Richard, *British Columbia Snowmobile Federation*, 253
Cronkrite, Della, *Victoria Epilepsy & Parkinson's Centre Society*, 1432
Cronkwright, Nancy, *ACUC International*, 7
Crook, Gail, *Canadian Health Information Management Association*, 402
Crook, Alice, *Animal Welfare Foundation of Canada*, 71
Crook, Robyn, *Archaeological Society of Alberta*, 76
Crooker, Barbara, *The Ninety-Nines Inc.*, 1578
Crooks, Donna, *Saskatchewan Lung Association*, 1269

Crooks, Dauna, *Cancer Advocacy Coalition of Canada*, 507
Crooks, Caroline, *Softball Nova Scotia*, 1332
Crooks, Holly, *La fédération des mouvements personne d'abord du Québec*, 716
Crookshanks, Laura, *Manitoba Genealogical Society Inc.*, 937
Crookshanks, Laura, *PFLAG Canada Inc.*, 1155
Crosby, Connie, *Canadian Association of Law Libraries*, 319
Crosby, Carolyn, *Oakville Art Society*, 1053
Cross, Alison, *Ontario Society for the Prevention of Cruelty to Animals*, 1105
Cross, Alex, *Health Association Nova Scotia*, 806
Cross, Clarke, *Consumer Health Products Canada*, 626
Cross, Bob, *Association of Accrediting Agencies of Canada*, 138
Cross, Ted, *Canadian Innovation Centre*, 412
Cross, Jeremy, *Coaches Association of Ontario*, 576
Cross, Liann, *Strathcona Christian Academy Society*, 1351
Cross, Troy, *Ovarian Cancer Canada*, 1133
Cross, Larry, *Association of Vancouver Island Coastal Communities*, 164
Crossan, Josephine, *Newfoundland & Labrador College of Physiotherapists*, 1017
Crosscombe, Jim, *Ontario Cycling Association*, 1076
Crossin, E. David, *Law Society of British Columbia*, 901
Crossley, Dave, *Planning Institute of British Columbia*, 1162
Crossman, Kim, *Ontario Sheet Metal Contractors Association*, 1104
Crossman, Angel, *Ontario Gymnastic Federation*, 1083
Croteau, Gerry, *Canadian AIDS Society*, 290
Croteau, Yanick, *NACE International*, 1572
Croteau, Gerry L., *AIDS Committee of Simcoe County*, 16
Crouse, Elizabeth, *Natural Products Marketing Council*, 999
Croutze, Randall, *Canadian Dental Association*, 376
Crow, Brian, *Independent School Bus Operators Association*, 833
Crowe, Val, *Canadian Pony Club*, 457
Crowe, Coralee, *Canadian Association for Williams Syndrome*, 307
Crowe, David, *Alberta Reappraising AIDS Society*, 43
Crowe, Susan, *Hornby Island Food Bank*, 821
Crowell, Beth, *Oromocto & Area Chamber of Commerce*, 1127
Crowell, Steven, *Nova Scotia Home Builders' Association*, 1046
Crowfoot, Bert, *Aboriginal Multi-Media Society*, 2
Crowhurst, Bob, *Middlesex, Oxford, Elgin Beekeepers' Association*, 965
Crowley, Val, *Canadian Authors Association*, 338
Crowson, Belinda, *Historical Society of Alberta*, 816
Crowson, Belinda, *Historical Society of Alberta*, 816
Crowther, Peter, *Big Brothers Big Sisters of Nova Scotia*, 210
Crowther, Kirk, *Canadian Down Syndrome Society*, 378
Crozier, Cheryl, *Volleyball Prince Edward Island*, 1438
Crozier, Sarah, *Heart & Stroke Foundation of Prince Edward Island Inc.*, 809
Cruden, John, *Environmental Law Institute*, 1524
Cruickshank, John, *Association de le communauté noire de Côte-des-Neiges inc.*, 102
Cruikshank, Bernie, *Friends of the Forestry Farm House Inc.*, 762

Cruse, Mike, *Hamilton Police Association*, 802
Crush, Terry, *Federation of Saskatchewan Surface Rights Association*, 726
Crutcher, Sandra, *Urban & Regional Information Systems Association*, 1601
Crute, Judy, *Golf Association of Ontario*, 777
Cruz, David, *Kamloops Immigrant Services*, 880
Cryderman, Eric, *Drainage Superintendents Association of Ontario*, 662
Cryne, Stephen, *Canadian Employee Relocation Council*, 381
Csank, Alex, *Alfa Romeo Club of Canada*, 53
Csergo, Zsuzsa, *Association for the Study of Nationalities*, 135
Csete, Sarolta, *Canadian Media Production Association*, 433
Csiba, Adriana, *Professional Engineers Ontario*, 1184
Cucci, Paul, *Ontario College of Social Workers & Social Service Workers*, 1072
Cuddemi, Nick, *Team Handball Ontario*, 1368
Cudmore, Valerie, *Candora Society of Edmonton*, 508
Cudmore, Ruth, *Ontario Association of Bovine Practitioners*, 1062
Cuenca, Leticia, *Québec Library Association*, 1198
Cuerrier, Susan, *Calgary Health Trust*, 272
Cuevas Barron, Gabriela, *Inter-Parliamentary Union*, 1567
Cuffling, Kevin, *Société d'horticulture de Saint-Lambert*, 1314
Cuillerier, Monique, *World Federalist Movement - Canada*, 1466
Culbert, Heather, *Doctors without Borders Canada*, 660
Culhane, Patrick, *Canadian Payroll Association*, 452
Cull, Stephen, *CharterAbility*, 552
Cullen, Christin, *The John Howard Society of Ontario*, 875
Cullen, Gail, *Risk & Insurance Management Society Inc.*, 1234
Cullen, Michael, *United Way/Centraide Sudbury & District*, 1418
Culley, Thea, *KidSport British Columbia*, 886
Cullingham, Elaine, *Girl Guides of Canada*, 773
Cullis, Tara, *David Suzuki Foundation*, 652
Cullis, Ian, *British Columbia Non-Profit Housing Association*, 248
Cumberbatch, Ruth, *Arts Etobicoke*, 85
Cumbo, Josie, *Order of Sons of Italy in Canada*, 1119
Cumming, Kerina, *Credit Association of Greater Toronto*, 639
Cummings, Harry, *Canadian Evaluation Society*, 383
Cummings, Garnet, *Brain Care Centre*, 225
Cummings Speirs, Carol, *Canadian Unitarian Council*, 499
Cundari, Aldo, *Villa Charities Inc. (Toronto District)*, 1434
Cundari, Rob, *Society for Technical Communication*, 1591
Cunha, Suzanne, *Casa dos Acores do Ontário*, 516
Cunningham, Dave, *Film & Video Arts Society Alberta*, 735
Cunningham, Richard, *Markham Board of Trade*, 952
Cunningham, Ian, *Council of Ontario Construction Associations*, 634
Cunningham, Bernice, *Streetsville Historical Society*, 1352
Cunningham, Leanne, *AIDS Vancouver Island*, 17
Cunningham, Ryan, *Native Earth Performing Arts Inc.*, 998
Cunningham, Andrew, *Canadian Institute of Financial Planners*, 415
Cunningham, Lorna, *PFLAG Canada Inc.*, 1155

Executive Name Index

Cunningham, Fiona, *Irish Dance Teacher's Association of Eastern Canada*, 864
Cunningham, Joan, *Okanagan Miniature Horse Club*, 1056
Cunningham, Kathleen, *British Columbia Law Institute*, 244
Cuq, Jean-Pierre, *Fédération internationale des professeurs de français*, 1525
Curcio, Daniel, *International Federation of Corporate Football*, 857
Curé, Gérard, *Fédération des aînés franco-manitobains inc.*, 711
Curl, Vivian, *The Community Foundation of Durham Region*, 597
Curleigh, Colin, *Parrsborough Shore Historical Society*, 1143
Curlew, Kenny, *Newfoundland & Labrador Table Tennis Association*, 1022
Curley, Ann, *Muskoka Steamship & Historical Society*, 985
Curman, Ivan, *Canadian Croatian Congress*, 373
Curran, Julie, *Scugog Chamber of Commerce*, 1287
Curran, Barry, *United Empire Loyalists' Association of Canada*, 1410
Curran, Pat, *An Cumann/The Irish Association of Nova Scotia*, 68
Curran, Jim, *Abbotsford Social Activity Association*, 1
Curran, Alicia, *KidSport Newfoundland & Labrador*, 887
Currey, Cathy, *Saskatchewan Bed & Breakfast Association*, 1259
Currie, Grant, *Squash Alberta*, 1347
Currie, Philip M., *Atlantic University Sport Association*, 186
Currie, Ian, *Creston & District Historical & Museum Society*, 642
Currie, Cheryl, *Post-Polio Network Manitoba Inc.*, 1168
Currie, Judy, *Saskatchewan Veterinary Medical Association*, 1277
Currie, William, *Archers Association of Nova Scotia*, 78
Currie, Rod, *Fredericton Fish & Game Association*, 759
Currie, Barbara, *Nurse Practitioners' Association of Nova Scotia*, 1052
Curry, Nora, *United Nations Association in Canada*, 1411
Curry, Graham, *Arts Etobicoke*, 85
Curry, Brennan, *Baseball Nova Scotia*, 198
Curry, Garry, *Vancouver Island Society for Disabled Artists*, 1427
Curtis, John, *PARN Your Community AIDS Resource Network*, 1143
Curtis, Andy, *Teachers of English to Speakers of Other Languages, Inc.*, 1597
Curtis, Shannon, *College of Family Physicians of Canada*, 585
Curtis, Amanda, *Canadian Automatic Merchandising Association*, 338
Curtis, Amanda, *Association of Canadian Search, Employment & Staffing Services*, 143
Curtis, Trudy, *Professional Petroleum Data Management Association*, 1186
Curtis, Janice, *Calgary Meals on Wheels*, 273
Curtis, Amanada, *National Association of Computer Consulting Business (Canada)*, 990
Curtis, Bill, *Biathlon Yukon*, 208
Curtis, Bill, *VeloNorth Cycling Club*, 1431
Curtis, John, *Wind Athletes Canada*, 1456
Curtiss, Bruce, *Mustard Seed Food Bank*, 986
Custer, Christine, *The Waterbird Society*, 1602
Custerra, Jeh, *Friends of Clayoquot Sound*, 761
Cuthbertson, Brent, *CAA British Columbia*, 267
Cutler, Ron, *The Anglican Church of Canada*, 70
Cutler, Joyce, *Canadian Society of Mayflower Descendants*, 484
Cutler, Brian, *Essex County Stamp Club (Windsor)*, 696
Cutti, Daniel, *Ordre des infirmières et infirmiers du Québec*, 1122
Cutting, Gerald, *Townshippers' Association*, 1393
Cutts, Danielle, *College of Family Physicians of Canada*, 585
Cymbaluk, Lidia, *Ukrainian Canadian Social Services (Toronto) Inc*, 1403
Cyngiser, Lior, *Hillel of Greater Toronto*, 815
Cyr, Mylène, *La Guilde des Musiciens/Musiciennes du Québec*, 794
Cyr, Mike, *Silent Voice Canada Inc.*, 1299
Cyr, Suzanne, *Windsor-Essex Down Syndrome Parent Association*, 1457
Cyr, Roseline, *Fédération des scouts de l'ouest*, 718
Cyr, Dennis, *British Columbia Bed & Breakfast Innkeepers Guild*, 233
Cyr, Carole, *Canadian Dairy Commission*, 375
Cyr, Gérald, *Association Québécoise des Loisirs Folkloriques*, 173
Cyr-Reid, Réjeanne, *Association coopérative d'économie familliale de Québec*, 98
Cyre, Tony, *Winnipeg Musicians' Association*, 1459
Czach, Liz, *Film Studies Association of Canada*, 735
Czerkas, Connie, *CADORA Ontario Association Inc.*, 269
Czerkas, Ashley, *CADORA Ontario Association Inc.*, 269
Czerny, Robert, *Ethics Practitioners' Association of Canada*, 697
Czerwinski, Edward, *Association of Registered Professional Foresters of New Brunswick*, 161
Czoli, Constantino, *Toronto Ukraina Sports Association*, 1388
Czukar, Gail, *Addictions & Mental Health Ontario*, 8
Czycz, Katharine, *Thermal Environmental Comfort Association*, 1375

D

D'Agaggio Lemaire, Nicole, *Académie européenne des sciences, des arts et des lettres*, 1485
D'Agostini, Leo, *Laborers' International Union of North America (AFL-CIO/CLC)*, 1569
d'Agostino, Steve, *Syndicat du personnel technique et professionnel de la Société des alcools du Québec (ind.)*, 1364
D'Alessandro, Tony, *Ontario Public Transit Association*, 1100
d'Amboise, Sébastien, *Patrouille de ski St-Jean*, 1146
D'amico, Lisa, *Fédération québécoise du loisir littéraire*, 731
D'Amour, Claire, *Canadian Academy of Periodontology*, 286
D'Amours, Louise, *Tourism Moncton*, 1390
D'Andrea, Andy, *The Society of Energy Professionals*, 1328
D'Angelo, Marco, *Ontario Traffic Council*, 1111
D'Angelo, Carmen, *Niagara Peninsula Conservation Authority*, 1025
D'Aoust, Angie, *Canadian Dental Hygienists Association*, 377
D'Aoust, Cindy, *Cruise Lines International Association, Inc.*, 1521
d'Aragon, Marc-Antione, *McGill Chamber Orchestra*, 955
d'Arc Auclair, Jeanne, *Congregation des Soeurs de Saint-Joseph de Saint-Vallier*, 612
d'Arc Umurungi, Jeanne, *Canadian Media Guild*, 432
D'Arcey, Sharon, *North Perth Chamber of Commerce*, 1032
D'Arcy, Brenna, *Maritime Association of Professional Sign Language Interpreters*, 950
D'Arras, Diane, *International Water Association*, 1566
D'Aubin, Jennifer, *Bridgetown & Area Chamber of Commerce*, 229
d'Auzac de Lamartinie, Brigitte, *Historica Canada*, 815
D'Avanzo, Tony, *Federation of North American Explorers*, 725
D'Avignon, Greg, *Business Council of British Columbia*, 266
D'Costa, Christina, *Canadian MedTech Manufacturers' Alliance*, 434
D'Elia, Len, *Professional Engineers Ontario*, 1184
d'Entremont, Louise, *Fédération des parents acadiens de la Nouvelle-Écosse*, 716
d'Entremont, Carmen, *Archives du Centre acadien*, 80
d'Eon, Kristin, *Snowboard Nova Scotia*, 1305
D'Hulster, Anna Maria, *The Geneva Association*, 1527
D'Intino, Joseph, *Tyndale St-Georges Community Centre*, 1401
D'Orangeville, Christian, *Canadian Kendo Federation*, 424
D'Orazio, Micah, *American Society of Safety Engineers*, 1502
D'Ornellas, Gary, *Avicultural Advancement Council of Canada*, 191
D'Sa, Kristina, *Special Olympics BC*, 1339
D'Souza, Joyce, *Real Estate Institute of Canada*, 1206
D'Souza, Sashya, *Toronto Financial Services Alliance*, 1384
D'Uva, Matthew, *International Association for the Study of Pain*, 1537
Da Cunha, Fernando, *Bricklayers, Masons Independent Union of Canada (CLC)*, 228
Da Ros, Greg, *Karate Nova Scotia*, 882
da Silva Porter, Maggie, *Canadian Association of Foodservice Professionals*, 315
Da Silva-Powell, Alexis, *Toronto Alliance for the Performing Arts*, 1381
Daborn, Lia A., *New Brunswick Dental Society*, 1007
Dabrowski, Ray, *Welsh Pony & Cob Society of Canada*, 1444
Dacey, Bernadette, *Chemical Institute of Canada*, 556
Dack, Brian, *BC Trappers' Association*, 202
Dackiw Mercier, Karen, *Association of Fundraising Professionals*, 1511
DaCosta, Lena, *Association of Early Childhood Educators Ontario*, 147
Dacyk, Amanda, *Canadian Council of Forest Ministers*, 368
Dadashi, Yassi, *OMID Foundation Canada*, 1058
Dadgostar, Bahram, *Canadian Federation of Business School Deans*, 386
Daffe, Lynn, *Law Society of Yukon*, 902
Dagenais, Louis, *Canadian Information Processing Society*, 411
Dagenais, Daniel, *Chambre de commerce des Jardins de Napierville*, 544
Dagenais, France, *Fédération des loisirs-danse du Québec*, 715
Dagenault, Richard, *Association des Sourds de Québec inc.*, 128
Dagg, Leslie, *Canadian Society of Hospital Pharmacists*, 484
Daggett, Harold, *International Longshoremen's Association (AFL-CIO/CLC)*, 1553
Dagher, May, *Association des pédiatres du Québec*, 122
Dagley, David, *Queens County Fish & Game Association*, 1200
Dagnino, Michelle, *Jane Finch Community & Family Centre*, 868
Dahdaly, John, *Ontario Limousine Owners Association*, 1089
Dahl, Marilyn, *Canadian Hard of Hearing Association*, 400
Dahl, Merv, *Risk & Insurance Management Society Inc.*, 1234
Dahl, Eric, *World Trade Centres Association*, 1608
Dahl, Shea, *Canadian Organization of Campus Activities*, 447
Dahms, Russ, *Edmonton Chamber of Voluntary Organizations*, 676
Daifallah, Adam, *Canadian Taxpayers Federation*, 492
Daigie, Fernand, *Architects' Association of New Brunswick*, 78
Daigle, Alain, *Corporation des maîtres mécaniciens en tuyauterie du Québec*, 630
Daigle, Deb, *Canadian Institute of Management*, 417
Daigle, Darlene, *Professional Engineers Ontario*, 1184
Daigle, Bernard, *Canadian Forestry Association of New Brunswick*, 392
Daigle, Jean-Yves, *International Peat Society - Canadian National Committee*, 859
Daigle, Gilles M., *Society of Composers, Authors & Music Publishers of Canada*, 1328
Daigle, Mona, *Canada Employment & Immigration Union*, 279
Daigle, Denis, *Richelieu International*, 1229
Daigneault, Luce, *Fédération interdisciplinaire de l'horticulture ornementale du Québec*, 721
Dailey, Melanie, *Scout Environmental*, 1286
Daitch, Richard, *NWT School Athletic Federation*, 1052
Dakins, Dion, *Fur Institute of Canada*, 765
Daku, Wendy, *Canadian Labour Congress*, 425
Dala, Peter, *Alberta Ballet*, 25
Dale, Ross, *Ontario Home Builders' Association*, 1086
Dale, Catherine, *Manitoba Dental Association*, 935
Dale, Anthony, *Ontario Hospital Association*, 1087
Dale, Amanda, *The Barbra Schlifer Commemorative Clinic*, 196
Dale, Judith, *Hastings County Law Association*, 804
Dale, Phil, *Ontario Association of Triathletes*, 1066
Dale, Veronica, *New Leaf Enterprises*, 1014
Dalen, Mary, *Meanskinisht Village Historical Association*, 956
Dalen-Brown, Charlene, *Canadian Morgan Horse Association*, 437
Dales, Brenda, *Peterborough Social Planning Council*, 1154
Daley, Ingrid, *Canadian Association of Critical Care Nurses*, 312
Dalgarno, Paula, *Welsh Pony & Cob Association of Ontario*, 1444
Dalgleish, Ryan, *Canadian Urethane Foam Contractors Association*, 500
Dalgleish, Ryan, *Manitoba Building Envelope Council*, 933
Dalgleish, Ryan, *Heating, Refrigeration & Air Conditioning Institute of Canada*, 810
Dalgleish, Laverne, *Manitoba Ozone Protection Industry Association*, 941
Dall'Antonia, Anthony, *Canadian Arm Wrestling Federation*, 295
Dallaire, Marco, *Chambre de commerce et d'industrie secteur Saint-Félicien inc.*, 548
Dallaire, Yannick, *Intervention régionale et information sur le sida en Estrie*, 862
Dallaire, Louis, *Reseau Biblio de l'Abitibi-Témiscamingue Nord-du-Québec*, 1218
Dallaire, Marie-Claude, *Association Jeannoise pour l'intégration sociale inc.*, 137
Dallaire, Michel, *La Fondation Émile-Nelligan*, 746
Dallaire, Mario, *Association des spécialistes en médecine interne du Québec*, 128
Dallaire, Roméo A., *Post Traumatic Stress Disorder Association*, 1167
Dalle, Esther, *Ontario Bobsleigh Skeleton Association*, 1068
Dalley, Jame, *Association of Manitoba Museums*, 151
Dalman, Christie, *Vatnabyggd Icelandic Club of Saskatchewan Inc.*, 1430

Executive Name Index

Dalpé, Lise, *Association coopérative d'économie familiale - Lanaudière*, 97
Dalton, Karen, *Canadian Public Relations Society Inc.*, 463
Dalton, Chris, *The Ontario Archaeological Society*, 1059
Dalton, Daintry, *Alliance of Canadian Cinema, Television & Radio Artists*, 58
Dalton, Robert, *Opticians Association of Canada*, 1116
Dalton, Patrick, *Air Currency Enhancement Society*, 19
Dalton, Patti, *London & District Labour Council*, 917
Dalton, Darrell, *Horse Industry Association of Alberta*, 822
Daly, Sharon, *Canadian Marketing Association*, 431
Daly, Patrick J., *Ontario Catholic School Trustees' Association*, 1070
Daly, Karen, *Institute of Law Clerks of Ontario*, 846
Daly, Lynn, *Christie-Ossington Neighbourhood Centre*, 568
Daly, Julian, *Boyle Street Community Services*, 221
Dalziel, Barbara, *Canadian Association for Sandplay Therapy*, 303
Damant, Krista, *Caledonia Regional Chamber of Commerce*, 270
Damar, Géraldine, *International Liver Cancer Association*, 1553
Damaren, C.J., *University of Toronto Institute for Aerospace Studies*, 1421
Damji, Ali, *Ontario Medical Students Association*, 1090
Dammrich, Thomas, *National Marine Manufacturers Association*, 1576
Damour, Carl, *Alberta College of Paramedics*, 29
Damphousse, François, *Non-Smokers' Rights Association*, 1028
Damptey, Nana Kojo, *Development & Peace*, 655
Damus, Martin, *Eastern Ontario Beekeepers' Association*, 670
Danas, Tony, *Circulation Management Association of Canada*, 570
Danchuk, Allane, *Human Resources Professionals Association*, 826
Dancyger, Alain, *Les Grands Ballets Canadiens de Montréal*, 781
Dandal, Flordeliz M., *Kababayan Multicultural Centre*, 879
Dandeno, Kevin, *Grey County Kiwanis Festival of Music*, 790
Dandewich, Greg, *Economic Development Winnipeg Inc.*, 673
Dandridge, Les, *Canadian Institute of Actuaries*, 414
Dandurand, Lise, *Mouvement national des québécoises et québécois*, 977
Daneau, Véronique, *AlterHéros*, 60
Daneault, Hélène, *Syndicat du personnel technique et professionnel de la Société des alcools du Québec (ind.)*, 1364
Danells, Carolyn, *Saint John Community Food Basket*, 1246
Danesi, Silvina, *Canadian Political Science Association*, 457
Dangerfield, Kristin, *Law Society of Manitoba*, 901
Daniel, Crystal, *Women's Legal Education & Action Fund*, 1463
Daniel, Brian, *Burnaby Arts Council*, 265
Daniels, Sandra, *Canadian Association of Gastroenterology*, 316
Daniels, Mike, *SPANCAN*, 1338
Daniels, Mark, *Klondike Snowmobile Association*, 892
Daniels-Smith, Linda, *Junior League of Hamilton-Burlington, Inc.*, 878
Danielson, Karen, *Saskatchewan Literacy Network*, 1269

Danilovich, John, *International Chamber of Commerce*, 1542
Dankert, Susan, *Pet Industry Joint Advisory Council*, 1153
Dankowich, Stephen, *Oakville Community Centre for Peace, Ecology & Human Rights*, 1053
Dann, Kathie, *SAIT Academic Faculty Association*, 1251
Danneffel, Andrew, *Port Moody Rock & Gem Club*, 1166
Dantas, Alison, *Canadian Chiropractic Association*, 356
Dantu, Sonia, *Alberta Equestrian Federation*, 34
Danylchuk, Lynette S., *International Society for the Study of Trauma & Dissociation*, 1559
Daoust, Caroline, *Ordre des dentistes du Québec*, 1121
Daoust, Nathalie, *Commission for Environmental Cooperation*, 593
Darboh, Julie, *COSTI Immigrant Services*, 632
Darby, Dennis, *Canadian Manufacturers & Exporters*, 429
Darby, Dennis, *Ontario Pharmacists' Association*, 1095
Darbyshire, Ron, *Beaumont Coin Discovery Group*, 203
Darbyshire, Ron, *Strathcona Coin Discovery Group*, 1351
Dardano, Ken, *United Way of Guelph, Wellington & Dufferin*, 1414
Dare, Malkin, *Society for Quality Education*, 1326
Darewych, Jurij, *Ukrainian Canadian Research & Documentation Centre*, 1402
Darewych, Daria, *Shevchenko Scientific Society of Canada*, 1296
Dargatz, Shirley, *United Empire Loyalists' Association of Canada*, 1410
Dargavel, Michael, *Ontario Fashion Exhibitors*, 1078
Dargavel, Michael, *Canadian Association of Exposition Management*, 313
Dargel, Ulli, *British Columbia Sporthorse - Sport Pony Breeders Group*, 255
Dargie, John, *Independent Financial Brokers of Canada*, 832
Dargis, Mario, *Association provinciale des constructeurs d'habitations du Québec inc.*, 168
Darling, Dan, *Canadian Cattlemen's Association*, 351
Darlington, Jonathan, *Vancouver Opera*, 1428
Darmody, Robert, *American Society of Mining & Reclamation*, 1501
Darnell, Chris J., *American Concrete Institute*, 1491
Darnley, Warren, *Caledon Chamber of Commerce*, 270
DaRosa, Paulo, *Canadian Association for Enterostomal Therapy*, 300
Darrow, Charles, *Royal Astronomical Society of Canada*, 1239
Dart, Brian, *Dominion Rabbit & Cavy Breeders Association*, 661
Dart, Bonnie, *Ontario Cavy Club*, 1070
Darveau, Richard, *Association québécoise de la quincaillerie et des matériaux de construction*, 170
Darvill, Amanda, *American Society for Bone & Mineral Research*, 1498
Darwin, Kim, *Sechelt & District Chamber of Commerce*, 1288
Dasenbrock, Manfred Alfonso, *World Council of Credit Unions, Inc.*, 1604
Dashney, Brenda, *Canadian Association for Laboratory Accreditation Inc.*, 301
DaSilva, Robert, *Broadcast Research Council of Canada*, 259
DaSilva, Elton, *Mennonite Brethren Church of Manitoba*, 960
DaSilva, Manny, *Association of Canadian Compliance Professionals*, 141

DaSilva-Gibbons, Regina, *Boys & Girls Clubs of Manitoba*, 222
Dastoor, Dolly, *L'Association Zoroastrianne du Québec*, 179
Dastur, Percy, *Ontario Zoroastrian Community Foundation*, 1114
Daub, Stacey, *Toronto Community Care Access Centre*, 1383
Daud, Aslam, *Ahmadiyya Muslim Jama'at Canada*, 15
Daud, Aslam, *Humanity First Canada*, 827
Daughton, David, *Community Legal Information Association of Prince Edward Island*, 600
Dauphinais, Pierre, *Association québécoise d'urbanisme*, 168
Dauphinee, Margo, *Nova Scotia Association of Architects*, 1040
Daus, Timothy, *Canadian Federation of Business School Deans*, 386
Daval-Bérillon, Marie-Chantal, *Fédération des parents francophones de l'Alberta*, 717
Dave, Smith, *Ecological Farmers of Ontario*, 672
Dave, Hopkins, *Saanich Historical Artifacts Society*, 1245
Davenport, Greg, *Ontario Brain Injury Association*, 1068
Davey, David, *Atlantic Turfgrass Research Foundation*, 186
Davey-Wiebe, Tammy, *Daily Bread Food Bank*, 648
Daviau, Debi, *The Professional Institute of the Public Service of Canada*, 1185
Daviault, France, *Automotive Industries Association of Canada*, 190
David, Michel, *Canadian Hearing Society*, 403
David, Marc, *Newfoundland Symphony Orchestra Association*, 1023
David, Jim, *Nova Scotia Progressive Conservative Association*, 1047
David, Cora, *Open Door Group*, 1114
David, Kenneth L., *Richmond County Disabled Association*, 1230
David, Geneviève, *Association des jardins du Québec*, 117
David, Marc, *Orchestre symphonique de Longueuil*, 1118
Davidge, Doug, *Yukon Underwater Diving Association*, 1480
Davids, Rebecca, *Ontario Society of Nutrition Professionals in Public Health*, 1107
Davidson, Kevin, *Abundance Canada*, 3
Davidson, Chuck, *The Manitoba Chambers of Commerce*, 933
Davidson, Janelle, *Moosomin Chamber of Commerce*, 974
Davidson, Paul J., *Inter-American Commercial Arbitration Commission*, 851
Davidson, Paul J., *Inter-American Commercial Arbitration Commission*, 851
Davidson, Roseann, *Fort McMurray Historical Society*, 753
Davidson, Dan, *Ontario Beekeepers' Association*, 1068
Davidson, Alex, *Canadian Amateur Wrestling Association*, 292
Davidson, Fraser, *Canadian Meteorological & Oceanographic Society*, 436
Davidson, Ronald, *Société pour les enfants handicapés du Québec*, 1322
Davidson, Paul, *Universities Canada*, 1418
Davidson, Ronald, *Fondation des maladies du coeur du Québec*, 745
Davidson, Alex, *Juvenile Diabetes Research Foundation Canada*, 878
Davidson, Dave, *Korea Veterans Association of Canada Inc., Heritage Unit*, 893
Davidson, Laura, *Canadian Bar Association*, 342
Davidson, Bette-Jean (B-J), *Canadian Thoroughbred Horse Society*, 495
Davidson, Tom, *Québec Competitive Festival of Music*, 1196

Davidson, Desarae, *Canadian Society of Hospital Pharmacists*, 483
Davidson, Suzanne, *United Empire Loyalists' Association of Canada*, 1410
Davidson, Mike, *Canadian Union of Public Employees*, 498
Davidson, Kathy, *Physiotherapy Education Accreditation Canada*, 1159
Davidson, Scott, *Ontario Funeral Service Association*, 1081
Davidson, Holly, *UNICEF Canada*, 1404
Davidson, Joy, *Arthritis Research Foundation*, 84
Davidson, Kim, *Ontario Percheron Horse Association Inc.*, 1095
Davidson Boles, Marian, *Roofing Contractors Association of Manitoba Inc.*, 1236
Davie, Brenda, *Alzheimer Society of Durham Region*, 62
Davie, Pearl, *Federation of Ontario Memorial Societies - Funeral Consumers Alliance*, 726
Davie, Laurie, *North Pacific Cannery - National Historic Site*, 1032
Davies, Joan MacKenzie, *Ontario Association of Social Workers*, 1066
Davies, McKenzie, *Boys & Girls Clubs of Alberta*, 221
Davies, Barb, *Golden Food Bank*, 776
Davies, Ross, *Ontario Association of Broadcasters*, 1062
Davies, Jean, *Carizon Family & Community Services*, 513
Davies, Bruce, *Central Okanagan Foundation*, 525
Davies, Trevor, *Canadian Union of Public Employees*, 498
Davies, Gwen, *Canadian Amputee Golf Association*, 292
Davies, Carol, *Artscape*, 86
Davies, Rob, *Alberta Barley Commission*, 25
Davies, Linda M., *Society of Local Government Managers of Alberta*, 1329
Davies, Donna, *Caledon East & District Historical Society*, 270
Davies, Kyle, *Respiratory Therapy Society of Ontario*, 1227
Davies, Mark, *Turkey Farmers of Canada*, 1400
Davies, Marylee, *British Columbia Society for the Prevention of Cruelty to Animals*, 254
Davies, P. Stratton, *American College of Chest Physicians*, 1491
Davis, Garnet, *Saskatchewan Lions Eye Bank*, 1269
Davis, Jacqueline, *First Nations Breast Cancer Society*, 738
Davis, Jen, *Nova Scotia Society of Occupational Therapists*, 1049
Davis, Barb, *Quinte Therapeutic Riding Association*, 1202
Davis, Richard, *Belleville & District Chamber of Commerce*, 204
Davis, Rebecca, *Bradford Board of Trade*, 224
Davis, Shawn, *Canadian Public Relations Society Inc.*, 463
Davis, Sheila, *British Columbia Federation of Foster Parent Associations*, 240
Davis, Melanie, *Physical & Health Education Canada*, 1158
Davis, Linda, *The Canadian Federation of Business & Professional Women's Clubs*, 385
Davis, Linda, *The Canadian Federation of Business & Professional Women's Clubs*, 385
Davis, Karen, *Saskatchewan Lung Association*, 1269
Davis, Marie-danielle, *Canadian Nuclear Association*, 442
Davis, Marie Adèle, *Canadian Paediatric Society*, 449
Davis, Benjamin, *Multiple Sclerosis Society of Canada*, 980
Davis, Brad, *Family Service Kent*, 704

Davis, Carolyn, *Catholic Cross Cultural Services*, 518
Davis, Greg, *Laborers' International Union of North America (AFL-CIO/CLC)*, 1568
Davis, Mary, *Special Olympics International*, 1596
Davis, Philip, *Professional Association of Residents in the Maritime Provinces*, 1182
Davis, Alexi, *Prospect Human Services*, 1189
Davis, Nancy, *North Pacific Anadromous Fish Commission*, 1031
Davis, Troy, *World Citizen Foundation*, 1604
Davis, Keitha, *Norfolk Historical Society*, 1028
Davis, Benjamin, *Royal College of Dentists of Canada*, 1241
Davis, Robert, *Council of the Haida Nation - Haida Fisheries Program*, 635
Davis, Marie Adèle, *Canadian Pediatric Foundation*, 452
Davis, Debbie, *Parkinson Society Central & Northern Ontario*, 1141
Davis, Alastair, *Habitat for Humanity Canada*, 797
Davis, Diana, *International Geosynthetics Society*, 1550
Davis, Kim, *Hearth, Patio & Barbecue Association of Canada*, 810
Davis, April, *International Society for Performance Improvement*, 1559
Davis, Anne, *Eastend Arts Council*, 669
Davis, Susan, *Yukon Territory Environmental Network*, 1480
Davis, Seth, *Geochemical Society*, 1527
Davis, Kelly, *St. John's International Women's Film Festival*, 1249
Davis, Mary Ellen K., *Association of College & Research Libraries*, 1511
Davis-Kerr, Carol, *Harry E. Foster Foundation*, 804
Davis-Murdoch, Sharon, *Health Association of African Canadians*, 806
Davison, Dwayne, *Lloydminster & District Fish & Game Association*, 915
Davison, Betty, *British Columbia Nature (Federation of British Columbia Naturalists)*, 247
Davison, Lori, *Hospital for Sick Children Foundation*, 823
Davison, Maggie, *Edmonton Economic Development Corporation*, 677
Davlut, Melanie, *TEAL Manitoba*, 1368
Daw, Christopher, *Canadian Association of Professional Immigration Consultants*, 329
Dawber, Andrea, *EcoSource Mississauga*, 673
Dawe, Roy, *Grand Orange Lodge of Canada*, 780
Dawe, David, *Mechanical Contractors Association of Newfoundland & Labrador*, 957
Dawe, Vickie, *Yukon Schools' Athletic Association*, 1480
Dawes, Wendy, *Kingston Lapidary & Mineral Club*, 889
Dawes, Sandra, *Canadian Cat Association*, 351
Dawson, Janice, *Speed Skating Canada*, 1341
Dawson, Barbara, *Society of the Sacred Heart*, 1594
Dawson, Karri, *True Sport Foundation*, 1399
Dawson, Mike, *Saskatchewan Recording Industry Association*, 1273
Dawson, Jim, *Transitions*, 1395
Dawson, Christine, *International Order of the King's Daughters & Sons*, 1554
Dawson, Tanya, *PFLAG Canada Inc.*, 1155
Dawson, Gary, *Biathlon Newfoundland & Labrador*, 207
Day, LeAnn, *Paint & Decorating Retailers Association*, 1582
Day, Rick, *Canadian Stamp Dealers' Association*, 490
Day, Al, *N'Amerind (London) Friendship Centre*, 986
Day, Edward, *Canadian Merchant Service Guild*, 435

Day, Robert D., *Renewable Natural Resources Foundation*, 1586
Day, Ken, *Pembroke District Construction Association*, 1149
Day, Anne, *Company of Women*, 608
Day, Sherry, *Association of Seafood Producers*, 162
Day-Stirk, Frances, *International Confederation of Midwives*, 1544
Dayler, Linda, *Catholic Family Services of Hamilton*, 518
Dayment, Stace, *Pacific Post Partum Support Society*, 1136
Dayton, Eric, *Canadian Philosophical Association*, 454
Daño, Neth, *ETC Group*, 697
De Angelis, Daniel, *Judo-Québec inc*, 877
De Baere, Rik Debal, *VZW Belgium-Canada*, 1601
De Bernardis, Esteban, *Canadian Standards Association*, 490
de Boer, Dirk, *Canadian Association of Geographers*, 316
de Boer, Margaret, *Indexing Society of Canada*, 834
de Bruyen, Theodore S., *Association internationale des études patristiques*, 1510
de Bruyn, Theodore S., *International Association of Patristic Studies*, 1539
De Caria, Joseph, *Acoustical Association Ontario*, 5
de Cesare, Christiane, *Illuminating Engineering Society of North America*, 1531
de Champlain, Andy, *TESL Nova Scotia*, 1373
de Champlain, Diane, *Association des Diplômés de Polytechnique*, 111
de Chantal, Anita, *Société de généalogie de la Jemmerais*, 1315
de Coninck Smith, Michael, *Canadian Contemporary Dance Theatre*, 364
De Cordova, Janette, *Edmonton Immigrant Services Association*, 677
De Croos, Laurie, *Prince George Alzheimer's Society*, 1179
De Faria, Julia, *Ontario Trial Lawyers Association*, 1111
De Filippis, Joseph, *Canadian Association of Provincial Court Judges*, 329
de Grandpré, Jocelyn, *Réseau des SADC et CAE*, 1220
De Gryse, Piet, *International Committee of Museums & Collections of Arms & Military History*, 1543
De Guire, Caroline, *Association québécoise des informaticiennes et informaticiens indépendants*, 173
de Hemptinne, Thérèse, *Commission internationale de diplomatique*, 1518
de Henry, Patrick, *International Union for Conservation of Nature*, 1563
de Jager, Julius, *Ontario Alliance of Christian Schools*, 1059
de Jong, Jeff, *USC Canada*, 1423
de Jong, Frank, *Yukon Green Party*, 1478
de Klerk, Wim, *International Confederation for Thermal Analysis & Calorimetry*, 1543
De Koven, Harriet, *The Friends of Fort York & Garrison Common*, 761
de la Cuesta, José Luis, *Association internationale de droit pénal*, 1509
de Laat, Paul, *Canadian Association for the Advancement of Netherlandic Studies*, 305
De Leemans, Pieter, *Société internationale pour l'étude de la philosophie médiévale*, 1589
de Leon, Gemma, *Retail, Wholesale & Department Store Union (AFL-CIO/CLC)*, 1586
De Leon-Casasola, Oscar, *American Society of Regional Anesthesia & Pain Medicine*, 1502
De Long, Karen, *Inclusion BC*, 832
De Luisa, Paul, *Community Living Greater Sudbury*, 602

De Manche, Maria, *Kolbe Eucharistic Apostolate*, 892
De Manche, Therese, *Kolbe Eucharistic Apostolate*, 892
De Marchi, Mario, *The Neocatechumenal Way*, 1003
de Montigny, Jazz, *Portage & District Arts Council*, 1166
de Montigny, Guillaume, *Association des Grands Frères et Grandes Soeurs du Québec*, 115
de Montmollin, Lorraine, *International Society of Physical & Rehabilitation Medicine*, 1561
De Pass, Deborah, *Canadian Masters Cross-Country Ski Association*, 431
De Pauw, Lars, *Orphan Well Association*, 1127
de Peña, Morgan, *Manitoba Baseball Association*, 932
de Pokomandy-Morin, Katia, *YWCA Canada*, 1482
de Raad, Lydia, *La Leche League International*, 1569
de Raadt, Jacqueline, *Applied Science Technologists & Technicians of British Columbia*, 74
de Repentigny, Chantal, *Fédération des Chambres immobilières du Québec*, 713
de Repentigny, France, *Association québécoise pour l'hygiène, la santé et la sécurité du travail*, 176
de Roodenbeke, Eric, *International Hospital Federation*, 1550
de Sanjose, Silvia, *International Papillomavirus Society*, 1555
de Shield, Andrea, *Toronto Community Employment Services*, 1383
de Silva, Shirley, *Sarnia Lambton Chamber of Commerce*, 1254
De Silva, Janet (Jan), *Toronto Region Board of Trade*, 1387
De Simone, Valeria, *Villa Charities Inc. (Toronto District)*, 1435
De Souza, Marian, *Canadian Bar Association*, 341
de Souza, Marina, *Canadian Concrete Masonry Producers Association*, 362
De Vos, Willem, *Society of Plastics Engineers*, 1594
de Vries, Jennifer, *International Association of Business Communicators*, 1538
de Vries, Joanne, *Fresh Outlook Foundation*, 760
de Waal, L., *IRC International Water & Sanitation Centre*, 1567
de Waal, Tom, *British Columbia Angus Association*, 230
de Wilde, Lisa, *Toronto International Film Festival Inc.*, 1385
de Wit, Robert, *Greater Vancouver Home Builders' Association*, 786
De Zordo, Alexander, *Pro Bono Québec*, 1181
Deacon, Paul, *Wiarton South Bruce Peninsula Chamber of Commerce*, 1453
Deacon, Kevin, *Ontario Brain Injury Association*, 1068
Deacon, Donnie, *Ottawa Chamber Orchestra*, 1129
Deagle-Gammon, Cathy, *Dartmouth Adult Services Centre*, 651
Deakin, Stephanie, *Professional Organizers in Canada*, 1186
Deakin-Thomas, Diana, *YMCA Canada*, 1471
Deal-Porter, Brettanie, *Special Olympics Yukon*, 1340
Dean, Bill, *Canadian Bible Society*, 343
Dean, Terry, *Canadian Lung Association*, 428
Dean, Amanda, *Insurance Bureau of Canada*, 849
Dean, Doleen, *Vancouver, Coast & Mountains Tourism Region*, 1429
Dean, Eric, *International Association of Bridge, Structural, Ornamental & Reinforcing Iron Workers (AFL-CIO)*, 1538
Dean, Ken, *Teamsters Canada (CLC)*, 1368

Deane, Patrick, *Council of Ontario Universities*, 635
Deane, Sheena, *Canadian Association of Pharmacy Technicians*, 326
Deans, Rosemary, *Manitoba Environmental Industries Association Inc.*, 936
Deans, Julia, *Futurpreneur Canada*, 765
Dear, Alfred, *St. Vincent & the Grenadines Association of Montreal Inc.*, 1251
DeBaker, April, *American Water Works Association*, 1504
Debergh, Karen, *Wallaceburg & District Chamber of Commerce*, 1440
Debicki, Ruth, *Sudbury Rock & Lapidary Society*, 1353
Debicki, Ed, *Sudbury Rock & Lapidary Society*, 1353
Debnath, Samir C., *Canadian Society for Horticultural Science*, 475
Debnath, Samir, *Newfoundland & Labrador Institute of Agrologists*, 1019
Deboeck, Brian, *BMW Clubs Canada*, 216
Deboisbriand, Marlene, *Boys & Girls Clubs of Québec*, 224
Deboisbriand, Marlene, *Boys & Girls Clubs of Canada*, 222
Debus, Johannes, *Canadian Opera Company*, 446
Decaens, Sebastien, *Nova Scotia Criminal Justice Association*, 1043
DeCator, Fred, *Ontario Home Builders' Association*, 1085
Decelles, Pierre, *Société de généalogie Saint-Hubert*, 1316
Decherf, Jonathan, *Chambre de commerce française au Canada - Section Québec*, 548
Decker, Kim, *YWCA Canada*, 1482
Decker, David, *Fish, Food & Allied Workers*, 739
Decker, Gay, *Trans Canada Trail Foundation*, 1394
Deckert, Mike, *Society of Tribologists & Lubrication Engineers*, 1594
DeCoste, Megan, *Child Find PEI Inc.*, 559
DeCoteau, Mary-Jo, *Rethink Breast Cancer*, 1228
DeCourcey, Michelle, *Recreation New Brunswick*, 1207
Decter, Ann, *YWCA Canada*, 1481
Decter, Michael, *Patients Canada*, 1145
Dedeluk, Ken M., *Computer Modelling Group*, 609
Dedrick, Tonya, *Screen Composers Guild of Canada*, 1287
Dee, Keith, *Community Living Ontario*, 604
Dees, Robert, *Livres Canada Books*, 915
DeFaveri, Annette, *British Columbia Library Association*, 245
deFaye, T.F., *Dominion of Canada Rifle Association*, 661
Defoort, Lisa, *Canadian Association of Agri-Retailers*, 308
DeGaetano, Richard, *Social Planning Toronto*, 1307
DeGagne, Nicolle, *Saskatchewan Association of Library Technicians, Inc.*, 1257
Degen, John, *The Writers' Union of Canada*, 1469
DeGrace, Karen, *New Brunswick Pharmaceutical Society*, 1011
Degray, Pierre, *Conseil provincial du soutien scolaire*, 620
DeGuire, Benoit, *Relance jeunes et familles*, 1217
DeHaan, Steve, *International Warehouse Logistics Association*, 1566
Dehaney, Carleen, *Boys & Girls Clubs of Canada*, 222
DeHaros, Carol, *Canadian Society of Cardiac Surgeons*, 481
DeHart, Jim, *Wilderness Tourism Association*, 1454
Dehdar, Feri, *Cerebral Palsy Association of British Columbia*, 538

Executive Name Index

Dehod, Rose, *Alberta Pharmacists' Association (RxA)*, 42
Dehtiar, Eitan, *Muscular Dystrophy Canada*, 982
Deichert, Debbie, *Alzheimer Society of Perth County*, 64
Deighton, Sheila, *Schizophrenia Society of Ontario*, 1284
DeJager, Tim, *Aquaculture Association of Canada*, 75
deJong, Audrey, *Craft & Hobby Association*, 1520
Dekinder, Darren, *Baseball Alberta*, 198
Dekker, Jennifer, *Association des professeurs de l'université d'Ottawa*, 125
Dekker, Chris, *Saskatchewan Trade & Export Partnership*, 1276
DeKort, Nicole, *Canada's Medical Technology Companies*, 282
Del Bigio, Marc, *Canadian Association of Neuropathologists*, 322
Del Col, Aldo, *Myeloma Canada*, 986
Del Gobbo, Luigi (Lou), *British Columbia Cancer Foundation*, 234
Del Grande, Karla, *Ontario Masters Athletics*, 1090
del Re, Renato Brun, *Hamilton Right to Life*, 802
Del Rio, Miguel, *Maison internationale de la Rive-Sud*, 927
Del Vecchio, Quentin, *Shipyard General Workers' Federation of British Columbia*, 1296
Delacroix, Céline, *Conservation Council of New Brunswick*, 622
Delage, Josée, *Société d'histoire de Sherbrooke*, 1311
Delage, Robert, *British Columbia Milk Marketing Board*, 246
Delainey, Bill, *Saskatchewan Professional Planners Institute*, 1272
DeLamirande, Patrick, *Fédération acadienne de la Nouvelle-Écosse*, 707
Delaney, Patrick J., *Petroleum Services Association of Canada*, 1154
Delaney, Patricia, *Fédération internationale des professions immobilières*, 1526
Delaney, Jan, *Better Business Bureau of Western Ontario*, 207
Delaney, Ken, *Canadian Steel Trade & Employment Congress*, 491
Delaney, Ed, *East Coast Trail Association*, 668
Delaney, Sandy, *Newfoundland & Labrador Association of Occupational Therapists*, 1016
Delaney, Dianne, *Prince Edward Island Draft Horse Association*, 1173
Delaney, Stephanie, *Canadian Disaster Restoration Group*, 378
Delaney, Sarah, *Foundation for Advancing Family Medicine of the College of Family Physicians of Canada*, 755
Delanoy, Sue, *Canadian Association of Elizabeth Fry Societies*, 313
Delany, Vicki, *The Crime Writers of Canada*, 642
Delany, Paul, *Kivalliq Chamber of Commerce*, 891
Delaquis, Rod, *Manitoba Percheron & Belgian Club*, 942
Delas, Olivier, *Société Québécoise de droit international*, 1323
DeLaura, Courtney, *Automotive Industries Association of Canada*, 190
DeLaurier, Stacey, *Ontario Brain Injury Association*, 1069
Delbridge, Christine, *Canadian Hydrographic Association*, 409
Deleenheer, Bernice, *Bow Island / Burdett District Chamber of Commerce*, 219
DeLeon, Raquel, *Urology Nurses of Canada*, 1423
Delesalle, Susan, *Innovate Calgary*, 839
Deleurme, Lise, *Chambre de commerce de Notre Dame*, 542

Delgado, Ana, *Canadian Society for Analytical Sciences & Spectroscopy*, 473
Delichte, Henry, *Jersey Canada*, 869
Deliencourt, Sylvie M., *Canadian College of Health Leaders*, 358
Delisle, Randy, *Société francophone de Victoria*, 1319
Delisle, Benoit, *Chambre de commerce de la MRC de L'Assomption*, 541
Delisle, André, *Société d'archéologie et de numismatique de Montréal*, 1309
Delisle, Frédérique, *Association québécoise pour le loisir des personnes handicapées*, 177
Dell'Anno, Gwen, *Alberta Camping Association*, 27
DeLombard, Marilee, *Western Québec Literacy Council*, 1450
Delon, Darius, *Risk & Insurance Management Society Inc.*, 1233
Delon, Darius, *Risk & Insurance Management Society Inc.*, 1234
Delong, Anne, *Durham Personal Computer Users' Club*, 665
Delorme, Connie, *Canadian Cutting Horse Association*, 375
Delorme, Janelle, *Development & Peace*, 654
Delorme, Carol, *South Stormont Chamber of Commerce*, 1336
Delorme, Lynne, *PFLAG Canada Inc.*, 1156
Delorme, Jean-Guy, *Fédération des chambres de commerce du Québec*, 713
DeLuca, Christopher, *Canadian Educational Researchers' Association*, 380
DeLuca, Christine, *Special Libraries Association*, 1596
Demand, Robert, *UNITE HERE Canada*, 1409
DeMarchi, Julie, *PFLAG Canada Inc.*, 1156
DeMatteo, Lina, *Association for Operations Management*, 134
Dembicki, Phil, *Canadian Union of Public Employees*, 498
Dembroski, David, *Interactive Ontario*, 851
DeMelo, Olga, *Professional Student Services Personnel*, 1186
DeMerchant, Colleen P., *Nuclear Insurance Association of Canada*, 1050
Demers, Jovette, *Oxy-jeunes*, 1134
Demers, Lisa, *Seva Canada Society*, 1292
Demers, Chantal, *Association des professionnels du chauffage*, 125
Demeter, Andrew, *Professional Engineers Ontario*, 1194
Demetrioff, Heather, *Manitoba School Boards Association*, 944
Demetrioff, Rory, *Ontario Association of Veterinary Technicians*, 1066
Demick, Jo-Anne, *Community Living Parry Sound*, 604
Demizio, Debbie, *The Bruce Trail Conservancy*, 261
Demma, Tom, *British Columbia Vegetable Marketing Commission*, 257
DeMoel, Debbie, *Provincial Women's Softball Association of Ontario*, 1191
Demontigny, Claude, *Fédération des syndicats de la santé et des services sociaux*, 719
Dempsey, Paul Stephen, *Institute of Air & Space Law*, 844
Dempsey, Brian, *Moncton Retriever Club*, 972
Dempsey, Carla, *Nova Scotia Real Estate Appraisers Association*, 1048
Dempsey, Ray, *Québec Shorthorn Association*, 1198
Dempsey, Colin, *Northern Air Transport Association*, 1034
Dempsey, Peter, *Niagara/Hamilton Association of Baptist Churches*, 1026
Dempsey, Gail, *Canadian Epilepsy Alliance*, 382
Dempsey, Stephen, *Offshore Energy Research Association of Nova Scotia*, 1055
Dempster, Darrell, *Nova Scotia School Athletic Federation*, 1048

Dempster, Dora, *The Royal Scottish Country Dance Society*, 1587
Demski, Allyson, *La Salle & District Chamber of Commerce*, 1251
Demulder, Bob, *The Nature Conservancy of Canada*, 999
Demuynck, Charles, *Oakville Chamber Orchestra*, 1053
Demyen, Aaron, *Saskatchewan Volleyball Association*, 1277
Denaburg, Jeff, *ARZA-Canada: The Zionist Voice of the Canadian Reform Movement*, 86
Denault, Johanne, *Canadian Association for Composite Structures & Materials*, 298
Denbak, Suzanne, *Whistler Resort Association*, 1452
Denbok, John, *SIM Canada*, 1299
Denbow, Jason, *Community Futures Saskatchewan*, 598
Denbrok, Jodi, *Manitoba Percheron & Belgian Club*, 942
Denburg, Elisha, *Canadian League of Composers*, 426
Denburg, Judah, *AllerGen NCE Inc.*, 54
Dendys, Jeanie, *Yukon Indian Hockey Association*, 1479
Denesha, Sherry, *Ontario Building Envelope Council*, 1070
Denhoff, Eric, *Canadian Hydrogen & Fuel Cell Association*, 409
Denholm, Jessica, *Family Services of Greater Vancouver*, 705
Denike, Alan, *Regina Musicians' Association*, 1212
Denike, Alan, *South Saskatchewan Youth Orchestra*, 1336
Denis, Frank, *Sail Nova Scotia*, 1246
Denluck, Barry, *British Columbia Bee Breeders' Association*, 233
Denney, Mike, *Canadian Country Music Association*, 372
Dennis, Martha, *Woodstock District Chamber of Commerce*, 1464
Dennis, Thea, *Samaritan House Ministries Inc.*, 1253
Dennis, Colin, *Institute of Food Technologists*, 1532
Dennis, Lynn, *Alberta Dressage Association*, 33
Denny, Jetta, *First Nations SchoolNet*, 739
DeNobile, Mark, *Canadian Football Hall of Fame & Museum*, 392
Dénommé, Pierre, *Sentier Urbain*, 1290
Denoncourt, Gisèle, *Mouvement national des québécoises et québécois*, 978
Denoncourt, Gisèle, *Société Saint-Jean-Baptiste du Centre du Québec*, 1325
Densmore, Chris, *Volleyball BC*, 1437
Densmore, Carla, *Hepatitis Outreach Society of Nova Scotia*, 812
Dent, Jonathan, *Canadian Bible Society*, 343
Dent, Jennifer, *The Public Affairs Association of Canada*, 1192
Dentelbeck, Chuck, *Canadian Lumber Standards Accreditation Board*, 428
Denton, Troy, *The New Brunswick Association of Respiratory Therapists Inc.*, 1005
Denty, Natasha, *Canadian Cancer Society*, 349
Denyer, Cathy, *Parks & Recreation Ontario*, 1142
Denys-Roulette, Melissa, *Manitoba Pulse & Soybean Growers Inc.*, 943
Denzel, Gene, *Richmond Hill Naturalists*, 1231
Deom, Joe, *Kanien'kehaka Onkwawen'na Raotitiohkwa Language & Cultural Centre*, 881
Depalme, Ray, *Salers Association of Canada*, 1251
DePete, Joe, *Air Line Pilots Association, International - Canada*, 19
Déquier, Réal, *Caisse Groupe Financier*, 270
Der Ghazarian, Salpi, *Armenian General Benevolent Union*, 83

Deraîche, Claude, *L'Association québécoise des centres de la petite enfance*, 172
Deranger, Eriel, *Sierra Club of Canada*, 1298
Derbyshire, Justin, *HelpAge International*, 1529
Derderian, Angel, *Armenian Relief Society of Canada, Inc.*, 83
Derewianchuk, Cathy, *Manitoba Amateur Broomball Association*, 928
Derewianchuk, Cathy, *Bowls Manitoba*, 220
Dergousoff, Brent, *College of Dental Surgeons of Saskatchewan*, 583
Dergousoff, Dale, *College of Optometrists of BC*, 587
Derkach, Larry, *National Council of Jewish Women of Canada*, 992
Derkach, Larry, *Jewish Family Services Edmonton*, 872
Derksen, Tanya, *Regina Symphony Orchestra*, 1212
Derkson, Vicky, *Mechanical Contractors Association of Alberta*, 956
Derome, Dominique, *National Building Envelope Council*, 991
Derome, Diane, *Fondation Desjardins*, 745
Derome, Bertrand, *L'Institut de développement de produits*, 841
DeRoose, Lorelie, *Saskatchewan Elocution & Debate Association*, 1264
Deroy, Gaston, *Les Chevaliers de Colomb du Québec, District No 37, Conseil 5198*, 557
Derrenbacker, Jr., Robert A., *Canadian Society of Biblical Studies*, 481
Derrick, Peter, *effect:hope*, 681
Derrick, Peter, *Saskatchewan Association of Medical Radiation Technologists*, 1257
Derrien, René, *Société des chefs, cuisiniers et pâtissiers du Québec*, 1317
Derulle, Joëlle, *Association québécoise du loisir municipal*, 176
Déry, Patrick, *Canadian Council of Insurance Regulators*, 368
Déry, Alberte, *Association québécoise de soins palliatifs*, 171
Déry, Gaston, *Opéra de Québec*, 1115
Derzko, Christine, *SIGMA Canadian Menopause Society*, 1298
Des Rivières, Marc, *Association québécoise des transports*, 175
Des Roches, Anne-Marie, *Canadian Conference of the Arts*, 363
Desai, Aakash, *Grey Highlands Chamber of Commerce*, 790
Desai, Nazir, *British Columbia Mainland Cricket League*, 246
Desaulniers, Lise, *Réseau FADOQ*, 1224
Desaulniers, Paulette, *Chambre de commerce francophone de Saint-Boniface*, 548
Desaulniers, Jacinthe, *Réseau des services de santé en français de l'Est de l'Ontario*, 1222
Desaulniers, Paulette, *Association des juristes d'expression française du Manitoba inc.*, 118
Desautels, Julie, *Association des bibliothèques publiques de la Montérégie*, 107
Desautels, Normand, *Fédération des caisses Desjardins du Québec*, 712
Desbien, Julie, *Alliance Française d'Ottawa*, 57
Desbiens, Anne-Marie, *Orchestre symphonique des jeunes de Montréal*, 1118
Desbiens, Michel, *Canadian Institute for Theatre Technology*, 414
Desbiens, Yves, *Association des Physiques Québécois*, 123
Deschambault, Donna, *Canine Federation of Canada*, 508
Deschamps, Leo, *Central Alberta Gliding Club*, 523
Deschamps, Alain, *Sports-Québec*, 1346
Deschamps, Claude, *Centre franco-ontarien de ressources pédagogiques*, 534
Deschamps, Richard, *Institut Nazareth et Louis-Braille*, 843
Deschênes, Hervé, *FPInnovations*, 757

Executive Name Index

Deschenes, Jacqueline, *Ontario Speed Skating Association*, 1108
Deschênes, Daniel, *Réseau des SADC et CAE*, 1221
Deschênes, Mathieu, *Société d'histoire de Louiseville inc.*, 1311
Deschênes, Gérard, *Maison internationale de la Rive-Sud*, 927
Desgagné, Serge, *Réseau des SADC et CAE*, 1221
Desgranges, Elisabeth, *Development & Peace*, 655
Deshaies, Paul, *Réseau du sport étudiant du Québec Cantons-de-l'Est*, 1222
Desharnais, Josée, *Chambre de commerce et d'industrie des Bois-Francs et de l'Érable*, 547
Desharnais, Cyndi, *Yukon Child Care Association*, 1477
Desharnais-Roy, Olivier, *Canadian Media Guild*, 432
Deshmukh, Archana, *Institute of Cultural Affairs International*, 846
Desiatnyk, Curtis, *Risk & Insurance Management Society Inc.*, 1234
Desjardin, Wanda, *Boys & Girls Clubs of Saskatchewan*, 224
Desjardins, Richard, *Maison Kekpart*, 927
Desjardins, Richard, *Boys & Girls Clubs of Québec*, 224
Desjardins, Marie-Claude, *Association coopérative d'économie familiale du Sud-Ouest de Montréal*, 98
Desjardins, David, *Association Museums New Brunswick*, 138
Desjardins, Anik, *Ringette Canada*, 1233
Desjardins, Louise, *Canadian Council on Animal Care*, 371
Desjardins, Carolle, *Société pour les enfants handicapés du Québec*, 1322
Desjardins, Raymond, *Société des établissements de plein air du Québec*, 1318
Desjardins, André, *Club cycliste de la Montérégie*, 574
Desjardins, David, *Canadian Association of Science Centres*, 332
Desjardins, Brian, *Danish Canadian National Museum Society*, 650
Desjardins, Brian, *Northwest Territories Tourism*, 1039
Desjardins, Martine, *Mouvement national des québécoises et québécois*, 977
Desjardins, Martin, *Association de taekwondo du Québec*, 104
Deslaurier, Jocelyn, *Fédération de cheerleading du Québec*, 708
Deslauriers, Hélène, *Réseau des SADC et CAE*, 1219
Deslauriers, Anne, *Hearth, Patio & Barbecue Association of Canada*, 810
Desmarais, Max, *Sail Manitoba*, 1246
Desmarais, Carolane, *Fédération des professionnelles et professionnels de l'éducation du Québec*, 718
Desmarais, Sophie, *Ami-e du Quartier*, 67
Desmarais, Hélène, *Réseau HEC Montréal*, 1224
Desmarais, Hélène, *Société d'investissement jeunesse*, 1314
Desmarais, Guy, *Canadian Bookkeepers Association*, 346
Desmarais, Margo, *PBA Society of Alberta*, 1146
Desnoyers, Danièle, *Le Carré des Lombes*, 515
Desnoyers, Pat, *L'Arche Western Region*, 78
Désourdie, Michel, *Syndicat des agents de la paix en services correctionnels du Québec*, 1362
DeSousa, Sharon, *Public Service Alliance of Canada*, 1193
DeSousa, Sharon, *Public Service Alliance of Canada*, 1193
Desparois, Marc, *International Federation of Broomball Associations*, 857

Després, Daniel, *Canadian Wood Truss Association*, 505
Després-Dubé, Caroll-Ann, *Association du Québec pour enfants avec problèmes auditifs*, 131
DesRochers, Rachelle, *Ontario Library Association*, 1089
Desrochers, Lise, *Chambre immobilière de la Haute Yamaska Inc.*, 550
Desrochers, Larry, *Manitoba Opera Association Inc.*, 941
Desrochers, Pierre, *Association canadienne des sciences régionales*, 95
Desrochers, Jacques, *Réseau du sport étudiant du Québec Montréal*, 1223
DesRoches, Judy, *Barrie Literacy Council*, 197
Desroches, Donald, *Réseau pour le développement de l'alphabétisme et des compétences*, 1225
DesRoches, Angele, *P.E.E.R.S. Alliance*, 1148
DesRoches, Anastasia, *Fédération des parents de l'Île-du-Prince-Édouard*, 716
Desroches, Maurice, *Chambre de commerce de Collette*, 540
Desrochers, Marili, *Association des collèges privés du Québec*, 109
Desrosiers, Etienne, *Vidéographe*, 1434
Desrosiers, Martin, *Children of the World Adoption Society Inc.*, 560
Desrosiers, Claire, *Hébergement la casa Bernard-Hubert*, 811
DesRosiers, Norma J., *Western Québec Literacy Council*, 1450
Desrosiers, Claudel P., *International Federation of Medical Students' Associations*, 1548
Desrosiers, Murielle, *Association des personnes handicapées physiques et sensorielles du secteur Joliette*, 123
Desrosiers, Tammy, *Saskatoon Parents of Twins & Triplets Organization*, 1280
Desrosiers, Gyslaine, *Secrétariat international des infirmières et infirmiers de l'espace francophone*, 1288
Dessureault, Sandra, *Mouvement national des québécoises et québécois*, 978
Detar, Ann, *Grey Highlands Chamber of Commerce*, 790
Detillieux, Gilbert, *Manitoba UNIX User Group*, 946
Dettweiler, Ben, *Waterloo Coin Society*, 1442
Deutch, Bill, *Faculty Association of the College of New Caledonia*, 701
Deutsch, Lorne, *Canadian Association of Foodservice Professionals*, 315
Deveau, Albert, *Goodwill, The Amity Group*, 778
Deveau, Andréa, *Société Saint-Thomas-d'Aquin*, 1325
Devereaux, Janis, *Skills/Compétences Canada*, 1303
Deverell, Frances, *Canadian Unitarians for Social Justice*, 499
Deverman, Ron, *National Association of Environmental Professionals*, 1573
Devers, Patricia, *North American Waterfowl Management Plan*, 1029
DeVicque, Marcia, *Glass Art Association of Canada*, 774
deViller, Clyde, *Fédération acadienne de la Nouvelle-Écosse*, 707
DeVito, Mark, *Villa Charities Inc. (Toronto District)*, 1435
Devits, Dean, *National Conferences of Firemen & Oilers (SEIU)*, 1575
Devitt, Crosby, *Grain Farmers of Ontario*, 779
Devlin, Lori, *Canadian Wood Pallet & Container Association*, 505
Devlin, Doug, *Police Martial Arts Association Inc.*, 1163
Devlin, Katherine, *Jean Tweed Treatment Centre*, 869
Devlin, Shaun, *Mutual Fund Dealers Association of Canada*, 986

Devoe, Ken, *Central Alberta Realtors Association*, 523
Devoe, Jim, *Congress of Aboriginal Peoples*, 613
Devonshire, Tashauna, *HIV/AIDS Resources and Community Health*, 817
DeVos, Jason, *Canadian Soccer Association*, 472
Devost, Mélanie, *Association québécoise des salons du livre*, 174
DeVries, John, *Ottawa Construction Association*, 1130
DeVries, Anita, *Ontario Home Builders' Association*, 1085
deVries, Lynn, *Back Country Horsemen of British Columbia*, 193
Dew, Rebecca, *Futurpreneur Canada*, 765
DeWaard, Ian, *Christian Labour Association of Canada*, 568
DeWaard, Ian, *Christian Labour Association of Canada*, 568
DeWaard, Ian, *Christian Labour Association of Canada*, 568
Dewan, Raylene, *Nova Scotia Society for the Prevention of Cruelty to Animals*, 1049
Dewar, Danielle, *Women's Legal Education & Action Fund*, 1463
Dewar, Donna, *Canadian Nurses Association*, 443
DeWeerd, Tim, *Compassion Canada*, 608
Dewey, John, *Federation of Prince Edward Island Municipalities Inc.*, 726
Dewinetz, Richard, *Galiano Island Chamber of Commerce*, 766
Dewit, Paula, *Chilliwack Symphony Orchestra & Chorus*, 564
DeWolfe, Nadine, *Psychological Association of Prince Edward Island*, 1192
DeWolff, Anna, *Okanagan Miniature Horse Club*, 1056
Dextraze, Gilles, *Association des Églises des frères mennonites du Québec*, 111
Dey Nuttall, Anita, *Canadian Circumpolar Institute*, 357
Deydey, Kim, *Saskatchewan Society of Medical Laboratory Technologists*, 1275
Deyell, Gerald M., *The Calgary Foundation*, 272
Deyglio, Victor S., *The Logistics Institute*, 917
Dhaliwal, Eden, *Access Copyright*, 5
Dhaliwal, Gagandeep, *Resident Doctors of British Columbia*, 1226
Dhaliwal, Ray, *Kamloops Multicultural Society*, 880
Dhaliwal, Navf, *Canadian Urban Institute*, 499
Dhaliwal, Sav, *Lower Mainland Local Government Association*, 920
Dhanani, Ashifa, *British Columbia Water & Waste Association*, 258
Dhanjal, Ranjit, *Food Allergy Canada*, 749
Dhatt, Rana, *Burnaby Multicultural Society*, 266
Dhawan, Rup, *Professional Engineers Ontario*, 1184
Dheilly, Stacie, *Risk & Insurance Management Society Inc.*, 1234
Dhesi, Christina, *The Appraisal Institute of Canada - British Columbia*, 75
Dhillon, Kulvinder Singh, *Maritime Sikh Society*, 951
Dhiman, Manjeet, *A.C.C.E.S. Employment*, 4
Di Carlo, Anna, *Communist Party of Canada (Marxist-Leninist)*, 595
Di Chiara, Elizabeth, *Canadian Society of Club Managers*, 482
Di Giovanni, Jérôme, *Alliance des communautés culturelles pour l'égalité dans la santé et les services sociaux*, 55
Di Iulio, Pal, *Villa Charities Inc. (Toronto District)*, 1435
Di Lallo, Wayne, *Wetaskiwin Chamber of Commerce*, 1451
Di Leo, Pina, *Dufferin Arts Council*, 664
Di Perna, Maria, *Association of Catholic Retired Administrators*, 144

Di Pietro, Yvonne, *Simcoe & District Chamber of Commerce*, 1299
Di Pietro, LUcy, *Heritage Toronto*, 813
Di Staulo, David, *General Conference of the Canadian Assemblies of God*, 769
Di Tomasso, Simone, *DanceSport Québec*, 650
Diabagaté, Siriki, *Association canadienne-française de Régina*, 96
Diachun, Dan, *The Appraisal Institute of Canada - Manitoba*, 75
Diamond, Ross, *Georgina Association for Community Living*, 771
Diamond, Robert, *Canadian Economics Association*, 379
Diamond, G. Scot, *St. Andrew's Society of Montréal*, 1248
Dias, Jerry, *UNIFOR*, 1405
Dias, Vitor, *Alberta Agricultural Economics Association*, 21
Diavolitsis, Evangelos, *Quickdraw Animation Society*, 1201
Diaz, Ian, *Fort McMurray Youth Soccer Association*, 753
Diaz, Beatriz, *Cátedra de Estudios sobre Canadá*, 1515
DiBartolomeo, Kathy, *Amherstburg Community Services*, 67
Dicaire, Trevor, *Starlight Children's Foundation Canada*, 1348
DiCamillo, Marietta, *Major League Baseball Players' Association (Ind.)*, 1569
Dichesne, Sara-Emmanuelle, *Association des journalistes indépendants du Québec*, 117
Dichon, Amanda, *Canadian Society of Soil Science*, 488
DiCicco, Vanessa, *Saskatchewan Association of Naturopathic Practitioners*, 1257
Dick, Greg, *Canadian Football League*, 392
Dick, Josephin, *Saskatchewan German Council Inc.*, 1266
Dick, Emmanuel, *National Council of Trinidad & Tobago Organizations in Canada*, 992
Dickenson, Christa, *Interactive Ontario*, 851
Dickey, Peter, *Huronia & District Beekeepers' Association*, 828
Dickie, Martha, *Ontario Minor Hockey Association*, 1091
Dickie, John, *Canadian Federation of Apartment Associations*, 385
Dicks, Andrea, *Community Foundations of Canada*, 598
Dickson, Kate, *Canadian Society for International Health*, 475
Dickson, Jason, *YMCA Canada*, 1472
Dickson, Nancy, *Burnaby Laphounds Club*, 266
Dickson, Paul, *Canadian National Federation of Independent Unions*, 439
Dickson, Jason, *Baseball Canada*, 198
Dickson, Andrew, *Manitoba Pork Council*, 942
DiClemente, Warren, *Ontario Hospital Association*, 1087
Didier, Martens, *Canadian Culinary Federation*, 374
DiDiomete, Franca, *Catholic Family Service of Ottawa*, 518
Didonato, Solidea, *Family of the Immaculate Heart of Mary*, 704
Didyk, Katie, *Times Change Women's Employment Service*, 1379
Diecidue, Frank, *Heating, Refrigeration & Air Conditioning Institute of Canada*, 810
Diehl, Rob, *Canadian Hard of Hearing Association*, 400
Dielen, Tom, *World Archery Federation*, 1603
Diemer, Ulli, *Connexions Information Sharing Services*, 613
Dieno, Linda, *CADORA British Columbia*, 268
Diessenes, Nicole, *Maison internationale de la Rive-Sud*, 927
Dieterich, Carrie, *Entertainment Merchants Association - International Head Office*, 1523
Dietrich, Mike, *Alberta Building Envelope Council (South)*, 27

Executive Name Index

Dietrich, Mike, *Navy League of Canada*, 1002
Dietschi, Ben, *Soundstreams Canada*, 1333
Dietz-Rathgeber, Lorie, *Melville Arts Council*, 960
Dieudonné, Nesly, *Recreation Vehicle Dealers Association of Canada*, 1208
Diewold, Bob, *Alberta Association of Rehabilitation Centres*, 25
Digby, Wayne, *Canadian Forage & Grassland Association*, 392
DiGiacomo, Jane, *Nelson & District Hospice Society*, 1003
DiGiovanni, Tony, *Landscape Ontario Horticultural Trades Association*, 898
Digout, Bev, *Parenting Education Saskatchewan*, 1140
Diki, Ngawang, *Canadian Tibetan Association of Ontario*, 495
Dillabaugh, Michael, *Local Government Management Association of British Columbia*, 917
Dille, Zoe, *Hart House Orchestra*, 804
Dillion, Terry, *Rowing Canada Aviron*, 1237
Dillon, Chantal G., *Hearst & Area Association for Community Living*, 808
Dillon, Jay, *Tilbury Chamber of Commerce*, 1379
Dillon, Valarie, *Scouts Canada*, 1286
Dillon, John R., *Business Council of Canada*, 267
Dillon, Patrick J., *Provincial Building & Construction Trades Council of Ontario*, 1190
Dillon, Justin, *National Association for Environmental Education (UK)*, 1572
Dillon, Wayne, *Hockey Development Centre for Ontario*, 817
Dillon, Patricia, *Mining Industry Human Resources Council*, 967
Dillon, Gord, *Prosthetics & Orthotics Association of British Columbia*, 1190
Dills, Kathleen, *Halton Hills Chamber of Commerce*, 800
DiLoreto, Erin, *Sculptors' Association of Alberta*, 1287
Dilwaria, Manoj, *Ontario Traffic Council*, 1111
Dimant, Frank, *League for Human Rights of B'nai Brith Canada*, 903
Dimant, Frank, *B'nai Brith Canada Institute for International Affairs*, 192
DiMenna, Jim, *Canadian Produce Marketing Association*, 460
Dimitroff, Darryl, *Mazda Sportscar Owners Club*, 954
Dimitrov, George, *Professional Engineers Ontario*, 1184
DiNardo, Ersilia, *Catholic Children's Aid Society of Hamilton*, 518
DiNatale, Nancy, *Catholic Children's Aid Society of Toronto*, 518
Dingwall, Robyn, *Grandview & District Chamber of Commerce*, 782
Diniz, Tony, *Child Development Institute*, 559
Dinka, Nicholas, *Grand Valley Trails Association*, 780
Dinnell, Beverley, *Association of Saskatchewan Home Economists*, 161
Dion, David, *Baseball New Brunswick*, 198
Dion, Martine, *Fédération du personnel de l'enseignement privé*, 720
Dion, Any-Claude, *Skate Canada*, 1301
Dion, Félix, *Fédération de volleyball du Québec*, 711
Dion, Michel, *Association des Grands Frères et Grandes Soeurs du Québec*, 115
Dion, Pierre, *Association des entrepreneurs en construction du Québec*, 112
Dion, Claire, *Independent Production Fund*, 833
Dion, Frédérick, *Association francophone des municipalités du Nouveau-Brunswick Inc.*, 135
Dion, Any-Claude, *Patinage Québec*, 1145
Dion, Carmen, *Point d'appui, centre d'aide et de prévention des agressions à caractère sexuel de Rouyn-Noranda*, 1163

Dionne, Valérie, *Société francophone de Victoria*, 1319
Dionne, Carole, *Association des Grands Frères et Grandes Soeurs du Québec*, 115
Dionne, Julie, *Canadian Dance Teachers' Association*, 375
Dionne, Jeff, *Canadian Society of Respiratory Therapists*, 487
Dionne, Isabelle, *Centraide Centre du Québec*, 522
Dionne, Julie, *Réseau du sport étudiant du Québec Chaudière-Appalaches*, 1222
Dionne, Louise, *Table des responsables de l'éducation des adultes et de la formation professionnelle des commissions scolaires du Québec*, 1366
Dionne, Louis, *Syndicat des producteurs en serre du Québec*, 1363
Dionne, Louise, *Centre femmes de Rimouski*, 531
Dionne, Justin, *Association provinciale des constructeurs d'habitations du Québec inc.*, 168
DiPenta, Joe, *The Leukemia & Lymphoma Society of Canada*, 909
DiPietro, Chris, *Canadian Condominium Institute*, 362
Distasio, Jino, *Institute of Urban Studies*, 847
Dittburner, Trask, *Canadian Security Association*, 469
Diverty, Brent, *Canadian Institute for Health Information*, 412
Divon, Elan, *Canadian Friends of the Hebrew University*, 395
Dixon, Brenda, *Association canadienne des ataxies familiales*, 92
Dixon, Dwight, *Western Retail Lumber Association*, 1450
Dixon, Jennifer, *Urban Development Institute of Canada*, 1422
Dixon, Dalyce, *Boys & Girls Clubs of British Columbia*, 222
Dixon, Brian, *Population Connection*, 1584
Dixon, Clarke, *Trent Valley Association of Baptist Churches*, 1397
Dixon, Deanna, *North American Waterfowl Management Plan*, 1029
Dixon, Deanna, *North American Waterfowl Management Plan*, 1029
Dixon, Cindy, *Alberta Community & Co-operative Association*, 30
Dixon, Neill, *Canadian Music Week Inc.*, 438
Dixon, David, *Toronto Fashion Incubator*, 1384
Do, Jennifer, *British Columbia Career Development Association*, 235
Doak, Doug, *The Anglican Church of Canada*, 69
Doan, Jon, *University of Lethbridge Faculty Association*, 1419
Doan, Anne, *The John Howard Society of Ontario*, 875
Doan, Andrew, *The Salvation Army in Canada*, 1253
Doan, Judy, *Alzheimer Society of Sarnia-Lambton*, 64
Doan-Crider, Diana, *International Association for Bear Research & Management*, 1536
Doane, Nancy, *East Hants Historical Society*, 668
Dobbelaar, Francis, *Ontario Processing Vegetable Growers*, 1097
Dobbie, Laura, *Peterborough Law Association*, 1153
Dobbie, Tim, *Goodwill, The Amity Group*, 778
Dobbin, Gary, *Association of Neighbourhood Houses BC*, 153
Dobbin, Kelly, *College of Midwives of Ontario*, 586
Dobbin, Michelle, *Canadian Association for Williams Syndrome*, 307
Dobbin, Mark, *Ireland Canada University Foundation*, 1567
Dobbs, Jim, *Canadian Institute for Theatre Technology*, 414

Dobinson, Wendy, *Ontario Electrical League*, 1077
Doblanko, Kiersten, *Professional Association of Residents of Alberta*, 1182
Dobmeier, Jeanette, *Canadian Sport Massage Therapists Association*, 490
Dobrowolski, Doug, *Association of Manitoba Municipalities*, 151
Dobson, Mark, *United Food & Commercial Workers Canada*, 1411
Dobson, Wendy, *Rotman Institute for International Business*, 1236
Dobson, Lindsay, *Canadian Poolplayers Association*, 458
Dobson, Kelly, *National Sunflower Association of Canada*, 996
Dodd, Doreen, *Saskatchewan Wildlife Federation*, 1278
Dodds, Derwood, *Melfort Real Estate Board*, 959
Dodds, Karen, *Science Teachers' Association of Ontario*, 1285
Dodds, Tom, *Sault Ste Marie Economic Development Corporation*, 1281
Dodge, Jim, *Association of Architectural Technologists of Ontario*, 139
Dodge, Randy, *Royal Astronomical Society of Canada*, 1238
Dodge, Dean, *YMCA Canada*, 1472
Dodia, Jaydipsinh K., *Indian Association for Canadian Studies*, 1531
Dodick, Rahn, *The Foundation Fighting Blindness*, 755
Dodjro, Komlanvi, *Alliance Française*, 57
Dodok, Mike, *Southwestern Ontario Beekeepers' Association*, 1338
Doebel-Atchison, Sabine, *Saskatchewan German Council Inc.*, 1266
Doell, Victoria, *Saskatchewan Association of Insolvency & Restructuring Professionals*, 1257
Doenz, Brad, *Alberta Hereford Association*, 37
Doering, Keith, *Ringette Association of Saskatchewan*, 1232
Doering, John, *Canadian Association for Graduate Studies*, 300
Doerksen, Mark, *Canadian Baptists of Western Canada*, 341
Doerksen, Linda, *Manitoba Brown Swiss Association*, 933
Doerksen, Olivia, *Insurance Brokers Association of Canada*, 848
Doerksen, Darlene, *Yukon Tourism Education Council*, 1480
Doerksen, Brad, *Friends of the Archibald*, 762
Doerksen, Phil, *Directors Guild of Canada*, 658
Dogra, Shanti, *Canada - Nova Scotia Offshore Petroleum Board*, 278
Dohan, Debbie, *Lupus Society of Manitoba*, 922
Doherty, Allen, *Animal Nutrition Association of Canada*, 71
Doherty, Shari, *Dress for Success*, 663
Doherty-Gilbert, Maggie, *Canadian Hearing Society*, 403
Doherty-Gilbert, Maggie, *Canadian Hearing Society*, 403
Doherty-Gilbert, Maggie, *Canadian Hearing Society*, 403
Doire, Marie-Claude, *Association du Syndrome de Turner du Québec*, 132
Doiron, Sherry, *New Brunswick Rugby Union*, 1011
Doiron, Aline, *Sooke Chamber of Commerce*, 1333
Doiron, Roger, *Fédération des aînées et aînés francophones du Canada*, 711
Doiron, Roger, *Association francophone des municipalités du Nouveau-Brunswick Inc.*, 135
Doiron, Line, *New Brunswick Association of Community Business Development Corporations*, 1005
Doka, Chris, *Saskatchewan Construction Association*, 1262

Doke, Charles, *Sealant & Waterproofing Association*, 1288
Dolan, Karen, *Kingston Arts Council*, 889
Dolan, Kim, *PARN Your Community AIDS Resource Network*, 1143
Dolan, Bill, *Prairie Conservation Forum*, 1169
Dolbec, Sylvie, *Alliance des professionels et des professionnelles de la Ville de Québec*, 56
Dolen, Conrad, *Peace Country Beef & Forage Association*, 1147
Dolez, Patricia, *Institute of Textile Science*, 847
Dolezsar, Richard, *Urban Municipal Administrators' Association of Saskatchewan*, 1422
Dolishny, Vanessa, *London Community Foundation*, 918
Doll, Dwayne, *Grande Prairie Soaring Society*, 781
Doll, Garret, *Alberta Schools' Athletic Association*, 46
Dollar, Fred, *Prince Edward Island Certified Organic Producers Co-op*, 1173
Dolter, Sean, *Model Forest of Newfoundland & Labrador*, 971
Domaradzki, George, *Rideau Valley Soaring*, 1232
Domer, Joan, *Alouette Field Naturalists*, 59
Dominguez, Rick, *Air Line Pilots Association, International - Canada*, 19
Domitruk, Daryl, *Manitoba Pulse & Soybean Growers Inc.*, 943
Domolewski, Marni, *East European Genealogical Society, Inc.*, 668
Domshy, Darlene, *Saskatchewan Youth in Care & Custody Network*, 1279
Don, Margaret, *Ottawa Valley Rock Garden & Horticultural Society*, 1132
don Wauchope, Andrew, *Canadian Association of Medical Biochemists*, 320
Donahue, Monica, *Food Banks Canada*, 749
Donald, Chris, *Catholic Health Association of Saskatchewan*, 520
Donald, Cathy, *Acupuncture Canada*, 7
Donald, Robert, *Canadian Council for Aviation & Aerospace*, 366
Donald, Richard, *Open Harbour Refugee Association*, 1114
Donaldson, Michelle, *The Lung Association of Nova Scotia*, 921
Donaldson, Al, *Boating Ontario*, 216
Donaldson, Billy, *Manitoba Organization of Disc Sports*, 941
Donat, Jean-Pierre, *Institut Tshakapesh*, 843
Doncaster, Deb, *Earth Day Canada*, 667
Donelle, Edgar, *Manitoba Association of Christian Home Schools*, 929
Donelon, Becky, *Alberta College of Paramedics*, 29
Donelon, Becky, *Alberta College of Paramedics*, 30
Dong Yue Zhang, Diana, *Chinese Medicine & Acupuncture Association of Canada*, 565
Donhauser, Carol, *Saskatchewan Music Festival Association Inc.*, 1270
Donihee, Jim, *Canadian Energy Pipeline Association*, 381
Donini, Andrea, *Covenant Foundation*, 637
Donison, Rob, *Qu'Appelle Valley Friendship Centre*, 1195
Donkers, Peter, *British Columbia Investment Agriculture Foundation*, 244
Donkin, Caroline, *Colleges Ontario*, 591
Donnan, Hugh, *Newfoundland Symphony Orchestra Association*, 1023
Donnell, Val, *Otter Valley Chamber of Commerce*, 1132
Donnelly, Peter, *International Society for Human & Animal Mycology*, 1558
Donnelly, Mitch, *AIESEC*, 18
Donnelly, Mary, *Ontario Horticultural Association*, 1086
Donnelly, Michele, *Oak Ridges Trail Association*, 1053

Executive Name Index

Donnelly, Eric, *Saskatchewan Wall & Ceiling Bureau Inc.*, 1277
Donnelly, Carlene, *Calgary Urban Project Society*, 275
Donnelly, Mike, *United Utility Workers' Association*, 1412
Donnelly, Michele, *Oak Ridges Moraine Foundation*, 1053
Donoghue, Ben, *Liaison of Independent Filmmakers of Toronto*, 909
Donovan, Shannon, *Football Canada*, 750
Donovan, Sherry, *Nova Scotia Home Builders' Association*, 1046
Donovan, Sue, *Epilepsy Ontario*, 694
Donovan, Mary Eileen, *Catholic Education Foundation of Ontario*, 518
Donovan, Michael, *Unparty: The Consensus-Building Party*, 1421
Donovan-Whitty, Judy, *Atlantic Therapeutic Touch Network*, 186
Dony, Bob, *Professional Engineers Ontario*, 1183
Doody, Alan, *PBA Society of Ontario*, 1146
Doohan, Anne, *American Association for Justice*, 1488
Dooks, David, *Canadian Institute of Quantity Surveyors - Maritimes*, 419
Dool, Ken, *Sail Canada*, 1245
Dooley, Martin, *McMaster University Faculty Association*, 956
Dooley, Lisa, *Canadian Celiac Association*, 352
Dooley, Suzanne, *Canadian Parks & Wilderness Society*, 451
Dooley, Calvin M., *American Chemistry Council*, 1491
Dopson, Cindy, *British Columbia Cancer Foundation*, 234
Dopson, Shane, *Information Services Vancouver*, 837
Dorais-Beauregard, Geneviève, *Centre de documentation sur l'éducation des adultes et la condition féminine*, 529
Doram, Shannon, *YMCA Canada*, 1471
Doram, Mark, *Edmonton's Food Bank*, 680
Doran, Sandy, *Saskatchewan Council for Archives & Archivists*, 1262
Doran, Nick, *Aerospace Heritage Foundation of Canada*, 11
Doran, Dan, *Prince Edward Island Association for Newcomers to Canada*, 1172
Doran, John Allen, *HRMS Professionals Association*, 824
Dorder, Alvin, *The Association of Ontario Locksmiths*, 155
Doré, Betty, *London & St. Thomas Association of Realtors*, 918
Doré, Claude, *Festival d'été de Québec*, 733
Dore, Sharon, *Canadian Association of Perinatal & Women's Health Nurses*, 325
Doré, Cam, *H.O.M.E. Society*, 819
Dorey, Dwight, *Congress of Aboriginal Peoples*, 613
Dorhofer, Bronwyn, *Art Libraries Society of North America*, 1506
Doricki, Greg, *Racquetball Ontario*, 1202
Dormody, Cathy, *Canadian Occupational Health Nurses Association*, 444
Dorn, Joanne, *Cerebral Palsy Association in Alberta*, 537
Dorn, Walter, *World Federalist Movement - Canada*, 1466
Dornan, Robert, *Animal Nutrition Association of Canada*, 71
Dornan, Lisa, *Hockey Canada*, 817
Dornan, Chris, *Triathlon Canada*, 1398
Dornian, Paul, *Calgary Philharmonic Society*, 274
Doroshuk, Bruce, *British Columbia Saw Filers Association*, 252
Dorothée, Girard, *Fibrose kystique Québec*, 733
Dorrington, Charla, *Nova Scotia Federation of Home & School Associations*, 1044

Dorrington, Charles W., *The Reformed Episcopal Church of Canada - Diocese of Western Canada & Alaska*, 1211
Dorrington, Cassandra, *Canadian Aboriginal & Minority Supplier Council*, 285
Dorsett, Matt, *Stettler Regional Board of Trade & Community Development*, 1350
Dorsett, Chris, *The Ocean Conservancy*, 1580
Dorval, Pierre, *L'Alliance des Caisses populaires de l'Ontario limitée*, 55
Dorval, Yves-Thomas, *Conseil du patronat du Québec*, 618
Dorval, Steve, *Syndicat de la fonction publique du Québec inc. (ind.)*, 1361
Dorval, Jean, *Société historique de Québec*, 1320
Dorval, Jean-Louis, *Club Optimiste de Rivière-du-Loup inc.*, 576
Doss, Joseph, *International Bottled Water Association*, 1541
Dossa, Anar, *College of Pharmacists of British Columbia*, 587
Dostie, Patricia, *Association pour l'intégration sociale d'Ottawa*, 166
Doucas, Flory, *Coalition québécoise pour le contrôle du tabac*, 578
Doucet, Nicole, *Centre des auteurs dramatiques*, 530
Doucet, Jean, *Canadian Urethane Foam Contractors Association*, 500
Doucet, Lola, *Bicycle Nova Scotia*, 208
Doucet, Robin, *Association québécoise des salons du livre*, 174
Doucet, Paula, *New Brunswick Nurses Union*, 1010
Doucet, Glen, *Hypertension Canada*, 829
Doucet, Patrick, *North Shore Forest Products Marketing Board*, 1032
Doucet, Daniel, *Fondation communautaire du Grand-Québec*, 743
Doucette, Rob, *Nova Scotia Veterinary Medical Association*, 1050
Doucette, Faye, *Funeral Service Association of Canada*, 764
Doucette, Joanthan, *Athletics Nova Scotia*, 181
Dougan, Kerridan, *Mission Association for Community Living*, 969
Dougan-McKenzie, Eusis, *Centre for Community Learning & Development*, 531
Doughart, JoAnn, *Canadian Celiac Association*, 352
Douglas, Debbie, *Ontario Council of Agencies Serving Immigrants*, 1075
Douglas, Kerri, *Ontario Funeral Service Association*, 1081
Douglas, Ted, *Saskatchewan Archaeological Society*, 1256
Douglas, Jennifer, *Peace Area Riding for the Disabled*, 1146
Douglas, Scott E., *South Wellington Coin Society*, 1336
Douglas, Heather, *Midwives Collective of Toronto*, 965
Douglas, Marianne S., *Canadian Circumpolar Institute*, 357
Douglas, Randy, *Alström Syndrome Canada*, 60
Douglas, Dave, *Concordia University Part-time Faculty Association*, 610
Douglas-Dungey, Wilma, *St. Leonard's Society of Canada*, 1250
Douglas-Matthews, Margaret, *Dania Home Society*, 650
Douglass, Patrick, *Army Cadet League of Canada*, 83
Douma, Trish, *Christian Labour Association of Canada*, 568
Doumbe, Odette, *Oasis Centre des femmes*, 1054
Doumont, Glen, *Elder Active Recreation Association*, 681
Dounoukos, Peter, *Northumberland Central Chamber of Commerce*, 1036

Doupe, Pearl, *Calgary United Soccer Association*, 275
Dourron, Magdalena, *IMCS Pax Romana*, 1531
Dourthe, Maeva, *J. Armand Bombardier Foundation*, 867
Doute, Stephanie, *International Association of Business Communicators*, 1538
Doutre, Diane, *Société d'Horticulture et d'Écologie de Brossard*, 1314
Dove, Brian, *Newfoundland & Labrador Drama Society*, 1018
Dove, Andrew, *Newfoundland & Labrador Amateur Bodybuilding Association*, 1015
Dover, Pegi, *Canadian Environmental Grantmakers' Network*, 382
Dovyak, Jeff, *Canadian Radiation Protection Association*, 465
Dow, Heather, *Canadian Association of Pathologists*, 325
Dow, Heather, *Canadian Association of Physical Medicine & Rehabilitation*, 327
Dow, Heather, *Operating Room Nurses Association of Canada*, 1115
Dow, Cindy, *Quinte West Chamber of Commerce*, 1202
Dowden, Cheryl, *ANKORS*, 71
Dowhaniuk, Ron, *United Way of Cambridge & North Dumfries*, 1413
Dowling, Pat, *The Canadian Federation of Business & Professional Women's Clubs*, 385
Dowling, Andrea, *Prince Edward Island Society for Medical Laboratory Science*, 1177
Dowling, Kristeva, *Parkinson Alberta Society*, 1141
Dowling, Steve, *Prince Edward Island Office of the Superintendent of Securities*, 1176
Downer, Doug, *Community Care Peterborough*, 596
Downer, Roger, *Vera Perlin Society*, 1431
Downes, Azzedine, *International Fund for Animal Welfare Canada*, 857
Downey, Diane, *Rideau Valley Conservation Authority*, 1231
Downham, James D., *Packaging Association of Canada*, 1136
Downing, Wendy, *The Garden Clubs of Ontario*, 767
Downs, Hugh, *National Space Society*, 1577
Downton, Anne, *Sweet Adelines International - Westcoast Harmony Chapter*, 1358
Downton, Beatrix, *Association for German Education in Calgary*, 133
Doyle, Kim, *Newfoundland & Labrador Occupational Therapy Board*, 1020
Doyle, Bill, *United Church of Canada*, 1409
Doyle, Pierre, *International Dairy Federation*, 1545
Doyle, Kristi, *Ontario Association of Architects*, 1061
Doyle, Mike, *Canadian Association of Geophysical Contractors*, 317
Doyle, Dianne, *Catholic Health Association of British Columbia*, 519
Doyle, Carol, *Liberal Party of Prince Edward Island*, 909
Doyle, David, *Glass, Molders, Pottery, Plastic & Allied Workers International Union (AFL-CIO/CLC)*, 1528
Doyle, Richard M., *The Vinyl Institute*, 1601
Doyle, Johanne, *Société d'histoire de La Prairie-de-la-Magdeleine*, 1310
Doyle, Ron, *Prince Edward Island Square & Round Dance Clubs*, 1177
Doyle, Joyce, *Prince Edward Island Square & Round Dance Clubs*, 1177
Doyle-MacBain, Lisa, *Prince Edward Island Automobile Dealers Association*, 1172
Doyon, Paul, *Fédération de l'UPA de la Beauce*, 709
Dozois, Charles, *Canadian Society of Microbiologists*, 485

Dracup, Pat, *Ontario Brain Injury Association*, 1069
Dragan Stojanovic, Daniel, *Seventh-day Adventist Church in Canada*, 1292
Dragasevich, Diane, *Serbian National Shield Society of Canada*, 1290
Drainville, Dennis Paul, *The Anglican Church of Canada*, 70
Drake, Patrice, *Canadian Association for Nursing Research*, 303
Drake, Heather, *Softball Prince Edward Island*, 1332
Draker, Jessica, *Mining Association of Canada*, 967
Dramnitzki, Lynn, *The Royal Scottish Country Dance Society*, 1587
Drapeau, Lucie, *Fondation de l'Hôpital Maisonneuve-Rosemont*, 744
Draper, Bill, *Field Botanists of Ontario*, 734
Draper, Diane, *Canadian Kennel Club*, 424
Draper, Daniel, *Carleton University Academic Staff Association*, 513
Draper, Harold, *National Association of Environmental Professionals*, 1573
Draper, Alice, *Ontario Association of Equine Practitioners*, 1063
Draskovic, Angela, *Yonge Street Mission*, 1473
Draude, Sandi, *Wakaw & District Board of Trade*, 1439
Drayton, Eric, *Barbados Cultural Association of British Columbia*, 196
Dreisziger, Nandor, *Hungarian Studies Association of Canada*, 827
Drennan, Rod, *North Okanagan Naturalists Club*, 1031
Dressler, Shirley L., *Canadian Postmasters & Assistants Association*, 458
Dreyfuss, Justin, *Society for Adolescent Health & Medicine*, 1589
Driedger, Nick, *Athabasca University Faculty Association*, 180
Driedger, Tim, *Grunthal & District Chamber of Commerce*, 792
Driedger, Andrea, *Canada Basketball*, 278
Drinan, James, *American Planning Association*, 1496
Dringen, Ralf, *International Society for Neurochemistry*, 1558
Driscoll, Bobbie, *Alberta Genealogical Society*, 36
Drisdelle, Ron, *Tourism Industry Association of New Brunswick Inc.*, 1390
Drisner, John, *Pentecostal Assemblies of Canada*, 1150
Drkulec, Vlad, *Chess Federation of Canada*, 556
Drodge, Wanda, *Community Food Sharing Association*, 597
Drohan, Paul V., *LifeSciences British Columbia*, 912
Drolet, Jean-François, *Chambre de commerce régionale de St-Raymond*, 549
Drolet, Doris, *Société historique de Québec*, 1320
Drolet, Sylvie, *Réseau des SADC et CAE*, 1220
Drolet, Stephane, *Association des handicapés adultes de la Mauricie*, 116
Drolet, Pierre, *Fondation de la greffe de moelle osseuse de l'Est du Québec*, 744
Drolet, Natalie, *West Coast Domestic Workers' Association*, 1444
Drope, Heather, *Nova Scotia Wild Flora Society*, 1050
Dror, Stephanie, *International Board on Books for Young People - Canadian Section*, 854
Drost, Alanna, *Lifewater Canada*, 912
Drost, Marietta, *L'Arche Ontario*, 77
Drought, Michael, *Alberta Amateur Wrestling Association*, 22
Drouillard, Bernard, *Bus History Association, Inc.*, 266
Drouin, Danny, *Huntington Society of Canada*, 828

Executive Name Index

Drouin, Jennifer, *Anglophones for Québec Independence*, 70
Drover, Mose, *Boys & Girls Clubs of Newfoundland & Labrador*, 223
Drover, Frances, *NL West SPCA*, 1027
Drown, Dale, *Guide Outfitters Association of British Columbia*, 793
Drown, Dale, *Métis Provincial Council of British Columbia*, 963
Drummond, James, *Antique Automobile Club of America*, 1505
Drummond, Alex, *Canadian Institute of Forestry*, 416
Drury, Robert, *Northwest Wall & Ceiling Bureau*, 1580
Drury, Karla, *Saskatchewan Racquetball Association*, 1273
Drury, Ryan, *Association of Fundraising Professionals*, 1512
Drutz, David, *Chai-Tikvah The Life & Hope Foundation*, 539
Drybrough, Kelly, *Port Alberni & District Labour Council*, 1165
Dryden, Sammy, *Estevan & District Labour Committee*, 697
Drysdale, Heather, *Osteoporosis Canada*, 1129
du Mont, Cynthia, *Boys & Girls Clubs of Ontario*, 223
Du Val, Lindsay, *Manitoba Medical Service Foundation Inc.*, 940
Dubanow, George, *Beekeepers' Association of Niagara Region*, 204
Dubé, Yvonne, *Association des Grands Frères et Grandes Soeurs du Québec*, 115
Dubé, Timothy, *Canadian Aviation Historical Society*, 340
Dubé, Rollande, *Fédération acadienne de la Nouvelle-Écosse*, 707
Dubé, Jean, *Association des médecins biochimistes du Québec*, 119
Dubé, Carolle, *Alliance du personnel professionnel et technique de la santé et des services sociaux*, 56
Dubé, Paul, *Merit Contractors Association of Newfoundland & Labrador*, 962
Dubé, Roch, *Mouvement québécois de la qualité*, 978
Dubé, Jacqueline, *Centre francophone d'informatisation des organisations*, 535
Dubé, Gilles, *Société d'histoire et de généalogie de Rivière-du-Loup*, 1312
Dubé, Francine, *Société québécoise de la schizophrénie*, 1323
Dubé, Jean Nicol, *Société de généalogie de la Beauce*, 1315
Dube, Diane, *Blue Water Chamber of Commerce*, 215
Dubeau, Laurier, *Canada China Business Council*, 278
Dubelaar, Jessica, *CUSO International*, 646
Dubiel, Marni, *Credit Counselling of Regional Niagara*, 639
Dubin, Richard, *Insurance Bureau of Canada*, 849
Dublenko, Connie, *Yukon Council on Aging*, 1478
Dubois, Christian G., *Chambre de commerce Canado-Suisse (Québec) Inc.*, 540
Dubois, Suzanne, *Canadian Cancer Society*, 349
Dubois, Nancy, *Canadian Fitness & Lifestyle Research Institute*, 390
Dubois, Mandy, *Portage Plains United Way*, 1167
Dubois, Madeleine, *Association pour l'intégration sociale d'Ottawa*, 166
Dubois, Paul, *Orienteering Québec*, 1126
Dubois, Luce, *Réseau des SADC et CAE*, 1220
Dubois, Stéphanie, *Association professionnelle des enseignantes et enseignants en commerce*, 167
Dubois, Sylvain, *Institute On Governance*, 848

Dubois, Alain, *Réseau du sport étudiant du Québec Abitibi-Témiscamingue*, 1222
Dubois, Lyne, *Réseau environnement*, 1223
Dubois, Francois, *Association des handicapés adultes de la Mauricie*, 116
Dubois, Gilles, *Fédération motocycliste du Québec*, 721
Dubois, Nancy, *Coalition for Active Living*, 578
Dubord, Julie, *Association touristique régionale du Saguenay-Lac-Saint-Jean*, 179
Dubreuil, Guillaum (Will), *The Canadian Chamber of Commerce*, 355
Dubrovsky, Tali, *Maccabi Canada*, 923
Dubs, Wayne, *Ontario Tenpin Bowling Association*, 1110
Dubuc, Denise, *Greniers de Joseph*, 789
Dubué, Cindy, *Ontario Secondary School Teachers' Federation*, 1103
Duce, David, *Eurographics - European Association for Computer Graphics*, 1524
Duceppe, Louise, *Théâtres associés inc.*, 1375
Ducharme, Hélène, *Association québécoise des marionnettistes*, 173
Ducharme, Isabelle, *Sports-Québec*, 1346
Ducharme, Denis, *Motor Dealers' Association of Alberta*, 975
Ducharme, Tracy, *Women Business Owners of Manitoba*, 1460
Ducharme, Isabelle, *Fédération de natation du Québec*, 710
Ducharme, Marc, *Réseau des SADC et CAE*, 1220
Ducharme, Anita, *National Aboriginal Diabetes Association Inc.*, 988
Duchesne, Susane, *International Board on Books for Young People - Canadian Section*, 854
Duchesne, Annie, *Canadian Public Health Association*, 462
Duchesne, Al, *Maritime Fire Chiefs' Association*, 950
Duchesne, Denis, *Association des experts en sinistre indépendants du Québec inc*, 113
Duchesne, Caroline, *Conseil régional de l'environnement de la Gaspésie et des Îles-de-la-Madeleine*, 620
Duchesne, Heidi, *Darts Prince Edward Island*, 651
Duchesneau, Roger, *Association du Québec pour l'intégration sociale / Institut québécois de la déficience intellectuelle*, 131
Duchesneau, Clémence, *Régionale Ringuette Rive-Sud*, 1213
Duchesneau, Suzanne, *Cercles de fermières du Québec*, 537
Duck, Glen, *Saskatchewan Association of Agricultural Societies & Exhibitions*, 1256
Duckworth, Helen, *Federation of Canadian Artists*, 722
Duckworth, Pam, *Saskatchewan Horse Federation*, 1267
Duclos, Pierre, *Société des écoles du monde du BI du Québec et de la francophonie*, 1318
Duclos, Marie-Noel, *Association de ringuette de Lotbinière*, 103
Dudas, Steven, *Lethbridge Soccer Association*, 908
Dudek, Greg, *Canadian Image Processing & Pattern Recognition Society*, 410
Dudek, Anna, *Canadian Society of Hospital Pharmacists*, 483
Dudek, Debra, *Association for Canadian Studies in Australia & New Zealand*, 1507
Dudfield, Brenda, *Volkssport Association of British Columbia*, 1437
Dudley, Kim, *Canadian Centre on Substance Use & Addiction*, 354
Dudych, Marissa, *University of Winnipeg Faculty Association*, 1421
Dueck, Gwen, *Saskatchewan Teachers' Federation*, 1276
Dueck Thiessen, Geoff, *Christian Labour Association of Canada*, 568
Duénez, Teresa, *Centre franco-ontarien de ressources pédagogiques*, 534

Duerksen, Everett, *Coaldale & District Chamber of Commerce*, 577
Dufault, Christopher P., *Ontario Institute of Agrologists*, 1087
Dufault, Gislaine, *Barreau de Montréal*, 197
Duff, Elizabeth, *Newfoundland & Labrador Credit Union*, 1018
Duffet, Charles, *Canadian Advanced Technology Alliance*, 288
Duffett, Emily, *Nova Scotia League for Equal Opportunities*, 1046
Duffey, Peter, *Canadian Air Traffic Control Association*, 291
Duffield, Nikki, *Sunrise Therapeutic Riding & Learning Centre*, 1355
Duffield, Siobhan, *Automobile Journalists Association of Canada*, 189
Duffield, Larry, *CARP*, 515
Duffin, Kelly, *Supply Chain Management Association - Ontario*, 1356
Duffy, Jane, *Institute for Performance & Learning*, 844
Duffy, Rick, *Canadian Parking Association*, 450
Duffy, Sheila, *Pacific Post Partum Support Society*, 1136
Duffy, Katie, *American Society for Bone & Mineral Research*, 1498
Dufour, Jules, *United Nations Association in Canada*, 1411
Dufour, Pierre, *L'Opéra de Montréal*, 1115
Dufour, Jean-Marc, *Association québécoise du transport aérien*, 176
Dufour, Valérie, *Canadian Association of University Teachers*, 335
Dufour, Renée, *Fédération des professionnelles et professionnels de l'éducation du Québec*, 718
Dufour, Lucie, *Fédération des professionnèles*, 717
DuFour, Pier, *Conseil québécois du théâtre*, 620
Dufour, Sylvianne, *Association touristique régionale du Saguenay-Lac-Saint-Jean*, 179
Dufour, Paul, *Richmond Orchestra & Chorus Association*, 1231
Dufour, Christyan, *Société des traversiers du Québec*, 1318
Dufour, Josée, *Société d'histoire de la MRC de l'Assomption*, 1310
Dufresne, Johanne, *Chambre de commerce St-Félix de Valois*, 549
Dufresne, François, *Association des spécialistes en médecine d'urgence du Québec*, 128
Dugan, Chris J., *Alberta Chambers of Commerce*, 28
Dugas, Dominique, *La cinémathèque québécoise*, 570
Duggan, Terry, *British Columbia Maritime Employers Association*, 246
Duguay, Rachelle, *Volleyball New Brunswick*, 1438
Duguid, Fiona, *Canadian Association for Studies in Co-operation*, 304
Duhamel, Cécile, *Société historique Cavelier-de-LaSalle*, 1319
Duhamel, Pierre, *Fondation de l'entrepreneurship*, 744
Duheme, Caroline, *Manitoba Real Estate Association*, 943
Duigou, Lynne, *Alberta Genealogical Society*, 36
Duigu, Leya, *Radio Television Digital News Association (Canada)*, 1203
Dujardin, Paul, *International Music Council*, 1553
Duke, Mel, *Masonic Foundation of Ontario*, 952
Duke, Chris, *Soil & Water Conservation Society*, 1595
Duke, Melvyn J., *Royal Arch Masons of Canada*, 1237
Duke, Valda, *Newfoundland & Labrador Nurse Practitioner Association*, 1020
Dukoff, Diane, *Embroiderers' Association of Canada, Inc.*, 686

Dumais, Denis, *Ottawa District Minor Hockey Association*, 1130
Dumais, Claudie, *Fédération du plongeon amateur du Québec*, 720
Dumais, Francis, *Réseau des SADC et CAE*, 1222
Dumanian, Julia, *Canadian Hearing Society*, 403
Dumaresq, Sydney, *Friends of Nature Conservation Society*, 761
Dumas, Renald, *Canadian Brown Swiss & Braunvieh Association*, 347
Dumas Pilon, Maxine, *College of Family Physicians of Canada*, 584
Dumelie,, Patrick, *Covenant Health*, 637
Dumond, Alex, *Biathlon Ontario*, 207
Dumont, Guillaume, *Association des médecins-psychiatres du Québec*, 120
Dumont, Jean-Pierre, *Ordre des architectes du Québec*, 1120
Dumont, Anne, *Association des archivistes du Québec*, 106
Dumont, Rébecca, *Fondation Centre de cancérologie Charles-Bruneau*, 743
Dumont, Bruce, *Métis Provincial Council of British Columbia*, 963
Dumont, Yves, *Association des Illustrateurs et Illustratrices du Québec*, 116
Dumont, Daphne, *Rowing PEI*, 1237
Dumouchel, Marilène, *Master Brewers Association of The Americas*, 1570
Dunbar, Virginia, *North Perth Chamber of Commerce*, 1032
Dunbar, Elizabeth, *CARP*, 515
Dunbar, Brian, *Eastern Canada Orchid Society*, 670
Dunbrack, Jeff, *Canadian Wheelchair Basketball Association*, 503
Duncan, Brad, *Saskatchewan Construction Association*, 1261
Duncan, Stephanie, *Stonewall & District Chamber of Commerce*, 1350
Duncan, Carmen, *Saskatchewan Heavy Construction Association*, 1267
Duncan, Sharon, *Appaloosa Horse Club of Canada*, 73
Duncan, Art, *Grand Orange Lodge of Canada*, 780
Duncan, James, *The Nature Conservancy of Canada*, 1000
Duncan, Nancy, *Enfant-Retour Québec*, 688
Duncan, Deborah, *Alberta Law Foundation*, 39
Duncan, Caryn, *Vancouver Women's Health Collective*, 1429
Duncan, Amy, *Prince Edward Island Curling Association*, 1173
Duncan, H. James, *Canadian Federation of Chiropractic Regulatory & Educational Accrediting Boards*, 386
Duncan, Donna, *Hincks-Dellcrest Treatment Centre & Foundation*, 815
Duncan, John, *Society for Existential & Phenomenological Theory & Culture*, 1326
Duncan, Alison, *Canadian Nutrition Society*, 444
Duncan, Natalie, *Central Beekeepers' Alliance*, 524
Duncan-He, Louis, *PFLAG Canada Inc.*, 1155
Dundas, Jill, *Canadian Camping Association*, 348
Dunfield, Malcolm M., *Ducks Unlimited Canada*, 663
Dunford, Cynthia, *Speed Skating Canada*, 1341
Dungate, Mike, *Chicken Farmers of Canada*, 557
Dunham, Candace, *Saskatchewan Golf Association Inc.*, 1266
Dunham, Jim, *Northwest Wall & Ceiling Bureau*, 1580
Duniewicz, Jolanta, *Polish-Jewish Heritage Foundation of Canada*, 1164
Dunkerley, George, *Pulaarvik Kablu Friendship Centre*, 1194

Executive Name Index

Dunlap, Ellen S., *American Antiquarian Society*, 1488
Dunlop, Martha, *Snowmobilers Association of Nova Scotia*, 1305
Dunlop, Betty, *Canadian Federation of University Women*, 389
Dunlop, Marg, *Learning Disabilities Association of Alberta*, 904
Dunlop, Peter, *Ancient, Free & Accepted Masons of Canada - Grand Lodge of Alberta*, 68
Dunlop, Jenna, *Canada's Oil Sands Innovation Alliance*, 282
Dunlop, Sam, *Canadian Belgian Blue Association*, 342
Dunn, Barbara M., *Canadian Society of Air Safety Investigators*, 479
Dunn, Mark, *Canadian Deaf Ice Hockey Federation*, 376
Dunn, Ashley, *Alberta Construction Association*, 31
Dunn, Dick, *Canadian Paper Money Society*, 449
Dunn, Bruce, *Kamloops Symphony*, 881
Dunn, Jeremy, *British Columbia Salmon Farmers Association*, 252
Dunn, Mathis, *Screen Actors Guild - American Federation of Television & Radio Artists*, 1588
Dunn, Tanya, *Ontario Centres of Excellence*, 1071
Dunn, Vikki, *Canadian Standards Association*, 490
Dunn, Dick, *Scarborough Coin Club*, 1282
Dunn, Lise, *Prader-Willi Syndrome Association of Alberta*, 1169
Dunn, Ronn, *North Okanagan Labour Council*, 1031
Dunn Lee, Janice, *International Atomic Energy Agency*, 1540
Dunne, Susan, *Altruvest Charitable Services*, 61
Dunnet, Margo, *British Columbia Camping Association*, 234
Dunnington, Georgina, *Canadian Bodybuilding Federation*, 345
Dunphy, Valerie, *Kidney Foundation of Canada*, 885
Dunsmore-Porter, Linda, *Saskatchewan Genealogical Society*, 1266
Duodu, Eugenia, *Visions of Science Network for Learning*, 1436
Duplessis, Marie-Josée, *Collectif des femmes immigrantes du Québec*, 581
Duplisea, David, *Saint John Region Chamber of Commerce*, 1247
Dupont, Nathalie, *Association des professionnels de la communication et du marketing*, 125
Dupont, Louise, *Alliance Chorale Manitoba*, 55
DuPont, Marie, *Conseil des arts et des lettres du Québec*, 617
Duport, Maurice, *Réseau FADOQ*, 1224
Dupré, Jean R., *Orchestre Métropolitain*, 1118
Dupuis, Jennifer, *C.A.R.E. Jeunesse*, 511
Dupuis, Wendy, *Financial Fitness Centre*, 737
Dupuis, Roxane, *Conseil jeunesse provincial (Manitoba)*, 619
Dupuis, Lee-Anne, *Community Living Essex County*, 602
Dupuis, Sylvain, *Chambre de commerce et d'industrie de Sorel-Tracy*, 546
Dupuis, Norm, *Alberta Forest Products Association*, 35
Dupuis, Serge, *Association of Professional Engineers & Geoscientists of New Brunswick*, 158
Dupuis, Jacqueline, *Greater Vancouver International Film Festival Society*, 787
Dupuis, Karine R., *Skills/Compétences Canada*, 1302
Dupuis, Patrick, *Association québécoise de Vol Libre*, 171
Dupuis, Robin, *Conseil québécois des arts médiatiques*, 620

Dupuis, Jason, *Almas Jiwani Foundation*, 59
Dupupet, Stéphane, *Association de Montréal pour la déficience intellectuelle*, 103
Duquenoy, Nafissatova, *Centre Communautaire Bon Courage De Place Benoît*, 526
Duquet, Michel, *Canadian Historical Association*, 405
Duquette, Esther, *Théatre la Seizième*, 1374
Duraisami, Peter, *The Scott Mission*, 1286
Durand, Ron, *International Fiscal Association Canada*, 857
Durand, Simon, *Union des cultivateurs franco-ontariens*, 1406
Durand, Louis-Gilles, *Institut de recherches cliniques de Montréal*, 842
Durdin, Martha, *Canadian Credit Union Association*, 372
Durham, Audry, *Trail & District Chamber of Commerce*, 1394
Durham, James, *Manitoba Association of Playwrights*, 931
Durieux, Wendy, *Alberta Music Festival Association*, 41
Durkee, David B., *Bakery, Confectionery, Tobacco Workers & Grain Millers International Union (AFL-CIO/CLC)*, 1514
Durnin-Richards, Debra, *Manitoba Association of Home Economists*, 930
Durocher, Greg, *Cambridge Chamber of Commerce*, 275
Durocher, Michel, *Fondation Mario-Racine*, 747
Durston, Jerry, *Child Evangelism Fellowship of Canada*, 559
Durston, Jerry, *Child Evangelism Fellowship of Canada*, 559
Dusek, Janice, *Scarborough Centre for Healthy Communities*, 1282
Dusik-Sharpe, Jodi, *Canadian Association of Neuroscience Nurses*, 322
Dussault, Pascale, *Regroupement des aveugles et amblyopes du Montréal métropolitain*, 1215
Dussault, Yves, *Association des naturopathes professionnels du Québec*, 120
Duteil, Gayle, *British Columbia Nurses' Union*, 248
Duthoit, Beverley, *Risk & Insurance Management Society Inc.*, 1234
Dutin, Philippe, *Alliance du personnel professionel et administratif de Ville de Laval*, 56
Dutton, Martin, *Learning Disabilities Association of Prince Edward Island*, 905
Dutton, Ben, *United Way of Fort McMurray*, 1414
Dutton, Diane, *Chartered Professionals in Human Resources of Alberta*, 554
Duval, Hélène, *Children of the World Adoption Society Inc.*, 560
Duval, Janie, *Fédération québécoise des sociétés Alzheimer*, 730
Duval, Hélène, *Centre Montérégien de réadaptation*, 536
Duval, Diane, *Ordre des hygiénistes dentaires du Québec*, 1121
Duval-Mace, Nicolas, *Association des clubs d'entrepreneurs étudiants du Québec*, 109
Duvot, Monique, *Société d'histoire et de généalogie de Shawinigan-sud*, 1313
DW, Ben, *Institute for Change Leaders*, 843
Dwyer, Colleen, *Rocky Mountain House & District Chamber of Commerce*, 1235
Dwyer, Mary, *Synchro Swim Ontario*, 1361
Dwyer, Kathryn, *Northwestern Ontario Sports Hall of Fame & Museum*, 1040
Dwyer, Paul-James, *Dance Oremus Danse*, 649
Dyas, Tom, *Kelowna Chamber of Commerce*, 883
Dyberg, Blair, *Alberta Walking Horse Association*, 51
Dybvig, Rick, *YOUTHLINK*, 1476

Dyck, Janice, *Hudson Bay Chamber of Commerce*, 824
Dyck, Jonathon, *Canadian Public Relations Society Inc.*, 463
Dyck, Cameron, *Association of Consulting Engineering Companies - Manitoba*, 146
Dyck, Carrie, *Canadian Linguistic Association*, 427
Dyck, Hedy, *British Columbia Landscape & Nursery Association*, 244
Dyck, Tim, *Evangelical Mennonite Conference*, 699
Dyck, Toban, *Manitoba Pulse & Soybean Growers Inc.*, 943
Dyer, Jeff, *Accessible Housing Society*, 5
Dyer, Shaun, *The John Howard Society of Saskatchewan*, 875
Dyer, Jeff, *Boys & Girls Clubs of Alberta*, 221
Dyer, William, *Canadian Institute for the Relief of Pain & Disability*, 413
Dyer, Alison, *Writers' Alliance of Newfoundland & Labrador*, 1468
Dyer, Lynn, *Foodservice & Packaging Institute*, 1526
Dyer, Denise, *Harmony, Inc.*, 804
Dyke, George, *Citroën Autoclub Canada*, 571
Dyke, Maureen, *Dominion Rabbit & Cavy Breeders Association*, 661
Dyke, Gary, *Ontario Municipal Administrators' Association*, 1092
Dykes, Barbara, *Institute of Packaging Professionals*, 1533
Dykstra, Sandra, *Hamilton Right to Life*, 802
Dykstra, Cam, *Alberta Federation of Labour*, 34
Dyson, Jane, *Disability Alliance British Columbia*, 658
Dyson, Rose Anne, *Canadians Concerned About Violence in Entertainment*, 506
Dzaman, Kirk, *Chilliwack Chamber of Commerce*, 563
Dzbik, Stan, *Victoria Labour Council*, 1433
Dziadyk, Darryl, *Calgary Zoological Society*, 275
Dzierzanowska, Basia, *Immigrant Services Association of Nova Scotia*, 830

E

E, Willie, *Special Olympics Ontario*, 1340
Eadie, Sharon Kathleen, *College of Occupational Therapists of Manitoba*, 587
Eadie, Patty, *College of Midwives of Manitoba*, 586
Eagles, James S., *Intercede International*, 851
Eagles, Tom, *The Royal Canadian Legion*, 1240
Eagles, Michelle, *St. John's Clean & Beautiful*, 1249
Eamon, James, *Law Society of Alberta*, 901
Earle, Nancy, *Bibliographical Society of Canada*, 208
Earle, Richard, *Canadian Institute of Stress*, 419
Earle, Kory, *Council of Canadians with Disabilities*, 633
Earle, Dave, *Construction Labour Relations Association of British Columbia*, 624
Earle, Jerry, *Newfoundland & Labrador Association of Public & Private Employees*, 1016
Earnshaw, Jacob, *Archaeological Society of British Columbia*, 76
Earnshaw, Ferguson, *Association of Professional Engineers & Geoscientists of Saskatchewan*, 159
East, Kevin, *Comox Valley Chamber of Commerce*, 607
Eastley, Ted, *Canadian Society of Association Executives*, 480
Eastlick, Denise, *Osoyoos Desert Society*, 1128
Easton, Charlie, *Federation of Canadian Artists*, 722
Eastwell, Doug, *Association of Quantity Surveyors of Alberta*, 160

Eastwood, Dianna, *The John Howard Society of Ontario*, 875
Eaton, Lisa, *Numeris*, 1051
Eaton, Richard, *Canadian Ski Patrol*, 471
Eaton, Bob, *Boating Ontario*, 216
Eaton, Chris, *World University Service of Canada*, 1467
Eaton, Jen, *Ontario Cycling Association*, 1076
Eayrs, Elizabeth, *Canadian Tinnitus Foundation*, 495
Ebbern, Jane, *Canadian Unitarian Council*, 499
Ebcas, Jr., Ben, *Filipino Canadian Catholic Charismatic Prayer Communities*, 735
Ebedes, Allan, *Excellence Canada*, 699
Eberhart, Greg, *Alberta College of Pharmacists*, 30
Eberle, Denise, *Bowls Saskatchewan Inc.*, 220
Ebert, Kevin, *Norquay & District Chamber of Commerce*, 1028
Eberts, Derrek, *Canadian Association of Geographers*, 316
Ebsworth, Nicholas, *Canadian Explosives Industry Association*, 383
Eburne, Mark, *Royal Astronomical Society of Canada*, 1239
Eby, Laura, *Yukon Curling Association*, 1478
Eby, Tom, *Association of Certified Fraud Examiners - Toronto Chapter*, 145
Echegaray-Benites, Christine, *Canadian Association of Critical Care Nurses*, 311
Ecker, Gayle, *Equine Guelph*, 694
Eckert, Mark, *Volleyball Canada*, 1437
Eckstein, Yechiel, *International Fellowship of Christians & Jews of Canada*, 857
Edding-Lee, Lauren, *Ontario Mental Health Foundation*, 1091
Eddy, Mike, *Snowmobilers Association of Nova Scotia*, 1305
Eddy, R. Bruce, *New Brunswick Law Foundation*, 1010
Eddy, Ron, *Rural Ontario Municipal Association*, 1244
Edelman, John, *Cayuga & District Chamber of Commerce*, 521
Eder, Tim A., *Great Lakes Commission*, 1528
Eder, Regine, *Errington Therapeutic Riding Association*, 695
Edey, Brian, *Swimming Canada*, 1359
Edgar, Cathie, *Directors Guild of Canada*, 658
Edgar, D. Walter, *Canadian Railroad Historical Association*, 465
Edgar, James, *Royal Astronomical Society of Canada*, 1238
Edgar, Laura, *Institute On Governance*, 848
Edgecomb, Beverly, *BC Alliance for Arts & Culture*, 201
Edgecombe, Nancy, *Nurse Practitioners' Association of Nova Scotia*, 1052
Edgecombe-Green, Barb, *Alberta Dressage Association*, 33
Edgington, Phyllis, *Cypress Hills Ability Centres, Inc.*, 647
Edillor, Elsie, *Urban Development Institute of Canada*, 1422
Edington, Barry, *Canadian Marfan Association*, 430
Edison, Joseph, *The World Job & Food Bank Inc.*, 1466
Edmiston, Greg, *Community Living North Halton*, 603
Edmiston, Laurie, *Canadian AIDS Treatment Information Exchange*, 290
Edmonds, Linda, *Fraserside Community Services Society*, 758
Edmonds, Ernie, *Brantford Lapidary & Mineral Society Inc.*, 227
Edmonds, Stuart, *Prostate Cancer Canada*, 1190
Edmunds, Casey, *Francophonie jeunesse de l'Alberta*, 757
Edstrom, Karen, *The Canadian Laser and Aesthetic Specialists Society*, 425
Edward, Ian, *Boys & Girls Clubs of Ontario*, 224

Executive Name Index

Edwardh, Joey, *Community Development Halton*, 597
Edwards, Sharleen, *Wheelchair Sports Alberta*, 1452
Edwards, David, *The Anglican Church of Canada*, 69
Edwards, Don, *Ontario Football Alliance*, 1081
Edwards, Craig, *Greater Vancouver Food Bank Society*, 786
Edwards, Kate, *Association of Canadian Publishers*, 143
Edwards, Gordon, *Canadian Coalition for Nuclear Responsibility*, 358
Edwards, Tanya, *Canadian Parks & Wilderness Society*, 451
Edwards, Colin, *Canadian Wind Energy Association*, 504
Edwards, Elizabeth, *Art Dealers Association of Canada Inc.*, 84
Edwards, Mike, *Cross Country Canada*, 643
Edwards, Ron, *Manitoba Table Tennis Association*, 946
Edwards, Derek, *Conservation Foundation of Greater Toronto*, 622
Edwards, Grant, *Indian Agricultural Program of Ontario*, 834
Edwards, Jeff, *Tofield & District Chamber of Commerce*, 1380
Edwards, David, *Education International*, 1522
Edwards, Patricia, *North American Waterfowl Management Plan*, 1029
Edwards, Laura, *Canadian Accredited Independent Schools Advancement Professionals*, 287
Edwards, MJ, *Grand Manan Museum Inc.*, 780
Edwards, Wayne, *Geneva Centre for Autism*, 769
Edwards, Kate, *International Game Developers Association*, 1549
Edwards, Wayne, *Canadian Anti-Counterfeiting Network*, 293
Edwards, Gord, *Alberta Water Council*, 51
Edwards, Cathy, *Canadian Association of Community Television Users & Stations*, 311
Edwards-Bentz, Robyn, *United Way of Regina*, 1416
Edwardson, Dean, *Sarnia-Lambton Environmental Association*, 1254
Eeles, Dennis, *Elevate NWO*, 684
Eelhart, Bryan, *Science for Peace*, 1285
Egan, Timothy M., *Canadian Gas Association*, 396
Egan, Christopher, *Financial Management Institute of Canada*, 737
Egger, Astrid, *Haida Gwaii Arts Council*, 798
Egger, Philippe, *Innovations et réseaux pour le développement*, 1532
Eggertson, Laura, *Adoption Council of Canada*, 8
Eggertson, Bill, *Canadian Association for Renewable Energies*, 303
Eggertson, Bill, *Earth Energy Society of Canada*, 667
Eggleton, Janet, *United Empire Loyalists' Association of Canada*, 1410
Eggli, Michelle, *Vancity Community Foundation*, 1424
Eglinski, Kim, *Fort Nelson & District Chamber of Commerce*, 753
Ehrent, Iris, *Canadian Magen David Adom for Israel*, 429
Ehrhardt, Amelia, *Dancemakers*, 649
Ehrlich, Tom, *Princess Margaret Cancer Foundation*, 1180
Ehrlick, Allan, *Arabian Horse Association of Eastern Canada*, 76
Eichel, Scott, *AirCrew Association - Western Canada Region*, 20
Eichenauer, Cedra, *Nakusp & District Chamber of Commerce*, 987
Eichler, Margrit, *Science for Peace*, 1285
Eilinger, Elisabeth, *Saskatchewan Association of Library Technicians, Inc.*, 1257
Eilinger, Elisabeth, *Swiss Club Saskatoon*, 1359

Eisebraun, Stefan, *German Canadian Association of Nova Scotia*, 772
Eisenberg, Seymour, *Canadian Magen David Adom for Israel*, 429
Eisenbraun, Corinne, *Dietitians of Canada*, 656
Eisenhauer, Janice, *Canadian Women for Women in Afghanistan*, 504
Eisenmann-Klein, Marita, *International Confederation for Plastic Reconstructive & Aesthetic Surgery*, 1543
Eisner, John D., *Credit Counselling Services of Atlantic Canada, Inc.*, 639
Eiswirth, Bernie, *Saskatchewan Federation of Police Officers*, 1265
Eiwanger, Jacqueline, *Softball Saskatchewan*, 1332
Ekosaari, Maija, *International Committee for Documentation of the International Council of Museums*, 1543
Ekstrand, Craig, *Model Aeronautics Association of Canada Inc.*, 970
El Hage, Georges, *World Fellowship of Orthodox Youth*, 1605
El Niaj, Husni Abou, *Muslim Association of New Brunswick*, 985
El Rashidy, Mohamed, *Canadian Arab Federation*, 294
El-Awadi, Ahmed, *Swimming Canada*, 1359
El-Bayoumi, Mohamed, *New Brunswick Chiropractors' Association*, 1006
El-Deir, Teraiz, *International Society for Augmentative & Alternative Communication*, 860
El-Hawary, Bette, *Swim Nova Scotia*, 1358
Elapatha, Indu, *Canadian Institute of Quantity Surveyors - British Columbia*, 419
Elaschuk, Patrick, *Hope for the Nations*, 821
Elbardouh, Hanan, *Islamic Association of Saskatchewan*, 864
Elbin, Susan, *The Waterbird Society*, 1602
Eldemire, Ann, *Acupuncture Canada*, 7
Elder, Louise, *Northwest Territories & Nunavut Construction Association*, 1037
Elder, Rhonda, *Red Deer & District Community Foundation*, 1209
Elder, Beverley, *Sidney Lions Food Bank*, 1298
Elderkin, Ann L., *American Society for Bone & Mineral Research*, 1498
Elenis, Tony, *Ontario Restaurant, Hotel & Motel Association*, 1101
Elford, Robin, *Federation of Calgary Communities*, 722
Elgazzar, Reda, *Manitoba Islamic Association*, 939
Elhalwagy, Mohamed, *The Nile Association of Ontario*, 1027
Elia, Christian D., *Catholic Civil Rights League*, 518
Elia, Christian, *Natural Family Planning Association*, 998
Elias, Kathleen, *Kootenay Society for Community Living*, 893
Elias, Choloe, *Hands on Summer Camp Society*, 803
Elias, Martine, *Myeloma Canada*, 986
Elkas, Lee, *Canadian College & University Food Service Association*, 358
Elkhal, Carole, *Foundation for Prader-Willi Research in Canada*, 756
Elkin, Lynn, *Yellowknife Association for Community Living*, 1471
Elkin, Lynn, *Special Olympics Northwest Territories*, 1340
Elkins, Fred, *Sign Association of Canada*, 1299
Elkins, Victor, *Hospital Employees' Union*, 823
Ell, Diane, *SaskCulture Inc.*, 1280
Ellacott, Lisa, *Community Living Thunder Bay*, 605
Ellard-Gray, Amy, *Out on the Shelf*, 1133
Ellenor, Douglas, *Christian Children's Fund of Canada*, 567
Ellerbeck, Carol, *Opticians of Manitoba*, 1116

Ellerman, Evelyn, *Alberta Women's Institutes*, 52
Elligott, Jason, *British Columbia Soccer Association*, 253
Elliot, Michael, *Alberta Federation of Police Associations*, 35
Elliot, Scott, *Fredericton Society for the Prevention of Cruelty to Animals*, 759
Elliot, Debbie, *Ontario Simmental Association*, 1104
Elliot, Carol Lee, *New Brunswick Genealogical Society Inc.*, 1009
Elliot, Richard, *Canadian HIV/AIDS Legal Network*, 406
Elliot, Virginia, *Association des diffuseurs culturels de l'Ile de Montréal*, 110
Elliott, Sherri, *South Queens Chamber of Commerce*, 1336
Elliott, Murray, *Alberta Weekly Newspapers Association*, 51
Elliott, Allistair, *Calgary Musicians Association*, 273
Elliott, David, *Ontario Genealogical Society*, 1082
Elliott, Bill, *FortWhyte Alive*, 754
Elliott, Jennifer, *Alberta Hospice Palliative Care Association*, 38
Elliott, Paul, *Ontario Secondary School Teachers' Federation*, 1103
Elliott, Brian, *Habitat for Humanity Canada*, 797
Elliott, Norma, *Women In Crisis (Algoma) Inc.*, 1461
Elliott, Mary, *Manitoba Hairstylists' Association*, 937
Elliott, Cheryl, *Financial Management Institute of Canada*, 737
Elliott, Debbie, *Downtown Truro Partnership*, 662
Elliott, Teresa, *Women That Hunt*, 1461
Elliott-Nielsen, Grace, *Tillicum Lelum Aboriginal Friendship Centre*, 1379
Ellis, Mark, *International Bar Association*, 1541
Ellis, Dale, *Orienteering Association of Nova Scotia*, 1126
Ellis, David, *Electrical Contractors Association of New Brunswick, Inc.*, 682
Ellis, Gary, *Canadian Independent Adjusters' Association*, 410
Ellis, Brian, *Canadian Printing Industries Association*, 460
Ellis, Dick, *Solid Waste Association of North America*, 1595
Ellis, Ted, *Canadian Country Music Association*, 372
Ellis, Chris, *The Ontario Archaeological Society*, 1060
Ellis, John, *Family Service Ontario*, 704
Ellis, Amber, *Earthroots*, 667
Ellis, Ryan, *TechConnex*, 1368
Ellis, Shawn, *Trent Port Historical Society*, 1397
Ellis, Jennifer, *GATEWAY Centre For Learning*, 767
Ellsworth, Susan, *United Empire Loyalists' Association of Canada*, 1410
Ellsworth, Katy, *Association of Canadian Deans of Education*, 142
Ellwood, Andy, *British North America Philatelic Society Ltd.*, 259
Elmhirst, Janice, *Canadian Phytopathological Society*, 455
Elson, Paul P., *Big Salmon River Anglers Association*, 210
Elson, Judith, *The Royal Commonwealth Society of Canada*, 1242
Elwood, R. Carter, *Canadian Association of Slavists*, 333
ElzingaCheng, Angela, *Greenest City*, 789
Emamally, Mohammud, *The Engineering Institute of Canada*, 688
Emberley, Geoff, *Professional Engineers & Geoscientists Newfoundland & Labrador*, 1183

Emerson, David, *Economic Developers Association of Canada*, 673
Emerson, Carolyn J., *NSERC Chair for Women in Science & Engineering*, 1050
Emery, Keith, *Credit Canada Debt Solutions, Inc.*, 639
Emery, Marc, *British Columbia Marijuana Party*, 246
Eminovski, Brian, *Licensed Paralegals Association (Ontario)*, 910
Emmett, Peter S., *Construction Specifications Canada*, 624
Emond, Lori, *Canadian Association of Pharmacy in Oncology*, 326
Émond, André, *Syndicat professionnel des scientifiques à pratique exclusive de Montréal*, 1365
Émond, Catherine, *Alliance numérique*, 58
Émond, Marie-Andrée, *Electric Mobility Canada*, 682
Emory, Leslie, *Ottawa Community Immigrant Services Organization*, 1130
Emrich, Hannes, *World Dance Council Ltd.*, 1604
Emslie, Jane, *Insurance Professionals of Calgary*, 850
Enault, Martin, *Revivre - Association Québécoise de soutien aux personnes souffrant de troubles anxieux, dépressifs ou bipolaires*, 1229
Endicott, Marie, *Society of Public Insurance Administrators of Ontario*, 1330
Eng, Mia, *International Coaching Federation*, 1542
Engel, Debbie, *Carizon Family & Community Services*, 513
Engel, Stephanie, *International Association of Business Communicators*, 1538
Engel, Gerry, *Trees Winnipeg*, 1397
Engel, Colleen, *Economic Developers Association of Manitoba*, 673
Engel, Timothy, *American Academy of Neurology*, 1488
Engell, Ann, *Norfolk Association for Community Living*, 1028
Engen, Kimberly, *Saskatchewan Registered Music Teachers' Association*, 1273
Engensperger, Peter M., *Canadian Association of Veterans in United Nations Peacekeeping*, 336
England, Denise, *Alberta Snowmobile Association*, 47
Englander, Cheryl, *ARZA-Canada: The Zionist Voice of the Canadian Reform Movement*, 86
Engle, William, *Association of Telehealth Service Providers*, 1513
English, Ann, *Association of Professional Engineers & Geoscientists of British Columbia*, 157
English, Peter, *Human Anatomy & Physiology Society*, 1530
English, Amanda, *Canadian Association of Staff Physician Recruiters*, 333
Englot, Kirk, *Saskatchewan Association of Social Workers*, 1258
Englund, Patty, *National Farmers Union*, 993
Enna, S.J., *International Union of Basic & Clinical Pharmacology*, 1564
Ennos, Bill, *British Columbia Amateur Hockey Association*, 230
Enns, John, *Animal Nutrition Association of Canada*, 71
Enns, Linda, *Vancouver Executives Association*, 1425
Enns, David, *Sustainable Development Technology Canada*, 1357
Enoch, Simon, *Canadian Centre for Policy Alternatives*, 354
Enretti-Zoppo, Cristina, *Personal Computer Club of Toronto*, 1152
Enright, Karen, *Digby & Area Board of Trade*, 656
Ensing, Elizabeth, *Association of Educators of Gifted, Talented & Creative Children in BC*, 147

Executive Name Index

Ensworth, Colin, *British Columbia Ringette Association*, 251
Entwistle, Melinda, *British Columbia Real Estate Association*, 250
Entwistle, Diane, *Boys & Girls Clubs of British Columbia*, 222
Entz, Peter, *Canadian Seed Trade Association*, 470
Envolden, Dennis, *Alberta Society of Artists*, 47
Epp, Ed, *Christian Blind Mission International*, 566
Epp, Len, *Manitoba Bison Association*, 932
Epstein, Risa, *Canadian Young Judaea*, 506
Erb, Blake, *American Society of Heating, Refrigerating & Air Conditioning Engineers*, 1500
Erb, Ryan, *United Way of Perth-Huron*, 1416
Ercolini, Michelle, *Ontario Federation of Home & School Associations Inc.*, 1079
Erdener, Ugur, *World Archery Federation*, 1603
Erdle, James C., *Computer Modelling Group*, 609
Erdle, Jim, *Computer Modelling Group*, 609
Erdmann, Ron, *Alberta Farm Fresh Producers Association*, 34
Ergang, Shawn, *Inclusion Alberta*, 831
Eric, Bégin, *Association professionnelle des entreprises en logiciels libres*, 167
Erickson, Chris, *International Brotherhood of Electrical Workers (AFL-CIO/CFL)*, 1542
Erickson, Deanna, *Association of Professional Engineers & Geoscientists of British Columbia*, 158
Erickson, Krista, *Commercial Seed Analysts Association of Canada Inc.*, 592
Erikson, Pam, *Aldergrove Daylily Society*, 53
Erin, Hinton, *Mannville & District Chamber of Commerce*, 948
Erjavec, Luc, *Restaurants Canada*, 1227
Erlichman, Stephen, *Canadian Coalition for Good Governance*, 357
Erman, Tracy, *Skills/Compétences Canada*, 1303
Erno, Mack, *Huntington Society of Canada*, 828
Ernst, Robert, *Vermilion & District Chamber of Commerce*, 1431
Ernst, Ellen, *International Association for Public Participation*, 1537
Errington, David, *Accessible Media Inc.*, 5
Ervin, Shelly, *UNITE HERE Canada*, 1409
Ervin-Ward, Anika, *Ontario Council of University Libraries*, 1075
Es Sabbar, Abdel Ilah, *Association de taekwondo du Québec*, 104
Esar, Robyn, *Canadian Council of Conservative Synagogues*, 368
Esau, Krista, *Canadian Pension & Benefits Institute*, 453
Escher, Emanuel, *Canadian Society of Pharmacology & Therapeutics*, 486
Escott, Irv, *Nature Saskatchewan*, 1001
Esedebe, Hilda, *Ontario Good Roads Association*, 1083
Eskelsen Garcia, Lily, *National Education Association*, 1576
Esmail, Zahra, *Association of Neighbourhood Houses BC*, 153
Esmail, Zahida, *Canadian College of Health Leaders*, 359
Eso, Mike, *Victoria Labour Council*, 1433
Espejo, Raul, *World Organisation of Systems & Cybernetics*, 1606
Esser, Jeffrey, *Government Finance Officers Association*, 1528
Essig, Ronald J., *American Fisheries Society*, 1493
Essington, Tim, *Alberta College of Paramedics*, 29
Esslinger, Bev, *The Society for Safe & Caring Schools & Communities*, 1326
Estable-Porter, Melanie, *Ontario Lung Association*, 1090

Esteves, Andrea, *Association of Canadian Faculties of Dentistry*, 142
Estey, Maggie, *New Brunswick Lung Association*, 1010
Estrella, John, *Scouts Canada*, 1286
Estwick, Ruth, *Ontario Home Builders' Association*, 1085
Etchegary, Grant, *Newfoundland Symphony Youth Orchestra*, 1023
Etherington, Murray, *CARP*, 514
Ethier, Stephan, *Laurier Teachers Union*, 900
Etkin, Rick, *Canadian Association of Professional Image Creators*, 329
Etkin, Maureen, *Elder Abuse Ontario*, 681
Etkin, Shannon, *Congregation Beth Israel - British Columbia*, 612
Eto, Dave, *British Columbia Dairy Association*, 238
Eubanks, Colleen, *Special Libraries Association*, 1596
Eva-Miller, Laurie, *Saskatchewan Cultural Society of the Deaf*, 1263
Evanochko, Cathy, *Tuberous Sclerosis Canada Sclérose Tubéreuse*, 1400
Evans, Gary, *Island Horse Council*, 865
Evans, Jennifer, *Ontario Association of Chiefs of Police*, 1062
Evans, Leslie, *Federation of Calgary Communities*, 722
Evans, Stephanie, *Wainwright & District Chamber of Commerce*, 1439
Evans, Colleen, *Campbell River & District Chamber of Commerce*, 276
Evans, Dave, *Greenwood Board of Trade*, 789
Evans, Gale, *Chartered Professional Accountants Canada*, 552
Evans, Bill, *Alberta Media Production Industries Association*, 40
Evans, Robert, *British Columbia Society of Landscape Architects*, 254
Evans, Russ, *Mechanical Contractors Association of Alberta*, 956
Evans, Arthur C., *American Psychological Association*, 1497
Evans, Kevin, *Physiotherapy Association of British Columbia*, 1159
Evans, Thomas, *International Society for Plant Pathology*, 1559
Evans, Ken, *Legal & District Chamber of Commerce*, 906
Evans, Clif, *Riverton & District Chamber of Commerce*, 1234
Evans, Matt John, *Ontario Students Against Impaired Driving*, 1109
Evans, Alex, *Alberta Dressage Association*, 33
Evans, Jim, *Ontario Standardbred Adoption Society*, 1109
Evans Maxwell, Megan, *Centre for Equality Rights in Accommodation*, 532
Evans-Good, Sonja, *Canadian Swiss Cultural Association*, 491
Evard, Virginia, *Sisters of St. Benedict*, 1301
Eveleigh, Laurie, *Island Technology Professionals*, 865
Evelyn, Joan Ann, *Canadian Association for Astrological Education*, 297
Even-Har, Meirav, *Recycling Council of Ontario*, 1209
Everett, Daneen, *Yellowknife Chamber of Commerce*, 1471
Everett, Anthony, *Northern British Columbia Tourism Association*, 1034
Everitt, Frank, *United Steelworkers Local 1-424*, 1412
Everley, Deborah, *Kenora Association for Community Living*, 883
Evreniadis, Abe, *Geneva Centre for Autism*, 769
Ewald, Eric, *American Society for Theatre Research*, 1499
Ewart, Susan, *Saskatchewan Trucking Association*, 1276
Ewert Fisher, Claire, *Mennonite Central Committee Canada*, 961

Ewing, Lynn, *Saskatchewan Registered Music Teachers' Association*, 1273
Excell, Oksana, *Western Transportation Advisory Council*, 1450
Exel, Deb, *Simcoe County Historical Association*, 1299
Exner, Kim, *Regina Regional Opportunities Commission*, 1212
Exner, Heidi, *AIDS Vancouver Island*, 17
Eyolfson, Owen, *Arborg Chamber of Commerce*, 76
Eyre, Roy, *Wycliffe Bible Translators of Canada, Inc.*, 1470
Ezako, Bryan, *KidSport Canada*, 886
Ezekiel, Ed, *Health Association Nova Scotia*, 806
Ezerins, Leo, *Canadian Football League Alumni Association*, 392

F

Fabbi, Nadine, *Association for Canadian Studies in the United States*, 1507
Fabbro, Ronald P., *Assembly of Catholic Bishops of Ontario*, 88
Fabbro, Joan, *Canadian Association of Pharmacy in Oncology*, 326
Faber, Susan, *United Way of Perth-Huron*, 1416
Fabian, Rita, *Television Bureau of Canada, Inc.*, 1370
Fabian, Nelson, *National Environmental Health Association*, 1576
Fabiano, Dolores, *Chamber of Commerce Niagara Falls, Canada*, 539
Fabiano, Dolores, *The Welland/Pelham Chamber of Commerce*, 1443
Fabius, Barb, *Lennox & Addington Association for Community Living*, 907
Faccio, Maria, *British Columbia's Children's Hospital Foundation*, 259
Facciolo, Vito, *Community Living Association for South Simcoe*, 600
Fadaie, Kian, *Canadian Hydrographic Association*, 410
Fadish, Larissa, *College of Medical Laboratory Technologists of Alberta*, 586
Faessler, Lana, *Laubach Literacy Ontario*, 900
Fafard, Katherine, *Association des libraires du Québec*, 118
Fafard, Bruce, *Edmonton & District Labour Council*, 675
Fagan, Gary A., *Canadian Liver Foundation*, 427
Fagan, Barb, *Canadian Association of Critical Care Nurses*, 311
Fagan, Kristina, *Canadian Association for Commonwealth Literature & Language Studies*, 298
Fagin Davis, Lisa, *Medieval Academy of America*, 1570
Fagnan, Shannon, *Caroline & District Chamber of Commerce*, 514
Fahey, Mark, *Project Management Institute*, 1585
Faille, Marie-Lou, *Syndicat des technicien(ne)s et artisan(e)s du réseau français de Radio-Canada (ind.)*, 1364
Fainstat, Tyler, *The John Howard Society of Ontario*, 875
Fair, Margaret, *Canadian Association for Young Children*, 307
Fair, Caryl, *Jersey Canada*, 869
Fair, Terry, *Cardiac Rehabilitation Network of Ontario*, 511
Fair, Maureen, *West Neighbourhood House*, 1446
Fairbairn, Heather, *DanceSport Atlantic*, 650
Fairbrother, Penny, *Canadian Celiac Association*, 352
Faires, Paul, *Ontario Farm & Country Accommodations Association*, 1078
Fairfield, Patti, *Ne'Chee Friendship Centre*, 1002

Fairley, Ann, *Ontario Motor Coach Association*, 1091
Fairley, John, *Community Living Windsor*, 606
Fairley, Laura, *Canadian Condominium Institute*, 362
Falconer, Chris, *Lutte NB Wrestling*, 923
Falconer, Chenelle, *Vancouver Island Construction Association*, 1426
Falconi, Robert J., *Canadian Standards Association*, 490
Falinger, Susan, *Pacific Salmon Commission*, 1136
Falk, Chad, *Manitoba High Schools Athletic Association*, 938
Falk, Gary, *Communitas Supportive Care Society*, 595
Falkenberg, Nancy, *Field Botanists of Ontario*, 734
Falkenham, Jennifer, *Campground Owners Association of Nova Scotia*, 277
Falkiner, Steve, *Foursquare Gospel Church of Canada*, 756
Fallin, Barbara, *Worldwatch Institute*, 1608
Fallis, Kathryn, *Canadian Institute of Plumbing & Heating*, 418
Fallis, David, *Opéra Atelier*, 1114
Falls, Kelly, *Canadian Sporting Goods Association*, 490
Famulak, Fiona, *British Columbia Construction Association*, 237
Fandrich, Bernie, *Lytton & District Chamber of Commerce*, 923
Fandrick, Melissa, *United Way of South Eastern Alberta*, 1417
Fanjoy, Lisa, *Ontario Council for University Lifelong Learning*, 1075
Fanjoy, John, *Nunavut Teachers' Association*, 1051
Fanner, Bernadette, *Alliance for Canadian New Music Projects*, 57
Fannin, Barb, *United Way of Durham Region*, 1414
Fanning, Chris, *The Jane Goodall Institute for Wildlife Research, Education & Conservation*, 1568
Fanton, Jonathan F., *American Academy of Arts & Sciences*, 1487
Faoro, Paul, *Canadian Union of Public Employees*, 498
Farah, Anis, *Laurentian University Faculty Association*, 900
Farah, Brigitte, *Metallurgy & Materials Society of the Canadian Institute of Mining, Metallurgy & Petroleum*, 962
Farber, Jill, *Autism Speaks Canada*, 189
Farber, Connie, *Indian & Metis Friendship Centre of Prince Albert*, 834
Farber, Bernie, *Mosaic Institute*, 975
Farfaras, Tom, *Grain Farmers of Ontario*, 779
Farha, Leilani, *Canada Without Poverty*, 281
Farha, Nancy, *The Farha Foundation*, 705
Faria, Jeremy, *Avicultural Advancement Council of Canada*, 191
Faria, Jeremy, *The Avian Preservation Foundation*, 190
Farid, Sara, *Development & Peace*, 654
Faris, Diane, *United Empire Loyalists' Association of Canada*, 1410
Faris, Paul D., *Home School Legal Defence Association of Canada*, 819
Faris, Ian, *Ottawa Chamber of Commerce*, 1129
Farley, Sylvia, *Manitoba Federation of Labour*, 936
Farley, Margaret, *Saskatchewan PeriOperative Registered Nurses' Group*, 1271
Farley-Chevrier, Francis, *Union des écrivaines et écrivains québécois*, 1406
Farmer, Monika, *Faculty Association of Medicine Hat College*, 700
Farmer, Ian, *Ontario Dental Association*, 1077
Farmer, Bob, *Canadian Federation of Pensioners*, 388
Farn, Nicole, *Change for Children Association*, 551

Executive Name Index

Farnes, David, *Radio Advisory Board of Canada*, 1202
Farquar, Donna, *British Columbia Aviation Council*, 233
Farquhar, Jo-Anne, *Motorcycle & Moped Industry Council*, 976
Farr, Bill, *Volunteer Red Deer*, 1439
Farr, Laura, *American Association of Naturopathic Physicians*, 1490
Farrell, Frances, *Nova Scotia Choral Federation*, 1042
Farrell, Floyd, *Society of Kabalarians of Canada*, 1329
Farrell, Aline, *Canadian Celiac Association*, 352
Farrell, Carl, *Canadian Association of SAS Users*, 332
Farrell, Sharon, *Saskatchewan Archaeological Society*, 1256
Farrell, Ashley, *Toronto Health Libraries Association*, 1385
Farrell, Alison, *Newfoundland & Labrador Health Libraries Association*, 1019
Farrell, Arnie, *Nova Scotia Minor Hockey Council*, 1047
Farrington, Carolyn, *Canadian College of Health Leaders*, 358
Farris, Carolyn, *Horse Council British Columbia*, 822
Farrow, Anna, *English Speaking Catholic Council*, 689
Farstad, Tim, *Canadian Luge Association*, 428
Faryon, Reta, *Canadian Cancer Society*, 349
Fash, Greg, *Atlantic Food & Beverage Processors Association*, 184
Fassier, Sébastien, *The Liberal Party of Canada*, 909
Fast, Russell, *Credit Union Central of Manitoba*, 641
Fast, Sue Ellen, *Interpretation Canada - A Professional Association for Heritage Interpretation*, 861
Fast, Joanna, *Canadian Sport Horse Association*, 490
Fatmi, Habib, *Pakistan Canada Association of Edmonton*, 1137
Faubert, André, *Fédération des aînées et aînés francophones du Canada*, 711
Faubert, Pierre, *Maison internationale de la Rive-Sud*, 927
Faucette, Craig, *Canadian Breast Cancer Network*, 347
Faucette, Trish, *CADORA Ontario Association Inc.*, 269
Faucher, Julie, *Corporation des officiers municipaux agréés du Québec*, 630
Faucher, Yvan, *Musée minéralogique et minier de Thetford Mines*, 982
Faucher, Charles, *Ordre des Podiatres du Québec*, 1123
Faucher, Jean, *Association de taekwondo du Québec*, 104
Faucher, Richard, *Burnaby Association for Community Inclusion*, 265
Fauchon, Sylvain, *Fédération de sociétés mutuelles d'assurance générale (Groupe promutuel)*, 710
Faulk, Teresa, *Canadian Agri-Marketing Association (Alberta)*, 290
Faulkner, Chris, *J. Douglas Ferguson Historical Research Foundation*, 867
Faulkner, Marcel, *Regroupement de parents de personnes ayant une déficience intellectuelle de Montréal*, 1214
Faulknor, Alison, *National Trust for Canada*, 996
Fauteux, Martha, *Canadian Catholic Campus Ministry*, 351
Fava, Matthew, *Canadian Music Centre*, 438
Favaloro, Sonja, *Organic Trade Association*, 1581
Favaro, Pat, *L'Arche Western Region*, 78
Favre, Julien, *Swiss Canadian Chamber of Commerce (Ontario) Inc.*, 1359

Fawcett, Karen, *Pacific Asia Travel Association (Eastern Canada Chapter)*, 1134
Fawcett, Mike, *British Columbia Construction Association*, 237
Fawcett, Penny, *UniforACL*, 1405
Fawcett, Robert O., *Real Estate Council of British Columbia*, 1205
Fawcett, Craig, *Industrial Fabrics Association International Canada*, 835
Fay, Jeanne, *Second Story Women's Centre*, 1288
Faye, Margaret, *Mycological Society of Toronto*, 986
Fayerman Noodelman, Brenda, *Na'amat Canada Inc.*, 987
Fayun Khan, Abdul, *British Columbia Muslim Association*, 247
Feal, Rosemary G., *Modern Language Association of America*, 1571
Feather, Joan, *Nature Saskatchewan*, 1001
Featherston, Sharry, *Canadian Association of Home & Property Inspectors*, 317
Featherstone, Mike, *Pacific Urchin Harvesters Association*, 1136
Febbrari, Stéphane, *Table d'Inter-Action du Quartier Peter-McGill*, 1365
Fecteau, Tony, *Association de Ringuette de Sainte-Marie*, 103
Fedchyshyn, Nick, *Friends of the Ukrainian Village Society*, 763
Feddena-Leonard, Susan, *Women in Film & Television Alberta*, 1461
Feddes, John, *Canadian Society for Bioengineering*, 473
Fedeli, Victor, *Ontario Progressive Conservative Party*, 1098
Fedick, Heather, *Embroiderers' Association of Canada, Inc.*, 685
Fedirko, Sarah, *Association of Fundraising Professionals*, 1512
Fedorak, Al, *The Christian & Missionary Alliance in Canada*, 566
Fedorak, Richard, *Canadian Digestive Health Foundation*, 378
Fedun, Larry, *Schizophrenia Society of Alberta*, 1283
Fedyk, Joanne, *Saskatchewan Waste Reduction Council*, 1277
Feeley, Patrick J., *Association of Fundraising Professionals*, 1511
Feeney, Carol, *Quinte Arts Council*, 1201
Feeney, Jeff, *Diving Plongeon Canada*, 660
Feeney, Lloyd, *Association d'informations en logements et immeubles adaptés*, 99
Feenstra, Kyle, *Canadian Children's Book Centre*, 356
Fefergrad, Irwin W., *Royal College of Dental Surgeons of Ontario*, 1241
Fehr, Ken, *Outlook & District Chamber of Commerce*, 1133
Fehr, Tracy, *Manitoba Lung Association*, 940
Fehr, Kim, *Pharmacy Technician Society of Alberta*, 1157
Fehr, Wendy, *CAUSE Canada*, 521
Fehr, Don, *National Hockey League Players' Association*, 994
Feigelstock, Avraham, *Kosher Check*, 894
Feil, Linda, *North Vancouver Community Arts Council*, 1033
Fejtek, Ian, *Canadian Aeronautics & Space Institute*, 289
Feldbruegge, Bill, *Health Sciences Association of Saskatchewan*, 807
Feldman, Jay, *Beyond Pesticides*, 1514
Felices-Luna, Pablo, *Carousel Players*, 514
Felicio, Joao Antonio, *International Trade Union Confederation*, 1563
Félix, Bernard, *Chez les français de L'Anse-à-Canards inc.*, 557
Félix, Robert, *Chez les français de L'Anse-à-Canards inc.*, 557
Fell, Carolyn, *Canadian Beverage Association*, 343
Fellner, Mark, *Swim-Natation Manitoba*, 1359

Fellows, Bob, *Thermal Insulation Association of Canada*, 1376
Fells, Ken, *Black Educators Association of Nova Scotia*, 213
Fels-Smith, Catherine, *Toronto Region Board of Trade*, 1387
Feltmate, Grant, *Nova Scotia Road Builders Association*, 1048
Felton, David R., *International Wine & Food Society*, 1567
Fendley, Darlene, *Ontario Home Builders' Association*, 1085
Fendt, Josef, *Fédération Internationale de Luge de Course*, 1525
Fenger, Michael, *Friends of Ecological Reserves*, 761
Feniak, John, *Wycliffe Bible Translators of Canada, Inc.*, 1470
Fenn, Kayla, *Human Resources Professionals Association*, 825
Fennell, Bill, *Nunavut Employees Union*, 1051
Fenner, Linda, *Society of Environmental Toxicology & Chemistry*, 1593
Fenske, Tom, *Laurentian University Staff Union*, 900
Fenske, Neil, *Western Independence Party of Saskatchewan*, 1450
Fenton, Blair, *Alberta Hereford Association*, 37
Fenton, Sharon, *Canadian Flooring, Cleaning & Restoration Association*, 391
Fenwick, George, *Calgary Youth Orchestra*, 275
Feral, Priscilla, *Friends of Animals*, 1527
Ferbey, Justin, *Yukon Aboriginal Sport Circle*, 1477
Ferdinandi, Mike, *British Columbia Golf Superintendents Association*, 242
Ferencz, Sarah, *Archives Association of Ontario*, 80
Fererko, Mary Ann, *Yorkton & District Labour Council*, 1474
Ferguson, Bruce, *Canadian Merchant Navy Veterans Association Inc.*, 435
Ferguson, Skit, *Consulting Engineers of Nova Scotia*, 625
Ferguson, Jamie, *Sport Nova Scotia*, 1345
Ferguson, Véronique, *New Brunswick Association of Dietitians*, 1005
Ferguson, Judy, *Central Alberta Realtors Association*, 523
Ferguson, Linda, *Canadian Council of Teachers of English Language Arts*, 370
Ferguson, Betty, *Junior Achievement Canada*, 877
Ferguson, Anne, *Canadian Cardiovascular Society*, 350
Ferguson, Anne, *Canadian Society of Cardiac Surgeons*, 481
Ferguson, Cori, *Supply Chain Management Association*, 1355
Ferguson, Doug, *Lifesaving Society*, 911
Ferguson, Tiffany, *MuchFACT*, 978
Ferguson, Scott, *World Trade Centre Atlantic Canada*, 1467
Ferguson, Rob, *Nova Scotia Archaeology Society*, 1040
Ferguson, Sara, *British Columbia Recreation & Parks Association*, 250
Ferguson, Barb, *Alzheimer Society of Calgary*, 62
Ferguson, Jason A., *New Brunswick Team Handball Federation*, 1013
Ferguson, Annie, *World Futures Studies Federation*, 1605
Ferguson, Steve, *Prince Edward Historical Society*, 1171
Ferguson, Todd, *Canada Employment & Immigration Union*, 279
Ferguson, Colin, *Travel Manitoba*, 1396
Ferguson, Elaine, *Child Care Connection Nova Scotia*, 558
Ferguson, Rick, *Environmental Bankers Association*, 1523
Ferguson, David, *Kaleidoscope Theatre Productions Society*, 880

Ferguson, Linsey, *Alpine Canada Alpin*, 59
Ferguson, Brad, *Edmonton Economic Development Corporation*, 677
Fergusson, Carol, *Canadian Progress Club*, 461
Ferini-Strambi, Luigi, *World Association of Sleep Medicine*, 1603
Fernandes, Roger, *Canadian Board of Marine Underwriters*, 345
Fernandes, Valerie, *Dying with Dignity*, 665
Fernandez, David, *Bibliographical Society of Canada*, 208
Fernandez, Mark, *Energy Action Council of Toronto*, 688
Fernandez, Edgar, *Professional Engineers Ontario*, 1184
Fernandez, Kevin, *Oakville Chamber Orchestra*, 1053
Fernando, John, *Canadian Society of Exploration Geophysicists*, 483
Fernando, Gerard, *Prince Edward Island Society for Medical Laboratory Science*, 1177
Fernando, Jo-Ann, *Canadian Association of Critical Care Nurses*, 312
Fernando, Mark, *American Sociological Association*, 1503
Fernando, Joseph, *Field Hockey Ontario*, 734
Ferne, Jessica, *International Development & Relief Foundation*, 856
Fernets, Debralee, *Canadian Liver Foundation*, 427
Ferrante, Tammy, *The Terry Fox Foundation*, 1372
Ferranto, Marcia, *National Court Reporters Association*, 1575
Ferrari, Pepita, *Documentary Organization of Canada*, 660
Ferrari, Maurizio, *International Federation of Clinical Chemistry & Laboratory Medicine*, 1547
Ferre, Ed, *British Columbia Transplant Society*, 257
Ferreira, Christa, *Project Management Institute*, 1585
Ferreira, Lidia, *FutureWatch Environment & Development Education Partners*, 765
Ferreira de Souza Dias, Braulio, *United Nations Environment Programme - Secretariat of the Convention on Biological Diversity*, 1412
Ferri, Joseph, *Canadian Association of Nordic Ski Instructors*, 323
Ferriani, Ivo, *Fédération internationale de bobsleigh et de tobogganing*, 1525
Ferrier, Camille, *Canadian Federation for the Humanities & Social Sciences*, 384
Ferrier, Miranda, *Ontario Personal Support Worker Association*, 1095
Ferris, Kevin, *Canadian Society for Chemical Technology*, 473
Ferris, Sean, *Habitat for Humanity Canada*, 797
Ferris, Carmen, *Manitoba Customer Contact Association, Inc.*, 935
Ferrish, Tyler, *Prince Edward Island Association of Medical Radiation Technologists*, 1172
Ferro, Orlando, *Quinte Immigrant Services*, 1201
Ferron, Grant, *Kin Canada*, 887
Ferron, Grant, *Scouts Canada*, 1287
Ferry, David, *ACTRA Fraternal Benefit Society*, 7
Fertig, Corbett, *Fox Creek Chamber of Commerce*, 756
Feser, Neil, *Alberta Northern Lights Wheelchair Basketball Society*, 41
Fesler, Douglas, *American Society for Bone & Mineral Research*, 1498
Fesyk, Justin, *Hockey Alberta*, 817
Fetch, Rick, *Whitecourt Fish & Game Association*, 1452
Fetherston, Richard, *St. John Ambulance*, 1249

Executive Name Index

Fetherston, Richard, *St. John Ambulance*, 1249

Fettes, Mark, *Universala Esperanto-Asocio*, 1601

Fevens, Kendra, *Sexual Health Centre Lunenburg County*, 1293

Fewer, Mark, *Professional Engineers & Geoscientists Newfoundland & Labrador*, 1183

Fey, Stéphanie, *Chantiers jeunesse*, 551

Fiala, Arden C., *Saskatchewan Families for Effective Autism Treatment*, 1265

Fiala, Calvin, *Saskatchewan Families for Effective Autism Treatment*, 1265

Fiallos, Luis, *Peruvian Horse Association of Canada*, 1152

Ficek, Rick, *Ex Libris Association*, 699

Fick, Mervin William, *Mississauga Choral Society*, 970

Ficocelli, Helen, *Alberta Association of Rehabilitation Centres*, 25

Fiddick, Denise, *Ashcroft & Area Food Bank*, 86

Fidler, Brian, *The Guild Society*, 794

Field, Alex, *Prince Edward Island Rugby Union*, 1177

Field, Debbie, *Foodshare Toronto*, 750

Field, John, *Pacific Salmon Commission*, 1136

Field, Chris, *Ontario High School Chess Association*, 1084

Fielding, Gayle, *Ontario Association of Orthodontists*, 1065

Fielding, Kim, *Embroiderers' Association of Canada, Inc.*, 686

Fieldon, Amy, *Chemainus & District Chamber of Commerce*, 555

Fields, Julia, *Chamber of Marine Commerce*, 539

Fiels, Keith, *American Library Association*, 1494

Fietje, Bill, *Associated Gospel Churches*, 89

Fietje, Bill, *Evangelical Fellowship of Canada*, 698

Fife, Amanda, *Canadian Authors Association*, 338

Fifield, Adele, *Canadian Society of Association Executives*, 480

Fifield, Adele, *Canadian Association of Radiologists*, 330

Figas, Jessica, *Welsh Pony & Cob Association of Ontario*, 1444

Figen, Musabay, *Turkish Community Heritage Centre of Canada*, 1400

Figge, Fran, *The Ontario Poetry Society*, 1096

Figueira, Elda, *Calgary Law Library Group*, 273

Fihser, Rod, *Canadian Federation of Aircraft Maintenance Engineers Associations*, 385

Filangi, Mary, *Women of the Word - Toronto*, 1461

Filbert, Karen, *Association of Fundraising Professionals*, 1511

Filella, Montserrat, *International Association of Environmental Analytical Chemistry*, 1538

Filiatrault, Marc, *Association des physiatres du Québec*, 123

Filiatrault, Melanie, *British Columbia Federation of Foster Parent Associations*, 240

Filiatrault, Louise, *United Nations Educational, Scientific & Cultural Organization: Canadian Commission for UNESCO*, 1412

Filice, Fabio, *Alberta Construction Association*, 31

Filice-Armenio, Sera, *St. Joseph's Healthcare Foundation*, 1249

Filion, Ghislaine, *Fédération des professionnelles et professionnels de l'éducation du Québec*, 718

Filion, Pierre, *Fédération de crosse du Québec*, 708

Filion, Judi, *British Columbia Government & Service Employees' Union*, 242

Filipow, Laura, *Cross Country Alberta*, 643

Filipowitsch, Mike, *Music NWT*, 984

Filippelli, James, *Your Political Party of BC*, 1475

Filippi, Fatima, *Rexdale Women's Centre*, 1229

Filippo, Miglior, *Canadian Society of Animal Science*, 480

Fillier, Travis, *Association of Professional Engineers & Geoscientists of Alberta*, 157

Fillion, Marla, *Construction Safety Association of Manitoba*, 624

Fillion, Maud, *Les Amis du Jardin botanique de Montréal*, 67

Fillion, Valerie, *Association de l'exploration minière de Québec*, 100

Fillion, Daniel, *Syndicat des producteurs de bois du Saguenay-Lac-Saint-Jean*, 1363

Fillmore, Gordon, *Thunder Bay Law Association*, 1378

Fillmore, Rick, *Back Country Horsemen of British Columbia*, 192

Filosa, Jean-Christophe, *Confédération des organismes familiaux du Québec*, 611

Filson, Gerald, *The Bahá'í Community of Canada*, 194

Filthaut, Blaine, *Maple Creek Chamber of Commerce*, 948

Fimrite, Deanna, *Army, Navy & Air Force Veterans in Canada*, 83

Finch, Robert, *Monarchist League of Canada*, 972

Finch, Bill, *Softball Manitoba*, 1331

Finch, Joy, *Environmental Information Association*, 1523

Findlay, Michael, *Canadian Association of Numismatic Dealers*, 323

Findlay, Scott, *Independent Financial Brokers of Canada*, 832

Findlay, C.E. (Ted), *Prairie Osteopathic Association*, 1169

Findlay, Teresa, *Fraser Lake Chamber of Commerce*, 757

Findura, John, *Regina Multicultural Council*, 1212

Finegood, Diane, *Michael Smith Foundation for Health Research*, 964

Fingard, Joel, *Manitoba Combative Sports Commission*, 934

Fink, Sarah, *Canadian National Exhibition Association*, 439

Finkbeiner, Doug, *Manitoba Paraplegia Foundation Inc.*, 942

Finkbeiner, Muriel, *Grey Wooded Forage Association*, 790

Finkelstein, Sarah, *Canadian Quaternary Association*, 464

Finkelstein, Janis, *ORT Canada*, 1127

Finkle, Pat, *Alzheimer Society Peterborough, Kawartha Lakes, Northumberland, & Haliburton*, 65

Finkler, Chava, *Newfoundland & Labrador Brain Injury Association*, 1017

Finlay, James, *Hamilton AIDS Network*, 800

Finlayson, Jock, *Business Council of British Columbia*, 266

Finlayson, Travis, *Prosthetics & Orthotics Association of British Columbia*, 1190

Finley, Richard J., *Army Cadet League of Canada*, 83

Finley, Katherine, *Organization of American Historians*, 1581

Finley, Ron, *Teamsters Canada (CLC)*, 1368

Finn, David, *Petroleum Research Newfoundland & Labrador*, 1154

Finn-Allen, Jeanne, *Saint John Naturalists' Club*, 1247

Finnegan, Paddy, *Master Brewers Association of The Americas*, 1570

Finnegan, Fatima, *Ontario Restaurant, Hotel & Motel Association*, 1102

Finnie, David, *Central 1 Credit Union*, 523

Finnie, Elizabeth, *Historical Society of St. Catharines*, 816

Finnie, James, *The Scots Society of Colchester*, 1286

Finnis, David, *Summerland Community Arts Council*, 1354

Finnson, Douglas, *Teamsters Canada Rail Conference*, 1368

Finseth, Doug, *Alberta Cattle Breeders Association*, 27

Finstad, Sarah, *American Marketing Association*, 1495

Fior, Michelle, *Calgary Marching Showband Association*, 273

Fiorilli, Lisa, *Canadian Independent Music Association*, 411

Firman, Marcus, *Ontario Water Works Association*, 1113

Firth, Tracey, *Canadian Animal Health Institute*, 293

Firth, Rick, *Hospice Palliative Care Ontario*, 823

Firth, Bonnie, *Human Resources Professionals Association*, 825

Fisch, Sarah, *Ontario Non-Profit Housing Association*, 1093

Fischer, Michael, *Hamilton Naturalists' Club*, 801

Fischer, Ingrid, *Canadian Co-operative Association*, 364

Fischer, Vern, *Better Business Bureau of Vancouver Island*, 206

Fischer, Wayne, *Heating, Refrigeration & Air Conditioning Institute of Canada*, 810

Fischer, David, *Canadian Society of Allergy & Clinical Immunology*, 480

Fischer, Silja, *International Music Council*, 1553

Fischer, Andy, *International Society for Telemedicine & eHealth*, 1559

Fischer-Kowalski, Marina, *International Society for Ecological Economics*, 1557

Fischetti, Tom, *Cruise Lines International Association, Inc.*, 1521

Fiset, Gigi, *Canadian Deaf Sports Association*, 376

Fisher, Jim, *Calgary Firefighters Burn Treatment Society*, 272

Fisher, Mark, *Entertainment Merchants Association - International Head Office*, 1523

Fisher, Peter, *Racquetball Ontario*, 1202

Fisher, Errol, *Canadian Home Builders' Association - Saskatchewan*, 407

Fisher, Jeff, *Urban Development Institute of Canada*, 1422

Fisher, David W., *Police Association of Nova Scotia*, 1163

Fisher, Paul D., *College of Licensed Practical Nurses of Newfoundland & Labrador*, 585

Fisher, Audrey, *Thunder Bay Indian Friendship Centre*, 1378

Fisher, Alan, *Alberta Professional Home Inspectors Society*, 43

Fisher, Susan, *Pembroke Kiwanis Music Festival*, 1149

Fisher, Sam, *American Council for Québec Studies*, 1492

Fisher, Rick, *Newfoundland & Labrador Table Tennis Association*, 1022

Fisher, Denise, *Alberta Cheerleading Association*, 28

Fisher, Cindy, *Ontario Native Education Counselling Association*, 1093

Fisher, Gary, *Trappers Association of Nova Scotia*, 1396

Fisk, Elizabeth, *Distress Centres Ontario*, 659

Fisk, John, *Wallace Center, Winrock International*, 1601

Fiske, Sylvia, *Osteoporosis Canada*, 1129

Fitch, E.S., *Royal United Services Institute of Vancouver Island*, 1243

Fitch, Vic, *Financial Executives International Canada*, 736

Fitch, Patrick, *Canadian Society of Hospital Pharmacists*, 484

Fitch, Wendy, *Museums Association of Saskatchewan*, 983

Fitchett, Colin, *Ontario Brain Injury Association*, 1069

Fitzgerald, Marika, *Canadian Neurological Society*, 441

Fitzgerald, Susan, *Ontario Hatcheries Association*, 1083

Fitzgerald, Gretchen, *Sierra Club of Canada*, 1298

Fitzgerald, Marika, *Canadian Neurological Sciences Federation*, 441

Fitzgerald, Jodi, *Human Resources Professionals Association*, 825

Fitzgerald, Guy, *Union québécoise de réhabilitation des oiseaux de proie*, 1408

Fitzgerald, Nadia, *Oro-Medonte Chamber of Commerce*, 1127

Fitzgerald, Sian, *HealthBridge Foundation of Canada*, 807

Fitzgerald, Dennis, *Campbell River Museum & Archives Society*, 276

Fitzgerald, JoAnne, *PFLAG Canada Inc.*, 1156

Fitzgerald, Darcy, *Alberta Pork*, 42

Fitzmier, John R., *American Academy of Religion*, 1488

Fitzpatrick, Stephen, *Canadian Credit Union Association*, 372

Fitzpatrick, Colleen, *Family Enterprise Xchange*, 703

Fitzpatrick, John, *American Hotel & Lodging Association*, 1494

Fitzpatrick, Glen, *Newfoundland-Labrador Federation of Cooperatives*, 1024

Fitzpatrick, Kenney, *Canadian Organization of Campus Activities*, 447

Fitzwilliam, Kathryn, *Breakfast Cereals Canada*, 227

Fixman, Laura, *Registered Massage Therapists' Association of Ontario*, 1213

Fixter, Kristina, *Junior Achievement Canada*, 877

Fizer, Janet-Marie, *Hay River Chamber of Commerce*, 805

Fjeldsted, John, *Manitoba Environmental Industries Association Inc.*, 936

Fladager, Larry, *Prince Albert & District Chamber of Commerce*, 1171

Flaherty, Marni, *Home Child Care Association of Ontario*, 819

Flaherty, Patti, *British Columbia Brain Injury Association*, 234

Flaig, Deb, *Association of Sign Language Interpreters of Alberta*, 162

Flamand, Kim, *Canadian Association of Foodservice Professionals*, 315

Flamand, Marcie, *British Columbia Crime Prevention Association*, 238

Flanagan, Terrence, *International Society of Arboriculture*, 1560

Flanagan, Michelle, *Central Beekeepers' Alliance*, 524

Flank, Steven, *Northwestern Ontario Prospectors Association*, 1039

Flaro, Haley, *Ability New Brunswick*, 2

Flasza, Donna, *Ontario Cooperative Education Association*, 1075

Flato, Gregory, *Canadian Meteorological & Oceanographic Society*, 436

Flatt, Julie L., *National Network for Mental Health*, 995

Flatts, Malcolm, *National Council of Barbadian Associations in Canada*, 991

Fleck, James D., *Business for the Arts*, 267

Fleck, Peter, *Calgary Philatelic Society*, 273

Fleckenstein, Kris, *Big Brothers Big Sisters of Alberta*, 209

Fleet, Greg, *The John Howard Society of Saskatchewan*, 875

Flegel, Peter, *Michaëlle Jean Foundation*, 964

Fleming, Sheila, *Ingersoll District Nature Club*, 838

Fleming, Gordon, *Association of Local Public Health Agencies*, 150

Fleming, Lindsay, *Canadian Pony Club*, 457

Fleming, Stephen, *Local Government Management Association of British Columbia*, 917

Executive Name Index

Fleming, Liz, *Association of Canadian Travel Agents - British Columbia & Yukon*, 144
Fleming, Patricia, *Earthwise Society*, 668
Fleming, Lee, *Pugwash & Area Chamber of Commerce*, 1194
Fleming, Ellie, *Voice of English-speaking Québec*, 1437
Flemington, Linda, *CARP*, 514
Flemming, Bob, *Fellowship of Evangelical Baptist Churches*, 731
Flemming, Kim, *Basketball New Brunswick*, 199
Flemming, Carrie, *Sisters of Charity of Halifax*, 1301
Flentge, Mary, *POWERtalk International*, 1584
Fleshner, Neil, *Canadian Urologic Oncology Group*, 500
Fletcher, Steve, *Automotive Recyclers of Canada*, 190
Fletcher, Cliff, *Free Methodist Church in Canada*, 759
Fletcher, Krystle, *Ontario Society for the Prevention of Cruelty to Animals*, 1106
Fletcher, Lesley, *The League of Canadian Poets*, 903
Fletcher, Andrea, *Real Estate Institute of Canada*, 1206
Fletcher, Cindy, *British Columbia Dental Hygienists' Association*, 238
Fletcher, Shelley, *People First of Canada*, 1151
Fletcher, Steve, *Ontario Automotive Recyclers Association*, 1067
Fletcher, Jonathan, *Ontario Association for Geographic & Environmental Education*, 1061
Fletcher, Paul, *Somenos Marsh Wildlife Society*, 1333
Fletcher, Susan, *Applegrove Community Complex*, 74
Fletcher, Paula, *Ralph Thornton Centre*, 1204
Fletcher-Stackhouse, Tannice, *Nurse Practitioners' Association of Ontario*, 1052
Flett, Jonathan, *Island Lake Tribal Council*, 865
Fleury, Jacqui, *Saskatchewan Association of Naturopathic Practitioners*, 1257
Fleury, Normand, *Société québécoise d'espéranto*, 1323
Fleury, Charles, *Canadian Union of Public Employees*, 498
Fleury, Ken, *Native Clan Organization Inc.*, 997
Flinn, Tyson, *New Brunswick Golf Association*, 1009
Flint, Shelly, *Calgary Exhibition & Stampede*, 272
Flint, David, *British Columbia Construction Association*, 237
Flitton, Corinne, *College of Massage Therapists of Ontario*, 586
Flood, Patrick, *Canadian Association for Dental Research*, 299
Flood, Glen, *Wrestling PEI*, 1468
Flood, David L., *Association for Healthcare Philanthropy*, 1508
Flood, Glen, *Football PEI*, 750
Flood, John, *Prince Edward Island Police Association*, 1176
Flottum, Kim, *Eastern Apicultural Society of North America, Inc.*, 1522
Floyd, Gordon, *National Alliance for Children & Youth*, 989
Floyd, Jim, *Nunavut Association of Landscape Architects*, 1051
Flumian, Maryantonett, *Institute On Governance*, 848
Flury, Chris, *Association of Professional Engineers & Geoscientists of British Columbia*, 158
Flury, Roger, *International Association of Music Libraries, Archives & Documentation Centres*, 1539
Flynn, Jennifer, *Legal Education Society of Alberta*, 906

Flynn, Ken, *Museum Association of Newfoundland & Labrador*, 983
Flynn, Debera, *Quality in Lifelong Learning Network*, 1195
Flynn, John, *Canadian Association for Social Work Education*, 304
Flynn, Lauren, *Canadian Biomaterials Society*, 344
Flys, André, *Toronto District Beekeepers' Association*, 1384
Focker, Klaas, *Community Arts Council of Richmond*, 595
Fodchuk, Kyle, *Association of Professional Engineers & Geoscientists of Alberta*, 157
Fogarty, Belinda, *Powell River Lapidary Club*, 1169
Fogwill, Allan, *Canadian Energy Research Institute*, 381
Foidart, Denis, *Childhood Cancer Canada Foundation*, 560
Fol, Alexandra, *LAUDEM, L'Association des musiciens liturgiques du Canada*, 900
Foley, Roger, *Association canadienne des ataxies familiales*, 92
Foley, Sophia, *Gulf of Maine Council on the Marine Environment*, 794
Foley, Sean, *Kingston Independent Nylon Workers Union*, 889
Folino, Frank, *Canadian Association of the Deaf*, 334
Folk, Doug, *Electrical Contractors Association of Saskatchewan*, 683
Folk, Colin, *Weyburn Group Home Society Inc*, 1451
Folk-Dawson, Janice, *Guelph & District Labour Council*, 792
Folkersen, Catherine, *Saskatchewan Canola Development Commission*, 1260
Folkes, Jennifer, *Synchro Newfoundland & Labrador*, 1361
Folkes Hanson, Tracy, *Canadian Society of Association Executives*, 480
Folkins, Neil, *Canadian Transplant Association*, 496
Follows, Robert C., *Altruvest Charitable Services*, 61
Fomproix, Nathalie, *International Union of Biological Sciences*, 1564
Fong, Traci, *Skate Canada*, 1302
Fong, Eric, *Canadian Population Society*, 458
Fontaine, Ed F., *Fellowship of Evangelical Baptist Churches*, 731
Fontaine, Pierre, *Parti communiste du Québec*, 1144
Fontaine, Shannon, *The Manitoba Tourism Education Council*, 946
Fontaine, Dan, *Economic Development Brandon*, 673
Fontaine, Daniel, *British Columbia Care Providers Association*, 235
Fontz, Jannel, *Filipino Students' Association of Toronto*, 735
Fooks, Cathy, *The Change Foundation*, 551
Foot, Duncan, *Halton Regional Police Association*, 800
Footz, Valerie, *Association of Parliamentary Libraries in Canada*, 155
Foran, Nancy, *Chartered Professional Accountants Canada*, 552
Foran, Vanessa, *Asthma Society of Canada*, 179
Foran, Lynda, *Nova Scotia Dental Assistants' Association*, 1044
Forand, Maryse, *Fédération des Associations de Musiciens-Éducateurs du Québec*, 712
Forbes, Inez, *Newspapers Atlantic*, 1024
Forbes, Ken, *Lumber & Building Materials Association of Ontario*, 920
Forbes, Linda, *Heritage Trust of Nova Scotia*, 813
Forbes, Cindy, *Canadian Medical Association*, 433
Forbes, Mary, *National Pensioners Federation*, 995

Forbes, Paula, *Catholic Family Services of Hamilton*, 518
Forbes, Kim, *Sault Ste Marie & 49th Field Regt. RCA Historical Society*, 1281
Forbes, Brian N., *National Council of Veteran Associations*, 992
Forbes, Miriam, *Certification Council of Early Childhood Educators of Nova Scotia*, 538
Ford, James E., *Scottish Rite Charitable Foundation of Canada*, 1286
Ford, Russ, *ASK! Community Information Centre (LAMP)*, 87
Ford, David, *Mount Forest District Chamber of Commerce*, 976
Ford, Jen, *ARMA Canada*, 82
Ford, Francine, *Canadian Association of Physicists*, 327
Ford, Ray, *Manitoba Water Well Association*, 947
Ford, Elizabeth, *Inuit Tapiriit Kanatami*, 862
Ford, Sarah, *World Federation of Hemophilia*, 1466
Ford, Carol, *Canadian University & College Conference Organizers Association*, 499
Ford, Carol, *General Practice Psychotherapy Association*, 769
Ford, Julie, *Interactive Advertising Bureau of Canada*, 851
Ford, Kristin, *Vernon BC Food Bank*, 1431
Ford, Russ, *Lakeshore Area Multi-Service Project*, 897
Forder, Doug, *Ontario Streams*, 1109
Foreman, Thomas, *Building Supply Industry Association of British Columbia*, 263
Foreman, Brent J., *Hamilton Community Foundation*, 801
Forest, Marc-André, *Chambre de commerce de Brandon*, 540
Forest, Andy, *Maker Kids*, 927
Forest, Éric, *Club timbres et monnaies de Sorel inc.*, 576
Forest, Marilyn, *Building Futures Employment Society*, 262
Forestell, Elizabeth, *Central Neighbourhood House*, 524
Forgeot D'Arc, Perrine, *L'Arche Québec*, 77
Forgeron, Don, *Insurance Bureau of Canada*, 849
Forget, Stéphane, *Fédération des chambres de commerce du Québec*, 713
Forget, Jean-Maurice, *Habitat for Humanity Canada*, 797
Forget, Stéphane, *Fédération des chambres de commerce du Québec*, 713
Forgues, Pierre, *Air Cadet League of Canada*, 19
Forgues, Claude, *Centraide Estrie*, 522
Forgues, Daniel, *Fondation des sourds du Québec inc.*, 745
Forhan, Carol, *Sisters Adorers of the Precious Blood*, 1300
Fornwald, Dennie, *Saskatchewan Outdoor & Environmental Education Association*, 1271
Foroughian, Maryam, *Goodwill Industries Essex Kent Lambton*, 777
Forrest, Ken, *Fredericton Tourism*, 759
Forrest, Joanne, *Paris & District Chamber of Commerce*, 1140
Forrester, Brian, *Gymnastics B.C.*, 795
Forsberg, Peter, *Conference of Defence Associations*, 612
Forsberg, Fran, *PFLAG Canada Inc.*, 1156
Forsman, Dwayne, *Paramedic Association of Canada*, 1138
Forsman, Nancey, *Baton Twirling Association of British Columbia*, 199
Forster, Dan, *Association of Fish & Wildlife Agencies*, 1511
Forsyth, Meghan, *Canadian Society for Traditional Music*, 479
Forsythe, Wayne, *Canadian Association of Geographers*, 316
Forsythe, Leslie, *Ontario Farm Fresh Marketing Association*, 1078

Forth, Ken, *Foreign Agricultural Resource Management Services*, 751
Fortier, Caroline, *Association des réalisateurs et réalisatrices du Québec*, 127
Fortier, Louis, *Association canadienne des juristes-traducteurs*, 94
Fortier, Robert, *Province of Québec Rifle Association*, 1190
Fortier, Maurice, *Syndicat de professionnelles et professionnels du gouvernement du Québec*, 1362
Fortier, Peter, *Foster Parents Association of Ottawa*, 755
Fortier, Huguette, *Ileostomy & Colostomy Association of Montréal*, 829
Fortier, Paul-André, *Fortier Danse-Création*, 754
Fortier, Ron, *Skills Unlimited*, 1302
Fortier, Jocelyn, *Société des traversiers du Québec*, 1318
Fortier, Gilles, *Association Trot & Amble du Québec*, 179
Fortier, Martin, *ArcticNet Inc.*, 81
Fortier, Louis, *ArcticNet Inc.*, 81
Fortier, Michael, *SIGMA Canadian Menopause Society*, 1298
Fortier, Nadège, *Canadian Children's Optimist Foundation*, 356
Fortin, Claude-Carrier, *Société de généalogie et d'archives de Rimouski*, 1316
Fortin, Luc, *La Guilde des Musiciens/Musiciennes du Québec*, 794
Fortin, Jean, *Terre sans frontières*, 1372
Fortin, Eric, *Badminton New Nouveau Brunswick*, 193
Fortin, Côme, *Association des médecins ophtalmologistes du Québec*, 120
Fortin, Jocelyne, *Association d'oto-rhino-laryngologie et de chirurgie cervico-faciale du Québec*, 99
Fortin, Michelle, *Options for Sexual Health*, 1117
Fortin, Lynda, *Syndicat des agents de maîtrise de TELUS (ind.)*, 1362
Fortin, Paul, *Club d'Ornithologie de Longueuil*, 574
Fortin, Caroline, *Mouvement Retrouvailles*, 978
Fortin, Jocelyne, *Ringuette-Québec*, 1233
Fortin, Chantal, *Réseau des SADC et CAE*, 1221
Fortin, Louise, *Société Provancher d'histoire naturelle du Canada*, 1323
Fortin, Christian, *Association professionnelle des techniciennes et techniciens en documentation du Québec*, 168
Fortin, Jean-Pierre, *Customs & Immigration Union*, 647
Fortin, Solange, *Conseil national Société de Saint-Vincent de Paul*, 619
Fortin, Jean-Mathieu, *Association coopérative d'économie familiale de la Péninsule*, 98
Fortin Thibault, Marie-Lyne, *Association de Ringuette de Longueuil*, 103
Fortman, Fred J., *American Society of Safety Engineers*, 1502
Foschi, Anna, *Vancouver & Lower Mainland Multicultural Family Support Services Society*, 1424
Foschini, Marie-Noëlle, *Éco-Quartier Sainte-Marie*, 673
Fossum, Sharilee, *Association of Professional Engineers & Geoscientists of Alberta*, 157
Foster, Rob, *Thunder Bay Field Naturalists*, 1378
Foster, Alison, *Greater Edmonton Library Association*, 783
Foster, Randy, *Canadian Grand Masters Fiddling Association*, 399
Foster, Barry, *The Anglican Church of Canada*, 69
Foster, Alice, *Association of Employees Supporting Education Services*, 147
Foster, Chris, *Boys & Girls Clubs of Ontario*, 224

Foster, Lisa, *Community Living Thunder Bay*, 605
Foster, Steve, *Chambre de commerce LGBT du Québec*, 549
Foster, Pam, *Canadian Association of University Teachers*, 335
Foster, Brian, *Operation Eyesight Universal*, 1115
Foster, Mike, *Association of Canadian Travel Agents - Ontario*, 144
Foster, Janet, *United Way of Halton Hills*, 1414
Foster, Sheila, *Calgary Canada-China Friendship Association*, 271
Foster, Jane, *Lennox & Addington Historical Society*, 907
Foster, David G., *American Cave Conservation Association*, 1491
Foster, Wendy, *International Association for Great Lakes Research*, 1536
Foster, Norma, *Karate BC*, 881
Foster, Ted, *Cannington & Area Historical Society*, 508
Foster, Lindsay, *Ottawa Flute Association*, 1130
Foster, Shari, *Alberta Baton Twirling Association*, 25
Foster, Janice, *North Okanagan Neurological Association*, 1031
Foster, Elvis, *Afro-Canadian Caribbean Association of Hamilton & District Inc.*, 13
Foster, Laura, *McMan Youth, Family & Community Services Association*, 956
Foster, Earl, *Ontario Rodeo Association*, 1102
Foster, Steve, *Conseil québécois des gais et lesbiennes du Québec*, 620
Foster, Darrell, *Kaye Nickerson Adult Service Centre*, 883
Fothergill, Janet, *Alliance for Canadian New Music Projects*, 57
Fougere, Dan, *Antigonish Chamber of Commerce*, 72
Fougère, Ginette, *Association of Registered Interior Designers of New Brunswick*, 161
Fougere, Tina, *Canadian National Autism Foundation*, 438
Fougere, Amanda, *4Korners Family Resource Center*, 756
Foullong, Karen, *University of Western Ontario Staff Association*, 1421
Fournier, Yvan, *The Christian & Missionary Alliance in Canada*, 566
Fournier, Marie Claude, *Association de la construction du Québec*, 101
Fournier, Benoit, *Canadian Ski Instructors' Alliance*, 471
Fournier, Elsa, *Association des physiatres du Québec*, 123
Fournier, Elsa, *Association des pneumologues de la province de Québec*, 123
Fournier, Luc, *Motorcycle & Moped Industry Council*, 976
Fournier, Luc, *Association des policières et policiers provinciaux du Québec*, 123
Fournier, Brad, *Alberta Diabetes Foundation*, 33
Fournier, Suzanne, *Action Nouvelle Vie*, 6
Fournier, Richard, *Canadian Remote Sensing Society*, 466
Fournier, Véronique, *Fondation Initia*, 746
Fournier, Jeff, *Nipissing Coin Club*, 1027
Fournier, Audrey, *Réseau TNO Santé en français*, 1226
Fournier, Serge, *Fédération du commerce (CSN)*, 720
Fournier, Annie, *Réseau des SADC et CAE*, 1220
Fournier, Martin, *Armateurs du Saint-Laurent*, 82
Fournier, Louise, *Project Management Institute*, 1585
Fournier, Jennifer, *Nurse Practitioner Association of Canada*, 1052
Fournier, Philippe, *Association québécoise des orthophonistes et des audiologistes*, 173

Fournier, Mireille, *Alliance du personnel professionel et administratif de Ville de Laval*, 56
Fowler, Ryan, *Saskatchewan Powerlifting Association*, 1272
Fowler, Julie, *Island Mountain Arts*, 865
Fowler, Ryan, *Canadian Powerlifting Union*, 459
Fowler, Cameron, *Canadian Bankers Association*, 341
Fowler, Michelle, *Canadian Dental Assistants Association*, 376
Fowler, Elisabeth, *Kidney Foundation of Canada*, 885
Fowler, Jennifer, *Central Vancouver Island Multicultural Society*, 525
Fowler, Jennifer, *Bereaved Families of Ontario*, 205
Fowler, Michelle, *Nova Scotia Dental Assistants' Association*, 1044
Fowler, Janeen, *British Columbia Family Child Care Association*, 240
Fowlow, Brian, *Labrador North Chamber of Commerce*, 894
Fox, Graham, *Institute for Research on Public Policy*, 844
Fox, Donna, *Block Parent Program of Canada*, 214
Fox, Lawrence, *Association of Independent Consultants*, 149
Fox, Tanya, *Camrose Chamber of Commerce*, 277
Fox, Stephenie, *Chartered Professional Accountants Canada*, 552
Fox, Bonnie, *Conservation Ontario*, 622
Fox, Lesley, *Fur-Bearer Defenders*, 765
Fox, Stephenie, *Birthright International*, 212
Fox, Sherry, *Canadian Sociological Association*, 489
Fox, Jeff, *YMCA Canada*, 1471
Fox, Delores, *National Association of Watch & Clock Collectors, Inc.*, 1574
Fox, Joyce, *Community Health Nurses of Canada*, 599
Fox, Judith, *The Terry Fox Foundation*, 1372
Fox, Mike, *Canadian Wood Truss Association*, 505
Fox-Robichaud, Alison, *Canadian Critical Care Society*, 373
Foy, Joe, *Wilderness Committee*, 1454
Fradet, Hélène, *Fédération des familles et amis de la personne atteinte de maladie mentale*, 715
Fradette, Allison, *Canadian Council of Motor Transport Administrators*, 369
Fradette Caron, Lisa, *Parcelles de tendresse*, 1139
Fragnito, Tony, *The Instrumentation, Systems & Automation Society of America*, 1534
Frame, Catherine, *The Royal Canadian Geographical Society*, 1239
Frampton, Gary, *Georgian Bay Steam & Antique Association*, 771
Franc, Christina, *Canadian Association of Fairs & Exhibitions*, 314
Franc, Christina, *Canadian Farm Writers' Federation*, 384
Franceschi, Susan, *American Water Works Association*, 1504
Francey, Christian, *Société francophone de Victoria*, 1319
Francey, Blair, *Audio Engineering Society*, 187
Francis, Andrew, *Association of Professional Engineers & Geoscientists of Alberta*, 157
Francis, Barb, *The Canadian Federation of Business & Professional Women's Clubs*, 385
Francis, Patricia, *International Trade Centre*, 1563
Francis, Robert, *Air Currency Enhancement Society*, 19
Francis, Sharon, *The Rainbow Society of Alberta*, 1203
Franco, Melissa, *Society of Fire Protection Engineers*, 1593

Francoeur, Aline, *Centre interdisciplinaire de recherches sur les activités langagières*, 535
Francoeur, Florent, *Ordre des conseillers en ressources humaines agréés*, 1121
Francoeur, Diane, *Fédération des médecins spécialistes du Québec*, 716
Francoeur, Rachelle, *Fédération franco-ténoise*, 721
Francoeur, Melody, *Back Country Horsemen of British Columbia*, 192
Francoeur, Nathalie, *Centre d'écoute Montérégie*, 528
Francois, Twyla, *Canadians for Ethical Treatment of Food Animals*, 507
Franjic, Nick, *Construction Specifications Canada*, 624
Frank, Greg, *British Columbia Association of School Business Officials*, 232
Frank, Roger, *International Society for Soil Mechanics & Geotechnical Engineering*, 1559
Frank, Anita, *Temporomandibular Joint Society of Canada*, 1370
Frankish, Matt, *Canadian Institute for Theatre Technology*, 414
Franklin, Leesa, *Canadian Association of Foodservice Professionals*, 315
Franklin, Linda, *Colleges Ontario*, 591
Franklin, Michelle, *Epilepsy Ontario*, 694
Franklin, Sharon, *Center for Health, Environment & Justice*, 1516
Frankling, Freddie, *GLOBE Foundation*, 775
Franklyn, Gaston, *Alzheimer Society of Windsor/Essex County*, 65
Frantz, Chris, *Canadian Ferry Association*, 389
Franz, Robert, *Alberta Genealogical Society*, 36
Franz, Robert, *Windsor Symphony Orchestra*, 1457
Franz Currie, Deborah, *Canadian Hemophilia Society*, 404
Fraser, Janine, *British Columbia Primary Teachers Association*, 249
Fraser, David, *IAESTE Canada (International Association for the Exchange of Students for Technical Experience)*, 829
Fraser, Duncan, *New Brunswick Institute of Agrologists*, 1009
Fraser, John, *Nova Scotia Powerlifting Association*, 1047
Fraser, Scott, *Ontario Tennis Association*, 1110
Fraser, Brian, *Food Banks Canada*, 749
Fraser, James E., *Canadian Association for Scottish Studies*, 303
Fraser, Éric, *Association de la construction du Québec*, 100
Fraser, Robert, *Ontario Professional Planners Institute*, 1098
Fraser, Glenn, *Childhood Cancer Canada Foundation*, 560
Fraser, Paul D.K., *International Commission of Jurists (Canadian Section)*, 855
Fraser, Jennifer, *Kidney Foundation of Canada*, 885
Fraser, Adam, *Nova Scotia Shorthorn Association*, 1048
Fraser, Kristy, *Nova Scotia Shorthorn Association*, 1048
Fraser, Jim, *Nova Scotia Cattle Producers*, 1042
Fraser, Cathie, *Research Council Employees' Association (Ind.)*, 1218
Fraser, Allison, *Nova Scotia Archaeology Society*, 1040
Fraser, Andrea, *Human Resources Professionals Association*, 826
Fraser, Janet, *Infertility Awareness Association of Canada*, 836
Fraser, Don, *Auditing Association of Canada*, 187
Fraser, Trevor, *Canadian Society of Hand Therapists*, 483
Fraser, Prentiss, *Women in Film & Television - Toronto*, 1461

Fraser, Sean, *Evergreen Theatre Society*, 699
Fraser, Robert B., *Canadian National Association of Real Estate Appraisers*, 438
Fraser, Kelly, *Canadian Association for Williams Syndrome*, 307
Fraser, W. Neil, *Clan Fraser Society of Canada*, 571
Fraser, Grant, *Travel Media Association of Canada*, 1396
Fraser, Mark, *National Golf Course Owners Association Canada*, 994
Fraser, Shelley, *British Columbia Sporthorse - Sport Pony Breeders Group*, 255
Fraser, Peter, *Horse Industry Association of Alberta*, 822
Fraser, Courtenay, *CADORA British Columbia*, 268
Fraser, Fil, *Canadian Communications Foundation*, 361
Fraser, Jeanette, *L'Arche Ontario*, 77
Fraser, Jeremy, *Alberta Social Credit Party*, 47
Fraser, John, *National NewsMedia Council*, 995
Frate, Nick, *CAEO Québec*, 270
Frater, Tammy, *Kipling Chamber of Commerce*, 890
Fratino, Andy, *The Leukemia & Lymphoma Society of Canada*, 909
Fray, Katherine J., *International Orthoptic Association*, 1554
Frayne, Les, *SHARE Agriculture Foundation*, 1294
Frayssignes, Christian, *International Wine & Food Society*, 1567
Frayssignes, Christian, *Belgian Canadian Business Chamber*, 204
Frazier, Margie, *Batten Disease Support & Research Association - Canadian Chapter*, 199
Freake, Lorne K., *Canadian Bible Society*, 343
Freake, Lorne K., *Canadian Bible Society*, 343
Fréchette, Johanne, *Association des éleveurs de chevaux Belge du Québec*, 111
Fréchette, François-Régis, *Ordre des infirmières et infirmiers du Québec*, 1122
Fréchette, Marie, *L'Arche Québec*, 77
Frederick, Smith, *Family History Society of Newfoundland & Labrador*, 703
Frederick, Barb, *Human Resources Professionals Association*, 826
Frederick, Peterson, *Black Coalition of Québec*, 213
Frederikse, Peggy, *Cecebe Waterways Association*, 521
Fredette, Cynthia, *Association des spécialistes du pneus et Mécanique du Québec*, 128
Fredette, Martin, *Association des Grands Frères et Grandes Soeurs du Québec*, 115
Fredette, Phil, *Funeral Service Association of Canada*, 764
Fredette, Sylvain, *Association des Scouts du Canada*, 127
Freeborn, John, *Canadian Picture Pioneers*, 455
Freed, Heather, *Canadian Association of Women Executives & Entrepreneurs*, 336
Freed, Susan, *Urology Nurses of Canada*, 1423
Freedman, Andrea, *The Centre for Israel & Jewish Affairs*, 533
Freelan, Sheldon, *Ontario Podiatric Medical Association*, 1096
Freeland, Alejandro, *Latino Canadian Cultural Association*, 900
Freeland, Neal, *Odawa Native Friendship Centre*, 1054
Freeman, Lynne, *Ontario Field Ornithologists*, 1080
Freeman, Barry, *Canadian Association for Theatre Research*, 306
Freeman, Diane, *Automotive Aftermarket Retailers of Ontario*, 189
Freeman, Judy, *Alliance for Canadian New Music Projects*, 56

Freeman, Mark, *Self-Help Resource Centre*, 1289
Freeman, Pharaoh, *One Full Circle*, 1058
Freeman, Tiina, *Northwest Wall & Ceiling Bureau*, 1580
Freeman, Melissa, *West Central Forage Association*, 1444
Freer, Elene J., *Muskoka Arts & Crafts Inc.*, 985
Freese, Manfred, *British Columbia Grapegrowers' Association*, 242
Freid, Loren, *Alzheimer Society of York Region*, 65
Freitag, Gabriele, *International Council for Central & East European Studies (Canada)*, 1544
Freitas de Quadros, Eda, *International Society for Rock Mechanics*, 1559
Frémond, Pascale, *Religions for Peace*, 1586
French, Douglas, *College of Psychologists of New Brunswick*, 589
French, Jasmine, *Grant MacEwan College Faculty Association*, 782
French, Beth, *Brockville & District Association for Community Involvement*, 260
French, Eileen, *Alberta Genealogical Society*, 36
French, Jason, *Holstein Canada*, 819
French, Debra, *Hamilton Philharmonic Youth Orchestra*, 802
French, Sylvia, *Fraser Valley Square & Round Dance Association*, 758
French, Gary E., *East Georgian Bay Historical Foundation*, 668
French, John, *British Columbia Fencing Association*, 241
French, David, *Electric Vehicle Council of Ottawa*, 682
French, Meg, *UNICEF Canada*, 1404
French, Lew, *Ontario Association for Geographic & Environmental Education*, 1061
French, Lola, *Canadian Association of Pregnancy Support Services*, 328
Frenette, Lucien, *Conseil régional de la culture Saguenay-Lac-Saint-Jean*, 621
Frenette, Gerry, *Canada's Medical Technology Companies*, 282
Frenette, Gerry, *Canadian MedTech Manufacturers' Alliance*, 434
Frenkel, Sophie, *Canadian Hadassah WIZO*, 399
Frenkel, Brian, *North Central Local Government Association*, 1030
Fresco, Theresa, *Fraser Basin Council*, 757
Freund, Cliff, *Manitoba Christmas Tree Growers Association*, 934
Freund, Dorothy, *Manitoba Christmas Tree Growers Association*, 934
Freund, Sherry, *Education Support Staff of the Ontario Secondary School Teachers' Federation - District 24 - Waterloo*, 680
Frey, Michele, *North American Society of Adlerian Psychology*, 1579
Freychet, Yannick, *Fédération des aînés Franco-Albertains*, 711
Frias, Cristina, *International Council for Canadian Studies*, 855
Frias, Rafael, *American Water Resources Association*, 1504
Fricker, Marc, *Canadian Space Society*, 489
Friday, Nancy, *Families for a Secure Future*, 701
Fridgen, Peter, *Building Envelope Council of Ottawa Region*, 262
Friebel, Ralph, *TEAM of Canada Inc.*, 1368
Friede, Joe, *Canadian Hypnosis Association*, 410
Friedrichkeit, Burke, *Brighton-Cramahe Chamber of Commerce*, 229
Friendly, Martha, *Childcare Resource & Research Unit*, 560
Friesen, Ronald G., *Continuing Legal Education Society of BC*, 627

Friesen, Dianne, *Winkler & District Chamber of Commerce*, 1458
Friesen, Randy, *MB Mission*, 954
Friesen, Connie, *The Canadian Federation of Business & Professional Women's Clubs*, 385
Friesen, Tom, *Hike Ontario*, 814
Friesen, Marcia, *Canadian Arabian Horse Registry*, 294
Friesen, Al, *The Marquis Project, Inc.*, 952
Friesen, Krista, *Canadian Plastics Industry Association*, 455
Friesen, Eva, *The Calgary Foundation*, 272
Friesen, Shannon, *YWCA Canada*, 1481
Friesen, Erin, *British Columbia Food Technologists*, 241
Friesen, Dorothy, *British Columbia Northern Real Estate Board*, 248
Friesen, Bob, *Farmers of North America Strategic Agriculture Institute*, 706
Frigon, Florence, *Société d'Horticulture et d'Écologie de Prévost*, 1314
Frigon, Lucie, *Canadian Society for Chemistry*, 473
Frigon, Simon, *Canadian Disaster Restoration Group*, 378
Frimpong, Adams, *Saskatchewan Institute of Agrologists*, 1268
Frise, David, *Swimming New Brunswick*, 1359
Frise, Peter, *AUTO21 Network of Centres of Excellence*, 189
Frisen, Sharlene, *Association of Professional Engineers & Geoscientists of Alberta*, 157
Frits, Vrijlandt, *Union internationale des associations d'alpinisme*, 1598
Fritter, Catherine, *Association of Consulting Engineering Companies - British Columbia*, 145
Fritz, Carrie, *Calgary Humane Society*, 272
Fritz, Richard (Rick) D., *The American Association of Petroleum Geologists*, 1490
Fritz, Earl M., *Canadian Junior Golf Association*, 423
Fritzshall, Fritzie, *Holocaust Memorial Foundation of Illinois*, 1530
Friz, Peter, *Geological Association of Canada*, 770
Froese, Dawn, *Big Brothers Big Sisters of Manitoba*, 209
Froese, Katrina, *Canadian Association of Nordic Ski Instructors*, 323
Froese, Peter, *Federation of Independent School Associations of BC*, 724
Froese, Terrance, *Saskatchewan Conference of Mennonite Brethren Churches*, 1261
Frojmovic, Michel, *Canadian Council on Social Development*, 371
Frolick, Michael, *Infrastructure Health & Safety Association*, 838
Fromme, Tom, *North Peace Applied Research Association*, 1032
Froncisz, Bartek, *Association of Polish Engineers in Canada*, 156
Frontini, Gian, *Kingston Orchid Society*, 889
Froome, Brenda, *Hamilton Stamp Club*, 802
Frost, Shelley, *Pacific National Exhibition*, 1135
Frost, Stan E., *Dominion of Canada Rifle Association*, 661
Frost, Larry, *Native Canadian Centre of Toronto*, 997
Frost, Richard L., *Winnipeg Foundation*, 1459
Frost, Yvette, *Nova Scotia Library Association*, 1046
Frost, Ken, *Association of Canadian Film Craftspeople*, 142
Frost, Doug, *Federation of Ontario Bed & Breakfast Accommodation*, 725
Frowley, Jody, *Baseball Canada*, 198
Fruetel, Karen, *Canadian Geriatrics Society*, 397
Fruitman, Mel, *Food Processors of Canada*, 750
Frulla, Liza, *Institut de tourisme et d'hôtellerie du Québec*, 842

Fruno, Greg, *Vancouver Museum Society*, 1427
Fry, Lori, *The Canadian Council of the Blind*, 370
Fry, Lorraine, *Non-Smokers' Rights Association*, 1028
Fry, Kathleen, *British Columbia Waterfowl Society*, 258
Fry, Lorraine, *Smoking & Health Action Foundation*, 1304
Frye, Tanya, *Canadian Veterinary Medical Association*, 501
Fryer, Brian, *Alberta Amateur Football Association*, 22
Fryer, Brian, *Great Lakes Institute for Environmental Research*, 782
Fryer, Greg, *Habitat for Humanity Canada*, 797
Fryett, Jim, *York Soaring Association*, 1474
Frymire Fleming, Ange, *Canadian Public Relations Society Inc.*, 463
Fuchsová, Marie, *Czech & Slovak Association of Canada*, 648
Fudge, Daphne, *Them Days Inc.*, 1375
Fudge, Brenda, *Canadian Psychiatric Association*, 461
Fugleberg, Todd, *Brandon University Faculty Association*, 226
Fuglem, Karla, *East Coast Trail Association*, 668
Fuhr, Justin, *Manitoba Association of Library Technicians*, 930
Fuhrer, Janet M., *Canadian Bar Association*, 341
Fujishige, Paul, *Transitions*, 1395
Fujita, Naoharu, *Japanese Association for Canadian Studies*, 1568
Fujiwara, Denise, *Fujiwara Dance Inventions*, 764
Fulan, Elio, *Richmond Hill Chamber of Commerce*, 1230
Fulcher, Andrew, *Canadian Condominium Institute*, 362
Fulcher, Owen, *Endurance Riders of Alberta*, 688
Fulford, Maggie, *Alberta College of Occupational Therapists*, 29
Fulford Hearn, Susan, *Canadian Nurses Foundation*, 443
Fullan, Michael, *Catholic Charities of The Archdiocese of Toronto*, 518
Fullan, Ron, *Insurance Councils of Saskatchewan*, 849
Fullard, Brent D., *Canadian Association of Income Trusts Investors*, 318
Fullarton, Nadine, *Construction Association of New Brunswick*, 623
Fullarton, Nadine, *Mechanical Contractors Association of New Brunswick*, 957
Fulleman, Mary, *LaHave Islands Marine Museum Society*, 895
Fuller, Jeff, *Canadian Association for Clinical Microbiology & Infectious Diseases*, 298
Fuller, Susanna, *Bicycle Nova Scotia*, 208
Fuller, Jon, *OMF International - Canada*, 1057
Fuller, Colleen, *Cowichan Valley Basket Society*, 637
Fuller, Andrew, *Ontario Association of Architects*, 1061
Fuller, Ana, *Local Government Management Association of British Columbia*, 917
Fuller, Lyda, *YWCA Canada*, 1482
Fuller, James, *Flowers Canada*, 741
Fuller, Shannon, *Cape Breton County Minor Hockey Association*, 509
Fuller, Michel, *Association des propriétaires canins de Prévost*, 126
Fullertown, Jane, *Canadian Museums Association*, 437
Fulmer, Ken, *Sheet Metal Contractors Association of Alberta*, 1295
Fülöp, Márta, *International Association for Cross-Cultural Psychology*, 1536
Fülöp, Tamas, *Société québécoise de gériatrie*, 1323

Fulton, Doug, *Western Canada Children's Wear Markets*, 1447
Fulton, Abigail, *British Columbia Construction Association*, 237
Fulton, Steve, *Ontario Genealogical Society*, 1082
Fulton, Diane, *Bowls British Columbia*, 220
Fultz, Aaron, *Society for Technical Communication*, 1591
Fung, Andy, *British Columbia Golf Association*, 242
Funk, Sandy, *Huntington Society of Canada*, 827
Funk, Sandra, *Huntington Society of Canada*, 828
Funk, Bill, *CancerCare Manitoba*, 508
Funk, Bob, *George Morris Centre*, 771
Funk, Mary Ann, *Living Bible Explorers*, 915
Funnell, Clark, *Resident Doctors of British Columbia*, 1226
Funt, Warren, *Investment Industry Regulatory Organization of Canada*, 863
Funt, Warren, *Investment Industry Regulatory Organization of Canada*, 863
Fuqua, John, *Pediatric Endocrine Society*, 1583
Furchner, Douglas, *Canadian Association of Veterans in United Nations Peacekeeping*, 335
Furlong, Alex, *Canadian Labour Congress*, 424
Furlong, Nancy, *Non-Academic Staff Association for the University of Alberta*, 1028
Furlong, Keith, *Interactive Gaming Council*, 851
Furlotte, Karen, *Lupus Ontario*, 921
Furmankiewicz, Frances, *Canadian Association of Foodservice Professionals*, 315
Furstenau, Sunna, *Icelandic National League of North America*, 829
Fyckes, Joy, *Reading Council for Literacy Advance in Montréal*, 1205
Fyfe, Kathy, *Epilepsy Association of Calgary*, 693
Fyfe, Toby, *Institute On Governance*, 848
Fyffe, Kathleen, *Saskatchewan Association of Naturopathic Practitioners*, 1257
Fyffe, Greg, *Canadian Association for Security & Intelligence Studies*, 303
Fykse Tveit, Olav, *World Council of Churches*, 1604
Fyles, Chris, *LakeCity Employment Services Association*, 896
Fyvie, Kathleen, *British Columbia Nurse Practitioner Association*, 248

G

Gabeli, Giulio, *General Conference of the Canadian Assemblies of God*, 769
Gabert, Carla, *Innisfail & District Chamber of Commerce*, 839
Gabert, Al, *Skills/Compétences Canada*, 1303
Gabinet, Gerry, *Economic Developers Association of Canada*, 673
Gaboury, Jacques, *Numeris*, 1051
Gaboury, Gilles, *Société Provancher d'histoire naturelle du Canada*, 1323
Gabriel, Leagh, *West Vancouver Chamber of Commerce*, 1446
Gabriel, Melodie, *Catholic Near East Welfare Association Canada*, 520
Gabriel, Tom, *Canadian Addiction Counsellors Certification Federation*, 288
Gabrys, Marcin, *Polish Association for Canadian Studies*, 1584
Gaceta, Georgia, *The Lord's Flock Charismatic Community*, 919
Gachanja, Michael, *East African Wild Life Society*, 1522
Gadansetti, Shifrah, *Canadian Alliance of Student Associations*, 291

Executive Name Index

Gadbois, Philippe, *Hotel Association of Canada Inc.,* 824
Gadbois, Michel, *Association Québécoise des dépanneurs en alimentation,* 172
Gaddy, Angie, *British Columbia Pharmacy Association,* 248
Gadhia, Atul, *Stroke Recovery Association of BC,* 1352
Gadoua, Carole, *Association coopérative d'économie familiale du Haut-Saint-Laurent,* 98
Gadoury, Jean-René Leblanc, *Association pour la voix études au Québec,* 167
Gaede, Lara, *Alberta Securities Commission,* 46
Gaetz, Steven, *St. John Ambulance,* 1249
Gaffney, George, *Rick Hansen Foundation,* 1231
Gage, Deanna, *Nicola Valley Community Arts Council,* 1026
Gage, Sandra, *Canadian Soccer Association,* 472
Gage, Rose, *Ag Energy Co-operative,* 13
Gagel, Mike P., *British Columbia School Trustees Association,* 252
Gagliardi, Carole, *Canadian Italian Business & Professional Association,* 423
Gaglione, Maria, *Association des professionnels et superviseurs de Radio-Canada,* 126
Gagne, Louis, *McLennan Chamber of Commerce,* 955
Gagné, Caroline, *Association des Grands Frères et Grandes Soeurs du Québec,* 115
Gagne, Andrea, *Sault Ste Marie Real Estate Board,* 1281
Gagné, Hélène, *Fondation des maladies du coeur du Québec,* 745
Gagné, Christine, *Syndicat professionnel des médecins du gouvernement du Québec (ind.),* 1365
Gagné, France, *Canadian Association of Veterans in United Nations Peacekeeping,* 336
Gagné, Daniel, *Association de Ringuette des Moulins,* 104
Gagné, Claude, *Association des pompiers de Laval,* 124
Gagne, Cheryl, *British Columbia Prader-Willi Syndrome Association,* 249
Gagnes, Frances, *International Confederation of Midwives,* 1544
Gagnier, Gilles, *The Royal Canadian Geographical Society,* 1239
Gagnon, John, *Bathurst & District Labour Council,* 199
Gagnon, Lloyd, *Canadian Association for Disabled Skiing - New Brunswick,* 299
Gagnon, Pâquerette, *La Fédération des commissions scolaires du Québec,* 713
Gagnon, Mario, *Fibrose kystique Québec,* 733
Gagnon, Marc-Olivier, *Chambre de commerce région de Mégantic,* 549
Gagnon, Denise, *Centre international de solidarité ouvrière,* 535
Gagnon, Alexis T., *American Society of Heating, Refrigerating & Air Conditioning Engineers,* 1500
Gagnon, Normande, *Association québécoise des personnes de petite taille,* 174
Gagnon, Terry, *Volleyball Alberta,* 1437
Gagnon, G., *Development & Peace,* 654
Gagnon, Steve, *The Canadian Corps of Commissionaires,* 365
Gagnon, Pierre-Claude, *Ordre des ingénieurs du Québec,* 1122
Gagnon, Denise, *Carrefour 50+ du Québec,* 515
Gagnon, Ruth, *Canadian Association of Elizabeth Fry Societies,* 313
Gagnon, Michel, *St. Leonard's Society of Canada,* 1250
Gagnon, Daniel, *Office du tourisme et des congrès de Québec,* 1055

Gagnon, Jean, *Fédération indépendante des syndicats autonomes,* 721
Gagnon, André, *Éco-Quartier Sainte-Marie,* 673
Gagnon, Mario, *Association des designers industriels du Québec,* 110
Gagnon, Pierre-Yves, *Fondation québécoise du cancer,* 748
Gagnon, Pierre-Yves, *Fondation québécoise du cancer,* 748
Gagnon, John, *New Brunswick Federation of Labour,* 1008
Gagnon, Andre, *National Association of Watch & Clock Collectors, Inc.,* 1575
Gagnon, Cathy, *Fédération québécoise des coopératives forestières,* 728
Gagnon, Chantal, *Softball Québec,* 1332
Gagnon, Marjorie, *Les bibliothèques publiques des régions de la Capitale-Nationale et Chaudière-Appalaches,* 208
Gagnon, Michel, *Association professionnelle des ingénieurs du gouvernement du Québec (ind.),* 167
Gagnon, Jean-Roch, *Réseau BIBLIO de la Côte-Nord,* 1218
Gagnon, Marie-Eve, *Association québécoise des auteurs dramatiques,* 171
Gagnon, Patrice, *Association des professionnels en développement économique du Québec,* 126
Gagnon, Jaquis, *Table des responsables de l'éducation des adultes et de la formation professionnelle des commissions scolaires du Québec,* 1366
Gagnon, Mélanie, *Syndicat des professeures et professeurs de l'Université du Québec à Rimouski,* 1363
Gagnon, Alain, *Syndicat national des employés de l'aluminium d'Arvida, inc.,* 1365
Gagnon, Penny, *Child Development Centre Society of Fort St. John & District,* 559
Gagnon, Richard, *Mouvement national des québécoises et québécois,* 977
Gagnon, Manon, *La Fondation Émile-Nelligan,* 746
Gagnon, Sophie, *Ordre des audioprothésistes du Québec,* 1120
Gagnon, Paul-André, *Association syndicale des employées de production et de service,* 178
Gagnon, Jacques, *La Fondation des Amis de la généalogie,* 744
Gagnon, Marie-Eve, *Société québécoise des auteurs dramatiques,* 1324
Gagnon, François, *Association des personnes handicapées physiques et sensorielles du secteur Joliette,* 123
Gagnon, L.P., *Saskatchewan Sailing Clubs Association,* 1274
Gagnon-Ducharme, Cédric, *Centre québécois du droit de l'environnement,* 536
Gagnon-Ouellet, Lucie, *Association canadienne des ataxies familiales,* 92
Gahagan, Jacqueline, *Canadian Public Health Association,* 462
Gahdia, Mayur, *Youth Science Canada,* 1476
Gainer, Lynn, *Ontario Genealogical Society,* 1082
Gainey, Anna, *The Liberal Party of Canada,* 909
Gainey, Anna, *Gainey Foundation,* 766
Gair, Bain, *Lillooet & District Chamber of Commerce,* 912
Gajewski, Bogdan, *Association of Polish Engineers in Canada,* 156
Gal, Susan, *Alberta Egg Producers' Board,* 33
Galbraith, Paul, *Canadian Luing Cattle Association,* 428
Gale, Francis, *Newfoundland & Labrador Ground Water Association,* 1019
Gale, Heather, *CanadaGAP,* 283
Galenzoski, Karen, *Covenant Health,* 637
Galette, Paige, *Les EssentiElles,* 696
Galezowska, Grazyna, *Canadian Polish Congress,* 456

Galgay, Jonathan, *George Street Association,* 771
Galiana, Patrisha, *The Garden Clubs of Ontario,* 767
Galibois, Stéphane, *Collaboration Santé Internationale,* 581
Galimberti, Joseph, *Canadian Steel Producers Association,* 491
Galioto, Riccarda, *Association of Medical Microbiology & Infectious Disease Canada,* 152
Gall, Dan, *Standardbred Canada,* 1348
Gall, Lori, *Ontario Brain Injury Association,* 1068
Gallagher, Heather, *Smithers District Chamber of Commerce,* 1304
Gallagher, Melanie, *Promotional Product Professionals of Canada Inc.,* 1189
Gallagher, Peter, *Architectural Woodwork Manufacturers Association of Canada - Ontario Chapter,* 79
Gallagher, Ellanore, *Canadian Society of Orthopaedic Technologists,* 485
Gallagher, Elizabeth Jane (BJ), *Soroptimist Foundation of Canada,* 1333
Gallagher, Bob, *YMCA Canada,* 1471
Gallagher, Brian A., *United Way Worldwide,* 1600
Gallagher, Ed, *Onoway & District Chamber of Commerce,* 1058
Gallant, Tammy, *New Brunswick Association for Community Living,* 1004
Gallant, Genevieve, *Development & Peace,* 655
Gallant, Paul, *Canadian College of Health Leaders,* 359
Gallant, Paul, *Canadian College of Health Leaders,* 359
Gallant, Karen, *Junior Achievement Canada,* 877
Gallant, Andre, *Junior Achievement Canada,* 877
Gallant, Rick, *Junior Achievement Canada,* 877
Gallant, Brian, *New Brunswick Liberal Association,* 1010
Gallant, Chris, *Recreation New Brunswick,* 1207
Gallant, Andre, *YMCA Canada,* 1471
Gallant, Karen, *Canadian Association for Leisure Studies,* 302
Gallant, Angela, *Gymnastics Nova Scotia,* 795
Gallant, Guy, *Fédération des producteurs de bovins du Québec,* 717
Gallant, Mélina, *Fédération des aînées et aînés francophones du Canada,* 711
Gallant, Roland, *Fédération des aînées et aînés francophones du Canada,* 711
Gallant, Francine, *Institut féminin francophone du Nouveau-Brunswick,* 842
Gallant, Marie, *Community Futures Development Association of British Columbia,* 598
Gallant, Joey, *Darts Prince Edward Island,* 651
Gallardo, Francisco, *Canadian Association of Medical Teams Abroad,* 321
Gallaway, Chris, *Alberta Federation of Labour,* 34
Galle, Peter, *International Liver Cancer Association,* 1553
Galleros, Leonora, *National Council of Philippine American Canadian Accountants,* 1575
Galliford, Mike, *British Columbia Cooperative Learning Provincial Specialist Association,* 237
Gallinati, Janet, *Parents Without Partners Inc.,* 1582
Gallop, Trina, *Evangelical Lutheran Church in Canada,* 698
Gallop, Chris, *Lacrosse New Brunswick,* 895
Galloway, Kristina, *Ontario Gymnastic Federation,* 1083
Galloway, Don, *Nunavut Speed Skating Association,* 1051

Galison, Dave, *Mood Disorders Society of Canada,* 973
Galluzzo, Rosa, *LOFT Community Services,* 917
Galpin-Nicholson, Alice, *Real Estate Institute of Canada,* 1206
Galskjot, Anette, *International Federation for Housing & Planning,* 1546
Galt, John, *Canadian Automatic Sprinkler Association,* 339
Galway, John, *The Harold Greenberg Fund,* 804
Gamache, Ginette, *Institut de médiation et d'arbitrage du Québec,* 841
Gambin-Walsh, Sherry, *Newfoundland & Labrador Association for Community Living,* 1015
Gamble, John D., *Association of Consulting Engineering Companies - Canada,* 146
Gamble, Debbie, *Island Writers' Association (P.E.I.),* 866
Gamble, Kellie, *Pipe Line Contractors Association of Canada,* 1160
Gamble, Jen, *Certified Organic Associations of British Columbia,* 538
Gamble-Arsenault, Debbie, *Maritime Model Horse Collectors & Showers Association,* 951
Gambrel, Rick, *British Columbia Psychological Association,* 250
Gamelli, Richard L., *International Society for Burn Injuries,* 1557
Gammage, Anne, *Ontario Ground Water Association,* 1083
Gammon, Anne-Marie, *Financial Executives International Canada,* 736
Gan, Bing, *Canadian Society of Plastic Surgeons,* 491
Gana, Beulah, *Saskatoon Open Door Society Inc.,* 1279
Gander, Lisa, *United Way of Morden & District Inc.,* 1415
Gander, Barry, *Canadian Technology Human Resources Board,* 493
Gandhi, Seva, *Institute of Cultural Affairs International,* 846
Gandilhon, Isabelle, *Association francophone pour le savoir,* 136
Ganem, Eduardo, *United Nations Environment Programme - Multilateral Fund for the Implementation of the Montréal Protocol,* 1412
Ganesh, Rea, *Children's Wish Foundation of Canada,* 562
Ganey, Patricia E., *Society of Toxicology,* 1594
Gangat, Shabbir, *Islamic Foundation of Toronto,* 864
Gangbar, Stephen, *Ontario Society of Periodontists,* 1107
Gange, Shirley, *Provincial Association of Resort Communities of Saskatchewan,* 1190
Ganley, Roger, *Model Aeronautics Association of Canada Inc.,* 970
Gannage, Gary, *Association of Management, Administrative & Professional Crown Employees of Ontario,* 151
Gannon, Carl, *Provincial Black Basketball Association,* 1190
Gannon, Carl, *Union of Veterans' Affairs Employees,* 1408
Gannon Jr., Louis (Lou), *African Nova Scotian Music Association,* 13
Gant, Rick, *Habitat for Humanity Canada,* 796
Ganter, Bea, *Lacombe Handicraft & Lapidary Guild,* 895
Gantous, Andres, *Canadian Academy of Facial Plastic & Reconstructive Surgery,* 286
Ganzert, Robin R., *American Humane Association,* 1494
Gänzle, Michael, *Canadian Institute of Food Science & Technology,* 415
Gao, Gloria, *Risk & Insurance Management Society Inc.,* 1234
Garand, Jean-Pierre, *Association nationale des camionneurs artisans inc.,* 138

Executive Name Index

Garber-Conrad, Martin, *Edmonton Community Foundation*, 676
Garbutt, Kenneth C., *Canadian Association of Veterans in United Nations Peacekeeping*, 336
Garcea, Laurie, *Learning Disabilities Association of Saskatchewan*, 905
Garceau, Louis-François, *Canadian Railroad Historical Association*, 465
Garceau, Pieere, *Conseil québécois de la franchise*, 620
Garcia, Anthony M. (Tony), *Foresters*, 751
García, Daniel, *Canadian Society of Association Executives*, 480
Gard, Paul, *Northwest Territories Softball*, 1038
Gardee, Ihsaan, *National Council of Canadian Muslims*, 991
Gardella, Ermanno, *Fédération internationale de bobsleigh et de tobogganing*, 1525
Garden, John, *Canadian Association of Drilling Engineers*, 312
Gardener, John, *Back Country Horsemen of British Columbia*, 193
Gardin, Mark, *Canadian Institute of Quantity Surveyors*, 419
Gardin, Melanie, *Ontario Brain Injury Association*, 1069
Gardiner, Gail, *Canadian Mental Health Association*, 435
Gardiner, Penny A., *Economic Developers Association of Canada*, 672
Gardiner, Heather, *Cowichan United Way*, 637
Gardiner, Penny, *Hamilton Technology Centre*, 802
Gardner, Jane, *Carousel Players*, 514
Gardner, Meggan, *Canadian Golf Hall of Fame & Museum*, 398
Gardner, Grant, *Canadian Network for Environmental Education & Communication*, 440
Gardner, Penny, *Badminton BC*, 193
Gardner, Tami, *Olds Regional Exhibition*, 1057
Gardner, Tracy, *Olds Regional Exhibition*, 1057
Gardon, Libby, *Consumer Health Organization of Canada*, 626
Garfield, Louise, *Arts Etobicoke*, 85
Garfinkel, Elliott, *Rose & Max Rady Jewish Community Centre*, 1236
Gargaro, Judy, *Etobicoke Philharmonic Orchestra*, 698
Gariépy, Julie, *Association québécoise de l'industrie du disque, du spectacle et de la vidéo*, 170
Gariépy, Sylvie, *Association des médecins ophtalmologistes du Québec*, 120
Gariépy, Marie-Josée, *Fondation de l'Hôpital de Montréal pour enfants*, 744
Gariépy, Jean, *Project Management Institute*, 1585
Garingalao, Marie, *University of the Philippines Alumni Association of Toronto*, 1420
Garland, Ryan, *Newfoundland Baseball*, 1023
Garland, Jennifer, *Art Libraries Society of North America*, 1506
Garneau, Brenda, *Junior Achievement Canada*, 877
Garneau, Matthew, *Literacy Coalition of New Brunswick*, 913
Garnett, Marguerite, *New Brunswick Genealogical Society Inc.*, 1008
Garnier, Glenda, *Model Forest of Newfoundland & Labrador*, 971
Garon, Marie, *Canadian Amateur Musicians*, 292
Garon, Alexandre, *Société d'histoire du Lac-St-Jean/Maison des Bâtisseurs*, 1312
Garone, Daniela, *Dignitas International*, 657
Garrah, Jeff, *Kingston Economic Development Corporation*, 889
Garrah, Larry, *Kingston Independent Nylon Workers Union*, 889
Garrard, Campbell, *Canadian Cutting Horse Association*, 375
Garrard, Ted, *Hospital for Sick Children Foundation*, 823

Garrett, Peter, *Innovate Calgary*, 839
Garrido, Lorena, *Ordre des sages-femmes du Québec*, 1124
Garries, Jennifer, *Leduc Regional Chamber of Commerce*, 906
Garrison, Michele, *Boundary District Arts Council*, 219
Garrison, Cynthia, *La Leche League International*, 1569
Garrity, Michael, *Alliance for the Wild Rockies*, 1487
Garro, Alicia, *Association for Canadian Studies in Argentina*, 1507
Garrod, Anne, *Community Living Essex County*, 601
Garshowitz, Paula, *College of Optometrists of Ontario*, 587
Gartland, Paul, *Fortress Louisbourg Association*, 754
Gartner, Tamara, *PFLAG Canada Inc.*, 1155
Garus, Jennifer, *Nova Scotia Dietetic Association*, 1044
Garvey, Julie, *Ontario Association of Residents' Councils*, 1066
Garvin, Myra, *Operation Harvest Sharing*, 1115
Garvin, Theresa, *Canadian Association of Geographers*, 316
Gaschler, Michael, *Insurance Brokers Association of Canada*, 848
Gashirabake, Moses, *Black Law Students' Association of Canada*, 213
Gasmo, Jason, *Association of Consulting Engineering Companies - Saskatchewan*, 146
Gaspar, Jayme, *Mississauga Heritage Foundation Inc.*, 970
Gasse, Valery, *Association des médecins spécialistes en santé communautaire du Québec*, 120
Gaston, Bev, *Union of Municipalities of New Brunswick*, 1407
Gates, Nadine, *Yarmouth County Historical Society*, 1470
Gates, Patrick, *Master Mariners of Canada*, 953
Gates, Rick, *Master Mariners of Canada*, 954
Gates, Debbie, *Canada's Medical Technology Companies*, 282
Gates, Debbie, *Canadian MedTech Manufacturers' Alliance*, 434
Gates, Heather, *American Society of Plastic Surgeons*, 1502
Gatien, Greg, *Brandon University School of Music*, 226
Gattiker, Melanie, *Lethbridge Symphony Orchestra*, 908
Gaudet, Frank, *Saskatchewan Badminton Association*, 1259
Gaudet, Lynn, *Canadian Association of Professional Immigration Consultants*, 329
Gaudet, Sylvie, *Fédération de l'industrie manufacturière (FIM-CSN)*, 709
Gaudet, Julien, *Association jeunesse fransaskoise*, 137
Gaudet, Charles, *Fédération des aînées et aînés francophones du Canada*, 711
Gaudet, Daniel, *Réseau des SADC et CAE*, 1221
Gaudet, Dorothy, *Eastern Charlotte Chamber of Commerce*, 670
Gaudette, Pamela, *Prairie Region Halfway House Association*, 1169
Gaudette, Jan, *Nova Scotia Golf Association*, 1045
Gaudette, Marco, *Association de la Construction Richelieu Yamaska*, 101
Gaudreau, Pierre, *Réseau d'aide aux personnes seiles et itinérantes de Montréal*, 1219
Gaudreault, Jérôme, *Association québécoise de prévention du suicide*, 171
Gaudreault, Gina, *Chambre immobilière de Québec*, 551
Gaudreault, Esther, *Association francophone pour le savoir*, 136

Gaudreault, Claire, *Association québécoise pour le loisir des personnes handicapées*, 177
Gaudreault-Martel, Julie, *Association des Grands Frères et Grandes Soeurs du Québec*, 115
Gaudry, Manon, *Association de neurochirurgie du Québec*, 103
Gaul, Alissa, *College of Naturopathic Doctors of Alberta*, 586
Gaulin, Jeff, *Canadian Association of Petroleum Producers*, 326
Gault, Gerry, *Grain Workers' Union, Local 333*, 779
Gauntlett, Rachel, *Esprit Orchestra*, 696
Gauthier, Mitch, *Credit Counselling Services of Cochrane District*, 640
Gauthier, Beth Corney, *Children's Wish Foundation of Canada*, 563
Gauthier, Gwenn, *Society for the Promotion of the Teaching of English as a Second Language in Quebec*, 1327
Gauthier, Carol, *Iroquois Falls Association for Community Living*, 864
Gauthier, David, *Atlantic Provinces Trial Lawyers Association*, 185
Gauthier, Julie, *Freight Carriers Association of Canada*, 759
Gauthier, Brigitte, *Canadian Dental Hygienists Association*, 377
Gauthier, Colette, *Learning Disabilities Association of Saskatchewan*, 905
Gauthier, Lise, *Fédération interdisciplinaire de l'horticulture ornementale du Québec*, 721
Gauthier, Ron, *Chartered Professionals in Human Resources Manitoba*, 554
Gauthier, Mélanie, *Canadian Association of Critical Care Nurses*, 311
Gauthier, Nathalie, *Ordre des infirmières et infirmiers du Québec*, 1122
Gauthier, Marie-Andrée, *Ordre des infirmières et infirmiers du Québec*, 1122
Gauthier, Gérald, *Railway Association of Canada*, 1203
Gauthier, Sue, *Saskatchewan Veterinary Medical Association*, 1277
Gauthier, Jean-René, *Société d'Horticulture et d'Écologie de Longueuil*, 1314
Gauthier, Mary, *Mechanical Contractors Association of Ottawa*, 957
Gauthier, Pierre, *Chemistry Industry Association of Canada*, 556
Gauthier, Marcel, *Thunder Bay Adventure Trails*, 1377
Gauthier, Luc, *Association des pompiers de Laval*, 124
Gauthier, Johanne, *Agape Food Bank*, 14
Gauthier, Jean-Marc, *Association québécoise pour le loisir des personnes handicapées*, 177
Gauthier, Alain, *Fédération québécoise des activités subaquatiques*, 728
Gauthier, Germaine, *Maison de Campagne & d'Entraide Communautaire du Lac*, 926
Gauthier, Maeva, *Explorer's Club (Canadian Chapter)*, 700
Gauthier, Jacques, *Société de généalogie de Lanaudière*, 1315
Gauthier, Natasha, *Canada's Public Policy Forum*, 283
Gauthier, Marie, *Association des psychothérapeutes psychanalytiques du Québec*, 127
Gauthier, David, *Genome Canada*, 769
Gauthier, Nancy, *Alberta Dressage Association*, 33
Gauthier, Paul-André, *Clinical Nurse Specialist Association of Ontario*, 574
Gauthier, Ninon, *International Association of Art Critics - Canada*, 854
Gauthier, Paule, *Canadian Dupuytren Society*, 379
Gauthier, Yvan, *Foundation of Greater Montreal*, 756

Gautrot, Jean-Jacques, *World Nuclear Association*, 1606
Gauvin, Holly, *Elevate NWO*, 684
Gauvin, Gaëtan, *Association du personnel administratif et professionnel de l'Université de Moncton*, 131
Gauvin, Pauline, *Canadian Office & Professional Employees Union*, 445
Gauvin, Louis, *Coalition québécoise pour le contrôle du tabac*, 578
Gaventa, William, *American Association on Intellectual & Developmental Disabilities*, 1490
Gavey, Linda, *Ontario Association of Committees of Adjustment & Consent Authorities*, 1063
Gavine, Kim, *Conservation Ontario*, 622
Gavrel, Gérard, *Electric Vehicle Council of Ottawa*, 682
Gavsie, Ronnie, *Trillium Gift of Life Network*, 1398
Gawronsky, Michelle, *Manitoba Government & General Employees' Union*, 937
Gaynor, Kim, *Vancouver Opera*, 1428
Gaze, Christopher, *Bard on the Beach Theatre Society*, 196
Gazley, Dave, *Tourism Vancouver/Greater Vancouver Convention & Visitors Bureau*, 1391
Gazzard, Nicholas, *Cooperative Housing Federation of Canada*, 628
Gazzola, Marino, *Canadian Catholic School Trustees' Association*, 351
Gbongbor, Andrew, *New Brunswick African Association Inc.*, 1004
Gearin, Seamus, *Canadian Decorators' Association*, 376
Geary, Jennifer, *The Trident Mediation Counselling & Support Foundation*, 1398
Gebre, Tefere, *American Federation of Labor & Congress of Industrial Organizations (AFL-CIO)*, 1493
Gebreab, Beth, *Eva's Initiatives for Homeless Youth*, 698
Geddert, Ron, *Canadian Association of Rent to Own Professionals*, 331
Geddes, Lisa, *Boating BC Association*, 216
Geddes, Ewan, *Ontario Association for Geographic & Environmental Education*, 1061
Geddes-Pfaff, Rosaire, *L'Arche Atlantic Region*, 77
Gee, Andrea, *Community Support Centre Haldimand-Norfolk*, 607
Gee, Sharon, *Dystonia Medical Research Foundation Canada*, 666
Gee, Ken, *Guelph Musicfest*, 793
Geertsma, Donna, *Marigold Enterprises Rehabilitation Services Society*, 949
Geffros, Scott, *Canadian Wood Pallet & Container Association*, 505
Geick, Steve, *Yukon Employees Union*, 1478
Geier, Bev, *Diamond Valley Chamber of Commerce*, 656
Geiger, John, *The Royal Canadian Geographical Society*, 1239
Geisler, Aaron, *Football Canada*, 750
Geiss, Bernie, *Canadian Society for Mucopolysaccharide & Related Diseases Inc.*, 477
Geist, Rose, *Israel Medical Association-Canadian Chapter*, 866
Geithner, Felix, *Wilderness Tourism Association of the Yukon*, 1454
Geitmann, Anja, *Canadian Society of Plant Biologists*, 487
Gekas, Michael, *Hellenic Canadian Board of Trade*, 811
Gelderman, Rosalie, *HelpAge Canada*, 812
Gélinas, François, *Société québécoise de spéléologie*, 1324
Gélinas, Serge, *Chambre de commerce et d'industrie du bassin de Chambly*, 547
Gélinas, Nathalie, *Ordre des infirmières et infirmiers du Québec*, 1122

Executive Name Index

Gélinas, Danielle, *Ordre des infirmières et infirmiers du Québec*, 1122
Gélinas, Micheline, *La Fédération des femmes acadiennes de la Nouvelle-Écosse*, 715
Gellatly, Dale, *Carizon Family & Community Services*, 513
Geller, Mitch, *Diving Plongeon Canada*, 660
Geller, Peter, *Association of Canadian Universities for Northern Studies*, 144
Gellhaus, Erin, *Alberta Alpine Ski Association*, 22
Gellner, Crystal, *Ringette Association of Saskatchewan*, 1232
Gelowitz, Christine, *Association of British Columbia Forest Professionals*, 140
Gelsomino, Mark, *Librarians Without Borders*, 910
Gelz, Des, *Animal Nutrition Association of Canada*, 71
Gemmell, Jay, *The John Howard Society of Ontario*, 875
Genaille, Sheila D., *Métis National Council of Women*, 963
Gendreau, Line, *Accessible Media Inc.*, 5
Gendron, Michelle, *Sports-Québec*, 1346
Gendron, Sylvain, *Syndicat québécois de la construction*, 1365
Gendron, Sylvain, *Syndicat de la fonction publique du Québec inc. (ind.)*, 1361
Gendron, Heather, *Art Libraries Society of North America*, 1506
Gendron, Agnes, *Cold Lake Native Friendship Centre*, 580
Gendron, Jennifer, *Lacrosse New Brunswick*, 895
Geneau, James, *Etobicoke Historical Society*, 697
Généreux, Bernard, *Fédération Québécoise des Municipalités*, 729
Genest, Danielle, *AIDS Saskatoon*, 17
Genest, Guy, *Réseau FADOQ*, 1224
Genest, Christian, *Association des statisticiennes et statisticiens du Québec*, 128
Gengatharan, Vinitha, *Agincourt Community Services Association*, 14
Gengatharan, Vinitha, *Agincourt Community Services Association*, 14
Genge, Catherine, *Luggage, Leathergoods, Handbags & Accessories Association of Canada*, 920
Genge, Dan, *Canadian Association of Snowboard Instructors*, 333
Gennings, Josh, *Canadian Institute for Theatre Technology*, 414
Genois, Réjean, *Tennis Québec*, 1371
Gensiorek, Vanessa, *Manitoba Community Newspapers Association*, 934
Gent, Derek, *Vancity Community Foundation*, 1424
Gentès, Mathieu, *Athletics Canada*, 181
Gentili, David, *Ontario Dental Association*, 1077
Genton, Kim, *Ontario Baton Twirling Association*, 1067
Geoffroy, Richard, *Association des Sourds de Lanaudière*, 128
Geoffroy, J. Gilles, *Société d'histoire Danville-Shipton*, 1310
Georgas, Marilynn, *Fitness New Brunswick*, 740
George, Martha, *Council of Ontario Construction Associations*, 634
George, Liliane, *GRAND Society*, 780
George, Chris, *Alberta Ballet*, 25
George, Torrie, *The Maritimes Energy Association*, 951
George, Phyllis, *Tecumseh Community Development Corporation*, 1369
George, Mike, *Southern First Nations Secretariat*, 1337
George, Vanessa, *Alberta Veterinary Technologist Association*, 51
George, Leonard, *Healing Our Spirit BC Aboriginal HIV/AIDS Society*, 805

George, Randy, *Project Management Institute*, 1585
George, Jim, *Institute of Packaging Professionals*, 1533
Georgescu, Maria, *Canadian Association of Optometrists*, 324
Georgopalis, Rene, *Archives Society of Alberta*, 81
Gerace, Rocco, *College of Physicians & Surgeons of Ontario*, 588
Gerard, Leo W., *United Steelworkers of America (AFL-CIO/CLC)*, 1600
Gerard, Lorraine, *British Columbia Hospice Palliative Care Association*, 243
Gerbasi, Jenny, *Federation of Canadian Municipalities*, 723
Gerber, Greg, *Society of Christian Schools in British Columbia*, 1328
Gerber, Sandy, *St. John Ambulance*, 1249
Gerber, Russ, *Christian Science*, 1517
Gerber, Gary, *Ontario Brain Injury Association*, 1069
Gerbig, Shelleen, *Smoky Applied Research & Demonstration Association*, 1305
Gerdts, Jennifer, *Food Allergy Canada*, 749
Gerein, Denise, *Chiropractors' Association of Saskatchewan*, 566
Gergatz, Megan, *Spina Bifida & Hydrocephalus Association of Northern Alberta*, 1342
Gerhardt, Lynne, *Nova Scotia Insurance Women's Association*, 1046
Gerlich-Fitzgerald, Krista, *BC Cheerleading Association*, 201
Gerlich-Fitzgerald, Krista, *Cheer Canada*, 555
Germain, Anne, *National Waste & Recycling Association*, 1577
Germain, Daniel, *Canadian Parking Association*, 450
German, Audrey, *Manitoba Antique Association*, 928
German, Peter, *International Centre for Criminal Law Reform & Criminal Justice Policy*, 854
Germiquet, Cori Lynn, *Habitat for Humanity Canada*, 796
Gérôme, Patrick, *Société des chefs, cuisiniers et pâtissiers du Québec*, 1317
Geroux, Denise, *Canadian Association of Critical Care Nurses*, 311
Gerow, Brad, *Kamloops & District Labour Council*, 880
Gerrard, Dennis, *Ontario Home Builders' Association*, 1086
Gerrard, Brock, *Saskatchewan Sports Hall of Fame & Museum*, 1276
Gerrard, John, *Habitat for Humanity Canada*, 797
Gerrie, Jamie, *Prince Rupert & District Chamber of Commerce*, 1179
Gerritsen, Susan, *Canadian Association of Critical Care Nurses*, 312
Gerritsen, Jennifer, *Youth Science Canada*, 1476
Gerrow, Jack D., *National Dental Examining Board of Canada*, 992
Gersdorff, Nicolas, *Canadian Crossroads International*, 373
Gerson, Marlene, *Jewish Community Foundation of Montréal*, 871
Gervais, Allison, *Synchro Manitoba*, 1360
Gervais, Bernard, *Canadian Owners & Pilots Association*, 448
Gervais, Bernard, *Association des Aviateurs et Pilotes de Brousse du Québec*, 106
Getz, Martina, *L'Arche Ontario*, 77
Gewurz, Brenda, *Jewish Community Foundation of Montréal*, 871
Ghabrial, Sarah, *Miss G Project*, 968
Ghadbane, Jim, *Canada's Advanced Internet Development Organization*, 282
Gharzai, Fatema, *American Society for Parenteral & Enteral Nutrition*, 1498
Ghazi Aissaoui, Mohamed, *Ordre des ingénieurs du Québec*, 1122
Ghiandoni, Vincenzo, *50 & Piu Enasco*, 735

Ghiz, Robert, *Canadian Wireless Telecommunications Association*, 504
Ghobros, Michael, *Project Management Institute*, 1585
Ghofrani, Surroosh, *Alberta Team Handball Federation*, 49
Ghosh, Anuradha (Ajay), *Association of Professional Engineers & Geoscientists of Alberta*, 157
Ghoussoub, Louise, *Information Services Vancouver*, 837
Giacomini, Rick, *Terrazzo, Tile & Marble Guild of Ontario, Inc.*, 1372
Giagkou, Anna, *Numeris*, 1051
Giakoumakis, Oura, *Qualicum Beach Chamber of Commerce*, 1195
Gialloreto, Robert, *Consumer Protection BC*, 626
Giammarco, Patsy, *Order of Sons of Italy in Canada*, 1119
Giannelia, Alex, *Canadian Institute of Geomatics*, 416
Gibb, Bill, *Canadian Society of Clinical Perfusion*, 482
Gibbens, Lynne M., *International Electrotechnical Commission - Canadian National Committee*, 857
Gibbins, Stefan, *Calgary Rock & Lapidary Club*, 274
Gibbon, Brian, *Ontario Field Ornithologists*, 1080
Gibbon, Brian, *Brereton Field Naturalists' Club Inc.*, 228
Gibbons, Kimberly, *Ontario Council for International Cooperation*, 1075
Gibbons, Del, *Associated Gospel Churches*, 89
Gibbons, Lorrie, *Pentecostal Assemblies of Canada*, 1150
Gibbons, Albert, *Royal Newfoundland Constabulary Association*, 1242
Gibbons, Ian, *Food for Life Canada*, 750
Gibbons, Jack, *Ontario Clean Air Alliance*, 1071
Gibbs, Brian, *Canadian Security Association*, 469
Gibbs, Lois Marie, *Center for Health, Environment & Justice*, 1516
Gibbs, Carmen, *Association acadienne des artistes professionnel.le.s du Nouveau-Brunswick*, 90
Gibeau, John, *Cloverdale & District Chamber of Commerce*, 574
Gibeau, Jean-Marc, *Agence municipale de financement et de développement des centres d'urgence 9-1-1 du Québec*, 14
Gibney, Laura, *Foothills Forage & Grazing Association*, 750
Gibran, Nicole S., *International Society for Burn Injuries*, 1557
Gibson, Janine, *Canadian Organic Growers Inc.*, 447
Gibson, Tammy, *Golf Manitoba Inc.*, 777
Gibson, Ken, *Alberta Construction Association*, 31
Gibson, Karien, *Justice for Children & Youth*, 878
Gibson, Dan, *American Political Science Association*, 1497
Gibson, Murray, *Manitoba Tobacco Reduction Alliance*, 946
Gibson, Jo-Anne, *Manitoba School Library Association*, 944
Gibson, Wayne, *Canadian Geotechnical Society*, 397
Gibson, Thomas J., *American Iron & Steel Institute*, 1494
Gibson, Jean, *Nature Nova Scotia (Federation of Nova Scotia Naturalists)*, 1000
Gibson, Jennifer L., *Joint Centre for Bioethics*, 875
Gibson, Deborah, *British Columbia Conservation Foundation*, 237
Gibson, Brooke, *Prader-Willi Syndrome Association of Alberta*, 1169

Gibson, Ernest, *The Factory: Hamilton Media Arts Centre*, 700
Gibson, Cathie, *New Westminster Hyack Festival Association*, 1015
Gibson, Caitlyn, *Society for Adolescent Health & Medicine*, 1589
Giddings, Alyssa, *Federation of Canadian Artists*, 723
Giddings, Kelly, *Manitoba Camping Association*, 933
Gidley, Jennifer, *World Futures Studies Federation*, 1605
Gidney, Marla, *Community Foundation of Prince Edward Island*, 598
Gidora, Timothy, *Communist Party of BC*, 594
Gieck, Alana, *Broadcast Educators Association of Canada*, 259
Giersch, Lynn, *Manitoba Water Well Association*, 947
Gies, Gary, *Alberta Construction Association*, 31
Giesbrecht, Don, *Canadian Child Care Federation*, 355
Giesbrecht, Ryan, *Manitoba Badminton Association*, 931
Giesbrecht, Monica, *Manitoba Association of Landscape Architects*, 930
Giesbrecht, Mike, *British Columbia Society of Respiratory Therapists*, 254
Giesen, Matt, *Aurora King Baseball Association*, 188
Gietz, Michelle, *Brooks & District Chamber of Commerce*, 260
Giffin, Todd, *Vegetable Growers' Association of Manitoba*, 1430
Giffin, Mark, *Canadian Powerlifting Union*, 459
Giffin, Geoff, *Atlantic Salmon Federation*, 186
Giffin, Greg, *Nova Central Ringette Association*, 1040
Gifford, Rhonda, *Ontario 5 Pin Bowlers' Association*, 1058
Gifford, Terry, *Certified Technicians & Technologists Association of Manitoba*, 538
Gifford, Terri-Lynn, *Bike to Work BC Society*, 211
Gifford, Mark, *Kiwassa Neighbourhood Services Association*, 892
Gifford, Alice, *Canadian Child Abuse Association*, 355
Gifford, Graham, *British Columbia Party*, 248
Gignac, Sylvie, *Société des technologues en nutrition*, 1318
Gignac, Lorraine, *Canadian Institute of Management*, 417
Gignac, Andrée, *Les Clubs 4-H du Québec*, 576
Gignac, Monique, *Canadian Arthritis Network*, 295
Gignac, Joan, *Aboriginal Head Start Association of British Columbia*, 2
Gignac, Kim, *Ontario Nonprofit Network*, 1094
Giguère, Alain, *Chambre de commerce de la région d'Acton*, 542
Giguère, Caroline, *Fédération québécoise des sociétés Alzheimer*, 730
Giguère, Francis, *The Canadian Corps of Commissionaires*, 365
Giguère, Anne, *Syndicat des professeures et professeurs de l'Université du Québec à Rimouski*, 1363
Giguère, Francine, *Fondation Ressources-Jeunesse*, 748
Giguère, Raymond, *Fédération des coopératives d'habitation Montérégiennes*, 714
Giguere, Jennifer, *Canadian Association of Defence & Security Industries*, 312
Giguère, Jean-Marie, *Fédération de l'UPA - Mauricie*, 709
Gilao, Mohamed, *Dejinta Beesha Multi-Service Centre*, 653
Gilbank, Sharon, *Prince Edward Island Aquaculture Alliance*, 1172
Gilbert, Jefferson, *Canadian Urban Libraries Council*, 500

Executive Name Index

Gilbert, Marie, *Secours aux lépreux (Canada) inc.*, 1288
Gilbert, Jen, *Ontario Camps Association*, 1070
Gilbert, Judi, *United Way of Quinte*, 1416
Gilbert, Donald, *Centre Psycho-Pédagogique de Québec Inc.*, 536
Gilbert, Paul-René, *Société d'histoire de Magog*, 1311
Giles, Amanda, *Boys & Girls Clubs of Ontario*, 223
Giles, Angela, *The Council of Canadians*, 633
Giles, Carla, *British Columbia Confederation of Parent Advisory Councils*, 237
Giles, Robert, *Toronto Transportation Society*, 1388
Gilgan, Peter, *Peter Gilgan Foundation*, 1153
Gilhespy, Beth, *The Bruce Trail Conservancy*, 261
Gilhula, Vicki, *Sudbury Arts Council*, 1353
Gilks, Rose, *SaskCulture Inc.*, 1280
Gill, Jasmine, *The Logistics Institute*, 917
Gill, Rodney, *Weyburn Chamber of Commerce*, 1451
Gill, Robert, *Army Cadet League of Canada*, 83
Gill, Nicolas, *Judo Canada*, 876
Gill, Dennis, *Newfoundland & Labrador Association for Community Living*, 1015
Gill, Goldi, *Ontario Dental Assistants Association*, 1077
Gill, Justine, *Canadian Anesthesiologists' Society*, 293
Gill, John, *National Screen Institute - Canada*, 996
Gill, Atma, *Peel Multicultural Council*, 1148
Gill, Kristy, *Variety - The Children's Charity of BC*, 1430
Gill, Heather, *Wildlife Rescue Association of British Columbia*, 1455
Gill, Jasmine, *World Literacy of Canada*, 1466
Gill, Alex, *Ontario Environment Industry Association*, 1078
Gill, Bruce, *Entomological Society of Ontario*, 690
Gill, Katelyn, *Jeunesse Acadienne et Francophone de l'Île-du-prince-Édouard*, 870
Gill, John D., *Le Bon Pilote inc.*, 217
Gill, Prem, *Creative BC*, 639
Gill, Joyce, *Société Saint-Thomas-d'Aquin*, 1325
Gill, Kamran, *Muslim Association of New Brunswick*, 985
Gill, Alex, *Canadian Environment Industry Association*, 381
Gillam, John, *Badminton Newfoundland & Labrador Inc.*, 193
Gillan, JoAnn, *Home Child Care Association of Ontario*, 819
Gillan, Jack, *Community Living Peterborough*, 604
Gillard, Art, *Fundy Stamp Collectors Club*, 764
Gillen, Lolly, *Squash Canada*, 1347
Gillespie, Michele, *Mackenzie Community Arts Council*, 924
Gillespie, Etelka, *Merritt & District Chamber of Commerce*, 962
Gillespie, Doreen, *Nova Scotia Society for the Prevention of Cruelty to Animals*, 1049
Gillespie, Duncan, *Canadian Training Institute*, 496
Gillespie, Sue, *Pathways to Education Canada*, 1145
Gillet, Brian, *Circulation Management Association of Canada*, 570
Gillette, Brenda, *Chilliwack Society for Community Living*, 563
Gillian-Bain, Gail, *Canadian Association of Business Incubation*, 309
Gilliard, Carol-Ann, *Hospitality Newfoundland & Labrador*, 823
Gillies, Jennifer, *Alzheimer Society Waterloo Wellington*, 66
Gillies, Donald, *Canadian Celtic Arts Association*, 353

Gillies, Joy, *Vernon Lapidary & Mineral Club*, 1431
Gillies, Nairn, *Saskatchewan Deaf & Hard of Hearing Services Inc.*, 1263
Gillis, Louise, *The Canadian Council of the Blind*, 370
Gillis, Claire, *Access Copyright*, 5
Gillis, Martin, *Provincial Dental Board of Nova Scotia*, 1190
Gillis, Rayna, *Ontario Good Roads Association*, 1083
Gillis, Edward, *The Professional Institute of the Public Service of Canada*, 1185
Gillis, Dianne, *Frasier Valley Orchid Society*, 758
Gillis, Margie, *Margie Gillis Dance Foundation*, 949
Gillis, John, *Liberal Party of Nova Scotia*, 909
Gillis, Sandra, *Talent Agents & Managers Association of Canada*, 1366
Gillis, Colin, *KidSport Nova Scotia*, 887
Gillivan, Jennifer, *IWK Health Centre Foundation*, 867
Gillson, Merv, *Canadian Institute of Underwriters*, 420
Gilman, Alec, *Automotive Recyclers Association of Manitoba*, 190
Gilman, Nicholas, *Montréal SPCA*, 973
Gilmer, Sheldon, *The Wesleyan Church of Canada - Central Canada District*, 1447
Gilmore, Shelley, *United Way of the Central Okanagan & South Okanagan/Similkameen*, 1417
Gilmour, Matthew W., *Canadian Association for Clinical Microbiology & Infectious Diseases*, 298
Gilmour, Darren, *The Royal Society of Canada*, 1243
Gilroy, Kevin, *Sask Sport Inc.*, 1254
Gilroy, Malcolm, *Lupus Canada*, 921
Gilson, Kelly, *United Way of Oxford*, 1416
Gilvesy, Bryan, *Alternative Land Use Services Canada*, 60
Gimigliano, Francesca, *International Society of Physical & Rehabilitation Medicine*, 1561
Gimore, Patricia, *Lymphoma Canada*, 923
Gin, Pascal, *Canadian Comparative Literature Association*, 361
Gingell, Susan, *Canadian Association for Commonwealth Literature & Language Studies*, 298
Gingell, Chris, *Alberta Dressage Association*, 33
Gingras, Stéphane, *Réseau québécois des groupes écologistes*, 1225
Gingras, Jonanne, *Fédération des professionnels et professionnelles de l'éducation du Québec*, 718
Gingras, Yolanda, *Société d'histoire de la MRC de l'Assomption*, 1310
Ginnish, Deborah, *Mi'kmaq Association for Cultural Studies*, 964
Ginter, Sally, *Ronald McDonald House Toronto*, 1235
Ginther, David, *OMF International - Canada*, 1058
Gionet, Théo, *Association des Pêcheurs de Longueuil*, 122
Gionet, Marc, *Falls Brook Centre*, 701
Giordan, Giuseppe, *Société internationale de sociologie des religions*, 1589
Giovanna Ruggieri, Maria, *Union mondiale des organisations féminines catholiques*, 1599
Gioventu, Tony, *Condominium Home Owners' Association of British Columbia*, 610
Giraldeau, Claudette, *Société de généalogie de Saint-Eustache*, 1315
Giraldeau, Denis, *Comité d'action Parc Extension*, 591
Giraldo, Lola, *Parliamentary Centre*, 1143
Girard, Sophie, *Fibrose kystique Québec*, 733
Girard, Véronic, *Chambre de commerce Témis-Accord*, 550

Girard, Jane, *New Brunswick Real Estate Association*, 1011
Girard, Gaëtan, *Canadian Ski Patrol*, 471
Girard, Luce, *Fondation québécoise du cancer*, 748
Girard, Brian, *Society of Professional Engineers & Associates*, 1330
Girard, Marlene, *Grands-Parents Tendresse*, 781
Girard, Christian, *Association franco-culturelle de Hay River*, 135
Girard, Jean-François, *Réseau des SADC et CAE*, 1220
Girard, Louise, *Association des cardiologues du Québec*, 108
Girard, François, *Recherches amérindiennes au Québec*, 1207
Girard, Jacques D., *Association des anciens élèves du collège Sainte-Marie*, 105
Girard, Jonathan, *University of British Columbia Symphony Orchestra*, 1419
Girard Riffou, Colette, *Centre de recherche et d'information en consommation de Port-Cartier*, 529
Girardeau, Lise, *Chambre immobilière de la Mauricie Inc.*, 550
Girardi, Carol, *Arts Council of Surrey*, 85
Girardot, Hélène, *Alliance Française de Calgary*, 57
Girdharry, Kevin, *Association of Home Appliance Manufacturers Canada Council*, 149
Girduckis, Emma, *Canadian Association of Management Consultants*, 320
Girling, Amanda, *HIV/AIDS Regional Services*, 817
Girouard, Jocelyn, *Chambre de commerce de Mont-Laurier*, 542
Girouard, Monica, *Manitoba Nurses' Union*, 941
Girouard, Yvan Noé, *Association des médias écrits communautaires du Québec*, 120
Girouard, Benoit, *Union Paysanne*, 1408
Giroux, Dan, *Community Living Glengarry*, 602
Giroux, Brian, *Scotia Fundy Mobile Gear Fishermen's Association*, 1286
Giroux, Jacques, *Canadian Aeronautics & Space Institute*, 289
Giroux, Michael, *Canadian Wood Council*, 505
Giroux, Nathalie, *Cancer Research Society*, 507
Giroux, Louis, *Club de marche moi mes souliers*, 575
Giroux, Monique, *Canadian Society for Traditional Music*, 479
Giroux, Jean-Philippe, *Opération Nez rouge*, 1116
Girvan, LoriAnn, *Artscape*, 86
Gitararen, Arutapani Peter, *Our Lady of Good Health Tamil Parish*, 1133
Gitcheva, Sashka, *British Columbia Rhythmic Sportive Gymnastics Federation*, 251
Gittens, Wendy, *Canadian Wheelchair Basketball Association*, 503
Gittens, JoAnne, *Intercultural Heritage Association*, 852
Gitzel, Tim, *World Nuclear Association*, 1606
Giusti, Dalila, *Canadian Acoustical Association*, 287
Givel, Jean-Claude, *International Society of Surgery*, 1561
Given, Mark, *Canadian Association of Medical Radiation Technologists*, 320
Given, James, *Seafarers' International Union of Canada (AFL-CIO/CLC)*, 1287
Gladu, J.P., *Canadian Council for Aboriginal Business*, 366
Gladue, Lawrence, *Frontiers Foundation*, 763
Glaicar, Jim, *Spruce City Wildlife Association*, 1346
Glanfield, Laurel, *Canadian Trakehner Horse Society*, 496
Glanville, Roderick, *Kaleidoscope Theatre Productions Society*, 880
Glaser, Ron, *Canadian Beef*, 342

Glaser, Tamar, *Na'amat Canada Inc.*, 987
Glassberg, Jeffrey, *North American Butterfly Association*, 1578
Glassco, Colin B., *Colin B. Glassco Charitable Foundation for Children*, 581
Glawson, Larry, *Manitoba Printmakers Association*, 942
Glazduri, Alex, *Ontario Dental Association*, 1077
Glazer, Sharon, *International Association for Cross-Cultural Psychology*, 1536
Glazier, Peter, *Ontario Lung Association*, 1090
Gleason, Bob, *Canadian Cat Association*, 351
Gledhill, Juanita, *Osteoporosis Canada*, 1128
Gleim, Phil, *Canadian Transplant Association*, 497
Gleisner, Kathy, *Alberta Genealogical Society*, 37
Glen, Ron, *Alberta Roadbuilders & Heavy Construction Association*, 44
Glen, Courtney, *Nova Scotia Archaeology Society*, 1040
Glen, Jim, *St Catharines Stamp Club*, 1248
Glen, Ian, *Wildlife Preservation Canada*, 1455
Glenday, Rob Walger, *Building Energy Management Manitoba*, 262
Glenn, Patricia, *Crohn's & Colitis Canada*, 642
Glenn, Daniel, *Atlantic Provinces Association of Landscape Architects*, 185
Glenn, Fran, *Tri-County Soccer Association*, 1398
Glennie, Dennis, *Saskatchewan Beekeepers Association*, 1259
Gliga, Basile, *Fondation roumaine de Montréal*, 748
Glizer, Victoria, *Canadian Artists' Representation Ontario*, 296
Gloade, Tammy, *Canadian Association of Elizabeth Fry Societies*, 313
Glofcheskie, Peter, *Wilno Heritage Society*, 1456
Glogowski, Konrad, *Pathways to Education Canada*, 1145
Glouchkow, Ellen, *Experiences Canada*, 700
Glover, Kelly, *Ronald McDonald House Charities of Canada*, 1235
Glover, Wayne, *Canadian Society of Safety Engineering, Inc.*, 488
Glover, Paul, *Association of Medical Microbiology & Infectious Disease Canada*, 152
Glumb, John C., *American Concrete Institute*, 1491
Glyptis, Stephanie, *Air & Waste Management Association*, 1486
Gnanam, Bala, *Building Owners & Managers Association Toronto*, 263
Gnarowski, Michael, *The Friends of Library & Archives Canada*, 761
Goa, Adele, *Alberta Genealogical Society*, 36
Goa, Kirsten, *La Leche League Canada*, 906
Goard, Marion, *Junior League of Hamilton-Burlington, Inc.*, 878
Gobeil, Chris, *Playwrights' Workshop Montréal*, 1162
Gobeil, Jean-Claude, *Association syndicale des employées de production et de service*, 178
Godbout, Patrick, *Speed Skating Canada*, 1341
Godbout, Laurent, *Fédération québécoise d'athlétisme*, 727
Godbout, Gaétan, *Société historique de la Côte-du-Sud*, 1320
Godbout, Danielle, *Association des commerçants de véhicules récréatifs du Québec*, 109
Goddard, Carol, *Big Brothers Big Sisters of Nova Scotia*, 210
Goddard, Bruce, *Canadian Association of Electroneurophysiology Technologists Inc.*, 312
Goddard, Lorraine, *United Way of Windsor-Essex County*, 1417

Goddard, Allan, Breton & District Historical Society, 228
Goddard, Jay, Boys & Girls Clubs of British Columbia, 222
Goddard, Carolyn, Stormont, Dundas & Glengarry Law Association, 1350
Godfrey, Robert, Prince Edward Island Federation of Agriculture, 1174
Godfrey, Eldon C., British North America Philatelic Society Ltd., 259
Godfrey, Doug, Municipal Law Enforcement Officers' Association, 981
Godfrey, Krista, Newfoundland & Labrador Library Association, 1020
Godfrey, Lynn, L'Arche Ontario, 77
Godin, Michel, Bathurst Volunteer Centre de Bénévolat Inc., 199
Godin, Caroline, MultiPrévention ASP: Association paritaire pour la santé et la sécurité au travail des secteurs: métal, électrique, habillement et imprimerie, 980
Godin, Mélanie, Agricultural Alliance of New Brunswick, 14
Godin, Lorraine, Ordre des ingénieurs du Québec, 1122
Godin, Louis, Fédération des médecins omnipraticiens du Québec, 716
Godlewska, Anne, Canadian Association of Geographers, 316
Godri, Cornelius, Winnipeg Musicians' Association, 1459
Godsall, Joseph, Canadian Motorcycle Association, 437
Godwin, Scott, Ontario Traffic Council, 1111
Goeres, Michael, Canadian Council of Ministers of the Environment, 368
Goertzen, Stan, Saskatoon City Police Association, 1279
Goetz, Jim, Canadian Beverage Association, 343
Goetz, Joe, Nova Scotia Beekeepers' Association, 1042
Goff, Corinne, Alliance for Canadian New Music Projects, 56
Goforth, Kelsey, Dying with Dignity, 665
Goggin, Valmai, Evergreen Theatre Society, 699
Gogolek, Vincent, British Columbia Freedom of Information & Privacy Association, 242
Goh, Chan Hon, Goh Ballet Society, 776
Goheen, Kevin, The Canadian Academy of Engineering, 286
Gokhale, Aneil, Toronto Community Foundation, 1383
Gokool, Shanaaz, Dying with Dignity, 665
Golby, Larry, Canadian Recreation Facilities Council, 465
Gold, Irving, Resident Doctors of Canada, 1226
Goldberg, Lyle, Canadian Society of Association Executives, 480
Goldberg, Jon M., The Atlantic Jewish Council, 184
Goldberg, Bryna, Israel Cancer Research Fund, 866
Goldberg, Elizabeth, Law Foundation of Ontario, 901
Goldberg, Mitchell, Canadian Association of Refugee Lawyers, 331
Golde, Peter, Canadian Mining Industry Research Organization, 437
Goldenberg, Bobbye, Family Counselling Centre of Cambridge & North Dumfries, 703
Goldfarb, Eldad, Jewish Community Centre of Greater Vancouver, 871
Goldfarb, Jeff, JVS of Greater Toronto, 879
Goldfeder, Matthew, American Council of Learned Societies, 1492
Goldfiner, Danielle, Not Far From The Tree, 1040
Goldhaber, Martin, Geochemical Society, 1527
Golding, Jasen, Association of Registered Professional Foresters of New Brunswick, 161
Golding, Linda, Northwest Territories & Nunavut Association of Professional Engineers & Geoscientists, 1037
Golding, Dawn, The Royal Canadian Legion, 1240
Goldman, Phil, Queen's University Faculty Association, 1200
Goldman, Claudia, Canadian Hadassah WIZO, 399
Goldman, Jennifer, Foodservice & Packaging Institute, 1526
Goldman, Charon, Toronto Hebrew Benevolent Society, 1385
Goldman-Brown, Rochelle, Chai-Tikvah The Life & Hope Foundation, 539
Goldrick, Jeanne Anne, The Garden Clubs of Ontario, 767
Goldsmid, Bruce, British Columbia Alpine Ski Association, 230
Goldstein, Yisroel Dovid, Hatzoloh Toronto, 804
Goldstein, Ellen, Forever Chai Foundation of Canada, 752
Goldstine, Elaine, The Centre for Israel & Jewish Affairs, 533
Goldsworthy, Nicole, Saskatchewan Association of Recreation Professionals, 1258
Goldthorp, Kevin, Mount Sinai Hospital Foundation, 976
Golfman, Jeff, Green Kids Inc., 788
Golfman, Noreen, St. John's International Women's Film Festival, 1249
Golick, Jill, Writers Guild of Canada, 1468
Goliger, Gabriella, Canadian Friends of Peace Now (Shalom Achshav), 395
Gollin, James D., Rainforest Action Network, 1586
Goluboff, Alan, Directors Guild of Canada, 658
Gomes, Francisco, World Aquaculture Society, 1603
Gomes, Elmer, Canadian Cancer Society, 349
Gomes da Silva, Josué C., International Textile Manufacturers Federation, 1562
Gomez, Franck, Association québécoise de canoë-kayak de vitesse, 169
Gomez, John, Ottawa Youth Orchestra Academy, 1132
Gomez-Insausti, Ricardo, Numeris, 1051
Gonçalves, Mario D., Conseil de l'enveloppe du bâtiment du Québec, 615
Goncalves, Renee, Canadian Safe School Network, 468
Gonda, Gabe, The Canadian Art Foundation, 295
Gonnason, Trevor, Risk & Insurance Management Society Inc., 1234
Gonsalves, Lynn, Junior Achievement Canada, 877
Gonthier, Ginette, Phobies-Zéro, 1157
Gonthier, Isabelle, Financial Planning Standards Council, 737
Gontovnick, Larry, Victoria Society for Humanistic Judaism, 1433
Gonzales, Mercedita, Association of Filipino Canadian Accountants, 148
Gonzales Soria, Julio, Inter-American Commercial Arbitration Commission, 851
Gonzalez, Beatriz, Canadian Crossroads International, 373
Gonzalez, Victor, Canadian Anesthesiologists' Society, 293
Gonzalez, Gladys, European Association of Geoscientists & Engineers, 1524
Gonzalez, Carmen, Alliance des communautés culturelles pour l'égalité dans la santé et les services sociaux, 55
Gonzalez, Daniel, Canadian Pastry Chefs Guild Inc., 451
Gooch, Peter, Ontario Council on Graduate Studies, 1075
Gooch, Daniel-Robert, Canadian Airports Council, 291
Gooch, Peter, Ontario Association of Deans of Education, 1063
Good, Elaine, Canadian Cutting Horse Association, 375
Good, Laura, Brockville & District Chamber of Commerce, 260
Good, Doug, Big Rideau Lake Association, 210
Good, James, Good Foundation Inc., 777
Goode, Glenn, Fellowship of Evangelical Baptist Churches, 731
Goodfeather, Kevin, Saskatchewan Deaf Sports Association, 1263
Goodfellow, Jessica, Canadian Federation of Agriculture, 384
Goodfellow, Robert, Amnesty International - Canadian Section (English Speaking), 68
Goodhue, Michelle & Bruce, Dystonia Medical Research Foundation Canada, 666
Goodine, Jennifer, Canadian Association of Municipal Administrators, 321
Goodleaf, Donna, First Nations Confederacy of Cultural Education Centres, 738
Goodman, Judy, Revelstoke Chamber of Commerce, 1228
Goodman, Teresa, International Commission on Illumination, 1542
Goodman, Kim, Manitoba Operating Room Nurses Association, 941
Goodman, Kevin, B'nai Brith Youth Organization, 192
Goodman, Dave, Emo Chamber of Commerce, 686
Goodman, Mary, Emo Chamber of Commerce, 686
Goodman, Kim, Environmental Information Association, 1523
Goodridge, Laureen, Manitoba Association of Optometrists, 930
Goodridge, Alan. Paddle Newfoundland & Labrador, 1137
Goodship, Stephen, Canadian Security Association, 469
Goodtrack, Terry, AFOA Canada, 12
Goodwin, Shelley, Association of Psychologists of Nova Scotia, 160
Goodwin, Roger, Schizophrenia Society of Alberta, 1283
Goodwin, Carry, Parrsboro & District Board of Trade, 1143
Goodwin, Doug, United Church of Canada, 1409
Goodwin, Gary, Ducks Unlimited Canada, 663
Goodwin, Terry. Probation Officers Association of Ontario, 1181
Goodwin, Michael, Office & Professional Employees International Union (AFL-CIO/CLC), 1580
Goodwin, Stephen, Human Resources Professionals Association, 825
Goodyear, Pam, The Salvation Army in Canada, 1253
Gooneratne, Felix, International Institute for Energy Conservation, 1551
Goossen, Tam, Urban Alliance on Race Relations, 1422
Goranson, Kevin, Friends of Music Therapy, 761
Gordey, Gordon, Alberta Ukrainian Dance Association, 50
Gordiano, Vicky, AIESEC, 18
Gordienko, Mark, International Longshore & Warehouse Union (CLC), 1553
Gordon, Kevin, Canadian Marketing Association, 431
Gordon, Christene, Alzheimer Society of Alberta & Northwest Territories, 61
Gordon, Britany, Canadian Lacrosse Association, 425
Gordon, Britany, Squash Canada, 1347
Gordon, Eileen, Canadian Celiac Association, 352
Gordon, Heather, Na'amat Canada Inc., 987
Gordon, William, Associated Manitoba Arts Festivals, Inc., 89
Gordon, Joyce, Parkinson Canada, 1141
Gordon, Sheldon, Canadian Friends of Peace Now (Shalom Achshav), 395
Gordon, Jeffrey A., American Birding Association, Inc., 1490
Gordon, Christine, BC Association for Individualized Technology and Supports, 201
Gordon, Martha, Réseau des SADC et CAE, 1220
Gordon, Aidan, Canadian Society for Engineering Management, 474
Gordon, Geoff, Ontario Vegetation Management Association, 1112
Gordon, Mark T., Mutual Fund Dealers Association of Canada, 986
Gordon, James, Freshwater Fisheries Society of British Columbia, 760
Gordon, Joyce, Neurological Health Charities Canada, 1004
Gordon, Zana, Fenestration Association of BC, 732
Gordon, Cathy, CADORA Ontario Association Inc., 269
Gore, Joanne, Xplor Canada Association, 1470
Goren, Ilaneet, Urban Alliance on Race Relations, 1422
Gorgerat, Karen, The Canadian Federation of Business & Professional Women's Clubs, 385
Gorham, Roberta, Appaloosa Horse Club of Canada, 73
Goriani, Mike, Canadian Italian Business & Professional Association, 423
Gorin, Robert David, Canadian Association of Provincial Court Judges, 329
Gorkoff, Jim, Royal Astronomical Society of Canada, 1239
Gorley, Al, McGregor Model Forest, 955
Gorman, Jennifer, Canadian Foundation for Masorti Judaism, 393
Gorman, Fred, Alberta Weekly Newspapers Association, 51
Gorman, Jennifer, United Way of Cochrane-Timiskaming, 1414
Gorman, Sean, Pride of Israel, 1170
Gorman, Jennifer, Mercaz-Canada, 961
Gorman, Marlene, YWCA Canada, 1481
Gorman, John A., Canadian Solar Industries Association, 489
Gormley, Michael A., Alberta Medical Association, 40
Gorrie, Jon, Alberta Sulphur Research Ltd., 48
Gorrie, Melissa, Alberta Environmental Network, 34
Gorsuch, Wanda, British Columbia Farm Industry Review Board, 240
Gortsos, George, Canadian Ball Hockey Association, 340
Gorveatt, Marg, Canadian Celiac Association, 352
Gorveatt, Brian, Royal Astronomical Society of Canada, 1238
Gorven, Kelly, Ontario Community Newspapers Association, 1073
Goseltine, Alexandra, BC Northern Real Estate Association, 202
Gosiewski, Sean, Alliance for Sustainability, 1487
Goslinkski, Matthew, Presbyterian Church in Canada, 1170
Gospodaric, Dori, Canadian Imaging Trade Association, 410
Gosselin, Mélanie, Conseil de la culture des Laurentides, 616
Gosselin, Guy, The Engineering Institute of Canada, 688
Gosselin, Jacques, Association des familles Gosselin, Inc., 113
Gosselin, William, Association des familles Gosselin, Inc., 113
Gosselin, Pierrette, The Professional Institute of the Public Service of Canada, 1185
Gosselin, Catherine, Syndicat des professeurs et professeures de l'Université du Québec à Montréal, 1364
Gosselin, Martine, Ordre des Podiatres du Québec, 1123

Executive Name Index

Gosselin, Aggie, *La chambre de commerce de Saint-Malo & District*, 543
Gosselin-Després, Catherine, *Canadian Paralympic Committee*, 449
Gossen, Cecilia, *Fort Calgary Society*, 752
Gossen, Randy, *World Petroleum Council*, 1607
Gotlieb, Walter, *Society of Gynecologic Oncologists of Canada*, 1329
Gotlieb, Todd, *Ontario Brain Injury Association*, 1069
Gots, Edward, *Youth Empowerment & Support Services*, 1475
Gottlieb, Lori, *Royal College of Dentists of Canada*, 1241
Gottlieb, Steven, *Boundless Adventures Association*, 219
Gottschalk, Tony, *Hearth, Patio & Barbecue Association of Canada*, 810
Goubko, Greg, *Toronto Renewable Energy Co-operative*, 1387
Goudou, Olivia, *Canadian Executive Service Organization*, 383
Goudoury, Michel, *Regroupement Pour-Valorisation*, 1216
Goudreau, Mitch, *Edmonton Numismatic Society*, 678
Goudy, Roger, *Amateur Athletic Union*, 1487
Gougen, Christine, *Bereaved Families of Ontario*, 205
Gougeon, Yves, *Action Intégration en Déficience Intellectuelle*, 6
Gough, Peter, *Society of Canadian Artists*, 1327
Gough, Tim, *Alberta Union of Provincial Employees*, 50
Gough, Linda, *College of Medical Radiation Technologists of Ontario*, 586
Gough, John, *GLOBE Foundation*, 775
Gouhin, Patrick, *The Instrumentation, Systems & Automation Society of America*, 1534
Gouie, Terry, *Canadian Council of Montessori Administrators*, 369
Goulah, Peter, *Belleville Police Association*, 204
Goulard, Jacynthe, *Ontario Disc Sports Association*, 1077
Gould, Denise, *Community Care Peterborough*, 596
Gould, Penny, *Stony Plain & District Chamber of Commerce*, 1350
Gould, Darrold, *Bide Awhile Animal Shelter Society*, 209
Gould, Peter, *Canadian Association of Neuropathologists*, 322
Gould, Ben, *Allen & Milli Gould Family Foundation*, 54
Gould, Lee, *Canadian Medical Foundation*, 434
Gould, Barbara, *National Magazine Awards Foundation*, 995
Gould, Peter, *Dairy Farmers of Ontario*, 648
Gould, Ian, *International Society of Chemotherapy for Infection & Cancer*, 1560
Gould, Kelly, *Human Resources Professionals of Newfoundland & Labrador*, 826
Gould, Chris, *Canadian Warmblood Horse Breeders Association*, 502
Gould-Thorpe, Joanna, *Avon Chamber of Commerce*, 191
Goulden, Jen, *Braille Literacy Canada*, 225
Goulden, Randy, *Yorkton Film Festival*, 1474
Goulding, John, *The Salvation Army in Canada*, 1253
Goulding, Paula, *Canadian Society of Association Executives*, 480
Goulet, Martin, *Water Polo Canada*, 1441
Goulet, Gilles, *Réseau des SADC et CAE*, 1220
Goulet, Nathalie, *Conseil d'intervention pour l'accès des femmes au travail*, 615
Goulet, Josée, *First Nations SchoolNet*, 739
Goulet, Paulette, *Association québécoise pour le loisir des personnes handicapées*, 177
Goulet, Tony, *Quesnel Tillicum Society Friendship Centre*, 1201

Goulet, Paulette, *Les Amis de la déficience intellectuelle Rive-Nord*, 67
Goulet, Mathieu, *Les AmiEs de la Terre de Québec*, 67
Goulet, Claude, *Collectif pour un Québec sans pauvreté*, 581
Goulet, Liza, *Philanthropic Foundations Canada*, 1157
Goulin, Lyanne, *Children's Wish Foundation of Canada*, 562
Goupil, Rémi, *Fédération des jeunes francophones du Nouveau-Brunswick Inc.*, 715
Goupil, Sébastien, *Canadian Commission for UNESCO*, 360
Gourdeau, Jean-Guy, *Fondation de l'Hôpital Général de Montréal*, 744
Gourdeau, Virginie, *Jeune chambre de commerce de Québec*, 870
Gourley, Philippa, *Council of Canadian Fire Marshals & Fire Commissioners*, 633
Gouthro Snow, Judy, *Haley Street Adult Services Centre Society*, 798
Gouveia, Wayne, *Air Transport Association of Canada*, 19
Gouveia, Zachary, *Professional Engineers Ontario*, 1185
Gouws, Daniel, *Occupational & Environmental Medical Association of Canada*, 1054
Gove, Alan, *Vancouver Symphony Society*, 1429
Govender, Kasari, *Women's Legal Education & Action Fund*, 1463
Gover, Jerome, *Canadian Hard of Hearing Association*, 400
Gow-Boyd, Pamela, *Canadian National Institute for the Blind*, 439
Gowda, Kempe S., *Canadian Association of Physicians of Indian Heritage*, 327
Gowie, Lynette, *Canadian Down Syndrome Society*, 378
Gowler, Scott, *Wasagaming Chamber of Commerce*, 1440
Gowridge, Kathy, *Fraser Valley Labour Council*, 758
Goyer, Guy, *Chambre de commerce de Sainte-Adèle*, 543
Goyer, Jean-Pierre, *Last Post Fund*, 899
Goyer, René, *Corporation des thanatologues du Québec*, 631
Goyer, Alex, *Fédération étudiante universitaire du Québec*, 720
Goyette, Robert, *Association québécoise des éditeurs de magazines*, 172
Goyette, Sylvie, *Association des arts thérapeutes du Québec*, 106
Grabosky, Kevin, *Syndicat des Agents Correctionnels du Canada (CSN)*, 1362
Graça Filho, Ary S., *International Volleyball Association*, 1566
Grace, Gord, *Ontario University Athletics*, 1112
Grace, Treena, *Heatherton Activity Centre*, 810
Gracey, Marion, *The Muttart Foundation*, 986
Gracie, Audrey, *The John Howard Society of Newfoundland & Labrador*, 874
Grad, Marya, *Forever Chai Foundation of Canada*, 752
Gradon, Jamie, *Canada West Foundation*, 281
Grady, D. Gary, *International Society of Friendship & Good Will*, 1560
Grady, Emily, *Canadian Avalanche Association*, 340
Graf, Rudy, *Automotive Aftermarket Retailers of Ontario*, 189
Graf, Jennifer, *Canadian Association of Critical Care Nurses*, 311
Graf, Jennifer, *Canadian Association of Critical Care Nurses*, 311
Graf, Peter, *Canadian Society for Brain, Behaviour & Cognitive Science*, 473
Grafstein, Mike, *Canadian Sport Massage Therapists Association*, 490
Grafton, Jill, *Nova Scotia Society for the Prevention of Cruelty to Animals*, 1049

Graham, Lynn, *Canadian Cutting Horse Association*, 375
Graham, Ivan, *Sussex & District Chamber of Commerce*, 1357
Graham, Alexander T., *Council for Exceptional Children*, 1520
Graham, Nicole, *Saskatchewan Association for Community Living*, 1256
Graham, Clyde, *Fertilizer Canada*, 733
Graham, Brian, *Saskatchewan Lung Association*, 1269
Graham, Cathy, *Kootenay Real Estate Board*, 892
Graham, Susan, *Voyageur Trail Association*, 1439
Graham, Heather, *Insurance Institute of Ontario*, 850
Graham, Gail, *Canadian College of Medical Geneticists*, 359
Graham, Wendy, *Newfoundland & Labrador Medical Association*, 1020
Graham, Skip, *St. Leonard's Society of Canada*, 1250
Graham, Franklin, *Samaritan's Purse Canada*, 1253
Graham, Tom, *Canadian Union of Public Employees*, 499
Graham, Ron, *Canadian Federal Pilots Association*, 384
Graham, JoAnne, *Association of New Brunswick Licensed Practical Nurses*, 153
Graham, Jane, *Ontario Commercial Fisheries' Association*, 1073
Graham, Patrick, *Seventh Step Society of Canada*, 1292
Graham, Andrew, *Ontario Soil & Crop Improvement Association*, 1108
Graham, Josie, *Canadian Innovation Centre*, 412
Graham, John, *American Society of Association Executives*, 1499
Graham, Richmond, *Institute of Certified Management Consultants of Saskatchewan*, 845
Graham, Susan, *Dartmouth Ringette Association*, 651
Graham, Roy, *Brewery, Winery & Distillery Workers Union - Local 300*, 228
Graham, Caroline, *Aquaculture Association of Canada*, 75
Graham, Florence, *British Columbia Registered Music Teachers' Association*, 251
Graham, Harold, *Brier Island Chamber of Commerce*, 229
Graham, Darcelle, *National Sunflower Association of Canada*, 996
Graham, Anna, *Catholic Action Montreal*, 517
Graham Walker, Ann, *Federation of British Columbia Writers*, 722
Grahamslaw, Colin, *World Curling Federation*, 1604
Grahlman, Doug, *Registered Insurance Brokers of Ontario*, 1213
Granado, Carlos, *Computer Modelling Group*, 609
Granat, Peter, *QMI - SAI Global*, 1195
Granata, Tania, *Alliance for Canadian New Music Projects*, 56
Grand'Maison, Roland, *Réseau Technoscience*, 1226
Grand-Maître, Jean, *Alberta Ballet*, 25
Grande, Laurie, *Alzheimer Society of Alberta & Northwest Territories*, 61
Grande, Jon, *International Game Developers Association*, 1549
Grandel, Bruce, *Alberta Horseshoe Pitchers Association*, 38
Grando, Sue, *Community Living Essex County*, 602
Granger, Christine, *Association québécoise de canoë-kayak de vitesse*, 169
Granger, Andrea, *Canadian Land Reclamation Association*, 425
Granger, Lucie, *Association pour la santé publique du Québec*, 167

Granger, Roland, *Association des fondations d'établissements de santé du Québec*, 114
Granger, Anique, *Association des professionnels de la chanson et de la musique*, 125
Granger, Daniel, *Jeux Olympiques Spéciaux du Québec Inc.*, 871
Granke, Robert, *Canadian Lutheran World Relief*, 428
Grant, Ursula, *Canadian Wireless Telecommunications Association*, 504
Grant, Chantelle, *Arts Etobicoke*, 85
Grant, Lee, *Canadian Association of Fire Chiefs*, 315
Grant, David, *Professional Engineers Ontario*, 1184
Grant, Sherry, *Nova Scotia Home Builders' Association*, 1046
Grant, Patricia, *College of Dental Hygienists of Nova Scotia*, 583
Grant, Jennifer, *Symphony New Brunswick*, 1360
Grant, Stewart, *Orchestre symphonique des jeunes du West Island*, 1118
Grant, Laura, *American Rhododendron Society*, 1497
Grant, Barry, *Medical Library Association*, 1570
Grant, Glenn, *Kamloops Wildlife Park Society*, 881
Grant, Beth, *Recreation Prince Edward Island*, 1208
Grant, Scott A., *Calgary Marching Showband Association*, 273
Grant, Lisa, *Alberta Lacrosse Association*, 39
Grant, John, *Trillium Party of Ontario*, 1399
Grant Fiander, Darlene, *Tourism Industry Association of Nova Scotia*, 1390
Grant-Walsh, Margie, *Big Brothers Big Sisters of Nova Scotia*, 210
Grantham, Tammy, *Alberta Genealogical Society*, 36
Grantham, Andrea, *Canadian Nutrition Society*, 444
Granton, John, *Canadian Thoracic Society*, 494
Granvig, Marianne, *Fédération mondiale des concours internationaux de musique*, 1526
Grasse, Daniel, *Grand Orange Lodge of Canada*, 780
Graszat, Karen, *Breast Cancer Action*, 227
Gratta, Domenic, *Catholic Children's Aid Society of Toronto*, 518
Gratton, Yves, *Canadian Meteorological & Oceanographic Society*, 436
Gratton, Pierre, *Mining Association of Canada*, 967
Gratton, Renée L., *Construction Resource Initiatives Council*, 624
Gratton, Jean-François, *Financial Markets Association of Canada*, 737
Gravani, Robert, *Institute of Food Technologists*, 1532
Gravel, François, *Canadian Society of Association Executives*, 480
Gravel, Florent, *Association des détaillants en alimentation du Québec*, 110
Gravel, Pierre, *Société d'histoire et de généalogie des Pays-d'en-Haut, inc.*, 1313
Graveline, Pierre, *Fondation Lionel-Groulx*, 747
Gravelle, Léo, *Voitures anciennes du Québec inc.*, 1437
Gravelle, Léo, *Canadian Forces Logistics Association - Montréal*, 392
Graves, David, *The CPR Stockholder's Society*, 638
Graves, Julie, *Canadian Society of Cardiac Surgeons*, 481
Graves, Shirley, *New Brunswick Genealogical Society Inc.*, 1008
Graves, Terry, *Temiskaming Environmental Action Committee*, 1370
Graves, Charles, *Saint John Naturalists' Club*, 1247

Graveson, Éric, *Chambre de commerce et d'industrie Magog-Orford*, 547
Gray, David, *BMW Clubs Canada*, 216
Gray, Sandra, *Arrowsmith Naturalists*, 84
Gray, Terri, *Community Living Oshawa / Clarington*, 604
Gray, Jean, *Alberta Genealogical Society*, 36
Gray, Devin, *Ontario Federation of School Athletic Associations*, 1080
Gray, Doug, *Ontario Genealogical Society*, 1082
Gray, Kerry, *Probation Officers Association of Ontario*, 1181
Gray, Maureen, *St. John Ambulance*, 1249
Gray, Corinne, *I.C.C. Foundation*, 829
Gray, Tim, *Environmental Defence*, 691
Gray, Rachel, *The Stop Community Food Centre*, 1350
Gray, David, *Eastern Ontario Beekeepers' Association*, 670
Gray Edwards, Karen, *American Sociological Association*, 1503
Graydon, Jay, *Centre for Effective Practice Inc.*, 532
Grayson, Scott, *Canadian Public Works Association*, 464
Grayson, Chris, *Community Living Upper Ottawa Valley*, 605
Grayson, Scott, *American Public Works Association*, 1497
Grayston, Corryn, *Salmon Arm & District Chamber of Commerce*, 1252
Greaney, Patrick, *Canadian Association of Movers*, 321
Greatrex, Geoffrey, *Canadian Committee of Byzantinists*, 361
Gréau, Pascaline, *Association franco-culturelle de Yellowknife*, 135
Greaves, Howard, *The Alcuin Society*, 53
Greaves, Lynn, *Saskatchewan Coalition for Tobacco Reduction*, 1261
Greaves, Helen, *South Okanagan Immigrant & Community Services*, 1335
Greaves, Jinny, *Prince Edward Island Literacy Alliance Inc.*, 1175
Grech, Jane, *Ontario Brain Injury Association*, 1068
Greco, Rebeca, *East Wellington Community Services*, 669
Greco, Alba, *Canadian Society of Orthopaedic Technologists*, 485
Greedy, Derek, *International Solid Waste Association*, 1562
Greeff, Stephanus, *Canadian Hearing Society*, 403
Greek, Mike, *Special Olympics Nova Scotia*, 1340
Greek, Richard, *The Ark/Lunenburg County Association for the Specially Challenged*, 81
Green, Gary, *The Crow's Nest Military Artifacts Association*, 644
Green, Clay, *The Waterbird Society*, 1602
Green, Brian, *Simon Fraser University Faculty Association*, 1300
Green, Shelley, *British Columbia Principals & Vice-Principals Association*, 249
Green, Kenneth P., *The Fraser Institute*, 757
Green, Anna, *British Columbia Purebred Sheep Breeders' Association*, 250
Green, Buzz, *Muscular Dystrophy Canada*, 982
Green, Don, *Canadian Country Music Association*, 372
Green, Ron, *New Brunswick Genealogical Society Inc.*, 1008
Green, Daniel, *Green Party of Canada*, 788
Green, Chris, *Postal History Society of Canada*, 1168
Green, Lyn, *Society for the Study of Egyptian Antiquities*, 1327
Green, Wayne, *United Way of the Fraser Valley*, 1417
Green, Howard, *British Columbia Podiatric Medical Association*, 249
Green, Terry, *South Okanagan Boundary Labour Council*, 1335

Green, Lori, *Massage Therapist Association of Saskatchewan*, 953
Green, Jeff, *Electrical Contractors Association of Quinte-St. Lawrence*, 683
Green, Kelly, *Canadian Canola Growers Association*, 349
Green, Kim, *The Capital Commission of Prince Edward Island Inc.*, 510
Green, Evan, *American Immigration Lawyers Association - Canadian Chapter*, 66
Green, Ian, *Northeast Highlands Chamber of Commerce*, 1034
Green, David, *Association of Chartered Industrial Designers of Ontario*, 145
Green, Kait, *Dress for Success*, 663
Green, Michael, *Canada Health Infoway*, 280
Green, Alistair, *Vancouver Island Society for Disabled Artists*, 1427
Green, Brenda, *Miniature Horse Association of Nova Scotia*, 966
Green, Phil, *Polyurethane Manufacturers Association*, 1584
Green, Stefanie, *Canadian Association of MAiD Assessors & Providers*, 320
Greenan, Blair, *Canadian Meteorological & Oceanographic Society*, 436
Greenaway, Aimee, *Nanaimo District Museum*, 987
Greenbaum, Mona, *Coalition des familles LGBT*, 577
Greenberg, Aaron, *Hillel of Greater Toronto*, 815
Greenberg, David, *Canadian Society for the Study of the Aging Male*, 478
Greene, Wendy, *Association canadienne des interprètes de conférence*, 90
Greene, Ronald, *Canadian Numismatic Research Society*, 442
Greene, Don H., *Institute of Industrial & Systems Engineers*, 1533
Greene, Angie, *Yarmouth & Area Chamber of Commerce*, 1470
Greene, Marion, *Ecojustice Canada Society*, 672
Greene, Terrance, *Community One Foundation*, 607
Greene, Dale, *Richmond Agricultural Society*, 1230
Greenfield, Tony, *Sunshine Coast Natural History Society*, 1355
Greenfield, Kirsten, *Canadian Hydrographic Association*, 409
Greenfield McManus, Elisabeth, *International Society for Burn Injuries*, 1557
Greenhalgh, Jennifer, *Fort Frances Chamber of Commerce*, 752
Greenhalgh, Chloe, *Dragon Boat Canada*, 662
Greenham, Merv, *Newfoundland & Labrador Table Tennis Association*, 1022
Greening, Laura, *Canadian Association of Insurance Women*, 319
Greenleaf Brassert, Amya, *Canadian Association of Women Executives & Entrepreneurs*, 336
Greenough, Dave, *Nova Scotia Table Tennis Association*, 1049
Greenough, Jim, *Cheer Canada*, 555
Greensides, Paul, *Canadian Association of Veterans in United Nations Peacekeeping*, 335
Greenstein, Howard, *College of Naturopathic Physicians of British Columbia*, 586
Greenstone, Warren, *Miriam Foundation*, 968
Greenstreet, Jodi, *CrossTrainers Canada*, 644
Greenwood, Robert, *Sun Ergos, A Company of Theatre & Dance*, 1354
Greenwood, Sally, *Genome Canada*, 769
Greenwood-Graham, Karyn, *Affected Families of Police Homicide*, 11
Greer, Dwight, *Ontario Institute of Agrologists*, 1087
Greer, Lori, *United Way of Stormont, Dundas & Glengarry*, 1417
Greer, John, *Canadian Concrete Pipe Association*, 362

Greer, Jolene, *West Nipissing Chamber of Commerce*, 1446
Greer, Darren, *The Identification Clinic*, 829
Greeson, Erin, *The Planetary Society*, 1584
Greetham, Georgia, *Yukon Conservation Society*, 1478
Greg, Constable, *Global Outreach Mission*, 775
Gregersen, Darrell, *CAMH Foundation*, 276
Gregg, Amber, *Quesnel & District Chamber of Commerce*, 1200
Gregg, Beverlee, *New Brunswick Genealogical Society Inc.*, 1009
Gregg, Randy, *FunTeam Alberta*, 765
Gregoire, Joanne, *Shaunavon Chamber of Commerce*, 1294
Grégoire, Geneviève, *Fédération québécoise des sociétés Alzheimer*, 730
Gregoire, Michael, *Association of Professional Engineers & Geoscientists of Manitoba*, 158
Grégoire, Martine, *Réseau FADOQ*, 1224
Grégoire, Maryse, *Ordre des infirmières et infirmiers du Québec*, 1122
Grégoire, Benoit, *Association des embouteilleurs d'eau du Québec*, 111
Grégoire, Normand, *La cinémathèque québécoise*, 570
Grégoire, Lucie, *Lucie Grégoire Danse*, 920
Gregorchuk, John, *Canadian Mineral Analysts*, 436
Gregorwich, Stephanie, *Young Alberta Book Society*, 1474
Gregory, Suzanne, *Chambre de commerce de Lac-Brome*, 542
Gregory, Mark, *Canadian Public Relations Society Inc.*, 463
Gregory, Ed, *Brewers Association of Canada*, 228
Gregory, Darrel, *Multiple Sclerosis Society of Canada*, 980
Gregory, Martha, *Ontario Music Festivals Association*, 1093
Gregotski, Francis, *AIDS Niagara*, 17
Greifer, Judith, *American Society of Pediatric Hematology / Oncology*, 1502
Greig, Kathy, *Canadian Association for Spiritual Care*, 304
Greisman, Lorie, *Storytelling Toronto*, 1351
Greiter, Nancy, *Ontario Home Economics Association*, 1086
Grella, Karen, *UNITE HERE Canada*, 1409
Grella-Mozejko, Piotr, *Edmonton Composers' Concert Society*, 676
Grenfell, Jenny, *Pacific Northwest Library Association*, 1135
Grenier, Nancy, *Chambre de commerce du Haut-Saint-François*, 544
Grenier, Pierre, *Institut de médiation et d'arbitrage du Québec*, 841
Grenier, Yvan, *Association des propriétaires de machinerie lourde du Québec inc.*, 126
Grenier, Paul, *Ontario Small Urban Municipalities*, 1105
Grenier, Styve, *Fraternité interprovinciale des ouvriers en électricité (CTC)*, 758
Grenier, Thérèse, *Réseau des SADC et CAE*, 1220
Grenier, Sylvie, *Ski Québec alpin*, 1302
Grenier, Christian, *Association québécoise de Vol Libre*, 171
Grenier-Denis, Eric, *Corporation des thérapeutes du sport du Québec*, 631
Grenon, Tami, *British Columbia Blind Sports & Recreation Association*, 234
Gresham, Robert, *Society of Tribologists & Lubrication Engineers*, 1594
Gresik, Warren, *St. Albert Firefighters - Union Local 2130*, 1248
Gress, Denise, *Saskatchewan Choral Federation*, 1261
Gress, Denise, *Association of Canadian Choral Communities*, 141
Gresty, Katelin, *Canadian Association of Cardiovascular Prevention & Rehabilitation*, 309

Gretton, Michael, *United Nations Association in Canada*, 1411
Greund Summerfield, Wendy, *Manitoba Heavy Construction Association*, 938
Grewal, Harjap, *The Council of Canadians*, 633
Grewal, Parm, *Richmond Multicultural Community Services*, 1231
Grewal, Parm, *Richmond Multicultural Community Services*, 1231
Grewal, Dilprit, *Sikh Foundation of Canada*, 1299
Grewall, Darsh, *British Columbia Ball Hockey Association*, 233
Greydanus, Jack, *Canadian Hatching Egg Producers*, 401
Griebenow, Gerhard, *German-Canadian Congress (Ontario)*, 772
Griesbach, Dorothy, *Canadian MedicAlert Foundation*, 434
Grieve, Corrine, *Canadian Down Syndrome Society*, 378
Griffen, Cheryl, *Ontario Society for the Prevention of Cruelty to Animals*, 1106
Griffin, Danielle, *AboutFace*, 3
Griffin, Gilly, *Canadian Council on Animal Care*, 371
Griffin, Jack, *Navy League of Canada*, 1002
Griffin, Dan, *United Empire Loyalists' Association of Canada*, 1410
Griffin, Sue, *ProMOTION Plus*, 1188
Griffin, Tyler, *Association of Professional Librarians of New Brunswick*, 159
Griffis, Ronald R., *Canadian Association of Veterans in United Nations Peacekeeping*, 335
Griffith, Gordon, *Canadian Council of Technicians & Technologists*, 370
Griffith, Gordon, *Canadian Meteorological & Oceanographic Society*, 435
Griffiths, Stella, *International ISBN Agency*, 1551
Griffiths, Jennifer, *Atlantic Planners Institute*, 184
Griffiths, Jeff, *Institute of Certified Management Consultants of Alberta*, 845
Griffiths, Carolyn, *Institution of Mechanical Engineers*, 1534
Griffiths, Dwight, *The Northern AIDS Connection Society*, 1034
Griffiths, Geoff, *Down Syndrome Research Foundation*, 661
Griffore, Anita, *Yellowknife Association for Community Living*, 1471
Grigg, Alex, *Music BC Industry Association*, 983
Grignon, Pascale, *McCord Museum of Canadian History*, 955
Grilli, Franca, *Caritas School of Life Therapeutic Community*, 513
Grimard, Daniel, *Fédération de basketball du Québec*, 708
Grimard, Marc, *Réseau des SADC et CAE*, 1221
Grimaud, Andrea, *Canadian Society for Civil Engineering*, 474
Grime, David, *Orangeville & District Real Estate Board*, 1117
Grimes, David, *World Meteorological Organization*, 1606
Grimes, Jessica, *Adult Literacy Council of Greater Fort Erie*, 9
Grimes, Brenda B., *Law Society of Newfoundland & Labrador*, 901
Grimm, Rick, *National Institute of Governmental Purchasing, Inc.*, 1576
Grimo, Bernice, *Society of Ontario Nut Growers*, 1330
Grimolfson, Tanis, *Riverton & District Friendship Centre*, 1234
Grimshaw, Rick, *Manitoba Building Officials Association*, 933
Grinberg, Agar, *Canadian Associates of Ben-Gurion University of the Negev*, 297
Grinspun, Doris, *Registered Nurses' Association of Ontario*, 1213

Grisé, Claire, *Fédération des aînées et aînés francophones du Canada*, 711
Griswold, Elizabeth, *Canadian Bottled Water Association*, 346
Groat, Lee A., *Mineralogical Association of Canada*, 966
Groat, Kirby, *Fort Simpson Chamber of Commerce*, 754
Grobe, Matt, *Geological Association of Canada*, 770
Grobelski, Giuliana, *International Catholic Deaf Association*, 854
Grod, Paul, *Ukrainian Canadian Congress*, 1402
Grod, Olya, *Ukrainian National Federation of Canada*, 1403
Grodkowska, Beata, *Canadian Polish Congress*, 456
Groeneveld, Henriette, *Mill Woods Society for Community Living*, 965
Groeneweg, Franck, *Saskatchewan Canola Development Commission*, 1260
Groleau, Marcel, *Union des producteurs agricoles*, 1406
Groleau, Lyse, *Television Bureau of Canada, Inc.*, 1370
Groleau, Jean, *Fondation de l'Ataxie Charlevoix-Saguenay*, 743
Gromaski, Gail, *Abbotsford Arts Council*, 1
Grona, Marnie, *Imagine Canada*, 830
Grondin, Claire, *Réseau du patrimoine franco-ontarien*, 1222
Grondin, Dan, *Association des motocyclistes gais du Québec*, 120
Gros, Georges, *Union internationale de la presse francophone*, 1598
Gros-Louis, Jocelyne, *Centre d'amitié autochtone du Québec*, 528
Groskorth, Elizabeth, *Alliance for Canadian New Music Projects*, 56
Gross, Ted, *Big Brothers Big Sisters of British Columbia*, 209
Grossberg, Michael, *American Society for Legal History*, 1498
Grossi, Ralph, *American Farmland Trust*, 1492
Grossman, Jim, *American Historical Association*, 1494
Grossman, Josh, *Toronto Downtown Jazz Society*, 1384
Grotkowski, Ali, *Greater Edmonton Library Association*, 783
Groulx, Josiane, *Centre intégré d'employabilité locale des Collines-de-l'Outaouais*, 535
Groulx, Loraine, *Corporation des entrepreneurs spécialisés du Grand Montréal inc.*, 630
Grove-Fanning,, William, *International Society for Environmental Ethics*, 1557
Grover, Caroline, *Kelowna Chamber of Commerce*, 883
Grover, Kelly, *Halifax Sexual Health Centre*, 799
Grover, Kelly, *Ovarian Cancer Canada*, 1133
Groves, Joanna, *International League of Dermatological Societies*, 1552
Groves, Elaina, *Children's Aid Society of the Districts of Sudbury & Manitoulin*, 561
Groves, Rob, *Risk & Insurance Management Society Inc.*, 1213
Gruber, Denise, *Community Living Cambridge*, 601
Gruber, Margaret, *Entomological Society of Saskatchewan*, 690
Grude, Jan K., *Canadian Association of Blue Cross Plans*, 309
Gruenagel, Anna-Lena, *Canadian German Chamber of Industry & Commerce Inc.*, 397
Grueter, Ellen, *Saskatchewan Canola Development Commission*, 1260
Gruetzner, Sara-Jane, *Fort Calgary Society*, 752
Grufman, Björn, *Bureau of International Recycling*, 1515
Grunau, Mara, *Centre for Suicide Prevention*, 534

Grundland, Pearl, *Association of Jewish Chaplains of Ontario*, 150
Grundy, Kevin, *Dalhousie Faculty Association*, 648
Grunerud, Élodie, *Association des francophones du nord-ouest de l'Ontario*, 114
Gruson, Geoff, *Police Sector Council*, 1163
Gryfe, David, *Canadian Memorial Chiropractic College*, 434
Gryn, Mary Ann, *Packaging Association of Canada*, 1136
Grynol, Susie, *Hotel Association of Canada Inc.*, 824
Grzesicki, Wieslaw, *Polish-Canadian Coin & Stamp Club "Troyak"*, 1164
Gu, Mingkun, *Greater Moncton Chinese Cultural Association*, 784
Guangmei, Zheng, *World Pheasant Association*, 1607
Guanzon, Ramon, *Association of Filipino Canadian Accountants*, 148
Guarin, Ulysses, *Seventh-day Adventist Church in Canada*, 1292
Guarnery, Mike, *Kimberley & District Chamber of Commerce*, 887
Guay, Andrée-Anne, *Fibrose kystique Québec*, 733
Guay, Rhonda, *ARMA Canada*, 82
Guay, Marc, *Food Banks Canada*, 749
Gucciardo, Dorotea, *Canadian Science & Technology Historical Association*, 468
Guderley, Helga, *Canadian Society of Zoologists*, 488
Gudgeon, Glenn, *Fédération de tir à l'arc du Québec*, 710
Guedes, Pedro, *Judo Ontario*, 876
Gueller, Bernhard, *Symphony Nova Scotia*, 1360
Guenette, Brandon, *Baseball Nova Scotia*, 198
Guénette, Jean-Sébastien, *Regroupement QuébecOiseaux*, 1216
Guénette, Suzanne, *Société historique de la région de Mont-Laurier*, 1320
Guénette, Daniel, *Association syndicale des employées de production et de service*, 178
Guenther, Lisa, *Canadian Farm Writers' Federation*, 384
Guérette, Yves, *Fraternité nationale des forestiers et travailleurs d'usine (CTC)*, 758
Guerico, Allison, *Manitoba Physiotherapy Association*, 942
Guérin, Arnold, *Fraternité interprovinciale des ouvriers en électricité (CTC)*, 758
Guerra, Laurie, *Autism Society of British Columbia*, 189
Guerra Salazar, René, *SalvAide*, 1252
Guerrero, Aisbel, *Association canadienne des interprètes de conférence*, 90
Guess, Deborah L., *National Association of Teachers of Singing*, 1574
Gueulette, Tricia, *Vocational Rehabilitation Association of Canada*, 1436
Gueulette, David, *Ontario Music Educators' Association*, 1093
Guevara, Denise, *Alberta Innovates*, 38
Guèvremont, Anne Marie, *BOMA Québec*, 217
Gugle, Yash, *Nova Scotia Cricket Association*, 1043
Guibourt, Christian, *Badminton Québec*, 194
Guidet, Rachel, *Les Conseillers en développement de l'employabilité*, 621
Guido, John, *L'Arche Ontario*, 77
Guilbault, Ginette, *Association des neurologues du Québec*, 121
Guilbert, Bernard, *Société d'histoire de Montarville*, 1311
Guillemette, Bianca, *Association canadienne des ataxies familiales*, 92
Guillemette, Micheline, *Réseau du sport étudiant du Québec, secteur Mauricie*, 1223
Guillot, Sandrine, *Association des médecins généticiens du Québec*, 119
Guillot, Frédérick, *Association des actuaires I.A.R.D.*, 105

Guimond, Jacques, *Association des propriétaires de machinerie lourde du Québec inc.*, 126
Guimond, Jean, *Association des médecins spécialistes en médecine nucléaire du Québec*, 120
Guimont, Wendy, *Music for Young Children*, 983
Guimont, Chantal, *Electric Mobility Canada*, 682
Guinan, Dan, *NEC Native Education College Society*, 1002
Guindon, Paul A., *The Canadian Corps of Commissionaires*, 365
Guinel, Fédéerique, *Canadian Botanical Association*, 346
Guiney, Jennifer, *Alberta Cheerleading Association*, 28
Guirguis, Rowayda, *International Napoleonic Society*, 858
Guise, Mary, *Provincial Nurse Educator Interest Group*, 1191
Guitard, Charles, *Association régionale de football Laurentides Lanaudière*, 177
Guiton, Bronwyn, *Special Libraries Association*, 1596
Gukamani-Abdulla, Jenny, *The Canadian Federation of Business & Professional Women's Clubs*, 385
Gul, Mohammed, *British Columbia Muslim Association*, 247
Gulezko, Nadia, *Canadian Law & Economics Association*, 425
Gullacher, David, *Prairie Agricultural Machinery Institute*, 1169
Gullacher, Darcy, *Biathlon Alberta*, 207
Gullick, John, *Canadian Power & Sail Squadrons (Canadian Headquarters)*, 459
Gulliford, Jim, *Soil & Water Conservation Society*, 1595
Gullino, M. Lodovica, *International Society for Plant Pathology*, 1559
Gulliver, Michael, *Start Right Coalition for Financial Literacy*, 1348
Gumpinger, Sarah, *Canadian Academic Accounting Association*, 285
Gunarajah, Dilani, *Canadian Tamils' Chamber of Commerce*, 492
Gunby, Sandy, *Canadian Pony Society*, 458
Gundermann, Glenn, *Toronto Users Group for Power Systems*, 1388
Gundry, John, *Ontario Home Builders' Association*, 1085
Gundu, Sarika, *Canadian Mental Health Association*, 434
Gunn, Ted, *Clan Gunn Society of North America - Eastern Canada Branch*, 571
Gunn, Louise, *Clan Gunn Society of North America - Eastern Canada Branch*, 571
Gunn, Angela, *Chartered Shorthand Reporters' Association of Ontario*, 555
Gunn, Joe, *CPJ Corp.*, 638
Gunn, Kendra, *Prince Edward Island Nurses' Union*, 1176
Gunn, Rae, *Recreation Nova Scotia*, 1207
Gunn, Dan, *Vancouver Island Advanced Technology Centre*, 1426
Gunn, Chan, *Institute for the Study & Treatment of Pain*, 844
Gunn, Aaron, *Canadian Taxpayers Federation*, 492
Gunn, Curt, *United Way of Cumberland County*, 1414
Gunn, Brian, *Wilderness Tourism Association*, 1454
Gunn, Tom, *Regional Occupation Centre Society*, 1213
Gunning, Trish, *Osteoporosis Canada*, 1128
Gunst, Ulla, *Association coopérative d'économie familliale de Québec*, 98
Gunter, Kirsten, *Ontario Arts Council*, 1060
Guo, Shibao, *Canadian Ethnic Studies Association*, 382
Gupta, Charu, *Manitoba School Counsellors' Association*, 944

Gupta, Amit, *Professional Engineers Ontario*, 1185
Gupta, Ravi, *World University Service of Canada*, 1467
Gupta, Arvind, *Mathematics of Information Technology & Complex Systems*, 954
Gupte, Sanjay, *Society for the Study of Pathophysiology of Pregnancy*, 1592
Guptill, Brian, *Grand Manan Fishermen's Association*, 780
Gurnett, Amy, *Local Government Management Association of British Columbia*, 917
Gurr, Nancy, *Trail Association for Community Living*, 1394
Gurría, Angel, *Organization for Economic Co-operation & Development*, 1581
Guse, Linda, *University of Manitoba Faculty Association*, 1420
Guse, Ronald, *College of Pharmacists of Manitoba*, 587
Gushue, Jennifer, *Canadian Health Information Management Association*, 402
Gushue, Emily, *Association of Newfoundland & Labrador Archives*, 154
Guss, David, *Canadian Society for Chemical Engineering*, 473
Gustafson, Arla, *Royal University Hospital Foundation*, 1243
Gustafson, Carmen, *Yukon Public Legal Education Association*, 1479
Gustafson, Nisse, *KickStart Disability Arts & Culture*, 884
Gustar, Gerry, *The Friends of Charleston Lake Park*, 760
Guthrie, Shaun, *CIO Association of Canada*, 570
Gutierrez, Andrea, *Ecojustice Canada Society*, 672
Gutray, Beverly, *Canadian Mental Health Association*, 435
Gutray, Bev, *From Grief To Action*, 763
Guttman, Deanna, *Peterborough Symphony Orchestra*, 1154
Guttormsson, Salín, *Manitoba Association of Medical Radiation Technologists*, 930
Gutzwiller, Barbara, *Federation of Swiss Association Executives*, 1526
Guy, Carolyn, *Atlantic Publishers Marketing Association*, 186
Guy, Rob, *Athletics Canada*, 181
Guy, Mary, *Dystonia Medical Research Foundation Canada*, 666
Guy, Bob, *Ontario Broiler Hatching Egg & Chick Commission*, 1069
Guy, Denyse, *Conseil canadien de la coopération et de la mutualité*, 613
Guy, Brad, *Building Materials Reuse Association*, 1514
Guy, Claire, *British Columbia School Superintendents Association*, 252
Guy, Denyse, *Co-operatives & Mutuals Canada*, 628
Guyn, Karla, *Ducks Unlimited Canada*, 663
Guyotjeannin, Olivier, *Commission internationale de diplomatique*, 1518
Guzik, Marta, *Institute of Public Administration of Canada*, 847
Guzman, Marco A., *Frontiers Foundation*, 763
Guzzo, Vincent, *Association des propriétaires de cinémas du Québec*, 126
Gyorkos, Doreen, *Canadian Hard of Hearing Association*, 400
Gyurkovits, Donald A., *Canadian Culinary Federation*, 373

H

Haaf, Stephanie M., *International Society for Magnetic Resonance in Medicine*, 1558
Haan, Maureen, *Canadian Council on Rehabilitation & Work*, 371
Haanstra, Christa, *The Change Foundation*, 551
Haas, Petra, *Sunshine Coast Community Services Society*, 1355

Executive Name Index

Haase, Mary, *College of Registered Psychiatric Nurses of Alberta*, 590
Haasper, Noranda, *Continental Automated Buildings Association*, 626
Habashi, Nagui, *Fédération québécoise des sociétés Alzheimer*, 729
Habbib, Michel M., *Association d'églises baptistes évangéliques au québec*, 99
Haber, Stuart, *Canadian Friends of Yeshiva University*, 395
Habib, George, *Ontario Lung Association*, 1089
Habib, George, *Ontario Respiratory Care Society*, 1101
Habrowski, Bartlomiej, *Polish National Union of Canada*, 1164
Hacault, Marcel L., *Canadian Agricultural Safety Association*, 290
Haché, Denise, *La Maison de la culture inc.*, 926
Haché, Michele, *Canadian Society of Association Executives*, 480
Haché, Gilles, *Chambre de commerce de la region de Cap-Pelé*, 542
Haché, Christian, *Mouvement national des québécoises et québécois*, 977
Hache, Ron, *Ontario Physique Association*, 1096
Hache, Angie, *Ontario Physique Association*, 1096
Hachette, Isabelle, *World Accord*, 1465
Hackl, Roland, *Teamsters Canada Rail Conference*, 1368
Hackman-Carty, Leann, *Economic Developers Alberta*, 672
Hadath, Wayne, *Recreational Aircraft Association*, 1208
Haddad, Camille, *New Brunswick Medical Society*, 1010
Haddad, Maha, *Professional Association of Residents & Interns of Manitoba*, 1182
Hadden, Sally, *American Society for Legal History*, 1498
Hadjigeorgiou, John, *Canadian Rock Mechanics Association*, 467
Hadley, Christina, *Special Olympics BC*, 1339
Hadzis, Maria, *Prison Fellowship Canada*, 1180
Haehnel, Kim, *Yukon Weightlifting Association*, 1481
Haendel, Angelika, *International Federation of Health Information Management Associations*, 1548
Haeni, Adrian, *Jersey Canada*, 869
Haeni, Adrian, *Jersey West*, 869
Haentjens, Marc, *Regroupement des éditeurs canadiens-français*, 1215
Hafso, Vern, *Alberta Senior Citizens Sport & Recreation Association*, 46
Haga, Susan, *Alberta Genealogical Society*, 36
Haga, Rick, *Carleton County Law Association*, 513
Hagan, Maureen, *The Canadian Association of Fitness Professionals*, 315
Hagar, Peter, *Gem & Mineral Federation of Canada*, 768
Hage, Marwan, *Canadian Football League Players' Association*, 392
Hage-Moussa, Rosine, *Society for Canadian Women in Science & Technology*, 1326
Hagedorn-Saupe, Monika, *International Committee for Documentation of the International Council of Museums*, 1543
Hagel, Gary M., *Richmond Caring Place Society*, 1230
Hagen, Barbara, *Canadian Association of Elizabeth Fry Societies*, 312
Hagens, John, *Community Living Sarnia-Lambton*, 605
Hager, Dan, *Port Renfrew Chamber of Commerce*, 1166
Hagerdal, Goran, *World Organization of the Scout Movement*, 1607
Hagerty, Loren, *S.A.L.T.S. Sail & Life Training Society*, 1252

Haggart, Jim, *Vancouver Paleontological Society*, 1428
Hagglund, Michelle, *College of Dietitians of Manitoba*, 584
Hagman, Al, *Evansburg & Entwistle Chamber of Commerce*, 699
Hagopian, Clara, *Armenian Relief Society of Canada, Inc.*, 83
Hagreen, Alison, *Prince George Brain Injured Group*, 1179
Hahn, Fred, *Canadian Union of Public Employees*, 498
Haiduk-Collier, Krista, *Community Living South Muskoka*, 605
Haig, Jill, *Registered Massage Therapists' Association of Ontario*, 1213
Haigh, Susan, *Canadian Association of Research Libraries*, 331
Haine, Marc, *Canadian Association of Foodservice Professionals*, 315
Haine, Marc, *Canadian Association of Foodservice Professionals*, 315
Haines, Sherry, *Brant United Way*, 227
Haines, Rhonda, *Sexual Health Centre Lunenburg County*, 1293
Haines, Karen, *First Nations Chiefs of Police Association*, 738
Hainsworth, Ray, *Central Canadian Federation of Mineralogical Societies*, 524
Hair, Ray, *American Federation of Musicians of the United States & Canada (AFL-CIO/CLC)*, 1493
Haire, Pamela, *West Lincoln Chamber of Commerce*, 1446
Haire, David, *Canadian Manufacturers & Exporters*, 430
Haj-Assaad, Lutfi, *Ontario Regional Poison Information Centre*, 1101
Hajek, Milos, *Edmonton Czech Language Society*, 676
Hakenson, Carlee, *Kenora & District Chamber of Commerce*, 883
Halani, John, *Vancouver Multicultural Society*, 1427
Halayko, Andrew, *Canadian Thoracic Society*, 494
Halcovitch, Dianne, *Ontario Trial Lawyers Association*, 1111
Haldane-Wilsone, C.R., *Masonic Foundation of Manitoba Inc.*, 952
Hale, Ivan, *HelpAge Canada*, 812
Hale, Paul A., *Canadian Association of Veterans in United Nations Peacekeeping*, 335
Hale, Ben, *International Society for Environmental Ethics*, 1557
Haley, John, *Adventive Cross Cultural Initiatives*, 10
Halfkenny-Zellas, Christine, *Canadian Association of Critical Care Nurses*, 311
Halford, Frank, *Ontario Brain Injury Association*, 1069
Halinda, Jennifer, *Dress for Success*, 663
Halkai, Errol, *Canadian Federation of Agriculture*, 384
Hall, Don, *Sault Naturalists*, 1281
Hall, Chris, *Master Mariners of Canada*, 953
Hall, Susan, *Boys & Girls Clubs of Ontario*, 223
Hall, Jessica, *Boys & Girls Clubs of New Brunswick*, 222
Hall, Terry, *Fibrose kystique Québec*, 733
Hall, Robyn, *Alberta Association of Academic Libraries*, 23
Hall, Amber, *Perth & District Chamber of Commerce*, 1152
Hall, Tara, *Ontario Home Builders' Association*, 1085
Hall, Brian, *Canadian Precast / Prestressed Concrete Institute*, 459
Hall, James, *Canadian Orthopaedic Foundation*, 448
Hall, Ken, *Canadian Children's Opera Company*, 356
Hall, Sharron, *Toronto & District Square & Round Dance Association*, 1381

Hall, Wayne, *Toronto & District Square & Round Dance Association*, 1381
Hall, Rick, *The Public Affairs Association of Canada*, 1192
Hall, Peter, *Royal Astronomical Society of Canada*, 1238
Hall, George, *Community Foundation of Lethbridge & Southwestern Alberta*, 597
Hall, Ken, *International Brotherhood of Teamsters (AFL-CIO/CLC)*, 1542
Hall, Dale, *Ducks Unlimited Inc.*, 1521
Hall, Jeff, *Ontario Food Protection Association*, 1080
Hall, Jamie, *Indian Agricultural Program of Ontario*, 834
Hall, Jeremy, *Institute of Certified Management Consultants of Saskatchewan*, 845
Hall, John, *Kamloops & District Labour Council*, 880
Hall, Gail, *Parry Sound Friendship Centre*, 1143
Hall, Donna, *Sunshine Coast Community Services Society*, 1355
Hall, Joe, *Centre for Child Development*, 531
Hall, Diana, *The Neil Squire Foundation*, 1002
Hall, Wayne, *Ontario Square & Round Dance Federation*, 1108
Hall, Glen, *Assiniboia & District Chamber of Commerce (SK)*, 88
Hall, Richard, *Institutional Limited Partners Association*, 848
Hall, Darryl, *Radius Child & Youth Services*, 1203
Hall, Richard, *Canada Korea Business Association*, 280
Hall, Earl, *Ontario Rural Softball Association*, 1103
Hall, Emily, *Canadian New Music Network*, 441
Hall, Barbara, *British Columbia Contract Cleaner's Association*, 237
Hall, Sarah, *Battle River Research Group*, 200
Hall, Mary T., *Safe Schools Manitoba*, 1245
Hall, Tom, *Office of the Superintendent of Securities of the Northwest Territories*, 1055
Hall Findlay, Martha, *Canada West Foundation*, 281
Hall-Cho, Vivien, *Treasury Management Association of Canada - Toronto*, 1396
Halladay, Laurel, *Alberta Historical Resources Foundation*, 37
Hallam, Rob, *Habitat for Humanity Canada*, 796
Hallatt, Phyllis, *Child Find Saskatchewan Inc.*, 560
Hallé, Marie-Paule, *Société généalogique de Châteauguay*, 1319
Hallen, Manjot, *The Liberal Party of Canada (British Columbia)*, 909
Haller, Robert, *Canadian Water & Wastewater Association*, 502
Haller, Martin, *Canadian Association of Veterans in United Nations Peacekeeping*, 336
Haller, Martin, *Manitoba Association of Fire Chiefs*, 929
Hallett, Sandra, *Olds College Faculty Association*, 1057
Hallett, Martin, *Wolfville Historical Society*, 1460
Hallett, Rebecca, *Entomological Society of Canada*, 690
Hallett DaSilva, Cassandra, *Canadian Teachers' Federation*, 493
Halliday, Bonnie, *Allied Arts Council of Spruce Grove*, 58
Halliday, Wally, *Ontario Home Builders' Association*, 1086
Halliwell, Chris, *Softball Prince Edward Island*, 1332
Halloran, Brenda, *Startup Canada*, 1348
Hallsworth, Suzanne, *Association of Fundraising Professionals*, 1512
Hallward, Graham F., *Alva Foundation*, 61
Hallworth, Frances, *United Way of St Catharines & District*, 1416

Halou, Sylvie, *Ski de fond Québec*, 1302
Halowaty, Justin, *Whitehorse Minor Hockey Association*, 1453
Halper, June, *Consortium of Multiple Sclerosis Centers*, 1519
Halpin, Roy, *Canadian Amateur Boxing Association*, 292
Halpin, Peter, *Association of Atlantic Universities*, 139
Halsall, Peter, *Canadian Urban Institute*, 499
Halsey, Jennifer, *The Instrumentation, Systems & Automation Society of America*, 1534
Halter, Allan, *Wetaskiwin Chamber of Commerce*, 1451
Halvorson, Sandi, *Parent Support Services Society of BC*, 1139
Halward, Keely, *Sunshine Coast Community Services Society*, 1355
Ham, Marlene, *Ontario Association of Interval & Transition Houses*, 1064
Hamade, Stéphane, *Ontario Undergraduate Student Alliance*, 1111
Hamalian Barsemian, Nelly, *Armenian Relief Society of Canada, Inc.*, 83
Hamamoto, Gail, *British Columbia Wheelchair Sports Association*, 258
Hamann, Stéphane, *Société des archives historiques de la région de l'Amiante*, 1317
Hambley, Ronald, *Winnipeg Construction Association*, 1458
Hamblin, Chrissie, *Alberta Weekly Newspapers Association*, 51
Hambling, Deb, *Canadian Girls Rodeo Association*, 398
Hambly, Keith, *Fife House*, 734
Hambly, Stephen, *Evangelical Order of Certified Pastoral Counsellors of America*, 699
Hambrook, Mark, *Miramichi Salmon Association*, 968
Hamé, Catherine, *New Democratic Party*, 1014
Hameed, Morad, *Trauma Association of Canada*, 1396
Hamel, Denis, *Chrysotile Institute*, 569
Hamel, Éliane, *Option consommateurs*, 1117
Hamel, Jocelyne, *Association of Neighbourhood Houses BC*, 153
Hamel, René, *Association de la construction du Québec*, 100
Hamel Migneaul, Suzanne, *A fleur de sein*, 740
Hamelin, Paul, *Community Living Huronia*, 603
Hamelmann, Ralph, *Rainbow Association of Canadian Artists (Spectra Talent Contest)*, 1203
Hames, Dorothy, *Dundalk Historical Society*, 664
Hames, Janie, *Ontario Trial Lawyers Association*, 1111
Hamil, Ty, *Agricultural Manufacturers of Canada*, 15
Hamill, Mona, *EDAM Performing Arts Society*, 674
Hamilton, Janice, *Manitoba Council for International Cooperation*, 934
Hamilton, Jacquie, *Castlegar & District Arts Council*, 517
Hamilton, Richard E. (Rick), *Christian Church (Disciples of Christ) in Canada*, 567
Hamilton, Dave, *Delta Chamber of Commerce*, 653
Hamilton, Ruth, *Kicking Horse Country Chamber of Commerce*, 884
Hamilton, Katie, *Basketball PEI*, 199
Hamilton, Ian, *Canadian Hard of Hearing Association*, 400
Hamilton, Ian, *Equitas - International Centre for Human Rights Education*, 695
Hamilton, Gary, *Western Retail Lumber Association*, 1450
Hamilton, Blair, *Cooperative Housing Federation of Canada*, 628
Hamilton, Jennifer, *Canadian Association of College & University Student Services*, 310

Executive Name Index

Hamilton, Murray, *Thames Valley Trail Association Inc.*, 1373
Hamilton, Lesley, *Canadian Association of Elizabeth Fry Societies*, 313
Hamilton, Rose, *Wildlife Rescue Association of British Columbia*, 1455
Hamilton, Lynn, *Alberta Diabetes Foundation*, 33
Hamilton, Dawn, *Breast Cancer Society of Canada*, 228
Hamilton, Robert (Bob), *WinSport Canada*, 1460
Hamilton, Michael, *The Royal Scottish Country Dance Society*, 1587
Hamilton, Doug, *Stratford Coin Club*, 1351
Hamilton, Rod, *College of Physiotherapists of Ontario*, 589
Hamilton, Gay, *Commonwealth Association for Public Administration & Management*, 593
Hamilton, Marilyn, *Young People's Theatre*, 1475
Hamilton, Britany, *Chartered Professionals in Human Resources Saskatchewan*, 554
Hamilton, Paulette, *Guid'amies franco-manitobaines*, 793
Hamilton, Glen, *Canadian Union of Brewery & General Workers, Local 325*, 498
Hamilton, Cheryl, *Association of Canadian Compliance Professionals*, 141
Hamlyn, Angela, *Canadian Institute of Mining, Metallurgy & Petroleum*, 418
Hamm, Rita R., *International Association for Impact Assessment*, 1537
Hamm, Eleonore, *Recreation Vehicle Dealers Association of Canada*, 1208
Hamm, Jess, *Saskatchewan Intercultural Association Inc.*, 1268
Hammersley, Bob, *St Thomas & District Chamber of Commerce*, 1251
Hamming, Jeremy, *Alberta Ski Jumping & Nordic Combined*, 47
Hammock, Janet, *PFLAG Canada Inc.*, 1156
Hammond, Sam, *Qualifications Evaluation Council of Ontario*, 1195
Hammond, Tom, *HIV/AIDS Resources and Community Health*, 817
Hammond, Vaughan, *Canadian Federation of Independent Business*, 387
Hammond, Stephanie, *Learning Disabilities Association of Yukon Territory*, 905
Hammond, Greg, *Manitoba Medical Service Foundation Inc.*, 940
Hammond, Sue, *Urology Nurses of Canada*, 1423
Hammond, Nancy, *Fondation de l'Ordre des infirmières et infirmiers du Québec*, 744
Hammond, Sam, *Elementary Teachers' Federation of Ontario*, 684
Hammond, Bruce, *American Society of Pediatric Hematology / Oncology*, 1502
Hammond-Thrasher, Josie, *Canadian Public Relations Society Inc.*, 463
Hammouche, Rabah, *Canadian Meteorological & Oceanographic Society*, 436
Hammoud, Mike, *Atlantic Convenience Store Association*, 183
Hamon, Tracy, *Saskatchewan Writers Guild*, 1278
Hamood, Faisal, *Association of Professional Engineers & Geoscientists of British Columbia*, 158
Hamoodi, Mary, *Shad Valley International*, 1294
Hampsey, Robert, *The Rainbow Alliance*, 1203
Hampson, Holly, *Québec Association of Independent Schools*, 1196
Hampson, Dennis, *Canadian Professional DJ Association Inc.*, 460
Hampton, Bettyanne, *North Peace Cultural Society*, 1032
Hampton, Jeff, *Comox Valley Food Bank Society*, 608
Hamre, Lee, *International Right of Way Association*, 1556

Hamsa, Ali, *Commonwealth Association for Public Administration & Management*, 593
Hancharek, Catharine, *Professional Engineers Ontario*, 1185
Hancharyk, Maureen, *Canadian Condominium Institute*, 362
Hanchate, Gangadhar, *Homeopathic Medical Association Of Canada*, 820
Hancock, Margaret, *Family Service Toronto*, 704
Hancock, Lorna, *Health Action Network Society*, 805
Hancock, B.J., *Canadian Association of Paediatric Surgeons*, 325
Hancock, Kristin, *College of Registered Nurses of Manitoba*, 589
Hancock, Margaret, *Oxfam Canada*, 1134
Hancock, Mark, *Canadian Union of Public Employees*, 498
Hancox, Amanda, *Dancer Transition Resource Centre*, 650
Hancox, Rick, *Financial & Consumer Services Commission*, 736
Handke, Stephen, *Ottawa Valley Historical Society*, 1132
Handley, Gerald, *Nature Saskatchewan*, 1001
Hands, Marian, *British Columbia Water & Waste Association*, 258
Handy, Karla, *Paddle Alberta*, 1137
Hanec, Cec, *Immigrant Centre Manitoba Inc.*, 830
Haner, Cindy, *Association of Visual Language Interpreters of Canada*, 164
Hanes, Jonathan M., *International Society of Biometeorology*, 1560
Hanes, Jane, *Canadian Society for Surgical Oncology*, 477
Hanes, Len, *Children's Hospital of Eastern Ontario Foundation*, 562
Haney, Patrick, *Canadian Hemochromatosis Society*, 404
Hanks, Katherine, *Canadian Institute of Management*, 417
Hanley, Lawrence J., *Amalgamated Transit Union (AFL-CIO/CLC)*, 1487
Hanley, Laura, *Community Living Guelph Wellington*, 602
Hanley, Jim, *Atlantic Canada Fish Farmers Association*, 182
Hanlon, Ward, *Canadian Federation of Independent Grocers*, 387
Hanlon, Julian, *Canadian Catholic School Trustees' Association*, 351
Hann, Ann Marie, *Coal Association of Canada*, 577
Hanna, Nader, *Canadian Bridge Federation*, 347
Hanna, Dominique, *Association des dermatologistes du Québec*, 110
Hanna, George P., *Shoe Manufacturers' Association of Canada*, 1297
Hanna, Pat, *Canadian Harvard Aircraft Association*, 401
Hanna, Suzanne, *Ontario Horticultural Association*, 1086
Hanna, Kate, *Junior League of Calgary*, 878
Hanna, Nadim, *Centre patronal de santé et sécurité du travail du Québec*, 536
Hannah, Brenda, *Alberta Association on Gerontology*, 25
Hannah, Robin, *Georgina Association for Community Living*, 771
Hannah, Linda, *The Nature Conservancy of Canada*, 1000
Hannah, Jody, *Canadian Society of Gastroenterology Nurses & Associates*, 483
Hannah, Scott, *Credit Counselling Society*, 640
Hannigan, Kathy, *Inverness County Centre for the Arts*, 862
Hannila, Sari S., *Canadian Association for Anatomy, Neurobiology, & Cell Biology*, 297
Hannon, Pat, *Harmony Foundation of Canada*, 803
Hanrahan, Susan, *Nova Scotia Designer Crafts Council*, 1044

Hans, Elisabeth, *Federation of New Brunswick Faculty Associations*, 725
Hanselman, Gail, *Ontario Association of Architects*, 1061
Hansen, Ted, *The Danish Club of Ottawa*, 650
Hansen, Dan, *Alberta Ready Mixed Concrete Association*, 43
Hansen, Lilia, *Fort St. John & District Chamber of Commerce*, 753
Hansen, Cato, *Model Aeronautics Association of Canada Inc.*, 970
Hansen, Glen, *Utility Contractors Association of Ontario, Inc.*, 1423
Hansen, Kim, *Canadian Professional Sales Association*, 460
Hansen, Gerry, *Infection & Prevention Control Canada*, 836
Hansen, Sally, *Myalgic Encephalomyelitis Association of Halton/Hamilton-Wentworth*, 986
Hansen, Sean, *Atlantic Marksmen Association*, 184
Hansen, Joey, *Association of Administrative & Professional Staff - University of British Columbia*, 139
Hansen, Rick, *Rick Hansen Foundation*, 1231
Hansford, Erika, *Professional Association of Internes & Residents of Newfoundland*, 1182
Hansman, Glen, *Vancouver Elementary School Teachers' Association*, 1425
Hansman, Glen, *British Columbia Teachers' Federation*, 256
Hansmann, Werner, *Eurographics - European Association for Computer Graphics*, 1524
Hanson, Vesti, *Saskatoon Musicians' Association*, 1279
Hanson, Cindy, *Canadian Research Institute for the Advancement of Women*, 467
Hanson, Jerry, *Child Evangelism Fellowship of Canada*, 559
Hanson, Brenda, *Child Evangelism Fellowship of Canada*, 559
Hanson, Arnold, *Family & Community Support Services Association of Alberta*, 702
Hanson, Gary, *Toronto Symphony Orchestra*, 1387
Hanson, Liz, *New Democratic Party*, 1014
Hanson, Jessica, *United Way of Durham Region*, 1414
Hanson, Tennys J.M., *Toronto General & Western Hospital Foundation*, 1385
Hanson, Vicki L., *Association for Computing Machinery*, 1508
Hanston, Eric, *Penticton & District Community Arts Council*, 1150
Hanus, George, *Greater Toronto Marketing Alliance*, 786
Happe, Suzanne, *Last Post Fund*, 899
Har-Tal, Helen, *Association of Americans & Canadians in Israel*, 1510
Harada, Laurie, *Food Allergy Canada*, 749
Haramincic, Arijana, *Family & Children's Services of Renfrew County*, 702
Harasyn, Keith, *American Society for Quality*, 1499
Harbour, Louise, *Action Life (Ottawa) Inc.*, 6
Harcourt, Laureen, *Grande Prairie Society for the Prevention of Cruelty to Animals*, 781
Hardcastle, Elizabeth, *American Academy of Religion*, 1488
Harder, Rose-Ann, *Manitoba Arts Network*, 929
Harder, Brian, *Fraser Valley Labour Council*, 758
Harder, Rick, *Watson Lake Chamber of Commerce*, 1443
Harder, John, *Evangelical Tract Distributors*, 699
Harder, Brian, *Back Country Horsemen of British Columbia*, 192
Hardie, Ken, *New Brunswick Federation of Woodlot Owners Inc.*, 1008
Hardie, Kristy, *Association of Municipal Administrators, Nova Scotia*, 152

Hardie, Steve, *Ontario Recreation Facilities Association*, 1100
Hardie, Susan, *Canadian Centre on Disability Studies*, 354
Hardie, Glenn, *Naval Museum of Alberta Society*, 1001
Hardie, Andy, *Nature Trust of New Brunswick*, 1001
Hardie, Diana, *Cycling British Columbia*, 647
Harding, Andrew, *Canadian Stuttering Association*, 491
Harding, Charles, *Threshold Ministries*, 1377
Harding, John, *Lethbridge & District Japanese Garden Society*, 907
Harding, Ashley, *Orienteering Association of Nova Scotia*, 1126
Harding, Bill, *Ontario Parks Association*, 1095
Harding, Carol, *United Empire Loyalists' Association of Canada*, 1410
Harding, Barb, *Seguin Arts Council*, 1289
Harding, John, *Canadian Association of Swine Veterinarians*, 334
Hardwick, Robert, *The Anglican Church of Canada*, 70
Hardy, Lisa, *Alberta Association of Agricultural Societies*, 23
Hardy, Beverly, *Family Enterprise Xchange*, 703
Hardy, Katie, *Canadian Psychiatric Association*, 461
Hardy, Tim, *Society of Composers, Authors & Music Publishers of Canada*, 1328
Hardy, Joëlle, *Société historique du Saguenay*, 1321
Hardy, Marc, *Réseau des SADC et CAE*, 1220
Hardy, Randy, *Métis Settlements General Council*, 963
Hardy, Terry, *Ontario Public Works Association*, 1100
Hardy, Michelle, *Saskatchewan Home Economics Teachers Association*, 1267
Hare, Kelly, *Children's Wish Foundation of Canada*, 563
Hare, John, *Comité maritime international*, 1518
Hare, Rob, *Canadian Hydrographic Association*, 409
Hare, Theresa, *Native Council of Nova Scotia*, 997
Hare, Laura, *Alzheimer Society of Belleville/Hastings/Quinte*, 62
Hare, Morgan, *Odawa Native Friendship Centre*, 1054
Hare, Kathy, *Canadian Nutrition Society*, 444
Haresnape, Peter, *Student Christian Movement of Canada*, 1352
Harford, Luke, *Brewers Association of Canada*, 228
Hargan, Kathryn, *Canadian Quaternary Association*, 464
Hargest, Paul, *Canadian Concrete Masonry Producers Association*, 362
Hargis, Anthony, *National Waste & Recycling Association*, 1577
Hargis, Eric R., *Epilepsy Foundation of America*, 1524
Hargreaves, Tara, *Radiation Safety Institute of Canada*, 1202
Hargreaves, Eric, *PFLAG Canada Inc.*, 1155
Hargreaves, Dagmar, *Dress for Success*, 663
Harkies, Coral, *Ontario Genealogical Society*, 1081
Harkins, Katharine, *The Donkey Sanctuary of Canada*, 661
Harkins, Jim, *F.A.S.T.*, 706
Harkness, Glenn, *Boys & Girls Clubs of Ontario*, 223
Harkonen, Harold, *Thunder Bay Adventure Trails*, 1377
Harland, Penny, *South Grenville Chamber of Commerce*, 1334
Harley, Catherine, *Canadian Association for Enterostomal Therapy*, 300
Harman, Donna A., *American Forest & Paper Association*, 1493

Executive Name Index

Harman, Joey, *On to Ottawa Historical Society*, 1058
Harmon, Allan, *Directors Guild of Canada*, 657
Harms, John, *Westerner Park*, 1450
Harms, Marion, *Kidney Foundation of Canada*, 885
Harms, Ted, *Canadian Cue Sport Association*, 373
Harmston, Richard, *South Asia Partnership Canada*, 1334
Harmston, Richard, *Group of 78*, 791
Harnish, Leslie, *Mainland South Heritage Society*, 926
Haron, Datuk Ir. Idris, *World Assembly of Youth*, 1603
Haroon, Max, *Society of Internet Professionals*, 1329
Harper, Bill, *Imagine Canada*, 830
Harper, Ben, *Professional Employees Association (Ind.)*, 1183
Harper, Roxanne, *Community Futures Yellowhead East*, 599
Harper, Colleen, *American Society for Parenteral & Enteral Nutrition*, 1498
Harper, John, *Manitoba Association for Business Economics*, 929
Harpley, Paul, *South Lake Simcoe Naturalists*, 1335
Harri, Deborah, *Manitoba Lung Association*, 940
Harrington, Rhonda, *The Salvation Army in Canada*, 1253
Harrington, Kevin, *Canadian Flag Association*, 391
Harrington, Nicholas, *Ontario Home Builders' Association*, 1085
Harrington, Michael, *Canadian Association for Conservation of Cultural Property*, 299
Harrington, Gerry, *Consumer Health Products Canada*, 626
Harrington, Alan, *Burlington Historical Society*, 265
Harriott, Nichelle, *Beyond Pesticides*, 1514
Harris, Andrew, *Canadian Association of Independent Life Brokerage Agencies*, 318
Harris, Pat, *Sherwood Park Fish & Game Association*, 1296
Harris, Jason, *Miramichi Chamber of Commerce*, 968
Harris, Kerry, *Grande Prairie Food Bank*, 781
Harris, Luke, *Newfoundland & Labrador Volleyball Association*, 1022
Harris, Julie, *Canadian Association of Heritage Professionals*, 317
Harris, Wendy, *Canadian Executive Service Organization*, 383
Harris, Allie, *Information Resource Management Association of Canada*, 837
Harris, Rosalyn, *Canadian Tarentaise Association*, 492
Harris, Gwen, *Gerontological Nursing Association of Ontario*, 772
Harris, Lorie, *The Ontario Archaeological Society*, 1059
Harris, Patty, *Ontario Association of Cemetery & Funeral Professionals*, 1062
Harris, Sandra, *The Leukemia & Lymphoma Society of Canada*, 909
Harris, Helen, *Ontario Non-Profit Housing Association*, 1093
Harris, Rebecca, *Ontario Association of Residences Treating Youth*, 1066
Harris, Stephanie, *Altona & District Chamber of Commerce*, 61
Harris, Dawn, *Niverville Chamber of Commerce*, 1027
Harris, John, *Metronome Canada*, 964
Harris, Leanne, *Environmental Managers Association of British Columbia*, 692
Harris, Wendy, *Back Country Horsemen of British Columbia*, 192
Harris, Brian, *Ontario Katahdin Sheep Association Inc.*, 1088
Harris, Elizabeth, *Atlantic Association of Prosthetists & Orthotists*, 182

Harris, Gillian, *People First Nova Scotia*, 1151
Harris-Wheatley, Janine, *Tecumseth & West Gwillimbury Historical Society*, 1369
Harrison, Trevor, *University of Lethbridge Faculty Association*, 1419
Harrison, James Jay, *Winnipeg Musicians' Association*, 1459
Harrison, Stuart, *Greater Peterborough Chamber of Commerce*, 785
Harrison, Pierre-Luc, *Chambre de commerce et industrie Mont-Joli-Mitis*, 548
Harrison, Laura, *Canadian Celiac Association*, 352
Harrison, Gordon, *Canadian National Millers Association*, 440
Harrison, Shaleeta, *Federation of British Columbia Writers*, 722
Harrison, Lucia, *Kitchener-Waterloo Multicultural Centre*, 891
Harrison, Erin, *Canadian Labour Congress*, 424
Harrison, Pamela, *Southern Alberta Health Libraries Association*, 1337
Harrison, Chris, *March of Dimes Canada*, 949
Harrison, Pamela, *Transition House Association of Nova Scotia*, 1395
Harrison, Lesley, *Central Coast Communications Society*, 524
Harrold, Lynne, *John Howard Society of Alberta*, 874
Harry, Denise, *ARMA Canada*, 82
Harsch, Harry, *The Canadian Corps of Commissionaires*, 365
Harsh, Ed, *New Music USA*, 1577
Hart, Shirley, *Middle River & Area Historical Society*, 964
Hart, Andrew, *Calgary Field Naturalists' Society*, 272
Hart, Ruth, *Nova Scotia Government Libraries Council*, 1045
Hart, Kori, *Ponoka & District Chamber of Commerce*, 1164
Hart, Cameron, *Saskatchewan Council for Archives & Archivists*, 1262
Hart, Nelson, *United Church of Canada*, 1409
Hart, Sarah, *Kidney Foundation of Canada*, 885
Hart, Melonie, *Ontario Association of Gastroenterology*, 1064
Hart, Anton, *Canadian Obesity Network*, 444
Hart, Alison, *ProMOTION Plus*, 1188
Hartemink, Aldred, *International Union of Soil Sciences*, 1565
Harter, Tom, *British Columbia Association of Agricultural Fairs & Exhibitions*, 231
Hartigan, Mo, *Bed & Breakfast Association of the Yukon*, 203
Hartin, Penny, *World Blind Union*, 1465
Hartlen, Donna, *Guillain-Barré Syndrome Foundation of Canada*, 794
Hartien, Mark, *Halifax Regional Police Association*, 799
Hartley, Donna, *The John Howard Society of Prince Edward Island*, 875
Hartley, Bonnie, *Community Association for Riding for the Disabled*, 596
Hartley, Corina, *Swimming Newfoundland & Labrador*, 1359
Hartley, Stephen, *PFLAG Canada Inc.*, 1155
Hartley, Linda, *Treasury Management Association of Canada - Toronto*, 1396
Hartman, Joey, *CoDevelopment Canada*, 580
Hartman, Steve, *Kivalliq Inuit Association*, 891
Hartman, Cindy, *Canadian Federation of Podiatric Medicine*, 388
Hartman, Joey, *Vancouver & District Labour Council*, 1424
Hartmann, Franz, *Toronto Environmental Alliance*, 1384
Hartmans, Peter, *United Church of Canada*, 1409
Hartner, Rinda, *Thyroid Foundation of Canada*, 1379
Hartog, Jim, *National Association of Watch & Clock Collectors, Inc.*, 1574

Hartt, Debbie, *Edmonton Dental Assistants Association*, 676
Hartwell, Linda, *Hotel Association of Canada Inc.*, 824
Harty, Valerie, *Alberta Federation of Rock Clubs*, 35
Harvard, Dawn, *Ontario Native Women's Association*, 1093
Harvey, Marcus, *Trent University Faculty Association*, 1397
Harvey, Chris, *Boys & Girls Clubs of Ontario*, 223
Harvey, Brenda, *Friends of Devonian Botanic Garden*, 761
Harvey, Dale, *Saskatchewan Association of Rural Municipalities*, 1258
Harvey, Laurie, *Nose Creek Valley Museum Society*, 1040
Harvey, Claire, *Conseil québécois sur le tabac et la santé*, 620
Harvey, Dany, *Association de Ringuette de Thetford*, 103
Harvey, Pascal, *Réseau des SADC et CAE*, 1220
Harvey, Deb, *Tourism London*, 1390
Harvey, Eric-Yves, *Société Provancher d'histoire naturelle du Canada*, 1323
Harvey, Frank, *Aerospace Heritage Foundation of Canada*, 11
Harvey, Patrice, *Syndicat national des employés de l'aluminium d'Alma inc.*, 1365
Harvey, Manon, *Canada Foundation for Innovation*, 279
Harvey, François, *Société des traversiers du Québec*, 1318
Harvey, David, *The Western Canada Group of Chartered Engineers*, 1448
Harvey, Allan, *Viking Economic Development Committee*, 1434
Harvey, Carol, *Nova Scotia Daylily Society*, 1043
Harvey, Moira, *Ontario Aerospace Council*, 1059
Harvey, Malcolm, *Coast Waste Management Association*, 579
Harvey, Dave, *Park People*, 1140
Harvie, Timothy, *Canadian Theological Society*, 494
Harvie, Melanie, *Canadian Taxpayers Federation*, 492
Harwood, Malcolm, *Manitoba Lung Association*, 940
Hasan, Farhat, *Council of Agencies Serving South Asians*, 632
Haskett, Denise, *L'Arche Western Region*, 78
Hasler, Paula, *Nova Scotia Society for the Prevention of Cruelty to Animals*, 1049
Hasquin, Hervé, *Union académique internationale*, 1598
Hassan, Hazim, *Ontario Hospital Association*, 1087
Hassan, Cheryl-Ann, *Ontario Brain Injury Association*, 1069
Hassanali, Meena, *Provision Coalition*, 1191
Hassard, Stacey, *Yukon Party*, 1479
Hassmiller, Bob, *National Association of College Auxiliary Services*, 1573
Hastings, Deborah, *Durham Region Law Association*, 665
Hastings, Donna, *Heart & Stroke Foundation of Alberta, NWT & Nunavut*, 808
Hastrup, Bjarne, *International Federation on Aging*, 857
Hasulo, Susanne, *Ontario Trial Lawyers Association*, 1111
Hatch, Christopher, *Mississauga Food Bank*, 970
Hatch, Emile, *Nunavut Teachers' Association*, 1051
Hateley, Donna, *Alberta Sports Hall of Fame & Museum*, 48
Hatfield, Gloria, *Gabriola Island Chamber of Commerce*, 766
Hatt, Jeremy, *Toronto Ornithological Club*, 1386

Hatt, Shauna, *Directors Guild of Canada*, 657
Hattendorf, Kai, *UFI - The Global Association of the Exhibition Industry*, 1598
Hatter, Bill, *National Darts Federation of Canada*, 992
Hattie, Chris, *Judo Nova Scotia*, 876
Hattle, Ron, *Wellington County Historical Society*, 1443
Hatzakos, Janice, *American Society for Information Science & Technology*, 1498
Hauck, Colleen, *Crohn's & Colitis Canada*, 642
Hauerslev, Marie, *International Federation of Medical Students' Associations*, 1548
Haugen, Sid, *Evangelical Lutheran Church in Canada*, 698
Haugen, Diane, *Dystonia Medical Research Foundation Canada*, 666
Haugh, Gord, *Community Living South Muskoka*, 605
Haughton, Andrea, *Kingston Symphony Association*, 890
Hauk, Alfred, *Ontario Association of Naturopathic Doctors*, 1065
Haukaas, Colleen, *Archaeological Society of Alberta*, 76
Hauser, Barbara, *Council of Ontario Universities*, 635
Hausman, Jonathan, *Canadian Council for the Americas*, 367
Hausner, Beatriz, *Literary Translators' Association of Canada*, 914
Haut, Kristine, *Alberta Horse Trials Association*, 38
Hauta, Patrick, *Canadian Society of Association Executives*, 480
Havaris, Eva, *Equestrian Canada*, 694
Haver, Ann, *Canadian Orthoptic Council*, 448
Haver, John, *Saskatchewan Rowing Association*, 1274
Haverkort, Nicole, *Solid Waste Association of North America*, 1595
Havill, Teresa, *Kidney Foundation of Canada*, 885
Hawco, Debbie, *Bay St. George Folk Arts Council*, 200
Hawco, Michelle, *PLEA Community Services Society of BC*, 1163
Hawco, Leanne, *Northeastern Alberta Aboriginal Business Association*, 1034
Hawes, Michael K., *Foundation for Educational Exchange Between Canada & the United States of America*, 755
Hawke, Wayne, *Essa & District Agricultural Society*, 696
Hawkes, Richard, *SCOPE for People with Cerebral Palsy*, 1588
Hawkes, Brent, *Metropolitan Community Church of Toronto*, 964
Hawkeswood, Marina, *Canadian Public Relations Society Inc.*, 463
Hawkesworth, Kathy, *Edmonton Community Foundation*, 676
Hawkins, Michael W., *The Anglican Church of Canada*, 70
Hawkins, Dianne, *Comox Valley Chamber of Commerce*, 607
Hawkins, Bruce, *Ontario Recreational Canoeing & Kayaking Association*, 1101
Hawkins, Kent, *Canadian Snack Food Association*, 472
Hawkins, Crawford, *Directors Guild of Canada*, 657
Hawkins, Cynthia, *The Toronto Mendelssohn Choir*, 1385
Hawkins, Louise, *The Maritimes Energy Association*, 951
Hawkins, Bud, *Princess Patricia's Canadian Light Infantry Association*, 1180
Hawkins, Raynald, *Lifesaving Society*, 911
Hawkins, Bryson, *AIDS Vancouver Island*, 17
Hawkins, Patty, *Embroiderers' Association of Canada, Inc.*, 686
Hawkins, Ann, *Ontario English Catholic Teachers' Association (CLC)*, 1078

Executive Name Index

Hawkins, Craig, *The Rainbow Society of Alberta*, 1203
Hawkins, Tammy, *Alberta Construction Safety Association*, 31
Hawkins, Marty, *Westport & Rideau Lakes Chamber of Commerce*, 1451
Hawley, David B., *United World Colleges*, 1418
Hawley, Rob, *Calgary Chamber of Commerce*, 271
Hawley, Kelly, *North Renfrew Family Services Inc.*, 1032
Hawley, Dawn, *Financial Planning Standards Council*, 737
Hawn, Esther, *Manitoba Society of Occupational Therapists*, 945
Haworth, Dawn, *Canadian Academy of Sport Medicine*, 287
Hawrelko, Donna, *Canadian Gemmological Association*, 396
Hawryluk, Graham, *Headingley Chamber of Commerce*, 805
Hawrysh, Brian, *British Columbia Wood Specialities Group Association*, 258
Hawthorne, Ron, *Slo-Pitch Ontario Association*, 1304
Hay, Graeme, *CFA Society Winnipeg*, 539
Hay, Jack, *Saskatchewan Agricultural Hall of Fame*, 1255
Hay, Terri, *Canadian Association for Pharmacy Distribution Management*, 303
Hay, Kim, *Royal Astronomical Society of Canada*, 1238
Hay, Greg, *Pulp & Paper Technical Association of Canada*, 1194
Hay, Sara, *PFLAG Canada Inc.*, 1155
Hay, Nairn, *Fundy Model Forest Network*, 764
Hayashi, Adam, *Cement Association of Canada*, 521
Hayday, Nolan, *Alberta Association of Prosthetists & Orthotists*, 24
Hayden, Lloyd, *Baie Verte & Area Chamber of Commerce*, 194
Hayduk, Chris, *Alberta Society of Radiologists*, 48
Hayes, Sue, *Annapolis Valley Chamber of Commerce*, 71
Hayes, Denise, *Southern Georgian Bay Chamber of Commerce*, 1337
Hayes, Gerard, *Canadian College & University Food Service Association*, 358
Hayes, Matt, *Association of Professional Engineers & Geoscientists of New Brunswick*, 158
Hayes, Maria, *Canadian Pension & Benefits Institute*, 453
Hayes, Janice, *YOUTHLINK*, 1476
Hayes, Scott, *Alberta Gymnastics Federation*, 37
Hayes, Christopher, *Heartwood Centre for Community Youth Development*, 810
Hayes, Ian, *Folklore Studies Association of Canada*, 742
Hayes, Anne-Marie, *Valley Family Resource Centre Inc.*, 1424
Hayes, Wally, *Canadian Knifemaker's Guild*, 424
Hayes, Anna-Marie, *The Atlantic Alliance of Family Resource Centres*, 182
Hayes, Chantale, *Paramedic Association of New Brunswick*, 1138
Hayes, Andrew, *Snowboard Nova Scotia*, 1305
Haynes, Sterling, *Canadian Authors Association*, 338
Hayos, Gabe, *Chartered Professional Accountants Canada*, 552
Hays, Fred, *Alberta Beef Producers*, 26
Hayter, Elaine, *Kidney Foundation of Canada*, 885
Hayter, Ron, *Edmonton International Baseball Foundation*, 678
Hayward, Sylvia, *Alberta Debate & Speech Association*, 32
Hayward, Sharon, *YMCA Canada*, 1472
Hayward, Tom, *Sonography Canada*, 1333

Hayward, Amy, *Paralympic Sports Association (Alberta)*, 1138
Hayward, Judi, *Canadian Horse Heritage & Preservation Society*, 408
Haywood, Kelly, *Huntsville, Lake of Bays Chamber of Commerce*, 828
Haywood-Farmer, David, *British Columbia Cattlemen's Association*, 235
Hazel, Craig, *Alliance for Chiropractic*, 57
Hazell, Stephen, *Nature Canada*, 999
Hazell, Lianne, *Red Deer Native Friendship Society*, 1209
Hazelton, Janet, *Nova Scotia Nurses' Union*, 1047
Hazen, Iris, *Greater Toronto Rose & Garden Horticultural Society*, 786
Hazlett, Mark, *Canadian Council for the Advancement of Education*, 367
Hazzard, David, *Pentecostal Assemblies of Canada*, 1150
Head, Chris, *Confederation of Meningitis Organizations*, 1519
Heagle, Heather, *Ontario Camps Association*, 1070
Heald, Ann, *British Columbia Dental Association*, 238
Healey, John, *The Christian & Missionary Alliance in Canada*, 566
Healey, Nancy, *St. John's Board of Trade*, 1249
Healy, Damien, *Basketball NWT*, 199
Heaman, Dan, *Risk & Insurance Management Society Inc.*, 1234
Heapy, Darcy, *Holstein Canada*, 819
Hearder-Moan, Wendy, *County of Perth Law Association*, 636
Hearn, Chris, *Master Mariners of Canada*, 953
Hearn, Christopher, *Master Mariners of Canada*, 954
Hearn, David, *The Christian & Missionary Alliance in Canada*, 566
Heath, Dianne, *British Columbia Association of Social Workers*, 232
Heath, Paul, *Royal Astronomical Society of Canada*, 1238
Heather, Glen, *Medicine Hat Fish & Game Association*, 958
Heather, Ken, *Faculty Association of Red Deer College*, 701
Heavisides, Terry, *Habitat for Humanity Canada*, 798
Hebda, Andrew, *Purebred Sheep Breeders Association of Nova Scotia*, 1194
Hébert, Suzanne, *Association des ingénieurs-professeurs des sciences appliquées*, 117
Hebert, Bob, *Boys & Girls Clubs of New Brunswick*, 222
Hebert, Larry, *Thunder Bay District Municipal League*, 1377
Hébert, Anne, *Conseil économique du Nouveau-Brunswick inc.*, 618
Hébert, Mélanie, *Chambre de commerce de Chibougamau*, 540
Hébert, Christian, *Architects' Association of New Brunswick*, 78
Hébert, Martine, *Canadian Federation of Independent Business*, 387
Hébert, Roger, *Association québécoise de l'épilepsie*, 169
Hebert, Todd, *Canadian Liver Foundation*, 427
Hébert, Pierre, *Fédération québécoise des revêtements de sol*, 729
Hebert, Denis, *Refrigeration Service Engineers Society (Canada)*, 1211
Hébert, Jessica, *Art Libraries Society of North America*, 1506
Hébert, Raymonde, *Association d'éducation préscolaire du Québec*, 99
Hébert, Michel, *Société historique de Dorval*, 1319
Hebert, Nadine, *New Brunswick Society of Cardiology Techologists*, 1012
Hebert, Terry, *Federation of Dance Clubs of New Brunswick*, 723

Hébert, Claude, *Association des personnes intéressées à l'aphasie et à l'accident vasculaire cérébral*, 123
Hébert-Daly, Éric, *Canadian Parks & Wilderness Society*, 450
Hecht, Jody, *Winnipeg Harvest Inc.*, 1459
Heck, Barry, *WinSport Canada*, 1460
Hecko, Barb, *Telecommunications Employees Association of Manitoba*, 1369
Hedar, Bernadette, *New Brunswick Musicians' Association, Local 815 of the American Federation of Musicians*, 1010
Hedlin, Catherine, *Child & Youth Care Association of Alberta*, 558
Hedlund, Scott, *Prosthetics & Orthotics Association of British Columbia*, 1190
Hedstrom, Heather, *The Salvation Army in Canada*, 1253
Heekin, Erin, *AFCOM*, 1486
Heeley, Warren J., *Heating, Refrigeration & Air Conditioning Institute of Canada*, 810
Heenan-Orr, Stephanie, *New Brunswick Genealogical Society Inc.*, 1008
Heeralal, Fareeda, *Association of Major Power Consumers in Ontario*, 151
Heerema, Helen, *Thunder Bay Law Association*, 1378
Heerema, Hank, *Kerby Centre for the 55 Plus*, 884
Heersink, Paul, *Canadian Cartographic Association*, 350
Heesen, Erika, *Librarians Without Borders*, 910
Hefferman, Sean, *Canadian Soccer Association*, 472
Heffernan, Mike, *Peterborough & the Kawarthas Association of Realtors Inc.*, 1153
Hefler, Donald, *HelpAge Canada*, 812
Hefler-Elson, Jennifer, *Labrador Friendship Centre*, 894
Heick, Caroline, *Canadian Institute for Health Information*, 412
Heick, Caroline, *Canadian Institute for Health Information*, 412
Heide, Rachel, *Canadian Aviation Historical Society*, 340
Heide, Rachel Lea, *Canadian Aviation Historical Society*, 340
Heidrich, Greg, *Society of Actuaries*, 1592
Heidsma, Melinda P., *AiMHi, Prince George Association for Community Living*, 19
Heighton, Ronnie, *Canadian Council of Professional Fish Harvesters*, 369
Heilbrunn, David, *Canadian Psychoanalytic Society*, 461
Heilman, Keith, *Youth Singers of Calgary*, 1476
Heim, Kathi, *Canadian Association of Elizabeth Fry Societies*, 312
Heim, Kathi, *Canadian Association of Elizabeth Fry Societies*, 313
Heim-Myers, Bev, *Huntington Society of Canada*, 827
Hein, Jane, *British Columbia Registered Music Teachers' Association*, 251
Heinen, Dick, *Christian Labour Association of Canada*, 567
Heinmiller, Kim, *Wellesley & District Board of Trade*, 1443
Heinrich, Paul, *Canadian College of Health Leaders*, 359
Heinrichs, Dana, *Canadian Deafblind Association (National)*, 376
Heinzelman, Bernice, *Quesnel & District Arts Council*, 1200
Heipel, Trent, *Walkerton Business Improvement Area*, 1440
Heise-Jensen, Katia, *Association de paralysie cérébrale du Québec*, 103
Heisler, Owen, *Covenant Health*, 637
Helbig, Johanna, *Coastal First Nations*, 579
Helbronner, Caroline, *International Pension & Employee Benefits Lawyers Association*, 859
Held, Daniel, *Centre for Jewish Education*, 533
Helder, Nathan, *Canadian Condominium Institute*, 362

Helderman, Amanda, *Association for Canadian Studies in the Netherlands*, 1507
Helgesen, Curtis, *Local Government Management Association of British Columbia*, 917
Hellewell, Tara, *Red Deer & District SPCA*, 1209
Helliwell, Jacob, *Association of Professional Economists of British Columbia*, 157
Hellsten-Bzovey, Laurie, *Canadian Educational Researchers' Association*, 380
Hellum, Hayley, *Boys & Girls Clubs of Alberta*, 221
Hellyer, Bill, *Canadian Ski Patrol*, 471
Helm, Christine, *Canadian Ferry Association*, 389
Helm Neima, Trish, *Prince Edward Island Physiotherapy Association*, 1176
Helmer, Doug, *Bio-dynamic Agricultural Society of British Columbia*, 211
Helmuth, Antje, *Health Libraries Association of British Columbia*, 806
Helsdon, Franca, *Global Business Travel Association (Canada)*, 774
Helwig, Steve, *Fort Erie Business Success & Loan Centre*, 752
Hemani, Ali R., *Canadian Association of Insolvency & Restructuring Professionals*, 318
Hemingson, Dustin, *Bashaw & District Chamber of Commerce*, 198
Hemingway, Dawn, *British Columbia Psychogeriatric Association*, 249
Hemmes, Marisa, *Canadian Land Reclamation Association*, 425
Hemminger, Carolyn, *Alzheimer Society Peterborough, Kawartha Lakes, Northumberland, & Haliburton*, 65
Hemminger, Carolyn, *Alzheimer Society Peterborough, Kawartha Lakes, Northumberland, & Haliburton*, 65
Hempel, Ronals, *Manitoba Underwater Council*, 946
Hemphill, Matt, *Potatoes New Brunswick*, 1168
Hemphill, Matt, *Potatoes New Brunswick*, 1168
Hemphill, Wanson, *Prince Edward Island Forest Improvement Association*, 1174
Hemphill, Wanson, *Prince Edward Island Forestry Training Corp.*, 1174
Hemsley, Clare, *Boys & Girls Clubs of Alberta*, 221
Hemsted, John, *Huronia Symphony Orchestra*, 828
Henbid, Kevin, *Chiropractors' Association of Saskatchewan*, 566
Hender, Cheryl, *Saskatchewan Environmental Industry & Managers' Association*, 1264
Hendershot, Holly, *Provision Coalition*, 1191
Henderson, Crystal, *Lakelands Association of Realtors*, 896
Henderson, Jane, *Boys & Girls Clubs of Newfoundland & Labrador*, 222
Henderson, Marjorie, *Canadian Public Relations Society Inc.*, 463
Henderson, Jason, *British Columbia Construction Association*, 237
Henderson, Graham, *Music Canada*, 983
Henderson, John, *Consumer Electronics Marketers of Canada: A Division of Electro-Federation Canada*, 625
Henderson, Susan, *Ontario Dental Assistants Association*, 1077
Henderson, Betty, *Elsa Wild Animal Appeal of Canada*, 685
Henderson, Linda, *Ripple Rock Gem & Mineral Club*, 1233
Henderson, Julie, *Ontario Soil & Crop Improvement Association*, 1108
Henderson, Russ, *Touch Football Ontario*, 1388
Henderson, Debby, *The Royal Scottish Country Dance Society*, 1587
Henderson, Michelle, *Canada Employment & Immigration Union*, 279

Executive Name Index

Henderson, Victoria, *Green Thumb Theatre for Young People*, 789
Henderson, Neville, *Ontario Provincial Trapshooting Association*, 1098
Henderson, Rob, *BioTalent Canada*, 212
Henderson, Allen, *National Association of Teachers of Singing*, 1574
Henderson, Jim, *Golden Horseshoe Beekeepers' Association*, 776
Henderson, Chris, *CADORA Ontario Association Inc.*, 269
Henderson, Jason, *Southern Interior Construction Association*, 1338
Hendin, Stephanie, *Canadian Hadassah WIZO*, 399
Hendrick, Pat, *Canadian Research Institute for the Advancement of Women*, 467
Hendricken-Eldershaw, Corrine, *Canadian Counselling & Psychotherapy Association*, 372
Hendricken-Eldershaw, Corrine, *Alzheimer Society of PEI*, 64
Hendrickson, Tim, *Cathedral Bluffs Symphony Orchestra*, 517
Hendrika, Maria, *Regina Transition Women's Society*, 1212
Hendrix, Ron, *Ontario Association of Cemetery & Funeral Professionals*, 1062
Heney, John, *Dystonia Medical Research Foundation Canada*, 666
Henheffer, Tom, *Canadian Journalists for Free Expression*, 423
Henkusens, Tiina, *Canadian Spice Association*, 489
Henley, Megan, *Music for Young Children*, 984
Henley, Judy, *Canadian Union of Public Employees*, 499
Henley, Marleen, *Wildrose Polio Support Society*, 1455
Henman, Pat, *Nelson & District Arts Council*, 1003
Hennessey, Dan, *Bridgewater & Area Chamber of Commerce*, 229
Hennessey, Teresa, *Pharmacy Technician Society of Alberta*, 1157
Hennessy, Michael, *Canadian Media Production Association*, 432
Hennessy, Michelle, *Canadian Contractors Association*, 364
Hennessy, Mary J., *Industrial Fabrics Association International*, 1531
Hennigar, Tammie, *Gabriola Island Chamber of Commerce*, 766
Hennigar, Michael, *EduNova*, 680
Henning, Randy, *Durham Regional Police Association*, 665
Henningsen, Nadine, *Canadian Home Care Association*, 408
Henri, Pierre, *Canadian Institute of Management*, 417
Henriques, Jackie, *Ontario 5 Pin Bowlers' Association*, 1058
Henry, Mary Kay, *Service Employees International Union (AFL-CIO/CLC)*, 1588
Henry, Jennifer, *KAIROS: Canadian Ecumenical Justice Initiatives*, 880
Henry, Shirley, *Pemberton & District Chamber of Commerce*, 1149
Henry, Mike, *Administrative Sciences Association of Canada*, 8
Henry, Sheila, *Saint John Real Estate Board Inc.*, 1247
Henry, Denyse, *Canadian Association of Ambulatory Care*, 308
Henry, Marian, *Manitoba Cheer Federation Inc.*, 933
Hensch, Barry, *Calgary Round-Up Band Association*, 274
Hensel, Gordon, *Alberta College of Optometrists*, 29
Henselmann, Branislav, *Ballet British Columbia*, 194
Henshaw, Liza, *Environmental Defense*, 1523
Henshaw, Cheryl, *Ontario Brain Injury Association*, 1069

Henson, Scott, *TEAM of Canada Inc.*, 1368
Hentschke, Liane, *International Society for Music Education*, 1558
Henzie, Kim, *Ontario Katahdin Sheep Association Inc.*, 1088
Hepburn, Catherine, *Alix Chamber of Commerce*, 54
Hepburn, Dave, *Canadian Home Builders' Association - Saskatchewan*, 408
Hepburn, Michele, *The 3C Foundation of Canada*, 1377
Hepburn, Michele, *IBD Foundation*, 829
Hepp, Mary Beth, *American Society of Neuroradiology*, 1501
Heppell, Aaron, *Society of Graphic Designers of Canada*, 1329
Heppler, Em (Matthew), *Ontario Public Interest Research Group*, 1099
Hepplewhite, Anne, *ARMA Canada*, 82
Hepworth, Lorne, *CropLife Canada*, 643
Herauf, Janine, *Dress for Success*, 663
Herbert, John, *Ontario Home Builders' Association*, 1085
Herbert, Cindy, *Nova Scotia Nurses' Union*, 1047
Herbert, Romi Chandra, *PeerNetBC*, 1148
Herbet, Cécile, *Société d'histoire du Témiscamingue*, 1312
Herchenson, Lorna, *British Columbia Fuchsia & Begonia Society*, 242
Herd, Larry, *Canadian Society of Exploration Geophysicists*, 483
Herd, Vicki, *Mensa Canada Society*, 961
Herechuk, Bryan, *Canadian College of Health Leaders*, 359
Herfindahl, Veronica, *Canadian Liver Foundation*, 427
Herget, Kelly, *Canadian Society of Hospital Pharmacists*, 484
Herhalt, John M., *Easter Seals Ontario*, 670
Herltein, Jacquie, *Calgary Women's Soccer Association*, 275
Herman, Deedee, *Ontario Lung Association*, 1090
Herman, Jonathan G., *Federation of Law Societies of Canada*, 724
Herman, Jacqueline, *Carcinoid NeuroEndocrine Tumour Society Canada*, 510
Herman, Carina, *Canadian Council of Practical Nurse Regulators*, 369
Herman, Eugene, *South Shore Wildlife Association*, 1336
Hermans, John, *Association of Professional Researchers for Advancement - Canada*, 160
Hermanson, Helmer, *Yukon RCMP Veteran's Association*, 1480
Hermolin, Maxine, *United Jewish Peoples' Order*, 1411
Hermus, Gregory, *Canadian Tourism Research Institute*, 496
Hernandez, Keith, *Community Development Council Durham*, 596
Herne, Priya, *Provincial Nurse Educator Interest Group*, 1191
Herniman, Richard, *Harrow Early Immigrant Research Society*, 804
Herold, Irene M.H., *Association of College & Research Libraries*, 1511
Heron, Craig, *York University Faculty Association*, 1474
Heron, James, *Japanese Canadian Cultural Centre*, 869
Heron, Rose, *God, Sex, & the Meaning of Life Ministry*, 776
Heroux, Denis, *Association of Architectural Technologists of Ontario*, 139
Herrera, Alice, *University of the Philippines Alumni Association of Toronto*, 1420
Herrick, Steve, *American Academy of Religion*, 1488
Herridge, Lesley, *United Nations Association in Canada*, 1411

Herrndorf, Peter, *National Arts Centre Orchestra of Canada*, 989
Herron, Shaun, *Canadian Information Processing Society*, 411
Herron, Marilynne, *Parkinson Alberta Society*, 1141
Herscovitch, Toby, *Na'amat Canada Inc.*, 987
Herscovitch, Alice, *The Montréal Holocaust Memorial Centre*, 972
Hervieux, Margot, *Peace Parkland Naturalists*, 1147
Hervot, Delphine, *Playwrights' Workshop Montréal*, 1162
Heschuk, Greg, *Manitoba Holiday Festival of the Arts Inc.*, 938
Hesje, Brenda, *Canadian Bar Association*, 342
Hesjedahl, Sue, *Older Adult Centres' Association of Ontario*, 1056
Hesketh, Ian, *Further Poultry Processors Association of Canada*, 765
Hesketh-Boles, Iris, *Association of Vancouver Island Coastal Communities*, 164
Hesketh-Boles, Iris, *Lower Mainland Local Government Association*, 920
Hess, Aart Schuurman, *Greater Vancouver Food Bank Society*, 786
Hess, Regitze Marianne, *International Federation for Housing & Planning*, 1546
Hess, John, *The Queen of Puddings Music Theatre Company*, 1199
Hess, Peter, *New Brunswick Aerospace & Defence Association*, 1004
Hessian, Elizabeth, *Certification Council of Early Childhood Educators of Nova Scotia*, 538
Hetherington, Jay, *Alberta Amateur Football Association*, 22
Hetherington, Stuart, *Comité maritime international*, 1518
Hetherington, Paul, *Baking Association of Canada*, 194
Hetram, Ann, *Canadian Society of Sugar Artistry*, 488
Hett, Bill, *Tillsonburg & District Multi-Service Centre*, 1379
Hettinga, Hanne, *Professional Engineers Ontario*, 1184
Hétu, Carl, *Catholic Near East Welfare Association Canada*, 520
Hetzel, Joseph R., *Door & Access Systems Manufacturers Association*, 1521
Hewitt, Tara, *Canadian Society for Aesthetic Plastic Surgery*, 472
Hewitt, David W., *United Church of Canada*, 1409
Hewitt, Khadijah, *Canadian Association for Laboratory Animal Science*, 302
Hewitt, Khadijah, *Canadian Association for Laboratory Animal Science*, 302
Hewitt, Dave, *Greater Vancouver International Film Festival Society*, 787
Hewitt, George, *Beaverton Thorah Eldon Historical Society*, 203
Hewitt, Ron, *Alberta Sailing Association*, 45
Hewittlo, Nancy, *Canadian Association of Foodservice Professionals*, 315
Hewko, Sarah, *Canadian Foundation for Dietetic Research*, 393
Hewlett, Margaret, *Richmond Food Bank Society*, 1230
Hewlett, Kristen, *Special Libraries Association*, 1596
Hewson, Tom, *Western Barley Growers Association*, 1447
Hewson, Karen, *Canadian Golf Hall of Fame & Museum*, 398
Hewton-Waters, Sue, *Alberta Dressage Association*, 33
Hext, Ted, *Sarnia & District Labour Council*, 1254
Heyer, Michelle, *Canadian Gerontological Nursing Association*, 397
Heyerdahl, Astrid, *Touchstones Nelson Museum of Art & History*, 1388

Heyl, Bryan, *Ontario Plumbing Inspectors Association*, 1096
Heyninck, Emanuela, *Society of Ontario Adjudicators & Regulators*, 1330
Heywood, Grant, *Stratford Musicians' Association, Local 418 of the American Federation of Musicians*, 1351
Heywood, Carol, *Canadian Society of Questers*, 487
Heywood, Vikki, *The Royal Society for the Encouragement of Arts, Manufactures & Commerce*, 1587
Hibbert, Nancy, *Canadian Pony Club*, 458
Hibbs, Carolyn, *Ontario Dental Assistants Association*, 1077
Hibbs, Elaine, *The Salvation Army START Program*, 1253
Hibma, Dick, *Conservation Ontario*, 622
Hicik, Andrew, *Local Government Management Association of British Columbia*, 917
Hickey, Joe E., *Prince Edward Island Association of Optometrists*, 1172
Hickey, Carolyn, *Newfoundland & Labrador Society for the Prevention of Cruelty to Animals*, 1022
Hickey, Bobby Jo, *Maritime Hereford Association*, 950
Hickey, Steve, *Centraide sud-ouest du Québec*, 523
Hickey, Mark, *Insurance Brokers Association of Canada*, 848
Hickey, Alexandra, *Ottawa Valley Health Libraries Association*, 1132
Hickman, Darrell, *Canadian Gelbvieh Association*, 396
Hickox, Jamie, *Squash Canada*, 1347
Hicks, David, *Computer Modelling Group*, 609
Hicks, Michael, *Fundy Trail Beagle Club*, 764
Hicks, Tim, *CARP*, 514
Hicks, Larry, *Geological Association of Canada*, 770
Hicks, Calvin, *New Brunswick Beekeepers Association*, 1006
Hicks, Kim, *YWCA Canada*, 1482
Hicks, Dawn, *Herb Society of Manitoba*, 812
Hicks, Grant, *Alberta Beekeepers Commission*, 26
Hicks, Barry, *Newfoundland & Labrador Table Tennis Association*, 1022
Hiebert, Sharon, *Association of Saskatchewan Realtors*, 161
Hiebert, Kerri, *Vocational Rehabilitation Association of Canada*, 1436
Hiebert, Mary Jane, *Association of Canadian Travel Agents - Manitoba & Nunavut*, 144
Hiebert, Ted, *Open Space Arts Society*, 1114
Hiebert, Lynda, *The Eckhardt-Gramatté Foundation*, 671
Hiemstra, Joan, *Global Village Nanaimo*, 775
Hierlihy, Mark, *Canadian Cancer Society*, 349
Higa, Kevin, *Financial Executives International Canada*, 736
Higenbottam, John, *Psychosocial Rehabilitation Canada*, 1192
Higenell, Peter, *Ontario Podiatric Medical Association*, 1096
Higginbotham, Ken, *Council of Forest Industries*, 633
Higgins, Peter, *Retail Council of Canada*, 1228
Higgins, Phil, *Havelock, Belmont, Methuen & District Chamber of Commerce*, 805
Higginson, Laralie, *Manitoba Ringette Association*, 943
Higgs, Laura, *Ontario Home Builders' Association*, 1086
Higgs, Blaine, *Progressive Conservative Party of New Brunswick*, 1187
Highcock, Bob, *Peninsula Field Naturalists*, 1149
Highway, Lynda, *Inter-Provincial Association on Native Employment*, 861
Hiland, Barb, *Community Living Peterborough*, 604

Executive Name Index

Hilborn, Vicki, *Professional Engineers Ontario*, 1184
Hilchie, Jayson, *Entertainment Software Association of Canada*, 690
Hildebrand, Ryan, *Winkler & District Chamber of Commerce*, 1458
Hildebrand, Glenn, *Canadian National Institute for the Blind*, 439
Hildebrand, Deb, *CADORA Ontario Association Inc.*, 269
Hildebrandt, Karen, *Alberta Association of Library Technicians*, 23
Hildebrandt, Kalamity, *Simon Fraser Public Interest Research Group*, 1300
Hildebtrandt, Henry, *Kenora Fellowship Centre*, 883
Hiley, Marjorie, *Flemingdon Community Legal Services*, 740
Hilford, Bonnie, *Alberta Municipal Clerks Association*, 40
Hilier, Wade, *Davenport-Perth Neighbourhood & Community Health Centre*, 651
Hill, Brad, *Irma Fish & Game Association*, 864
Hill, Tina, *Big Brothers Big Sisters of Ontario*, 210
Hill, Aaron, *North Hastings Community Integration Association*, 1031
Hill, Rick, *Community Living Walkerton & District*, 606
Hill, Dwayne, *Vulcan & District Chamber of Commerce*, 1439
Hill, Stephen, *Fredericton Chamber of Commerce*, 758
Hill, Jessica, *College of Family Physicians of Canada*, 585
Hill, Terry, *International Organization for Standardization*, 1554
Hill, William, *Flax Council of Canada*, 740
Hill, Brenda, *Alzheimer Society of Alberta & Northwest Territories*, 61
Hill, Mark, *Craft & Hobby Association*, 1520
Hill, Penny, *Council of Private Investigators - Ontario*, 635
Hill, D'Arcy, *Volleyball Yukon*, 1438
Hill, Jane, *Numeris*, 1051
Hill, Leslie, *HIV Community Link*, 816
Hill, Karen, *The Avon Trail*, 191
Hill, Simone, *Association for Mineral Exploration British Columbia*, 134
Hill, Kathryn Ann, *Family Service Centre of Ottawa-Carleton*, 704
Hill, Ana, *Catholic Family Services of Peel Dufferin*, 519
Hill, Maggie, *Real Estate Institute of Canada*, 1206
Hill, Caitlin, *Ecological Farmers of Ontario*, 672
Hill, Carol, *Hamilton Regional Indian Centre*, 802
Hill, Richard B., *American Society for Information Science & Technology*, 1498
Hill, Maggie, *Real Estate Institute of British Columbia*, 1205
Hill, Kim, *Saskatchewan Food Processors Association*, 1265
Hill, Michael, *Stephen Leacock Associates*, 1349
Hill, Lesley, *Batshaw Youth & Family Centres*, 199
Hill, Michael, *Heart & Stroke Foundation of Alberta, NWT & Nunavut*, 808
Hill, Deirdre, *Maxville & District Chamber of Commerce*, 954
Hill, Violet, *Native Fishing Association*, 998
Hill, Penny, *Association of Certified Fraud Examiners - Toronto Chapter*, 145
Hill, Elizabeth, *Canadian-Cuban Friendship Association Toronto*, 506
Hill, Phyllis, *Jake Thomas Learning Centre*, 867
Hill, Greg, *Campbell River & District Association for Community Living*, 276
Hill, Charlene, *TelecomPioneers*, 1597
Hill, Lorraine, *Alberta Dressage Association*, 33

Hill, Lorraine, *Alberta Dressage Association*, 33
Hill, Aimee, *Alberta Music Industry Association*, 41
Hill-Lehr, Andria, *Canadian Counselling & Psychotherapy Association*, 372
Hillcox, Brenda, *Alberta Deaf Sports Association*, 32
Hillier, Kirk, *The Acadian Entomological Society*, 4
Hillier, Heather, *Newfoundland & Labrador Veterinary Medical Association*, 1022
Hillier, Scott, *Junior Achievement Canada*, 877
Hillier, Melissa, *United Way of Leeds & Grenville*, 1415
Hillier, Rick, *The Vimy Foundation*, 1435
Hillier, Lynette, *Dr. H. Bliss Murphy Cancer Care Foundation*, 662
Hillier, David, *St Catharines Stamp Club*, 1248
Hillier, Greg, *Golf Newfoundland & Labrador*, 777
Hillier, Steven, *Canadian Association of Defence & Security Industries*, 312
Hilliker, Arthur, *York University Faculty Association*, 1474
Hillis-Krause, Anita, *Haldimand-Norfolk Literacy Council*, 798
Hills, Philip, *Association of Christian Schools International*, 1511
Hills, Marla, *Westward Goals Support Services Inc.*, 1451
Hills, Bev, *Kwakiutl District Council*, 894
Hillyard, Jason, *Chartered Professional Accountants of Newfoundland & Labrador*, 553
Hillyer, Dan, *Tofield & District Chamber of Commerce*, 1380
Hilton, Andrew (Sandy), *Chartered Professional Accountants Canada*, 552
Hilts, Michelle, *Canadian Organization of Medical Physicists*, 447
Hiltz, Fred, *The Primate's World Relief & Development Fund*, 1171
Hiltz, Fred, *The Anglican Church of Canada*, 69
Hiltz, Doug, *Canadian Forestry Association of New Brunswick*, 392
Hiltz, Matt, *New Brunswick Nurses Union*, 1010
Hiltz, Wayne, *Manitoba Chicken Producers*, 933
Hiltz, Tammy, *People First Nova Scotia*, 1151
Himbeault, Donald, *Nature Manitoba*, 1000
Himelfarb, Alex, *World Wildlife Fund - Canada*, 1468
Hinchey, Garrett, *NWT Squash*, 1052
Hind, Michael, *Tri-Cities Chamber of Commerce Serving Coquitlam, Port Coquitlam & Port Moody*, 1398
Hindley, Rob, *Canadian National Institute for the Blind*, 439
Hindley, James, *Central Coast Communications Society*, 524
Hindmarsh, Wayne, *The Canadian Council for Accreditation of Pharmacy Programs*, 366
Hinds, John, *Canadian Community Newspapers Association*, 361
Hinds, John, *Newspapers Canada*, 1024
Hinds, Tammy, *Lupus SK Society*, 922
Hinds, Susanna, *Association of American Publishers*, 1510
Hine, Susan, *Darts Ontario*, 651
Hines, Betty-Anne, *Canadian Hemophilia Society*, 404
Hing Man, Shu, *Chinese Canadian National Council*, 564
Hinse, Maurizia, *Alberta Weekly Newspapers Association*, 51
Hinsperger, Chris, *Ottawa Valley Tourist Association*, 1132
Hinter, Ross, *Alberta Trappers' Association*, 50
Hinton, Julie, *Similkameen Okanagan Organic Producers Association*, 1300
Hinton, Louisette, *Congress of Union Retirees Canada*, 613
Hinton, Nacole B., *American Chemistry Council*, 1491

Hippolt-Squair, Gisela, *Association of Professional Engineers & Geoscientists of Alberta*, 157
Hird, Jim, *Canadian Haflinger Association*, 400
Hirji, Sheherazade, *Canadian Women's Foundation*, 505
Hirokawa, Nobutaka, *International Federation for Cell Biology*, 1546
Hirowatari, Mark, *Canadian Bible Society*, 343
Hirsch, Dave, *Friends of the Earth International*, 1527
Hirsch, Jeff, *Federation of Law Societies of Canada*, 724
Hirsch, Marianne, *Modern Language Association of America*, 1571
Hirschhaut, Richard S., *Holocaust Memorial Foundation of Illinois*, 1529
Hirst, Brad, *Rugby Manitoba*, 1244
Hirt, Ilana, *The Canadian Society for the Weizmann Institute of Science*, 479
Hirtle, Chris, *Canadian Society for Medical Laboratory Science*, 476
Hiscocks, Mandy, *Ontario Public Interest Research Group*, 1099
Hitchins, Nancy, *Canadian Consumer Specialty Products Association*, 364
Hitchlock, Norma, *Registered Insurance Brokers of Ontario*, 1213
Hitkari, Jason, *Canadian Fertility & Andrology Society*, 389
Hitscherich, Helmut, *Ontario Trail Riders Association*, 1111
Hizaka, Maureen, *Canadian Hardware & Housewares Manufacturers' Association*, 401
Hjorngaard, Marilia, *Newcastle & District Chamber of Commerce*, 1015
Hladik, Gale, *Winnipeg Association of Non-Teaching Employees*, 1458
Hladun, Marianne, *Public Service Alliance of Canada*, 1193
Hladun, Marianne, *Public Service Alliance of Canada*, 1193
Hlady, Andrea, *Castle-Crown Wilderness Coalition*, 517
Hlus, Barbara, *Ukrainian Canadian Congress*, 1402
Hlusko, Christina, *Better Business Bureau of Eastern & Northern Ontario & the Outaouais*, 206
Hnatiuk, Jeff, *Sport Manitoba*, 1344
Ho, Minh, *Spina Bifida & Hydrocephalus Association of Southern Alberta*, 1342
Ho, Laina, *International College of Traditional Chinese Medicine of Vancouver*, 855
Ho, Amelia, *British Columbia Table Tennis Association*, 255
Ho, Wilson, *Immigrant Services Calgary*, 830
Ho, Jacqui, *Canadian Society of Gastroenterology Nurses & Associates*, 483
Ho, Jimmy, *Canadian Dental Protective Association*, 377
Ho, Wilfred, *National Taekwon-Do Federation*, 996
Ho, Mimi, *British Columbia Registered Music Teachers' Association*, 251
Ho, Emmanuel, *Controlled Release Society*, 1520
Ho Ng, Chi, *Canadian Academic Accounting Association*, 285
Hoa, Suong V., *Canadian Association for Composite Structures & Materials*, 298
Hoadley, Don, *Colchester Community Workshops Foundation*, 580
Hoar, Bill, *Canadian Vintage Motorcycle Group*, 501
Hoare, Wendy, *Canadian Association of Numismatic Dealers*, 323
Hobart, Janie, *Thebacha Chamber of Commerce*, 1375
Hobbins, Cindy, *Community Living Peterborough*, 604
Hobbs, Stephanie, *Simcoe/Muskoka Literacy Network*, 1300
Hobbs, Matt, *Toronto Financial Services Alliance*, 1384

Hobbs, Brian, *Association of Fundraising Professionals*, 1512
Hobbs-Blyth, Sarah, *Planned Parenthood of Toronto*, 1161
Hobby, Ric, *International Alliance of Dietary/Food Supplement Associations*, 1535
Hocaluk, Steve, *Sports Car Club of British Columbia*, 1346
Hocevar, Mike, *Canadian Hard of Hearing Association*, 400
Hoch, Ruth, *Thames Valley Trail Association Inc.*, 1373
Hochstein, Philip, *Independent Contractors & Businesses Association of British Columbia*, 832
Hochstein, Terence, *Potato Growers of Alberta*, 1168
Hochu, Carol, *Canadian Plastics Industry Association*, 455
Hockey, David, *Great Divide Trails Association*, 782
Hockin, Jill, *Prader-Willi Syndrome Association of Alberta*, 1169
Hodder, Stacey, *Hike Ontario*, 814
Hodge, John, *Motorsport Club of Ottawa*, 976
Hodge, Laurie, *Alberta Assessors' Association*, 22
Hodge, Andrew, *Canadian Culinary Federation*, 374
Hodge, Peter, *Ontario Trucking Association*, 1111
Hodge, Barbara Anne, *Canadian Burn Survivors Community*, 347
Hodge, Barbara-Anne, *Mamingwey Burn Survivor Society*, 928
Hodges, Jean, *Parents, Families & Friends of Lesbians & Gays*, 1582
Hodgett, Simon, *Canadian IT Law Association*, 423
Hodgin, Tanya, *Racquetball Ontario*, 1202
Hodgins, Glenn, *Canadian Music Centre*, 438
Hodgins, Rob, *Architectural Woodwork Manufacturers Association of Canada - Southern Alberta*, 80
Hodgins, Douglas, *Gem & Mineral Federation of Canada*, 768
Hodgins, Jean, *Vancouver Recital Society*, 1428
Hodgins, Valerie, *Windsor/Essex County Parents of Multiple Births Association*, 1457
Hodgson, Karen, *Canadian Adult Recreational Hockey Association*, 288
Hodgson, Chris, *Ontario Mining Association*, 1091
Hodgson, George, *Insurance Brokers Association of Canada*, 848
Hodgson, Emily, *Canadian Federation of Medical Students*, 388
Hoedeman, Anouk, *Dutch-Canadian Association Ottawa Valley/Outaouais*, 665
Hoefer, Tom, *Northwest Territories & Nunavut Chamber of Mines*, 1037
Hoekenga, Virginia, *National Association for Environmental Management*, 1572
Hoekstra, Greg, *The Greater Vancouver Board of Trade*, 786
Hoeppner, Dirk, *The Green Party of Manitoba*, 788
Hoevenaars, Rick, *Central 1 Credit Union*, 523
Hoey, Keith, *Burlington Chamber of Commerce*, 265
Hofbauer, Maria, *Lanark County Therapeutic Riding Program*, 897
Hoff, Shannon, *Canadian Society for Continental Philosophy*, 474
Hoffa, James P., *International Brotherhood of Teamsters (AFL-CIO/CLC)*, 1542
Hoffart, Brian, *Saskatchewan Outfitters Association*, 1271
Hoffberger, Lisa, *Alcoholic Beverage Medical Research Foundation*, 1487
Hoffman, Carolyn, *Saskatchewan Registered Nurses' Association*, 1273
Hoffman, Mary C., *Coffin-Lowry Syndrome Foundation*, 1518

Executive Name Index

Hoffman, Carolyn, *Hawk Migration Association of North America*, 1529
Hoffman, Benjamin, *Canadian International Institute of Applied Negotiation*, 422
Hoffman, Evan, *Canadian International Institute of Applied Negotiation*, 422
Hoffman, Tom, *The Order of United Commercial Travelers of America*, 1119
Hoffman, Joseph, *The Order of United Commercial Travelers of America*, 1119
Hoffman, Brian, *Concrete Precasters Association of Ontario*, 610
Hoffmann, Phillip, *Literacy Alberta*, 913
Hogan, Brian, *Windsor & District Labour Council*, 1456
Hogan, Bill, *Aquatic Federation of Canada*, 75
Hogan, Kathy, *Urban Development Institute of Canada*, 1422
Hogan, Chris, *Newfoundland & Labrador Environment Network*, 1018
Hogan, Andrew, *Canadian Association of Freediving & Apnea*, 316
Hogben, Alia, *Canadian Council of Muslim Women*, 369
Hogenson, Daryl, *Cardston Historical Society*, 511
Hogg, Frances, *Presbyterian Church in Canada*, 1170
Hogg, Ian, *Prince Edward Island Rifle Association*, 1176
Hogg, Cathy, *Public School Boards' Association of Alberta*, 1193
Hogg, Alan, *Boxing Manitoba*, 220
Hogg, Robert, *The Canadian Association for HIV Research*, 301
Hoggan, James, *David Suzuki Foundation*, 652
Hogue, Edward E., *World Safety Organization*, 1607
Hohman, Peter G., *Insurance Institute of Canada*, 849
Hohol, David, *Centre for Newcomers Society of Calgary*, 533
Hojjati, Mehdi, *Canadian Association for Composite Structures & Materials*, 298
Holbrook, Greg, *Canadian Federal Pilots Association*, 384
Holdaway, Lorraine, *Canadian Palomino Horse Association*, 449
Holden, Miles, *Vintage Road Racing Association*, 1435
Holden, Paul, *Burnaby Board of Trade*, 266
Holden, Linda, *Newfoundland & Labrador Right to Life Association*, 1021
Holden, Michelle, *Gateway Research Organization*, 767
Holder, Ed, *Sunshine Dreams for Kids*, 1355
Holdsworth, Sandra, *Canadian Transplant Association*, 497
Hole, Ken, *Boissevain & District Chamber of Commerce*, 217
Holebrook, Caroline, *International Society for Affective Disorders*, 1557
Holfeld, Mark, *Saskatchewan Municipal Hail Insurance Association*, 1270
Holinda, Dan, *Canadian Cancer Society*, 349
Holitzki, Greg, *Kitikmeot Regional Board of Trade*, 891
Hollahan, Roger, *Association of Seafood Producers*, 162
Holland, Marjorie, *Princeton Community Arts Council*, 1180
Holland, Dan, *International Institute of Fisheries Economics & Trade*, 1551
Holland, Kline, *Architectural Glass & Metal Contractors Association*, 79
Holland, Jordanne, *Concerned Friends of Ontario Citizens in Care Facilities*, 609
Holland, Thomas, *Cross Country Canada*, 643
Holland, Camilla, *Royal Manitoba Theatre Centre*, 1242
Holland, Byron, *Canadian Internet Registration Authority*, 422
Hollett, Lynette, *The Lung Association of Nova Scotia*, 921

Hollett, Charmaine, *Osteoporosis Canada*, 1128
Hollinger, Martha, *Saskatchewan Waste Reduction Council*, 1277
Hollingshead, Stephanie, *Big Brothers Big Sisters of British Columbia*, 209
Hollins, Leah, *Canadian Blood Services*, 344
Hollins, Deborah, *Nanaimo Family Life Association*, 988
Holloway, Ian, *Canadian Institute of Resources Law*, 419
Holloway, Gordon, *Royal New Brunswick Rifle Association Inc.*, 1242
Hollowell, Ray, *Canadian Hockey League*, 406
Holm, Marilyn, *Juvenile Diabetes Research Foundation Canada*, 879
Holm, Kai, *International Masters Games Association*, 1553
Holm, Jens V., *International Masters Games Association*, 1553
Holman, Shawn, *Speed Skating Canada*, 1341
Holman, Katie, *Ontario Horse Trials Association*, 1086
Holman, George, *Atlin Board of Trade*, 187
Holman, Jennifer, *Canadian Transplant Association*, 496
Holmes, David, *International Union of Painters & Allied Trades*, 1565
Holmes, Jonathan L., *Independent Telecommunications Providers Association*, 834
Holmes, Lynne, *Enderby & District Chamber of Commerce*, 687
Holmes, Jeff, *St. Andrews Chamber of Commerce*, 1248
Holmes, Ken, *Canadian Association of Drilling Engineers*, 312
Holmes, Rebecca, *Family Enterprise Xchange*, 703
Holmes, Susan, *Canadian Cancer Society*, 349
Holmes, Matthew, *Magazines Canada*, 925
Holmes, Kate, *United Way of Milton*, 1415
Holmes, Carol, *The Writers' Guild of Alberta*, 1469
Holmes, Doug, *South Okanagan Immigrant & Community Services*, 1335
Holmes, Tami, *Sarnia & District Humane Society*, 1254
Holmes, Kelly, *Resource Assistance for Youth*, 1227
Holmes, Margot, *Vancouver Island Symphony*, 1427
Holmes, Elizabeth, *Eastern Ontario Model Forest*, 670
Holmes, Jeanne, *Canada Dance Festival Society*, 278
Holmes, Bev, *Michael Smith Foundation for Health Research*, 964
Holmes, Martha, *Shelburne Association Supporting Inclusion*, 1295
Holmes-Tuor, Penny, *Canadian Blood Services*, 345
Holmquist, Bruce, *Canadian Simmental Association*, 470
Holmwood, Andy, *Biathlon Canada*, 207
Holness, Duncan, *Bowls Saskatchewan Inc.*, 220
Holoboff, Melissa, *South Peace Community Arts Council*, 1335
Holoboff, Chris, *Parrot Association of Canada*, 1143
Holod, Tracy, *Community Living Manitoba*, 603
Holowka, Taryn, *U.S. Green Building Council*, 1601
Holst, Haldis, *Education International*, 1522
Holst, Michelle, *Mortgage Investment Association of British Columbia*, 975
Holt, Rush D., *American Association for the Advancement of Science*, 1489
Holtby, Anna, *Alberta Recreation & Parks Association*, 44
Holter, Erika, *Real Estate Institute of Canada*, 1205
Holton, Helen, *Central Okanagan Community Food Bank*, 525

Holtslander, Cathy, *National Farmers Union*, 993
Holtslander, Cathy, *National Farmers Foundation*, 993
Holuboch, Wendy, *Edson & District Chamber of Commerce*, 680
Holubowich, Greg, *Edmonton Fire Fighters Union*, 677
Holzschuh Sator, Monika, *Queen's University Faculty Association*, 1200
Homan, Don, *Canadian Student Leadership Association*, 491
Homel, David, *Québec Writers' Federation*, 1199
Homel, Gene, *Peretz Centre for Secular Jewish Culture*, 1152
Homer, Alicia, *Metro Toronto Movement for Literacy*, 963
Homer, Bruce, *Garth Homer Society*, 767
Hominuk, Darell, *Multiple Sclerosis Society of Canada*, 980
Hominuk, Peter, *Assemblée de la francophonie de l'Ontario*, 88
Hon, Teresa, *American Public Works Association*, 1497
Hone, Susan, *Barth Syndrome Foundation of Canada*, 197
Honeywell, Peter, *Ottawa Arts Council*, 1129
Hong, Al, *Ontario 5 Pin Bowlers' Association*, 1058
Hood, Barbara, *NWT Seniors' Society*, 1052
Hood, Chris, *Paramedic Association of Canada*, 1138
Hood, Chris, *Paramedic Association of New Brunswick*, 1138
Hood, Colin, *New Brunswick Physiotherapy Association*, 1011
Hood, Grant, *Local Government Administrators of the Northwest Territories*, 916
Hoodless, Karen, *Association of Canadian Ergonomists*, 142
Hooey, Jane, *The Bob Rumball Centre for the Deaf*, 216
Hoogendoorn, Ben, *Canadian Food for the Hungry International*, 391
Hook, Adrienne, *Canadian Institute for the Relief of Pain & Disability*, 413
Hook, Tomas, *International Association for Great Lakes Research*, 1536
Hooles, Richard, *Toronto Transportation Society*, 1388
Hooper, Jim, *British Columbia School Counsellors' Association*, 252
Hooper, Shauna, *Threshold Ministries*, 1377
Hooper, Elizabeth, *Canadian Society of Clinical Chemists*, 481
Hooper, Jay, *World Wildlife Fund - Canada*, 1468
Hooper, Sonya, *Early Childhood Development Association of Prince Edward Island*, 666
Hooper, Mary, *London Insurance Professionals Association*, 918
Hope, David, *The Actors' Fund of Canada*, 7
Hope, Marty, *Canadian Business Aviation Association*, 348
Hope, Amy, *Master Brewers Association of The Americas*, 1569
Hope, Len, *Congress of Union Retirees Canada*, 613
Hope, Amy, *Controlled Release Society*, 1520
Hope, Ian, *Alberta Automotive Recyclers & Dismantlers Association*, 25
Hopfauf, Anita, *Schizophrenia Society of Saskatchewan*, 1284
Hopgood, Jane, *Artscape*, 86
Hopgood, Susan, *Education International*, 1522
Hopkin, Jacqueline, *Wikwemikong Anishinabe Association for Community Living*, 1453
Hopkins, Robyn, *Canadian Dermatology Association*, 377
Hopkins, John, *Regina & District Chamber of Commerce*, 1211
Hopkins, Sareena, *Canadian Career Development Foundation*, 350

Hopkins, Eric, *CAA British Columbia*, 267
Hopkins, Jim B., *Canadian Society of Safety Engineering, Inc.*, 488
Hopkins, Paul, *Esperanto Association of Canada*, 695
Hopkins, Sheryl, *Soroptimist Foundation of Canada*, 1333
Hopkins, Amanda, *The Writers' Trust of Canada*, 1469
Hopkins, Susan, *Concerned Educators Allied for a Safe Environment*, 1519
Hopkins, Coralie, *Association of New Brunswick Massage Therapists*, 154
Hopkins, Mark, *Nova Scotia Band Association*, 1042
Hopkins, Sandy, *Habitat for Humanity Canada*, 796
Hopkins, Ken, *School Lunch Association*, 1284
Hopkinson, Claire, *Toronto Arts Foundation*, 1382
Hopkinson, Claire, *Toronto Arts Council*, 1381
Hopkyns, David, *Credit Institute of Canada*, 641
Hoppe, Mason, *American Society of Heating, Refrigerating & Air Conditioning Engineers*, 1500
Hoppe, Dan, *American Library Association*, 1494
Hopper, Linda, *Osteoporosis Canada*, 1128
Hoque, Kazi, *Settlement Assistance & Family Support Services*, 1292
Horbal, Russ, *Sport Medicine & Science Council of Manitoba Inc.*, 1344
Horel, Robin, *Canadian Poultry & Egg Processors Council*, 458
Horgan, John, *New Democratic Party*, 1014
Horiuchi, Masatsugu, *International Society of Hypertension*, 1560
Horn, Michiel, *Canadian Association for the Advancement of Netherlandic Studies*, 305
Horne, Bill, *Ottawa Independent Writers*, 1131
Horne, Dawn, *Insurance Institute of Northern Alberta*, 849
Horne, Kat, *Institute for Change Leaders*, 843
Horner, Barbara, *Huntington Society of Canada*, 828
Horner, Eldon, *Federation of Ontario Law Associations*, 726
Hornsby, Richard, *Cultural Human Resources Council*, 645
Hornsby, Richard, *Music/Musique NB*, 984
Hornstein, Marty, *Jewish Family Services - Calgary*, 871
Horsman, Doug, *Royal Canadian Army Service Corps Association-(Atlantic Region)*, 1239
Horstman, Ig, *Rotman Institute for International Business*, 1237
Horth, Sylvie, *Ringuette 96 Montréal-Nord-Est*, 1233
Horting, Karen, *Society of Women Engineers*, 1594
Horton, Sue, *Canadian Association for Graduate Studies*, 300
Horton, Wendy, *Youth Without Shelter*, 1476
Horton, Kim, *Miniature Horse Association of Nova Scotia*, 966
Horvath, Gaspar, *Black Creek Conservation Project*, 213
Horvath, Steve, *Radiation Safety Institute of Canada*, 1202
Horvath, John R., *Canadian Association of Veterans in United Nations Peacekeeping*, 336
Horwath, Andrea, *New Democratic Party*, 1014
Horwich, Jim, *Parkinson Society Maritime Region*, 1141
Horwitz, Robert, *Oraynu Congregation for Humanistic Judaism*, 1117
Horwood, Kathleen, *Congregational Christian Churches in Canada*, 613
Hos, Hajni, *New Canadians Centre Peterborough Immigrant Services*, 1014
Hosanna, Trevor, *Hockey Northwestern Ontario*, 818

Executive Name Index

Hoscheit, Steve, *Trillium Health Partners Foundation*, 1398
Hosein, Salisha, *Canadian Investor Relations Institute*, 422
Hosein, Trisha, *Visions of Science Network for Learning*, 1436
Hosken, Cathie, *Ontario Society for the Prevention of Cruelty to Animals*, 1106
Hoskins, Kevin, *Association québécoise pour le loisir des personnes handicapées*, 177
Hossack-Scott, Lisa, *CADORA Ontario Association Inc.*, 269
Hosseiny, Fardous, *Canadian Mental Health Association*, 434
Hou, Feng, *Canadian Population Society*, 458
Houdayer, Julie-Anne, *Association of Fundraising Professionals*, 1512
Houde, Ghislain, *Association des consultants et laboratoires experts*, 110
Houde, Raymond, *Counselling & Support Services of S.D. & G.*, 636
Houde, Normand, *Société de généalogie de la Mauricie et des Bois-Francs*, 1315
Houde, Mario, *Syndicat des professeurs et professeures de l'Université du Québec à Montréal*, 1364
Houdeib, Mazen, *Communauté Laotienne du Québec*, 594
Hough, Arthur, *Squash Alberta*, 1347
Hough, Frank, *Master Mariners of Canada*, 953
Hough, Barbara, *Skate Canada*, 1301
Hough, Lucy, *West Coast Environmental Law*, 1445
Hougham, Alison, *British Columbia Teacher Regulation Branch*, 255
Houghton, Ed, *Ontario Municipal Water Association*, 1092
Houghton, Ted, *British Columbia Speed Skating Association*, 254
Hould, Caroline, *Association sportive des sourds du Québec inc.*, 178
Houle, Nancy, *Canadian Condominium Institute*, 362
Houle, Denis, *Association des constructeurs de routes et grands travaux du Québec*, 110
Houle, Julie, *Centre canadien d'arbitrage commercial*, 526
Houle, Suzanne, *Société généalogique canadienne-française*, 1319
Houle, Ginette, *Fédération de l'industrie manufacturière (FIM-CSN)*, 709
Houle, Laureen, *Athabasca Native Friendship Centre Society*, 180
Houle-LeSarge, Jocelyne, *Institut québécois de planification financière*, 843
Hounsell, Cindy, *Réseau du sport étudiant du Québec Côte-Nord*, 1223
House, John, *Canadian Dove Association*, 378
House, David, *Canadian Dove Association*, 378
House, Rowena, *Craft Council of Newfoundland & Labrador*, 638
House, Christopher, *Toronto Dance Theatre*, 1384
House, Amy, *Alliance of Canadian Cinema, Television & Radio Artists*, 58
House, Betty, *Atlantic Canada Fish Farmers Association*, 182
House, Emma, *The Publishers Association*, 1586
House, Sherry, *The Appraisal Institute of Canada - Newfoundland & Labrador*, 75
Houser, Jeff, *Atlantic Division, CanoeKayak Canada*, 183
Houston, Bill, *Lundy's Lane Historical Society*, 920
Houston, Sandra, *Arts Council of Sault Ste Marie & District*, 85
Houston, Sandy, *George Cedric Metcalf Charitable Foundation*, 770
Houston, Lisa, *North Algoma Literacy Coalition*, 1028
Houston, Lisa, *Canada-Japan Society of Toronto*, 283

Houze, Graham, *Professional Engineers Ontario*, 1185
Hovakimian, Abgar, *Armenian Holy Apostolic Church - Canadian Diocese*, 83
Howard, Vivian, *Canadian Association for Information Science*, 301
Howard, Sherry, *Carberry Plains Arts Council*, 510
Howard, Murray, *George Bray Sports Association*, 770
Howard, Mike, *British Columbia Technology Education Association*, 256
Howard, Ashley, *Saskatchewan Curling Association*, 1263
Howard, Jock, *Alberta Genealogical Society*, 36
Howard, Maria, *Alzheimer Society of British Columbia*, 62
Howard, Samantha, *Canadian Federation of Independent Business*, 387
Howard, Donna, *Ontario Federation of School Athletic Associations*, 1080
Howard, Claire, *The Canadian Society for the Weizmann Institute of Science*, 479
Howard, Gloria, *United Empire Loyalists' Association of Canada*, 1410
Howard, Robert, *United Way of Durham Region*, 1414
Howard, Steve, *Habitat for Humanity Canada*, 797
Howard Baker, Jane, *Inner City Angels*, 839
Howard-Tripp, Micheal, *College of Physicians & Surgeons of Saskatchewan*, 588
Howchin, Maxine, *Arts Council of Surrey*, 85
Howcroft, Ian, *Canadian Manufacturers & Exporters*, 430
Howe, Dan, *Special Olympics BC*, 1339
Howe, Meghan, *Canadian Children's Book Centre*, 355
Howe, Alan, *Manitoba Water & Wastewater Association*, 947
Howe, Darlene, *Richmond Gem & Mineral Society*, 1230
Howe, Cathy, *Bereaved Families of Ontario*, 205
Howe, Valerie, *Gardiner Centre*, 767
Howe-Bundy, Germaine, *Nova Scotia Association of Black Social Workers*, 1041
Howell, Rose Marie, *Investment Property Owners Association of Nova Scotia Ltd.*, 863
Howell, David W., *Hamilton Law Association*, 801
Howell, Philip, *Canadian Council of Insurance Regulators*, 368
Howell, Fran, *DES Action USA*, 1521
Howell, Doris, *Canadian Association of Psychosocial Oncology*, 330
Howerter, David, *Ducks Unlimited Canada*, 663
Howes, Hilary, *New Brunswick Society for the Prevention of Cruelty to Animals*, 1012
Howes, Lauren, *Canadian Filmmakers Distribution Centre*, 390
Howes, Nicole, *Operation Springboard*, 1116
Howie, Wes, *Royal Astronomical Society of Canada*, 1238
Howie, Bruce, *Society of Plastics Engineers*, 1594
Howland, Kathy, *Bridgetown & Area Historical Society*, 229
Howland, Wink, *Saskatchewan Beekeepers Association*, 1259
Howland, Sharon, *Recycling Council of Alberta*, 1208
Hoyle, Alice, *Alberta Genealogical Society*, 37
Hoyles, Cathy, *Canadian College of Health Leaders*, 359
Hoyles, John, *Canadian Bar Association*, 341
Hoyt, Evelyn, *Moncton Retriever Club*, 972
Hrab, Roy, *Ontario Energy Association*, 1077
Hraynyk, Jason, *Golf Association of Ontario*, 777
Hrebeniuk, Darcy, *Saskatchewan/Manitoba Gelbvieh Association*, 1279

Hrehoruk, Bobby, *Volunteer Management Professionals of Canada*, 1439
Hrubecky, George, *Mississauga Choral Society*, 970
Hrudka, Christine, *Pharmacists' Association of Saskatchewan, Inc.*, 1157
Hrycenko-Luhova, Zorianna, *Ukrainian Canadian Congress*, 1402
Hrycyna, Brad, *Royal United Services Institute of Regina*, 1243
Hryniuk-Adamov, Carol, *Manitoba Reading Association*, 943
Hryshko, Gayle, *The Regional Health Authorities of Manitoba*, 1212
Hsieh, William, *Canadian Meteorological & Oceanographic Society*, 436
Hsu, Annie, *CropLife Canada*, 643
Hsueh, Po-Ren, *International Society of Chemotherapy for Infection & Cancer*, 1560
Huang, Danny, *Whitchurch-Stouffville Chamber of Commerce*, 1452
Hubbard, Janine, *Association of Psychology Newfoundland & Labrador*, 160
Hubbard, Michael, *Master Mariners of Canada*, 953
Hubbard, W. David, *Council of Better Business Bureaus*, 1520
Hubbard, Fern, *College of Dietitians of British Columbia*, 584
Hubbart, Larry, *Canadian Poolplayers Association*, 458
Hubberten, Hans-W., *International Permafrost Association*, 1555
Huber, Uli, *Canadian Federation of Aircraft Maintenance Engineers Associations*, 384
Huber, Arron, *Saskatchewan Shorthorn Association*, 1274
Huber, Gwen, *British Columbia Association for Regenerative Agriculture*, 231
Huber, Tim, *Law Society of Saskatchewan*, 902
Huberman, Anita, *Surrey Board of Trade*, 1357
Hubert, Gérald, *Fédération québécoise des sociétés Alzheimer*, 730
Hubert, Ollivier, *Institut d'histoire de l'Amérique française*, 841
Hubich, Larry, *Saskatchewan Federation of Labour*, 1265
Hubick, Robert, *Museums Association of Saskatchewan*, 983
Hubley, Norm, *Canadian Baptist Ministries*, 341
Huchet, Thibaut X., *Master Brewers Association of The Americas*, 1570
Huckaby, Jody M., *Parents, Families & Friends of Lesbians & Gays*, 1582
Hucul, Carlie, *British Columbia Water & Waste Association*, 258
Hucul, Tracy, *Green Action Centre*, 788
Hudak, Tim, *Ontario Real Estate Association*, 1100
Huddart, Stephen, *The J.W. McConnell Family Foundation*, 879
Hudler, Richard, *Queer Ontario*, 1200
Hudon, Paul-Henri, *Société d'histoire de la Seigneurie de Chambly*, 1311
Hudon, Élizabeth, *Chambre de commerce Kamouraska-L'Islet*, 549
Hudon, Dave, *Architectural Woodwork Manufacturers Association of Canada - Manitoba*, 79
Hudson, Lynne, *Canadian Cancer Society*, 348
Hudson, Nan, *Canadian Institute of Cultural Affairs*, 415
Hudson, Kent, *Insurance Institute of Prince Edward Island*, 850
Hudson, Linda, *Writers' Federation of Nova Scotia*, 1469
Hudson, Trevor, *Hypertension Canada*, 829
Hudson, Brenda, *College of Physical Therapists of British Columbia*, 588
Hudson, Angela, *Conseil national Société de Saint-Vincent de Paul*, 619
Hudson, Paul, *Halifax Regional CAP Association*, 799

Hudson, Derek, *Edmonton Economic Development Corporation*, 677
Hudson, Kent, *Community Foundation of Prince Edward Island*, 598
Hudson Stewart, Jennifer, *Lac du Bonnet & District Chamber of Commerce*, 894
Huebel, Norm, *Chemistry Industry Association of Canada*, 556
Huebner, Gerald, *Home School Legal Defence Association of Canada*, 819
Huel, Chad, *Saskatchewan Band Association*, 1259
Huesing, Elaine, *International Medical Informatics Association*, 1553
Huff, Marilyn, *Geological Association of Canada*, 770
Huff, Bob, *Habitat for Humanity Canada*, 796
Huffman, William, *Inuit Art Foundation*, 862
Huffman, Carrie, *Yukon Registered Nurses Association*, 1480
Hufford, Steve, *Society for Information Management*, 1590
Huggins, Dan, *Ontario Water Works Association*, 1113
Hughes, Tom, *Canadian Farm Animal Care Trust*, 384
Hughes, Jim, *Campaign Life Coalition*, 276
Hughes, Debbie, *Project Ploughshares*, 1188
Hughes, Mike, *Threshold Ministries*, 1377
Hughes, Delia E., *Fox Valley Chamber of Commerce*, 756
Hughes, Dave, *Ontario Association of Broadcasters*, 1062
Hughes, Kevin, *Professional Engineers Ontario*, 1184
Hughes, Sandy, *Canadian Network for Innovation in Education*, 441
Hughes, Sheila, *Canadian Liver Foundation*, 427
Hughes, Sheila, *Canadian Liver Foundation*, 427
Hughes, Sheila, *Canadian Liver Foundation*, 427
Hughes, Dede, *National Association of Women in Construction*, 1575
Hughes, Melissa, *Organic Trade Association*, 1581
Hughes, David, *The Natural Step Canada*, 999
Hughes, Richard, *Hastings County Historical Society*, 804
Hughes, Shawn, *Ontario Association for Geographic & Environmental Education*, 1061
Hughes, Caroline, *Oakville Chamber of Commerce*, 1053
Hughes, Robert, *Orienteering New Brunswick*, 1126
Hughes, Susan, *Alberta Dressage Association*, 33
Hughes, Stephanie, *Association of Fundraising Professionals*, 1512
Hughes, David, *Great White North Franchisee Association*, 782
Hughes-Newman, Misty, *Telecommunications Employees Association of Manitoba*, 1369
Hughson, Barry, *National Ballet of Canada*, 991
Hugonnier, Bernard, *Fédération québécoise du canot et du kayak*, 730
Huhn, Arlene, *Alzheimer Society of Alberta & Northwest Territories*, 61
Hull, David, *Cranbrook & District Chamber of Commerce*, 638
Hull, Ashley, *Powell River & District United Way*, 1169
Hull, Tracy L., *American Society of Colon & Rectal Surgeons*, 1499
Hull-Jacquin, Marc, *The Shelter Movers of Toronto*, 1295
Hulme, Carl, *Canadian Carpet Institute*, 350
Hulsker, Fie, *Alberta Sailing Association*, 45
Hum, Lillian, *British Columbia's Children's Hospital Foundation*, 259
Humar, Atul, *Canadian Society of Transplantation*, 488

Executive Name Index

Humber, Troy, *Canadian Condominium Institute*, 362
Humble, John, *UNICEF Canada*, 1405
Hume, Todd, *Niagara Falls Coin Club*, 1025
Hummel, Lauren, *Ontario Library Association*, 1089
Hummel, Erica, *Tourism Prince George*, 1390
Humphrey, Dawnette, *Girl Guides of Canada*, 773
Humphrey, Hector, *Canada West Foundation*, 281
Humphrey, Donna, *Canadian Society of Otolaryngology - Head & Neck Surgery*, 485
Humphrey, J. Steven, *National Association of Watch & Clock Collectors, Inc.*, 1574
Humphrey, Kevin, *Canadian Institute for Theatre Technology*, 414
Humphrey, Cheryl, *Swim Alberta*, 1358
Humphrey, Mary, *The Jane Goodall Institute for Wildlife Research, Education & Conservation*, 1568
Humphreys, Kathy, *Kamloops Symphony*, 881
Humphries, Carole, *Acoustic Neuroma Association of Canada*, 5
Humphries, Mark, *Elkhorn Chamber of Commerce*, 685
Hunchuk, Leslie, *Canadian Registry of Tennessee Walking Horse*, 466
Hundal, Ranbir, *Federal Liberal Association of Nunavut*, 706
Hundersmarck, Fred, *Gravelbourg Chamber of Commerce*, 782
Hunks, Glenn, *Saskatchewan Blind Sports Association Inc.*, 1260
Hunsberger, Bob, *George Morris Centre*, 771
Hunt, Murray, *Rideau Valley Field Naturalists*, 1232
Hunt, Daryl, *Rimbey Fish & Game Association*, 1232
Hunt, Simon, *Nanton & District Chamber of Commerce*, 988
Hunt, Susan, *Petroleum Research Newfoundland & Labrador*, 1154
Hunt, Andrea, *Calgary Wildlife Rehabilitation Society*, 275
Hunt, Brian A., *Canadian Public Accountability Board*, 462
Hunter, Brianna, *The J.W. McConnell Family Foundation*, 879
Hunter, DeAnn, *Big Brothers Big Sisters of Alberta*, 209
Hunter, Sean, *Boys & Girls Clubs of Alberta*, 221
Hunter, Kyle, *Canadian Amateur Wrestling Association*, 292
Hunter, Sylvia, *Nova Scotia Society for the Prevention of Cruelty to Animals*, 1049
Hunter, Linda, *Canadian Information Processing Society*, 411
Hunter, Malcolm, *The Foundation Fighting Blindness*, 755
Hunter, Dave, *United Empire Loyalists' Association of Canada*, 1410
Hunter, Jane, *Embroiderers' Association of Canada, Inc.*, 686
Hunter, Jayne, *Literacy Nova Scotia*, 914
Hunter, Terry, *Vancouver Moving Theatre*, 1427
Hunter, David, *Scottish Studies Foundation Inc.*, 1286
Hunter, Stephen, *Disabled Sailing Association of B.C.*, 658
Hunter, Shawn, *National Golf Course Owners Association Canada*, 994
Hunter, Donna, *Manitoba Welsh Pony & Cob Association*, 947
Hunter, Brenda, *Manitoba Percheron & Belgian Club*, 942
Hunter, Bruce, *Pacific Western Athletic Association*, 1136
Hunter, V. Diane, *Hunter Family Foundation*, 827
Hunting, Rachel, *Townshippers' Association*, 1393

Huntingford, Guy, *Building Industry & Land Development Calgary Region*, 262
Huntley, Marlene, *Horticulture Nova Scotia*, 822
Huntley, Anthony E., *Armed Forces Pensioners'/Annuitants' Association of Canada*, 82
Huntus, Larry, *Kitimat, Terrace & District Labour Council*, 891
Huot, Gilles, *Cabbagetown Preservation Association*, 268
Hur, Selene, *Association of Professional Researchers for Advancement - Canada*, 160
Hurd, Andrew, *Ontario Road Builders' Association*, 1102
Hureau, Laura, *Yukon Employees Union*, 1478
Hurford, Tara, *Development & Peace*, 654
Hurl, Chris, *Society for Socialist Studies*, 1326
Hurlburt, Kate, *Alberta & Northwest Territories Lung Association*, 21
Hurley, Mike, *Business Professional Association of Canada*, 267
Hurley, Michael, *Canadian Union of Public Employees*, 498
Hurley, Dave, *Habitat for Humanity Canada*, 796
Hursh, Kevin, *Inland Terminal Association of Canada*, 838
Hurst, Don, *Manitoba Heavy Construction Association*, 938
Hurst, Russel, *CropLife Canada*, 643
Hurst, Melvin, *Canadian Music Festival Adjudicators' Association*, 438
Hurst, Geoff, *Chisholm Services for Children*, 566
Hurst, Mel, *Prologue to the Performing Arts*, 1188
Hurtubise, Michelle, *Canadian Association of Community Health Centres*, 311
Hurwitz, Sandy, *Technion Canada*, 1368
Husain, Ashfaq (Kash), *Institute of Electrical & Electronics Engineers Inc. - Region 7*, 846
Husband, Brian, *Plumbing Officials' Association of British Columbia*, 1163
Husbands, Winston, *AIDS Committee of Toronto*, 16
Husch Foote, Sherri, *Early Childhood Intervention Program (ECIP) Sask. Inc.*, 667
Hushion, Nancy, *The Gershon Iskowitz Foundation*, 773
Huskins, Bonnie, *Faculty Association of University of Saint Thomas*, 701
Hussain, Taghrid, *The John Howard Society of Ontario*, 875
Hussain, Murad, *Professional Engineers Ontario*, 1184
Hussey, Maureen, *College of Opticians of Alberta*, 587
Husten, Heidi, *Southern Georgian Bay Chamber of Commerce*, 1338
Huszka, Emery, *National Farmers Union*, 993
Hutchens, Derrick, *Newfoundland & Labrador Association of Insolvency & Restructuring Professionals*, 1016
Hutchens, Don, *Salmonid Association of Eastern Newfoundland*, 1252
Hutcheon, Brent, *National Golf Course Owners Association Canada*, 993
Hutchins, Tracey, *Taoist Tai Chi Society of Canada*, 1367
Hutchinson, Tanis, *Manitoba Community Newspapers Association*, 934
Hutchinson, Fred, *Association of Nova Scotia Land Surveyors*, 154
Hutchinson, Ron, *Realtors Association of Edmonton*, 1206
Hutchinson, Dawn, *British Columbia Society of Laboratory Science*, 254
Hutchinson, Aaron, *Symphony on the Bay*, 1360
Hutchinson, Peter, *North Atlantic Salmon Conservation Organization*, 1579
Hutchinson, Brian, *Canadian Association of Home & Property Inspectors*, 317

Hutchinson, Linda, *Affirm United*, 12
Hutchison, Carmela, *Council of Canadians with Disabilities*, 633
Hutchison, Craig, *Concerned Children's Advertisers*, 609
Hutniak, David, *LandlordBC*, 898
Hutson, Eric, *Laborers' International Union of North America (AFL-CIO/CLC)*, 1568
Hutt, Sally, *Sport New Brunswick*, 1345
Hutt, Howard, *Canadian Bureau for the Advancement of Music*, 347
Hutt, Carter, *Snow Crab Fishermans Inc.*, 1305
Hutt, Lisa, *Canadian Hays Converter Association*, 401
Hutt, Lisa, *Canadian Luing Cattle Association*, 428
Hutt, Lisa, *Canadian Pinzgauer Association*, 455
Hutt Temoana, Mamie, *Pender Island Chamber of Commerce*, 1149
Hutton, Joan, *Canadian Society of Cinematographers*, 481
Hutton, Brad E., *Guelph Arts Council*, 793
Hutton, John, *The John Howard Society of Manitoba*, 874
Hutton, Ron, *New Brunswick Roofing Contractors Association, Inc.*, 1011
Hutton, Mike, *Manitoba Athletic Therapists Association Inc.*, 931
Hutton, Virginia, *Breast Cancer Society of Canada*, 228
Hutton, Jonathan, *UNEP - World Conservation Monitoring Centre*, 1598
Hutzal, Ron, *Full Gospel Business Men's Fellowship in Canada*, 764
Huxman, Jesse, *Abundance Canada*, 3
Huybers, Richard, *Cross Country Ski Association of Manitoba*, 644
Huza, Joseph, *Chambre de commerce de l'Ouest-de-l'Ile de Montréal*, 541
Hwang, Kum Suk, *Korean Senior Citizens Society of Toronto*, 893
Hyatt, Mel, *Power Workers' Union*, 1169
Hyde, Cheryl, *Alberta Municipal Clerks Association*, 40
Hyde-Lay, Robyn, *Health Law Institute*, 806
Hyder Ali, Amyn, *WaterCan*, 1442
Hyer, Bruce, *Green Party of Canada*, 788
Hykaway, Adrian, *Canadian Dexter Cattle Association*, 377
Hyland, Ray, *Explorer's Club (Canadian Chapter)*, 700
Hyland, Sylvia, *Institute for Safe Medication Practices Canada*, 844
Hylland, Sue, *Canada Games Council*, 279
Hyman, Neil H., *American Society of Colon & Rectal Surgeons*, 1499
Hynd, Bill, *Social Justice Cooperative Newfoundland & Labrador*, 1306
Hyndman, Pat, *Appaloosa Horse Club of Canada*, 73
Hynes, Marcus, *Multifaith Action Society*, 979
Hynes, Corinne, *Association of Professional Researchers for Advancement - Canada*, 160
Hyrorijiw, Clint, *Photographic Historical Society of Canada*, 1157
Hyslop, Carol, *The North Cumberland Historical Society*, 1030
Hyvarinen, Joy, *Foundation for International Environmental Law & Development*, 1527
Hyvärinen, Anne, *International Society of Indoor Air Quality & Climate*, 1561
Hᵢyer, Poul-Erik, *Badminton World Federation*, 1513

I

l'Anson, Cindy, *Woodview Mental Health & Autism Services*, 1464
Iacobacci, Mario, *Canadian Transportation Research Forum*, 497
Iacobucci, Frank, *NABET 700 CEP*, 987
Iacoe, Tina, *Ontario Public Buyers Association*, 1098

Iampieri, Donna, *Hockey Canada Foundation*, 817
Iannaccio, Amanda, *Canadian Society of Hospital Pharmacists*, 483
Iannicca, Nando, *Credit Valley Conservation Foundation*, 641
Iannuzzi, Perry, *Canadian Automobile Sport Clubs - Ontario Region Inc.*, 340
Ianson, Alina, *Canadian Hadassah WIZO*, 399
Iavicoli, Sergio, *International Commission on Occupational Health*, 1543
Ibbetson, Norma, *Canadian Lawyers Insurance Association*, 426
Ibrahim, Riz, *Canadian Education & Research Institute for Counselling*, 379
Iceton, Ann, *Okanagan Miniature Horse Club*, 1056
Idlout-Sudlovenick, Hagar, *Qikiqtani Inuit Association*, 1194
Idris, Salman, *Manitoba Islamic Association*, 939
Igartua, Karine J., *Association des médecins-psychiatres du Québec*, 120
Igartua, Karine J., *Centre d'orientation sexuelle de l'université McGill*, 528
Ignatiuk, Jordan, *Nature Saskatchewan*, 1000
Igoe, Liz, *Operation Springboard*, 1116
Igonia, Barbette, *British Columbia Electrical Association*, 239
Ihaza, Apollinaire, *Canadian Executive Service Organization*, 383
Iida, Hiroyuki, *International Computer Games Association*, 1543
Ikenaka, Kazuhiro, *International Society for Neurochemistry*, 1558
Ilarion, , *Ukrainian Orthodox Church of Canada*, 1403
Ilich, Sasha, *Ontario Underwater Council*, 1112
Ilkiw, Stephen, *Financial Executives International Canada*, 736
Illerbrun, Carolyn, *Grain Services Union (CLC)*, 779
Ilott, Kevin, *Association of Professional Engineers & Geoscientists of British Columbia*, 158
Ilson, Ray, *Canadian Radiation Protection Association*, 465
Imam, Ayesha, *Greenpeace International*, 1529
Imata, Katsuji, *CIVICUS: World Alliance for Citizen Participation*, 1517
Immenhauser, Adrian, *International Association of Sedimentologists*, 1540
Imo, Jennifer, *National Association of Towns & Townships*, 1574
Imrie, Diane, *Northwestern Ontario Sports Hall of Fame & Museum*, 1040
Ince, Stefanie, *Dystonia Medical Research Foundation Canada*, 666
Inch, John, *Health Association Nova Scotia*, 806
Inch, Jeanne, *Canadian Conservation Institute*, 363
Infeld, Jonathan, *Congregation Beth Israel - British Columbia*, 612
Ingall, Michelle, *Pacific Riding for Developing Abilities*, 1136
Ingebrigtson, Karen, *Firefly*, 738
Ingersoll, Ruth, *Community Development Council of Quinte*, 596
Ingham, April, *Pacific Peoples' Partnership*, 1136
Inglis, Lesley, *Community Foundations of Canada*, 598
Ingraham, Carol, *Nova Scotia Road Builders Association*, 1048
Ingram, Susan, *Big Brothers Big Sisters of Ontario*, 210
Ingram, Sarah, *Canadian Urban Transit Association*, 500
Ingram, Susan, *Canadian Comparative Literature Association*, 361
Ingram, Tara, *Northern Ontario Native Tourism Association*, 1035
Ingrao, Leonard, *London Community Orchestra*, 918

Executive Name Index

Ingrao, Len, *London Youth Symphony*, 919
Ingratta, Frank, *George Morris Centre*, 771
Ingratta, Jen, *CADORA Ontario Association Inc.*, 270
Ings, Joanne, *Prince Edward Island Lung Association*, 1175
Ingwersen, June, *World Small Animal Veterinary Association*, 1467
Inhaber, Susan, *Na'amat Canada Inc.*, 987
Inkila, Liz, *Cross Country Ski Ontario*, 644
Inkpen, Linda, *College of Physicians & Surgeons of Newfoundland & Labrador*, 588
Innes, Cathy, *Canadian Tenpin Federation, Inc.*, 494
Innes, C. Peter, *Victoria Medical Society*, 1433
Innes, Dave, *Natural History Society of Newfoundland & Labrador*, 999
Inouye, Nikki, *North Okanagan Labour Council*, 1031
Insigne, Erlinda, *Filipino Canadian Association of Vaughan*, 735
Intven, Laurie, *YWCA Canada*, 1481
Inward, Sharyn, *Green Communities Canada*, 788
Ip, Gordon, *Professional Engineers Ontario*, 1185
Ippolito, Daniel, *General Conference of the Canadian Assemblies of God*, 768
Iranitalab, Roya, *Association of Professional Engineers & Geoscientists of Alberta*, 157
Irick, Brett, *Windsor Coin Club*, 1456
Irish, Gordon, *Information Resource Management Association of Canada*, 837
Irizawa, Naomi, *Association of Ontario Land Economists*, 155
Iron, Larry, *Meadow Lake Tribal Council*, 956
Irons, Leona, *National Aboriginal Lands Managers Association*, 989
Ironstone, Penelope, *Canadian Communication Association*, 361
Irvin, Donna, *Canadian Neurological Sciences Federation*, 441
Irvin, Emma, *Institute for Work & Health*, 844
Irvin, William Robert (Bob), *American Rivers*, 1497
Irvine, Terry, *Oliver Community Arts Council*, 1057
Irvine, Orion, *Canadian Labour Congress*, 425
Irvine, Seana, *Evergreen*, 699
Irvine, Karen, *Millbrook & District Chamber of Commerce*, 966
Irving, David M., *The Anglican Church of Canada*, 70
Irving, Todd, *Sail Canada*, 1245
Irving, Don, *Frontiers Foundation*, 764
Irving, Michael C., *The Child Abuse Survivor Monument Project*, 558
Irving, Jacob, *Canadian Hydropower Association*, 410
Irwin, John W., *Threshold Ministries*, 1377
Irwin, Trish, *Collingwood Chamber of Commerce*, 591
Irwin, Tim, *Huntington Society of Canada*, 828
Irwin, Linda, *British Columbia Transplant Society*, 257
Irwin, Judy, *Ontario Long Term Care Association*, 1089
Irwin, Jim, *Manitoba Rural Tourism Association Inc.*, 943
Irwin, Michelle, *British Columbia Farm Industry Review Board*, 240
Irwin, Ross W., *Canadian Meter Study Group*, 436
Irwin, Clare, *Pollination Guelph*, 1164
Irwin Gisbon, Mary, *The Anglican Church of Canada*, 69
Isaac, Gemma, *Canadian Association of Music Therapists*, 322
Isaac, Karen, *British Columbia Aboriginal Child Care Society*, 279
Isaacs, Lisa, *Canadian Insurance Accountants Association*, 420
Isaacs, Marc D., *The Canadian Maritime Law Association*, 430

Isaacs, Milt, *Association of Canadian Financial Officers*, 142
Isaacs, Milt, *Air Canada Pilots Association*, 19
Isaak, Lloyd, *Meewasin Valley Authority*, 959
Isabel, Ginette, *Réseau des SADC et CAE*, 1222
Isabella, Louis, *Allergy/Asthma Information Association*, 54
Isabelle, Chantal, *Fédération des harmonies et des orchestres symphoniques du Québec*, 715
Isard, Brian, *Canadian Wood Pallet & Container Association*, 505
Isenberg, Sid, *Canadian Fence Industry Association*, 389
Isenor, Jessica, *Canadian Counselling & Psychotherapy Association*, 372
Isenor, Gerry, *Solid Waste Association of North America*, 1595
Ishak, Philippine, *Windsor Women Working with Immigrant Women*, 1457
Ishmael, Azam, *The Liberal Party of Canada*, 909
Isidro, Jorge, *Movement for Marriage Enrichment*, 978
Isidro, Elsa, *Movement for Marriage Enrichment*, 978
Iskandar, Youssef, *Association of Professional Engineers & Geoscientists of Alberta*, 157
Iskov, Bunny, *The Ontario Poetry Society*, 1096
Islam, Debbie, *Alzheimer Society of Simcoe County*, 65
Ismail, Hazra, *British Columbia Muslim Association*, 247
Itiveh, Emmanuel, *Black Business Initiative*, 213
Ius, Ivan, *Ontario Association for Geographic & Environmental Education*, 1061
Ivan, Maureen, *Canadian Curly Horse Association*, 375
Ivanco, Michael, *Society of Professional Engineers & Associates*, 1330
Ivankine, Alex, *Oceana Canada*, 1054
Ivany, Laura, *Newfoundland Symphony Youth Orchestra*, 1023
Iverson, Melana, *Multicultural Association of Saint John Inc.*, 979
Ivey, Kathy, *Canadian College of Health Leaders*, 358
Ivey, Rosamond, *Richard Ivey Foundation*, 1229
Ivey, Richard W., *Richard Ivey Foundation*, 1229
Ivic, Alex, *Dog Guides Canada*, 660
Ivison, John, *Society of Fire Protection Engineers*, 1593
Ivol, Ann, *Ostomy Canada Society*, 1129
Ivonoffski, Vrenia, *Toronto Association of Acting Studios*, 1382
Ivy, Michael, *Apeetogosan (Metis) Development Inc.*, 73
Iwanaka, Derek, *Greater Vancouver Japanese Canadian Citizens' Association*, 787
Iwaniw, Aubrey, *Smart Commute*, 1304
Iwaskow, Don, *North Central Labour Council of British Columbia*, 1030
Izatt, Chris, *Canadian Security Association*, 469

J

Jabat, John, *Canadian Tinnitus Foundation*, 495
Jabbour, Raymond, *Québec Lung Association*, 1198
Jabra, Lina, *Royal Canadian Academy of Arts*, 1239
Jabs, Alan, *International Federation of Broomball Associations*, 857
Jack, Les, *Canadian Cutting Horse Association*, 375
Jack, Chantalle, *Health Libraries Association of British Columbia*, 806

Jack, Barb, *Canadian Chianina Association*, 355
Jackett, Suzanne, *Bragg Creek Chamber of Commerce*, 224
Jackman, Edward, *Canadian Catholic Historical Association - English Section*, 351
Jackman, April, *Agricultural Manufacturers of Canada*, 15
Jackman, Victoria, *Hal Jackman Foundation*, 798
Jacknisky, Tom, *American Society of Heating, Refrigerating & Air Conditioning Engineers*, 1500
Jackson, John, *Canadian Institute of Marketing*, 417
Jackson, Rod, *Greater Barrie Chamber of Commerce*, 782
Jackson, Fiona, *Association canadienne des ataxies familiales*, 92
Jackson, Peter, *Canadian Automobile Sport Clubs - Ontario Region Inc.*, 340
Jackson, Sherry, *Canadian Pony Club*, 458
Jackson, Russell, *Newfoundland & Labrador Volleyball Association*, 1022
Jackson, Michelle, *Speech-Language & Audiology Canada*, 1341
Jackson, Peter, *Canadian Meteorological & Oceanographic Society*, 436
Jackson, Susan, *Canadian Public Health Association*, 462
Jackson, Anne, *Canadian Public Works Association*, 464
Jackson, Robin, *Canadian Federation of University Women*, 389
Jackson, Cynthia, *Québec Angus Association*, 1195
Jackson, Fawn, *Canadian Cattlemen's Association*, 351
Jackson, Greg, *Ontario Pollution Control Equipment Association*, 1097
Jackson, Joan, *Recreation Vehicle Dealers Association of Canada*, 1208
Jackson, David, *Risk & Insurance Management Society Inc.*, 1234
Jackson, Bob, *Public Service Alliance of Canada*, 1193
Jackson, Suzanne, *Institute of Cultural Affairs International*, 846
Jackson, Michael, *Canadian Professional Sales Association*, 460
Jackson, Tim, *Nova Scotia Library Association*, 1046
Jackson, Sue, *Swim Nova Scotia*, 1358
Jackson, Tim, *Aquaculture Association of Canada*, 75
Jackson, Viki, *Marmot Recovery Foundation*, 952
Jackson, Lois, *Atlantic Health Promotion Research Centre*, 184
Jackson, Margaret A., *The Freda Centre for Research on Violence Against Women & Children*, 758
Jackson, Rona, *Manitoba Sign Association*, 944
Jackson, Vanda, *Nova Scotia Trails Federation*, 1050
Jackson, Tim, *Lacrosse New Brunswick*, 895
Jackson, Adam, *Pragmora*, 1169
Jackson, Adrienne, *Canadian Public Accountability Board*, 462
Jacob, Jason, *East Kootenay Chamber of Mines*, 668
Jacob, Jeremy, *Canadian Association of Medical Cannabis Dispensaries*, 320
Jacob Edwards, Rosslyn, *Dance Ontario Association*, 649
Jacobi, Shannon, *Alberta Occupational Health Nurses Association*, 41
Jacobs, Jenny, *Canadian Hemophilia Society*, 404
Jacobs, Patricia, *University Settlement*, 1421
Jacobs, Brad, *Cape Breton Regional Hospital Foundation*, 510
Jacobs, Katherine, *Ontario Construction Secretariat*, 1074

Jacobsen, Jim, *Creston Valley Chamber of Commerce*, 642
Jacobsen, Wayne, *Canadian Association of Police Educators*, 327
Jacobson, Anna, *International Orienteering Federation*, 1554
Jacobson, Paul, *Canadian Association for Business Economics*, 297
Jacobson, Guy, *Softball Saskatchewan*, 1332
Jacoby, Neil, *Alzheimer Society of Toronto*, 65
Jacques, Johanne, *Réseau des SADC et CAE*, 1219
Jacques, Vecerina, *O Vertigo Danse*, 1053
Jaffey, Marina, *Canadian Public Relations Society Inc.*, 463
Jaffray, Don, *Social Planning & Research Council of Hamilton*, 1306
Jafri, Nuzhat, *Canadian Council of Muslim Women*, 369
Jagasar, Rohan, *Medical Device Reprocessing Association of Ontario*, 958
Jaglal, Susan, *Canadian Society for Epidemiology & Biostatistics*, 474
Jagoda, Kalinga, *Canadian Transportation Research Forum*, 497
Jahn, Gordon, *Prince Albert & District Chamber of Commerce*, 1171
Jahn, Gina, *AFCOM*, 1486
Jain, Sushil, *South Asian Centre of Windsor*, 1334
Jakeway, George, *OMF International - Canada*, 1057
Jakobsen, Morten, *Lucknow & District Chamber of Commerce*, 920
Jakop, Heidi, *Administrators of Volunteer Resources BC*, 8
Jakubec, Debra, *Edmonton Federation of Community Leagues*, 677
Jalbert, Michel, *Association of Canadian Pension Management*, 143
Jalloh, Bashir, *Saskatchewan Association of Medical Radiation Technologists*, 1257
Jaltema, Elaine, *Provincial Intermediate Teachers' Association*, 1191
Jambrosic, Rudy, *Ontario Physique Association*, 1096
James, Glenda, *Saskatchewan Brain Injury Association*, 1260
James, Rusty, *Brantford Musicians' Association*, 227
James, Richard, *Wiccan Church of Canada*, 1453
James, Kelvin, *World Darts Federation*, 1604
James, Michelle, *Canadian Public Relations Society Inc.*, 463
James, Mary, *Association for Vaccine Damaged Children*, 135
James, Harry N., *Canadian Association of Token Collectors*, 334
James, Anne, *The Canadian Corps of Commissionaires*, 365
James, Sean, *Association of Professional Engineers & Geoscientists of New Brunswick*, 158
James, Bonnie, *Canadian Die Casters Association*, 378
James, Annette, *Fredericton Society for the Prevention of Cruelty to Animals*, 759
James, June, *Ontario Genealogical Society*, 1082
James, Jim (Harold), *Canadian Association of Veterans in United Nations Peacekeeping*, 336
James, Susan, *Lillooet Tribal Council*, 912
James, Michael, *Ringette PEI*, 1233
James, Alex, *Design Exchange*, 654
James, Marina R., *Economic Development Winnipeg Inc.*, 673
James, Paul, *Brantford Stamp Club*, 227
James, Patrice, *Independent Filmmakers' Co-operative of Ottawa*, 832
James, McConnell, *Canada - United States Trade Center*, 1515
James, Mary Jane, *Sexual Assault Centre of Edmonton*, 1293

Executive Name Index

James, Scott, *The Arts & Letters Club*, 85
James, Bonnie, *Armed Forces Pensioners'/Annuitants' Association of Canada*, 82
James, Krista, *British Columbia Law Institute*, 244
James, Rachel, *Door & Access Systems Manufacturers Association*, 1521
Jamieson, Larry, *New Brunswick Teachers' Association*, 1013
Jamieson, Gene, *Native Canadian Centre of Toronto*, 997
Jamieson, Roberta, *Indspire*, 835
Jamieson, Devon, *CADORA Ontario Association Inc.*, 269
Jamison, Kelly, *Canadian Society of Exploration Geophysicists*, 483
Jamroz, Agata, *Risk & Insurance Management Society Inc.*, 1234
Janeck, Amy, *College of Psychologists of British Columbia*, 589
Janes, Diane, *Canadian Network for Innovation in Education*, 441
Janes, Glenda, *St. John Ambulance*, 1249
Janes, Matt, *North America Railway Hall of Fame*, 1029
Jang, Mike, *Chinese Cultural Centre*, 564
Jang, Queenie, *International Society for Cellular Therapy*, 860
Jannetta, Patti, *Canadian Association for the Advancement of Music & the Arts*, 305
Janow, Joel, *Public Legal Education Association of Saskatchewan, Inc.*, 1192
Jansen, Nic, *Hockey New Brunswick*, 818
Jansen, Tatjana, *The Vancouver Art Therapy Institute*, 1425
Jansen, Dolf, *Blue Mountains Chamber of Commerce*, 215
Janson, Beth, *Academy of Canadian Cinema & Television*, 3
Janssen, Margaret, *Ontario Home Builders' Association*, 1085
Janssens, Dominique, *Canadian Society for Engineering Management*, 474
Jansson, Jason, *Ontario Basketball*, 1067
Janz, Carolyn, *Alberta Insurance Council*, 38
Janzen, Howard, *Calgary Society of Organists*, 274
Janzen, Christine, *Manitoba Library Association*, 940
Janzen, Henry, *Hart House Orchestra*, 804
Janzen, Kathy, *Association of the Chemical Profession of Alberta*, 163
Janzen, Ben, *British Columbia Milk Marketing Board*, 246
Janzen, Rich, *Centre for Community Based Research*, 531
Janzen, Abe, *Mennonite Central Committee Canada*, 960
Japp, Leah, *Saskatchewan Outdoor & Environmental Education Association*, 1271
Jarabek, Adrienne, *Canadian Council on International Law*, 371
Jardine, Mary, *Reflexology Association of Canada*, 1210
Jardine, Amparo, *Trans Canada Trail Foundation*, 1394
Jarvis, George, *Block Parent Program of Canada*, 215
Jarvis, Susan, *Ontario Professional Foresters Association*, 1097
Jarvis, Marshall, *Ontario English Catholic Teachers' Association (CLC)*, 1078
Jarvis, Beverly, *Building Industry & Land Development Calgary Region*, 262
Jarvis, Patrick, *Canadian Snowboard Federation*, 472
Jarvis, Jeff, *Alberta Snowboard Association*, 47
Jaskela, Norma, *Epilepsy Association of Calgary*, 693
Jaskiewicz, Matthew, *Toronto Sinfonietta*, 1387
Jasper, Justin, *Valleyview & District Chamber of Commerce*, 1424
Jasper, Kellen, *Motion Picture Theatre Association of Central Canada*, 975
Jass, Janak, *Unison Health & Community Services*, 1408
Jassal, Avtar, *College of Chiropractors of British Columbia*, 583
Jassem, Peter, *Polish-Jewish Heritage Foundation of Canada*, 1164
Jaton, Cindy, *Association des jeunes ruraux du Québec*, 117
Jaucian, Arthur, *Multicultural Association of Fredericton*, 978
Jaumain, Serge, *Centre d'Études Nord-Américaines de l'Université Libre de Bruxelles*, 1516
Jawad, Atheer, *American Society for Quality*, 1498
Jay, Shirley Smedley, *Prince Edward Island Home & School Federation Inc.*, 1175
Jay, Kimberley, *College of Licensed Practical Nurses of PEI*, 585
Jean, Martin, *Canadian Ski Instructors' Alliance*, 471
Jean, Michaëlle, *Organisation internationale de la Francophonie*, 1581
Jean, Sylvie, *Association pour le développement de la personne handicapée intellectuelle du Saguenay*, 167
Jean, Louis-Joseph, *Expo agricole de Chicoutimi*, 700
Jean-Baptiste, Alfred, *Centre for Community Learning & Development*, 531
Jean-Baptiste, Alfred, *Toronto Centre for Community Learning & Development*, 1383
Jean-Gilles, Joseph, *Groupe d'action pour la prévention de la transmission du VIH et l'éradication du Sida*, 791
Jean-Louis, Bonnie, *Hawkesbury & Region Chamber of Commerce*, 805
Jean-Vézina, Jonathan, *Association renaissance des personnes traumatisées crâniennes du Saguenay-Lac-Saint-Jean*, 178
Jeanneau, Jocelyne, *Association du Syndrome de Turner du Québec*, 132
Jecmen, Frantisek, *Masaryk Memorial Institute Inc.*, 952
Jedig, Diana, *Ontario Association of Community Futures Development Corporations*, 1063
Jedrych, Andrzej, *Association of Polish Engineers in Canada*, 156
Jedwab, Jack, *Association for Canadian Studies*, 133
Jeethan, Tara, *Edmonton Dental Assistants Association*, 676
Jeeva, Zeib, *International Development & Relief Foundation*, 856
Jeeves, Beverly, *Newcastle Village & District Historical Society*, 1015
Jefferies, Dan, *Alberta Freestyle Ski Association*, 36
Jeffers, Larry, *Golden Prairie Arts Council*, 776
Jefferson, Arthur, *Nova Scotia Ground Water Association*, 1045
Jefferson, Glen E., *Exhibitions Association of Nova Scotia*, 699
Jefferson, Ross, *Tourism Saint John*, 1391
Jefferson, Ross, *Destination Halifax*, 654
Jeffery, Betty, *University of Prince Edward Island Faculty Association*, 1420
Jeffery, Jill, *Urology Nurses of Canada*, 1423
Jeffery, Julie, *Northwest Territories Amateur Speed Skating Association*, 1037
Jeffery, Pamela, *Women's Executive Network*, 1462
Jeffrey, Leslie, *AIDS Saint John*, 17
Jeffrey, Robert, *Retirement Planning Association of Canada*, 1228
Jeffrey, Rick, *Coast Forest Products Association*, 579
Jeffrey, Robert, *Canadian Institute of Financial Planners*, 415
Jeffrey, Deborah, *First Nations SchoolNet*, 739
Jeffrey, Ursula, *Wilno Heritage Society*, 1456
Jeffrey, Shaun, *Manitoba Pest Management Association*, 942
Jeffreys, Mike, *PLEA Community Services Society of BC*, 1163
Jeffries, Matthew, *Cycling Canada Cyclisme*, 647
Jegatheesan, Vathanan, *Canadian Tamil Youth Development Centre*, 492
Jelavic, Matthew, *Canadian Institute of Management*, 417
Jeliazkov, Heather, *British Columbia Museums Association*, 246
Jelinek, Julie, *Lions Foundation of Canada*, 913
Jelinek, Julie, *Dog Guides Canada*, 660
Jemison, Kyla, *Canadian Association of Music Libraries, Archives & Documentation Centres*, 321
Jemison, Lisa, *Editors' Association of Canada*, 675
Jeneroux, Jayne, *College of Podiatric Physicians of Alberta*, 589
Jeneroux, Jayne, *Canadian Podiatric Medical Association*, 456
Jenkins, Nicole, *Newfoundland & Labrador Association of Medical Radiation Technologists*, 1016
Jenkins, Jody, *Association of Registered Professional Foresters of New Brunswick*, 161
Jenkins, Erica, *Medical Society of Prince Edward Island*, 958
Jenkins, Samantha, *Canadian Association of Pharmacy Technicians*, 326
Jennejohn, Dana, *The Association of Social Workers of Northern Canada*, 162
Jenner, Valerie, *Alberta CGIT Association*, 28
Jennett, Sue, *Canadian Celiac Association*, 352
Jennex, Steve, *Nova Scotia Dental Association*, 1044
Jennex, Ramona, *Tourette Syndrome Foundation of Canada*, 1389
Jennings, Dorothy, *College of Registered Psychiatric Nurses of British Columbia*, 590
Jennings, Matt, *British Columbia Fishing Resorts & Outfitters Association*, 241
Jennings, Dawn, *Canadian Society of Hospital Pharmacists*, 484
Jennings, Tim, *Shaw Festival*, 1295
Jennings, Sara, *Whistler Food Bank*, 1452
Jensen, Kalin, *Greater Edmonton Library Association*, 783
Jensen, Melissa, *Ontario School Library Association*, 1103
Jensen, Karla, *Local Government Management Association of British Columbia*, 917
Jensen, Heather, *Public Legal Education Association of Saskatchewan, Inc.*, 1192
Jensen, Joanne, *Saskatchewan Genealogical Society*, 1266
Jensen, Katrina, *AIDS Vancouver Island*, 17
Jensen, Sarah, *Archives Association of British Columbia*, 80
Jensen, Maureen, *Ontario Securities Commission*, 1104
Jenson, Mari, *Women in Capital Markets*, 1460
Jeong, Bae Kim, *Korean Senior Citizens Society of Toronto*, 893
Jeppesen, Ruth, *Sisters of Charity of Halifax*, 1301
Jeramaz-Larson, Kathy, *Institutional Limited Partners Association*, 848
Jeremian, Anna, *The College of Naturopaths of Ontario*, 586
Jergl, Charles, *Daily Bread Food Bank*, 648
Jermer, Jöran, *International Research Group on Wood Protection*, 1556
Jermy, Gary, *Burford Township Historical Society*, 265
Jerome, Darren, *Ottawa Independent Writers*, 1131
Jerome, Olivier, *Myeloma Canada*, 986
Jerrett, Robert, *Association of Translators & Interpreters of Saskatchewan*, 163
Jesmer, Marc, *Mactaquac Country Chamber of Commerce*, 924
Jespersen, Sandy, *Canadian Athletic Therapists Association*, 338
Jessani, Faizal, *Edmonton Construction Association*, 676
Jesseman, Rebecca, *Canadian Centre on Substance Use & Addiction*, 354
Jessome, Joan, *Nova Scotia Government & General Employees Union*, 1045
jetté, Nicole, *Front commun des personnes assistées sociales du Québec*, 763
Jetté, Mathieu-Henri, *Mouvement national des québécoises et québécois*, 977
Jetyter, Marilyn, *Medicine Hat Rock & Lapidary Club*, 959
Jeune, Patrick, *ARMA Canada*, 82
Jew, Karen, *British Columbia Council for Exceptional Children*, 237
Jewell, Louisa, *Canadian Positive Psychology Association*, 458
Jewett, L.C., *College of Physicians & Surgeons of British Columbia*, 588
Jewett, Susan, *Access Counselling & Family Services*, 5
Jewitt, Mike, *Calgary Marching Showband Association*, 273
Jezewski, Meghan, *Vancouver Island Public Interest Research Group*, 1426
Jha, Sudhir, *Northwest Territories & Nunavut Association of Professional Engineers & Geoscientists*, 1036
Jhajj, Raj, *Peel Multicultural Council*, 1148
Jhass, Bimal, *Field Hockey Ontario*, 734
Ji, Chris, *Association of Dental Technologists of Ontario*, 146
Jiang, Lei, *Alberta Table Tennis Association*, 49
Jijian, Tara, *Saskatchewan Liberal Association*, 1269
Jimenez, Angie, *Forever Young Seniors Society*, 752
Jivraj, Ashif, *Broadcast Educators Association of Canada*, 259
Jiwa, Famida, *Osteoporosis Canada*, 1128
Jiwan, Moe, *ReelWorld Film Festival*, 1210
Jiwani, Salima, *Canadian Academy of Audiology*, 285
Jiwani, Almas, *United Nations Entity for Gender Equality & the Empowerment of Women - National Committee Canada*, 1412
Jiwani, Almas, *Almas Jiwani Foundation*, 59
Joanasie, David, *National Inuit Youth Council*, 994
Joanis, Lise, *Hearst, Mattice - Val Côté & Area Chamber of Commerce*, 808
Job, Iov, *Russian Orthodox Church in Canada*, 1244
Jobe, Lana, *Brant Historical Society*, 226
Jobin, Audrey, *Chambre de commerce et d'industrie de Dolbeau-Mistassini*, 545
Jobin, Jacques, *Association des compagnies de théâtre*, 109
Jobity, Sharon, *Ontario Centres of Excellence*, 1071
Jocelyn, Scott, *Manitoba Restaurant & Food Services Association*, 943
Jocelyn, Matthew, *The Canadian Stage Company*, 490
Jocksch, Adam, *Canadian Underwater Games Association*, 498
Jodoin, Isabelle, *Association des firmes de génie-conseil - Québec*, 114
Jodoin, Amanda, *Pancreatic Cancer Canada Foundation*, 1138
Joe, Francyne, *Native Women's Association of Canada*, 998
Joffre, Michael, *Montreal Numismatic Society*, 973
Joffre, Michael, *Lakeshore Coin Club*, 897
Johannes, Aaron, *Spectrum Society for Community Living*, 1340
Johansen, James, *Association of Professional Engineers & Geoscientists of Alberta*, 157

Executive Name Index

Johansen, Cynthia, *College of Registered Nurses of British Columbia*, 589
Johansen, Christopher, *Mackenzie & District Museum Society*, 924
Johanson, Adel, *Forever Young Seniors Society*, 752
John, Parker, *Investment Funds Institute of Canada*, 863
John, Peggy, *British Columbia Transplant Society*, 257
John, Herb, *National Pensioners Federation*, 995
John, Crystal, *Nova Scotia Association of Black Social Workers*, 1041
Johns, Lawrie, *Basketball BC*, 198
Johns, Jill, *Probation Officers Association of Ontario*, 1181
Johns, Brian, *Ontario Liberal Party*, 1088
Johnson, Deana, *Council on Aging, Windsor - Essex County*, 636
Johnson, John E., *The Council on Aging of Ottawa*, 636
Johnson, Michelle, *AIDS Coalition of Nova Scotia*, 16
Johnson, Martin, *Firefighters Burn Fund Inc.*, 738
Johnson, Corol, *Smithers Community Services Association*, 1304
Johnson, Penelope, *Oliver Community Arts Council*, 1057
Johnson, Geoffrey, *Ontario Senior Games Association*, 1104
Johnson, Dave, *Armed Forces Communications & Electronics Association (Canada)*, 82
Johnson, Colin R., *The Anglican Church of Canada*, 70
Johnson, Colin, *The Anglican Church of Canada*, 69
Johnson, Susan, *Evangelical Lutheran Church in Canada*, 698
Johnson, Kevin, *Pentecostal Assemblies of Canada*, 1150
Johnson, Mark, *Seventh-day Adventist Church in Canada*, 1292
Johnson, Katherine, *Community Torchlight Guelph/Wellington/Dufferin*, 607
Johnson, Brenda, *Spruce Grove & District Chamber of Commerce*, 1346
Johnson, Paul A., *Sault Ste Marie Chamber of Commerce*, 1281
Johnson, Peter, *Society for Treatment of Autism*, 1327
Johnson, Arianna, *Wood Buffalo Food Bank*, 1463
Johnson, Weyman, *Multiple Sclerosis International Federation*, 1571
Johnson, Valerie, *Canadian Agricultural Economics Society*, 289
Johnson, Mary Alice, *Canadian Organic Growers inc.*, 447
Johnson, Jeff, *Canadian Baton Twirling Federation*, 342
Johnson, Glen, *Canadian Football League*, 392
Johnson, Steve, *Canadian Aerophilatelic Society*, 289
Johnson, N.J., *The Canadian Society for Mesopotamian Studies*, 476
Johnson, Jim, *Confederation of University Faculty Associations of British Columbia*, 611
Johnson, Justin, *Fédération de la jeunesse canadienne-française inc.*, 709
Johnson, Al, *Financial Executives International Canada*, 736
Johnson, Bart, *Canadian College of Health Leaders*, 359
Johnson, Nancy, *Jane Austen Society of North America*, 868
Johnson, Bev, *Federation of Medical Women of Canada*, 724
Johnson, Sylvia, *Métis Nation of Alberta*, 963
Johnson, Jana, *NACE International*, 1572
Johnson, David, *The Liberal Party of Canada (Manitoba)*, 909

Johnson, Lori, *Algoma Kinniwabi Travel Association*, 53
Johnson, Jennifer, *The Greater Vancouver Board of Trade*, 786
Johnson, Barb, *Schizophrenia Society of New Brunswick*, 1284
Johnson, Peter R., *Conference of Great Lakes & St. Lawrence Governors & Premiers*, 1519
Johnson, Jim, *National Association of Watch & Clock Collectors, Inc.*, 1574
Johnson, Jodie, *United Way Alberta Northwest*, 1413
Johnson, Steve, *Sport Medicine Council of Alberta*, 1344
Johnson, Linda, *Nova Scotia Co-operative Council*, 1043
Johnson, Kenneth G., *Great Lakes Commission*, 1528
Johnson, Kathy, *Barrington & Area Chamber of Commerce*, 197
Johnson, Stan, *United Steelworkers of America (AFL-CIO/CLC)*, 1600
Johnson, Barbara, *Candlelighters Simcoe Parents of Children with Cancer*, 508
Johnson, Joyce, *Walpole Island Heritage Centre*, 1440
Johnson, Beth, *International Centre for Sustainable Cities*, 855
Johnson, Catherine, *C.G. Jung Foundation of Ontario*, 539
Johnson, Peggy, *Rainy River District Municipal Association*, 1204
Johnson, Jody, *Alberta Pharmacists' Association (RxA)*, 42
Johnson, Robert, *Association des professeur(e)s à temps partiel de l'Université d'Ottawa*, 124
Johnson, Kathy, *Centre for Indigenous Environmental Resources, Inc.*, 532
Johnson, Darryl, *Atlantic Floor Covering Association*, 184
Johnson, Pat, *McMan Youth, Family & Community Services Association*, 956
Johnson, J'Lynn, *Lighthouse Mission*, 912
Johnson, Margaret, *Canadian Association of Independent Credit Counselling Agencies*, 318
Johnson, Heather, *Canadian International Grains Institute*, 421
Johnson, Bruce, *Farm & Ranch Safety & Health Association*, 705
Johnson, Keegan, *Foundation for Prader-Willi Research in Canada*, 756
Johnson, Ellie, *Smart Serve Ontario*, 1304
Johnson, Kristie, *PFLAG Canada Inc.*, 1155
Johnson, Wendy, *Worldwide Association of Business Coaches*, 1468
Johnson, Jeff, *Association for Financial Professionals*, 1508
Johnson, Robert, *National Association for Information Destruction*, 1573
Johnson, John, *Sustainable Kingston*, 1358
Johnson, Debra, *American Society of Plastic Surgeons*, 1502
Johnson, Vicki, *North American Piedmontese Association*, 1579
Johnson, Monique, *Cheer Nova Scotia*, 555
Johnson, Audrey, *St. Josephine Bakhita Black Heritage*, 1497
Johnson, Thomas J., *Eskasoni Fish & Wildlife Commission*, 695
Johnson, Leah, *Nova Scotia Amateur Bodybuilding Association*, 1040
Johnson, Chris, *Nova Scotia Amateur Bodybuilding Association*, 1040
Johnson, Bryan, *Newfoundland & Labrador Deaf Sports Association*, 1018
Johnson, Jay D., *Door & Access Systems Manufacturers Association*, 1521
Johnson-Smith, Kim, *Soil & Water Conservation Society*, 1595
Johnston, Philippe, *CIO Association of Canada*, 570
Johnston, Catherine, *Advanced Card Technology Association of Canada*, 10

Johnston, Heather, *Carp Agricultural Society*, 515
Johnston, Will, *Canadian Physicians for Life*, 454
Johnston, John, *Ontario Milk Transport Association*, 1091
Johnston, Natasha, *Ringette Canada*, 1233
Johnston, Terra, *Alberta Society for the Prevention of Cruelty to Animals*, 47
Johnston, Stuart, *Canadian Independent Music Association*, 411
Johnston, Kathy, *Canadian Physicians for Aid & Relief*, 454
Johnston, Jill, *Manitoba Real Estate Association*, 943
Johnston, Heather A., *Government Finance Officers Association*, 1528
Johnston, Richard, *Alberta Medical Association*, 40
Johnston, Geoffrey, *Canadian Orthopaedic Foundation*, 448
Johnston, Greg, *Songwriters Association of Canada*, 1333
Johnston, Rochelle, *Canadian Society of Hospital Pharmacists*, 484
Johnston, David W., *Canadian Association for Pharmacy Distribution Management*, 303
Johnston, John W., *Royal Canadian Institute*, 1240
Johnston, Ilene, *Saskatchewan Genealogical Society*, 1266
Johnston, Christine, *Society for the Study of Egyptian Antiquities*, 1327
Johnston, Michelle, *The Society of Energy Professionals*, 1328
Johnston, Wade, *Chisholm Services for Children*, 566
Johnston, Graeme, *British Columbia Ferry & Marine Workers' Union (CLC)*, 241
Johnston, Wes, *Canadian Solar Industries Association*, 489
Johnston, Laurie, *Ontario Retirement Communities Association*, 1102
Johnston, Ryan, *Newfoundland & Labrador College of Physiotherapists*, 1017
Johnston, Andrew, *Saskatchewan Playwrights Centre*, 1272
Johnston, Steve, *Northern Ramblers Car Club Inc.*, 1035
Johnston, Natasha, *International Ringette Federation - Canada*, 859
Johnston, John, *Land Improvement Contractors of Ontario*, 897
Johnston, Laura-Lynn, *Vegetarians of Alberta Association*, 1430
Johnston, Lindsay, *Canadian Circumpolar Institute*, 357
Johnston, Brett, *Structural Pest Management Association of British Columbia*, 1352
Johnston, John, *Canadian Soybean Council*, 489
Johnston, Mary, *College & University Retiree Associations of Canada*, 582
Johnston, Heather, *Dignitas International*, 657
Johnstone, Scott, *Greater Langley Chamber of Commerce*, 784
Johnstone, Brenda, *Manitoba Magazine Publishers Association*, 940
Jokinen, Nancy, *British Columbia Psychogeriatric Association*, 249
Jolicoeur, Marcel H., *Chambre de commerce de Val-d'Or*, 543
Jolicoeur, Ganga, *Midwives Association of British Columbia*, 965
Jolicoeur, Elizabeth, *Calgary Horticultural Society*, 272
Jolin, Claudette, *Chambre de commerce et d'industrie de Malartic*, 546
Jolin, Gisèle, *Syndicat des professionnelles et professionnels municipaux de Montréal*, 1364
Jolly, Elaine, *SIGMA Canadian Menopause Society*, 1298
Jolly, Brent, *National NewsMedia Council*, 995
Jonah, Brian, *Canadian Association of Road Safety Professionals*, 331

Jonasson, Kris, *British Columbia Golf Association*, 242
Jonathan, Kim, *Federation of Saskatchewan Indian Nations*, 726
Joncas, Gilles, *Canadian Astronomical Society*, 337
Joncas, Jean-François, *Association d'orthopédie du Québec*, 99
Joncas, Danielle, *Association des pathologistes du Québec*, 122
Joncas, Robert, *SportMedBC*, 1345
Joncas, Robert, *Canadian Snowboard Federation*, 472
Jones, Chris, *Canadian Wireless Telecommunications Association*, 504
Jones, Miriam, *Association of University of New Brunswick Teachers*, 163
Jones, Steven, *Fellowship of Evangelical Baptist Churches*, 731
Jones, Robin, *The Appraisal Institute of Canada - Ontario*, 75
Jones, Gareth, *Canadian Centre for Occupational Health & Safety*, 353
Jones, Alan, *International Plant Propagators Society, Inc.*, 1555
Jones, Alonzo, *Association of Architectural Technologists of Ontario*, 139
Jones, Kitty, *Alberta Orienteering Association*, 42
Jones, Barry, *Automotive Parts Manufacturers' Association*, 190
Jones, Patti, *Canadian Security Association*, 469
Jones, Laura, *Canadian Federation of Independent Business*, 387
Jones, Lovella, *Canadian Institute of Plumbing & Heating*, 419
Jones, Donalee, *Manitoba Simmental Association*, 944
Jones, Matthew, *Timmins Symphony Orchestra*, 1380
Jones, Yolanda, *Ontario Public Interest Research Group*, 1099
Jones, Newton B., *International Brotherhood of Boilermakers, Iron Ship Builders, Blacksmiths, Forgers & Helpers (AFL-CIO)*, 1541
Jones, Linda, *Canadian Union of Public Employees*, 499
Jones, Manina, *Association of Canadian College & University Teachers of English*, 141
Jones, Leanne, *Prince George Alzheimer's Society*, 1179
Jones, Tim, *Artscape*, 86
Jones, Jacqueline, *UNICEF Canada*, 1405
Jones, Faye, *Health Record Association of British Columbia*, 807
Jones, Elizabeth, *North Shore Multicultural Society*, 1033
Jones, Stanley, *Heritage Belleville*, 812
Jones, Afan, *Yukon Orienteering Association*, 1479
Jones, David, *Electronic Frontier Canada Inc.*, 683
Jones, Russell, *International Geosynthetics Society*, 1550
Jones, Matthew, *Kitchener-Waterloo Chamber Orchestra*, 890
Jones, Cailyn, *Saskatchewan Egg Producers*, 1264
Jones, Caitlin, *Western Front Society*, 1449
Jones, Katherine, *Alberta Foster Parent Association*, 35
Jones, Maureen, *Ontario Association of Student Financial Aid Administrators*, 1066
Jones, Michael, *Saskatchewan Arts Board*, 1256
Jones, Maria, *Financial Markets Association of Canada*, 737
Jones, Louise C., *Eastern Shores Independent Association for Support Personnel*, 671
Jones, David, *College of Respiratory Therapists of Ontario*, 590
Jones, Joanne, *PFLAG Canada Inc.*, 1156

Executive Name Index

Jones, Craig, *National Organization for the Reform of Marijuana Laws Canada*, 995
Jones, Scott, *Micah House*, 964
Jones, Eric, *Friends of the Central Experimental Farm*, 762
Jones, Fred L., *Helicopter Association of Canada*, 811
Jones, Joyce, *American Galloway Breeders Association*, 66
Jones, Kathy, *Industrial Fabrics Association International Canada*, 835
Jones, Kimberly, *Polarettes Gymnastics Club*, 1163
Jones, Bruce, *NWT Squash*, 1052
Jones-Harmer, Alicia, *Canadian Association of Critical Care Nurses*, 312
Jonescu Lisitza, Sylvia, *Moving Images Distribution*, 978
Jonkman, Frank, *Drainage Superintendents Association of Ontario*, 662
Jonkov, Anthony, *American Society of Heating, Refrigerating & Air Conditioning Engineers*, 1500
Jonsson, Egon, *Institute of Health Economics*, 846
Jopson, Geoff, *West Vancouver Community Foundation*, 1447
Jordaan, Bernard, *United Senior Citizens of Ontario Inc.*, 1412
Jordan, Teresa, *Community Living Kawartha Lakes*, 603
Jordan, Don, *Alliance of Canadian Cinema, Television & Radio Artists*, 58
Jordan, Natalie, *American Numismatic Society*, 1496
Jordan, David, *First Vancouver Theatre Space Society*, 739
Jordan, Teresa, *Community Living Haliburton County*, 602
Jordan, Beth, *Assaulted Women's Helpline*, 87
Jordan, Jim, *Association of Administrators of English Schools of Québec*, 139
Jordan, Nicole, *International Lilac Society*, 1552
Jörgen, Bengt, *Ballet Jörgen*, 195
Jorgensen, Sven E., *International Society for Ecological Modelling*, 1557
Jorgensen, Eric, *Manitoba Nurses' Union*, 941
Jorgenson, Cheryl, *Port McNeill & District Chamber of Commerce*, 1166
Jorgenson, Michael, *Canadian Hardware & Housewares Manufacturers' Association*, 401
Joseph, Pascal, *The City of Greater Sudbury Developmental Services*, 571
Joseph, Michelle, *Aplastic Anemia & Myelodysplasia Association of Canada*, 73
Joseph, Marina, *Parkinson Canada*, 1141
Joseph, Soby, *Jesus Youth Canada*, 870
Joseph, Reg, *BioTalent Canada*, 212
Josephson, Belinda, *Canadian Counselling & Psychotherapy Association*, 372
Joshi, Amit, *Nova Scotia Cricket Association*, 1043
Joshua, Maria, *Ontario Independent Insurance Adjusters' Association*, 1087
Josst, John, *Austrian Canadian Edelweiss Club of Regina Inc*, 188
Jost, Allanna, *College of Occupational Therapists of Nova Scotia*, 587
Jotham, Matthew, *Guelph Police Association Inc.*, 793
Joubert, Ray, *Saskatchewan College of Pharmacists*, 1261
Joudrey, Andrew, *Nova Scotia Home Builders' Association*, 1046
Joudrey, Stephen, *South Shore Wildlife Association*, 1336
Jourdain, Stéphanie, *Association des handicapés adultes de la Côte-Nord*, 116
Journoud, Mélanie, *College of Dietitians of British Columbia*, 584
Jovicevic, Stanka, *College of Optometrists of BC*, 587
Jowett, Ed, *Canadian Iris Society*, 422
Joy, Jodi, *Nature Canada*, 999
Joy, Anne, *Embroiderers' Association of Canada, Inc.*, 685
Joyce, Penny, *Diving Plongeon Canada*, 659
Joynt, Shawna, *Manitoba Deaf Sports Association Inc.*, 935
Jsespersen, Blake, *Financial Markets Association of Canada*, 737
Juan, Pablo Crespo Vasquez, *Canadian Association for Latin American & Caribbean Studies*, 302
Jubinville, Chantale, *Association Québécoise de chirurgie*, 169
Jud, Brian, *Small Publishers Association of North America*, 1589
Judah Chevron, Janeen, *Society of Petroleum Engineers*, 1593
Judas, Walt, *Tourism Industry Association of British Columbia*, 1389
Judd, Carol, *Canadian Pony Club*, 457
Judd, Maria, *Canadian Foundation for Healthcare Improvement*, 393
Judd, Robert, *American Musicological Society*, 1495
Judge, Nicole, *Ontario Farm Fresh Marketing Association*, 1078
Judge, Rahatjan, *Saskatchewan Economics Association*, 1264
Judson, Susan, *Prince Edward Island Association of Optometrists*, 1172
Judson, Tim, *Nuclear Information & Resource Service*, 1580
Juhasz, Matthew, *Salmon Arm - Salvation Army Food Bank*, 1252
Julian, Bruce, *The Royal Canadian Legion*, 1240
Julien, Pierre-Yves, *Canadian Association of Blue Cross Plans*, 309
Julien, Peter, *Canadian Society of Atherosclerosis, Thrombosis & Vascular Biology*, 481
Julien, Pierre, *Québec Society of Lipidology, Nutrition & Metabolism Inc.*, 1199
Julien, Donald M., *Confederacy of Mainland Mi'kmaq*, 610
Julien, Josée, *Tourisme Montérégie*, 1393
Julott, Darryl, *Canadian Booksellers Association*, 346
Juneau, Yves, *Association des stations de ski du Québec*, 128
Juneja, Roma, *Hike Ontario*, 814
Junek, Wade, *Canadian Academy of Child & Adolescent Psychiatry*, 285
Junemann, Gregory J., *International Federation of Professional & Technical Engineers (AFL-CIO/CLC)*, 1549
Jung, Jason, *Applied Science Technologists & Technicians of British Columbia*, 74
Juravel, Annemarie, *German-Canadian Association of Alberta*, 772
Jurkash, John, *Government Finance Officers Association*, 1528
Jurkovic, Leah, *Colleges and Institutes Canada*, 590
Jury, Eric, *TechNova*, 1369
Juteau, Laurent, *Association québécoise pour le loisir des personnes handicapées*, 176
Jutras, Pierre, *Canadian Institute of Management*, 417
Jutras, Valérie, *Association pour l'intégration sociale (Région des Bois-Francs)*, 166
Juutiand, Patti, *Canadian Horse Breeders' Association*, 408
Juvet, David, *Advocis*, 11

K

Kaarid, Anne, *Storytellers of Canada*, 1350
Kaarsoo, Karin, *Biathlon Alberta*, 207
Kaattari, Tamara, *Literacy Link South Central*, 914
Kaba, Aysha, *Focus Humanitarian Assistance Canada*, 742
Kabat, Pavel, *International Institute for Applied Systems Analysis*, 1551
Kabatoff, Eldeen, *Learning Disabilities Association of Saskatchewan*, 905
Kabildjanov, Alisher, *National Aboriginal Diabetes Association Inc.*, 988
Kabis, Cynthia, *Chambre de commerce et d'industrie Thérèse-De Blainville*, 548
Kablutsiak, Kevin, *Inuit Community Centre*, 862
Kabranov, Ognian, *Royal Astronomical Society of Canada*, 1238
Kachaje, Rachel, *Disabled Peoples' International*, 658
Kacsuta, Keith, *The John Howard Society of Ontario*, 875
Kafka, Erika, *London Multiple Births Association*, 918
Kagan, Rachel, *Food & Consumer Products of Canada*, 749
Kagan, Leilani, *The Dream Factory*, 662
Kageorge, John, *Canadian Public Relations Society Inc.*, 463
Kahnert, Peter, *The Writers' Trust of Canada*, 1469
Kahrovic, Anne-Marie, *International Society for Magnetic Resonance in Medicine*, 1558
Kail, Greg, *American Water Works Association*, 1504
Kain, Karen, *National Ballet of Canada*, 991
Kaiser, Betty Jo, *Calgary Children's Foundation*, 271
Kaiser, Keith, *Ontario Ringette Association*, 1102
Kaiser, Randy, *Canadian Welsh Black Cattle Society*, 503
Kaiser, Dave, *Alberta Hotel & Lodging Association*, 38
Kaiser, Magdalena, *Wine Country Ontario*, 1458
Kaiser, Joe, *Nova Scotia Union of Public & Private Employees (CCU)*, 1050
Kakabadse, Yolanda, *WWF International*, 1608
Kako, Nelly, *Société culturelle régionale Les Chutes*, 1309
Kakouros, Frank, *Canadian Billiards & Snooker Association*, 343
Kalaria, Raj, *International Society for Vascular Behavioural & Cognitive Disorders*, 1560
Kalawarny, Garry, *Canadian Institute of Management*, 417
Kaliberda, Natalia, *Canadian Energy Efficiency Alliance*, 381
Kalin Zader, Kara, *Synchro BC*, 1360
Kalina, Ian, *Boys & Girls Clubs of British Columbia*, 222
Kalinski, Norman, *Manitoba Welsh Pony & Cob Association*, 947
Kallai, Peter, *Canadian Printable Electronics Industry Association*, 459
Kallaste-Kruzelecky, Ann, *L'Association des artistes Baltes à Montréal*, 106
Kallendorf, Craig, *International Association for Neo-Latin Studies*, 1537
Kalles, Anne, *Technion Canada*, 1368
Kallsen, Susan, *Canadian Manufacturers & Exporters*, 429
Kalsi, Tanjeet, *British Columbia Road Builders & Heavy Construction Association*, 251
Kaluzny, Wanda, *Orchestre de chambre de Montréal*, 1118
Kalytuk, Patty, *Association of Saskatchewan Realtors*, 161
Kamanye, Anne-Marie, *African Medical & Research Foundation Canada*, 13
Kamblé, Sangita, *Canadian Occupational Therapy Foundation*, 444
Kamelchuk, Dave, *Canadian Blonde d'Aquitaine Association*, 344
Kamensek, Jill, *Canadian Association of Neuroscience Nurses*, 322
Kaminski, Jacek, *Canadian Polish Congress*, 456
Kaminski, June, *Canadian Nursing Informatics Association*, 443
Kampen, Dan, *Fraser Valley Egg Producers' Association*, 757
Kamstra-Cooper, Krista, *Turner's Syndrome Society*, 1400
Kamuk, Bettina, *International Solid Waste Association*, 1562
Kan, Sharon, *Ottawa Chinese Community Services Centre*, 1129
Kan, Wendy, *Canadian Journalism Foundation*, 423
Kanagasabai, Sabitha, *Joint Forum of Financial Market Regulators*, 875
Kanani, Zahida, *GLOBE Foundation*, 775
Kanbayashi, Ikuo, *Canadian Ice Carvers' Society*, 410
Kandiuk, Mary, *York University Faculty Association*, 1474
Kandola, Manny, *Alliance of Canadian Cinema, Television & Radio Artists*, 58
Kane, Kevin, *Association of Academic Staff - University of Alberta*, 138
Kane, Jo-Ann, *Association des collections d'entreprises*, 109
Kang, Surinder Singh, *Maritime Sikh Society*, 951
Kang, Inky, *British Columbia Psychological Association*, 250
Kania, Scott, *Earthwatch Institute*, 1522
Kanmacher, Kim, *YMCA Canada*, 1472
Kannon, Karen, *Alianza Hispano-Canadiense Ontario*, 54
Kanojia, Amanda, *The Royal Society for the Encouragement of Arts, Manufactures & Commerce*, 1587
Kant, Shashi, *Commonwealth Forestry Association - Canadian Chapter*, 593
Kanter, Michelle, *Carolinian Canada Coalition*, 514
Kanters, Bart, *Concrete Ontario*, 610
Kantrowitz, Ted, *Canadian GeoExchange Coalition*, 397
Kanwar, Asha S., *The Commonwealth of Learning*, 594
Kaplan, Joel B., *British Columbia Council for Families*, 238
Kaplan, Gilla, *Heiser Program for Research in Leprosy & Tuberculosis*, 1529
Kaplan, Annie, *Association of Hemophilia Clinic Directors of Canada*, 149
Kaplanek, Barbara, *Kitchener-Waterloo Symphony Youth Orchestra*, 891
Kapodrawee, Abdullah, *Canadian Council of Muslim Theologians*, 369
Kapovic, Brady, *Canadian Western Agribition Association*, 503
Kappele, Ross, *Investment Funds Institute of Canada*, 863
Kapronczai, Paulo, *Alberta Freestyle Ski Association*, 36
Kaptyn, Ramona, *CARP*, 515
Kapur, Atul, *Physicians for a Smoke-Free Canada*, 1158
Kapur, Sandy, *Canadian Society of Allergy & Clinical Immunology*, 480
Kapusta, Vivian, *Canadian Quilters' Association*, 464
Karabelnicoff, Ariel, *Canadian Associates of Ben-Gurion University of the Negev*, 297
Karajaberlian, Suzanne, *Environmental Defence*, 691
Karakasis, Dean, *Building Owners & Managers Association of Ottawa*, 263
Karami, Hisham, *Canadian Institute of Food Science & Technology*, 415
Karapita, John, *Ontario Trial Lawyers Association*, 1111
Karasik, Arthur, *Ontario Rheumatology Association*, 1102
Karasin, Keith, *Canadian Cancer Society*, 349
Kardaris, Maria, *Canadian Academy of Geriatric Psychiatry*, 286
Karen, Peters, *Manitoba Eco-Network Inc.*, 936
Karen, Hemingway, *Marguerite Bourgeoys Family Centre Fertility Care Programme*, 949

Executive Name Index

Karg, Ludwig, *International Network for Environmental Management*, 1553
Kargard, April, *Fuse Collective*, 765
Karim, Fawzia, *Building Owners & Managers Association Toronto*, 263
Karim, Abdool, *Canadian Association of Medical Device Reprocessing*, 320
Karim, Rahim, *Canadian Memorial Chiropractic College*, 434
Kariya, Paul, *Pacific Salmon Foundation*, 1136
Karklins, Karlis, *Society of Bead Researchers*, 1592
Karlzen, Eric, *Evansburg & Entwistle Chamber of Commerce*, 699
Karok, Shannon, *Insurance Institute of Saskatchewan*, 850
Karp, Rick, *Whitehorse Chamber of Commerce*, 1453
Karras, Ron, *BC Assocation for Crane Safety*, 201
Karsh, Jacob, *Canadian Rheumatology Association*, 467
Karthaus, Detlef, *Esperanto-Toronto*, 695
Karunakaran, Siva, *Saskatchewan Medical Association*, 1270
Kary, Sandra, *Catholic Health Association of Saskatchewan*, 520
Kashton, Maxine, *Winnipeg Chamber of Commerce*, 1458
Kasirer, Nicholas, *Foundation for Legal Research*, 756
Kasp, Gladys, *Promotional Product Professionals of Canada Inc.*, 1189
Kasper, Tony, *Calgary Co-operative Memorial Society*, 271
Kasperskaya, Zhanna, *International Council of AIDS Service Organizations*, 855
Kasperski, Kim, *Alberta Orienteering Association*, 42
Kasperski, Janet, *Ontario Psychological Association*, 1098
Kassabian, Louise, *College of Optometrists of Ontario*, 587
Kassam, Shayda, *Institute of Certified Management Consultants of British Columbia*, 845
Kassam, Tahzeem, *DIVERSEcity Community Resources Society*, 659
Kassam-Kara, Roxanna, *Ronald McDonald House Charities of Canada*, 1235
Kassie, Roshini, *New Brunswick Lung Association*, 1010
Kassirer, Jay, *Healthy Indoors Partnership*, 807
Kast, W. Martin, *International Papillomavirus Society*, 1555
Kaster, Dwayne, *Walkerton Business Improvement Area*, 1440
Kastern, Chandra, *Red Deer Symphony Orchestra*, 1210
Kastner, Terry, *Northwest Wall & Ceiling Bureau*, 1580
Katanik, Lorraine, *Ontario Network of Employment Skills Training Projects*, 1093
Katchelewa, Shimbi, *Centre des ressources sur la non-violence inc*, 531
Kater, Julia, *Association of English Language Publishers of Québec*, 148
Katulski, David, *Congregation of St. Basil*, 613
Katz, Robert, *Canadian Dental Protective Association*, 377
Katz, Andrea, *Manitoba Rowing Association*, 943
Katz, Linda, *Polyurethane Manufacturers Association*, 1584
Kauffman-Lambert, Nancy, *Alzheimer Society Waterloo Wellington*, 66
Kaufman, Rocky, *Bengough Agricultural Society*, 205
Kaufman, Audrey, *Am Shalom*, 66
Kaulius, Jo-Anne, *Law Foundation of British Columbia*, 900
Kaun, Joan, *College of the Rockies Faculty Association*, 590

Kaur Dhaliwal, Rupinder, *World Sikh Organization of Canada*, 1467
Kaur Randhawa, Jasbir, *World Sikh Organization of Canada*, 1467
Kaustinen, Fred, *Ontario Association of Police Services Boards*, 1065
Kautto, Ginger, *National Shevchenko Musical Ensemble Guild of Canada*, 996
Kauzman, Adel, *Royal College of Dentists of Canada*, 1241
Kavanagh, Ruth, *Canadian Fire Alarm Association*, 390
Kavanagh, Gwen, *CARP*, 514
Kavanagh, Dawna, *British Columbia Registered Music Teachers' Association*, 251
Kavanaugh, Martha, *Canso Historical Society*, 509
Kavanaugh, Charles, *Maritime Fire Chiefs' Association*, 950
Kawaguchi, Gary, *Japanese Canadian Cultural Centre*, 869
Kawamura, Leslie, *Jodo Shinshu Buddhist Temples of Canada*, 873
Kay, Jean, *Canadian Authors Association*, 338
Kay, Lori, *Ontario Genealogical Society*, 1082
Kay, Lynda, *Northumberland United Way*, 1036
Kay, Cheryl, *LaCloche Foothills Chamber of Commerce*, 895
Kaye, Pam, *Sussex & District Chamber of Commerce*, 1357
Kaye, Darcie, *Westgen*, 1451
Kazina, Sydney, *Manitoba Camping Association*, 933
Kdouh, Louis, *Parents partenaires en éducation*, 1140
Kealey, G.S., *Canadian Committee on Labour History*, 361
Kealey, Greg, *Ontario Association of Triathletes*, 1066
Kean, Sarah, *Professional Association of Internes & Residents of Newfoundland*, 1182
Keane, Kathleen, *Association for Bright Children (Ontario)*, 132
Keane, Tony, *International Facility Management Association*, 1546
Keane, Sue, *Auditing Association of Canada*, 187
Kear, Celine, *Jane Austen Society of North America*, 868
Keating, Roger, *Nova Scotia Tennis Association*, 1050
Keating, Michael, *New Brunswick Association of Nursing Homes, Inc.*, 1005
Keating, Caroll-Ann, *Le Réseau d'enseignement francophone à distance du Canada*, 1219
Keating, Frank, *American Bankers Association*, 1490
Keats, Patrice, *Canadian Counselling & Psychotherapy Association*, 372
Keats, Lindsay, *Professional Engineers Ontario*, 1184
Keats, Tony, *Municipalities Newfoundland & Labrador*, 982
Kebe, Kent, *Radium Hot Springs Chamber of Commerce*, 1203
Keddy, Steven, *PFLAG Canada Inc.*, 1155
Kedron, Peter, *Canadian Association of Geographers*, 316
Kee, Anne-Marie, *Canadian Accredited Independent Schools*, 287
Kee, Peggy, *Canadian Association for Population Therapeutics*, 303
Keefe, Birdene, *Midwives Association of Saskatchewan*, 965
Keefer, Michael, *Society for Ecological Restoration International*, 1590
Keelaghan, James, *Georgian Bay Folk Society*, 771
Keeler, Barry, *Last Post Fund*, 899
Keen, Rob, *Forests Ontario*, 752
Keenan, Alvin, *Canadian Horticultural Council*, 408
Keenan, Susan, *Street Haven at the Crossroads*, 1352

Keenan, William J., *International Pediatric Association*, 1555
Keenlyside, David L., *Prince Edward Island Museum & Heritage Foundation*, 1176
Keeping, Janet, *The Green Party of Alberta*, 788
Keeping, Jeff, *Canadian Football League Players' Association*, 392
Keess, Leigh, *Saskatchewan Bodybuilding Association*, 1260
Kegie, Sandra, *Federation of Mutual Fund Dealers*, 725
Keglowitsch, Suzanne, *American Saddlebred Horse Association of Alberta*, 66
Kehler, Joyce, *Youth in Care in Ontario*, 1476
Kehler, Connie, *Saskatchewan Herb & Spice Association*, 1267
Kehoe, Victoria, *Distress Centre of Durham Region*, 659
Kehoe, Annabel, *British Columbia Rugby Union*, 252
Kehoe, Carol, *Hamilton Philharmonic Orchestra*, 801
Kehoe, Scott, *The Leukemia & Lymphoma Society of Canada*, 909
Kehrig, Rachel, *Saskatchewan Pulse Growers*, 1273
Keibel, Angela, *Volunteer Alberta*, 1438
Keil, T.J., *Building Industry & Land Development Alberta*, 262
Keilback, Christine, *Canadian Hemophilia Society*, 404
Keill, Linda, *Lupus Ontario*, 921
Keim, Mike, *Respiratory Therapy Society of Ontario*, 1227
Keith, Gary, *Canadian Plowing Organization*, 456
Keith, Jack, *Halifax Foundation*, 799
Keiver, Wendy, *Alberta School Councils' Association*, 45
Kelava, Wanita, *Canadian-Croatian Chamber of Commerce*, 506
Kelderman, Dianne, *Nova Scotia Co-operative Council*, 1043
Kell, Kevin, *Royal Astronomical Society of Canada*, 1238
Kellard, Crystal, *Alliston & District Chamber of Commerce*, 59
Kelleppan, Areni, *Green Calgary*, 788
Keller, Amanda, *C.A.R.E. Jeunesse*, 511
Keller, Kris, *Kawartha Chamber of Commerce & Tourism*, 882
Keller, Suzanne, *World Society for Ekistics*, 1607
Keller, Monica, *Canadian Property Tax Association, Inc.*, 461
Keller, Peter, *International Council of Museums*, 1545
Keller, James, *Lutheran Bible Translators of Canada Inc.*, 922
Keller, Egon, *Canadian Pastry Chefs Guild Inc.*, 452
Keller, Donna, *CADORA Ontario Association Inc.*, 269
Keller-Hobson, Doug, *Hope Air*, 821
Kellett, Patrick H., *United Association of Journeymen & Apprentices of the Plumbing & Pipe Fitting Industry of the United States & Canada*, 1599
Kellett, Malinda, *Northwest Territories Law Foundation*, 1038
Kelley, Greg, *Canadian Association of Professional Conservators*, 328
Kelley, Rebecca, *Canadian Association for Young Children*, 307
Kelley, Becky, *Canadian Association for Young Children*, 307
Kellington, Ronda, *Acupuncture Canada*, 7
Kelln, Diane, *Catholic Women's League of Canada*, 520
Kellogg, Emily, *Association of Canadian Publishers*, 143
Kells, Catherine, *Canadian Society of Cardiac Surgeons*, 481

Kells, Laureen, *Saskatchewan Registered Music Teachers' Association*, 1273
Kelly, Kathy, *Manitoba Society of Occupational Therapists*, 945
Kelly, Kevin, *National Court Reporters Association*, 1575
Kelly, Barbara, *British Columbia Library Trustees' Association*, 245
Kelly, Lizz, *New Westminster Chamber of Commerce*, 1015
Kelly, Trish, *Greater Vancouver Food Bank Society*, 786
Kelly, Danielle, *Canadian Public Relations Society Inc.*, 463
Kelly, John, *Ontario Fruit & Vegetable Growers' Association*, 1081
Kelly, Mike, *Golf Association of Ontario*, 777
Kelly, Dan, *Canadian Condominium Institute*, 362
Kelly, Dan, *Canadian Federation of Independent Business*, 387
Kelly, Jon E., *Responsible Gambling Council (Ontario)*, 1227
Kelly, Seán, *Canadian Psychological Association*, 462
Kelly, Cathy, *Canadian Association for University Continuing Education*, 307
Kelly, Marie, *Ontario Nurses' Association*, 1094
Kelly, Sean, *Canada - Newfoundland & Labrador Offshore Petroleum Board*, 278
Kelly, Monique, *Daughters of Isabella*, 651
Kelly, Michael, *Clean Water Action*, 1517
Kelly, Sheila, *Saskatchewan Sports Hall of Fame & Museum*, 1276
Kelly, Pat, *Blomidon Naturalists Society*, 215
Kelly, Myranda, *Jeunesse Acadienne et Francophone de l'Île-du-prince-Édouard*, 870
Kelly, Lesley, *Canadian Agri-Marketing Association (Saskatchewan)*, 290
Kelly, Charles, *Concrete B.C.*, 610
Kelly, Jennifer, *Mining Industry NL*, 967
Kelly, Ryan, *SailNL*, 1246
Kelly, Jeff, *Flowercart*, 741
Kelman, Jill, *Alliance for Canadian New Music Projects*, 56
Kelman, Les, *Jewish Genealogical Society of Toronto*, 872
Kelman, Les, *Oraynu Congregation for Humanistic Judaism*, 1117
Kelner, Reid, *Manitoba Hotel Association*, 938
Kelsch, Dan, *Prairie Apparel Market*, 1169
Kelsey, Brenda, *Myasthenia Gravis Association of British Columbia*, 986
Kelusky, Ron, *Public Services Health & Safety Association*, 1193
Kembhavi, Sandeep, *Nepali Children's Education Project*, 1003
Kemmett, Sue, *Yukon Conservation Society*, 1478
Kemp, Shelley, *Learning Disabilities Association of Saskatchewan*, 905
Kemp, Randy, *The Royal Canadian Regiment Association*, 1241
Kempster, Amy, *Greenspace Alliance of Canada's Capital*, 789
Kendall, Stephen, *Presbyterian Church in Canada*, 1170
Kendall, Sandra, *Ontario Health Libraries Association*, 1084
Kendall, Susannah, *Canadian Association for Conservation of Cultural Property*, 299
Kendrick Burk, Lacy, *International Foster Care Organisation*, 1549
Kenedy, Margie, *Association of Professional Archaeologists*, 156
Kenequanash, Margaret, *Shibogama First Nations Council*, 1296
Kenkel, Jeffrey M., *American Society for Aesthetic Plastic Surgery*, 1497
Kennedy, Helen, *Egale Canada*, 681
Kennedy, Mark, *Association of Christian Schools International*, 1510
Kennedy, Gordon, *Canadian Fraternal Association*, 394

Executive Name Index

Kennedy, Ed, *Toronto Professional Fire Fighters Association*, 1386
Kennedy, Nadine, *Lanark County Food Bank*, 897
Kennedy, Teresa J., *International Council of Associations for Science Education*, 1545
Kennedy, Lloyd, *Ontario Creamerymen's Association*, 1076
Kennedy, Jennifer, *Alzheimer Society of Alberta & Northwest Territories*, 61
Kennedy, Arthur, *Learning Enrichment Foundation*, 905
Kennedy, Lindsay, *Canadian Literacy & Learning Network*, 427
Kennedy, John, *Saskatchewan Cultural Exchange Society*, 1263
Kennedy, John, *Canada - Newfoundland & Labrador Offshore Petroleum Board*, 278
Kennedy, Bonnie, *Canadian Association for Prior Learning Assesment*, 303
Kennedy, Kathryn, *Center for Plant Conservation*, 1516
Kennedy, Nancy, *Saskatchewan Library Trustees' Association*, 1269
Kennedy, Nancy, *Canadian Iris Society*, 422
Kennedy, Dave, *Professional Locksmith Association of Alberta*, 1186
Kennedy, Shawn E., *Canadian Association of Veterans in United Nations Peacekeeping*, 335
Kennedy, Susan, *God, Sex, & the Meaning of Life Ministry*, 776
Kennedy, Jim, *Windsor Electrical Contractors Association*, 1456
Kennedy, Stewart, *The Royal Scottish Country Dance Society*, 1587
Kennedy, Matt, *Boxing Ontario*, 220
Kennedy, Jean, *International Foster Care Organisation*, 1549
Kennedy, Joan, *Seasons Centre for Grieving Children*, 1288
Kennedy, Anna, *Canadian Lymphedema Framework*, 429
Kennedy, Jacky, *Green Communities Canada*, 788
Kennedy, Floyd, *Back Country Horsemen of British Columbia*, 192
Kennedy, Louise, *CADORA Ontario Association Inc.*, 269
Kennedy, Gerard, *Centre for Transportation Engineering & Planning*, 534
Kennedy, Karyn, *Boost Child & Youth Advocacy Centre*, 218
Kennedy, Barbara, *Cardiac Health Foundation of Canada*, 510
Kennedy-Baker, Jodie, *CADORA British Columbia*, 268
Kennell, Fred, *Concrete Manitoba*, 610
Kennelly, Wendy, *The Terry Fox Foundation*, 1372
Kennett, Betty, *Hampton Food Basket & Clothing Centre Inc.*, 802
Kenney, Padraic, *Association for Slavic, East European, & Eurasian Studies*, 1509
Kenney, Jason, *United Conservative Association*, 1410
Kennis, Lorri, *Human Resources Professionals Association*, 825
Kennish, Janet, *The Garden Clubs of Ontario*, 767
Kenny, Patrick, *Canada Games Council*, 279
Kenny, Beth Ann, *Federation of Health Regulatory Colleges of Ontario*, 724
Kenny, Diane, *Alliance Française Halifax*, 57
Kenny, Stephanie, *Professional Association of Residents of Ontario*, 1182
Kenny, Kay, *Volunteer Central Society*, 1438
Kenoyer, J. Mark, *Society of Bead Researchers*, 1592
Kense, Frank, *Canadian Council on Africa*, 370
Kent, Diane, *Ontario Herbalists Association*, 1084
Kent, Andrea, *Renewable Industries Canada*, 1217
Kent, Lynne, *Learning Disabilities Association of British Columbia*, 904
Kent, Jodi, *Canadian Association of Electroneurophysiology Technologists Inc.*, 312
Kent, Sandy, *Judo BC*, 876
Kent, C. Adèle, *National Judicial Institute*, 994
Kent, Holly, *Ontario Book Publishers Organization*, 1068
Kenyon, Candace, *Canadian Orthopaedic Nurses Association*, 448
Keogh, Tobias, *Canadian AIDS Society*, 290
Keohane, Sé, *Green Communities Canada*, 788
Keon, Jim, *Canadian Generic Pharmaceutical Association*, 397
Keough, Patrick, *West Nipissing Chamber of Commerce*, 1446
Keown, Melissa, *Canadian Society of Cardiac Surgeons*, 481
Keown, Eileen, *Orchestras Mississauga*, 1117
Kepper, Shirley, *UNICEF Canada*, 1405
Keppler, Stephen, *Intermodal Association of North America*, 1534
Kerasiotis, Effie, *Hellenic Community of Vancouver*, 812
Kerbel, Howard, *Toronto Downtown Jazz Society*, 1384
Kerby, Debra, *Canadian Feed The Children*, 389
Kerby, Zane, *American Society of Travel Agents*, 1503
Kerby, Morgan, *Human Resources Professionals of Durham*, 826
Keri, Alen, *Concrete Ontario*, 610
Kerik, Fran, *Canadian Registry of Tennessee Walking Horse*, 466
Kerkhoven, Phyllis, *Osteoporosis Canada*, 1129
Kern, Harry, *Yukon River Marathon Paddlers Association*, 1480
Kernaghan, Kevin, *Alberta Plastics Recycling Association*, 42
Kerns, Samuel, *American Forest & Paper Association*, 1493
Kerr, Hasell, *OMF International - Canada*, 1057
Kerr, Joanna, *Greenpeace Canada*, 789
Kerr, Leslie, *Northern Ontario Curling Association*, 1035
Kerr, Andrew, *Geological Association of Canada*, 770
Kerr, Skip, *Environmental Services Association of Alberta*, 692
Kerr, Jessica, *Canadian Group Psychotherapy Association*, 399
Kerr, John, *Canadian Business Press*, 348
Kerr, John, *Wellington Law Association*, 1444
Kerr, Allan, *Canadian Militaria Preservation Society*, 436
Kerr, Shelagh, *Electronics Product Stewardship Canada*, 684
Kerr, Jennifer, *Institutional Limited Partners Association*, 848
Kerr, Gregg, *Triathlon Nova Scotia*, 1398
Kerrigan, Christopher, *Alva Foundation*, 61
Kerslake, Su, *Alberta Provincial Council*, 43
Kersten, Arend, *Flamborough Chamber of Commerce*, 740
Keselman, Harvey, *Manitoba Orchid Society*, 941
Keshavji, Ashifa, *College of Pharmacists of British Columbia*, 587
Keshavmurthy, Prashant, *Canadian Asian Studies Association*, 296
Keshen, Bryan, *Reena*, 1210
Keshen, Robert, *Toronto Association of Law Libraries*, 1382
Kesic, Vesna, *European Society of Gynaecological Oncology*, 1524
Kester, Carlton, *National Association of Addiction Treatment Providers*, 1573
Kesteris, Andris, *Baltic Federation in Canada*, 195
Kesteris, Andris, *Latvian National Federation in Canada*, 900

Ketcheson, Graham, *Paddle Canada*, 1137
Ketilson, Neil, *Sask Pork*, 1254
Ketterling, Pat, *Swimming New Brunswick*, 1359
Kettle, David, *Commonwealth War Graves Commission - Canadian Agency*, 594
Kettles, Patty, *Automotive Industries Association of Canada*, 190
Kevin, Day, *Canadian Captive Insurance Association*, 350
Key, Shannon, *BC School Sports*, 202
Key, Rob, *Professional Association of Residents of Alberta*, 1182
Key, Robert, *Muskoka-Parry Sound Beekeepers' Association*, 985
Keydash, Mary, *International Society for Magnetic Resonance in Medicine*, 1558
Keyes, Stan, *Canadian Payday Loan Association*, 452
Khachan, Ali, *United Nations Association in Canada*, 1411
Khadaroo, Nawshad, *Credit Institute of Canada*, 640
Khadaroo, Nawshad, *Canadian Credit Institute Educational Foundation*, 372
Khairi, Vahid, *Société canadienne-française de radiologie*, 1309
Khales, Hanane, *DisAbled Women's Network of Canada*, 658
Khalfan, Al-Azhar, *Institute of Corporate Directors*, 845
Khalfan, Al-Azhar, *Global Network of Director Institutes*, 775
Khaloo, Azam, *Pakistan Canada Association of Calgary*, 1137
Khami, Mana, *Regional HIV/AIDS Connection*, 1212
Khan, Osaed, *Manitoba Islamic Association*, 939
Khan, Azam, *Association of Professional Engineers & Geoscientists of Alberta*, 157
Khan, Tariq, *Pakistan Canada Association of Calgary*, 1137
Khan, Yasmin, *Social Planning Toronto*, 1307
Khan, Nadia, *Hypertension Canada*, 829
Khan, Compton, *Georgian Bay Native Friendship Centre*, 771
Khan, Kamran, *Project Management Institute*, 1585
Khan, Sanjida, *Pathways to Education Canada*, 1145
Khan, Fazal, *College of Opticians of Ontario*, 587
Khan, Sahaban, *Scarborough Cricket Association*, 1282
Khan, Azhar (Sam), *Saskatchewan Cricket Association*, 1262
Khan, David, *Alberta Liberal Party*, 39
Khan Malik, Lal, *Ahmadiyya Muslim Jama'at Canada*, 15
Khandal, R.K., *World Association of Industrial & Technological Research Organizations*, 1603
Khaper, Shelley, *Science Teachers' Association of Ontario*, 1285
Kharod, Mandip, *TD Friends of the Environment Foundation*, 1367
Khelfaoui, Mahdi, *Canadian Science & Technology Historical Association*, 468
Kherani, Amin, *Canadian Retina Society*, 467
Khetrapal, Shoba, *Public Accountants Council for the Province of Ontario*, 1192
Khiani, Gobind, *Association of Professional Engineers & Geoscientists of Alberta*, 157
Khokhar, Perveen, *Our Harbour*, 1132
Khoury, Joseph, *Association de paralysie cérébrale du Québec*, 103
Khoury, Michael, *The Israel Economic Mission to Canada*, 866
Khoury, Rebecca, *Taekwondo Canada*, 1366
Khudorozhkova, Kseniia, *Building Owners & Managers Association Toronto*, 263
Kiang, Josephine, *Federation of Chinese Canadian Professionals (Ontario)*, 723
Kianza, Nola, *Canadian Council on Africa*, 370

Kianza, Chris, *Canadian Council on Africa*, 370
Kidd, Nancy, *American Sociological Association*, 1503
Kidd, Bill, *Toronto Chapter of the International Association of Printing House Craftsmen*, 1383
Kiddell, Charlotte, *Canadian Federation of Students*, 388
Kidder, Annie, *People for Education*, 1151
Kidder, Ruth, *Alberta Aboriginal Women's Society*, 21
Kidder, Rushworth M., *Institute for Global Ethics (Canada)*, 843
Kidney, Pam, *Synchro Nova Scotia*, 1361
Kidston, Paul, *Feed Nova Scotia*, 731
Kidston, Paul, *Kidney Foundation of Canada*, 885
Kiell, David, *Landscape Newfoundland & Labrador*, 898
Kielly, Janet, *Law Foundation of Newfoundland & Labrador*, 901
Kienast, Jeff, *Organic Crop Improvement Association (International)*, 1581
Kierstead, Mike, *Newspapers Atlantic*, 1024
Kierstead, Andrew, *Saint John Gallery Association*, 1247
Kiesenhofer, Tony, *Table Tennis Canada*, 1366
Kihn, Roberta, *Association of Neighbourhood Houses BC*, 153
Kilbride, Andria, *Ontario Band Association*, 1067
Kilby, Leanne, *Canadian Association of Elizabeth Fry Societies*, 313
Kilgallon, Patty, *Children's Cottage Society*, 561
Kilkenny, Chloe, *Osteoporosis Canada*, 1128
Kim, Dong-One, *International Labour & Employment Relations Association*, 1551
Kim, Eun-Shik, *International Association for Ecology*, 1536
Kim, Ellie, *ARMA Canada*, 82
Kim, Kyong-ae, *College of Registered Psychiatric Nurses of British Columbia*, 590
Kim, Kyong-ae, *College of Registered Psychiatric Nurses of B.C.*, 590
Kim, Harold, *Canadian Society of Allergy & Clinical Immunology*, 480
Kim, David, *Resident Doctors of British Columbia*, 1226
Kim, Younghoon David, *World Energy Council*, 1604
Kim, John C.H., *Canada Korea Business Association*, 280
Kim, Song Chul, *WTF Taekwondo Federation of British Columbia*, 1469
Kim, Sang-Im, *Korean Senior Citizens Society of Toronto*, 893
Kim, Sarah, *Women's Missionary Society*, 1463
Kim, Perry, *Canadian Frailty Network*, 394
Kimak, Brett, *Edmonton CFA Society*, 675
Kimball, Jay, *Insurance Brokers Association of Canada*, 848
Kimberley-Young, Rhonda, *Ontario Teachers' Federation*, 1110
Kimmerly, Ian, *Canadian Stamp Dealers' Association*, 490
Kimmins, Ted, *Northwest Territories Biathlon Association*, 1037
Kimpton, Daniel, *Association des avocats et avocates de province*, 106
Kincaid, Ali, *Skills/Compétences Canada*, 1303
Kinch, Jack, *Ontario Society for the Prevention of Cruelty to Animals*, 1106
Kinch, Brenda, *British Columbia Therapeutic Recreation Association*, 257
Kincler, Jack, *Canadian Institute for Jewish Research*, 412
Kind, Julie, *Alberta 5 Pin Bowlers' Association*, 21
Kindrachuk, Slawko, *Ukrainian Canadian Congress*, 1402
Kindt, Teena, *Alzheimer Society of Niagara Region*, 63
Kines, David, *MuchFACT*, 978

Executive Name Index

Kinew, Wab, *New Democratic Party*, 1014
King, Marie Ellen, *Congrégation des Soeurs de Sainte-Anne*, 612
King, Nancy, *Comox Valley Therapeutic Riding Society*, 608
King, Carman, *Soccer Nova Scotia*, 1305
King, Sylvie, *Athletics Canada*, 181
King, Charlotte, *Canadian Authors Association*, 338
King, Colin, *The Canadian Corps of Commissionaires*, 365
King, Catherine, *Fertilizer Canada*, 733
King, Wayne, *Canadian Hearing Society*, 403
King, Rachel, *Co-operative Education & Work-Integrated Learning Canada*, 627
King, Jim, *Financial Executives International Canada*, 736
King, Gordon, *Navy League of Canada*, 1002
King, Jeff, *Society of Composers, Authors & Music Publishers of Canada*, 1328
King, Barry, *Community Museums Association of Prince Edward Island*, 606
King, Sara, *Archives Society of Alberta*, 81
King, Bruce, *Institute of Power Engineers*, 847
King, Colin, *Atlantic Provinces Athletic Therapists Association*, 185
King, Janet, *Kids Now*, 886
King, Doug, *Ontario Monument Builders Association*, 1091
King, Patrick, *Nova Scotia College of Physiotherapists*, 1043
King, Maureen, *Congress of Union Retirees Canada*, 613
King, Lois, *Sussex Sharing Club*, 1357
King, Shelley, *Aquaculture Association of Canada*, 75
King, Myron, *Northeast Avalon ACAP, Inc.*, 1034
King, Richard, *British Columbia Egg Marketing Board*, 239
King, Joanne, *PFLAG Canada Inc.*, 1155
King, Patricia, *Fishermen & Scientists Research Society*, 740
King, Fritz Burns, *Halifax Employers Association*, 799
King, Kristina, *International Society for Magnetic Resonance in Medicine*, 1558
King, Andrea, *Society of Cardiovascular Anesthesiologists*, 1592
King, Michael, *Alberta Katahdin Sheep Association*, 38
King, Darlene, *Canadian National Baton Twirling Association*, 439
King, Andy, *Caregivers Alberta*, 512
King Kottman, Lana, *Schizophrenia Society of Alberta*, 1283
Kingdon, Marilyn, *Canadian Hard of Hearing Association*, 400
Kingdon, Rose, *The Canadian Press*, 459
Kinghorn, Russ, *Engineers Canada*, 689
Kinghorne, Elizabeth Ann (Libby), *Atlantic Provinces Trial Lawyers Association*, 185
Kingsbury, Kori, *Cardiac Care Network of Ontario*, 510
Kingsbury, Fanny, *Association québécoise de pédagogie collégiale*, 171
Kingsley, Adam, *Intellectual Property Institute of Canada*, 851
Kingsley, Adam, *Consumer Health Products Canada*, 626
Kingsmill, Terry, *Ontario Institute of Agrologists*, 1087
Kingston, Brian, *Ottawa Economics Association*, 1130
Kingston, Brian, *Business Council of Canada*, 267
Kingston, Joan, *Chemical Institute of Canada*, 556
Kingston, Kathryn, *Special Libraries Association*, 1596
Kingston, Fred, *Northwest Atlantic Fisheries Organization*, 1036
Kingston, Bob, *Agriculture Union*, 15
Kingston, Joan, *Canadian Society for Chemistry*, 473

Kingyens, Donette, *Athabasca University Students' Union*, 180
Kinnear, Gary, *Kamloops, Revelstoke, Okanagan & District Building & Construction Trades Council*, 881
Kinney, Brenda, *Nurses Association of New Brunswick*, 1052
Kinniburgh, Robert, *Canadian Association of Orthodontists*, 324
Kinniburgh, David, *Canadian Society of Clinical Chemists*, 481
Kinoshameg, Samantha, *Barrie Native Friendship Centre*, 197
Kinsman, Amanada, *Childhood Cancer Canada Foundation*, 560
Kinsman, Terri, *Strathmore & District Chamber of Commerce*, 1352
Kirby, Matt, *Professional Engineers Ontario*, 1184
Kirby, Sean, *Mining Association of Nova Scotia*, 967
Kirby, Mel, *Festival Chorus of Calgary*, 733
Kirby, Jacqueline, *Apparel BC*, 74
Kirejczyk, Juliusz, *Canadian Polish Congress*, 456
Kirk, Doug, *Ontario Association of Broadcasters*, 1062
Kirk, Tosha, *Vividata*, 1436
Kirk, Bob, *Printing Equipment & Supply Dealers' Association of Canada*, 1180
Kirk, Diane, *New Brunswick Gymnastics Association*, 1009
Kirk, Jacqueline, *Canadian Association for the Study of Educational Administration*, 306
Kirk, John, *British Columbia Scientific Cryptozoology Club*, 253
Kirk, Mary Anne, *Manitoba Trail Riding Club Inc.*, 946
Kirk, Ken, *Habitat for Humanity Canada*, 797
Kirk, Rebecca, *Literacy Central Vancouver Island*, 913
Kirk, Bob, *Canadian Printing Industries Scholarship Trust Fund*, 460
Kirkby, Judy, *Canadian Trakehner Horse Society*, 496
Kirke, Bob, *Canadian Apparel Federation*, 294
Kirkham, Allen, *Canadian Hearing Instrument Practitioners Society*, 403
Kirkham, Allen, *College of Hearing Aid Practitioners of Alberta*, 585
Kirkness, Ryan, *Manitoba Hotel Association*, 938
Kirkpatrick, Sherry, *Canadian Association of Exposition Management*, 313
Kirkpatrick, Gwen, *Huron Perth Association of Realtors*, 828
Kirkpatrick, Eunice, *YMCA Canada*, 1472
Kirkpatrick, James, *The American Astronautical Society*, 1490
Kirkpatrick, Karin, *Family Services of Greater Vancouver*, 705
Kirkpatrick, Robert, *Canadian Fallen Firefighters Foundation*, 383
Kirkpatrick, Rick, *New Brunswick Dart Association*, 1007
Kirkwood, Bonnie, *WaterCan*, 1442
Kirkwood, Rod, *Northwest Territories Association of Architects*, 1037
Kirkwood, Karen, *Alberta Chicken Producers*, 28
Kirkwood-Whyte, Karen, *United Way of Chatham-Kent County*, 1413
Kirkwood-Whyte, Karen, *Information Tilbury & Help Centre*, 837
Kirouac, Barb, *Community Living Dryden-Sioux Lookout*, 601
Kirpaul, Dalip, *La Fédération Québécoise du Cricket Inc.*, 731
Kirshin, Toby, *College of Family Physicians of Canada*, 584
Kirton, Krys, *Epilepsy & Seizure Association of Manitoba*, 693
Kirton, Daryl, *British Columbia Hereford Association*, 243

Kirwan, Joe, *Melville & District Chamber of Commerce*, 959
Kischak, Steve, *The Association of Ontario Locksmiths*, 155
Kisel, Dave, *Ontario Sledge Hockey Association*, 1105
Kish, Jocelyn, *Appaloosa Horse Club of Canada*, 73
Kisil, Anna, *International Organization of Ukrainian Communities "Fourth Wave"*, 859
Kisilevich, Leanne, *Alberta College of Speech-Language Pathologists & Audiologists*, 30
Kislowicz, Linda, *Jewish Federations of Canada - UIA*, 872
Kissel, Julie, *Glendon & District Business Alliance*, 774
Kissinger, Ed, *Calgary Field Naturalists' Society*, 272
Kistabish, Oscar, *Centre d'amitié autochtone de Val-d'Or*, 527
Kitamura, Yutaka, *International Commission of Agricultural & Biosystems Engineering*, 1542
Kitchen, Katie, *Manitoba Society of Occupational Therapists*, 945
Kitchen, Hugh, *Yukon Chamber of Mines*, 1477
Kitchen, Susan, *Coaches Association of Ontario*, 576
Kitchin, Paul, *Career Colleges Ontario*, 511
Kite, Gisele, *Canadian Organization of Medical Physicists*, 447
Kiteley, Heather, *Guaranteed Funeral Deposits of Canada*, 792
Kitty, Darlene, *Indigenous Physicians Association of Canada*, 835
Kituyi, Mukhisa, *United Nations Conference on Trade & Development*, 1599
Kitz, Sheila, *Alberta Rural Municipal Administrators Association*, 45
Kivisild, Emma, *KickStart Disability Arts & Culture*, 884
Kjearsgaard, Faye, *Danish Canadian National Museum Society*, 650
Klaassen, Eric V., *North American Die Casting Association*, 1579
Klass, Mike, *Hockey Alberta*, 817
Klassen, Matthew, *La Ronge & District Chamber of Commerce*, 1236
Klassen, Neil, *Certified Technicians & Technologists Association of Manitoba*, 538
Klassen, Glenn, *Lethbridge Symphony Orchestra*, 908
Klassen, Marie, *Lakehead Social Planning Council*, 896
Klassen, Ken, *Manitoba Association of School Superintendents*, 931
Klassen, Ray, *Seton Portage/Shalalth District Chamber of Commerce*, 1292
Klassen, Leighton, *Architectural & Building Technologists Association of Manitoba Inc.*, 78
Klassen, Laurie, *Trochu Chamber of Commerce*, 1399
Klassen, Curtis, *Living Bible Explorers*, 915
Klassen, Carly, *Alberta Music Industry Association*, 41
Klatt, Jason, *Canadian Celiac Association*, 353
Klein, Lorretta, *Alberta Association of Professional Paralegals*, 24
Klein, Seth, *Canadian Centre for Policy Alternatives*, 354
Klein, Marina, *Canadian HIV Trials Network*, 405
Klein, Shauna, *Child Development Institute*, 559
Klein, Christina, *Canadian Horticultural Therapy Association*, 408
Klein, Debbie, *Edmonton Community Legal Centre*, 676
Klein, Allan, *American Society of Echocardiography*, 1499
Klein Leighton, Talia, *The Association for the Soldiers of Israel*, 135

Klein Leighton, Talia, *The Canadian Zionist Cultural Association*, 506
Kleine, Lennart P., *The Swedish-Canadian Chamber of Commerce*, 1358
Kleinedler, Steve, *Dictionary Society of North America*, 1521
Kleiner, David, *Canadian Friends of Bikur Cholim Hospital*, 395
Kleinman, Robert A., *Jewish Community Foundation of Montréal*, 871
Kleinmann, Rami, *Canadian Friends of the Hebrew University*, 395
Klemky, Daniel, *Building Owners & Managers Association of British Columbia*, 263
Klemmer, Daris, *Nurse Practitioners Association of Alberta*, 1052
Klenk, Frank, *Model Aeronautics Association of Canada Inc.*, 971
Klie, Erica, *Marketing Research & Intelligence Association*, 951
Klim, Edward J., *International Snowmobile Manufacturers Association*, 1557
Kline, Daniel, *British Columbia Society for Male Survivors of Sexual Abuse*, 254
Kljenak, Diana, *Ontario Psychiatric Association*, 1098
Kloepper, Alan, *Alberta Educational Facilities Administrators Association*, 33
Klohn, Peter, *Financial & Consumer Services Commission*, 736
Klomp, Jamie, *Human Resources Professionals Association*, 826
Kloosterman, Mary, *YMCA Canada*, 1472
Kloppenburg, Camille, *Toronto Parents of Multiple Births Association*, 1386
Klotz-Ritter, Jennifer, *Make-A-Wish Canada*, 927
Klugman, Iain, *Communitech*, 595
Klukas, Andrew, *Western Convenience Store Association*, 1449
Klumper, Alice, *Manitoba Association of Library Technicians*, 930
Klymkiw, Slawko, *Canadian Film Centre*, 390
Klynstra, Jenna, *Alberta Roadbuilders & Heavy Construction Association*, 44
Kmet, Lori, *College of Medical Laboratory Technologists of Alberta*, 586
Knaapen, Jacoba, *Toronto Alliance for the Performing Arts*, 1381
Knapman, Andrew, *Vancouver Grain Exchange*, 1425
Knapp, Millie, *Association for Native Development in the Performing & Visual Arts*, 134
Knapp, Stephen, *Canadian Copper & Brass Development Association*, 365
Knapp, Bob, *The Bruce Trail Conservancy*, 261
Knapp, Laura, *Toronto Association of Law Libraries*, 1382
Knapp, Barry, *Association of Fundraising Professionals*, 1512
Kneen, Sharon, *Marwayne & District Chamber of Commerce*, 952
Knell, Lyn, *Peruvian Horse Association of Canada*, 1152
Knickle, David, *Illuminating Engineering Society of North America*, 1531
Knierim, Justus (Gus), *Grey, Bruce, Dufferin, & Simcoe Postal History Study Group*, 790
Knight, Christine, *Association of BC Drama Educators*, 140
Knight, Mel, *National Environmental Health Association*, 1576
Knight, Dawn, *Manitoba Association for Art Education*, 929
Knight, Greg, *Lacrosse Nova Scotia*, 895
Knight, Wade, *Ontario Woodlot Association*, 1114
Knight, Kathy, *Information & Communication Technologies Association of Manitoba*, 836
Knight, Tamara, *British Columbia Amateur Bodybuilding Association*, 230
Knight, Keith, *Canadian Christian Business Federation*, 356

Executive Name Index

Knispel, Doug, *Ontario Jiu-Jitsu Association*, 1088
Knoch, John, *Canadian College of Health Leaders*, 358
Knoch, Marilynn, *British Columbia Printing & Imaging Association*, 249
Knor, Lana, *Green Acres Art Centre*, 788
Knorr, Wayne, *Canadian Public Relations Society Inc.*, 463
Knorr, Dietrich, *International Union of Food Science & Technology*, 861
Knott, Stephen, *International Longshoremen's Association (AFL-CIO/CLC)*, 1553
Knott, Whitney, *Thunder Bay Indian Friendship Centre*, 1378
Knott, Teresa, *Medical Library Association*, 1570
Knott, Lyall, *Rick Hansen Foundation*, 1231
Knous, Gloria, *Canadian Hard of Hearing Association*, 401
Knowles, Jill, *Skate Canada*, 1302
Knox, Larry, *Bear River Board of Trade*, 202
Knox, Mark, *Nipawin & District Chamber of Commerce*, 1027
Knox, Alex, *International Flying Farmers*, 1549
Knudsen, Debie, *Fairview & District Chamber of Commerce*, 701
Knudsen, Colin, *Red Lake District Chamber of Commerce*, 1210
Knutson, Glenna, *Lakehead University Faculty Association*, 896
Knutson, Sonja, *TESL Newfoundland & Labrador*, 1372
Knutson, Dan, *Saskatchewan Building Officials Association Inc.*, 1260
Ko, Ken, *Queen's University Faculty Association*, 1100
Kobly, Ken, *Alberta Chambers of Commerce*, 28
Kobrynsky, Marusia, *Svoboda Dance Festival Association*, 1358
Koch, Niels Elers, *International Union of Forest Research Organizations*, 1564
Koch, Katherine, *Canadian Children's Book Centre*, 356
Koch, Stephanie, *Canadian Society of Orthopaedic Technologists*, 485
Koch, Lloyd, *Pembroke Kiwanis Music Festival*, 1149
Kochan, Matthew, *Manitoba Medical Students' Association*, 940
Kochendorfer, Larry, *Evangelical Lutheran Church in Canada*, 698
Kocher, Lyn, *Health Employers Association of British Columbia*, 806
Kochhar, Vim, *Canadian Foundation for Physically Disabled Persons*, 394
Kochisarli, Jolaine, *Alberta School Councils' Association*, 45
Koe, Ed, *Society of Fire Protection Engineers*, 1593
Koehler, Marlaine, *Waterfront Regeneration Trust*, 1442
Koenig, Mark, *Parrot Association of Canada*, 1143
Koenigsfest, Ian, *Radio Television Digital News Association (Canada)*, 1203
Koerner, Michael M., *Royal Conservatory Orchestra*, 1242
Koester, Lynee, *American Academy of Neurology*, 1488
Koetting, Phyllis DeRosa, *McMaster University Faculty Association*, 956
Koff, John, *The Facial Pain Association*, 1525
Kofman, Michelle, *Two/Ten Charity Trust of Canada Inc.*, 1401
Kofsky, Debra, *Karate Manitoba*, 881
Kogi, Kazutaka, *International Commission on Occupational Health*, 1543
Koh, François, *Georgian Bay Symphony*, 771
Kohler, Barry, *Aerospace Industries Association of Canada*, 11
Kohler, Betsy, *North American Association of Central Cancer Registries, Inc.*, 1578

Kohli, Deepak, *Canadian Association of Professional Immigration Consultants*, 329
Kohlruss, Colleen, *Chicken Farmers of Saskatchewan*, 558
Koizumi, Junji, *International Union of Anthropological & Ethnological Sciences*, 1563
Kokesch, Audrey, *Alberta Dressage Association*, 33
Kokesh, Dianne, *Canadian Federation of Junior Leagues*, 387
Kokkonen, Ray, *Canadian Peacekeeping Veterans Association*, 452
Kokkonen, Ray, *Biathlon Nouveau-New Brunswick*, 207
Koks, Howard, *The Dream Factory*, 662
Koks, Howard, *Parkinson Society Manitoba*, 1141
Kolaitis, Gerry, *Canadian Transportation Research Forum*, 497
Kolarevic, Branko, *Canadian Architectural Certification Board*, 295
Kolasky, Norman, *Roncesvalles Macdonell Residents' Association*, 1236
Kolb, Jared, *Cycle Toronto*, 647
Kolbuc, Zoë, *Sustainable Development Technology Canada*, 1357
Koldyk, Diana, *Canadian Lutheran World Relief*, 428
Kolesar, Mark, *Calgary Seniors' Resource Society*, 274
Kolesnichenko, Ludmila, *Canadian Ukrainian Immigrant Aid Society*, 498
Kolga, Marcus, *Estonian Central Council in Canada*, 697
Kolisnyk, Alice, *Red Deer Food Bank Society*, 1209
Kolitsas, Spiro, *Saskatchewan College of Pharmacists*, 1261
Kolla, Michelle, *Council of Yukon First Nations*, 635
Kolodychuk, Philip, *Canadian Sheep Federation*, 470
Kolton, Anne, *American Chemistry Council*, 1491
Koltutsky, Carolyn, *McMan Youth, Family & Community Services Association*, 956
Kolwich, Tracy, *Ovarian Cancer Canada*, 1134
Kolwich, Tracy, *Ovarian Cancer Canada*, 1134
Komar, Cyndee, *Northwestern Ontario Prospectors Association*, 1039
Komiotis, Wendy, *Metropolitan Action Committee on Violence Against Women & Children*, 964
Komlen, Milé, *Canadian Association for the Prevention of Discrimination & Harassment in Higher Education*, 305
Komm, Janey, *British Columbia Association for Marriage & Family Therapy*, 231
Kompter, Gerhard, *Central Ontario Orchid Society*, 525
Komuro, Tetsuo, *Toronto Japanese Association of Commerce & Industry*, 1385
Komuro-Lee, Ikuko, *Canadian Association for Japanese Language Education*, 301
Kondaj, Ruki, *Albanian Canadian Community Association*, 21
Kondra, Peter, *Ukrainian Self-Reliance League of Canada*, 1403
Koneczny, Chet, *Lacrosse Nova Scotia*, 895
Koneva, Elena, *Choirs Ontario*, 566
Kong, Veronica, *Canadian Association of Medical Teams Abroad*, 321
König Sarkis, Marcelo, *Professional Engineers Ontario*, 1184
Konkle, Wynnie, *Rare Breeds Canada*, 1204
Konkle, Charlotte, *Ontario Tenpin Bowling Association*, 1110
Kono, Chieko, *The Japan Foundation, Toronto*, 868
Konoé, Tadateru, *International Federation of Red Cross & Red Crescent Societies*, 1549
Konotopsky, Ryan, *Canadian Energy Law Foundation*, 381

Konstant, Louis, *Medical Device Reprocessing Association of Ontario*, 958
Konstantynova, Iryna, *Ontario Equestrian Federation*, 1078
Konzelmann, Dolly, *Customer Service Professionals Network*, 646
Kook, Tony, *WTF Taekwondo Federation of British Columbia*, 1469
Koolen, Emily, *Human Resources Professionals Association*, 825
Koolhaas, Paul, *Canadian Association of Numismatic Dealers*, 323
Koonar, Saifa, *Alberta Children's Hospital Foundation*, 28
Koop, Lois, *Lakes District Festival Association*, 896
Koop, Alan, *Canadian Laboratory Suppliers Association*, 424
Koopmans, Andy, *Association of Municipal Managers, Clerks & Treasurers of Ontario*, 152
Kootstra, Tom, *Alberta Milk*, 40
Kopchinski, Robert J., *Art Libraries Society of North America*, 1506
Koperwas, Cheryl, *Technion Canada*, 1368
Kopinski, Jason, *American Academy of Neurology*, 1488
Kopp, Jerry, *Ancient, Free & Accepted Masons of Canada - Grand Lodge of Alberta*, 68
Kopp, Wesley D., *Canadian Association of Veterans in United Nations Peacekeeping*, 336
Koppe, Maxine, *North Central Local Government Association*, 1030
Kopperson, Brent, *Windfall Ecology Centre*, 1456
Korchinski, Kevin, *Organization of Saskatchewan Arts Councils*, 1126
Korek, Gregg, *Canadian Association of Fairs & Exhibitions*, 314
Korell, Alan, *Municipal Engineers Association*, 981
Koren, Oscar, *Canadian Meteorological & Oceanographic Society*, 436
Korkka, Janne, *Nordic Association for Canadian Studies*, 1578
Kornet, Lou, *Paperboard Packaging Council*, 1582
Koroluk, Karen, *Saskatchewan Reading Council*, 1273
Korolyova, Yuliana, *Ontario Gymnastic Federation*, 1083
Koropatnick, Grant, *Association of Professional Engineers & Geoscientists of Manitoba*, 158
Kortenhorst, Jules, *The Rocky Mountain Institute*, 1587
Kortright, Bob, *Toronto Field Naturalists*, 1384
Korvela, Kaj, *The Organization for Bipolar Affective Disorder*, 1125
Korytko, Zane, *YMCA Canada*, 1472
Kosak, Mark, *Alberta Colleges Athletic Conference*, 30
Kosar, Justin, *Saskatchewan College of Pharmacists*, 1261
Koshman, Sheri, *Canadian Society of Hospital Pharmacists*, 484
Koskamp-Bergeron, Tracy, *Alzheimer Society of Timmins/Porcupine District*, 65
Koslowsky, Ron, *Canadian Manufacturers & Exporters*, 430
Kosowan, Lynda, *Scarborough Women's Centre*, 1283
Koss, Johann, *Right to Play*, 1232
Kossel, Diane, *Dufferin Peel Educational Resource Workers' Association*, 664
Kostachuk, Carol, *Maple Ridge Lapidary Club*, 948
Kostakis, Lisa, *Albion Neighbourhood Services*, 52
Kostelka, Peter, *International Ombudsman Institute*, 1554
Koster, Andrew, *Brant Family & Children's Services*, 226

Koster, Andrew, *Child Welfare League of Canada*, 560
Kostoff, John B., *Ontario Catholic Supervisory Officers' Association*, 1070
Kostuck, Jessica, *Association of Fundraising Professionals*, 1512
Kotak, Brian, *Manitoba Model Forest*, 940
Kotar, Kimberley, *Canadian Transverse Myelitis Association*, 497
Kotecha, Jyoti, *Queen's University International Centre*, 1200
Kothary, Hitesh, *British Columbia's Children's Hospital Foundation*, 259
Kothringer, Ed, *Ontario Network of Employment Skills Training Projects*, 1093
Kotsopoulos, Chris, *Children's Wish Foundation of Canada*, 562
Kotwal, Ashok, *Canada India Village Aid Association*, 280
Kouchaji, Loulia, *Global Automakers of Canada*, 774
Koughan, Gemma, *Sport PEI Inc.*, 1345
Koughan, Gemma, *Coaches Association of PEI*, 577
Kouhestaninejad, Medhi, *Canadian Labour Congress*, 425
Kouidri, Selma, *DisAbled Women's Network of Canada*, 658
Koundakjian, Vicken, *Royal Heraldry Society of Canada*, 1242
Koutouki, Kostantia, *International Law Association - Canadian Branch*, 858
Kovach, Liz, *Manitoba Camping Association*, 933
Kovach, Krysia (Christine), *Polish Combatants Association - Winnipeg*, 1164
Kovacs, Sasha, *Canadian Association for Theatre Research*, 306
Kovacs, Paul, *Institute for Catastrophic Loss Reduction*, 843
Koval, Pat, *Canada-India Business Council*, 283
Koval, John J., *Statistical Society of Canada*, 1348
Kovari, Tibor, *Toronto Council of Hazzanim (Cantors)*, 1383
Kovesi, Thomas, *Ontario Thoracic Society*, 1110
Kovich, Tammy, *Ontario Public Interest Research Group*, 1099
Kowalchuk, Darlene, *Assiniboia & District Arts Council*, 88
Kowalchuk, Lisa, *Medicine Hat & District Chamber of Commerce*, 958
Kowalchuk, Walter, *Canadian Power & Sail Squadrons (Canadian Headquarters)*, 459
Kowalchuk, Candace, *Child & Family Services of Western Manitoba*, 558
Kowalczuk, Terry, *Counterpoint Community Orchestra*, 636
Kowalik, Carly, *Bereaved Families of Ontario*, 205
Kowalski, Susan, *Dauphin & District Allied Arts Council Inc.*, 651
Kowalski, Ryszard, *Canadian Federation of University Women*, 389
Kowaz, Andrea, *College of Psychologists of British Columbia*, 589
Kozak, Tracy, *Petroleum Accountants Society of Canada*, 1154
Kozeij, Tamara Anna, *Esperanto Association of Canada*, 695
Kozera, Tanya, *College of Physiotherapists of Manitoba*, 588
Kozera, Lorraine, *Canadian Square & Round Dance Society*, 490
Kozera, John, *Canadian Square & Round Dance Society*, 490
Kozey, Stephen W., *Federation of Aboriginal Foster Parents*, 722
Koziak, Leanne, *Vinok Worldance*, 1435
Kozloff, David, *Juvenile Diabetes Research Foundation Canada*, 878
Kozlovsky, Michel, *Orchestre symphonique des jeunes Philippe-Filion*, 1119

Executive Name Index

Kozma, Ed, *Canadian Automatic Merchandising Association*, 338
Kozole, Carolyn, *Shiatsu Therapy Association of Ontario*, 1296
Kraemer, Maureen, *Health Sciences Association of Saskatchewan*, 807
Kraft, Wendy, *Kitimat Chamber of Commerce*, 891
Kraglund, Kevin, *Edmonton & District Council of Churches*, 675
Krahn, Dale, *British Columbia Chicken Growers' Association*, 236
Krainyk, Kim, *Redvers Chamber of Commerce*, 1210
Krajnc, Anita, *Toronto Pig Save*, 1386
Kramble, Scott, *FunTeam Alberta*, 765
Kramer, Noami, *Canadian-Scandinavian Foundation*, 507
Kramer, Randy, *Prosthetics & Orthotics Association of British Columbia*, 1190
Kramers, Peter, *The Canadian Corps of Commissionaires*, 365
Kranjac, Paul, *Lunenfeld-Tanenbaum Research Institute*, 921
Krantz, Frederick, *Canadian Institute for Jewish Research*, 412
Kranz, Dory, *National Alopecia Areata Foundation*, 1572
Kraus, John, *Northumberland Orchestra Society*, 1036
Kraus, Werner, *Alliance internationale de tourisme*, 1487
Kraus, Steve, *Northwest Territories Medical Association*, 1038
Kraus, Lisa, *Likely & District Chamber of Commerce*, 912
Krause, Pam, *Calgary Sexual Health Centre*, 274
Krause, Axel, *British Columbia Bee Breeders' Association*, 233
Krause, Jeffrey M., *Society of Manufacturing Engineers - Canada Office*, 1330
Krauss, Angela, *Saskatchewan Trade & Export Partnership*, 1276
Krauss, Tracy, *InScribe Christian Writers' Fellowship*, 839
Krautwurst, Udo, *Canadian Anthropology Society*, 293
Kravchenko, Volodymyr, *Canadian Institute of Ukrainian Studies*, 420
Kravitz, Roberta A., *International Society for Magnetic Resonance in Medicine*, 1558
Krawchuk, Andrii, *International Council for Central & East European Studies (Canada)*, 1544
Krayden, Janet, *Grain Growers of Canada*, 779
Kreddig, Lynette, *Alberta Katahdin Sheep Association*, 38
Kredentser, Marcia, *The Professional Institute of the Public Service of Canada*, 1185
Kreider, Ryan, *Association for the Study of Nationalities*, 135
Kreiger, Nicole, *Nova Scotia Association of REALTORS*, 1041
Krejci, David, *Grain Elevator & Processing Society*, 1528
Krelic, Jean-Claude, *Society of Motion Picture & Television Engineers*, 1593
Krell, Marnie, *Canada's Sports Hall of Fame*, 283
Kremeniuk, Sharon, *Saskatchewan Lung Association*, 1269
Kremeniuk, Terry, *Canadian Bison Association*, 344
Krens, Carla, *Eagle Valley Arts Council*, 666
Kress, Vicky, *Alberta Irrigation Projects Association*, 38
Kresta, Stanya, *Edmonton Czech Language Society*, 676
Kretz, Rod, *Waterton Park Chamber of Commerce & Visitors Association*, 1442
Kreuger, Diane, *Independent Living Canada*, 833
Kreuzburg, Paula, *International Caterers Association*, 1542

Krewda, Lisa, *Consulting Engineers of Alberta*, 625
Krieger, Kit, *British Columbia Principals & Vice-Principals Association*, 249
Krieger, Mitchell, *Victoria Symphony Society*, 1434
Krieger, Nina, *Vancouver Holocaust Centre Society - A Museum for Education & Remembrance*, 1426
Krieger, Sarah, *Alzheimer Society of Belleville/Hastings/Quinte*, 62
Kriegler, Andrew J., *Investment Industry Regulatory Organization of Canada*, 863
Kriel, Louie, *College of Dental Surgeons of Saskatchewan*, 583
Krievins, Alex, *Easter Seals Canada*, 669
Kripki, Zenon, *Canadian Federation of Engineering Students*, 386
Krips, Darwin, *Alberta Band Association*, 25
Kristalovich, Del L., *North Island Wildlife Recovery Association*, 1031
Kristiansen, Kimberley, *Lake Country Chamber of Commerce*, 895
Kristiansen, Kristian, *Canadian Norwegian Business Association*, 1515
Kristie, Marg, *Nova Scotia Music Educators' Association*, 1047
Kristjanson, Liz, *Carl Orff Canada Music for Children*, 513
Kristjansson, Ron, *Provincial Exhibition of Manitoba*, 1190
Kroeger, Les, *Saskatchewan Bison Association*, 1259
Kroeker, Laurie, *Lupus Foundation of Ontario*, 921
Kroeker, Harry, *Southern Interior Local Government Association*, 1338
Kroeker-Hall, Jennifer, *Canadian Association of Road Safety Professionals*, 331
Kroening, Brittany, *Alberta Dressage Association*, 33
Kroetsch, Gina, *Alberta College of Occupational Therapists*, 29
Kroft, Ed, *The Royal Philatelic Society of Canada*, 1242
Kroll, Sherri, *Middlesex Community Living*, 965
Kroll, Robert, *The Speech & Stuttering Institute*, 1341
Kroll, Paul F., *African Violet Society of Canada*, 13
Kroll, Deborah, *American Society for Bone & Mineral Research*, 1498
Krolop, Sebastian, *Healthcare Information & Management Systems Society*, 1529
Kromand, Ben, *Danish Canadian Club of Calgary*, 650
Kron, David, *Cerebral Palsy Association of Manitoba Inc.*, 538
Krone, Alyssa, *Lakeland Agricultural Research Association*, 896
Kronick, Jonathan, *Canadian Paediatric Society*, 449
Kronick, Adam, *Ontario Camps Association*, 1070
Kronis, Jules, *Canadian Friends of Boys Town Jerusalem*, 395
Kroon, Alex, *Learning Enrichment Foundation*, 905
Kropp, Rhonda, *Centre for Immunization & Respiratory Infectious Diseases*, 532
Krotz, Paul, *Canadian Hockey League*, 406
Krowitz, Penny, *Act To End Violence Against Women*, 6
Krueger, Angela, *Big Brothers Big Sisters of Yukon*, 210
Kruger, Jonathon, *World Confederation for Physical Therapy*, 1604
Kruger, Lianne, *Historical Society of Alberta*, 816
Kruger, Catherine, *Perioperative Registered Nurses Association of British Columbia*, 1152
Krupp, Fred, *Environmental Defense*, 1523
Kruschner, Mark, *Product Care Association*, 1181

Kruse, Naomi, *Manitoba Association of Parent Councils*, 931
Kruse, Jean, *Canadian Thoroughbred Horse Society*, 495
Kruse, Inga, *The Royal Canadian Legion*, 1240
Kruse, Richard, *International Bible Correspondence School*, 854
Kruspel, Jamie, *American Society of Heating, Refrigerating & Air Conditioning Engineers*, 1500
Kruyt, Peter, *Canada China Business Council*, 278
Kruzel, Hugh, *CARP*, 515
Kryschuk, Brenda, *Viscount Cultural Council Inc.*, 1435
Krystofiak, Doug, *College of Alberta Professional Foresters*, 582
Krzic, Maja, *Canadian Society of Soil Science*, 488
Kshyk, Clifford, *Southern Interior Construction Association*, 1338
Kuan, Erin, *Multiple Sclerosis Society of Canada*, 980
Kub, John, *Manitoba Ozone Protection Industry Association*, 941
Kucher, Elaine, *Vegreville & District Chamber of Commerce*, 1430
Kucheran, Robert, *International Union of Painters & Allied Trades*, 1565
Kuchma, Robin, *Ontario Society for the Prevention of Cruelty to Animals*, 1105
Kudeba, Wendy, *Kidney Foundation of Canada*, 885
Kudloo, Rebecca, *Pauktuutit Inuit Women of Canada*, 1146
Kudlowsky, Margaret, *Red Lake & District Association for Community Living*, 1210
Kuefler, Misty, *Canadian Association for Williams Syndrome*, 307
Kuehn, Linda, *Serena Canada*, 1290
Kuehn, Wolf, *Canadian Institute of Gemmology*, 416
Kuellmer, Jim, *Bruce Peninsula Environment Group*, 261
Kuemper, Val, *Saskatchewan Music Educators Association*, 1270
Kuffner, Lynn, *Saskatchewan College of Physical Therapists*, 1261
Kugler, Danette, *Ridge Meadows Association of Community Living*, 1232
Kugler, Kyle, *Hockey North*, 818
Kugler, Henry, *Canadian Bar Insurance Association*, 342
Kuglitsch, Franz G., *International Union of Geodesy & Geophysics*, 1564
Kuhlenbaumer, Dawn, *Ontario Brain Injury Association*, 1069
Kuhr, Linda, *Back Country Horsemen of British Columbia*, 193
Kuhr, Peter, *Back Country Horsemen of British Columbia*, 193
Kuiper, Wendy, *YWCA of Banff Programs & Services*, 1482
Kuiper, Eva, *Information Systems Security Association*, 1532
Kuipers, Albert, *Grey Wooded Forage Association*, 790
Kulchitsky, Lynne, *Risk & Insurance Management Society Inc.*, 1234
Kulik, Irving, *Canadian Criminal Justice Association*, 373
Kulkarni, S.A., *International Commission on Irrigation & Drainage*, 1543
Kullman, Chris, *Epilepsy & Seizure Association of Manitoba*, 693
Kulmala, Peggy, *Canadian Public Relations Society Inc.*, 463
Kulmala, Rory, *British Columbia Construction Association*, 237
Kulmala, Rory, *Vancouver Island Construction Association*, 1426
Kumagai, Mayumi, *Orillia Youth Symphony Orchestra*, 1126
Kumar, Eshwar, *Canadian Association of Provincial Cancer Agencies*, 329

Kumar, Prem, *Friends of the Third World*, 763
Kumaranayake, Lilani, *Immigrant Services Association of Nova Scotia*, 830
Kummen, Kathleen, *Canadian Association for Young Children*, 307
Kumove, Shirley, *Toronto Jewish Film Society*, 1385
Kump, Gail, *Association of American Publishers*, 1510
Kunder, Will, *United Church of Canada*, 1409
Kunert, Debbie, *CFA Society Calgary*, 538
Kuntz, Anita, *Music for Young Children*, 984
Kuntz, Matthew, *Edmonton Association of the Deaf*, 675
Kunzelman, Richard, *Lighthouse Mission*, 912
Kuraite-Lasiene, Joana, *The Lithuanian Canadian Community*, 914
Kurbis, Rhonda, *Saskatchewan 5 Pin Bowlers' Association*, 1255
Kurian, Joseph, *Canadian Association of Physicians of Indian Heritage*, 327
Kurilecz, Peter, *ARMA International*, 1505
Kurkul, Doug, *American Foundry Society*, 1493
Kurowski, George, *Manitoba Ozone Protection Industry Association*, 941
Kurtz, Sheri, *Business Professional Association of Canada*, 267
Kurtz, Jim, *Foam Lake & District Chamber of Commerce*, 1
Kurys, J.G., *World Federation of Ukrainian Engineering Societies*, 1466
Kurz, Gwen, *Dryden District Chamber of Commerce*, 663
Kushner, Stephen, *Merit Contractors Association of Alberta*, 962
Kusunoki, Koichi, *International Association for Earthquake Engineering*, 1536
Kutikov, Olga, *Multiple Birth Families Association*, 979
Kutschker, Tracey, *Shuswap District Arts Council*, 1297
Kutulakos, Sarah, *Canada China Business Council*, 278
Kuwabara, Bruce, *Canadian Centre for Architecture*, 353
Kuylenstierna, Johan, *Stockholm Environment Institute*, 1597
Kuzik, Sarah, *Thunder Bay Minor Football Association*, 1378
Kuzmynskyi, Volodymyr, *International Foster Care Organisation*, 1549
Kuzyk, Monica, *Canadian Independent Adjusters' Association*, 410
Kuzyshyn, Oksana, *League of Ukrainian Canadian Women*, 903
Kvakic, Kristen, *AIDS Vancouver Island*, 17
Kvarnstrom, Michele, *Northwest Wildlife Preservation Society*, 1039
Kvern, Brent, *College of Physicians & Surgeons of Manitoba*, 588
Kwan, Cheuk, *Toronto Association for Democracy in China*, 1382
Kwan, Linda, *Alberta Taekwondo Association*, 49
Kwasnicki, Andrea, *Diabetes Canada*, 655
Kwesiga, Charles, *World Association of Industrial & Technological Research Organizations*, 1603
Kwok, Angela, *British Columbia Centre for Ability*, 235
Kwok, Glen, *Fédération mondiale des concours internationaux de musique*, 1526
Kwok, Anita, *The Supreme Master Ching Hai Meditation Association of Ontario*, 1357
Kwon, Nancy, *Canadian Federation of Independent Grocers*, 387
Kwon, Steve, *Korean Students' Association of Canada*, 894
Kyle, Scott, *Consulting Engineers of Nova Scotia*, 625
Kyle, Gordon, *Community Living Ontario*, 604
Kyle, Kenneth, *Miramichi Salmon Association*, 968

Kynoch, Brent, *Environmental Information Association*, 1523
Kyriakis, George, *Ability Online Support Network*, 2
Kyte, Christopher J., *Food Processors of Canada*, 750
Kyte, Jack, *Pictou County Chamber of Commerce*, 1159

L

L'Africain, Louise, *L'Association de la Neurofibromatose du Québec*, 101
L'Arrivee, Louis, *Canadian Katahdin Sheep Association Inc.*, 424
L'Arrivee, Jean, *Saskatchewan Katahdin Sheep Association Inc.*, 1268
L'Espérance, Gilles, *Centre de caractérisation microscopique des matériaux*, 528
L'Espérance, Claude, *Chambre de commerce et du tourisme du Grand Caraquet*, 548
L'Hebreux, Michel, *Société historique de Saint-Romuald*, 1320
L'Heureux, Pierre, *Association des collèges privés du Québec*, 109
L'Heureux, Rob, *Geological Association of Canada*, 770
L'Heureux, Paul, *The Speech & Stuttering Institute*, 1341
L'Heureux, Richard, *Association des anciens élèves du collège Sainte-Marie*, 105
L'Hirondelle, Kristy, *Lakeland District Soccer Association*, 896
L'Hoir, Peggy, *Alliance for Canadian New Music Projects*, 57
L'Italien, Lyne, *Conseil régional de la culture Saguenay-Lac-Saint-Jean*, 621
L'Italien, Isabelle, *Conseil québécois des arts médiatiques*, 620
L., Marco, *Alcooliques Anonymes du Québec*, 53
La Brèque, Marie-Paule, *Société d'histoire des Six Cantons*, 1312
La Brie, Léo, *Canadian Society for the Study of Names*, 478
La Chapelle, Jennifer, *Ontario Public Library Association*, 1099
La Couture, Mélanie, *Fondation Institut de Cardiologie de Montréal*, 746
La Couture, Jean, *Regroupement des assureurs de personnes à charte du Québec*, 1215
La France, Kerienne, *Trees Winnipeg*, 1397
La Haye, Michèle, *Confédération québécoise des coopératives d'habitation*, 611
La Madrid, Teodora S., *Our Lady of the Rosary of Manaoag Evangelization Group*, 1133
La Pierre King, Tamara, *Ontario Association of Architects*, 1061
La Point, Michele, *Kicking Horse Country Chamber of Commerce*, 884
La Roche, Stéphan, *Conseil des arts et des lettres du Québec*, 617
La Rochelle, Julie, *Chambre de commerce et d'industrie de la Vallée-du-Richelieu*, 545
La Rocque, Cloée, *Association des jeunes travailleurs et travailleuses de Montréal inc*, 117
La Rosa, Salvo, *Children's Tumor Foundation*, 1517
Laar, Win, *Niagara Falls Nature Club*, 1025
LaBarre, Guillaume, *Ordre des agronomes du Québec*, 1120
Labbé, Nancy, *Chambre de commerce et d'industrie Nouvelle-Beauce*, 547
Labbe, Roland, *Boxing Alberta*, 220
Labchuk, Camille, *Animal Justice*, 70
Labeaume, Régis, *Association internationale des maires francophones - Bureau à Québec*, 136
Labelle, Diane, *Canadian Guild of Crafts*, 399
Labelle, Patrick, *Fédération des médecins résidents du Québec inc. (ind.)*, 716

Labelle, Luc, *Chambre de la sécurité financière*, 550
Labelle, Francois, *Manitoba Pulse & Soybean Growers Inc.*, 943
Laberge, Nicole, *Fibrose kystique Québec*, 733
Laberge, Mark, *National Retriever Club of Canada*, 996
Laberge, Monique, *Association de paralysie cérébrale du Québec*, 103
Laberge, Normand, *Association médicale du Québec*, 137
Laberge, Monique, *Musée minéralogique et minier de Thetford Mines*, 982
Laberge, Gabriel, *La fédération des mouvements personne d'abord du Québec*, 716
Labersweiler, Deb, *Saskatchewan Construction Association*, 1262
LaBillios-Slocum, Carol, *New Brunswick Aboriginal Peoples Council*, 1004
Labindao, Caring, *Filipino Canadian Catholic Charismatic Prayer Communities*, 735
Labonne, Paul, *Atelier d'histoire Hochelaga-Maisonneuve*, 179
Labonté, Sarina, *Community Living Grimsby, Lincoln & West Lincoln*, 602
Labonté, René, *L'Association de spina-bifida et d'hydrocéphalie du Québec*, 104
Labonté, André, *Association des expositions agricoles du Québec*, 113
Labow, Rosalind, *Canadian Biomaterials Society*, 344
LaBranche, Paul, *Building Owners & Managers Association of British Columbia*, 478
Labrecque, Bernard, *Canadian Hydrographic Association*, 410
Labrecque, Jacques, *Conseil francophone de la chanson*, 618
Labrecque, Julie, *Regroupement des jeunes chambres de commerce du Québec*, 1215
Labrecque, Geneviève, *Regroupement pour la Trisomie 21*, 1216
Labrecque King, Lynn, *Alberta College of Social Workers*, 30
Labrie, Marco, *Carrefour de solidarité internationale inc.*, 515
Labrie, Marise, *Canadian Highland Cattle Society*, 405
Labrie, Geneviève, *Coalition des femmes de l'Alberta*, 578
LaBrie, Ashley, *AthletesCAN*, 180
Lacalamita, Paul, *The Catholic Principals' Council of Ontario*, 520
Lacasse, Richard, *Société de coopération pour le développement international*, 1314
Lacasse, Gary, *Canadian AIDS Society*, 290
Lacasse, Eve-Marie, *Fédération des femmes du Québec*, 715
Lacasse, Louise, *Groupe Brosse Art*, 791
Laccasse, Rémi, *Fédération des astronomes amateurs du Québec*, 712
Lacelle, Paul, *Lanark County Beekeepers' Association*, 897
Lacenaire, Della Collette, *Fédération des femmes acadiennes et francophones du Nouveau-Brunswick*, 715
Lacerte, Paul, *British Columbia Association of Aboriginal Friendship Centres*, 231
Lacerte, Yves, *Canadian Association of Veterans in United Nations Peacekeeping*, 336
Lacey, Graham, *Boating Ontario*, 216
Lacey, Peter, *Transport Action Canada*, 1395
Lacey, Robert, *International Allied Printing Trades Association*, 1535
Lacey, Kevin, *Canadian Taxpayers Federation*, 493
Lacey, Allan, *Alberta Magazine Publishers Association*, 39
Lachaine, Yves, *Club Kiwanis Chibougamau*, 575
Lachance, Patrice, *Academy of Canadian Cinema & Television*, 4
LaChance, Laura, *Canadian Down Syndrome Society*, 378

Lachance, Lisa, *Children and Youth in Challenging Contexts Network*, 560
Lachance, Nadine, *Chambre de commerce et d'industrie Vaudreuil-Soulanges*, 548
Lachance, Georgette, *Association des neurotraumatisés de l'Outaouais*, 121
Lachance, Kelly, *Association of Fundraising Professionals*, 1512
Lachapelle, Diane, *Synchro-Québec*, 1361
Lachapelle, Jocelyne, *Association québécoise de lutte contre la pollution atmosphérique*, 170
Lachapelle, Guy, *International Political Science Association*, 859
Lachetti, Pierre, *College of Applied Biology British Columbia*, 582
Lackie, Donna, *Government Services Union*, 778
Lacombe, Sid, *Canadian Peace Alliance*, 452
Lacombe, Richard, *Association canadienne d'éducation de langue française*, 90
Lacombe, Jacques, *Orchestre symphonique de Trois-Rivières*, 1118
Lacombe, Darcy, *Madawaska Valley Association for Community Living*, 925
Lacombe, Gabriel, *Société Saint-Jean-Baptiste du Centre du Québec*, 1325
Lacombe, Claudette, *Farming Smarter*, 706
Lacoste, Dominique, *Association québécoise des transports*, 175
Lacourse, Michel, *Association des personnes handicapées physiques et sensorielles du secteur Joliette*, 123
Lacourse, Paul, *Halton Regional Police Association*, 800
Lacouture, Yves, *Syndicat des professeurs de l'Université Laval*, 1364
Lacroix, Yvan, *Association québécoise des industries de nutrition animale et céréalière*, 173
Lacroix, Yves, *Animal Nutrition Association of Canada*, 71
Lacroix, Alexandre, *Canadian Carpet Institute*, 350
Lacroix, Nadyne, *International Council for Canadian Studies*, 855
Lacroix, Francine, *Société Huntington du Québec*, 1321
Lacroix, Jean-Michel, *Association française d'études canadiennes*, 1509
Lacroix, Norbert, *Club des ornithologues de Québec inc.*, 575
Lacroix, Jean, *Association québécoise pour la maîtrise de l'énergie*, 176
Lacroix, Laurier, *Académie des lettres du Québec*, 3
Lacroix, Lisanne, *Association of Professional Executives of the Public Service of Canada*, 159
Lacroix, Véronique, *Ensemble contemporain de Montréal*, 690
Lacroix, Yann, *Centre de la Communauté sourde du Montréal métropolitain*, 529
Lacroix, Karine, *Chambre de commerce de l'Est de Portneuf*, 541
Lacroix, Linda, *Northwestern Ontario Insurance Professionals*, 1039
Lacy, William, *Quesnel & District Chamber of Commerce*, 1200
Laden, Francine, *International Society for Environmental Epidemiology*, 1557
Laden, Francine, *International Society for Environmental Epidemiology*, 1557
Ladines, Yoly, *Markham Federation of Filipino Canadians*, 952
Ladouceur, Nathalie, *La fédération des mouvements personne d'abord du Québec*, 716
Ladurantaye, Karyn, *The Professional Institute of the Public Service of Canada*, 1185
Lafantaisie, Josianne, *Réseau environnement*, 1223
Laflamme, Yvon, *Chambre de commerce Bellechasse-Etchemins*, 540

Laflamme, Maryse, *Association des bibliothèques de l'Ontario-Franco*, 107
Laflamme, Marc, *Association des directeurs municipaux du Québec*, 111
Laflamme, Tristan, *Canadian Marine Pilots' Association*, 430
Laflamme, Sylvain, *Bureau régional d'action sida (Outaouais)*, 265
Laflèche, Marc, *Union des cultivateurs franco-ontariens*, 1406
Lafleur, Maxime, *Association du Québec pour enfants avec problèmes auditifs*, 131
Lafleur, Jean-François, *Assemblée parlementaire de la Francophonie (Section canadienne)*, 88
Lafon Simard, Pierre Antoine, *Théâtre du Trillium*, 1374
Lafond, Chantal, *Chambre de commerce et d'industrie du Coeur-du-Québec*, 547
Lafond, Kim, *Chambre de commerce et d'industrie de Maniwaki & Vallée de la Gatineau*, 546
Lafond, André, *Société Philatelique de Québec*, 1322
Lafond, Jean-Daniel, *Michaëlle Jean Foundation*, 964
Lafontaine, Yvan, *Fédération québécoise de camping et de caravaning inc.*, 727
Lafontaine, Darlene, *AFOA Canada*, 12
Lafontaine, Carl, *Association provinciale des constructeurs d'habitations du Québec inc.*, 168
Lafontaine, Pierre, *National Winter Sports Association*, 997
Laforest, Suzanne, *Association sportive des sourds du Québec inc.*, 178
Laforest, Stéphane, *Orchestre symphonique de Sherbrooke*, 1118
Laforest, Pierre, *Club violettes Longueuil*, 576
Laforest, Jacques, *Le centre jeunesse de Québec*, 536
Laforest, Guylaine, *Association québécoise pour le loisir des personnes handicapées*, 177
Lafortune, Jean-Marie, *Fédération québécoise des professeures et professeurs d'université*, 729
Laframboise, Kelly, *Commonwealth Games Canada*, 594
Laframboise, France, *Ordre des infirmières et infirmiers du Québec*, 1122
Laframboise, Jacques, *Canadian Air Cushion Technology Society*, 290
Lafrance, Roger, *Association coopérative d'économie familiale - Montérégie-est*, 97
Lafrance, Sylvain, *Chambre de commerce du Transcontinental*, 544
LaFrance, David B., *American Water Works Association*, 1504
Lafrance, Luc, *Fédération des transporteurs par autobus*, 719
Lafrance, Jessica, *Canadian Association for Conservation of Cultural Property*, 299
Lafrance, Robert, *Réseau des SADC et CAE*, 1221
Lafrance, Rick, *Progressive Conservative Party of New Brunswick*, 1187
Lafrenière, Lorraine, *Coaching Association of Canada*, 577
Lafrenière, Normand, *Canadian Association of Mutual Insurance Companies*, 322
LaFreniere, Lara, *Women Expanding Business Network of Lanark County*, 1460
Lafreniere, Rheal, *Canadian Association of Professional Apiculturists*, 328
Lagacé, Eve, *Association des bibliothèques publiques du Québec*, 107
Lagacé, Michel, *Société historique de Saint-Boniface*, 1320
Lagace, Paul, *Kamloops Immigrant Services*, 880
Lagace, Marjolaine, *DanceSport Québec*, 650
LaGrange, Shaun, *Pentathlon Canada*, 1150
LaGrange, Adrianna, *Alberta Catholic School Trustees Association*, 27

Executive Name Index

LaGrange, Shaun, *Ontario Modern Pentathalon Association*, 1091
Lagrois, Yvette, *Truck Training Schools Association of Ontario Inc.*, 1399
Lagueux, Richard, *Chambre de commerce de Tring-Jonction*, 543
Lah, Thomas, *Technology Services Industry Association*, 1597
LaHaye, Roland, *Canadian Criminal Justice Association*, 373
Lahey, Beth, *Canadian Institute of Management*, 417
Lahey, Beth, *Canadian Institute of Management*, 417
Lahey, Rhona, *Canadian Association of Optometrists*, 324
Lahey, Dawn, *Canadian Union of Public Employees*, 498
Lahiton, Damien, *New Brunswick Curling Association*, 1007
Lahuis, Marjan, *Canadian Environment Industry Association*, 381
Lai, Vivien, *Alberta Association on Gerontology*, 25
Lai, Tak-Ng, *Canadian Sinfonietta Youth Orchestra*, 471
Lai, Holman, *North American Association of Asian Professionals Vancouver*, 1029
Laidlaw, Margaret, *Cranbrook Society for Community Living*, 638
Laidlaw, John, *Ontario Soil & Crop Improvement Association*, 1108
Laine, Joan Margaret, *Alberta Association of Midwives*, 24
Laing, David, *Baseball BC*, 198
Laing, Tony, *Penticton & District Society for Community Living*, 1151
Laing, Robert, *British Columbia Real Estate Association*, 250
Laing, Nancy, *The Royal Scottish Country Dance Society*, 1587
Laird, Jacquie, *Prince Edward Island Women's Institute*, 1178
Laird, Hugh, *Interior Systems Contractors Association of Ontario*, 852
Laird, Scott, *Canadian Association of Veterans in United Nations Peacekeeping*, 336
Lait, Ken, *The Naval Officers' Association of Canada*, 1001
Lajambe, Suzanne, *The John Howard Society of Ontario*, 875
Lajeunesse, Patrick, *Canadian Quaternary Association*, 464
Lajeunesse, Marie, *Master Brewers Association of The Americas*, 1570
Lajeunesse, Michel, *Centre d'aide personnes traumatisées crâniennes et handicapées physiques Laurentides*, 527
Lajeunesse Zingg, Jeannette, *Opéra Atelier*, 1114
Lajoie, Sylvian, *Fibrose kystique Québec*, 733
Lajoie, François, *Programme d'aide aux membres du barreau*, 1187
Lajoie, Marie-Hélène, *Canadian Association of Municipal Administrators*, 321
Lajoie, Alain, *Via Prévention*, 1432
Lajoie, Claire, *Syndicat des agricultrices de la Côte-du-Sud*, 1362
Lajoie, Gesele, *Bully B'Ware*, 264
Lajoie, Cheryl, *Metro (Toronto) Association of Family Resource Programs*, 963
Lajoie, Mathieu, *Association des personnes accidentées cérébro-vasculaires, aphasiques et traumatisées crânio-cérébrales du Bas-Saint-Laurent*, 122
Lake, Terry, *Community Living Cambridge*, 601
Lake, Michael, *The Royal Commonwealth Society*, 1587
Lake, David, *American Political Science Association*, 1497
Lake, Bill, *Limestone Beekeepers Guild*, 912
Laker, Elisha, *York Region Family Services (Markham)*, 1473
Lakevold, Courtney, *Archaeological Society of Alberta*, 76

Lakha-Evin, Mezaun, *Cerebral Palsy Association in Alberta*, 537
Lakhani, Amin, *Association of International Physicians & Surgeons of Ontario*, 149
Lalancette, Clément, *Fédération des producteurs de pommes de terre du Québec*, 717
Lalancette, Régine, *Fédération des coopératives d'habitation du Royaume Saguenay Lac-Saint-Jean*, 714
Lalancette, Réjeanne, *Mouvement du Renouveau charismatique*, 977
Lalancette, Guy, *Théâtre des épinettes*, 1374
Lalande, Lise, *Fédération québécoise des sociétés Alzheimer*, 730
Lalande, HUbert, *Centre franco-ontarien de ressources pédagogiques*, 534
Laliberté, Manon, *Conseil de la culture des régions de Québec et de Chaudière-Appalaches*, 616
Laliberté, André, *Canadian Asian Studies Association*, 296
Laliberte, Rodney, *College of Alberta Denturists*, 582
Laliberté, Marc, *Aboriginal Sport & Wellness Council of Ontario*, 2
Laliberté, Éric, *Réseau des SADC et CAE*, 1221
Laliberté, Jean-François, *Réseau des SADC et CAE*, 1221
Laliberté, Mélissa, *Société de développement économique du Saint-Laurent*, 1315
Lalitananda, Swami, *Yasodhara Ashram Society*, 1470
Lallement, Fabienne, *Fédération internationale des professeurs de français*, 1525
Lalli, Brian, *British Columbia Ferry & Marine Workers' Union (CLC)*, 241
Lalonde, David, *American Foundry Society*, 1493
Lalonde, Pascal, *Canadian Anesthesiologists' Society*, 293
Lalonde, Heather, *Economic Developers Council of Ontario Inc.*, 673
Lalonde, Marie, *Ontario Museum Association*, 1092
Lalonde, Stephanie, *United Way of Stormont, Dundas & Glengarry*, 1417
Lalonde, Luc, *Fédération des policiers et policières municipaux du Québec (ind.)*, 717
Lalonde, Étienne, *Fondation des étoiles*, 745
Lalonde, Bob, *Entomological Society of British Columbia*, 690
Lalonde, Pierre, *Canadian Horse Breeders' Association*, 408
Lalsingh, Sushila, *National United Professional Association of Trained Homeopaths*, 997
Laluk, Sheena, *Yukon Broomball Association*, 1477
Lalumière, Yves, *Tourisme Montréal/Office des congrès et du tourisme du Grand Montréal*, 1393
Lalumière, Lucie, *Interactive Ontario*, 851
Lam, Melanie, *Simon Fraser University Faculty Association*, 1300
Lam, Chris, *British Columbia Lung Association*, 245
Lam, Amy, *Chinese Canadian National Council*, 564
Lam, Tannie, *Associated Manitoba Arts Festivals, Inc.*, 89
Lam, Fred, *Hong Kong Trade Development Council*, 1530
Lam, Allan, *Institute for the Study & Treatment of Pain*, 844
Lam, Stephen, *International Federation of Human Genetics Societies*, 1548
Lam, Amy, *Chartered Professional Accountants of British Columbia*, 553
Lamacchia, Aaron, *Peace Region Internet Society*, 1147
Lamanque, Johanne, *Insurance Bureau of Canada*, 849

Lamanque, Johanne, *Groupement des assureurs automobiles*, 792
Lamarche, Maxime, *Fédération du baseball amateur du Québec*, 720
Lamarche, Jean-François, *Fédération québécoise des sociétés Alzheimer*, 729
Lamarche, Jean-Luc, *Canadian Ski Patrol*, 471
Lamarche, Nancy, *The Professional Institute of the Public Service of Canada*, 1185
Lamarche, Francine, *Association québécoise de soins palliatifs*, 171
Lamarche, Jacques, *Association des parents ayants droit de Yellowknife*, 121
Lamarche, Hugo, *Association des pompiers de Laval*, 124
Lamarche, Marcèle, *Association d'entraide Le Chaînon inc.*, 99
Lamarre, Claude, *Association des propriétaires de Saint-Bruno*, 126
Lamarre, Philippe, *Société des designers graphiques du Québec*, 1317
Lamarre, Chantal, *Association de parents d'enfant trisomique-21 de Lanaudière*, 103
Lamarre, Chantal, *Comité d'action des citoyennes et citoyens de Verdun*, 591
Lamarre-Renaud, Thierry, *Association des Perfusionnistes du Québec Inc.*, 122
Lamas, Luís, *International Society for Rock Mechanics*, 1559
Lamb, Marg, *Lundy's Lane Historical Society*, 920
Lamb, Paddy, *Canadian Artists Representation*, 295
Lamb, Wesley, *Ontario Industrial Roofing Contractors' Association*, 1087
Lamb, Mary, *Pelham Historical Society*, 1149
Lamb, Patrick, *Copyright Visual Arts*, 628
Lambert, Phyllis, *Canadian Centre for Architecture*, 353
Lambert, Nadine, *Fédération de la santé et des services sociaux*, 710
Lambert, Valerie, *Big Brothers Big Sisters of British Columbia*, 209
Lambert, Claudia, *Association des Grands Frères et Grandes Soeurs du Québec*, 115
Lambert, Sylvain, *Québec Simmental Association*, 1199
Lambert, Manon, *Ordre des pharmaciens du Québec*, 1123
Lambert, Rick, *Manitoba Tobacco Reduction Alliance*, 946
Lambert, Michel, *Réseau d'action et de communication pour le développement international*, 1218
Lambert, Ruth, *PFLAG Canada Inc.*, 1156
Lambert, Adrian, *Canadian Trail & Mountain Running Association*, 496
Lambert, Tim, *Egg Farmers of Canada*, 681
Lambertini, Marco, *WWF International*, 1608
Lambie, Rosemary, *United Church of Canada*, 1409
Lambie, Carol, *Waypoint Centre for Mental Health Care*, 1443
Lamboo, Susan, *Coaching Manitoba*, 577
Lambourne, Jan, *Teulon Chamber of Commerce*, 1373
Lamer, Antonio, *Canadian Battlefields Foundation*, 342
Lamerson, Cheryl, *South Shore Genealogical Society*, 1336
Lamese, Elana, *Probation Officers Association of Ontario*, 1181
Lamm, Chris, *Concerned Educators Allied for a Safe Environment*, 1519
Lammens, Mark, *Saskatchewan Sailing Clubs Association*, 1274
Lammey, John, *Risk & Insurance Management Society Inc.*, 1234
Lammi, Brenda, *Canadian College of Health Leaders*, 359
Lamont, Lori, *Academy of Canadian Executive Nurses*, 4
Lamont, Jocelyn, *Candlelighters Childhood Cancer Support Programs, Inc.*, 508
Lamont, Dougald, *Manitoba Liberal Party*, 939

Lamontagne, Mario, *Chambre de commerce et d'industrie de Shawinigan*, 546
LaMontagne, Jason, *Canadian Public Relations Society Inc.*, 463
Lamontagne, Lynne, *Service familial de Sudbury*, 1291
Lamontagne, Paule, *Les Amis du Jardin botanique de Montréal*, 67
Lamontagne, Jacques, *Canadian Office & Professional Employees Union*, 444
Lamontagne, Blake, *Spinal Cord Injury Saskatchewan*, 1344
Lamontagne, Isabelle, *Regroupement de Bouches à Oreilles*, 1214
Lamontagne, Michel, *Association des résidents du Lac Écho*, 127
Lamonte, Jean-Pierre, *Société historique de Bellechasse*, 1319
Lamothe, Denis, *Chambre de commerce Mont-Saint-Bruno*, 549
Lamothe, Danielle, *Canadian Society of Association Executives*, 480
Lamothe, Annie, *Association des Grands Frères et Grandes Soeurs du Québec*, 115
Lamothe, Juanita, *Forever Young Seniors Society*, 752
Lamothe, Nancy, *L'Arche Québec*, 77
Lamour, Anthony, *Ski Québec alpin*, 1302
Lamoureux, Marie, *Jeunesses Musicales du Canada*, 871
Lamoureux, Marc, *Saint Mary's University Faculty Union*, 1247
Lamoureux, Francine, *Fédération du personnel de l'enseignement privé*, 720
Lamoureux, Rachelle, *Ontario Society for the Prevention of Cruelty to Animals*, 1106
Lamoureux, François, *Association des médecins spécialistes en médecine nucléaire du Québec*, 120
Lamoureux, Francois, *Canadian Association of Nuclear Medicine*, 323
Lamoureux, Linda, *Teulon Chamber of Commerce*, 1373
Lamourie, Tracy, *Canadian Coalition Against the Death Penalty*, 357
Lampron, Alain, *Fédération de l'industrie manufacturière (FIM-CSN)*, 709
Lampson, Sarah, *Canadian Association of Research Administrators*, 331
Lamswood, Harrison, *Newfoundland & Labrador Table Tennis Association*, 1022
Lamy, Jean-Pierre, *Association québécoise de la gestion parasitaire*, 170
Lanari, Robert, *Recherches amérindiennes au Québec*, 1207
Lancaster, Joyce, *Weed Science Society of America*, 1602
Lancaster, Phil, *Native Women's Transition Centre Inc.*, 998
Lancastle, Keith, *Appraisal Institute of Canada*, 74
Lance, Peter M., *Cordage Institute*, 1520
Lanctin, Sam, *New Brunswick Pharmaceutical Society*, 1011
Lanctot, Jeff, *Ontario Brain Injury Association*, 1069
Lanctôt, Sophie, *Société Logique*, 1321
Landals, Duane, *Alberta Veterinary Medical Association*, 50
Landau, Stacy, *SPRINT Senior Care*, 1346
Landers, Stephanie, *Ontario Waterpower Association*, 1113
Landeryou, Tim, *Squash Alberta*, 1347
Landeryou, Tim, *Saskatchewan Racquetball Association*, 1273
Landin, Stacey, *Moose Jaw & District Labour Council*, 974
Landing, Sydney, *BC School Sports*, 202
Landon, Todd, *Port Hardy & District Chamber of Commerce*, 1166
Landra, Jeannine, *Vides Canada*, 1434
Landreville, Marie-Eve, *Association des jeunes Barreaux du Québec*, 117
Landriault, Erik, *Access Alliance Multicultural Health & Community Services*, 4

Executive Name Index

Landriault, Sylvie, *Carrefour jeunesse emploi du Pontiac*, 515
Landrigan, David, *Canadian Cancer Society*, 349
Landrigan, Jim, *Association of Professional Engineers of Prince Edward Island*, 159
Landry, Jacques, *Cycling Canada Cyclisme*, 647
Landry, Germain, *Athletics New Brunswick*, 181
Landry, Andrien, *Judo Canada*, 876
Landry, John, *Construction Association of New Brunswick*, 623
Landry, Pierre-Éric, *Canadian Association of Oral & Maxillofacial Surgeons*, 324
Landry, Serge, *Canadian Labour Congress*, 424
Landry, Daniel, *Syndicat de la fonction publique du Québec inc. (ind.)*, 1361
Landry, Jacques, *Association des artistes peintres affiliés de la Rive-Sud*, 106
Landry, Jacques, *Fédération des professionnelles et professionnels de l'éducation du Québec*, 718
Landry, Gary, *Federation of Foster Families of Nova Scotia*, 724
Landry, Chantal, *Habitat for Humanity Canada*, 796
Landry, Jean-Yves, *Société d'histoire de Sainte-Foy*, 1311
Landry, Mike, *Ontario Lawn Bowls Association*, 1088
Landry, Alain, *North Shore Forest Products Marketing Board*, 1032
Landry, Marcel, *Mouvement national des québécoises et québécois*, 977
Landry, Serge, *Laurier Teachers Union*, 900
Landry, Natalie, *New Brunswick Crafts Council*, 1007
Landry, Roxane, *Status of Women Council of the Northwest Territories*, 1349
Landry, Robert, *Katimavik*, 882
Landry, Clemency, *Blonde d'Aquitaine du Québec*, 215
Landry, Maureen, *Blonde d'Aquitaine du Québec*, 215
Landry, Haidee, *Canadian Quarter Horse Association*, 464
Landry, Paul, *Canadian Deaf Golf Association*, 376
Landry, Eric, *Association des professionnels à l'outillage municipal*, 125
Landry, John, *Bowhunters Association of Nova Scotia*, 219
Landry-Bigelow, Jackie, *Orchestre symphonique des jeunes du West Island*, 1118
Landstrom, William, *Métis Nation of Alberta*, 963
Lane, Gene, *Annapolis Region Community Arts Council*, 71
Lane, Chandra, *Bow Island / Burdett District Chamber of Commerce*, 219
Lane, Jennifer, *Entertainment Merchants Association - International Head Office*, 1523
Lane, Jack, *Alberta Golf Association*, 37
Lane, Carolyn, *Real Property Association of Canada*, 1206
Lane, Jill, *Alberta Association of Landscape Architects*, 23
Lane, Nadine, *New Brunswick Competitive Festival of Music Inc.*, 1007
Lane, Neil G., *Pipe Line Contractors Association of Canada*, 1160
Lane, Oliver, *Society Promoting Environmental Conservation*, 1331
Lane, Chris, *Canadian Western Agribition Association*, 503
Lane, Debbie, *SaskCentral*, 1280
Lane, Jill, *Canadian Aerial Applicators Association*, 288
Lane, Darlene, *American Concrete Institute*, 1492
Lang, Rob, *National Automotive Trades Association of Canada*, 991

Lang, Lynette, *Saskatchewan Genealogical Society*, 1266
Lang, Duval, *Alliance of Canadian Cinema, Television & Radio Artists*, 58
Lang, Bill, *Esquimalt Chamber of Commerce*, 696
Lang, Susan, *Association of School Business Officials of Alberta*, 162
Lang, Denise, *Lymphovenous Association of Ontario*, 923
Lang, Mary Ann, *Central Ontario Orchid Society*, 525
Lang, Susan, *Orillia & District Chamber of Commerce*, 1126
Langbroek, Casey, *Bibles for Missions Foundation*, 208
Langdon, Lois, *Ontario Home Builders' Association*, 1085
Langdon, Nikki, *The Neil Squire Foundation*, 1003
Langdon, Susan, *Toronto Fashion Incubator*, 1384
Lange, Elke, *Arts Council of the Central Okanagan*, 85
Lange, Joan, *National Farmers Union*, 993
Lange, Carola, *German-Canadian Congress (Manitoba) Inc.*, 772
Lange, Barbara, *Society of Motion Picture & Television Engineers*, 1593
Lange, Lisa, *People for the Ethical Treatment of Animals*, 1583
Lange, Clifford, *Saskatchewan Underwater Council*, 1277
Lange, Joan, *National Farmers Foundation*, 993
Langelier, Rino, *Association québécoise de racquetball*, 171
Langen, Geof, *Community Legal Education Association (Manitoba) Inc.*, 600
Langendyk, Tammy, *London Multiple Births Association*, 918
Langevin, Louis, *Randonneurs du Saguenay*, 1204
Langevin, Louise, *Association québécoise pour le loisir des personnes handicapées*, 177
Langevin, Vincent, *La fédération des mouvements personne d'abord du Québec*, 716
Langford, Rachel, *Association of Early Childhood Educators Ontario*, 147
Langford, Don, *Métis Child & Family Services Society (Edmonton)*, 963
Langille, Chrystine, *Ajax-Pickering Board of Trade*, 20
Langille, Chrystine, *Ontario Association of Naturopathic Doctors*, 1065
Langille, Leola, *Canadian Home & School Federation*, 406
Langille, Leola, *New Brunswick Federation of Home & School Associations, Inc.*, 1008
Langille, Anne, *WIL Employment Connections*, 1453
Langille, Marlene, *Clydesdale Horse Association of Canada*, 576
Langlais, Jean-François, *Development & Peace*, 655
Langlais, Gilles, *Chambre immobilière de l'Abitibi-Témiscamingue Inc.*, 550
Langley, Charles H., *International Genetics Federation*, 1550
Langley, Alan M., *Association of Certified Forensic Investigators of Canada*, 145
Langlois, Steve, *Association paritaire pour la santé et la sécurité du travail - Secteur Affaires municipales*, 165
Langlois, Alex, *Canadian Marketing Association*, 431
Langlois, Charles, *Conseil des industriels laitiers du Québec inc.*, 617
Langlois, Norm, *Windsor-Essex County Real Estate Board*, 1457
Langlois, Alain, *Le Réseau d'enseignement francophone à distance du Canada*, 1219

Langlois, Pierre, *Chambre de commerce de la MRC de la Matapédia*, 542
Langlois, Ginette, *Fédération des professionnèles*, 717
Langlois, Serge, *Association des chirurgiens dentistes du Québec*, 109
Langlois, Étienne, *Association des compagnies de théâtre*, 109
Langlois, Claudia, *Canadian Association of Montessori Teachers*, 321
Langlois Saulnier, Linda, *Fondation Marie-Ève Saulnier*, 747
Langman, Erin, *Saskatchewan Health Libraries Association*, 1267
Langmann, Jeanette, *Art Dealers Association of Canada Inc.*, 84
Langstaff, Shelley, *Vocational Rehabilitation Association of Canada*, 1436
Langston, Linda, *Ontario Trial Lawyers Association*, 1111
Languedoc, Geoff, *Canadian Aeronautics & Space Institute*, 289
Lanigan, Betty, *Amputee Society of Ottawa & District*, 68
Lanigan, Troy, *Canadian Taxpayers Federation*, 492
Lanoue, Madeleine, *Congrégation des Soeurs de Sainte-Anne*, 612
Lanoue, Josée, *TECHNOCompétences*, 1369
Lansink, Laura, *Food Banks British Columbia*, 749
Lantaigne, Julie, *Réseau franco-santé du Sud de l'Ontario*, 1224
Lanteigne, Jean, *Canadian Council of Professional Fish Harvesters*, 369
Lanteigne, Kat, *BloodWatch*, 215
Lanthier, Clément, *Calgary Zoological Society*, 275
Lanthier, Sylviane, *Fédération des communautés francophones et acadienne du Canada*, 713
Lanthier, Nancy, *BC Alliance for Arts & Culture*, 201
Lantuit, Hugues, *International Permafrost Association*, 1555
Lantz, Josh, *Association of Great Lakes Outdoor Writers*, 1512
Lantz, Dan, *Scout Environmental*, 1286
Lanz, Marlene, *Métis Nation of Alberta*, 963
Lanz, Dustyn, *Responsible Investment Association*, 1227
Lao, Marietta, *Institute of Asian Research*, 844
Lapalme, Claude, *Red Deer Symphony Orchestra*, 1210
Lapchinski, Ernest, *The Friends of Bon Echo Park*, 760
Lapensée, Roch, *House of Commons Security Services Employees Association*, 824
Lapensée, Normande, *Club d'ornithologie de Mirabel*, 574
Lapensee, Michel, *Canadian Disaster Restoration Group*, 378
Laperle, Dominique, *Société canadienne d'histoire de l'Église Catholique - Section française*, 1307
Lapidus, Sidney, *American Antiquarian Society*, 1488
Lapierre, Gilles, *Association d'églises baptistes évangéliques au québec*, 99
Lapierre, François, *Réseau FADOQ*, 1224
Lapierre, Mylène, *Chartered Professional Accountants of New Brunswick*, 553
LaPierre, Mike, *Canadian Association of Smallmouth Anglers*, 333
Laplante, Louise, *Community Living Espanola*, 601
Laplante, Daniel, *Centraide Richelieu-Yamaska*, 523
Laplante, Lucie, *Avocats Hors Québec*, 191
Laplante, Pierre, *Tourisme Bas-Saint-Laurent*, 1392
Laplante, Mario, *Réseau environnement*, 1223
Laplante, Pascal, *St. Lawrence Valley Natural History Society*, 1250
Lapointe, Pierre, *FPInnovations*, 757

LaPointe, Marc, *Cycling Association of the Yukon*, 647
Lapointe, Sylvie J., *International Social Service Canada*, 860
LaPointe, Cathy, *British Columbia Wall & Ceiling Association*, 257
Lapointe, Katherine, *Canadian University Press*, 499
Lapointe, Ginette, *Réseau FADOQ*, 1224
Lapointe, Steven, *Association des urologues du Québec*, 130
Lapointe, Jean-Pierre, *Ileostomy & Colostomy Association of Montréal*, 829
Lapointe, Jean-Louis, *Crane Rental Association of Canada*, 639
Lapointe, Francine, *Groupe export agroalimentaire Québec - Canada*, 792
Lapointe, Michel, *Association des directeurs généraux des services de santé et des services sociaux du Québec*, 111
Lapointe, Daniel, *Association québécoise des allergies alimentaires*, 171
Lapointe, André, *FloraQuebeca*, 741
Lapointe, Debbie, *Manitoba Pest Management Association*, 942
Lapointe-Manseau, Pascale, *Chambre de commerce du Grand Joliette*, 544
Laporte, Nathalie, *Canadian Association of University Business Officers*, 334
Laporte, Jean-François, *Chambre de commerce et d'industrie Berthier-D'Autray*, 545
Laporte, André, *Association des avocats et avocates représentant les bénéficiaires des régimes d'indemnisation publics*, 107
Laporte, François, *Teamsters Canada (CLC)*, 1368
Laporte, Pierre, *Société de développement des entreprises culturelles*, 1314
Laporte, Manon, *Enviro-Accès Inc.*, 691
Lapostolle, Lynn, *Association pour la recherche au collégial*, 166
Lapp, Jim, *L'Arche Western Region*, 78
Lapper, Robert G. W., *Law Society of Upper Canada*, 902
Lappin, Dave, *H.O.M.E. Society*, 819
Laprise, Serge, *Canadian Ski Patrol*, 471
Laprise, Renee, *Island Media Arts Co-op*, 865
Laprise, Jean-Roch, *Service budgétaire populaire de St-Félicien*, 1291
Lapworth, Daina, *Early Childhood Intervention Program (ECIP) Sask. Inc.*, 667
Laquerre, Lyne, *Alliance Française de Calgary*, 57
Laramée, Richard, *Fondation maman Dion*, 747
Lardjane, Mahmoud, *Canadian Society for Civil Engineering*, 474
Lardner, Janice, *Squash Ontario*, 1347
Lareau, Suzanne, *Vélo Québec*, 1431
Larin, Sheila, *Association of Professional Researchers for Advancement - Canada*, 160
LaRiviere, David, *PAVED Arts*, 1146
Lariviere, Alain, *Association de la fibromyalgie région Ile-De-Montréal*, 101
Larizza, Joe, *Toronto Association of Systems & Software Quality*, 1382
Larmond, JoAnne, *Canadian Gemmological Association*, 396
Larney, Elinor, *College of Occupational Therapists of Ontario*, 587
Laroche, Jacques, *Association de la santé et de la sécurité des pâtes et papiers et des industries de la forêt du Québec*, 102
Laroche, France, *Conseil des arts de Montréal*, 617
Laroche, Ron, *Community Living Ontario*, 604
Laroche, François, *Canadian Hemophilia Society*, 404
Laroche, Maryse, *Bureau local d'intervention traitant du SIDA*, 264
Laroche, Mélanie, *Chambre de commerce et d'industrie MRC de Deux-Montagne*, 547

Executive Name Index

Laroche, Miranda, *Grande Prairie Friendship Centre*, 781
Larochelle, Michel, *Association de paralysie cérébrale du Québec*, 103
Larochelle, Serge, *Fédération québécoise du loisir littéraire*, 731
Larochelle, Julie, *Association des neurotraumatisés de l'Outaouais*, 121
Larock, Mike, *Association of British Columbia Forest Professionals*, 140
Larocque, Claudette, *Learning Disabilities Association of Canada*, 904
Larocque, Yves, *Bureau des regroupements des artistes visuels de l'Ontario*, 264
Laroque, Colin, *Canadian Association of Geographers*, 316
Larose, Anik, *Association du Québec pour l'intégration sociale / Institut québécois de la déficience intellectuelle*, 131
Larose, Marie-Claire, *Réseau des SADC et CAE*, 1220
Larose, Benoit, *Canada's Medical Technology Companies*, 282
LaRose, Patti, *CrossTrainers Canada*, 644
Larouche, Liliane, *Fondation des maladies du coeur du Québec*, 745
Larouche, Carole, *Kidney Foundation of Canada*, 885
Larouche, Marguerite, *Club des ornithologues de Québec inc.*, 575
Larouche, Alain, *Tourisme Cantons-de-l'Est*, 1392
Larouche, Dany, *Jeunes en partage*, 870
Larrivée, Doris, *Barreau de Montréal*, 197
Larsen, Denise, *Hope Studies Central*, 821
Larsen, Danielle, *Alberta Athletic Therapists Association*, 25
Larsen, Christine, *Women in Film & Television Vancouver*, 1461
Larsen, Paul, *Prince Edward Island Hog Commodity Marketing Board*, 1174
Larson, Jennifer, *Canadian Cerebral Palsy Sports Association*, 355
Larson, Roger, *Canadian Faculties of Agriculture & Veterinary Medicine*, 383
Larson, John, *American Farmland Trust*, 1492
Larson, Paula, *Canadian Women Voters Congress*, 505
Larson, Patti, *Revelstoke Community Connections Food Bank*, 1228
Lartey, Anna, *International Union of Nutritional Sciences*, 1565
Larue, Marie, *Institut de recherche Robert-Sauvé en santé et en sécurité du travail*, 842
LaRusic, Bernie, *Federation of Senior Citizens & Pensioners of Nova Scotia*, 726
Larwood, Brent, *Saskatchewan Snowboard Association*, 1275
Lasby, Cathy, *Ontario Plowmen's Association*, 1096
Lasek, Phil, *Professional Engineers Ontario*, 1184
Lash, Rob, *Plant Engineering & Maintenance Association of Canada*, 1162
Laskaris, Lia, *Animal Alliance of Canada*, 70
Laskey, David, *New Brunswick Genealogical Society Inc.*, 1009
Laskey, Dave, *United Empire Loyalists' Association of Canada*, 1410
Laskin, Monty, *Caledon Community Services*, 270
Laskoski, Andrew, *Ontario Athletic Therapists Association*, 1067
Lasnier, Jean-François, *L'Ordre des comptables professionels agréés du Québec*, 1120
Lassen, Moira, *Ontario Weightlifting Association*, 1113
Lassen, Jeane, *Yukon Weightlifting Association*, 1481
Lastra, Jane, *Canadian Association of Student Financial Aid Administrators*, 334
Laszlo, Stewart, *Canadian Society of Association Executives*, 480

Laszlo, Shannon, *Canadian Plastics Industry Association*, 455
Latendresse, Rhonda, *Epilepsy Ontario*, 694
Latendresse, Rhonda, *Ontario Brain Injury Association*, 1069
Latendresse, Nathalie, *Association des médecins hématologistes-oncologistes du Québec*, 119
Laterreur, Daniel, *Syndicat des travailleurs de la construction du Québec (CSD)*, 1364
Latham, Linda, *Professional Engineers Ontario*, 1183
Latham, Julia, *Easter Seals New Brunswick*, 669
Lathan, Gary, *Schizophrenia Society of Alberta*, 1283
Lathlin, Don, *Swampy Cree Tribal Council*, 1358
Latimer, Catherine, *The John Howard Society of Canada*, 874
Latimer, Christine, *Valemount & Area Chamber of Commerce*, 1424
Latimer, Michael, *Canadian Beef Breeds Council*, 342
Latoski, Ann-Marie, *Vecova Centre for Disability Services & Research*, 1430
Latour, Gilles, *Canadian Education Association*, 380
Latour, Benoit, *Club de trafic de Québec*, 575
Latrace, Kevan, *Canadian National Baton Twirling Association*, 439
Latraverse, Pierre, *Fédération québécoise des chasseurs et pêcheurs*, 728
Latraverse, Guy, *Revivre*, 1228
Latreille, Francine, *Judo Canada*, 876
Latreille, France, *Union des consommateurs*, 1406
Latreille, Philippe, *Parrainage civique Montréal*, 1143
Latreille, Hélène, *Foundation of Greater Montreal*, 756
Latta, Tammy, *Canadian Association of Foodservice Professionals*, 315
Latta, Lynn, *Society for Treatment of Autism*, 1327
Latta, Bud, *Solid Waste Association of North America*, 1595
Lattanzio, Joseph, *Registered Massage Therapists' Association of British Columbia*, 1213
Lattmann, Gerry, *Canada BIM Council Inc.*, 278
Lau, Victor, *Canadian Office & Professional Employees Union*, 445
Lau, Breda, *Alberta Athletic Therapists Association*, 25
Lau, Jonathan, *Landlord's Self-Help Centre*, 898
Lau, Chris, *Maison Plein Coeur*, 927
Lauchlan, Anneisa, *Calgary Association of Self Help*, 271
Laugalys, Erica, *The College of Naturopaths of Ontario*, 586
Laughlen, Geri, *The Garden Clubs of Ontario*, 767
Laughren, Chris, *Orienteering Ontario Inc.*, 1126
Laughren, Josh, *Oceana Canada*, 1054
Lauren, Philip, *PFLAG Canada Inc.*, 1155
Laurence, Mira, *Victoria Epilepsy & Parkinson's Centre Society*, 1432
Laurencelle, Suzanne, *Fondation québécoise de la maladie coeliaque*, 748
Laurendeau, Alain, *Mission Old Brewery*, 969
Laurent, Régine, *Fédération interprofessionnelle de la santé du Québec*, 721
Laurent, Claude, *Ordre professionnel de la physiothérapie du Québec*, 1124
Laurent, Michel, *Regroupement des Sourds de Chaudière-Appalaches*, 1216
Laurenzi, Nathalie, *MultiPrévention*, 980
Laureti, David, *Fédération des chambres de commerce du Québec*, 713

Laurich, Sarah, *Atikokan Native Friendship Centre*, 181
Laurie, Jeremy, *Development & Peace*, 654
Laurie-Lean, Justyna, *Mining Association of Canada*, 967
Laurin, Isabelle, *Association canadienne-française de l'Alberta*, 96
Laurin, Fernand, *Club informatique de Longueuil*, 575
Laurin, Claudine, *Fédération des OSBL d'habitation de Montréal*, 716
Laurin, Ginette, *O Vertigo Danse*, 1053
Laurin, Claudine, *Réseau québécois des OSBL d'habitation*, 1225
Lauson, Doug, *Federation of Independent School Associations of BC*, 724
Lauzière, Marcel, *Lawson Foundation*, 902
Lauzon, Sylvie, *Diabète Québec*, 655
Lauzon, François, *Préventex - Association paritaire du textile*, 1170
Lauzon, Jo-Ann, *Fédération québécoise de l'autisme*, 727
Lauzon, Gaëtan, *Canadian Hardwood Plywood & Veneer Association*, 401
Lauzon, Marcel, *Canadian Ski Patrol*, 471
Lauzon, Joanne, *Canadian Nurses Association*, 443
Lauzon, Daniel, *Chemins du soleil*, 556
Lauzon, Rebecca, *Human Resources Professionals Association*, 825
Lauzon, Curtis, *Judo New Brunswick*, 876
Lauzon, Jules, *Chemistry Industry Association of Canada*, 556
Lauzon, Ryan, *Canadian Wheelchair Basketball Association*, 503
Lauzon, Chantal, *Association sectorielle: Fabrication d'équipement de transport et de machines*, 178
Lauzon, Hélène, *Conseil patronal de l'environnement du Québec*, 619
Lauzon, Denis, *Club d'ornithologie de Mirabel*, 574
Lauzon, Gaëtan, *Architectural Woodwork Manufacturers Association of Canada - Québec*, 80
Lauzon-Gosselin, Maude, *Enviro-Accès Inc.*, 691
Lavack, Ginette, *Centre culturel franco-manitobain*, 526
Lavack, Annie, *Parent Support Services Society of BC*, 1139
Lavallee, Brian, *Association of Professional Engineers & Geoscientists of New Brunswick*, 158
Lavallée, Martin, *Association des juristes pour l'avancement de la vie artistique*, 118
Lavallée, Denise, *Association coopérative d'économie familiale - Rive-Sud de Québec*, 97
Lavallée, Daniel Paul, *Ski Québec alpin*, 1302
Lavallée, Nicolas, *Fédération des associations étudiantes du campus de l'université de Montréal*, 712
Lavallée, Nathalie, *National Golf Course Owners Association Canada*, 993
Laveau, Dave, *Société touristique des Autochtones du Québec*, 1325
Lavender, Leigh Anne, *Madoc & District Chamber of Commerce*, 925
Lavenir, Marie-Laure, *International Council on Monuments & Sites*, 1545
Laver, Ross H., *Business Council of Canada*, 267
Laverdière, Marco, *Ordre des optométristes du Québec*, 1123
Laverdure, Katelyn, *Alberta Beef Producers*, 26
Laverdure, Martin, *Club des débrouillards*, 575
Lavergne, Claude, *Réseau des SADC et CAE*, 1219
Lavers, Dominique, *Newfoundland Equestrian Association*, 1023
Lavery, Michael J., *Alliance for Audited Media*, 56

LaVie, Marie, *Eastern Prince Edward Island Chamber of Commerce*, 670
Lavigne, Danielle, *Mosaïque centre d'action bénévole et communautaire*, 975
Lavigne, Richard, *Confédération des Organismes de Personnes Handicapées du Québec*, 611
Lavigne, Josée, *Association québécoise des troubles d'apprentissage - section Outaouais*, 175
Lavigne, Suzanne, *Canine Federation of Canada*, 508
Laviolette, Brenda, *Community Living Dundas County*, 601
Laviolette, Michelle, *Association des médecins spécialistes en médecine nucléaire du Québec*, 120
Laviolette, Lance, *Society of Canadian Ornithologists*, 1327
Laviolette, Ralph, *Huron East Chamber of Commerce*, 828
Laviolette, Doug, *Civic Institute of Professional Personnel*, 571
Lavoie, Lyne, *Association coopérative d'économie familiale de l'Ile-Jésus*, 97
Lavoie, Yves, *Association des personnes handicapées de Charlevoix inc.*, 122
Lavoie, Ghislain, *College of Family Physicians of Canada*, 584
Lavoie, Suzanne, *Association de la santé et de la sécurité des pâtes et papiers et des industries de la forêt du Québec*, 102
Lavoie, Chris, *Better Business Bureau of Western Ontario*, 207
Lavoie, André, *Insitut canadien des économistes en construction - Québec*, 840
Lavoie, Eve, *Centraide Bas St-Laurent*, 522
Lavoie, Mathieu, *Syndicat des agents de la paix en services correctionnels du Québec*, 1362
Lavoie, Éric, *Fédération des professionnelles et professionnels de l'éducation du Québec*, 718
Lavoie, Marc, *Fédération d'escrime du Québec*, 708
Lavoie, P., *University of Toronto Institute for Aerospace Studies*, 1421
Lavoie, Patrick, *American Society of Plumbing Engineers*, 1502
Lavoie, André, *Assemblée parlementaire de la Francophonie*, 88
Lavoie, Martin, *Canada Pork International*, 280
Lavoie, Linda, *Fédération de l'UPA - Abitibi-Témiscamingue*, 709
Lavoie, Marc, *Société historique acadienne de la Baie Sainte-Marie*, 1319
Lavoie, Daniel, *École internationale de français*, 672
Lavoie, Doris, *National Dental Hygiene Certification Board*, 992
Lavoir, Lise, *Mouvement national des québécoises et québécois*, 978
Lavorato, Aaron, *Alberta Amateur Baseball Council*, 22
Lavrencic, Natalia, *Canadian Association of Critical Care Nurses*, 312
Lavrencic, Rome, *British Columbia Association of Teachers of Modern Languages*, 233
Law, Janet, *Delta Arts Council*, 653
Law, Stephen, *Mount Allison Faculty Association*, 976
Law, Judith, *Anxiety Disorders Association of British Columbia*, 72
Lawford, John, *The Public Interest Advocacy Centre*, 1192
Lawler, Bob, *Credit Counselling of Regional Niagara*, 639
Lawler, Nancy, *Elementary Teachers' Federation of Ontario*, 684
Lawler, Colleen, *Society of Cardiovascular Anesthesiologists*, 1592
Lawless, Justin, *Prince Edward Island Cattle Producers*, 1173
Lawless, Maura, *The 519 Church St. Community Centre*, 740

Executive Name Index

Lawless-Ajibade, Sarah, *TD Friends of the Environment Foundation*, 1367
Lawley, Michael, *Muskoka Tourism*, 985
Lawlor, Julie, *West Shore Chamber of Commerce*, 1446
Lawlor, Brad, *Soccer Nova Scotia*, 1305
Lawn, Patti, *Chilliwack Community Arts Council*, 563
Lawrence, Sharon, *Penticton & District Community Arts Council*, 1150
Lawrence, Nathan, *Northwestern Ontario Associated Chambers of Commerce*, 1039
Lawrence, Chris, *Better Business Bureau of Central & Northern Alberta*, 206
Lawrence, Donna, *Student Christian Movement of Canada*, 1352
Lawrence, Sara, *Real Estate Institute of Canada*, 1206
Lawrence, Jennifer, *College of Dental Hygienists of British Columbia*, 583
Lawrence, Leah, *Sustainable Development Technology Canada*, 1357
Lawrence, Doug, *Information Systems Security Association*, 1532
Lawrence-Fisher, Ute, *Post Traumatic Stress Disorder Association*, 1167
Lawrie, Robert, *Canadian Cancer Society*, 348
Lawrie, Dawn, *Health Record Association of British Columbia*, 807
Laws, Bob, *Alexandra Writers' Centre Society*, 53
Lawson, James, *Jockey Club of Canada*, 873
Lawson, Carol, *Action Volunteers for Animals*, 7
Lawson, Debra, *Second Harvest*, 1288
Lawson, Chris, *Canadian Association of Labour Media*, 319
Lawson, Kate, *Ontario Confederation of University Faculty Associations*, 1074
Lawson, Donald G., *The Counselling Foundation of Canada*, 636
Lawson, Bruce, *The Counselling Foundation of Canada*, 636
Lawson, Dave, *Lethbridge Association for Community Living*, 907
Lawson, Dean, *Darts Alberta*, 651
Lawton, Fraser, *The Anglican Church of Canada*, 69
Lawton, Hilary, *Canadian Public Relations Society Inc.*, 463
Lay, Eric, *Canadian Association of Wireless Internet Service Providers*, 336
Laycock, Anthony, *Criminal Lawyers' Association*, 642
Laycock, Lisa, *Horse Council British Columbia*, 822
Laycock, Anthony, *Reinsurance Research Council*, 1217
Laycock, Anthony, *Wood Energy Technology Transfer Inc.*, 1463
Laycock, Anthony, *Canadian Association of Psychosocial Oncology*, 330
Laycock, Anthony, *Global Commercial Insurers' Association*, 775
Laycraft, Dennis, *Canadian Cattlemen's Association*, 351
Lazar, Mark, *International Wine & Food Society*, 1567
Lazare, Jerry, *Chawkers Foundation*, 555
Lazarovits, Kathy, *East York - Scarborough Reading Association*, 669
Le Bouyonnec, Stéphane, *Coalition Avenir Québec*, 577
Le Clainche, Yvonnick, *Canadian Meteorological & Oceanographic Society*, 436
Le Gros, Francois-Xavier, *World Veterinary Poultry Association*, 1608
Le Guilcher, Jean Paul, *Model Aeronautics Association of Canada Inc.*, 971
Le Jeune, Cliff, *Dance Nova Scotia*, 649
Le Nabat, Marv, *Saskatoon Society for the Prevention of Cruelty to Animals Inc.*, 1280
le Nobel, J. Christian, *Family Services of Greater Vancouver*, 705

Le Saux, Nicole, *Immunize Canada*, 831
Le Sueur, Richard, *Kiwanis International (Western Canada District)*, 892
Le Vay, Paul, *Association des juristes d'expression française de l'Ontario*, 117
Leach, Tammy, *Alberta Continuing Care Association*, 31
Leach, Catherine, *Sunshine Coast Community Services Society*, 1355
Leach, Lori, *Horse Trials New Brunswick*, 822
Leach, Gary, *Explorers & Producers Association of Canada*, 700
Leach, Kelly, *Big Brothers Big Sisters of Eastern Newfoundland*, 209
Leader, Clarice, *Telecommunities Canada Inc.*, 1369
Leadley, Brenda, *BC Alliance for Arts & Culture*, 201
Leahy, Maura, *Distance Riders of Manitoba Association*, 659
Leaman, Bruce M., *International Pacific Halibut Commission*, 1554
Lear, Andrea, *Manitoba Veterinary Medical Association*, 946
Leard, Jonathan, *Big Brothers Big Sisters of Nova Scotia*, 210
Leard, Darla, *Canadian Labour Congress*, 425
Leavens, Jon, *Alzheimer Society of Belleville/Hastings/Quinte*, 62
Leavitt, Beverly J., *Canada East Equipment Dealers' Association*, 278
Leavitt, Tracey, *Millet & District Historical Society*, 966
Lebans, Anne, *Canadian Public Health Association - NB/PEI Branch*, 462
LeBeau, François, *Canadian Team Handball Federation*, 493
Lebeau, Ghislain, *Société d'histoire de la Haute Gaspésie*, 1310
Lebeau, Élisabeth, *Association des techniciens en santé animale du Québec*, 129
Lebeau, Martin, *Ontario Opticians Association*, 1094
Lebel, Audrey, *Chambre de commerce de Mont-Laurier*, 542
Lebel, Jean, *International Development Research Centre*, 856
Lebel, Émilie, *Chambre de commerce de St-Jean-de-Dieu*, 543
Lebel, Alain, *Association Québécoise pour la Santé Mentale des Nourrisson*, 176
Lebel, Sylvain, *Association Sportive de Ringuette Brossard*, 178
LeBelle-Déjario, Nadine, *Baton New Brunswick*, 199
LeBerge, Brian, *Hinton & District Chamber of Commerce*, 815
LeBlanc, Danièle, *Jeunesses Musicales du Canada*, 871
LeBlanc, Tracie, *Covenant House Toronto*, 637
LeBlanc, Miguel, *New Brunswick Association of Social Workers*, 1006
LeBlanc, Nathalie, *Société culturelle Sud-Acadie*, 1309
Leblanc, Fernande, *Soeurs missionnaires de Notre-Dame des Anges*, 1331
LeBlanc, Daniel M., *Boys & Girls Clubs of New Brunswick*, 222
LeBlanc, Alex, *New Brunswick Multicultural Council*, 1010
Leblanc, Michel, *Chambre de commerce du Montréal métropolitain*, 544
Leblanc, Kieran, *Book Publishers Association of Alberta*, 218
LeBlanc, Gabriel (Gabe), *Athletics New Brunswick*, 181
LeBlanc, Allen, *CODE*, 580
LeBlanc, Charlie, *New Brunswick Wildlife Federation*, 1013
LeBlanc, Aubrey, *Ontario Building Officials Association Inc.*, 1070
LeBlanc, Claude, *Réseau FADOQ*, 1224
LeBlanc, Monique, *Insurance Institute of New Brunswick*, 849

LeBlanc, Fred, *Ontario Professional Fire Fighters Association*, 1097
LeBlanc, Joan, *Gulf of Maine Council on the Marine Environment*, 794
Leblanc, Nicole, *Société de généalogie des Cantons de l'Est*, 1316
LeBlanc, Darrell, *Nova Scotia School Athletic Federation*, 1048
LeBlanc, Gérald, *Atlantic Episcopal Assembly*, 183
LeBlanc, Jacques B., *Fondation CHU Dumont Foundation*, 743
Leblanc, Pierre-Luc, *Éleveurs de volailles du Québec*, 684
LeBlanc, Albert E., *Chambre de commerce de la region de Cap-Pelé*, 542
LeBlanc, Maggie, *Association de Dards du Québec inc.*, 100
Leblanc, Michel, *World Trade Centre Montréal*, 1467
LeBlanc, Jérémie, *Canada Employment & Immigration Union*, 279
Leblanc, Mario, *Tourisme Côte-Nord*, 1392
LeBlanc, Lorraine, *Société Alzheimer Society Sudbury-Manitoulin*, 1307
LeBlanc, Maurice D., *Family Service Moncton Inc.*, 704
LeBlanc, Lynn, *Saint John Deaf & Hard of Hearing Services, Inc*, 1246
Leblanc, Brigitte, *Réseau du sport étudiant du Québec Côte-Nord*, 1223
LeBlanc, Sylvie, *Aguasabon Chamber of Commerce*, 15
Leblanc, Virginie, *Regroupement des jeunes chambres de commerce du Québec*, 1215
LeBlanc, Wayne, *Sudbury & District Beekeepers' Association*, 1353
LeBlanc, Heather, *New Brunswick Physique & Figure Association*, 1011
LeBlanc, Jean, *New Brunswick Physique & Figure Association*, 1011
LeBlanc-Lebel, Francine, *Ontario Teachers' Federation*, 1110
LeBlank, Léo-Guy, *Canadian Condominium Institute*, 362
Leblond, Sylvie, *Association de la construction du Québec*, 100
Leblond, Paul H., *British Columbia Scientific Cryptozoology Club*, 252
Leblond, Simon, *Syndicat de la relève agricole d'Abitibi-Témiscamingue*, 1362
Leblond, Claude, *Fondation Émergence inc.*, 746
Leboeuf, Sylvain, *Syndicat des employés en radio-télédiffusion de Télé-Québec (CSQ)*, 1363
Leboeuf, Reynald, *Maisons Adrianna*, 927
LeBoutillier, John, *Tennis Canada*, 1371
Lebrasseur, Lyne, *Réseau des SADC et CAE*, 1220
LeBreux, Pierre, *Association québécoise pour le loisir des personnes handicapées*, 177
Lebrun, Gilles, *Victoria Lapidary & Mineral Society*, 1433
LeCavalier, Norm, *Greater Westside Board of Trade*, 787
LeChien, R.H., *Association of Millwrighting Contractors of Ontario Inc.*, 152
Lecker, Sheri, *Adsum for Women & Children*, 9
Leckie, Kent, *Bobcaygeon & Area Chamber of Commerce*, 217
Leckie, Anne, *Silver Trail Chamber of Commerce*, 1299
LeClair, Don, *Baseball PEI*, 198
Leclair, Paul, *Sault Ste Marie Musicians' Association*, 1281
LeClair, Tracey, *Winnipeg Youth Orchestras*, 1460
LeClaire, Alison, *Arctic Council*, 81
Leclerc, Roselyne, *Centre de formation à la coopération interculturelle du Québec*, 529
Leclerc, Lucie, *Volleyball Canada*, 1438
Leclerc, Julie, *The Canadian Federation of Business & Professional Women's Clubs*, 386

Leclerc, Patrick, *Canadian Urban Transit Association*, 500
Leclerc, Marie-Claude, *Regroupement des organismes de bassins versants du Québec*, 1215
Leclerc, André, *Kéroul, Tourisme pour personnes à capacité physique restreinte*, 884
Leclerc, Gaston, *Association québécoise d'information scolaire et professionnelle*, 168
Leclerc, Stéphanie-Claude, *Les Amis de la déficience intellectuelle Rive-Nord*, 67
Leclerc, Cindra, *Manitoba Water Polo Association Inc.*, 947
Leclerc, Valérie, *Association du transport urbain du Québec*, 132
Leclerc, Geneviève, *The Transplantation Society*, 1395
Lecompte, Anne Marie, *Canadian College of Health Leaders*, 359
Lecompte, Isabelle, *Synchro Canada*, 1360
Lecoq, Sophie, *Association des bibliothèques de droit de Montréal*, 107
Lecours, Lucie, *Chambre de commerce d'industrie Les Moulins*, 540
Ledi-Thom, Arlene, *Health & Safety Conference Society of Alberta*, 805
Leduc, Pierre-Paul, *Festivals et Événements Québec*, 733
Leduc, Jacques, *Canadian Institute of Actuaries*, 414
Leduc, François, *Canadian Office & Professional Employees Union*, 444
Leduc, Roxanne, *Réseau santé en français Terre-Neuve-et-Labrador*, 1226
Leduc, André, *Association des alternatives en santé mentale de la Montérégie*, 105
Leduc, Hélène, *Table des responsables de l'éducation des adultes et de la formation professionnelle des commissions scolaires du Québec*, 1366
Leduc, Pierre-Paul, *Société des attractions touristiques du Québec*, 1317
Leduc, Gilles, *Partage Humanitaire*, 1143
Leduc, Andrew, *Information Technology Association of Canada*, 837
Leduc, Isabelle, *Réseau québécois des OSBL d'habitation*, 1225
Ledwidge, Marc, *Association of Canadian Mountain Guides*, 143
Lee, Barbara, *Elora Arts Council*, 685
Lee, A. Grant, *Canadian Institute of Marketing*, 417
Lee, Patti, *Parksville & District Chamber of Commerce*, 1142
Lee, Sharon, *Ontario Association of Food Banks*, 1064
Lee, Bill, *International Federation of Hardware & Housewares Association*, 1548
Lee, Sally, *Canadian Artists' Representation Ontario*, 296
Lee, Diane, *Consulting Engineers of Ontario*, 625
Lee, Susan, *Association of Local Public Health Agencies*, 150
Lee, Chuck, *Alberta Whitewater Association*, 52
Lee, Brian, *Saskatchewan Golf Association Inc.*, 1266
Lee, Gale, *Canadian Executive Service Organization*, 383
Lee, Kevin, *Canadian Home Builders' Association*, 106
Lee, Joan, *Chinese Canadian National Council*, 564
Lee, Thealzel, *Learning Disabilities Association of Canada*, 904
Lee, Carmen, *Hong Kong-Canada Business Association*, 820
Lee, Mary, *Health Association Nova Scotia*, 806
Lee, Karen, *Multiple Sclerosis Society of Canada*, 980
Lee, Bonny, *Dance Nova Scotia*, 649
Lee, Rebecca, *Support Enhance Access Service Centre*, 1356

Executive Name Index

Lee, Isa, *The Cross-Cultural Community Services Association*, 644
Lee, Robert, *Ontario Pollution Control Equipment Association*, 1097
Lee, Elsa, *Institute for Performance & Learning*, 844
Lee, Tiffany, *Canadian Society of Hospital Pharmacists*, 484
Lee, Ted, *Tourism Vancouver/Greater Vancouver Convention & Visitors Bureau*, 1391
Lee, John, *Regina Regional Opportunities Commission*, 1212
Lee, Joan, *Vecova Centre for Disability Services & Research*, 1430
Lee, Dennis, *Alberta College of Acupuncture & Traditional Chinese Medicine*, 28
Lee, Christopher, *Canadian Association of Medical Oncologists*, 320
Lee, Kevin, *British Columbia Ferry & Marine Workers' Union (CLC)*, 241
Lee, John, *Indefinite Arts Society*, 832
Lee, David, *British Columbia Team Handball Federation*, 256
Lee, Jim, *International Association of Fire Fighters (AFL-CIO/CLC)*, 1538
Lee, Leonard, *Pender Harbour & District Chamber of Commerce*, 1149
Lee, Sharon, *Allergy/Asthma Information Association*, 54
Lee, Richard, *Korean-Canadian Symphony Orchestra*, 894
Lee, Susan, *Certified Professional Trainers Network*, 538
Lee, Sandra, *British Columbia Registered Music Teachers' Association*, 251
Lee, Ellie, *Canadian Association of Ambulatory Care*, 308
Lee, Olive, *Essa Historical Society*, 696
Lee, Kate, *Canadian Arthritis Network*, 295
Lee, Kevin, *Scadding Court Community Centre*, 1282
Lee, Peter A., *Pediatric Endocrine Society*, 1583
Lee, Daniel, *Korean Canadian Cultural Association of the Greater Toronto Area*, 893
Lee, Chi-Guhn, *Association of Korean Canadian Scientists & Engineers*, 150
Lee, Chris, *Inspirit Foundation*, 840
Lee, Deryk, *Public Works Association of British Columbia*, 1194
Lee, Jason, *Association of Fundraising Professionals*, 1511
Lee, Richard, *Halifax Wildlife Association*, 799
Lee, S.K., *BC Chinese Music Association*, 201
Lee Garcia, Erica, *Professional Engineers Ontario*, 1184
Lee McKenzie, Dawn, *REALTORS Association of Grey Bruce Owen Sound*, 1206
Lee Williams, Tonya, *ReelWorld Film Festival*, 1210
Leech, Andrew, *New Brunswick Association of Real Estate Appraisers*, 1005
Leech, Garry, *Cape Breton University Centre for International Studies*, 510
Leech, John, *Applied Science Technologists & Technicians of British Columbia*, 74
Leeder, Emma, *Ontario Association of Triathletes*, 1066
Leek, Gord, *Royal Alberta United Services Institute*, 1237
Leekam, Cathy, *Multicultural History Society of Ontario*, 979
Leekha, Gurpreet, *British Columbia Doctors of Optometry*, 239
Leeman, Ed, *Boating Ontario*, 216
Leenhouts, Pieter, *Ontario Woodlot Association*, 1114
Lees, Rebecca, *German Canadian Business Association*, 772
Leese, Greg, *Association of Architectural Technologists of Ontario*, 139
Leese, Dave, *Lansdowne Outdoor Recreational Development Association*, 899

Leeson, Jon, *Canadian Institute of Plumbing & Heating*, 418
Leewes, Gerrit, *Alberta Camping Association*, 27
Lefebre, Michelle, *Alberta Association of Landscape Architects*, 23
Lefebvre, Serge, *Association des directeurs généraux des commissions scolaires du Québec*, 111
Lefebvre, Jean-François, *Football Canada*, 750
Lefebvre, Jean, *Restaurants Canada*, 1227
Lefebvre, Marie-Eve, *Association des obstétriciens et gynécologues du Québec*, 121
Lefebvre, Fleur-Ange, *Federation of Medical Regulatory Authorities of Canada*, 724
Lefebvre, Serge, *Fédération des producteurs d'oeufs de consommation du Québec*, 717
Lefebvre, Claire, *La coopérative de Solidarité de Répit et d'Etraide*, 627
Lefebvre, Francine, *L'Atelier des lettres*, 180
Lefebvre, Léo, *Toronto Users Group for Power Systems*, 1388
Lefebvre, François, *Société québécoise du dahlia*, 1324
Lefebvre, Johanne, *Association de Laval pour la déficience intellectuelle*, 102
Lefebvre, Fleur-Ange, *Federation of Medical Regulatory Authorities of Canada*, 724
Lefebvre, Melissa, *Alberta Bodybuilding Association*, 26
Lefol, Laurette, *Fondation fransaskoise*, 746
Lefort, Angus, *Conseil coopératif acadien de la Nouvelle-Écosse*, 614
Lefrançois, Danielle, *Advertising Standards Canada*, 10
Lefrancq, Philip, *Electro-Federation Canada*, 683
Legal, Michael, *Canadian Society of Hospital Pharmacists*, 484
Légaré, Gaétan, *Association nationale des camionneurs artisans inc.*, 138
Légaré, Yves, *Société des Auteurs de Radio, Télévision et Cinéma*, 1317
Légaré, Luc, *Syndicat de la fonction publique du Québec inc. (ind.)*, 1361
Légaré, Hélène, *Coalition des organismes communautaires québécois de lutte contre le sida*, 578
Légaré, Pauline, *Réseau santé albertain*, 1225
Legaree, Ian, *Arctic Winter Games International Committee*, 81
LeGates, Marlene, *Women's International League for Peace & Freedom*, 1462
Legault, Jacques, *Fédération des syndicats de l'action collective*, 719
Legault, Gilles, *Canadian Institute of Plumbing & Heating*, 419
Legault, Chantal, *Chambre immobilière de l'Outaouais*, 550
Legault, Ellen, *Insurance Institute of Ontario*, 850
Legault, Paul E., *Secours aux lépreux (Canada) inc.*, 1288
Legault, Maryse, *Secours aux lépreux (Canada) inc.*, 1288
Legault, Véronique, *Commission nationale des parents francophones*, 593
Legault, Victor, *Fédération des dentistes spécialistes du Québec*, 714
Legault, François, *Coalition Avenir Québec*, 577
Legault, Yves, *Tourisme Laval*, 1393
Legault, Margo, *Literacy Volunteers of Quebec*, 914
Legault, Michel, *Fédération des coopératives d'habitation de la Mauricie et du Centre-du-Québec*, 714
Legault, Elaine, *Conseil des organismes francophones de la région de Durham*, 617
Legendre, Grégoire, *Opéra de Québec*, 1115
Leger, Paul A., *Bus History Association, Inc.*, 266
Léger, André, *Canadian Cancer Society*, 349

Léger, Rhéal, *Canadian Hard of Hearing Association*, 400
Léger, Pierre, *Canadian Manufacturers & Exporters*, 429
Leger, Lisa, *Osteoporosis Canada*, 1128
Léger, Marie-Hélène, *Association québécoise pour l'évaluation d'impacts*, 176
Léger, Sylvie, *Action Intégration en Déficience Intellectuelle*, 6
Leger, Don, *New Brunswick Candlepin Bowlers Association*, 1006
Léger, Bernice, *New Brunswick Dental Assistants Association*, 1007
Légère, Daniel, *Canadian Union of Public Employees*, 498
Legg, Peter, *International Geosynthetics Society*, 1550
Legge, Kevin, *Newfoundland Baseball*, 1023
Legge, Matthew, *Canadian Friends Service Committee*, 395
Legge, Adam, *Calgary Chamber of Commerce*, 271
Leggett-Bachand, Nancy, *Pro Bono Québec*, 1181
Leggett-Bachand, Nancy, *Fondation québécoise pour l'alphabétisation*, 748
Leggott, Mark, *L.M. Montgomery Institute*, 916
Legrand, Stéphane, *Chambre de commerce du Haut-Richelieu*, 544
Legris, Mary Ann, *Alberta Genealogical Society*, 36
Legros-Kelly, Joanne, *Osteoporosis Canada*, 1128
Legrow, Bruce, *Canadian Masters Cross-Country Ski Association*, 431
Leguerrier, Gabriele, *Agricultural Institute of Canada*, 15
Lehigh, Sheana, *Physiotherapy Association of British Columbia*, 1159
Lehman, Ed, *Regina Peace Council*, 1212
Lehman, Patti, *Ontario Brain Injury Association*, 1069
Lehmkuhl, Ursula, *Association for Canadian Studies in German-Speaking Countries*, 1507
Lehodey, Germaine, *Fédération des aînées et aînés francophones du Canada*, 711
Lehr, Diane, *Alberta Genealogical Society*, 37
Lehr, Sharon Paulette, *Canadian College of Health Leaders*, 359
Lei, Judy, *Association of Canadian Pension Management*, 143
Leib, Melissa, *Saskatchewan Lung Association*, 1269
Leiba, Sheldon, *Mississauga Board of Trade*, 970
Leibel, Rhea, *Society of Graphic Designers of Canada*, 1329
Leibgott, Laura, *Southern Ontario Orchid Society*, 1338
Leicht-Eckardt, Elisabeth, *International Federation for Home Economics*, 1546
Leigh, Tamara, *Canadian Farm Writers' Federation*, 384
Lein, Daryl, *Lakehead Stamp Club*, 896
Leinbach, Bea, *Kitsilano Showboat Society*, 891
Leinweber, Daryl, *Calgary Minor Soccer Association*, 273
Leipsic, Greg, *Junior Achievement Canada*, 877
Leiska, Ray, *Base Borden Soaring*, 197
Leitch, Ted, *London Numismatic Society*, 918
Leitner, Gerald, *International Federation of Library Associations & Institutions*, 1548
Lelarge, Isabelle, *Société de développement des périodiques culturels québécois*, 1315
Lelièvre, Katia, *Syndicat des employé(e)s de magasins et de bureau de la Société des alcools du Québec (ind.)*, 1362
Lelièvre, Nicole, *Association des embouteilleurs d'eau du Québec*, 111
Lelliott, Cindy, *Nova Scotia Library Association*, 1046
Leloup, Marie, *Army Cadet League of Canada*, 83

Lemaire, Ron, *Canadian Produce Marketing Association*, 460
Lemaire, Guylaine, *Canadian Amateur Musicians*, 292
Lemauviel, Colin, *North Battleford & District Labour Council*, 1030
Lemay, Céline, *Banque d'yeux nationale, inc.*, 196
Lemay, Carmen, *Alberta Construction Association*, 31
Lemay, Pierre, *Association des policières et policiers provinciaux du Québec*, 123
Lemay, Catherine, *Le Centre jeunesse de la Montérégie*, 536
Lemay, Gilbert, *Association de vitrerie et fenestrations du Québec*, 104
Lemay, Claude, *Information Technology Association of Canada*, 837
Lemay, Stéphane P., *Research & Development Institute for the Agri-Environment*, 1218
Lemcke, Bonnie, *Toronto Association for Business Economics Inc.*, 1382
Lemelin, Richard, *Association des véhicules électriques du Québec*, 130
Lemercier, Pascal, *Chambre de commerce secteur ouest de Portneuf*, 549
Lemière, Catherine, *Canadian Thoracic Society*, 494
Lemieux, Francis, *Canadian Bible Society*, 343
Lemieux, Guillaume, *Cement Association of Canada*, 521
Lemieux, Tristan, *Orchestre symphonique de Québec*, 1118
Lemieux, Carole, *Centraide Haute-Côte-Nord/Manicouagan*, 522
Lemieux, Louise, *Conseil régional FTQ Québec et Chaudière-Appalaches*, 621
Lemieux, Julie, *Réseau des SADC et CAE*, 1220
Lemieux, Martine, *Chambre de commerce du Témiscouata*, 544
Lemieux, Michel, *Association québécoise des éducatrices et éducateurs spécialisés en arts plastiques*, 172
Lemieux, Pierre, *Research & Development Institute for the Agri-Environment*, 1218
Lemieux, Guy, *Regroupement des associations de personnes traumatisées craniocérébrales du Québec*, 1215
Lemieux, Valerie, *Catherine Donnelly Foundation*, 517
Lemire, Denise, *Fédération des aînés et des retraités francophones de l'Ontario*, 711
Lemire, Francine, *College of Family Physicians of Canada*, 584
Lemire, Raymonde, *Canadian Carpet Institute*, 350
Lemire, Paul, *Canadian Culinary Federation*, 374
Lemire, Rhonda, *Recreation Nova Scotia*, 1207
Lemire, Daniel, *La Société Numismatique de Québec*, 1322
Lemiski, Walter, *Canadian Depression Glass Association*, 377
Lemkay, Dave, *Canadian Forestry Association*, 392
Lemke, Deana, *Yukon Law Foundation*, 1479
Lemmon, Rhonda, *Alberta Walking Horse Association*, 51
LeMoine, Jeff, *Canadian Automobile Association South Central Ontario*, 339
LeMoine, Joyce, *Rug Hooking Guild of Nova Scotia*, 1244
Lemoine, Gérald, *Comité condition féminine Baie-James*, 591
Lemon, Sue, *CFA Society Toronto*, 539
Lemon, Anne, *The Garden Clubs of Ontario*, 767
Lemon, Brian, *Manitoba Beef Producers*, 932
Lemonde, Jean, *Association québécoise pour le loisir des personnes handicapées*, 177
Lemonde, Pierre, *Conseil des relations internationales de Montréal*, 618

Executive Name Index

Lenardon, Theresa, *Local Government Management Association of British Columbia*, 917
Lender, Dee, *Ontario Association of Residents' Councils*, 1066
Lendsay, Kelly, *Indigenous Works*, 835
Lenehan, Nick, *Gymnastics Nova Scotia*, 795
Leney, Stella, *Fondation Hydro-Québec pour l'environnement*, 746
Leng, Ray, *Muskoka Pioneer Power Association*, 985
Lenkinski, Lionel, *Canadian Dental Protective Association*, 377
Lennea, Coralie, *Saskatchewan Society of Occupational Therapists*, 1275
Lennon, Charlie, *Education International*, 1522
Lennon, Doreen, *Western Independent Adjusters' Association*, 1450
Lennon, Susan, *Society for Research in Child Development*, 1591
Lennox, Ashley, *Smiths Falls & District Chamber of Commerce*, 1304
Lennox, Peter, *Canadian Society of Plastic Surgeons*, 487
Lennox, Victoria, *Startup Canada*, 1348
Leo, Jr., Frank, *Canadian Conference of Catholic Bishops*, 363
Leon, Mark, *American Library Association*, 1494
Leon, Judith, *Senior Link*, 1290
Leon, Kenny, *Ottawa Chamber of Commerce*, 1129
Léonard, Pierre, *Association des enseignantes et des enseignants franco-ontariens*, 112
Leonard, Bill, *Canadian Committee on MARC*, 361
Leonard, Mike, *British Columbia Maritime Employers Association*, 246
Leonard, Michael T., *Ontario Building Officials Association Inc.*, 1070
Leonard, Mieke, *Yukon Registered Nurses Association*, 1480
Léonard, Chantal, *Canadian Nurses Protective Society*, 443
Leonard, Bill, *Family & Children's Services of the District of Rainy River*, 702
Léonard, Carol J., *Canadian Society for the Study of Names*, 478
Leonard, Annie, *Greenpeace USA*, 1529
Leonard, Michael, *Credit Unions Atlantic Canada*, 641
Leonard, Bill, *Ability New Brunswick*, 2
Leonard, Kevin, *The EJLB Foundation*, 681
Léonard, Roxanne, *ÉquiLibre - Groupe d'action sur le poids*, 694
Leonard, Christine, *Information Technology Association of Canada*, 837
Leonard, Roseanne, *Atlantic Association of CBDCs*, 182
Leonardi, Louise, *Canadian Families & Corrections Network*, 384
Leonardis, Nina, *ARMA Canada*, 82
Leong, Michael, *Canadian Film Institute*, 390
Leong, Brenda, *British Columbia Securities Commission*, 253
Leong, Sylvia, *Urban & Regional Information Systems Association*, 1601
Leong, Leslie, *Yukon Art Society*, 1477
Leonoff, Arthur, *Canadian Psychoanalytic Society*, 461
Lepage, Nathalie, *Centraide Outaouais*, 523
Lepage, Ginette, *Conseil de la culture du Bas-Saint-Laurent*, 616
Lepage, Diane, *Ottawa Field-Naturalists' Club*, 1130
Lepage, Michel, *Société Provancher d'histoire naturelle du Canada*, 1323
Lepage, Lucia, *Association pour les applications pédagogiques de l'ordinateur au postsecondaire*, 167
LePage, Pierre, *Canadian Association of Tour Operators*, 334
Lepage, Roger, *Fondation fransaskoise*, 746
Lepage, Gilles, *Société d'histoire et de généalogie de Verdun*, 1313

LePage, Marc, *Genome Canada*, 769
LePage, Marc, *Genome Canada*, 769
Lépine, Gérald, *Réseau FADOQ*, 1224
Lépine, Hélène, *YWCA Canada*, 1481
Lépine dos Santos, Kristen, *Association of Canadian Ergonomists*, 142
Lepko, Jennifer, *YWCA Canada*, 1481
Lepp, Jacquie, *Communitas Supportive Care Society*, 595
Leppard, John, *Stroll of Poets Society*, 1352
Lequin, Lucie, *Concordia University Faculty Association*, 610
Lerigny, Steve, *Chilliwack & District Real Estate Board*, 563
Lerman-Elmaleh, Amy, *Colon Cancer Canada*, 591
Leroux, Janice, *Big Brothers Big Sisters of Ontario*, 210
Leroux, John, *Architects' Association of New Brunswick*, 78
Leroux, Mathieu, *Québec Lung Association*, 1198
Leroux, Carole, *Syndicat professionnel des ingénieurs d'Hydro-Québec*, 1365
Leroux, Jeremy, *Manitoba Hotel Association*, 938
Les, Willetta, *Canadian Hard of Hearing Association*, 400
Lesage, Gilles, *Société historique de Saint-Boniface*, 1320
Lesage, Frédéric, *Association de Ringuette de Sept-Îles*, 103
Lesanko, Chris, *Saskatchewan Lacrosse Association*, 1268
LeSergent, Jodi, *United Way of Trail & District*, 1417
Lesiw, Bob, *Toronto Users Group for Power Systems*, 1388
Leske, Sandy, *Alberta Civil Trial Lawyers' Association*, 28
Leskun, Jim, *Multilingual Association of Regina, Inc.*, 979
Leslie, Jennifer, *Community Living St. Marys & Area Association*, 605
Leslie, Edward F., *New Brunswick Society of Certified Engineering Technicians & Technologists*, 1012
Leslie, Sarah, *Ontario Speed Skating Association*, 1108
Leslie, Sharon, *Canadian Association for Social Work Education*, 304
Leslies, Sue, *Ontario Horse Racing Industry Association*, 1086
Lespérance, Michel, *Autorité des marchés financiers*, 190
Lessard, Roch, *Conseil régional FTQ Québec et Chaudière-Appalaches*, 621
Lessard, Jocelyn, *Fédération québécoise des coopératives forestières*, 728
Lessard, Sandie, *Canadian Hospice Palliative Care Association*, 409
Lessard, Johanne, *Association Renaissance de la région de l'Amiante*, 178
Lessard, Guy, *Association québécoise des directeurs et directrices d'établissement d'enseignement retraités*, 172
Lessard, Chantal, *Association des personnes en perte d'autonomie de Chibougamau inc. & Jardin des aînés*, 122
Lessels, Craig, *Canadian Hydrographic Association*, 410
Lessels, Christina, *Ontario Women's Health Network*, 1113
Lessoway, Vickie, *British Columbia Ultrasonographers' Society*, 257
Lestage, François, *Association des Aménagistes Régionaux du Québec*, 105
Lester, Brian, *Regional HIV/AIDS Connection*, 1212
Lester, Peter, *Film Studies Association of Canada*, 735
Lester, Michelle, *Provincial Farm Women's Association*, 1191
Lestition Burke, Amy, *Special Libraries Association*, 1596

Lesurf, Craig, *Council of Ontario Construction Associations*, 634
Leszner, Paul, *Canadian Council for Reform Judaism*, 367
Letain, Karen, *Invest Ottawa*, 862
Letendre, Cory, *Calgary Minor Soccer Association*, 273
Letendre, Luc, *Tourisme Baie-James*, 1392
Letham, Stacie, *North Shore Multicultural Society*, 1033
Lethbridge, Glenn, *Ontario Sailing*, 1103
Letizia, Pat, *Alberta Ecotrust Foundation*, 33
Letofsky, Karen, *Canadian Association for Suicide Prevention*, 304
Letofsky, Karen, *Distress Centres of Toronto*, 659
Letofsky, Karen, *Distress Centres Ontario*, 659
Létouneau, David, *Ringuette St-Hubert*, 1233
Letourneau, Joe, *Wetaskiwin Chamber of Commerce*, 1451
Létourneau, Gina, *Canadian Academic Accounting Association*, 285
Létourneau, Jacques, *Confédération des syndicats nationaux*, 611
Létourneau, Robert, *Société historique et généalogique de Trois-Pistoles, inc.*, 1321
Letourneau, Sara, *Battle River Soccer Association*, 200
Létourneau, Stéphane, *Institut de recherches cliniques de Montréal*, 842
Létourneau, Guylaine, *Chambre de commerce Témiscaming-Kipawa*, 550
Letourneaux, Francois, *Foundation for Legal Research*, 756
Lett, Steven, *International Cospas-Sarsat Programme*, 855
Letude, Suzie, *Darts British Columbia Association*, 651
Leu, Rosemary, *West Ottawa Board of Trade*, 1446
Leung, Linden, *Volleyball Canada*, 1437
Leung, Cindy, *GLOBE Foundation*, 775
Leung, Eve, *Toronto Association of Law Libraries*, 1382
Leung, Thomas In-Sing, *Culture Regeneration Research Society*, 645
Leurer, Tim, *Rural Municipal Administrators' Association of Saskatchewan*, 1244
Leushen, Laurel, *Saskatchewan Dietitians Association*, 1263
Leuwers, Daniel, *Association internationale de la critique littéraire*, 1509
Levac, Mélanie, *Canadian Propane Association*, 461
Levac, Joanne, *Eastern Ontario Beekeepers' Association*, 670
Leval, Kim, *Northwest Coalition for Alternatives to Pesticides*, 1580
Levasseur, Denis, *North Bay Police Association*, 1030
Levasseur, Hélène, *Centre Anti-Poison du Québec*, 1072
Léveillé, Michel, *Canadian Red Cross*, 466
Léveillé, Diane, *La fédération des mouvements personne d'abord du Québec*, 716
Levenston, Michael, *City Farmer - Canada's Office of Urban Agriculture*, 571
Leveque, Nancy, *Ontario Genealogical Society*, 1082
Lever, Shannon, *Brock University Faculty Association*, 260
Leversage, Jill, *Mr. & Mrs. P.A. Woodward's Foundation*, 978
Leversedge, Eileen, *Music for Young Children*, 984
Leverty, Robert, *Ontario Historical Society*, 1084
Levesque, Nicole, *Société culturelle régionale Les Chutes*, 1309
Lévesque, Marie-France, *Conseil régional de la culture et des communications de la Côte-Nord*, 621
Lévesque, Louis, *Fédération Québécoise de Dynamophilie*, 727

Lévesque, Claudette, *Canadian Heritage Information Network*, 405
Lévesque, Marie-Claude, *Chambre de commerce et d'industrie de Varennes*, 546
Lévesque, Martine, *Association des directeurs généraux des municipalités du Québec*, 111
Levesque, Roger, *Canadian Masters Cross-Country Ski Association*, 431
Levesque, Pascale, *Alberta Orienteering Association*, 42
Lévesque, Sylvie, *Fédération des associations de familles monoparentales et recomposées du Québec*, 712
Levesque, Gino, *Écrivains Francophones d'Amérique*, 674
Lévesque, Maurice, *Archery Association of New Brunswick*, 78
Lévesque, Normand, *Réseau pour le développement de l'alphabétisme et des compétences*, 1225
Levesque, Claude J.G., *Federal Association of Security Officials*, 706
Lévesque, Jocelyn, *Réseau des SADC et CAE*, 1220
Lévesque, Mélanie, *Association des Acupuncteurs du Québec*, 105
Lévesque, Lucette, *Société d'histoire et de généalogie des Quatre Lieux*, 1313
Lévesque, Marie-Claire, *L'Institut canadien de Québec*, 840
Levesque, Guy, *Canada Foundation for Innovation*, 279
Lévesque, François, *Fédération québécoise de naturisme*, 728
Lévesque, Sylvie, *Association des familles monoparentales et recomposées de l'Outaouais*, 113
Levesque, Christine, *Valley Chamber of Commerce*, 1424
Lévesque, Myriam, *Syndicat des employés et employées des syndicats et des organismes collectifs du Québec*, 1363
Lévesque, Sylvain, *Association des garderies privées du Québec*, 114
Lévesque, Marie-Paule, *Association Marie-Reine de Chibougamau*, 137
Lévesque, Jean-Guy, *Fédération québécoise de biathlon*, 727
Lévesque, Louis, *Finance Montréal*, 736
Levi, John, *International Warehouse Logistics Association*, 1566
Levine, Ronn, *Specialized Information Publishers Association*, 1596
Levine, Renee, *Canadian Society of Medical Evaluators*, 484
Levine, Ben, *Immigrant & Multicultural Services Society*, 830
Levine-Clark, Marjorie, *North American Conference on British Studies*, 1578
Levinson, P., *Vancouver Holocaust Centre Society - A Museum for Education & Remembrance*, 1426
Levinson, Leesa, *Lights, Camera, Access!*, 912
Lévis, Stéphane, *Fédération du personnel de l'enseignement privé*, 720
LeVoir, Koren, *Tennessee Walking Horse Association of Western Canada*, 1370
Levy, David N.L., *International Computer Games Association*, 1543
Levy, Roanie, *Access Copyright*, 5
Levy, Gary, *Federation of Canada-China Friendship Associations*, 722
Levy, Gary, *Federation of Canada-China Friendship Associations - Ottawa Chapter*, 722
Levy, Shauna, *Design Exchange*, 654
Levy, Michael H., *Plastics Foodservice Packaging Group*, 1584
Levy, Leonard, *Lookout Emergency Aid Society*, 919
Levy, Moses, *Asper Foundation*, 87
Lewarne, Andrew, *Registered Massage Therapists' Association of Ontario*, 1213

Executive Name Index

Lewchuk, Allana, *Saskatchewan Institute of Agrologists*, 1268
Lewington, Jane, *Conservation Ontario*, 622
Lewis, Scott, *Greater Moncton Chamber of Commerce*, 784
Lewis, Doug, *International Social Service*, 1557
Lewis, Christina, *Ontario Dairy Council*, 1076
Lewis, Terry, *Diabetes Canada*, 656
Lewis, André, *Royal Winnipeg Ballet*, 1243
Lewis, John M., *International Alliance of Theatrical Stage Employees, Moving Picture Technicians, Artists & Allied Crafts of the U.S., Its Territories & Canada*, 1535
Lewis, Jason, *Manitoba Association of Medical Radiation Technologists*, 930
Lewis, Ashley, *Sport Physiotherapy Canada*, 1345
Lewis, Maureen, *Moorelands Community Services*, 973
Lewis, Shiata, *One Full Circle*, 1058
Lewis, Gail, *South Norwich Historical Society*, 1335
Lewis, Loretta, *Burin Peninsula Chamber of Commerce*, 265
Lewis, Brian, *Canada's Medical Technology Companies*, 282
Lewis, Martha Jane, *British Columbia Coalition to Eliminate Abuse of Seniors*, 236
Lewis, Brian, *Canadian MedTech Manufacturers' Alliance*, 434
Lewis, John, *LEAD Canada Inc.*, 903
Lewis, Norm, *Canadian Titanic Society*, 495
Lewis, Leota, *Weymouth Historical Society*, 1451
Lewis, Daniel, *Saskatchewan College of Paramedics*, 1261
Lewis, Stacy, *Tennis Yukon Association*, 1371
Lewis, Leanne, *Helping Other Parents Everywhere Inc.*, 812
Lewis, Amy, *Pancreatic Cancer Canada Foundation*, 1138
Lewko, Richard, *Ontario College of Teachers*, 1072
Lewkowicz, Antoni G., *International Permafrost Association*, 1555
Lewycky, Dennis, *Social Planning Council of Winnipeg*, 1306
Leyten, Linda, *Oxford Regional Labour Council*, 1134
Leyton, Marco, *Canadian College of Neuropsychopharmacology*, 360
Li, Jianan, *International Society of Physical & Rehabilitation Medicine*, 1561
Li, Mary, *Arctic Institute of North America*, 81
Li, Iris, *Canadian Anesthesiologists' Society*, 293
Li, Diana Tong, *Chinese Medicine & Acupuncture Association of Canada*, 565
Li, Xixi, *Service à la famille chinoise du Grand Montréal*, 1291
Li, Oscar, *Judo Manitoba*, 876
Li, Jenny, *British Columbia Food Technolgists*, 241
Liao, Qing, *Canadian Meteorological & Oceanographic Society*, 435
Liard, Alain, *Ordre des Géologues du Québec*, 1121
Liard, Hélène, *Société d'histoire de Sherbrooke*, 1311
Libby, John A., *Canadian Association of Personal Property Appraisers*, 325
Libby, Eileen, *Law Foundation of Saskatchewan*, 901
Libman, Rachel, *Holocaust Education Centre*, 819
Liboro, Rheea, *University of the Philippines Alumni Association of Toronto*, 1420
Libralato, Carla, *Canadian Business Aviation Association*, 348
Lichtenstein, Mark, *National Recycling Coalition, Inc.*, 1577
Lichtner, Horst, *International Ice Hockey Federation*, 1551

Lickers-Sage, Cynthia, *Dance Ontario Association*, 649
Lidington, Jasmin, *Canadian Association of General Surgeons*, 316
Lieb, Glynnis, *Alberta Federation of Labour*, 34
Lieb, Glynnis, *Canadian Union of Public Employees*, 498
Lieber, H. Stephen, *Healthcare Information & Management Systems Society*, 1529
Lieberman, Anne, *National Audubon Society, Inc.*, 1575
Liebow, Ed, *American Anthropological Association*, 1488
Liebrecht, Angel, *Saskatchewan Registered Music Teachers' Association*, 1273
Liebrecht, Darrell, *SaskTel Pioneers*, 1280
Lieff, Susan, *Canadian Association for Medical Education*, 302
Lieffers, Vic, *Association of University Forestry Schools of Canada*, 163
Lightfoot, Geraldine, *POWERtalk International*, 1584
Lightning, Marlene, *United Church of Canada*, 1409
Lightning-Earle, Koren, *Indigenous Bar Association*, 834
Likely, Zak, *Prince Edward Island Snowboard Association*, 1177
Lilauwala, Nicole, *Toronto Community Foundation*, 1383
Lilbourne, Lucia, *Middlesex Federation of Agriculture*, 965
Lilgert, Karl, *Boundary Organic Producers Association*, 219
Liliefeldt, Raine, *YWCA Canada*, 1481
Lillico, Craig, *Canadian National Institute for the Blind*, 439
Lim, Marc Brian, *Junior Chamber International*, 1568
Lim, Kitack, *International Maritime Organization*, 1553
Lima, Paul, *Canadian Heritage Information Network*, 405
Lima, Ileana, *Canadian Snack Food Association*, 472
Limacher, Lori, *Alberta Association of Marriage & Family Therapy*, 24
Limbertie, Wendy, *Community Folk Art Council of Toronto*, 597
Limoges, Michel, *Chambre de Commerce Bois-des-Filion - Lorraine*, 540
Limoges, Isabelle, *Fondation des maladies mentales*, 745
Limón, Lavinia, *U.S. Committee for Refugees & Immigrants*, 1601
Lin, Yongtao, *Southern Alberta Health Libraries Association*, 1337
Lin, Hannah, *YWCA Canada*, 1481
Lin Heng, Lye, *Asia-Pacific Centre for Environmental Law*, 1506
Lin Lim, Poh, *Manitoba Gerontological Nurses' Association*, 937
Linares, Nancy, *Association of Retail Travel Agents*, 1513
Lincourt, Raoul, *Action des Chrétiens pour l'abolition de la torture*, 6
Lincourt, Pierre, *Association québécoise des écoles de français langue étrangère*, 172
Lind, Jens, *Royal Danish Guards Association of Western Canada*, 1242
Linder, David, *Madonna House Apostolate*, 925
Linder, David, *Alberta Securities Commission*, 46
Lindhout, Julie, *Atlantic Council of Canada*, 183
Lindop, Peter, *Institute of Professional Bookkeepers of Canada*, 847
Lindsay, Jason, *Association of Professional Engineers of Prince Edward Island*, 159
Lindsay, David, *Forest Products Association of Canada*, 751
Lindsay, David, *Council of Ontario Universities*, 635

Lindsay, Lloyd, *Bereaved Families of Ontario*, 205
Lindsay, Heather, *Intrepid Theatre Co. Society*, 862
Lindsay, Don, *British Columbia's Children's Hospital Foundation*, 259
Lindsay, Sheryl, *Sistering - A Woman's Place*, 1300
Lindsay, Cindy, *Community Foundations of Canada*, 598
Lindsay-MacLeod, Anne, *Organization of Military Museums of Canada*, 1126
Lindstrom, Darrell, *Canadian Association of Foodservice Professionals*, 315
Lindstrom, Harold, *Ontario Home Builders' Association*, 1086
Ling, Jim, *National Retriever Club of Canada*, 996
Ling, Joan, *Nova Scotia Teachers Union*, 1049
Ling, Chris, *Environmental Studies Association of Canada*, 692
Ling, Kevin, *Grain Workers' Union, Local 333*, 779
Ling, Jason, *Prince Edward Island Trucking Sector Council*, 1178
Linington, Jamie, *Slave Lake Native Friendship Centre*, 1303
Linka, Ruth, *Association of Book Publishers of British Columbia*, 140
Linkie, Coellen, *Professional Engineers Ontario*, 1184
Linkiewicz, Rob, *Ontario Society of Occupational Therapists*, 1107
Linney, Bob, *Federation of Law Societies of Canada*, 724
Linstead, Gilbert, *Fisheries Council of Canada*, 740
Linton, Mark, *National Transportation Brokers Association*, 996
Linzey, Doug, *Nature Nova Scotia (Federation of Nova Scotia Naturalists)*, 1000
Lio, Attilio, *The Children's Aid Foundation of York Region*, 560
Lior, Karen, *Toronto Workforce Innovation Group*, 1388
Liosis, Connie, *Wild Rose Ball Hockey Association*, 1454
Lipinski, Gary, *Métis Nation of Ontario*, 963
Lipoczi, Ana-Maria, *Canadian Music Centre*, 438
Lipsen, Linda, *American Association for Justice*, 1488
Lirette, Yvon, *La Société historique du Cap-Rouge*, 1321
Lisak, Robert, *Consortium of Multiple Sclerosis Centers*, 1519
Lisée, Jean-François, *Parti québécois*, 1144
Liss, David, *Museum of Contemporary Canadian Art*, 983
Lissimore, Marilyn, *Terrace & District Community Services Society*, 1371
List, Cary, *Financial Planning Standards Council*, 737
Lister, Linda, *Community Living Stormont County*, 605
Litchfield, Laura, *Hearth, Patio & Barbecue Association of Canada*, 810
Liteplo, Jonathan, *Christian Blind Mission International*, 566
Litke, Karen, *Saskatchewan College of Psychologists*, 1261
Litster, Chris, *Ecological Farmers of Ontario*, 672
Little, Jack, *Edmonton Heritage Festival Association*, 677
Little, Becky, *Lethbridge Naturalists' Society*, 908
Little, Gregg, *Ontario Refrigeration & Air Conditioning Contractors Association*, 1101
Little, Kenneth, *Watch Tower Bible & Tract Society of Canada*, 1441
Little, Ingrid, *Ontario Association of Landscape Architects*, 1064
Little, Samantha, *Orchestra Toronto*, 1117

Little, Betsy, *Alzheimer Society London & Middlesex*, 61
Little, Jayne, *Massage Therapist Association of Saskatchewan*, 953
Little, Judy, *American Guild of Variety Artists (AFL-CIO)*, 1494
Little, Ginette, *New Brunswick Continuing Legal Education*, 1007
Little, Rob, *AthletesCAN*, 180
Little, Marion, *PEERS Victoria Resource Society*, 1148
Little, Dianne, *Canadian Registry of Tennessee Walking Horse*, 466
Little, Neil, *Centre for Transportation Engineering & Planning*, 534
Littleford, Holly, *Vancouver Youth Symphony Orchestra Society*, 1429
Littlejohn, David, *Greater Nanaimo Chamber of Commerce*, 784
Littlejohn, Dale, *Community Energy Association*, 597
Littlejohns, Carl, *Ontario Rural Softball Association*, 1103
Littleton, Jeff H., *American Society of Heating, Refrigerating & Air Conditioning Engineers*, 1500
Litwin, Val, *British Columbia Chamber of Commerce*, 235
Litwin, Val, *Whistler Chamber of Commerce*, 1452
Litwin, Greg, *Tofield & District Chamber of Commerce*, 1380
Litwinski, Rob, *Hockey Alberta*, 817
Litz, Christina, *Canadian Football League*, 392
Liu, Zhen, *Asthma Society of Canada*, 179
Liu, Meilan, *Professional Engineers Ontario*, 1184
Liu, Lin, *Chinese Medicine & Acupuncture Association of Canada*, 565
Liu, D., *Opera.ca*, 1115
Liu, Loretta, *Emmaus Canada*, 686
Lively Jones, Kelly, *East Coast Aquarium Society*, 668
Liverman, David, *Newfoundland & Labrador Cricket Association*, 1018
Livingston, Kathleen, *Saskatchewan Environmental Industry & Managers' Association*, 1264
Livingstone, Amber, *North Bay Food Bank*, 1030
Livingstone, J.L. (John), *The Canadian Corps of Commissionaires*, 365
Livingstone, Troy, *Island Technology Professionals*, 865
Livingstone, Dustin, *Canadian Society of Orthopaedic Technologists*, 485
Livingstone, Dalbert, *Automotive Recyclers Association of Atlantic Canada*, 190
Lizon, Amanda, *AboutFace*, 3
Lizon, Władysław, *Canadian Polish Congress*, 456
Ljubicic, Jo-Anne, *Ontario Volleyball Association*, 1112
Llewellyn, Gareth, *Royal City Field Naturalists*, 1241
Llewellyn, Bethan, *The Kitchener & Waterloo Community Foundation*, 890
Llewellyn, Kristina, *Canadian History of Education Association*, 405
Llewelyn, Elwyn, *Conseil du troisième âge de Saint-Lambert*, 618
Lloyd, Simon, *Archives Council of Prince Edward Island*, 80
Lloyd, Conor, *Canadian Public Relations Society Inc.*, 463
Lloyd, David, *Alberta Institute of Agrologists*, 38
Lloyd, Ian, *Association of British Columbia Land Surveyors*, 140
Lloyd, Gordon, *Chemistry Industry Association of Canada*, 556
Lloyd, B., *Northwatch*, 1036
Lloyd, Mark, *Electrical Construction Association of Hamilton*, 682

Executive Name Index

Lloyd, Philip, *Ontario Undergraduate Student Alliance*, 1111
Lloyd, Anita, *STRIDE*, 1352
Lloyd, Angela, *Triathlon Manitoba*, 1398
Lloyd, Diane, *Association of Fundraising Professionals*, 1512
Loat, Alison, *The Canadian Club of Toronto*, 357
Lobel, Art, *Grand Masters Curling Association Ontario*, 780
Loblaw, Cathy, *Ronald McDonald House Charities of Canada*, 1235
Locas, France, *Association des professionnels en gestion philanthropique*, 126
Locas, France, *Association de Laval pour la déficience intellectuelle*, 102
Lochanski, Laura, *Lawn Bowls Association of Alberta*, 902
Locher, Caroline, *Fédération professionnelle des journalistes du Québec*, 727
Lock, Henri, *Student Christian Movement of Canada*, 1352
Lock, Randy, *Canadian College of Health Leaders*, 359
Locke, Brenda, *Registered Massage Therapists' Association of British Columbia*, 1213
Lockhart, Kirbey, *Lake Country Chamber of Commerce*, 895
Lockner, Mia, *World Confederation for Physical Therapy*, 1604
Lockwood, Frank, *Audio Engineering Society*, 187
Lockwood, Érika, *St. Patrick's Society of Richmond & Vicinity*, 1250
Loder, Colleen, *Boys & Girls Clubs of Newfoundland & Labrador*, 223
Loder, James, *National Association of Career Colleges*, 990
Lodge, Isabelle, *Chambre de commerce et d'entrepreneuriat des Sources*, 545
Loeb, Matthew D., *International Alliance of Theatrical Stage Employees, Moving Picture Technicians, Artists & Allied Crafts of the U.S., Its Territories & Canada*, 1535
Loeffelholz, Maureen, *Saskatchewan Registered Music Teachers' Association*, 1273
Loehr, Marilyn, *British Columbia Deaf Sports Federation*, 238
Loerchner, Wolfgang, *Canadian Knifemaker's Guild*, 424
Loeters, Michael, *Toronto Insurance Conference*, 1385
Loewen, Tracey, *Prairie Theatre Exchange*, 1170
Loewen, Kevin, *Brandon Police Association*, 226
Loewen, Andrew, *Canadian Union of Public Employees*, 499
Loewen, Liz, *MBTelehealth Network*, 955
Loewen, Shirley, *Youth for Christ Canada*, 1475
Loewen, Mark, *Northwest Mennonite Conference*, 1036
Loewen, Andrea, *First Pacific Theatre Society*, 739
Loewen, Christina, *Opera.ca*, 1115
Loewen, Paul, *Alberta Conference of Mennonite Brethren Churches*, 31
Loewen, Richard, *Import Vintners & Spirits Association*, 831
Loewen Mauritz, Marilyn, *Central 1 Credit Union*, 523
Loewer, Jason, *Saskatchewan Abilities Council*, 1255
Loffredi, Angelo, *Canadian International Freight Forwarders Association*, 421
Loffredi, Angelo, *Canadian International Freight Forwarders Association*, 421
Lofstrom, Karin, *Canadian Association for the Advancement of Women & Sport & Physical Activity*, 305
Loft, Fonda, *Symphony on the Bay*, 1360

Loftsgard, Tia, *Canada Organic Trade Association*, 280
Logan, David, *Health Employers Association of British Columbia*, 806
Logan, Vickie, *Community Living St. Marys & Area Association*, 605
Logan, Marcus, *Information Oakville*, 837
Logan, Gail, *Renfrew County United Way*, 1217
Logan, Louise, *Parachute*, 1138
Logan, Lorraine, *The Council of Senior Citizens Organization of British Columbia*, 635
Logies, David, *Canadian Percheron Association*, 453
Logins, Nicky, *British Columbia Association of Family Resource Programs*, 231
Loh, Justina, *Disability Alliance British Columbia*, 658
Lohr, Jason, *College of Dental Technologists of Alberta*, 583
Lohrenz, Marilyn, *Saskatchewan Registered Music Teachers' Association*, 1273
Loiseau, Véronique, *Chambre de commerce et d'industrie française au canada*, 547
Loisel, Steeve, *Fédération des professionnelles et professionnels de l'éducation du Québec*, 718
Loisel, Anick, *Conseil de la culture de la Gaspésie*, 616
Lojk, Begonia, *Canadian General Standards Board*, 397
Lok, Johnathan, *Canadian Institute of Forestry*, 416
Lokker, Yvette, *Canadian Investor Relations Institute*, 422
Lomas-McGee, Kathi, *YMCA Canada*, 1471, 1472
Lombard, Alan, *Association provinciale des enseignantes et enseignants du Québec*, 168
Lombardi, Daniel, *People First of Ontario*, 1151
Lombardo, Anthony, *Canadian Association on Gerontology*, 337
Lombardo, Angelo, *Ontario Federation of Anglers & Hunters*, 1079
Lomond, Ted, *Newfoundland & Labrador Environmental Industry Association*, 1018
Loncar, Terese M., *Academy of Management*, 1485
London, Jason, *Recycling Council of Alberta*, 1208
Long, Marc, *Chambre de commerce de la région d'Edmundston*, 542
Long, Mary, *Multiple Sclerosis Society of Canada*, 980
Long, Barbara, *New Brunswick Federation of Music Festivals Inc.*, 1008
Long, Barbara, *Federation of Canadian Music Festivals*, 723
Long, Todd, *Manitoba Council for Exceptional Children*, 934
Long, Helena, *Unity & District Chamber of Commerce*, 1418
Long, Helen, *Canadian Health Food Association*, 401
Long, Margo, *Youth Empowerment & Support Services*, 1475
Long, Kerrie, *Edmonton International Film Festival Society*, 678
Long, Scott, *Music Nova Scotia*, 984
Long, Grady, *Bowling Federation of Alberta*, 219
Longard, Jeff, *Canadian Luing Cattle Association*, 428
Longboat, Dan, *Jake Thomas Learning Centre*, 867
Longchamps, Louis, *Organisme de développement d'affaires commerciales et économiques*, 1125
Longley, Blair T., *Marijuana Party*, 949
Longley, Gayle, *RBC Foundation*, 1204
Longman, Jenanne, *Fusion: The Ontario Clay & Glass Association*, 765

Longman, Alana, *Welsh Pony & Cob Society of Saskatchewan*, 1444
Longo, Cori, *Canadian Labour Congress*, 425
Longpré, Jean-Marc, *Association québécoise des informaticiennes et informaticiens indépendants*, 173
Longridge, Tom, *British Columbia School Superintendents Association*, 252
Lonsbury, Jerry, *Crowsnest Pass Symphony*, 645
Loo, Debbie, *British Columbia Association of Mathematics Teachers*, 232
Looker, Ron, *Manitoba Darts Association Inc.*, 935
Loomans, Cassandra, *Ontario Agri Business Association*, 1059
Loomer, Diana, *Association of Professional Engineers & Geoscientists of New Brunswick*, 158
Loomer, Martin, *The Duke Ellington Society - Toronto Chapter #40*, 664
Loomis, Keanin, *Hamilton Chamber of Commerce*, 801
Loomis, Beverly, *United Empire Loyalists' Association of Canada*, 1410
Loosemore, Tracy, *Children's Health Foundations*, 561
Loosemore, Deborah, *Association of Fundraising Professionals*, 1512
Lopes, David, *Architects Association of Prince Edward Island*, 78
Lopes, Mario, *Professional Property Managers Association Inc.*, 1186
Lopez, Lori, *Canadian Adult Recreational Hockey Association*, 288
Lopez, Cyril, *British Columbia Pharmacy Association*, 248
López, Esther, *United Food & Commercial Workers' International Union*, 1599
Lord, Éric, *Culture Mauricie*, 645
Lord, Jean-Marc, *Comité de solidarité/Trois-Rivières*, 592
Lord, Gaétan, *Canadian Association of Nordic Ski Instructors*, 322
Lord, Gaetan, *Canadian Association of Nordic Ski Instructors*, 323
Lord, Iris, *Kidney Foundation of Canada*, 885
Lord, Brendan, *Choir Alberta*, 566
Lord, Justin, *Buy-Side Investment Management Association*, 267
Loree, Terri, *Alberta Reined Cow Horse Association*, 44
Lorenc, Christopher, *Manitoba Heavy Construction Association*, 938
Lorenz, Jodi, *Ringette Association of Saskatchewan*, 1232
Lorenz, Lisseth, *Institute of Cultural Affairs International*, 846
Loreto, Nora, *Canadian Association of Labour Media*, 319
Lorimer, Janet, *Community Living Oakville*, 604
Lorimer, Conor, *British Columbia Camping Association*, 234
Loring, Nigel, *Alberta Alpine Ski Association*, 22
Lorman, Corinne, *Fondation québécoise du cancer*, 748
Lormé-Gulbrandsen, Renee, *British Columbia Sustainable Energy Association*, 255
Lorna, Hunt, *Airdrie Chamber of Commerce*, 20
Lortie, Anne, *Association des neurologues du Québec*, 121
Lortie, Jean, *Confédération des syndicats nationaux*, 611
Lortie, Michelle, *Fédération québécoise de handball olympique*, 727
Lorway, Robin, *Skills/Compétences Canada*, 1303
Losier, Frances, *Ringette Canada*, 1233
Lotakow, Mike, *Polish North American Trucking Association*, 1164
Lotherington, Priscilla, *Investment Property Owners Association of Cape Breton*, 863

Lothian, Heather, *Alberta Bicycle Association*, 26
Lothian, Derek, *Insurance Brokers Association of Canada*, 848
Lotinga, Stephen, *The Publishers Association*, 1586
Lott, Brent, *Winnipeg's Contemporary Dancers*, 1460
Lotto, Andrew, *Cardiac Rehabilitation Network of Ontario*, 511
Loubert, Roger, *ArtsConnect - Tri-Cities Regional Arts Council*, 86
Louch, Scott, *Goodwill Industries*, 777
Loudon, Jonathan, *Association of Chartered Industrial Designers of Canada*, 145
Louer, Alain, *Nature Manitoba*, 1000
Lougheed, Tim, *Canadians for Health Research*, 507
Lougheed, Tim, *Science Writers & Communicators of Canada*, 1285
Lougheed, Stephen, *Alberta Research Council Inc.*, 44
Loughlin, Katherine, *Alberta Milk*, 40
Loughlin, Thomas G., *American Society of Mechanical Engineers*, 1500
Loughry, Craig, *Golf Association of Ontario*, 777
Loughton, Lorna, *Alberta Family History Society*, 34
Louie, Gorman, *Canadian Society of Plastic Surgeons*, 487
Louie, Kim, *Red Road HIV/AIDS Network*, 1210
Lounds, John, *The Nature Conservancy of Canada*, 999
Lourdel, Olivier, *Groupe d'entraide à l'intention des personnes séropositives, itinérantes et toxicomanes*, 791
Loureiro, Joe, *Casa do Benfica*, 516
Lourie, Bruce, *Richard Ivey Foundation*, 1229
Love, David, *Bird Studies Canada*, 212
Love, Ondina, *Canadian Dental Hygienists Association*, 377
Love, Drew, *Canadian Interuniversity Sport*, 422
Love, Rick, *The Royal Canadian Legion*, 1240
Love, Barbara, *Canadian Investor Protection Fund*, 422
Love, Erin, *The Canadian Association for HIV Research*, 301
Love, Shauna, *Ontario Council on Articulation and Transfer*, 1075
Love, Jered, *Lions Legacy International*, 913
Lovegrove, Mike, *Canadian Institute of Plumbing & Heating*, 418
Lovegrove, Wendy, *Brampton Horticultural Society*, 226
Lovelace, Karen, *Canadian Pension & Benefits Institute*, 453
Lovelace, W. Scott, *International Heavy Haul Association*, 1550
Loveless, Evan, *Wilderness Tourism Association*, 1454
Lovell, Phyllis, *Bruce Grey Child & Family Services*, 260
Lovell, Kelly, *Federation of Ontario Law Associations*, 726
Lovett, Allan, *Chamber of Commerce of Brantford & Brant*, 539
Lovrics, Margit, *Hungarian Studies Association of Canada*, 827
Low, Erin, *Alberta Construction Association*, 31
Low, Karen, *Merit Contractors Association of Saskatchewan*, 962
Low, Becky, *Rumble Productions Society*, 1244
Low, Travis, *Parkinson Society Saskatchewan*, 1142
Lowden, Brenda, *CAA British Columbia*, 267
Lowe, Louise, *Canadian Diamond Drilling Association*, 378
Lowe, Chris, *Juvenile Diabetes Research Foundation Canada*, 879
Lowe, Barbara, *College of Registered Psychiatric Nurses of Alberta*, 590

Executive Name Index

Lowe, Brian, *BioNova*, 211
Lowell Graber, Dan, *Mennonite Church Canada*, 961
Lowery, Dave, *Calgary & Area Medical Staff Society*, 270
Lowi-Young, Mimi, *Ontario Neurotrauma Foundation*, 1093
Lowther, Shaun, *Alberta Soccer Association*, 47
Lowther, Kenneth W., *Canadian Association of Veterans in United Nations Peacekeeping*, 336
Lowther, Wayne, *Alberta Square & Round Dance Federation*, 48
Lowther, Helen, *Alberta Square & Round Dance Federation*, 48
Lowther-Doiron, Rachel, *Prince Edward Island Pharmacy Board*, 1176
Loyer, Dale, *Canadian Association for Disabled Skiing - Alberta*, 299
Loyer, Josée, *Association des femmes d'assurance de Montréal*, 114
Lozovsky-Burns, Natasha, *Community Arts Council of Richmond*, 595
Lubarsky, Ron, *Canadian Council for Reform Judaism*, 367
Lubinski, Robert, *Toronto Transportation Society*, 1388
Lubitz, K., *Ultralight Pilots Association of Canada*, 1404
Luborsky, Fran, *Canadian Hadassah WIZO*, 399
Luc, Jean, *International Judo Federation*, 1551
Lucas, Shirley, *Alzheimer Society of Newfoundland & Labrador*, 63
Lucas, Greg, *Basketball Saskatchewan*, 199
Lucas, Lesley, *Real Estate Institute of Canada*, 1205
Lucas, Wayne, *Canadian Union of Public Employees*, 498
Lucas, Sheri, *SaskCentral*, 1280
Lucas, Paul, *Life Sciences Ontario*, 911
Lucas, Elizabeth, *Soroptimist International of the Americas*, 1595
Lucas, G. Brent, *Help for Headaches*, 812
Lucas, Jerry, *March of Dimes Canada*, 949
Luchak, Taras, *Manitoba Chiropractors' Association*, 934
Luciano, Douglas, *Canadian Welding Bureau*, 503
Luck, Matt, *Community Living Kingston*, 603
Luckman, Michele, *ISACA*, 1567
Lucko, Tim, *Risk & Insurance Management Society Inc.*, 1234
Lucsko, David, *Society for the History of Technology*, 1591
Luddington, Shelly, *Nova Scotia Recreation Professionals in Health*, 1048
Ludgate, Brian, *OMF International - Canada*, 1058
Ludke, Ron, *Lutheran Association of Missionaries & Pilots*, 922
Ludwig, Jim, *Mackenzie Applied Research Assciation*, 924
Luebke, Dana, *Sun Ergos, A Company of Theatre & Dance*, 1354
Luff, Glenn, *Manitoba Snowboard Association*, 944
Luft, Andrea, *Children's Heart Society*, 562
Lugar, Katherine, *American Hotel & Lodging Association*, 1494
Lui, Grace, *Building Industry & Land Development Calgary Region*, 262
Luipasco, Neil, *Association of Fundraising Professionals*, 1512
Luk, Keith, *International Society for the Study of the Lumbar Spine*, 1559
Luk, Winnie, *Inside Out Toronto LGBT Film & Video Festival*, 840
Lukacs, Martin, *Canadian Association of Labour Media*, 319
Lukezic, Boris, *North American Die Casting Association*, 1579
Lukian, Maegan, *Recycling Council of Alberta*, 1208

Lukings, Rob, *Child Evangelism Fellowship of Canada*, 559
Lukinuk, Tim, *North of Superior Tourism Association*, 1031
Lukinuk, Lori, *Ontario Physical & Health Education Association*, 1095
Lukszova, Miriam, *Whitehorse Cross Country Ski Club*, 1453
Lumia, Ivy, *Canadian Centre for Occupational Health & Safety*, 353
Lumley, Heather, *St. Leonard's Society of Canada*, 1250
Lumsden, Paul, *Peterborough Historical Society*, 1153
Lund, Ron, *Association canadienne des annonceurs inc.*, 92
Lund, Ronald S., *Association of Canadian Advertisers Inc.*, 140
Lund, John D., *Archives Association of Ontario*, 80
Lund, Craig, *American Marketing Association*, 1495
Lund, Daryl, *International Union of Food Science & Technology*, 861
Lund, Lisa, *Pathways to Education Canada*, 1145
Lund, Annika, *Salt Spring Community Centre Food Bank*, 1252
Lundale, Keith, *Eriksdale & District Chamber of Commerce*, 695
Lunden, Susan, *National Audubon Society, Inc.*, 1575
Lundmark, Deborah, *Canadian Contemporary Dance Theatre*, 364
Lundrigan, Cheryl, *Canadian Information Processing Society*, 411
Lundrigan, Jaime, *Child & Youth Care Association of Newfoundland & Labrador*, 558
Lunn, Andrew, *New Brunswick Roofing Contractors Association, Inc.*, 1011
Lunzer, Bernard J., *The Newspaper Guild (AFL-CIO/CLC)*, 1577
Luoma, Kaarina, *Mid-Toronto Community Services*, 965
Lupien, Richard, *Société Pro Musica Inc.*, 1322
Luppens, Wannes, *Cross Country British Columbia*, 643
Lurz, Donna, *Canadian Swiss Cultural Association*, 491
Luscher, Denise, *Canadian Racing Pigeon Union Inc.*, 464
Lushinton, Mike, *Biathlon Nouveau-New Brunswick*, 207
Lusk, Judy, *PFLAG Canada Inc.*, 1155
Lussier, Jocelyn, *Fédération Québécoise des Intervenants en Sécurité Incendie*, 729
Lussier, Christian, *Association des pathologistes du Québec*, 122
Lussier, Mathieu, *Canadian Amateur Musicians*, 292
Lussier, Sylvie, *Société des Auteurs de Radio, Télévision et Cinéma*, 1317
Lussier, Jacinthe, *Réseau du sport étudiant du Québec Laurentides-Lanaudière*, 1223
Lussier, Tom, *The Catholic Foundation of Manitoba*, 519
Lussier, Richard, *Canadian Electricity Association*, 380
Lussier, Jean-François, *Association des commerçants de véhicules récréatifs du Québec*, 109
Lussier, Patrick, *Association Québec Snowboard*, 168
Lustig, Al, *New Brunswick Signallers Association*, 1012
Luten, Trevor E., *Canadian Association of Veterans in United Nations Peacekeeping*, 335
Lutes, Michael, *Civil Constables Association of Nova Scotia*, 571
Luther, Wendy, *EduNova*, 680
Luthy, Genevieve, *Alberta Association of Academic Libraries*, 23

Lutz, Kiomi, *Building Owners & Managers Association of British Columbia*, 263
Lux, Tamelynda, *Family Enterprise Xchange*, 703
Lux, Norman, *Association of Quantity Surveyors of Alberta*, 160
Luxen, Diane, *Alberta Dressage Association*, 33
Luymes, Martin, *Heating, Refrigeration & Air Conditioning Institute of Canada*, 810
Luzi, Italo Joe, *Ontario Association of Property Standards Officers Inc.*, 1065
Luzia, Jennifer, *Synchro Alberta*, 1360
Ly, Sang-Kiet, *Greater Victoria Chamber of Commerce*, 787
Lychowyd, Sandy, *The John Howard Society of Ontario*, 875
Lyn-Harrison, Jodie, *Physical & Health Education Canada*, 1158
Lynch, Walker, *Walker Lynch Foundation*, 1439
Lynch, Michael, *Discovery Islands Chamber of Commerce*, 658
Lynch, David, *Good Shepherd Refuge Social Ministries*, 777
Lynch, James G., *The Canadian Corps of Commissionaires*, 365
Lynch, Jennifer, *Ontario Home Builders' Association*, 1086
Lynch, Dan, *Canadian Transportation Research Forum*, 497
Lynch, Doug, *East Hants Historical Society*, 668
Lynch, Elaine, *American Anthropological Association*, 1488
Lynch, Sandra, *Environmental Services Association of Nova Scotia*, 692
Lynch, Barrie, *Supply Chain Management Association - British Columbia*, 1356
Lynch, Cynthia, *FilmOntario*, 735
Lynn, Marnie, *Children's Aid Society of Toronto*, 561
Lyon, Brent, *Association of Professional Engineers & Geoscientists of British Columbia*, 158
Lyon, Jennifer, *Epilepsy Ontario*, 694
Lyon, Jonathon, *Health Sciences Centre Foundation*, 807
Lyon, Meloni, *Brain Injury Association of Alberta*, 225
Lyon, Allyn, *Yukon Underwater Diving Association*, 1480
Lyons, John, *PARN Your Community AIDS Resource Network*, 1143
Lyons, Daniel T., *Board of Canadian Registered Safety Professionals*, 216
Lyons, Ed, *Association of Professional Engineers & Geoscientists of British Columbia*, 158
Lyons, Janette, *Canadian Institute for the Relief of Pain & Disability*, 413
Lyons, Penny, *Seva Canada Society*, 1292
Lyons, Shannon, *Alberta Cattle Feeders' Association*, 27
Lyons, Dawn, *Pathways to Education Canada*, 1145
Lyons, Michael, *La Jeunesse Youth Orchestra*, 870
Lyseng, Orrin, *Alberta Alliance on Mental Illness & Mental Health*, 21
Lythgoe, Sherry, *Newfoundland & Labrador Physiotherapy Association*, 1021
Lyttle, Wendy Sue, *North West Commercial Travellers' Association*, 1033
Lytton, Stephen, *British Columbia Aboriginal Network on Disability Society*, 229

M

Ma, Jonas, *Chinese Canadian National Council*, 564
Ma, David, *Canadian Nutrition Society*, 444
Maadarani, Saousan, *Canadian Association of Second Language Teachers*, 332

Maahs, David M., *International Society for Pediatric & Adolescent Diabetes*, 1558
Maamo, Ethel, *Best Buddies Canada*, 206
Maass, Randy, *Timmins Coin Club*, 1380
Mabbott, Mel, *Alberta Reined Cow Horse Association*, 44
Mabilais, Stéphane, *Société de Promotion et de Diffusion des Arts et de la Culture*, 1317
Mabilleau, Philippe, *Société Québécoise de Psilogie inc*, 1323
Maboungou, Zab, *Cercle d'expression artistique Nyata Nyata*, 537
Mac Donald, Garry, *Brantford & District Labour Council*, 227
Macabenta, Lucy, *National Council of Philippine American Canadian Accountants*, 1575
Macallum, Linda, *Okotoks Arts Council*, 1056
MacAlpine, Karen, *Boys & Girls Clubs of New Brunswick*, 222
Macaulay, Elizabeth, *Canadian Council on International Law*, 371
Macaulay, Mary, *Atlantic Concrete Association*, 183
MacBride, Geoff, *Ontario Paramedic Association*, 1095
MacCallum, Barbara, *Canadian Counselling & Psychotherapy Association*, 371
MacCallum, Michelle, *Women's Network PEI*, 1463
MacCartney, Gerry, *London Chamber of Commerce*, 918
MacConnell, Patrick, *Brain Injury Association of Nova Scotia*, 225
MacCormac, Shaun, *Prince Edward Island Teachers' Federation*, 1178
MacCormack, Gerald, *Prince Edward Island School Athletic Association*, 1177
MacCready-Williams, Nancy, *Doctors Nova Scotia*, 660
MacCuish, Derek, *Social Justice Committee*, 1305
MacCullough, Wayne R., *Canadian Association of Veterans in United Nations Peacekeeping*, 335
MacDermid, Val, *PEDVAC Foundation*, 1147
MacDermott, Wendy, *United Way of Greater Saint John Inc.*, 1414
MacDonald, Kevin A., *Legal Information Society of Nova Scotia*, 906
MacDonald, Ann Marie, *Mood Disorders Association of Ontario*, 973
MacDonald, John, *PEI Powerlifting Association*, 1149
MacDonald, John, *Canadian Register of Health Service Psychologists*, 466
MacDonald, Peter, *Big Brothers Big Sisters of New Brunswick*, 210
MacDonald, Michele, *Boys & Girls Clubs of Prince Edward Island*, 224
MacDonald, Tiffany, *Children's Wish Foundation of Canada*, 563
MacDonald, Donna, *Carleton Place & District Chamber of Commerce & Visitor Centre*, 513
MacDonald, Anna, *Canadian Public Relations Society Inc.*, 463
MacDonald, Paul, *Prince Edward Island Institute of Agrologists*, 1175
MacDonald, Marian, *Army Cadet League of Canada*, 83
MacDonald, Melanie, *Association of Municipal Administrators of New Brunswick*, 152
MacDonald, Charlie, *Blind Sports Nova Scotia*, 214
MacDonald, Don, *Scouts Canada*, 1286, 1287
MacDonald, Doug, *Scouts Canada*, 1286, 1287
MacDonald, Ken, *HIV Network of Edmonton Society*, 816
MacDonald, Paul, *Family Enterprise Xchange*, 703
MacDonald, G. Edward, *Canadian Catholic Historical Association - English Section*, 351
MacDonald, Bruce, *Imagine Canada*, 830
Macdonald, Janice, *Dietitians of Canada*, 656

Executive Name Index

MacDonald, Kate, *Ontario Society for the Prevention of Cruelty to Animals*, 1105
MacDonald, Lorin, *Canadian Hard of Hearing Association*, 400
MacDonald, Annie Lee, *Canadian Hard of Hearing Association*, 401
MacDonald, Andrea, *Canadian Association of Importers & Exporters*, 318
MacDonald, Robert, *The Lung Association of Nova Scotia*, 921
MacDonald, Corinne, *Canadian Operational Research Society*, 446
MacDonald, Ernie, *Canadian Picture Pioneers*, 455
MacDonald, Tracy, *International Sanitary Supply Association Canada*, 860
MacDonald, Watson, *Prince Edward Island Ground Water Association*, 1174
Macdonald, Danny, *Association des établissements privés conventionnés - santé services sociaux*, 113
MacDonald, Patty, *Canadian College of Health Leaders*, 359
Macdonald, Greg, *Illuminating Engineering Society of North America*, 1531
MacDonald, Mary, *Association of Commercial & Industrial Contractors of PEI*, 145
MacDonald, Melissa, *College of Physicians & Surgeons of Prince Edward Island*, 588
MacDonald, Mary Susan, *Mensa Canada Society*, 961
MacDonald, Bob, *Mining Society of Nova Scotia*, 967
Macdonald, Jerry, *The College & Association of Registered Nurses of Alberta*, 581
MacDonald, Isaac, *Liberal Party of Prince Edward Island*, 909
Macdonald, Brock, *Recycling Council of British Columbia*, 1208
MacDonald, Melanie, *Society of Graphic Designers of Canada*, 1329
Macdonald, Shelley, *Canadian Hotel Marketing & Sales Executives*, 409
MacDonald, Betty, *Union of Nova Scotia Municipalities*, 1408
MacDonald, Andrea, *United Way of Prince Edward Island*, 1416
MacDonald, Sherry, *Canadian Scholarship Trust Foundation*, 468
MacDonald, Sheila Lund, *Law Foundation of Prince Edward Island*, 901
MacDonald, Troy, *Canada - Nova Scotia Offshore Petroleum Board*, 278
MacDonald, Gail, *Federation of Canadian Electrolysis Associations*, 723
MacDonald, Dawn, *Nova Scotia Recreation Professionals in Health*, 1048
Macdonald, Nathan, *Heritage Society of British Columbia*, 813
Macdonald, Arlene, *Canadian Society for the Study of Religion*, 478
MacDonald, W. Brock, *Canadian Association for the Study of Discourse & Writing*, 306
Macdonald, Ian, *Canadian Professional Sales Association*, 460
MacDonald, Connie, *YWCA Canada*, 1481
MacDonald, Chris, *Maritime Regional CGIT Committee*, 951
MacDonald, Joe, *COSTI Immigrant Services*, 632
MacDonald, Ross, *SportAbility BC*, 1345
MacDonald, Connie, *YWCA of Banff Programs & Services*, 1482
MacDonald, Mary, *World Wildlife Fund - Canada*, 1468
MacDonald, Beverly, *Eastern Veterinary Technician Association*, 671
Macdonald, Meaghan, *Habitat for Humanity Canada*, 797
MacDonald, Mandy, *Manitoba Association of Visual Language Interpreters*, 931
MacDonald, Monica, *Pier 21 Society*, 1159
MacDonald, Cailin, *Pier 21 Society*, 1159
MacDonald, Christina, *BC Rural & Multigrade Teachers' Association*, 202
Macdonald, Laurie, *Vintners Quality Alliance*, 1435
MacDonald, Denise, *Alberta Carriage Driving Association*, 27
MacDonald, Andrea, *Historic Sites Association of Newfoundland & Labrador*, 815
Macdonald, Ian, *Association of Professional Geoscientists of Ontario*, 159
MacDonald, Robin, *Ontario Students Against Impaired Driving*, 1109
MacDonald, Nathan B., *Electronics Product Stewardship Canada*, 684
MacDonald, Kim, *Federation of Medical Regulatory Authorities of Canada*, 724
MacDonald, Ophelia Lynn, *Canadian Association of Physicians with Disabilities*, 327
MacDonald, Chantal, *Bell Aliant Pioneers*, 204
MacDonald, Nancy, *American Saddlebred Horse Association of Ontario*, 67
MacDonald, Mavis, *Miniature Horse Association of Canada*, 966
MacDonald, Corey, *The Metal Working Association of New Brunswick*, 962
MacDonald, Pat, *Canadian Association of Foot Care Nurses*, 315
MacDonald, Susan, *Canadian Society of Palliative Care Physicians*, 486
MacDonald-Dewhirst, Portia, *Canadian Agricultural Human Resource Council*, 289
MacDonell, Glenn, *Special Olympics Ontario*, 1340
MacDonnell, Janet, *The Pharmacy Examining Board of Canada*, 1157
MacDougall, Diane, *Schizophrenia Society of Nova Scotia*, 1284
MacDougall, Camilla, *Athletics New Brunswick*, 181
MacDougall, Lisa, *Prince Edward Island Home & School Federation Inc.*, 1175
MacDougall, Bruce, *Federation of Prince Edward Island Municipalities Inc.*, 726
MacDougall, Patrick, *Jersey Canada*, 869
MacDougall, Bruce, *Digital Nova Scotia*, 656
MacDougall, Susan, *Canadian Connemara Pony Society*, 363
MacDuff, Colin, *Canadian Institute for Theatre Technology*, 414
MacEachern, Morah, *Nova Scotia Physiotherapy Association*, 1047
Macedo, Maria Alice, *La Maison des Açores du Québec*, 926
Macedo, Paul, *Aboriginal Multi-Media Society*, 2
Macedo, Paul, *Council for Advancement of Native Development Officers*, 632
Macerollo, Joseph, *Classical Accordion Society of Canada*, 572
MacEwan, Joan, *Clan MacLeod Societies of Canada*, 572
MacEwen, Todd, *Canadian Home Builders' Association - Prince Edward Island*, 407
MacEwen, Debbie, *Real Estate Institute of Canada*, 1206
MacEwen, Allison, *Canadian Automobile Insurance Rate Regulators Association*, 339
Macey, Anne, *Canadian Organic Growers Inc.*, 447
MacFadden, Gordon, *Saskatchewan Brain Injury Association*, 1260
Macfarland, Jonathan, *Canadian Alliance of British Pensioners*, 291
MacFarlane, Claudia, *Nova Scotia Union of Public & Private Employees (CCU)*, 1050
MacFarlane, John H., *London Health Sciences Foundation*, 918
MacFarlane, Devon, *Canadian Professional Association for Transgender Health*, 460
Macfie, Norman, *The Royal Commonwealth Society of Canada*, 1242
Macfie, Norman, *The Royal Commonwealth Society of Canada*, 1242
MacGillivray, Angus, *Heritage Association of Antigonish*, 812
MacGillivray, Betty, *Canadian Hard of Hearing Association*, 400
MacGillivray, Nancy, *Ontario Association of Children's Aid Societies*, 1062
MacGillivray, Nancy, *Halton Children's Aid Society*, 800
MacGillivray, Cameron, *Enform*, 688
MacGillivray, Chris, *Prince Edward Island Draft Horse Association*, 1173
MacGregor, Ian, *Croquet Canada*, 643
Macgregor, Alex, *International Society of City & Regional Planners*, 1560
MacGregor, Jim, *PFLAG Canada Inc.*, 1155
Machado, José, *La Maison des Açores du Québec*, 926
Machat, Karl, *Audio Engineering Society*, 187
Machell, Catherine, *Sisters of the Child Jesus*, 1301
Macherel Rey, Anne, *Association francophone internationale des directeurs d'établissements scolaires*, 1509
Machniak, Linda, *Battlefords Chamber of Commerce*, 200
Maciejowski, Chris, *Parkinson Society Southwestern Ontario*, 1142
Maciel, Jane, *Canadian Investor Relations Institute*, 422
MacIlwaine, Paula I., *American Water Works Association*, 1504
MacInnes, Karen, *Port Sydney/Utterson & Area Chamber of Commerce*, 1166
MacInnis, Sandra, *Canadian Council on Animal Care*, 371
MacInnis, Breanne, *Ringette PEI*, 1233
MacInnis, Jim, *The Royal Canadian Regiment Association*, 1241
MacInnis, Allen, *Young People's Theatre*, 1475
MacInnis, Roy, *Traditional Archers Association of Nova Scotia*, 1394
MacInnis-Langley, Stephanie, *Nova Scotia Advisory Council on the Status of Women*, 1040
MacIntosh, Clarke, *Royal Academy of Dance Canada*, 1237
MacIntosh, Davin, *Cross Country Canada*, 643
MacIntosh, Clark, *Nova Scotia Public Interest Research Group*, 1047
MacIntosh, Pam, *Horse Trials Nova Scotia*, 822
MacIntosh, Jane, *CADORA Ontario Association Inc.*, 269
MacIntyre, Shannon, *Greater Innisfil Chamber of Commerce*, 783
Macintyre, Dorothy, *Canadian Celiac Association*, 352
MacIntyre, Scott, *NACE International*, 1572
MacIntyre, Dave, *YMCA Canada*, 1472
MacIsaac, Menna, *Heart & Stroke Foundation of Nova Scotia*, 809
MacIsaac, Gary, *Union of British Columbia Municipalities*, 1407
MacIsaac, Shaun, *Legal Archives Society of Alberta*, 906
MacIssac, Ian, *Prince Edward Island Marketing Council*, 1175
MacIver, Don, *Alberta 5 Pin Bowlers' Association*, 21
Mack, Cameron, *Wildlife Habitat Canada*, 1454
Mack, Sheryl, *Athletics Alberta*, 181
Mack, Lis, *Partners FOR the Saskatchewan River Basin*, 1144
MacKay, Kathryn, *Liaison of Independent Filmmakers of Toronto*, 909
MacKay, Sharla, *British Columbia Funeral Association*, 242
Mackay, Davida, *Nova Scotia Real Estate Appraisers Association*, 1048
Mackay, Lori, *Canadian Union of Public Employees*, 498
MacKay, Kelly, *Travel and Tourism Research Association (Canada Chapter)*, 1396
MacKay, Todd, *Canadian Taxpayers Federation*, 493
MacKay, Fergie, *Pictou County Historical Society*, 1159
MacKay, Ian, *Re:Sound Music Licensing Company*, 1204
Mackay, Crystal, *Farm & Food Care Canada*, 705
MacKeen, Heather, *Canadian Society of Hospital Pharmacists*, 484
MacKeigan, Emily, *CanoeKayak Canada*, 509
MacKeigan, Katherine, *Provincial Fitness Unit of Alberta*, 1191
MacKeil, Catherine, *Women's Inter-Church Council of Canada*, 1462
Mackellar, Nicole, *Grain Farmers of Ontario*, 779
Mackenzie, Amy, *Canadian Counselling & Psychotherapy Association*, 372
MacKenzie, Melissa, *Canadian Morgan Horse Association*, 437
MacKenzie, Kent, *Canadian Society for Vascular Surgery*, 479
MacKenzie, Kelly, *Silent Voice Canada Inc.*, 1299
Mackenzie, Ann, *Canadian Professional Sales Association*, 460
Mackenzie, Jay, *Magrath & District Chamber of Commerce*, 925
Mackenzie, Heather, *The Terry Fox Foundation*, 1372
Mackenzie, Murray, *Endurance Riders Association of British Columbia*, 687
MacKenzie, Meagan, *Spinal Cord Injury (Prince Edward Island)*, 1342
MacKenzie, Ruth, *Canadian Association of Gift Planners*, 317
MacKenzie, Erin, *Prince Edward Island Pharmacists Association*, 1176
MacKenzie, Adrianna, *Pathways to Education Canada*, 1145
Mackenzie, Vince, *Maritime Fire Chiefs' Association*, 950
MacKenzie, David, *Truckers Association of Nova Scotia*, 1399
MacKenzie, Mack, *PFLAG Canada Inc.*, 1156
Mackenzie, Cathy, *PFLAG Canada Inc.*, 1155
Mackenzie, Heather, *People First Nova Scotia*, 1151
MacKenzien, Michael, *Canadian Snowbird Association*, 472
Mackey, Jeff, *Canadian Urban Transit Association*, 500
Mackie, Robyn, *Calgary Association of the Deaf*, 271
Mackie, Craig, *Prince Edward Island Association for Newcomers to Canada*, 1172
Mackin, Alan, *Tennis Newfoundland & Labrador*, 1371
MacKinnon, Karen, *Flin Flon & District Chamber of Commerce*, 740
MacKinnon, Jeffrey, *Windsor-Essex Regional Chamber of Commerce*, 1457
MacKinnon, Nancy, *Prince Edward Island Badminton Association*, 1172
MacKinnon, Don, *Better Business Bureau Serving the Atlantic Provinces*, 207
MacKinnon, Kari, *Manitoba Professional Planners Institute*, 942
MacKinnon, Marysa, *Canadian Institute of Traffic & Transportation*, 420
MacKinnon, Barbara, *New Brunswick Lung Association*, 1010
MacKinnon, Rob, *Ontario Ground Water Association*, 1083
MacKinnon, Marilyn, *Learning Disabilities Association of Manitoba*, 904
MacKinnon, Shannon, *Huntington Society of Canada*, 828
MacKinnon, Andrew, *Illuminating Engineering Society of North America*, 1531
MacKinnon, Marie-France, *Consumer Health Products Canada*, 626
MacKinnon, Rick, *Prince Edward Island School Athletic Association*, 1177

Executive Name Index

MacKinnon, Blair, *Prince Edward Island Building & Construction Trades Council*, 1172

MacKinnon, Jim, *London Building & Construction Trades Council*, 918

MacKinnon, Jyl, *Dalhousie Medical Research Foundation*, 648

Mackinnon, Heather, *The Royal Commonwealth Society of Canada*, 1242

MacKinnon, Lynn, *Nature Trust of New Brunswick*, 1001

MacKinnon, Amy, *Paralympic Sports Association (Alberta)*, 1138

MacKinnon, Cindy, *Destination Eastern & Northumberland Shores*, 654

MacKinnon, David, *Steel Structures Education Foundation*, 1349

MacKinnon, Janice, *OmbudService for Life & Health Insurance*, 1057

MacKinnon, Laddie, *Master Bowlers' Association of British Columbia*, 953

Mackison, Bruce, *Collingwood & District Historical Society*, 591

Macklem, Paul, *Government Finance Officers Association of British Columbia*, 778

Macknee, Judy, *Family & Community Support Services Association of Alberta*, 702

Mackneson, Heather, *Central Ontario Developmental Riding Program*, 525

Mackwood, Wayne, *Society of Tribologists & Lubrication Engineers*, 1594

MacLachlan, Ian, *Canadian Association of Geographers*, 316

MacLachlan, Kate, *Association of Professional Engineers & Geoscientists of Saskatchewan*, 159

MacLachlan, James, *College of Physicians & Surgeons of Nova Scotia*, 588

MacLachlan, Michaela, *Central Nova Women's Resource Centre*, 524

MacLaine, Kirsten, *Canadian Music Educators' Association*, 438

MacLaren, Alfred, *Accelerated Christian Education Canada*, 4

MacLauchlan, Wade, *Liberal Party of Prince Edward Island*, 909

MacLauchlan, Sherry, *Concerned Children's Advertisers*, 609

MacLean, Valerie, *British Columbia Apartment Owners & Managers Association*, 230

Maclean, Neil, *Lakeland College Faculty Association*, 896

Maclean, Rosie, *Canadian Association of Foodservice Professionals*, 315

Maclean, J.R., *Canadian Authors Association*, 338

Maclean, Jody, *Canadian Business Aviation Association*, 348

MacLean, Beckie, *Prince Edward Island Humane Society*, 1175

MacLean, David, *Canadian Manufacturers & Exporters*, 429

MacLean, Chuck, *Peel Family Services*, 1148

MacLean, Vanessa, *Risk & Insurance Management Society Inc.*, 1234

MacLean, Brandi, *Resident Doctors of British Columbia*, 1226

MacLean, Dave, *Cornwall Police Association*, 629

MacLean, Sharon, *Oshawa & District Coin Club*, 1127

MacLean, Neil, *Canadian Captive Insurance Association*, 350

MacLean, Richard, *Football Nova Scotia Association*, 750

MacLean, Debra-Ann, *TOPS Club, Inc.*, 1598

MacLean, Barb, *Family Caregivers of British Columbia*, 702

Maclean, Deb, *Snowboard Nova Scotia*, 1305

MacLean, Donna, *Inverness Cottage Workshop*, 862

MacLean, Karen, *Nova Scotia Amateur Bodybuilding Association*, 1040

MacLean, Ron, *Prince Edward Island Police Association*, 1176

MacLean, Donnie, *People First Nova Scotia*, 1151

MacLean-Evans, Leah, *Saskatchewan Writers Guild*, 1278

MacLellan, Nate, *Judo Alberta*, 876

MacLennan, John, *Union of National Defence Employees*, 1407

MacLennan, Lynne, *Atlantic Standardbred Breeders Association*, 186

MacLennan, Dan, *Alberta Construction Safety Association*, 31

MacLennan, Lynne, *Atlantic Standardbred Breeders Association*, 186

MacLeod, Peggy, *Middle River & Area Historical Society*, 964

MacLeod, Flora, *The John Howard Society of Nova Scotia*, 874

MacLeod, Diane, *Boys & Girls Clubs of Ontario*, 223

MacLeod, J. William, *The Scots*, 1286

MacLeod, Ida, *Manitoba Cooperative Honey Producers Ltd.*, 934

MacLeod, Beverly, *Association of Consulting Engineering Companies - Saskatchewan*, 146

MacLeod, Alison, *Association of Professional Engineers & Geoscientists of British Columbia*, 158

MacLeod, Katherine, *Engineers Nova Scotia*, 689

MacLeod, Christy, *Canadian Home Builders' Association - British Columbia*, 407

MacLeod, Lynne, *Canadian Mountain Arts Foundation*, 437

MacLeod, Don, *Huronia Symphony Orchestra*, 828

MacLeod, A. Donald, *Canadian Society of Presbyterian History*, 487

MacLeod, Ray, *Association of Prince Edward Island Libraries*, 156

Macleod, Frances, *AIDS Coalition of Cape Breton*, 15

MacLeod, Lisa, *Burin Peninsula Chamber of Commerce*, 265

MacLeod, Foster, *Police Martial Arts Association Inc.*, 1163

MacLeod, Norman, *Clean Air Strategic Alliance*, 573

MacLeod, Cedric, *New Brunswick Cattle Producers*, 1006

Macleod, Marg, *Digital Imaging Association*, 656

MacLeod, Bryan, *Clean Energy British Columbia*, 573

MacLeod, Tawna, *Skills/Compétences Canada*, 1303

MacLeod, Bonnie, *Bear River Historical Society*, 203

MacLeod, Hugh, *Canadian Patient Safety Institute*, 452

MacLeod, John, *Ontario Disc Sports Association*, 1077

MacMackin, Bill, *Athletics New Brunswick*, 181

MacMillan, Don, *Oxfam Canada*, 1134

MacMillan, Lorna, *Saskatchewan Physiotherapy Association*, 1272

MacMillan, Ian, *National Association of Computer Consulting Business (Canada)*, 990

MacMillan-Murphy, James P., *Canadian Association of Veterans in United Nations Peacekeeping*, 336

MacMullin, Craig, *Centre for Entrepreneurship Education & Development Inc.*, 532

Macnab, Elizabeth, *Ontario Society of Senior Citizens' Organizations*, 1108

Macnab, Catherine, *Planned Parenthood Ottawa*, 1162

MacNeil, Maureen, *Association of Parent Support Groups in Ontario Inc.*, 155

MacNeil, Paula Eileen, *Association of Fundraising Professionals*, 1512

MacNeill, Ron, *Prince Edward Island Golf Association*, 1174

MacNeill, Eric, *British Columbia Culinary Arts Specialist Association*, 238

MacNevin, Darren, *Darts Prince Edward Island*, 651

MacNutt, Catherine, *Canadian Association of Exposition Management*, 313

Maconachie, Tracey, *Life Science Association of Manitoba*, 911

Macoun, Jeff, *London Chamber of Commerce*, 918

MacPhail, Linda, *Alberta Sports & Recreation Association for the Blind*, 48

MacPhail, Don, *Saint John Naturalists' Club*, 1247

MacPhail, John, *Yukon Soccer Association*, 1480

MacPhail, Mark, *Nova Scotia Arm Wrestling Association*, 1040

MacPhail, Victoria, *Pollination Guelph*, 1164

MacPhee, Janet, *Canadian AIDS Society*, 290

MacPhee, Richard, *The Brothers of the Good Shepherd*, 260

MacPherson, Lindsay, *Music BC Industry Association*, 983

MacPherson, Natalie, *Nova Scotia Government Libraries Council*, 1045

MacPherson, Daryl, *The Wesleyan Church of Canada - Central Canada District*, 1447

MacPherson, Sandra, *Glace Bay Food Bank Society*, 774

MacPherson, Brian, *Commonwealth Games Canada*, 594

MacPherson, Grant, *Construction Association of Prince Edward Island*, 623

Macpherson, Gord, *Electrical Association of Manitoba Inc.*, 682

MacPherson, Chad, *Saskatchewan Stock Growers Association*, 1276

MacPherson, Ian, *Prince Edward Island Fishermen's Association Ltd.*, 1174

MacPherson, George, *Shipyard General Workers' Federation of British Columbia*, 1296

MacPherson, Donald, *Canadian Drug Policy Coalition*, 379

MacPherson, Paige, *Canadian Taxpayers Federation*, 493

MacPherson, Doug, *Congress of Union Retirees Canada*, 613

MacPherson, Doug, *Steelworkers Organization of Active Retirees*, 1349

MacPherson, Phyllis, *Lake Country Food Assistance Society*, 896

MacQuarrie, Patricia, *The Writers' Guild of Alberta*, 1469

Macrae, Barb, *Learning Disabilities Association of Yukon Territory*, 905

MacRae, Erin, *Jean Tweed Treatment Centre*, 869

Macrae, Findlay, *Acadia Entrepreneurship Centre*, 4

MacTavish, John, *HIV/AIDS Regional Services*, 817

MacTavish, Jennifer, *Ontario Sheep Marketing Agency*, 1104

MacVicar, Wes, *Foundation for Education Perth Huron*, 755

MacWilliams, Kelly, *Prince Edward Island Association of Social Workers*, 1172

Madahbee, Patrick, *Union of Ontario Indians*, 1408

Madan, Emmanuel, *Independent Media Arts Alliance*, 833

Madara, James L., *American Medical Association*, 1495

Madden, Andrea, *Maple Ridge Pitt Meadows Chamber of Commerce*, 949

Madden, Signy, *United Way Central & Northern Vancouver Island*, 1413

Madden, Sean, *Ontario Undergraduate Student Alliance*, 1111

Madden, Michael, *Alexandria & District Chamber of Commerce*, 53

Madder, Bill, *Association of Saskatchewan Realtors*, 161

Maddigan, Matilda, *Petroleum Research Newfoundland & Labrador*, 1154

Madeira, Mike, *West Elgin Chamber of Commerce*, 1445

Madeley, Mary-Ellen, *Greater Innisfil Chamber of Commerce*, 783

Mader, Randy, *Canadian Simmental Association*, 470

Mader, Marianne, *Maker Kids*, 927

Maderer, Roni, *Na'amat Canada Inc.*, 987

Madore, Nathalie, *Club de photographie L'Oeil qui voit de Saint-Hubert*, 575

Madrigga, Michelle, *British Columbia Association of Insolvency & Restructuring Professionals*, 232

Madryga, Jack, *Kamloops Wildlife Park Society*, 881

Madsen, Carol, *Parent Support Services Society of BC*, 1139

Madsen, Christopher, *Canadian Nautical Research Society*, 440

Madsen, MaryAnne, *British Columbia Tenpin Bowling Association*, 256

Maeda, Kenji, *Greater Vancouver Professional Theatre Alliance*, 787

Maeder, Chris, *Business Professional Association of Canada*, 267

Maekawan, Takaaki, *International Commission of Agricultural & Biosystems Engineering*, 1542

Maendel, Jake, *Manitoba Beekeepers' Association*, 932

Maeren, Mandy, *Canadian Rental Association*, 467

Magalas, Mel, *Lyndhurst Seeleys Bay & District Chamber of Commerce*, 923

Magalhaes, Connie, *Little People of Manitoba*, 915

MaGarrey, Tim, *Ontario Amateur Wrestling Association*, 1059

Magee, Eugene, *Sydney & Louisbourg Railway Historical Society*, 1360

Mager, Michael R., *CAA Manitoba*, 268

Maggrah, Brad, *Ontario Coalition of Aboriginal Peoples*, 1071

Maggs, Derek, *The Friends of Bon Echo Park*, 760

Magidson, Stan, *Institute of Corporate Directors*, 845

Magidson, Stan, *Alberta Securities Commission*, 46

Magjarevic, Ratko, *International Federation for Medical & Biological Engineering*, 1547

Maglione, Julio C., *International Amateur Swimming Federation*, 1535

Maglione, Julio Cesar, *Pan American Sports Organization*, 1582

Magnan, Paul, *Manitoba Lacrosse Association*, 939

Magnanensi, Giorgio, *Vancouver New Music*, 1428

Magnus, Brian K., *The United Brethren Church in Canada*, 1409

Magnuson, Ruth, *Manitoba Interfaith Welcome Place*, 939

Magnuson-Ford, Erika, *Terrace & District Chamber of Commerce*, 1371

Maguire, Sheila, *Lytton & District Chamber of Commerce*, 923

Maguire, Gail, *Credit Institute of Canada*, 641

Maguire, Mike, *Lifesaving Society*, 911

Maguire, Molly, *Playwrights' Workshop Montréal*, 1162

Maguire, Catherine, *CADORA Ontario Association Inc.*, 269

Maguire MacKnight, Charlene, *Big Brothers Big Sisters of New Brunswick*, 209

Magyarody, Tom, *Ontario Medical Association*, 1090

Mah, Herman, *Downtown Vancouver Association*, 662

Mah, Randall, *Wycliffe Bible Translators of Canada, Inc.*, 1470

Mah, Emmay, *Dignitas International*, 657

Executive Name Index

Mah, Andy, *Nordic Combined Ski Canada*, 1028
Mahanna, Mike, *National Association for Environmental Management*, 1572
Mahar, Shari, *Community Integration Services Society*, 599
Maharaj, Varoun, *Canadian Tamil Youth Development Centre*, 492
Mahboob, Sana, *Association of Fundraising Professionals*, 1512
Mahdian, Parisa, *Professional Engineers Ontario*, 1184
Mahdy, Medhat, *YMCA Canada*, 1472
Mahendramohan, Sagaana, *Canadian Tamil Professionals Association*, 492
Maher, Kathy, *Canadian Public Relations Society Inc.*, 463
Maheu, John, *Association of Ontario Road Supervisors*, 155
Maheu, André, *Association québécoise de la gestion parasitaire*, 170
Maheux, Daniel L., *Canadian Postmasters & Assistants Association*, 458
Mahfoudhi, Omar, *Islamic Care Centre*, 864
Mahlman, Melanie, *Victoria Hospitals Foundation*, 1432
Mahmood, Nasir, *Muslim Association of New Brunswick*, 985
Mahon, Paul, *Canadian Life & Health Insurance Association Inc.*, 426
Mahon, Kate, *Trauma Association of Canada*, 1396
Mahon, Sandy, *Funeral & Cremation Services Council of Saskatchewan*, 764
Mahoney, Patrick, *Canadian Lawyers Insurance Association*, 426
Mahoney, Anne Louise, *Editors' Association of Canada*, 674
Maidment, Michael, *Ottawa Food Bank*, 1130
Maidment, Glenn, *Tire and Rubber Association of Canada*, 1380
Maidment, Kennedie, *Canadian Nursing Students' Association*, 443
Maidment, Glenn, *Tire Stewardship BC Association*, 1380
Maier, Lenore, *PAVED Arts*, 1146
Maier, Dionne, *Churchill Park Family Care Society*, 569
Maier, Martin, *American Concrete Institute*, 1492
Mailer, Allison, *British Columbia Sports Hall of Fame & Museum*, 255
Mailhot, Alain, *Association des restaurateurs du Québec*, 127
Mailhot, Monique, *Opération Nez rouge*, 1116
Maillé, Nathalie, *Conseil des arts de Montréal*, 617
Maillet, Roxanne, *Greater Moncton Real Estate Board Inc.*, 784
Maillet, Jacques, *Focolare Movement - Canada*, 741
Mailloux, Jacques S., *Canadian Association for Photographic Art*, 303
Mailloux, Jean-Marc, *Société d'histoire et de généalogie Maria-Chapdelaine*, 1313
Main, Tim, *Canadian Institute of Plumbing & Heating*, 418
Main, David, *BIOTECanada*, 212
Mainella, Monique, *Society for the Promotion of the Teaching of English as a Second Language in Quebec*, 1327
Mainguy, Louise, *La Société historique du Cap-Rouge*, 1321
Mains, Howard, *Association of Equipment Manufacturers - Canada*, 148
Mainville, Kenn, *Association of Fundraising Professionals*, 1512
Mair, Heather, *Canadian Association for Leisure Studies*, 302
Mair, Aaron, *Sierra Club*, 1589
Maira, Arun, *HelpAge International*, 1529
Mairs, Lil, *Douglas College Faculty Association*, 661
Maisonneuve, Éric, *Réseau Hommes Québec*, 1224

Maitland, Karen, *Ecological Farmers of Ontario*, 672
Maitland, Leslie, *Heritage Ottawa*, 813
Maitland Muir, Cheryl, *Business Council of British Columbia*, 266
Majek, Stephen, *Association of Alberta Agricultural Fieldmen*, 139
Majewski, Cathy, *Red Lake District Chamber of Commerce*, 1210
Majkic, Sandra, *Transportation Association of Canada*, 1395
Major, Jacques, *Out-of-Home Marketing Association of Canada*, 1133
Mak, Shirley, *Asia-Pacific Centre for Environmental Law*, 1506
Makanjuola, Ayo D., *Black Business Initiative*, 213
Mäkelä, Markku, *International Peat Society*, 1555
Maki, Lynn, *United Church of Canada*, 1409
Maki, Tina, *Association of Professional Engineers & Geoscientists of Saskatchewan*, 159
Makin, Lisa, *Fort Saskatchewan Chamber of Commerce*, 754
Makkar, Sanjay, *Indo-Canada Chamber of Commerce*, 835
Makowski, Ann, *Society for Environmental Graphic Design*, 1590
Makrides, Carl, *Canada - Nova Scotia Offshore Petroleum Board*, 278
Maks, Amanda, *Greater Montreal Athletic Association*, 784
Malacket, Andréanne, *Association du jeune barreau de Montréal*, 131
Malakoe, Garth, *Northwest Territories Association of Provincial Court Judges*, 1037
Malange, Ramsay, *British Columbia Association of Family Resource Programs*, 231
Malboeuf, Myra, *Ile-a-la-Crosse Friendship Centre Inc.*, 829
Malbon, Neil, *Alberni Valley Chamber of Commerce*, 21
Malcolm, Brenda, *Girl Guides of Canada*, 773
Malcolm, Luke, *Canadian Security Association*, 469
Malcolm, Claire, *Heaven Can Wait Equine Rescue*, 810
Malcolmson, Kelly, *Manitoba Rowing Association*, 943
Malcomson, Peter, *Ontario Tennis Association*, 1110
Malden, Cheryl, *American Library Association*, 1494
Male, Peter, *Pacific National Exhibition*, 1135
Malek, Allan H., *Ontario Pharmacists' Association*, 1095
Malenfant, Karine, *Chambre de commerce de la MRC de Rivière-du-Loup*, 542
Malépart, Pierrette, *Centre d'information communautaire et de dépannage Ste-Marie*, 528
Malette, Cathi, *Canadian Association of Wireless Internet Service Providers*, 336
Malfatti, Giulio, *York University Staff Association*, 1474
Malhotra, Anju, *Association for Financial Professionals - Ottawa*, 133
Malik, Naeem, *Ottawa Muslim Association*, 1131
Malik, Daniel, *Toronto Financial Services Alliance*, 1384
Malik, Ausma, *Atkinson Charitable Foundation*, 182
Malik, Farah, *Atkinson Charitable Foundation*, 182
Malisani, Debbie, *Provincial Women's Softball Association of Ontario*, 1191
Malixi, Lita, *Magnificat Charismatic Prayer Community*, 925
Malkhassian, Seta, *Armenian Relief Society of Canada, Inc.*, 83
Malkiewicz, Joanna, *Canadian Association for Young Children*, 307

Malkin, Helen, *The Montréal Holocaust Memorial Centre*, 972
Malkin, Albert, *Ontario Association for Behaviour Analysis*, 1061
Malkoske, Jessica, *Crossreach Adult Day Centre*, 644
Malkowski, Gary, *Canadian Hearing Society*, 403
Mall, Sohail, *College of Chiropodists of Ontario*, 583
Mallari, Marlo, *National Council of Philippine American Canadian Accountants*, 1575
Mallet, Michel, *Canadian Association of University Teachers of German*, 335
Mallet, Lisette, *La Société d'histoire de Toronto*, 1312
Mallett, Ken, *Nova Scotia Prospectors Association*, 1047
Mallette, Judy, *Community Living South Huron*, 605
Mallette, Sylvie, *Association sectorielle services automobiles*, 178
Mallette, Michel, *Association Québécoise des Loisirs Folkloriques*, 173
Malley, Fred, *Canadian Culinary Federation*, 374
Malley, Terry, *New Brunswick Aerospace & Defence Association*, 1004
Malli, Nicky, *Applied Science Technologists & Technicians of British Columbia*, 74
Mallin, Jayne, *Rexdale Community Legal Services*, 1229
Mallin, Barry, *Manitoba Association of School Psychologists Inc.*, 931
Mallinson, Michael, *Ontario Spondylitis Association*, 1108
Mallon, Kevin, *Orchestra Toronto*, 1117
Mallory, Bill, *Atlantic Salmon Federation*, 186
Mallory, Connie, *Ontario Society for the Prevention of Cruelty to Animals*, 1105
Mallove, Cathy, *Ontario Prader-Willi Syndrome Association*, 1097
Malmas, Shamin, *Archives Society of Alberta*, 81
Malo, José, *Association québécoise de sports pour paralytiques cérébraux*, 171
Malone, Judi, *Psychologists Association of Alberta*, 1192
Malone, Dan, *Foster Parent Support Services Society*, 755
Malone, Tom, *Medical Group Management Association of Canada*, 958
Maloney, Samantha, *Canadian Celiac Association*, 352
Maloney, Lana, *Alberta Construction Association*, 31
Maloney, Joseph, *International Brotherhood of Boilermakers, Iron Ship Builders, Blacksmiths, Forgers & Helpers (AFL-CIO)*, 1541
Maloney, Elaine L., *Canadian Circumpolar Institute*, 357
Malottke, Brenda, *American Society for Bone & Mineral Research*, 1498
Maltais, Éric, *Association des employés de l'Université de Moncton*, 112
Maltais, Valérie, *Association de la Rivière Ste-Marguerite Inc.*, 102
Maltman, Brian, *General Insurance OmbudService*, 769
Malvea, Samuel, *India Rainbow Community Services of Peel*, 834
Malzer, Jen, *Canadian Institute of Transportation Engineers*, 420
Mamane, Joelle, *Jewish Community Foundation of Montréal*, 871
Mammel, Suzanne, *Ontario Home Builders' Association*, 1085
Manarin, Karen, *Villa Charities Inc. (Toronto District)*, 1435
Manastyrsky, Peter, *Manitoba Riding for the Disabled Association Inc.*, 943
Manchon, Augustin, *Strategic Leadership Forum*, 1351

Manchul, Kristy, *Canadian Society of Exploration Geophysicists*, 483
Mancinelli, Joseph S., *Laborers' International Union of North America (AFL-CIO/CLC)*, 1569
Mancini, Cathy, *Canadian Association of Gastroenterology*, 316
Mancini, Anthony, *Atlantic Episcopal Assembly*, 184
Mander, Lisa, *Horse Council British Columbia*, 822
Mandziuk, Steven, *Canadian Bar Association*, 341
Mandziuk, Glenn, *Thompson Okanagan Tourism Association*, 1376
Manery, Sue, *Southern Alberta Community Living Association*, 1337
Manglapus, Adonis, *Canadian Society of Ophthalmic Registered Nurses*, 485
Manguian Chahinian, Lucy, *Armenian Relief Society of Canada, Inc.*, 83
Manhas, Rosie, *Vancouver Island Construction Association*, 1426
Manhussier, Gloria, *Canadian Association for Williams Syndrome*, 307
Mani, Mahesh, *Children's Hospital of Eastern Ontario Foundation*, 562
Maniate, Matthew, *Child Evangelism Fellowship of Canada*, 559
Manibal, Jean François, *Tennis Québec*, 1371
Manji, Nimet, *Ontario Heritage Trust*, 1084
Manki, Salman, *CAA British Columbia*, 267
Mankis, Larissa, *Rugby Ontario*, 1244
Mankow, Ethel, *Tennessee Walking Horse Association of Western Canada*, 1370
Manley, Dustin, *Canadian Public Relations Society Inc.*, 463
Manley, John, *Business Council of Canada*, 267
Mann, John W., *FPInnovations*, 757
Mann, Linda, *Mount Saint Vincent University Faculty Association*, 976
Mann, Kevin, *American Water Works Association*, 1504
Mann, Kelly, *BC Games Society*, 201
Mann, Doug, *Saskatchewan Hereford Association*, 1267
Mann, Ann, *College of Licensed Practical Nurses of Nova Scotia*, 585
Mann, Richard, *Canadian Society for the Study of Religion*, 478
Mann, Amanda, *Pharmacy Technician Society of Alberta*, 1157
Mann, Debbie, *Festivals & Events Ontario*, 733
Mann, James, *Farmers of North America*, 705
Manness, Garth, *Credit Union Central of Manitoba*, 641
Manness, Kathy, *Strathroy & District Chamber of Commerce*, 1352
Manness, Jessica, *Distance Riders of Manitoba Association*, 658
Manning, Jimmy, *Inuit Art Foundation*, 862
Manning, Genevieve, *Sail Canada*, 1246
Manning, Roger, *Immigrant Services - Guelph Wellington*, 830
Manning, Lee, *Manitoba Association of Health Care Professionals*, 930
Manning, Laurissa, *Black Business Initiative*, 213
Manningham, Robert, *Atelier habitation Montréal*, 180
Manns, Braden, *Canadian Society of Nephrology*, 485
Manns, Robert L., *Canadian Association of Veterans in United Nations Peacekeeping*, 335
Manocchio, Nick, *Villa Charities Inc. (Toronto District)*, 1435
Manoka, Zina, *Association de la fibromyalgie de la Montérégie*, 101
Manola, Evelina, *IMCS Pax Romana*, 1531
Manookian, Berge, *Tekeyan Armenian Cultural Association*, 1369
Manoosingh, Rawle, *Manitoba Cricket Association*, 935

Executive Name Index

Manoukian, Nathalie, *Armenian Relief Society of Canada, Inc.*, 83
Manovil, Rafael, *International Nuclear Law Association*, 1553
Mansell, Tracy, *Kerry's Place Autism Services*, 884
Manset, Nadine, *Canadian Astronomical Society*, 337
Mansfield, Nancy, *Bide Awhile Animal Shelter Society*, 209
Manson, Anne, *Manitoba Chamber Orchestra*, 933
Manson, Alan, *Institute of Space & Atmospheric Studies*, 847
Manson, Rob, *Football Nova Scotia Association*, 750
Manson, Larry, *Rideau Environmental Action League*, 1231
Manson, Jeff, *Nunavut Securities Office*, 1051
Mansoory, Shahzad, *British Columbia Muslim Association*, 247
Manteuffel, Sarah, *Ontario Association of Landscape Architects*, 1064
Mantha, Robert, *Canadian Federation of Business School Deans*, 386
Mantha, John, *Association of Prince Edward Island Land Surveyors*, 156
Mantha, Luc, *Pathways to Education Canada*, 1145
Manthorne, Jackie, *Canadian Cancer Survivor Network*, 349
Mantle, Brenda, *Missing Children Society of Canada*, 968
Manton, Danielle, *Association des juristes d'expression française de l'Ontario*, 117
Mantovani, Diego, *Canadian Biomaterials Society*, 344
Manuel, Leslie, *Canadian Society of Hospital Pharmacists*, 484
Manuel, Jackie, *Newfoundland & Labrador Construction Safety Association*, 1018
Manuge, Lana, *Canadian Culinary Federation*, 374
Manz, Deb, *Alberta College & Association of Chiropractors*, 28
Manz, Liane, *Canadian Association of Critical Care Nurses*, 311
Manzer, Audrey, *Federation for Scottish Culture in Nova Scotia*, 721
Manzini, Lisa, *Physical Education in British Columbia*, 1158
Manzoor Ahmed, Rana, *Ahmadiyya Muslim Jama'at Canada*, 15
Mapara, Amy, *Canadian Red Cross*, 466
Mar, Darryl, *Victoria Jazz Society*, 1433
Maracle, Mae, *Aboriginal Tourism Association of Southern Ontario*, 2
Maracle, Ken, *Jake Thomas Learning Centre*, 867
Marage, Jade, *Meeting Professionals International*, 1571
Marah, Braye, *Harbourfront Centre*, 803
Maramieri, Anthoney, *Alberta Insurance Council*, 38
Maranda, Marg, *New Brunswick Curling Association*, 1007
Maranda, Erin, *Fitness New Brunswick*, 740
Maranda, Bruno, *Association des médecins généticiens du Québec*, 119
Marasigan, Jaime, *Block Rosary Group of Ontario*, 215
Marble, Allan, *Genealogical Association of Nova Scotia*, 15
Marble, Allen, *Genealogical Institute of The Maritimes*, 768
Marburg, Jerome, *College of Dental Surgeons of British Columbia*, 583
Marceau, Jean-François, *Judo-Québec inc*, 877
Marceau, Christiane, *Ottawa Carleton Ultimate Association*, 1129
Marceau, Bruno, *Chorale Les Voix de la Vallée du Cuivre de Chibougamau inc.*, 566
Marcel, Dumais, *Société catholique de la Bible*, 1309

Marcelino, Erin, *Credit Institute of Canada*, 641
Marcell, Dale, *British Columbia Refederation Party*, 250
March, Michael, *Renfrew County Law Association*, 1217
March-McCuish, Faith, *United Church of Canada*, 1409
Marchand, Raylene, *H.R. MacMillan Space Centre Society*, 824
Marchand, Matt, *Windsor-Essex Regional Chamber of Commerce*, 1457
Marchand, Raynard, *Canada Safety Council*, 280
Marchand, Claire, *Canadian Music Centre*, 438
Marchand, André, *Corporation des bijoutiers du Québec*, 629
Marchand, Bruno, *Centraide Québec*, 523
Marchand, Jason, *Northern Ontario Hockey Association*, 1035
Marchand, Jacques, *Orchestre symphonique régional Abitibi-Témiscamingue*, 1119
Marchand, Lori, *Western Canada Theatre Company Society*, 1448
Marchand, Chantal, *Association des gestionnaires des établissements de santé et des services sociaux*, 115
Marchand, Linda, *Association patronale des entreprises en construction du Québec*, 165
Marchand, Linda, *Association provinciale des constructeurs d'habitations du Québec inc.*, 168
Marchand, Valerie, *Canadian Nutrition Society*, 444
Marchand, Gael, *Yukon Aboriginal Sport Circle*, 1476
Marchand, Dawn, *Canadian Bar Insurance Association*, 342
Marchanfd, Gaël, *Aikido Yukon Association*, 18
Marchant-Short, Sheila, *Association of Registered Nurses of Prince Edward Island*, 161
Marchi, Sergio, *Canadian Electricity Association*, 380
Marchildon, Gilles, *Reflet Salvéo*, 1210
Marcil, Mathieu, *Association des professionnels des arts de la scène du Québec*, 125
Marcil, Daniel, *Handball Association of Nova Scotia*, 802
Marcolongo, Tullia, *International Association for Medical Assistance to Travellers*, 853
Marconato, Vince, *St. Leonard's Society of Canada*, 1250
Marcos, M.A., *The Coptic Orthodox Church (Canada)*, 628
Marcotte, Viviane, *Canadian Property Tax Association, Inc.*, 461
Marcotte, Louis, *Financial Executives International Canada*, 736
Marcotte, François, *Canadian Amateur Musicians*, 92
Marcotte, Suzanne, *Société d'histoire de la Rivière du Nord inc.*, 1310
Marcotullio, Tracy, *Oromocto & Area SPCA*, 1127
Marcoux, Sylvie, *Association québécoise des salons du livre*, 174
Marcoux, Marie-Hélène, *Association québécoise des professeures de français*, 174
Marcoux, Louis-Etienne, *Canadian Orthoptic Council*, 448
Marcoux, Yves, *Conseil régional FTQ Québec et Chaudière-Appalaches*, 621
Marcoux, Lise, *Ontario Brain Injury Association*, 1069
Marcucci, Waldy, *Little Faces of Panama Association*, 915
Marculescu, Cornel, *International Amateur Swimming Federation*, 1535
Marcus, Paul, *Association of Independent Consultants*, 149
Marcus, Esther, *London Jewish Federation*, 918
Marentette, Elise, *Human Resources Professionals Association*, 825

Marget, Laurence, *Groupe de recherche en animation et planification économique*, 791
Margets, Juan, *International Tennis Federation*, 1562
Margie, Lewis, *Newfoundland & Labrador Laubach Literacy Council*, 1019
Margolin, David A., *American Society of Colon & Rectal Surgeons*, 1499
Maria, Lepage, *Alliance des femmes de la francophonie canadienne*, 56
Maria, Salvati, *Adult Literacy Council of Greater Fort Erie*, 9
Mariash, Christa, *Folklorama*, 742
Marien, Rémi, *Conseil jeunesse francophone de la Colombie-Britannique*, 618
Marimuthu, Perm, *Association of Canadian Film Craftspeople*, 142
Marin, Marc, *College of Veterinarians of Ontario*, 590
Marin, Richard, *Réseau des SADC et CAE*, 1220
Marin, Ronald, *Fédération des Associations et Corporations en Construction du Québec*, 712
Marincola, John, *Society for Classical Studies*, 1589
Marineau, Dennis, *Alberta Bobsleigh Association*, 26
Marinho, Raquel, *Canadian Team Handball Federation*, 493
Marining, Rod, *British Columbia Environmental Network*, 240
Marino, Ron, *Upper Canada District Canadian Horse Breeders*, 1422
Marinoske, Sonja, *Western Canadian Miniature Horse Club*, 1448
Marinovich, John, *Bay of Quinte Dental Society*, 200
Marion, Giselle, *Northwest Territories Archives Council*, 1037
Marion, Julie, *Canadian Heritage Information Network*, 405
Marion, Mathieu, *Canadian Philosophical Association*, 454
Marion, Rick, *Royal Astronomical Society of Canada*, 1239
Marion, Gail, *Pembroke Symphony Orchestra*, 1149
Marion, Kelly, *Vancouver Island Construction Association*, 1426
Marion, Lisa, *Kingston & District Labour Council*, 888
Marit, Ina, *Saskatchewan Association of Rural Municipalities*, 1258
Marjanac, Jovan, *Serbian Orthodox Church - Orthodox Diocese of Canada*, 1290
Mark-Eng, Karline, *Western Forestry Contractors Association*, 1449
Mark-Eng, Karline, *Association of Fundraising Professionals*, 1512
Markarian, Michael, *The Humane Society of the United States*, 1530
Markens, Ben, *Paperboard Packaging Council*, 1582
Markens, Jennie, *Paperboard Packaging Council*, 1582
Markes, Hope, *Kiwanis International (Eastern Canada & the Caribbean District)*, 892
Market, Helmut, *Canadian Culinary Federation*, 374
Markham, Chris, *Ontario Physical & Health Education Association*, 1095
Markham, J. David, *International Napoleonic Society*, 858
Markin, Patricia, *Peace-Laird Regional Arts Council*, 1147
Markle, Kerri, *Canadian Heavy Oil Association*, 404
Markotic, Lorraine, *Canadian Society for Continental Philosophy*, 474
Markowitz, Robin, *Lymphoma Canada*, 923
Markowski, Mike, *Saskatchewan Archaeological Society*, 1256
Marks, Joanna, *Financial Fitness Centre*, 737

Marks, Linda, *Nova Scotian Institute of Science*, 1050
Marks, Raissa, *New Brunswick Environmental Network*, 1008
Marks, Scott, *International Association of Fire Fighters (AFL-CIO/CLC)*, 1538
Markus, Elizabeth, *Richmond Orchid Club*, 1231
Marleau, Lynne, *Canadian College of Health Leaders*, 359
Marler, Dave, *Canadian Football Hall of Fame & Museum*, 392
Marles, Roger, *Hispanic Canadian Arts & Culture Association*, 815
Marlier, Thierry, *Meeting Professionals International*, 1571
Marling, Dwayne, *Prairie Theatre Exchange*, 1170
Marling, Shauna, *Skate Canada*, 1301
Marling, Dwayne, *Restaurants Canada*, 1227
Marmei, Jana, *Association of Independent Corrugated Converters*, 149
Marmer, Max, *United Synagogue Youth*, 1412
Marois, Alain, *Alliance des professeures et professeurs de Montréal*, 56
Marois Blanchet, Catherine, *Fédération de cheerleading du Québec*, 708
Marolla, Carmen, *British Columbia Paralegal Association*, 248
Marquis, Robert, *Geological Association of Canada*, 770
Marquis, Dominique, *Société canadienne d'histoire de l'Église Catholique - Section française*, 1307
Marquis, Dominique, *Institut d'histoire de l'Amérique française*, 841
Marquis, Gilbert, *Fédération de l'UPA - Bas-Saint-Laurent*, 709
Marquis, Pierre, *National Electricity Roundtable*, 993
Marr, Jean, *Houston Chamber of Commerce*, 824
Marr, Lucille, *Canadian Society of Church History*, 481
Marrero, Ric, *Association of Canadian Pension Management*, 143
Marriner, Sunny, *Ottawa Rape Crisis Centre*, 1131
Marriott, Cathy, *Alberta Genealogical Society*, 36
Marsden, Sandra, *Canadian Sugar Institute*, 491
Marsh, Ina, *Clarenville Area Chamber of Commerce*, 572
Marsh, Lois, *Canadian Public Relations Society Inc.*, 463
Marsh, Kevin, *Royal College of Dental Surgeons of Ontario*, 1241
Marsh, Glenda, *College of Pharmacists of Manitoba*, 587
Marsh, Marcia, *World Wildlife Fund - USA*, 1608
Marsh, Jennie, *Ontario Skeet Shooting Association*, 1104
Marsh, Maggie, *Sargeant Bay Society*, 1253
Marsh, Lois, *Canadian Steel Door Manufacturers Association*, 491
Marsh, Lois, *Canadian Centre for Ethics & Corporate Policy*, 353
Marsh, Mike, *Nova Scotia Construction Sector Council - Industrial-Commercial-Institutional*, 1043
Marshall, J., *Coronach Community Chamber of Commerce*, 629
Marshall, Kelly, *Summerland Chamber of Commerce*, 1354
Marshall, Candy, *Prince Albert & District Association of Realtors*, 1171
Marshall, Joe B., *Union of Nova Scotia Indians*, 1407
Marshall, John, *York Pioneer & Historical Society*, 1473
Marshall, Dennis, *Canadian Adventist Teachers Network*, 288

Executive Name Index

Marshall, Anne, *Canadian Feed The Children*, 389
Marshall, Carolyn, *Nova Scotia Hospice Palliative Care Association*, 1046
Marshall, Steve, *Canadian Printing Ink Manufacturers' Association*, 460
Marshall, Roy, *Ontario Brain Injury Association*, 1069
Marshall, Mike, *Alberta Amateur Speed Skating Association*, 22
Marshall, Sarah, *Ontario Tender Fruit Producers Marketing Board*, 1110
Marshall, Thomas, *Community Social Services Employers' Association*, 607
Marshall, David, *Fraser Basin Council*, 757
Marshall, Ian, *Vancouver Consultants*, 1425
Marsman-Murphy, Veronica, *Nova Scotia Association of Black Social Workers*, 1041
Martel, Alayne, *Ringette Canada*, 1233
Martel, Nathalie, *Ordre des ingénieurs du Québec*, 1122
Martel, Manon, *Association of Canadian Travel Agents - Québec*, 144
Martel, Claude, *Sierra Club of Canada*, 1298
Martel, Guy, *Centre de formation en entreprise et récupération Normand-Maurice*, 529
Martel, Émile, *Académie des lettres du Québec*, 3
Martel, Nicole, *Association québécoise des technologies*, 175
Martel, Maryse, *Association du syndrome de Down de L'Estrie*, 131
Martel, Céline, *Association québécoise des traumatisés crâniens*, 175
Martell, Sherry, *Truro & Colchester Chamber of Commerce*, 1400
Martell, Jeremy, *Nova Scotia Association of Architects*, 1040
Martell, Sharleen, *Women That Hunt*, 1461
Martelli, Dale, *British Columbia Social Studies Teachers Association*, 254
Martens, Rod, *Canadian Organic Growers Inc.*, 447
Martens, Floyd, *Canadian School Boards Association*, 468
Martens, Aaron D., *Legal Education Society of Alberta*, 906
Martens, Harold, *Saskatchewan Stock Growers Association*, 1276
Martens, Marilyn, *Saskatchewan Soil Conservation Association*, 1275
Martens, Ace, *Canadian Institute for Theatre Technology*, 414
Martens-Funk, Christina, *Saskatchewan Association for Community Living*, 1256
Martin, Shane, *Alberta Powerlifting Union*, 42
Martin, Nathalie, *Conseil de l'enveloppe du bâtiment du Québec*, 615
Martin, Kyla, *Children's Wish Foundation of Canada*, 562
Martin, Kyla, *Children's Wish Foundation of Canada*, 562
Martin, Stephanie, *Stratford Musicians' Association, Local 418 of the American Federation of Musicians*, 1351
Martin, Béatrice, *Canadian Association of Foodservice Professionals*, 315
Martin, Francis, *Chambre de commerce de Rawdon*, 542
Martin, Barb, *American Water Works Association*, 1504
Martin, Blain W., *Association of Ontario Land Surveyors*, 155
Martin, Keith, *Association of Professional Engineers & Geoscientists of British Columbia*, 158
Martin, Claudette, *Canadian 4-H Council*, 284
Martin, Glenn, *Canadian Hard of Hearing Association*, 400
Martin, Deborah, *Canadian Hearing Society*, 403
Martin, Keith, *Canadian International Council*, 421
Martin, Sue, *Renfrew County Real Estate Board*, 1217

Martin, Dianne, *Registered Practical Nurses Association of Ontario*, 1214
Martin, Annette, *Canadian Nurses Foundation*, 443
Martin, Danièle J., *Fondation Hôpital Charles-LeMoyne*, 746
Martin, Sydney, *American Numismatic Society*, 1496
Martin, Wanda, *Saskatchewan Public Health Association Inc.*, 1272
Martin, Ronald, *Association des Pompiers de Montréal inc.*, 124
Martin, André, *Fondation de la faune du Québec*, 744
Martin, Michael, *Ontario Association of Archers Inc.*, 1061
Martin, Rhowena, *Canadian Centre on Substance Use & Addiction*, 354
Martin, Eric, *Swim Ontario*, 1359
Martin, Michael S., *Canadian Association of Veterans in United Nations Peacekeeping*, 336
Martin, Judy, *Batshaw Youth & Family Centres*, 199
Martin, David, *Mennonite Church Canada*, 961
Martin, Vicki, *Alberta Registered Music Teachers' Association*, 44
Martin, Jane, *American Society for Quality*, 1499
Martin, Loranne, *Trans Canada Yellowhead Highway Association*, 1395
Martin, Richard, *Fédération des aînées et aînés francophones du Canada*, 711
Martin, Mary, *Cabbagetown Preservation Association*, 268
Martin, Louis, *Turkey Farmers of New Brunswick*, 1400
Martin, Patrice-Guy, *Réseau ACTION TI*, 1218
Martin, Sylvie, *Council of Atlantic Ministers of Education & Training*, 632
Martin, Marc, *Association France-Québec*, 1509
Martin, Rhonda, *Joint Centre for Bioethics*, 875
Martin, Dawn, *Pharmacists' Association of Saskatchewan, Inc.*, 1157
Martin, Gaston, *Canadian Transplant Association*, 497
Martin, Berthe, *Association générale des insuffisants rénaux*, 136
Martin, Jean-C., *Club canadien de Toronto*, 574
Martin, Candace, *Edmonton Insurance Association*, 678
Martin, Angela, *Friends of Mashkinonje Park*, 761
Martin, Kim, *Gerontological Nursing Association of British Columbia*, 772
Martin, Roger, *Martin Prosperity Institute*, 952
Martin-Lindsay, Irene, *Alberta Senior Citizens' Housing Association*, 46
Martindale, Barb, *Caledonia Regional Chamber of Commerce*, 270
Martindale, Tony, *Minor Hockey Alliance of Ontario*, 968
Martineau, Julie, *Conseil régional de la culture de l'Outaouais*, 621
Martineau, Luc, *Festivals et Événements Québec*, 733
Martineau, Sylvain, *Festivals et Événements Québec*, 733
Martineau, France, *Canadian Linguistic Association*, 217
Martineau, Lucie, *Syndicat de la fonction publique du Québec inc. (ind.)*, 1361
Martineau, Jean, *Fédération des professionnelles et professionnels de l'éducation du Québec*, 718
Martineau, Suzanne, *Soeurs de Sainte-Marie de Namur*, 1331
Martineau, Céline, *Association des Sourds de l'Estrie Inc.*, 128
Martineau, Alain, *Mouvement national des québécoises et québécois*, 977
Martinek, David, *Canadian Electricity Association*, 380

Martinez, Hellen, *Association of Translators & Interpreters of Alberta*, 163
Martinez, J. Eduardo, *Information Resource Management Association of Canada*, 837
Martinez, Mark, *Pulp & Paper Centre*, 1194
Martinez Cruz, Medardo, *Canadian Theosophical Association*, 494
Martini-Wong, Gary, *Canadian Franchise Association*, 394
Martins, Sandra, *British Columbia Historical Federation*, 243
Martins, Susan, *Paperboard Packaging Council*, 1582
Martinuea, Jamie, *Canadian Culinary Federation*, 374
Martinuk, Joel, *Yorkton Chamber of Commerce*, 1474
Martodam, Yvonne, *Vecova Centre for Disability Services & Research*, 1430
Martselos, Peter, *Thebacha & Wood Buffalo Astronomical Society*, 1375
Marubashi, Sharon, *Japanese Canadian Cultural Centre*, 869
Maruschak, Patricia, *Canadian Lutheran World Relief*, 428
Marvin, Chris, *Canadian Association on Water Quality*, 337
Mary, Gay, *West Kootenay District Labour Council*, 1445
MaryMoon, Pashta, *Canadian Integrative Network for Death Education & Alternatives*, 420
Marynuik, Eleanor, *British Columbia Maritime Employers Association*, 246
Marzetti, Ruth, *BC Association for Individualized Technology and Supports*, 201
Marzolf, Helen, *Open Space Arts Society*, 1114
Mascall, Jennifer, *Mascall Dance*, 952
Mascarin, Marty, *North of Superior Film Association*, 1031
Mascle, Christian, *Association des professeurs de l'École Polytechnique de Montréal*, 124
Masi, Joe, *Association of Manitoba Municipalities*, 151
Masiel, Mary, *Vermilion Forks Field Naturalists*, 1431
Mask, Teenie, *Wilno Heritage Society*, 1456
Maskell, Donna, *Canadian Home Builders' Association - British Columbia*, 407
Maslowski, Brandy, *Penticton & Wine Country Chamber of Commerce*, 1151
Maslowsky, Jerry, *Variety - The Children's Charity of Manitoba, Tent 58 Inc.*, 1430
Masmoudi, Radhouane, *Association des ingénieurs-professeurs des sciences appliquées*, 117
Masnyk, Katya, *Canadian Alliance of Physiotherapy Regulators*, 291
Mason, Becky, *Timmins & Area Women in Crisis Support & Information Centre on Violence Against Women*, 1380
Mason, Mike, *Association of Professional Engineers & Geoscientists of British Columbia*, 158
Mason, David, *Canadian Electrical Contractors Association*, 380
Mason, Jill, *Yukon Teachers' Association*, 1480
Mason, Joanne, *Alberta Native Friendship Centres Association*, 41
Mason, Kaley, *Canadian Society for Traditional Music*, 479
Mason, Gillian, *ABC Life Literacy Canada*, 1
Mason, Juliet, *International Association of Fire Fighters (AFL-CIO/CLC)*, 1538
Mason, Kendall, *Atlantic Canada Water & Wastewater Association*, 182
Mason, Anne, *Administrative & Professional Staff Association*, 8
Massé, Bruno, *Réseau québécois des groupes écologistes*, 1225
Masse, Yollande, *Société d'histoire de la MRC de l'Assomption*, 1310
Massel, Heather, *Alberta School Boards Association*, 45

Massey, Michael, *Edmonton Youth Orchestra Association*, 680
Massey, Jacqueline M., *Bowen Island Arts Council*, 219
Massey, Sylvia, *Chemainus Harvest House Society Food Bank*, 556
Massicotte, Lisa, *Association des intervenants en dépendance du Québec*, 117
Massie, Dominique, *Québec Lung Association*, 1198
Massie, Jennifer, *Elder Active Recreation Association*, 681
Massie, Ruth, *Council of Yukon First Nations*, 635
Massip, Isabelle, *Catholic Family Service of Ottawa*, 518
Masson, Paul, *Alberta Ready Mixed Concrete Association*, 43
Masson, Marc, *Assemblée communautaire fransaskoise*, 87
Masson, Richard, *Société généalogique canadienne-française*, 1319
Masson, Alain, *Cross Country Yukon*, 644
Masson, Martin, *Mouvement d'information et d'entraide dans la lutte contre le sida à Québec*, 977
Masson, Steve, *Manitoba-Saskatchewan Prospectors & Developers Association*, 948
Massouh, Devon Lee, *Human Resources Professionals Association*, 825
Masswohl, John, *Canadian Cattlemen's Association*, 351
Masters, Gordon, *Ontario Association of Architects*, 1061
Masters, Susan, *Western Institute for the Deaf & Hard of Hearing*, 1450
Masters, Allan, *Canadian Institute of Forestry, Newfoundland & Labrador*, 416
Masters, John, *Trotskyist League of Canada*, 1399
Masters-Boyne, Anne, *Canadian Occupational Health Nurses Association*, 444
Masterson, Bob, *Chemistry Industry Association of Canada*, 556
Mastervick, Greg, *Alberta Broomball Association*, 26
Mastlezav, Blair, *Heating, Refrigeration & Air Conditioning Institute of Canada*, 810
Maston, Thomas, *Canadian College of Health Leaders*, 359
Mastrella, John, *Canadian Public Accountability Board*, 462
Mastromonaco, Denis, *Orchestras Mississauga*, 1117
Mastromonaco, Denis, *York Symphony Orchestra Inc.*, 1474
Masuda, Naoko, *Society of Graphic Designers of Canada*, 1329
Masut, Ana, *International Council of Design*, 856
Matas, James A., *American Society for Aesthetic Plastic Surgery*, 1497
Matchim, Lisa, *Institute of Law Clerks of Ontario*, 846
Matejcic, Andrew, *The Canadian Association for HIV Research*, 301
Matejovsky, Lukas, *Alberta Agricultural Economics Association*, 21
Matern, Richard, *Daily Bread Food Bank*, 648
Mateus, Gentil, *Community Social Services Employers' Association*, 607
Matheos, Kathleen, *Canadian Society for the Study of Higher Education*, 478
Mather, Kerrie, *Airports Council International - Asia-Pacific Region*, 1486
Mather, Duane, *Enform*, 688
Mather, David, *Boys & Girls Clubs of Canada Foundation*, 222
Matheson, Albert, *Clan Matheson Society of Nova Scotia*, 572
Matheson, Melanie, *Manitoba Writers' Guild Inc.*, 947
Matheson, Heather, *Prince County Hospital Foundation*, 1171

Executive Name Index

Matheson, Al, *Federation for Scottish Culture in Nova Scotia*, 721
Matheson, Lynn, *New Brunswick Coalition of Transition Houses/Centres for Abused Women*, 1007
Mathew, Eddie, *Army Cadet League of Canada*, 83
Mathew, George, *CARP*, 515
Mathew, Xavier, *Jesus Youth Canada*, 870
Mathews, Julie, *Community Legal Education Ontario*, 600
Mathews, Jim, *National Association of Railroad Passengers*, 1573
Mathiason, Garrett, *Saskatchewan Rowing Association*, 1274
Mathieson, Chris, *Interpretation Canada - A Professional Association for Heritage Interpretation*, 861
Mathieu, Greg, *Cycling Canada Cyclisme*, 647
Mathieu, David, *Association de neurochirurgie du Québec*, 103
Mathieu, Sylvain, *Association provinciale des constructeurs d'habitations du Québec inc.*, 168
Mathurin, Dickens, *Centre Sportif de la Petite Bourgogne*, 536
Matiation, Nicole, *On Screen Manitoba*, 1058
Matichuk, Adam, *Saskatchewan Wildlife Federation*, 1278
Matier, Gerald, *Insurance Council of British Columbia*, 849
Matson, Mark, *Hamilton District Society for Disabled Children*, 801
Matsuoka, Rob, *Alberta Lacrosse Association*, 39
Matsushita, Sarah, *Ontario Nonprofit Network*, 1094
Matsutani, Grace, *British Columbia Public Interest Advocacy Centre*, 250
Matt, Faye, *Special Olympics Saskatchewan*, 1340
Matte, Darren, *Golf Association of Ontario*, 777
Matte, Lisa, *Diabetes Canada*, 655, 656
Matte, Laurent, *Ordre des conseillers et conseillères d'orientation du Québec*, 1121
Matte, Simon, *Association des recycleurs de pièces d'autos et de camions*, 127
Matte-Stotyn, Michelle, *Canadian Sport Parachuting Association*, 490
Matteau, Marie-Pier, *Chambre de commerce et d'industries de Trois-Rivières*, 548
Matten, Jaime, *British Columbia Federation of Labour*, 241
Matthew, Keith, *Council for Advancement of Native Development Officers*, 632
Matthews, Eddie, *Royal United Services Institute of Regina*, 1243
Matthews, Cheryl, *Children's Wish Foundation of Canada*, 563
Matthews, Wendy, *Community Living Brantford*, 600
Matthews, Dawna, *Canadian Condominium Institute*, 362
Matthews, Heather, *Canadian Independent Adjusters' Association*, 410
Matthews, Michael, *Meetings & Conventions Prince Edward Island*, 959
Matthews, Don, *Federation of Ontario Bed & Breakfast Accommodation*, 725
Matthews, Chris, *Ontario Gay & Lesbian Chamber of Commerce*, 1081
Matthews, Tom, *Hillfield-Strathallan College Foundation*, 815
Matthews, Hans, *Canadian Aboriginal Minerals Association*, 285
Matthews, Brendan, *Canadian Snowboard Federation*, 472
Matthiessen, Beverley D., *Alberta Committee of Citizens with Disabilities*, 30
Matthon, Natalie, *Fédération de voile du Québec*, 710
Mattock, Chris, *Calgary Meals on Wheels*, 273
Matton, Dawna, *Insurance Institute of Ontario*, 850

Matton, Marie-Claude, *Concours de musique du Canada inc.*, 610
Mattson, Erica, *British Columbia Museums Association*, 246
Mattson, Kathy J., *Industrial Fabrics Association International*, 1531
Matwick, Leesa, *British Columbia Wall & Ceiling Association*, 257
Mauch, Anne, *Council of Forest Industries*, 634
Mauger, Suzanne, *Association Gaspé-Jersey & Guernesey*, 136
Maung Htoo, Tin, *Canadian Friends of Burma*, 395
Maurer, Charles E., *Knights of Columbus*, 1568
Maurice, Peter, *Association des marchands de machines aratoires de la province de Québec*, 119
Maurice, Suzanne, *Canadian Association of Occupational Therapists*, 323
Maurice, John, *Nunavut Speed Skating Association*, 1051
Mauroy, Martine, *Association des cinémas parallèles du Québec*, 109
Mausberg, Burkhard, *Friends of the Greenbelt Foundation*, 762
Mavriplis, Cahterine, *NSERC Chair for Women in Science & Engineering*, 1050
Mavropoulos, Antonis, *International Solid Waste Association*, 1562
Mawani, Farah, *Canadian Authors Association*, 338
Mawani, Mina, *Crohn's & Colitis Canada*, 642
Mawani, Mina, *Greater Toronto CivicAction Alliance*, 785
Mawby, Sandra, *South Simcoe Community Information Centre*, 1336
Mawhinney, David, *Council of Archives New Brunswick*, 632
Mawlam, Laurie, *Autism Canada*, 188
Mawson, Douglas, *Group 25 Model Car Builders' Club*, 790
Maxim, Bev, *Batten Disease Support & Research Association - Canadian Chapter*, 199
Maxwell, Glynis, *Information Burlington*, 837
Maxwell, Maxine, *Alberta Genealogical Society*, 36
Maxwell, John, *AIDS Committee of Toronto*, 16
Maxwell, Ann, *Vocational Rehabilitation Association of Canada*, 1436
May, Ian, *Western Canadian Shippers' Coalition*, 1449
May, Tim, *Crowsnest Pass Chamber of Commerce*, 644
May, Marie, *Canadian Association of Women Executives & Entrepreneurs*, 336
May, Phil, *Canadian Picture Pioneers*, 455
May, Shelley, *Ontario Parks Association*, 1095
May, Elizabeth, *Green Party of Canada*, 788
May, Karen, *Texada Island Chamber of Commerce*, 1373
May, Barbara, *Alberta Racquetball Association*, 43
Mayba, Ihor, *The Great Herd of Bisons of the Fertile Plains*, 782
Maychak, Matt, *Canadian Football League*, 392
Mayer, Pierre, *Association des pneumologues de la province de Québec*, 123
Mayer, Uri, *University of Toronto Symphony Orchestra*, 1421
Mayer, Alina, *Emunah Women of Canada*, 687
Mayer, Carole, *Canadian Association of Psychosocial Oncology*, 330
Mayer, Amanda, *Lawson Foundation*, 902
Mayes, Bill, *Drainage Superintendents Association of Ontario*, 662
Mayes, Sarah, *Operation Lifesaver*, 1116
Mayhew, Lori, *Canadian Office & Professional Employees Union*, 445
Mayhew, Lori, *New Westminster & District Labour Council*, 1015
Mayhill, Stacey L., *AIDS Committee of North Bay & Area*, 16
Maynard, Doug, *Canadian Association of Paediatric Health Centres*, 325

Maynard, Matthew, *Canadian Hemophilia Society*, 404
Maynard, Hugh, *Canadian Farm Writers' Federation*, 384
Mayne, Brad, *International Association of Venue Managers, Inc.*, 1540
Maynes, Clifford, *Green Communities Canada*, 788
Mayo, Kim, *Chartered Professional Accountants of Newfoundland & Labrador*, 553
Mayr, John, *British Columbia College of Social Workers*, 236
Mayrand, Michel, *Fédération des professionnelles et professionnels de l'éducation du Québec*, 718
Mayrand, Robert, *Service Intégration Travail Outaouais*, 1291
Mayrand, Errold, *Réseau des SADC et CAE*, 1219
Mayrand, Karine, *Réseau du sport étudiant du Québec Lac Saint-Louis*, 1223
Mayrand, Elaine, *Maison Plein Coeur*, 927
Mayrand, Andrée, *Autorité des marchés financiers*, 190
Maystruck, Gary, *Financial Executives International Canada*, 736
Mazaheri, Seti, *Insurance Institute of Southern Alberta*, 850
Maze, Patrick, *Saskatchewan Teachers' Federation*, 1276
Mazerolle, Don, *Karate New Brunswick*, 882
Mazhar Shafi, Danial, *AIESEC*, 18
Maziade, Richard, *Réseau québécois des OSBL d'habitation*, 1225
Mazier, Dan, *Keystone Agricultural Producers*, 884
Mazik, Denise, *Abundance Canada*, 3
Mazumder, Tapan, *The Toronto-Calcutta Foundation*, 1388
Mazur, Daniel, *Manitoba Association of Prosthetists & Orthotists*, 931
Mazurenko, Marcie, *Alberta Trappers' Association*, 50
Mazurkiewicz, Anna, *Canadian Polish Congress*, 456
Mazurkiewicz, Anna, *Canadian Polish Congress*, 456
Mazzola, Michael, *Institutional Limited Partners Association*, 848
McAdam, Devin, *PAVED Arts*, 1146
McAlear, Rob, *Edmonton Symphony Orchestra*, 679
McAlear, Maureen, *Cornwall Township Historical Society*, 629
McAlister, Marc, *Free Methodist Church in Canada*, 759
McAlister, Alyson, *The Salvation Army START Program*, 1253
McAllan, Andrew, *Canada Green Building Council*, 279
McAllister, Sherri, *McMan Youth, Family & Community Services Association*, 956
McAlorum, Shannon, *Newfoundland & Labrador Health Libraries Association*, 1019
McAlpine, Sandy, *Coffee Association of Canada*, 580
McAlpine, Ric, *Canadian Union of Public Employees*, 498
McArdle, André, *Canadian Intergovernmental Conference Secretariat*, 421
McArthur, Blanca, *Ontario Society of Medical Technologists*, 1107
McArthur, Michael, *Swim Yukon*, 1359
McAulay, Tom, *Positive Living BC*, 1167
McAuley, Rob, *Toronto Autosport Club*, 1382
McAuley, Tricia, *Saskatoon Society for the Prevention of Cruelty to Animals Inc.*, 1280
McAuley, Paul, *Spiritans, the Congregation of the Holy Ghost*, 1344
McAuley, Paul, *Emmaus Canada*, 686
McAuslan, Kevin, *Mycological Society of Toronto*, 986
McAvity, John G., *Canadian Museums Association*, 437

McAvoy, Lynette, *Health Sciences Association of Alberta*, 807
McBain, Douglas, *Western Barley Growers Association*, 1447
McBeath, James, *Northwest Wildlife Preservation Society*, 1039
McBride, Karen, *Canadian Bureau for International Education*, 347
McBride, Boyd, *SOS Children's Villages Canada*, 1333
McBride, Judith, *British Columbia Association of Healthcare Auxiliaries*, 232
McBride, Robert C., *United Empire Loyalists' Association of Canada*, 1410
McBride, Ronald F., *Canadian Association of Veterans in United Nations Peacekeeping*, 336
McBride, Chris, *Spinal Cord Injury British Columbia*, 1343
McBride, Andrew, *Alberta Lacrosse Association*, 39
McBridge, Rikki, *Insurance Brokers Association of Canada*, 848
McCabe, Philip, *International Federation of Beekeepers' Associations*, 1547
McCabe, Don, *Ontario Federation of Agriculture*, 1079
McCabe, Meghan, *Canadian Academy of Recording Arts & Sciences*, 286
McCabe, Larry, *Ontario Small Urban Municipalities*, 1105
McCabe, Michael, *New Brunswick Racquetball Association*, 1011
McCafferty, Leo R., *American Society for Aesthetic Plastic Surgery*, 1497
McCaffrey, Greg, *CARP*, 514
McCaffrey, Craig, *Eastern Ontario Beekeepers' Association*, 670
McCagg, Darrell, *Heating, Refrigeration & Air Conditioning Institute of Canada*, 810
McCahan, Susan, *Canadian Engineering Education Association*, 381
McCaie, Roger, *Credit Institute of Canada*, 640
McCaig, Scott, *L'Ordinariat militaire Catholique Romain du Canada*, 1119
McCain, Geoff, *Clean Nova Scotia Foundation*, 573
McCalder, Brian, *British Columbia Athletics*, 233
McCall, Jeremy, *Okanagan Similkameen Parks Society*, 1056
McCall, Jeremy, *Outdoor Recreation Council of British Columbia*, 1133
McCall, Matt, *Royal Astronomical Society of Canada*, 1239
McCallum, Helen, *Consumers International*, 1520
McCallum, Alicia, *Prince Edward Island Pharmacy Board*, 1176
McCallum, Marnie, *Risk & Insurance Management Society Inc.*, 1234
McCallum, Tom, *Lambton County Developmental Services*, 897
McCallum, John, *Miniature Horse Club of Ontario*, 967
McCallum, Jake, *Pacific Western Athletic Association*, 1136
McCallum, Wade, *Triathlon Nova Scotia*, 1398
McCalmont, Joseph, *Society of St. Vincent de Paul - Toronto Central Council*, 1331
McCammon, Scott, *Milton Chamber of Commerce*, 966
McCamus, John, *Legal Aid Ontario*, 906
McCann, John, *Master Mariners of Canada*, 953
McCann, Kevin, *Royal Canadian Numismatic Association*, 1241
McCann, Louis, *PIJAC Canada*, 1159
McCann, Louis, *Pet Industry Joint Advisory Council*, 1153
McCann Sauter, Paige, *Rehabilitation Society of Southwestern Alberta*, 1216
McCannell, Scott, *Professional Employees Association (Ind.)*, 1183

Executive Name Index

McCarney, Patricia, *World Council on City Data*, 1465
McCarrey, Maryan, *Resident Doctors of Canada*, 1226
McCarrick, Lee Anthony, *Conference of Great Lakes & St. Lawrence Governors & Premiers*, 1519
McCarron, Patricia, *Parent Finders Ottawa*, 1139
McCarron, Lynne, *United Way of Cape Breton*, 1413
McCarron, Douglas J., *United Brotherhood of Carpenters & Joiners of America (AFL-CIO/CLC)*, 1599
McCarter, Katherine S., *Ecological Society of America*, 1522
McCarthy, Shannon, *United Church of Canada*, 1409
McCarthy, Christopher, *Prince Edward Island Chiropractic Association*, 1173
McCarthy, Anthony J., *Canadian Culinary Federation*, 374
McCarthy, Marta, *Association of Canadian Choral Communities*, 141
McCarthy, Francine, *Canadian Association of Palynologists*, 325
McCarthy, David, *Central Alberta Soccer Association*, 524
McCarthy, Michele, *The St. George's Society of Toronto*, 1248
McCarthy, Grace M., *CHILD Foundation*, 560
McCarthy, Bud, *Edmonton Fire Fighters Union*, 677
McCarthy, Devin, *Canadian Electricity Association*, 380
McCarthy, Don, *Atlantic Pest Management Association*, 184
McCarthy, Dana, *Canadian Deaf Golf Association*, 376
McCarthy, Shawn, *Canadian Committee for World Press Freedom*, 360
McCarthy-Flynn, Jennifer, *Pacific Immigrant Resources Society*, 1135
McCartney-Cameron, Maureen, *Alberta Civil Trial Lawyers' Association*, 28
McCarty, Ben L., *Canadian Federation of Aircraft Maintenance Engineers Associations*, 384
McCarty, Michael, *Society of Composers, Authors & Music Publishers of Canada*, 1328
McCarville, Carolyn, *Prince Edward Island Society for Medical Laboratory Science*, 1177
McCarville, Matthew, *Prince Edward Island Eco-Net*, 1173
McCaskill, Don, *Addictions Foundation of Manitoba*, 8
McCauley, Steve, *The Pollution Probe Foundation*, 1164
McCauley, Gordon, *LifeSciences British Columbia*, 912
McCauley, Karen, *International Lilac Society*, 1552
McCauley, Jennifer, *L'Arche Ontario*, 77
McClary, Glenn, *Mount Pleasant Group*, 976
McClean, Yolanda, *Coalition of Black Trade Unionists*, 578
McClellan, Cheryl, *Arthritis Society*, 84
McClelland, Deb, *Greater Kamloops Chamber of Commerce*, 783
McClelland, Andrew, *Québec Farmers' Association*, 1197
McClelland, Anne, *Canadian Copyright Institute*, 365
McClelland, Michael, *ICOMOS Canada*, 829
McClements, Mike, *Wood Manufacturing Council*, 1463
McClemont, Tim, *Hamilton AIDS Network*, 800
McClenaghan, Thom, *Friends of the Coves Subwatershed Inc.*, 762
McClew, Martha, *The Terry Fox Foundation*, 1372
McClinchey, Scott, *North American Lincoln Red Association*, 1579

McClintock, Kelly, *Saskatchewan Hockey Association*, 1267
McClintock Wilson, Connie, *Société historique de la Vallée de la Châteauguay*, 1320
McCloy, Kerry, *Kidney Foundation of Canada*, 885
McClure, Cheryle, *Appaloosa Horse Club of Canada*, 73
McClure, Peter, *North West Commercial Travellers' Association*, 1033
McClure, Heather, *Saint Elizabeth Health Care*, 1246
McClure, Michelle, *Ability Online Support Network*, 2
McClymont, Terri, *Prince George Recycling & Environmental Action Planning Society*, 1179
McClymont, Kim, *Volunteer Alberta*, 1438
McColgan, Katherine, *Canadian Association of Research Libraries*, 331
McColl, Duncan, *Prince George Backcountry Recreation Society*, 1179
McCollister, Gus, *Peruvian Horse Association of Canada*, 1152
McConchie, Mary, *Embroiderers' Association of Canada, Inc.*, 686
McConnachie, Terri, *Canadian Home Builders' Association - Northern British Columbia*, 407
McConnell, Greg, *Canadian Federal Pilots Association*, 384
McConnell, Andre, *LakeCity Employment Services Association*, 896
McConnell, Sheri, *Canadian Association for Social Work Education*, 304
McCooey, Martin, *Canadian Fence Industry Association*, 389
McCord, Blake, *Association of Professional Engineers & Geoscientists of Alberta*, 157
McCorkell, Elizabeth, *Amethyst Scottish Dancers of Nova Scotia*, 67
McCorkle, James, *African Literature Association*, 1486
McCormack, Ken, *Automotive Retailers Association of British Columbia*, 190
McCormack, Scott, *Alberta School Boards Association*, 45
McCormack, Scott, *Canadian Maine-Anjou Association*, 429
McCormack, Mike, *Toronto Police Association*, 1386
McCormack, Margaret, *AIDS Committee of Durham Region*, 16
McCormack, Paul, *Ontario Brain Injury Association*, 1069
McCormack, Pat, *Child Care Connection Nova Scotia*, 558
McCormack, Eric, *Canadian Square & Round Dance Society*, 490
McCormack, Neil, *Ontario Pipe Trades Council*, 1096
McCormick, Ray, *Financial Executives International Canada*, 736
McCormick, Amanda, *Catholic Women's League of Canada*, 520
McCormick, Joanne, *Nova Scotia Lighthouse Preservation Society*, 1047
McCorquodale, David, *Science Atlantic*, 1285
McCort, Kevin, *Vancouver Foundation*, 1425
McCourt, Jeff, *Canadian Culinary Federation*, 374
McCoy, Tim, *Canadian Baptists of Ontario & Quebec*, 341
McCoy, Kelly, *Ontario Home Builders' Association*, 1086
McCoy, Susan, *Bereavement Ontario Network*, 205
McCoy, Lesley, *Ontario Equestrian Federation*, 1078
McCoy, Charline, *Cities of New Brunswick Association*, 570
McCoy, Elaine, *Macleod Institute*, 924
McCracken, Tim, *British Columbia Science Teachers' Association*, 252
McCracken, Molly, *Canadian Centre for Policy Alternatives*, 354

McCracken, Jamie, *Ontario Hospital Association*, 1087
McCracken, Beth, *Registered Practical Nurses Association of Ontario*, 1214
McCracken, Lynette, *High River & District Chamber of Commerce*, 814
McCraig, John, *United County Beekeepers*, 1410
McCray, Kevin, *National Ground Water Association*, 1576
McCrea, Frank, *Association of Professional Computer Consultants - Canada*, 157
McCrea, Trudie, *Wasaga Beach Chamber of Commerce*, 1440
McCready, Jim, *Eastern Ontario Model Forest*, 670
McCreary, Al, *British Columbia Hotel Association*, 243
McCrimmon, Karen, *Clans & Scottish Societies of Canada*, 572
McCrosky, Judy, *SF Canada*, 1293
McCuaig, Cathie, *Alberta Underwater Council*, 50
McCue, Chris, *British Columbia Environment Industry Association*, 239
McCue, Lorna, *Ontario Healthy Communities Coalition*, 1084
McCue, Rosamond, *Bear River Historical Society*, 203
McCullagh, Bruce, *Further Poultry Processors Association of Canada*, 765
McCullagh, Karen, *Boys & Girls Clubs of Canada*, 222
McCullagh, John, *Canadian AIDS Treatment Information Exchange*, 290
McCulloch, Tony, *British Association for Canadian Studies*, 1514
McCulloch, John, *Pacific Salmon Commission*, 1136
McCulloch, Jamie, *Canadian Association for Disabled Skiing - Alberta*, 299
McCullough, Elizabeth, *Canadian Institute of Plumbing & Heating*, 418
McCullough, Barry, *Literary & Historical Society of Québec*, 914
McCullough, Jamie, *Experiences Canada*, 700
McCullough, S., *Saint John Coin Club*, 1246
McCullough, Tracy, *Entre Nous Femmes Housing Society*, 691
McCullough, Gail, *East York Learning Experience*, 669
McCurry, Carole, *Manitoba Reading Association*, 943
McCusker, Anna, *The Scleroderma Society of Ontario*, 1285
McCusker, Anna, *Scleroderma Canada*, 1285
McCutchan, Don, *Saint Elizabeth Health Care*, 1246
McCutcheon, Sean, *Canadian Amateur Musicians*, 292
McCutcheon, Peter, *Royal College of Dentists of Canada*, 1241
McCutcheon, Laurent, *Gai Écoute inc.*, 766
McDadi, Hatem, *Tennis Canada*, 1371
McDaniel, Michael, *Pacific National Exhibition*, 1135
McDaniel, Lon S., *World Safety Organization*, 1607
McDavid, Kristina, *Council of Prairie & Pacific University Libraries*, 635
McDavid, Kristina, *Health Libraries Association of British Columbia*, 806
McDermid, Gary, *Helicopter Association of Canada*, 811
McDermott, Valerie, *Canadian Pony Club*, 457
McDermott, Dan, *Sierra Club of Canada*, 1298
McDevitt, Krista, *New Brunswick Association of Optometrists*, 1005
McDiarmid, Sheryl, *Canadian Vascular Access Association*, 501
McDiarmid, Don, *Alzheimer Society of Lanark County*, 63
McDiarmid, Theresa, *Iyengar Yoga Association of Canada*, 867

McDonald, Stephanie, *Edmonton Humane Society for the Prevention of Cruelty to Animals*, 677
McDonald, Leslie, *Manitoba Association of Library Technicians*, 930
McDonald, Jamie D., *Melville & District Agri-Park Association Inc.*, 959
McDonald, Cindy, *Portage la Prairie & District Chamber of Commerce*, 1167
McDonald, Mary Ruth, *Ontario Institute of Agrologists*, 1087
McDonald, Ron, *American Water Works Association*, 1504
McDonald, Jayne, *British Columbia Diving*, 239
McDonald, Lisa, *Canadian Association of Exposition Management*, 313
McDonald, Susan, *Construction Association of New Brunswick*, 623
McDonald, Gerard, *Professional Engineers Ontario*, 1183
McDonald, Bob, *Association of Professional Engineers & Geoscientists of Saskatchewan*, 159
McDonald, Leah, *Nova Scotia Society for the Prevention of Cruelty to Animals*, 1049
McDonald, Christina, *Manitoba Forestry Association Inc.*, 937
McDonald, Scott, *British Columbia Lung Association*, 245
McDonald, Lisa, *Prospectors & Developers Association of Canada*, 1189
McDonald, Karen, *Seniors Association of Greater Edmonton*, 1290
McDonald, Shannon, *Nova Scotia College of Respiratory Therapists*, 1043
McDonald, Esther, *Camrose Association for Community Living*, 277
McDonald, Anne, *Canadian Occupational Therapy Foundation*, 444
McDonald, Connie, *Canadian Holistic Nurses Association*, 406
McDonald, Shane, *Manitoba Association of Registered Respiratory Therapists, Inc.*, 931
McDonald, Michael, *Canadian Alliance of Student Associations*, 291
McDonald, Elizabeth, *Canadian Energy Efficiency Alliance*, 381
McDonald, Patrick, *Green Thumb Theatre for Young People*, 789
McDonald, Cameron, *Edmonton Inner City Housing Society*, 678
McDonald, Anne, *British Columbia Registered Music Teachers' Association*, 251
McDonald, Brian, *Professional Golfers' Assocation of British Columbia*, 1185
McDonald, Heather, *LOFT Community Services*, 917
McDonald, Lynn, *National Initiative for the Care of the Elderly*, 994
McDonald, Ben, *Canadian Arctic Resources Committee*, 295
McDonald, Alison, *Nova Scotia Physiotherapy Association*, 1047
McDonald, Janette, *Agricultural Research & Extension Council of Alberta*, 15
McDonald, Linda, *Association of Alberta Coordinated Action for Recycling Enterprises*, 139
McDonell, Glenda, *Clan Donald Canada*, 571
McDonnell, Dan, *Canadian Hard of Hearing Association*, 400
McDonnell, John, *Canadian Parks & Wilderness Society*, 451
McDonnell, Spence, *Interactive Ontario*, 851
McDonough Dolmaya, Julie, *Association canadienne de traductologie*, 92
McDougall, Norma, *Sparwood & District Chamber of Commerce*, 1339
McDougall, Danine, *Canadian Masonry Contractors' Association*, 431
McDougall, John, *Alberta Research Council Inc.*, 44
McDougall, John, *Alberta Research Council Inc.*, 44

Executive Name Index

McDougall, Mike, *Klondike Placer Miners' Association*, 892
McDowell, Jim, *Peel Regional Labour Council*, 1148
McDowell, Phil, *Boys & Girls Clubs of Canada*, 222
McDowell, Neemet, *Canadian Society of Consultant Pharmacists*, 482
McDuff, Louis, *Association des personnes handicapées de la Vallée du Richelieu*, 123
McEachern, Ryan, *Mining Suppliers Trade Association Canada*, 967
McEachern, Sean, *Saskatchewan Urban Municipalities Association*, 1277
McEachern, Andrea, *Canadian Land Reclamation Association*, 425
McEachern, Darlene, *Canadian Association of Elizabeth Fry Societies*, 313
McEachern, Joan, *Manitoba Association of Non-Teaching Employees*, 930
McEachern, Kelsey, *New Brunswick Society of Cardiology Techologists*, 1012
McEachern, Sue, *Variety Club of Northern Alberta, Tent 63*, 1430
McEllrath, Robert, *International Longshore & Warehouse Union (CLC)*, 1553
McElman, Melody, *Saint John SPCA Animal Rescue*, 1247
McElroy, Tom, *Canadian Meteorological & Oceanographic Society*, 436
McEneaney, Neil, *Numeris*, 1051
McEwan, Lloyd, *Fenelon Falls Stamp Club*, 732
McEwan, Lesley, *Physical Culture Association of Alberta*, 1158
McEwen, Michael, *North American Broadcasters Association*, 1029
McEwen, Kristyn, *Moose Jaw Humane Society Inc.*, 974
McEwen, Gary, *Manitoba Historical Society*, 938
McFadden, Cassie, *British Columbia Library Association*, 245
McFadden, Tom, *Canadian Deafblind Association (National)*, 376
McFadden, Andy, *Canadian Society for Surgical Oncology*, 477
McFadden, Sean, *Alzheimer Society of Leeds-Grenville*, 63
McFadden, Jeff, *Chatham-Kent Labour Council*, 555
McFadden, Nan, *Canadian Union of Public Employees*, 498
McFadyen, Marissa, *British Columbia Lung Association*, 245
McFadyen, Teresa, *Licensed Practical Nurses Association of British Columbia*, 910
McFall, Tom, *Alberta Craft Council*, 32
McFarland, Jenna, *Calgary Wildlife Rehabilitation Society*, 275
McFarlane, Kyle, *Golf Association of Ontario*, 777
McFarlane, Julie, *Canadian Tooling & Machining Association*, 495
McFarlane, Ian, *Ontario Principals' Council*, 1097
McFarlane, Brian, *USC Canada*, 1423
McFarlane, Brian, *Kensington Foundation*, 883
McFarlane, Anne, *Canadian Institute for Health Information*, 412
McFarlane, Becky, *Ontario Council of Alternative Businesses*, 1075
McFarlane-Burton, Joy, *Federation of Canadian Music Festivals*, 723
McFaull, Dan, *International Society for Performance Improvement*, 1559
McFee, Dale, *Canadian Association of Chiefs of Police*, 310
McFetridge, Heather, *Comox Valley Child Development Association*, 607
McGann, Larry, *International Union of Elevator Constructors*, 1564
McGann, Locksley, *Heritage Agricultural Society*, 812

McGann, Twyla, *Alberta Diabetes Foundation*, 33
McGarry, Niamh, *Canadian ADHD Resource Alliance*, 288
McGarvey, Doug, *Champlain Coin Club*, 551
McGaughey, Jane, *Canadian Association for Irish Studies*, 301
McGeachie, Erin, *Canadian Society of Cardiac Surgeons*, 481
McGee, Timothy E., *Law Society of British Columbia*, 901
McGifford, Lisa, *University of Winnipeg Faculty Association*, 1421
McGill, Jennifer, *Canadian Credit Union Association*, 372
McGill, Stephanie, *Ontario Brain Injury Association*, 1069
McGill, James D., *Canadian Association for Mine & Explosive Ordnance Security*, 302
McGillis, Greg, *Public Service Alliance of Canada*, 1193
McGillivray, Jennifer, *Sudbury Symphony Orchestra Association Inc.*, 1353
McGinn, Tom, *New Brunswick Road Builders & Heavy Construction Association*, 1011
McGinn, Ralph, *Farm & Ranch Safety & Health Association*, 705
McGinnis, Dorothy, *Manitoba School Library Association*, 944
McGiven, Derek, *Community Living Wallaceburg*, 606
McGlogan, Carol, *Electro-Federation Canada*, 683
McGoldrick, Owen, *Alberta Wilderness Association*, 52
McGonigle, Wanda, *Ontario Aboriginal Lands Association*, 1058
McGowan, Richard, *Emmanuel International Canada*, 686
McGowan, Gil, *Alberta Federation of Labour*, 34
McGowan, Carly, *Independent Production Fund*, 833
McGowan, R. Gordon, *Canadian Militaria Preservation Society*, 436
McGrane, David, *New Democratic Party*, 1014
McGrath, Vaughan, *Fort Saskatchewan Minor Sports Association*, 754
McGrath, Kevin, *Model Aeronautics Association of Canada Inc.*, 970
McGrath, Caitlin, *Canadian Association of Pharmacy Students & Interns*, 326
McGrath, Kelly, *Jeunesse Acadienne et Francophone de l'Île-du-prince-Édouard*, 870
McGrath, Susan, *Refugee Research Network*, 1211
McGrath-Gaudet, Erin, *Canadian Federation of Independent Business*, 387
McGraw, Pierre, *New Brunswick Arts Board*, 1004
McGraw, Harold, *International Chamber of Commerce*, 1542
McGreal, Shirley, *International Primate Protection League*, 1556
McGregor, Lynda, *Foundation for Education Perth Huron*, 755
McGregor, Trevor, *Community Living Stratford & Area*, 605
McGregor, Glenn, *International Society of Biometeorology*, 1560
McGregor, Heather, *YWCA Canada*, 1482
McGregor, Rosanna, *Cariboo Friendship Society*, 512
McGregor, Orla, *Insurance Professionals of Calgary*, 850
McGuinness, Karen L., *Mutual Fund Dealers Association of Canada*, 986
McGuire, Mike, *Youth in Care Canada*, 1476
McGuire, Noreene, *Nova Scotia Ground Water Association*, 1045
McGuire, Heather, *Canadian Railway Club*, 465
McGuire, Michael, *Association ontarienne des Sourd(e)s francophones*, 164

McIlroy, Jessica, *British Columbia Sustainable Energy Association*, 255
McIlveen, Bill, *Field Botanists of Ontario*, 734
McIlwaine, Brenda, *Prince Edward Island Golf Association*, 1174
McIlwaine, Bob, *Canadian Lifeboat Institution*, 427
McIlwraith, Ciaran, *Eastern Canadian Galloway Association*, 670
McInerney, Betty, *Mechanical Contractors Association of Manitoba*, 957
McInnis, Peter, *Saint Francis Xavier Association of University Teachers*, 1246
McInnis, Debbie, *United Way of Greater Moncton & Southeastern New Brunswick*, 1414
McIntee, Gina, *Haldimand-Norfolk Literacy Council*, 798
McIntosh, Lisa, *H.R. MacMillan Space Centre Society*, 824
McIntosh, Sarah, *Canadian Association of Management Consultants*, 320
McIntosh, Christopher, *St. Leonard's Society of Canada*, 1250
McIntosh, Sue, *British Columbia Coalition to Eliminate Abuse of Seniors*, 236
McIntosh, Don, *Cornwall Township Historical Society*, 629
McIntyre, David, *Chinook Musical Society*, 565
McIntyre, Doug, *Vulcan & District Fish & Game Club*, 1439
McIntyre, Mary, *Canadian Bookbinders & Book Artists Guild*, 346
McIntyre, Carl, *South Dundas Chamber of Commerce*, 1334
McIntyre, Greg, *Institute of Certified Management Consultants of Alberta*, 845
McIntyre, Gerry, *Canadian Educational Resources Council*, 380
McIntyre, John, *Aurora Historical Society, Inc.*, 187
McIntyre, Paula, *International Association for Great Lakes Research*, 1536
McIntyre, Jennifer, *Canadian Society of Gastroenterology Nurses & Associates*, 483
McIntyre, Dayna, *Vegetarians of Alberta Association*, 1430
McIntyre, Julie, *Canadian Artists' Representation British Columbia*, 296
McIntyre, Danielle, *Interfaith Food Bank Society of Lethbridge*, 852
McIsaac, Steve, *Inside Education*, 839
McIsaac, Geoff, *Polyurethane Manufacturers Association*, 1584
McIsaac, Elizabeth, *Maytree Foundation*, 954
McIver, Christine, *Kids Cancer Care Foundation of Alberta*, 886
McIvor, R.A. (Dick), *Maintenance, Engineering & Reliability (MER) Society*, 926
McKay, Adèle, *Canadian Organic Growers Inc.*, 447
McKay, Janet, *ADR Institute of Canada*, 9
McKay, Raine, *Craft Council of British Columbia*, 638
McKay, Shelley, *Forests Ontario*, 752
McKay, Kevin, *Partners International*, 1144
McKay, Alex, *Sex Information & Education Council of Canada*, 1292
McKay, Gerry, *Independent First Nations' Alliance*, 833
McKay, Frank, *Windigo First Nations' Council*, 1456
McKay, Elspeth, *Operation Come Home*, 1115
McKay, Robert, *Ontario Brain Injury Association*, 1069
McKay, Duane, *Council of Canadian Fire Marshals & Fire Commissioners*, 633
McKay, Ivan, *Sarnia Rock & Fossil Club*, 1254
McKay, Eugene, *AFOA Canada*, 12
McKay, Dianne, *PFLAG Canada Inc.*, 1156
McKay, Wendy, *Nurse Practitioners' Association of Ontario*, 1052
McKay-Panos, Linda, *Alberta Civil Liberties Research Centre*, 28

McKeagan, Richard, *Mechanical Contractors Association of Canada*, 956
McKeagan, Richard, *National Trade Contractors Coalition of Canada*, 996
McKechnie, Brenda, *College of Physiotherapists of Manitoba*, 589
McKenchie, Ann, *Applegrove Community Complex*, 74
McKee, Denise, *Autism Society Northwest Territories*, 189
McKee, Darren, *Saskatchewan School Boards Association*, 1274
McKee, Phillip, *Ontario Hockey Federation*, 1084
McKee, Denise, *NWT Disabilities Council*, 1052
McKee, Chris, *Manitoba Amateur Bodybuilding Association*, 928
McKee, Dave, *Communist Party of Canada (Ontario)*, 595
McKee-Protopapas, Sheila, *Wilfrid Laurier University Faculty Association*, 1455
McKeen, Ken, *Heavy Equipment & Aggregate Truckers Association of Manitoba*, 810
McKeen, Alice, *Welsh Pony & Cob Association of Ontario*, 1444
McKeever, Paul, *Freedom Party of Ontario*, 759
McKeil, Jeff, *University of Victoria Faculty Association*, 1421
McKellar, John, *Toronto Arts Foundation*, 1381
McKellar, Lyle, *Schizophrenia Society of Alberta*, 1283
McKellar, Ross, *Treherne Chamber of Commerce*, 1397
McKellar, Lyle, *School Sport Canada*, 1284
McKelvy, Jason, *MacGregor Chamber of Commerce*, 924
McKendry, Lisa, *Association of Employees Supporting Education Services*, 147
McKenna, Catherine, *Canadian Council of Ministers of the Environment*, 368
McKenna, John, *Air Transport Association of Canada*, 19
McKenna, Janice, *Yellowknife Association for Community Living*, 1471
McKenna, Vicki, *Ontario Nurses' Association*, 1094
McKenna, Terrence, *Cursillo Movement of the Archdiocese of Toronto*, 646
McKenna, Mike, *BC Construction Safety Alliance*, 201
McKenna, Joe, *Supply Chain Management Association - Nova Scotia*, 1356
McKenna, Alex, *The Canadian Association of Naturopathic Doctors*, 322
McKenna, Dawn, *Down Syndrome Research Foundation*, 661
McKenna, Mike, *Canadian Fallen Firefighters Foundation*, 383
McKenzie, Brian, *Canadian Hearing Society*, 403
McKenzie, Brian, *Canadian Hearing Society*, 403
McKenzie, Donald, *The Canadian Press*, 459
McKenzie, Dianne, *Epilepsy Ontario*, 693
McKenzie, Jan, *The Ninety-Nines Inc.*, 1578
McKenzie, Jennifer, *New Democratic Party*, 1014
McKenzie, Beth, *Real Estate Institute of Canada*, 1206
McKenzie, Owen, *Manitoba Funeral Service Association*, 937
McKenzie, Nicole, *Entomological Society of Ontario*, 690
McKenzie, Alan, *Clan Mackenzie Society of Canada*, 572
McKenzie, Karlee, *Canadian Nursing Students' Association*, 443
McKenzie, Stéphanie, *Club de natation Natchib inc.*, 575
McKenzie, Kevin, *Canadian Association of Interventional Cardiology*, 319
McKenzie, Rhoni, *Manitoba Team Handball Federation*, 946

Executive Name Index

McKenzie Jansen, Catherine, *Scottish Studies Foundation Inc.*, 1286
McKeown, Steve, *Airport Management Council of Ontario*, 20
McKeown, Fiona, *The Arts & Letters Club*, 85
McKernan, James, *Canadian Institute for Theatre Technology*, 414
McKerr, Lynda, *Community Care Peterborough*, 596
McKerral, Jen, *Cultural Industries Ontario North*, 645
McKibbon, Candace, *British Columbia Aviation Council*, 233
McKibbon, Vicki, *Atlantic Provinces Trucking Association*, 185
McKie, Duncan, *Foundation Assisting Canadian Talent on Recordings*, 755
McKiernan, Helen, *Friends of The Canadian War Museum*, 762
McKietiuk, Lori, *College of Audiologists and Speech-Language Pathologists of Manitoba*, 582
McKietiuk, Lori, *Association of Manitoba Land Surveyors*, 151
McKillop, Darcy, *Sport New Brunswick*, 1345
McKim, Bill, *Ontario Municipal Management Institute*, 1092
McKim, Blake, *Employment & Education Centre*, 687
McKimm, Mayland, *Canadian Association of Provincial Court Judges*, 329
McKinley, Karen, *Ontario Brain Injury Association*, 1069
McKinnon, Mark, *Ontario Professional Fire Fighters Association*, 1097
McKinnon, Heather, *St. Albert Family Resource Centre*, 1247
McKinstry, E. Richard, *Ephemera Society of Canada*, 693
McKivett, Paul, *College of Denturists of British Columbia*, 583
McKnight, Michael, *United Way of the Lower Mainland*, 1417
McKnight, Kim, *Water Ski & Wakeboard British Columbia*, 1441
McKye, Karen, *The Bahá'í Community of Canada*, 194
McLachlan, Barbara, *InformOntario*, 838
McLachlan, Lorraine, *Canadian Franchise Association*, 394
McLachlan, Glenda, *Quetico Foundation*, 1201
McLagan, Jim, *Canadian Institute of Steel Construction*, 419
McLagan, Lorna, *Historical Association of Annapolis Royal*, 816
McLain, Steve, *Recreation Facilities Association of British Columbia*, 1207
McLaren, Brian, *Thunder Bay Field Naturalists*, 1378
McLaren, Lindsay, *Alberta Public Health Association*, 43
McLaren, Patricia Genoe, *Administrative Sciences Association of Canada*, 8
McLaren, Sarah, *Junior Farmers' Association of Ontario*, 878
McLaren, Amanda, *The Canadian Federation of Business & Professional Women's Clubs*, 385
McLaren, Scott, *Canadian Society of Church History*, 481
McLaren, Maura, *Real Estate Institute of Canada*, 1205
McLaren, Marilyn, *United Way of Winnipeg*, 1417
McLarty, Susan, *Nature Manitoba*, 1000
McLarty, Jeff, *United Way of Lethbridge & South Western Alberta*, 1415
McLauchlin, Rob, *ARMA Canada*, 82
McLaughlin, Claire, *Canadian Child Care Federation*, 355
McLaughlin, Becky, *Glass & Architectural Metals Association*, 774
McLaughlin, Blair, *United Way/Centraide (Central NB) Inc.*, 1418

McLaughlin, Peter, *Gulf of Maine Council on the Marine Environment*, 794
McLaughlin, Don, *Global, Environmental & Outdoor Education Council*, 775
McLaughlin, Kristine, *New Brunswick Society of Cardiology Techologists*, 1012
McLaughlin, Peter, *Carleton-Victoria Arts Council*, 513
McLaughlin, Barb, *Nova Scotia Beekeepers' Association*, 1042
McLean, Mandy, *College of Psychologists of New Brunswick*, 589
McLean, Marg, *Community Living St. Marys & Area Association*, 605
McLean, Ian, *Greater Kitchener & Waterloo Chamber of Commerce*, 784
McLean, Sheri, *Electrical Contractors Association of Alberta*, 682
McLean, Alistair, *Hostelling International - Canada*, 823
McLean, Mark, *Toronto Real Estate Board*, 1387
McLean, Rose, *Institute of Municipal Assessors*, 846
McLean, Paul, *The McLean Foundation*, 955
McLean, Cindy, *College of Occupational Therapists of British Columbia*, 586
McLean, Don, *Conserver Society of Hamilton & District Inc.*, 623
McLean, Ernie, *The Professional Institute of the Public Service of Canada*, 1185
McLean, Linda, *Inn From the Cold Society*, 838
McLean, Christy, *Literacy Coalition of New Brunswick*, 913
McLean, Megan, *Governance Professionals of Canada*, 778
McLean, Sheila, *Human Resources Association of Nova Scotia*, 825
McLean, Helen, *Donner Canadian Foundation*, 661
McLean, Andy, *East Coast Music Association*, 668
McLean, Brian, *Achilles Canada*, 5
Mclean, Murdo, *Harrow & Colchester Chamber of Commerce*, 804
McLean, Don, *Friends of Red Hill Valley*, 762
McLean, Rachel, *Foothills Forage & Grazing Association*, 750
McLellan, Steve, *Saskatchewan Chamber of Commerce*, 1260
McLellan, Harry, *Kidney Foundation of Canada*, 885
McLellan, Jennifer, *Elora Environment Centre*, 685
McLellan, Cindy, *Archives Association of British Columbia*, 80
McLellan, Bill, *Merit Contractors Association of Nova Scotia*, 962
McLellan, Troy, *Canadian Self Storage Association*, 470
McLellan, Stephanie, *Laurier Teachers Union*, 900
McLellan, Alyson, *Bully B'Ware*, 264
McLennan, Donna, *The Leukemia & Lymphoma Society of Canada*, 909
McLeod, Doug, *Alberta Genealogical Society*, 36
McLeod, Cindy, *Alzheimer Society of Alberta & Northwest Territories*, 61
McLeod, Andrew, *Association of Professional Engineers & Geoscientists of New Brunswick*, 158
McLeod, James, *Learning Enrichment Foundation*, 905
McLeod, Katie, *The Endometriosis Network*, 687
McLeod, Ron, *Greater Vancouver Community Services Society*, 786
McLeod, Liz, *Manitoba College of Registered Social Workers*, 934
McLeod, Michael, *Highland Shores Children's Aid*, 814
McLeod, Sheldon, *Manitoba Environmental Industries Association Inc.*, 936

McLeod, Stephen, *Saskatchewan Martial Arts Association*, 1270
McLeod Tipple, Judy, *Clan MacLeod Societies of Canada*, 572
McLister, Jack, *Ontario Dental Association*, 1077
McMahon, Patricia, *Youth in Care in Ontario*, 1476
McMahon, Sheila, *Ontario Federation of Indian Friendship Centres*, 1079
McMahon, Donna, *Canadian Society for Chemical Technology*, 473
McMahon, Sheila, *United Native Friendship Centre*, 1412
McMahon, Karen, *PFLAG Canada Inc.*, 1156
McMain, Karen, *International Orthoptic Association*, 1554
McManus, Mark, *United Association of Journeymen & Apprentices of the Plumbing & Pipe Fitting Industry of the United States & Canada*, 1599
McManus, Patrick, *Ontario Sewer & Watermain Construction Association*, 1104
McManus, Sean, *Manitoba Music*, 941
McMaster, Brian, *Canadian Tenpin Federation, Inc.*, 494
McMaster, Donna, *Ontario Rock Garden Society*, 1102
McMechan, Fred, *Williams Lake Field Naturalists*, 1455
McMenamie, Logan, *The Anglican Church of Canada*, 69
McMillan, Susan, *The Salvation Army in Canada*, 1252
McMillan, Ken, *Canadian Hydrographic Association*, 409
McMillan, Ann, *Canadian Meteorological & Oceanographic Society*, 436
McMillan, Tim, *Canadian Association of Petroleum Producers*, 326
McMillan, Chuck, *Canadian Technical Asphalt Association*, 493
McMillan, Tannis, *Kidney Foundation of Canada*, 885
McMillan, Neil, *Saskatchewan Mining Association*, 1270
McMillan, Michelle, *Youth Ballet & Contemporary Dance of Saskatchewan Inc.*, 1475
McMillan, Ross, *Tides Canada Foundation*, 1379
McMillan-Evans, Judy, *Community Futures Network Society of Alberta*, 598
McMorris, Mike, *Beef Improvement Ontario*, 204
McMorrow, Thomas, *Canadian Law & Society Association*, 426
McMullan, Marilyn, *Manitoba 5 Pin Bowlers' Association*, 928
McMullen, Brian, *Kingston Construction Association*, 889
McMullen, Glen, *Central Ontario Beekeepers' Association*, 525
McMullin, Anne, *Urban Development Institute of Canada*, 1422
McMurchy, Jim, *Archaeological Society of Alberta*, 76
McMurter, Lola, *Ontario Lung Association*, 1090
McMurter, Lola, *Ontario Lung Association*, 1090
McMurtry, Mike, *Field Botanists of Ontario*, 734
McMurtry, Andrew, *The Royal Commonwealth Society of Canada*, 1242
McNab, Paul, *Dental Association of Prince Edward Island*, 653
McNab, Guy, *Rehabilitation Society of Southwestern Alberta*, 1216
McNabb, Gloria, *Evangelical Lutheran Church in Canada*, 698
McNabb, Sally, *Manitoba Amateur Wrestling Association*, 928
McNabb, Edward, *Royal Heraldry Society of Canada*, 1242

McNabb, Rob, *Canadian Cattlemen's Association*, 351
McNagny, Kelly, *AllerGen NCE Inc.*, 54
McNair, Andrew, *Insurance Brokers Association of Canada*, 848
McNally, Chris, *Canadian Construction Association*, 363
McNally, Len, *Heiser Program for Research in Leprosy & Tuberculosis*, 1529
McNamara, Jamie, *Council of Catholic School Superintendents of Alberta*, 633
McNary, Lois, *Special Olympics BC*, 1339
McNaughton, Shirley, *Blissymbolics Communication International*, 214
McNea, Amanda, *Boys & Girls Clubs of Nova Scotia*, 223
McNee-Baker, Lisa, *Boys & Girls Clubs of Ontario*, 223
McNeil, Valerie, *Saint John East Food Bank Inc.*, 1247
McNeil, Kate, *Water Ski & Wakeboard Alberta*, 1441
McNeil, Stephen, *Liberal Party of Nova Scotia*, 909
McNeil, Shelly, *Immunize Canada*, 831
McNeil, Natasha, *EduNova*, 680
McNeill, Lindsey, *Alberta Media Production Industries Association*, 40
McNeill, Patricia, *Manitoba Association of Cheerleading*, 929
McNestry, Lois, *British Columbia Career College Association*, 235
McNicoll, John, *Alberta Construction Association*, 31
McNicoll, John, *Edmonton Construction Association*, 676
McNiven, Cathy, *Lincoln Chamber of Commerce*, 912
McNiven, Bruce, *Drummond Foundation*, 663
McNulty, Gord, *Canadian Aviation Historical Society*, 340
McNulty, Laura, *National Association of PeriAnesthesia Nurses of Canada*, 990
McNutt, Mitch, *Fortress Louisbourg Association*, 754
McNutt, John, *Junior Achievement Canada*, 877
McNutt, Albert, *The Northern AIDS Connection Society*, 1034
McPhail, Paul, *Independent Assemblies of God International - Canada*, 832
McPhail, Ellen, *PEI Sailing Association*, 1149
McPhedran Waitzer, Jon, *Head & Hands*, 805
McPhee, W.R. (Bob), *Calgary Opera Association*, 273
McPhersen, Arran, *International Council for the Exploration of the Sea*, 1544
McPherson, Clayton, *Canadian Institute of Management*, 417
McPherson, Ryan, *Supply Chain Management Association - New Brunswick*, 1356
McPherson, Marilyn, *Alberta Funeral Services Regulatory Board*, 36
McPherson, Russ, *Saskatchewan Economic Development Association*, 1264
McPherson, Mary, *Association of Fundraising Professionals*, 1512
McQuaid, Melissa, *College of Family Physicians of Canada*, 584
McQuaid, Randy, *Peterborough Numismatic Club*, 1154
McQuaid, Peggy, *CADORA Ontario Association Inc.*, 269
McQuaker, Joe, *Geological Association of Canada*, 770
McQuarrie, Alan, *Community Counselling Centre of Nipissing*, 596
McQuarrie, Colleen, *The Canadian College of Naturopathic Medicine*, 360
McQueen, Melissa, *Canadian Vascular Access Association*, 501
McQueen, Lynn, *Canadian Actors' Equity Association (CLC)*, 288
McQueen, Gary, *Canadian Space Society*, 489

Executive Name Index

McQuiggan, Joanne, *Lions Quest Canada - The Centre for Positive Youth Development*, 913
McRae, Sandy, *London & Middlesex Historical Society*, 918
McRae, Brad, *Ontario Skeet Shooting Association*, 1104
McRae, Jean, *Inter-Cultural Association of Greater Victoria*, 851
McRae, Jane, *International Centre for Sustainable Cities*, 855
McReynolds, Kathy, *Futurpreneur Canada*, 765
McRitchie, Lori, *Airdrie Food Bank*, 20
McRitchie, Lori, *Food Banks Alberta Association*, 749
McRoberts, Marnie, *Canadian Wheelchair Sports Association*, 504
McSherry, Karin, *Cross Country Ski Association of Manitoba*, 644
McSorley, Tom, *Canadian Film Institute*, 390
McSweeney, Michael, *Cement Association of Canada*, 521
McTaggart, Jackie, *Dominion Automobile Association Limited*, 660
McTaggart, Ev, *The McLean Foundation*, 955
McTaggart, Donna, *Calgary Folk Club*, 272
McTaggart, Kerri, *Resource Industry Suppliers Association*, 1227
McTavish, Kevin, *Saskatchewan Association for Community Living*, 1256
McTavish, Jill, *Southwestern Ontario Health Libraries & Information Network*, 1338
McTavish, Darlene, *Project Management Institute*, 1585
McTavish, Scott, *Pumphouse Theatres Society*, 1194
McTiernan-Gamble, Anne, *Canadian Cancer Society*, 349
McVey, John, *Bechtel Foundation of Canada*, 203
McWhinney, David, *Canadian Energy Research Institute*, 381
McWilliam, David, *Alberta Land Surveyors' Association*, 39
McWilliams, James, *SAIT Academic Faculty Association*, 1251
Mead, Mary, *Elder Abuse Ontario*, 681
Mead, Dan, *Orthotics Prosthetics Canada*, 1127
Meades, Susan, *PFLAG Canada Inc.*, 1156
Meadows, Michael, *International Geographic Union*, 1550
Meadows Forgeron, Tradina, *Multicultural Association of the Greater Moncton Area*, 979
Meagher, Jane, *Canadian Tax Foundation*, 492
Meakin, Jonathan, *Writers' Federation of Nova Scotia*, 1469
Meaney, Heather, *Music for Young Children*, 984
Mearns, Michael, *AFOA Canada*, 12
Mears, Emira, *Physiotherapy Association of British Columbia*, 1159
Meawasige, Marie, *N'swakamok Native Friendship Centre*, 987
Meban, Karen, *The Canadian Federation of Business & Professional Women's Clubs*, 386
Medd, Kari, *Alberta Therapeutic Recreation Association*, 50
Medhurst, Gina, *Kootenay Lake Chamber of Commerce*, 892
Medichkov, Elizabeth, *United Macedonians Organization of Canada*, 1411
Medley, Heather, *The Garden Clubs of Ontario*, 766
Mednick, Fred, *Teachers Without Borders*, 1597
Medwell, Caroline, *Ontario Community Newspapers Association*, 1073
Medwidsky, Tamara, *Canadian Amateur Wrestling Association*, 292
Medynski, Jolene, *Nurse Practitioners Association of Alberta*, 1052

Mee, Janet, *Canadian Association of College & University Student Services*, 310
Meech, Judith, *International Union of Food Science & Technology*, 861
Meehan, Brian, *Museum London*, 983
Meek, Gerry, *CanLearn Society for Persons with Learning Difficulties*, 508
Meeker, Mike, *Northern Ontario Aquaculture Association*, 1035
Meekins, Marcie, *Springhill & Area Chamber of Commerce*, 1346
Meeks, Michael, *Cardston & District Chamber of Commerce*, 511
Meems, Alice, *Church Library Association of Ontario*, 569
Meerakker, Tony, *Society of Motion Picture & Television Engineers*, 1593
Mees, Anna, *Bowls Canada Boulingrin*, 220
Meessen, Chantal, *Association québécoise de gérontologie*, 169
Meffe, Jean-Charles, *Football Québec*, 750
Megarity, Eric, *Cities of New Brunswick Association*, 570
Mégie, Marie-Françoise, *Médecins francophones du Canada*, 957
Megill, William, *Coastal Ecosystems Research Foundation*, 579
Meguerian, John, *CARP*, 514
Megyesi, Kim, *Big Brothers Big Sisters of Saskatchewan*, 210
Meharry, Isabel, *Kerry's Place Autism Services*, 884
Mehdi, Syed, *The College of Naturopaths of Ontario*, 586
Mehdipour, Saeed, *Association of Professional Engineers & Geoscientists of British Columbia*, 158
Mehendale, Trivi, *Halton Multicultural Council*, 800
Mehra, Vibhuti, *AIDS Committee of York Region*, 17
Mehta, Kavita, *Association of Family Health Teams of Ontario*, 148
Mehta, Krishan, *Association of Fundraising Professionals*, 1512
Meier, Gail, *Pathways Abilities Society*, 1145
Meier-Duthie, Pamela, *Canada Employment & Immigration Union*, 279
Meijer, Yolanda, *Habitat for Humanity Canada*, 796
Meilleur, Juli, *Children's Wish Foundation of Canada*, 563
Meincke, Peter, *The Royal Commonwealth Society of Canada*, 1242
Meinecke, Angel, *PBA Society of Canada*, 1146
Meinema, Paul, *United Food & Commercial Workers Canada*, 1411
Meiorin, John, *Bricklayers, Masons Independent Union of Canada (CLC)*, 228
Meisner, Lorne, *Baptist General Conference of Canada*, 196
Meisner, Lorne, *Baptist General Conference of Canada*, 196
Meixner, Scott, *Underwater Council of British Columbia*, 1404
Melakuova, Eva, *Canadian Association of Management Consultants*, 320
Melamed, Ken, *Green Party of Canada*, 788
Melançon, Sylvain, *Conseil communautaire Beausoleil*, 614
Melanson, Gail, *Nova Scotia Society for the Prevention of Cruelty to Animals*, 1049
Melanson, Brad, *Saint John SPCA Animal Rescue*, 1247
Melanson, Bob, *Yukon Amateur Radio Association*, 1477
Melanson, Marilyn, *Nova Scotia Stamp Club*, 1049
Melanson, Brian, *Yukon Trappers Association*, 1480
Melanson, Durline, *Historical Association of Annapolis Royal*, 816
Melanson, Jennifer, *Greyhound Pets of Atlantic Canada Society*, 790

Melanson, Janice, *Atlantic Canadian Organic Regional Network*, 183
Melchionna, Pina, *Canadian Institute of Traffic & Transportation*, 419
Meldrum, Bill, *Orienteering Québec*, 1126
Melia, Rick, *Alberta Rugby Football Union*, 45
Melia, Paul, *Canadian Centre for Ethics in Sport*, 353
Melin, Jonas, *Hotel Association of Vancouver*, 824
Melkert, Susan, *Family Services Perth-Huron*, 705
Mellafont, Rhonda, *Association of Professional Engineers & Geoscientists of British Columbia*, 158
Melles, Amanuel, *Couchiching Institute on Public Affairs*, 632
Mellett, Rebecca, *Canadian Evaluation Society*, 383
Mellish, Ron, *Ontario Association for Marriage & Family Therapy*, 1061
Mellor, Lindsay, *Fraser Valley Symphony Society*, 758
Mellos, Christina, *Cardiac Health Foundation of Canada*, 510
Mellott, John D., *Plastic Loose Fill Council*, 1584
Melnychuk, Ken, *Alberta Men's Wear Agents Association*, 40
Melnyk, Anatoliy, *Orthodox Church in America Archdiocese of Canada*, 1127
Melo, Nancy, *Vancity Community Foundation*, 1424
Melrose, Camilla, *Clean Nova Scotia Foundation*, 573
Meltzer, Jed, *Esperanto-Toronto*, 695
Melville, Frances, *Children's Health Foundation of Vancouver Island*, 561
Melville, Douglas, *Ombudsman for Banking Services & Investments*, 1057
Melville, John, *Accessible Media Inc.*, 5
Ménard, Paul, *Hockey Québec*, 818
Ménard, Marie, *Association paritaire pour la santé et la sécurité du travail - Imprimerie et activités connexes*, 165
Ménard, Frédéric, *Canadian Ski Marathon*, 471
Ménard, Christiane, *Canadian Society of Respiratory Therapists*, 487
Menard, Dan, *Alberta Aquaculture Association*, 22
Ménard, Danny, *Association des techniciens en santé animale du Québec*, 129
Ménard, Lyne, *Kéroul, Tourisme pour personnes à capacité physique restreinte*, 884
Menard, Shari, *Simcoe/Muskoka Literacy Network*, 1300
Menard Dumas, Pierre-Olivier, *Canadian Transport Lawyers Association*, 497
Menard-Penner, Lynda, *Community Living Dryden-Sioux Lookout*, 601
Menchenton, Lillian, *Canadian Hard of Hearing Association*, 400
Mendelson, Edna, *Crohn's & Colitis Canada*, 643
Mendelson, Edna, *Crohn's & Colitis Canada*, 642
Mendelson, Mark, *Canadian Associates of Ben-Gurion University of the Negev*, 297
Mendes, Carlos, *University of Waterloo Staff Association*, 1421
Mendez, Margarita, *Nellie's Shelter*, 1003
Mendez, Israel, *Canadian College of Health Leaders*, 359
Mendez, Malika, *Urban Alliance on Race Relations*, 1422
Mendoza, Carol, *World Aquaculture Society*, 1603
Menec, Verena, *Canadian Association on Gerontology*, 337
Mengel, Michael, *Canadian Society of Transplantation*, 488
Mensah, Nana, *Children's Miracle Network*, 562

Mensinga, Sid, *West Toronto Stamp Club*, 1446
Menzies, Meghan, *Community Living Manitoba*, 603
Menzies, Charles, *Canadian Anthropology Society*, 293
Merali, Zul, *Canadian Depression Research & Intervention Network*, 377
Mercado, Romeo, *Forever Young Seniors Society*, 752
Mercer, David, *Mount Pearl-Paradise Chamber of Commerce*, 976
Mercer, Chris, *Canadian University & College Counselling Association*, 499
Mercer, Greg, *One Parent Families Association of Canada*, 1058
Mercer, Christopher, *Lifesaving Society*, 911
Mercer, Paul, *Gideons International in Canada*, 773
Mercer, Robert, *Professional Association of Internes & Residents of Newfoundland*, 1182
Mercer, Tammy, *British Columbia Competitive Trail Riders Association*, 236
Mercer, Don, *Consumers Council of Canada*, 626
Mercer, Norm, *Newfoundland & Labrador Prospectors Association*, 1021
Mercieca, Charles, *International Association of Educators for World Peace - USA*, 1538
Mercier, Véronique, *Association de la construction du Québec*, 101
Mercier, Bernard, *Insitut canadien des économistes en construction - Québec*, 840
Mercier, Lucie, *Association canadienne-française de l'Ontario, Mille-îles*, 96
Mercier, Paul, *Illuminating Engineering Society of North America*, 1531
Mercier, Nathalie, *Confédération québécoise des coopératives d'habitation en Outaouais*, 611
Mercier, Nathalie, *Association provinciale des constructeurs d'habitations du Québec inc.*, 168
Mercier, Jean-Paul, *Association mototocycliste Chibougamau Chapais*, 137
Mercier, Karen, *Alberta Dressage Association*, 33
Mercure, Gilles, *Réseau des SADC et CAE*, 1222
Mercury, Rosemarie, *Canadian Association of Black Lawyers*, 309
Meredith, Mimi, *Society of Environmental Toxicology & Chemistry*, 1593
Mereu, R.F., *Southern Ontario Seismic Network*, 1338
Mereweather, Cher, *Provision Coalition*, 1191
Merikanskas, Mauricio, *World ORT Union*, 1607
Merk, Sebastian, *Benevolent & Protective Order of Elks of Canada*, 205
Merkl, Andreas, *The Ocean Conservancy*, 1580
Merkley, Bob, *Canadian Shorthorn Association*, 470
Merkowsky, Dan, *Recreation Vehicle Dealers Association of Canada*, 1208
Merola, Kanys, *TB Vets*, 1367
Merrell, Dennis, *Alberta Weekly Newspapers Association*, 51
Merrell, Bill, *National Association of Review Appraisers & Mortgage Underwriters*, 1574
Merrier, Paula, *Association for Financial Professionals - Vancouver*, 133
Merrill, Rick, *Children's Miracle Network*, 562
Merriman, Lynnette, *La Ronge & District Chamber of Commerce*, 1236
Merritt, Ian, *Ontario Association of Cemetery & Funeral Professionals*, 1062
Merritt, Jody, *Human Resources Professionals Association*, 826
Merritt, Fred, *Canadian Musical Reproduction Rights Agency*, 438
Merzetti, Tony, *New Brunswick Filmmakers' Co-op*, 1008

Meshack, Samuel W., *World Association for Christian Communication*, 1465
Meshwork, Lindy, *ORT Canada*, 1127
Mesih, Connie, *Ontario Municipal Tax & Revenue Association*, 1092
Meski, Driss, *International Commission for the Conservation of Atlantic Tunas*, 1542
Messely, Louis, *Club des ornithologues de Québec inc.*, 575
Messenger, Cynthia, *University of Toronto Faculty Association*, 1420
Messenger, Michael, *World Vision Canada*, 1467
Messenger, Pat, *PFLAG Canada Inc.*, 1155
Messer-Engel, Karen, *Saskatchewan College of Psychologists*, 1261
Messer-Lepage, Jacquie, *Saskatchewan College of Paramedics*, 1261
Messier, Hélène, *Association québécoise de la production médiatique*, 170
Messier, Christine, *CUSO International*, 646
Messinger, Marra, *Jewish Free Loan Toronto*, 872
Meste, Sylvie, *Conseil québécois du théâtre*, 620
Metatawabin, Shannin, *National Aboriginal Capital Corporations Association*, 988
Metcalf, Allan A., *American Dialect Society*, 1492
Metcalf, Beth, *Parkinson Alberta Society*, 1141
Metcalfe, Selina, *Environmental Educators' Provincial Specialist Association*, 691
Metcalfe, Lois, *Canadian Institute of Quantity Surveyors*, 419
Metcalfe, Lois, *Canadian Institute of Quantity Surveyors - Ontario*, 419
Metcalfe, Donna, *Mississauga Real Estate Board*, 970
Metherell, Joni, *YMCA Canada*, 1471
Méthot, Nicolas, *Association québécoise pour le loisir des personnes handicapées*, 177
Métivier, Michel, *Chambre de commerce et d'industrie St-Jérôme*, 548
Metlej, Samir, *Diman Association Canada (Lebanese)*, 657
Metouilli, Faouzi, *Moroccan Association of Toronto*, 974
Metz, Bernhard, *Association for Canadian Studies in German-Speaking Countries*, 1507
Metzger, Willard, *Mennonite Church Canada*, 961
Meunier, Jean-Patrice, *Association de la presse francophone*, 102
Meunier, Kim, *Recreation Prince Edward Island*, 1208
Meurice, Stephen, *The Canadian Press*, 459
Meurling, Sara, *Professional Association of Canadian Theatres*, 1182
Meyer, Evelyn, *International Arthurian Society - North American Branch*, 1535
Meyer, Patrick E., *Federation of Canadian Artists*, 722
Meyer, William, *Renewable Industries Canada*, 1217
Meyer, Geri, *Credit Institute of Canada*, 641
Meyer, David, *Saskatchewan Archaeological Society*, 1256
Meyer, Dustin, *Association for Financial Professionals - Edmonton*, 133
Meyers, Amanda, *American Political Science Association*, 1497
Mezzarobba, Dianna, *British Columbia Literacy Council*, 245
Mharapara, Primrose, *Canadian Association of Critical Care Nurses*, 312
Mian, Aamir, *Schizophrenia Society of Ontario*, 1284
Miano, Tiziana, *Italian Cultural Institute (Istituto Italiano di Cultura)*, 867
Miazga, Susan, *Swim Saskatchewan*, 1359
Michael, Lorraine, *New Democratic Party*, 1014
Michael, Baddeley, *Canadian Captive Insurance Association*, 350
Michael, Patrick, *Yukon Arts Centre*, 1477

Michaels, Sean, *Community Living Manitoba*, 603
Michalenko, Carm, *Saskatoon Community Foundation*, 1279
Michaud, Serge, *Special Olympics Yukon*, 1340
Michaud, Chantal, *Ordre des ingénieurs du Québec*, 1122
Michaud, Jean-Luc, *New Brunswick Society of Certified Engineering Technicians & Technologists*, 1012
Michaud, Terrie, *Catholic Health Association of Saskatchewan*, 520
Michaud, Adrien, *Centre Jean-Claude Malépart*, 536
Michaud, Steve, *Dairy Farmers of New Brunswick*, 648
Michaud, Dany, *Société québécoise de récupération et de recyclage*, 1323
Michaud, Nadia, *Association des juristes d'expression française du Nouveau-Brunswick*, 118
Michaud, Harold, *Association des juristes d'expression française du Nouveau-Brunswick*, 118
Michaud, Elaine, *Les EssentiElles*, 696
Michaudville, Bonnie, *Hamiota Chamber of Commerce*, 802
Michel, Viviane, *Femmes autochtones du Québec inc.*, 732
Micheli, Serge, *Ontario Fashion Exhibitors*, 1078
Micheli, Serge, *Canadian Association of Exposition Management*, 313
Micheli, Serge, *Canadian Toy Association / Canadian Toy & Hobby Fair*, 496
Michelin, Heather, *Lord Reading Law Society*, 919
Michnik, Brad, *Saskatchewan Trade & Export Partnership*, 1276
Michols, Dann, *Thousand Islands Watershed Land Trust*, 1377
Michrowski, Andrew, *Planetary Association for Clean Energy, Inc.*, 1161
Mickanuck, Penny, *John Howard Society of Alberta*, 874
Mickeloff, Al, *Canadian Warplane Heritage*, 502
Mickelthwate, Alexander, *Winnipeg Symphony Orchestra Inc.*, 1459
Micucci, Lori, *Canadian Golf Superintendents Association*, 398
Middlebrook, Ken, *Canadian Association for Laboratory Accreditation Inc.*, 302
Middlebrough, David, *Alberta Target Archers Association*, 49
Middler, Anne, *Yukon Conservation Society*, 1478
Middleton, Andrew, *Ponoka & District Chamber of Commerce*, 1164
Middleton, Catherine, *Directors Guild of Canada*, 658
Middleton, Catherine, *Directors Guild of Canada*, 658
Middleton, Amy, *Provincial Health Ethics Network*, 1191
Middleton, Marguerite, *Swimming Prince Edward Island*, 1359
Middleton, Janice, *The Garden Clubs of Ontario*, 766
Middleton, Manna, *Association of Early Childhood Educators of Alberta*, 147
Midgley, Clare, *International Federation for Research in Women's History*, 1547
Midgley, James (Jamie), *Chartered Professional Accountants of British Columbia*, 553
Mielczarek, Leanne, *Lupus Canada*, 921
Mifflin, Glenn, *CUSO International*, 646
Migicovsky, Manny, *Canadian Correspondence Chess Association*, 366
Migone, Andrea, *Institute of Public Administration of Canada*, 847
Mihok, Peter, *World Chambers Federation*, 1604

Mikalishen, Stephanie, *British Columbia Camping Association*, 234
Mike, Jesse, *National Inuit Youth Council*, 994
Mike, McCann, *VeloNorth Cycling Club*, 1431
Miki, Art, *Japanese Cultural Association of Manitoba*, 869
Miki, Art, *Asian Heritage Society of Manitoba*, 87
Mikkelsen, Dave, *Society for Treatment of Autism*, 1327
Mikkelsen, Naja, *International Arctic Science Committee*, 1535
Mikkila, Dagmar, *Association of Unity Churches Canada*, 163
Mikkola, Raymond, *Last Post Fund*, 899
Milanetti, Nick, *Ontario Catholic School Trustees' Association*, 1070
Milburn, Cynthia, *Epilepsy Ontario*, 693
Milbury, Calvin, *New Brunswick Innovation Foundation*, 1009
Mileham, Doug, *Appaloosa Horse Club of Canada*, 73
Miles, Val, *University of Saskatchewan Arts Council*, 1420
Miles, Pamela, *Abundance Canada*, 3
Miles, Brian, *Appaloosa Horse Club of Canada*, 73
Miles, Melody, *Hamilton Niagara Haldimand Brant Community Care Access Centre*, 801
Miles, Diana, *Law Society of Upper Canada*, 902
Milford, Lynne, *CADORA Ontario Association Inc.*, 269
Milito, Gino, *Canadian Italian Business & Professional Association of Ottawa*, 423
Milla, Stephanie, *AIDS Programs South Saskatchewan*, 17
Millan, Kim, *Oakville & Milton Humane Society*, 1053
Millan, Kim, *Ontario Society for the Prevention of Cruelty to Animals*, 1106
Millar, Jeff, *Devon & District Chamber of Commerce*, 655
Millar, Danielle, *Gravenhurst Chamber of Commerce/Visitors Bureau*, 782
Millar, Jim, *Port Moody Heritage Society*, 1166
Millar, Sydney, *Canadian Association for the Advancement of Women & Sport & Physical Activity*, 305
Millar, Jim, *Moose Jaw Real Estate Board*, 974
Millar, Joan, *Jane Austen Society of North America*, 868
Millar, Seanna, *Hospital for Sick Children Foundation*, 823
Millar, Kerri-Rae, *Western Canadian Association of Bovine Practitioners*, 1448
Millar, Lawrence, *Southeast Environmental Association*, 1337
Millard, Eleanor, *Canadian Grandparents' Rights Association*, 399
Millard, Michele, *Refugee Research Network*, 1211
Miller, Patti, *Canada Grains Council*, 279
Miller, Cheryl, *Arts Council of the Central Okanagan*, 85
Miller, Sheila, *University of Calgary Faculty Association*, 1419
Miller, Doug, *Social Justice Committee*, 1305
Miller, Sarah, *Atlantic Association of Applied Economists*, 182
Miller, Carmen, *Chase & District Chamber of Commerce*, 555
Miller, Kim, *Powell River Chamber of Commerce*, 1169
Miller, Chaz, *National Waste & Recycling Association*, 1577
Miller, Kathleen, *International Council of Ophthalmology*, 1545
Miller, Moreen, *Ontario Stone, Sand & Gravel Association*, 1109
Miller, Patti, *Canola Council of Canada*, 509
Miller, Lynn, *Special Olympics Ontario*, 1340
Miller, Maureen, *Sport North Federation*, 1345
Miller, Don, *Canadian Bible Society*, 343

Miller, Christine, *Manitoba Heavy Construction Association*, 938
Miller, Donna, *Canadian Co-operative Association*, 364
Miller, Jennifer, *Saskatchewan Lung Association*, 1269
Miller, Nicole, *Paperboard Packaging Council*, 1582
Miller, Chris, *Canadian Parks & Wilderness Society*, 451
Miller, Dave, *Atlantic Provinces Trucking Association*, 185
Miller, Carling, *Kind Space*, 888
Miller, Kristi, *Junior Achievement Canada*, 877
Miller, Tania, *Victoria Symphony Society*, 1434
Miller, André, *The Ontario Archaeological Society*, 1060
Miller, Dale, *Lifesaving Society*, 911
Miller, James, *Tourism Industry Association of Nova Scotia*, 1390
Miller, Lucy, *United Way of Calgary & Area*, 1413
Miller, Karly, *Manitoba Gymnastics Association*, 937
Miller, Klara, *Gymnastics Saskatchewan*, 795
Miller, John, *Muskoka Steamship & Historical Society*, 985
Miller, Lukas, *Saskatchewan Health Libraries Association*, 1267
Miller, Dianne, *Society of Gynecologic Oncologists of Canada*, 1329
Miller, Shirley, *Southern First Nations Secretariat*, 1337
Miller, Lynn, *Anxiety Disorders Association of Canada*, 72
Miller, Thomas H., *International Association of Fire Fighters (AFL-CIO/CLC)*, 1538
Miller, Ann, *Canadian Association for the Study of International Development*, 306
Miller, Candice, *British Columbia Therapeutic Riding Association*, 257
Miller, David, *World Wildlife Fund - Canada*, 1468
Miller, Joan, *Collingwood & District Historical Society*, 591
Miller, Lois, *Saskatchewan Environmental Industry & Managers' Association*, 1264
Miller, David, *Independent Canadian Extrusion Workers Union*, 832
Miller, Keith, *Creation Science of Saskatchewan Inc.*, 639
Miller, Sarah, *Dog Guides Canada*, 660
Miller, Gary, *Congregation Beth Israel - British Columbia*, 612
Miller, Nicole, *FAST (Fighting Antisemitism Together)*, 706
Miller, Jeff, *Installation, Maintenance & Repair Sector Council & Trade Association*, 840
Miller, Johathan, *Prison Fellowship Canada*, 1180
Miller, Mark E., *Manitoba Ozone Protection Industry Association*, 941
Miller, Corey, *Nova Scotia Nature Trust*, 1047
Miller, Rosalyn, *Delta Family Resource Centre*, 653
Miller, Ken, *Canadian Belgian Blue Association*, 342
Miller, Garth, *Triathlon New Brunswick*, 1398
Miller, Peter, *Interactive Ontario*, 851
Miller, Earl, *International Association of Art Critics - Canada*, 854
Miller, Rachel, *Chartered Professional Accountants of Alberta*, 552
Miller, Jenn, *Atkinson Charitable Foundation*, 182
Miller-Sanford, Brenda, *Grain Farmers of Ontario*, 779
Millette, Robert, *Association des ingénieurs municipaux du Québec*, 116
Millette, Dianne, *Physiotherapy Alberta - College + Association*, 1158
Millette, Jackie, *Canadian Pediatric Foundation*, 452
Millette, Réjean, *Société québécoise des hostas et des hémérocalles*, 1324

Executive Name Index

Milley, Danielle, *Ontario Medical Association*, 1090
Milley, Gary, *Recreation Newfoundland & Labrador*, 1207
Milley, Karen, *Credit Counselling Services of Newfoundland & Labrador*, 640
Millian, Mike, *Private Motor Truck Council of Canada*, 1180
Millier, Harvey, *Merit Contractors Association of Manitoba*, 962
Milligan, Bill, *Appaloosa Horse Club of Canada*, 73
Milligan, Edward, *Spinal Cord Injury British Columbia*, 1343
Milligan, Doug, *Horse Industry Association of Alberta*, 822
Milligan, Beverley, *Media Access Canada*, 957
Milliken, Peter, *United Empire Loyalists' Association of Canada*, 1410
Milliken, Peter A. S., *The Order of St. Lazarus*, 1119
Millington, Dinara, *Canadian Energy Research Institute*, 381
Millions, Noel, *Canadian Association of Petroleum Landmen*, 326
Millman, Dorothy, *ARZA-Canada: The Zionist Voice of the Canadian Reform Movement*, 86
Mills, John, *Manitoba Society of Artists*, 944
Mills, Wes, *Apostolic Church of Pentecost of Canada Inc.*, 73
Mills, Becky, *Windsor-Essex Therapeutic Riding Association*, 1457
Mills, Pat, *East Hants & District Chamber of Commerce*, 668
Mills, Susan, *Grand Bend & Area Chamber of Commerce*, 779
Mills, Brian, *Financial Services Commission of Ontario*, 737
Mills, Julie, *Canadian Crossroads International*, 373
Mills, Larry, *Canadian Red Cross*, 466
Mills, Cathie, *The Bruce Trail Conservancy*, 261
Mills, Lauralee, *Canadian Fjord Horse Association*, 391
Mills, Laura Lee, *Canadian Palomino Horse Association*, 449
Mills, Jamey, *Public Service Alliance of Canada*, 1193
Mills, Lorna, *Career Colleges Ontario*, 511
Mills, Don, *Novia Scotia Sports Hall of Fame*, 1050
Mills, Shirley, *Ontario Bison Association*, 1068
Mills, Gerry, *Immigrant Services Association of Nova Scotia*, 830
Mills, Sharon, *New Brunswick Sailing Association*, 1011
Mills, Stan, *TelecomPioneers of Alberta*, 1369
Mills, Laura Lee, *Canine Federation of Canada*, 508
Mills, Laura Lee, *Canadian Horse Breeders' Association*, 408
Mills, Laura Lee, *Canadian Finnsheep Breeders' Association*, 390
Mills, Laura Lee, *Canadian Katahdin Sheep Association Inc.*, 424
Millson, Dana, *The Ontario Archaeological Society*, 1059
Milne, Cheryl, *Canadian Coalition for the Rights of Children*, 358
Milne, Garry, *Military Collectors Club of Canada*, 965
Milne, Noella, *UNICEF Canada*, 1404
Milne, Jon, *Invest Ottawa*, 862
Milner, Colin, *International Council on Active Aging*, 856
Milner, Julie, *International Council on Active Aging*, 856
Milner, Helen, *International Political Science Association*, 859
Milord, Isabelle, *FaunENord*, 706
Milroy, Carol, *PFLAG Canada Inc.*, 1155
Milsom, David, *Ontario Field Ornithologists*, 1080

Milton, Martin, *Bureau international des poids et mesures*, 1515
Milton, John, *Ontario Recreation Facilities Association*, 1100
Milton, John, *Canadian Recreation Facilities Council*, 465
Milway, James, *Catholic Missions in Canada*, 520
Milway, James, *Newman Centre Catholic Chaplaincy and Parish*, 1024
Min, Jason, *Canadian Fertility & Andrology Society*, 389
Min-yang Wang, Eric, *International Ergonomics Association*, 1546
Mina, Petros, *Cypriot Federation of Canada*, 647
Minard, Lance, *Greater Woodstock Chamber of Commerce*, 787
Minas, David, *Financial Executives International Canada*, 736
Mincer, Harvey, *Shaarei Tefillah*, 1293
Mineault, Shelley, *The Canadian Association for HIV Research*, 301
Ming Sun, Sophia, *China Canada Investment Association*, 564
Mingo, Joyce, *Central Nova Tourist Association*, 524
Minhas, Sudip, *Windsor Women Working with Immigrant Women*, 1457
Miniely, Donna, *Thyroid Foundation of Canada*, 1379
Minigh, Howard, *Croplife International*, 1520
Mink, Georges, *International Council for Central & East European Studies (Canada)*, 1544
Minnick, Matthew, *Professional Engineers Ontario*, 1184
Minniti, Samuel, *The St. George's Society of Toronto*, 1248
Minsky, Adam, *UJA Federation of Greater Toronto*, 1402
Mintram, Bill, *Saskatoon Indian & Métis Friendship Centre*, 1279
Mintz, James, *Canadian Public Health Association*, 462
Minuk, David, *Judo Manitoba*, 876
Minz, Elana, *Jewish Chamber of Commerce*, 871
Mion, Alfred, *Essex-Kent Cage Bird Society*, 696
Mion, Nicole, *Springboard Dance*, 1346
Miousse, Denis, *Centraide Duplessis*, 522
Mir, Furakh, *Meningitis Relief Canada*, 960
Miranda, Lily, *Filipino Canadian Association of Vaughan*, 735
Mireau, Colleen, *Association of Professional Engineers & Geoscientists of Alberta*, 157
Miriguay, David, *Institute of Chartered Secretaries & Administrators - Canadian Division*, 845
Miriguay, David, *Canadian Council of Cardiovascular Nurses*, 368
Mirkovic, Dragan, *Newfoundland & Labrador Soccer Association*, 1021
Mirolla, Michael, *Ontario Book Publishers Organization*, 1068
Miron, Ernie, *Manitoba Chiropractors' Association*, 934
Mirza, Ali, *Ontario Chamber of Commerce*, 1071
Mirza, Sami, *Islamic Association of Nova Scotia*, 864
Mirza, Shabana, *Association of Dental Technologists of Ontario*, 146
Mirza, Raza M., *National Initiative for the Care of the Elderly*, 994
Misdrahi, Marian, *Centre de prévention de la radicalisation menant à la violence*, 529
Mish, Janette, *Saskatchewan Katahdin Sheep Association Inc.*, 1268
Mishra, Mamta, *World Literacy of Canada*, 1466
Miskiman, Wes, *Alberta Snowboard Association*, 47

Miskiw, John, *York Regional Police Association*, 1473
Misner, Judy, *Psoriasis Society of Canada*, 1191
Missori, Joe, *Laborers' International Union of North America (AFL-CIO/CLC)*, 1569
Misthios, Costas, *Greek Orthodox Metropolis of Toronto (Canada)*, 788
Mistry, Vanisha, *Football Canada*, 750
Mistry, Reena, *British Columbia Food Technolgists*, 241
Mitchell, Julie, *South Coast District Labour Council*, 1334
Mitchell, Cecil, *Nova Scotia Horseshoe Players Association*, 1046
Mitchell, Paul, *Central Ontario Musicians' Association*, 525
Mitchell, Hugh, *Western Fair Association*, 1449
Mitchell, Bob, *Basketball Alberta*, 198
Mitchell, Grant, *Athletics Manitoba*, 181
Mitchell, Ian, *Scouts Canada*, 1286
Mitchell, Gary, *British Columbia Historical Federation*, 243
Mitchell, Catherine, *Manitoba Heavy Construction Association*, 938
Mitchell, Chris, *The Canadian Corps of Commissionaires*, 365
Mitchell, Marilyn, *Huntington Society of Canada*, 827
Mitchell, Evan, *Kingston Symphony Association*, 890
Mitchell, Evan, *Kitchener-Waterloo Symphony Youth Orchestra*, 891
Mitchell, Robert J., *United Way of Central Alberta*, 1413
Mitchell, Eric, *Canadian Aviation Artists Assocation*, 340
Mitchell, Wendy, *Responsible Investment Association*, 1227
Mitchell, Jewell, *YWCA Canada*, 1481
Mitchell, Adam, *Canadian Institute for Theatre Technology*, 413
Mitchell, Rebecca, *Human Resources Professionals Association*, 826
Mitchell, Brent, *Yonge Street Mission*, 1473
Mitchell, Andy, *Canadian Association of Former Parliamentarians*, 315
Mitchell, Arthur, *Habitat for Humanity Canada*, 798
Mitchell, Prabha, *Women Entrepreneurs of Saskatchewan Inc.*, 1460
Mitchell, Keri, *Theatre Alberta Society*, 1373
Mitchell, Laurie, *La Jeunesse Youth Orchestra*, 871
Mitchell, Andrea, *Insurance Women's Association of Western Manitoba*, 850
Mitchell, Don, *Sault Ste Marie Economic Development Corporation*, 1281
Mitchell, Pierre, *Association québécoise des traumatisés craniens*, 175
Mitchell, Brian, *Trade Facilitation Office Canada*, 1394
Mitchell, Mack C., *Alcoholic Beverage Medical Research Foundation*, 1487
Mitchell, Jean, *British Columbia Contact Centre Association*, 237
Mitchell, David J., *Canada's Public Policy Forum*, 282
Mitchell, Winna, *Campbell River & District Association for Community Living*, 276
Mitchell, David, *Calgary Chamber of Voluntary Organizations*, 271
Mitchell, Derek, *Camping Association of Nova Scotia & PEI*, 277
Mitchell, Pierre, *Association québécoise des traumatisés crâniens*, 175
Mitchell, Darryl, *BC Taekwondo Association*, 202
Mitchell, Mallory, *Manitoba Cheer Federation Inc.*, 933
Mitchell, Lorraine, *Biathlon Manitoba*, 207
Mitchell, Peter, *Canadian Deaf Golf Association*, 376
Mitchell-Matheson, Heather, *Horse Industry Association of Alberta*, 822

Mitchell-Walker, Brian, *Affirm United*, 12
Mitchener, Hugh, *Canadian Amateur Softball Association*, 292
Mitges, George, *Ontario Institute of Agrologists*, 1087
Mithcelmore, Kara, *Marketing Research & Intelligence Association*, 951
Mitman, Gregg, *American Society for Environmental History*, 1498
Mitra, Trini, *Opéra Atelier*, 1114
Mitrani, Michael, *Earth Island Institute*, 1522
Mitrow, Carolyn, *Ski Hawks Ottawa*, 1302
Mittal, Ajai Kumar, *World Blind Union*, 1465
Mitton, Donald, *Canadian Association for Humane Trapping*, 301
Mitton, Rachel, *Association of Registered Interior Designers of New Brunswick*, 161
Mitton, Charlie, *Ridgetown & South East Kent Chamber of Commerce*, 1232
Miyano, Mai, *DanceSport Atlantic*, 650
Miyashita, Debbie, *British Columbia Welsh Pony & Cob Association*, 258
Miyazaki, Donald, *Professional Golfers' Assocation of British Columbia*, 1185
Mlieczko, Emily, *Early Childhood Educators of British Columbia*, 667
Mlynarek, Jacek, *Groupe CTT Group*, 791
Moatti, Bonnie, *Pride of Israel*, 1170
Moauro, Pat, *CARP*, 514
Mobbs, Deborah, *Blue Mountain Foundation for the Arts*, 215
Mobbs, Verle, *Canadian Music Week Inc.*, 438
Moberg-Parker, Tine, *BC Sailing Association*, 202
Mochkin, Berel, *Chabad Lubavitch Youth Organization*, 539
Modolo, Gregoria, *Association de la construction du Québec*, 101
Modrovsky, Bernadette, *Huntington Society of Canada*, 828
Moeller, Lorraine, *Boys & Girls Clubs of Saskatchewan*, 224
Moeller, Lorraine, *Boys & Girls Clubs of Saskatchewan*, 224
Moen, Timothy, *The Libertarian Party of Canada*, 909
Moen, Wayne, *Old Strathcona Foundation*, 1056
Moffat, Lynda, *St. Albert & District Chamber of Commerce*, 1247
Moffat, William, *Aboriginal Firefighters Association of Canada*, 2
Moffat, Shannon, *Ontario Brain Injury Association*, 1068
Moffat, Susan, *Tarragon Theatre*, 1367
Moffatt, Lynn, *Alzheimer Society of Kenora/Rainy River Districts*, 63
Moffatt, Kelly, *Edmonton Reptile & Amphibian Society*, 679
Moffitt, Scott, *BioNova*, 211
Mogado, Marlene, *University of the Philippines Alumni Association of Toronto*, 1420
Moggach, Bob, *Photo Marketing Association International - Canada*, 1157
Mohammed, Eleanor, *Alberta Professional Planners Institute*, 43
Mohammed, Rafi, *Manitoba Dental Association*, 935
Mohammed, Peter, *Integrated Vegetation Management Association of British Columbia*, 850
Mohammed, Hakim, *British Columbia Muslim Association*, 247
Mohammed, Mostafa, *British Columbia Muslim Association*, 247
Mohan, Charles A., *United Mitochondrial Disease Foundation*, 1599
Mohan, Dilani, *Miss G Project*, 968
Mohan, Jr., Charles A., *United Mitochondrial Disease Foundation*, 1599
Mohideen, Fazal, *Ontario Rifle Association*, 1102
Mohindra, Neil, *Canadian Association of Pension Supervisory Authorities*, 325

Executive Name Index

Mohr, Cindy, *Fort St. John Association for Community Living*, 753
Mohr, Gregory, *Evangelical Lutheran Church in Canada*, 698
Mohr, Jeremy, *Saskatchewan Council for Archives & Archivists*, 1262
Mohr, Tom, *The Ontario Archaeological Society*, 1060
Mohr, Christine, *Options: Services to Communities Society*, 1117
Mohseni, Madjid, *Canadian Society for Chemical Engineering*, 473
Moineau, Genevieve, *Association of Faculties of Medicine of Canada*, 148
Moir, Judy, *Ontario Brain Injury Association*, 1069
Moisan, Yves, *British Columbia Paralegal Association*, 248
Moist, Kelly, *Canadian Union of Public Employees*, 498
Mojor, Jennifer, *Association Carrefour Famille Montcalm*, 96
Mok, Helen, *Calgary Law Library Group*, 273
Mokssit, Abdalah, *World Meteorological Organization*, 1606
Molcak, Josh, *Petroleum Accountants Society of Canada*, 1154
Molczanski, Mark, *Free Methodist Church in Canada*, 759
Mole, Sally, *Ucluelet Chamber of Commerce*, 1402
Molenaar, Tammie, *Community Living Manitoulin*, 603
Molendyk, Brenda, *McBride & District Chamber of Commerce*, 955
Molendyk, Eric, *Tetra Society of North America*, 1373
Moleschi, Marshall, *Canadian Foundation for Pharmacy*, 393
Molgat, Anne, *Regroupement des éditeurs canadiens-français*, 1215
Molina, Adriana, *Credit Canada Debt Solutions, Inc.*, 639
Molina, Patricia, *ACUC International*, 7
Molina, Catherine, *Guelph Symphony Orchestra*, 793
Mollenhauer, John G., *Council of Ontario Construction Associations*, 634
Moller, Lars, *World Health Organization Partnership for Health in the Criminal Justice Sytem*, 1606
Mollison, Marty, *Navy League of Canada*, 1002
Molloy, Sean J., *Canadian College of Health Leaders*, 359
Molloy, Sheila, *Massage Therapy Association of Manitoba Inc.*, 953
Molloy, Bernie, *Bell Aliant Pioneers*, 204
Molnar, Marc, *CODE*, 580
Molnar, Emily, *Ballet British Columbia*, 194
Moloney, Jane, *Canadian Association of Community Health Centres*, 311
Mombourquette, Amanda, *Strait Area Chamber of Commerce*, 1351
Mombourquette, Chad, *Halifax Hurricanes Ringette Association*, 799
Mombourquette, Sarah, *Australian Cattle Dog Rescue of Ontario*, 188
Mona, Laurie, *American Association of Neuromuscular & Electrodiagnostic Medicine*, 1490
Monaco, Carolyn, *Canadian Deafblind Association (National)*, 376
Monaco, Jerry, *Ontario Plumbing Inspectors Association*, 1096
Monaco-Wells, Nella, *West Grey Chamber of Commerce*, 1445
Monaghan, William, *Canadian Foundry Association*, 394
Monaghan, Dale, *Goodwill Industries of Alberta*, 778
Moncada, Sam, *Canadian Hardware & Housewares Manufacturers' Association*, 401
Moncada, Sam, *Canadian Office Products Association*, 445

Monden, Kim, *Community Living St. Marys & Area Association*, 605
Mondeville, Michelle, *Coal Association of Canada*, 577
Moner-Banet, Jean-Luc, *World Lottery Association*, 1606
Monette, Louis, *Association de bienfaisance et de retraite des policiers et policières de la ville de Montréal*, 99
Monette, Jocelyn, *Catholic Biblical Association of Canada*, 517
Monette, Céline, *Médecins francophones du Canada*, 957
Monette, Pascal, *Association de la recherche industrielle du Québec*, 102
Monette, Pierre, *Réseau des SADC et CAE*, 1222
Money, Ken, *National Space Society*, 1577
Monforton, Linda, *Ducks Unlimited Canada*, 663
Monge, Todd, *West Coast Environmental Law*, 1445
Mongeau, Catherine, *Corporation des bibliothécaires professionnels du Québec*, 629
Mongeau, René, *Ordre des agronomes du Québec*, 1120
Mongeau, Richard, *Fédération équestre du Québec inc.*, 720
Mongeau, José, *Association de médiation familiale du Québec*, 102
Mongeau, Jean-Pierre, *The Transplantation Society*, 1395
Mongeon, Philippe, *Canadian Association for Information Science*, 301
Mongeon, Line, *Microscopical Society of Canada*, 964
Monger, Leslie, *Community Living Welland Pelham*, 606
Mongrain, Parise, *Dancer Transition Resource Centre*, 650
Mongrain, Maurice, *Association de planification fiscale et financière*, 103
Monier, Christine, *L'Arche Western Region*, 78
Moniz, Tiffany, *Promotional Product Professionals of Canada Inc.*, 1189
Monk, Gary, *Human Resources Professionals Association*, 825
Monk, Sarah, *Alberta Bobsleigh Association*, 26
Monkman, Linda, *Nicola Valley & District Food Bank*, 1026
Monks, Alice, *Saskatchewan CGIT Committee*, 1260
Monnerie, Annick, *Association française d'études canadiennes*, 1509
Monnin, Christian, *Société de la francophonie manitobaine*, 1316
Monnon Dempsey, Karen, *The National Council of Women of Canada*, 992
Monson, Marty, *Barbershop Harmony Society*, 1514
Mont, Ken, *Canadian Picture Pioneers*, 455
Montano, Gloria, *NSERC Chair for Women in Science & Engineering*, 1050
Monteith, Ken, *Coalition des organismes communautaires québécois de lutte contre le sida*, 578
Monteith, Lee, *Canadian Lowline Cattle Association*, 428
Montgomery, Regina H., *American Economic Association*, 1492
Montgomery, Don, *Auctioneers Association of Alberta*, 187
Montina, Lyndsay, *Boys & Girls Clubs of Alberta*, 221
Montmarquette, Daniel, *Polio Québec*, 1163
Montney, Sheila, *Manitoba Cultural Society of the Deaf*, 935
Montopoli, Peter, *Canadian Soccer Association*, 472
Montour, Ken, *Canadian Council for Aboriginal Business*, 366
Montour, Claire, *Fédération de la santé du Québec - CSQ*, 710

Montour, Pam, *Chiefs of Ontario*, 558
Montpellier, Ryan, *Mining Industry Human Resources Council*, 967
Montpetit, Zoée, *BC Rainbow Alliance of the Deaf*, 202
Montreuil, Carol, *Canadian Fuels Association*, 396
Monture, Janis, *Woodland Cultural Centre*, 1464
Montvydas, Nancy, *Soroptimist International of the Americas*, 1595
Montwieler, William, *Industrial Truck Association*, 1531
Mood, Melissa, *Boys & Girls Clubs of Alberta*, 221
Moody, Robert, *British Columbia Institute of Agrologists*, 244
Moody, Neil, *Canadian Home Builders' Association - British Columbia*, 406
Moody, Tim, *Canadian Amateur Musicians*, 292
Moon, Kristine, *Unity & District Chamber of Commerce*, 1418
Mooney, Colleen, *Boys & Girls Clubs of Ontario*, 223
Mooney, Natasha, *Canadian Society of Nutrition Management*, 485
Mooney, Kevin, *Funeral Information & Memorial Society of Guelph*, 764
Moons, Maryann, *Financial Executives International Canada*, 736
Moorcroft, Brittany, *Brewers Association of Canada*, 228
Moore, Fran, *DeBolt & District Pioneer Museum Society*, 652
Moore, Adele, *Prince Edward Island Association of Exhibitions*, 1172
Moore, Tammy, *ALS Society of Canada*, 60
Moore, Robert, *Canadian Security Association*, 469
Moore, Cam, *Canadian Association of Geophysical Contractors*, 317
Moore, Peter, *Canadian Corrugated Containerboard Association*, 366
Moore, Lana, *Saskatchewan Dietitians Association*, 1263
Moore, Mike, *Manitoba Home Builders' Association*, 938
Moore, Jane, *Canadian Association of Critical Care Nurses*, 311
Moore, Daniel, *Family & Children's Services of Guelph & Wellington County*, 702
Moore, Samuel, *Physicians Services Inc. Foundation*, 1158
Moore, Randy, *Alzheimer Society of Thunder Bay*, 65
Moore, Donna, *Alberta Trappers' Association*, 50
Moore, Belinda, *Australian Society of Association Executives Ltd.*, 1513
Moore, Judy, *Community Arts Council of Greater Victoria*, 595
Moore, Tanya, *Association de Ringuette Lévis*, 104
Moore, Sean, *London Orchid Society*, 918
Moore, Monica, *Pesticide Action Network North America*, 1583
Moore, Steve, *Georgeville Historical Society*, 771
Moore, Rick, *National Association for PET Container Resources*, 1573
Moore, Dave, *Cross Country New Brunswick*, 643
Moore, Glyn, *Ontario Powerlifting Association*, 1097
Moore, Don, *Canadian Transportation Equipment Association*, 497
Moore, Gary, *Grace Communion International Canada*, 779
Moore, Gordon, *Nova Scotia Hearing & Speech Foundation*, 1045
Moore-Wright, Jonathan, *Project Management Institute*, 1585
Moores, David, *Drainage Superintendents Association of Ontario*, 662

Moores, Catherine, *Newfoundland & Labrador Fur Breeders Association*, 1019
Moorhouse, Andy, *Makivik Corporation*, 927
Mooring, Teri, *British Columbia Teachers' Federation*, 256
Moors, Dave, *AIDS Saskatoon*, 17
Moors, David, *Canadian Fire Safety Association*, 390
Mopoho, Raymond, *Atlantic Provinces Linguistic Association*, 185
Morabito, Cathy, *Music for Young Children*, 984
Morales, Karen, *Northwest Wall & Ceiling Bureau*, 1580
Moran, Kimberly, *Children's Mental Health Ontario*, 562
Moran, Hugh, *Ontario Petroleum Institute Inc.*, 1095
Moran, Linsay, *Women's Executive Network*, 1462
Moran, John, *Cole Foundation*, 581
Moraru, Ortansa, *Society of Canadian Artists*, 1327
Morawetz, Claudia, *West Coast Amateur Musicians' Society*, 1444
Morbia, Rita, *Inter Pares*, 851
Morden, Marie, *Canadian Manufacturers & Exporters*, 429
Morden, Barb, *Essex County Orchid Society*, 696
More, Kevin, *Society for Information Management*, 1590
Moreau, Robert, *Conseil économique du Nouveau-Brunswick inc.*, 618
Moreau, Lisa, *Canadian Media Production Association*, 433
Moreau, Michèle, *Canadian Institute for the Administration of Justice*, 413
Moreau, Elizabeth, *Canadian Paediatric Society*, 449
Moreau, Luce, *Fondation du CHUM*, 746
Moreau, Richard, *Tourisme Chaudière-Appalaches*, 1392
Moreau, Elizabeth, *Canadian Pediatric Foundation*, 452
Moreau, André, *Société d'histoire de Warwick*, 1312
Moreau, Marc, *Canadian Association of Medical Teams Abroad*, 321
Moreau, Luce, *Association of Fundraising Professionals*, 1512
Morel, Melanie, *Elora Arts Council*, 685
Morel, Louise, *Canadian Philosophical Association*, 454
Morel, Daniel, *Audition Québec*, 187
Moreland, Al, *St Catharines Association for Community Living*, 1248
Moreland, Marim, *Physical & Health Education Canada*, 1158
Moreland, Bill, *BeautyCouncil*, 203
Moreland, Vickie, *Community Living Port Colborne-Wainfleet*, 604
Morell, Arlene, *Canadian Home & School Federation*, 406
Morency, Marie-Josée, *Chambre de commerce du Saguenay-Le Fjord*, 544
Morency, Catherine, *Chambre de commerce de Disraéli*, 541
Moreno, Alejandro, *Frequency Co-ordination System Association*, 760
Moreno, Juan Antonio, *International Commission for the Conservation of Atlantic Tunas*, 1542
Morey, David, *Jersey Canada*, 869
Morgan, Sharon, *Manitoba Association of Women's Shelters*, 931
Morgan, Doug, *Association of New Brunswick Land Surveyors*, 153
Morgan, Jordi, *Canadian Federation of Independent Business*, 387
Morgan, Dudley, *Canadian Mental Health Association*, 435
Morgan, Elizabeth, *Canadian Polish Congress*, 456
Morgan, Nancy, *Theatre Nova Scotia*, 1374

Executive Name Index

Morgan, Laurie, *Almost Home*, 59
Morgan, Rachel, *Ontario Society of Nutrition Professionals in Public Health*, 1107
Morgan, Cyril, *Mission Bon Accueil*, 969
Morgan, Wayne, *Community Heritage Ontario*, 599
Morgan, Steve, *Canadian Association for Health Services & Policy Research*, 301
Morgan, Annette, *Dze L K'ant Friendship Centre Society*, 666
Morgan, Anne, *Recreation & Parks Association of the Yukon*, 1207
Morgan, Lael, *Halifax Sport & Social Club*, 799
Morgan, Roger, *Saskatchewan High Schools Athletic Association*, 1267
Morgan, Tracy, *Wellington Waterloo Dufferin Health Library Network*, 1444
Morgan Clark, Katherine, *Manitoba Association of Insurance Professionals*, 930
Morhart, Christa, *United Way of Estevan*, 1414
Moriarity, David, *An Cumann/The Irish Association of Nova Scotia*, 68
Moriarity, Ed, *Mining Industry NL*, 967
Morice, Erin, *Halifax Library Association*, 799
Morikawa, Junko, *International Confederation for Thermal Analysis & Calorimetry*, 1543
Morin, Louise, *Fédération sportive de ringuette du Québec*, 731
Morin, Angela, *Atlantic Provinces Association of Landscape Architects*, 185
Morin, Luc, *Conseil de coopération de l'Ontario*, 615
Morin, Dan, *Canadian Neurological Society*, 441
Morin, Dan, *Canadian Society of Clinical Neurophysiologists*, 482
Morin, Geneviève, *Canadian Amateur Musicians*, 292
Morin, Janelle, *Alberta Federation of Labour*, 34
Morin, Dan, *Canadian Neurological Sciences Federation*, 441
Morin, Jacques, *Canadian Office & Professional Employees Union*, 445
Morin, Dave, *American Society of Plumbing Engineers*, 1502
Morin, Pierre, *Canadian Vocational Association*, 501
Morin, Philippe, *Association des juristes d'expression française du Nouveau-Brunswick*, 118
Morin, Bruno, *Société canadienne-française de radiologie*, 1309
Morin, Luc, *Skills/Compétences Canada*, 1303
Morin, Renee, *Society of Plastics Engineers*, 1594
Morin, Albert André, *Order of Malta - Canadian Association*, 1119
Morin, Paul, *Association québécoise des troubles d'apprentissage - section Outaouais*, 175
Morin, Isabelle, *Association des professionnels en gestion philanthropique*, 126
Morin, Frédéric, *Association des médecins rhumatologues du Québec*, 120
Morin, Sylvie, *L'Arche Québec*, 77
Morin-Chain, Hélène, *Community Living North Bay*, 603
Morinville, Lori, *Confederation of Alberta Faculty Associations*, 611
Morisset, Louis, *Canadian Securities Administrators*, 469
Morisset, Louis, *Autorité des marchés financiers*, 190
Morissette, Claudia, *Jeunesses Musicales du Canada*, 871
Morissette, Martine, *Carrefour jeunesse emploi de l'Outaouais*, 515
Morissette, France, *Association féminine d'éducation et d'action sociale*, 132
Morissette, Joe, *Badminton Canada*, 193
Morland, Richard, *Northwest Territories Chamber of Commerce*, 1038

Morley, Stephen, *Ontario Association of Certified Engineering Technicians & Technologists*, 1062
Morley, Dianne, *Canadian Association of Critical Care Nurses*, 311
Morley, Karen, *Alzheimer Society of Durham Region*, 62
Morley, David, *UNICEF Canada*, 1404
Morneau, Nathalie, *Fédération des éducateurs et éducatrices physiques enseignants du Québec*, 714
Morneau-Sénéchal, Antoine, *POPIR-Comité logement (St-Henri, Petite Bourgogne, Ville Émard, Côte St-Paul)*, 1165
Möröy, Tarik, *Institut de recherches cliniques de Montréal*, 842
Moroz, Ted, *The Leukemia & Lymphoma Society of Canada*, 908
Moroz, Bob, *Manitoba Association of Health Care Professionals*, 930
Morrell, Michelle, *Architectural Woodwork Manufacturers Association of Canada*, 79
Morrell, Rick, *Saskatchewan Eco-Network*, 1264
Morrell, Louis M., *American Birding Association, Inc.*, 1490
Morris, Sandra, *Boys & Girls Clubs of Ontario*, 223
Morris, Darryl, *Kerrobert Chamber of Commerce*, 884
Morris, Thelma, *Tikinagan Child & Family Services*, 1379
Morris, Andrew, *Canadian Association for Laboratory Accreditation Inc.*, 302
Morris, Sandra, *Boys & Girls Clubs of Canada*, 222
Morris, Peter, *Deep River Symphony Orchestra*, 652
Morris, Rick, *The College of Psychologists of Ontario*, 589
Morris, Robyn, *Association for Canadian Studies in Australia & New Zealand*, 1507
Morris, Brenda, *British Columbia Dental Hygienists' Association*, 238
Morris, Jennifer, *Conservation International*, 1519
Morris, Margretta, *National Recycling Coalition, Inc.*, 1577
Morris, Victoria, *Saskatchewan Co-operative Association*, 1262
Morris, Kelly, *Palliative Manitoba*, 1137
Morris, John C., *American Thyroid Association*, 1504
Morris, Ross, *Pacific Urchin Harvesters Association*, 1136
Morris, Shawn, *Essex County Cattlemen's Association*, 696
Morris, Shelley, *Economic Developers Association of Manitoba*, 673
Morris, John B., *Society of Toxicology*, 1594
Morris-Reade, Janet, *Association of Service Providers for Employability & Career Training*, 162
Morrisette, Eve, *Centre Montérégien de réadaptation*, 536
Morrison, Hailee, *Women's Legal Education & Action Fund*, 1463
Morrison, Al, *Camosun College Faculty Association*, 276
Morrison, Randall, *Canadian Billiards & Snooker Association*, 343
Morrison, Gerald, *Mennonite Economic Development Associates Canada*, 961
Morrison, Andrew, *The Acadian Entomological Society*, 4
Morrison, Jeff, *Canadian Housing & Renewal Association*, 409
Morrison, Katie, *Canadian Parks & Wilderness Society*, 450
Morrison, Francois, *Canadian Ski Instructors' Alliance*, 471
Morrison, Andrea, *Federated Women's Institutes of Ontario*, 707
Morrison, Ian, *Friends of Canadian Broadcasting*, 760

Morrison, Karen, *Canadian Association of Medical Radiation Technologists*, 320
Morrison, Deborah, *Experiences Canada*, 700
Morrison, Peter, *Recreation New Brunswick*, 1207
Morrison, Janice, *Health Sciences Association of British Columbia*, 807
Morrison, Don, *Bimose Tribal Council*, 211
Morrison, Brian, *Prince Edward Island Cattle Producers*, 1173
Morrison, Matt, *Pacific NorthWest Economic Region*, 1582
Morrison, Shannon, *Canadian Taxpayers Federation*, 492
Morrison, Andy, *Arctic Co-operatives Limited*, 81
Morrison, President, *Association for Financial Professionals - Calgary*, 133
Morrison, Duncan, *Manitoba Forage & Grassland Association*, 937
Morrison Nicholls, Marlene, *Lindsay & District Chamber of Commerce*, 912
Morrisseau, Johanne, *Syndicat du personnel technique et professionnel de la Société des alcools du Québec (ind.)*, 1364
Morrissette, Pierre, *Centre d'action bénévole de Montréal*, 527
Morrissey, Cathie, *Jamaican Self-Help Organization*, 868
Morrissey, Susan, *Edmonton Social Planning Council*, 679
Morrissey, Harold, *Syndicat des agents de maîtrise de TELUS (ind.)*, 1362
Morrissey, Corryn, *Atlantic Canada Cruise Association*, 182
Morrow, Max, *Professional Engineers Ontario*, 1184
Morrow, Jenny, *Canadian Down Syndrome Society*, 378
Morrow, Martin, *Canadian Theatre Critics Association*, 494
Morrow, Terry, *Canadian Belgian Horse Association*, 342
Morse, Jonathan C., *Master Brewers Association of The Americas*, 1570
Morse, Paul, *Unifor87-M*, 1405
Morselli, Carlo, *Centre international de criminologie comparée*, 535
Morson, Frank, *Credit Institute of Canada*, 641
Mortensen, Elaine, *The Canadian Federation of Business & Professional Women's Clubs*, 385
Mortimer, John, *Canadian LabourWatch Association*, 425
Mortimer-Gibson, Shana, *Action Volunteers for Animals*, 7
Morton, Karen, *Community Care Peterborough*, 596
Morton, Kendra, *Canadian Cancer Society*, 349
Morton, Evan, *Tweed & Area Historical Society*, 1400
Morton, Cheryl, *Canadian Association of Insurance Women*, 319
Morton, Fabienne, *Canadian Association of Perinatal & Women's Health Nurses*, 325
Morton, Ruth, *Multiple Births Guelph-Wellington*, 980
Morton, Jake, *Mercy for Animals Canada*, 961
Morzenti, Patricia, *Lupus Canada*, 921
Mosca, Michael, *Canadian Picture Pioneers*, 455
Moscovitch, David, *Shaare Zion Congregation*, 1293
Mosel, Dorrie, *Miniature Horse Association of Nova Scotia*, 966
Moser, Robert, *Sheet Harbour & Area Chamber of Commerce & Civic Affairs*, 1295
Moser, Lori, *Canadian Cancer Society Research Institute*, 349
Moses, Znaimer, *VISION TV*, 1436
Moses, Lionel E., *Shaare Zion Congregation*, 1293
Moskal, Alexis, *Ontario Brain Injury Association*, 1069

Moskalyk, Chris, *Fort McMurray Realtors Association*, 753
Moskowitz, Steven L., *Antique Automobile Club of America*, 1505
Moskowitz, David, *Ontario Special Constable Association*, 1108
Mosonyi, Attila, *Ontario Table Tennis Association*, 1109
Moss, Darcy, *Grande Prairie Regional College Academic Staff Association*, 781
Moss, Ian, *Badminton Ontario*, 194
Moss, Ian, *Gymnastics Canada Gymnastique*, 795
Moss, Bradley, *Theatre Network (1975) Society*, 1374
Moss, Eileen, *Kingston Lapidary & Mineral Club*, 889
Mosseler, Isabel, *Literacy Alliance of West Nipissing*, 913
Mosser, Kevin, *Canada Pork International*, 280
Mossey, Don, *Historical Automobile Society of Canada, Inc.*, 816
Mostyn, Michael, *B'nai Brith Canada*, 192
Mota, Grace, *International Institute for Sustainable Development*, 858
Mottard, Geneviève, *L'Ordre des comptables professionnels agréés du Québec*, 1120
Mottard, Benoît, *Association provinciale des constructeurs d'habitations du Québec inc.*, 168
Mottard, Benoit, *Association provinciale des constructeurs d'habitations du Québec inc.*, 168
Mouait, Amanda, *Junior League of Edmonton*, 878
Mouat, Mike, *Equestrian Canada*, 694
Moubarak, Louis, *Canada World Youth*, 281
Moubayed, Farida, *Légion de Marie - Senatus de Montréal*, 906
Moudakis, John, *Ontario Society of Professional Engineers*, 1108
Mouflier, Kevin, *Tourism Industry Association of PEI*, 1390
Mougeot, Laurent, *Saskatchewan Urban Municipalities Association*, 1277
Moulton, Anne, *Canadian Association of Nephrology Nurses & Technologists*, 322
Moulton, Paul, *Edmonton Arts Council*, 675
Moulton, Joy, *Halifax Regional Cerebral Palsy Association*, 799
Moulton, Angie, *Canadian Society for Chemistry*, 473
Moulton, Lynne, *Alberta Gerontological Nurses Association*, 37
Moumouni, Charles, *Centre international de documentation et d'échanges de la francophonie*, 537
Mount, Carl, *South Lake Community Futures Development Corporation*, 1335
Mount, Jeff, *Mutual Fund Dealers Association of Canada*, 986
Mountain, Jim, *National Trust for Canada*, 996
Mountain, Shelley, *Canadian Hemophilia Society*, 404
Moura, Antonio Divino, *World Meteorological Organization*, 1606
Mournier, Gérard, *Cercle de la finance internationale de Montréal*, 537
Mousseau, Darrell, *Canadian College of Neuropsychopharmacology*, 360
Moustacalis, Anthony, *Criminal Lawyers' Association*, 642
Moutquin, Geneviève, *L'Arche Québec*, 77
Mowat, Farley, *Sea Shepherd Conservation Society*, 1287
Mowat, Marny, *Bracebridge Chamber of Commerce*, 224
Mowat, Debbie, *Master Brewers Association of The Americas*, 1570
Mowat, Sandi, *Manitoba Nurses' Union*, 941
Mowat, Tara, *Cycling British Columbia*, 647
Mowat, Peter, *Deep Roots Music Cooperative*, 652
Mowatt, Ashley, *Canadian Association of Critical Care Nurses*, 311

Mowbray, Jan, *Milton Historical Society*, 966
Moyes, Maureen, *Editors' Association of Canada*, 674
Moyse, Cyril, *College of Physicians & Surgeons of Prince Edward Island*, 588
Mozayani, Natalia, *Radiation Safety Institute of Canada*, 1202
Mozur, Mike, *Society of Environmental Toxicology & Chemistry*, 1593
Mozzon, Robert, *Thunder Bay Community Foundation*, 1377
Mrema, Elizabeth, *United Nations Environment Programme*, 1600
Mrozewski, Andrzej H., *Canadian Polish Congress*, 456
Mudimbe, V.Y., *International African Institute*, 1535
Mueller, Darlene, *Canadian Society for Transfusion Medicine*, 479
Mueller, Sylvia, *InformOntario*, 838
Mueller, Fred, *National Association for Surface Finishing*, 1573
Mueller, Dianne, *Institute of Professional Bookkeepers of Canada*, 847
Mueller, Lisa, *Edmonton Dental Assistants Association*, 676
Mueller, Mark, *Water Ski - Wakeboard Manitoba*, 1441
Mueller, Thomas, *Canada Green Building Council*, 279
Mufti, Aftab, *Structural Innovation & Monitoring Technologies Resources Centre*, 1352
Muir, Don, *Presbyterian Church in Canada*, 1170
Muir, Justin, *Malaspina Printmakers Society*, 927
Muir, Alan, *Parkinson Society of Eastern Ontario*, 1141
Muise, Randy, *People First Nova Scotia*, 1151
Mukasa, Samuel, *Geochemical Society*, 1527
Mukesh Sharma, Mike, *Ontario Association of Radiology Managers*, 1065
Mukhida, Karim, *Canadian Pain Society*, 449
Mukwavi, Bernard, *Baptist General Conference of Canada*, 196
Mulder, Michele, *Alzheimer Society of Alberta & Northwest Territories*, 61
Mulders, Annemieke, *Status of Women Council of the Northwest Territories*, 1349
Muldowney, Marie, *Canadian Securities Institute*, 469
Mulhern, Gerrard F., *Ontario Concrete Pipe Association*, 1074
Mulka, John, *Canadian National Institute for the Blind*, 439
Mulka, John, *Canadian National Institute for the Blind*, 439
Mulkani, Liberty, *Vancouver Humane Society*, 1426
Mullally, Sasha, *Canadian Society for the History of Medicine*, 477
Mullaly, Kelly, *Canadian 4-H Council*, 284
Mullen, Dave, *Canada's Venture Capital & Private Equity Association*, 283
Mullen, Dan, *Nova Scotia Mink Breeders' Association*, 1047
Mullen, Nelson G., *Canadian Association of Veterans in United Nations Peacekeeping*, 336
Mullen, Maurine, *Weymouth Historical Society*, 1451
Muller, Michael, *Yukon Badminton Association*, 1477
Muller, Nathalie, *Ringette Canada*, 1233
Muller, Elmi, *The Transplantation Society*, 1395
Mulligan, Brock, *Alberta Forest Products Association*, 35
Mulligan, Marlene, *Canadian Cancer Society*, 349
Mulligan, Shane, *Cement Association of Canada*, 521
Mulligan, Terry B., *Mining Suppliers, Contractors & Consultants Association of BC*, 968

Mullin, Debbie, *New Brunswick Dart Association*, 1007
Mullinder, John, *Paper & Paperboard Packaging Environmental Council*, 1138
Mullins, Debbie, *Cape Breton Professional Musicians Association, AFM Local 355*, 509
Mullins, Rosemary, *The John Howard Society of Newfoundland & Labrador*, 874
Mulroney, Greg, *Association for Operations Management*, 134
Mulroney, Greg, *Structural Pest Management Association of Ontario*, 1352
Multhaup, Gerhard, *Canadian Society of Pharmacology & Therapeutics*, 486
Mulvale, Catherine, *Canadian Digestive Health Foundation*, 378
Mulveney, Shelagh, *Canadian Ski Instructors' Alliance*, 471
Muma, Pam, *Ontario Provincial Trapshooting Association*, 1098
Mumm, David, *Saskatchewan Meat Processors' Association*, 1270
Muncaster, David, *American Society for Quality*, 1499
Munday, Brian, *Alberta Land Surveyors' Association*, 39
Mundell, Terry, *Greater Toronto Hotel Association*, 786
Mundy, Karen, *Canadian Global Campaign for Education*, 398
Munford, Robert, *Insurance Institute of Ontario*, 850
Munger, Martin, *Kidney Foundation of Canada*, 885
Munger-Perry, Lise, *Navy League of Canada*, 1002
Munic, Jagoda, *Friends of the Earth International*, 1527
Munkittrick-Colton, Janna, *Ontario Puppetry Association*, 1100
Munn, Tracy, *Brandon Humane Society*, 226
Munro, Gary, *CIO Association of Canada*, 570
Munro, Ron, *Dufferin Board of Trade*, 664
Munro, Shanna, *Restaurants Canada*, 1227
Munro, Matthew, *New Brunswick Association of Insolvency & Restructuring Professionals*, 1005
Munro, Zoë, *Conference of Great Lakes & St. Lawrence Governors & Premiers*, 1519
Munro, Barry, *Canadian Spinal Research Organization*, 489
Munro, Ian, *Ontario Regional Common Ground Alliance*, 1101
Munroe, Allan, *AFOA Canada*, 12
Munsil, Janet, *Intrepid Theatre Co. Society*, 862
Munson, Anne P., *National Association of College Auxiliary Services*, 1573
Munton, Barb, *Canadian Rose Society*, 468
Munyaradzi, Chenje, *United Nations Environment Programme*, 1600
Muranko, Starr, *Canadian Alliance of Dance Artists*, 291
Murano, Cristina, *Lace Up Your Cleats*, 895
Murat, Michelle, *Hearth, Patio & Barbecue Association of Canada*, 810
Murch, Heather, *Parry Sound Area Chamber of Commerce*, 1143
Murcutt, Paul, *Canadian Condominium Institute*, 362
Murdoch, Tammy, *College of Registered Nurses of Manitoba*, 589
Murdoch, Cindy, *Canadian Labour Congress*, 425
Murdock, Jean, *Fédération nationale des enseignants et des enseignantes du Québec*, 722
Murgic, Ivan, *Greater Toronto Apartment Association*, 785
Murie, Andrew, *MADD Canada*, 925
Murison, Laurie, *Grand Manan Whale & Seabird Research Station*, 780
Murjani, Maria, *Canadian Institute of Traffic & Transportation*, 420

Murko, Wendy, *College of Midwives of Ontario*, 586
Murphy, Brett, *Big Brothers Big Sisters of New Brunswick*, 209
Murphy, Margo, *Conception Bay Area Chamber of Commerce*, 609
Murphy, Judy, *Safety Services Manitoba*, 1245
Murphy, Bill, *Newfoundland & Labrador Basketball Association*, 1017
Murphy, Mary Ann, *CARP*, 515
Murphy, Elizabeth, *Nova Scotia Society for the Prevention of Cruelty to Animals*, 1049
Murphy, Elizabeth, *Nova Scotia Society for the Prevention of Cruelty to Animals*, 1049
Murphy, Donna, *Canadian Independent Music Association*, 411
Murphy, David, *Denturist Society of Prince Edward Island*, 654
Murphy, Helen, *Universities Canada*, 1418
Murphy, Laurie, *Multiple Sclerosis Society of Canada*, 980
Murphy, Elizabeth, *Theatre Nova Scotia*, 1374
Murphy, Jennifer, *Canadian Association of Elizabeth Fry Societies*, 313
Murphy, Allan, *Canadian Propane Association*, 461
Murphy, Lisa, *St. John Ambulance*, 1249
Murphy, Mike, *Cowichan United Way*, 637
Murphy, Doug, *Canadian Council of Insurance Regulators*, 368
Murphy, Nadia, *Canadian Orthopaedic Residents Association*, 448
Murphy, Colleen, *Saskatchewan Institute of Agrologists*, 1268
Murphy, Randy, *East Coast Trail Association*, 668
Murphy, Darlene, *Indefinite Arts Society*, 832
Murphy, Julie, *Archery Association of New Brunswick*, 78
Murphy, Kate, *Junior League of Halifax*, 878
Murphy, Sallie, *Halifax Area Leisure & Therapeutic Riding Association*, 798
Murphy, Kevin, *Hotel Association of Prince Edward Island*, 824
Murphy, Sandra, *Associés bénévoles qualifiés au service des jeunes*, 179
Murphy, Frank, *Ontario Brain Injury Association*, 1069
Murphy, Frank R., *Jeunes canadiens pour une civilisation chrétienne*, 870
Murphy, Jane, *Trans Canada Trail Foundation*, 1394
Murphy, Andrew, *Inside Out Toronto LGBT Film & Video Festival*, 840
Murphy, Shawn, *Ontario Undergraduate Student Alliance*, 1112
Murphy, Leroy, *Human Resources Professionals of Newfoundland & Labrador*, 826
Murphy, Barb, *CADORA British Columbia*, 269
Murphy, Cailey, *British Columbia Hotel Association*, 243
Murphy, Colette, *Atkinson Charitable Foundation*, 182
Murphy Hilliard, Janet, *Chicken Farmers of Prince Edward Island*, 557
Murphy-Collins, Ruby, *Atlantic Provinces Trucking Association*, 185
Murray, Bruce, *Association for the Rehabilitation of the Brain Injured*, 135
Murray, Kelly, *Vélo New Brunswick*, 1431
Murray, Lisa, *Community Care for South Hastings*, 596
Murray, Dianne, *Information Markham*, 837
Murray, Dave, *Abbotsford Food Bank & Christmas Bureau*, 1
Murray, Katrina, *World Arabian Horse Organization*, 1603
Murray, Alyson, *Canadian Public Relations Society Inc.*, 463
Murray, Keith, *Alberta Forest Products Association*, 35
Murray, Marybeth, *Arctic Institute of North America*, 81

Murray, Scott, *Canadian Carwash Association*, 350
Murray, Debbie, *Association of Canadian Port Authorities*, 143
Murray, Martha, *Cement Association of Canada*, 521
Murray, Susan, *Forest Products Association of Canada*, 751
Murray, Dave, *Canadian Water Resources Association*, 503
Murray, Joanne, *The John Howard Society of New Brunswick, Inc.*, 874
Murray, Larry, *The Royal Canadian Legion*, 1240
Murray, Cindy, *United Way of Durham Region*, 1414
Murray, Tanya, *United Way of Regina*, 1416
Murray, Julie, *Canadian Society for Eighteenth-Century Studies*, 474
Murray, Glen R., *The Pembina Institute*, 1149
Murray, Pat, *Newfoundland & Labrador Public Health Association*, 1021
Murray, Roger, *Knights of Pythias - Domain of British Columbia*, 892
Murray, Nick, *Prince Edward Island Sports Hall of Fame & Museum Inc.*, 1177
Murray, Carol, *British Columbia Co-operative Association*, 237
Murray, Sarah, *Drainage Superintendents Association of Ontario*, 662
Murray, Barb, *Canadian Captive Insurance Association*, 350
Murray, John, *Dufferin Child & Family Services*, 664
Murray, Ty, *Professional Bull Riders Inc*, 1585
Murray, Kate, *Real Estate Council of Ontario*, 1205
Murray, Larry, *Canada's Public Policy Forum*, 282
Murray, Jean, *Canadian Safe Boating Council*, 468
Murray, Cate, *Stem Cell Network*, 1349
Murray, Andrea, *Ontario Agri-Food Technologies*, 1059
Murray, Gordon, *Wood Pellet Association of Canada*, 1463
Murray, Donald, *Manitoba Securities Commission*, 944
Murray, Aaron, *Saskatchewan Economics Association*, 1264
Murray-MacDonell, Sandra, *Canadian Collegiate Athletic Association*, 360
Murry, Sean, *Canadian Mineral Analysts*, 436
Murtland, Dave, *Heating, Refrigeration & Air Conditioning Institute of Canada*, 810
Murumets, Kelly D., *Tennis Canada*, 1371
Murynowicz, Ryszard, *Association of Polish Engineers in Canada*, 156
Musacchio, Robert, *American College of Chest Physicians*, 1491
Musehl, Stephen, *Alzheimer Society of Grey-Bruce*, 62
Musgrave, Karen, *Alpine Saskatchewan*, 60
Musoke, Carol Nabanoba, *Canadian Institute of Food Science & Technology*, 416
Mussar, Keith, *Canadian Association of Importers & Exporters*, 318
Mustard, Cameron, *Institute for Work & Health*, 844
Mustello, Randi, *International Trademark Association*, 1563
Mutaher, Ahmed, *Baking Association of Canada*, 194
Mutford, John, *Northwest Territories Library Association*, 1038
Muth, Steve, *High River & District Chamber of Commerce*, 814
Mutoigo, Ida, *World Renew*, 1467
Muxlow, Sheila, *The Council of Canadians*, 633
Muzaffar, Aysha, *Canadian Water Quality Association*, 502
Muzio, Linda, *Canadian Holistic Nurses Association*, 406

Executive Name Index

Muzychka, Ivan, *Canadian Council for the Advancement of Education*, 367
Muzyczka, Alex, *Gillam Chamber of Commerce*, 773
Muzyka, Daniel, *The Conference Board of Canada*, 612
Muzyka, Daniel, *Natural Sciences & Engineering Research Council of Canada*, 999
Mwanzia, Kithio, *Guelph Chamber of Commerce*, 793
Myall, Natalie, *Société d'histoire de la MRC de l'Assomption*, 1310
Mychasiw, Cynamon, *United Way of Brandon & District Inc.*, 1413
Myer, Rabin, *Canadian Transport Lawyers Association*, 497
Myers, David, *Ringette Alberta*, 1232
Myers, John, *Ontario Jaguar Owners Association*, 1088
Myers, Shona, *International Association for Ecology*, 1536
Myers, Rollo, *The Architectural Conservancy of Ontario*, 78
Myers, Paul, *Canadian Meteorological & Oceanographic Society*, 436
Myers, Susan, *Association of Holocaust Organizations*, 1512
Myers, Melanie, *Golden Women's Resource Centre Society*, 777
Myers, Clinton, *Prince Edward Island Trucking Sector Council*, 1178
Myers, Paula, *Association of Family Health Teams of Ontario*, 148
Myggland, Dale, *Canadian Horse Breeders' Association*, 408
Myggland, Dale, *Canadian Horse Breeders' Association*, 408
Myggland-Carter, Leanne, *Canadian Authors Association*, 338
Myhill, Tracey, *Shoal Lake & District Chamber of Commerce*, 1296
Myler, Louise, *Association des fermières de l'Ontario*, 114
Myles, Elizabeth, *Kidney Foundation of Canada*, 885
Myner, Dominique, *Canadian Association of Paralegals*, 325
Mynott, Clive, *West Vancouver Municipal Employees Association*, 1447
Mynttinen, Juha, *Toronto Finnish-Canadian Seniors Centre*, 1384
Myo, Dorothy, *First Nations Confederacy of Cultural Education Centres*, 738
Myrah, Jamie, *Canadian Society for Mucopolysaccharide & Related Diseases Inc.*, 477
Myrdal, Randy, *Manitoba Provincial Handgun Association*, 942
Myre, Stéphanie, *Réseau environnement*, 1223
Myrer, Heather, *Nova Scotia Equestrian Federation*, 1044
Myrick, Stephanie, *Spinal Cord Injury Alberta*, 1343
Myroniuk, Bob, *Real Estate Council of Alberta*, 1205
Myslik, Stephanie, *CADORA Ontario Association Inc.*, 269
Myung, Hwa Sun, *Ontario Taekwondo Association*, 1109
Mzoughi, Othman, *Association des fonctionnaires issus des communautés culturelles*, 114

N

Nadeau, Jean-Philippe, *Association coopérative d'économie familiale du Grand-Portage*, 98
Nadeau, Catherine, *ARMA Canada*, 82
Nadeau, Sonia, *Fédération québécoise des sociétés Alzheimer*, 730
Nadeau, Pierre, *Association des firmes de génie-conseil - Québec*, 114
Nadeau, Jacques, *Canadian Association of Provincial Court Judges*, 329
Nadeau, Steven, *Ontario Soil & Crop Improvement Association*, 1108
Nadeau, Symphonie, *International Log Builders' Association*, 858
Nadeau, Thérèse, *Association des psychothérapeutes psychanalytiques du Québec*, 127
Nadeau, Patrick, *Ottawa Riverkeeper*, 1131
Nadeau, Louise, *Canadian Foundation on Fetal Alcohol Research*, 394
Nadeau, Monique, *L'Appui pour les proches aidants d'aînés*, 75
Nadel, Steven, *American Council for an Energy-Efficient Economy*, 1492
Nadon, Pam, *Canadian Society of Orthopaedic Technologists*, 485
Naeem, Khalid, *Ahmadiyya Muslim Jama'at Canada*, 15
Naftzger, David, *Conference of Great Lakes & St. Lawrence Governors & Premiers*, 1519
Nafziger, Gloria, *Sojourn House*, 1332
Nagano, Kent, *Orchestre symphonique de Montréal*, 1118
Nagel, Sonja, *Duncan-Cowichan Chamber of Commerce*, 664
Nagel, Edward, *Technion Canada*, 1368
Nagel, Kari, *Canadian Association for Young Children*, 307
Nagel, Linda J., *Advertising Standards Canada*, 10
Nagendran, Jay, *Association of Professional Engineers & Geoscientists of Alberta*, 157
Nagle, Stacy A., *Manitoba Bar Association*, 932
Nagy, Suzanna, *Royal Astronomical Society of Canada*, 1239
Nagy, Dave, *Society of Graphic Designers of Canada*, 1329
Nagy, Nick, *Canadian Plywood Association*, 456
Nagy, Carol, *Hospice Niagara*, 822
Nagy, Andy, *Western Canada Tire Dealers Association*, 1448
Nahabedian, Paul, *Canadian Armenian Business Council Inc.*, 295
Nahal, Tamara, *Association of Medical Microbiology & Infectious Disease Canada*, 152
Nahanee, Teressa, *Conayt Friendship Society*, 609
Nahirniak, Kristy, *CADORA Ontario Association Inc.*, 269
Nahwegahbow, Theresa, *Nistawoyou Association Friendship Centre*, 1027
Naidoo, Kumi, *Amnesty International*, 1505
Naidoo, Jennifer, *Ethiopiaid*, 697
Naik, Saurabh, *Toronto Cricket Umpires' & Scorers' Association*, 1383
Nair, Vijayan N., *International Statistical Institute*, 1562
Nair, Lynsay, *Saskatchewan Association of Licensed Practical Nurses*, 1257
Nair, Raman, *Amma Foundation of Canada*, 68
Nairn, Ernie, *Assiniboia Chamber of Commerce (MB)*, 88
Nairn, Judy, *Hospice of Waterloo Region*, 822
Naizghi, Eyob, *Multilingual Orientation Service Association for Immigrant Communities*, 979
Najem, Elmustapha, *Syndicat des professeures et professeurs de l'Université du Québec en Outaouais*, 1363
Nakagawa, Bob, *College of Pharmacists of British Columbia*, 587
Nakata, Zoé, *Shwachman-Diamond Syndrome Canada*, 1297
Namagoose, Bill, *Grand Council of the Crees*, 779
Nana, Larisse, *Professional Engineers Ontario*, 1184
Nance, Margit, *British Columbia Hang Gliding & Paragliding Association*, 243
Nance, Margit, *Hang Gliding & Paragliding Association of Canada*, 803
Nancekivell, Greg, *Drainage Superintendents Association of Ontario*, 662
Nanibush, Sarah, *University of Toronto Native Students Association*, 1421
Nanni, Chris, *Seed Corn Growers of Ontario*, 1289
Nantais, Mark A., *Canadian Vehicle Manufacturers' Association*, 501
Naphin, Paul, *Gas Processing Association Canada*, 767
Napier, Sara, *United Way of Halifax Region*, 1414
Napier, Marilyn, *Native Women's Association of the Northwest Territories*, 998
Napier, Mark, *National Hockey League Alumni Association*, 994
Napoli, Gemma, *Canadian Association of Elizabeth Fry Societies*, 313
Napoli, Gemma, *Ontario Community Justice Association*, 1073
Naqvi, Raza, *Saskatchewan Cricket Association*, 1262
Naraine, Brian, *Villa Charities Inc. (Toronto District)*, 1435
Naraine, Suresh, *Ontario Lung Association*, 1090
Narayanan, Unni, *American Academy for Cerebral Palsy & Developmental Medicine*, 1487
Narbonne, Manon, *Canadian GeoExchange Coalition*, 397
Narro-Perez, Rodrigo, *Ontario Undergraduate Student Alliance*, 1112
Narula, Raymond, *General Conference of the Canadian Assemblies of God*, 769
Naruse, Susumu, *International Association of Ports & Harbours*, 1539
Narveson, Jan, *Kitchener-Waterloo Chamber Music Society*, 890
Narveson, Jean, *Kitchener-Waterloo Chamber Music Society*, 890
Nas, Peter J.M., *International Union of Anthropological & Ethnological Sciences*, 1563
Nash, Tana, *Canadian Association for Suicide Prevention*, 304
Nash, Gail, *West Shore Arts Council*, 1446
Nash, Alison, *Canadian Condominium Institute*, 362
Nash, Ted, *Prostate Cancer Canada*, 1190
Naslund, Jo-Anne, *Canadian Children's Book Centre*, 356
Nason, Curt, *Royal Astronomical Society of Canada*, 1238
Nason, Jim, *LOFT Community Services*, 917
Nat, Vinder, *Canadian Association of Ambulatory Care*, 308
Natale, Isabel, *Canadian Institute of Chartered Business Valuators*, 414
Nath, Gautam, *Multicultural Marketing Society of Canada*, 979
Nathoo, Al-Noor Nenshi, *Provincial Health Ethics Network*, 1191
Nau, Werner, *European Photochemistry Association*, 1524
Naugler, Ted, *Professional Engineers Ontario*, 1185
Naugler, Stephenie, *Medical Device Reprocessing Association of Ontario*, 958
Nault, Johanne, *Alliance autochtone du Québec*, 55
Nault, Aline, *L'Association de spina-bifida et d'hydrocéphalie du Québec*, 104
Nault, Marc, *Compton County Historical Museum Society*, 609
Nault, Gillian, *Saskatchewan Dental Assistants' Association*, 1263
Naumovski, Lou, *Canada Eurasia Russia Business Association*, 279
Naus, Lauren, *The Champlain Society*, 551
Nauss, Carol, *Chester Municipal Heritage Society*, 557
Navaratnam, Sri, *CancerCare Manitoba*, 508
Navarro, Yuri, *National Angel Capital Organization*, 989
Navarro-Genie, Marco, *Atlantic Institute for Market Studies*, 184
Navazesh, Shasha (Shaun), *Artisan Bakers' Quality Alliance*, 85
Navetta, Jean-Marie, *Parents, Families & Friends of Lesbians & Gays*, 1582
Nawar, Selma, *Lebanese Canadian Heritage Association*, 905
Nawaz, Ammar, *Professional Engineers Ontario*, 1185
Nawrocki, Andrzej, *The Western Canada Group of Chartered Engineers*, 1448
Nawrot, Piotr, *Canadian Polish Congress*, 456
Naylor, Pamela, *Canadian Bar Association*, 342
Naylor, Pamela, *Law Society of the Northwest Territories*, 902
Nayman, Ira, *SF Canada*, 1293
Nazir, Abu, *Muslim Association of Canada*, 985
Ndoutoum, Jean-Pierre, *Institut de la Francophonie pour le développement durable*, 841
Neal, Kathi, *Manitoba Lung Association*, 940
Neal, Bruce, *Manitoba Federation of Independent Schools Inc.*, 936
Neal, Tara, *United Way of Oakville*, 1415
Neal, David, *Reach for the Rainbow*, 1205
Neale, Mary, *Seniors Peer Helping Program*, 1290
Neapole, Jacqueline, *Canadian Research Institute for the Advancement of Women*, 467
Neapole, Jackie, *Feminist Alliance for International Action*, 731
Neary, Rhonda, *Newfoundland & Labrador Construction Association*, 1017
Neary, Jennifer, *Scouts Canada*, 1287
Neary, Michael, *Cross Country Alberta*, 643
Neault, Hélène, *Sidaction Mauricie*, 1298
Neault, Kathleen, *Association de parents pour l'adoption québécoise*, 103
Nebesio, Bohdan, *Canadian Association of Slavists*, 333
Nebesio, Bohdan, *Canadian Association of Slavists*, 333
Nechita, Luciana, *Automotive Industries Association of Canada*, 190
Ned, Murray, *Pacific Salmon Commission*, 1136
Nedelec, Paul, *Construction Maintenance & Allied Workers Canada*, 624
Neden, Janice, *Learning Assistance Teachers' Association*, 903
Nederpel, Barb, *Kamloops & District Labour Council*, 880
Nedkov, Matey, *Canada Bulgaria Business Network*, 278
Nedumpara, Rappai, *Family Prayer Mission (Ontario)*, 704
Needham, H.G., *Canadian Battlefields Foundation*, 342
Needles, Jane, *The Québec Drama Federation*, 1197
Neef, Alexander, *Canadian Opera Company*, 446
Neeposh, David, *Réseau des SADC et CAE*, 1220
Nef Ojeda, Gabriela, *FunTeam Alberta*, 765
Negre, Leandro, *Fédération internationale de hockey*, 1525
Neigel, Wayne, *Alberta Broomball Association*, 26
Neil, Paula, *Hospice Palliative Care Ontario*, 823
Neil, Diane, *Saskatchewan Registered Music Teachers' Association*, 1273
Neil, Garry, *International Network for Cultural Diversity*, 858
Neill, Kathy, *The John Howard Society of Ontario*, 875
Neill, Jeff, *The Welland/Pelham Chamber of Commerce*, 1443
Neill, Jay, *Ontario Tennis Association*, 1110
Neilson, Lydia E., *National ME/FM Action Network*, 995

Executive Name Index

Neilson, Mary Ellen, *Association for the Rehabilitation of the Brain Injured*, 135
Neilson, Richard, *Rainy River Beekeepers' Association*, 1204
Neish, Rob, *Canoe Kayak New Brunswick*, 508
Neitzel, Leonardo, *Lutheran Church - Canada*, 922
Nel, Marijke, *Nova Scotia Tennis Association*, 1050
Nel, Leenta, *Perioperative Registered Nurses Association of British Columbia*, 1152
Nelson, Rhonda, *Starbright Children's Development Centre*, 1348
Nelson, Gordon, *Vulcan Business Development Society*, 1439
Nelson, S., *Coronach Community Chamber of Commerce*, 629
Nelson, Douglas, *British Columbia Cancer Foundation*, 234
Nelson, Dave, *Canadian Mental Health Association*, 435
Nelson, Karen, *Learning Disabilities Association of Newfoundland & Labrador Inc.*, 904
Nelson, Doug, *Ontario Recovery Group Inc.*, 1100
Nelson, Bob, *Royal Astronomical Society of Canada*, 1238
Nelson, Melissa, *The Newspaper Guild (AFL-CIO/CLC)*, 1577
Nelson, Donna, *Stephan G. Stephansson Icelandic Society*, 1349
Nelson, Wendy, *Canadian Artists' Representation Saskatchewan*, 296
Nelson, Mark, *Ontario Equestrian Federation*, 1078
Nelson, Doug, *Provincial Towing Association (Ontario)*, 1191
Nelson, Karen, *Greater Moncton Society for the Prevention of Cruelty to Animals*, 784
Nelson, Laura, *Alberta Bottle Depot Association*, 26
Nelson, Fiona, *Alberta Professional Outfitters Society*, 43
Nelson, Danny, *Vision of Love Ministry - Canada*, 1436
Nelson, Norman, *Sooke Philharmonic Society*, 1333
Nelson, Patrick, *Canadian Association of Physician Assistants*, 327
Nemchin, Tamara, *Canadian Association of University Business Officers*, 334
Néméh, Francine, *Fédération des coopératives d'habitation intermunicipale du Montréal métropolitain*, 714
Nemeth, Hillary, *Canadian Hemophilia Society*, 404
Nemkovich, Jennifer, *American College of Chest Physicians*, 1491
Nemtin, Andrea, *Inspirit Foundation*, 840
Nemtin Levine, Sheila, *Canadian Hadassah WIZO*, 399
Nenson, Garry, *Canadian National Institute for the Blind*, 439
Nepinak, Derek, *Assembly of Manitoba Chiefs*, 88
Nepinak, Josie, *Awo Taan Healing Lodge Society*, 191
Nepton, André, *Réseau des SADC et CAE*, 1221
Nerbas, Tim, *Saskatchewan Soil Conservation Association*, 1275
Nero, Michel, *Softball Québec*, 1332
Neron, Maryse, *Kidney Foundation of Canada*, 885
Nesbitt, Sandy, *Alberta Rugby Football Union*, 45
Ness, Steven D., *Surety Association of Canada*, 1357
Neth, Michael, *Alberta College of Speech-Language Pathologists & Audiologists*, 30
Netten, Linda, *Durham Personal Computer Users' Club*, 665

Neufeld, Robert, *Manitoba Choral Association*, 934
Neufeld, Travis, *Saskatchewan Association for Community Living*, 1256
Neufeld, Eric, *Manitoba Genealogical Society Inc.*, 937
Neufeld, Naomi, *Swan Valley Chamber of Commerce*, 1358
Neufeld, Larry, *La Crete & Area Chamber of Commerce*, 642
Neuman, Pat, *The Rotary Club of Toronto*, 1236
Neumann, Randy, *Environmental Services Association of Alberta*, 692
Neumann, Ken, *United Steelworkers of America (AFL-CIO/CLC)*, 1600
Neumann, Mary, *Canadian Albacore Association*, 291
Neumann, Helen, *Cell Stress Society International*, 1516
Neven, Jeffrey, *Homestead Christian Care*, 820
Nevert, Michèle, *Syndicat des professeurs et professeures de l'Université du Québec à Montréal*, 1364
Nevidon, Vince, *Grand River Beekeepers' Association*, 780
Neville, George, *Historical Society of Ottawa*, 816
Neville, Rosemary, *Ladies' Morning Musical Club*, 895
Neville, Helen, *King Chamber of Commerce*, 888
Nevin, Caroline, *Canadian Bar Association*, 341
Nevins, Maureen, *Almonte in Concert*, 59
New, Bev, *Métis Nation of Alberta*, 963
New, Gemma, *Hamilton Philharmonic Orchestra*, 801
Newberry, Darren, *Saskatchewan Wildlife Federation*, 1278
Newbigging, Ted, *Ontario Brain Injury Association*, 1068
Newburgh, Marc, *Hillel of Greater Toronto*, 815
Newcombe, Chad, *Theatre Calgary*, 1374
Newcombe, Ron, *Prince Edward Island Draft Horse Association*, 1173
Newell, Sylvia, *Canadian Association of Railway Suppliers*, 330
Newell, Andrée, *Fédération de la jeunesse franco-ontarienne*, 709
Newell, Keith, *Lincoln County Law Association*, 912
Newell, Katherine, *Guysborough County Inshore Fishermen's Association*, 795
Newhall, Amy W., *Middle East Studies Association of North America*, 1571
Newkirk, Ingrid E., *People for the Ethical Treatment of Animals*, 1583
Newman, Rob, *Sport BC*, 1344
Newman, Ira, *Canadian Society for Aesthetics*, 473
Newman, Patrick, *Cooperative Housing Federation of Canada*, 628
Newman, Paul J., *Council of Forest Industries*, 633
Newman, David, *Canadian Association of College & University Student Services*, 310
Newman, Barbara, *Medieval Academy of America*, 1570
Newman, Louise, *Canadian Society for Civil Engineering*, 474
Newman, John, *Habitat for Humanity Canada*, 796
Newman, Roberta, *Emunah Women of Canada*, 687
Newnham, Michael, *Peterborough Symphony Orchestra*, 1154
Newnham, Michael, *Symphony New Brunswick*, 1360
Newnham, Dave, *Tim Horton Children's Foundation*, 1379
Newsome, Paul, *Vintage Locomotive Society Inc.*, 1435

Newsome, Linda, *Cremona Water Valley & District Chamber of Commerce*, 641
Newson, Rob, *Hockey PEI*, 818
Newton, Edie, *Children's Wish Foundation of Canada*, 563
Newton, Alana, *Ladysmith Chamber of Commerce*, 895
Newton, Shawn, *First Unitarian Congregation of Toronto*, 739
Newton, Christie, *College of Family Physicians of Canada*, 584
Newton, Jim, *Diabetes Canada*, 655
Newton, Denyse, *Alzheimer Society of Durham Region*, 62
Newton, Blain, *Healthcare Information & Management Systems Society*, 1529
Newton, Kimberly, *Nurse Practitioners' Association of Nova Scotia*, 1052
Newton, Tom, *Western Association of Broadcasters*, 1447
Ney, Kimberley, *Financial Planning Standards Council*, 737
Neysmith, Mark, *Syme-Woolner Neighbourhood & Family Centre*, 1360
Nézet-Séguin, Yannick, *Orchestre Métropolitain*, 1118
Ng, Priscilla, *The Logistics Institute*, 917
Ng, Vyda, *Canadian Unitarian Council*, 499
Ng, Oliver, *Presbyterian Church in Canada*, 1170
Ng, Sandra, *Ontario Association of Optometrists*, 1065
Ng, Michelle, *Canadian Executive Service Organization*, 383
Ng, Charles, *North West Commercial Travellers' Association*, 1033
Ng, Carmen, *EcoWatch Canada*, 673
Ng, Mary, *Ontario Society of Artists*, 1107
Ng, Helen, *World Council on City Data*, 1465
Ng-A-Fook, Nicholas, *Canadian Society for the Study of Education*, 478
Ngai, Cliff, *Bradford Board of Trade*, 224
Ngo, Anh, *North American Broadcasters Association*, 1029
Nguyen, Travis, *Association of Professional Engineers & Geoscientists of British Columbia*, 158
Nguyen, Nam, *British Columbia Surgical Society*, 255
Nguyen, Huong, *Ontario Electrical League*, 1077
Nguyen, Manh, *Vietnamese Association, Toronto*, 1434
Nguyen, Kathy, *Tellus Institute*, 1598
Nguyen, Bao, *Centre for Comparative Literature*, 531
Nhan, Frank, *Chinese Canadian Chiropractic Society*, 564
Ni Mheadhra, Dairine, *The Queen of Puddings Music Theatre Company*, 1199
Niang, Sokhna Fatim, *African Students Association of Concordia*, 13
Niangoran, Jean-Marie, *Canadian Association of Gift Planners*, 317
Niazi, Adeena, *Afghan Women's Counselling & Integration Community Support Organization*, 12
Nichiporik, Kellie, *Lakeland Agricultural Research Association*, 896
Nichol, June, *Huntington Society of Canada*, 828
Nichol, Kevin, *Toronto Transportation Society*, 1388
Nichol, Matt, *Manitoba Funeral Service Association*, 937
Nichol, Sheila, *Pittsburgh Historical Society*, 1161
Nicholas, Teri, *British Columbia's Children's Hospital Foundation*, 259
Nicholas, Latrica (Terry), *British Columbia Aboriginal Lands Managers*, 229
Nicholls, Jamie, *Squash Ontario*, 1347
Nicholls, Chris, *Gibsons & District Chamber of Commerce*, 773

Nicholls, John, *Confederation of Alberta Faculty Associations*, 611
Nicholls, Pat, *Ontario Women's Hockey Association*, 1113
Nicholls, Christopher, *Mutual Fund Dealers Association of Canada*, 986
Nicholls, Kathleen, *Nunavut Arts & Crafts Association*, 1051
Nicholov, Bill, *Macedonian Human Rights Movement International*, 923
Nichols, Christy, *Alberta Association of Library Technicians*, 23
Nichols, Christina, *Canadian Council of Archives*, 367
Nichols, Jim, *Canadian Association of Home & Property Inspectors*, 318
Nichols, Dave, *Sarnia Concert Association*, 1254
Nichols, William O., *The Society of Professional Accountants of Canada*, 1330
Nichols, Russell, *Compton Historical Society*, 609
Nicholson, Jody, *VALID Association*, 1424
Nicholson, Judy, *Saskatchewan Library Association*, 1269
Nicholson, Jane, *Annapolis District Board of Trade*, 71
Nicholson, Bruce, *Burlington Chamber of Commerce*, 265
Nicholson, Debbi, *Greater Sudbury Chamber of Commerce*, 785
Nicholson, Sindy, *Saskatchewan Forestry Association*, 1265
Nicholson, James B., *Directors Guild of Canada*, 657
Nicholson, Carl, *Ontario Council of Agencies Serving Immigrants*, 1075
Nicholson, Linda Jean, *Prince Edward Island Senior Citizens Federation Inc.*, 1177
Nicholson, Veronica, *Timmins Native Friendship Centre*, 1380
Nicholson, Charlene, *Chamber of Commerce of Brantford & Brant*, 539
Nicholson, Nancy, *Ontario Brain Injury Association*, 1069
Nicholson, Leah, *Calgary Society of Independent Filmmakers*, 274
Nicholson, Bonnie, *Saskatchewan Registered Music Teachers' Association*, 1273
Nicholson, Shelly, *Delburne & District Chamber of Commerce*, 653
Nicholson, Eldred, *Prince Edward Island Harness Racing Industry Association*, 1174
Nicholson, Steve, *Canadian Wild Turkey Federation*, 504
Nickel, Irm, *Abundance Canada*, 3
Nickel, Jodi, *Canadian Association for Teacher Education*, 305
Nickel, Debbie, *BeautyCouncil*, 203
Nickel, Frank, *First Pacific Theatre Society*, 739
Nickel, Murray, *International Mennonite Health Association Inc.*, 858
Nickerson, Michael, *Canadian Institute of Food Science & Technology*, 415
Nickerson, Mike, *Sustainability Project*, 1357
Nickerson, Jamie, *Triathlon Price Edward Island*, 1398
Nickle, Bev, *Osteoporosis Canada*, 1128
Nickle, Danny, *United Way of Quinte*, 1416
Nicol, Lucie, *Association québécoise des salons du livre*, 174
Nicol, Peter, *Gymnastics Canada Gymnastique*, 795
Nicol, Lynda, *Canadian Association of Agri-Retailers*, 308
Nicol, Laurie, *Ontario Independent Meat Processors*, 1087
Nicol, Ann, *Alberta Association of Rehabilitation Centres*, 25
Nicolaison, Iris, *Ajax-Pickering Board of Trade*, 20
Nicoll, Jim, *Canadian Information Processing Society*, 411

Executive Name Index

Nicolle, Leanne, *Big Brothers Big Sisters of Ontario*, 210
Nicolson, Carl, *Catholic Centre for Immigrants - Ottawa + CIC Foundation*, 517
Nicotine, Janice, *National Native Addictions Partnership Foundation*, 995
Niebergall, Stu, *Canadian Home Builders' Association - Saskatchewan*, 408
Niebylski, Mark, *World Hypertension League*, 1466
Niedermier, Paulette, *Canadian Association of Importers & Exporters*, 318
Niehenke, Edward C., *IEEE Microwave Theory & Techniques Society*, 1530
Nielsen, Pernille, *Red Deer Danish Canadian Club*, 1209
Nielsen, Gladys, *Canadian Hard of Hearing Association*, 400
Nielsen, Christine, *Canadian Society for Medical Laboratory Science*, 476
Nielsen, Svend E., *Danish Canadian National Museum Society*, 650
Nielsen, Paul, *Northwestern Ontario Prospectors Association*, 1039
Nieman, Peter, *Association des accidentés cérébro-vasculaires et traumatisés crâniens de l'Estrie*, 105
Niemczyk, Ilona, *Multiple Sclerosis Society of Canada*, 980
Niemi, Fo, *Center for Research-Action on Race Relations*, 522
Nigam, Sonya, *Canadian Association for the Prevention of Discrimination & Harassment in Higher Education*, 305
Nightingale, Jon, *Canadian Information Processing Society*, 411
Nightingale, Scott, *Salmonid Association of Eastern Newfoundland*, 1252
Nigro, Joseph J., *Sheet Metal Workers' International Association (AFL-CIO/CFL)*, 1589
Nigro, Sandra, *Modular Housing Association Prairie Provinces*, 971
Nihei, Kathy, *Wild Bird Care Centre*, 1453
Nihoul, Michèle, *Chambre de commerce et de tourisme de St-Adolphe-d'Howard*, 548
Nijmeh, Anthony, *Association for Operations Management*, 134
Nikbakht, Abbas, *Association of Professional Engineers & Geoscientists of British Columbia*, 158
Nikkel, Joanne, *Canadian Association of Electroneurophysiology Technologists Inc.*, 312
Nikleva, Steve, *Canadian Dance Teachers' Association*, 375
Nikolai, Alfred, *Habitat for Humanity Canada*, 796
Nikolaou, Konstantin, *Greek Orthodox Community of East Vancouver*, 788
Nikoniuk, Rik, *Lac La Biche & District Chamber of Commerce*, 894
Nilsen Sparks, Laurel, *Archaeological Institute of America*, 1505
Nilson, Kevin, *Environmental Careers Organization of Canada*, 691
Nilsson, Joanne, *Army Cadet League of Canada*, 83
Nilsson, Kathy, *Building Industry & Land Development Alberta*, 262
Nimara, Mariana, *Cerebral Palsy Association in Alberta*, 537
Nimmons, Holly, *Coalition for Music Education in Canada*, 578
Niquette, Nathalie, *GRIS-Mauricie/Centre-du-Québec*, 790
Nisha Zuber, Khatoon, *British Columbia Muslim Association*, 247
Nishiyama, Jason, *Royal Astronomical Society of Canada*, 1238
Niskala, Brenda, *Saskatchewan Publishers Group*, 1272
Nitz, Sarah, *Edmonton Dental Assistants Association*, 676

Nixon, Bree, *Port Hope & District Chamber of Commerce*, 1166
Nixon, Steven, *Saskatchewan Weekly Newspapers Association*, 1278
Nixon, Ryan, *Alberta Building Officials Association*, 27
Nixon, Keith, *SaskCentral*, 1280
Njagi Runguma, Sebastian, *CIVICUS: World Alliance for Citizen Participation*, 1517
Nkala, Njabulo, *Black Business Initiative*, 213
Nkapnang, Isabelle, *Association canadienne-française de Régina*, 96
Noakes, Doug, *Saskatchewan Manitoba Galloway Association*, 1269
Nobili, Alan, *Alliance Française du Manitoba*, 57
Noble, Owen, *Lloydminster Agricultural Exhibition Association*, 916
Noble, Ryan, *North York Harvest Food Bank*, 1033
Noble, Bob, *Pentathlon Canada*, 1150
Noble, CJ, *Canadian Parks & Recreation Association*, 450
Noble, Penny, *Bike to Work BC Society*, 211
Noble, Louise, *Alzheimer Society of Lanark County*, 63
Noble, Louise, *Alzheimer Society of Leeds-Grenville*, 63
Noble, Jodi, *British Columbia Dental Hygienists' Association*, 238
Noble, Rusty, *Jasper Park Chamber of Commerce*, 869
Noble, Lois, *Saskatchewan Registered Music Teachers' Association*, 1273
Noble, Terry, *Alberta Association of Police Governance*, 24
Noble, Nicka, *Ontario Rainbow Alliance of the Deaf*, 1100
Noddin, Donna, *Massage Therapists' Association of Nova Scotia*, 953
Nodwell, Lisa, *Canadian Society of Hospital Pharmacists*, 484
Noël, Thomas, *College of Optometrists of Ontario*, 587
Noël, Marie-Josée, *Fédération du personnel de l'enseignement privé*, 720
Noel, Greg, *Newfoundland & Labrador Lung Association*, 1020
Noël, Andrée, *Canadian Broadcast Standards Council*, 347
Noël, Jacques, *Fédération des clubs de croquet du Québec*, 713
Noel, Jean-Marc, *Canadian Military Colleges Faculty Association*, 436
Noël, Marie-Lou, *Chambre de commerce de Shippagan inc.*, 543
Noël, Michèle, *La Fondation des Auberges du coeur*, 744
Noftle, Gary, *Boys & Girls Clubs of Newfoundland & Labrador*, 223
Noiseux, Jacqueline, *L'Association française des municipalités de l'Ontario*, 135
Nokleby, Scott, *Commission canadienne pour la théorie des machines et des mécanismes*, 593
Nolan, Mark, *Alberta Association of Landscape Architects*, 23
Nolan, Tracey, *Canadian Accredited Independent Schools*, 287
Nolan, Kelly, *St. Leonard's Society of Canada*, 1250
Nolet, Marc, *Fédération des professionnelles et professionnels de l'éducation du Québec*, 718
Nolin, Eugene, *Community Living Mississauga*, 603
Nolin, Maryse, *Association des optométristes du Québec*, 121
Noll, Phillip, *Congregational Christian Churches in Canada*, 613
Nolleau, Olivier, *Chambre de commerce et de tourisme de Gaspé*, 548
Nollet, André, *Tourisme Mauricie*, 1393
Noma, Ken, *National Association of Japanese Canadians*, 990

Nome, Helge, *Rocky Native Friendship Society*, 1235
Noonan, Jane, *The Ireland Funds, Canada*, 863
Noonan, Jan, *God, Sex, & the Meaning of Life Ministry*, 776
Noonan, Lisa, *Muskoka Lakes Association*, 985
Noone, Chris, *AdvantAge Ontario*, 10
Noordeloos, Koos, *International Industry Working Group*, 1551
Noordermeer, Xavier, *Community Living Windsor*, 606
Noot, Ed, *Society of Christian Schools in British Columbia*, 1328
Nopper, Roger, *Heiltsuk Tribal Council*, 811
Norberg, Alison, *Manitoba Crafts Council*, 935
Nord, Doug, *Association for Canadian Studies in the United States*, 1507
Nordal, Cliff, *The Michener Institute for Applied Health Sciences*, 964
Norden, Karyn, *Alberta Genealogical Society*, 36
Nordenstrom, Jay, *NAIMA Canada*, 987
Nordhaus, William D., *American Economic Association*, 1492
Nordheim, Alfred, *International Genetics Federation*, 1550
Nordin, Dave, *Canadian Society of Exploration Geophysicists*, 483
Nordin, Sundae, *Community Kitchen Program of Calgary*, 599
Norman, Jackie, *Safety Services Nova Scotia*, 1245
Norman, Corrina, *Quesnel & District Child Development Centre Association*, 1200
Norman-Bain, Janet, *Prince Edward Island Roadrunners Club*, 1177
Normand, Louise, *Canadian Hard of Hearing Association*, 400
Normand, Sandy, *Catholic Health Association of Saskatchewan*, 520
Normand, Gabrielle, *Association québécoise des interprètes du patrimoine*, 173
Normand, Jérôme, *Environnement jeunesse*, 693
Normand, Pierre, *Canada Foundation for Innovation*, 279
Normand, Amélie, *Association forestières du sud du Québec*, 135
Normand, Jérôme, *Front commun québécois pour une gestion écologique des déchets*, 763
Normand-Charbonneau, Lorraine, *Fédération québécoise des directions d'établissements d'enseignement*, 728
Normandeau, Édith, *Association des architectes paysagistes du Québec*, 105
Normandin, Kyle, *Association for Preservation Technology International*, 1509
Norn, Tammie, *Ontario Insurance Adjusters Association*, 1088
Noronha, James, *Special Olympics Ontario*, 1340
Noronha, Ligia, *United Nations Environment Programme*, 1600
Norris, Craig, *Saanich Peninsula Chamber of Commerce*, 1245
Norris, Jim, *Friends of Music Therapy*, 761
Norris, William, *Tafelmusik Baroque Orchestra & Chamber Choir*, 1366
Norris, Colleen, *Canadian Association of Pharmacy Technicians*, 326
Norris, Shelly, *Calgary Women's Emergency Shelter Association*, 275
Norris, Paul, *Ontario Waterpower Association*, 1113
Norris, Shelley, *Chinook Applied Research Association*, 565
Norsworthy, Stephen, *American Society of Heating, Refrigerating & Air Conditioning Engineers*, 1500
Northam, Tammy, *Bladder Cancer Canada*, 214

Northcott, Jasmine, *Water Ski & Wakeboard Canada*, 1442
Northcott, David, *Vanier Institute of The Family*, 1429
Northcott, Teri, *Helicopter Association of Canada*, 811
Northcott, Allan, *Max Bell Foundation*, 954
Northey Argue, Sharie, *Clan Mackenzie Society of Canada*, 571
Northup, Robert, *Ancient, Free & Accepted Masons of Canada - Grand Lodge of Nova Scotia*, 69
Norton, Debbie, *Northumberland Salmon Protection Association*, 1036
Norton, Ryan, *Society for Adolescent Health & Medicine*, 1589
Norton Scott, Nicole, *Chartered Professionals in Human Resources Saskatchewan*, 554
Noseworthy, Ken, *Canadian Institute of Management*, 417
Noseworthy, Chris, *Greater Corner Brook Board of Trade*, 783
Noseworthy, Mark, *Newfoundland & Labrador Curling Association*, 1018
Nosko, Susan, *North Bay Real Estate Board*, 1030
Nosko, Mike, *International Sanitary Supply Association Canada*, 860
Noster, Jan, *Construction Maintenance & Allied Workers Canada*, 624
Nosworthy, Kate, *Taekwondo Canada*, 1366
Notarandrea, Rita, *Canadian Centre on Substance Use & Addiction*, 354
Notley, Raelynn, *Boys & Girls Clubs of Alberta*, 221
Notley, Rachel, *New Democratic Party*, 1014
Nott, Joy, *Canadian Association of Importers & Exporters*, 318
Nott, Mel, *Manitoba Municipal Administrators' Association Inc.*, 941
Nott, Joy, *Electronics Import Committee*, 684
Noureldin, Ash, *Big Brothers Big Sisters of Saskatchewan*, 210
Novak, Lance, *Canadian Kennel Club*, 424
Novak, Thomas, *Dignity Winnipeg Dignité*, 657
Novak, Sarah, *Canadian Western Agribition Association*, 503
Novak, Ruth, *Cyclic Vomiting Syndrome Association*, 1521
Novak, Pam, *Atlantic Wildlife Institute*, 186
Novakowski, Ebony, *Manitoba Association of Library Technicians*, 930
Novakowski, Michelle, *Canadian Association of Elizabeth Fry Societies*, 312
Novakowski, Kristi, *Canadian College of Professional Counsellors & Psychotherapists*, 360
Novecosky, Joe, *Alberta Cattle Feeders' Association*, 27
Novecosky, Joe, *Independent Power Producers Society of Alberta*, 833
Nowak, Nathan, *Canadian Tinnitus Foundation*, 495
Nowakowski, Camila C.D., *Theresians International - Canada*, 1375
Nowicki, Victor, *Canadian Environmental Certification Approvals Board*, 381
Nowinka, Jaroslaw, *Canadian Polish Congress*, 456
Nudelman, André, *Canadian Council for the Americas - British Columbia*, 367
Nugent, Bianca, *Association francophone à l'éducation des services à l'enfance de l'Ontario*, 135
Nummi, Kimberli, *Alberta Cattle Feeders' Association*, 27
Nunn, Cara, *North Okanagan Organic Association*, 1031
Nursall, Alan, *Edmonton Space & Science Foundation*, 679
Nursey, Paul, *Tourism Victoria/Greater Victoria Visitors & Convention Bureau*, 1392
Nurvo, Anja, *Local Government Management Association of British Columbia*, 917

Executive Name Index

Nussbaum, Gerald, *Pacific Life Bible College*, 1135
Nutt, Darrell, *Stratford Coin Club*, 1351
Nyberg, Gail, *Daily Bread Food Bank*, 648
Nyczai, Debra, *Humboldt & District Chamber of Commerce*, 827
Nye, Bill, *The Planetary Society*, 1584
Nygren, Margaret A., *American Association on Intellectual & Developmental Disabilities*, 1490
Nykiforuk, Ross, *Saskatoon Musicians' Association*, 1279
Nyman, Jacline A., *United Way of Canada - Centraide Canada*, 1413
Nyquist, Michelle, *Dauphin & District Allied Arts Council Inc.*, 651
Nywening, Clarence, *Christian Farmers Federation of Ontario*, 567

O

O'Brien, Gary, *Block Watch Society of British Columbia*, 215
O'Brien, Lana, *Association of BC Drama Educators*, 140
O'Brien, Megan, *Manitoba Library Association*, 939
O'Brien, Lynne, *Sunrise Therapeutic Riding & Learning Centre*, 1355
O'Brien, Sue, *Thompson Crisis Centre*, 1376
O'Brien, Judy, *Ontario Society for the Prevention of Cruelty to Animals*, 1106
O'Brien, Lorraine, *Canadian Hard of Hearing Association*, 400
O'Brien, Jordan, *Catholic Teachers Guild*, 520
O'Brien, Paul, *Newfoundland & Labrador Dental Board*, 1018
O'Brien, Jim, *Kidney Foundation of Canada*, 885
O'Brien, Dan, *Ontario Simmental Association*, 1104
O'Brien, Mike, *Royal Astronomical Society of Canada*, 1238
O'Brien, J. Robert, *Canadian Association of Veterans in United Nations Peacekeeping*, 335
O'Brien, Bill, *North York Coin Club*, 1033
O'Brien, Steve, *Cross Country PEI*, 643
O'Brien, Bassima Jurdak, *Association of Translators & Interpreters of Nova Scotia*, 163
O'Brien, John, *Thompson Rivers University Open Learning Faculty Association*, 1376
O'Brien, Chris, *Accessible Media Inc.*, 5
O'Brien, Suzanne, *Council on Palliative Care*, 636
O'Brien, Tanya, *Chartered Professional Accountants of Prince Edward Island*, 553
O'Brien, John, *Office of the Superintendent of Securities of Newfoundland & Labrador*, 1055
O'Brien Leggott, Trina, *Association of Prince Edward Island Libraries*, 156
O'Bright, Michele, *Ontario School Bus Association*, 1103
O'Bryan, Raymond J., *American Chemistry Council*, 1491
O'Byrne, Nicole, *Canadian Law & Society Association*, 426
O'Carroll, Thomas, *British Canadian Chamber of Trade & Commerce*, 229
O'Carroll, Paul, *Canadian Aerial Applicators Association*, 288
O'Connell, Blanche, *Archelaus Smith Historical Society*, 78
O'Connell, Mary, *Boys & Girls Clubs of Canada*, 222
O'Connell, Rosalind, *Canadian Ophthalmological Society*, 446
O'Connell, Mark, *Interac Association*, 851
O'Connell, April, *AllerGen NCE Inc.*, 54
O'Connell, Candice, *Responsible Dog Owners of Canada*, 1227
O'Connell, Paula, *Nova Scotia Arm Wrestling Association*, 1040

O'Connor, Mary-Rose, *Ontario Library Association*, 1089
O'Connor, Brenda, *Canadian Credit Union Association*, 372
O'Connor, Laurie, *Saskatoon Food Bank & Learning Centre*, 1279
O'Connor, Carolyn, *Easter Seals Ontario*, 670
O'Connor, Lori, *Ontario Association of Library Technicians*, 1064
O'Connor, Desmond, *Ininew Friendship Centre*, 838
O'Connor, Jeanne, *Harmony, Inc.*, 804
O'Connor, Brenda, *Saskatchewan Baton Twirling Association*, 1259
O'Doherty, Lori, *Toronto Academy of Dentistry*, 1381
O'Donnell, Shannon, *Information Orillia*, 837
O'Donnell, Janet, *Libra House Inc.*, 910
O'Donnell, Kate, *Special Libraries Association*, 1596
O'Donnell, Bill, *Central Ontario Standardbred Association*, 525
O'Donnell, Shyla, *Wolastoqey Tribal Council Inc.*, 1460
O'Donoghue, Linda, *Canadian Association for Young Children*, 307
O'Donoghue, Sheila, *Ontario Pioneers*, 1096
O'Donovan, Kevin, *National Golf Course Owners Association Canada*, 994
O'Dwyer, Paddy, *International Amateur Theatre Association*, 1535
O'Flaherty, Deirdre, *College of Family Physicians of Canada*, 584
O'Flaherty, Ron, *Atlantic Collegiate Athletic Association*, 183
O'Halloran, Marea, *Island Technology Professionals*, 865
O'Halloran, Sally, *North Bay Police Association*, 1030
O'Hanley, Carol, *United Way of Prince Edward Island*, 1416
O'Hanlon, Martin, *The Newspaper Guild (AFL-CIO/CLC)*, 1577
O'Hara, Gilles, *Association des cardiologues du Québec*, 108
O'Hara, Patrick, *Canadian Insurance Claims Managers Association*, 420
O'Hara, Kevin, *Institute of Housing Management*, 846
O'Hara, Jessica, *Academic Pediatric Association*, 1485
O'Hara-Leman, Maureen, *Canadian Association for Disabled Skiing*, 299
O'Hare, Colleen, *Royal Astronomical Society of Canada*, 1238
O'Hare, Debbie, *Manitoba Government & General Employees' Union*, 937
O'Keefe, Aldonna, *Bay St. George Folk Arts Council*, 200
O'Keefe, Jeff, *Canada - Newfoundland & Labrador Offshore Petroleum Board*, 278
O'Keefe, Michele, *Canada Basketball*, 278
O'Keefe, Edward, *WineAmerica*, 1602
O'Keefe, Mary Jo, *Arts Council of the North Okanagan*, 85
O'Keeffe, Caroline, *Master Insulators' Association of Ontario Inc.*, 953
O'Leary, Jim, *Canadian Church Press*, 356
O'Leary, Eugene, *Eastern Fishermen's Federation*, 670
O'Leary, Eugene, *Guysborough County Inshore Fishermen's Association*, 795
O'Leary-Coughlan, Patricia, *Irish Canadian Cultural Association of New Brunswick*, 864
O'Loughlin, Chloe, *British Columbia Spaces for Nature*, 254
O'Malley, Cleave, *Algoma Cattlemen's Association*, 53
O'Mara, Collin, *National Wildlife Federation*, 1577
O'Neil, Sandra, *Community Living Dundas County*, 601
O'Neil, Karyn, *AIDS Committee of Windsor*, 16
O'Neil, Diane, *Stroke Recovery Association of Manitoba Inc.*, 1352

O'Neil, Maureen, *Canadian Foundation for Healthcare Improvement*, 393
O'Neil, Denise, *Kitimat Community Services Society*, 891
O'Neil King, Rawlson, *Continental Automated Buildings Association*, 626
O'Neill, Liz, *Big Brothers Big Sisters of Alberta*, 209
O'Neill, Liz, *Boys & Girls Clubs of Alberta*, 221
O'Neill, Eileen, *Water Environment Federation*, 1601
O'Neill, Karen, *Canadian Paralympic Committee*, 449
O'Neill, Shane, *Benevolent Irish Society of Prince Edward Island*, 205
O'Neill, George, *Hamilton-Burlington & District Real Estate Board*, 802
O'Neill, Donna, *British Columbia Society of Laboratory Science*, 254
O'Neill, Chantel, *Canadian Labour Congress*, 425
O'Neill, Blair, *Water Ski Wakeboard Nova Scotia*, 1442
O'Neill, Marie, *British Columbia Miniature Horse Club*, 246
O'Neill, Cindy, *Inverness Cottage Workshop*, 862
O'Rafferty, Jessica, *Ontario Association of Architects*, 1061
O'Regan, Jeannie, *Starlight Children's Foundation Canada*, 1348
O'Reilly, Carol, *Greater Moncton Chamber of Commerce*, 784
O'Reilly, Heather, *Professional Association of Internes & Residents of Newfoundland*, 1182
O'Reilly, Stephen, *Canadian Institute for Health Information*, 412
O'Reilly, Shawn, *The Canadian Association of Naturopathic Doctors*, 322
O'Reilly, Robert, *The Canadian Don't Do Drugs Society*, 378
O'Reilly, Jim, *Chawkers Foundation*, 555
O'Riordan, Brian, *College of Audiologists & Speech-Language Pathologists of Ontario*, 582
O'Rourke, Helen, *Newfoundland & Labrador Association for Community Living*, 1015
O'Rourke, Stacy, *Canada - Nova Scotia Offshore Petroleum Board*, 278
O'Rourke, Brian, *Canadian Agency for Drugs & Technologies in Health*, 289
O'Rourke, Brian, *United Steelworkers Local 1-424*, 1412
O'Rourke, Robert, *Association of Psychologists of the Northwest Territories*, 160
O'Shaughnessy, Lynn, *National Judicial Institute*, 994
O'Shea, Mona, *Prince Edward Island Nurses' Union*, 1176
O'Shea, Kevin, *Public Legal Information Association of Newfoundland*, 1192
O'Sullivan, Paddy, *Sudbury Arts Council*, 1353
O'Sullivan, Terry, *Laborers' International Union of North America (AFL-CIO/CLC)*, 1568
O'Sullivan, Frank, *Society of Deaf & Hard of Hearing Nova Scotians*, 1328
O'Toole, David, *Canadian Institute for Health Information*, 412
O'Toole, Sarah, *Antigonish Culture Alive*, 72
O-Connor, Aime, *Canadian Business Aviation Association*, 347
Oakden, Larry, *Hamiota Chamber of Commerce*, 802
Oakes, Lester, *International Association for Educational & Vocational Guidance*, 853
Oakes, Les, *Alberta Equestrian Federation*, 34
Oakie, Rob, *Music PEI*, 984
Oakley, Nancy, *Yukon Historical & Museums Association*, 1479
Oana, Michelle, *Myeloma Canada*, 986
Oates, Sara, *World Wildlife Fund - Canada*, 1468
Oates, John, *Skills/Compétences Canada*, 1302

Oatway, Judith, *Associated Manitoba Arts Festivals, Inc.*, 89
Oatway, Shannon, *Victoria Epilepsy & Parkinson's Centre Society*, 1432
Obad, Joe, *Canadian Avalanche Association*, 340
Obal, T., *Association of the Chemical Profession of Ontario*, 163
Obed, Natan, *Inuit Tapiriit Kanatami*, 862
Obermann, Elisa, *Marine Renewables Canada*, 950
Obermann, Elisa, *Marine Renewables Canada*, 950
Oberth, Ron, *Organization of Canadian Nuclear Industries*, 1125
Oberto, Giacomo, *International Association of Judges*, 1539
Obeyesekere, Upali, *Canada-Sri Lanka Business Council*, 284
Oblin, Rhonda, *Waswanipi Cree Model Forest*, 1441
Obregón, Idalia, *Belgian Canadian Business Chamber*, 204, 229
Occhionero, Tonia, *Canadian Association of Midwives*, 321
Ochocka, Joanna, *Centre for Community Based Research*, 531
Ochoski, Judy, *Ontario Home Builders' Association*, 1085
Ockedahl, Bianca, *Judo Yukon*, 876
Ocopnick, Elliot, *Receivables Management Assocation of Canada Inc.*, 1206
Odegard, Larry W., *College of Veterinarians of British Columbia*, 590
Odell, Rose, *Ontario Horticultural Association*, 1086
Odnokon, Quinten, *Vanscoy & District Agricultural Society*, 1429
Odoom, Isaac, *African Students Association - Univeristy of Alberta*, 13
Odorico, Frank, *Denturist Association of Ontario*, 654
Oechslin, Erwin, *Canadian Adult Congenital Heart Network*, 288
Oehler, Tim, *Saskatchewan Martial Arts Association*, 1270
Oesch, Grace, *Ontario Simmental Association*, 1104
Oetter, Heidi, *College of Physicians & Surgeons of British Columbia*, 588
Oettgen, Hannelore, *Health Initiatives for Youth Hamilton*, 806
Off, Terry, *Goodwill Industries*, 777
Offet Gartner, Kathy, *Canadian Counselling & Psychotherapy Association*, 372
Ogale, Aruna, *Bereaved Families of Ontario*, 205
Oger, Derek, *Conservatory Canada*, 622
Ogilvie, Rob, *Canadian Baptists of Western Canada*, 341
Ogilvie, Peter, *Athletics Alberta*, 181
Ogilvie, Scott, *Archery Canada Tir à l'Arc*, 78
Ogilvie, Louise, *Canadian Institute for Health Information*, 412
Ogilvy, David, *Canadian Association of Movers*, 321
Ogra, Anahita, *Zoroastrian Society of Ontario*, 1482
Ogryzlo, Kathy, *Alberta Dressage Association*, 33
Ogunyemi, Boluwaji, *Resident Doctors of British Columbia*, 1226
Oh, Jay, *Canada Korea Business Association*, 280
Ohayon, Charles, *Independent Production Fund*, 833
Ohlson, Rob, *Operation Eyesight Universal*, 1115
Ohman, Viveka, *White Rock & Surrey Naturalists*, 1452
Ohno, Yoshihiro, *International Commission on Illumination*, 1542
Oickle, Irene, *Alberta Family History Society*, 34

Executive Name Index

Oikawa, Toshi, *The Garden Clubs of Ontario*, 767
Oishi, Gerrad, *Habitat for Humanity Canada*, 796
Okere, Michelle, *Association of Fundraising Professionals*, 1512
Okihiro, Fran, *Canadian Thoroughbred Horse Society*, 495
Okomba-Deparice, Herman, *Centre de prévention de la radicalisation menant à la violence*, 529
Olafsen, Soo, *Canadian Sport Horse Association*, 490
Olafson, Candace, *Morden & District Chamber of Commerce*, 974
Olan-MacLean, Sheila, *Ontario Coalition for Better Child Care*, 1071
Olanski, Bernie, *Dive Ontario*, 659
Oldfield, Christine, *Volunteer Centre of Guelph/Wellington*, 1438
Oldman, Jonathan, *The Bloom Group*, 215
Oleffe, Grégory, *Belgian Canadian Business Chamber*, 204
Oleksuk, Iris, *Manitoba Trail Riding Club Inc.*, 946
Oleksyn, Deanne, *Saskatchewan College of Opticians*, 1261
Oler, Samantha, *Association of Professional Engineers & Geoscientists of Alberta*, 157
Oler, Ralph, *Alberta Metallic Silhouette Association*, 40
Oler, Kathy, *Alberta Metallic Silhouette Association*, 40
Olesky, Luba, *Manitoba Society of Artists*, 944
Oligny, Bernard, *Association québécoise pour le loisir des personnes handicapées*, 177
Olinder Eriksson, Katarina, *International Society for the Study of the Lumbar Spine*, 1559
Oliphant, Darcy, *Ontario Agri Business Association*, 1059
Oliva, Vincent, *Association des radiologistes du Québec*, 127
Olivastri, Beatrice, *Friends of the Earth Canada*, 762
Oliveira, Joe, *British Columbia Powerlifting Association*, 249
Oliveira, Paul, *Bowling Proprietors' Association of Canada*, 219
Oliver, Stephen, *Niagara Association of REALTORS*, 1024
Oliver, Christine, *Canadian Committee on Cataloguing*, 361
Oliver, Matthew, *Association of Professional Engineers & Geoscientists of Alberta*, 157
Oliver, John, *Canadian Institute of Energy (British Columbia)*, 415
Oliver, Fraser, *Northwest Territories Teachers' Association*, 1038
Oliver, Susan, *Canadian Society of Cardiac Surgeons*, 481
Oliver, Kerry L., *Law Foundation of Nova Scotia*, 901
Oliver, Leslie, *Black Cultural Society for Nova Scotia*, 213
Oliver, Joe, *Speed Skate New Brunswick*, 1341
Oliver, Shannon, *Cameco Capitol Arts Centre*, 276
Oliveria, Julie, *People, Words & Change*, 1152
Olivier, Jérémie, *Action Nouvelle Vie*, 6
Olivier, Lévesque, *Foosball Québec*, 750
Olkovich, Nick, *Canadian Theological Society*, 494
Ollenberger, Glenn, *Canadian Association of Nuclear Medicine*, 323
Olmstead, Cathryn, *Smithers Community Services Association*, 1304
Olmstead, Helen, *Canadian Celiac Association*, 352
Olmstead, Denie, *Building Industry & Land Development Alberta*, 262
Olmstead, Stuart, *Carberry & District Chamber of Commerce*, 510
Olsen, Steph, *Boys & Girls Clubs of Alberta*, 221

Olsen, Starr, *Community Living Quinte West*, 604
Olsen, Sharon, *Alberta Genealogical Society*, 36
Olsen, Connie, *Pentathlon Alberta*, 1150
Olsen, Kim, *Canadian Council of Professional Fish Harvesters*, 369
Olsen, Susan, *British Columbia Registered Music Teachers' Association*, 251
Olsen, Hope, *Alberta Dressage Association*, 33
Olsmats, Carl, *World Packaging Organization*, 1607
Olson, Christyann, *Alberta Wilderness Association*, 52
Olson, Rob, *Manitoba Wildlife Federation*, 947
Olson, Everett, *Manitoba Simmental Association*, 944
Olson, Leah, *Agricultural Manufacturers of Canada*, 15
Olson, David, *College of Chiropractors of British Columbia*, 583
Olson, Rose, *Saskatchewan Turkey Producers' Marketing Board*, 1276
Olson-Sutton, Judith, *International Society for Business Education*, 1557
Olstead, Jodi, *British Columbia School Trustees Association*, 252
Olszewski, Roman, *Athletics Ontario*, 181
Olthof, Ed, *Nelson & District Chamber of Commerce*, 1003
Olver, John, *International Society of Physical & Rehabilitation Medicine*, 1561
Olynyk, Jill, *Calgary Health Trust*, 272
Omell, Penny, *Downtown Business Association of Edmonton*, 661
Omichinski, Dave, *Portage la Prairie & District Chamber of Commerce*, 1167
Omokanye, Akim, *Peace Country Beef & Forage Association*, 1147
Onagi, Jackie, *NSERC Chair for Women in Science & Engineering*, 1050
Ondrick, James, *Association for Canadian Studies*, 133
Ongoiba, Fanta, *Africans in Partnership Against AIDS*, 13
Ono, Jay, *Vancouver TheatreSports League*, 1429
Onofrychuk, Brad, *Habitat for Humanity Canada*, 797
Ontko, Ken, *CAA British Columbia*, 267
Onufriu, Vicki, *Société d'histoire régionale Deux-Montagnes*, 1314
Onuschak, Katarina, *Canadian Association of Professional Immigration Consultants*, 329
Onyskow, Barbara, *Women in Food Industry Management*, 1461
Oostenbrink, Jim, *Christian Labour Association of Canada*, 568
Opala, Andrew, *Royal Astronomical Society of Canada*, 1238
Opashinov, Mark, *Macedonian Human Rights Movement International*, 923
Openshaw, Lauren, *Special Olympics BC*, 1339
Opyr, Mary, *Lethbridge Symphony Orchestra*, 908
Oravec, Don, *The Writers' Trust of Canada*, 1469
Orcherton, Steve, *Child Find British Columbia*, 559
Ord, Jeff, *Freestyle Skiing Ontario*, 759
Orellana, Albert, *Governance Professionals of Canada*, 778
Orford, Lori, *Manitoba Association of Personal Care Home Social Workers*, 931
Organ, Jim, *Heavy Civil Association of Newfoundland & Labrador, Inc.*, 810
Orlando, Dean, *Trout Unlimited Canada*, 1399
Ormsby, Kevin, *Community One Foundation*, 607
Ornburn, Cheryl Lou, *Canadian Tour Guide Association of British Columbia*, 495
Ornyik, Roman, *Association of Saskatchewan Forestry Professionals*, 161

Orosz, Drew, *Ontario Institute of Agrologists*, 1087
Orozco-Marquez, Maria, *Population Connection*, 1584
Orr, Tim, *Canadian College of Health Leaders*, 359
Orr, Gordon, *Tourism Windsor Essex Pelee Island*, 1392
Orr, Bob, *UNIFOR*, 1405
Orr, Joan, *Doggone Safe*, 660
Orr, Doug, *Alberta Dressage Association*, 33
Orr, Sandi, *Darts Alberta*, 651
Orrbine, Elaine, *Canadian Association of Paediatric Health Centres*, 325
Orser, Karen, *Big Brothers Big Sisters of Alberta*, 209
Orser, Richard, *Central Carleton Chamber of Commerce*, 524
Orszulak, Ben, *National Association of Watch & Clock Collectors, Inc.*, 1575
Ortega-Nuere, Cristina, *World Leisure & Recreation Association*, 1606
Orysik, John, *Coastal Jazz & Blues Society*, 579
Osborne, Deanne, *Association of Canadian Travel Agencies*, 144
Osborne, Joyce, *Bruce County Historical Society*, 260
Osborne, Carolyn, *Mariners' House of Montréal*, 950
Osborne, John, *Canadian Society of Medievalists*, 485
Oscapella, Eugene, *Canadian Foundation for Drug Policy*, 393
Oscarson, Stéphanie, *Association des Diplômés de Polytechnique*, 111
Osgood, Marlaine, *Alliance for Canadian New Music Projects*, 56
Oshanyk, Yvonne, *Hinton Friendship Centre*, 815
Osinchuk, Myka, *Alberta Cancer Foundation*, 27
Osip, Linda, *Canadian Call Management Association*, 348
Osland, Paul, *Canadian Masters Athletic Association*, 431
Osmak, Laurianne, *Wakaw & District Board of Trade*, 1439
Osmok, Paula, *The John Howard Society of Ontario*, 874
Ossowski, Robert, *Conseil national Société de Saint-Vincent de Paul*, 619
Ostafichuk, Tara, *Alberta Bodybuilding Association*, 26
Ostergaard, Hanne, *Canadian Society for Immunology*, 475
Ostermeier, Ron, *British Columbia Archery Association*, 230
Ostin, Marvin, *Technion Canada*, 1368
Ostojski, Mieczyslaw S., *World Meteorological Organization*, 1606
Ostrander, Ingrid, *Victoria Orchid Society*, 1433
Ostridge, Sheri, *Canadian Public Relations Society Inc.*, 463
Ostrom, Ron, *Northwest Territories Tourism*, 1039
Ostrosser, Melissa, *Junior League of Toronto*, 878
Oswald, Gary B., *Skate Canada*, 1301
Oswald, Colton, *Alberta College of Acupuncture & Traditional Chinese Medicine*, 28
Oswald, Patricia, *Canadians for Ethical Treatment of Food Animals*, 507
Oswick-Kearney, Tammy, *Canadian 4-H Council*, 284
Othberg, Sandra, *Maritime Limousin Association*, 951
Otis, Alain, *Canadian Translators, Terminologists & Interpreters Council*, 496
Ottenbreit, Alana, *Cross Country Saskatchewan*, 644
Ottenbreit, Alana, *Alpine Saskatchewan*, 60
Ottenbreit, Alana, *Biathlon Saskatchewan*, 208

Otto, Stephen, *The Friends of Fort York & Garrison Common*, 761
Otto, Brian, *Barley Council of Canada*, 196
Ottoni, Eduardo, *First Vancouver Theatre Space Society*, 739
Ouanès, Abdeljelil, *Chambre de commerce Canado-Tunisienne*, 540
Oucharek-Deo, Michelle, *British Columbia Art Therapy Association*, 230
Oud, Fred, *Pulp & Paper Employee Relations Forum*, 1194
Ouedraogo, Alain, *L'Arche Québec*, 77
Ouellet, Bertrand, *Assemblée des évêques catholiques du Québec*, 88
Ouellet, Josiane, *Société de développement des périodiques culturels québécois*, 1315
Ouellet, Brigitte, *Society for the Study of Egyptian Antiquities*, 1327
Ouellet, Emile, *Association québécoise de joueurs d'échecs handicapeés visuels*, 169
Ouellet, Monica, *Association des Gestionnaires de l'information de la santé du Québec*, 115
Ouellet, Yves, *Canadian Office & Professional Employees Union*, 445
Ouellet, Martin, *Réseau des SADC et CAE*, 1221
Ouellet, Serge, *Réseau des SADC et CAE*, 1221
Ouellet, Martine, *Bloc québécois*, 214
Ouellet, Serge, *Société de généalogie Gaspésie-Les Îles*, 1316
Ouellet, Aubert, *Patrimoine et Culture du Portage*, 1145
Ouellet, Yves, *Fédération des travailleurs et travailleuses du Québec - Construction*, 719
Ouellet, Chantal, *Association des gestionnaires de ressources bénévoles du Québec*, 115
Ouellet, Louise, *Alliance des professionels et des professionnelles de la Ville de Québec*, 56
Ouellet-LeBlanc, Mylène, *Société des Jeux de l'Acadie inc.*, 1318
Ouellette, Sarah, *New Denmark Historical Society*, 1014
Ouellette, Rachelle, *Restigouche County Volunteer Action Association Inc.*, 1228
Ouellette, Brigitte, *Association des juristes d'expression française du Nouveau-Brunswick*, 118
Ouellette, Alain, *Association des Sourds de l'Estrie Inc.*, 128
Ouellette, Peter, *Conseil national Société de Saint-Vincent de Paul*, 619
Ouellette, Jim, *Oliver Food Bank*, 1057
Ouellette, Allyson, *New Brunswick Interscholastic Athletic Association*, 1010
Ouellette, Gail, *Regroupement québécois des maladies orphelines*, 1216
Oughton, Dale, *Heart & Stroke Foundation of Saskatchewan*, 809
Oughtred, Lindsay, *Kids Up Front*, 886
Ouimet, Rock, *Canadian Masters Cross-Country Ski Association*, 431
Ouimet, Renée, *Canadian Mental Health Association*, 435
Ouimet, Catherine, *Association du jeune barreau de Montréal*, 131
Ouimet, Steve, *Chambre de commerce de la Haute-Gaspésie*, 541
Oulton, Michael D, *The Anglican Church of Canada*, 70
Oumarou, Moussa, *International Labour & Employment Relations Association*, 1551
Oundjian, Peter, *Toronto Symphony Orchestra*, 1387
Outhit, Allison, *Foundation Assisting Canadian Talent on Recordings*, 755
Outwater, Edwin, *Kitchener-Waterloo Symphony Orchestra Association Inc.*, 891
Ouzilleau, Gabrielle, *Fondation des maladies du coeur du Québec*, 745

Executive Name Index

Overbeek, Christian, *Fédération des producteurs de cultures commerciales du Québec*, 717
Overbo, Wayne, *Canadian College of Health Leaders*, 359
Overgaard, Sune, *Federation of Danish Associations in Canada*, 723
Overholt, Christopher, *Canadian Olympic Committee*, 445
Overton, Clare, *Living Positive Resource Centre, Okanagan*, 915
Overwater, Greg, *Global Automakers of Canada*, 774
Ovington, Ken, *Ontario Pork Producers' Marketing Board*, 1097
Owen, Bridgett, *Association for Facilities Engineering*, 1508
Owen, Rochelle, *Ecology Action Centre*, 672
Owen, Kevin, *Canadian Home Builders' Association*, 1085
Owen, David, *Kinsmen Foundation of British Columbia & Yukon*, 890
Owen, Liz, *Parents, Families & Friends of Lesbians & Gays*, 1582
Owen, Tara, *Alberta Craft Council*, 32
Owen, Sherri, *Ontario Society for Environmental Education*, 1105
Owens, Oscar, *Amalgamated Transit Union (AFL-CIO/CLC)*, 1487
Owens, Kenda, *Interior Designers Association of Saskatchewan*, 852
Owens, Nicole, *Dance Manitoba Inc.*, 649
Oxley, Renee, *YWCA Canada*, 1481
Oxman, Ellen, *Nanaimo, Duncan & District Labour Council*, 988
Oxner, Gidget, *Nova Scotia Equestrian Federation*, 1044
Ozaruk, Janet, *Kitchener-Waterloo Field Naturalists*, 890
Ozemoyah, Peter, *Knights of St. John International - Canada*, 892
Ozolins, Chris, *Ontario Disc Sports Association*, 1077
Ozon, John, *Canadian Institute of Plumbing & Heating*, 418
Ozorio, Stephanie, *Canadian Hearing Society*, 403
Ozunko, Randy, *Manitoba Milk Prices Review Commission*, 940

P

Paas, Jocelyn, *Science Teachers' Association of Ontario*, 1285
Pablo Estable, Luis, *Ordre des ingénieurs du Québec*, 1122
Pace, Nadia, *Canadian Urological Association*, 500
Pace, William, *World Federalist Movement*, 1605
Pace, Teresa, *Aerospace & Electronic Systems Society*, 1485
Pace, William R., *Coalition for International Criminal Court*, 1517
Pacella, Maria, *Skills/Compétences Canada*, 1303
Pacelle, Wayne, *The Humane Society of the United States*, 1530
Pacey, Lucille, *Children's Arts Umbrella Association*, 561
Pacey, Katrina, *Pivot Legal Society*, 1161
Pach, Amanda, *Fertilizer Canada*, 733
Pacheco, Tony, *Community Living Association (Lanark County)*, 600
Pacheco, Laura, *Financial Executives International Canada*, 736
Pacho, Mercedes, *Independent Media Arts Alliance*, 833
Packham, Joanne, *Red Deer & District Community Foundation*, 1209
Pacukiewicz, Christine, *British Columbia Competitive Trail Riders Association*, 236
Paddick, Christy, *Institute of Public Administration of Canada*, 847

Paddock, Earl, *Calgary Round-Up Band Association*, 274
Paddock, Suzanne, *Toronto PWA Foundation*, 1386
Padgett, Lisa, *Bereavement Authority of Ontario*, 205
Padilla, Jennifer, *Academic Pediatric Association*, 1485
Padmos, Andrew, *The Royal College of Physicians & Surgeons of Canada*, 1241
Paduh, Bojan, *Electronic Recycling Association*, 683
Paech, Gail, *Associated Medical Services Inc.*, 89
Paetkau, Eric, *Saskatoon Symphony Society*, 1280
Paez, Nestor, *Canadian Columbian Professional Association*, 360
Pagani, Marco, *Community Foundation of Ottawa*, 598
Page, Cassie, *Manitoba Association of Library Technicians*, 930
Page, Susan, *Associated Gospel Churches*, 89
Page, Liz, *International Board on Books for Young People*, 1541
Page, David, *Canadian Hemophilia Society*, 404
Page, Devon, *Ecojustice Canada Society*, 672
Paiement, Sherri, *Canadian Home Builders' Association - British Columbia*, 407
Paige, Alan, *Tourism Victoria/Greater Victoria Visitors & Convention Bureau*, 1392
Paina, Corrado, *Italian Chamber of Commerce of Ontario*, 866
Painchaud, Martine, *Union des municipalités du Québec*, 1406
Painchaud, Jacques, *Association des policières et policiers provinciaux du Québec*, 123
Pais, Vanita, *AWIC Community & Social Services*, 191
Pais, Charles, *La Fédération Québécoise du Cricket Inc.*, 731
Paisley, Barry, *Canadian Security Association*, 469
Paisley, Catherine, *Canadian Association of Science Centres*, 332
Paisley, Kate, *Canadian Automobile Insurance Rate Regulators Association*, 339
Pal, Faythe, *Canadian Institute of Marketing*, 417
Pal Verma, Dharam, *National Association of Canadians of Origins in India*, 990
Palace Churchill, Barbara, *The Manitoba Law Foundation*, 939
Palardy, Isabelle, *Association des cadres des centres de la petite enfance*, 108
Palecek, Mike, *Canadian Union of Postal Workers*, 498
Paleczny, Kelly, *Ontario Public Transit Association*, 1100
Palejs, Dzintra, *L'Association des artistes Baltes à Montréal*, 106
Palen, George, *Paradise Hill Chamber of Commerce*, 1138
Palermo, Johanne, *Canadian Urban Transit Association*, 500
Palit, Arun, *The Toronto-Calcutta Foundation*, 1388
Palladino, Carol, *Revelstoke Arts Council*, 1228
Pallen, Lori, *Ontario Lung Association*, 1090
Pallister, Kent, *Calgary Combative Sports Commission*, 271
Pallister, Brian, *Progressive Conservative Party of Manitoba*, 1187
Pallotta, Sue, *CADORA Ontario Association Inc.*, 269
Pallotto, Carmela, *Catholic Charities of The Archdiocese of Toronto*, 518
Palmantier, Emma, *Canadian Aboriginal AIDS Network*, 285
Palmantier, Emma, *Prince George Native Friendship Centre*, 1179
Palmer, Michelle, *Community Living Elgin*, 601

Palmer, Linda, *Canadian Society of Cardiac Surgeons*, 481
Palmer, Michelle, *Ontario Public Buyers Association*, 1098
Palmer, Lurlean, *Spina Bifida & Hydrocephalus Association of Prince Edward Island*, 1342
Palmer, Sara L., *Middle East Studies Association of North America*, 1571
Palmer, Michelle, *Community Living London*, 603
Palmer, Christopher, *Chebucto Symphony Orchestra*, 555
Palmer, Glenda, *Volkssport Association of Alberta*, 1437
Palmer, Steven, *Canadian Association for Latin American & Caribbean Studies*, 302
Palmer, Sherrol, *Canadian Association of Ambulatory Care*, 308
Palmer, Steve, *Collaborative Centre for Justice & Safety*, 581
Palmer, Iain, *College of Podiatrists of Manitoba*, 589
Palmeter, Isabel, *West Hants Historical Society*, 1445
Paloschi, Vico, *Amici dell'Enotria Toronto*, 67
Paluck, Holly, *Regina Multicultural Council*, 1212
Palusci, Oriana, *Italian Association for Canadian Studies*, 1568
Paluzzi, Ron, *Canadian Football Officials Association*, 392
Palz, Barb, *College of Licensed Practical Nurses of Manitoba*, 585
Pancoast, Rochelle, *Canadian Wind Energy Association*, 504
Panesar, Ravinder, *Professional Engineers Ontario*, 1184
Paniak, Vince, *BMW Clubs Canada*, 216
Paniati, Jeffrey, *Institute of Transportation Engineers*, 1534
Panichella, Palmina, *Chambre de commerce et d'industrie de Montréal-Nord*, 546
Panko, Andy, *Canadian Railroad Historical Association*, 465
Pankov, Gradimir, *Les Grands Ballets Canadiens de Montréal*, 781
Pankovich, Jim, *Canadian Junior Football League*, 423
Pannell, Jane, *Association of Visual Language Interpreters of Canada*, 164
Panning, Sue, *Canmore Folk & Blues Club*, 508
Panozzo, Jack, *HelpAge Canada*, 812
Panteluk, Jen, *Junior Achievement Canada*, 877
Panteluk, Laura, *College of Registered Psychiatric Nurses of Manitoba*, 590
Panthakee, Dara, *Zoroastrian Society of Ontario*, 1482
Panting, Nancy, *Blankets for Canada Society Inc.*, 214
Panton, David, *Community Museums Association of Prince Edward Island*, 606
Paolucci, Cecelia, *United Way of Peel Region*, 1416
Papa, Luisa, *Canadian Italian Business & Professional Association*, 423
Papaionnou, John, *American Foundry Society*, 1493
Papavinasam, Sankara, *NACE International*, 1572
Papenburg, Ellen, *Memorial Society of Kitchener-Waterloo & Area*, 960
Papin, Danielle, *Canadian Masters Cross-Country Ski Association*, 431
Papoff, Sarah, *Council of Ontario Drama & Dance Educators*, 635
Papp, Peter, *Big Brothers Big Sisters of Ontario*, 210
Papp, Theresa (Therri), *Professional Photographers of Canada*, 1186
Papple, James, *TESL Ontario*, 1373
Papy, Jan, *International Association for Neo-Latin Studies*, 1537

Paquet, Emilie, *Chambre de commerce de Sept-Îles*, 543
Paquet, Stephane, *Canadian Culinary Federation*, 374
Paquet, Mary, *Prince Edward Island Museum & Heritage Foundation*, 1176
Paquet, Mario, *Association longueuilloise des photographes amateurs*, 137
Paquet, Michel, *Fédération des centres de ressourcement Chrétien*, 713
Paquette, Chantal, *Intégration communautaire Cochrane Association for Community Living*, 850
Paquette, Hélène, *Chambre de commerce de Cowansville et région*, 540
Paquette, Marcelle, *Diabète Québec*, 655
Paquette, Line, *Ordre des ingénieurs du Québec*, 1122
Paquette, Line, *Ordre des ingénieurs du Québec*, 1122
Paquette, Line, *Ordre des ingénieurs du Québec*, 1122
Paquette, Michaël, *Ordre des ingénieurs du Québec*, 1122
Paquette, Gilber, *Hebdos Québec*, 811
Paquette, Patrick D., *Association des microbiologistes du Québec*, 120
Paquette, Luc, *Union of Environment Workers*, 1407
Paquette, Larry, *Original Hockey Hall of Fame & Museum*, 1126
Paquette, Gilbert, *Conseil de la souveraineté du Québec*, 616
Paquette, Pierre, *CADORA Ontario Association Inc.*, 269
Paquette, Michel, *Canadian Race Communications Association*, 464
Paquette, Joan, *People First Nova Scotia*, 1151
Paquette-Rivard, Marie, *Margaret Morris Method (Canada)*, 949
Paquin, Pierre, *Ordre des chiropraticiens du Québec*, 1120
Paquin, Mélanie, *Chambre de commerce St-Jean-de-Matha*, 549
Paquin, Audrey, *Association des Grands Frères et Grandes Soeurs du Québec*, 115
Parada, Franklin, *Association of Dental Technologists of Ontario*, 146
Paradis, Hélène, *Chambre de commerce de Val-d'Or*, 544
Paradis, Jean, *Insitut canadien des économistes en construction - Québec*, 840
Paradis, Serge, *Canadian Ski Patrol*, 471
Paradis, Martine, *Fondation des maladies du coeur du Québec*, 745
Paradis, Laurie, *Manitoba Antique Association*, 928
Paradis, Marney, *Skookum Jim Friendship Centre*, 1303
Paradis, Régis, *Ordre des infirmières et infirmiers auxiliaires du Québec*, 1121
Paradis, Louise, *Réseau des SADC et CAE*, 1219
Paradis, François, *Union of Postal Communications Employees*, 1408
Paradis, Esther, *Association montérégienne de la surdité inc.*, 137
Paradis, Jeanne d'Arc, *Centre de la Communauté sourde du Montréal métropolitain*, 529
Paradis, Patrice, *L'Arche Québec*, 77
Paradowski, Cheryl, *Supply Chain Management Association*, 1355
Parakin, Lyndon, *Autism Calgary Association*, 188
Parapuf, Alina, *Association des Perfusionnistes du Québec Inc.*, 122
Paraskevas, Steven, *Canadian Association of Transplantation*, 334
Paré, France, *Chambre de commerce de Mont-Tremblant*, 542
Paré, Dominic, *Chambre de commerce de St-Jules-de-Beauce*, 543

Executive Name Index

Paré, Annie, *Canadian Public Relations Society Inc.*, 463
Paré, Marie-Claude, *Fondation CHU de Québec*, 743
Paré, Nathalie, *Centre d'adaptation de la main-d'œuvre aérospatiale du Québec*, 527
Paré, Yvon, *Association professionnelle des écrivains de la Sagamie-Côte-Nord*, 167
Parent, Henri-Louis, *Institut Voluntas Dei*, 843
Parent, Ed, *Windsor Police Association*, 1457
Parent, Jean-François, *Tel-Aide Outaouais*, 1369
Parent, Diane, *Association paritaire pour la santé et la sécurité du travail du secteur affaires sociales*, 165
Parent, Jennifer, *Consulting Engineers of Ontario*, 625
Parent, Marc, *The Canadian Corps of Commissionaires*, 365
Parent, Marc, *The Canadian Corps of Commissionaires*, 365
Parent, Denis, *Canadian Culinary Federation*, 374
Parent, Serge-Étienne, *Carrefour de solidarité internationale inc.*, 515
Parent, Jean-François, *Association québécoise des cadres scolaires*, 172
Parent, Josée, *Association des gastro-entérologues du Québec*, 115
Parent, Guy, *Insurance Brokers Association of Canada*, 848
Parent, Debbie, *Yukon Learn Society*, 1479
Parent, Patrick, *Fédération des éducateurs et éducatrices physiques enseignants du Québec*, 714
Parent, Pascal, *Canadian Association of Home & Property Inspectors*, 317
Parent, Réjean, *Syndicat des conseillères et conseillers de la CSQ*, 1362
Parent, Johanne, *Canine Federation of Canada*, 508
Parenteau, Madeleine, *Société du patrimoine de Boucherville*, 1319
Parenteau-Lebeuf, Marie-Claude, *Association professionnelle des designers d'intérieur du Québec*, 167
Parhar, Parveen, *British Columbia Road Builders & Heavy Construction Association*, 252
Paribello, Carlo, *Fragile X Research Foundation of Canada*, 757
Parikh, Manasi, *Canadian Public Health Association*, 462
Paris, Deb, *Canadian Celiac Association*, 353
Parish, Murray, *Canadian Association of Home & Property Inspectors*, 318
Parisian, Bruce, *Victoria Native Friendship Centre*, 1433
Parisian, Edie, *Manitoba Baton Twirling Sportive Association*, 932
Parisien, Kara, *Canadian Water & Wastewater Association*, 502
Parisotto, Marco, *Ontario Philharmonic*, 1095
Park, Michael, *Antiquarian Booksellers' Association of Canada*, 72
Park, Rory, *Tennis Saskatchewan*, 1371
Park, Brad, *United Way of Oakville*, 1415
Park, Gordon, *Kneehill Historical Society*, 892
Park, Alice, *Kneehill Historical Society*, 892
Park, Lynda, *Association for Slavic, East European, & Eurasian Studies*, 1509
Park, James M., *Glaucoma Research Society of Canada*, 774
Park, Paige, *Alberta Summer Swimming Association*, 48
Parke, Audrey, *Lloydminster Native Friendship Centre*, 916
Parker, Martin, *Peterborough Field Naturalists*, 1153
Parker, Elaine, *Canadian Society of Air Safety Investigators*, 479
Parker, C. Andrew, *Nova Scotia Fruit Growers' Association*, 1045
Parker, Darron, *Canadian Security Association*, 469

Parker, Sue, *Association of Early Childhood Educators Ontario*, 147
Parker, Gary, *Klondike Visitors Association*, 892
Parker, Taryn, *Yukon Church Heritage Society*, 1477
Parker, Mary Ellen, *Alzheimer Society of Chatham-Kent*, 62
Parker, Pamela, *Atlantic Canada Fish Farmers Association*, 182
Parker, Maureen, *Writers Guild of Canada*, 1468
Parker, Kip, *Cataraqui Archaeological Research Foundation*, 517
Parker, Scott D., *NORA, An Association of Responsible Recyclers*, 1578
Parker, Yvonne, *Learning Centre for Georgina*, 903
Parker, Vince, *Canadian Children's Optimist Foundation*, 356
Parkes, Philip, *CADORA Ontario Association Inc.*, 269
Parkins, Ilya, *Women's & Gender Studies et Recherches Féministes*, 1461
Parkinson, Monica, *Golden District Arts Council*, 776
Parkinson, Sean, *University of the Fraser Valley Faculty & Staff Association*, 1420
Parkinson, Nick, *YMCA Canada*, 1471
Parkinson, Dave, *Canadian Coalition Against the Death Penalty*, 357
Parkinson, Arlene, *Association of Kootenay & Boundary Local Governments*, 150
Parks, Trevor, *Architectural Woodwork Manufacturers Association of Canada - Manitoba*, 79
Parmar, Navjeet, *Regina Immigrant Women Centre*, 1212
Parmegiani, Sandra, *Canadian Society for Italian Studies*, 476
Parnell, Nathalie, *Timmins Family Counselling Centre, Inc.*, 1380
Parnell, Jeff, *Power Workers' Union*, 1169
Parr, Janene, *Home Child Care Association of Ontario*, 819
Parr, David, *Friends of The Canadian War Museum*, 762
Parr, Andrew, *The College of Naturopaths of Ontario*, 586
Parr, Dianne, *Ontario Council for Exceptional Children*, 1075
Parrell, Nicole, *Newfoundland & Labrador Federation of Agriculture*, 1018
Parris, Sylvia, *Multicultural Association of Nova Scotia*, 979
Parrish, Sandra, *Campbell River Museum & Archives Society*, 276
Parrott, Joan, *Municipality of Port Hope Historical Society*, 982
Parrott, Sharron, *The Therapeutic Touch Network of Ontario*, 1375
Parry, Lenetta, *Central Okanagan Community Food Bank*, 525
Parry, Evalyn, *Buddies in Bad Times Theatre*, 261
Parsley, Sherry, *Community Living Hamilton*, 602
Parslow, Joyce, *Canadian Beef*, 342
Parslow, Patti, *Appaloosa Horse Club of Canada*, 73
Parson, Michelle, *Toronto Arts Foundation*, 1381
Parson, Patrick, *Ballet Creole*, 194
Parsons, Katharine, *The Waterbird Society*, 1602
Parsons, Harold, *Boys & Girls Clubs of Ontario*, 223
Parsons, Trish, *Kitimat Chamber of Commerce*, 891
Parsons, Kristin, *Mission Regional Chamber of Commerce*, 969
Parsons, Wendy, *Leamington District Chamber of Commerce*, 903
Parsons, Calvin, *Saskatchewan Beekeepers Association*, 1259

Parsons, Stephen, *Assembly of BC Arts Councils*, 88
Parsons, Peter, *Blind Sports Nova Scotia*, 214
Parsons, Leanne, *Hamilton AIDS Network*, 800
Parsons, Donna, *Association of Engineering Technicians & Technologists of Newfoundland & Labrador*, 147
Parsons, Andy, *Newfoundland & Labrador Association of Public & Private Employees*, 1016
Parsons, Mark, *Economics Society of Northern Alberta*, 673
Parsons, Todd, *Union of Northern Workers*, 1407
Parsons, Sean, *Ontario Brain Injury Association*, 1069
Parsons, Mary, *CHILD Foundation*, 560
Parsons, Jennifer, *Welsh Pony & Cob Society of Canada*, 1444
Parsons, Leah, *Rehtaeh Parsons Society*, 1217
Parsons, Chanae, *Nova Scotia Association of Black Social Workers*, 1041
Parton, Sue, *Lake Abitibi Model Forest*, 895
Partridge, David, *Oxford-Brant Association of Baptist Churches*, 1134
Partridge, Sophie, *Yukon Foundation*, 1478
Partridge, Allan, *Canada BIM Council Inc.*, 278
Pasaoa, Edna, *Canadian Association of Ambulatory Care*, 308
Pasay, Rachael, *Alberta Amputee Sports & Recreation Association*, 22
Pascal, Gerald, *Centre des ressources sur la non-violence inc*, 531
Pasetka, Mark, *Canadian Association of Pharmacy in Oncology*, 326
Pasieczka, Liz, *Beausejour & District Chamber of Commerce*, 203
Pasildo, Gloria, *Filipino Canadian Association of Vaughan*, 735
Pasnak, Josh, *Special Olympics BC*, 1339
Pass, Andrea, *Footprints Dance Project Society of Alberta*, 751
Passinger, Megan, *National Waste & Recycling Association*, 1577
Passmore, Bob, *Alberta Building Envelope Council (South)*, 27
Passmore, Sandy, *Dunnville Chamber of Commerce*, 664
Paszkowski, Dan, *Canadian Vintners Association*, 501
Patacairk, Blair, *Invest Ottawa*, 862
Patava, James, *World Council on City Data*, 1465
Pate, Heather, *The Royal Scottish Country Dance Society*, 1587
Pate, Barbara, *The Terry Fox Foundation*, 1372
Patel, Nina Jane, *Dancer Transition Resource Centre*, 650
Patel, Vispi, *Zoroastrian Society of Ontario*, 1482
Patel, Ken K., *Council of Better Business Bureaus*, 1520
Patel, Hardik, *Alberta Diabetes Foundation*, 33
Patel, Nadir, *Association of Professional Executives of the Public Service of Canada*, 159
Patel, Ismail, *British Columbia Muslim Association*, 247
Patelos, Effie, *Art Libraries Society of North America*, 1506
Patenaude, Yves, *Association des professeures et professeurs de la Faculté de médecine de l'Université de Sherbrooke*, 124
Patenaude, Carole Anne, *Autism Society Alberta*, 189
Patenaude, Val, *Maple Ridge Museum & Community Archives*, 948
Patenaude, Francine, *Tourisme Cantons-de-l'Est*, 1392
Pater, Suzanne, *The Appraisal Institute of Canada - Prince Edward Island*, 75
Paterson, Shelagh, *Ontario Library Association*, 1089

Paterson, David, *The Canadian Chamber of Commerce*, 355
Paterson, Brent, *Canadian National Committee for Irrigation & Drainage*, 439
Paterson, Shelagh, *Canadian Federation of Library Associations*, 388
Paterson, Josh, *British Columbia Civil Liberties Association*, 236
Paterson, Kent, *YMCA Canada*, 1471
Paterson, Donald C., *The Paterson Foundation*, 1145
Paterson, Carleigh, *Back Country Horsemen of British Columbia*, 192
Patey, Agnes, *St Anthony & Area Chamber of Commerce*, 1248
Patey, Anthony, *Newfoundland & Labrador Dental Association*, 1018
Patey, Tony, *Malton Neighbourhood Services*, 928
Pathy, Constance V., *Ladies' Morning Musical Club*, 895
Patmore, Glenys, *Clay Tree Society for People with Developmental Disabilities*, 572
Patoine, Claude, *Ligue de dards Ungava*, 912
Paton, John F., *Alberta Schools' Athletic Association*, 46
Paton, Richard, *Chemistry Industry Association of Canada*, 556
Patrician, Michael W., *Canadian Association of Orthodontists*, 324
Patrick, Jeff, *Skate Canada*, 1301
Patrick, Alison, *United Way of Chatham-Kent County*, 1413
Patrick, Sarah, *Cabbagetown Community Arts Centre*, 268
Patrick, Ed, *Toronto Press & Media Club*, 1386
Patrick, Amelie, *Debden & District Chamber of Commerce*, 652
Patrick, Trisha, *Literacy Council York-Simcoe*, 914
Patrick, Caitlyn, *Canadian Nursing Students' Association*, 443
Patrick, Robert, *Coalition on the Niagara Escarpment*, 578
Patrick-MacDonald, Tambra, *United Way of Quinte*, 1416
Patrocinio, Horacio, *Canadian College of Physicists in Medicine*, 360
Patry, Pierre, *Confédération des syndicats nationaux*, 611
Patry, Michele, *Alberta Amateur Softball Association*, 22
Patry, Fernand, *Association des intervenantes et des intervenants en soins spirituels du Québec*, 117
Patry, Gilles G., *Canada Foundation for Innovation*, 279
Patry, Michel, *Réseau HEC Montréal*, 1224
Patsis, Marion, *Spinal Cord Injury British Columbia*, 1343
Patterson, Linda, *Block Parent Program of Canada*, 214
Patterson, Krista, *West Kootenay Regional Arts Council*, 1445
Patterson, Kevin, *Nova Scotia Curling Association*, 1043
Patterson, Brian J., *Ontario Safety League*, 1103
Patterson, Meaghan, *Alberta Museums Association*, 41
Patterson, McKensi, *Business Council of Canada*, 267
Patterson, Jason, *AIDS Committee of Toronto*, 16
Patterson, Peter, *Canadian Ski Patrol*, 471
Patterson, Gina, *Clean Nova Scotia Foundation*, 573
Patterson, Lorraine, *Council on Drug Abuse*, 636
Patterson, Suzanne, *Institute of Public Administration of Canada*, 847
Patterson, Sandra, *Junior Achievement Canada*, 877
Patterson, Carlena, *Canadian Sheep Federation*, 470

Patterson, Jennifer, *Economic Developers Council of Ontario Inc.*, 673
Patterson, Steve, *Calgary & Area Medical Staff Society*, 270
Patterson, Tiffannie, *Three Hills & District Chamber of Commerce*, 1377
Patterson, Garth, *Western Grains Research Foundation*, 1449
Patterson-Elden, Chante, *Recreation Facilities Association of British Columbia*, 1207
Pattison, Marilyn, *World Federation of Occupational Therapists*, 1605
Patton, Andrew, *Canadian Kennel Club*, 424
Paugh, Mike, *Boys & Girls Clubs of British Columbia*, 222
Paugh, Keith, *Canadian Council of Professional Fish Harvesters*, 369
Pauk, Alex, *Esprit Orchestra*, 696
Paul, Brenda, *Boys & Girls Clubs of Newfoundland & Labrador*, 223
Paul, Cori, *Alberta Water Polo Association*, 51
Paul, Ileana, *Canadian Linguistic Association*, 427
Paul, Wendy, *Dystonia Medical Research Foundation Canada*, 666
Paul, Dunne, *Family History Society of Newfoundland & Labrador*, 703
Paul Hargrove, Rebecca Paul, *World Lottery Association*, 1606
Paulen, Lisa, *International Trademark Association*, 1563
Paulencu, Don, *Baseball Canada*, 198
Paulic, Lovro, *Mining Association of Manitoba Inc.*, 967
Paulin, Francine, *Association of Canadian Port Authorities*, 143
Paull, Michael, *Fort Edmonton Foundation*, 752
Paulovich, Nora, *North Peace Applied Research Association*, 1032
Paulse, Sharon, *The Leukemia & Lymphoma Society of Canada*, 909
Paulson, Gary, *The Canadian Corps of Commissionaires*, 366
Paulson, Dianne, *Health & Safety Conference Society of Alberta*, 805
Pauzé, Lee, *The Friends of Algonquin Park*, 760
Pavanelli, Rosa, *Public Services International*, 1585
Pavelich, Craig, *Simon Fraser Public Interest Research Group*, 1300
Pavkovic, Jessica, *Family Enterprise Xchange*, 703
Pavlica, Dusanka, *Canadian Physicians for Aid & Relief*, 454
Pavlis, Stefan, *South Peace Community Resources Society*, 1335
Pavlov, Pattie, *Jasper Park Chamber of Commerce*, 869
Pawlikowski, Jackie, *Kincardine & District Chamber of Commerce*, 888
Pawlovich, Paula, *St. Elias Chamber of Commerce*, 1248
Pawlowicz, Chris, *BMW Clubs Canada*, 216
Payeur, Sebastien, *Pas de la rue*, 1144
Payeur, Claire, *Réseau du patrimoine franco-ontarien*, 1222
Payler, Katie, *YMCA Canada*, 1472
Payn, Valerie, *Halifax Chamber of Commerce*, 799
Payne, Keith, *Canadian Association of Nordic Ski Instructors*, 323
Payne, Sue, *Scarborough Philharmonic Orchestra*, 1282
Payne, Wes, *Manitoba Nurses' Union*, 941
Payne, Angie, *Canadian Society of Hospital Pharmacists*, 484
Payne, Gordon, *Risk & Insurance Management Society Inc.*, 1234
Payne, Adrian, *Royal Astronomical Society of Canada*, 1239
Payne, Kimberley, *Physiotherapy Association of British Columbia*, 1159
Payne, Peter, *British Columbia Technology Industries Association*, 256

Payne, Keith, *Newfoundland & Labrador Outfitters Association*, 1020
Payne, Christine, *Alberta Association of Family School Liaison Workers*, 23
Payne, Patricia, *Orphan Well Association*, 1127
Pazerniuk, Elizabeth, *Polish Combatants Association - Winnipeg*, 1164
Pazzaglia, Sharon, *Niagara Region Sexual Assault Centre*, 1025
Peach, Cyril, *Canadian Hard of Hearing Association*, 400
Peacock, Clementine, *Canadian Association of Independent Life Brokerage Agencies*, 318
Peacock, Chris, *The Sharing Place - Orillia & District Food Bank*, 1294
Peacock, Catherine, *Hampton Food Basket & Clothing Centre Inc.*, 802
Peacock, Ken, *Business Council of British Columbia*, 266
Peacock, Ken, *Natural Products Marketing Council*, 999
Peale, David, *International Order of the King's Daughters & Sons*, 1554
Pearce, Dylan, *Film & Video Arts Society Alberta*, 735
Pearce, Alexandra, *Indexing Society of Canada*, 834
Pearce, Suzanne, *Kwantlen Faculty Association*, 894
Pearce, George, *Creation Science Association of British Columbia*, 639
Pearce, Marni, *The Society for Safe & Caring Schools & Communities*, 1326
Pearce, Stephen, *Western Regional Advocacy Group Society*, 1450
Pearce, Matthew, *Mission Old Brewery*, 969
Pearce Rayner, Emily, *Fertilizer Canada*, 733
Pearcy, Dan, *Grande Prairie & District Chamber of Commerce*, 781
Pearcy, Margaret, *Canadian Public Relations Society Inc.*, 463
Pearen, Suzanne, *Canadian Institute for Child & Adolescent Psychoanalytic Psychotherapy*, 412
Pearlman, Miriam, *ARZA-Canada: The Zionist Voice of the Canadian Reform Movement*, 86
Pearse, Colleen, *South Essex Community Centre*, 1334
Pearse, Bill, *Quinte - Saint Lawrence Building & Construction Trades Council*, 1201
Pearson, Valerie, *Saskatchewan Agricultural Hall of Fame*, 1255
Pearson, Josée, *Fédération québécoise des sociétés Alzheimer*, 730
Pearson, Isabelle, *Judo Canada*, 876
Pearson, Jamie, *Probation Officers Association of Ontario*, 1181
Pearson, Christine, *Canadian Association of Wound Care*, 337
Pearson, Victoria, *Road Scholar*, 1586
Pearson, Cindy, *British Columbia Technology Industries Association*, 256
Pearson, Beth, *Registered Insurance Brokers of Ontario*, 1213
Pearson, Erin, *Insurance Council of Manitoba*, 849
Pearson, Iris Yong, *PeerNetBC*, 1148
Pearson, Amanda, *International WWOOF Association*, 1567
Pearson, Hilary, *Philanthropic Foundations Canada*, 1157
Peart, Bob, *Sierra Club of Canada*, 1298
Peason, Glen, *London Food Bank*, 918
Peat, Sharon, *New West Theatre Society*, 1014
Peat, John P., *Canadian Hemerocallis Society*, 404
Peck, Stephen, *World Organization of the Scout Movement*, 1607
Peck, Steve, *Used Car Dealers Association of Ontario*, 1423
Peck, Julie, *Canadian Association of Home & Property Inspectors*, 317
Peck, Eben, *American Society of Travel Agents*, 1503

Peck, Ryan, *HALCO*, 798
Peck, Steven, *Green Roofs for Healthy Cities*, 789
Peckford, Grant, *Learning Centre for Georgina*, 903
Peckham, June, *Canadian Society of Gastroenterology Nurses & Associates*, 483
Pecson, Kaitlyn, *Canadian Down Syndrome Society*, 378
Pedden, Cathy, *Big Brothers Big Sisters of Manitoba*, 209
Peddle, Geoff, *The Anglican Church of Canada*, 69
Peddle, John, *International Personnel Management Association - Canada*, 859
Peddle, Lori, *The Maritimes Energy Association*, 951
Peddle, Joanne, *Newfoundland & Labrador Operating Room Nurses Association*, 1020
Pedelty, Sarah, *North American Lincoln Red Association*, 1579
Peden, Verena, *Canadian Brown Swiss & Braunvieh Association*, 347
Pedersen, Catheryn, *Tiger Hills Arts Association Inc.*, 1379
Pedersen, Kirsten, *British Columbia Farm Industry Review Board*, 240
Pedersen, Soren, *International Commission of Agricultural & Biosystems Engineering*, 1542
Pedersen, Tim, *Architectural Woodwork Manufacturers Association of Canada - Atlantic*, 79
Pederson, Doug, *Saskatchewan Soccer Association Inc.*, 1275
Pédot, Isabelle, *Alliance Française Halifax*, 57
Peebles, Peter, *Water Ski & Wakeboard Alberta*, 1441
Peek, Mikk, *McMan Youth, Family & Community Services Association*, 955
Peek, Vinetta, *Chartered Professional Accountants of British Columbia*, 553
Peel, Tim, *Canadian Circulations Audit Board Inc.*, 357
Peers, Jennifer, *Alberta Dressage Association*, 33
Peets, Christine, *Professional Writers Association of Canada*, 1187
Peever, Dick, *Boating Ontario*, 216
Pegg, Bill, *Kitchener Sports Association*, 890
Peggs, Elizabeth, *International Geosynthetics Society*, 1550
Peirce, Casey, *Association for Mountain Parks Protection & Enjoyment*, 134
Pekor, Bernie, *American Concrete Institute*, 1491
Pekow, Cynthia, *International Council for Laboratory Animal Science*, 1544
Péladeau, Isabelle, *Association québécoise des professeurs de français*, 174
Pelangio, Pauline, *Sudbury Real Estate Board*, 1353
Pelham, Judy, *Canadian Philosophical Association*, 454
Pelkey, Nadja, *Arts Council Windsor & Region*, 85
Pelkey, Dean, *Association of British Columbia Forest Professionals*, 140
Pelland, Philippe, *Fédération québécoise du canot et du kayak*, 730
Pelland, Jacques, *Optimist International Canada*, 1116
Pelland, Jacques, *Canadian Children's Optimist Foundation*, 356
Pellarin, Steve, *Small Business Centre*, 1304
Pelle Hanlon, Deborah, *Canadian Institute of Chartered Business Valuators*, 414
Pellegrom, Daniel, *Sustainable Forestry Initiative Inc.*, 1597
Pellerin, Guy, *Association des services de réhabilitation sociale du Québec inc.*, 128
Pellerin, Alain, *Conference of Defence Associations*, 612
Pellerin, Catherine, *Société historique de la Côte-Nord*, 1320

Pellerine, Patricia, *Nova Scotia Dental Association*, 1044
Pellerine, Moira, *Meeting Professionals International*, 1570
Pelletier, Diane, *Kenora Association for Community Living*, 883
Pelletier, Sylvie, *Association des Allergologues et Immunologues du Québec*, 105
Pelletier, Jennifer, *NSERC Chair for Women in Science & Engineering*, 1050
Pelletier, Simon, *Canadian Marine Pilots' Association*, 430
Pelletier, Denis, *Ordre professionnel de la physiothérapie du Québec*, 1124
Pelletier, Frédérick, *La cinémathèque québécoise*, 570
Pelletier, Lucie, *Hébergement la casa Bernard-Hubert*, 811
Pelletier, Geneviève, *Le Cercle Molière*, 537
Pelletier, René, *Société d'histoire et de généalogie de la Matapédia*, 1312
Pelletier, Manon, *Regroupement des artistes en arts visuels du Québec (ind.)*, 1214
Pelletier, Catherine, *Parents-Unis Lanaudière*, 1140
Pelletier, Claude A., *Madawaska Forest Products Marketing Board*, 924
Pelletier, Lyne, *Amicale des Sommeliers du Québec*, 67
Pelletier, Claudia-Lynn, *Association des personnes intéressées à l'aphasie et à l'accident vasculaire cérébral*, 123
Pelletier, Pierre, *Société d'histoire régionale de Chibougamau*, 1313
Pelletier, Denise, *Saskatchewan Aboriginal Land Technicians*, 1255
Pellowe, John, *Canadian Council of Christian Charities*, 368
Pelly, Kyle, *Ontario Blind Sports Association*, 1068
Pelly, Kyle, *Ontario Colleges Athletic Association*, 1073
Péloffy, Karine, *Centre québécois du droit de l'environnement*, 536
Péloquin, Claude, *Canadian Ski Council*, 471
Péloquin, Mireille, *Fédération des parents francophones de l'Alberta*, 717
Péloquin-Antoun, Claudette, *Ordre professionnel des diététistes Québec*, 1124
Pelser, Kerry, *Canadian Association of Broadcast Consultants*, 309
Peltola, Brent, *Partners in Research*, 1144
Peltz, Lee, *Association of Professional Engineers & Geoscientists of British Columbia*, 158
Pelyk, Mike, *National Hockey League Alumni Association*, 994
Penaud, Patrice, *Canadian Management Centre*, 429
Pendea, Florin, *Canadian Association of Palynologists*, 325
Pendergast, Garry, *Revelstoke Arts Council*, 1228
Pendergast, Karen, *North Bay Police Association*, 1030
Pendlebury, Matthew, *Real Estate Institute of Canada*, 1206
Pendrill, Linda, *Canadian Investor Protection Fund*, 422
Peng, Frank, *Inclusion BC*, 832
Pengelly, Steve, *Canadian Bar Association*, 342
Pengelly, Bianca, *Canadian Liver Foundation*, 427
Penk-O'Donnell, Deirdre, *Western Canada Irish Dancing Teachers Association*, 1448
Penn, John S., *International Society for Eye Research*, 1558
Penna, Phillip, *Ontario Environmental Network*, 1078
Pennefather-O'Brien, Elizabeth, *Faculty Association of Medicine Hat College*, 700
Pennell, Melissa, *Canadian Public Relations Society Inc.*, 463

Executive Name Index

Pennell, Tim, *Southern Interior Local Government Association*, 1338
Penner, Harold, *Abundance Canada*, 3
Penner, Michael, *Big Brothers Big Sisters of Manitoba*, 209
Penner, Dylan, *ACT for the Earth*, 6
Penner, Kailey, *Manitoba Hereford Association*, 938
Penner, Shirley, *Youth Singers of Calgary*, 1476
Penner, Lori, *Winkler & District United Way*, 1458
Penner, Lori, *Insurance Women's Association of Western Manitoba*, 850
Penney, Kay, *Girl Guides of Canada*, 773
Penney, Karl, *Royal Astronomical Society of Canada*, 1238
Penney, Greg, *National Literacy & Health Program*, 994
Penney, Jeff, *Economic Developers Alberta*, 672
Penney, Catharine, *Immigrant Services Association of Nova Scotia*, 830
Penny, David J., *Corrugated Steel Pipe Institute*, 631
Penny, Joss, *British Columbia Lodging & Campgrounds Association*, 245
Penny, Leslie, *Alberta Hospice Palliative Care Association*, 38
Pennylegion, Anne, *Saskatchewan Library Association*, 1269
Pente, Catherine, *New Brunswick Association of Occupational Therapists*, 1005
Penzo, Paul, *Association of Canadian Corporations in Translation & Interpretation*, 141
Pepall, George, *Kitchener-Waterloo Philatelic Society*, 891
Pepe, Paul, *Tourism Thunder Bay*, 1391
Pepin, Fred, *Langley Heritage Society*, 899
Pepin, Michelle, *Alzheimer Society of Durham Region*, 62
Pépin, Daniel, *Syndicat des pompiers et pompières du Québec (CTC)*, 1363
Pepin, Mireille, *Fédération des coopératives d'habitation de la Mauricie et du Centre-du-Québec*, 714
Pepin, Geneviève, *Conseil du bâtiment durable du Canada - Québec*, 618
Peppas, Nicholas A., *International Union of Societies for Biomaterials Science & Engineering*, 1565
Pepper, Gordon, *Saskatchewan Filmpool Co-operative*, 1265
Pepper, Michael, *Travel Industry Council of Ontario*, 1396
Pepperell, John, *Hearing Foundation of Canada*, 808
Peppin, Carolyn, *Basketball New Brunswick*, 199
Peralta, Gonzalo, *Languages Canada*, 899
Peralta, Eloisa, *Association of Filipino Canadian Accountants in British Columbia*, 148
Percival, Kent, *University of Guelph Professional Staff Association*, 1419
Percy, Ingrid Mary, *Canadian Artists Representation*, 295
Percy, Kevin, *Wood Buffalo Environmental Association*, 1463
Perdaus, Ahmad Faizal, *International Council of Voluntary Agencies*, 1545
Perdue, Jeff, *National Association of College Auxiliary Services*, 1573
Perea, P.J., *Association of Great Lakes Outdoor Writers*, 1512
Pereboom, Carly, *Port Hardy & District Chamber of Commerce*, 1166
Pereira, Joao Alves, *Fédération Internationale de Camping, Caravanning et Autocaravaning*, 1525
Pereira, Idalia Ivon, *Action for Healthy Communities*, 6
Perelman, Dell, *American Chemistry Council*, 1491

Perera, Mohan, *Canada-Sri Lanka Business Council*, 284
Peresa, Lili-Anna, *Centraide du Grand Montréal*, 522
Peretz, Daniel, *Canadian Federation of Medical Students*, 388
Pereyra-Rojas, Milagros, *Latin American Studies Association*, 1569
Perez, Andrew, *Canadian Bankers Association*, 341
Perez, Meredith, *Canadian Sheet Steel Building Institute*, 470
Perez, Jr, Javier, *Amalgamated Transit Union (AFL-CIO/CLC)*, 1487
Pergantis, Paula, *Food & Consumer Products of Canada*, 749
Perih, Jennifer, *Western Transportation Advisory Council*, 1450
Perin, Roberto, *Canadian Society for Italian Studies*, 476
Peringer, Marylyn, *Ontario Folk Dance Association*, 1080
Peris, Rohini, *Association pour la santé environnementale du Québec*, 166
Perizzolo, Leonara, *50 & Piu Enasco*, 734
Perkel, Patricia, *National NewsMedia Council*, 995
Perkins, Kevin, *Farm Radio International*, 705
Perkins, Stan, *World Masters Athletics*, 1606
Perkins, Stasia, *Southern Alberta Curling Association*, 1337
Perkins, Kim, *Special Olympics BC*, 1339
Perkinson, Walter, *Standardbred Breeders of Ontario Association*, 1347
Perks, Warren, *British Columbia Construction Association*, 237
Perley, Michael, *The Ontario Campaign for Action on Tobacco*, 1070
Permack, Michael, *Canadian Cancer Society*, 349
Perna, Jennifer, *International Caterers Association*, 1542
Pero, Robert, *New Brunswick Building Officials Association*, 1006
Perrault, Sylvie, *Association des Architectes en pratique privée du Québec*, 105
Perrault, Denis, *Corporation des services d'ambulance du Québec*, 630
Perrault, Anie, *BIOQuébec*, 211
Perrault, Jacques, *Fondation Tourisme Jeunesse*, 748
Perrault, Danielle, *Réseau FADOQ*, 1224
Perrault, Jean-François, *Professional Photographers of Canada*, 1186
Perrault, Isabelle, *Association des familialistes de Québec*, 113
Perrault, Isabelle, *Canadian Society for the History of Medicine*, 477
Perrault, Normand, *Fédération québécoise de ballon sur glace*, 727
Perrault, Sophie, *Association québécoise de la distribution de fruits et légumes*, 170
Perrault, Jacques, *Association des professionnels en exposition du Québec*, 126
Perrault, Isabelle, *International Society for the History of Medicine - Canadian Section*, 860
Perrella, Elvira, *Victoria International Development Education Association*, 1432
Perrier, Richard, *Sheridan Park Association*, 1296
Perrin, Janne, *Chilliwack Field Naturalists*, 563
Perrin, Dennis, *Christian Labour Association of Canada*, 567
Perrin, Dennis, *Christian Labour Association of Canada*, 568
Perrin, Dennis, *Christian Labour Association of Canada*, 567
Perrin, Dennis, *Christian Labour Association of Canada*, 568
Perritt, Lesia, *Ukrainian Women's Association of Canada*, 1403
Perron, Madeleine, *Conseil de la culture de L'Abitibi-Témiscamingue*, 615
Perron, Sylvain, *Chambre de commerce Haute-Yamaska et Région*, 548

Perron, Sylvie, *Association coopérative d'économie familiale des Basses Laurentides*, 98
Perron, Éric, *Société de développement des périodiques culturels québécois*, 1315
Perron, Michel, *Société des musées québécois*, 1318
Perron, Richard, *Syndicat de professionnelles et professionnels du gouvernement du Québec*, 1362
Perron, Jacques, *La Compagnie des philosophes*, 608
Perron, Christian, *Futurpreneur Canada*, 765
Perron, Nicolas, *Association québécoise pour l'hygiène, la santé et la sécurité du travail*, 176
Perron, Leonie, *Canadian Council on Africa*, 370
Perrone, Anthony, *United Food & Commercial Workers' International Union*, 1599
Perrotta, Kim, *Canadian Association of Physicians for the Environment*, 327
Perruzza, Sandro, *Ontario Society of Professional Engineers*, 1107
Perry, Patricia, *Bonnyville & District Fine Arts Society*, 217
Perry, Christina, *TESL Prince Edward Island*, 1373
Perry, Clair, *Royal Astronomical Society of Canada*, 1238
Perry, David, *College of Psychologists of British Columbia*, 589
Perry, Wendy, *Human Resources Professionals Association*, 826
Perry, Rhonda, *Réseau des SADC et CAE*, 1221
Perry, Joan, *British Columbia Ground Water Association*, 242
Perry, Linda, *Vela Microboard Association of British Columbia*, 1430
Perry, Kevin, *NAID Canada*, 987
Perry, Nalani, *Offshore Energy Research Association of Nova Scotia*, 1055
Persaud, Ravi, *Vocational Rehabilitation Association of Canada*, 1436
Persaud, Praim, *Cricket Council of Ontario*, 642
Persechino, Tony, *Canadian Railway Club*, 465
Pérusse, Claude, *Association des physiciens et ingénieurs biomédicaux du Québec*, 123
Peschken, Christine, *Canadian Network for Improved Outcomes in Systemic Lupus Erythematosus*, 440
Peski, Michael S., *Canadian Adult Recreational Hockey Association*, 288
Pestrak, Judy, *Manitoba Association of Architects*, 929
Pesun, Simona, *Canadian Academy of Endodontics*, 286
Petch, Paul, *Ontario Numismatic Association*, 1094
Petelle, Pierre, *CropLife Canada*, 643
Petelycky, Ashley, *Terrazzo Tile & Marble Association of Canada*, 1372
Peter, Dinsdale, *YMCA Canada*, 1471
Peter, Bradley, *Alberta Lake Management Society*, 39
Peter, Noel, *Eastern Ontario Beekeepers' Association*, 670
Peters, Janelle, *Boys & Girls Clubs of Alberta*, 221
Peters, Linda, *Steinbach Chamber of Commerce*, 1349
Peters, Dave, *Newmarket Chamber of Commerce*, 1024
Peters, Michelle, *Association of Manitoba Book Publishers*, 151
Peters, Anna, *Operation Springboard*, 1116
Peters, Arthur, *ShareLife*, 1294
Peters, Ann, *Northwest Wildlife Preservation Society*, 1039
Peters, Mary-Lynn, *Alzheimer Society of Peel*, 64

Peters, David, *Northwest Mennonite Conference*, 1036
Peters, Menno, *Manitoba Non-Profit Housing Association*, 941
Peters, Cheryl, *Living Bible Explorers*, 915
Peters, Don, *Mennonite Central Committee Canada*, 960
Peters, Gene, *Back Country Horsemen of British Columbia*, 193
Peters, Doris, *Helping Spirit Lodge Society*, 812
Peters, Shawn, *Saskatchewan Bodybuilding Association*, 1260
Petersen, Jennifer, *Children's Wish Foundation of Canada*, 562
Petersen, Joanne, *Saskatchewan Registered Nurses' Association*, 1273
Petersen, Charles, *Youth Flight Canada*, 1475
Petersen, Dianne, *Kids Kottage Foundation*, 886
Petersen-Banfield, Lis, *Scandinavian Society of Nova Scotia*, 1282
Peterson, Ken, *Lethbridge Fish & Game Association*, 908
Peterson, Kristina, *Ontario Chiropractic Association*, 1071
Peterson, Andreas, *Ontario Association of Committees of Adjustment & Consent Authorities*, 1063
Peterson, Wayne, *Ontario Sheet Metal Contractors Association*, 1104
Peterson, Wayne, *Construction Employers Coordinating Council of Ontario*, 624
Peterson, Craig, *Missing Children Society of Canada*, 968
Peterson, Rhonda, *Debden & District Chamber of Commerce*, 652
Peterson, Leon, *NWT Seniors' Society*, 1052
Peterson, Don, *Freshwater Fisheries Society of British Columbia*, 760
Petersons, Vilnis, *Latvian National Federation in Canada*, 900
Petersson, Sandra, *Alberta Law Reform Institute*, 39
Petit, Marlene, *Canadian Propane Association*, 461
Petit, Dawn, *Pain Society of Alberta*, 1137
Petitclerc, Julien, *Vertes boisées du fjord*, 1431
Petitpas, Lise, *Corporation des bijoutiers du Québec*, 629
Petitti, John, *Scouts Canada*, 1286
Petkau, Christine, *Summerland Chamber of Commerce*, 1354
Petkov, Plamen, *Canadian Federation of Independent Business*, 387
Petley, Shelley, *POWERtalk International*, 1584
Peto, Karen, *Manitoba Association of Women's Shelters*, 931
Peto, Karen, *YWCA Canada*, 1481
Petovar, Shelly, *Canadian Pension & Benefits Institute*, 453
Petracek-Kolb, Jennifer, *YMCA Canada*, 1472
Petrauskas, Chris, *Alpine Club of Canada*, 59
Petretta, Davide, *Council of Ontario Construction Associations*, 634
Petricone, Ivana, *ARCH Disability Law Centre*, 76
Petrie, Kate, *Carman & Community Chamber of Commerce*, 514
Petrie, Trish, *Truro & Colchester Chamber of Commerce*, 1400
Petrie, Lloyd, *Cosmetology Association of Nova Scotia*, 631
Petrie, Jennifer, *Nova Scotia Badminton Association*, 1041
Petrie, David, *Professional Writers Association of Canada*, 1187
Petrie, Jim, *Alberta Union of Provincial Employees*, 50
Petrie, Deborah, *Manitoba Regional Lily Society*, 943
Pétrin, Serge, *Généalogie Abitibi-Témiscamingue*, 768

Executive Name Index

Petrini, Carlo, *Slow Food*, 1589
Petrone, Richard, *Canadian Geophysical Union*, 397
Petrongolo, Remo, *Ontario Recreation Facilities Association*, 1100
Petrov, Annemarie, *Edmonton Symphony Orchestra*, 679
Petrovic, Vasilj, *Professional Engineers Ontario*, 1184
Petryk, Henryk, *International Union of Theoretical & Applied Mechanics*, 1565
Petryshen, John, *Parkinson Alberta Society*, 1141
Petterson, Kathy, *Alberta Organic Producers Association*, 41
Petursdottir, Thorunn, *Manitoba Funeral Service Association*, 937
Petzold, Sheila, *USC Canada*, 1423
Pew, Jonathan, *Freshwater Fisheries Society of British Columbia*, 760
Pexman, Penny, *Canadian Society for Brain, Behaviour & Cognitive Science*, 473
Peyton, Sterling, *Labrador North Chamber of Commerce*, 894
Peña, Fidel, *The Advertising & Design Club of Canada*, 10
Pfeifer, Judy, *Yorkton Real Estate Association Inc.*, 1474
Pflieger, Lisa, *Financial Planning Standards Council*, 737
Phady, Khan, *World Amateur Muay Thai Association of Canada*, 1465
Pham, Thu, *British Columbia Food Technolgists*, 241
Pham, Huong, *Assaulted Women's Helpline*, 87
Phaneuf, Don, *AIDS Committee of Toronto*, 16
Phaneuf, Gordon, *Child Welfare League of Canada*, 560
Phare, Garth, *Pemberton & District Chamber of Commerce*, 1149
Phare, Merrell-Ann, *Centre for Indigenous Environmental Resources, Inc.*, 532
Phelan, Deanna, *New Brunswick Equestrian Association*, 1008
Phelps, Fred, *Canadian Association of Social Workers*, 333
Phelps, Fred, *Canadian Social Work Foundation*, 472
Phelps, Ann, *Canadian International Dragon Boat Festival Society*, 421
Phelps, Marjorie, *Kitimat Food Bank*, 891
Phibbs, Rick, *Greater Fort Erie Chamber of Commerce*, 783
Philibert, Michel, *Fédération des chambres de commerce du Québec*, 713
Philie, Patrice, *Canadian Philosophical Association*, 454
Philipovsky, Carlos, *Consulting Engineers of the Northwest Territories*, 625
Philipp, Rob, *Fraser Valley Real Estate Board*, 758
Philipp, Lois, *Northern Youth Abroad Program*, 1035
Philips, Shirley, *Arthritis Society*, 84
Phillip, Jan, *Biggar & District Arts Council*, 211
Phillip, Stewart, *Union of British Columbia Indian Chiefs*, 1407
Phillips, Lori, *HIV West Yellowhead Society*, 817
Phillips, Donald, *The Anglican Church of Canada*, 70
Phillips, Robert C., *Hagersville & District Chamber of Commerce*, 798
Phillips, Jenne, *Child Evangelism Fellowship of Canada*, 559
Phillips, Carson, *Holocaust Education Centre*, 819
Phillips, Suzanne, *National Eating Disorder Information Centre*, 992
Phillips, Christina, *Stratford Tourism Alliance*, 1351
Phillips, Donna, *N'Amerind (London) Friendship Centre*, 986
Phillips, Kelley, *TechConnex*, 1368

Phillips, Dave, *Earth Island Institute*, 1522
Phillips, Sue, *Niagara Peninsula Electrical Contractors Association*, 1025
Phillips, Alex, *The Van Horne Institute for International Transportation & Regulatory Affairs*, 1424
Phillips, Tom, *Habitat for Humanity Canada*, 797
Phillips, Wayne, *Canadian Dam Association*, 375
Phillips, Amanda, *Professional Petroleum Data Management Association*, 1186
Phillips, James D., *Can-Am Border Trade Alliance*, 1515
Phillips, Debra M., *American Chemistry Council*, 1491
Phillips, Louise, *British Columbia Registered Music Teachers' Association*, 251
Phillips, Jessie, *Ontario Prader-Willi Syndrome Association*, 1097
Phillips, Heather, *Canadian Association of Specialized Kinesiology*, 333
Phillips, Diane, *Wood Buffalo Environmental Association*, 1463
Philp, John, *Wellspring Cancer Support Foundation*, 1444
Philpitt, Candace, *Compensation Employees' Union (Ind.)*, 609
Phimister, Lesley, *Manitoba Naturopathic Association*, 941
Phinney, Jackie, *Maritimes Health Libraries Association*, 951
Phinney, Patricia, *The Salvation Army in Canada*, 1253
Phinney, Alison, *Canadian Association on Gerontology*, 337
Phinney, Chris, *Save Ontario Shipwrecks*, 1281
Phipps, Erica, *Canadian Partnership for Children's Health & Environment*, 451
Phord-Toy, Lesley, *International Game Developers Association*, 1549
Pia-Comella, Jelena, *Coalition for International Criminal Court*, 1517
Pialasse, Jean-Philippe, *Association des chercheurs et chercheures étudiants en médecine*, 108
Piao, Marina, *Council of Ontario Universities*, 635
Piasta, Andy, *PFLAG Canada Inc.*, 1156
Picard, Valérie, *Conseil des arts de Hearst*, 617
Picard, André, *Canadian Pension & Benefits Institute*, 453
Picard, Jean-Pierre, *Canadian Academy of Periodontology*, 286
Picard, Marc, *L'Association de spina-bifida et d'hydrocéphalie du Québec*, 104
Picard, Magali, *Public Service Alliance of Canada*, 1193
Picard, Magali, *Public Service Alliance of Canada*, 1193
Picard, France, *Centre de recherche et d'intervention interuniversitaire sur l'éducation et la vie au travail*, 530
Picard, Ghislain, *Assemblée des premières nations du Québec et du Labrador*, 88
Picard, Rejean, *The Ontario Greenhouse Alliance*, 1083
Picard, Serge, *Association chasse & pêche de Chibougamau*, 96
Picard, Jocelyn, *Association des personnes handicapées physiques et sensorielles du secteur Joliette*, 123
Picard, Hélène, *ZAP Montérégie*, 1482
Picciano, Filomena, *Canadian Society of Nephrology*, 485
Picco Garland, Deborah, *Quidi Vidi Rennie's River Development Foundation*, 1201
Piché, Nicole, *Carrefour Tiers-Monde*, 516
Piche, Terry, *Ontario Recreation Facilities Association*, 1100
Piché, Suzanne M., *Centraide Laurentides*, 522
Piche, Christine, *Biathlon Ontario*, 207

Pichelin, Marie-Noël, *Société québécoise de la rédaction professionnelle*, 1323
Pichette, David, *Club 'Les Pongistes d'Ungava'*, 574
Pick, Amanda, *Missing Children Society of Canada*, 968
Pick, Shelley, *Brain Injury Association of Nova Scotia*, 225
Pickard, LuAnn, *Urology Nurses of Canada*, 1422
Pickard, David, *Canadian Deaf Curling Association*, 376
Pickerell, Syd, *British Columbia Farm Machinery & Agriculture Museum Association*, 240
Pickering, Christine, *Alfa Romeo Club of Canada*, 53
Pickering, Ken, *Coastal Jazz & Blues Society*, 579
Pickering, Larry K., *Infectious Diseases Society of America*, 1531
Pickthorne, Sharon, *Back Country Horsemen of British Columbia*, 192
Pickthorne, Sharon, *Back Country Horsemen of British Columbia*, 193
Pierce, Anna, *Chamber of Commerce Niagara Falls, Canada*, 539
Piercey, Matthew, *Canadian Cancer Society*, 349
Piercey, Melodie, *Fencing - Escrime New Brunswick*, 732
Piercey, Ron, *Bakery, Confectionery, Tobacco Workers & Grain Millers International Union (AFL-CIO/CLC)*, 1514
Piercy, Wendy, *Supply Chain Management Association - New Brunswick*, 1356
Pierno, Theresa, *National Parks Conservation Association*, 1577
Pieroni, Danielle, *Chartered Professional Accountants of New Brunswick*, 553
Pierre-Pierre, Valérie, *African & Caribbean Council on HIV/AIDS in Ontario*, 12
Piers, George, *New Brunswick Association of Food Banks*, 1005
Piesena, Aleksandras, *L'Association des artistes Baltes à Montréal*, 106
Pietroniro, Elise, *Canadian Cartographic Association*, 350
Pietropaolo, Cristina, *Storytelling Toronto*, 1351
Pigeon, Jean, *Fondation Santé Gatineau*, 748
Pighin, Karen, *Maple Ridge Pitt Meadows Arts Council*, 948
Pigott, Pierre, *Financial Executives International Canada*, 736
Pigott, Jim, *Northwest Wildlife Preservation Society*, 1039
Pihack, Brian, *Royal Astronomical Society of Canada*, 1238
Pihack, Brian, *Royal Astronomical Society of Canada*, 1238
Pihèwa Karoue, Edouard, *IMCS Pax Romana*, 1531
Pijl, Stan, *Canadian Vaping Association*, 500
Pike, Sara, *Armed Forces Communications & Electronics Association (Canada)*, 82
Pike, Wayne, *The Royal Canadian Legion*, 1240
Pike, Bryan, *West Coast Book Prize Society*, 1444
Pike, Allison, *Alberta School Councils' Association*, 45
Pike, Graham, *Central Vancouver Island Multicultural Society*, 525
Pike, Jeffrey, *Canadian Council of Independent Laboratories*, 368
Pike, Denise, *Newfoundland & Labrador Federation of School Councils*, 1019
Pike, Wayne, *Prince Edward Island Harness Racing Industry Association*, 1174
Pike, Wayne, *Maritime Breeders Association*, 950
Pike, Wayne, *Prince Edward Island Colt Stakes Association*, 1173

Pike, Wayne, *Prince Edward Island Standardbred Horseowners' Association*, 1177
Pike, Lisa, *New Brunswick Physiotherapy Association*, 1011
Pike, Lisa, *Newfoundland & Labrador Physiotherapy Association*, 1021
Pikel, John, *Manitoba Environmental Industries Association Inc.*, 936
Piksa, Ron, *International Association of Bridge, Structural, Ornamental & Reinforcing Iron Workers (AFL-CIO)*, 1538
Pilc-Levine, Miriam, *Canadian Friends of the Hebrew University*, 395
Pilgrim, Kate, *The T. R. Meighen Foundation*, 1365
Pilgrim, Craig, *Stop Abuse in Families Society*, 1350
Pilip, Ken, *Consulting Engineers of Alberta*, 625
Pillainayagam, Jude, *Canadian Information Processing Society*, 411
Pillay, Som, *Grande Prairie Regional College Academic Staff Association*, 781
Pillay, Intheran, *Saskatchewan Medical Association*, 1270
Piller, Dean, *British Columbia Golf Superintendents Association*, 242
Piller, Madi, *Toronto Animated Image Society*, 1381
Pilon, Chantal, *Chambre de commerce et d'industrie Rimouski-Neigette*, 547
Pilon, Darlene, *Canadian Council of Technicians & Technologists*, 370
Pilon, Brigitte, *Council of Canadian Law Deans*, 633
Pilon, Biff, *Sudbury Stamp Club*, 1353
Pilon, Cliff, *Ontario Motor Vehicle Industry Council*, 1091
Pilon, David, *Canadian Depression Research & Intervention Network*, 377
Pilote, Jacqueline, *Syndicat professionnel des ingénieurs d'Hydro-Québec*, 1365
Pilote, Édith, *Association des professionnels en électrolyse et soins esthétiques du Québec*, 126
Pilote, Marie-Pier, *Réseau indépendant des diffuseurs d'événements artistiques unis*, 1225
Pimentel, Stephanie, *Ontario Library Association*, 1089
Pimentel, Maria, *Promotional Product Professionals of Canada Inc.*, 1189
Pimm, Chad, *Canadian Contractors Association*, 364
Pinard, Andrée, *Financial Executives International Canada*, 736
Pinard, Daniel, *L'Association du Québec de l'Institut canadien des évaluateurs*, 131
Pinco, Raymond, *St. Albert Historical Society*, 1248
Pincox, Carol, *Fondation des maladies du coeur du Québec*, 745
Pinder, Adam, *Council of Ontario Construction Associations*, 634
Pine, George, *AIDS Vancouver Island*, 17
Pineau, Alain, *Canadian Conference of the Arts*, 363
Pineau, Brett W., *Native Friendship Centre of Montréal Inc.*, 998
Pineau, Olivier, *Karate Canada*, 881
Pineault, Geneviève, *Association des théâtres francophones du Canada*, 129
Pineault, Geneviève, *Théâtre du Nouvel-Ontario*, 1374
Pink, Darrel, *Nova Scotia Barristers' Society*, 1042
Pinkerton, Donald, *The Association of Maritime Arbitrators of Canada*, 151
Pinkney, Rick, *Canadian Arm Wrestling Federation*, 295
Pinkney, Rick, *Nova Scotia Arm Wrestling Association*, 1040
Pinks, Stuart, *Canada - Nova Scotia Offshore Petroleum Board*, 278

Executive Name Index

Pinks, Jennifer, *Offshore Energy Research Association of Nova Scotia*, 1055
Pinnock, Stephen, *Best Buddies Canada*, 206
Pinto, Rowena, *Canadian Cancer Society*, 349
Pinto, Fred, *Ontario Professional Foresters Association*, 1097
Pinto, Darlene, *Canadian Centre on Substance Use & Addiction*, 354
Pinto, B. Mario, *Natural Sciences & Engineering Research Council of Canada*, 999
Pipon, Lisette, *Association des radiologistes du Québec*, 127
Pippy, Doreen, *Prince Edward Island Dietetic Association*, 1173
Pirani, Alamin, *Scouts Canada*, 1286
Piraux, Jade, *CFA Society Calgary*, 538
Pirbhai, Mariam, *Canadian Association for Commonwealth Literature & Language Studies*, 298
Pires, Sandra, *CIVICUS: World Alliance for Citizen Participation*, 1517
Pirti, Andy, *Makivik Corporation*, 927
Pisani, Ray R., *Canadian Association of Blue Cross Plans*, 309
Pisarzowski, Gerald, *Greater Toronto Marketing Alliance*, 786
Piskur, Michael, *Conference of Great Lakes & St. Lawrence Governors & Premiers*, 1519
Pismenny, Lorrie, *Winnipeg Ostomy Association*, 1459
Pister, Jayson, *Sport Parachute Association of Saskatchewan*, 1345
Pitblado, Jamie, *Children's Arts Umbrella Association*, 561
Pitcairn, Matt, *Richmond Chamber of Commerce*, 1230
Pitchen, Christian, *La cinémathèque québécoise*, 570
Pitcher, Jeff, *Theatre Newfoundland Labrador*, 1374
Pitcher, Marcel, *Newfoundland & Labrador Independent Adjusters' Association*, 1019
Pitcher, Twila, *Manitoba Cycling Association*, 935
Pither, Kerry, *Canadian Labour Congress*, 424
Pitkin, Bruce, *Theatre Ontario*, 1375
Piton, Caitlyn, *Scouts Canada*, 1286
Pitotti, Melissa, *International Council of Voluntary Agencies*, 1545
Pitre, Louise, *Sexual Assault Centre London*, 1292
Pitre, Mike A., *Canadian Culinary Federation*, 374
Pitre, Louise, *Family Service Thames Valley*, 704
Pitrini, Alfredo, *Italian Cultural Society of Edmonton*, 867
Pitt, Don, *Distress Line Sarnia*, 659
Pitt, Kathleen, *Nature Saskatchewan*, 1001
Pittman, Emily, *Newfoundland & Labrador Snowboard Association*, 1021
Pitts, Charles, *Canadian Oncology Societies*, 446
Pitts Diedrichs, Carol, *Association of Research Libraries*, 1513
Pityn, Kim, *Mennonite Economic Development Associates Canada*, 961
Pizioli, Tiffany, *Canadian Urological Association*, 500
Pizzo, Ron, *Alternative Dispute Resolution Atlantic Institute*, 60
Place, Teresa, *British Columbia Institute of Technology Faculty & Staff Association*, 244
Plache, Burkhard, *Halifax Field Naturalists*, 799
Plaetinck, Chantal, *Canadian Health Information Management Association*, 402
Plagge, Jeff L., *American Bankers Association*, 1490
Plamondon, Jean A., *Fédération québécoise du canot et du kayak*, 730
Plamondon, Jonathan, *Force Jeunesse*, 751
Plandowski, Wendy, *Lloydminster Region Health Foundation*, 916

Planet, Marie-Claire, *Ruiter Valley Land Trust*, 1244
Planetta, Tara, *Nova Scotia College of Respiratory Therapists*, 1043
Planka, Daniela, *Canadian Amateur Musicians*, 292
Plant, Fred R., *Canadian Independent Adjusters' Association*, 410
Plant, Laura, *Tourism Industry Association of British Columbia*, 1389
Plante, Yourianne, *Fédération de la relève agricole du Québec*, 709
Plante, Ybo, *Back Country Horsemen of British Columbia*, 192
Plantinga, Duane, *Association of Independent Schools & Colleges in Alberta*, 149
Plaskett, Rita, *Financial Executives International Canada*, 736
Plasse, Lillian, *Association des médecins gériatres du Québec*, 119
Plasse, Lillian, *Association des néphrologues du Québec*, 120
Platana, Janine, *Saskatchewan Athletics*, 1259
Plato, Earl, *Bertie Historical Society*, 206
Platt, Brent, *Association of Fundraising Professionals*, 512
Platts, David, *Groupe de recherche et d'intervention sociale*, 792
Platz, Randee, *Local Government Management Association of British Columbia*, 917
Playdon, Kathy, *Canadian Finnsheep Breeders' Association*, 390
Playford, Schuyler, *Church Council on Justice & Corrections*, 569
Playford, Tomasin, *Saskatchewan Archaeological Society*, 1256
Pleasant, Michael, *United Association of Journeymen & Apprentices of the Plumbing & Pipe Fitting Industry of the United States & Canada*, 1599
Plecash, Mike, *Canadian Door Institute of Dealers, Manufacturers & Distributors*, 378
Plessas, Monique, *Canadian Association for Williams Syndrome*, 307
Plessas, John, *Canadian Association for Williams Syndrome*, 307
Plett, Nicola, *Living Bible Explorers*, 915
Plewes, Joyanne, *ALS Society of British Columbia*, 60
Plitt, Cameron N., *Alberta Medical Association*, 40
Plouffe, Isabelle, *Chambre de commerce de Mont-Tremblant*, 542
Ploughman, Michelle, *Newfoundland & Labrador Brain Injury Association*, 1017
Plourde, Stephan, *Canadian College of Health Leaders*, 359
Plukov, Andy, *Macedonian Human Rights Movement International*, 923
Plumbtree, Jennifer, *CADORA Ontario Association Inc.*, 269
Plummer, Mallory, *South Queens Chamber of Commerce*, 1336
Plummer, Richard, *Family Enterprise Xchange*, 703
Plumridge, Nancy, *Association of Municipalities of Ontario*, 153
Pocha, Mitchell, *Cranbrook & District Arts Council*, 638
Pocock, Steve, *British Columbia Shellfish Growers Association*, 253
Podrebarac, Joseph, *Professional Engineers Ontario*, 1184
Podruzny, David, *Chemistry Industry Association of Canada*, 556
Poe, Christine, *Casting Directors Society of Canada*, 516
Poehlmann, Mike, *Alberta Boilers Safety Association*, 26
Poffley, Vicki, *Alzheimer Society of Kingston, Frontenac, Lennox & Addington*, 63
Pogas, Dean, *British Columbia Non-Profit Housing Association*, 248

Pogoryelova, Lyudmyla, *Taras H. Shevchenko Museum & Memorial Park Foundation*, 1367
Pohl, Tanya, *Synchro Saskatchewan*, 1361
Pohl, Daniella, *Fraser Valley Labour Council*, 758
Pohland, Liz, *Society for Technical Communication*, 1591
Pohlmann, Corinne, *Canadian Federation of Independent Business*, 387
Pohrebnuk, Patricia, *Manitoba Forestry Association Inc.*, 937
Poirier, Jim S., *Pentecostal Assemblies of Canada*, 1150
Poirier, Mitch, *Greater Bathurst Chamber of Commerce*, 783
Poirier, Isabelle, *Chambre de commerce du grand de Châteauguay*, 544
Poirier, Karinne, *Chambre de commerce de St-Donat*, 543
Poirier, Chantal, *Ringette New Brunswick*, 1233
Poirier, Stephanie, *Canadian Wood Pallet & Container Association*, 505
Poirier, Jo-Anne, *Victorian Order of Nurses for Canada*, 1434
Poirier, Marcus, *Canadian Concrete Masonry Producers Association*, 362
Poirier, Roger, *Association canadienne des métiers de la truelle, section locale 100 (CTC)*, 94
Poirier, Claude, *Canadian Association of Professional Employees*, 328
Poirier, Nicole, *La coopérative de Solidarité de Répit et d'Etraide*, 627
Poirier, Faye, *Federation of Aboriginal Foster Parents*, 722
Poirier, Paula, *Trauma Association of Canada*, 1396
Poirier, Francine, *Fédération des aînées et aînés francophones du Canada*, 711
Poirier, Matthew, *Canadian Finance & Leasing Association*, 390
Poirier, Rhéal, *Council of Atlantic Ministers of Education & Training*, 632
Poirier, Genevieve, *Dze L K'ant Friendship Centre Society*, 666
Poirier, Pierre, *Paramedic Association of Canada*, 1138
Poirier, Isabelle, *Minalliance*, 966
Poirier, Julie, *Club Richelieu Boréal de Chibougamau*, 576
Poirier, Wendi James, *Prince Edward Island Federation of Foster Families*, 1174
Poirier, Rick, *Antique Motorcycle Club of Manitoba Inc.*, 72
Poirier, Véronique, *Service budgétaire populaire des Sources*, 1291
Poirier-Sinclair, Lisa, *L'Arche Atlantic Region*, 77
Poisson, Christiane, *Greniers de Joseph*, 789
Poisson, Eric, *Société d'histoire régionale Deux-Montagnes*, 1314
Poisson, Marie-Josée, *Alliance des massothérapeutes du Québec*, 56
Poitras, Audrey, *Métis Nation of Alberta*, 963
Poitras, Germain, *Navy League of Canada*, 1002
Poitras, Rick, *Federation of Aboriginal Foster Parents*, 722
Poitras, Jacques, *Fédération québécoise de philatélie*, 728
Poitras, Martine, *Comité logement Rosemont*, 592
Poitras, Louise, *New Brunswick Maple Syrup Association*, 1010
Polak, Steven, *Municipal Pension Retirees Association*, 981
Polakoff, Jeff, *The Nature Conservancy of Canada*, 1000
Polegi, Juanita, *Yorkton Chamber of Commerce*, 1474
Policicchio, John, *Community Living Algoma*, 600

Poliquin, André, *Société des orchidophiles de Montréal*, 1318
Polischuk, Patricia, *YWCA Canada*, 1481
Polivka, Jan, *Whitehorse Cross Country Ski Club*, 1453
Polk, Josephine, *Action Volunteers for Animals*, 7
Polka, Erin, *Canadian Nuclear Association*, 442
Polkosnik, Suzanne, *Legal Aid Society of Alberta*, 906
Pollard, Lynn, *White Rock & Surrey Naturalists*, 1452
Pollard, Brooke, *Ajax-Pickering Board of Trade*, 20
Pollett, Craig, *Municipalities Newfoundland & Labrador*, 982
Pollit, Dan, *Canadian Association of Orthodontists*, 324
Pollock, Greg, *Advocis*, 11
Pollock, Bill, *International Union, United Automobile, Aerospace & Agricultural Implement Workers of America*, 1565
Pollock, Adam, *Saskatoon Heritage Society*, 1279
Pollock, Courtney, *Canadian Wheelchair Basketball Association*, 503
Pollock, Bradley, *Thunder Bay Adventure Trails*, 1377
Polski, Sharon, *Pincher Creek Allied Arts Council*, 1160
Polson, Lylas, *Frontiers Foundation*, 764
Polsoni, Daniela, *Ontario Sewer & Watermain Construction Association*, 1104
Polunin, Nicholas V.C., *Foundation for Environmental Conservation*, 1527
Pomerleau, Johanne, *Fédération des professionnelles et professionnels de l'éducation du Québec*, 718
Pomerleau, Claire, *Fédération de l'UPA de la Montérégie*, 709
Pona, Natalie, *Ottawa Humane Society*, 1130
Ponce de Leon, Catalina, *Royal College of Dentists of Canada*, 1241
Pond, Peter, *World Arabian Horse Organization*, 1603
Pond, Brian M., *New Brunswick Beekeepers Association*, 1006
Pond, Val, *Northwest Territories Broomball Association*, 1037
Pond, Allison, *A.C.C.E.S. Employment*, 4
Pons, Pamela, *Unemployed Help Centre*, 1404
Pontbriand, Michel, *Risk & Insurance Management Society Inc.*, 1234
Pontbriand, Chantal, *Museum of Contemporary Canadian Art*, 983
Ponte, Marcie, *Working Women Community Centre*, 1464
Pontin, Jackie, *Association of Administrative Professionals*, 139
Poole, Jim, *Maritime Shorthorn Association*, 951
Poole, Lynn, *Maritime Shorthorn Association*, 951
Poole, Jennifer, *Self-Help Resource Centre*, 1289
Poole, Krista, *CanLearn Society for Persons with Learning Difficulties*, 508
Poole, Nancy, *British Columbia Centre of Excellence for Women's Health*, 235
Poole, Joanne, *Back Country Horsemen of British Columbia*, 193
Poole-Cotnam, Lynn, *Ontario Coalition for Better Child Care*, 1071
Poolton, Sandra, *Music for Young Children*, 984
Poon, Monica, *Canadian Association of Professional Immigration Consultants*, 329
Pop, John, *Southwestern Ontario Gliding Association*, 1338
Popal, Karen, *Learning Disabilities Association of Alberta*, 904
Popazzi, Rob, *GAMA International Canada*, 766

Executive Name Index

Popel, Curtis, *Architectural Woodwork Manufacturers Association of Canada - Manitoba*, 79
Popescu, Mary-Ane, *Ontario Association for Family Mediation*, 1061
Popham, Elizabeth, *Canadian Celiac Association*, 352
Popik, Amanda, *Association for Financial Professionals - Edmonton*, 133
Popoff, Brad, *Prince George Construction Association*, 1179
Popoff, Anne, *Belgian Canadian Business Chamber*, 204
Popov, Bonnie, *Canadian Rope Skipping Federation*, 468
Popplewell, Bill, *Cochrane & District Chamber of Commerce*, 580
Porath, Amy, *Canadian Centre on Substance Use & Addiction*, 354
Porcher, Richard, *Law Society of Manitoba*, 901
Porcher, Cyndi, *RESOLVE: Research & Education for Solutions to Violence & Abuse*, 1226
Porlier, Lucille, *Association québécoise pour le loisir des personnes handicapées*, 177
Porr, Caroline, *Canadian Association for Nursing Research*, 303
Porte, Moira, *Plum Coulee & District Chamber of Commerce*, 1163
Portelli, Sharon, *Association of Registered Interior Designers of Ontario*, 161
Porten, Sebastian, *Alberta Triathlon Association*, 50
Porteous, Doug, *Partners FOR the Saskatchewan River Basin*, 1144
Porteous, Tracy, *Ending Violence Association of British Columbia*, 687
Porteous, Carol, *Alberta Dressage Association*, 33
Porter, Gordon, *Canadian Association for Community Living*, 298
Porter, Mary, *Child Evangelism Fellowship of Canada*, 559
Porter, Sandra, *Toronto Lawyers Association*, 1385
Porter, Barb, *College of Physicians & Surgeons of Saskatchewan*, 588
Porter, Tess, *Children's Aid Society of Ottawa*, 561
Porter, Diana M., *Alberta Law Foundation*, 39
Porter, Tim, *Conference of New England Governors & Eastern Canadian Premiers*, 612
Porter, Tim, *Council of Atlantic Premiers*, 633
Porter, Christine, *AIDS Coalition of Cape Breton*, 15
Porter, Kevin, *UNITE HERE Canada*, 1408
Porter, Gina, *Urology Nurses of Canada*, 1422, 1423
Porter, Gary, *Laubach Literacy Ontario*, 900
Porter, Kim, *Aboriginal Tourism Association of Southern Ontario*, 2
Porter, Wendy, *CANGRANDS Kinship Support*, 508
Porter, David, *Bluegrass Music Association of Canada*, 215
Porter, Theresa, *Saskatchewan Baton Twirling Association*, 1259
Porter, Marilyn, *Social Justice Cooperative Newfoundland & Labrador*, 1306
Portigal, Lawrie, *Volunteer BC*, 1438
Portlock, Peter, *Alberta Funeral Services Regulatory Board*, 36
Portnoff, Morrie, *Royal Astronomical Society of Canada*, 1238
Posluns, James, *Royal College of Dentists of Canada*, 1241
Possia, Jodi, *Paramedic Association of Manitoba*, 519
Post, Dave, *Canadian 5 Pin Bowlers' Association*, 285
Post, Arthur, *Thunder Bay Symphony Orchestra Association*, 1378

Posterski, Diane, *Ontario College Administrative Staff Associations*, 1072
Postill, Karen, *Crossfield Chamber of Commerce*, 644
Postma, Will, *The Primate's World Relief & Development Fund*, 1171
Postma, Hazel, *Human Rights Internet*, 826
Postma, Joey, *Water Polo Nova Scotia*, 1441
Postma, Dan, *Cardus Institute*, 511
Potentier, Doug, *Co-operatives & Mutuals Canada*, 628
Pothier, Michelle, *Ontario Gymnastic Federation*, 1083
Pothier, Harold, *Council of Canadian Fire Marshals & Fire Commissioners*, 633
Pothitos, George, *Neptune Theatre Foundation*, 1003
Potié, Francis, *Canadian Association of Second Language Teachers*, 332
Potje, Dave, *Ontario Printing & Imaging Association*, 1097
Potkonjak, Billie, *Canadian Liver Foundation*, 427
Potsiou, Chryssy, *International Federation of Surveyors*, 1549
Pott, Derek, *Construction Safety Association of Manitoba*, 624
Potten, Dave, *Thames Valley Trail Association Inc.*, 1373
Potten, Greg, *New Brunswick & Prince Edward Island Independent Adjusters' Association*, 1004
Potter, Terri, *College of Family Physicians of Canada*, 584
Potter, Roderic, *American Society of Heating, Refrigerating & Air Conditioning Engineers*, 1500
Potter, Bruce, *Consulting Engineers of Ontario*, 625
Potter, Wendy, *Baby's Breath*, 192
Potter, Wilma, *Credit Institute of Canada*, 641
Potter, Drew, *Canadian Chiropractic Research Foundation*, 356
Potter, Wendy, *Alliance for Canadian New Music Projects*, 57
Potter, Mark, *Original Hockey Hall of Fame & Museum*, 1126
Potter, Andrew, *Vaccine & Infectious Disease Organization*, 1423
Potter, Stephanie, *Christian Medical & Dental Society of Canada*, 568
Potter, Talia, *Folk Festival Society of Calgary*, 742
Potter, John, *Summer Street*, 1354
Pottie, Christina, *Library Boards Association of Nova Scotia*, 910
Pottier, Gerald, *Health Association Nova Scotia*, 806
Pottinger, Elizabeth, *National Eating Disorder Information Centre*, 992
Pottle, Bridget, *Saskatchewan Lacrosse Association*, 1268
Potts, Lee, *Crowsnest Pass Society for the Prevention of Cruelty to Animals*, 645
Potts, Geraldine, *Nechi Training, Research & Health Promotions Institute*, 1002
Potts, Carl, *Saskatchewan Pulse Growers*, 1273
Potts, Donny, *PFLAG Canada Inc.*, 1155
Potts, Alan, *CanoeKayak Canada Western Ontario Division*, 509
Potvin, Véronique, *Association des Grands Frères et Grandes Soeurs du Québec*, 115
Potvin, Annie, *Réseau des SADC et CAE*, 1220
Potvin, Lynn, *Guillain-Barré Support Group of Canada*, 794
Potvin, Pierre, *Société historique Pierre-de-Saurel inc.*, 1321
Potvin, Jean Mathieu, *Corporations des assureurs directs de dommage*, 631
Pouderoux, Julie, *Alliance Française de Calgary*, 57

Poudrier, Mario, *Association des professionnels et superviseurs de Radio-Canada*, 126
Poudyal, Shyam, *Cerebral Palsy Association in Alberta*, 537
Pouget, Stephanie L., *Amherstburg Historic Sites Association*, 67
Poulin, François, *Action des Chrétiens pour l'abolition de la torture*, 6
Poulin, Francis, *Association des juristes d'expression française de la Saskatchewan*, 118
Poulin, Cathy, *Chambre de commerce de St-Frédéric*, 543
Poulin, Yvan, *Canadian Association of Provincial Court Judges*, 329
Poulin, Martin, *Canadian Medical & Biological Engineering Society*, 433
Poulin, Nicole, *Société d'histoire du Haut-Richelieu*, 1312
Poulin, Roger, *Sudbury Rock & Lapidary Society*, 1353
Poulin, Valérie, *Association pour l'intégration sociale - Région Beauce-Sartigan*, 166
Poulin, Manon, *Syndicat des agricultrices de la Beauce*, 1362
Poulin, Carl, *Chambre de commerce de l'Est de Montréal*, 541
Pouliot, Sylvie, *Réseau des SADC et CAE*, 1221
Pouliot, Brigitte, *Réseau des SADC et CAE*, 1221
Pouliot, Thomas, *Confédération des associations d'étudiants et étudiantes de l'Université Laval*, 611
Pouliot, Eric, *Canadian Meat Science Association*, 432
Poulter, Neil, *International Society of Hypertension*, 1560
Poupart, Julie, *Canadian Association for Neuroscience*, 302
Pouplot, Daniel, *Fédération québécoise de la marche*, 727
Povill, Michelle Billy, *Women in Film & Television Vancouver*, 1461
Povolo, Beatrice, *Food Allergy Canada*, 749
Powderly, William G., *Infectious Diseases Society of America*, 1531
Powell, Geoff, *Winnipeg Executives Association*, 1458
Powell, Geoff, *Recreation Vehicle Dealers Association of Canada*, 1208
Powell, Martha, *London Community Foundation*, 918
Powell, David, *Canadian Finance & Leasing Association*, 390
Powell, Bruce, *Association of Internet Marketing & Sales*, 149
Powell, Geri, *Powell River Sunshine Coast Real Estate Board*, 1169
Powell, Catherine, *North of Superior Film Association*, 1031
Powell, Monica, *Association of Fundraising Professionals*, 1512
Powell, Mike, *Canadian American Law Enforcement Organization*, 1515
Powell, William, *Graham Boeckh Foundation*, 779
Power, Lawrence, *Southern Kings & Queens Food Bank Inc.*, 1338
Power, Mike, *Newfoundland & Labrador Soccer Association*, 1021
Power, Diane, *Canadian Home & School Federation*, 406
Power, Colin, *Newfoundland & Labrador Society for Medical Laboratory Science*, 1021
Power, Edward, *International Brotherhood of Boilermakers, Iron Ship Builders, Blacksmiths, Forgers & Helpers (AFL-CIO)*, 1541
Power, Bernadine, *Newfoundland & Labrador Association of Public & Private Employees*, 1016

Power, Cheryl, *ALS Society of Newfoundland & Labrador*, 60
Power, Glenda, *Pharmacists' Association of Newfoundland & Labrador*, 1156
Power, Terry, *National Association of Computer Consulting Business (Canada)*, 990
Power, Mike, *Yukon Prospectors' Association*, 1479
Power, Jenn, *L'Arche Atlantic Region*, 76
Power, Richard, *Thebacha & Wood Buffalo Astronomical Society*, 1375
Powers, Vincent, *Canadian Organic Growers Inc.*, 446
Powers, Tim, *Rugby Canada*, 1244
Powers-Dunlop, Marcia, *Girl Guides of Canada*, 773
Poweska, Sonya, *Guelph Arts Council*, 793
Powlowski, Siobhan, *Pacific Peoples' Partnership*, 1136
Poznansky, Mark J., *Genome Canada*, 769
Pozzobon, Marco, *Association of Canadian Travel Agencies*, 144
Prachar, Thomas, *Lutheran Church - Canada*, 922
Prahalis, Steve, *Society of Manufacturing Engineers - Canada Office*, 1330
Prairie, Yves, *International Society of Limnology*, 1561
Prajapat, Mahesh, *Children's Aid Society of Toronto*, 561
Pranger, John, *Animal Defence & Anti-Vivisection Society of BC*, 70
Prasad, Sandeep, *Action Canada for Sexual Health & Rights*, 6
Prashad, Geeta, *Canadian Society of Association Executives*, 480
Praski, Sheri, *Solid Waste Association of North America*, 1595
Prat, Margaret, *Vancouver Orchid Society*, 1428
Pratt, Jody, *Kent Centre Chamber of Commerce*, 883
Pratt, Patrice, *Canadian Co-operative Association*, 364
Pratt, Bill, *Manitoba Lung Association*, 940
Pratt, Bob, *Ontario Principals' Council*, 1097
Pratt, Michel, *Société historique et culturelle du Marigot inc.*, 1321
Pratt, Donna, *Canadian Society of Gastroenterology Nurses & Associates*, 483
Pratt, Donna, *Canadian Society of Gastroenterology Nurses & Associates*, 483
Pratt, Adrienne, *L'Association communautaire francophone de St-Jean*, 97
Pratt, Bill, *Canadian Antique Phonograph Society*, 294
Pratt, Shannon, *Prince Edward Island Business Women's Association*, 1173
Pratte, Karin, *Professional Engineers Ontario*, 1184
Pratte, Jean Paul, *Pas de la rue*, 1145
Pratte, Marilou, *Technoscience Estrie*, 1369
Pravibhavan, Pravilal, *Karate Ontario*, 882
Prawdzik, Kari, *Parkland Crisis Centre & Women's Shelter*, 1142
Prebble, Peter, *Saskatchewan Environmental Society*, 1265
Predoi, Roxana, *Ovarian Cancer Canada*, 1134
Preece, Carol, *Saskatchewan School Library Association*, 1274
Preece, Jim, *Building Owners & Managers Institute of Canada*, 263
Prefasi, Alexandra, *Aspergers Society of Ontario*, 87
Préfontaine, Éric, *Ski Québec alpin*, 1302
Pregel, Ingrid, *United Way of Kitchener-Waterloo & Area*, 1415
Prègent, Sophie, *Union des artistes*, 1406
Prégent, Karyne, *Fédération CSN - Construction (CSN)*, 708
Premi, David, *Hamilton Arts Council*, 801
Prenevost, Marc, *Institut de réadaptation en déficience physique de Québec*, 842

Executive Name Index

Prentice, Barry, *Canadian Transportation Research Forum*, 497, 567, 568
Prentis, Dave, *Public Services International*, 1585
Presant-Jahn, Wendy, *Saskatchewan Association of Naturopathic Practitioners*, 1257
Prescott, Terry, *Nova Scotia Cattle Producers*, 1042
Prestage, Norm, *Canadian Northern Society*, 441
Prestie, Mike, *College of Dental Surgeons of Saskatchewan*, 583
Preston, Jennifer, *Canadian Friends Service Committee*, 395
Preston, Rebecca, *Chambre de commerce du Grand Tracadie-Sheila*, 544
Preston, Jennifer, *Quaker Aboriginal Affairs Committee*, 1195
Preston, Rick, *Urban Development Institute Greater Edmonton Chapter*, 1422
Preston, Carmen, *Kin Canada Foundation*, 888
Pretlove, David, *Cabbagetown Preservation Association*, 268
Pretorius, Fred, *Office of the Yukon Superintendent of Securities*, 1055
Pretty, Lisa, *College of Physiotherapists of Ontario*, 589
Prévéreault, Dave, *Chambre de commerce de Manicouagan*, 542
Previsich, John, *United Transportation Union (AFL-CIO/CLC)*, 1600
Prévost, Colette, *York Region Children's Aid Society*, 1473
Prévost, Michel, *Société d'histoire de l'Outaouais inc.*, 1310
Pribac, Simon, *Canadian Slovenian Chamber of Commerce*, 472
Price, Ron, *Abbotsford International Air Show Society*, 1
Price, Avis, *Algonquin Arts Council*, 54
Price, Roy, *World Darts Federation*, 1604
Price, Andrew, *Scouts Canada*, 1286
Price, Stephanie, *Engineers Canada*, 689
Price, Michael, *Professional Engineers Ontario*, 1183
Price, Dorothy, *Canadian Foundation for Physically Disabled Persons*, 394
Price, Anita, *Ronald McDonald House Toronto*, 1235
Price, Goronwy, *Canadian School Boards Association*, 468
Price, Anita, *Association of Nova Scotia Museums*, 154
Price, Mimi, *YMCA Canada*, 1473
Price, Elaine, *Newfoundland & Labrador Association of Public & Private Employees*, 1016
Price, Doug, *Ontario Competitive Trail Riding Association Inc.*, 1074
Price, Russell, *Ontario Association of Pathologists*, 1065
Price, Janice, *Banff Centre for Arts & Creativity*, 195
Price, Marlene, *Central Beekeepers' Alliance*, 524
Priddle, Margot, *Newfoundland & Labrador Pharmacy Board*, 1021
Priddy, Elsie, *Canadian Connemara Pony Society*, 363
Pries-Klassen, Darren, *Abundance Canada*, 3
Priestley, Glenn, *Northern Air Transport Association*, 1034
Prieur, Richard, *Association nationale des éditeurs de livres*, 138
Prieur, Benoit, *Association des distributeurs exclusifs de livres en langue française inc.*, 111
Prieur, Christine, *Windsor/Essex County Parents of Multiple Births Association*, 1457
Prihoda, Richard F., *Association des avocats de la défense de Montréal*, 106
Primeau, Denis, *Canadian Security Association*, 469

Primerano, Anthony, *Laborers' International Union of North America (AFL-CIO/CLC)*, 1569
Primus, Michelle, *Alternative Land Use Services Canada*, 61
Prince, Suzie, *Ordre des médecins vétérinaires du Québec*, 1123
Prince, Norman, *Dignity Canada Dignité*, 657
Prince, Metzi, *Petroleum Research Newfoundland & Labrador*, 1154
Pringle, J.W. (Jim), *Alberta Curling Federation*, 32
Pringle, Dorothy, *Associated Medical Services Inc.*, 89
Prins, Tom, *The Canadian Corps of Commissionaires*, 365
Prins, Wayne, *Christian Labour Association of Canada*, 567
Prinzen, Dave, *Canadian Milking Shorthorn Society*, 436
Prior, Gail, *Ontario Senior Games Association*, 1104
Prior, Bonnie, *The Appraisal Institute of Canada - Ontario*, 75
Priowirjanto, Gatot Hari, *Southeast Asian Ministers of Education Organization*, 1595
Priske, Tanya, *Centre for Women in Business*, 534
Prisley, Dale, *Canadian Vintage Motorcycle Group*, 501
Pristanski, Bill, *The Terry Fox Foundation*, 1372
Pritchard, Dawna, *Aurora House*, 188
Pritchard, Andrew, *North Okanagan Labour Council*, 1031
Pritchard, Heather, *Slow Food Canada*, 1304
Pritchett, Newton, *Association of Engineering Technicians & Technologists of Newfoundland & Labrador*, 147
Prittie, Don, *Boating BC Association*, 216
Privett, John, *The Anglican Church of Canada*, 69
Probert, Debra, *Vancouver Humane Society*, 1426
Prockert, Brent, *Canadian Culinary Federation*, 374
Procyk, Christine, *Creelman Agricultural Society*, 641
Prodan, Miles, *British Columbia Wine Institute*, 258
Prodivus, Victoria, *German-Canadian Congress (Manitoba) Inc.*, 772
Proft, Norm, *Skate Canada*, 1301
Prokopchuk, Shauna, *Canadian Land Reclamation Association*, 425
Prokopchuk, Shauna, *Canadian Information Processing Society*, 411
Prokopchuk, Pat, *Saskatchewan Ski Association - Skiing for Disabled*, 1275
Proll, Cathy, *Canadian Deafblind Association (National)*, 376
Pronovost, Éric, *Fédération du personnel de soutien scolaire (CSQ)*, 720
Pronovost, Janet, *National Aboriginal Forestry Association*, 989
Pronovost, Steve, *Conseil régional de l'environnement de la Gaspésie et des Îles-de-la-Madeleine*, 620
Prosofsky, Patti, *Hanley Agricultural Society*, 803
Prosperi, Louie, *Institute of Professional Bookkeepers of Canada*, 847
Prosser, Chris, *The Literacy Group of Waterloo Region*, 914
Protor Duax, Kathryn, *National Association of Teachers of Singing*, 1574
Proud, Karen, *Consumer Health Products Canada*, 626
Proudfoot, Kelly, *Music Yukon*, 984
Proulx, Hélène, *Association du Québec pour enfants avec problèmes auditifs*, 131
Proulx, Martine, *Association of Consulting Engineering Companies - Canada*, 146
Proulx, Sylvain, *Fédération québécoise d'athlétisme*, 727

Proulx, Jennifer, *Canadian College of Health Leaders*, 359
Proulx, Stéphane, *Association sportive et communautaire du Centre-Sud*, 178
Proulx, Richard, *Les Kilomaîtres de LaSalle*, 887
Proulx, Anne-Marie, *Chambre de commerce de Gatineau*, 541
Proulx, Marie Josee, *Canadian Horse Breeders' Association*, 408
Proulx, Martin, *Kapuskasing & District Chamber of Commerce*, 881
Proulx, Laurent, *Procure Alliance*, 1181
Proulx-Daigle, Susie, *New Brunswick Union*, 1013
Proulx-Kenzle, Francine, *PFLAG Canada Inc.*, 1156
Prouse, Dennis, *CropLife Canada*, 643
Prousky, Brian, *Jewish Family & Child*, 871
Proussalidis, Daniel, *Cardus Institute*, 511
Prout, Lawrence, *Children's Hospital Foundation of Manitoba*, 562
Prout, Cara, *Alberta Turkey Producers*, 50
Prout, Tom, *Ausable Bayfield Conservation Foundation*, 188
Provencher, Janick, *Fédération de pétanque du Québec*, 710
Provencher, Doris, *Association des groupes d'intervention en défense de droits en santé mentale du Québec*, 116
Provencher, Léo-Paul, *Réseau Hommes Québec*, 1224
Provis, Paul, *Risk & Insurance Management Society Inc.*, 1234
Provost, Chantal, *Chambre de commerce et d'industrie de Laval*, 545
Provost, Katherine, *Atelier de Formation Socioprofessionnelle de la Petite-Nation*, 180
Provost, Jean-Rémy, *Revivre - Association Québécoise de soutien aux personnes souffrant de troubles anxieux, dépressifs ou bipolaires*, 1229
Provost, Jean-Rémy, *Revivre*, 1228
Provost, Allison, *Independent Association of Support Staff*, 832
Prowten, Dave, *Juvenile Diabetes Research Foundation Canada*, 878
Prud'homme, Danis, *Réseau FADOQ*, 1224
Prud'homme, Barb, *Ontario Public Health Association*, 1099
Prud'Homme, Josée, *Ordre professionnel des inhalothérapeutes du Québec*, 1124
Pruden, Connie, *Canadian Institute of Plumbing & Heating*, 418
Pruden, Kari, *Saskatchewan Association of Licensed Practical Nurses*, 1257
Prudham, Scott, *University of Toronto Faculty Association*, 1420
Pruett-Jones, Melinda, *American Ornithological Society*, 1496
Pruneau, Christine, *L'Association des orthopédagogues du Québec inc.*, 121
Pruner, Michael, *British Columbia Association of Mathematics Teachers*, 232
Pruski, Kris, *Canadian Society for Horticultural Science*, 475
Pryor, Miranda, *Newfoundland Aquaculture Industry Association*, 1022
Pryse, Michael J., *Evangelical Lutheran Church in Canada*, 698
Prytuliak, Stephanie, *Canadian Security Association*, 469
Psomopoulos, Panayis, *World Society for Ekistics*, 1607
Ptack, Lisa, *Canadian IT Law Association*, 423
Puchailo, Renee, *Alberta Association of Clinic Managers*, 23
Puchhammer-Sédillot, Jutta, *Canadian Viola Society*, 501
Puddester, Leigh, *Gardiner Centre*, 767
Puderak, Danylo, *Ukrainian Canadian Congress*, 1402
Puehse, Alona, *Open Door Group*, 1114
Puetz, Paula, *Canadian Dance Teachers' Association*, 375

Puhl, Jeff, *Mortgage Investment Association of British Columbia*, 975
Puhvel, Kris, *The Friends of Killarney Park*, 761
Pulford, Paul, *Wilfrid Laurier University Symphony Orchestra*, 1455
Pulham, Adrian, *Chartered Institute of Public Finance & Accountancy*, 1516
Pulins, Sara, *Ontario Physiotherapy Association*, 1096
Pullen, Carolyn, *Canadian Nurses Association*, 443
Punch, Donna, *Canadian Society of Ophthalmic Registered Nurses*, 485
Puppin, Giorgio, *Italian Chamber of Commerce in Canada - West*, 866
Pura, Talia, *Alliance of Canadian Cinema, Television & Radio Artists*, 58
Purcell, Anita, *Book & Periodical Council*, 218
Purcell, Anita, *Canadian Authors Association*, 338
Purcell, Bryan, *The John Howard Society of Newfoundland & Labrador*, 874
Purcell, Karen, *Biathlon Nova Scotia*, 207
Purcer, Carol, *Rowing Canada Aviron*, 1237
Purchase, Don, *National Association of Watch & Clock Collectors, Inc.*, 1575
Purdy, Kathryn, *East Coast Aquarium Society*, 668
Purdy, William, *Alberta Fire Chiefs Association*, 35
Purdy, Kelvin, *Beaver Party of Canada*, 203
Purgathofer, Werner, *Eurographics - European Association for Computer Graphics*, 1524
Purin, Sam, *Wilderness Tourism Association*, 1454
Pursell, Terry, *North York General Foundation*, 1033
Purser, Don, *Institute of Power Engineers*, 847
Pursey, Carl, *Prince Edward Island Federation of Labour*, 1174
Purves, Lynn, *Dalhousie Faculty Association*, 648
Purvis, Alison, *Radius Child & Youth Services*, 1203
Purvs, Arvids, *Toronto Latvian Concert Association*, 1385
Pushman, Paul J., *Ontario Building Envelope Council*, 1070
Puttock, Shirley, *Boys & Girls Clubs of Alberta*, 221
Pyc, Greg, *The Neil Squire Foundation*, 1002
Pye, Gordon, *Canadian Paraplegic Association (Nova Scotia)*, 450
Pye, Brittany, *Triathlon New Brunswick*, 1398
Pym, David, *Canadian Snowsports Association*, 472
Pynch-Worthylake, Nancy, *Nova Scotia School Boards Association*, 1048
Pyne, Chester, *Cape Breton University Faculty Association*, 510
Pyne, Deborah, *British Columbia Golf Association*, 242
Pynkoski, Marshall, *Opéra Atelier*, 1114
Pyper, Bert, *Alberta Beach & District Chamber of Commerce*, 25
Pyrch, Karla, *Lethbridge Chamber of Commerce*, 908
Pyrih, Lorna, *Jane Austen Society of North America*, 868

Q

Qiu, Michael, *Association of Professional Engineers & Geoscientists of British Columbia*, 158
Quach, Veronica, *Ontario Association of Art Galleries*, 1062
Quackenbush, Sarah, *Catholic Health Sponsors of Ontario*, 520
Quagliara, Mary Ann, *Markham Board of Trade*, 952
Qualey, Blair, *BCADA - The New Car Dealers of BC*, 202

Executive Name Index

Quan, Nancy, *Canadian Catholic Campus Ministry*, 351
Quarry, Andrew, *Society for Technical Communication*, 1591
Queen, Alyson, *Canadian Ferry Association*, 389
Queen, Rosanne, *Scleroderma Association of British Columbia*, 1285
Quenneville, Camille, *Canadian Mental Health Association*, 435
Quenneville, Julie, *McGill University Health Centre Foundation*, 955
Quenneville, Brenda, *Amelia Rising Sexual Assault Centre of Nipissing*, 66
Quernby, Karen, *Alzheimer Society of Muskoka*, 63
Quesnel, Nicole, *Association des services de réhabilitation sociale du Québec inc.*, 128
Quesnel, Maurice, *Chambre de commerce Baie-des-Chaleurs*, 540
Queval, Muriel, *Mennonite Central Committee Canada*, 961
Queval, Claude, *Mennonite Central Committee Canada*, 961
Quevillon, Pete, *Sport BC*, 1344
Quick, Jim, *Aerospace Industries Association of Canada*, 11
Quick Rajala, Heather, *Jessie's Hope Society*, 870
Quickert, Lia, *Ontario Council on Articulation and Transfer*, 1075
Quies, Brenda, *Illuminating Engineering Society of North America*, 1531
Quigley, Cynthia, *Association of Fundraising Professionals*, 1512
Quilao, Don, *Filipino Canadian Catholic Charismatic Prayer Communities*, 735
Quilty, Heather, *Registered Veterinary Technologists & Technicians of Canada*, 1214
Quin, Emma, *Ontario Crafts Council*, 1076
Quin, Dennis, *Child Evangelism Fellowship of Canada*, 559
Quinlan, Susanne, *Gleaners Food Bank*, 774
Quinn, Darin, *New Brunswick Association of Speech-Language Pathologists & Audiologists*, 1006
Quinn, Ben, *Association of Neighbourhood Houses BC*, 153
Quinn, Kevin, *Canadian Amateur Softball Association*, 292
Quinn, Dorena, *Numeris*, 1051
Quinn, Anthony, *CARP*, 515
Quinn, Anthony, *CARP*, 514
Quinn, Wendy, *Canadian Hemophilia Society*, 404
Quinn, Karen, *Learning Disabilities Association of Ontario*, 905
Quinn, Nolan, *United Way of Stormont, Dundas & Glengarry*, 1417
Quinn, Barry, *Ontario Professional Fire Fighters Association*, 1097
Quinn, Christopher J., *American Optometric Association*, 1496
Quinn, Louise, *Quebec English Literacy Alliance*, 1197
Quinn, Chris, *Edmonton Community Foundation*, 676
Quinn Graham, Laura, *Prince Edward Island Association of Family Resource Programs*, 1172
Quinsey, John, *Yukon Canoe & Kayak Club*, 1477
Quintal, Shauna, *Lac La Biche Disability Services*, 895
Quintal, Michel, *Fédération québécoise de camping et de caravaning inc.*, 727
Quintas, Diane, *Réseau du mieux-être francophone du Nord de l'Ontario*, 1222
Quinton, Sarah, *ALS Society of Alberta*, 60
Quintyn, Michelle, *Goodwill Industries*, 777
Quiring, Nancy, *United Food & Commercial Workers Canada*, 1411
Quish, Margaret, *International Council of AIDS Service Organizations*, 855

Quist, Becky, *Nature Saskatchewan*, 1000
Quiñonez, Carlos, *Canadian Association of Public Health Dentistry*, 330
Quocksister, Vikki, *Yukon Federation of Labour*, 1478
Quon, Verna, *Edmonton Chamber Music Society*, 675
Quong, Ken, *Yukon Medical Association*, 1479
Quraishi, Ajaz, *Lakeland United Way*, 896
Qureshi, Salman, *Manitoba Islamic Association*, 939
Qureshi, Tan, *Cricket Council of Ontario*, 642

R

Rabbani, Roya, *Immigrant Services - Guelph Wellington*, 830
Rabbior, Gary, *Canadian Foundation for Economic Education*, 393
Rabideau, Monique, *Dancer Transition Resource Centre*, 650
Rabinowicz, Jane, *USC Canada*, 1423
Racanelli, Joe, *Master Painters & Decorators Association*, 954
Racca, Roberto, *Canadian Acoustical Association*, 287
Race, Doug, *Schizophrenia Society of Alberta*, 1283
Racette, Jim, *Canadian Society of Exploration Geophysicists*, 483
Racette, Ray J., *Canadian College of Health Leaders*, 358
Rach, Karen, *Yukon Speech-Language Pathology & Audiology Association*, 1480
Rachold, Volker, *International Arctic Science Committee*, 1535
Rachwalski, Tony, *Community Living Temiskaming South*, 605
Rachynski, Charlene, *Lakeland Agricultural Research Association*, 896
Racicot, Michel, *United Empire Loyalists' Association of Canada*, 1410
Racicot, Henriette, *Association du syndrome de Down de L'Estrie*, 131
Racine, Sophie, *Service budgétaire Lac-Saint-Jean-Est*, 1291
Racine, Normand, *Fédération des Chambres immobilières du Québec*, 713
Racine, Lisanne, *Syndicat du personnel technique et professionnel de la Société des alcools du Québec (ind.)*, 1364
Racine, Jean-Luc, *Fédération des aînées et aînés francophones du Canada*, 711
Racine, Marie-Pier, *Société de développement économique du Saint-Laurent*, 1315
Racine, Bruno, *Société d'histoire de Longueuil*, 1311
Racine, Robert, *Fédération de l'UPA de la Montérégie*, 709
Racine, Simon, *Vrac environnement group d'action et de recherche en développement durable*, 1439
Radano, Michael, *Society of Translators & Interpreters of British Columbia*, 1331
Radchenko, Vladimir, *North Pacific Anadromous Fish Commission*, 1031
Radcliffe, Katherina, *Vintners Quality Alliance*, 1435
Rade, Bryan, *Nova Scotia Association of Naturopathic Doctors*, 1041
Radford, Greg, *International Association for Impact Assessment*, 1537
Radford, Sharon, *Real Estate Institute of Canada*, 1206
Radford, Paul E., *Nova Scotia Securities Commission*, 1048
Radice, Martha, *Canadian Anthropology Society*, 293
Radke, Lori, *Multiple Sclerosis Society of Canada*, 980
Radtke-Jardine, Jennifer, *Operating Room Nurses Association of Nova Scotia*, 1115
Radyo, Vera, *North Shore Multicultural Society*, 1033

Rae, Sheryl, *Wild Rose Agricultural Producers*, 1454
Rae, Andrew, *Canadian Marine Pilots' Association*, 430
Rae, Nataly, *Fondation communautaire du Grand-Québec*, 743
Raedler, Thomas, *Alberta Psychiatric Association*, 43
Rafferty, John M., *Canadian National Institute for the Blind*, 439
Rafferty, Jim, *Appaloosa Horse Club of Canada*, 73
Rafferty, Meghan, *Environmental Action Barrie - Living Green*, 691
Rafi, Shazia Z., *Parliamentarians for Global Action*, 1583
Rafuse, Judy, *Annapolis Valley Chamber of Commerce*, 71
Rafuse, Eileen, *L'Héritage de L'Ile Rouge*, 813
Ragagnin, Lou, *Chartered Professional Accountants Canada*, 552
Rago, Elvira, *Financial Executives International Canada*, 736
Rahal, Edgar, *Canadian Culinary Federation*, 374
Rahamatulla, Mohammad, *British Columbia Muslim Association*, 247
Rahbar, Shahrzad, *Industrial Gas Users Association*, 835
Rahbar, Hamid, *Vitesse*, 1436
Rahman, Mahbubur, *Nova Scotia Public Interest Research Group*, 1047
Rahme, Ziyad, *Sustainable Development Technology Canada*, 1357
Rahrig, Philip G., *American Galvanizers Association*, 1493
Raic, Maya, *Chambre de l'assurance de dommages*, 550
Raickovic, Mladen, *The Advertising Club of Toronto*, 10
Rail, Laurie, *Bereaved Families of Ontario*, 205
Raine, Charlotte, *Saskatchewan School Library Association*, 1274
Raines, Chris, *Oceanside Community Arts Council*, 1054
Rainey, Grahame, *British Columbia Teacher-Librarians' Association*, 255
Rainey, Grahame, *British Columbia Science Teachers' Association*, 252
Rainnie, Stephanie, *Big Brothers Big Sisters of Prince Edward Island*, 210
Rainville, André, *Association des firmes de génie-conseil - Québec*, 114
Rainville, Martine, *Corporation l'Espoir*, 631
Rainville, Jacqueline, *Association de la Construction Richelieu Yamaska*, 101
Rainville, Bobby, *Association provinciale des constructeurs d'habitations du Québec inc.*, 168
Rainville, Josee, *Myeloma Canada*, 986
Raja, Srinivasa, *International Association for the Study of Pain*, 1537
Rajaraman, Sharon, *Field Hockey Nova Scotia*, 734
Rajendra, Kumar, *Toronto Users Group for Power Systems*, 1388
Rajotte, Tasmin, *Quakers Fostering Justice*, 1195
Rajotte, Stéphanie, *Réseau québécois des OSBL d'habitation*, 1225
Rakuson, Kerry, *Greater Moncton Real Estate Board Inc.*, 784
Ralliaram, Ratan, *Cancer Care Ontario*, 507
Ralph, Randy, *Newfoundland & Labrador Amateur Wrestling Association*, 1015
Ralph, Trina, *Kidney Foundation of Canada*, 885
Ralph, Joel, *Canada's History*, 282
Ralph, Penney, *Newfoundland & Labrador Nurse Practitioner Association*, 1020
Ramage, Mike, *Saskatchewan Baseball Association*, 1259
Ramage, Lindsay, *British Columbia Veterinary Technologists Association*, 257

Ramage, Dianne, *Pacific Salmon Foundation*, 1136
Ramanujam, Mahesh, *U.S. Green Building Council*, 1601
Ramarui, Jennifer, *The Oceanography Society*, 1580
Rambeau, Debbie, *Hockey Eastern Ontario*, 818
Ramberg, Michele, *Canadian Association of Professional Image Creators*, 329
Ramey, Rowley, *Seasons Centre for Grieving Children*, 1288
Ramgobin, Danny, *The St. George's Society of Toronto*, 1248
Ramina, Inguna, *Muskoka Steamship & Historical Society*, 985
Ramirez, Oscar, *Chambre de commerce Latino-américaine du Québec*, 549
Ramji, Rubina, *Canadian Society for the Study of Religion*, 478
Ramkissoon, Roger, *Association of Municipal Managers, Clerks & Treasurers of Ontario*, 152
Rammlmair, Dieter, *International Council for Applied Mineralogy*, 1544
Ramos, Ben, *Recycling Council of British Columbia*, 1208
Ramos, Duberlis, *Hispanic Development Council*, 815
Ramos-Javellana, Pia, *Registered Practical Nurses Association of Ontario*, 1214
Rampeneaux, Sandrine, *Chambre de commerce MRC du Rocher-Percé*, 549
Rampersad, Naline, *Almas Jiwani Foundation*, 59
Ramphos, Steve, *Greek Orthodox Metropolis of Toronto (Canada)*, 788
Ramsay, Sue, *Council of Ontario Construction Associations*, 634
Ramsay, Brent, *Many Rivers Counselling & Support Services*, 948
Ramsay, Fiona, *College of Registered Psychiatric Nurses of B.C.*, 590
Ramsay, Brian, *Canadian Football League Players' Association*, 392
Ramsden, Bruce, *Ontario Podiatric Medical Association*, 1096
Ramsey, Bonnie, *Canadian Katahdin Sheep Association Inc.*, 424
Ramsfjell, Bent Ånund, *World Curling Federation*, 1604
Ramshaw, Spencer, *Mining Suppliers Trade Association Canada*, 967
Ramzanali, Rizwana, *Kidney Foundation of Canada*, 886
Ranalli, Melissa, *Nature Saskatchewan*, 1000
Rance, John, *Orienteering Association of British Columbia*, 1126
Ranchoux, Jason, *Junior Chamber International Canada*, 878
Rand, Tom, *Nova Scotian Institute of Science*, 1050
Rand, Leslie, *Alzheimer Society London & Middlesex*, 61
Randall, Bob, *Bowling Federation of Canada*, 219
Randall, Chris, *Paddle Manitoba*, 1137
Randall, John, *Illuminating Engineering Society of North America*, 1531
Randall, Michèle E., *Bibliographical Society of America*, 1514
Randel, Don M., *American Academy of Arts & Sciences*, 1487
Randell, Annie, *Qalipu Mi'kmaq First Nations Band*, 1194
Rangam, Mary Ann, *Ontario Professional Planners Institute*, 1098
Ranganathan, Radha, *International Seed Federation*, 1556
Rangel, Gabriela, *Association camadienne des interprètes de conférence*, 90
Rangeley, Robert, *Oceana Canada*, 1054
Ranger, Louise, *North Vancouver Chamber of Commerce*, 1033

Executive Name Index

Ranger, Serge, *Chambre de commerce régionale de Windsor*, 549
Rangooni, Justin, *Electricity Distributors Association*, 683
Ranick, Bob, *Southern Ontario Thunderbird Club*, 1338
Rankin, Jerry, *St. John Ambulance*, 1248
Rankin, Jude, *Institute of Power Engineers*, 847
Rankin, Bruce, *John Gordon Home*, 873
Rankin, Ian, *Toronto Bicycling Network*, 1382
Rankin, Susan, *Grande Prairie & Area Association of Realtors*, 781
Rankin, Darrell, *Communist Party of Canada (Manitoba)*, 595
Rankin, Naomi, *Communist Party of Canada (Alberta)*, 594
Rants, Bill, *Canada's National Firearms Association*, 282
Rao, Max, *Ontario Pollution Control Equipment Association*, 1097
Raouf, Naglaa, *Arab Community Centre of Toronto*, 76
Raphael, Bert, *Canadian Committee of Lawyers & Jurists for World Jewry*, 361
Rapoport, Mark, *Canadian Academy of Geriatric Psychiatry*, 286
Rapp, Barry, *Saskatchewan Institute of Agrologists*, 1268
Rappell, Gabriela, *Sierra Youth Coalition*, 1298
Ras, Michael, *Federation of Ontario Law Associations*, 726
Rasaiah, Angela, *Sault Symphony Association*, 1281
Rashdi, Maheen A., *International Development & Relief Foundation*, 856
Rasheed, Amir, *Anxiety Disorders Association of British Columbia*, 72
Rasiulis, Michelle, *Ontario Public Buyers Association*, 1098
Raskin, Paul, *Tellus Institute*, 1598
Rasmussen, Diana, *ALS Society of Manitoba*, 60
Rasmussen, Regan, *British Columbia Art Teachers' Association*, 230
Rasode, Barinder, *National Institute for Cannabis Health & Education*, 994
Rastall, Mary, *Sarnia Rock & Fossil Club*, 1254
Rastoul, Pierre, *Société d'histoire de Magog*, 1311
Rasussen, Mitch, *Greater Toronto Apartment Association*, 785
Raszmann, Bruce, *Ontario Numismatic Association*, 1094
Rataic-Lang, Joan, *Toronto Lawyers Association*, 1385
Ratcliff, Pam, *Inclusion BC*, 832
Ratcliffe, Brian, *London Food Bank*, 918
Ratcliffe, Susan, *The Architectural Conservancy of Ontario*, 78
Rath, Tom, *Southern Kings Arts Council*, 1338
Rath, Thomas, *Saskatchewan Cheerleading Association*, 1261
Rathgeb Smith, Steven, *American Political Science Association*, 1497
Rathi, Dinesh, *Canadian Association for Information Science*, 301
Rathjen, Heidi, *Coalition québécoise pour le contrôle du tabac*, 578
Rathwell, Sean, *Alberta Fencing Association*, 35
Ratsoy, Sheri, *Parkland Food Bank*, 1142
Ratté, Jasmine, *Urban & Regional Information Systems Association*, 1601
Ratthé, Priscilla, *Auxiliaires bénévoles de l'Hôpital de Chibougamau*, 190
Rattink, Shelley, *Central Vancouver Island Orchid Society*, 525
Rattray, Rita, *New Brunswick Institute of Agrologists*, 1009
Rattray, Dougal, *Québec Farmers' Association*, 1197
Ratzlaff, Leonard, *Richard Eaton Singers*, 1229
Rau, Uwe, *Goethe-Institut (Toronto)*, 776

Rauh, Susan, *Local Government Management Association of British Columbia*, 917
Rault, Linda, *Little Bits Therapeutic Riding Association*, 915
Rausch, Ryan, *Alberta Snowboard Association*, 47
Rauscher, Robert, *Canada's Medical Technology Companies*, 282
Rauscher, Donna, *Niagara Cattlemen's Association*, 1024
Rautava, Tanya, *Finnish Canadian Rest Home Association*, 738
Raven, Meg, *Canadian Children's Book Centre*, 356
Raven, Doug, *Ontario Veterinary Medical Association*, 1112
Ravenhill, Michael, *David Foster Foundation*, 651
Ravnsborg, Glenn, *Animal Nutrition Association of Canada*, 71
Rawal, Sheetal, *Miss G Project*, 968
Rawson, Julie, *Northeast Organic Farming Association*, 1580
Ray, Christie, *Prince George Chamber of Commerce*, 1179
Ray, Patricia, *Canadian Curling Association*, 374
Ray, Marcia, *Canadian Union of Public Employees*, 499
Ray, Stuart, *Alberta Association of Recreation Facility Personnel*, 24
Ray, Geoff, *Northwest Territories Recreation & Parks Association*, 1038
Raymer, Sandy, *Southern Georgian Bay Association of REALTORS*, 1337
Raymond, Mélanie, *Fondation Richelieu International*, 748
Raymond, Danielle, *Association des parents fransaskois*, 122
Raymond, Kim, *Canadian Fence Industry Association*, 389
Raymond, Steve, *Chambre de commerce et d'industrie de Mirabel*, 546
Raymond, Michel, *Canadian Manufacturers & Exporters*, 430
Raymond, Paul, *Epilepsy Ontario*, 693
Raymond, Gordie, *Maritime Hereford Association*, 950
Raymond, Myriam, *Carrefour d'Actions Populaires*, 515
Raymond, Melinda, *New Clarence-Rockland Chamber of Commerce*, 1014
Raymond, Frédéric, *Fédération québécoise pour le saumon atlantique*, 731
Raymond, Paul-André, *La fédération des mouvements personne d'abord du Québec*, 716
Raymond, Susan, *Equine Guelph*, 695
Raymond-Millett, Rita, *Alliance for Canadian New Music Projects*, 57
Raynault, Guy, *Société Saint-Jean-Baptiste de Montréal*, 1324
Rayner, Adam, *Kingston & Area Real Estate Association*, 888
Rayner, John, *Canadian Association of Rhodes Scholars*, 331
Rayner, Jessica, *Slocan District Chamber of Commerce*, 1303
Razafimbahiny, Maggy, *Fédération culturelle canadienne-française*, 708
Rea, Carol, *Appaloosa Horse Club of Canada*, 73
Read, Barb, *Parksville & District Association for Community Living*, 1142
Read, Gayle, *National Farmers Union*, 993
Read, Don, *Prince Edward Island Vegetable Growers Co-op Association*, 1178
Read, Laurel, *Sport Manitoba*, 1344
Read, John K., *Ernest C. Manning Awards Foundation*, 695
Read, Gilles, *Centre de la Communauté sourde du Montréal métropolitain*, 529
Read, Lavon, *British Columbia Miniature Horse Club*, 246
Reade, Janice, *Music for Young Children*, 983

Reading, Francis, *Bereaved Families of Ontario*, 205
Ready, Susan, *Theatre New Brunswick*, 1374
Ready, Jolan, *Forum for Intercultural Leadership & Learning*, 754
Ready, Mike, *Canadian Haflinger Association*, 400
Realffe, Pamela, *Missisquoi Historical Society*, 969
Reardon, Regina C., *International Foundation of Employee Benefit Plans*, 1549
Reardon, Tom, *Business & Institutional Furniture Manufacturer's Association*, 1515
Reaume, Christie, *Association of Visual Language Interpreters of Canada*, 164
Reaume, Sarah, *Habitat for Humanity Canada*, 797
Reaume, Byron, *Back to the Bible Canada*, 193
Rebeck, Kevin, *Manitoba Federation of Labour*, 936
Rebel, Bruce, *Association of Home Appliance Manufacturers Canada Council*, 149
Rebelo, José, *Carrefour de ressources en interculturel*, 515
Rebman, Brenda, *Canadian College of Health Leaders*, 359
Rebman, Brenda, *Canadian College of Health Leaders*, 359
Rebolledo, Patricia, *Horizons of Friendship*, 821
Reboulis, Marilou, *Canadian Institute of Mining, Metallurgy & Petroleum*, 418
Recsky, Keith, *Association of Professional Engineers & Geoscientists of British Columbia*, 158
Rector, Shelley, *Cumberland Museum Society*, 646
Recupero, Mario, *Ontario Table Soccer Association*, 1109
Reddekopp, Anne, *Catholic Health Association of Saskatchewan*, 520
Redden, Kara, *Pool & Hot Tub Council of Canada*, 1165
Redeker, Jolanda, *Canadian Home Builders' Association - British Columbia*, 407
Redelback, Margo, *Alberta Irrigation Projects Association*, 38
Reder, Eric, *Wilderness Committee*, 1454
Redfern, Heather, *The Cultch*, 645
Redford, Allan, *Little People of Ontario*, 915
Redhead, Sheila, *Greater Victoria Youth Orchestra*, 787
Redin, Karl, *Ontario Steelheaders*, 1109
Redman, Karen, *Habitat for Humanity Canada*, 797
Redmile, Robert D., *The Christian Episcopal Church of Canada*, 567
Redmond, Mike, *New Democratic Party*, 1014
Redmond, Jackie, *Ontario Competitive Trail Riding Association Inc.*, 1074
Redmond, Margaret, *Assiniboine Park Conservancy*, 89
Redmond, Adam, *Canadian Deaf Golf Association*, 376
Redpath, Fraser, *Canadian Simmental Association*, 470
Reece, Tove, *Voice for Animals Humane Society*, 1437
Reed, Marla, *Dawson Creek Society for Community Living*, 652
Reed, Allan, *British Columbia Association of School Business Officials*, 232
Reed, Joel, *New Brunswick Liberal Association*, 1010
Reed, Alyson, *Linguistic Society of America*, 1569
Reed, Ron, *First Pacific Theatre Society*, 739
Reed, Cindy G., *Saskatchewan Dental Therapists Association*, 1263
Reedie, Craig, *World Anti-Doping Agency*, 1465
Reekie, Mel, *Canadian Charolais Association*, 355

Rees, Dave, *Canadian Masters Cross-Country Ski Association*, 431
Rees, Terry, *Federation of Ontario Cottagers' Associations*, 725
Rees, Bonnie G., *IODE Canada*, 863
Rees, Richard, *Chartered Professional Accountants of British Columbia*, 553
Rees, Richard, *Chartered Professional Accountants of the Yukon*, 554
Reesor, Sheila, *Toronto Insurance Conference*, 1385
Reesor, Peter, *Owen Sound & District Chamber of Commerce*, 1134
Reesor, Garth, *L'Arche Western Region*, 78
Reeve, Alana, *Canadian Bible Society*, 343
Reeve, Jessica, *Ontario Association of Library Technicians*, 1064
Reeve, Marilyn, *Flowercart*, 741
Reeves, Eleanor, *Beachville District Historical Society*, 202
Reeves, Mona, *Prescott Group*, 1170
Regalado, Sophie, *Canadian Health Libraries Association*, 402
Regan, Ron, *Association of Fish & Wildlife Agencies*, 1511
Regas, Diane, *Environmental Defense*, 1523
Regehr, Sharon, *Medicine Hat Fibre Arts Society*, 958
Regendanz, Liane, *St. Stephen's Community House*, 1251
Reggi, Nick, *Refrigeration Service Engineers Society (Canada)*, 1211
Reghai, Bahija, *National Council on Canada-Arab Relations*, 992
Regiec, Alex, *Winnipeg Association of Public Service Officers*, 1458
Régimbal, Roger, *Canadian Association of Retired Teachers*, 331
Régis, Jacques, *International Electrotechnical Commission - Canadian National Committee*, 857
Regis, Romy, *Réseau environnement*, 1223
Regular, Alice, *Labrador West Chamber of Commerce*, 894
Rehberg, Cathy, *Stratford Tourism Alliance*, 1351
Rehbinder, Jean, *World Fellowship of Orthodox Youth*, 1605
Rehead, Cheryl, *Connect Society - D.E.A.F. Services*, 613
Rehman, Anis, *Canada-Pakistan Association of the National Capital Region*, 284
Rehwald, Gerry, *Creston Valley Prospectors & Lapidary Club*, 642
Reib, Sharon, *Churchill Park Family Care Society*, 569
Reichardt, Bernie, *Hockey Manitoba*, 818
Reiche, Christopher, *Canadian League of Composers*, 426
Reichrath, Silke, *Peacebuild: The Canadian Peacebuilding Network*, 1147
Reid, Brian, *United Nations Association in Canada*, 1411
Reid, Don, *Ontario Research Council on Leisure*, 1101
Reid, Jeff, *SeCan Association*, 1288
Reid, Peter, *Convention of Atlantic Baptist Churches*, 627
Reid, Dave, *Salmo & District Chamber of Commerce*, 1251
Reid, Fiona, *The Actors' Fund of Canada*, 7
Reid, Pat, *Edmonton Combative Sports Commission*, 676
Reid, Allan, *Canadian Academy of Recording Arts & Sciences*, 286
Reid, John, *Canadian Advanced Technology Alliance*, 288
Reid, Marilyn, *Canadian Hearing Society*, 403
Reid, Jenn, *Prince Edward Island Veterinary Medical Association*, 1178
Reid, Darrell, *Heart & Stroke Foundation of Ontario*, 809
Reid, Tracy, *Ontario Brown Swiss Association*, 1069
Reid, John, *Canadian Music Centre*, 438

Reid, David, *Royal Winnipeg Ballet*, 1243
Reid, Stephen, *Police Association of Ontario*, 1163
Reid, Colin, *YMCA Canada*, 1473
Reid, Diana, *Professional Convention Management Association - Canada West Chapter*, 1183
Reid, Herbert Ross, *Canadian Association of Veterans in United Nations Peacekeeping*, 336
Reid, Susanna, *The Maitland Trail Association*, 927
Reid, Ruby, *British Columbia Aboriginal Network on Disability Society*, 229
Reid, Nick, *Ontario Water Works Association*, 1113
Reid, Sandra, *Alberta Cultural Society of the Deaf*, 32
Reid, Rick, *Supply Chain Management Association - Manitoba*, 1356
Reid, John, *Gorsebrook Research Institute for Atlantic Canada Studies*, 778
Reid, Sharon, *Women In Crisis (Algoma) Inc.*, 1461
Reid, Terry, *Accessible Media Inc.*, 5
Reid, Peter, *Back Country Horsemen of British Columbia*, 193
Reid, Rose, *Welsh Pony & Cob Association of Ontario*, 1444
Reid, Tom, *Ski Jumping Canada*, 1302
Reid, Miriam, *British Columbia Tenpin Bowling Association*, 256
Reid, Mark, *PBA Society of Atlantic*, 1146
Reid Burlinguette, Shannon, *Alberta Dressage Association*, 33
Reid Crichton, Pat, *Multicultural Council of Windsor & Essex County*, 979
Reid-Kuecks, Brenda, *Ecotrust Canada*, 673
Reider, Jon, *Canadian Friends of the Hebrew University*, 395
Reidstra, Lesley, *New College Alumni Association*, 1014
Reidy, John, *Diabetes Canada*, 655
Reidy, Carol, *Canadian Society of Gastroenterology Nurses & Associates*, 483
Reilander, David, *Catholic Missions in Canada*, 520
Reilly, Paul, *Institute of Communication Agencies*, 845
Reilly, Nolan, *Canadian Oral History Association*, 446
Reilly, Edward T., *American Management Association*, 1495
Reilly-King, Fraser, *Canadian Council for International Co-operation*, 366
Reimbold, Sue, *American College of Chest Physicians*, 1491
Reimer, Melanie, *Manitoba Ringette Association*, 943
Reimer, Carolyn, *Family Enterprise Xchange*, 703
Reimer, Tom, *The Canadian Corps of Commissionaires*, 365
Reimer, Maggie, *The Canadian Federation of Business & Professional Women's Clubs*, 385
Reimer, Paul, *Opimian Society*, 1116
Reimer, Willy, *Canadian Conference of Mennonite Brethren Churches*, 363
Reimer, Rodney, *Ontario Amputee & Les Autres Sports Association*, 1059
Rein, Kristi, *Pharmacy Technician Society of Alberta*, 1157
Reindl, Bob, *Saskatchewan Athletics*, 1259
Reine, Corinne, *Hudson Bay Chamber of Commerce*, 824
Reinert, Chris, *Association of Quantity Surveyors of Alberta*, 160
Reinhardt, Maryann, *British Columbia Paralegal Association*, 248
Reinhardt, Mark, *Environmental Abatement Council of Ontario*, 691
Reinsbakken, Morgan, *British Columbia Art Therapy Association*, 230

Reisenleitner, Markus, *Canadian Comparative Literature Association*, 361
Reiss, Warren, *North American Society for Oceanic History*, 1579
Reissner, Gerhard, *International Association of Judges*, 1539
Reistetter, Andrew, *National Elevator & Escalator Association*, 993
Reiter, Lori, *Kids Kottage Foundation*, 886
Reithmayer, Sheila, *Solid Waste Association of North America*, 1595
Reitz, Beth, *Boys & Girls Clubs of Alberta*, 221
Rekhson, Vlad, *Alberta Chess Association*, 28
Relihan, Dan, *Canadian Association of Career Educators & Employers*, 310
Remedios, Francis, *Edmonton Jazz Society*, 678
Remillard, Donna, *Post-Polio Network Manitoba Inc.*, 1168
Rémillard, André, *CPE du Carrefour*, 638
Remin, Rod, *Canadian Speckle Park Association*, 489
Rempel, Murray, *Sarnia Minor Athletic Association*, 1254
Rempel, Errol, *The Christian & Missionary Alliance in Canada*, 566
Rempel, Dale, *Learning Disabilities Association of Saskatchewan*, 905
Rempel, Rick, *Niagara Region Orchid Society*, 1025
Rempel, Scott, *Western Canadian Miniature Horse Club*, 1448
Rempel, Shawn, *Saskatchewan Triathlon Association Corporation*, 1276
Rempel-Patrick, Cindi, *Steinbach Arts Council*, 1349
Renaud, Harry, *Whitchurch-Stouffville Chamber of Commerce*, 1452
Renaud, Nicholas, *Canadian Counselling & Psychotherapy Association*, 372
Renaud, Louise, *Chambre immobilière de Lanaudière Inc.*, 551
Renaud, Sylvianne, *Société pour les enfants handicapés du Québec*, 1322
Renaud, Claude, *Fédération acadienne de la Nouvelle-Écosse*, 707
Renaud, Diane, *Breast Cancer Society of Canada*, 228
Renaud, Marie, *Lo-Se-Ca Foundation*, 919
Renaud, Sylvie, *Canadian Association for Social Work Education*, 304
Renauer, Laurie, *Slave Lake & District Chamber of Commerce*, 1303
Rendell, Tim, *Early Music Vancouver*, 667
René de Cotret, Emanuelle, *Special Libraries Association*, 1596
Reniers, Paul, *British Columbia Institute of Technology Faculty & Staff Association*, 244
Renihan, Colleen, *American Musicological Society*, 1496
Renke, Brygeda, *Association of Academic Staff - University of Alberta*, 138
Renken, Suzanne, *Tillsonburg District Chamber of Commerce*, 1379
Renné, David, *International Solar Energy Society*, 1562
Renneberg, Nicole, *Saskatchewan Athletic Therapists Association*, 1259
Rennehan, George, *Nova Scotia Swordfish Association*, 1049
Renner, Gregor, *International Society for Augmentative & Alternative Communication*, 860
Rennette, Terry, *IAMAW District 78*, 829
Renney, Tom, *Hockey Canada*, 817
Rennick, Candace, *Canadian Union of Public Employees*, 498
Rennie, Brenda, *University of Lethbridge Faculty Association*, 1419
Renschler, Doreen, *Alliance for Canadian New Music Projects*, 56
Renshaw, Pat, *Canadian Association of Professional Pet Dog Trainers*, 329
Rentmeister, Doug, *Sport North Federation*, 1345

Renton, Jean, *Alberta Maine-Anjou Association*, 39
Renwick, Nicole, *Memorial Society of British Columbia*, 960
Renyo, Jenny, *Insurance Institute of Nova Scotia*, 849
Renzullo, Carm, *Lower Mainland Independent Secondary School Athletic Association*, 920
Reoch, Lorraine, *United Empire Loyalists' Association of Canada*, 1410
Repnow, Sylvia, *Shuswap Rock Club*, 1297
Repuski, Michelle, *Goodwill Industries Essex Kent Lambton*, 777
Resulaj, Eglantina, *Afghan Women's Counselling & Integration Community Support Organization*, 12
Resuli, Estref, *Eaglesland Albanian Society of BC*, 666
Reszczynski, Annette, *Social Planning Council of Sudbury Region*, 1306
Reszel, Rozanne E., *Canadian Investor Protection Fund*, 422
Rettie, Claire, *Victoria READ Society*, 1433
Reuber, Derwyn L., *Canadian Council of Independent Laboratories*, 368
Revenco, Kim, *Union of Calgary Co-op Employees*, 1407
Revez, Jean, *Association des études du Proche-Orient ancien*, 113
Rewa, Oksana, *Ukrainian Canadian Congress*, 1402
Reyerse, Robert, *Harrison Agassiz Chamber of Commerce*, 804
Reynar, Gert, *Leduc & District Food Bank Association*, 906
Reyners, Patrick, *International Nuclear Law Association*, 1553
Reynolds, Bill, *International Association for Literary Journalism Studies*, 853
Reynolds, Margaret, *Association of Book Publishers of British Columbia*, 140
Reynolds, Jenna, *Asthma Society of Canada*, 179
Reynolds, Kathleen, *Synchro Saskatchewan*, 1361
Reynolds, Joyce, *Restaurants Canada*, 1227
Reynolds, Edward, *British Columbia Association of Kinesiologists*, 232
Reynolds, Harry, *International Association for Bear Research & Management*, 1536
Reynolds, Beth, *Toronto Arts Council*, 1381
Reynolds, Jeanette, *Greyhound Pets of Atlantic Canada Society*, 790
Reynolds, Gunta, *The Latvian Relief Society of Canada*, 900
Reynolds, Jennifer, *Toronto Financial Services Alliance*, 1384
Reyolds, Justin, *Canadian Fence Industry Association*, 389
Rezansoff, Bob, *Pacific Salmon Commission*, 1136
Rheault, Pierre-Daniel, *Société professionnelle des auteurs et des compositeurs du Québec*, 1322
Rhéaume, Pierre, *Chambre de commerce de la grande région de Saint-Hyacinthe*, 541
Rhissa, Zakary, *Les banques alimentaires du Québec*, 196
Rho, Sarom, *Ontario Public Interest Research Group*, 1099
Rhodenizer, Tosha, *RA Stamp Club*, 1202
Rhodenizer, Tosha, *The Recreation Association*, 1207
Rhodes, Sheri, *Alberta Teachers of English as a Second Language*, 49
Rhodes, Brenda, *Bracebridge Chamber of Commerce*, 224
Rhodes, Gerald, *Alberta Association of Municipal Districts & Counties*, 24
Rhodes, Marcia, *World at Work*, 1603
Rhodes, Cindy, *Interior Running Association*, 852
Rhuland, Elizabeth, *Shelburne & Area Chamber of Commerce*, 1295

Rhyant Mal, Carla, *Alberta Professional Outfitters Society*, 43
Rhyndress, Bud, *Yellowknife Shooting Club*, 1471
Ribeiro, Natalia, *TESL New Brunswick*, 1372
Riberdy, Nicole, *Jeunesse du Monde*, 870
Ricard, Mélanie, *Chambre de commerce et d'industrie du Haut St-Maurice*, 547
Ricard, Charles, *Association des directeurs municipaux du Québec*, 111
Ricard, Caroline, *Association québécoise de la dysphasie*, 170
Ricard, Josée, *Fédération des associations étudiantes du campus de l'université de Montréal*, 712
Ricchio, Chelsea, *Healthy Minds Canada*, 808
Ricci Bitti, Francesco, *International Tennis Federation*, 1562
Ricci-Thode, Vanessa, *Canadian Authors Association*, 338
Riccoboni, Lou, *Canadian National Energy Alliance*, 439
Rice, Pamela, *Girl Guides of Canada*, 773
Rice, Sandra, *The Salvation Army in Canada*, 1253
Rice, Darlene, *Boys & Girls Clubs of Newfoundland & Labrador*, 222
Rice, Kevin, *Atlantic Provinces Art Gallery Association*, 185
Rice, Linda, *The Canadian Federation of Business & Professional Women's Clubs*, 385
Rice, Ken, *North Bay Police Association*, 1030
Rice, Carolyn, *New Westminster & District Labour Council*, 1015
Rice, Matt, *Mercy for Animals Canada*, 961
Rich, Curt, *North American Insulation Manufacturers Association*, 1579
Richard, Marie-Josée, *Association du Québec pour enfants avec problèmes auditifs*, 131
Richard, Alain, *Fédération Québécoise des Intervenants en Sécurité Incendie*, 729
Richard, Martin, *Canadian Paralympic Committee*, 449
Richard, Jill, *Alberta Tennis Association*, 50
Richard, Pierre, *Association des fabricants de meubles du Québec inc.*, 113
Richard, Andrea, *Canadian Association of Public Health Dentistry*, 330
Richard, Fred, *Grand Chapter, R.A.M. of Nova Scotia*, 779
Richard, Louise, *Association des orchestres de jeunes du Québec inc.*, 121
Richard, Marc L., *New Brunswick Law Foundation*, 1010
Richard, Karen, *School Sports Newfoundland & Labrador*, 1284
Richard, Kenn, *Native Child & Family Services of Toronto*, 997
Richard, Denis, *La Coop Fédérée*, 627
Richard, Évangéline, *Tourisme Lanaudière*, 1392
Richard, Julie-Anne, *Réseau indépendant des diffuseurs d'événements artistiques unis*, 1224
Richard, Marc, *Fraternité des Policiers et Policières de la Ville de Québec*, 758
Richard, Amélie, *Association québécoise pour le loisir des personnes handicapées*, 177
Richard, Viviane, *Mouvement national des québécoises et québécois*, 977
Richard, Marc L., *Law Society of New Brunswick*, 901
Richard, Shawn, *Canadian Association of Black Lawyers*, 309
Richard, Elisabeth, *L'Arche Québec*, 77
Richards, Dave, *Cordage Institute*, 1520
Richards, Marnie, *Brampton Arts Council*, 225
Richards, Kerry, *Community of Christ - Canada East Mission*, 606
Richards, Karen, *Community Living Newmarket/Aurora District*, 603
Richards, Rand, *Whitecourt & District Chamber of Commerce*, 1452
Richards, Tanya, *Canadian Pony Club*, 457

Executive Name Index

Richards, Lorraine, *Heavy Civil Association of Newfoundland & Labrador, Inc.*, 810
Richards, Bob, *Alberta Provincial Rifle Association*, 43
Richards, Gabrielle, *Canadian Tax Foundation*, 492
Richards, Sue, *Contagious Mountain Bike Club*, 626
Richards-Conley, Holly, *Ontario Home Builders' Association*, 1085
Richardson, Glenn, *Toronto Entomologists Association*, 1384
Richardson, Angela, *Boys & Girls Clubs of Alberta*, 221
Richardson, Alan J., *Canadian Academic Accounting Association*, 285
Richardson, Joel, *Canadian Manufacturers & Exporters*, 430
Richardson, Frank, *Nova Scotia Veterinary Medical Association*, 1050
Richardson, Jeff, *United Way/Centraide (Central NB) Inc.*, 1418
Richardson, Paul, *The Bible League of Canada*, 208
Richardson, Douglas, *Association of American Geographers*, 1510
Richardson, Susan, *Ontario Art Therapy Association*, 1060
Richardson, Hartley, *Assiniboine Park Conservancy*, 89
Richardson, Nelli, *Revelstoke Women's Shelter Society*, 1228
Richardson, David, *African Enterprise (Canada)*, 13
Richardson, Mark, *Canadian Council on Ecological Areas*, 371
Richardson, Amanda, *Manitoba Pest Management Association*, 942
Richelhoff, Jerald, *Health & Safety Conference Society of Alberta*, 805
Richer, Anne, *Canadian Centre on Substance Use & Addiction*, 354
Richer, Thérèse, *Mouvement d'information et d'entraide dans la lutte contre le sida à Québec*, 977
Richer, Philippe, *Association des juristes d'expression française du Manitoba inc.*, 118
Richer, Andre, *AFOA Canada*, 12
Richey, Denise, *Canada Employment & Immigration Union*, 279
Richler, Neil, *Jewish Genealogical Society of Toronto*, 872
Richman, Joy M., *Canadian Association for Dental Research*, 299
Richmond, Tammy, *The Canadian Federation of Business & Professional Women's Clubs*, 386
Richmond, Tiffany, *Alberta Angus Association*, 22
Richmond, Geraldine, *American Association for the Advancement of Science*, 1489
Richmond, Sarah, *Vancouver Association of Law Libraries*, 1425
Richter, Tonia, *Chetwynd & District Chamber of Commerce*, 557
Richter, Janet, *Association of Ontario Snowboarders*, 155
Rick, Bates, *Canadian Wildlife Federation*, 504
Rickards, Pamela, *Canadian Warplane Heritage*, 502
Rickards, Tracey, *Canadian Public Health Association - NB/PEI Branch*, 462
Ricketts, Frank, *Newfoundland & Labrador Environmental Industry Association*, 1018
Riddell, Louise Ann, *Ontario Municipal Human Resources Association*, 1092
Riddell, Ron, *YMCA Canada*, 1471
Riddell, Joyce, *Manitoba School Library Association*, 944
Riddell, Jan, *Saint John Naturalists' Club*, 1247
Riddell, M. Gatz, *American Association of Bovine Practitioners*, 1489
Riddle, Deborah, *Canadian Association of Elizabeth Fry Societies*, 313

Rideout, Gerry, *Cross Country Newfoundland & Labrador*, 643
Rideout, Debbie, *College of Family Physicians of Canada*, 585
Rideout, Yvonne, *Snowmobilers of Manitoba Inc.*, 1305
Rideout, Arthur, *College of Physicians & Surgeons of Newfoundland & Labrador*, 588
Rideout, Linda, *Newfoundland & Labrador Federation of Labour*, 1019
Rideout, Kira, *Baie Verte & Area Chamber of Commerce*, 194
Rideout, Melvin, *Newfoundland & Labrador Federation of Agriculture*, 1018
Rideout, Jason, *Horseshoe Canada*, 822
Rideout, Jason, *Horseshoe New Brunswick*, 822
Rider, Fran, *Ontario Women's Hockey Association*, 1113
Rider, Steven C., *Industrial Fabrics Association International*, 1531
Ridge, Robert, *Canadian MedicAlert Foundation*, 434
Ridgway, Kevan, *Vancouver, Coast & Mountains Tourism Region*, 1429
Ridha, Ibtihal, *Automotive Industries Association of Canada*, 190
Ridout, Renee, *AthletesCAN*, 180
Rieber, Cybelle, *P.E.E.R.S. Alliance*, 1148
Rieck, Mark, *International Right of Way Association*, 1556
Rieck Buckley, Christine, *Canadian Nurses Foundation*, 443
Rieder, Michael, *Canadian Society of Pharmacology & Therapeutics*, 486
Riedle, Jennifer, *Canadian Actors' Equity Association (CLC)*, 288
Riedstra, Marie, *National Chinchilla Breeders of Canada*, 991
Riehl, Greg, *Canadian AIDS Society*, 290
Riehl-Fitzsimmons, Belinda, *Saskatchewan Archaeological Society*, 1256
Riel, Jennifer, *Martin Prosperity Institute*, 952
Riemer, Pierce, *World Petroleum Council*, 1607
Riemer, Joan, *Prairie Rock & Gem Society*, 1169
Ries, Lori, *Community Futures Saskatchewan*, 598
Rifai, Taleb D., *World Tourism Organization*, 1608
Rifkind, Lewis, *Yukon Conservation Society*, 1478
Rigby, Peter, *The Wesleyan Church of Canada - Central Canada District*, 1447
Rigby, Judy, *College of Dental Technologists of Ontario*, 583
Rigby, Joe, *Conseil national Société de Saint-Vincent de Paul*, 619
Rigg, Lacey, *YMCA Canada*, 1471
Riggs, Sherry, *Canadian Association for Young Children*, 307
Riggs, Joan, *Anxiety Disorders Association of Ontario*, 72
Rightmyer, Susan, *Greater Toronto Water Garden & Horticultural Society*, 786
Rigmaiden, Kenneth E., *International Union of Painters & Allied Trades*, 1565
Rigney, Reed, *Alberta Blonde d'Aquitaine Association*, 26
Rijsberman, Frank, *Consultative Group on International Agricultural Research*, 1519
Rikley, Darlene, *Operating Room Nurses of Alberta Association*, 1115
Riley, Paul, *Association of Neighbourhood Houses BC*, 153
Riley, Lorne F., *Canadian Forestry Accreditation Board*, 392
Riley, Gina Lori, *Gina Lori Riley Dance Enterprises*, 773
Rinaldi, Roberto, *Canadian Italian Business & Professional Association*, 423
Rincon, Alberto, *Halton Peel Hispanic Association*, 800
Ring, Rory, *Sault Ste Marie Chamber of Commerce*, 1281

Ring, Lesley, *Canadian Cancer Society*, 349
Rintoul, R. Chad, *Association of British Columbia Land Surveyors*, 140
Riopel, Janet M., *Edmonton Chamber of Commerce*, 676
Riopel, Dianne, *Ojibway & Cree Cultural Centre*, 1055
Riopelle, RJ, *Brain Injury Association of Canada*, 225
Rioux, Pierre, *Société de généalogie et d'archives de Rimouski*, 1316
Rioux, Gaston, *Fédération des comités de parents du Québec inc.*, 713
Rioux, Catherine, *Association québécoise de prévention du suicide*, 171
Rioux, Marie-Claude, *Fédération acadienne de la Nouvelle-Écosse*, 707
Rioux, Sheldon, *Sign Association of Canada*, 1299
Rioux, Mikaël, *Coop kayak des Îles*, 627
Rioux, Emmanuel, *La Société historique du Cap-Rouge*, 1321
Rioux, Yvanho, *Réseau des SADC et CAE*, 1221
Rioux, Raynald, *Association des familles Rioux d'Amérique inc.*, 113
Rioux, Sylvie, *Société de protection des plantes du Québec*, 1317
Rioux, Simon-Pierre, *Association des véhicules électriques du Québec*, 130
Riseboro, Caroline, *Plan Canada*, 1161
Riseley, Ian H.S., *Rotary International*, 1587
Risenrough, Rhonda, *The Terry Fox Foundation*, 1372
Ritcey, Ray, *The Maritimes Energy Association*, 951
Ritch, John B., *World Nuclear Association*, 1606
Ritcher, Serge, *Fédération des clubs de motoneigistes du Québec*, 713
Ritchi, Paul, *Federation of North American Explorers*, 725
Ritchie, Jocelyn, *Battlefords Agricultural Society*, 200
Ritchie, Ray, *Association of Professional Engineers & Geoscientists of New Brunswick*, 158
Ritchie, Sherrill, *Lupus Ontario*, 921
Ritchie, Kevin, *Rural Municipal Administrators' Association of Saskatchewan*, 1244
Ritchie, Dave, *International Association of Machinists & Aerospace Workers*, 1539
Ritchie, Geoffrey, *Private Capital Markets Association of Canada*, 1180
Ritsema, Cathy, *Alzheimer Society of Huron County*, 63
Ritson, Karen, *Alliance of Canadian Cinema, Television & Radio Artists*, 58
Rittenhouse, Rick, *Auctioneers Association of Ontario*, 187
Ritter, Leonard, *Canadian Network of Toxicology Centres*, 441
Ritter, David, *Canadian Jewellers Association*, 423
Ritter, Jean, *British Columbia Registered Music Teachers' Association*, 251
Riva, Leslie, *National Dental Assisting Examining Board*, 992
Rivard, Pierre, *Le Centre culturel francophone de Vancouver*, 527
Rivard, Mathieu, *Muniscope*, 982
Rivard, David, *Children's Aid Society of Toronto*, 561
Rivera, Gladis, *Association of Neighbourhood Houses BC*, 153
Rivera, Soraya, *Association of Power Producers of Ontario*, 156
Rivera-Gamarra, Julio, *Corporation culturelle Latino-Américaine de l'Amitié*, 629
Rivers, Bruce, *Covenant House Toronto*, 637
Rivers, Emily, *AboutFace*, 3
Rivers, Corinne, *York Region Law Association*, 1473
Rivest, Linda, *La Société d'histoire de la Rivière-du-Nord*, 1310

Rivet, Christophe, *ICOMOS Canada*, 829
Rivet, Serge, *Real Estate Institute of Canada*, 1206
Rivière, Renée, *Ordre des infirmières et infirmiers du Québec*, 1122
Rivington, Kristie, *Jersey Canada*, 869
Rix-Moore, Dawn, *College of Licensed Practical Nurses of PEI*, 585
Rizzi, Marco, *International Association of Patristic Studies*, 1539
Rizzuti, Franco, *Canadian Federation of Medical Students*, 388
Roach, Cassandra, *Schizophrenia Society of Ontario*, 1284
Roach, Tom, *Atlantic Federation of Musicians, Local 571*, 184
Roach, Ereka, *Sport Physiotherapy Canada*, 1345
Roach-Ganaway, Maggie, *Caregivers Nova Scotia*, 512
Roantree, Rhonda, *Ontario Maple Syrup Producers' Association*, 1090
Roark, Tim, *Environmental Health Foundation of Canada*, 692
Robb, Ian, *UNITE HERE Canada*, 1408
Robb, Sylvia, *Urology Nurses of Canada*, 1423
Robb, Stephen, *Richmond Delta Youth Orchestra*, 1230
Robb, Fraser, *East Shore Internet Society*, 668
Robbins, Heather, *Manitoba Society of Artists*, 944
Robbins, Joanne, *Saugeen Shores Chamber of Commerce*, 1281
Robbins, Rachel, *Toronto Symphony Youth Orchestra*, 1387
Robbins, Keith, *Poultry Industry Council*, 1168
Robbins, Linda, *Burford Township Historical Society*, 265
Robbins, Rebekah, *MusicNL*, 984
Robbins, Sarah, *Canadian Nutrition Society*, 444
Robbins, Nancy, *Community Futures West Yellowhead*, 598
Roberage, Carole, *Alliance des cadres de l'État*, 55
Roberge, Jérémie, *Carrefour de solidarité internationale inc.*, 515
Roberge, Louise, *Tea Association of Canada*, 1367
Roberge, Sophie, *Association des orchestres de jeunes de la Montérégie*, 121
Roberge, Sylvie, *Palais Montcalm*, 1137
Robert, François, *Canadian Paralympic Committee*, 449
Robert, Diane, *Fédération québécoise du loisir littéraire*, 731
Robert, Yves, *Collège des médecins du Québec*, 582
Robert, Josianne, *Canadian Committee of Graduate Students in Education*, 361
Robert, Isabelle, *Orienteering Québec*, 1126
Robert, André-P., *Réseau Québec-France*, 1225
Robert, Enrique, *Birchmount Bluffs Neighbourhood Centre*, 212
Robert, Terry, *Fraser Basin Council*, 757
Robert, Andrew, *Manitoba Library Trustees Association*, 940
Roberto, Claude M., *Edmonton (Alberta) Nerve Pain Association*, 675
Roberts, Jeffrey, *Irritable Bowel Syndrome Self Help & Support Group*, 864
Roberts, Mike, *British Columbia School Trustees Association*, 252
Roberts, William, *Confederation of Resident & Ratepayer Associations*, 611
Roberts, Stacie, *Jockey Club of Canada*, 873
Roberts, Ben, *International Federation of Landscape Architects*, 1548
Roberts, Emma, *Canadian Pain Society*, 449
Roberts, Jane, *International Association of University Professors of English*, 1540
Roberts, Mark, *Tennis BC*, 1370
Roberts, Russ, *Canadian Advanced Technology Alliance*, 288

Roberts, Paula, *Canadian Cancer Society*, 348
Roberts, Rob, *The Canadian Press*, 459
Roberts, Trevor, *International Schizophrenia Foundation*, 860
Roberts, Tom, *AFCOM*, 1486
Roberts, Yvette, *Canadian Mathematical Society*, 432
Roberts, Nancy, *Canadian College of Health Leaders*, 359
Roberts, Jeff, *Canadian Fertility & Andrology Society*, 389
Roberts, Ada, *Canadian Indigenous Nurses Association*, 411
Roberts, Hayley, *Canadian Association of Pharmacy Technicians*, 326
Roberts, Terry L., *International Plant Nutrition Institute*, 1555
Roberts, Marle, *Canadian Union of Public Employees*, 498
Roberts, Marc, *Oxford Child & Youth Centre*, 1134
Roberts, Carter S., *World Wildlife Fund - USA*, 1608
Roberts, Cecil, *United Mine Workers of America (CLC)*, 1599
Roberts, Elizabeth, *Human Resources Professionals Association*, 826
Roberts, Joy, *Musagetes Foundation*, 982
Roberts, Ron, *Canadian Office & Professional Employees Union*, 445
Roberts, Paul, *Ontario Water Ski Association*, 1113
Roberts, Brittney, *Human Anatomy & Physiology Society*, 1530
Roberts, Lindsay, *Synchro Yukon Association*, 1361
Roberts, Susan, *Canadian Association of Aesthetic Medicine*, 308
Roberts, Ruth A., *Society of Toxicology*, 1594
Roberts, Patricia L., *American Society of Colon & Rectal Surgeons*, 1499
Roberts-Joseph, Avice, *Fédération de Netball du Québec*, 710
Robertson, Gail, *Cowichan Valley Arts Council*, 637
Robertson, Larry, *The Anglican Church of Canada*, 70
Robertson, Scott, *Boys & Girls Clubs of Ontario*, 223
Robertson, Pam, *Brockville & District Chamber of Commerce*, 260
Robertson, James, *International Wine & Food Society*, 1567
Robertson, Doug, *Western Barley Growers Association*, 1447
Robertson, Janelle, *Diabetes Canada*, 655
Robertson, Charlynne, *Clean Nova Scotia Foundation*, 573
Robertson, Brian, *Canadian Galloway Association*, 396
Robertson, Erica, *Canadian Psychoanalytic Society*, 461
Robertson, Michael, *Microscopical Society of Canada*, 964
Robertson, Greg, *Society of Canadian Ornithologists*, 1327
Robertson, Duncan, *Television Bureau of Canada, Inc.*, 1370
Robertson, Robyn D., *Traffic Injury Research Foundation*, 1394
Robertson, Wayne, *Law Foundation of British Columbia*, 900
Robertson, Craig, *Environmental Services Association of Alberta*, 692
Robertson, Bonnie, *New Brunswick Equestrian Association*, 1008
Robertson, Denise, *Island Deaf & Hard of Hearing Centre*, 865
Robertson, Carla, *Ontario Brain Injury Association*, 1069
Robertson, Andrea, *Shock Trauma Air Rescue Society*, 1296
Robertson, Lauri Sue, *Disability Awareness Consultants*, 658

Robertson, William F., *Disability Awareness Consultants*, 658
Robertson, Randle, *Burgess Shale Geoscience Foundation*, 265
Robertson, Jaye, *Progressive Housing Society*, 1187
Robertson, Donna, *Canadian Cable Systems Alliance*, 348
Robertson, Liz, *Canadian Association of Farm Advisors*, 314
Robichau, Bernie, *Canadian Ski Patrol*, 471
Robichaud, Denis, *Canadian Federation of Independent Business*, 387
Robichaud, Daniel J., *New Brunswick Denturists Society*, 1007
Robichaud, André, *Société d'histoire de Lachine*, 1311
Robichaud, Carol, *Association of Image Consultants International Canada*, 149
Robichaud, Peter, *The Canadian Woodlands Forum*, 505
Robichaud, Jacques, *Chambre de commerce Kent-Sud*, 549
Robichaud, Raymond, *Canadian Horse Breeders' Association*, 408
Robicheau, Brigette, *Canadian Association for Community Living - Clare Branch*, 298
Robidoux, Marie C., *Alberta Women Entrepreneurs*, 52
Robidoux, Raphaëlle, *Association des neurotraumatisés de l'Outaouais*, 121
Robillard, Jamie, *Ontario Ball Hockey Association*, 1067
Robillard, Mireille, *La Trame*, 1394
Robinchaud, Darren, *Electric Vehicle Council of Ottawa*, 682
Robinette, Katie, *Healthy Minds Canada*, 808
Robins, Clayton, *Canadian 4-H Council*, 284
Robins, Shane, *Manitoba Conservation Districts Association*, 934
Robinson, Ron, *Nelson & District Arts Council*, 1003
Robinson, Michael, *Winnipeg Association of Public Service Officers*, 1458
Robinson, Kelsey, *Wainwright & District Chamber of Commerce*, 1439
Robinson, Karen, *Manitouwadge Economic Development Corporation*, 948
Robinson, Charla, *Thunder Bay Chamber of Commerce*, 1377
Robinson, Janice, *Catholic Children's Aid Society of Toronto*, 518
Robinson, Lee, *Marketing Research & Intelligence Association*, 951
Robinson, Mary, *Prince Edward Island Federation of Agriculture*, 1174
Robinson, Eunice, *British Columbia Genealogical Society*, 242
Robinson, Marie-Therese, *Canadian Association of Optometrists*, 324
Robinson, Jay, *British Columbia Chiropractic Association*, 236
Robinson, Jan, *College of Veterinarians of Ontario*, 590
Robinson, David, *Canadian Association of University Teachers*, 335
Robinson, Frances, *Indexing Society of Canada*, 834
Robinson, Ira, *Canadian Institute for Jewish Research*, 412
Robinson, Bev, *Junior Achievement Canada*, 877
Robinson, Tom, *Holstein Canada*, 819
Robinson, Charla, *Northwestern Ontario Municipal Association*, 1039
Robinson, Myles, *Canadian Cosmetic, Toiletry & Fragrance Association*, 366
Robinson, Steven, *Ontario Restaurant, Hotel & Motel Association*, 1101
Robinson, Kris, *Canadian Midwifery Regulators Consortium*, 436
Robinson, John, *New Brunswick Soil & Crop Improvement Association*, 1012
Robinson, David, *Linguistic Society of America*, 1569

Robinson, Christine, *Canadian Energy Workers' Association*, 381
Robinson, Bruce, *Canadian Freestyle Ski Association*, 394
Robinson, Susan, *Health Sciences Centre Foundation*, 807
Robinson, Joanne, *Jamaican Ottawa Community Association*, 867
Robinson, Bill, *Novia Scotia Sports Hall of Fame*, 1050
Robinson, Christopher, *Royal College of Dentists of Canada*, 1241
Robinson, Ann, *Osgoode Twp. Historical Society*, 1127
Robinson, B.A., *Ontario Consultants on Religious Tolerance*, 1074
Robinson, Peter, *David Suzuki Foundation*, 652
Robinson, Amber, *Centre for Child Development*, 531
Robinson, Brenda, *Family Service Moncton Inc.*, 704
Robinson, Frances, *British Columbia Prader-Willi Syndrome Association*, 249
Robinson, Bill, *Employees' Association Hammond Manufacturing Company Ltd.*, 687
Robinson, Sarah, *Ontario Society of Chiropodists*, 1107
Robinson, Susan M., *Law Society of Prince Edward Island*, 902
Robinson, Kasia, *Architectural Woodwork Manufacturers Association of Canada - Saskatchewan*, 80
Robinson, Ira, *Canadian Society for Jewish Studies*, 476
Robinson, Peter, *Community Energy Association*, 597
Robinson, Erin, *Fraser Basin Council*, 757
Robinson, Sandy, *Manitoba Pulse & Soybean Growers Inc.*, 943
Robison, Ron, *Western Hockey League*, 1450
Robison, Ron, *Canadian Hockey League*, 406
Robitaille, Louis, *Les Ballets Jazz de Montréal*, 195
Robitaille, Claude, *Canadian Institute of Plumbing & Heating*, 419
Robitaille, Chantal, *Fédération des professionnelles et professionnels de l'éducation du Québec*, 718
Robitaille, Denis, *Regroupement des offices d'habitation du Québec*, 1215
Robitaille, Dominic, *Fédération québécoise des jeux récréatifs*, 729
Robles, Flavia, *Kidney Foundation of Canada*, 885
Roblesky, Lori, *Soroptimist Foundation of Canada*, 1333
Robski, Cathie, *Insurance Brokers Association of Canada*, 848
Robson, Keitha, *Timmins Chamber of Commerce*, 1380
Robson, William B.P., *C.D. Howe Institute*, 521
Robson, Marian, *The Chartered Institute of Logistics & Transport in North America*, 552
Robson, Tom, *Manitoba Wall & Ceiling Association*, 947
Robyn, Raymond, *M2/W2 Association - Restorative Christian Ministries*, 923
Rocchi, Franco, *Conseil régional des personnes âgées italo-canadiennes de Montréal*, 621
Rocco, Patricia, *Ontario Art Education Association*, 1060
Roche, Hélène, *Building Envelope Council of Ottawa Region*, 262
Roche, Kelly, *Canadian Labour Congress*, 424
Rochefort, Terry, *CAMPUT*, 277
Rochefort, Carol, *Canadian Society of Physician Executives*, 486
Rocheleau, Jean-Claude, *Alliance québécoise des techniciens de l'image et du son*, 58
Rochelle, Anna, *Recycling Council of British Columbia*, 1208

Rochette, Hélène, *Regroupement des artistes en arts visuels du Québec (ind.)*, 1214
Rochon, Irénée, *Orthodox Church in America Archdiocese of Canada*, 1127
Rochon, François, *Association des collections d'entreprises*, 109
Rochon, Martin, *Canadian Council of Motor Transport Administrators*, 369
Rochon, Jennifer, *Ontario Modern Language Teachers Association*, 1091
Rochon, Louis-Philippe, *La cinémathèque québécoise*, 570
Rochon, Fernand, *Les Chevaliers de Colomb du Québec*, 557
Rochon, Benoit, *Wikimedia Canada*, 1453
Rock, Brian, *Québec Federation of Home & School Associations Inc.*, 1197
Rock, Gail, *Canadian Apheresis Group*, 294
Rockett, Frank, *Ontario Society for the Prevention of Cruelty to Animals*, 1106
Rockwell, Robyn, *Canadian Society of Hospital Pharmacists*, 483
Rodall, Leona, *Harbourfront Community Centre*, 803
Rodd, Donald, *Ancient, Free & Accepted Masons of Canada - Grand Lodge of Prince Edward Island*, 69
Rodd-Nielsen, Elise, *Canadian Association for Enterostomal Therapy*, 300
Rodé, Britny, *Real Estate Institute of Canada*, 1205
Rode, Bethany, *Canadian Society of Gastroenterology Nurses & Associates*, 483
Rode, Tiffany, *National Association of Addiction Treatment Providers*, 1573
Rodenberg, Frances, *Animal Welfare Foundation of Canada*, 71
Rodenburg, Frances, *Agricultural Institute of Canada Foundation*, 15
Rodgers, Ruth, *Pastel Artists Canada*, 1145
Rodgers, Bruce, *Canadian International Freight Forwarders Association*, 421
Rodgers, Mark, *Habitat for Humanity Canada*, 796
Rodgers, Evan, *Landmark & Community Chamber of Commerce*, 898
Rodgers, Guy, *English-Language Arts Network*, 689
Rodier, Pier, *Compagnie vox théâtre*, 608
Rodman, Geri, *Inter-Varsity Christian Fellowship*, 862
Rodo, Vince, *Ontario Public Transit Association*, 1100
Rodrigo, Stan, *Gethsemane Ministries*, 773
Rodrigue, Robert, *Confédération des organismes familiaux du Québec*, 611
Rodrigue, Robert, *Mouvement québécois des vacances familiales inc.*, 978
Rodrigue, David, *St. Lawrence Valley Natural History Society*, 1250
Rodrigue, Maxime, *Association provinciale des constructeurs d'habitations du Québec inc.*, 168
Rodrigues, Mirabelle, *Foundation for International Training*, 755
Rodriguez, Gabriella C., *Association for Facilities Engineering*, 1508
Rodriguez, Juan, *ACUC International*, 7
Rody, Douglas, *Yukon Teachers' Association*, 1480
Roe, K. Keith, *American Society of Mechanical Engineers*, 1500
Roe, Karen, *Construction Association of Rural Manitoba Inc.*, 624
Roebuck, Robert, *Mission Aviation Fellowship of Canada*, 969
Roebuck, I. Hillel, *Ontario Association of Architects*, 1061
Roebuck, David, *Northwest Territories Teachers' Association*, 1038
Roed, Tyler, *Boys & Girls Clubs of Alberta*, 221
Roediger, David, *American Studies Association*, 1503
Roel, Gustave, *Réseau du sport étudiant du Québec*, 1222

Executive Name Index

Roelof Polling, Jan, *International Orthoptic Association*, 1554
Roemich, Brenden, *The Salvation Army in Canada*, 1253
Roeser, Paul, *Society of Motion Picture & Television Engineers*, 1593
Rogalski, Alex, *PAVED Arts*, 1146
Rogalsky, Dave, *Church of the Good Shepherd*, 569
Roger, Andrew, *International Society for Evolutionary Protistology*, 860
Roger, Michael A., *Naval Club of Toronto*, 1001
Roger, Ivan, *APCHQ - Montréal Métropolitain*, 73
Rogers, Claire, *Crowsnest Pass Chamber of Commerce*, 644
Rogers, Dan, *Greater Vernon Chamber of Commerce*, 787
Rogers, Linda, *Greater Bathurst Chamber of Commerce*, 783
Rogers, Gerry, *Huron Chamber of Commerce - Goderich, Central & North Huron*, 828
Rogers, Heather, *Alberta School Boards Association*, 45
Rogers, Pamela, *Federation of Music Festivals of Nova Scotia*, 725
Rogers, Joe, *Children's Aid Society of the District of Nipissing & Parry Sound*, 561
Rogers, Blake, *Tourism Industry Association of the Yukon*, 1390
Rogers, Robert, *United Empire Loyalists' Association of Canada*, 1410
Rogers, Carolyn, *Canadian Council of Insurance Regulators*, 368
Rogers, Neil, *Yarmouth & Area Chamber of Commerce*, 1470
Rogers, Bob, *Canadian Hemochromatosis Society*, 404
Rogers, Sean, *Bamfield Marine Sciences Centre*, 195
Rogers, Dean, *Porcupine Prospectors & Developers Association*, 1165
Rogers Healey, Robynne, *Canadian Society of Church History*, 481
Rogerson, Nancy, *Music for Young Children*, 984
Rogerson, Jo-Anne, *Ontario Association of Cemetery & Funeral Professionals*, 1062
Rogerson, Garth, *Red River Exhibition Association*, 1210
Rogov, Sergei, *Russian Association of Canadian Studies*, 1588
Rogowsky, Brad, *Manitoba Association of Library Technicians*, 930
Rogoza, Christina, *Acupuncture Canada*, 7
Rogucki, Marisa, *The Shepherds' Trust*, 1295
Roh, Phillip, *Atkinson Charitable Foundation*, 182
Rohan, Shannon, *Shareholder Association for Research & Education*, 1294
Rohani, Farid, *The Laurier Institution*, 900
Rohn, Rob, *HeliCat Canada*, 811
Rohrmann, Axel, *Saskatchewan College of Podiatrists*, 1261
Rois, Judy, *Anglican Foundation of Canada*, 70
Rolfe, Brent, *Niagara Support Services*, 1026
Rolfe, Sigrid, *Prince Edward Island Rape & Sexual Assault Centre*, 1176
Rolingher, Sol, *Lieutenant Governor's Circle on Mental Health & Addiction*, 910
Rolland, Daniel, *Association des policières et policiers provinciaux du Québec*, 123
Rolland, Marie-Pierre, *Orchestre symphonique de Laval*, 1118
Rolland-Porucks, Shelley, *Renfrew County United Way*, 1217
Rollheiser, Pamela, *Saskatchewan Registered Music Teachers' Association*, 1273
Rollins, Matt, *Alberta Golf Association*, 37
Rollins, Lisa, *Canadian Energy Research Institute*, 381
Rollins, William (Bill), *Model Aeronautics Association of Canada Inc.*, 970

Rollo, Alicia, *Canadian Institute of Actuaries*, 414
Roloson, Deb, *Woodstock & District Developmental Services*, 1464
Rolston, Terence, *Focus on the Family Canada*, 742
Romain, Carole, *Alliance autochtone du Québec*, 55
Roman, Lori, *Salt Institute*, 1588
Romaniuk, Bohdan (Don), *International Telecommunications Society*, 1562
Romano, Tony, *Greater Toronto Marketing Alliance*, 786
Romanoff, Lesley, *Parent Cooperative Preschools International*, 1139
Romanovych, Andy, *Manitoba Cycling Association*, 935
Romanow, Carol, *Directors Guild of Canada*, 657
Romanuck, Wally, *Saskatoon City Police Association*, 1279
Romard, Kyla, *Nova Scotia Dental Association*, 1044
Rome, Susan, *Georgina Association for Community Living*, 771
Romeo, C. Lynn, *Uniform Law Conference of Canada*, 1405
Romeril, Sue, *Canadian Dance Teachers' Association*, 375
Romero, Luis, *Canadian Welding Bureau*, 503
Romizuddin, Muhammed, *Muslim Community of Québec*, 985
Romkey, Sarah, *Archives Association of British Columbia*, 80
Romoff, Mark, *The Canadian Council for Public-Private Partnerships*, 367
Romphf, Karla, *Ontario Ringette Association*, 1102
Romstad, Svein, *Fédération Internationale de Luge de Course*, 1525
Romund, Grace, *Manitoba Association of Health Information Providers*, 930
Ronan, Stella, *Orléans Chamber of Commerce*, 1127
Ronan, Paul, *Ontario Trails Council*, 1111
Ronan, Doug, *Ontario Seaplane Association*, 1103
Ronan, Paul, *Ontario Parks Association*, 1095
Rondeau, Joël, *Caisse Groupe Financier*, 270
Rondeau, Jon, *Segal Centre for the Performing Arts at the Saidye*, 1289
Rondeau, Maryse, *Association d'éducation préscolaire du Québec*, 99
Rondeau-Bernier, Johanne, *Community Living Timmins Intégration Communautaire*, 605
Roney, Bruce, *Ottawa Humane Society*, 1130
Rönnberg, Barbro, *International Orienteering Federation*, 1554
Ronson, Alison, *Canadian Parks & Wilderness Society*, 451
Rooke, Marg, *Block Parent Program of Canada*, 215
Rooke, Barry, *National Campus & Community Radio Association*, 991
Rooke, Lorraine, *Association des intervenantes et des intervenants en soins spirituels du Québec*, 117
Rooks-Trotzuk, Angela, *Lloydminster Interval Home Society*, 916
Roome, Catherine, *British Columbia Safety Authority*, 252
Rooney, Larry, *Phoenix Community Works Foundation*, 1157
Rooney, Shirley, *Newfoundland Horticultural Society*, 1023
Rooney, Janice, *Toronto Law Office Management Association*, 1385
Roos, Hank, *Abbotsford-Mission Nature Club*, 1
Roos, Jane, *Canadian Athletes Now Fund*, 337
Roose, Mikeal L., *International Society of Citriculture*, 1560
Roosma, Gary, *OMF International - Canada*, 1057
Roots, James, *Canadian Association of the Deaf*, 334

Ropcean, Ryan, *Alberta Water & Wastewater Operators Association*, 51
Ropchan, Richard, *Ontario Minor Hockey Association*, 1091
Roquet, François, *Air Transport Association of Canada*, 19
Roquet, Louis L., *Canada Media Fund*, 280
Rork, Lorri, *Community Care Peterborough*, 596
Rosa, Brigitte, *Carrefour communautaire de Chibougamau*, 515
Rosati, Mike, *Liberal Party of Canada (Ontario)*, 909
Rosato, Melissa, *FogQuest*, 742
Rose, Don, *Master Mariners of Canada*, 954
Rose, Tom, *Bay St. George Chamber of Commerce*, 200
Rose, Kevin, *Economic Developers Association of Canada*, 673
Rose, Mark, *Muniscope*, 982
Rose, Sarah, *New Brunswick Aboriginal Women's Council*, 1004
Rose, Bruce, *Manitoba Horse Council Inc.*, 938
Rose, Jeff, *Enform*, 688
Rose, Richard, *Tarragon Theatre*, 1367
Rose, Bruce, *Manitoba Water Polo Association Inc.*, 947
Rose, Bruce, *Manitoba Customer Contact Association, Inc.*, 935
Rose, Pat, *Union of Calgary Co-op Employees*, 1407
Rose, Yannick, *Club canadien de Toronto*, 574
Rose, Leanna, *British Columbia Centre of Excellence for Women's Health*, 235
Rose, Ken, *Westport & Rideau Lakes Chamber of Commerce*, 1451
Rose, Amanda, *Construction Owners Association of Alberta*, 624
Rose, Brenda, *Alberta Bodybuilding Association*, 26
Rose, Lee, *Community Foundations of Canada*, 598
Rose-Krasnor, Linda, *Brock University Faculty Association*, 260
Rosen, Hartley, *Environmental Youth Alliance*, 693
Rosen, Al, *Cobequid Arts Council*, 579
Rosen, Michael, *Tree Canada Foundation*, 1397
Rosenberg, Judith, *Community Torchlight Guelph/Wellington/Dufferin*, 607
Rosenberg, Paul, *Calgary Exhibition & Stampede*, 272
Rosenberg, Richard, *Electronic Frontier Canada Inc.*, 683
Rosenberger, Katie, *Affiliation of Multicultural Societies & Service Agencies of BC*, 11
Rosenberh, Meir, *Mizrachi Organization of Canada*, 970
Rosenblum, Norman, *Canadian Society for Clinical Investigation*, 474
Rosenfeld, Mark, *Ontario Confederation of University Faculty Associations*, 1074
Rosenfeld, Mark, *Ontario Confederation of University Faculty Associations*, 1074
Rosenfeldt, Gary, *Victims of Violence*, 1432
Rosenke, Rosey, *Wilberforce Project*, 1453
Rosensweig, David, *Canadian Dressage Owners & Riders Association*, 379
Rosenthal, Caroline, *Association for Canadian Studies in German-Speaking Countries*, 1507
Rosenthal, Stephen M., *Pediatric Endocrine Society*, 1583
Roslyn, Leighton, *Community Living Greater Sudbury*, 602
Ross, Tammy, *Community Care Peterborough*, 596
Ross, Jeanne, *Chemainus & District Chamber of Commerce*, 555
Ross, Krista, *Fredericton Chamber of Commerce*, 758
Ross, Shelley, *Medical Women's International Association*, 958
Ross, Marie-Josée, *MultiPrévention ASP: Association paritaire pour la santé et la sécurité au travail des secteurs: métal, électrique, habillement et imprimerie*, 980
Ross, Bob, *Aplastic Anemia & Myelodysplasia Association of Canada*, 73
Ross, Sheryl, *Restaurants Canada*, 1227
Ross, Rick, *Canadian Water Resources Association*, 503
Ross, Ian, *Canadian Association of Oral & Maxillofacial Surgeons*, 324
Ross, Sylvie, *Parents partenaires en éducation*, 1140
Ross, Heather, *Canadian Cardiovascular Society*, 350
Ross, Henrietta, *Ontario Association of Credit Counselling Services*, 1063
Ross, Adam, *Lifesaving Society*, 911
Ross, Ken, *Tourism Industry Association of Canada*, 1389
Ross, Dan, *Toronto Police Association*, 1386
Ross, Henrietta, *Canadian Association of Credit Counselling Services*, 311
Ross, Andrew, *Canadian Association of Nuclear Medicine*, 323
Ross, Roseanne, *Timmins Native Friendship Centre*, 1380
Ross, Greg, *Rocky Mountain Naturalists*, 1235
Ross, Chris, *Association des Pompiers de Montréal inc.*, 124
Ross, Andy, *Canadian Office & Professional Employees Union*, 445
Ross, Alan, *British Columbia Courthouse Library Society*, 238
Ross, Joëlle, *Tourisme Gaspésie*, 1392
Ross, Joan, *Nova Scotia College of Physiotherapists*, 1043
Ross, Brad, *Minnedosa Chamber of Commerce*, 968
Ross, Stéphane, *Alliance internationale des employé(e)s de scène, de théâtre et de cinéma*, 57
Ross, John, *Registered Professional Foresters Association of Nova Scotia*, 1214
Ross, Shelley, *Canadian Association for Medical Education*, 302
Ross, Marian, *Canadian Payday Loan Association*, 452
Ross, Jenelle, *March of Dimes Canada*, 949
Ross, Sally E., *Ontario Golf Superintendents' Association*, 1083
Ross, Shawn, *Nova Scotia Arm Wrestling Association*, 1040
Ross-Arseneault, Hélène, *La Fondation canadienne du rein, section Chibougamau*, 743
Ross-Smith, Denny, *Small Water Users Association of BC*, 1304
Rossano, Joseph, *Canadian Security Association*, 469
Rossant, Janet, *The Gairdner Foundation*, 766
Rosser, Doug, *Canadian Federation of Mental Health Nurses*, 388
Rosseth, Lynn, *Foodservice & Packaging Institute*, 1526
Rossetti, Ros, *The Bruce Trail Conservancy*, 261
Rossetti, Brian, *Master Bowlers' Association of Alberta*, 953
Rossi, Rocco, *Ontario Chamber of Commerce*, 1071
Rossi, Kimberly, *Ontario Traffic Council*, 1111
Rossiter, Ashley, *Newfoundland & Labrador Association of Speech-Language Pathologists & Audiologists*, 1016
Rossner, Marilyn, *International Institute of Integral Human Sciences*, 858
Rossner, Marilyn Z., *Spiritual Science Fellowship/International Institute of Integral Human Sciences*, 1344
Rosu-Sieza, Luciana, *Bulimia Anorexia Nervosa Association*, 264
Rosval, Kim, *American Society of Heating, Refrigerating & Air Conditioning Engineers*, 1500
Rotchild, Leor, *Canadian Business for Social Responsibility*, 348

Executive Name Index

Roter, George, *Engineers Without Borders*, 689
Roth, Lauren, *Adventive Cross Cultural Initiatives*, 10
Roth, Jessica, *Leduc Regional Chamber of Commerce*, 906
Roth, Shirley, *Sexsmith & District Chamber of Commerce*, 1292
Roth, Judith, *Canadian Institute of Chartered Business Valuators*, 414
Roth, Melissa, *Teaching Support Staff Union*, 1368
Roth, Stephanie, *Skills/Compétences Canada*, 1303
Rothfuss, Barry, *Atlantic Wildlife Institute*, 186
Rothman, Avram, *Aish Thornhill Community Shul & Learning Centre*, 20
Rothon, Robert, *La Fédération des francophones de la Colombie-Britannique*, 715
Rothwell, Jillann, *Ontario Association of Library Technicians*, 1064
Rothwell, Kathleen, *Caregivers Nova Scotia*, 512
Rotstein, Stephen, *Financial Planning Standards Council*, 737
Rotter, David B., *Association of Children's Prosthetic-Orthotic Clinics*, 1510
Rouan, Judith, *Fédération du Québec pour le planning des naissances*, 720
Rouben, Denise, *Canadian Nuclear Society*, 442
Rouleau, Hans, *Association of Registrars of the Universities & Colleges of Canada*, 161
Rouleau, André, *Centre local de développement Rouyn-Noranda*, 536
Rouleau, Denis, *La Troupe du Jour*, 1399
Rouleau, Émilie, *L'Écluse des Laurentides*, 671
Roundpoint, Russell, *Native North American Traveling College*, 998
Roundpoint, Russell, *Mohawk Council of Akwesasne*, 971
Rourke, Tanja, *University of the Fraser Valley Faculty & Staff Association*, 1420
Rous, Chris, *Arts Council of Sault Ste Marie & District*, 85
Rouse, Kirsten, *Atlantic Salmon Federation*, 186
Roussain, James, *Archives Association of Ontario*, 80
Rousseau, Guillaume, *SPCA of Western Québec*, 1339
Rousseau, Megan, *Canadian Institute of Chartered Business Valuators*, 414
Rousseau, Natalie, *Orchestre symphonique de Trois-Rivières*, 1118
Rousseau, Carmen, *Société d'histoire d'Amos*, 1310
Rousseau, Peter L., *American Economic Association*, 1492
Rousseau, Larry, *Public Service Alliance of Canada*, 1193
Rousseau, Monique, *Réseau du patrimoine franco-ontarien*, 1222
Rousseau, Yvonne, *Allergy/Asthma Information Association*, 54
Rousseau, Richard, *HRMS Professionals Association*, 824
Rousseau, Robert, *RÉZO*, 1229
Rousselet, Denyse, *Association québécoise des traumatisés crâniens*, 175
Roussety, Daniel, *Canadian Amateur Musicians*, 292
Routhier, Michel, *Conseil régional FTQ Saguenay-Lac-St-Jean-Chibougamau-Chapais*, 621
Routledge, Steve, *Newfoundland & Labrador Curling Association*, 1018
Routledge, Doug, *Council of Forest Industries*, 633
Routledge, Bryan, *Western Finance Association*, 1602
Routly, Bob, *Tavistock Chamber of Commerce*, 1367

Roux, Jean-Baptiste, *Alliance Française de Calgary*, 57
Roux, Clive, *Society for Environmental Graphic Design*, 1590
Rowan, Andrew, *The Humane Society of the United States*, 1530
Rowat, Theresa, *Réseau des services d'archives du Québec*, 1222
Rowbotham, Michael, *International Association for the Study of Pain*, 1537
Rowbotham, Wayne, *Orillia & District Construction Association*, 1126
Rowe, Darrell, *St. Leonard's Society of Canada*, 1250
Rowe, Craig, *Canada - Newfoundland & Labrador Offshore Petroleum Board*, 277
Rowe, Darrell, *Ontario Halfway House Association*, 1083
Rowe, Sheldon, *United Way Alberta Northwest*, 1413
Rowe, Penelope M., *Community Sector Council, Newfoundland & Labrador*, 607
Rowe, Sandra, *Canadian Horse Breeders' Association*, 408
Rowell, Petra, *Nature Alberta*, 999
Rowland, Douglas S., *Friends of The Canadian War Museum*, 762
Rowland, Phil, *The Western Stock Growers' Association*, 1450
Rowlands, Fiona, *Canadian Association for Young Children*, 307
Rowlands, Alison, *Canadian Association of Critical Care Nurses*, 311
Rowlands, Joyce, *College of Registered Psychotherapists of Ontario*, 590
Rowledge, Joseph, *Bell Aliant Pioneers*, 204
Rowley, Liz, *Communist Party of Canada*, 594
Rowley, Saskia, *Canadian Church Press*, 356
Rowsell, Harold, *Shelter for Helpless Animals in Distress*, 1295
Rowsell, Leona, *Insurance Institute of Newfoundland & Labrador Inc.*, 849
Roxborough Brown, Dianne, *New Brunswick Choral Federation*, 1006
Roxburgh, Kathryn, *Jersey Canada*, 869
Roxburgh, Doug, *Alberta Maine-Anjou Association*, 39
Roxburgh, Bruce, *Green Communities Canada*, 788
Roy, Anne-Marie, *Association pour la promotion des services documentaires scolaires*, 166
Roy, Yoland, *Fédération québécoise du théâtre amateur*, 731
Roy, Carole, *Canadian Association for the Study of Adult Education*, 306
Roy, Michael, *Fibrose kystique Québec*, 733
Roy, Nathalie, *Chambre de commerce de Saint-Georges*, 543
Roy, Jane, *London Food Bank*, 918
Roy, Sheila, *Appraisal Institute of Canada*, 74
Roy, Ivan, *Association des MBA du Québec*, 119
Roy, Francis, *Association de la construction du Québec*, 100
Roy, Graeme, *The Canadian Press*, 459
Roy, Margaret, *Dystonia Medical Research Foundation Canada*, 666
Roy, Anne, *Association québécoise de l'épilepsie*, 169
Roy, Monic, *Réseau FADOQ*, 1224
Roy, Sylvain, *Ontario Psychological Association*, 1098
Roy, Yves, *Municipal Law Enforcement Officers' Association*, 981
Roy, Maya, *Newcomer Women's Services Toronto*, 1015
Roy, Myrella, *Canadian Society of Hospital Pharmacists*, 483
Roy, Brendon, *Royal Astronomical Society of Canada*, 1239
Roy, Sylvain, *Centraide KRTB-Côte-du-Sud*, 522
Roy, Nichol, *Alberta College of Combined Laboratory & X-Ray Technologists*, 29

Roy, Lise, *Centre St-Pierre*, 536
Roy, Joëlle, *Association québécoise des avocats et avocates de la défense*, 171
Roy, Amy, *Ontario Community Justice Association*, 1073
Roy, Jean, *Société canadienne d'histoire de l'Église Catholique - Section française*, 1307
Roy, Lisa, *Learning for a Sustainable Future*, 905
Roy, Maya, *YWCA Canada*, 1481
Roy, Toe-Blake, *Bibles & Literature in French Canada*, 208
Roy, Mike, *New Brunswick Outfitters Association Inc.*, 1011
Roy, Andreé, *Réseau des SADC et CAE*, 1221
Roy, Denis, *Institut de cardiologie de Montréal*, 841
Roy, Valérie, *Regroupement québécois des organismes pour le développement de l'employabilité*, 1216
Roy, Jean-Yves, *Institut national d'optique*, 843
Roy, Geneviève, *Tourisme Laval*, 1393
Roy, Alain, *Association maritime du Québec*, 137
Roy, Jean Stéphane, *Théâtre la Catapulte*, 1374
Roy, Kishone Tony, *British Columbia Non-Profit Housing Association*, 248
Roy, Réjean, *L'arc-en-ciel littéraire*, 76
Roy, Bruce, *Horse Industry Association of Alberta*, 822
Roy, Bill, *Canadian Registry of Tennessee Walking Horse*, 466
Roy, Julie, *Alberta Percheron Club*, 42
Roy, Cyril, *PEI Cricket Association*, 1148
Roy, Alexandra, *Karate Canada*, 881
Roy-Brenneis, Derek, *Emil Skarin Fund*, 686
Roy-Patenaude, Nathalie, *Appraisal Institute of Canada*, 74
Roy-Wsiaki, Genevieve, *Manitoba Association for Behaviour Analysis*, 208
Royal, Marie, *Société d'histoire et de généalogie de Salaberry*, 1313
Roybedy, Melanie, *New Brunswick Association of Medical Radiation Technologists*, 1005
Royce, Diana, *AllerGen NCE Inc.*, 54
Royea, Arlene, *Brome County Historical Society*, 260
Royer, Donald, *Parasports Québec*, 1139
Royer, Donald, *Canadian Wheelchair Sports Association*, 504
Royer, Ronald, *Scarborough Philharmonic Orchestra*, 1282
Royko, Lee, *CARP*, 514
Royle, Catherine, *Vancouver Island Miniature Horse Club*, 1426
Roze, Lucas, *New Brunswick Building Officials Association*, 1006
Rozman, Erin, *Douglas College Faculty Association*, 661
Ruano, Jessica, *Canadian Council for International Co-operation*, 366
Rubel, Julie, *Gerontological Nursing Association of Ontario*, 772
Rubin, Lisa, *Segal Centre for the Performing Arts at the Saidye*, 1289
Rubin, Shira, *Nova Scotia Amateur Bodybuilding Association*, 1040
Rubinstein, Mark, *Alpine Canada Alpin*, 59
Rubuliak, Deena, *University of British Columbia Faculty Association*, 1419
Rudderham, Cheryl, *Nova Scotia Forest Technicians Association*, 1045
Ruddiman, Alan, *Doctors of BC*, 660
Ruddock, Janice, *Taste of Nova Scotia*, 1367
Ruddock, Laura, *Covenant Foundation*, 637
Ruddy, Anne, *World at Work*, 1603
Rude-Weisman, Bonnie, *Psychologists Association of Alberta*, 1192
Rudelich, Ron, *Covenant Health*, 637
Rudin, Jonathan, *Aboriginal Legal Services of Toronto*, 2
Rudko, Lauren, *Canadian Urban Transit Association*, 500
Rudland, Rand, *Sargeant Bay Society*, 1253

Rudy, Harold, *Ontario Soil & Crop Improvement Association*, 1108
Rudy, Harold, *Ontario Seed Growers Association*, 1104
Rudzitis, Mara, *L'Association des artistes Baltes à Montréal*, 106
Rueger, Trevor, *Alberta Playwrights' Network*, 42
Ruehlen, Perry, *Disaster Recovery Institute Canada*, 658
Ruehlicke, Frank, *Canadian Micro-Mineral Association*, 436
Ruest, Tina, *Development & Peace*, 654
Ruetz, John P., *Catholic Health Sponsors of Ontario*, 520
Ruf, Cory, *Dying with Dignity*, 665
Ruggera, Alessandro, *Italian Cultural Institute (Istituto Italiano di Cultura)*, 866
Ruggero, Sue, *Ontario Society for Environmental Management*, 1105
Ruggle, Richard, *Organization of Military Museums of Canada*, 1126
Ruivo, Sergio, *Federation of Portuguese Canadian Business & Professionals Inc.*, 726
Ruiz, Crystal, *American Ornithological Society*, 1496
Ruiz-Pilarte, Claudio, *Hispanic Canadian Heritage Council*, 815
Rukhledev, Valery, *International Committee of Sports for the Deaf*, 1543
Rumball, David E., *Royal Heraldry Society of Canada*, 1242
Rumball, Derek, *Bob Rumball Foundation for the Deaf*, 217
Rumscheidt, Natalie, *Coaching Association of Canada*, 577
Runciman, Mark C., *Royal Botanical Gardens*, 1239
Rundle, Bob, *Association of Professional Engineers & Geoscientists of Alberta*, 157
Rundle, Jami, *Governor General's Performing Arts Awards Foundation*, 778
Runkle, Nathan, *Mercy for Animals Canada*, 961
Rupasinghe, H.P. Vasantha, *Canadian Institute of Food Science & Technology*, 415
Rupert, Bob, *Ontario Fire Buff Associates*, 1080
Rupp, Melanie, *Canadian Pony Club*, 457
Rupp, David W., *Canadian Institute in Greece*, 414
Ruse, Kim, *Calgary Women's Emergency Shelter Association*, 275
Rusel, Walter, *Ukrainian Genealogical & Historical Society of Canada*, 1403
Rusen, Stephanie, *Canadian Hadassah WIZO*, 399
Rush, John, *International Society for Affective Disorders*, 1557
Rushowick, Geoffrey, *Nature Saskatchewan*, 1001
Rushton, Shelby, *Lifesaving Society*, 911
Rushton, Amber, *Ontario Association of Emergency Managers*, 1063
Rusinek, Dahlia, *National Council of Jewish Women of Canada*, 992
Rusonik, Ellie, *Geneva Centre for Autism*, 769
Russel, Dunbar, *Canadian Blood Services*, 344, 345
Russell, Ron, *Saint Mary's University Faculty Union*, 1247
Russell, Ken, *Pentecostal Assemblies of Canada*, 1150
Russell, Dianne, *Flin Flon & District Chamber of Commerce*, 740
Russell, Betty, *Blenheim & District Chamber of Commerce*, 214
Russell, Mike, *Canadian Association of Exposition Management*, 313
Russell, Todd, *Saskatchewan Building Officials Association Inc.*, 1260
Russell, Jim, *Huntington Society of Canada*, 828
Russell, Rebecca, *Ontario Recreation Facilities Association*, 1100

Executive Name Index

Russell, Jim, *United Way of Peterborough & District*, 1416
Russell, Michele, *Canadian Progress Charitable Foundation*, 460
Russell, Cheryl, *Gymnastics Saskatchewan*, 795
Russell, Carmen, *American Sociological Association*, 1503
Russell, Ian, *Investment Industry Association of Canada*, 863
Russell, Sandy, *Schneider Office Employees' Association*, 1284
Russell, Tamara, *Attractions Ontario*, 187
Russell, Steve, *American Chemistry Council*, 1491
Russell, Glen, *Newfoundland & Labrador Brain Injury Association*, 1017
Russell, Colin, *Kamloops Exploration Group*, 880
Russo, Dino, *Ontario Refrigeration & Air Conditioning Contractors Association*, 1101
Russo, Frank, *Canadian Acoustical Association*, 287
Russo, Ben, *Northwest Territories Association of Architects*, 1037
Russwurm, Reg, *Municipal Engineers Association*, 981
Russwurm, Reg, *Ontario Water Works Association*, 1113
Rust, Scott, *British Columbia Floor Covering Association*, 241
Ruston, Richard, *People First of Ontario*, 1151
Ruszkowski, Jean-Paul, *Parliamentary Centre*, 1142
Ruta, Andrzej M., *Polish Combatants Association*, 1164
Ruth, Micki, *Canadian Association of Police Governance*, 328
Rutherford, Sally, *Canadian Association for Graduate Studies*, 300
Rutherford, Janice, *Manitoba Percheron & Belgian Club*, 942
Rutledge, Melanie, *Magazines Canada*, 925
Rutledge, Mark, *Society of Graphic Designers of Canada*, 1329
Rutsey, William P., *Canadian Gaming Association*, 396
Ruttan, Stephen, *Friends of Ecological Reserves*, 761
Rutten, Stuart, *Darts Ontario*, 651
Rutter, Blair, *Western Canadian Wheat Growers*, 1449
Ruttman, Kelly, *Environmental Information Association*, 1523
Ruzic, Tamara, *Saskatchewan Organization for Heritage Languages Inc.*, 1271
Ruzicka, John, *Alberta Percheron Club*, 42
Ruzicka, Karen, *Alberta Percheron Club*, 42
Ryall, Lorne, *Manitoba Association of Optometrists*, 930
Ryall, Shauna, *Canadian Society of Cardiology Technologists Inc.*, 481
Ryall, Shauna, *Cardiology Technologists' Association of British Columbia*, 511
Ryall, Patrick, *Nova Scotian Institute of Science*, 1050
Ryan, Loretta, *Association of Local Public Health Agencies*, 150
Ryan, Don, *Canadian Amateur Wrestling Association*, 292
Ryan, Lionel, *Professional Engineers Ontario*, 1184
Ryan, Loretta, *Ontario Professional Planners Institute*, 1098
Ryan, Jamie, *New Brunswick Real Estate Association*, 1011
Ryan, Glenda, *Canadian Association of Cardio-Pulmonary Technologists*, 309
Ryan, Patrick, *Risk & Insurance Management Society Inc.*, 1234
Ryan, Eileen, *British Columbia Art Teachers' Association*, 230
Ryan, Derek J., *Canadian Chito-Ryu Karate-Do Association*, 356

Ryan, Colleen, *Pathways to Education Canada*, 1145
Ryan, Carole Ann, *Skills/Compétences Canada*, 1303
Ryan, Elizabeth, *National Association for Environmental Management*, 1572
Ryan, Basil, *Atlantic Association of Community Business Development Corporations*, 182
Ryan, Carey, *Offshore Energy Research Association of Nova Scotia*, 1055
Ryan, Dominic, *Canadian Institute for Neutron Scattering*, 413
Ryan, Kim, *Saskatchewan Freestyle Ski Incorporated*, 1265
Ryan, Derek J., *Karate Newfoundland & Labrador*, 882
Ryan, Jylene, *Biathlon Nova Scotia*, 207
Ryba, Thomas, *International Husserl & Phenomenological Research Society*, 1550
Rybuck, Cory, *Manitoba Egg Farmers*, 936
Rydell, Catherine M., *American Academy of Neurology*, 1488
Ryder, Guy, *International Labour Organization*, 1552
Rydzik, Suzanne, *Association pour l'intégration sociale d'Ottawa*, 166
Ryeland, Andrew, *Parry Sound Area Chamber of Commerce*, 1143
Ryffel, Hans, *Edmonton Radial Railway Society*, 679
Ryland, Al, *Glass & Architectural Metals Association*, 774
Rymberg, Gustavo, *Hamilton Jewish Federation*, 801
Rymer, Roy R.R., *Model Aeronautics Association of Canada Inc.*, 970
Ryshpan, Arden R., *Canadian Actors' Equity Association (CLC)*, 288
Ryterband, Eva, *Fenestration Canada*, 732

S

Sa'd, Randy, *Floorball Canada*, 741
Saa, Ann, *Immigrant & Multicultural Services Society*, 830
Saas, Lynne, *Provincial Association of Resort Communities of Saskatchewan*, 1190
Sabados, Darcie, *Vegreville & District Chamber of Commerce*, 1430
Sabattis, Joe, *Atlantic Region Aboriginal Lands Association*, 186
Sabean, Doris, *Music for Young Children*, 984
Sabeski, Patti, *Manitoba Baton Twirling Sportive Association*, 932
Sablatnig, Al, *Aerospace Heritage Foundation of Canada*, 11
Sablok, Akash, *The Society of Notaries Public of British Columbia*, 1330
Sabourin, Rénald, *PIJAC Canada*, 1159
Sabourin, Rénald, *Pet Industry Joint Advisory Council*, 1153
Sabourin, Serge, *Fédération de gymnastique du Québec*, 708
Sabourin, Françoise, *Soeurs de Sainte-Marie de Namur*, 1331
Sabourin, Francine, *Ordre des administrateurs agréés du Québec*, 1120
Sabourin, Yvan, *Ensemble vocal Ganymède*, 690
Sabraw, Colleen, *Early Childhood Intervention Program (ECIP) Sask. Inc.*, 667
Saby, Tamara, *Habitat for Humanity Canada*, 796
Saccani, Petra, *Italian Chamber of Commerce in Canada - West*, 866
Sachdev, Brenda, *Trillium Automobile Dealers' Association*, 1398
Sachdev, Neelu, *Regina Immigrant Women Centre*, 1212
Sachvie, Lauren, *Squash Ontario*, 1347
Sactouris, Hélène, *Chambre de commerce de Cowansville et région*, 540
Sacy, Hubert, *Éduc'alcool*, 680
Sade, Danielle, *Canadian Federation of Aromatherapists*, 385

Sadej, Andrzej, *Judo Canada*, 876
Sader, Naeem, *Islamic Association of Saskatchewan*, 864
Sadhra, Ruminder, *Burnaby Multicultural Society*, 266
Sadler, Roby, *Oraynu Congregation for Humanistic Judaism*, 1117
Sado, Anne, *Toronto Region Board of Trade*, 1387
Sadoun, Joseph, *Canadian Association of Broadcast Consultants*, 309
Safarian, Mona, *Ontario Cooperative Education Association*, 1075
Safer, Jordan, *Toronto Blues Society*, 1382
Safer, Jordan, *Music Managers Forum Canada*, 984
Sagar, Bob, *Yukon Orienteering Association*, 1479
Sage, Leslie, *Canadian Astronomical Society*, 337
Sageau, Julie, *Ordre des ingénieurs du Québec*, 1122
Sagel, Debbie, *University of Regina Faculty Association*, 1420
Sagin, Donna, *Swift Current Agricultural & Exhibition Association*, 1358
Sahib, Gurdwara, *Khalsa Diwan Society*, 884
Sahib, Iltaf, *British Columbia Muslim Association*, 247
Sahota, Satinder, *Support Organization for Trisomy 18, 13 & Related Disorders*, 1356
Sahota, Surrinder S., *Canadian Associated Air Balance Council*, 297
Sahota, Neelam, *DIVERSEcity Community Resources Society*, 659
Saikaley, Laila, *Army, Navy & Air Force Veterans in Canada*, 83
Sailer, Steve, *Denturist Association of Canada*, 653
Saine, André, *Québec Association of Naturopathic Medicine*, 1196
Saini, Ranjit, *Cricket Canada*, 642
Sainsbury, Kristin, *Stratford Tourism Alliance*, 1351
Saint-Aubin, Claire L., *Société historique de Joliette-De Lanaudière*, 1320
Saint-Georges, Andrée, *Conseil de la culture de Lanaudière*, 616
Saint-Pierre, Josée, *Fondation des étoiles*, 745
St. Amand, Mike, *Canadian Catholic School Trustees' Association*, 351
St. Amant, Debbie, *The Regional Health Authorities of Manitoba*, 1212
St. Croix, Gail, *Newfoundland & Labrador Association for Community Living*, 1015
St. Croix, Robyn, *Canadian Association of Pharmacy Students & Interns*, 326
St. Denis, Diane, *Canada West Universities Athletic Association*, 281
St. George, Gerry, *Canadian National Railways Police Association (Ind.)*, 440
St. Germain, Judy, *Urology Nurses of Canada*, 1423
St. Germain, Penny, *Temagami & District Chamber of Commerce*, 1370
St. Godard, Jo-Anne, *Recycling Council of Ontario*, 1209
St. Hilaire, Ashley, *Canadian Organic Growers Inc.*, 446
St. Jean, Noel, *College of Alberta Professional Foresters*, 582
St. Jean, Carrie, *PEI Teacher-Librarians' Association*, 1149
St. John, John, *Canadian Culinary Federation*, 374
St. John, Neil, *Canadian Centre for Ethics & Corporate Policy*, 353
Ste-Marie, Eddie, *Canadian Labour Congress*, 425
Ste-Marie, Janique, *Ordre des hygiénistes dentaires du Québec*, 1121
St. Onge, Elizabeth, *Osteoporosis Canada*, 1128
Saintonge, Martin, *Canadian Institute for Theatre Technology*, 414

St. Onge, Trish, *Catholic Family Services of Saskatoon*, 519
St. Onge, Jordan, *Saskatchewan Amateur Speed Skating Association*, 1255
Sakaki, Claire, *Bard on the Beach Theatre Society*, 196
Salam, Khaled, *AIDS Committee of Ottawa*, 16
Salamon, Boris, *Ukrainian Fraternal Society of Canada*, 1403
Saldivar, Juan, *Project Management Institute*, 1585
Sale, Geoff, *Applied Science Technologists & Technicians of British Columbia*, 74
Salée, Daniel, *Société québécoise de science politique*, 1324
Salen, Warren, *Melfort & District Chamber of Commerce*, 959
Sales, Cherry-Lyn, *Ontario Good Roads Association*, 1083
Salesse, Isabelle, *Association franco-yukonnaise*, 136
Salesse, Isabelle, *Réseau pour le développement de l'alphabétisme et des compétences*, 1225
Saley, Samantha, *Ontario Brain Injury Association*, 1069
Saliba, Soraya, *McMan Youth, Family & Community Services Association*, 956
Saliga, Pauline, *Society of Architectural Historians*, 1592
Salisbury, Jaki, *Chartered Institute of Public Finance & Accountancy*, 1516
Salkeld, Mark, *Petroleum Services Association of Canada*, 1154
Sallete, Nadia, *International Association for Medical Assistance to Travellers*, 853
Salloum, Doug, *Canadian Society for Civil Engineering*, 474
Sallows, Robert, *Canadian Transplant Association*, 496
Sallstrom, Linda, *St Paul & District Chamber of Commerce*, 1251
Sallustio-Jarvis, Gioia, *Coalition des femmes de l'Alberta*, 578
Salmon, Chuck, *Association of British Columbia Land Surveyors*, 140
Salmon, Ruth, *Canadian Aquaculture Industry Alliance*, 294
Salois, Manon, *International Association of Infant Massage Canada*, 854
Salonga Tapia, Carmelita, *Southeast Asia-Canada Business Council*, 1337
Saloojee, Anver, *Ryerson Faculty Association*, 1244
Salsberg, Jan, *Ontario Genealogical Society*, 1082
Salsman, Theresa, *Real Estate Institute of Canada*, 1206
Salsman, Gayle, *College of Occupational Therapists of Nova Scotia*, 587
Salter Dorland, Anne, *Sudbury Manitoulin Children's Foundation*, 1353
Saltman, Roger, *American Association of Bovine Practitioners*, 1489
Saltonstall, Peter L., *National Organization for Rare Disorders, Inc.*, 1577
Saltz, Renato, *American Society for Aesthetic Plastic Surgery*, 1497
Salvador, Robert, *Society of Fire Protection Engineers*, 1593
Salvador, Leonora, *Association of Filipino Canadian Accountants*, 148
Salvadori, Mario, *Eucharistic Apostles of the Divine Mercy*, 698
Salvatore, David, *Manitoba Real Estate Association*, 943
Salvatori, Michael, *Ontario College of Teachers*, 1072
Salvini, Julia, *Canadian Institute of Transportation Engineers*, 420
Salzman, Heather, *Beaverton Thorah Eldon Historical Society*, 203
Sam-Foh, Claude, *Emmaus Canada*, 686
Samad, Taimur, *Islamic Association of Saskatchewan*, 864

Executive Name Index

Samdup, Carole, *Canada Tibet Committee*, 280
Samelo, Maria Evelyn, *Canadian Institute of Food Science & Technology*, 415
Sametz, Peter, *Saskatchewan Orchestral Association, Inc.*, 1270
Sami, Fahad, *Canadian Association of Medical Radiation Technologists*, 320
Sammut, Grace, *Resorts Ontario*, 1226
Sampaio, Nathalie, *Alliance du personnel professionel et administratif de Ville de Laval*, 56
Sampley, Gary, *Edmonton Epilepsy Association*, 677
Sampson, Jan, *Chartered Professional Accountants of British Columbia*, 553
Samray, Jean-François, *Association québécoise de la production d'énergie renouvelable*, 170
Samson, Robert A., *International Union of Microbiological Societies*, 1564
Samson, Roger, *Resource Efficient Agricultural Production*, 1227
Samson, Yvon, *Fédération acadienne de la Nouvelle-Écosse*, 707
Samson, Isabelle, *Association des médecins spécialistes en santé communautaire du Québec*, 120
Samson, Nancy, *British Columbia Turkey Farms*, 257
Samson, Gilbert, *Société d'histoire régionale de Lévis*, 1313
Samson, Linda, *Ordre des opticiens d'ordonnances du Québec*, 1123
Samusevich, Alla, *Association of Consulting Engineering Companies - British Columbia*, 145
Samworth, Clare, *Medico-Legal Society of Toronto*, 959
Samworth, Phillioa, *Medico-Legal Society of Toronto*, 959
San Jose, Mia, *Canadian Education Association*, 380
Sánchez, Julia, *Canadian Council for International Co-operation*, 366
Sanchez, Andrea E., *International Facility Management Association*, 1546
Sanchez, Diego, *Parents, Families & Friends of Lesbians & Gays*, 1582
Sanchez, Maritza, *Jessie's - The June Callwood Centre for Young Women*, 870
Sanchez, Paolo, *Association of Filipino Canadian Accountants in British Columbia*, 148
Sancho, U. Leebert, *Guyana Cultural Association of Montréal*, 794
Sand, Kathy, *Canada Employment & Immigration Union*, 279
Sand, Gordon, *John Howard Society of Alberta*, 874
Sande, Jennifer, *Manitoba League of Persons with Disabilities*, 939
Sander, Nicole, *Canadian Deafblind Association (National)*, 376
Sanders, Nick, *Fort McMurray Chamber of Commerce*, 753
Sanders, Garth, *Concrete Sask*, 610
Sanders, Nora, *United Church of Canada*, 1409
Sanders, Paula, *Independent Living Canada*, 833
Sanders, Alvin, *Alliance of Canadian Cinema, Television & Radio Artists*, 58
Sanders, Madeleine, *Project Management Institute*, 1585
Sanders, Michelle, *Ontario Commercial Rabbit Growers' Association*, 1073
Sanders, Richard, *Coalition to Oppose the Arms Trade*, 579
Sanderson, Stanley (Sam), *Construction Association of Prince Edward Island*, 623
Sanderson, Lauranne, *Canadian Agricultural Safety Association*, 290
Sandford, Dave, *Ontario Gymnastic Federation*, 1083

Sandhals, Lyric, *Northwest Territories Volleyball Association*, 1039
Sandhals, Lyric, *Northwest Territories Soccer Association*, 1038
Sandholm, Phillipa, *World Federation of the Deaf*, 1605
Sandhu, Pria, *Resident Doctors of British Columbia*, 1226
Sandhu, Sudhir, *Manitoba Building & Construction Trades Council*, 933
Sandino, Daysi, *Canadian Society of Gastroenterology Nurses & Associates*, 483
Sandler, Jordan, *Canadian Association of Management Consultants*, 320
Sandler, Mark J., *Law Foundation of Ontario*, 901
Sandor, Mihaela, *Réseau environnement*, 1223
Sandron, Brigitte, *Travel Manitoba*, 1396
Sandul, Shirley, *Project Adult Literacy Society*, 1187
Sandusky, Vincent R., *Sheet Metal & Air Conditioning Contractors' National Association*, 1588
Sandvold, Laura, *Canadian Dental Hygienists Association*, 377
Sandy, Surranna, *Skills for Change*, 1302
Sanford, Jenniffer, *Block Watch Society of British Columbia*, 215
Sanford, Lorraine, *British Columbia Angus Association*, 230
Sanford, Kathy, *Canadian Association for the Study of Women & Education*, 306
Sanford, Cindy, *Canadian Association for Williams Syndrome*, 307
Sanford, John, *Council on Palliative Care*, 636
Sangha, Purdeep, *Social Planning & Research Council of Hamilton*, 1306
Sangha, Harmale, *British Columbia Business Educators Association*, 234
Sanghera, Kanwaljit, *Information Services Vancouver*, 837
Sangster, Michael, *Canadian AIDS Society*, 290
Sanguinetti, Dominique, *Arts Etobicoke*, 85
Sangwoo Kim, David, *Korean Canadian Society of London*, 893
Sankar, Sharon E., *Association of Professional Engineers & Geoscientists of Manitoba*, 158
Sankey, Linda, *South Okanagan Similkameen Brain Injury Society*, 1335
Sankey, John, *Pesticide Education Network*, 1153
Santacruz, Victor, *Canadian Nursery Landscape Association*, 442
Santamaria, Alicia, *Ontario Society for the Prevention of Cruelty to Animals*, 1106
Santerre-Bélec, Laurence, *Association des techniciens en santé animale du Québec*, 129
Santhakumar, Vadivelu, *Canadian Tamil Congress*, 492
Santiago, Rod, *Abbotsford Community Services*, 1
Santiago, Karyn, *Communitas Supportive Care Society*, 595
Santonja, Rafael, *International Federation of Bodybuilding & Fitness*, 1547
Santoro, Sabrina, *British Columbia Salmon Farmers Association*, 252
Santoro, M. Gabriella, *Cell Stress Society International*, 1516
Santoro, Miléna, *Association internationale des études québécoises*, 136
Santos, Nimfa, *Association of Filipino Canadian Accountants*, 148
Santos, Ana, *Central Coast Chamber of Commerce*, 524
Santucci, Joanne, *Hamilton Food Share*, 801
Sanz de Acedo, Etienne, *International Trademark Association*, 1563
Saporta, Adam, *Canadian Association of Ambulatory Care*, 308
Saptel, Frank, *Canadian Labour International Film Festival*, 425

Sarabura, Philip, *Brantford Symphony Orchestra Association Inc.*, 227
Saranchuk, Susan, *Canadian Society of Cinematographers*, 481
Saratsiotis, Fotios, *Learning Enrichment Foundation*, 905
Saravanamuttoo, Colin, *Canadian Ski Patrol*, 471
Sarcevic, Ado, *Red Deer City Soccer Association*, 1209
Sardinha, Joe, *British Columbia Fruit Growers' Association*, 242
Saretsky, Laura, *Heritage Society of British Columbia*, 813
Sarfin, Ian, *Canadian Culinary Federation*, 374
Sargent, Tim, *Jersey Canada*, 869
Sargent, Mike, *Natural Resources Union*, 999
Sargent, Tasha, *North American Waterfowl Management Plan*, 1029
Sargent, Tasha, *North American Waterfowl Management Plan*, 1029
Sargent, Chantal, *Consulting Engineers of Alberta*, 625
Sarian, Lilian, *Armenian Relief Society of Canada, Inc.*, 83
Saric, Sandra, *Information & Communications Technology Council of Canada*, 836
Sark-Carr, Tiffany, *First Nations Confederacy of Cultural Education Centres*, 738
Sarkesian, Teresa, *Electricity Distributors Association*, 683
Sarkissian, Varsenig, *Armenian Relief Society of Canada, Inc.*, 83
Sarmiento, Antonio, *Cameco Capitol Arts Centre*, 276
Sarna, C. Scott, *Association of Professional Engineers & Geoscientists of Manitoba*, 158
Sarnese, Mel, *The Ontario Poetry Society*, 1096
Sarny, Dominique, *Assemblée communautaire fransaskoise*, 87
Sarracini, Diane, *North American Recycled Rubber Association*, 1029
Sarrazin, Janik, *Association d'oto-rhino-laryngologie et de chirurgie cervico-faciale du Québec*, 99
Sartorelli, Brian, *Council of Private Investigators - Ontario*, 635
Sasaki, Mari, *Calgary Japanese Community Association*, 273
Sashaw, Keith, *Association of Consulting Engineering Companies - British Columbia*, 145
Sasouni, Renette, *Reach Canada*, 1205
Sass, Brigitte, *Focolare Movement - Canada*, 741
Satgunaraj, Suba, *Centre for Immigrant & Community Services*, 532
Sather, Tanya, *Burnaby Association for Community Inclusion*, 265
Satin, Tracy, *Okanagan Historical Society*, 1055
Sattar Rahimi, Abdul, *Muslim Association of New Brunswick*, 985
Sattin, Allan J., *Sport Dispute Resolution Centre of Canada*, 1344
Sattler, Lisa, *Association of Home Appliance Manufacturers Canada Council*, 149
Saucier, Julie, *L'Institut d'assurance de dommages du Québec*, 841
Saucier, Healther, *Alberta Simmental Association*, 46
Saucier, Marc-André, *Centre de la Communauté sourde du Montréal métropolitain*, 529
Sauder, Allan, *Mennonite Economic Development Associates Canada*, 961
Sauder, Kim, *Federated Women's Institutes of Ontario*, 707
Sauer, Dave, *Winnipeg Labour Council*, 1459
Sauer, Elaine, *Evangelical Lutheran Church in Canada*, 698
Sauerlender, Darrel, *Accessible Media Inc.*, 5
Sauks, Robyn, *Association of Sign Language Interpreters of Alberta*, 162

Saul, Graham, *Nature Canada*, 999
Saul, Mike, *Salmon Arm Bay Nature Enhancement Society*, 1252
Sauliner, Nathalie, *Kidney Foundation of Canada*, 885
Saull, John W., *International Federation of Airworthiness*, 1547
Saulnier, Marcel, *Chambre de commerce de Clare*, 540
Saulnier, Christine, *Canadian Centre for Policy Alternatives*, 354
Saulnier, Carole, *Association des archivistes du Québec*, 106
Saulnier, Charles, *Association des Gestionnaires de l'information de la santé du Québec*, 115
Saulnier-Taylor, Mary, *Coverdale Centre for Women Inc.*, 637
Sault, Debbie, *Thunder Bay Indian Friendship Centre*, 1378
Saumier Demers, Marylène, *Société francophone de Victoria*, 1319
Saunders, Richard, *Cree-Naskapi Commission*, 641
Saunders, Betty, *Boys & Girls Clubs of Newfoundland & Labrador*, 223
Saunders, Brad, *Community Living Toronto*, 605
Saunders, Weena, *James Bay Association for Community Living*, 868
Saunders, Bill, *Belleville & District Chamber of Commerce*, 204
Saunders, Phil, *Canadian Public Relations Society Inc.*, 463
Saunders, Jeffrey, *Anthroposophical Society in Canada*, 72
Saunders, Dave, *Canadian Celiac Association*, 352
Saunders, Kathy, *Canadian Institute of Plumbing & Heating*, 418
Saunders, Glenn, *International Personnel Management Association - Canada*, 859
Saunders, Scott, *Council of Ontario Construction Associations*, 634
Saunders, L. Duncan, *Canadian Society for International Health*, 475
Saunders, Liz, *Horse Council British Columbia*, 822
Saunders, Rick, *Royal Astronomical Society of Canada*, 1238
Saunders, David, *The War Amputations of Canada*, 1440
Saunders, Angela, *Lunenburg Marine Museum Society*, 921
Saunders, Marcey, *Human Resources Professionals Association*, 825
Saunders, Mark, *Field Hockey BC*, 734
Saunders, Linda, *Friends of The Moncton Hospital Foundation*, 763
Saunders, Darren, *Coalition sida des sourds du Québec*, 579
Saunders, Danny, *Ultimate Canada*, 1404
Saunders, Brenda, *Dress for Success*, 663
Saunders, Sue, *CADORA Ontario Association Inc.*, 269
Saundry, Peter D., *National Council for Science & the Environment*, 1575
Sautner, Linda, *Alberta Bison Association*, 26
Sauvage, Suzanne, *McCord Museum of Canadian History*, 955
Sauvageau, Philippe, *Conseil de la culture des régions de Québec et de Chaudière-Appalaches*, 616
Sauvageau, Philippe, *Association québécoise des salons du livre*, 174
Sauvageau, Jean, *Federation of New Brunswick Faculty Associations*, 725
Sauvageau, Normand, *Association des procureurs de cours municipales du Québec*, 124
Sauvageau, Denis, *Association provinciale des constructeurs d'habitations du Québec inc.*, 168
Sauvé, Jeff, *Field Hockey Canada*, 734
Sauvé, Conrad, *Canadian Red Cross*, 466

Executive Name Index

Sauvé, Jean-Luc, *Canadian Ski Patrol*, 471
Sauvé, Dorianne, *Ontario Physiotherapy Association*, 1096
Sauvé, Karol, *Aviron Québec*, 191
Sauvé, Daniel, *Association des professionnels de la chanson et de la musique*, 125
Sauvey, Robert, *Dance Umbrella of Ontario*, 649
Savage, Rob, *Colleges Ontario*, 591
Savage, Lynda, *Ontario Association of Archers Inc.*, 1061
Savage, Judy, *Lions Gate Hospital Foundation*, 913
Savage, Jade, *Société d'entomologie du Québec*, 1310
Savage, Christy, *Ottawa South Community Association*, 1131
Savage, Doug, *Miniature Horse Club of Ontario*, 967
Savard, Marc, *Association des maîtres couvreurs du Québec*, 118
Savard, Michèle, *Conseil des directeurs médias du Québec*, 617
Savard, Caroline, *Société de criminologie du Québec*, 1314
Savard, Gabriel, *Office du tourisme et des congrès de Québec*, 1055
Savard, Jasmin, *Union des municipalités du Québec*, 1406
Savard, Caroline, *Carrefour de ressources en interculturel*, 515
Savard, Roland, *Association québécoise des parents d'enfants handicapés visuels*, 174
Savard, Jacques, *Radio Amateur Québec inc.*, 1202
Savard, Michel, *Association des médecins vétérinaires praticiens du Québec*, 120
Savard, Marc, *APCHQ - Montréal Métropolitain*, 73
Savard, Martine, *Association provinciale des constructeurs d'habitations du Québec inc.*, 168
Savary, Gilles, *Fortier Danse-Création*, 754
Savignac Dufour, Patrice, *Fédération des médecins résidents du Québec inc. (ind.)*, 716
Savitsky, Ellen, *Ontario Association of Architects*, 1061
Saviye, Sombo, *Association of Family Health Teams of Ontario*, 148
Savja, Raheem, *College of Opticians of British Columbia*, 587
Savoia, Vince, *The Tema Conter Memorial Trust*, 1370
Savoie, Carole, *La Maison de la culture inc.*, 926
Savoie, Véronique, *Chambre de commerce et du tourisme du Grand Caraquet*, 548
Savoie, Jean-Eudes, *New Brunswick Association of Nursing Homes, Inc.*, 1005
Savoie, Yves, *Multiple Sclerosis Society of Canada*, 980
Savoie, Guy, *Association des parents et amis de la personne atteinte de maladie mentale Rive-Sud*, 122
Savoie, Martin, *Sports Laval*, 1346
Savoie-Levesque, Veronique, *Société culturelle de la Baie des Chaleurs*, 1309
Savoy, George, *Savoy Foundation Inc.*, 1282
Saw, Janine, *British Columbia Association of Agricultural Fairs & Exhibitions*, 231
Sawa, Victor, *Regina Symphony Orchestra*, 1212
Sawatsky, Melissa, *Bulkley Valley Community Arts Council*, 264
Sawatzky, Dave, *Barrhead & District Chamber of Commerce*, 197
Sawatzky, Tammy, *Canadian Public Relations Society Inc.*, 463
Sawatzky, Russell, *Claresholm & District Chamber of Commerce*, 572
Sawelo, Victor, *Manitoba Historical Society*, 938
Sawler, Mark, *Horticulture Nova Scotia*, 822

Sawler, Vince, *All Terrain Vehicle Association of Nova Scotia*, 54
Sawyer, Rick, *Doctors Manitoba*, 660
Sawyer, Paula, *Indigenous Works*, 835
Sawyers, Utcha, *Boys & Girls Clubs of Ontario*, 223
Saxena, Anurag, *Canadian Association for Medical Education*, 302
Saxon, Chad, *Manitoba Beef Producers*, 932
Sayeau, Nancy, *Quinte Immigrant Services*, 1201
Sayers, Gail, *Ojibway Power Toboggan Association*, 1055
Sayward, Cheryl, *Southern Alberta Brain Injury Society*, 1337
Sbardella, Christine, *Ontario Coalition for Better Child Care*, 1071
Scace, Susan, *The Henry White Kinnear Foundation*, 812
Scaife, Fred R., *Red Deer Food Bank Society*, 1209
Scalella, Luis Alberto, *Fédération internationale des associations de producteurs de films*, 1525
Scaletta, Todd, *Chartered Professional Accountants of Manitoba*, 553
Scammell, Kim, *Catholic Women's League of Canada*, 520
Scanlon, David, *British Columbia Mountaineering Club*, 246
Scantlebury, Fraser, *United Way of Lanark County*, 1415
Scapillati, Nicholas, *FarmFolk CityFolk*, 706
Scaplen, Graeme, *New Brunswick Merit Contractors Association*, 1010
Scaramuzza, Andrea, *International Society for Pediatric & Adolescent Diabetes*, 1558
Scarborough, Debbie, *South Okanagan Women in Need Society*, 1335
Scarborough, Michelle, *National Angel Capital Organization*, 989
Scarlett, Rod, *Canadian Honey Council*, 408
Scarlett, Christie, *Churchill Park Family Care Society*, 569
Scarlett, Brenda, *Ontario Association for Geographic & Environmental Education*, 1061
Scarlett, Tracey, *Alberta Women Entrepreneurs*, 52
Scarrow, Roberta, *Centre Wellington Chamber of Commerce*, 536
Scassa, Cristina, *Etobicoke Humane Society*, 697
Schaaf, Tina-Marie, *Oshawa-Whitby Kiwanis Music & Theatre Festival*, 1128
Schaafsma, Jeff, *Risk & Insurance Management Society Inc.*, 1234
Schaal, Barbara A., *American Association for the Advancement of Science*, 1489
Schachtler, Linda, *Elizabeth House*, 685
Schacter, Brent, *Canadian Association of Provincial Cancer Agencies*, 329
Schadle, Lauren, *Financial Planning Association*, 1526
Schaefer, Anna, *Markland Homes Association*, 952
Schaeffer, Glenn, *Lutheran Church - Canada*, 922
Schafer, Ernie, *Mirror & District Museum Association*, 968
Schaffer, Martin, *Universala Esperanto-Asocio*, 1601
Schaffer, Peter, *Model Aeronautics Association of Canada Inc.*, 970
Schaffer, Don, *Local Government Management Association of British Columbia*, 917
Schaffner, Amanda, *British Columbia Association of Agricultural Fairs & Exhibitions*, 231
Schafler, Naomi, *Ontario Track 3 Ski Association for the Disabled*, 1110
Schaitberger, Harold A., *International Association of Fire Fighters (AFL-CIO/CLC)*, 1538

Schanck, Daniel, *Association des enterprises spécialiseés en eau du Québec*, 112
Schank, Doreen, *Alberta Genealogical Society*, 37
Schattmann, Sarah, *Canadian Federation of University Women*, 389
Schaub, Rene, *Alberta Target Archers Association*, 49
Schaufelberger, Bryce, *BC People First Society*, 202
Scheeder, Donna, *International Federation of Library Associations & Institutions*, 1548
Scheer, Andrew, *Conservative Party of Canada*, 622
Scheinberg, Stephen, *Canadian Friends of Peace Now (Shalom Achshav)*, 395
Scheinert, Michael F., *Association of Jewish Seniors*, 150
Schell, Susan, *Kawartha Lakes Real Estate Association*, 882
Schell, Karen, *Editors' Association of Canada*, 674
Schellenberger, Matt, *Edmonton Construction Association*, 676
Schemenauer, Robert, *FogQuest*, 742
Schepers, Rob, *Creston Valley Chamber of Commerce*, 642
Schepp, Jeannette, *Human Resources Professionals Association*, 826
Scherer, Alice, *Society of Bead Researchers*, 1592
Scherr, Laurel, *Spina Bifida & Hydrocephalus Association of South Saskatchewan*, 1342
Scherrer, Steve, *Skate Canada*, 1302
Schers, Tricia, *UNICEF Canada*, 1405
Schettler, Wendy, *Alzheimer Manitoba*, 61
Schibli, Ernie, *Social Justice Committee*, 1305
Schiele, Gordon, *Calgary Numismatic Society*, 273
Schilds, Danny, *British Columbia Summer Swimming Association*, 255
Schimmer, Aaron, *Canadian Hematology Society*, 404
Schina, Sonia, *British Columbia Archery Association*, 230
Schindler, Christian P., *International Textile Manufacturers Federation*, 1562
Schindler, Pia, *Kidney Foundation of Canada*, 885
Schipper, Steven, *Royal Manitoba Theatre Centre*, 1242
Schlamp, Wendolyn, *YWCA Canada*, 1481
Schlegl, Heide, *Ontario Traffic Council*, 1111
Schleicher, Peter, *Athletes International*, 180
Schlenker, Murray, *Medicine Hat Real Estate Board Co-operative Ltd.*, 958
Schley, Lorna, *Quesnel Naturalists*, 1200
Schley, Justin, *Greater Nanaimo Chamber of Commerce*, 784
Schlitter, Terry, *Alberta College of Combined Laboratory & X-Ray Technologists*, 29
Schlosser, Chris, *Canadian Donkey & Mule Association*, 378
Schlosser, Francine, *Canadian Council for Small Business & Entrepreneurship*, 367
Schmaltz, Valerie, *Alberta Rural Municipal Administrators Association*, 45
Schmalz, Curtis, *Hanover Chamber of Commerce*, 803
Schmeiser, John, *Canada West Equipment Dealers Association*, 281
Schmid, Fredi, *International Skating Union*, 1556
Schmid, Alariss, *Alzheimer Society of Alberta & Northwest Territories*, 61
Schmid, Matthew G., *Canadian College of Physicists in Medicine*, 360
Schmid, Hans, *Right to Quiet Society*, 1232
Schmid, Ruth B., *Controlled Release Society*, 1520
Schmidt, Ali, *St. Walburg Chamber of Commerce*, 1251
Schmidt, Katharine, *Food Banks Canada*, 749
Schmidt, Michael, *Alberta Water Well Drilling Association*, 51

Schmidt, Bonnie, *Let's Talk Science*, 907
Schmidt, Jonathan, *Forum for Intercultural Leadership & Learning*, 754
Schmidt, Ron, *Medicine Hat Coin & Stamp Club*, 958
Schmidt, Maria, *Canadian Association of Hepatology Nurses*, 317
Schmidt, Andy, *Newfoundland & Labrador Lacrosse Association*, 1019
Schmiedge, Dean, *Kabuki Syndrome Network Inc.*, 880
Schmiedge, Margot, *Kabuki Syndrome Network Inc.*, 880
Schmitt, Fernando, *International Academy of Cytology*, 1535
Schnarr, Dave, *Centre for Family Business*, 532
Schneider, Sharry, *Summerland Community Arts Council*, 1354
Schneider, Heather, *Community Living Welland Pelham*, 606
Schneider, Lynda, *Parksville & District Chamber of Commerce*, 1142
Schneider, Blake, *Saskatchewan Construction Safety Association Inc.*, 1262
Schneider, Karen, *Canadian Masonry Contractors' Association*, 431
Schneider, Marilyn, *Manitoba Water Well Association*, 947
Schneider, Melissa, *United Way Elgin-St. Thomas*, 1413
Schneider, Thomas W., *International Erosion Control Association*, 1546
Schneider, Gary, *Environmental Coalition of Prince Edward Island*, 691
Schnekenburger, Norma, *West Elgin Historical & Genealogical Society*, 1445
Schnobb, Philippe, *Association du transport urbain du Québec*, 132
Schnurr, Amy, *BurlingtonGreen Environmental Association*, 265
Schoel, Gerald, *Association de médiation familiale du Québec*, 102
Schoen, Carol, *Canada East Equipment Dealers' Association*, 278
Schoenfeld, Jason, *Concrete Precasters Association of Ontario*, 610
Schoettler, Rodney, *Saskatchewan Municipal Hail Insurance Association*, 1270
Schofield, Richard, *Scarborough Historical Society*, 1282
Schofield, Aurel, *Société Santé en français*, 1325
Schofield, Rick, *Community Heritage Ontario*, 599
Schola, Al, *Saskatchewan Institute of Agrologists*, 1268
Scholl-Buckwald, Steve, *Pesticide Action Network North America*, 1583
Schollar, Kia, *Canoe Kayak Saskatchewan*, 509
Scholz, Mark A., *Canadian Association of Oilwell Drilling Contractors*, 324
Schoock, Carlene, *Sign Association of Canada*, 1299
Schooley, Kevin, *Ontario Berry Growers' Association*, 1068
Schoonheyt, Mike, *Fort York Food Bank*, 754
Schorr, Brian, *Association of Environmental Engineering & Science Professors*, 1511
Schott, Ben Yu, *Athletics Yukon*, 181
Schous, Leslie A., *Canadian Postmasters & Assistants Association*, 458
Schout, Ron, *Federation of Canadian Naturists*, 723
Schrader, David, *Congregational Christian Churches in Canada*, 613
Schram, Stefanie, *Martin Prosperity Institute*, 952
Schreiber, Rick, *Canadian Association for the Study of the Liver*, 306
Schreiner, Mike, *The Green Party of Ontario*, 789
Schrenk, Manfred, *International Society of City & Regional Planners*, 1560

Executive Name Index

Schrie, Niki, *Canadian Institute for Neutron Scattering*, 413
Schriemer, Gerry, *Saskatchewan Emergency Medical Services Association*, 1264
Schroder, Gary, *Québec Family History Society*, 1197
Schroeder, Fredric, *World Blind Union*, 1465
Schroeder, Deanna, *Alberta Funeral Service Association*, 36
Schroeder, Marie, *Ontario Home Builders' Association*, 1086
Schroeder, Trudy, *Winnipeg Symphony Orchestra Inc.*, 1459
Schroeder, Bonnie, *Canadian Coalition for Seniors Mental Health*, 358
Schroeder, Rose, *Back Country Horsemen of British Columbia*, 193
Schroeder, Rose, *Back Country Horsemen of British Columbia*, 193
Schroeder, Lacey, *Saskatchewan Triathlon Association Corporation*, 1276
Schrum, Michael W, *Environmental Information Association*, 1523
Schryver, Donna, *Saskatchewan Katahdin Sheep Association Inc.*, 1268
Schubert, Lori, *Québec Writers' Federation*, 1199
Schubert, François, *BioTalent Canada*, 212
Schuelle, Nadine, *Saskatchewan Association of Veterinary Technologists, Inc.*, 1258
Schuett, Robbie, *Liberal Party of Canada in Alberta*, 909
Schuett, Mark, *Swim BC*, 1358
Schular, Kevin, *Baptist General Conference of Canada*, 196
Schule, Al, *Langdon & District Chamber of Commerce*, 898
Schuler, Vaughn, *Calgary Danish Businessmen's Association*, 271
Schuler, Mark, *Operation Springboard*, 1116
Schull, Michael, *Institute for Clinical Evaluative Sciences*, 843
Schulte, Dave, *Vancouver Consultants*, 1425
Schultz, Robin, *Ingersoll District Chamber of Commerce*, 838
Schultz, Nick, *Canadian Association of Petroleum Producers*, 326
Schultz, Caroline, *Ontario Nature*, 1093
Schultz, Robert, *Urban & Regional Information Systems Association*, 1601
Schultz, Dean, *Swim Alberta*, 1358
Schultz, Sharon, *Canadian Institutional Research & Planning Association*, 420
Schultz, Crystal, *Pharmacy Technician Society of Alberta*, 1157
Schultz, Amber, *Alberta Association of the Deaf*, 25
Schultz, Tom, *Pest Management Association of Alberta*, 1152
Schultz, Âge, *Multinational Association for Supportive Care in Cancer*, 1571
Schulz, Valerie, *Grenville County Historical Society*, 790
Schulz, Al, *Chemistry Industry Association of Canada*, 556
Schupp, Cora, *British Columbia & Yukon Community Newspapers Association*, 229
Schurman-Smith, Lisa, *Prince County Hospital Foundation*, 1171
Schuster, Catherine, *The Canadian Council for Accreditation of Pharmacy Programs*, 366
Schuster, Eric, *Pest Management Association of Alberta*, 1152
Schutte, Alta, *International Society of Hypertension*, 1560
Schutz, Scott, *Volleyball Nunavut*, 1438
Schutz, Amanda, *Society of Graphic Designers of Canada*, 1329
Schuurmans, Frank, *Civil Air Search & Rescue Association*, 571
Schwandt, Jillian Arkles, *Sexual Health Centre Saskatoon*, 1293
Schwanen, Daniel, *C.D. Howe Institute*, 521
Schwanky, T.J., *Outdoor Writers of Canada*, 1133

Schwann, Pamela, *Saskatchewan Mining Association*, 1270
Schwark, Gordon, *Michael Smith Foundation for Health Research*, 964
Schwartz, Marilyn, *Na'amat Canada Inc.*, 987
Schwartz, Stacey, *Swift Current United Way*, 1358
Schwartz, Agatha, *Hungarian Studies Association of Canada*, 827
Schwartz, Bernard, *Association of Jewish Chaplains of Ontario*, 150
Schwartz, Ken, *Two Planks & a Passion Theatre Company*, 1401
Schwartz, Audrey, *Active Support Against Poverty*, 7
Schwartz, Bunnie, *Colon Cancer Canada*, 591
Schwartz, Jeffrey, *Consolidated Credit Counseling Services of Canada, Inc.*, 623
Schwartz, Jeff, *Credit Association of Greater Toronto*, 639
Schwartz, Jeff, *Jacob's Ladder - The Canadian Foundation for Control of Neurodegenerative Disease*, 867
Schwartz, Ellen, *Jacob's Ladder - The Canadian Foundation for Control of Neurodegenerative Disease*, 867
Schwass, Tammy, *Canadian Public Relations Society Inc.*, 463
Schwass, Tammy, *Alberta Plastics Recycling Association*, 42
Schwass, Dave, *Alberta Plastics Recycling Association*, 42
Schweer, Bonnie, *Alberta Galloway Association*, 36
Schweiger, Christoph, *Fédération Internationale de Luge de Course*, 1525
Schweighardt, Mike, *British Columbia Ball Hockey Association*, 233
Schwersensky, Javier, *Winnipeg Humane Society*, 1459
Schwieger, Melodie, *American Saddlebred Horse Association of Canada*, 66
Sciara, Sephora, *Toronto Insurance Women's Association*, 1385
Sclar, Casey, *American Public Gardens Association*, 1497
Scocchia, Susanna, *Ontario Cooperative Education Association*, 1075
Scoffield, Heather, *The Canadian Press*, 459
Scoles, Margaret, *International Organic Inspectors Association*, 1554
Scollan, Clyde, *Construction Labour Relations Association of British Columbia*, 624
Scoot, Derrick, *The Canadian Philatelic Society of Great Britain*, 1515
Scorca, Marc A., *Opera America Inc.*, 1580
Scotchmer, Carolyn, *TD Friends of the Environment Foundation*, 1367
Scott, Christine, *Kinsight*, 890
Scott, Jennifer, *Simon Fraser University Faculty Association*, 1300
Scott, Sheri, *Community Living Kingston*, 603
Scott, Shelley, *Flamborough Information & Community Services*, 740
Scott, Helen, *Canadian Association of Foodservice Professionals*, 315
Scott, Tony, *Vulcan & District Chamber of Commerce*, 1439
Scott, Debra, *Newmarket Chamber of Commerce*, 1024
Scott, Knox, *Institute of Communication Agencies*, 845
Scott, Kelly, *British Columbia Road Builders & Heavy Construction Association*, 251
Scott, Rosalind, *Better Business Bureau of Vancouver Island*, 206
Scott, Robert, *Alberta Land Surveyors' Association*, 39
Scott, Katherine, *Canadian Council on Social Development*, 371
Scott, Betty Lou, *Maritime Aberdeen Angus Association*, 950
Scott, Randy, *Canadian Welsh Black Cattle Society*, 503

Scott, Janice, *Society of Composers, Authors & Music Publishers of Canada*, 1328
Scott, Angela, *Association of Electromyography Technologists of Canada*, 147
Scott, Sean, *Construction Safety Association of Manitoba*, 1264
Scott, Rebecca J., *American Society for Legal History*, 1498
Scott, Laura, *American Lung Association*, 1495
Scott, Terry, *Canadian Harvard Aircraft Association*, 401
Scott, Jeff, *Canadian Blood Services*, 344, 345
Scott, Craig, *Ecology North*, 672
Scott, Suzanne, *Prince Edward Island Crafts Council*, 1173
Scott, John F.T., *George Morris Centre*, 771
Scott, Wendy, *Alternative Dispute Resolution Atlantic Institute*, 60
Scott, Marianne, *The Friends of Library & Archives Canada*, 761
Scott, Calum, *Family Services of Greater Vancouver*, 705
Scott, Sandra, *Alberta Research Council Inc.*, 44
Scott, John, *Association des surintendants de golf du Québec*, 129
Scott, Marianne, *Canadian Writers' Foundation Inc.*, 506
Scott, Terrylynn, *Ontario Pinzgauer Breeders Association*, 1096
Scott Lafontaine, Geneviève, *Chambre de commerce et d'industrie de la MRC de Maskinongé*, 545
Scott-Perez, Myrna, *Society of Tribologists & Lubrication Engineers*, 1594
Scotti, Susan, *Business Council of Canada*, 267
Scotti, Susan, *Canadian Film Institute*, 390
Scrimgeour, Gray, *Northern Canada Study Group*, 1034
Scull, John, *Cowichan Valley Naturalists' Society*, 638
Scully, Joe, *Ontario Rodeo Association*, 1102
Sculthorpe, David, *Heart & Stroke Foundation of Canada*, 808
Seabright, Glenn, *Springdale & Area Chamber of Commerce*, 1346
Seaby, Chelsea, *Multiple Sclerosis Society of Canada*, 980
Seager, John, *Population Connection*, 1584
Seaman, Alfred, *Squash Nova Scotia*, 1347
Searle, Deanna, *Boys & Girls Clubs of Ontario*, 223
Searles, John, *Community Development Halton*, 597
Searles Jones, Janis, *The Ocean Conservancy*, 1580
Sears, Joye, *Eastern Veterinary Technician Association*, 671
Sears, Jessica, *Canadian Sport Massage Therapists Association*, 490
Sears, J. Michael, *TelecomPioneers of Canada*, 1369
Sears, Cynthia L., *Infectious Diseases Society of America*, 1531
Sebree, Val, *Alberta Katahdin Sheep Association*, 38
Sebunya, Kaddu, *African Wildlife Foundation*, 1486
Seccia, Maria Cristina, *Association of Italian Canadian Writers*, 150
Secco, Mary, *Epilepsy Ontario*, 694
Seckel, Allan, *Doctors of BC*, 660
Secker, John, *Canadian Australian Chamber of Commerce*, 1515
Secondi, John, *Canadian Textile Association*, 494
Secondiak, Brent, *Medicine Hat Police Association*, 958
Secord, Melissa, *Ontario Association of Optometrists*, 1065
Secord, Scott, *Canadian Hard of Hearing Association*, 400

Secord, Sharon, *Canadian Institute for Theatre Technology*, 414
Sedaca, Jorge, *Chosen People Ministries (Canada)*, 566
Seddon, Cindi, *Bully B'Ware*, 264
Sedfawi, Tony, *Canadian Association for Spiritual Care*, 304
Sedivy, Julie, *The Writers' Guild of Alberta*, 1469
Sedlickas, Arlene, *Newfoundland & Labrador Association of Public & Private Employees*, 1016
Seeber, Tim, *Prince Edward Island Hog Commodity Marketing Board*, 1174
Seechurn, Shiv, *Canadian Institute of Marketing*, 417
Seeley, Tracie, *Saskatoon Society for the Prevention of Cruelty to Animals Inc.*, 1280
Seely, Andrew, *Canadian Association of Thoracic Surgeons*, 334
Seely, Jan, *New Brunswick Special Care Home Association Inc.*, 1013
Seepersad, Sharon, *Ontario Association of Chiefs of Police*, 1062
Sefton, Andrew, *Ontario Painting Contractors Association*, 1094
Segal, Joel, *Jewish Community Foundation of Montréal*, 871
Segal, Hugh, *Atlantic Council of Canada*, 183
Segall, Kevin, *Canadian Institute of Food Science & Technology*, 415
Segatto, Bianca, *Canadian Transplant Association*, 496
Segovia, Gil, *Saskatchewan Archery Association*, 1256
Séguin, Michel, *Squash Québec*, 1347
Séguin, Yves, *Centre d'intervention et de prévention en toxicomanie de l'Outaouais*, 528
Séguin, Sylvie, *Chambre de commerce et d'industrie de St-Laurent-Mont-Royal*, 546
Séguin, Kevin, *Association des Grands Frères et Grandes Soeurs du Québec*, 115
Séguin, Marc, *Canadian Media Production Association*, 433
Seguin, Yves, *Industrial Gas Users Association*, 835
Séguin, Daniel, *Canadian Overseas Telecommunications Union*, 448
Séguin, Loriane, *Comité Social Centre-Sud*, 592
Seguin, Larry, *Nickel Belt Coin Club*, 1026
Seguin, Rick, *Ontario Greenhouse Vegetable Growers*, 1083
Seguin, Bob, *Niagara Economic Development*, 1025
Séguin, Michel, *Balle au mur Québec*, 194
Seguin, Sylvain, *Helicopter Association of Canada*, 811
Sehgal, Tushar, *Nova Scotia Cricket Association*, 1043
Sehl, Ted, *The John Howard Society of Ontario*, 875
Seib, Gary, *Nature Saskatchewan*, 1001
Seib, Jennifer, *Russell & District Chamber of Commerce*, 1244
Seibold, Claire, *Saskatchewan Registered Music Teachers' Association*, 1273
Seidel, Robert P., *Society of Motion Picture & Television Engineers*, 1593
Seidelman, Perry, *Jewish Historical Society of BC*, 872
Seidler, Roy, *Manitoba Association of School Business Officials*, 931
Seidlitz, Sandra, *TOPS Club, Inc.*, 1598
Seitinger, Heinz, *Austrian-Canadian Society*, 1513
Sekhar, Kripa, *South Asian Women's Centre*, 1334
Sekhon, Baljinder, *Peel Multicultural Council*, 1148
Sekhon, Manji, *Project Management Institute*, 1585
Sekiguchi, Takashi, *Japan Automobile Manufacturers Association of Canada*, 868

Executive Name Index

Sekopet, Nino, *Dying with Dignity*, 665
Self, Neil, *Positive Living BC*, 1167
Self, Gordon, *Covenant Health*, 637
Seligmann, Peter, *Conservation International*, 1519
Seline, Megan, *Appalachian Teachers' Association*, 73
Selinger, Georgina, *Gem & Mineral Federation of Canada*, 768
Sell, Stephen, *Ontario Electrical League*, 1077
Sellar, Steve, *Lakehead Japanese Cultural Association*, 896
Sellar, Melanie, *Librarians Without Borders*, 910
Selley, Debbie, *Canadian Tax Foundation*, 492
Sellwood, Ron, *Circulation Management Association of Canada*, 570
Selman, Roger, *Ramara & District Chamber of Commerce*, 1204
Selvamani, Senthill, *Newfoundland & Labrador Cricket Association*, 1018
Semaniuk, Irene, *Ukrainian Youth Association of Canada*, 1404
Semenchuk, Glen, *Cumulative Environmental Management Association*, 646
Semeniuk, Sharon, *College of Medical Laboratory Technologists of Alberta*, 586
Semenoff, Andy, *Kamloops, Revelstoke, Okanagan & District Building & Construction Trades Council*, 881
Semeschuk, Darci, *Souris & Glenwood Chamber of Commerce*, 1334
Semmler, Sarah, *Entomological Society of Manitoba Inc.*, 690
Semotok, Cheryl, *CADORA Ontario Association Inc.*, 269
Sen, Shom, *CAA British Columbia*, 267
Senaratne, Uditha, *Professional Engineers Ontario*, 1184
Senécal, Jean-Luc, *Association des médecins cliniciens enseignants de Montréal*, 119
Sénécal, Émilie, *St. Lawrence Valley Natural History Society*, 1250
Sénéchal, Yvon, *Canadian Welding Bureau*, 503
Sénéchal, Yvon, *Canadian Welding Bureau*, 503
Sénéchal, Pierre-Paul, *Mouvement national des québécoises et des québécois*, 977
Senft, Barry, *Grain Farmers of Ontario*, 779
Senger, Sherri, *Boys & Girls Clubs of Alberta*, 221
Senghera, Rikki, *Association of Women in Finance*, 164
Senior, Kevin, *Canadian Independent Bicycle Retailers Association*, 410
Senkovich, Vlado, *World Safety Organization*, 1607
Senkus, Roman, *Canadian Institute of Ukrainian Studies*, 420
Sennanyana, Sean, *Professional Engineers Ontario*, 1185
Senneville, Caroline, *Fédération nationale des enseignants et des enseignantes du Québec*, 722
Sentes, Corey, *Canadian Western Agribition Association*, 503
Senthilnathan, Thamia, *Canadian Tamil Youth Development Centre*, 492
Senzilet, Linda, *Canadian Hadassah WIZO*, 399
Seong, Hwan Yong, *Ontario Taekwondo Association*, 1109
September, Che, *Nishnawbe - Gamik Friendship Centre*, 1027
Septon, Paula, *Biathlon Nouveau-New Brunswick*, 207
Sereda, Cyndi, *Big Brothers Big Sisters of Ontario*, 210
Sereda, Rhonda, *Bowling Federation of Saskatchewan*, 219
Seretis, George, *Greek Orthodox Metropolis of Toronto (Canada)*, 788
Serink, Wendy, *Boys & Girls Clubs of Alberta*, 221

Serino, Peter, *Ontario Industrial Roofing Contractors' Association*, 1087
Sermeus, Kurt, *Montréal Soaring Council*, 973
Serran, Jamie, *Council of Nova Scotia Archives*, 634
Serrano, Maria, *Social Planning Toronto*, 1306
Serrick, Cyril, *Canadian Society of Clinical Perfusion*, 482
Servais, Yves, *Association des marchands dépanneurs et épiciers du Québec*, 119
Serviss-Low, Erika, *Yukon Registered Nurses Association*, 1480
Servos, Mark, *Canadian Water Network*, 502
Serwin, Marcin, *Catholic Youth Studio - KSM Inc.*, 521
Sesar, Stephen, *Human Resources Professionals Association*, 825
Setaram, Sharmila, *Amnesty International - Canadian Section (English Speaking)*, 68
Seth, Nikhil, *Division of Sustainable Development*, 1521
Sethi, Baljit, *Immigrant & Multicultural Services Society*, 830
Sethna, Zahra, *International Institute for Sustainable Development*, 858
Sethuram, Shannon, *Stem Cell Network*, 1349
Seto, Karen, *Canadian Liver Foundation*, 427
Seto, Debbie, *Alzheimer Society of Ottawa & Renfrew County*, 64
Settembrini, Carlo, *Italian Cultural Institute (Istituto Italiano di Cultura)*, 867
Setterington, Ken, *World Literacy of Canada*, 1466
Settle, Martin, *USC Canada*, 1423
Setzkorn, Matt, *Ontario Farmland Trust*, 1078
Sevcik, Karen, *Alberta Liberal Party*, 39
Sevestre, Mark, *National Aboriginal Trust Officers Association*, 989
Sewell, Gregg, *Construction Labour Relations Association of British Columbia*, 624
Sewell, Mike, *Lupus Society of Alberta*, 922
Sexsmith, Stephanie, *Lumby Chamber of Commerce*, 920
Sexsmith, Mary, *Canadian Haflinger Association*, 400
Sexsmith, David, *Ontario Woodlot Association*, 1114
Seyler, John, *Canadian Independent Adjusters' Association*, 410
Seymour, Kevin, *Ontario Field Ornithologists*, 1080
Seymour, Bill, *Alzheimer Society of Sarnia-Lambton*, 64
Seys, Wendy, *Yamaska Literacy Council*, 1470
Sfeir, Marsha, *Springtide Resources*, 1346
Shackell, Doug, *Canadian Public Relations Society Inc.*, 463
Shadrack, Andy, *Association of Kootenay & Boundary Local Governments*, 150
Shah, Abbad, *Association of Professional Engineers & Geoscientists of British Columbia*, 158
Shah, Rupal, *Alliance for South Asian AIDS Prevention*, 57
Shah, Yaqoob, *British Columbia Muslim Association*, 247
Shah, Rohan, *Toronto Cricket Umpires' & Scorers' Association*, 1383
Shakya, Armila C., *Trans-Himalayan Aid Society*, 1395
Shallit, Jeffrey, *Electronic Frontier Canada Inc.*, 683
Shaman, Phil, *Child & Family Services of Western Manitoba*, 558
Shambrock, Dave, *Manitoba Food Processors Association*, 936
Shamisa, Abdallah, *Windsor Islamic Association*, 1456
Shan, Rodney Li Pi, *Canadian Association of Physical Medicine & Rehabilitation*, 327
Shan, Neethan, *Council of Agencies Serving South Asians*, 632
Shand, Douglas B., *Sou'wester Coin Club*, 1333

Shank, Denis, *Council of Ontario Construction Associations*, 634
Shanken, Ezra S., *Jewish Federation of Greater Vancouver*, 872
Shanks, Amy, *Boys & Girls Clubs of New Brunswick*, 222
Shanks, Ruth, *Associated Country Women of the World*, 1507
Shanks, Craig, *Manitoba Independent Insurance Adjusters' Association*, 939
Shanmugavadivel, Shan, *Canadian Tamil Medical Association*, 492
Shann, Samantha, *World Federation of Occupational Therapists*, 1605
Shannon, Terry, *International Union of Elevator Constructors*, 1564
Shannon, Shelly, *Peace River & District Chamber of Commerce*, 1147
Shannon, Heather, *Canadian Society of Nutrition Management*, 485
Shannon, Joanne, *London & St. Thomas Association of Realtors*, 918
Shannon, Elizabeth, *Royal Canadian College of Organists*, 1239
Shannon, Meg, *Professional Association of Canadian Theatres*, 1182
Shannon, Diane, *United Way of Fort McMurray*, 1414
Shannon, Greg, *Association of Fundraising Professionals*, 1512
Shantz, Jill, *Professional Photographers of Canada*, 1186
Shantz, Ralph, *The Pennsylvania German Folklore Society of Ontario*, 1178
Shapiro, Mark, *Prince Edward Island Symphony Society*, 1178
Shardlow, Karen, *Ontario Community Newspapers Association*, 1073
Sharief, Tanveer, *Canadian Association of Professional Immigration Consultants*, 329
Shariff, Khalil Z., *Aga Khan Foundation Canada*, 14
Sharkey, Shirley, *Dystonia Medical Research Foundation Canada*, 666
Sharkey, Shirlee, *Saint Elizabeth Health Care*, 1246
Sharkey, Annette, *Social Planning Council for the North Okanagan*, 1306
Sharkey, Priscilla, *Clan Donald Canada*, 571
Sharkey, Daryl, *Mechanical Service Contractors of Canada*, 957
Sharma, Rajni, *Canadian Art Therapy Association*, 295
Sharma, Muneesh, *Building Owners & Managers Association of British Columbia*, 263
Sharma, Anand, *Canadian Condominium Institute*, 362
Sharma, Rohit, *Canadian Board of Registration of Electroencephalograph Technologists Inc.*, 345
Sharma, Arya M., *Canadian Obesity Network*, 444
Sharp, Mike, *Peel Regional Police Association*, 1148
Sharp, Caroline, *Canadian Fencing Federation*, 389
Sharp, Anne, *Applied Science Technologists & Technicians of British Columbia*, 74
Sharp, Marsha, *Dietitians of Canada*, 656
Sharp, Alan, *Saskatchewan Athletics*, 1259
Sharpe, Jan, *Greater Summerside Chamber of Commerce*, 785
Sharpe, Elizabeth A., *Canadian Society of Landscape Architects*, 484
Sharpe, Jason, *Insurance Brokers Association of Canada*, 848
Sharpe, Elizabeth A., *Canadian Association for Child & Play Therapy*, 297
Sharpe, Dawn, *Recreation Newfoundland & Labrador*, 1207
Sharpe, Andrew, *Centre for the Study of Living Standards*, 534
Sharpe, Doreen, *Friends of Ferris Provincial Park*, 761

Sharpe, John, *Partners for Youth*, 1144
Sharples, Betsy, *Ontario Trucking Association*, 1111
Sharren, Martin, *Alberta Fish & Game Association*, 35
Shatosky, Rick, *Enform*, 688
Shaughnessy, Richard, *International Society of Indoor Air Quality & Climate*, 1561
Shaw, Ian, *Ottawa Independent Writers*, 1131
Shaw, Bruce, *Community Living South Huron*, 605
Shaw, Nancy, *Greater Oshawa Chamber of Commerce*, 784
Shaw, Danielle, *Skate Canada*, 1302
Shaw, Liana, *Canadian Pony Club*, 457
Shaw, Patrick, *Canadian Security Association*, 469
Shaw, Tracy, *Canadian Association of Recycling Industries*, 330
Shaw, Nancy, *Durham Region Association of REALTORS*, 665
Shaw, Terry, *Manitoba Trucking Association*, 946
Shaw, Karen, *College of Physicians & Surgeons of Saskatchewan*, 588
Shaw, Trish, *Judo Prince Edward Island*, 876
Shaw, David Evans, *American Association for the Advancement of Science*, 1489
Shaw, Mike, *British Columbia Alternate Education Association*, 230
Shaw, Tony, *Recreational Canoeing Association BC*, 1208
Shaw, Doug, *Archaeological Society of Alberta*, 76
Shaw, Mike, *Canadian Blood Services*, 344, 345
Shaw, Edward, *Canadian Association for Disabled Skiing - Alberta*, 299
Shaw, Robert, *Parkinson Society Maritime Region*, 1141
Shaw, Kathleen, *The Friends of Library & Archives Canada*, 761
Shaw, Robert, *Vancouver Electric Vehicle Association*, 1425
Shaw, Russell, *Canadian Institute of Underwriters*, 420
Shaw, Mary, *West Niagara Second Stage Housing & Counselling*, 1446
Shaw, Amelia, *International Association for Public Participation Canada*, 853
Shaw-Swettenham, Kelly, *The Recreation Association*, 1207
Shaw-White, Tanya, *PFLAG Canada Inc.*, 1155
Shawana, Brian, *Cree-Naskapi Commission*, 641
Shchukina, Tatiana, *Russian Association of Canadian Studies*, 1588
Shea, Emma, *Canadian Public Relations Society Inc.*, 463
Shea, Michael, *Catholic Health Alliance of Canada*, 519
Shea, Jim, *Council for Continuing Pharmaceutical Education*, 632
Shea, Joe, *Little League Canada*, 915
Shea, Clara, *Atlantic Canada Water & Wastewater Association*, 182
Shea, Canon Derwyn, *Ontario Association of Former Parliamentarians*, 1064
Sheach, David, *British Columbia Association for Charitable Gaming*, 231
Sheahan, Terry, *Skate Canada*, 1301
Sheard, T. Scott, *Association of Strategic Alliance Professionals - Toronto Chapter*, 162
Shearer, Brenna, *Manitoba Society of Pharmacists Inc.*, 945
Shearer, Heather, *Bike Ottawa*, 211
Shearon, Paul, *International Federation of Professional & Technical Engineers (AFL-CIO/CLC)*, 1549
Shearon, Kimberly, *Ecojustice Canada Society*, 672
Sheather, Steve, *Receivables Management Assocation of Canada Inc.*, 1206

Executive Name Index

Sheather, Craig, *British Columbia Disc Sports*, 238
Shedden, Catherine, *Canadian Association of Communicators in Education*, 310
Shedden, Sylvia, *Latvian Canadian Cultural Centre*, 900
Sheddy, Ossie, *Alberta Weekly Newspapers Association*, 51
Sheehan, Peter, *Innkeepers Guild of Nova Scotia*, 839
Sheehan, Charity, *Special Olympics Prince Edward Island*, 1340
Sheffer, Andra, *Independent Production Fund*, 833
Sheffield, John, *Canadian Stamp Dealers' Association*, 490
Sheffield, Jim, *Council of Ontario Construction Associations*, 634
Sheffield, John W., *International Association for Hydrogen Energy*, 1537
Sheffield, Aartje, *Judo Ontario*, 876
Sheffield, Steve, *Judo Ontario*, 876
Sheidlower, Jesse, *American Dialect Society*, 1492
Sheila, Bourque, *Canadian Meteorological & Oceanographic Society*, 435
Sheils, Steve, *The Brampton Board of Trade*, 225
Sheinbaum, Naomi, *Canadian Magen David Adom for Israel*, 429
Sheldrick, Karin, *Council of Ontario Construction Associations*, 634
Shelley, Alexander, *National Arts Centre Orchestra of Canada*, 989
Shelly, Neil, *Alberta Forest Products Association*, 35
Shelly, Neil, *Construction Owners Association of Alberta*, 624
Shelswell, Michelle, *Ontario Association of Child & Youth Care*, 1062
Shelton, Nick, *Professional Engineers Ontario*, 1185
Shelton, Sharon, *Tropicana Community Services Organization*, 1399
Shelton, Norman, *The Royal Canadian Legion*, 1240
Shelvin, Carol, *Canadian Council of Insurance Regulators*, 368
Sheney, Sherri, *Consumer Health Products Canada*, 626
Shenton, Margaret, *Canadian Hard of Hearing Association*, 400
Shepard, Bruce, *Archaeological Society of Alberta*, 76
Shephard, Denise, *Sydenham Field Naturalists*, 1359
Shepherd, Robert R., *Nova Scotia Association of Social Workers*, 1041
Shepherd, Deborah, *Canadian Pony Club*, 457
Shepherd, Lucia, *Ontario Community Newspapers Association*, 1073
Shepherd, Catherine, *Alberta Association of Travel Health Professionals*, 25
Shepherdson, Dar, *Community of Christ - Canada East Mission*, 607
Shepherdson, Evanne, *Insurance Professionals of Calgary*, 850
Sheppard, Vince, *Big Brothers Big Sisters of Manitoba*, 209
Sheppard, Christine, *Library Association of Alberta*, 910
Sheppard, Steve, *Canadian Society of Agronomy*, 479
Sheppard, Diane, *Freight Carriers Association of Canada*, 759
Sheppard, Michael, *Judo Prince Edward Island*, 876
Sheppard, Christopher, *St. John's Native Friendship Centre*, 1249
Sheppard, Paula, *Newfoundland & Labrador Organization of Women Entrepreneurs*, 1020
Sheppy, Bobbi, *Canadian Society of Gastroenterology Nurses & Associates*, 483
Sher, Desirée, *British Columbia Neurofibromatosis Foundation*, 247
Sher, Graham D., *Canadian Blood Services*, 344
Sheramy, Rona, *Association for Jewish Studies - USA*, 1508
Sherar, Michael, *Cancer Care Ontario*, 507
Sherazi, Bilal, *Professional Engineers Ontario*, 1185
Sheremeta, Peter, *The Terry Fox Foundation*, 1372
Sheridan, Bob, *Lillooet & District Chamber of Commerce*, 912
Sheridan, Shawn, *Numeris*, 1051
Sheridan, Paul, *Greater Toronto Electrical Contractors Association*, 786
Sheridan, Kim, *Peruvian Horse Association of Canada*, 1152
Sherk, Lloyd, *Grande Prairie Soaring Society*, 781
Sherkawi, Tracy, *High Prairie & Area Chamber of Commerce*, 814
Sherlen, Karina, *Indonesia Canada Chamber of Commerce*, 1531
Sherlock, Christopher, *British Columbia Association of Laboratory Physicians*, 232
Sherman, Louise, *Oraynu Congregation for Humanistic Judaism*, 1117
Sherman, Keith, *Severn Sound Environmental Association*, 1292
Sherman, Recinda, *North American Association of Central Cancer Registries, Inc.*, 1578
Sherrer, Norma, *Québec Women's Institutes*, 1199
Sherrer, Bettyanne, *Canadian Society of Professional Event Planners*, 487
Sherri, Joe, *Maltese-Canadian Federation Inc.*, 928
Sherris, Martin, *Greater Kingston Chamber of Commerce*, 783
Sherritt-Fleming, Lori, *Children's Writers & Illustrators of British Columbia Society*, 563
Sherrod, Lonnie, *Society for Research in Child Development*, 1591
Sherry, Karen, *POWERtalk International*, 1584
Shershen, Gene, *Inventors Association of Ottawa*, 862
Sherwood, Don, *Atlantic Building Supply Dealers Association*, 182
Sherwood, Tom, *Student Christian Movement of Canada*, 1352
Sherwood, Betty, *Jewish Historical Society of Southern Alberta*, 873
Sheta, Sherif, *CIO Association of Canada*, 570
Shevalier, Alex, *Calgary & District Labour Council*, 270
Shevalier, Maurice, *Association of the Chemical Profession of Alberta*, 163
Sheweli, Olya, *Council of Ukrainian Credit Unions of Canada*, 635
Shi, Dayi, *Buddhist Association of Canada - Cham Shan Temple*, 261
Shi, Andi, *Chinese Professionals Association of Canada*, 565
Shields, Stacy, *Pacific National Exhibition*, 1135
Shields, Chris, *Canadian Society for Psychomotor Learning & Sport Psychology*, 477
Shields, Reg, *Navy League of Canada*, 1002
Shields, Roy, *Denesoline Corporation Ltd.*, 653
Shier, Blair, *Further Poultry Processors Association of Canada*, 765
Shier, Carl, *Lifesaving Society*, 911
Shiffman, Barry, *Banff International String Quartet Competition*, 195
Shifman, Brian, *Vaughan Chamber of Commerce*, 1430
Shigetomi, Elaine, *Care Institute of Safety & Health Inc.*, 511
Shija, William F., *Commonwealth Parliamentary Association*, 1518
Shilton, Don, *Langley Arts Council*, 899
Shim, Youn Young, *Association of Korean Canadian Scientists & Engineers*, 150
Shimoda, Kimiko, *Rosetown & District Chamber of Commerce*, 1236
Shin, Hyun-Ju, *Korean Senior Citizens Society of Toronto*, 893
Shinewald, Benjamin L,, *Building Owners & Managers Association - Canada*, 262
Shinn, Bryan, *International Bottled Water Association*, 1541
Shipman, Nancy, *Canadian Council on Social Development*, 371
Shipton, Jodi, *Coronation Chamber of Commerce*, 629
Shkordoff, Lara, *Miss G Project*, 968
Shockey, Ben, *Canadian Alliance of Dance Artists*, 291
Shoctor, Debby, *The Centre for Israel & Jewish Affairs*, 533
Shoebridge, Micheline, *One World Arts*, 1058
Shoemaker, Dean, *Flowers Canada Growers*, 741
Shoffey, Valerie, *Canadian Association of Geographers*, 316
Shold, Clayton, *Merry Go Round Children's Foundation*, 962
Shoop, Barry, *Institute of Electrical & Electronics Engineers Inc.*, 1532
Shoranick, Mostafa, *British Columbia Muslim Association*, 247
Shore, Maynard, *Jobs Unlimited*, 873
Shore, Elliott, *Association of Research Libraries*, 1513
Shore, Nancy, *Canadian Association of Gift Planners*, 317
Shore, Richard, *Anxiety Disorders Association of Manitoba*, 72
Shores, John, *International Catholic Deaf Association*, 854
Shorsky, Shawn, *Water Ski & Wakeboard British Columbia*, 1441
Short, Paul, *Seniors for Nature Canoe Club*, 1290
Short, Paul, *Canadian Sphagnum Peat Moss Association*, 489
Short, Doug, *Northern Alberta Institute of Technology Academic Staff Association*, 1034
Short, Mike, *Boating BC Association*, 216
Short, Paul, *International Peat Society - Canadian National Committee*, 859
Short, Christine, *Financial Executives International Canada*, 736
Short, John, *Alberta Sport Connection*, 48
Short, Bernadette, *Irish Dance Teacher's Association of Eastern Canada*, 864
Shortall, Brian, *Newfoundland & Labrador School Boards Association*, 1021
Shortall, Christopher, *Solid Waste Association of North America*, 1595
Shortall, Mary, *Newfoundland & Labrador Federation of Labour*, 1019
Shortill, Dave, *South Cowichan Chamber of Commerce*, 1334
Shortreed, John, *Institute for Risk Research*, 844
Shortt, Joan, *Alberta Genealogical Society*, 37
Shortt, Pam, *Association canadienne des ataxies familiales*, 92
Shortt, Kevin, *Canadian Space Society*, 489
Shortt, Paul, *Canadian Junior Football League*, 423
Showchuk, Tony, *Canadian Employee Assistance Program Association*, 380
Showers, Dave, *BC Lacrosse Association*, 201
Shpyth, Al, *Saskatchewan Environmental Industry & Managers' Association*, 1264
Shrinath Dwivedi, Acharya, *Multifaith Action Society*, 979
Shriver, Ann L., *International Institute of Fisheries Economics & Trade*, 1551
Shtym, Mary Ann, *Association de joueurs de bridge de Boucherville*, 100
Shuckburgh, Kevin, *Alberta Maine-Anjou Association*, 39
Shufelt, Martha, *Yamaska Literacy Council*, 1470
Shugarman, Julie, *National Association of Women & the Law*, 990
Shuja, Fahad, *Ontario Good Roads Association*, 1083
Shujah, Sarah, *Ontario College & University Library Association*, 1072
Shukla, Manoj, *Professional Engineers Ontario*, 1185
Shukla, Baijul, *Ontario Society of Professional Engineers*, 1108
Shuler, Elizabeth, *American Federation of Labor & Congress of Industrial Organizations (AFL-CIO)*, 1493
Shulist, Karen, *Tuberous Sclerosis Canada Sclérose Tubéreuse*, 1400
Shulman, William L., *Association of Holocaust Organizations*, 1512
Shumanty, Rufteen, *Association des démographes du Québec*, 110
Shurish, William, *Quad County Support Services*, 1195
Shurko, Lynda, *Alberta Association of Library Technicians*, 23
Shuster, Ellie, *Learning Disabilities Association of Alberta*, 904
Shuster, Henry, *Sholem Aleichem Community Inc.*, 1297
Shvetsova, Ludmila, *International Women's Forum*, 1567
Shwec, Michael, *Ukrainian Youth Association of Canada*, 1404
Shymko, Lisa, *Canadian Friends of Ukraine*, 395
Siani, Sheren Anwar, *Canadian Nursing Students' Association*, 443
Siddle, Jeffery, *Global, Environmental & Outdoor Education Council*, 775
Sider, Doug, *Brethren in Christ*, 228
Sidhu, Kanwal K, *Maritime Sikh Society*, 951
Sidhu, Nimmi, *Canadian Dermatology Association*, 377
Sidiropoulos, Jimmy, *Hellenic Canadian Congress of BC*, 811
Sidloski, Tannis, *Canadian Association of Critical Care Nurses*, 311
Sidoryk, Michael, *Lloydminster Agricultural Exhibition Association*, 916
Siebert, Jared, *Free Methodist Church in Canada*, 759
Siebes, Philippe, *Fondation québécoise de la déficience intellectuelle*, 747
Siemens, Spencer, *Vanderhoof Chamber of Commerce*, 1429
Siemens, Scott, *ADR Institute of Canada*, 9
Siemens, Ryan, *Mennonite Church Canada*, 961
Sifoued, Hinda, *Association provinciale des constructeurs d'habitations du Québec inc.*, 168
Sigmeth, Donna, *Law Society of Saskatchewan*, 902
Sigouin, Mélanie, *Festivals et Événements Québec*, 733
Sigouin, Daniel, *Réseau de développement économique et d'employabilité Ontario*, 1219
Sihvonen, Irene, *A.C.C.E.S. Employment*, 4
Sikand, Meenu, *Centre for Independent Living in Toronto*, 532
Sikes, David E., *International Sanitary Supply Association, Inc.*, 1556
Siklos, Mary, *Holocaust Education Centre*, 819
Sikora, Lindsey, *Canadian Health Libraries Association*, 402
Sikura, R. Glenn, *Canadian Thoroughbred Horse Society*, 495
Silas, Linda, *Canadian Federation of Nurses Unions*, 388
Silber, Simi, *Credit Institute of Canada*, 641
Silberer, Zsolt, *American Water Works Association*, 1504
Sile, Astride, *The Latvian Relief Society of Canada*, 900
Silliker, Roy, *New Brunswick Construction Safety Association*, 1007

Executive Name Index

Silnicki, Adrienne, *Canadian Health Coalition*, 401
Silpola, Jaakko, *International Peat Society*, 1555
Silva, E.N., *World's Poultry Science Association*, 1608
Silva, Angelica, *Nova Scotian Institute of Science*, 1050
Silva, Jun, *The Lord's Flock Charismatic Community*, 919
Silva, Cynthia, *The Lord's Flock Charismatic Community*, 919
Silva Filho, Carlos, *International Solid Waste Association*, 1562
Silver, Jack, *Guitar Society of Toronto*, 794
Silver, Sandy, *Yukon Liberal Party*, 1479
Silver, Erica, *Canadian Public Relations Society Inc.*, 463
Silver, Adam, *The Centre for Israel & Jewish Affairs*, 533
Silver, Rafael, *Operation Springboard*, 1116
Silver, Adam, *Bernard Betel Centre for Creative Living*, 205
Silver, David, *W. Maurice Young Centre for Applied Ethics*, 1439
Silver, Patricia, *Infertility Network*, 836
Silver, John, *Community Financial Counselling Services*, 597
Silverberg, Sarah, *Canadian Federation of Medical Students*, 388
Silverstone, Martin, *Atlantic Salmon Federation*, 186
Silverstone, Denise, *Boys & Girls Clubs of Canada*, 222
Silverstone, Ron, *Association of Administrators of English Schools of Québec*, 139
Silverthorn, Mary Anne, *Canadian Association of Police Governance*, 328
Silverthorne, Judith, *Saskatchewan Writers Guild*, 1278
Silverton, Mike, *Computer-Using Educators of BC*, 609
Silzer, Stacey, *Saskatchewan Broomball Association*, 1260
Sim, Christina, *Yukon Registered Nurses Association*, 1480
Sim, Maggie, *Embroiderers' Association of Canada, Inc.*, 686
Sim, Evelyn, *North Peace Historical Society*, 1032
Sim, Gary, *L'Arche Foundation*, 77
Simard, Luc, *Société de coopération pour le développement international*, 1314
Simard, Charles, *Centre de services Guigues*, 530
Simard, Jean-François, *Association de la construction du Québec*, 101
Simard, Michel C., *Canadian Institute of Actuaries*, 414
Simard, Diane, *Union des municipalités du Québec*, 1406
Simard, Martin, *Société d'histoire et d'archéologie du Témiscouata*, 1312
Simard, Christian, *Nature Québec*, 1000
Simard, Louis, *Fédération ski nautique et planche Québec*, 731
Simard, Monique, *Société de développement des entreprises culturelles*, 1314
Simard, Danielle, *Réseau des SADC et CAE*, 1221
Simard, Cyril, *Société internationale du réseau ÉCONOMUSÉE et Société ÉCONOMUSÉE du Québec*, 1321
Simard, Pierre, *Vancouver Island Symphony*, 1427
Simard, Pierre, *Syndicat des travailleurs énergie électrique nord*, 1364
Simard, Johanne, *Association des gestionnaires des établissements de santé et des services sociaux*, 115
Simard, Jean, *Aluminium Association of Canada*, 61
Simard, Régis, *Table jamésienne de concertation minière*, 1366

Siméon, Geneviève, *Association pour la promotion des droits des personnes handicapées*, 166
Simic, Sanja, *Robert L. Conconi Foundation*, 1234
Simmonds, Claudia, *Canadian Home Builders' Association - New Brunswick*, 407
Simmons, Brian S., *Association of Christian Schools International*, 1510
Simmons, Melanie, *Canadian Public Relations Society Inc.*, 463
Simmons, Chris, *Canadian Handball Association*, 400
Simmons, Dave, *Holstein Canada*, 819
Simmons, Karl, *Canadian Institute for Theatre Technology*, 414
Simmons, Rod, *Kamloops Wildlife Park Society*, 881
Simms, Joe, *TechNova*, 1369
Simms, Nigel, *Ducks Unlimited Canada*, 663
Simms, Meaghen, *Peace Brigades International (Canada)*, 1147
Simms, Ann, *American Planning Association*, 1496
Simon, Paula, *Family Enterprise Xchange*, 703
Simon, Florence, *Canadian Zionist Federation*, 506
Simon, Deborah, *Ontario Community Support Association*, 1073
Simon, Daphne, *Society of Ontario Adjudicators & Regulators*, 1330
Simon, Robert J., *American Chemistry Council*, 1491
Simonds, Robert, *Canadian Association of Fire Chiefs*, 315
Simone, Andrew, *Canadian Food for Children*, 391
Simone, Joan, *Canadian Food for Children*, 391
Simone, Joan, *Silent Children's Mission*, 1299
Simone, Andrew, *Silent Children's Mission*, 1299
Simoneau, Pierre, *Human Resources Association of New Brunswick*, 825
Simons, Tony, *World Agroforestry Centre*, 1602
Simons, Joanne, *Casey House Hospice Inc.*, 516
Simons, Penelope, *Human Rights Research & Education Centre*, 826
Simonsen, Gary, *The Canadian Real Estate Association*, 465
Simonson, Bryan, *National Electricity Roundtable*, 993
Simpson, Michael, *One Sky*, 1058
Simpson, Bernie, *Canadian Association for Disabled Skiing - National Capital Division*, 299
Simpson, Don, *Schizophrenia Society of Alberta*, 1283
Simpson, David J., *Facility Association*, 700
Simpson, Kari, *East Wellington Community Services*, 669
Simpson, Debbie, *Air Transport Association of Canada*, 19
Simpson, Susan, *Canadian Federation of Junior Leagues*, 387
Simpson, Louise, *Saskatchewan Weekly Newspapers Association*, 1278
Simpson, Ritchie, *Prince Edward Island Real Estate Association*, 1176
Simpson, Cathy, *Annapolis Valley Real Estate Board*, 71
Simpson, Carl, *Canadian Society for Aesthetics*, 473
Simpson, Danièle, *Union des écrivaines et écrivains québécois*, 1406
Simpson, Fred N., *Brotherhood of Maintenance of Way Employes (AFL-CIO/CLC)*, 1514
Simpson, Douglas, *Canadian Philosophy of Education Society*, 454
Simpson, Colin, *Insurance Brokers Association of Canada*, 848

Simpson, Robin, *College of Optometrists of BC*, 587
Simpson, Susan, *Ladies' Golf Union*, 1569
Simpson, Carolyn, *British Columbia Art Therapy Association*, 230
Simpson, Al J., *Canadian Association of Veterans in United Nations Peacekeeping*, 336
Simpson, Noel, *Smoky Lake & District Chamber of Commerce*, 1305
Simpson, Kevin, *Dignity Vancouver Dignité*, 657
Simpson, Pierre, *Théâtre Action*, 1373
Simpson, Jill, *PFLAG Canada Inc.*, 1156
Simpson, Jennifer, *International Titanium Association*, 1563
Simpson, Mike, *Fraser Basin Council*, 757
Sims, Norman, *International Association for Literary Journalism Studies*, 853
Sims, Natalie, *Greater Oshawa Chamber of Commerce*, 784
Sims, Elliot, *Canadian Federation of Independent Business*, 387
Sims, David, *Cycling PEI*, 647
Simundson, Peter, *Ontario Military Vehicle Association*, 1091
Simzer, Sherri, *Employment & Education Centre*, 687
Sinclair, Jim, *Pacific Cinémathèque Pacifique*, 1135
Sinclair, David, *Ontario Refrigeration & Air Conditioning Contractors Association*, 1101
Sinclair, Arthur, *Professional Engineers Ontario*, 1184
Sinclair, Stacey, *Financial Executives International Canada*, 736
Sinclair, Bruce, *Canadian Sheep Breeders' Association*, 470
Sinclair, Paul, *Canadian Association of Gastroenterology*, 316
Sinclair, Maureen, *Ontario Parks Association*, 1095
Sinclair, Toni, *Canadian Association of Elizabeth Fry Societies*, 313
Sinclair, Gordon, *Kingston Historical Society*, 889
Sinclair, Ron, *Glanbrook Heritage Society*, 774
Sinclair, Jim, *Indian & Metis Friendship Centre of Winnipeg Inc.*, 834
Sinclair, Irvin, *Keewatin Tribal Council*, 883
Sinclair, Shane, *Canadian Association of Psychosocial Oncology*, 330
Sinclair, Sherry, *British Columbia Association of Family Resource Programs*, 231
Sinclair, Peter, *Loaves & Fishes Community Food Bank*, 916
Sinclair, Noel, *Yukon Film Society*, 1478
Sinclair, Don, *Ontario Cerebral Palsy Sports Association*, 1071
Sindwani, Seema, *Ontario Society of Occupational Therapists*, 1107
Sine, Geoff, *Manitoba Motor Dealers Association*, 941
Singbeil, Donna, *Canadian Condominium Institute*, 362
Singer, Jennifer, *Alberta Construction Trucking Association*, 31
Singer, Ron, *CARP*, 514
Singer, Ilana, *Canadian Investor Protection Fund*, 422
Singer Neuvelt, Carol, *National Association for Environmental Management*, 1572
Singh, Rose, *British Columbia Paralegal Association*, 248
Singh, Tajinder, *International Organization of Securities Commissions*, 1554
Singh, Sanjit, *The Appraisal Institute of Canada - Alberta*, 74
Singh, Anjani, *Association of Neighbourhood Houses BC*, 153
Singh, Mary, *Lutte NB Wrestling*, 923
Singh, Santokh, *Canadian Botanical Association*, 346

Singh, Asha, *The Canadian Federation of Business & Professional Women's Clubs*, 385
Singh, Jagmeet, *New Democratic Party*, 1014
Singh, Judy, *Canadian Tax Foundation*, 492
Singh, Bhupinder, *Ontario Sikh & Gurudwara Council*, 1104
Singh, Kultar, *Ontario Sikh & Gurudwara Council*, 1104
Singh, Balkaran, *Ontario Sikh & Gurudwara Council*, 1104
Singh, Jagdev, *Ontario Sikh & Gurudwara Council*, 1104
Singh, Davindra, *Sikh Foundation of Canada*, 1299
Singh, Bea, *Brockville & District Multicultural Council Inc.*, 260
Singh, Mukhbir, *World Sikh Organization of Canada*, 1467
Singh, Mala, *Ontario Asphalt Pavement Council*, 1061
Singh, Karan, *PFLAG Canada Inc.*, 1155
Singh, Loretta, *Saskatchewan Dental Therapists Association*, 1263
Singh, Kultar, *Ontario Floorball Association*, 1080
Singh Mann, Jagdeep, *World Sikh Organization of Canada*, 1467
Singleton, Pat, *Cambridge Self-Help Food Bank*, 275
Singleton, Michael, *Sustainable Buildings Canada*, 1357
Sinha, Mrinalini, *Association for Asian Studies - USA*, 1507
Sinha, Rajiv, *Edmonton Immigrant Services Association*, 677
Siniscalchi, Raffaela, *Ingénieurs Sans Frontières Québec*, 838
Sinker, Eric, *ViaSport*, 1432
Sinkewicz, Paul, *Saskatoon Youth Orchestra*, 1280
Sipkens, Jennifer, *Alberta Society of Professional Biologists*, 47
Sir, Paul, *Basketball Alberta*, 198
Sirard, Benoit, *Association Hôtellerie Québec*, 136
Sirgey, David J., *Freight Carriers Association of Canada*, 759
Sirman, Hilary, *Centre for Suicide Prevention*, 534
Sirnaik, Lalita, *Canadian Finance & Leasing Association*, 390
Sirois, Anne, *Directors Guild of Canada*, 657
Sirois, Tanya, *Regroupement des centres d'amitié autochtone du Québec*, 1215
Sirois-Caouette, Benjamin, *Ressources Saint-Jean-Vianney*, 1227
Sironi, Camilla, *Conseil du patronat du Québec*, 618
Sirrs, Eric, *Alberta Association of Insolvency & Restructuring Professionals*, 23
Sisk, Nadine, *CropLife Canada*, 643
Sisk, Kurtis, *Heart & Stroke Foundation of New Brunswick*, 809
Sismondohan, Piero, *International Seed Federation*, 1556
Sisso, Shmuel, *World ORT Union*, 1607
Sisson, Lindy, *Maple Ridge Pitt Meadows Arts Council*, 948
Sissons, Jennifer, *The Royal Scottish Country Dance Society*, 1587
Siu, Michelle, *Jane Austen Society of North America*, 868
Siu, Megan, *Edmonton Law Libraries Association*, 678
Siu, Eric, *Canada Chinese Computer Association*, 278
Siu, Eugenia, *The Transplantation Society*, 1395
Sivakumar, Preethy, *Good Jobs for All Coalition*, 777
Sivapalan, Ram, *Canada Employment & Immigration Union*, 279
Sivertson, Joanne, *Saskatchewan Medical Association*, 1270

Executive Name Index

Sjoberg, Stephen, *Volunteer Grandparents*, 1439
Sjodin, Serena, *Lloydminster Chamber of Commerce*, 916
Sjodin, Rob, *Peruvian Horse Association of Canada*, 1152
Sjoholm, Anki, *CADORA British Columbia*, 269
Sjostrom, Mary, *Union of British Columbia Municipalities*, 1407
Skakun, Stephanie, *Canadian Mental Health Association*, 435
Skalesky, Sheri, *Selkirk & District Chamber of Commerce*, 1289
Skalos, John, *Myasthenia Gravis Association of British Columbia*, 986
Skanes, Leah, *Glace Bay Literacy Council*, 774
Skeats, Terry, *Patrimoine Huntingville*, 1145
Skeikheldin, Ferdose, *Manitoba Islamic Association*, 939
Skelly, Jennifer, *Canadian Nurse Continence Advisors Association*, 442
Skelton, Melissa M., *The Anglican Church of Canada*, 69
Skelton, Carmen, *Canadian Occupational Health Nurses Association*, 444
Skender, Jackie, *Volleyball Canada*, 1437
Skene, Dave, *Global Youth Volunteer Network*, 775
Skerritt, Ginelle, *Warden Woods Community Centre*, 1440
Skerten, Jamie, *Model Aeronautics Association of Canada Inc.*, 971
Skidmore, James M., *Canadian Association of University Teachers of German*, 335
Skiera, Jim, *International Society of Arboriculture*, 1560
Skihar, Craig, *Sport Parachute Association of Saskatchewan*, 1345
Skillings, Roger, *Tennis BC*, 1370
Skinner, James, *Adlerian Psychology Association of British Columbia*, 8
Skinner, George, *Canadian Mental Health Association*, 435
Skinner, Ron, *Yorkton Real Estate Association Inc.*, 1474
Skinner, Scott, *Clean Nova Scotia Foundation*, 573
Skinner, Jill, *Sexual Health Centre Lunenburg County*, 1293
Skinner, Doug, *Big Brothers Big Sisters of Eastern Newfoundland*, 209
Skipper, Chrisandra, *Canadian Catholic Campus Ministry*, 351
Skjerdal, Keith, *Saskatchewan Provincial Rifle Association Inc.*, 1272
Sklar, Brian, *Regina Musicians' Association*, 1212
Skoczylas, Alexandra, *Opéra Atelier*, 1114
Skof, Matt, *Ottawa Police Association*, 1131
Skolnik, Bill, *American Federation of Musicians of the United States & Canada (AFL-CIO/CLC)*, 1493
Skolnik, Bill, *Directors Guild of Canada*, 658
Skomedal, Anne, *Dystonia Medical Research Foundation Canada*, 666
Skone, Susan, *Canadian Navigation Society*, 440
Skoretz, Larise, *Saskatchewan Emergency Medical Services Association*, 1264
Skorupsky, Anna, *Holocaust Education Centre*, 819
Skosnik, Jeff, *LC Line Contractors' Association of BC*, 902
Skotnicki, Greg, *Nursery Sod Growers' Association of Ontario*, 1052
Skrba, Gordana, *Ontario Federation for Cerebral Palsy*, 1079
Skvoretz, John, *International Network for Social Network Analysis*, 1553
Sky, Sheila, *Associated Designers of Canada*, 89
Sky, Laura, *SkyWorks Charitable Foundation*, 1303
Slaats, Shirley, *Quest Centre Community Initiatives*, 1200

Slack, Robert, *Canadian Snowbird Association*, 472
Slager, Chris, *International Titanium Association*, 1563
Slaight, Annabel, *The Ladies of the Lake*, 895
Slaight, Annabel, *Shaw Rocket Fund*, 1295
Slaney, Sheri, *Canadian Institute of Plumbing & Heating*, 418
Slaney, Brenda, *The Royal Canadian Legion*, 1240
Slater, Kerry, *British Columbia & Yukon Community Newspapers Association*, 229
Slater, John D., *The Canadian Corps of Commissionaires*, 365
Slater, Dennis, *Association of Equipment Manufacturers - Canada*, 148
Slater, Gary, *Canadian Association for Graduate Studies*, 300
Slater, Vanessa, *North Durham Social Development Council*, 1030
Slater, Alison, *Southern Interior Local Government Association*, 1338
Slattery, Shari, *Association of Fundraising Professionals*, 1512
Slauenwhite, Lisa, *Canadian Association of Foodservice Professionals*, 315
Slauenwhite, Barry, *Compassion Canada*, 608
Slaunwhite, Susan, *Prescott Group*, 1170
Slavin, Danielle, *Association of Women in Finance*, 164
Slawecki, Eva, *Canadian Society for International Health*, 475
Slayton, Philip, *The Canadian Centre/International P.E.N.*, 354
Sledz, Janice, *Alberta Teachers' Association*, 49
Slessor, Doreen, *Stop Abuse in Families Society*, 1350
Slight, Colleen, *Manitoba Library Consortium Inc.*, 940
Slike, Alyssa, *The Dream Factory*, 662
Slingbeil, Terrie, *Horseshoe Ontario*, 822
Slipchuk, Mike, *Skate Canada*, 1301
Slipec, Jim, *Canadian Meteorological & Oceanographic Society*, 436
Slipp, Larry, *Turkey Farmers of New Brunswick*, 1400
Sliz, Edward, *Canadian Polish Congress*, 456
Sloan, Kelly, *Natural Health Practitioners of Canada Association*, 999
Sloan, Chris, *Canada Employment & Immigration Union*, 279
Sloan, Christina, *Canadian Hockey League*, 406
Sloan, Kelly, *Natural Health Practitioners of Canada*, 999
Sloan, Lawrence, *American Industrial Hygiene Association*, 1494
Sloat, Melanie, *Mactaquac Country Chamber of Commerce*, 924
Sloboda, Antin, *Catholic Near East Welfare Association Canada*, 520
Slobodian, Glen, *Surrey Food Bank*, 1357
Slobodian, Terrance M, *Christian Children's Fund of Canada*, 567
Slobodin, Brent, *Humane Society Yukon*, 826
Slofstra, Ruthanne, *Global Youth Volunteer Network*, 775
Slomp, Mike, *Alberta Milk*, 40
Slone, Eric, *Environmental Health Association of Nova Scotia*, 692
Slubowski, Tadeusz, *Alliance of Cancer Consultants*, 58
Slusky, Alan, *Psychological Association of Manitoba*, 1192
Slywka, Brandi, *Prince Albert Exhibition Association*, 1171
Smale, Bryan, *Ontario Research Council on Leisure*, 1101
Smale, Ron, *Ontario Soccer Association*, 1105
Small, Gail, *Jewish Immigrant Aid Services of Canada*, 873
Small, Niamh, *Vancouver Recital Society*, 1428
Smallegange, Gerry, *Conservation Halton Foundation*, 622

Smallwood, Sandy, *Canadian Association of Police Governance*, 328
Smallwood, Lee, *Inuvik Chamber of Commerce*, 862
Smart, Rosemary, *Canadian Swine Breeders' Association*, 491
Smeaton, Darlene, *Multicultural Association of Kenora & District*, 978
Smeland, Jordan, *Natural Gas Employees' Association*, 998
Smelkowska, Malgorzata, *The Hunger Project Canada*, 827
Smellink, Marja, *Community Living Dundas County*, 601
Smethurst, Bill, *Victorian Order of Nurses for Canada*, 1434
Smigelsky, Donna, *Ukrainian Fraternal Society of Canada*, 1403
Smillie, Ruth, *Globe Theatre Society*, 775
Smit, Becky, *The Green Party of Ontario*, 789
Smith, Patrick, *The Renascent Centres for Alcoholism & Drug Addiction*, 1217
Smith, Mary-Ann, *Baseball Ontario*, 198
Smith, Julia, *Women's Musical Club of Toronto*, 1463
Smith, Timothy, *Guitar Society of Toronto*, 794
Smith, Stuart, *Swift Current Agricultural & Exhibition Association*, 1358
Smith, George, *Congregation of St. Basil*, 613
Smith, Franklin, *International Society for Augmentative & Alternative Communication*, 860
Smith, Craig, *Help Fill a Dream Foundation of Canada*, 812
Smith, Bryan "BJ", *Alberta Cowboy Poetry Association*, 32
Smith, Stephen B., *Canadian Association for Corporate Growth, Toronto Chapter*, 133
Smith, Betty, *Canadian Institute of Management*, 417
Smith, Adam M., *Villa Charities Inc. (Toronto District)*, 1435
Smith, Penny, *Community Association for Riding for the Disabled*, 596
Smith, Amanda, *Community Care Peterborough*, 596
Smith, Rod, *Concrete Sask*, 610
Smith, Delores, *Canadian Association of Foodservice Professionals*, 315
Smith, Lezlie, *Canadian Association of Foodservice Professionals*, 315
Smith, Devyn, *Spruce Grove & District Chamber of Commerce*, 1346
Smith, Janis, *Swan Hills Chamber of Commerce*, 1358
Smith, Anthony, *Chester Municipal Chamber of Commerce*, 557
Smith, Mike, *Lunenburg Board of Trade*, 920
Smith, Angela, *Greater Charlottetown & Area Chamber of Commerce*, 783
Smith, Autumn, *Haliburton Highlands Chamber of Commerce*, 798
Smith, Matt, *Kincardine & District Chamber of Commerce*, 888
Smith, Gillian, *Toronto Public Library Foundation*, 1386
Smith, Violet, *Ponoka Food Bank*, 1164
Smith, Annie, *McCreary Centre Society*, 955
Smith, Bill, *United Church of Canada*, 1409
Smith, Mary Lou, *Canadian League Against Epilepsy*, 426
Smith, Shelly, *ARMA Canada*, 82
Smith, Jack, *Canada Safety Council*, 280
Smith, Wally, *Dairy Farmers of Canada*, 648
Smith, David, *Amnesty International - Canadian Section (English Speaking)*, 68
Smith, Allen, *Association of Neighbourhood Houses BC*, 153
Smith, Eric, *Canadian Amateur Wrestling Association*, 292
Smith, Annie, *Synchro BC*, 1360
Smith, Brendan, *Alberta Tennis Association*, 50
Smith, Arlene, *Canadian Authors Association*, 338

Smith, Karen, *Better Business Bureau of Saskatchewan*, 206
Smith, David, *Professional Engineers Ontario*, 1183
Smith, Lila, *The Canadian Federation of Business & Professional Women's Clubs*, 385
Smith, Marja, *Ontario Society for the Prevention of Cruelty to Animals*, 1106
Smith, Elizabeth, *Fertilizer Canada*, 733
Smith, Howard, *Gas Processing Association Canada*, 767
Smith, Linda, *Canadian Home Builders' Association - New Brunswick*, 407
Smith, Megan, *Canadian Institute of Forestry*, 416
Smith, Debbie, *Canadian Lung Association*, 428
Smith, Pat, *Saskatchewan Lung Association*, 1269
Smith, Liz, *New Brunswick Lung Association*, 1010
Smith, Bernadette, *Canadian Management Centre*, 429
Smith, Patrick, *Canadian Mental Health Association*, 434
Smith, K.L. (Ken), *Canadian Nuclear Society*, 442
Smith, Susan, *Easter Seals Ontario*, 670
Smith, Scott, *Ontario Trucking Association*, 1111
Smith, Jewelles, *Council of Canadians with Disabilities*, 633
Smith, N. Arthur, *GS1 Canada*, 792
Smith, Alison, *Council of Ontario Construction Associations*, 634
Smith, Sheila, *Canadian Association of Orthodontists*, 324
Smith, Heather, *Canadian Teachers' Federation*, 493
Smith, Frank, *National Educational Association of Disabled Students*, 993
Smith, Neil, *Association of Canadian Search, Employment & Staffing Services*, 143
Smith, Steve, *Health Association Nova Scotia*, 806
Smith, Glyn J., *Christian Health Association of Alberta*, 567
Smith, Elaine, *Huntington Society of Canada*, 828
Smith, Barb, *Junior Achievement Canada*, 877
Smith, Marlene, *Kidney Foundation of Canada*, 886
Smith, Jane, *Canadian Bar Association*, 342
Smith, Rob, *Canadian Angus Association*, 293
Smith, Julie, *Ontario Angus Association*, 1059
Smith, Gerry, *Canadian Association of Blue Cross Plans*, 309
Smith, Pamela, *Canadian Society of Orthopaedic Technologists*, 485
Smith, Lisa, *Multiple Sclerosis Society of Canada*, 980
Smith, Barbara, *National Youth Orchestra Canada*, 997
Smith, Janis, *Ontario Folk Dance Association*, 1080
Smith, Luke, *National Campus & Community Radio Association*, 991
Smith, Danielle, *Nature NB*, 1000
Smith, Fred, *Newfoundland Historical Society*, 1023
Smith, Sue, *College of Registered Nurses of Nova Scotia*, 589
Smith, Heather, *United Nurses of Alberta*, 1412
Smith, Heather, *United Nurses of Alberta*, 1412
Smith, Brian, *Woodgreen Community Centre*, 1464
Smith, James, *Ontario Good Roads Association*, 1083
Smith, Craig, *Canada East Equipment Dealers' Association*, 278
Smith, Douglas, *Canadian Railroad Historical Association*, 465
Smith, Cindy, *Spina Bifida & Hydrocephalus Association of Northern Alberta*, 1342

Executive Name Index

Smith, Paul, *United Empire Loyalists' Association of Canada*, 1410
Smith, Anne, *United Way of the Alberta Capital Region*, 1417
Smith, Jessica, *United Way of Pictou County*, 1416
Smith, Yvonne, *YMCA Canada*, 1472
Smith, Yvonne, *YMCA Canada*, 1473
Smith, Bruce R., *Glass, Molders, Pottery, Plastic & Allied Workers International Union (AFL-CIO/CLC)*, 1528
Smith, Jeff, *Food Allergy Canada*, 749
Smith, Drew, *Ontario Association of Orthodontists*, 1065
Smith, Carey, *Bereavement Authority of Ontario*, 205
Smith, Shawn I., *Canadian Northern Society*, 441
Smith, Wendy, *Ontario Physiotherapy Association*, 1096
Smith, Kevin, *Goodwill Industries Essex Kent Lambton*, 777
Smith, Anne, *Canadian Remote Sensing Society*, 466
Smith, Andrew, *Campaign Against Arms Trade*, 1515
Smith, Christine, *Seva Canada Society*, 1292
Smith, Brad, *Mainland Nova Scotia Building & Construction Trades Council*, 926
Smith, Chloe, *The Publishers Association*, 1586
Smith, Kathy, *American Forest & Paper Association*, 1493
Smith, Joan-Dianne, *Canadian Group Psychotherapy Association*, 399
Smith, David, *Canadian Chito-Ryu Karate-Do Association*, 356
Smith, Paul F., *Softball Newfoundland & Labrador*, 1332
Smith, Robin, *Georgina Chamber of Commerce*, 771
Smith, Janice, *Canada's Sports Hall of Fame*, 283
Smith, Doug, *Ontario Masters Athletics*, 1090
Smith, Steve, *Canadian Office & Professional Employees Union*, 445
Smith, Dwight, *Canadian Trapshooting Association*, 497
Smith, Billy, *American Society of Plumbing Engineers*, 1502
Smith, Gabrielle, *Multilingual Orientation Service Association for Immigrant Communities*, 979
Smith, Juliet, *Airdrie & District Soccer Association*, 20
Smith, Michael, *1000 Islands Gananoque Chamber of Commerce*, 1058
Smith, Brian, *General Church of the New Jerusalem in Canada*, 768
Smith, Susanne, *Essential Skills Ontario*, 696
Smith, Lorne R., *Markham District Historical Society*, 952
Smith, Peter, *Ottawa Valley Curling Association*, 1132
Smith, Kim, *Ontario Brain Injury Association*, 1069
Smith, Peter M., *International Curling Information Network Group*, 856
Smith, Ian, *Hincks-Dellcrest Treatment Centre & Foundation*, 815
Smith, P.S., *Institute for Folklore Studies in Britain & Canada*, 1532
Smith, Phil, *Australian Association for Environmental Education*, 1513
Smith, Barbara (Bobbi) R., *American Thyroid Association*, 1504
Smith, Jennifer, *Women Entrepreneurs of Saskatchewan Inc.*, 1460
Smith, Jennifer, *Institute On Governance*, 848
Smith, Karen Dickenson, *Family Services of Greater Vancouver*, 705
Smith, Don, *Canadian Health Food Association*, 401
Smith, Liz, *Fish Harvesters Resource Centres*, 739

Smith, Tammy, *Canadian Investor Protection Fund*, 422
Smith, Wayne, *Historic Restoration Society of Annapolis County*, 815
Smith, Cheri, *Kinark Child & Family Services*, 888
Smith, Rich, *Alberta Beef Producers*, 26
Smith, Stephen, *Progressive Conservative Party of New Brunswick*, 1187
Smith, Glenn, *Direction Chrétienne*, 657
Smith, Llewellyn, *New Brunswick Scottish Cultural Association Inc.*, 1012
Smith, Wayne, *Fisher Branch & District Chamber of Commerce*, 739
Smith, Sheila, *Ovarian Cancer Canada*, 1133
Smith, Dave, *Canadian Transplant Association*, 496
Smith, Linda, *Canadian Association of Cardiovascular Prevention & Rehabilitation*, 309
Smith, Harold, *The Canadian Addison Society*, 288
Smith, Bonnie, *Canadian Reiki Association*, 466
Smith, Michael, *Australian Bankers' Association Inc.*, 1513
Smith, Fraser, *Canadian Coalition for Fair Digital Access*, 357
Smith, Christina, *Wellspring Cancer Support Foundation*, 1444
Smith, Colleen, *Ontario Agri-Food Education Inc.*, 1059
Smith, Tanya, *Bikes Without Borders*, 211
Smith, Glyn, *Pain Society of Alberta*, 1137
Smith, Carla, *Healthcare Information & Management Systems Society*, 1529
Smith, Earl, *Prince Edward Island Harness Racing Industry Association*, 1174
Smith, Rob, *Canadian Pinzgauer Association*, 455
Smith, Donna, *Alberta Pinzgauer Association*, 42
Smith, Karin, *Back Country Horsemen of British Columbia*, 193
Smith, Cindie, *Caregivers Nova Scotia*, 512
Smith, Michael, *BC Taekwondo Association*, 202
Smith, Dave, *Saskatchewan Karate Association*, 1268
Smith, Dallas, *Manitoba Lacrosse Association*, 939
Smith, Liris, *Physiotherapy Association of Yukon*, 1159
Smith, Sonya, *Association of Fundraising Professionals*, 1512
Smith-Darrell, Donna, *Health Association of African Canadians*, 806
Smith-Walsh, Gwen, *The Terry Fox Foundation*, 1372
Smith-Windsor, Kent, *Greater Saskatoon Chamber of Commerce*, 785
Smits, Elizabeth, *Urology Nurses of Canada*, 1422
Smitten, Don, *Alberta Motor Association*, 40
Smola, Catherine, *Centre for Study of Insurance Operations*, 534
Smout, Jennifer A., *Municipal Law Departments Association of Ontario*, 981
Smudits, Alfred, *International Research Institute for Media, Communication & Cultural Development*, 1556
Smyth, Keith, *Olds College Faculty Association*, 1057
Smyth, Patrick, *Canadian Energy Pipeline Association*, 381
Smythe, Kim, *Greater Nanaimo Chamber of Commerce*, 784
Snagg, Rose, *Ontario Ringette Association*, 1102
Sneesby, Jennifer, *Portage Plains United Way*, 1167
Snelgrove, Toby, *Mayne Island Community Chamber of Commerce*, 954
Snell, Spencer, *Golf Canada Foundation*, 777

Snetselaar, Betty Lou, *Lambton County Historical Society*, 897
Snider, Ellen, *New Brunswick Association of Occupational Therapists*, 1005
Snider, Laurie, *Canadian Adult Recreational Hockey Association*, 288
Sniegowski, Wojciech, *Canada-Poland Chamber of Commerce of Toronto*, 284
Snip, Rika, *Lethbridge Community College Faculty Association*, 908
Snively, Jen, *Beef Farmers of Ontario*, 204
Snoddon, Katy, *Ontario Brain Injury Association*, 1069
Snoek, Daniel, *PFLAG Canada Inc.*, 1155
Snook, Laureen, *Saskatchewan Association of Landscape Architects*, 1257
Snow, Terry W., *The Pentecostal Assemblies of Newfoundland & Labrador*, 1150
Snowdon, Daniel, *International Continence Society*, 1544
Snyder, Laurie, *Daily Bread Food Bank*, 648
Snyder, Tanya, *The Literary Press Group of Canada*, 914
Snyder, Ruth, *InScribe Christian Writers' Fellowship*, 839
So, Justin, *Newfoundland & Labrador Fencing Association*, 1019
Soave, Luciana, *Association multi-ethnique pour l'intégration des personnes handicapées*, 138
Sobey, Paul, *Canadian Society of Addiction Medicine*, 479
Sobkowich, Wade, *Western Grain Elevator Association*, 1449
Sobol, Heidi, *Canadian Association of Professional Conservators*, 328
Sobotkiewicz, Roger, *Financial & Consumer Affairs Authority of Saskatchewan*, 736
Soby, Lynn, *International Union of Pure & Applied Chemistry*, 1565
Soda, Lee, *Agincourt Community Services Association*, 14
Soderstrom, Carl, *Alberta Union of Provincial Employees*, 50
Soever, Leslie, *Arthritis Health Professions Association*, 84
Sofin, Andrew, *Québec Association of Marriage & Family Therapy*, 1196
Sohi, Manjit S., *Building Officials' Association of British Columbia*, 262
Soholt, Trent, *Nova Scotia Construction Sector Council - Industrial-Commercial-Institutional*, 1043
Sok, Soyuth, *YMCA Canada*, 1471
Sokoloski, Robin, *Playwrights Guild of Canada*, 1162
Sokolove, Jennifer, *Pesticide Action Network North America*, 1583
Solar, Donald, *Canadian College of Health Leaders*, 359
Solbrekken, Ken, *Pentecostal Assemblies of Canada*, 1150
Solbrekken, Max, *Solbrekken Evangelistic Association of Canada*, 1332
Solbrekken, Donna, *Solbrekken Evangelistic Association of Canada*, 1332
Solda, Cindy, *Association of Vancouver Island Coastal Communities*, 164
Soldo, Edward, *Canadian Institute of Transportation Engineers*, 420
Solek, Robert, *Canadian Association of Pharmacy Technicians*, 326
Soles, John, *Society of Rural Physicians of Canada*, 1330
Solntseff, June, *The Garden Clubs of Ontario*, 767
Solo, Dalia, *Fondation des maladies du coeur du Québec*, 745
Solomon, Jack, *Ininew Friendship Centre*, 838
Solomon, Alex, *Blind River Chamber of Commerce*, 214
Solomon, Lawrence, *Consumer Policy Institute*, 626
Solomon, Ari, *Mercy for Animals Canada*, 961
Solomos, Angela, *Yonge Street Mission*, 1473

Soltis, Reina, *People First of Ontario*, 1151
Soltys, Pearl, *Manitoba Society of Occupational Therapists*, 945
Solymar, Bernie, *Norfolk Field Naturalists*, 1028
Solymar, Bernie, *Asparagus Farmers of Ontario*, 87
Somani, Moe, *SOHO Business Group*, 1332
Somascanthan, Priya, *Canadian Bioethics Society*, 343
Somersall, Marla, *Prince Edward Island Humane Society*, 1175
Somerville, Clark, *Federation of Canadian Municipalities*, 723
Somerville, Sheri, *Atlantic Chamber of Commerce*, 183
Somerville, Margaret, *McGill Centre for Medicine, Ethics & Law*, 955
Sommer, Ryan, *Alberta College of Occupational Therapists*, 29
Sommer, Angela, *Williams Lake & District Chamber of Commerce*, 1455
Sommer, Elise, *Professional Petroleum Data Management Association*, 1186
Sommers, Cathy, *Foodservice Consultants Society International - Canadian Chapter*, 750
Sommers, Andrew, *Antique Automobile Club of America*, 1505
Son, Grace, *Newcomer Women's Services Toronto*, 1015
Sonier, Faye, *Canadian Physicians for Life*, 454
Sonier, Joanne, *Alzheimer Society of Moncton*, 63
Sonmen, Janice, *Canadian Institute of Child Health*, 415
Sonnema, Bradley, *College of Podiatric Physicians of Alberta*, 589
Sonntag, Armella, *Development & Peace*, 655
Sonshine, Fran, *Canadian Society for Yad Vashem*, 479
Sood, Vivek, *Neighbourhood Pharmacy Association of Canada*, 1002
Sookman, Rosemary, *Embroiderers' Association of Canada, Inc.*, 686
Sookraj, Nyron, *Catholic Children's Aid Society of Toronto*, 518
Soolanayakanahally, Raju, *Poplar Council of Canada*, 1165
Sooley-Perley, Jill, *Canadian Association of Principals*, 328
Soong, George, *Pulp & Paper Centre*, 1194
Sopha, Keith, *Canadian Association of Environmental Management*, 313
Sopkow, Tracy, *Covenant Foundation*, 637
Sora, April, *International Women of Saskatoon*, 861
Sorbara, Christina, *The Sam Sorbara Charitable Foundation*, 1253
Sorensen, Maibrit, *West Kootenay Women's Association*, 1445
Sorichetti, Beth, *Daily Bread Food Bank*, 648
Sorland, Rolf H., *Innovation Norway*, 839
Soroka, Melana, *Canadian Council for the Advancement of Education*, 367
Soroka, Shmuli, *Shaarei Tefillah*, 1293
Soroka, Tomasz, *Polish Association for Canadian Studies*, 1584
Sossin, Lorne, *Reena*, 1210
Soteroff, Sarah, *Martin Prosperity Institute*, 952
Soublière, Jean-Pierre, *Harmony Foundation of Canada*, 803
Soucy, Pierre, *Fédération québécoise des sociétés de généalogie*, 730
Soucy, Denise, *Association paritaire pour la santé et la sécurité du travail - Secteur Affaires municipales*, 165
Soucy, Claude, *Ordre des ingénieurs du Québec*, 1122
Soucy, Francine, *Chambre immobilière des Laurentides*, 551
Soucy, Paul-Emile, *Fédération des agriculteurs et agricultrices francophones du Nouveau-Brunswick*, 711

Executive Name Index

Soukup, David, *American Society of Mechanical Engineers*, 1500
Soulas, Caroline, *Association CFA Montréal*, 96
Soulet, Marc-Henry, *Association internationale des sociologues de langue française*, 1510
Soulière, Jean-Guy, *National Association of Federal Retirees*, 990
Soulière, Madelaine, *Conseil national Société de Saint-Vincent de Paul*, 619
Soulières, Daniel, *Danse-Cité inc*, 650
Soulis, Marisa, *Heating, Refrigeration & Air Conditioning Institute of Canada*, 810
Soumahoro, Youenn, *Conseil des industriels laitiers du Québec inc.*, 617
Sousa, Eduarda, *Association of Early Childhood Educators Ontario*, 147
Sousa, Mona, *Canadian Association of Pharmacy Technicians*, 326
Sousa, Damiao, *La Maison des Açores du Québec*, 926
Soussi, Anass, *Syndicat des producteurs de chèvres du Québec*, 1363
Soutar, Juanita, *Canadian Progress Club*, 461
South, Darlene, *Saskatchewan Construction Association*, 1262
South, Valerie, *Headache Network Canada*, 805
Southam, Tim, *Directors Guild of Canada*, 657
Southam, Brenda, *Real Estate Institute of Canada*, 1206
Southam, Brenda, *Real Estate Institute of British Columbia*, 1205
Southwood, Mike, *Alberta Milk*, 40
Southwood, Jeanette M., *Engineers Canada*, 689
Souza, Mike, *North Shore Numismatic Society*, 1033
Sowa, Victor, *Canadian Geotechnical Society*, 397
Sowter, Shelley, *Vanscoy & District Agricultural Society*, 1429
Sozo, Espavo, *The Platinum Party of Employers Who Think & Act to Increase Awareness*, 1162
Spacek, Alan, *Federation of Northern Ontario Municipalities*, 725
Spadafore, Ron, *Ontario Registered Music Teachers' Association*, 1101
Spady, Sheri, *Canadian Hemophilia Society*, 404
Spaetzel, Don, *Canadian Institute of Management*, 417
Spafford, Charlotte, *British Columbia Art Therapy Association*, 230
Spaidal, Chris, *St. Albert Soccer Association*, 1248
Spain, Jackie, *East Kootenay District Labour Council*, 668
Spalding, Shauna, *Community Living Dryden-Sioux Lookout*, 601
Sparkes, Lynn, *Janeway Children's Hospital Foundation*, 868
Sparks, Sherry, *New Brunswick Building Officials Association*, 1006
Sparks, Rosemary, *BuildForce Canada*, 261
Sparks, Donna, *People First Nova Scotia*, 1151
Sparling, Cheryl, *Greater Arnprior Chamber of Commerce*, 782
Sparling, Michele, *Parents for Children's Mental Health*, 1140
Spatari, Sam, *Canadian Italian Business & Professional Association*, 423
Spaulding, Neil, *Hamilton Philharmonic Orchestra*, 801
Spayne, Jacqueline, *Canadian Association of Radiation Oncology*, 330
Speagle, Mary, *Canadian Association of Professional Regulatory Affairs*, 329
Spear, Colin, *International Industry Working Group*, 1551
Spear, Mike, *Genome Canada*, 769
Specht, Vicki, *Wabamun District Chamber of Commerce Society*, 1439

Specht, Elisabeth, *Northwest Territories & Nunavut Dental Association*, 1037
Specic, Angie, *Crohn's & Colitis Canada*, 642
Spector, Shira, *Arts Etobicoke*, 85
Spedding, Susan M., *Commonwealth Association of Surveying & Land Economy*, 1518
Spedding, Dave, *UNICEF Canada*, 1404
Spedding, Michael, *International Union of Basic & Clinical Pharmacology*, 1564
Speer, Ty, *Tourism Vancouver/Greater Vancouver Convention & Visitors Bureau*, 1391
Speer, John, *Red River Apiarists' Association*, 1210
Speer, Christina, *Niijkiwenhwag - Friends of Lake Superior Park*, 1027
Speevak, Paula, *Volunteer Canada*, 1438
Speir, Marc, *Allied Beauty Association*, 59
Speirs, Dave, *Hong Kong-Canada Business Association*, 820
Spelliscy, Richard, *College of Alberta Psychologists*, 582
Spence, Sheila, *Saskatchewan Association of Optometrists*, 1257
Spence, Daniel, *Sierra Club of Canada*, 1298
Spence, Walter, *Keewatin Tribal Council*, 883
Spence, Debbie, *Yoga Association of Alberta*, 1473
Spencer, Metta, *Science for Peace*, 1285
Spencer, Sally, *Youth Assisting Youth*, 1475
Spencer, Dallas, *Estevan Exhibition Association*, 697
Spencer, Sonya, *The John Howard Society of Ontario*, 875
Spencer, Terry, *Association of Educational Researchers of Ontario*, 147
Spencer, Phil, *Toronto Railway Historical Association*, 1386
Spencer, Anthony Peter, *Lawn Bowls Association of Alberta*, 902
Spencer, Nicole, *Northwest Territories Society for the Prevention of Cruelty to Animals*, 1038
Spencer, Marleen, *Canadian Society of Gastroenterology Nurses & Associates*, 483
Spencer, Cheryl, *Canadian Hospice Palliative Care Association*, 409
Spencer, Gail, *University of Waterloo Staff Association*, 1421
Spencer, Ian, *Recreation & Parks Association of the Yukon*, 1207
Spencer, Debbie, *Canadian Speckle Park Association*, 489
Spencer, Myles, *Rugby Canada*, 1244
Spencer, Megan, *Cheer Nova Scotia*, 555
Spencer-Miller, Karen, *Alberta West Realtors' Association*, 52
Spicer, Darcy, *Sheet Metal Contractors Association of Alberta*, 1295
Spicer, Geneviève, *CODE*, 580
Spieker, Hans, *World Ploughing Organization*, 1607
Spiers, Graeme, *Canadian Society for Analytical Sciences & Spectroscopy*, 473
Spilchak, Peter, *Norman Wells & District Chamber of Commerce*, 1028
Spina, Louisa, *Canadian Water & Wastewater Association*, 502
Spina, Marg, *Southern Interior Local Government Association*, 1338
Spindel, Andria, *March of Dimes Canada*, 949
Spinello, Joe, *Association des Physiques Québécois*, 123
Spinks, Nora, *Vanier Institute of The Family*, 1429
Spinnato, JoAnn, *American Water Works Association*, 1504
Spitale, Sal, *Society for Ecological Restoration International*, 1590
Spittal, Robin, *Writers' Federation of Nova Scotia*, 1469
Spivey, Norman, *National Association of Teachers of Singing*, 1574

Splinter, Angela, *Trucking Human Resources Canada*, 1399
Spoelstra, Marg, *Autism Ontario*, 188
Sponchia, Ange, *Atikokan Chamber of Commerce*, 181
Sponder, Marta, *The Oakville, Milton & District Real Estate Board*, 1054
Spooner, Stephen, *Institute of Certified Management Consultants of British Columbia*, 845
Spottiswood, Christine, *Gateway Association*, 767
Spradley, Candace, *International Society for Magnetic Resonance in Medicine*, 1558
Sprague, Cheryl, *Windsor-Essex Children's Aid Society*, 1457
Spring, Clarence, *College of Dental Technologists of Alberta*, 583
Springett, Isobell, *CADORA British Columbia*, 268
Springfield, Janice, *Deaf Children's Society of B.C.*, 652
Sprogin, Karl, *Arts Etobicoke*, 85
Sproston, Andy, *Rare Breeds Canada*, 1204
Sproul, Peter, *Community Living Kingston*, 603
Sproule, Laurie Lee, *Church Library Association of Ontario*, 569
Sproule, Robert, *Canadian Arabian Horse Registry*, 294
Sproule, Joanne, *Association of Hearing Instrument Practitioners of Ontario*, 149
Sproule, Gordon, *Merit OpenShop Contractors Association of Ontario*, 962
Spurr, Ken, *Credit Institute of Canada*, 641
Spurrell, Kris, *Exploits Regional Chamber of Commerce*, 700
Spyksma, Darren, *Society of Christian Schools in British Columbia*, 1328
Spyridakou, Chrysa, *International Association of Physicians in Audiology*, 1539
Squarey, Lesley, *Nova Scotia Dental Association*, 1044
Squartecchia, Catia, *50 & Piu Enasco*, 734
Squibb, Marilyn, *Federation of Broomball Associations of Ontario*, 722
Squire, Tiana, *Alberta Soccer Association*, 47
Squire, Roberta, *United Way of Northern BC*, 1415
Squires, Jacqui, *Canadian Manufacturers & Exporters*, 430
Squires, Glenn, *Tourism Industry Association of Nova Scotia*, 1390
Squires, Denise, *Horseshoe Saskatchewan Inc.*, 822
Squires, Debbie, *Newfoundland & Labrador Palliative Care Association*, 1020
Srinath, Ingrid, *CIVICUS: World Alliance for Citizen Participation*, 1517
Sripathi, Geetika, *Mercy for Animals Canada*, 961
Srivastava, Lalit, *Canadian College of Neuropsychopharmacology*, 360
Sroczynska, Krystyna, *Association of Polish Engineers in Canada*, 156
Srour, Akram, *International Federation of Corporate Football*, 857
St-Amour, Line, *Boys & Girls Clubs of Canada*, 222
St-Arnaud, André, *Cercles des jeunes naturalistes*, 537
St-Arnault, Luc, *Cercle de la finance internationale de Montréal*, 537
St-Cyr, Sylvain, *Ringuette Boucherville*, 1233
St-Denis-Lachaîne, Rachèle, *Association des fermières de l'Ontario*, 114
St-Engo, Martine, *Association francophone à l'éducation des services à l'enfance de l'Ontario*, 135
St-Georges, Darquise, *Club de l'âge d'or Les intrépides de Chibougamau*, 574
St-Germain, Jean-Paul, *Development & Peace*, 655
St-Hilaire, André, *Société Provancher d'histoire naturelle du Canada*, 1323

St-Hilaire, Édith, *Association coopérative d'économie familiale - Rive-Sud de Québec*, 97
St-Hilaire, Joseph-Anne, *Association des alternatives en santé mentale de la Montérégie*, 105
St-Jacques, André, *Fédération québécoise de la montagne et de l'escalade*, 727
St-Jacques, Marc, *Théâtres unis enfance jeunesse*, 1375
St-Jacques, Gaston, *Mouvement national des québécoises et québécois*, 977
St-Jacques, Coquille, *Association des motocyclistes gais du Québec*, 120
St-Jean, Patricia, *Groupement des assureurs automobiles*, 792
St-Jean, Georges, *Union of National Employees*, 1407
St-Jean, Francine, *Carrefour jeunesse-emploi Papineau*, 516
St-Jean, Pierre, *Corporation des approvisionneurs du Québec*, 629
St-Laurent, Maurice, *Association des médecins gériatres du Québec*, 119
St-Laurent, Mario, *Conseil de l'industrie forestière du Québec*, 615
St-Laurent, Sandra, *Partenariat communauté en santé*, 1143
St-Laurent, Mélanie, *Association des compagnies de théâtre*, 109
St-Laurent, Mathieu, *International Political Science Association*, 859
St-Louis, Shane, *Volleyball Nova Scotia*, 1438
St-Martin, Armelle, *Canadian Society for Eighteenth-Century Studies*, 474
St-Maurice, J.-P., *Institute of Space & Atmospheric Studies*, 847
St-Onge, Pascale, *Fédération nationale des communications (CSN)*, 721
St-Onge, Sylvain, *Carrefour d'entraide de Drummond*, 515
St-Onge, Marc, *Association québécoise pour le loisir des personnes handicapées*, 176
St-Pierre, Martin, *Chambre de commerce et d'industrie de Shawinigan*, 546
St-Pierre, Sonia, *Association coopérative d'économie familiale du Grand-Portage*, 98
St-Pierre, Patrice, *Réseau FADOQ*, 1224
St-Pierre, Nathalie, *Canadian Propane Association*, 461
St-Pierre, Rémy, *Real Estate Institute of Canada*, 1206
St-Pierre, Martin, *Centraide Saguenay-Lac St-Jean*, 523
St-Pierre, Léna, *Réseau des SADC et CAE*, 1221
St-Pierre, Alain, *Association des centres jeunesse du Québec*, 108
St-Pierre, Yves, *Société d'histoire de Weedon*, 1312
St-Pierre, France, *Association du syndrome de Down de L'Estrie*, 131
St-Pierre, Marjolaine, *Early Childhood Care & Education New Brunswick*, 666
St-Pierre, Lynda, *L'Arche Québec*, 77
St.Amand, Sean, *Ontario Brain Injury Association*, 1068
Stacey, Edith, *Edmonton Musicians' Association*, 678
Stacey, Jeremy, *Professional Association of Canadian Theatres*, 1182
Stacey, Joanne, *PFLAG Canada Inc.*, 1155
Stack, Kelly, *Essex Community Services*, 696
Stack, Marianna, *Canadian Association of Elizabeth Fry Societies*, 313
Stade, Phil, *Alberta Soaring Council*, 47
Stadelbauer, Kelly, *Association of Ontario Midwives*, 155
Stadelbauer-Sampa, Cheryl-Ann, *United Church of Canada*, 1409
Stadnick, Carla, *Saskatchewan Land Surveyors' Association*, 1268
Stadnyk, Peter M., *Dance Oremus Danse*, 649
Stajic, Janina, *Canadian Public Relations Society Inc.*, 463

Executive Name Index

Staley, Christine, *Canadian Corporate Counsel Association*, 365
Stamatakis, Tom, *Canadian Police Association*, 456
Stamatakis, Tom, *British Columbia Police Association*, 249
Stamper, Kory, *Dictionary Society of North America*, 1521
Standeven, Heidi, *Red Road HIV/AIDS Network*, 1210
Stanfield, Angus, *The Royal Canadian Legion*, 1240
Stanfield, Susan, *Spectrum Society for Community Living*, 1340
Stanford, Mark, *Newfoundland & Labrador Lacrosse Association*, 1019
Stang, Tim, *Canadian Fencing Federation*, 389
Stang, Steve, *Professional Engineers Ontario*, 1185
Stang, Colette, *Saskatchewan Pro Life Association*, 1272
Stanger, Linda L., *College of Licensed Practical Nurses of Alberta*, 585
Stanhope, Joe, *Association of Vancouver Island Coastal Communities*, 164
Staniland, Emily, *Editors' Association of Canada*, 674
Stankovic, Silvia, *Human Resources Professionals Association*, 825
Stanley, Marni, *Vancouver Island University Faculty Association*, 1427
Stanley, Rob, *The Society of Energy Professionals*, 1328
Stanley, Joanne, *Canadian Women in Communications*, 505
Stanley, Heather, *Clearwater & District Food Bank Society*, 573
Stanley, Margaret, *International Papillomavirus Society*, 1555
Stanley-Young, Donna, *The Registered Nurses Association of the Northwest Territories & Nunavut*, 1213
Stannard, Kevin, *Lupus Ontario*, 922
Stanoev, George, *Newfoundland & Labrador Athletics Association*, 1017
Stanowski, Margaret, *Operation Springboard*, 1116
Stansfield, Katherine, *College of Registered Nurses of Manitoba*, 589
Stansislawski, Sheila, *Civic Institute of Professional Personnel*, 571
Stanton, Jim, *Royal United Services Institute - Vancouver Society*, 1243
Stanton, Kim, *Women's Legal Education & Action Fund*, 1463
Stanzel, Roger, *Canadian Society of Clinical Perfusion*, 482
Staples, Rick, *Tunnelling Association of Canada*, 1400
Staples, Blaine, *Alberta Farm Fresh Producers Association*, 34
Stapleton, Stan, *Union of Solicitor General Employees*, 1408
Stapleton, Donna, *Child Care Connection Nova Scotia*, 558
Stapleton, Allan, *Nova Scotia Construction Labour Relations Association Limited*, 1043
Staresina, Colleen, *Block Watch Society of British Columbia*, 215
Stark, Margarite, *Canadian 4-H Council*, 284
Stark, Laura, *Saskatchewan Association of Naturopathic Practitioners*, 1257
Stark, Kate, *Dixon Hall*, 660
Stark, Christine, *Northern Ontario Darts Association*, 1035
Starke, Alison, *Alberta Central*, 27
Starlight, Yvette, *Impact Society*, 831
Starrett, Dave, *Easter Seals Canada*, 669
Starrett, Tracey, *Human Resources Professionals Association*, 825
Starrett, Tracey, *Human Resources Professionals of Durham*, 826
Start, Bonnie, *Lloydminster Native Friendship Centre*, 916
Startup, Mark, *Retail Council of Canada*, 1228

Starzynski, John, *Mood Disorders Society of Canada*, 973
Stasiuk, Jacqueline, *Portage Friendship Centre Inc.*, 1166
Stastna, Marketa, *Canadian Lung Association*, 428
Stathonikos, Damian, *British Columbia Real Estate Association*, 250
Statia, Basil, *Guyanese Canadian Cultural Association of BC*, 794
Stationwala, Ata, *Saskatchewan College of Podiatrists*, 1261
Staubitzer, Derek, *Parkinson Society Newfoundland & Labrador*, 1141
Stauch, Warren, *Waterloo Regional Heritage Foundation*, 1442
Stauffer, Sheila, *Cornerstone Counselling Society of Edmonton*, 629
Stav, Lesley, *Canadian Culinary Federation*, 374
Staviss, Marcus, *Ontario Dental Association*, 1077
Stavness, Alyn, *Canadian Society of Hospital Pharmacists*, 484
Staz, Ardeth, *Curriculum Services Canada*, 646
Stead-Coyle, Barbara, *Muscular Dystrophy Canada*, 982
Steciw, Orest, *League of Ukrainian Canadians*, 903
Stecyk, Fran, *Armstrong-Spallumcheen Chamber of Commerce*, 83
Stedall, Shelley, *Municipal Finance Officers' Association of Ontario*, 981
Stedwill, Robert, *Canadian Society of Environmental Biologists*, 483
Steele, Victoria, *Arts Ottawa East-Est*, 86
Steele, Peggy, *Oakville Symphony Orchestra*, 1054
Steele, Greg, *Federation of Law Reform Agencies of Canada*, 724
Steele, David, *Earthsave Canada*, 667
Steele, Barbara, *Lower Mainland Local Government Association*, 920
Steele, Craig, *NABET 700 CEP*, 987
Steele, Jana, *International Pension & Employee Benefits Lawyers Association*, 859
Steen, Rachel, *Risk & Insurance Management Society Inc.*, 1234
Steenman-Marcusse, Conny J., *Association for Canadian Studies in the Netherlands*, 1507
Steensma, Monique, *Mediate BC Society*, 957
Steenstra, RJ, *Tourism Red Deer*, 1391
Steer, Andrew, *World Resources Institute*, 1607
Steeve, Jamison, *Martin Prosperity Institute*, 952
Steeves, Jessica, *Association of Professional Engineers & Geoscientists of British Columbia*, 158
Steeves, Marc, *Association of Professional Engineers & Geoscientists of New Brunswick*, 158
Steeves, Arnold, *Canadian Goat Society*, 398
Steeves, Paula, *New Brunswick Society of Medical Laboratory Technologists*, 1012
Steeves, C.A., *University of Toronto Institute for Aerospace Studies*, 1421
Steeves, Kristen, *Chartered Professional Accountants of New Brunswick*, 553
Stefani, Scott, *ViaSport*, 1432
Stefanko, Alix-Rae, *Manitoba Library Association*, 939
Stefanko, Alix-Rae, *Canadian Federation of Library Associations*, 388
Stefanów, Jan J., *Catholic Biblical Federation*, 1515
Steffenson, Darrell, *Manitoba Arm Wrestling Association*, 929
Steffes, Peter, *Heating, Refrigeration & Air Conditioning Institute of Canada*, 810
Stein, Nicci, *The Teresa Group*, 1371
Stein, Barry D., *Colorectal Cancer Association of Canada*, 591

Steinbrenner, Larry, *Archaeological Society of Alberta*, 76
Steinburg, Barry, *Consulting Engineers of Ontario*, 625
Steinebach, Elizabeth, *Artists in Stained Glass*, 85
Steiner, Achim, *United Nations Environment Programme*, 1600
Steiner, Jessica, *Wildlife Preservation Canada*, 1455
Steiner, Achim, *United Nations Development Programme*, 1600
Steinhoff, Barbara, *Ontario Society for the Prevention of Cruelty to Animals*, 1107
Steinhoff, Mary, *United Empire Loyalists' Association of Canada*, 1410
Steinmann, Roger, *The Canadian Addison Society*, 288
Stellinga, Anita, *United Way of Peel Region*, 1416
Stenberg, Robert, *Alberta Maine-Anjou Association*, 39
Stencill, Todd, *Elliot Lake & District Chamber of Commerce*, 685
Stengel, Angie, *American Society of Regional Anesthesia & Pain Medicine*, 1502
Stephanson, Stella, *Vatnabyggd Icelandic Club of Saskatchewan Inc.*, 1430
Stephen, Klinck, *Lutheran Laymen's League of Canada*, 922
Stephen, Alex, *Portfolio Management Association of Canada*, 1167
Stephen, Hibbs, *The Salvation Army START Program*, 1253
Stephens, Margaret, *Community Arts Council of Richmond*, 595
Stephens, Mark, *Association of Professional Engineers & Geoscientists of British Columbia*, 158
Stephens, Sandy, *Canadian Printing Industries Association*, 460
Stephens, Keith, *Nature Saskatchewan*, 1001
Stephens, John F., *American Studies Association*, 1503
Stephens, Dave, *Middlesex-Lambton-Huron Association of Baptist Churches*, 965
Stephens, Sheryl, *Fédération de Netball du Québec*, 710
Stephens, Geoffrey, *Ontario Road Builders' Association*, 1102
Stephenson, Lonnie R., *International Brotherhood of Electrical Workers (AFL-CIO/CFL)*, 1542
Stephenson, Leah, *Association of Ontario Health Centres*, 154
Stephenson, Kish, *Alpine Club of Canada*, 59
Stephenson, Gordon, *Canadian Hereford Association*, 405
Stephenson, Linda M., *The Nature Conservancy of Canada*, 1000
Stephenson, Linda, *The Nature Conservancy of Canada*, 1000
Stephenson, Linda, *The Nature Conservancy of Canada*, 1000
Stephenson, Linda, *The Nature Conservancy of Canada*, 1000
Stephenson, Kathryn, *Tourism Simcoe County*, 1391
Stephenson, Karie, *United Way of Durham Region*, 1414
Stephenson, Janelle, *Wildlife Rescue Association of British Columbia*, 1455
Stephenson, Karen, *Thunderbird Friendship Centre*, 1378
Stephenson, Greg, *Thunder Bay Police Association*, 1378
Stephenson, Ryan, *Victorian Studies Association of Western Canada*, 1434
Stephenson, Robyn, *The Association of School Transportation Services of British Columbia*, 162
Stephenson, Barb, *Wild Rose Draft Horse Association*, 1454
Stepleton, Jared, *Canadian Paper Money Society*, 449

Steppan, Mat, *Association of Science & Engineering Technology Professionals of Alberta*, 162
Steranka, Marilyn, *Saskatchewan Professional Planners Institute*, 1272
Sterdnica, Marilyn, *The Appraisal Institute of Canada - Saskatchewan*, 75
Steringa, Erinn, *WaterCan*, 1442
Sterken, Elisabeth, *Infant Feeding Action Coalition*, 836
Sterling, Jamie, *Canadian Association of Nordic Ski Instructors*, 323
Sterling, Ray, *Associated Research Centres for the Urban Underground Space*, 89
Stern, Susan, *The Canadian Society for the Weizmann Institute of Science*, 478
Stern, Norman, *Canadian Zionist Federation*, 506
Stern, Hartley, *The Canadian Medical Protective Association*, 434
Stetic, Dan, *Alberta Team Handball Federation*, 49
Stetson, Alanna, *Prince Edward Island Association of Optometrists*, 1172
Steven, Jennifer, *Tofino-Long Beach Chamber of Commerce*, 1381
Steven, David, *Canadian League Against Epilepsy*, 426
Steven, Chris, *Family & Children's Services Niagara*, 701
Steven, Tony, *Australian Society of Association Executives Ltd.*, 1513
Stevens, Sharon, *Arusha Centre Society*, 86
Stevens, Ken, *Manitoba Diving Association*, 935
Stevens, Dave, *British Columbia Environmental Network*, 240
Stevens, Janet, *Canadian Amateur Musicians*, 292
Stevens, Cyndi, *Port Alberni Friendship Center*, 1165
Stevens, Sinclair M., *Progressive Canadian Party*, 1187
Stevens, Sara, *Pine Tree Potters Guild*, 1160
Stevens, Emile, *Electric Vehicle Society*, 682
Stevens, Holly, *Saskatchewan Physical Education Association*, 1271
Stevens, Anitra, *Athletics Nova Scotia*, 181
Stevens, Maria, *Association of Corporate Travel Executives Inc. Canada*, 146
Stevens, Sherri, *Women's Executive Network*, 1462
Stevens, Sherri, *Canadian Board Diversity Council*, 345
Stevenson, Dallas, *Comox Valley Community Arts Council*, 608
Stevenson, Liliane, *Union mondiale des organisations féminines catholiques*, 1599
Stevenson, R. Lynn, *Canadian Foundation for Healthcare Improvement*, 393
Stevenson, David, *Association of Saskatchewan Forestry Professionals*, 161
Stevenson, Tracy, *ParaSport & Recreation PEI*, 1139
Stevenson, Angie, *Saskatchewan Early Childhood Association*, 1264
Stevenson, Alec, *Artscape*, 86
Stevenson, Derek, *New West Theatre Society*, 1014
Stevenson, Elaine, *Ontario Lawn Bowls Association*, 1088
Stewart, Marlena, *Nanaimo Association for Community Living*, 987
Stewart, Phil, *Prince Edward Island Fencing Association*, 1174
Stewart, Harry, *Welcome Friend Association*, 1443
Stewart, Kathryn, *International Council on Alcohol, Drugs & Traffic Safety*, 1545
Stewart, Mark, *Lethbridge Lacrosse Association*, 908
Stewart, Christy, *Canadian Hackney Society*, 399
Stewart, Sharleen, *Service Employees International Union (AFL-CIO/CLC)*, 1588

Stewart, Beth, *Thunder Bay District Municipal League*, 1377
Stewart, Darren, *Melita & District Chamber of Commerce*, 959
Stewart, Fraser, *Energy Action Council of Toronto*, 688
Stewart, C. James, *College of Family Physicians of Canada*, 585
Stewart, Scott, *Architects Association of Prince Edward Island*, 78
Stewart, Brett, *Cycling Canada Cyclisme*, 647
Stewart, Ann, *Casey House Hospice Inc.*, 516
Stewart, Shirley, *Canadian Celiac Association*, 352
Stewart, Wendy, *Canadian Celiac Association*, 352
Stewart, Robert, *New Brunswick Association of Nursing Homes, Inc.*, 1005
Stewart, John, *Canadian Nuclear Association*, 442
Stewart, Jane, *Central Ontario Industrial Relations Institute*, 525
Stewart, Robert, *Catholic Health Association of New Brunswick*, 520
Stewart, Ruth, *Na'amat Canada Inc.*, 987
Stewart, Dave, *Beef Farmers of Ontario*, 204
Stewart, Jeremy, *Prince George Symphony Orchestra Society*, 1179
Stewart, Robert, *Sons of Scotland Benevolent Association*, 1333
Stewart, Carol, *College of Alberta Denturists*, 582
Stewart, Darryl, *Toronto Sheet Metal Contractors Association*, 1387
Stewart, Caroline, *Prospect Human Services*, 1189
Stewart, Tracy, *Physiotherapy Association of British Columbia*, 1159
Stewart, Coreena, *Mennonite Church Canada*, 961
Stewart, Frances, *Urology Nurses of Canada*, 1423
Stewart, Hilary, *Manitoba Beekeepers' Association*, 932
Stewart, Don, *Millarville Racing & Agricultural Society*, 965
Stewart, Robyn, *Western Canadian Music Alliance*, 1449
Stewart, Tim, *St. Albert Firefighters - Union Local 2130*, 1248
Stewart, Jon, *Vasculitis Foundation Canada*, 1430
Stewart, Lorraine, *College of Alberta Psychologists*, 582
Stewart, Janice, *Truro Art Society*, 1400
Stewart, Donna, *Storytellers of Canada*, 1350
Stewart, Shane, *Community Futures Network Society of Alberta*, 598
Stewart, Duane, *Welsh Pony & Cob Society of Canada*, 1444
Stewart, Alissa, *Saskatchewan Cheerleading Association*, 1261
Stewart, James, *British Columbia Association of Broadcasters*, 231
Stewart, Karen, *Public Works Association of British Columbia*, 1194
Stewart, Jessica, *Pancreatic Cancer Canada Foundation*, 1138
Stewart-Belisle, Kelly, *Armed Forces Communications & Electronics Association (Canada)*, 82
Stewart-Verger, Ruth, *Storytellers of Canada*, 1350
Steyn, Doug G., *Canadian Meteorological & Oceanographic Society*, 435
Stezenko, Dan, *Habitat for Humanity Canada*, 797
Stieb, Tammy, *University of Saskatchewan Faculty Association*, 1420
Stiefel, Barry, *Association for Canadian Jewish Studies*, 132
Stiemer, Robert, *Council of Ontario Construction Associations*, 634
Stienburg, Mary, *Eastern Shore Ringette Association*, 671

Stigter, Shelley, *Schizophrenia Society of Alberta*, 1283
Stilborn, Lisa, *Canadian Fuels Association*, 396
Stiles, Paul, *Beef Farmers of Ontario*, 204
Stiles, Marit, *New Democratic Party*, 1014
Stiles, Brandy, *Spinal Cord Injury British Columbia*, 1343
Stiltzenberger, Betty, *Echo-Edson Cultural Heritage Organization*, 671
Stimmell, Carole, *The Ontario Archaeological Society*, 1060
Stinnissen, Peter, *Canadian Nursing Students' Association*, 443
Stinson, Bob, *CARP*, 514
Stinson, Al, *Canadian Institute of Forestry*, 416
Stinson, David, *Organization of Military Museums of Canada*, 1126
Stinson, Kathy, *Victoria Cool Aid Society*, 1432
Stinson, Jean, *Red Deer Action Group*, 1209
Stinson, Paul, *Alberta Biotechnology Association*, 26
Stintz, Karen, *Variety - The Children's Charity (Ontario)*, 1429
Stipp, Ron, *Canadian Labour Congress*, 425
Stirling, Bill, *Newfoundland & Labrador Association of Realtors*, 1016
Stirling, Roger C., *Seafood Producers Association of Nova Scotia*, 1288
Stirling, Bill, *Copian*, 628
Stirling, Jim, *Hamilton Industrial Environmental Association*, 801
Stith, Dan, *Alberta Sport Parachuting Association*, 48
Stitt, Mark, *American Society of Heating, Refrigerating & Air Conditioning Engineers*, 1500
Stitz, Klaus, *Canada's Medical Technology Companies*, 282
Stocco, Lisa, *Canadian Public Relations Society Inc.*, 463
Stock, Rene, *Saskatchewan Genealogical Society*, 1266
Stockdale, David, *Table Tennis Yukon*, 1366
Stocker, Simon, *European Solidarity Towards Equal Participation of People*, 1524
Stocking, Luke, *Development & Peace*, 655
Stockley, Johanna, *Seasons Centre for Grieving Children*, 1288
Stocks, John C., *National Education Association*, 1576
Stocks, Ron, *Alberta Electrical League*, 33
Stockwell, Grant, *CAA British Columbia*, 267
Stoesz, Conrad, *Manitoba Mennonite Historical Society*, 940
Stokes, Nancy, *Jane Austen Society of North America*, 868
Stokes, Kathy, *Manitoba Genealogical Society Inc.*, 937
Stokes, Alex, *Alberta Falconry Association*, 34
Stokesbury, Bria, *Kings Historical Society*, 888
Stoll, Tamara, *Insurance Bureau of Canada*, 849
Stoll, Benjamin, *Réso Santé Colombie Britannique*, 1226
Stoltz, Keith, *Canada East Equipment Dealers' Association*, 278
Stoncius, Victoria, *Canadian Icelandic Horse Federation*, 410
Stone, Ken, *Canadian Oilseed Processors Association*, 445
Stone, Dennis, *Canadian Baptists of Western Canada*, 341
Stone, Karen, *Alberta College of Medical Diagnostic & Therapeutic Technologists*, 29
Stone, Kelly, *Canadian Association of Family Resource Programs*, 314
Stone, Cathy, *Canadian Parents for French*, 450
Stone, James, *College of Physicians & Surgeons of Alberta*, 588
Stone, Greg, *Conservation International*, 1519
Stone, Jeff, *Kamloops Wildlife Park Society*, 881

Stone, Cheryl, *North Okanagan Labour Council*, 1031
Stonechild, Jason, *Saskatchewan Federation of Police Officers*, 1265
Stonefish, Geoff, *Association of Iroquois & Allied Indians*, 149
Stoneking, Kristin, *Fellowship of Reconciliation*, 1526
Stones, David, *Royal Canadian Armoured Corps Association*, 1239
Stoodley, Alison, *Newfoundland & Labrador Organization of Women Entrepreneurs*, 1020
Storch, Jason, *Association of Alberta Agricultural Fieldmen*, 139
Storen, Ken, *Ontario Occupational Health Nurses Association*, 1094
Storey, Mark, *James Bay Association for Community Living*, 868
Storie-Pugh, Sarah, *International Association of Professional Congress Organizers*, 1540
Storm, Svend Aage, *Royal Danish Guards Association of Western Canada*, 1242
Storrs, Cheryl, *Kiwanis International (Western Canada District)*, 892
Stos, Carol, *Women's Legal Education & Action Fund*, 1463
Stott, Mark, *Mutual Fund Dealers Association of Canada*, 986
Stout, Bruce, *Vancouver Electric Vehicle Association*, 1425
Stovall, Tyler E., *American Historical Association*, 1494
Stover, Tim, *Motorcycle & Moped Industry Council*, 976
Stovin, Elaine, *British Columbia Cattlemen's Association*, 235
Stow, Laura, *Starlight Children's Foundation Canada*, 1348
Strachan, Paul, *Air Canada Pilots Association*, 19
Strack, Maria, *Canadian Geophysical Union*, 397
Stradiotti, Leo, *Council of Marine Carriers*, 634
Strand, Katie, *National Association of Addiction Treatment Providers*, 1573
Strasser, Lezlie, *Cornwall & Area Chamber of Commerce*, 629
Strathdee, Mike, *Abundance Canada*, 3
Stratton, Bill, *Durham Regional Labour Council*, 665
Stratton, Wayne, *Englehart & District Chamber of Commerce*, 689
Straub, Gary, *John Howard Society of Alberta*, 874
Straus, Kathy, *Woodstock & District Developmental Services*, 1464
Strauss, Jonathan, *Occupational & Environmental Medical Association of Canada*, 1054
Straw, Will, *McGill Institute for the Study of Canada*, 955
Strebly, Johnathon, *Society of Graphic Designers of Canada*, 1329
Streich-Poser, Kim, *Children's Aid Society of Algoma*, 560
Strelioff, Angela, *Regina Therapeutic Recreation Association*, 1212
Stremes, David, *Bytown Railway Society*, 267
Stremlaw, Greg, *Canadian Sport Tourism Alliance*, 490
Strickland, Jeff, *Pacific National Exhibition*, 1135
Strickland, Jason, *Clarenville Area Chamber of Commerce*, 572
Strickland, Sean, *Ontario Construction Secretariat*, 1074
Strickland, Will, *Urban Music Association of Canada*, 1422
Strike, Leslie, *Royal Astronomical Society of Canada*, 1238
Strike, Carol, *The Canadian Association for HIV Research*, 301
Stringer, Mike, *Canadian Institute of Plumbing & Heating*, 418

Stroeher, Virginia, *Association of Professors of Bishop's University*, 160
Strohschein, Arlin, *Canadian Welsh Black Cattle Society*, 503
Strom, Brian, *Canadian Institute for Conflict Resolution*, 412
Stromar, Janice, *Vancouver Island Real Estate Board*, 1427
Stromberg, Carol, *British Columbia Registered Music Teachers' Association*, 251
Stromner, Calli, *Alberta Triathlon Association*, 50
Stronach, Belinda, *The Belinda Stronach Foundation*, 204
Strong, Beryth, *Association of Manitoba Museums*, 151
Strong, Suzette, *Markham Stouffville Hospital Foundation*, 952
Strong, Heather, *The Terry Fox Foundation*, 1372
Strooband, Kevin, *Ontario Society for the Prevention of Cruelty to Animals*, 1106
Strooband, Kevin, *Lincoln County Humane Society*, 912
Stroock, Lucy, *Concerned Educators Allied for a Safe Environment*, 1519
Stroock, Lucy, *Concerned Educators Allied for a Safe Environment*, 1519
Strotmann, Geoff, *Model Aeronautics Association of Canada Inc.*, 970
Strub, Arnold, *Stoney Creek Chamber of Commerce*, 1350
Strus, William J., *SUS Foundation of Canada*, 1357
Struthers, David, *Cranbrook & District Chamber of Commerce*, 638
Stuart, Alexandria, *Autism Society of British Columbia*, 189
Stuart, Terry, *British Columbia Supercargoes' Association*, 255
Stuart, Ian A., *Turks & Caicos Development Organization of Canada*, 1400
Stuart, Shirley, *Buckskinners Muzzleloading Association, Limited*, 261
Stuart, Roberta, *Council of Parent Participation Preschools in British Columbia*, 635
Stubbs, Darrin, *Grande Prairie & District Association for Persons with Developmental Disabilities*, 781
Stubbs, Etti, *Association of Jewish Libraries (Toronto)*, 150
Stuckey, Nan, *Big Brothers Big Sisters of Ontario*, 210
Stueck, Gordon, *Leader Board of Trade*, 903
Stuempfle, Stephen, *Society for Ethnomusicology*, 1590
Stuhl, Connie, *Alberta Genealogical Society*, 36
Stumo-Langer, Nick, *Institute for Local Self-Reliance*, 1532
Stumpf-Allen, Craig, *Edmonton Community Foundation*, 676
Stumph, David, *Council of Science Editors*, 1520
Stunzi, Shirley, *Calgary Combative Sports Commission*, 271
Sturchio, Neil, *Geochemical Society*, 1527
Sturk-Nadeau, Chantal, *Economic Development Winnipeg Inc.*, 673
Styles, Doug, *Military Collectors Club of Canada*, 965
Styles, Linda, *Cumberland Equal Rights for the Disabled*, 645
Styre, Wanda, *The Appraisal Institute of Canada - Saskatchewan*, 75
Suchan, Laura, *Oshawa Historical Society*, 1128
Suchar, Lynette, *Saskatchewan Environmental Society*, 1265
Sudbury, Brian, *Alberta 5 Pin Bowlers' Association*, 21
Sudchak, Carol, *Canadian Home Builders' Association - British Columbia*, 407
Sue, Kidd, *Canadian Catholic Campus Ministry*, 351

Executive Name Index

Sue-Ping, Marina, *Schizophrenia Society of Ontario*, 1284
Suess, David, *Canadian Manufacturers & Exporters*, 429
Suffern, Lori, *Vaughan Chamber of Commerce*, 1430
Suffield, Trevor, *On Screen Manitoba*, 1058
Sufi, Khalil, *Hilal Committee of Metropolitan Toronto & Vicinity*, 814
Suggett, Brenda, *Canadian Association of Road Safety Professionals*, 331
Sugumar, Ganesan, *Canada-Sri Lanka Business Council*, 284
Suk, Millie, *American Association of Neuromuscular & Electrodiagnostic Medicine*, 1490
Suleman, Alykhan, *New Circles Community Services*, 1014
Sulis, Jim, *Canadian Aviation Historical Society*, 340
Sullivan, Gerry, *Placentia Area Chamber of Commerce*, 1161
Sullivan, Marjorie, *Alzheimer Society Canada*, 61
Sullivan, Jacqui, *Canadian Association for Laboratory Animal Science*, 302
Sullivan, Sherry, *Cement Association of Canada*, 521
Sullivan, Veronica, *Society for Information Management*, 1590
Sullivan, Marcy, *Ducks Unlimited Canada*, 663
Sullivan, Derek, *Last Post Fund*, 899
Sullivan, John, *Doctors Nova Scotia*, 660
Sullivan, Dee, *People, Words & Change*, 1152
Sullivan, Sarah, *AIDS Vancouver Island*, 17
Sullivan, Warren, *Royal Newfoundland Constabulary Association*, 1242
Sullivan, David, *Manitoba Brain Injury Association Inc.*, 932
Sullivan, Nevan, *Ottawa Carleton Ultimate Association*, 1129
Sullivan, Anne T., *Association for Preservation Technology International*, 1509
Sullivan, Keith, *Fish, Food & Allied Workers*, 739
Sullivan, Michael, *Canadian Transplant Association*, 496
Sullivan, Marie-Eve, *Triathlon Québec*, 1398
Sullivan, Katie, *International Emissions Trading Association*, 1546
Sullivan, Nicole, *Canadian Horse Breeders' Association*, 408
Sullivan, Mike, *Canadian Common Ground Alliance*, 361
Sultanem, Khalil, *Association des radio-oncologues du Québec*, 127
Sumi, Kim, *Ontario Association of Architects*, 1061
Summach, Jay, *Edmonton Construction Association*, 676
Summerhill, Louise R., *Birthright International*, 212
Summers, Steven, *Gas Processing Association Canada*, 767
Summers, Bill, *Colleges Ontario*, 591
Summers, Marcie, *Positive Women's Network*, 1168
Summers, Craig, *Port Alberni Association for Community Living*, 1165
Summers, Paul N., *World Presidents' Organization*, 1607
Summers, Mike, *Boxing Newfoundland & Labrador*, 220
Summerside, Lyse, *Mosaïque centre d'action bénévole et communautaire*, 975
Summerville, Chris, *Manitoba Schizophrenia Society, Inc.*, 944
Summerville, Chris, *Schizophrenia Society of Canada*, 1283
Summerville, Donna, *Ontario Brain Injury Association*, 1068
Sumner, Janet, *Canadian Parks & Wilderness Society*, 451
Sundaramoorthy, Jovita, *Diabetes Canada*, 655

Sundell, Karyn, *Electrical Contractors Association of Thunder Bay*, 683
Sunder, Chitra, *AWIC Community & Social Services*, 191
Sundevic, Linda, *Long Term & Continuing Care Association of Manitoba*, 919
Sundstrom, Kathi, *Decidedly Jazz Danceworks*, 652
Sundt, Thoralf M., *American Association for Thoracic Surgery*, 1489
Sunner, Joginder Singh, *Khalsa Diwan Society*, 884
Suokonautio, Miia, *YWCA Canada*, 1481
Super, Betsy, *American Political Science Association*, 1497
Suppa, Ralph, *Canadian Institute of Plumbing & Heating*, 418
Suppa, Bruno M., *COSTI Immigrant Services*, 631
Suppa, Matthew, *Academy of Management*, 1485
Suraci, Michael, *Ontario Cycling Association*, 1076
Surbey, Val, *Manitoba Down Syndrome Society*, 936
Surette, Susanne, *Canadian Health Information Management Association*, 402
Surette, Clarence, *The Ontario Archaeological Society*, 1060
Surette, Lisette, *Fédération des femmes acadiennes et francophones du Nouveau-Brunswick*, 715
Surette, Jean, *Music/Musique NB*, 984
Surma, Teena, *Algonquin Arts Council*, 54
Surprenant, Richard, *Alberta Sulphur Research Ltd.*, 48
Surprenant, Yves, *Fédération de tennis de table du Québec*, 710
Surprenant, Loretta, *Eastern Apicultural Society of North America, Inc.*, 1522
Surtees, Jeff, *Trout Unlimited Canada*, 1399
Surti, Russi, *Zoroastrian Society of Ontario*, 1482
Surujbali, Serena, *Boys & Girls Clubs of Ontario*, 223
Susanto, Pauline, *Catholic Charismatic Renewal Council, Toronto*, 518
Sushilnikova, Oxana, *Apparel Quebec*, 74
Sushko, O., *World Federation of Ukrainian Women's Organizations*, 1466
Susko, Allyson, *Schizophrenia Society of Ontario*, 1284
Sutcliffe, Joan, *The Ontario Poetry Society*, 1096
Sutdhibhasilp, Noulmook, *Asian Community AIDS Services*, 87
Sutherland, Mike, *Winnipeg Police Association*, 1459
Sutherland, John K., *Atlantic Dairy Council*, 183
Sutherland, John K., *Nova Scotia Automobile Dealers' Association*, 1041
Sutherland, John K., *Nova Scotia College of Chiropractors*, 1042
Sutherland, Lori, *Nova Scotia Society for the Prevention of Cruelty to Animals*, 1049
Sutherland, Janet, *Canadian Lung Association*, 428
Sutherland, Janet, *Canadian Thoracic Society*, 494
Sutherland, Lisa Jean, *College of Physicians & Surgeons of New Brunswick*, 588
Sutherland, John K., *Recreation Vehicle Dealers Association of Canada*, 1208
Sutherland, David, *The Royal Nova Scotia Historical Society*, 1242
Sutherland, Barbara, *Association of Canadian Travel Agents - Alberta & NWT*, 144
Sutherland, Peter, *Canada-Arab Business Council*, 283
Sutherland, Joan, *Prince George Native Friendship Centre*, 1179
Sutherland, Janet, *Canadian Respiratory Health Professionals*, 467

Sutherland, Margaret, *POWERtalk International*, 1584
Sutherland, Katherine, *Open Learning at Thompson Rivers University*, 1114
Sutherland, Bonnie, *Nova Scotia Nature Trust*, 1047
Sutherland, Gillian, *Alberta Dressage Association*, 33
Sutherland, Chip, *Radio Starmaker Fund*, 1203
Sutherland-Allan, Jaqi, *PFLAG Canada Inc.*, 1156
Sutter, Sandra, *Aboriginal Friendship Centre of Calgary*, 2
Suttie, Margaret, *Reading Council for Literacy Advance in Montréal*, 1205
Sutton, Vanessa, *Ottawa Symphony Orchestra Inc.*, 1132
Sutton, James, *Canadian Association of Importers & Exporters*, 318
Sutton, Camilla, *Women in Capital Markets*, 1460
Sutton, Stephanie, *CADORA British Columbia*, 268
Sutton, Dean, *Canadian Deaf Curling Association*, 376
Sutton, Teresa, *Helderleigh Foundation*, 811
Svarich, Brigitte, *Energy Council of Canada*, 688
Svenningson, Victor, *Canadian Institute for Theatre Technology*, 414
Svetanoff, Rachel, *International Student Pugwash*, 1562
Svigir, Beba, *Calgary Immigrant Women's Association*, 273
Svoboda, Carl, *The Green Party of Alberta*, 788
Swackhammer, Susan, *Elementary Teachers' Federation of Ontario*, 684
Swail, David, *Canadian Publishers' Council*, 464
Swain, Marcel, *Lu'ma Native Housing Society*, 920
Swaine, Sue, *Racquetball Ontario*, 1202
Swaine, Laura, *Heartwood Centre for Community Youth Development*, 810
Swallow, Cheryl, *Canadian Cancer Society*, 349
Swamp, Jerry, *First Nations Chiefs of Police Association*, 738
Swan, Andy, *Community Living Kincardine & District*, 603
Swan, Bill, *Canadian Society of Children's Authors, Illustrators & Performers*, 481
Swan, Sue, *American Lung Association*, 1495
Swan, Oliver, *International Union of Bricklayers & Allied Craftworkers (AFL-CIO/CFL)*, 1564
Swan, Roger, *Alberta Reappraising AIDS Society*, 43
Swan, Jessica, *National Association of Addiction Treatment Providers*, 1573
Swanson, Janis, *Thunder Bay Regional Arts Council*, 1378
Swanson, Karen, *Saskatchewan Diving*, 1263
Sward, Emily Beckett, *Junior League of Toronto*, 878
Swatridge, Stephen, *Carizon Family & Community Services*, 513
Swayne, David, *College & University Retiree Associations of Canada*, 582
Swayzer, Natalie, *Canadian Network for Environmental Education & Communication*, 440
Swedlove, Wendy, *Canadian Tourism Human Resource Council*, 495
Sweeney, Peggy, *Ontario Principals' Council*, 1097
Sweeney, Peter, *YMCA Canada*, 1473
Sweeney, Christopher, *The Vimy Foundation*, 1435
Sweeney, Debora, *British Columbia's Children's Hospital Foundation*, 259
Sweet, Wade, *Prince Edward Island Veterinary Medical Association*, 1178
Sweet, Geri, *Manitoba Horse Council Inc.*, 938

Sweetlove, Jim A., *Conservation Halton Foundation*, 622
Sweetman, Fleur, *Vancouver Pro Musica Society*, 1428
Swenson, Rick, *Progressive Conservative Party of Saskatchewan*, 1187
Swerid, Cathy, *Saskatchewan Registered Music Teachers' Association*, 1273
Swetlishoff, Stephanie, *Union of Spiritual Communities of Christ*, 1408
Swidnicki, Joni, *Manitoba Women's Institutes*, 947
Swidrovich, Jaris, *Canadian Society of Hospital Pharmacists*, 484
Swift, Lorraine, *Change for Children Association*, 551
Swift, Megan, *Canadian Association of Slavists*, 333
Swinden, Scott, *Canadian Federation of Earth Sciences*, 386
Swindlehurst, Dave, *Canadian Ski Patrol*, 471
Swinemar, Dianne, *Feed Nova Scotia*, 731
Swinimer, Hope, *Hope for Wildlife Society*, 821
Swinnen, Johan, *International Association of Agricultural Economists*, 1538
Swinton, Ian, *Simcoe & District Chamber of Commerce*, 1299
Swinton, Andrea, *Hearing Foundation of Canada*, 808
Swinton, Andrea, *Ontario Mental Health Foundation*, 1091
Switzer, Doug, *Ontario Motor Coach Association*, 1091
Switzer, Colette, *Alberta Media Production Industries Association*, 40
Switzer, Doug, *Motor Coach Canada*, 975
Switzer-McIntyre, Sharon, *Physiotherapy Education Accreditation Canada*, 1159
Swonek, Raymond, *Alberta Public Housing Administrators' Association*, 43
Swords, Brian, *Scarboro Foreign Mission Society*, 1282
Swystun, Lenore, *Saskatchewan Environmental Industry & Managers' Association*, 1264
Sy, Elhadj As, *International Federation of Red Cross & Red Crescent Societies*, 1549
Sy, Mame Moussa, *Centre Communautaire Bon Courage De Place Benoît*, 526
Sych, Darrin, *Saskatoon Region Association of REALTORS*, 1280
Sychuk, Bruce E., *British Columbia Sheet Metal Association*, 253
Sydorenko, Nadia, *Ukrainian Canadian Congress*, 1402
Syed, Farukh, *Pakistani Canadian Cultural Association of British Columbia*, 1137
Syed, Hasanat Ahmad, *Human Rights & Race Relations Centre*, 826
Sylvester, Bruce, *Radiation Safety Institute of Canada*, 1202
Sylvester, Doug, *Biathlon Saskatchewan*, 208
Sylvestervich, John, *Durham Personal Computer Users' Club*, 665
Sylvestre, Jean-François, *Syndicat de la fonction publique du Québec inc. (ind.)*, 1361
Sylvestre, Andréanne, *Katimavik*, 882
Sylvestre, Eric, *Meadow Lake Tribal Council*, 956
Syme, Brent, *Southern Alberta Curling Association*, 1337
Symes, Kevin, *Canadian Deafblind Association (National)*, 376
Symmonds, Celina, *Medicine Hat & District Food Bank*, 958
Symsyk, Meg, *Music Managers Forum Canada*, 984
Synnott, Bernard, *Fondation du barreau du Québec*, 745
Syrette, Cathy, *Indian Friendship Centre in Sault Ste Marie*, 834
Syrota, Tracey, *The Association of School Transportation Services of British Columbia*, 162

Executive Name Index

Syslak, Anne-Marie, *Canadian Parks & Wilderness Society*, 450
Sysyn, Frank E., *Canadian Institute of Ukrainian Studies*, 420
Szabolcs, Natasha, *Canadian Association of Pharmacy Students & Interns*, 326
Szalankiewicz, Cyprian, *Startup Canada*, 1348
Szasz, Andrew, *Alzheimer Society of Oxford*, 64
Szczepanski, Elizabeth, *Canadian Polish Congress*, 456
Szekrenyes, Julius, *Society for the Study of Egyptian Antiquities*, 1327
Szentmiklossy, Frank, *Island Horse Council*, 865
Szeverenyi, Victor, *Tourism Burlington*, 1389
Szkotnicki, Jean, *Canadian Animal Health Institute*, 293
Sztain, David, *Historical Society of Alberta*, 816
Szubelak, Aleksandra, *Ukrainian World Congress*, 1404
Szuck, Maryanne, *Society for the Preservation of Old Mills - Canadian Chapter*, 1326
Szwajcer, Andrea, *Manitoba Association of Health Information Providers*, 930
Szwaluk, Lesia, *Ukrainian Canadian Foundation of Taras Shevchenko*, 1402

T

Tabachnick, Marcus, *Québec English School Boards Association*, 1197
Tabor, Karen, *Old Strathcona Foundation*, 1056
Tabor, Don, *Cumberland County Genealogical Society*, 645
Tachejian, Annie, *Armenian Relief Society of Canada, Inc.*, 83
Tachuk, Rick, *Canadian Council of Technicians & Technologists*, 370
Tadashi Oshima, Ken, *Society of Architectural Historians*, 1592
Taggart, Jim, *Canadian Electrical Manufacturers Representatives Association*, 380
Taggart, Leigh, *Habitat for Humanity Canada*, 797
Taggart, Lauren, *American Society for Bone & Mineral Research*, 1498
Taggart, Adrian, *BC Freestyle Ski Association*, 201
Tagoe, Albert, *Association of Professional Engineers & Geoscientists of Alberta*, 157
Tahir, Hassan, *British Columbia Muslim Association*, 247
Tahori, Salaheddine, *Moroccan Association of Toronto*, 974
Tai, Sabrina, *American Society of Heating, Refrigerating & Air Conditioning Engineers*, 1500
Tai, Lui, *Professional Engineers Ontario*, 1185
Taillefer, Bobbi, *Manitoba Teachers' Society*, 946
Taillefer, Fernand O., *Canadian Association of Veterans in United Nations Peacekeeping*, 335
Tailleur, Danielle, *Children's Heart Society*, 562
Taillon, Serge, *Chambre de commerce et d'industrie de Roberval*, 546
Taillon, Peggy, *Canadian Council on Social Development*, 371
Taillon, Gerry, *CNBC*, 576
Tainsh, Brian, *Canadian Crop Hail Association*, 373
Tait, Ian, *Delta Chamber of Commerce*, 653
Tait, Rob, *British Columbia Ringette Association*, 251
Tait, Patricia, *Meeting Professionals International*, 1570
Tak, Devendra, *CIVICUS: World Alliance for Citizen Participation*, 1517
Takacs, April, *Stroke Recovery Association of Manitoba Inc.*, 1352

Takala, Paul, *Canadian Urban Libraries Council*, 500
Takala, Paul, *Canadian Federation of Library Associations*, 388
Takashi, Ishida, *The Japan Foundation, Toronto*, 868
Takayesu, Roy, *Timmins Symphony Orchestra*, 1380
Takeda, Sadao, *International Organization for Standardization*, 1554
Talaee, Alireza, *Association of Professional Engineers & Geoscientists of British Columbia*, 158
Talbot, Solange, *Société de généalogie de Québec*, 1315
Talbot, Colleen, *Spina Bifida & Hydrocephalus Association of Canada*, 1342
Talbot, Colleen, *Spina Bifida & Hydrocephalus Association of British Columbia*, 1341
Talbot, Lucie, *Syndicat des agricultrices du Centre du Québec*, 1362
Talha Patel, Mohammed, *British Columbia Mainland Cricket League*, 246
Talitzaine, Suzanne, *Port Hardy Harvest Food Bank*, 1166
Tallim, Jane, *Media Smarts*, 957
Talman, Jean, *Canadian Association for Irish Studies*, 301
Talman, Jean, *Canadian Celtic Arts Association*, 353
Talmey, Sue, *Canadian Association for Community Living*, 298
Talsma, Stephanie, *Physical & Health Education Canada*, 1158
Tam, David, *Hong Kong-Canada Business Association*, 820
Tam, Bill, *British Columbia Technology Industries Association*, 256
Tam, Karen, *Toronto Financial Services Alliance*, 1384
Tam, David, *Chinese Real Estate Professionals Association of British Columbia*, 565
Tamachi, Shabira, *Oxford County Law Association*, 1134
Tambeau, Stephanie, *Canadian Health Information Management Association*, 402
Tamblyn, Giulliana, *United Nations Association in Canada*, 1411
Tammen, Abby, *National Association of College Auxiliary Services*, 1573
Tamr, Radwan, *Professional Engineers Ontario*, 1185
Tamr, Radwan, *Windsor Islamic Association*, 1456
Tamura, Michael, *Quest Support Services Inc.*, 1200
Tan, Doreen, *Master Painters & Decorators Association*, 954
Tan, Howard, *Federation of Chinese Canadian Professionals (Québec)*, 723
Tanaka, Stewart, *Judo Canada*, 876
Tanchak, Shenda, *Federation of Health Regulatory Colleges of Ontario*, 724
Tanchak, Shenda, *College of Physiotherapists of Ontario*, 589
Tancock, Theresa, *Canadian Deafblind Association (National)*, 376
Tang, Ian, *College of Family Physicians of Canada*, 584
Tang, Elizabeth, *Canadian Public Relations Society Inc.*, 463
Tang, Gengmin, *Canadian Society of Chinese Medicine & Acupuncture*, 481
Tang, Sammy, *ASM International - Calgary Chapter*, 87
Tanguay, Pierre, *Chambre immobilière de Saint-Hyacinthe Inc.*, 551
Tanguay, Micheline, *Canadian Amateur Musiciens*, 292
Tanguay, Claude, *Syndicat des professeurs de l'État du Québec (ind.)*, 1364
Tanguay, Maxime, *Association provinciale des constructeurs d'habitations du Québec inc.*, 168

Tanguay, Robert, *Fondation communautaire du Grand-Québec*, 743
Tanguay, Christian, *Centre communautaire des gais et lesbiennes de Montréal*, 526
Tanguay-Labrosse, Hubert, *Orchestre symphonique des jeunes de Sherbrooke*, 1118
Tanguy, Julie, *Association des jeunes bègues de Québec*, 117
Tankoano, Fimba, *Fédération des centres d'action bénévole du Québec*, 713
Tanner, Jennifer, *211 Southwest Ontario*, 1401
Tanner, Karen, *AIDS New Brunswick*, 17
Tanner, Annette, *Wilderness Committee*, 1454
Tanner, Loretta, *Alzheimer Society of Durham Region*, 62
Tanner, Scott, *Judo Nova Scotia*, 876
Tansley, Keith, *Community Living Mississauga*, 603
Taparti, Marianne, *Pulaarvik Kablu Friendship Centre*, 1194
Tapaungai, Quvianatiliaq, *Aiviq Hunters & Trappers Organization*, 20
Tapley, Jane, *International Orthoptic Association*, 1554
Tapp-McDougall, Caroline, *Canadian Abilities Foundation*, 285
Taqtaq, Abe, *Frontier Duty Free Association*, 763
Tarantino-Dean, Christie, *Institute of Food Technologists*, 1532
Taraschuk, Landon, *Manitoba Coin Club*, 934
Tarasick, Madeliene, *Canadian Women for Women in Afghanistan*, 504
Tarbell, Reaghan, *Kanien'kehaka Onkwawen'na Raotitiohkwa Language & Cultural Centre*, 881
Tardif, Gaétan, *Canadian Paralympic Committee*, 449
Tardif, Richard, *Québec Community Newspaper Association*, 1196
Tardif, André, *Réseau du patrimoine franco-ontarien*, 1222
Tardif, Claude, *Association des maisons de commerce extérieur du Québec*, 118
Tardiff, Deb, *Manitoba Environmental Industries Association Inc.*, 936
Tardiff, André, *Groupe régional d'intervention social - Québec*, 792
Targett, John, *Canadian Association for Pharmacy Distribution Management*, 303
Tarini, Natalie, *Canadian Wood Council*, 505
Tarini, Mike, *North Bay Police Association*, 1030
Tariq Kamal, Syed, *British Columbia Muslim Association*, 247
Taris, Sian, *Oakville & District Chamber of Commerce*, 1053
Tarko, Michel, *Justice Institute of British Columbia*, 878
Tarkyth, Dène, *Geological Association of Canada*, 769
Tarnavskyj, Maria, *United Ukrainian Charitable Trust*, 1412
Tarnowski, Rose Marie, *Tourism Thunder Bay*, 1391
Tarshis, Ellen, *Community Living Victoria*, 606
Tarvudd, Ruth, *Lupus Ontario*, 922
Taschuk, Cindy, *Rocky Mountain House & District Chamber of Commerce*, 1235
Tass, Thomas, *World Border Organization*, 1465
Tastsoglou, Evangelia, *Canadian Ethnic Studies Association*, 382
Tataryn, Tamara, *Ukrainian Youth Association of Canada*, 1404
Tate, Dave, *Manitoba Teachers' Society*, 946
Tate, Teresa, *Quadra Island Food Bank*, 1195
Tatsuoka, Fumio, *International Geosynthetics Society*, 1559
Tauber, Fred, *Edmonton Stamp Club*, 679
Taulu, Tracey, *Trauma Association of Canada*, 1396
Taupier, Natalie, *Aphasie Rive-Sud*, 73

Taurins-Crawford, Larissa, *Canadian Alliance of Dance Artists*, 291
Tavares, Maria, *First Portuguese Canadian Cultural Centre*, 739
Tavuchis, Alex, *Canadian Home Builders' Association - British Columbia*, 407
Tayler, Jim, *Whitewater Ontario*, 1453
Taylor, Bonnie, *Manitoba Society of Artists*, 944
Taylor, Cavelle, *Newfoundland & Labrador Darts Association*, 1018
Taylor, Gareth, *Scottish Rite Charitable Foundation of Canada*, 1286
Taylor, Leitta, *College of Audiologists and Speech-Language Pathologists of Manitoba*, 582
Taylor, Sheldon, *Boys & Girls Clubs of Ontario*, 224
Taylor, Glenn, *Community Living Durham North*, 601
Taylor, Paul, *Vulcan Business Development Society*, 1439
Taylor, Robert, *Centreville Chamber of Commerce*, 537
Taylor, R. N. (Neil), *International Society for Soil Mechanics & Geotechnical Engineering*, 1559
Taylor, Hugh, *International Council of Ophthalmology*, 1545
Taylor, Marilyn, *Arrow Lakes Historical Society*, 84
Taylor, Ian, *Ontario Minor Hockey Association*, 1091
Taylor, Nancy, *Tennis Newfoundland & Labrador*, 1371
Taylor, Bill, *Atlantic Salmon Federation*, 186
Taylor, Jill, *Canadian Association of Heritage Professionals*, 317
Taylor, Karen, *Applied Science Technologists & Technicians of British Columbia*, 74
Taylor, Margi, *Canadian Independent Telephone Association*, 411
Taylor, Maureen, *Canadian Institute of Food Science & Technology*, 416
Taylor, Troy, *Restaurants Canada*, 1227
Taylor, Rodney, *Pool & Hot Tub Council of Canada*, 1165
Taylor, Robert P., *Institute of Public Administration of Canada*, 847
Taylor, Dana, *Mechanical Contractors Association of British Columbia*, 956
Taylor, S. Mark, *Canadian Society of Otolaryngology - Head & Neck Surgery*, 485
Taylor, Nancy, *Municipal Finance Officers' Association of Ontario*, 981
Taylor, Nancy, *Local Government Management Association of British Columbia*, 917
Taylor, Cynthia, *Canadian Federation of Music Teachers' Associations*, 388
Taylor, Janet, *Canadian Association of Critical Care Nurses*, 311
Taylor, Peter D., *Ontario Genealogical Society*, 1081
Taylor, James R., *The Royal Philatelic Society of Canada*, 1242
Taylor, Jennifer, *Tourism Industry Association of Canada*, 1389
Taylor, Kathleen, *Hospital for Sick Children Foundation*, 823
Taylor, D., *UNITE HERE*, 1599
Taylor, Mike, *Telecommunications Employees Association of Manitoba*, 1369
Taylor, Mark, *Canadian Academy of Facial Plastic & Reconstructive Surgery*, 286
Taylor, Noreen, *Saint Elizabeth Health Care*, 1246
Taylor, Tobi, *Atlantic Canada Fish Farmers Association*, 182
Taylor, Steven, *Sjogren's Syndrome Foundation Inc.*, 1589
Taylor, Jim, *Downtown Business Association of Edmonton*, 661
Taylor, T.V., *Judo Saskatchewan*, 876
Taylor, Sandy, *Judo Saskatchewan*, 876

Executive Name Index

Taylor, Kelly, *Ontario Horticultural Association*, 1086
Taylor, Rod, *Christian Heritage Party of Canada*, 567
Taylor, Pam, *The New Brunswick Association of Respiratory Therapists Inc.*, 1005
Taylor, Whitney, *Governor General's Performing Arts Awards Foundation*, 778
Taylor, Ron, *Newfoundland & Labrador Association of Technology Industries*, 1016
Taylor, Liz, *Tourism Red Deer*, 1391
Taylor, Paul, *Mortgage Professionals Canada*, 975
Taylor, Heidi, *Playwrights Theatre Centre*, 1162
Taylor, Peter, *British Columbia Food Technolgists*, 241
Taylor, Skye Crawford, *Association of Early Childhood Educators of Newfoundland & Labrador*, 147
Taylor, Greg, *Solo Swims of Ontario Inc.*, 1332
Taylor, Cynthia, *British Columbia Registered Music Teachers' Association*, 251
Taylor, Cynthia, *British Columbia Registered Music Teachers' Association*, 251
Taylor, Adam, *Habitat Acquisition Trust*, 796
Taylor, Earle, *Canadian Organization of Campus Activities*, 447
Taylor, Tracey, *Saskatchewan Dental Assistants' Association*, 1263
Taylor, Ally, *Law Society of Alberta*, 901
Taylor, David, *British Columbia Vegetable Marketing Commission*, 257
Taylor, Lori, *PFLAG Canada Inc.*, 1155
Taylor, Cheryl, *Lake Simcoe Region Conservation Foundation*, 896
Taylor, Barbara, *Newfoundland & Labrador Women's Institutes*, 1022
TAylor, Dave, *Calgary Sledge Hockey Association*, 274
Taylor, Crispin, *American Society of Plant Biologists*, 1502
Taylor, Rod, *Christian Heritage Party of British Columbia*, 567
Taylor, Adam, *Underwater Council of British Columbia*, 1404
Taylor, Keith, *Gateway Research Organization*, 767
Taylor, Bruce, *British Columbia Tenpin Bowling Association*, 256
Taylor, Kim, *Canadian Society of Palliative Care Physicians*, 486
Taylor, Trish, *Association of Fundraising Professionals*, 1512
Taylor, Cathy, *Ontario Nonprofit Network*, 1094
Taylor-Vaisey, Nick, *Canadian Association of Journalists*, 319
Tchatat, Léonie, *La Passerelle - Intégration et Développement Économique*, 1145
Tchorz, Linda, *Parksville & District Chamber of Commerce*, 1142
Teal, Al, *Trenton Care & Share Food Bank*, 1397
Teare, Scott A., *World Organization of the Scout Movement*, 1607
Teasdale, Bryan, *Local Government Management Association of British Columbia*, 917
Teather, Andria, *The Jane Goodall Institute of Canada*, 868
Tebworth, Barbara, *Quinte Construction Association*, 1201
Tedeschi, George, *International Brotherhood of Teamsters (AFL-CIO/CLC)*, 1542
Tedesco-Derouchie, Dani, *Cornwall & District Real Estate Board*, 629
Teed, Deb, *Family & Community Support Services Association of Alberta*, 702
Teegee, Mary, *British Columbia Aboriginal Child Care Society*, 229
Teeple, Erin, *Fernie & District Arts Council*, 732
Teeple, Wayne, *Armed Forces Communications & Electronics Association (Canada)*, 82

Teeple, Charlotte, *Canadian Children's Book Centre*, 355
Teichman, Allan, *Canadian Actors' Equity Association (CLC)*, 288
Teichreb, Rhonda, *Vocational Rehabilitation Association of Canada*, 1436
Teichroeb, Laurel, *Saskatchewan Registered Music Teachers' Association*, 1273
Teigen, Erin, *Alcoholic Beverage Medical Research Foundation*, 1487
Teixeira, Michael, *Ability Online Support Network*, 2
Tejada, Alfonso, *International Watercolour Society - Canada*, 861
Telego, Tacy, *Environmental Bankers Association*, 1523
Telego, D. Jeffrey, *Environmental Bankers Association*, 1523
Telford, John, *United Association of Journeymen & Apprentices of the Plumbing & Pipe Fitting Industry of the United States & Canada*, 1599
Telford, Sheila, *Canadian Alliance of British Pensioners*, 291
Temansja, Giovanni, *Asian Community AIDS Services*, 87
Temkin, Mitchell, *Garth Homer Society*, 767
Temple-Smith, Joyce, *Malton Neighbourhood Services*, 928
Templeton, Jane, *Muskoka Lakes Chamber of Commerce*, 985
Templin, Marjorie, *Sparwood & District Chamber of Commerce*, 1338
Ten Broek, Alied, *Alberta Alpine Ski Association*, 22
ten Kortenaar, Neil, *Canadian Association for Commonwealth Literature & Language Studies*, 298
ten Kortenaar, Neil, *Centre for Comparative Literature*, 531
TenBruggencate, Anita, *Ontario Standardbred Adoption Society*, 1109
Tennant, Doug, *Semiahmoo House Society*, 1290
Tennant, Alan, *Calgary Real Estate Board Cooperative Limited*, 274
Téodori, Johanne, *Parrainage civique Montréal*, 1143
Teodoro, Durvalina, *Portuguese Club of London*, 1167
Teperman, Lee, *Society of Rural Physicians of Canada*, 1330
Terbasket, Edna, *Ki-Low-Na Friendship Society*, 887
Terbasket, Delphine, *Interior Indian Friendship Society*, 852
Teresinski, Jerome, *Association of Polish Engineers in Canada*, 156
Terezakis, Paras, *Kinesis Dance Society*, 888
Ternes, Tara, *Alberta Electrical League*, 33
Terp, Eva, *Federation of Danish Associations in Canada*, 724
Terrault, Guy, *Syndicat des travailleurs de la construction du Québec (CSD)*, 1364
Terreberry, Theresa, *Community Living Welland Pelham*, 606
Terrence, Heather, *Financial Planning Standards Council*, 737
Terriff, Beth, *The Canadian Doukhobor Society*, 378
Terrillon-Mackay, Louise, *Canadian Institute for Mediterranean Studies*, 413
Terrio, Rick, *London Police Association*, 919
Terry, Bernadette, *Armed Forces Communications & Electronics Association (Canada)*, 82
Terry, Wendy, *The Workers' Educational Association of Canada*, 1464
Terry, Linda, *Social Planning Council of Cambridge & North Dumfries*, 1306
Tersakian, Maral, *Institut du cancer de Montréal*, 842
Tersigni, Livia, *Insurance Institute of Ontario*, 850

Tersigni, Livia, *Insurance Institute of Ontario*, 850
Tersigni-Paltrinieri, Mary, *Dress for Success*, 663
Terzariol, Carla, *Trial Lawyers Association of British Columbia*, 1397
Tessier, Daniel, *Comité régional d'éducation pour le développement international de Lanaudière*, 592
Tessier, Pierre, *Ordre des arpenteurs-géomètres du Québec*, 1120
Tessier, Dominic, *Institute of Textile Science*, 847
Tessier, Elizabeth, *Orchestre symphonique de Québec*, 1118
Tessier, Scott, *Canada - Newfoundland & Labrador Offshore Petroleum Board*, 277
Tessier, Marc-André, *Union des cultivateurs franco-ontariens*, 1406
Tessier, Nathalie, *Association Carrefour Famille Montcalm*, 96
Tessier, Marjolaine, *Fondation Jeanne-Crevier*, 746
Testin, Frank, *Dignity Canada Dignité*, 657
Teti, Arlene, *Canadian Cancer Society*, 348
Tetley, Adrianna, *Association of Ontario Health Centres*, 154
Tétrault, Robert, *Syndicat des professeures et professeurs de l'Université de Sherbrooke*, 1363
Tétrault, Éric, *Canadian Manufacturers & Exporters*, 429
Tétrault, Robert, *Association des juristes d'expression française du Manitoba inc.*, 118
Tetreault, Caroline, *Association of Visual Language Interpreters of Canada*, 164
Tétreault, Jean-Claude, *Canadian Board of Examiners for Professional Surveyors*, 345
Tetreault, Caroline, *Westcoast Association of Visual Language Interpreters*, 1447
Tétreault, Jean-Claude, *Association of Canada Lands Surveyors*, 140
Tew, Ryan, *Foothills Research Institute*, 751
Tezel, Handan, *Canadian Society for Chemical Engineering*, 473
Thacker, Amy, *Cariboo Chilcotin Coast Tourism Association*, 512
Thacker, John R., *National Conferences of Firemen & Oilers (SEIU)*, 1575
Thacker, Molly, *American Studies Association*, 1503
Thakar, Tushar, *Toronto Cricket Umpires' & Scorers' Association*, 1383
Thaleshvar, Hansa, *Hindu Society of Alberta*, 815
Thambiah, Kaylee, *Intellectual Property Institute of Canada*, 851
Thames, Carol, *Doorsteps Neighbourhood Services*, 661
Than, Wuchow, *Hamilton Stamp Club*, 802
Thao, Mai, *Canadian Management Centre*, 429
Thauvette-Poupart, Andrée, *Société québécoise des psychothérapeutes professionnels*, 1324
Thawar, Tasleem, *The Canadian Centre/International P.E.N.*, 354
Thebaud, Craig, *Prince Albert & District Labour Council*, 1171
Théberge, Sylvie, *Festivals et Événements Québec*, 733
Théberge, Martin, *Fédération culturelle acadienne de la Nouvelle-Écosse*, 708
Theil, Chuck, *International Alliance of Theatrical Stage Employees, Moving Picture Technicians, Artists & Allied Crafts of the U.S., Its Territories & Canada*, 1535
Theiss, Ronny, *Professional Engineers Ontario*, 1184
Thémens, Jocelyn, *Fondation des maladies du coeur du Québec*, 745
Theobald, Tobias, *Telecommunications Employees Association of Manitoba*, 1369
Theodore, Charlene, *Canadian Association of Black Lawyers*, 309

Théôret, Janie, *Société canadienne d'histoire de l'Église Catholique - Section française*, 1307
Théorêt, Jonathan, *Groupe de recherche appliquée en macroécologie*, 791
Theriault, Joseph, *Saint John & District Labour Council*, 1246
Thériault, Donald, *L'Ordinariat militaire Catholique Romain du Canada*, 1119
Theriault, Carole, *Kapuskasing, Cochrane & District Association for Community Living*, 881
Thériault, Stéphane, *Chambre de commerce de Lévis*, 542
Thériault, Bernard-Marie, *Société d'histoire de la Rivière Saint-Jean incorporée*, 1310
Theriault, Greg, *Ontario Blind Sports Association*, 1068
Thériault, Camille H., *Fédération des caisses populaires acadiennes*, 712
Thériault, Serge A., *Christian Catholic Church Canada*, 567
Thériault, Line, *Fédération des professionnelles et professionnels de l'éducation du Québec*, 718
Thériault, Benoît, *Réseau des SADC et CAE*, 1221
Thériault, Pierre-Antoine, *Société de protection des plantes du Québec*, 1317
Thériault, Carole, *Centre d'aide et de lutte contre les agressions à caractère sexuel de Granby*, 527
Thériault, Laurier, *Richelieu International*, 1229
Thériault, Christian, *Association patronale des entreprises en construction du Québec*, 165
Thériault McGraw, Geneviève, *Commission de la Médiathèque Père-Louis-Lamontagne*, 593
Therrien, Jasmine, *Chambre de commerce Duparquet*, 544
Therrien, Aaron, *Building Owners & Managers Association Toronto*, 263
Therrien, Robert, *Conseil de la Coopération de la Saskatchewan*, 615
Therrien, Rachel, *La fédération des mouvements personne d'abord du Québec*, 716
Thiagarajan, Bhaskar, *Down Syndrome Association of Toronto*, 661
Thibaudeau, Roxanne, *Fédération des aînées et aînés francophones du Canada*, 711
Thibault, Héléne, *Fédération québécoise des sociétés Alzheimer*, 730
Thibault, Ghislaine, *Association québécoise des salons du livre*, 174
Thibault, Mark, *Tennis New Brunswick*, 1371
Thibault, Nicole, *Canadian Parents for French*, 450
Thibault, Martin, *Canadian Bar Association*, 342
Thibault, Laurier, *Réseau des cégeps et des collèges francophones du Canada*, 1219
Thibault, Debbie, *Federation of Foster Families of Nova Scotia*, 724
Thibault, Alain, *Canadian Association of Direct Response Insurers*, 312
Thibault, Verona, *Saskatchewan Economic Development Association*, 1264
Thibeault, Raynald, *Association des directeurs généraux des commissions scolaires du Québec*, 711
Thibeault, Caroline, *Chambre de commerce et d'Industrie de la région de Coaticook*, 545
Thibeault, Annie, *Chambre de commerce et d'industrie de St-Joseph-de-Beauce*, 546
Thibodeau, Manon, *Fondation des maladies du coeur du Québec*, 745
Thibodeau, Serge Patrice, *Regroupement des éditeurs canadiens-français*, 1215
Thibodeau, Tina, *Crossroads for Women Inc.*, 644
Thibodeau, Henri, *Association Carrefour Famille Montcalm*, 96

Executive Name Index

Thibodeau, Susan, *Bridge Adult Service Society*, 228
Thick, Amanda, *Saskatchewan Construction Association*, 1261
Thiel, Shelley, *Chartered Professional Accountants of Saskatchewan*, 554
Thiele, Cindy, *CADORA British Columbia*, 268
Thielen, Joe, *American Water Works Association*, 1504
Thiessen, Janis, *Canadian Oral History Association*, 446
Thiessen, Ron, *Canadian Parks & Wilderness Society*, 451
Thiessen, Dana, *Financial Executives International Canada*, 736
Thiessen, Harvey, *Operation Mobilization Canada*, 1116
Thiessen, Tom, *Building Owners & Managers Association of Manitoba*, 263
Thiessen, Richard, *Mennonite Historical Society of Canada*, 961
Thiessen, Wyndham, *L'Arche Western Region*, 78
Thiessen, Rob, *British Columbia Conference of MB Churches*, 237
Thinh, Lê Minh, *Communauté vietnamienne au Canada, région de Montréal*, 594
Third, Bruce, *Morris & District Chamber of Commerce*, 974
Thirlwall, Gale, *Chemical Institute of Canada*, 556
Thirlwall, Gale, *Canadian Society for Chemistry*, 473
Thisdel, Nicolas, *Canadian Ski Patrol*, 471
Thistle, Linda, *Yukon Church Heritage Society*, 1477
Thivierge, Louis, *Chambre de commerce et d'industrie de Thetford Mines*, 546
Thivierge, Renée, *Canadian Ski Patrol*, 471
Thivierge, Nicole, *Club de marche de Québec*, 574
Tholen, Michael L., *American Concrete Institute*, 1491
Tholl, Bill, *HealthCareCAN*, 807
Thom, Brian, *The Christian & Missionary Alliance in Canada*, 566
Thom, Ken, *Ontario Wheelchair Sports Association*, 1113
Thomas, Jasmin, *Ottawa Economics Association*, 1130
Thomas, D. Karl, *The Apostolic Church in Canada*, 73
Thomas, Chris, *Schizophrenia Society of Alberta*, 1283
Thomas, Geoff, *Canadian Cutting Horse Association*, 375
Thomas, Dave, *College of Family Physicians of Canada*, 585
Thomas, Joy, *Chartered Professional Accountants Canada*, 552
Thomas, Christen, *The Literary Press Group of Canada*, 914
Thomas, Shannon, *Canadian Down Syndrome Society*, 378
Thomas, Ann, *Canadian Institute of Public Health Inspectors*, 419
Thomas, Bradley, *Real Estate Board of the Fredericton Area Inc.*, 1205
Thomas, Roy, *The Canadian Society for Mesopotamian Studies*, 476
Thomas, Karen, *Kidney Foundation of Canada*, 885
Thomas, Jamie, *Beef Farmers of Ontario*, 204
Thomas, Wanda, *Nova Scotia College of Medical Laboratory Technologists*, 1042
Thomas, Laura, *Niagara Youth Orchestra Association*, 1026
Thomas, Deirdre, *Kawartha-Haliburton Children's Aid Society*, 883
Thomas, Val, *Nature Saskatchewan*, 1001
Thomas, Russell, *United Way of Fort McMurray*, 1414
Thomas, Anne, *Alberta Innovates*, 38
Thomas, Sajiev, *Canadian Dental Therapists Association*, 377

Thomas, Merv, *Canadian Aboriginal AIDS Network*, 285
Thomas, Shane, *AIDS Vancouver Island*, 18
Thomas, Ben, *Archaeological Institute of America*, 1505
Thomas, Heather, *Ontario Society of Nutrition Professionals in Public Health*, 1107
Thomas, Warren (Smokey), *Ontario Public Service Employees Union*, 1100
Thomas, Cathie, *South Shore Chamber of Commerce*, 1336
Thomas, Betty, *Oxford Philatelic Society*, 1134
Thomas, Tony, *Mi'kmaq Native Friendship Centre*, 964
Thomas, Christine, *Vancouver Association for the Survivors of Torture*, 1425
Thomas, Steve, *Airdrie & District Soccer Association*, 20
Thomas, Julie, *Healing Our Nations*, 805
Thomas, Fred, *Williams Lake Stampede Association*, 1455
Thomas, Isaac, *Native Earth Performing Arts Inc.*, 998
Thomas, Barbara, *The Canadian Council on Continuing Education in Pharmacy*, 371
Thomas, Brian, *Boot'n Bonnet British Car Club*, 218
Thomas, Linda, *Boot'n Bonnet British Car Club*, 218
Thomas, Samantha, *Status of Women Council of the Northwest Territories*, 1349
Thomas, Jim, *ETC Group*, 697
Thomas, Della, *Saskatchewan Rental Housing Industry Association*, 1274
Thomas, Yvonne, *Jake Thomas Learning Centre*, 867
Thomas, Patrick, *Apparel Human Resources Council*, 74
Thomas, Laura M., *Dundas Valley Orchestra*, 664
Thomas, Rhonda, *Newfoundland & Labrador Provincial Association of Family Resource Centres*, 1021
Thomas, David, *Ontario Floorball Association*, 1080
Thomas, Marilyn, *New Boundaries*, 1004
Thomas, Bob, *SHARE Agriculture Foundation*, 1294
Thomas, Allard, *Canadian Deaf Curling Association*, 376
Thomas, Kevin, *Shareholder Association for Research & Education*, 1294
Thomas Ryan, Shannon, *Black Coalition for AIDS Prevention*, 213
Thome, Edie, *Association for Mineral Exploration British Columbia*, 134
Thome, Mike, *Edmonton District Soccer Association*, 677
Thomopson, David, *Canadian College of Health Leaders*, 359
Thompson, Julia, *Wildlife Habitat Canada*, 1454
Thompson, C. Vincella, *Keyano College Faculty Association*, 884
Thompson, Linda, *Township of Clarence Minor Hockey Association*, 1393
Thompson, Todd, *Canadian Grand Masters Fiddling Association*, 399
Thompson, Holly, *Girl Guides of Canada*, 773
Thompson, Michael, *The Anglican Church of Canada*, 69
Thompson, Samara, *Dance Ontario Association*, 649
Thompson, John, *Carleton County Historical Society, Inc.*, 513
Thompson, Stephen, *Canadian Authors Association*, 338
Thompson, Jim, *Canadian Business Aviation Association*, 348
Thompson, Irene, *Canadian Celiac Association*, 352
Thompson, Lisa, *Ontario Horse Trials Association*, 1086
Thompson, Sally, *Canadian Condominium Institute*, 362

Thompson, Michael, *Realtors Association of Edmonton*, 1206
Thompson, Wanda, *Canadian Wood Council*, 505
Thompson, Jim, *Dominion of Canada Rifle Association*, 661
Thompson, Leslee, *Accreditation Canada*, 5
Thompson, Warren, *Institute of Certified Management Consultants of Manitoba*, 845
Thompson, Anne, *Jane Austen Society of North America*, 868
Thompson, Katie, *Lupus SK Society*, 922
Thompson, Robert, *Newfoundland & Labrador Medical Association*, 1020
Thompson, Ingrid, *The Pollution Probe Foundation*, 1164
Thompson, Tanya, *Professional Photographers of Canada*, 1186
Thompson, Verna, *Saskatchewan Genealogical Society*, 1266
Thompson, Johanna, *Wildlife Rescue Association of British Columbia*, 1455
Thompson, Katie, *BullyingCanada Inc.*, 264
Thompson, Terry, *Naval Museum of Alberta Society*, 1001
Thompson, Jennie, *Association of Prince Edward Island Libraries*, 156
Thompson, Rob, *Thunder Bay Minor Football Association*, 1378
Thompson, Carole, *Junior League of Halifax*, 878
Thompson, Diane, *The American Astronautical Society*, 1490
Thompson, Terry, *Agricultural Adaptation Council*, 14
Thompson, Woodroe, *Church of God of Prophecy in Canada*, 569
Thompson, Winston, *Healing Our Spirit BC Aboriginal HIV/AIDS Society*, 805
Thompson, Shirley, *Environmental Studies Association of Canada*, 692
Thompson, Mary-Ellen, *Ontario Brain Injury Association*, 1068
Thompson, Brent, *Speed Skate Nova Scotia*, 1341
Thompson, Terry, *Human Anatomy & Physiology Society*, 1530
Thompson, David, *Habitat for Humanity Canada*, 797
Thompson, Virginia, *Youth Flight Canada*, 1475
Thompson, Patrick, *Field Hockey Nova Scotia*, 734
Thompson, Allen, *International Society for Environmental Ethics*, 1557
Thompson, Sylvia, *Alberta Foster Parent Association*, 35
Thompson, Don, *Law Society of Alberta*, 901
Thompson, Derrick, *Irish Loop Chamber of Commerce*, 864
Thompson, Jack, *Calgary Motor Dealers Association*, 273
Thompson, Jim, *National Golf Course Owners Association Canada*, 993
Thompson, Stephen, *Community of Christ - Canada West Mission*, 607
Thompson, Lyle, *Yukon Shooting Federation*, 1480
Thompson, Maureen, *Pediatric Endocrine Society*, 1583
Thompson, Louise, *British Columbia Hotel Association*, 243
Thompson, Patrick, *Row Nova Scotia*, 1237
Thompson, Melanie, *Northwest Territories Softball*, 1038
Thompson, Colleen, *Biathlon Nova Scotia*, 207
Thompson, Buck, *Olds Regional Exhibition*, 1057
Thompson, Roosevelt, *Pork Producers Association of Newfoundland & Labrador*, 1165
Thompson, Patricia, *Atkinson Charitable Foundation*, 182

Thompson Frost, Katrina, *Alliance for Canadian New Music Projects*, 56
Thomsen, Jo-Ann, *Meetings & Conventions Prince Edward Island*, 959
Thomson, Bill, *Burnaby Arts Council*, 265
Thomson, Ron, *TESL Canada Federation*, 1372
Thomson, Janet, *Woodstock & District Developmental Services*, 1464
Thomson, Doug, *Florenceville-Bristol Chamber of Commerce*, 741
Thomson, Janice, *Niagara-on-the-Lake Chamber of Commerce*, 1026
Thomson, Carol, *Alberta Genealogical Society*, 36
Thomson, Joanne, *Canadian Lacrosse Association*, 425
Thomson, David J., *Ontario Association of Certified Engineering Technicians & Technologists*, 1062
Thomson, Jay, *Canadian Media Production Association*, 433
Thomson, Tammy, *Canadian Dental Assistants Association*, 376
Thomson, Monty, *Shorthorn Breeders of Manitoba Inc.*, 1297
Thomson, Debra M., *Canadian Anesthesiologists' Society*, 293
Thomson, Sarah, *Orchestras Canada*, 1117
Thomson, Rosemary, *Okanagan Symphony Society*, 1056
Thomson, James P., *Harry E. Foster Foundation*, 804
Thomson, Katie, *Judo BC*, 876
Thomson, Gareth, *Alberta Council for Environmental Education*, 31
Thomson, Donna, *Ontario Brain Injury Association*, 1069
Thomson, Neil, *Student Legal Services of Edmonton*, 1353
Thomson, Douglas C., *Canadian Orthopaedic Association*, 448
Thomson, Drew, *Law Society of Alberta*, 901
Thomson, Patricia, *Stanley Park Ecology Society*, 1348
Thomson, Robin, *Atlantic Division, CanoeKayak Canada*, 183
Thomson, Nancy, *Trail & Ultra Running Association Of The Yukon*, 1394
Thomson, Brad, *Ontario Amateur Softball Association*, 1059
Thor, Kristin, *The Ontario Archaeological Society*, 1060
Thor, Kari-Ann, *Recreational Canoeing Association BC*, 1208
Thorassie, Peter, *Keewatin Tribal Council*, 883
Thorburn, Marisa, *Save a Family Plan*, 1281
Thoresen, Lynnette, *Alberta Summer Swimming Association*, 48
Thorkelson, Myra, *Prince Edward Island Association for Newcomers to Canada*, 1172
Thorn, Jami, *Moose Jaw Real Estate Board*, 974
Thorn, Rosalind, *Prince George Construction Association*, 1179
Thorne, Perry, *Canadian Association of Movers*, 321
Thorne, Philip, *Maritime Hereford Association*, 950
Thorne, Jim, *Money Mentors*, 972
Thorne, Dana, *Archives Association of Ontario*, 80
Thorne, Dianna, *Embroiderers' Association of Canada, Inc.*, 685
Thorne, Bob, *Bramalea Stamp Club*, 225
Thorne, Margo, *Northwest Territories Tourism*, 1039
Thorne, Walter, *Kitimat Valley Naturalists*, 891
Thornley, Mary, *Canadian Agri-Marketing Association*, 290
Thornton, Lynn, *Victoria International Development Education Association*, 1432
Thornton, Meredith, *Timberline Trail & Nature Club*, 1379

Executive Name Index

Thornton, Jane, *Canadian Guide Dogs for the Blind*, 399
Thornton, Mark, *North Grenville Chamber of Commerce*, 1031
Thornton, Kelly, *Judo Alberta*, 876
Thorp, Marion, *Grimsby & District Chamber of Commerce*, 790
Thorp, Lynn, *Clean Water Action*, 1517
Thorson, Stephanie, *The Pollution Probe Foundation*, 1164
Thorson, Shaun, *Skills Canada*, 1302
Thorson, Shaun, *Skills/Compétences Canada*, 1302
Thorsteinson, Janet, *Canadian Association of Defence & Security Industries*, 312
Thorvaldson, Darryl, *Canadian Athletic Therapists Association*, 338
Thostenson, Grace, *United Utility Workers' Association*, 1412
Thouin, Daniel, *Mouvement d'éducation et de défense des actionnaires*, 977
Throop, Paul "Boomer", *Canadian Ski Marathon*, 471
Thubodeau, Éric, *Réseau des SADC et CAE*, 1220
Thunstrom, Gayla, *Northern Territories Federation of Labour*, 1035
Thunstrom, Sheldon, *Alberta College of Paramedics*, 29
Thurber, Elizabeth, *Fredericton Community Services Inc.*, 759
Thurston, Clive, *Ontario General Contractors Association*, 1082
Thurston, Robert, *Ontario Hereford Association*, 1084
Thurston, Molly, *North Okanagan Organic Association*, 1031
Tibaldo, Emma, *Playwrights' Workshop Montréal*, 1162
Tibbe, Erika, *Pitch-In Canada*, 1160
Tibbo, Marg, *Canadian Association for Disabled Skiing - Newfoundland & Labrador Division*, 299
Tiberini, Rina, *Villa Charities Inc. (Toronto District)*, 1435
Tibollo, Michael, *Canadian Italian Heritage Foundation*, 423
Tice, Michelle, *ViaSport*, 1432
Tickell, Crispin, *Climate Institute*, 1517
Tickner, Jerry, *Cariboo Chilcotin Child Development Centre Association*, 512
Tiefenbach, Wilf, *Polio Regina*, 1163
Tiegs, Lorrie, *Canadian Northern Society*, 441
Tiegs, Dean, *Canadian Northern Society*, 441
Tiernay, Joseph W., *Ontario Good Roads Association*, 1083
Tierney, William, *International Federation of Bodybuilding & Fitness*, 1547
Tierney, Chris, *International Wine & Food Society*, 1567
Tierney, Keith B., *Canadian Society of Zoologists*, 488
Tiessen, Jeff, *ParaSport Ontario*, 1139
Tijam, Rose, *University of the Philippines Alumni Association of Toronto*, 1420
Tiller, Heidi, *Saskatchewan Construction Safety Association Inc.*, 1262
Tillett, Shirley E., *Association of Consulting Engineering Companies - Manitoba*, 146
Tillett, Shirley, *Real Estate Institute of Canada*, 1206
Tillett, Shirley, *Professional Property Managers Association Inc.*, 1186
Tilley, Annice, *Kirkland Lake Association for Community Living*, 890
Tilley, Keith, *Canadian Business Aviation Association*, 348
Tilley, Scott, *Ontario Trucking Association*, 1111
Tilley, Lynda, *Moorelands Community Services*, 973
Tilley, Tony, *National Health Union*, 994
Tilley-Russell, Susan, *Arthritis Society*, 84
Tilroe, Bram, *Aviation Alberta*, 191
Tilson, Renate, *TESL Ontario*, 1373

Tilson, Melodie, *Non-Smokers' Rights Association*, 1028
Timar, Hal, *Nunavut Economic Developers Association*, 1051
Timbers, Samantha, *COSTI Immigrant Services*, 632
Timlin, Cathy, *Community Living West Northumberland*, 606
Timmerman, Peter, *Canadian Feed The Children*, 389
Timmermans, Steven, *Christian Reformed Church in North America*, 568
Timmings, Carol, *Registered Nurses' Association of Ontario*, 1213
Timmons, Les, *Canadian Cutting Horse Association*, 375
Timney, Brian, *Council of Ontario Universities*, 635
Timpano, Vince, *United Way Toronto & York Region*, 1417
Tinani, Naresh, *Canadian Society of Clinical Perfusion*, 482
Tinckam, Kathryn, *Canadian Society of Transplantation*, 488
Tingle, Florenda, *Ontario Public School Boards Association*, 1099
Tingley-Holt, Evelyn, *Boys & Girls Clubs of New Brunswick*, 222
Tinglin, Winston, *Social Planning Toronto*, 1306
Tinker, Scott W., *The American Association of Petroleum Geologists*, 1490
Tinman, Katrina, *Manitoba Schizophrenia Society, Inc.*, 944
Tippet-Fagyas, Shelagh, *The Leukemia & Lymphoma Society of Canada*, 908
Tipton, Lilla, *Inclusion Powell River Soceity*, 832
Tirone, Tony, *Kidney Foundation of Canada*, 885
Tirpak, Jon D., *ASM International*, 1506
Tisdale, Ellen, *Manitoba Library Association*, 940
Titanich, Fred, *Canadian Automobile Association Saskatchewan*, 339
Titcomb, Bert, *Transport Action Canada*, 1395
Titizian, Connie, *Armenian Relief Society of Canada, Inc.*, 83
Titus, Carmen, *Big Brothers Big Sisters of Ontario*, 210
Titus, Chris, *New Brunswick Competitive Festival of Music Inc.*, 1007
Titus, Anne, *Embroiderers' Association of Canada, Inc.*, 686
Titus, Michael W., *Canadian Association of Veterans in United Nations Peacekeeping*, 336
Titus, Robert F.M., *Canadian Association of Veterans in United Nations Peacekeeping*, 335
Titus, Cindy, *The Dream Factory*, 662
Titus, C. Richard, *Kitchen Cabinet Manufacturers Association*, 1568
Titus, Doug, *Big Game Society of Nova Scotia*, 210
Tjipto, Yatti, *Access Alliance Multicultural Health & Community Services*, 4
Tkach, Darren, *Saskatchewan Cerebral Palsy Association*, 1260
To, Allan, *Supply Chain Management Association - Alberta*, 1355
Tobin, Debbi, *Epilepsy Association of Nova Scotia*, 693
Tobin, Mary Anne, *St. John's Kiwanis Music Festival*, 1249
Todd, Trevor, *Consumers' Association of Canada*, 626
Todd, James, *United Way Elgin-St. Thomas*, 1413
Todd, Jeff, *UBC Alumni Association*, 1401
Todd, Wes, *Canada Employment & Immigration Union*, 279
Todd, Bobbie, *Calgary Society of Independent Filmmakers*, 274

Todd, Nicolas, *Canadian Association of Defence & Security Industries*, 312
Todoschuk, Ted, *Canadian Carbonization Research Association*, 350
Todson, Ron, *Fraser Valley Real Estate Board*, 758
Toepfer, Sandi, *Alberta College of Combined Laboratory & X-Ray Technologists*, 29
Toering, Rudy, *Canadian Business Aviation Association*, 347
Toews, Cam, *Brandon Real Estate Board*, 226
Toews, Lorraine, *Southern Alberta Health Libraries Association*, 1337
Toffner, Greg, *Ontario Association of Medical Radiation Sciences*, 1065
Toguri, Allan, *Society of Urologic Surgeons of Ontario*, 1331
Toher, Drew, *Beyond Pesticides*, 1514
Tokarchuk, Jim, *Soil Conservation Council of Canada*, 1332
Tokay, Eric, *Habitat for Humanity Canada*, 796
Tokos, Jim, *The Canadian Council of the Blind*, 370
Toledo, Dinoi, *Latino Canadian Cultural Association*, 900
Toll, Haley, *Canadian Art Therapy Association*, 295
Tollefson, Treva, *Weyburn Agricultural Society*, 1451
Tollefson, Laurie, *Canadian National Committee for Irrigation & Drainage*, 439
Toller, Brian, *Community Foundation of Ottawa*, 598
Tolley, Delano, *Lakeland Industry & Community Association*, 896
Tolmie, Helen, *Chilliwack Society for Community Living*, 563
Toma, Ward, *Alberta Canola Producers Commission*, 27
Tomalin, Barry, *South Queens Chamber of Commerce*, 1336
Tomasevic, Sam, *B.C. Horseshoe Association*, 201
Tomaszewski, Maciej, *International Society of Hypertension*, 1560
Tomberlin, Jerry, *Canadian Federation of Business School Deans*, 386
Tomcko, Kristen, *211 Ontario North*, 1401
Tomic, Vasilije, *Serbian Orthodox Church - Orthodox Diocese of Canada*, 1290
Tomilson, Trevor, *Construction Association of New Brunswick*, 623
Tomkinson, John, *Alberta Catholic School Trustees Association*, 27
Tomko, George, *International Council on Global Privacy & Security, By Design*, 856
Tomlin, Jessica, *MATCH International Women's Fund*, 954
Tomm, Ian, *HeliCat Canada*, 811
Tommasel, Marco, *Canadian Masonry Contractors' Association*, 431
Tomney, Sue, *YWCA Canada*, 1481
Tompkins, Gary, *University of Regina Faculty Association*, 1420
Tompkins, Lisa, *Retail Advertising & Marketing Club of Canada*, 1228
Tompkins, Keiren, *Nova Scotia Government & General Employees Union*, 1045
Tompkins, Karen, *Joubert Syndrome & Related Disoarders Foundation*, 1568
Tompkins, Caroline, *Forum for International Trade Training*, 754
Toms, Bridget, *Jane Austen Society of North America*, 868
Tomsons, Sandra, *Canadian Society for the Study of Practical Ethics*, 478
Tonelli, Patricia, *Association de Montréal pour la déficience intellectuelle*, 103
Toner, Pat, *New Brunswick Institute of Agrologists*, 1009
Toner, Denise, *Canadian Urological Association*, 500
Tonkinson, Anthony, *Association of Canadian Travel Agents - Alberta & NWT*, 144

Tonkovic, Laura, *Ontario Catholic Supervisory Officers' Association*, 1070
Tooke, Susan, *Canadian Artists' Representation Maritimes*, 296
Toombs, Jayne, *Prince Edward Island Association of Optometrists*, 1172
Toomey, Tom, *Ottawa Philatelic Society*, 1131
Toomsalu, Harnald, *Hamilton Folk Arts Heritage Council*, 801
Toone, Joan, *Post-Polio Awareness & Support Society of BC*, 1168
Toone, Mark, *Lunenfeld-Tanenbaum Research Institute*, 921
Topalovich, Maria, *Screen Composers Guild of Canada*, 1287
Topham, Christopher, *Canadian Association of Medical Radiation Technologists*, 320
Topham, Colin, *Canadian Special Crops Association*, 489
Topley, Earle, *Canadian Association of Veterans in United Nations Peacekeeping*, 336
Topliss, Heather, *Kirkland Lake Association for Community Living*, 890
Topolnitsky, Terry, *Alberta Development Officers Association*, 32
Topping, John, *Climate Institute*, 1517
Topple, George, *Canadian Aviation Historical Society*, 340
Topps, David, *Huntsville & Lake of Bays Railway Society*, 828
Torfason, Louise, *Winnipeg Clinic Employees Association*, 1458
Toribio, Ester, *Markham Federation of Filipino Canadians*, 952
Torjman, Sherri, *Caledon Institute of Social Policy*, 270
Torkko, Keira, *Coaching Association of Canada*, 577
Torner, Carles, *PEN International*, 1583
Torrance, Trish, *Canadian Fluid Power Association*, 391
Torrance, Trish, *Canadian Process Control Association*, 460
Torrance, Joshua, *Canadian Society of Hospital Pharmacists*, 484
Torraville, David, *The Anglican Church of Canada*, 69
Torrens, Kathy, *Ontario Water Polo Association Incorporated*, 1113
Torres, Ana, *Canadian Blood & Marrow Transplant Group*, 344
Torres, Mary Ann, *International Council of AIDS Service Organizations*, 855
Torry, Brian, *Roncesvalles Macdonell Residents' Association*, 1236
Toscano, Alison, *CIO Association of Canada*, 570
Toscano, Maria, *Children's Wish Foundation of Canada*, 563
Tosczak, Robin, *Victoria Labour Council*, 1433
Tosczak, Kari, *Chicken Farmers of Saskatchewan*, 558
Tose, Aggie, *Ontario Home Builders' Association*, 1085
Tose, Barbara, *British Isles Family History Society of Greater Ottawa*, 259
Tosine, Helle, *Royal Canadian Institute*, 1240
Toso, Giuseppe, *Fogolârs Federation of Canada*, 742
Tostenson, Ian, *British Columbia Restaurant & Foodservices Association*, 251
Toth, Adrian, *Canadian Water & Wastewater Association*, 502
Toth, Les, *British Columbia Federation of Foster Parent Associations*, 240
Toth, Jack, *Impact Society*, 831
Toth, Susan, *Professional Organizers in Canada*, 1186
Toth, Christina, *Fraser Basin Council*, 757
Toucas, Marion, *Service budgétaire et communautaire de Chicoutimi inc*, 1291
Touchette, Charlie, *North American Farmers' Direct Marketing Association, Inc.*, 1579

Executive Name Index

Toulouse, Jo-Ann, *Centre indien cri de Chibougamau*, 535
Toupin, Harley P., *Saskatchewan Safety Council*, 1274
Toupin, Luc, *Association québécoise du loisir municipal*, 176
Toupin, Marie, *Fondation québécoise du cancer*, 748
Toupin, Luc, *Association québécoise des arénas et des installations récréatives et sportives*, 171
Toupin, Zoë, *Yukon Film Society*, 1478
Tourangeau, Éric, *Chambre de commerce de Mont-Laurier*, 542
Tourigny, Thérèse, *Fédération des sociétés d'horticulture et d'écologie du Québec*, 719
Tousignant, Philippe, *Social Justice Committee*, 1305
Tousignant, Hélène, *Chambre de commerce et d'industrie de la région de Richmond*, 545
Tousignant, Daniel, *Chambre de commerce Mont-Saint-Bruno*, 549
Tousignant, Bruno, *Kidney Foundation of Canada*, 885
Tousignant, Gérald, *Fédération québécoise de tir*, 728
Toussaint, Vicky, *Société de protection des plantes du Québec*, 1317
Touzel, Pierre, *Association des clubs d'entrepreneurs étudiants du Québec*, 109
Touzin, Alexandre, *Chambre de commerce Témis-Accord*, 550
Tovey, Bramwell, *Vancouver Symphony Society*, 1429
Towell, Philip, *British Columbia Welsh Pony & Cob Association*, 258
Towler, Patricia (Patti), *Chartered Professional Accountants of Nova Scotia*, 553
Townsend, Craig, *ArtsConnect - Tri-Cities Regional Arts Council*, 86
Townsend, Patty, *Canadian Seed Trade Association*, 470
Townsend, Stanley, *Canadian Culinary Federation*, 374
Townsend, Kendra, *The Pharmacy Examining Board of Canada*, 1157
Townsend, Teresa, *Urban & Regional Information Systems Association*, 1601
Townsley, John, *Canadian Society of Exploration Geophysicists*, 483
Toye, Mike, *Canadian CED Network*, 352
Toyer, Wendy, *ALS Society of British Columbia*, 60
Toze, Sandra, *Dalhousie University School of Information Management Associated Alumni*, 648
Tozer, David, *Canadian Toy Collectors' Society Inc.*, 496
Tracey, Karen, *Northern Ontario Aquaculture Association*, 1035
Tracogna, John, *Toronto Zoo*, 1388
Tracy, Tony, *Canadian Labour Congress*, 424
Traer, Jennifer, *Canadian Institute of Traffic & Transportation*, 420
Traer, Rick, *Canadian Sport Tourism Alliance*, 490
Trafford, Joyce, *Carp Agricultural Society*, 515
Trafford, Dave, *The Canadian Council for Public-Private Partnerships*, 367
Trafton, Jackie, *Building Supply Industry Association of British Columbia*, 263
Trainer, Maria, *CropLife Canada*, 643
Trainor, Bob, *Therapeutic Ride Algoma*, 1375
Trainor, Donna, *Saskatchewan Union of Nurses*, 1277
Traister, Bryce, *Canadian Association for American Studies*, 297
Trakalo, Len, *Ontario Numismatic Association*, 1094
Trakalo, Len, *Brantford Numismatic Society*, 227
Tran, Lien, *Association of Professional Engineers & Geoscientists of British Columbia*, 158

Tran, Vivian, *Canadian Economics Association*, 379
Tran, Van-Nha, *Association des vietnamiens de Sherbrooke*, 130
Tranberg, Janice, *CropLife Canada*, 643
Trappenberg, Thomas, *Green Party of Nova Scotia*, 789
Trask, Brent, *The Christian & Missionary Alliance in Canada*, 566
Trask, Arlene, *Early Childhood Intervention Program (ECIP) Sask. Inc.*, 667
Trask, Peter, *International Personnel Management Association - Canada*, 859
Trask, Jason, *Saskatchewan College of Paramedics*, 1261
Trask-Soltesz, Chelsie, *Certified Dental Assistants of BC*, 538
Travers, Jodi, *Electrical Contractors Association of Ontario*, 683
Travers, Scott, *The Society of Energy Professionals*, 1328
Travors, Mark, *Thermal Insulation Association of Alberta*, 1376
Treadwell, Brian, *Parkinson Alberta Society*, 1141
Treble, Doug, *Crystal City & District Chamber of Commerce*, 645
Treeby, Graeme S., *Special Needs Planning Group*, 1339
Treede, Rolf-Detlef, *International Association for the Study of Pain*, 1537
Treleaven, John, *Hong Kong-Canada Business Association*, 820
Tremblay, Sylvie, *Children of the World Adoption Society Inc.*, 560
Tremblay, Diane, *Entraide familiale de l'Outaouais inc.*, 690
Tremblay, Marc, *English Additional Language Learners Provincial Specialist Association*, 689
Tremblay, Louise, *Ordre des ergothérapeutes du Québec*, 1121
Tremblay, Lisette, *Fibrose kystique Québec*, 733
Tremblay, Sylvia, *British Columbia Council for Families*, 237
Tremblay, Sylvie Ann, *Chambre de commerce de l'Ile d'Orléans*, 541
Tremblay, Jeannot, *Chambre de commerce et d'industrie de Roberval*, 546
Tremblay, Pascale, *Association des cadres municipaux de Montréal*, 108
Tremblay, Louis, *Ordre des ingénieurs du Québec*, 1122
Tremblay, Bernard, *Fédération des cégeps*, 712
Tremblay, Valérie, *Holstein Canada*, 819
Tremblay, Dan, *Quinte Symphony*, 1202
Tremblay, Ginette, *Alliance autochtone du Québec*, 5
Tremblay, Michael, *Innovative Medicines Canada*, 839
Tremblay, André, *Conseil de l'industrie forestière du Québec*, 615
Tremblay, Louis Claude, *Centre canadien de leadership en éducation*, 526
Tremblay, Suzanne, *Club photo Évasion*, 576
Tremblay, Isabelle, *Canadian Society for Eighteenth-Century Studies*, 474
Tremblay, Christian, *Chambre des notaires du Québec*, 550
Tremblay, Germain, *Lake Superior Coin Club*, 896
Tremblay, Pierre, *Théâtres unis enfance jeunesse*, 1375
Tremblay, Denis, *Association de l'industrie électrique du Québec*, 100
Tremblay, Marie-Ellen, *Fédération de l'industrie manufacturière (FIM-CSN)*, 709
Tremblay, Michel, *Société Santé en français*, 1325
Tremblay, Charles, *Quebec Association of Insolvency & Restructuring Professionals*, 1196

Tremblay, Marc, *Association des démographes du Québec*, 110
Tremblay, Michel, *Alliance Française d'Ottawa*, 57
Tremblay, Carol, *Legal & District Chamber of Commerce*, 906
Tremblay, Sylvie, *Fondation des pompiers du Québec pour les grands brûlés*, 745
Tremblay, Sylvie, *Les programmes éducatifs JA Québec*, 1187
Tremblay, Chantal, *Mouvement national des québécoises et québécois*, 977
Tremblay, Dominique, *Boîte à science - Conseil du loisir scientifique du Québec*, 217
Tremblay, Donald, *Association de chasse et pêche nordique, inc.*, 100
Tremblay, Érick, *Fédération des trappeurs gestionnaires du Québec*, 719
Tremblay, Lucie, *Association québécoise des infirmières et intervenants en recherche clinique*, 173
Tremblay, Nicole, *Regroupement des associations de personnes traumatisées craniocérébrales du Québec*, 1214
Tremblay, Louise, *Semiahmoo Foundation*, 1289
Tremblay, Alain, *Écomusée de l'Au-Delà*, 672
Trembley, Tara, *College of Dental Technologists of Alberta*, 583
Trempe, Eliane, *Canadian Therapeutic Riding Association*, 494
Trempe, Carole, *Association des cadres supérieurs de la santé et des services sociaux du Québec*, 108
Trenholm, Brian, *Cumberland Museum Society*, 646
Trépanier, Monique, *Moisson Mauricie/Centre-du-Québec*, 971
Trépanier, Daniel, *Canadian Amateur Boxing Association*, 292
Trepanier, Jason, *Volleyball Nova Scotia*, 1438
Trépanier, Julie, *Statistical Society of Canada*, 1348
Trépanier, François, *Tourisme Montérégie*, 1393
Trépanier, Guy, *Réseau des SADC et CAE*, 1221
Trépanier, Nicole, *Société de développement économique du Saint-Laurent*, 1315
Trepasso, Jennifer, *Ontario Brain Injury Association*, 1069
Treutler, Theresa, *Television Bureau of Canada, Inc.*, 1370
Treverton, Susan, *Community Living Prince Edward (County)*, 604
Trew, Stuart, *The Council of Canadians*, 633
Trew, David, *North Saskatchewan Watershed Alliance*, 1032
Triantafilou, Jim, *Brampton Caledon Community Living*, 226
Triassi, Emanuele, *Italian Chamber of Commerce in Canada*, 866
Tribe, Christine, *Canadian Arabian Horse Registry*, 294
Tribe, Laura, *OpenMedia Engagement Network*, 1114
Trimboli, Alberto, *World Federation for Mental Health*, 1605
Triollet, Karine, *Action-Gardien, la table de concertation communautaire de Pointe-Saint-Charles*, 7
Tripp, Douglas, *Canadian Institute for Energy Training*, 412
Triska, Ollie, *EmployAbilities*, 686
Trogdon, Eric, *Ontario Parks Association*, 1095
Troian, Halyna, *Canadian Board of Marine Underwriters*, 345
Troke, Jamie, *Quinte & District Association of REALTORS Inc.*, 1201
Troke, Ray, *Bonavista Historic Townscape Foundation*, 217
Trombley, Adam, *Planned Lifetime Advocacy Network*, 1161

Tromp, Ginny, *British Columbia Golf Superintendents Association*, 242
Tronrud, Tory, *Thunder Bay Historical Museum Society*, 1378
Tross, Michael, *YOUTHLINK*, 1476
Trost, Claus, *Ontario Home Builders' Association*, 1085
Troszko, Mary, *Community Legal Education Association (Manitoba) Inc.*, 600
Trott, Ally, *British Columbia Water & Waste Association*, 258
Trotter, Martin, *Canadian Association of Pathologists*, 325
Trotter, Sarah, *Canadian Hard of Hearing Association*, 400
Trottier, Carmen, *Association des intervenants en toxicomanie du Québec inc.*, 117
Trottier, Ginette, *Parkinson Society of Eastern Ontario*, 1141
Trowbridge, David, *Clean North*, 573
Trowsdale, Ronald T., *The Royal Canadian Legion*, 1240
Troy, Bill, *American Society for Quality*, 1498
Troyer, Brent, *Canadian Red Angus Promotion Society*, 465
Truant, Tracy, *Canadian Association of Nurses in Oncology*, 323
Truax, Morgan, *Northern Alberta Health Libraries Association*, 1034
Trude, Della, *Ontario Tenpin Bowling Association*, 1110
Trudeau, Wendy, *Canadian International Freight Forwarders Association*, 421
Trudeau, Gilles, *International Society for Labour & Social Security Law - Canadian Chapter*, 860
Trudeau, Justin, *The Liberal Party of Canada*, 909
Trudeau, Jean, *Association des golfeurs professionnels du Québec*, 115
Trudeau, Julie, *Association québécoise de la déficience intellectuelle de la région de Sorel*, 101
Trudeau, Johanne, *Baking Association of Canada*, 194
Trudeau, Michel, *Syndicat professionnel des scientifiques de l'IREQ*, 1365
Trudeau, Roseann, *Tweed Chamber of Commerce*, 1400
Trudeau, Miranda, *CADORA Ontario Association Inc.*, 269
Trudel, Dominic, *Conseil montérégien de la culture et des communications*, 619
Trudel, Claude, *Fédération des associations de familles du Québec*, 711
Trudel, Marie-Edith, *Association coopérative d'économie familiale - Rive-Sud de Montréal*, 97
Trudel, Colette, *Association paritaire pour la santé et la sécurité du travail - Administration provinciale*, 164
Trudel, Anne-Marie, *Association québécoise des salons du livre*, 174
Trudel, André, *Association de la construction du Québec*, 100
Trudel, Sandy, *Economic Development Brandon*, 673
Trudel, Louise, *Conseil pédagogique interdisciplinaire du Québec*, 619
Trudel, Dominic, *Conseil québécois de la musique*, 620
Trudel, Camille, *Société des attractions touristiques du Québec*, 1317
Trudel, Amélie, *Association québécoise pour l'hygiène, la santé et la sécurité du travail*, 176
Trudel, Pierre, *Recherches amérindiennes au Québec*, 1207
Trudel, Alain, *Orchestre symphonique de Laval*, 1118
Trudel, Suzanne, *Alberta Magazine Publishers Association*, 39
Trudelle, Monique, *Alzheimer Society of Alberta & Northwest Territories*, 61
Trueman, Debbie, *Nanaimo District Museum*, 987

Executive Name Index

Trueman, Anne, *Canadian Media Production Association*, 433
Trueman, Stephen, *Risk & Insurance Management Society Inc.*, 1234
Trumka, Richard, *American Federation of Labor & Congress of Industrial Organizations (AFL-CIO)*, 1493
Trumpler, Angie, *Miniature Horse Club of Ontario*, 967
Trus, David, *Miniature Horse Association of Canada*, 966
Truscott, Richard, *Canadian Federation of Independent Business*, 387
Truscott, Richard, *Canadian Federation of Independent Business*, 387
Trussell, Dawn, *Canadian Association for Leisure Studies*, 302
Tryhuba, Janet, *Fort Edmonton Foundation*, 752
Tryon, Barbara, *Nova Scotia Society for the Prevention of Cruelty to Animals*, 1049
Tsang, Winnie, *Association for Image & Information Management International - 1st Canadian Chapter*, 133
Tsang, Tammy, *North American Association of Asian Professionals Vancouver*, 1029
Tsang, Tony, *Biathlon BC*, 207
Tsaprailis, Haralampos, *NACE International*, 1572
Tse, Simon, *Canadian Association of Foodservice Professionals*, 315
Tse, John, *Canada Chinese Computer Association*, 278
Tse, Mark, *Petroleum Tank Management Association of Alberta*, 1154
Tsedryk, Egor, *Atlantic Provinces Linguistic Association*, 185
Tsehai, Fikre M., *Canadian Lutheran World Relief*, 428
Tsomo, Tsering, *Canadian Tibetan Association of Ontario*, 495
Tsouras, Melanie, *Occupational & Environmental Medical Association of Canada*, 1054
Tubman, Kent, *Renfrew & Area Chamber of Commerce*, 1217
Tubrett, Glenn, *Canadian Institute for NDE*, 413
Tuccaro, Tammie, *Northeastern Alberta Aboriginal Business Association*, 1034
Tucker, Bruce, *Waterloo Regional Police Association*, 1442
Tucker, Cheryl, *Association of Workers' Compensation Boards of Canada*, 164
Tucker, Albert, *Funeral Advisory & Memorial Society*, 764
Tucker, Liz, *Canadian Pony Club*, 457
Tucker, John, *Broadcast Executives Society*, 259
Tucker, Una, *Newfoundland & Labrador Association for Community Living*, 1015
Tucker, Tracy, *Canadian Environmental Law Association*, 382
Tucker, Tina, *Canadian Bar Association*, 342
Tucker, Peter, *Association of Canadian Mountain Guides*, 143
Tucker, Neal, *Bonavista Area Chamber of Commerce*, 217
Tucker, Edouard, *Québec Black Medical Association*, 1196
Tucker, Dean, *Karate Alberta Association*, 881
Tuckey, Bryan, *Building Industry & Land Development Association*, 262
Tudor, Dean, *Wine Writers' Circle of Canada*, 1458
Tudorache, Nancy, *Global Business Travel Association (Canada)*, 774
Tuer, Jane, *Project READ Literacy Network Waterloo-Wellington*, 1188
Tuffnail, John, *Woodstock Coin Club*, 1464
Tufts, Gordo, *Canadian Transportation Research Forum*, 497
Tugwell, Cindy, *Heritage Winnipeg Corp.*, 814
Tukkiapik, Jobie, *Makivik Corporation*, 927

Tulk, Bertram, *Atlantic Provinces Special Education Authority*, 185
Tulk, Craig, *Hockey Newfoundland & Labrador*, 818
Tulk, Glenda, *MusicNL*, 984
Tulloch, John, *Eastern Apicultural Society of North America, Inc.*, 1522
Tume, Vincent, *Society of Professional Engineers & Associates*, 1330
Tumilowicz, Viktoria, *Brantford Regional Real Estate Association Inc.*, 227
Tunley, Rayne, *Canadian Society of Painters in Water Colour*, 486
Tunney, Bill, *Hamilton Baseball Umpires' Association*, 801
Turack, Jennifer, *Canadian Liver Foundation*, 427
Turbide, Yves, *Association des auteures et des auteurs de l'Ontario français*, 106
Turchansky, Chris, *Edmonton CFA Society*, 675
Turcott, Sam, *Disability Alliance British Columbia*, 658
Turcotte, Bruno, *Chambre de commerce de Ste-Justine*, 543
Turcotte, Lynne, *Canadian Celiac Association*, 352
Turcotte, Marie-Bois, *Réseau FADOQ*, 1224
Turcotte, Robert, *Association d'orthopédie du Québec*, 99
Turcotte, Renée, *New Brunswick Hospice Palliative Care Association*, 1009
Turcotte, Camille, *Association pour l'enseignement de la science et de la technologie au Québec*, 165
Turcotte, Sylvain, *Fédération québécoise des centres communautaires de loisir inc.*, 728
Turcotte, Marie-Andrée, *Fédération des coopératives d'habitation du Royaume Saguenay Lac-Saint-Jean*, 714
Turenne, Roger, *Nature Manitoba*, 1000
Turgeon, Léopold, *Conseil québécois du commerce de détail*, 620
Turgeon, Robert, *Héritage Montréal*, 813
Turgeon, Michel, *Coalition sida des sourds du Québec*, 579
Turgeon, Jacynthe, *L'Association des orthopédagogues du Québec inc.*, 121
Turk, Ellen, *Canadian Gift Association*, 398
Turmel, Patrick, *Société de philosophie du Québec*, 1316
Turnbull, Laas, *CARP*, 514
Turnbull, Joan, *Canadian Pension & Benefits Institute*, 453
Turnbull, Susan, *College of Psychologists of British Columbia*, 589
Turnbull, David, *Canadian Courier & Logistics Association*, 372
Turner, Elsie, *Clan Lamont Society of Canada*, 571
Turner, Jo Ann, *Oliver Community Arts Council*, 1057
Turner, Jim, *Boys & Girls Clubs of Ontario*, 223
Turner, Rhodina, *Boys & Girls Clubs of Ontario*, 223
Turner, JoAnne, *Boys & Girls Clubs of Ontario*, 223
Turner, Tina, *Ontario Football Alliance*, 1081
Turner, Jim, *Community Living Atikokan*, 600
Turner, Jill, *Saskatchewan Agricultural Graduates' Association Inc.*, 1255
Turner, Peter, *Yukon Chamber of Commerce*, 1477
Turner, Bonnie, *Sales & Marketing Executives of Vancouver*, 1251
Turner, Monika, *Association of Municipalities of Ontario*, 153
Turner, Jessica, *Parent Support Services Society of BC*, 1139
Turner, Donna, *Canadian Association of Recycling Industries*, 330
Turner, Robert, *Chamber of Marine Commerce*, 539
Turner, Mary Kate, *Canadian Society of Orthopaedic Technologists*, 485

Turner, Mark, *Saskatoon Symphony Society*, 1280
Turner, Ashleigh, *Options for Sexual Health*, 1117
Turner, Malcolm, *Newfoundland & Labrador Camping Association*, 1017
Turner, Gayleen, *Association of Saskatchewan Home Economists*, 161
Turner, Joan, *Gem & Mineral Federation of Canada*, 768
Turner, Martha, *Downtown Legal Services*, 662
Turner, Lee, *Atlantic Food & Beverage Processors Association*, 184
Turner, Dominic, *International Continence Society*, 1544
Turner, Karen, *Incident Prevention Association of Manitoba*, 831
Turner Shoemaker, Victoria, *Canadian Ornamental Plant Foundation*, 448
Turney, Sandy, *Lions Foundation of Canada*, 913
Turney, Evelina, *Kidney Foundation of Canada*, 886
Turney, Lisa, *Beef Farmers of Ontario*, 204
Turney, Sandy, *Dog Guides Canada*, 660
Turney, Jayme, *Toronto Public Spaces Initiative*, 1386
Turp, Daniel, *Association québécoise de doit constitutionel*, 169
Turpin, Alain, *Canadian Deaf Sports Association*, 376
Turrittin, Tony, *Transport Action Canada*, 1395
Turrone, Peter, *Newman Centre Catholic Chaplaincy and Parish*, 1024
Turtle, Gordon, *Chartered Professional Accountants of Alberta*, 552
Turton, Justin, *Outlook & District Chamber of Commerce*, 1133
Turvey, Natalie, *Canadian Journalism Foundation*, 423
Tuskin, Jo Ann M., *Clans & Scottish Societies of Canada*, 572
Tuskin, Jo Ann, *United Empire Loyalists' Association of Canada*, 1410
Tutching, Meredith, *Ontario Library Association*, 1089
Tutschek, Alex, *Chartered Accountants' Education Foundation of Alberta*, 552
Tutthill, Mike, *Rainbow Resource Centre*, 1203
Tveitane, Vanessa, *Community Futures Development Association of British Columbia*, 598
Twarog, Daniel, *North American Die Casting Association*, 1579
Tweedie, Pat, *Tetra Society of North America*, 1373
Twigg, John, *BC First Party*, 201
Twohig, Peter, *Canadian Society for the History of Medicine*, 477
Twohig, Peter L., *Gorsebrook Research Institute for Atlantic Canada Studies*, 778
Tyagi, Pree, *Alberta College of Medical Diagnostic & Therapeutic Technologists*, 29
Tyagi, Avinash C., *International Commission on Irrigation & Drainage*, 1543
Tyler, Tony, *International Air Transport Association*, 853
Tyler, Susan, *Organic Crop Improvement Association - New Brunswick*, 1125
Tyler, Matthew, *Windsor & District Baseball Umpires Association*, 1456
Tymchyshyn, Donovan, *Vecova Centre for Disability Services & Research*, 1430
Tymieniecka, Anna-Teresa, *International Husserl & Phenomenological Research Society*, 1550
Tynning, Ryan, *Mechanical Contractors Association of Saskatchewan Inc.*, 957
Tyrrell, Alex, *Parti Vert du Québec*, 1144
Tyson, Dave, *Information Systems Security Association*, 1532
Tywoniuk, Laura, *Barrhead Gem Seekers*, 197
Tzanakopoulos, Antonios, *International Law Association*, 1552

U

Uchatius, Susanna, *Theatre Terrific Society*, 1375
Udemgba, Ijeoma, *International Women of Saskatoon*, 861
Uditsky, Bruce, *Inclusion Alberta*, 831
Udod, Taras, *Ukrainian Orthodox Church of Canada*, 1403
Uffer-Marcolongo, Assunta, *International Association for Medical Assistance to Travellers*, 853
Ukrainetz, Sheri, *Central Interior Regional Arts Council*, 524
Ullmann, Barbara, *Glaucoma Research Society of Canada*, 774
Ulmer, Barry, *Chronic Pain Association of Canada*, 568
Umar, Suli, *Canadian Business Aviation Association*, 348
Underhill, Kevin, *Field Hockey Canada*, 734
Underhill, Jeffrey, *Association of Professional Engineers & Geoscientists of New Brunswick*, 158
Underhill, Heather, *Family Service Canada*, 704
Underhill, Lauren, *Mayne Island Community Chamber of Commerce*, 954
Underhill, Janine, *Albert County Chamber of Commerce*, 21
Underschultz, Grant, *Alberta Deaf Sports Association*, 32
Underwood, Fran, *Association of Interior Designers of Nova Scotia*, 149
Underwood, Vanessa, *Junior Achievement Canada*, 877
Underwood, Pat, *Canadian Association of Occupational Therapists*, 323
Underwood, Ene, *Habitat for Humanity Canada*, 797
Underwood, Rudy, *American Chemistry Council*, 1491
Unger, Greg, *Big Brothers Big Sisters of Manitoba*, 209
Unger, Ron, *Saskatchewan Genealogical Society*, 1266
Unger, Jason, *The Environmental Law Centre (Alberta) Society*, 692
Unger, Geri, *Society for Conservation Biology*, 1590
Unite, Erlinda, *Filipino Association of Nova Scotia*, 735
Unrau, Marilyn, *Music for Young Children*, 984
Unrau, Janelle, *Saskatchewan Association of Architects*, 1485
Unrau, Sara, *Canadian Association of Critical Care Nurses*, 311
Unrau, Samuel, *Manitoba Wheelchair Sports Association*, 947
Unryn, Cherylle, *Osteoporosis Canada*, 1129
Unvoas, Arlene, *Swift Current Creek Watershed Stewards*, 1358
Uppal, Manjeet, *Vancouver Island University Faculty Association*, 1427
Upshall, Christy, *Our Place (Peel)*, 1133
Upshall, Phil, *Canadian Depression Research & Intervention Network*, 377
Upshaw, Robert, *Black Educators Association of Nova Scotia*, 213
Upton, Leslie, *British Columbia Philatelic Society*, 249
Uranowski, Andrew, *Durham Chamber Orchestra*, 665
Urbanowicz, Nancy, *Academy of Management*, 1485
Urias, César, *Canada Pork International*, 280
Uribe, Sherry, *National Emergency Nurses Association*, 993
Urquhart, Brian, *London Police Association*, 919
Urquhart, Sue, *Canadian Arts Presenting Association*, 296
Urquhart, Diane, *Social Planning Council of Ottawa*, 1306

Executive Name Index

Urquhart, Steven, *Association for Canadian & Québec Literatures*, 132

Urquhart, Martin, *Military Collectors Club of Canada*, 965

Urquhart, Pierre, *Chambre de commerce et de tourisme de la Vallée de Saint-Sauveur/Piedmont*, 548

Ursacki, Drew, *Ontario Undergraduate Student Alliance*, 1111

Ursu, Nicole, *Canadian Institute of Plumbing & Heating*, 419

Usher, Bill, *Golden District Arts Council*, 776

Usher, John, *University of Lethbridge Faculty Association*, 1419

Usmanali, Reaz, *American Society of Heating, Refrigerating & Air Conditioning Engineers*, 1500

Usyk, Wolodymyr, *Ukrainian Youth Association of Canada*, 1404

Utgoff, Margaret, *Girl Guides of Canada*, 773

Uttaro, Bethany, *Canadian Meat Science Association*, 432

Utting, Peter, *United Nations Research Institute for Social Development*, 1600

Uwiera, Trina, *Canadian Society of Otolaryngology - Head & Neck Surgery*, 485

Uytterhagen, Shelley, *Carthy Foundation*, 516

V

Vaadeland, Gord, *Canadian Parks & Wilderness Society*, 451

Vaage, Lesley, *Schizophrenia Society of Alberta*, 1283

Vaaja, Nina Buvang, *Arctic Council*, 81

Vaartstra, Carrie, *Rimbey Chamber of Commerce*, 1232

Vaas, Susanne, *Canadian Media Production Association*, 433

Vaccaro, Joe, *Ontario Home Builders' Association*, 1085

Vachon, Pierre, *L'Opéra de Montréal*, 1115

Vachon, Ruth, *Réseau des femmes d'affaires du Québec inc.*, 1219

Vachon, Jocelyn, *Ordre professionnel des inhalothérapeutes du Québec*, 1124

Vachon, Pierrette, *Mouvement des femmes Chrétiennes*, 977

Vachon, Lucie, *Société d'histoire de Weedon*, 1312

Vachon, Léandre, *Société de généalogie de Longueuil*, 1315

Vachon, Mélanie, *Association pour l'intégration sociale (Rouyn-Noranda) inc.*, 166

Vachon, Michel, *Association des médecins omnipraticiens de Montréal*, 120

Vachon, Sébastien, *Association des actuaires I.A.R.D.*, 105

Vachon, Ruth, *Réseau Femmes Québec*, 1224

Vaddapalli, Nalini, *Law Society of Nunavut*, 902

Vadeika, John, *Swim Ontario*, 1359

Vadnais, Patty, *Fernie Chamber of Commerce*, 732

Vagianos, Andrea, *Toronto Dance Theatre*, 1384

Vagneux, Luc, *Ordre des ingénieurs du Québec*, 1122

Vail, Kevin, *Canadian Marine Pilots' Association*, 430

Vaillancourt, Lise, *Centre des auteurs dramatiques*, 530

Vaillancourt, Jean-Guy, *Groupe de recherche en écologie sociale*, 791

Vaillancourt, Katherine, *Association of Administrative Professionals*, 139

Vaillancourt, Daryl, *North Bay & District Humane Society*, 1030

Vaillancourt, Daryl, *Ontario Society for the Prevention of Cruelty to Animals*, 1106

Vaillancourt, Laura, *Ontario Philharmonic*, 1095

Vaillancourt, Regis, *Ontario College of Pharmacists*, 1072

Vaillancourt, Stéphane, *YMCA Canada*, 1472

Vaillancourt, Pauline, *Chants Libres, compagnie lyrique de création*, 552

Vaillancourt, Joé, *La fédération des mouvements personne d'abord du Québec*, 716

Vaillant, Marie, *Multiple Sclerosis Society of Canada*, 980

Vaillant, Linda, *Canadian Society of Hospital Pharmacists*, 484

Vaillant, Linda, *Association des pharmaciens des établissements de santé du Québec*, 123

Vaillant, Kevin, *Air Canada Pilots Association*, 19

Vaira, Vike-Freiberga, *Club de Madrid*, 1517

Vajda, Lexi, *Canadian Alliance of Dance Artists*, 291

Valade, Gilles, *Wilderness Tourism Association*, 1454

Valcour, Lance, *Canadian Interoperability Technology Interest Group*, 422

Vale, Edward, *Peterborough Field Naturalists*, 1153

Vale, Geoffrey, *Master Mariners of Canada*, 954

Valenti, Jennifer, *Community Living North Bay*, 603

Valentine, Pamela, *Alberta Innovates*, 38

Valentine, Betty, *Waypoint Centre for Mental Health Care*, 1443

Valéry, Vlad, *Salon du livre de Toronto et Festival des écrivains*, 1252

Vales, Jennifer, *Coalition des associations de consommateurs du Québec*, 577

Valin, Stewart, *Polio Québec*, 1163

Valiquet, Jehan, *Société du droit de reproduction des auteurs, compositeurs et éditeurs au Canada (SODRAC 2003) inc.*, 1319

Valiquette, Danielle, *Canadian Pony Club*, 457

Valiquette, Leo, *Canadian Printable Electronics Industry Association*, 459

Vallance, Greg, *Marathon & District Chamber of Commerce*, 949

Vallée, Daniel, *Préventex - Association paritaire du textile*, 1170

Vallée, Cynthia, *Association québécoise des industries de nutrition animale et céréalière*, 173

Vallée, Andrée, *Réseau FADOQ*, 1224

Vallée, Robert, *World Organisation of Systems & Cybernetics*, 1606

Vallée, Louis, *Société d'histoire de Sillery*, 1311

Vallée, Karen, *Family Supports Institute Ontario*, 705

Vallée, Martin, *Mon Réseau Plus, Association professionnelle des massothérapeutes spécialisés du Québec inc.*, 971

Vallega, Adalberto, *International Geographic Union*, 1550

Vallentin, Jeff, *United Way of Burlington & Greater Hamilton*, 1413

Vallentin, Jeff, *United Way of Burlington & Greater Hamilton*, 1413

Vallières, Hélène, *Société de généalogie de Drummondville*, 1315

Valters, Peter, *Scouts Canada*, 1286

Valverde, Sharon, *Environmental Bankers Association*, 1523

Van Aert Pattrosson, Dana, *Manitoba Association of Library Technicians*, 930

Van Akker, Sherrie, *British Columbia Registered Music Teachers' Association*, 251

Van Amelsvoort-Barran, Ric, *Canadian Health Information Management Association*, 402

van Beek, Jac, *Canadian Association of Management Consultants*, 320

Van Begin, Gino, *International Council for Local Environmental Initiatives*, 1544

van Belzen, Nico, *International Dairy Federation*, 1545

Van Berkel, Ryan, *Archers & Bowhunters Association of Manitoba*, 78

van Bryce, Teresa, *Horse Industry Association of Alberta*, 822

Van Buren, Mary, *Canadian Construction Association*, 363

van Bylandt, Katrina, *British Columbia Lung Association*, 245

Van Caelenberg, Bert, *International Federation of Employees in Public Service*, 1547

Van Camp, Debbie, *Family Enterprise Xchange*, 703

Van De Crommenacker, Corinne, *Enderby & District Chamber of Commerce*, 687

van de Vijver, Fons, *International Association for Cross-Cultural Psychology*, 1536

van den Boom, Fieny, *Chilliwack Chamber of Commerce*, 563

van den Bosch, Paul, *Alberta Home Education Association*, 37

Van Den Heuvel, Carolyn, *Nova Scotia Institute of Agrologists*, 1046

van den Heuvel, Chris, *Nova Scotia Federation of Agriculture*, 1044

van den Hoogen, Suzanne, *Atlantic Provinces Library Association*, 185

Van Der Heyden, Barb, *Big Brothers Big Sisters of Ontario*, 210

van der Heyden, André, *Belgian Canadian Business Chamber*, 204

van der Leest, Michel, *IRC International Water & Sanitation Centre*, 1567

van der Made, Elly, *Ontario Public Transit Association*, 1100

van der Ree, Dororthy, *Matsqui Sumas Abbotsford Museum Society*, 954

van der Veer, Gerrit, *Special Interest Group on Computer Human Interaction*, 1339

Van der Vuur, Colin, *Fellowship of Evangelical Baptist Churches*, 731

Van Deurzen, Joyce, *Kidney Foundation of Canada*, 885

van Deusen, Natalie, *Association for the Advancement of Scandinavian Studies in Canada*, 134

Van Deventer, Paul, *Meeting Professionals International*, 1570

Van Deynze, David, *Canadian Crop Hail Association*, 373

van Dyk, Peter, *North Queens Board of Trade*, 1032

Van Dyke, Stanley, *Musquodoboit Trailways Association*, 986

Van Geyn, Christine, *Canadian Taxpayers Federation*, 493

Van Gyzen, Sharon, *Allergy/Asthma Information Association*, 54

Van Iderstine, Anne, *Nova Scotia Government Libraries Council*, 1045

Van Iderstine, Peter R., *Canadian Association of Veterans in United Nations Peacekeeping*, 336

Van Kessel, Karla, *Colleges Ontario*, 591

Van Keulen, Ron, *Alberta Amateur Baseball Council*, 22

Van Knoll, John, *Regina Therapeutic Riding Association*, 1212

Van Kommer, Rob, *CurlManitoba Inc.*, 646

van Krimpen, Ada, *International Statistical Institute*, 1562

Van Laer, Annelies, *Ressources Saint-Jean-Vianney*, 1227

van Leeuwen, Henk, *Boys & Girls Clubs of Nova Scotia*, 223

van Leeuwen, Henk, *Easter Seals Nova Scotia*, 669

van Leeuwen, Fred, *Education International*, 1522

Van Leeuwen, John, *Habitat for Humanity Canada*, 797

Van Loo, William, *Belgian Canadian Business Chamber*, 204

Van Looyen, Dale, *Project Management Institute*, 1585

van Manen, Frank, *International Association for Bear Research & Management*, 1536

Van Massenhoven, John, *Headingley Chamber of Commerce*, 805

Van Minsel, Patrick, *Peachland Chamber of Commerce*, 1147

Van Neutegem, Andy, *Canadian Wheelchair Sports Association*, 504

Van Nostrand, Dick, *Dawson City Chamber of Commerce*, 652

Van Oosterhout, Joep, *Dignitas International*, 657

van Rooijen, Gijs, *Dutch Canadian Business Club of Calgary*, 665

Van Sant, Donna, *African Canadian Continuing Education Society*, 12

Van Schel, Louis, *Association internationale permanente des congrès de navigation*, 1510

Van Schoor, Vanessa, *Dignitas International*, 657

Van Sickle, Christina, *Ontario College of Social Workers & Social Service Workers*, 1072

Van Sluys, Shawn, *Musagetes Foundation*, 982

van Spronsen, Tom, *Dawson Creek Construction Association*, 652

Van Steinburg, Terri, *Kwantlen Faculty Association*, 894

Van Stempvoort, Alice, *Alliance for Canadian New Music Projects*, 56

Van Tassel, Lyn, *Association of Registered Interior Designers of New Brunswick*, 161

Van Toen, Jane, *Probation Officers Association of Ontario*, 1181

van Tuijl, Ronald, *International Trademark Association*, 1563

van Uden, Renee, *South Okanagan Boundary Labour Council*, 1335

van Veldhoven, Pum, *Carleton University Academic Staff Association*, 513

Van Vliet, Cornelius, *Ontario Home Builders' Association*, 1085

Van Vliet, Simon, *Association des journalistes indépendants du Québec*, 1117

van Vugt, Greg, *British Columbia Teachers for Peace & Global Education*, 256

Van Wolde, Joan, *Red Deer City Soccer Association*, 1209

van Zanden, Jan Luiten, *International Economic History Association*, 1546

Van't Schip, Ron, *Powell River & District Labour Council*, 1168

Vance, Geraldine, *British Columbia Pharmacy Association*, 248

Vance, Deb, *American Galloway Breeders Association*, 66

Vandal, Francine, *Association des Grands Frères et Grandes Soeurs du Québec*, 115

Vandal, Daniel, *Chambre immobilière des Laurentides*, 551

Vandal, Roland, *Boxing Manitoba*, 220

Vandebelt, Rob, *Christian Stewardship Services*, 568

Vandebelt, Rob, *Sunrise Therapeutic Riding & Learning Centre*, 1355

Vandelinder, Christine, *The Appraisal Institute of Canada - Alberta*, 74

Vandeloo, Tom, *Canadian Netherlands Business & Professional Association Inc.*, 440

Vanden Hoek, Jason, *Chinook Regional Hospital Foundation*, 565

Vandenberg, Helen, *Canadian Association for the History of Nursing*, 305

Vandenberg, John, *Supply Chain Management Association - Northwest Territories*, 1356

Vandenberghe, Maureen, *Tillsonburg & District Multi-Service Centre*, 1379

Vandepoele, Joanne, *Dauphin & District Chamber of Commerce*, 651

Vander Heiden, Marie, *Association of Professional Biology*, 156

Vander Heyden, Jen, *Canadian Hearing Society*, 403

Vander Hooft, Kelly, *Interior Designers of Alberta*, 852

Executive Name Index

Vander Ploeg, Casey, *Alberta Cattle Feeders' Association*, 27
Vander Voet, Tony, *Ontario Society of Artists*, 1107
VanderBent, Susan D., *Ontario Home Care Association*, 1086
VanderBerg, Kristen, *World Renew*, 1467
VanderGriendt, Sherry, *Lethbridge & District Humane Society*, 907
Vandermarel, Maureen, *Ontario Beekeepers' Association*, 1068
VanDerMeer, Katie, *American Musicological Society*, 1495
Vandermeersch, Ivan, *Federation of European Direct & Interactive Marketing*, 1526
Vanderschaeghe, Jennifer, *Central Alberta AIDS Network Society*, 523
Vandersteen, Bev, *Fort Nelson & District Chamber of Commerce*, 753
Vandervalk, Stephen, *Grain Growers of Canada*, 779
Vanderwekken, Ken, *Trail Riding Alberta Conference*, 1394
VanderWielen, Henry, *Essa & District Agricultural Society*, 696
Vanderzweerde, Robert, *Trail Riders of the Canadian Rockies*, 1394
VanDeurzen, Joyce, *Kidney Foundation of Canada*, 885
Vandezande, Ben, *Indian Métis Christian Fellowship*, 834
Vandressen, Monique, *Associaçao Brasileira de Estudos Canadense*, 1506
Vanessen, Joe, *South Delta Food Bank*, 1334
Vangen, Jeff, *Medicine Hat Soccer Association*, 959
Vanier, Véronique, *Bureau local d'intervention traitant du SIDA*, 264
Vanier, JY, *Alberta Plastics Recycling Association*, 42
Vanini, Pat, *Association of Municipalities of Ontario*, 152
Vansen, Allen, *Rugby Canada*, 1244
Vanstone, Kaneena, *Manitoba Sport Parachute Association*, 945
Vantrepote, Michele, *Starlight Children's Foundation Canada*, 1348
Vanzessen, Tymen, *Holstein Canada*, 819
Vardy, Gerard, *Canadian Counselling & Psychotherapy Association*, 372
Varekamp, Linda, *Toronto Renewable Energy Co-operative*, 1387
Varey, Matt, *Juvenile Diabetes Research Foundation Canada*, 878
Varghese, Thomas, *Jesus Youth Canada*, 870
Varin, Marguerite, *Chambre de commerce et d'industrie d'Argenteuil*, 545
Varma, Bhavana, *United Way of Kingston, Frontenac, Lennox & Addington*, 1415
Varner, Merrill, *Canadian Institute of Quantity Surveyors - Maritimes*, 419
Varner, Jan, *United Way of Kitchener-Waterloo & Area*, 1415
Vasil, Nancy, *Canadian Academy of Geriatric Psychiatry*, 286
Vasiliou, William, *Association of Certified Fraud Examiners - Toronto Chapter*, 145
Vassallo, Gary, *Windsor Association for the Deaf*, 1456
Vaudreuil, François, *Centrale des syndicats démocratiques*, 525
Vaudry, Catherine, *Fédération québécoise des sociétés Alzheimer*, 730
Vaughan, Lloyd, *Council of Private Investigators - Ontario*, 635
Vaughan, Murray, *Canadian Home Furnishings Alliance*, 408
Vaughan, Scott, *International Institute for Sustainable Development*, 858
Vaughn Strebly, Jonathan, *Society of Graphic Designers of Canada*, 1329
Vaugrante, Béatrice, *Amnistie internationale, Section canadienne (Francophone)*, 68

Vautour, Kathy, *Restigouche County Society for the Prevention of Cruelty to Animals*, 1228
Vautour, Paul, *Multicultural Association of the Greater Moncton Area*, 979
Vazalinskas, John, *L'Association des artistes Baltes à Montréal*, 106
Veale, Jordan, *Manitoba Association of Medical Radiation Technologists*, 930
Vecchiarelli, Cindy, *Essa & District Agricultural Society*, 696
Vecchio-Scandinavo, Filomena, *Communion & Liberation Canada*, 594
Vecchione, Bob, *National Association of Collegiate Directors of Athletics*, 1573
Veeneman, Sharon, *Canadian Association for Disabled Skiing - Alberta*, 299
Veenstra, Terrence Lee, *Society of Tribologists & Lubrication Engineers*, 1594
Veenstra, Richard, *Service universitaire canadien outre-mer*, 1292
Veenstra, Richard, *Fondation Jules et Paul-Émile Léger*, 747
Veer, Ken, *Irma Fish & Game Association*, 864
Vegh, Stephanie, *Hamilton Arts Council*, 800
Vehrs, Mary Anne, *Freight Carriers Association of Canada*, 759
Vehrs, Kris, *Association of Zoos & Aquariums*, 1513
Veillard, Jeremy, *Canadian Institute for Health Information*, 412
Veillette, André, *Institut de recherches cliniques de Montréal*, 842
Veilleux, Yanie, *Vintage Road Racing Association*, 1435
Veilleux, Pierre, *Association des policières et policiers provinciaux du Québec*, 123
Veilleux, François, *Chambre de commerce de Beauceville*, 540
Veilleux, Francis, *Bluewater Recycling Association*, 216
Veilleux, Denis, *Regroupement des associations de personnes traumatisées craniocérébrales du Québec*, 1214
Veitch, Peyton, *Canadian Federation of Students*, 388
Vekay, Iryn, *Greater Vancouver Food Bank Society*, 786
Velarde, Daniel, *Canadiana*, 506
Velarde, Daniel, *George Grant Society*, 770
Velasquez, Layla, *Canadian Bible Society*, 343
Velcoff, Jackie, *Building Industry & Land Development Alberta*, 262
Veldhuis, Niels, *The Fraser Institute*, 757
Veldhuyzen, Val, *Building Industry & Land Development Calgary Region*, 262
Velikonja, Diana, *Ontario Brain Injury Association*, 1068
Vella, Anthony, *Malta Band Club, Inc.*, 928
Veller, Christy, *Macklin Chamber of Commerce*, 924
Veltri, Anna, *Le Collège du Savoir*, 582
Venables, Brian, *The Salvation Army in Canada*, 1253
Venditti, Jennifer, *BMW Clubs Canada*, 216
Venditto, Christine, *Association québécoise pour l'hygiène, la santé et la sécurité du travail*, 176
Veneklasen, Rose, *Middle East Studies Association of North America*, 1571
Venn, David, *Community Foundations of Canada*, 1968
Venne, Marie-Marthe, *Chambre de commerce de Saint-Côme*, 543
Venne, Rachelle, *Institute for the Advancement of Aboriginal Women*, 844
Venneri, Marie-France, *Canadian Construction Women*, 363
Vennes, Richard, *Fédération des syndicats de l'action collective*, 179
Vennes, Richard, *Syndicat des employés et employées des syndicats et des organismes collectifs du Québec*, 1363
Vent, Gail, *Skills/Compétences Canada*, 1302

Ventor, Derek, *Ontario Rowing Association*, 1102
Ventrell, Marvin, *National Association of Addiction Treatment Providers*, 1573
Ventress, Donna, *Canadian Institute for the Administration of Justice*, 413
Ventry, Mark, *Ontario Co-operative Association*, 1074
Venus, Henny, *Ontario Society for the Prevention of Cruelty to Animals*, 1105
Veraguth, Gion, *International Ice Hockey Federation*, 1551
Verbaas, Heather, *Alberta College of Paramedics*, 30
Verbeek, Tessa, *Canadian Limousin Association*, 427
Verbeek, Linda, *Alpine Garden Club of BC*, 59
Vercouteren, Frank, *Blenheim & District Chamber of Commerce*, 214
Verdeflor-Alvarado, Amor, *Shareholder Association for Research & Education*, 1294
Verdon, Karina, *Ordre des urbanistes du Québec*, 1124
Verdone, Gerry, *Brampton Real Estate Board*, 226
Vere, Isobel, *British Columbia Bison Association*, 234
Veresh, Tim, *The John Howard Society of British Columbia*, 874
Veresh, Tim, *British Columbia Criminal Justice Association*, 238
Veresh, Tim, *PLEA Community Services Society of BC*, 1163
Vergalito, Vilma, *50 & Piu Enasco*, 734
Vergara, Patri, *International Council for Laboratory Animal Science*, 1544
Vergara, Anyela, *Centre de soutien entr'Aidants*, 530
Verge, Mike, *Ontario Refrigeration & Air Conditioning Contractors Association*, 1101
Verge, Robert, *Canadian Centre for Fisheries Innovation*, 353
Verhulst, Katie, *Prince Edward Island Occupational Therapy Society*, 1176
Veri, Adam, *Port Dover Board of Trade*, 1166
Veri, Heidi, *Association of Registered Graphic Designers of Ontario*, 161
Verigin, Barry, *Union of Spiritual Communities of Christ*, 1408
Verkaik, Jason, *Ontario Fruit & Vegetable Growers' Association*, 1081
Verklan, Yvonne, *Canadian Society of Gastroenterology Nurses & Associates*, 483
Verleun, Peter, *Prince Edward Island Cattle Producers*, 1173
Vermette, Audrey, *ICOM Museums Canada*, 829
Vermette, Maryse, *Éco Entreprises Québec*, 671
Vermeulen, Matt, *Elora Environment Centre*, 685
Vernier, Shana, *Conseil des arts de Hearst*, 617
Vernon, Mark, *Architectural Institute of British Columbia*, 79
Vernon, J.E. (Jerry), *Canadian Aviation Historical Society*, 340
Vernon, Sally, *London Community Orchestra*, 918
Vernon, Timothy, *Pacific Opera Victoria*, 1135
Verrall, Brian, *Ontario Occupational Health Nurses Association*, 1094
Verreault, Nancy, *Association of Electromyography Technologists of Canada*, 147
Verreault, Pierre, *Canadian Council of Professional Fish Harvesters*, 369
Verreault, Karine, *Centre multiethnique de Québec*, 536
Verret, G., *Canadian Society of Forensic Science*, 483
Verret, Johanne, *Fédération de l'industrie manufacturière (FIM-CSN)*, 709
Verrillo, Josie, *National Congress of Italian-Canadians*, 991

Verroeulst, Christiane, *Réseau indépendant des diffuseurs d'événements artistiques unis*, 1225
Versavel, Neil, *Canadian Sheep Breeders' Association*, 470
Verschoor, Karla, *Inclusion BC*, 832
Verst, Paul, *International Warehouse Logistics Association*, 1566
Verville, Martin, *Centre de formation en entreprise et récupération Normand-Maurice*, 529
Verville, Renée, *Ordre des psychoéducateurs et psychoéducatrices du Québec*, 1123
Vescera, Mauro, *Italian Cultural Centre Society*, 866
Vesely, Carolyn, *Ontario Arts Council*, 1060
Vesin, Patrick, *Judo-Québec inc*, 877
Vesta, Marie, *Association of Personal Computer Users Groups*, 1513
Vetter, Mary A., *Canadian Association of Palynologists*, 325
Vezeau, Joan, *Lighthouse Mission*, 912
Vézina, Ginette, *Association québécoise des salons du livre*, 174
Vézina, Pierre, *Conseil de l'industrie forestière du Québec*, 615
Vézina, Nathalie, *Association québécoise de doit comparé*, 169
Vezina, Alain, *International Council for the Exploration of the Sea*, 1544
Vézina, Michel, *Fédération des aînées et aînés francophones du Canada*, 711
Vézina, Véronique, *Confédération des Organismes de Personnes Handicapées du Québec*, 611
Vézina, Michel, *Fondation fransaskoise*, 746
Vézina, France, *Association du transport urbain du Québec*, 132
Vézina-Doré, Émilie, *Action Patrimoine*, 7
Veziroglu, T. Nejat, *International Association for Hydrogen Energy*, 1537
Via, Steven, *American Water Works Association*, 1504
Viau, Celine, *Ordre des évaluateurs agréés du Québec*, 1121
Viau, Stéphane, *Association pour l'intégration communautaire de l'Outaouais*, 165
Vicé, Otto, *Projet 10*, 1188
Vickers, Cheryl, *Juvenile Diabetes Research Foundation Canada*, 879
Vickery, Emily, *Triathlon British Columbia*, 1397
Viczko, April, *Associated Designers of Canada*, 89
Vidershpan, Valery, *Canadian Council of Technicians & Technologists*, 370
Vidinovski, Luby, *Macedonian Human Rights Movement International*, 923
Vidler, Cam, *Business Council of Canada*, 267
Viegas, Norman, *Association of Science & Engineering Technology Professionals of Alberta*, 162
Viegas Guerreiro, Maria, *Portuguese Canadian Seniors Foundation*, 1167
Vieira, Verónica, *International Society for Environmental Epidemiology*, 1557
Viel, Claude, *Fédération des producteurs de bovins du Québec*, 717
Viel, Cécile, *Association des implantés cochléaires du Québec*, 116
Vielh, Philippe, *International Academy of Cytology*, 1535
Vieni, Mary, *Addus*, 8
Vienneau, Gilles, *Société Santé et Mieux-être en français du Nouveau-Brunswick*, 1325
Viens, Mario, *Association Québécoise de chirurgie*, 169
Viens, Val, *Smoky River Regional Chamber of Commerce*, 1305
Vigneault, Alexandre, *Ordre des ingénieurs du Québec*, 1122
Vigneault, Eric, *Canadian Association of Radiation Oncology*, 330

Executive Name Index

Vigneault, Francine, *Association québécoise pour le loisir des personnes handicapées*, 177
Vigon, Carolyne, *Canadian Fire Safety Association*, 390
Vigon, Carolyne, *Door & Hardware Institute in Canada*, 661
Vigon, Bruce, *Society of Environmental Toxicology & Chemistry*, 1593
Vigon, Carolyne, *Institute of Housing Management*, 846
Vihvelin, Liisa, *Peace Country Beef & Forage Association*, 1147
Villecourt, Guy, *Similkameen Okanagan Organic Producers Association*, 1300
Villefranche, Marjorie, *Maison D'Haiti*, 926
Villemure, Sylvie, *Chambre de commerce et d'industrie Beauharnois-Valleyfield-Haut Saint-Laurent*, 545
Villeneuve, Yolaine, *Conseil des industriels laitiers du Québec inc.*, 617
Villeneuve, Marie-Sophie, *Development & Peace*, 655
Villeneuve, Debbie, *Canadian Interuniversity Sport*, 422
Villeneuve, Mike, *Canadian Nurses Association*, 443
Villeneuve, Denis, *Ordre des ingénieurs forestiers du Québec*, 1123
Villeneuve, Dominique, *Association des agences de publicité du Québec*, 105
Villeneuve, Luc, *Petits frères des pauvres*, 1154
Villeneuve, Gilles, *Auto Sport Québec*, 189
Villeneuve, Johanne, *Table des responsables de l'éducation des adultes et de la formation professionnelle des commissions scolaires du Québec*, 1366
Villeneuve, Julie, *Association québécoise pour le tourisme équestre et l'équitation de loisir du Québec*, 177
Villeneuve, Donald, *Fédération québécoise de biathlon*, 727
Vince, John, *CIO Association of Canada*, 570
Vince, Gary, *Canadian International Freight Forwarders Association*, 421
Vincent, Kevin, *Convention of Atlantic Baptist Churches*, 627
Vincent, Alana, *Sioux Lookout Chamber of Commerce*, 1300
Vincent, Jean-Guy, *Canadian Pork Council*, 458
Vincent, Julie, *Water Environment Association of Ontario*, 1441
Vincent, Lisa, *International Confederation of Principals*, 1544
Vincenten, Pauline, *Friends of the Earth International*, 1527
Vine, Cathy, *Voices for Children*, 1437
Vinet-Roy, Anne, *Association canadienne d'éducation de langue française*, 90
Vinette, Michel, *Society of Plastics Engineers*, 1594
Vint, Cosmin, *Romanian Orthodox Deanery of Canada*, 1235
Viola, Carlo, *Information Technology Association of Canada*, 837
Vipond, Dee, *Risk & Insurance Management Society Inc.*, 1234
Vipond, Gary, *United Way of Sault Ste Marie & District*, 1417
Vipond, Tony, *Ontario Association on Developmental Disabilities*, 1067
Virone, Danielle, *Italian Chamber of Commerce in Canada*, 866
Visintin, George, *Italian Chamber of Commerce of Ontario*, 866
Vissers, Henry, *Nova Scotia Federation of Agriculture*, 1044
Vitales, Nechane, *Association of Filipino Canadian Accountants*, 148
Vittal, Anu, *Mississauga Arts Council*, 969
Vittiglio, Mario, *Institute of Municipal Assessors*, 846

Vivian, John, *Newfoundland & Labrador Nurses' Union*, 1020
Vivian-Book, Lynn, *Newfoundland & Labrador Public Health Association*, 1021
Vizer, Andy, *Cement Association of Canada*, 521
Vizer, Marius, *International Judo Federation*, 1551
Vlooswyk, Anton, *Alberta Building Envelope Council (South)*, 27
Vlug, Leanor, *Greater Vancouver Association of the Deaf*, 786
Voce, Graham, *International Institute for Conservation of Historic & Artistic Works*, 1551
Vodicka, Christy, *Melfort Agricultural Society*, 959
Voegeli-Bleiker, Heidi, *Holstein Canada*, 819
Voegeli-Bleiker, Heidi, *Alberta Salers Association*, 45
Vogel, Tim, *Canadian Paint & Coatings Association*, 449
Vogelaar, Karen, *Brooks & District Chamber of Commerce*, 260
Vogt, Khrista, *Medicine Hat & District Chamber of Commerce*, 958
Vogt, Julie, *Ottawa Safety Council*, 1131
Vogt, Geoff, *YMCA Canada*, 1473
Vogt, Alyshia, *Family Caregivers of British Columbia*, 702
Voilquin, Laure, *Centraide Gatineau-Labelle-Hautes-Laurentides*, 522
Voinerchuk, Genadi, *Canada Employment & Immigration Union*, 279
Voisine, Pierre, *Canadian Association of Fire Chiefs*, 315
Voith, Michael Robert, *The Canadian Corps of Commissionaires*, 365
Volans, Cathy, *Cooperative Housing Federation of Canada*, 628
Volino, Cornelia, *Canadian Culinary Federation*, 374
Volk, Lois, *Canadian Association of Women Executives & Entrepreneurs*, 336
Vollans, Leroy, *Kamloops, Revelstoke, Okanagan & District Building & Construction Trades Council*, 881
Vollet, Kevin, *Saskatchewan High Schools Athletic Association*, 1267
Vollman, Ardene Robinson, *Canadian Public Health Association*, 462
Vollmer, Karl, *Canoe Kayak Nova Scotia*, 509
Volpe, Flavio, *Automotive Parts Manufacturers' Association*, 190
Volpé, Linda, *Porc NB Pork*, 1165
Von Doellen, Joe, *Vanderhoof Chamber of Commerce*, 1429
von Fuchs, Ruth, *The Right to Die Society of Canada*, 1232
von Hausen, Ingrid, *Canadian Trakehner Horse Society*, 496
von Keitz, Michael, *Chess Federation of Canada*, 556
von Sass, Carola, *Alberta Forest Products Association*, 35
von Schellwitz, Mark, *Restaurants Canada*, 1227
Vonn, Micheal, *British Columbia Civil Liberties Association*, 236
Vos, Jonathan, *Prince Edward Island Soccer Association*, 1177
Voss, Brent, *South Okanagan Boundary Labour Council*, 1335
Voth, Matt, *Manitoba Sign Association*, 944
Votour, Nancy, *Lupus New Brunswick*, 921
Votta-Bleeker, Lisa, *Canadian Psychological Association*, 462
Voyer, Kathleen, *Chambre de commerce et d'industrie Lac-Saint-Jean-Est*, 547
Voyer, Normand, *Sous-Traitance Industrielle Québec*, 1334
Voyer-Léger, Catherine, *Regroupement des éditeurs canadiens-français*, 1215
Vreman, Tim, *Ontario Association of Cemetery & Funeral Professionals*, 1062

Vrieselaar, Tim, *Alberta Farm Fresh Producers Association*, 34
Vrionis, Tania, *Multiple Sclerosis Society of Canada*, 980
Vu, Catherine, *Saskatchewan School Boards Association*, 1274
Vuillemot, Valerie, *Ringette PEI*, 1233
Vuillemot, Valerie, *Gymnastics PEI*, 795
Vukelich, Goranka, *Association of Early Childhood Educators Ontario*, 147
Vukelj, Simon, *Children's Tumor Foundation*, 1517
Vukosavovic, Marko, *Academy of Management*, 1485
Vuyk, Wendy, *Pathways to Education Canada*, 1145
Vyas, Varun, *Atlantic Federation of Musicians, Local 571*, 184
Vyrostko, Barbara, *Community Living Welland Pelham*, 606

W

Wach, Frances, *Saskatchewan Society for the Prevention of Cruelty to Animals*, 1275
Wachtel, Dina, *Canadian Friends of the Hebrew University*, 395
Waddell, Stephen, *Alliance of Canadian Cinema, Television & Radio Artists*, 58
Waddell, Chris, *Ontario Rowing Association*, 1102
Waddell, William, *Northeast Modern Language Association*, 1579
Wadden, Kevin, *Canadian Association of Veterans in United Nations Peacekeeping*, 336
Waddington, Lyal, *Saskatchewan Square & Round Dance Federation*, 1276
Waddington, Carmel, *Saskatchewan Square & Round Dance Federation*, 1276
Waddy, Susan, *Aquaculture Association of Canada*, 75
Wade, Casey, *CanoeKayak Canada*, 509
Wade, Mike, *Society of Toxicology of Canada*, 1331
Wade, Shawn M., *The Royal Commonwealth Society of Canada*, 1242
Wade, Joy, *Aquaculture Association of Canada*, 75
Wade, Anne, *Centre for the Study of Learning & Performance*, 534
Wadee, Oday, *Professional Engineers Ontario*, 1184
Wadel, Don, *The John Howard Society of Ontario*, 875
Wadman, Barbara, *Newfoundland & Labrador Sexual Assault Crisis & Prevention Centre Inc.*, 1021
Wadsworth, Jessica, *Canadian Alliance of Dance Artists*, 291
Waeland, Pamela, *Alzheimer Society Ontario*, 65
Wagar, Wes, *Castor Fish & Game Association*, 517
Wagenaer, Lucien, *Kent Coin Club*, 883
Wagers, Michael, *International Association of Chiefs of Police*, 1538
Wagg, David, *Basketball Nova Scotia*, 199
Wagg, Adrian, *The Canadian Continence Foundation*, 364
Wagler, Steve, *New Hamburg Board of Trade*, 1014
Wagman, K., *Leader Board of Trade*, 903
Wagman, Morty, *Canadian Association for Israel Philately*, 301
Wagner, Mary, *Toronto Renewable Energy Co-operative*, 1387
Wagner, E., *New Apostolic Church Canada*, 1004
Wagner, Belinda, *Saskatchewan Cattle Breeders Association*, 1260
Wagner, Anton, *Canadian Theatre Critics Association*, 494
Wagner, Michael, *Canadian Association of Orthodontists*, 324

Wagner, Diane, *Learning Disabilities Association of Ontario*, 905
Wagner, Belinda, *Canadian Shorthorn Association*, 470
Wagner, Karyn, *Canadian Society of Plastic Surgeons*, 487
Wagner, Hugh J., *Grain Services Union (CLC)*, 779
Wagner, Belinda, *Saskatchewan Livestock Association*, 1269
Wagner, Joy, *Pancreatic Cancer Canada Foundation*, 1174
Wagner Arbus, Joy, *Israel Cancer Research Fund*, 866
Wagner-Miller, Carrie, *Boys & Girls Clubs of Canada*, 222
Wahl, Judith, *Advocacy Centre for the Elderly*, 10
Wahl, Joan, *Alberta Genealogical Society*, 37
Wahl, Bettina, *Sandford Fleming Foundation*, 1253
Waight, Elizabeth, *Municipal Law Departments Association of Ontario*, 981
Waindubence, Gordon, *Union of Ontario Indians*, 1408
Waines, Jordan, *Muskoka Steamship & Historical Society*, 985
Wainikka, Trish, *Manitoba Quality Network*, 943
Wainstein, Pablo, *Cu Nim Gliding Club*, 645
Wainwright, Paul, *Musicians' Association of Victoria & the Islands, Local 247, AFM*, 984
Wainwright, Kaitlin, *Heritage Toronto*, 813
Waisman, Malcolm, *Social Planning Council of Kitchener-Waterloo*, 1306
Waite, Peter, *Pension Investment Association of Canada*, 1150
Waite, Elizabeth, *Canadian Academy of Child & Adolescent Psychiatry*, 285
Waite, Peter, *Canadian Bond Investors' Association*, 346
Waithe, Frances, *Desta Black Youth Network*, 654
Wakefield, Wesley H., *The Bible Holiness Movement*, 208
Wakefield, Christina, *Archives Association of Ontario*, 80
Wakelam, Gary, *College of Dental Technologists of Alberta*, 583
Wakem, Beverley A., *International Ombudsman Institute*, 1554
Wakimets, Stephen, *Alberta Pioneer Railway Association*, 12
Walchuk, Rob, *Canadian Masonry Contractors' Association*, 431
Walczyk, Barbara, *Children's Miracle Network*, 562
Walden, Wayne, *Ingersoll District Nature Club*, 838
Waldner, Laurel, *Saskatchewan Wildlife Federation*, 1278
Waldon, Seana, *Community Association for Riding for the Disabled*, 596
Waldron, Brad, *Air & Waste Management Association*, 1486
Wales, Don, *Red Deer River Naturalists*, 1209
Wales, Leah, *Human Resources Professionals Association*, 825
Walford, Nigel, *Commonwealth Geographical Bureau*, 1518
Walicka, Maria, *Polish Teachers Association in Canada*, 1164
Walker, Liz, *White Rock & Surrey Naturalists*, 1452
Walker, Louise, *Squamish Chamber of Commerce*, 1346
Walker, Jerry, *Haliburton Highlands Chamber of Commerce*, 798
Walker, Orland, *Saskatchewan Charolais Association*, 1261
Walker, Valerie, *Business Council of Canada*, 267
Walker, Glen, *AIDS Niagara*, 17
Walker, David, *Canadian Association of Provincial Court Judges*, 329

Executive Name Index

Walker, Greg, *Continental Automated Buildings Association*, 626
Walker, Ryan, *Saskatchewan Professional Planners Institute*, 1272
Walker, James, *Physicians for a Smoke-Free Canada*, 1158
Walker, Nelson, *Royal Astronomical Society of Canada*, 1239
Walker, Crystal, *Centre for Suicide Prevention*, 534
Walker, Brenda, *College of Registered Dental Hygienists of Alberta*, 589
Walker, Stan, *Golden Rock & Fossil Club*, 776
Walker, Ron, *Canadian Native Friendship Centre*, 440
Walker, Channing, *Christian Science*, 1517
Walker, Bill, *Safety Services New Brunswick*, 1245
Walker, Jennifer, *Carleton County Law Association*, 513
Walker, Janet, *Canada's History*, 282
Walker, Darryl, *British Columbia Government & Service Employees' Union*, 242
Walker, Alexandra, *Island Deaf & Hard of Hearing Centre*, 865
Walker, Wendy, *Alberta Amateur Speed Skating Association*, 22
Walker, Ron, *Alberta Texas Longhorn Association*, 50
Walker, Kathy, *New Brunswick Society of Cardiology Techologists*, 1012
Walker, Terry, *Velo Halifax Bicycle Club*, 1431
Walker, Kent, *Prince Edward Island Baseball Umpires Association*, 1172
Walker, Elaine, *Saskatchewan Darts Association*, 1263
Walker, Adam, *New Brunswick Physique & Figure Association*, 1011
Walker, Heather, *Canadian Automobile Insurance Rate Regulators Association*, 339
Walkowiak, Anna, *Société québécoise de récupération et de recyclage*, 1323
Walkowska, Urszula, *Canadian Polish Congress*, 456
Wall, Heather, *Kindersley Chamber of Commerce*, 888
Wall, Jackie, *Estevan Chamber of Commerce*, 697
Wall, Lori, *Basketball New Brunswick*, 199
Wall, Diane, *Epilepsy & Seizure Association of Manitoba*, 693
Wall, Emily, *Anglican Foundation of Canada*, 70
Wall, Jack, *Cape Breton Island Building & Construction Trades Council*, 509
Wall, Heidi, *Kitchener-Waterloo Kiwanis Music Festival*, 891
Wall, Brad, *Saskatchewan Party*, 1271
Wallace, Jacqueline, *British Columbia Association of Medical Radiation Technologists*, 232
Wallace, Dee, *Manitoba Library Association*, 940
Wallace, Debbie, *Mackenzie Chamber of Commerce*, 924
Wallace, Nancy, *Business Council of Canada*, 267
Wallace, Tod, *Manitoba Beef Cattle Performance Association*, 932
Wallace, Bruce, *National Wildlife Federation*, 1577
Wallace, Thomas (Tom) E.S., *Federation for Scottish Culture in Nova Scotia*, 721
Wallace, Robert K., *Real Estate Board of Greater Vancouver*, 1205
Wallace, Brian, *Back Country Horsemen of British Columbia*, 192
Wallace, Brian, *Back Country Horsemen of British Columbia*, 193
Wallace, Suzanne, *CADORA British Columbia*, 269
Wallace-Gero, Nancy, *Community Living Essex County*, 601
Waller, Ann, *Canadian National Federation of Independent Unions*, 439

Walling, Savannah, *Vancouver Moving Theatre*, 1427
Wallner, Bryan L., *Roofing Contractors Association of British Columbia*, 1236
Walls, Barbara, *New Brunswick Lung Association*, 1010
Walls, Michael P., *American Chemistry Council*, 1491
Walls-Carr, Michelle, *Windsor Association for the Deaf*, 1456
Walmsley, Sharon, *Canadian HIV Trials Network*, 405
Walmsley, Katie, *Portfolio Management Association of Canada*, 1167
Walmsley, Jason, *British Columbia Miniature Horse Club*, 246
Walsh, Michael, *Associated Designers of Canada*, 89
Walsh, Renée, *Catholic Children's Aid Society of Toronto*, 518
Walsh, Lindsay, *Ontario Basketball*, 1067
Walsh, Bob, *Newfoundland & Labrador Athletics Association*, 1017
Walsh, Alison, *Newfoundland & Labrador Athletics Association*, 1017
Walsh, Anya, *Autism Society of British Columbia*, 189
Walsh, Nathalie, *Autism Society of PEI*, 189
Walsh, Michael, *Continuing Care Association of Nova Scotia*, 627
Walsh, Marie Annik, *Association des avocats et avovates en droit familial du Québec*, 107
Walsh, Pegeen, *Ontario Public Health Association*, 1099
Walsh, Susan, *USC Canada*, 1423
Walsh, Shawna, *British Columbia Ferry & Marine Workers' Union (CLC)*, 241
Walsh, Eileen Mary, *Sisters Adorers of the Precious Blood*, 1300
Walsh, Peter, *Alberta Rowing Association*, 45
Walsh, Brian, *Ontario Steam & Antique Preservers Association*, 1109
Walsh, Ron, *Chicken Farmers of Newfoundland & Labrador*, 557
Walsh, Alexandra, *Ottawa Chamber of Commerce*, 1129
Walsh, Dean, *Community Living North Frontenac*, 603
Walsh, Shane, *Ontario Home Respiratory Services Association*, 1086
Walsh, Susan, *Geneva Centre for Autism*, 769
Walsh, Allyn, *Canadian Association for Medical Education*, 302
Walsh, Vera, *Newfoundland Dental Assistants Association*, 1023
Walsh, Gary, *Karate Nova Scotia*, 882
Walsh, Michael, *Friends of Dismas*, 761
Walsh McGuire, Penny, *Greater Charlottetown & Area Chamber of Commerce*, 783
Walston, Lori Lee, *Canadian Association of Hepatology Nurses*, 317
Walter, Ross, *Model "A" Owners of Canada Inc.*, 970
Walter, Scott, *CODE*, 580
Walter, Scott, *Canadian Organization for Development through Education*, 447
Walter, Martin, *Australian Football League Ontario*, 188
Walters, Harold, *Newfoundland & Labrador Curling Association*, 1018
Walters, Wanda, *Carleton County Law Association*, 513
Walters, Janet, *Town of York Historical Society*, 1393
Walters, Jeff, *Flowers Canada*, 741
Walters, Brenda, *Master Bowlers' Association of Ontario*, 953
Walthers, Robert, *Canadian Jiu-jitsu Council*, 423
Walthert, Henry, *Wood Preservation Canada*, 1463
Waltman, Marla, *Jewish Genealogical Society of Toronto*, 872
Walton, Priscilla L., *Canadian Association for American Studies*, 297

Walton, Kim, *Quickdraw Animation Society*, 1201
Walton, Bryan, *Alberta Cattle Feeders' Association*, 27
Walton, Marj, *Swim Saskatchewan*, 1359
Walton, Theresa, *Edmonton CFA Society*, 675
Wamback, Trevor, *Baseball Nova Scotia*, 198
Wang, Daniel, *Chambre de commerce francophone de Vancouver*, 548
Wang, Quiju, *International Association of Physicians in Audiology*, 1539
Wang, Christa, *Association of Neighbourhood Houses BC*, 153
Wang, Flora, *Canadian Sugar Institute*, 491
Wang, Vicky, *Canadian Association of Occupational Therapists*, 323
Wankel, Joan, *Logan Lake Arts Council*, 917
Wanless, Judy, *Community Association for Riding for the Disabled*, 596
Wannamaker, Heather, *Human Resources Professionals Association*, 826
Wanner, Denise, *Regina Exhibition Association Ltd.*, 1211
Wanner, Judy, *CADORA Ontario Association Inc.*, 269
Wanuch, Ray, *Council for Advancement of Native Development Officers*, 632
Warcup, Margaret, *Kitimat Child Development Centre*, 891
Ward, Helen, *Kids First Parent Association of Canada*, 886
Ward, Bernadette, *Oakville Arts Council*, 1053
Ward, Casey, *Regina Policemen Association Inc.*, 1212
Ward, Kevin, *Northumberland Central Chamber of Commerce*, 1036
Ward, William, *Canadian Meteorological & Oceanographic Society*, 436
Ward, Katherine, *Motion Picture Association - Canada*, 975
Ward, Dale, *Manitoba Cooperative Association (MCA) Inc.*, 934
Ward, Jill, *Young People's Theatre*, 1475
Ward, Margo, *Didsbury Chamber of Commerce*, 656
Ward, Heather, *Manitoba Egg Farmers*, 936
Ward, Ken, *Strathcona Christian Academy Society*, 1351
Ward, Pat, *Nova Scotia Hereford Club*, 1045
Ward, Donna, *Consort & District Chamber of Commerce*, 623
Ward, Paige L., *Mutual Fund Dealers Association of Canada*, 986
Ward, Bob, *Legal Aid Ontario*, 906
Ward, Heather, *British Columbia Miniature Horse Club*, 246
Ward, Marc, *Karate Alberta Association*, 881
Ward, Russ, *Concerned Children's Advertisers*, 609
Ward, Brian, *Canadian Association for Immunization Research & Evaluation*, 301
Ward-Pereira, Amanda, *Algoma District Law Association*, 53
Warda, Stanislaw, *Canadian Polish Congress*, 456
Ware, Bob, *Canadian Association of Veterans in United Nations Peacekeeping*, 336
Wareham, Catherine, *Canadian Association of Police Educators*, 327
Warga, Brent, *Manitoba Association of Insolvency & Restructuring Professionals*, 930
Warick, Ruth, *Canadian Hard of Hearing Association*, 400
Warick, Ruth, *Western Institute for the Deaf & Hard of Hearing*, 1450
Waring, Jennifer, *Canadian New Music Network*, 441
Warkentin, Bruce, *Taber & District Chamber of Commerce*, 1365
Warkentin, Germaine, *Toronto Renaissance & Reformation Colloquium*, 1387
Warkentin, Marvin, *Royal Astronomical Society of Canada*, 1238

Warkentin, Ken, *Mennonite Church Canada*, 961
Warner, Denny, *Saanich Peninsula Chamber of Commerce*, 1245
Warner, Stephen M., *Industrial Fabrics Association International*, 1531
Warnock, Richard, *Alberta Motor Transport Association*, 40
Warnock, Julie, *Northwest Territories Tourism*, 1039
Warnock, Dean, *Folk Festival Society of Calgary*, 742
Warr, Brian, *Atlantic Building Supply Dealers Association*, 182
Warren, Jamie, *Canadian Counselling & Psychotherapy Association*, 372
Warren, Janelle, *Ontario Good Roads Association*, 1083
Warren, Deborah, *AIDS Moncton*, 17
Warren, Carol, *International Federation for Home Economics*, 1546
Warren, Brian, *Start2Finish*, 1348
Warrick, Gary, *Canadian Archaeological Association*, 294
Warris, Peter, *Prince Edward Island Aquaculture Alliance*, 1172
Warshawski, Tom, *Childhood Obesity Foundation*, 560
Wartenberg Kagan, Ute, *American Numismatic Society*, 1496
Warth, Peter, *Central Canada Broadcast Engineers*, 524
Wartman, Mark, *The Nature Conservancy of Canada*, 1000
Warwick, Art, *Thunder Bay Community Foundation*, 1377
Warwick, Will, *Hanna & District Chamber of Commerce*, 803
Warwick, Ian, *Association of Fundraising Professionals*, 1512
Wasacase, Jacqui, *Saskatchewan Council for International Co-operation*, 1262
Waschuk, Mike, *Saskatchewan Land Surveyors' Association*, 1268
Washburn, Sarah, *Institute of Packaging Professionals*, 1533
Washer, Jim, *Canadian Cattle Breeders' Association*, 351
Washer, Jim, *Canadian Livestock Records Corporation*, 428
Wasilewski, Barb, *Manitoba Public Health Association*, 943
Waslen, Patrick, *Football BC*, 750
Wasylenko, Karen, *Health Sciences Association of Saskatchewan*, 807
Wasylyshen, Sharla, *The Canadian Federation of Business & Professional Women's Clubs*, 386
Watanabe, Natalie, *Ensemble contemporain de Montréal*, 690
Waters, Pierre, *Association québécoise du loisir municipal*, 176
Waters, Rosanne, *Canadian Alliance of Student Associations*, 291
Waters, Kelly, *The Battlefords Music Festival*, 200
Watkins, Jennifer, *Dance Ontario Association*, 649
Watkins, George, *Ontario Sportfishing Guides' Association*, 1108
Watkins, Judith, *The Bronte Historical Society*, 260
Watling, David, *Baseball New Brunswick*, 198
Watsa, Prem, *Horatio Alger Association of Canada*, 821
Watson, Jean, *Clan Lamont Society of Canada*, 571
Watson, Linda, *Wilfrid Laurier University Faculty Association*, 1455
Watson, Michele, *Information Durham*, 837
Watson, Sandra, *Aurora Chamber of Commerce*, 187
Watson, Kent, *Canadian Society of Soil Science*, 488

Executive Name Index

Watson, Chris, *Canadian Racing Pigeon Union Inc.*, 464
Watson, Kathleen, *Saskatchewan Ground Water Association*, 1267
Watson, Ian, *Canadian Academy of Endodontics*, 286
Watson, Sarah, *Canadian Mathematical Society*, 432
Watson, Grant, *Canadian Thoroughbred Horse Society*, 495
Watson, Michele, *United Way of Durham Region*, 1414
Watson, Kathy, *Western Association of Broadcast Engineers*, 1447
Watson, Paul, *Sea Shepherd Conservation Society - USA*, 1588
Watson, Brent, *Alberta Bowhunters Association*, 26
Watson, Bev, *Dreams Take Flight*, 662
Watson, Jayne, *National Arts Centre Foundation*, 989
Watson, Karen, *Bowen Island Arts Council*, 219
Watson, Jennifer, *Canadian Feed The Children*, 389
Watson, Jim, *Oxford Philatelic Society*, 1134
Watson, Christine, *British Columbia Veterinary Technologists Association*, 257
Watson, Steve, *EFILE Association of Canada*, 681
Watson, Karin, *Creative BC*, 639
Watson, Kellie, *Saskatchewan Dental Hygienists' Association*, 1263
Watson, Grant, *Bio-dynamic Agricultural Society of British Columbia*, 211
Watson, Heather, *Farm Management Canada*, 705
Watson, Brenda, *Canadian Partnership for Consumer Food Safety Education*, 451
Watson, Robert, *Information Technology Association of Canada*, 837
Watson, Ellen, *Evangelical Medical Aid Society Canada*, 698
Watson, April, *Canadian Horse Breeders' Association*, 408
Watson, Jessica, *West Central Forage Association*, 1444
Watson, Jeanne, *International Society for Emotion Focused Therapy*, 860
Watson, Carol, *Edmonton Community Foundation*, 676
Watson-Borg, Brian, *YMCA Canada*, 1472
Watt, Josh, *Manitoba School Boards Association*, 944
Watt, Fergus, *World Federalist Movement - Canada*, 1466
Watt, Bob, *Law Foundation of Saskatchewan*, 901
Watt, Eric, *Rick Hansen Foundation*, 1231
Wattam, Chris, *BC Soccer Referees Association*, 202
Watters, Craig, *Goodwill Industries Essex Kent Lambton*, 778
Watters, Ryan, *Canadian Junior Football League*, 423
Watters, Michelle, *AUTO21 Network of Centres of Excellence*, 189
Watterson, Mary S., *College of Traditional Chinese Medicine Practitioners & Acupuncturists of British Columbia*, 590
Wattling, Shari, *Theatre Calgary*, 1374
Watts, Jack, *Manitoba Society of Artists*, 944
Watts, Susan, *Canadian Crossroads International*, 373
Watts, Victoria, *Canadian Hemophilia Society*, 404
Watts, Sharon, *Real Estate Board of the Fredericton Area Inc.*, 1205
Watts, Peter, *Master Brewers Association of The Americas*, 1570
Watts, Sherry, *Canadian Masters Athletic Association*, 431
Watts, Jonathan, *Canada-Cuba Sports & Cultural Festivals*, 283

Watts, Jessica, *Friends of the Greater Sudbury Public Library*, 762
Watts-Rynard, Sarah, *Canadian Apprenticeship Forum*, 294
Waugh, Earl, *PFLAG Canada Inc.*, 1155
Waugh, Garry, *Ontario Amateur Softball Association*, 1059
Wavell, Susan, *Community Living Haldimand*, 602
Way, Robert, *Association of Newfoundland Land Surveyors*, 154
Way, Nikki, *Alberta Environmental Network*, 34
Way, Brad, *Napanee & District Chamber of Commerce*, 988
Waycott, Debbie, *Nova Scotia Forestry Association*, 1045
Wayland, Bridget, *Alternative Land Use Services Canada*, 60
Waylett, Belinda, *Canadian Vascular Access Association*, 501
Waytowich, Samantha, *Canadian Society for Chemical Technology*, 473
Weale, John, *The Association of Maritime Arbitrators of Canada*, 151
Wear, Laurie, *Edmonton Zone Medical Staff Association*, 680
Weary, Walter, *Toronto Field Naturalists*, 1384
Weasel Head, Yolande, *Sik-ooh-kotoki Friendship Society*, 1299
Weatherbee, Jamie, *New Brunswick Road Builders & Heavy Construction Association*, 1011
Weatherwax, Enid M., *International Union of Pure & Applied Chemistry*, 1565
Weaver, Carol Ann, *Association of Canadian Women Composers*, 144
Weaver, LaMar, *Red Lake District Chamber of Commerce*, 1210
Weaver, Andrew, *Green Party Political Association of British Columbia*, 789
Weaver, Lynn, *Cowichan Intercultural Society*, 637
Webb, Steve, *Computer Modelling Group*, 609
Webb, Hilary, *Equestrian Association for the Disabled*, 694
Webb, D., *Masonry Industry Employers Council of Ontario*, 952
Webb, Greg, *Bancroft & District Chamber of Commerce, Tourism & Information Centre*, 195
Webb, Marianne, *Canadian Association of Professional Conservators*, 328
Webb, Audrey, *Canadian Celiac Association*, 352
Webb, Terry, *Canadian Hard of Hearing Association*, 400
Webb, Karen, *Community Microskills Development Centre*, 606
Webb, Dennis, *Outdoor Recreation Council of British Columbia*, 1133
Webb, David, *Alberta Egg Producers' Board*, 33
Webb, Lesley, *Waterloo Historical Society*, 1442
Webb, Terry, *Northwestern Ontario Building & Construction Trades Council*, 1039
Webb, Brian, *Edmonton Arts Council*, 675
Webb, Linda, *Sleeping Children Around the World*, 1303
Webb, Heather, *Women in Film & Television - Toronto*, 1461
Webb, Brian, *Brian Webb Dance Co.*, 228
Webb, Cara, *British Columbia Registered Music Teachers' Association*, 251
Webb, Annabel, *Justice for Girls*, 878
Webb, Derek, *Canadian Environment Industry Association*, 381
Webb, Morgan, *Commercial Seed Analysts Association of Canada Inc.*, 592
Webber, Bob, *Canadian Baptists of Western Canada*, 341
Webber, Mike, *Crystal City & District Chamber of Commerce*, 645
Webber, June, *Coady International Institute*, 577

Webber, Tara, *Canadian Security Association*, 469
Webber, Paula, *Roofing Contractors Association of Nova Scotia*, 1236
Webber, Andy S., *Nova Scotia Rifle Association*, 1048
Webber, Judy, *Union of Nova Scotia Municipalities*, 1408
Webber-Gallagher, Karla, *New Democratic Party*, 1014
Weber, Cassy, *MindFuel*, 966
Weber, George, *Accreditation Canada*, 5
Weber, Rebecca, *Human Resources Professionals Association*, 825
Weber, Mark, *Customs & Immigration Union*, 647
Weber, Lee, *Bamfield Marine Sciences Centre*, 195
Weber, Sascha, *Yukon Mine Training Association*, 1479
Webster, Mary Jane, *Prince Edward Island Real Estate Association*, 1176
Webster, Scott, *Federation of Mountain Clubs of British Columbia*, 725
Webster, Lorne, *Simmental Association of British Columbia*, 1300
Webster, Barrie, *Memorial Society of British Columbia*, 960
Webster, Donna, *Lac La Biche Canadian Native Friendship Centre*, 894
Webster, John, *Vancouver Aboriginal Friendship Centre Society*, 1424
Webster, Nancy J., *Young People's Theatre*, 1475
Webster, Peter, *Row Nova Scotia*, 1237
Webster, Shannon, *Baton Twirling Association of British Columbia*, 199
Wedge, Pip, *Canadian Communications Foundation*, 361
Wedlake, Adam, *Basketball Manitoba*, 198
Wedlake, Susan, *Nova Scotia College of Pharmacists*, 1042
Wedzinga, Julie, *Professional Engineers Ontario*, 1184
Weedmark, Kevin, *Moosomin Chamber of Commerce*, 974
Weekes, Lacey, *Nature Saskatchewan*, 1000
Weening, Chris, *Architectural Woodwork Manufacturers Association of Canada - Southern Alberta*, 80
Wege, Pat, *Manitoba Child Care Association*, 933
Wehlau, Amelia, *Funeral Consumers Advocacy of London & Windsor*, 764
Wei, Wan-Jung, *International Organization of Scenographers, Theatre Architects & Technicians*, 1554
Weicker, Nancy F., *Canadian Swine Exporters Association*, 491
Weidlich, Kevin, *Edmonton Economic Development Corporation*, 677
Weidner, Marion, *Schizophrenia Society of Alberta*, 1283
Weigand, Richard, *Kingston Stamp Club*, 889
Weightman, Kenny, *Fédération des clubs de fers du Québec*, 713
Weihs, Jean, *Ex Libris Association*, 699
Weil, Edward J., *Canadian Association of Veterans in United Nations Peacekeeping*, 336
Weimer, Mitch, *Canadian Healthcare Engineering Society*, 403
Weinreb, Lorne, *Addus*, 8
Weinstein, David, *Canadian Standards Association*, 490
Weir, Michelle, *Advanced Card Technology Association of Canada*, 10
Weir, Robert, *Canadian Association for the Practical Study of Law in Education*, 305
Weir, Cliff, *Gananoque Food Bank*, 766
Weir, Jim, *Manitoba Institute of Agrologists*, 939
Weir, Russell, *Canadian Culinary Federation*, 374

Weir, Jessie, *Canadian Brown Swiss & Braunvieh Association*, 347
Weir, Jesse, *Canadian Guernsey Association*, 399
Weir, Glenn, *Saskatchewan Hotel & Hospitality Association*, 1268
Weir, Kathy, *Tourism Industry Association of New Brunswick Inc.*, 1390
Weir, Cathy, *Ontario Brain Injury Association*, 1068
Weir, Sally, *American Society of Pediatric Hematology / Oncology*, 1502
Weir, Jerry, *Manitoba Hotel Association*, 938
Weisbart, Marilyn, *Canadian Hadassah WIZO*, 400
Weiser, Judy, *International PhotoTherapy Association*, 859
Weisfeld, Gabi, *Canadian Friends of Bar-Ilan University*, 394
Weiss, Joanne, *Assiniboia & District Arts Council*, 88
Weiss, Melanie, *Big Brothers Big Sisters of Saskatchewan*, 210
Weiss, Karen, *Winnipeg Chamber of Commerce*, 1458
Weiss, Sherry, *Canadian Kennel Club*, 424
Weiss, Fred, *Samaritan's Purse Canada*, 1253
Weiss, Shelly K., *Canadian Sleep Society*, 472
Weiss, Karl, *Association des médecins microbiologistes-infectiologues du Québec*, 119
Weiss, Ed, *Toronto Bicycling Network*, 1382
Weiss, Fred, *Billy Graham Evangelistic Association of Canada*, 211
Weisz, Daniel, *Ontario Association of Insolvency & Restructuring Professionals*, 1064
Weisz, Aryella, *Emunah Women of Canada*, 687
Weitzman, Elaine, *The Hanen Centre*, 803
Welch, Mara, *Promotional Product Professionals of Canada Inc.*, 1189
Welch, Angela, *Canadian Celiac Association*, 352
Welch, Dottie, *Square & Round Dance Federation of Nova Scotia*, 1347
Welch, Stephen J., *American College of Chest Physicians*, 1491
Welcher, Sohani, *Nova Scotia Gerontological Nurses Association*, 1045
Welford, Philip, *Stem Cell Network*, 1349
Welin, Leslie, *Clements Centre Society*, 573
Welke, Jill, *Saskatchewan School Boards Association*, 1274
Wellens, Brigitte, *Voice of English-speaking Québec*, 1437
Weller, Andrew, *Kidney Cancer Canada Association*, 885
Welling, Frank, *Ontario Brain Injury Association*, 1069
Wellon, Chris, *Newfoundland & Labrador Judo Association*, 1019
Wells, David, *Pentecostal Assemblies of Canada*, 1150
Wells, Carol, *Ostomy Canada Society*, 1129
Wells, Ron, *Ontario Hereford Association*, 1084
Wells, Sarah, *Transportation Association of Canada*, 1395
Wells, Graham, *The Galpin Society*, 1527
Wells, Bill, *Alberta Recreation & Parks Association*, 44
Wells, Stephanie, *ABC Life Literacy Canada*, 1
Wells, Scott, *Qikiqtani Inuit Association*, 1194
Wells, Pamela, *Association of Occupational Health Nurses of Newfoundland & Labrador*, 154
Welner, Chris, *Alberta Magazine Publishers Association*, 39
Welsh, Michael, *ADR Institute of Canada*, 9
Welsh, Katrina, *Open Door Group*, 1114
Welwood, Clayton, *British Columbia Libertarian Party*, 244
Wen, Eric, *Peel Multicultural Council*, 1148
Wendaferew, Aklilu, *Good Shepherd Refuge Social Ministries*, 777

Executive Name Index

Wendelgass, Robert, *Clean Water Action*, 1517
Wendt, Brain, *Ontario Seaplane Association*, 1103
Wendy, Aylsworth, *Society of Motion Picture & Television Engineers*, 1593
Wengler, Ursula, *Ontario Plumbing Inspectors Association*, 1096
Wenn, Ray, *Dental Association of Prince Edward Island*, 653
Wennekes, Kevin, *Canadian Advanced Technology Alliance*, 288
Wensley, Marina, *Saskatchewan Registered Music Teachers' Association*, 1273
Wentworth, Rand, *Land Trust Alliance*, 1569
Wentzell, Janice, *Association of Municipal Administrators, Nova Scotia*, 152
Wentzell, Kevin, *Atlantic Turfgrass Research Foundation*, 186
Wenzler, Mark, *National Parks Conservation Association*, 1577
Werb, Dan, *International Centre for Science in Drug Policy*, 854
Weremy, Andrew, *Winnipeg Association of Public Service Officers*, 1458
Werry, Dave, *Basketball Saskatchewan*, 199
Wert, Shell-Lee, *Community Care for South Hastings*, 596
Wervers, Debbie, *Canadian Union of Public Employees*, 499
Wes, Savill, *Nordic Combined Ski Canada*, 1028
Wesley, Lucette, *BC Lymphedema Association*, 201
Wesselius, Carol Ann, *Thunder Bay Real Estate Board*, 1378
Wesslen, Shirley, *Alberta Walking Horse Association*, 51
West, Jamie, *Sudbury & District Labour Council*, 1353
West, Mary, *Chipman Community Care Inc.*, 565
West, Cheryl, *Cardiology Technologists' Association of British Columbia*, 511
West, Dave, *Alberni Valley Rock & Gem Club*, 21
West, Vanessa, *Positive Living North: No kheyoh t'sih'en t'sehena Society*, 1168
West, Faye, *Information & Communications Technology Council of Canada*, 836
West, Kelly, *Kerry's Place Autism Services*, 884
West, Chris, *Baffin Regional Chamber of Commerce*, 194
West, Kevin, *Almas Jiwani Foundation*, 59
Westcott, Donalda, *Nova Scotia Music Educators' Association*, 1047
Westendrop, Carlos, *Club de Madrid*, 1517
Westerberg, Eric, *Drainage Superintendents Association of Ontario*, 662
Westerberg, Eric, *Drainage Superintendents Association of Ontario*, 662
Westerberg, Mark, *British Columbia Tenpin Bowling Association*, 256
Westerhof, Bill, *Field Botanists of Ontario*, 734
Westerlind, Brian, *Paperboard Packaging Council*, 1582
Westerlund, Dianne, *Chinook Applied Research Association*, 565
Westermark, Lisa, *British Columbia Epilepsy Society*, 240
Westgate, Carmen, *Chetwynd & District Chamber of Commerce*, 557
Westin, Allison, *Association of Professional Engineers & Geoscientists of British Columbia*, 158
Westin, Lisa, *Canadian Society of Gastroenterology Nurses & Associates*, 483
Westlake, Larry, *Professional Engineers Ontario*, 1184
Westlake, Bob, *College of Dental Technologists of Alberta*, 583
Westlands, Dawn, *British Columbia Aboriginal Child Care Society*, 229

Westlands, Dawn, *British Columbia Aboriginal Child Care Society*, 229
Westling, Dustin, *International Live Events Association Canada*, 858
Westman, Bobbi, *Alberta Dance Alliance*, 32
Weston, Lorianne, *Canadian Public Relations Society Inc.*, 463
Weston, Dianne, *Nova Scotia School Athletic Federation*, 1048
Weston-Bernstein, Lois, *Temiskaming Shores & Area Chamber of Commerce*, 1370
Westwell, Norman A., *Canadian Association of Veterans in United Nations Peacekeeping*, 336
Westwood, Richard, *Trees Winnipeg*, 1397
Wetsch, David, *British Columbia Hotel Association*, 243
Wetstein, Cheryl, *Canada-Israel Cultural Foundation*, 283
Wetteland, Wendy, *New Brunswick Aboriginal Peoples Council*, 1004
Wetter, Graham, *Alberta Central*, 27
Wever, Gerry, *Federation of Broomball Associations of Ontario*, 722
Wexler-Charow, Doris, *Na'amat Canada Inc.*, 987
Weylie, Donald, *Association for Financial Professionals - Vancouver*, 133
Weyman, Norman G., *New Brunswick Musicians' Association, Local 815 of the American Federation of Musicians*, 1010
Weyman, Brandon, *New Brunswick Musicians' Association, Local 815 of the American Federation of Musicians*, 1010
Weymark, Jennifer, *Archives Association of Ontario*, 80
Whale, Cameron, *March of Dimes Non-Profit Housing Corporation*, 949
Whale, Tyler, *Ontario Agri-Food Technologies*, 1059
Whalen, Cynthia, *Newfoundland & Labrador College of Dietitians*, 1017
Whalen, Ed, *Canadian Institute of Steel Construction*, 419
Whalen, Garry, *UNITE HERE Canada*, 1408
Whaley, Carrie, *Association for Childhood Education International*, 1508
Whalley, Tim, *Scarborough Arts Council*, 1282
Whang, Kil Yeo, *Korean Senior Citizens Society of Toronto*, 893
Wharton, Dolores, *Mining Suppliers Trade Association Canada*, 967
Wharton, Mark, *The Publishers Association*, 1586
Wheaton, Neville, *Maritime Fire Chiefs' Association*, 950
Wheeldon, Dale, *British Columbia Economic Development Association*, 239
Wheeldon, Linda, *Canadian Counselling & Psychotherapy Association*, 372
Wheeler, Louise, *British Columbia Rugby Union*, 252
Wheeler, Garry, *Multiple Sclerosis Society of Canada*, 980
Wheeler, Bruce, *Society for Research on Nicotine & Tobacco*, 1591
Whelan, Gerald, *Canadian Media Guild*, 432
Whelan, Karyn, *Newfoundland & Labrador Nurses' Union*, 1020
Whelan, Mike, *Supply Chain Management Association*, 1355
Whelan, Ed, *Canadian Union of Public Employees*, 498
Whelan, Tensie, *Rainforest Alliance*, 1586
Whelan, John, *Healthcare Information & Management Systems Society*, 1529
Whetstone, James, *Ontario Association of Consultants, Counsellors, Psychometrists & Psychotherapists*, 1063
Whetstone, Terri, *4Cs Foundation*, 756
Whetter, Kevin, *International Arthurian Society - North American Branch*, 1535
Whidden, Shannon, *Thunder Bay Symphony Orchestra Association*, 1378

Whidden, John, *Wolfville Historical Society*, 1460
Whidden, Mark, *Halifax Hurricanes Ringette Association*, 799
Whiffen, Sandra, *Habitat for Humanity Canada*, 796
Whillans, Barb, *Appaloosa Horse Club of Canada*, 73
Whipp, Nancy, *Chartered Professional Accountants of New Brunswick*, 553
Whissell, Jeff, *Alberta Pharmacists' Association (RxA)*, 42
White, Kathryn, *United Nations Association in Canada*, 1411
White, Harry, *Sources Foundation*, 1334
White, Merle, *Rocky Native Friendship Society*, 1235
White, John, *Canadian Billiards & Snooker Association*, 343
White, Janet, *Canadian Association of Neuroscience Nurses*, 322
White, Michael, *Mennonite Economic Development Associates Canada*, 961
White, Pat, *Community Living Stratford & Area*, 605
White, Chris, *Canadian Credit Union Association*, 372
White, Roseann, *Deer Lake Chamber of Commerce*, 652
White, Dan, *Meaford Chamber of Commerce*, 956
White, Rebecca, *Smiths Falls & District Chamber of Commerce*, 1304
White, Liz, *Animal Alliance of Canada*, 70
White, David, *College of Family Physicians of Canada*, 584
White, Lawrence, *Alpine Club of Canada*, 59
White, Susan, *British Columbia Golf Association*, 242
White, John, *Canadian Automobile Dealers' Association*, 339
White, Marcela, *Canadian Brain Tumour Tissue Bank*, 347
White, Len, *Engineers Nova Scotia*, 689
White, Zack, *Professional Engineers Ontario*, 1184
White, Chris, *Canadian Meat Council*, 432
White, Gil, *Saskatchewan Wildlife Federation*, 1278
White, Barry, *Catholic Teachers Guild*, 520
White, Chris, *Geological Association of Canada*, 769
White, Daryl, *Historical Society of Alberta*, 816
White, Jerrold, *Institute of Certified Management Consultants of Atlantic Canada*, 845
White, Stacey, *Canadian Sheep Breeders' Association*, 470
White, Matthew, *Early Music Vancouver*, 667
White, Marilyn, *Canadian Association of Critical Care Nurses*, 311
White, Elizabeth, *St. Leonard's Society of Canada*, 1250
White, Allison, *Maple Ridge Museum & Community Archives*, 948
White, Bradley Kenneth, *The Royal Canadian Legion*, 1240
White, Robert, *St. John Ambulance*, 1248
White, Christopher, *Canadian Hotel Marketing & Sales Executives*, 409
White, Tammy, *Food Allergy Canada*, 749
White, Carol, *Gymnastics Newfoundland & Labrador Inc.*, 795
White, Marc I., *Canadian Institute for the Relief of Pain & Disability*, 413
White, Jan, *Alzheimer Society of Kingston, Frontenac, Lennox & Addington*, 63
White, Brian S., *British Columbia Environment Industry Association*, 239
White, Tony, *Rossburn & District Chamber of Commerce*, 1236
White, Nancy, *The Royal Scottish Country Dance Society*, 1587
White, Barrie, *Edmonton Interdistrict Youth Soccer Association*, 678

White, Rick, *Canadian Canola Growers Association*, 349
White, Dave, *Headingley Chamber of Commerce*, 805
White, Donna, *The Terry Fox Foundation*, 1372
White, David, *Screen Actors Guild - American Federation of Television & Radio Artists*, 1588
White, Judy, *Canadian Plywood Association*, 456
White, Marina, *Newfoundland & Labrador Brain Injury Association*, 1017
White, Mandy, *Historic Sites Association of Newfoundland & Labrador*, 815
White, Derek, *The Church Lads' Brigade*, 569
White, Cindy, *Corporation des Chemins Craig et Gosford*, 629
White, Gord, *Association of Professional Geoscientists of Ontario*, 159
White, Adrian, *Sydney & Area Chamber of Commerce*, 1360
White, Peter, *World Business Council for Sustainable Development*, 1603
White, Sharon, *British Columbia Liberal Party*, 244
White, Liz, *Animal Protection Party of Canada*, 71
White, Jennifer, *Prince Edward Island Massage Therapy Association*, 1175
White, Amanda, *Marine Renewables Canada*, 950
White, Jeff, *Saint John Jeux Canada Games Foundation Inc.*, 1247
White, Bill, *New Brunswick Dart Association*, 1007
White, Alida, *Max Bell Foundation*, 954
Whitefield, Valerie, *ARZA-Canada: The Zionist Voice of the Canadian Reform Movement*, 86
Whitehead, Lois, *Science Atlantic*, 1285
Whitehead, Bill, *Trans-Canada Advertising Agency Network*, 1395
Whitehead, Diane, *Association for Childhood Education International*, 1508
Whitehead, Ron, *Superior International Junior Hockey League*, 1355
Whitehouse, Taya, *Early Childhood Educators of British Columbia*, 667
Whitehouse, Lynn, *Greater Langley Chamber of Commerce*, 784
Whitehouse, Caroline, *Entomological Society of Alberta*, 690
Whitehurst, Ken, *Consumers Council of Canada*, 626
Whitelaw, Steve, *Centre for Study of Insurance Operations*, 534
Whitelaw, Anne, *Universities Art Association of Canada*, 1418
Whitelaw, Scott, *The Scots Society of Colchester*, 1286
Whiteman, Rob, *Chartered Institute of Public Finance & Accountancy*, 1516
Whiteside, Jennifer, *Hospital Employees' Union*, 823
Whitfield, Linda, *Travel Manitoba*, 1396
Whitfield, Jennifer, *Atlantic Mission Society*, 184
Whitford, Belinda, *Northwest Territories Biathlon Association*, 1037
Whiting, Ariane, *Canadian Public Relations Society Inc.*, 463
Whiting, Pat, *International Commission of Jurists (Canadian Section)*, 855
Whiting, Roxanne, *Sign Language Interpreters of the National Capital*, 1299
Whiting, Wayne, *Beaver Party of Canada*, 203
Whiting, Leona, *Beaver Party of Canada*, 203
Whitley, Mary, *Canadian Masters Cross-Country Ski Association*, 431
Whitley, Jess, *Canadian Association for Educational Psychology*, 300
Whitlock, Christine, *Women Who Excel Inc.*, 1461
Whitlow, Paula, *Woodland Cultural Centre*, 1464

Executive Name Index

Whitmarsh, Luanne, *Kerby Centre for the 55 Plus*, 884
Whitmire, Dewey, *American Society of Safety Engineers*, 1502
Whitmore, Donald, *Structural Innovation & Monitoring Technologies Resources Centre*, 1352
Whitney, Erin, *Newfoundland & Labrador Folk Arts Society*, 1019
Whitson, Bryndis, *The Van Home Institute for International Transportation & Regulatory Affairs*, 1424
Whittaker, Sue, *Osoyoos & District Arts Council*, 1128
Whittaker, Brady, *Alberta Forest Products Association*, 35
Whittaker, Kevin, *McGill University Non Academic Certified Association*, 955
Whittal, Natalie, *Tilbury Chamber of Commerce*, 1379
Whittle, George, *New Brunswick Veterinary Medical Association*, 1013
Whittle, Peter, *Newfoundland & Labrador Federation of School Councils*, 1019
Whittle, Lynn, *Back Country Horsemen of British Columbia*, 193
Whittles, Mary Lou, *Kenaston & District Chamber of Commerce*, 883
Whittleton, Marg, *Embroiderers' Association of Canada, Inc.*, 686
Whitwell, Jane, *Arabian Horse Association of Eastern Canada*, 76
Whitworth, John, *The Bruce Trail Conservancy*, 261
Whyte, Heather, *Chartered Professional Accountants Canada*, 552
Whyte, Garth, *Fertilizer Canada*, 732
Whyte, Althea, *AdvantAge Ontario*, 10
Whyte, Scott, *College of Audiologists & Speech-Language Pathologists of Ontario*, 582
Whyte, Linda, *Operating Room Nurses Association of Ontario*, 1115
Wick, Don, *Ontario Delphinium Club*, 1076
Wicke, Brandon, *The Guild Society*, 794
Wickens, Terry, *Korea Veterans Association of Canada Inc., Heritage Unit*, 893
Wickens, Jenna, *CrossTrainers Canada*, 644
Wickens, Laurie, *Shag Harbour Incident Society*, 1294
Wickes, Erica, *Interior Designers Institute of British Columbia*, 852
Wickham, Sandra, *British Columbia Amateur Bodybuilding Association*, 230
Wicklum, Dan, *Canada's Oil Sands Innovation Alliance*, 282
Wicks, Clayton, *Swift Current & District Chamber of Commerce*, 1358
Wicks, Ross, *PFLAG Canada Inc.*, 1155
Wickstrom, Gaby, *Port McNeill & District Chamber of Commerce*, 1166
Wickstrom, Dawn, *The Advertising & Design Club of Canada*, 10
Wickwire, Levi, *Society for Ecological Restoration International*, 1590
Widajat, Sukwan, *Radio Amateurs of Canada Inc.*, 1202
Widdis, Vonni, *Schizophrenia Society of Saskatchewan*, 1284
Wideman, Tracy, *Affiliation of Multicultural Societies & Service Agencies of BC*, 11
Wiebe, Joyce, *Burrows Trail Arts Council*, 266
Wiebe, Diane, *Baptist General Conference of Canada*, 196
Wiebe, Amie, *Canadian Bible Society*, 343
Wiebe, Annette, *Brandon Real Estate Board*, 226
Wiebe, Ron, *Child Evangelism Fellowship of Canada*, 559
Wiebe, John, *Association of Canadian Choral Communities*, 141
Wiebe, Valerie, *CancerCare Manitoba*, 508
Wiebe, John, *Environmental Careers Organization of Canada*, 691
Wiebe, John D., *GLOBE Foundation*, 775

Wiebe, Ron, *Supply Chain Management Association - British Columbia*, 1356
Wiebe, Gerald, *Riverbend District Chamber of Commerce*, 1234
Wiebe, Tim, *L'Arche Western Region*, 78
Wiebe, Frank A., *Thomas Sill Foundation Inc.*, 1376
Wiechnik, Chris, *Saskatchewan Physiotherapy Association*, 1272
Wiegerink, Robin, *American Society of Echocardiography*, 1499
Wiener, Robin K., *Institute of Scrap Recycling Industries, Inc.*, 1534
Wienold, Peter, *British Columbia Drama Association*, 239
Wiens, Clint, *Saskatchewan Sheep Breeders' Association*, 1274
Wiens, Colleen, *South Okanagan Boundary Labour Council*, 1335
Wiens, Kathy, *Manitoba Runners' Association*, 943
Wiens, Alana, *Ontario Council on Articulation and Transfer*, 1075
Wiernik, Neil, *Breast Cancer Society of Canada*, 228
Wiersma, Maynard, *Christian Stewardship Services*, 568
Wiersma, Jon, *Scouts Canada*, 1287
Wiersma, Jon, *Scouts Canada*, 1287
Wiesenfeld, Matt, *Canadian Institute of Plumbing & Heating*, 418
Wieser, Shelly, *Brain Injury Association of Alberta*, 225
Wiffen, Gord, *Bowling Proprietors' Association of BC*, 219
Wigbels, Lyn D., *The American Astronautical Society*, 1490
Wigdor, Ted, *Electricity Distributors Association*, 683
Wigg, Bonnie, *Nova Scotia Association of REALTORS*, 1041
Wiggins, Donna, *Canadian National Millers Association*, 440
Wiggins, Susan, *Interior Designers of Canada*, 852
Wiggins, Melanie, *Canadian Association of Nephrology Nurses & Technologists*, 322
Wight, Leanne, *Frontenac Law Association*, 763
Wightman, Faye, *Canadian Cancer Society*, 349
Wightman, John, *Nova Scotia Prospectors Association*, 1047
Wightman, Gregory, *Public Works Association of British Columbia*, 1194
Wigwas, Mariah, *Oshki Anishnawbeg Student Association*, 1128
Wijeratne, Dinuk, *Nova Scotia Youth Orchestra*, 1050
Wijesinghe, Anna-Maria, *Union of British Columbia Municipalities*, 1407
Wijewickreme, Nilmini, *British Columbia Food Technolgists*, 241
Wik, Brian, *Alberta Association of Optometrists*, 24
Wikdahl, Kathy, *Golden Prairie Arts Council*, 776
Wikkerink, Joan, *Holstein Canada*, 819
Wiland, Virve, *Woodland Cultural Centre*, 1464
Wilbee, Jeff, *Canadian Addiction Counsellors Certification Federation*, 288
Wilbur, Sara, *Grand River Conservation Foundation*, 780
Wilcock, Ruth, *Ontario Brain Injury Association*, 1068
Wilcocks, Wayne, *Sarnia Rock & Fossil Club*, 1254
Wilcox, Christopher, *Scotia Chamber Players*, 1286
Wilcox, Tara, *Atlantic Canada Pipe Band Association*, 182
Wilcox, Ian, *Upper Thames River Conservation Authority*, 1422
Wild, Matthew, *Tetra Society of North America*, 1373

Wilde, Lisa, *Canadian Baton Twirling Federation*, 342
Wilde, Chrystalla, *Association of Registered Interior Designers of New Brunswick*, 161
Wildfong, Bob, *Seeds of Diversity Canada*, 1289
Wilding, Carol, *Chartered Professional Accountants of Ontario*, 553
Wildman, Timothy, *Institute of Certified Management Consultants of Manitoba*, 845
Wildman, Brett, *Canadian Angus Association*, 293
Wiles, Jessica, *Canadian Authors Association*, 338
Wiley, Sarah, *Outward Bound Canada*, 1133
Wiley, Scott D., *American Society of Association Executives*, 1499
Wiley, Caroline, *Manitoba Food Processors Association*, 936
Wilfert, Bryon, *Richmond Hill Chamber of Commerce*, 1230
Wilker, Laura, *International Federation of Accountants*, 1547
Wilker, Chelsea, *Saskatchewan Association of Medical Radiation Technologists*, 1257
Wilkie, Douglas R., *Master Brewers Association of The Americas*, 1570
Wilkie, Colleen, *Canadian Group Psychotherapy Association*, 399
Wilkie, Karen, *Carthy Foundation*, 516
Wilkins, Kathy, *Shaunavon Chamber of Commerce*, 1294
Wilkins, Robert C., *The Canadian Maritime Law Association*, 430
Wilkins, Deb, *Compassion Canada*, 608
Wilkins, Robert, *United Empire Loyalists' Association of Canada*, 1410
Wilkins, Susan P., *International Association for Impact Assessment - Western & Northern Canada*, 853
Wilkins, Janice, *Pediatric Endocrine Society*, 1583
Wilkinson, Keith, *Canadian Unitarian Council*, 499
Wilkinson, Don, *Community Living York South*, 606
Wilkinson, Ian, *Saskatchewan Abilities Council*, 1255
Wilkinson, John, *Sault Symphony Association*, 1281
Wilkinson, Christopher, *Symphony Nova Scotia*, 1360
Wilkinson, Donna, *Saskatchewan Camping Association*, 1260
Wilkinson, Gloria, *Community Planning Association of Alberta*, 607
Wilkinson, Janis, *Ontario Sustainable Energy Association*, 1109
Wilkinson, Susan, *Rowing British Columbia*, 1237
Will, Alysone, *Canadian Association for Laboratory Animal Science*, 302
Will, Fabian, *Eastern Townships Resource Centre*, 671
Willans, Carole, *Canadian Hard of Hearing Association*, 401
Willans, Carole, *Canadian Hard of Hearing Association*, 401
Willbond, Billy, *International Community for Relief of Suffering & Starvation Canada*, 855
Willcock, Don, *Peterborough Historical Society*, 1153
Willcocks, Ann, *British Columbia Netball Association*, 247
Willems, John, *Ontario Community Newspapers Association*, 1073
Willems, Judy, *Alzheimer Society of Niagara Region*, 63
Willems, Melisse L., *College of Dietitians of Ontario*, 584
Willemsen, Mathieu, *International Committee of Museums & Collections of Arms & Military History*, 1543
Willemsen, Kristin, *Consumer Health Products Canada*, 626

Willemsma, Glenda, *Ontario Federation of Teaching Parents*, 1080
Willer, Dave, *Historical Society of St. Catharines*, 816
Willet, Hugh, *Ottawa Baptist Association*, 1129
Williams, Michael, *Canadian Association of Independent Life Brokerage Agencies*, 318
Williams, Trish, *Special Olympics Newfoundland & Labrador*, 1340
Williams, Tina, *Arts Mosaic*, 86
Williams, Shawna, *Association of British Columbia Teachers of English as an Additional Language*, 140
Williams, Kelly, *Kenora Association for Community Living*, 883
Williams, Keith E., *Underwriters' Laboratories of Canada*, 1404
Williams, Jeff, *Canadian Association of Foodservice Professionals*, 315
Williams, Bradley, *Red Deer Chamber of Commerce*, 1209
Williams, Pam, *Greater Charlottetown & Area Chamber of Commerce*, 783
Williams, Glenn, *The Brampton Board of Trade*, 226
Williams, Rhian, *Canadian Society of Association Executives*, 480
Williams, Chris, *Canadian Public Relations Society Inc.*, 463
Williams, Marie-Josée, *Fédération québécoise des sociétés Alzheimer*, 730
Williams, Matt, *Association of Canadian Publishers*, 143
Williams, Danielle, *Canadian Pony Club*, 457
Williams, Shelley, *HIV Network of Edmonton Society*, 816
Williams, Cheryl, *British Columbia Doctors of Optometry*, 239
Williams, Gary, *Canadian Aviation Historical Society*, 340
Williams, Gary, *Canadian Aviation Historical Society*, 340
Williams, Russell, *Diabetes Canada*, 655
Williams, Heather, *Canadian 4-H Council*, 284
Williams, Ruby, *Hong Kong-Canada Business Association*, 820
Williams, Kristin, *Junior Achievement Canada*, 877
Williams, Gar, *Salers Association of Canada*, 1251
Williams, Duncan, *Mechanical Contractors Association of Nova Scotia*, 957
Williams, Sheila, *Acupuncture Canada*, 7
Williams, Bill, *United Native Nations Society*, 1412
Williams, Donald, *Vividata*, 1436
Williams, Lesley, *Prospectors & Developers Association of Canada*, 1189
Williams, Paul, *Society of Graphic Designers of Canada*, 1329
Williams, Randy, *Tourism Calgary*, 1389
Williams, Toni, *Niagara Falls Tourism*, 1025
Williams, Dennis, *International Union, United Automobile, Aerospace & Agricultural Implement Workers of America*, 1565
Williams, Ed, *Canada - Newfoundland & Labrador Offshore Petroleum Board*, 277
Williams, Patrick, *British Columbia International Commercial Arbitration Centre*, 244
Williams, Jodi, *Synchro PEI*, 1361
Williams, Marlene, *British Columbia Seniors Living Association*, 253
Williams, Debbie, *Hiiye'yu Lelum Society House of Friendship*, 814
Williams, Kai, *International Wildlife Rehabilitation Council*, 1567
Williams, Elaine, *Wildlife Preservation Canada*, 1455
Williams, Mary, *Palliative Manitoba*, 1137
Williams, Mita, *Ontario Library & Information Technology Association*, 1088
Williams, Denise, *Sylvan Lake Chamber of Commerce*, 1360

Executive Name Index

Williams, Laura, *Central British Columbia Railway & Forest Industry Museum Society*, 524
Williams, Anthony, *Canadian Institute of Financial Planners*, 415
Williams, April, *Canadian Association for Williams Syndrome*, 307
Williams, Shawn, *Saskatchewan Lacrosse Association*, 1268
Williams, Mitch, *Thorsby & District Chamber of Commerce*, 1376
Williams, Ollie, *Northwest Territories Soccer Association*, 1038
Williams, Shayne, *Lookout Emergency Aid Society*, 919
Williams, Kimberly, *Resident Doctors of Canada*, 1226
Williams, Duncan, *Construction Association of Nova Scotia*, 623
Williams, Hayley, *Paris & District Chamber of Commerce*, 1140
Williams, Suzanne, *Canadian Writers' Foundation Inc.*, 506
Williams, Chris, *Interactive Advertising Bureau of Canada*, 851
Williams, Tracy, *Canadian Association for Supported Employment*, 304
Williams, Siân, *International Primary Care Respiratory Group*, 1555
Williams, Melanie, *Canada Fox Breeders' Association*, 279
Williams, Pamela, *CADORA British Columbia*, 268
Williams, Pam, *CADORA British Columbia*, 268
Williams, Rheal, *New Brunswick Camping Association*, 1006
Williams, Paul, *Golden Opportunities Vocational Rehabilitation Centre Workshop*, 776
Williams, Sue, *Foreign Agricultural Resource Management Services*, 751
Williams, Lauretta, *Canadian Lactation Consultant Association*, 425
Williams Whitt, Kelly, *Association canadienne des relations industrielles*, 94
Williamson, Nadia, *Regina & District Chamber of Commerce*, 1211
Williamson, Frank, *Easter Seals Canada*, 669
Williamson, Astra, *Association of Certified Fraud Examiners - Toronto Chapter*, 145
Williamson, Patricia, *British Columbia Registered Music Teachers' Association*, 251
Williamson, M. Jane, *Canadian Public Accountability Board*, 462
Willington, Garett, *Society of Kabalarians of Canada*, 1329
Willis, George, *Canadian Society of Cinematographers*, 481
Willis, Debbie, *Campbell River & District Food Bank*, 276
Willison, Martin, *Canadian Parks & Wilderness Society*, 451
Willms, Ed, *Ontario Conference of Mennonite Brethren Churches*, 1074
Willock, James, *Special Interest Group on Computer Human Interaction*, 1339
Willouby, Vic, *Alberta Genealogical Society*, 37
Wills, Donna, *Arthritis Society*, 84
Wills, Maureen, *Brantford Symphony Orchestra Association Inc.*, 227
Wills, Brett, *Provision Coalition*, 1191
Willsie, Irene, *Social Planning & Research Council of BC*, 1306
Willsie, Julie, *Ontario Brain Injury Association*, 1069
Willson, Margaret, *Osteoporosis Canada*, 1129
Willson, Jo-Ann, *College of Chiropractors of Ontario*, 583
Wilm, Jim, *Saskatchewan Genealogical Society*, 1266
Wilmot, Lesley, *Oceana Canada*, 1054

Wilsgard, Jon, *Local Government Management Association of British Columbia*, 917
Wilson, Linda, *Association d'isolation du Québec*, 99
Wilson, Caroline, *College of Audiologists and Speech-Language Pathologists of Manitoba*, 582
Wilson, Russ, *Associated Gospel Churches*, 89
Wilson, HC, *The Atlantic District of The Wesleyan Church*, 183
Wilson, Misha, *North Vancouver Chamber of Commerce*, 1033
Wilson, Doug, *Parrsboro & District Board of Trade*, 1143
Wilson, George, *Waskesiu Chamber of Commerce*, 1440
Wilson, Jodie, *Canadian International Freight Forwarders Association*, 421
Wilson, Don, *Bobsleigh Canada Skeleton*, 217
Wilson, Cairine, *Chartered Professional Accountants Canada*, 552
Wilson, Chris, *Swimming Canada*, 1359
Wilson, Jo-Anne, *Canadian Celiac Association*, 352
Wilson, Lara, *Canadian Council of Archives*, 367
Wilson, Jane, *Professional Engineers Ontario*, 1184
Wilson, Mathew, *Canadian Manufacturers & Exporters*, 429
Wilson, Anita, *Canadian Water & Wastewater Association*, 502
Wilson, Gary, *Association of Canadian Universities for Northern Studies*, 144
Wilson, Mickey, *Pride Centre of Edmonton*, 1170
Wilson, Don, *Grand Orange Lodge of Canada*, 780
Wilson, Ian, *Local Government Management Association of British Columbia*, 917
Wilson, Eric, *Friends of Chamber Music*, 760
Wilson, Donegal, *British Columbia Snowmobile Federation*, 253
Wilson, Linda, *St. Leonard's Society of Canada*, 1250
Wilson, Douglas, *Bytown Railway Society*, 267
Wilson, Rob, *Nature Saskatchewan*, 1001
Wilson, Elaine, *Spina Bifida & Hydrocephalus Association of Ontario*, 1342
Wilson, Doug, *The M.S.I. Foundation*, 978
Wilson, Don, *Lunenburg Heritage Society*, 921
Wilson, Michael, *International Foundation of Employee Benefit Plans*, 1549
Wilson, Archie, *Federation of Broomball Associations of Ontario*, 722
Wilson, Jim, *Canadian Institute for Theatre Technology*, 414
Wilson, Chris, *Alzheimer Society of Nova Scotia*, 64
Wilson, Gillian, *The Royal Scottish Country Dance Society*, 1587
Wilson, Bob, *Mississauga-Etobicoke Coin Stamp & Collectibles Club*, 970
Wilson, Doretta, *Society for Quality Education*, 1326
Wilson, Doreen, *North Lanark Historical Society*, 1031
Wilson, Reg, *Project Management Institute*, 1585
Wilson, Cole, *Saskatchewan Physical Education Association*, 1271
Wilson, Bernadette, *Saskatoon Youth Orchestra*, 1280
Wilson, Todd, *Canadian Junior Football League*, 423
Wilson, Philip, *Kingston Kiwanis Music Festival*, 889
Wilson, Laura, *Ontario Wheelchair Sports Association*, 1113
Wilson, Andria, *Inside Out Toronto LGBT Film & Video Festival*, 840
Wilson, Maggie, *McMaster University Staff Association*, 956

Wilson, Rod, *Arctic Co-operatives Limited*, 81
Wilson, Tim, *Triathlon Canada*, 1397
Wilson, Melanie, *PFLAG Canada Inc.*, 1155
Wilson, Jim, *Canadian Lyme Disease Foundation*, 429
Wilson, Jenine, *Ontario Handball Association*, 1083
Wilson, Lee-Anne, *Master Bowlers' Association of British Columbia*, 953
Wilson, John, *Interior Running Association*, 852
Wilson, Terry, *People First Nova Scotia*, 1151
Wilson, Jules, *Federation of B.C. Youth in Care Networks*, 722
Wilson, Gary, *Coastal First Nations*, 579
Wilson-Smith, Anthony, *Historica Canada*, 815
Wiltermuth, Dustin, *Association of Professional Engineers & Geoscientists of Alberta*, 157
Wiltshire, John, *Canadian Marketing Association*, 430
Wiltsie, Cathy, *Alberta Professional Outfitters Society*, 43
Wimmer, Chris, *Association of Professional Engineers & Geoscientists of Saskatchewan*, 159
Wimmer, Harold P., *American Lung Association*, 1495
Windbiel, Coreen, *Surrey Association for Community Living*, 1357
Windeler, Eric, *Jack.org*, 867
Windrum, Robert, *Canadian Lesbian & Gay Archives*, 426
Windsor, Alice, *Langham Cultural Society*, 898
Wing, Cathy, *Media Smarts*, 957
Wing, Margaret, *Alberta Pharmacists' Association (RxA)*, 42
Winichakul, Thongchai, *Association for Asian Studies - USA*, 1507
Winkel, Michelle, *Canadian Art Therapy Association*, 295
Winkler, Monica, *Canadian Council on Rehabilitation & Work*, 371
Winkler, Jamie, *Chatham-Kent Real Estate Board*, 555
Winnicky, Kim, *Music Yukon*, 984
Winninger, Diana, *Canadian Amateur Musicians*, 292
Winquist, Donna-Mae, *MacEwan Staff Association*, 924
Winski, Linda, *Alberta Genealogical Society*, 36
Winsor, Reg, *Newfoundland & Labrador Arts Council*, 1015
Winsor, Jennifer, *NWT Disabilities Council*, 1052
Winter, Pam, *Canadian Hardware & Housewares Manufacturers' Association*, 401
Winter, Susan, *Consumer Electronics Marketers of Canada: A Division of Electro-Federation Canada*, 625
Winter, Edward, *Northwest Coalition for Alternatives to Pesticides*, 1580
Winter, Alan E., *Genome Canada*, 769
Winterburn, Darlene, *British Columbia Shellfish Growers Association*, 253
Winters, Rod, *Building Owners & Managers Association - Nova Scotia*, 263
Winters, Shelley, *Union of Calgary Co-op Employees*, 1407
Winterton, Stephanie, *London Community Foundation*, 918
Winterton, Rochelle, *BC Lacrosse Association*, 201
Wintrup, Lainie, *Ringette Nova Scotia*, 1233
Wipfli, Susan, *Canadian Llama & Alpaca Association*, 428
Wiqvist, Weine, *International Solid Waste Association*, 1562
Wirtzfeld, Debrah, *Canadian Association of General Surgeons*, 316
Wisdom, Sheila, *Windsor Symphony Orchestra*, 1457

Wiseman, Roy, *Municipal Information Systems Association of Canada*, 981
Wiseman, Glenn, *Saskatchewan Genealogical Society*, 1266
Wishart, Pam, *Aplastic Anemia & Myelodysplasia Association of Canada*, 73
Wishart, Rick, *Canadian Network for Environmental Education & Communication*, 440
Wishlow, Alex, *The Canadian Doukhobor Society*, 378
Wishnowski, Dennis, *Alberta Shorthorn Association*, 46
Wisleski, Linda, *Canadian Institute of Underwriters*, 420
Wismer, Anne, *United Way of Oxford*, 1416
Wisse, Jan, *Simmental Association of British Columbia*, 1300
Wiszniowski, Barry, *Canadian Society of Air Safety Investigators*, 479
Withers, Jill, *Canadian Thoroughbred Horse Society*, 495
Withey, Jane, *Community Legal Education Ontario*, 600
Witney, Beth, *Ontario Association of Optometrists*, 1065
Witt, T., *New Apostolic Church Canada*, 1004
Wittens, Elly, *Manitoba Arts Council*, 929
Wittig, Herbert H., *German-Canadian Mardi Gras Association Inc.*, 772
Wittmaack, Shannon, *Temiskaming Law Association*, 1370
Wittrock, Virginia, *Canadian Meteorological & Oceanographic Society*, 436
Wlodarczyk, Janet, *Transportation Association of Canada*, 1395
Wodchis, Ellen, *Ontario Public Health Association*, 1099
Wodelet, Krista, *Orchestras Canada*, 1117
Wodoslawsky, George, *Oro-Medonte Chamber of Commerce*, 1127
Woermke, Mark, *Catholic Teachers Guild*, 520
Wojcichowsky, Genaya, *Saskatchewan Early Childhood Association*, 1264
Wolach, Jo, *Cross Country Alberta*, 643
Wolbaum, Dianne, *Saskatchewan Safety Council*, 1274
Wolday, Azaria, *Northwood Neighbourhood Services*, 1040
Wolf, Gary, *Recreational Aircraft Association*, 1208
Wolf, Lauren, *North West Library Federation*, 1033
Wolf, Lynda, *Palliative Manitoba*, 1137
Wolfbeiss, Petra, *Ontario Municipal Social Services Association*, 1092
Wolfe, Eric, *Canadian Payments Association*, 452
Wolfe, Heather, *Canadian College of Health Leaders*, 358
Wolfe, Brian, *Community Living Alternatives Society*, 600
Wolfe, Scott, *Canadian Association of Community Health Centres*, 311
Wolfenden, Haley, *Canadian Association for the Advancement of Women & Sport & Physical Activity*, 305
Wolfenden, Dan, *Squash Canada*, 1347
Wolfenden, Brian, *Canadian Aerophilatelic Society*, 289
Wolfsdorf, Joseph, *International Society for Pediatric & Adolescent Diabetes*, 1558
Wolfus, Bev, *Eastview Neighbourhood Community Centre*, 671
Wolfwood, Theresa, *The Barnard-Boecker Centre Foundation*, 196
Wollbaum, Myla, *Pharmacists' Association of Saskatchewan, Inc.*, 1157
Woloshyn, Doug, *Financial Executives International Canada*, 736
Woloz, Steve, *Model Aeronautics Association of Canada Inc.*, 971
Wolsey, Shair, *Crohn's & Colitis Canada*, 643
Wolski, Kim, *British Columbia Dance Educators' Association*, 238

Executive Name Index

Wolter, Jake, *Canadian Kitchen Cabinet Association*, 424
Wolters, Peter, *Prince Edward Island Soccer Association*, 1177
Wolters, Beth, *L'Arche Atlantic Region*, 76
Woltjer, Gavin, *Librarians Without Borders*, 910
Wolverton, Jamie, *New Brunswick Sports Hall of Fame*, 1013
Wombold, Marion, *Alberta Funeral Services Regulatory Board*, 36
Wondra, Dave, *International Coaching Federation*, 1542
Wong, Maria Paola, *Casa - Pueblito*, 516
Wong, Ilsa, *Women's Soccer Assocation of Lethbridge*, 1463
Wong, Linda, *Eye Bank of BC*, 700
Wong, Mila, *The City of Greater Sudbury Developmental Services*, 571
Wong, John H., *Alberta Neurosurgical Society*, 41
Wong, Sandra, *Association of Ontario Health Centres*, 154
Wong, Nancy, *Canadian Wheelchair Sports Association*, 504
Wong, Corrie, *British Columbia Golf Association*, 242
Wong, Kevin, *Canadian Institute of Plumbing & Heating*, 418
Wong, Debora, *British Columbia Lung Association*, 245
Wong, Victor, *Chinese Canadian National Council*, 564
Wong, Lloyd, *Chinese Canadian National Council*, 564
Wong, Betty, *Chinese Canadian National Council*, 564
Wong, Bonita, *Hong Kong-Canada Business Association*, 820
Wong, Albert, *Junior Achievement Canada*, 877
Wong, Peggy, *Cathedral Bluffs Symphony Orchestra*, 517
Wong, Bonnie, *Hong Fook Mental Health Association*, 820
Wong, Cassandra, *Parkdale Community Information Centre*, 1140
Wong, Kevin, *Canadian Water Quality Association*, 502
Wong, King Sang, *Chinese Medicine & Acupuncture Association of Canada*, 565
Wong, Anita, *EcoSource Mississauga*, 673
Wong, Suzanna, *Global, Environmental & Outdoor Education Council*, 775
Wong, Happy, *American Society of Plumbing Engineers*, 1502
Wong, Letty, *Occupational Hygiene Association of Ontario*, 1054
Wong, Stephanie, *Mon Sheong Foundation*, 971
Wong, Linda, *Canadian Society of Ophthalmic Registered Nurses*, 485
Wong, Anthony, *Alberta Colleges Athletic Conference*, 30
Wong, Robert, *Creative BC*, 639
Wong, Lilly, *Alberta Society of Surveying & Mapping Technologies*, 48
Wong, Edy, *Centre for International Business Studies*, 533
Wong, Sandra, *Toronto Bicycling Network*, 1382
Wong, Rita, *Emily Carr University of Art & Design Faculty Association*, 686
Wong-Martinez, Carlos G., *Manitoba Library Consortium Inc.*, 940
Wong-Rieger, Durhane, *Canadian Organization for Rare Disorders*, 447
Wong-Tam, Kristyn, *Chinese Canadian National Council*, 564
Wong-Tam, Moy, *Centre for Immigrant & Community Services*, 532
Woo, Julia, *Association of Neighbourhood Houses BC*, 153
Woo, Jay, *Canadian Automobile Association South Central Ontario*, 339

Woo, Jeffrey, *Saskatchewan Table Tennis Association Inc.*, 1276
Woo, Walt, *North American Association of Asian Professionals Vancouver*, 1029
Wood, Peter, *West Kootenay Naturalists Association*, 1445
Wood, Laurel, *Big Brothers Big Sisters of Alberta*, 209
Wood, Rebecca, *Calgary Chamber of Commerce*, 271
Wood, Barbara, *CoDevelopment Canada*, 580
Wood, Matt, *Canadian Public Relations Society Inc.*, 463
Wood, Ted, *Amnesty International - Canadian Section (English Speaking)*, 68
Wood, J.B., *Technology Services Industry Association*, 1597
Wood, Sue, *Canadian 4-H Council*, 284
Wood, Kathryn, *Canadian Golf Superintendents Association*, 398
Wood, Robert, *Pool & Hot Tub Council of Canada*, 1165
Wood, Nicole, *Saskatchewan Association of Veterinary Technologists, Inc.*, 1258
Wood, Dean, *Historical Society of Alberta*, 816
Wood, Sharon, *Kids Help Phone*, 886
Wood, Tracy, *Canadian Maine-Anjou Association*, 429
Wood, Gary, *British Columbia Shorthorn Association*, 253
Wood, Tracy, *Canadian Association of Elizabeth Fry Societies*, 313
Wood, Berni, *Professional Photographers of Canada*, 1186
Wood, Marlene, *Tourism Sarnia Lambton*, 1391
Wood, James B., *International Alliance of Theatrical Stage Employees, Moving Picture Technicians, Artists & Allied Crafts of the U.S., Its Territories & Canada*, 1535
Wood, Jo-Ann, *North Shore Hospice Society*, 1033
Wood, Richard, *Kosher Check*, 894
Wood, Jim, *Canadian Oil Heat Association*, 445
Wood, Barry T., *Canadian Association of Veterans in United Nations Peacekeeping*, 335
Wood, Lester, *Margaree Salmon Association*, 949
Wood, Jeff, *Speed Skate PEI*, 1341
Wood, Scott, *Halifax Amateur Radio Club*, 798
Wood Edwards, Linda, *Canadian Institute of Plumbing & Heating*, 418
Wood Edwards, Linda, *LUE-42 Enterprises*, 920
Wood-Tweel, Michele, *Chartered Professional Accountants Canada*, 552
Woodacre, Bevan, *Prince County Hospital Foundation*, 1171
Woodall, Pam, *Nanton & District Chamber of Commerce*, 988
Woodard, Amanda, *College of Family Physicians of Canada*, 584
Woodburn, Rick, *Canadian Association of Crown Counsel*, 312
Woodbury, David, *New Democratic Party*, 1014
Woodbury, Robert, *Sculptors' Association of Alberta*, 1287
Woodcock, Maxine, *Manitoba Genealogical Society Inc.*, 937
Woodcock, Loretta, *British Columbia Spaces for Nature*, 254
Woodcock, Andy, *Canadian Machinery Vibration Association*, 429
Woodfine, Gail, *Municipalities Newfoundland & Labrador*, 982
Woodford, Ashley, *Canadian Bar Association*, 342
Woodgett, Jim, *Lunenfeld-Tanenbaum Research Institute*, 921
Woodhouse, Linda, *Canadian Physiotherapy Association*, 455

Woodhouse, David, *Arts Council of the North Okanagan*, 85
Woodill, Holly, *Nova Scotia Trails Federation*, 1050
Woodland, Kerry, *Big Brothers Big Sisters of Alberta*, 209
Woodman, Steve, *Family & Children's Services of Frontenac, Lennox & Addington*, 702
Woodman, Pam, *Landscape Nova Scotia*, 898
Woodman, Steve, *Biathlon Prince Edward Island*, 208
Woodrow, Joan, *Newfoundland Federation of Music Festivals*, 1023
Woods, Doug, *Ontario Field Ornithologists*, 1080
Woods, George, *International Academy of Law & Mental Health*, 853
Woods, Debbie, *The John Howard Society of Ontario*, 875
Woods, Nick, *International ISBN Agency*, 1551
Woods, Jennifer, *ARMA Canada*, 82
Woods, Kelly, *Association of Neighbourhood Houses BC*, 153
Woods, Percy J., *Building Owners & Managers Association of Edmonton*, 263
Woods, Jaclyn, *Alzheimer Society of Thunder Bay*, 65
Woods, Moira, *Manitoba Holiday Festival of the Arts Inc.*, 938
Woods, Peter, *Hockey Manitoba*, 818
Woods, Jennifer, *Ending Violence Association of British Columbia*, 687
Woods, Dave, *Saskatchewan Snowboard Association*, 1275
Woodside, Connie, *Junior Achievement Canada*, 877
Woodward, Carla, *Alberta Diabetes Foundation*, 33
Woodward, Bill, *Middlesex Law Association*, 965
Woodward, Renata, *Nature Trust of New Brunswick*, 1001
Woodward, Christopher, *Mr. & Mrs. P.A. Woodward's Foundation*, 978
Woodward, Ron, *Alberta Council on Admissions & Transfer*, 31
Woolaver, Florence, *Nova Scotia Association of Naturopathic Doctors*, 1041
Wooles, Richard, *Cycling British Columbia*, 647
Woolford, Penny, *Canadian Tax Foundation*, 492
Woollatt, Mike, *Canada's Venture Capital & Private Equity Association*, 283
Woolley, Frances, *Canadian Economics Association*, 379
Woolridge, Tony, *Petroleum Research Newfoundland & Labrador*, 1154
Woolsey, Lorna, *Canada Fox Breeders' Association*, 279
Woolsey, Lorna, *Canadian Finnsheep Breeders' Association*, 390
Woolsey, Lorna, *Canadian Katahdin Sheep Association Inc.*, 424
Worden, Sean, *Nature Manitoba*, 1000
Work, Craig, *Association of Professional Engineers & Geoscientists of British Columbia*, 158
Worku, Yeshihareg, *Ethiopian Association in the Greater Toronto Area & Surrounding Regions*, 697
Worland, Ian, *Society of Trust & Estate Practitioners*, 1331
World, Charles, *Edmonton Bicycle & Touring Club*, 675
Worms, Terri, *Canadian Hays Converter Association*, 401
Wornell, Jonathan, *Karate BC*, 881
Wörner, Johann-Dietrich, *European Space Agency*, 1524
Worobec, Kathy, *Alberta Council for Environmental Education*, 31
Woroch, Patricia, *Immigrant Services Society of BC*, 830

Worrall, Patsy, *British Columbia Cancer Foundation*, 234
Worrell, Jim, *Saskatchewan Archaeological Society*, 1256
Worrick, Amy, *Trenton Art Club*, 1397
Worsfold, Roly, *Model Aeronautics Association of Canada Inc.*, 970
Worsfold, Pauline, *Canadian Federation of Nurses Unions*, 388
Worsnop, Connie, *Ontario Baton Twirling Association*, 1067
Worster, Jocelyn, *L'Arche Atlantic Region*, 77
Worthen, Larry, *Christian Medical & Dental Society of Canada*, 568
Worthington, Ian, *Fédération québécoise des sociétés Alzheimer*, 730
Worthy, Matt, *Canadian Association of Petroleum Land Administration*, 325
Wosk, Becky, *Music BC Industry Association*, 983
Woudsma, Carole Ann, *Canadian Transportation Research Forum*, 497
Wournell, Dar, *Alliance for Equality of Blind Canadians*, 57
Wowk, Dave, *Virden Community Chamber of Commerce*, 1435
Woytowich, Ron, *Kikinahk Friendship Centre*, 887
Wozniak, Kim, *Manitoba Dental Hygienists Association*, 935
Wraggett, Anne, *Canadian Celiac Association*, 352
Wray, Bruce, *Alzheimer Society London & Middlesex*, 61
Wright, Kristi, *Psychology Association of Saskatchewan*, 1192
Wright, Brian, *Lethbridge Oldtimers Sports Association*, 908
Wright, Kathy, *Boundary Country Regional Chamber of Commerce*, 219
Wright, Nicola, *Board of Canadian Registered Safety Professionals*, 216
Wright, John, *Canadian Management Centre*, 429
Wright, Ann, *Canadian Dental Hygienists Association*, 377
Wright, Keith, *Grand Orange Lodge of Canada*, 780
Wright, Larry, *British Columbia Society of Laboratory Science*, 254
Wright, Leslie, *Meeting Professionals International*, 1571
Wright, Kathy, *Alzheimer Society of Ottawa & Renfrew County*, 64
Wright, Elizabeth, *Newfoundland & Labrador Public Health Association*, 1021
Wright, Kitty, *The Brontë Society*, 1514
Wright, J.M., *The Canadian Philatelic Society of Great Britain*, 1515
Wright, Sandra, *Compensation Employees' Union (Ind.)*, 609
Wright, Miriam, *The Royal Scottish Country Dance Society*, 1587
Wright, Catherine, *The Royal Scottish Country Dance Society*, 1587
Wright, Irene, *Eastern Charlotte Chamber of Commerce*, 670
Wright, Nathan, *Information Services Vancouver*, 837
Wright, Nancy, *GLOBE Foundation*, 775
Wright, Simona, *Northeast Modern Language Association*, 1579
Wright, Rosalind, *Society of Deaf & Hard of Hearing Nova Scotians*, 1328
Wright, Bruce, *Vancouver Art Gallery Association*, 1424
Wright, Kim, *AllerGen NCE Inc.*, 54
Wright, Alexandra, *Canadian Association for Social Work Education*, 304
Wright, Ashley, *Newfoundland & Labrador Cheerleading Athletics*, 1017
Wright, Cameron, *Canadian Music Week Inc.*, 438
Wrigley-Thomas, Constance, *Canadian Society of Association Executives*, 480

Executive Name Index

Wrigley-Thomas, Constance, *NAIOP Greater Toronto*, 987
Wroe, Paul, *Canadian Picture Pioneers*, 455
Wrolstad, Andrew, *Manitoba Sign Association*, 944
Wu, Jianhong, *Canadian Applied & Industrial Mathematics Society*, 294
Wu, Dennis, *Cross Country British Columbia*, 643
Wudrick, Kim, *Football Canada*, 750
Wueppelmann, William, *Canadiana*, 506
Wujcik, Andrew, *Alberta Ukrainian Dance Association*, 50
Wulff, Michelle, *Block Watch Society of British Columbia*, 215
Wurm, Jack, *Retail, Wholesale & Department Store Union (AFL-CIO/CLC)*, 1586
Wyand, Michelle, *Prince Edward Island Pharmacy Board*, 1176
Wyant, Martin, *Share Family & Community Services Society*, 1294
Wyatt, Betty, *Saskatchewan Shorthorn Association*, 1274
Wyatt, Bob, *The Muttart Foundation*, 986
Wycks, Brendan, *Canadian Association of Financial Institutions in Insurance*, 315
Wyles, David F., *Bruce Grey Child & Family Services*, 260
Wylie, Pamela, *The Appraisal Institute of Canada - Manitoba*, 75
Wylie, Douglas, *Canadian Fallen Firefighters Foundation*, 383
Wyllie, Patricia, *Nova Scotia Egg Producers*, 1044
Wynberg, Joe, *Landscape New Brunswick Horticultural Trades Association*, 898
Wynn-Williams, Andrew, *Canadian Manufacturers & Exporters*, 430
Wynne, Kathleen, *Ontario Liberal Party*, 1088
Wynnyczuk, Peter, *Ontario Urban Forest Council*, 1112
Wynnyk, Mike, *Blue Line Racing Association*, 215
Wynters, Chris, *Alberta Music Industry Association*, 41
Wyss, Jessica, *German Canadian Association of Nova Scotia*, 772
Wyton, Carmen, *Canadian Society of Association Executives*, 480
Wyton, Carmen, *Building Industry & Land Development Alberta*, 262
Wyvill, Brian, *Eurographics - European Association for Computer Graphics*, 1524

X

Xavier, Cindy, *Telemiracle/Kinsmen Foundation Inc.*, 1369
Xinsheng, Zhang, *International Union for Conservation of Nature*, 1563
Xiwu, Zhang, *World Coal Institute*, 1604
Xu, Zhenghe, *Metallurgy & Materials Society of the Canadian Institute of Mining, Metallurgy & Petroleum*, 962
Xuereb, Marc, *Waterloo Regional Labour Council*, 1442

Y

Yabit, François, *Northwood Neighbourhood Services*, 1040
Yaciuk, Bob, *Trillium Party of Ontario*, 1399
Yada, Rickey, *International Union of Food Science & Technology*, 861
Yakabuski, Mark, *Canadian Association of Insolvency & Restructuring Professionals*, 318
Yake, Marianne, *Richmond Hill Naturalists*, 1231
Yakimchuk, Heather, *Drayton Valley & District Chamber of Commerce*, 662
Yakimec, Tim, *Edmonton Opera Association*, 678
Yako, Louise, *British Columbia Trucking Association*, 257
Yalden, Rob, *Equitas - International Centre for Human Rights Education*, 695
Yale, Janet, *Arthritis Society*, 84
Yamada, Jitsuhiro, *Lions Clubs International*, 1569
Yamashita, Satoshi, *Manitoba Brain Injury Association Inc.*, 932
Yamkowy, Brenda, *Grande Prairie & Region United Way*, 781
Yamkowy, Brenda, *United Way Alberta Northwest*, 1413
Yan, CY, *OMF International - Canada*, 1057
Yan, Joyce, *British Columbia Freedom of Information & Privacy Association*, 242
Yan, Han, *Canadian Federation of Medical Students*, 388
Yan, Judith, *Guelph Symphony Orchestra*, 793
Yang, Jae, *International Union of Soil Sciences*, 1565
Yang, Heidi, *Association of Professional Engineers & Geoscientists of Alberta*, 157
Yang, Margaret, *Chinese Professionals Association of Canada*, 565
Yanko, Paula, *Thompson Chamber of Commerce*, 1376
Yankova, Diana, *Central European Association for Canadian Studies*, 1516
Yannakidis, Debby, *Gander & Area Chamber of Commerce*, 766
Yanofsky, Deena, *Association of Canadian Map Libraries & Archives*, 142
Yantz, Darcy, *Canadian Welding Bureau*, 503
Yap, George, *WaterCan*, 1442
Yap, George, *WaterCan*, 1442
Yaple, Charles H., *Coalition for Education in the Outdoors*, 1517
Yarascavitch, Ronald, *Royal College of Dental Surgeons of Ontario*, 1241
Yarema, Megan, *Canada Without Poverty*, 281
Yaremko, Vance, *Smoky Applied Research & Demonstration Association*, 1305
Yarhi, Manuela, *National Advertising Benevolent Society*, 989
Yarnold, David, *National Audubon Society, Inc.*, 1575
Yaschuk, Michelle, *Early Childhood Intervention Program (ECIP) Sask. Inc.*, 667
Yashinsky, Dan, *Ontario Prader-Willi Syndrome Association*, 1097
Yates, John, *Association of Canadian University Presses*, 144
Yates, Louise, *Regina Humane Society Inc.*, 1211
Yates, Suzan, *Waterford & Townsend Historical Society*, 1442
Yates, Jani, *Les normes canadiennes de la publicité*, 1028
Yates, Myron, *Big Brothers Big Sisters of Prince Edward Island*, 210
Yates, Catherine, *Association of Fundraising Professionals*, 1511
Yau, Daisey, *Chinese Cultural Centre*, 564
Yaw Kotoka Amuzu, Matthias, *Catholic Charismatic Renewal Council, Toronto*, 518
Yazbeck, David, *Canadian Artists Representation*, 295
Yazdanfar, Bahman, *Canadians' Choice Party*, 507
Yazdani, Arash, *Professional Engineers Ontario*, 1184
Ye, Ying, *Windsor Women Working with Immigrant Women*, 1457
Yearous, Kim, *South Western Alberta Teachers' Convention Association*, 1336
Yearwood, Louise, *Jane Austen Society of North America*, 868
Yeasting, Nicole, *Vancouver International Children's Festival*, 1426
Yehl, Victoria, *Geological Association of Canada*, 769
Yellow Face, Lance, *Treaty & Aboriginal Land Stewards Association of Alberta*, 1396
Yen, Mike, *Toronto Entertainment District Residental Association*, 1384
Yeo, Matt, *Northern Alberta Curling Association*, 1034
Yeo, Jennie, *Korean Students' Association of Canada*, 894
Yeoh, Lin Lin, *World Organization of the Scout Movement*, 1607
Yetman, Gerard, *AIDS Committee of Newfoundland & Labrador*, 16
Yetman, William, *Toronto Community Care Access Centre*, 1383
Yeung, Sonia, *Eye Bank of BC*, 700
Yeung, Paul, *Canadian Counselling & Psychotherapy Association*, 372
Yeung, Rosie, *Pathways to Education Canada*, 1145
Yeung, Paul, *Fountain of Love & Life*, 756
Ygartua, Lotta, *Canada China Business Council*, 278
Yip, Alana, *American Society of Heating, Refrigerating & Air Conditioning Engineers*, 1500
Yip, Grace, *Alliance for Canadian New Music Projects*, 56
Yiu, Donna, *Canadian Investor Protection Fund*, 422
Yochim, Jason, *Saskatoon Region Association of REALTORS*, 1280
Yochim, Dwight, *Truck Loggers Association*, 1399
Yong, Li, *United Nations Industrial Development Organization*, 1600
Yoo, John, *Canadian Society of Otolaryngology - Head & Neck Surgery*, 485
York, Lorne, *Prospect Human Services*, 1189
Yorke, Andrew, *Canadian Association of Blue Cross Plans*, 309
Yorke, Ekua, *Sickle Cell Foundation of Alberta*, 1298
Young, David, *Sources Foundation*, 1334
Young, Wendy, *Community Arts Council of Prince George & District*, 595
Young, Paul, *Queen's University Faculty Association*, 1200
Young, Paul, *Queen's University Faculty Association*, 1200
Young, Robert, *Winnipeg Association of Public Service Officers*, 1458
Young, David, *ARMA Canada*, 82
Young, Judi Michelle, *Sculptors Society of Canada*, 1287
Young, Rene, *National Automotive Trades Association of Canada*, 991
Young, Jane, *Canadian Botanical Association*, 346
Young, Robert, *Canadian Hard of Hearing Association*, 400
Young, Andrew, *Planning Institute of British Columbia*, 1162
Young, Alan, *Canadian Public Works Association*, 464
Young, John H., *Canadian Society of Church History*, 481
Young, Graham, *Geological Association of Canada*, 769
Young, Sean, *Canadian College of Medical Geneticists*, 359
Young, Vicki, *Manitoba Chamber Orchestra*, 933
Young, Carole, *Osteoporosis Canada*, 1129
Young, Nora J., *Prince Edward Island Museum & Heritage Foundation*, 1176
Young, Christine, *YMCA Canada*, 1472
Young, Marnie, *United Way Alberta Northwest*, 1413
Young, Lorna, *Chemistry Industry Association of Canada*, 556
Young, David, *Wilderness Canoe Association*, 1454
Young, Gillian, *The Royal Scottish Country Dance Society*, 1587
Young, Garnet, *Blind River Chamber of Commerce*, 214
Young, Robert, *Pelham Historical Society*, 1149
Young, Jean, *Rivers & District Chamber of Commerce*, 1234
Young, Bradley, *National Aboriginal Forestry Association*, 989
Young, Judith, *Margaret M. Allemang Centre for the History of Nursing*, 949
Young, Troy, *Attractions Ontario*, 187
Young, Tom, *Société internationale du réseau ÉCONOMUSÉE et Société ÉCONOMUSÉE du Québec*, 1321
Young, Michael, *Canada Pork International*, 280
Young, Julia, *Canadian Association of Ambulatory Care*, 308
Young, Jeffrey, *Franco-Jeunes de Terre-Neuve et du Labrador*, 757
Young, Sharon, *Canadian Breast Cancer Network*, 347
Young, Ben, *Urban Development Institute of Nova Scotia*, 1422
Young, Allan, *International Society for Affective Disorders*, 1557
Young, Lynn, *CADORA Ontario Association Inc.*, 269
Young, Ross, *Corridor Community Options for Adults*, 631
Young, Kam, *Ontario DanceSport*, 1076
Young, Michelle, *Almas Jiwani Foundation*, 59
Young-Crook, Michele, *National Aboriginal Trust Officers Association*, 989
Youngblud, Nicolas, *Alberta Water Polo Association*, 51
Younger, Calvin, *Big Brothers Big Sisters of Ontario*, 210
Youngson, Cera, *Canadian 4-H Council*, 285
Yousuf Esha, Samina, *Ontario Public Interest Research Group*, 1099
Youzwa, Terry, *Canola Council of Canada*, 509
Yu, Jiannan, *Cardiology Technologists' Association of British Columbia*, 511
Yu, Pauline, *American Council of Learned Societies*, 1492
Yuan-Su, Lin, *Canadian Association of Foodservice Professionals*, 315
Yudelson, Joan, *Financial Planning Standards Council*, 737
Yuen, Anila Lee, *Centre for Newcomers Society of Calgary*, 533
Yuen, Chui Kin, *SIGMA Canadian Menopause Society*, 1298
Yui, Andrew, *Hong Kong Trade Development Council*, 1530
Yuill, Stephanie, *Interpretation Canada - A Professional Association for Heritage Interpretation*, 861
Yuke, Reagan, *Canadian Society of Technical Analysts*, 488
Yuksel, Nesé, *SIGMA Canadian Menopause Society*, 1298
Yule, Linda, *United Way of North Okanagan Columbia Shuswap*, 1415
Yung, Jennifer, *Canadian Board of Marine Underwriters*, 345
Yung, Troy, *Canadian Agencies Practicing Marketing Activation*, 289
Yungblut, Doug, *Ontario Institute of Agrologists*, 1087
Yungwirth, Joe, *Saskatchewan Construction Association*, 1262
Yurick, Mark, *Alberta Teachers' Association*, 49
Yurij, Metropolitan, *Ukrainian Orthodox Church of Canada*, 1403
Yurychuk, Darrel, *Earthsave Canada*, 667
Yussuf, Samira, *CODA International Training*, 1518
Yussuff, Hassan, *Canadian Labour Congress*, 424
Yves, Bissonnette, *Société généalogique canadienne-française*, 1319

Z

Z'Graggen, Jocelyne, *Canadian Association for Williams Syndrome*, 307

Executive Name Index

Zaat, Patricia, *International Fund for Animal Welfare Canada*, 857
Zabava, Isabela, *Coast Foundation Society*, 579
Zabel, Paul, *Lutheran Church - Canada*, 922
Zabinsky, Tony, *Fort St. John & District Chamber of Commerce*, 753
Zabolotney, Jacqueline, *Association of Saskatchewan Realtors*, 161
Zaborski Breton, Visnja, *Canadian Parks & Recreation Association*, 450
Zaccarelli, Wayne, *Amalgamated Conservation Society*, 66
Zachariah, Coty, *Canadian Federation of Students*, 388
Zacharie, Dwayne, *First Nations Chiefs of Police Association*, 738
Zadarnowski, Ewa L., *Polish Canadian Women's Federation*, 1164
Zagar, Mirna, *Dance Centre*, 649
Zagar, Mima, *The Dance Centre*, 649
Zagari, Tammy, *Information & Communication Technologies Association of Manitoba*, 836
Zahn, Catherine, *Centre for Addiction & Mental Health*, 531
Zahn, Scott, *Nakiska Alpine Ski Association*, 987
Zahra, Yves, *Tourisme Centre-du-Québec*, 1392
Zajac, George, *Canadian Association of Certified Planning Technicians*, 310
Zakaib, Daniel D., *Canadian Association of Personal Property Appraisers*, 325
Zakaluzny, Roman, *Ukrainian Canadian Civil Liberties Association*, 1402
Zakhidov, Marat, *International Society for Human Rights*, 1558
Zakoor, Colleen, *Community Living Newmarket/Aurora District*, 603
Zaks-Walker, Linda, *Ontario College of Teachers*, 1072
Zalik, Sharon, *Canadian Friends of the Hebrew University*, 395
Zalman, Amy, *World Future Society*, 1605
Zambonin, Susan, *Habitat for Humanity Canada*, 797
Zambory, Tracy, *Saskatchewan Union of Nurses*, 1277
Zamojc, Kristen, *Ontario Pharmacists' Association*, 1095
Zamvrano-Nieto, Diego R., *Venezuelan Association for Canadian Studies*, 1431
Zanardo, Ivana, *Catholic Family Services of Toronto*, 519
Zanatta, Mirella, *Association of Image Consultants International Canada*, 149
Zanchettin, Vilma, *Risk & Insurance Management Society Inc.*, 1234
Zandbergen, Jeremy, *Association of Professional Engineers & Geoscientists of British Columbia*, 158
Zandbergen, Peter, *Professional Engineers Ontario*, 1184
Zander, Otto, *Professional Engineers Ontario*, 1185
Zanotti, Daniele, *United Way Toronto & York Region*, 1417

Zapfe, Werner, *Good Shepherd Refuge Social Ministries*, 777
Zaplitny, Kathy, *Chartered Professional Accountants of Manitoba*, 553
Zappala, Paul, *Title Insurance Industry Association of Canada*, 1380
Zarate, Soraya, *Réseau des SADC et CAE*, 1220
Zardini, Mirko, *Canadian Centre for Architecture*, 353
Zarecki, Mark, *Jewish Immigrant Aid Services of Canada*, 873
Zarecki, Mark, *Jewish Family Services of Ottawa-Carleton*, 872
Zarif, Sashar, *Dance Ontario Association*, 649
Zarins, Harry, *Brain Injury Association of Canada*, 225
Zarrugr, Baset, *Mount Royal Staff Association*, 976
Zaruba, David, *Pacific Bluegrass Heritage Society*, 1135
Zasowski, Krystyna, *Marguerite Bourgeoys Family Centre Fertility Care Programme*, 949
Zatyko, Barbara, *Magazines Canada*, 925
Zatylny, Wendy, *Association of Canadian Port Authorities*, 143
Zatylny, Jane, *Western Magazine Awards Foundation*, 1450
Zatzman, Steven, *Baron de Hirsch Hebrew Benevolent Society*, 197
Zaugg, Michael, *Pro Coro Canada*, 1181
Zawadski, Brian, *Nunavut Harvesters Association*, 1051
Zawierucha, Robert, *Polish Alliance of Canada*, 1163
Zayid, Ismail, *Arab Canadian Association of the Atlantic Provinces*, 76
Zbib, Ahmad, *Arthritis Society*, 84
Zbily, Albert, *International Federation of Corporate Football*, 857
Zdunic, Allan, *Occupational First Aid Attendants Association of British Columbia*, 1054
Zealand, Gord, *Yukon Fish & Game Association*, 1478
Zealand, Gordon, *Yukon Golf Association*, 1478
Zeb, Amir, *British Columbia Muslim Association*, 247
Zebiere, Lori, *Manitoba Society of Artists*, 944
Zebruck, Richard, *Judo Yukon*, 876
Zecher, Carla, *Renaissance Society of America*, 1586
Zedel, Len, *Canadian Meteorological & Oceanographic Society*, 436
Zehr, Keith, *William W. Creighton Youth Services*, 1455
Zelaya, Walter, *Moelle Épinière et Motricité Québec*, 971
Zelaya, Walter, *Fondation pour la recherche sur la moelle épinière*, 747
Zellars, Rachel, *Girls Action Foundation*, 774
Zelmanovits, Jill, *Girl Guides of Canada*, 773
Zerehi, Sima Sahar, *Qikiqtani Inuit Association*, 1194
Zeschuk, Pauline, *Gem & Mineral Federation of Canada*, 768

Zhang, Hui, *Chinese Medicine & Acupuncture Association of Canada*, 565
Zhang, Hao, *World University Service of Canada*, 1467
Zhang, Jin, *Vancouver Philharmonic Orchestra*, 1428
Zhang, Ze, *Canadian Biomaterials Society*, 344
Zhao, Yonggan, *Chinese Canadian National Council*, 564
Zhou, Linda, *The World Job & Food Bank Inc.*, 1466
Zhou, Jing, *Canadian Association of Ambulatory Care*, 308
Zhu, Jani, *Society of Fire Protection Engineers*, 1593
Ziavras, Helen, *Thalassemia Foundation of Canada*, 1373
Zieba, Agata, *Canadian Association for Community Living*, 298
Ziegner, Kelly, *United Way of London & Middlesex*, 1415
Zigelstein-Yip, Jodi, *Human Resources Professionals Association*, 826
Zilinsky, Deanne, *Manitoba Five Pin Bowling Federation, Inc.*, 936
Zimmer, Ronald J., *Continental Automated Buildings Association*, 626
Zimmer, Lynn, *YWCA Canada*, 1481
Zimmerling, Todd, *Alberta Conservation Association*, 31
Zimmerman, Shelly, *Lloydminster Society for the Prevention of Cruelty to Animals*, 916
Zimmerman, Debbie, *Grape Growers of Ontario*, 782
Zimmerman, Blair, *British Columbia Floorball Federation*, 241
Zimmermann, Lothar, *German-Canadian Historical Association Inc.*, 772
Zimmermann, Elisabeth, *YWCA Canada*, 1481
Zimmermann, Monika, *International Council for Local Environmental Initiatives*, 1544
Zimmermann, Wolfgang, *National Institute of Disability Management & Research*, 994
Zinabou, Maike, *Huntington Society of Canada*, 828
Zinck, Janice, *Canadian Mineral Processors Society*, 437
Zinger, Nathalie, *The Nature Conservancy of Canada*, 1000
Ziniak, Madeline, *Canadian Ethnic Media Association*, 382
Zinkowski, Sandy, *Athletic Therapy Association of British Columbia*, 181
Zinman, Shirley, *Funeral Advisory & Memorial Society*, 764
Ziola, Cheryl, *Urban Development Institute of Canada*, 1422
Ziomek, Anna, *College of Physicians & Surgeons of Manitoba*, 588
Zizian, Daniel, *Conférence des recteurs et des principaux des universités du Québec*, 612
Zizian, Daniel, *Centre patronal de santé et sécurité du travail du Québec*, 536
Zlomislic, Erica, *Jesuit Development Office*, 870
Znaimer, Moses, *CARP*, 514

Zoccole, Art, *2-Spirited People of the First Nations*, 1401
Zoellner, Jean, *L'Église Réformée du Québec*, 681
Zohary, Tamar, *International Society of Limnology*, 1561
Zohner, Troy, *North Central Labour Council of British Columbia*, 1030
Zoldy, Derek, *Tunnelling Association of Canada*, 1400
Zolinski, Doug, *Saskatchewan Rowing Association*, 1274
Zornberg, Jorge G., *International Geosynthetics Society*, 1550
Zorzos, Sonia, *Ontario Environment Industry Association*, 1078
Zottola, Amedeo, *Ontario Pharmacists' Association*, 1095
Zuba, Angela, *Building Industry & Land Development Alberta*, 262
Zuccarelli, Diego, *50 & Piu Enasco*, 735
Zuccon, Johnny, *Professional Engineers Ontario*, 1183
Zuckerman, Shelley, *North York Community House*, 1033
Zufelt-Baxter, Wendy, *Shad Valley International*, 1294
Zuhair El-Khateeb, Mohamad, *Muslim World League - Canada*, 986
Zukewich, Tara, *Construction Safety Association of Manitoba*, 624
Zukowski, Donna, *Canadian Association of Hepatology Nurses*, 317
Zulkoskey, Anna-Beth, *Saskatchewan Amateur Wrestling Association*, 1255
Zumwalt, Bryan, *American Chemistry Council*, 1491
Zupan, Leon, *Alberta Chamber of Resources*, 28
Zurakowski, Jocelyn, *United Way of Saskatoon & Area*, 1417
Zurba, Tammy, *Manitoba Genealogical Society Inc.*, 937
Zussman, David, *Canadian Centre for Ethics in Sport*, 353
Zutis, Robyn, *Ontario Traffic Council*, 1111
Zvanitajs, C.J., *Family Enterprise Xchange*, 703
Zwart, Johannes, *Community Futures West Yellowhead*, 598
Zweifel, Tracy, *Sagitawa Friendship Centre*, 1245
Zwickel, Jon, *Canadian Resort Development Association*, 467
Zwicker, Gwen, *Greater Sackville Chamber of Commerce*, 785
Zwiers, Jon, *Alberta Beekeepers Commission*, 26
Zwozdesky, Willi, *British Columbia Choral Federation*, 236

Geographic Index

- Canadian associations indexed only
- Headquarters, along with branches, divisions, chapters, etc. are listed
- Name of provinces are presented alphabetically, followed by constituent cities & towns, also in alphabetical order
- Each entry is accompanied by a page number which points you to the corresponding listing

Alberta

Airdrie
Airdrie & District Soccer Association, 20
Airdrie Chamber of Commerce, 20
Airdrie Food Bank, 20
Alberta Electrical League, 33
Alberta Simmental Association, 46
Association of Christian Schools International-Western Canada Office, 1510
Boys & Girls Clubs of Alberta-Boys & Girls Club of Airdrie, 221
Canadian 4-H Council-Alberta - Airdrie Office, 284
Horse Industry Association of Alberta, 822
Nose Creek Valley Museum Society, 1040
Professional Locksmith Association of Alberta, 1186
Western Barley Growers Association, 1447

Alberta Beach
Alberta Beach & District Chamber of Commerce, 25

Alix
Alberta Dressage Association-Parkland Area Chapter, 33
Alix Chamber of Commerce, 54

Ardrossan
Canadian Pony Club-Alberta North, 457
Canadian Chemical Producers' Association-Alberta Regional Office, 556

Ashmont
Ashmont & District Agricultural Society, 86

Athabasca
Athabasca & District Chamber of Commerce, 180
Athabasca Native Friendship Centre Society, 180
Athabasca University Faculty Association, 180

Banff
Association for Mountain Parks Protection & Enjoyment, 134
Banff & Lake Louise Tourism, 195
Banff Centre for Arts & Creativity, 195
Banff Food Bank Association, 195
Banff International String Quartet Competition, 195
YWCA Canada-YWCA Banff, 1481
YWCA of Banff Programs & Services, 1482

Barrhead
Barrhead & District Chamber of Commerce, 197
Barrhead Animal Rescue Society, 197
Barrhead Association for Community Living, 197
Barrhead Gem Seekers, 197

Bashaw
Bashaw & District Chamber of Commerce, 198
Boys & Girls Clubs of Alberta-Boys & Girls Club of Bashaw & Area, 221

Beaverlodge
Beaverlodge Chamber of Commerce, 203
Beaverlodge Food Bank, 203

Beiseker
Beiseker & District Chamber of Commerce, 204

Berwyn
Berwyn & District Chamber of Commerce, 206

Black Diamond
Alberta Dressage Association, 33
Alberta Soaring Council, 47

Boys & Girls Clubs of Alberta-Boys & Girls Club of the Foothills, 221

Blackfalds
Alberta Walking Horse Association, 51
Blackfalds & District Chamber of Commerce, 214
Calgary Faceter's Guild, 272
Global Youth Volunteer Network, 775

Blairmore
Boys & Girls Clubs of Alberta-Boys & Girls Club of Crowsnest Pass, 221
Crowsnest Pass Allied Arts Association, 644
Crowsnest Pass Chamber of Commerce, 644
Crowsnest Pass Society for the Prevention of Cruelty to Animals, 645
Crowsnest Pass Symphony, 645

Bluffton
Bluffton & District Chamber of Commerce, 216
Canadian Sheep Breeders' Association, 470
Recycling Council of Alberta, 1208

Bonnyville
Bonnyville & District Chamber of Commerce, 217
Bonnyville & District Fine Arts Society, 217
Bonnyville Canadian Native Friendship Centre, 217
Boys & Girls Clubs of Alberta-Boys & Girls Club of Bonnyville, 221
Glendon & District Business Alliance, 774
Lakeland Agricultural Research Association, 896
Lakeland District Soccer Association, 896
Lakeland Industry & Community Association, 896
Métis Nation of Alberta-Regional Office - Zone 2, 963

Bow Island
Bow Island / Burdett District Chamber of Commerce, 219

Bowden
Bowden Historical Society, 219

Boyle
Boyle & District Chamber of Commerce, 220
Boyle Food Bank Association, 221

Bragg Creek
Bragg Creek Chamber of Commerce, 224
Canadian Murray Grey Association, 437

Breton
Breton & District Chamber of Commerce, 228
Breton & District Historical Society, 228

Brocket
Treaty & Aboriginal Land Stewards Association of Alberta, 1396

Brooks
Alberta Genealogical Society-Brooks & District Branch, 36
Animal Nutrition Association of Canada-Alberta Division, 71
Brooks & District Chamber of Commerce, 260
Calgary Catholic Immigration Society-Brooks & County Immigration Services, 271
Realtors Association of South Central Alberta, 1206
SPEC Association for Children & Families, 1339

Bruderheim
Society of Local Government Managers of Alberta, 1329

Calgary
Ability Society of Alberta, 2
Aboriginal Friendship Centre of Calgary, 2
Abundance Canada-Calgary Office, 3
Accessible Housing Society, 5
Alberta Amateur Baseball Council, 22
Alberta Amateur Speed Skating Association, 22
Alberta Amputee Sports & Recreation Association, 22
Alberta Association of Academic Libraries, 23
Alberta Association of Clinic Managers, 23
Alberta Association of Marriage & Family Therapy, 24
Alberta Association of Midwives, 24
Alberta Association of Police Governance, 24
Alberta Association of Rehabilitation Centres, 24
Alberta Athletic Therapists Association, 25
Alberta Ballet, 25
Alberta Barley Commission, 25
Alberta Beef Producers, 25
Alberta Bobsleigh Association, 26
Alberta Bowhunters Association, 26
Alberta Building Envelope Council (South), 26
Alberta Cattle Breeders Association, 27
Alberta Cattle Feeders' Association, 27
Alberta Central, 27
Alberta CGIT Association, 28
Alberta Children's Hospital Foundation, 28
Alberta Civil Liberties Research Centre, 28
Alberta College of Acupuncture & Traditional Chinese Medicine, 28
The Alberta Community Crime Prevention Association, 30
Alberta Conference of Mennonite Brethren Churches, 30
Alberta Construction Association-Calgary Construction Association, 31
Alberta Construction Trucking Association, 31
Alberta Council for Exceptional Children, 31
Alberta Debate & Speech Association, 32
Alberta Easter Seals Society, 33
Alberta Ecotrust Foundation, 33
Alberta Egg Producers' Board, 33
Alberta Equestrian Federation, 34
Alberta Family Child Care Association, 34
Alberta Family History Society, 34
Alberta Family Mediation Society, 34
Alberta Federation of Rock Clubs, 35
Alberta Floor Covering Association, 35
Alberta Food Processors Association, 35
Alberta Freestyle Ski Association, 36
Alberta Golf Association, 37
Alberta Gymnastics Federation, 37
Alberta Hospice Palliative Care Association, 38
Alberta Insurance Council-Calgary Office, 38
Alberta Law Foundation, 39
Alberta Luge Association, 39
Alberta Magazine Publishers Association, 39
Alberta Neurosurgical Society, 41
Alberta Pioneer Auto Club, 42
Alberta Plastics Recycling Association, 42
Alberta Playwrights' Network, 42
Alberta Powerlifting Union, 42
Alberta Professional Home Inspectors Society, 43
Alberta Provincial Rifle Association, 43
Alberta Psychiatric Association, 43
Alberta Real Estate Association, 43
Alberta Reappraising AIDS Society, 43
Alberta Research Council Inc.-Calgary Office, 44
Alberta Roofing Contractors Association, 44
Alberta Rural Municipal Administrators Association, 45
Alberta Sailing Association, 45

Alberta Salers Association, 45
Alberta Securities Commission, 46
Alberta Senior Citizens Sport & Recreation Association, 46
The Alberta Seventh Step Society, 46
Alberta Ski Jumping & Nordic Combined, 46
Alberta Snowboard Association, 47
Alberta Social Credit Party, 47
Alberta Society of Artists, 47
Alberta Society of Artists-TREX Southwest Office, 47
Alberta Society of Professional Biologists, 47
Alberta Society of Surveying & Mapping Technologies, 48
Alberta Speleological Society, 48
Alberta Sports & Recreation Association for the Blind, 48
Alberta Sulphur Research Ltd., 48
Alberta Therapeutic Recreation Association, 50
Alberta Water Polo Association, 51
Alberta Wilderness Association, 52
Alberta Women Entrepreneurs-Calgary Office, 52
Alcoholics Anonymous-Calgary - Central Service Office, 52
Alexandra Writers' Centre Society, 53
Alliance for Canadian New Music Projects-Contemporary Showcase - Calgary, 56
Alliance Française de Calgary, 57
Alliance of Canadian Cinema, Television & Radio Artists-ACTRA Alberta, 58
Alpine Canada Alpin, 59
ALS Society of Alberta, 60
Alzheimer Society of Calgary, 62
American Society of Heating, Refrigerating & Air Conditioning Engineers-Southern Alberta Chapter
Ancient, Free & Accepted Masons of Canada - Grand Lodge of Alberta, 68
The Anglican Church of Canada-Diocese of Calgary, 69
Apostolic Church of Pentecost of Canada Inc., 73
Appaloosa Horse Club of Canada-Calgary Regional Appaloosa Club, 73
The Appraisal Institute of Canada - Alberta, 74
Archaeological Society of Alberta-Calgary Centre, 76
L'Arche Western Region, 77
L'Arche Western Region-L'Arche Calgary, 78
Architectural Woodwork Manufacturers Association of Canada - Southern Alberta, 80
Arctic Institute of North America, 81
ARMA Canada-Calgary Chapter, 82
Arthritis Society-Alberta/NWT Division, 84
Arusha Centre Society, 86
ASM International - Calgary Chapter, 87
Association camadienne des interprètes de conférence, 90
Association for Financial Professionals - Calgary, 133
Association for German Education in Calgary, 133
Association for Literature, Environment, & Culture in Canada, 133
Association for the Rehabilitation of the Brain Injured, 135
Association of Alberta Agricultural Fieldmen, 139
Association of Fundraising Professionals-Calgary & Area Chapter
The Association of Professional Engineers & Geoscientists of Alberta-Calgary Branch, 157
Autism Calgary Association, 188
Autism Society Alberta, 188

Geographic Index / Alberta - Calgary

Awo Taan Healing Lodge Society, 191
B'nai Brith Youth Organization-Northwest Canada Region, 192
Badminton Alberta, 193
Barley Council of Canada, 196
Beef Cattle Research Council, 203
Better Business Bureau Serving Southern Alberta & East Kootenay, 207
Biathlon Alberta, 207
Big Brothers Big Sisters of Alberta-Big Brothers Big Sisters of Calgary & Area, 209
Billy Graham Evangelistic Association of Canada, 211
Block Parent Program of Canada-Alberta Block Parent Association, 214
BMW Clubs Canada-Southern Alberta BMW Club, 216
Bobsleigh Canada Skeleton, 217
Boys & Girls Clubs of Alberta-Boys & Girls Club of Calgary, 221
Building Industry & Land Development Calgary Region, 262
Calgary & Area Medical Staff Society, 270
Calgary & District Labour Council, 270
Calgary & District Target Shooters Association, 270
Calgary Aboriginal Arts Awareness Society, 270
Calgary Alpha House Society, 271
Calgary Association of Self Help, 271
Calgary Association of the Deaf, 271
Calgary Catholic Immigration Society, 271
Calgary Catholic Immigration Society-Margaret Chisholm Resettlement Centre, 271
Calgary Chamber of Commerce, 271
Calgary Chamber of Voluntary Organizations, 271
Calgary Children's Foundation, 271
Calgary Chinese Cultural Society, 271
Calgary Combative Sports Commission, 271
Calgary Community Living Society, 271
Calgary Co-operative Memorial Society, 271
Calgary Danish Businessmen's Association, 271
Calgary Exhibition & Stampede, 271
Calgary Field Naturalists' Society, 272
Calgary Firefighters Burn Treatment Society, 272
Calgary Folk Club, 272
Calgary Food Bank, 272
The Calgary Foundation, 272
Calgary Health Trust, 272
Calgary Horticultural Society, 272
Calgary Humane Society, 272
Calgary Immigrant Women's Association, 272
Calgary Japanese Community Association, 273
Calgary Law Library Group, 273
Calgary Marching Showband Association, 273
Calgary Meals on Wheels, 273
Calgary Minor Soccer Association, 273
Calgary Motor Dealers Association, 273
Calgary Musicians Association, 273
Calgary Numismatic Society, 273
Calgary Opera Association, 273
Calgary Philatelic Society, 273
Calgary Philharmonic Society, 273
Calgary Real Estate Board Cooperative Limited, 274
Calgary Residential Rental Association, 274
Calgary Rock & Lapidary Club, 274
Calgary Round-Up Band Association, 274
Calgary Seniors' Resource Society, 274
Calgary Sexual Health Centre, 274
Calgary Soccer Federation, 274
Calgary Society of Independent Filmmakers, 274
Calgary Society of Organists, 274
Calgary Stetson Show Band, 274
Calgary United Soccer Association, 275
Calgary Urban Project Society, 275
Calgary Vietnamese Canadian Association, 275
Calgary Wildlife Rehabilitation Society, 275
Calgary Women's Emergency Shelter Association, 275
Calgary Women's Soccer Association, 275
Calgary Youth Orchestra, 275

Calgary Zoological Society, 275
Canada West Equipment Dealers Association, 281
Canada West Foundation, 281
Canada's Oil Sands Innovation Alliance, 282
Canada's Sports Hall of Fame, 283
Canadian Alliance of British Pensioners-British Pensioners Association of Western Canada, 291
Canadian Amputee Golf Association, 292
Canadian Association for Disabled Skiing, 299
Canadian Association for Disabled Skiing - Alberta-Calgary Zone, 299
Canadian Association for Young Children-Alberta/North West Territories, 307
Canadian Association of Aquarium Clubs, 308
Canadian Association of Child Neurology, 310
Canadian Association of Drilling Engineers, 312
Canadian Association of Elizabeth Fry Societies-Elizabeth Fry Society of Calgary, 312
Canadian Association of Geophysical Contractors, 317
Canadian Association of Oilwell Drilling Contractors, 324
Canadian Association of Petroleum Land Administration, 325
Canadian Association of Petroleum Landmen, 326
Canadian Association of Petroleum Producers, 326
Canadian Association of Veterans in United Nations Peacekeeping-Calgary Chapter, 335
Canadian Association of Wooden Money Collectors, 336
Canadian Athletic Therapists Association, 337
Canadian Aviation Historical Society-Calgary Chapter, 340
Canadian Baptists of Western Canada, 341
Canadian Baptists of Western Canada-Alberta & NWT Regional Office, 341
Canadian Bar Association-Alberta Branch, 341
Canadian Beef-Western Office, 342
Canadian Beef Breeds Council, 342
Canadian Blood Services-Calgary, 344
Canadian Cancer Society-Alberta & Northwest Territories Division, 349
Canadian Cattlemen's Association, 351
Canadian Celiac Association-Calgary Chapter, 352
The Canadian Chamber of Commerce-Calgary Office, 355
Canadian Charolais Association, 355
Canadian Child Abuse Association, 355
Canadian Chiropractic Examining Board, 356
Canadian Clean Power Coalition, 357
Canadian Common Ground Alliance, 361
Canadian Condominium Institute-CCI-South Alberta Chapter, 362
Canadian Contractors Association, 364
The Canadian Corps of Commissionaires-Southern Alberta Division, 365
Canadian Council of Professional Certification-Calgary - Western Canada Regional Office, 369
Canadian Cue Sport Association, 373
Canadian Culinary Federation-Calgary Branch, 374
Canadian Down Syndrome Society, 378
Canadian Energy Pipeline Association, 381
Canadian Energy Research Institute, 381
Canadian Environmental Certification Approvals Board, 381
Canadian Environmental Technology Advancement Corporation - West, 382
Canadian Ethnic Studies Association, 382
Canadian Federation of Business & Professional Women's Clubs-Calgary, 385
Canadian Federation of Independent Business-Alberta & Northwest Territories Office, 387
Canadian Federation of Independent Business-Calgary Office, 387

Canadian Friends of the Hebrew University-Calgary Chapter, 395
Canadian Fuels Association-Western Division, 396
Canadian Gelbvieh Association, 396
Canadian Geophysical Union, 397
Canadian Girls Rodeo Association, 398
Canadian Hard of Hearing Association-Alberta - Calgary Branch, 400
Canadian Hays Converter Association, 401
Canadian Heavy Oil Association, 403
Canadian Hereford Association, 404
Canadian HIV Trials Network-Prairie Region, 405
Canadian Institute of Chartered Business Planners, 414
Canadian Institute of Management-Alberta - Southern Branch, 417
Canadian Institute of Plumbing & Heating-Calgary, Alberta Region, 418
Canadian Institute of Resources Law, 419
Canadian Limousin Association, 427
Canadian Liver Foundation-Southern Alberta/Calgary/Edmonton Chapter, 427
Canadian Llama & Alpaca Association, 428
Canadian Luge Association, 428
Canadian Magen David Adom for Israel-Calgary Chapter, 429
Canadian Maine-Anjou Association, 429
Canadian Marketing Association-Calgary Chapter, 431
Canadian Masonry Contractors' Association-Masonry Contractors' Association of Alberta, Southern Region, 431
Canadian Music Centre-Prairie Region, 438
Canadian Neurological Sciences Federation, 441
Canadian Neurological Society, 441
Canadian Orienteering Federation, 447
Canadian Parks & Wilderness Society-Calgary - Southern Alberta Chapter, 450
Canadian Pension & Benefits Institute-Southern Alberta Region, 453
Canadian Political Science Students' Association, 457
Canadian Powerlifting Union, 459
The Canadian Press-Calgary Bureau, 459
Canadian Progress Club-Stampede City, 461
Canadian Propane Association-Calgary Office, 461
Canadian Public Relations Society Inc.-CPRS Calgary, 463
Canadian Railroad Historical Association-Calgary & South-Western Division, 465
The Canadian Red Cross Society-Western Zone Office, 468
Canadian Simmental Association, 470
Canadian Society for Continental Philosophy, 474
The Canadian Society for the Weizmann Institute of Science-Calgary Office, 479
Canadian Society of Addiction Medicine, 479
Canadian Society of Clinical Neurophysiologists, 482
Canadian Society of Exploration Geophysicists, 483
Canadian Society of Gastroenterology Nurses & Associates-Calgary Chapter, 483
Canadian Society of Orthopaedic Technologists-Alberta Chapter, 485
Canadian Society of Petroleum Geologists, 486
Canadian Taxpayers Federation-Alberta, 493
Canadian Thoroughbred Horse Society-Alberta Division, 495
Canadian Well Logging Society, 503
Canadian Women for Women in Afghanistan, 504
Canadian Women's Foundation-Calgary Office, 505
Canadian Wood Truss Association, 505
Canadian Worker Co-operative Federation, 505
CanLearn Society for Persons with Learning Difficulties, 508
Caribbean Community Council of Calgary, 512

Carthy Foundation, 516
CAUSE Canada, 521
The Centre for Israel & Jewish Affairs-Calgary Jewish Federation, 533
Centre for Newcomers Society of Calgary, 533
Centre for Suicide Prevention, 534
Centre for Transportation Engineering & Planning, 534
Cerebral Palsy Association in Alberta, 537
CFA Society Calgary, 538
Chartered Professional Accountants of Alberta, 552
Chartered Professionals in Human Resources of Alberta, 554
Child Evangelism Fellowship of Canada-Child Evangelism Fellowship of Alberta, 559
Children's Cottage Society, 561
Children's Wish Foundation of Canada-Alberta & N.W.T. Chapter - Calgary, 562
Chinese Canadian National Council-AB - Calgary Chinese Community Service Association, 564
Chinook Musical Society, 565
The Christian & Missionary Alliance in Canada-Western Canadian District (WCD) Office, 566
Christian Labour Association of Canada-Calgary Regional Office, 567
Churchill Park Family Care Society, 569
Clan MacLeod Societies of Canada-Southern Alberta Branch, 572
Coal Association of Canada, 577
Colin B. Glassco Charitable Foundation for Children, 581
College & Association of Respiratory Therapists of Alberta, 581
College of Naturopathic Doctors of Alberta, 586
Community Kitchen Program of Calgary, 599
Computer Modelling Group, 609
Construction Labour Relations - An Alberta Association, 624
Credit Counselling Society-Calgary, 640
Credit Institute of Canada-Calgary Chapter, 641
Cricket Alberta, 642
Crohn's & Colitis Canada-Alberta/NWT Region, 642
Danish Canadian Club of Calgary, 650
Decidedly Jazz Danceworks, 652
Developmental Disabilities Resource Centre of Calgary, 655
Canadian Diabetes Association-Calgary & District Branch, 655
Directors Guild of Canada-Alberta District Council, 657
Dress for Success-Calgary, 663
Dystonia Medical Research Foundation Canada-Alberta - Calgary Support Group, 666
Ecojustice Canada Society-Alberta Office, 672
Economic Developers Alberta, 672
Electronic Recycling Association, 683
Embroiderers' Association of Canada, Inc.-Alberta - Calgary Guild of Needle & Fibre Arts, 685
Enform, 688
Environmental Careers Organization of Canada, 691
Epilepsy Association of Calgary, 693
Ernest C. Manning Awards Foundation, 695
Evergreen Theatre Society, 699
Explorers & Producers Association of Canada, 700
Family Enterprise Xchange-FEX Calgary, 703
Fédération des scouts de l'ouest, 718
Federation of Calgary Communities, 722
Federation of Canada-China Friendship Associations, 722
Festival Chorus of Calgary, 733
Field Hockey Alberta, 734
Folk Festival Society of Calgary, 742
Foothills Library Association, 750
Foothills Orchid Society, 751
Footprints Dance Project Society of Alberta, 751
Fort Calgary Society, 752
The Fraser Institute-Calgary Office, 757

Friends of the Oldman River, 763
Fuse Collective, 765
Futurpreneur Canada-Alberta Office, 765
Gas Processing Association Canada, 767
Genome Canada-Genome Alberta, 769
Glass & Architectural Metals Association, 774
Grand Orange Lodge of Canada-Grand Orange Lodge of Western Canada, 780
Great Divide Trails Association, 782
Green Calgary, 788
The Green Party of Alberta, 788
GS1 Canada-Calgary Office, 792
Habitat for Humanity Canada-Alberta - Southern Alberta, 796
Harry & Martha Cohen Foundation, 804
Health & Safety Conference Society of Alberta, 805
Heart & Stroke Foundation of Alberta, NWT & Nunavut, 808
Heritage Park Society, 813
Historical Society of Alberta, 816
Historical Society of Alberta-Chinook Country Historical Society, 816
HIV Community Link, 816
Hockey Canada-Calgary Office, 817
Hockey Canada Foundation, 817
Hong Kong-Canada Business Association-Calgary Section Office, 820
Hunter Family Foundation, 827
Huntington Society of Canada-Southern Alberta Resource Centre, 828
Immigrant Services Calgary, 830
Impact Society, 831
Indefinite Arts Society, 832
Independent Power Producers Society of Alberta, 833
Inn From the Cold Society, 838
Innovate Calgary, 839
Inside Education-Calgary, 839
Insurance Institute of Southern Alberta, 850
Insurance Professionals of Calgary, 850
International Association for Impact Assessment - Western & Northern Canada, 853
International Association of Business Communicators-Calgary Chapter
International Association of Science & Technology for Development, 854
International Brotherhood of Boilermakers, Iron Ship Builders, Blacksmiths, Forgers & Helpers (AFL-CIO)-Calgary (Lodge 146), 1541
Investment Industry Regulatory Organization of Canada-Calgary Office, 863
Italian Chamber of Commerce in Canada - West-Calgary Office, 866
Jewish Family Services - Calgary, 871
Jewish Historical Society of Southern Alberta, 872
John Howard Society of Alberta-Calgary, 874
Jump Alberta, 877
Junior Achievement of Canada-Junior Achievement of Southern Alberta, 877
Junior League of Calgary, 878
Justice Centre for Constitutional Freedoms, 878
Juvenile Diabetes Research Foundation-Calgary, 878
Karate Alberta Association, 881
Kerby Centre for the 55 Plus, 884
The Kidney Foundation of Canada-Southern Alberta Branch, 885
Kids Cancer Care Foundation of Alberta, 886
Kids Help Phone-Alberta/Northwest Territories, 886
Law Society of Alberta, 901
Legal Archives Society of Alberta, 906
The Leukemia & Lymphoma Society of Canada-Prairies/Territories Branch - Calgary, 909
Library Association of Alberta, 910
Literacy Alberta, 913
Lupus Society of Alberta, 922
Macleod Institute, 924
The Magic of Christmas, 925
Max Bell Foundation, 954

McMan Youth, Family & Community Services Association-Calgary, 955
Mechanical Contractors Association of Alberta, 956
Mennonite Central Committee Canada-MCC Alberta, 960
Métis Nation of Alberta-Regional Office - Zone 3, 963
Military Collectors Club of Canada, 965
MindFuel, 966
Missing Children Society of Canada, 968
Money Mentors, 972
Motion Picture Theatre Association of Alberta, 975
Mount Royal Staff Association, 976
Multiple Sclerosis Society of Canada-Calgary & Area Chapter, 980
Music for Young Children-Alberta, 983
Mutual Fund Dealers Association of Canada-Prairie Regional Office, 986
NACE International-Canadian Region - Calgary Section, 1572
Nakiska Alpine Ski Association, 987
National Electricity Roundtable, 993
The Nature Conservancy of Canada-Alberta, 999
Naval Museum of Alberta Society, 1001
Netball Alberta, 1003
Nordic Combined Ski Canada, 1028
Operation Eyesight Universal, 1115
Operation Eyesight Universal-Vancouver Regional Office, 1115
The Order of United Commercial Travelers of America, 1119
The Organization for Bipolar Affective Disorder, 1125
Orphan Well Association, 1127
Osteoporosis Canada-Calgary - Alberta Chapter, 1128
Ovarian Cancer Canada-Western Regional Office, 1134
Paddle Alberta, 1136
Pakistan Canada Association of Calgary, 1137
Parkinson Alberta Society, 1141
Patronato INAS (Canada)-Calgary Office, 1145
The Pembina Institute, 1149
Petroleum Accountants Society of Canada, 1154
Petroleum Services Association of Canada, 1154
Petroleum Technology Alliance Canada, 1154
PFLAG Canada Inc.-Calgary Chapter, 1155
Poison & Drug Information Service, 1163
Polanie-Polish Song & Dance Association, 1163
Prairie Osteopathic Association, 1169
Prairie Region Halfway House Association, 1169
Prairie Saengerbund Choir Association, 1169
Prairieaction Foundation, 1170
Printing & Graphics Industries Association of Alberta, 1180
Professional Petroleum Data Management Association, 1186
Project Management Institute-Southern Alberta
Prospect Human Services, 1189
Public Service Alliance of Canada-Calgary Branch, 1193
Pumphouse Theatres Society, 1194
Quickdraw Animation Society, 1201
The Rainbow Society of Alberta-Calgary, 1203
Real Estate Council of Alberta, 1205
Real Estate Institute of Canada-Alberta - Calgary Chapter, 1205
REHOBOTH Christian Ministries-Calgary Branch, 1216
Risk & Insurance Management Society Inc., 1233
Risk & Insurance Management Society Inc.-Southern Alberta Chapter, 1234
Royal Alberta United Services Institute, 1237
Royal Astronomical Society of Canada-Calgary Centre, 1238
The Royal Canadian Legion-Alberta & NWT Command, 1240

Royal Danish Guards Association of Western Canada, 1242
The Royal Scottish Country Dance Society-Calgary Branch, 1587
SAIT Academic Faculty Association, 1251
Salers Association of Canada, 1251
Samaritan's Purse Canada, 1253
Schizophrenia Society of Alberta-Calgary & Area Chapter, 1283
Scouts Canada-Manitoba Council, 1286
Scouts Canada-Chinook Council, 1286
SEEDS Foundation, 1289
Seventh Step Society of Canada, 1292
Shaw Rocket Fund, 1295
Sheet Metal Contractors Association of Alberta, 1295
Shock Trauma Air Rescue Society, 1296
Ski Jumping Canada, 1302
Society for Technical Communication-Alberta Chapter, 1591
Society for the Study of Egyptian Antiquities-Calgary Chapter, 1327
Society for Treatment of Autism, 1327
Society of Graphic Designers of Canada-Alberta South Chapter, 1329
Society of Kabalarians of Canada-Calgary, 1329
Southern Alberta Brain Injury Society, 1337
Southern Alberta Curling Association, 1337
Southern Alberta Health Libraries Association, 1337
Southern Alberta Post Polio Support Society, 1337
Spina Bifida & Hydrocephalus Association of Southern Alberta, 1342
Spinal Cord Injury Alberta-Calgary, 1343
Springboard Dance, 1346
Squash Alberta, 1347
Starlight Starbright Children's Foundation Canada-Calgary Chapter, 1348
Taoist Tai Chi Society of Canada-Western Region, 1367
TEAM of Canada Inc., 1368
The Terry Fox Foundation-Alberta/NWT/Nunavut Office, 1372
TESL Canada Federation, 1372
Theatre Calgary, 1374
Thermal Insulation Association of Alberta, 1375
Tourism Calgary, 1389
Trail Riders of the Canadian Rockies, 1394
Trout Unlimited Canada, 1399
Twins, Triplets & More Association of Calgary, 1400
UNICEF Canada-UNICEF Alberta, 1404
Union of Calgary Co-op Employees, 1407
United Conservative Association, 1410
United Empire Loyalists' Association of Canada-Calgary Branch, 1410
United Nations Association in Canada-Calgary, 1411
United Nurses of Alberta-Southern Alberta Regional Office, 1412
United Utility Workers' Association, 1412
United Way of Calgary & Area, 1413
University of Calgary Faculty Association, 1419
The Van Horne Institute for International Transportation & Regulatory Affairs, 1424
Vecova Centre for Disability Services & Research, 1430
Western Association of Broadcast Engineers, 1447
Western Association of Broadcasters, 1447
Western Canada Tire Dealers Association, 1448
Western Hockey League, 1449
WinSport Canada, 1460
Women in a Home Office, 1460
Women in Film & Television Alberta, 1461
The World Job & Food Bank Inc., 1466
World Organization of Building Officials, 1466
Writers Guild of Alberta-Calgary Office, 1469
Wycliffe Bible Translators of Canada, Inc., 1470
YMCA Canada-YMCA Calgary, 1471
Youth Singers of Calgary, 1476

YWCA Canada-YWCA Calgary, 1481

Camrose
Alberta Genealogical Society-Camrose Branch, 36
Boys & Girls Clubs of Alberta-Camrose Boys & Girls Club, 221
Camrose & District Food Bank, 277
Camrose Arts Society, 277
Camrose Association for Community Living, 277
Camrose Chamber of Commerce, 277
Canadian Heartland Training Railway, 403
Canadian Northern Society, 441
Central Alberta Soccer Association, 523
College of Hearing Aid Practitioners of Alberta, 585
Habitat for Humanity Canada-Alberta - Camrose, 796
Kiwanis International (Western Canada District), 892
Schizophrenia Society of Alberta-Camrose & Area Chapter, 1283

Canmore
Alberta Alpine Ski Association, 22
Alberta Council for Environmental Education, 31
Alberta Municipal Clerks Association, 40
Alpine Club of Canada, 59
Association of Canadian Mountain Guides, 142
Banff World Television Festival Foundation, 196
Biathlon Canada, 207
Bow Valley Food Bank, 219
Canadian Association for Disabled Skiing - Alberta-Rocky Mountain Zone, 299
Canadian Association of Nordic Ski Instructors-Mountain Region - AB & NT, 323
Canadian Masters Cross-Country Ski Association-Alberta, 431
Canadian Mountain Arts Foundation, 437
Canmore Folk & Blues Club, 508
Cross Country Canada, 643
Malcolm Scottish Society, 927
National Winter Sports Association, 997
Tourism Canmore Kananaskis, 1389
The Trident Mediation Counselling & Support Foundation, 1398

Cardston
Cardston & District Chamber of Commerce, 511
Cardston Historical Society, 511

Caroline
Caroline & District Chamber of Commerce, 514

Carseland
Canadian Senior Pro Rodeo Association, 470

Carstairs
Carstairs & District Historical Society, 516
Carstairs Chamber of Commerce, 516

Carvel
Canadian Association of Veterans in United Nations Peacekeeping-Stony Plain Chapter, 336

Castor
Alberta Shorthorn Association, 46
Alliance for Canadian New Music Projects-Contemporary Showcase - East Central Alberta, 56

Clarence Creek
Township of Clarence Minor Hockey Association, 1393

Claresholm
Appaloosa Horse Club of Canada, 73
Claresholm & District Chamber of Commerce, 572

Coaldale
Coaldale & District Chamber of Commerce, 577
REHOBOTH Christian Ministries-Coaldale Branch, 1216
South Western Alberta Teachers' Convention Association, 1336

Geographic Index / Alberta - Cochrane

Cochrane
Alberta Association of Recreation Facility Personnel, 24
Alberta Orienteering Association, 41
Boys & Girls Clubs of Alberta-Boys & Girls Club of Cochrane and Area, 221
Canadian Recreation Facilities Council, 465
CNBC, 576
Cochrane & District Chamber of Commerce, 579
Community Futures Network Society of Alberta, 598
Outdoor Writers of Canada, 1133
Western Canada Water, 1448

Cold Lake
Alberta Dressage Association-Cold Lake Area Chapter, 33
Cold Lake Native Friendship Centre, 580
Cold Lake Regional Chamber of Commerce, 580
Lakeland United Way, 896

Consort
Consort & District Chamber of Commerce, 623

Coronation
Coronation Chamber of Commerce, 629

Cremona
Cremona Water Valley & District Chamber of Commerce, 641

Crossfield
Canadian Speckle Park Association, 489
Crossfield Chamber of Commerce, 644

Crowsnest Pass
Crowsnest Community Support Society, 644

DeBolt
DeBolt & District Pioneer Museum Society, 652

Delburne
Delburne & District Chamber of Commerce, 653

Derwent
Alberta Maine-Anjou Association, 39

Devon
Alberta Research Council Inc.-Devon Branch, 44
Devon & District Chamber of Commerce, 655
Edmonton Dental Assistants Association, 676

Didsbury
Didsbury & District Historical Society, 656
Didsbury Chamber of Commerce, 656
Holstein Canada-Alberta Branch, 819
Jersey Canada-West, 869
Mount View Special Riding Association, 976
Northwest Mennonite Conference, 1036

Drayton Valley
Beehive Support Services Association, 204
Canadian Ski Patrol-Drayton Valley - Mountain Division, 471
Drayton Valley & District Chamber of Commerce, 662
Tennessee Walking Horse Association of Western Canada, 1370

Drumheller
Badlands Historical Centre, 193
Drumheller & District Chamber of Commerce, 663

Eckville
Eckville & District Chamber of Commerce, 671

Edgerton
Edgerton & District Chamber of Commerce, 674
Edgerton & District Historical Society, 674

Edmonton
Aboriginal Multi-Media Society, 2
Action for Healthy Communities, 6
Action on Smoking & Health, 6
ADR Institute of Canada-ADR Institute of Alberta, 9
AIESEC-Edmonton, 18

Alberta & Northwest Territories Lung Association, 21
Alberta Agricultural Economics Association, 21
Alberta Alliance on Mental Illness & Mental Health, 21
Alberta Amateur Football Association, 22
Alberta Amateur Softball Association, 22
Alberta Amateur Wrestling Association, 22
Alberta Assessment Consortium, 22
Alberta Assessors' Association, 22
Alberta Association of Agricultural Societies, 23
Alberta Association of Architects, 23
Alberta Association of Fund Raising Executives, 23
Alberta Association of Insolvency & Restructuring Professionals, 23
Alberta Association of Landscape Architects, 23
Alberta Association of Library Technicians, 23
Alberta Association of Optometrists, 24
Alberta Association of Professional Paralegals, 24
Alberta Association of the Deaf, 25
Alberta Association of Travel Health Professionals, 25
Alberta Association on Gerontology, 25
Alberta Associations for Bright Children, 25
Alberta Aviation Museum Association, 25
Alberta Baton Twirling Association, 25
Alberta Beekeepers Commission, 26
Alberta Bicycle Association, 26
Alberta Biotechnology Association, 26
Alberta Bodybuilding Association, 26
Alberta Boilers Safety Association, 26
Alberta Bottle Depot Association, 26
Alberta Broomball Association, 26
Alberta Building Officials Association, 27
Alberta Camping Association, 27
Alberta Cancer Foundation, 27
Alberta Canola Producers Commission, 27
Alberta Catholic School Trustees Association, 27
Alberta Cerebral Palsy Sport Association, 27
Alberta Chamber of Resources, 28
Alberta Chambers of Commerce, 28
Alberta Cheerleading Association, 28
Alberta Chess Association, 28
Alberta Chicken Producers, 28
Alberta Civil Trial Lawyers' Association, 28
Alberta College & Association of Chiropractors, 28
Alberta College of Medical Diagnostic & Therapeutic Technologists, 29
Alberta College of Occupational Therapists, 29
Alberta College of Optometrists, 29
Alberta College of Pharmacists, 30
Alberta College of Social Workers, 30
Alberta College of Speech-Language Pathologists & Audiologists, 30
Alberta Colleges Athletic Conference, 30
Alberta Committee of Citizens with Disabilities, 30
Alberta Construction Association, 31
Alberta Construction Association-Edmonton Construction Association, 31
Alberta Construction Safety Association, 31
Alberta Continuing Care Association, 31
Alberta Council on Admissions & Transfer, 31
Alberta Council on Aging, 31
Alberta Craft Council, 32
Alberta Criminal Justice Association, 32
Alberta Cultural Society of the Deaf, 32
Alberta Curling Federation, 32
Alberta Dance Alliance, 32
Alberta Deaf Sports Association, 32
Alberta Dental Association & College, 32
Alberta Diabetes Foundation, 32
Alberta Dressage Association-Edmonton Area Chapter, 33
Alberta Environmental Network, 33
Alberta Farmers' Market Association, 34
Alberta Federation of Labour, 34
Alberta Federation of Police Associations, 34
Alberta Federation of Shooting Sports, 35
Alberta Fencing Association, 35
Alberta Fish & Game Association, 35

Alberta Forest Products Association, 35
Alberta Foster Parent Association, 35
Alberta Foundation for the Arts, 35
Alberta Funeral Services Regulatory Board, 36
Alberta Genealogical Society, 36
Alberta Genealogical Society-Edmonton Branch, 36
Alberta Gerontological Nurses Association, 37
Alberta Greenhouse Growers Association, 37
Alberta Historical Resources Foundation, 37
Alberta Hotel & Lodging Association, 38
Alberta Innovates, 38
Alberta Institute of Agrologists, 38
Alberta Insurance Council, 38
Alberta Lake Management Society, 39
Alberta Land Surveyors' Association, 39
Alberta Law Reform Institute, 39
Alberta Liberal Party, 39
Alberta Library Trustees Association, 39
Alberta Media Production Industries Association, 39
Alberta Medical Association, 40
Alberta Men's Wear Agents Association, 40
Alberta Milk, 40
Alberta Motor Association, 40
Alberta Museums Association, 40
Alberta Music Industry Association, 41
Alberta Native Friendship Centres Association, 41
Alberta Native Plant Council, 41
Alberta Northern Lights Wheelchair Basketball Society, 41
Alberta Occupational Health Nurses Association, 41
Alberta Party, 42
Alberta Pharmacists' Association (RxA), 42
Alberta Pioneer Railway Association, 42
Alberta Pork, 42
Alberta Professional Planners Institute, 43
Alberta Provincial Council, 43
Alberta Public Health Association, 43
Alberta Public Housing Administrators' Association, 43
Alberta Ready Mixed Concrete Association, 43
Alberta Recreation & Parks Association, 44
Alberta Registered Music Teachers' Association, 44
Alberta Research Council Inc., 44
Alberta Restorative Justice Association, 44
Alberta Roadbuilders & Heavy Construction Association, 44
Alberta Rowing Association, 45
Alberta Rugby Football Union, 45
Alberta Safety Council, 45
Alberta School Boards Association, 45
Alberta School Councils' Association, 45
Alberta School Learning Commons Council, 45
Alberta Schools' Athletic Association, 46
Alberta Senior Citizens' Housing Association, 46
Alberta Snowmobile Association, 47
Alberta Soccer Association, 47
Alberta Society for the Prevention of Cruelty to Animals, 47
Alberta Society of Radiologists, 47
Alberta Sport Connection, 48
Alberta Sport Parachuting Association, 48
Alberta Sprint Racing Canoe Association, 48
Alberta Summer Swimming Association, 48
Alberta Table Tennis Association, 48
Alberta Taekwondo Association, 49
Alberta Teachers of English as a Second Language, 49
Alberta Teachers' Association, 49
Alberta Team Handball Federation, 49
Alberta Tennis Association, 49
Alberta Triathlon Association, 50
Alberta Turkey Producers, 50
Alberta Ukrainian Dance Association, 50
Alberta Underwater Council, 50
Alberta Union of Provincial Employees, 50
Alberta Urban Municipalities Association, 50
Alberta Veterinary Medical Association, 50
Alberta Veterinary Technologist Association, 50
Alberta Wall & Ceiling Association, 51

Alberta Water & Wastewater Operators Association, 51
Alberta Water Council, 51
Alberta Weekly Newspapers Association, 51
Alberta Whitewater Association, 52
Alberta Women Entrepreneurs, 52
Alcoholics Anonymous-Edmonton - AA Central Office, 52
ALIGN Association of Community Services, 54
Allergy/Asthma Information Association-AAIA Prairies/NWT/Nunavut, 54
Alliance Française d'Edmonton, 57
Alpaca Livestock Producers & Cooperators Association, 59
ALS Society of Alberta-Edmonton Chapter, 60
Alzheimer Society of Alberta & Northwest Territories, 61
Alzheimer Society of Alberta & Northwest Territories-Edmonton & Area Chapter, 61
American Society of Heating, Refrigerating & Air Conditioning Engineers-Northern Alberta Chapter, 1500
The Anglican Church of Canada-Diocese of Edmonton, 69
Apeetogosan (Metis) Development Inc., 73
Archaeological Society of Alberta, 76
L'Arche Western Region-L'Arche Edmonton, 78
Architectural Woodwork Manufacturers Association of Canada, 79
Architectural Woodwork Manufacturers Association of Canada - Northern Alberta, 79
Archives Society of Alberta, 80
ARMA Canada-Edmonton Chapter, 82
Army, Navy & Air Force Veterans in Canada-Alberta Provincial Command, 83
Association canadienne-française de l'Alberta, 96
Association for Financial Professionals - Edmonton, 133
Association of Academic Staff - University of Alberta, 138
Association of Canadian Travel Agents - Alberta & NWT, 144
Association of Early Childhood Educators of Alberta, 147
Association of Independent Schools & Colleges in Alberta, 149
Association of Parliamentary Libraries in Canada, 155
Association of Polish Engineers in Canada-Edmonton Branch, 156
Association of Professional Engineers & Geoscientists of Alberta, 157
Association of Quantity Surveyors of Alberta, 160
Association of School Business Officials of Alberta, 161
Association of Science & Engineering Technology Professionals of Alberta, 162
Association of Sign Language Interpreters of Alberta, 162
Association of the Chemical Profession of Alberta, 162
Association of Translators & Interpreters of Alberta, 163
Association of University Forestry Schools of Canada, 163
Athabasca University Students' Union, 180
Athletics Alberta, 181
Aviation Alberta, 190
Baptist General Conference of Canada, 196
Baptist General Conference of Canada-Baptist General Conference in Alberta (BGCA), 196
Baseball Alberta, 198
Basketball Alberta, 198
Beaumont Coin Discovery Group, 203
Beaverhill Bird Observatory, 203
Better Business Bureau of Central & Northern Alberta, 206
Big Brothers Big Sisters of Alberta-Big Brothers Big Sisters of Edmonton & Area, 209
BMW Clubs Canada-Northern Alberta BMW Club, 216
Book Publishers Association of Alberta, 218
Bowling Federation of Alberta, 219

Geographic Index / Alberta - Edmonton

Boxing Alberta, 220
Boyle Street Community Services, 221
Boys & Girls Clubs of Alberta, 221
Boys & Girls Clubs of Alberta-Boys & Girls Clubs of Edmonton & Area, 221
Brain Care Centre, 225
Brian Webb Dance Co., 228
Building Industry & Land Development Alberta, 262
Building Industry & Land Development Alberta-Edmonton Region, 262
Building Owners & Managers Association of Edmonton, 263
BullyingCanada Inc.-Alberta Office, 264
Butler Family Foundation, 267
Canada's National Firearms Association, 282
Canadian Academy of the History of Pharmacy, 287
Canadian Aerial Applicators Association, 288
Canadian Assembly of Narcotics Anonymous, 296
Canadian Association for Disabled Skiing - Alberta, 299
Canadian Association for Disabled Skiing - Alberta-Edmonton Zone, 299
Canadian Association for the Study of the Liver, 306
Canadian Association for Williams Syndrome-CAWS - Alberta, 307
Canadian Association of Blue Cross Plans-Alberta Blue Cross, 309
Canadian Association of Critical Care Nurses-Greater Edmonton Chapter, 311
Canadian Association of Elizabeth Fry Societies-Elizabeth Fry Society of Edmonton, 313
Canadian Association of Medical Teams Abroad, 321
Canadian Association of Slavists, 333
Canadian Association of Veterans in United Nations Peacekeeping-Edmonton Chapter, 336
Canadian Authors Association-Edmonton (Alberta Branch), 338
Canadian Bible Society-North Alberta District Office, 343
Canadian Bible Society-South Alberta District Office, 343
Canadian Blood Services-Edmonton, 344
Canadian Celiac Association-Edmonton Chapter, 352
Canadian Children's Book Centre-Edmonton, 356
Canadian Circumpolar Institute, 357
Canadian College of Emergency Medical Services, 358
Canadian College of Neuropsychopharmacology, 360
Canadian Committee on Labour History, 361
Canadian Condominium Institute-CCI-North Alberta Chapter, 362
The Canadian Corps of Commissionaires-Northern Alberta, Northwest Territories & Nunavut Division, 365
Canadian Council on Africa-Western Office, 370
Canadian Culinary Federation-Edmonton Branch, 374
Canadian Energy Workers' Association, 381
Canadian Federation of AME Associations-Western AME Association, 385
Canadian Fence Industry Association-Western, 389
Canadian Friends of the Hebrew University-Edmonton Chapter, 395
Canadian Hard of Hearing Association-Alberta - Edmonton Branch, 400
Canadian Hemophilia Society-Alberta Chapter, 404
Canadian Information Processing Society-Alberta Chapter, 411
Canadian Institute of Management-Alberta - Northern & NWT Branch, 417
Canadian Institute of Plumbing & Heating-Edmonton, Alberta, Region, 418
Canadian Institute of Ukrainian Studies, 420
Canadian Land Reclamation Association, 425
Canadian Manufacturers & Exporters-Alberta Division, 429
Canadian Masonry Contractors' Association-Masonry Contractors' Association of Alberta, Northern Region, 431
Canadian Meat Science Association, 432
Canadian Mental Health Association-Alberta Division, 434
Canadian Militaria Preservation Society, 436
Canadian National Institute for the Blind-Alberta-Northwest Territories Division, 439
Canadian Native Friendship Centre, 440
Canadian Obesity Network, 444
Canadian Office & Professional Employees Union-Region 3 - Local 458, 445
Canadian Orthopaedic Nurses Association, 448
Canadian Orthopractic Manual Therapy Association, 448
Canadian Parks & Wilderness Society-Edmonton - Northern Alberta Chapter, 451
Canadian Patient Safety Institute, 452
Canadian Pension & Benefits Institute-Northern Alberta Region, 453
Canadian Physiological Society, 454
Canadian Polish Congress-Alberta Branch, 456
The Canadian Press-Edmonton Bureau, 459
Canadian Public Relations Society Inc.-CPRS Edmonton, 463
Canadian Search Dog Association, 469
Canadian Society for Pharmaceutical Sciences, 477
Canadian Society of Association Executives-Edmonton Chapter, 480
Canadian Society of Gastroenterology Nurses & Associates-Edmonton Chapter, 483
Canadian Society of Orthopaedic Technologists-Northtechs Chapter, 485
Canadian Society of Patristic Studies, 486
Canadian Standards Association-Western Region, 490
Canadian Union of Public Employees-Alberta Division, 498
Canadian Welding Bureau-Alberta Region, 503
Candora Society of Edmonton, 508
Caregivers Alberta, 512
Castor Fish & Game Association, 517
Catalyst Theatre Society of Alberta, 517
Centre for International Business Studies, 533
The Centre for Israel & Jewish Affairs-Jewish Federation of Edmonton, 533
Change for Children Association, 551
Chartered Accountants' Education Foundation of Alberta, 552
Chartered Professional Accountants of Alberta-Edmonton Office, 552
Cheer Canada, 555
Child & Youth Care Association of Alberta, 558
Children's Heart Society, 562
Children's Wish Foundation of Canada-Alberta & N.W.T. Chapter - Edmonton, 562
Chinese Medicine & Acupuncture Association of Canada-Alberta Chapter, 565
Choir Alberta, 566
Christian Health Association of Alberta, 567
Christian Labour Association of Canada-Edmonton Regional Office, 567
Chronic Pain Association of Canada, 568
Clean Air Strategic Alliance, 572
Coalition des femmes de l'Alberta, 577
The College & Association of Registered Nurses of Alberta, 581
College of Alberta Denturists, 582
College of Alberta Professional Foresters, 582
College of Alberta Psychologists, 582
College of Dental Technologists of Alberta, 583
College of Dietitians of Alberta, 584
College of Family Physicians of Canada-Alberta College of Family Physicians, 584
College of Licensed Practical Nurses of Alberta, 585
College of Medical Laboratory Technologists of Alberta, 586
College of Opticians of Alberta, 587
College of Physicians & Surgeons of Alberta, 588
College of Registered Dental Hygienists of Alberta, 589
College of Registered Psychiatric Nurses of Alberta, 589
Commonwealth Association of Museums, 593
Communist Party of Canada (Alberta), 594
Community of Christ - Canada West Mission, 607
Community Planning Association of Alberta, 607
Compass Centre for Sexual Wellness, 608
Confederation of Alberta Faculty Associations, 611
Connect Society - D.E.A.F. Services, 613
Conseil national Société de Saint-Vincent de Paul-Edmonton, 619
Construction Labour Relations - An Alberta Association-Edmonton Office, 624
Construction Owners Association of Alberta, 624
Consulting Engineers of Alberta, 625
Cornerstone Counselling Society of Edmonton, 628
Cosmopolitan Music Society, 631
Council for Advancement of Native Development Officers, 632
The Council of Canadians-Prairies, 633
Couples for Christ Canada-Couples for Christ Edmonton, 636
Covenant Foundation, 637
Covenant Health, 637
The CPR Stockholder's Society, 638
Credit Counselling Society-Edmonton, 640
Cross Country Alberta, 643
Darts Alberta, 651
Development & Peace-Alberta/Mackenzie, 654
Canadian Diabetes Association-Edmonton & District Branch, 655
Downtown Business Association of Edmonton, 661
Ducks Unlimited Canada-Alberta Provincial Office, 664
Economics Society of Northern Alberta, 673
Edmonton & District Council of Churches, 675
Edmonton & District Labour Council, 675
Edmonton (Alberta) Nerve Pain Association, 675
Edmonton Aboriginal Senior Centre, 675
Edmonton Arts Council, 675
Edmonton Association of the Deaf, 675
Edmonton Bicycle & Touring Club, 675
Edmonton CFA Society, 675
Edmonton Chamber Music Society, 675
Edmonton Chamber of Commerce, 675
Edmonton Chamber of Voluntary Organizations, 676
Edmonton Classical Guitar Society, 676
Edmonton Combative Sports Commission, 676
Edmonton Community Foundation, 676
Edmonton Community Legal Centre, 676
Edmonton Community Networks, 676
Edmonton Composers' Concert Society, 676
Edmonton Construction Association, 676
Edmonton Czech Language Society, 676
Edmonton District Soccer Association, 677
Edmonton Economic Development Corporation, 677
Edmonton Economic Development Corporation-Edmonton Tourism, 677
Edmonton Epilepsy Association, 677
Edmonton Executives Association, 677
Edmonton Federation of Community Leagues, 677
Edmonton Fire Fighters Union, 677
Edmonton Folk Music Festival, 677
Edmonton Heritage Festival Association, 677
Edmonton Humane Society for the Prevention of Cruelty to Animals, 677
Edmonton Immigrant Services Association, 677
Edmonton Inner City Housing Society, 677
Edmonton Insurance Association, 678
Edmonton Interdistrict Youth Soccer Association, 678
Edmonton International Baseball Foundation, 678
Edmonton International Film Festival Society, 678
Edmonton Japanese Community Association, 678
Edmonton Jazz Society, 678
Edmonton Kiwanis Music Festival, 678
Edmonton Law Libraries Association, 678
Edmonton Minor Soccer Association, 678
Edmonton Motor Dealers' Association, 678
Edmonton Musicians' Association, 678
Edmonton Numismatic Society, 678
Edmonton Opera Association, 678
Edmonton Police Association, 678
Edmonton Radial Railway Society, 679
Edmonton Reptile & Amphibian Society, 679
Edmonton Social Planning Council, 679
Edmonton Space & Science Foundation, 679
Edmonton Stamp Club, 679
Edmonton Symphony Orchestra, 679
Edmonton Twin & Triplet Club, 679
Edmonton Weavers' Guild, 679
Edmonton Youth Orchestra Association, 679
Edmonton's Food Bank, 680
Electrical Contractors Association of Alberta, 682
Embroiderers' Association of Canada, Inc.-Alberta - Edmonton Needlecraft Guild, 685
Emil Skarin Fund, 686
EmployAbilities, 686
Enokhok Development Corporation Ltd., 689
Entomological Society of Alberta, 690
The Environmental Law Centre (Alberta) Society, 692
Environmental Services Association of Alberta, 692
Evangelical Lutheran Church in Canada-Synod of Alberta & the Territories, 698
Evangelical Tract Distributors, 699
Family & Community Support Services Association of Alberta, 702
Fédération des aînés Franco-Albertains, 711
Fédération des parents francophones de l'Alberta, 717
Fellowship of Evangelical Baptist Churches in Canada-Fellowship Prairies, 731
Film & Video Arts Society Alberta, 735
Food Beverage Canada, 749
Foresters-Edmonton, 751
Fort Edmonton Foundation, 752
FPInnovations-Edmonton Division, 757
Francophonie jeunesse de l'Alberta, 757
Friends of Devonian Botanic Garden, 761
Friends of the Third World, 763
Friends of the Ukrainian Village Society, 763
FunTeam Alberta, 765
Gem & Mineral Federation of Canada-Alberta Federation of Rock Clubs, 768
Geological Association of Canada-Edmonton Section, 770
Geotechnical Society of Edmonton, 771
German Canadian Cultural Association, 772
German-Canadian Association of Alberta, 772
Girl Guides of Canada-Guides du Canada-Alberta, Northwest Territories & Yukon Council, 773
Global, Environmental & Outdoor Education Council, 775
Goodwill Industries of Alberta, 778
Grant MacEwan College Faculty Association, 782
Greater Edmonton Library Association, 783
Greenpeace Canada-Edmonton Office, 789
Habitat for Humanity Canada-Alberta - Edmonton, 796
Health Law Institute, 806
Health Sciences Association of Alberta, 807
Heart & Stroke Foundation of Alberta, NWT & Nunavut-Edmonton Office, 808
Hindu Society of Alberta, 815

Geographic Index / Alberta - Edson

Historical Society of Alberta-Edmonton & District Historical Society, 816
HIV Network of Edmonton Society, 816
Hong Kong-Canada Business Association-Edmonton Section Office, 820
Hope Studies Central, 821
Huntington Society of Canada-Northern Alberta Resource Centre, 828
Hussar Fish & Game Association, 828
Inclusion Alberta, 831
InScribe Christian Writers' Fellowship, 839
Inside Education, 839
Institute for Stuttering Treatment & Research & the Communication Improvement Program, 844
Institute for the Advancement of Aboriginal Women, 844
Institute of Health Economics, 846
Insurance Brokers Association of Canada-Insurance Brokers Association of Alberta, 848
Insurance Bureau of Canada-Alberta & the North, 849
Insurance Institute of Northern Alberta, 849
Interior Designers of Alberta, 852
International Brotherhood of Boilermakers, Iron Ship Builders, Blacksmiths, Forgers & Helpers (AFL-CIO)-Edmonton (Lodge 146)
International Personnel Management Association - Canada-Alberta & North Chapter, 859
Italian Cultural Society of Edmonton, 867
Jewish Family Services Edmonton, 871
John Howard Society of Alberta, 874
John Howard Society of Alberta-Edmonton, 874
Judo Alberta, 875
Junior Achievement of Canada-Junior Achievement of Northern Alberta & Northwest Territories, 877
Junior League of Edmonton, 878
Juvenile Diabetes Research Foundation-Edmonton, 879
The Kidney Foundation of Canada-Northern Alberta & The Territories Branch, 885
Kids First Parent Association of Canada, 886
Kids Kottage Foundation, 886
KidSport Alberta, 886
Landscape Alberta Nursery Trades Association, 898
Last Post Fund-Alberta Branch, 899
Law Society of Alberta-Edmonton Office, 901
Lawn Bowls Association of Alberta, 902
Learning Disabilities Association of Alberta, 903
Learning Disabilities Association of Alberta-Edmonton Chapter, 904
Legal Aid Society of Alberta, 906
Legal Education Society of Alberta, 906
The Leukemia & Lymphoma Society of Canada-Prairies/Territories Branch - Edmonton, 909
Liberal Party of Canada in Alberta, 909
Lieutenant Governor's Circle on Mental Health & Addiction, 910
Lifesaving Society-Alberta & North West Territories Branch, 911
The Lithuanian Society of Edmonton, 915
Little Bits Therapeutic Riding Association, 915
Living Positive, 915
LUE-42 Enterprises, 920
Lutheran Association of Missionaries & Pilots, 922
Lutheran Church - Canada-Alberta-British Columbia District, 922
MacEwan Staff Association, 924
Madonna House Apostolate-Edmonton, 925
Mahatma Gandhi Canadian Foundation for World Peace, 925
McMan Youth, Family & Community Services Association, 955
Meeting Professionals International-Greater Edmonton Chapter, 1571
Memorial Society of Edmonton & District, 960
Merit Contractors Association of Alberta, 962
Métis Child & Family Services Society (Edmonton), 962

Métis Nation of Alberta, 963
Métis Nation of Alberta-Regional Office - Zone 4, 963
Métis Settlements General Council, 963
Mill Woods Society for Community Living, 965
Motor Dealers' Association of Alberta, 975
The M.S.I. Foundation, 978
Multiple Sclerosis Society of Canada-Alberta & Northwest Territories Division, 980
The Muttart Foundation, 986
NACE International-Canadian Region - Edmonton Section, 1572
National Council of Jewish Women of Canada-Edmonton Section, 992
Native Counselling Services of Alberta, 997
Natural Gas Employees' Association, 998
Natural Health Practitioners of Canada, 998
Natural Health Practitioners of Canada Association, 999
Nature Alberta, 999
New Democratic Party-Alberta NDP, 1014
Non-Academic Staff Association for the University of Alberta, 1028
North American Waterfowl Management Plan-Arctic Goose Joint Venture (AGJV), 1029
North American Waterfowl Management Plan-Prairie Habitat Joint Venture (PHJV), 1029
North Saskatchewan Watershed Alliance, 1032
Northern Alberta Curling Association, 1034
Northern Alberta Health Libraries Association, 1034
Northern Alberta Institute of Technology Academic Staff Association, 1034
Old Strathcona Foundation, 1056
Orchid Soceity of Alberta, 1119
Pain Society of Alberta, 1137
Pakistan Canada Association of Edmonton, 1137
Paralympic Sports Association (Alberta), 1138
Parkinson Alberta Society-Edmonton Office, 1141
Patronato INAS (Canada)-Edmonton Office, 1145
Pax Natura Society for Rehabilitation of the Deaf, 1146
PBA Society of Alberta, 1146
PBA Society of Atlantic, 1146
PBA Society of Canada, 1146
PBA Society of Ontario, 1146
The Pembina Institute-Edmonton Office, 1149
Pentecostal Assemblies of Canada-Alberta & Northwest Territories Office, 1150
Pet Therapy Society of Northern Alberta, 1153
Petroleum Tank Management Association of Alberta, 1154
PFLAG Canada Inc.-Edmonton Chapter, 1155
Pharmacy Technician Society of Alberta, 1157
Physical Culture Association of Alberta, 1158
Physiotherapy Alberta - College + Association, 1158
Pool & Hot Tub Council of Canada-Alberta Chapter, 1165
Poplar Council of Canada, 1165
Prader-Willi Syndrome Association of Alberta, 1169
Pride Centre of Edmonton, 1170
Princess Patricia's Canadian Light Infantry Association, 1180
Pro Coro Canada, 1181
Professional Association of Residents of Alberta, 1182
The Professional Institute of the Public Service of Canada-Alberta & Northwest Territories Regional Office, 1185
Project Adult Literacy Society, 1187
Project Management Institute-Northern Alberta
Provincial Fitness Unit of Alberta, 1191
Provincial Health Ethics Network, 1191
Psychologists Association of Alberta, 1192
Public School Boards' Association of Alberta, 1193
Public Service Alliance of Canada-Edmonton Branch, 1193

The Rainbow Society of Alberta, 1203
Realtors Association of Edmonton, 1206
Recreation Vehicle Dealers Association of Canada-Recreation Vehicle Dealers Association of Alberta, 1208
Réseau santé albertain, 1225
Rhythmic Gymnastics Alberta, 1229
Richard Eaton Singers, 1229
Ringette Alberta, 1232
Royal Astronomical Society of Canada-Edmonton Centre, 1238
Russian Orthodox Church in Canada, 1244
St. John Ambulance-Alberta Council, 1249
The Salvation Army in Canada-Edmonton - Alberta & Northern Territories Division, 1253
Saskatchewan Nursery Landscape Association, 1270
Schizophrenia Society of Alberta-Edmonton & Area Chapter, 1283
Scouts Canada-Northern Lights Council, 1287
Sculptors' Association of Alberta, 1287
Seniors Association of Greater Edmonton, 1290
Serena Canada-Alberta Branch, 1290
Sexual Assault Centre of Edmonton, 1292
Shock Trauma Air Rescue Society-Edmonton Base, 1296
Sickle Cell Foundation of Alberta, 1298
Sierra Club of Canada-Prairie Chapter, 1298
Skate Canada-Alberta/NWT/Nunavut Section, 1301
Skills/Compétences Canada-Alberta, 1302
The Society for Safe & Caring Schools & Communities, 1326
Society of Graphic Designers of Canada-Alberta North Chapter, 1329
Society of Kabalarians of Canada-Edmonton, 1329
Solbrekken Evangelistic Association of Canada, 1332
Special Olympics Alberta, 1339
Spina Bifida & Hydrocephalus Association of Northern Alberta, 1342
Spinal Cord Injury Alberta, 1342
Sport Medicine Council of Alberta, 1344
Strathcona Coin Discovery Group, 1351
Stroll of Poets Society, 1352
Student Legal Services of Edmonton, 1352
Supply Chain Management Association - Alberta, 1355
Swim Alberta, 1358
Synchro Alberta, 1360
Telephone Historical Centre, 1369
Theatre Alberta Society, 1373
Theatre Network (1975) Society, 1374
Toxics Watch Society of Alberta, 1394
Trans Canada Yellowhead Highway Association, 1394
Ukrainian Canadian Congress-Alberta Provincial Council, 1402
Ukrainian Orthodox Church of Canada-Western Eparchy, 1403
Ukrainian Women's Association of Canada, 1403
Ukrainian Youth Association of Canada-Edmonton Branch, 1404
Uncles & Aunts at Large, 1404
UNIFOR-Edmonton, 1405
UNITE HERE Canada, 1408
UNITE HERE Canada-Edmonton-Calgary Chapter, 1408
United Church of Canada-Alberta & Northwest Conference, 1409
United Empire Loyalists' Association of Canada-Edmonton Branch, 1410
United Nations Association in Canada-Edmonton, 1411
United Nurses of Alberta, 1412
United Way of the Alberta Capital Region, 1417
University of Alberta Library & Information Studies Alumni Association, 1419
University of Alberta South East Asian Students' Association, 1419
University of Alberta Students' Union, 1419
Urban & Regional Information Systems Association-URISA Alberta, 1601

Urban Development Institute Greater Edmonton Chapter, 1422
Variety Club of Northern Alberta, Tent 63, 1430
Vegetarians of Alberta Association, 1430
Vinok Worldance, 1435
Voice for Animals Humane Society, 1436
Volleyball Alberta, 1437
Volunteer Alberta, 1438
Water Ski & Wakeboard Alberta, 1441
Western Boreal Growth & Yield Association, 1447
Western Independent Adjusters' Association, 1450
Wheelchair Sports Alberta, 1452
Wilberforce Project, 1453
Wildrose Polio Support Society, 1455
The Writers' Guild of Alberta, 1469
YMCA Canada-YMCA of Northern Alberta - Edmonton, 1471
Yoga Association of Alberta, 1473
Young Alberta Book Society, 1474
Youth Empowerment & Support Services, 1475
YWCA Canada-YWCA Edmonton, 1481

Edson
Boys & Girls Clubs of Alberta-Boys & Girls Club of Edson & District, 221
Echo-Edson Cultural Heritage Organization, 671
Edson & District Chamber of Commerce, 680
Edson Friendship Centre, 680
Supporting Choices of People Edson, 1356

Elk Point
Elk Point Chamber of Commerce, 685

Entwistle
West Central Forage Association, 1444

Evansburg
Evansburg & Entwistle Chamber of Commerce, 699

Fairview
Fairview & District Chamber of Commerce, 701
Peace Country Beef & Forage Association, 1147

Falher
Falher Chamber of Commerce, 701
Falher Friendship Corner Association, 701
Smoky Applied Research & Demonstration Association, 1304
Smoky River Regional Chamber of Commerce, 1305

Fawcett
Alberta Clydesdale & Shire Association, 28

Foremost
Foremost & District Chamber of Commerce, 751

Forestburg
Battle River Research Group, 199

Fort MacLeod
Fort Macleod & District Chamber of Commerce, 752
Fort Macleod Historical Association, 752

Fort McMurray
Alberta Construction Association-Fort McMurray Construction Association, 31
Alberta Genealogical Society-Fort McMurray Branch, 36
Alzheimer Society of Alberta & Northwest Territories-Fort McMurray - Wood Buffalo Chapter, 61
Boys & Girls Clubs of Alberta-Fort McMurray Boys & Girls Club, 221
Christian Labour Association of Canada-Fort McMurray Regional Office, 568
Cumulative Environmental Management Association, 646
Fort McMurray Association for Community Living, 752
Fort McMurray Chamber of Commerce, 753
Fort McMurray Historical Society, 753

Fort McMurray Realtors Association, 753
Fort McMurray Society for the Prevention of Cruelty to Animals, 753
Fort McMurray Youth Soccer Association, 753
Habitat for Humanity Canada-Alberta - Wood Buffalo, 796
Keyano College Faculty Association, 884
Nistawoyou Association Friendship Centre, 1027
Northeastern Alberta Aboriginal Business Association, 1034
The Salvation Army START Program, 1253
United Way of Fort McMurray, 1414
Wood Buffalo Environmental Association, 1463
Wood Buffalo Food Bank, 1463
YMCA Canada-YMCA of Northern Alberta - Wood Buffalo, 1473

Fort Saskatchewan
American Saddlebred Horse Association of Alberta, 66
Boys & Girls Clubs of Alberta-Boys & Girls Club of Fort Saskatchewan, 221
Fort Saskatchewan Chamber of Commerce, 753
Fort Saskatchewan Fish & Game Association, 754
Fort Saskatchewan Historical Society, 754
Fort Saskatchewan Minor Sports Association, 754
Tri-County Soccer Association, 1398

Fort Vermilion
Fort Vermilion & Area Board of Trade, 754
Mackenzie Applied Research Assciation, 924

Fox Creek
Fox Creek Chamber of Commerce, 756

Gibbons
Bon Accord/Gibbons Food Bank, 217

Grande Cache
Grande Cache Chamber of Commerce, 780

Grande Prairie
Alberta Construction Association-Grande Prairie Construction Association, 31
Alberta Genealogical Society-Grande Prairie & District Branch, 36
Alzheimer Society of Alberta & Northwest Territories-Grande Prairie Chapter, 61
Army Cadet League of Canada-Alberta Branch, 83
Building Industry & Land Development Alberta-Grande Prairie Region, 262
Canadian Institute of Food Science & Technology-Alberta Section, 415
Grande Prairie & Area Association of Realtors, 781
Grande Prairie & District Association for Persons with Developmental Disabilities, 781
Grande Prairie & District Chamber of Commerce, 781
Grande Prairie & Region United Way, 781
Grande Prairie Food Bank, 781
Grande Prairie Friendship Centre, 781
Grande Prairie Museum, 781
Grande Prairie Regional College Academic Staff Association, 781
Grande Prairie Society for the Prevention of Cruelty to Animals, 781
Heart & Stroke Foundation of Alberta, NWT & Nunavut-Grande Prairie Office, 808
Historical Society of Alberta-Peace Country Historical Society, 816
HIV North Society, 817
John Howard Society of Alberta-Grande Prairie, 874
Northwest Peace Soccer Association, 1036
Parkinson Alberta Society-Grande Prairie Office, 1141
Peace Area Riding for the Disabled, 1146
Peace Curling Association, 1147
Peace Parkland Naturalists, 1147
The Rainbow Society of Alberta-Grande Prairie Office, 1203

REHOBOTH Christian Ministries-Grande Prairie Branch, 1217
Shock Trauma Air Rescue Society-Grande Prairie Base, 1296
Spinal Cord Injury Alberta-Grande Prairie, 1343
United Way Alberta Northwest, 1412
Wolverines Wheelchair Sports Association, 1460

Grimshaw
Grimshaw & District Chamber of Commerce, 790

Hanna
Hanna & District Chamber of Commerce, 803
Hanna Museum & Pioneer Village, 803

Hardisty
Alberta Hereford Association, 37

High Level
High Level & District Chamber of Commerce, 814
High Level Native Friendship Centre, 814

High Prairie
High Prairie & Area Chamber of Commerce, 814
High Prairie Association for Community Living, 814
High Prairie Native Friendship Centre, 814
Marigold Enterprises Rehabilitation Services Society, 949
Peace Country Beef & Forage Association-High Prairie Office, 1147

High River
Calgary Catholic Immigration Society-Foothills Community Immigrant Services, 271
High River & District Chamber of Commerce, 814

Hinton
Alberta West Realtors' Association, 51
Community Futures West Yellowhead, 598
Foothills Research Institute, 751
Hinton & District Chamber of Commerce, 815
Hinton Friendship Centre, 815
HIV West Yellowhead Society, 817
Medical Group Management Association of Canada, 958
Yellowhead Emergency Shelter for Women Society, 1470

Holden
Alberta Square & Round Dance Federation, 48

Hythe
Grande Prairie Soaring Society, 781

Iddesleigh
Rainy Hills Historical Society, 1204

Innisfail
Canadian Cutting Horse Association, 375
Innisfail & District Chamber of Commerce, 839
McMan Youth, Family & Community Services Association-Central Alberta, 956

Irma
Irma & District Chamber of Commerce, 864
Irma Fish & Game Association, 864

Jasper
Jasper Environmental Association, 869
Jasper Park Chamber of Commerce, 869

Kelsey
Alberta Farm Fresh Producers Association, 34

Killam
Killam & District Chamber of Commerce, 887

La Crete
La Crete & Area Chamber of Commerce, 642

Lac La Biche
Lac La Biche & District Chamber of Commerce, 894
Lac La Biche Canadian Native Friendship Centre, 894

Lac La Biche Disability Services, 894
Métis Nation of Alberta-Regional Office - Zone 1, 963

Lacombe
Lacombe & District Chamber of Commerce, 895
Lacombe Handicraft & Lapidary Guild, 895
Trail Riding Alberta Conference, 1394
Wild Rose Agricultural Producers, 1454

Lake Newell Resort
Alberta Educational Facilities Administrators Association, 33

Langdon
Langdon & District Chamber of Commerce, 898

Leduc
Agricultural Research & Extension Council of Alberta, 15
Alberta Texas Longhorn Association, 50
Association of Alberta Coordinated Action for Recycling Enterprises, 139
Battle River Soccer Association, 200
Boys & Girls Clubs of Alberta-Boys & Girls Club of Leduc, 221
Canadian Brown Swiss & Braunvieh Association-Alberta Braunveih Association, 347
Council of Catholic School Superintendents of Alberta, 633
Leduc & District Food Bank Association, 906
Leduc Regional Chamber of Commerce, 906
Model Aeronautics Association of Canada Inc.-Alberta Zone, 970
Wetaskiwin Chamber of Commerce, 1451

Legal
Legal & District Chamber of Commerce, 906

Lethbridge
Alberta 5 Pin Bowlers' Association, 21
Alberta Construction Association-Lethbridge Construction Association, 31
Alberta Dressage Association-Chinook Country Chapter, 33
Alberta Falconry Association, 34
Alberta Genealogical Society-Lethbridge & District Branch, 36
Alberta Irrigation Projects Association, 38
Alberta Metallic Silhouette Association, 40
Alzheimer Society of Alberta & Northwest Territories-Lethbridge & Area Chapter, 61
Archaeological Society of Alberta-Lethbridge Centre, 76
L'Arche Western Region-L'Arche Lethbridge, 78
Association for Canadian & Québec Literatures, 132
Birthright International-Lethbridge Chapter, 212
Blankets for Canada Society Inc., 214
Boys & Girls Clubs of Alberta-Boys & Girls Club of Lethbridge & District, 221
Building Industry & Land Development Alberta-Lethbridge Region, 262
Canadian Association of Geographers-Western Division, 316
Canadian Blood Services-Lethbridge, 344
Canadian Culinary Federation-Lethbridge Branch, 374
Canadian Hard of Hearing Association-Alberta - Lethbridge Branch, 400
Canadian Tenpin Federation, Inc., 493
Canadian Water Resources Association, 503
Chinook Regional Hospital Foundation, 565
Community Foundation of Lethbridge & Southwestern Alberta, 597
Conseil national Société de Saint-Vincent de Paul-Western Regional Council, 619
Farming Smarter, 706
Fort Whoop-up Interpretive Society, 754
Habitat for Humanity Canada-Alberta - Lethbridge, 796
Heart & Stroke Foundation of Alberta, NWT & Nunavut-Lethbridge Office, 808
Historical Society of Alberta-Lethbridge Historical Society, 816
Interfaith Food Bank Society of Lethbridge, 852

John Howard Society of Alberta-Lethbridge, 874
Lethbridge & District Association of Realtors, 907
Lethbridge & District Humane Society, 907
Lethbridge & District Japanese Garden Society, 907
Lethbridge & District Pro-Life Association, 907
Lethbridge Association for Community Living, 907
Lethbridge Chamber of Commerce, 907
Lethbridge Community College Faculty Association, 908
Lethbridge Fish & Game Association, 908
Lethbridge Handicraft Guild, 908
Lethbridge HIV Connection, 908
Lethbridge Lacrosse Association, 908
Lethbridge Naturalists' Society, 908
Lethbridge Oldtimers Sports Association, 908
Lethbridge Soccer Association, 908
Lethbridge Soup Kitchen Association, 908
Lethbridge Symphony Orchestra, 908
Lethbridge Therapeutic Riding Association, 908
New Beginnings Association of Southern Alberta, 1004
New West Theatre Society, 1014
Parkinson Alberta Society-Lethbridge Office, 1141
Prairie Conservation Forum, 1169
Quest Support Services Inc., 1200
Rehabilitation Society of Southwestern Alberta, 1216
Rehablitation Society of Southwestern Alberta-JobLinks Employment Centre, 1216
Schizophrenia Society of Alberta-Lethbridge & Area Chapter, 1283
Sik-ooh-kotoki Friendship Society, 1299
Southern Alberta Community Living Association, 1337
Spinal Cord Injury Alberta-Lethbridge, 1343
Sunny South District Soccer Association, 1354
United Way of Lethbridge & South Western Alberta, 1415
University of Lethbridge Faculty Association, 1419
Women's Soccer Assocation of Lethbridge, 1463
YMCA Canada-YMCA of Lethbridge, 1472
YWCA Canada-YWCA Lethbridge & District, 1481

Lloydminster
Alberta Construction Association-Lloydminster Construction Association, 31
Canadian Donkey & Mule Association, 378
Lloydminster & District Fish & Game Association, 915
Lloydminster & District United Way, 916
Lloydminster Chamber of Commerce, 916
Realtors Association of Lloydminster & District, 1206
Saskatchewan Registered Music Teachers' Association-Lloydminster Branch, 1273

Lougheed
Alberta Water Well Drilling Association, 51

Lyalta
Peruvian Horse Association of Canada, 1152

Magrath
Magrath & District Chamber of Commerce, 925

Mallaig
Mallaig Chamber of Commerce, 928

Manning
Appaloosa Horse Club of Canada-Mighty Peace Appaloosa Club, 73
Manning & District Chamber of Commerce, 948
North Peace Applied Research Association, 1032

Mannville
Mannville & District Chamber of Commerce, 948

Markerville
Alberta Percheron Club, 42

Geographic Index / Alberta - Marwayne

Stephan G. Stephansson Icelandic Society, 1349

Marwayne
Marwayne & District Chamber of Commerce, 952

McLennan
McLennan Chamber of Commerce, 955

Medicine Hat
Alberta Construction Association-Medicine Hat Construction Association, 31
Alberta Genealogical Society-Medicine Hat & District Branch, 36
Alzheimer Society of Alberta & Northwest Territories-Medicine Hat & Area - Palliser Chapter, 61
Bridges Family Programs Association, 228
Building Industry & Land Development Alberta-Medicine Hat & District, 262
Faculty Association of Medicine Hat College, 700
Grasslands Naturalists, 782
Heart & Stroke Foundation of Alberta, NWT & Nunavut-Medicine Hat Office, 808
John Howard Society of Alberta-Medicine Hat, 874
McMan Youth, Family & Community Services Association-Southern Alberta, 956
Medicine Hat & District Chamber of Commerce, 958
Medicine Hat & District Food Bank, 958
Medicine Hat Coin & Stamp Club, 958
Medicine Hat Fibre Arts Society, 958
Medicine Hat Fish & Game Association, 958
Medicine Hat Police Association, 958
Medicine Hat Real Estate Board Co-operative Ltd., 958
Medicine Hat Rock & Lapidary Club, 958
Medicine Hat Soccer Association, 959
Medicine Hat Society for the Prevention of Cruelty to Animals, 959
Parkinson Alberta Society-Medicine Hat Office, 1141
The Royal Scottish Country Dance Society-Medicine Hat Branch
Schizophrenia Society of Alberta-Medicine Hat & Area Chapter, 1283
Spinal Cord Injury Alberta-Medicine Hat, 1343
Unisphere Global Resource Centre, 1408
United Way of South Eastern Alberta, 1417
YMCA Canada-YMCA of Medicine Hat, 1472

Millard
Canadian Registry of Tennessee Walking Horse, 466

Millarville
Millarville Racing & Agricultural Society, 965

Millet
Millet & District Chamber of Commerce, 966
Millet & District Historical Society, 966

Mirror
Mirror & District Museum Association, 968

Morinville
Morinville & District Chamber of Commerce, 974

Nanton
Nanton & District Chamber of Commerce, 988

New Norway
Canadian Red Angus Promotion Society, 465

Nisku
Alberta Association of Municipal Districts & Counties, 24
Alberta Bison Association, 26
Bison Producers of Alberta, 212
Enform: The Safety Association for the Upstream Oil & Gas Industry-Nisku Training Facility, 688
Resource Industry Suppliers Association, 1227

Okotoks
Alberta Dressage Association-Calgary Area Chapter, 33
Cu Nim Gliding Club, 645
Foothills Forage & Grazing Association, 750
Okotoks & District Chamber of Commerce, 1056
Okotoks Arts Council, 1056
The Western Stock Growers' Association, 1450

Olds
Alberta Angus Association, 22
Alberta Pinzgauer Association, 42
Alberta Reined Cow Horse Association, 44
Boys & Girls Clubs of Alberta-Boys & Girls Club of Olds & Area, 221
Canadian Pinzgauer Association, 455
Olds & District Chamber of Commerce, 1057
Olds College Faculty Association, 1057
Olds Regional Exhibition, 1057

Onoway
Onoway & District Chamber of Commerce, 1058

Oyen
Chinook Applied Research Association, 565
Oyen & District Chamber of Commerce, 1134

Peace River
Alberta Aboriginal Women's Society, 21
Alberta Genealogical Society-Peace River & District Branch, 37
The Anglican Church of Canada-Diocese of Athabasca, 69
Métis Nation of Alberta-Regional Office - Zone 6, 963
Peace River & District Chamber of Commerce, 1147
Sagitawa Friendship Centre, 1245

Picture Butte
Picture Butte & District Chamber of Commerce, 1159

Pincher Creek
Castle-Crown Wilderness Coalition, 516
Mennonite Church Canada-Mennonite Church Alberta, 961
Napi Friendship Association, 988
Oldman River Antique Equipment & Threshing Club, 1057
Pincher Creek & District Chamber of Commerce, 1160
Pincher Creek Allied Arts Council, 1160
Pincher Creek Humane Society, 1160

Ponoka
Boys & Girls Clubs of Alberta-Boys & Girls Club of Wolf Creek, 221
Ponoka & District Chamber of Commerce, 1164
Ponoka Food Bank, 1164

Priddis
Canadian Angelman Syndrome Society, 293
Sun Ergos, A Company of Theatre & Dance, 1354

Provost
Archaeological Society of Alberta-Bodo Archaeological Society, 76
Provost & District Chamber of Commerce, 1191

Ranfurly
Ranfurly & District Recreation & Agricultural Society, 1204

Raymond
Raymond Chamber of Commerce, 1204

Red Deer
Active Parenting Canada, 7
Alberta Aquaculture Association, 22
Alberta Band Association, 25
Alberta Construction Association-Red Deer Construction Association, 31
Alberta Funeral Service Association, 36
Alberta Galloway Association, 36
Alberta Genealogical Society-Red Deer & District Branch, 37
Alberta Sports Hall of Fame & Museum, 48
Alliance for Canadian New Music Projects-Contemporary Showcase - Red Deer, 56
Alzheimer Society of Alberta & Northwest Territories-Red Deer & Central Alberta Chapter, 61
Association of Fundraising Professionals-Central Alberta Chapter
Auctioneers Association of Alberta, 187
Big Brothers Big Sisters of Alberta-Big Brothers Big Sisters of Red Deer & District, 209
Boys & Girls Clubs of Alberta-Boys & Girls Clubs of Red Deer & District, 221
Brain Injury Association of Alberta, 225
Building Industry & Land Development Alberta-Central Alberta, 262
Canadian Association of Pregnancy Support Services, 328
Canadian Blood Services-Red Deer, 345
Canadian Dance Teachers Association-Alberta Branch, 375
Canadian Occupational Health Nurses Association, 444
Central Alberta AIDS Network Society, 523
Central Alberta Realtors Association, 523
Central Alberta Women's Outreach Society, 524
Dress for Success-Central Alberta, 663
Epilepsy Association of Calgary-Central Alberta Office, 693
Faculty Association of Red Deer College, 700
Habitat for Humanity Canada-Alberta - Red Deer, 796
Heart & Stroke Foundation of Alberta, NWT & Nunavut-Red Deer Office, 808
Historical Society of Alberta-Central Alberta Historical Society, 816
Hockey Alberta, 817
Interpretation Canada - A Professional Association for Heritage Interpretation, 861
John Howard Society of Alberta-Red Deer, 874
Learning Disabilities Association of Alberta-Red Deer Chapter, 904
Massage Therapist Association of Alberta, 953
Master Bowlers' Association of Alberta, 953
Master Bowlers' Association of Canada, 953
Memorial Society of Red Deer & District, 960
Parkinson Alberta Society-Red Deer Office, 1141
Parkland Community Living & Supports Society, 1142
Red Deer & District Allied Arts Council, 1209
Red Deer & District Community Foundation, 1209
Red Deer & District SPCA, 1209
Red Deer Action Group, 1209
Red Deer Chamber of Commerce, 1209
Red Deer City Soccer Association, 1209
Red Deer Danish Canadian Club, 1209
Red Deer Food Bank Society, 1209
Red Deer Native Friendship Society, 1209
Red Deer River Naturalists, 1209
Red Deer Symphony Orchestra, 1209
Schizophrenia Society of Alberta, 1283
Schizophrenia Society of Alberta-Red Deer & Area Chapter, 1283
Tourism Red Deer, 1390
United Way of Central Alberta, 1413
Volunteer Central Society, 1438
Volunteer Red Deer, 1439
Westerner Park, 1450
The Yellow Dog Project, 1470

Red Deer County
Alberta Horse Trials Association, 37

Redwater
Alberta Carriage Driving Association, 27
Redwater & District Chamber of Commerce, 1210

Rimbey
Canadian Luing Cattle Association, 428
Rimbey Chamber of Commerce, 1232

Rimbey Fish & Game Association, 1232
Rimbey Historical Society, 1232

Rocky Mountain House
Boys & Girls Clubs of Alberta-Clearwater Boys & Girls Club, 221
Grey Wooded Forage Association, 790
Peruvian Horse Association of Canada-Peruvian Horse Club of Alberta, 1152
Rocky Mountain House & District Chamber of Commerce, 1235
Rocky Native Friendship Society, 1235
Westward Goals Support Services Inc., 1451

Rocky Rapids
Alberta Genealogical Society-Drayton Valley Branch, 36

Rocky View
Alberta Motor Transport Association, 40

Rocky View County
Canadian Angus Association, 293

Saddle Lake
Boys & Girls Clubs of Alberta-Saddle Lake Boys & Girls Club, 221

Sangudo
Alberta Development Officers Association, 32

Sexsmith
Huntington Society of Canada-Northern Alberta Chapter - Peace Country, 828
Sexsmith & District Chamber of Commerce, 1292

Sherwood Park
Alberta College of Combined Laboratory & X-Ray Technologists, 29
Alberta College of Paramedics, 29
Alberta Conservation Association, 31
Alberta Conservation Tillage Society II, 31
Alberta Lacrosse Association, 38
Alberta Sign Association, 46
Boys & Girls Clubs of Alberta-Boys & Girls Club of Strathcona County, 221
Canadian Honey Council, 408
Canadian Podiatric Medical Association, 456
College of Podiatric Physicians of Alberta, 589
Modular Housing Association Prairie Provinces, 971
National Taekwon-Do Federation, 996
Robin Hood Association for the Handicapped, 1235
Sherwood Park & District Chamber of Commerce, 1296
Sherwood Park District Soccer Association, 1296
Sherwood Park Fish & Game Association, 1296
Solid Waste Association of North America-Northern Lights Chapter, 1595
Strathcona Christian Academy Society, 1351
Strathcona Food Bank, 1351

Siksika
AFOA Canada-AFOA Alberta, 12

Slave Lake
Boys & Girls Clubs of Alberta-Boys & Girls Club of Slave Lake, 221
Lesser Slave Lake Indian Regional Council, 907
Métis Nation of Alberta-Regional Office - Zone 5, 963
Slave Lake & District Chamber of Commerce, 1303
Slave Lake Native Friendship Centre, 1303

Smoky Lake
Smoky Lake & District Chamber of Commerce, 1305

Spruce Grove
Allied Arts Council of Spruce Grove, 58
Association of Fundraising Professionals-Edmonton & Area Chapter, 1512
Canadian Association for Sandplay Therapy, 303

Canadian Horse Breeders' Association-Rocky Mountain District, 408
Nurse Practitioners Association of Alberta, 1052
Parkland Food Bank, 1142
Spruce Grove & District Chamber of Commerce, 1346

Spruce View
Danish Canadian National Museum Society, 650
Dickson Store Museum Society, 656

St Albert
Alberta Association of Family School Liaison Workers, 23
Alberta Automotive Recyclers & Dismantlers Association, 25
Alberta Racquetball Association, 43
Alberta Sheep Breeders Association, 46
Alberta Shorthand Reporters Association, 46
Alliance for Canadian New Music Projects-Contemporary Showcase - Edmonton, 56
Canadian Progress Club-Alberta North Zone, 461
Canadian Sphagnum Peat Moss Association, 489
Edmonton Tumbleweed Lapidary Club, 679
Food Banks Alberta Association, 749
Lo-Se-Ca Foundation, 919
Nechi Training, Research & Health Promotions Institute, 1002
St. Albert & District Chamber of Commerce, 1247
St. Albert Family Resource Centre, 1247
St. Albert Firefighters - Union Local 2130, 1247
St. Albert Fish & Game Association, 1248
St. Albert Historical Society, 1248
St. Albert Soccer Association, 1248
Stop Abuse in Families Society, 1350
Transitions, 1395
Volkssport Association of Alberta, 1437

St Paul
Boys & Girls Clubs of Alberta-Boys & Girls Club of St. Paul & District, 221
Mannawanis Native Friendship Centre, 948
St Paul & District Chamber of Commerce, 1250
St. Paul Abilities Network, 1251
Spinal Cord Injury Alberta-St. Paul, 1343

Stand Off
Kainai Chamber of Commerce, 880

Stettler
Boys & Girls Clubs of Alberta-Stettler & District Boys & Girls Club, 221
Buffalo Lake Naturalists Club, 261
Stettler Regional Board of Trade & Community Development, 1350

Stony Plain
Alberta Community & Co-operative Association, 30
Alberta Professional Outfitters Society, 43
Canadian Finnsheep Breeders' Association, 390
Heritage Agricultural Society, 812
REHOBOTH Christian Ministries, 1216
REHOBOTH Christian Ministries-Stony Plain Branch, 1217
Stony Plain & District Chamber of Commerce, 1350

Strathmore
Community Futures Wild Rose, 598
Strathmore & District Chamber of Commerce, 1351

Strome
Strome & District Historical Society, 1352

Sturgeon County
Alberta Organic Producers Association, 41

Sundre
Alberta Cowboy Poetry Association, 32
Sundre Chamber of Commerce, 1354

Sunnybrook
Canadian Curly Horse Association, 375

Swan Hills
Swan Hills Chamber of Commerce, 1358

Sylvan Lake
Sylvan Lake Chamber of Commerce, 1360

Taber
Potato Growers of Alberta, 1168
Taber & District Chamber of Commerce, 1365

Tees
Canadian Pony Club-Alberta Central, 457

Thorhild
Thorhild Chamber of Commerce, 1376

Thorsby
Thorsby & District Chamber of Commerce, 1376

Three Hills
Kneehill Historical Society, 892
REHOBOTH Christian Ministries-Three Hills Branch, 1217
Three Hills & District Chamber of Commerce, 1377

Tofield
Helios Nudist Association, 811
Tofield & District Chamber of Commerce, 1380
Tofield Historical Society, 1381

Trochu
Trochu Chamber of Commerce, 1399

Turner Valley
Diamond Valley Chamber of Commerce, 656
Sheep Creek Arts Council, 1295
Wild Rose Draft Horse Association, 1454

Valleyview
Valleyview & District Chamber of Commerce, 1424

Vegreville
Alberta Katahdin Sheep Association, 38
Alberta Research Council Inc.-Vegreville Branch, 44
VALID Association, 1424
Vegreville & District Chamber of Commerce, 1430

Vermilion
FOCUS, 741
Lakeland College Faculty Association, 896
Vermilion & District Chamber of Commerce, 1431

Viking
Viking Economic Development Committee, 1434

Vilna
Vilna & District Chamber of Commerce, 1435

Vulcan
Vulcan & District Chamber of Commerce, 1439
Vulcan & District Fish & Game Club, 1439
Vulcan Business Development Society, 1439
Western Canadian Miniature Horse Club, 1448

Wabamun
Wabamun District Chamber of Commerce Society, 1439

Wainwright
Battle River Historical Society, 199
Canadian Association of Veterans in United Nations Peacekeeping-Wainwright Chapter, 336
Wainwright & District Chamber of Commerce, 1439

Waterton Park
Waterton Natural History Association, 1442
Waterton Park Chamber of Commerce & Visitors Association, 1442

Westerose
Pigeon Lake Regional Chamber of Commerce, 1159

Westlock
Alberta Blonde d'Aquitaine Association, 26
Alberta Trappers' Association, 50
Gateway Research Organization, 767
Westlock & District Chamber of Commerce, 1451

Wetaskiwin
Alberta Genealogical Society-Wetaskiwin Branch, 37
Boys & Girls Clubs of Alberta-Boys & Girls Club of Wetaskiwin, 221
Canada's Aviation Hall of Fame, 282
Wetaskiwin & District Association for Community Service, 1451

Whitecourt
Boys & Girls Clubs of Alberta-Boys & Girls Club of Whitecourt, 221
Community Futures Yellowhead East, 599
Whitecourt & District Chamber of Commerce, 1452
Whitecourt Fish & Game Association, 1452

Worsley
Worsley Chamber of Commerce, 1468

British Columbia

100 Mile House
Cedar Crest Society for Community Living, 521
100 Mile & District Arts Council, 1058
100 Mile House Food Bank Society, 1058
South Cariboo Chamber of Commerce, 1334

150 Mile House
British Columbia Environmental Network, 240

Abbotsford
Abbotsford Arts Council, 1
Abbotsford Chamber of Commerce, 1
Abbotsford Community Services, 1
Abbotsford Downtown Business Association, 1
Abbotsford Female Hockey Association, 1
Abbotsford Food Bank & Christmas Bureau, 1
Abbotsford International Air Show Society, 1
Abbotsford Social Activity Association, 1
Abbotsford-Mission Nature Club, 1
Abundance Canada-Abbotsford Office, 3
Alcoholics Anonymous-Abbotsford - Intergroup Committee, 52
American Saddlebred Horse Association of British Columbia, 66
Back to the Bible Canada, 193
BC Taekwondo Association, 202
British Columbia Blueberry Council, 234
British Columbia Broiler Hatching Egg Producers' Association, 234
British Columbia Chicken Growers' Association, 236
British Columbia Conference of MB Churches, 237
British Columbia Cranberry Marketing Commission, 238
British Columbia Egg Marketing Board, 239
British Columbia Hog Marketing Commission, 243
British Columbia Milk Marketing Board, 246
British Columbia Muslim Association-Abbotsford Branch, 247
British Columbia Speed Skating Association, 254
British Columbia Automobile Association-Abbotsford Branch, 267
Canadian Federation of Business & Professional Women's Clubs-Abbotsford, 385
Canadian Food for the Hungry International, 391
Canadian Home Builders' Association - British Columbia-Fraser Valley, 407
Communitas Supportive Care Society, 595
Credit Counselling Society-Abbotsford, 640
Fraser Valley Egg Producers' Association, 757
Fraser Valley Symphony Society, 758
Gem & Mineral Federation of Canada-British Columbia Lapidary Society, 768
Habitat for Humanity Canada-British Columbia - Upper Fraser Valley Society, 796
H.O.M.E. Society, 819
Kinsmen Foundation of British Columbia & Yukon, 890
M2/W2 Association - Restorative Christian Ministries, 923
Matsqui Sumas Abbotsford Museum Society, 954
MB Mission, 954
Mennonite Central Committee Canada-MCC British Columbia, 960
Mennonite Historical Society of Canada, 961
Métis Provincial Council of British Columbia, 963
MSA Society for Community Living, 978
Raspberry Industry Development Council, 1204
Serena Canada-British Columbia Branch, 1290
United Way of the Fraser Valley, 1417
University of the Fraser Valley Faculty & Staff Association, 1420

Agassiz
Agassiz-Harrison Community Services, 14

Aldergrove
British Columbia Hereford Association, 243
CADORA British Columbia-Country CADORA Chapter, 268
Heating, Refrigeration & Air Conditioning Institute of Canada-British Columbia - Regional Chapter, 810
Horse Council British Columbia, 822
Languages Canada, 899

Alert Bay
U'mista Cultural Society, 1401

Armstrong
Armstrong-Spallumcheen Chamber of Commerce, 83
British Columbia Angus Association, 230
Okanagan Miniature Horse Club, 1055
Peruvian Horse Association of Canada-Peruvian Horse Club of BC, 1152

Ashcroft
Ashcroft & Area Food Bank, 86
Ashcroft & District Chamber of Commerce, 86
British Columbia Science Teachers' Association, 252
Canadian Association of Elizabeth Fry Societies-South Cariboo Elizabeth Fry Society, 313

Atlin
Atlin Board of Trade, 187

Balfour
Small Water Users Association of BC, 1304

Bamfield
Bamfield Chamber of Commerce, 195
Bamfield Marine Sciences Centre, 195

Barriere
Barriere & District Chamber of Commerce, 197
Barriere & District Food Bank Society, 197
British Columbia Women's Institutes, 258

Belcarra
Association of Neighbourhood Houses BC-Sasamat Outdoor Centre, 153

Bella Bella
Heiltsuk Tribal Council, 811

Bella Coola
Central Coast Communications Society, 524

Blind Bay
South Shuswap Chamber of Commerce, 1336

Bowen Island
Bowen Island Arts Council, 219
Bowen Island Chamber of Commerce, 219

Geographic Index / British Columbia - Brentwood Bay

Bowen Nature Club, 219

Brentwood Bay
Saanich Native Heritage Society, 1245
Victoria Therapeutic Riding Association, 1434

Brisco
British Columbia Charolais Association, 236

Burnaby
Adala - Canadian Arab Justice Committee, 7
AIESEC-Simon Fraser University, 18
American Society of Heating, Refrigerating & Air Conditioning Engineers-British Columbia Chapter, 1500
L'Arche Western Region-L'Arche Greater Vancouver, 78
Architectural Woodwork Manufacturers Association of British Columbia, 79
Assembly of BC Arts Councils, 88
Association des professeurs de français des universités et collèges canadiens, 124
Association of Canadian Film Craftspeople, 142
Association of Professional Engineers & Geoscientists of British Columbia, 157
Athletic Therapy Association of British Columbia, 180
Autism Society of British Columbia, 189
Automotive Retailers Association of British Columbia, 190
B.C. Horseshoe Association, 201
BC Lacrosse Association, 201
BC School Sports, 202
Biophysical Society of Canada, 211
Brewery, Winery & Distillery Workers Union - Local 300, 228
British Columbia Association of People Who Stutter, 232
British Columbia Athletics, 233
British Columbia Bailiffs Association, 233
British Columbia Care Providers Association, 234
British Columbia Confederation of Parent Advisory Councils, 236
British Columbia Dairy Association, 238
British Columbia Dental Hygienists' Association, 238
British Columbia Electrical Association, 239
British Columbia Federation of Foster Parent Associations, 240
British Columbia Government & Service Employees' Union, 242
British Columbia Institute of Technology Faculty & Staff Association, 244
British Columbia Muslim Association-Burnaby Branch, 247
British Columbia Nurses' Union, 248
British Columbia Party, 248
British Columbia Professional Fire Fighters' Burn Fund, 249
British Columbia Road Builders & Heavy Construction Association, 251
British Columbia Wrestling Association, 258
Burnaby Arts Council, 265
Burnaby Association for Community Inclusion, 265
Burnaby Board of Trade, 265
Burnaby Laphounds Club, 266
Burnaby Multicultural Society, 266
Burnaby Volunteer Centre Society, 266
CAA British Columbia, 267
Canadian Aviation Historical Society-Vancouver Chapter, 340
Canadian Baptists of Western Canada-British Columbia & Yukon Regional Office, 341
Canadian Council of Practical Nurse Regulators, 369
Canadian Council of Professional Geoscientists, 370
Canadian Hard of Hearing Association-British Columbia - HEAR Branch, 400
Canadian Home Builders' Association - British Columbia, 406
Canadian Institute of Management-British Columbia & Yukon Branch, 417

Canadian Office & Professional Employees Union-Region 4 - Local 378, 445
Canadian Philosophy of Education Society, 454
Canadian Union of Public Employees-British Columbia Division, 498
CanoeKayak BC, 509
Catholic Health Association of British Columbia, 519
Chartered Professional Accountants Canada-Burnaby Office, 552
Chinese Canadian Writers' Association, 564
College of Licensed Practical Nurses of BC, 585
The Commonwealth of Learning, 594
Council of Marine Carriers, 634
Council of Parent Participation Preschools in British Columbia, 635
Culture Regeneration Research Society, 645
Curl BC, 646
Dania Home Society, 650
Deaf Children's Society of B.C., 652
Down Syndrome Research Foundation, 661
Electrical Contractors Association of BC, 682
50 & Piu Enasco, 734
Football BC, 750
Grandparents Raising Grandchildren - British Columbia, 781
Greater Vancouver Japanese Canadian Citizens' Association, 787
Greater Vancouver Regional District Employees' Union, 787
Habitat for Humanity Canada-British Columbia - Greater Vancouver, 796
Health Action Network Society, 805
Hospital Employees' Union, 823
Immigrant Services Society of BC-Burnaby - LINC & Settlement Services, 831
Immigrant Services Society of BC-Burnaby - Settlement & Career Services, 830
Independent Contractors & Businesses Association of British Columbia, 832
International Brotherhood of Boilermakers, Iron Ship Builders, Blacksmiths, Forgers & Helpers (AFL-CIO)-Burnaby (Vancouver Lodge 359), 1541
International Union of Painters & Allied Trades (AFL-CIO/CFL)-District Council 28 - British Columbia
Juvenile Diabetes Research Foundation-Vancouver, 879
Karate BC, 881
The Kidney Foundation of Canada-British Columbia & Yukon Branch, 885
Korean Businessmen's Cooperative Association of British Columbia, 893
Lifesaving Society-British Columbia & Yukon Branch, 911
Master Painters & Decorators Association, 954
Mechanical Contractors Association of British Columbia, 956
Medical Women's International Association, 958
Multiple Sclerosis Society of Canada-British Columbia & Yukon Division, 980
National Automotive Trades Association of Canada, 991
National Building Envelope Council, 991
The Neil Squire Foundation, 1002
New Democratic Party-British Columbia NDP, 1014
New Westminster & District Labour Council, 1015
Pacific Northwest Library Association, 1135
Pacific Post Partum Support Society, 1136
Pacific Society of Nutrition Management, 1136
Parent Support Services Society of BC, 1139
Portuguese Canadian Seniors Foundation, 1167
posAbilities Association of BC, 1167
Progressive Housing Society, 1187
Prosthetics & Orthotics Association of British Columbia, 1190
St. Leonard's Youth & Family Services Society, 1250
The Salvation Army in Canada-Burnaby - British Columbia Division, 1253

Sign Association of Canada-British Columbia Chapter, 1299
Simon Fraser Public Interest Research Group, 1300
Simon Fraser University Faculty Association, 1300
Skate Canada-British Columbia/Yukon Section, 1301
Social Planning & Research Council of BC, 1306
Southeast Asia-Canada Business Council, 1337
Special Olympics BC, 1339
SportMedBC, 1345
Synchro BC, 1360
Teaching Support Staff Union, 1367
Terrazzo Tile & Marble Association of Canada-Burnaby (Western Branch), 1372
The Terry Fox Foundation, 1372
The Terry Fox Foundation-International, 1372
UNITE HERE Canada-Vancouver & Vicinity Chapter, 1409
United Church of Canada-British Columbia Conference, 1409
United Way of the Lower Mainland, 1417
Vancouver & Lower Mainland Multicultural Family Support Services Society, 1424
Variety - The Children's Charity of BC, 1429
Volleyball BC, 1437
Volunteer Grandparents, 1438
West Coast Amateur Musicians' Society, 1444
Wildlife Rescue Association of British Columbia, 1455

Burns Lake
Burns Lake & District Chamber of Commerce, 266
Burns Lake Christian Supportive Society, 266

Cache Creek
Cache Creek Chamber of Commerce, 268

Campbell River
AIDS Vancouver Island-Campbell River Office, 17
British Columbia Conservative Party, 237
British Columbia Salmon Farmers Association, 252
Campbell River & Courtenay District Labour Council, 276
Campbell River & District Association for Community Living, 276
Campbell River & District Chamber of Commerce, 276
Campbell River & District Food Bank, 276
Campbell River & District United Way, 276
Campbell River Museum & Archives Society, 276
Immigrant Welcome Centre, 831
Kwakiutl District Council, 894
Musgamagw Tsawataineuk Tribal Council, 983
Ripple Rock Gem & Mineral Club, 1233
Strathcona Park Lodge & Outdoor Education Centre, 1351
United Native Nations Society, 1412

Canoe
British Columbia Welsh Pony & Cob Association, 258

Castlegar
Castlegar & District Arts Council, 517
Castlegar & District Chamber of Commerce, 517
Kootenay Society for Community Living, 892

Central Saanich
British Columbia Folklore Society, 241

Chase
Chase & District Chamber of Commerce, 555
Open Door Group-Chase & District Satellite Office, 1114

Chemainus
British Columbia Katahdin Sheep Association, 244
Chemainus & District Chamber of Commerce, 555

Chemainus Harvest House Society Food Bank, 555

Chetwynd
Chetwynd & District Chamber of Commerce, 557
Tansi Friendship Centre Society, 1366

Chilliwack
Alpine Garden Club of BC, 59
Animal Nutrition Association of Canada-British Columbia Division, 71
Bibles for Missions Foundation, 208
British Columbia Economic Development Association, 239
British Columbia Rifle Association, 251
British Columbia Automobile Association-Chilliwack Branch, 267
Canadian Hard of Hearing Association-British Columbia - BC Main Chapter, 400
Canadian Hard of Hearing Association-British Columbia - Chilliwack Branch, 400
Canadian Hard of Hearing Association-British Columbia - BC Parents' Branch, 400
Chilliwack & District Real Estate Board, 563
Chilliwack Chamber of Commerce, 563
Chilliwack Community Arts Council, 563
Chilliwack Field Naturalists, 563
Chilliwack Society for Community Living, 563
Chilliwack Symphony Orchestra & Chorus, 563
National Emergency Nurses Association, 993
Pacific Riding for Developing Abilities-Chilliwack Branch, 1136
Simmental Association of British Columbia, 1300
Teachers of Home Economics Specialist Association, 1367
United Empire Loyalists' Association of Canada-Chilliwack Branch, 1410
YMCA Canada-YMCA of Greater Vancouver - Chilliwack, 1471

Christina Lake
Christina Lake Chamber of Commerce, 568

Clearwater
Clearwater & District Chamber of Commerce, 573
Clearwater & District Food Bank Society, 573

Cloverdale
Air Line Pilots Association, International - Canada-Vancouver Regional Office, 19
Cloverdale & District Chamber of Commerce, 574
Credit Institute of Canada-British Columbia Chapter, 640

Cobble Hill
Coast Waste Management Association, 579
Holstein Canada-British Columbia Branch, 819

Colwood
Vancouver Island Rock & Alpine Garden Society, 1427

Comox
British Columbia Honey Producers Association, 243
British Columbia Shellfish Growers Association, 253
Embroiderers' Association of Canada, Inc.-British Columbia - Comox Valley Needlearts Guild, 685
Performing Arts BC, 1152

Coombs
Society for Organic Urban Land Care, 1326

Coquitlam
ArtsConnect - Tri-Cities Regional Arts Council, 86
Association Provinciale des Professeurs d'Immersion et du Programme Francophone, 168
British Columbia Association for Behaviour Analysis, 231
British Columbia Libertarian Party, 244

Geographic Index / British Columbia - Kamloops

British Columbia Teacher-Librarians' Association, 255
Burke Mountain Naturalists, 265
British Columbia Automobile Association-Coquitlam Branch, 267
Canadian Merchant Service Guild (CLC)-Western Branch, 435
Clan MacLeod Societies of Canada-Vancouver Branch, 572
Immigrant Services Society of BC-Coquitlam - Settlement Services, 830
Immigrant Services Society of BC-Coquitlam - LINC, 830
Immigrant Services Society of BC-Coquitlam - Career & Settlement Services, 830
Kinsight, 890
Licensed Practical Nurses Association of British Columbia, 910
Share Family & Community Services Society, 1294
Sisters of the Child Jesus, 1301
Step-By-Step Child Development Society, 1349
Tri-Cities Chamber of Commerce Serving Coquitlam, Port Coquitlam & Port Moody, 1398
United Food & Commercial Workers Canada-Western Canada, 1411
World Organization Ovulation Method Billings Inc., 1466
WTF Taekwondo Federation of British Columbia, 1469

Courtenay
AIDS Vancouver Island-Courtenay/Comox Office, 17
L'Arche Western Region-L'Arche Comox Valley, 78
Bowls British Columbia, 220
British Columbia Automobile Association-Courtenay, 267
CADORA British Columbia-Courtenay CADORA Chapter, 268
Canadian Culinary Federation-North Vancouver Island, 374
Church Library Association of British Columbia, 569
Comox Valley Chamber of Commerce, 607
Comox Valley Child Development Association, 607
Comox Valley Community Arts Council, 607
Comox Valley Food Bank Society, 608
Comox Valley Therapeutic Riding Society, 608
Comox Valley United Way, 608
Courtenay & District Historical Society, 637
Courtenay Gem & Mineral Club, 637
Habitat for Humanity Canada-British Columbia - Vancouver Island North, 796
North Island College Faculty Association, 1031

Cranbrook
ANKORS Kootenay Boundary Aids Network, Outreach & Support Society-East Kootenay Regional Office, 71
Boys & Girls Clubs of British Columbia-Cranbrook Boys & Girls Club, 222
Canadian Disaster Child Care Society, 378
College of the Rockies Faculty Association, 590
Cranbrook & District Arts Council, 638
Cranbrook & District Chamber of Commerce, 638
Cranbrook Archives, Museum & Landmark Foundation, 638
Cranbrook Food Bank Society, 638
Cranbrook Society for Community Living, 638
East Kootenay Chamber of Mines, 668
East Kootenay District Labour Council, 668
Music for Young Children-British Columbia & Western United States, 983
PFLAG Canada Inc.-Kimberley Chapter, 1155
PFLAG Canada Inc.-Cranbrook Chapter, 1155
Rocky Mountain Naturalists, 1235
United Way of East Kootenay, 1414

Crawford Bay
East Shore Internet Society, 668
Kootenay Lake Chamber of Commerce, 892

Creston
The Canadian Doukhobor Society, 378
Creston & District Historical & Museum Society, 641
Creston Valley Chamber of Commerce, 642
Creston Valley Prospectors & Lapidary Club, 642

Cumberland
Cumberland Chamber of Commerce, 645
Wilderness Tourism Association, 1454

Dawson Creek
Canadian Shire Horse Association, 470
Dawson Creek & District Chamber of Commerce, 652
Dawson Creek Construction Association, 652
Dawson Creek Society for Community Living, 652
Nawican Friendship Centre, 1002
Peace Region Internet Society, 1147
South Peace Community Arts Council, 1335
South Peace Community Resources Society, 1335
Timberline Trail & Nature Club, 1379

Dease Lake
Dease Lake & District Chamber of Commerce, 652
Dze L K'ant Friendship Centre Society-Dease Lake Location, 666

Delta
Adult Basic Education Association of British Columbia, 9
Airspace Action on Smoking & Health, 20
Association of Canadian Deans of Education, 141
British Columbia Ball Hockey Association, 233
British Columbia Bottle & Recycling Depot Association, 234
British Columbia Golf Association, 242
British Columbia Therapeutic Riding Association, 257
British Columbia Waterfowl Society, 258
British Columbia Weightlifting Association, 258
British Columbia Automobile Association-Delta Branch, 267
Canadian Ball Hockey Association, 340
Canadian Plastics Industry Association-Western Region, 456
Delta Arts Council, 653
Delta Chamber of Commerce, 653
Delta Community Living Society, 653
Delta Rockhound Gem & Mineral Club, 653
Earthwise Society, 668
Endurance Riders Association of British Columbia, 687
North American Waterfowl Management Plan-Pacific Birds Habitat Joint Venture, 1029
North American Waterfowl Management Plan-Canadian Intermountain Joint Venture (CIJV), 1029
Scleroderma Association of British Columbia, 1285
South Delta Food Bank, 1334
Unparty: The Consensus-Building Party, 1421
Western Canadian Shippers' Coalition, 1449

Denny Island
Central Coast Chamber of Commerce, 524

Duncan
Aboriginal Head Start Association of British Columbia, 2
Alberni Valley Soaring Association, 21
Clan MacLeod Societies of Canada-Vancouver Island Branch, 572
Clements Centre Society, 573
Cowichan Intercultural Society, 637
Cowichan Therapeutic Riding Association, 637
Cowichan United Way, 637
Cowichan Valley Arts Council, 637
Cowichan Valley Basket Society, 637
Cowichan Valley Naturalists' Society, 637
Duncan-Cowichan Chamber of Commerce, 664

Hiiye'yu Lelum Society House of Friendship, 814
Islands Organic Producers Association, 866
Pulp & Paper Employee Relations Forum, 1194
Somenos Marsh Wildlife Society, 1333

Elkford
Elkford Chamber of Commerce, 685

Enderby
Enderby & District Arts Council, 687
Enderby & District Chamber of Commerce, 687
Enderby & District Museum Society, 687

Errington
North Island Wildlife Recovery Association, 1031

Falkland
Falkland Chamber of Commerce, 701

Fernie
Canadian Home Builders' Association - British Columbia-Rocky Mountain, 407
Elk Valley Society for Community Living, 685
Fernie & District Arts Council, 732
Fernie & District Historical Society, 732
Fernie Chamber of Commerce, 732

Field
Burgess Shale Geoscience Foundation, 265

Fort Langley
British Columbia Farm Machinery & Agriculture Museum Association, 240
Fellowship of Evangelical Baptist Churches in Canada-Fellowship Pacific, 731
Langley Heritage Society, 899

Fort Nelson
Fort Nelson & District Chamber of Commerce, 753
Fort Nelson Aboriginal Friendship Society, 753

Fort St James
Community Arts Council of Fort St. James, 595
Fort St. James Chamber of Commerce, 753

Fort St John
British Columbia Bison Association, 233
Child Development Centre Society of Fort St. John & District, 558
Christian Labour Association of Canada-Fort St. John/Northeastern BC Regional Office, 568
Enform: The Safety Association for the Upstream Oil & Gas Industry-British Columbia Office, 688
Fort St. John & District Chamber of Commerce, 753
Fort St. John Association for Community Living, 753
Fort St. John Community Arts Council, 753
North Peace Cultural Society, 1032
North Peace Historical Society, 1032
Northern Rockies Alaska Highway Tourism Association, 1035
Peace Valley Environment Association, 1147

Francois Lake
Lakes District Festival Association, 896

Fraser Lake
Fraser Lake Chamber of Commerce, 757

Gabriola
British Columbia Bee Breeders' Association, 233
Gabriola Island Chamber of Commerce, 765

Galiano Island
Galiano Island Chamber of Commerce, 766
Galiano Rod & Gun Club, 766

Gambier Island
International PhotoTherapy Association, 859

Garibaldi Highlands
Squamish Food Bank, 1346
Swim BC, 1358

Gibsons
British Columbia Spaces for Nature, 254
Denturist Association of British Columbia, 653
Gibsons & District Chamber of Commerce, 773
Open Door Group-Gibsons Satellite Office, 1114
Sunshine Coast Labour Council, 1355

Gitlaxt'aamiks
Nisga'a Lisims Government, 1027

Gold River
Gold River Chamber of Commerce, 776

Golden
Golden District Arts Council, 776
Golden Food Bank, 776
Golden Rock & Fossil Club, 776
Golden Women's Resource Centre Society, 776
Kicking Horse Country Chamber of Commerce, 884

Grand Forks
Boundary District Arts Council, 219
Boundary Organic Producers Association, 219
British Columbia Grapegrowers' Association, 242
Habitat for Humanity Canada-British Columbia - Southeast BC, 796
Union of Spiritual Communities of Christ, 1408
United Nations Association in Canada-Kootenay Region, 1411

Greenwood
Greenwood Board of Trade, 789

Harrison Hot Springs
Harrison Agassiz Chamber of Commerce, 804

Hazelton
Gitxsan Treaty Office, 774

Heriot Bay
Quadra Island Food Bank, 1195

Hope
Hope & District Chamber of Commerce, 820
Hope Food Bank, 821
Tillicum Centre - Hope Association for Community Living, 1379

Hornby Island
Hornby Island Food Bank, 821

Houston
Dze L K'ant Friendship Centre Society-Houston Location, 666
Houston Chamber of Commerce, 824
Houston Link to Learning, 824

Hudson's Hope
Hudson's Hope Museum, 824
Peace-Laird Regional Arts Council, 1147

Invermere
Association of BC First Nations Treatment Programs, 140
British Columbia Aboriginal Lands Managers, 229
Columbia Valley Chamber of Commerce, 591
Windermere District Historical Society, 1456

Kamloops
Aboriginal Agricultural Education Society of British Columbia, 2
Administrative Sciences Association of Canada, 8
Association of Registrars of the Universities & Colleges of Canada, 161
Boys & Girls Clubs of British Columbia-Boys & Girls Club of Kamloops, 221
British Columbia Cattlemen's Association, 235
British Columbia Drama Association, 239
British Columbia Fishing Resorts & Outfitters Association, 241
British Columbia Native Women's Association, 247
British Columbia Target Sports Association, 255
British Columbia Veterinary Technologists Association, 257

Geographic Index / British Columbia - Kaslo

British Columbia Automobile Association-Kamloops Branch, 267
Canadian Association of Elizabeth Fry Societies-Kamloops & District Elizabeth Fry Society, 313
Canadian Celiac Association-Kamloops Chapter, 352
Canadian Cutting Horse Association-British Columbia, 375
Canadian Home Builders' Association - British Columbia-Central Interior, 407
Canadian Safe Cannabis Society, 468
First Nations Agricultural Lending Association, 738
FogQuest, 742
Fraser Basin Council-Thompson Regional Office, 757
Greater Kamloops Chamber of Commerce, 783
Habitat for Humanity Canada-British Columbia - Kamloops, 796
Heart & Stroke Foundation of B.C. & Yukon-Kamloops Area Office - Kamloops/Cariboo, 808
Interior Indian Friendship Society, 852
Kamloops & District Labour Council, 880
Kamloops & District Real Estate Association, 880
Kamloops Exploration Group, 880
Kamloops Foodbank & Outreach Society, 880
Kamloops Immigrant Services, 880
Kamloops Multicultural Society, 880
Kamloops Naturalist Club, 880
Kamloops Society for Community Living, 880
Kamloops Symphony, 880
Kamloops Wildlife Park Society, 881
Kamloops, Revelstoke, Okanagan & District Building & Construction Trades Council, 881
Model Aeronautics Association of Canada Inc.-British Columbia & Yukon Zone, 970
Ontario University Registrars' Association, 1112
Open Door Group-Kamloops North Shore Office, 1114
Open Door Group-Kamloops South Shore Office, 1114
Open Learning at Thompson Rivers University, 1114
PFLAG Canada Inc.-Kamloops Chapter, 1155
Southern Interior Local Government Association, 1338
Thompson Rivers University Faculty Association, 1376
Thompson, Nicola, Cariboo United Way, 1376
Western Canada Theatre Company Society, 1448

Kaslo
YMCA Canada-YMCA-YWCA of Kamloops, 1473
Kaslo & Area Chamber of Commerce, 882
Langham Cultural Society, 898

Kelowna
Allergy/Asthma Information Association-AAIA BC/Yukon, 54
Alliance for Equality of Blind Canadians, 57
The Anglican Church of Canada-Diocese of Kootenay, 69
Arts Council of the Central Okanagan, 85
Associated Gospel Churches-Canada West Office, 89
Association of Fundraising Professionals-Okanagan Chapter
Big Brothers Big Sisters of British Columbia-Big Brothers Big Sisters of the Okanagan, 209
Boys & Girls Clubs of British Columbia-Okanagan Boys & Girls Clubs, 222
British Columbia Amateur Bodybuilding Association, 230
British Columbia Construction Association-Southern Interior Construction Association, 237
British Columbia Fruit Growers' Association, 242
British Columbia Herb Growers Association, 243
British Columbia Muslim Association-Kelowna Branch, 247
British Columbia Prader-Willi Syndrome Association, 249
British Columbia Snowboard Association, 253
British Columbia Wine Institute, 258
British Columbia Automobile Association-Kelowna Branch, 267
Canadian Association of Elizabeth Fry Societies-Central Okanagan Elizabeth Fry Society, 312
Canadian Blood Services-Kelowna, 344
Canadian Celiac Association-Kelowna Chapter, 352
Canadian Culinary Federation-Okanagan Branch, 374
Canadian Home Builders' Association - British Columbia-Central Okanagan, 407
Canadian Masters Cross-Country Ski Association-British Columbia, 431
Canadian Society of Gastroenterology Nurses & Associates-Okanagan Chapter, 483
Central Okanagan Community Food Bank, 524
Central Okanagan Foundation, 525
Central Okanagan Naturalists Club, 525
Christian Labour Association of Canada-Kelowna/Southern Interior, BC Regional Office, 568
Credit Counselling Society-Kelowna, 640
EFILE Association of Canada, 681
Embroiderers' Association of Canada, Inc.-British Columbia - Okanagan Guild of Needlearts, 685
Entomological Society of British Columbia, 690
Family Enterprise Xchange-FEX Okanagan, 703
Habitat for Humanity Canada-British Columbia - Okanagan, 796
Health Record Association of British Columbia, 807
Heart & Stroke Foundation of B.C. & Yukon-Kelowna Area Office - Okanagan/Kootenays, 808
Home Inspectors Association BC, 819
Hope for the Nations, 821
Kelowna & District Stamp Club, 883
Kelowna Chamber of Commerce, 883
Ki-Low-Na Friendship Society, 887
Living Positive Resource Centre, Okanagan, 915
North Okanagan Labour Council, 1031
Okanagan Mainline Real Estate Board, 1055
Okanagan Symphony Society, 1056
Osteoporosis Canada-Kelowna Chapter, 1128
Pathways Abilities Society, 1145
Southern Interior Construction Association, 1338
Starbright Children's Development Centre, 1348
Thompson Okanagan Tourism Association, 1376
Tourism Kelowna, 1390
United Way of the Central Okanagan & South Okanagan/Similkameen, 1417
Urban Development Institute of Canada-Okanagan, 1422
Waldorf School Association of Kelowna, 1439
YMCA Canada-YMCA of Okanagan, 1471

Keremeos
British Columbia Snowmobile Federation, 253
Similkameen Chamber of Commerce, 1300
Similkameen Okanagan Organic Producers Association, 1300

Kimberley
Kimberley & District Chamber of Commerce, 887
Kimberley Arts Council - Centre 64 Society, 887
Kimberley Helping Hands Food Bank, 887
Kootenay Rockies Tourism, 892

Kitimat
Kitimat Chamber of Commerce, 891
Kitimat Child Development Centre, 891
Kitimat Community Services Society, 891
Kitimat Food Bank, 891
Kitimat Valley Naturalists, 891
Meningitis BC, 960

Kitwanga
Meanskinisht Village Historical Association, 956

Kootenay Bay
Yasodhara Ashram Society, 1470

Ladysmith
Ladysmith Chamber of Commerce, 895
Ladysmith Food Bank, 895
Provincial CGIT Board of BC, 1190

Lake Country
Fresh Outlook Foundation, 760
Lake Country Chamber of Commerce, 895

Lake Cowichan
British Columbia Golf Superintendents Association, 242
Cowichan Lake District Chamber of Commerce, 637

Langley
Aldergrove Daylily Society, 53
Baptist General Conference of Canada-British Columbia Baptist Conference (BCBC), 196
Basketball BC, 198
British Columbia Amateur Softball Association, 230
British Columbia Association of Family Resource Programs, 231
British Columbia Aviation Council, 233
British Columbia Ground Water Association, 242
British Columbia Municipal Safety Association, 246
British Columbia Sporthorse - Sport Pony Breeders Group, 255
British Columbia Trucking Association, 257
British Columbia Wood Specialities Group Association, 258
British Columbia Automobile Association-Langley Branch, 267
Canadian Society of Church History, 481
Christian Labour Association of Canada-Vancouver/Lower Mainland Regional Office, 568
Concrete B.C., 610
Farm & Ranch Safety & Health Association, 705
Fenestration Association of BC, 732
Focus on the Family Canada, 742
Fraser Valley Labour Council, 757
Fraser Valley Rock & Gem Club, 758
Frasier Valley Orchid Society, 758
Greater Langley Chamber of Commerce, 784
Immigrant Services Society of BC-Langley - Settlement & Career Services, 830
Jersey Canada-British Columbia, 869
Langley & Aldergrove Food Bank, 898
Langley Arts Council, 899
Langley Association for Community Living, 899
Langley District Help Network, 899
Langley Field Naturalists Society, 899
Motion Picture Theatre Association of British Columbia, 975
Pacific Riding for Developing Abilities, 1136
Pentecostal Assemblies of Canada-British Columbia & Yukon District Office, 1150
Professional Photographers of Canada-Professional Photographers of Canada - British Columbia Region, 1186
Roofing Contractors Association of British Columbia, 1236
Signal Hill, 1299
Society of Christian Schools in British Columbia, 1328
Vela Microboard Association of British Columbia, 1430
Western Employers Labour Relations Association, 1449
Wycliffe Bible Translators of Canada, Inc.-Western Canada Office, 1470
Youth for Christ Canada, 1475

Lazo
Canadian Hard of Hearing Association-British Columbia - Comox Valley, 400

Lengley
Canadian Association of Freediving & Apnea, 316

Likely
Likely & District Chamber of Commerce, 912

Lillooet
Lillooet & District Chamber of Commerce, 912
Lillooet Food Bank, 912
Lillooet Tribal Council, 912
Open Door Group-Lillooet Office, 1114

Logan Lake
Canadian Association for Photographic Art, 303
Logan Lake Arts Council, 917

Lone Butte
Community Enhancement & Economic Development Society, 597

Lumby
Lumby Chamber of Commerce, 920

Lytton
Lytton & District Chamber of Commerce, 923
Lytton Community Food Bank, 923

Mackenzie
Mackenzie & District Museum Society, 924
Mackenzie Chamber of Commerce, 924
Mackenzie Community Arts Council, 924

Madeira Park
Pender Harbour & District Chamber of Commerce, 1149

Maple Ridge
Aboriginal Firefighters Association of Canada, 2
Alouette Field Naturalists, 59
British Columbia Federation of Foster Parent Associations, 240
British Columbia Nurse Practitioner Association, 248
British Columbia Powerlifting Association, 249
British Columbia Automobile Association-Maple Ridge, 267
Canadian Hemophilia Society-British Columbia Chapter, 404
Hominum, 820
Immigrant Services Society of BC-Maple Ridge - LINC, Settlement & Career Services, 830
Maple Ridge Lapidary Club, 948
Maple Ridge Museum & Community Archives, 948
Maple Ridge Pitt Meadows Arts Council, 948
Ridge Meadows Association of Community Living, 1232

Mayne Island
Mayne Island Community Chamber of Commerce, 954

McBride
McBride & District Chamber of Commerce, 955

Merritt
Clan MacLeod Societies of Canada-British Columbia Interior Branch, 572
Conayt Friendship Society, 609
Merritt & District Chamber of Commerce, 962
Nicola Valley & District Food Bank, 1026
Nicola Valley Community Arts Council, 1026
Nicola Valley Museum Archives Association, 1026

Midway
Boundary Country Regional Chamber of Commerce, 218

Mill Bay
The Company of Master Mariners of Canada-Vancouver Island Division, 954
South Cowichan Chamber of Commerce, 1334

Milner
Westgen, 1450

Mission
British Columbia Shake & Shingle Association, 253
Canadian Federation of Business & Professional Women's Clubs-Mission, 385
Community Futures Development Association of British Columbia, 598
District of Mission Arts Council, 659
Mission Association for Community Living, 968
Mission Community Services Food Centre, 969
Mission Heritage Association, 969
Mission Indian Friendship Centre, 969
Mission Regional Chamber of Commerce, 969
Sports Car Club of British Columbia, 1345

Nakusp
Arrow Lakes Historical Society, 84
Nakusp & District Chamber of Commerce, 987

Nanaimo
AIDS Vancouver Island-Nanaimo Office, 17
Autism Society of British Columbia-Nanaimo Branch, 189
Beaver Party of Canada, 203
Boys & Girls Clubs of British Columbia-Boys & Girls Clubs of Central Vancouver Island, 222
British Columbia Ferry & Marine Workers' Union (CLC), 241
British Columbia Muslim Association-Nanaimo Branch, 247
British Columbia Automobile Association-Nanaimo Branch, 267
CADORA British Columbia-Mid-Island CADORA Chapter, 268
Canadian Home Builders' Association - British Columbia-Vancouver Island, 407
Canadian Public Relations Society Inc.-CPRS Vancouver Island, 463
Central Vancouver Island Multicultural Society, 525
Central Vancouver Island Orchid Society, 525
Clay Tree Society for People with Developmental Disabilities, 572
Credit Counselling Society of British Columbia-Nanaimo, 640
Global Village Nanaimo, 775
Greater Nanaimo Chamber of Commerce, 784
Habitat for Humanity Canada-British Columbia - Mid-Vancouver Island, 796
Heart & Stroke Foundation of B.C. & Yukon-Vancouver Island Area Office - Nanaimo, 808
Island Deaf & Hard of Hearing Centre-Nanaimo Branch Office, 865
Literacy Central Vancouver Island, 913
Loaves & Fishes Community Food Bank, 916
Marmot Recovery Foundation, 952
Mid-Island Coin Club, 965
Nanaimo Association for Community Living, 987
Nanaimo Community Foundation, 987
Nanaimo District Museum, 987
Nanaimo Family Life Association, 988
Nanaimo Historical Society, 988
Nanaimo Volunteer and Information Centre Society, 988
Nanaimo, Duncan & District Labour Council, 988
Tillicum Lelum Aboriginal Friendship Centre, 1379
Tourism Nanaimo, 1390
United Way Central & Northern Vancouver Island, 1413
Vancouver Island Construction Association-Nanaimo Office, 1426
Vancouver Island Crisis Society, 1426
Vancouver Island Real Estate Board, 1426
Vancouver Island Symphony, 1427
Vancouver Island University Faculty Association, 1427

Nanoose Bay
Canadian Pony Club-British Columbia Islands, 457
Parent Support Services Society of BC-Central Island Office, 1139

Nelson
ANKORS, 71
British Columbia Technology Education Association, 256
British Columbia Automobile Association-Nelson Branch, 268
Chamber of Mines of Eastern British Columbia, 539
The Friends of West Kootenay Parks Society, 763
Kootenay Real Estate Board, 892
Nelson & District Arts Council, 1003
Nelson & District Chamber of Commerce, 1003
Nelson & District Hospice Society, 1003
Touchstones Nelson Museum of Art & History, 1388
West Kootenay District Labour Council, 1445
West Kootenay Regional Arts Council, 1445
West Kootenay Women's Association, 1445
WWOOF Canada, 1469

New Denver
Slocan District Chamber of Commerce, 1303
Valhalla Wilderness Society, 1424

New Westminster
Anxiety Disorders Association of British Columbia, 72
BC Construction Safety Alliance, 201
BC Lymphedema Association, 201
Bowling Proprietors' Association of BC, 219
British Columbia Contract Cleaner's Association, 237
British Columbia Deaf Sports Federation, 238
British Columbia Safety Authority, 252
British Columbia Automobile Association-New Westminster Branch, 268
Canadian Association of Elizabeth Fry Societies-Elizabeth Fry Society of Greater Vancouver, 313
Canadian Association of Hepatology Nurses, 317
Canadian Deafblind Association (National)-British Columbia Chapter, 376
Canadian Lacrosse Hall of Fame, 425
Canadian Lutheran World Relief-Western Regional Office, 428
College of Denturists of British Columbia, 583
Community Living Society, 605
Condominium Home Owners' Association of British Columbia, 610
Construction Labour Relations Association of British Columbia, 624
Credit Counselling Society, 640
Darts British Columbia Association, 651
Douglas College Faculty Association, 661
Evangelical Lutheran Church in Canada-British Columbia Synod, 698
Federation of B.C. Youth in Care Networks, 722
Fraserside Community Services Society, 758
Gerontological Nursing Association of British Columbia, 772
Health Sciences Association of British Columbia, 807
HOPE International Development Agency, 821
Immigrant Services Society of BC-New Westminster - LINC, Settlement & Career Services, 830
Inclusion BC, 831
Justice Institute of British Columbia, 878
New Westminster Chamber of Commerce, 1015
New Westminster Hyack Festival Association, 1015
North West Library Federation, 1033
Orienteering Association of British Columbia, 1126
Pacific Urchin Harvesters Association, 1136
Structural Pest Management Association of British Columbia, 1352
Supply Chain Management Association - British Columbia, 1355
UNIFOR-New Westminster, 1405
Victorian Studies Association of Western Canada, 1434
Westcoast Association of Visual Language Interpreters, 1447

North Saanich
Saanich Peninsula Chamber of Commerce, 1245

North Vancouver
Animal Defence & Anti-Vivisection Society of BC, 70
Association of Image Consultants International Canada, 149
British Columbia Bed & Breakfast Innkeepers Guild, 233
British Columbia Brain Injury Association, 234
British Columbia Floorball Federation, 241
British Columbia Muslim Association-North Shore Branch, 247
British Columbia Nature (Federation of British Columbia Naturalists), 247
British Columbia Paralegal Association, 248
British Columbia Podiatric Medical Association, 249
British Columbia Supercargoes' Association, 255
British Columbia Automobile Association-North Vancouver, 268
Canadian Association for Young Children-British Columbia/Yukon, 307
Canadian Association of Aesthetic Medicine, 308
Canadian Association of Music Therapists-Music Therapy Association of British Columbia, 322
Canadian Hard of Hearing Association-British Columbia - North Shore Branch, 400
Canadian Plywood Association, 456
Canadian Shiatsu Society of British Columbia, 470
Canadian Society for Mucopolysaccharide & Related Diseases Inc., 477
Capilano University Faculty Association, 510
College of Veterinarians of British Columbia, 590
Jane Austen Society of North America-British Columbia - Vancouver Chapter, 868
Lions Gate Hospital Foundation, 913
Lynn Canyon Ecology Centre, 923
Native Courtworker & Counselling Association of BC, 997
North Shore ConneXions Society, 1032
North Shore Disability Resource Centre Association, 1032
North Shore Hospice Society, 1032
North Shore Multicultural Society, 1033
North Vancouver Community Arts Council, 1033
Red Road HIV/AIDS Network, 1210
St. Leonard's Society of Canada-St. Leonard's Society of North Vancouver, 1250
Save Your Skin Foundation, 1282
SOHO Business Group, 1332

Old Masset
Council of the Haida Nation - Haida Fisheries Program, 635

Oliver
Oliver Community Arts Council, 1057
Oliver Food Bank, 1057
Open Door Group-Oliver Office, 1114
South Okanagan Chamber Of Commerce, 1335

Osoyoos
Oliver-Osoyoos Naturalists, 1057
Open Door Group-Osoyoos Satellite Office, 1114
Osoyoos & District Arts Council, 1128
Osoyoos Desert Society, 1128
Osoyoos Food Bank, 1128

Parksville
Arrowsmith Naturalists, 84
Canadian Art Therapy Association, 295
Canadian Hypnosis Association, 410
Errington Therapeutic Riding Association, 695
Model Aeronautics Association of Canada Inc.-British Columbia Coastal Zone, 970
Oceanside Community Arts Council, 1054
Osteoporosis Canada-Mid-Island Chapter, 1128
Parksville & District Association for Community Living, 1142
Parksville & District Chamber of Commerce, 1142
Parksville & District Rock & Gem Club, 1142
Parksville Golden Oldies Sports Association, 1142
Salvation Army Mt. Arrowsmith Community Ministries - Food Bank, 1253

Peachland
Peachland Chamber of Commerce, 1147
Peachland Food Bank, 1147

Pemberton
Pemberton & District Chamber of Commerce, 1149

Pender Island
Pender Island Chamber of Commerce, 1149
Pender Island Field Naturalists, 1149

Penticton
British Columbia Society of Electroneurophysiology Technologists, 254
British Columbia Automobile Association-Penticton Branch, 268
Canadian Home Builders' Association - British Columbia-South Okanagan, 407
Penticton & District Community Arts Council, 1150
Penticton & District Community Resources Society, 1150
Penticton & District Society for Community Living, 1150
Penticton & Wine Country Chamber of Commerce, 1151
South Okanagan Boundary Labour Council, 1335
South Okanagan Immigrant & Community Services, 1335
South Okanagan Real Estate Board, 1335
South Okanagan Similkameen Brain Injury Society, 1335
South Okanagan Women in Need Society, 1335

Pitt Meadows
British Columbia Philatelic Society, 248
Canadian Dance Teachers Association-British Columbia Branch, 375
Maple Ridge Pitt Meadows Chamber of Commerce, 948

Port Alberni
Alberni District Historical Society, 21
Alberni Valley Chamber of Commerce, 21
Alberni Valley Coin Club, 21
Alberni Valley Rock & Gem Club, 21
British Columbia Purebred Sheep Breeders' Association, 250
British Columbia Welsh Pony & Cob Association-Vancouver Island Region, 258
Canadian Society of Professionals in Disability Management, 487
Community Arts Council of the Alberni Valley, 595
National Institute of Disability Management & Research, 994
PFLAG Canada Inc.-Alberni Chapter, 1155
Port Alberni & District Labour Council, 1165
Port Alberni Association for Community Living, 1165
Port Alberni Friendship Center, 1165

Port Clements
Port Clements Historical Society, 1165

Port Coquitlam
Alliance of Cancer Consultants, 58
Archives Association of British Columbia, 80
BC Hands & Voices, 201
British Columbia Archery Association, 230
British Columbia Fuchsia & Begonia Society, 242
British Columbia Square & Round Dance Federation, 255
Canada West Universities Athletic Association, 281

Geographic Index / British Columbia - Port Edward

Community Integration Services Society, 599
Credit Counselling Society of British Columbia-Port Coquitlam, 640
Foursquare Gospel Church of Canada, 756
Heart & Stroke Foundation of B.C. & Yukon-Fraser North & East Area Office - Tri-Cities/Fraser Valley/Burnaby/New Westminster, 808
Immigrant Services Society of BC-Port Coquitlam - LINC, 830
New Westminster Historical Society, 1015
The Terry Fox Foundation-British Columbia/Yukon Office, 1372

Port Edward
North Pacific Cannery - National Historic Site, 1032

Port Hardy
AIDS Vancouver Island-Port Hardy Office, 18
Port Hardy & District Chamber of Commerce, 1166
Port Hardy Harvest Food Bank, 1166

Port McNeill
Port McNeill & District Chamber of Commerce, 1166

Port Moody
British Columbia Lodging & Campgrounds Association, 245
Bully B'Ware, 264
Canadian Institute of Energy (British Columbia), 415
College of Registered Psychiatric Nurses of B.C., 590
College of Registered Psychiatric Nurses of British Columbia, 590
Port Moody Heritage Society, 1166
Port Moody Rock & Gem Club, 1166

Port Renfrew
Port Renfrew Chamber of Commerce, 1166
Vancouver Island Community Forest Action Network, 1426

Pouce Coupe
Pouce Coupe & District Museum & Historical Society, 1168

Powell River
Inclusion Powell River Soceity, 832
Powell River & District Labour Council, 1168
Powell River & District United Way, 1168
Powell River Chamber of Commerce, 1169
Powell River Lapidary Club, 1169
Powell River Sunshine Coast Real Estate Board, 1169
Recreation Facilities Association of British Columbia, 1207

Prince George
Active Support Against Poverty, 7
AiMHi, Prince George Association for Community Living, 18
Autism Society of British Columbia-Prince George Branch, 189
BC Northern Real Estate Association, 201
BC Trappers' Association, 202
Big Brothers Big Sisters of British Columbia-Big Brothers Big Sisters of Prince George, 209
Boxing BC Association, 220
British Columbia Association of School Psychologists, 232
British Columbia Construction Association-Northern Regional Construction Association, 237
British Columbia Muslim Association-Prince George Branch, 247
British Columbia Northern Real Estate Board, 248
British Columbia Paleontological Alliance, 248
British Columbia Automobile Association-Prince George Branch, 268
CADORA British Columbia-North Central - Skeena CADORA Chapter, 268
Canadian Association for Supported Employment, 304

Canadian Association of Elizabeth Fry Societies-Prince George & District Elizabeth Fry Society, 313
Canadian Association of Veterans in United Nations Peacekeeping-Prince George & Northern British Columbia Chapter, 336
Canadian Blood Services-Prince George, 345
Canadian Home Builders' Association - British Columbia-Northern BC, 407
Canadian Home Builders' Association - Northern British Columbia, 407
Canadian Railroad Historical Association-Prince George-Nechako-Fraser Division, 465
Carefree Society, 511
Cariboo Action Training Society, 512
Central British Columbia Railway & Forest Industry Museum Society, 524
Community Arts Council of Prince George & District, 595
Faculty Association of the College of New Caledonia, 701
Fraser Basin Council-Upper Fraser Regional Office, 757
Heart & Stroke Foundation of B.C. & Yukon-Prince George Area Office Northern BC/Yukon, 808
Immigrant & Multicultural Services Society, 830
McGregor Model Forest, 955
North Central Labour Council of British Columbia, 1030
North Central Local Government Association, 1030
Northern British Columbia Tourism Association, 1034
Parent Support Services Society of BC-Prince George Office, 1139
Perioperative Registered Nurses Association of British Columbia, 1152
PFLAG Canada Inc.-Prince George Chapter, 1156
Positive Living North: No kheyoh t'sih'en t'sehena Society, 1168
Prince George Alzheimer's Society, 1178
Prince George Backcountry Recreation Society, 1179
Prince George Brain Injured Group, 1179
Prince George Chamber of Commerce, 1179
Prince George Construction Association, 1179
Prince George Native Friendship Centre, 1179
Prince George Naturalists Club, 1179
Prince George Parents of Twins & Triplets Association, 1179
Prince George Recycling & Environmental Action Planning Society, 1179
Prince George Symphony Orchestra Society, 1179
Royal Astronomical Society of Canada-Prince George Centre, 1238
Spinal Cord Injury British Columbia-Prince George, 1343
Spruce City Wildlife Association, 1346
Tourism Prince George, 1390
United Steelworkers Local 1-424, 1412
United Way of Northern BC, 1415
YMCA Canada-YMCA of Northern BC - Prince George, 1472

Prince Rupert
Friendship House Association of Prince Rupert, 763
Northern Native Fishing Corporation, 1035
Prince Rupert & District Chamber of Commerce, 1179
Prince Rupert Association for Community Living, 1179
Prince Rupert Fire Museum Society, 1179
Prince Rupert Labour Council, 1180
World Wildlife Fund - Canada-Prince Rupert, 1468

Princeton
Princeton & District Chamber of Commerce, 1180
Princeton Community Arts Council, 1180
Vermilion Forks Field Naturalists, 1431

Qualicum Beach
Canadian National Association of Real Estate Appraisers, 438
Embroiderers' Association of Canada, Inc.-British Columbia - Arrowsmith Needle Arts, 685
Qualicum Beach Chamber of Commerce, 1195
Wilderness Committee-Vancouver Island - Mid-Island Office, 1454

Quathiaski Cove
Discovery Islands Chamber of Commerce, 658

Queen Charlotte
Haida Gwaii Arts Council, 798

Quesnel
British Columbia Broadband Association, 234
Quesnel & District Arts Council, 1200
Quesnel & District Chamber of Commerce, 1200
Quesnel & District Child Development Centre Association, 1200
Quesnel & District Labour Council, 1200
Quesnel Community Living Association, 1200
Quesnel Naturalists, 1200
Quesnel Tillicum Society Friendship Centre, 1200

Radium Hot Springs
Radium Hot Springs Chamber of Commerce, 1203

Revelstoke
Canadian Avalanche Association, 340
Canadian Railroad Historical Association-Selkirk Division, 465
HeliCat Canada, 811
Revelstoke Arts Council, 1228
Revelstoke Chamber of Commerce, 1228
Revelstoke Community Connections Food Bank, 1228
Revelstoke Women's Shelter Society, 1228
Shuswap Columbia District Labour Council, 1297
Wood Pellet Association of Canada, 1463

Richmond
ALS Society of British Columbia, 60
ALS Society of British Columbia-North Central Island Chapter, 60
Ambulance Paramedics of British Columbia, 66
The Appraisal Institute of Canada - British Columbia, 74
Armenian Relief Society of Canada, " Inc.-Vancouver Chapter: ""Araz""", 83
Baton Twirling Association of British Columbia, 199
BC Chinese Soccer Federation, 201
BC Sailing Association, 202
BCADA - The New Car Dealers of BC, 202
Boating BC Association, 216
British Columbia Chiropractic Association, 236
British Columbia Council for Exceptional Children, 237
British Columbia Fencing Association, 241
British Columbia Genealogical Society, 242
British Columbia Muslim Association, 246
British Columbia Muslim Association-Richmond Branch, 247
British Columbia Registered Music Teachers' Association-Richmond Branch, 251
British Columbia Table Tennis Association, 255
British Columbia Water Polo Association, 258
Building Officials' Association of British Columbia, 262
British Columbia Automobile Association-Richmond Branch, 268
Canadian Association for Williams Syndrome-CAWS - British Columbia, 307
Canadian Association of Foodservice Professionals, 315
Canadian Federation of AME Associations-Pacific AME Association, 385
Canadian Federation of Music Teachers' Associations, 388
Canadian Geotechnical Society, 397

Canadian Hearing Instrument Practitioners Society, 403
Canadian Hemochromatosis Society, 404
Canadian Lifeboat Institution, 427
Canadian Manufacturers & Exporters-British Columbia Division, 429
Canadian Sablefish Association, 468
Canadian Standards Association-Pacific Region, 490
Chinese Canadian Table Tennis Federation, 564
Chinese Cultural Centre-Richmond Office, 564
Chinese Federation of Commerce of Canada, 565
Chiu Chow Benevolent Association of BC Canada, 566
The Christian Episcopal Church of Canada, 567
College of Chiropractors of British Columbia, 583
College of Dental Technicians of British Columbia, 583
Community Arts Council of Richmond, 595
Compensation Employees' Union (Ind.), 608
Couples for Christ Canada-Couples for Christ Vancouver, 636
Creative Jewellers Guild of BC, 639
Heart & Stroke Foundation of B.C. & Yukon-Richmond Office - Richmond/South Delta, 808
Henan Fellowship Association of Canada, 812
Immigrant Services Society of BC-Richmond - LINC & Settlement Services, 830
Immigrant Services Society of BC-Richmond - LINC, 830
Industry Training Authority, 835
Jodo Shinshu Buddhist Temples of Canada, 873
KidSport British Columbia, 886
Lower Mainland Local Government Association, 920
Numeris-Western Office, 1051
Professional Golfers' Assocation of British Columbia, 1185
QMI-Vancouver, 1195
Recreation Vehicle Dealers Association of Canada, 1208
Richmond Caring Place Society, 1230
Richmond Chamber of Commerce, 1230
Richmond Chinese Community Society, 1230
Richmond Delta Youth Orchestra, 1230
Richmond Food Bank Society, 1230
Richmond Gem & Mineral Society, 1230
Richmond Multicultural Community Services, 1231
Richmond Orchestra & Chorus Association, 1231
Richmond Orchid Club, 1231
Richmond Society for Community Living, 1231
Rick Hansen Foundation, 1231
Rowing British Columbia, 1237
Sport BC, 1344
Syrian Canadian Council-Vancouver Office, 1365
Underwriters' Laboratories of Canada-Vancouver Site, 1404
Union of British Columbia Municipalities, 1407
Vancouver Paleontological Society, 1428
Western Regional Advocacy Group Society, 1450
World Vision Canada-British Columbia Office, 1467

Roberts Creek
Canadian Horse Heritage & Preservation Society, 408

Saanichton
AirCrew Association - Western Canada Region, 20
British Columbia Amateur Hockey Association, 230
International Community for Relief of Suffering & Starvation Canada, 855
Saanich Historical Artifacts Society, 1245
Worldwide Association of Business Coaches, 1468

Salmo
Salmo & District Chamber of Commerce, 1251
Salmo Community Resource Society, 1251

Salmon Arm
Canadian Society of Questers, 487
Recreation Vehicle Dealers Association of Canada-Recreation Vehicle Dealers Association of British Columbia, 1208
Salmon Arm - Salvation Army Food Bank, 1252
Salmon Arm & District Chamber of Commerce, 1252
Salmon Arm Bay Nature Enhancement Society, 1252
Shuswap Area Family Emergency Society, 1297
Shuswap Association for Community Living, 1297
Shuswap District Arts Council, 1297
Shuswap Naturalists, 1297
Shuswap Tourism, 1297

Salt Spring Island
CADORA British Columbia-Salt Spring CADORA Chapter, 269
Canadian Organic Growers Inc.-Island Natural Growers (Gulf Islands), 446
Rare Breeds Canada-Island Heritage Livestock, 1204
Salt Spring Community Centre Food Bank, 1252
Salt Spring Island Chamber of Commerce, 1252

Scotch Creek
North Shuswap Chamber of Commerce, 1033

Sechelt
Habitat for Humanity Canada-British Columbia - Sunshine Coast, 796
Open Door Group-Sechelt Office, 1114
Royal Astronomical Society of Canada-Sunshine Coast Centre, 1239
Sargeant Bay Society, 1253
Sechelt & District Chamber of Commerce, 1288
Sunshine Coast Arts Council, 1355
Sunshine Coast Community Services Society, 1355
Sunshine Coast Natural History Society, 1355

Seton Portage
Seton Portage/Shalalth District Chamber of Commerce, 1292

Shawnigan Lake
British Columbia Miniature Horse Club, 246
Vancouver Island Miniature Horse Club, 1426

Sicamous
Eagle Valley Arts Council, 666
Sicamous & District Chamber of Commerce, 1297

Sidney
Association of British Columbia Land Surveyors, 140
Canadian Hydrographic Association-Pacific Branch, 410
North Pacific Marine Science Organization, 1032
Organization of Military Museums of Canada, 1125
Post-Polio Awareness & Support Society of BC, 1168
The Royal Commonwealth Society of Canada-Vancouver Island, 1242
Sidney Lions Food Bank, 1298

Smithers
Bulkley Valley Community Arts Council, 264
Dze L K'ant Friendship Centre Society, 666
One Sky, 1058
Smithers Community Services Association, 1304
Smithers District Chamber of Commerce, 1304

Sooke
Canadian Merchant Navy Veterans Association Inc., 435
Sooke Chamber of Commerce, 1333

Sooke Food Bank Society, 1333
Sooke Philharmonic Society, 1333

Sorrento
Back Country Horsemen of British Columbia, 192
Shuswap Rock Club, 1297

South Surrey
Canadian Authors Association-Vancouver Branch, 338
Canadian Resort Development Association, 467

Sparwood
Local Government Management Association of British Columbia-Rocky Mountain Chapter, 917
Sparwood & District Chamber of Commerce, 1338

Squamish
Immigrant Services Society of BC-Squamish - LINC & Assessment Services, 830
Sea to Sky Free-Net Association, 1287
Squamish & District Labour Committee, 1346
Squamish Chamber of Commerce, 1346

Stewart
Stewart Historical Society, 1350
Stewart-Hyder International Chamber of Commerce, 1350

Summerland
Okanagan Similkameen Parks Society, 1056
Summerland Chamber of Commerce, 1354
Summerland Community Arts Council, 1354
Summerland Food Bank & Resource Centre, 1354
Summerland Museum & Heritage Society, 1354

Surrey
African Canadian Continuing Education Society, 12
AIESEC-Kwantlen, 18
American Foundry Society-British Columbia Chapter, 1493
Applied Science Technologists & Technicians of British Columbia, 74
Arts Council of Surrey, 85
Association of Neighbourhood Houses BC-Alexandra, 153
Badminton BC, 193
Barbados Cultural Association of British Columbia, 196
Baseball BC, 198
Block Watch Society of British Columbia, 215
British Columbia Association for Charitable Gaming, 231
British Columbia Association of Agricultural Fairs & Exhibitions, 231
British Columbia Career College Association, 235
British Columbia Conservation Foundation, 237
British Columbia Crime Prevention Association, 238
British Columbia Diving, 238
British Columbia Family Child Care Association, 240
British Columbia Floor Covering Association, 241
British Columbia Landscape & Nursery Association, 244
British Columbia Library Trustees' Association, 245
British Columbia Mainland Cricket League, 246
British Columbia Muslim Association-Surrey Delta Branch, 247
British Columbia Muslim Association-Surrey East Branch, 247
British Columbia Paint Manufacturers' Association, 248
British Columbia Printing & Imaging Association, 249
British Columbia Refederation Party, 250
British Columbia Registered Music Teachers' Association, 250
British Columbia Sheet Metal Association, 253
British Columbia Shorthorn Association, 253

British Columbia Turkey Farms, 257
British Columbia Vegetable Marketing Commission, 257
British Columbia Wall & Ceiling Association, 257
Building Supply Industry Association of British Columbia, 263
British Columbia Automobile Association-Surrey, 268
Canadian Association for School Health, 303
Canadian Association of Independent Credit Counselling Agencies, 318
Canadian Association of Private Language Schools, 328
Canadian Blood Services-Surrey, 345
Canadian Grandparents' Rights Association, 399
Canadian Institute of Plumbing & Heating-British Columbia Region, 418
Canadian Society of Hand Therapists, 483
Canadian Society of Palliative Care Physicians, 486
Canadian Thoroughbred Horse Society-British Columbia Division, 495
Canadian Tinnitus Foundation, 495
Centre for Child Development, 531
Child Evangelism Fellowship of Canada-Child Evangelism Fellowship of British Columbia, 559
The Christian & Missionary Alliance in Canada-Canadian Pacific District (CPD) Office, 566
Co-Dependents Recovery Society, 580
The Council of Senior Citizens Organization of British Columbia, 635
Creation Science Association of British Columbia, 639
Credit Counselling Society-Surrey - Guildford, 640
Credit Counselling Society of British Columbia-Delta - Surrey, 640
DIVERSEcity Community Resources Society, 659
Ducks Unlimited Canada-British Columbia Provincial Office, 664
Eaglesland Albanian Society of BC, 666
Environmental Health Foundation of Canada, 692
Food Banks British Columbia, 749
Fraser Valley Real Estate Board, 758
Frontiers Foundation-North Western Office, 764
Grace Communion International Canada, 779
Greater Vancouver Home Builders' Association, 786
Guide Outfitters Association of British Columbia, 793
Heart & Stroke Foundation of B.C. & Yukon-Surrey Area Office - Surrey/Langley/Whiterock/Cloverdale/Aldergrove/North Delta, 808
Institute of Professional Bookkeepers of Canada, 847
Kwantlen Faculty Association, 894
Last Post Fund-British Columbia Branch, 899
LC Line Contractors' Association of BC, 902
Master Bowlers' Association of British Columbia, 953
National Advertising Benevolent Society-NABS West, 989
Options: Services to Communities Society, 1117
Options: Services to Communities Society-Newton Office, 1117
Pacific Life Bible College, 1135
Pakistani Canadian Cultural Association of British Columbia, 1137
Parents Without Partners Inc.-Coquitlam Chapter, 1582
The Royal Canadian Legion-British Columbia/Yukon Command, 1240
Semiahmoo Foundation, 1289
Semiahmoo House Society, 1289
Surrey Association for Community Living, 1357
Surrey Board of Trade, 1357
Surrey Food Bank, 1357

Surrey Symphony Society, 1357
Sweet Adelines International - Westcoast Harmony Chapter, 1358
Thermal Environmental Comfort Association, 1375
Volkssport Association of British Columbia, 1437

Tahsis
Tahsis Chamber of Commerce, 1366

Tatla Lake
Gelbvieh Association of Alberta/BC, 768

Telkwa
Bulkley Valley Naturalists, 264
Christian Heritage Party of British Columbia, 567

Terrace
The Anglican Church of Canada-Diocese of Caledonia, 69
British Columbia School Counsellors' Association, 252
Kermode Friendship Society, 884
Kitimat, Terrace & District Labour Council, 891
Skeena Valley Naturalists, 1302
Terrace & District Chamber of Commerce, 1371
Terrace & District Community Services Society, 1371

Tofino
First Nations Environmental Network, 738
Friends of Clayoquot Sound, 760
Tofino-Long Beach Chamber of Commerce, 1381

Trail
Association of Kootenay & Boundary Local Governments, 150
Trail & District Chamber of Commerce, 1394
Trail Association for Community Living, 1394
United Way of Trail & District, 1417
West Kootenay Naturalists Association, 1445

Tsawwassen
Naut'sa mawt Resource Group, 1001

Ucluelet
Ucluelet Chamber of Commerce, 1402

Valemount
Valemount & Area Chamber of Commerce, 1423

Vananda
Texada Island Chamber of Commerce, 1373

Vancouver
Adlerian Psychology Association of British Columbia, 8
Administrative & Professional Staff Association, 8
Administrators of Volunteer Resources BC, 8
ADR Institute of Canada-British Columbia Arbitration & Mediation Institute, 9
Adult Educators' Provincial Specialist Association, 9
Adult Learning Development Association, 9
Aerospace Industry Association of British Columbia, 11
Affiliation of Multicultural Societies & Service Agencies of BC, 11
African Enterprise (Canada), 13
The AIDS Foundation of Canada, 17
AIDS Vancouver, 17
AIESEC-University of British Columbia, 18
Alcoholics Anonymous-Whitehorse - Whitehorse Intergroup, 53
Alcoholics Anonymous-Vancouver - Greater Vancouver Intergroup Society, 53
The Alcuin Society, 53
Alliance of Canadian Cinema, Television & Radio Artists-ACTRA BC Branch - Union of B.C. Performers, 58
Alzheimer Society of British Columbia, 62
American Concrete Institute-British Columbia Chapter, 1492

Geographic Index / British Columbia - Vancouver

American Marketing Association-British Columbia Chapter, 1495
American Society of Plumbing Engineers-British Columbia Chapter, 1502
Amnesty International - Canadian Section (English Speaking)-Vancouver Regional Office, 68
Ancient, Free & Accepted Masons of Canada - Grand Lodge of British Columbia & Yukon, 68
The Anglican Church of Canada-Diocese of New Westminster, 69
Apparel BC, 73
Architectural Institute of British Columbia, 79
ARMA Canada-Vancouver Chapter, 82
Army, Navy & Air Force Veterans in Canada-British Columbia Provincial Command, 83
Art Libraries Society of North America-Northwest Chapter
Arthritis Society-British Columbia / Yukon Division, 84
Asia Pacific Foundation of Canada, 86
Association for Mineral Exploration British Columbia, 134
Association of Administrative & Professional Staff - University of British Columbia, 138
Association of BC Drama Educators, 140
Association of Book Publishers of British Columbia, 140
Association of British Columbia Forest Professionals, 140
Association of British Columbia Teachers of English as an Additional Language, 140
Association of Canadian Faculties of Dentistry, 142
Association of Consulting Engineering Companies - British Columbia, 145
Association of Educators of Gifted, Talented & Creative Children in BC, 147
Association of Fundraising Professionals-Vancouver Chapter, 1512
Association of Neighbourhood Houses BC, 153
Association of Neighbourhood Houses BC-Cedar Cottage, 153
Association of Neighbourhood Houses BC-Frog Hollow, 153
Association of Neighbourhood Houses BC-Gordon House, 153
Association of Neighbourhood Houses BC-Kitsilano House, 153
Association of Neighbourhood Houses BC-Mount Pleasant, 153
Association of Neighbourhood Houses BC-South Vancouver, 153
Association of Professional Economists of British Columbia, 157
Association of Visual Language Interpreters of Canada, 164
Association of Women in Finance, 164
Australia-New Zealand Association, 188
Ballet British Columbia, 194
Bard on the Beach Theatre Society, 196
BC Adaptive Snowsports, 200
BC Alliance for Arts & Culture, 200
BC Assocation for Crane Safety, 201
BC Association for Individualized Technology and Supports, 201
BC Chinese Music Association, 201
BC First Party, 201
BC Freestyle Ski Association, 201
BC Soccer Referees Association, 202
BC Society of Transition Houses, 202
BeautyCouncil, 203
Better Business Bureau of Mainland BC, 206
The Bible Holiness Movement, 208
The Bible Holiness Movement, 208
Big Brothers Big Sisters of British Columbia-Big Brothers of Greater Vancouver, 209
Bike to Work BC Society, 211
Bio-dynamic Agricultural Society of British Columbia, 211
Birthright International-Vancouver Chapter, 212
The Bloom Group, 215
BMW Clubs Canada-BMW Car Club of BC, 216

Boys & Girls Clubs of British Columbia-Boys & Girls Clubs of South Coast B.C., 222
British Columbia & Yukon Community Newspapers Association, 229
British Columbia Alpine Ski Association, 229
British Columbia Alternate Education Association, 230
British Columbia Apartment Owners & Managers Association, 230
British Columbia Art Teachers' Association, 230
British Columbia Art Therapy Association, 230
British Columbia Association for Marriage & Family Therapy, 231
British Columbia Association for Regenerative Agriculture, 231
British Columbia Association of Healthcare Auxiliaries, 231
British Columbia Association of Insolvency & Restructuring Professionals, 232
British Columbia Association of Kinesiologists, 232
British Columbia Association of Mathematics Teachers, 232
British Columbia Association of Medical Radiation Technologists, 232
British Columbia Association of School Business Officials, 232
British Columbia Association of Social Workers, 232
British Columbia Association of Speech-Language Pathologists & Audiologists, 233
British Columbia Association of Teachers of Modern Languages, 233
British Columbia Blind Sports & Recreation Association, 234
British Columbia Business Educators Association, 234
British Columbia Cancer Foundation, 234
British Columbia Career Development Association, 235
British Columbia Centre for Ability, 235
British Columbia Centre for Ability Association, 235
British Columbia Centre of Excellence for Women's Health, 235
British Columbia Chamber of Commerce, 235
British Columbia Choral Federation, 236
British Columbia Civil Liberties Association, 236
British Columbia Coalition to Eliminate Abuse of Seniors, 236
British Columbia College of Social Workers, 236
British Columbia Construction Association-Vancouver Regional Construction Association, 237
British Columbia Contact Centre Association, 237
British Columbia Co-operative Association, 237
British Columbia Cooperative Learning Provincial Specialist Association, 237
British Columbia Council for Families, 237
British Columbia Courthouse Library Society, 238
British Columbia Criminal Justice Association, 238
British Columbia Culinary Arts Specialist Association, 238
British Columbia Dance Educators' Association, 238
British Columbia Dental Association, 238
British Columbia Disc Sports, 238
British Columbia Doctors of Optometry, 239
British Columbia Drug & Poison Information Centre, 239
British Columbia Environment Industry Association, 239
British Columbia Epilepsy Society, 240
British Columbia Federation of Labour, 240
British Columbia Food Technologists, 241
British Columbia Freedom of Information & Privacy Association, 241
British Columbia Hospice Palliative Care Association, 243
British Columbia Hotel Association, 243

British Columbia Industrial Designer Association, 244
British Columbia International Commercial Arbitration Centre, 244
British Columbia Law Institute, 244
British Columbia Liberal Party, 244
British Columbia Library Association, 244
British Columbia Library Association Library Technicians' & Assistants' Section, 245
British Columbia Lions Society for Children with Disabilities, 245
British Columbia Literacy Council, 245
British Columbia Lung Association, 245
British Columbia Lupus Society, 245
British Columbia Marijuana Party, 246
British Columbia Maritime Employers Association, 246
British Columbia Mountaineering Club, 246
British Columbia Music Educators' Association, 246
British Columbia Muslim Association-Vancouver Branch, 247
British Columbia Naturopathic Association, 247
British Columbia Non-Profit Housing Association, 247
British Columbia Pharmacy Association, 248
British Columbia Play Therapy Association, 249
British Columbia Police Association, 249
British Columbia Primary Teachers Association, 249
British Columbia Principals & Vice-Principals Association, 249
British Columbia Provincial Renal Agency, 249
British Columbia Psychogeriatric Association, 249
British Columbia Psychological Association, 249
British Columbia Public Interest Advocacy Centre, 250
British Columbia Real Estate Association, 250
British Columbia Recreation & Parks Association, 250
British Columbia Restaurant & Foodservices Association, 251
British Columbia Rhythmic Sportive Gymnastics Federation, 251
British Columbia Ringette Association, 251
British Columbia Rugby Union, 252
British Columbia Schizophrenia Society, 252
British Columbia School Superintendents Association, 252
British Columbia School Trustees Association, 252
British Columbia Seafood Alliance, 253
British Columbia Securities Commission, 253
British Columbia Seniors Living Association, 253
British Columbia Shorthand Reporters Association, 253
British Columbia Soccer Association, 253
British Columbia Social Studies Teachers Association, 253
British Columbia Society for Male Survivors of Sexual Abuse, 254
British Columbia Society for the Prevention of Cruelty to Animals, 254
British Columbia Society of Laboratory Science, 254
British Columbia Society of Landscape Architects, 254
British Columbia Society of Prosthodontists, 254
British Columbia Society of Respiratory Therapists, 254
British Columbia Sports Hall of Fame & Museum, 255
British Columbia Summer Swimming Association, 255
British Columbia Surgical Society, 255
British Columbia Teacher Regulation Branch, 255
British Columbia Teachers for Peace & Global Education, 256
British Columbia Teachers of English Language Arts, 256
British Columbia Teachers' Federation, 256

British Columbia Technology Industries Association, 256
British Columbia Therapeutic Recreation Association, 256
British Columbia Transplant Society, 257
British Columbia Ultrasonographers' Society, 257
British Columbia Video Relay Services Committee, 257
British Columbia Water & Waste Association, 257
British Columbia Wheelchair Sports Association, 258
British Columbia's Children's Hospital Foundation, 259
British Columbia-Yukon Halfway House Association, 259
British Exservicemen's Association, 259
Building Owners & Managers Association of British Columbia, 263
BullyingCanada Inc.-British Columbia Office, 264
Business Council of British Columbia, 266
British Columbia Automobile Association-Vancouver - Broadway Branch, 268
British Columbia Automobile Association-Vancouver - Kerrisdale Branch, 268
CADORA British Columbia-Vancouver - Richmond CADORA Chapter, 269
Canada China Business Council-Vancouver Office, 278
Canada Employment & Immigration Union-British Columbia & Yukon Regional Office, 279
Canada Health Infoway-Vancouver, 280
Canada India Village Aid Association, 280
Canada Korea Business Association, 280
Canada Taiwan Trade Association, 280
Canada-China Bilateral Cooperation Association, 283
The Canada-Japan Society of British Columbia, 283
Canada-Singapore Business Association, 284
Canadian Aboriginal AIDS Network, 285
Canadian Actors' Equity Association (CLC)-Western Office, 288
Canadian Alliance of Dance Artists-West Chapter, 291
Canadian Artists' Representation British Columbia, 295
Canadian Assembly of Narcotics Anonymous-British Columbia Region, 296
Canadian Association for Immunization Research & Evaluation, 301
Canadian Association for the Prevention of Discrimination & Harassment in Higher Education, 305
Canadian Association of Blue Cross Plans-Pacific Blue Cross, 309
Canadian Association of Medical Cannabis Dispensaries, 320
Canadian Association of Nordic Ski Instructors-Pacific Region - BC & YT, 323
Canadian Association of Nurses in HIV/AIDS Care, 323
Canadian Association of Nurses in Oncology, 323
Canadian Association of Sexual Assault Centres, 333
Canadian Bar Association-British Columbia Branch, 341
Canadian Bible Society-British Columbia District Office, 343
Canadian Blind Sports Association Inc., 344
Canadian Blood & Marrow Transplant Group, 344
Canadian Blood Services-Vancouver - Oak Street, 345
Canadian Blood Services-Vancouver - Standard Life, 345
Canadian Cancer Society-British Columbia & Yukon Division, 349

Canadian Celiac Association-Vancouver Chapter, 353
Canadian Centre for Policy Alternatives-British Columbia Office, 354
Canadian Centre for Studies in Publishing, 354
Canadian Children's Book Centre-Vancouver, 356
Canadian Condominium Institute-CCI-Vancouver Chapter, 362
Canadian Construction Women, 363
The Canadian Corps of Commissionaires-British Columbia Division, 365
Canadian Council for the Americas - British Columbia, 367
Canadian Croatian Congress, 373
Canadian Culinary Federation-Vancouver Branch, 374
Canadian Drug Policy Coalition, 379
Canadian Federation of Independent Business-British Columbia Office, 387
Canadian Freestyle Ski Association, 394
Canadian Friends of Bar-Ilan University-Western Region, 394
Canadian Friends of the Hebrew University-Vancouver Chapter, 395
Canadian Fujianese Friendship Association, 396
Canadian Genetic Diseases Network, 397
Canadian Hadassah WIZO-Vancouver, 399
Canadian Hard of Hearing Association-British Columbia - Vancouver Branch, 400
Canadian HIV Trials Network, 405
Canadian HIV Trials Network-Pacific Region, 405
Canadian Horticultural Therapy Association, 408
Canadian Hydrogen & Fuel Cell Association, 409
Canadian Information Processing Society-British Columbia Chapter, 411
Canadian Institute for the Relief of Pain & Disability, 413
Canadian Institute of Gemmology, 416
Canadian Institute of Public Health Inspectors, 419
Canadian International Dragon Boat Festival Society, 421
Canadian International Freight Forwarders Association, Inc.-Western Division, 421
Canadian Labour Congress-Pacific Regional Office, 425
Canadian LabourWatch Association, 425
Canadian Liver Foundation-British Columbia/Yukon Chapter, 427
Canadian Magen David Adom for Israel-Vancouver Chapter, 429
Canadian Masonry Contractors' Association-British Columbia & Yukon Chapter, 431
Canadian Melanoma Foundation, 434
Canadian Mental Health Association-British Columbia Division, 434
Canadian Mortgage Brokers Association, 437
Canadian Music Centre-British Columbia Region, 438
Canadian National Institute for the Blind-British Columbia-Yukon Division, 439
Canadian Parks & Wilderness Society-Vancouver - British Columbia Chapter, 451
Canadian Pension & Benefits Institute-Pacific Region, 453
Canadian Poetry Association, 456
Canadian Polish Congress-British Columbia Branch, 456
The Canadian Press-Vancouver Bureau, 459
Canadian Psychoanalytic Society-CPS Western Canadian Branch, 461
Canadian Public Relations Society Inc.-CPRS Vancouver, 463
Canadian Railroad Historical Association-Pacific Coast Division, 465
Canadian Snowboard Federation, 472
Canadian Snowsports Association, 472

Canadian Society for Brain, Behaviour & Cognitive Science, 473
The Canadian Society for the Weizmann Institute of Science-Vancouver Office, 479
Canadian Society of Air Safety Investigators, 479
Canadian Society of Biblical Studies, 481
Canadian Society of Hospital Pharmacists-British Columbia, 484
Canadian Taxpayers Federation-British Columbia, 493
Canadian Tour Guide Association of British Columbia, 495
Canadian Underwater Games Association, 498
Canadians for Ethical Treatment of Food Animals, 507
Cardiology Technologists' Association of British Columbia, 511
Care Institute of Safety & Health Inc., 511
Cement Association of Canada-Western Region (Vancouver), 521
Cement Association of Canada-Western Region (Vancouver & Calgary), 521
Central 1 Credit Union, 523
Le Centre culturel francophone de Vancouver, 526
Cerebral Palsy Association of British Columbia, 537
Certified Dental Assistants of BC, 538
CFA Society Vancouver, 539
Chambre de commerce francophone de Vancouver, 548
Chartered Professional Accountants of British Columbia, 553
Chartered Professional Accountants of the Yukon, 554
Chartered Professionals in Human Resources of British Columbia & Yukon, 554
Canadian Chemical Producers' Association-British Columbia Regional Office, 556
CHILD Foundation, 560
Childhood Cancer Canada Foundation-British Columbia Childhood Cancer Parent's Association, 560
Childhood Obesity Foundation, 560
Children's Arts Umbrella Association, 561
Children's Wish Foundation of Canada-British Columbia & Yukon Chapter, 562
Children's Writers & Illustrators of British Columbia Society, 563
Chinese Benevolent Association of Vancouver, 564
Chinese Cultural Centre, 564
Chinese Real Estate Professionals Association of British Columbia, 565
Chown Adult Day Care Centre, 566
Chris Spencer Foundation, 566
Circle of Eagles Lodge, 570
Citizens Concerned About Free Trade-Vancouver Office, 570
City Farmer - Canada's Office of Urban Agriculture, 571
Clean Energy British Columbia, 573
Coalition of BC Businesses, 578
Coast Forest Products Association, 579
Coast Foundation Society, 579
Coastal First Nations, 579
Coastal Jazz & Blues Society, 579
CoDevelopment Canada, 580
College of Dental Surgeons of British Columbia, 583
College of Dietitians of British Columbia, 584
College of Family Physicians of Canada-British Columbia College of Family Physicians, 584
College of Massage Therapists of British Columbia, 585
College of Midwives of British Columbia, 586
College of Naturopathic Physicians of British Columbia, 586
College of Opticians of British Columbia, 587
College of Optometrists of BC, 587
College of Pharmacists of British Columbia, 587
College of Physical Therapists of British Columbia, 587

College of Physicians & Surgeons of British Columbia, 588
College of Psychologists of British Columbia, 589
College of Registered Nurses of British Columbia, 589
College of Traditional Chinese Medicine Practitioners & Acupuncturists of British Columbia, 590
Communist Party of BC, 594
Community Energy Association, 597
Community Legal Assistance Society, 599
Community Legal Assistance Society-British Columbia Human Rights Clinic, 600
Community Social Services Employers' Association, 607
Computer-Using Educators of BC, 609
Confederation of University Faculty Associations of British Columbia, 611
Congregation Beth Israel - British Columbia, 612
Conseil jeunesse francophone de la Colombie-Britannique, 618
Construction Maintenance & Allied Workers Canada, 624
Continuing Legal Education Society of BC, 627
Cooperative Housing Federation of British Columbia, 628
Cooperative Housing Federation of Canada-British Columbia Region, 628
The Council of Canadians-British Columbia & Yukon, 633
Council of Forest Industries, 633
Council of Post Secondary Library Directors, British Columbia, 635
Council of Prairie & Pacific University Libraries, 635
Craft Council of British Columbia, 638
Creative BC, 639
Credit Counselling Society-Vancouver, 640
Credit Counselling Society of British Columbia-Burnaby, 640
Crohn's & Colitis Canada-British Columbia/Yukon Region, 642
Crossreach Adult Day Centre, 644
The Cultch, 645
Cycling British Columbia, 647
Dance Centre, 648
The Dance Centre, 649
Dancer Transition Resource Centre-British Columbia, 650
David Suzuki Foundation, 651
Development & Peace-British Columbia & Yukon, 654
Dignity Vancouver Dignité, 657
Directors Guild of Canada-British Columbia District Council, 657
Disability Alliance British Columbia, 658
Disabled Sailing Association of B.C., 658
Doctors of BC, 660
Downtown Vancouver Association, 662
Dress for Success-Vancouver, 663
Drug Prevention Network of Canada, 663
Dunbar Lapidary Club, 664
Early Childhood Educators of British Columbia, 666
Early Music Vancouver, 667
Earthsave Canada, 667
Ecojustice Canada Society, 672
Ecotrust Canada, 673
EDAM Performing Arts Society, 674
Edith Lando Charitable Foundation, 674
Editors' Association of Canada-British Columbia, 674
Educators for Distributed Learning PSA (British Columbia), 680
Emily Carr University of Art & Design Faculty Association, 686
End Legislated Poverty, 687
Ending Violence Association of British Columbia, 687
English Additional Language Learners Provincial Specialist Association, 689
Entre Nous Femmes Housing Society, 690

Environmental Educators' Provincial Specialist Association, 691
Environmental Managers Association of British Columbia, 692
Environmental Youth Alliance, 692
Evergreen-Vancouver Office, 699
Eye Bank of BC, 700
Family Enterprise Xchange-FEX Vancouver Region, 703
Family Services of Greater Vancouver, 704
FarmFolk CityFolk, 706
La Fédération des francophones de la Colombie-Britannique, 715
Fédération des parents francophones de Colombie-Britannique, 716
Federation of Aboriginal Foster Parents, 722
Federation of British Columbia Writers, 722
Federation of Canadian Artists, 722
Federation of Independent School Associations of BC, 724
Federation of Mountain Clubs of British Columbia, 725
Field Hockey BC, 734
Field Hockey Canada, 734
15th Field Artillery Regiment Museum & Archives Society, 734
Finnish Canadian Rest Home Association, 738
First Nations Breast Cancer Society, 738
First Pacific Theatre Society, 739
First Vancouver Theatre Space Society, 739
FPInnovations-Vancouver Division, 757
Fraser Basin Council, 757
Fraser Basin Council-Greater Vancouver Sea to Sky Regional Office (GVSS), 757
The Fraser Institute, 757
The Freda Centre for Research on Violence Against Women & Children, 758
Friends of Chamber Music, 760
From Grief To Action, 763
Fur-Bearer Defenders, 765
Canadian Youth Business Foundation-British Columbia Office, 765
Genome Canada-Genome British Columbia, 769
Geological Association of Canada-Vancouver (Cordilleran) Section, 770
GI (Gastrointestinal) Society, 773
Girl Guides of Canada-Guides du Canada-British Columbia Council, 773
GLOBE Foundation, 775
Goh Ballet Society, 776
Grain Workers' Union, Local 333, 779
Greater Vancouver Association of the Deaf, 786
The Greater Vancouver Board of Trade, 786
Greater Vancouver Community Services Society, 786
Greater Vancouver Food Bank Society, 786
Greater Vancouver International Film Festival Society, 786
Greater Vancouver Professional Theatre Alliance, 787
Greater Vancouver Taiwanese Canadian Association, 787
Greek Orthodox Community of East Vancouver, 787
Green Thumb Theatre for Young People, 789
Greenpeace Canada-Vancouver Office, 789
Guyanese Canadian Cultural Association of BC, 794
Gymnastics B.C., 795
Hamber Foundation, 800
Hang Gliding & Paragliding Association of Canada, 803
Hastings Centre Rockhounds, 804
Healing Our Spirit BC Aboriginal HIV/AIDS Society, 805
Health Employers Association of British Columbia, 806
Heart & Stroke Foundation of British Columbia & Yukon, 808
Heart & Stroke Foundation of B.C. & Yukon-Coastal Vancouver Area Office - Vancouver/North Shore, 808
Hellenic Canadian Congress of BC, 811
Hellenic Community of Vancouver, 811

Geographic Index / British Columbia - Vancouver

Helping Spirit Lodge Society, 812
Hong Kong-Canada Business Association, 820
Hong Kong-Canada Business Association-Vancouver Section Office, 820
Hostelling International - Canada-Pacific Mountain Region, 823
Hotel Association of Vancouver, 824
Hoy Ping Benevolent Association of Canada - Vancouver Branch, 824
H.R. MacMillan Space Centre Society, 824
Hub for Active School Travel, 824
Huntington Society of Canada-British Columbia Chapter, 827
Immigrant Services Society of BC, 830
Immigrant Services Society of BC-Vancouver - Language & Career College, 831
Import Vintners & Spirits Association, 831
Inland Refugee Society of BC, 838
Institute for Global Ethics (Canada), 843
Institute for the Study & Treatment of Pain, 844
Institute of Asian Research, 844
Insurance Brokers Association of Canada-Insurance Brokers Association of British Columbia, 848
Insurance Bureau of Canada-British Columbia, Saskatchewan & Manitoba Office, 849
Insurance Council of British Columbia, 849
Insurance Institute of British Columbia, 849
Integrated Vegetation Management Association of British Columbia, 850
Interactive Gaming Council, 851
Interior Designers Institute of British Columbia, 852
International Centre for Criminal Law Reform & Criminal Justice Policy, 854
International Centre for Sustainable Cities, 855
International College of Traditional Chinese Medicine of Vancouver, 855
International Council on Active Aging, 856
International Longshore & Warehouse Union (CLC)-Canadian Office, 1553
International Longshoremen's Association (AFL-CIO/CLC)-Canadian Division, 1553
International Society for Cellular Therapy, 860
International Society for Performance Improvement-Vancouver Chapter, 1559
International Wine & Food Society-Vancouver Branch, 1567
Investment Industry Regulatory Organization of Canada-Vancouver Office, 863
Italian Chamber of Commerce in Canada - West, 866
Italian Cultural Centre Society, 866
Jessie's Hope Society, 870
Jewish Community Centre of Greater Vancouver, 871
Jewish Federation of Greater Vancouver, 872
Jewish Genealogical Institute of British Columbia, 872
Jewish Historical Society of BC, 872
The John Howard Society of British Columbia, 874
Judo BC, 876
Junior Achievement of Canada-Junior Achievement of British Columbia, 877
Khalsa Diwan Society, 884
KickStart Disability Arts & Culture, 884
Kids Help Phone-British Columbia/Yukon, 886
Kinesis Dance Society, 888
Kitsilano Showboat Society, 891
Kiwassa Neighbourhood Services Association, 892
Korean Society of British Columbia for Fraternity & Culture, 893
Kosher Check, 894
Langara Faculty Association, 898
The Laurier Institution, 900
Law Foundation of British Columbia, 900
Law Society of British Columbia, 901
Learning Assistance Teachers' Association, 903
Leave Out Violence-British Columbia, 905
Lee's Benevolent Association of Canada, 906
Legal Services Society, 906
The Leon & Thea Koerner Foundation, 907
Lesbian & Gay Immigration Task Force, 907

The Leukemia & Lymphoma Society of Canada-British Columbia/Yukon Branch, 909
The Liberal Party of Canada (British Columbia), 909
Lifeforce Foundation, 911
LifeSciences British Columbia, 911
Lookout Emergency Aid Society, 919
Lu'ma Native Housing Society, 920
Madonna House Apostolate-Vancouver, 925
Malaspina Printmakers Society, 927
Marine Insurance Association of British Columbia, 949
Mascall Dance, 952
The Company of Master Mariners of Canada-Vancouver Division, 954
Mathematics of Information Technology & Complex Systems, 954
McCreary Centre Society, 955
Mediate BC Society, 957
Meeting Professionals International-British Columbia Chapter, 1570
MEFM Myalgic Encephalomyelitis & Fibromyalgia Society of British Columbia, 959
Memorial Society of British Columbia, 960
Michael Smith Foundation for Health Research, 964
Midwives Association of British Columbia, 965
Mining Association of British Columbia, 967
Mining Suppliers, Contractors & Consultants Association of BC, 967
Modern Baroque Opera Society, 971
Mood Disorders Association of British Columbia, 973
Mortgage Investment Association of British Columbia, 975
Moving Images Distribution, 978
Mr. & Mrs. P.A. Woodward's Foundation, 978
Multifaith Action Society, 979
Multilingual Orientation Service Association for Immigrant Communities, 979
Muscular Dystrophy Canada-Western Canada Regional Office, 982
Music BC Industry Association, 983
Mutual Fund Dealers Association of Canada-Pacific Regional Office, 986
Myasthenia Gravis Association of British Columbia, 986
Na'amat Canada Inc.-Vancouver Council, 987
NACE International-Canadian Region - British Columbia Section, 1572
National Association of Watch & Clock Collectors, Inc.-British Columbia Chapter, 1574
National Council of Jewish Women of Canada-Vancouver Section, 992
National Institute for Cannabis Health & Education, 994
Native Investment & Trade Association, 998
Nature Vancouver, 1001
NEC Native Education College Society, 1002
North American Association of Asian Professionals Vancouver, 1029
North Pacific Anadromous Fish Commission, 1031
North Vancouver Chamber of Commerce, 1033
Northwest Territories & Nunavut Dental Association, 1037
Northwest Wildlife Preservation Society, 1039
NSERC Chair for Women in Science & Engineering-British Columbia/Yukon, 1050
Occupational First Aid Attendants Association of British Columbia, 1054
Open Door Group, 1114
Open Door Group-Vancouver Downtown Eastside - VCC Office, 1114
Open Door Group-Vancouver Downtown Eastside - Hastings Office, 1114
OpenMedia Engagement Network, 1114
Options for Sexual Health, 1117
Outdoor Recreation Council of British Columbia, 1133
Ovarian Cancer Canada-Pacific-Yukon Regional Office, 1134

Oxfam Canada-British Columbia & Yukon Regional Office, 1134
Pacific Association of First Nations' Women, 1134
Pacific Bluegrass Heritage Society, 1135
Pacific Cinémathèque Pacifique, 1135
Pacific Corridor Enterprise Council, 1135
Pacific Immigrant Resources Society, 1135
Pacific Institute for the Mathematical Sciences, 1135
Pacific National Exhibition, 1135
Pacific Riding for Developing Abilities-Vancouver Branch, 1136
Pacific Salmon Commission, 1136
Pacific Salmon Foundation, 1136
Pan American Hockey Federation, 1138
Parkinson Society British Columbia, 1141
PeerNetBC, 1148
The Pembina Institute-Vancouver Office, 1149
People's Law School, 1151
Peretz Centre for Secular Jewish Culture, 1152
Physical Education in British Columbia, 1158
Physiotherapy Association of British Columbia, 1158
Pivot Legal Society, 1161
Planned Lifetime Advocacy Network, 1161
Planning Institute of British Columbia, 1162
Playwrights Theatre Centre, 1162
PLEA Community Services Society of BC, 1162
Positive Living BC, 1167
Positive Women's Network, 1168
Product Care Association, 1181
The Professional Institute of the Public Service of Canada-British Columbia & Yukon Regional Office, 1185
ProMOTION Plus, 1188
Public Service Alliance of Canada-British Columbia Branch, 1193
Public Service Alliance of Canada-Vancouver Branch, 1193
Public Service Alliance of Canada-Vancouver Satellite Office, 1193
Public Works Association of British Columbia, 1193
Pulp & Paper Centre, 1194
Pulp, Paper & Woodworkers of Canada, 1194
Radio Television Digital News Association (Canada), 1203
Real Estate Board of Greater Vancouver, 1205
Real Estate Council of British Columbia, 1205
Real Estate Institute of British Columbia, 1205
Real Estate Institute of Canada-British Columbia Chapter - The Real Estate Institute of British Columbia, 1206
Recreational Canoeing Association BC, 1208
Recycling Council of British Columbia, 1208
Registered Massage Therapists' Association of British Columbia, 1213
Resident Doctors of British Columbia, 1226
Réso Santé Colombie Britannique, 1226
Restaurants Canada-Western Canada Office, 1227
Retail Council of Canada-Western Office, 1228
Right to Quiet Society, 1232
Robert L. Conconi Foundation, 1234
Robson Street Business Association, 1235
Royal Astronomical Society of Canada-Vancouver Centre, 1239
Royal City Field Naturalists, 1241
The Royal Commonwealth Society of Canada-British Columbia Mainland Branch, 1242
The Royal Scottish Country Dance Society-Vancouver Branch, 1587
Royal United Services Institute - Vancouver Society, 1243
Rumble Productions Society, 1244
St. John Ambulance-British Columbia & Yukon Council, 1249
Scouts Canada-British Columbia - Yukon Operations Centre, 1286
Sea Shepherd Conservation Society, 1287
Seicho-No-Ie Toronto Centre-Seicho-No-Ie Vancouver Centre, 1289
Seva Canada Society, 1292

Shareholder Association for Research & Education, 1294
Shipyard General Workers' Federation of British Columbia, 1296
SIGMA Canadian Menopause Society, 1298
Skills/Compétences Canada-British Columbia, 1303
Society for Canadian Women in Science & Technology, 1325
Society for Technical Communication-Canada West Coast Chapter, 1591
Society of Composers, Authors & Music Publishers of Canada-West Coast Division, 1328
Society of Kabalarians of Canada, 1329
The Society of Notaries Public of British Columbia, 1330
Society of Translators & Interpreters of British Columbia, 1331
Society Promoting Environmental Conservation, 1331
Solid Waste Association of North America-Pacific Chapter - BC & Yukon, 1595
Special Interest Group on Computer Human Interaction, 1339
Spectrum Society for Community Living, 1340
Spina Bifida & Hydrocephalus Association of British Columbia, 1341
Spinal Cord Injury British Columbia, 1343
SportAbility BC, 1345
Squash British Columbia, 1347
Stanley Park Ecology Society, 1348
Starlight Starbright Children's Foundation Canada-British Columbia Chapter, 1348
Stroke Recovery Association of BC, 1352
Taiwan Trade Center, Vancouver, 1366
Taiwanese Canadian Cultural Society, 1366
Taoist Tai Chi Society of Canada-Pacific Region, 1367
Tara Canada Network Association, 1367
TB Vets, 1367
Teachers of Inclusive Education - British Columbia, 1367
Teamsters Canada (CLC)-Western Region, 1368
Tennis BC, 1370
Tetra Society of North America, 1373
Théâtre la Seizième, 1374
Theatre Terrific Society, 1375
Tides Canada Foundation, 1379
Tourism Industry Association of British Columbia, 1389
Tourism Vancouver/Greater Vancouver Convention & Visitors Bureau, 1391
Trans-Himalayan Aid Society, 1395
Trial Lawyers Association of British Columbia, 1397
Triathlon British Columbia, 1397
Truck Loggers Association, 1399
UBC Alumni Association, 1401
Ultimate Canada, 1404
Underwater Archaeological Society of British Columbia, 1404
UNICEF Canada-UNICEF British Columbia, 1405
Union of British Columbia Indian Chiefs, 1406
United Empire Loyalists' Association of Canada-Vancouver Branch, 1410
United Nations Association in Canada-Vancouver Office, 1411
University of British Columbia Faculty Association, 1419
University of British Columbia Symphony Orchestra, 1419
Urban & Regional Information Systems Association-British Columbia Chapter
Urban Development Institute of Canada, 1422
Vancity Community Foundation, 1424
Vancouver & District Labour Council, 1424
Vancouver Aboriginal Friendship Centre Society, 1424
Vancouver Art Gallery Association, 1424
The Vancouver Art Therapy Institute, 1425
Vancouver Association for the Survivors of Torture, 1425

Vancouver Association of Law Libraries, 1425
Vancouver Ballet Society, 1425
Vancouver Chinatown Business Improvement Area Society, 1425
Vancouver Community College Faculty Association, 1425
Vancouver Community Network, 1425
Vancouver Consultants, 1425
Vancouver Electric Vehicle Association, 1425
Vancouver Elementary School Teachers' Association, 1425
Vancouver Executives Association, 1425
Vancouver Foundation, 1425
Vancouver Grain Exchange, 1425
Vancouver Holocaust Centre Society - A Museum for Education & Remembrance, 1425
Vancouver Humane Society, 1426
Vancouver International Children's Festival, 1426
Vancouver Japanese Gardeners Association, 1427
Vancouver Jewish Film Centre Society, 1427
Vancouver Maritime Museum, 1427
Vancouver Moving Theatre, 1427
Vancouver Multicultural Society, 1427
Vancouver Museum Society, 1427
Vancouver Musicians' Association, 1427
Vancouver New Music, 1427
Vancouver Numismatic Society, 1428
Vancouver Opera, 1428
Vancouver Orchid Society, 1428
Vancouver Philharmonic Orchestra, 1428
Vancouver Pro Musica Society, 1428
Vancouver Rape Relief & Women's Shelter, 1428
Vancouver Recital Society, 1428
Vancouver Second Mile Society, 1428
Vancouver Soaring Association, 1428
Vancouver Society of Immigrant & Visible Minority Women, 1428
Vancouver Status of Women, 1428
Vancouver Symphony Society, 1429
Vancouver TheatreSports League, 1429
Vancouver Women's Health Collective, 1429
Vancouver Youth Symphony Orchestra Society, 1429
Vancouver, Coast & Mountains Tourism Region, 1429
VanDusen Botanical Garden Association, 1429
Vetta Chamber Music Society, 1431
ViaSport, 1432
ViaSport-Coaches ViaSport, 1432
Vocational Rehabilitation Association of Canada-British Columbia Society, 1436
Volunteer BC, 1438
W. Maurice Young Centre for Applied Ethics, 1439
WE Charity-Western Canada Office, 1443
West Coast Book Prize Society, 1444
West Coast Domestic Workers' Association, 1444
West Coast Environmental Law, 1444
West Coast Railway Association, 1445
Western Canada Children's Wear Markets, 1447
Western Canadian Opera Society, 1449
Western Forestry Contractors Association, 1449
Western Front Society, 1449
Western Institute for the Deaf & Hard of Hearing, 1450
Western Magazine Awards Foundation, 1450
Western Red Cedar Lumber Association, 1450
Western Silvicultural Contractors' Association, 1450
Western Transportation Advisory Council, 1450
Wilderness Committee, 1454
Women in Film & Television Vancouver, 1461
Women's Legal Education & Action Fund-West Coast LEAF, 1463
World Wildlife Fund - Canada-Vancouver, 1468
YMCA Canada-YMCA of Greater Vancouver, 1472
Your Political Party of BC, 1475
YWCA Canada-YWCA Metro Vancouver, 1482

Vanderhoof
Vanderhoof Chamber of Commerce, 1429

Vernon
Arts Council of the North Okanagan, 85
British Columbia Saw Filers Association, 252
British Columbia Automobile Association-Vernon Branch, 268
CADORA British Columbia-Okanagan CADORA Chapter, 268
Canadian 4-H Council-British Columbia, 284
Canadian College of Professional Counsellors & Psychotherapists, 360
Certified Organic Associations of British Columbia, 538
Commercial Seed Analysts Association of Canada Inc., 592
Cross Country British Columbia, 643
First Nations Friendship Centre, 738
Greater Vernon Chamber of Commerce, 787
North Okanagan Naturalists Club, 1031
North Okanagan Neurological Association, 1031
North Okanagan Organic Association, 1031
O'Keefe Ranch & Interior Heritage Society, 1053
Okanagan Historical Society, 1055
Ontario DX Association, 1077
People's Memorial Society of BC & Vancouver Island Memorial Society, 1152
Social Planning Council for the North Okanagan, 1306
Tourism Vernon, 1391
United Way of North Okanagan Columbia Shuswap, 1415
Vernon BC Food Bank, 1431
Vernon Japanese Cultural Society, 1431
Vernon Jubilee Hospital Foundation, 1431
Vernon Lapidary & Mineral Club, 1431
Vernon Women's Transition House Society, 1431

Victoria
AIDS Vancouver Island, 17
AIESEC-Victoria, 18
Alcoholics Anonymous-Victoria - AA Central Office, 53
ALS Society of British Columbia-Victoria Chapter, 60
Amalgamated Conservation Society, 66
The Anglican Church of Canada-Diocese of British Columbia, 69
Archaeological Society of British Columbia, 76
ARMA Canada-Vancouver Island Chapter, 82
Army Cadet League of Canada-British Columbia Branch, 83
Association of Complementary & Integrative Physicians of BC, 145
Association of Fundraising Professionals-Vancouver Island Chapter, 1512
Association of Professional Biology, 156
Association of Service Providers for Employability & Career Training, 162
Association of Vancouver Island Coastal Communities, 163
The Barnard-Boecker Centre Foundation, 196
BC Games Society, 201
Better Business Bureau of Vancouver Island, 206
Big Brothers Big Sisters of British Columbia-Big Brothers Big Sisters of Victoria & Area, 209
BMW Clubs Canada-Vancouver Island BMW Club, 216
Boys & Girls Clubs of British Columbia-Boys & Girls Club Services of Greater Victoria, 222
British Columbia Aboriginal Network on Disability Society, 229
British Columbia Association of Aboriginal Friendship Centres, 231
British Columbia Association of Clinical Counsellors, 231
British Columbia Association of Professionals with Disabilities, 232
British Columbia Chess Federation, 236
British Columbia Competitive Trail Riders Association, 236
British Columbia Construction Association, 237
British Columbia Construction Association-Vancouver Island Construction Association, 237
British Columbia Farm Industry Review Board, 240
British Columbia Funeral Association, 242
British Columbia Historical Federation, 243
British Columbia Institute of Agrologists, 244
British Columbia Investment Agriculture Foundation, 244
British Columbia Lions Society for Children with Disabilities-Victoria Office, 245
British Columbia Museums Association, 246
British Columbia Muslim Association-Victoria Branch, 247
British Columbia Neurofibromatosis Foundation, 247
British Columbia Railway Historical Association, 250
British Columbia Sustainable Energy Association, 255
British Columbia Automobile Association-Victoria - Broadmead Branch, 268
British Columbia Automobile Association-Victoria - Downtown Branch, 268
CADORA British Columbia, 268
Camosun College Faculty Association, 276
Canadian Aboriginal Veterans & Serving Members Association, 285
Canadian Agricultural Economics Society, 289
Canadian Association for Neuroscience, 302
Canadian Association of MAiD Assessors & Providers, 320
Canadian Association of Professionals with Disabilities, 329
Canadian Association of Veterans in United Nations Peacekeeping-MCpl Mark Isfeld Memorial Chapter, 336
Canadian Aviation Artists Assocation, 340
Canadian Blood Services-Victoria, 345
Canadian Celiac Association-Victoria Chapter, 353
The Canadian Corps of Commissionaires-Victoria, the Islands & Yukon Division, 365
Canadian Culinary Federation-Victoria Branch, 374
Canadian Institute for Health Information-CIHI Victoria, 412
Canadian Numismatic Research Society, 442
The Canadian Press-Victoria Bureau, 459
Canadian Railroad Historical Association-Esquimalt & Nanaimo Division, 465
Canadian Society for Education through Art, 474
Canadian Student Leadership Association, 491
Canadian Technical Asphalt Association, 493
Capital Region Beekeepers Association, 510
Child Find British Columbia, 559
Children's Health Foundation of Vancouver Island, 561
Les Clefs d'Or Canada, 573
College of Applied Biology British Columbia, 582
College of Dental Hygienists of British Columbia, 583
College of Occupational Therapists of British Columbia, 586
Community Arts Council of Greater Victoria, 595
Community Living Victoria, 606
Conseil national Société de Saint-Vincent de Paul-Vancouver Island, 619
Consumer Protection BC, 626
Credit Counselling Society of British Columbia-Victoria, 640
David Foster Foundation, 651
Ecoforestry Institute Society, 671
Environmental Health Association of British Columbia, 691
Esquimalt Chamber of Commerce, 696
Eurographics - European Association for Computer Graphics-Canada Branch, 1524

Family Caregivers of British Columbia, 702
Foster Parent Support Services Society, 755
Freshwater Fisheries Society of British Columbia, 760
Friends of Ecological Reserves, 761
Garth Homer Society, 767
Goldstream Food Bank Society, 777
Government Finance Officers Association of British Columbia, 778
Greater Victoria Chamber of Commerce, 787
Greater Victoria Philatelic Society, 787
Greater Victoria Youth Orchestra, 787
Green Party Political Association of British Columbia, 789
Habitat Acquisition Trust, 795
Habitat for Humanity Canada-British Columbia - Victoria, 796
Hands on Summer Camp Society, 803
Harmony Foundation of Canada, 803
Health Libraries Association of British Columbia, 806
Heart & Stroke Foundation of B.C. & Yukon-Victoria Office, 808
Help Fill a Dream Foundation of Canada, 812
Heritage Society of British Columbia, 813
Inter-Cultural Association of Greater Victoria, 851
International Brotherhood of Boilermakers, Iron Ship Builders, Blacksmiths, Forgers & Helpers (AFL-CIO)-Victoria (Lodge 191), 1541
Intrepid Theatre Co. Society, 862
Island Deaf & Hard of Hearing Centre, 865
Kaleidoscope Theatre Productions Society, 880
LandlordBC, 898
Learning Disabilities Association of British Columbia, 904
Local Government Management Association of British Columbia, 916
Musicians' Association of Victoria & the Islands, Local 247, AFM, 984
Mustard Seed Food Bank, 986
The Nature Conservancy of Canada-British Columbia, 1000
Navy League of Canada-Vancouver Island, 1002
North Central Library Federation, 1030
Northern Canada Study Group, 1034
Open Space Arts Society, 1114
Pacific Institute for Sport Excellence, 1135
Pacific Opera Victoria, 1135
Pacific Peoples' Partnership, 1135
Pacific States-British Columbia Oil Spill Task Force, 1136
Parent Support Services Society of BC-Victoria Office, 1139
PEERS Victoria Resource Society, 1148
PFLAG Canada Inc.-Victoria Chapter, 1156
The Platinum Party of Employers Who Think & Act to Increase Awareness, 1162
Plumbing Officials' Association of British Columbia, 1163
Private Forest Landowners Association, 1180
Professional Employees Association (Ind.), 1183
Project Management Institute-Vancouver Island
Public Health Association of British Columbia, 1192
Public Service Alliance of Canada-Victoria Branch, 1193
Rowing Canada Aviron, 1237
Royal Astronomical Society of Canada-Victoria Centre, 1239
Royal Canadian Artillery Association, 1239
Royal Canadian Naval Benevolent Fund-Western Committee, 1241
The Royal Scottish Country Dance Society-Vancouver Island Branch
Royal United Services Institute of Vancouver Island, 1243
S.A.L.T.S. Sail & Life Training Society, 1252
Sierra Club of Canada-British Columbia Chapter, 1298
Socialist Party of Canada, 1307
Société francophone de Victoria, 1319

Geographic Index / British Columbia - Wells

Special Olympics BC-Victoria, 1339
Student Christian Movement of Canada-Western Region, 1352
Tire Stewardship BC Association, 1380
Tourism Victoria/Greater Victoria Visitors & Convention Bureau, 1391
Triathlon Canada, 1397
United Empire Loyalists' Association of Canada-Victoria Branch, 1410
United Nations Association in Canada-Victoria Office, 1411
United World Colleges, 1418
University of Victoria Faculty Association, 1421
Urban Development Institute of Canada-Capital Region, 1422
Vancouver Island Advanced Technology Centre, 1426
Vancouver Island Construction Association, 1426
Vancouver Island Prostate Cancer Research Foundation, 1426
Vancouver Island Public Interest Research Group, 1426
Vancouver Island Society for Disabled Artists, 1427
Victoria Canada-China Friendship Association, 1432
Victoria Cool Aid Society, 1432
Victoria Epilepsy & Parkinson's Centre Society, 1432
Victoria Hospitals Foundation, 1432
Victoria International Development Education Association, 1432
Victoria Jazz Society, 1432
Victoria Labour Council, 1433
Victoria Lapidary & Mineral Society, 1433
Victoria Medical Society, 1433
Victoria Native Friendship Centre, 1433
Victoria Natural History Society, 1433
Victoria Numismatic Society, 1433
Victoria Orchid Society, 1433
Victoria READ Society, 1433
Victoria Real Estate Board, 1433
Victoria Society for Humanistic Judaism, 1433
Victoria Symphony Society, 1433
Victoria Youth Empowerment Society, 1434
Water Ski & Wakeboard British Columbia, 1441
West Shore Arts Council, 1446
West Shore Chamber of Commerce, 1446
Wilderness Committee-Victoria Office & Outreach Centre, 1454
X Changes Artists' Gallery & Studios Society, 1470
YMCA Canada-YMCA-YWCA of Greater Vancouver Island, 1472

Wells
Island Mountain Arts, 865
Wells & District Chamber of Commerce, 1444

West Kelowna
Greater Westside Board of Trade, 787
Municipal Pension Retirees Association, 981

West Vancouver
Aboriginal Tourism Association of British Columbia, 2
AFOA Canada-AFOA British Columbia, 12
British Columbia Aboriginal Child Care Society, 229
British Columbia Automobile Association-West Vancouver Branch, 268
First Nations SchoolNet-British Columbia Region, 739
German Canadian Business Association, 772
Lapidary Club of West Vancouver, 899
Native Brotherhood of British Columbia, 997
Native Fishing Association, 998
West Vancouver Chamber of Commerce, 1446
West Vancouver Community Arts Council, 1446
West Vancouver Community Foundation, 1447
West Vancouver Municipal Employees Association, 1447

Westbank
Canadian Authors Association-Kelowna (Okanagan Branch), 338

Canadian Lyme Disease Foundation, 428

Whistler
Canadian Home Builders' Association - British Columbia-Sea to Sky, 407
Whistler Chamber of Commerce, 1452
Whistler Food Bank, 1452
Whistler Resort Association, 1452

White Rock
Canadian Women Voters Congress, 505
Osteoporosis Canada-Surrey / White Rock Chapter, 1129
Pitch-In Canada, 1160
Sources Foundation, 1333
South Surrey & White Rock Chamber of Commerce, 1336

Williams Lake
Boys & Girls Clubs of British Columbia-Boys & Girls Club of Williams Lake & District, 222
Cariboo Chilcotin Child Development Centre Association, 512
Cariboo Chilcotin Coast Tourism Association, 512
Cariboo Friendship Society, 512
Central Interior Regional Arts Council, 524
Fraser Basin Council-Cariboo-Chilcotin Regional Office, 757
Thompson Rivers University Faculty Association-Williams Lake, 1376
Williams Lake & District Chamber of Commerce, 1455
Williams Lake Field Naturalists, 1455
Williams Lake Stampede Association, 1455

Winfield
Gem & Mineral Federation of Canada, 768
Lake Country Food Assistance Society, 895

Winlaw
Vaccination Risk Awareness Network Inc., 1423

Zeballos
Zeballos Board of Trade, 1482

Manitoba

Altona
Altona & District Chamber of Commerce, 61
Prairie Fruit Growers Association, 1169

Arborg
Arborg Chamber of Commerce, 76

Ashern
Ashern & District Chamber of Commerce, 86

Austin
Manitoba Brown Swiss Association, 933

Baldur
Canadian Pony Club, 457
Manitoba Beekeepers' Association, 932

Beausejour
Beausejour & District Chamber of Commerce, 203
Soil Conservation Council of Canada, 1332

Birtle
Birtle & District Chamber of Commerce, 212

Blumenort
Holstein Canada-Manitoba Branch, 819

Boissevain
Boissevain & District Chamber of Commerce, 217

Brandon
Addictions Foundation of Manitoba-Western Region Office, 8
American Saddlebred Horse Association of Canada, 66
The Anglican Church of Canada-Diocese of Brandon, 69
Appaloosa Horse Club of Canada-Manitoba Appaloosa Club, 73
Brandon Chamber of Commerce, 226

Brandon Friendship Centre, 226
Brandon Humane Society, 226
Brandon Police Association, 226
Brandon Real Estate Board, 226
Brandon University Faculty Association, 226
Brandon University School of Music, 226
Canadian 4-H Council-Manitoba, 284
Canadian Association of Fairs & Exhibitions, 314
Canadian Association of Geographers-Prairie Division, 316
Canadian Association of Police Educators, 327
Canadian Association of Veterans in United Nations Peacekeeping-Spr Christopher Holopina Chapter, 336
Canadian Blood Services-Brandon, 344
Canadian Celiac Association-Manitoba - West Chapter, 352
Canadian Forage & Grassland Association, 392
Child & Family Services of Western Manitoba, 558
Construction Association of Rural Manitoba Inc., 623
Ducks Unlimited Canada-Manitoba Provincial Office, 664
Economic Development Brandon, 673
Manitoba Conservation Districts Association, 934
Manitoba Genealogical Society Inc.-South West Branch, 937
Manitoba Hereford Association, 938
Manitoba Independent Insurance Adjusters' Association, 939
Manitoba Women's Institutes, 947
The Marquis Project, Inc., 952
Parkinson Society Manitoba-Brandon/Westman Office, 1141
PFLAG Canada Inc.-Brandon - Brandon / Westman Chapter, 1155
Provincial Exhibition of Manitoba, 1190
Samaritan House Ministries Inc., 1253
Sexuality Education Resource Centre Manitoba-Brandon Office, 1293
Society for Manitobans with Disabilities Inc.-Westman Regional Office, 1326
United Way of Brandon & District Inc., 1413
YMCA Canada-YMCA of Brandon, 1471
YWCA Canada-YWCA Brandon, 1481
YWCA Westman Women's Shelter, 1482

Carberry
Carberry & District Chamber of Commerce, 510
Carberry Plains Arts Council, 510
Manitoba Beef Cattle Performance Association, 932

Carman
Canadian Phytopathological Society, 455
Carman & Community Chamber of Commerce, 514
Golden Prairie Arts Council, 776
Manitoba Pulse & Soybean Growers Inc., 943
National Sunflower Association of Canada, 996

Carroll
Manitoba Welsh Pony & Cob Association-Keystone Region, 947

Cartwright
Manitoba Simmental Association, 944

Churchill
Churchill Chamber of Commerce, 569

Crystal City
Crystal City & District Chamber of Commerce, 645

Cypress River
Cypress River Chamber of Commerce, 647

Dauphin
Dauphin & District Allied Arts Council Inc., 651
Dauphin & District Chamber of Commerce, 651
Dauphin Friendship Centre, 651
Manitoba Genealogical Society Inc.-Dauphin Branch, 937

Parkland Crisis Centre & Women's Shelter, 1142
Society for Manitobans with Disabilities Inc.-Parkland Regional Office, 1326
West Region Tribal Council Cultural Education Centre, 1446

Deloraine
Deloraine & District Chamber of Commerce, 653

East Selkirk
Carl Orff Canada Music for Children, 513

East St Paul
Heavy Equipment & Aggregate Truckers Association of Manitoba, 810
International Brotherhood of Boilermakers, Iron Ship Builders, Blacksmiths, Forgers & Helpers (AFL-CIO)-Winnipeg (Lodge 555), 1541

Elie
Elie Chamber of Commerce, 685

Elkhorn
Elkhorn Chamber of Commerce, 685

Eriksdale
Eriksdale & District Chamber of Commerce, 695

Falcon Beach
Falcon, West Hawk & Caddy Lakes Chamber of Commerce, 701

Fisher Branch
Fisher Branch & District Chamber of Commerce, 739

Flin Flon
Flin Flon & District Chamber of Commerce, 740
Flin Flon Aboriginal Friendship Association Inc., 741
Manitoba-Saskatchewan Prospectors & Developers Association, 948

Gardenton
Friends of the Ukrainian Village Society-Ukrainian Museum & Village Society Inc., 763

Gillam
Gillam Chamber of Commerce, 773

Gimli
Icelandic National League of North America, 829

Gladstone
Shorthorn Breeders of Manitoba Inc., 1297

Grande Pointe
Music for Young Children-Manitoba, 983

Grandview
Grandview & District Chamber of Commerce, 781

Grunthal
Grunthal & District Chamber of Commerce, 792

Hamiota
Hamiota Chamber of Commerce, 802
Manitoba Square & Round Dance Federation, 945

Hartney
Hartney & District Chamber of Commerce, 804

Headingley
Headingley Chamber of Commerce, 805

Holland
Tiger Hills Arts Association Inc., 1379

Ile des Chênes
Wildlife Haven Rehabilitation Centre, 1454

Inwood
Manitoba Bison Association, 932

Kenton
Manitoba Percheron & Belgian Club, 942
Manitoba Welsh Pony & Cob Association, 947

Geographic Index / Manitoba - Winnipeg

Killarney
Killarney & District Chamber of Commerce, 887

La Salle
Animal Nutrition Association of Canada-Manitoba Division, 71
La Salle & District Chamber of Commerce, 1251

Lac du Bonnet
Canadian Liver Foundation-Manitoba Chapter, 427
Lac du Bonnet & District Chamber of Commerce, 894

Lake Audy
Manitoba Rural Tourism Association Inc., 943

Lake Manitoba First Nation
Manitoba Indian Education Association Inc., 939

Landmark
Landmark & Community Chamber of Commerce, 898

Leaf Rapids
Leaf Rapids Chamber of Commerce, 903

Lynn Lake
Lynn Lake Friendship Centre, 923

MacGregor
MacGregor Chamber of Commerce, 924

McCreary
Burrows Trail Arts Council, 266

Melita
Melita & District Chamber of Commerce, 959

Miniota
Organic Producers Association of Manitoba Co-operative Inc., 1125

Minnedosa
Minnedosa Chamber of Commerce, 968

Moosehorn
Grahamdale Community Development Corporation, 779

Morden
Morden & District Chamber of Commerce, 974
Society for Manitobans with Disabilities Inc.-Central Regional Office, 1326
United Way of Morden & District Inc., 1415

Morris
Manitoba Association of School Business Officials, 931
Morris & District Chamber of Commerce, 974

Neepawa
Canadian Porphyria Foundation Inc., 458
Manitoba Genealogical Society Inc.-Beautiful Plains, 937
Manitoba Holiday Festival of the Arts Inc., 938
Manitoba Regional Lily Society, 943
Margaret Laurence Home, Inc., 949
Neepawa & District Chamber of Commerce, 1002
Neepawa & District United Way, 1002
Viscount Cultural Council Inc., 1435

Nesbitt
Rare Breeds Canada, 1204

Niverville
Niverville Chamber of Commerce, 1027

Notre Dame de Lourdes
Chambre de commerce de Notre Dame, 542

Oak Bank
Canadian Square & Round Dance Society, 490

Oak Bluff
Canadian Association of Medical Device Reprocessing, 320

Oakville
Child Find Canada Inc., 559
Oakville & District Chamber of Commerce, 1053

Onanole
Wasagaming Chamber of Commerce, 1440

Petersfield
Saskatchewan Manitoba Galloway Association, 1269

Pinawa
Canadian Society of Agronomy, 479
Canadian Society of Soil Science, 488
Pinawa Chamber of Commerce, 1160

Pine Falls
Manitoba Model Forest, 940

Plum Coulee
Plum Coulee & District Chamber of Commerce, 1163

Portage la Prairie
Accelerated Christian Education Canada, 4
Association of Manitoba Municipalities, 151
Big Brothers Big Sisters of Manitoba-Big Brothers Big Sisters of Portage la Prairie, 209
Insurance Women's Association of Western Manitoba, 850
Manitoba Association of Fire Chiefs, 929
Manitoba Water & Wastewater Association, 947
Portage & District Arts Council, 1166
Portage Friendship Centre Inc., 1166
Portage Industrial Exhibition Association, 1166
Portage la Prairie & District Chamber of Commerce, 1167
Portage La Prairie Real Estate Board, 1167
Portage Plains United Way, 1167
Prairie Agricultural Machinery Institute-Portage la Prairie, 1169
Vegetable Growers' Association of Manitoba, 1430

Pukatawagan
Mamawehetowin Crisis Centre, 928

Rivers
Rivers & District Chamber of Commerce, 1234

Riverton
Riverton & District Chamber of Commerce, 1234
Riverton & District Friendship Centre, 1234

Roblin
Roblin & District Chamber of Commerce, 1235

Rossburn
Rossburn & District Chamber of Commerce, 1236

Russell
Russell & District Chamber of Commerce, 1244

Saint-Boniface
Chambre de commerce francophone de Saint-Boniface, 548
Conseil communauté en santé du Manitoba, 614
Conseil jeunesse provincial (Manitoba), 619
Development & Peace-Manitoba, 654
Fédération des aînés franco-manitobains inc., 711
Société historique de Saint-Boniface, 1320

Saint-Malo
La chambre de commerce de Saint-Malo & District, 543

Saint-boniface
Société de la francophonie manitobaine, 1316

Scanterbury
AFOA Canada-AFOA Manitoba, 12
Manitoba Uske, 946

Selkirk
Manitoba Forage & Grassland Association, 937
Selkirk & District Chamber of Commerce, 1289
Selkirk Friendship Centre, 1289
Society for Manitobans with Disabilities Inc.-Interlake Regional Office, 1326

Seven Sisters Falls
Canadian Association of Farm Advisors, 314

Shamattawa
Shamattawa Crisis Centre, 1294

Shoal Lake
Shoal Lake & District Chamber of Commerce, 1296

Souris
Souris & Glenwood Chamber of Commerce, 1334

St Alphonse
Jersey Canada-Manitoba, 869

St Georges
Blue Water Chamber of Commerce, 215

St Pierre Jolys
St. Pierre Chamber of Commerce, 1251

Ste Anne
Gospel Tract & Bible Society, 778

Ste Rose du Lac
Ste Rose & District Chamber of Commerce, 1349

Steinbach
Embroiderers' Association of Canada, Inc., 685
Evangelical Mennonite Conference, 699
Manitoba Sign Association, 944
Society for Manitobans with Disabilities Inc.-Eastman Regional Office, 1326
Steinbach Arts Council, 1349
Steinbach Chamber of Commerce, 1349

Stonewall
Ducks Unlimited Canada, 663
Stonewall & District Chamber of Commerce, 1350

Swan River
Elbert Chartrand Friendship Centre, 681
Manitoba Genealogical Society Inc.-Swan Valley Branch, 937
Swan Valley Chamber of Commerce, 1358

Teulon
Green Acres Art Centre, 788
Teulon Chamber of Commerce, 1373

The Pas
Aurora House, 187
The Pas & District Chamber of Commerce, 1144
The Pas Arts Council Inc., 1144
The Pas Friendship Centre Inc., 1145
Swampy Cree Tribal Council, 1358

Thompson
Addictions Foundation of Manitoba-Northern Region Office, 8
Boys & Girls Clubs of Manitoba-Thompson Boys & Girls Club, 222
Keewatin Tribal Council, 883
Ma-Mow-We-Tak Friendship Centre Inc., 928
Society for Manitobans with Disabilities Inc.-Northern Regional Office, 1326
Thompson Chamber of Commerce, 1376
Thompson Crisis Centre, 1376
YWCA Canada-YWCA Thompson, 1481

Treherne
Treherne Chamber of Commerce, 1397

Victoria Beach
PFLAG Canada Inc.-Winnipeg Chapter, 1156

Virden
Arts Mosaic, 85
Virden Community Chamber of Commerce, 1435

Wasagaming
Wasagaming Community Arts Inc., 1440

Winkler
Big Brothers Big Sisters of Manitoba-Big Brothers Big Sisters of Morden-Winkler, 209
Canadian Association of School Social Workers & Attendance Counsellors, 332
Childhood Cancer Canada Foundation-Manitoba - Candlelighters Childhood Cancer Support Group, 560
Manitoba Association of Women's Shelters, 931
South Central Committee on Family Violence, Inc., 1334
Winkler & District Chamber of Commerce, 1458
Winkler & District United Way, 1458

Winnipeg
Abundance Canada, 3
Addictions Foundation of Manitoba, 8
Addictions Foundation of Manitoba-Winnipeg Region Office, 8
Advertising Association of Winnipeg Inc., 10
Age & Opportunity Inc., 14
AIESEC-Manitoba, 18
Alcoholics Anonymous-Winnipeg - Manitoba Central Office, 53
Alliance Chorale Manitoba, 55
Alliance Française du Manitoba, 57
Alliance of Canadian Cinema, Television & Radio Artists-ACTRA Manitoba, 58
ALS Society of Manitoba, 60
Alzheimer Manitoba, 61
American Concrete Institute-Manitoba Chapter, 1492
The Anglican Church of Canada-Diocese of Rupert's Land, 70
Antiquarian Booksellers' Association of Canada, 72
Antique Automobile Club of America-Lord Selkirk Region
Antique Motorcycle Club of Manitoba Inc., 72
Anxiety Disorders Association of Manitoba, 72
The Appraisal Institute of Canada - Manitoba, 75
L'Arche Western Region-L'Arche Winnipeg, 78
Archers & Bowhunters Association of Manitoba, 78
Architectural & Building Technologists Association of Manitoba Inc., 78
Architectural Woodwork Manufacturers Association of Canada - Manitoba, 79
Arctic Co-operatives Limited, 81
ARMA Canada-Winnipeg Chapter, 82
Army, Navy & Air Force Veterans in Canada-Manitoba & Northwestern Ontario Provincial Command, 83
Arthritis Society-Manitoba / Nunavut Division, 84
Artists in Healthcare Manitoba, 85
Asper Foundation, 87
Assembly of Manitoba Chiefs, 88
Assiniboia Chamber of Commerce (MB), 88
Assiniboine Park Conservancy, 88
Associated Manitoba Arts Festivals, Inc., 89
Association des juristes d'expression française du Manitoba inc., 118
Association for Manitoba Archives, 133
Association for Vaccine Damaged Children, 135
Association of Christian Churches in Manitoba, 145
Association of Consulting Engineering Companies - Manitoba, 146
Association of Employees Supporting Education Services, 147
Association of Fundraising Professionals-Manitoba Chapter, 1512
Association of Manitoba Book Publishers, 151
Association of Manitoba Hydro Staff & Supervisory Employees, 151
Association of Manitoba Land Surveyors, 151
Association of Manitoba Museums, 151
Association of Professional Engineers & Geoscientists of Manitoba, 158
Association of Translators, Terminologists & Interpreters of Manitoba, 163
Athletics Manitoba, 181
Autism Society Manitoba, 189
Automotive Recyclers Association of Manitoba, 190
B'nai Brith Canada-Midwest Region, 192

Geographic Index / Manitoba - Winnipeg

B'nai Brith Youth Organization-Red River Region, 192
Ballon sur glace Broomball Canada, 195
Baptist General Conference of Canada-Baptist General Conference of Central Canada, 196
Basketball Manitoba, 198
Better Business Bureau of Manitoba & Northwest Ontario, 206
Biathlon Manitoba, 207
Big Brothers Big Sisters of Manitoba-Big Brothers Big Sisters of Winnipeg, 209
Block Parent Program of Canada-Block Parent Program of Winnipeg, 214
BMW Clubs Canada-BMW Club of Manitoba, 216
Bowls Manitoba, 220
Boxing Manitoba, 220
Boys & Girls Clubs of Manitoba-Boys & Girls Clubs of Winnipeg, 222
Brewing & Malting Barley Research Institute, 228
Building Energy Management Manitoba, 261
Building Owners & Managers Association of Manitoba, 263
CAA Manitoba, 268
Caisse Groupe Financier, 270
Calypso Association of Manitoba, 275
Canada Employment & Immigration Union-Manitoba, Saskatchewan, Alberta, Northwest Territories & Nunavut Regional Office, 279
Canada Grains Council, 279
Canadian Academy of Endodontics, 286
Canadian Agricultural Safety Association, 289
Canadian Agri-Marketing Association (Manitoba), 290
Canadian Artists' Representation Manitoba, 296
Canadian Associates of Ben-Gurion University of the Negev-Winnipeg Office, 297
Canadian Association for Anatomy, Neurobiology, & Cell Biology, 297
Canadian Association for Clinical Microbiology & Infectious Diseases, 297
Canadian Association for Williams Syndrome-CAWS - Manitoba, 307
Canadian Association of Agri-Retailers, 308
Canadian Association of Blue Cross Plans-Manitoba Blue Cross, 309
Canadian Association of Broadcast Consultants, 309
Canadian Association of Cardiovascular Prevention & Rehabilitation, 309
Canadian Association of Electroneurophysiology Technologists Inc., 312
Canadian Association of Elizabeth Fry Societies-Elizabeth Fry Society of Manitoba, 313
Canadian Association of Foot Care Nurses, 315
Canadian Association of Home & Property Inspectors-Manitoba Chapter, 317
Canadian Association of Paediatric Surgeons, 325
Canadian Association of Pharmacy in Oncology, 326
Canadian Association of Student Financial Aid Administrators, 334
Canadian Association of Veterans in United Nations Peacekeeping-LGen. R.R. Crabbe Chapter, 336
Canadian Aviation Historical Society-Manitoba Chapter, 340
Canadian Band Association, 340
Canadian Bar Association-Manitoba Branch, 342
Canadian Bible Society-Manitoba District Office, 343
Canadian Blood Services-Winnipeg, 345
Canadian Cancer Society-Manitoba Division, 349
Canadian Canola Growers Association, 349
Canadian Celiac Association-Manitoba Chapter, 352
Canadian Centre for Policy Alternatives-Manitoba Office, 354

Canadian Centre on Disability Studies, 354
Canadian Children's Book Centre-Winnipeg, 356
Canadian College of Health Leaders-Manitoba Regional Chapter, 359
Canadian Condominium Institute-CCI-Manitoba Chapter, 362
Canadian Conference of Mennonite Brethren Churches, 363
The Canadian Corps of Commissionaires-Manitoba Division, 365
Canadian Council for Small Business & Entrepreneurship, 367
Canadian Council of Ministers of the Environment, 368
Canadian Council of Teachers of English Language Arts, 370
Canadian Culinary Federation-Winnipeg Branch, 374
Canadian Employee Assistance Program Association, 380
Canadian Engineering Education Association, 381
Canadian Federation of AME Associations-Central AME Association, 384
Canadian Federation of Business & Professional Women's Clubs-Winnipeg Central, 386
Canadian Federation of Independent Business-Manitoba & Yukon Office, 387
Canadian Foodgrains Bank, 391
Canadian Friends of the Hebrew University-Winnipeg Chapter, 395
Canadian Hard of Hearing Association-Manitoba Chapter, 400
Canadian Hemophilia Society-Hemophilia Manitoba, 404
Canadian Information Processing Society-Manitoba Chapter, 411
Canadian Institute of Food Science & Technology-Manitoba Section, 415
Canadian Institute of Management-Manitoba - Winnipeg Branch, 417
Canadian Institute of Plumbing & Heating-Manitoba Region, 418
Canadian International Grains Institute, 421
Canadian Lutheran World Relief, 428
Canadian Manufacturers & Exporters-Manitoba Division, 430
Canadian Marketing Association-Manitoba Chapter, 431
Canadian Masonry Contractors' Association-Manitoba Masonry Contractors' Association, 431
Canadian Masters Cross-Country Ski Association-Manitoba, 431
Canadian Mental Health Association-Manitoba Division, 435
Canadian Midwifery Regulators Consortium, 436
Canadian Mineral Analysts, 436
Canadian National Institute for the Blind-Manitoba Division, 439
Canadian Network for Environmental Education & Communication, 440
Canadian Network for Improved Outcomes in Systemic Lupus Erythematosus, 440
Canadian Office & Professional Employees Union-Region 3 - Local 342, 445
Canadian Oilseed Processors Association, 445
Canadian Oral History Association, 446
Canadian Organic Growers Inc.-Organic Food Council of Manitoba, 447
Canadian Paraplegic Association (Manitoba), 449
Canadian Parks & Wilderness Society-Winnipeg - Manitoba Chapter, 451
Canadian Pension & Benefits Institute-Manitoba Region, 453
Canadian Polish Congress-Manitoba Branch, 456
The Canadian Press-Winnipeg Bureau, 459
Canadian Public Relations Society Inc.-CPRS Manitoba, 463
Canadian Rental Association, 467

Canadian Society for Eighteenth-Century Studies, 474
Canadian Society of Association Executives-Manitoba Chapter, 480
Canadian Society of Cardiology Technologists Inc., 481
Canadian Society of Hospital Pharmacists-Manitoba, 484
Canadian Society of Orthopaedic Technologists-Manitoba Chapter, 485
Canadian Special Crops Association, 489
Canadian Thoroughbred Horse Society-Manitoba Division, 495
Canadian Union of Public Employees-Manitoba Division, 498
Canadian Welding Bureau-Western Region, 503
Canadian Zionist Federation-Midwest Region, 506
CancerCare Manitoba, 508
Canola Council of Canada, 509
The Catholic Foundation of Manitoba, 519
Catholic Health Association of Manitoba, 519
Catholic Women's League of Canada, 520
Centre culturel franco-manitobain, 526
Centre for Indigenous Environmental Resources, Inc., 532
The Centre for Israel & Jewish Affairs-Jewish Federation of Winnipeg, 533
Le Cercle Molière, 537
Cerebral Palsy Association of Manitoba Inc., 538
Certified Technicians & Technologists Association of Manitoba, 538
CFA Society Winnipeg, 539
The Chartered Institute of Logistics & Transport in North America-Manitoba Region, 552
Chartered Professional Accountants of Manitoba, 553
Chartered Professionals in Human Resources Manitoba, 554
Child Evangelism Fellowship of Canada, 559
Child Evangelism Fellowship of Canada-Child Evangelism Fellowship of Manitoba, 559
Children's Hospital Foundation of Manitoba, 562
Children's Wish Foundation of Canada-Manitoba & Nunavut Chapter, 563
Chinese Medicine & Acupuncture Association of Canada-Manitoba Chapter, 565
Christian Labour Association of Canada-Winnipeg Regional Office, 568
Coaching Manitoba, 577
College of Audiologists and Speech-Language Pathologists of Manitoba, 582
College of Dietitians of Manitoba, 584
College of Family Physicians of Canada-Manitoba College of Family Physicians, 584
College of Licensed Practical Nurses of Manitoba, 585
College of Midwives of Manitoba, 586
College of Occupational Therapists of Manitoba, 586
College of Pharmacists of Manitoba, 587
College of Physicians & Surgeons of Manitoba, 588
College of Physiotherapists of Manitoba, 588
College of Podiatrists of Manitoba, 589
College of Registered Nurses of Manitoba, 589
College of Registered Psychiatric Nurses of Manitoba, 590
Communist Party of Canada (Manitoba), 594
Community Financial Counselling Services, 597
Community Futures Manitoba Inc., 598
Community Legal Education Association (Manitoba) Inc., 600
Community Living Manitoba, 603
Concrete Manitoba, 610
Conseil de développement économique des municipalités bilingues du Manitoba, 615
Construction Safety Association of Manitoba, 624
Controlled Release Society-Canadian Local Chapter, 1520

Cooperative Housing Federation of Canada-Prairie Region, 628
Council of Canadians with Disabilities, 633
Couples for Christ Canada-Couples for Christ Winnipeg, 636
Credit Counselling Society-Winnipeg, 640
Credit Institute of Canada-Manitoba Chapter, 641
Credit Union Central of Manitoba, 641
Crohn's & Colitis Canada-Manitoba/Saskatchewan/Nunavut Region, 643
Cross Country Ski Association of Manitoba, 644
CurlManitoba Inc., 646
Dairy Farmers of Manitoba, 648
Dance Manitoba Inc., 649
Denturist Association of Manitoba, 653
Canadian Diabetes Association-Manitoba & Nunavut Regional Leadership Centre, 655
Dignity Winnipeg Dignité, 657
Doctors Manitoba, 660
The Dream Factory, 662
East European Genealogical Society, Inc., 668
The Eckhardt-Gramatté Foundation, 671
Economic Developers Association of Manitoba, 673
Economic Development Winnipeg Inc., 673
Electrical Association of Manitoba Inc., 682
Embroiderers' Association of Canada, Inc.-Manitoba - Winnipeg Embroiderers' Guild, 685
Entomological Society of Manitoba Inc., 690
Epilepsy & Seizure Association of Manitoba, 693
Evangelical Covenant Church of Canada, 698
Evangelical Lutheran Church in Canada, 698
Evangelical Lutheran Church in Canada-Manitoba/Northwestern Ontario Synod, 698
Family Mediation Manitoba, 704
Fédération des associations de juristes d'expression française de common law, 712
Federation of Law Reform Agencies of Canada, 724
Fibromyalgia Support Group of Winnipeg, Inc., 733
Filipino Canadian Technical Professionals Association of Manitoba, Inc., 735
Fire Fighters Historical Society of Winnipeg, Inc., 738
Firefighters Burn Fund Inc., 738
First Nations SchoolNet-Manitoba Region, 739
Flax Council of Canada, 740
Folklorama, 742
FortWhyte Alive, 754
Francofonds inc., 757
Free Vietnamese Association of Manitoba, 759
Frontiers Foundation-Manitoba Office, 763
Funeral Planning & Memorial Society of Manitoba, 764
Canadian Youth Business Foundation-Manitoba Office, 765
Gem & Mineral Federation of Canada-Rock of Ages Lapidary Club, 768
Geological Association of Canada-Winnipeg Section, 770
German Canadian Cultural Association of Manitoba Inc., 772
German Society of Winnipeg, 772
German-Canadian Congress (Manitoba) Inc., 772
Girl Guides of Canada-Guides du Canada-Manitoba Council, 773
Golf Manitoba Inc., 777
The Great Herd of Bisons of the Fertile Plains, 782
Green Action Centre, 788
Green Kids Inc., 788
The Green Party of Manitoba, 788
Habitat for Humanity Canada-Manitoba, 796
Health Sciences Centre Foundation, 807
Heart & Stroke Foundation of Manitoba, 808
Heating, Refrigeration & Air Conditioning Institute of Canada-Manitoba - Regional Chapter, 810

Herb Society of Manitoba, 812
Heritage Winnipeg Corp., 813
Hockey Manitoba, 818
Hong Kong-Canada Business Association-Winnipeg Section Office, 820
Huntington Society of Canada-Manitoba Chapters, 827
Huntington Society of Canada-Manitoba Resource Centre, 828
Illuminating Engineering Society of North America-Winnipeg Section, 1531
Immigrant Centre Manitoba Inc., 830
Incident Prevention Association of Manitoba, 831
Indian & Metis Friendship Centre of Winnipeg Inc., 834
Indigenous Physicians Association of Canada, 835
Indspire-Winnipeg Office, 835
Infection & Prevention Control Canada, 836
Information & Communication Technologies Association of Manitoba, 836
Injured Workers Association of Manitoba Inc., 838
Institute of Urban Studies, 847
Insurance Brokers Association of Canada-Insurance Brokers Association of Manitoba, 848
Insurance Council of Manitoba, 849
Insurance Institute of Manitoba, 849
International Institute for Sustainable Development, 858
International Mennonite Health Association Inc., 858
Inter-Provincial Association on Native Employment, 861
Island Lake Tribal Council, 865
Japanese Cultural Association of Manitoba, 869
Jewish Child & Family Services, 871
Jewish Foundation of Manitoba, 872
Jewish Heritage Centre of Western Canada Inc., 872
The Joe Brain Foundation, 873
The John Howard Society of Manitoba, 874
Judo Manitoba, 876
Junior Achievement of Canada-Junior Achievement of Manitoba, 877
Juvenile Diabetes Research Foundation-Winnipeg, 879
Kali-Shiva AIDS Services, 880
Karate Manitoba, 881
Keystone Agricultural Producers, 884
The Kidney Foundation of Canada-Manitoba Branch, 885
Kids Help Phone-Manitoba, 886
KidSport Canada, 886
KidSport Manitoba, 886
Korean Society of Manitoba, 893
Law Society of Manitoba, 901
League for Human Rights of B'nai Brith Canada-Winnipeg Office, 903
Learning Disabilities Association of Manitoba, 904
The Liberal Party of Canada (Manitoba), 909
Life Science Association of Manitoba, 910
Life's Vision, 911
Lifesaving Society-Manitoba Branch, 911
Lighthouse Mission, 912
Lions Eye Bank of Manitoba & Northwest Ontario, Incorporated, 913
Little People of Manitoba, 915
Living Bible Explorers, 915
Long Term & Continuing Care Association of Manitoba, 919
Lupus Society of Manitoba, 922
Lutheran Church - Canada, 922
Lutheran Church - Canada-Central District, 922
Mamingwey Burn Survivor Society, 928
Manitoba & Northwestern Ontario CGIT Association, 928
Manitoba 5 Pin Bowlers' Association, 928
Manitoba Aboriginal Education Counselling Association Inc., 928
Manitoba Amateur Bodybuilding Association, 928

Manitoba Amateur Broomball Association, 928
Manitoba Amateur Wrestling Association, 928
Manitoba Animal Health Technologists Association, 928
Manitoba Antique Association, 928
Manitoba Arts Council, 929
Manitoba Arts Network, 929
Manitoba Association for Behaviour Analysis, 929
Manitoba Association for Medical Laboratory Science, 929
Manitoba Association for Volunteer Administration, 929
Manitoba Association of Architects, 929
Manitoba Association of Asian Physicians, 929
Manitoba Association of Christian Home Schools, 929
Manitoba Association of Friendship Centres, 929
Manitoba Association of Health Care Professionals, 929
Manitoba Association of Health Information Providers, 930
Manitoba Association of Home Economists, 930
Manitoba Association of Insolvency & Restructuring Professionals, 930
Manitoba Association of Landscape Architects, 930
Manitoba Association of Library Technicians, 930
Manitoba Association of Medical Radiation Technologists, 930
Manitoba Association of Non-Teaching Employees, 930
Manitoba Association of Optometrists, 930
Manitoba Association of Parent Councils, 930
Manitoba Association of Personal Care Home Social Workers, 931
Manitoba Association of Playwrights, 931
Manitoba Association of Registered Respiratory Therapists, Inc., 931
Manitoba Association of School Psychologists Inc., 931
Manitoba Association of School Superintendents, 931
Manitoba Association of Sheet Metal & Air Handling Contractors Inc., 931
Manitoba Association of Visual Language Interpreters, 931
Manitoba Athletic Therapists Association Inc., 931
Manitoba Badminton Association, 931
Manitoba Ball Hockey Association, 931
Manitoba Band Association, 932
Manitoba Bar Association, 932
Manitoba Baseball Association, 932
Manitoba Beef Producers, 932
Manitoba Blind Sports Association, 932
Manitoba Blues Society Inc., 932
Manitoba Brain Injury Association Inc., 932
Manitoba Building & Construction Trades Council, 933
Manitoba Building Envelope Council, 933
Manitoba Building Officials Association, 933
Manitoba Camping Association, 933
Manitoba Cardiac Institute (Reh-Fit) Inc., 933
Manitoba Chamber Orchestra, 933
The Manitoba Chambers of Commerce, 933
Manitoba Cheer Federation Inc., 933
Manitoba Chicken Producers, 933
Manitoba Child Care Association, 933
Manitoba Chiropractors' Association, 933
Manitoba Choral Association, 934
Manitoba Christmas Tree Growers Association, 934
Manitoba Coin Club, 934
Manitoba College of Registered Social Workers, 934
Manitoba Combative Sports Commission, 934
Manitoba Community Newspapers Association, 934
Manitoba Cooperative Association (MCA) Inc., 934
Manitoba Cooperative Honey Producers Ltd., 934

Manitoba Council for Exceptional Children, 934
Manitoba Council for International Cooperation, 934
Manitoba Crafts Council, 934
Manitoba Cricket Association, 935
Manitoba Criminal Justice Association, 935
Manitoba Cultural Society of the Deaf, 935
Manitoba Customer Contact Association, Inc., 935
Manitoba Cycling Association, 935
Manitoba Darts Association Inc., 935
Manitoba Deaf Sports Association Inc., 935
Manitoba Dental Assistants Association, 935
Manitoba Dental Association, 935
Manitoba Dental Hygienists Association, 935
Manitoba Diving Association, 935
Manitoba Down Syndrome Society, 935
Manitoba Eco-Network Inc., 936
Manitoba Egg Farmers, 936
Manitoba Environment Officers Association Inc., 936
Manitoba Environmental Industries Association Inc., 936
Manitoba Federation of Independent Schools Inc., 936
Manitoba Federation of Labour, 936
Manitoba Fencing Association, 936
Manitoba Five Pin Bowling Federation, Inc., 936
Manitoba Food Processors Association, 936
Manitoba Forestry Association Inc., 937
Manitoba Freestyle Ski Association, 937
Manitoba Funeral Service Association, 937
Manitoba Genealogical Society Inc., 937
Manitoba Genealogical Society Inc.-Southeast & Winnipeg Branch, 937
Manitoba Gerontological Nurses' Association, 937
Manitoba Government & General Employees' Union, 937
Manitoba Gymnastics Association, 937
Manitoba Hairstylists' Association, 937
Manitoba Hang Gliding Association, 937
Manitoba Heavy Construction Association, 937
Manitoba High Schools Athletic Association, 938
Manitoba Historical Society, 938
Manitoba Home Builders' Association, 938
Manitoba Horse Council Inc., 938
Manitoba Indian Cultural Education Centre, 939
Manitoba Institute of Agrologists, 939
Manitoba Interfaith Welcome Place, 939
Manitoba Islamic Association, 939
Manitoba Lacrosse Association, 939
The Manitoba Law Foundation, 939
Manitoba League of Persons with Disabilities, 939
Manitoba Liberal Party, 939
Manitoba Library Association, 939
Manitoba Library Consortium Inc., 940
Manitoba Lung Association, 940
Manitoba Magazine Publishers Association, 940
Manitoba Medical Service Foundation Inc., 940
Manitoba Medical Students' Association, 940
Manitoba Mennonite Historical Society, 940
Manitoba Métis Federation, 940
Manitoba Milk Prices Review Commission, 940
Manitoba Motor Dealers Association, 940
Manitoba Municipal Administrators' Association Inc., 941
Manitoba Music, 941
Manitoba Naturopathic Association, 941
Manitoba Non-Profit Housing Association, 941
Manitoba Nurses' Union, 941
Manitoba Opera Association Inc., 941
Manitoba Orchid Society, 941
Manitoba Organization of Disc Sports, 941
Manitoba Orienteering Association Inc., 941
Manitoba Ozone Protection Industry Association, 941
Manitoba Paddling Association Inc., 942
Manitoba Paraplegia Foundation Inc., 942
Manitoba Physiotheraphy Association, 942
Manitoba Poison Control Centre, 942
Manitoba Pork Council, 942
Manitoba Printmakers Association, 942

Manitoba Professional Painting Contractors Association, 942
Manitoba Professional Planners Institute, 942
Manitoba Provincial Handgun Association, 942
Manitoba Provincial Rifle Association Inc., 942
Manitoba Public Health Association, 942
Manitoba Quality Network, 943
Manitoba Reading Association, 943
Manitoba Real Estate Association, 943
Manitoba Restaurant & Food Services Association, 943
Manitoba Riding for the Disabled Association Inc., 943
Manitoba Ringette Association, 943
Manitoba Rowing Association, 943
Manitoba Runners' Association, 943
Manitoba Schizophrenia Society, Inc., 943
Manitoba School Boards Association, 944
Manitoba School Counsellors' Association, 944
Manitoba School Library Association, 944
Manitoba Securities Commission, 944
Manitoba Snowboard Association, 944
Manitoba Soaring Council, 944
Manitoba Society of Artists, 944
Manitoba Society of Occupational Therapists, 945
Manitoba Society of Pharmacists Inc., 945
Manitoba Speed Skating Association, 945
Manitoba Sport Parachute Association, 945
Manitoba Sports Hall of Fame & Museum, 945
Manitoba Table Tennis Association, 945
Manitoba Teachers' Society, 946
Manitoba Tenpin Federation, 946
Manitoba Tobacco Reduction Alliance, 946
The Manitoba Tourism Education Council, 946
Manitoba Trail Riding Club Inc., 946
Manitoba Trucking Association, 946
Manitoba Underwater Council, 946
Manitoba UNIX User Group, 946
Manitoba Used Car Dealers Association, 946
Manitoba Veterinary Medical Association, 946
Manitoba Volleyball Association, 946
Manitoba Wall & Ceiling Association, 947
Manitoba Water Polo Association Inc., 947
Manitoba Water Well Association, 947
Manitoba Wheelchair Sports Association, 947
Manitoba Wildlife Federation, 947
Manitoba Writers' Guild Inc., 947
Masonic Foundation of Manitoba Inc., 952
Massage Therapy Association of Manitoba Inc., 953
Master Brewers Association of The Americas-District Western Canada, 1570
MB Mission-Central Canada, 954
MBTelehealth Network, 955
Mechanical Contractors Association of Manitoba, 957
Mennonite Brethren Church of Manitoba, 960
Mennonite Church Canada, 961
Mennonite Church Canada-Mennonite Church Manitoba, 961
Mensa Canada Society, 961
Merit Contractors Association of Manitoba, 962
Mineral Society of Manitoba, 966
Mining Association of Manitoba Inc., 967
Mood Disorders Association of Manitoba, 973
Mother of Red Nations Women's Council of Manitoba, 975
Multiple Sclerosis Society of Canada-Manitoba Division, 980
Na'amat Canada Inc.-Winnipeg Council, 987
National Aboriginal Diabetes Association Inc., 988
National Association of Canadian Optician Regulators, 989
National Association of Japanese Canadians, 990
National Council of Jewish Women of Canada, 992
National Council of Jewish Women of Canada-Winnipeg Section, 992
National Screen Institute - Canada, 996
Native Addictions Council of Manitoba, 997
Native Clan Organization Inc., 997
Native Orchid Conservation Inc., 998

Native Women's Transition Centre Inc., 998
The Nature Conservancy of Canada-Manitoba, 1000
Nature Manitoba, 1000
Navy League of Canada-Manitoba, 1002
New Democratic Party-Manitoba NDP, 1014
North American Wild Fur Shippers Council, 1030
NSERC Chair for Women in Science & Engineering-Prairie Region, 1050
Occupational & Environmental Medical Association of Canada, 1054
On Screen Manitoba, 1058
Opticians Association of Canada, 1116
Opticians of Manitoba, 1116
Osteoporosis Canada-Winnipeg - Manitoba Chapter, 1129
Paddle Manitoba, 1137
Palliative Manitoba, 1137
Paramedic Association of Manitoba, 1138
Parents Without Partners Inc.-Stepping Stone (Winnipeg) Chapter
Parkinson Society Manitoba, 1141
Patronato INAS (Canada)-Winnipeg Office, 1146
Pentecostal Assemblies of Canada-Manitoba & Northwest Ontario District Office, 1150
People First of Canada, 1151
Philippine Association of Manitoba, Inc., 1157
Physical & Health Educators of Manitoba, 1158
Polish Combatants Association - Winnipeg, 1164
Post-Polio Network Manitoba Inc., 1168
Prairie Apparel Market, 1169
Prairie Theatre Exchange, 1170
Professional Association of Residents & Interns of Manitoba, 1182
The Professional Institute of the Public Service of Canada-Manitoba/Saskatchewan Regional Office, 1185
Professional Interior Designers Institute of Manitoba, 1185
Professional Property Managers Association Inc., 1186
Progressive Conservative Party of Manitoba, 1187
Project Management Institute-Manitoba
Project Peacemakers, 1187
Provincial Council of Women of Manitoba Inc., 1190
Psychological Association of Manitoba, 1191
Public Service Alliance of Canada-Prairies Branch, 1193
Public Service Alliance of Canada-Winnipeg Branch, 1193
Racquetball Canada, 1202
Racquetball Manitoba Inc., 1202
Rainbow Resource Centre, 1203
Real Estate Institute of Canada-Manitoba Chapter, 1206
Recreation Vehicle Dealers Association of Canada-Recreation Vehicle Dealers Association of Manitoba, 1208
Red River Apiarists' Association, 1210
Red River Exhibition Association, 1210
Reflexology Association of Canada, 1210
The Regional Health Authorities of Manitoba, 1212
RESOLVE: Research & Education for Solutions to Violence & Abuse, 1226
Resource Assistance for Youth, 1226
Restaurants Canada-Manitoba-Saskatchewan Office, 1227
Rhythmic Gymnastics Manitoba Inc., 1229
Roofing Contractors Association of Manitoba Inc., 1236
Rose & Max Rady Jewish Community Centre, 1236
Royal Astronomical Society of Canada-Winnipeg Centre, 1239
The Royal Canadian Legion-Manitoba & Northwest Ontario Command, 1240
The Royal Commonwealth Society of Canada-Winnipeg Branch, 1242
Royal Manitoba Theatre Centre, 1242

The Royal Scottish Country Dance Society-Winnipeg Branch
Royal Winnipeg Ballet, 1243
Rugby Manitoba, 1244
Safe Schools Manitoba, 1245
Safety Services Manitoba, 1245
Sail Manitoba, 1246
St. John Ambulance-Manitoba Council, 1249
The Salvation Army in Canada-Winnipeg - Prairie Division, 1253
Schizophrenia Society of Canada, 1283
Serena Canada-Manitoba Branch, 1290
Sexuality Education Resource Centre Manitoba, 1293
Sholem Aleichem Community Inc., 1297
Sisters of St. Benedict, 1301
Skate Canada-Manitoba Section, 1301
Skills Unlimited, 1302
Skills/Compétences Canada-Manitoba, 1303
Snowmobilers of Manitoba Inc., 1305
Social Planning Council of Winnipeg, 1306
Society for Manitobans with Disabilities Inc., 1326
Society for Manitobans with Disabilities Inc.-Wheelchair Services, 1326
Society for Manitobans with Disabilities Inc.-SMD Self-Help Clearinghouse, 1326
Society for Socialist Studies, 1326
Softball Manitoba, 1331
Special Olympics Manitoba, 1339
Spina Bifida & Hydrocephalus Association of Canada, 1341
Spina Bifida Association of Manitoba, 1342
Sport Manitoba, 1344
Sport Medicine & Science Council of Manitoba Inc., 1344
Squash Manitoba, 1347
Stroke Recovery Association of Manitoba Inc., 1352
Structural Innovation & Monitoring Technologies Resources Centre, 1352
Supply Chain Management Association - Manitoba, 1356
Swim-Natation Manitoba, 1359
Synchro Manitoba, 1360
Taekwondo Manitoba, 1366
TEAL Manitoba, 1368
Telecommunications Employees Association of Manitoba, 1369
Telecommunities Canada Inc., 1369
Tennis Manitoba, 1371
The Terry Fox Foundation-Manitoba Office, 1372
Thomas Sill Foundation Inc., 1376
Trager Canada, 1394
Travel Manitoba, 1396
Treaty & Aboriginal Rights Research Centre of Manitoba Inc., 1397
Trees Winnipeg, 1397
Triathlon Manitoba, 1398
Ukrainian Canadian Congress, 1402
Ukrainian Canadian Foundation of Taras Shevchenko, 1402
Ukrainian Fraternal Society of Canada, 1403
Ukrainian Orthodox Church of Canada, 1403
Ukrainian Youth Association of Canada-Winnipeg Branch, 1404
UNICEF Canada-UNICEF Prairies, 1405
UNIFOR-Winnipeg, 1405
United Church of Canada-All Native Circle Conference, 1409
United Church of Canada-Manitoba & Northwestern Ontario Conference, 1409
United Empire Loyalists' Association of Canada-Manitoba Branch, 1410
United Nations Association in Canada-Winnipeg Office, 1411
United Way of Winnipeg, 1417
University of Manitoba Faculty Association, 1419
University of Winnipeg Faculty Association, 1421
Variety - The Children's Charity of Manitoba, Tent 58 Inc., 1430
Vintage Locomotive Society Inc., 1435

Vocational Rehabilitation Association of Canada-Manitoba Society, 1436
Voices: Manitoba's Youth in Care Network, 1437
Water Ski - Wakeboard Manitoba, 1441
Western Canada Roadbuilders & Heavy Construction Association, 1448
Western Canadian Music Alliance, 1449
Western Grain Elevator Association, 1449
Western Retail Lumber Association, 1450
Wilderness Committee-Manitoba Field Office, 1454
Winnipeg Association of Non-Teaching Employees, 1458
Winnipeg Association of Public Service Officers, 1458
Winnipeg Chamber of Commerce, 1458
Winnipeg Construction Association, 1458
Winnipeg Executives Association, 1458
Winnipeg Film Group, 1458
Winnipeg Foundation, 1459
Winnipeg Gliding Club, 1459
Winnipeg Harvest Inc., 1459
Winnipeg Humane Society, 1459
Winnipeg Labour Council, 1459
Winnipeg Musicians' Association, 1459
Winnipeg Ostomy Association, 1459
Winnipeg Philatelic Society, 1459
Winnipeg Police Association, 1459
Winnipeg Real Estate Board, 1459
Winnipeg Symphony Orchestra Inc., 1459
Winnipeg Vegetarian Association, 1459
Winnipeg Youth Orchestras, 1459
Winnipeg's Contemporary Dancers, 1460
Women Business Owners of Manitoba, 1460
Women's Enterprise Centre of Manitoba, 1462
YMCA Canada-YMCA-YWCA of Winnipeg, 1471

New Brunswick

Arthurette
Victoria County Society for the Prevention of Cruelty to Animals, 1432

Balmoral
Canadian Business Aviation Association-Atlantic Provinces Chapter, 348
Canadian Masters Cross-Country Ski Association-New Brunswick, 431

Bathurst
Bathurst & District Labour Council, 199
Bathurst Volunteer Centre de Bénévolat Inc., 199
College of Family Physicians of Canada-New Brunswick College of Family Physicians, 584
Fédération des femmes acadiennes et francophones du Nouveau-Brunswick, 715
Greater Bathurst Chamber of Commerce, 783
Nepisiguit Salmon Association, 1003
New Brunswick Association of Community Business Development Corporations, 1004
New Brunswick Outfitters Association Inc., 1011
North Shore Forest Products Marketing Board, 1032

Bayswater
New Brunswick Special Care Home Association Inc., 1012

Benoit
Cross Country New Brunswick, 643

Blacks Harbour
Charlotte Seafood Employees Association, 552

Boiestown
Miramichi Board of Trade, 968

Bouctouche
Bouctouche Chamber of Commerce, 218

Burtts Corner
Grand Orange Lodge of Canada-Grand Orange Lodge of New Brunswick, 780

Cambridge-Narrows
Washademoak Region Chamber of Commerce, 1440

Campbellton
Campbellton Regional Chamber of Commerce, 276
Restigouche County Volunteer Action Association Inc., 1228
Société culturelle de la Baie des Chaleurs, 1309

Cap-Pelé
Chambre de commerce de la region de Cap-Pelé, 542

Caraquet
Association des juristes d'expression française du Nouveau-Brunswick-Péninsule acadienne, 118
Centre de Bénévolat de la Péninsule Acadienne Inc., 528
Chambre de commerce et du tourisme du Grand Caraquet, 548
Fédération des caisses populaires acadiennes, 712
New Brunswick Denturists Society, 1007
Théâtre populaire d'Acadie, 1375

Centre Village
New Brunswick Aerospace & Defence Association, 1004

Centreville
Centreville Chamber of Commerce, 537

Chamcook
Atlantic Salmon Federation, 186

Chipman
Chipman Community Care Inc., 565

Collette
Chambre de commerce de Collette, 540

Cookville
Atlantic Wildlife Institute, 186

Dalhousie
New Brunswick Genealogical Society Inc.-Restigouche Branch, 1009
Restigouche County Society for the Prevention of Cruelty to Animals, 1227

Dartmouth
Atlantic Convenience Store Association, 183

Dieppe
Association francophone des parents du Nouveau-Brunswick, 135
Athletics New Brunswick, 181
Atlantic Building Supply Dealers Association, 182
Atlantic Provinces Trucking Association, 185
Boys & Girls Clubs of New Brunswick-Boys & Girls Club of Dieppe, 222
Buckskinners Muzzleloading Association, Limited, 261
Canadian Hard of Hearing Association-New Brunswick - Moncton Branch, 400
New Brunswick Senior Citizens Federation Inc., 1012
Public Service Alliance of Canada-Moncton Branch, 1193
Skate Canada-New Brunswick Section, 1301

Dorchester
Westmorland Historical Society, 1451

Douglas
Association of Municipal Administrators of New Brunswick, 152
Illuminating Engineering Society of North America-Fiddlehead Section
Irish Canadian Cultural Association of New Brunswick, 864

Dufferin
Boys & Girls Clubs of New Brunswick-Boys & Girls Club of Charlotte County, 222

Edmundston
Association des juristes d'expression française du Nouveau-Brunswick-Madawaska, 118
Atelier RADO Inc., 180
Canadian Association for Disabled Skiing - New Brunswick, 299
Chambre de commerce de la région d'Edmundston, 542
Fédération des agriculteurs et agricultrices francophones du Nouveau-Brunswick, 711
Madawaska Forest Products Marketing Board, 924
New Brunswick Chamber of Commerce, 1006

Elsipogtog
New Brunswick Aboriginal Women's Council, 1004

Florenceville
Carleton-Victoria Forest Products Marketing Board & Wood Producers Association, 513
Multicultural Association of Carleton County Inc., 978

Florenceville-Bristol
Florenceville-Bristol Chamber of Commerce, 741

Fredericton
Ability New Brunswick, 1
The Acadian Entomological Society, 4
AFOA Canada-AFOA Atlantic, 12
Agricultural Alliance of New Brunswick, 14
AIDS New Brunswick, 17
Alzheimer Society of New Brunswick, 63
American Concrete Institute-Atlantic Chapter
The Anglican Church of Canada-Diocese of Fredericton, 69
Apple Growers of New Brunswick, 74
ARMA Canada-New Brunswick Chapter, 82
Arthritis Society-New Brunswick Division, 84
Association des bibliothécaires professionnel(le)s du Nouveau-Brunswick, 107
Association des enseignantes et des enseignants francophones du Nouveau-Brunswick, 112
Association Museums New Brunswick, 138
Association of New Brunswick Land Surveyors, 153
Association of New Brunswick Licensed Practical Nurses, 153
Association of New Brunswick Massage Therapists, 154
Association of Professional Engineers & Geoscientists of New Brunswick, 158
Association of Professional Librarians of New Brunswick, 159
Association of Registered Interior Designers of New Brunswick, 161
Association of Registered Professional Foresters of New Brunswick, 161
Association of University of New Brunswick Teachers, 163
Atlantic Provinces Chambers of Commerce-Fredericton, 183
Atlantic Planners Institute, 184
Baseball New Brunswick, 198
Basketball New Brunswick, 198
Boys & Girls Clubs of New Brunswick-Boys & Girls Club of Fredericton, 222
BullyingCanada Inc., 264
Canadian Association of Municipal Administrators, 321
Canadian Bar Association-New Brunswick Branch, 342
Canadian Celiac Association-Fredericton Chapter, 352
Canadian Condominium Institute-CCI-New Brunswick Chapter, 362
Canadian Crafts Federation, 372
Canadian Deafblind Association (National)-Canadian Deafblind Association - New Brunswick Inc., 376
Canadian Education & Training Accreditation Commission, 379
Canadian Federation of AME Associations-AME Association (Atlantic) Inc., 384
Canadian Forestry Association of New Brunswick, 392
Canadian Home Builders' Association - New Brunswick, 407
Canadian Home Builders' Association - New Brunswick-Greater Fredericton, 407
Canadian Manufacturers & Exporters-New Brunswick & Prince Edward Island Division, 430
Canadian Mental Health Association-New Brunswick Division, 435
Canadian Parks & Wilderness Society-Fredericton - New Brunswick Chapter, 451
The Canadian Press-Fredericton Bureau, 459
Canadian Union of Public Employees-New Brunswick Division, 498
Canoe Kayak New Brunswick, 508
Central Beekeepers' Alliance, 524
Chicken Farmers of New Brunswick, 557
Cities of New Brunswick Association, 570
College of Psychologists of New Brunswick, 589
Commission canadienne pour la théorie des machines et des mécanismes, 593
Conservation Council of New Brunswick, 621
Construction Association of New Brunswick, 623
Construction Association of New Brunswick-Fredericton Northwest Construction Association, 623
Construction Technology Centre Atlantic, 625
Copian, 628
Corporation des traducteurs, traductrices, terminologues et interprètes du Nouveau-Brunswick, 631
Council of Archives New Brunswick, 632
Council of Canadian Fire Marshals & Fire Commissioners, 633
Credit Counselling Services of Atlantic Canada-New Brunswick - Fredericton, 639
Canadian Diabetes Association-New Brunswick Region, 655
Ducks Unlimited Canada-New Brunswick Provincial Office, 664
Early Childhood Care & Education New Brunswick, 666
Easter Seals New Brunswick, 669
Electrical Contractors Association of New Brunswick, Inc., 682
Embroiderers' Association of Canada, Inc.-N.B. - Embroiderers' Guild of Fredericton, 686
Faculty Association of University of Saint Thomas, 701
Federation of Dance Clubs of New Brunswick, 723
Federation of New Brunswick Faculty Associations, 725
Financial & Consumer Services Commission-Fredericton, 736
Fitness New Brunswick, 740
Fredericton Anti-Poverty Association, 758
Fredericton Chamber of Commerce, 758
Fredericton Community Services Inc., 759
Fredericton Fish & Game Association, 759
Fredericton Police Association, 759
Fredericton Sexual Assault Crisis Centre, 759
Fredericton Society for the Prevention of Cruelty to Animals, 759
Fredericton Tourism, 759
Green Party of New Brunswick, 788
Gulf of Maine Council on the Marine Environment, 794
Habitat for Humanity Canada-New Brunswick - Fredericton Area Inc., 796
Hockey New Brunswick, 818
Insurance Brokers Association of Canada-Insurance Brokers Association of New Brunswick, 848
International Personnel Management Association - Canada-New Brunswick Chapter, 859
Jobs Unlimited, 873
Judo New Brunswick, 876
Junior Achievement of Canada-Junior Achievement of New Brunswick, 877
The Kidney Foundation of Canada-Atlantic Canada Branch, 885
KidSport New Brunswick, 886
The Kindness Club, 888
Law Society of New Brunswick, 901
Learning Disabilities Association of New Brunswick, 904
Lifesaving Society-New Brunswick Branch, 911
Literacy Coalition of New Brunswick, 913
Multicultural Association of Fredericton, 978
The Nature Conservancy of Canada-New Brunswick, 1000
Nature NB, 1000
Nature Trust of New Brunswick, 1001
The Neil Squire Foundation-Atlantic Regional Office, 1002
New Brunswick & Prince Edward Island Independent Adjusters' Association, 1004
New Brunswick Aboriginal Peoples Council, 1004
New Brunswick Arts Board, 1004
New Brunswick Association for Community Living, 1004
New Brunswick Association of Family Resource Centres, 1005
New Brunswick Association of Nursing Homes, Inc., 1005
New Brunswick Association of Occupational Therapists, 1005
New Brunswick Association of Optometrists, 1005
New Brunswick Association of Real Estate Appraisers, 1005
New Brunswick Association of Social Workers, 1006
New Brunswick Building Officials Association, 1006
New Brunswick Candlepin Bowlers Association, 1006
New Brunswick Cattle Producers, 1006
New Brunswick Chiropractors' Association, 1006
New Brunswick Choral Federation, 1006
New Brunswick Christmas Tree Growers Co-op Ltd., 1006
New Brunswick Continuing Legal Education, 1007
New Brunswick Crafts Council, 1007
New Brunswick Dental Society, 1007
New Brunswick Egg Marketing Board, 1007
New Brunswick Equestrian Association, 1008
New Brunswick Federation of Home & School Associations, Inc., 1008
New Brunswick Federation of Woodlot Owners Inc., 1008
New Brunswick Filmmakers' Co-op, 1008
New Brunswick Forest Products Association Inc., 1008
New Brunswick Fruit Growers Association Inc., 1008
New Brunswick Genealogical Society Inc., 1008
New Brunswick Golf Association, 1009
New Brunswick Ground Search & Rescue Association, 1009
New Brunswick Hospice Palliative Care Association, 1009
New Brunswick Innovation Foundation, 1009
New Brunswick Institute of Agrologists, 1009
New Brunswick Interscholastic Athletic Association, 1009
New Brunswick Latino Association, 1010
New Brunswick Law Foundation, 1010
New Brunswick Liberal Association, 1010
New Brunswick Lung Association, 1010
New Brunswick Medical Society, 1010
New Brunswick Multicultural Council, 1010
New Brunswick Nurses Union, 1010
New Brunswick Pharmacists' Association, 1011
New Brunswick Real Estate Association, 1011
New Brunswick Road Builders & Heavy Construction Association, 1011
New Brunswick Rugby Union, 1011
New Brunswick Sailing Association, 1011
New Brunswick Salmon Council, 1011
New Brunswick Scottish Cultural Association Inc., 1012
New Brunswick Society for the Prevention of Cruelty to Animals, 1012
New Brunswick Society of Certified Engineering Technicians & Technologists, 1012
New Brunswick Soil & Crop Improvement Association, 1012
New Brunswick Sports Hall of Fame, 1013
New Brunswick Teachers' Association, 1013
New Brunswick Union, 1013
New Brunswick Women's Institute, 1013
New Brunswick Youth in Care Network, 1013
New Democratic Party-New Brunswick NDP, 1014
Nurses Association of New Brunswick, 1052
Paramedic Association of New Brunswick, 1138
Partners for Youth, 1144
People's Alliance of New Brunswick, 1151
Porc NB Pork, 1165
Progressive Conservative Party of New Brunswick, 1187
Real Estate Board of the Fredericton Area Inc., 1205
Recreation New Brunswick, 1207
Rowing New Brunswick Aviron, 1237
Royal New Brunswick Rifle Association Inc., 1242
Safety Services New Brunswick, 1245
St. John Ambulance-New Brunswick Council, 1249
Scouts Canada-New Brunswick Council, 1287
Skills/Compétences Canada-New Brunswick, 1303
Société d'histoire de la Rivière Saint-Jean incorporée, 1310
Special Olympics New Brunswick, 1339
Sport New Brunswick, 1344
Supply Chain Management Association - New Brunswick, 1356
Swimming New Brunswick, 1359
Tennis New Brunswick, 1371
The Terry Fox Foundation-New Brunswick/PEI Office, 1372
Theatre New Brunswick, 1374
Tourism Industry Association of New Brunswick Inc., 1390
Turkey Farmers of New Brunswick, 1400
United Way/Centraide (Central NB) Inc., 1418
Volleyball New Brunswick, 1438
Wolastoqey Tribal Council Inc., 1460
Writers' Federation of New Brunswick, 1468
YMCA Canada-YMCA of Fredericton, 1472

Fredericton Junction
Sunbury West Historical Society, 1354

Gagetown
Gagetown & Area Chamber of Commerce, 766

Glassville
Falls Brook Centre, 701

Grand Bay
Saint John Coin Club, 1246

Grand Falls
New Brunswick Funeral Directors & Embalmers Association, 1008
New Brunswick Maple Syrup Association, 1010
Potatoes New Brunswick, 1168
Potatoes NB-Grand Falls, 1168
Société culturelle régionale Les Chutes, 1309
Valley Chamber of Commerce, 1424

Grand Manan
Boys & Girls Clubs of New Brunswick-Grand Manan Boys & Girls Club, 222
Eastern Fishermen's Federation, 670
Grand Manan Fishermen's Association, 779
Grand Manan Museum Inc., 780
Grand Manan Tourism Association & Chamber of Commerce, 780
Grand Manan Whale & Seabird Research Station, 780

Grand-Barachois
Institut féminin francophone du Nouveau-Brunswick, 842

Grand-Digue
Chambre de commerce Kent-Sud, 549

Grand-Sault
Association des juristes d'expression française du Nouveau-Brunswick-Victoria-Carleton, 118

Hampton
Hampton Area Chamber of Commerce, 802
Hampton Food Basket & Clothing Centre Inc., 802
King's County Historical Society, 888

Hanwell
Fencing - Escrime New Brunswick, 732

Hartland
Central Carleton Chamber of Commerce, 524

Haut-Saint-Antoine
Fédération des scouts de l'Atlantique, 718

Havelock
New Brunswick Shorthorn Breeders Association, 1012

Hillgrove
Atlantic Canada Trail Riding Association, 182

Hillsborough
Albert County Chamber of Commerce, 21
Canadian Railroad Historical Association-New Brunswick Division, 465

Keswick Ridge
Holstein Canada-New Brunswick Branch, 819
Lacrosse New Brunswick, 895

Kingsclear
Atlantic Region Aboriginal Lands Association, 186

Kingston
New Brunswick Dart Association, 1007

Lakeside
Horse Trials New Brunswick, 822

Lamèque
Association coopérative des pêcheurs de l'Île ltée, 98
Chambre de commerce des Iles Lamèque et Miscou inc., 544

Letang
Atlantic Canada Fish Farmers Association, 182

Long Reach
Appaloosa Horse Club of Canada-New Brunswick Appaloosa Horse Club, 73

Lower Cove
Fundy Model Forest Network, 764

Lower Kingsclear
New Brunswick Association of Food Banks, 1005

Lutes Mountain
Moncton Retriever Club, 972

Memramcook
Development & Peace-Nouveau-Brunswick, 654
New Brunswick Association of Medical Radiation Technologists, 1005
New Brunswick Society of Medical Laboratory Technologists, 1012
Ringette New Brunswick, 1233

Miramichi
Alzheimer Society of Miramichi, 63
Association of Professional Engineers & Geoscientists of New Brunswick-Northeastern Branch, 158
Big Brothers Big Sisters of New Brunswick-Big Brothers Big Sisters of Miramichi, 209
Boys & Girls Clubs of New Brunswick-Boys & Girls Club Miramichi, 222
Catholic Health Association of New Brunswick, 520
Commission de la Médiathèque Père-Louis-Lamontagne, 593
Conseil communautaire Beausoleil, 614
Miramichi Chamber of Commerce, 968
Miramichi Historical Society, Inc., 968
New Brunswick Association of Naturopathic Doctors, 1005
New Brunswick Genealogical Society Inc.-Miramichi Branch, 1009
PFLAG Canada Inc.-Miramichi Chapter, 1155
Schizophrenia Society of New Brunswick, 1283
Softball NB Inc., 1331

Moncton
Ability New Brunswick-Moncton, 2
AIDS Moncton, 17
Alzheimer Society of Moncton, 63
American Society of Heating, Refrigerating & Air Conditioning Engineers-New Brunswick/PEI Chapter
Archery Association of New Brunswick, 78
Association acadienne des artistes professionnel.le.s du Nouveau-Brunswick inc., 89
Association des bibliothécaires, des professeures et professeurs de l'Université de Moncton, 107
Association des employés de l'Université de Moncton, 112
Association des juristes d'expression française du Nouveau-Brunswick, 118
Association des juristes d'expression française du Nouveau-Brunswick-Westmorland, 118
Association du personnel administratif et professionnel de l'Université de Moncton, 131
Association of Consulting Engineering Companies - New Brunswick, 146
Atlantic Provinces Chambers of Commerce-Moncton, 183
The Atlantic District of The Wesleyan Church, 183
Atlantic Food & Beverage Processors Association, 184
Big Brothers Big Sisters of New Brunswick-Big Brothers Big Sisters of Moncton, 209
Birthright International-Moncton Chapter, 212
Boys & Girls Clubs of New Brunswick-Boys & Girls Club of Moncton, 222
Canada Employment & Immigration Union-New Brunswick & Prince Edward Island Regional Office, 279
Canada Fox Breeders' Association, 279
Canadian Association of Blue Cross Plans-Medavie Blue Cross/Atlantic Blue Cross Care/Service Croix Bleue de l'Atlantique, 309
Canadian Association of University Teachers of German, 335
Canadian Bible Society-Prince Edward Island District Office, 343
Canadian Bible Society-New Brunswick District Office, 343
Canadian Bible Society-Nova Scotia District Office, 343
Canadian Blood Services-Moncton, 344
Canadian Celiac Association-Moncton Chapter, 352
Canadian Federation of Business & Professional Women's Clubs-Greater Moncton, 385
Canadian Federation of Independent Business-New Brunswick Office, 387
Canadian Home Builders' Association - New Brunswick-Greater Moncton, 407
Canadian Institute of Plumbing & Heating-Atlantic Region, 418
Canadian Labour Congress-Atlantic Regional Office, 424
Canadian Liver Foundation-Moncton Chapter, 427
Canadian National Institute for the Blind-New Brunswick Division, 439
Canadian Poetry Association-Atlantic Canada, 456
Chartered Professional Accountants of New Brunswick, 553
Child Evangelism Fellowship of Canada-Child Evangelism Fellowship - Atlantic, 559
Conseil économique du Nouveau-Brunswick inc., 618
Conseil pour le développement de l'alphabétisme et des compétences des adultes du Nouveau-Brunswick, 619
Construction Association of New Brunswick-Moncton Northeast Construction Association, 623
Credit Counselling Services of Atlantic Canada-New Brunswick - Moncton, 639
Crossroads for Women Inc., 644
Dorchester & Westmorland Literacy Council, 661
Family Service Moncton Inc., 704
Fédération des jeunes francophones du Nouveau-Brunswick Inc., 715
Fondation CHU Dumont Foundation, 743
Food Depot Alimentaire, Inc., 749
Friends of The Moncton Hospital Foundation, 763
Greater Moncton Chamber of Commerce, 784
Greater Moncton Real Estate Board Inc., 784
Greater Moncton Society for the Prevention of Cruelty to Animals, 784
Habitat for Humanity Canada-New Brunswick - Moncton, 796
Human Resources Association of New Brunswick, 825
Illuminating Engineering Society of North America-Northumberland Section
Insurance Institute of New Brunswick, 849
Intercultural Heritage Association, 852
The John Howard Society of New Brunswick, Inc.-Southeastern New Brunswick, 874
Laubach Literacy New Brunswick, 900
Learning Disabilities Association of New Brunswick-Moncton Chapter, 904
Lupus New Brunswick, 921
Mechanical Contractors Association of New Brunswick, 957
Moncton Area Lawyers' Association, 972
Moncton Coin Club, 972
Multicultural Association of the Greater Moncton Area, 979
Music for Young Children-New Brunswick & Prince Edward Island, 984
Music/Musique NB, 984
The New Brunswick Association of Respiratory Therapists Inc., 1005
New Brunswick Association of Speech-Language Pathologists & Audiologists, 1006
New Brunswick Federation of Labour, 1008
New Brunswick Pharmaceutical Society, 1011
New Brunswick Wildlife Federation, 1013
Numeris-Moncton Office, 1051
Les Productions DansEncorps Inc., 1181
Project Management Institute-New Brunswick
Schizophrenia Society of New Brunswick-Moncton Chapter, 1284
Soccer New Brunswick, 1305
Société nationale de l'Acadie, 1322
Société Santé et Mieux-être en français du Nouveau-Brunswick, 1325
Spina Bifida & Hydrocephalus Association of New Brunswick, 1342
Théâtre l'Escaouette, 1374
Tourism Moncton, 1390
UNIFOR-Moncton, 1405
United Way of Greater Moncton & Southeastern New Brunswick, 1414
YMCA Canada-YMCA of Greater Moncton, 1472
YWCA Canada-YWCA Moncton, 1481

Morrisdale
Professional Photographers of Canada-Professional Photographers of Canada - Atlantic Region, 1186

Nackawic
Mactaquac Country Chamber of Commerce, 924

New Brandon
National Association of PeriAnesthesia Nurses of Canada, 990

New Denmark
New Denmark Historical Society, 1014

New Maryland
Fredericton Numismatic Society, 759

Newcastle Centre
New Brunswick Curling Association, 1007

Old Ridge
Horseshoe New Brunswick, 822

Oromocto
New Brunswick Signallers Association, 1012
Oromocto & Area Chamber of Commerce, 1127
Oromocto & Area SPCA, 1127
Oromocto & Surrounding Area Food & Clothing Bank, 1127

Petit-Rocher
Association francophone des municipalités du Nouveau-Brunswick Inc., 135
Société de l'Acadie du Nouveau-Brunswick, 1316
Société des Jeux de l'Acadie inc., 1318

Petitcodiac
Boys & Girls Clubs of New Brunswick-Petitcodiac Boys & Girls Club, 222

Pine Glen
Cavalier Riding Club Ltd., 521

Pointe-Verte
New Brunswick Massotherapy Association, 1010

Port Elgin
PEDVAC Foundation, 1147

Quispamsis
Alliance for Canadian New Music Projects-Contemporary Showcase - St. John/Kennebecasis Valley, 56
Association of Canadian Travel Agencies - Atlantic, 144
Canadian Cable Systems Alliance, 348
Ontario Cooperative Education Association, 1074

Red Bank Queens County
Canadian Home & School Federation, 406

Rexton
Union of Municipalities of New Brunswick, 1407

Richibucto
Kent Centre Chamber of Commerce, 883
Kent County Community Volunteer Action Organization, 884

Ripples
New Brunswick Sportfishing Association, 1013

Riverview
Atlantic Tire Dealers Association, 186
Boys & Girls Clubs of New Brunswick-Boys & Girls Club of Riverview, 222
Canadian Culinary Federation, 373
Credit Unions Atlantic Canada-Riverview Office, 641
Fundy Stamp Collectors Club, 764
The Metal Working Association of New Brunswick, 962
New Brunswick Association of Dietitians, 1005
New Brunswick Genealogical Society Inc.-Southeastern Branch, 1009
Police Martial Arts Association Inc., 1163

Vélo New Brunswick, 1431

Rogersville
Chambre de commerce de Rogersville, 542
Comité de bénévolat de Rogersville, 591

Rothesay
College of Physicians & Surgeons of New Brunswick, 588
Danish Canadian Society of Saint John, 650
The Company of Master Mariners of Canada-Fundy Division, 953
Multicultural Association of Saint John Inc., 979
New Brunswick Solid Waste Association, 1012

Rowena
National Farmers Union-Maritimes - Taxation Office, 993

Sackville
Atlantic Canadian Organic Regional Network, 183
Canadian Association for Williams Syndrome-CAWS - New Brunswick, 307
Greater Sackville Chamber of Commerce, 785
Mount Allison Faculty Association, 976
North American Waterfowl Management Plan-Black Duck Joint Venture (BDJV), 1029
North American Waterfowl Management Plan-Eastern Habitat Joint Venture (EHJV), 1029
PFLAG Canada Inc.-Sackville - Sackville NB / Amherst NS Chapter, 1156
United Church of Canada-Maritime Conference, 1409

Saint John
AIDS Saint John, 17
Ancient, Free & Accepted Masons of Canada - Grand Lodge of New Brunswick, 69
L'Arche Atlantic Region-L'Arche Saint-John, 77
Association of Visual Language Interpreters of New Brunswick, 164
Association régionale de la communauté francophone de Saint-Jean inc., 177
Bell Aliant Pioneers, 204
Boxing New Brunswick Boxe, 220
Boys & Girls Clubs of New Brunswick-Boys & Girls Club of Saint John Inc., 222
Canadian Assembly of Narcotics Anonymous-Canada Atlantic Region, 296
Canadian Association of Elizabeth Fry Societies-Elizabeth Fry Society of Saint John, 313
Canadian Automobile Association Atlantic, 339
Canadian Aviation Historical Society-New Brunswick Chapter, 340
Canadian Blood Services-Saint John, 345
Canadian Cancer Society-New Brunswick Division, 349
The Canadian Corps of Commissionaires-New Brunswick & Prince Edward Island Division, 365
Canadian Hard of Hearing Association-New Brunswick Chapter, 400
Canadian Hemophilia Society-New Brunswick Chapter, 404
Canadian Home Builders' Association - New Brunswick-Saint John Region, 407
Canadian Public Relations Society Inc.-CPRS New Brunswick, 463
Cerebral Palsy Foundation (St. John) Inc., 538
Children's Wish Foundation of Canada-New Brunswick Chapter, 563
Chinese Cultural Association of Saint John, 564
Construction Association of New Brunswick-Saint John, 623
Convention of Atlantic Baptist Churches, 627
Coverdale Centre for Women Inc., 637
Credit Counselling Services of Atlantic Canada, Inc., 639
Financial & Consumer Services Commission, 736
Fundy Trail Beagle Club, 764
Girl Guides of Canada-Guides du Canada-New Brunswick & Prince Edward Island Council, 773
Habitat for Humanity Canada-New Brunswick - Saint John, 796
Heart & Stroke Foundation of New Brunswick, 808
Independence Plus Inc., 832
International Brotherhood of Boilermakers, Iron Ship Builders, Blacksmiths, Forgers & Helpers (AFL-CIO)-Saint John (Lodge 73), 1541
The John Howard Society of New Brunswick, Inc., 874
Landscape New Brunswick Horticultural Trades Association, 898
Learning Disabilities Association of New Brunswick-Saint John Chapter (LDASJ), 904
Legal Aid New Brunswick, 906
Muslim Association of New Brunswick, 985
New Brunswick Association of Insolvency & Restructuring Professionals, 1005
New Brunswick Competitive Festival of Music Inc., 1007
New Brunswick Genealogical Society Inc.-Saint John Branch, 1009
New Brunswick Historical Society, 1009
New Brunswick Musicians' Association, Local 815 of the American Federation of Musicians, 1010
New Brunswick Roofing Contractors Association, Inc., 1011
New Brunswick Veterinary Medical Association, 1013
Opticians Association of New Brunswick, 1116
PFLAG Canada Inc.-Saint John Chapter, 1156
Royal Astronomical Society of Canada-New Brunswick Centre, 1238
The Royal Canadian Legion-New Brunswick Command, 1240
Saint John & District Labour Council, 1246
Saint John Alzheimer Society, 1246
Saint John Community Food Basket, 1246
Saint John Deaf & Hard of Hearing Services, Inc, 1246
Saint John East Food Bank Inc., 1246
Saint John Gallery Association, 1247
Saint John Jeux Canada Games Foundation Inc., 1247
Saint John Jewish Historical Society, 1247
Saint John Law Society, 1247
Saint John Naturalists' Club, 1247
Saint John Real Estate Board Inc., 1247
Saint John Region Chamber of Commerce, 1247
Saint John SPCA Animal Rescue, 1247
Schizophrenia Society of New Brunswick-Saint John Chapter, 1284
Symphony New Brunswick, 1360
Synchro New Brunswick, 1360
TESL New Brunswick, 1372
Threshold Ministries, 1377
Tourism Saint John, 1391
Triathlon New Brunswick, 1398
United Empire Loyalists' Association of Canada-New Brunswick Branch, 1410
United Way of Greater Saint John Inc., 1414
YMCA Canada-YMCA of Greater Saint John, 1471

Saint-Antoine-de-Kent
A coeur joie Nouveau-Brunswick Inc., 580

Saint-Louis-de-Kent
Chambre de Commerce de Saint Louis de Kent, 542

Saint-Quentin
Chambre de commerce de Saint-Quentin Inc., 543

Sainte Phillippe
New Brunswick Beekeepers Association, 1006

Salisbury
Boys & Girls Clubs of New Brunswick-Boys & Girls Club of Salisbury, 222
Canadian Plowing Organization, 456

Shediac
Greater Shediac Chamber of Commerce, 785
J. Douglas Ferguson Historical Research Foundation, 867
Maritime Fishermen's Union (CLC), 950
New Brunswick Dental Assistants Association, 1007

Shippagan
Chambre de commerce de Shippagan inc., 543
International Peat Society - Canadian National Committee, 859
La Maison de la culture inc., 926

Shédiac
Société culturelle Sud-Acadie, 1309

Somerville
Federation of Canadian Music Festivals, 723

South Beach Kings
Organic Crop Improvement Association - New Brunswick, 1125

South Esk
Miramichi Salmon Association, 968
Northumberland Salmon Protection Association, 1036

Springsfield
Embroiderers' Association of Canada, Inc.-N.B. - Pleasant Valley Stitchers, 686

St Andrews
Aquaculture Association of Canada, 75
New Brunswick Genealogical Society Inc.-Charlotte Branch, 1008
St. Andrews Chamber of Commerce, 1248

St André Leblanc
Army Cadet League of Canada-New Brunswick Branch, 83

St Antoine
New Brunswick Library Trustees' Association, 1010

St George
Eastern Charlotte Chamber of Commerce, 670

St Martins
St. Martins & District Chamber of Commerce, 1250

St Stephen
New Brunswick Coalition of Transition Houses/Centres for Abused Women, 1007
St. Stephen Area Chamber of Commerce, 1251
Volunteer Centre of Charlotte County Inc., 1438

St-Martin de Restigouche
New Brunswick Ground Water Association, 1009

Sussex
Animal Nutrition Association of Canada-Atlantic Division, 71
Architects' Association of New Brunswick, 78
Canadian Home Builders' Association - New Brunswick-Sussex, 407
Dairy Farmers of New Brunswick, 648
Kennebecasis Naturalists' Society, 883
Sussex & District Chamber of Commerce, 1357
Sussex Sharing Club, 1357

Tide Head
Baton New Brunswick, 199

Tracadie-Sheila
Chambre de commerce du Grand Tracadie-Sheila, 544

Trout Brook
Biathlon Nouveau-New Brunswick, 207

Upper Cloverdale
New Brunswick Gymnastics Association, 1009

Upper Kingsclear
Orienteering New Brunswick, 1126
Wild Blueberry Association of North America, 1453

Waterford
New Brunswick Environmental Network, 1007

Waterville
Carleton-Victoria Arts Council, 513

Woodstock
The Atlantic Alliance of Family Resource Centres, 182
Canadian 4-H Council-New Brunswick, 284
Carleton County Historical Society, Inc., 513
Carleton Literacy Council, 513
Greater Woodstock Chamber of Commerce, 787
PFLAG Canada Inc.-Woodstock Chapter, 1156
Valley Family Resource Centre Inc., 1424

Newfoundland & Labrador

Baie Verte
Baie Verte & Area Chamber of Commerce, 194

Bay Roberts
Spinal Cord Injury Newfoundland & Labrador-Bay Roberts, 1343

Bedford
Merit Contractors Association of Nova Scotia, 962

Bell Island
Boys & Girls Clubs of Newfoundland & Labrador-Wabana Boys & Girls Club, 223

Benoits Cove
Newfoundland Native Women's Association, 1023

Bishops Falls
Canadian Hard of Hearing Association-Newfoundland - Exploits Valley Branch, 400

Bonavista
Bonavista Area Chamber of Commerce, 217
Bonavista Historic Townscape Foundation, 217

Botwood
Boys & Girls Clubs of Newfoundland & Labrador-Boys & Girls Club of Botwood, 222

Buchans
Boys & Girls Clubs of Newfoundland & Labrador-James Hornell Boys & Girls Club - Buchans, 223

Calvert
Canadian 4-H Council-Newfoundland, 284

Cavendish
Canadian Hemophilia Society-Newfoundland & Labrador Chapter, 404

Channel-Port-aux-Basques
Channel Port Aux Basques & Area Chamber of Commerce, 551

Clarenville
Clarenville Area Chamber of Commerce, 572

Conception Bay South
Conception Bay Area Chamber of Commerce, 609
Rowing Newfoundland, 1237

Corner Brook
ALS Society of Newfoundland & Labrador, 60
The Anglican Church of Canada-Diocese of Western Newfoundland, 70
Canadian Association of Nordic Ski Instructors-Atlantic Region, 322
Canadian Association of Veterans in United Nations Peacekeeping-Western Newfoundland Chapter, 336
Canadian Blood Services-Corner Brook, 344
Canadian Hard of Hearing Association-Newfoundland - Western NL Branch, 400
Canadian Institute of Forestry, Newfoundland & Labrador, 416

Credit Counselling Services of Newfoundland & Labrador-Corner Brook Office, 640
Greater Corner Brook Board of Trade, 783
Holstein Canada-Nova Scotia & Newfoundland Branch, 819
The John Howard Society of Newfoundland-Corner Brook, 874
Model Forest of Newfoundland & Labrador, 971
Newfoundland & Labrador Association of Public & Private Employees-Western Office, 1016
Newfoundland & Labrador Laubach Literacy Council, 1019
Newfoundland & Labrador Outfitters Association, 1020
NL West SPCA, 1027
Qalipu Mi'kmaq First Nations Band, 1194
Salmon Preservation Association for the Waters of Newfoundland, 1252
Spinal Cord Injury Newfoundland & Labrador-Corner Brook, 1343
Theatre Newfoundland Labrador, 1374
YMCA Canada-YMCA of Western Newfoundland - Humber Community, 1472

Deer Lake
Deer Lake Chamber of Commerce, 652

Doyles
Newfoundland & Labrador Ground Water Association, 1019

Fogo
Fogo Island Folk Alliance, 742

Forteau
Labrador Straits Chamber of Commerce, 894

Gander
The Anglican Church of Canada-Diocese of Central Newfoundland, 69
Boys & Girls Clubs of Newfoundland & Labrador-Gander Boys & Girls Club, 222
Canadian Hard of Hearing Association-Newfoundland - Gander Branch, 400
Gander & Area Chamber of Commerce, 766
Gander & Area Society for the Prevention of Cruelty to Animals, 766
Newfoundland & Labrador Drama Society, 1018
Spinal Cord Injury Newfoundland & Labrador-Gander, 1343

Goulds
Newfoundland & Labrador Provincial Association of Family Resource Centres, 1021

Grand Falls-Windsor
Environment Resources Managament Association, 691
Exploits Regional Chamber of Commerce, 700
Exploits Valley Society for the Prevention of Cruelty to Animals, 700
Hockey Newfoundland & Labrador, 818
Newfoundland & Labrador Association of Public & Private Employees-Central Office, 1016
Spinal Cord Injury Newfoundland & Labrador-Grand Falls - Windsor, 1343
YMCA Canada-YMCA of Exploits Valley, 1472

Happy Valley-Goose Bay
Canadian Hard of Hearing Association-Newfoundland - Happy Valley Goose Bay Branch, 400
Labrador Friendship Centre, 894
Labrador Literacy Information & Action Network, 894
Labrador Native Women's Association, 894
Labrador North Chamber of Commerce, 894
Libra House Inc., 909
Spinal Cord Injury Newfoundland & Labrador-Happy Valley - Labrador Office, 1343
Them Days Inc., 1375

Holyrood
International Brotherhood of Boilermakers, Iron Ship Builders, Blacksmiths, Forgers & Helpers (AFL-CIO)-Holyrood (Lodge 203), 1541

Kippens
Bay St. George Folk Arts Council, 200

L'Anse-à-Canards
Chez les français de L'Anse-à-Canards inc., 557

Labrador City
Canadian Hard of Hearing Association-Newfoundland - Labrador West Branch, 400
Cross Country Newfoundland & Labrador, 643
Labrador West Chamber of Commerce, 894

Lewisporte
Ducks Unlimited Canada-Newfoundland & Labrador Provincial Office, 664
Lewisporte & Area Chamber of Commerce, 909

Logy Bay
Newfoundland & Labrador Amateur Bodybuilding Association, 1015

Lourdes
L'Héritage de L'Ile Rouge, 813

Marystown
Burin Peninsula Chamber of Commerce, 265
South Coast District Labour Council, 1334
Spinal Cord Injury Newfoundland & Labrador-Marystown, 1343

Mount Pearl
Alzheimer Society of Newfoundland & Labrador, 63
Association of Allied Health Professionals: Newfoundland & Labrador (Ind.), 139
Association of Engineering Technicians & Technologists of Newfoundland & Labrador, 147
Bell Aliant Pioneers-Newfoundland and Labrador, 204
Canadian Hard of Hearing Association-Newfoundland & Labrador Chapter, 400
Heart & Stroke Foundation of Newfoundland & Labrador, 809
International Personnel Management Association - Canada, 859
Mount Pearl-Paradise Chamber of Commerce, 976
Navy League of Canada-Newfoundland & Labrador, 1002
Newfoundland & Labrador Construction Safety Association, 1017
Newfoundland & Labrador Deaf Sports Association, 1018
Newfoundland & Labrador Dental Association, 1018
Newfoundland & Labrador Federation of Agriculture, 1018
Newfoundland & Labrador Independent Adjusters' Association, 1019
Newfoundland & Labrador Institute of Agrologists, 1019
Newfoundland & Labrador Prospectors Association, 1021
Newfoundland & Labrador Rugby Union, 1021
Newfoundland & Labrador Veterinary Medical Association, 1022
Safety Services Newfoundland & Labrador, 1245
St. John Ambulance-Newfoundland Council, 1249
School Milk Foundation of Newfoundland & Labrador, 1284
Skills/Compétences Canada-Newfoundland & Labrador, 1303
The Terry Fox Foundation-Newfoundland & Labrador, 1372

Norris Arm
Boys & Girls Clubs of Newfoundland & Labrador-Norris Arm Boys & Girls Club, 223

Paradise
Canada Employment & Immigration Union-Newfoundland & Labrador Regional Office, 279
Gymnastics Newfoundland & Labrador Inc., 795
KidSport Newfoundland & Labrador, 887
Newfoundland & Labrador Athletics Association, 1017
Newfoundland & Labrador Basketball Association, 1017
Newfoundland & Labrador Volleyball Association, 1022
Scouts Canada-Newfoundland & Labrador Council, 1287
Search & Rescue Volunteer Association of Canada, 1288
Skate Canada-Newfoundland/Labrador Section, 1301
Swimming Newfoundland & Labrador, 1359
Synchro Newfoundland & Labrador, 1360
United Nations Association in Canada-St. John's, 1411

Pasadena
Canadian Quilters' Association, 464
Newfoundland & Labrador Camping Association, 1017
Pasadena Chamber of Commerce, 1145

Placentia
Placentia Area Chamber of Commerce, 1161

Plum Point
Straits-St. Barbe Chamber of Commerce, 1351

Point Leamington
Pork Producers Association of Newfoundland & Labrador, 1165

Portugal Cove-St. Philips
Chinese Medicine & Acupuncture Association of Canada-Newfoundland Chapter, 565

Springdale
Springdale & Area Chamber of Commerce, 1346

St Alban's
Newfoundland Aquaculture Industry Association-St. Alban's Office, 1022

St Anthony
Boys & Girls Clubs of Newfoundland & Labrador-St. Anthony & Area Boys & Girls Club, 223
St Anthony & Area Chamber of Commerce, 1248

St. John's
AIDS Committee of Newfoundland & Labrador, 16
Alcoholics Anonymous-St. John's - Central Office, 53
Alliance of Canadian Cinema, Television & Radio Artists-ACTRA Newfoundland, 58
The Anglican Church of Canada-Diocese of Eastern Newfoundland & Labrador, 69
The Appraisal Institute of Canada - Newfoundland & Labrador, 75
ARMA Canada-Newfoundland Chapter, 82
Arthritis Society-Newfoundland & Labrador Division, 84
L'Association communautaire francophone de St-Jean, 97
Association for New Canadians, 134
Association of Early Childhood Educators of Newfoundland & Labrador, 147
Association of Fundraising Professionals-Newfoundland & Labrador Chapter, 1512
Association of Midwives of Newfoundland & Labrador, 152
Association of Newfoundland & Labrador Archives, 154
Association of Newfoundland Land Surveyors, 154
Association of Occupational Health Nurses of Newfoundland & Labrador, 154
Association of Psychology Newfoundland & Labrador, 160
Association of Seafood Producers, 162
Atlantic Provinces Athletic Therapists Association, 185
Autism Society Newfoundland & Labrador, 189
Badminton Newfoundland & Labrador Inc., 193
Bicycle Newfoundland & Labrador, 208
Big Brothers Big Sisters of Eastern Newfoundland, 209
Boys & Girls Clubs of Newfoundland & Labrador-Boys & Girls Club of St. John's, 222
Canada - Newfoundland & Labrador Offshore Petroleum Board, 277
Canadian Applied & Industrial Mathematics Society, 294
Canadian Association for Disabled Skiing - Newfoundland & Labrador Division, 299
Canadian Association for Nursing Research, 302
Canadian Bar Association-Newfoundland Branch, 342
Canadian Bible Society-Newfoundland & Labrador District Office, 343
Canadian Blood Services-St. John's, 345
Canadian Cancer Society-Newfoundland & Labrador Division, 349
Canadian Celiac Association-Newfoundland & Labrador Chapter, 352
Canadian Centre for Fisheries Innovation, 353
Canadian Condominium Institute-CCI-Newfoundland & Labrador Chapter, 362
The Canadian Corps of Commissionaires-Newfoundland & Labrador Division, 365
Canadian Epilepsy Alliance, 382
Canadian Federation of Independent Business-Newfoundland & Labrador Office, 387
Canadian Home Builders' Association - Newfoundland Labrador, 407
Canadian Information Processing Society-Newfoundland & Labrador Chapter, 411
Canadian Institute for Health Information-CIHI St. John's, 412
Canadian Institute of Management-Newfoundland & Labrador Branch, 417
Canadian Institute of Plumbing & Heating-Newfoundland Region, 418
Canadian Manufacturers & Exporters-Newfoundland & Labrador Division, 430
Canadian Mental Health Association-Newfoundland & Labrador Division, 435
Canadian National Institute for the Blind-Newfoundland & Labrador Division, 439
Canadian Parks & Wilderness Society-St. John's - Newfoundland & Labrador Chapter, 451
The Canadian Press-St. John's Bureau, 459
Canadian Society of Hospital Pharmacists-Newfoundland & Labrador, 484
Canadian Union of Public Employees-Newfoundland & Labrador Division, 498
Cerebral Palsy Association of Newfoundland & Labrador, 538
Chartered Professional Accountants of Newfoundland & Labrador, 553
Chicken Farmers of Newfoundland & Labrador, 557
Child & Youth Care Association of Newfoundland & Labrador, 558
Child Find Newfoundland & Labrador, 559
Childhood Cancer Canada Foundation-Candlelighters Newfoundland & Labrador, 560

Children's Wish Foundation of Canada-Newfoundland & Labrador Chapter, 563
Chinese Canadian National Council-Nfld. - Chinese Association of Newfoundland & Labrador, 564
The Church Lads' Brigade, 569
College of Family Physicians of Canada-Newfoundland & Labrador Chapter, 584
College of Licensed Practical Nurses of Newfoundland & Labrador, 585
College of Physicians & Surgeons of Newfoundland & Labrador, 588
Community Food Sharing Association, 597
Community Sector Council, Newfoundland & Labrador, 607
Construction Labour Relations Association of Newfoundland & Labrador, 624
Consulting Engineers of Newfoundland & Labrador, 625
Craft Council of Newfoundland & Labrador, 638
Credit Counselling Services of Newfoundland & Labrador, 640
The Crow's Nest Military Artifacts Association, 644
Dairy Farmers of Newfoundland & Labrador, 648
Denturist Association of Newfoundland & Labrador, 653
Canadian Diabetes Association-Newfoundland & Labrador Regional Leadership Centre, 656
Dr. H. Bliss Murphy Cancer Care Foundation, 662
East Coast Trail Association, 668
Easter Seals Newfoundland & Labrador, 669
Family History Society of Newfoundland & Labrador, 703
La Fédération des francophones de Terre-Neuve et du Labrador, 715
Fédération des parents francophones de Terre-Neuve et du Labrador, 717
Fish Harvesters Resource Centres, 739
Fish, Food & Allied Workers, 739
Franco-Jeunes de Terre-Neuve et du Labrador, 757
Gardiner Centre, 767
Geological Association of Canada, 769
Geological Association of Canada-Newfoundland & Labrador Section, 770
George Street Association, 771
Girl Guides of Canada-Guides du Canada-Newfoundland & Labrador Council, 773
Golf Newfoundland & Labrador, 777
Habitat for Humanity Canada-Newfoundland & Labrador, 796
Heavy Civil Association of Newfoundland & Labrador, Inc., 810
Heritage Foundation of Newfoundland & Labrador, 813
Historic Sites Association of Newfoundland & Labrador, 815
Hospitality Newfoundland & Labrador, 823
Human Resources Professionals of Newfoundland & Labrador, 826
Insurance Brokers Association of Canada-Insurance Brokers Association of Newfoundland, 848
Insurance Institute of Newfoundland & Labrador Inc., 849
The International Grenfell Association, 857
Interpreting Services of Newfoundland & Labrador Inc., 861
Janeway Children's Hospital Foundation, 868
The John Howard Society of Newfoundland & Labrador, 874
Junior Achievement of Canada-Junior Achievement of Newfoundland and Labrador, 877
Korean Association of Newfoundland & Labrador, 893
Landscape Newfoundland & Labrador, 898

Last Post Fund-Newfoundland-Labrador Branch, 899
Law Foundation of Newfoundland & Labrador, 900
Law Society of Newfoundland & Labrador, 901
Learning Disabilities Association of Newfoundland & Labrador Inc., 904
Liberal Party of Newfoundland & Labrador, 909
Lifesaving Society-Newfoundland & Labrador Branch, 911
Lupus Newfoundland & Labrador, 921
The Company of Master Mariners of Canada-Newfoundland & Labrador Division, 954
Mechanical Contractors Association of Newfoundland & Labrador, 957
Merit Contractors Association of Newfoundland & Labrador, 962
Mining Industry NL, 967
Municipalities Newfoundland & Labrador, 982
Museum Association of Newfoundland & Labrador, 982
Music for Young Children-Newfoundland & Labrador, 984
MusicNL, 984
Natural History Society of Newfoundland & Labrador, 999
The Nature Conservancy of Canada-Newfoundland & Labrador, 1000
New Brunswick Physiotherapy Association, 1011
New Democratic Party-Newfoundland & Labrador NDP, 1014
Newfoundland & Labrador Arts Council, 1015
Newfoundland & Labrador Association for Community Living, 1015
Newfoundland & Labrador Association of Insolvency & Restructuring Professionals, 1015
Newfoundland & Labrador Association of Medical Radiation Technologists, 1016
Newfoundland & Labrador Association of Occupational Therapists, 1016
Newfoundland & Labrador Association of Optometrists, 1016
Newfoundland & Labrador Association of Public & Private Employees, 1016
Newfoundland & Labrador Association of Realtors, 1016
Newfoundland & Labrador Association of Respiratory Therapists, 1016
Newfoundland & Labrador Association of Social Workers, 1016
Newfoundland & Labrador Association of Speech-Language Pathologists & Audiologists, 1016
Newfoundland & Labrador Association of Technology Industries, 1016
Newfoundland & Labrador Association of the Deaf, 1016
Newfoundland & Labrador Brain Injury Association, 1017
Newfoundland & Labrador Cheerleading Athletics, 1017
Newfoundland & Labrador Chiropractic Association, 1017
Newfoundland & Labrador College of Dietitians, 1017
Newfoundland & Labrador College of Physiotherapists, 1017
Newfoundland & Labrador Construction Association, 1017
Newfoundland & Labrador Credit Union, 1018
Newfoundland & Labrador Curling Association, 1018
Newfoundland & Labrador Dental Board, 1018
Newfoundland & Labrador Environment Network, 1018
Newfoundland & Labrador Environmental Industry Association, 1018
Newfoundland & Labrador Federation of Labour, 1018
Newfoundland & Labrador Federation of School Councils, 1019

Newfoundland & Labrador Fencing Association, 1019
Newfoundland & Labrador Folk Arts Society, 1019
Newfoundland & Labrador Health Libraries Association, 1019
Newfoundland & Labrador Judo Association, 1019
Newfoundland & Labrador Lacrosse Association, 1019
Newfoundland & Labrador Library Association, 1019
Newfoundland & Labrador Lung Association, 1020
Newfoundland & Labrador Massage Therapists' Association, 1020
Newfoundland & Labrador Medical Association, 1020
Newfoundland & Labrador Multicultural Council Inc., 1020
Newfoundland & Labrador Nurses' Union, 1020
Newfoundland & Labrador Occupational Therapy Board, 1020
Newfoundland & Labrador Organization of Women Entrepreneurs, 1020
Newfoundland & Labrador Palliative Care Association, 1020
Newfoundland & Labrador Pharmacy Board, 1021
Newfoundland & Labrador Public Health Association, 1021
Newfoundland & Labrador Right to Life Association, 1021
Newfoundland & Labrador School Boards Association, 1021
Newfoundland & Labrador Sexual Assault Crisis & Prevention Centre Inc., 1021
Newfoundland & Labrador Soccer Association, 1021
Newfoundland & Labrador Society for Medical Laboratory Science, 1021
Newfoundland & Labrador Society for the Prevention of Cruelty to Animals, 1021
Newfoundland & Labrador Teachers' Association, 1022
Newfoundland & Labrador Wildlife Federation, 1022
Newfoundland & Labrador Women's Institutes, 1022
Newfoundland Aquaculture Industry Association, 1022
Newfoundland Association of Architects, 1022
Newfoundland Cancer Treatment & Research Foundation, 1023
Newfoundland Dental Assistants Association, 1023
Newfoundland Equestrian Association, 1023
Newfoundland Federation of Music Festivals, 1023
Newfoundland Historical Society, 1023
Newfoundland Horticultural Society, 1023
Newfoundland Symphony Orchestra Association, 1023
Newfoundland Symphony Youth Orchestra, 1023
Newfoundland-Labrador Federation of Cooperatives, 1024
Noia, 1027
Northeast Avalon ACAP, Inc., 1034
NSERC Chair for Women in Science & Engineering-WISE (Women in Science & Engineering) Newfoundland & Labrador, 1050
Office of the Superintendent of Securities of Newfoundland & Labrador, 1055
Paddle Newfoundland & Labrador, 1137
Paramedic Association of Newfoundland & Labrador, 1138
Parkinson Society Newfoundland & Labrador, 1141
The Pentecostal Assemblies of Newfoundland & Labrador, 1150
People First of Newfoundland & Labrador, 1151
Petroleum Research Newfoundland & Labrador, 1154

Pharmacists' Association of Newfoundland & Labrador, 1156
Planned Parenthood - Newfoundland & Labrador Sexual Health Centre, 1161
Professional Association of Internes & Residents of Newfoundland, 1182
Professional Engineers & Geoscientists Newfoundland & Labrador, 1183
Project Management Institute-Newfoundland & Labrador
Protected Areas Association of Newfoundland & Labrador, 1190
Provincial Farm Women's Association, 1190
Public Legal Information Association of Newfoundland, 1192
Public Service Alliance of Canada-St. John's Branch, 1193
Quidi Vidi Rennie's River Development Foundation, 1201
Recreation Newfoundland & Labrador, 1207
Réseau santé en français Terre-Neuve-et-Labrador, 1226
Royal Astronomical Society of Canada-St. John's Centre, 1238
The Royal Canadian Legion-Newfoundland & Labrador Command, 1240
The Royal Commonwealth Society of Canada-Newfoundland Branch, 1242
Royal Newfoundland Constabulary Association, 1242
The Royal Scottish Country Dance Society-St. John's Branch, 1587
SailNL, 1246
St. John's Board of Trade, 1249
St. John's Clean & Beautiful, 1249
St. John's International Women's Film Festival, 1249
St. John's Kiwanis Music Festival, 1249
St. John's Native Friendship Centre, 1249
Salmonid Association of Eastern Newfoundland, 1252
The Salvation Army in Canada-St. John's - Newfoundland & Labrador Division, 1253
Schizophrenia Society of Newfoundland & Labrador, 1284
School Lunch Association, 1284
School Sports Newfoundland & Labrador, 1284
Seniors Resource Centre Association of Newfoundland & Labrador Inc., 1290
Single Parent Association of Newfoundland, 1300
Social Justice Cooperative Newfoundland & Labrador, 1305
Softball Newfoundland & Labrador, 1332
Special Olympics Newfoundland & Labrador, 1340
Spinal Cord Injury Newfoundland & Labrador, 1343
Sport Newfoundland & Labrador, 1345
Squash Newfoundland & Labrador Inc., 1347
Student Christian Movement of Canada-Eastern Region, 1352
Supply Chain Management Association - Newfoundland & Labrador, 1356
Tennis Newfoundland & Labrador, 1371
TESL Newfoundland & Labrador, 1372
Triathlon Newfoundland & Labrador, 1398
UNIFOR-St. John's, 1405
United Church of Canada-Newfoundland & Labrador Conference, 1409
Vera Perlin Society, 1431
Visual Artists Newfoundland & Labrador, 1436
World Wildlife Fund - Canada-St. John's, 1468
Writers' Alliance of Newfoundland & Labrador, 1468
YMCA Canada-YMCA of Newfoundland & Labrador, 1472
YWCA Canada-YWCA St. John's, 1481

St. Philips
Newfoundland Association of Visual Language Interpreters, 1022

Steady Brook
Newfoundland & Labrador Snowboard Association, 1021

Geographic Index / Newfoundland & Labrador - Stephenville

Stephenville
Bay St. George Chamber of Commerce, 200
Canadian Masters Cross-Country Ski Association, 431
Canadian Masters Cross-Country Ski Association-Newfoundland/Labrador, 431
The John Howard Society of Newfoundland-Stephenville, 874
Newfoundland & Labrador Criminology & Corrections Association, 1018

Torbay
Canadian Association for Williams Syndrome-CAWS - Newfoundland, 307
Karate Newfoundland & Labrador, 882

Trepassey
Irish Loop Chamber of Commerce, 864

Trinity
Ceta-Research Inc., 538
Trinity Historical Society Inc., 1399

Upper Island Cove
Boys & Girls Clubs of Newfoundland & Labrador-Upper Island Cove Boys & Girls Club, 223

Winterton
Newfoundland & Labrador Funeral Services Association, 1019

Nova Scotia

Amherst
Amherst & Area Chamber of Commerce, 67
Bridge Adult Service Society, 228
Cumberland County Genealogical Society, 645
Cumberland Museum Society, 645
Ducks Unlimited Canada-Nova Scotia Provincial Office, 664
Maritime Lumber Bureau, 951
Nova Scotia School Counsellor Association, 1048
Sexual Health Centre for Cumberland County, 1293
United Way of Cumberland County, 1414
YMCA Canada-YMCA of Cumberland, 1471

Annapolis Royal
Annapolis District Board of Trade, 71
Annapolis Region Community Arts Council, 71
Clean Annapolis River Project, 573
Historic Restoration Society of Annapolis County, 815
Historical Association of Annapolis Royal, 815

Antigonish
Antigonish Ceilidh Association, 72
Antigonish Chamber of Commerce, 72
Antigonish Culture Alive, 72
Antigonish Highland Society, 72
Antigonish Therapeutic Riding Association, 72
L'Arche Atlantic Region-L'Arche Antigonish, 76
Canadian Association for Community Living - Antigonish, 298
Canadian Dental Therapists Association, 377
Coady International Institute, 577
Denturist Society of Nova Scotia, 654
Development & Peace-Nova Scotia/New Brunswick/PEI/Newfoundland & Labrador, 654
Fédération acadienne de la Nouvelle-Écosse-Société Acadienne Sainte-Croix, 707
Heatherton Activity Centre, 810
Heritage Association of Antigonish, 812
Nova Scotia Society for the Prevention of Cruelty to Animals-Antigonish Branch, 1049
Saint Francis Xavier Association of University Teachers, 1246

Aylesford
Annapolis Valley Real Estate Board, 71
Beehive Adult Service Centre, Inc., 204
Canadian Association of Professional Apiculturists, 328

Barrington
Barrington & Area Chamber of Commerce, 197
Cape Sable Historical Society, 510

Bear River
Bear River Historical Society, 202

Bedford
Atlantic Pest Management Association, 184
Breast Cancer Action Nova Scotia, 227
Canada Health Infoway-Halifax, 280
Canadian Pension & Benefits Institute-Atlantic Region, 453
College of Family Physicians of Canada-Nova Scotia College of Family Physicians, 585
Diman Association Canada (Lebanese), 657
Fellowship of Evangelical Baptist Churches in Canada-Fellowship Atlantic, 731
Canadian Youth Business Foundation-Atlantic Office, 765
Health Association Nova Scotia-Bedford Office, 806
Junior Achievement of Canada-Junior Achievement of Nova Scotia, 877
Juvenile Diabetes Research Foundation-Halifax Region, 879
Kids Help Phone-Atlantic Region, 886
Nova Scotia Golf Association, 1045
Réseau Santé - Nouvelle-Écosse, 1225
United Food & Commercial Workers Canada-Atlantic Canada, 1411

Berwick
Berwick Food Bank, 206

Bible Hill
Canadian 4-H Council-Nova Scotia, 284
Nova Scotia Cattle Producers, 1042
Nova Scotia Federation of Agriculture, 1044
Nova Scotia Institute of Agrologists, 1046
Pork Nova Scotia, 1165
Women's Institutes of Nova Scotia, 1462

Birch Grove
Port Morien Wildlife Association, 1166

Boutiliers Point
Orchid Society of Nova Scotia, 1119

Bridgetown
Bridgetown & Area Chamber of Commerce, 229
Bridgetown & Area Historical Society, 229

Bridgewater
Acadia Entrepreneurship Centre-Bridgewater, 4
The Ark/Lunenburg County Association for the Specially Challenged, 81
Bridgewater & Area Chamber of Commerce, 229
Health Association Nova Scotia-Southern Region Office, 806
Library Boards Association of Nova Scotia, 910
PFLAG Canada Inc.-Bridgewater Chapter, 1155
Sexual Health Centre Lunenburg County, 1293
Shelter for Helpless Animals in Distress, 1295
Society for Muscular Dystrophy Information International, 1326
YMCA Canada-YMCA of Southwest Nova Scotia - Lunenburg County, 1472

Brookfield
Women That Hunt, 1461

Caledonia
North Queens Board of Trade, 1032

Camperdown
South Shore Wildlife Association, 1336

Canning
Two Planks & a Passion Theatre Company, 1401

Canso
Canso Historical Society, 509
Guysborough County Inshore Fishermen's Association, 795

Charlottetown
Atlantic Provinces Art Gallery Association, 184

Cherry Brook
Black Cultural Society for Nova Scotia, 213
Health Association of African Canadians, 806

Chester
Chester Municipal Chamber of Commerce, 556
Chester Municipal Heritage Society, 557
Friends of Nature Conservation Society, 761
Lighthouse Food Bank Society, 912
Nova Scotia Salmon Association, 1048
The Royal Commonwealth Society of Canada-Nova Scotia Branch, 1242

Chester Basin
Atlantic Canada Cruise Association, 182

Cheticamp
Cheticamp Association for Community Living, 557
Fédération acadienne de la Nouvelle-Écosse-Société Saint-Pierre, 707
La Société Saint-Pierre, 1325

Church Point
Canadian Association for Community Living - Clare Branch, 298

Chéticamp
Conseil coopératif acadien de la Nouvelle-Écosse, 614

Clarks Harbour
Archelaus Smith Historical Society, 78

Cole Harbour
Cole Harbour Rural Heritage Society, 581

Dartmouth
Air Currency Enhancement Society, 19
ALS Society of New Brunswick & Nova Scotia, 60
Amethyst Scottish Dancers of Nova Scotia, 67
Architectural Woodwork Manufacturers Association of Canada - Atlantic, 79
ARMA Canada-Nova Scotia Chapter, 82
Association of Nova Scotia Land Surveyors, 154
Association of Professional Geoscientists of Nova Scotia, 159
Atlantic Canada Water & Wastewater Association, 182
Atlantic Division, CanoeKayak Canada, 183
Atlantic Marksmen Association, 184
Atlantic Provinces Association of Landscape Architects, 185
Atlantic Provinces Numismatic Association, 185
Atlantic Therapeutic Touch Network, 186
Bide Awhile Animal Shelter Society, 208
Big Brothers Big Sisters of Nova Scotia-Big Brothers Big Sisters of Greater Halifax, 210
Boys & Girls Clubs of Nova Scotia-Boys & Girls Clubs of Greater Halifax, 223
Canadian Association of Elizabeth Fry Societies-Elizabeth Fry Society of Mainland Nova Scotia, 313
Canadian Celiac Association-Nova Scotia Chapter, 352
Canadian Condominium Institute-CCI-Nova Scotia Chapter, 362
Canadian Hydrographic Association-Atlantic Branch, 409
Canadian Institute of Quantity Surveyors - Maritimes, 419
Canadian Mental Health Association-Nova Scotia Division, 435
The Canadian Red Cross Society-Atlantic Zone Office, 466
Canadian Welding Bureau-Atlantic Region, 503
Children's Wish Foundation of Canada-Nova Scotia Chapter, 563
Christian Medical & Dental Society of Canada, 568
Clean Nova Scotia Foundation, 573
Construction Association of Nova Scotia, 623
Credit Counselling Services of Atlantic Canada-Nova Scotia - Dartmouth, 639
Dartmouth Adult Services Centre, 650
Dartmouth N.S. Family History Centre, 651
Digital Nova Scotia, 656
DIRECTIONS Council for Vocational Services Society, 657
Doctors Nova Scotia, 660
East Coast Aquarium Society, 668
Environmental Services Association of Nova Scotia, 692
Fédération acadienne de la Nouvelle-Écosse, 707
Fédération acadienne de la Nouvelle-Écosse-Conseil communautaire du Grand-Havre, 707
Fédération culturelle acadienne de la Nouvelle-Écosse, 708
La Fédération des femmes acadiennes de la Nouvelle-Écosse, 715
Fédération des parents acadiens de la Nouvelle-Écosse, 716
Federation of Foster Families of Nova Scotia, 724
Habitat for Humanity Canada-Nova Scotia, 796
Halifax Chamber of Commerce, 798
Halifax Professional Fire Fighters Association, 799
Halifax Regional Coin Club, 799
Halifax Regional Police Association, 799
Healing Our Nations, 805
Hepatitis Outreach Society of Nova Scotia, 812
Hockey Nova Scotia, 818
The Identification Clinic, 829
Insurance Institute of Nova Scotia, 849
Islamic Association of Nova Scotia, 864
LakeCity Employment Services Association, 896
Landscape Nova Scotia, 898
Maritime Fire Chiefs' Association, 950
The Maritimes Energy Association, 951
The Company of Master Mariners of Canada-Maritimes Division, 953
Mechanical Contractors Association of Nova Scotia, 957
Multiple Sclerosis Society of Canada-Atlantic Division, 980
Muscular Dystrophy Canada-Atlantic Regional Office, 982
NACE International-Canadian Region - Atlantic Canada Section
Northwest Atlantic Fisheries Organization, 1036
Nova Scotia Association of Black Social Workers, 1040
Nova Scotia Association of REALTORS, 1041
Nova Scotia College of Medical Laboratory Technologists, 1042
Nova Scotia College of Physiotherapists, 1042
Nova Scotia Construction Labour Relations Association Limited, 1043
Nova Scotia Construction Safety Association, 1043
Nova Scotia Federation of Home & School Associations, 1044
Nova Scotia Government & General Employees Union, 1045
Nova Scotia Ground Water Association, 1045
Nova Scotia Insurance Women's Association, 1046
Nova Scotia Minor Hockey Council, 1047
Nova Scotia Nurses' Union, 1047
Nova Scotia Prospectors Association, 1047
Nova Scotia Real Estate Commission, 1048
Nova Scotia Rifle Association, 1048
Nova Scotia Road Builders Association, 1048
Nova Scotia School Boards Association, 1048
Nova Scotia Society for the Prevention of Cruelty to Animals, 1049
Nova Scotia Society for the Prevention of Cruelty to Animals-Dartmouth Branch, 1049
Osteoporosis Canada-Dartmouth - Nova Scotia Chapter, 1128
Pharmacy Association of Nova Scotia, 1157
Police Association of Nova Scotia, 1163
The Royal Canadian Legion-Nova Scotia/Nunavut Command, 1240
Safety Services Nova Scotia, 1245
St. John Ambulance-Nova Scotia/PEI Council, 1249

Schizophrenia Society of Nova Scotia, 1284
Scouts Canada-Nova Scotia Council, 1287
Seafood Producers Association of Nova Scotia, 1288
Self-Help Connection Clearinghouse Association, 1289
Shooting Federation of Nova Scotia, 1297
Sign Association of Canada-Atlantic Provinces Chapter, 1298
Skills/Compétences Canada-Nova Scotia, 1303
Société internationale du réseau ÉCONOMUSÉE et Société ÉCONOMUSÉE du Québec-Bureau de l'Atlantique, 1321
Society of Bastet, 1327
Society of Composers, Authors & Music Publishers of Canada-Atlantic Division, 1328
Taste of Nova Scotia, 1367
TechNova, 1369
UNICEF Canada-UNICEF Atlantic, 1404
United Way of Halifax Region, 1414
Velo Halifax Bicycle Club, 1431

Debert
Wild Blueberry Producers Association of Nova Scotia, 1454

Digby
Conway Workshop Association, 627
Digby & Area Board of Trade, 656

Donkin
Navy League of Canada-Cape Breton, 1001

East Mountain
Colchester Highland Games & Gathering Society, 580
The Scots Society of Colchester, 1286

East Preston
Boys & Girls Clubs of Nova Scotia-Boys & Girls Club of Preston, 223

Eastern Passage
Spina Bifida & Hydrocephalus Association of Nova Scotia, 1342

Enfield
Canadian Hemophilia Society-Nova Scotia Chapter, 404
Corridor Community Options for Adults, 631
East Hants & District Chamber of Commerce, 668

Eskasoni
Eskasoni Fish & Wildlife Commission, 695

Freeport
Islands Historical Society, 866

George's River
Canadian Association of Veterans in United Nations Peacekeeping-MGen. Lewis W. Mackenzie Chapter, 336

Glace Bay
Cape Breton Chamber of Voluntary Organizations, 509
Centre for Adults in Progressive Employment Society, 531
Glace Bay Food Bank Society, 774
Glace Bay Literacy Council, 774
Spina Bifida & Hydrocephalus Association of Nova Scotia-Cape Breton Chapter, 1342
United Mine Workers of America (CLC)-Canada, 1599
United Mine Workers of America (CLC)-District 26, 1599

Greenfield
Water Ski Wakeboard Nova Scotia, 1442

Greenwood
Canadian Association of Veterans in United Nations Peacekeeping-William C. Hall VC, Greenwood Chapter, 336

Guysborough
Guysborough Historical Society, 795
Mulgrave Road Theatre Foundation, 978

Halifax
ADR Institute of Canada-ADR Atlantic Institute, 9
Adsum for Women & Children, 9
African Nova Scotian Music Association, 13
AIDS Coalition of Nova Scotia, 15
AIESEC-Halifax, 18
Alcoholics Anonymous-Halifax Central Office, 52
All Terrain Vehicle Association of Nova Scotia, 54
Alliance Française Halifax, 57
Alliance of Canadian Cinema, Television & Radio Artists-ACTRA Maritimes, 58
Alternative Dispute Resolution Atlantic Institute, 60
Alzheimer Society of Nova Scotia, 64
An Cumann/The Irish Association of Nova Scotia, 68
Ancient, Free & Accepted Masons of Canada - Grand Lodge of Nova Scotia, 69
The Anglican Church of Canada-Diocese of Nova Scotia & Prince Edward Island, 70
Aquaculture Association of Nova Scotia, 75
Arab Canadian Association of the Atlantic Provinces, 75
L'Arche Atlantic Region-L'Arche Halifax, 77
Archers Association of Nova Scotia, 78
Arthritis Society-Nova Scotia Division, 84
Association of Atlantic Universities, 139
Association of Fundraising Professionals-Nova Scotia Chapter
Association of Interior Designers of Nova Scotia, 149
Association of Municipal Administrators, Nova Scotia, 152
Association of Nigerians in Nova Scotia, 154
Association of Nova Scotia Museums, 154
Association of Psychologists of Nova Scotia, 160
Association of Translators & Interpreters of Nova Scotia, 163
Athletics Nova Scotia, 181
Atlantic Association of Applied Economists, 182
Atlantic Canada Centre for Environmental Science, 182
Atlantic Canada Pipe Band Association, 182
Atlantic Concrete Association, 183
Atlantic Dairy Council, 183
Atlantic Episcopal Assembly, 183
Atlantic Federation of Musicians, Local 571, 184
The Atlantic Film Festival Association, 184
Atlantic Filmmakers Cooperative, 184
Atlantic Fishing Industry Alliance, 184
Atlantic Halfway House Association, 184
Atlantic Health Promotion Research Centre, 184
Atlantic Institute for Market Studies, 184
The Atlantic Jewish Council, 184
Atlantic Motion Picture Exhibitors Association, 184
Atlantic Provinces Economic Council, 185
Atlantic Provinces Library Association, 185
Atlantic Provinces Linguistic Association, 185
Atlantic Provinces Special Education Authority, 185
Atlantic Provinces Trial Lawyers Association, 185
Atlantic Publishers Marketing Association, 186
Atlantic University Sport Association, 186
Autism Nova Scotia, 188
Baron de Hirsch Hebrew Benevolent Society, 196
Baseball Nova Scotia, 198
Basketball Nova Scotia, 199
Bell Aliant Pioneers-Nova Scotia, 204
Better Business Bureau Serving the Atlantic Provinces, 207
Biathlon Nova Scotia, 207
Bicycle Nova Scotia, 208
BioNova, 211
Birthright International-Halifax Chapter, 212
Black Business Initiative, 213
Black Educators Association of Nova Scotia, 213
BMW Clubs Canada-Atlantic Canada Chapter, 216
Brain Injury Association of Nova Scotia, 225
Building Owners & Managers Association - Nova Scotia, 263
Campground Owners Association of Nova Scotia, 277
Camping Association of Nova Scotia & PEI, 277
Canada - Nova Scotia Offshore Petroleum Board, 278
Canadian Artists' Representation Maritimes, 296
Canadian Association for Disabled Skiing - Nova Scotia, 299
Canadian Association of Geographers-Atlantic Division, 316
Canadian Association of Insurance Women, 318
Canadian Association of Neuroscience Nurses, 322
Canadian Association of Smallmouth Anglers, 333
Canadian Bar Association-Nova Scotia Branch, 342
Canadian Blood Services-Halifax, 344
Canadian Board for Respiratory Care Inc., 345
Canadian Cancer Society-Nova Scotia Division, 349
Canadian Centre for Policy Alternatives-Nova Scotia Office, 354
Canadian Children's Book Centre-Halifax, 356
The Canadian Corps of Commissionaires-Nova Scotia Division, 365
Canadian Culinary Federation-Halifax Branch, 374
Canadian Energy Law Foundation, 381
Canadian Federation of Earth Sciences, 386
Canadian Federation of Independent Business-Nova Scotia Office, 387
Canadian Federation of Junior Leagues, 387
Canadian HIV Trials Network-Atlantic Region, 405
Canadian Information Processing Society-Nova Scotia Chapter, 411
Canadian Lebanon Society of Halifax, 426
Canadian Liver Foundation-Atlantic Canada Chapter, 427
Canadian Manufacturers & Exporters-Nova Scotia Division, 430
Canadian Media Guild-Halifax Regional Office, 432
Canadian National Institute for the Blind-Nova Scotia-PEI Division, 439
Canadian Paraplegic Association (Nova Scotia), 450
Canadian Parks & Wilderness Society-Halifax - Nova Scotia Chapter, 451
The Canadian Press-Halifax Bureau, 459
Canadian Progress Club-Halifax Cornwallis, 461
Canadian Public Relations Society Inc.-CPRS Nova Scotia, 463
Canadian Society of Association Executives-Nova Scotia Chapter, 480
Canadian Taxpayers Federation-Atlantic Canada, 493
Canoe Kayak Nova Scotia, 508
Caregivers Nova Scotia, 512
Centre for Entrepreneurship Education & Development Inc., 532
Centre for Women in Business, 534
Certification Council of Early Childhood Educators of Nova Scotia, 538
Chartered Professional Accountants of Nova Scotia, 553
Chebucto Community Net, 555
Chebucto Symphony Orchestra, 555
Child Care Connection Nova Scotia, 558
Child Find Nova Scotia, 559
Children and Youth in Challenging Contexts Network, 560
Chinese Canadian National Council-NS - Chinese Society of Nova Scotia, 564
Chinese Medicine & Acupuncture Association of Canada-Nova Scotia Chapter, 565
Chisholm Services for Children, 566
Coastal Zone Canada Association, 579
College of Dental Hygienists of Nova Scotia, 583
College of Licensed Practical Nurses of Nova Scotia, 585
College of Occupational Therapists of Nova Scotia, 587
College of Physicians & Surgeons of Nova Scotia, 588
College of Registered Nurses of Nova Scotia, 589
Community Foundation of Nova Scotia, 597
Conference of New England Governors & Eastern Canadian Premiers, 612
Conseil national Société de Saint-Vincent de Paul-Halifax Particular Council, 619
Consulting Engineers of Nova Scotia, 625
Continuing Care Association of Nova Scotia, 626
Cooperative Housing Federation of Canada-Atlantic Region, 628
Cosmetology Association of Nova Scotia, 631
Council of Atlantic Ministers of Education & Training, 632
Council of Atlantic Premiers, 633
The Council of Canadians-Atlantic, 633
Council of Nova Scotia Archives, 634
Credit Unions Atlantic Canada, 641
Cross Country Nova Scotia, 643
Dalhousie Faculty Association, 648
Dalhousie Medical Research Foundation, 648
Dalhousie University School of Information Management Associated Alumni, 648
Dance Nova Scotia, 649
Destination Halifax, 654
Canadian Diabetes Association-Nova Scotia Leadership Centre, 656
Directors Guild of Canada-Atlantic Regional District Council, 657
Disabled Individuals Alliance, 658
Dress for Success, 662
East Coast Music Association, 668
Easter Seals Nova Scotia, 669
Ecology Action Centre, 672
EduNova, 680
Engineers Nova Scotia, 689
Entrepreneurs with Disabilities Network, 691
Environmental Health Association of Nova Scotia, 692
Epilepsy Association of Nova Scotia, 693
Exhibitions Association of Nova Scotia, 699
Family Service Association of Halifax, 704
Feed Nova Scotia, 731
Fencing Association of Nova Scotia, 732
Field Hockey Nova Scotia, 734
Fishermen & Scientists Research Society, 740
Football Nova Scotia Association, 750
4Cs Foundation, 756
Freestyle Ski Nova Scotia, 759
Gem & Mineral Federation of Canada-Nova Scotia Mineral & Gem Society, 768
Genealogical Association of Nova Scotia, 768
Genealogical Institute of The Maritimes, 768
Genome Canada-Genome Atlantic, 769
German Canadian Association of Nova Scotia, 771
Girl Guides of Canada-Guides du Canada-Nova Scotia Council, 773
Gorsebrook Research Institute for Atlantic Canada Studies, 778
Green Party of Nova Scotia, 789
Gymnastics Nova Scotia, 795
Halifax Amateur Radio Club, 798
Halifax Citadel Regimental Association, 799
Halifax County United Soccer Club, 799
Halifax Employers Association, 799
Halifax Field Naturalists, 799
Halifax Foundation, 799
Halifax Library Association, 799
Halifax North West Trails Association, 799
Halifax Regional Cerebral Palsy Association, 799
Halifax Sexual Health Centre, 799
Halifax Sport & Social Club, 799

Halifax Transition House Association - Bryony House, 799
Halifax Wildlife Association, 799
Halifax-Dartmouth Automobile Dealers' Association, 800
Health Association Nova Scotia, 805
Heart & Stroke Foundation of Nova Scotia, 809
Heartwood Centre for Community Youth Development, 810
Heritage Trust of Nova Scotia, 813
Hong Kong-Canada Business Association-Atlantic Office, 820
Hostelling International - Canada-Atlantic Region, 823
Hotel Association of Nova Scotia, 824
Human Resources Association of Nova Scotia, 825
Huntington Society of Canada-Nova Scotia & PEI Resource Centre, 828
Immigrant Services Association of Nova Scotia, 830
Independent Living Nova Scotia, 833
Insurance Brokers Association of Canada-Insurance Brokers Association of Nova Scotia, 848
Insurance Bureau of Canada-Atlantic Canada Office, 849
International Oceans Institute of Canada, 858
International Society for Evolutionary Protistology, 860
Interprovincial School Development Association, 861
Investment Property Owners Association of Nova Scotia Ltd., 863
Islamic Information Foundation, 864
Italian Canadian Cultural Association of Nova Scotia, 866
IWK Health Centre Foundation, 867
Junior League of Halifax, 878
Karate Nova Scotia, 882
KidSport Nova Scotia, 887
Lacrosse Nova Scotia, 895
Last Post Fund-Nova Scotia Branch, 899
Law Foundation of Nova Scotia, 901
Leave Out Violence-Nova Scotia, 905
Legal Information Society of Nova Scotia, 906
The Leukemia & Lymphoma Society of Canada-Atlantic Canada Branch, 909
Liberal Party of Nova Scotia, 909
Lifesaving Society-Nova Scotia Branch, 911
The Lung Association of Nova Scotia, 921
Mainland Nova Scotia Building & Construction Trades Council, 926
Mainland South Heritage Society, 926
Marine Renewables Canada, 950
Marine Renewables Canada-Atlantic Office, 950
Maritime Association of Professional Sign Language Interpreters, 950
Maritime Sikh Society, 951
Maritimes Health Libraries Association, 951
Massage Therapists' Association of Nova Scotia, 953
Master Mariners of Canada, 953
Meeting Professionals International-Atlantic Canada Chapter, 1570
Men for Change, 960
Mi'kmaq Native Friendship Centre, 964
Mount Saint Vincent University Faculty Association, 976
Multicultural Association of Nova Scotia, 979
Music Nova Scotia, 984
The Nature Conservancy of Canada-Nova Scotia, 1000
Nature Nova Scotia (Federation of Nova Scotia Naturalists), 1000
Neptune Theatre Foundation, 1003
New Democratic Party-Nova Scotia NDP, 1014
New Leaf Enterprises, 1014
Newspapers Atlantic, 1024
Nordic Walking Nova Scotia, 1028
Nova Scotia Advisory Council on the Status of Women, 1040
Nova Scotia Amateur Bodybuilding Association, 1040
Nova Scotia Archaeology Society, 1040

Nova Scotia Association for Community Living, 1040
Nova Scotia Association of Architects, 1040
Nova Scotia Association of Insolvency & Restructuring Professionals, 1041
Nova Scotia Association of Medical Radiation Technologists, 1041
Nova Scotia Association of Optometrists, 1041
Nova Scotia Association of Social Workers, 1041
Nova Scotia Automobile Dealers' Association, 1041
Nova Scotia Badminton Association, 1041
Nova Scotia Band Association, 1041
Nova Scotia Barristers' Society, 1042
Nova Scotia Child Care Association, 1042
Nova Scotia Choral Federation, 1042
Nova Scotia College of Chiropractors, 1042
Nova Scotia College of Pharmacists, 1042
Nova Scotia College of Respiratory Therapists, 1043
Nova Scotia Construction Sector Council - Industrial-Commercial-Institutional, 1043
Nova Scotia Council for the Family, 1043
Nova Scotia Criminal Justice Association, 1043
Nova Scotia Curling Association, 1043
Nova Scotia Deaf Sports Association, 1043
Nova Scotia Dental Assistants' Association, 1044
Nova Scotia Dental Association, 1044
Nova Scotia Designer Crafts Council, 1044
Nova Scotia Dietetic Association, 1044
Nova Scotia Equestrian Federation, 1044
Nova Scotia Federation of Anglers & Hunters, 1044
Nova Scotia Federation of Labour, 1044
Nova Scotia Gerontological Nurses Association, 1045
Nova Scotia Hearing & Speech Foundation, 1045
Nova Scotia Home Builders' Association, 1045
Nova Scotia Home Builders' Association-Central Nova, 1046
Nova Scotia Independent Adjusters' Association, 1046
Nova Scotia League for Equal Opportunities, 1046
Nova Scotia Library Association, 1046
Nova Scotia Lighthouse Preservation Society, 1047
The Nova Scotia Mineral & Gem Society, 1047
Nova Scotia Nature Trust, 1047
Nova Scotia Physiotherapy Association, 1047
Nova Scotia Progressive Conservative Association, 1047
Nova Scotia Public Interest Research Group, 1047
Nova Scotia Real Estate Appraisers Association, 1048
Nova Scotia Rugby Football Union, 1048
Nova Scotia School Athletic Federation, 1048
Nova Scotia Securities Commission, 1048
Nova Scotia Society of Occupational Therapists, 1049
Nova Scotia Swordfish Association, 1049
Nova Scotia Table Tennis Association, 1049
Nova Scotia Teachers Union, 1049
Nova Scotia Tennis Association, 1049
Nova Scotia Trails Federation, 1050
Nova Scotia Union of Public & Private Employees (CCU), 1050
Nova Scotia Wild Flora Society, 1050
Nova Scotia Wool Marketing Board, 1050
Nova Scotia Youth Orchestra, 1050
Nova Scotian Institute of Science, 1050
Novia Scotia Sports Hall of Fame, 1050
Nurse Practitioners' Association of Nova Scotia, 1052
Offshore Energy Research Association of Nova Scotia, 1055
OMF International - Canada-Atlantic Region, 1057
Open Harbour Refugee Association, 1114
Orienteering Association of Nova Scotia, 1126

Ovarian Cancer Canada-Atlantic Regional Office, 1134
Parkinson Society Maritime Region, 1141
Pathways to Education Canada-Pathways to Education - Halifax-Spryfield, 1145
Pier 21 Society, 1159
Prescott Group, 1170
Professional Association of Residents in the Maritime Provinces, 1182
The Professional Institute of the Public Service of Canada-Nova Scotia/New Brunswick/Newfoundland/Prince Edward Island Regional Office, 1185
Project Management Institute-Nova Scotia Provincial Black Basketball Association, 1190
Provincial Dental Board of Nova Scotia, 1190
Psoriasis Society of Canada, 1191
Public Health Association of Nova Scotia, 1192
Public Service Alliance of Canada-Atlantic Branch, 1193
Public Service Alliance of Canada-Halifax Branch, 1193
Real Estate Institute of Canada-Nova Scotia Chapter, 1206
Recreation Nova Scotia, 1207
Recreational Vehicle Dealers Association of Canada-Atlantic Recreation Vehicle Dealers Association, 1208
Restaurants Canada-Atlantic Canada Office, 1227
Ringette Nova Scotia, 1233
Row Nova Scotia, 1237
Royal Astronomical Society of Canada-Halifax Centre, 1238
The Royal Nova Scotia Historical Society, 1242
Sail Nova Scotia, 1246
Saint Mary's University Faculty Union, 1247
St. Leonard's Society of Canada-Shelter Nova Scotia, 1250
The Salvation Army in Canada-Halifax - Maritime Division, 1253
Scandinavian Society of Nova Scotia, 1282
Science Atlantic, 1285
Scotia Chamber Players, 1285
The Scots, 1286
Sierra Club of Canada-Atlantic Chapter, 1298
Sisters of Charity of Halifax, 1300
Skate Canada-Nova Scotia Section, 1302
Snowboard Nova Scotia, 1305
Snowmobilers Association of Nova Scotia, 1305
Soccer Nova Scotia, 1305
Society of Deaf & Hard of Hearing Nova Scotians, 1328
Softball Nova Scotia, 1332
Solid Waste Association of North America-Atlantic Canada Chapter
Special Olympics Nova Scotia, 1340
Speech & Hearing Association of Nova Scotia, 1340
Speed Skate Nova Scotia, 1341
Sport Nova Scotia, 1345
Squash Nova Scotia, 1347
Supply Chain Management Association - Nova Scotia, 1356
Swim Nova Scotia, 1358
Symphony Nova Scotia, 1360
Synchro Nova Scotia, 1361
Taoist Tai Chi Society of Canada-Atlantic Region, 1367
TelecomPioneers of Canada, 1369
The Terry Fox Foundation-Nova Scotia Office, 1372
TESL Nova Scotia, 1372
Theatre Nova Scotia, 1374
Tourism Industry Association of Nova Scotia, 1390
Transition House Association of Nova Scotia, 1395
Trauma Association of Canada, 1396
Triathlon Nova Scotia, 1398
UNIFOR-Halifax Office, 1405
UniforACL, 1405
Union of Nova Scotia Municipalities, 1407
United Empire Loyalists' Association of Canada-Nova Scotia Branch, 1410

Urban Development Institute of Nova Scotia, 1422
Visual Arts Nova Scotia, 1436
Volleyball Nova Scotia, 1438
Water Polo Nova Scotia, 1441
World Trade Centre Atlantic Canada, 1467
World Wildlife Fund - Canada-Halifax, 1468
Writers' Federation of Nova Scotia, 1468
YMCA Canada-YMCA of Greater Halifax/Dartmouth, 1472
YWCA Canada-YWCA Halifax, 1481

Hants County
Nova Scotia Daylily Society, 1043

Hantsport
Hantsport & Area Historical Society, 803

Head Chezzetcook
Chezzetcook Historical Society, 557

Head Jeddore
Eastern Shore Fisherman's Protective Association, 670

Heatherton
Miniature Horse Association of Nova Scotia, 966

Hopewell
Clydesdale Horse Association of Canada, 576

Hubbards
Atlantic Collegiate Athletic Association, 183
Canadian Bioethics Society, 343
Nova Scotia Mackerel Fishermen's Association, 1047

Ingonish
Northeast Highlands Chamber of Commerce, 1034

Ingramport
Mining Association of Nova Scotia, 967

Inverness
Inverness Cottage Workshop, 862
Inverness County Centre for the Arts, 862

Kentville
Annapolis Valley Chamber of Commerce, 71
Big Brothers Sisters of Nova Scotia-Big Brothers Sisters of the Annapolis Valley, 210
Chicken Farmers of Nova Scotia, 557
Community Living Alternatives Society, 600
Health Association Nova Scotia-Central Region Office, 806
Horticulture Nova Scotia, 822
Kings Historical Society, 888
Nova Scotia Fruit Growers' Association, 1045
Nova Scotia Home Builders' Association-Annapolis Valley, 1046
Survivors of Abuse Recovering, 1357

LaHave
LaHave Islands Marine Museum Society, 895
Lunenburg County Historical Society, 921

Lakeside
Nova Scotia Hospice Palliative Care Association, 1046

Lansdowne
Lansdowne Outdoor Recreational Development Association, 899

Lawrencetown
Carleton Road Industries Association, 513
Halifax Area Leisure & Therapeutic Riding Association, 798
Square & Round Dance Federation of Nova Scotia, 1346

Lewis Lake
Nova Scotia Stamp Club, 1049

Liverpool
Nova Scotia Guides Association, 1045
Nova Scotia Society for the Prevention of Cruelty to Animals-Queens Branch, 1049
Queens County Fish & Game Association, 1200

Geographic Index / Nova Scotia - Truro

Queens County Historical Society, 1200
South Queens Chamber of Commerce, 1336

Louisbourg
Fortress Louisbourg Association, 754
Sydney & Louisburg Railway Historical Society, 1360

Lower Sackville
Bowhunters Association of Nova Scotia, 219
Building Futures Employment Society, 262
Clan Matheson Society of Nova Scotia, 572
Coalition for a Smoke-Free Nova Scotia, 578
Crohn's & Colitis Canada-Atlantic Canada Region, 642
DanceSport Atlantic, 650
Federation for Scottish Culture in Nova Scotia, 720
The John Howard Society of Nova Scotia, 874
Navy League of Canada-Nova Scotia Mainland, 1002
Nova Scotia Arm Wrestling Association, 1040
Nova Scotia Association of Naturopathic Doctors, 1041
Nova Scotia Veterinary Medical Association, 1050

Lower Truro
Dairy Farmers of Nova Scotia, 648

Lunenburg
Federation of Music Festivals of Nova Scotia, 725
Lunenburg Board of Trade, 920
Lunenburg County Wildlife Association, 921
Lunenburg Heritage Society, 921
Lunenburg Marine Museum Society, 921
Nova Scotia Cricket Association, 1043
Second Story Women's Centre, 1288
South Shore Genealogical Society, 1336

Maccan
Cumberland Equal Rights for the Disabled, 645

Mahone Bay
Mahone Bay & Area Chamber of Commerce, 926

Maitland
East Hants Historical Society, 668

Margaree Centre
Margaree Salmon Association, 949

McKay Siding
Nova Scotia Beekeepers' Association, 1042

Membertou
First Nations SchoolNet-Atlantic Region, 738
Union of Nova Scotia Indians, 1407

Middle Musquodoboit
Jersey Canada-Atlantic, 869

Middle Sackville
Canadian Burn Survivors Community, 347

Middleton
Annapolis Valley Historical Society, 71

Millbrook
Central Nova Tourist Association, 524

Milton
Queens Association for Supported Living, 1200

Mount Uniacke
Canadian Horse Breeders' Association-Atlantic District, 408
Roofing Contractors Association of Nova Scotia, 1236

Mulgrave
Atlantic Association of CBDCs, 182
Atlantic Association of Community Business Development Corporations, 182

Musquodoboit Harbour
Eastern Shore Volunteer Food Bank, 671
Greyhound Pets of Atlantic Canada Society, 790
Musquodoboit Trailways Association, 986

Traditional Archers Association of Nova Scotia, 1394

New Glasgow
Big Brothers Big Sisters of Nova Scotia-Big Brothers Big Sisters of Pictou County, 210
Canadian Progress Charitable Foundation, 460
Canadian Progress Club, 460
Credit Counselling Services of Atlantic Canada-Nova Scotia - New Glasgow, 640
Destination Eastern & Northumberland Shores, 654
Health Association Nova Scotia-Northern Region Office, 806
Nova Scotia Society for the Prevention of Cruelty to Animals-Pictou Branch, 1049
Pictou County Centre for Sexual Health, 1159
Pictou County Chamber of Commerce, 1159
Pictou County Historical Society, 1159
Summer Street, 1354
United Way of Pictou County, 1416
YMCA Canada-YMCA of Pictou County, 1472

New Minas
Flowercart, 741

New Ross
Maritime Hereford Association, 950
Trappers Association of Nova Scotia, 1396

New Waterford
Army, Navy & Air Force Veterans in Canada-Nova Scotia Provincial Command, 84

North Sydney
Haley Street Adult Services Centre Society, 798
North Sydney Historical Society, 1033

Orangedale
L'Arche Atlantic Region, 76

Parrsboro
Parrsboro & District Board of Trade, 1143
Parrsborough Shore Historical Society, 1143

Petit de Grat
Fédération acadienne de la Nouvelle-Écosse-Centre communautaire La Picasse, 707
Richmond County Disabled Association, 1230

Pictou
Canadian Union of Public Employees-Nova Scotia Division, 498
Federation of Canadian Electrolysis Associations, 723
Maritime Regional CGIT Committee, 951

Pointe-De-L'ÉGlise
Société historique acadienne de la Baie Sainte-Marie, 1319

Pointe-de-l'Église
Archives du Centre acadien, 80
Chambre de commerce de Clare, 540

Port Hastings
Port Hastings Historical Society, 1166

Port Hawkesbury
Regional Occupation Centre Foundation, 1212
Regional Occupation Centre Society, 1213
Strait Area Chamber of Commerce, 1351

Port Hood
Atlantic Standardbred Breeders Association, 186
Atlantic Standardbred Breeders Association, 186
Eastern Veterinary Technician Association, 671

Port Williams
Canadian Institute of Management-Maritime Branch, 417
Nova Scotia Music Educators' Association, 1047

Prospect Bay
Canadian Association for Young Children, 307

Pugwash
The North Cumberland Historical Society, 1030
Pugwash & Area Chamber of Commerce, 1194
Seagull Foundation, 1288

Riverport
Nova Scotia Society for the Prevention of Cruelty to Animals-Lunenburg Branch, 1049

Sackville
Clan Lamont Society of Canada, 571
Sackville Rivers Association, 1245

Saulnierville
Fédération acadienne de la Nouvelle-Écosse-Société acadienne de Clare, 707
Nova Scotia Society for the Prevention of Cruelty to Animals-La Baie Branch, 1049

Scotsburn
Farmers' Markets of Nova Scotia Cooperative Ltd., 706

Seaforth
Hope for Wildlife Society, 821

Shag Harbour
Chapel Hill Historical Society, 552
Shag Harbour Incident Society, 1294
Sou'wester Coin Club, 1333

Shearwater
PFLAG Canada Inc.-Halifax Chapter, 1155

Sheet Harbour
Gerald Hardy Memorial Society, 771
Seacoast Trail Arts Association, 1287
Sheet Harbour & Area Chamber of Commerce & Civic Affairs, 1295

Shelburne
Black Loyalist Heritage Society, 213
Shelburne & Area Chamber of Commerce, 1295
Shelburne Association Supporting Inclusion, 1295
Shelburne County Genealogical Society, 1295
Shelburne Historical Society, 1295

Sherbrooke
St Mary's River Association, 1250

Springhill
Golden Opportunities Vocational Rehabilitation Centre Workshop, 776
Springhill & Area Chamber of Commerce, 1346

Stewaicke
Royal Canadian Army Service Corps Association-(Atlantic Region), 1239

Stewiacke
Nova Forest Alliance, 1040

Sydney
AIDS Coalition of Cape Breton, 15
Beaton Institute, 203
Boys & Girls Clubs of Nova Scotia-Boys & Girls Clubs of Cape Breton, 223
Canadian Association of Elizabeth Fry Societies-Elizabeth Fry Society of Cape Breton, 313
Canadian Blood Services-Sydney, 345
Canadian Society for Traditional Music, 479
Cape Breton Centre for Sexual Health, 509
Cape Breton Injured Workers' Association, 509
Cape Breton Island Building & Construction Trades Council, 509
Cape Breton Island Wildlife Association, 509
Cape Breton Professional Musicians Association, AFM Local 355, 509
Cape Breton Regional Hospital Foundation, 509
Cape Breton University Centre for International Studies, 510
Cape Breton University Faculty Association, 510
Community Involvement of the Disabled, 599
Credit Counselling Services of Atlantic Canada-Nova Scotia - Sydney, 640

Fédération acadienne de la Nouvelle-Écosse-Community education center Étoile de l'Acadie, 707
Federation of Senior Citizens & Pensioners of Nova Scotia, 726
Horizon Achievement Centre, 821
Investment Property Owners Association of Cape Breton, 863
Mi'kmaq Association for Cultural Studies, 964
Mining Society of Nova Scotia, 967
Nova Scotia Powerlifting Association, 1047
Nova Scotia Recreation Professionals in Health, 1048
Nova Scotia Society for the Prevention of Cruelty to Animals-Cape Breton Branch, 1049
Old Sydney Society, 1056
PFLAG Canada Inc.-Sydney Chapter, 1156
Autism Treatment Services of Canada-Nova Scotia - Society for Treatment of Autism, 1327
Sydney & Area Chamber of Commerce, 1359
Tourism Cape Breton, 1389
UNIFOR-Sydney, 1405
United Way of Cape Breton, 1413
YMCA Canada-YMCA of Cape Breton, 1471

Sydney River
Cape Breton County Minor Hockey Association, 509

Tantallon
Halifax Association of Vegetarians, 798

Tatamagouche
Innkeepers Guild of Nova Scotia, 839

Timberlea
Music for Young Children-Nova Scotia, 984
Pool & Hot Tub Council of Canada-Atlantic Chapter, 1165
Rug Hooking Guild of Nova Scotia, 1243

Trenton
Clan Donald Canada, 571

Truro
Atlantic Turfgrass Research Foundation, 186
Boys & Girls Clubs of Nova Scotia-Boys & Girls Club of Truro & Colchester, 223
Bridges, 228
Canadian Society for Horticultural Science, 475
The Canadian Woodlands Forum, 505
Central Nova Women's Resource Centre, 524
Civil Constables Association of Nova Scotia, 571
Cobequid Arts Council, 579
Colchester Community Workshops Foundation, 580
Colchester Historical Society, 580
Colchester-East Hants Public Library Foundation, 580
Community Enhancement Association, 597
Confederacy of Mainland Mi'kmaq, 610
Credit Counselling Services of Atlantic Canada-Nova Scotia - Truro, 640
Downtown Truro Partnership, 662
Forest Nova Scotia, 751
Horse Trials Nova Scotia, 822
Literacy Nova Scotia, 914
Maritime Aboriginal Peoples Council, 950
Native Council of Nova Scotia, 997
Natural Products Marketing Council, 999
The Northern AIDS Connection Society, 1034
Nova Scotia Co-operative Council, 1043
Nova Scotia Egg Producers, 1044
Nova Scotia Forest Technicians Association, 1045
Nova Scotia Forestry Association, 1045
Nova Scotia Native Women's Society, 1047
Nova Scotia Society for the Prevention of Cruelty to Animals-Colchester Branch, 1049
Pentecostal Assemblies of Canada-Maritime District Office, 1150
People First Nova Scotia, 1151
Purebred Sheep Breeders Association of Nova Scotia, 1194

Geographic Index / Nova Scotia - Truro Heights

Registered Professional Foresters Association of Nova Scotia, 1214
Truckers Association of Nova Scotia, 1399
Truro & Colchester Chamber of Commerce, 1399
Truro Art Society, 1400

Truro Heights
International Brotherhood of Boilermakers, Iron Ship Builders, Blacksmiths, Forgers & Helpers (AFL-CIO)-Truro (Lodge 73), 1541

Tusket
Fédération acadienne de la Nouvelle-Écosse-Conseil acadien de Par-en-Bas, 707

Upper Mount Thom
Maritime Aberdeen Angus Association, 950

Valley
Embroiderers' Association of Canada, Inc.-N.S. - Marigold Guild of Needle Arts, 686

Waterville
Nova Scotia Mink Breeders' Association, 1047
Nova Scotia Society for the Prevention of Cruelty to Animals-Kings Branch, 1049

Waverley
Atlantic Floor Covering Association, 184

West Pubnico
Société historique de Pubnico-Ouest, 1320

West River Station
Nova Scotia Shorthorn Association, 1048

Westport
Brier Island Chamber of Commerce, 229

Weymouth
Weymouth Historical Society, 1451

Whycocomagh
L'Arche Atlantic Region-L'Arche Cape Breton, 77

Windsor
Atlantic Chamber of Commerce, 183
Avon Chamber of Commerce, 191
Big Game Society of Nova Scotia, 210
Conservation Enforcement Officers Association of Nova Scotia, 622
New Boundaries, 1004
Nova Scotia Society for the Prevention of Cruelty to Animals-Hants Branch, 1049
People First Nova Scotia-Windsor Chapter, 1151
West Hants Historical Society, 1445

Wolfville
Acadia Entrepreneurship Centre, 4
Acadia Entrepreneurship Centre-Wolfville - Innovation & Incubation Services, 4
Acadia Environmental Society, 4
Acadia University Faculty Association, 4
Appaloosa Horse Club of Canada-Appaloosa Horse Club of Nova Scotia, 73
L'Arche Atlantic Region-L'Arche Homefires, 77
Atlantic Conference of Independent Schools, 183
Blomidon Naturalists Society, 215
Deep Roots Music Cooperative, 652
Wolfville Historical Society, 1460

Yarmouth
Boys & Girls Clubs of Nova Scotia-Boys & Girls Club of Yarmouth, 223
Handicapped Organization Promoting Equality, 803
Kaye Nickerson Adult Service Centre, 883
National Seafood Sector Council, 996
Nova Scotia Fish Packers Association, 1044
Nova Scotia Society for the Prevention of Cruelty to Animals-Yarmouth Branch, 1049
PFLAG Canada Inc.-Yarmouth Chapter, 1156
Scotia Fundy Mobile Gear Fishermen's Association, 1286
Tri-County Women's Centre, 1398

Yarmouth & Area Chamber of Commerce, 1470
Yarmouth County Historical Society, 1470
Yarmouth Food Bank Society, 1470
YMCA Canada-YMCA of Yarmouth, 1473

Northwest Territories

Fort Providence
Zhahti Koe Friendship Centre, 1482

Fort Simpson
Fort Simpson Chamber of Commerce, 754

Fort Smith
Association des francophones de Fort Smith, 114
NWT School Athletic Federation, 1052
Thebacha & Wood Buffalo Astronomical Society, 1375
Thebacha Chamber of Commerce, 1375

Hay River
Association franco-culturelle de Hay River, 135
Hay River Chamber of Commerce, 805
Soaring Eagle Friendship Centre, 1305

Inuvik
AFOA Canada-AFOA Northwest Territories, 12
Association des francophones du delta du Mackenzie, 114
Inuvik Chamber of Commerce, 862
World Wildlife Fund - Canada-Inuvik, 1468

Lutsel K'e
Denesoline Corporation Ltd., 653

Norman Wells
Norman Wells & District Chamber of Commerce, 1028
Norman Wells Historical Society, 1028

Yellowknife
The Anglican Church of Canada-Diocese of the Arctic, 69
Association des parents ayants droit de Yellowknife, 121
Association franco-culturelle de Yellowknife, 135
Association of Northwest Territories Speech Language Pathologists & Audiologists, 154
Association of Psychologists of the Northwest Territories, 160
The Association of Social Workers of Northern Canada, 162
Autism Society Northwest Territories, 189
Basketball NWT, 199
Canadian Bar Association-Northwest Territories, 342
Canadian Hard of Hearing Association-Northwest Territories - Yellowknife Branch, 400
Canadian Parks & Wilderness Society-Yellowknife - Northwest Territories Chapter, 451
Canadian Public Health Association - NWT/Nunavut Branch, 462
Certified General Accountants Association of the Northwest Territories & Nunavut, 538
CMA Canada - Northwest Territories & Nunavut, 576
Consulting Engineers of the Northwest Territories, 625
Denturist Association of Northwest Territories, 654
Ducks Unlimited Canada-Northwest Territories Office, 664
Ecology North, 672
Fédération franco-ténoise, 721
Great Slave Snowmobile Association, 782
Habitat for Humanity Canada-Northwest Territories, 796
Hockey North, 818
Institute of Chartered Accountants of the Northwest Territories & Nunavut, 845
The John Howard Society of Northwest Territories, 874
KidSport Northwest Territories, 887

Law Society of the Northwest Territories, 902
Learning Disabilities Association of The Northwest Territories, 905
Local Government Administrators of the Northwest Territories, 916
Music NWT, 984
Native Communications Society of the Northwest Territories, 997
Native Women's Association of the Northwest Territories, 998
Northern Air Transport Association, 1034
Northern Frontier Visitors Association, 1035
Northern Territories Federation of Labour, 1035
Northwest Territories & Nunavut Association of Professional Engineers & Geoscientists, 1036
Northwest Territories & Nunavut Chamber of Mines, 1037
Northwest Territories & Nunavut Construction Association, 1037
Northwest Territories 5 Pin Bowlers' Association, 1037
Northwest Territories Amateur Speed Skating Association, 1037
Northwest Territories Archives Council, 1037
Northwest Territories Arts Council, 1037
Northwest Territories Association of Architects, 1037
Northwest Territories Association of Communities, 1037
Northwest Territories Association of Landscape Architects, 1037
Northwest Territories Association of Provincial Court Judges, 1037
Northwest Territories Badminton Association, 1037
Northwest Territories Broomball Association, 1037
Northwest Territories Chamber of Commerce, 1037
Northwest Territories Curling Association, 1038
Northwest Territories Federal Liberal Association, 1038
Northwest Territories Law Foundation, 1038
Northwest Territories Library Association, 1038
Northwest Territories Medical Association, 1038
Northwest Territories Recreation & Parks Association, 1038
Northwest Territories Ski Division, 1038
Northwest Territories Soccer Association, 1038
Northwest Territories Society for the Prevention of Cruelty to Animals, 1038
Northwest Territories Softball, 1038
Northwest Territories Teachers' Association, 1038
Northwest Territories Tennis Association, 1038
Northwest Territories Tourism, 1039
Northwest Territories Volleyball Association, 1039
Northwest Territories/Nunavut Council of Friendship Centres, 1039
NWT Disabilities Council, 1052
NWT Seniors' Society, 1052
Office of the Superintendent of Securities of the Northwest Territories, 1055
Prince of Wales Northern Heritage Centre, 1179
Public Service Alliance of Canada-Yellowknife Branch, 1193
The Registered Nurses Association of the Northwest Territories & Nunavut, 1213
Réseau TNO Santé en français, 1226
St. John Ambulance-NWT & Nunavut Council, 1249
Skills/Compétences Canada-Northwest Territories, 1303
Special Olympics Northwest Territories, 1340
Sport North Federation, 1345
Status of Women Council of the Northwest Territories, 1349
Supply Chain Management Association - Northwest Territories, 1356
Tides Canada Foundation-Yellowknife Office, 1379
Union of Northern Workers, 1407

Yellowknife Association for Community Living, 1470
Yellowknife Chamber of Commerce, 1471
Yellowknife Real Estate Board, 1471
Yellowknife Shooting Club, 1471
YWCA Canada-YWCA NWT, 1482

Nunavut

Arctic Bay
Arctic Bay Housing Association, 81

Cambridge Bay
Enokhok Development Corporation Ltd.-Enokhok Inn & Suites - Campbridge Bay, 690

Cape Dorset
Aiviq Hunters & Trappers Organization, 20

Iqaluit
Ajjiit Nunavut Media Association, 20
Arctic Co-operatives Limited-Nunavut Regional Office, 81
Association des francophones du Nunavut, 114
Baffin Regional Chamber of Commerce, 194
Habitat for Humanity Canada-Nunavut - Iqaluit, 796
Iqaluit Chamber of Commerce, 863
Judo Nunavut, 876
Law Society of Nunavut, 901
Nunasi Corporation, 1051
Nunavummi Disabilities Makinnasuaqtiit Society, 1051
Nunavut Arts & Crafts Association, 1051
Nunavut Association of Landscape Architects, 1051
Nunavut Economic Developers Association, 1051
Nunavut Employees Union, 1051
Nunavut Library Association, 1051
Nunavut Securities Office, 1051
Nunavut Speed Skating Association, 1051
Nunavut Teachers' Association, 1051
Nunavut Tourism, 1051
Public Service Alliance of Canada-Northern Branch, 1193
Qikiqtani Inuit Association, 1194
Réseau de Santé en Français au Nunavut, 1219
Skills/Compétences Canada-Nunavut, 1303
Volleyball Nunavut, 1438
World Wildlife Fund - Canada-Iqaluit, 1468
YWCA Canada-YWCA Agvvik Nunavut, 1481

Kugluktuk
Kugluktuk Chamber of Commerce, 894

Pond Inlet
Mittimatalik Hunters' & Trappers' Organization, 970

Rankin Inlet
Kivalliq Chamber of Commerce, 891
Kivalliq Inuit Association, 891
Nunavut Curling Association, 1051
Nunavut Harvesters Association, 1051
Pamiqsaiji Association for Community Living, 1138
Pulaarvik Kablu Friendship Centre, 1194

Ontario

Acton
Field Botanists of Ontario, 733
Ontario Vegetation Management Association, 1112
Professional Golfers' Association of Canada, 1185
South Wellington Coin Society, 1336

Agincourt
Coalition for Music Education in Canada, 578

Ahkwesahsne
Native North American Traveling College, 998

Ailsa Craig
Craft & Hobby Association-Canada Chapter, 1520

Ajax
Advanced Card Technology Association of Canada, 9
Ajax-Pickering Board of Trade, 20
Community Development Council Durham, 596
Community Living Ajax-Pickering & Whitby, 600
Credit Institute of Canada-Toronto Chapter, 641
Daughters of Isabella, 651
God, Sex, & the Meaning of Life Ministry, 776
Habitat for Humanity Canada-Durham Region, Ontario, 797
Huntington Society of Canada-East Central Ontario Resource Centre, 827
Independent Lumber Dealers Co-operative, 833
International Union of Elevator Constructors (AFL-CIO/CFL)-Local 50 - Toronto
Militia of the Immaculata Canada, 965
Movement for Marriage Enrichment, 978
National Transportation Brokers Association, 996
Ontario Association of Fire Chiefs, 1063
SPANCAN, 1338
Touch Football Ontario, 1388

Akwesasne
Native Women's Association of Canada, 998

Alexandria
Alexandria & District Chamber of Commerce, 53
Canadian Society of Professional Event Planners, 487
Community Living Glengarry, 602

Alliston
Alliston & District Chamber of Commerce, 59
The Bruce Trail Conservancy-Dufferin Hi-Land, 261
Community Living Association for South Simcoe, 600
Ontario Creamerymen's Association, 1076
South Simcoe Community Information Centre, 1336
Welsh Pony & Cob Society of Canada, 1444

Almonte
Almonte in Concert, 59
Canadian Federation of Pensioners, 388
Mississippi Mills Chamber of Commerce, 970

Alton
Canadian Independent Telephone Association, 411

Amaranth
Dominion Rabbit & Cavy Breeders Association, 661
Pentathlon Canada, 1150

Amherstburg
Amherstburg Chamber of Commerce, 67
Amherstburg Community Services, 67
Amherstburg Historic Sites Association, 67
CADORA Ontario Association Inc.-Windsor - Essex CADORA Chapter, 270
Canadian Vintage Motorcycle Group, 501
Community Living Essex County-Amherstburg - Channel Office, 601
Helping Unite Grandparents & Grandchildren, 812
Marsh Collection Society, 952

Amherstview
Canadian Association of Veterans in United Nations Peacekeeping-Kingston Limestone Chapter, 336

Ancaster
Ancaster Community Services, 68
Canadian Blood Services-Ancaster, 344
Hike Ontario, 814
Ontario Alliance of Christian Schools, 1059
Ontario Association of Cemetery & Funeral Professionals, 1062
Pastel Artists Canada, 1145

Photo Marketing Association International - Canada, 1157
Réseau franco-santé du Sud de l'Ontario, 1224

Appleton
North Lanark Historical Society, 1031

Apsley
Community Care Peterborough-Apsley Office, 596

Arkona
Arkona & Area Historical Society, 81

Arnprior
L'Arche Ontario-L'Arche Arnprior, 77
Boston Terrier Rescue Canada, 218
Greater Arnprior Chamber of Commerce, 782
Ontario Society for the Prevention of Cruelty to Animals-Arnprior Branch (Affiliate), 1105
Universities Art Association of Canada, 1418

Arthur
Arthur & District Chamber of Commerce, 84
Independent School Bus Operators Association, 833
Southwestern Ontario Gliding Association, 1338

Arva
Middlesex, Oxford, Elgin Beekeepers' Association, 965
SARI Therapeutic Riding, 1254

Ashburn
Canadian Society of Presbyterian History, 487

Atikokan
Atikokan Chamber of Commerce, 181
Atikokan Native Friendship Centre, 181
Community Living Atikokan, 600
Family & Children's Services of the District of Rainy River-Atikokan Office, 702
Northern Ontario Curling Association, 1035

Aurora
Alzheimer Society of York Region, 65
Aurora Chamber of Commerce, 187
Aurora Historical Society, Inc., 187
Aurora King Baseball Association, 188
Canadian Business Aviation Association-Ontario Chapter, 348
Canadian Hard of Hearing Association-Ontario - York Branch, 400
Canadian Office & Professional Employees Union-Region 2 - Local 131, 445
Human Resources Professionals Association-York Region Chapter, 826
Kerry's Place Autism Services, 884
Kerry's Place Autism Services-Central Region, 884
Oak Ridges Trail Association, 1053
Ontario Canoe Kayak Sprint Racing Affiliation, 1070
Ontario Farm Fresh Marketing Association, 1078
Ontario Municipal Tax & Revenue Association, 1092
Ontario Streams, 1109
Pine Tree Potters Guild, 1160
The Royal Canadian Legion-Ontario Command, 1240
Trillium Party of Ontario, 1398
Windfall Ecology Centre, 1456

Bailieboro
Mirabel Morgan Special Riding Centre, 968

Bala
Muskoka Lakes Chamber of Commerce, 985

Balderson
American Saddlebred Horse Association of Ontario, 66

Bancroft
Algonquin Arts Council, 53
Alzheimer Society of Belleville/Hastings/Quinte-North Hastings, 62
Bancroft & District Chamber of Commerce, Tourism & Information Centre, 195

Bancroft District Real Estate Board, 195
Bancroft Gem & Mineral Club, 195
Highland Shores Children's Aid-North Hastings, 814
North Hastings Community Integration Association, 1031

Barrie
AIDS Committee of Simcoe County, 16
Alcoholics Anonymous-Barrie - Barrie & Area Intergroup, 52
Alzheimer Society of Simcoe County, 65
Am Shalom, 66
Barrie & District Association of REALTORS Inc., 197
Barrie Gem & Mineral Society Inc., 197
Barrie Literacy Council, 197
Barrie Native Friendship Centre, 197
Barrie Post Polio Association, 197
Big Brothers Big Sisters of Ontario-Big Brothers Big Sisters of Barrie & District, 210
Block Parent Program of Canada, 214
Brereton Field Naturalists' Club Inc., 228
Canada East Equipment Dealers' Association, 278
Canadian Association of Elizabeth Fry Societies-Elizabeth Fry Society of Simcoe County, 313
Canadian Association of Veterans in United Nations Peacekeeping-Central Ontario Chapter, 335
Canadian Blood Services-Barrie, 344
Canadian Condominium Institute-CCI-Huronia Chapter, 362
Canadian Culinary Federation-Muskoka Branch, 374
Canadian Education Exchange Foundation, 380
Canadian Farm Animal Care Trust, 384
Canadian Hearing Society-Barrie Office, 403
Canadian Institute of Management, 416
Canadian Institute of Management-Ontario - Lake Simcoe Branch, 417
Canadian Pastry Chefs Guild Inc., 451
Candlelighters Simcoe Parents of Children with Cancer, 508
Catholic Family Services of Simcoe County, 519
La Clé d'la Baie en Huronie - Association culturelle francophone, 572
Council of Ontario Construction Associations-Barrie Construction Association, 634
Ducks Unlimited Canada-Ontario Provincial Office, 664
Epilepsy Ontario-Simcoe County, 694
Georgian Bay Steam & Antique Association, 771
Greater Barrie Chamber of Commerce, 782
Habitat for Humanity Canada-Ontario - Huronia, 797
Heart & Stroke Foundation of Ontario-Barrie Office, 809
Human Resources Professionals Association-Barrie & District Chapter, 825
Huronia Symphony Orchestra, 828
Information Barrie, 836
International Machine Cancel Research Society of Canada, 858
The John Howard Society of Ontario-Simcoe & Muskoka, 875
Ontario Genealogical Society-Simcoe County Branch, 1082
Ontario Home Builders' Association-Simcoe County, 1086
Ontario Jiu-Jitsu Association, 1088
Ontario Provincial Police Association, 1098
Ontario Society for the Prevention of Cruelty to Animals-Barrie Branch, 1105
Registered Deposit Brokers Association, 1213
Saint Elizabeth Health Care-Barrie - North Simcoe Muskoka Service Delivery Centre, 1246
Seasons Centre for Grieving Children, 1288
Simcoe County Historical Association, 1299
Simcoe County Law Association, 1299
Simcoe Muskoka Family Connexions, 1300

Simcoe Women's Wellness Centre Corporation, 1300
Spinal Cord Injury Ontario-Barrie Office, 1343
Tuberous Sclerosis Canada Sclérose Tubéreuse, 1400
Women's Association of the Mining Industry of Canada, 1461
YMCA Canada-YMCA of Simcoe/Muskoka - Barrie, 1471

Barry's Bay
Madawaska Valley Association for Community Living, 924
Wilno Heritage Society, 1456

Bath
Ontario Healthcare Housekeepers' Association Inc., 1084
Thyroid Foundation of Canada, 1378

Battersea
Limestone Beekeepers Guild, 912

Bayfield
Bayfield & Area Chamber of Commerce, 200

Beachville
Beachville District Historical Society, 202

Beamsville
The Bruce Trail Conservancy-Niagara, 261
Canadian Association of Veterans in United Nations Peacekeeping-Niagara Chapter, 336
Community Living Grimsby, Lincoln & West Lincoln, 602
Community Living Grimsby, Lincoln & West Lincoln-Beamsville - C.D. Hopkins Centre, 602
Lincoln Chamber of Commerce, 912
Niagara West Employment & Learning Resource Centres, 1026
West Niagara Second Stage Housing & Counselling, 1446

Beaverton
Beaverton District Chamber of Commerce, 203
Beaverton Thorah Eldon Historical Society, 203
Federation of Health Regulatory Colleges of Ontario, 724

Beeton
Circulation Management Association of Canada, 570
Ontario Daylily Society, 1076
Ontario Society for the Prevention of Cruelty to Animals-Alliston Branch (Affiliate), 1105
Wings & Heros, 1458

Belle River
Lakeshore Community Services, 897

Belleville
Alzheimer Society of Belleville/Hastings/Quinte, 62
Alzheimer Society of Hastings - Prince Edward, 62
Belleville & District Chamber of Commerce, 204
Belleville Police Association, 204
Canadian Hearing Society-Belleville Office, 403
Community Care for South Hastings, 596
Community Development Council of Quinte, 596
Counselling Services of Belleville & District, 636
Denturist Association of Canada, 653
Gleaners Food Bank, 774
Habitat for Humanity Canada-Ontario - Prince Edward-Hastings, 797
Hastings County Law Association, 804
Heart & Stroke Foundation of Ontario-Belleville Office, 809
Heritage Belleville, 812
Highland Shores Children's Aid, 814
The John Howard Society of Ontario-Belleville, 874
K3C Community Counselling Centres-K3C Credit Counselling Belleville, 879
Kerry's Place Autism Services-Eastern Office, 884
Mood Disorders Society of Canada, 973

Geographic Index / Ontario - Belwood

Ontario Brain Injury Association-Belleville, 1068
Ontario Home Builders' Association-Quinte, 1085
Ontario Lung Association-Kingston Office (Kingston & the Thousand Islands), 1090
Ontario Lung Association-Belleville Office (Hastings & Prince Edward Counties), 1090
Ontario Society for the Prevention of Cruelty to Animals-Quinte Branch (Affiliate), 1106
Quinte Arts Council, 1201
Quinte Construction Association, 1201
Quinte Immigrant Services, 1201
Quinte Labour Council, 1201
Quinte Symphony, 1201
United Church of Canada-Bay of Quinte Conference, 1409
United Nations Association in Canada-Quinte & District, 1411
United Way of Quinte, 1416
YMCA Canada-YMCA of Central East Ontario - Belleville, 1471

Belwood
Ontario Farm & Country Accommodations Association, 1078
York Soaring Association, 1473

Binbrook
Binbrook Agricultural Society, 211
Glanbrook Heritage Society, 774
International Police Association - Canada, 859

Blenheim
Blenheim & District Chamber of Commerce, 214
Ontario Commercial Fisheries' Association, 1073
Save Ontario Shipwrecks, 1281

Blezard Valley
Full Gospel Business Men's Fellowship in Canada, 764

Blind River
Blind River Chamber of Commerce, 214
Children's Aid Society of Algoma-Blind River Office, 560
Ontario Paramedic Association, 1094

Bloomfield
Canadian Celiac Association-Belleville & Quinte Chapter, 352
Canadian Urban Libraries Council, 500

Bobcaygeon
Bobcaygeon & Area Chamber of Commerce, 217

Bognor
Ontario Brown Swiss Association, 1069

Bolton
Association of Veterans & Friends of the Mackenzie-Papineau Battalion, International Brigades in Spain, 164
Caledon Chamber of Commerce, 270
Caledon Community Services, 270
Canadian Printing Industries Scholarship Trust Fund, 460
Catholic Family Services of Peel Dufferin-Caledon Branch, 519
National Marine Manufacturers Association Canada, 995
Printing Equipment & Supply Dealers' Association of Canada, 1180

Bond Head
Tecumseth & West Gwillimbury Historical Society, 1369

Borden
Base Borden Soaring, 197
Electrical & Mechanical Engineering Association, 682

Bothwell
Autism Canada, 188
Bothwell-Zone & District Historical Society, 218
Southern First Nations Secretariat, 1337

Bowmanville
Canadian Christian Relief & Development Association, 356
Master Bowlers' Association of Ontario, 953
Society of Public Insurance Administrators of Ontario, 1330

Bracebridge
Alzheimer Society of Muskoka, 63
Bracebridge Chamber of Commerce, 224
Bracebridge Historical Society, 224
Canadian Hearing Society-Muskoka Office, 403
Canadian Supply Chain Sector Council, 491
Community Living South Muskoka, 605
Muskoka Arts & Crafts Inc., 985
Muskoka Community Futures Development Corporation, 985
Muskoka Pioneer Power Association, 985
Ontario Agencies Supporting Individuals with Special Needs, 1059
Ontario Recovery Group Inc., 1100
Ontario Society for the Prevention of Cruelty to Animals-Muskoka Branch, 1106
Provincial Towing Association (Ontario), 1191
YWCA Canada-Community YWCA Muskoka, 1481

Bradford
Bradford Board of Trade, 224
CrossTrainers Canada, 644
Drainage Superintendents Association of Ontario, 662

Brampton
A.C.C.E.S. Employment-Brampton, 4
Boys & Girls Clubs of Ontario-Boys & Girls Club of Peel, 223
Brampton Arts Council, 225
The Brampton Board of Trade, 225
Brampton Caledon Community Living, 226
Brampton Horticultural Society, 226
Brampton Real Estate Board, 226
BullyingCanada Inc.-Ontario Office, 264
Canadian Association of Elizabeth Fry Societies-Elizabeth Fry Society of Peel Halton, 313
Canadian Corrugated Containerboard Association, 366
Canadian Depression Glass Association, 377
Canadian Federation of Business & Professional Women's Clubs-Ontario, 385
Canadian Federation of Business & Professional Women's Clubs-Brampton, 385
Canadian Institute for Child & Adolescent Psychoanalytic Psychotherapy, 412
Canadian Textile Association, 494
Catholic Cross Cultural Services-Brampton, 518
Catholic Family Services of Peel Dufferin-Brampton Branch, 519
Church of Jesus Christ of Latter-day Saints - Canada, 569
Citroën Autoclub Canada, 571
Le Collège du Savoir, 582
COSTI Immigrant Services-Brampton & Caledon Employment Centre, 632
COSTI Immigrant Services-Brampton - Language, Employment & Settlement Services, 632
Cricket Council of Ontario, 642
Fragile X Research Foundation of Canada, 757
Heart & Stroke Foundation of Ontario-Peel Office, 809
The John Howard Society of Ontario-Peel, Halton & Dufferin, 875
Karate Ontario, 882
Knights of St. John International - Canada, 892
Mary Undoer of Knots, 952
Meningitis Relief Canada, 960
National Chinchilla Breeders of Canada, 991
The Nile Association of Ontario, 1027
Oasis Centre des femmes-Brampton, 1054
Ontario Association of Police Services Boards, 1065
Ontario Pioneers, 1096
Ontario Waste Management Association, 1112
Paper & Paperboard Packaging Environmental Council, 1138
Partners International, 1144
Peel Law Association, 1148
Peel Music Festival, 1148
Peel Regional Police Association, 1148
Pool & Hot Tub Council of Canada, 1164
Respiratory Therapy Society of Ontario, 1227
St. Leonard's Society of Canada-St. Leonard's House Peel, 1250
St. Mary's Prayer Group, 1250
Spectra Helpline, 1340
Twins Plus Association of Brampton, 1400

Brantford
Alzheimer Society of Brant, 62
Association of Polish Engineers in Canada-Hamilton Branch, 156
Boys & Girls Clubs of Ontario-Boys & Girls Clubs of Brantford, 223
Brant Family & Children's Services, 226
Brant Historical Society, 226
Brant Skills Centre, 226
Brant United Way, 226
Brantford & District Labour Council, 227
Brantford Lapidary & Mineral Society Inc., 227
Brantford Musicians' Association, 227
Brantford Numismatic Society, 227
Brantford Police Association, 227
Brantford Regional Real Estate Association Inc., 227
Brantford Stamp Club, 227
Brantford Symphony Orchestra Association Inc., 227
Brantwood Foundation, 227
Canadian Association of Physicians of Indian Heritage, 327
Canadian Hearing Society-Brantford Office, 403
Canadian Society of Orthopaedic Technologists-Graham Bell Chapter, 485
Career Colleges Ontario, 511
Chamber of Commerce of Brantford & Brant, 539
Child Evangelism Fellowship of Canada-Child Evangelism Fellowship of Ontario, 559
Community Living Brantford, 600
Congregational Christian Churches in Canada, 613
Family Counselling Centre of Brant, Inc., 703
Habitat for Humanity Canada-Ontario - Brant-Norfolk, 796
Haldimand-Norfolk Information Centre, 798
Hamilton Niagara Haldimand Brant Community Care Access Centre, 801
Heart & Stroke Foundation of Ontario-Brantford Office, 809
Heating, Refrigeration & Air Conditioning Institute of Canada-Ontario - Brant/Haldimand/Norfolk Chapter, 810
Holstein Canada, 819
Kiwanis International (Eastern Canada & the Caribbean District), 891
The Ontario Archaeological Society Inc.-Hamilton Chapter, 1060
Ontario Genealogical Society-Brant County Branch, 1081
Ontario Home Builders' Association-Brantford, 1085
Ontario Lung Association-Hamilton Office (Hamilton, Brant County, Niagara, Haldimand & Norfolk Counties, & Waterloo & Wellington Regions), 1090
Ontario Lung Association-Brantford Office (Brant County), 1090
Ontario Society for the Prevention of Cruelty to Animals-Brant County Branch (Affliate), 1105
Ontario Steelheaders, 1109
Solo Swims of Ontario Inc., 1332
Woodland Cultural Centre, 1464

Brechin
Ramara & District Chamber of Commerce, 1204

Breslau
Heating, Refrigeration & Air Conditioning Institute of Canada-Ontario - Waterloo/Wellington Chapter, 810
Recreational Aircraft Association, 1208
Society for the Preservation of Old Mills - Canadian Chapter, 1326

Bridgenorth
Smith-Ennismore Historical Society, 1304

Bright
Ultralight Pilots Association of Canada, 1404

Bright's Grove
Association of Italian Canadian Writers, 150

Brighton
Brighton-Cramahe Chamber of Commerce, 229
Farmers' Markets Ontario, 706
The Friends of Presqu'ile Park, 761
Save Our Heritage Organization, 1281

Brockton
Ontario Home Builders' Association-Saugeen, 1086

Brockville
Alzheimer Society of Leeds-Grenville, 63
Brockville & District Association for Community Involvement, 260
Brockville & District Chamber of Commerce, 260
Brockville & District Multicultural Council Inc., 260
Canadian Hearing Society-Brockville Sub-Office, 403
Employment & Education Centre, 687
Family & Children's Services of Lanark, Leeds & Grenville, 702
Grand Orange Lodge of Canada-Grand Orange Lodge of Ontario East, 780
Habitat for Humanity Canada-Ontario - Thousand Islands, 797
Heart & Stroke Foundation of Ontario-Brockville Office, 809
K3C Community Counselling Centres-K3C Credit Counselling Brockville, 879
Ontario Genealogical Society-Leeds & Grenville Branch, 1082
Ontario Society for the Prevention of Cruelty to Animals-Leeds & Grenville Branch, 1106
Operation Harvest Sharing, 1115
PFLAG Canada Inc.-Brockville Chapter, 1155
Professional Engineers Ontario-Thousand Islands, 1185
Rideau-St. Lawrence Real Estate Board, 1232
United Way of Leeds & Grenville, 1415
YMCA Canada-YMCA of Bockville & Area, 1471

Brussels
Ontario Commercial Rabbit Growers' Association, 1073
Ontario's Finest Inns & Spas, 1114

Buckhorn
Central Ontario Beekeepers' Association, 525
Community Care Peterborough-Harvey Office, 596

Burgessville
Canadian Haflinger Association, 400

Burks Falls
Cecebe Waterways Association, 521

Burlington
Access Counselling & Family Services, 5
Acclaim Health-Burlington, 5
Associated Gospel Churches, 89
Automotive Aftermarket Retailers of Ontario, 189
Burlington Chamber of Commerce, 265
Burlington Historical Society, 265
BurlingtonGreen Environmental Association, 265
Canadian Association of Chemical Distributors, 310
Canadian Association on Water Quality, 337

Canadian Blood Services-Burlington, 344
Canadian Condominium Institute-CCI-Golden Horseshoe Chapter, 362
Canadian Deafblind Association (National), 376
Canadian Dental Protective Association, 377
Canadian Hydrographic Association-Central Branch, 409
Canadian Institute of Underwriters, 420
Canadian Office & Professional Employees Union-Region 2 - Local 290, 445
Canadian Polish Congress-Hamilton Branch, 456
Canadian Reiki Association, 466
Children's Education Funds Inc., 561
The Christian & Missionary Alliance in Canada-Central Canadian District (CCD) Office, 566
Christian Reformed Church in North America, 568
Citizens Opposed to Paving the Escarpment, 570
Community Development Halton, 596
Conservation Halton Foundation, 622
Corsa Ontario, 631
The Easter Seal Society (Ontario)-Western Region - Burlington / Mississauga / Oakville, 670
Evangelical Medical Aid Society Canada, 698
Evangelical Order of Certified Pastoral Counsellors of America, 699
Field Hockey Ontario, 734
Food for Life Canada, 749
Foresters-Burlington, 751
The Garden Clubs of Ontario-Burlington, 766
Global Business Travel Association (Canada), 774
Halton Children's Aid Society, 800
Halton District Educational Assistants Association, 800
Heart & Stroke Foundation of Ontario-Halton Region Office, 809
Information Burlington, 836
Institute of Power Engineers, 846
International Brotherhood of Boilermakers, Iron Ship Builders, Blacksmiths, Forgers & Helpers (AFL-CIO)-Burlington (Toronto Lodge 128)
Islamic Relief Canada, 865
Junior League of Hamilton-Burlington, Inc., 878
The Literacy Council of Burlington, 913
Model Aeronautics Association of Canada Inc., 970
Morgan Sports Car Club of Canada, 974
Myalgic Encephalomyelitis Association of Halton/Hamilton-Wentworth, 986
NAIOP Greater Toronto, 987
Ontario Dental Hygienists' Association, 1077
Ontario Funeral Service Association, 1081
Ontario Municipal Human Resources Association, 1092
Ontario Professional Fire Fighters Association, 1097
Ontario Public Transit Association, 1100
Ontario Tenpin Bowling Association, 1110
Ontario Trial Lawyers Association, 1111
Ontario University Athletics, 1112
Orchid Society of Royal Botanical Gardens, 1119
Pentecostal Assemblies of Canada-Western Ontario District Office, 1150
Pioneer Clubs Canada Inc., 1160
The Royal Scottish Country Dance Society-Burlington Branch
Start2Finish, 1348
Symphony on the Bay, 1360
Tourism Burlington, 1389
United Way of Burlington & Greater Hamilton-Burlington Office, 1413
Woodview Mental Health & Autism Services, 1464
World Renew, 1467

Caledon
The Bruce Trail Conservancy-Caledon Hills, 261

Canadian Network for Respiratory Care, 441
Clan MacLeod Societies of Canada, 572
Ontario Association of Archers Inc., 1061
SHARE Agriculture Foundation, 1294
Whole Village, 1453

Caledon East
Caledon East & District Historical Society, 270
Older Adult Centres' Association of Ontario, 1056

Caledonia
Caledonia Regional Chamber of Commerce, 270
Community Support Centre Haldimand-Norfolk, 607
The Royal Scottish Country Dance Society-Hamilton Branch

Calgary
The Canadian Federation of Business & Professional Women's Clubs, 385

Callander
Canadian Office & Professional Employees Union-Region 2 - Local 24, 445
Skate Canada-Northern Ontario Section, 1302

Cambridge
Alzheimer Society Waterloo Wellington, 65
Armenian Relief Society of Canada, Inc.-Cambridge Chapter: "Meghri", 83
Art Libraries Society of North America-Ontario Chapter
Baseball Ontario, 198
CADORA Ontario Association Inc.-Glanbrook CADORA Chapter, 269
Cambridge Association of Realtors Inc., 275
Cambridge Chamber of Commerce, 275
Cambridge Self-Help Food Bank, 275
Cambridge Tourism, 275
Canadian Association of Snowboard Instructors, 333
Canadian Partnership for Consumer Food Safety Education, 451
Canadian Sheet Steel Building Institute, 470
Canadian Tooling & Machining Association, 495
Christian Labour Association of Canada-Kitchener/Cambridge/Waterloo Regional Office, 568
Community Living Cambridge, 600
Corrugated Steel Pipe Institute, 631
Council of Ontario Construction Associations-Grand Valley Construction Association, 634
Family Counselling Centre of Cambridge & North Dumfries, 703
Fellowship of Evangelical Baptist Churches in Canada-FEB Central, 731
Grand River Conservation Foundation, 780
Guelph Creative Arts Association, 793
Holstein Canada-Ontario Branch, 819
Kin Canada, 887
Kin Canada Foundation, 887
Lions Quest Canada - The Centre for Positive Youth Development, 913
The Literacy Group of Waterloo Region, 914
Ontario Federation of Independent Schools, 1079
Ontario Hockey Federation, 1084
Ontario Mutual Insurance Association, 1093
Ontario Society for the Prevention of Cruelty to Animals-Cambridge & District Branch (Affiliate), 1105
Order of Sons of Italy in Canada, 1119
Siding & Window Dealers Association of Canada, 1298
Social Planning Council of Cambridge & North Dumfries, 1306
Tire and Rubber Association of Canada, 1380
United Way of Cambridge & North Dumfries, 1413
Vasculitis Foundation Canada, 1430
Waterloo Regional Police Association, 1442
World Amateur Muay Thai Association of Canada, 1465
YMCA Immigrant & Community Services, 1473

YWCA Canada-YWCA Cambridge, 1482

Cameron
Heaven Can Wait Equine Rescue, 810

Campbellford
Campbellford/Seymour Heritage Society, 276
Community Living Campbellford/Brighton, 601
Friends of Ferris Provincial Park, 761
Trent Hills & District Chamber of Commerce, 1397

Campbellville
Arabian Horse Association of Eastern Canada, 76
Canadian National Federation of Independent Unions, 439
Central Ontario Standardbred Association, 525
Doggone Safe, 660
Ontario Standardbred Adoption Society, 1109
Serbian Orthodox Church - Orthodox Diocese of Canada, 1290

Cannifton
Hastings County Historical Society, 804
Quinte & District Association of REALTORS Inc., 1201

Cannington
Cannington & Area Historical Society, 508
Information Brock, 836

Capreol
Canadian Aboriginal Minerals Association, 285

Cargill
Ontario Hereford Association, 1084

Carleton Place
CADORA Ontario Association Inc.-Ottawa Area CADORA Chapter, 269
Canadian Co-operative Wool Growers Ltd., 364
Canadian Radiation Protection Association, 464
Carleton Place & Beckwith Historical Society, 513
Carleton Place & District Chamber of Commerce & Visitor Centre, 513
Community Living Association (Lanark County), 600
Lanark County Beekeepers' Association, 897
Lanark County Food Bank, 897
The Lanark County Museums Network, 897
Lanark County Therapeutic Riding Program, 897
LifeCanada, 911
United Way of Lanark County, 1415
Women Expanding Business Network of Lanark County, 1460

Carlisle
United Church of Canada-Hamilton Conference, 1409

Carp
Carp Agricultural Society, 515
Construction Resource Initiatives Council, 624
Huntley Township Historical Society, 828
International Association of Hydrogeologists - Canadian National Chapter, 854
Ontario Blonde d'Aquitaine Association, 1068
Ottawa Philatelic Society, 1131

Cayuga
Cayuga & District Chamber of Commerce, 521
Community Living Haldimand, 602
Ontario Association of Committees of Adjustment & Consent Authorities, 1063

Chalk River
Canadian Institute for Neutron Scattering, 413

Chapleau
The Children's Aid Society of the Districts of Sudbury & Manitoulin-Chapleau Office, 561
Intégration communautaire Chapleau Community Living, 850

Charlottetown
Ducks Unlimited Canada-Prince Edward Island Provincial Office, 664

Chatham
AIDS Committee of Windsor-AIDS Support Chatham-Kent, 16
Alliance for Canadian New Music Projects-Contemporary Showcase - Chatham, 56
Alzheimer Society of Chatham-Kent, 62
Big Brothers Big Sisters of Ontario-Big Brothers Big Sisters of Chatham-Kent, 210
Canadian Hearing Society-Chatham-Kent Office, 403
Canadian Liver Foundation-Chatham/Kent Chapter, 427
Canadian Sport Massage Therapists Association, 490
Chatham Outreach for Hunger, 555
Chatham Railroad Museum Society, 555
Chatham-Kent Chamber of Commerce, 555
Chatham-Kent Labour Council, 555
Chatham-Kent Real Estate Board, 555
Christian Labour Association of Canada-Southwestern Ontario Regional Office, 568
Community Living Chatham-Kent, 601
Family Service Kent, 704
Habitat for Humanity Canada-Ontario - Chatham-Kent, 796
Heart & Stroke Foundation of Ontario-Chatham-Kent Office, 809
Independent Assemblies of God International - Canada, 832
Junior Achievement of Canada-Junior Achievement of Southwestern Ontario, 877
Kent Coin Club, 883
Kent County Cattlemen's Association, 884
Kent County Stamp Club, 884
Ontario Brain Injury Association-Chatham, 1068
Ontario Genealogical Society-Kent County Branch, 1082
Ontario Home Builders' Association-Chatham Kent, 1085
Ontario Muzzle Loading Association, 1093
Ontario Society for the Prevention of Cruelty to Animals-Kent Branch, 1105
Seed Corn Growers of Ontario, 1288
Southwestern Ontario Beekeepers' Association, 1338
UNIFOR-Chatham Office, 1405
United Way of Chatham-Kent County, 1413
YMCA Canada-YMCAs across Southwestern Ontario - Chatham—Kent, 1471

Chatsworth
Ontario Competitive Trail Riding Association Inc., 1073

Chelmsford
CADORA Ontario Association Inc.-Greater Sudbury Chapter, 269
Huntington Society of Canada-Northern Ontario Resource Centre, 828

Chesley
Chesley & District Chamber of Commerce, 556

Clarence Creek
Union des cultivateurs franco-ontariens, 1406

Clinton
Alzheimer Society of Huron County, 63

Cloyne
The Friends of Bon Echo Park, 760

Cobourg
Automobile Journalists Association of Canada, 189
Cobourg & District Historical Society, 579
Community Living West Northumberland, 606
Habitat for Humanity Canada-Ontario - Northumberland, 797
Highland Shores Children's Aid-Cobourg, 814
Horizons of Friendship, 821
Info Northumberland, 836
Northumberland Central Chamber of Commerce, 1036

Geographic Index / Ontario - Cochrane

Northumberland Hills Association of Realtors, 1036
Northumberland Orchestra Society, 1036
Northumberland United Way, 1036
Pentecostal Assemblies of Canada-Eastern Ontario District Office, 1150
Receivables Insurance Association of Canada, 1206
YMCA Canada-YMCA of Northumberland, 1472

Cochrane
The Anglican Church of Canada-Diocese of Moosonee, 69
Ininew Friendship Centre, 838
Intégration communautaire Cochrane Association for Community Living, 850
Lake Abitibi Model Forest, 895

Coldwater
Canadian Self Storage Association, 470

Collingwood
Alpine Ontario Alpin, 59
Association of Ontario Snowboarders, 155
Biathlon Ontario, 207
Blue Mountain Foundation for the Arts, 215
The Bruce Trail Conservancy-Blue Mountains, 261
Canadian Ski Instructors' Alliance-Ontario, 471
Collingwood & District Historical Society, 591
Collingwood Chamber of Commerce, 591
Community Connection, 596
E3 Community Services, 666
The Georgian Triangle Tourist Association & Tourist Information Centre, 771
Habitat for Humanity Canada-Ontario - South Georgian Bay, 797
Ontario Municipal Water Association, 1092
Southern Georgian Bay Association of REALTORS, 1337
Toronto Entomologists Association, 1384
YMCA Canada-YMCA of Simcoe/Muskoka - Collingwood, 1471

Combermere
Dance Oremus Danse, 649
Madonna House Apostolate, 925

Concord
Canadian Friends of Bar-Ilan University, 394
Forever Chai Foundation of Canada, 752
Humanity First Canada, 827
Knights Hospitallers, Sovereign Order of St. John of Jerusalem, Knights of Malta, Grand Priory of Canada, 892
Maccabi Canada, 923
MasonryWorx, 952
Ontario Association for Impact Assessment, 1061
Ontario Ball Hockey Association, 1067
Ontario Genealogical Society, 1081
Ontario Genealogical Society-Elgin County Branch, 1082
Ontario Genealogical Society-Sault & District Branch, 1082
Sign Association of Canada-Ontario Chapter, 1299
Skate Canada-Central Ontario Section, 1301
Terrazzo Tile & Marble Association of Canada, 1371
Terrazzo, Tile & Marble Guild of Ontario, Inc., 1372
Universal Youth Foundation, 1418

Connaught
The Kidney Foundation of Canada-Timmins-Porcupine Chapter, 886

Consecon
Peruvian Horse Association of Canada-Ontario Peruvian Horse Association, 1152

Cookstown
Huronia & District Beekeepers' Association, 828

Cornwall
Agape Food Bank, 14
Alzheimer Society of Cornwall & District, 62
Bereaved Families of Ontario-Cornwall, 205
Boys & Girls Clubs of Ontario-Boys & Girls Club of Cornwall/SDG, 223
Canadian Association for Mine & Explosive Ordnance Security, 302
Canadian Collegiate Athletic Association, 360
Canadian Hearing Society-Cornwall Office, 403
Community Living Stormont County, 605
Cornwall & Area Chamber of Commerce, 629
Cornwall & District Labour Council, 629
Cornwall & District Real Estate Board, 629
Cornwall Police Association, 629
Counselling & Support Services of S.D. & G., 636
Economic Developers Council of Ontario Inc., 673
First Nations Chiefs of Police Association, 738
Habitat for Humanity Canada-Ontario - Seaway Valley, 797
Heart & Stroke Foundation of Ontario-Cornwall Office, 809
K3C Community Counselling Centres-K3C Credit Counselling Cornwall, 879
Mohawk Council of Akwesasne, 971
Ontario Society for the Prevention of Cruelty to Animals-Stormont, Dundas & Glengarry Branch, 1106
Regnum Christi Movement, 1214
Saint Elizabeth Health Care-Cornwall - Eastern Counties Service Delivery Centre, 1246
Stormont, Dundas & Glengarry Historical Society, 1350
Stormont, Dundas & Glengarry Law Association, 1350
United Way of Stormont, Dundas & Glengarry, 1417

Courtice
Canadian Automotive Repair & Service Council, 340

Curve Lake
National Aboriginal Lands Managers Association, 989

Dashwood
Community Living South Huron, 605

Deep River
Deep River Symphony Orchestra, 652
North Renfrew Family Services Inc., 1032

Delaware
Canadian Association of Nephrology Nurses & Technologists, 322

Deseronto
Community Care for South Hastings-Deseronto Office, 596
Ontario Trails Council, 1111

Dorchester
Electrical Contractors Association of London, 682

Downsview
Ontario Christian Music Assembly, 1071

Drayton
Canadian Fence Industry Association, 389
Ontario Tire Dealers Association, 1110

Dresden
Science Teachers' Association of Ontario, 1285

Dryden
Canadian Office & Professional Employees Union-Region 2 - Local 521, 445
Community Living Dryden-Sioux Lookout, 601
Dryden District Chamber of Commerce, 663
Dryden Native Friendship Centre, 663
Family & Children's Services of the District of Rainy River-Dryden Office, 702

Dundas
Canadian Celiac Association-Hamilton/Burlington Chapter, 352
Canadian Lactation Consultant Association, 425

Centre for Excellence in Emergency Preparedness, 532
The Garden Clubs of Ontario-Dundas, 766
Ontario Nurses' Association-Hamilton Office, 1094
World Small Animal Veterinary Association, 1467

Dunnville
Dunnville Chamber of Commerce, 664
Haldimand-Norfolk Literacy Council-Dunnville Office & Adult Learning Centre, 798

Durham
West Grey Chamber of Commerce, 1445

Duro
CADORA Ontario Association Inc.-Kawartha Lakes Dressage Chapter, 269

East Garafraxa
Community Living Dufferin, 601

Eganville
Canadian International Institute of Applied Negotiation, 421

Elliot Lake
Algoma-Manitoulin & District Labour Council, 53
Canadian Hearing Society-Elliot Lake Office, 403
Children's Aid Society of Algoma-Elliot Lake Office, 561
Elliot Lake & District Chamber of Commerce, 685

Elmira
Canadian Council of Christian Charities, 368
Ontario Hatcheries Association, 1083
Woolwich Community Services, 1464

Elmvale
East Georgian Bay Historical Foundation, 668

Elora
Canadian Society of Otolaryngology - Head & Neck Surgery, 485
Elora Arts Council, 685
Elora Environment Centre, 685
Family & Children's Services of Guelph & Wellington County-County Office, 702
Ontario Potato Board, 1097

Embro
London Soaring Club, 919

Emo
Emo Chamber of Commerce, 686
Ontario Institute of Agrologists-Northern Branch, 1087

Englehart
Englehart & District Chamber of Commerce, 689

Ennismore
Community Care Peterborough-Chemung Office, 596

Erin
Canadian Process Control Association, 460
East Wellington Community Services, 669
Ontario Society for the Prevention of Cruelty to Animals-Upper Credit Branch (Affiliate), 1107

Espanola
Community Living Espanola, 601
LaCloche Foothills Chamber of Commerce, 895

Essex
Canadian Rope Skipping Federation, 468
Community Living Essex County, 601
Essex Community Services, 696
Essex County Cattlemen's Association, 696
Windsor-Essex Therapeutic Riding Association, 1457

Exeter
Ausable Bayfield Conservation Foundation, 188
Sheet Metal Workers' International Association (AFL-CIO/CFL)-Canadian Office, 1589

South Huron Chamber of Commerce, 1334

Fenelon Falls
Associated Environmental Site Assessors of Canada Inc., 89
Fenelon Falls & District Chamber of Commerce, 732
Heating, Refrigeration & Air Conditioning Institute of Canada-Ontario - Kawartha Lakes Chapter, 810
PFLAG Canada Inc.-Fenelon Falls Chapter, 1155

Fergus
Centre Wellington Chamber of Commerce, 536
Ontario Angus Association, 1059
Wellington County Historical Society, 1443

Finch
Alström Syndrome Canada, 60

Flamborough
Flamborough Chamber of Commerce, 740
Hamilton Technology Centre, 802

Flesherton
Grey Highlands Chamber of Commerce, 790
South-East Grey Support Services, 1337

Fonthill
CADORA Ontario Association Inc.-Dressage Niagara Chapter, 269
Friends of Short Hills Park, 762
Pelham Historical Society, 1149

Foresters Falls
Whitewater Historical Society, 1453

Fort Erie
Adult Literacy Council of Greater Fort Erie, 9
Community Living Fort Erie, 602
Fort Erie Business Success & Loan Centre, 752
Fort Erie Native Friendship Centre, 752
Freight Carriers Association of Canada, 759
Greater Fort Erie Chamber of Commerce, 783
Intercede International, 851
Niagara Falls Coin Club, 1025
Ontario Brain Injury Association-Fort Erie, 1068
Ontario Society for the Prevention of Cruelty to Animals-Fort Erie Branch (Affiliate), 1105
YMCA Canada-YMCA of Niagara - Fort Erie, 1472

Fort Frances
Community Living Fort Frances & District, 602
Family & Children's Services of the District of Rainy River-Fort Frances Office, 702
Fort Frances & District Labour Council, 752
Fort Frances Chamber of Commerce, 752
United Native Friendship Centre, 1412
United Native Friendship Centre-Circle of Life Centre, 1412

Fort William First Nation
Ontario Native Women's Association, 1093

Foxboro
Ontario Association of Quick Printers, 1065

Frankford
Ontario Artist Blacksmith Association, 1060

Freelton
Canadian Recreational Vehicle Association, 465

Gananoque
Canadian Council of Muslim Women, 369
Family & Children's Services of Lanark, Leeds & Grenville-Gananoque Office, 702
Gananoque Food Bank, 766
1000 Islands Gananoque Chamber of Commerce, 1058
Ontario Society for the Prevention of Cruelty to Animals-Gananoque Branch (Affiliate), 1105

Georgetown
Barth Syndrome Foundation of Canada, 197
Canadian Association for the Practical Study of Law in Education, 305
Canadian Flooring, Cleaning & Restoration Association, 391

Canadian Institute of Marketing, 417
Distress Centre North Halton, 659
Ontario Environmental Network, 1078
Ontario Professional Foresters Association, 1097
United Way of Halton Hills, 1414
Watch Tower Bible & Tract Society of Canada, 1441

Geraldton
Geraldton Chamber of Commerce, 771
Superior Greenstone Association for Community Living, 1355
Thunderbird Friendship Centre, 1378

Glen Robertson
Society of Canadian Ornithologists, 1327

Glencoe
Ontario Association of Agricultural Societies, 1061
Quest Centre Community Initiatives, 1200

Gloucester
British North America Philatelic Society Ltd., 259
Canadian Amateur Wrestling Association, 292
Canadian Association of Veterans in United Nations Peacekeeping, 335
Canadian Philosophical Association, 454
Children's Aid Society of Ottawa, 561
Federation of Danish Associations in Canada, 723
Gloucester Historical Society, 775
International Order of the King's Daughters & Sons-Ontario Branch, 1554
National Association of Women & the Law, 990

Goderich
Habitat for Humanity Canada-Ontario - Huron County, 797
Huron Chamber of Commerce - Goderich, Central & North Huron, 828
The Maitland Trail Association, 927
Ontario Association of Emergency Managers, 1063
Ontario Genealogical Society-Huron County Branch, 1082
Ontario Home Builders' Association-Bluewater, 1085
Ontario Municipal Administrators' Association, 1092
Ontario Society for the Prevention of Cruelty to Animals-Huron County Branch, 1105
Tourism Goderich, 1389

Gogama
Gogama Chamber of Commerce, 776

Gormley
Ontario Amateur Softball Association, 1059

Grand Bend
Grand Bend & Area Chamber of Commerce, 779

Gravenhurst
Gravenhurst Chamber of Commerce/Visitors Bureau, 782
Habitat for Humanity Canada-Ontario - Ontario Gateway North, 797
Learning for Living South Muskoka, 905
Muskoka Steamship & Historical Society, 985

Grimsby
The Bible League of Canada, 208
Canadian Association of Credit Counselling Services, 311
Canadian Call Management Association, 348
Christian Labour Association of Canada-Niagara/Hamilton/Brant Regional Office, 568
Community Living Grimsby, Lincoln & West Lincoln-Grimsby - Livingston Resource Centre, 602
Community Living Grimsby, Lincoln & West Lincoln-Grimsby - Employment Services, 602
Grimsby & District Chamber of Commerce, 790
The Ontario Greenhouse Alliance, 1083

Guelph
Ag Energy Co-operative, 13
Agricultural Adaptation Council, 14
AIESEC-Guelph, 18
Alcoholics Anonymous-Guelph - Central West District 3, 52
Alliance for Chiropractic, 57
Alzheimer Society of Waterloo Wellington-Guelph Office, 66
Animal Nutrition Association of Canada-Ontario Agri Business Association, 71
Beef Farmers of Ontario, 204
Beef Improvement Ontario, 204
Canadian Animal Health Institute, 293
Canadian Association for Child & Play Therapy, 297
Canadian Association for Scottish Studies, 303
Canadian Association of Environmental Management, 313
Canadian Blood Services-Guelph, 344
Canadian Brown Swiss & Braunvieh Association, 347
Canadian Christian Business Federation, 356
Canadian College & University Food Service Association, 358
Canadian Depression Research & Intervention Network, 377
Canadian Farm Builders Association, 384
Canadian Guernsey Association, 399
Canadian Hearing Society-Guelph Office, 403
Canadian Meat Goat Association, 432
Canadian Meter Study Group, 436
Canadian Network of Toxicology Centres, 441
Canadian Ornamental Plant Foundation, 448
Canadian Sheep Federation, 470
Canadian Society for Italian Studies, 476
Canadian Society of Plant Biologists, 486
Canadian Soybean Council, 489
Canadian Therapeutic Riding Association, 494
Central Ontario Orchid Society, 525
Chess Federation of Canada, 556
Christian Farmers Federation of Ontario, 567
Church Library Association of Ontario, 569
College of Veterinarians of Ontario, 590
Community Living Guelph Wellington, 602
Community of Christ - Canada East Mission, 606
Community Torchlight Guelph/Wellington/Dufferin, 607
The Crime Writers of Canada, 642
The Donkey Sanctuary of Canada, 661
EastGen, 671
Ecological Farmers of Ontario, 672
Employees' Association Hammond Manufacturing Company Ltd., 687
Equine Guelph, 694
Family & Children's Services of Guelph & Wellington County, 702
Family & Children's Services of Guelph & Wellington County-Shelldale Centre Branch, 702
Family Counselling & Support Services for Guelph-Wellington, 702
Farm & Food Care Canada, 705
Farm & Food Care Ontario, 705
Fellowship of Evangelical Baptist Churches, 731
Flowers Canada Growers, 741
Funeral Information & Memorial Society of Guelph, 764
George Morris Centre, 770
Gideons International in Canada, 773
Grain Farmers of Ontario, 779
Guelph & District Labour Council, 792
Guelph & District Real Estate Board, 792
Guelph Arts Council, 792
Guelph Chamber of Commerce, 793
Guelph Food Bank, 793
Guelph Hiking Trail Club, 793
Guelph Historical Society, 793
Guelph International Resource Centre, 793
Guelph Musicfest, 793
Guelph Police Association Inc., 793
Guelph Symphony Orchestra, 793
Guelph-Wellington Women in Crisis, 793

Habitat for Humanity Canada-Ontario - Wellington Dufferin Guelph, 797
Heart & Stroke Foundation of Ontario-Guelph Office, 809
HIV/AIDS Resources and Community Health, 817
Immigrant Services - Guelph Wellington, 830
International Association for Medical Assistance to Travellers-Guelph Office, 853
International Credential Assessment Service of Canada, 856
Jersey Canada, 869
Jersey Canada-Ontario, 869
Junior Farmers' Association of Ontario, 878
Land Improvement Contractors of Ontario, 897
Mission Aviation Fellowship of Canada, 969
Multiple Births Guelph-Wellington, 980
Municipal Law Enforcement Officers' Association, 981
Municipal Waste Association, 981
Musagetes Foundation, 982
Mushrooms Canada, 983
National Farmers Union-Ontario Office, 993
Nursery Sod Growers' Association of Ontario, 1052
Ontario Agri Business Association, 1059
Ontario Agri-Food Technologies, 1059
Ontario Association of Equine Practitioners, 1063
Ontario Association of Veterinary Technicians, 1066
Ontario Broiler Hatching Egg & Chick Commission, 1069
Ontario Campus Radio Organization, 1070
Ontario Co-operative Association, 1074
Ontario Farmland Trust, 1078
Ontario Federation of Agriculture, 1079
Ontario Football Alliance, 1080
Ontario Fruit & Vegetable Growers' Association, 1081
Ontario Genealogical Society-Wellington County Branch, 1082
Ontario Goat Breeders Association, 1083
Ontario Golf Superintendents' Association, 1083
Ontario Home Builders' Association-Guelph & District, 1085
Ontario Independent Meat Processors, 1087
Ontario Institute of Agrologists, 1087
Ontario Milk Transport Association, 1091
Ontario Plowmen's Association, 1096
Ontario Pork Producers' Marketing Board, 1097
Ontario Public Interest Research Group-OPIRG Guelph, 1099
Ontario Seed Growers Association, 1104
Ontario Sheep Marketing Agency, 1104
Ontario Shuffleboard Association, 1104
Ontario Society for the Prevention of Cruelty to Animals-Guelph Branch (Affiliate), 1105
Ontario Soil & Crop Improvement Association, 1108
Ontario Veal Association, 1112
Out on the Shelf, 1133
Parents Without Partners Inc.-Royal City Chapter, 1582
Patronato INAS (Canada)-Guelph Office, 1145
Pollination Guelph, 1164
Provision Coalition, 1191
Soil & Water Conservation Society-Ontario Chapter, 1595
Solid Waste Association of North America-Ontario Chapter, 1595
Spinal Cord Injury Ontario-Waterloo-Wellington Office, 1344
The United Brethren Church in Canada, 1409
United Way of Guelph, Wellington & Dufferin, 1414
University of Guelph Food Service Employees Association, 1419
University of Guelph Professional Staff Association, 1419
Volunteer Centre of Guelph/Wellington, 1438
Wellington Law Association, 1443
Wildlife Preservation Canada, 1455
YMCA Canada-YMCA-YWCA of Guelph, 1473

Hagersville
Hagersville & District Chamber of Commerce, 798
National Aboriginal Trust Officers Association, 989
Ontario Institute of Agrologists-Long Point Branch, 1087

Haileybury
Community Living Temiskaming South, 605
Friends of the Haileybury Heritage Museum, 762
Temiskaming Law Association, 1370

Haliburton
Community Living Haliburton County, 602
Haliburton Highlands Chamber of Commerce, 798
Haliburton Highlands Guild of Fine Arts, 798
Kawartha-Haliburton Children's Aid Society-Haliburton, 883
Ontario Home Builders' Association-Haliburton County, 1085

Halton Hills
Canadian Concrete Pipe Association, 362
Halton Hills Chamber of Commerce, 800

Hamilton
Afro-Canadian Caribbean Association of Hamilton & District Inc., 13
AIESEC-McMaster, 18
Alcoholics Anonymous-Hamilton - Central Office, 52
Allen & Milli Gould Family Foundation, 54
AllerGen NCE Inc., 54
Alzheimer Society of Hamilton Halton, 62
American Foundry Society-Ontario Chapter, 1493
Ancient, Free & Accepted Masons of Canada - Grand Lodge in the Province of Ontario, 68
The Anglican Church of Canada-Diocese of Niagara, 70
L'Arche Ontario-L'Arche Hamilton, 77
Australian Cattle Dog Rescue of Ontario, 188
Bach Elgar Choir, 192
Bereaved Families of Ontario-South Central Region, 205
Boys & Girls Clubs of Ontario-Boys & Girls Clubs of Hamilton, 223
The Brothers of the Good Shepherd, 260
The Bruce Trail Conservancy, 261
The Bruce Trail Conservancy-Toronto, 261
CADORA Ontario Association Inc., 269
Canadian Assembly of Narcotics Anonymous-Hamilton Area, 296
Canadian Association for Humane Trapping, 301
Canadian Association of Certified Planning Technicians, 310
Canadian Association of Elizabeth Fry Societies-Elizabeth Fry Society of Hamilton, 313
Canadian Association of Veterans in United Nations Peacekeeping-Buffalo 461 Chapter (Hamilton), 335
Canadian Botanical Conservation Network, 346
Canadian Carbonization Research Association, 350
Canadian Centre for Occupational Health & Safety, 353
Canadian Church Press, 356
The Canadian Corps of Commissionaires-Hamilton Division, 365
Canadian Council of University Physical Education & Kinesiology Administrators, 370
Canadian Dressage Owners & Riders Association, 378
Canadian Fabry Association, 383
Canadian Football Hall of Fame & Museum, 391
Canadian Football League Alumni Association, 392
Canadian Hard of Hearing Association-Ontario - Hamilton Branch, 400
Canadian Hearing Society-Hamilton Office, 403
Canadian Institute for NDE, 413

Geographic Index / Ontario - Hampton

Canadian Institute for Research in Nondestructive Examination, 413
Canadian Institute of Management-Ontario - Hamilton Branch, 417
Canadian Motorcycle Association, 437
Canadian Nurse Continence Advisors Association, 442
Canadian Office & Professional Employees Union-Region 2 - Local 527, 445
Canadian Payday Loan Association, 452
Canadian Public Relations Society Inc.-CPRS Hamilton, 463
Canadian Society for Medical Laboratory Science, 476
Canadian Vascular Access Association, 501
Cardus Institute, 511
Catholic Children's Aid Society of Hamilton, 518
Catholic Family Services of Hamilton, 518
CHARGE Syndrome Canada, 552
Coalition on the Niagara Escarpment, 578
Community Information Hamilton, 599
Community Living Hamilton, 602
Conserver Society of Hamilton & District Inc., 623
Council of Ontario Construction Associations-Hamilton-Halton Construction Association, 634
Credit Counselling Society-Hamilton, 640
Development & Peace-Ontario - Southwestern, 655
Dundas Valley Orchestra, 664
Economic Developers Association of Canada, 672
Electrical Construction Association of Hamilton, 682
Evergreen-Hamilton Office, 699
The Factory: Hamilton Media Arts Centre, 700
50 & Piu Enasco-Hamilton Office, 734
Friends of Red Hill Valley, 762
The Garden Clubs of Ontario, 766
The Garden Clubs of Ontario-Hamilton, 767
Golden Horseshoe Co-operative Housing Federation, 776
Goodwill, The Amity Group, 778
GRAND Society-Hamilton Chapter, 780
Habitat for Humanity Canada-Ontario - Hamilton, 797
Hamilton AIDS Network, 800
Hamilton Arts Council, 800
Hamilton Chamber of Commerce, 801
Hamilton Community Foundation, 801
Hamilton District Society for Disabled Children, 801
Hamilton Folk Arts Heritage Council, 801
Hamilton Industrial Environmental Association, 801
Hamilton Jewish Federation, 801
Hamilton Law Association, 801
Hamilton Naturalists' Club, 801
Hamilton Philharmonic Orchestra, 801
Hamilton Philharmonic Youth Orchestra, 801
Hamilton Police Association, 802
Hamilton Program for Schizophrenia, 802
Hamilton Regional Indian Centre, 802
Hamilton Right to Life, 802
Hamilton Stamp Club, 802
Hamilton-Brantford Building & Construction Trades Council, 802
Hamilton-Burlington & District Real Estate Board, 802
Head-of-the-Lake Historical Society, 805
Health Initiatives for Youth Hamilton, 806
Heart & Stroke Foundation of Ontario-Hamilton Office, 809
Hillfield-Strathallan College Foundation, 815
Homestead Christian Care, 820
Human Resources Professionals Association-Hamilton Chapter, 825
National Optics Institute-Ontario Branch, 843
Insurance Institute of Ontario-Hamilton/Niagara Chapter, 850
International Curling Information Network Group, 856
International Union of Operating Engineers (AFL-CIO/CFL)-Local 772

The John Howard Society of Ontario-Hamilton, Burlington & Area, 875
Korean Business Association, 893
Laborers' International Union of North America (AFL-CIO/CLC)-Canada - Central & Eastern Office
Masonic Foundation of Ontario, 952
McMaster University Faculty Association, 956
McMaster University Retirees Association, 956
McMaster University Staff Association, 956
Micah House, 964
NACE International-Canadian Region - National Capital Section, 1572
National Academy Orchestra, 989
Ontario Association of Medical Radiation Sciences, 1064
Ontario Automotive Recyclers Association, 1067
Ontario Brain Injury Association-Hamilton-Wentworth, 1068
Ontario Disc Sports Association, 1077
Ontario Federation of Home & School Associations Inc., 1079
Ontario Gang Investigators Association, 1081
Ontario Genealogical Society-Hamilton Branch, 1082
Ontario Home Builders' Association-Hamilton - Halton, 1085
Ontario Home Care Association, 1086
Ontario Industrial Fire Protection Association, 1087
Ontario Public Interest Research Group-OPIRG McMaster, 1099
Ontario Puppetry Association, 1100
Ontario Sailing, 1103
Ontario Society for the Prevention of Cruelty to Animals-Hamilton / Burlington Branch (Affiliate), 1105
Ontario Undergraduate Student Alliance-McMaster University Students Union, 1111
Osteoporosis Canada-Hamilton - Hamilton-Burlington Chapter, 1128
Parents Without Partners Inc.-New Dawn Chapter, 1582
Pathways to Education Canada-Pathways to Education - Hamilton, 1145
Patronato INAS (Canada)-Hamilton Office, 1146
Royal Arch Masons of Canada, 1237
Royal Botanical Gardens, 1239
Saint Elizabeth Health Care-Hamilton - Hamilton, Niagara, Haldimand & Brant Service Delivery Centre, 1246
St. Joseph's Healthcare Foundation, 1249
St. Leonard's Society of Canada-St. Leonard's Society of Hamilton, 1250
Schizophrenia Society of Ontario-Hamilton/Niagara Region, 1284
Scleroderma Canada, 1285
The Scleroderma Society of Ontario, 1285
Scottish Rite Charitable Foundation of Canada, 1286
Social Planning & Research Council of Hamilton, 1306
Society of Tribologists & Lubrication Engineers-Hamilton Section
Spinal Cord Injury Ontario-Hamilton Office, 1343
Tourism Hamilton, 1389
Truck Training Schools Association of Ontario Inc., 1399
United Empire Loyalists' Association of Canada-Hamilton Branch, 1410
United Nations Association in Canada-Hamilton, 1411
United Way of Burlington & Greater Hamilton, 1413
Women Who Excel Inc., 1461
YMCA Canada-YMCA of Hamilton/Burlington/Brantford, 1472
YWCA Canada-YWCA Hamilton, 1481

Hampton
Ontario Skeet Shooting Association, 1104

Hanmer
Nickel Belt Coin Club, 1026

Hannon
Canadian Palomino Horse Association, 449

Hanover
Guelph Equine Area Rescue Stables, 793
Hanover Chamber of Commerce, 803
REALTORS Association of Grey Bruce Owen Sound, 1206

Harley
Burford Township Historical Society, 265

Harriston
Minto Chamber of Commerce, 968

Harrow
Harrow & Colchester Chamber of Commerce, 804
Harrow Early Immigrant Research Society, 804

Harrowsmith
Ontario Camelids Association, 1070

Hartington
Association of Administrative Professionals, 139

Havelock
Community Care Peterborough-Havelock Office, 596
Havelock, Belmont, Methuen & District Chamber of Commerce, 805

Hawkesbury
Hawkesbury & Region Chamber of Commerce, 805

Hearst
Conseil des arts de Hearst, 617
Hearst & Area Association for Community Living, 808
Hearst, Mattice - Val Côté & Area Chamber of Commerce, 808
Réseau du patrimoine franco-ontarien-La Vieille Branche, 1222

Hillsburgh
Canadian Institute of Plumbing & Heating-Ontario Region, 418
Ontario School Counsellors' Association, 1103
Upper Canada District Canadian Horse Breeders, 1421

Hornepayne
Children's Aid Society of Algoma-Hornepayne Office, 561

Huntsville
Association of Certified Forensic Investigators of Canada, 145
Community Living Huntsville, 602
Huntsville & Lake of Bays Railway Society, 828
Huntsville, Lake of Bays Chamber of Commerce, 828
Lakelands Association of Realtors, 896
Music for Young Children-Ontario - Central, 984
Muskoka-Parry Sound Beekeepers' Association, 985

Huron Park
Bluewater Recycling Association, 215

Ilderton
Ontario Association For Students At Risk, 1061

Ingersoll
Ingersoll District Chamber of Commerce, 838
Ingersoll District Nature Club, 838

Ingleside
Clan MacLeod Societies of Canada-Glengarry Ontario Branch, 572
Lost Villages Historical Society, 919
South Stormont Chamber of Commerce, 1336

Innerkip
Ontario Rural Softball Association, 1103

Innisfil
Greater Innisfil Chamber of Commerce, 783

Iroquois Falls
Iroquois Falls & District Chamber of Commerce, 864
Iroquois Falls Association for Community Living, 864
Iroquois Falls Historical Society, 864

Jordan
Museums of Niagara Association, 983

Kagawong
Algoma Manitoulin Environmental Awareness, 53

Kakabeka Falls
Thunder Bay District Municipal League, 1377

Kanata
Canadian Air Cushion Technology Society, 290
Canadian Association of Chiefs of Police, 310
Canadian Association of Principals, 328
Canadian College of Physicists in Medicine, 360
Canadian Council on Social Development, 371
Canadian Forestry Accreditation Board, 392
Canadian Interoperability Technology Interest Group, 422
Canadian Navigation Society, 440
Canadian Organization of Medical Physicists, 447
Canadian Remote Sensing Society, 466
Mining Industry Human Resources Council, 967
Music for Young Children, 983
The Royal Scottish Country Dance Society-Ottawa Branch, 1587
SeCan Association, 1288
The 3C Foundation of Canada, 1377
West Ottawa Board of Trade, 1446

Kapuskasing
Federation of Northern Ontario Municipalities, 725
Kapuskasing & District Chamber of Commerce, 881
Kapuskasing Friendship Centre, 881
Kapuskasing, Cochrane & District Association for Community Living, 881

Kearney
Spinal Cord Injury Ontario-Muskoka Office, 1343

Keene
Ontario Aboriginal Lands Association, 1058

Keewatin
The Anglican Church of Canada-Diocese of Keewatin, 69

Kemptville
Eastern Ontario Model Forest, 670
Family & Children's Services of Lanark, Leeds & Grenville-Kemptville Office, 702
North Grenville Chamber of Commerce, 1031
North Grenville Historical Society, 1031
Ontario Berry Growers' Association, 1068
Ontario Maple Syrup Producers' Association, 1090
Ontario Woodlot Association, 1114
Registered Veterinary Technologists & Technicians of Canada, 1214
Responsible Dog Owners of Canada, 1227
Sonography Canada, 1333

Kenora
Alzheimer Society of Kenora/Rainy River Districts, 63
Bimose Tribal Council, 211
Family & Children's Services of the District of Rainy River, 702
Firefly, 738
Kenora & District Chamber of Commerce, 883
Kenora Association for Community Living, 883
Kenora Fellowship Centre, 883
Lake of the Woods Adult Learning Line, 896
Lake of the Woods Ojibway Cultural Centre, 896
Model Aeronautics Association of Canada Inc.-Manitoba/Northwestern Ontario Zone, 970

Multicultural Association of Kenora & District, 978
Ne'Chee Friendship Centre, 1002
Northwest Ontario Sunset Country Travel Association, 1036
Northwestern Ontario Insurance Professionals, 1039
Probation Officers Association of Ontario-Northwest Branch, 1181

Keswick
Eczema Society of Canada, 674
Georgina Chamber of Commerce, 771
International Fellowship of Christians & Jews of Canada, 857
Learning Centre for Georgina, 903
South Lake Community Futures Development Corporation, 1335

Killaloe
Community Resource Centre (Killaloe) Inc., 607
The Friends of Bonnechere Parks, 760

Killarney
The Friends of Killarney Park, 761

Kilworthy
Muskoka Tourism, 985

Kincardine
Community Living Kincardine & District, 603
Kincardine & District Chamber of Commerce, 888

King City
Canadian Alopecia Areata Foundation, 292
Canadian Association for Disabled Skiing - Ontario, 300
The Tema Conter Memorial Trust, 1370

Kingston
AIESEC-Queen's, 18
Almost Home, 59
Alzheimer Society of Kingston, Frontenac, Lennox & Addington, 63
American Musicological Society-New York - St. Lawrence Chapter
The Anglican Church of Canada-Diocese of Ontario, 70
Association canadienne-française de l'Ontario, Mille-Îles, 96
Association of Fundraising Professionals-South Eastern Ontario Chapter, 1512
Bereaved Families of Ontario-Kingston, 205
Boys & Girls Clubs of Ontario-Boys & Girls Club of Kingston & Area, 223
Canadian Assessment, Vocational Evaluation & Work Adjustment Society, 297
Canadian Association of Elizabeth Fry Societies-Elizabeth Fry Society of Kingston, 313
Canadian Association of Pathologists, 325
Canadian Association of Physical Medicine & Rehabilitation, 327
Canadian Astronomical Society, 337
Canadian Blood Services-Kingston, 344
Canadian College of Medical Geneticists, 359
The Canadian Corps of Commissionaires-Kingston Division, 365
Canadian Council for the Advancement of Education, 367
Canadian Culinary Federation-Kingston Branch, 374
Canadian Families & Corrections Network, 383
Canadian Frailty Network, 394
Canadian Hard of Hearing Association-Ontario - Kingston Hard of Hearing Club, 400
Canadian Healthcare Engineering Society, 402
Canadian Hearing Society-Kingston Regional Office, 403
Canadian Military Colleges Faculty Association, 436
Canadian Peacekeeping Veterans Association, 452
Canadian Quaternary Association, 464
Canadian Railroad Historical Association-Kingston Division, 465
Canadian Society for Engineering Management, 474
Canadian Society for Mechanical Engineering, 476
Canadian Society of Clinical Chemists, 481
Canadian Society of Cytology, 482
Canadian University & College Counselling Association, 499
Cataraqui Archaeological Research Foundation, 517
Community Foundation for Kingston & Area, 597
Community Living Kingston, 603
Dress for Success-Kingston, 663
The Easter Seal Society (Ontario)-Eastern Region - Kingston, 670
Electrical Contractors Association of Quinte-St. Lawrence, 683
Embroiderers' Association of Canada, Inc.-Ontario - Cataraqui Guild of Needle Arts, 686
Employees' Union of St. Mary's of the Lake Hospital - CNFIU Local 3001, 687
Epilepsy Ontario-Southeastern Ontario, 694
Family & Children's Services of Frontenac, Lennox & Addington, 701
The Friends of Frontenac Park, 761
Frontenac County Schools Museum Association, 763
Frontenac Law Association, 763
The Great Lakes Marine Heritage Foundation, 782
Greater Kingston Chamber of Commerce, 783
Habitat for Humanity Canada-Ontario - Kingston Limestone Region, 797
Heart & Stroke Foundation of Ontario-Kingston Office, 809
HIV/AIDS Regional Services, 817
Human Resources Professionals Association-Kingston & District, 825
Human Resources Professionals Association-Kingston District, 825
International Fiscal Association Canada, 857
The John Howard Society of Canada, 874
The John Howard Society of Ontario-Kingston & District, 875
K3C Community Counselling Centres, 879
The Kidney Foundation of Canada-Kingston Chapter, 885
Kingston & Area Real Estate Association, 888
Kingston & District Labour Council, 888
Kingston Arts Council, 888
Kingston Association of Museums, Art Galleries & Historic Sites, 889
Kingston Construction Association, 889
Kingston Economic Development Corporation, 889
Kingston Field Naturalists, 889
Kingston Historical Society, 889
Kingston Independent Nylon Workers Union, 889
Kingston Kiwanis Music Festival, 889
Kingston Lapidary & Mineral Club, 889
Kingston Orchid Society, 889
Kingston Police Association, 889
Kingston Stamp Club, 889
Kingston Symphony Association, 889
Kingston Youth Orchestra, 890
Ontario Association of Pathologists, 1065
Ontario Brain Injury Association-Kingston, 1068
Ontario Consultants on Religious Tolerance, 1074
Ontario Genealogical Society-Kingston Branch, 1082
Ontario Home Builders' Association-Kingston, 1085
Ontario Nurses' Association-Kingston Office, 1094
Ontario Public Interest Research Group-OPIRG Kingston, 1099
Ontario Society for the Prevention of Cruelty to Animals-Kingston Branch (Affliate), 1106
Ontario Undergraduate Student Alliance-Alma Mater Society at Queen's University, 1111
Original Hockey Hall of Fame & Museum, 1126
Paddle Canada, 1137
Pathways to Education Canada-Pathways to Education - Kingston, 1145
PFLAG Canada Inc.-Kingston Chapter, 1155
Pittsburgh Historical Society, 1160
Psychosocial Rehabilitation Canada, 1192
Public Service Alliance of Canada-Kingston Branch, 1193
Queen's University Faculty Association, 1199
Queen's University International Centre, 1200
Rideau Trail Association, 1231
Royal Astronomical Society of Canada-Kingston Centre, 1238
The Royal Scottish Country Dance Society-Kingston Branch, 1587
Sail Canada, 1245
Saint Elizabeth Health Care-Kingston - South East Service Delivery Centre, 1246
Sexual Assault Centre Kingston Inc., 1292
Spinal Cord Injury Ontario-Kingston Office, 1343
Sustainable Kingston, 1358
Telephone Aid Line Kingston, 1369
United Empire Loyalists' Association of Canada-Kingston Branch, 1410
United Way of Kingston, Frontenac, Lennox & Addington, 1414
Urology Nurses of Canada, 1422
Wind Athletes Canada, 1456
World Association of Societies of Pathology and Laboratory Medicine, 1465
YMCA Canada-YMCA of Kingston, 1472

Kingsville
Historic Vehicle Society of Ontario, 815
Jack Miner Migratory Bird Foundation, Inc., 867
Royal Astronomical Society of Canada-Windsor Centre, 1239

Kirkland Lake
Canadian Office & Professional Employees Union-Region 2 - Local 429, 445
Kirkland Lake Association for Community Living, 890
Kirkland Lake District Chamber of Commerce, 890
Northern Prospectors Association, 1035

Kitchener
Abundance Canada-Kitchener Office, 3
AIDS Committee of Cambridge, Kitchener/Waterloo & Area, 16
Alzheimer Society of Waterloo Wellington-Kitchener Office, 66
Association of Polish Engineers in Canada-Kitchener Branch, 156
Association of Unity Churches Canada, 163
Audio Engineering Society, 187
Bereaved Families of Ontario-Midwestern Region, 205
Better Business Bureau of Mid-Western & Central Ontario, 206
Canadian Addiction Counsellors Certification Federation, 288
Canadian Assembly of Narcotics Anonymous-Golden Triangle Area, 296
Canadian Association of Elizabeth Fry Societies-Elizabeth Fry Society for the Regional Municipality of Waterloo, 312
Canadian Bible Society-Southwestern Ontario District Office, 343
Canadian Coalition for Genetic Fairness, 357
Canadian Hearing Society-Waterloo Regional Office, 403
Canadian Institute of Transportation Engineers, 420
Canadian Laboratory Suppliers Association, 424
Canadian Polish Congress-Kitchener Branch, 456
Carizon Family & Community Services, 513
Central Ontario Developmental Riding Program, 525
Central Ontario Musicians' Association, 525
Chinese Canadian National Council-ON - Central Ontario Chinese Cultural Centre, 564
Church of the Good Shepherd, 569
College & University Retiree Associations of Canada, 581
Communitech, 595
Distress Centres Ontario, 659
Education Support Staff of the Ontario Secondary School Teachers' Federation - District 24 - Waterloo, 680
Electronic Frontier Canada Inc., 683
Environmental Education Ontario, 691
Epilepsy Ontario-Waterloo/Wellington, 694
Evangelical Lutheran Church in Canada-Eastern Synod, 698
Food Bank of Waterloo Region, 749
The Garden Clubs of Ontario-Kitchener-Waterloo, 767
German-Canadian Business & Professional Association of Kitchener-Waterloo, 772
German-Canadian Congress (Ontario), 772
Greater Kitchener & Waterloo Chamber of Commerce, 783
Grey, Bruce, Dufferin, & Simcoe Postal History Study Group, 790
Heart & Stroke Foundation of Ontario-Kitchener Office, 809
Hospice of Waterloo Region, 822
Huntington Society of Canada, 827
Huntington Society of Canada-Toronto Chapter, 828
Huntington Society of Canada-West Central Ontario Resource Centre, 828
Infant & Toddler Safety Association, 836
Insurance Institute of Ontario-Conestoga Chapter, 850
The John Howard Society of Ontario-Waterloo - Wellington, 875
Junior Achievement of Canada-Junior Achievement of Waterloo Region, 877
Juvenile Diabetes Research Foundation-Waterloo, 879
The Kitchener & Waterloo Community Foundation, 890
Kitchener Sports Association, 890
Kitchener-Waterloo Field Naturalists, 890
Kitchener-Waterloo Multicultural Centre, 891
Kitchener-Waterloo Parents of Multiple Births Association, 891
Kitchener-Waterloo Philatelic Society, 891
Kitchener-Waterloo Symphony Orchestra Association Inc., 891
Kitchener-Waterloo Symphony Youth Orchestra, 891
Korea Veterans Association of Canada Inc., Heritage Unit, 893
The Literacy Group of Waterloo Region-Kitchener Branch, 914
Lupus Ontario-Kitchener Branch, 921
Lutheran Bible Translators of Canada Inc., 922
Lutheran Church - Canada-East District, 922
Lutheran Laymen's League of Canada, 922
MB Mission-Eastern Canada, 954
Memorial Society of Kitchener-Waterloo & Area, 960
Mennonite Central Committee Canada-MCC Ontario, 960
Mennonite Church Canada-Mennonite Church Eastern Canada, 961
Municipal Equipment & Operations Association (Ontario) Inc., 981
Old Chrysler Corporation Auto Club, 1056
Ontario Brain Injury Association-Waterloo-Wellington, 1069
Ontario Concrete Pipe Association, 1074
Ontario Genealogical Society-Waterloo Region Branch, 1082
Ontario Home Builders' Association-Waterloo Region, 1086
Ontario Rodeo Association, 1102
Ontario Society for the Prevention of Cruelty to Animals-Kitchener-Waterloo Branch (Affiliate), 1106
Pathways to Education Canada-Pathways to Education - Kitchener, 1145
Planned Parenthood Waterloo Region, 1162

Geographic Index / Ontario - Komoka

Project Management Institute-Canada's Technology Triangle, 1585
Project READ Literacy Network Waterloo-Wellington, 1188
Reception House Waterloo Region, 1206
Schneider Office Employees' Association, 1284
Social Planning Council of Kitchener-Waterloo, 1306
UNIFOR-Kitchener, 1405
Waterloo Historical Society, 1442
Waterloo Regional Heritage Foundation, 1442
Waterloo Regional Labour Council, 1442
YMCA Canada-YMCAs of Cambridge & Kitchener-Waterloo, 1473
YWCA Canada-YWCA Kitchener-Waterloo, 1481

Komoka
United Empire Loyalists' Association of Canada-London & Western Ontario Branch, 1410

Lakefield
Community Care Peterborough-Lakefield Office, 596
Kawartha Chamber of Commerce & Tourism, 882
Ontario Society for Environmental Education, 1105
Ontario Speed Skating Association, 1108

Lambton Shores
The Friends of Pinery Park, 761

Lanark
Ontario Modern Language Teachers Association, 1091
Sustainability Project, 1357

Lansdowne
The Friends of Charleston Lake Park, 760
Thousand Islands Watershed Land Trust, 1376

Laurentian Valley
Ontario Home Builders' Association-Renfrew County, 1085

Leamington
Community Living Essex County-Leamington - Southshore Office, 601
Leamington District Chamber of Commerce, 903
Ontario Greenhouse Vegetable Growers, 1083
South Essex Community Centre, 1334

Lefaivre
Canadian Belgian Blue Association, 342

Lindsay
Alzheimer Society Peterborough, Kawartha Lakes, Northumberland, & Haliburton-Kawartha Lakes & Haliburton Office, 65
Alzheimer Society of Peterborough & Area-Lindsay Office, 65
Association of Hearing Instrument Practitioners of Ontario, 148
Boys & Girls Clubs of Ontario-Boys & Girls Clubs of Kawartha Lakes, 223
Canadian Oil Heat Association, 445
Community Living Kawartha Lakes, 603
John Howard Society of Ontario-Kawartha Lakes & Haliburton, 875
Kawartha Lakes Real Estate Association, 882
Kawartha-Haliburton Children's Aid Society-Lindsay, 883
Lindsay & District Chamber of Commerce, 912
The Ontario Archaeological Society Inc.-Peterborough Chapter, 1060
Ontario Society for the Prevention of Cruelty to Animals-Kawartha Lakes Branch (Affiliate), 1105
United Way for the City of Kawartha Lakes, 1413
Victoria County Historical Society, 1432

Lions Head
Barrow Bay & District Sports Fishing Association, 197

Bruce Peninsula Environment Group, 261

Listowel
CADORA Ontario Association Inc.-Conestoga CADORA Chapter, 269
North Perth Chamber of Commerce, 1032

Little Current
Northern Ontario Aquaculture Association, 1035

London
Addiction Services of Thames Valley, 8
AIESEC-Western, 18
Alliance for Canadian New Music Projects-Contemporary Showcase - London, 56
Alzheimer Society London & Middlesex, 61
The Anglican Church of Canada-Diocese of Huron, 69
The Apostolic Church in Canada, 73
L'Arche Ontario-L'Arche London, 77
Association of Canadian College & University Teachers of English, 141
Association of Iroquois & Allied Indians, 149
Association of Polish Engineers in Canada-London Branch, 156
Automotive Recyclers of Canada, 190
Bereaved Families of Ontario-London - Southwest Region, 205
Better Business Bureau of Western Ontario, 207
Boys & Girls Clubs of Ontario-Boys & Girls Club of London, 223
Brain Tumour Foundation of Canada, 225
Canadian Association for American Studies, 297
Canadian Association for Dental Research, 299
Canadian Association for Young Children-Ontario, 307
Canadian Association of Critical Care Nurses, 311
Canadian Association of Music Therapists, 321
Canadian Blood Services-London, 344
Canadian Brain Tumour Tissue Bank, 346
Canadian Celiac Association-London Chapter, 352
Canadian Committee of Byzantinists, 360
Canadian Condominium Institute-CCI-London & Area Chapter, 362
Canadian Deaf Golf Association, 376
Canadian Federation of Business & Professional Women's Clubs-London, 385
Canadian Health Information Management Association, 402
Canadian Hearing Society-London Regional Office, 403
Canadian Image Processing & Pattern Recognition Society, 410
Canadian Institute of Management-Ontario - London Branch, 417
Canadian Knifemaker's Guild, 424
Canadian Magen David Adom for Israel-London Chapter, 429
Canadian Office & Professional Employees Union-Region 2 - Local 473, 445
Canadian Organization of Campus Activities, 447
Canadian Society of Clinical Perfusion, 482
Canadian Stamp Dealers' Association, 490
Carolinian Canada Coalition, 514
Centre for Research on Violence Against Women & Children, 533
Child & Parent Resource Institute, 558
Children's Health Foundations, 561
Chinese Canadian National Council-ON - CCNC London, 564
Chinese Medicine & Acupuncture Association of Canada, 565
Colleges Ontario-Heads, Libraries and Learning Resources (HLLR), 591
Community Living London, 603
Compassion Canada, 608
Conservatory Canada, 622
Council of Ontario Construction Associations-London & District Construction Association, 634

Credit Counselling Society-London, 640
Dads Can, 648
Dominion Automobile Association Limited, 660
The Easter Seal Society (Ontario)-Western Region - London, 670
Epilepsy Ontario-London & Area, 693
Epilepsy Ontario-Windsor/Essex County, 694
Family Enterprise Xchange-FEX Southwestern Ontario, 703
Family Service Thames Valley, 704
Freedom Party of Ontario, 759
Friends of the Coves Subwatershed Inc., 762
Funeral Consumers Advocacy of London & Windsor, 764
The Garden Clubs of Ontario-London, 767
Good Foundation Inc., 777
Goodwill Industries, 777
Habitat for Humanity Canada-Ontario - Heartland Ontario, 797
Heart & Stroke Foundation of Ontario-London Office, 809
Help for Headaches, 812
Home School Legal Defence Association of Canada, 819
Hong Kong-Canada Business Association-London Section Office, 820
Human Resources Professionals Association-London & District Chapter, 825
Indian Agricultural Program of Ontario-Western/Southern Office, 834
Infant Feeding Action Coalition, 836
Institute for Catastrophic Loss Reduction-London Office, 843
Institute of Electrical & Electronics Engineers Inc. - Region 7, 846
Insurance Institute of Ontario-Southwestern Ontario Chapter, 850
Jane Austen Society of North America-Ontario - London Chapter, 868
John Gordon Home, 873
The John Howard Society of Ontario-London & District, 875
Junior Achievement of Canada-Junior Achievement of London & District, 877
Juvenile Diabetes Research Foundation-London, 879
The Kidney Foundation of Canada-Southwestern Ontario Chapter, 885
Korean Canadian Society of London, 893
Let's Talk Science, 907
Literacy Link South Central, 914
London & District Labour Council, 917
London & Middlesex Historical Society, 917
London & St. Thomas Association of Realtors, 918
London Building & Construction Trades Council, 918
London Chamber of Commerce, 918
London Community Foundation, 918
London Community Orchestra, 918
London Food Bank, 918
London Health Sciences Foundation, 918
London Jewish Federation, 918
London Multiple Births Association, 918
London Musicians' Association, 918
London Numismatic Society, 918
London Orchid Society, 918
London Police Association, 919
London Regional Resource Centre for Heritage & the Environment, 919
London Youth Symphony, 919
London-Middlesex Children's Aid Society, 919
McIlwraith Field Naturalists, 955
Middlesex Law Association, 965
Museum London, 983
N'Amerind (London) Friendship Centre, 986
The Nature Conservancy of Canada-Ontario, 1000
Ontario Amputee & Les Autres Sports Association, 1059
The Ontario Archaeological Society Inc.-London Chapter, 1060
Ontario Art Therapy Association, 1060
Ontario Brain Injury Association-London, 1069
Ontario Dental Assistants Association, 1077

Ontario Genealogical Society-London-Middlesex County Branch, 1082
Ontario Home Builders' Association-London, 1085
Ontario Horticultural Association, 1086
Ontario Lung Association-London Office (Bluewater-Thames Valley), 1090
Ontario Nurses' Association-London Office, 1094
Ontario Petroleum Institute Inc., 1095
Ontario Processing Vegetable Growers, 1097
Ontario Rett Syndrome Association, 1102
Ontario Society for the Prevention of Cruelty to Animals-London Branch (Affiliate), 1106
Ontario Square & Round Dance Federation, 1108
Ontario Therapeutic Riding Association, 1110
Ontario Undergraduate Student Alliance-University Students' Council at the University of Western Ontario, 1112
Osteoporosis Canada-London - London & Thames Valley Chapter, 1128
Parkinson Society Southwestern Ontario, 1142
Partners in Research, 1144
Patronato INAS (Canada)-London Office, 1146
PFLAG Canada Inc.-London Chapter, 1155
Physiotherapy Education Accreditation Canada, 1159
Pillar Nonprofit Network, 1160
Portuguese Club of London, 1167
Professional Engineers Ontario-Western Regional Office, 1185
Project Management Institute-South Western Ontario, 1585
Public Service Alliance of Canada-London Branch, 1193
Public Service Alliance of Canada-Toronto Branch, 1193
Regional HIV/AIDS Connection, 1212
Royal Astronomical Society of Canada-London Centre, 1238
The Royal Scottish Country Dance Society-London Branch
Saint Elizabeth Health Care-London - South West Service Delivery Centre, 1246
St. Leonard's Society of Canada-St. Leonard's Community Services of London & Region, 1250
The Salvation Army in Canada-London - Ontario Great Lakes Division, 1253
Save a Family Plan, 1281
Scouts Canada-Southwestern Ontario Administrative Centre, 1287
Sexual Assault Centre London, 1292
Sisters Adorers of the Precious Blood, 1300
Skate Canada-Western Ontario Section, 1302
Small Business Centre, 1304
South West Community Care Access Centre, 1336
Southern Ontario Seismic Network, 1338
Southern Ontario Thunderbird Club, 1338
Southwestern Ontario Health Libraries & Information Network, 1338
Spinal Cord Injury Ontario-London Office, 1343
Sunshine Dreams for Kids, 1355
Syrian Canadian Council-London Office, 1365
Thames Region Ecological Association, 1373
Thames Valley Trail Association Inc., 1373
Tourism London, 1390
UNIFOR-London Office, 1405
United Church of Canada-London Conference, 1409
United Way of London & Middlesex, 1415
University of Western Ontario Staff Association, 1421
University of Western Ontario Symphony Orchestra, 1421
Upper Thames River Conservation Authority, 1422
Western Fair Association, 1449
WIL Employment Connections, 1453
YMCA Canada-YMCA of Western Ontario - London, 1472

Longlac
Longlac Chamber of Commerce, 919
Réseau du patrimoine franco-ontarien-Joseph-Marie-Couture, 1222

Lucknow
Lucknow & District Chamber of Commerce, 920

Lyn
The Wesleyan Church of Canada - Central Canada District, 1447

Lyndhurst
Lyndhurst Seeleys Bay & District Chamber of Commerce, 923

Maberly
EcoPerth, 673

Madoc
Canadian Jiu-jitsu Council, 423
Madoc & District Chamber of Commerce, 925
The Palyul Foundation of Canada, 1137

Mallorytown
Ontario Fencing Association, 1080

Manitouwadge
Canadian Association of Public Health Dentistry, 330
Manitouwadge Economic Development Corporation, 948

Manotick
Canadian Association of Prawn Producers, 328
Canadian Guide Dogs for the Blind, 399
Eastern Ontario Beekeepers' Association, 670
Groundfish Enterprise Allocation Council, 790
Rideau Chamber of Commerce, 1231
Rideau Valley Conservation Authority, 1231
Rideau Valley Soaring, 1232

Maple
Ahmadiyya Muslim Jama'at Canada, 15
Australian Wine Society of Toronto, 188
Canadian Fence Industry Association-Ontario, 389
Family of the Immaculate Heart of Mary, 704

Marathon
Canadian Office & Professional Employees Union-Region 2 - Local 151, 445
Marathon & District Chamber of Commerce, 949

Marberly
Ontario Lawn Bowls Association, 1088

Markham
Allstate Foundation of Canada, 59
ALS Society of Canada, 60
Association of Dental Technologists of Ontario, 146
Block Rosary Group of Ontario, 215
Bowling Federation of Canada, 219
Bowling Proprietors' Association of Canada, 219
Bowling Proprietors' Association of Ontario, 219
Canada Chinese Computer Association, 278
Canada's History, 282
Canadian Academy of Geriatric Psychiatry, 286
Canadian ADHD Resource Alliance, 288
Canadian Association of Bariatric Physicians & Surgeons, 308
Canadian Association of Radiation Oncology, 330
Canadian Automatic Sprinkler Association, 338
Canadian Bottled Water Association, 346
Canadian Caribbean Amateur Golfers Association, 350
Canadian Cartographic Association, 350
Canadian Condominium Institute, 362
Canadian Condominium Institute-CCI-Toronto & Area Chapter, 362
Canadian Door Institute of Dealers, Manufacturers & Distributors, 378
Canadian Fire Alarm Association, 390
Canadian Fire Safety Association, 390
Canadian Geriatrics Society, 397
Canadian Institute of Management-Ontario - Toronto Branch, 417
Canadian Institute of Quantity Surveyors, 419
Canadian Institute of Quantity Surveyors - British Columbia, 419
Canadian Institute of Quantity Surveyors - Ontario, 419
Canadian Institute of Steel Construction, 419
Canadian League Against Epilepsy, 426
Canadian Liver Foundation-Toronto/GTA Chapter, 427
Canadian Polo Association, 457
Canadian Security Association, 469
Canadian Society for Transfusion Medicine, 479
Canadian Steel Construction Council, 490
Canadian Syringomyelia Network, 491
Canadian Test Centre Inc., 494
Canadian Union of Public Employees-Ontario Division, 498
Centre for ADHD Awareness, Canada, 531
Centre for Immigrant & Community Services of Ontario-York Region Immigrant Youth Centre, 532
Centre for Information & Community Services of Ontario-Markham South Welcome Centre, 532
China Canada Investment Association, 564
Chinese Canadian National Council-ON - Chinese Canadians for Equity in York Region, 564
Christian Children's Fund of Canada, 567
Christian Stewardship Services, 568
CIO Association of Canada, 570
Community Living York South-Markham Office, 606
COSTI Immigrant Services-Markham North - Language, Settlement & Skills Training Services, 632
COSTI Immigrant Services-Markham - Enhanced Language Training Services, 632
Customer Service Professionals Network, 646
effect:hope, 680
Epilepsy Canada, 693
Foresters-Markham, 751
Foundation for International Training, 755
Friends of Dismas, 761
Hungarian Canadian Engineers' Association, 827
Hypertension Canada, 829
Information Markham, 837
Innovation & Technology Association of Ontario, 839
Kinark Child & Family Services, 888
LOMA Canada, 917
Markham Board of Trade, 951
Markham District Historical Society, 952
Markham Federation of Filipino Canadians, 952
Markham Stouffville Hospital Foundation, 952
Motorcycle & Moped Industry Council, 975
Mycological Society of Toronto, 986
Ontario Association of Broadcasters, 1062
Ontario Association of Gastroenterology, 1064
Ontario Association of Residences Treating Youth, 1065
Ontario Association of School Business Officials, 1066
Ontario Athletic Therapists Association, 1067
Ontario Band Association, 1067
Ontario Jaguar Owners Association, 1088
Ontario Taekwondo Association, 1109
The Pennsylvania German Folklore Society of Ontario, 1149
Professional Engineers Ontario-York, 1185
Professional Writers Association of Canada, 1187
Royal Canadian Numismatic Association, 1241
Saint Elizabeth Health Care, 1246
Saint Elizabeth Health Care-Markham - Central Service Delivery Centre, 1246
St. Josephine Bakhita Black Heritage, 1249
Society of Manufacturing Engineers - Canada Office, 1330
Steel Structures Education Foundation, 1349
TechConnex, 1368
Toronto Law Office Management Association, 1385
Trillium Automobile Dealers' Association, 1398
Vides Canada, 1434
Xplor Canada Association, 1470
Youth Bowling Canada, 1475

Maryhill
Historical Society of St. Boniface & Maryhill Community, 816

Matheson
Black River-Matheson Chamber of Commerce, 213

Mattawa
Canadian Forestry Association, 392
Canadian Institute of Forestry, 416

Maxville
Maxville & District Chamber of Commerce, 954

McArthurs Mills
CANGRANDS Kinship Support, 508

Meaford
The Bruce Trail Conservancy-Beaver Valley, 261
Meaford Chamber of Commerce, 956
Miniature Horse Club of Ontario, 966
Parrot Association of Canada, 1143

Merrickville
Canadian Anti-Money Laundering Institute, 293
Ontario East Tourism Association, 1077

Metcalfe
Canadian Hackney Society, 399

Midhurst
Embroiderers' Association of Canada, Inc.-Ontario - Simcoe County Embroidery Guild, 686
United Way of Greater Simcoe County, 1414

Midland
Boys & Girls Clubs of Ontario-Boys & Girls Club of North Simcoe, 223
Canadian Society for the Prevention of Cruelty to Children, 477
Community Health Nurses of Canada, 599
Community Living Huronia, 602
GATEWAY Centre For Learning, 767
Georgian Bay Native Friendship Centre, 771
The Ontario Archaeological Society Inc.-Huronia Chapter, 1060
Severn Sound Environmental Association, 1292
Southern Georgian Bay Chamber of Commerce, 1337
YMCA Canada-YMCA of Simcoe/Muskoka - Midland, 1472

Millbrook
Community Care Peterborough-Millbrook Office, 596
Millbrook & Cavan Historical Society, 965
Millbrook & District Chamber of Commerce, 965

Milton
Canadian Nursery Landscape Association, 442
Canadian Welding Bureau, 503
Canadian Welding Bureau-Ontario Region, 503
Carers ARK, 512
Clan MacLeod Societies of Canada-Central Ontario Branch, 572
Community Living North Halton, 603
Landscape Ontario Horticultural Trades Association, 898
Milton Chamber of Commerce, 966
Milton Historical Society, 966
Ontario Agri-Food Education Inc., 1059
Ontario Association of Triathletes, 1066
Ontario Beekeepers' Association, 1067
Ontario Cycling Association, 1076
Ontario Electric Railway Historical Association, 1077
Ontario Parks Association, 1095
Ontario Steam & Antique Preservers Association, 1109
Ontario Veterinary Medical Association, 1112
Private Motor Truck Council of Canada, 1180
STRIDE, 1352
United Way of Milton, 1415
Water Environment Association of Ontario, 1441

Mindemoya
Community Living Manitoulin, 603

Minesing
Association of Christian Schools International-Eastern Canada Office
Tourism Simcoe County, 1391

Miramichi
New Brunswick Construction Safety Association, 1007

Mississauga
Aboriginal Sport & Wellness Council of Ontario, 2
A.C.C.E.S. Employment-Mississauga, 4
Afghan Women's Counselling & Integration Community Support Organization-Mississauga, 12
Air Canada Pilots Association, 19
Alliance for Canadian New Music Projects-Contemporary Showcase - Mississauga, 56
Allied Beauty Association, 58
Alzheimer Society of Peel, 64
American Society of Heating, Refrigerating & Air Conditioning Engineers-Toronto Chapter
Amma Foundation of Canada, 68
Animal Aid Foundation, 70
Armenian Relief Society of Canada, Inc.-Mississauga Chapter: "Arakasd", 83
Association canadienne des sciences régionales, 95
Association for Canadian Educational Resources, 132
Association of Architectural Technologists of Ontario, 139
Association of Canadian Search, Employment & Staffing Services, 143
Association of Canadian Travel Agencies, 143
Association of Canadian Travel Agents - British Columbia & Yukon, 144
Association of Canadian Travel Agents - Manitoba & Nunavut, 144
Association of Canadian Travel Agents - Ontario, 144
Association of Condominium Managers of Ontario, 145
Association of Municipal Managers, Clerks & Treasurers of Ontario, 152
Association of Polish Engineers in Canada-Mississauga Branch, 156
Association of Professional Researchers for Advancement - Canada, 160
Association of Workers' Compensation Boards of Canada, 164
Baking Association of Canada, 194
Bereaved Families of Ontario, 205
Bereaved Families of Ontario-Halton/Peel, 205
Board of Canadian Registered Safety Professionals, 216
Canadian Adult Congenital Heart Network, 288
Canadian Association for the Advancement of Music & the Arts, 305
Canadian Association of Home & Property Inspectors-Ontario Association of Home Inspectors (OAHI), 318
Canadian Association of Movers, 321
Canadian Association of Pharmacy Technicians, 326
Canadian Association of Professional Pet Dog Trainers, 329
Canadian Association of Professional Regulatory Affairs, 329
Canadian Association of Token Collectors, 334
Canadian Automatic Merchandising Association, 338
Canadian Baptist Ministries, 341
Canadian Beef, 342
Canadian Blood Services-Mississauga, 344
Canadian Board of Marine Underwriters, 345

Geographic Index / Ontario - Monetville

Canadian Cat Association, 351
Canadian Celiac Association, 352
Canadian Cosmetic, Toiletry & Fragrance Association, 366
Canadian Dance Teachers' Association, 375
Canadian Dance Teachers Association-Ontario Branch, 375
Canadian Federation of Aircraft Maintenance Engineers Associations, 384
Canadian Federation of AME Associations-Ontario AME Association, 385
Canadian Food for Children, 391
Canadian Foundation for Pharmacy, 393
Canadian Hearing Society-Mississauga, 403
Canadian Home Care Association, 408
Canadian Home Furnishings Alliance, 408
Canadian Information Processing Society, 411
Canadian Institute of Financial Planners, 415
Canadian Institute of Iridology, 416
Canadian International Freight Forwarders Association, Inc.-Central Division, 421
Canadian Manufacturers & Exporters, 429
Canadian Manufacturers & Exporters-Ontario Division, 430
Canadian Marfan Association, 430
Canadian Masonry Contractors' Association, 431
Canadian Masonry Contractors' Association-Ontario Masonry Contractors' Association, 431
Canadian Music Week Inc., 438
Canadian Plastics Industry Association, 455
Canadian Ready Mixed Concrete Association, 465
The Canadian Red Cross Society-Ontario Zone Office, 466
Canadian Slovak League, 472
Canadian Snack Food Association, 472
Canadian Sociological Association, 488
Canadian Spice Association, 489
Canadian Tire Dealers Association, 495
Canadian Urethane Foam Contractors Association, 500
Canadian Vaping Association, 500
Carefirst Seniors & Community Services Association-Mississauga On-Site Drop-In Service, 511
Catholic Biblical Association of Canada, 517
Catholic Cross Cultural Services-Mississauga, 518
Catholic Family Services of Peel Dufferin, 519
Central 1 Credit Union-Mississauga - Ontario Region, 523
Children's Aid Society of the Region of Peel, 561
Chinese Canadian Chiropractic Society, 564
Christian Labour Association of Canada, 567
Christian Labour Association of Canada-GTA/Central/Northern Ontario Regional Office, 568
Church of God of Prophecy in Canada, 569
Classical Accordion Society of Canada, 572
College of Family Physicians of Canada, 584
Community Living Mississauga, 603
Concrete Ontario, 610
Construction Employers Coordinating Council of Ontario, 624
Consumer Electronics Marketers of Canada: A Division of Electro-Federation Canada, 625
COSTI Immigrant Services-Mississauga Centre, 632
Credit Valley Conservation Foundation, 641
Dairy Farmers of Ontario, 648
Denturist Association of Ontario, 654
Dufferin Peel Educational Resource Workers' Association, 664
EcoSource Mississauga, 673
Eden Community Food Bank, 674
Epilepsy Ontario-Halton Peel Hamilton Region, 693
Family Prayer Mission (Ontario), 704
Federation of Chinese Canadian Professionals (Ontario), 723
Food Banks Canada, 749

Foreign Agricultural Resource Management Services, 751
Foundation for Advancing Family Medicine of the College of Family Physicians of Canada, 755
Free Methodist Church in Canada, 759
Great White North Franchisee Association, 782
Habitat for Humanity Canada-Ontario - Halton-Mississauga, 797
Heating, Refrigeration & Air Conditioning Institute of Canada, 810
Heating, Refrigeration & Air Conditioning Institute of Canada-Ontario - Greater Toronto Area Chapter, 810
Human Resources Professionals Association-Peel Chapter, 826
Illuminating Engineering Society of North America-Toronto Section
Independent Financial Brokers of Canada, 832
India Rainbow Community Services of Peel, 834
Information Technology Association of Canada, 837
Infrastructure Health & Safety Association, 838
International Brotherhood of Electrical Workers-Canadian Office, 1542
Islamic Propagation Centre of Ontario, 865
The Kidney Foundation of Canada-Ontario Branch, 885
The Kidney Foundation of Canada-Hamilton & District Chapter, 885
The Kidney Foundation of Canada-Western Ontario Chapter, 886
The Kidney Foundation of Canada-Niagara & District Chapter, 885
Little Faces of Panama Association, 915
Lumber & Building Materials Association of Ontario, 920
Lymphoma Canada, 923
Malta Band Club, Inc., 928
Malton Neighbourhood Services, 928
Masonry Industry Employers Council of Ontario, 952
Master Insulators' Association of Ontario Inc., 953
Mazda Sportscar Owners Club, 954
Meeting Professionals International-Toronto Chapter, 1570
Mining Suppliers Trade Association Canada, 967
Mississauga Arts Council, 969
Mississauga Board of Trade, 969
Mississauga Choral Society, 970
Mississauga Food Bank, 970
Mississauga Heritage Foundation Inc., 970
Mississauga Real Estate Board, 970
Mississauga-Etobicoke Coin Stamp & Collectibles Club, 970
Morning Light Ministry, 974
Muslim Association of Canada, 985
Muslim World League - Canada, 985
National Association of Computer Consulting Business (Canada), 990
National Elevator & Escalator Association, 993
National Floor Covering Association, 993
National Pensioners Federation, 995
National United Professional Association of Trained Homeopaths, 996
North York Coin Club, 1033
Occupational Hygiene Association of Ontario, 1054
OMF International - Canada, 1057
Ontario Asphalt Pavement Council, 1060
Ontario Association of Property Standards Officers Inc., 1065
Ontario Brain Injury Association-Mississauga, 1069
Ontario Catholic Supervisory Officers' Association, 1070
Ontario Dairy Council, 1076
Ontario General Contractors Association, 1082
Ontario Insurance Adjusters Association, 1088
Ontario Kinesiology Association, 1088
Ontario Masonry Contractors' Association, 1090
Ontario Military Vehicle Association, 1091

Ontario Pollution Control Equipment Association, 1096
Ontario Psychiatric Association, 1098
Ontario Refrigeration & Air Conditioning Contractors Association, 1101
Ontario Restaurant, Hotel & Motel Association, 1101
Ontario Road Builders' Association, 1102
Ontario Safety League, 1103
Ontario School Bus Association, 1103
Ontario Sewer & Watermain Construction Association, 1104
Ontario Society of Chiropodists, 1107
Ontario Stone, Sand & Gravel Association, 1109
Ontario Women's Hockey Association, 1113
Orchestras Mississauga, 1117
Osteoporosis Canada-Mississauga Chapter, 1128
Ostomy Canada Society, 1129
Our Place (Peel), 1133
Parents Without Partners Inc.-Mississauga Valley Chapter
Patronato INAS (Canada)-Mississauga Office, 1146
Peel Committee Against Woman Abuse, 1147
Peel Family Services, 1147
Peel HIV/AIDS Network, 1148
Peel Multicultural Council, 1148
Peel Regional Labour Council, 1148
Pentecostal Assemblies of Canada, 1150
Plant Engineering & Maintenance Association of Canada, 1162
Polish Alliance of Canada, 1163
Polish North American Trucking Association, 1164
Prison Fellowship Canada, 1180
Project Management Institute-Lakeshore
Registered Practical Nurses Association of Ontario, 1213
Retirement Planning Association of Canada, 1228
Royal Astronomical Society of Canada-Mississauga Centre, 1238
The Royal Commonwealth Society of Canada-Toronto Branch, 1242
Saint Elizabeth Health Care-Mississauga - Peel Service Delivery Centre, 1246
Sheridan Park Association, 1296
Shwachman-Diamond Syndrome Canada, 1297
Skate Ontario, 1302
Social Planning Council of Peel, 1306
Society of Incentive & Travel Executives of Canada, 1329
Society of Professional Engineers & Associates, 1330
Standardbred Canada, 1347
Streetsville Historical Society, 1352
Surety Association of Canada, 1357
Sustainable Urban Development Association, 1358
Teamsters Canada (CLC)-Central Region, 1368
Teamwork Children's Services International, 1368
Toronto Association of Systems & Software Quality, 1382
Toronto Cat Rescue, 1383
Toronto Press & Media Club, 1386
Tourette Syndrome Foundation of Canada, 1388
Travel Industry Council of Ontario, 1396
Trillium Health Partners Foundation, 1398
Turkey Farmers of Canada, 1400
Ukrainian Orthodox Church of Canada-Eastern Eparchy, 1403
UNIFOR-Mississauga, 1405
United Way of Peel Region, 1416
Women in Food Industry Management, 1461
Workplace Safety & Prevention Services, 1464
World Vision Canada, 1467

Monetville
Friends of Mashkinonje Park, 761

Mono
Dufferin Board of Trade, 664

Taoist Tai Chi Society of Canada-The International Centre, 1367

Moonbeam
Canadian Office & Professional Employees Union-Region 2 - Local 523, 445

Moosonee
James Bay Association for Community Living, 868
Moosonee Native Friendship Centre, 974

Morpeth
The Friends of Rondeau Park, 762

Morrisburg
Community Living Dundas County, 601
South Dundas Chamber of Commerce, 1334
United Empire Loyalists' Association of Canada-St. Lawrence Branch, 1410

Mossley
Mossley Post Heritage & Citizenship Society, 975

Mount Brydges
Middlesex Federation of Agriculture, 965
National Association of Watch & Clock Collectors, Inc.-Southwestern Ontario, 1575

Mount Forest
Mount Forest District Chamber of Commerce, 976

Mount Hope
Canadian Warplane Heritage, 502
Equestrian Association for the Disabled, 694

Napanee
Heating, Refrigeration & Air Conditioning Institute of Canada-Ontario - Loyalist Chapter, 810
Lennox & Addington Association for Community Living, 907
Lennox & Addington County Law Association, 907
Lennox & Addington Historical Society, 907
Napanee & District Chamber of Commerce, 988
Napanee Sports Association, 988
Ontario College Administrative Staff Associations, 1072
Ontario Society for the Prevention of Cruelty to Animals-Lennox & Addington Branch, 1106

Naughton
Ontario Native Education Counselling Association, 1093

Nepean
Adventive Cross Cultural Initiatives, 10
Alliance for Canadian New Music Projects-Contemporary Showcase - Ottawa/Carleton, 56
Association of Applied Geochemists, 139
Bowls Canada Boulingrin, 220
Canada-Israel Cultural Foundation-Ottawa Chapter, 283
Canadian Aerophilatelic Society, 289
Canadian Catholic School Trustees' Association, 351
Canadian Physicians for Life, 454
Credit Canada Debt Solutions, Inc.-SOS Dettes - Solutions à l'endettement, 639
National ME/FM Action Network, 995
National Union of Public & General Employees, 996
Ontario Nurses' Association-Ottawa Office, 1094
Ottawa Safety Council, 1131
Royal Astronomical Society of Canada-Ottawa Centre, 1238
Shooting Federation of Canada, 1297
Squash Canada, 1347
United Empire Loyalists' Association of Canada-Sir Guy Carleton Branch, 1410
Wild Bird Care Centre, 1453

Nestleton Station
Greater Toronto Water Garden & Horticultural Society, 786
Ontario Delphinium Club, 1076

New Hamburg
Canadian Trakehner Horse Society, 496
New Hamburg Board of Trade, 1014

New Liskeard
Ontario College of Reflexology, 1072
Temiskaming Cattlemen's Association, 1370
Temiskaming Environmental Action Committee, 1370
Temiskaming Multiple Births, 1370
Temiskaming Shores & Area Chamber of Commerce, 1370

Newcastle
Adventist Development & Relief Agency Canada, 10
Harry E. Foster Foundation, 804
Newcastle & District Chamber of Commerce, 1015
Newcastle Village & District Historical Society, 1015

Newmarket
Arthritis Health Professions Association, 84
Bereaved Families of Ontario-York Region, 205
Boys & Girls Clubs of Ontario-Boys & Girls Clubs of York Region, 223
Canadian Association of Montessori Teachers, 321
Canadian Hearing Society-Simcoe York Regional Office, 403
Canadian Rheumatology Association, 467
Canadian University & College Conference Organizers Association, 499
Community Living Newmarket/Aurora District, 603
Conservation Ontario, 622
General Practice Psychotherapy Association, 769
Heart & Stroke Foundation of Ontario-York Region North Office, 809
Independent Telecommunications Providers Association, 833
International Live Events Association Canada, 858
The John Howard Society of Ontario-York Region, 875
Lake Simcoe Region Conservation Foundation, 896
Literacy Council York-Simcoe, 913
Lupus Canada, 921
Newmarket Chamber of Commerce, 1024
Oak Ridges Moraine Foundation, 1053
Ontario Rheumatology Association, 1102
Ontario Society for the Prevention of Cruelty to Animals-Provincial Education & Animal Centre, 1106
Ontario Society for the Prevention of Cruelty to Animals-Ontario SPCA Centre Veterinary Hospital Spay/Neuter Services, 1106
Ontario Society for the Prevention of Cruelty to Animals-Bruce Grey Branch, 1105
Women's Support Network of York Region, 1463
York Region Children's Aid Society, 1473
York Region Law Association, 1473
York Regional Police Association, 1473

Niagara Falls
The Association of Professional Accounting & Tax Consultants Inc., 156
Boys & Girls Clubs of Ontario-Boys & Girls Club of Niagara, 223
Branscombe Family Foundation, 226
Canadian Institute of Management-Ontario - Niagara Branch, 417
Chamber of Commerce Niagara Falls, Canada, 539
Family & Children's Services Niagara-Niagara Falls Branch, 701
Friends of Music Therapy, 761
The Garden Clubs of Ontario-Niagara, 767
Greek-Canadian Cultural Centre, 788
Lundy's Lane Historical Society, 920
Niagara Falls Nature Club, 1025
Niagara Falls Tourism, 1025
Niagara Region Orchid Society, 1025
Ontario Society for the Prevention of Cruelty to Animals-Niagara Falls Branch (Affiliate), 1106
Parent Cooperative Preschools International, 1139
Professional Hockey Players' Association, 1185
Project Share, 1188
Royal Astronomical Society of Canada-Niagara Centre, 1238
United Way of Niagara Falls & Greater Fort Erie, 1415

Niagara-on-the-Lake
Niagara Regional Native Centre, 1026
Niagara-on-the-Lake Bed & Breakfast Association Inc., 1026
Niagara-on-the-Lake Chamber of Commerce, 1026
Shaw Festival, 1294
Society of Ontario Nut Growers, 1330

Nipigon
Top of Lake Superior Chamber of Commerce, 1381

Nobleton
Heralds of the Gospel, 812

Noelville
Ontario Lumber Manufacturers' Association, 1089

North Bay
AIDS Committee of North Bay & Area, 16
Airport Management Council of Ontario, 20
L'Alliance des Caisses populaires de l'Ontario limitée, 55
Almaguin-Nipissing Travel Association, 59
Alzheimer Society of North Bay & District, 63
Amelia Rising Sexual Assault Centre of Nipissing, 66
L'Arche Ontario-L'Arche North Bay, 77
Canadian College of Health Leaders-Southwestern Ontario Regional Chapter, 359
Canadian Diamond Drilling Association, 377
Canadian Hearing Society-North Bay Office, 403
Canadian Office & Professional Employees Union-Region 2 - Local 529, 445
Children's Aid Society of the District of Nipissing & Parry Sound, 561
Community Counselling Centre of Nipissing, 596
Community Living North Bay, 603
Crisis Centre North Bay, 642
Nipissing Environmental Watch, 1027
Nipissing Law Association, 1027
North Bay & District Chamber of Commerce, 1030
North Bay & District Humane Society, 1030
North Bay Food Bank, 1030
North Bay Indian Friendship Centre, 1030
North Bay Police Association, 1030
North Bay Real Estate Board, 1030
Northern Ontario Hockey Association, 1035
Northwatch, 1036
Ontario Brain Injury Association-North Bay, 1069
Ontario Genealogical Society-Nipissing Branch, 1082
Ontario Home Builders' Association-North Bay & District, 1085
Ontario Society for the Prevention of Cruelty to Animals-North Bay Branch (Affiliate), 1106
Réseau du patrimoine franco-ontarien-Jean-Nicolet, 1222
Sisters of Saint Joseph of Sault Ste Marie, 1301
Union of Ontario Indians, 1408
United Church of Canada-Manitou Conference, 1409
YMCA Canada-YMCA of Northeastern Ontario - North Bay, 1472

Northbrook
Sasha's Legacy Equine Rescue, 1254

Norwich
Ontario CGIT Association, 1071
Ontario Home Builders' Association-Oxford County, 1085

Norwood
Community Care Peterborough-Norwood Office, 596
Ontario Katahdin Sheep Association Inc., 1088

Oakville
Acclaim Health, 5
Association for Bright Children (Ontario), 132
Brethren in Christ, 228
The Bronte Historical Society, 260
CAMPUT, 277
Canadian Association for Spiritual Care, 304
Canadian Association of Gastroenterology, 316
Canadian Association of Genetic Counsellors, 316
Canadian Association of School System Administrators, 332
Canadian Colombian Professional Association, 360
Canadian Convenience Stores Association, 364
The Canadian Corps of Commissionaires-Great Lakes-Toronto Division, 365
Canadian Digestive Health Foundation, 378
Canadian Explosive Technicians' Association, 383
Canadian Fluid Power Association, 391
Canadian Golf Hall of Fame & Museum, 398
Canadian Society of Gastroenterology Nurses & Associates, 483
CharterAbility, 552
Clan Mackenzie Society of Canada, 571
Community Living Oakville, 604
Company of Women, 608
Credit Institute of Canada-Hamilton & District Chapter, 641
DEBRA Canada, 652
Dog Guides Canada, 660
Family Enterprise Xchange, 703
Family Enterprise Xchange-FEX Central Ontario, 703
F.A.S.T., 706
Golf Canada, 777
Golf Canada Foundation, 777
Halton Family Services, 800
Halton Mississauga Youth Orchestra, 800
Halton Multicultural Council, 800
Halton Peel Hispanic Association, 800
Halton Regional Police Association, 800
Headache Network Canada, 805
Information Oakville, 837
International Union of Food Science & Technology, 861
Irish Dance Teacher's Association of Eastern Canada, 864
Lions Foundation of Canada, 913
Lotus Car Club of Canada, 919
MADD Canada, 925
Monarchist League of Canada, 971
Municipal Engineers Association, 980
Oakville & Milton Humane Society, 1053
Oakville Art Society, 1053
Oakville Arts Council, 1053
Oakville Chamber of Commerce, 1053
Oakville Chamber Orchestra, 1053
Oakville Community Centre for Peace, Ecology & Human Rights, 1053
Oakville Distress Centre, 1053
Oakville Historical Society, 1053
Oakville Symphony Orchestra, 1053
The Oakville, Milton & District Real Estate Board, 1054
Ontario Association of Library Technicians, 1064
Ontario Convenience Store Association, 1074
Ontario Council for Exceptional Children, 1075
Ontario Good Roads Association, 1083
Ontario Public Supervisory Officers' Association, 1100
Ontario Public Works Association, 1100
Ontario Retirement Communities Association, 1102
Ontario Society for the Prevention of Cruelty to Animals-Oakville Branch (Affiliate), 1106
Ontario Zoroastrian Community Foundation, 1114
Pipe Line Contractors Association of Canada, 1160
Professional Engineers Ontario-Oakville, 1184
Radius Child & Youth Services, 1203
Royal Astronomical Society of Canada-Hamilton Centre, 1238
Schizophrenia Society of Ontario-Halton / Peel Region, 1284
South Peel Naturalists' Club, 1336
United Way of Oakville, 1415
Utility Contractors Association of Ontario, Inc., 1423
The Women's Centre, 1462
YMCA Canada-YMCA of Oakville, 1472

Odessa
PFLAG Canada Inc.-Belleville - Quinte Chapter, 1155

Omemee
Ontario Home Economics Association, 1086

Orangeville
Alzheimer Society of Dufferin County, 62
Canadian Flag Association, 391
Catholic Family Services of Peel Dufferin-Orangeville Branch, 519
Dufferin Arts Council, 664
Dufferin Child & Family Services, 664
Ontario Home Builders' Association-Greater Dufferin, 1085
Ontario Modern Pentathalon Association, 1091
Ontario Society for the Prevention of Cruelty to Animals-Orangeville & District Branch, 1106
Orangeville & District Real Estate Board, 1117

Orillia
Canadian Authors Association, 338
Federation of Ontario Bed & Breakfast Accommodation, 725
Ganaraska Hiking Trail Association, 766
Information Orillia, 837
Mariposa Folk Foundation, 950
Ontario Nurses' Association-Orillia Office, 1094
Ontario Society for the Prevention of Cruelty to Animals-Orillia Branch, 1106
Orillia & District Chamber of Commerce, 1126
Orillia & District Construction Association, 1126
Orillia Youth Symphony Orchestra, 1126
Resorts Ontario, 1226
The Sharing Place - Orillia & District Food Bank, 1294
Simcoe/Muskoka Literacy Network, 1300
Stephen Leacock Associates, 1349
YMCA Canada-YMCA of Simcoe/Muskoka - Orillia, 1472

Orléans
Association ontarienne des Sourd(e)s francophones, 164
Canadian Association of Veterans in United Nations Peacekeeping-Colonel John Gardam Chapter, 335
Canadian Aviation Historical Society-Ottawa Chapter, 340
Canadian Curling Association, 374
Canadian Printing Industries Association, 459
Canadian Society for Bioengineering, 473
Canadian Society of Allergy & Clinical Immunology, 479
Industrial Gas Users Association, 835
International Academy of Energy, Minerals & Materials, 852
Orléans Chamber of Commerce, 1126

Oro
Oro-Medonte Chamber of Commerce, 1127

Oro Station
Heating, Refrigeration & Air Conditioning Institute of Canada-Ontario - Huronia Chapter, 810

Orton
Ontario Pinzgauer Breeders Association, 1096

Oshawa
AIDS Committee of Durham Region, 16
Alcoholics Anonymous-Oshawa - Lakeshore Intergroup, 52
Alzheimer Society of Durham Region, 62
Bereaved Families of Ontario-Durham Region, 205
Boys & Girls Clubs of Ontario-Boys & Girls Club of Durham, 223
Canadian Adventist Teachers Network, 288
Canadian Association for Astrological Education, 297
Canadian Association for Community Living, 298
Canadian Association of Provincial Court Judges, 329
Canadian Blood Services-Oshawa, 344
Canadian Hearing Society-Durham Regional Office, 403
Canadian Polish Congress-Oshawa Branch, 456
Canadian Shooting Sports Association, 470
Chinese Medicine & Acupuncture Association of Canada-Ontario Office, 565
Community Living Oshawa / Clarington, 604
Conseil des organismes francophones de la région de Durham, 617
Cursillo Movement of the Archdiocese of Toronto, 646
Durham Deaf Services, 665
Durham Personal Computer Users' Club, 665
Durham Region Association of REALTORS, 665
Durham Region Law Association, 665
Durham Regional Labour Council, 665
Durham Youth Orchestra, 665
Greater Oshawa Chamber of Commerce, 784
Information Durham, 837
The John Howard Society of Ontario-Durham Region, 875
K3C Community Counselling Centres-K3C Credit Counselling Oshawa, 879
Literacy Council of Durham Region, 913
Ontario Brain Injury Association-Oshawa, 1069
Ontario Halfway House Association, 1083
Ontario Home Builders' Association-Durham Region, 1085
Ontario Municipal Management Institute, 1092
Ontario Philharmonic, 1095
Ontario Undergraduate Student Alliance-Trent in Oshawa Students Association, 1112
Oshawa Historical Society, 1128
PFLAG Canada Inc.-Oshawa - Durham Region / Oshawa Chapter, 1155
Seventh-day Adventist Church in Canada, 1292
United Way of Durham Region, 1414
YWCA Canada-YWCA Durham, 1481

Oshweken
Indspire, 835

Ottawa
Aboriginal Tourism Association of Southern Ontario, 2
Academy of Canadian Executive Nurses, 4
Accreditation Canada, 5
Action Canada for Sexual Health & Rights, 6
Action Life (Ottawa) Inc., 6
Adoption Council of Canada, 8
Advanced Coronary Treatment (ACT) Foundation of Canada, 10
Aerospace Industries Association of Canada, 11
Affirm United, 11
AFOA Canada, 12
Aga Khan Foundation Canada, 14
Agricultural Institute of Canada, 14
Agricultural Institute of Canada Foundation, 15
Agriculture Union, 15
AIDS Committee of Ottawa, 16
AIESEC-Ottawa, 18
Air Cadet League of Canada, 19
Air Force Association of Canada, 19
Air Line Pilots Association, International - Canada, 19
Air Transport Association of Canada, 19
Al-Anon Family Groups (Canada), Inc., 21
Alberta Association of Prosthetists & Orthotists, 24
Alcoholics Anonymous-Ottawa - Ottawa Area Intergroup, 52
Alliance canadienne des responsables et enseignants en français (langue maternelle), 55
Alliance des femmes de la francophonie canadienne, 55
Alliance des radios communautaires du Canada, 56
Alliance Française, 57
Alliance Française d'Ottawa, 57
Alliance of Canadian Cinema, Television & Radio Artists-ACTRA Ottawa, 58
Almas Jiwani Foundation, 59
Alzheimer Society of Ottawa & Renfrew County, 64
American Galloway Breeders Association, 66
American Society of Heating, Refrigerating & Air Conditioning Engineers-Ottawa Valley Chapter
Amnesty International - Canadian Section (English Speaking), 68
Amputee Society of Ottawa & District, 68
The Anglican Church of Canada-Diocese of Ottawa, 70
Animal Defence League of Canada, 70
Animal Nutrition Association of Canada, 70
Animal Welfare Foundation of Canada, 71
Anxiety Disorders Association of Ontario, 72
Appraisal Institute of Canada, 74
Aquatic Federation of Canada, 75
L'Arche Ontario-L'Arche Ottawa, 77
Archery Canada Tir à l'Arc, 78
Arctic Council, 81
ARMA Canada-Ottawa, 82
Army Cadet League of Canada, 83
Army, Navy & Air Force Veterans in Canada, 83
Arts Ottawa East-Est, 86
Assemblée de la francophonie de l'Ontario, 87
Assemblée parlementaire de la Francophonie (Section canadienne), 88
Assembly of First Nations, 88
Association canadienne de traductologie, 92
Association canadienne des professeurs d'immersion, 94
Association de la presse francophone, 101
Association des auteurs et des auteurs de l'Ontario français, 106
Association des enseignantes et des enseignants franco-ontariens, 112
Association des juristes d'expression française de l'Ontario, 117
Association des professeur(e)s à temps partiel de l'Université d'Ottawa, 124
Association des professeurs de l'université d'Ottawa, 125
Association des professionnels de la chanson et de la musique, 125
Association des théâtres francophones du Canada, 129
Association des universités de la francophonie canadienne, 130
L'Association du Québec de l'Institut canadien des évaluateurs, 131
Association for Bahá'í Studies, 132
Association for Financial Professionals - Ottawa, 133
L'Association française des municipalités de l'Ontario, 135
Association francophone à l'éducation des services à l'enfance de l'Ontario, 135
Association of Canada Lands Surveyors, 140
Association of Canadian Archivists, 141
Association of Canadian Financial Officers, 142
Association of Canadian Port Authorities, 143
Association of Canadian Universities for Northern Studies, 144
Association of Consulting Engineering Companies - Canada, 145
Association of Equipment Manufacturers - Canada, 148
Association of Faculties of Medicine of Canada, 148
Association of Faculties of Pharmacy of Canada, 148
Association of Fundraising Professionals-Ottawa Chapter, 1512
Association of Home Appliance Manufacturers Canada Council, 149
Association of Medical Microbiology & Infectious Disease Canada, 151
Association of Professional Executives of the Public Service of Canada, 159
Association of Professional Recruiters of Canada, 159
Association of Translators & Interpreters of Ontario, 163
Association pour l'intégration sociale d'Ottawa, 166
Association québécoise de doit comparé, 169
AthletesCAN, 180
Athletics Canada, 181
Atlantic Association of Prosthetists & Orthotists, 182
Automotive Industries Association of Canada, 189
Badminton Canada, 193
Bahá'í Community of Ottawa, 194
Barbados Ottawa Association, 196
Baseball Canada, 198
Bereaved Families of Ontario-Ottawa Region, 205
Better Business Bureau of Eastern & Northern Ontario & the Outaouais, 206
Big Brothers Big Sisters of Ontario-Big Brothers Big Sisters of Ottawa, 210
Bike Ottawa, 211
BioTalent Canada, 211
BIOTECanada, 212
Birthright International-Ottawa Chapter, 212
BMW Clubs Canada-BMW Car Club of Ottawa, 216
Boys & Girls Clubs of Ontario-Boys & Girls Club of Ottawa, 223
Brain Injury Association of Canada, 225
Breast Cancer Action, 227
Brewers Association of Canada, 228
British Isles Family History Society of Greater Ottawa, 259
Bruce House, 260
BuildForce Canada, 261
Building Envelope Council of Ottawa Region, 262
Building Owners & Managers Association of Ottawa, 263
Bureau des regroupements des artistes visuels de l'Ontario, 264
Business Council of Canada, 266
Bytown Railway Society, 267
Caledon Institute of Social Policy, 270
Campaign for Nuclear Phaseout, 276
Canada Dance Festival Society, 278
Canada Employment & Immigration Union, 278
Canada Foundation for Innovation, 279
Canada Games Council, 279
Canada Green Building Council, 279
Canada Organic Trade Association, 280
Canada Pork International, 280
Canada Safety Council, 280
Canada Without Poverty, 281
Canada's Accredited Zoos & Aquariums, 281
Canada's Advanced Internet Development Organization, 281
Canada's Public Policy Forum, 282
CanadaGAP, 283
Canada-Pakistan Association of the National Capital Region, 283
Canadian 4-H Council, 284
Canadian 5 Pin Bowlers' Association, 285
Canadian Academy of Child & Adolescent Psychiatry, 285
The Canadian Academy of Engineering, 286
Canadian Academy of Periodontology, 286
Canadian Academy of Psychiatry & the Law, 286
Canadian Academy of Sport Medicine, 287
Canadian Acoustical Association, 287
Canadian Adult Recreational Hockey Association, 288
Canadian Advanced Technology Alliance, 288
Canadian Aeronautics & Space Institute, 288
Canadian Agency for Drugs & Technologies in Health, 289
Canadian Agricultural Human Resource Council, 289
Canadian AIDS Society, 290
Canadian Air Traffic Control Association, 291
Canadian Airports Council, 291
Canadian Alliance of Student Associations, 291
Canadian Alliance on Mental Illness & Mental Health, 291
Canadian Amateur Musicians-Ottawa-Gatineau Region, 292
Canadian Amateur Softball Association, 292
Canadian Apheresis Group, 294
Canadian Apparel Federation, 294
Canadian Apprenticeship Forum, 294
Canadian Aquaculture Industry Alliance, 294
Canadian Architectural Certification Board, 295
Canadian Arctic Resources Committee, 295
Canadian Artists Representation, 295
Canadian Arts Presenting Association, 296
Canadian Association for Business Economics, 297
Canadian Association for Conservation of Cultural Property, 298
Canadian Association for Curriculum Studies, 299
Canadian Association for Disabled Skiing - National Capital Division, 299
Canadian Association for Educational Psychology, 300
Canadian Association for Enterostomal Therapy, 300
Canadian Association for Graduate Studies, 300
Canadian Association for Health Services & Policy Research, 300
The Canadian Association for HIV Research, 301
Canadian Association for Laboratory Accreditation Inc., 301
Canadian Association for Medical Education, 302
Canadian Association for Prior Learning Assesment, 303
Canadian Association for Renewable Energies, 303
Canadian Association for Security & Intelligence Studies, 303
Canadian Association for Social Work Education, 304
Canadian Association for Teacher Education, 304
Canadian Association for the Advancement of Women & Sport & Physical Activity, 305
Canadian Association for the Study of Adult Education, 306
Canadian Association for the Study of Educational Administration, 306
Canadian Association for the Study of Indigenous Education, 306
Canadian Association for the Study of International Development, 306
Canadian Association for the Study of Women & Education, 306
Canadian Association of Apheresis Nurses, 308
Canadian Association of Broadcasters, 309
Canadian Association of Communicators in Education, 310
Canadian Association of Defence & Security Industries, 312
Canadian Association of Elizabeth Fry Societies, 312

Geographic Index / Ontario - Ottawa

Canadian Association of Elizabeth Fry Societies-Elizabeth Fry Society of Ottawa, 313
Canadian Association of Elizabeth Fry Societies-Council of Elizabeth Fry Societies of Ontario, 312
Canadian Association of Family Resource Programs, 314
Canadian Association of Film Distributors & Exporters, 314
Canadian Association of Fire Chiefs, 315
Canadian Association of Former Parliamentarians, 315
Canadian Association of Foundations of Education, 315
Canadian Association of General Surgeons, 316
Canadian Association of Gift Planners, 317
Canadian Association of Heritage Professionals, 317
Canadian Association of Home & Property Inspectors, 317
Canadian Association of Learned Journals, 319
Canadian Association of Medical Biochemists, 320
Canadian Association of Medical Oncologists, 320
Canadian Association of Medical Radiation Technologists, 320
Canadian Association of Mutual Insurance Companies, 322
Canadian Association of Nuclear Medicine, 323
Canadian Association of Occupational Therapists, 323
Canadian Association of Occupational Therapists - British Columbia, 324
Canadian Association of Optometrists, 324
Canadian Association of Oral & Maxillofacial Surgeons, 324
Canadian Association of Paediatric Health Centres, 325
Canadian Association of Perinatal & Women's Health Nurses, 325
Canadian Association of Physician Assistants, 327
Canadian Association of Physicists, 327
Canadian Association of Police Governance, 327
Canadian Association of Professional Conservators, 328
Canadian Association of Professional Employees, 328
Canadian Association of Radiologists, 330
Canadian Association of Railway Suppliers, 330
Canadian Association of Recycling Industries, 330
Canadian Association of Regulated Importers, 331
Canadian Association of Research Administrators, 331
Canadian Association of Research Libraries, 331
Canadian Association of Retired Teachers, 331
Canadian Association of Schools of Nursing, 332
Canadian Association of Second Language Teachers, 332
Canadian Association of Social Workers, 333
Canadian Association of Statutory Human Rights Agencies, 333
Canadian Association of the Deaf, 334
Canadian Association of Thoracic Surgeons, 334
Canadian Association of Transplantation, 334
Canadian Association of University Business Officers, 334
Canadian Association of University Teachers, 335
Canadian Association of Wireless Internet Service Providers, 336
Canadian Automobile Association North & East Ontario, 339
Canadian Automobile Dealers' Association-Ottawa Office, 339
Canadian Aviation Historical Society, 340

Canadian Bankers Association-Ottawa Office, 341
Canadian Bar Association, 341
Canadian Battlefields Foundation, 342
Canadian Bible Society-Eastern Ontario District Office, 343
Canadian Bible Society-Northern Ontario District Office, 343
Canadian Biogas Association, 343
Canadian Blonde d'Aquitaine Association, 344
Canadian Blood Services, 344
Canadian Blood Services-Ottawa - Alta Vista Dr. - National Fundraising Office, 344
Canadian Blood Services-Ottawa, 344
Canadian Board of Examiners for Professional Surveyors, 345
Canadian Breast Cancer Network, 347
Canadian Broadcast Standards Council, 347
Canadian Bureau for International Education, 347
Canadian Business Aviation Association, 347
Canadian Cancer Survivor Network, 349
Canadian Cardiovascular Society, 350
Canadian Career Development Foundation, 350
Canadian Caregiver Coalition, 350
Canadian Carpet Institute, 350
Canadian Cattlemen's Association-Ottawa Office, 351
Canadian Celiac Association-Ottawa Chapter, 352
Canadian Centre for Ethics in Sport, 353
Canadian Centre for Policy Alternatives, 354
Canadian Centre on Substance Use & Addiction, 354
Canadian Cerebral Palsy Sports Association, 354
The Canadian Chamber of Commerce, 355
Canadian Child Care Federation, 355
Canadian Coalition for Fair Digital Access, 357
Canadian College of Health Leaders, 358
Canadian Commission for UNESCO, 360
Canadian Committee for World Press Freedom, 360
Canadian Committee of Graduate Students in Education, 361
Canadian Committee on MARC, 361
Canadian Community Reinvestment Coalition, 361
Canadian Condominium Institute-CCI-Eastern Ontario Chapter, 362
Canadian Conference of Catholic Bishops, 362
Canadian Conference of the Arts, 363
Canadian Conservation Institute, 363
Canadian Construction Association, 363
Canadian Consumer Specialty Products Association, 363
Canadian Co-operative Association, 364
The Canadian Corps of Commissionaires, 365
The Canadian Corps of Commissionaires-Ottawa Division, 365
Canadian Council for Aviation & Aerospace, 366
Canadian Council for International Co-operation, 366
Canadian Council for Tobacco Control, 367
Canadian Council of Archives, 367
Canadian Council of Cardiovascular Nurses, 367
Canadian Council of Forest Ministers, 368
Canadian Council of Independent Laboratories, 368
Canadian Council of Motor Transport Administrators, 369
Canadian Council of Professional Fish Harvesters, 369
Canadian Council of Technicians & Technologists, 370
The Canadian Council of the Blind, 370
Canadian Council on Africa, 370
Canadian Council on Animal Care, 370
Canadian Council on International Law, 371
Canadian Counselling & Psychotherapy Association, 371
Canadian Credit Union Association-Ottawa Office, 373

Canadian Criminal Justice Association, 373
Canadian Dairy Commission, 375
Canadian Dental Assistants Association, 376
Canadian Dental Association, 376
Canadian Dental Hygienists Association, 377
Canadian Dermatology Association, 377
Canadian Dexter Cattle Association, 377
Canadian Disaster Restoration Group, 378
Canadian Educational Researchers' Association, 380
Canadian Electricity Association, 380
Canadian Energy Efficiency Alliance, 381
Canadian Environmental Network, 382
Canadian Ethnocultural Council, 382
Canadian Faculties of Agriculture & Veterinary Medicine, 383
Canadian Fallen Firefighters Foundation, 383
Canadian Federal Pilots Association, 384
Canadian Federation for the Humanities & Social Sciences, 384
Canadian Federation of Agriculture, 384
Canadian Federation of Apartment Associations, 385
Canadian Federation of Engineering Students, 386
Canadian Federation of Friends of Museums, 386
Canadian Federation of Humane Societies, 386
Canadian Federation of Library Associations, 387
Canadian Federation of Medical Students, 388
Canadian Federation of Nurses Unions, 388
Canadian Federation of Students, 388
Canadian Federation of University Women, 388
Canadian Fencing Federation, 389
Canadian Ferry Association, 389
Canadian Film Institute, 390
Canadian Fitness & Lifestyle Research Institute, 390
Canadian Fjord Horse Association, 391
Canadian Foundation for Climate & Atmospheric Sciences, 393
Canadian Foundation for Drug Policy, 393
Canadian Foundation for Healthcare Improvement, 393
Canadian Foundry Association, 394
Canadian Friends of Burma, 395
Canadian Friends of the Hebrew University-Ottawa Chapter, 395
Canadian Fuels Association, 395
Canadian Galloway Association, 396
Canadian Gas Association, 396
Canadian Global Campaign for Education, 398
Canadian Goat Society, 398
Canadian Grand Masters Fiddling Association, 398
Canadian Hadassah WIZO-Ottawa, 399
Canadian Hard of Hearing Association, 400
Canadian Hard of Hearing Association-Ontario - National Capital Region, 400
Canadian Hatching Egg Producers, 401
Canadian Health Coalition, 401
Canadian Hearing Society-Ottawa Regional Office, 403
Canadian Hematology Society, 404
Canadian Historical Association, 405
Canadian HIV Trials Network-Ontario Region, 405
Canadian Hoisting & Rigging Safety Council, 406
Canadian Home Builders' Association, 406
Canadian Horticultural Council, 408
Canadian Hospice Palliative Care Association, 409
Canadian Housing & Renewal Association, 409
Canadian Hydrographic Association-Ottawa Branch, 409
Canadian Hydropower Association, 410
Canadian Icelandic Horse Federation, 410
Canadian Indigenous Nurses Association, 411
Canadian Institute for Conflict Resolution, 412
Canadian Institute for Health Information, 412
Canadian Institute for Mediterranean Studies-Ottawa, 413
Canadian Institute of Actuaries, 414

Canadian Institute of Child Health, 414
Canadian Institute of Geomatics, 416
Canadian Institute of Management-Ontario - Ottawa Valley Branch, 417
Canadian Institute of Planners, 418
Canadian Intergovernmental Conference Secretariat, 420
Canadian Internet Registration Authority, 422
Canadian Interuniversity Sport, 422
Canadian ISBN Agency, 422
Canadian Italian Business & Professional Association of Ottawa, 423
Canadian Katahdin Sheep Association Inc., 423
Canadian Kitchen Cabinet Association, 424
Canadian Labour Congress, 424
Canadian Lacrosse Association, 425
Canadian Life & Health Insurance Association Inc.-Ottawa Office, 426
Canadian Life Insurance Medical Officers Association, 426
Canadian Literacy & Learning Network, 427
Canadian Livestock Records Corporation, 428
Canadian Lumber Standards Accreditation Board, 428
Canadian Lung Association, 428
Canadian Magen David Adom for Israel-Ottawa Chapter, 429
Canadian Manufactured Housing Institute, 429
The Canadian Marine Industries and Shipbuilding Association, 430
Canadian Marine Pilots' Association, 430
Canadian Marketing Association-Ottawa Chapter, 431
Canadian Mathematical Society, 431
Canadian Meat Council, 432
Canadian Media Production Association, 432
Canadian Medical & Biological Engineering Society, 433
Canadian Medical Association, 433
Canadian Medical Foundation, 434
The Canadian Medical Protective Association, 434
Canadian Mental Health Association, 434
Canadian Merchant Service Guild, 435
Canadian Meteorological & Oceanographic Society, 435
Canadian Mineral Processors Society, 437
Canadian Museums Association, 437
Canadian National Committee for Irrigation & Drainage, 439
Canadian National Millers Association, 440
Canadian Nautical Research Society, 440
Canadian Network for Innovation in Education, 440
Canadian Network of National Associations of Regulators, 441
Canadian Network to Abolish Nuclear Weapons, 441
Canadian Nuclear Association, 442
Canadian Nurses Association, 442
Canadian Nurses Foundation, 443
Canadian Nurses Protective Society, 443
Canadian Nursing Informatics Association, 443
Canadian Nursing Students' Association, 443
Canadian Nutrition Society, 443
Canadian Occupational Therapy Foundation, 444
Canadian Office & Professional Employees Union-Region 2 - Local 225, 445
Canadian Olympic Committee-Ottawa, 445
Canadian Olympic Hall of Fame, 446
Canadian Operational Research Society, 446
Canadian Ophthalmological Society, 446
Canadian Organic Growers Inc., 446
Canadian Organization for Development through Education, 447
Canadian Owners & Pilots Association, 448
Canadian Paediatric Society, 449
Canadian Paint & Coatings Association, 449
Canadian Paralympic Committee, 449
Canadian Parents for French, 450
Canadian Parking Association, 450
Canadian Parks & Recreation Association, 450
Canadian Parks & Wilderness Society, 450

Canadian Parks & Wilderness Society-Ottawa - Ottawa Valley Chapter, 451
Canadian Pasta Manufacturers Association, 451
Canadian Payments Association, 452
Canadian Pediatric Foundation, 452
Canadian Pharmacists Association, 453
Canadian Physiotherapy Association, 454
Canadian Piedmontese Association, 455
Canadian Police Association, 456
Canadian Political Science Association, 457
Canadian Population Society, 458
Canadian Pork Council, 458
Canadian Postmasters & Assistants Association, 458
Canadian Post-MD Education Registry, 458
Canadian Poultry & Egg Processors Council, 458
Canadian Precast / Prestressed Concrete Institute, 459
The Canadian Press-Ottawa Bureau, 459
Canadian Printable Electronics Industry Association, 459
Canadian Produce Marketing Association, 460
Canadian Professional Association for Transgender Health, 460
Canadian Propane Association, 461
Canadian Psychiatric Association, 461
Canadian Psychoanalytic Society-Ottawa Psychoanalytic Society, 461
Canadian Psychological Association, 462
Canadian Public Health Association, 462
Canadian Public Relations Society Inc.-CPRS Ottawa-Gatineau, 463
Canadian Public Works Association, 464
The Canadian Real Estate Association, 465
Canadian Red Cross, 465
Canadian Red Poll Cattle Association, 466
Canadian Research Institute for the Advancement of Women, 467
Canadian Resident Matching Service, 467
Canadian Respiratory Health Professionals, 467
Canadian Retina Society, 467
Canadian Roofing Contractors' Association, 468
Canadian Science & Technology Historical Association, 468
Canadian Seed Growers' Association, 469
Canadian Seed Trade Association, 470
Canadian Ski Patrol, 471
Canadian Skin Patient Alliance, 471
Canadian Soccer Association, 472
Canadian Social Work Foundation, 472
Canadian Society for Analytical Sciences & Spectroscopy, 473
Canadian Society for Chemical Engineering, 473
Canadian Society for Chemical Technology, 473
Canadian Society for Chemistry, 473
Canadian Society for Clinical Investigation, 474
Canadian Society for Epidemiology & Biostatistics, 474
Canadian Society for Exercise Physiology, 475
Canadian Society for International Health, 475
Canadian Society for Molecular Biosciences, 476
Canadian Society for Psychomotor Learning & Sport Psychology, 477
Canadian Society for the History of Medicine, 477
Canadian Society for the Study of Education, 478
Canadian Society for the Study of Higher Education, 478
Canadian Society for the Study of Religion, 478
Canadian Society for Vascular Surgery, 479
Canadian Society of Cardiac Surgeons, 481
Canadian Society of Customs Brokers, 482
Canadian Society of Endocrinology & Metabolism, 482
Canadian Society of Forensic Science, 483
Canadian Society of Hospital Pharmacists, 483
Canadian Society of Hospital Pharmacists-Ontario, 484
Canadian Society of Internal Medicine, 484

Canadian Society of Landscape Architects, 484
Canadian Society of Mayflower Descendants, 484
Canadian Society of Microbiologists, 485
Canadian Society of Physician Executives, 486
Canadian Society of Respiratory Therapists, 487
Canadian Society of Transplantation, 488
Canadian Solar Industries Association, 489
Canadian Sport Tourism Alliance, 490
Canadian Steel Producers Association, 491
Canadian Supply Chain Food Safety Coalition, 491
Canadian Teachers' Federation, 493
Canadian Technology Human Resources Board, 493
Canadian Thoracic Society, 494
Canadian Tourism Human Resource Council, 495
Canadian Tourism Research Institute, 495
Canadian Toy Testing Council, 496
Canadian Translators, Terminologists & Interpreters Council, 496
Canadian Tribute to Human Rights, 497
Canadian Union of Postal Workers, 498
Canadian Union of Public Employees, 498
Canadian Unitarians for Social Justice, 499
Canadian Urban Transit Association-Ottawa Office, 500
Canadian Veterinary Medical Association, 501
Canadian Vintners Association, 501
Canadian Viola Society, 501
Canadian Vocational Association, 501
Canadian Volkssport Federation, 501
Canadian Water & Wastewater Association, 502
Canadian Welsh Black Cattle Society, 503
Canadian Wheelchair Basketball Association, 503
Canadian Wheelchair Sports Association, 503
Canadian Wildlife Federation, 504
Canadian Wind Energy Association, 504
Canadian Wireless Telecommunications Association, 504
Canadian Women in Communications, 505
Canadian Wood Council, 505
Canadian Wood Pallet & Container Association, 505
Canadian Writers' Foundation Inc., 506
Canadiana, 506
Cancer Research Society Inc.-Ottawa, 507
Candlelighters Childhood Cancer Support Programs, Inc., 508
Cannabis Canada Association, 508
Canoe Kayak Ontario, 509
CanoeKayak Canada, 509
CARE Canada, 511
Carleton County Law Association, 513
Carleton University Academic Staff Association, 513
Catholic Centre for Immigrants - Ottawa + CIC Foundation, 517
Catholic Family Service of Ottawa, 518
Catholic Health Alliance of Canada, 519
Catholic Near East Welfare Association Canada, 520
Cement Association of Canada, 521
Centre canadien de leadership en éducation, 526
Centre de services Guigues, 530
Centre for Canadian Language Benchmarks, 531
Centre for Immunization & Respiratory Infectious Diseases, 532
The Centre for Israel & Jewish Affairs-Jewish Federation of Ottawa, 533
Centre for the Study of Living Standards, 534
Centre franco-ontarien de ressources pédagogiques, 534
Chamber of Marine Commerce, 539
The Chartered Institute of Logistics & Transport in North America, 552
The Chartered Institute of Logistics & Transport in North America-Pacific Region, 552
Chartered Professional Accountants Canada-Ottawa Office, 552

Chartered Professionals in Human Resources, 554
Chemical Institute of Canada, 556
Chemistry Industry Association of Canada, 556
Chess & Math Association-Ottawa Branch, 556
Chicken Farmers of Canada, 557
Child Care Providers Resource Network of Ottawa-Carleton, 558
Child Welfare League of Canada, 560
Children's Hospital of Eastern Ontario Foundation, 562
Children's Wish Foundation of Canada-National Capital Region, 563
Chinese Canadian National Council-ON - CCNC Ottawa, 564
Christian Heritage Party of Canada, 567
Christian Labour Association of Canada-Ottawa/Eastern Ontario Regional Office, 568
Church Council on Justice & Corrections, 569
Civic Institute of Professional Personnel, 571
Clan MacLeod Societies of Canada-Ottawa Branch, 572
Climate Action Network - Canada, 573
Coaching Association of Canada, 577
Coalition for Active Living, 578
Coalition of Rail Shippers, 578
Coalition to Oppose the Arms Trade, 579
CODE, 580
Colleges and Institutes Canada, 590
Commission canadienne d'histoire militaire, 592
Commission nationale des parents francophones, 593
Commonwealth Association for Public Administration & Management, 593
Commonwealth Games Canada, 593
Commonwealth Parliamentary Association-Canadian Branch
Commonwealth War Graves Commission - Canadian Agency, 594
Community Foundation of Ottawa, 597
Community Foundations of Canada, 598
Community Information Centre of Ottawa, 599
Compagnie vox théâtre, 608
The Comparative & International Education Society of Canada, 608
The Conference Board of Canada, 611
Conference of Defence Associations, 612
Congress of Aboriginal Peoples, 613
Congress of Union Retirees Canada, 613
Conseil canadien de la coopération et de la mutualité, 613
Conseil de coopération de l'Ontario, 615
Conseil national Société de Saint-Vincent de Paul, 619
Conseil national Société de Saint-Vincent de Paul-Ottawa Central Council, 619
Conservative Party of Canada, 622
Consumer Health Products Canada, 626
Continental Automated Buildings Association, 626
Cooperative Housing Federation of Canada, 628
Co-operatives & Mutuals Canada, 628
Copyright Visual Arts, 628
Council of Canadian Academies, 633
Council of Canadian Law Deans, 633
The Council of Canadians, 633
The Council on Aging of Ottawa, 635
CPJ Corp., 638
Credit Counselling Society-Ottawa, 640
Cree-Naskapi Commission, 641
CropLife Canada, 643
Cultural Human Resources Council, 645
CUSO International, 646
Customs & Immigration Union, 646
Cycling Canada Cyclisme, 647
Dairy Farmers of Canada, 648
The Danish Club of Ottawa, 650
Democracy Watch, 653
Development & Peace-Ontario - Eastern, 655
Canadian Diabetes Association-Ottawa & District Branch, 656
Dignity Canada Dignité, 657
Disabled Peoples' International, 658

Distress Centre of Ottawa & Region, 659
Diving Plongeon Canada, 659
Dominion of Canada Rifle Association, 660
Dr. James Naismith Basketball Foundation, 662
Dress for Success-Ottawa, 663
Dutch-Canadian Association Ottawa Valley/Outaouais, 665
The Easter Seal Society (Ontario)-Eastern Region - Ottawa, 670
Ecojustice Canada Society-Ecojustice Environmental Law Clinic at the University of Ottawa, 672
Editors' Association of Canada-National Capital Region, 674
Egg Farmers of Canada, 681
Electric Vehicle Council of Ottawa, 682
Electricity Human Resources Canada, 683
Embroiderers' Association of Canada, Inc.-Ontario - Ottawa Valley Guild of Stitchery, 686
Energy Council of Canada, 688
The Engineering Institute of Canada, 688
Engineers Canada, 689
Engineers Canada, 689
Entomological Society of Canada, 690
Entomological Society of Ontario, 690
Environmental Health Association of Ontario, 692
Epilepsy Ontario-Ottawa-Carleton, 694
Equestrian Canada, 694
ETC Group, 697
Ethics Practitioners' Association of Canada, 697
Ethiopiaid, 697
Evangelical Fellowship of Canada-Centre for Faith & Public Life, 698
Experiences Canada, 699
Family Enterprise Xchange-FEX Ottawa, 703
Family Service Canada, 704
Family Service Centre of Ottawa-Carleton, 704
Farm Management Canada, 705
Farm Radio International, 705
Farmers of North America Strategic Agriculture Institute-Ottawa Office, 706
Federal Association of Security Officials, 706
Federal Liberal Association of Nunavut, 706
Fédération culturelle canadienne-française, 708
Fédération de la jeunesse canadienne-française inc., 709
Fédération de la jeunesse franco-ontarienne, 709
Fédération des aînés et aînés francophones du Canada, 711
Fédération des aînés et des retraités francophones de l'Ontario, 711
Fédération des communautés francophones et acadienne du Canada, 713
Federation of Canada-China Friendship Associations - Ottawa Chapter, 722
Federation of Canadian Municipalities, 723
Federation of Law Societies of Canada, 724
Federation of Medical Regulatory Authorities of Canada, 724
Federation of Medical Regulatory Authorities of Canada, 724
Federation of Medical Women of Canada, 724
Feminist Alliance for International Action, 731
Fenestration Canada, 732
Fertilizer Canada, 732
Fertilizer Safety & Security Council, 733
Financial Management Institute of Canada, 737
Fire Prevention Canada, 738
First Nations Child & Family Caring Society of Canada, 738
First Nations Confederacy of Cultural Education Centres, 738
Fisheries Council of Canada, 739
Flowers Canada, 741
Fondation franco-ontarienne, 746
Fondation Richelieu International, 748
Food Processors of Canada, 750
Football Canada, 750
Forest Products Association of Canada, 751
Forum for International Trade Training, 754
Forum of Federations, 755
Foster Parents Association of Ottawa, 755

Geographic Index / Ontario - Ottawa

Foundation for Educational Exchange Between Canada & the United States of America, 755
Foundation for Legal Research, 755
Freight Management Association of Canada, 759
Frequency Co-ordination System Association, 760
The Friends of Library & Archives Canada, 761
Friends of The Canadian War Museum, 762
Friends of the Central Experimental Farm, 762
Friends of the Earth Canada, 762
Frontier Duty Free Association, 763
Funeral Service Association of Canada, 764
Fur Institute of Canada, 765
Further Poultry Processors Association of Canada, 765
Gatineau Gliding Club, 768
Genome Canada, 769
Geomatics Industry Association of Canada, 770
George Grant Society, 770
Government Services Union, 778
Governor General's Performing Arts Awards Foundation, 778
Grain Growers of Canada, 779
Grand Council of the Crees-Bureau de Ottawa, 779
GRAND Society-Ottawa Chapter, 780
Green Party of Canada, 788
Greenspace Alliance of Canada's Capital, 789
Group of 78, 791
Gymnastics Canada Gymnastique, 795
Habitat for Humanity Canada-Ontario - Greater Ottawa, 797
Harold Crabtree Foundation, 804
Health Care Public Relations Association, 806
Health Charities Coalition of Canada, 806
HealthBridge Foundation of Canada, 807
HealthCareCAN, 807
Healthy Indoors Partnership, 807
Heart & Stroke Foundation of Canada, 808
Heart & Stroke Foundation of Ontario-Ottawa Office, 809
Helicopter Association of Canada, 811
HelpAge Canada, 812
Heritage Ottawa, 813
Historical Society of Ottawa, 816
Hockey Canada, 817
Hockey Eastern Ontario, 817
Hong Kong-Canada Business Association-Ottawa Section Office, 820
Hostelling International - Canada, 823
Hotel Association of Canada Inc., 823
House of Commons Security Services Employees Association, 824
Human Concern International, 824
Human Rights Internet, 826
Human Rights Research & Education Centre, 826
Humanist Canada, 826
IAESTE Canada (International Association for the Exchange of Students for Technical Experience), 829
IBD Foundation, 829
I.C.C. Foundation, 829
ICOM Museums Canada, 829
ICOMOS Canada, 829
Illuminating Engineering Society of North America-National Capital Section
Immigrant Women Services Ottawa, 831
Immunize Canada, 831
Independent Filmmakers' Co-operative of Ottawa, 832
Independent Living Canada, 833
Indigenous Bar Association, 834
Industrial Fabrics Association International Canada, 835
Information & Communications Technology Council of Canada, 836
Information Systems Security Association-Ottawa Chapter, 1532
Information Technology Association of Canada-Ottawa Office, 837
InformCanada, 838
Inner Peace Movement of Canada, 839
Innovative Medicines Canada, 839

Institute of Chartered Secretaries & Administrators - Canadian Division, 845
Institute of Professional Management, 847
Institute On Governance, 848
Insurance Bureau of Canada-Ottawa Office, 849
Insurance Institute of Ontario-Ottawa Chapter, 850
Intellectual Property Institute of Canada, 850
Inter Pares, 851
Inter-American Commercial Arbitration Commission-Canadian National Section, 851
International Academy of Science, Engineering & Technology, 853
International Association for Educational & Vocational Guidance, 853
International Association of Fire Fighters (AFL-CIO/CLC)-Canadian Office, 1538
International Cheese Council of Canada, 855
International Commission of Jurists (Canadian Section), 855
International Commission on Radiological Protection, 855
International Council for Canadian Studies, 855
International Development Research Centre, 856
International Electrotechnical Commission - Canadian National Committee, 857
International Fund for Animal Welfare Canada, 857
International Ringette Federation - Canada, 859
International Social Service Canada, 860
International Society for the History of Medicine - Canadian Section, 860
International Union of Bricklayers & Allied Craftworkers (AFL-CIO/CFL)-Canadian Office, 1564
Inuit Community Centre, 862
Inuit Tapiriit Kanatami, 862
Inventors Association of Ottawa, 862
Invest Ottawa, 862
Islamic Care Centre, 864
Jaku Konbit, 867
Jamaican Ottawa Community Association, 867
Jewish Family Services of Ottawa-Carleton, 872
Jewish Immigrant Aid Services of Canada, 873
JMJ Children's Fund of Canada Inc, 873
The John Howard Society of Ontario-Ottawa, 875
Judo Canada, 876
Junior Achievement of Canada-Junior Achievement of Ottawa, 877
K3C Community Counselling Centres-K3C Credit Counselling Ottawa - Carling Ave., 879
K3C Community Counselling Centres-K3C Credit Counselling Ottawa - McArthur Ave., 879
The Kidney Foundation of Canada-Eastern Ontario Chapter, 885
Kind Space, 888
Korean Canadian Association of Ottawa, 893
Learning Disabilities Association of Canada, 904
The Leukemia & Lymphoma Society of Canada-Ontario Branch - Ottawa, 909
The Liberal Party of Canada, 909
The Libertarian Party of Canada, 909
Little League Canada, 915
Livres Canada Books, 915
Madonna House Apostolate-Ottawa, 925
Manitoba Association of Prosthetists & Orthotists, 931
The Company of Master Mariners of Canada-Capital Division, 953
MATCH International Women's Fund, 954
Mechanical Contractors Association of Canada, 956
Mechanical Contractors Association of Ottawa, 957
Mechanical Service Contractors of Canada, 957
Media Smarts, 957
Medical Council of Canada, 958
Métis Nation of Ontario, 963
Métis National Council, 963

Michaëlle Jean Foundation, 964
Miniature Horse Association of Canada, 966
Mining Association of Canada, 967
MiningWatch Canada, 968
Motorsport Club of Ottawa, 976
Multiple Birth Families Association, 979
Murray Grey International, Incorporated, 982
Music for Young Children-Ontario - Eastern, 984
Na'amat Canada Inc.-Ottawa Council, 987
NAIMA Canada, 987
National Aboriginal Capital Corporations Association, 988
National Aboriginal Forestry Association, 988
National Alliance for Children & Youth, 989
National Arts Centre Foundation, 989
National Arts Centre Orchestra of Canada, 989
National Association of Canadians of Origins in India, 990
National Association of Career Colleges, 990
National Association of Federal Retirees, 990
National Association of Friendship Centres, 990
National Association of Pharmacy Regulatory Authorities, 990
National Campus & Community Radio Association, 991
National Capital FreeNet, 991
National Congress of Italian-Canadians-National Capital Region, 991
National Council of Canadian Filipino Associations, 991
National Council of Canadian Muslims, 991
National Council of Veteran Associations, 992
The National Council of Women of Canada, 992
National Council on Ethics in Human Research, 992
National Dental Assisting Examining Board, 992
National Dental Examining Board of Canada, 992
National Dental Hygiene Certification Board, 992
National Educational Association of Disabled Students, 993
National Golf Course Owners Association Canada, 993
National Health Union, 994
National Inuit Youth Council, 994
National Judicial Institute, 994
National Literacy & Health Program, 994
National Organization of Immigrant & Visible Minority Women of Canada, 995
National Press Club of Canada Foundation, 995
National Trade Contractors Coalition of Canada, 996
National Trust for Canada, 996
Natural Resources Union, 999
Natural Sciences & Engineering Research Council of Canada, 999
The Natural Step Canada, 999
Nature Canada, 999
The Naval Officers' Association of Canada, 1001
Navy League of Canada, 1001
The Neil Squire Foundation-Central Regional Office, 1002
New Beginnings for Youth, 1004
New Democratic Party, 1014
Non-Smokers' Rights Association-Ottawa, 1028
Northern Youth Abroad Program, 1035
The North-South Institute, 1036
NSERC Chair for Women in Science & Engineering, 1050
NSERC Chair for Women in Science & Engineering-Ontario, 1050
Odawa Native Friendship Centre, 1054
The Olde Forge Community Resource Centre, 1056
One World Arts, 1058
The Ontario Archaeological Society Inc.-Ottawa Chapter, 1060
Ontario Bobsleigh Skeleton Association, 1068
Ontario Brain Injury Association-Ottawa, 1069
Ontario Cerebral Palsy Sports Association, 1071

Ontario Genealogical Society-Ottawa Branch, 1082
Ontario Home Builders' Association-Greater Ottawa, 1085
Ontario Luge Association, 1089
Ontario Lung Association-Ottawa Office (Ottawa, Renfrew County, & Cornwall Area), 1090
Ontario Public Interest Research Group-OPIRG Carleton, 1099
Ontario Society for the Prevention of Cruelty to Animals-Ottawa Branch (Affiliate), 1106
Ontario Weightlifting Association, 1113
Operation Come Home, 1115
Operation Lifesaver, 1115
Operative Plasterers' & Cement Masons' International Association of the US & Canada (AFL-CIO/CFL) - Canadian Office, 1116
Order of Malta - Canadian Association, 1119
The Order of St. Lazarus, 1119
L'Ordinariat militaire Catholique Romain du Canada, 1119
Orthodox Church in America Archdiocese of Canada, 1127
Orthotics Prosthetics Canada, 1127
Ottawa & District Labour Council, 1129
Ottawa Arts Council, 1129
Ottawa Association of People Who Stutter, 1129
Ottawa Baptist Association, 1129
Ottawa Carleton Ultimate Association, 1129
Ottawa Chamber of Commerce, 1129
Ottawa Chamber Orchestra, 1129
Ottawa Chinese Community Services Centre, 1129
Ottawa Community Immigrant Services Organization, 1130
Ottawa Construction Association, 1130
Ottawa District Minor Hockey Association, 1130
Ottawa Duck Club, 1130
Ottawa Economics Association, 1130
Ottawa Field-Naturalists' Club, 1130
Ottawa Food Bank, 1130
Ottawa Humane Society, 1130
Ottawa Independent Writers, 1130
Ottawa Japanese Community Association Inc., 1131
Ottawa Muslim Association, 1131
Ottawa New Car Dealers Association, 1131
Ottawa Numismatic Society, 1131
Ottawa Orchid Society, 1131
Ottawa Police Association, 1131
Ottawa Rape Crisis Centre, 1131
Ottawa Real Estate Board, 1131
Ottawa Riverkeeper, 1131
Ottawa South Community Association, 1131
Ottawa Sports Hall of Fame Inc., 1131
Ottawa Symphony Orchestra Inc., 1132
Ottawa Tamil Seniors Association, 1132
Ottawa Tourism, 1132
Ottawa Valley Curling Association, 1132
Ottawa Valley Health Libraries Association, 1132
Ottawa Valley Rock Garden & Horticultural Society, 1132
Ottawa Youth Orchestra Academy, 1132
Oxfam Canada, 1134
Paramedic Association of Canada, 1138
Parent Finders Ottawa, 1139
Parents partenaires en éducation, 1140
Parkinson Society of Eastern Ontario, 1141
Parliamentary Centre, 1142
Pathways to Education Canada-Pathways to Education - Ottawa, 1145
Pauktuutit Inuit Women of Canada, 1146
Peace & Environment Resource Centre, 1146
Peace Brigades International (Canada), 1146
Peacebuild: The Canadian Peacebuilding Network, 1147
People, Words & Change, 1152
Pet Industry Joint Advisory Council, 1153
PFLAG Canada Inc., 1155
PFLAG Canada Inc.-Ottawa Chapter, 1155
Physical & Health Education Canada, 1158
Physicians for a Smoke-Free Canada, 1158

Physicians for Global Survival (Canada), 1158
PIJAC Canada, 1159
Planetary Association for Clean Energy, Inc., 1161
Planned Parenthood Ottawa, 1161
Police Sector Council, 1163
A Post Psychiatric Leisure Experience, 1167
Postal History Society of Canada, 1168
Probation Officers Association of Ontario-Eastern Branch, 1181
Professional Association of Foreign Service Officers, 1182
Professional Engineers Ontario-Ottawa, 1184
The Professional Institute of the Public Service of Canada, 1185
The Professional Institute of the Public Service of Canada-National Capital Region, 1185
Professional Surveyors Canada, 1186
Progressive Canadian Party, 1187
Project Management Institute-Ottawa Valley Outaouais
The Public Interest Advocacy Centre, 1192
Public Service Alliance of Canada, 1193
Public Service Alliance of Canada-National Capital Region Branch, 1193
Public Service Alliance of Canada-Ottawa Branch, 1193
RA Stamp Club, 1202
Radio Advisory Board of Canada, 1202
Radio Amateurs of Canada Inc., 1202
Railway Association of Canada, 1203
Reach Canada, 1204
Real Estate Institute of Canada-Ontario - Ottawa Chapter, 1206
REAL Women of Canada, 1206
The Recreation Association, 1207
Regroupement des éditeurs canadiens-français, 1215
Regroupement des personnes vivant avec le VIH-sida de Québec et la région, 1215
Renewable Industries Canada, 1217
Research Council Employees' Association (Ind.), 1218
Réseau de développement économique et d'employabilité Ontario, 1219
Réseau des cégeps et des collèges francophones du Canada, 1219
Réseau des services de santé en français de l'Est de l'Ontario, 1222
Réseau du patrimoine franco-ontarien, 1222
Réseau pour le développement de l'alphabétisation et des compétences, 1225
Resident Doctors of Canada, 1226
Richelieu International, 1229
Rideau Trail Association-Ottawa Rideau Trail Club, 1231
Ringette Canada, 1232
Royal Architectural Institute of Canada, 1237
The Royal Canadian Geographical Society, 1239
The Royal Canadian Legion, 1240
Royal Canadian Mounted Police Veterans' Association, 1240
Royal Canadian Naval Benevolent Fund, 1240
The Royal College of Physicians & Surgeons of Canada, 1241
The Royal Commonwealth Society of Canada, 1241
The Royal Commonwealth Society of Canada-Ottawa Branch, 1242
Royal Heraldry Society of Canada, 1242
The Royal Society of Canada, 1242
Saint Elizabeth Health Care-Ottawa - Champlain Service Delivery Centre, 1246
St. John Ambulance, 1248
St. John Ambulance-Federal District Council (Ottawa Area), 1249
St. Leonard's Society of Canada, 1250
SalvAide, 1252
Saskatchewan Association of Prosthetists & Orthotists, 1257
Schizophrenia Society of Ontario-Ottawa Region, 1284
Scouts Canada, 1286
Scouts Canada-Northern Ontario Council, 1287
Scouts Canada-Voyageur Council, 1286
Senate Protective Service Employees Association, 1290
Serena Canada, 1290
Serena Canada-Ontario Branch, 1290
Sexual Assault Support Centre Ottawa, 1293
Sierra Club of Canada, 1298
Sierra Youth Coalition, 1298
Sign Language Interpreters of the National Capital, 1299
Skate Canada, 1301
Ski Hawks Ottawa, 1302
Skills Canada, 1302
Skills/Compétences Canada, 1302
Sledge Hockey of Canada, 1303
Soaring Association of Canada, 1305
Social Planning Council of Ottawa, 1306
Société Santé en français, 1325
Society for the Study of Architecture in Canada, 1327
Society of Fire Protection Engineers-National Capital Region
Society of Graphic Designers of Canada, 1329
Society of Gynecologic Oncologists of Canada, 1329
Society of Obstetricians & Gynaecologists of Canada, 1330
Soeurs de Sainte-Marie de Namur, 1331
SOS Children's Villages Canada, 1333
South Asia Partnership Canada, 1334
Speech-Language & Audiology Canada, 1341
Speed Skating Canada, 1341
Spinal Cord Injury Canada, 1343
Spinal Cord Injury Ontario-Ottawa Office, 1343
Startup Canada, 1348
Statistical Society of Canada, 1348
Stem Cell Network, 1349
Student Christian Movement of Canada-Central Region, 1352
Sustainable Development Technology Canada, 1357
Swimming Canada, 1359
Synchro Canada, 1360
Table Tennis Canada, 1366
Teamsters Canada Rail Conference, 1368
Tel-Aide Outaouais, 1369
Théâtre Action, 1373
Théâtre de la Vieille 17, 1374
Théâtre du Trillium, 1374
Théâtre la Catapulte, 1374
Thermal Insulation Association of Canada, 1376
Tourism Industry Association of Canada, 1389
Trade Facilitation Office Canada, 1394
Traffic Injury Research Foundation, 1394
Transport Action Canada, 1395
Transportation Association of Canada, 1395
Travel and Tourism Research Association (Canada Chapter), 1396
Tree Canada Foundation, 1397
Trucking Human Resources Canada, 1399
True Sport Foundation, 1399
Turner's Syndrome Society, 1400
Ukrainian Canadian Civil Liberties Association, 1402
Ukrainian Youth Association of Canada-Ottawa Branch, 1404
Underwriters' Laboratories of Canada-Ottawa Site, 1404
UNICEF Canada-UNICEF Carleton, 1405
UNIFOR-Ottawa, 1405
UNIFOR-Ottawa, 1405
Uniform Law Conference of Canada, 1405
L'Union culturelle des Franco-Ontariennes, 1406
Union of Canadian Transportation Employees, 1407
Union of Environment Workers, 1407
Union of National Defence Employees, 1407
Union of National Employees, 1407
Union of Postal Communications Employees, 1408
Union of Solicitor General Employees, 1408
Union of Taxation Employees, 1408
Union of Veterans' Affairs Employees, 1408
UNITE HERE Canada-Ottawa Chapter, 1408
United Association of Journeymen & Apprentices of the Plumbing & Pipe Fitting Industry of the U.S. & Canada (AFL-CIO/CFL)-Canadian Office
United Nations Association in Canada, 1411
United Nations Association in Canada-National Capital Region, 1411
United Nations Educational, Scientific & Cultural Organization: Canadian Commission for UNESCO, 1411
United Nations Entity for Gender Equality & the Empowerment of Women - National Committee Canada, 1412
United Nations High Commissioner for Refugees, 1412
United Way of Canada - Centraide Canada, 1413
United Way/Centraide Ottawa, 1418
Universities Canada, 1418
USC Canada, 1423
USC Canada, 1423
Vanier Institute of The Family, 1429
Victims of Violence, 1432
Victorian Order of Nurses for Canada, 1434
Vietnamese Canadian Federation, 1434
Vitesse, 1436
Volleyball Canada, 1437
Volunteer Canada, 1438
Volunteer Circle of the National Gallery of Canada, 1438
The War Amputations of Canada, 1440
Water Polo Canada, 1441
Water Ski & Wakeboard Canada, 1441
WaterCan, 1442
Wildlife Habitat Canada, 1454
Women's Business Network of Ottawa, 1462
Wood Manufacturing Council, 1463
Wood Preservation Canada, 1463
World Border Organization, 1465
World Federalist Movement - Canada, 1465
World Sikh Organization of Canada, 1467
World University Service of Canada, 1467
World Wildlife Fund - Canada-Ottawa, 1468
YMCA Canada-YMCA-YWCA of the National Capital Region, 1471
Youth in Care Canada, 1475

Otterville
South Norwich Historical Society, 1335

Owen Sound
Alzheimer Society of Grey-Bruce, 62
Bruce Grey Child & Family Services, 260
The Bruce Trail Conservancy-Sydenham, 261
Community Living Owen Sound & District, 604
Federation of Ontario Law Associations, 725
The Garden Clubs of Ontario-Georgian Bay, 767
Georgian Bay Folk Society, 771
Georgian Bay Symphony, 771
Grey County Kiwanis Festival of Music, 790
Grey County Law Association, 790
Habitat for Humanity Canada-Ontario - Grey Bruce, 797
Heart & Stroke Foundation of Ontario-Owen Sound Office, 809
Ontario Genealogical Society-Bruce & Grey Branch, 1081
Ontario Home Builders' Association-Grey - Bruce, 1085
Owen Sound & District Chamber of Commerce, 1134
YMCA Canada-YMCA of Owen Sound Grey Bruce, 1471

Palgrave
Christmas Tree Farmers of Ontario, 568

Palmer Rapids
Boundless Adventures Association, 219

Paris
Canadian Deafblind Association (National)-Ontario Chapter, 376
Central Canada Broadcast Engineers, 524
Paris & District Chamber of Commerce, 1140

Parry Sound
Alliance for Canadian New Music Projects-Contemporary Showcase - Parry Sound, 56
Artists in Stained Glass, 85
Community Living Parry Sound, 604
Community Living Parry Sound-Addie St. Residence, 604
Parry Sound & Area Association of REALTORS, 1143
Parry Sound Area Chamber of Commerce, 1143
Parry Sound Friendship Centre, 1143

Pembroke
Boys & Girls Clubs of Ontario-Boys & Girls Clubs of Pembroke, 223
Canadian Office & Professional Employees Union-Region 2 - Local 103, 444
Community Living Upper Ottawa Valley, 605
Family & Children's Services of Renfrew County, 702
Ontario Society for the Prevention of Cruelty to Animals-Renfrew Branch, 1106
Ottawa Valley Historical Society, 1132
Ottawa Valley Tourist Association, 1132
Pembroke Area Field Naturalists, 1149
Pembroke District Construction Association, 1149
Pembroke Kiwanis Music Festival, 1149
Pembroke Symphony Orchestra, 1149
Renfrew County Child Poverty Action Network, 1217
Renfrew County Law Association, 1217
Renfrew County Real Estate Board, 1217
Renfrew County United Way, 1217
Sisters of Saint Joseph of Pembroke, 1301
Start Right Coalition for Financial Literacy, 1348
Upper Ottawa Valley Chamber of Commerce, 1422

Penetanguishene
Boating Ontario, 216
Dive Ontario, 659
The Friends of Awenda Park, 760
Independent Canadian Extrusion Workers Union, 832
Southern Georgian Bay Chamber of Commerce-Penetanguishene Tourist Information Centre, 1338
Waypoint Centre for Mental Health Care, 1443

Perth
Alzheimer Society of Lanark County, 63
Ontario Home Builders' Association-Lanark - Leeds, 1085
Perth & District Chamber of Commerce, 1152
Rideau Trail Association-Central Rideau Trail Club, 1231
Rideau Valley Field Naturalists, 1231

Petawawa
The Royal Canadian Regiment Association, 1241

Peterborough
Alcoholics Anonymous-Peterborough - Kawartha District Intergroup, 52
Alzheimer Society Peterborough, Kawartha Lakes, Northumberland, & Haliburton, 65
Bereaved Families of Ontario-Peterborough, 205
Canadian Association of Elizabeth Fry Societies-Elizabeth Fry Society of Peterborough, 313
Canadian Association of Veterans in United Nations Peacekeeping-Peterborough Chapter, 336
Canadian Authors Association-Peterborough (Peterborough & Area Branch), 338
Canadian Blood Services-Peterborough, 345
The Canadian Continence Foundation, 364
Canadian Hearing Society-Peterborough Office, 403
Canadian Institute of Food Science & Technology-Ontario Section, 416
Community Care Peterborough, 596

Community Counselling & Resource Centre, 596
Community Living Peterborough, 604
Council of Ontario Construction Associations-Peterborough Construction Association, 634
Down Syndrome Association of Ontario, 661
Employees Association of Milltronics - CNFIU Local 3005, 686
Epilepsy Ontario-Peterborough & Area, 694
Federation of Ontario Cottagers' Associations, 725
Greater Peterborough Chamber of Commerce, 784
Green Communities Canada, 788
Habitat for Humanity Canada-Ontario - Peterborough & Kawartha Region, 797
Heart & Stroke Foundation of Ontario-Peterborough Office, 809
Jamaican Self-Help Organization, 867
The John Howard Society of Ontario-Peterborough, 875
Junior Achievement of Canada-Junior Achievement of Peterborough, Lakeland & Muskoka, 877
Kawartha Sexual Assault Centre, 882
Kawartha World Issues Centre, 882
Kawartha-Haliburton Children's Aid Society, 882
Literacy Ontario Central South, 914
New Canadians Centre Peterborough Immigrant Services, 1013
Ontario Brain Injury Association-Peterborough, 1069
Ontario Federation of Anglers & Hunters, 1079
Ontario Genealogical Society-Kawartha Branch, 1082
Ontario Home Builders' Association-Peterborough & The Kawarthas, 1085
Ontario Public Interest Research Group-OPIRG Peterborough, 1099
Ontario Society for the Prevention of Cruelty to Animals-Peterborough Branch (Affiliate), 1106
Ontario Waterpower Association, 1113
Orchestras Canada, 1117
Osteoporosis Canada-Peterborough Chapter, 1128
PARD Therapeutic Riding, 1139
PARN Your Community AIDS Resource Network, 1143
People First of Ontario-Peterborough Chapter, 1151
Peterborough & District Labour Council, 1153
Peterborough & the Kawarthas Association of Realtors Inc., 1153
Peterborough & the Kawarthas Tourism, 1153
Peterborough Field Naturalists, 1153
Peterborough Historical Society, 1153
Peterborough Law Association, 1153
Peterborough Numismatic Club, 1153
Peterborough Police Association, 1154
Peterborough Social Planning Council, 1154
Peterborough Symphony Orchestra, 1154
St. Leonard's Society of Canada-St. Leonard's Society of Peterborough, 1250
Schizophrenia Society of Ontario-Peterborough/Durham Region, 1284
Sisters of Saint Joseph of Peterborough, 1301
Soroptimist Foundation of Canada, 1333
Trent University Faculty Association, 1397
United Way of Peterborough & District, 1416
YMCA Canada-YMCA of Central East Ontario - Peterborough, 1472
YWCA Canada-YWCA Peterborough Haliburton, 1481

Petrolia
CADORA Ontario Association Inc.-London Chapter, 269
Lambton County Developmental Services, 897
Lambton County Historical Society, 897
Petrolia Discovery, 1155

Pickering
Alianza Hispano-Canadiense Ontario, 54
Architectural Glass & Metal Contractors Association, 78
Camping in Ontario, 277
Canadian Federation of Business & Professional Women's Clubs-Durham, 385
The Canadian Laser and Aesthetic Specialists Society, 425
Canadian Paper Money Society, 449
Children's Wish Foundation of Canada, 562
Children's Wish Foundation of Canada-Ontario Chapter, 563
FIRST Robotics Canada, 739
Helping Other Parents Everywhere Inc., 812
International Dyslexia Association-Ontario Branch
Neurofibromatosis Society of Ontario, 1003
One Parent Families Association of Canada, 1058
Ontario Aerospace Council, 1058
Ontario Curling Association, 1076
Organization of Canadian Nuclear Industries, 1125
Pharmaceutical Advertising Advisory Board, 1156
Pickering Naturalists, 1159
Project Management Institute-Durham Highlands
Scarborough Coin Club, 1282
Youth Science Canada, 1476

Picton
Community Living Prince Edward (County), 604
The Friends of Sandbanks Park, 762
Highland Shores Children's Aid-Picton, 814
Picton United Church County Food Bank, 1159
Prince Edward County Arts Council, 1171
Prince Edward County Chamber of Tourism & Commerce, 1171

Plantagenet
Valoris for Children & Adults of Prescott-Russell, 1424

Plattsville
Canadian Dove Association, 378

Pointe-au-Baril-Station
Pointe-au-Baril Chamber of Commerce, 1163

Poland
Association of Polish Engineers in Canada-Ottawa Branch, 156

Port Carling
Muskoka Lakes Association, 985
Muskoka Ratepayers' Association, 985

Port Colborne
Community Living Port Colborne-Wainfleet, 604
Operation Mobilization Canada, 1116
Port Colborne Community Association for Research Extension, 1165
Port Colborne-Wainfleet Chamber of Commerce, 1165

Port Dover
ACUC International, 7
Port Dover Board of Trade, 1165

Port Elgin
Canadian Agri-Marketing Association, 290
Canadian Agri-Marketing Association (Alberta), 290
The Friends of MacGregor Point, 761
Saugeen Shores Chamber of Commerce, 1280
UNIFOR-Port Elgin Office (Family Education Centre), 1405

Port Hope
Cameco Capitol Arts Centre, 276
Canadian Cosmetics Careers Association Inc., 366
La Jeunesse Youth Orchestra, 870
Municipality of Port Hope Historical Society, 982
Ontario Institute of Agrologists-Quinte Branch, 1087
Ontario Society for the Prevention of Cruelty to Animals-Northumberland Branch (Affiliate), 1106
Port Hope & District Chamber of Commerce, 1166
Willow Beach Field Naturalists, 1455

Port McNicoll
Ontario Society for the Prevention of Cruelty to Animals-Midland & District Branch, 1106

Port Perry
Appaloosa Horse Club of Canada-Kawartha Regional Appaloosa Horse Club, 73
Canadian Morgan Horse Association, 437
Community Living Durham North, 601
Scugog Chamber of Commerce, 1287
Whitewater Ontario, 1453

Port Robinson
Niagara Support Services, 1026

Port Rowan
Bird Studies Canada, 212
United Empire Loyalists' Association of Canada-Grand River Branch, 1410

Port Severn
Southeast Georgian Bay Chamber of Commerce, 1337

Port Sydney
Hearth, Patio & Barbecue Association of Canada, 809
Port Sydney/Utterson & Area Chamber of Commerce, 1166

Portland
Big Rideau Lake Association, 210

Powassan
Richmond Club of Toronto, 1230

Prescott
Grenville County Historical Society, 789
Skate Canada-Eastern Ontario Section, 1301
South Grenville Chamber of Commerce, 1334

Princeton
Canadian Pony Society, 458

Procton Station
Dundalk Historical Society, 664

Puslinch
Canadian National Baton Twirling Association, 438
Eastern Canadian Galloway Association, 670
Poultry Industry Council, 1168
Sunrise Therapeutic Riding & Learning Centre, 1354

Queenston
Ontario Monument Builders Association, 1091

Queensville
Magnificat Charismatic Prayer Community, 925

Rainy River
Rainy River & District Chamber of Commerce, 1204

Rama
Ogemawahj Tribal Council, 1055

Red Lake
Family & Children's Services of the District of Rainy River-Red Lake Office, 702
Red Lake & District Association for Community Living, 1210
Red Lake District Chamber of Commerce, 1210
Red Lake Indian Friendship Centre, 1210

Renfrew
Armed Forces Pensioners'/Annuitants' Association of Canada, 82
Association of Accrediting Agencies of Canada, 138
Canadian Die Casters Association, 378
Canadian Evaluation Society, 383
Community Living Renfrew County South, 604
Family & Child Services of Renfrew County-Renfrew Office, 702
Ontario Powerlifting Association, 1097
Renfrew & Area Chamber of Commerce, 1217
Renfrew & District Food Bank, 1217
Renfrew & District Historical Society, 1217
Upper Ottawa Valley Beekeepers' Association, 1422
Vocational Rehabilitation Association of Canada, 1436

Richmond
Canadian Sport Horse Association, 489
Earth Energy Society of Canada, 667
Richmond Agricultural Society, 1229
Tunnelling Association of Canada, 1400

Richmond Hill
AIDS Committee of York Region, 17
Aplastic Anemia & Myelodysplasia Association of Canada, 73
L'Arche Foundation, 77
L'Arche Ontario-L'Arche Daybreak, 77
Architectural Woodwork Manufacturers Association of Canada - Ontario Chapter, 79
Arts Richmond Hill, 86
Association of Jewish Libraries (Toronto), 150
ATM Industry Association Canada Region, 187
Canadian Federation of Aromatherapists, 385
Canadian Junior Golf Association, 423
Canadian Spinal Research Organization, 489
Carefirst Seniors & Community Services Association-York Region Community Services Centre, 511
Community Living York South, 606
COSTI Immigrant Services-Richmond Hill - Language, Settlement & Skills Training Services, 632
Council of Ontario Construction Associations-Toronto Construction Association, 634
Environmental Abatement Council of Ontario, 691
Epilepsy Ontario-York Region, 694
Evangelical Fellowship of Canada, 698
Federation of North American Explorers, 725
Filipino Canadian Catholic Charismatic Prayer Communities, 735
Foundation for Prader-Willi Research in Canada, 756
Fountain of Love & Life, 756
Heart & Stroke Foundation of Ontario-York South Office, 809
Huntington Society of Canada-Individual & Family Services, 827
Institute of Municipal Assessors, 846
Mon Sheong Foundation, 971
Motor Carrier Passenger Council of Canada, 975
Ontario Arms Collectors' Association, 1060
Ontario Association of Residents' Councils, 1066
Ontario Brain Injury Association-Richmond Hill, 1069
Ontario Equestrian Federation, 1078
Ontario Floorball Association, 1080
Ontario Horse Trials Association, 1086
Ontario Minor Hockey Association, 1091
Ontario Sheet Metal Contractors Association, 1104
Ontario Table Tennis Association, 1109
Ontario Urban Forest Council, 1112
PFLAG Canada Inc.-Richmond Hill - York Region Chapter, 1156
Resilient Flooring Contractors Association of Ontario, 1226
Richmond Hill Chamber of Commerce, 1230
Richmond Hill Naturalists, 1230
Rugby Canada, 1244
Sealant & Waterproofing Association, 1288
Service Employees International Union (AFL-CIO/CLC)-SEIU Healthcare
Toronto District Beekeepers' Association, 1384
Toronto Montessori Institute, 1386
Toronto Sheet Metal Contractors Association, 1387
Turkish Community Heritage Centre of Canada, 1400
York Symphony Orchestra Inc., 1474

Ridgetown
Ridgetown & South East Kent Chamber of Commerce, 1232

Ridgeway
Bertie Historical Society, 206
Lupus Foundation of Ontario, 921

Rockland
Canadian Sport Parachuting Association, 490
New Clarence-Rockland Chamber of Commerce, 1014

Rockton
SOSA Gliding Club, 1333

Rockwood
Canadian 4-H Council-Ontario, 284
Standardbred Breeders of Ontario Association, 1347

Rodney
West Elgin Chamber of Commerce, 1445
West Elgin Historical & Genealogical Society, 1445

Roslin
CADORA Ontario Association Inc.-Quinte St. Lawrence CADORA Chapter, 269

Rosseau
Seguin Arts Council, 1289

Russell
Federation of Broomball Associations of Ontario, 722

Rutherglen
Bluegrass Music Association of Canada, 215

Saint-Eugène
Association des fermières de l'Ontario, 114

Saint-Hyacinthe
Institute of Textile Science, 847

Sarnia
Alzheimer Society of Sarnia-Lambton, 64
Boys & Girls Clubs of Ontario-Boys & Girls Club of Sarnia-Lambton, 223
Breast Cancer Society of Canada, 228
Canadian Blood Services-Sarnia, 345
Canadian Hearing Society-Sarnia Office, 403
Canadian Institute of Management-Ontario - Sarnia Branch, 417
Canadian Liver Foundation-Sarnia/Lambton/London Chapter, 427
Chinese Canadian National Council-ON - Lambton Chinese Canadian Association, 564
Community Living Sarnia-Lambton, 605
Council of Ontario Construction Associations-Sarnia Construction Association, 634
Distress Line Sarnia, 659
Financial Fitness Centre-Sarnia Office, 737
Goodwill Industries Essex Kent Lambton, 777
Habitat for Humanity Canada-Ontario - Sarnia/Lambton, 797
Heart & Stroke Foundation of Ontario-Sarnia Office, 809
Information Sarnia Lambton, 837
International Symphony Orchestra of Sarnia, Ontario & Port Huron, Michigan, 861
International Symphony Orchestra Youth String Ensemble, 861
The John Howard Society of Ontario-Sarnia & Lambton, 875
The Kidney Foundation of Canada-Sarnia-Lambton Chapter, 885
Lambton Wildlife Inc., 897
Ontario Brain Injury Association-Sarnia-Lambton, 1069
Ontario Genealogical Society-Lambton County Branch, 1082
Ontario Home Builders' Association-Sarnia Lambton, 1085
Ontario Society for the Prevention of Cruelty to Animals-Sarnia Branch (Affiliate), 1106
Patronato INAS (Canada)-Sarnia Office, 1146
PFLAG Canada Inc.-Sarnia - Sarnia / Bluewater Chapter, 1156
Sarnia & District Humane Society, 1254
Sarnia & District Labour Council, 1254
Sarnia Building Trades Council, 1254
Sarnia Concert Association, 1254
Sarnia Lambton Chamber of Commerce, 1254
Sarnia Minor Athletic Association, 1254
Sarnia-Lambton Environmental Association, 1254
Sarnia-Lambton Real Estate Board, 1254
Sexual Assault Survivors' Centre - Sarnia-Lambton, 1293
Tecumseh Community Development Corporation, 1369
Tourism Sarnia Lambton, 1391
UNIFOR-Sarnia, 1405
United Way of Sarnia-Lambton, 1416
YMCA Canada-YMCAs across Southwestern Ontario - Sarnia—Lambton, 1472

Sauble Beach
Sauble Beach Chamber of Commerce, 1280

Sault Ste Marie
Algoma Arts Festival Association, 53
Algoma District Law Association, 53
Algoma Kinniwabi Travel Association, 53
Alzheimer Society of Sault Ste. Marie & District of Algoma, 64
The Anglican Church of Canada-Diocese of Algoma, 69
Arts Council of Sault Ste Marie & District, 85
Canadian Hearing Society-Sault Ste. Marie Regional Office, 403
Canadian Office & Professional Employees Union-Region 2 - Local 26, 445
Children's Aid Society of Algoma, 560
Clean North, 573
Community Living Algoma, 600
Council of Ontario Construction Associations-Sault Ste Marie Construction Association, 634
Credit Counselling Service of Sault Ste. Marie & District, 639
The Easter Seal Society (Ontario)-Northern Region - Sault Ste. Marie, 670
Habitat for Humanity Canada-Ontario - Sault Ste Marie, 797
Heart & Stroke Foundation of Ontario-Sault Ste. Marie Office, 809
Indian Friendship Centre in Sault Ste Marie, 834
The John Howard Society of Ontario-Sault Ste Marie & District, 875
The Kidney Foundation of Canada-Sault Ste Marie Chapter, 885
Model Aeronautics Association of Canada Inc.-Northern Ontario Zone, 970
Ontario Bailiff Association, 1067
Ontario Brain Injury Association-Sault Ste Marie, 1069
Ontario Lung Association-Sault Ste Marie Office (Algoma Area), 1090
Ontario Society for the Prevention of Cruelty to Animals-Sault Ste. Marie Branch (Affiliate), 1106
Sault Naturalists, 1281
Sault Ste. Marie Music Festival, 1281
Sault Ste Marie & 49th Field Regt. RCA Historical Society, 1281
Sault Ste Marie Chamber of Commerce, 1281
Sault Ste Marie Economic Development Corporation, 1281
Sault Ste Marie Musicians' Association, 1281
Sault Ste Marie Police Association, 1281
Sault Ste Marie Real Estate Board, 1281
Sault Symphony Association, 1281
Spinal Cord Injury Ontario-Sault St. Marie Office, 1344
Therapeutic Ride Algoma, 1375
United Way of Sault Ste Marie & District, 1417
Voyageur Trail Association, 1439
Women In Crisis (Algoma) Inc., 1460
YMCA Canada-YMCA of Sault Ste Marie, 1472

Schomberg
CADORA Ontario Association Inc.-Caledon CADORA Chapter, 269
Canadian Belgian Horse Association, 342
King Chamber of Commerce, 888
Silent Children's Mission, 1299

Seaforth
Foundation for Education Perth Huron, 755
Huron East Chamber of Commerce, 828
Saint Elizabeth Health Care-Seaforth - Huron Service Delivery Centre, 1246

Selwyn
Ontario Cavy Club, 1070

Shannonville
Canadian Race Communications Association, 464

Sharbot Lake
Community Living North Frontenac, 603

Sharon
East Gwillimbury Chamber of Commerce, 668
Toronto Autosport Club, 1382

Shelburne
Active Living Coalition for Older Adults, 7

Simcoe
Alzheimer Society of Haldimand Norfolk, 62
Asparagus Farmers of Ontario, 87
Canadian Titanic Society, 495
Demeter Canada, 653
Embroiderers' Association of Canada, Inc.-Ontario - Norfolk's Own Needle Arts Guild, 686
Haldimand-Norfolk Literacy Council, 798
Norfolk Association for Community Living, 1028
Norfolk County Agricultural Society, 1028
Norfolk Field Naturalists, 1028
Norfolk Historical Society, 1028
Ontario Ginseng Growers Association, 1082
Ontario Home Builders' Association-Haldimand Norfolk, 1085
Ontario Society for the Prevention of Cruelty to Animals-Simcoe & District Branch (Affiliate), 1106
Simcoe & District Chamber of Commerce, 1299
Simcoe & District Real Estate Board, 1299
United Way of Haldimand-Norfolk, 1414

Sioux Lookout
Family & Children's Services of the District of Rainy River-Sioux Lookout Office, 702
First Nations SchoolNet-Ontario Region, 739
Independent First Nations' Alliance, 832
Nishnawbe - Gamik Friendship Centre, 1027
Ojibway Power Toboggan Association, 1055
Shibogama First Nations Council, 1296
Sioux Lookout Chamber of Commerce, 1300
Tikinagan Child & Family Services, 1379
Wawatay Native Communications Society, 1443
Windigo First Nations' Council, 1456

Smiths Falls
Canadian Railroad Historical Association-Rideau Valley Division, 465
Ontario Society for the Prevention of Cruelty to Animals-Lanark Branch (Affiliate), 1106
PFLAG Canada Inc.-Carleton Place/Lanark Chapter, 1155
Rideau Environmental Action League, 1231
Smiths Falls & District Chamber of Commerce, 1304
Smiths Falls & District Historical Society, 1304

Smithville
West Lincoln Chamber of Commerce, 1445
West Lincoln Historical Society & Archives, 1446

Southampton
Bruce County Historical Society, 260

St Agatha
Carizon Family & Community Services-St. Agatha Office, 513

St Andrews
Cornwall Township Historical Society, 629

St Catharines
AIDS Niagara, 17
Alzheimer Society of Niagara Region, 63
Armenian Relief Society of Canada, Inc.-St. Catharines Chapter: "Araz", 83
Association of Day Care Operators of Ontario, 146
Baby's Breath, 192
Brock University Faculty Association, 259
Canada's National Bible Hour, 282
Canadian Accredited Independent Schools, 287
Canadian Authors Association-Niagara Branch, 338
Canadian Blood Services-St Catharines, 345
Canadian Celiac Association-St Catharines Chapter, 352
Canadian Economics Association, 379
Canadian Polish Congress-Niagara Branch, 456
Canadian Polish Society, 457
Canadian Railroad Historical Association-Niagara Division, 465
Carousel Players, 514
Central Ontario Network for Black History, 525
Council of Ontario Construction Associations-Niagara Construction Association, 634
Credit Counselling of Regional Niagara, 639
Distress Centre Niagara Inc., 659
Family & Children's Services Niagara, 701
50 & Piu Enasco-St. Catharines Office, 734
Film Studies Association of Canada, 735
Folk Arts Council of St Catharines, 742
Global Outreach Mission, 775
Greater Niagara Chamber of Commerce, 784
Habitat for Humanity Canada-Ontario - Niagara, 797
Heart & Stroke Foundation of Ontario-Niagara District Office, 809
Historical Society of St. Catharines, 816
Hospice Niagara, 822
Human Resources Professionals Association-Niagara Chapter, 825
Information Niagara, 837
The John Howard Society of Ontario-Niagara, 875
Lincoln County Humane Society, 912
Lincoln County Law Association, 912
Model Aeronautics Association of Canada Inc.-Middle Ontario Zone, 970
National Network for Mental Health, 995
Niagara Action for Animals, 1024
Niagara Association of REALTORS, 1024
Niagara Peninsula Electrical Contractors Association, 1025
Niagara Peninsula Geological Society, 1025
Niagara Region Sexual Assault Centre, 1025
Niagara Youth Orchestra Association, 1026
Ontario Brain Injury Association-St. Catharines, 1069
Ontario Home Builders' Association-Niagara, 1085
Ontario Public Buyers Association, 1098
Ontario Public Interest Research Group-OPIRG Brock, 1099
Ontario Society for the Prevention of Cruelty to Animals-Lincoln Branch (Affiliate), 1106
Ontario Undergraduate Student Alliance-Brock University Students' Union, 1111
Osteoporosis Canada-St. Catharines - Niagara Chapter, 1129
Parents for Children's Mental Health, 1140
Peninsula Field Naturalists, 1149
PFLAG Canada Inc.-Niagara Chapter, 1155
Professional Engineers Ontario-Niagara, 1184
Promoting Awareness of RSD & CRPS in Canada, 1188
St Catharines & District Labour Council, 1248
St Catharines Association for Community Living, 1248
St Catharines Stamp Club, 1248
Slo-Pitch Ontario Association, 1303
UNIFOR-St Catharines, 1405

United Way of St Catharines & District, 1416
YMCA Canada-YMCA of Niagara - St Catharines, 1472
YWCA Canada-YWCA Niagara Region, 1481

St George
Federated Women's Institutes of Canada, 706
Tim Horton Children's Foundation, 1379

St Isidore
PFLAG Canada Inc.-Cornwall Chapter, 1155

St Marys
Community Living St. Marys & Area Association, 604
Ontario Bison Association, 1068
Strategic Leadership Forum, 1351
Stratford Musicians' Association, Local 418 of the American Federation of Musicians, 1351

St Mitchell
Korean Canadian Association of Waterloo & Wellington, 893

St Thomas
Community Living Elgin, 601
George Bray Sports Association, 770
North America Railway Hall of Fame, 1029
Ontario Association of Community Futures Development Corporations, 1063
Ontario Home Builders' Association-St. Thomas & Elgin, 1085
Ontario Rifle Association, 1102
St Thomas & District Chamber of Commerce, 1251
United Way Elgin-St. Thomas, 1413
YMCA Canada-YMCA of Western Ontario - St Thomas—Elgin, 1472
YWCA Canada-YWCA St. Thomas-Elgin, 1481

Staffa
Ontario Simmental Association, 1104

Stirling
Indian Agricultural Program of Ontario, 834
Quinte Beekeepers' Association, 1201
Quinte Therapeutic Riding Association, 1202
United Empire Loyalists' Association of Canada-Bay of Quinte Branch, 1410

Stittsville
Association of Corporate Travel Executives Inc. Canada, 146
Heating, Refrigeration & Air Conditioning Institute of Canada-Ontario - National Capital Region Chapter, 810
Human Resources Professionals Association-Ottawa Chapter, 826

Stoney Creek
Armenian Relief Society of Canada, Inc.-Hamilton Chapter: "Arev", 83
Canadian Association of Numismatic Dealers, 323
Canadian Culinary Federation-Hamilton Branch, 374
Canadian Football League Players' Association, 392
Canadian National Autism Foundation, 438
Federated Women's Institutes of Ontario, 706
Hamilton Food Share, 801
Heating, Refrigeration & Air Conditioning Institute of Canada-Ontario - Golden Horseshoe Chapter, 810
Juvenile Diabetes Research Foundation-Hamilton, 879
PFLAG Canada Inc.-Stoney Creek - Hamilton Chapter, 1156
Racquetball Ontario, 1202
Society of Canadian Cine Amateurs, 1327
Stoney Creek Chamber of Commerce, 1350
Stoney Creek Historical Society, 1350
Ukrainian Self-Reliance League of Canada, 1403

Stouffville
Canadian Examiners in Optometry, 383
Christian Blind Mission International, 566
Emmanuel International Canada, 686
Ontario Genealogical Society-York Region Branch, 1082
Ontario Society for the Prevention of Cruelty to Animals, 1105
Special Needs Planning Group, 1339
Whitchurch-Stouffville Chamber of Commerce, 1452

Straffordville
Otter Valley Chamber of Commerce, 1132

Stratford
Alzheimer Society of Perth County, 64
L'Arche Ontario-L'Arche Stratford, 77
The Avon Trail, 191
Community Living Stratford & Area, 605
County of Perth Law Association, 636
Family Services Perth-Huron, 705
Heart & Stroke Foundation of Ontario-Stratford Office, 809
Huron Perth Association of Realtors, 828
Minor Hockey Alliance of Ontario, 968
Ontario Bean Growers Association, 1067
Ontario Genealogical Society-Perth County Branch, 1082
Ontario Home Builders' Association-Stratford & Area, 1086
Ontario Lung Association-Stratford Office (Huron-Perth), 1090
Prince Edward Island Pharmacists Association, 1176
Rotary Club of Stratford Charitable Foundation, 1236
Stratford & District Chamber of Commerce, 1351
Stratford & District Labour Council, 1351
Stratford Coin Club, 1351
Stratford Tourism Alliance, 1351
United Way of Perth-Huron, 1416
YMCA Canada-YMCA of Stratford—Perth, 1473

Strathroy
Auctioneers Association of Ontario, 187
Middlesex Community Living, 965
Ontario Ground Water Association, 1083
Strathroy & District Chamber of Commerce, 1352

Stratton
Rainy River Beekeepers' Association, 1204

Streetsville
Canadian Federation of Business & Professional Women's Clubs-Mississauga, 385
Ontario Genealogical Society-Halton-Peel Branch, 1082

Sturgeon Falls
Community Living West Nipissing, 606
Literacy Alliance of West Nipissing, 913
West Nipissing Chamber of Commerce, 1446

Sudbury
L'Arche Ontario-L'Arche Sudbury, 77
Canadian Association of Elizabeth Fry Societies-Elizabeth Fry Society of Sudbury, 313
Canadian Association of Science Centres, 332
Canadian Blood Services-Sudbury - National Contact Centre, 345
Canadian Blood Services-Sudbury, 345
Canadian College of Health Leaders-NEON Lights (Northeastern Ontario) Regional Chapter, 359
Canadian Federation of Business & Professional Women's Clubs-Greater Sudbury, 385
Canadian Hard of Hearing Association-Ontario - Sudbury Branch, 400
Canadian Hearing Society-Sudbury Regional Office, 403
Canadian Mining Industry Research Organization, 437
Canadian Polish Congress-Sudbury Branch, 456
Spinal Cord Injury Ontario-Sudbury, 505
Centre franco-ontarien de folklore, 534
Child Find Ontario-Northern Ontario Office, 559
Children's Aid Society of the Districts of Sudbury & Manitoulin, 561
The City of Greater Sudbury Developmental Services, 571
Classical Association of Canada, 572
Community Living Greater Sudbury, 602
Council of Ontario Construction Associations-Northeastern Ontario Construction Association, 634
Cultural Industries Ontario North, 645
The Easter Seal Society (Ontario)-Northern Region - Sudbury, 670
Friends of the Greater Sudbury Public Library, 762
Greater Sudbury Chamber of Commerce, 785
Heart & Stroke Foundation of Ontario-Sudbury Office, 809
Inner City Home of Sudbury, 839
The John Howard Society of Ontario-Sudbury, 875
Laurentian University Faculty Association, 900
Laurentian University Staff Union, 900
Maintenance, Engineering & Reliability (MER) Society, 926
Memorial Society of Northern Ontario, 960
Municipal Law Departments Association of Ontario, 981
N'swakamok Native Friendship Centre, 986
National Retriever Club of Canada, 996
Northeastern Ontario Building & Construction Trades Council, 1034
Northeastern Ontario Tourism, 1034
Northern Ontario Darts Association, 1035
Ontario Brain Injury Association-Sudbury & District, 1069
Ontario Genealogical Society-Sudbury District Branch, 1082
Ontario Home Builders' Association-Sudbury & District, 1086
Ontario Nurses' Association-Sudbury Office, 1094
Ontario Society for the Prevention of Cruelty to Animals-Sudbury & District Branch, 1106
Public Service Alliance of Canada-Sudbury Branch, 1193
Réseau ACCESS Network, 1218
Réseau du mieux-être francophone du Nord de l'Ontario, 1222
St. Leonard's Society of Canada-Larch Halfway House of Sudbury, 1250
Service familial de Sudbury, 1291
Social Planning Council of Sudbury Region, 1306
Société Alzheimer Society Sudbury-Manitoulin, 1307
Sudbury & District Labour Council, 1353
Sudbury Arts Council, 1353
Sudbury Community Service Centre Inc., 1353
Sudbury Manitoulin Children's Foundation, 1353
Sudbury Real Estate Board, 1353
Sudbury Stamp Club, 1353
Sudbury Symphony Orchestra Association Inc., 1353
Sudbury Tourism, 1353
Sudbury Youth Orchestra Inc., 1353
Théâtre du Nouvel-Ontario, 1374
UNIFOR-Sudbury, 1405
United Way/Centraide Sudbury & District, 1418
Village International Sudbury, 1435
YMCA Canada-YMCA of Northeastern Ontario - Sudbury, 1473
YWCA Canada-YWCA Sudbury, 1481

Sutton West
Family Services York Region (Georgina), 705
Georgina Association for Community Living, 771
South Lake Simcoe Naturalists, 1335

Tamworth
Canadian Association of Specialized Kinesiology, 333

Tavistock
Canadian Transplant Association, 496
Pagan Federation International - Canada, 1137
Tavistock Chamber of Commerce, 1367

Tecumseh
Community Living Essex County-Tecumseh - Northshore Office, 602

Temagami
Temagami & District Chamber of Commerce, 1370

Terrace Bay
Aguasabon Chamber of Commerce, 15

Thamesville
Centre for Indigenous Sovereignty, 532

Thessalon
Welcome Friend Association, 1443

Thornbury
Blue Mountains Chamber of Commerce, 215

Thorndale
Association of Ontario Road Supervisors, 155

Thornhill
Act To End Violence Against Women, 6
Aish Thornhill Community Shul & Learning Centre, 20
Anthroposophical Society in Canada, 72
Association of Independent Consultants, 149
The Bahá'í Community of Canada, 194
Canadian Association for Israel Philately, 301
Canadian Automobile Association, 339
Canadian Automobile Association South Central Ontario, 339
Canadian Automobile Dealers' Association, 339
Canadian Committee of Lawyers & Jurists for World Jewry, 361
Canadian IT Law Association, 422
Ephemera Society of Canada, 693
Eucharistic Apostles of the Divine Mercy, 698
Grand Masters Curling Association Ontario, 780
Iraqi Jewish Association of Ontario, 863
Jewish Family & Child-Thornhill Branch - Family Resource Centre & Clothing Cupboard, 871
Reena, 1210
Reinforcing Steel Institute of Ontario, 1217
Southern African Jewish Association of Canada, 1337
Temporomandibular Joint Society of Canada, 1370
Two/Ten Charity Trust of Canada Inc., 1401
Urban & Regional Information Systems Association-URISA Ontario, 1601

Thornton
Essa & District Agricultural Society, 696
Essa Historical Society, 696

Thorold
Canadian Automobile Association Niagara, 339
Canadian Society of Orthopaedic Technologists-Niagara Chapter, 485
Niagara Economic Development, 1025
Niagara Regional Labour Council, 1025
Ontario Brain Injury Association, 1068
Ontario Genealogical Society-Niagara Peninsula Branch, 1082
Provincial Women's Softball Association of Ontario, 1191
St. Catharines Coin Club, 1248
Toronto & District Square & Round Dance Association, 1381
United Empire Loyalists' Association of Canada-Col. John Butler Branch, 1410

Thunder Bay
Alzheimer Society of Thunder Bay, 65
Appaloosa Horse Club of Canada-Thunder Bay Appaloosa Club, 73
Association des francophones du nord-ouest de l'Ontario, 114
Big Brothers Big Sisters of Ontario-Big Brothers Big Sisters of Thunder Bay, 210
Boys & Girls Clubs of Ontario-Boys & Girls Clubs of Thunder Bay, 223

Canadian Association of Elizabeth Fry Societies-Elizabeth Fry Society of Northwestern Ontario, 313
Canadian Association of Veterans in United Nations Peacekeeping-Camp Maple Leaf Chapter, 335
Canadian Celiac Association-Thunder Bay Chapter, 353
Canadian Condominium Institute-CCI-Northwestern Ontario Chapter, 362
Canadian Council of Snowmobile Organizations, 370
Canadian Hearing Society-Thunder Bay Regional Office, 403
Canadian Injured Workers Alliance, 411
Canadian Office & Professional Employees Union-Region 2 - Local 81, 445
Canadian Office & Professional Employees Union-Region 2 - Local 96, 445
Canadian Office & Professional Employees Union-Region 2 - Local 236, 445
Canadian Office & Professional Employees Union-Region 2 - Local 454, 445
Canadian Polish Congress-Thunder Bay Branch, 456
Community Living Thunder Bay, 605
Council of Ontario Construction Associations-Construction Association of Thunder Bay, 634
Cross Country Ski Ontario, 644
The Easter Seal Society (Ontario)-Northern Region - Thunder Bay, 670
Electrical Contractors Association of Thunder Bay, 683
Elevate NWO, 684
The Friends of Sleeping Giant, 762
Habitat for Humanity Canada-Ontario - Thunder Bay, 797
Heart & Stroke Foundation of Ontario-Thunder Bay Office, 809
Hockey Northwestern Ontario, 818
Human Resources Professionals Association-Northwestern Ontario Chapter, 826
International Brotherhood of Boilermakers, Iron Ship Builders, Blacksmiths, Forgers & Helpers (AFL-CIO)-Thunder Bay (Lodge 555), 1541
The John Howard Society of Ontario-Thunder Bay & District, 875
The Kidney Foundation of Canada-Northern Superior Chapter - Thunder Bay, 885
Lake Superior Coin Club, 896
Lakehead Japanese Cultural Association, 896
Lakehead Social Planning Council, 896
Lakehead Stamp Club, 896
Lakehead University Faculty Association, 896
Lifewater Canada, 912
Multicultural Association of Northwestern Ontario, 979
North of Superior Film Association, 1031
North of Superior Tourism Association, 1031
Northern Ontario Native Tourism Association, 1035
Northwestern Ontario Air Search & Rescue Association, 1039
Northwestern Ontario Associated Chambers of Commerce, 1039
Northwestern Ontario Municipal Association, 1039
Northwestern Ontario Prospectors Association, 1039
Northwestern Ontario Sports Hall of Fame & Museum, 1039
Northwestern Ontario Technology Association, 1040
The Ontario Archaeological Society Inc.-Thunder Bay Chapter, 1060
Ontario Brain Injury Association-Thunder Bay, 1069
Ontario Council for University Lifelong Learning, 1075
Ontario Genealogical Society-Thunder Bay District Branch, 1082

Ontario Home Builders' Association-Thunder Bay, 1086
Ontario Nurses' Association-Thunder Bay Office, 1094
Ontario Prospectors Association, 1098
Ontario Society for the Prevention of Cruelty to Animals-Thunder Bay Branch (Affiliate), 1106
Oshki Anishnawbeg Student Association, 1128
The Paterson Foundation, 1145
Public Service Alliance of Canada-Thunder Bay Branch, 1193
Royal Astronomical Society of Canada-Thunder Bay Centre, 1239
Saint Elizabeth Health Care-Thunder Bay - North West Service Delivery Centre, 1246
Scandinavian Home Society of Northwestern Ontario, 1282
Spinal Cord Injury Ontario-Thunder Bay Office, 1344
Superior International Junior Hockey League, 1355
Thunder Bay & District Labour Council, 1377
Thunder Bay Adventure Trails, 1377
Thunder Bay Beekeepers' Association, 1377
Thunder Bay Chamber of Commerce, 1377
Thunder Bay Community Foundation, 1377
Thunder Bay Counselling Centre, 1377
Thunder Bay Field Naturalists, 1377
Thunder Bay Historical Museum Society, 1378
Thunder Bay Indian Friendship Centre, 1378
Thunder Bay Law Association, 1378
Thunder Bay Minor Football Association, 1378
Thunder Bay Multicultural Association, 1378
Thunder Bay Musicians' Association, 1378
Thunder Bay Police Association, 1378
Thunder Bay Real Estate Board, 1378
Thunder Bay Regional Arts Council, 1378
Thunder Bay Sexual Assault / Sexual Abuse Counselling & Crisis Centre, 1378
Thunder Bay Symphony Orchestra Association, 1378
Tourism Thunder Bay, 1391
211 Ontario North, 1401
UNIFOR-Thunder Bay, 1405
William W. Creighton Youth Services, 1455
Women's & Gender Studies et Recherches Féministes, 1461

Tilbury
Information Tilbury & Help Centre, 837
Tilbury Chamber of Commerce, 1379

Tillsonburg
Canadian Association of Veterans in United Nations Peacekeeping-LCpl David W. Young Chapter, 336
Canadian Harvard Aircraft Association, 401
Canadian Racing Pigeon Union Inc., 464
Model Aeronautics Association of Canada Inc.-Southwest Ontario Zone, 971
Ontario Flue-Cured Tobacco Growers' Marketing Board, 1080
Tillsonburg & District Association for Community Living, 1379
Tillsonburg & District Multi-Service Centre, 1379
Tillsonburg District Chamber of Commerce, 1379
Tillsonburg District Real Estate Board, 1379

Timmins
AFOA Canada-AFOA Ontario, 12
Alzheimer Society of Timmins/Porcupine District, 65
Canadian Hearing Society-Timmins Office, 403
Community Living Timmins Intégration Communautaire, 605
Credit Counselling Services of Cochrane District, 640
Epilepsy Ontario-Timmins, 694
Heart & Stroke Foundation of Ontario-Timmins Office, 809
Medical Device Reprocessing Association of Ontario, 958
North Eastern Ontario Family & Children's Services, 1030
Ojibway & Cree Cultural Centre, 1055

Ontario Brain Injury Association-Timmins, 1069
Ontario Nurses' Association-Timmins Office, 1094
Ontario Registered Music Teachers' Association, 1101
Ontario Society for the Prevention of Cruelty to Animals-Timmins Branch (Affiliate), 1106
Porcupine Prospectors & Developers Association, 1165
Timmins & Area Women in Crisis Support & Information Centre on Violence Against Women, 1379
Timmins Chamber of Commerce, 1380
Timmins Coin Club, 1380
Timmins Family Counselling Centre, Inc., 1380
Timmins Native Friendship Centre, 1380
Timmins Symphony Orchestra, 1380
Timmins, Cochrane & Timiskaming District Association of REALTORS, 1380
United Way of Cochrane-Timiskaming, 1413
YMCA Canada-YMCA of Timmins, 1471

Tobermory
The Bruce Trail Conservancy-Peninsula, 261
Tobermory & District Chamber of Commerce, 1380

Toronto
Abbeyfield Houses Society of Canada, 1
ABC Life Literacy Canada, 1
Ability Online Support Network, 2
Aboriginal Legal Services of Toronto, 2
AboutFace, 3
Academy of Canadian Cinema & Television, 3
A.C.C.E.S. Employment, 4
A.C.C.E.S. Employment-Scarborough, 4
A.C.C.E.S. Employment-North York, 4
Access Alliance Multicultural Health & Community Services, 4
Access Alliance Multicultural Health & Community Services-AccessPoint on Danforth, 4
Access Alliance Multicultural Health & Community Services-AccessPoint on Jane, 4
Access Alliance Multicultural Health & Community Services-Neighbourhood Centre, 4
Access Copyright, 4
Accessible Media Inc., 5
Achilles Canada, 5
Acoustic Neuroma Association of Canada, 5
Acoustical Association Ontario, 5
ACT for the Earth, 5
Active Healthy Kids Canada, 7
The Actors' Fund of Canada, 7
ACTRA Fraternal Benefit Society, 7
Acupuncture Canada, 7
Adam Mickiewicz Foundation of Canada, 7
Addictions & Mental Health Ontario, 8
Addus, 8
Adoption Council of Ontario, 8
ADR Institute of Canada, 9
ADR Institute of Canada-ADR Institute of Ontario, Inc., 9
Adult Children of Alcoholics, 9
The Advertising & Design Club of Canada, 10
Advertising Standards Canada, 10
Advocacy Centre for the Elderly, 10
The Advocates' Society, 11
Advocis, 11
Aerospace Heritage Foundation of Canada, 11
Afghan Association of Ontario, 12
Afghan Women's Counselling & Integration Community Support Organization, 12
Afghan Women's Counselling & Integration Community Support Organization-North York, 12
Afghan Women's Counselling & Integration Community Support Organization-Scarborough, 12
Africa Inland Mission International (Canada), 12
African & Caribbean Council on HIV/AIDS in Ontario, 12
African Canadian Heritage Association, 12
African Canadian Social Development Council, 12

African Community Health Services, 13
African Medical & Research Foundation Canada, 13
Africans in Partnership Against AIDS, 13
Agincourt Community Services Association, 14
Agincourt Community Services Association, 14
AIDS Committee of Toronto, 16
AIESEC, 18
AIESEC-Ryerson, 18
AIESEC-Toronto, 18
AIESEC-York, 18
Air Line Pilots Association, International - Canada-Toronto Contract Office, 19
Albanian Canadian Community Association, 21
Albion Neighbourhood Services, 52
Alcoholics Anonymous (GTA Intergroup), 52
Alfa Romeo Club of Canada, 53
Allergy, Asthma & Immunology Society of Ontario, 54
Allergy/Asthma Information Association, 54
Allergy/Asthma Information Association-AAIA Ontario/Québec/Atlantic, 54
Alliance for Audited Media, 56
Alliance for Canadian New Music Projects, 56
Alliance for Canadian New Music Projects-Contemporary Showcase - Toronto, 57
Alliance for South Asian AIDS Prevention, 57
Alliance of Canadian Cinema, Television & Radio Artists, 58
Alliance of Canadian Cinema, Television & Radio Artists-ACTRA Toronto, 58
Alliance of Credential Evaluation Services of Canada, 58
Alternative Land Use Services Canada, 60
Altruvest Charitable Services, 61
Alva Foundation, 61
Alzheimer Society Canada, 61
Alzheimer Society of Toronto, 65
Alzheimer Society Ontario, 65
American Concrete Institute-Ontario Chapter, 1492
American Federation of Musicians of the United States & Canada (AFL-CIO/CLC)-Canadian Office, 1493
American Immigration Lawyers Association - Canadian Chapter, 66
American Marketing Association-Toronto Chapter, 1495
Amici dell'Enotria Toronto, 67
Amnesty International - Canadian Section (English Speaking)-Toronto Office, 68
The Anglican Church of Canada, 69
The Anglican Church of Canada-Diocese of Toronto, 70
Anglican Foundation of Canada, 70
Animal Alliance of Canada, 70
Animal Justice, 70
Animal Protection Party of Canada, 71
ANNISAA Organization of Canada, 71
Antisemitism Must End Now, 72
Applegrove Community Complex, 74
The Appraisal Institute of Canada - Ontario, 75
Arab Community Centre of Toronto, 76
ARCH Disability Law Centre, 76
L'Arche Ontario, 77
L'Arche Ontario-L'Arche Toronto, 77
The Architectural Conservancy of Ontario, 78
Archives Association of Ontario, 80
ARK II, 81
Armenian Canadian Medical Association of Ontario, 82
Armenian Community Centre of Toronto, 83
Armenian General Benevolent Union, 83
Armenian Relief Society of Canada, " Inc.-Toronto Chapter: ""Roubina"""", 83
Army Cadet League of Canada-Ontario Branch, 83
Army, Navy & Air Force Veterans in Canada-Ontario Provincial Command, 84
Art Dealers Association of Canada Inc., 84
Arthritis Research Foundation, 84
Arthritis Society, 84
Arthritis Society-Ontario Division, 84
Artisan Bakers' Quality Alliance, 85

The Arts & Letters Club, 85
Arts Etobicoke, 85
Artscape, 86
ARZA-Canada: The Zionist Voice of the Canadian Reform Movement, 86
Asian Community AIDS Services, 87
ASK! Community Information Centre (LAMP), 87
Aspergers Society of Ontario, 87
Assaulted Women's Helpline, 87
Assembly of Catholic Bishops of Ontario, 88
Associated Designers of Canada, 89
Associated Medical Services Inc., 89
Associated Senior Executives of Canada Ltd., 89
Association des bibliothèques de l'Ontario-Franco, 107
Association for Corporate Growth, Toronto Chapter, 133
Association for Native Development in the Performing & Visual Arts, 134
Association for Operations Management, 134
The Association for the Soldiers of Israel, 135
Association of Canadian Advertisers Inc., 140
Association of Canadian Choral Communities, 141
Association of Canadian Corporations in Translation & Interpretation, 141
Association of Canadian Distillers, 142
Association of Canadian Ergonomists, 142
Association of Canadian Industrial Designers, 142
Association of Canadian Pension Management, 143
Association of Canadian Publishers, 143
Association of Canadian University Presses, 144
Association of Canadian Women Composers, 144
Association of Career Professionals International, 144
Association of Certified Fraud Examiners - Toronto Chapter, 145
Association of Chartered Industrial Designers of Ontario, 145
Association of Early Childhood Educators Ontario, 147
Association of Educational Researchers of Ontario, 147
Association of Family Health Teams of Ontario, 148
Association of Filipino Canadian Accountants, 148
Association of Fundraising Professionals-Greater Toronto Chapter
Association of Hemophilia Clinic Directors of Canada, 149
Association of Independent Corrugated Converters, 149
Association of International Physicians & Surgeons of Ontario, 149
Association of Internet Marketing & Sales, 149
Association of Jewish Chaplains of Ontario, 150
Association of Jewish Seniors, 150
Association of Korean Canadian Scientists & Engineers, 150
Association of Latvian Craftsmen in Canada, 150
Association of Local Public Health Agencies, 150
Association of Major Power Consumers in Ontario, 151
Association of Management, Administrative & Professional Crown Employees of Ontario, 151
Association of Mature Canadians, 151
Association of Millwrighting Contractors of Ontario Inc., 152
Association of Municipalities of Ontario, 152
Association of Ontario Health Centres, 154
Association of Ontario Land Economists, 155
Association of Ontario Land Surveyors, 155
The Association of Ontario Locksmiths, 155
Association of Ontario Midwives, 155

Association of Parent Support Groups in Ontario Inc., 155
Association of Polish Engineers in Canada, 155
Association of Polish Engineers in Canada-Toronto Branch, 156
Association of Power Producers of Ontario, 156
Association of Professional Archaeologists, 156
Association of Professional Computer Consultants - Canada, 157
Association of Professional Geoscientists of Ontario, 159
Association of Registered Graphic Designers of Ontario, 160
Association of Registered Interior Designers of Ontario, 161
Association of Regular Baptist Churches (Canada), 161
Association of the Chemical Profession of Ontario, 163
Asthma Society of Canada, 179
Athletics Ontario, 181
Atkinson Charitable Foundation, 182
Atlantic Council of Canada, 183
Attractions Ontario, 187
Australian Football League Ontario, 188
Autism Ontario, 188
Autism Speaks Canada, 189
Automobile Protection Association-Toronto Office, 189
Automotive Parts Manufacturers' Association, 190
AWIC Community & Social Services, 191
Azrieli Foundation, 191
B'nai Brith Canada, 192
B'nai Brith Canada Institute for International Affairs, 192
B'nai Brith Youth Organization, 192
Badminton Ontario, 193
BALANCE for Blind Adults, 194
Ballet Creole, 194
Ballet Jörgen, 194
Baltic Federation in Canada, 195
The Barbra Schlifer Commemorative Clinic, 196
Baycrest Foundation, 200
Beach Hebrew Institute, 202
Belgian Canadian Business Chamber, 204
Bereaved Families of Ontario-Toronto, 205
Bereavement Authority of Ontario, 205
Bernard Betel Centre for Creative Living, 205
Best Buddies Canada, 206
Bibliographical Society of Canada, 208
Big Brothers Big Sisters of Canada, 209
Big Brothers & Big Sisters of Ontario-Big Brothers & Big Sisters of Toronto, 210
Bikes Without Borders, 211
Birchmount Bluffs Neighbourhood Centre, 212
Birth Control & Venereal Disease Information Centre, 212
Birthright International, 212
Black Business & Professional Association, 213
Black Coalition for AIDS Prevention, 213
Black Creek Conservation Project, 213
Bladder Cancer Canada, 214
Blind Sailing Association of Canada, 214
Blissymbolics Communication International, 214
BloodWatch, 215
BMW Clubs Canada-Trillium Chapter, 216
The Bob Rumball Centre for the Deaf, 216
Bob Rumball Foundation for the Deaf, 217
Book & Periodical Council, 218
Boost Child & Youth Advocacy Centre, 218
Bosnian Canadian Relief Association, 218
Bosnian Islamic Association, 218
Boxing Ontario, 220
Boys & Girls Clubs of Canada, 222
Boys & Girls Clubs of Canada Foundation, 222
Boys & Girls Clubs of Ontario-Albion Boys & Girls Club, 223
Boys & Girls Clubs of Ontario-Braeburn Boys & Girls Club, 224
Boys & Girls Clubs of Ontario-Boys & Girls Club of East Scarborough, 223
Boys & Girls Clubs of Ontario-Dovercourt Boys & Girls Club, 224

Boys & Girls Clubs of Ontario-St. Alban's Boys & Girls Club, 224
Boys & Girls Clubs of Ontario-Toronto Kiwanis Boys & Girls Clubs, 224
Boys & Girls Clubs of Ontario-Boys & Girls Clubs of West Scarborough, 223
Boys & Girls Clubs of Ontario-Eastview (Toronto) Boys & Girls Club, 224
Braille Literacy Canada, 224
Breakfast Cereals Canada, 227
Breakfast for Learning, 227
Bricklayers, Masons Independent Union of Canada (CLC), 228
British Canadian Chamber of Trade & Commerce, 229
British Council - Canada, 259
British Israel World Federation (Canada) Inc., 259
The British Methodist Episcopal Church of Canada, 259
Broadcast Executives Society, 259
Broadcast Research Council of Canada, 259
Buddhist Association of Canada - Cham Shan Temple, 261
Buddies in Bad Times Theatre, 261
Building Industry & Land Development Association, 262
Building Owners & Managers Association - Canada, 262
Building Owners & Managers Association Toronto, 263
Building Owners & Managers Institute of Canada, 263
Bukas Loob sa Diyos Covenant Community, 264
Burn Survivors Association, 265
Business Development Centre (Toronto), 267
Business for the Arts, 267
Buy-Side Investment Management Association, 267
Cabbagetown Community Arts Centre, 268
Cabbagetown Preservation Association, 268
CADORA Ontario Association Inc.-Toronto CADORA Chapter, 269
Call2Recycle Canada, Inc., 275
CAMH Foundation, 276
Campaign Life Coalition, 276
Canada - Albania Business Council, 277
Canada Basketball, 278
Canada BIM Council Inc., 278
Canada Bulgaria Business Network, 278
Canada China Business Council, 278
Canada Employment & Immigration Union-Ontario Regional Office, 279
Canada Eurasia Russia Business Association, 279
Canada Health Infoway-Toronto, 280
Canada Israel Experience Centre, 280
Canada Media Fund, 280
Canada World Youth-Toronto Office, 281
Canada's Medical Technology Companies, 282
Canada's Venture Capital & Private Equity Association, 283
Canada-Arab Business Council, 283
Canada-Finland Chamber of Commerce, 283
Canada-India Business Council, 283
Canada-Israel Cultural Foundation, 283
Canada-Poland Chamber of Commerce of Toronto, 284
Canada-Sri Lanka Business Council, 284
Canadian Abilities Foundation, 285
Canadian Aboriginal & Minority Supplier Council, 285
Canadian Academic Accounting Association, 285
Canadian Academy of Audiology, 285
Canadian Academy of Facial Plastic & Reconstructive Surgery, 286
Canadian Academy of Recording Arts & Sciences, 286
Canadian Actors' Equity Association (CLC), 287
The Canadian Addison Society, 288
Canadian Agencies Practicing Marketing Activation, 289

Canadian AIDS Treatment Information Exchange, 290
Canadian Albacore Association, 291
Canadian Alliance of British Pensioners, 291
Canadian Alliance of Dance Artists, 291
Canadian Alliance of Physiotherapy Regulators, 291
Canadian Amateur Musicians-Toronto Region, 292
Canadian Anesthesiologists' Society, 292
Canadian Anti-Counterfeiting Network, 293
Canadian Antique Phonograph Society, 293
Canadian Arab Federation, 294
The Canadian Art Foundation, 295
Canadian Arthritis Network, 295
Canadian Artists' Representation Ontario, 296
Canadian Assembly of Narcotics Anonymous-Ontario Region, 297
Canadian Associates of Ben-Gurion University of the Negev, 297
Canadian Association for Food Studies, 300
Canadian Association for Free Expression, 300
Canadian Association for Japanese Language Education, 301
Canadian Association for Laboratory Animal Science, 302
Canadian Association for Latin American & Caribbean Studies, 302
Canadian Association for Population Therapeutics, 303
Canadian Association for Size Acceptance, 304
Canadian Association for the Study of Discourse & Writing, 306
Canadian Association for Williams Syndrome-CAWS - Ontario, 307
Canadian Association of Acupuncture & Traditional Chinese Medicine, 307
Canadian Association of Ambulatory Care, 308
Canadian Association of Black Journalists, 308
Canadian Association of Black Lawyers, 308
Canadian Association of Blue Cross Plans, 309
Canadian Association of Blue Cross Plans-Ontario Blue Cross, 309
Canadian Association of Business Incubation, 309
Canadian Association of Cardio-Pulmonary Technologists, 309
Canadian Association of Career Educators & Employers, 309
Canadian Association of College & University Student Services, 310
Canadian Association of Community Health Centres, 311
Canadian Association of Critical Care Nurses-Toronto Chapter, 312
Canadian Association of Crown Counsel, 312
Canadian Association of Direct Response Insurers, 312
Canadian Association of Elizabeth Fry Societies-Toronto Elizabeth Fry Society, 313
Canadian Association of Exposition Management, 313
Canadian Association of Financial Institutions in Insurance, 314
The Canadian Association of Fitness Professionals, 315
Canadian Association of Geographers-Ontario Division, 316
Canadian Association of Importers & Exporters, 318
Canadian Association of Income Trusts Investors, 318
Canadian Association of Independent Life Brokerage Agencies, 318
Canadian Association of Insolvency & Restructuring Professionals, 318
Canadian Association of Journalists, 319
Canadian Association of Labour Media, 319
Canadian Association of Law Libraries, 319
Canadian Association of Management Consultants, 320
Canadian Association of Music Libraries, Archives & Documentation Centres, 321
The Canadian Association of Naturopathic Doctors, 322

Geographic Index / Ontario - Toronto

Canadian Association of Orthodontists, 324
Canadian Association of Pension Supervisory Authorities, 325
Canadian Association of Personal Property Appraisers, 325
Canadian Association of Pharmacy Students & Interns, 326
Canadian Association of Physicians for the Environment, 327
Canadian Association of Physicians with Disabilities, 327
Canadian Association of Professional Academic Librarians, 328
Canadian Association of Professional Image Creators, 328
Canadian Association of Professional Immigration Consultants, 329
Canadian Association of Professional Speakers, 329
Canadian Association of Provincial Cancer Agencies, 329
Canadian Association of Psychosocial Oncology, 330
Canadian Association of Refugee Lawyers, 330
Canadian Association of Rhodes Scholars, 331
Canadian Association of SAS Users, 331
Canadian Association of Tour Operators, 334
Canadian Association of Wholesale Sales Representatives, 336
Canadian Association of Women Executives & Entrepreneurs, 336
Canadian Association of Wound Care, 337
Canadian Association on Gerontology, 337
Canadian Athletes Now Fund, 337
Canadian Automobile Sport Clubs - Ontario Region Inc., 339
Canadian Aviation Historical Society-Toronto Chapter, 340
Canadian Bankers Association, 341
Canadian Baptists of Ontario & Québec, 341
Canadian Bar Association-Ontario Bar Association, 342
Canadian Bar Insurance Association, 342
Canadian Baton Twirling Federation, 342
Canadian Beverage Association, 342
Canadian Bible Society, 343
Canadian Bible Society-Central Ontario District Office, 343
Canadian Bible Society-Central Ontario District Office, 343
Canadian Blood Services-Toronto - College St., 345
Canadian Blood Services-Toronto - Bay & Bloor, 345
Canadian Blood Services-Toronto - King Street, 345
Canadian Board Diversity Council, 345
Canadian Board of Registration of Electroencephalograph Technologists Inc., 345
Canadian Bond Investors' Association, 345
Canadian Bookbinders & Book Artists Guild, 346
Canadian Bookkeepers Association, 346
Canadian Booksellers Association, 346
Canadian Brain Tumour Consortium, 346
Canadian Bureau for the Advancement of Music, 347
Canadian Business for Social Responsibility, 348
Canadian Business Press, 348
Canadian Camping Association, 348
Canadian Cancer Society, 348
Canadian Cancer Society-Ontario Division, 349
Canadian Cancer Society Research Institute, 349
Canadian Capital Markets Association, 349
Canadian Carwash Association, 350
Canadian Casting Federation, 350
Canadian Catholic Campus Ministry, 351
Canadian Catholic Historical Association - English Section, 351
Canadian Catholic Historical Association - English Section-History Office, 351
Canadian Celiac Association-Toronto Chapter, 353
Canadian Celtic Arts Association, 353
Canadian Centre for Ethics & Corporate Policy, 353
Canadian Centre for Victims of Torture, 354
Canadian Centre for Wellbeing, 354
The Canadian Centre/International P.E.N., 354
The Canadian Chamber of Commerce-Toronto Office, 355
Canadian Chihuahua Rescue & Transport, 355
Canadian Children's Book Centre, 355
Canadian Children's Opera Company, 356
Canadian Chiropractic Association, 356
Canadian Chiropractic Research Foundation, 356
Canadian Chito-Ryu Karate-Do Association, 356
Canadian Circulations Audit Board Inc., 357
Canadian Civil Liberties Association, 357
The Canadian Club of Toronto, 357
Canadian Coalition Against the Death Penalty, 357
Canadian Coalition for Farm Animals, 357
Canadian Coalition for Good Governance, 357
Canadian Coalition for Seniors Mental Health, 358
Canadian Coalition for the Rights of Children, 358
The Canadian College of Naturopathic Medicine, 360
Canadian Columbian Professional Association, 360
Canadian Community Newspapers Association, 361
Canadian Comparative Literature Association, 361
Canadian Concrete Masonry Producers Association, 362
Canadian Contemporary Dance Theatre, 364
Canadian Copper & Brass Development Association, 364
Canadian Copyright Institute, 365
Canadian Corporate Counsel Association, 365
Canadian Corps Association, 365
Canadian Council for Aboriginal Business, 366
The Canadian Council for Accreditation of Pharmacy Programs, 366
The Canadian Council for Public-Private Partnerships, 366
Canadian Council for Reform Judaism, 367
Canadian Council for the Americas, 367
The Canadian Council of Churches, 368
Canadian Council of Conservative Synagogues, 368
Canadian Council of Insurance Regulators, 368
Canadian Council of Montessori Administrators, 369
Canadian Council of Muslim Theologians, 369
Canadian Council of Professional Certification, 369
Canadian Council on Africa-Toronto - Central Office, 370
Canadian Council on Rehabilitation & Work, 371
Canadian Country Music Association, 372
Canadian Courier & Logistics Association, 372
Canadian Credit Institute Educational Foundation, 372
Canadian Credit Union Association, 372
Canadian Critical Care Society, 373
Canadian Crossroads International, 373
Canadian Culinary Federation-Toronto Branch, 374
Canadian Cultural Society of The Deaf, Inc., 374
Canadian Decorators' Association, 376
The Canadian Don't Do Drugs Society, 378
Canadian Education & Research Institute for Counselling, 379
Canadian Education Association, 379
Canadian Educational Resources Council, 380
Canadian Electric Wheelchair Hockey Association, 380
Canadian Electrical Manufacturers Representatives Association, 380
Canadian Employee Relocation Council, 380
Canadian Environment Industry Association, 381
Canadian Environmental Grantmakers' Network, 382
Canadian Environmental Law Association, 382
Canadian ETF Association, 382
Canadian Ethnic Media Association, 382
Canadian Executive Service Organization, 383
Canadian Fanconi Anemia Research Fund, 384
Canadian Federation of Business & Professional Women's Clubs-North Toronto, 385
Canadian Federation of Chiropractic Regulatory & Educational Accrediting Boards, 386
Canadian Federation of Independent Business, 386
Canadian Federation of Independent Business-Ontario Office, 387
Canadian Federation of Independent Grocers, 387
Canadian Federation of Mental Health Nurses, 388
Canadian Feed The Children, 389
Canadian Film Centre, 390
Canadian Filmmakers Distribution Centre, 390
Canadian Finance & Leasing Association, 390
Canadian Food Exporters Association, 391
Canadian Football League, 392
Canadian Foundation for AIDS Research, 392
Canadian Foundation for Dietetic Research, 393
Canadian Foundation for Economic Education, 393
Canadian Foundation for Masorti Judaism, 393
Canadian Foundation for Physically Disabled Persons, 394
Canadian Foundation for Ukrainian Studies, 394
Canadian Foundation on Fetal Alcohol Research, 394
Canadian Franchise Association, 394
Canadian Friends of Bikur Cholim Hospital, 394
Canadian Friends of Boys Town Jerusalem, 395
Canadian Friends of Peace Now (Shalom Achshav), 395
Canadian Friends of the Hebrew University, 395
Canadian Friends of the Hebrew University-Toronto Chapter, 395
Canadian Friends of Ukraine, 395
Canadian Friends of Yeshiva University, 395
Canadian Friends Service Committee, 395
Canadian Fuels Association-Ontario Division, 396
Canadian Fuels Association-Eastern Canada Division, 396
Canadian Gaming Association, 396
Canadian Gemmological Association, 396
Canadian Generic Pharmaceutical Association, 397
Canadian German Chamber of Industry & Commerce Inc., 397
Canadian Gift Association, 398
Canadian Golf Superintendents Association, 398
Canadian Group Psychotherapy Association, 399
Canadian Hadassah WIZO, 399
Canadian Hadassah WIZO-Toronto, 399
Canadian Hardware & Housewares Manufacturers' Association, 401
Canadian Harm Reduction Network, 401
Canadian Health Food Association, 401
Canadian Health Libraries Association, 402
Canadian Hearing Society, 403
Canadian Hearing Society-Toronto (Central) Region, 403
Canadian Hemerocallis Society, 404
Canadian Hemophilia Society-Hemophilia Ontario, 404
Canadian HIV Trials Network-Toronto & Area Office, 405
Canadian HIV/AIDS Legal Network, 405
Canadian Hockey League, 406
Canadian Hotel Marketing & Sales Executives, 409
Canadian Hydrographic Association, 409
Canadian Imaging Trade Association, 410
Canadian Independent Adjusters' Association, 410
Canadian Independent Bicycle Retailers Association, 410
Canadian Independent Music Association, 410
Canadian Information Centre for International Credentials, 411
The Canadian Institute, 412
Canadian Institute for Advanced Research, 412
Canadian Institute for Energy Training, 412
Canadian Institute for Health Information-CIHI Toronto, 412
Canadian Institute for Mediterranean Studies, 412
Canadian Institute for Theatre Technology-Ontario Section, 414
Canadian Institute of Bookkeeping, 414
Canadian Institute of Chartered Business Valuators, 414
Canadian Institute of Cultural Affairs, 415
Canadian Institute of Food Science & Technology, 415
Canadian Institute of Plumbing & Heating, 418
Canadian Institute of Traffic & Transportation, 419
Canadian Institute of Ukrainian Studies-Toronto Office, 420
Canadian Insurance Accountants Association, 420
Canadian Insurance Claims Managers Association, 420
Canadian International Air Show, 421
Canadian International Council, 421
Canadian International Freight Forwarders Association, 421
Canadian Investor Protection Fund, 422
Canadian Investor Relations Institute, 422
Canadian Jesuits International, 423
Canadian Jewellers Association, 423
Canadian Journalism Foundation, 423
Canadian Journalists for Free Expression, 423
Canadian Kennel Club, 424
Canadian Kennel Club Foundation, 424
Canadian Labour Congress-Ontario Regional Office, 424
Canadian Law & Economics Association, 425
Canadian Lawyers Insurance Association, 426
Canadian League of Composers, 426
Canadian Lesbian & Gay Archives, 426
Canadian Life & Health Insurance Association Inc., 426
Canadian Linguistic Association, 427
Canadian Liver Foundation, 427
Canadian Lymphedema Framework, 429
Canadian Machinery Vibration Association, 429
Canadian Magen David Adom for Israel-Toronto Chapter, 429
Canadian Management Centre, 429
Canadian Marketing Association, 430
Canadian Media Directors' Council, 432
Canadian Media Guild, 432
Canadian MedicAlert Foundation, 434
Canadian MedTech Manufacturers' Alliance, 434
Canadian Memorial Chiropractic College, 434
Canadian Mental Health Association-Ontario Division, 435
Canadian Music Centre, 438
Canadian Music Centre-Ontario Region, 438
Canadian Music Festival Adjudicators' Association, 438
Canadian Musical Reproduction Rights Agency, 438
Canadian National Exhibition Association, 439
Canadian National Institute for the Blind, 439
Canadian National Institute for the Blind-Ontario Division, 439
Canadian Natural Health Association, 440
Canadian Netherlands Business & Professional Association Inc., 440
Canadian Nuclear Society, 442

Geographic Index / Ontario - Toronto

Canadian Office & Professional Employees Union-Region 2 - Local 343, 445
Canadian Office & Professional Employees Union-Region 2 - Local 468, 445
Canadian Office & Professional Employees Union-Region 2 - Local 550, 445
Canadian Office Products Association, 445
Canadian Olympic Committee, 445
Canadian Opera Company, 446
Canadian Organization for Rare Disorders, 447
Canadian Orthopaedic Foundation, 448
Canadian Out-of-Home Measurement Bureau, 448
Canadian Pain Society, 449
Canadian Parks & Wilderness Society-Toronto - CPAWS Wildlands League Chapter, 451
Canadian Partnership for Children's Health & Environment, 451
Canadian Payroll Association, 452
Canadian Peace Alliance, 452
Canadian Pension & Benefits Institute-Ontario Region, 453
Canadian Peregrine Foundation, 453
Canadian Physicians for Aid & Relief, 454
Canadian Picture Pioneers, 455
Canadian PKU and Allied Disorders Inc., 455
Canadian Polish Congress, 456
Canadian Polish Congress-Toronto Branch, 456
Canadian Polish Foundation, 457
Canadian Positive Psychology Association, 458
Canadian Power & Sail Squadrons (Canadian Headquarters), 459
The Canadian Press, 459
Canadian Private Copying Collective, 460
Canadian Professional DJ Association Inc., 460
Canadian Professional Sales Association, 460
Canadian Property Tax Association, Inc., 461
Canadian Psychoanalytic Society-Toronto Psychoanalytic Society, 461
Canadian Public Accountability Board, 462
Canadian Public Relations Society Inc., 462
Canadian Public Relations Society Inc.-CPRS Toronto, 463
Canadian Publishers' Council, 464
Canadian Race Relations Foundation, 464
Canadian Railroad Historical Association-Toronto & York Division, 465
Canadian Retransmission Collective, 467
Canadian Rock Mechanics Association, 467
Canadian Rose Society, 468
Canadian Safe Boating Council, 468
Canadian Safe School Network, 468
Canadian Scholarship Trust Foundation, 468
Canadian Securities Institute, 469
Canadian Securities Institute Research Foundation, 469
Canadian Security Traders Association, Inc., 469
Canadian Sinfonietta Youth Orchestra, 470
Canadian Slovenian Chamber of Commerce, 472
Canadian Snowbird Association, 472
Canadian Soccer Association-Technical Office, 472
The Canadian Society for Mesopotamian Studies, 476
Canadian Society for Surgical Oncology, 477
Canadian Society for the History & Philosophy of Science, 477
Canadian Society for the Protection of Nature in Israel, 477
Canadian Society for the Study of Practical Ethics, 478
Canadian Society for the Study of the Aging Male, 478
The Canadian Society for the Weizmann Institute of Science-Toronto Office, 479
Canadian Society for Yad Vashem, 479
Canadian Society of Association Executives, 480
Canadian Society of Association Executives-Ontario (Trillium) Chapter, 480
Canadian Society of Children's Authors, Illustrators & Performers, 481

Canadian Society of Chinese Medicine & Acupuncture, 481
Canadian Society of Cinematographers, 481
Canadian Society of Club Managers, 482
Canadian Society of Environmental Biologists, 482
Canadian Society of Gastroenterology Nurses & Associates-Greater Toronto Chapter, 483
Canadian Society of Medical Evaluators, 484
Canadian Society of Nutrition Management, 485
Canadian Society of Ophthalmic Registered Nurses, 485
Canadian Society of Orthopaedic Technologists, 485
Canadian Society of Painters in Water Colour, 486
Canadian Society of Safety Engineering, Inc., 487
Canadian Society of Sugar Artistry, 488
Canadian Society of Teachers of the Alexander Technique, 488
Canadian Society of Technical Analysts, 488
Canadian Space Society, 489
Canadian Sporting Goods Association, 490
The Canadian Stage Company, 490
Canadian Standards Association, 490
Canadian Steel Door Manufacturers Association, 491
Canadian Steel Trade & Employment Congress, 491
Canadian Stuttering Association, 491
Canadian Sugar Institute, 491
Canadian Tamil Congress, 492
Canadian Tamil Medical Association, 492
Canadian Tamil Professionals Association, 492
Canadian Tamil Youth Development Centre, 492
Canadian Tamils' Chamber of Commerce, 492
Canadian Tax Foundation, 492
Canadian Taxpayers Federation-Ontario, 493
Canadian Theatre Critics Association, 494
Canadian Thoroughbred Horse Society, 494
Canadian Thoroughbred Horse Society-Québec Division, 495
Canadian Thoroughbred Horse Society-Ontario Division, 495
Canadian Tibetan Association of Ontario, 495
Canadian Toy Association / Canadian Toy & Hobby Fair, 496
Canadian Toy Collectors' Society Inc., 496
Canadian Training Institute, 496
Canadian Transport Lawyers Association, 497
Canadian Trucking Alliance, 497
Canadian Ukrainian Immigrant Aid Society, 498
Canadian Union of Brewery & General Workers, Local 325, 498
Canadian Unitarian Council, 499
Canadian University Music Society, 499
Canadian University Press, 499
Canadian Urban Institute, 499
Canadian Urban Transit Association, 500
Canadian Vehicle Manufacturers' Association, 501
Canadian Water Quality Association, 502
Canadian Women's Foundation, 505
Canadian Young Judaea, 506
The Canadian Zionist Cultural Association, 506
Canadian Zionist Federation, 506
Canadian Zionist Federation-Central Region, 506
Canadian-Croatian Chamber of Commerce, 506
Canadian-Cuban Friendship Association Toronto, 506
Canadian-Palestinian Education Exchange, 506
Canadians Concerned About Violence in Entertainment, 506
Canadians for Clean Prosperity, 506
Canadians of Bangladeshi Origin, 507
Canadians' Choice Party, 507
Cancer Advocacy Coalition of Canada, 507
Cancer Care Ontario, 507
CANDU Owners Group Inc., 508
CanoeKayak Canada Western Ontario Division, 509

Carcinoid NeuroEndocrine Tumour Society Canada, 510
Cardiac Care Network of Ontario, 510
Cardiac Health Foundation of Canada, 510
Cardiac Rehabilitation Network of Ontario, 510
Carefirst Seniors & Community Services Association, 511
Carefirst Seniors & Community Services Association-South Toronto Office, Helen Lam Community Service Centre, 511
Carefirst Seniors & Community Services Association-Supportive Housing Services, Alexandra Park, 511
Carefirst Seniors & Community Services Association-Supportive Housing Services, Tam O'Shanter, 511
CARP, 514
Casa - Pueblito, 516
Casa Cultural Peruana, 516
Casa do Benfica, 516
Casa dos Acores do Ontário, 516
Casey House Hospice Inc., 516
Cathedral Bluffs Symphony Orchestra, 517
Catherine Donnelly Foundation, 517
Catholic Charismatic Renewal Council, Toronto, 517
Catholic Charities of The Archdiocese of Toronto, 518
Catholic Children's Aid Society of Toronto, 518
Catholic Children's Aid Society of Toronto-South Toronto Branch, 518
Catholic Children's Aid Society of Toronto-North West Toronto Branch, 518
Catholic Children's Aid Society of Toronto-East Toronto Branch, 518
Catholic Children's Aid Society of Toronto-Scarborough Branch, 518
Catholic Civil Rights League, 518
Catholic Cross Cultural Services, 518
Catholic Cross Cultural Services-Scarborough Region, 518
Catholic Education Foundation of Ontario, 518
Catholic Family Services of Toronto, 519
Catholic Family Services of Toronto-North Toronto Office, 519
Catholic Health Sponsors of Ontario, 520
Catholic Missions in Canada, 520
The Catholic Principals' Council of Ontario, 520
Catholic Teachers Guild, 520
Catholic Youth Studio - KSM Inc., 521
C.D. Howe Institute, 521
Cement Association of Canada-Ontario Region, 521
Central 1 Credit Union-Toronto Office, 523
Central Canadian Federation of Mineralogical Societies, 524
Central Neighbourhood House, 524
Central Ontario Industrial Relations Institute, 525
LA Centre for Active Living, 531
Centre for Addiction & Mental Health, 531
Centre for Community Learning & Development, 531
Centre for Comparative Literature, 531
Centre for Effective Practice Inc., 532
Centre for Equality Rights in Accommodation, 532
Centre for Immigrant & Community Services, 532
Centre for Immigrant & Community Services of Ontario-LINC Centre, 532
Centre for Information & Community Services of Ontario-North York Office, 532
Centre for Information & Community Services of Ontario-Woodside Square LINC Centre, 532
Centre for Information & Community Services of Ontario-Toronto Integrated Service Centre, 532
Centre for Independent Living in Toronto, 532
Centre for Inquiry Canada, 533
The Centre for Israel & Jewish Affairs, 533
Centre for Jewish Education, 533
The Centre for Peace in the Balkans, 533
Centre for Research on Latin America & The Caribbean, 533

Centre for Spanish Speaking Peoples, 533
Centre for Study of Insurance Operations, 534
Centre francophone de Toronto, 535
Certified Professional Trainers Network, 538
CFA Society Toronto, 538
C.G. Jung Foundation of Ontario, 539
Chaeo Chow Association of Eastern Canada, 539
Chai-Tikvah The Life & Hope Foundation, 539
The Champlain Society, 551
The Change Foundation, 551
Chartered Professional Accountants Canada, 552
Chartered Professional Accountants of Ontario, 553
Chartered Shorthand Reporters' Association of Ontario, 554
Chawkers Foundation, 555
Canadian Chemical Producers' Association-Ontario Regional Office, 556
Chess & Math Association-Toronto Branch, 556
Chiefs of Ontario, 558
The Child Abuse Survivor Monument Project, 558
Child Care Advocacy Association of Canada, 558
Child Development Institute, 559
Child Find Ontario, 559
Childcare Resource & Research Unit, 560
Childhood Cancer Canada Foundation, 560
Children's Aid Society of Toronto, 561
Children's International Summer Villages (Canada) Inc., 562
Children's Mental Health Ontario, 562
Children's Resource & Consultation Centre of Ontario, 562
Children's Safety Association of Canada, 562
China Council for the Promotion of International Trade - Canadian Office, 564
Chinese Canadian National Council, 564
Chinese Canadian National Council-ON - CCNC Toronto, 564
Chinese Canadian National Council-British Columbia - United Chinese Community Enrichment Service Society, 564
Chinese Cultural Centre of Greater Toronto, 564
Chinese Family Services of Ontario, 565
Chinese Professionals Association of Canada, 565
Choirs Ontario, 566
Chosen People Ministries (Canada), 566
The Christian & Missionary Alliance in Canada, 566
Christie-Ossington Neighbourhood Centre, 568
Church of Scientology of Toronto, 569
Citizen Scientists, 570
Citizens Concerned About Free Trade-Toronto Office, 570
Citizens' Environment Watch, 570
Clan Farquharson Association of Canada, 571
Clan Fraser Society of Canada, 571
Clans & Scottish Societies of Canada, 572
Classical & Medieval Numismatic Society, 572
Clinical Nurse Specialist Association of Ontario, 574
Club canadien de Toronto, 574
Coaches Association of Ontario, 576
Coalition for Gun Control, 578
Coalition of Black Trade Unionists, 578
Coffee Association of Canada, 580
College of Audiologists & Speech-Language Pathologists of Ontario, 582
College of Chiropodists of Ontario, 583
College of Chiropractors of Ontario, 583
College of Dental Technologists of Ontario, 583
College of Denturists of Ontario, 583
College of Dietitians of Ontario, 584
College of Family Physicians of Canada-Ontario College of Family Physicians, 585
College of Massage Therapists of Ontario, 585
College of Medical Radiation Technologists of Ontario, 586
College of Midwives of Ontario, 586
The College of Naturopaths of Ontario, 586

College of Nurses of Ontario, 586
College of Occupational Therapists of Ontario, 587
College of Opticians of Ontario, 587
College of Optometrists of Ontario, 587
College of Physicians & Surgeons of Ontario, 588
College of Physiotherapists of Ontario, 589
The College of Psychologists of Ontario, 589
College of Registered Psychotherapists of Ontario, 590
College of Respiratory Therapists of Ontario, 590
Colleges Ontario, 591
Colon Cancer Canada, 591
Colorectal Cancer Association of Canada, 591
Commonwealth Forestry Association - Canadian Chapter, 593
Communicative Disorders Assistant Association of Canada, 594
Communist Party of Canada, 594
Communist Party of Canada (Ontario), 595
Community Action Resource Centre, 595
Community Association for Riding for the Disabled, 596
Community Folk Art Council of Toronto, 597
Community Heritage Ontario, 599
Community Information Fairview, 599
Community Legal Education Ontario, 600
Community Living Ontario, 604
Community Living Toronto, 605
Community Microskills Development Centre, 606
Community One Foundation, 607
Compost Council of Canada, 609
Concerned Children's Advertisers, 609
Concerned Friends of Ontario Citizens in Care Facilities, 609
Confederation of Resident & Ratepayer Associations, 611
Congregation of Missionaries of the Precious Blood, Atlantic Province, 613
Congregation of St. Basil, 613
Connexions Information Sharing Services, 613
Conseil national Société de Saint-Vincent de Paul-Toronto Central Council, 619
Conservation Council of Ontario, 622
Conservation Foundation of Greater Toronto, 622
Consolidated Credit Counseling Services of Canada, Inc., 623
Construction Specifications Canada, 624
Consulting Engineers of Ontario, 625
Consumer Health Organization of Canada, 625
Consumer Policy Institute, 626
Consumers Council of Canada, 626
Contact Point, 626
Co-operative Education & Work-Integrated Learning Canada, 627
Cooperative Housing Federation of Canada-Ontario Region, 628
Co-operative Housing Federation of Toronto, 628
The Coptic Orthodox Church (Canada), 628
Corbrook Awakening Abilities, 628
COSTI Immigrant Services, 631
COSTI Immigrant Services-Corvetti Education Centre, 632
COSTI Immigrant Services-Toronto - Employment Services, 632
COSTI Immigrant Services-Jane St. Hub, 632
COSTI Immigrant Services-North York Centre, 632
COSTI Immigrant Services-Reception Centre, 632
COSTI Immigrant Services-Caledonia Centre, 632
Costume Society of Ontario, 632
Couchiching Institute on Public Affairs, 632
Council for Automotive Human Resources, 632
Council of Agencies Serving South Asians, 632
The Council of Canadians-Ontario, Québec, Nunavut, 633
Council of Ministers of Education, Canada, 634

Council of Ontario Construction Associations, 634
Council of Ontario Universities, 635
Council of Outdoor Educators of Ontario, 635
Council of Private Investigators - Ontario, 635
Council of Ukrainian Credit Unions of Canada, 635
Council on Drug Abuse, 636
The Counselling Foundation of Canada, 636
Counterpoint Community Orchestra, 636
Couples For Christ Foundation for Family & Life, 636
Couples For Christ, 636
Covenant House Toronto, 637
CP24 CHUM Christmas Wish, 638
Credit Association of Greater Toronto, 639
Credit Canada Debt Solutions, Inc., 639
Credit Counselling Canada, 639
Credit Counselling Society-Toronto, 640
Credit Institute of Canada, 640
Criminal Lawyers' Association, 642
Crohn's & Colitis Canada, 642
Crohn's & Colitis Canada-Ontario Region, 643
Croquet Canada, 643
The Cross-Cultural Community Services Association, 644
Cryonics Society of Canada, 645
Curriculum Services Canada, 646
CUSO International-Toronto Office, 646
Cycle Toronto, 647
Cypriot Federation of Canada, 647
Cystic Fibrosis Canada, 647
Czech & Slovak Association of Canada, 648
Daily Bread Food Bank, 648
Dance Ontario Association, 649
Dance Umbrella of Ontario, 649
Dancemakers, 649
Dancer Transition Resource Centre, 649
Davenport-Perth Neighbourhood & Community Health Centre, 651
Dejinta Beesha Multi-Service Centre, 652
Delta Family Resource Centre, 653
Design Exchange, 654
Development & Peace-Ontario - Central, 654
Diabetes Canada, 655
Canadian Diabetes Association-GTA Regional Leadership Centre, 655
Dial-a-Tutor, 656
Dietitians of Canada, 656
Digital Health Canada, 656
Digital Imaging Association, 656
Dignitas International, 656
Dignity Toronto Dignité, 657
Direct Sellers Association of Canada, 657
Directors Guild of Canada, 657
Directors Guild of Canada-Ontario District Council, 658
Directors Guild of Canada-Saskatchewan District Council, 658
Directors Guild of Canada-Manitoba District Council, 657
Disability Awareness Consultants, 658
Disaster Recovery Institute Canada, 658
Discalced Carmelite Secular Order - Canada, 658
Distress Centres of Toronto, 659
Dixon Hall, 660
Doctors without Borders Canada, 660
Documentary Organization of Canada, 660
Donner Canadian Foundation, 661
Door & Hardware Institute in Canada, 661
Doorsteps Neighbourhood Services, 661
Down Syndrome Association of Toronto, 661
Downtown Legal Services, 661
Dragon Boat Canada, 662
Dress for Success-Toronto, 663
Drinks Ontario, 663
Driving School Association of Ontario, 663
Dutch Canadian Association of Greater Toronto Inc., 665
Dying with Dignity, 665
Dystonia Medical Research Foundation Canada, 665
Earth Day Canada, 667
Earthroots, 667

East Toronto Community Legal Services, 668
East York - Scarborough Reading Association, 669
East York Historical Society, 669
East York Learning Experience, 669
Easter Seals Canada, 669
Easter Seals Ontario, 669
Eastview Neighbourhood Community Centre, 671
Ecojustice Canada Society-Toronto Office, 672
Editors' Association of Canada, 674
Editors' Association of Canada-Toronto, 674
Egale Canada, 681
Elder Abuse Ontario, 681
Electric Vehicle Society, 682
Electrical Contractors Association of Ontario, 682
Electro-Federation Canada, 683
Electronics Import Committee, 683
Electronics Product Stewardship Canada, 684
Elementary Teachers' Federation of Ontario, 684
Eli Bay Relaxation Response Institute, 684
Elsa Wild Animal Appeal of Canada, 685
Embroiderers' Association of Canada, Inc.-Ontario - Toronto Guild of Stitchery, 686
Empire Club of Canada, 686
Emunah Women of Canada-Toronto Chapter, 687
Enactus Canada, 687
The Endometriosis Network, 687
Energy Action Council of Toronto, 688
Energy Probe Research Foundation, 688
Engineers Without Borders, 689
Entertainment Software Association of Canada, 690
Environmental Defence, 691
Epilepsy Ontario, 693
Epilepsy Ontario-Toronto, 694
Eritrean Canadian Community Centre of Metropolitan Toronto, 695
Esprit Orchestra, 695
Essential Skills Ontario, 696
Estonian Central Council in Canada, 697
Estonian Evangelical Lutheran Church Consistory, 697
Ethiopian Association in the Greater Toronto Area & Surrounding Regions, 697
Etobicoke Historical Society, 697
Etobicoke Humane Society, 697
Etobicoke Philharmonic Orchestra, 697
European Union Chamber of Commerce in Toronto, 698
Eva's Initiatives for Homeless Youth, 698
Evangel Hall Mission, 698
Eventing Canada [!], 699
Evergreen, 699
Ex Libris Association, 699
Excellence Canada, 699
Eye Bank of Canada - Ontario Division, 700
Facility Association, 700
The Fair Rental Policy Organization of Ontario, 701
Fair Vote Canada, 701
Families for a Secure Future, 701
Family Day Care Services (Toronto), 703
Family Service Ontario, 704
Family Service Toronto, 704
Family Supports Institute Ontario, 705
Federation of Canadian Naturists, 723
Federation of Canadian Turkish Associations, 723
Federation of Metro Tenants' Associations, 725
Federation of Mutual Fund Dealers, 725
Federation of Ontario Public Libraries, 726
Federation of Portuguese Canadian Business & Professionals Inc., 726
Fife House, 734
50 & Piu Enasco-Toronto Office, 735
Filipino Students' Association of Toronto, 735
FilmOntario, 735
Financial Executives International Canada, 736
Financial Markets Association of Canada, 737
Financial Planning Standards Council, 737
Financial Services Commission of Ontario, 737

Findhelp Information Services, 737
First Portuguese Canadian Cultural Centre, 739
First Unitarian Congregation of Toronto, 739
The 519 Church St. Community Centre, 740
Flavour Manufacturers Association of Canada, 740
Flemingdon Community Legal Services, 740
Flemingdon Neighbourhood Services, 740
Floorball Canada, 741
Focolare Movement - Canada, 741
Focus Humanitarian Assistance Canada, 741
Food & Consumer Products of Canada, 749
Food Allergy Canada, 749
Foodservice Consultants Society International - Canadian Chapter, 750
Foodshare Toronto, 750
Forests Ontario, 751
Fort York Food Bank, 754
Forum for Intercultural Leadership & Learning, 754
Foundation Assisting Canadian Talent on Recordings, 755
The Foundation Fighting Blindness, 755
Foundation for the Study of Objective Art, 756
The Fraser Institute-Toronto Office, 757
Fred Victor Centre, 758
Freestyle Skiing Ontario, 759
Friends of Canadian Broadcasting, 760
The Friends of Fort York & Garrison Common, 761
Friends of Simon Wiesenthal Centre for Holocaust Studies - Canada, 762
Friends of the Greenbelt Foundation, 762
Frontiers Foundation, 763
Fujiwara Dance Inventions, 764
Funeral Advisory & Memorial Society, 764
Fung Loy Kok Institute of Taoism, 764
Furriers Guild of Canada, 765
Fusion: The Ontario Clay & Glass Association, 765
FutureWatch Environment & Development Education Partners, 765
Futurpreneur Canada, 765
The Gairdner Foundation, 766
GAMA International Canada, 766
The Garden Clubs of Ontario-Toronto Japanese Garden, 767
The Garden Clubs of Ontario-Milne House, 767
The Garden Clubs of Ontario-Toronto, 767
Gay Fathers of Toronto, 768
Gem & Mineral Club of Scarborough, 768
General Church of the New Jerusalem in Canada, 768
General Insurance OmbudService, 769
Genesis Research Foundation, 769
Geneva Centre for Autism, 769
Genome Canada-Ontario Genomics Institute, 769
George Cedric Metcalf Charitable Foundation, 770
German-Canadian Mardi Gras Association Inc., 772
Gerontological Nursing Association of Ontario, 772
The Gershon Iskowitz Foundation, 772
Girl Guides of Canada, 773
Girl Guides of Canada-Guides du Canada-Ontario Council, 773
Glaucoma Research Society of Canada, 774
Global Automakers of Canada, 774
Global Commercial Insurers' Association, 774
Global Network of Director Institutes, 775
Goethe-Institut (Toronto), 776
Good Shepherd Refuge Social Ministries, 777
Gordon Foundation, 778
Governance Professionals of Canada, 778
Grand Orange Lodge of Canada, 780
GRAND Society, 780
Greater Toronto Al-Anon Information Services, 785
Greater Toronto Apartment Association, 785
Greater Toronto CivicAction Alliance, 785
Greater Toronto Electrical Contractors Association, 785
Greater Toronto Hotel Association, 786

Greater Toronto Marketing Alliance, 786
Greater Toronto Rose & Garden Horticultural Society, 786
Greek Community of Toronto, 787
Greek Orthodox Metropolis of Toronto (Canada), 788
The Green Party of Ontario, 789
Green Roofs for Healthy Cities, 789
Greenest City, 789
Greenpeace Canada, 789
GS1 Canada, 792
Guaranteed Funeral Deposits of Canada, 792
Guillain-Barré Support Group of Canada, 794
Habitat for Humanity Canada, 796
Habitat for Humanity Canada-Ontario - Greater Toronto Area, 797
Hal Jackman Foundation, 798
HALCO, 798
The Hanen Centre, 803
Harbourfront Centre, 803
Harbourfront Community Centre, 803
Harmony Foundation of Canada-Greater Toronto Chapter, MegaCity Chorus, 804
Harmony Foundation of Canada-East York Chapter, Barbershoppers, 803
The Harold Greenberg Fund, 804
Harry A. Newman Memorial Foundation, 804
Hart House Orchestra, 804
Hashomer Hatzair Canada, 804
Hatzoloh Toronto, 804
Healthy Minds Canada, 807
Hearing Foundation of Canada, 808
Heart & Stroke Foundation of Ontario, 809
Heart & Stroke Foundation of Ontario-Chinese Canadian Council, 809
Heart & Stroke Foundation of Ontario-Toronto Office, 809
Hellenic Canadian Board of Trade, 811
The Henry White Kinnear Foundation, 812
Heritage Toronto, 813
Heritage York, 814
Hilal Committee of Metropolitan Toronto & Vicinity, 814
Hillel of Greater Toronto, 814
Hincks-Dellcrest Treatment Centre & Foundation, 815
Hincks-Dellcrest Centre-Gail Appel Institute, 815
Hincks-Dellcrest Centre-Treatment Centre, 815
Hispanic Canadian Heritage Council, 815
Hispanic Development Council, 815
Historica Canada, 815
HMWN (Holy Mother World Networks) Radio Maria, 817
Hockey Development Centre for Ontario, 817
Hola, 818
Holocaust Education Centre, 818
Home Child Care Association of Ontario, 819
Homeopathic Medical Association Of Canada, 820
Hong Fook Mental Health Association, 820
Hong Fook Mental Health Association-Downton Branch, 820
Hong Kong Trade Development Council-Toronto Office
Hong Kong-Canada Business Association-Toronto Section Office, 820
Hope Air, 821
Hospice Palliative Care Ontario, 823
Hospital Auxiliaries Association of Ontario, 823
Hospital for Sick Children Foundation, 823
HRMS Professionals Association, 824
Human Resources Professionals Association, 825
Human Rights & Race Relations Centre, 826
Hungarian Canadian Cultural Centre, 827
Hungarian Studies Association of Canada, 827
The Hunger Project Canada, 827
IAMAW District 78, 829
Imagine Canada, 829
Immigrant Women's Health Centre, 831
Independent Practice Nurses Interest Group, 833
Independent Production Fund, 833
Indexing Society of Canada, 834

Indo-Canada Chamber of Commerce, 835
Indspire-Toronto Office, 835
Industrial Accident Victims Group of Ontario, 835
Infertility Network, 836
Information Resource Management Association of Canada, 837
Inner City Angels, 838
Innovation Norway, 839
Inside Out Toronto LGBT Film & Video Festival, 839
Inspirit Foundation, 840
Installation, Maintenance & Repair Sector Council & Trade Association, 840
Institute for Catastrophic Loss Reduction, 843
Institute for Change Leaders, 843
Institute for Clinical Evaluative Sciences, 843
Institute for Optimizing Health Outcomes, 843
Institute for Performance & Learning, 844
Institute for Safe Medication Practices Canada, 844
Institute for Work & Health, 844
Institute of Certified Management Consultants of Alberta, 845
Institute of Certified Management Consultants of Atlantic Canada, 845
Institute of Certified Management Consultants of British Columbia, 845
Institute of Certified Management Consultants of Manitoba, 845
Institute of Certified Management Consultants of Saskatchewan, 845
Institute of Communication Agencies, 845
Institute of Corporate Directors, 845
Institute of Cultural Affairs International, 846
Institute of Cultural Affairs International-ICA Canada, 846
Institute of Housing Management, 846
Institute of Law Clerks of Ontario, 846
Institute of Public Administration of Canada, 847
Institutional Limited Partners Association, 848
Insurance Brokers Association of Canada, 848
Insurance Brokers Association of Canada-Insurance Brokers Association of Ontario, 848
Insurance Bureau of Canada, 848
Insurance Bureau of Canada-Insurance Information Services & Investigative Services, 849
Insurance Institute of Canada, 849
Insurance Institute of Ontario, 849
Insurance Institute of Ontario-Cambrian Shield Chapter, 850
Insurance Institute of Ontario-Kawartha/Durham Chapter, 850
Insurance Institute of Prince Edward Island, 850
Integrity Toronto, 850
Interac Association, 851
Interactive Advertising Bureau of Canada, 851
Interactive Ontario, 851
Interior Designers of Canada, 852
International Alliance of Theatrical Stage Employees, Moving Picture Technicians, Artists & Allied Crafts of the U.S., Its Territories & Canada-Toronto Office, 1535
International Association for Literary Journalism Studies, 853
International Association for Medical Assistance to Travellers, 853
International Association of Business Communicators-Toronto Chapter
International Association of Machinists & Aerospace Workers-Canadian Office, 1539
International Atomic Energy Agency-IAEA Regional Office in Canada, 1540
International Bible Correspondence School, 854
International Board on Books for Young People - Canadian Section, 854
International Centre for Science in Drug Policy, 854
International Council of AIDS Service Organizations, 855
International Development & Relief Foundation, 856

International Federation of Professional & Technical Engineers (AFL-CIO/CLC)-Canadian Office - Local 160
International Federation on Aging, 857
International Institute of Concern for Public Health, 858
International Napoleonic Society, 858
International Network for Cultural Diversity, 858
International Organization of Ukrainian Communities "Fourth Wave", 859
International Pension & Employee Benefits Lawyers Association, 859
International Relief Agency Inc., 859
International Schizophrenia Foundation, 860
International Society for Augmentative & Alternative Communication, 860
International Society for Emotion Focused Therapy, 860
Interval House, 861
Inter-Varsity Christian Fellowship, 862
Inuit Art Foundation, 862
Investment Funds Institute of Canada, 862
Investment Industry Association of Canada, 863
Investment Industry Regulatory Organization of Canada, 863
IODE Canada, 863
Iranian Community Association of Ontario, 863
Iraqi Canadian Society of Ontario, 863
The Ireland Funds, Canada, 863
Ireland-Canada Chamber of Commerce, 863
Irritable Bowel Syndrome Self Help & Support Group, 864
Is Five Foundation, 864
Islamic Foundation of Toronto, 864
Israel Aliyah Center, 866
Israel Cancer Research Fund, 866
The Israel Economic Mission to Canada, 866
Israel Medical Association-Canadian Chapter, 866
Italian Chamber of Commerce of Ontario, 866
Italian Cultural Institute (Istituto Italiano di Cultura), 866
Iyengar Yoga Association of Canada, 867
Jack.org, 867
Jacob's Ladder - The Canadian Foundation for Control of Neurodegenerative Disease, 867
Jamaican Canadian Association, 867
Jane Austen Society of North America, 868
Jane Finch Community & Family Centre, 868
The Jane Goodall Institute of Canada, 868
Japan Automobile Manufacturers Association of Canada, 868
Japan External Trade Organization (Toronto), 868
The Japan Foundation, Toronto, 868
The Japan Society Canada, 869
Japanese Canadian Cultural Centre, 869
Jean Tweed Treatment Centre, 869
The Jerrahi Sufi Order of Canada, 869
Jessie's - The June Callwood Centre for Young Women, 870
Jesuit Development Office, 870
Jewellers Vigilance Canada Inc., 871
Jewish Family & Child, 871
Jewish Family & Child-Downtown Branch, 871
Jewish Family & Child-Toronto Branch - Jerome D. Diamond Adolescent Centre, 871
Jewish Federations of Canada - UIA, 872
Jewish Free Loan Toronto, 872
Jewish Genealogical Society of Toronto, 872
Jewish Information Service of Greater Toronto, 873
Jews for Jesus, 873
Jews for Judaism, 873
Jockey Club of Canada, 873
Jockeys Benefit Association of Canada, 873
The John Howard Society of Ontario, 874
The John Howard Society of Ontario-The John Howard Society of Toronto, 875
John Milton Society for the Blind in Canada, 875
Joint Centre for Bioethics, 875
Joint Forum of Financial Market Regulators, 875
Judo Ontario, 876
Junior Achievement Canada, 877

Junior Achievement of Canada-Junior Achievement of Central Ontario, 877
Junior Chamber International Canada, 877
Junior League of Toronto, 878
Justice for Children & Youth, 878
Juvenile Diabetes Research Foundation Canada, 878
Juvenile Diabetes Research Foundation-Toronto-York, 879
JVS of Greater Toronto, 879
JVS of Greater Toronto-Toronto North, 879
JVS of Greater Toronto-Jane-Finch, 879
JVS of Greater Toronto-Bathurst Finch, 879
JVS of Greater Toronto-Al Green Resource Centre, 879
Kababayan Multicultural Centre, 879
KAIROS: Canadian Ecumenical Justice Initiatives, 880
Kashmiri Canadian Council, 882
Kashruth Council of Canada, 882
Kenneth M Molson Foundation, 883
Kensington Foundation, 883
Kerry's Place Autism Services-Kerry's Place Toronto, 884
Kidney Cancer Canada Association, 884
Kids Help Phone, 886
Kids Help Phone-Ontario, 886
Kids Now, 886
Kids Up Front, 886
KidSport Ontario, 887
Kiwanis Music Festival Association of Greater Toronto, 892
Kolbe Eucharistic Apostolate, 892
Korean Canadian Cultural Association of the Greater Toronto Area, 893
Korean Canadian Women's Association, 893
Korean Senior Citizens Society of Toronto, 893
Korean-Canadian Symphony Orchestra, 894
Kurdish Community & Information Centre of Toronto, 894
Ladies' Orange Benevolent Association of Canada, 895
Laidlaw Foundation, 895
Lakeshore Area Multi-Service Project, 896
LAMP Community Health Centre, 897
Landlord's Self-Help Centre, 898
Language Industry Association, 899
Lao Association of Ontario, 899
Last Post Fund-Ontario Branch, 899
Latino Canadian Cultural Association, 900
Latvian Canadian Cultural Centre, 900
Latvian National Federation in Canada, 900
The Latvian Relief Society of Canada, 900
Law Foundation of Ontario, 901
Law Society of Upper Canada, 902
Law Union of Ontario, 902
Lawson Foundation, 902
League for Human Rights of B'nai Brith Canada, 903
League for Human Rights of B'nai Brith Canada-Ontario Region Office, 903
The League of Canadian Poets, 903
League of Ukrainian Canadian Women, 903
League of Ukrainian Canadians, 903
Learning Disabilities Association of Ontario, 904
Learning Enrichment Foundation, 905
Learning for a Sustainable Future, 905
Leave Out Violence Everywhere, 905
Legal Aid Ontario, 906
Legislative Recording & Broadcast Association, 906
Lesbian & Gay Immigration Task Force-LEGIT - Toronto, 907
The Leukemia & Lymphoma Society of Canada, 908
The Leukemia & Lymphoma Society of Canada-Ontario Branch, 909
Liaison of Independent Filmmakers of Toronto, 909
Liberal Party of Canada (Ontario), 909
Life Sciences Ontario, 911
Lifesaving Society, 911
Lifesaving Society-Ontario & Nunavut Branch, 911
Lights, Camera, Access!, 912

Geographic Index / Ontario - Toronto

The Literary Press Group of Canada, 914
The Lithuanian Canadian Community, 914
Lithuanian Community Association of Toronto, 914
Lithuanian-Canadian Foundation, 915
Little People of Ontario, 915
LOFT Community Services, 917
The Logistics Institute, 917
The Lord's Flock Charismatic Community, 919
Luggage, Leathergoods, Handbags & Accessories Association of Canada, 920
Lunenfeld-Tanenbaum Research Institute, 921
Lupus Ontario, 921
Lymphovenous Association of Ontario, 923
Macedonian Human Rights Movement International, 923
The Mackenzie Institute, 924
Madonna House Apostolate-Toronto, 925
Magazines Canada, 925
Maggie's: The Toronto Sex Workers Action Project, 925
Make-A-Wish Canada, 927
Maker Kids, 927
Maltese Veterans Association of Canada, 928
Maltese-Canadian Federation Inc., 928
Maltese-Canadian Society of Toronto, Inc., 928
March of Dimes Canada, 949
March of Dimes Non-Profit Housing Corporation, 949
Margaret M. Allemang Centre for the History of Nursing, 949
Marguerite Bourgeoys Family Centre Fertility Care Programme, 949
Marketing Research & Intelligence Association, 951
Markland Homes Association, 952
Martin Prosperity Institute, 952
Masaryk Memorial Institute Inc., 952
Massey Centre for Women, 953
Master Brewers Association of The Americas-Ontario District
The Company of Master Mariners of Canada-Great Lakes Division, 953
Maytree Foundation, 954
The McLean Foundation, 955
Media Access Canada, 957
Medical Marijuana Association, 958
Medico-Legal Society of Toronto, 959
Mercaz-Canada, 961
Mercy for Animals Canada, 961
Merit OpenShop Contractors Association of Ontario, 962
Merry Go Round Children's Foundation, 962
The Metal Arts Guild of Canada, 962
Metro (Toronto) Association of Family Resource Programs, 963
Metro Toronto Chinese & Southeast Asian Legal Clinic, 963
Metro Toronto Movement for Literacy, 963
Metronome Canada, 963
Metropolitan Action Committee on Violence Against Women & Children, 964
Metropolitan Community Church of Toronto, 964
The Michener Institute for Applied Health Sciences, 964
Mid-Toronto Community Services, 965
Midwives Collective of Toronto, 965
Miss G Project, 968
Missing Children Society of Canada-Toronto Office, 968
Missionary Sisters of The Precious Blood of North America, 969
Mizrachi Organization of Canada, 970
Model "A" Owners of Canada Inc., 970
Mood Disorders Association of Ontario, 973
Mooredale Youth Concert Orchestra, 973
Moorelands Community Services, 973
Mortgage Professionals Canada, 975
Mosaic Institute, 975
Motion Picture Association - Canada, 975
Motor Coach Canada, 975
Mount Sinai Hospital Foundation, 976
MuchFACT, 978
Multicultural History Society of Ontario, 979

Multiple Sclerosis Society of Canada, 980
Multiple Sclerosis Society of Canada-Ontario & Nunavut Division, 980
The Municipal Chapter of Toronto IODE, 980
Municipal Finance Officers' Association of Ontario, 981
Municipal Information Systems Association of Canada, 981
Muniscope, 982
Muscular Dystrophy Canada, 982
Muscular Dystrophy Canada-Ontario & Nunavut Regional Office, 982
Museum of Contemporary Canadian Art, 983
Music Canada, 983
Music Managers Forum Canada, 984
Mutual Fund Dealers Association of Canada, 986
Myalgic Encephalomyelitis Association of Ontario, 986
Na'amat Canada Inc.-Toronto Council, 987
NABET 700 CEP, 987
NACE International-Canadian Region - Toronto Section, 1572
NAID Canada, 987
Nar-Anon Family Groups of Ontario, 988
National Action Committee on the Status of Women, 989
National Advertising Benevolent Society, 989
National African Integration & Families of Ontario, 989
National Angel Capital Organization, 989
National Association of Major Mail Users, Inc., 990
National Association of Watch & Clock Collectors, Inc.-Toronto Chapter
National Ballet of Canada, 991
The National Citizens Coalition, 991
National Congress of Italian-Canadians, 991
National Council of Barbadian Associations in Canada, 991
National Council of Jewish Women of Canada-Toronto Section, 992
National Council of Trinidad & Tobago Organizations in Canada, 992
National Crowdfunding Association of Canada, 992
National Eating Disorder Information Centre, 992
National Hockey League Alumni Association, 994
National Hockey League Players' Association, 994
National Information Program on Antibiotics, 994
National Initiative for the Care of the Elderly, 994
National Institute of Broadcasting, 994
National Magazine Awards Foundation, 994
National NewsMedia Council, 995
National Reading Campaign, Inc., 995
National Shevchenko Musical Ensemble Guild of Canada, 996
National Youth Orchestra Canada, 997
Native Canadian Centre of Toronto, 997
Native Child & Family Services of Toronto, 997
Native Earth Performing Arts Inc., 998
Native Women's Resource Centre of Toronto, 998
Natural Family Planning Association, 998
The Nature Conservancy of Canada, 999
Naval Club of Toronto, 1001
Navy League of Canada-Ontario, 1002
Neighbourhood Information Post, 1002
Neighbourhood Pharmacy Association of Canada, 1002
Nellie's Shelter, 1003
Nellie's (Women's Hostels Inc.)-Outreach Office, 1003
Nepali Children's Education Project, 1003
Neurological Health Charities Canada, 1004
New Circles Community Services, 1014
New College Alumni Association, 1014
New Democratic Party-Ontario NDP, 1014
Newcomer Women's Services Toronto, 1015

Newcomer Women's Services Toronto-Newcomer Employment Services Toronto (NEST), 1015
Newman Centre Catholic Chaplaincy and Parish, 1024
Newspapers Canada, 1024
Nickel Institute, 1026
Non-Smokers' Rights Association, 1028
Les normes canadiennes de la publicité, 1028
North American Broadcasters Association, 1029
North American Native Plant Society, 1029
North West Commercial Travellers' Association, 1033
North York Community House, 1033
North York General Foundation, 1033
North York Harvest Food Bank, 1033
Northern Finance Association, 1035
Northern Ramblers Car Club Inc., 1035
Northwood Neighbourhood Services, 1040
Not Far From The Tree, 1040
Nuclear Insurance Association of Canada, 1050
Numeris, 1050
Nurse Practitioners' Association of Ontario, 1052
Oasis Centre des femmes, 1054
Occupational Health Clinics for Ontario Workers, 1054
Oceana Canada, 1054
The Older Women's Network, 1056
Olivet New Church, 1057
OmbudService for Life & Health Insurance, 1057
Ombudsman for Banking Services & Investments, 1057
OMID Foundation Canada, 1058
Ontario 5 Pin Bowlers' Association, 1058
Ontario Amateur Wrestling Association, 1059
The Ontario Archaeological Society, 1059
The Ontario Archaeological Society Inc.-Toronto Chapter, 1060
Ontario Arts Council, 1060
Ontario Association for Behaviour Analysis, 1061
Ontario Association for Family Mediation, 1061
Ontario Association for Geographic & Environmental Education, 1061
Ontario Association of Acupuncture & Traditional Chinese Medicine, 1061
Ontario Association of Architects, 1061
Ontario Association of Art Galleries, 1062
Ontario Association of Certified Engineering Technicians & Technologists, 1062
Ontario Association of Chiefs of Police, 1062
Ontario Association of Child & Youth Care, 1062
Ontario Association of Children's Aid Societies, 1062
Ontario Association of Children's Rehabilitation Services, 1062
Ontario Association of Community Care Access Centres, 1063
Ontario Association of Consultants, Counsellors, Psychometrists & Psychotherapists, 1063
Ontario Association of Deans of Education, 1063
Ontario Association of Food Banks, 1064
Ontario Association of Former Parliamentarians, 1064
Ontario Association of Insolvency & Restructuring Professionals, 1064
Ontario Association of Interval & Transition Houses, 1064
Ontario Association of Landscape Architects, 1064
Ontario Association of Medical Laboratories, 1064
Ontario Association of Naturopathic Doctors, 1065
Ontario Association of Optometrists, 1065
Ontario Association of Prosthetists & Orthotists, 1065
Ontario Association of Sign Language Interpreters, 1066
Ontario Association of Social Workers, 1066

Ontario Association of Speech-Language Pathologists & Audiologists, 1066
Ontario Association of Trading Houses, 1066
Ontario Association on Developmental Disabilities, 1067
Ontario Ballet Theatre, 1067
Ontario Baton Twirling Association, 1067
Ontario Black History Society, 1068
Ontario Blind Sports Association, 1068
Ontario Book Publishers Organization, 1068
Ontario Brain Injury Association-Toronto, 1069
Ontario Building Envelope Council, 1069
The Ontario Campaign for Action on Tobacco, 1070
Ontario Camps Association, 1070
Ontario Catholic School Trustees' Association, 1070
Ontario Centres of Excellence, 1070
Ontario Chamber of Commerce, 1071
Ontario Chiropractic Association, 1071
Ontario Clean Air Alliance, 1071
Ontario Coalition Against Poverty, 1071
Ontario Coalition for Abortion Clinics, 1071
Ontario Coalition for Better Child Care, 1071
Ontario Coalition of Rape Crisis Centres, 1072
Ontario College & University Library Association, 1072
Ontario College of Pharmacists, 1072
Ontario College of Social Workers & Social Service Workers, 1072
Ontario College of Teachers, 1072
Ontario Colleges Athletic Association, 1073
Ontario Community Newspapers Association, 1073
Ontario Community Support Association, 1073
Ontario Confederation of University Faculty Associations, 1074
Ontario Construction Secretariat, 1074
Ontario Council for International Cooperation, 1075
Ontario Council of Agencies Serving Immigrants, 1075
Ontario Council of Alternative Businesses, 1075
Ontario Council of University Libraries, 1075
Ontario Council on Articulation and Transfer, 1075
Ontario Council on Graduate Studies, 1075
Ontario Craft Brewers, 1075
Ontario Crafts Council, 1075
Ontario Criminal Justice Association, 1076
Ontario Crown Attorneys Association, 1076
Ontario Dental Association, 1077
Ontario Electrical League, 1077
Ontario Energy Association, 1077
Ontario English Catholic Teachers' Association (CLC), 1077
Ontario Environment Industry Association, 1078
Ontario Fashion Exhibitors, 1078
Ontario Federation for Cerebral Palsy, 1079
Ontario Federation of Indian Friendship Centres, 1079
Ontario Federation of Labour, 1079
Ontario Federation of School Athletic Associations, 1079
Ontario Federation of Teaching Parents, 1080
Ontario Field Ornithologists, 1080
Ontario Fire Buff Associates, 1080
Ontario Fly & Bait Casting Association, 1080
Ontario Food Protection Association, 1080
Ontario Forest Industries Association, 1081
Ontario Foundation for Visually Impaired Children Inc., 1081
Ontario Gay & Lesbian Chamber of Commerce, 1081
Ontario Gerontology Association, 1082
Ontario Gymnastic Federation, 1083
Ontario Health Libraries Association, 1084
Ontario Healthy Communities Coalition, 1084
Ontario Herbalists Association, 1084
Ontario Heritage Trust, 1084
Ontario High School Chess Association, 1084
Ontario HIV Treatment Network, 1084
Ontario Home Builders' Association, 1085
Ontario Home Respiratory Services Association, 1086

Ontario Homeopathic Association, 1086
Ontario Horse Racing Industry Association, 1086
Ontario Hospital Association, 1086
Ontario Independent Insurance Adjusters' Association, 1087
Ontario Industrial Roofing Contractors' Association, 1087
Ontario Labour-Management Arbitrators Association, 1088
Ontario Lacrosse Association, 1088
Ontario Liberal Party, 1088
Ontario Library & Information Technology Association, 1088
Ontario Library Association, 1088
Ontario Library Boards' Association, 1089
Ontario Limousine Owners Association, 1089
Ontario Long Term Care Association, 1089
Ontario Lung Association, 1089
Ontario Lung Association-Toronto Office (Greater Toronto Area West), 1090
Ontario Masters Athletics, 1090
Ontario Medical Association, 1090
Ontario Medical Students Association, 1090
Ontario Mental Health Foundation, 1090
Ontario Mining Association, 1091
Ontario Motor Coach Association, 1091
Ontario Motor Vehicle Industry Council, 1091
Ontario Municipal Social Services Association, 1092
Ontario Museum Association, 1092
Ontario Music Festivals Association, 1093
Ontario Nature, 1093
Ontario Network of Employment Skills Training Projects, 1093
Ontario Neurotrauma Foundation, 1093
Ontario Non-Profit Housing Association, 1093
Ontario Nonprofit Network, 1094
Ontario Nurses' Association, 1094
Ontario Occupational Health Nurses Association, 1094
Ontario Opticians Association, 1094
Ontario Pharmacists' Association, 1095
Ontario Physical & Health Education Association, 1095
Ontario Physiotherapy Association, 1096
Ontario Plumbing Inspectors Association, 1096
Ontario Podiatric Medical Association, 1096
The Ontario Poetry Society, 1096
Ontario Prader-Willi Syndrome Association, 1097
Ontario Principals' Council, 1097
Ontario Printing & Imaging Association, 1097
Ontario Professional Planners Institute, 1098
Ontario Progressive Conservative Party, 1098
Ontario Psychological Association, 1098
Ontario Public Health Association, 1098
Ontario Public Interest Research Group, 1099
Ontario Public Interest Research Group-OPIRG York, 1099
Ontario Public Library Association, 1099
Ontario Public School Boards Association, 1099
Ontario Public Service Employees Union, 1099
Ontario Rainbow Alliance of the Deaf, 1100
Ontario Real Estate Association, 1100
Ontario Recreation Facilities Association, 1100
Ontario Recreational Canoeing & Kayaking Association, 1101
Ontario Regional Poison Information Centre, 1101
Ontario Respiratory Care Society, 1101
Ontario Ringette Association, 1102
Ontario Rock Garden Society, 1102
Ontario Rowing Association, 1102
Ontario School Library Association, 1103
Ontario Secondary School Teachers' Federation, 1103
Ontario Securities Commission, 1104
Ontario Senior Games Association, 1104
Ontario Sikh & Gurudwara Council, 1104
Ontario Small Urban Municipalities, 1105
Ontario Society for Environmental Management, 1105
Ontario Society for the Prevention of Cruelty to Animals-Etobicoke Branch (Affiliate), 1105

Ontario Society for the Prevention of Cruelty to Animals-Toronto Branch (Affiliate), 1107
Ontario Society of Artists, 1107
Ontario Society of Medical Technologists, 1107
Ontario Society of Nutrition Professionals in Public Health, 1107
Ontario Society of Occupational Therapists, 1107
Ontario Society of Periodontists, 1107
Ontario Society of Professional Engineers, 1107
Ontario Society of Psychotherapists, 1108
Ontario Society of Senior Citizens' Organizations, 1108
Ontario Spondylitis Association, 1108
Ontario Students Against Impaired Driving, 1109
Ontario Summer Theatre Association, 1109
Ontario Sustainable Energy Association, 1109
Ontario Teachers' Federation, 1110
Ontario Tennis Association, 1110
Ontario Thoracic Society, 1110
Ontario Track 3 Ski Association for the Disabled, 1110
Ontario Traffic Council, 1110
The Ontario Trillium Foundation, 1111
Ontario Trucking Association, 1111
Ontario Trucking Association-Education Foundation, 1111
Ontario Undergraduate Student Alliance, 1111
Ontario Underwater Council, 1112
Ontario Volleyball Association, 1112
Ontario Water Polo Association Incorporated, 1113
Ontario Water Ski Association, 1113
Ontario Water Works Association, 1113
Ontario Wheelchair Sports Association, 1113
Ontario Women's Health Network, 1113
Ontario Women's Justice Network, 1113
Opéra Atelier, 1114
Opera.ca, 1115
Operation Springboard, 1116
Operation Springboard-Employment Services, 1116
Operation Springboard-North Beaches Residence, 1116
Operation Springboard-Blue Jays Lodge, 1116
Operation Springboard-Terry Fox House, 1116
Operation Springboard-Diversion Office - Old City Hall, 1116
Operation Springboard-Diversion Office - Scarborough Ct., 1116
Operation Springboard-Aris Kaplanis Centre for Youth, Resource Room & Attendance Program, 1116
Opportunity For Advancement, 1116
Oraynu Congregation for Humanistic Judaism, 1117
Orchestra Toronto, 1117
ORT Canada, 1127
Osteoporosis Canada, 1128
Our Lady of Good Health Tamil Parish, 1133
Our Lady of the Rosary of Manaoag Evangelization Group, 1133
Out-of-Home Marketing Association of Canada, 1133
Outward Bound Canada, 1133
Ovarian Cancer Canada, 1133
Ovarian Cancer Canada-Ontario Regional Office, 1134
Oxfam Canada-Toronto Regional Office & National Fundraising Office, 1134
Pacific Asia Travel Association (Eastern Canada Chapter), 1134
Packaging Association of Canada, 1136
Pancreatic Cancer Canada Foundation, 1138
Parachute, 1138
ParaSport Ontario, 1139
Parent Action on Drugs, 1139
Parents as First Educators, 1140
Park People, 1140
Parkdale Community Information Centre, 1140
Parkdale Community Legal Services, 1140
Parkdale Focus Community Project, 1140
Parkdale Intercultural Association, 1140
Parkdale Neighbourhood Land Trust, 1141

Parkinson Canada, 1141
Parkinson Society Central & Northern Ontario, 1141
Parks & Recreation Ontario, 1142
La Passerelle - Intégration et Développement Économique, 1145
Pathways to Education Canada, 1145
Patients Canada, 1145
Patronato INAS (Canada), 1145
The Pembina Institute-Toronto Office, 1149
Pension Investment Association of Canada, 1150
People for Education, 1151
Periodical Marketers of Canada, 1152
Personal Computer Club of Toronto, 1152
Pet Food Association of Canada, 1153
Peter Gilgan Foundation, 1153
PFLAG Canada Inc.-Toronto Chapter, 1156
The Pharmacy Examining Board of Canada, 1157
Phoenix Community Works Foundation, 1157
Photographic Historical Society of Canada, 1157
Physicians Services Inc. Foundation, 1158
Pilot Parents, 1160
Plan Canada, 1161
Planned Parenthood of Toronto, 1161
Plast Ukrainian Youth Association of Canada, 1162
Playwrights Guild of Canada, 1162
Police Association of Ontario, 1163
Polish Army Veterans Association of America, 1163
Polish Combatants Association, 1164
Polish National Union of Canada, 1164
Polish Teachers Association in Canada, 1164
Polish-Jewish Heritage Foundation of Canada, 1164
The Pollution Probe Foundation, 1164
Pontifical Mission Societies, 1164
Portfolio Management Association of Canada, 1167
Post Traumatic Stress Disorder Association, 1167
Positive Youth Outreach, 1168
Power Workers' Union, 1169
Pragmora, 1169
Presbyterian Church in Canada, 1170
Pride of Israel, 1170
The Primate's World Relief & Development Fund, 1170
Princess Margaret Cancer Foundation, 1180
Prisoners' HIV/AIDS Support Action Network, 1180
Private Capital Markets Association of Canada, 1180
Pro Bono Law Ontario, 1180
Probation Officers Association of Ontario, 1181
Probe International, 1181
Professional Association of Canadian Theatres, 1181
Professional Association of Residents of Ontario, 1182
Professional Engineers Government of Ontario, 1183
Professional Engineers Ontario, 1183
Professional Engineers Ontario-Toronto Humber, 1185
The Professional Institute of the Public Service of Canada-Ontario Regional Office, 1185
Professional Organizers in Canada, 1186
Professional Student Services Personnel, 1186
Project Management Institute-Toronto
Prologue to the Performing Arts, 1188
Prospectors & Developers Association of Canada, 1189
Prosserman Jewish Community Centre, 1189
Prostate Cancer Canada, 1189
Provincial Building & Construction Trades Council of Ontario, 1190
Provincial Nurse Educator Interest Group, 1191
Public Accountants Council for the Province of Ontario, 1192
The Public Affairs Association of Canada, 1192

Public Service Alliance of Canada-Ontario Branch, 1193
Public Services Health & Safety Association, 1193
QMI - SAI Global, 1194
Quaker Aboriginal Affairs Committee, 1195
Quakers Fostering Justice, 1195
Qualifications Evaluation Council of Ontario, 1195
The Queen of Puddings Music Theatre Company, 1199
Queer Ontario, 1200
Quetico Foundation, 1201
Radiation Safety Institute of Canada, 1202
Radio Starmaker Fund, 1202
The Rainbow Alliance, 1203
Ralph Thornton Centre, 1204
RBC Foundation, 1204
Re:Sound Music Licensing Company, 1204
Reach for the Rainbow, 1205
Real Estate Council of Ontario, 1205
Real Estate Institute of Canada, 1205
Real Estate Institute of Canada-Ontario - Toronto Chapter, 1206
Real Property Association of Canada, 1206
reBOOT Canada, 1206
Receivables Management Assocation of Canada Inc., 1206
Recycling Council of Ontario, 1208
ReelWorld Film Festival, 1210
Reflet Salvéo, 1210
Refrigeration Service Engineers Society (Canada), 1211
Refugee Research Network, 1211
Registered Insurance Brokers of Ontario, 1213
Registered Massage Therapists' Association of Ontario, 1213
Registered Nurses' Association of Ontario, 1213
Reinsurance Research Council, 1217
The Renascent Centres for Alcoholism & Drug Addiction, 1217
Réseau des femmes du sud de l'Ontario, 1219
Responsible Gambling Council (Ontario), 1227
Responsible Investment Association, 1227
Restaurants Canada, 1227
Retail Advertising & Marketing Club of Canada, 1228
Retail Council of Canada, 1228
Rethink Breast Cancer, 1228
The Retired Teachers of Ontario, 1228
Rexdale Community Legal Services, 1229
Rexdale Women's Centre, 1229
Richard III Society of Canada, 1229
Richard Ivey Foundation, 1229
The Right to Die Society of Canada, 1232
The Right to Life Association of Toronto & Area, 1232
Right to Play, 1232
Risk & Insurance Management Society Inc.-Ontario Chapter, 1234
Riverdale Immigrant Women's Centre, 1234
Romanian Children's Relief, 1235
Ronald McDonald House Charities of Canada, 1235
Ronald McDonald House Toronto, 1235
Roncesvalles Macdonell Residents' Association, 1235
The Rosary Apostolate, Inc., 1236
The Rotary Club of Toronto, 1236
Rotman Institute for International Business, 1236
Royal Academy of Dance Canada, 1237
Royal Agricultural Winter Fair Association, 1237
Royal Astronomical Society of Canada, 1238
Royal Astronomical Society of Canada-Toronto Centre, 1239
Royal Canadian Academy of Arts, 1239
Royal Canadian Armoured Corps Association, 1239
Royal Canadian College of Organists, 1239
Royal Canadian Institute, 1240
Royal Canadian Military Institute, 1240
Royal College of Dental Surgeons of Ontario, 1241
Royal College of Dentists of Canada, 1241

Geographic Index / Ontario - Toronto

Royal Conservatory Orchestra, 1242
The Royal Philatelic Society of Canada, 1242
The Royal Scottish Country Dance Society-Toronto Branch, 1587
Rugby Ontario, 1244
Rural Ontario Municipal Association, 1244
Ryerson Faculty Association, 1244
Saint Elizabeth Health Care-Toronto - Toronto Central Service Delivery Centre, 1246
St. Andrew's Society of Toronto, 1248
St. Christopher House, 1248
The St. George's Society of Toronto, 1248
St. John Ambulance-Ontario Council, 1249
St. John's Cathedral Polish Catholic Church, 1249
St. Stephen's Community House, 1251
Salesian Cooperators, Association of St. Benedict Centre, 1251
Salon du livre de Toronto et Festival des écrivains, 1252
The Salvation Army in Canada, 1252
The Salvation Army in Canada-Toronto - Ontario Central East Division, 1253
Sanctuary, 1253
Sandbox Project, 1253
Sar-El Canada, 1253
Save the Children Canada, 1281
Scadding Court Community Centre, 1282
Scarboro Foreign Mission Society, 1282
Scarborough Arts Council, 1282
Scarborough Centre for Healthy Communities, 1282
Scarborough Historical Society, 1282
Scarborough Muslim Association, 1282
Scarborough Philharmonic Orchestra, 1282
Scarborough Women's Centre, 1283
Schizophrenia Society of Ontario, 1284
Science for Peace, 1285
Science Writers & Communicators of Canada, 1285
The Scott Mission, 1286
Scottish Studies Foundation Inc., 1286
Scout Environmental, 1286
Scouts Canada-Central Ontario Service Centre, 1286
Screen Composers Guild of Canada, 1287
Sculptors Society of Canada, 1287
Second Harvest, 1288
Seicho-No-Ie Toronto Centre, 1289
Self-Help Resource Centre, 1289
Senior Link, 1290
Seniors for Nature Canoe Club, 1290
Seniors in Need, 1290
Seniors Peer Helping Program, 1290
Serbian National Shield Society of Canada, 1290
Settlement Assistance & Family Support Services, 1292
Sex Information & Education Council of Canada, 1292
Shaarei Tefillah, 1293
ShareLife, 1294
ShareOwner Education Inc., 1294
Sheena's Place, 1295
The Shelter Movers of Toronto, 1295
The Shepherds' Trust, 1295
Shevchenko Scientific Society of Canada, 1296
Shiatsu Therapy Association of Ontario, 1296
Sickle Cell Association of Ontario, 1297
Sierra Club of Canada-Ontario Chapter, 1298
Sikh Foundation of Canada, 1299
Silent Voice Canada Inc., 1299
SIM Canada, 1299
Sistering - A Woman's Place, 1300
Sivananda Ashram Yoga Camp-Sivananda Yoga Vedanta Centre, 1301
Skills for Change, 1302
SkyWorks Charitable Foundation, 1303
Sleeping Children Around the World, 1303
Smart Commute, 1304
Smart Serve Ontario, 1304
Smoking & Health Action Foundation, 1304
Social Planning Toronto, 1306
Social Planning Toronto-York/West Toronto Office, 1307

Social Planning Toronto-Etobicoke Office, 1307
Società Unita, 1307
La Société d'histoire de Toronto, 1311
Society for Quality Education, 1326
Society for the Study of Egyptian Antiquities, 1327
Society of Canadian Artists, 1327
Society of Composers, Authors & Music Publishers of Canada, 1328
The Society of Energy Professionals, 1328
Society of Internet Professionals, 1329
Society of Ontario Adjudicators & Regulators, 1330
The Society of Professional Accountants of Canada, 1330
Society of St. Vincent de Paul - Toronto Central Council, 1330
Society of Trust & Estate Practitioners, 1331
Society of Urologic Surgeons of Ontario, 1331
Softball Ontario, 1332
Sojourn House, 1332
Somali Immigrant Women's Association, 1332
Songwriters Association of Canada, 1333
Sons of Scotland Benevolent Association, 1333
Soundstreams Canada, 1333
South Asian Women's Centre, 1334
South Etobicoke Community Legal Services, 1334
Southern Ontario Cocaine Anonymous, 1338
Special Olympics Canada, 1339
Special Olympics Ontario, 1340
The Speech & Stuttering Institute, 1340
Spina Bifida & Hydrocephalus Association of Ontario, 1342
Spinal Cord Injury Ontario, 1343
Spinal Cord Injury Ontario-Toronto - West Office, 1344
Spinal Cord Injury Ontario-Mississauga/Halton; Peel/Dufferin Office, 1343
Spiritans, the Congregation of the Holy Ghost, 1344
Sport Physiotherapy Canada, 1345
Springtide Resources, 1346
SPRINT Senior Care, 1346
Squash Ontario, 1347
Steelworkers Organization of Active Retirees, 1349
The Stop Community Food Centre, 1350
Storytellers of Canada, 1350
Storytelling Toronto, 1350
Street Haven at the Crossroads, 1352
Structural Pest Management Association of Ontario, 1352
Student Christian Movement of Canada, 1352
Supply Chain Management Association, 1355
Supply Chain Management Association - Ontario, 1356
Support Enhance Access Service Centre, 1356
SUS Foundation of Canada, 1357
Sustainable Buildings Canada, 1357
The Swedish-Canadian Chamber of Commerce, 1358
Swim Ontario, 1359
Swiss Canadian Chamber of Commerce (Ontario) Inc., 1359
Syme-Woolner Neighbourhood & Family Centre, 1360
Synchro Swim Ontario, 1361
Syrian Canadian Council-Toronto Office, 1365
The T. R. Meighen Foundation, 1365
Taekwondo Canada, 1366
Tafelmusik Baroque Orchestra & Chamber Choir, 1366
Taiwan Entrepreneurs Society Taipei/Toronto, 1366
Talent Agents & Managers Association of Canada, 1366
Tamil Eelam Society of Canada, 1366
Tamil Writers' Association of Canada, 1366
Taoist Tai Chi Society of Canada, 1366
Taras H. Shevchenko Museum & Memorial Park Foundation, 1367
Tarragon Theatre, 1367
TD Friends of the Environment Foundation, 1367

Tea Association of Canada, 1367
Technion Canada, 1368
Television Bureau of Canada, Inc., 1370
Tennis Canada, 1370
The Teresa Group, 1371
The Terry Fox Foundation-Ontario Office, 1372
TESL Ontario, 1373
Thalassemia Foundation of Canada, 1373
Théâtre français de Toronto, 1374
Theatre Ontario, 1374
The Therapeutic Touch Network of Ontario, 1375
Theresians International - Canada, 1375
Thorncliffe Neighbourhood Office, 1376
Tides Canada Foundation-Toronto Office, 1379
Times Change Women's Employment Service, 1379
Title Insurance Industry Association of Canada, 1380
Toronto & York Region Labour Council, 1381
Toronto Academy of Dentistry, 1381
Toronto Action for Social Change, 1381
Toronto Alliance for the Performing Arts, 1381
Toronto Animated Image Society, 1381
Toronto Area Gays & Lesbians Phoneline & Crisis Counselling, 1381
Toronto Art Therapy Institute, 1381
Toronto Arts Council, 1381
Toronto Arts Foundation, 1381
Toronto Association for Business Economics Inc., 1382
Toronto Association for Democracy in China, 1382
Toronto Association for Learning & Preserving the History of WWII in Asia, 1382
Toronto Association of Acting Studios, 1382
Toronto Association of Law Libraries, 1382
Toronto Association of Synagogue & Temple Administrators, 1382
Toronto Baptist Ministries, 1382
Toronto Bicycling Network, 1382
Toronto Blues Society, 1382
Toronto Canada-China Friendship Association, 1383
Toronto Centre for Community Learning & Development, 1383
Toronto Chapter of the International Association of Printing House Craftsmen, 1383
Toronto Coin Club, 1383
Toronto Community Care Access Centre, 1383
Toronto Community Employment Services, 1383
Toronto Community Foundation, 1383
The Toronto Consort, 1383
Toronto Council Fire Native Cultural Centre, 1383
Toronto Council of Hazzanim (Cantors), 1383
Toronto Crime Stoppers, 1383
Toronto Curling Association, 1383
Toronto Dance Theatre, 1383
Toronto Downtown Jazz Society, 1384
Toronto Environmental Alliance, 1384
Toronto Fashion Incubator, 1384
Toronto Field Naturalists, 1384
Toronto Film Society, 1384
Toronto Financial Services Alliance, 1384
Toronto Finnish-Canadian Seniors Centre, 1384
Toronto Free-Net, 1384
Toronto Gaelic Learners Association, 1384
Toronto General & Western Hospital Foundation, 1385
Toronto Health Libraries Association, 1385
Toronto Hebrew Benevolent Society, 1385
Toronto Insurance Conference, 1385
Toronto Insurance Women's Association, 1385
Toronto International Film Festival Inc., 1385
Toronto Japanese Association of Commerce & Industry, 1385
Toronto Jewish Film Society, 1385
Toronto Lawyers Association, 1385
The Toronto Mendelssohn Choir, 1385
Toronto Musicians' Association, 1386
Toronto Paramedic Association, 1386
Toronto Parents of Multiple Births Association, 1386

Toronto Police Accountability Coalition, 1386
Toronto Police Association, 1386
Toronto Professional Fire Fighters Association, 1386
Toronto Public Library Foundation, 1386
Toronto PWA Foundation, 1386
Toronto Railway Historical Association, 1386
Toronto Real Estate Board, 1386
Toronto Region Board of Trade, 1387
Toronto Region Board of Trade-West End Office, 1387
Toronto Renaissance & Reformation Colloquium, 1387
Toronto Renewable Energy Co-operative, 1387
Toronto Sinfonietta, 1387
Toronto Sportsmen's Association, 1387
Toronto Symphony Orchestra, 1387
Toronto Symphony Youth Orchestra, 1387
Toronto Transportation Society, 1388
Toronto Ukraina Sports Association, 1388
Toronto Users Group for Power Systems, 1388
Toronto Vegetarian Association, 1388
Toronto Workforce Innovation Group, 1388
Toronto Zoo, 1388
Toronto's Hare Krishna Centre, 1388
The Toronto-Calcutta Foundation, 1388
Tourism Toronto, 1391
Town of York Historical Society, 1393
T.P.U.G., 1394
Trans-Canada Advertising Agency Network, 1395
Travel Health Insurance Association of Canada, 1396
Travel Media Association of Canada, 1396
Travellers' Aid Society of Toronto, 1396
Trillium Gift of Life Network, 1398
Tropicana Community Services Organization, 1399
Trotskyist League of Canada, 1399
Turks & Caicos Development Organization of Canada, 1400
2-Spirited People of the First Nations, 1401
UJA Federation of Greater Toronto, 1402
Ukrainian Canadian Congress-Toronto Branch, 1402
Ukrainian Canadian Research & Documentation Centre, 1402
Ukrainian Canadian Social Services (Toronto) Inc, 1403
Ukrainian Democratic Youth Association, 1403
Ukrainian National Federation of Canada, 1403
Ukrainian War Veterans Association of Canada, 1403
Ukrainian Women's Association of Canada-Toronto Branch, 1403
Ukrainian World Congress, 1403
Ukrainian Youth Association of Canada, 1404
Underwriters' Laboratories of Canada, 1404
UNICEF Canada, 1404
UNICEF Canada-UNICEF Ontario - Toronto, 1405
UNIFOR, 1405
Unifor87-M, 1405
Union des Artistes (FIA) - Bureau de Toronto, 1406
Union of Injured Workers of Ontario, 1407
Unison Health & Community Services, 1408
UNITE HERE Canada-Toronto Chapter, 1408
United Church of Canada, 1409
United Church of Canada-Toronto Conference, 1409
United Church of Canada Foundation, 1409
United Empire Loyalists' Association of Canada, 1410
United Empire Loyalists' Association of Canada-Governor Simcoe Branch, 1410
United Empire Loyalists' Association of Canada-Toronto Branch, 1410
United Food & Commercial Workers Canada, 1410
United Generations Ontario, 1411
United Jewish Peoples' Order, 1411
United Macedonians Organization of Canada, 1411

United Nations Association in Canada-Toronto Office, 1411
United Senior Citizens of Ontario Inc., 1412
United Steelworkers of America (AFL-CIO/CLC)-USWA Canadian National Office, 1600
United Synagogue of Conservative Judaism, Canadian Region, 1412
United Synagogue Youth, 1412
United Ukrainian Charitable Trust, 1412
United Way Toronto & York Region, 1417
Unity for Autism, 1418
University of the Philippines Alumni Association of Toronto, 1420
University of Toronto Faculty Association, 1420
University of Toronto Institute for Aerospace Studies, 1420
University of Toronto Native Students Association, 1421
University of Toronto Symphony Orchestra, 1421
University of Toronto, Faculty of Information Alumni Association, 1421
University Settlement, 1421
Urban Alliance on Race Relations, 1422
Urban Music Association of Canada, 1422
Used Car Dealers Association of Ontario, 1423
Variety - The Children's Charity (Ontario), 1429
VHA Home HealthCare, 1431
Vietnamese Association, Toronto, 1434
Villa Charities Inc. (Toronto District), 1434
Villa Charities Inc. (Toronto District)-Columbus Centre, 1435
Villa Charities Inc. (Toronto District)-VITA Community Living Services, 1435
Villa Charities Inc. (Toronto District)-Villa Colombo Services for Seniors, 1435
Vintners Quality Alliance, 1435
Vision Institute of Canada, 1435
VISION TV, 1436
Visions of Science Network for Learning, 1436
Vocational Rehabilitation Association of Canada-Ontario Society, 1436
VOICE for Hearing Impaired Children, 1437
Voices for Children, 1437
Volunteer Management Professionals of Canada, 1439
The W. Garfield Weston Foundation, 1439
Walker Lynch Foundation, 1439
Walker Mineralogical Club, 1439
Warden Woods Community Centre, 1440
Waterfront Regeneration Trust, 1442
WE Charity, 1443
Welfare Committee for the Assyrian Community in Canada, 1443
Wellspring Cancer Support Foundation, 1444
The West Bend Community Association, 1444
West Neighbourhood House, 1446
West Scarborough Neighbourhood Community Centre, 1446
West Toronto Junction Historical Society, 1446
West Toronto Stamp Club, 1446
Weston Historical Society, 1451
The White Ribbon Campaign, 1452
Wiccan Church of Canada, 1453
Wilderness Canoe Association, 1454
Wilderness Committee-Toronto Office, 1454
William Morris Society of Canada, 1455
Willowdale Community Legal Services, 1455
Wireless Toronto, 1460
Women for Recreation, Information & Business, 1460
Women in Capital Markets, 1460
Women in Film & Television - Toronto, 1461
Women's Art Association of Canada, 1461
Women's Executive Network, 1462
Women's Healthy Environments Network, 1462
Women's Inter-Church Council of Canada, 1462
Women's Legal Education & Action Fund, 1462
Women's Musical Club of Toronto, 1463
Wong Kung Har Wun Sun Association, 1463
Wood Energy Technology Transfer Inc., 1463
Woodgreen Community Centre, 1463
The Workers' Educational Association of Canada, 1464

Working Women Community Centre, 1464
World Animal Protection, 1465
World Association for Christian Communication, 1465
World Blind Union, 1465
World Council on City Data, 1465
World Federation of Chiropractic, 1466
World Federation of Ukrainian Engineering Societies, 1466
World Federation of Ukrainian Women's Organizations, 1466
World Literacy of Canada, 1466
World Wildlife Fund - Canada, 1468
Writers Guild of Canada, 1468
The Writers' Trust of Canada, 1469
The Writers' Union of Canada, 1469
WushuCanada, 1469
WushuOntario, 1469
Wycliffe Bible Translators of Canada, Inc.-Eastern Region Office, 1470
YMCA Canada, 1471
YMCA Canada-YMCA of Greater Toronto, 1472
Yonge Street Mission, 1473
York Pioneer & Historical Society, 1473
York University Faculty Association, 1474
York University Staff Association, 1474
Young People's Theatre, 1474
Youth Assisting Youth, 1475
Youth Challenge International, 1475
Youth Flight Canada, 1475
Youth Now on Track Program, 1476
Youth Without Shelter, 1476
YOUTHLINK, 1476
YOUTHLINK-North West Scarborough Youth Centre, 1476
YOUTHLINK-Pathways to Education - Scarborough Village, 1476
YWCA Canada, 1481
YWCA Canada-YWCA Toronto, 1482
YWCA December 6 Fund of Toronto, 1482
Zane Cohen Centre for Digestive Diseases Familial Gastrointestinal Cancer Registry, 1482
ZOOCHECK Canada Inc., 1482
Zoroastrian Society of Ontario, 1482

Tottenham
Canadian Iris Society, 422
Great Lakes Gliding Club, 782
Historical Automobile Society of Canada, Inc., 816
Ontario Association for Marriage & Family Therapy, 1061
Tottenham & District Horticultural Association, 1388

Trenton
Bay of Quinte Dental Society, 200
Community Living Quinte West, 604
Highland Shores Children's Aid-Quinte West, 814
Ontario Genealogical Society-Quinte Branch, 1082
Quinte West Chamber of Commerce, 1202
Royal Astronomical Society of Canada-Belleville Centre, 1238
St. Leonard's Society of Canada-St. Leonard's Home Trenton, 1250
Trent Port Historical Society, 1397
Trenton Art Club, 1397
Trenton Care & Share Food Bank, 1397

Tweed
Tweed & Area Historical Society, 1400
Tweed Chamber of Commerce, 1400

Unionville
Action Volunteers for Animals, 7
The Avian Preservation Foundation, 190
Avicultural Advancement Council of Canada, 191
Ontario Association of Dental Specialists, 1063
York Region Athletic Association, 1473
York Region Family Services (Markham), 1473

Uxbridge
Canadian Electrical Contractors Association, 380
Golf Association of Ontario, 777
Uxbridge Chamber of Commerce, 1423
Uxbridge Historical Centre, 1423

Val Caron
Sudbury Rock & Lapidary Society, 1353

Vaughan
Canadian Pest Management Association, 453
The Children's Aid Foundation of York Region, 560
Children's Miracle Network, 562
COSTI Immigrant Services-Vaughan Centre, 632
COSTI Immigrant Services-Vaughan - Language, Settlement & Skills Training Services, 632
Couples for Christ Canada, 636
Electricity Distributors Association, 683
Jewish Family & Child-York Region Branch, 871
Licensed Paralegals Association (Ontario), 910
Ontario Regional Common Ground Alliance, 1101
Ontario Soccer Association, 1105
Residential Construction Council of Ontario, 1226
The Sam Sorbara Charitable Foundation, 1253
Vaughan Chamber of Commerce, 1430
Villa Charities Inc. (Toronto District)-Villa Colombo Vaughan - Di Poce Centre, 1435

Vernon
Osgoode Twp. Historical Society, 1127

Vineland
Grape Growers of Ontario, 782
Ontario Conference of Mennonite Brethren Churches, 1074
Ontario Tender Fruit Producers Marketing Board, 1110
Wine Country Ontario, 1457

Wabigoon
Ontario Coalition of Aboriginal Peoples, 1071

Walkerton
Community Living Walkerton & District, 606
Quality in Lifelong Learning Network, 1195
Walkerton Business Improvement Area, 1440

Wallaceburg
Community Living Wallaceburg, 606
Concrete Precasters Association of Ontario, 610
International Union, United Automobile, Aerospace & Agricultural Implement Workers of America-UAW Local 251 - Wallaceburg, ON, 1565
Society of Tribologists & Lubrication Engineers-Toronto Section, 1594
Sydenham Field Naturalists, 1359
Wallaceburg & District Chamber of Commerce, 1440
Wallaceburg & District Historical Society, Inc., 1440
Wallaceburg Arts Council, 1440
Walpole Island Heritage Centre, 1440

Wardsville
Quad County Support Services, 1195

Warsaw
PFLAG Canada Inc.-Peterborough Chapter, 1156
Spinal Cord Injury Ontario-Peterborough Office, 1343

Wasaga Beach
The Friends of Nancy Island Historic Site & Wasaga Beach Park, 761
Multiple Births Canada, 979
Wasaga Beach Chamber of Commerce, 1440

Washago
Ontario Sportfishing Guides' Association, 1108

Waterdown
Flamborough Information & Community Services, 740
PFLAG Canada Inc.-Halton Region Chapter, 1155

Waterford
Ontario Percheron Horse Association Inc., 1095
Waterford & Townsend Historical Society, 1442

Waterloo
AIESEC-Laurier, 18
Canadian Association for Commonwealth Literature & Language Studies, 298
Canadian Association for Leisure Studies, 302
Canadian Association for Suicide Prevention, 304
Canadian Blood Services-Kitchener-Waterloo, 344
Canadian Celiac Association-Kitchener/Waterloo Chapter, 352
Canadian Communication Association, 361
Canadian Federation of Podiatric Medicine, 388
Canadian Fraternal Association, 394
Canadian Innovation Centre, 411
Canadian Institute of Management-Ontario - Grand Valley Branch, 417
Canadian Lutheran World Relief-Eastern Regional Office, 428
Canadian Micro-Mineral Association, 436
Canadian Peony Society, 453
Canadian School Libraries, 468
Canadian Water Network, 502
Centre for Community Based Research, 531
Centre for Family Business, 532
City of Waterloo Staff Association, 571
Education Assistants Association of the Waterloo Region District School Board, 680
Environmental Studies Association of Canada, 692
Family Mediation Canada, 703
Focus for Ethnic Women, 741
Grand Valley Trails Association, 780
Habitat for Humanity Canada-Ontario - Waterloo Region, 797
Horseshoe Ontario, 822
Human Resources Professionals Association-Grand Valley Chapter, 825
Institute for Risk Research, 844
International Geographical Union - Canadian Committee, 857
Kitchener-Waterloo Chamber Music Society, 890
Kitchener-Waterloo Chamber Orchestra, 890
Kitchener-Waterloo Kiwanis Music Festival, 890
Laubach Literacy Ontario, 900
Meningitis Research Foundation of Canada, 960
Mennonite Economic Development Associates Canada, 961
New Apostolic Church Canada, 1004
Ontario Association of Student Financial Aid Administrators, 1066
Ontario Numismatic Association, 1094
Ontario Public Interest Research Group-Waterloo PIRG, 1099
Ontario Research Council on Leisure, 1101
Ontario Undergraduate Student Alliance-Federation of Students, University of Waterloo, 1111
Ontario Undergraduate Student Alliance-Wilfrid Laurier University Students' Union, 1112
Project Ploughshares, 1188
Royal Astronomical Society of Canada-Kitchener/Waterloo Centre, 1238
The Royal Scottish Country Dance Society-Kitchener-Waterloo Branch
Sandford Fleming Foundation, 1253
Seeds of Diversity Canada, 1289
Shad Valley International, 1293
Skills/Compétences Canada-Ontario, 1303
United Way of Kitchener-Waterloo & Area, 1415
University of Waterloo Staff Association, 1421
Waterloo Coin Society, 1442
Waterloo, Wellington, Dufferin & Grey Building & Construction Trades Council, 1442

Wilfrid Laurier University Faculty Association, 1455
Wilfrid Laurier University Symphony Orchestra, 1455
World Accord, 1465

Wawa
Children's Aid Society of Algoma-Wawa Office, 561
Niijkiwenhwag - Friends of Lake Superior Park, 1027
North Algoma Literacy Coalition, 1028

Welland
Big Brothers Big Sisters of Ontario-Big Brothers Big Sisters of South Niagara, 210
Community Living Welland Pelham, 606
Family & Children's Services Niagara-Welland Branch, 701
Niagara Cattlemen's Association, 1024
Niagara Peninsula Conservation Authority, 1025
Niagara Region Police Association, 1025
Ontario Society for the Prevention of Cruelty to Animals-Welland Branch (Affiliate), 1107
Réseau du patrimoine franco-ontarien-Niagara, 1222
Sisters of the Sacred Heart of Ragusa, 1301
United Way South Niagara, 1417
Welland County Law Association, 1443
The Welland/Pelham Chamber of Commerce, 1443
Your Life Counts, 1475

Wellandport
Gethsemane Ministries, 773

Wellesley
Wellesley & District Board of Trade, 1443

Wellington
Boys & Girls Clubs of P.E.I.-Wellington & Area Boys & Girls Club, 224
Canadian Association for the Advancement of Netherlandic Studies, 305
Prince Edward Historical Society, 1171

West Lorne
West Elgin Nature Club, 1445

Westport
Westport & Rideau Lakes Chamber of Commerce, 1451

Wheatley
Canadian Wild Turkey Federation, 504

Whitby
Auditing Association of Canada, 187
Canadian Society for Aesthetic Plastic Surgery, 472
The Christian & Missionary Alliance in Canada-Eastern Canadian District (ECD) Office, 566
The Community Foundation of Durham Region, 597
Conference of Independent Schools (Ontario), 612
Distress Centre of Durham Region, 659
Durham Parents of Multiples, 665
Durham Regional Police Association, 665
Epilepsy Ontario-Durham Region, 693
Guillain-Barré Syndrome Foundation of Canada, 794
Heart & Stroke Foundation of Ontario-Durham Regional Office, 809
Human Resources Professionals Association-Durham Chapter, 825
Human Resources Professionals of Durham, 826
International Sanitary Supply Association Canada, 859
North American Recycled Rubber Association, 1029
Ontario Association of Radiology Managers, 1065
Ontario Basketball, 1067
Ontario Cheerleading Federation, 1071

Ontario Genealogical Society-Durham Region Branch, 1081
Ontario Pipe Trades Council, 1096
Ontario Shorthorn Association, 1104
Ontario Society for the Prevention of Cruelty to Animals-Durham Region Branch (Affiliate), 1105
Oshawa-Durham Rape Crisis Centre, 1128
Oshawa-Whitby Kiwanis Music & Theatre Festival, 1128
Roller Sports Canada, 1235
Saint Elizabeth Health Care-Whitby - Central East Service Delivery Centre, 1246
Welsh Pony & Cob Association of Ontario, 1444
Whitby Chamber of Commerce, 1452

White River
White River District Historical Society, 1452

Whitney
The Friends of Algonquin Park, 760

Wiarton
Bruce Peninsula Association for Community Living, 260
Wiarton South Bruce Peninsula Chamber of Commerce, 1453

Wikwemikong
Wikwemikong Anishinabe Association for Community Living, 1453

Willowdale
Ontario Historical Society, 1084

Wilsonville
Jake Thomas Learning Centre, 867

Windsor
AIDS Committee of Windsor, 16
AIESEC-Windsor, 18
Alzheimer Society of Windsor/Essex County, 65
Armenian Relief Society of Canada, Inc.-Windsor Chapter: "Roubina", 83
Arts Council Windsor & Region, 85
Assisted Living Southwestern Ontario, 89
Association of Fundraising Professionals-Canada South Chapter
AUTO21 Network of Centres of Excellence, 189
Bulimia Anorexia Nervosa Association, 264
Bus History Association, Inc., 266
Canadian Association of Moldmakers, 321
Canadian Blood Services-Windsor, 345
Canadian Condominium Institute-CCI-Windsor - Essex County Chapter, 362
Canadian Culinary Federation-Windsor Branch, 374
Canadian Hearing Society-Windsor Regional Office, 403
Canadian Liver Foundation-Windsor/Essex Chapter, 427
Canadian Polish Congress-Windsor Branch, 456
Canadian Transportation Equipment Association, 497
CanAm Indian Friendship Centre of Windsor, 507
Citizens' Environment Alliance, 570
Community Living Windsor, 606
Council of Ontario Construction Associations-Windsor Construction Association, 634
Council on Aging, Windsor - Essex County, 636
The Easter Seal Society (Ontario)-Western Region - Windsor / Sarnia, 670
Essex County Orchid Society, 696
Essex Law Association, 696
Essex-Kent Cage Bird Society, 696
Family Services Windsor-Essex Counselling & Advocacy Centre, 705
Financial Fitness Centre, 736
Gina Lori Riley Dance Enterprises, 773
Great Lakes Institute for Environmental Research, 782
Habitat for Humanity Canada-Ontario - Windsor-Essex, 797
Heart & Stroke Foundation of Ontario-Windsor Office, 809

Heating, Refrigeration & Air Conditioning Institute of Canada-Ontario - Essex/Kent/Lambton Chapter, 810
InformOntario, 838
IntegrityLink, 850
The John Howard Society of Ontario-Windsor - Essex County, 875
The Kidney Foundation of Canada-Windsor & District Chapter, 886
Kiwanis Music Festival of Windsor/Essex County, 892
Lupus Ontario-Windsor Branch, 922
Madonna House Apostolate-Windsor, 925
Multicultural Council of Windsor & Essex County, 979
The Ontario Archaeological Society Inc.-Windsor Chapter, 1060
Ontario Brain Injury Association-Windsor-Essex, 1069
Ontario Genealogical Society-Essex County Branch, 1082
Ontario Home Builders' Association-Windsor Essex, 1086
Ontario Lung Association-Windsor Office (Windsor-Essex & Chatham-Kent Area), 1090
Ontario Nurses' Association-Windsor Office, 1094
Ontario Public Interest Research Group-OPIRG Windsor, 1099
Ontario Society for the Prevention of Cruelty to Animals-Windsor-Essex Branch (Affiliate), 1107
Réseau du patrimoine franco-ontarien-La Pionnière du Sud-Ouest (Belle Rivière), 1222
Saint Elizabeth Health Care-Windsor - Erie St. Clair Service Delivery Centre, 1246
St. Leonard's Society of Canada-St. Leonard's House Windsor, 1250
Sexual Assault Crisis Centre of Essex County Inc., 1293
South Asian Centre of Windsor, 1334
Spinal Cord Injury Ontario-Windsor Office, 1344
Tourism Windsor Essex Pelee Island, 1392
211 Southwest Ontario, 1401
Unemployed Help Centre, 1404
UNIFOR-Windsor Office, 1405
United Empire Loyalists' Association of Canada-Bicentennial Branch, 1410
United Way of Windsor-Essex County, 1417
Windsor & District Black Coalition of Canada, 1456
Windsor & District Labour Council, 1456
Windsor Association for the Deaf, 1456
Windsor Coin Club, 1456
Windsor Electrical Contractors Association, 1456
Windsor Federation of Musicians, 1456
Windsor Islamic Association, 1456
Windsor Orchid Society, 1457
Windsor Police Association, 1457
Windsor Public Library Adult Literacy Program, 1457
Windsor Symphony Orchestra, 1457
Windsor University Faculty Association, 1457
Windsor Women Working with Immigrant Women, 1457
Windsor/Essex County Parents of Multiple Births Association, 1457
Windsor-Essex Children's Aid Society, 1457
Windsor-Essex County Real Estate Board, 1457
Windsor-Essex Down Syndrome Parent Association, 1457
Windsor-Essex Regional Chamber of Commerce, 1457
YMCA Canada-YMCA of Western Ontario - Windsor, 1471

Wolfe Island
Boot'n Bonnet British Car Club, 218

Woodbridge
AdvantAge Ontario, 10
Association of Canadian Compliance Professionals, 141
Canada-Cuba Sports & Cultural Festivals, 283

Canadian Association for Pharmacy Distribution Management, 303
Canadian Italian Heritage Foundation, 423
Canadian Ski Council, 471
Caritas School of Life Therapeutic Community, 512
Community Living York South-Vaughan Office, 606
Cricket Canada, 642
50 & Piu Enasco-Woodbridge Office, 735
Fogolârs Federation of Canada, 742
Guild of Industrial, Commercial & Institutional Accountants, 794
Interior Systems Contractors Association of Ontario, 852
Mechanical Contractors Association of Ontario, 957
Ontario Building Officials Association Inc., 1070
Ontario Formwork Association, 1081
Ontario Painting Contractors Association, 1094
Patronato INAS (Canada)-Woodbridge Office, 1146
Sign Association of Canada, 1298

Woodland
International Airborne Geophysics Safety Association, 853

Woodlawn
Métis National Council of Women, 963

Woodstock
Alzheimer Society of Oxford, 64
Bereavement Ontario Network, 205
Canadian Swine Breeders' Association, 491
Canadian Swine Exporters Association, 491
Canadian Transportation Research Forum, 497
Children's Aid Society of Oxford County, 561
Festivals & Events Ontario, 733
Friends of the Orphans, Canada, 763
Ontario Genealogical Society-Oxford County Branch, 1082
Oxford Child & Youth Centre, 1134
Oxford County Geological Society, 1134
Oxford County Law Association, 1134
Oxford Philatelic Society, 1134
Oxford Regional Labour Council, 1134
Professional Photographers of Canada, 1186
Saint Elizabeth Health Care-Woodstock - Oxford County Service Delivery Centre, 1246
United Way of Oxford, 1415
Woodstock & District Developmental Services, 1464
Woodstock Coin Club, 1464
Woodstock District Chamber of Commerce, 1464
Woodstock Field Naturalists, 1464
Woodstock-Ingersoll & District Real Estate Board, 1464

Woodview
Antique Automobile Club of America-Ontario Region

Youngs Point
Professional Association of Volunteer Leaders Ontario, 1183

Zephyr
Southern Ontario Orchid Society, 1338

Zurich
Zurich & District Chamber of Commerce, 1482

Prince Edward Island

Alberton
Snow Crab Fishermans Inc., 1305

Borden-Carleton
Canadian Hard of Hearing Association-Prince Edward Island Chapter, 401

Cardigan
Chicken Farmers of Prince Edward Island, 557

Charlottetown
Alzheimer Society of PEI, 64

Ancient, Free & Accepted Masons of Canada - Grand Lodge of Prince Edward Island, 69
The Appraisal Institute of Canada - Prince Edward Island, 75
Architects Association of Prince Edward Island, 78
Archives Council of Prince Edward Island, 80
ARMA Canada-Prince Edward Island Chapter, 82
Arthritis Society-Prince Edward Island Division, 84
Association of Commercial & Industrial Contractors of PEI, 145
Association of Consulting Engineering Companies - Prince Edward Island, 146
Association of Prince Edward Island Land Surveyors, 156
Association of Prince Edward Island Libraries, 156
Association of Professional Engineers of Prince Edward Island, 159
Association of Registered Nurses of Prince Edward Island, 161
Athletics PEI, 181
Autism Society of PEI, 189
Baseball PEI, 198
Basketball PEI, 199
Bell Aliant Pioneers-Prince Edward Island, 204
Benevolent Irish Society of Prince Edward Island, 205
Big Brothers Big Sisters of Prince Edward Island, 210
Boys & Girls Clubs of P.E.I.-Boys & Girls Club of Charlottetown, 224
Brain Injury Coalition of Prince Edward Island, 225
Canadian 4-H Council-Prince Edward Island, 284
Canadian Bar Association-Prince Edward Island Branch, 342
Canadian Blood Services-Charlottetown, 344
Canadian Cancer Society-Prince Edward Island Division, 349
Canadian Celiac Association-Prince Edward Island Chapter, 352
Canadian Culinary Federation-Prince Edward Island Branch, 374
Canadian Federation of Independent Business-Prince Edward Island Office, 387
Canadian Hemophilia Society-Prince Edward Island Chapter, 404
Canadian Home Builders' Association - Prince Edward Island, 407
Canadian Institute of Food Science & Technology-Atlantic Section, 415
Canadian Mental Health Association-Prince Edward Island Division, 435
Canadian Union of Public Employees-Prince Edward Island Division, 498
The Capital Commission of Prince Edward Island Inc., 510
Charlottetown Area Baseball Association, 552
Chartered Professional Accountants of Prince Edward Island, 553
Children's Wish Foundation of Canada-Prince Edward Island Chapter, 563
Chinese Canadian Association of Prince Edward Island, 564
Coaches Association of PEI, 576
College of Family Physicians of Canada-Prince Edward Island Chapter, 585
College of Licensed Practical Nurses of PEI, 585
College of Physicians & Surgeons of Prince Edward Island, 588
Community Foundation of Prince Edward Island, 598
Community Legal Information Association of Prince Edward Island, 600
Community Museums Association of Prince Edward Island, 606
Construction Association of Prince Edward Island, 623
Cooper Institute, 627

Credit Counselling Services of Atlantic Canada-Prince Edward Island - Charlottetown, 640
Credit Unions Atlantic Canada-Charlottetown Office, 641
Cycling PEI, 647
Dental Association of Prince Edward Island, 653
Dental Council of Prince Edward Island, 653
Canadian Diabetes Association-Prince Edward Island Region, 656
Early Childhood Development Association of Prince Edward Island, 666
Environmental Coalition of Prince Edward Island, 691
Fédération culturelle de L'Ile-du-Prince-Édouard inc., 708
Federation of Prince Edward Island Municipalities Inc., 726
German-Canadian Historical Association Inc., 772
Greater Charlottetown & Area Chamber of Commerce, 783
Green Party of Prince Edward Island, 789
Gymnastics PEI, 795
Habitat for Humanity Canada-Prince Edward Island, 797
Health Association of PEI, 806
Heart & Stroke Foundation of Prince Edward Island Inc., 809
Hockey PEI, 818
Hospice Palliative Care Association of Prince Edward Island, 823
Hotel Association of Prince Edward Island, 824
Insurance Brokers Association of Canada-Insurance Brokers Association of Prince Edward Island, 848
Island Fitness Council, 865
Island Horse Council, 865
Island Media Arts Co-op, 865
Island Nature Trust, 865
Island Technology Professionals, 865
Island Writers' Association (P.E.I.), 866
The John Howard Society of Prince Edward Island, 875
Judo Prince Edward Island, 876
Junior Achievement of Canada-Junior Achievement of P.E.I., 877
The Kidney Foundation of Canada-Prince Edward Island Chapter, 885
KidSport PEI, 887
Latin American Mission Program, 899
Law Foundation of Prince Edward Island, 901
Law Society of Prince Edward Island, 902
Learning Disabilities Association of Prince Edward Island, 905
Liberal Party of Prince Edward Island, 909
Lifesaving Society-Prince Edward Island Branch, 911
L.M. Montgomery Institute, 916
Lupus PEI, 922
Maritime Breeders Association, 950
Maritime Model Horse Collectors & Showers Association, 951
Meetings & Conventions Prince Edward Island, 959
Music PEI, 984
Native Council of Prince Edward Island, 997
The Nature Conservancy of Canada-Prince Edward Island, 1000
New Democratic Party-PEI NDP, 1014
ParaSport & Recreation PEI, 1138
P.E.E.R.S. Alliance, 1148
PEI Field Hockey Association, 1148
PEI People First, 1148
PEI Teacher-Librarians' Association, 1149
Prince Edward Island Alpine Ski Association, 1171
Prince Edward Island Aquaculture Alliance, 1171
Prince Edward Island Association for Newcomers to Canada, 1172
Prince Edward Island Association of Exhibitions, 1172
Prince Edward Island Association of Medical Radiation Technologists, 1172

Prince Edward Island Association of Optometrists, 1172
Prince Edward Island Association of Social Workers, 1172
Prince Edward Island Automobile Dealers Association, 1172
Prince Edward Island Badminton Association, 1172
Prince Edward Island Building & Construction Trades Council, 1172
Prince Edward Island Business Women's Association, 1172
Prince Edward Island Cattle Producers, 1173
Prince Edward Island Cerebral Palsy Association Inc., 1173
Prince Edward Island Certified Organic Producers Co-op, 1173
Prince Edward Island Chiropractic Association, 1173
Prince Edward Island College of Physiotherapists, 1173
Prince Edward Island Colt Stakes Association, 1173
Prince Edward Island Council of People with Disabilities, 1173
Prince Edward Island Crafts Council, 1173
Prince Edward Island Curling Association, 1173
Prince Edward Island Dietetic Association, 1173
Prince Edward Island Eco-Net, 1173
Prince Edward Island Federation of Agriculture, 1174
Prince Edward Island Federation of Foster Families, 1174
Prince Edward Island Federation of Labour, 1174
Prince Edward Island Fencing Association, 1174
Prince Edward Island Fishermen's Association Ltd., 1174
Prince Edward Island Five Pin Bowlers Association Inc., 1174
Prince Edward Island Flying Association, 1174
Prince Edward Island Genealogical Society Inc., 1174
Prince Edward Island Golf Association, 1174
Prince Edward Island Harness Racing Industry Association, 1174
Prince Edward Island Hockey Referees Association, 1174
Prince Edward Island Hog Commodity Marketing Board, 1174
Prince Edward Island Home & School Federation Inc., 1175
Prince Edward Island Humane Society, 1175
Prince Edward Island Institute of Agrologists, 1175
Prince Edward Island Lawn Bowling Association, 1175
Prince Edward Island Literacy Alliance Inc., 1175
Prince Edward Island Lung Association, 1175
Prince Edward Island Marketing Council, 1175
Prince Edward Island Massage Therapy Association, 1175
Prince Edward Island Museum & Heritage Foundation, 1175
Prince Edward Island Nurses' Union, 1176
Prince Edward Island Occupational Therapy Society, 1176
Prince Edward Island Office of the Superintendent of Securities, 1176
Prince Edward Island Rape & Sexual Assault Centre, 1176
Prince Edward Island Real Estate Association, 1176
Prince Edward Island Rifle Association, 1176
Prince Edward Island Right to Life Association, 1176
Prince Edward Island Road Builders & Heavy Construction Association, 1177
Prince Edward Island Roadrunners Club, 1177
Prince Edward Island Rugby Union, 1177
Prince Edward Island Senior Citizens Federation Inc., 1177
Prince Edward Island Soccer Association, 1177

Prince Edward Island Society for Medical Laboratory Science, 1177
Prince Edward Island Speech & Hearing Association, 1177
Prince Edward Island Sports Hall of Fame & Museum Inc., 1177
Prince Edward Island Square & Round Dance Clubs, 1177
Prince Edward Island Standardbred Horseowners' Association, 1177
Prince Edward Island Symphony Society, 1178
Prince Edward Island Table Tennis Association, 1178
Prince Edward Island Teachers' Federation, 1178
Prince Edward Island Tennis Association, 1178
Prince Edward Island Trucking Sector Council, 1178
Prince Edward Island Union of Public Sector Employees, 1178
Prince Edward Island Vegetable Growers Co-op Association, 1178
Prince Edward Island Veterinary Medical Association, 1178
Prince Edward Island Wildlife Federation, 1178
Prince Edward Island Women's Institute, 1178
Progressive Conservative Association of Prince Edward Island, 1187
Public Service Alliance of Canada-Charlottetown Branch, 1193
Queen Elizabeth Hospital Foundation, 1199
Racquetball PEI, 1202
Recreation Prince Edward Island, 1207
Ringette PEI, 1233
Rowing PEI, 1237
Royal Astronomical Society of Canada-Charlottetown Centre, 1238
The Royal Canadian Legion-Prince Edward Island Command, 1240
The Royal Commonwealth Society of Canada-Prince Edward Island Branch, 1242
Schizophrenia Society of Prince Edward Island, 1284
Scottish Settlers Historical Society, 1286
Scouts Canada-Prince Edward Island Council, 1287
Skate Canada-Prince Edward Island Section, 1302
Skills/Compétences Canada-Prince Edward Island, 1303
Société Saint-Thomas-d'Aquin-Comité du Carrefour Isle-Saint-Jean, 1325
Softball Prince Edward Island, 1332
Special Olympics Prince Edward Island, 1340
Speed Skate PEI, 1341
Spina Bifida & Hydrocephalus Association of Prince Edward Island, 1342
Spinal Cord Injury (Prince Edward Island), 1342
Sport PEI Inc., 1345
Swimming Prince Edward Island, 1359
Synchro PEI, 1361
TESL Prince Edward Island, 1373
Tourism Industry Association of PEI, 1390
Triathlon Price Edward Island, 1398
United Way of Prince Edward Island, 1416
University of Prince Edward Island Faculty Association, 1420
Vocational Rehabilitation Association of Canada-Atlantic Society, 1436
Volleyball Prince Edward Island, 1438
Women's Network PEI, 1463
World Potato Congress, 1466
Wrestling PEI, 1468

Cornwall
Canadian Milking Shorthorn Society, 436
Prince Edward Island Ground Water Association, 1174
Prince Edward Island Karate Association, 1175

Crapaud
Prince Edward Island Pharmacy Board, 1176
South Shore Chamber of Commerce, 1336

Ellerslie
PEI Shellfish Association, 1149

Geographic Index / Prince Edward Island - Emerald

Emerald
Bedeque Bay Environmental Management Association, 203

Fortune
Société Saint-Thomas-d'Aquin-Le comité acadien et francophone de l'Est, 1325

Frenchfort
Holstein Canada-Prince Edward Island Branch, 819

Glenfinnan
Navy League of Canada-Prince Edward Island, 1002

Hunter River
Biathlon Prince Edward Island, 207

Johnston's River
Child Find PEI Inc., 559

Kensington
Kensington & Area Chamber of Commerce, 883
Kensington & Area Tourist Association, 883
Kensington Cooperative Association Ltd, 883
Prince Edward Island Funeral Directors & Embalmers Association, 1174

Lennox Island
Aboriginal Women's Association of Prince Edward Island, 3

Montague
Denturist Society of Prince Edward Island, 654
Eastern Prince Edward Island Chamber of Commerce, 670
Prince Edward Island Beekeepers' Cooperative Association, 1172
Prince Edward Island Canoe Kayak Association, 1173
Southeast Environmental Association, 1337
Southern Kings & Queens Food Bank Inc., 1338
Southern Kings Arts Council, 1338

Mount Stewart
Canadian Public Relations Society Inc.-CPRS Prince Edward Island, 463

Rustico
Société Saint-Thomas-d'Aquin-Conseil Acadien de Rustico, 1325

Souris
Cross Country PEI, 643
Eastern Kings Health Foundation Inc., 670
Prince Edward Island Wildlife Federation-Souris & Area, 1178

Stratford
Canadian Association of Veterans in United Nations Peacekeeping-Prince Edward Island Chapter, 336
Canadian Aviation Historical Society-Prince Edward Island "Carl F. Burke, MBE" Chapter, 340
Medical Society of Prince Edward Island, 958
Prince Edward Island Association for Community Living, 1172
Prince Edward Island Kiwanis Music Festival Association, 1175
Small Investor Protection Association, 1304

Summerside
Alcoholics Anonymous-Prince Edward Island - Green Acres Intergroup, 52
ALS Society of PEI, 60
Boys & Girls Clubs of P.E.I.-Boys & Girls Club of Summerside, 224
East Prince Youth Development Centre, 668
Embroiderers' Association of Canada, Inc.-P.E.I. - Island Treasures Needleart Guild, 686
Fédération des parents de l'Ile-du-Prince-Édouard, 716
Greater Summerside Chamber of Commerce, 785
Jeunesse Acadienne et Francophone de l'Île-du-prince-Édouard, 870
Music for Young Children-Prince Edward Island Sunrise Program, 984
National Farmers Union-Maritimes - NFU Financial Services, 993
Prince County Hospital Foundation, 1171
Prince Edward Island Association of Family Resource Programs, 1172
Prince Edward Island School Athletic Association, 1177
Société Saint-Thomas-d'Aquin, 1325
Société Saint-Thomas-d'Aquin-Comité régional la Belle-Alliance ltée, 1325
Summerside & Area Minor Hockey Association, 1354

Tignish
Société Saint-Thomas-d'Aquin-Le Conseil Rév. S.-E.-Perrey, 1325

Vernon Bridge
United Empire Loyalists' Association of Canada-Abegweit Branch, 1410

Wellington
Chambre de commerce acadienne et francophone de l'Ile-du-Prince-Édouard, 539
Réseau Santé en français I.-P.-É, 1226
Société Saint-Thomas-d'Aquin-Conseil scolaire-communautaire Évangéline, 1325

Wellington Station
Conseil de la coopération de L'Ile-du-Prince-Édouard, 615

York
Prince Edward Island Forestry Training Corp., 1174

York Point
PEI Sailing Association, 1149

York-Covehead
Prince Edward Island Forest Improvement Association, 1174

Québec

Acton Vale
Chambre de commerce de la région d'Acton, 542
Réseau des SADC et CAE-SADC de la région d'Acton inc., 1220
Société d'histoire des Six Cantons, 1312

Alma
Chambre de commerce et d'industrie Lac-Saint-Jean-Est, 547
Conseil régional de la culture Saguenay-Lac-Saint-Jean, 621
Fédération québécoise des sociétés Alzheimer-Sagamie, 730
Maison de Campagne & d'Entraide Communautaire du Lac, 926
Mouvement national des québécoises et québécois-SNQ du Saguenay/Lac-Saint-Jean, 977
Ordre des infirmières et infirmiers du Québec-Ordre régional des infirmières et infirmiers de Saguenay—Lac-Saint-Jean/Nord-du-Québec, 1122
Réseau BIBLIO du Saguenay-Lac-Saint-Jean, 1218
Réseau des SADC et CAE-SADC Lac-Saint-Jean-Est inc., 1221
FADOQ - Mouvement des aînés du Québec-Région Saguenay - Lac-St-Jean - Ungava, 1224
Service budgétaire Lac-Saint-Jean-Est, 1291
Société d'histoire du Lac-St-Jean/Maison des Bâtisseurs, 1312
Syndicat des travailleurs énergie électrique nord, 1364
Syndicat national des employés de l'aluminium d'Alma inc., 1365

Amos
L'Arche Québec-L'Arche Abitibi-Témiscamingue, 77
Association du Québec pour enfants avec problèmes auditifs-AQEPA Abitibi-Témiscamingue, 131
Chambre de Commerce et d'Industrie du Centre-Abitibi, 547
Maison du Tourisme, 927
Réseau des SADC et CAE-SADC Harricana inc., 1221
Société d'histoire d'Amos, 1310

Amqui
Chambre de commerce de la MRC de la Matapédia, 541
Fédération des professionnelles et professionnels de l'éducation du Québec-Syndicat des professionnelles et professionnels de l'éducation du Bas St-Laurent (SPPEBSL), 718
Réseau des SADC et CAE-SADC Matapédia inc., 1221
Société d'histoire et de généalogie de la Matapédia, 1312

Anjou
APCHQ - Montréal Métropolitain, 73
Association de la construction du Québec, 100
Association de la construction du Québec-Région Métropolitaine, 101
Association des denturologistes du Québec, 110
Association des entrepreneurs en construction du Québec, 112
Association nationale des peintres - locale 99, 138
Association paritaire pour la santé et la sécurité du travail - Imprimerie et activités connexes, 164
Association pour l'enseignement de la science et de la technologie au Québec, 165
Association provinciale des constructeurs d'habitations du Québec inc., 168
Association provinciale des constructeurs d'habitations du Québec inc.-Montréal métropolitain, 168
Association québécoise des directeurs et directrices d'établissement d'enseignement retraités, 172
Fédération des policiers et policières municipaux du Québec (ind.), 717
Fédération québécoise des coopératives en milieu scolaire-Bureau d'Anjou, 728
Fédération québécoise des directions d'établissements d'enseignement, 728
Fédération québécoise des revêtements de sol, 729
Illuminating Engineering Society of North America-Montréal Section
Ordre des Podiatres du Québec, 1123
Ordre professionnel de la physiothérapie du Québec, 1124
Syndicat interprovincial des ferblantiers et couvreurs, la section locale 2016 à la FTQ-Construction, 1364

Asbestos
Réseau des SADC et CAE-SADC des Sources, 1221
Service budgétaire populaire des Sources, 1291
Société d'histoire d'Asbestos, 1310

Baie d'Urfe
Canadian Anthropology Society, 293
Shoe Manufacturers' Association of Canada, 1296

Baie-Comeau
Association des handicapés adultes de la Côte-Nord, 116
Association du Québec pour enfants avec problèmes auditifs-AQEPA Côte-Nord, 131
Association pour la protection des intérêts des consommateurs de la Côte-Nord, 166
Association québécoise pour le loisir des personnes handicapées-ARLPH Côte-Nord, 177
Centraide Haute-Côte-Nord/Manicouagan, 522
Chambre de commerce de Manicouagan, 542
Conseil régional de Baie Comeau (Manicouagan) - Bureau régional FTQ Côte Nord, 620
Conseil régional de la culture et des communications de la Côte-Nord, 621
Fédération de l'industrie manufacturière (FIM-CSN)-Baie-Comeau, 709
Model Aeronautics Association of Canada Inc.-Québec Zone, 970
Mouvement national des québécoises et québécois-SNQ de la Côte-Nord, 977
Réseau des SADC et CAE-SADC Manicouagan, 1221
FADOQ - Mouvement des aînés du Québec-Région Côte-Nord, 1224
Société historique de la Côte-Nord, 1320
Tourisme Côte-Nord, 1392

Baie-Saint-Paul
Centre d'information et de recherche en consommation de Charlevoix-Ouest, 528
Chambre de commerce de Charlevoix, 540
Réseau des SADC et CAE-SADC de Charlevoix, 1220

Beaconsfield
L'Association Zoroastrianne du Québec, 179
Canadian Association of Interventional Cardiology, 319
Canadian Aviation Historical Society-Montréal Chapter, 340
Canadian Explosives Industry Association, 383

Beauceville
Chambre de commerce de Beauceville, 540
Réseau des SADC et CAE-CAE Beauce-Chaudière inc, 1219

Beauport
Le centre jeunesse de Québec, 536
Fondation des sourds du Québec inc., 745
Fondation Edward Assh, 746

Beaupré
Association des grands-parents du Québec, 115

Bedford
Association des marchands de machines aratoires de la province de Québec, 119

Beloeil
L'Arche Québec-L'Arche Beloeil, 77
L'Arche Québec-L'Arche Joliette, 77
Association de la Vallée-du-Richelieu pour la déficience intellectuelle, 102
Association des chefs en sécurité incendie du Québec, 108
Association des personnes handicapées de la Vallée du Richelieu, 123
Association des Traumatisés cranio-cérébraux de la Montérégie, 129
Chambre de commerce et d'industrie de la Vallée-du-Richelieu, 545
Maison de la famille de la Vallée du Richelieu, 926
Réseau des SADC et CAE-CAE Capital, 1219
Voitures anciennes du Québec inc., 1437

Berthierville
Chambre de commerce et d'industrie Berthier-D'Autray, 545
Réseau des SADC et CAE-SADC de Autray-Joliette, 1220

Blainville
Association des herboristes de la province de Québec, 116
Association québécoise pour le tourisme équestre et l'équitation de loisir du Québec, 177
Canadian Tire Coupon Collectors Club, 495
Centraide Laurentides, 522

Moisson Laurentides, 971

Bois-des-Filion
Chambre de Commerce Bois-des-Filion - Lorraine, 540

Boisbriand
Association des médias écrits communautaires du Québec, 120
CAA-Québec-Boisbriand, 268

Bolton Centre
Chambre de commerce Vallée de la Missisquoi, 550

Bonaventure
Association coopérative d'économie familiale de la Péninsule-Centre de services de Bonaventure, 98
Chambre de commerce Baie-des-Chaleurs, 540
Conseil de la culture de la Gaspésie, 615
Conseil régional de l'environnement de la Gaspésie et des Îles-de-la-Madeleine, 620
Fédération québécoise des sociétés Alzheimer-Gaspésie/Iles-De-La-Madeleine, 730

Boucherville
American Society of Heating, Refrigerating & Air Conditioning Engineers-Chapitre Montréal Chapter, 1500
Association Béton Québec, 90
Association de joueurs de bridge de Boucherville, 100
Association des concessionnaires Ford du Québec, 109
Association des Numismates et des Philatélistes de Boucherville, 121
Canadian Association for Composite Structures & Materials, 298
Club de photo de Boucherville, 575
Fédération québécoise de camping et de caravaning inc., 727
Fondation Jeanne-Crevier, 746
Ringuette Boucherville, 1233
Société d'histoire des Iles-Percées, 1312
Société d'horticulture et d'écologie de Boucherville, 1314
Société du patrimoine de Boucherville, 1319
Society of Plastics Engineers-Québec Section, 1594
Syndicat professionnel des scientifiques de l'IREQ, 1365

Bromont
Aéroclub des cantons de l'est, 11
Association québécoise pour l'hygiène, la santé et la sécurité du travail, 176
BIOQuébec, 211

Brossard
Action Intégration en Déficience Intellectuelle, 6
Amis de la Bibliothèque de Brossard Georgette-Lepage, 67
Association des bibliothèques publiques de la Montérégie, 107
Association maritime du Québec, 137
Association sectorielle services automobiles, 178
Association Sportive de Ringuette Brossard, 178
CAA-Québec-Brossard, 268
Child Evangelism Fellowship of Canada-Québec - Association Évangile & Enfance, 559
Club informatique de Brossard, 575
Conseil régional FTQ du Richelieu - Bureau régional FTQ - Montérégie, 621
Corporation des infirmiers et infirmières de salle d'opération du Québec, 630
Fédération des caisses Desjardins du Québec-Rive-Sud de Montréal, 712
Groupe Brosse Art, 791
Maison internationale de la Rive-Sud, 927
Organisme d'autoréglementation du courtage immobilier du Québec, 1125
Préventex - Association paritaire du textile, 1170

Société d'Horticulture et d'Écologie de Brossard, 1314
Tourisme Montérégie, 1393
ZAP Montérégie, 1482

Bécancour
Chambre de commerce et d'industrie du Coeur-du-Québec, 547
Réseau des SADC et CAE-SADC Nicolet-Bécancour inc., 1221

Cabano
Société d'histoire et d'archéologie du Témiscouata, 1312

Cadillac
Frontiers Foundation-Québec Office, 764

Campbell's Bay
Carrefour jeunesse emploi du Pontiac, 515
Réseau des SADC et CAE-SADC Pontiac CFDC, 1221

Cantley
Centre intégré d'employabilité locale des Collines-de-l'Outaouais, 535

Cap Rouge
Chinese Medicine & Acupuncture Association of Canada-Québec Chapter, 565

Cap-aux-Meules
Chambre de commerce des Îles-de-la-Madeleine, 544
Réseau des SADC et CAE-SADC des Iles-de-la-Madeleine, 1221
Tourisme Îles-de-la-Madeleine, 1393

Cap-des-Rosiers
Chambre de Commerce de Cap-des-Rosiers, 540

Caplan
Association québécoise pour le loisir des personnes handicapées-URLS Gaspésie/Iles de la Madeleine, 177

Carleton
Chambre de commerce de Carleton, 540

Carleton-sur-Mer
Mouvement national des québécoises et québécois-SN Gaspésie/Iles-de-la-Madeleine, 977

Chambly
ARMA Canada, 81
Centre d'écoute Montérégie, 528
Chambre de commerce et d'industrie du bassin de Chambly, 547
Société d'histoire de la Seigneurie de Chambly, 1311

Chandler
Chambre de commerce MRC du Rocher-Percé, 549
Réseau des SADC et CAE-SADC du Rocher-Percé, 1221

Charlemagne
Fondation maman Dion, 747

Charlesbourg
Association des malentendants Québécois, 118
Association pour l'intégration sociale (Région de Québec), 166
Société historique de Charlesbourg, 1319

Charny
Les bibliothèques publiques des régions de la Capitale-Nationale et Chaudière-Appalaches, 208
Canadian Railroad Historical Association-Charny Division, 465
Réseau BIBLIO du Québec, 1218

Chelsea
Gatineau Valley Historical Society, 768

Chibougamau
Alcooliques Anonymes Groupe La Vallée du Cuivre, 53

Association chasse & pêche de Chibougamau, 96
Association des personnes en perte d'autonomie de Chibougamau inc. & Jardin des aînés, 122
Association Marie-Reine de Chibougamau, 137
Association mototocycliste Chibougamau Chapais, 137
Auxiliaires bénévoles de l'Hôpital de Chibougamau, 190
Carrefour communautaire de Chibougamau, 515
Centre de Femmes Les Elles du Nord, 529
Centre de plein air du Mont Chalco, 529
Centre indien cri de Chibougamau, 535
Cercle des Fermières - Chibougamau, 537
Chambre de commerce de Chibougamau, 540
Les Chevaliers de Colomb du Québec, District No 37, Conseil 5198, 557
Chorale Les Voix de la Vallée du Cuivre de Chibougamau inc., 566
Club 'Les Pongistes d'Ungava', 574
Club d'astronomie Quasar de Chibougamau, 574
Club d'auto-neige Chibougamau inc., 574
Club de golf Chibougamau-Chapais inc., 574
Club de karaté Shotokan Chibougamau, 574
Club de l'âge d'or Les intrépides de Chibougamau, 574
Club de natation Natchib inc., 575
Club de patinage artistique Les lames givrées inc., 575
Club Kiwanis Chibougamau, 575
Club Lions de Chibougamau, 575
Club nautique de Chibougamau inc., 575
Club Richelieu Boréal de Chibougamau, 576
Comité condition féminine Baie-James, 591
FaunEnord, 706
Fédération des professionnelles et professionnels de l'éducation du Québec-Syndicat des professionnelles et professionnels de commissions scolaires du Lac St-Jean, Pays-des-Bleuets et Baie-James (SPPLPB), 718
A fleur de sein, 737
La Fondation canadienne du rein, section Chibougamau, 743
Jeunes en partage, 870
Ligue de dards Ungava, 912
La Mine d'Or, entreprise d'insertion sociale, 966
Mouvement du Renouveau charismatique, 977
Parcelles de tendresse, 1139
Patrouille de ski St-Jean, 1146
Regroupement de Bouches à Oreilles, 1214
Réseau des SADC et CAE-SADC Chibougamau-Chapais inc, 1220
Société d'histoire régionale de Chibougamau, 1313
Table jamésienne de concertation minière, 1366
Théâtre des épinettes, 1374
Tourisme Baie-James, 1392

Chicoutimi
AIESEC-Chicoutimi, 18
Association du Québec pour enfants avec problèmes auditifs-AQEPA Saguenay, 131
Association pour le développement de la personne handicapée intellectuelle du Saguenay, 167
Association professionnelle des écrivains de la Sagamie-Côte-Nord, 167
Association provinciale des constructeurs d'habitations du Québec inc.-Saguenay, 168
Association québécoise de l'épilepsie-Épilepsie régionale pour personnes épileptiques de la région 02, 169
Association québécoise pour le loisir des personnes handicapées-ARLPH Saguenay/Lac St-Jean, 177
Association touristique régionale du Saguenay-Lac-Saint-Jean, 179
Centraide Saguenay-Lac St-Jean, 523
Chambre de commerce du Saguenay-Le Fjord, 544

Children of the World Adoption Society Inc.-Saguenay - Lac-St-Jean Office, 560
Expo agricole de Chicoutimi, 700
Fédération des coopératives d'habitation du Royaume Saguenay Lac-Saint-Jean, 714
Fédération des infirmières et infirmiers du Québec-FIQ - Saguenay/Lac St-Jean, 721
Fondation des maladies du coeur du Québec-Saguenay/Lac Saint-Jean, 745
The Kidney Foundation of Canada-Saguenay/Lac Saint-Jean Chapter, 885
Mouvement d'information, d'éducation et d'entraide dans la lutte contre le sida, 977
Orchestre symphonique du Saguenay-Lac-St-Jean, 1119
Québec Association of Insolvency & Restructuring Professionals, 1196
Randonneurs du Saguenay, 1204
Réseau du sport étudiant du Québec Saguenay-Lac St-Jean, 1223
Service budgétaire et communautaire de Chicoutimi inc, 1291
Société de généalogie du Saguenay, inc., 1316
Société historique du Saguenay, 1321
Syndicat des professeures et professeurs de l'Université du Québec à Chicoutimi, 1363
United Nations Association in Canada-Saguenay/Lac-St-Jean, 1411
Vertes boisées du fjord, 1431

Chomedey
Les Missions des Soeurs Missionnaires du Christ-Roi, 969

Chénéville
International Society for Research in Palmistry Inc., 860

Châteauguay
Centre d'aide et de lutte contre les agressions à caractère sexuel de Châteauguay, 527
Chambre de commerce du grand de Châteauguay, 544
Réseau québécois des OSBL d'habitation-Montérégie & de l'Estrie, 1225
Société généalogique de Châteauguay, 1319

Coaticook
Chambre de commerce et d'Industrie de la région de Coaticook, 545
Réseau des SADC et CAE-SADC région de Coaticook, 1221
Société d'histoire de Coaticook, 1310

Compton
Association des éleveurs de chevaux Belge du Québec, 111
Compton Historical Society, 609

Cookshire-Eaton
Compton County Historical Museum Society, 609

Courcelette
Army Cadet League of Canada-Ligue des cadets de l'armée du Canada (Québec), 83
Navy League of Canada-Québec, 1002

Cowansville
Chambre de commerce de Cowansville et région, 540
Yamaska Literacy Council, 1470

Côte Saint-Luc
Emunah Women of Canada, 687
Model Aeronautics Association of Canada Inc.-St. Lawrence Zone, 971

Danville
Chambre de commerce et d'entrepreneuriat des Sources, 544
Société d'histoire Danville-Shipton, 1310

Deux-Montagnes
4Korners Family Resource Center, 756

Disraéli
Chambre de commerce de Disraéli, 540

Dolbeau-Mistassini
Association des Grands Frères Grandes Soeurs du Québec-Grands Frères Grandes Soeurs du Lac St-Jean Nord, 115
Chambre de commerce et d'industrie de Dolbeau-Mistassini, 545
Réseau des SADC et CAE-SADC Maria-Chapdelaine, 1221
Service budgétaire et communautaire de la MRC Maria-Chapdelaine, 1291
Société d'histoire et de généalogie Maria-Chapdelaine, 1313

Dollard des Ormeaux
CARP-Montréal - Metro West Chapter, 514
Eastern Canada Orchid Society, 670

Dollard-des-Ormeaux
African Violet Society of Canada, 13
Réseau du sport étudiant du Québec Lac Saint-Louis, 1223
Société québécoise du dahlia, 1324

Donnacona
Réseau des SADC et CAE-SADC Portneuf, 1221

Dorval
Canadian Business Aviation Association-Québec Chapter, 348
Canadian Transverse Myelitis Association, 497
Canadian Urological Association, 500
Dreams Take Flight, 662
Fondation des maladies du coeur du Québec-Ouest de Montréal, 745
Infertility Awareness Association of Canada, 836
Lakeshore Stamp Club Inc., 897
Scouts Canada-Québec Council, 1287
Société historique de Dorval, 1319
Starlight Children's Foundation Canada, 1348
Starlight Starbright Children's Foundation Canada-Montréal Chapter, 1348

Drummondville
Association des clubs d'entrepreneurs étudiants du Québec, 109
Association provinciale des constructeurs d'habitations du Québec inc.-Centre du Québec, 168
Birthright International-Drummondville Chapter, 212
Canadian Federation of Orthotherapists, 388
Carrefour d'entraide de Drummond, 515
Centraide Centre du Québec, 522
Chambre de commerce et d'industrie de Drummond, 545
Chambre immobilière Centre du Québec Inc., 550
Conseil FTQ Drummondville, 618
Fédération des caisses Desjardins du Québec-Centre-du-Québec, 712
Fédération des coopératives d'habitation de la Mauricie et du Centre-du-Québec, 714
La fédération des mouvements personne d'abord du Québec-Drummondville, 716
GRIS-Mauricie/Centre-du-Québec, 790
Mon Réseau Plus, Association professionnelle des massothérapeutes spécialisés du Québec inc., 971
Mouvement national des québécoises et québécois-SSJB du Centre-du-Québec, 978
Réseau des SADC et CAE-CAE de Drummond, 1219
Société de généalogie de Drummondville, 1315
Société Saint-Jean-Baptiste du Centre du Québec, 1324
Syndicat de la fonction publique du Québec inc. (ind.)-Centre du Québec-Estrie-Mauricie, 1361
UNIFOR-Drummondville, 1405

Duparquet
Chambre de commerce Duparquet, 544

Durham-Sud
Québec Angus Association, 1195

Syndicat des agricultrices du Centre du Québec, 1362

East Angus
Chambre de commerce du Haut-Saint-François, 544
Réseau des SADC et CAE-SADC du Haut-Saint-François, 1221

East Broughton
Chambre de commerce East Broughton, 544

Farnham
Regroupement Pour-Valorisation, 1216

Ferme-Neuve
Chambre de commerce de Ferme-Neuve, 541

Fermont
Chambre de Commerce de Fermont, 541

Forestville
Chambre de commerce de Forestville, 541

Gaspé
Association coopérative d'économie familiale de la Péninsule-Centre de services de Gaspé, 98
Association des capitaines propriétaires de Gaspésie inc, 108
Association Gaspé-Jersey & Guernesey, 136
Chambre de commerce et de tourisme de Gaspé, 548
Regroupement des femmes de la Côte-de-Gaspé, 1215
Réseau des SADC et CAE-SADC de Gaspé, 1220
FADOQ - Mouvement des aînés du Québec-Région Gaspésie Iles-de-la-Madeleine, 1224
Société de généalogie Gaspésie-Les Îles, 1316
TechnoCentre éolien, 1368

Gatineau
Alliance autochtone du Québec, 54
L'Arche Québec-L'Arche Agapè, 77
Association coopérative d'économie familiale de l'Outaouais, 98
Association coopérative d'économie familiale de l'Outaouais, 97
Association de la construction du Québec-Région de l'Outaouais / Abitibi / Nord-Ouest du Québec, 100
Association des Grands Frères Grandes Soeurs du Québec-Grands Frères Grandes Soeurs de l'Outaouais, 115
Association des neurotraumatisés de l'Outaouais, 121
Association du Patrimoine d'Aylmer, 131
Association pour l'intégration communautaire de l'Outaouais, 165
Association provinciale des constructeurs d'habitations du Québec inc.-Outaouais, 168
Association québécoise de l'épilepsie-Épilepsie Outaouais, 169
Association québécoise des interprètes du patrimoine, 173
Association québécoise des salons du livre-Outaouais, 174
Association québécoise des troubles d'apprentissage - section Outaouais, 175
Association québécoise pour le loisir des personnes handicapées-URLS Outaouais, 177
Bureau régional d'action sida (Outaouais), 264
CAA-Québec-Gatineau, 268
Canadian Association of Administrators of Labour Legislation, 307
Canadian Association of Nordic Ski Instructors, 322
Canadian Committee on Cataloguing, 361
Canadian Council on Ecological Areas, 371
Canadian Dyslexia Association, 379
Canadian General Standards Board, 396
Canadian Hard of Hearing Association-Québec Chapter, 401
Canadian Hard of Hearing Association - Outaouais Branch, 401

Canadian Heritage Information Network, 405
Canadian Register of Health Service Psychologists, 466
Canadian Society for the Study of Names, 478
Carrefour jeunesse emploi de l'Outaouais, 515
Carrefour jeunesse-emploi Papineau, 516
Centraide Outaouais, 523
Centre d'intervention et de prévention en toxicomanie de l'Outaouais, 528
Les Centres jeunesse de l'Outaouais, 537
Chambre de commerce de Gatineau, 541
Chambre immobilière de l'Outaouais, 550
Christian Catholic Church Canada, 566
Confédération québécoise des coopératives d'habitation en Outaouais, 611
Conseil régional de la culture de l'Outaouais, 620
Conseil régional FTQ de l'Outaouais, 621
Development & Peace-Québec - Gatineau/Ottawa (French), 655
Entraide familiale de l'Outaouais inc., 690
Envol SRT, 693
Federal Libraries Coordination Secretariat, 706
Fédération des caisses Desjardins du Québec-Outaouais, 712
Fédération des professionnelles et professionnels de l'éducation du Québec-Syndicat du personnel professionnel des commissions scolaires de l'Outaouais (SPPCSO), 718
Fédération des infirmières et infirmiers du Québec-FIQ - Outaouais, 721
Fédération québécoise des sociétés Alzheimer-Outaouais québécois, 730
First Nations SchoolNet, 738
Fondation des maladies du coeur du Québec-Outaouais, 745
Fondation québécoise du cancer-Hôtellerie de l'Outaouais, 748
Fondation Santé Gatineau, 748
Groupe gai de l'Outaouais, 792
International Watercolour Society - Canada, 861
The Kidney Foundation of Canada-Outaouais-Québécois Chapter, 885
Mouvement national des québécoises et québécois-SNQ de l'Outaouais, 977
National Council on Canada-Arab Relations, 992
North American Bird Conservation Initiative Canada, 1029
North American Waterfowl Management Plan, 1029
Ordre des infirmières et infirmiers du Québec-Ordre régional des infirmières et infirmiers de l'Outaouais, 1122
Oxygène, 1134
Public Service Alliance of Canada-Section de Gatineau, 1193
Réseau des SADC et CAE-SADC de Papineau inc., 1220
Réseau du patrimoine de Gatineau et de l'Outaouais, 1222
Réseau du sport étudiant du Québec Outaouais, 1223
FADOQ - Mouvement des aînés du Québec-Région Outaouais, 1224
Réseau québécois des OSBL d'habitation-Outaouais, 1225
Service Intégration Travail Outaouais, 1291
Société d'histoire de l'Outaouais inc., 1310
Société de généalogie de l'Outaouais, 1315
SPCA of Western Québec, 1339
Tourisme Outaouais, 1393
UNIFOR-Gatineau, 1405

Georgeville
Georgeville Historical Society, 771

Granby
Association coopérative d'économie familiale - Montérégie-est, 97
Association de paralysie cérébrale du Québec-Bureau de Granby, 103
Association des alternatives en santé mentale de la Montérégie, 105
Association des Physiques Québécois, 123

Association québécoise de l'épilepsie-Épilepsie Granby et régions, 169
Association québécoise de soins palliatifs, 171
Centrale des syndicats démocratiques-Richelieu - Yamaska, 525
Centre d'aide et de lutte contre les agressions à caractère sexuel de Granby, 527
Chambre de commerce Haute-Yamaska et Région, 548
Chambre immobilière de la Haute Yamaska Inc., 550
Conseil de la transformation agroalimentaire et des produits de consommation, 616
Conseil régional FTQ de la Haute-Yamaska - Bureau régional FTQ - Montérégie, 621
Fédération des professionnelles et professionnels de l'éducation du Québec-Syndicat des professionnelles et professionnels de Richelieu Yamaska (SPPRY), 718
Fédération Québécoise des Intervenants en Sécurité Incendie, 728
Fédération des sociétés Alzheimer-Granby et Région, 730
Réseau des SADC et CAE-CAE Haute-Yamaska et région inc., 1219
Société d'histoire de la Haute-Yamaska, 1310

Greenfield Park
Association des cadres supérieurs de la santé et des services sociaux du Québec, 108
Association des parents et amis de la personne atteinte de maladie mentale Rive-Sud, 122
Association québécoise des parents d'enfants handicapés visuels, 173
Fondation Hôpital Charles-LeMoyne, 746
Orchestre symphonique de Longueuil, 1118
Pavillon Marguerite de Champlain, 1146
Société d'histoire de Greenfield Park, 1310
South Shore Reading Council, 1336
Syndicat de la fonction publique du Québec inc. (ind.)-Montérégie, 1361
The Terry Fox Foundation-Québec Office, 1372

Hampstead
Canadian Coalition for Nuclear Responsibility, 357

Harrington
Canadian Amateur Musicians, 292

Havre-Saint-Pierre
Centre de recherche et d'information en consommation de Port-Cartier-Havre-Saint-Pierre, 530

Hull
Syndicat des professeures et professeurs de l'Université du Québec en Outaouais, 1363

Huntingdon
Société historique de la Vallée de la Châteauguay, 1320

Ile-des-Soeurs
Association québécoise du chauffage au mazout, 175
Chambre immobilière de Québec, 551
Chambre immobilière du Grand Montréal, 551
Fédération des Chambres immobilières du Québec, 713

Iles de Soeurs
Electric Mobility Canada, 681

Inukjuak
Makivik Corporation-Inukjuak Office, 927

Inverness
The Celtic Way, 521

Isle-aux-Coudres
Société des traversiers du Québec-Traverse Isle-aux-Coudres-St-Joseph-de-la-Rive, 1318

Joliette
Association coopérative d'économie familiale - Lanaudière, 97
Association des fondations d'établissements de santé du Québec, 114

Association des personnes handicapées physiques et sensorielles du secteur Joliette, 123
Association des Sourds de Lanaudière, 128
Association québécoise pour le loisir des personnes handicapées-ARLPH Lanaudière, 177
Centraide Lanaudière, 522
Chambre de commerce du Grand Joliette, 544
Chambre immobilière de Lanaudière Inc., 551
Comité régional d'éducation pour le développement international de Lanaudière, 592
Conseil de la culture de Lanaudière, 616
Fédération de l'industrie manufacturière (FIM-CSN)-Joliette, 709
La fédération des mouvements personne d'abord du Québec-Joliette, 716
Fédération québécoise des sociétés Alzheimer-Lanaudière, 730
Mouvement national des québécoises et québécois-SNQ de Lanaudière, 977
Parents-Unis Lanaudière, 1140
FADOQ - Mouvement des aînés du Québec-Région Lanaudière, 1224
Société de généalogie de Lanaudière, 1315
Société historique de Joliette-De Lanaudière, 1319

Jonquière
Association de la construction du Québec-Région Saguenay / Lac St-Jean, 101
Association pour la promotion des droits des personnes handicapées, 166
Association québécoise des écoles de français langue étrangère, 172
Association québécoise des salons du livre-Saguenay-Lac-St-Jean, 174
Association renaissance des personnes traumatisées crâniennes du Saguenay-Lac-Saint-Jean, 178
Le Syndicat canadien des employées et employés professionnels et de bureau-Region 1 - Section locale 526, 444
Centrale des syndicats démocratiques-Saguenay - Lac St-Jean, 525
Chambre immobilière du Saguenay-Lac St-Jean Inc., 551
Conseil régional FTQ Saguenay-Lac-St-Jean-Chibougamau-Chapais, 621
Fédération indépendante des syndicats autonomes-Saguenay, 721
Service budgétaire communautaire de Jonquière, 1291
Syndicat de la fonction publique du Québec inc. (ind.)-Saguenay - Lac-St-Jean - Chibougamau - Charlevoix - Houte-Côte-Nord, 1361
Syndicat des producteurs de bois du Saguenay-Lac-Saint-Jean, 1363
Syndicat national des employés de l'aluminium d'Arvida, inc., 1365
UNIFOR-Jonquière, 1405

Kahnawake
Femmes autochtones du Québec inc., 731
Kanien'kehaka Onkwawen'na Raotitiohkwa Language & Cultural Centre, 881
National Aboriginal Circle Against Family Violence, 988

Kamouraska
Le Berceau de Kamouraska inc., 205

Kingsey Falls
Association des Poneys Welsh & Cob au Québec, 124

Kinnear's Mills
Grand Orange Lodge of Canada-Grand Orange Lodge of Québec, 780
Héritage Kinnear's Mills, 813

Kipawa
Chambre de commerce Témiscaming-Kipawa, 550

Kirkland
Association des Grands Frères Grandes Soeurs du Québec-Grands Frères Grandes Soeurs de l'Ouest de l'île, 115
Association provinciale des enseignantes et enseignants du Québec, 168
Canadian Railway Club, 465
Quintiles IMS Canada, 1202

Knowlton
Brome County Historical Society, 260

Kuujjuaq
Makivik Corporation, 927
Réseau des SADC et CAE-Nunavik Investment Corporation, 1220

Kuujjuaraapik
Makivik Corporation-Kuujjuaraapik Office, 927

L'Assomption
Canadian Association of Paralegals, 325
Société d'histoire de la MRC de l'Assomption, 1310

L'Ile-Bizard
Association des professionnels en exposition du Québec, 126

L'Isle-Verte
Société de conservation de la Baie de l'Isle-Verte, 1314

L'Isle-aux-Grues
Société des traversiers du Québec-Traverse Isle aux Grues-Montmagny, 1318

L'Orignal
Canadian Correspondence Chess Association, 366

La Baie
Réseau des SADC et CAE-SADC du Fjord inc., 1221
Service budgétaire populaire de La Baie et du Bas Saguenay, 1291

La Malbaie
Association des personnes handicapées de Charlevoix inc., 122
Association touristique régionale de Charlevoix, 178
Regroupement pour l'intégration sociale de Charlevoix, 1216
Service alimentaire et aide budgétaire de Charlevoix-Est, 1291
Service alimentaire et aide budgétaire de Charlevoix-Est, 1291

La Pocatière
Centraide KRTB-Côte-du-Sud, 522
Chambre de commerce Kamouraska-L'Islet, 548
Réseau des SADC et CAE-SADC Kamouraska, 1221
Société historique de la Côte-du-Sud, 1320
Syndicat des agricultrices de la Côte-du-Sud, 1362

La Prairie
Association des personnes handicapées de la Rive-Sud Ouest, 122
Société d'histoire de La Prairie-de-la-Magdeleine, 1310
Terre sans frontières, 1372

La Sarre
Association des Grands Frères Grandes Soeurs du Québec-Grands Frères Grandes Soeurs d'Abitibi Ouest, 115
Chambre de commerce et d'industrie d'Abitibi-Ouest, 545
Réseau des SADC et CAE-SADC Abitibi-Ouest, 1220

La Tuque
Chambre de commerce et d'industrie du Haut St-Maurice, 547
Réseau des SADC et CAE-SADC du Haut-Saint-Maurice inc., 1221

LaSalle
Associaça Portuguesa de LaSalle, 89
Association of Teachers of English in Québec, 162
Boys & Girls Clubs of Québec-Boys & Girls Club of LaSalle, 224
Corporation l'Espoir, 631
Les Kilomaîtres de LaSalle, 887
Master Brewers Association of The Americas-District Eastern Canada
Patronato INAS (Canada)-La Salle Office, 1146
Single Persons Association of Montréal, 1300
Société historique Cavelier-de-LaSalle, 1319

Labrecque
Fédération des professionnelles et professionnels de l'éducation du Québec-Syndicat des professionnelles et professionnels de l'éducation du Saguenay (SPPÉS), 718

Lac-Brome
Chambre de commerce de Lac-Brome, 542
Townshippers' Association-Lac-Brome Office, 1393

Lac-Mégantic
Chambre de commerce région de Mégantic, 549
Réseau des SADC et CAE-SADC région de Mégantic, 1221

Lac-Sergent
Frères de Notre-Dame de la Miséricorde, 760

Lachine
Association de Dards du Québec inc., 100
Comité logement de Lacine-Lasalle, 592
Congrégation des Soeurs de Sainte-Anne, 612
Lachine Black Community Association, 895
Société d'histoire de Lachine, 1311

Lachute
Bibles & Literature in French Canada, 208
Chambre de commerce et d'industrie d'Argenteuil, 545
La fédération des mouvements personne d'abord du Québec-Lachute, 716
Union Paysanne, 1408

Laterrière
Réseau québécois des OSBL d'habitation-Saguenay, Lac St-Jean, Chibougamau, Chapais & Côte-Nord, 1225

Laurier-Station
Réseau des SADC et CAE-SADC de Lotbinière, 1220

Laval
Armenian Relief Society of Canada, " Inc.-Laval Chapter: ""Shoushi""", 83
Association de balle des jeunes handicapés de Laval-Laurentides-Lanaudière, 99
Association de Laval pour la déficience intellectuelle, 102
Association de loisirs pour personnes handicapées psychiques de Laval, 102
Association des Aviateurs et Pilotes de Brousse du Québec, 106
Association des entrepreneurs de systèmes intérieurs du Québec, 112
Association des jeunes bègues de Québec, 117
Association des maîtres couvreurs du Québec, 118
Association des physiciens et ingénieurs biomédicaux du Québec, 123
Association des pompiers de Laval, 124
Association des spécialistes du pneus et Mécanique du Québec, 128
Association nationale des distributeurs aux petites surfaces alimentaires, 138
Association pour aînés résidant à Laval, 165
Association québécoise de commercialisation de poissons et de fruits de mer, 169
Association québécoise de la fibromyalgie, 170
Association québécoise des informaticiennes et informaticiens indépendants, 173
Association québécoise pour le loisir des personnes handicapées-ARLPH Laval, 177
Association régionale de ringuette Laval, 177
Associations touristiques régionales associées du Québec, 179
Baptist General Conference of Canada-Baptist General Conference - Eastern Expansion, 196
CAA-Québec-Laval, 268
Canadian Fence Industry Association-Québec, 389
Canadian Institute of Food Science & Technology-Québec Section, 416
Le Syndicat canadien des employées et employés professionnels et de bureau-Region 1 - Section locale 577, 444
Canadian Welding Bureau-Québec Region, 503
Chambre de commerce et d'industrie de Laval, 545
Children of the World Adoption Society Inc., 560
Club d'observateurs d'oiseaux de Laval, 574
Les Clubs 4-H du Québec, 576
Clubs 4-H du Québec, 576
College of Family Physicians of Canada-Collège québécois des médecins de famille, 584
Conseil national du meuble, 619
Conseil québécois de la franchise, 620
Entre-amis Lavallois inc, 691
Fédération de soccer du Québec, 710
Fédération des caisses Desjardins du Québec-Laval-Laurentides, 712
La fédération des mouvements personne d'abord du Québec-Laval, 716
Fédération québécoise des sociétés Alzheimer-Laval, 730
Floorball Québec, 741
Fondation des maladies du coeur du Québec-Laval/Laurentides/Lanaudière, 745
Gymn-eau Laval inc, 795
Hebdos Québec, 810
Laurier Teachers Union, 900
Montréal Science Fiction & Fantasy Association, 973
Myeloma Canada, 986
L'Office de Certification Commerciale du Québec Inc., 1054
Orchestre symphonique de Laval, 1118
Osteoporosis Canada-Laval - Greater Montreal Chapter, 1128
Packaging Association of Canada-Québec Office, 1136
Partage Humanitaire, 1143
Québec Ball Hockey Association, 1196
Regroupement des associations de personnes traumatisées craniocérébrales du Québec, 1214
Regroupement des Marocains au Canada, 1215
Regroupement pour l'intégration dans la communauté de Rivière-des-Prairies, 1216
FADOQ - Mouvement des aînés du Québec-Région Laval, 1224
Réseau québécois des OSBL d'habitation-Laval, Laurentides & Lanaudière, 1225
Société d'histoire et de généalogie de l'Ile Jésus, 1312
Sports Laval, 1346
Teamsters Canada (CLC), 1368
Tourisme Laval, 1393

LeMoyne
Association québécoise des professeurs de français, 174
Mosaïque centre d'action bénévole et communautaire, 975

Lennoxville
Québec Anglophone Heritage Network, 1195

Les Escoumins
Association de chasse et pêche nordique, inc., 100
Fondation des maladies du coeur-Côte-Nord, 745
Réseau des SADC et CAE-SADC Haute-Côte-Nord inc., 1221

Limoilou
Organisation québécoise des personnes atteintes de cancer, 1125

Listuguj First Nation
First Nation Lands Managers Association of Québec & Labrador, 738

Longueuil
Action Nouvelle Vie, 6
Alliance du personnel professionnel et technique de la santé et des services sociaux, 56
Association coopérative d'économie familiale - Rive-Sud de Montréal, 97
Association d'éducation préscolaire du Québec, 99
Association d'informations en logements et immeubles adaptés, 99
Association de la fibromyalgie de la Montérégie, 101
Association de Ringuette de Longueuil, 103
Association des artistes peintres de Longueuil, 106
Association des directeurs généraux des commissions scolaires du Québec, 111
Association des gestionnaires des établissements de santé et des services sociaux, 115
Association des goélands de Longueuil, 115
Association des intervenants en toxicomanie du Québec inc., 117
Association des parents et des handicapés de la Rive-Sud métropolitaine, 122
Association des Pêcheurs de Longueuil, 122
Association des professionnels du chauffage, 125
Association des usagers du transport adapté de Longueuil, 130
Association Et si c'était moi, 132
Association Hôtellerie Québec, 136
Association longueuilloise des photographes amateurs, 137
Association québécoise de joueurs d'échecs handicapeés visuels, 169
Association québécoise de la quincaillerie et des matériaux de construction, 170
Bouffe pour tous/Moisson Longueuil, 218
Camping Québec, 277
Canadian Institute of Management-Québec - Montréal Branch, 417
Le Syndicat canadien des employées et employés professionnels et de bureau-Region 1 - Section locale 578, 444
Carrefour pour Elle, 516
Le Centre de soutien en santé mentale - Montérégie, 530
Centre des Femmes de Longueuil, 530
Le Centre jeunesse de la Montérégie, 536
Cercles de fermières du Québec, 537
Chambre de commerce et d'industrie de la Rive-Sud, 545
Club cycliste de la Montérégie, 574
Club d'Ornithologie de Longueuil, 574
Club informatique de Longueuil, 575
Club violettes Longueuil, 576
Conseil montérégien de la culture et des communications, 619
Conseil pédagogique interdisciplinaire du Québec, 619
Éleveurs de porcs du Québec, 684
Éleveurs de volailles du Québec, 684
Fédération de la relève agricole du Québec, 709
Fédération des agricultrices du Québec, 711
Fédération des apiculteurs du Québec, 711
Fédération des Associations de Musiciens-Éducateurs du Québec, 712
Fédération des coopératives d'habitation Montérégiennes, 714
Fédération des producteurs acéricoles du Québec, 717
Fédération des producteurs d'agneaux et moutons du Québec, 717
Fédération des producteurs d'oeufs de consommation du Québec, 717
Fédération des producteurs de bovins du Québec, 717
Fédération des producteurs de cultures commerciales du Québec, 717
Fédération des producteurs de pommes de terre du Québec, 717
Fédération des producteurs forestiers du Québec, 717
Fédération québécoise des sociétés Alzheimer-Rive-Sud, 730
Fondation Cardio-Montérégienne, 743
Fondation des maladies du coeur du Québec-Rive-Sud/Montérégie, 745
Groupe d'entraide G.E.M.E., 791
Hébergement la casa Bernard-Hubert, 811
Institut Nazareth et Louis-Braille, 843
Insurance Brokers Association of Canada-Regroupement des cabinets de courtage d'assurance du Québec, 848
Maison Kekpart, 927
Mouvement action chômage de Longueuil, 976
Mouvement Retrouvailles, 978
MultiPrévention, 980
MultiPrévention ASP: Association paritaire pour la santé et la sécurité au travail des secteurs: métal, électrique, habillement et imprimerie, 980
Office municipal d'habitation de Longueuil, 1055
Ordre des denturologistes du Québec, 1121
Pentecostal Assemblies of Canada-Québec District Office, 1150
Les producteurs de lait du Québec, 1181
Québec Farmers' Association, 1197
Réseau des femmes d'affaires du Québec inc., 1219
Réseau du sport étudiant du Québec Montérégie, 1223
Ressources Saint-Jean-Vianney, 1227
Société d'histoire de Longueuil, 1311
Société d'Horticulture et d'Écologie de Longueuil, 1314
Société de généalogie de Longueuil, 1315
Société de généalogie Saint-Hubert, 1316
Société des écoles du monde du BI du Québec et de la francophonie, 1317
Société des professeurs d'histoire du Québec inc., 1318
Société historique et culturelle du Marigot inc., 1321
Syndicat des producteurs de chèvres du Québec, 1363
Syndicat des producteurs en serre du Québec, 1363
Table de développement de la production biologique, 1365
Taoist Tai Chi Society of Canada-Eastern Region, 1367
Union des producteurs agricoles, 1406
Union québécoise du bison, 1408
Les Vieux Brachés de Longueuil, 1434

Loretteville
Association des traumatisés cranio-cérébraux des deux rives (Québec-Chaudière-Appalaches), 129

Louiseville
Chambre de commerce et d'industrie de la MRC de Maskinongé, 545
Réseau des SADC et CAE-SADC de la MRC de Maskinongé, 1220
Société d'histoire de Louiseville inc., 1311

LéVis
Centre d'aide et de lutte contre les agressions à caractère sexuel de la Rive-Sud, 527

Lévis
Alliance Québécoise du Psoriasis, 58
Association coopérative d'économie familiale - Rive-Sud de Québec, 97
Association québécoise pour le loisir des personnes handicapées-ARLPH Chaudière-Appalaches, 176
Chambre de commerce de Lévis, 542
Club de trafic de Lévis, 575
Conseil québécois de la coopération et de la mutualité, 620
Fédération des caisses Desjardins du Québec, 712
Fédération des caisses Desjardins du Québec-Québec-Rive-Sud, 712
Fédération des professionnelles et professionnels de l'éducation du Québec-Syndicat du personnel professionnel de l'éducation Chaudière-Appalaches (SPPÉCA), 718
Fondation Les oiseleurs du Québec inc., 747
Ordre des infirmières et infirmiers du Québec-Ordre régional des infirmières et infirmiers de Chaudière-Appalaches, 1122
Société d'histoire régionale de Lévis, 1313
Société historique Alphonse-Desjardins, 1319

Magog
Appalachian Teachers' Association, 73
Association des orthésistes et prothésistes du Québec, 121
Association des professionnels en développement économique du Québec, 126
Chambre de commerce et d'industrie Magog-Orford, 547
Réseau des SADC et CAE-CAE Memphrémagog inc., 1219
Société d'histoire de Magog, 1311
Syndicat des ouvriers du textile de Magog, 1363

Malartic
Chambre de commerce et d'industrie de Malartic, 545

Maniwaki
AFOA Canada-AFOA Québec, 12
Carrefour Jeunesse Emploi Vallée-de-la-Gatineau, 516
Chambre de commerce et d'industrie de Maniwaki & Vallée de la Gatineau, 546
Réseau des SADC et CAE-SADC Vallée-de-la-Gatineau, 1222

Mansonville
Ruiter Valley Land Trust, 1244

Maria
Association des TCC (le traumatisme cranio-cérébral) et ACV (un accident vasculaire cérébral) de la Gaspésie et des Îles-de-la-Madeleine Inc., 129
Fédération des caisses Desjardins du Québec-Gaspésie/Iles-de-la-Madeleine, 712

Marieville
Chambre de commerce au Coeur de la Montérégie, 539
Société d'histoire de la Seigneurie de Monnoir, 1311

Mascouche
Association de parents d'enfant trisomique-21 de Lanaudière, 103
Association de Ringuette des Moulins, 104
Association of Canadian Travel Agents - Québec, 144
Fédération des caisses Desjardins du Québec-Lanaudière, 712

Matagami
Réseau des SADC et CAE-SADC Matagami, 1221

Matane
Association coopérative d'économie familiale de la Péninsule, 98
Chambre de commerce région de Matane, 549
Fédération québécoise des sociétés Alzheimer-Bas St-Laurent, 729
Réseau des SADC et CAE-SADC de la région de Matane, 1220
Société d'histoire et de généalogie de Matane, 1312
Société des traversiers du Québec-Traverse Matane-Baie-Comeau-Godbout, 1318
Syndicat de la fonction publique du Québec inc. (ind.)-Bas Saint-Laurent - Côte Nord - Gaspésie et les Iles, 1361

McMasterville
Association des psychothérapeutes pastoraux du Canada, 126

Melbourne
Richmond County Historical Society, 1230

Mirabel
Chambre de commerce et d'industrie de Mirabel, 546
Club d'ornithologie de Mirabel, 574
Réseau des SADC et CAE-CAE Rive-Nord, 1220
Tourisme Laurentides, 1392

Mont-Joli
Centraide Bas St-Laurent, 522
Chambre de commerce et industrie Mont-Joli-Mitis, 548
Réseau des SADC et CAE-SADC La Mitis, 1221
Tourisme Gaspésie, 1392

Mont-Laurier
Centraide Gatineau-Labelle-Hautes-Laurentides, 522
Chambre de commerce de Mont-Laurier, 542
Mouvement national des québécoises et québécois-SNQ des Hautes-Rivières, 977
Réseau des SADC et CAE-SADC d'Antoine-Labelle, 1220
Société historique de la région de Mont-Laurier, 1320

Mont-Royal
Association des distributeurs exclusifs de livres en langue française inc., 111
The Christian & Missionary Alliance in Canada-St. Lawrence District (SLD) Office, 566
Lebanese Canadian Heritage Association, 905
Procure Alliance, 1181

Mont-Saint-Hilaire
Association de Ringuette de Vallée-du-Richelieu, 103
Canadian Institute for Theatre Technology-Québec Section, 414
Société d'histoire de Beloeil - Mont-Saint-Hilaire, 1310
Société québécoise de psychologie du travail, 1323

Mont-Tremblant
Chambre de commerce de Mont-Tremblant, 542
FADOQ - Mouvement des aînés du Québec-Région Laurentides, 1224

Montebello
International Log Builders' Association, 858

Montmagny
Centrale des syndicats démocratiques-Montmagny - Bas St-Laurent, 525
Chambre de commerce de Montmagny, 542
Réseau des SADC et CAE-CAE Montmagny-L'Islet, 1219

Montréal
Académie de musique du Québec, 3
Académie des lettres du Québec, 3
Academy of Canadian Cinema & Television-Montréal Office, 4
Action Autonomie, 6
Action Centre-Ville, 6
Action des Chrétiens pour l'abolition de la torture, 6

Action-Gardien, la table de concertation communautaire de Pointe-Saint-Charles, 7
Advertising Standards Canada-Québec, 10
Aéro Montréal, 11
African & Caribbean Students' Network of Montréal, 12
African Legacy, 13
African Students Association of Concordia, 13
AFS Interculture Canada, 13
Agence universitaire de la Francophonie, 14
AIESEC-Concordia, 18
AIESEC-École des Hautes Études Commerciales, 18
AIESEC-McGill, 18
AIESEC-Université du Québec à Montréal, 18
Al-Anon Montréal, 21
Alcoholics Anonymous-Montréal - Intergroupe de Montréal, 52
Alcooliques Anonymes du Québec, 53
Alliance des chorales du Québec, 55
Alliance des communautés culturelles pour l'égalité dans la santé et les services sociaux, 55
Alliance des professeures et professeurs de Montréal, 56
Alliance internationale des employé(e)s de scène, de théâtre et de cinéma, 57
Alliance numérique, 58
Alliance of Canadian Cinema, Television & Radio Artists-ACTRA Montréal, 58
Alliance québécoise des techniciens de l'image et du son, 58
ALS Society of Québec, 60
AlterHéros, 60
Aluminium Association of Canada, 61
American Society of Plumbing Engineers-Chapitre de Montréal, 1502
Amicale des Sommeliers du Québec, 67
Les Amis du centre canadien d'architecture, 67
Les Amis du Jardin botanique de Montréal, 67
Amis et propriétaires de maisons anciennes du Québec, 68
Amnistie internationale, Section canadienne (Francophone), 68
The Anglican Church of Canada-Diocese of Montréal, 69
Anxiety Disorders Association of Canada, 72
APER Santé et services sociaux, 73
Apparel Human Resources Council, 74
Apparel Québec, 74
L'Appui pour les proches aidants d'aînés, 75
ARC - Aînés et retraités de la communauté, 76
L'arc-en-ciel littéraire, 76
L'Arche Québec-L'Arche Montréal, 77
ARMA Canada-Montréal Chapter, 82
Armenian Relief Society of Canada, Inc., 83
Armenian Relief Society of Canada, " Inc.-Montréal Chapter: ""Sosse""", 83
Art Libraries Society of North America-Montréal, Ottawa & Québec Chapter, 1506
Arthritis Society-Québec Division, 84
Assemblée des évêques catholiques du Québec, 88
Associaça Portuguesa Do Canadà, 89
Associaça Portuguesa Espirito Santo, 89
Associaçao dos Pais, 89
Associated Research Centres for the Urban Underground Space, 89
Association canadienne des annonceurs inc., 92
Association canadienne des ataxies familiales, 92
Association canadienne des juristes-traducteurs, 93
Association canadienne des métiers de la truelle, section locale 100 (CTC), 94
Association CFA Montréal, 96
Association coopérative d'économie familiale de l'est de Montréal, 97
Association coopérative d'économie familiale du Nord de Montréal, 98
Association coopérative d'économie familiale du Sud-Ouest de Montréal, 98
Association d'églises baptistes évangéliques au québec, 99

Association d'entraide des avocats de Montréal, 99
Association d'entraide Le Chaînon inc., 99
Association d'isolation du Québec, 99
Association d'orthopédie du Québec, 99
Association d'oto-rhino-laryngologie et de chirurgie cervico-faciale du Québec, 99
Association de bienfaisance et de retraite des policiers et policières de la ville de Montréal, 99
Association de l'Agricotourism et du Tourisme Gourmand, 100
Association de l'industrie électrique du Québec, 100
Association de la fibromyalgie région Ile-De-Montréal, 101
L'Association de la Neurofibromatose du Québec, 101
Association de la recherche industrielle du Québec, 102
Association de le communauté noire de Côte-des-Neiges inc., 102
Association de médiation familiale du Québec, 102
Association de Montréal pour la déficience intellectuelle, 102
Association de neurochirurgie du Québec, 103
Association de paralysie cérébrale du Québec-Bureau de Montréal, 103
Association de Parents de Jumeaux et de Triplés de la région de Montréal, 103
Association de planification fiscale et financière, 103
Association de soccer du Sud-Ouest de Montréal, 104
L'Association de spina-bifida et d'hydrocéphalie du Québec, 104
L'Association de spina-bifida et d'hydrocéphalie du Québec-A.S.B.H. Région Montréal, 104
Association de taekwondo du Québec, 104
Association de vol à voile Champlain, 104
Association des Acupuncteurs du Québec, 105
Association des agences de publicité du Québec, 105
Association des Allergologues et Immunologues du Québec, 105
Association des Architectes en pratique privée du Québec, 105
Association des architectes paysagistes du Québec, 105
Association des arts thérapeutes du Québec, 106
Association des assistant(e)s-dentaires du Québec, 106
Association des avocats de la défense de Montréal, 106
Association des avocats en droit de la jeunesse, 106
Association des avocats et avocates représentant les bénéficiaires des régimes d'indemnisation publics, 107
Association des avocats et avovates en droit familial du Québec, 107
Association des bénévoles du don de sang, 107
Association des bibliothèques de droit de Montréal, 107
Association des bibliothèques de la santé affiliées à l'Université de Montréal, 107
Association des bibliothèques publiques du Québec, 107
Association des Boulangers Artisans du Québec, 107
Association des brasseurs du Québec, 108
Association des cadres municipaux de Montréal, 108
Association des camps du Québec inc., 108
Association des cardiologues du Québec, 108
Association des centres jeunesse du Québec, 108
Association des chiropraticiens du Québec, 108
Association des chirurgiens dentistes du Québec, 109
Association des cinémas parallèles du Québec, 109
Association des collèges privés du Québec, 109

Association des commerçants de véhicules récréatifs du Québec, 109
Association des conseils des médecins, dentistes et pharmaciens du Québec, 109
Association des conseils en gestion linguistique Inc., 109
Association des constructeurs de routes et grands travaux du Québec-Bureau de Montréal, 110
Association des démographes du Québec, 110
Association des dermatologistes du Québec, 110
Association des designers industriels du Québec, 110
Association des détaillants en alimentation du Québec, 110
Association des Diplômés de Polytechnique, 110
Association des directeurs généraux des services de santé et des services sociaux du Québec, 111
Association des économistes québécois, 111
Association des Églises des frères mennonites du Québec, 111
Association des enterprises spécialiseés en eau du Québec, 112
Association des entrepreneurs en maçonnerie du Québec, 112
Association des établissements privés conventionnés - santé services sociaux, 113
Association des études du Proche-Orient ancien, 113
Association des experts en sinistre indépendants du Québec, 113
Association des fabricants de meubles du Québec inc., 113
Association des familles Gosselin, Inc., 113
Association des familles monoparentales et recomposées de l'Outaouais, 113
Association des firmes de génie-conseil - Québec, 114
Association des garderies privées du Québec, 114
Association des gastro-entérologues du Québec, 114
Association des groupes d'intervention en défense de droits en santé mentale du Québec, 116
Association des hypnologues du Québec, 116
Association des Illustrateurs et Illustratrices du Québec, 116
Association des ingénieurs municipaux du Québec, 116
Association des intervenantes et des intervenants en soins spirituels du Québec, 117
Association des intervenants en dépendance du Québec, 117
Association des jeunes Barreaux du Québec, 117
Association des journalistes indépendants du Québec, 117
Association des juristes pour l'avancement de la vie artistique, 118
Association des lesbiennes et des gais sur Internet, 118
Association des libraires du Québec, 118
Association des MBA du Québec, 119
Association des médecins biochimistes du Québec, 119
Association des médecins cliniciens enseignants de Montréal, 119
Association des médecins endocrinologues du Québec, 119
Association des médecins généticiens du Québec, 119
Association des médecins gériatres du Québec, 119
Association des médecins hématologistes-oncologistes du Québec, 119
Association des médecins microbiologistes-infectiologues du Québec, 119
Association des médecins ophtalmologistes du Québec, 120

Association des médecins rhumatologues du Québec, 120
Association des médecins spécialistes en médecine nucléaire du Québec, 120
Association des médecins spécialistes en santé communautaire du Québec, 120
Association des médecins-psychiatres du Québec, 120
Association des microbiologistes du Québec, 120
Association des motocyclistes gais du Québec, 120
Association des néphrologues du Québec, 120
Association des neurologues du Québec, 120
Association des obstétriciens et gynécologues du Québec, 121
Association des optométristes du Québec, 121
L'Association des orthopédagogues du Québec inc., 121
Association des parents catholiques du Québec, 121
Association des pathologistes du Québec, 122
Association des pédiatres du Québec, 122
Association des pères gais de Montréal inc., 122
Association des Perfusionnistes du Québec Inc., 122
Association des pharmaciens des établissements de santé du Québec, 123
Association des physiatres du Québec, 123
Association des pneumologues de la province de Québec, 123
Association des Pompiers de Montréal inc., 124
Association des producteurs maraîchers du Québec, 124
Association des professeurs de l'École Polytechnique de Montréal, 124
Association des professionnels à l'outillage municipal, 125
Association des professionnels de la communication et du marketing, 125
Association des professionnels des arts de la scène du Québec, 125
Association des professionnels en gestion philanthropique, 126
Association des professionnels en santé du travail, 126
Association des professionnels et superviseurs de Radio-Canada, 126
Association des propriétaires de cinémas du Québec, 126
Association des propriétaires du Québec inc., 126
Association des psychothérapeutes psychanalytiques du Québec, 127
Association des radiodiffuseurs communautaires du Québec, 127
Association des radiologistes du Québec, 127
Association des radio-oncologues du Québec, 127
Association des réalisateurs et réalisatrices de Télé-Québec, 127
Association des réalisateurs et réalisatrices du Québec, 127
Association des restaurateurs du Québec, 127
Association des Scouts du Canada, 127
Association des services de réhabilitation sociale du Québec inc., 128
Association des sexologues du Québec, 128
Association des spécialistes en chirurgie plastique et esthétique du Québec, 128
Association des spécialistes en médecine d'urgence du Québec, 128
Association des spécialistes en médecine interne du Québec, 128
Association des sports pour aveugles de Montréal, 128
Association des surintendants de golf du Québec, 129
Association des syndicats de copropriété du Québec, 129
Association des techniciens en santé animale du Québec, 129
Association des technologues en agroalimentaire, 129

Geographic Index / Québec - Montréal

Association des urologues du Québec, 130
Association des véhicules électriques du Québec, 130
Association des veuves de Montréal inc., 130
Association du camionnage du Québec inc., 130
Association du jeune barreau de Montréal, 130
Association du Québec pour enfants avec problèmes auditifs, 131
Association du Québec pour enfants avec problèmes auditifs-AQEPA Gaspésie - Iles-de-la-Madeleine, 131
Association du Québec pour enfants avec problèmes auditifs-AQEPA Montréal Régional, 131
Association du Québec pour enfants avec problèmes auditifs-AQEPA Outaouais, 131
Association du Québec pour l'intégration sociale / Institut québécois de la déficience intellectuelle, 131
Association du Syndrome de Sjogren, Inc, 131
Association du transport urbain du Québec, 132
Association féminine d'éducation et d'action sociale, 132
Association for Canadian Jewish Studies, 132
Association for Canadian Studies, 133
Association francophone pour le savoir, 135
Association générale des insuffisants rénaux, 136
Association industrielle de l'est de Montréal, 136
Association mathématique du Québec, 137
Association médicale du Québec, 137
Association montréalaise des directions d'établissement scolaire, 137
Association multi-ethnique pour l'intégration des personnes handicapées, 137
Association nationale des éditeurs de livres, 138
Association of Administrators of English Schools of Québec, 139
Association of Canadian Map Libraries & Archives, 142
Association of Early Childhood Educators of Québec, 147
Association of English Language Publishers of Québec, 148
Association of Islamic Charitable Projects, 149
Association of Jewish Day Schools, 150
Association of Jewish Libraries (Montréal), 150
Association of Legal Court Interpreters & Translators, 150
The Association of Maritime Arbitrators of Canada, 151
Association of Polish Engineers in Canada-Montréal Branch, 156
Association paritaire pour la santé et la sécurité du travail - Secteur Affaires municipales, 165
Association paritaire pour la santé et la sécurité du travail du secteur affaires sociales, 165
Association patronale des entreprises en construction du Québec, 165
Association pour l'avancement des sciences et des techniques de la documentation, 165
Association pour la prévention de la contamination de l'air et du sol, 166
Association pour la promotion des services documentaires scolaires, 166
Association pour la recherche au collégial, 166
Association pour la santé publique du Québec, 166
Association pour la voix études au Québec, 167
Association professionnelle des designers d'intérieur du Québec, 167
Association professionnelle des entreprises en logiciels libres, 167
Association provinciale des constructeurs d'habitations du Québec inc.-Abitibi-Témiscamingue, 168
Association Québec Snowboard, 168
Association québécoise d'urbanisme, 168
Association québécoise de canoë-kayak de vitesse, 169
Association Québécoise de chirurgie, 169

Association québécoise de défense des droits des personnes retraitées et préretraitées, 169
Association québécoise de gérontologie, 169
Association québécoise de l'épilepsie, 169
Association québécoise de l'industrie de la peinture, 170
Association québécoise de l'industrie du disque, du spectacle et de la vidéo, 170
Association québécoise de la dysphasie, 170
Association québécoise de la gestion parasitaire, 170
Association québécoise de la production d'énergie renouvelable, 170
Association québécoise de la production médiatique, 170
Association québécoise de pédagogie collégiale, 170
Association québécoise de promotion du tourisme socioculturel, 171
Association québécoise de racquetball, 171
Association québécoise de sports pour paralytiques cérébraux, 171
Association québécoise des arénas et des installations récréatives et sportives, 171
Association québécoise des auteurs dramatiques, 171
Association québécoise des avocats et avocates de la défense, 171
Association québécoise des avocats et avocates en droit de l'immigration, 171
L'Association québécoise des centres de la petite enfance, 172
Association québécoise des critiques de cinéma, 172
Association Québécoise des dépanneurs en alimentation, 172
Association québécoise des éditeurs de magazines, 172
Association québécoise des enseignantes et des enseignants du primaire, 172
Association québécoise des enseignants de français langue seconde, 172
Association québécoise des infirmières et intervenants en recherche clinique, 173
Association québécoise des joueurs de dames, 173
Association québécoise des marionnettistes, 173
Association québécoise des organismes de coopération internationale, 173
Association québécoise des orthophonistes et des audiologistes, 173
Association québécoise des personnes de petite taille, 174
Association québécoise des pharmaciens propriétaires, 174
Association québécoise des phytothérapeutes, 174
Association québécoise des salons du livre-Montréal, 174
Association québécoise des technologies, 174
Association québécoise des transports, 175
Association québécoise des traumatisés craniens, 175
Association québécoise des traumatisés crâniens, 175
Association québécoise des troubles d'apprentissage, 175
Association québécoise des utilisateurs de l'ordinateur au primaire-secondaire, 175
Association québécoise du loisir municipal, 175
Association Québécoise du Lymphoedème, 176
Association québécoise Plaidoyer-Victimes, 176
Association québécoise pour la maîtrise de l'énergie, 176
Association québécoise pour le loisir des personnes handicapées-AlterGo, 176
Association québécoise pour le loisir des personnes handicapées-ARLPH de la Capitale-Nationale, 177
Association sectorielle: Fabrication d'équipement de transport et de machines, 178

Association sportive des aveugles du Québec inc., 178
Association sportive des sourds du Québec inc., 178
Association sportive et communautaire du Centre-Sud, 178
Association Trot & Amble du Québec, 179
Associés bénévoles qualifiés au service des jeunes, 179
Atelier d'histoire Hochelaga-Maisonneuve, 179
L'Atelier des lettres, 180
Atelier habitation Montréal, 180
Athletes International, 180
Athmajothi Tamils Association, 181
Au bas de l'échelle, 187
Au Coup de pouce Centre-Sud inc., 187
Audition Québec, 187
Auto Sport Québec, 189
Automobile Protection Association, 189
Autorité des marchés financiers-Montréal, 190
Aux Prismes Plein air et culture, 190
Avataq Cultural Institute, 190
Aviron Québec, 191
Avocats Hors Québec, 191
B'nai Brith Canada-Québec Region, 192
Badminton Québec, 194
Balle au mur Québec, 194
Les Ballets Jazz de Montréal, 195
Banda de nossa Senhora dos Milagres, 195
Les banques alimentaires du Québec, 196
Barreau de Montréal, 197
Bechtel Foundation of Canada, 203
Bi Unité Montréal, 207
La Biennale de Montréal, 209
The Bimetallic Question, 211
Birks Family Foundation, 212
Black Coalition of Québec, 213
Black Community Resource Centre, 213
Black Studies Centre, 213
Black Theatre Workshop, 213
Bloc québécois, 214
BMW Clubs Canada, 216
BMW Clubs Canada-BMW Club of Québec, 216
Les Bolides, 217
BOMA Québec, 217
Le Bon Pilote inc., 217
Boys & Girls Clubs of Québec-Dawson Boys & Girls Club, 224
Brian Bronfman Family Foundation, 228
British Council - Canada-Montréal Office, 259
CAA-Québec-Montréal, 268
CAEO Québec, 270
Canada China Business Council-Montréal Office, 278
Canada Employment & Immigration Union-Bureaux régionaux du Québec, 279
Canada Health Infoway, 280
Canada Tibet Committee, 280
Canada World Youth, 281
Canada's Medical Technology Companies-Québec Office, 282
Canadian Acquirer's Association, 287
Canadian Amateur Boxing Association, 292
Canadian Armenian Business Council Inc., 295
Canadian Asian Studies Association, 296
Canadian Assembly of Narcotics Anonymous-Narcotiques Anonymes, 296
Canadian Associates of Ben-Gurion University of the Negev-Montréal Office, 297
Canadian Association for Irish Studies, 301
Canadian Association for Young Children-Québec, 307
Canadian Association of Blue Cross Plans-Québec Blue Cross/Croix Bleue du Québec, 309
Canadian Association of Elizabeth Fry Societies-Société Elizabeth Fry du Québec, 313
Canadian Association of Geographers, 316
Canadian Association of Home & Property Inspectors-Association des inspecteurs en bâtiments du Québec (AIBQ), 317
Canadian Association of Midwives, 321
Canadian Bankers Association-Montréal Office, 341

Association du barreau canadien-Division du Québec, 342
Canadian Cancer Society-Division du Québec, 349
Canadian Centre for Architecture, 353
The Canadian Chamber of Commerce-Montréal Office, 355
Canadian Children's Optimist Foundation, 356
The Canadian Corps of Commissionaires-Division du Québec, 365
The Canadian Corps of Commissionaires-Division de Montréal, 365
Canadian Crossroads International-Montréal Office, 373
Canadian Deaf Sports Association, 376
Canadian Executive Service Organization-Montréal, 383
Canadian Federation of Business School Deans, 386
Canadian Federation of Independent Business-Bureau du Québec, 387
Canadian Fertility & Andrology Society, 389
Canadian Friends of Bar-Ilan University-Eastern Region, 394
Canadian Friends of Beth Hatefutsoth, 394
Canadian Friends of the Hebrew University-Montréal Chapter, 395
The Canadian Fur Trade Development Institute, 396
Canadian GeoExchange Coalition, 397
Canadian German Chamber of Industry & Commerce Inc.-Montréal, 397
Canadian Guild of Crafts, 399
Canadian Hadassah WIZO-Montréal, 399
Canadian Hemophilia Society, 404
Canadian Hemophilia Society-Section Québec, 404
Canadian HIV Trials Network-Québec Region, 405
Canadian Information Processing Society-Réseau Action TI, 411
Canadian Institute for Health Information-CIHI Montréal, 412
Canadian Institute for Jewish Research, 412
Canadian Institute for the Administration of Justice, 413
Canadian Institute for Theatre Technology, 413
Canadian Institute of Plumbing & Heating-Québec Region, 418
Canadian Institutional Research & Planning Association, 420
Canadian International Freight Forwarders Association, Inc.-Eastern Division, 421
Canadian Italian Business & Professional Association, 423
Canadian Kendo Federation, 424
Canadian Labour Congress-Québec Regional Office, 425
Canadian Life & Health Insurance Association Inc.-Montréal Office, 426
Canadian Liver Foundation-Montréal Chapter, 427
Canadian Magen David Adom for Israel, 429
Canadian Manufacturers & Exporters-Association des manufacturiers et des exportateurs du Québec, 429
The Canadian Maritime Law Association, 430
Canadian Marketing Association-Association du marketing relationne, 431
Canadian Masonry Contractors' Association-Association des entrepreneurs en maçonnerie du Québec, 431
Canadian Mental Health Association-Division du Québec, 435
Canadian Music Centre-Région du Québec, 438
Canadian National Institute for the Blind-Division du Québec, 439
Canadian National Railways Police Association (Ind.), 440
Canadian New Music Network, 441
Canadian Office & Professional Employees Union, 444
Le Syndicat canadien des employées et employés professionnels et de bureau-Region 1 - Section locale 434, 444

Le Syndicat canadien des employées et employés professionnels et de bureau-Region 1 - Section locale 463, 444
Le Syndicat canadien des employées et employés professionnels et de bureau-Region 1 - Section locale 480, 444
Le Syndicat canadien des employées et employés professionnels et de bureau-Region 1 - Section locale 571, 444
Le Syndicat canadien des employées et employés professionnels et de bureau-Region 1 - Section locale 573, 444
Le Syndicat canadien des employées et employés professionnels et de bureau-Region 1 - Section locale 574, 444
Le Syndicat canadien des employées et employés professionnels et de bureau-Region 1 - Section locale 575, 444
Le Syndicat canadien des employées et employés professionnels et de bureau-Region 1 - Section locale 610, 444
Le Syndicat canadien des employées et employés professionnels et de bureau-Region 1 - Section locale 611, 444
Le Syndicat canadien des employées et employés professionnels et de bureau-Region 1 - Section locale 1012, 444
Canadian Olympic Committee-Montréal, 445
Canadian Orthopaedic Residents Association, 448
Canadian Overseas Telecommunications Union, 448
Canadian Parks & Wilderness Society-Montréal - Québec Chapter, 451
Canadian Pediatric Endocrine Group, 452
Canadian Pension & Benefits Institute, 453
Canadian Pension & Benefits Institute-Québec Region, 453
Canadian Picture Pioneers-Montréal - Les Pionniers du cinéma du Québec, 455
Canadian Polish Congress-Québec Branch, 456
The Canadian Press-Montréal Bureau, 459
Canadian Psychoanalytic Society, 461
Canadian Psychoanalytic Society-Société psychanalytique de Montréal, 461
Canadian Psychoanalytic Society-Québec English Branch, 461
Canadian Public Relations Society Inc.-CPRS Québec, 463
Canadian School Boards Association, 468
Canadian Securities Administrators, 469
The Canadian Securities Institute-Bureau de Montréal, 469
Canadian Ski Instructors' Alliance, 471
Canadian Sleep Society, 472
Canadian Society for Civil Engineering, 473
Canadian Society for Jewish Studies, 476
Canadian Society of Hospital Pharmacists-Québec, 484
Canadian Society of Nephrology, 485
Canadian Society of Plastic Surgeons, 487
Canadian Tax Foundation-Québec Office, 492
Canadian Union of Public Employees-Québec Division, 499
Canadian Urologic Oncology Group, 500
Canadian Zionist Federation-Eastern Region, 506
Canadian-Scandinavian Foundation, 507
Cancer Research Society, 507
Caribbean Students' Society of McGill University, 512
Le Carré des Lombes, 515
Carrefour de ressources en interculturel, 515
Casa do Ribatejo, 516
Catholic Action Montreal, 517
CDC Centre-Sud, 521
Center for Research-Action on Race Relations, 522
Centraide du Grand Montréal, 522
Centrale des syndicats démocratiques-Montréal, 525
Centrale des syndicats du Québec, 525
Centre Afrika, 526
Centre canadien d'arbitrage commercial, 526

Centre canadien d'étude et de coopération internationale, 526
Centre Communautaire Bon Courage De Place Benoît, 526
Centre communautaire des gais et lesbiennes de Montréal, 526
Centre d'action bénévole de Montréal, 527
Centre d'action sida Montréal (Femmes), 527
Centre d'adaptation de la main-d'oeuvre aérospatiale du Québec, 527
Centre d'animation de développement et de recherche en éducation, 528
Centre d'éducation et d'action des femmes de Montréal, 528
Centre d'entraide et de ralliement familial, 528
Centre d'information communautaure et de dépannage Ste-Marie, 528
Centre d'orientation sexuelle de l'université McGill, 528
Centre de caractérisation microscopique des matériaux, 528
Centre de documentation sur l'éducation des adultes et la condition féminine, 529
Centre de la Communauté sourde du Montréal métropolitain, 529
Centre de prévention de la radicalisation menant à la violence, 529
Centre de réadaptation Constance-Lethbridge, 529
Centre de recherche interdisciplinaire sur la violence familiale et la violence faite aux femmes, 530
Centre de ressources et d'intervention pour hommes abusés sexuellement dans leur enfance, 530
Centre de solidarité lesbienne, 530
Centre des auteurs dramatiques, 530
Centre des femmes de Montréal, 530
Centre des ressources sur la non-violence inc, 530
The Centre for Israel & Jewish Affairs-Québec Region, 533
Centre for Study of Insurance Operations-Montréal Office, 534
Centre for the Study of Learning & Performance, 534
Centre francophone d'informatisation des organisations-Bureau à Montréal, 535
Centre international de criminologie comparée, 535
Centre international de solidarité ouvrière, 535
Centre international pour la prévention de la criminalité, 535
Centre interuniversitaire de recherche en économie quantitative, 535
Centre Jean-Claude Malépart, 536
Centre patronal de santé et sécurité du travail du Québec, 536
Centre québécois du droit de l'environnement, 536
Centre Sportif de la Petite Bourgogne, 536
Centre St-Pierre, 536
Centro Comunitàrio Divino Espírito Santo, 537
Cercle d'expression artistique Nyata Nyata, 537
Cercle de la finance internationale de Montréal, 537
Cercles des jeunes naturalistes, 537
Chabad Lubavitch Youth Organization, 539
Chambre de commerce Canada-Pologne, 540
Chambre de commerce Canado-Suisse (Québec) Inc., 540
Chambre de commerce Canado-Tunisienne, 540
Chambre de commerce de l'Est de Montréal, 541
Chambre de commerce du Montréal métropolitain, 544
Chambre de commerce et d'industrie de Montréal-Nord, 546
Chambre de commerce et d'industrie de St-Laurent-Mont-Royal, 546
Chambre de commerce et d'industrie du Sud-Ouest de Montréal, 547
Chambre de commerce et d'industrie française au canada, 547

Chambre de commerce Latino-américaine du Québec, 549
Chambre de commerce LGBT du Québec, 549
Chambre de l'assurance de dommages, 550
Chambre de la sécurité financière, 550
Chambre des huissiers de justice du Québec, 550
Chambre des notaires du Québec, 550
Chantiers jeunesse, 551
Chants Libres, compagnie lyrique de création, 551
Chartered Professional Accountants Canada-Montréal Office, 552
Chemins du soleil, 556
Chess'n Math Association, 556
Chez Doris, 557
Children's Wish Foundation of Canada-Bureau de Montréal, 563
Chinese Neighbourhood Society of Montréal, 565
Chrysotile Institute, 568
Church Council on Justice & Corrections-Le Conseil Des Églises Pour La Justice Et La Criminologie (CEJC) Québec, 569
La cinémathèque québécoise, 569
CIRANO, 570
Club de plein air Les Aventuriers, 575
Club des débrouillards, 575
Clube Oriental Português de Montreal, 576
Clube Portugal de Montreal, 576
Coalition Avenir Québec, 577
Coalition des associations de consommateurs du Québec, 577
Coalition des organismes communautaires québécois de lutte contre le sida, 578
Coalition for Gun Control-Bureau de Montréal, 578
Coalition québécoise pour le contrôle du tabac, 578
Coalition sida des sourds du Québec, 578
Cole Foundation, 581
Collectif des femmes immigrantes du Québec, 581
Collège des médecins du Québec, 582
Comité d'action Parc Extension, 591
Comité des orphelins victimes d'abus, 592
Comité des personnes atteintes du VIH du Québec, 592
Comité logement du Plateau Mont-Royal, 592
Comité logement Rosemont, 592
Comité québécois femmes et développement, 592
Comité régional des associations pour la déficience intellectuelle, 592
Comité Social Centre-Sud, 592
Commission for Environmental Cooperation, 593
Communauté Laotienne du Québec, 594
Communauté sépharade unifiée du Québec, 594
Communauté vietnamienne au Canada, région de Montréal, 594
Communication & Natural Logic International Society, 594
Communion & Liberation Canada, 594
Communist Party of Canada (Marxist-Leninist), 595
La Compagnie des philosophes, 608
Compagnie Marie Chouinard, 608
Concordia Caribbean Students' Union, 609
Concordia University Faculty Association, 609
Concordia University Part-time Faculty Association, 610
Concours de musique du Canada inc., 610
Confédération des Organismes de Personnes Handicapées du Québec, 611
Confédération des organismes familiaux du Québec, 611
Confédération des syndicats nationaux, 611
Conférence des recteurs et des principaux des universités du Québec, 612
Confrérie de la librairie ancienne du Québec, 612
Congrégation de Sainte-Croix - Les Frères de Sainte-Croix, 612

Congress of Black Lawyers & Jurists of Québec, 613
Conseil central du Montréal métropolitain, 614
Conseil communautaire Notre-Dame-de-Grâce, 614
Conseil d'intervention pour l'accès des femmes au travail, 615
Conseil de l'enveloppe du bâtiment du Québec, 615
Conseil de presse du Québec, 616
Conseil des arts de Montréal, 617
Conseil des directeurs médias du Québec, 617
Conseil des métiers d'art du Québec (ind.), 617
Conseil des relations internationales de Montréal, 617
Conseil du bâtiment durable du Canada - Québec, 618
Conseil du patronat du Québec, 618
Conseil interprofessionnel du Québec, 618
Conseil patronal de l'environnement du Québec, 619
Conseil provincial du soutien scolaire, 619
Conseil québécois de la musique, 620
Conseil québécois des arts médiatiques, 620
Conseil québécois des gais et lesbiennes du Québec, 620
Conseil québécois du commerce de détail, 620
Conseil québécois du théâtre, 620
Conseil québécois sur le tabac et la santé, 620
Conseil régional des personnes âgées italo-canadiennes de Montréal, 621
Conseil régional FTQ Montréal Métropolitain, 621
Les Conseillers en développement de l'employabilité, 621
La Coop Fédérée, 627
Corporation culturelle Latino-Américaine de l'Amitié, 629
Corporation de développement économique communautaire Centre-Sud/Plateau Mont-Royal, 629
Corporation des bibliothécaires professionnels du Québec, 629
Corporation des entrepreneurs généraux du Québec, 630
Corporation des entrepreneurs spécialisés du Grand Montréal inc., 630
Corporation des entreprises de traitement de l'air et du froid, 630
Corporation des maîtres électriciens du Québec, 630
Corporation des maîtres mécaniciens en tuyauterie du Québec, 630
Corporation des propriétaires immobiliers du Québec, 630
Corporation des thérapeutes du sport du Québec, 631
Council for Black Aging, 632
Council for Continuing Pharmaceutical Education, 632
Council on Palliative Care, 636
CPE du Carrefour, 638
Crohn's & Colitis Canada-Bureau du Québec, 642
Curling Québec, 646
CUSO International-Atlantic Regional Office, 646
CUSO International-Québec Regional Office, 646
Cyclo-Nature, 647
Dairy Farmers of Canada-Montréal Office, 648
Dancer Transition Resource Centre-Québec, 650
DanceSport Québec, 650
Danse-Cité inc, 650
Desta Black Youth Network, 654
Development & Peace, 654
Development & Peace-Québec - Montréal, 655
Diabète Québec, 655
Direction Chrétienne, 657
Directors Guild of Canada-Conseil du Québec, 657
DisAbled Women's Network of Canada, 658
Doctors without Borders Canada-Québec Office, 660

Geographic Index / Québec - Montréal

Drummond Foundation, 663
Éco Entreprises Québec, 671
Écomusée de l'Au-Delà, 672
Éco-Quartier Sainte-Marie, 673
Écrivains Francophones d'Amérique, 674
Éduc'alcool, 680
L'Église Réformée du Québec, 681
The EJLB Foundation, 681
Eldee Foundation, 681
Elizabeth House, 685
Énergie Solaire Québec, 688
Enfant-Retour Québec, 688
English Speaking Catholic Council, 689
English-Language Arts Network, 689
Ensemble contemporain de Montréal, 690
Ensemble vocal Ganymède, 690
Entraide Léo-Théorêt, 690
Enviro-Accès Inc.-Montréal, 691
Environnement jeunesse, 693
ÉquiLibre - Groupe d'action sur le poids, 694
Equitas - International Centre for Human Rights Education, 695
ERS Training & Development Corporation, 695
Esperanto Association of Canada, 695
The Farha Foundation, 705
Fédération autonome du collégial (ind.), 707
Fédération CSN - Construction (CSN), 708
Fédération d'escrime du Québec, 708
Fédération de basketball du Québec, 708
Fédération de cheerleading du Québec, 708
Fédération de crosse du Québec, 708
Fédération de golf du Québec, 708
Fédération de gymnastique du Québec, 708
Fédération de l'industrie manufacturière (FIM-CSN), 708
Fédération de la santé du Québec - CSQ, 709
Fédération de la santé et des services sociaux, 710
Fédération de lutte olympique du Québec, 710
Fédération de natation du Québec, 710
Fédération de Netball du Québec, 710
Fédération de pétanque du Québec, 710
Fédération de rugby du Québec, 710
Fédération de tennis de table du Québec, 710
Fédération de tir à l'arc du Québec, 710
Fédération de voile du Québec, 710
Fédération de volleyball du Québec, 710
Fédération de Water-Polo du Québec, 711
Fédération des associations de familles monoparentales et recomposées du Québec, 711
Fédération des Associations et Corporations en Construction du Québec, 712
Fédération des associations étudiantes du campus de l'université de Montréal, 712
Fédération des astronomes amateurs du Québec, 712
Fédération des caisses Desjardins du Québec-Montréal, 712
Fédération des cégeps, 712
Fédération des centres d'action bénévole du Québec, 712
Fédération des chambres de commerce du Québec, 713
Fédération des chambres de commerce du Québec, 713
Fédération des clubs de croquet du Québec, 713
Fédération des clubs de fers du Québec, 713
Fédération des clubs de motoneigistes du Québec, 713
Fédération des coopératives d'habitation intermunicipale du Montréal métropolitain, 714
Fédération des employées et employés de services publics inc. (CSN), 714
Fédération des enseignants de cégeps, 714
Fédération des établissements d'enseignement privés, 714
Fédération des femmes du Québec, 715
Fédération des harmonies et des orchestres symphoniques du Québec, 715
Fédération des intervenantes en petite enfance du Québec, 715
Fédération des loisirs-danse du Québec, 715

Fédération des maisons d'hébergement pour femmes, 715
Fédération des médecins résidents du Québec inc. (ind.), 716
Fédération des médecins spécialistes du Québec, 716
Fédération des OSBL d'habitation de Montréal, 716
Fédération des professionnèles, 717
Fédération des professionnelles et professionnels de l'éducation du Québec, 718
Fédération des professionnelles et professionnels de l'éducation du Québec-Syndicat des professionnelles et professionnels du milieu de l'éducation de Montréal (SPPMÉM), 718
Fédération des sociétés d'histoire du Québec, 719
Fédération des sociétés d'horticulture et d'écologie du Québec, 719
Fédération des syndicats de l'action collective, 719
Fédération des syndicats de la santé et des services sociaux, 719
Fédération des travailleurs et travailleises du Québec, 719
Fédération des travailleurs et travailleuses du Québec - Construction, 719
Fédération du baseball amateur du Québec, 719
Fédération du commerce (CSN), 720
Fédération du personnel de l'enseignement privé, 720
Fédération du personnel de soutien scolaire (CSQ), 720
Fédération du personnel professionnel des collèges, 720
Fédération du plongeon amateur du Québec, 720
Fédération du Québec pour le planning des naissances, 720
Fédération équestre du Québec inc., 720
Fédération étudiante universitaire du Québec, 720
Fédération indépendante des syndicats autonomes-Montréal, 721
Fédération interprofessionnelle de la santé du Québec, 721
Fédération motocycliste du Québec, 721
Fédération nationale des communications (CSN), 721
Fédération nationale des enseignants et des enseignantes du Québec, 721
Federation of Chinese Canadian Professionals (Québec), 723
Federation of Teachers of Jewish Schools, 726
Fédération professionnelle des journalistes du Québec, 726
Fédération québécoise d'athlétisme, 727
Fédération québécoise de ballon sur glace, 727
Fédération Québécoise de Boxe Olympique, 727
Fédération québécoise de canoë-kayak d'eau vives, 727
Fédération québécoise de handball olympique, 727
Fédération québécoise de l'autisme, 727
Fédération québécoise de la marche, 727
Fédération québécoise de la montagne et de l'escalade, 727
Fédération québécoise de naturisme, 727
Fédération québécoise de philatélie, 728
Fédération québécoise de tir, 728
Fédération québécoise des activités subaquatiques, 728
Fédération québécoise des échecs, 728
Fédération québécoise des jeux récréatifs, 729
Fédération québécoise des laryngectomisés, 729
Fédération québécoise des massothérapeutes, 729
Fédération québécoise des professeures et professeurs d'université, 729

Fédération québécoise des revêtements de sol, 729
Fédération québécoise des sociétés Alzheimer, 729
Fédération québécoise des sociétés Alzheimer-Société Alzheimer Society Montréal, 730
Fédération québécoise des sports cyclistes, 730
Fédération québécoise du canot et du kayak, 730
La Fédération Québécoise du Cricket Inc., 730
Fédération québécoise du loisir littéraire, 731
Fédération ski nautique et planche Québec, 731
Fédération sportive de ringuette du Québec, 731
Festivals et Événements Québec, 733
Fibrose kystique Québec, 733
Filarmónica Portuguesa de Montreal, 735
Finance Montréal, 735
FloraQuébeca, 741
Folklore Canada International, 742
Fondation Alfred Dallaire, 742
Fondation Centre de cancérologie Charles-Bruneau, 743
Fondation CHU Sainte-Justine, 743
Fondation de l'Ataxie Charlevoix-Saguenay, 743
Fondation de l'Hôpital de Montréal pour enfants, 744
Fondation de l'Hôpital du Sacré-Coeur de Montréal, 744
Fondation de l'Hôpital Général de Montréal, 744
Fondation de l'Hôpital Maisonneuve-Rosemont, 744
Fondation de l'Ordre des infirmières et infirmiers du Québec, 744
Fondation de la banque d'yeux du Québec inc., 744
La Fondation des Auberges du coeur, 744
Fondation des aveugles du Québec, 744
Fondation des étoiles, 744
Fondation des maladies du coeur du Québec, 745
Fondation des maladies mentales, 745
Fondation des pompiers du Québec pour les grands brûlés-Montréal, 745
Fondation Desjardins, 745
Fondation du barreau du Québec, 745
Fondation du CHUM, 745
Fondation Émergence inc., 746
La Fondation Émile-Nelligan, 746
Fondation Hydro-Québec pour l'environnement, 746
Fondation Institut de Cardiologie de Montréal, 746
Fondation Jules et Paul-Émile Léger, 746
Fondation Lionel-Groulx, 747
Fondation Lucie et André Chagnon, 747
Fondation Mario-Racine, 747
Fondation Père-Ménard, 747
Fondation pour enfants diabétiques, 747
Fondation pour l'aide aux travailleuses et travailleurs accidentés, 747
Fondation pour la recherche sur la moelle épinière, 747
Fondation québécoise de la déficience intellectuelle, 747
Fondation québécoise de la maladie coeliaque, 747
Fondation québécoise du cancer, 748
Fondation québécoise du cancer-Hôtellerie de Montréal, 748
Fondation québécoise en environnement, 748
Fondation québécoise pour l'alphabétisation, 748
Fondation Ressources-Jeunesse, 748
Fondation roumaine de Montréal, 748
Fondation Sommeil: Association de personnes atteintes de déficiences reliées au sommeil, 748
Fondation Tourisme Jeunesse, 748
Football Québec, 750
Force Jeunesse, 751
Fortier Danse-Création, 754
Forum francophone des affaires, 754

Foundation of Catholic Community Services Inc., 756
Foundation of Greater Montreal, 756
The Fraser Institute-Montréal Office, 757
Fraternité interprovinciale des ouvriers en électricité (CTC), 758
Front commun des personnes assistées sociales du Québec, 763
Front commun québécois pour une gestion écologique des déchets, 763
The Fur Council of Canada, 765
Canadian Youth Business Foundation-Québec Office, 765
Gai Écoute inc., 766
Gainey Foundation, 766
Garrod Association, 767
Genome Canada-Génome Québec, 769
Girl Guides of Canada-Guides du Canada-Québec Council, 773
Girls Action Foundation, 774
Goethe-Institut (Montréal), 776
Graham Boeckh Foundation, 779
Grand Chapter, Royal Arch Masons of Québec, 779
Grand Council of the Crees-Bureau de Montréal, 779
Grand Lodge of Québec - Ancient, Free & Accepted Masons, 779
Les Grands Ballets Canadiens de Montréal, 781
Greater Montreal Athletic Association, 784
Greenpeace Canada-Montréal Office, 789
Groupe CDH, 791
Groupe d'action pour la prévention de la transmission du VIH et l'éradication du Sida, 791
Groupe d'aide et d'information sur le harcèlement sexuel au travail de la province de Québec, 791
Groupe d'entraide à l'intention des personnes séropositives, itinérantes et toxicomanes, 791
Groupe de droit collaboratif du Québec, 791
Groupe de recherche appliquée en macroécologie, 791
Groupe de recherche en écologie sociale, 791
Groupe de recherche et d'intervention sociale, 791
Groupe intervention vidéo, 792
Le groupe multimédia du Canada, 792
Groupement des assureurs automobiles, 792
GS1 Canada-Montréal Office, 792
La Guilde des Musiciens/Musiciennes du Québec, 794
Gustav Levinschi Foundation, 794
Habitat for Humanity Canada-Québec, 797
Handicap International Canada, 802
Head & Hands, 805
Heating, Refrigeration & Air Conditioning Institute of Canada-Québec - Montréal Chapter, 810
Hébergements de l'envol, 811
L'Héritage canadien du Québec, 813
Héritage Montréal, 813
Hockey Québec, 818
Holy Face Association, 819
Hong Kong-Canada Business Association-Montréal Section Office, 820
Horatio Alger Association of Canada, 821
Hors sentiers, 821
Hostelling International - Canada-Québec & Ontario Region, 823
Humane Society International/Canada, 826
Ileostomy & Colostomy Association of Montreal, 829
Independent Media Arts Alliance, 833
Independent Production Fund-Québec Office, 833
Information Technology Association of Canada-Montréal Office, 837
Ingénieurs Sans Frontières Québec, 838
L'Institut d'assurance de dommages du Québec, 841
Institut d'histoire de l'Amérique française, 841
Institut de cardiologie de Montréal, 841

Geographic Index / Québec - Montréal

Institut de coopération pour l'éducation des adultes, 841
L'Institut de développement de produits, 841
Institut de médiation et d'arbitrage du Québec, 841
Institut de recherche en biologie végétale, 842
Institut de recherche Robert-Sauvé en santé et en sécurité du travail, 842
Institut de recherches cliniques de Montréal, 842
Institut de tourisme et d'hôtellerie du Québec, 842
Institut du cancer de Montréal, 842
Institut québécois de planification financière, 843
Institute for Research on Public Policy, 844
Institute of Air & Space Law, 844
Insurance Bureau of Canada-Québec Office, 849
Inter-loge, 852
International Academy of Law & Mental Health, 853
International Air Transport Association, 853
International Association of Art Critics - Canada, 853
International Brotherhood of Boilermakers, Iron Ship Builders, Blacksmiths, Forgers & Helpers (AFL-CIO)-Montréal (Lodge 271), 1541
International Civil Aviation Organization: Legal Affairs & External Relations Bureau, 855
International Cospas-Sarsat Programme, 855
International Council of Design, 855
International Federation of Broomball Associations, 857
International Federation of Corporate Football, 857
International Financial Centre of Montréal, 857
International Institute of Integral Human Sciences, 858
International Law Association - Canadian Branch, 858
International Political Science Association, 859
International Society for Labour & Social Security Law - Canadian Chapter, 860
Investment Funds Institute of Canada-Bureau du Québec - Le Conseil des fonds d'investissement du Québec, 863
Investment Industry Regulatory Organization of Canada-Bureau de Montréal, 863
The Israel Economic Mission to Canada-Montréal, 866
Italian Chamber of Commerce in Canada, 866
J. Armand Bombardier Foundation, 867
Jamaica Association of Montréal Inc., 867
Jerusalem Foundation of Canada Inc, 869
Jeune chambre de commerce de Montréal, 870
Jeunesse Lambda, 870
Jeunesses Musicales du Canada, 871
Jeux Olympiques Spéciaux du Québec Inc., 871
Jewish Chamber of Commerce, 871
Jewish Community Council of Montreal, 871
Jewish Community Foundation of Montréal, 871
Jewish General Hospital Foundation, 872
Jewish Immigrant Aid Services of Canada-Agence Ometz, 873
Jewish Information Referral Service Montréal, 873
Judo Canada-National Training Centre, 876
Judo-Québec inc, 876
Junior Achievement of Canada-Junior Achievement of Québec, 877
Juvenile Diabetes Research Foundation-Québec, 879
The J.W. McConnell Family Foundation, 879
Karate Canada, 881
Karaté Québec, 882
Katimavik, 882
Kéroul, Tourisme pour personnes à capacité physique restreinte, 884
Kidney Foundation of Canada, 885
The Kidney Foundation of Canada-Division du Québec, 885
Kids Help Phone-Québec, 886
Korean Community of Greater Montréal, 893

Ladies' Morning Musical Club, 895
Last Post Fund, 899
LAUDEM, L'Association des musiciens liturgiques du Canada, 900
League for Human Rights of B'nai Brith Canada-Montréal Office, 903
Leave Out Violence-Québec, 905
Lebanese Syrian Canadian Ladies Aid Society, 905
Légion de Marie - Senatus de Montréal, 906
Leucan - Association pour les enfants atteints de cancer, 908
The Leukemia & Lymphoma Society of Canada-Québec Branch, 909
Lifesaving Society-Québec Branch, 911
Ligue des propriétaires de Montréal, 912
Literacy Volunteers of Québec, 914
Literary Translators' Association of Canada, 914
Lord Reading Law Society, 919
Louise Bédard Danse, 919
Lucie Grégoire Danse, 920
Maison Amaryllis, 926
La Maison Benoit Labre, 926
Maison D'Haïti, 926
La Maison des Açores du Québec, 926
Maison du Parc, 927
Maison Plein Coeur, 927
Maisons Adrianna, 927
Makivik Corporation-Montréal Office, 927
Margie Gillis Dance Foundation, 949
Marijuana Party, 949
Mariners' House of Montréal, 950
The Company of Master Mariners of Canada-Montréal Division, 954
McCord Museum of Canadian History, 955
McGill Centre for Medicine, Ethics & Law, 955
McGill Chamber Orchestra, 955
McGill Institute for the Study of Canada, 955
McGill University Health Centre Foundation, 955
McGill University Non Academic Certified Association, 955
Médecins francophones du Canada, 957
Meeting Professionals International-Montréal/Québec, 1571
Megantic County Historical Society, 959
Mennonite Central Committee Canada-MCC Québec, 961
Mères avec pouvoir, 961
Méta d'âme, 962
Metallurgy & Materials Society of the Canadian Institute of Mining, Metallurgy & Petroleum, 962
Microscopical Society of Canada, 964
Minalliance, 966
Miriam Foundation, 968
Mission Bon Accueil, 969
Mission Old Brewery, 969
Moelle Épinière et Motricité Québec, 971
The Molson Family Foundation, 971
Montréal Association for the Blind, 972
Montréal Council of Women, 972
Montréal Danse, 972
Montréal Field Naturalists Club, 972
The Montréal Holocaust Memorial Centre, 972
Montreal Numismatic Society, 973
Montréal Soaring Council, 973
Montréal SPCA, 973
Mouvement ATD Quart Monde Canada, 976
Mouvement contre le viol et l'inceste, 976
Mouvement d'éducation et de défense des actionnaires, 977
Mouvement d'éducation populaire et d'action communautaire du Québec, 977
Mouvement national des québécoises et québécois, 977
Mouvement national des québécoises et québécois-SSJB de Montréal, 978
Mouvement québécois de la qualité, 978
Mouvement québécois des vacances familiales inc., 978
Multiple Sclerosis Society of Canada-Division du Québec, 980
Muscular Dystrophy Canada-Québec Regional Office, 982

Musicaction, 984
Muslim Community of Québec, 985
Muslim Council of Montréal, 985
Na'amat Canada Inc., 987
Na'amat Canada Inc.-Montréal Council, 987
National Council of Jamaicans & Supportive Organizations in Canada, 991
Native Friendship Centre of Montréal Inc., 998
The Nature Conservancy of Canada-Québec, 1000
New Democratic Party-Québec NDP, 1014
Non-Smokers' Rights Association-Montréal, 1028
Numeris-Montréal Office, 1051
O Vertigo Danse, 1052
OmbudService for Life & Health Insurance-Montréal Office, 1057
One Full Circle, 1058
L'Opéra de Montréal, 1114
Opimian Society, 1116
Optimist International Canada, 1116
Option consommateurs, 1117
Orchestre de chambre de Montréal, 1117
Orchestre Métropolitain, 1118
Orchestre symphonique de Montréal, 1118
Orchestre symphonique des jeunes de Montréal, 1118
Ordre des acupuncteurs de Québec, 1119
Ordre des administrateurs agréés du Québec, 1119
Ordre des agronomes du Québec, 1120
Ordre des architectes du Québec, 1120
Ordre des audioprothésistes du Québec, 1120
Ordre des chimistes du Québec, 1120
Ordre des chiropraticiens du Québec, 1120
L'Ordre des comptables professionels agréés du Québec, 1120
Ordre des conseillers en ressources humaines agréés, 1120
Ordre des conseillers et conseillères d'orientation du Québec, 1121
Ordre des dentistes du Québec, 1121
Ordre des ergothérapeutes du Québec, 1121
Ordre des évaluateurs agréés du Québec, 1121
Ordre des Géologues du Québec, 1121
Ordre des hygiénistes dentaires du Québec, 1121
Ordre des infirmières et infirmiers auxiliaires du Québec, 1121
Ordre des infirmières et infirmiers du Québec, 1121
Ordre des infirmières et infirmiers du Québec-Ordre régional des infirmières et infirmiers de Montréal/Laval, 1122
Ordre des ingénieurs du Québec, 1122
Ordre des opticiens d'ordonnances du Québec, 1123
Ordre des optométristes du Québec, 1123
Ordre des orthophonistes et audiologistes du Québec, 1123
Ordre des pharmaciens du Québec, 1123
Ordre des psychoéducateurs et psychoéducatrices du Québec, 1123
L'Ordre des psychologues du Québec, 1123
Ordre des sages-femmes du Québec, 1123
Ordre des techniciens et techniciennes dentaires du Québec, 1124
Ordre des technologues professionnels du Québec, 1124
Ordre des traducteurs, terminologues et interprètes agréés du Québec, 1124
Ordre des urbanistes du Québec, 1124
Ordre professionnel des diététistes Québec, 1124
Ordre professionnel des inhalothérapeutes du Québec, 1124
Ordre professionnel des sexologues du Québec, 1124
Ordre professionnel des technologistes médicaux du Québec, 1124
Ordre professionnel des travailleurs sociaux du Québec, 1125
Organisation multiressources pour les personnes atteintes de cancer, 1125
ORT Canada-Montréal Office, 1127

Outremangeurs Anonymes, 1133
Ovarian Cancer Canada-Québec Regional Office, 1134
Oxy-jeunes, 1134
Parasports Québec, 1139
Parlimage CCF, 1143
Parrainage civique Montréal, 1143
Parti communiste du Québec, 1143
Parti communiste révolutionnaire, 1144
Parti libéral du Québec, 1144
Parti marxiste-léniniste du Québec, 1144
Parti québécois, 1144
Parti Vert du Québec, 1144
Pas de la rue, 1144
Pathways to Education Canada-Pathways to Education - Montréal-Verdun, 1145
Patinage Québec, 1145
Patronato INAS (Canada)-Montréal Office, 1146
Petites-Mains, 1154
Petits frères des pauvres, 1154
Philanthropic Foundations Canada, 1157
Place Vermeil, 1161
Playwrights' Workshop Montréal, 1162
Polio Québec, 1163
Polish-Jewish Heritage Foundation of Canada-Montréal Chapter, 1164
POPIR-Comité logement (St-Henri, Petite Bourgogne, Ville Émard, Côte St-Paul), 1165
Prevention CDN/NDG, 1170
Pro Bono Québec, 1181
The Professional Institute of the Public Service of Canada-Québec Regional Office, 1185
Programme Action Réfugiés Montréal, 1187
Programme d'aide aux membres du barreau, 1187
Les programmes éducatifs JA Québec, 1187
Project Chance, 1187
Project Genesis, 1187
Project Management Institute-Montréal
Projet 10, 1188
Projet d'Intervention auprès des mineurs-res prostitués-ées, 1188
Projet T.R.I.P., 1188
Promotional Product Professionals of Canada Inc., 1188
Public Service Alliance of Canada-Section provinciale du Québec, 1193
Public Service Alliance of Canada-Section de Montréal, 1193
Pulp & Paper Products Council, 1194
Pulp & Paper Technical Association of Canada, 1194
Québec Association of Baptist Churches, 1195
Québec Association of Independent Schools, 1196
Québec Association of Naturopathic Medicine, 1196
Québec Black Medical Association, 1196
Québec Board of Black Educators, 1196
The Québec Drama Federation, 1197
Québec English Literacy Alliance, 1197
Québec English School Boards Association, 1197
Québec Federation of Home & School Associations Inc., 1197
Québec Federation of the Blind Inc., 1197
Québec Library Association, 1198
Québec Lung Association, 1198
Québec Public Interest Research Group - McGill, 1198
Québec Thistle Council Inc., 1199
Québec Writers' Federation, 1199
Québec-Labrador Foundation (Canada) Inc., 1199
Radio Amateur Québec inc., 1202
Randonnées plein air du Québec, 1204
Reading Council for Literacy Advance in Montréal, 1205
Recherches amérindiennes au Québec, 1207
Recreation Vehicle Dealers Association of Canada-Recreation Vehicle Dealers Association of Québec, 1208
Regroupement de parents de personnes ayant une déficience intellectuelle de Montréal, 1214

Regroupement des Aidantes et Aidants Naturel(le)s de Montréal, 1214
Regroupement des artistes en arts visuels du Québec (ind.), 1214
Regroupement des assureurs de personnes à charte du Québec, 1215
Regroupement des aveugles et amblyopes du Montréal métropolitain, 1215
Regroupement des jeunes chambres de commerce du Québec, 1215
Regroupement pour la Trisomie 21, 1216
Regroupement provincial des maisons d'hébergement et de transition pour femmes victimes de violence conjugale, 1216
Regroupement québécois de la danse, 1216
Regroupement québécois des maladies orphelines, 1216
Regroupement québécois des organismes pour le développement de l'employabilité, 1216
Regroupement QuébecOiseaux, 1216
Relance jeunes et familles, 1217
Réseau ACTION TI, 1218
Réseau d'action et de communication pour le développement international, 1218
Réseau d'aide aux personnes seiles et itinérantes de Montréal, 1218
Le Réseau d'enseignement francophone à distance du Canada, 1219
Réseau des lesbiennes du Québec, 1219
Réseau des services d'archives du Québec, 1222
Réseau des services d'archives du Québec-Réseau de diffusion des archives du Québec, 1222
Réseau du sport étudiant du Québec, 1222
Réseau du sport étudiant du Québec Montréal, 1223
Réseau environnement, 1223
Réseau FADOQ, 1223
FADOQ - Mouvement des aînés du Québec-Région Ile de Montréal, 1224
Réseau Femmes Québec, 1224
Réseau HEC Montréal, 1224
Réseau Hommes Québec, 1224
Réseau indépendant des diffuseurs d'événements artistiques unis, 1224
Réseau québécois des groupes écologistes, 1225
Réseau québécois des OSBL d'habitation, 1225
Réseau québécois pour l'inclusion social des personnnes sourdes et malentendantes, 1225
Réseau Tara Canada (Québec), 1226
Réseau Technoscience, 1226
Restaurants Canada-Québec Office, 1227
Revivre, 1228
Revivre - Association Québécoise de soutien aux personnes souffrant de troubles anxieux, dépressifs ou bipolaires, 1228
RÉZO, 1229
Ringuette-Québec, 1233
Risk & Insurance Management Society Inc.-Québec Chapter, 1234
Royal Astronomical Society of Canada-Montréal Centre - Centre francophone de Montréal, 1238
Royal Astronomical Society of Canada-Montréal Centre - English, 1238
The Royal Canadian Legion-Direction du Québec, 1240
The Royal Commonwealth Society of Canada-Montréal Branch, 1242
The Royal Scottish Country Dance Society-Montréal Branch
La rue des femmes, 1243
St. Andrew's Society of Montréal, 1248
St. John Ambulance-Québec Council, 1249
St. Leonard's Society of Canada-Maison "Crossroads"" de la Société St-Léonard de Montréal, 1250
St. Vincent & the Grenadines Association of Montreal Inc., 1251
The Salvation Army in Canada-Montréal - Québec Division, 1253
Sar-El Canada-Montréal, 1253

Seafarers' International Union of Canada (AFL-CIO/CLC), 1287
Secours aux lépreux (Canada) inc., 1288
Secrétariat international des infirmières et infirmiers de l'espace francophone, 1288
Segal Centre for the Performing Arts at the Saidye, 1289
Sentier Urbain, 1290
Serena Canada-Québec Branch, 1290
Service à la famille chinoise du Grand Montréal, 1291
Service universitaire canadien outre-mer, 1291
Sexual Health Network of Québec Inc., 1293
Shaare Zion Congregation, 1293
Shipping Federation of Canada, 1296
SIDALYS, 1298
Sierra Club of Canada-Québec Chapter, 1298
Sign Association of Canada-Québec Chapter, 1299
Sivananda Ashram Yoga Camp-Centre Sivananda de Yoga Vedanta de Montréal, 1301
Skate Canada-Fédération de patinage artistique du Québec, 1301
Ski Québec alpin, 1302
Social Justice Committee, 1305
Société Canada-Japon de Montréal, 1307
Société canadienne de la sclérose en plaques (Division du Québec), 1308
Société canadienne-française de radiologie, 1309
Société catholique de la Bible, 1309
Société d'archéologie et de numismatique de Montréal, 1309
Société d'entomologie du Québec, 1309
Société d'histoire de la Côte-des-Neiges, 1310
Société d'investissement jeunesse, 1314
Société de criminologie du Québec, 1314
Société de développement des entreprises culturelles, 1314
Société de développement des périodiques culturels québécois, 1314
Société de philosophie du Québec, 1316
Société de Promotion et de Diffusion des Arts et de la Culture, 1316
Société des attractions touristiques du Québec, 1317
Société des Auteurs de Radio, Télévision et Cinéma, 1317
Société des chefs, cuisiniers et pâtissiers du Québec, 1317
Société des collectionneurs d'estampes de Montréal, 1317
Société des designers graphiques du Québec, 1317
Société des musées québécois, 1318
Société des orchidophiles de Montréal, 1318
Société du droit de reproduction des auteurs, compositeurs et éditeurs au Canada (SODRAC 2003) inc., 1318
Société généalogique canadienne-française, 1319
Société historique de Rivière-des-Prairies, 1320
Société historique de Saint-Henri, 1320
Société Huntington du Québec, 1321
Société Logique, 1321
Société Parkinson du Québec, 1322
Société pour les enfants handicapés du Québec, 1322
Société Pro Musica Inc., 1322
Société professionnelle des auteurs et des compositeurs du Québec, 1322
Société québécoise d'espéranto, 1323
Société Québécoise de droit international, 1323
Société québécoise de la rédaction professionnelle, 1323
Société québécoise de la schizophrénie, 1323
Société Québécoise de Psilogie inc, 1323
Société québécoise de récupération et de recyclage-Bureau à Montréal, 1323
Société québécoise de science politique, 1324
Société québécoise de spéléologie, 1324
Société québécoise des auteurs dramatiques, 1324

Société québécoise des hostas et des hémérocalles, 1324
Société québécoise des psychothérapeutes professionnels, 1324
Société québécoise pour l'étude de la religion, 1324
Société québécoise pour la défense des animaux, 1324
Société Saint-Jean-Baptiste de Montréal, 1324
Society for the Promotion of the Teaching of English as a Second Language in Québec, 1326
Society for the Study of Egyptian Antiquities-Chapitre de Montréal, 1327
Society of Composers, Authors & Music Publishers of Canada-Québec Division, 1328
Society of Toxicology of Canada, 1331
Soeurs missionnaires de Notre-Dame des Anges, 1331
Softball Québec, 1332
Sous-Traitance Industrielle Québec, 1334
Special Libraries Association-Eastern Canada
Spiritual Science Fellowship/International Institute of Integral Human Sciences, 1344
Sport Dispute Resolution Centre of Canada, 1344
Sport Jeunesse, 1344
Sports-Québec, 1346
Squash Québec, 1347
Suicide Action Montréal, 1353
Synchro-Québec, 1361
Syndicat de la fonction publique du Québec inc. (ind.)-Montréal - Laval, 1361
Syndicat des Agents Correctionnels du Canada (CSN), 1362
Syndicat des agents de la paix en services correctionnels du Québec, 1362
Syndicat des employé(e)s de magasins et de bureau de la Société des alcools du Québec (ind.), 1362
Syndicat des employés en radio-télédiffusion de Télé-Québec (CSQ), 1363
Syndicat des pompiers et pompières du Québec (CTC), 1363
Syndicat des professeurs de l'État du Québec (ind.), 1363
Syndicat des professeurs et professeures de l'Université du Québec à Montréal, 1364
Syndicat des professionnelles et professionnels municipaux de Montréal, 1364
Syndicat des professionnels et des techniciens de la santé du Québec, 1364
Syndicat des technicien(ne)s et artisan(e)s du réseau français de Radio-Canada (ind.), 1364
Syndicat des technologues en radiologie du Québec, 1364
Syndicat du personnel technique et professionnel de la Société des alcools du Québec (ind.), 1364
Association nationale des ferblantiers et couvreurs, section locale 2020 (CTC)-Montréal, 1364
Syndicat professionnel des homéopathes du Québec, 1365
Syndicat professionnel des ingénieurs d'Hydro-Québec, 1365
Syndicat professionnel des scientifiques à pratique exclusive de Montréal, 1365
Syrian Canadian Council, 1365
Table d'Inter-Action du Quartier Peter-McGill, 1365
Table de concertation du faubourg Saint-Laurent, 1365
Technion Canada-Montréal Office, 1368
TECHNOCompétences, 1369
Tekeyan Armenian Cultural Association, 1369
Television Bureau of Canada, Inc.-Montréal Branch Office, 1370
Tennis Canada-Montréal, 1371
Tennis Québec, 1371
Thalidomide Victims Association of Canada, 1373
Théâtres associés inc., 1375
Théâtres unis enfance jeunesse, 1375

Tourisme Montréal/Office des congrès et du tourisme du Grand Montréal, 1393
La Trame, 1394
Trans Canada Trail Foundation, 1394
The Transplantation Society, 1395
T.R.E.E. Foundation for Youth Development, 1397
Triathlon Québec, 1398
Tyndale St-Georges Community Centre, 1401
Tyndale St-Georges Community Centre-Des Seigneurs Branch, 1401
Ukrainian Canadian Congress-Montréal Branch, 1402
Ukrainian Youth Association of Canada-Montréal Branch, 1404
Underwriters' Laboratories of Canada-Montréal Site, 1404
UNICEF Canada-UNICEF Québec - Montréal, 1405
UNIFOR-Montréal Office, 1405
Union des artistes, 1406
Union des consommateurs, 1406
Union des écrivaines et écrivains québécois, 1406
Union des municipalités du Québec, 1406
Union des philatélistes de Montréal, 1406
Union des tenanciers de bars du Québec, 1406
United Church of Canada-Synode Montréal & Ottawa Conference, 1409
United Empire Loyalists' Association of Canada-Heritage Branch, 1410
United Food & Commercial Workers Canada-Québec Council, 1411
United Nations Association in Canada-Greater Montréal Office, 1411
United Nations Environment Programme - Multilateral Fund for the Implementation of the Montréal Protocol, 1412
United Nations Environment Programme - Secretariat of the Convention on Biological Diversity, 1412
Universal Negro Improvement Association of Montreal, 1418
Urban & Regional Information Systems Association-URISA Québec, 1601
Vélo Québec, 1431
Via Prévention, 1431
Vidéographe, 1434
The Vimy Foundation, 1435
Vrac environnement group d'action et de recherche en développement durable, 1439
Vues d'Afriques - Les Journées du cinéma africain et créole, 1439
Walkley Centre, 1440
WE Charity-Québec Office, 1443
Westhaven-Elmhurst Community Association, 1451
Westmount Historical Association, 1451
Wikimedia Canada, 1453
Women's Centre of Montréal, 1462
World Anti-Doping Agency, 1465
World Federation of Hemophilia, 1466
World Trade Centre Montréal, 1467
World Wildlife Fund - Canada-Montréal, 1468
YMCA Canada-YMCAs of Québec, 1472
Youth Media Alliance, 1476
YWCA Canada-Y des femmes de Montréal, 1481
Zoological Society of Montréal, 1482

Montréal-Nord
Association des Grands Frères Grandes Soeurs du Québec-Grands Frères Grandes Soeurs du Grand Montréal, 115

Morin-Heights
La coopérative de Solidarité de Répit et d'Etraide, 627

Nemaska
Grand Council of the Crees, 779

Neuville
Association professionnelle des techniciennes et techniciens en documentation du Québec, 167

New Carlisle
Eastern Shores Independent Association for Support Personnel, 671

New Richmond
Réseau des SADC et CAE-SADC Baie-des-Chaleurs, 1220

Normandin
Chambre de commerce et d'industrie du secteur Normandin, 547

North Hatley
Patrimoine Huntingville, 1145

Notre-Dame-des-Pins
Syndicat des agricultrices de la Beauce, 1362

Notre-Dame-du-Bon-Conseil
Blonde d'Aquitaine du Québec, 215

Notre-Dame-du-Nord
Chambre de commerce Notre-Dame-du-Nord, 549

Notre-Dame-du-Portage
Patrimoine et Culture du Portage, 1145

Ormstown
Canadian Farm Writers' Federation, 384
LEAD Canada Inc., 902

Otterburn Park
Le Syndicat canadien des employées et employés professionnels et de bureau-Region 1 - Section locale 576, 444

Outremont
L'Arche Canada, 77
L'Arche Québec, 77
Armenian Holy Apostolic Church - Canadian Diocese, 83
Association Internationale pour le Développement de l'Apnée Canada, 136
Le Syndicat canadien des employées et employés professionnels et de bureau-Region 1 - Section locale 579, 444
Fédération des dentistes spécialistes du Québec, 714

Papineauville
Canadian Ski Marathon, 471
Chambre de commerce Vallée de la Petite-Nation, 550

Paspébiac
Association québécoise de l'épilepsie-Épilepsie Gaspésie-sud, 169
Fédération des professionnelles et professionnels de l'éducation du Québec-Syndicat des professionnelles et professionnels scolaires de la Gaspésie et des Îles-de-la-Madeleine (SPPGIM), 718

Percé
Office de Tourisme du Rocher-Percé, 1055

Piedmont
Chambre immobilière des Laurentides, 551

Pierrefonds
Associaça Portuguesa do West Island, 89

Pincourt
Corporation des praticiens en médecine douce du Canada, 630

Pohénégamook
FADOQ-Région Bas St-Laurent, 1224

Pointe Claire
Québec Community Newspaper Association, 1196

Pointe-Claire
Association des diffuseurs culturels de l'Ile de Montréal, 110
Ballet West, 195
CAA-Québec-Pointe-Claire, 268
Canadian Dupuytren Society, 379
Canadian Standards Association-Eastern Region, 490
Chambre de commerce de l'Ouest-de-l'Ile de Montréal, 541
Editors' Association of Canada-Québec/Région de l'Atlantique, 674
Embroiderers' Association of Canada, Inc.-Québec - Lakeshore Creative Stitchery Guild/La Guilde des Travaux á l'Aiguille du Lakeshore, 686
FPInnovations, 756
Independent Association of Support Staff, 832
Lakeshore Coin Club, 897
Orchestre symphonique des jeunes du West Island, 1118
QMI-Montréal, 1195
Québec Competitive Festival of Music, 1196
Québec Family History Society, 1197

Pointe-à-la-Croix
Société historique Machault, 1321

Pont-Rouge
Chambre de commerce de l'Est de Portneuf, 541

Port-Cartier
Centre de recherche et d'information en consommation de Port-Cartier, 529
Chambre de commerce de Port-Cartier, 542

Princeville
Association des jeunes ruraux du Québec, 117
Tourisme Centre-du-Québec, 1392

Prévost
Association des propriétaires canins de Prévost, 126
Association des résidents du Lac Renaud, 127
Société d'Horticulture et d'Écologie de Prévost, 1314

Québec
Action Patrimoine, 6
Agence municipale de financement et de développement des centres d'urgence 9-1-1 du Québec, 14
AIESEC-Laval, 18
Alcoholics Anonymous-Québec - Northeast Area of Québec Central Office, 52
Alliance des cadres de l'État, 55
American Concrete Institute-Eastern Ontario & Québec Chapter, 1492
American Society of Heating, Refrigerating & Air Conditioning Engineers-Chapitre de Québec Chapter, 1500
American Society of Plumbing Engineers-Québec, 1502
Les AmiEs de la Terre de Québec, 67
The Anglican Church of Canada-Diocese of Québec, 70
Apprenp'tits Numismates, 75
L'Arche Québec-L'Arche l'Étoile, 77
ArcticNet Inc., 81
Armateurs du Saint-Laurent, 82
Assemblée parlementaire de la Francophonie, 88
Association canadienne d'éducation de langue française, 90
Association canadienne des relations industrielles, 94
Association coopérative d'économie familiale de Québec, 98
Association coopérative d'économie familliale de Québec, 98
Association de la construction du Québec-Région de Québec, 101
Association de la santé et de la sécurité des pâtes et papiers et des industries de la forêt du Québec, 102
Association de la sécurité de l'information du Québec, 102
Association de vitrerie et fenestrations du Québec, 102
Association des Aménagistes Régionaux du Québec, 105
Association des archéologues du Québec, 105
Association des archivistes du Québec, 105
Association des chercheurs et chercheures étudiants en médecine, 108
Association des constructeurs de routes et grands travaux du Québec, 110
Association des directeurs généraux des municipalités du Québec, 111
Association des directeurs municipaux du Québec, 111
Association des employées et employés du gouvernement du Québec, 112
Association des expositions agricoles du Québec, 113
Association des familialistes de Québec, 113
Association des fonctionnaires issus des communautés culturelles, 115
Association des gestionnaires de ressources bénévoles du Québec, 115
Association des Grands Frères Grandes Soeurs du Québec-Grands Frères Grandes Soeurs de Québec, 115
Association des guides touristiques de Québec, 116
Association des handicapés respiratoires de Québec, 116
Association des implantés cochléaires du Québec, 116
Association des jardins du Québec, 117
Association des marchands dépanneurs et épiciers du Québec, 119
Association des médecins cliniciens enseignants de Laval, 119
Association des médecins vétérinaires praticiens du Québec, 120
Association des personnes intéressées à l'aphasie et à l'accident vasculaire cérébral, 123
Association des professionnels en électrolyse et soins esthétiques du Québec, 126
Association des Sourds de Québec inc., 128
Association des statisticiennes et statisticiens du Québec, 128
Association du Québec pour enfants avec problèmes auditifs-AQEPA Québec Métro, 131
Association internationale des études québécoises, 136
Association internationale des maires francophones - Bureau à Québec, 136
Association minière du Québec, 137
Association nationale des camionneurs artisans inc., 138
Association paritaire pour la santé et la sécurité du travail - Administration provinciale, 164
Association pétrolière et gazière du Québec, 165
Association pour les applications pédagogiques de l'ordinateur au postsecondaire, 167
Association professionnelle des ingénieurs du gouvernement du Québec (ind.), 167
Association provinciale des constructeurs d'habitations du Québec inc.-Québec, 168
Association québécoise d'information scolaire et professionnelle, 168
Association québécoise de doit constitutionel, 169
Association québécoise de l'épilepsie-Épilepsie - Section de Québec, 169
Association québécoise de l'industrie de la pêche, 170
Association québécoise de prévention du suicide, 171
Association québécoise de Vol Libre, 171
Association québécoise des cadres scolaires, 171
Association québécoise des salons du livre-Québec, 174
Association québécoise du personnel de direction des écoles, 176
Association québécoise du transport aérien, 176
Association québécoise pour l'évaluation d'impacts, 176
Asthme et allergies Québec, 179
Augustines de la Miséricorde de Jésus, 187
Autorité des marchés financiers, 190
Avocats sans frontières Canada, 191
Boîte à science - Conseil du loisir scientifique du Québec, 217
Boys & Girls Clubs of Québec-Régional des maisons de jeunes de Québec, 224
CAA Québec, 268
CAA-Québec-Québec, 268
CAA-Québec-Québec (Place de la Cité), 268
Canadian Association of Neuropathologists, 322
Canadian Bible Society-Québec District Office, 343
Canadian Masters Cross-Country Ski Association-Québec, 431
Canadian Merchant Service Guild (CLC)-Eastern Branch, 435
Canadian Photonic Industry Consortium, 454
The Canadian Press-Québec Bureau, 459
Canadian Society of Atherosclerosis, Thrombosis & Vascular Biology, 480
Canadian Society of Zoologists, 488
Carnaval de Québec, 514
Carrefour Tiers-Monde, 516
Carrefour Tiers-Monde-Boutique ÉquiMonde, 516
Centraide Québec, 523
Centrale des syndicats démocratiques, 525
Centrale des syndicats du Québec-Bureau de Québec, 526
Centre Anti-Poison du Québec, 526
Centre d'amitié autochtone du Québec, 527
Centre d'entrepreneuriat et PME, 528
Centre de formation et de consultation en métiers d'art, 529
Centre de recherche et d'intervention interuniversitaire sur l'éducation et la vie au travail, 530
Centre de valorisation du patrimoine vivant, 530
Centre francophone d'informatisation des organisations, 534
Centre interdisciplinaire de recherches sur les activités langagières, 535
Centre international de documentation et d'échanges de la francophonie, 535
Centre multiethnique de Québec, 536
Centre Psycho-Pédagogique de Québec Inc., 536
Chambre de commerce et d'industrie de Québec, 546
Chambre de commerce française au Canada - Section Québec, 548
Children's Wish Foundation of Canada-Bureau de Québec, 563
Clan Gunn Society of North America - Eastern Canada Branch, 571
Club de marche de Québec, 574
Club des ornithologues de Québec inc., 575
A Coeur d'Homme, 580
Collaboration Santé Internationale, 581
Collectif pour un Québec sans pauvreté, 581
Comité des citoyens et citoyennes du quartier Saint-Sauveur, 592
Compagnie de danse Migrations, 608
Confédération des associations d'étudiants et étudiantes de l'Université Laval, 610
Confédération québécoise des coopératives d'habitation, 611
Congregation des Soeurs de Saint-Joseph de Saint-Vallier, 612
Conseil de la culture des régions de Québec et de Chaudière-Appalaches, 616
Conseil des arts et des lettres du Québec, 617
Conseil régional FTQ Québec et Chaudière-Appalaches, 621
Corporation des concessionnaires d'automobiles du Québec inc., 630
Corporation des officiers municipaux agréés du Québec, 630
Corporation des services d'ambulance du Québec, 630
Corporation des thanatologues du Québec, 630
Corporation du patrimoine et du tourisme religieux de Québec, 631
Corporations des assureurs directs de dommage, 631
Development & Peace-Québec - Québec, 655

Ducks Unlimited Canada-Québec Provincial Office, 664
Fédération de l'industrie manufacturière (FIM-CSN)-Québec, 709
Fédération de sociétés mutuelles d'assurance générale (Groupe promutuel), 710
Fédération des associations de familles du Québec, 711
Fédération des centres de ressourcement Chrétien, 713
Fédération des comités de parents du Québec inc., 713
La Fédération des commissions scolaires du Québec, 713
Fédération des coopératives de Québec, Chaudière-Appalaches, 714
Fédération des familles et amis de la personne atteinte de maladie mentale, 715
La fédération des mouvements personne d'abord du Québec-Québec Métropolitain, 716
Fédération des professionnelles et professionnels de l'éducation du Québec-Syndicat du personnel professionnel des commissions scolaires de la Région de Québec (SPPRÉQ), 718
Fédération des secrétaires professionnelles du Québec, 718
Fédération des Syndicats de l'Enseignement, 719
Fédération des transporteurs par autobus, 719
Fédération des trappeurs gestionnaires du Québec, 719
Fédération indépendante des syndicats autonomes, 721
Fédération des infirmières et infirmiers du Québec-FIQ - Québec, 721
Fédération québécoise de biathlon, 727
Fédération québécoise des centres communautaires de loisir inc., 728
Fédération québécoise des chasseurs et pêcheurs, 728
Fédération québécoise des coopératives en milieu scolaire, 728
Fédération québécoise des coopératives forestières, 728
Fédération québécoise des sociétés Alzheimer-Québec, 730
Fédération québécoise des sociétés de généalogie, 730
Fédération québécoise pour le saumon atlantique, 731
Fédérations de l'UPA de Lévis Bellechasse, Rive Nord, Lotbinière-Mégantic, 731
Festival d'été de Québec, 733
Fibrose kystique Québec-Section Québec, 733
Folklore Studies Association of Canada, 742
Fondation CHU de Québec, 743
Fondation communautaire du Grand-Québec, 743
Fondation de l'entrepreneurship, 743
Fondation de la faune du Québec, 744
Fondation de la greffe de moelle osseuse de l'Est du Québec, 744
Fondation des maladies du coeur du Québec-La Capitale, 745
Fondation des pompiers du Québec pour les grands brûlés, 745
Fondation Dufresne et Gauthier, 746
FPInnovations-Québec Division, 757
Fraternité des Policiers et Policières de la Ville de Québec, 758
GEOIDE Network, 769
Grand Council of the Crees-Bureau de Québec, 779
Groupe de recherche en animation et planification économique, 791
Groupe gai de l'Université Laval, 792
Groupe régional d'intervention social - Québec, 792
Hautes études internationales, 804
L'Institut canadien de Québec, 840
L'Institut d'assurance de dommages du Québec-Bureau de Québec, 841

Institut de la Francophonie pour le développement durable, 841
Institut de réadaptation en déficience physique de Québec, 841
Institut national d'optique, 843
Institut Séculier Pie X, 843
Jeffery Hale Community Services in English, 869
Jeune Barreau de Québec, 870
Jeune chambre de commerce de Québec, 870
Jeunes canadiens pour une civilisation chrétienne, 870
Jeunesse du Monde, 870
The Kidney Foundation of Canada-Québec Chapter, 885
Literary & Historical Society of Québec, 914
Maison des femmes de Québec inc., 926
Makivik Corporation-Québec City Office, 927
Messagères de Notre-Dame de l'Assomption, 962
Mineralogical Association of Canada, 966
Moisson Québec, 971
Mouvement d'information et d'entraide dans la lutte contre le sida à Québec, 977
Mouvement des femmes Chrétiennes, 977
Mouvement national des québécoises et québécois-SNQ de la Capitale, 977
MultiPrévention-Québec, 980
Nature Québec, 1000
North American Waterfowl Management Plan-Sea Duck Joint Venture (SDJV), 1029
Office du tourisme et des congrès de Québec, 1055
Opéra de Québec, 1115
Opération Nez rouge, 1116
Orchestre symphonique de Québec, 1118
Orchidophiles de Québec, 1119
Ordre des arpenteurs-géomètres du Québec, 1120
Ordre des infirmières et infirmiers du Québec-Ordre régional des infirmières et infirmiers de Québec, 1122
Ordre des ingénieurs forestiers du Québec, 1123
Osteoporosis Canada-Québec - Québec City Chapter, 1129
Palais Montcalm, 1137
Public Service Alliance of Canada-Section de Québec, 1193
Québec dans le monde, 1196
Regroupement des offices d'habitation du Québec, 1215
Regroupement des organismes de bassins versants du Québec, 1215
Research & Development Institute for the Agri-Environment, 1218
Réseau de la coopération du travail du Québec, 1219
Réseau des SADC et CAE, 1219
Réseau du sport étudiant du Québec Chaudière-Appalaches, 1220
Réseau québécois de l'asthme et de la MPOC, 1225
Réseau québécois des OSBL d'habitation-Québec, Chaudière-Appalaches, 1225
Royal Astronomical Society of Canada-Centre de Québec, 1238
Skills/Compétences Canada-Compétences Québec, 1303
Société d'histoire de Sillery, 1311
Société de coopération pour le développement international, 1314
Société de développement économique du Saint-Laurent, 1315
Société de généalogie de Québec, 1315
Société de protection des forêts contre les insectes et maladies, 1317
Société des communicateurs du Québec, 1317
Société des établissements de plein air du Québec, 1318
Société des technologies en nutrition, 1318
Société des traversiers du Québec, 1318
Société des traversiers du Québec-Traverse Québec-Lévis, 1318

Société historique de Québec, 1320
La Société historique du Cap-Rouge, 1320
Société internationale du réseau ÉCONOMUSÉE et Société ÉCONOMUSÉE du Québec, 1321
La Société Numismatique de Québec, 1322
Société Philatelique de Québec, 1322
Société Provancher d'histoire naturelle du Canada, 1322
Société québécoise d'ethnologie, 1323
Société québécoise de récupération et de recyclage, 1323
Syndicat de la fonction publique du Québec inc. (ind.), 1361
Syndicat de la fonction publique du Québec inc. (ind.)-Québec - Chaudière-Appalaches, 1361
Syndicat de professionnelles et professionnels du gouvernement du Québec, 1362
Syndicat des conseillères et conseillers de la CSQ, 1362
Syndicat des employés et employées des syndicats et des organismes collectifs du Québec, 1363
Syndicat des professeurs de l'Université Laval, 1364
Syndicat des travailleurs de la construction du Québec (CSD), 1364
Syndicat interprovincial des ferblantiers et couvreurs, la section locale 2016-Québec, 1364
Table des responsables de l'éducation des adultes et de la formation professionnelle des commissions scolaires du Québec, 1366
UNIFOR-Québec Office, 1405
Union des Artistes (FIA) - Bureau de Québec, 1406
United Nations Association in Canada-Québec Office, 1411
Vert l'Aventure Plein Air, 1431
Viol-secours inc., 1435
Voice of English-speaking Québec, 1437
YWCA Canada-YWCA Québec, 1482

Rawdon
Chambre de commerce de Rawdon, 542
Tourisme Lanaudière, 1392

Repentigny
Les Amis de la déficience intellectuelle Rive-Nord, 67
Canadian Literary & Artistic Association, 427
Canadian Transplant Association-Québec Region, 497
Chambre de commerce de la MRC de L'Assomption, 541
Conseil de la souveraineté du Québec, 616

Richmond
Chambre de commerce et d'industrie de la région de Richmond, 545
Réseau des SADC et CAE-CAE Val-St-François, 1220

Rigaud
Professional Photographers of Canada-Photographes professionnels du Québec, 1186

Rimouski
Association coopérative d'économie familiale - Rimouski-Neigette et Mitis, 97
Association de la construction du Québec-Région Bas-St-Laurent - Gaspésie - Les Iles, 100
Association des personnes accidentées cérébro-vasculaires, aphasiques et traumatisées cranio-cérébrales du Bas-Saint-Laurent, 122
Association du Québec pour enfants avec problèmes auditifs-AQEPA Bas-Saint-Laurent, 131
Association provinciale des constructeurs d'habitations du Québec inc.-Est-du-Québec, 168
Association québécoise des salons du livre-Rimouski, 174

Association québécoise pour le loisir des personnes handicapées-URLS Bas St-Laurent, 177
Canadian Hydrographic Association-Québec Branch, 410
Carrefour 50+ du Québec, 515
Centre femmes de Rimouski, 531
Chambre de commerce et d'industrie Rimouski-Neigette, 547
Club de marche de Rimouski, 574
Club de Numismates du Bas-St-Laurent, 575
Conseil de la culture du Bas-Saint-Laurent, 616
Conseil régional FTQ Bas St-Laurent - Gaspésie-Îles-de-la-Madeleine, 621
Fédération de l'UPA - Bas-Saint-Laurent, 709
Fédération des caisses Desjardins du Québec-Bas St-Laurent, 712
Fédération des infirmières et infirmiers du Québec-FIQ - Gaspésie Bas St-Laurent, 721
Fondation des maladies du coeur du Québec-Bas St-Laurent et Gaspésie, 745
Mouvement national des québécoises et québécois-SN de l'Est du Québec, 977
Ordre des infirmières et infirmiers du Québec-Ordre régional des infirmières et infirmiers du Bas-Saint-Laurent/Gaspésie-Iles-de-la-Madeleine, 1122
Réseau des SADC et CAE-SADC de la Neigette, 1220
Réseau du sport étudiant du Québec Est-du-Québec, 1223
Société de généalogie et d'archives de Rimouski, 1316
Syndicat des agents de maîtrise de TELUS (ind.), 1362
Syndicat des professeures et professeurs de l'Université du Québec à Rimouski, 1363

Rivière-Bleue
Chambre de commerce du Transcontinental, 544

Rivière-Héva
Fédération des professionnelles et professionnels de l'éducation du Québec-Syndicat des professionnelles et professionnels en milieu scolaire du Nord-Ouest (SPPMSNO), 718

Rivière-du-Loup
Association coopérative d'économie familiale du Grand-Portage, 98
Centre de formation à la coopération interculturelle du Québec, 529
Chambre de commerce de la MRC de Rivière-du-Loup, 542
Club Optimiste de Rivière-du-Loup inc., 576
Fédération des professionnelles et professionnels de l'éducation du Québec-Syndicat des professionnelles et professionnels des commissions scolaires du Grand-Portage (SPGP), 718
Réseau des SADC et CAE-SADC de la MRC de Rivière-du-Loup, 1220
Réseau québécois des OSBL d'habitation-Bas-St-Laurent, de la Gaspésie & des Iles, 1225
Société d'histoire et de généalogie de Rivière-du-Loup, 1312
Tourisme Bas-Saint-Laurent, 1392

Roberval
Association des Grands Frères Grandes Soeurs du Québec-Grands Frères Grandes Soeurs du Domaine du Roy, 115
Association du Québec pour enfants avec problèmes auditifs-AQEPA Lac-Saint-Jean, 131
Association Jeannoise pour l'intégration sociale inc., 136
Chambre de commerce et d'industrie de Roberval, 546
Réseau des SADC et CAE-SADC Lac-Saint-Jean Ouest inc., 1221

Rosemère
Fédération des employés du préhospitaliers du Québec, 714
Real Estate Institute of Canada-Québec Chapter, 1206

Rougemont
Société d'histoire et de généalogie des Quatre Lieux, 1313

Rouyn-Noranda
Association coopérative d'économie familiale - Abitibi-Témiscamingue, 97
Association de l'exploration minière de Québec, 100
Association des Grands Frères Grandes Soeurs du Québec-Grands Frères Grandes Soeurs de Rouyn-Noranda, 115
Association des traumatisés crâniens de l'Abitibi-Témiscamingue (Le Pilier), 129
Association pour l'intégration sociale (Rouyn-Noranda) inc., 166
Association québécoise de l'épilepsie-Épilepsie Abitibi-Témiscamingue, 169
Association québécoise des salons du livre-Abitibi-Témiscamingue, 174
Association québécoise pour le loisir des personnes handicapées-ARLPH Abitibi-Témiscamingue, 176
Centre local de développement Rouyn-Noranda, 536
Chambre de commerce et d'industrie de Rouyn-Noranda, 546
Chambre immobilière de l'Abitibi-Témiscamingue Inc., 550
Collectif féministe Rouyn-Noranda/Centre de femmes "Entre-Femmes", 581
Conseil de la culture de L'Abitibi-Témiscamingue, 615
Conseil régional FTQ Abitibi-Témiscamingue - Nord-du-Québec, 621
Fédération de l'industrie manufacturière (FIM-CSN)-Rouyn-Noranda, 709
Fédération de l'UPA - Abitibi-Témiscamingue, 709
Fédération des infirmières et infirmiers du Québec-FIQ - Abitibi-Témiscamingue, 721
Fédération québécoise des sociétés Alzheimer-Rouyn-Noranda, 730
Généalogie Abitibi-Témiscamingue, 768
Mouvement national des québécoises et québécois-SNQ d'Abitibi-Témiscamingue et du Nord-du-Québec inc., 977
Orchestre symphonique régional Abitibi-Témiscamingue, 1119
Ordre des infirmières et infirmiers du Québec-Ordre régional des infirmières et infirmiers de l'Abitibi-Témiscamingue, 1122
Point d'appui, centre d'aide et de prévention des agressions à caractère sexuel de Rouyn-Noranda, 1163
Reseau Biblio de l'Abitibi-Témiscamingue Nord-du-Québec, 1218
Réseau des SADC et CAE-SADC de Rouyn-Noranda, 1220
FADOQ - Mouvement des aînés du Québec-Région Abitibi-Témiscamingue, 1224
Société d'histoire de Rouyn-Noranda, 1311
Syndicat de la fonction publique du Québec inc. (ind.)-Abitibi - Témiscamingue - Nord du Québec, 1361
Syndicat de la relève agricole d'Abitibi-Témiscamingue, 1362
Tourisme Abitibi-Témiscamingue, 1392

Roxboro
West Island Black Community Association, 1445

Sacré-Coeur
Association de la Rivière Ste-Marguerite Inc., 102

Saguenay
CAA-Québec-Saguenay, 268
Fédération de l'industrie manufacturière (FIM-CSN)-Saguenay, 709
Fédération des caisses Desjardins du Québec-Saguenay-Lac-Saint-Jean-Charlevoix, 712

Saint Leonard
Patronato INAS (Canada)-Saint Leonard Office, 1146

Saint-Adolphe-d'Howard
Chambre de commerce et de tourisme de St-Adolphe-d'Howard, 548

Saint-Alphonse de Granby
Association provinciale des constructeurs d'habitations du Québec inc.-Haute-Yamaska, 168

Saint-Alphonse-Rodriguez
Réseau des SADC et CAE-SADC Matawinie inc., 1221
Société pour les enfants handicapés du Québec-Camp Papillon, 1322

Saint-Ambroise
Réseau des SADC et CAE-SADC du Haut-Saguenay, 1221

Saint-André-Avellin
Atelier de Formation Socioprofessionnelle de la Petite-Nation, 179

Saint-Antonin
Children of the World Adoption Society Inc.-Lower St. Lawrence - Gaspé Office, 560

Saint-Augustin-de-Desmaures
Association des professeurs de Campus Notre-Dame-de-Foy, 124

Saint-Basile-le-Grand
Alliance des massothérapeutes du Québec, 56

Saint-Bruno
Canine Federation of Canada, 508
Chambre de commerce Mont-Saint-Bruno, 549
Club de curling Mont-Bruno, 574
Club photo Évasion, 576

Saint-Bruno-de-Montarville
Association des artistes peintres affiliés de la Rive-Sud, 106
Canadian Forces Logistics Association - Montréal, 392
Société d'histoire de Montarville, 1311

Saint-Bruno-sur-Richelieu
Association des propriétaires de Saint-Bruno, 126
Club informatique Mont-Bruno, 575

Saint-Casimir
Société d'histoire et de généalogie de Saint-Casimir, 1312

Saint-Charles-de-Bellechasse
Société historique de Bellechasse, 1319

Saint-Charles-de-Drummond
Fédération québécoise des sociétés Alzheimer-Centre du Québec, 729

Saint-Chrysostome
Québec Women's Institutes, 1199

Saint-Constant
Association de ringuette Roussillon, 104
Canadian Railroad Historical Association, 465

Saint-Côme
Chambre de commerce de Saint-Côme, 542

Saint-Côme-Linière
Chambre de commerce de St-Côme-Linière, 543

Saint-Donat
Rhinoceros Party, 1229

Saint-Donat-de-Montcalm
Association québécoise des éducatrices et éducateurs spécialisés en arts plastiques, 172
Chambre de commerce de St-Donat, 543

Saint-Donat-de-Rimouski
Canadian Highland Cattle Society, 405

Saint-Eustache
Chambre de commerce et d'industrie MRC de Deux-Montagne, 547
La fédération des mouvements personne d'abord du Québec-Saint-Eustache, 716
Société d'histoire régionale Deux-Montagnes, 1313
Société de généalogie de Saint-Eustache, 1315

Saint-Félicien
Chambre de commerce et d'industrie secteur Saint-Félicien inc., 547
Service budgétaire populaire de St-Félicien, 1291

Saint-Félix-d'Otis
Association chasse et pêche du Lac Brébeuf, 96

Saint-Félix-de-Valois
Chambre de commerce St-Félix de Valois, 549

Saint-Frédéric
Chambre de commerce de St-Frédéric, 543

Saint-Gabriel
Chambre de commerce de Brandon, 540

Saint-Georges
Association pour l'intégration sociale - Région Beauce-Sartigan, 165
Association provinciale des constructeurs d'habitations du Québec inc.-Beauce-Appalaches, 168
Centrale des syndicats démocratiques-Beauce, 525
Chambre de commerce de Saint-Georges, 543
Fédération de l'UPA de la Beauce, 709
Société de généalogie de la Beauce, 1315

Saint-Germain
Québec Simmental Association, 1198

Saint-Gédéon
Association féminine d'éducation et d'action sociale-Saguenay-Lac-St-Jean-Chibougamau, 132

Saint-Hippolyte
Association des résidents du Lac Écho, 127
Canadian Association for Williams Syndrome-CAWS - Québec, 307

Saint-Hubert
Les Amis du vitrail, 67
Aphasie Rive-Sud, 73
Association Sclérose en Plaques Rive-Sud, 178
Black Academic Scholarship Fund, 212
Centre de réadaptation et dépendance le virage, 529
Centre de soutien entr'Aidants, 530
Centre Montérégien de réadaptation, 536
Club de photographie L'Oeil qui voit de Saint-Hubert, 575
L'Écrit Tôt de Saint-Hubert, 674
Fédération des professionnelles et professionnels de l'éducation du Québec-Syndicat des professionnelles et professionnels de la Montérégie (SPM), 718
Fondation Marie-Ève Saulnier, 747
Greniers de Joseph, 789
Guyana Cultural Association of Montréal, 794
Ordre des infirmières et infirmiers du Québec-Ordre régional des infirmières et infirmiers de la Montérégie, 1122
Ringuette St-Hubert, 1233
Société d'histoire de Saint-Hubert, 1311

Saint-Hyacinthe
Animal Nutrition Association of Canada-Québec Division, 71
Association de la Construction Richelieu Yamaska, 101
Association des Grands Frères Grandes Soeurs du Québec-Grands Frères Grandes Soeurs de la Montérégie, 115
Association des procureurs de cours municipales du Québec, 124
Association professionnelle des enseignantes et enseignants en commerce, 167
Association québécoise des industries de nutrition animale et céréalière, 173
Association québécoise pour le loisir des personnes handicapées-Zone loisir Montérégie, 177
Ayrshire Breeders Association of Canada, 191
Canadian Cattle Breeders' Association, 351
Centraide Richelieu-Yamaska, 523
Centre d'Histoire de Saint-Hyacinthe, 528
Chambre de commerce de la grande région de Saint-Hyacinthe, 541
Chambre immobilière de Saint-Hyacinthe Inc., 551
Les Chevaliers de Colomb du Québec, 557
Conseil des entrepreneurs agricoles, 617
Fédération de l'UPA de la Montérégie, 709
Fédération des caisses Desjardins du Québec-Montérégie, 712
Fédération interdisciplinaire de l'horticulture ornementale du Québec, 721
Fédération québécoise des sociétés Alzheimer-Maskoutains-Vallée des Patriotes, 730
Fondation Initia, 746
Groupe CTT Group, 791
Holstein Canada-Section de Québec, 819
Jersey Canada-Québec, 869
Mouvement national des québécoises et québécois-SSJB de Richelieu/Yamaska, 978
Ordre des médecins vétérinaires du Québec, 1123
FADOQ - Mouvement des aînés du Québec-Région Richelieu-Yamaska, 1224
Ringuette St-Hyacinthe, 1233
Société St-Jean-Baptiste Richelieu-Yamaska, 1325
Syndicat québécois de la construction, 1365
Union québécoise de réhabilitation des oiseaux de proie, 1408

Saint-Jacques
Réseau des SADC et CAE-SADC Achigan-Montcalm inc., 1220

Saint-Jean-Chrysostome
Association des fabricants et détaillants de l'industrie de la cuisine du Québec, 113

Saint-Jean-de-Dieu
Chambre de commerce de St-Jean-de-Dieu, 543

Saint-Jean-de-Matha
Chambre de commerce St-Jean-de-Matha, 549

Saint-Jean-sur-Richelieu
Association de la construction du Québec-Région Montérégie, 101
Association de paralysie cérébrale du Québec-Bureau de Saint-Jean-sur-Richelieu, 103
Association de parents pour l'adoption québécoise, 103
Association des embouteilleurs d'eau du Québec, 111
Association des golfeurs professionnels du Québec, 115
Association montérégienne de la surdité inc., 137
Association Québécoise pour la Santé Mentale des Nourrisson, 176
Canadian Association of Veterans in United Nations Peacekeeping-Succursale MGén Alain R. Forand, 336
Chambre de commerce du Haut-Richelieu, 544
Corporation des approvisionneurs du Québec, 629

Fédération québécoise des sociétés Alzheimer-Haut-Richelieu, 730
Mouvement national des québécoises et québécois-SNQ Richelieu/Saint-Laurent, 977
Réseau des SADC et CAE-CAE Haute-Montérégie, 1219
FADOQ - Mouvement des aînés du Québec-Région Rive-Sud-Suroît, 1224
Savoy Foundation Inc., 1282
Société d'histoire du Haut-Richelieu, 1312

Saint-Joseph-de-Beauce
Chambre de commerce et d'industrie de St-Joseph-de-Beauce, 546

Saint-Jules
Chambre de commerce de St-Jules-de-Beauce, 543

Saint-Jérôme
Alcoholics Anonymous-Québec - Northwest Area of Québec Central Office, 52
Ami-e du Quartier, 67
Association de la Fibromyalgie des Laurentides, 101
Association des artistes en arts visuels de Saint-Jérôme, 106
Association des Grands Frères Grandes Soeurs du Québec-Grands Frères Grandes Soeurs de La Porte du Nord, 115
Association des recycleurs de pièces d'autos et de camions, 127
Association québécoise pour le loisir des personnes handicapées-ARLPH Laurentides, 177
Canadian Ski Patrol-Québec Division, 471
Carrefour d'Actions Populaires, 515
Centre d'aide personnes traumatisées crâniennes et handicapées physiques Laurentides, 527
Centre sida amitié, 536
Chambre de commerce et d'industrie St-Jérôme, 548
Conseil de la culture des Laurentides, 616
La fédération des mouvements personne d'abord du Québec-Saint-Jérôme, 716
Fédération des professionnelles et professionnels de l'éducation du Québec-Syndicat des professionnelles et professionnels de l'éducation des Laurentides-Lanaudière (SPPÉLL), 718
FTQ Laurentides-Lanaudière, 764
Grands-Parents Tendresse, 781
Mouvement national des québécoises et québécois-SNQ des Laurentides, 977
Ordre des infirmières et infirmiers du Québec-Ordre régional des infirmières et infirmiers de Laurentides/Lanaudière, 1122
Société d'histoire de la Rivière du Nord inc., 1310
La Société d'histoire de la Rivière-du-Nord, 1310
Société de généalogie des Laurentides, 1316
Syndicat de la fonction publique du Québec inc. (ind.)-Laurentides - Lanaudière - Outaouais, 1361

Saint-Lambert
Association des orchestres de jeunes de la Montérégie, 121
Canadian International DX Club, 421
Canadian Theosophical Association, 494
Conseil des industriels laitiers du Québec inc., 617
Conseil du troisième âge de Saint-Lambert, 618
La Fédération québécoise des organismes communautaires Famille, 729
Our Harbour, 1132
Société chorale de Saint-Lambert, 1309
Société d'horticulture de Saint-Lambert, 1314
Société histoire de Mouillepied, 1319

Saint-Lazare
Association syndicale des employées de production et de service, 178

Saint-Lin-Laurentides
Association Carrefour Famille Montcalm, 96
Chambre de commerce Saint-Lin-Laurentides, 549

Saint-Léon-de-Standon
Association québécoise de lutte contre la pollution atmosphérique, 170
Réseau des SADC et CAE-SADC Bellechasse-Etchemins, 1220

Saint-Léonard
Action Dignité de Saint-Léonard, 6
Association des consultants et laboratoires experts, 110
Association des massologues et techniciens en massage du Canada - Association des massothérapeutes professionnels du Québec, 119
Association québécoise de la distribution de fruits et légumes, 170
Association québécoise des allergies alimentaires, 171
CAA-Québec-Saint-Léonard, 268
Chambre de commerce de St-Léonard, 543
Canadian Chemical Producers' Association-Québec Regional Office, 556
General Conference of the Canadian Assemblies of God, 768
Insitut canadien des économistes en construction - Québec, 840
National Congress of Italian-Canadians-Congrès national des Italo-Canadiens du Québec, 991
Ordre des technologues en imagerie médicale, en radio-oncologie et en élétrophysiologie médicale du Québec, 1124

Saint-Malachie
L'Arche Québec-L'Arche Le Printemps, 77

Saint-Marc-des-Carrières
Chambre de commerce secteur ouest de Portneuf, 549

Saint-Martin
Chambre de commerce St-Martin de Beauce, 549

Saint-Michel-des-Saints
Chambre de commerce de la Haute-Matawinie, 541

Saint-Narcisse-de-Beaurivage
Association de ringuette de Lotbinière, 103

Saint-Nicolas
Regroupement des Sourds de Chaudière-Appalaches, 1215
Tourisme Chaudière-Appalaches, 1392

Saint-Pierre-Ile-d'Orléans
Chambre de commerce de l'Ile d'Orléans, 541

Saint-Raymond
Chambre de commerce régionale de St-Raymond, 549

Saint-Romuald
Mouvement national des québécoises et québécois-SNQ de Chaudière-Appalaches, 977
Société historique de Saint-Romuald, 1320

Saint-Rédempteur
Association de Ringuette Lévis, 104

Saint-Rémi
Chambre de commerce des Jardins de Napierville, 544
Fédération de l'UPA de la Montérégie-Bureau de Saint-Rémi, 709

Saint-Sauveur
Architectural Woodwork Manufacturers Association of Canada - Québec, 80
Association pour la santé environnementale du Québec, 166
Canadian Hardwood Plywood & Veneer Association, 401
Chambre de commerce et de tourisme de la Vallée de Saint-Sauveur/Piedmont, 548
L'Écluse des Laurentides, 671
Ski de fond Québec, 1302
Société d'histoire et de généalogie des Pays-d'en-Haut, inc., 1313

Saint-Stanislas
Réseau des SADC et CAE-SADC Vallée de la Batiscan, 1222

Saint-Stanislas-de-Champlain
Société d'histoire St-Stanislas inc., 1314

Saint-Sébastien
Société d'histoire et généalogie du granit, 1313

Saint-Tite
Société d'histoire de Saint-Tite, 1311

Sainte-Adèle
Chambre de commerce de Sainte-Adèle, 543
Réseau des SADC et CAE-SADC des Laurentides, 1221

Sainte-Agathe-des-Monts
Fédération québécoise des sociétés Alzheimer-Laurentides, 730

Sainte-Anne-de-Bellevue
Ecological Agriculture Projects, 672
Resource Efficient Agricultural Production, 1227
St. Lawrence Valley Natural History Society, 1250

Sainte-Anne-des-Monts
Carrefour-Ressources, 516
Centraide Gaspésie Îles-de-la-Madeleine, 522
Chambre de commerce de la Haute-Gaspésie, 541
Réseau des SADC et CAE-SADC de la Haute-Gaspésie, 1220
Société d'histoire de la Haute Gaspésie, 1310

Sainte-Barbe
Association Québécoise des Loisirs Folkloriques, 173

Sainte-Clare
Chambre de commerce Bellechasse-Etchemins, 540

Sainte-Cécile-de-Masham
Canadian Association of Community Television Users & Stations, 311

Sainte-Foy
Académie de Réflexologie du Québec, 3
Association des propriétaires de machinerie lourde du Québec inc., 126
Banque d'yeux nationale, inc., 196
Canadian Orthoptic Council, 448
Canadian Psychoanalytic Society-Société psychanalytique de Québec, 461
Club de vol à voile de Québec, 575
Conseil de l'industrie forestière du Québec, 615
Fédération de Patinage de Vitesse du Québec, 710
Fédération Québécoise des Municipalités, 729
Québec Society of Lipidology, Nutrition & Metabolism Inc., 1199
FADOQ - Mouvement des aînés du Québec-Régions de Québec et Chaudière-Appalaches, 1224
Société d'histoire de Sainte-Foy, 1311
Syndicat professionnel des médecins du gouvernement du Québec (ind.), 1365

Sainte-Julie
Association de la construction du Québec-Région Montérégie - Bureau de Ste-Julie, 101
Association des policières et policiers provinciaux du Québec, 123
Corporation des bijoutiers du Québec, 629
Groupe export agroalimentaire Québec - Canada, 792
Phobies-Zéro, 1157
Société de généalogie de la Jemmerais, 1315

Sainte-Julienne
Chambre de commerce de Ste-Julienne, 543

Sainte-Justine
Chambre de commerce de Ste-Justine, 543

Sainte-Lucie-des-Laurentides
Association des jeunes travailleurs et travailleuses de Montréal inc, 117

Sainte-Marie
Chambre de commerce et d'industrie Nouvelle-Beauce, 547
Fédération des caisses Desjardins du Québec-Chaudière-Appalaches, 712
Fédération québécoise des sociétés Alzheimer-Chaudière-Appalaches, 730
La Société historique de Nouvelle-Beauce, 1320

Sainte-Thérèse
Alliance des gais et lesbiennes Laval-Laurentides, 56
Associaça Portuguesa de Ste-Thérèse, 89
Association coopérative d'économie familiale des Basses Laurentides, 98
Association de la construction du Québec-Région Laval / Laurentides, 101
Chambre de commerce et d'industrie Thérèse-De Blainville, 548
La fédération des mouvements personne d'abord du Québec-Sainte-Thérèse, 716
Réseau du sport étudiant du Québec Laurentides-Lanaudière, 1223
Société d'histoire et de généalogie des Mille-Iles, 1313

Sainte-Thérèse-de-Blainville
Fondation Diane Hébert Inc, 745

Sainte-Victoire-de-Sorel
Vintage Road Racing Association, 1435

Sainte-Émélie-de-l'Énergie
Chambre de commerce Ste-Émélie-de-l'Énergie, 549

Salaberry-de-Valleyfield
Association coopérative d'économie familiale du Haut-Saint-Laurent, 98
Canadian Boating Federation, 345
Centraide sud-ouest du Québec, 523
Chambre de commerce et d'industrie Beauharnois-Valleyfield-Haut Saint-Laurent, 545
Conseil régional FTQ du Suroît - Bureau régional FTQ - Montérégie, 621
Fédération québécoise des sociétés Alzheimer-Suroît, 730
Réseau des SADC et CAE-SADC du Suroît-Sud, 1221
Société d'histoire et de généalogie de Salaberry, 1313

Senneterre
Réseau des SADC et CAE-SADC Barraute-Senneterre-Quévillon inc, 1220

Sept-Iles
Association de la construction du Québec-Région Nord-Est du Québec, 101
Association québécoise de l'épilepsie-Épilepsie Côte-Nord, 169
Association québécoise des salons du livre-Côte-Nord, 174
Centraide Duplessis, 522
Centre de recherche et d'information en consommation de Port-Cartier-Sept-Iles, 530
Chambre de commerce de Sept-Îles, 543
Conseil régional FTQ Sept-Îles et Côte-Nord - Bureau régional FTQ Côte Nord, 621
Fédération des professionnelles et professionnels de l'éducation du Québec-Syndicat des professionnelles et professionnels du Nord-Est du Québec (SPPNEQ), 718
Fédération québécoise des sociétés Alzheimer-Côte-Nord, 730

Fraternité nationale des forestiers et travailleurs d'usine (CTC), 758
Ordre des infirmières et infirmiers du Québec-Ordre régional des infirmières et infirmiers de la Côte-Nord, 1122
Réseau BIBLIO de la Côte-Nord, 1218
Réseau des SADC et CAE-SADC Côte-Nord inc., 1220
Réseau du sport étudiant du Québec Côte-Nord, 1222

Shawinigan
Chambre de commerce et d'industrie de Shawinigan, 546
Fédération des infirmières et infirmiers du Québec-FIQ - Mauricie Bois-Francs, 721
Orchestre symphonique des jeunes Philippe-Filion, 1118
Réseau des SADC et CAE-SADC Centre-de-la-Mauricie, 1220
Service de protection et d'information du consommateur, 1291
Société d'histoire et de généalogie de Shawinigan-sud, 1313
Tourisme Mauricie, 1393

Shawville
Pontiac Chamber of Commerce, 1164
Society of Rural Physicians of Canada, 1330
Western Québec Literacy Council, 1450

Sherbrooke
AIESEC-Sherbrooke, 18
Army, Navy & Air Force Veterans in Canada-Québec Provincial Command, 84
Association coopérative d'économie familiale - Estrie, 97
Association de la construction du Québec-Région Estrie, 101
Association de paralysie cérébrale du Québec, 103
Association de Sherbrooke pour la déficience intellectuelle, 104
L'Association de spina-bifida et d'hydrocéphalie du Québec-A.S.B.H. Région Estrie, 104
Association des accidentés cérébro-vasculaires et traumatisés crâniens de l'Estrie, 104
Association des compagnies de théâtre, 109
Association des Gestionnaires de l'information de la santé du Québec, 115
Association des Grands Frères Grandes Soeurs du Québec-Grands Frères Grandes Soeurs de l'Estrie, 115
Association des ingénieurs-professeurs des sciences appliquées, 116
Association des personnes handicapés visuels de l'Estrie, inc, 123
Association des professeures et professeurs de la Faculté de médecine de l'Université de Sherbrooke, 124
Association des Sourds de l'Estrie Inc., 128
Association des vietnamiens de Sherbrooke, 130
Association du Québec pour enfants avec problèmes auditifs-AQEPA Estrie, 131
Association du syndrome de Down de L'Estrie, 131
Association forestières du sud du Québec, 135
Association of Professors of Bishop's University, 160
Association professionnelle des pharmaciens salariés du Québec, 167
Association provinciale des constructeurs d'habitations du Québec inc.-Estrie, 168
Association québécoise des salons du livre-Estrie, 174
Association québécoise pour le loisir des personnes handicapées-ARLPH Estrie, 177
Boys & Girls Clubs of Québec-Club Garçons et Filles - Local des jeunes des Jardins Fleuris, 224
Boys & Girls Clubs of Québec-Repaire jeunesse de Sherbrooke - Ascot, 224
CAA-Québec-Sherbrooke, 268
Canadian Society of Animal Science, 480
Canadian Team Handball Federation, 493

Carrefour de solidarité internationale inc., 515
Centraide Estrie, 522
Centrale des syndicats démocratiques-Estrie, 525
Chambre de commerce de Sherbrooke, 543
Chambre immobilière de l'Estrie inc., 550
Comité du patrimoine paysager estrien, 592
Conseil central de l'Estrie (CSN), 614
Conseil francophone de la chanson, 618
Conseil régional FTQ Estrie, 621
Destination Sherbrooke, 654
Eastern Townships Resource Centre, 671
Enviro-Accès Inc., 691
Fédération de l'industrie manufacturière (FIM-CSN)-Sherbrooke, 709
Fédération des caisses Desjardins du Québec-Estrie, 712
Fédération des coopératives d'habitation de l'Estrie, 714
Fédération des éducateurs et éducatrices physiques enseignants du Québec, 714
Fédération des professionnelles et professionnels de l'éducation du Québec-Syndicat des professionnelles et professionnels des commissions scolaires de l'Estrie (SPPCSE), 718
Fédération des infirmières et infirmiers du Québec-FIQ - Estrie, 721
Fédération Québécoise de Dynamophilie, 727
Fédération québécoise des sociétés Alzheimer-Estrie, 730
Fédération québécoise du théâtre amateur, 731
Fondation Caritas-Sherbrooke inc., 743
Fondation des maladies du coeur du Québec-Estrie, 745
Fondation québécoise du cancer-Hôtellerie de l'Estrie, 748
Intervention régionale et information sur le sida en Estrie, 862
Lennoxville-Ascot Historical & Museum Society, 907
Orchestre symphonique de Sherbrooke, 1118
Orchestre symphonique des jeunes de Sherbrooke, 1118
Ordre des infirmières et infirmiers du Québec-Ordre régional des infirmières et infirmiers de l'Estrie, 1122
Organisme de développement d'affaires commerciales et économiques, 1125
Réseau du sport étudiant du Québec Cantons-de-l'Est, 1222
FADOQ - Mouvement des aînés du Québec-Région Estrie, 1224
Réseau Québec-France, 1225
Sentiers de l'estrie, 1290
Sherbrooke Snow Shoe Club, 1296
Société d'histoire de Sherbrooke, 1311
Société de généalogie des Cantons de l'Est, 1315
Société québécoise de gériatrie, 1323
Syndicat des employées de soutien de l'Université de Sherbrooke, 1362
Syndicat des professeures et professeurs de l'Université de Sherbrooke, 1363
Technoscience Estrie, 1369
Tourisme Cantons-de-l'Est, 1392
Townshippers' Association, 1393
United Empire Loyalists' Association of Canada-Little Forks Branch, 1410

Sorel-Tracy
Association de la déficience intellectuelle de la région de Sorel, 101
Chambre de commerce et d'industrie de Sorel-Tracy, 546
Club timbres et monnaies de Sorel inc., 576
Fédération de l'industrie manufacturière (FIM-CSN)-Sorel-Tracy, 709
Réseau des SADC et CAE-SADC Pierre-De Saurel, 1221
Société des traversiers du Québec-Traverse Sorel-St-Ignace-de-Loyola, 1318
Société historique Pierre-de-Saurel inc., 1321

St-Armand
Centre historique de St-Armand, 535

St-François-de-la-Rivière-du-Sud
Société de Conservation du Patrimoine de Saint-François-de-la-Rivière-du-Sud inc., 1314

Stanbridge East
Missisquoi Historical Society, 969

Stanstead
Stanstead Historical Society, 1348

Ste-Catharine-de-la-Jacques-Cartier
Association Hereford du Québec, 136

Ste-Catherine-de-la-J-Cartier
Chambre de Commerce de la Jacques-Cartier, 541

Tadoussac
Société des traversiers du Québec-Traverse Tadoussac-Baie-Ste-Catherine, 1318

Terrebonne
Association des naturopathes professionnels du Québec, 120
Association des orchestres de jeunes du Québec inc., 121
Association des stations de ski du Québec, 128
Association régionale de football Laurentides Lanaudière, 177
CAA-Québec-Terrebonne, 268
Chambre de commerce d'industrie Les Moulins, 540

Thetford Mines
Association coopérative d'économie familiale - Appalaches, Beauce, Etchemins, 97
Association de Ringuette de Thetford, 103
Association des Grands Frères Grandes Soeurs du Québec-Grands Frères Grandes Soeurs des Appalaches, 115
Association Renaissance de la région de l'Amiante, 177
Chambre de commerce et d'industrie de Thetford Mines, 546
Corporation des Chemins Craig et Gosford, 629
Mouvement national des québécoises et québécois-SNQ de la région de Thetford, 977
Musée minéralogique et minier de Thetford Mines, 982
Province of Québec Rifle Association, 1190
Réseau des SADC et CAE-SADC de l'Amiante, 1220
Société de généalogie et d'histoire de la région de Thetford-Mines, 1316
Société des archives historiques de la région de l'Amiante, 1317

Tring-Jonction
Chambre de commerce de Tring-Jonction, 543

Trois-Pistoles
Association des familles Rioux d'Amérique inc., 113
Coop kayak des îles, 627
Réseau des SADC et CAE-SADC des Basques inc., 1221
Société historique et généalogique de Trois-Pistoles, inc., 1321

Trois-Rivières
L'Arche Québec-L'Arche Mauricie, 77
Association de la construction du Québec-Région de la Mauricie - Bois-Francs - Lanaudière - Centre-du-Québec, 100
Association des avocats et avocates de province, 106
Association des handicapés adultes de la Mauricie, 116
Association des traumatisés cranio-cérébraux Mauricie-Centre-du-Québec, 130
Association du Québec pour enfants avec problèmes auditifs-AQEPA Mauricie/Centre du Québec, 131
Association provinciale des constructeurs d'habitations du Québec inc.-Mauricie-Lanaudière, 168
Association québécoise des salons du livre, 174

Association québécoise des salons du livre-Trois-Rivières, 174
Association québécoise pour le loisir des personnes handicapées, 176
Association québécoise pour le loisir des personnes handicapées-URLS Mauricie, 177
Boys & Girls Clubs of Québec-Maison Coup De Pouce Trois-Rivières, 224
CAA-Québec-Trois-Rivières, 268
Centraide Mauricie, 522
Centrale des syndicats démocratiques-Mauricie, 525
Centre d'intervention budgétaire et sociale de la Mauricie, 528
Centre d'organisation mauricien de services et d'éducation populaire, 528
Les Centres jeunesse de la Mauricie et du Centre de Québec, 537
Chambre de commerce et d'industries de Trois-Rivières, 548
Chambre immobilière de la Mauricie Inc., 550
Club de marche moi mes souliers, 575
Comité de solidarité/Trois-Rivières, 592
Conseil régional FTQ de la Mauricie et du Centre-du-Québec - Bureau régional FTQ - Mauricie et Centre du Québec, 621
Culture Mauricie, 645
École internationale de français, 672
Fédération de l'UPA - Mauricie, 709
Fédération des caisses Desjardins du Québec-Mauricie, 712
La fédération des mouvements personne d'abord du Québec-Mauricie, 716
Fédération des professionnelles et professionnels de l'éducation du Québec-Syndicat du personnel professionnel de l'éducation du Coeur et du Centre du Québec (SPPECCQ), 718
Fédération du personnel professionnel des universités et de la recherche, 720
Fédération nationale des services de préparation au mariage, 722
Fondation des maladies du coeur du Québec-Mauricie/Centre du Québec, 745
Fondation québécoise du cancer-Hôtellerie de la Mauricie, 748
Institut Voluntas Dei, 843
Moisson Mauricie/Centre-du-Québec, 971
Mouvement national des québécoises et québécois-SSJB de la Mauricie, 977
Les Oblates Missionnaires de Marie Immaculée, 1054
Orchestre symphonique de Trois-Rivières, 1118
Ordre des infirmières et infirmiers du Québec-Ordre régional des infirmières et infirmiers de Mauricie/Centre-du-Québec, 1122
Parents-secours du Québec inc., 1140
Réseau des SADC et CAE-CAE LaPrade Trois-Rivières, 1219
Réseau du sport étudiant du Québec, secteur Mauricie, 1223
FADOQ - Mouvement des aînés du Québec-Région Mauricie, 1224
Réseau québécois des OSBL d'habitation-Mauricie - Centre-du-Québec, 1225
Sidaction Mauricie, 1298
Société canadienne d'histoire de l'Église Catholique - Section française, 1307
Société de généalogie de la Mauricie et des Bois-Francs, 1315
Syndicat des professeurs et des professeures de l'Université du Québec à Trois-Rivières, 1364
UNIFOR-Trois Rivières, 1405

Témiscouata-sur-le-Lac
Chambre de commerce du Témiscouata, 544
Réseau des SADC et CAE-SADC de Témiscouata, 1220

Uashat
Institut Tshakapesh, 843

Geographic Index / Québec - Val Morin

Val Morin
Sivananda Ashram Yoga Camp, 1301

Val-David
Association du Syndrome de Turner du Québec, 132

Val-d'Or
Centraide Abitibi Témiscamingue et Nord-du-Québec, 522
Centre d'amitié autochtone de Val-d'Or, 527
Chambre de commerce de Val-d'Or, 543
Fédération des caisses Desjardins du Québec-Abitibi-Témiscamingue - Nord du Québec, 712
Fédération québécoise des sociétés Alzheimer-Val d'or, 730
Réseau des SADC et CAE-SADC Vallée-de-l'Or, 1222
Société d'histoire et de généalogie de Val-d'Or, 1313

Valcourt
Association des bibliothèques publiques de l'Estrie, 107
Chambre de commerce de Valcourt et Région, 543

Valleyfield
Credit Institute of Canada-Montréal/Québec City Chapter, 641

Varennes
Association des entomologistes amateurs du Québec inc., 112
Chambre de commerce et d'industrie de Varennes, 546

Vaudreuil-Dorion
Association provinciale des constructeurs d'habitations du Québec inc.-Montérégie-Suroît, 168
Chambre de commerce et d'industrie Vaudreuil-Soulanges, 548
Mouvement national des québécoises et québécois-SNQ du Suroît, 977

Verdun
Associated Gospel Churches-Québec Office, 89
Association des locataires de l'Ile-des-Soeurs, 118
The Canadian Red Cross Society-Division du Québec, 466
Comité d'action des citoyennes et citoyens de Verdun, 591
Société d'histoire et de généalogie de Verdun, 1313

Victoriaville
Association coopérative d'économie familiale des Bois-Francs, 98
Association pour l'intégration sociale (Région des Bois-Francs), 166
Association provinciale des constructeurs d'habitations du Québec inc.-Bois-Francs, 168
Association québécoise pour le loisir des personnes handicapées-ARLPH Centre du Québec, 176
Bureau local d'intervention traitant du SIDA, 264
Canadian CED Network, 351
Canadian Horse Breeders' Association, 408
Centrale des syndicats démocratiques-Centre du Québec, 525
Centre de formation en entreprise et récupération Normand-Maurice, 529
Chambre de commerce et d'industrie des Bois-Francs et de l'Érable, 546
Réseau des SADC et CAE-SADC Arthabaska-Érable inc., 1220
FADOQ - Mouvement des aînés du Québec-Région Centre-du-Québec, 1224
Tournoi de Soccer de Victoriaville, 1393

Ville Mont-Royal
Canadian Council on Africa-Québec Office, 370
Montréal Gem & Mineral Club, 972

Ville Saint-Laurent
Fédération des professionnelles et professionnels de l'éducation du Québec-Syndicat des professionnelles et professionnels de l'Ouest de Montréal (SPPOM), 718

Ville-Marie
Association des parents d'enfants handicapés du Témiscamingue inc., 122
Chambre de commerce Témis-Accord, 549
Réseau des SADC et CAE-SADC du Témiscamingue, 1221
Société d'histoire du Témiscamingue, 1312

Vimont
Association coopérative d'économie familiale de l'Ile-Jésus, 97

Warwick
Société d'histoire de Warwick, 1312

Waswanipi
Réseau des SADC et CAE-Eeyou Economic Group, 1220
Waswanipi Cree Model Forest, 1440

Weedon
Chambre de commerce de la région de Weedon, 542
Société d'histoire de Weedon, 1312

Wendake
Assemblée des premières nations du Québec et du Labrador, 88
First Nations Education Council, 738
First Nations SchoolNet-Québec Region, 739
Regroupement des centres d'amitié autochtone du Québec, 1215
Société de communication Atikamekw-Montagnais, 1314
Société touristique des Autochtones du Québec, 1325

Westmount
Association des maisons de commerce extérieur du Québec, 118
Association des médecins omnipraticiens de Montréal, 119
Association G.R.A.N.D., 136
Batshaw Youth & Family Centres, 199
Canadian Institute of Mining, Metallurgy & Petroleum, 417
Canadian Orthopaedic Association, 448
Canadian Society for Aesthetics, 473
Canadians for Health Research, 507
Fédération des médecins omnipraticiens du Québec, 716
International Society for Research in Palmistry Inc.-Consultation Center, 860
Québec Association of Marriage & Family Therapy, 1196

Windsor
Chambre de commerce régionale de Windsor, 549

Saskatchewan

Aberdeen
Canadian Botanical Association, 346

Alameda
Alameda Agricultural Society, 21

Arborfield
Arborfield Board of Trade, 76

Assiniboia
Assiniboia & District Arts Council, 88
Assiniboia & District Chamber of Commerce (SK), 88

Aylsham
Aylsham & District Board of Trade, 191

Balcarres
Nature Saskatchewan-Fort Qu'Appelle Branch, 1001

Battleford
Development & Peace-Saskatchewan, 655
Saskatchewan Registered Music Teachers' Association-Battleford Branch, 1273

Bengough
Bengough Agricultural Society, 205

Big River
Big River Chamber of Commerce, 210

Biggar
Alliance for Canadian New Music Projects-Contemporary Showcase - West Central Saskatchewan, 57
Biggar & District Arts Council, 210
Biggar & District Chamber of Commerce, 211
Saskatchewan Genealogical Society-Biggar Branch, 1266

Blaine Lake
Blaine Lake & District Chamber of Commerce, 214
Ukrainian Genealogical & Historical Society of Canada, 1403

Briercrest
Saskatchewan Genealogical Society-Moose Jaw Branch, 1266

Buffalo Narrows
Buffalo Narrows Chamber of Commerce, 261
Buffalo Narrows Friendship Centre, 261

Canora
Canora Arts Council, 509

Carlyle
Moose Mountain Friendship Centre, 974
Saskatchewan Shorthorn Association, 1274

Carnduff
Saskatchewan Genealogical Society-Southeast Branch, 1266

Caronport
Friends of the Archibald, 762

Carrot River
Carrot River & District Board of Trade, 516

Central Butte
Saskatchewan Genealogical Society-Central Butte Branch, 1266

Ceylon
Saskatchewan Genealogical Society-Pangman Branch, 1266

Choiceland
Choiceland & District Chamber of Commerce, 566

Coronach
Coronach Community Chamber of Commerce, 629

Cowessess
Saskatchewan Aboriginal Land Technicians, 1255

Craven
Saskatchewan Outdoor & Environmental Education Association, 1271

Creelman
Creelman Agricultural Society, 641
Saskatchewan Genealogical Society-Weyburn Branch, 1266

Cudworth
Saskatchewan Music Educators Association, 1270

Cut Knife
Cut Knife Chamber of Commerce, 647

Debden
Debden & District Chamber of Commerce, 652

Eastend
Eastend & District Chamber of Commerce, 669
Eastend Arts Council, 669

Eatonia
Eatonia & District Chamber of Commerce, 671
Eatonia Arts Council, 671

Edam
Canadian Lowline Cattle Association, 428
Edam & District Board of Trade, 674

Elbow
Inland Terminal Association of Canada, 838
Provincial Association of Resort Communities of Saskatchewan, 1190
Saskatchewan Wildlife Federation-Elbow & District Wildlife Federation, 1278

Endeavour
Western Independence Party of Saskatchewan, 1450

Esterhazy
Esterhazy & District Chamber of Commerce, 696

Estevan
Estevan & District Labour Committee, 696
Estevan Arts Council, 697
Estevan Chamber of Commerce, 697
Estevan Exhibition Association, 697
Music for Young Children-Saskatchewan, 984
Saskatchewan Bodybuilding Association, 1260
United Way of Estevan, 1414

Eston
Eston Arts Council, 697
Prairie West Historical Society Inc., 1170
Saskatchewan Genealogical Society-West Central Branch, 1266

Fillmore
Canadian Cutting Horse Association-Saskatchewan, 375

Foam Lake
Foam Lake & District Chamber of Commerce, 741

Fort Qu'Appelle
Fort Qu'Appelle & District Chamber of Commerce, 753
Qu'Appelle Valley Friendship Centre, 1195
Saskatchewan Deaf Sports Association, 1263

Fox Valley
Fox Valley Chamber of Commerce, 756

Goodsoil
Goodsoil & District Chamber of Commerce, 777

Grasswood
Saskatoon Society for the Prevention of Cruelty to Animals Inc., 1280

Gravelbourg
Assemblée communautaire fransaskoise-Bureau de Gravelbourg, 87
Gravelbourg Chamber of Commerce, 782

Gull Lake
Saskatchewan Dental Therapists Association, 1263

Harris
Saskatchewan Physical Education Association, 1271
Welsh Pony & Cob Society of Saskatchewan, 1444

Herbert
Herbert & District Chamber of Commerce, 812

Hudson Bay
Hudson Bay Chamber of Commerce, 824
Saskatchewan Charolais Association, 1260
Saskatchewan/Manitoba Gelbvieh Association, 1279
Urban Municipal Administrators' Association of Saskatchewan, 1422

Humboldt
Canadian Dance Teachers Association-Saskatchewan Branch, 375

Humboldt & District Chamber of Commerce, 827
Humboldt & District Labour Council, 827
Prairie Agricultural Machinery Institute, 1169

Ile-a-la-Crosse
Ile-a-la-Crosse Friendship Centre Inc., 829

Indian Head
Nature Saskatchewan-Indian Head Natural History Society, 1001
Saskatchewan Soil Conservation Association, 1275

Kamsack
Kamsack & District Arts Council, 881
Kamsack & District Chamber of Commerce, 881

Kenaston
Creation Science of Saskatchewan Inc., 639
Kenaston & District Chamber of Commerce, 883
Saskatchewan Dental Assistants' Association, 1263

Kerrobert
Kerrobert Chamber of Commerce, 884

Kindersley
Community Futures Saskatchewan, 598
Early Childhood Intervention Program (ECIP) Sask. Inc.-Kindersley - West Central ECIP Inc., 667
Kindersley Chamber of Commerce, 888
PFLAG Canada Inc.-Kindersley Chapter, 1155

Kinistino
Kinistino & District Chamber of Commerce, 890

Kipling
Kipling Chamber of Commerce, 890
Saskatchewan Lions Eye Bank, 1269

La Ronge
Early Childhood Intervention Program (ECIP) Sask. Inc.-La Ronge - Children North ECIP Inc., 667
First Nations SchoolNet-Saskatchewan & Alberta Region, 739
Kikinahk Friendship Centre, 887
La Ronge & District Chamber of Commerce, 1236

Lake Lenore
AgriVenture Global Ltd, 15

Landis
Landis & District Chamber of Commerce, 897

Langenburg
Langenburg & District Chamber of Commerce, 898

Lanigan
Saskatchewan Registered Music Teachers' Association-East Central Branch, 1273

Leader
Leader Board of Trade, 903

Lloydminster
Early Childhood Intervention Program (ECIP) Sask. Inc.-Lloydminster - Midwest Family Connections, 667
Habitat for Humanity Canada-Saskatchewan - Lloydminster, 797
Lloydminster Agricultural Exhibition Association, 916
Lloydminster German Heritage Society Inc., 916
Lloydminster Interval Home Society, 916
Lloydminster Native Friendship Centre, 916
Lloydminster Region Health Foundation, 916
Lloydminster Society for the Prevention of Cruelty to Animals, 916

Lone Rock
Federation of Saskatchewan Surface Rights Association, 726

Lumsden
Lumsden & District Chamber of Commerce, 920

South Saskatchewan Youth Orchestra, 1336

Macklin
Macklin Chamber of Commerce, 924

Maidstone
Maidstone & District Chamber of Commerce, 926

Mankota
Saskatchewan Genealogical Society-Grasslands Branch, 1266

Maple Creek
Cypress Hills Registered Horse Breeders' Association, 647
Maple Creek Chamber of Commerce, 948

Martensville
Baptist General Conference of Canada-Baptist General Conference in Saskatchewan, 196

Maryfield
Saskatchewan Genealogical Society-Pipestone Branch, 1266
United Empire Loyalists' Association of Canada-Saskatchewan Branch, 1410

Mazenod
Saskatchewan Provincial Rifle Association Inc., 1272

McTaggart
Nature Saskatchewan-Weyburn Nature Society, 1001

Meadow Lake
Early Childhood Intervention Program (ECIP) Sask. Inc.-Meadow Lake - Meadow Lake & Area Early Childhood Services Inc., 667
Meadow Lake & District Chamber of Commerce, 956
Meadow Lake Tribal Council, 956

Melfort
Melfort & District Chamber of Commerce, 959
Melfort Agricultural Society, 959
Melfort Real Estate Board, 959
Saskatchewan Genealogical Society-North-East Branch, 1266

Melville
Melville & District Agri-Park Association Inc., 959
Melville & District Chamber of Commerce, 959
Melville Arts Council, 959
Melville Dance Association, 960
Saskatchewan Martial Arts Association, 1269

Meskanaw
Canadian Chianina Association, 355

Moose Jaw
Canadian Dam Association, 375
Canadian Quarter Horse Association, 464
Early Childhood Intervention Program (ECIP) Sask. Inc.-Moose Jaw - South Central ECIP Inc., 667
The John Howard Society of Saskatchewan-Moose Jaw, 875
Moose Jaw & District Chamber of Commerce, 973
Moose Jaw & District Food Bank, 973
Moose Jaw & District Labour Council, 973
Moose Jaw Exhibition Company Ltd., 974
Moose Jaw Humane Society Inc., 974
Moose Jaw Multicultural Council, 974
Moose Jaw Music Festival, 974
Moose Jaw Real Estate Board, 974
Progressive Conservative Party of Saskatchewan, 1187
The Royal Scottish Country Dance Society-Saskatchewan Branch
Saskatchewan Association of Chiropodists, 1257
Saskatchewan Association of Recreation Professionals, 1258
Saskatchewan Construction Association-Moose Jaw Construction Association, 1261
Saskatchewan Wildlife Federation, 1278

Saskatchewan Wildlife Federation-Moose Jaw Wildlife Federation, 1278
YMCA Canada-YMCA of Moose Jaw, 1471

Moosomin
Moosomin Chamber of Commerce, 974

Muskoday
National Native Addictions Partnership Foundation, 995

Nipawin
Nipawin & District Chamber of Commerce, 1027
Nipawin Exhibition Association Inc., 1027

Norquay
Norquay & District Chamber of Commerce, 1028

North Battleford
Association of Battlefords Realtors, 139
Battlefords Agricultural Society, 200
Battlefords Chamber of Commerce, 200
Battlefords Indian & Métis Friendship Centre, 200
Battlefords Interval House Society, 200
The Battlefords Music Festival, 200
Battlefords United Way Inc., 200
Boys & Girls Clubs of Saskatchewan-Battlefords Boys & Girls Club, 224
Early Childhood Intervention Program (ECIP) Sask. Inc.-North Battleford - Battlefords ECIP Inc., 667
North Battleford & District Labour Council, 1030
Saskatchewan Genealogical Society-Battlefords Branch, 1266
Svoboda Dance Festival Association, 1358

North Weyburn
Saskatchewan Powerlifting Association, 1272

Outlook
Outlook & District Chamber of Commerce, 1133

Paradise Hill
Paradise Hill Chamber of Commerce, 1138

Pilot Butte
Ranch Ehrlo Society, 1204

Preeceville
Nature Saskatchewan-Kelsey Ecological Society, 1001

Prince Albert
The Anglican Church of Canada-Diocese of Saskatchewan, 70
Association of Saskatchewan Forestry Professionals, 161
Canadian Association for Williams Syndrome, 307
Canadian Association for Williams Syndrome-CAWS - Saskatchewan, 307
Childhood Cancer Canada Foundation-SK - Candlelighters - Prince Albert, 560
Early Childhood Intervention Program (ECIP) Sask. Inc.-Prince Albert - Prince Albert ECIP Inc., 667
Gem & Mineral Federation of Canada-Mid Pro Rock & Gem Society, 768
Habitat for Humanity Canada-Saskatchewan - Prince Albert, 797
Indian & Metis Friendship Centre of Prince Albert, 834
Learning Disabilities Association of Saskatchewan-Prince Albert Branch, 905
Merit Contractors Association of Saskatchewan, 962
Mid-Pro Rock & Gem Society, 965
Native Coordinating Council, 997
Nature Saskatchewan-Nature Prince Albert, 1001
Nurse Practitioners of Saskatchewan, 1052
PFLAG Canada Inc.-Prince Albert Chapter, 1156
Prince Albert & District Association of Realtors, 1171

Prince Albert & District Chamber of Commerce, 1171
Prince Albert & District Labour Council, 1171
Prince Albert Exhibition Association, 1171
Prince Albert Model Forest Association Inc., 1171
Saskatchewan Association of Insolvency & Restructuring Professionals, 1257
Saskatchewan Building Officials Association Inc., 1260
Saskatchewan Construction Association-Prince Albert Construction Association, 1262
Saskatchewan Forestry Association, 1265
Saskatchewan Genealogical Society-Prince Albert Branch, 1266
Saskatchewan Registered Music Teachers' Association-Prince Albert Branch, 1273
Tourism Prince Albert, 1390
YWCA Canada-YWCA Prince Albert, 1481

Quill Lake
Saskatchewan Katahdin Sheep Association Inc., 1268

Radisson
Riverbend District Chamber of Commerce, 1234

Radville
Radville Chamber of Commerce, 1203

Redvers
Redvers Chamber of Commerce, 1210

Regina
Agricultural Manufacturers of Canada, 15
AIDS Programs South Saskatchewan, 17
Alcoholics Anonymous-Regina - Central Office, 52
Alliance for Canadian New Music Projects-Contemporary Showcase - Regina, 56
Alliance of Canadian Cinema, Television & Radio Artists-ACTRA Saskatchewan, 58
Alpine Saskatchewan, 59
ALS Society of Saskatchewan, 60
Alzheimer Society of Saskatchewan Inc., 64
American Society of Heating, Refrigerating & Air Conditioning Engineers-Regina Chapter, 1500
Appaloosa Horse Club of Canada-Saskatchewan Appaloosa Club, 73
The Appraisal Institute of Canada - Saskatchewan, 75
Architectural Heritage Society of Saskatchewan, 79
Army Cadet League of Canada-Saskatchewan Branch, 83
Assemblée communautaire fransaskoise, 87
Association canadienne-française de Régina, 96
Association des juristes d'expression française de la Saskatchewan, 118
Association for the Advancement of Scandinavian Studies in Canada, 134
Association of Consulting Engineering Companies - Saskatchewan, 146
Association of Fundraising Professionals-Regina Chapter, 1512
Association of Professional Engineers & Geoscientists of Saskatchewan, 158
Association of Regina Realtors, 160
Association of Translators & Interpreters of Saskatchewan, 163
Austrian Canadian Edelweiss Club of Regina Inc, 188
Basketball Saskatchewan, 199
Benevolent & Protective Order of Elks of Canada, 204
Better Business Bureau of Saskatchewan, 206
Biathlon Saskatchewan, 208
Big Brothers Big Sisters of Saskatchewan-Big Brothers Big Sisters of Regina & Area, 210
Birthright International-Regina Chapter, 212
BMW Clubs Canada-BMW Club of Saskatchewan, 216
Bowling Federation of Saskatchewan, 219
Bowls Saskatchewan Inc., 220

Geographic Index / Saskatchewan - Regina

Boxing Saskatchewan, 220
Canadian Agri-Marketing Association (Saskatchewan), 290
Canadian Artists' Representation Saskatchewan, 296
Canadian Association for the History of Nursing, 305
Canadian Association of Home & Property Inspectors-Saskatchewan Chapter, 318
Canadian Association of Palynologists, 325
Canadian Association of Programs in Public Administration, 329
Canadian Association of Veterans in United Nations Peacekeeping-South Saskatchewan Chapter, 336
Canadian Automobile Association Saskatchewan, 339
Canadian Aviation Historical Society-Regina "Roland Groome" Chapter, 340
Canadian Baptists of Western Canada-Heartland Regional Office, 341
Canadian Bison Association, 344
Canadian Blood Services-Regina, 345
Canadian Bridge Federation, 347
Canadian Business Aviation Association-Saskatchewan Chapter, 348
Canadian Cancer Society-Saskatchewan Division, 349
Canadian Celiac Association-Regina Chapter, 352
Canadian Centre for Policy Alternatives-Saskatchewan Office, 354
Canadian Condominium Institute-CCI-South Saskatchewan Chapter, 362
The Canadian Corps of Commissionaires-South Saskatchewan Division, 365
Canadian Cowboys' Association, 372
Canadian Crop Hail Association, 373
Canadian Culinary Federation-Regina Branch, 374
Canadian Federation of Business & Professional Women's Clubs-Regina, 386
Canadian Federation of Independent Business-Saskatchewan Office, 387
Canadian Hard of Hearing Association-Saskatchewan - Regina Branch, 401
Canadian Home Builders' Association - Saskatchewan-Regina & Region, 407
Canadian Information Processing Society-Saskatchewan Chapter, 411
Canadian Institute of Plumbing & Heating-Saskatchewan Region, 419
Canadian Labour Congress-Prairie Regional Office, 425
Canadian Mental Health Association-Saskatchewan Division, 435
Canadian National Institute for the Blind-Saskatchewan Division, 439
Canadian Office & Professional Employees Union-Region 2 - Local 491, 445
Canadian Office & Professional Employees Union-Region 3 - Local 397, 445
The Canadian Press-Regina Bureau, 459
Canadian Public Relations Society Inc.-CPRS Regina, 463
Canadian Shorthorn Association, 470
Canadian Society of Orthopaedic Technologists-Wascana Chapter, 485
Canadian Taxpayers Federation, 492
Canadian Taxpayers Federation-Prairies (Saskatchewan & Manitoba), 493
Canadian Union of Public Employees-Saskatchewan Division, 499
Canadian Western Agribition Association, 503
Chartered Professional Accountants of Saskatchewan, 553
Chartered Professionals in Human Resources Saskatchewan, 554
Child Evangelism Fellowship of Canada-Child Evangelism Fellowship of Saskatchewan, 559
Childhood Cancer Canada Foundation-SK - Regina Candlelighters, 560

Chinese Medicine & Acupuncture Association of Canada-Saskatchewan Chapter, 565
Chiropractors' Association of Saskatchewan, 565
The Christian & Missionary Alliance in Canada-Canadian Midwest District (CMD) Office, 566
Collaborative Centre for Justice & Safety, 581
Concrete Sask, 610
Conflict Resolution Saskatchewan, 612
Conseil culturel fransaskois, 614
Conseil de la Coopération de la Saskatchewan, 615
Crane Rental Association of Canada, 638
Credit Counselling Society-Regina, 640
Cross Country Saskatchewan, 643
Dress for Success-Regina, 663
Ducks Unlimited Canada-Saskatchewan Provincial Office, 664
Early Childhood Intervention Program (ECIP) Sask. Inc., 667
Early Childhood Intervention Program (ECIP) Sask. Inc.-Regina - Regina Region ECIP, 667
Embroiderers' Association of Canada, Inc.-Saskatchewan - Regina Stitchery Guild, 686
Family Enterprise Xchange-FEX Regina, 703
Financial & Consumer Affairs Authority of Saskatchewan, 736
Fondation fransaskoise, 746
Funeral & Cremation Services Council of Saskatchewan, 764
Girl Guides of Canada-Guides du Canada-Saskatchewan Council, 773
Globe Theatre Society, 775
Grain Services Union (CLC), 779
Gymnastics Saskatchewan, 795
Habitat for Humanity Canada-Saskatchewan - Regina, 798
Hong Kong-Canada Business Association-Saskatchewan Section Office, 820
Indian Métis Christian Fellowship, 834
Insurance Brokers Association of Canada-Insurance Brokers Association of Saskatchewan, 848
Insurance Councils of Saskatchewan, 849
Insurance Institute of Saskatchewan, 850
International Brotherhood of Boilermakers, Iron Ship Builders, Blacksmiths, Forgers & Helpers (AFL-CIO)-Regina (Lodge 555), 1541
International Personnel Management Association - Canada-Saskatchewan Chapter, 859
The John Howard Society of Saskatchewan, 875
Juvenile Diabetes Research Foundation-South Saskatchewan, 879
Kabuki Syndrome Network Inc., 879
The Kidney Foundation of Canada-Regina & District Chapter, 885
Kids Help Phone-Saskatchewan, 886
KidSport Saskatchewan, 887
Law Foundation of Saskatchewan, 901
Law Society of Saskatchewan, 902
Learning Disabilities Association of Saskatchewan-Regina Branch, 905
Lifesaving Society-Saskatchewan Branch, 911
Madonna House Apostolate-Regina, 925
Multilingual Association of Regina, Inc., 979
Multiple Sclerosis Society of Canada-Saskatchewan Division, 980
Museums Association of Saskatchewan, 983
National Orgnization For The Reform Of Marijuana Laws Canada-NORML Saskatchewan, 995
The Nature Conservancy of Canada-Saskatchewan, 1000
Nature Saskatchewan, 1000
Nature Saskatchewan-Nature Regina, 1001
Navy League of Canada-Saskatchewan, 1002
The Neil Squire Foundation-Prairie Regional Office, 1002

New Democratic Party-Saskatchewan NDP, 1014
Nurse Practitioner Association of Canada, 1051
Organization of Saskatchewan Arts Councils, 1126
Osteoporosis Canada-Regina Chapter, 1129
PFLAG Canada Inc.-Regina Chapter, 1156
Pharmacists' Association of Saskatchewan, Inc., 1156
Planned Parenthood Regina, 1162
Polio Regina, 1163
Prairie Rock & Gem Society, 1169
Project Management Institute-Regina/South Saskatchewan, 1585
Psychology Association of Saskatchewan, 1192
Public Service Alliance of Canada-Regina Branch, 1193
Regina & District Chamber of Commerce, 1211
Regina & District Food Bank Inc., 1211
Regina & District Labour Council, 1211
Regina Coin Club, 1211
Regina Exhibition Association Ltd., 1211
Regina Gliding & Soaring Club, 1211
Regina Humane Society Inc., 1211
Regina Immigrant Women Centre, 1211
Regina Multicultural Council, 1212
Regina Musicians' Association, 1212
Regina Philatelic Club, 1212
Regina Policemen Association Inc., 1212
Regina Regional Opportunities Commission, 1212
Regina Symphony Orchestra, 1212
Regina Therapeutic Recreation Association, 1212
Regina Therapeutic Riding Association, 1212
Registered Psychiatric Nurses Association of Saskatchewan, 1214
Ringette Association of Saskatchewan, 1232
Risk & Insurance Management Society Inc.-Saskatchewan Chapter, 1234
Romanian Orthodox Deanery of Canada, 1235
Royal Astronomical Society of Canada-Regina Centre, 1238
The Royal Canadian Legion-Saskatchewan Command, 1240
Royal United Services Institute of Regina, 1243
St. John Ambulance-Saskatchewan Council, 1249
The Salvation Army in Canada-Regina Office, 1253
Sask Sport Inc., 1254
Saskatchewan 5 Pin Bowlers' Association, 1254
Saskatchewan Abilities Council-Regina Branch, 1255
Saskatchewan Amateur Speed Skating Association, 1255
Saskatchewan Applied Science Technologists & Technicians, 1255
Saskatchewan Arts Board, 1256
Saskatchewan Association for Multicultural Education, 1256
Saskatchewan Association of Agricultural Societies & Exhibitions, 1256
Saskatchewan Association of Health Organizations, 1257
Saskatchewan Association of Landscape Architects, 1257
Saskatchewan Association of Licensed Practical Nurses, 1257
Saskatchewan Association of Medical Radiation Technologists, 1257
Saskatchewan Association of Naturopathic Practitioners, 1257
Saskatchewan Association of Rural Municipalities, 1258
Saskatchewan Association of Social Workers, 1258
Saskatchewan Association of Speech-Language Pathologists & Audiologists, 1258
Saskatchewan Athletic Therapists Association, 1258
Saskatchewan Automobile Dealers Association, 1259
Saskatchewan Badminton Association, 1259

Saskatchewan Baseball Association, 1259
Saskatchewan Bison Association, 1259
Saskatchewan Broomball Association, 1260
Saskatchewan Camping Association, 1260
Saskatchewan Cattle Breeders Association, 1260
Saskatchewan CGIT Committee, 1260
Saskatchewan Chamber of Commerce, 1260
Saskatchewan Cheerleading Association, 1261
Saskatchewan Choral Federation, 1261
Saskatchewan Coalition for Tobacco Reduction, 1261
Saskatchewan College of Paramedics, 1261
Saskatchewan College of Pharmacists, 1261
Saskatchewan College of Podiatrists, 1261
Saskatchewan College of Psychologists, 1261
Saskatchewan Construction Association, 1261
Saskatchewan Construction Association-Regina Construction Association, 1262
Saskatchewan Construction Safety Association Inc., 1262
Saskatchewan Council for Archives & Archivists, 1262
Saskatchewan Council for International Co-operation, 1262
Saskatchewan Cultural Exchange Society, 1262
Saskatchewan Curling Association, 1263
Saskatchewan Cycling Association, 1263
Saskatchewan Darts Association, 1263
Saskatchewan Deaf & Hard of Hearing Services Inc., 1263
Saskatchewan Dietitians Association, 1263
Saskatchewan Diving, 1263
Saskatchewan Egg Producers, 1264
Saskatchewan Elocution & Debate Association, 1264
Saskatchewan Environmental Industry & Managers' Association, 1264
Saskatchewan Federation of Labour, 1265
Saskatchewan Field Hockey Association, 1265
Saskatchewan Filmpool Co-operative, 1265
Saskatchewan Genealogical Society, 1265
Saskatchewan Genealogical Society-Regina Branch, 1266
Saskatchewan Government & General Employees' Union, 1266
Saskatchewan Heavy Construction Association, 1267
Saskatchewan High Schools Athletic Association, 1267
Saskatchewan History & Folklore Society Inc., 1267
Saskatchewan Hockey Association, 1267
Saskatchewan Horse Breeders Association, 1267
Saskatchewan Horse Federation, 1267
Saskatchewan Hotel & Hospitality Association, 1267
Saskatchewan Independent Insurance Adjusters' Association, 1268
Saskatchewan Joint Board Retail, Wholesale & Department Store Union, 1268
Saskatchewan Lacrosse Association, 1268
Saskatchewan Land Surveyors' Association, 1268
Saskatchewan Liberal Association, 1268
Saskatchewan Library Association, 1269
Saskatchewan Library Trustees' Association, 1269
Saskatchewan Livestock Association, 1269
Saskatchewan Mining Association, 1270
Saskatchewan Motion Picture Industry Association, 1270
Saskatchewan Municipal Hail Insurance Association, 1270
Saskatchewan Music Festival Association Inc., 1270
Saskatchewan Orchestral Association, Inc., 1270
Saskatchewan Organization for Heritage Languages Inc., 1270
Saskatchewan Palliative Care Association, 1271
Saskatchewan Parks & Recreation Association, 1271

Saskatchewan Party, 1271
The Saskatchewan Poetry Society, 1272
Saskatchewan Pro Life Association, 1272
Saskatchewan Professional Planners Institute, 1272
Saskatchewan Provincial Mediation Board, 1272
Saskatchewan Public Health Association Inc., 1272
Saskatchewan Publishers Group, 1272
Saskatchewan Recording Industry Association, 1273
Saskatchewan Registered Music Teachers' Association, 1273
Saskatchewan Registered Music Teachers' Association-Regina Branch, 1273
Saskatchewan Registered Nurses' Association, 1273
Saskatchewan Safety Council, 1274
Saskatchewan School Boards Association, 1274
Saskatchewan Snowboard Association, 1275
Saskatchewan Soccer Association Inc., 1275
Saskatchewan Society of Medical Laboratory Technologists, 1275
Saskatchewan Sports Hall of Fame & Museum, 1275
Saskatchewan Stock Growers Association, 1276
Saskatchewan Swine Breeders' Association, 1276
Saskatchewan Trade & Export Partnership, 1276
Saskatchewan Trucking Association, 1276
Saskatchewan Union of Nurses, 1277
Saskatchewan Urban Municipalities Association, 1277
Saskatchewan Voice of People with Disabilities, Inc., 1277
Saskatchewan Volleyball Association, 1277
Saskatchewan Wildlife Federation-Regina Wildlife Federation, 1278
Saskatchewan Writers Guild, 1278
Saskatchewan Youth in Care & Custody Network, 1279
SaskCentral, 1280
SaskCulture Inc., 1280
SaskTel Pioneers, 1280
Schizophrenia Society of Saskatchewan, 1284
School Sport Canada, 1284
Scouts Canada-Saskatchewan Council, 1287
Skate Canada-Saskatchewan Section, 1302
Softball Saskatchewan, 1332
South Saskatchewan Community Foundation Inc., 1336
Special Olympics Saskatchewan, 1340
Spina Bifida & Hydrocephalus Association of South Saskatchewan, 1342
Spina Bifida & Hydrocephalus Association of Saskatchewan-South Chapter, 1342
Spinal Cord Injury Saskatchewan-Regina, 1344
Swim Saskatchewan, 1359
Synchro Saskatchewan, 1361
Tennis Saskatchewan, 1371
The Terry Fox Foundation-Saskatchewan Office, 1372
Theatre Saskatchewan, 1375
UNIFOR-Regina, 1405
UNITE HERE Canada-Regina Chapter, 1408
United Church of Canada-Saskatchewan Conference, 1409
United Way of Regina, 1416
University of Regina Faculty Association, 1420
Vocational Rehabilitation Association of Canada-Saskatchewan Society, 1436
Water Polo Saskatchewan Inc., 1441
Women Entrepreneurs of Saskatchewan Inc.-Regina Office, 1460
YMCA Canada-YMCA of Regina, 1472
Youth Ballet & Contemporary Dance of Saskatchewan Inc., 1475
YWCA Canada-YWCA Regina, 1481

Regina Beach
Saskatchewan Snowmobile Association, 1275

Rocanville
Rocanville & District Museum Society Inc., 1235

Rosetown
Rosetown & District Chamber of Commerce, 1236
Saskatchewan Registered Music Teachers' Association-West Central Branch, 1273

Rosthern
Station Arts Centre Cooperative, 1348

Saltcoats
Nature Saskatchewan-Yellowhead Flyway Birding Trail Association, 1001

Saskatoon
Aboriginal Friendship Centres of Saskatchewan, 2
Abundance Canada-Saskatoon Office, 3
Administrative & Supervisory Personnel Association, 8
ADR Institute of Canada-ADR Institute of Saskatchewan Inc., 9
AFOA Canada-AFOA Saskatchewan, 12
Afro-Caribbean Cultural Association of Saskatchewan Inc., 13
AIDS Saskatoon, 17
AIESEC-Saskatoon, 18
Alcoholics Anonymous-Saskatoon - Saskatoon Central Office, 53
The Anglican Church of Canada-Diocese of Saskatoon, 70
Animal Nutrition Association of Canada-Saskatchewan Division, 71
L'Arche Western Region-L'Arche Saskatoon, 78
Architectural Woodwork Manufacturers Association of Canada - Saskatchewan, 80
Army, Navy & Air Force Veterans in Canada-Saskatchewan Provincial Command, 84
Arthritis Society-Saskatchewan Division, 84
Association des parents fransaskois, 122
Association jeunesse fransaskoise, 137
Association of Fundraising Professionals-Saskatoon Chapter
Association of Saskatchewan Realtors, 161
Big Brothers Big Sisters of Saskatchewan-Big Brothers Big Sisters of Saskatoon, 210
Boys & Girls Clubs of Saskatchewan-Boys & Girls Clubs of Saskatoon, 224
Canadian 4-H Council-Saskatchewan, 285
Canadian Arm Wrestling Federation, 295
Canadian Artists' Representation Saskatchewan-Saskatoon Office, 296
Canadian Association for Commonwealth Literature & Language Studies, 298
Canadian Association for Studies in Co-operation, 304
Canadian Association for University Continuing Education, 306
Canadian Association of Blue Cross Plans-Saskatchewan Blue Cross, 309
Canadian Association of Elizabeth Fry Societies-Elizabeth Fry Society of Saskatchewan, 313
Canadian Association of Veterans in United Nations Peacekeeping-North Saskatchewan Chapter, 336
Canadian Bar Association-Saskatchewan Branch, 342
Canadian Bible Society-Saskatchewan District Office, 343
Canadian Blood Services-Saskatoon, 345
Canadian Celiac Association-Saskatoon Chapter, 352
Canadian Condominium Institute-CCI-North Saskatchewan Chapter, 362
Canadian Connemara Pony Society, 363
The Canadian Corps of Commissionaires-North Saskatchewan Division, 365
The Canadian Council on Continuing Education in Pharmacy, 371
Canadian Deafblind Association (National)-Saskatchewan Chapter, 376
Canadian Federation of Business & Professional Women's Clubs-Saskatoon, 386
Canadian Hemophilia Society-Hemophilia Saskatchewan, 404
Canadian History of Education Association, 405
Canadian Home Builders' Association - Saskatchewan, 407
Canadian Home Builders' Association - Saskatchewan-Saskatoon & Region, 408
Canadian Institute of Management-Saskatchewan - Saskatoon/Regina Branch, 417
Canadian Masonry Contractors' Association-Saskatchewan Masonry Institute, 431
Canadian Massage Therapist Alliance, 431
Canadian Masters Cross-Country Ski Association-Saskatchewan, 431
Canadian Parks & Wilderness Society-Saskatoon - Saskatchewan Chapter, 451
Canadian Pony Club-Saskatchewan, 458
Canadian Society for Immunology, 475
Canadian Theological Society, 494
Canadian Thoroughbred Horse Society-Saskatchewan Division, 495
Canadian Warmblood Horse Breeders Association, 502
Canoe Kayak Saskatchewan, 509
Catholic Family Services of Saskatoon, 519
Catholic Health Association of Saskatchewan, 520
Chicken Farmers of Saskatchewan, 557
Child Find Saskatchewan Inc., 559
Children's Hospital Foundation of Saskatchewan, 562
Children's Wish Foundation of Canada-Saskatchewan Chapter, 563
Christian Labour Association of Canada-Saskatoon Regional Office, 568
Citizens Concerned About Free Trade, 570
College of Dental Surgeons of Saskatchewan, 583
College of Family Physicians of Canada-Saskatchewan College of Family Physicians, 585
College of Physicians & Surgeons of Saskatchewan, 588
Credit Institute of Canada-Saskatchewan Chapter, 641
Dance Saskatchewan Inc., 649
Dental Technicians Association of Saskatchewan, 653
Canadian Diabetes Association-North Saskatchewan Regional Leadership Centre, 656
Dress for Success-Saskatoon, 663
Early Childhood Intervention Program (ECIP) Sask. Inc.-Saskatoon - Prairie Hills ECIP Inc., 667
Entomological Society of Saskatchewan, 690
Epilepsy Saskatoon, 694
Evangelical Lutheran Church in Canada-Saskatchewan Synod, 698
Family Enterprise Xchange-FEX Saskatoon, 703
Farmers of North America, 705
Farmers of North America Strategic Agriculture Institute, 705
Fédération des aînés fransaskois, 711
Federation of Saskatchewan Indian Nations, 726
Federation of Saskatchewan Indian Nations-Office of Treaty Governance Processes, 726
Fibromyalgia Association of Saskatchewan, 733
Friends of the Forestry Farm House Inc., 762
Funeral Advisory & Memorial Society of Saskatchewan, 764
Canadian Youth Business Foundation-Saskatchewan Office, 765
Genome Canada-Genome Prairie, 769
Greater Saskatoon Chamber of Commerce, 785
Habitat for Humanity Canada-Saskatchewan - Saskatoon, 798
Health Sciences Association of Saskatchewan, 807
Heart & Stroke Foundation of Saskatchewan, 809
Horseshoe Saskatchewan Inc., 822
Huntington Society of Canada-Saskatoon & Area, 828
Indigenous Works, 835
Institute of Space & Atmospheric Studies, 847
Interior Designers Association of Saskatchewan, 852
International Women of Saskatoon, 861
Islamic Association of Saskatchewan, 864
The John Howard Society of Saskatchewan-Saskatoon, 875
Junior Achievement of Canada-Junior Achievement of Saskatchewan, 877
Juvenile Diabetes Research Foundation-Saskatoon, 879
The Kidney Foundation of Canada-Saskatchewan Branch, 885
Last Post Fund-Saskatchewan Branch, 899
Learning Disabilities Association of Saskatchewan, 905
The Leukemia & Lymphoma Society of Canada-Prairies/Territories Branch - Saskatoon, 909
Lupus SK Society, 922
Massage Therapist Association of Saskatchewan, 953
Mechanical Contractors Association of Saskatchewan Inc., 957
Meewasin Valley Authority, 959
Mennonite Central Committee Canada-MCC Saskatchewan, 961
Mennonite Church Canada-Mennonite Church Saskatchewan, 961
Métis Nation - Saskatchewan, 963
National Farmers Foundation, 993
National Farmers Union, 993
Nature Saskatchewan-Saskatoon Nature Society, 1001
Neurofibromatosis Association of Saskatchewan, 1003
Osteoporosis Canada-Saskatoon Chapter, 1129
Our Lady of The Prairies Foundation, 1133
Oxfam Canada-Saskatoon - Prairies Regional Office, 1134
Parenting Education Saskatchewan, 1140
Parkinson Society Saskatchewan, 1141
Partners FOR the Saskatchewan River Basin, 1144
PAVED Arts, 1146
Pentecostal Assemblies of Canada-Saskatchewan District Office, 1150
Persons Living with AIDS Network of Saskatchewan Inc., 1152
PFLAG Canada Inc.-Saskatoon Chapter, 1156
Prince Albert Gliding & Soaring Club, 1171
Project Management Institute-North Saskatchewan
Public Legal Education Association of Saskatchewan, Inc., 1192
Public Service Alliance of Canada-Saskatoon Branch, 1193
Radiation Safety Institute of Canada-National Laboratories, 1202
Réseau Santé en français de la Saskatchewan, 1225
Royal Astronomical Society of Canada-Saskatoon Centre, 1239
Royal University Hospital Foundation, 1243
Rushnychok Ukrainian Folk Dancing Association, 1244
The Salvation Army in Canada-Saskatoon Office, 1253
Sask Pork, 1254
Saskatchewan Abilities Council, 1255
Saskatchewan Abilities Council-Saskatoon Branch, 1255
Saskatchewan Agricultural Graduates' Association Inc., 1255
Saskatchewan Agricultural Hall of Fame, 1255
Saskatchewan Amateur Wrestling Association, 1255

Geographic Index / Saskatchewan - Shaunavon

Saskatchewan Archaeological Society, 1256
Saskatchewan Archaeological Society-Saskatchewan Association of Professional Archaeologists, 1256
Saskatchewan Archaeological Society-Saskatoon Archaeological Society, 1256
Saskatchewan Association for Community Living, 1256
Saskatchewan Association of Architects, 1256
Saskatchewan Association of Library Technicians, Inc., 1257
Saskatchewan Association of Optometrists, 1257
Saskatchewan Association of Rehabilitation Centres, 1258
Saskatchewan Association of School Councils, 1258
Saskatchewan Association of Veterinary Technologists, Inc., 1258
Saskatchewan Athletics, 1259
Saskatchewan Baton Twirling Association, 1259
Saskatchewan Black Powder Association, 1259
Saskatchewan Blind Sports Association Inc., 1259
Saskatchewan Brain Injury Association, 1260
Saskatchewan Canola Development Commission, 1260
Saskatchewan Cerebral Palsy Association, 1260
Saskatchewan College of Opticians, 1261
Saskatchewan College of Physical Therapists, 1261
Saskatchewan Conference of Mennonite Brethren Churches, 1261
Saskatchewan Construction Association-Saskatoon Construction Association, 1262
Saskatchewan Co-operative Association, 1262
Saskatchewan Council for Educators of Non-English Speakers, 1262
Saskatchewan Craft Council, 1262
Saskatchewan Cultural Society of the Deaf, 1263
Saskatchewan Deaf & Hard of Hearing Services-Saskatoon Office, 1263
Saskatchewan Dental Hygienists' Association, 1263
Saskatchewan Eco-Network, 1264
Saskatchewan Economic Development Association, 1264
Saskatchewan Economics Association, 1264
Saskatchewan Emergency Medical Services Association, 1264
Saskatchewan Environmental Society, 1264
Saskatchewan Fencing Association, 1265
Saskatchewan Food Processors Association, 1265
Saskatchewan Genealogical Society-Saskatoon Branch, 1266
Saskatchewan German Council Inc., 1266
Saskatchewan Golf Association Inc., 1266
Saskatchewan Graphic Arts Industries Association, 1266
Saskatchewan Ground Water Association, 1266
Saskatchewan Herb & Spice Association, 1267
Saskatchewan Home Based Educators, 1267
Saskatchewan Institute of Agrologists, 1267
Saskatchewan Intercultural Association Inc., 1268
Saskatchewan Karate Association, 1268
Saskatchewan Literacy Network, 1269
Saskatchewan Lung Association, 1269
Saskatchewan Medical Association, 1270
Saskatchewan Orchid Society, 1270
Saskatchewan Outfitters Association, 1271
Saskatchewan Physiotherapy Association, 1272
Saskatchewan Playwrights Centre, 1272
Saskatchewan Prevention Institute, 1272
Saskatchewan Pulse Growers, 1273
Saskatchewan Registered Music Teachers' Association-Saskatoon Branch, 1273
Saskatchewan Rental Housing Industry Association, 1274
Saskatchewan Rowing Association, 1274

Saskatchewan School Library Association, 1274
Saskatchewan Sheep Breeders' Association, 1274
Saskatchewan Ski Association - Skiing for Disabled, 1274
Saskatchewan Society for Education through Art, 1275
Saskatchewan Society for the Prevention of Cruelty to Animals, 1275
Saskatchewan Society of Occupational Therapists, 1275
Saskatchewan Squash, 1276
Saskatchewan Table Tennis Association Inc., 1276
Saskatchewan Teachers' Federation, 1276
Saskatchewan Triathlon Association Corporation, 1276
Saskatchewan Turkey Producers' Marketing Board, 1276
Saskatchewan Underwater Council, 1276
Saskatchewan Veterinary Medical Association, 1277
Saskatchewan Wall & Ceiling Bureau Inc., 1277
Saskatchewan Waste Reduction Council, 1277
Saskatchewan Water & Wastewater Association, 1277
Saskatchewan Weekly Newspapers Association, 1278
Saskatchewan Wheelchair Sports Association, 1278
Saskatchewan Wildlife Federation-Saskatoon Wildlife Federation, 1278
Saskatoon & District Labour Council, 1279
Saskatoon City Police Association, 1279
Saskatoon Civic Middle Management Association, 1279
Saskatoon Coin Club, 1279
Saskatoon Community Foundation, 1279
Saskatoon Crisis Intervention Service, 1279
Saskatoon Farmers' Markets, 1279
Saskatoon Food Bank & Learning Centre, 1279
Saskatoon Heritage Society, 1279
Saskatoon Indian & Métis Friendship Centre, 1279
Saskatoon Lapidary & Mineral Club, 1279
Saskatoon Musicians' Association, 1279
Saskatoon Open Door Society Inc., 1279
Saskatoon Parents of Twins & Triplets Organization, 1280
Saskatoon Region Association of REALTORS, 1280
Saskatoon Senior Citizens Action Now Inc., 1280
Saskatoon Soaring Club, 1280
Saskatoon Symphony Society, 1280
Saskatoon Youth Orchestra, 1280
Schizophrenia Society of Saskatchewan-Saskatoon Chapter, 1284
Serena Canada-Saskatchewan Branch, 1291
Sexual Health Centre Saskatoon, 1293
SF Canada, 1293
Sign Association of Canada-Saskatchewan Chapter, 1299
Skills/Compétences Canada-Saskatchewan, 1303
Autism Treatment Services of Canada-Saskatchewan - Autism Services, 1327
Society of Graphic Designers of Canada-Saskatchewan North Chapter, 1329
Spina Bifida & Hydrocephalus Association of Saskatchewan-North Chapter, 1342
Spinal Cord Injury Saskatchewan, 1344
Supply Chain Management Association - Saskatchewan, 1356
Swiss Club Saskatoon, 1359
Telemiracle/Kinsmen Foundation Inc., 1369
Tourism Saskatoon, 1391
La Troupe du Jour, 1399
Ukrainian Canadian Congress-Saskatchewan Provincial Council, 1402
United Way of Saskatoon & Area, 1416
University of Saskatchewan Arts Council, 1420
University of Saskatchewan Faculty Association, 1420

Vaccine & Infectious Disease Organization, 1423
Western Canadian Association of Bovine Practitioners, 1448
Western Canadian Wheat Growers, 1449
Western Grains Research Foundation, 1449
Women Entrepreneurs of Saskatchewan Inc., 1460
YMCA Canada-YMCA of Saskatoon, 1472
YWCA Canada-YWCA Saskatoon, 1481

Shaunavon
Cypress Hills Ability Centres, Inc., 647
Saskatchewan Families for Effective Autism Treatment, 1265
Shaunavon Arts Council, 1294
Shaunavon Chamber of Commerce, 1294

Shellbrook
Canadian Tarentaise Association, 492

Silton
La Leche League Canada, 905

Spiritwood
Spiritwood Chamber of Commerce, 1344

St Walburg
St. Walburg Chamber of Commerce, 1251

St-Isidor-de-Bellevue
Assemblée communautaire fransaskoise-Bureau de St-Isidore de Bellevue, Domrémy et St Louis, 87

Swift Current
Association of Saskatchewan Home Economists, 161
Early Childhood Intervention Program (ECIP) Sask. Inc.-Swift Current - Swift Current ECIP Inc., 667
Nature Saskatchewan-Southwest Naturalists, 1001
Saskatchewan Abilities Council-Swift Current Branch, 1255
Saskatchewan Genealogical Society-Swift Current Branch, 1266
Saskatchewan Registered Music Teachers' Association-Swift Current Branch, 1273
Swift Current & District Chamber of Commerce, 1358
Swift Current Agricultural & Exhibition Association, 1358
Swift Current Creek Watershed Stewards, 1358
Swift Current United Way, 1358

Tisdale
Early Childhood Intervention Program (ECIP) Sask. Inc.-Tisdale - North East ECIP Inc., 667
Tisdale & District Chamber of Commerce, 1380

Unity
Unity & District Chamber of Commerce, 1418

Vanscoy
Vanscoy & District Agricultural Society, 1429

Vibank
Holstein Canada-Saskatchewan Branch, 819

Vonda
Vonda Chamber of Commerce, 1439

Wakaw
Wakaw & District Board of Trade, 1439

Warman
Judo Saskatchewan, 876
Saskatchewan Archery Association, 1256
Saskatchewan Council for Exceptional Children, 1262

Waskesiu Lake
Waskesiu Chamber of Commerce, 1440

Watrous
Watrous & District Chamber of Commerce, 1442
Watrous Area Arts Council, 1442

Watson
Watson & District Chamber of Commerce, 1443

Weyburn
Early Childhood Intervention Program (ECIP) Sask. Inc.-Weyburn - Weyburn & Area ECIP Inc., 667
Early Childhood Intervention Program (ECIP) Sask. Inc.-Weyburn - Holy Family RCSSD 140, 667
Enform: The Safety Association for the Upstream Oil & Gas Industry-Saskatchewan Office, 688
Midwives Association of Saskatchewan, 965
Real Estate Institute of Canada-Saskatchewan Chapter, 1206
Saskatchewan Early Childhood Association, 1263
Saskatchewan Hereford Association, 1267
Saskatchewan Wildlife Federation-Weyburn Wildlife Federation, 1278
Weyburn & District Labour Council, 1451
Weyburn & District United Way, 1451
Weyburn Agricultural Society, 1451
Weyburn Chamber of Commerce, 1451

White City
Canadian Pension & Benefits Institute-Saskatchewan Region, 453

Wilcox
Rural Municipal Administrators' Association of Saskatchewan, 1244

Wymark
Saskatchewan Meat Processors' Association, 1270

Wynyard
Wynyard & District Chamber of Commerce, 1470

Yorkton
Boys & Girls Clubs of Saskatchewan-Boys & Girls Club of Yorkton, 224
Early Childhood Intervention Program (ECIP) Sask. Inc.-Yorkton - Parkland ECIP Inc., 667
Nature Saskatchewan-Yorkton Natural History Society, 1001
PFLAG Canada Inc.-Yorkton - East Central Chapter, 1156
Sask Taekwondo, 1254
Saskatchewan Abilities Council-Yorkton Branch, 1255
Saskatchewan Aboriginal Women's Circle Corporation, 1255
Saskatchewan Band Association, 1259
Saskatchewan Beekeepers Association, 1259
Saskatchewan Genealogical Society-Yorkton Branch, 1266
Saskatchewan Professional Fire Fighters Burn Unit Fund, 1272
Saskatchewan Reading Council, 1273
Saskatchewan Registered Music Teachers' Association-Yorkton Branch, 1273
Tourism Yorkton, 1392
Yorkton & District Labour Council, 1474
Yorkton & District United Way Inc., 1474
Yorkton Chamber of Commerce, 1474
Yorkton Film Festival, 1474
Yorkton Friendship Centre, 1474
Yorkton Real Estate Association Inc., 1474
Yorkton Society for the Prevention of Cruelty to Animals Inc., 1474

Zenon Park
Zenon Park Board of Trade, 1482

Yukon Territory

Dawson City
Dawson City Chamber of Commerce, 652
Klondike Visitors Association, 892
Many Rivers Counselling & Support Services-Dawson City, 948

Faro
Faro Humane Society, 706

Haines Junction
Many Rivers Counselling & Support Services-Haines Junction, 948
St. Elias Chamber of Commerce, 1248
TESL Yukon, 1373

Mayo
Silver Trail Chamber of Commerce, 1299

Teslin
Teslin Regional Chamber of Commerce, 1373

Watson Lake
Many Rivers Counselling & Support Services-Watson Lake, 948
Watson Lake Chamber of Commerce, 1443

Whitehorse
Aikido Yukon Association, 18
The Anglican Church of Canada-Diocese of the Yukon, 70
Association franco-yukonnaise, 136
Association of Professional Engineers of Yukon, 159
Association of Yukon Communities, 164
Athletics Yukon, 181
Autism Yukon, 189
Bed & Breakfast Association of the Yukon, 203
Biathlon Yukon, 208
Big Brothers Big Sisters of Yukon, 210
Blood Ties Four Directions Centre, 215
Boys & Girls Clubs of Yukon, 224
Canada-Yukon Business Service Centre, 284
Canadian Bar Association-Yukon Branch, 342
Canadian Masters Cross-Country Ski Association-Yukon, 431
Canadian Mental Health Association-Yukon Division, 435
Canadian Parks & Wilderness Society-Whitehorse - Yukon Chapter, 451
Consulting Engineers of Yukon, 625
Contagious Mountain Bike Club, 626
Council of Yukon First Nations, 635
Cross Country Yukon, 644
Cycling Association of the Yukon, 647
Ducks Unlimited Canada-Yukon Territory Office, 664
Elder Active Recreation Association, 681
Equine Association of Yukon, 694
Les EssentiElles, 696
Golden Age Society, 776
The Guild Society, 794
Habitat for Humanity Canada-Yukon, 798
Hockey Yukon, 818
Humane Society Yukon, 826
Jazz Yukon, 869
Judo Yukon, 876
Klondike Placer Miners' Association, 892
Klondike Snowmobile Association, 892
Law Society of Yukon, 902
Learning Disabilities Association of Yukon Territory, 905
Madonna House Apostolate-Whitehorse, 925
Many Rivers Counselling & Support Services, 948
Mediation Yukon Society, 957
Medical Laboratory Science Association of Yukon, 958
Music Yukon, 984
New Democratic Party-Yukon NDP, 1014
Northern Film & Video Industry Association, 1034
Office of the Yukon Superintendent of Securities, 1055
Partenariat communauté en santé, 1143
People First Society of Yukon, 1151
Polarettes Gymnastics Club, 1163
Public Service Alliance of Canada-Whitehorse Branch, 1193
Recreation & Parks Association of the Yukon, 1207
St. John Ambulance-Yukon Branch, 1249
Skills/Compétences Canada-Yukon, 1303
Skookum Jim Friendship Centre, 1303
Softball Yukon, 1332
Special Olympics Yukon, 1340
Sport Yukon, 1345
Swim Yukon, 1359
Synchro Yukon Association, 1361
Table Tennis Yukon, 1366
Tourism Industry Association of the Yukon, 1390
Trail & Ultra Running Association Of The Yukon, 1394
VeloNorth Cycling Club, 1431
Volleyball Yukon, 1438
Whitehorse Chamber of Commerce, 1452
Whitehorse Cross Country Ski Club, 1453
Whitehorse Glacier Bears Swim Club, 1453
Whitehorse Minor Hockey Association, 1453
Whitehorse Minor Soccer Association, 1453
Whitehorse Women's Hockey Association, 1453
Wilderness Tourism Association of the Yukon, 1454
Yukon Aboriginal Sport Circle, 1476
Yukon Aboriginal Women's Council, 1477
Yukon Agricultural Association, 1477
Yukon Amateur Radio Association, 1477
Yukon Amateur Speed Skating Association, 1477
Yukon Art Society, 1477
Yukon Arts Centre, 1477
Yukon Association for Community Living, 1477
Yukon Badminton Association, 1477
Yukon Broomball Association, 1477
Yukon Chamber of Commerce, 1477
Yukon Chamber of Mines, 1477
Yukon Child Care Association, 1477
Yukon Church Heritage Society, 1477
Yukon Conservation Society, 1477
Yukon Contractors Association, 1478
Yukon Council of Archives, 1478
Yukon Council on Aging, 1478
Yukon Curling Association, 1478
Yukon Denturist Association, 1478
Yukon Employees Union, 1478
Yukon Federation of Labour, 1478
Yukon Film Society, 1478
Yukon First Nations Culture & Tourism Association, 1478
Yukon Fish & Game Association, 1478
Yukon Foundation, 1478
Yukon Freestyle Ski Association, 1478
Yukon Golf Association, 1478
Yukon Green Party, 1478
Yukon Gymnastics Association, 1478
Yukon Historical & Museums Association, 1478
Yukon Horse & Rider Association, 1479
Yukon Indian Hockey Association, 1479
Yukon Law Foundation, 1479
Yukon Learn Society, 1479
Yukon Liberal Party, 1479
Yukon Medical Association, 1479
Yukon Mine Training Association, 1479
Yukon Order of Pioneers, 1479
Yukon Orienteering Association, 1479
Yukon Outdoors Club, 1479
Yukon Outfitters' Association, 1479
Yukon Party, 1479
Yukon Prospectors' Association, 1479
Yukon Public Legal Education Association, 1479
Yukon RCMP Veteran's Association, 1479
Yukon Real Estate Association, 1480
Yukon Registered Nurses Association, 1480
Yukon River Marathon Paddlers Association, 1480
Yukon Schools' Athletic Association, 1480
Yukon Shooting Federation, 1480
Yukon Soccer Association, 1480
Yukon Sourdough Rendezvous Society, 1480
Yukon Speech-Language Pathology & Audiology Association, 1480
Yukon Teachers' Association, 1480
Yukon Territory Environmental Network, 1480
Yukon Tourism Education Council, 1480
Yukon Trappers Association, 1480

Mailing List Index

- Canadian and foreign associations that rent mailing lists of members, listed by subject
- An entry may appear under more than one subject
- Each entry is accompanied by a page number which points you to the corresponding listing in the alphabetical listings of both Canadian and foreign associations
- Contact association for more information on rental fees, etc.

Acadians
Fédération des communautés francophones et acadienne du Canada, 713

Accounting
Canadian Academic Accounting Association, 285

Administrative Assistants
International Association of Administrative Professionals, 1537

Administrative Sciences
Association canadienne des sciences régionales, 95

Adult Education
Centre de documentation sur l'éducation des adultes et la condition féminine, 529

Advertising
The Advertising Club of Toronto, 10
Canadian Marketing Association, 430
National Advertising Benevolent Society, 989

Africa
African Medical & Research Foundation Canada, 13

African Studies
African Literature Association, 1486

Aging
Association québécoise de défense des droits des personnes retraitées et préretraitées, 169
Canadian Association on Gerontology, 337
International Federation on Aging, 857
Mid-Toronto Community Services, 965
Réseau FADOQ, 1223

Agricultural Economics
International Association of Agricultural Economists, 1537

Agriculture
Alberta Conservation Tillage Society II, 31
Fédération de l'UPA de la Beauce, 709
Fédérations de l'UPA de Lévis Bellechasse, Rive Nord, Lotbinière-Mégantic, 731
International Peat Society - Canadian National Committee, 859
Melville & District Agri-Park Association Inc., 959
Western Barley Growers Association, 1447

Agriculture & Youth
Association des jeunes ruraux du Québec, 117

Agroforestry
World Agroforestry Centre, 1602

Air Cadets
Air Cadet League of Canada, 19

Alumni
National Hockey League Alumni Association, 994

Alzheimer's Disease
Alzheimer Society Ontario, 65

American Studies
American Studies Association, 1503

Animal Rights Movement
People for the Ethical Treatment of Animals, 1583
Sea Shepherd Conservation Society - USA, 1588

Animal Welfare
Edmonton Humane Society for the Prevention of Cruelty to Animals, 677
ZOOCHECK Canada Inc., 1482

Anthropology & Ethnology
Canadian Sociological Association, 488

Antiquities
Archaeological Institute of America, 1505

Aquaculture
American Fisheries Society, 1493

Aquariums
Association of Zoos & Aquariums, 1513

Arab Countries
Middle East Studies Association of North America, 1571

Archaeology
Archaeological Institute of America, 1505

Architectural Conservation
Action Patrimoine, 6

Architecture
Alberta Association of Architects, 23
Architectural Institute of British Columbia, 79
Manitoba Association of Architects, 929
Union internationale des architectes, 1598

Art
The Canadian Art Foundation, 295

Arts & Crafts
Ontario Crafts Council, 1075

Arts Councils
Arts Richmond Hill, 86
Conseil de la culture de L'Abitibi-Témiscamingue, 615
Conseil de la culture de Lanaudière, 616
Conseil régional de la culture et des communications de la Côte-Nord, 621
Red Deer & District Allied Arts Council, 1209

Asia
Pacific Asia Travel Association (Eastern Canada Chapter), 1134

Associations
American Society of Association Executives, 1499

Athletics
Amateur Athletic Union, 1487
Athletics New Brunswick, 181
British Columbia Athletics, 233

Atmosphere
Sierra Club of Canada, 1298

Auditing
ISACA, 1567

Auditoriums
International Association of Venue Managers, Inc., 1540

Autism
Autism Nova Scotia, 188

Automobile Clubs
Auto Sport Québec, 189

Automobiles
Automobile Journalists Association of Canada, 189

Automotive Industry
Ontario Automotive Recyclers Association, 1067

Aviation
Association québécoise de Vol Libre, 171

Bands, Musical
Ontario Band Association, 1067

Bankruptcy
Ontario Association of Insolvency & Restructuring Professionals, 1064

Baseball
Newfoundland Baseball, 1022

Basketball
Newfoundland & Labrador Basketball Association, 1017

Beads
Society of Bead Researchers, 1592

Beekeeping
Canadian Honey Council, 408
Ontario Beekeepers' Association, 1067

Bible
Catholic Biblical Association of Canada, 517

Bibliographers
Bibliographical Society of America, 1514

Bicycling
Canadian Independent Bicycle Retailers Association, 410
Cycling British Columbia, 647
Saskatchewan Cycling Association, 1263

Bilingualism
Canadian Parents for French, 450

Biochemistry
Canadian Society for Molecular Biosciences, 476

Biotechnology
BIOTECanada, 212

Birds
American Birding Association, Inc., 1490
Bird Studies Canada, 212

Blindness
Canadian Blind Sports Association Inc., 344
Christian Blind Mission International, 566

Boards of Education
Canadian School Boards Association, 468

Boards of Trade
Edam & District Board of Trade, 674
Mississauga Board of Trade, 969
Toronto Region Board of Trade, 1387

Book Trade
Antiquarian Booksellers' Association of Canada, 72
Association des distributeurs exclusifs de livres en langue française inc., 111
Canadian Booksellers Association, 346

Botany
American Public Gardens Association, 1497

Breeding
Ayrshire Breeders Association of Canada, 191
Fédération des producteurs de bovins du Québec, 717
Ontario Brown Swiss Association, 1069

Building Inspection
New Brunswick Building Officials Association, 1006

Building Materials
British Columbia Shake & Shingle Association, 253

Business
International Association of Business Communicators,
Canadian Corporate Counsel Association, 365
Canadian Management Centre, 429
International Association of Business Communicators, 1538
Ontario Council of Alternative Businesses, 1075

Business Travel
Society of Incentive & Travel Executives of Canada, 1329

Camping
Alberta Camping Association, 27
Association des camps du Québec inc., 108
British Columbia Camping Association, 234

Canada & Canadian Studies
Association for Canadian Studies, 133
Canada's History, 282
The Council of Canadians, 633

Cardiology
Canadian Cardiovascular Society, 350

Caribbeans & the Caribbean
Centre for Research on Latin America & The Caribbean, 533

Catholics & Catholicism
Catholic Biblical Association of Canada, 517

Cattle
Ayrshire Breeders Association of Canada, 191
Fédération des producteurs de bovins du Québec, 717
Ontario Brown Swiss Association, 1069

Chambers of Commerce
Assiniboia Chamber of Commerce (MB), 88
Atikokan Chamber of Commerce, 181
Big River Chamber of Commerce, 210
Bouctouche Chamber of Commerce, 218
British Columbia Chamber of Commerce, 235
Burlington Chamber of Commerce, 265
Burnaby Board of Trade, 265
Cambridge Chamber of Commerce, 275
Chambre de commerce de Clare, 540
Chambre de commerce de la MRC de Rivière-du-Loup, 542
Chambre de commerce de Valcourt et Région, 543
Chambre de commerce des Îles-de-la-Madeleine, 544
Chambre de commerce et d'industrie de Laval, 545
Chambre de commerce et d'industrie de Québec, 546
Chambre de commerce et d'industrie secteur Saint-Félicien inc., 547
Chambre de commerce St-Martin de Beauce, 549
Dawson Creek & District Chamber of Commerce, 652
Georgina Chamber of Commerce, 771
Greater Kingston Chamber of Commerce, 783
Greater Kitchener & Waterloo Chamber of Commerce, 783
Greater Peterborough Chamber of Commerce, 784
Greater Westside Board of Trade, 787
Halton Hills Chamber of Commerce, 800
Hamilton Chamber of Commerce, 801
Kelowna Chamber of Commerce, 883
Kimberley & District Chamber of Commerce, 887
Kitimat Chamber of Commerce, 891
Kugluktuk Chamber of Commerce, 894
London Chamber of Commerce, 918
The Manitoba Chambers of Commerce, 933
Melfort & District Chamber of Commerce, 959
Niagara-on-the-Lake Chamber of Commerce, 1026
Parksville & District Chamber of Commerce, 1142
Penticton & Wine Country Chamber of Commerce, 1151
Red Deer Chamber of Commerce, 1209
Regina & District Chamber of Commerce, 1211
Richmond Hill Chamber of Commerce, 1230
Saanich Peninsula Chamber of Commerce, 1245

Mailing List Index / Chemical Engineering

St Thomas & District Chamber of Commerce, 1251
Sarnia Lambton Chamber of Commerce, 1254
Scugog Chamber of Commerce, 1287
Southern Georgian Bay Chamber of Commerce, 1337
Spruce Grove & District Chamber of Commerce, 1346
Thompson Chamber of Commerce, 1376
Vanderhoof Chamber of Commerce, 1429
Vulcan & District Chamber of Commerce, 1439
Weyburn Chamber of Commerce, 1451
Whitehorse Chamber of Commerce, 1452

Chemical Engineering
Chemical Institute of Canada, 556

Chemical Industry
Canadian Consumer Specialty Products Association, 363
National Association of the Chemistry Industry, 1574

Chemistry
Chemical Institute of Canada, 556

Child Welfare
Child Welfare League of Canada, 560

Children
Canadian Paediatric Society, 449

Children - Diseases
British Columbia Lions Society for Children with Disabilities, 245

Chiropractic Health Care
British Columbia Chiropractic Association, 236

Choral Music
Bach Elgar Choir, 192
National Association of Teachers of Singing, 1574

Christian Education
Ontario Alliance of Christian Schools, 1059

Christians & Christianity
Action des Chrétiens pour l'abolition de la torture, 6
Association internationale des études patristiques, 1509
Brethren in Christ, 228
Christian Blind Mission International, 566

Commerce
GS1 Canada, 792

Communications
BIOTECanada, 212
International Association of Business Communicators, 1538

Community Development
Canadian Institute of Planners, 418
Federation of Canadian Municipalities, 723
Horizons of Friendship, 821
USC Canada, 1423

Community Information Services
Community Care Peterborough, 596
Community Connection, 596
Community Information Centre of Ottawa, 599
Findhelp Information Services, 737
Haldimand-Norfolk Information Centre, 798
Jewish Information Referral Service Montréal, 873
South Essex Community Centre, 1334
211 Southwest Ontario, 1401
Volunteer Centre of Guelph/Wellington, 1438

Community Planning
Saskatchewan Professional Planners Institute, 1272

Compensation Management
World at Work, 1603

Composers
Foundation Assisting Canadian Talent on Recordings, 755

Computer Software
Association québécoise des technologies, 174

Computers
ARMA Canada, 81
The Instrumentation, Systems & Automation Society of America, 1534
ISACA, 1567

Conflict Resolution
Peace & Justice Studies Association, 1583

Conservation of Natural Resources
Alberta Conservation Tillage Society II, 31
International Peat Society - Canadian National Committee, 859
National Wildlife Federation, 1577
USC Canada, 1423

Construction Industry
Alberta Construction Association, 31
Association of Construction Inspectors, 1511
Canadian Home Builders' Association - New Brunswick, 407
Construction Specifications Canada, 624
Nova Scotia Home Builders' Association, 1045
Orillia & District Construction Association, 1126

Consultants & Consulting
Association des firmes de génie-conseil - Québec, 114
Association of Consulting Engineering Companies - Canada, 145

Contractors
Corporation des maîtres électriciens du Québec, 630
Electrical Association of Manitoba Inc., 682
Electrical Contractors Association of BC, 682

Copyright
Intellectual Property Institute of Canada, 850

Counselling
British Columbia Association of Clinical Counsellors, 231
Maison de Campagne & d'Entraide Communautaire du Lac, 926

Cricket
Cricket Council of Ontario, 642

Crime
Victims of Violence, 1432

Crisis Intervention Services
Distress Centres of Toronto, 659

Critics
Association internationale de la critique littéraire, 1509

Cultural Affairs
Société des attractions touristiques du Québec, 1317

Culture
Conseil de la culture du Bas-Saint-Laurent, 616
Italian Cultural Institute (Istituto Italiano di Cultura), 866

Dance
Melville Dance Association, 960
O Vertigo Danse, 1052

Dental Surgery
College of Dental Surgeons of British Columbia, 583
Royal College of Dental Surgeons of Ontario, 1241

Dentistry
College of Dental Surgeons of British Columbia, 583
Dental Association of Prince Edward Island, 653
New Brunswick Dental Society, 1007
Nova Scotia Dental Association, 1044
Ordre des dentistes du Québec, 1121

Denturism
Denturist Association of Canada, 653

Design
Society of Graphic Designers of Canada, 1329

Developing Countries
Christian Blind Mission International, 566
Horizons of Friendship, 821
Inter Pares, 851

Development Education
Canadian Bureau for International Education, 347

Developmentally Disabled Persons
British Columbia Lions Society for Children with Disabilities, 245
Community Living Mississauga, 603
Community Living South Huron, 605
Inclusion BC, 831

Dietitians & Nutritionists
Nova Scotia Dietetic Association, 1044
Prince Edward Island Dietetic Association, 1173

Direct Marketing
Canadian Marketing Association, 430
Data & Marketing Association, 1521

Disabled Persons
Canadian Abilities Foundation, 285
North Shore Disability Resource Centre Association, 1032

Disorders
Irritable Bowel Syndrome Self Help & Support Group, 864

Doors & Windows
Door & Access Systems Manufacturers Association, 1521

Down Syndrome
Down Syndrome Association of Toronto, 661

Drilling
Canadian Diamond Drilling Association, 377

Drunk Driving
MADD Canada, 925

East European Studies
Canadian Association of Slavists, 333

Ecology
Conservation Council of New Brunswick, 621
Ecological Society of America, 1522
John E. Mack Institute, 1568
Sierra Club of Canada, 1298
World Agroforestry Centre, 1602
World Wildlife Fund - Canada, 1468

Economic Development
Association canadienne des sciences régionales, 95
Economic Developers Association of Canada, 672
Fondation de l'entrepreneurship, 743
Horizons of Friendship, 821
Niagara Economic Development, 1025

Economics
American Economic Association, 1492
Connexions Information Sharing Services, 613
International Institute of Fisheries Economics & Trade, 1551
Responsible Investment Association, 1227

Education
Canadian Bureau for International Education, 347
Centre de documentation sur l'éducation des adultes et la condition féminine, 529
International Arthurian Society - North American Branch, 1535
International Association of Educators for World Peace - USA, 1538
Peace & Justice Studies Association, 1583

Electrical Engineering
Illuminating Engineering Society of North America, 1530

Electrical Industry
Corporation des maîtres électriciens du Québec, 630
Electrical Association of Manitoba Inc., 682
Electrical Contractors Association of BC, 682

Electronic Data Interchange
GS1 Canada, 792

Electronic Instruments
The Instrumentation, Systems & Automation Society of America, 1534

Emergency Housing
Adsum for Women & Children, 9

Employment
Regroupement québécois des organismes pour le développement de l'employabilité, 1216

Energy
Canadian Institute of Energy (British Columbia), 415

Engineering
Applied Science Technologists & Technicians of British Columbia, 74
Association des firmes de génie-conseil - Québec, 114
Association des ingénieurs municipaux du Québec, 116
Association for Facilities Engineering, 1508
Association of Consulting Engineering Companies - Canada, 145
Association of Environmental Engineering & Science Professors, 1511
NACE International, 1571
Society of Fire Protection Engineers, 1593
Society of Tribologists & Lubrication Engineers, 1594

English Language
American Dialect Society, 1492
Association of Canadian College & University Teachers of English, 141
Québec Community Newspaper Association, 1196

English as a Second Language
Association of British Columbia Teachers of English as an Additional Language, 140

Entertainment
Association québécoise de l'industrie du disque, du spectacle et de la vidéo, 170

Entomology
Entomological Society of Saskatchewan, 690

Environment
Alberta Environmental Network, 33
British Columbia Environmental Network, 240
Connexions Information Sharing Services, 613
Greenpeace USA, 1529
Muniscope, 982
NACE International, 1571
Sierra Club of Canada, 1298
Worldwatch Institute, 1608

Environment Industry
Association of Environmental Engineering & Science Professors, 1511
Environmental Services Association of Nova Scotia, 692
National Association of Environmental Professionals, 1573

Environmental Biology
Canadian Society of Environmental Biologists, 482

Environmental Health
International Society for Environmental Epidemiology, 1557

Environmental Law
The Environmental Law Centre (Alberta) Society, 692

Epilepsy & Related Disorders
Epilepsy Saskatoon, 694

Equestrian Sports & Activities
Equestrian Canada, 694
Manitoba Horse Council Inc., 938
Ontario Competitive Trail Riding Association Inc., 1073
Ontario Equestrian Federation, 1078

Esperanto
Esperanto Association of Canada, 695
International Society of Friendship & Good Will, 1560

Executives
American Society of Association Executives, 1499

Canadian Association of Women Executives & Entrepreneurs, 336
Society of Incentive & Travel Executives of Canada, 1329

Exhibitions & Fairs
Association des professionnels en exposition du Québec, 126
Festivals et Événements Québec, 733
German-Canadian Mardi Gras Association Inc., 772
Vancouver Jewish Film Centre Society, 1427

Facility Management
International Facility Management Association, 1546

Family
Metro (Toronto) Association of Family Resource Programs, 963

Family Therapy
Alberta Association of Marriage & Family Therapy, 24

Farms & Farming
Alberta Conservation Tillage Society II, 31
Association des jeunes ruraux du Québec, 117
Fédération de l'UPA de la Beauce, 709
Fédérations de l'UPA de Lévis Bellechasse, Rive Nord, Lotbinière-Mégantic, 731

Festivals
Festivals et Événements Québec, 733
Intrepid Theatre Co. Society, 862
Vancouver Jewish Film Centre Society, 1427

Film
Association des réalisateurs et réalisatrices du Québec, 127
Canadian Film Institute, 390

Finance
Cercle de la finance internationale de Montréal, 537
Responsible Investment Association, 1227

Fire Fighting
Canadian Association of Fire Chiefs, 315

Fire Protection & Prevention
Society of Fire Protection Engineers, 1593

Fisheries
American Fisheries Society, 1493
International Institute of Fisheries Economics & Trade, 1551

Fisheries Science
American Fisheries Society, 1493

Flags
Canadian Flag Association, 391

Folk Dancing
Fraser Valley Square & Round Dance Association, 758

Folk Music
Canadian Society for Traditional Music, 479
Folk Festival Society of Calgary, 742

Folklore
Folklore Studies Association of Canada, 742

Food Industry
Association des détaillants en alimentation du Québec, 110

Football
Canadian Football League, 392
Football Nova Scotia Association, 750
Ontario Football Alliance, 1080

Forest Industries
Conseil de l'industrie forestière du Québec, 615

Forestry
North Shore Forest Products Marketing Board, 1032
World Agroforestry Centre, 1602

Foster Parents
British Columbia Federation of Foster Parent Associations, 240

Foundations
African Medical & Research Foundation Canada, 13
The Canadian Art Foundation, 295
Canadian Liver Foundation, 427
Canadian Ornamental Plant Foundation, 448
Canadian Orthopaedic Foundation, 448
Fondation des maladies mentales, 745
Foundation Assisting Canadian Talent on Recordings, 755

Founding
American Foundry Society, 1493
Canadian Foundry Association, 394

Francophones in Canada
Fédération des communautés francophones et acadienne du Canada, 713
Hebdos Québec, 810

Fraternal Organizations
Knights of Pythias - Domain of British Columbia, 892

French Language
Association canadienne d'éducation de langue française, 90
Association des distributeurs exclusifs de livres en langue française inc., 111
Association des juristes d'expression française de la Saskatchewan, 118
Canadian Parents for French, 450
Société de développement des périodiques culturels québécois, 1314

Funeral Planning
Corporation des thanatologues du Québec, 630

Geography
Association of American Geographers, 1510

Germany
German-Canadian Mardi Gras Association Inc., 772

Gerontology
Canadian Association on Gerontology, 337

Gifted Children
Association of Educators of Gifted, Talented & Creative Children in BC, 147

Global Governance
Institute for Planetary Synthesis, 1532
World Federalist Movement - Canada, 1465
Worldwatch Institute, 1608

Goats
Syndicat des producteurs de chèvres du Québec, 1363

Golf
British Columbia Golf Association, 242
Professional Golfers' Association of Canada, 1185

Government
National Institute of Governmental Purchasing, Inc., 1576
The Public Affairs Association of Canada, 1192

Grains
Grain Elevator & Processing Society, 1528
Western Barley Growers Association, 1447

Graphic Arts & Design
Society of Graphic Designers of Canada, 1329

Great Lakes
Citizens' Environment Alliance, 570

HIV/AIDS
AIDS Saint John, 17
Intervention régionale et information sur le sida en Estrie, 862

Hairdressing
Allied Beauty Association, 58

Hard of Hearing
Island Deaf & Hard of Hearing Centre, 865
Réseau québécois pour l'inclusion social des personnnes sourdes et malentendantes, 1225

Health
Association des intervenantes et des intervenants en soins spirituels du Québec, 117
Health Association Nova Scotia, 805
The Regional Health Authorities of Manitoba, 1212

Health Care
African Medical & Research Foundation Canada, 13

Health Care Facilities
HealthCareCAN, 807

Health Professionals
Canadian Register of Health Service Psychologists, 466

Hearing Impaired
Canadian Association of the Deaf, 334
Island Deaf & Hard of Hearing Centre, 865

Heritage
Action Patrimoine, 6

Hiking
American Hiking Society, 1494

History
American Historical Association, 1494
American Society for Legal History, 1498
Canada's History, 282
Canadian Oral History Association, 446
Canadian Science & Technology Historical Association, 468
Friends Historical Association, 1527
International Arthurian Society - North American Branch, 1535
Multicultural History Society of Ontario, 979
Newfoundland Historical Society, 1023
Organization of American Historians, 1581
Société d'histoire du Témiscamingue, 1312

Hockey
Canadian Hockey League, 406
Hockey Alberta, 817
Hockey Development Centre for Ontario, 817
Hockey Québec, 818
National Hockey League Alumni Association, 994

Home Care
Ontario Community Support Association, 1073

Honey
Canadian Honey Council, 408

Horses
Equestrian Canada, 694
Manitoba Horse Council Inc., 938
Ontario Equestrian Federation, 1078
Peruvian Horse Association of Canada, 1152
Standardbred Canada, 1347

Horseshoe Pitching
Nova Scotia Horseshoe Players Association, 1046

Horticulture
American Public Gardens Association, 1497
Canadian Ornamental Plant Foundation, 448

Hospitality Industry
Ontario Farm & Country Accommodations Association, 1078

Hospitals
HealthCareCAN, 807
International Hospital Federation, 1550

Hotels & Motels
Hotel Association of Canada Inc., 823

Housing
Canadian Housing & Renewal Association, 409
Muniscope, 982
Ontario Coalition Against Poverty, 1071

Human Resources
BIOTECanada, 212
Forum for International Trade Training, 754
International Personnel Management Association - Canada, 859
International Society for Performance Improvement, 1558
Ordre des conseillers en ressources humaines agréés, 1120

Human Rights
Amnesty International - Canadian Section (English Speaking),
B'nai Brith Canada, 192
Canadian Committee of Lawyers & Jurists for World Jewry, 361
Social Justice Committee, 1305

Humanities
Association for Canadian Studies, 133
Association of Canadian College & University Teachers of English, 141

Hypertension
World Hypertension League, 1466

Immigrants
Kamloops Immigrant Services, 880
Ontario Council of Agencies Serving Immigrants, 1075

Independent Schools
Ontario Alliance of Christian Schools, 1059
Québec Association of Independent Schools, 1196

Industrial Design
Association of Canadian Industrial Designers, 142

Industrial Engineering
Association for Facilities Engineering, 1508
Institute of Industrial & Systems Engineers, 1533

Industrial Materials, Advanced
ASM International, 1506

Information Technology
GS1 Canada, 792
Information Systems Security Association, 1532
International Association of Business Communicators, 1538
Ontario Library & Information Technology Association, 1088

Interior Design
Association professionnelle des designers d'intérieur du Québec, 167
Interior Designers Institute of British Columbia, 852

International Cooperation
Horizons of Friendship, 821
Inter Pares, 851
International Society of Friendship & Good Will, 1560
International Student Pugwash, 1562
Social Justice Committee, 1305

International Law
American Society of International Law, 1500

International Relations
Canadian Bureau for International Education, 347
Canadian Commission for UNESCO, 360
Connexions Information Sharing Services, 613
World Federalist Movement - Canada, 1465

International Relief
Doctors without Borders Canada, 660

International Trade
Forum for International Trade Training, 754
World Trade Centre Montréal, 1467

Investment
Investment Property Owners Association of Nova Scotia Ltd., 863
Responsible Investment Association, 1227

Italian Canadians & Italy
Italian Cultural Institute (Istituto Italiano di Cultura), 866

Jewellery
Canadian Jewellers Association, 423
Society of Bead Researchers, 1592

Jewish People
Hashomer Hatzair Canada, 804
Jewish Information Referral Service Montréal, 873
Vancouver Jewish Film Centre Society, 1427

Jewish Studies
Aish Thornhill Community Shul & Learning Centre, 20

Journalism
Automobile Journalists Association of Canada, 189
Canadian Association of Journalists, 319
Canadian University Press, 499
Hebdos Québec, 810

Judaism
Aish Thornhill Community Shul & Learning Centre, 20
B'nai Brith Canada, 192
Canadian Committee of Lawyers & Jurists for World Jewry, 361

Kinesiology
Ontario Kinesiology Association, 1088

LGBTQ
Lace Up Your Cleats, 895

Labour Relations
Association canadienne des relations industrielles, 94
Ordre des conseillers en ressources humaines agréés, 1120

Labour Unions
Association des réalisateurs et réalisatrices du Québec, 127
British Columbia Nurses' Union, 248
Syndicat de professionnelles et professionnels du gouvernement du Québec, 1362

Lacrosse
Canadian Lacrosse Association, 425

Land Surveying
Association of Manitoba Land Surveyors, 151
Ordre des arpenteurs-géomètres du Québec, 1120

Land Use
World Agroforestry Centre, 1602

Landscape Architecture
Manitoba Association of Landscape Architects, 930

Language Disorders
International Society for Augmentative & Alternative Communication, 860

Language Teaching
Association canadienne d'éducation de langue française, 90

Languages
American Dialect Society, 1492
Esperanto Association of Canada, 695
Modern Language Association of America, 1571

Latin America
Centre for Research on Latin America & The Caribbean, 533

Law
American Society for Legal History, 1498
Canadian Corporate Counsel Association, 365

Lawyers
Association des juristes d'expression française de la Saskatchewan, 118
Canadian Committee of Lawyers & Jurists for World Jewry, 361

Learned Societies
American Sociological Association, 1503
American Studies Association, 1503
Archaeological Institute of America, 1505
Association internationale des études patristiques, 1509
Association of Canadian College & University Teachers of English, 141
Bibliographical Society of America, 1514
Canadian Association of Slavists, 333
Canadian Political Science Association, 457
Canadian Psychological Association, 462
Canadian Science & Technology Historical Association, 468
Canadian Sociological Association, 488
International Political Science Association, 859
Medieval Academy of America, 1570
Organization of American Historians, 1581

Librarians
Association des bibliothécaires professionnel(le)s du Nouveau-Brunswick, 107

Libraries
Canadian Urban Libraries Council, 500
Ontario College & University Library Association, 1072
Ontario Library & Information Technology Association, 1088

Lighting
Illuminating Engineering Society of North America, 1530

Linguistics
American Dialect Society, 1492

Literature
African Literature Association, 1486
International Arthurian Society - North American Branch, 1535

Liver & Biliary Tract Diseases
Canadian Liver Foundation, 427

Livestock
Canadian Hackney Society, 399

Long Term Care Facilities
HealthCareCAN, 807
Ontario Long Term Care Association, 1089

Lumber Industry
Conseil de l'industrie forestière du Québec, 615

Management
American Society of Association Executives, 1499
Canadian Management Centre, 429
Canadian Society of Association Executives, 480
Canadian Urban Libraries Council, 500
International Association of Venue Managers, Inc., 1540

Manufacturing
Association for Operations Management, 134
Door & Access Systems Manufacturers Association, 1521

Maps
Antiquarian Booksellers' Association of Canada, 72

Marine Mammals
Sea Shepherd Conservation Society - USA, 1588

Marine Trades
The Canadian Marine Industries and Shipbuilding Association, 430
Vancouver Maritime Museum, 1427

Marketing
Canadian Marketing Association, 430

Martial Arts
Karate New Brunswick, 881

Materials Management
National Institute of Governmental Purchasing, Inc., 1576

Mathematics
Canadian Mathematical Society, 431

Measuring Instruments
The Instrumentation, Systems & Automation Society of America, 1534

Meat
Fédération des producteurs de bovins du Québec, 717
Saskatchewan Meat Processors' Association, 1270

Medical Libraries
Canadian Health Libraries Association, 402

Medical Radiation
Ordre des technologues en imagerie médicale, en radio-oncologie et en élétrophysiologie médicale du Québec, 1124

Medicine
Doctors of BC, 660
New Brunswick Medical Society, 1010

Medieval Studies
International Arthurian Society - North American Branch, 1535
Medieval Academy of America, 1570

Mental Health
American Psychological Association, 1497
Fondation des maladies mentales, 745

Metal Industries
American Foundry Society, 1493

Missions & Missionaries
Christian Blind Mission International, 566

Molding (Founding)
American Foundry Society, 1493

Molecular Biology
Canadian Society for Molecular Biosciences, 476

Multiculturalism
Multicultural Association of Northwestern Ontario, 979
Multicultural History Society of Ontario, 979
North Shore Multicultural Society, 1033

Municipal Government
Alberta Urban Municipalities Association, 50
Association des ingénieurs municipaux du Québec, 116
Association francophone des municipalités du Nouveau-Brunswick Inc., 135
Corporation des officiers municipaux agréés du Québec, 630
Federation of Canadian Municipalities, 723
Municipalities Newfoundland & Labrador, 982
Saskatchewan Urban Municipalities Association, 1277
Union des municipalités du Québec, 1406

Museums
O'Keefe Ranch & Interior Heritage Society, 1053
Vancouver Maritime Museum, 1427

Music
Association québécoise de l'industrie du disque, du spectacle et de la vidéo, 170
Canadian Society for Traditional Music, 479
Classical Accordion Society of Canada, 572

Music Festivals
Canadian Music Festival Adjudicators' Association, 438
Federation of Canadian Music Festivals, 723

Music Teachers
Alberta Registered Music Teachers' Association, 44

Musicians
Sault Ste Marie Musicians' Association, 1281

Muslims
Muslim World League - Canada, 985

Native Peoples
Association for Native Development in the Performing & Visual Arts, 134

Newspapers
British Columbia & Yukon Community Newspapers Association, 229
Circulation Management Association of Canada, 570
Hebdos Québec, 810
Québec Community Newspaper Association, 1196

Nurses
British Columbia Nurses' Union, 248
Canadian Orthopaedic Nurses Association, 448
Independent Practice Nurses Interest Group, 833

Nursing Homes
Ontario Long Term Care Association, 1089

Nutrition
Nova Scotia Dietetic Association, 1044
Prince Edward Island Dietetic Association, 1173

Occupational Health & Safety
Canadian Society of Safety Engineering, Inc., 487
Occupational Hygiene Association of Ontario, 1054

Occupational Therapy
Canadian Association of Occupational Therapists, 323
Canadian Association of Occupational Therapists - British Columbia, 324
New Brunswick Association of Occupational Therapists, 1005
Ontario Society of Occupational Therapists, 1107
Saskatchewan Society of Occupational Therapists, 1275

Offenders (Criminal) & Ex-Offenders
The John Howard Society of Ontario, 874

Office Employees
International Association of Administrative Professionals, 1537

Oil
NORA, An Association of Responsible Recyclers, 1578

Opera
Opera America Inc., 1580

Ophthalmology
Canadian Ophthalmological Society, 446

Opticians
Ordre des opticiens d'ordonnances du Québec, 1123

Optometry
American Optometric Association, 1496
College of Optometrists of Ontario, 587

Oral Surgeons
College of Dental Surgeons of British Columbia, 583
Royal College of Dental Surgeons of Ontario, 1241

Orchestras
Ensemble contemporain de Montréal, 690
International Symphony Orchestra of Sarnia, Ontario & Port Huron, Michigan, 861
Orchestras Mississauga, 1117

Organ Retrieval & Donation
Canadian Liver Foundation, 427

Orienteering
Canadian Orienteering Federation, 447

Orthopaedics
Canadian Orthopaedic Foundation, 448
Canadian Orthopaedic Nurses Association, 448

Pain
International Association for the Study of Pain, 1537

Pakistani Canadians
Pakistan Canada Association of Edmonton, 1137

Parents
British Columbia Federation of Foster Parent Associations, 240
Canadian Parents for French, 450

Patents
Intellectual Property Institute of Canada, 850

Peace
Canadian Peace Alliance, 452
Institute for Planetary Synthesis, 1532
International Association of Educators for World Peace - USA, 1538
Peace & Justice Studies Association, 1583

World Federalist Movement - Canada, 1465

Peat
International Peat Society - Canadian National Committee, 859

Performing Arts
American Society for Theatre Research, 1499
Association for Native Development in the Performing & Visual Arts, 134
Association québécoise des marionnettistes, 173
Canadian Arts Presenting Association, 296
Intrepid Theatre Co. Society, 862
Melville Dance Association, 960
O Vertigo Danse, 1052
Toronto Alliance for the Performing Arts, 1381

Periodicals & Magazines
Société de développement des périodiques culturels québécois, 1314

Pharmacology
Canadian Society of Pharmacology & Therapeutics, 486

Pharmacy
Association québécoise des pharmaciens propriétaires, 174

Physical Education & Training
Fédération des éducateurs et éducatrices physiques enseignants du Québec, 714

Physicians
Collège des médecins du Québec, 582
College of Physicians & Surgeons of New Brunswick, 588
College of Physicians & Surgeons of Prince Edward Island, 588
College of Physicians & Surgeons of Saskatchewan, 588
Doctors of BC, 660
Doctors without Borders Canada, 660

Planning
Alberta Professional Planners Institute, 43
American Planning Association, 1496
Canadian Institute of Planners, 418

Plastics
Canadian Plastics Industry Association, 455

Playwriting
Playwrights Guild of Canada, 1162

Podiatry
Canadian Podiatric Medical Association, 456

Political Organizations
Nova Scotia Progressive Conservative Association, 1047

Political Science
Canadian Political Science Association, 457
International Political Science Association, 859

Poverty
Ontario Coalition Against Poverty, 1071
Réseau d'action et de communication pour le développement international, 1218

Printing Industries
Association des enseignants en infographie et en imprimerie du Québec, 112

Production Control
Association for Operations Management, 134

Professional Development
International Society for Performance Improvement, 1558

Property Management
Investment Property Owners Association of Nova Scotia Ltd., 863

Psychology
American Psychological Association, 1497
Canadian Psychological Association, 462
Canadian Register of Health Service Psychologists, 466
John E. Mack Institute, 1568
L'Ordre des psychologues du Québec, 1123
Psychologists Association of Alberta, 1192

Public Administration
Muniscope, 982
Ontario Association of Committees of Adjustment & Consent Authorities, 1063
The Public Affairs Association of Canada, 1192

Public Libraries
Canadian Urban Libraries Council, 500

Publishing
Association of Book Publishers of British Columbia, 140
Association of Canadian Publishers, 143
Association of Canadian University Presses, 144
Playwrights Guild of Canada, 1162
Specialized Information Publishers Association, 1596

Puppetry
Association québécoise des marionnettistes, 173

Purchasing
National Institute of Governmental Purchasing, Inc., 1576
Ontario Public Buyers Association, 1098

Québec
Office du tourisme et des congrès de Québec, 1055
Québec dans le monde, 1196
Société des attractions touristiques du Québec, 1317

Race Relations
B'nai Brith Canada, 192
Center for Research-Action on Race Relations, 522
Kamloops Immigrant Services, 880

Racquetball
Racquetball Canada, 1202

Radio Broadcasting
Foundation Assisting Canadian Talent on Recordings, 755

Radiology
Canadian Association of Radiologists, 330

Railroads & Railways
National Association of Railroad Passengers, 1573

Rainforests
Rainforest Alliance, 1586

Real Estate
Investment Property Owners Association of Nova Scotia Ltd., 863

Recording Industry
Association québécoise de l'industrie du disque, du spectacle et de la vidéo, 170
Foundation Assisting Canadian Talent on Recordings, 755

Records Management
ARMA Canada, 81

Recycling
NORA, An Association of Responsible Recyclers, 1578
Ontario Automotive Recyclers Association, 1067
Resource Recycling Inc., 1586

Refugees
U.S. Committee for Refugees & Immigrants, 1601

Regional Development
Association canadienne des sciences régionales, 95

Rehabilitation
The John Howard Society of Ontario, 874
Vocational Rehabilitation Association of Canada, 1436

Religion
Association des intervenantes et des intervenants en soins spirituels du Québec, 117

Religious Society of Friends
Friends Historical Association, 1527

Research
American Society for Theatre Research, 1499
Canadian Institute for Research in Nondestructive Examination, 413
Centre for Research on Latin America & The Caribbean, 533
International Research Group on Wood Protection, 1556
Muniscope, 982
Peace & Justice Studies Association, 1583
Society of Bead Researchers, 1592
World Agroforestry Centre, 1602

Retail Trade
International Federation of Hardware & Housewares Association, 1548

Retirement
Association québécoise de défense des droits des personnes retraitées et préretraitées, 169

Rivers & Streams
Black Creek Conservation Project, 213

Romanian Canadians & Romania
Fondation roumaine de Montréal, 748

Safety Engineering
American Society of Safety Engineers, 1502
Canadian Society of Safety Engineering, Inc., 487

Science
Canadian Science & Technology Historical Association, 468
International Student Pugwash, 1562

Sculpture
Sculptors Society of Canada, 1287

Seafood
International Institute of Fisheries Economics & Trade, 1551

Secretaries
International Association of Administrative Professionals, 1537

Security Services
Information Systems Security Association, 1532

Senior Citizens
Association québécoise de défense des droits des personnes retraitées et préretraitées, 169
Mid-Toronto Community Services, 965
Réseau FADOQ, 1223

Sex Therapy
Association des sexologues du Québec, 128

Shipbuilding
The Canadian Marine Industries and Shipbuilding Association, 430

Skiing
Association des stations de ski du Québec, 128
Canadian Freestyle Ski Association, 394
Canadian Ski Council, 471

Small Business
Fondation de l'entrepreneurship, 743

Snowboarding
Canadian Ski Council, 471

Snowmobiles
British Columbia Snowmobile Federation, 253

Soccer
Lace Up Your Cleats, 895

Social Development
Réseau d'action et de communication pour le développement international, 1218

Social Policy
Social Justice Committee, 1305

Social Services
Alberta Association of Marriage & Family Therapy, 24
Mid-Toronto Community Services, 965

Regroupement québécois des organismes pour le développement de l'employabilité, 1216
Youth in Care Canada, 1475

Social Work
Maison de Campagne & d'Entraide Communautaire du Lac, 926

Sociology
American Sociological Association, 1503
Canadian Sociological Association, 488

Soil Science
Alberta Conservation Tillage Society II, 31
International Union of Soil Sciences, 1565

Space Sciences
National Space Society, 1577
The Planetary Society, 1584

Speakers
Canadian Association of Professional Speakers, 329

Speech Disorders
International Society for Augmentative & Alternative Communication, 860

Speech-Language Pathologists & Audi
Alberta College of Speech-Language Pathologists & Audiologists, 30
New Brunswick Association of Speech-Language Pathologists & Audiologists, 1006

Sports
Amateur Athletic Union, 1487

Sports for the Disabled
Canadian Blind Sports Association Inc., 344

Sports, Amateur
Hockey Alberta, 817
Hockey Québec, 818
Newfoundland Baseball, 1022

Standards
Canadian Evaluation Society, 383

Statistics
International Statistical Institute, 1562

Storytelling
Canadian Oral History Association, 446

Students
International Student Pugwash, 1562

Surgeons
College of Physicians & Surgeons of New Brunswick, 588
College of Physicians & Surgeons of Prince Edward Island, 588
College of Physicians & Surgeons of Saskatchewan, 588

Sustainable Development
American Fisheries Society, 1493
International Institute of Fisheries Economics & Trade, 1551
Muniscope, 982
USC Canada, 1423
Wildlife Habitat Canada, 1454

Swimming
Swimming Canada, 1359
Synchro BC, 1360

Table Tennis
Alberta Table Tennis Association, 48
Saskatchewan Table Tennis Association Inc., 1276
Table Tennis Canada, 1366

Teaching
Association des enseignants en infographie et en imprimerie du Québec, 112
Association of British Columbia Teachers of English as an Additional Language, 140
Association of Canadian College & University Teachers of English, 141
Association of Educators of Gifted, Talented & Creative Children in BC, 147
National Association of Teachers of Singing, 1574

Technicians & Technologists
Applied Science Technologists & Technicians of British Columbia, 74
Ordre des technologues en imagerie médicale, en radio-oncologie et en élétrophysiologie médicale du Québec, 1124
Ordre des technologues professionnels du Québec, 1124

Technology
Advanced Card Technology Association of Canada, 9
ASM International, 1506
Canadian Science & Technology Historical Association, 468
International Student Pugwash, 1562

Telecommunications
Canadian Wireless Telecommunications Association, 504

Television Broadcasting
Association des réalisateurs et réalisatrices du Québec, 127

The Arts
Canadian Arts Presenting Association, 296
Yukon Art Society, 1477

The Middle East
Middle East Studies Association of North America, 1571

Theatre
American Society for Theatre Research, 1499
Intrepid Theatre Co. Society, 862
Toronto Alliance for the Performing Arts, 1381

Therapeutic Riding
Pacific Riding for Developing Abilities, 1136

Torture
Action des Chrétiens pour l'abolition de la torture, 6
Canadian Centre for Victims of Torture, 354

Tourism
Muskoka Tourism, 985
Niagara Economic Development, 1025
North of Superior Tourism Association, 1031
Office du tourisme et des congrès de Québec, 1055
Ontario Farm & Country Accommodations Association, 1078
Tourism Industry Association of Nova Scotia, 1390
Tourism Toronto, 1391
Tourisme Montérégie, 1393

Trade
International Institute of Fisheries Economics & Trade, 1551

Trade Marks
Intellectual Property Institute of Canada, 850

Transportation
Association québécoise des transports, 175
Atlantic Provinces Trucking Association, 185
Canadian Council of Motor Transport Administrators, 369
National Association of Railroad Passengers, 1573
The Van Horne Institute for International Transportation & Regulatory Affairs, 1424

Travel Industry
Association of Canadian Travel Agencies - Atlantic, 144
Association of Canadian Travel Agents - Québec, 144
Northwest Ontario Sunset Country Travel Association, 1036
Pacific Asia Travel Association (Eastern Canada Chapter), 1134

Tribology & Lubrication
Society of Tribologists & Lubrication Engineers, 1594

Trucks & Trucking
Atlantic Provinces Trucking Association, 185
British Columbia Trucking Association, 257

Turkish Canadians
Federation of Canadian Turkish Associations, 723

United Nations
Canadian Commission for UNESCO, 360
World Federalist Movement - Canada, 1465

Universities & Colleges
Association of Canadian College & University Teachers of English, 141
Association of Canadian University Presses, 144
Association of Registrars of the Universities & Colleges of Canada, 161
Canadian University Press, 499

University & College Libraries
Ontario College & University Library Association, 1072

Urban Planning
Canadian Institute of Planners, 418
Muniscope, 982

Vacation Industry
Ontario Farm & Country Accommodations Association, 1078

Veterinary Medicine
College of Veterinarians of Ontario, 590
Manitoba Veterinary Medical Association, 946
Newfoundland & Labrador Veterinary Medical Association, 1022

Video
Association québécoise de l'industrie du disque, du spectacle et de la vidéo, 170
Foundation Assisting Canadian Talent on Recordings, 755

Violence
Association québécoise Plaidoyer-Victimes, 176
Victims of Violence, 1432

Visual Arts
Association for Native Development in the Performing & Visual Arts, 134

Volleyball
Volleyball Alberta, 1437
Volleyball Canada, 1437
Volleyball Prince Edward Island, 1438

Water Resources
American Water Resources Association, 1504

Wilderness
Sierra Club of Canada, 1298

Wildlife
Canadian Wildlife Federation, 504
National Wildlife Federation, 1577
Wildlife Habitat Canada, 1454

Wildlife Conservation
Association of Zoos & Aquariums, 1513
Sea Shepherd Conservation Society - USA, 1588
Sierra Club of Canada, 1298
Toronto Zoo, 1388
World Wildlife Fund - Canada, 1468
ZOOCHECK Canada Inc., 1482

Wine
Wine Writers' Circle of Canada, 1458

Women
Centre de documentation sur l'éducation des adultes et la condition féminine, 529
Inter Pares, 851
Lace Up Your Cleats, 895
National Action Committee on the Status of Women, 989

Women in Business, Industry & Trade
Canadian Association of Women Executives & Entrepreneurs, 336
Centre de documentation sur l'éducation des adultes et la condition féminine, 529
Women Who Excel Inc., 1461

Women in Crisis
Adsum for Women & Children, 9

Women in Professions
Canadian Association of Women Executives & Entrepreneurs, 336

Wood
International Research Group on Wood Protection, 1556

Writers
Wine Writers' Circle of Canada, 1458

Young Offenders
The John Howard Society of Ontario, 874

Youth
Hashomer Hatzair Canada, 804
World Assembly of Youth, 1603
Youth in Care Canada, 1475

Zionism
Hashomer Hatzair Canada, 804

Zoos
Association of Zoos & Aquariums, 1513
Toronto Zoo, 1388
ZOOCHECK Canada Inc., 1482

Registered Charitable Organizations Index

- Canadian and foreign associations that identify themselves as registered charitable organizations, listed by subject
- An entry may appear under more than one subject
- Each entry is accompanied by a page number which points you to the corresponding listing in the alphabetical listings of both Canadian and foreign associations

ALS
ALS Society of Alberta, 60
ALS Society of British Columbia, 60
ALS Society of Canada, 60
ALS Society of Manitoba, 60
ALS Society of New Brunswick & Nova Scotia, 60
ALS Society of Newfoundland & Labrador, 60
ALS Society of PEI, 60
ALS Society of Québec, 60
ALS Society of Saskatchewan, 60

Acadians
Association acadienne des artistes professionnel.le.s du Nouveau-Brunswick inc., 89
Beaton Institute, 203
Conseil coopératif acadien de la Nouvelle-Écosse, 614
Fédération culturelle acadienne de la Nouvelle-Écosse, 708
Fédération des communautés francophones et acadienne du Canada, 713
Fédération des parents acadiens de la Nouvelle-Écosse, 716
Société de l'Acadie du Nouveau-Brunswick, 1316
Société des Jeux de l'Acadie inc., 1318
Société nationale de l'Acadie, 1322
La Société Saint-Pierre, 1325
Société Saint-Thomas-d'Aquin, 1325

Accessibility
Accessible Housing Society, 5
March of Dimes Non-Profit Housing Corporation, 949

Accident Prevention
Association paritaire pour la santé et la sécurité du travail - Imprimerie et activités connexes, 164
Association sectorielle: Fabrication d'équipement de transport et de machines, 178
Canadian Centre for Occupational Health & Safety, 353
Industrial Accident Victims Group of Ontario, 835
MultiPrévention, 980

Accountants, Chartered
Certified General Accountants Association of the Northwest Territories & Nunavut, 538

Acoustic Neuroma
Acoustic Neuroma Association of Canada, 5

Acoustics
Canadian Acoustical Association, 287

Actors
The Actors' Fund of Canada, 7

Acupuncture
Association des Acupuncteurs du Québec, 105

Addiction
Addictions & Mental Health Ontario, 8
Centre for Addiction & Mental Health, 531
Council on Drug Abuse, 636
F.A.S.T., 706
Native Addictions Council of Manitoba, 997
Nechi Training, Research & Health Promotions Institute, 1002
Parent Action on Drugs, 1139
The Renascent Centres for Alcoholism & Drug Addiction, 1217

Adoption
Adoption Council of Canada, 8
Adoption Council of Ontario, 8
Ontario Standardbred Adoption Society, 1109

Adult Education
Canadian Association for the Study of Adult Education, 306
Canadian Literacy & Learning Network, 427
Institut de coopération pour l'éducation des adultes, 841
Learning Centre for Georgina, 903
Learning Enrichment Foundation, 905
Literacy Link South Central, 914
Niagara West Employment & Learning Resource Centres, 1026
People, Words & Change, 1152
Project Adult Literacy Society, 1187
Project READ Literacy Network Waterloo-Wellington, 1188
Simcoe/Muskoka Literacy Network, 1300
Society for Personal Growth, 1326

Advertising
Association des agences de publicité du Québec, 105
National Advertising Benevolent Society, 989
Les normes canadiennes de la publicité, 1028

Aeronautics
International Federation of Airworthiness, 1547

Aerospace Engineering
Aerospace Heritage Foundation of Canada, 11
Centre d'adaptation de la main-d'oeuvre aérospatiale du Québec, 527

Aerospace Industries
Centre d'adaptation de la main-d'oeuvre aérospatiale du Québec, 527

Afghans in Canada
Afghan Women's Counselling & Integration Community Support Organization, 12

Africa
Africa Inland Mission International (Canada), 12
African Enterprise (Canada), 13
African Medical & Research Foundation Canada, 13
Aga Khan Foundation Canada, 14
Teamwork Children's Services International, 1368
Vues d'Afriques - Les Journées du cinéma africain et créole, 1439

African Canadians
Africans in Partnership Against AIDS, 13

African Studies
International African Institute, 1535

Aging
Alberta Council on Aging, 31
Canadian Association on Gerontology, 337
The Council on Aging of Ottawa, 635
Council on Aging, Windsor - Essex County, 636
HelpAge Canada, 812
Mid-Toronto Community Services, 965
Réseau FADOQ, 1223
The Shepherds' Trust, 1295

Agricultural Economics
Alberta Agricultural Economics Association, 21

Agricultural Equipment & Machinery
Agricultural Manufacturers of Canada, 15
Association des marchands de machines aratoires de la province de Québec, 119
British Columbia Farm Machinery & Agriculture Museum Association, 240
Oldman River Antique Equipment & Threshing Club, 1057
Prairie Agricultural Machinery Institute, 1169

Agricultural Exhibitions
Lloydminster Agricultural Exhibition Association, 916
Royal Agricultural Winter Fair Association, 1237

Agriculture
Agricultural Alliance of New Brunswick, 14
Agricultural Institute of Canada Foundation, 15
Alameda Agricultural Society, 21
Alliance for Sustainability, 1487
American Farmland Trust, 1492
Association des technologues en agroalimentaire, 129
Bengough Agricultural Society, 205
Biggar & District Agricultural Society, 210
Canadian Organic Growers Inc., 446
Canadian Plowing Organization, 456
Carp Agricultural Society, 515
Essa & District Agricultural Society, 696
FarmFolk CityFolk, 706
Federated Women's Institutes of Canada, 706
Fédération des agriculteurs et agricultrices francophones du Nouveau-Brunswick, 711
Groupe export agroalimentaire Québec - Canada, 792
Heritage Agricultural Society, 812
International Federation of Organic Agriculture Movements, 1548
The Marquis Project, Inc., 952
Melfort Agricultural Society, 959
Pesticide Action Network North America, 1583
Resource Efficient Agricultural Production, 1227
Richmond Agricultural Society, 1229
Saskatchewan Agricultural Hall of Fame, 1255
Saskatchewan Soil Conservation Association, 1275
Swift Current Agricultural & Exhibition Association, 1358
Syndicat des agricultrices de la Côte-du-Sud, 1362
Syndicat des agricultrices du Centre du Québec, 1362
Syndicat des producteurs en serre du Québec, 1363
Wallace Center, Winrock International, 1601
Weyburn Agricultural Society, 1451

Agriculture & Youth
Canadian 4-H Council, 284

Agrochemicals
Croplife International, 1520
Northwest Coalition for Alternatives to Pesticides, 1580

Agronomists
Ordre des agronomes du Québec, 1120

Air Cadets
Air Cadet League of Canada, 19

Air Safety
Canadian Owners & Pilots Association, 448

Air Transportation
Association québécoise du transport aérien, 176
Hope Air, 821

Aircraft
Canadian Federal Pilots Association, 384
Canadian Warplane Heritage, 502

Alcoholism
Addictions & Mental Health Ontario, 8
Al-Anon Family Groups (Canada), Inc., 21
Alcoholics Anonymous (GTA Intergroup), 52
Canadian Centre on Substance Use & Addiction, 354
Centre for Addiction & Mental Health, 531
Éduc'alcool, 680
Jean Tweed Treatment Centre, 869
Nechi Training, Research & Health Promotions Institute, 1002
The Renascent Centres for Alcoholism & Drug Addiction, 1217

Allergies
Allergy/Asthma Information Association, 54
Asthme et allergies Québec, 179
Environmental Health Association of Ontario, 692
Food Allergy Canada, 749

Alumni
National Hockey League Alumni Association, 994

Alzheimer's Disease
Alzheimer Manitoba, 61
Alzheimer Society Canada, 61
Alzheimer Society London & Middlesex, 61
Alzheimer Society of Alberta & Northwest Territories, 61
Alzheimer Society of British Columbia, 62
Alzheimer Society of Calgary, 62
Alzheimer Society of Chatham-Kent, 62
Alzheimer Society of Cornwall & District, 62
Alzheimer Society of Dufferin County, 62
Alzheimer Society of Durham Region, 62
Alzheimer Society of Grey-Bruce, 62
Alzheimer Society of Haldimand Norfolk, 62
Alzheimer Society of Hamilton Halton, 62
Alzheimer Society of Hastings - Prince Edward, 62
Alzheimer Society Peterborough, Kawartha Lakes, Northumberland, & Haliburton,
Alzheimer Society of Kenora/Rainy River Districts, 63
Alzheimer Society of Kingston, Frontenac, Lennox & Addington, 63
Alzheimer Society of Leeds-Grenville, 63
Alzheimer Society of Moncton, 63
Alzheimer Society of Muskoka, 63
Alzheimer Society of Newfoundland & Labrador, 63
Alzheimer Society of Niagara Region, 63
Alzheimer Society of North Bay & District, 63
Alzheimer Society of Nova Scotia, 64
Alzheimer Society of Ottawa & Renfrew County, 64
Alzheimer Society of Oxford, 64
Alzheimer Society of Peel, 64
Alzheimer Society of PEI, 64
Alzheimer Society of Perth County, 64
Alzheimer Society of Sarnia-Lambton, 64
Alzheimer Society of Saskatchewan Inc., 64
Alzheimer Society of Sault Ste. Marie & District of Algoma, 64
Alzheimer Society of Simcoe County, 65
Alzheimer Society of Thunder Bay, 65
Alzheimer Society of Timmins/Porcupine District, 65
Alzheimer Society of Toronto, 65
Alzheimer Society of Windsor/Essex County, 65
Alzheimer Society of York Region, 65
Alzheimer Society Ontario, 65
Alzheimer Society Peterborough, Kawartha Lakes, Northumberland, & Haliburton, 65
Alzheimer Society Waterloo Wellington, 65
Fédération québécoise des sociétés Alzheimer, 729
Prince George Alzheimer's Society, 1178
Saint John Alzheimer Society, 1246
Scottish Rite Charitable Foundation of Canada, 1286

American Studies
American Studies Association, 1503

Anglicans
The Anglican Church of Canada, 69
Anglican Foundation of Canada, 70

The Christian Episcopal Church of Canada, 567

Animal Rights Movement
Friends of Animals, 1527
Fur-Bearer Defenders, 765
Lifeforce Foundation, 911
People for the Ethical Treatment of Animals, 1583
Sea Shepherd Conservation Society - USA, 1588
Society for the Prevention of Cruelty to Animals International, 1592

Animal Science
International Association for Bear Research & Management, 1535
Westgen, 1450

Animal Welfare
Action Volunteers for Animals, 7
Alberta Society for the Prevention of Cruelty to Animals, 47
Animal Aid Foundation, 70
Animal Welfare Foundation of Canada, 71
ARK II, 81
Barrhead Animal Rescue Society, 197
Bide Awhile Animal Shelter Society, 208
British Columbia Society for the Prevention of Cruelty to Animals, 254
Calgary Humane Society, 272
Canadian Association for Humane Trapping, 301
Canadian Chihuahua Rescue & Transport, 355
Canadian Farm Animal Care Trust, 384
Canadian Federation of Humane Societies, 386
Edmonton Humane Society for the Prevention of Cruelty to Animals, 677
Elsa Wild Animal Appeal of Canada, 685
Etobicoke Humane Society, 697
Fort McMurray Society for the Prevention of Cruelty to Animals, 753
Fredericton Society for the Prevention of Cruelty to Animals, 759
Grande Prairie Society for the Prevention of Cruelty to Animals, 781
Greater Moncton Society for the Prevention of Cruelty to Animals, 784
International Primate Protection League, 1556
The Kindness Club, 888
Lethbridge & District Humane Society, 907
Lincoln County Humane Society, 912
Lloydminster Society for the Prevention of Cruelty to Animals, 916
Medicine Hat Society for the Prevention of Cruelty to Animals, 959
New Brunswick Society for the Prevention of Cruelty to Animals, 1012
Newfoundland & Labrador Society for the Prevention of Cruelty to Animals, 1021
Niagara Action for Animals, 1024
North Bay & District Humane Society, 1030
North Island Wildlife Recovery Association, 1031
Northwest Territories Society for the Prevention of Cruelty to Animals, 1038
Nova Scotia Society for the Prevention of Cruelty to Animals, 1049
Oakville & Milton Humane Society, 1053
Ontario Society for the Prevention of Cruelty to Animals, 1105
Ontario Standardbred Adoption Society, 1109
Oromocto & Area SPCA, 1127
Ottawa Humane Society, 1130
Pincher Creek Humane Society, 1160
Prince Edward Island Humane Society, 1175
Red Deer & District SPCA, 1209
Regina Humane Society Inc., 1211
Saint John SPCA Animal Rescue, 1247
Sarnia & District Humane Society, 1254
Société québécoise pour la défense des animaux, 1324
Society for the Prevention of Cruelty to Animals International, 1592
SPCA of Western Québec, 1339
Victoria County Society for the Prevention of Cruelty to Animals, 1432
Wildlife Haven Rehabilitation Centre, 1454
Wildlife Rescue Association of British Columbia, 1455
Winnipeg Humane Society, 1459
World Animal Protection, 1465
ZOOCHECK Canada Inc., 1482

Animation
Quickdraw Animation Society, 1201

Anthropology & Ethnology
International Council for Archaeozoology, 1544
Société québécoise d'ethnologie, 1323

Antique Automobiles & Trucks
Historic Vehicle Society of Ontario, 815

Antiques
Oldman River Antique Equipment & Threshing Club, 1057

Antiquities
Archaeological Institute of America, 1505
Society for the Study of Egyptian Antiquities, 1327

Aphasia
Association des personnes intéressées à l'aphasie et à l'accident vasculaire cérébral, 123

Aplastic Anemia/Myelodysplasia Synd
Aplastic Anemia & Myelodysplasia Association of Canada, 73

Aquaculture
Aquaculture Association of Canada, 75
Association québécoise de commercialisation de poissons et de fruits de mer, 169

Aquariums
Canada's Accredited Zoos & Aquariums, 281

Aquatic Sports
Diving Plongeon Canada, 659
Manitoba Underwater Council, 946

Arab Canadians
Arab Canadian Association of the Atlantic Provinces, 75

Arab Countries
Middle East Studies Association of North America, 1571

Arbitration
ADR Institute of Canada, 9
Centre canadien d'arbitrage commercial, 526

Archaeology
Archaeological Institute of America, 1505
Archaeological Society of Alberta, 76
Association des archéologues du Québec, 105
Canadian Archaeological Association, 294
The Canadian Society for Mesopotamian Studies, 476
Cataraqui Archaeological Research Foundation, 517
International Council for Archaeozoology, 1544
Nova Scotia Archaeology Society, 1040
The Ontario Archaeological Society, 1059
Saskatchewan Archaeological Society, 1256
Société d'archéologie et de numismatique de Montréal, 1309
Société d'histoire de la Haute Gaspésie, 1310
Society for the Study of Egyptian Antiquities, 1327

Archery
Archery Canada Tir à l'Arc, 78

Architectural Conservation
Amis et propriétaires de maisons anciennes du Québec, 68
The Architectural Conservancy of Ontario, 78
Canadian Northern Society, 441
The Friends of Fort York & Garrison Common, 761
Nova Scotia Lighthouse Preservation Society, 1047

Architecture
Architectural Woodwork Manufacturers Association of British Columbia, 79
Canadian Centre for Architecture, 353
National Trust for Canada, 996
Société Logique, 1321

Archives
Alberni District Historical Society, 21
Archives Association of British Columbia, 80
Association of Newfoundland & Labrador Archives, 154
Campbell River Museum & Archives Society, 276
Canadian Council of Archives, 367
Canadian Lesbian & Gay Archives, 426
Council of Nova Scotia Archives, 634
15th Field Artillery Regiment Museum & Archives Society, 734
The Friends of Library & Archives Canada, 761
King's County Historical Society, 888
Kings Historical Society, 888
Legal Archives Society of Alberta, 906
Missisquoi Historical Society, 969
Nicola Valley Museum Archives Association, 1026
Summerland Museum & Heritage Society, 1354
Touchstones Nelson Museum of Art & History, 1388
Ukrainian Canadian Research & Documentation Centre, 1402

Archivists
Association des archivistes du Québec, 105

Arctic Region
Association of Canadian Universities for Northern Studies, 144

Armed Forces
Armed Forces Communications & Electronics Association (Canada), 82

Armenians & Armenia
Armenian General Benevolent Union, 83
Armenian Holy Apostolic Church - Canadian Diocese, 83
International Association for Armenian Studies, 1535

Army Cadets
Army Cadet League of Canada, 83

Art
Artists in Healthcare Manitoba, 85
Association des collections d'entreprises, 109
Calgary Aboriginal Arts Awareness Society, 270
The Canadian Art Foundation, 295
Inuit Art Foundation, 862
Oakville Art Society, 1053
Saskatchewan Filmpool Co-operative, 1265
Women's Art Association of Canada, 1461

Art Education
PAVED Arts, 1146

Art Festivals
Associated Manitoba Arts Festivals, Inc., 89

Art Galleries
Association Museums New Brunswick, 138
Bowen Island Arts Council, 219
Museum London, 983
Museum of Contemporary Canadian Art, 983
Touchstones Nelson Museum of Art & History, 1388
Volunteer Circle of the National Gallery of Canada, 1438

Art Therapy
Toronto Art Therapy Institute, 1381
The Vancouver Art Therapy Institute, 1425

Arthritis & Rheumatism
Arthritis Health Professions Association, 84
Arthritis Society, 84

Artisans
The Metal Arts Guild of Canada, 962

Artists
Alberta Society of Artists, 47
Association acadienne des artistes professionnel.le.s du Nouveau-Brunswick inc., 89
Association des artistes en arts visuels de Saint-Jérôme, 106
Canadian Mountain Arts Foundation, 437
Federation of Canadian Artists, 722
Manitoba Society of Artists, 944
The Metal Arts Guild of Canada, 962

Arts & Crafts
Alberta Craft Council, 32
Canadian Crafts Federation, 372
Canadian Guild of Crafts, 399
Craft Council of British Columbia, 638
Embroiderers' Association of Canada, Inc., 685
Georgian Bay Folk Society, 771
Haliburton Highlands Guild of Fine Arts, 798
Manitoba Crafts Council, 934
Nova Scotia Designer Crafts Council, 1044
Ontario Crafts Council, 1075
Saskatchewan Craft Council, 1262
William Morris Society of Canada, 1455

Arts Councils
Abbotsford Arts Council, 1
Algonquin Arts Council, 53
Allied Arts Council of Spruce Grove, 58
Annapolis Region Community Arts Council, 71
Arts Council of Sault Ste Marie & District, 85
Arts Council of the Central Okanagan, 85
Arts Etobicoke, 85
Arts Mosaic, 85
Arts Ottawa East-Est, 86
ArtsConnect - Tri-Cities Regional Arts Council, 86
Assembly of BC Arts Councils, 88
Assiniboia & District Arts Council, 88
Bowen Island Arts Council, 219
Brampton Arts Council, 225
Burnaby Arts Council, 265
Burrows Trail Arts Council, 266
Central Interior Regional Arts Council, 524
Community Arts Council of Greater Victoria, 595
Community Arts Council of Richmond, 595
Community Arts Council of the Alberni Valley, 595
Comox Valley Community Arts Council, 607
Conseil de la culture de L'Abitibi-Témiscamingue, 615
Conseil de la culture de Lanaudière, 616
Conseil de la culture des Laurentides, 616
Conseil montérégien de la culture et des communications, 619
Conseil régional de la culture et des communications de la Côte-Nord, 621
Conseil régional de la culture Saguenay-Lac-Saint-Jean, 621
Cranbrook & District Arts Council, 638
Crowsnest Pass Allied Arts Association, 644
Dauphin & District Allied Arts Council Inc., 651
Delta Arts Council, 653
District of Mission Arts Council, 659
Eastend Arts Council, 669
Enderby & District Arts Council, 687
Estevan Arts Council, 697
Eston Arts Council, 697
Fernie & District Arts Council, 732
Guelph Arts Council, 792
Hamilton Arts Council, 800
Hamilton Folk Arts Heritage Council, 801
Kamsack & District Arts Council, 881
Kingston Arts Council, 888
Langham Cultural Society, 898
Mackenzie Community Arts Council, 924
Manitoba Arts Network, 929
Maple Ridge Pitt Meadows Arts Council, 948
Melville Arts Council, 959
Mississauga Arts Council, 969
New Brunswick Arts Board, 1004
Newfoundland & Labrador Arts Council, 1015
Nicola Valley Community Arts Council, 1026
Oakville Arts Council, 1053
Oceanside Community Arts Council, 1054
Oliver Community Arts Council, 1057
Organization of Saskatchewan Arts Councils, 1126
Osoyoos & District Arts Council, 1128
The Pas Arts Council Inc., 1144
Peace-Laird Regional Arts Council, 1147
Pincher Creek Allied Arts Council, 1160
Portage & District Arts Council, 1166

Prince Edward County Arts Council, 1171
Quinte Arts Council, 1201
Scarborough Arts Council, 1282
Seguin Arts Council, 1289
Société culturelle de la Baie des Chaleurs, 1309
Société culturelle régionale Les Chutes, 1309
Société culturelle Sud-Acadie, 1309
Sudbury Arts Council, 1353
Summerland Community Arts Council, 1354
Sunshine Coast Arts Council, 1355
Thunder Bay Regional Arts Council, 1378
Toronto Arts Council, 1381
Toronto Arts Foundation, 1381
Wallaceburg Arts Council, 1440
Wasagaming Community Arts Inc., 1440
Watrous Area Arts Council, 1442
West Kootenay Regional Arts Council, 1445
West Vancouver Community Arts Council, 1446

Asia
Aga Khan Foundation Canada, 14
Support Enhance Access Service Centre, 1356

Asian Canadians
Alliance for South Asian AIDS Prevention, 57
Asian Community AIDS Services, 87

Asthma
Allergy/Asthma Information Association, 54
Asthma Society of Canada, 179
Asthme et allergies Québec, 179
Canadian Network for Respiratory Care, 441

Astronomy
Fédération des astronomes amateurs du Québec, 712
H.R. MacMillan Space Centre Society, 824
Royal Astronomical Society of Canada, 1238

At-Risk Youth
Our Place (Peel), 1133

Athletics
B2ten, 192
Canadian Wheelchair Basketball Association, 503
Fédération québécoise d'athlétisme, 727
Greater Montreal Athletic Association, 784
Hamber Foundation, 800
Réseau du sport étudiant du Québec Abitibi-Témiscamingue, 1222
Réseau du sport étudiant du Québec Laurentides-Lanaudière, 1223
Réseau du sport étudiant du Québec Montréal, 1223
Réseau du sport étudiant du Québec Saguenay-Lac St-Jean, 1223

Atlantic Provinces
Fédération des scouts de l'Atlantique, 718
Québec-Labrador Foundation (Canada) Inc., 1199
Seagull Foundation, 1288
Them Days Inc., 1375

Atmosphere
Sierra Club of Canada, 1298

Audiology
Association québécoise des orthophonistes et des audiologistes, 173

Autism
Aspergers Society of Ontario, 87
Autism Canada, 188
Autism Nova Scotia, 188
Autism Ontario, 188
Autism Society Alberta, 188
Autism Society Manitoba, 189
Autism Society Newfoundland & Labrador, 189
Autism Society of British Columbia, 189
Canadian National Autism Foundation, 438
Fédération québécoise de l'autisme, 727
Geneva Centre for Autism, 769
Kerry's Place Autism Services, 884
Society for Treatment of Autism, 1327
Unity for Autism, 1418

Autoimmune Diseases
Endometriosis Association, Inc., 1523

Automobile Clubs
Lotus Car Club of Canada, 919
Sports Car Club of British Columbia, 1345

Automobile Dealers
Association des concessionnaires Ford du Québec, 109
Corporation des concessionnaires d'automobiles du Québec inc., 630
Motor Dealers' Association of Alberta, 975

Aviation
Canada's Aviation Hall of Fame, 282
Canadian Aviation Historical Society, 340
Canadian Navigation Society, 440
Canadian Owners & Pilots Association, 448
International Federation of Airworthiness, 1547
Mission Aviation Fellowship of Canada, 969
Youth Flight Canada, 1475

Baha'i Faith
Association for Bahá'í Studies, 132
The Bahá'í Community of Canada, 194

Baking Industry
Société des chefs, cuisiniers et pâtissiers du Québec, 1317

Ballet
Alberta Ballet, 25
Ballet British Columbia, 194
Ballet Jörgen, 194
Les Ballets Jazz de Montréal, 195
Les Grands Ballets Canadiens de Montréal, 781
Ontario Ballet Theatre, 1067
Royal Winnipeg Ballet, 1243
Vancouver Ballet Society, 1425
Youth Ballet & Contemporary Dance of Saskatchewan Inc., 1475

Bands, Musical
Alberta Band Association, 25
Atlantic Canada Pipe Band Association, 182
Calgary Round-Up Band Association, 274
Canadian Band Association, 340
Manitoba Band Association, 932
Ontario Band Association, 1067
Saskatchewan Band Association, 1259

Baptists
Baptist General Conference of Canada, 196
Canadian Baptists of Western Canada, 341
CNBC, 576
Convention of Atlantic Baptist Churches, 627

Barbershop Quartets
Barbershop Harmony Society, 1514

Baseball
Baseball Canada, 198
Little League Canada, 915

Basketball
Alberta Northern Lights Wheelchair Basketball Society, 41
Basketball Saskatchewan, 199
Canada Basketball, 278
Canadian Wheelchair Basketball Association, 503
Dr. James Naismith Basketball Foundation, 662
Fédération de basketball du Québec, 708
Newfoundland & Labrador Basketball Association, 1017

Baton Twirling
Canadian Baton Twirling Federation, 342

Bereavement
Bereaved Families of Ontario, 205
Bereavement Ontario Network, 205
Canadian Hospice Palliative Care Association, 409

Biathlon
Biathlon Canada, 207

Bible
The Bible Holiness Movement, 208
The Bible League of Canada, 208
Canadian Bible Society, 343
Catholic Biblical Association of Canada, 517
Full Gospel Business Men's Fellowship in Canada, 764
Gideons International in Canada, 773
Lutheran Bible Translators of Canada Inc., 922
Société catholique de la Bible, 1309
Wycliffe Bible Translators of Canada, Inc., 1470

Bicycling
Fédération québécoise des sports cyclistes, 730

Bilingualism
Canadian Parents for French, 450
Parents partenaires en éducation, 1140

Biodiversity
International Union of Biological Sciences, 1564
Rare Breeds Canada, 1204

Bioethics
Canadian Bioethics Society, 343
Canadian College of Medical Geneticists, 359

Biology
Institut de recherche en biologie végétale, 842
International Union of Biological Sciences, 1564

Biomedical Research
Partners in Research, 1144

Biotechnology
BIOQuébec, 211

Birds
The Avian Preservation Foundation, 190
Beaverhill Bird Observatory, 203
Bird Studies Canada, 212
British Columbia Waterfowl Society, 258
Club d'observateurs d'oiseaux de Laval, 574
Fondation Les oiseleurs du Québec inc., 747
Grand Manan Whale & Seabird Research Station, 780
Jack Miner Migratory Bird Foundation, Inc., 867
National Audubon Society, Inc., 1575
Ontario Field Ornithologists, 1080
Pembroke Area Field Naturalists, 1149
Regroupement QuébecOiseaux, 1216
Society of Canadian Ornithologists, 1327
Toronto Ornithological Club, 1386
World Pheasant Association, 1607

Bishops
Assemblée des évêques catholiques du Québec, 88
Canadian Conference of Catholic Bishops, 362

Black Canadians
Black Academic Scholarship Fund, 212
Black Cultural Society for Nova Scotia, 213
Black Educators Association of Nova Scotia, 213
Black Theatre Workshop, 213
Ontario Black History Society, 1068

Blindness
Canadian Deafblind Association (National), Accessible Media Inc., 5
Alberta Sports & Recreation Association for the Blind, 48
Alliance for Equality of Blind Canadians, 57
Association des sports pour aveugles de Montréal, 128
BALANCE for Blind Adults, 194
British Columbia Blind Sports & Recreation Association, 234
Canadian Blind Sports Association Inc., 344
The Canadian Council of the Blind, 370
Canadian Deafblind Association (National), 376
Canadian National Institute for the Blind, 439
Christian Blind Mission International, 566
John Milton Society for the Blind in Canada, 875
Ontario Blind Sports Association, 1068
Québec Federation of the Blind Inc., 1197
Seva Canada Society, 1292

Blood Transfusion
Association des bénévoles du don de sang, 107

Boards of Education
Fédération des Syndicats de l'Enseignement, 719
Québec English School Boards Association, 1197

Boards of Trade
Stettler Regional Board of Trade & Community Development, 1350

Boating
Canadian Power & Sail Squadrons (Canadian Headquarters), 459
Sail Canada, 1245

Bobsledding & Luge
Alberta Bobsleigh Association, 26
Bobsleigh Canada Skeleton, 217

Bodybuilding
International Federation of Bodybuilding & Fitness, 1547

Book Arts
The Alcuin Society, 53
Canadian Bookbinders & Book Artists Guild, 346

Book Trade
Association des distributeurs exclusifs de livres en langue française inc., 111
Association des libraires du Québec, 118
Association professionnelle des écrivains de la Sagamie-Côte-Nord, 167
Canadian Children's Book Centre, 355

Botany
International Society for Plant Pathology, 1559
VanDusen Botanical Garden Association, 1429

Bowling
Alberta 5 Pin Bowlers' Association, 21
Canadian 5 Pin Bowlers' Association, 285

Boys & Girls Clubs
Boys & Girls Clubs of Canada, 222

Brain
Brain Tumour Foundation of Canada, 225

Brain Injury
Association for the Rehabilitation of the Brain Injured, 135
Association québécoise des traumatisés craniens, 175
Brain Care Centre, 225
Manitoba Brain Injury Association Inc., 932
Saskatchewan Brain Injury Association, 1260
South Okanagan Similkameen Brain Injury Society, 1335
Southern Alberta Brain Injury Society, 1337

Breastfeeding
La Leche League Canada, 905

Breeding
Fédération des producteurs de bovins du Québec, 717
Rare Breeds Canada, 1204
Westgen, 1450

Brewing Industry
The Molson Family Foundation, 971

British Isles
British Council - Canada, 259
British Isles Family History Society of Greater Ottawa, 259

Broadcasting
Back to the Bible Canada, 193
Women in Film & Television - Toronto, 1461
Youth Media Alliance, 1476

Broomball
Ballon sur glace Broomball Canada, 195

Buddhism
Jodo Shinshu Buddhist Temples of Canada, 873
The Palyul Foundation of Canada, 1137
Yasodhara Ashram Society, 1470

Building Materials
Association québécoise de la quincaillerie et des matériaux de construction, 170
British Columbia Shake & Shingle Association, 253

Building Trades
Building Envelope Council of Ottawa Region, 262

Burns & Scalds
British Columbia Professional Fire Fighters' Burn Fund, 249
Burn Survivors Association, 265
Calgary Firefighters Burn Treatment Society, 272
Firefighters Burn Fund Inc., 738
Fondation des pompiers du Québec pour les grands brûlés, 745

Business
AIESEC, 18
Association des clubs d'entrepreneurs étudiants du Québec, 109
Canadian Association of University Business Officers, 334
Canadian Council for Aboriginal Business, 366
Organisme de développement d'affaires commerciales et économiques, 1125
Robson Street Business Association, 1235
Shad Valley International, 1293

Business Education
Association professionnelle des enseignantes et enseignants en commerce, 167
Junior Achievement Canada, 877
Réseau HEC Montréal, 1224

Caisses populaires
Société historique Alphonse-Desjardins, 1319

Camping
Alberta Camping Association, 27
Association des camps du Québec inc., 108
Canadian Camping Association, 348
Fédération québécoise du canot et du kayak, 730

Canada & Canadian Studies
Associaçao Brasileira de Estudos Canadense, 1506
Association for Canadian Jewish Studies, 132
Association for Canadian Studies, 133
Association for Canadian Studies in China, 1507
Association for Canadian Studies in the Netherlands, 1507
Association for Canadian Studies in the United States, 1507
Association française d'études canadiennes, 1509
British Association for Canadian Studies, 1514
Canada's History, 282
Historica Canada, 815
The Laurier Institution, 900
McGill Institute for the Study of Canada, 955
Organization of Military Museums of Canada, 1125
Pier 21 Society, 1159

Cancer
Lymphoma Canada,
Alberta Cancer Foundation, 27
Bladder Cancer Canada, 214
Breast Cancer Action, 227
Breast Cancer Action Nova Scotia, 227
Breast Cancer Society of Canada, 228
British Columbia Cancer Foundation, 234
Canadian Association of Provincial Cancer Agencies, 329
Canadian Cancer Society, 348
Cancer Research Society, 507
Candlelighters Simcoe Parents of Children with Cancer, 508
Carcinoid NeuroEndocrine Tumour Society Canada, 510
Dr. H. Bliss Murphy Cancer Care Foundation, 662
Fondation Centre de cancérologie Charles-Bruneau, 743
Fondation de la greffe de moelle osseuse de l'Est du Québec, 744
Fondation québécoise du cancer, 748
Israel Cancer Research Fund, 866
Kidney Cancer Canada Association, 884
Kids Cancer Care Foundation of Alberta, 886
The Leukemia & Lymphoma Society of Canada, 908
Lymphoma Canada, 923
Lymphovenous Association of Ontario, 923
Newfoundland Cancer Treatment & Research Foundation, 1023
Organisation multiressources pour les personnes atteintes de cancer, 1125
Organisation québécoise des personnes atteintes de cancer, 1125
Ovarian Cancer Canada, 1133
Pancreatic Cancer Canada Foundation, 1138
Procure Alliance, 1181
Rethink Breast Cancer, 1228
The Terry Fox Foundation, 1372
The 3C Foundation of Canada, 1377
Wellspring Cancer Support Foundation, 1444

Canoeing & Rafting
Association québécoise de canoë-kayak de vitesse, 169
Canoe Kayak Saskatchewan, 509
Fédération québécoise du canot et du kayak, 730
Outward Bound Canada, 1133
Paddle Canada, 1137
Paddle Manitoba, 1137

Cardiology
Cardiac Health Foundation of Canada, 510
International Society of Hypertension, 1560

Career Counselling
Canadian Education & Research Institute for Counselling, 379

Caribbeans & the Caribbean
Canadian-Cuban Friendship Association Toronto, 506
Jamaican Canadian Association, 867

Carpentry
Fraternité nationale des forestiers et travailleurs d'usine (CTC), 758

Catholics & Catholicism
Assemblée des évêques catholiques du Québec, 88
Association des parents catholiques du Québec, 121
Block Rosary Group of Ontario, 215
Bukas Loob sa Diyos Covenant Community, 264
Canadian Catholic Campus Ministry, 351
Canadian Conference of Catholic Bishops, 362
Carizon Family & Community Services, 513
Catholic Action Montreal, 517
Catholic Biblical Association of Canada, 517
Catholic Biblical Federation, 1515
Catholic Charities of The Archdiocese of Toronto, 518
Catholic Children's Aid Society of Hamilton, 518
Catholic Children's Aid Society of Toronto, 518
Catholic Education Foundation of Ontario, 518
Catholic Family Service of Ottawa, 518
Catholic Family Services of Peel Dufferin, 519
Catholic Family Services of Simcoe County, 519
Catholic Family Services of Toronto, 519
Catholic Health Alliance of Canada, 519
Catholic Health Association of Manitoba, 519
Catholic Health Association of Saskatchewan, 520
Catholic Missions in Canada, 520
Christian Catholic Church Canada, 566
Congregation of Missionaries of the Precious Blood, Atlantic Province, 613
Couples For Christ Foundation for Family & Life, 636
Couples For Christ, 636
Covenant Foundation, 637
Cursillo Movement of the Archdiocese of Toronto, 646
Daughters of Isabella, 651
Development & Peace, 654
English Speaking Catholic Council, 689
Family Prayer Mission (Ontario), 704
Federation of North American Explorers, 725
Gethsemane Ministries, 773
HMWN (Holy Mother World Networks) Radio Maria, 817
Madonna House Apostolate, 925
Marguerite Bourgeoys Family Centre Fertility Care Programme, 949
The Neocatechumenal Way, 1003
Newman Centre Catholic Chaplaincy and Parish, 1024
Order of Malta - Canadian Association, 1119
L'Ordinariat militaire Catholique Romain du Canada, 1119
Our Lady of Good Health Tamil Parish, 1133
Pontifical Mission Societies, 1164
Regnum Christi Movement, 1214
The Rosary Apostolate, Inc., 1236
ShareLife, 1294
The Shepherds' Trust, 1295
Silent Children's Mission, 1299
Società Unita, 1307
Société catholique de la Bible, 1309
Society of St. Vincent de Paul - Toronto Central Council, 1330
Society of the Sacred Heart, 1594

Cats
Toronto Cat Rescue, 1383

Cattle
Fédération des producteurs de bovins du Québec, 717

Celiac Disease
Canadian Celiac Association, 352
Fondation québécoise de la maladie coeliaque, 747

Celtic Culture & Peoples
Beaton Institute, 203

Central America
Friends of the Orphans, Canada, 763

Cerebral Palsy
Alberta Cerebral Palsy Sport Association, 27
British Columbia Centre for Ability Association, 235
Canadian Cerebral Palsy Sports Association, 354
Cerebral Palsy Association of Manitoba Inc., 538
Cerebral Palsy Association of Newfoundland & Labrador, 538
Child Development Centre Society of Fort St. John & District, 558
Ontario Federation for Cerebral Palsy, 1079
Prince Edward Island Cerebral Palsy Association Inc., 1173
Quesnel & District Child Development Centre Association, 1200
Saskatchewan Cerebral Palsy Association, 1260
SportAbility BC, 1345

Chamber Music
Friends of Chamber Music, 760
Kitchener-Waterloo Chamber Music Society, 890
Manitoba Chamber Orchestra, 933
McGill Chamber Orchestra, 955
Oakville Chamber Orchestra, 1053
Scotia Chamber Players, 1285
Soundstreams Canada, 1333

Chambers of Commerce
Abbotsford Chamber of Commerce, 1
Airdrie Chamber of Commerce, 20
Antigonish Chamber of Commerce, 72
Atikokan Chamber of Commerce, 181
Biggar & District Chamber of Commerce, 211
Carleton Place & District Chamber of Commerce & Visitor Centre, 513
Chambre de commerce de Beauceville, 540
Chambre de commerce de Charlevoix, 540
Chambre de commerce de Chibougamau, 540
Chambre de commerce de Ferme-Neuve, 541
Chambre de Commerce de Fermont, 541
Chambre de commerce de l'Est de la Beauce, 541
Chambre de commerce de la grande région de Saint-Hyacinthe, 541
Chambre de commerce de la MRC de la Matapédia, 541
Chambre de commerce de la MRC de Rivière-du-Loup, 542
Chambre de commerce de la région de Weedon, 542
Chambre de commerce de Saint-Côme, 542
Chambre de commerce de Ste-Julienne, 543
Chambre de commerce de Sept-Îles, 543
Chambre de commerce de St-Donat, 543
Chambre de commerce de St-Frédéric, 543
Chambre de commerce des Jardins de Napierville, 544
Chambre de commerce des Îles-de-la-Madeleine, 544
Chambre de commerce du Haut-Saint-François, 544
Chambre de commerce du Montréal métropolitain, 544
Chambre de commerce et d'industrie de Dolbeau-Mistassini, 545
Chambre de commerce et d'Industrie de la région de Coaticook, 545
Chambre de commerce et d'industrie de la région de Richmond, 545
Chambre de commerce et d'industrie de Laval, 545
Chambre de commerce et d'industrie de Maniwaki & Vallée de la Gatineau, 546
Chambre de commerce et d'industrie de Montréal-Nord, 546
Chambre de commerce et d'industrie de Roberval, 546
Chambre de commerce et d'industrie de St-Laurent-Mont-Royal, 546
Chambre de commerce et d'industrie française au canada, 547
Chambre de commerce et d'industrie MRC de Deux-Montagne, 547
Chambre de commerce et d'industrie Nouvelle-Beauce, 547
Chambre de commerce et d'industrie Rimouski-Neigette, 547
Chambre de commerce et d'industrie secteur Saint-Félicien inc., 547
Chambre de commerce et de tourisme de Gaspé, 548
Chambre de commerce francophone de Saint-Boniface, 548
Chambre de commerce St-Félix de Valois, 549
Chambre de commerce St-Martin de Beauce, 549
Chambre de commerce Témis-Accord, 549
La Crete & Area Chamber of Commerce, 642
Delta Chamber of Commerce, 653
Elkford Chamber of Commerce, 685
Evansburg & Entwistle Chamber of Commerce, 699
Fort Frances Chamber of Commerce, 752
Gabriola Island Chamber of Commerce, 765
Gander & Area Chamber of Commerce, 766
Greater Kitchener & Waterloo Chamber of Commerce, 783
High Level & District Chamber of Commerce, 814
Mackenzie Chamber of Commerce, 924
Melville & District Chamber of Commerce, 959
Northwest Territories Chamber of Commerce, 1037
Organisme de développement d'affaires commerciales et économiques, 1125
The Pas & District Chamber of Commerce, 1144
Pigeon Lake Regional Chamber of Commerce, 1159
Ponoka & District Chamber of Commerce, 1164
Portage la Prairie & District Chamber of Commerce, 1167
Ridgetown & South East Kent Chamber of Commerce, 1232
Rocky Mountain House & District Chamber of Commerce, 1235
Silver Trail Chamber of Commerce, 1299
Spruce Grove & District Chamber of Commerce, 1346
Squamish Chamber of Commerce, 1346

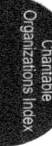

Registered Charitable Organizations Index / Christians & Christianity

Tofino-Long Beach Chamber of Commerce, 1381
Truro & Colchester Chamber of Commerce, 1399
Vermilion & District Chamber of Commerce, 1431
West Lincoln Chamber of Commerce, 1445
Westport & Rideau Lakes Chamber of Commerce, 1451
Yukon Chamber of Commerce, 1477

Charities
Abundance Canada, 3
Altruvest Charitable Services, 61
Calgary Health Trust, 272
Canadian Council of Christian Charities, 368
Canadian Food for Children, 391
Children's Cottage Society, 561
Children's Health Foundations, 561
Children's Hospital Foundation of Manitoba, 562
Children's Hospital Foundation of Saskatchewan, 562
Daughters of Isabella, 651
HMWN (Holy Mother World Networks) Radio Maria, 817
Humanity First Canada, 827
Imagine Canada, 829
IODE Canada, 863
The Magic of Christmas, 925
Phoenix Community Works Foundation, 1157
reBOOT Canada, 1206
Yonge Street Mission, 1473

Chefs
Société des chefs, cuisiniers et pâtissiers du Québec, 1317

Chemical Industry
Croplife International, 1520

Chess
Canadian Correspondence Chess Association, 366
Chess Federation of Canada, 556
Fédération québécoise des échecs, 728

Child Abuse
Boost Child & Youth Advocacy Centre, 218
Canadian Child Abuse Association, 355
The Child Abuse Survivor Monument Project, 558
Chisholm Services for Children, 566
Foster Parent Support Services Society, 755
Metropolitan Action Committee on Violence Against Women & Children, 964
Mouvement contre le viol et l'inceste, 976
Parent Support Services Society of BC, 1139
Parents-Unis Lanaudière, 1140
Viol-secours inc., 1435

Child Care
Canadian Child Care Federation, 355
Family Day Care Services (Toronto), 703
Manitoba Child Care Association, 933
Starbright Children's Development Centre, 1348
Step-By-Step Child Development Society, 1349

Child Psychology
Native Child & Family Services of Toronto, 997

Child Welfare
Alva Foundation, 61
Canadian Feed The Children, 389
Canadian Society for the Prevention of Cruelty to Children, 477
Catholic Children's Aid Society of Hamilton, 518
Catholic Children's Aid Society of Toronto, 518
Catholic Family Services of Saskatoon, 519
Child Development Institute, 559
Child Welfare League of Canada, 560
Children's Aid Society of Ottawa, 561
Children's Aid Society of the District of Nipissing & Parry Sound, 561
Children's Aid Society of the Districts of Sudbury & Manitoulin, 561
Children's Aid Society of the Region of Peel, 561
Chisholm Services for Children, 566
Family & Children's Services Niagara, 701
Family & Children's Services of Frontenac, Lennox & Addington, 701
Foster Parent Support Services Society, 755
Friends of the Orphans, Canada, 763
Halton Children's Aid Society, 800
Highland Shores Children's Aid, 814
Infant & Toddler Safety Association, 836
Jewish Family & Child, 871
Kids Help Phone, 886
McMan Youth, Family & Community Services Association, 955
Native Child & Family Services of Toronto, 997
Nova Scotia Council for the Family, 1043
Parent Support Services Society of BC, 1139
Saskatchewan Prevention Institute, 1272
Silent Children's Mission, 1299
Sudbury Manitoulin Children's Foundation, 1353
UNICEF Canada, 1404
WE Charity, 1443
York Region Children's Aid Society, 1473

Childbirth
Birthright International, 212
International Confederation of Midwives, 1543
Pacific Post Partum Support Society, 1136

Children
Active Healthy Kids Canada, 7
Air Canada Foundation, 19
Alberta Children's Hospital Foundation, 28
Association des Grands Frères et Grandes Soeurs du Québec, 115
Association des parents et amis de la personne atteinte de maladie mentale Rive-Sud, 122
Association du Québec pour enfants avec problèmes auditifs, 131
Big Brothers Big Sisters of Alberta, 209
Big Brothers Big Sisters of British Columbia, 209
Big Brothers Big Sisters of Canada, 209
Big Brothers Big Sisters of Eastern Newfoundland, 209
Big Brothers Big Sisters of Manitoba, 209
Big Brothers Big Sisters of New Brunswick, 209
Big Brothers Big Sisters of Nova Scotia, 210
Big Brothers Big Sisters of Ontario, 210
Big Brothers Big Sisters of Saskatchewan, 210
Boost Child & Youth Advocacy Centre, 218
Breakfast for Learning, 227
British Columbia's Children's Hospital Foundation, 259
Canadian Academy of Child & Adolescent Psychiatry, 285
Canadian Association for Young Children, 307
Canadian Children's Book Centre, 355
Canadian Children's Opera Company, 356
Canadian Institute of Child Health, 414
Casa - Pueblito, 516
Centre for Child Development, 531
Les Centres jeunesse de l'Outaouais, 537
Change for Children Association, 551
Child Development Centre Society of Fort St. John & District, 558
Child Evangelism Fellowship of Canada, 559
Children's Arts Umbrella Association, 561
Children's Cottage Society, 561
Children's Health Foundation of Vancouver Island, 561
Children's Health Foundations, 561
Children's Hospital Foundation of Manitoba, 562
Children's Hospital Foundation of Saskatchewan, 562
Children's Hospital of Eastern Ontario Foundation, 562
Children's Mental Health Ontario, 562
Children's Miracle Network, 562
Children's Wish Foundation of Canada, 562
Christian Children's Fund of Canada, 567
Colin B. Glassco Charitable Foundation for Children, 581
Compassion Canada, 608
Deaf Children's Society of B.C., 652
The Dream Factory, 662
Dreams Take Flight, 662
Early Childhood Intervention Program (ECIP) Sask. Inc., 667
Enfant-Retour Québec, 688
Fondation Centre de cancérologie Charles-Bruneau, 743
Fondation de l'Hôpital de Montréal pour enfants, 744
Forever Chai Foundation of Canada, 752
Gustav Levinschi Foundation, 794
Gymn-eau Laval inc, 795
Help Fill a Dream Foundation of Canada, 812
Justice for Children & Youth, 878
Kids First Parent Association of Canada, 886
Kids Kottage Foundation, 886
Kids Now, 886
Kids Up Front, 886
The Kindness Club, 888
Lawson Foundation, 902
Make-A-Wish Canada, 927
Maker Kids, 927
Moorelands Community Services, 973
Ontario Association of Children's Rehabilitation Services, 1062
Oxford Child & Youth Centre, 1134
Parachute, 1138
Pontifical Mission Societies, 1164
Quesnel & District Child Development Centre Association, 1200
The Rainbow Society of Alberta, 1203
Ranch Ehrlo Society, 1204
Right to Play, 1232
Romanian Children's Relief, 1235
Ronald McDonald House Charities of Canada, 1235
St. Leonard's Youth & Family Services Society, 1250
Sandbox Project, 1253
Save the Children Canada, 1281
School Lunch Association, 1284
Seasons Centre for Grieving Children, 1288
Sleeping Children Around the World, 1303
Société pour les enfants handicapés du Québec, 1322
SOS Children's Villages Canada, 1333
Starlight Children's Foundation Canada, 1348
Sudbury Manitoulin Children's Foundation, 1353
Sunshine Dreams for Kids, 1355
Teamwork Children's Services International, 1368
The Teresa Group, 1371
Vancouver International Children's Festival, 1426
Variety - The Children's Charity of Manitoba, Tent 58 Inc., 1430
Victoria Youth Empowerment Society, 1434
Vides Canada, 1434
VOICE for Hearing Impaired Children, 1437
Voices for Children, 1437
Youth Assisting Youth, 1475
Youth Media Alliance, 1476

Children - Diseases
Ability Online Support Network, 2
British Columbia Centre for Ability Association, 235
British Columbia Lions Society for Children with Disabilities, 245
Candlelighters Simcoe Parents of Children with Cancer, 508
CHILD Foundation, 560
Childhood Obesity Foundation, 560
Children's Wish Foundation of Canada, 562
Dreams Take Flight, 662
Fondation des étoiles, 744
Help Fill a Dream Foundation of Canada, 812
Hospital for Sick Children Foundation, 823
Kids Cancer Care Foundation of Alberta, 886
Make-A-Wish Canada, 927
Ronald McDonald House Toronto, 1235

China
Carefirst Seniors & Community Services Association, 511
Centre for Immigrant & Community Services, 532
Chinese Cultural Centre, 564
Chinese Cultural Centre of Greater Toronto, 564
Chinese Family Services of Ontario, 565
Federation of Chinese Canadian Professionals (Ontario), 723
Hoy Ping Benevolent Association of Canada - Vancouver Branch, 824
Ottawa Chinese Community Services Centre, 1129

Chinese Canadians
Hoy Ping Benevolent Association of Canada - Vancouver Branch, 824
Richmond Chinese Community Society, 1230
Service à la famille chinoise du Grand Montréal, 1291

Chiropractic Health Care
Canadian Chiropractic Research Foundation, 356
Ordre des chiropraticiens du Québec, 1120

Choral Music
Alliance des chorales du Québec, 55
Bach Elgar Choir, 192
Canadian Children's Opera Company, 356
Choir Alberta, 566
Festival Chorus of Calgary, 733
Manitoba Choral Association, 934
New Brunswick Choral Federation, 1006
Northumberland Orchestra Society, 1036
Prairie Saengerbund Choir Association, 1169
Pro Coro Canada, 1181
Richard Eaton Singers, 1229
Sweet Adelines International - Westcoast Harmony Chapter, 1358
The Toronto Mendelssohn Choir, 1385
Youth Singers of Calgary, 1476

Christian Education
Canadian Catholic Campus Ministry, 351
Catholic Education Foundation of Ontario, 518
Child Evangelism Fellowship of Canada, 559
Partners International, 1144
Pioneer Clubs Canada Inc., 1160
Sisters of St. Benedict, 1301

Christian Science in Canada
Creation Science Association of British Columbia, 639
Creation Science of Saskatchewan Inc., 639

Christians & Christianity
Action des Chrétiens pour l'abolition de la torture, 6
Adventist Development & Relief Agency Canada, 10
Adventive Cross Cultural Initiatives, 10
The Bible League of Canada, 208
Bibles for Missions Foundation, 208
Brethren in Christ, 228
British Israel World Federation (Canada) Inc., 259
Canadian Bible Society, 343
Canadian Council of Christian Charities, 368
Canadian Foodgrains Bank, 391
Catholic Health Alliance of Canada, 519
The Christian & Missionary Alliance in Canada, 566
Christian Blind Mission International, 566
Christian Catholic Church Canada, 566
Christian Children's Fund of Canada, 567
The Christian Episcopal Church of Canada, 567
Christian Health Association of Alberta, 567
Christian Stewardship Services, 568
Congregational Christian Churches in Canada, 613
Direction Chrétienne, 657
Evangelical Medical Aid Society Canada, 698
Focus on the Family Canada, 742
Institut Séculier Pie X, 843
Institut Voluntas Dei, 843
Intercede International, 851
International Fellowship of Christians & Jews of Canada, 857
Inter-Varsity Christian Fellowship, 862
Living Bible Explorers, 915
M2/W2 Association - Restorative Christian Ministries, 923
Pacific Life Bible College, 1135

Registered Charitable Organizations Index / Churches

Project Peacemakers, 1187
REHOBOTH Christian Ministries, 1216
Samaritan House Ministries Inc., 1253
Samaritan's Purse Canada, 1253
Seventh-day Adventist Church in Canada, 1292
Sisters of St. Benedict, 1301
World Association for Christian Communication, 1465
World Renew, 1467

Churches
Apostolic Church of Pentecost of Canada Inc., 73
Armenian Holy Apostolic Church - Canadian Diocese, 83
Associated Gospel Churches, 89
Association of Unity Churches Canada, 163
The Canadian Council of Churches, 368
Christian Church (Disciples of Christ) in Canada, 567
Church Council on Justice & Corrections, 569
Church of God of Prophecy in Canada, 569
Congregational Christian Churches in Canada, 613
General Conference of the Canadian Assemblies of God, 768
The Reformed Episcopal Church of Canada - Diocese of Western Canada & Alaska, 1210
Spiritual Science Fellowship/International Institute of Integral Human Sciences, 1344
The United Brethren Church in Canada, 1409
Yukon Church Heritage Society, 1477

Citizens' Groups
Environmental Defence, 691

Citizenship
Immigrant Centre Manitoba Inc., 830
Saskatoon Open Door Society Inc., 1279

Civil Service Employees
Association des directeurs municipaux du Québec, 111

Classical Studies
Classical Association of Canada, 572

Climate
Canadian Foundation for Climate & Atmospheric Sciences, 393
Climate Institute, 1517
Tides Canada Foundation, 1379

Climate Change
Saskatchewan Environmental Society, 1264

Clothing
Groupe CTT Group, 791
MultiPrévention, 980
New Circles Community Services, 1014

Coaching
Coaching Association of Canada, 577

Collecting
Association des collections d'entreprises, 109
Club des collectionneurs d'épinglettes Inc., 575

Colostomy
Ileostomy & Colostomy Association of Montréal, 829

Commerce
The Royal Society for the Encouragement of Arts, Manufactures & Commerce, 1587

Communications
Armed Forces Communications & Electronics Association (Canada), 82
Blissymbolics Communication International, 214
Parlimage CCF, 1143

Community Centres
Applegrove Community Complex, 74
Birchmount Bluffs Neighbourhood Centre, 212
Carrefour-Ressources, 516
Central Neighbourhood House, 524
Christie-Ossington Neighbourhood Centre, 568
Community Action Resource Centre, 595
Davenport-Perth Neighbourhood & Community Health Centre, 651
Delta Community Living Society, 653
Dixon Hall, 660
Doorsteps Neighbourhood Services, 661
Eastview Neighbourhood Community Centre, 671
Fédération québécoise des centres communautaires de loisir inc., 728
The 519 Church St. Community Centre, 740
Flemingdon Neighbourhood Services, 740
Harbourfront Community Centre, 803
Jane Finch Community & Family Centre, 868
Jewish Federation of Greater Vancouver, 872
Kababayan Multicultural Centre, 879
Kitimat Community Services Society, 891
Lakeshore Area Multi-Service Project, 896
Native Women's Resource Centre of Toronto, 998
North York Community House, 1033
Project Share, 1188
Ralph Thornton Centre, 1204
St. Stephen's Community House, 1251
Scadding Court Community Centre, 1282
Scarborough Centre for Healthy Communities, 1282
La Société Saint-Pierre, 1325
Sudbury Community Service Centre Inc., 1353
Syme-Woolner Neighbourhood & Family Centre, 1360
Warden Woods Community Centre, 1440
YMCA Canada, 1471

Community Development
Action for Healthy Communities, 6
Applegrove Community Complex, 74
Arusha Centre Society, 86
Association of Neighbourhood Houses BC, 153
Association régionale de la communauté francophone de Saint-Jean inc., 177
Birchmount Bluffs Neighbourhood Centre, 212
The Calgary Foundation, 272
Community Development Council Durham, 596
Community Development Halton, 596
Community Foundation for Kingston & Area, 597
Community Foundation of Lethbridge & Southwestern Alberta, 597
Community Foundation of Prince Edward Island, 598
Compassion Canada, 608
Davenport-Perth Neighbourhood & Community Health Centre, 651
Delta Family Resource Centre, 653
Dixon Hall, 660
Doorsteps Neighbourhood Services, 661
Edmonton Community Foundation, 676
Fondation communautaire du Grand-Québec, 743
Foundation of Greater Montreal, 756
Fred Victor Centre, 758
Frontiers Foundation, 763
Hamilton Community Foundation, 801
Harbourfront Community Centre, 803
Horizons of Friendship, 821
Jane Finch Community & Family Centre, 868
Jewish Community Foundation of Montréal, 871
The Kitchener & Waterloo Community Foundation, 890
Learning Enrichment Foundation, 905
London Community Foundation, 918
Nanaimo Family Life Association, 988
North York Community House, 1033
PeerNetBC, 1148
SkyWorks Charitable Foundation, 1303
United Way/Centraide (Central NB) Inc., 1418
USC Canada, 1423
World Renew, 1467
Youth Challenge International, 1475

Community Information Services
Access Alliance Multicultural Health & Community Services, 4
Agincourt Community Services Association, 14
Ancaster Community Services, 68
Caledon Community Services, 270
Centre for Immigrant & Community Services, 532
Community Action Resource Centre, 595
Community Care Peterborough, 596
Community Connection, 596
Community Information Centre of Ottawa, 599
Community Information Hamilton, 599
Community Resource Centre (Killaloe) Inc., 607
Community Support Centre Haldimand-Norfolk, 607
East Wellington Community Services, 669
Essex Community Services, 696
Findhelp Information Services, 737
Flamborough Information & Community Services, 740
Fraserside Community Services Society, 758
Haldimand-Norfolk Information Centre, 798
Info Northumberland, 836
Information Niagara, 837
Information Services Vancouver, 837
Information Tilbury & Help Centre, 837
InformOntario, 838
Jewish Federation of Greater Vancouver, 872
Malton Neighbourhood Services, 928
The Olde Forge Community Resource Centre, 1056
Ottawa Chinese Community Services Centre, 1129
Parkdale Community Information Centre, 1140
Port Colborne Community Association for Research Extension, 1165
Rose & Max Rady Jewish Community Centre, 1236
Social Planning Council of Kitchener-Waterloo, 1306
South West Community Care Access Centre, 1336
Thorncliffe Neighbourhood Office, 1376
Tillsonburg & District Multi-Service Centre, 1379
211 Southwest Ontario, 1401
Volunteer Centre of Guelph/Wellington, 1438

Community Planning
Community Sector Council, Newfoundland & Labrador, 607

Community Safety
Ontario Community Justice Association, 1073

Composers
Edmonton Composers' Concert Society, 676
Musicaction, 984
Société du droit de reproduction des auteurs, compositeurs et éditeurs au Canada (SODRAC 2003) inc., 1318
Société professionnelle des auteurs et des compositeurs du Québec, 1322
Songwriters Association of Canada, 1333

Computers
Canadian Information Processing Society, 411
Centre francophone d'informatisation des organisations, 534
The Instrumentation, Systems & Automation Society of America, 1534
reBOOT Canada, 1206

Confectionery Industry
Association nationale des distributeurs aux petites surfaces alimentaires, 138

Conflict Resolution
Canadian Institute for Conflict Resolution, 412

Conservation of Historic & Artistic
Community Heritage Ontario, 599
The Friends of Fort York & Garrison Common, 761
Heritage Ottawa, 813
National Trust for Canada, 996
Ontario Heritage Trust, 1084

Conservation of Natural Resources
Alberta Conservation Association, 31
British Columbia Spaces for Nature, 254
Clean Annapolis River Project, 573
Conservation International, 1519
The Cousteau Society, 1520
Earthwatch Institute, 1522
FarmFolk CityFolk, 706
Fondation Les oiseleurs du Québec inc., 747
Friends of Clayoquot Sound, 760
Friends of Ecological Reserves, 761
Grand River Conservation Foundation, 780
Jack Miner Migratory Bird Foundation, Inc., 867
Kamloops Wildlife Park Society, 881
National Audubon Society, Inc., 1575
Ontario Federation of Anglers & Hunters, 1079
Partners FOR the Saskatchewan River Basin, 1144
Pollination Guelph, 1164
Protected Areas Association of Newfoundland & Labrador, 1190
Réseau environnement, 1223
St. Lawrence Valley Natural History Society, 1250
Saskatchewan Soil Conservation Association, 1275
SEEDS Foundation, 1289
Soil Conservation Council of Canada, 1332
Sustainable Forestry Initiative Inc., 1597
UNEP - World Conservation Monitoring Centre, 1598
USC Canada, 1423
Valhalla Wilderness Society, 1424
WWF International, 1608

Construction Industry
APCHQ - Montréal Métropolitain, 73
Association de la Construction Richelieu Yamaska, 101
Association des constructeurs de routes et grands travaux du Québec, 110
Construction Association of Rural Manitoba Inc., 623

Consultants & Consulting
Association of Independent Consultants, 149

Consumer Protection
Association pour la protection des intérêts des consommateurs de la Côte-Nord, 166
Canadian Partnership for Consumer Food Safety Education, 451
Centre d'information et de recherche en consommation de Charlevoix-Ouest, 528

Contractors
Association des maîtres couvreurs du Québec, 118
Corporation des entrepreneurs spécialisés du Grand Montréal inc., 630

Cooperative Housing
Association des syndicats de copropriété du Québec, 129
Confédération québécoise des coopératives d'habitation, 611
Fédération des coopératives d'habitation du Royaume Saguenay Lac-Saint-Jean, 714

Cooperative Movement
Conseil canadien de la coopération et de la mutualité, 613
Conseil de la Coopération de la Saskatchewan, 615

Copyright
Société du droit de reproduction des auteurs, compositeurs et éditeurs au Canada (SODRAC 2003) inc., 1318

Corporate Planning
Canadian Centre for Ethics & Corporate Policy, 353

Correctional Services
Canadian Families & Corrections Network, 383
Church Council on Justice & Corrections, 569
M2/W2 Association - Restorative Christian Ministries, 923
St. Leonard's Society of Canada, 1250
Syndicat des agents de la paix en services correctionnels du Québec, 1362

Counselling
A.C.C.E.S. Employment, 4
The Barbra Schlifer Commemorative Clinic, 196
British Columbia Society for Male Survivors of Sexual Abuse, 254
Canadian Career Development Foundation, 350
Catholic Family Services of Saskatoon, 519
Centre d'aide et de lutte contre les agressions à caractère sexuel de Châteauguay, 527

Cornerstone Counselling Society of Edmonton, 628
Counselling Services of Belleville & District, 636
Family Counselling Centre of Cambridge & North Dumfries, 703
Family Service Kent, 704
Family Services Perth-Huron, 705
Family Services Windsor-Essex Counselling & Advocacy Centre, 705
Fondation Diane Hébert Inc, 745
Halton Family Services, 800
JVS of Greater Toronto, 879
McMan Youth, Family & Community Services Association, 955
Nanaimo Family Life Association, 988
Native Courtworker & Counselling Association of BC, 997
North Renfrew Family Services Inc., 1032
Signal Hill, 1299
South Peace Community Resources Society, 1335
Timmins Family Counselling Centre, Inc., 1380

Courts
Canadian Criminal Justice Association, 373

Credit Counselling
Association coopérative d'économie familiale - Abitibi-Témiscamingue, 97
Association coopérative d'économie familiale - Appalaches, Beauce, Etchemins, 97
Association coopérative d'économie familiale - Estrie, 97
Association coopérative d'économie familiale - Lanaudière, 97
Association coopérative d'économie familiale - Montérégie-est, 97
Association coopérative d'économie familiale - Rive-Sud de Québec, 97
Association coopérative d'économie familiale de l'est de Montréal, 97
Association coopérative d'économie familiale des Basses Laurentides, 98
Association coopérative d'économie familiale des Bois-Francs, 98
Association coopérative d'économie familiale du Sud-Ouest de Montréal, 98
Association coopérative d'économie familiale Rimouski-Neigette et Mitis, 98
Canadian Association of Credit Counselling Services, 311
Carizon Family & Community Services, 513
Carrefour-Ressources, 516
Catholic Family Services of Peel Dufferin, 519
Community Counselling & Resource Centre, 596
Community Counselling Centre of Nipissing, 596
Community Financial Counselling Services, 597
Consolidated Credit Counseling Services of Canada, Inc., 623
Credit Canada Debt Solutions, Inc., 639
Credit Counselling of Regional Niagara, 639
Credit Counselling Service of Sault Ste. Marie & District, 639
Credit Counselling Services of Cochrane District, 640
Family Counselling & Support Services for Guelph-Wellington, 702
Family Service Kent, 704
Family Services Perth-Huron, 705
Financial Fitness Centre, 736
Halton Family Services, 800
K3C Community Counselling Centres, 879
Ontario Association of Credit Counselling Services, 1063
Option consommateurs, 1117
Service budgétaire et communautaire de Chicoutimi inc, 1291
Service budgétaire Lac-Saint-Jean-Est, 1291
Sudbury Community Service Centre Inc., 1353
Thunder Bay Counselling Centre, 1377

Crime
British Columbia Crime Prevention Association, 238

Centre international pour la prévention de la criminalité, 535
The Mackenzie Institute, 924
Victims of Violence, 1432

Criminology
British Columbia Crime Prevention Association, 238
Canadian Training Institute, 496

Crisis Intervention Services
Battlefords Interval House Society, 200
CAEO Québec, 270
Canadian Association of Sexual Assault Centres, 333
Community Torchlight Guelph/Wellington/Dufferin, 607
Crisis Centre North Bay, 642
Distress Centre of Durham Region, 659
Distress Centre of Ottawa & Region, 659
Distress Centres Ontario, 659
Distress Line Sarnia, 659
Fédération des maisons d'hébergement pour femmes, 715
Fredericton Sexual Assault Crisis Centre, 759
Gai Écoute inc., 766
Kawartha Sexual Assault Centre, 882
Kids Help Phone, 886
Niagara Region Sexual Assault Centre, 1025
Oakville Distress Centre, 1053
Ontario Coalition of Rape Crisis Centres, 1072
Oshawa-Durham Rape Crisis Centre, 1128
Ottawa Rape Crisis Centre, 1131
Prince Edward Island Rape & Sexual Assault Centre, 1176
Réseau des femmes du sud de l'Ontario, 1219
Sexual Assault Centre Kingston Inc., 1292
Sexual Assault Centre London, 1292
Sexual Assault Crisis Centre of Essex County Inc., 1293
Sexual Assault Support Centre Ottawa, 1293
South Okanagan Women In Need Society, 1335
Spectra Helpline, 1340
Suicide Action Montréal, 1353
Tel-Aide Outaouais, 1369
Timmins & Area Women in Crisis Support & Information Centre on Violence Against Women, 1379
Vancouver Island Crisis Society, 1426
Vancouver Rape Relief & Women's Shelter, 1428
Victoria Cool Aid Society, 1432
Youth Empowerment & Support Services, 1475
YWCA Westman Women's Shelter, 1482

Critics
Association internationale de la critique littéraire, 1509
Association québécoise des critiques de cinéma, 172

Croatians & Croatia
Canadian Croatian Congress, 373

Crohn's & Colitis
CHILD Foundation, 560
Crohn's & Colitis Canada, 642
IBD Foundation, 829

Cross-Cultural Communication
Coady International Institute, 577
The Comparative & International Education Society of Canada, 608
CUSO International, 646
Kawartha World Issues Centre, 882
Pier 21 Society, 1159
Unisphere Global Resource Centre, 1408

Cubans & Cuba
Canadian-Cuban Friendship Association Toronto, 506

Culinary Arts
Société des chefs, cuisiniers et pâtissiers du Québec, 1317

Cultural Affairs
Canadian Institute of Cultural Affairs, 415
Société des attractions touristiques du Québec, 1317

Cultural Exchanges
AFS Interculture Canada, 13
Saskatchewan Cultural Exchange Society, 1262

Culture
Black Cultural Society for Nova Scotia, 213
Canada-Israel Cultural Foundation, 283
The Canadian Zionist Cultural Association, 506
Le Centre culturel francophone de Vancouver, 526
Chinese Cultural Centre of Greater Toronto, 564
Comité culturel "La Chaussée", 591
Conseil culturel fransaskois, 614
Conseil de la culture de la Gaspésie, 615
Conseil de la culture du Bas-Saint-Laurent, 616
Culture Mauricie, 645
Folklore Canada International, 742
Heritage Park Society, 813
Institute of Cultural Affairs International, 846
Kanien'kehaka Onkwawen'na Raotitiohkwa Language & Cultural Centre, 881
Kings Historical Society, 888
Latvian Canadian Cultural Centre, 900
The Laurier Institution, 900
La Maison de la culture inc., 926
North Peace Cultural Society, 1032
Ojibway & Cree Cultural Centre, 1055
Segal Centre for the Performing Arts at the Saidye, 1289
Société de conservation de la Baie de l'Isle-Verte, 1314
Société Saint-Jean-Baptiste du Centre du Québec, 1324
U'mista Cultural Society, 1401
Viscount Cultural Council Inc., 1435
Woodland Cultural Centre, 1464

Curling
Curling Québec, 646

Cystic Fibrosis
Cystic Fibrosis Canada, 647
Fibrose kystique Québec, 733

Cytology
Canadian Society of Cytology, 482

Czech Canadians
Masaryk Memorial Institute Inc., 952

DES Exposure
DES Action USA, 1521

Dams
Probe International, 1181

Dance
The Actors' Fund of Canada, 7
Alberta Dance Alliance, 32
Ballet Creole, 194
Brian Webb Dance Co., 228
Canada Dance Festival Society, 278
Le Carré des Lombes, 515
Cercle d'expression artistique Nyata Nyata, 537
Compagnie de danse Migrations, 608
Dance Centre, 648
The Dance Centre, 649
Dance Nova Scotia, 649
Dance Oremus Danse, 649
Dance Saskatchewan Inc., 649
Dancemakers, 649
Dancer Transition Resource Centre, 649
EDAM Performing Arts Society, 674
Fortier Danse-Création, 754
Harbourfront Centre, 803
Kinesis Dance Society, 888
Margie Gillis Dance Foundation, 949
Montréal Danse, 972
O Vertigo Danse, 1052
Opéra Atelier, 1114
Les Productions DansEncorps Inc., 1181
Regroupement québécois de la danse, 1216
Springboard Dance, 1346
Sun Ergos, A Company of Theatre & Dance, 1354
Toronto Dance Theatre, 1383
Vancouver Moving Theatre, 1427
Winnipeg's Contemporary Dancers, 1460

Danish Canadians & Denmark
Dania Home Society, 650
Danish Canadian National Museum Society, 650
Dickson Store Museum Society, 656

Darts
Association de Dards du Québec inc., 100

Day Care - Adult
Chown Adult Day Care Centre, 566
Crossreach Adult Day Centre, 644

Day Care - Children
Canadian Child Care Federation, 355
Manitoba Child Care Association, 933

Death & Dying
Canadian Hospice Palliative Care Association, 409
Dying with Dignity, 665

Debating
Alberta Debate & Speech Association, 32
Saskatchewan Elocution & Debate Association, 1264

Defence
Conference of Defence Associations, 612

Democracy
Parliamentary Centre, 1142

Dentistry
Association des conseils des médecins, dentistes et pharmaciens du Québec, 109
Ordre des dentistes du Québec, 1121

Dermatology
Association des dermatologistes du Québec, 110

Design
Nova Scotia Designer Crafts Council, 1044
Society of Graphic Designers of Canada, 1329

Developing Countries
African Enterprise (Canada), 13
Aga Khan Foundation Canada, 14
Almas Jiwani Foundation, 59
The Belinda Stronach Foundation, 204
Canadian Crossroads International, 373
Canadian Food for Children, 391
Canadian Physicians for Aid & Relief, 454
CARE Canada, 511
Carrefour de solidarité internationale inc., 515
Change for Children Association, 551
Christian Blind Mission International, 566
CODA International Training, 1518
CODE, 580
Colin B. Glassco Charitable Foundation for Children, 581
Collaboration Santé Internationale, 581
Comité de solidarité/Trois-Rivières, 592
Compassion Canada, 608
CUSO International, 646
Dignitas International, 656
Ethiopiaid, 697
Farm Radio International, 705
Fondation Edward Assh, 746
Foundation for International Training, 755
Horizons of Friendship, 821
Humanity First Canada, 827
The Hunger Project Canada, 827
Inter Pares, 851
The Marquis Project, Inc., 952
MATCH International Women's Fund, 954
Mennonite Central Committee Canada, 960
Nepali Children's Education Project, 1003
Oxfam Canada, 1134
Plan Canada, 1161
The Primate's World Relief & Development Fund, 1170
Probe International, 1181
Save a Family Plan, 1281
Sleeping Children Around the World, 1303
SOS Children's Villages Canada, 1333
Terre sans frontières, 1372
WaterCan, 1442
World Vision Canada, 1467
Youth Challenge International, 1475

Registered Charitable Organizations Index / Development Education

Development Education
Canadian Bureau for International Education, 347
Centre canadien d'étude et de coopération internationale, 526
Coady International Institute, 577
CODE, 580
Comité régional d'éducation pour le développement international de Lanaudière, 592
CUSO International, 646
Development & Peace, 654
Innovations et réseaux pour le développement, 1532
Kawartha World Issues Centre, 882
MATCH International Women's Fund, 954
One World Arts, 1058
Société de coopération pour le développement international, 1314
Victoria International Development Education Association, 1432

Developmentally Disabled Persons
Action Intégration en Déficience Intellectuelle, 6
AiMHi, Prince George Association for Community Living, 18
L'Arche Atlantic Region, 76
L'Arche Canada, 77
L'Arche Foundation, 77
L'Arche Ontario, 77
L'Arche Québec, 77
L'Arche Western Region, 77
Association de Montréal pour la déficience intellectuelle, 102
Association de Sherbrooke pour la déficience intellectuelle, 104
Association du syndrome de Down de L'Estrie, 131
Association pour l'intégration communautaire de l'Outaouais, 165
Association pour l'intégration sociale - Région Beauce-Sartigan, 165
Association pour l'intégration sociale (Rouyn-Noranda) inc., 166
Association pour l'intégration sociale d'Ottawa, 166
Barrhead Association for Community Living, 197
Beehive Support Services Association, 204
Best Buddies Canada, 206
Bridges Family Programs Association, 228
British Columbia Lions Society for Children with Disabilities, 245
Brockville & District Association for Community Involvement, 260
Calgary Community Living Society, 271
Camrose Association for Community Living, 277
Canadian Association for Community Living, 298
CanLearn Society for Persons with Learning Difficulties, 508
Chilliwack Society for Community Living, 563
Clements Centre Society, 573
Community Living Ajax-Pickering & Whitby, 600
Community Living Algoma, 600
Community Living Alternatives Society, 600
Community Living Association (Lanark County), 600
Community Living Atikokan, 600
Community Living Brantford, 600
Community Living Cambridge, 600
Community Living Dryden-Sioux Lookout, 601
Community Living Dufferin, 601
Community Living Durham North, 601
Community Living Elgin, 601
Community Living Espanola, 601
Community Living Essex County, 601
Community Living Fort Erie, 602
Community Living Fort Frances & District, 602
Community Living Greater Sudbury, 602
Community Living Guelph Wellington, 602
Community Living Haldimand, 602
Community Living Huntsville, 602
Community Living Huronia, 602
Community Living Kawartha Lakes, 603
Community Living Kingston, 603
Community Living London, 603
Community Living Manitoulin, 603
Community Living Mississauga, 603
Community Living Newmarket/Aurora District, 603
Community Living North Bay, 603
Community Living North Halton, 603
Community Living Oakville, 604
Community Living Ontario, 604
Community Living Oshawa / Clarington, 604
Community Living Parry Sound, 604
Community Living Peterborough, 604
Community Living Prince Edward (County), 604
Community Living Quinte West, 604
Community Living Sarnia-Lambton, 605
Community Living Society, 605
Community Living South Huron, 605
Community Living Stormont County, 605
Community Living Stratford & Area, 605
Community Living Thunder Bay, 605
Community Living Toronto, 605
Community Living Upper Ottawa Valley, 605
Community Living Victoria, 606
Community Living Wallaceburg, 606
Community Living West Nipissing, 606
Community Living West Northumberland, 606
Community Living York South, 606
Corporation l'Espoir, 631
Cranbrook Society for Community Living, 638
Crowsnest Community Support Society, 644
Developmental Disabilities Resource Centre of Calgary, 655
E3 Community Services, 666
Early Childhood Intervention Program (ECIP) Sask. Inc., 667
Families for a Secure Future, 701
Fondation québécoise de la déficience intellectuelle, 747
Fort St. John Association for Community Living, 753
Gateway Association, 767
Harry E. Foster Foundation, 804
Hearst & Area Association for Community Living, 808
Homestead Christian Care, 820
Inclusion Alberta, 831
Inclusion BC, 831
Inclusion Powell River Soceity, 832
Indefinite Arts Society, 832
Independence Plus Inc., 832
Intégration communautaire Cochrane Association for Community Living, 850
James Bay Association for Community Living, 868
Kamloops Society for Community Living, 880
Kenora Association for Community Living, 883
Kinsight, 890
Lethbridge Association for Community Living, 907
Lo-Se-Ca Foundation, 919
Madawaska Valley Association for Community Living, 924
McMan Youth, Family & Community Services Association, 955
Middlesex Community Living, 965
Mill Woods Society for Community Living, 965
Mission Association for Community Living, 968
MSA Society for Community Living, 978
New Brunswick Association for Community Living, 1004
Newfoundland & Labrador Association for Community Living, 1015
Niagara Support Services, 1026
Norfolk Association for Community Living, 1028
North Hastings Community Integration Association, 1031
Our Harbour, 1132
Pamiqsaiji Association for Community Living, 1138
Parkland Community Living & Supports Society, 1142
Parrainage civique Montréal, 1143
PEI People First, 1148
Penticton & District Society for Community Living, 1150
People First Nova Scotia, 1151
People First of Canada, 1151
People First of Ontario, 1151
Prince Edward Island Association for Community Living, 1172
Quad County Support Services, 1195
Quesnel Community Living Association, 1200
Red Deer Action Group, 1209
Red Lake & District Association for Community Living, 1210
Regroupement de parents de personnes ayant une déficience intellectuelle de Montréal, 1214
REHOBOTH Christian Ministries, 1216
St Catharines Association for Community Living, 1248
Saskatchewan Association for Community Living, 1256
Saskatchewan Association of Rehabilitation Centres, 1258
Semiahmoo Foundation, 1289
Skills Unlimited, 1302
Society of St. Vincent de Paul - Toronto Central Council, 1330
Superior Greenstone Association for Community Living, 1355
Surrey Association for Community Living, 1357
Vela Microboard Association of British Columbia, 1430
Vera Perlin Society, 1431
Yellowknife Association for Community Living, 1470

Diabetes
Alberta Diabetes Foundation, 32
Diabetes Canada, 655
Juvenile Diabetes Research Foundation Canada, 878

Dietitians & Nutritionists
College of Dietitians of Ontario, 584

Diplomatic & Consular Service
Commission internationale de diplomatique, 1518

Disabled Persons
Alberta Cerebral Palsy Sport Association, 27
Alberta Committee of Citizens with Disabilities, 30
Alberta Easter Seals Society, 33
ARCH Disability Law Centre, 76
Association de balle des jeunes handicapés de Laval-Laurentides-Lanaudière, 99
Association des alternatives en santé mentale de la Montérégie, 105
Association des personnes handicapées de la Rive-Sud Ouest, 122
Association des personnes handicapés visuels de l'Estrie, inc, 123
Association multi-ethnique pour l'intégration des personnes handicapées, 137
Association pour la promotion des droits des personnes handicapées, 166
BC Association for Individualized Technology and Supports, 201
Bridges Family Programs Association, 228
British Columbia Aboriginal Network on Disability Society, 229
Canadian Abilities Foundation, 285
Canadian Centre on Disability Studies, 354
Canadian Cerebral Palsy Sports Association, 354
Canadian Council on Rehabilitation & Work, 371
Canadian Foundation for Physically Disabled Persons, 394
Carefree Society, 511
Carleton Road Industries Association, 513
Centre de services Guigues, 530
Centre for Child Development, 531
Centre for Independent Living in Toronto, 532
Community Care for South Hastings, 596
Community Involvement of the Disabled, 599
Confédération des Organismes de Personnes Handicapées du Québec, 611
Disability Alliance British Columbia, 658
Disabled Peoples' International, 658
Early Childhood Intervention Program (ECIP) Sask. Inc., 667
Easter Seals Canada, 669
Easter Seals New Brunswick, 669
Easter Seals Nova Scotia, 669
Easter Seals Ontario, 669
Elk Valley Society for Community Living, 685
EmployAbilities, 686
FOCUS, 741
Fort McMurray Association for Community Living, 752
Goodwill Industries, 777
Goodwill Industries Essex Kent Lambton, 777
Goodwill Industries of Alberta, 778
Gustav Levinschi Foundation, 794
Handicap International Canada, 802
Handicapped Organization Promoting Equality, 803
High Prairie Association for Community Living, 814
Independence Plus Inc., 832
Kinsmen Foundation of British Columbia & Yukon, 890
Lac La Biche Disability Services, 894
Lights, Camera, Access!, 912
Manitoba League of Persons with Disabilities, 939
March of Dimes Canada, 949
March of Dimes Non-Profit Housing Corporation, 949
National Institute of Disability Management & Research, 994
North Shore Disability Resource Centre Association, 1032
NWT Disabilities Council, 1052
Ontario Prader-Willi Syndrome Association, 1097
Ontario Track 3 Ski Association for the Disabled, 1110
Open Door Group, 1114
The Order of United Commercial Travelers of America, 1119
Paralympic Sports Association (Alberta), 1138
Prince Edward Island Council of People with Disabilities, 1173
Professional Association of Therapeutic Horsemanship International, 1584
Reach for the Rainbow, 1205
Red Deer Action Group, 1209
Reena, 1210
Regroupement pour l'intégration sociale de Charlevoix, 1216
Rehabilitation Society of Southwestern Alberta, 1216
Robin Hood Association for the Handicapped, 1235
Saskatchewan Abilities Council, 1255
Saskatchewan Voice of People with Disabilities, Inc., 1277
The Shepherds' Trust, 1295
Société Logique, 1321
Société pour les enfants handicapés du Québec, 1322
Society for Manitobans with Disabilities Inc., 1326
Special Needs Planning Group, 1339
SportAbility BC, 1345
Step-By-Step Child Development Society, 1349
Sunrise Therapeutic Riding & Learning Centre, 1354
Tetra Society of North America, 1373
Theatre Terrific Society, 1375
VALID Association, 1424
The War Amputations of Canada, 1440

Disarmament
Physicians for Global Survival (Canada), 1158

Diseases
Association of Medical Microbiology & Infectious Disease Canada, 151
Barth Syndrome Foundation of Canada, 197
Batten Disease Support & Research Association - Canadian Chapter, 199
Brain Tumour Foundation of Canada, 225

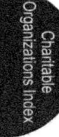

British Columbia Prader-Willi Syndrome Association, 249
The Canadian Addison Society, 288
Canadian Lyme Disease Foundation, 428
Canadian Society for Mucopolysaccharide & Related Diseases Inc., 477
Canadian Syringomyelia Network, 491
CHARGE Syndrome Canada, 552
Fédération québécoise des laryngectomisés, 729
Foundation for Prader-Willi Research in Canada, 756
Fragile X Research Foundation of Canada, 757
Huntington Society of Canada, 827
Jacob's Ladder - The Canadian Foundation for Control of Neurodegenerative Disease, 867
Meningitis Relief Canada, 960
Meningitis Research Foundation of Canada, 960
Ontario Prader-Willi Syndrome Association, 1097
Partners in Research, 1144
Prader-Willi Syndrome Association of Alberta, 1169
Promoting Awareness of RSD & CRPS in Canada, 1188
Regroupement québécois des maladies orphelines, 1216
Société Huntington du Québec, 1321
Thalassemia Foundation of Canada, 1373
Tuberous Sclerosis Canada Sclérose Tubéreuse, 1400

Disorders
Association des personnes intéressées à l'aphasie et à l'accident vasculaire cérébral, 123
Association du Syndrome de Sjogren, Inc, 131
Association/Troubles de l'Humeur et d'Anxiété au Québec, 179
Barth Syndrome Foundation of Canada, 197
Canadian Alopecia Areata Foundation, 292
Canadian Association for Clinical Microbiology & Infectious Diseases, 297
Canadian Association for Williams Syndrome, 307
Canadian Hemochromatosis Society, 404
Canadian Organization for Rare Disorders, 447
Canadian Porphyria Foundation Inc., 458
Cyclic Vomiting Syndrome Association, 1521
The Facial Pain Association, 1525
Fibromyalgia Association of Saskatchewan, 733
Fibromyalgia Support Group of Winnipeg, Inc., 733
Guillain-Barré Syndrome Foundation of Canada, 794
International Society for Affective Disorders, 1557
Joubert Syndrome & Related Disoarders Foundation, 1568
Kabuki Syndrome Network Inc., 879
Lymphovenous Association of Ontario, 923
National Alopecia Areata Foundation, 1572
Scleroderma Association of British Columbia, 1285
Sickle Cell Association of Ontario, 1297
Sjogren's Syndrome Foundation Inc., 1589
Society for Muscular Dystrophy Information International, 1326
Support Organization for Trisomy 18, 13 & Related Disorders, 1356
Tuberous Sclerosis Canada Sclérose Tubéreuse, 1400
Vasculitis Foundation Canada, 1430

Distance Education
Canadian Network for Innovation in Education, 440
Le Réseau d'enseignement francophone à distance du Canada, 1219

Diving
British Columbia Diving, 238
Diving Plongeon Canada, 659
Fédération québécoise des activités subaquatiques, 728
Manitoba Underwater Council, 946

Divorce
Family Mediation Canada, 703

Dogs
Boston Terrier Rescue Canada, 218
Canadian Chihuahua Rescue & Transport, 355
Canadian Kennel Club Foundation, 424

Domestic Violence
Crossroads for Women Inc., 644
Metropolitan Action Committee on Violence Against Women & Children, 964
The Shelter Movers of Toronto, 1295
Springtide Resources, 1346
Stop Abuse in Families Society, 1350
Viol-secours inc., 1435

Donkeys & Mules
The Donkey Sanctuary of Canada, 661

Doors & Windows
Association de vitrerie et fenestrations du Québec, 104

Doukhobors
The Canadian Doukhobor Society, 378

Down Syndrome
Canadian Down Syndrome Society, 378
Down Syndrome Association of Ontario, 661
Down Syndrome Association of Toronto, 661
Down Syndrome Research Foundation, 661
Manitoba Down Syndrome Society, 935
Windsor-Essex Down Syndrome Parent Association, 1457

Drama
British Columbia Drama Association, 239
Carousel Players, 514
Centre des auteurs dramatiques, 530
Manitoba Association of Playwrights, 931
The Québec Drama Federation, 1197
Theatre Nova Scotia, 1374

Drug Abuse
Addictions & Mental Health Ontario, 8
Canadian Centre on Substance Use & Addiction, 354
The Canadian Don't Do Drugs Society, 378
Centre for Addiction & Mental Health, 531
Council on Drug Abuse, 636
From Grief To Action, 763
Jean Tweed Treatment Centre, 869
Nechi Training, Research & Health Promotions Institute, 1002
Parent Action on Drugs, 1139
The Renascent Centres for Alcoholism & Drug Addiction, 1217

Drunk Driving
MADD Canada, 925

Ducks
Ducks Unlimited Canada, 663

Dyslexia
International Dyslexia Association, Canadian Dyslexia Association, 379

Dystonia
Dystonia Medical Research Foundation Canada, 665

Early Childhood Education
Association of Early Childhood Educators Ontario, 147
Quesnel & District Child Development Centre Association, 1200

Eastern Europe
East European Genealogical Society, Inc., 668

Eating Disorders
Bulimia Anorexia Nervosa Association, 264
National Eating Disorder Information Centre, 992

Ecology
Conservation Council of New Brunswick, 621
Conservation Council of Ontario, 622
Conservation Halton Foundation, 622
David Suzuki Foundation, 651
Ecoforestry Institute Society, 671
Ecological Farmers of Ontario, 672
Fédération des sociétés d'horticulture et d'écologie du Québec, 719
Friends of Ecological Reserves, 761
Friends of the Earth Canada, 762
Groupe de recherche en écologie sociale, 791
International Federation of Organic Agriculture Movements, 1548
International Union of Biological Sciences, 1564
John E. Mack Institute, 1568
Lifeforce Foundation, 911
The Nature Conservancy of Canada, 999
Niagara Peninsula Conservation Authority, 1025
Partners FOR the Saskatchewan River Basin, 1144
Québec-Labrador Foundation (Canada) Inc., 1199
Réseau québécois des groupes écologistes, 1225
Sierra Club of Canada, 1298
Society Promoting Environmental Conservation, 1331
Thames Region Ecological Association, 1373
World Wildlife Fund - Canada, 1468
Yukon Conservation Society, 1477

Economic Assistance (Domestic)
Canada India Village Aid Association, 280
Canadian Lutheran World Relief, 428
Canadian-Cuban Friendship Association Toronto, 506
Catholic Charities of The Archdiocese of Toronto, 518
Firefighters Burn Fund Inc., 738
Jamaican Self-Help Organization, 867
Jewish Free Loan Toronto, 872
Oxfam Canada, 1134
The Primate's World Relief & Development Fund, 1170
Romanian Children's Relief, 1235
Ronald McDonald House Charities of Canada, 1235
St. Andrew's Society of Toronto, 1248
Samaritan's Purse Canada, 1253
Saskatoon Open Door Society Inc., 1279
Save the Children Canada, 1281
Sleeping Children Around the World, 1303
SOS Children's Villages Canada, 1333
SOS Children's Villages Canada, 1333
Victoria Cool Aid Society, 1432
World Vision Canada, 1467

Economic Development
Centre local de développement Rouyn-Noranda, 536
Conseil canadien de la coopération et de la mutualité, 613
Conseil de la Coopération de la Saskatchewan, 615
Fondation de l'entrepreneurship, 743
Horizons of Friendship, 821
Mennonite Economic Development Associates Canada, 961
Société de développement économique du Saint-Laurent, 1315

Economics
Association des économistes québécois, 111
Canada West Foundation, 281
Canadian Foundation for Economic Education, 393
Centre for the Study of Living Standards, 534
The Fraser Institute, 757
Groupe de recherche en animation et planification économique, 791
International Institute of Fisheries Economics & Trade, 1551
The North-South Institute, 1036
Société Saint-Thomas-d'Aquin, 1325

Ecumenism
The Canadian Council of Churches, 368
Forum for Intercultural Leadership & Learning, 754
John Milton Society for the Blind in Canada, 875
Student Christian Movement of Canada, 1352
VISION TV, 1436
World Association for Christian Communication, 1465

Editors
Canadian Journalism Foundation, 423

Education
Académie européenne des sciences, des arts et des lettres, 1485
African Enterprise (Canada), 13
AFS Interculture Canada, 13
AIESEC, 18
American Academy of Religion, 1488
Associated Medical Services Inc., 89
L'Association des orthopédagogues du Québec inc., 121
Association des Scouts du Canada, 127
Association québécoise des cadres scolaires, 171
Black Educators Association of Nova Scotia, 213
Boîte à science - Conseil du loisir scientifique du Québec, 217
Canadian Association for Social Work Education, 304
Canadian Association for Teacher Education, 304
Canadian Association for University Continuing Education, 306
Canadian Association of Principals, 328
Canadian Association of Schools of Nursing, 332
Canadian Bureau for International Education, 347
Canadian Education & Research Institute for Counselling, 379
Canadian Education Association, 379
Canadian Film Centre, 390
Canadian Foundation for Economic Education, 393
Canadian Network for Environmental Education & Communication, 440
Canadian Organization for Development through Education, 447
Canadian Post-MD Education Registry, 458
Canadian Society for the Study of Education, 478
Canadian Society for the Study of Higher Education, 478
CanLearn Society for Persons with Learning Difficulties, 508
Catholic Association of Religious & Family Life Educators of Ontario, 517
Catholic Family Services of Toronto, 519
Centre d'animation de développement et de recherche en éducation, 528
Centre femmes de Rimouski, 531
Centre for Inquiry Canada, 533
Chawkers Foundation, 555
The Comparative & International Education Society of Canada, 608
Council of Ontario Universities, 635
Credit Institute of Canada, 640
Dance Oremus Danse, 649
Dorchester & Westmorland Literacy Council, 661
Earthwatch Institute, 1522
Ecological Farmers of Ontario, 672
ERS Training & Development Corporation, 695
Fédération des parents francophones de l'Alberta, 717
Fédération des professionnelles et professionnels de l'éducation du Québec, 718
Fédération québécoise des directions d'établissements d'enseignement, 728
Foundation for Education Perth Huron, 755
Hamber Foundation, 800
Hands on Summer Camp Society, 803
Humanist Canada, 826
Indspire, 835
International Society for Music Education, 1558
Inter-Varsity Christian Fellowship, 862
The Jane Goodall Institute of Canada, 868
Learning Enrichment Foundation, 905
The Mackenzie Institute, 924

National Reading Campaign, Inc., 995
Nechi Training, Research & Health Promotions Institute, 1002
Nepali Children's Education Project, 1003
Ontario Trucking Association,
Outdoor Recreation Council of British Columbia, 1133
Pacific Life Bible College, 1135
Pathways to Education Canada, 1145
PeerNetBC, 1148
People for Education, 1151
Road Scholar, 1586
SEEDS Foundation, 1289
Société des écoles du monde du BI du Québec et de la francophonie, 1317
Société historique Alphonse-Desjardins, 1319
Société Québécoise de Psilogie inc, 1323
Society for Quality Education, 1326
Toronto Montessori Institute, 1386
United World Colleges, 1418
Universities Canada, 1418
Visions of Science Network for Learning, 1436
The W. Garfield Weston Foundation, 1439
The Workers' Educational Association of Canada, 1464
Working Women Community Centre, 1464
Youth Flight Canada, 1475

Educational Media
Centre franco-ontarien de ressources pédagogiques, 534
Manitoba Indian Cultural Education Centre, 939
SkyWorks Charitable Foundation, 1303
Youth Media Alliance, 1476

Egypt
Society for the Study of Egyptian Antiquities, 1327

Eighteenth-Century Studies
Canadian Society for Eighteenth-Century Studies, 474

Electric Power
Association de l'industrie électrique du Québec, 100

Electrical Engineering
Institute of Electrical & Electronics Engineers Inc. - Region 7, 846

Electrolysis
Association des professionnels en électrolyse et soins esthétiques du Québec, 126

Electronic Engineering
Institute of Electrical & Electronics Engineers Inc. - Region 7, 846

Electronic Instruments
The Instrumentation, Systems & Automation Society of America, 1534

Electronics Industry
Armed Forces Communications & Electronics Association (Canada), 82

Embroidery
Embroiderers' Association of Canada, Inc., 685

Emergency Housing
Adsum for Women & Children, 9
Almost Home, 59
Battlefords Interval House Society, 200
Calgary Women's Emergency Shelter Association, 275
Chez Doris, 557
Covenant House Toronto, 637
Evangel Hall Mission, 698
Fédération des maisons d'hébergement pour femmes, 715
Halifax Transition House Association - Bryony House, 799
Inn From the Cold Society, 838
Kenora Fellowship Centre, 883
Lookout Emergency Aid Society, 919
Mission Bon Accueil, 969
Nellie's Shelter, 1003
La rue des femmes, 1243
South Okanagan Women in Need Society, 1335

Emergency Services
Focus Humanitarian Assistance Canada, 741
Hampton Food Basket & Clothing Centre Inc., 802
New Brunswick Association of Food Banks, 1005
Occupational First Aid Attendants Association of British Columbia, 1054
Oromocto & Surrounding Area Food & Clothing Bank, 1127
St. John Ambulance, 1248

Employee Counselling
Unemployed Help Centre, 1404

Employment
A.C.C.E.S. Employment, 4
Conseil d'intervention pour l'accès des femmes au travail, 615
Dress for Success, 662
EmployAbilities, 686
Flowercart, 741
Goodwill Industries, 777
Goodwill Industries Essex Kent Lambton, 777
Goodwill Industries of Alberta, 778
Horizon Achievement Centre, 821
Jobs Unlimited, 873
Ontario Network of Employment Skills Training Projects, 1093
Open Door Group, 1114
Port Colborne Community Association for Research Extension, 1165
Regional Occupation Centre Foundation, 1212
Shelburne Association Supporting Inclusion, 1295
Thunder Bay Counselling Centre, 1377
Times Change Women's Employment Service, 1379

Endometriosis
Endometriosis Association, Inc., 1523

Energy
Association québécoise pour la maîtrise de l'énergie, 176
Community Energy Association, 597
Energy Probe Research Foundation, 688
Institut de la Francophonie pour le développement durable, 841
Planetary Association for Clean Energy, Inc., 1161
SEEDS Foundation, 1289
World Nuclear Association, 1606

Energy Conservation
Elora Environment Centre, 685
Energy Probe Research Foundation, 688

Engineering
American Society of Mining & Reclamation, 1501
Association des ingénieurs-professeurs des sciences appliquées, 116
Association of Professional Engineers of Prince Edward Island, 159
The Canadian Academy of Engineering, 286
The Engineering Institute of Canada, 688
Hungarian Canadian Engineers' Association, 827
L'Institut de développement de produits, 841
NACE International, 1571
Ordre des ingénieurs forestiers du Québec, 1123
Visions of Science Network for Learning, 1436

English Language
Catholic Action Montreal, 517
English Speaking Catholic Council, 689
Newcomer Women's Services Toronto, 1015
Québec Writers' Federation, 1199

English as a Second Language
Association of British Columbia Teachers of English as an Additional Language, 140
Folk Arts Council of St Catharines, 742
Haldimand-Norfolk Literacy Council, 798
Project Adult Literacy Society, 1187
Society for the Promotion of the Teaching of English as a Second Language in Quebec, 1326

TESL Nova Scotia, 1372
Victoria READ Society, 1433

Enterostomy
Ostomy Canada Society, 1129
Winnipeg Ostomy Association, 1459

Entertainment
Canadian Film Centre, 390

Entomology
Association des entomologistes amateurs du Québec inc., 112
Entomological Society of Manitoba Inc., 690
Société d'entomologie du Québec, 1309
Toronto Entomologists Association, 1384

Environment
Alberta Ecotrust Foundation, 33
American Society for Environmental History, 1498
American Society of Mining & Reclamation, 1501
Les AmiEs de la Terre de Québec, 67
British Columbia Spaces for Nature, 254
Canadian Network for Environmental Education & Communication, 440
Canadian Society for the Protection of Nature in Israel, 477
Carthy Foundation, 516
Chawkers Foundation, 555
Conservation Council of Ontario, 622
Conservation Foundation of Greater Toronto, 622
Conserver Society of Hamilton & District Inc., 623
CUSO International, 646
David Suzuki Foundation, 651
Earth Day Canada, 667
Earthsave Canada, 667
East Coast Trail Association, 668
EcoSource Mississauga, 673
Ecotrust Canada, 673
Elora Environment Centre, 685
Environmental Action Barrie - Living Green, 691
Environmental Defence, 691
FarmFolk CityFolk, 706
Fondation québécoise en environnement, 748
Friends of Clayoquot Sound, 760
Friends of the Central Experimental Farm, 762
Friends of the Earth Canada, 762
Grand River Conservation Foundation, 780
Greenpeace USA, 1529
Groupe de recherche en écologie sociale, 791
Habitat Acquisition Trust, 795
Harmony Foundation of Canada, 803
Heartwood Centre for Community Youth Development, 810
Island Nature Trust, 865
Kamloops Wildlife Park Society, 881
The Kindness Club, 888
Lambton Wildlife Inc., 897
Manitoba Eco-Network Inc., 936
Marine Renewables Canada, 950
The Marquis Project, Inc., 952
NACE International, 1571
The Nature Conservancy of Canada, 999
Nature Trust of New Brunswick, 1001
Niagara Peninsula Conservation Authority, 1025
Ontario Public Health Association, 1098
Outdoor Recreation Council of British Columbia, 1133
Peace & Environment Resource Centre, 1146
The Pembina Institute, 1149
Petroleum Tank Management Association of Alberta, 1154
The Pollution Probe Foundation, 1164
Protected Areas Association of Newfoundland & Labrador, 1190
Réseau environnement, 1223
Réseau québécois des groupes écologistes, 1225
Ruiter Valley Land Trust, 1244
Saskatchewan Environmental Society, 1264
Sierra Club of Canada, 1298
Society Promoting Environmental Conservation, 1331

TD Friends of the Environment Foundation, 1367
Tellus Institute, 1597
Tides Canada Foundation, 1379
USC Canada, 1423
Valhalla Wilderness Society, 1424
The W. Garfield Weston Foundation, 1439
Worldwatch Institute, 1608

Environmental & Outdoor Education
Boundless Adventures Association, 219
Council of Outdoor Educators of Ontario, 635
Evergreen, 699
Green Kids Inc., 788
Inside Education, 839
National Association for Environmental Education (UK), 1572
Peterborough Field Naturalists, 1153
Seagull Foundation, 1288
VanDusen Botanical Garden Association, 1429

Environmental Biology
Canadian Society of Environmental Biologists, 482

Environmental Health
Environmental Health Association of British Columbia, 691
Environmental Health Association of Ontario, 692
Environmental Health Foundation of Canada, 692
International Institute of Concern for Public Health, 858
National Environmental Health Association, 1576

Environmental Law
Canadian Institute of Resources Law, 419
Centre québécois du droit de l'environnement, 536
Ecojustice Canada Society, 672
The Environmental Law Centre (Alberta) Society, 692
West Coast Environmental Law, 1444

Environmental Management
Alberta Lake Management Society, 39

Environmental Policy
The Fraser Institute, 757

Epilepsy & Related Disorders
Association québécoise de l'épilepsie, 169
British Columbia Epilepsy Society, 240
Canadian Epilepsy Alliance, 382
Edmonton Epilepsy Association, 677
Epilepsy & Seizure Association of Manitoba, 693
Epilepsy Association of Calgary, 693
Epilepsy Association of Nova Scotia, 693
Epilepsy Canada, 693
Epilepsy Foundation of America, 1524
Epilepsy Ontario, 693
Epilepsy Saskatoon, 694
Victoria Epilepsy & Parkinson's Centre Society, 1432

Equal Opportunity Employment
Nova Scotia League for Equal Opportunities, 1046

Equestrian Sports & Activities
Equestrian Association for the Disabled, 694
Equestrian Canada, 694
Fédération équestre du Québec inc., 720
Ontario Horse Trials Association, 1086
Professional Association of Therapeutic Horsemanship International, 1584

Equipment & Machinery
Association sectorielle: Fabrication d'équipement de transport et de machines, 178

Ergonomics
Commonwealth Human Ecology Council, 1518

Esperanto
Esperanto Association of Canada, 695
Société québécoise d'espéranto, 1323

Ethics
Canadian Centre for Ethics & Corporate Policy, 353

Ethiopian Canadians
Ethiopian Association in the Greater Toronto Area & Surrounding Regions, 697

Evangelism
African Enterprise (Canada), 13
Billy Graham Evangelistic Association of Canada, 211
Child Evangelism Fellowship of Canada, 559
Community of Christ - Canada East Mission, 606
Emmanuel International Canada, 686
Evangelical Covenant Church of Canada, 698
Evangelical Fellowship of Canada, 698
Evangelical Mennonite Conference, 699
Foursquare Gospel Church of Canada, 756
Independent Assemblies of God International - Canada, 832
MB Mission, 954
Solbrekken Evangelistic Association of Canada, 1332
TEAM of Canada Inc., 1368
Threshold Ministries, 1377

Executives
Canadian Executive Service Organization, 383

Exhibitions & Fairs
Battlefords Agricultural Society, 200
Canadian Association of Fairs & Exhibitions, 314
Prince Albert Exhibition Association, 1171
Richmond Agricultural Society, 1229
Royal Agricultural Winter Fair Association, 1237
UFI - The Global Association of the Exhibition Industry, 1598
Vancouver Jewish Film Centre Society, 1427
Western Fair Association, 1449
Westerner Park, 1450

Export Trade
Groupe export agroalimentaire Québec - Canada, 792

Eye Banks
Eye Bank of BC, 700
Eye Bank of Canada - Ontario Division, 700
Fondation de la banque d'yeux du Québec inc., 744
Lions Eye Bank of Manitoba & Northwest Ontario, Incorporated, 913
Saskatchewan Lions Eye Bank, 1269

Eye Diseases & Disorders
The Foundation Fighting Blindness, 755
Glaucoma Research Society of Canada, 774
Operation Eyesight Universal, 1115
Vision Institute of Canada, 1435

Facial Disfigurement
AboutFace, 3

Facility Management
International Facility Management Association, 1546

Faculty & Staff Associations
Association du personnel administratif et professionnel de l'Université de Moncton, 131
Syndicat des professeurs et des professeures de l'Université du Québec à Trois-Rivières, 1364

Family
British Columbia Council for Families, 237
Calgary Community Living Society, 271
Canadian Association of Family Resource Programs, 314
Canadian Families & Corrections Network, 383
Carrefour-Ressources, 516
Catholic Family Services of Saskatoon, 519
Children's Aid Society of the Region of Peel, 561
Confédération des organismes familiaux du Québec, 611
Elizabeth House, 685
Family & Children's Services of Guelph & Wellington County, 702
Family Services of Greater Vancouver, 704
Fédération nationale des services de préparation au mariage, 722
4Korners Family Resource Center, 756
Jewish Family & Child, 871
Jewish Family Services - Calgary, 871
Jewish Family Services Edmonton, 871
Jewish Family Services of Ottawa-Carleton, 872
Kids First Parent Association of Canada, 886
Mouvement québécois des vacances familiales inc., 978
Nova Scotia Council for the Family, 1043
St. Leonard's Youth & Family Services Society, 1250
Save a Family Plan, 1281
South Peace Community Resources Society, 1335
Vanier Institute of The Family, 1429

Family Planning
Action Canada for Sexual Health & Rights, 6
Compass Centre for Sexual Wellness, 608
Halifax Sexual Health Centre, 799
Health Initiatives for Youth Hamilton, 806
Jessie's - The June Callwood Centre for Young Women, 870
Marguerite Bourgeoys Family Centre Fertility Care Programme, 949
Natural Family Planning Association, 998
Options for Sexual Health, 1117
Pictou County Centre for Sexual Health, 1159
Planned Parenthood of Toronto, 1161
Planned Parenthood Ottawa, 1161
Planned Parenthood Waterloo Region, 1162
Serena Canada, 1290
Sexual Health Centre Lunenburg County, 1293
Sexual Health Network of Québec Inc., 1293
YWCA of Banff Programs & Services, 1482

Family Therapy
Carizon Family & Community Services, 513
Catholic Family Service of Ottawa, 518
Catholic Family Services of Peel Dufferin, 519
Catholic Family Services of Simcoe County, 519
Catholic Family Services of Toronto, 519
Child & Family Services of Western Manitoba, 558
Community Counselling Centre of Nipissing, 596
Family Counselling & Support Services for Guelph-Wellington, 702
Family Mediation Canada, 703
Family Service Toronto, 704
Family Services York Region (Georgina), 705
Native Child & Family Services of Toronto, 997
Peel Family Services, 1147
Service familial de Sudbury, 1291
Stop Abuse in Families Society, 1350
Thunder Bay Counselling Centre, 1377

Farms & Farming
American Farmland Trust, 1492
Association des fermières de l'Ontario, 114
Cercles de fermières du Québec, 537
Ecological Farmers of Ontario, 672
Farm & Food Care Canada, 705
Farm Radio International, 705
Friends of the Central Experimental Farm, 762
International Federation of Organic Agriculture Movements, 1548
National Farmers Foundation, 993
Union des cultivateurs franco-ontariens, 1406
USC Canada, 1423
World Ploughing Organization, 1607

Fathers
Association des pères gais de Montréal inc., 122
Dads Can, 648

Fencing
Canadian Fencing Federation, 389
Saskatchewan Fencing Association, 1265

Fertility & Infertility (Human)
Canadian Fertility & Andrology Society, 389
Infertility Awareness Association of Canada, 836
Infertility Network, 836
Serena Canada, 1290

Festivals
Associated Manitoba Arts Festivals, Inc., 89
Bard on the Beach Theatre Society, 196
The Battlefords Music Festival, 200
Carnaval de Québec, 514
Edmonton Heritage Festival Association, 677
Edmonton International Film Festival Society, 678
Fédération culturelle acadienne de la Nouvelle-Écosse, 708
Folk Arts Council of St Catharines, 742
Greater Vancouver International Film Festival Society, 786
Harbourfront Centre, 803
Intrepid Theatre Co. Society, 862
Kingston Kiwanis Music Festival, 889
Oshawa-Whitby Kiwanis Music & Theatre Festival, 1128
Salon du livre de Toronto et Festival des écrivains, 1252
Toronto International Film Festival Inc., 1385
Vancouver Jewish Film Centre Society, 1427
Vues d'Afriques - Les Journées du cinéma africain et créole, 1439
Yorkton Film Festival, 1474

Fibromyalgia Syndrome
Association de la Fibromyalgie des Laurentides, 101
Fibromyalgia Association of Saskatchewan, 733
Fibromyalgia Support Group of Winnipeg, Inc., 733
National ME/FM Action Network, 995

Field Hockey
Field Hockey Alberta, 734
Field Hockey Canada, 734

Film
Academy of Canadian Cinema & Television, 3
The Actors' Fund of Canada, 7
Association des propriétaires de cinémas du Québec, 126
Association québécoise des critiques de cinéma, 172
The Atlantic Film Festival Association, 184
Canadian Film Centre, 390
Canadian Film Institute, 390
Canadian Picture Pioneers, 455
La cinémathèque québécoise, 569
Edmonton International Film Festival Society, 678
Film & Video Arts Society Alberta, 735
Greater Vancouver International Film Festival Society, 786
Liaison of Independent Filmmakers of Toronto, 909
National Screen Institute - Canada, 996
New Brunswick Filmmakers' Co-op, 1008
Pacific Cinémathèque Pacifique, 1135
Parlimage CCF, 1143
PAVED Arts, 1146
Saskatchewan Filmpool Co-operative, 1265
Toronto Film Society, 1384
Toronto International Film Festival Inc., 1385
Toronto Jewish Film Society, 1385
Vues d'Afriques - Les Journées du cinéma africain et créole, 1439
Winnipeg Film Group, 1458
Women in Film & Television - Toronto, 1461
Yorkton Film Festival, 1474

Finance
Association de planification fiscale et financière, 103
Canadian Tax Foundation, 492
Christian Stewardship Services, 568

Financial Services Industry
Consolidated Credit Counseling Services of Canada, Inc., 623
Credit Institute of Canada, 640
Edmonton CFA Society, 675
Institut québécois de planification financière, 843
Ontario Association of Credit Counselling Services, 1063
Service budgétaire et communautaire de Chicoutimi inc, 1291

Fire Fighting
Association des chefs en sécurité incendie du Québec, 108
Association des Pompiers de Montréal inc., 124
Canadian Fallen Firefighters Foundation, 383
Fire Fighters Historical Society of Winnipeg, Inc., 738
Firefighters Burn Fund Inc., 738
Prince Rupert Fire Museum Society, 1179

Fire Protection & Prevention
Fire Prevention Canada, 738

Firearms
Dominion of Canada Rifle Association, 660
Fédération québécoise de tir, 728
Shooting Federation of Canada, 1297

First Aid
Advanced Coronary Treatment (ACT) Foundation of Canada, 10
Occupational First Aid Attendants Association of British Columbia, 1054
St. John Ambulance, 1248

Fish & Game
Salmon Preservation Association for the Waters of Newfoundland, 1252
Whitecourt Fish & Game Association, 1452

Fisheries
Atlantic Salmon Federation, 186
International Institute of Fisheries Economics & Trade, 1551
Nova Scotia Salmon Association, 1048
Oceana Canada, 1054

Fishing & Angling
Association de la Rivière Ste-Marguerite Inc., 102
Edmonton Trout Fishing Club, 679
Ontario Federation of Anglers & Hunters, 1079

Floor Covering Industry
Fédération québécoise des revêtements de sol, 729

Flowers
American Rhododendron Society, 1497
Canadian Rose Society, 468
FloraQuebeca, 741
North American Native Plant Society, 1029
Société québécoise du dahlia, 1324

Folk Arts
Community Folk Art Council of Toronto, 597
Folk Arts Council of St Catharines, 742
Georgian Bay Folk Society, 771

Folk Dancing
British Columbia Square & Round Dance Federation, 255
The Royal Scottish Country Dance Society, 1587

Folk Music
Canadian Society for Traditional Music, 479
Canmore Folk & Blues Club, 508
Edmonton Folk Music Festival, 677
Folk Festival Society of Calgary, 742
Georgian Bay Folk Society, 771

Folklore
British Columbia Folklore Society, 241
Canadian Nautical Research Society, 440
Centre franco-ontarien de folklore, 534
Folklore Canada International, 742
Folklore Studies Association of Canada, 742

Food Banks
Agape Food Bank, 14
Airdrie Food Bank, 20
Atelier RADO Inc., 180
Banff Food Bank Association, 195
Les banques alimentaires du Québec, 196
Beaverlodge Food Bank, 203

Registered Charitable Organizations Index / Food Industry

Bow Valley Food Bank, 219
Boyle Food Bank Association, 221
Calgary Food Bank, 272
Cambridge Self-Help Food Bank, 275
Campbell River & District Food Bank, 276
Camrose & District Food Bank, 277
Central Okanagan Community Food Bank, 524
Chemainus Harvest House Society Food Bank, 555
Community Kitchen Program of Calgary, 599
Comox Valley Food Bank Society, 608
Cowichan Valley Basket Society, 637
East Wellington Community Services, 669
Edmonton's Food Bank, 680
Feed Nova Scotia, 731
Food Bank of Waterloo Region, 749
Food Banks Alberta Association, 749
Food Banks Canada, 749
Food Depot Alimentaire, Inc., 749
Food for Life Canada, 749
Foodshare Toronto, 750
Fort York Food Bank, 754
Gananoque Food Bank, 766
Glace Bay Food Bank Society, 774
Gleaners Food Bank, 774
Golden Food Bank, 776
Goldstream Food Bank Society, 777
Greater Vancouver Food Bank Society, 786
Guelph Food Bank, 793
Hamilton Food Share, 801
Hampton Food Basket & Clothing Centre Inc., 802
Humanity First Canada, 827
Inner City Home of Sudbury, 839
Interfaith Food Bank Society of Lethbridge, 852
Lanark County Food Bank, 897
Leduc & District Food Bank Association, 906
Lethbridge Soup Kitchen Association, 908
Lighthouse Food Bank Society, 912
London Food Bank, 918
Medicine Hat & District Food Bank, 958
Mission Community Services Food Centre, 969
Mississauga Food Bank, 970
Moisson Laurentides, 971
Moisson Mauricie/Centre-du-Québec, 971
Moisson Québec, 971
Mustard Seed Food Bank, 986
New Brunswick Association of Food Banks, 1005
North Bay Food Bank, 1030
North York Harvest Food Bank, 1033
Ontario Association of Food Banks, 1064
Oromocto & Surrounding Area Food & Clothing Bank, 1127
Ottawa Food Bank, 1130
Parkland Food Bank, 1142
Picton United Church County Food Bank, 1159
Port Hardy Harvest Food Bank, 1166
Project Share, 1188
Regina & District Food Bank Inc., 1211
Richmond Food Bank Society, 1230
Saint John Community Food Basket, 1246
Saskatoon Food Bank & Learning Centre, 1279
School Lunch Association, 1284
Second Harvest, 1288
The Sharing Place - Orillia & District Food Bank, 1294
Squamish Food Bank, 1346
The Stop Community Food Centre, 1350
Strathcona Food Bank, 1351
Summerland Food Bank & Resource Centre, 1354
Surrey Food Bank, 1357
Sussex Sharing Club, 1357
Vernon BC Food Bank, 1431
Winnipeg Harvest Inc., 1459
Wood Buffalo Food Bank, 1463
Yarmouth Food Bank Society, 1470

Food Industry
Conseil de la transformation agroalimentaire et des produits de consommation, 616
Farm & Food Care Canada, 705

Food Science
Canadian Foundation for Dietetic Research, 393
Canadian Partnership for Consumer Food Safety Education, 451
Fondation Initia, 746

Football
Canadian Football Hall of Fame & Museum, 391
Football Canada, 750

Footwear
Two/Ten Charity Trust of Canada Inc., 1401

Foreign Aid
Adventist Development & Relief Agency Canada, 10
Canadian Lutheran World Relief, 428
Hope for the Nations, 821
Intercede International, 851
Save the Children Canada, 1281
Vides Canada, 1434

Forest Industries
Central British Columbia Railway & Forest Industry Museum Society, 524

Forestry
Canadian Forestry Association, 392
Canadian Forestry Association of New Brunswick, 392
Ecoforestry Institute Society, 671
Forests Ontario, 751
Friends of the Forestry Farm House Inc., 762
Madawaska Forest Products Marketing Board, 924
Manitoba Forestry Association Inc., 937
Nova Scotia Forestry Association, 1045
Ordre des ingénieurs forestiers du Québec, 1123
Saskatchewan Forestry Association, 1265
Sustainable Forestry Initiative Inc., 1597
Trees Winnipeg, 1397

Foster Parents
Alberta Foster Parent Association, 35
British Columbia Federation of Foster Parent Associations, 240
Federation of Foster Families of Nova Scotia, 724
International Foster Care Organisation, 1549
Plan Canada, 1161
Prince Edward Island Federation of Foster Families, 1174

Foundations
ABC Life Literacy Canada, 1
Active Healthy Kids Canada, 7
ADR Institute of Canada, 9
Advanced Coronary Treatment (ACT) Foundation of Canada, 10
Aerospace Heritage Foundation of Canada, 11
African Medical & Research Foundation Canada, 13
Aga Khan Foundation Canada, 14
Agricultural Institute of Canada Foundation, 15
Air Canada Foundation, 19
Alberta Cancer Foundation, 27
Alberta Children's Hospital Foundation, 28
Alberta Diabetes Foundation, 32
Alberta Ecotrust Foundation, 33
Alberta Law Foundation, 39
Allen & Milli Gould Family Foundation, 54
Allstate Foundation of Canada, 59
Almas Jiwani Foundation, 59
Alva Foundation, 61
Anglican Foundation of Canada, 70
Animal Aid Foundation, 70
Animal Welfare Foundation of Canada, 71
Asper Foundation, 87
Atkinson Charitable Foundation, 182
The Avian Preservation Foundation, 190
Azrieli Foundation, 191
Baby's Breath, 192
Banff World Television Festival Foundation, 196
Baycrest Foundation, 200
The Belinda Stronach Foundation, 204
Bibles for Missions Foundation, 208
Birks Family Foundation, 212
Brain Tumour Foundation of Canada, 225
Branscombe Family Foundation, 226
Brantwood Foundation, 227
Breakfast for Learning, 227
Brian Bronfman Family Foundation, 228
British Columbia Cancer Foundation, 234
British Columbia Neurofibromatosis Foundation, 247
British Columbia's Children's Hospital Foundation, 259
Butler Family Foundation, 267
The Calgary Foundation, 272
CAMH Foundation, 276
Canada West Foundation, 281
Canada-Israel Cultural Foundation, 283
Canadian Alopecia Areata Foundation, 292
The Canadian Art Foundation, 295
Canadian Athletes Now Fund, 337
Canadian Battlefields Foundation, 342
Canadian Children's Optimist Foundation, 356
Canadian Chiropractic Research Foundation, 356
The Canadian Continence Foundation, 364
Canadian Digestive Health Foundation, 378
Canadian Fallen Firefighters Foundation, 383
Canadian Foundation for AIDS Research, 392
Canadian Foundation for Climate & Atmospheric Sciences, 393
Canadian Foundation for Masorti Judaism, 393
Canadian Foundation for Pharmacy, 393
Canadian Foundation for Ukrainian Studies, 394
Canadian Institute for the Relief of Pain & Disability, 413
Canadian Kennel Club Foundation, 424
Canadian Liver Foundation, 427
Canadian Lyme Disease Foundation, 428
Canadian Medical Foundation, 434
Canadian MedicAlert Foundation, 434
Canadian National Autism Foundation, 438
Canadian Nurses Foundation, 443
Canadian Occupational Therapy Foundation, 444
Canadian Orthopaedic Foundation, 448
Canadian Porphyria Foundation Inc., 458
Canadian Progress Charitable Foundation, 460
Canadian Scholarship Trust Foundation, 468
Canadian Social Work Foundation, 472
Canadian Writers' Foundation Inc., 506
Canadian-Scandinavian Foundation, 507
Cape Breton Regional Hospital Foundation, 509
Carthy Foundation, 516
Catherine Donnelly Foundation, 517
Catholic Education Foundation of Ontario, 518
Central Okanagan Foundation, 525
C.G. Jung Foundation of Ontario, 539
Chai-Tikvah The Life & Hope Foundation, 539
Chawkers Foundation, 555
CHILD Foundation, 560
Children's Health Foundations, 561
Children's Hospital Foundation of Manitoba, 562
Children's Hospital Foundation of Saskatchewan, 562
Children's Hospital of Eastern Ontario Foundation, 562
Children's Tumor Foundation, 1516
Children's Wish Foundation of Canada, 562
Chinook Regional Hospital Foundation, 565
Chris Spencer Foundation, 566
Clean Nova Scotia Foundation, 573
Coast Foundation Society, 579
Colchester-East Hants Public Library Foundation, 580
Cole Foundation, 581
Colin B. Glassco Charitable Foundation for Children, 581
Community Foundation for Kingston & Area, 597
The Community Foundation of Durham Region, 597
Community Foundation of Lethbridge & Southwestern Alberta, 597
Community Foundation of Nova Scotia, 597
Community Foundation of Ottawa, 597
Community Foundation of Prince Edward Island, 598
Community Foundations of Canada, 598
Conservation Foundation of Greater Toronto, 622
Conservation Halton Foundation, 622
CP24 CHUM Christmas Wish, 638
Cranbrook Archives, Museum & Landmark Foundation, 638
Crohn's & Colitis Canada, 642
Cystic Fibrosis Canada, 647
Dalhousie Medical Research Foundation, 648
David Foster Foundation, 651
David Suzuki Foundation, 651
Down Syndrome Research Foundation, 661
Dr. H. Bliss Murphy Cancer Care Foundation, 662
Dr. James Naismith Basketball Foundation, 662
Dreams Take Flight, 662
Drummond Foundation, 663
Dystonia Medical Research Foundation Canada, 665
East Georgian Bay Historical Foundation, 668
Easter Seals Nova Scotia, 669
Eastern Kings Health Foundation Inc., 670
Ecotrust Canada, 673
Edith Lando Charitable Foundation, 674
Edmonton Community Foundation, 676
Eldee Foundation, 681
Energy Probe Research Foundation, 688
Epilepsy Foundation of America, 1524
Equitas - International Centre for Human Rights Education, 695
Evergreen, 699
The Farha Foundation, 705
Farm & Food Care Canada, 705
Fondation Alfred Dallaire, 742
Fondation Caritas-Sherbrooke inc., 743
Fondation Centre de cancérologie Charles-Bruneau, 743
Fondation CHU de Québec, 743
Fondation CHU Dumont Foundation, 743
Fondation CHU Sainte-Justine, 743
Fondation de l'Hôpital de Montréal pour enfants, 744
Fondation de l'Hôpital du Sacré-Coeur de Montréal, 744
Fondation de l'Hôpital Général de Montréal, 744
Fondation de l'Hôpital Maisonneuve-Rosemont, 744
Fondation de la banque d'yeux du Québec inc., 744
Fondation des étoiles, 744
Fondation des maladies du coeur du Québec, 745
Fondation des pompiers du Québec pour les grands brûlés, 745
Fondation Desjardins, 745
Fondation Diane Hébert Inc, 745
Fondation du CHUM, 745
Fondation Dufresne et Gauthier, 746
Fondation Edward Assh, 746
Fondation franco-ontarienne, 746
Fondation Hôpital Charles-LeMoyne, 746
Fondation Initia, 746
Fondation Institut de Cardiologie de Montréal, 746
Fondation Jeanne-Crevier, 746
Fondation Lionel-Groulx, 747
Fondation Père-Ménard, 747
Fondation québécoise de la déficience intellectuelle, 747
Fondation québécoise de la maladie coeliaque, 747
Fondation québécoise en environnement, 748
Fondation Santé Gatineau, 748
Fondation Tourisme Jeunesse, 748
Fort Edmonton Foundation, 752
The Foundation Fighting Blindness, 755
Foundation for Advancing Family Medicine of the College of Family Physicians of Canada, 755
Foundation for Education Perth Huron, 755
Foundation for Educational Exchange Between Canada & the United States of America, 755
Foundation for Legal Research, 755

Foundation for Prader-Willi Research in Canada, 756
Foundation of Greater Montreal, 756
Francofonds inc., 757
Friends of The Moncton Hospital Foundation, 763
Frontiers Foundation, 763
Gainey Foundation, 766
The Gairdner Foundation, 766
Genesis Research Foundation, 769
Golf Canada Foundation, 777
Good Foundation Inc., 777
Gordon Foundation, 778
Governor General's Performing Arts Awards Foundation, 778
Graham Boeckh Foundation, 779
Grand River Conservation Foundation, 780
The Great Lakes Marine Heritage Foundation, 782
Gustav Levinschi Foundation, 794
Hal Jackman Foundation, 798
Halifax Foundation, 799
Hamber Foundation, 800
Hamilton Community Foundation, 801
Harmony Foundation of Canada, 803
Harold Crabtree Foundation, 804
Harry & Martha Cohen Foundation, 804
Harry A. Newman Memorial Foundation, 804
Harry E. Foster Foundation, 804
Health Sciences Centre Foundation, 807
Hearing Foundation of Canada, 808
Heart & Stroke Foundation of British Columbia & Yukon, 808
Heart & Stroke Foundation of Canada, 808
Heart & Stroke Foundation of Manitoba, 808
Heart & Stroke Foundation of Nova Scotia, 809
Heart & Stroke Foundation of Ontario, 809
Heart & Stroke Foundation of Prince Edward Island Inc., 809
Heart & Stroke Foundation of Saskatchewan, 809
Helderleigh Foundation, 811
Help Fill a Dream Foundation of Canada, 812
The Henry White Kinnear Foundation, 812
Heritage Foundation of Newfoundland & Labrador, 813
Hockey Canada Foundation, 817
Hospital for Sick Children Foundation, 823
Hunter Family Foundation, 827
IBD Foundation, 829
I.C.C. Foundation, 829
Independent Production Fund, 833
Indspire, 835
Inuit Art Foundation, 862
Islamic Foundation of Toronto, 864
Islamic Information Foundation, 864
IWK Health Centre Foundation, 867
J. Armand Bombardier Foundation, 867
J. Douglas Ferguson Historical Research Foundation, 867
Jack Miner Migratory Bird Foundation, Inc., 867
Janeway Children's Hospital Foundation, 868
Jewish Community Foundation of Montréal, 871
Jewish Foundation of Manitoba, 872
Jewish General Hospital Foundation, 872
The Joe Brain Foundation, 873
Joubert Syndrome & Related Disoarders Foundation, 1568
Juvenile Diabetes Research Foundation Canada, 878
The J.W. McConnell Family Foundation, 879
Kenneth M Molson Foundation, 883
Kensington Foundation, 883
Kidney Foundation of Canada, 885
Kids Cancer Care Foundation of Alberta, 886
Kids Kottage Foundation, 886
Kin Canada Foundation, 887
Kinsmen Foundation of British Columbia & Yukon, 890
The Kitchener & Waterloo Community Foundation, 890
Laidlaw Foundation, 895
Law Foundation of British Columbia, 900
Law Foundation of Ontario, 901
Lawson Foundation, 902

Learning Enrichment Foundation, 905
The Leon & Thea Koerner Foundation, 907
Lifeforce Foundation, 911
Lions Foundation of Canada, 913
Lions Gate Hospital Foundation, 913
Lithuanian-Canadian Foundation, 915
Lloydminster Region Health Foundation, 916
London Community Foundation, 918
London Health Sciences Foundation, 918
Lo-Se-Ca Foundation, 919
Lupus Foundation of Ontario, 921
Mahatma Gandhi Canadian Foundation for World Peace, 925
Make-A-Wish Canada, 927
Margie Gillis Dance Foundation, 949
Markham Stouffville Hospital Foundation, 952
Masonic Foundation of Manitoba Inc., 952
Masonic Foundation of Ontario, 952
Max Bell Foundation, 954
Maytree Foundation, 954
McGill University Health Centre Foundation, 955
The McLean Foundation, 955
Meningitis Research Foundation of Canada, 960
Michaëlle Jean Foundation, 964
Mississauga Heritage Foundation Inc., 970
The Molson Family Foundation, 971
Mount Sinai Hospital Foundation, 976
Mr. & Mrs. P.A. Woodward's Foundation, 978
The M.S.I. Foundation, 978
MuchFACT, 978
Mulgrave Road Theatre Foundation, 978
The Muttart Foundation, 986
Nanaimo Community Foundation, 987
National Alopecia Areata Foundation, 1572
National Arts Centre Foundation, 989
National Farmers Foundation, 993
National Psoriasis Foundation - USA, 1577
National Trust for Canada, 996
Neptune Theatre Foundation, 1003
Newfoundland Cancer Treatment & Research Foundation, 1023
Newman Centre Catholic Chaplaincy and Parish, 1024
Niagara Peninsula Conservation Authority, 1025
Northwest Territories Law Foundation, 1038
Old Strathcona Foundation, 1056
Ontario Mental Health Foundation, 1090
Ontario Trucking Association - Education Foundation, 1111
Our Lady of The Prairies Foundation, 1133
The Palyul Foundation of Canada, 1137
Pancreatic Cancer Canada Foundation, 1138
Parkinson Society Saskatchewan, 1141
The Paterson Foundation, 1145
Peter Gilgan Foundation, 1153
Phoenix Community Works Foundation, 1157
Physicians Services Inc. Foundation, 1158
The Pollution Probe Foundation, 1164
Prairieaction Foundation, 1170
Prince County Hospital Foundation, 1171
Prince Edward Island Museum & Heritage Foundation, 1175
Princess Margaret Cancer Foundation, 1180
Québec-Labrador Foundation (Canada) Inc., 1199
Queen Elizabeth Hospital Foundation, 1199
Quetico Foundation, 1201
Reena, 1210
Regional Occupation Centre Foundation, 1212
Richard Ivey Foundation, 1229
Rick Hansen Foundation, 1231
Robert L. Conconi Foundation, 1234
Rotary Club of Stratford Charitable Foundation, 1236
Royal University Hospital Foundation, 1243
Saint John Jeux Canada Games Foundation Inc., 1247
St. Andrew's Society of Toronto, 1248
St. Joseph's Healthcare Foundation, 1249
The Sam Sorbara Charitable Foundation, 1253
Saskatoon Community Foundation, 1279
Savoy Foundation Inc., 1282

Scottish Rite Charitable Foundation of Canada, 1286
Scottish Studies Foundation Inc., 1286
Seagull Foundation, 1288
SEEDS Foundation, 1289
Semiahmoo Foundation, 1289
Seva Foundation, 1588
Sjogren's Syndrome Foundation Inc., 1589
SkyWorks Charitable Foundation, 1303
Société internationale du réseau ÉCONOMUSÉE et Société ÉCONOMUSÉE du Québec, 1321
Soroptimist Foundation of Canada, 1333
South Saskatchewan Community Foundation Inc., 1336
The Speech & Stuttering Institute, 1340
Starlight Children's Foundation Canada, 1348
Sunshine Dreams for Kids, 1355
SUS Foundation of Canada, 1357
The T. R. Meighen Foundation, 1365
TD Friends of the Environment Foundation, 1367
Telemiracle/Kinsmen Foundation Inc., 1369
The Terry Fox Foundation, 1372
Thomas Sill Foundation Inc., 1376
Thunder Bay Community Foundation, 1377
Thyroid Foundation of Canada, 1378
Tides Canada Foundation, 1379
Toronto Arts Foundation, 1381
Toronto Community Foundation, 1383
Toronto General & Western Hospital Foundation, 1385
Toronto Public Library Foundation, 1386
Toronto PWA Foundation, 1386
The Toronto-Calcutta Foundation, 1388
Trans Canada Trail Foundation, 1394
T.R.E.E. Foundation for Youth Development, 1397
The Trident Mediation Counselling & Support Foundation, 1398
Trillium Health Partners Foundation, 1398
True Sport Foundation, 1399
Ukrainian Canadian Foundation of Taras Shevchenko, 1402
United Church of Canada Foundation, 1409
United Way of Canada - Centraide Canada, 1413
Vancity Community Foundation, 1424
Vancouver Foundation, 1425
Vernon Jubilee Hospital Foundation, 1431
Victoria Hospitals Foundation, 1432
The W. Garfield Weston Foundation, 1439
Walker Lynch Foundation, 1439
Wellspring Cancer Support Foundation, 1444
West Coast Environmental Law, 1444
West Vancouver Community Foundation, 1447
Winnipeg Foundation, 1459
Youth Science Canada, 1476

France
Association France-Québec, 1509

Francophones in Canada
Alliance des femmes de la francophonie canadienne, 55
Alliance Française, 57
Alliance Française d'Ottawa, 57
Alliance Française de Calgary, 57
Alliance Française du Manitoba, 57
Alliance Française Halifax, 57
Assemblée communautaire fransaskoise, 87
Association canadienne-française de l'Alberta, 96
Association des francophones du nord-ouest de l'Ontario, 114
Association des professionnels de la chanson et de la musique, 125
Association des universités de la francophonie canadienne, 130
Association francophone des parents du Nouveau-Brunswick, 135
Association franco-yukonnaise, 136
Association internationale des maires francophones - Bureau à Québec, 136
Association jeunesse fransaskoise, 137
Centre culturel franco-manitobain, 526

Le Centre culturel francophone de Vancouver, 526
Centre franco-ontarien de folklore, 534
Centre franco-ontarien de ressources pédagogiques, 534
Centre francophone de Toronto, 535
La Clé d'la Baie en Huronie - Association culturelle francophone, 572
Club canadien de Toronto, 574
Coalition des femmes de l'Alberta, 577
Conseil culturel fransaskois, 614
Conseil des organismes francophones de la région de Durham, 617
Conseil jeunesse francophone de la Colombie-Britannique, 618
Conseil jeunesse provincial (Manitoba), 619
Fédération culturelle acadienne de la Nouvelle-Écosse, 708
Fédération de la jeunesse canadienne-française inc., 709
Fédération de la jeunesse franco-ontarienne, 709
Fédération des agriculteurs et agricultrices francophones du Nouveau-Brunswick, 711
Fédération des aînés et des retraités francophones de l'Ontario, 711
Fédération des aînés franco-manitobains inc., 711
Fédération des aînés fransaskois, 711
Fédération des communautés francophones et acadienne du Canada, 713
La Fédération des francophones de la Colombie-Britannique, 715
Fédération des jeunes francophones du Nouveau-Brunswick Inc., 715
Fédération des parents francophones de Colombie-Britannique, 716
Fédération des parents francophones de l'Alberta, 717
Fédération des scouts de l'Atlantique, 718
Fondation franco-ontarienne, 746
Fondation fransaskoise, 746
Fondation Lionel-Groulx, 747
Francophonie jeunesse de l'Alberta, 757
Institut d'histoire de l'Amérique française, 841
Jeunesse Acadienne et Francophone de l'Île-du-prince-Édouard, 870
Oasis Centre des femmes, 1054
Société de l'Acadie du Nouveau-Brunswick, 1316
Société de la francophonie manitobaine, 1316
Société francophone de Victoria, 1319
Société généalogique canadienne-française, 1319
L'Union culturelle des Franco-Ontariennes, 1406
Union des cultivateurs franco-ontariens, 1406

Fraternal Organizations
Ancient, Free & Accepted Masons of Canada - Grand Lodge of Nova Scotia, 69
Benevolent & Protective Order of Elks of Canada, 204
Canadian Progress Club, 460
Kin Canada Foundation, 887
Knights Hospitallers, Sovereign Order of St. John of Jerusalem, Knights of Malta, Grand Priory of Canada, 892
Knights of Columbus, 1568
Mission Aviation Fellowship of Canada, 969
Order of Malta - Canadian Association, 1119
The Order of United Commercial Travelers of America, 1119

Free-Nets
Chebucto Community Net, 555
Edmonton Community Networks, 676

French Immersion Programs
Parents partenaires en éducation, 1140

French Language
Agence universitaire de la Francophonie, 14
Alliance canadienne des responsables et enseignants en français (langue maternelle), 55
Alliance Française, 57

Registered Charitable Organizations Index / French Media

Alliance Française d'Ottawa, 57
Alliance Française de Calgary, 57
Alliance Française du Manitoba, 57
Alliance Française Halifax, 57
Association canadienne d'éducation de langue française, 90
Association des auteurs et des auteurs de l'Ontario français, 106
Association des distributeurs exclusifs de livres en langue française inc., 111
Association des juristes d'expression française de l'Ontario, 117
Association des juristes d'expression française de la Saskatchewan, 118
Association des juristes d'expression française du Manitoba inc., 118
Association des juristes d'expression française du Nouveau-Brunswick, 118
Association internationale des sociologues de langue française, 1510
Association québécoise des professeurs de français, 174
Canadian Parents for French, 450
Conseil pour le développement de l'alphabétisme et des compétences des adultes du Nouveau-Brunswick, 619
Fédération internationale des professeurs de français, 1525
Forum francophone des affaires, 754
Institut de la Francophonie pour le développement durable, 841
Parents partenaires en éducation, 1140
Regroupement des éditeurs canadiens-français, 1215
Le Réseau d'enseignement francophone à distance du Canada, 1219
Salon du livre de Toronto et Festival des écrivains, 1252
Société Saint-Jean-Baptiste du Centre du Québec, 1324
Théâtre français de Toronto, 1374
Union internationale de la presse francophone, 1598

French Media
Association de la presse francophone, 101
Vues d'Afriques - Les Journées du cinéma africain et créole, 1439

Friedreich's Ataxia
Association canadienne des ataxies familiales,
Association canadienne des ataxies familiales,
Association canadienne des ataxies familiales, 92

Friends of Groups
The Friends of Algonquin Park, 760
Friends of Animals, 1527
The Friends of Bon Echo Park, 760
The Friends of Charleston Lake Park, 760
Friends of Clayoquot Sound, 760
Friends of Devonian Botanic Garden, 761
Friends of Ecological Reserves, 761
Friends of the Earth Canada, 762
Friends of the Forestry Farm House Inc., 762
Friends of the Greater Sudbury Public Library, 762

Fruit & Vegetables
Association québécoise de la distribution de fruits et légumes, 170

Fundraising
British Columbia's Children's Hospital Foundation, 259
Children's Miracle Network, 562
Covenant Foundation, 637
Imagine Canada, 829
The International Grenfell Association, 857
UNICEF Canada, 1404

Funeral Planning
Federation of Ontario Memorial Societies - Funeral Consumers Alliance, 726
Last Post Fund, 899
Memorial Society of Edmonton & District, 960
Memorial Society of Red Deer & District, 960

Fur Trade
Canadian Association for Humane Trapping, 301
Fur-Bearer Defenders, 765
Yukon Trappers Association, 1480

Furniture Industry
Association des fabricants de meubles du Québec inc., 113

Gambling
Canadian Centre on Substance Use & Addiction, 354
Responsible Gambling Council (Ontario), 1227

Gas
Enform, 688
Petroleum Tank Management Association of Alberta, 1154

Gastroenterology
Canadian Digestive Health Foundation, 378

Gems
Bancroft Gem & Mineral Club, 195
Edmonton Tumblewood Lapidary Club, 679
Fraser Valley Rock & Gem Club, 758
Medicine Hat Rock & Lapidary Club, 958

Genealogy
Alberta Family History Society, 34
Association des familles Rioux d'Amérique inc., 113
British Columbia Genealogical Society, 242
British Isles Family History Society of Greater Ottawa, 259
Clan Lamont Society of Canada, 571
Clan Mackenzie Society of Canada, 571
Clans & Scottish Societies of Canada, 572
East European Genealogical Society, Inc., 668
Fédération des associations de familles du Québec, 711
Fédération québécoise des sociétés de généalogie, 730
Gatineau Valley Historical Society, 768
Genealogical Association of Nova Scotia, 768
Harrow Early Immigrant Research Society, 804
Historic Restoration Society of Annapolis County, 815
Jewish Genealogical Society of Toronto, 872
Kings Historical Society, 888
Manitoba Genealogical Society Inc., 937
New Brunswick Genealogical Society Inc., 1008
Norfolk Historical Society, 1028
Ontario Genealogical Society, 1081
Prince Edward Island Genealogical Society Inc., 1174
Québec Family History Society, 1197
The Royal Nova Scotia Historical Society, 1242
Saskatchewan Genealogical Society, 1265
Shelburne County Genealogical Society, 1295
Société d'histoire et de généalogie de l'Ile Jésus, 1312
Société d'histoire et de généalogie de la Matapédia, 1312
Société d'histoire et de généalogie de Matane, 1312
Société d'histoire et de généalogie de Rivière-du-Loup, 1312
Société d'histoire et de généalogie de Saint-Casimir, 1312
Société d'histoire et de généalogie de Salaberry, 1313
Société d'histoire et de généalogie Maria-Chapdelaine, 1313
Société de généalogie de la Beauce, 1315
Société de généalogie de la Jemmerais, 1315
Société de généalogie de Québec, 1315
Société de généalogie de Saint-Eustache, 1315
Société de généalogie des Cantons de l'Est, 1315
Société de généalogie des Laurentides, 1316
Société de généalogie du Saguenay, inc., 1316
Société de généalogie et d'archives de Rimouski, 1316
Société de généalogie et d'histoire de la région de Thetford-Mines, 1316
Société de généalogie Gaspésie-Les Îles, 1316

Société de généalogie Saint-Hubert, 1316
Société généalogique canadienne-française, 1319
Société historique du Saguenay, 1321
Société historique et généalogique de Trois-Pistoles, inc., 1321
Tweed & Area Historical Society, 1400
Ukrainian Genealogical & Historical Society of Canada, 1403
United Empire Loyalists' Association of Canada, 1410

Genetic Diseases & Disorders
Huntington Society of Canada, 827
Shwachman-Diamond Syndrome Canada, 1297
Société Huntington du Québec, 1321

Geology
Mineralogical Association of Canada, 966

German Canadians
Association for German Education in Calgary, 133
Prairie Saengerbund Choir Association, 1169

Gerontology
Alberta Association on Gerontology, 25
Association québécoise de gérontologie, 169
Canadian Association on Gerontology, 337
Canadian Gerontological Nursing Association, 397
Gerontological Nursing Association of Ontario, 772
Gustav Levinschi Foundation, 794
Société québécoise de gériatrie, 1323

Gifted Children
Alberta Associations for Bright Children, 25
Association for Bright Children (Ontario), 132

Global Governance
Forum of Federations, 755
Worldwatch Institute, 1608

Global Warming
Climate Institute, 1517

Golf
Association des surintendants de golf du Québec, 129
Canadian Golf Hall of Fame & Museum, 398
Fédération de golf du Québec, 708
Golf Canada Foundation, 777

Government
Association des employées et employés du gouvernement du Québec, 112
Commonwealth Parliamentary Association, 1518

Graduate Studies
Canadian Association for Graduate Studies, 300

Grandparents
CANGRANDS Kinship Support, 508

Graphic Arts & Design
Société des designers graphiques du Québec, 1317
Society of Graphic Designers of Canada, 1329

Great Lakes
Citizens' Environment Alliance, 570
The Great Lakes Marine Heritage Foundation, 782

Greek Canadians
Greek Community of Toronto, 787
Greek-Canadian Cultural Centre, 788

Guide Dogs
Canadian Guide Dogs for the Blind, 399

Guides
Association des Scouts du Canada, 127
Girl Guides of Canada, 773

Gymnastics
Gymnastics Canada Gymnastique, 795

HIV/AIDS
Africans in Partnership Against AIDS, 13
AIDS Committee of Cambridge, Kitchener/Waterloo & Area, 16
AIDS Committee of Durham Region, 16
AIDS Committee of Newfoundland & Labrador, 16
AIDS Committee of Ottawa, 16
AIDS Committee of Simcoe County, 16
AIDS Committee of Toronto, 16
AIDS Committee of Windsor, 16
AIDS Moncton, 17
AIDS New Brunswick, 17
AIDS Niagara, 17
AIDS Programs South Saskatchewan, 17
AIDS Saint John, 17
AIDS Saskatoon, 17
AIDS Vancouver Island, 17
Alliance for South Asian AIDS Prevention, 57
ANKORS, 71
Asian Community AIDS Services, 87
Blood Ties Four Directions Centre, 215
Bruce House, 260
Bureau local d'intervention traitant du SIDA, 264
Canadian AIDS Society, 290
Canadian AIDS Treatment Information Exchange, 290
Canadian Association of Nurses in HIV/AIDS Care, 323
Canadian Foundation for AIDS Research, 392
Canadian HIV/AIDS Legal Network, 405
Casey House Hospice Inc., 516
Centre sida amitié, 536
Coalition des organismes communautaires québécois de lutte contre le sida, 578
Coalition sida des sourds du Québec, 578
Comité des personnes atteintes du VIH du Québec, 592
CUSO International, 646
Dignitas International, 656
Elevate NWO, 684
The Farha Foundation, 705
Fife House, 734
Healing Our Spirit BC Aboriginal HIV/AIDS Society, 805
HIV Community Link, 816
HIV Network of Edmonton Society, 816
HIV/AIDS Regional Services, 817
HIV/AIDS Resources and Community Health, 817
Intervention régionale et information sur le sida en Estrie, 862
Kali-Shiva AIDS Services, 880
Living Positive, 915
Living Positive Resource Centre, Okanagan, 915
Maggie's: The Toronto Sex Workers Action Project, 925
Maison Amaryllis, 926
Mouvement d'information, d'éducation et d'entraide dans la lutte contre le sida, 977
P.E.E.R.S. Alliance, 1148
Positive Living BC, 1167
Positive Women's Network, 1168
Sidaction Mauricie, 1298
The Teresa Group, 1371
Toronto PWA Foundation, 1386
2-Spirited People of the First Nations, 1401

Haitian Canadians & Haiti
Friends of the Orphans, Canada, 763

Halls of Fame
Alberta Sports Hall of Fame & Museum, 48
British Columbia Sports Hall of Fame & Museum, 255
Canada's Aviation Hall of Fame, 282
Canadian Football Hall of Fame & Museum, 391
Canadian Golf Hall of Fame & Museum, 398
Manitoba Sports Hall of Fame & Museum, 945
New Brunswick Sports Hall of Fame, 1013
North America Railway Hall of Fame, 1029
Northwestern Ontario Sports Hall of Fame & Museum, 1039
Prince Edward Island Sports Hall of Fame & Museum Inc., 1177
Saskatchewan Agricultural Hall of Fame, 1255
Saskatchewan Sports Hall of Fame & Museum, 1275

Handball
Canadian Team Handball Federation, 493
New Brunswick Team Handball Federation, 1013

Hard of Hearing
Canadian Hard of Hearing Association, 400
Canadian Hearing Society, 403
Hearing Foundation of Canada, 808
Island Deaf & Hard of Hearing Centre, 865
Réseau québécois pour l'inclusion social des personnnes sourdes et malentendantes, 1225
Saskatchewan Deaf & Hard of Hearing Services Inc., 1263
Speech & Hearing Association of Nova Scotia, 1340
Western Institute for the Deaf & Hard of Hearing, 1450
World Federation of the Deaf, 1605

Hazardous Wastes
Center for Health, Environment & Justice, 1516

Head Injury
Association québécoise des traumatisés craniens, 175

Health
Action Canada for Sexual Health & Rights, 6
Action on Smoking & Health, 6
Active Healthy Kids Canada, 7
Alzheimer Manitoba, 61
Les Amis de la déficience intellectuelle Rive-Nord, 67
Association des intervenantes et des intervenants en soins spirituels du Québec, 117
Barth Syndrome Foundation of Canada, 197
BC Lymphedema Association, 201
Canadian Association for Enterostomal Therapy, 300
Canadian Council for Tobacco Control, 367
Canadian Dupuytren Society, 379
Canadian Institute of Child Health, 414
Canadian Lymphedema Framework, 429
Canadian Natural Health Association, 440
Canadian Red Cross, 465
Canadian Society for International Health, 475
Canadians for Health Research, 507
CHARGE Syndrome Canada, 552
Children's Health Foundation of Vancouver Island, 561
Christian Children's Fund of Canada, 567
Collaboration Santé Internationale, 581
Gymn-eau Laval inc, 795
Hamber Foundation, 800
Health Action Network Society, 805
Health Sciences Centre Foundation, 807
Kidney Cancer Canada Association, 884
LAMP Community Health Centre, 897
McCreary Centre Society, 955
Ontario Healthy Communities Coalition, 1084
Partage Humanitaire, 1143
Patients Canada, 1145
Physical & Health Education Canada, 1158
Physicians for Global Survival (Canada), 1158
Sandbox Project, 1253
Simcoe Women's Wellness Centre Corporation, 1300
The 3C Foundation of Canada, 1377

Health Care
Advanced Coronary Treatment (ACT) Foundation of Canada, 10
African Medical & Research Foundation Canada, 13
Artists in Healthcare Manitoba, 85
Canadian Association of Medical Teams Abroad, 321
Canadian MedicAlert Foundation, 434
Carefirst Seniors & Community Services Association, 511
Catholic Health Alliance of Canada, 519
Catholic Health Association of Manitoba, 519
Catholic Health Association of Saskatchewan, 520
Christian Health Association of Alberta, 567
Dignitas International, 656
East Wellington Community Services, 669
Eastern Kings Health Foundation Inc., 670
Evangelical Medical Aid Society Canada, 698
Mr. & Mrs. P.A. Woodward's Foundation, 978
Patients Canada, 1145
Saint Elizabeth Health Care, 1246
Saskatchewan Association of Health Organizations, 1257
The 3C Foundation of Canada, 1377
VHA Home HealthCare, 1431

Health Care Facilities
Accreditation Canada, 5
Association des établissements privés conventionnés - santé services sociaux, 113
Association of Ontario Health Centres, 154
Baycrest Foundation, 200
Children's Mental Health Ontario, 562
Dr. H. Bliss Murphy Cancer Care Foundation, 662
Fondation Santé Gatineau, 748
HealthCareCAN, 807
Immigrant Women's Health Centre, 831
Infection & Prevention Control Canada, 836
Lions Gate Hospital Foundation, 913
Lloydminster Region Health Foundation, 916
Ontario Association of Children's Rehabilitation Services, 1062
The Renascent Centres for Alcoholism & Drug Addiction, 1217

Health Professionals
Alliance du personnel professionnel et technique de la santé et des services sociaux, 56
Armenian Canadian Medical Association of Ontario, 82
Canadian Tamil Medical Association, 492

Health Records
Association des Gestionnaires de l'information de la santé du Québec, 115

Hearing
Association du Québec pour enfants avec problèmes auditifs, 131
BC Hands & Voices, 201
Canadian Hard of Hearing Association, 400
Canadian Hearing Society, 403
Connect Society - D.E.A.F. Services, 613
Interpreting Services of Newfoundland & Labrador Inc., 861
Saskatchewan Deaf & Hard of Hearing Services Inc., 1263
Speech & Hearing Association of Nova Scotia, 1340
Speech-Language & Audiology Canada, 1341
VOICE for Hearing Impaired Children, 1437

Hearing Aid Industry
Association des implantés cochléaires du Québec, 116

Hearing Impaired
Accessible Media Inc., 5
Alberta Association of the Deaf, 25
Alberta Cultural Society of the Deaf, 32
Association des malentendants Québécois, 118
Association des Sourds de l'Estrie inc., 128
Association des Sourds de Québec inc., 128
Association montérégienne de la surdité inc., 137
BC Hands & Voices, 201
British Columbia Deaf Sports Federation, 238
Canadian Association of the Deaf, 334
Canadian Cultural Society of The Deaf, Inc., 374
Canadian Deaf Ice Hockey Federation, 376
Canadian Deaf Sports Association, 376
Canadian Deafblind Association (National), 376
Canadian Hearing Society, 403
Centre de la Communauté sourde du Montréal métropolitain, 529
Connect Society - D.E.A.F. Services, 613
Deaf Children's Society of B.C., 652
Deafness Advocacy Association Nova Scotia, 652
Durham Deaf Services, 665
Edmonton Association of the Deaf, 675
Fondation des sourds du Québec inc., 745
Greater Vancouver Association of the Deaf, 786
Hands on Summer Camp Society, 803
Hearing Foundation of Canada, 808
International Committee of Sports for the Deaf, 1543
Island Deaf & Hard of Hearing Centre, 865
Pax Natura Society for Rehabilitation of the Deaf, 1146
Regroupement des Sourds de Chaudière-Appalaches, 1215
Saint John Deaf & Hard of Hearing Services, Inc, 1246
Saskatchewan Deaf & Hard of Hearing Services Inc., 1263
Saskatchewan Deaf Sports Association, 1263
Silent Voice Canada Inc., 1299
Western Institute for the Deaf & Hard of Hearing, 1450
World Federation of the Deaf, 1605

Heart Diseases
Canadian Society of Atherosclerosis, Thrombosis & Vascular Biology, 480
Fondation des maladies du coeur du Québec, 745
Fondation Institut de Cardiologie de Montréal, 746
Heart & Stroke Foundation of Alberta, NWT & Nunavut, 808
Heart & Stroke Foundation of British Columbia & Yukon, 808
Heart & Stroke Foundation of Canada, 808
Heart & Stroke Foundation of Manitoba, 808
Heart & Stroke Foundation of Nova Scotia, 809
Heart & Stroke Foundation of Ontario, 809
Heart & Stroke Foundation of Prince Edward Island Inc., 809
Heart & Stroke Foundation of Saskatchewan, 809

Height
Association québécoise des personnes de petite taille, 174
Little People of Manitoba, 915
Little People of Ontario, 915

Hematology
Association des médecins hématologistes-oncologistes du Québec, 119

Hemophilia
Canadian Hemophilia Society, 404

Hepatitis
Canadian AIDS Treatment Information Exchange, 290
Living Positive Resource Centre, Okanagan, 915
P.E.E.R.S. Alliance, 1148

Heraldry
Royal Heraldry Society of Canada, 1242

Heritage
Aerospace Heritage Foundation of Canada, 11
Association québécoise des interprètes du patrimoine, 173
Campbellford/Seymour Heritage Society, 276
Canada's Aviation Hall of Fame, 282
Canadian Italian Heritage Foundation, 423
Canadian Northern Society, 441
Canadian Warplane Heritage, 502
Chester Municipal Heritage Society, 557
Cole Harbour Rural Heritage Society, 581
Community Heritage Ontario, 599
Conservation Foundation of Greater Toronto, 622
Dickson Store Museum Society, 656
Edmonton Heritage Festival Association, 677
Edmonton Radial Railway Society, 679
Fortress Louisbourg Association, 754
The Friends of Fort York & Garrison Common, 761
Grande Prairie Museum, 781
The Great Lakes Marine Heritage Foundation, 782
Hamilton Folk Arts Heritage Council, 801
Harrow Early Immigrant Research Society, 804
Heritage Foundation of Newfoundland & Labrador, 813
Héritage Montréal, 813
Heritage Ottawa, 813
Heritage Toronto, 813
Heritage Trust of Nova Scotia, 813
Heritage Winnipeg Corp., 813
Heritage York, 814
Historic Sites Association of Newfoundland & Labrador, 815
Huntsville & Lake of Bays Railway Society, 828
J. Douglas Ferguson Historical Research Foundation, 867
Jewish Historical Society of BC, 872
Langley Heritage Society, 899
Lunenburg Heritage Society, 921
Mainland South Heritage Society, 926
Manitoba Indian Cultural Education Centre, 939
Marsh Collection Society, 952
Mississauga Heritage Foundation Inc., 970
Mossley Post Heritage & Citizenship Society, 975
National Trust for Canada, 996
Nova Scotia Lighthouse Preservation Society, 1047
Old Strathcona Foundation, 1056
Old Sydney Society, 1056
Ontario Heritage Trust, 1084
Organization of Military Museums of Canada, 1125
Pier 21 Society, 1159
Port Moody Heritage Society, 1166
Prince Edward Island Museum & Heritage Foundation, 1175
Saskatoon Heritage Society, 1279
Sault Ste Marie & 49th Field Regt. RCA Historical Society, 1281
Save Our Heritage Organization, 1281
Stephan G. Stephansson Icelandic Society, 1349
Them Days Inc., 1375
Ukrainian Canadian Research & Documentation Centre, 1402
United Empire Loyalists' Association of Canada, 1410
Westmount Historical Association, 1451
York Pioneer & Historical Society, 1473
Yukon Church Heritage Society, 1477

Heritage Language Programs
Manitoba Indian Cultural Education Centre, 939
Saskatchewan Organization for Heritage Languages Inc., 1270

Hiking
The Avon Trail, 191
The Bruce Trail Conservancy, 261
East Coast Trail Association, 668
Federation of Mountain Clubs of British Columbia, 725
Fédération québécoise de la marche, 727
Ganaraska Hiking Trail Association, 766
Grand Valley Trails Association, 780
Hike Ontario, 814
Ontario Trails Council, 1111
Rideau Trail Association, 1231
Thames Valley Trail Association Inc., 1373
Trans Canada Trail Foundation, 1394
Voyageur Trail Association, 1439

Hinduism
Hindu Society of Alberta, 815

History
Alberni District Historical Society, 21
American Society for Environmental History, 1498
Amherstburg Historic Sites Association, 67
Archelaus Smith Historical Society, 78
Archives du Centre acadien, 80
Arrow Lakes Historical Society, 84
Associated Medical Services Inc., 89
Atelier d'histoire Hochelaga-Maisonneuve, 179
Aurora Historical Society, Inc., 187
Battle River Historical Society, 199

Registered Charitable Organizations Index / Hockey

Bear River Historical Society, 202
Beaverton Thorah Eldon Historical Society, 203
Bothwell-Zone & District Historical Society, 218
Bowden Historical Society, 219
Bracebridge Historical Society, 224
Brant Historical Society, 226
Breton & District Historical Society, 228
Bridgetown & Area Historical Society, 229
British Columbia Historical Federation, 243
British Columbia Railway Historical Association, 250
Brome County Historical Society, 260
Bruce County Historical Society, 260
Burford Township Historical Society, 265
Burlington Historical Society, 265
Bytown Railway Society, 267
Cabbagetown Preservation Association, 268
Canada's History, 282
Canadian Association for the History of Nursing, 305
Canadian Aviation Historical Society, 340
Canadian Historical Association, 405
Canadian Nautical Research Society, 440
Canadian Railroad Historical Association, 465
Canadian Science & Technology Historical Association, 468
Canadiana, 506
Cannington & Area Historical Society, 508
Cardston Historical Society, 511
Carleton Place & Beckwith Historical Society, 513
Carstairs & District Historical Society, 516
The Champlain Society, 551
Chapel Hill Historical Society, 552
Chatham Railroad Museum Society, 555
Cobourg & District Historical Society, 579
Colchester Historical Society, 580
Commission internationale de diplomatique, 1518
Community Heritage Ontario, 599
Compton County Historical Museum Society, 609
Cornwall Township Historical Society, 629
Courtenay & District Historical Society, 637
Cranbrook Archives, Museum & Landmark Foundation, 638
Creston & District Historical & Museum Society, 641
Cumberland Museum Society, 645
Dartmouth Historical Association, 651
Didsbury & District Historical Society, 656
East Georgian Bay Historical Foundation, 668
East Hants Historical Society, 668
Edgerton & District Historical Society, 674
Edmonton Radial Railway Society, 679
Etobicoke Historical Society, 697
Fédération des sociétés d'histoire du Québec, 719
Fire Fighters Historical Society of Winnipeg, Inc., 738
Fondation Lionel-Groulx, 747
Fort Edmonton Foundation, 752
Fort Macleod Historical Association, 752
Fort McMurray Historical Society, 753
Fort Saskatchewan Historical Society, 754
Fort Whoop-up Interpretive Society, 754
Friends Historical Association, 1527
The Friends of Fort York & Garrison Common, 761
Friends of the Forestry Farm House Inc., 762
Gatineau Valley Historical Society, 768
Glanbrook Heritage Society, 774
Grenville County Historical Society, 789
Guelph Historical Society, 793
Guysborough Historical Society, 795
Hanna Museum & Pioneer Village, 803
Hantsport & Area Historical Society, 803
Harrow Early Immigrant Research Society, 804
Hastings County Historical Society, 804
Heritage Toronto, 813
Historic Restoration Society of Annapolis County, 815
Historical Society of Alberta, 816
Historical Society of Ottawa, 816
Hudson's Hope Museum, 824

Huntley Township Historical Society, 828
Huntsville & Lake of Bays Railway Society, 828
Institut d'histoire de l'Amérique française, 841
International Society for the History of Medicine - Canadian Section, 860
Iroquois Falls Historical Society, 864
J. Douglas Ferguson Historical Research Foundation, 867
Jewish Heritage Centre of Western Canada Inc., 872
Jewish Historical Society of BC, 872
Jewish Historical Society of Southern Alberta, 872
King's County Historical Society, 888
Kings Historical Society, 888
Kneehill Historical Society, 892
Lambton County Historical Society, 897
Legal Archives Society of Alberta, 906
Literary & Historical Society of Québec, 914
London & Middlesex Historical Society, 917
Lost Villages Historical Society, 919
Markham District Historical Society, 952
Marsh Collection Society, 952
Matsqui Sumas Abbotsford Museum Society, 954
Millet & District Historical Society, 966
Milton Historical Society, 966
Missisquoi Historical Society, 969
Museum London, 983
Muskoka Steamship & Historical Society, 985
National Trust for Canada, 996
Naval Museum of Alberta Society, 1001
New Brunswick Historical Society, 1009
Newfoundland Historical Society, 1023
Norfolk Historical Society, 1028
The North Cumberland Historical Society, 1030
North Lanark Historical Society, 1031
North Peace Historical Society, 1032
Okanagan Historical Society, 1055
Old Strathcona Foundation, 1056
Old Sydney Society, 1056
Ontario Black History Society, 1068
Ontario Electric Railway Historical Association, 1077
Ontario Historical Society, 1084
Organization of American Historians, 1581
Osgoode Twp. Historical Society, 1127
Ottawa Valley Historical Society, 1132
Parrsborough Shore Historical Society, 1143
Petrolia Discovery, 1155
Photographic Historical Society of Canada, 1157
Pier 21 Society, 1159
Port Clements Historical Society, 1165
Port Hastings Historical Society, 1166
Pouce Coupe & District Museum & Historical Society, 1168
Prairie West Historical Society Inc., 1170
Renfrew & District Historical Society, 1217
Richmond County Historical Society, 1230
Rimbey Historical Society, 1232
The Royal Nova Scotia Historical Society, 1242
Saanich Historical Artifacts Society, 1245
Saint John Jewish Historical Society, 1247
St. Albert Historical Society, 1248
Sault Ste Marie & 49th Field Regt. RCA Historical Society, 1281
Scarborough Historical Society, 1282
Shelburne Historical Society, 1295
Smith-Ennismore Historical Society, 1304
Société d'histoire de Beloeil - Mont-Saint-Hilaire, 1310
Société d'histoire de la Haute Gaspésie, 1310
Société d'histoire de la Haute-Yamaska, 1310
Société d'histoire de La Prairie-de-la-Magdeleine, 1310
Société d'histoire de la Rivière du Nord inc., 1310
Société d'histoire de la Seigneurie de Chambly, 1311
Société d'histoire de Lachine, 1311
Société d'histoire de Longueuil, 1311
Société d'histoire de Sainte-Foy, 1311
Société d'histoire de Sherbrooke, 1311
Société d'histoire de Sillery, 1311

La Société d'histoire de Toronto, 1311
Société d'histoire de Warwick, 1312
Société d'histoire de Weedon, 1312
Société d'histoire du Haut-Richelieu, 1312
Société d'histoire du Lac-St-Jean/Maison des Bâtisseurs, 1312
Société d'histoire et de généalogie de l'Ile Jésus, 1312
Société d'histoire et de généalogie de la Matapédia, 1312
Société d'histoire et de généalogie de Matane, 1312
Société d'histoire et de généalogie de Rivière-du-Loup, 1312
Société d'histoire et de généalogie de Saint-Casimir, 1312
Société d'histoire et de généalogie de Salaberry, 1313
Société d'histoire et de généalogie de Shawinigan-sud, 1313
Société d'histoire et de généalogie de Val-d'Or, 1313
Société d'histoire et de généalogie des Mille-Iles, 1313
Société d'histoire et de généalogie des Quatre Lieux, 1313
Société d'histoire et de généalogie Maria-Chapdelaine, 1313
Société d'histoire régionale de Lévis, 1313
Société d'histoire régionale Deux-Montagnes, 1313
Société d'histoire St-Stanislas inc., 1314
Société de conservation de la Baie de l'Isle-Verte, 1314
Société de généalogie et d'histoire de la région de Thetford-Mines, 1316
Société historique acadienne de la Baie Sainte-Marie, 1319
Société historique Alphonse-Desjardins, 1319
Société historique de Bellechasse, 1319
Société historique de Charlesbourg, 1319
Société historique de Dorval, 1319
Société historique de Joliette-De Lanaudière, 1319
Société historique de la Côte-Nord, 1320
Société historique de la région de Mont-Laurier, 1320
La Société historique de Nouvelle-Beauce, 1320
Société historique de Pubnico-Ouest, 1320
Société historique de Québec, 1320
Société historique de Rivière-des-Prairies, 1320
Société historique de Saint-Boniface, 1320
La Société historique du Cap-Rouge, 1320
Société historique du Saguenay, 1321
Société historique et culturelle du Marigot inc., 1321
Société historique et généalogique de Trois-Pistoles, inc., 1321
Société historique Machault, 1321
Société historique Pierre-de-Saurel inc., 1321
South Norwich Historical Society, 1335
Stanstead Historical Society, 1348
Stewart Historical Society, 1350
Stoney Creek Historical Society, 1350
Stormont, Dundas & Glengarry Historical Society, 1350
Streetsville Historical Society, 1352
Strome & District Historical Society, 1352
Telephone Historical Centre, 1369
Them Days Inc., 1375
Thunder Bay Historical Museum Society, 1378
Toronto Railway Historical Association, 1386
Touchstones Nelson Museum of Art & History, 1388
Town of York Historical Society, 1393
Trent Port Historical Society, 1397
Tweed & Area Historical Society, 1400
United Empire Loyalists' Association of Canada, 1410
Victoria County Historical Society, 1432
Vintage Locomotive Society Inc., 1435
Wallaceburg & District Historical Society, Inc., 1440
Waterloo Historical Society, 1442

Wellington County Historical Society, 1443
West Coast Railway Association, 1445
West Hants Historical Society, 1445
West Toronto Junction Historical Society, 1446
Westmount Historical Association, 1451
Windermere District Historical Society, 1456
Wolfville Historical Society, 1460
Yarmouth County Historical Society, 1470
York Pioneer & Historical Society, 1473
Yukon Historical & Museums Association, 1478

Hockey
Calgary Sledge Hockey Association, 274
Canadian Adult Recreational Hockey Association, 288
Canadian Deaf Ice Hockey Federation, 376
Canadian Electric Wheelchair Hockey Association, 380
Hockey Canada Foundation, 817
National Hockey League Alumni Association, 994

Holocaust & Holocaust Studies
Canadian Society for Yad Vashem, 479
Friends of Simon Wiesenthal Centre for Holocaust Studies - Canada, 762
Vancouver Holocaust Centre Society - A Museum for Education & Remembrance, 1425

Home & School Associations
British Columbia Confederation of Parent Advisory Councils, 236
Canadian Home & School Federation, 406
Manitoba Association of Parent Councils, 930
Ontario Federation of Home & School Associations Inc., 1079
Québec Federation of Home & School Associations Inc., 1197
Saskatchewan Association of School Councils, 1258

Home Care
Carefirst Seniors & Community Services Association, 511
Caregivers Alberta, 512
Carers ARK, 512
Community Care for South Hastings, 596
Family Caregivers of British Columbia, 702
Ontario Community Support Association, 1073
Saint Elizabeth Health Care, 1246
VHA Home HealthCare, 1431
Victorian Order of Nurses for Canada, 1434

Home Economics
International Federation for Home Economics, 1546

Home Schooling
Saskatchewan Home Based Educators, 1267

Homeopathy
Syndicat professionnel des homéopathes du Québec, 1365

Horse Racing
Ontario Standardbred Adoption Society, 1109

Horses
Association des éleveurs de chevaux Belge du Québec, 111
Equestrian Canada, 694
Fédération équestre du Québec inc., 720
Ontario Standardbred Adoption Society, 1109
Peruvian Horse Association of Canada, 1152
World Arabian Horse Organization, 1603

Horticulture
Les Amis du Jardin botanique de Montréal, 67
Brampton Horticultural Society, 226
Conserver Society of Hamilton & District Inc., 623
Fédération des sociétés d'horticulture et d'écologie du Québec, 719
Friends of Devonian Botanic Garden, 761
North American Native Plant Society, 1029
Ontario Horticultural Association, 1086
VanDusen Botanical Garden Association, 1429

Hospice Care
British Columbia Hospice Palliative Care Association, 243
Casey House Hospice Inc., 516
Hospice Niagara, 822
Hospice of Waterloo Region, 822
Nelson & District Hospice Society, 1003
North Shore Hospice Society, 1032
Palliative Manitoba, 1137

Hospital Auxiliaries
Hospital Auxiliaries Association of Ontario, 823

Hospitals
Accreditation Canada, 5
Alberta Children's Hospital Foundation, 28
CAMH Foundation, 276
Cape Breton Regional Hospital Foundation, 509
Children's Hospital Foundation of Manitoba, 562
Children's Hospital Foundation of Saskatchewan, 562
Children's Hospital of Eastern Ontario Foundation, 562
Children's Miracle Network, 562
Chinook Regional Hospital Foundation, 565
Covenant Foundation, 637
Fondation CHU de Québec, 743
Fondation CHU Dumont Foundation, 743
Fondation CHU Sainte-Justine, 743
Fondation de l'Hôpital de Montréal pour enfants, 744
Fondation de l'Hôpital du Sacré-Coeur de Montréal, 744
Fondation de l'Hôpital Général de Montréal, 744
Fondation de l'Hôpital Maisonneuve-Rosemont, 744
Fondation du CHUM, 745
Friends of The Moncton Hospital Foundation, 763
Gustav Levinschi Foundation, 794
HealthCareCAN, 807
Hospital for Sick Children Foundation, 823
Infection & Prevention Control Canada, 836
International Hospital Federation, 1550
IWK Health Centre Foundation, 867
Janeway Children's Hospital Foundation, 868
Jewish General Hospital Foundation, 872
Lions Gate Hospital Foundation, 913
Lloydminster Region Health Foundation, 916
London Health Sciences Foundation, 918
Markham Stouffville Hospital Foundation, 952
McGill University Health Centre Foundation, 955
Mount Sinai Hospital Foundation, 976
Prince County Hospital Foundation, 1171
Queen Elizabeth Hospital Foundation, 1199
Royal University Hospital Foundation, 1243
St. Joseph's Healthcare Foundation, 1249
Saskatchewan Association of Health Organizations, 1257
Toronto General & Western Hospital Foundation, 1385
Trillium Health Partners Foundation, 1398
Vernon Jubilee Hospital Foundation, 1431
Victoria Hospitals Foundation, 1432

Hostelling
Fondation Tourisme Jeunesse, 748

Hotels & Motels
Association Hôtellerie Québec, 136
Innkeepers Guild of Nova Scotia, 839
International Hotel & Restaurant Association, 1550

Housing
Abbeyfield Houses Society of Canada, 1
Association d'entraide Le Chaînon inc., 99
Bruce House, 260
Edmonton Inner City Housing Society, 677
Entre Nous Femmes Housing Society, 690
Fife House, 734
Habitat for Humanity Canada, 796
Hong Fook Mental Health Association, 820
Lookout Emergency Aid Society, 919
Regroupement des offices d'habitation du Québec, 1215

Human Resources
Foundation for International Training, 755
International Association for Human Resource Information Management, 1536

Human Rights
Alberta Civil Liberties Research Centre, 28
Amnesty International - Canadian Section (English Speaking), 68
ARCH Disability Law Centre, 76
Association pour la promotion des droits des personnes handicapées, 166
B'nai Brith Canada, 192
British Columbia Civil Liberties Association, 236
Canadian Association of Statutory Human Rights Agencies, 333
The Canadian Centre/International P.E.N., 354
Canadian Journalists for Free Expression, 423
Canadian Tribute to Human Rights, 497
Centre for Inquiry Canada, 533
Centre international pour la prévention de la criminalité, 535
CPJ Corp., 638
CUSO International, 646
Disabled Peoples' International, 658
Equitas - International Centre for Human Rights Education, 695
Handicap International Canada, 802
Human Rights Internet, 826
League for Human Rights of B'nai Brith Canada, 903
Nova Scotia League for Equal Opportunities, 1046
PEN International, 1583
Social Justice Committee, 1305

Humanism
Humanist Canada, 826
The Royal Society of Canada, 1242

Humanities
American Society for Environmental History, 1498
Association for Canadian Studies, 133
Canadian Historical Association, 405
Classical Association of Canada, 572
Emil Skarin Fund, 686
Union académique internationale, 1598

Hungarian Canadians
Hungarian Canadian Cultural Centre, 827
Hungarian Canadian Engineers' Association, 827

Hunger
Canadian Food for the Hungry International, 391
Canadian Foodgrains Bank, 391
Chatham Outreach for Hunger, 555
Foodshare Toronto, 750
The Hunger Project Canada, 827

Hunting
Ontario Federation of Anglers & Hunters, 1079

Huntington's Disease
Huntington Society of Canada, 827
Société Huntington du Québec, 1321

Hydrocephalus
L'Association de spina-bifida et d'hydrocéphalie du Québec, 104
Spina Bifida & Hydrocephalus Association of British Columbia, 1341
Spina Bifida & Hydrocephalus Association of Northern Alberta, 1342
Spina Bifida & Hydrocephalus Association of Nova Scotia, 1342
Spina Bifida & Hydrocephalus Association of Ontario, 1342
Spina Bifida & Hydrocephalus Association of Prince Edward Island, 1342

Hydrography
International Federation of Hydrographic Societies, 1548

Hypertension
International Society of Hypertension, 1560

Icelanders & Iceland
Stephan G. Stephansson Icelandic Society, 1349

Ileitis
Crohn's & Colitis Canada, 642

Ileostomy
Ileostomy & Colostomy Association of Montréal, 829

Illustrators & Illustration
Association des Illustrateurs et Illustratrices du Québec, 116

Immigrants
A.C.C.E.S. Employment, 4
Afghan Women's Counselling & Integration Community Support Organization, 12
Association of Americans & Canadians in Israel, 1510
The Barbra Schlifer Commemorative Clinic, 196
Calgary Immigrant Women's Association, 272
Canadian Council for Refugees,
Centre for Immigrant & Community Services, 532
Collectif des femmes immigrantes du Québec, 581
DIVERSEcity Community Resources Society, 659
Edmonton Immigrant Services Association, 677
Ethiopian Association in the Greater Toronto Area & Surrounding Regions, 697
Folk Arts Council of St Catharines, 742
Harrow Early Immigrant Research Society, 804
Hong Fook Mental Health Association, 820
Immigrant & Multicultural Services Society, 830
Immigrant Services Calgary, 830
Immigrant Services Society of BC, 830
Immigrant Women's Health Centre, 831
Inter-Cultural Association of Greater Victoria, 851
Jewish Immigrant Aid Services of Canada, 873
Kababayan Multicultural Centre, 879
Malton Neighbourhood Services, 928
Multilingual Orientation Service Association for Immigrant Communities, 979
Ontario Council of Agencies Serving Immigrants, 1075
Ottawa Community Immigrant Services Organization, 1130
Pacific Immigrant Resources Society, 1135
Richmond Multicultural Community Services, 1231
Saskatoon Open Door Society Inc., 1279
Windsor Women Working with Immigrant Women, 1457
Working Women Community Centre, 1464

Immigration
Catholic Cross Cultural Services, 518
International Social Service Canada, 860
Pier 21 Society, 1159

Immunology
Canadian Society for Immunology, 475

Incontinence
The Canadian Continence Foundation, 364
International Continence Society, 1544

Independent Schools
Ontario Federation of Independent Schools, 1079
Youth Ballet & Contemporary Dance of Saskatchewan Inc., 1475

India
India Rainbow Community Services of Peel, 834
The Toronto-Calcutta Foundation, 1388

Industrial Design
Association de la recherche industrielle du Québec, 102

Industrial Engineering
Association de la recherche industrielle du Québec, 102

Industrial Waste
Center for Health, Environment & Justice, 1516

Infant Mortality
Baby's Breath, 192

Infants
Early Childhood Intervention Program (ECIP) Sask. Inc.,
Baby's Breath, 192
Les Centres jeunesse de l'Outaouais, 537
Early Childhood Intervention Program (ECIP) Sask. Inc., 667
Infant & Toddler Safety Association, 836

Infection Control
Infection & Prevention Control Canada, 836

Information Science
Association québécoise des troubles d'apprentissage - section Outaouais, 175
Canadian Information Processing Society, 411
Centre femmes de Rimouski, 531

Information Technology
Armed Forces Communications & Electronics Association (Canada), 82
Association de la sécurité de l'information du Québec, 102
Canadian Information Processing Society, 411

Injured Workers
Industrial Accident Victims Group of Ontario, 835
Injured Workers Association of Manitoba Inc., 838

Insurance Industry
L'Institut d'assurance de dommages du Québec, 841
Insurance Brokers Association of Canada, 848
Insurance Institute of Northern Alberta, 849

Insurance, Life
Chambre de la sécurité financière, 550

Interior Design
Association of Interior Designers of Nova Scotia, 149
Association professionnelle des designers d'intérieur du Québec, 167

International Cooperation
CARE Canada, 511
Carrefour de solidarité internationale inc., 515
Casa - Pueblito, 516
Centre canadien d'étude et de coopération internationale, 526
Change for Children Association, 551
CoDevelopment Canada, 580
CUSO International, 646
Development & Peace, 654
Earthwatch Institute, 1522
HOPE International Development Agency, 821
Horizons of Friendship, 821
Innovations et réseaux pour le développement, 1532
Institute of Cultural Affairs International, 846
Inter Pares, 851
Jamaican Self-Help Organization, 867
Jeunesse du Monde, 870
Manitoba Council for International Cooperation, 934
The Marquis Project, Inc., 952
The North-South Institute, 1036
Oxfam Canada, 1134
Partners International, 1144
Saskatchewan Council for International Co-operation, 1262
Scarboro Foreign Mission Society, 1282
Seva Canada Society, 1292
Social Justice Committee, 1305
Société de coopération pour le développement international, 1314
World Vision Canada, 1467

International Law
Canadian Council on International Law, 371

International Relations
Association Canado-Américaine, 1507
Canadian Bureau for International Education, 347
Canadian International Council, 421

Centre canadien d'étude et de coopération internationale, 526
Institut de la Francophonie pour le développement durable, 841
Institute of Cultural Affairs International, 846
Parliamentary Centre, 1142
SOS Children's Villages Canada, 1333
United Nations Association in Canada, 1411

International Relief
Adventist Development & Relief Agency Canada, 10
Canadian Association for Mine & Explosive Ordnance Security, 302
Canadian Feed The Children, 389
Canadian Foodgrains Bank, 391
Canadian Lutheran World Relief, 428
Canadian Organization for Development through Education, 447
CARE Canada, 511
Doctors without Borders Canada, 660
HelpAge International, 1529
Hope for the Nations, 821
International Community for Relief of Suffering & Starvation Canada, 855
Islamic Relief Canada, 865
Nepali Children's Education Project, 1003
Operation Eyesight Universal, 1115
Probe International, 1181
Save the Children Canada, 1281
Seva Canada Society, 1292
Vides Canada, 1434
The World Job & Food Bank Inc., 1466
World Renew, 1467

International Trade
World Trade Centre Montréal, 1467

Internet
Ability Online Support Network, 2
Chebucto Community Net, 555
Edmonton Community Networks, 676

Interpreters
Canadian Translators, Terminologists & Interpreters Council, 496
Corporation des traducteurs, traductrices, terminologues et interprètes du Nouveau-Brunswick, 631

Inuit
I.C.C. Foundation, 829
Inuit Art Foundation, 862
Makivik Corporation, 927
Northern Youth Abroad Program, 1035
Pauktuutit Inuit Women of Canada, 1146

Inventory Control
AIM Global, 1486

Investment
Mouvement d'éducation et de défense des actionnaires, 977
National Aboriginal Trust Officers Association, 989
Réseau des SADC et CAE, 1219

Ireland
The Ireland Funds, Canada, 863

Irish Studies
Canadian Association for Irish Studies, 301

Islam
Ahmadiyya Muslim Jama'at Canada, 15
Islamic Care Centre, 864
Islamic Foundation of Toronto, 864
Islamic Information Foundation, 864
Islamic Propagation Centre of Ontario, 865

Israel
Association of Americans & Canadians in Israel, 1510
Canada-Israel Cultural Foundation, 283
Canadian Associates of Ben-Gurion University of the Negev, 297
Canadian Foundation for Masorti Judaism, 393
Canadian Friends of Peace Now (Shalom Achshav), 395
Canadian Friends of Yeshiva University, 395
Canadian Institute for Jewish Research, 412
Canadian Magen David Adom for Israel, 429
Canadian Society for the Protection of Nature in Israel, 477
The Canadian Society for the Weizmann Institute of Science, 478
The Canadian Zionist Cultural Association, 506
Forever Chai Foundation of Canada, 752
Israel Cancer Research Fund, 866
Mizrachi Organization of Canada, 970

Italian Canadians & Italy
Canadian Italian Heritage Foundation, 423
Canadian Society for Italian Studies, 476
Conseil régional des personnes âgées italo-canadiennes de Montréal, 621
Villa Charities Inc. (Toronto District), 1434

Jamaican Canadians
Jamaican Canadian Association, 867
Jamaican Self-Help Organization, 867

Japanese Canadians
Japanese Canadian Cultural Centre, 869
Société Canada-Japon de Montréal, 1307

Jazz
Les Ballets Jazz de Montréal, 195
Coastal Jazz & Blues Society, 579
Jazz Yukon, 869
Toronto Downtown Jazz Society, 1384

Jesuits
Canadian Jesuits International, 423
Jesuit Development Office, 870

Jewellery
Corporation des bijoutiers du Québec, 629

Jewish People
Antisemitism Must End Now, 72
Asper Foundation, 87
Azrieli Foundation, 191
Bernard Betel Centre for Creative Living, 205
Canadian Hadassah WIZO, 399
The Centre for Israel & Jewish Affairs, 533
Emunah Women of Canada, 687
Hamilton Jewish Federation, 801
Hashomer Hatzair Canada, 804
International Fellowship of Christians & Jews of Canada, 857
Jewish Child & Family Services, 871
Jewish Community Foundation of Montréal, 871
Jewish Family & Child, 871
Jewish Family Services - Calgary, 871
Jewish Family Services Edmonton, 871
Jewish Family Services of Ottawa-Carleton, 872
Jewish Federation of Greater Vancouver, 872
Jewish Free Loan Toronto, 872
Jewish Genealogical Society of Toronto, 872
Jewish Heritage Centre of Western Canada Inc., 872
Jewish Historical Society of BC, 872
Jewish Historical Society of Southern Alberta, 872
Jewish Immigrant Aid Services of Canada, 873
JVS of Greater Toronto, 879
London Jewish Federation, 918
Na'amat Canada Inc., 987
National Council of Jewish Women of Canada, 992
Reena, 1210
Rose & Max Rady Jewish Community Centre, 1236
Saint John Jewish Historical Society, 1247
Segal Centre for the Performing Arts at the Saidye, 1289
Toronto Jewish Film Society, 1385
UJA Federation of Greater Toronto, 1402
Vancouver Jewish Film Centre Society, 1427

Jewish Studies
Aish Thornhill Community Shul & Learning Centre, 20
Canadian Institute for Jewish Research, 412

Journalism
Association de la presse francophone, 101
Canadian Journalism Foundation, 423
Canadian Journalists for Free Expression, 423
Conseil de presse du Québec, 616
Professional Writers Association of Canada, 1187
Union internationale de la presse francophone, 1598

Judaism
Aish Thornhill Community Shul & Learning Centre, 20
Am Shalom, 66
Association for Canadian Jewish Studies, 132
B'nai Brith Canada, 192
Canadian Foundation for Masorti Judaism, 393
The Centre for Israel & Jewish Affairs, 533
Chosen People Ministries (Canada), 566
Emunah Women of Canada, 687
Jewish Foundation of Manitoba, 872
Jews for Jesus, 873
Kosher Check, 894
League for Human Rights of B'nai Brith Canada, 903
Mizrachi Organization of Canada, 970
Oraynu Congregation for Humanistic Judaism, 1117
Shaare Zion Congregation, 1293
World ORT Union, 1607

Kayaking
Association québécoise de canoë-kayak de vitesse, 169
Canoe Kayak Saskatchewan, 509
Paddle Canada, 1137

Kidney Disorders & Diseases
Kidney Cancer Canada Association, 884
Kidney Foundation of Canada, 885

Korean Canadians & Korea
Korea Veterans Association of Canada Inc., Heritage Unit, 893
Korean Senior Citizens Society of Toronto, 893

Kosher Food
Kosher Check, 894

LGBTQ
Association des pères gais de Montréal inc., 122
CAEO Québec, 270
Canadian Lesbian & Gay Archives, 426
Community One Foundation, 607
The 519 Church St. Community Centre, 740
Gai Écoute inc., 766
Kind Space, 888
Metropolitan Community Church of Toronto, 964
PFLAG Canada Inc., 1155
Rainbow Resource Centre, 1203
Toronto Area Gays & Lesbians Phoneline & Crisis Counselling, 1381
2-Spirited People of the First Nations, 1401

Laboratory Medicine
College of Medical Laboratory Technologists of Alberta, 586

Labour
Association des jeunes travailleurs et travailleuses de Montréal inc, 117
Centre for the Study of Living Standards, 534
Centre international de solidarité ouvrière, 535

Labour Councils
Conseil central de l'Estrie (CSN), 614
Conseil économique du Nouveau-Brunswick inc., 618
Conseil régional FTQ Estrie, 621
Conseil régional FTQ Saguenay-Lac-St-Jean-Chibougamau-Chapais, 621

Labour Relations
Association canadienne des relations industrielles, 94

Labour Unions
Alliance du personnel professionnel et technique de la santé et des services sociaux, 56
Association des policières et policiers provinciaux du Québec, 123
Association nationale des peintres - locale 99, 138
Canadian Federal Pilots Association, 384
Canadian Overseas Telecommunications Union, 448
Confédération des syndicats nationaux, 611
Fédération des employées et employés de services publics inc. (CSN), 714
Fédération des professionnèles, 717
Fédération des professionnelles et professionnels de l'éducation du Québec, 718
Fédération des Syndicats de l'Enseignement, 719
Fédération du personnel de l'enseignement privé, 720
Fédération du personnel de soutien scolaire (CSQ), 720
Fédération indépendante des syndicats autonomes, 721
Fraternité nationale des forestiers et travailleurs d'usine (CTC), 758
International Longshore & Warehouse Union (CLC), 1553
Professional Writers Association of Canada, 1187
Société professionnelle des auteurs et des compositeurs du Québec, 1322
Syndicat des agents de la paix en services correctionnels du Québec, 1362
Syndicat professionnel des homéopathes du Québec, 1365
Syndicat professionnel des médecins du gouvernement du Québec (ind.), 1365
Teamsters Canada (CLC), 1368

Lacrosse
Canadian Lacrosse Association, 425

Land Mines
Canadian Association for Mine & Explosive Ordnance Security, 302

Land Reclamation
American Society of Mining & Reclamation, 1501
Canadian Society of Soil Science, 488

Land Use
American Farmland Trust, 1492
American Society of Mining & Reclamation, 1501
Canadian Society of Soil Science, 488

Landlords
Ligue des propriétaires de Montréal, 912

Landscape Architecture
International Federation of Landscape Architects, 1548

Language Disorders
International Society for Augmentative & Alternative Communication, 860
Speech & Hearing Association of Nova Scotia, 1340
The Speech & Stuttering Institute, 1340

Language Teaching
Alliance Française, 57
Alliance Française d'Ottawa, 57
Alliance Française du Manitoba, 57
Alliance Française Halifax, 57
Association canadienne d'éducation de langue française, 90
Association canadienne des professeurs d'immersion, 94
Fédération internationale des professeurs de français, 1525
Parents partenaires en éducation, 1140

Languages
Esperanto Association of Canada, 695
Parents partenaires en éducation, 1140
Société québécoise d'espéranto, 1323

Lao Canadians
Lao Association of Ontario, 899

Latvian Canadians & Latvia
Latvian Canadian Cultural Centre, 900

Registered Charitable Organizations Index / Marine Biology

The Latvian Relief Society of Canada, 900
Toronto Latvian Concert Association, 1385

Law
Alberta Law Foundation, 39
ARCH Disability Law Centre, 76
Association d'entraide Le Chaînon inc., 99
British Columbia Law Institute, 244
Canadian Association of Elizabeth Fry Societies, 312
Canadian Council on International Law, 371
Canadian Criminal Justice Association, 373
Canadian HIV/AIDS Legal Network, 405
Canadian Institute for the Administration of Justice, 413
Church Council on Justice & Corrections, 569
Community Legal Information Association of Prince Edward Island, 600
Foundation for Legal Research, 755
International Centre for Criminal Law Reform & Criminal Justice Policy, 854
Justice for Children & Youth, 878
Law Foundation of British Columbia, 900
Law Foundation of Ontario, 901
Legal Archives Society of Alberta, 906
National Association of Women & the Law, 990
National Judicial Institute, 994
Northwest Territories Law Foundation, 1038
Ontario Community Justice Association, 1073
The Public Interest Advocacy Centre, 1192

Law Libraries
Association des bibliothèques de droit de Montréal, 107

Lawn Bowling
Bowls Canada Boulingrin, 220

Lawyers
Association des juristes d'expression française de l'Ontario, 117
Association des juristes d'expression française de la Saskatchewan, 118
Association des juristes d'expression française du Manitoba inc., 118
Association des juristes d'expression française du Nouveau-Brunswick, 118
Barreau de Montréal, 197

Learned Societies
American Studies Association, 1503
Anthroposophical Society in Canada, 72
Archaeological Institute of America, 1505
Associaçao Brasileira de Estudos Canadense, 1506
Association for Bahá'í Studies, 132
Association for Canadian Studies in China, 1507
Canadian Association for Irish Studies, 301
Canadian Education Association, 379
Canadian Historical Association, 405
Canadian Institute for Mediterranean Studies, 412
Canadian Philosophical Association, 454
Canadian Political Science Association, 457
Canadian Science & Technology Historical Association, 468
The Canadian Society for Mesopotamian Studies, 476
Canadian Society for the Study of Education, 478
Canadian Society for the Study of Higher Education, 478
Canadian Society for the Study of Names, 478
Dictionary Society of North America, 1521
International Association for Armenian Studies, 1535
International Political Science Association, 859
The Ontario Archaeological Society, 1059
Organization of American Historians, 1581
Royal Astronomical Society of Canada, 1238
Royal Canadian Institute, 1240
The Royal Society of Canada, 1242
Société québécoise d'ethnologie, 1323
Society for Socialist Studies, 1326
Society for the Study of Egyptian Antiquities, 1327

Learning Disabilities
Adult Learning Development Association, 9
Association de Montréal pour la déficience intellectuelle, 102
Association québécoise des troubles d'apprentissage, 175
Canadian Dyslexia Association, 379
Learning Disabilities Association of Alberta, 903
Learning Disabilities Association of Canada, 904
Learning Disabilities Association of Manitoba, 904
Learning Disabilities Association of New Brunswick, 904
Learning Disabilities Association of Newfoundland & Labrador Inc., 904
Learning Disabilities Association of Ontario, 904
Learning Disabilities Association of Prince Edward Island, 905
Learning Disabilities Association of Saskatchewan, 905
Learning Disabilities Association of Yukon Territory, 905
Victoria READ Society, 1433

Leather Industry
Two/Ten Charity Trust of Canada Inc., 1401

Lebanese Canadians & Lebanon
Lebanese Syrian Canadian Ladies Aid Society, 905

Legal Clinics
Advocacy Centre for the Elderly, 10
ARCH Disability Law Centre, 76
Au bas de l'échelle, 187
The Barbra Schlifer Commemorative Clinic, 196
Community Legal Education Ontario, 600
Parkdale Community Legal Services, 1140
Rexdale Community Legal Services, 1229
South Etobicoke Community Legal Services, 1334
Student Legal Services of Edmonton, 1352

Legal Education
Advocacy Centre for the Elderly, 10
Community Legal Education Association (Manitoba) Inc., 600
Community Legal Education Ontario, 600
Legal Information Society of Nova Scotia, 906
Women's Legal Education & Action Fund, 1462

Leprosy
Heiser Program for Research in Leprosy & Tuberculosis, 1529
Secours aux lépreux (Canada) inc., 1288

Leukemia
The Leukemia & Lymphoma Society of Canada, 908

Librarians
Canadian Association of Professional Academic Librarians, 328
Ex Libris Association, 699

Libraries
Association des bibliothèques publiques du Québec, 107
British Columbia Library Association, 244
Canadian Association of Professional Academic Librarians, 328
Canadian Association of Research Libraries, 331
Colchester-East Hants Public Library Foundation, 580
Commission de la Médiathèque Père-Louis-Lamontagne, 593
Ex Libris Association, 699
The Friends of Library & Archives Canada, 761
Friends of the Greater Sudbury Public Library, 762
Manitoba Library Association, 939
National Reading Campaign, Inc., 995
North West Library Federation, 1033
Nova Scotia Library Association, 1046
Ontario College & University Library Association, 1072
Ontario Library Association, 1088
Saskatchewan Library Association, 1269
Toronto Public Library Foundation, 1386
Woodland Cultural Centre, 1464

Library Science
Canadiana, 506

Library Technicians
Association professionnelle des techniciennes et techniciens en documentation du Québec, 167

Library Trustees
British Columbia Library Trustees' Association, 245
Ontario Library Boards' Association, 1089

Lifesaving
Lifesaving Society, 911

Lifestyle
Commonwealth Human Ecology Council, 1518

Linguistics
Canadian Society for the Study of Names, 478

Literacy
ABC Life Literacy Canada, 1
Adult Literacy Council of Greater Fort Erie, 9
Barrie Literacy Council, 197
Brant Skills Centre, 226
Canadian Literacy & Learning Network, 427
CODE, 580
Conseil pour le développement de l'alphabétisme et des compétences des adultes du Nouveau-Brunswick, 619
Copian, 628
Dorchester & Westmorland Literacy Council, 661
Fondation québécoise pour l'alphabétisation, 748
GATEWAY Centre For Learning, 767
Haldimand-Norfolk Literacy Council, 798
Houston Link to Learning, 824
John Howard Society of Ontario,
Kitimat Community Services Society, 891
Learning Enrichment Foundation, 905
Literacy Alberta, 913
Literacy Central Vancouver Island, 913
Literacy Coalition of New Brunswick, 913
The Literacy Council of Burlington, 913
Literacy Council of Durham Region, 913
Literacy Council York-Simcoe, 913
The Literacy Group of Waterloo Region, 914
Literacy Link South Central, 914
Metro Toronto Movement for Literacy, 963
Niagara West Employment & Learning Resource Centres, 1026
North Algoma Literacy Coalition, 1028
People, Words & Change, 1152
Prince Edward Island Literacy Alliance Inc., 1175
Project Adult Literacy Society, 1187
Project READ Literacy Network Waterloo-Wellington, 1188
Quality in Lifelong Learning Network, 1195
Reading Council for Literacy Advance in Montréal, 1205
Saskatchewan Literacy Network, 1269
Simcoe/Muskoka Literacy Network, 1300
Victoria READ Society, 1433
Western Québec Literacy Council, 1450
World Literacy of Canada, 1466
Wycliffe Bible Translators of Canada, Inc., 1470
Yamaska Literacy Council, 1470
Young Alberta Book Society, 1474
Yukon Learn Society, 1479

Literary Appreciation
Bard on the Beach Theatre Society, 196
The Bronte Historical Society, 260
The Brontë Society, 1514

Literature
Association professionnelle des écrivains de la Sagamie–Côte-Nord, 167
The Bronte Historical Society, 260
The Brontë Society, 1514
Fédération québécoise du loisir littéraire, 731
La Fondation Émile-Nelligan, 746
Literary & Historical Society of Québec, 914
Québec Writers' Federation, 1199
Young Alberta Book Society, 1474

Lithuanian Canadians
Lithuanian-Canadian Foundation, 915

Liver & Biliary Tract Diseases
Canadian Liver Foundation, 427

Livestock
Canadian Bison Association, 344
Rare Breeds Canada, 1204

Long Term Care Facilities
AdvantAge Ontario, 10
Canadian Hospice Palliative Care Association, 409
Concerned Friends of Ontario Citizens in Care Facilities, 609
La coopérative de Solidarité de Répit et d'Etraide, 627
HealthCareCAN, 807
Kensington Foundation, 883

Longshoremen
International Longshore & Warehouse Union (CLC), 1553

Lumber Industry
Syndicat des producteurs de bois du Saguenay-Lac-Saint-Jean, 1363

Lung Disorders & Diseases
Alberta & Northwest Territories Lung Association, 21
American Lung Association, 1495
British Columbia Lung Association, 245
Canadian Lung Association, 428
Canadian Thoracic Society, 494
The Lung Association of Nova Scotia, 921
Manitoba Lung Association, 940
New Brunswick Lung Association, 1010
Newfoundland & Labrador Lung Association, 1020
Ontario Lung Association, 1089
Ontario Respiratory Care Society, 1101
Ontario Thoracic Society, 1110
Prince Edward Island Lung Association, 1175
Québec Lung Association, 1198
Saskatchewan Lung Association, 1269

Lupus Erythematosus
British Columbia Lupus Society, 245
Lupus Canada, 921
Lupus Foundation of Ontario, 921
Lupus Newfoundland & Labrador, 921
Lupus Ontario, 921
Lupus SK Society, 922
Lupus Society of Alberta, 922
Lupus Society of Manitoba, 922

Lutheran Church
Canadian Lutheran World Relief, 428
Evangelical Lutheran Church in Canada, 698
Lutheran Laymen's League of Canada, 922

Management
Association des Aménagistes Régionaux du Québec, 105
Canadian Association of University Business Officers, 334
Ordre des administrateurs agréés du Québec, 1119

Management Consultants
Institute of Certified Management Consultants of Saskatchewan, 845

Manufacturing
Agricultural Manufacturers of Canada, 15
The Royal Society for the Encouragement of Arts, Manufactures & Commerce, 1587

Marfan Syndrome
Canadian Marfan Association, 430

Marine Biology
Canadian Meteorological & Oceanographic Society, 435
Grand Manan Whale & Seabird Research Station, 780

Marine Engineering
Marine Renewables Canada, 950

Marine Mammals
Grand Manan Whale & Seabird Research Station, 780
Sea Shepherd Conservation Society - USA, 1588

Mariners
Mariners' House of Montréal, 950

Maritime Law
Canadian Nautical Research Society, 440

Marketing
Canadian Institute of Marketing, 417

Marketing Boards & Commissions
Madawaska Forest Products Marketing Board, 924

Martial Arts
International Judo Federation, 1551
Judo Yukon, 876
Judo-Québec inc, 876
Karate BC, 881

Massage Therapy
Alliance des massothérapeutes du Québec, 56
Association des massologues et techniciens en massage du Canada - Association des massothérapeutes professionnels du Québec, 119
Fédération québécoise des massothérapeutes, 729

Materials Management
AIM Global, 1486

Mathematics
Association mathématique du Québec, 137
Canadian Mathematical Society, 431
Visions of Science Network for Learning, 1436

Measuring Instruments
The Instrumentation, Systems & Automation Society of America, 1534

Meat
Canadian Bison Association, 344
Fédération des producteurs de bovins du Québec, 717

Mechanical Engineering
Canadian Society for Mechanical Engineering, 476
Corporation des maîtres mécaniciens en tuyauterie du Québec, 630

Media
Accessible Media Inc., 5
Canadian Journalism Foundation, 423
Conseil des directeurs médias du Québec, 617
Lights, Camera, Access!, 912
Rumble Productions Society, 1244
Saskatchewan Filmpool Co-operative, 1265

Mediation
ADR Institute of Canada, 9
Centre canadien d'arbitrage commercial, 526

Medical Assistance
Canadian Physicians for Aid & Relief, 454
International Association for Medical Assistance to Travellers, 853
Operation Eyesight Universal, 1115
Secours aux lépreux (Canada) inc, 1288
Telemiracle/Kinsmen Foundation Inc., 1369

Medical Care
Hope Air, 821

Medical Devices
Association des implantés cochléaires du Québec, 116

Medical Genetics
Canadian College of Medical Geneticists, 359

Medical Research
Canadian Chiropractic Research Foundation, 356
Canadian Foundation for AIDS Research, 392
Canadian Institute for the Relief of Pain & Disability, 413
Canadians for Health Research, 507
Dalhousie Medical Research Foundation, 648
Dystonia Medical Research Foundation Canada, 665
Fondation de l'Ordre des infirmières et infirmiers du Québec, 744
Fondation des étoiles, 744
Fondation Initia, 746
The Foundation Fighting Blindness, 755
Institute for the Study & Treatment of Pain, 844
Israel Cancer Research Fund, 866
The Leukemia & Lymphoma Society of Canada, 908
The M.S.I. Foundation, 978

Medical Schools
Association of Faculties of Medicine of Canada, 148

Medical Specialists
Association d'oto-rhino-laryngologie et de chirurgie cervico-faciale du Québec, 99
Association des dermatologistes du Québec, 110
Association des médecins hématologistes-oncologistes du Québec, 119
Association des médecins ophtalmologistes du Québec, 120
Association des spécialistes en médecine interne du Québec, 128
The Royal College of Physicians & Surgeons of Canada, 1241
Société canadienne-française de radiologie, 1309

Medical Technology
College of Medical Laboratory Technologists of Alberta, 586

Medicine
Associated Medical Services Inc., 89
Association des conseils des médecins, dentistes et pharmaciens du Québec, 109
Association médicale du Québec, 137
Canadian Medical Foundation, 434
Canadian MedicAlert Foundation, 434
Canadian Society of Transplantation, 488
International Society for the History of Medicine - Canadian Section, 860
The M.S.I. Foundation, 978

Meditation
Réseau Tara Canada (Québec), 1226
Sivananda Ashram Yoga Camp, 1301
Tara Canada Network Association, 1367
Yasodhara Ashram Society, 1470

Mediterranean
Canadian Institute for Mediterranean Studies, 412

Meetings & Conventions
Westerner Park, 1450

Men
British Columbia Society for Male Survivors of Sexual Abuse, 254

Mennonites
Evangelical Mennonite Conference, 699
International Mennonite Health Association Inc., 858
MB Mission, 954
Mennonite Central Committee Canada, 960
Mennonite Church Canada, 961
Mennonite Economic Development Associates Canada, 961

Mental Health
AiMHi, Prince George Association for Community Living, 18
Anxiety Disorders Association of Canada, 72
Anxiety Disorders Association of Manitoba, 72
Anxiety Disorders Association of Ontario, 72
Aspergers Society of Ontario, 87
Association de loisirs pour personnes handicapées psychiques de Laval, 102
Association des alternatives en santé mentale de la Montérégie, 105
Association des parents et amis de la personne atteinte de maladie mentale Rive-Sud, 122
Association/Troubles de l'Humeur et d'Anxiété au Québec, 179
Calgary Association of Self Help, 271
CAMH Foundation, 276
Canadian Mental Health Association, 434
Centre for Addiction & Mental Health, 531
C.G. Jung Foundation of Ontario, 539
Chai-Tikvah The Life & Hope Foundation, 539
Child Development Institute, 559
Children's Mental Health Ontario, 562
Fédération des familles et amis de la personne atteinte de maladie mentale, 715
Flowercart, 741
Graham Boeckh Foundation, 779
Healthy Minds Canada, 807
Hong Fook Mental Health Association, 820
Horizon Achievement Centre, 821
Jack.org, 867
Kenora Association for Community Living, 883
Mood Disorders Association of British Columbia, 973
Mood Disorders Association of Manitoba, 973
Mood Disorders Association of Ontario, 973
Ontario Mental Health Foundation, 1090
The Organization for Bipolar Affective Disorder, 1125
Pacific Post Partum Support Society, 1136
Post Traumatic Stress Disorder Association, 1167
Regional Occupation Centre Foundation, 1212
Responsible Gambling Council (Ontario), 1227
Revivre - Association Québécoise de soutien aux personnes souffrant de troubles anxieux, dépressifs ou bipolaires, 1228
Scottish Rite Charitable Foundation of Canada, 1286
Shelburne Association Supporting Inclusion, 1295
Society of St. Vincent de Paul - Toronto Central Council, 1330
Toronto Art Therapy Institute, 1381
World Federation for Mental Health, 1605

Mesopotamian Studies
The Canadian Society for Mesopotamian Studies, 476

Metabolic Diseases
Canadian PKU and Allied Disorders Inc., 455
Québec Society of Lipidology, Nutrition & Metabolism Inc., 1199

Metal Arts
The Metal Arts Guild of Canada, 962

Meteorology
Canadian Meteorological & Oceanographic Society, 435
Climate Institute, 1517

Methodists
The Bible Holiness Movement, 208

Mexico
Friends of the Orphans, Canada, 763

Microbiology
Canadian Association for Clinical Microbiology & Infectious Diseases, 297

Microreproduction
Canadiana, 506

Midwives
International Confederation of Midwives, 1543

Migraine
Headache Network Canada, 805
Help for Headaches, 812

Military
Conference of Defence Associations, 612
15th Field Artillery Regiment Museum & Archives Society, 734
L'Ordinariat militaire Catholique Romain du Canada, 1119
Organization of Military Museums of Canada, 1125
Princess Patricia's Canadian Light Infantry Association, 1180
Royal Canadian Artillery Association, 1239
Royal United Services Institute of Regina, 1243

Military Weapons
Canadian Association for Mine & Explosive Ordnance Security, 302

Millwork
Architectural Woodwork Manufacturers Association of British Columbia, 79

Mineralogy
Bancroft Gem & Mineral Club, 195
Mineralogical Association of Canada, 966
Musée minéralogique et minier de Thetford Mines, 982

Mining
American Society of Mining & Reclamation, 1501
Association minière du Québec, 137
Mineralogical Association of Canada, 966
Musée minéralogique et minier de Thetford Mines, 982

Minorities
Vancouver & Lower Mainland Multicultural Family Support Services Society, 1424

Missing Children
Child Find British Columbia, 559
Child Find Canada Inc., 559
Child Find Ontario, 559
Child Find PEI Inc., 559
Child Find Saskatchewan Inc., 559
Missing Children Society of Canada, 968

Missions & Missionaries
Adventive Cross Cultural Initiatives, 10
Africa Inland Mission International (Canada), 12
The Bible Holiness Movement, 208
Canadian Jesuits International, 423
The Christian & Missionary Alliance in Canada, 566
Christian Blind Mission International, 566
Fondation Père-Ménard, 747
Institut Voluntas Dei, 843
Intercede International, 851
International Mennonite Health Association Inc., 858
MB Mission, 954
Les Missions des Soeurs Missionnaires du Christ-Roi, 969
Operation Mobilization Canada, 1116
Pentecostal Assemblies of Canada, 1150
Pontifical Mission Societies, 1164
Soeurs missionnaires de Notre-Dame des Anges, 1331
Wycliffe Bible Translators of Canada, Inc., 1470
Yonge Street Mission, 1473

Monuments
Canadian Tribute to Human Rights, 497

Morris, William
William Morris Society of Canada, 1455

Mothers
Forever Chai Foundation of Canada, 752
International Confederation of Midwives, 1543

Motorcycles
Association des motocyclistes gais du Québec, 120

Mountaineering
Alpine Club of Canada, 59
Federation of Mountain Clubs of British Columbia, 725
Fédération québécoise de la montagne et de l'escalade, 727

Multiculturalism
Beaton Institute, 203
Brockville & District Multicultural Council Inc., 260
Burnaby Multicultural Society, 266
Central Vancouver Island Multicultural Society, 525
Centre multiethnique de Québec, 536
Community Folk Art Council of Toronto, 597
Immigrant & Multicultural Services Society, 830
Institute of Cultural Affairs International, 846

Inter-Cultural Association of Greater Victoria, 851
New Brunswick Multicultural Council, 1010
Parkdale Intercultural Association, 1140
Peel Multicultural Council, 1148
Regina Multicultural Council, 1212
Richmond Multicultural Community Services, 1231
Saskatchewan Intercultural Association Inc., 1268
Vancouver Multicultural Society, 1427
Welfare Committee for the Assyrian Community in Canada, 1443

Multifaith
Multifaith Action Society, 979

Multiple Births
Association de Parents de Jumeaux et de Triplés de la région de Montréal, 103
Multiple Birth Families Association, 979

Multiple Sclerosis
Multiple Sclerosis Society of Canada,
Multiple Sclerosis International Federation, 1571
Multiple Sclerosis Society of Canada, 980
Société canadienne de la sclérose en plaques (Division du Québec), 1308

Municipal Government
Association des Aménagistes Régionaux du Québec, 105
Association internationale des maires francophones - Bureau à Québec, 136
Halifax Foundation, 799
Municipalities Newfoundland & Labrador, 982
Union des municipalités du Québec, 1406

Muscular Dystrophy
Muscular Dystrophy Canada, 982
Society for Muscular Dystrophy Information International, 1326

Museums
Alberta Museums Association, 40
Alberta Pioneer Railway Association, 42
Alberta Sports Hall of Fame & Museum, 48
Association Museums New Brunswick, 138
Association of Manitoba Museums, 151
Brant Historical Society, 226
British Columbia Farm Machinery & Agriculture Museum Association, 240
British Columbia Museums Association, 246
British Columbia Sports Hall of Fame & Museum, 255
Campbell River Museum & Archives Society, 276
Canadian Centre for Architecture, 353
Canadian Federation of Friends of Museums, 386
Canadian Football Hall of Fame & Museum, 391
Canadian Golf Hall of Fame & Museum, 398
Canadian Railroad Historical Association, 465
Cardston Historical Society, 511
Central British Columbia Railway & Forest Industry Museum Society, 524
Compton County Historical Museum Society, 609
Creston & District Historical & Museum Society, 641
Danish Canadian National Museum Society, 650
DeBolt & District Pioneer Museum Society, 652
Enderby & District Museum Society, 687
15th Field Artillery Regiment Museum & Archives Society, 734
Grande Prairie Museum, 781
Historical Society of Ottawa, 816
ICOM Museums Canada, 829
LaHave Islands Marine Museum Society, 895
Mackenzie & District Museum Society, 924
Manitoba Sports Hall of Fame & Museum, 945
Margaret Laurence Home, Inc., 949
McCord Museum of Canadian History, 955
Mirror & District Museum Association, 968
Missisquoi Historical Society, 969

Musée minéralogique et minier de Thetford Mines, 982
Museum Association of Newfoundland & Labrador, 982
Museum London, 983
Museum of Contemporary Canadian Art, 983
Museums Association of Saskatchewan, 983
Nanaimo District Museum, 987
Nicola Valley Museum Archives Association, 1026
North Peace Historical Society, 1032
Northwestern Ontario Sports Hall of Fame & Museum, 1039
O'Keefe Ranch & Interior Heritage Society, 1053
Old Sydney Society, 1056
Ontario Museum Association, 1092
Organization of Military Museums of Canada, 1125
Petrolia Discovery, 1155
Port Clements Historical Society, 1165
Pouce Coupe & District Museum & Historical Society, 1168
Prince Edward Island Museum & Heritage Foundation, 1175
Prince Edward Island Sports Hall of Fame & Museum Inc., 1177
Prince Rupert Fire Museum Society, 1179
Rocanville & District Museum Society Inc., 1235
Saskatchewan Sports Hall of Fame & Museum, 1275
Save Our Heritage Organization, 1281
Société historique Alphonse-Desjardins, 1319
Société internationale du réseau ÉCONOMUSÉE et Société ÉCONOMUSÉE du Québec, 1321
La Société Saint-Pierre, 1325
Stephan G. Stephansson Icelandic Society, 1349
Summerland Museum & Heritage Society, 1354
Touchstones Nelson Museum of Art & History, 1388
U'mista Cultural Society, 1401
Vancouver Museum Society, 1427
Yukon Historical & Museums Association, 1478

Music
Académie de musique du Québec, 3
Alliance for Canadian New Music Projects, 56
Atlantic Canada Pipe Band Association, 182
The Battlefords Music Festival, 200
BC Chinese Music Association, 201
Calgary Society of Organists, 274
Canadian Academy of Recording Arts & Sciences, 286
Canadian Bureau for the Advancement of Music, 347
Canadian Music Centre, 438
Canadian Society for Traditional Music, 479
Canadian University Music Society, 499
Canmore Folk & Blues Club, 508
Concours de musique du Canada inc., 610
Conseil québécois de la musique, 620
Conservatory Canada, 622
Cosmopolitan Music Society, 631
Early Music Vancouver, 667
Edmonton Composers' Concert Society, 676
The Galpin Society, 1527
International Society for Music Education, 1558
Jeunesses Musicales du Canada, 871
Ladies' Morning Musical Club, 895
Metronome Canada, 963
MuchFACT, 978
Musicaction, 984
National Shevchenko Musical Ensemble Guild of Canada, 996
Oshawa-Whitby Kiwanis Music & Theatre Festival, 1128
Pro Coro Canada, 1181
Royal Canadian College of Organists, 1239
Sarnia Concert Association, 1254
Société Pro Musica Inc., 1322
The Toronto Consort, 1383
Toronto Latvian Concert Association, 1385
Vancouver Moving Theatre, 1427
Vancouver New Music, 1427

Vancouver Pro Musica Society, 1428
Women's Musical Club of Toronto, 1463

Music Festivals
Associated Manitoba Arts Festivals, Inc., 89
Edmonton Folk Music Festival, 677
Kiwanis Music Festival Association of Greater Toronto, 892
New Brunswick Competitive Festival of Music Inc., 1007
Prince Edward Island Kiwanis Music Festival Association, 1175
Saskatchewan Music Festival Association Inc., 1270

Music Teachers
Canadian Federation of Music Teachers' Associations, 388
International Society for Music Education, 1558

Musicians
Canadian Amateur Musicians, 292
West Coast Amateur Musicians' Society, 1444

Muslims
Ahmadiyya Muslim Jama'at Canada, 15
Islamic Foundation of Toronto, 864
Islamic Information Foundation, 864
Islamic Propagation Centre of Ontario, 865
Ottawa Muslim Association, 1131
Scarborough Muslim Association, 1282

Myalgic Encephalomyelitis
Myalgic Encephalomyelitis Association of Halton/Hamilton-Wentworth, 986
Myalgic Encephalomyelitis Association of Ontario, 986
National ME/FM Action Network, 995

Myasthenia Gravis
Myasthenia Gravis Association of British Columbia, 986

NATO
Atlantic Council of Canada, 183

Names
Canadian Society for the Study of Names, 478

Native Development Corporations
Makivik Corporation, 927

Native Friendship Centres
Atikokan Native Friendship Centre, 181
Barrie Native Friendship Centre, 197
Battlefords Indian & Métis Friendship Centre, 200
Brandon Friendship Centre, 226
Canadian Native Friendship Centre, 440
CanAm Indian Friendship Centre of Windsor, 507
Centre d'amitié autochtone du Québec, 527
Cold Lake Native Friendship Centre, 580
Dauphin Friendship Centre, 651
Dze L K'ant Friendship Centre Society, 666
Edson Friendship Centre, 680
First Nations Friendship Centre, 738
Fort Nelson Aboriginal Friendship Society, 753
Georgian Bay Native Friendship Centre, 771
Interior Indian Friendship Society, 852
Kermode Friendship Society, 884
Ki-Low-Na Friendship Society, 887
Lloydminster Native Friendship Centre, 916
Manitoba Association of Friendship Centres, 929
Mannawanis Native Friendship Centre, 948
Mi'kmaq Native Friendship Centre, 964
Mission Indian Friendship Centre, 969
Napi Friendship Association, 988
Native Canadian Centre of Toronto, 997
Native Friendship Centre of Montréal Inc., 998
Ne'Chee Friendship Centre, 1002
Niagara Regional Native Centre, 1026
Odawa Native Friendship Centre, 1054
Qu'Appelle Valley Friendship Centre, 1195
Quesnel Tillicum Society Friendship Centre, 1200
Red Lake Indian Friendship Centre, 1210
Regroupement des centres d'amitié autochtone du Québec, 1215
Riverton & District Friendship Centre, 1234

United Native Friendship Centre, 1412
Vancouver Aboriginal Friendship Centre Society, 1424

Native Peoples
British Columbia Aboriginal Network on Disability Society, 229
Calgary Aboriginal Arts Awareness Society, 270
Canadian Council for Aboriginal Business, 366
Canadian Indigenous Nurses Association, 411
Edmonton Aboriginal Senior Centre, 675
Femmes autochtones du Québec inc., 731
Indspire, 835
Jake Thomas Learning Centre, 867
James Bay Association for Community Living, 868
Kanien'kehaka Onkwawen'na Raotitiohkwa Language & Cultural Centre, 881
Manitoba Association of Friendship Centres, 929
Manitoba Indian Cultural Education Centre, 939
National Aboriginal Trust Officers Association, 989
Native Addictions Council of Manitoba, 997
Native Canadian Centre of Toronto, 997
Native Child & Family Services of Toronto, 997
Native Courtworker & Counselling Association of BC, 997
Native Earth Performing Arts Inc., 998
Niagara Regional Native Centre, 1026
Ojibway & Cree Cultural Centre, 1055
Quaker Aboriginal Affairs Committee, 1195
Regroupement des centres d'amitié autochtone du Québec, 1215
2-Spirited People of the First Nations, 1401
U'mista Cultural Society, 1401
Woodland Cultural Centre, 1464

Native Women
Femmes autochtones du Québec inc., 731
Native Women's Resource Centre of Toronto, 998
Pauktuutit Inuit Women of Canada, 1146

Natural History
Natural History Society of Newfoundland & Labrador, 999
Nature Saskatchewan, 1000
Nature Vancouver, 1001
St. Lawrence Valley Natural History Society, 1250
Société Provancher d'histoire naturelle du Canada, 1322
Waterton Natural History Association, 1442

Natural Products Industry
Canadian Organic Growers Inc., 446
International Federation of Organic Agriculture Movements, 1548

Naturalists
Blomidon Naturalists Society, 215
Brereton Field Naturalists' Club Inc., 228
Burke Mountain Naturalists, 265
Calgary Field Naturalists' Society, 272
Central Okanagan Naturalists Club, 525
Cercles des jeunes naturalistes, 537
Cole Harbour Rural Heritage Society, 581
Grasslands Naturalists, 782
Halifax Field Naturalists, 799
Hamilton Naturalists' Club, 801
Ingersoll District Nature Club, 838
Kamloops Naturalist Club, 880
Kingston Field Naturalists, 889
Kitchener-Waterloo Field Naturalists, 890
National Audubon Society, Inc., 1575
Nature Alberta, 999
Nature Canada, 999
Nature Manitoba, 1000
Nature NB, 1000
Nature Nova Scotia (Federation of Nova Scotia Naturalists), 1000
Nature Québec, 1000
Niagara Falls Nature Club, 1025
North Okanagan Naturalists Club, 1031
Ontario Field Ornithologists, 1080
Ontario Nature, 1093
Osoyoos Desert Society, 1128

Ottawa Field-Naturalists' Club, 1130
Pembroke Area Field Naturalists, 1149
Peninsula Field Naturalists, 1149
Peterborough Field Naturalists, 1153
Red Deer River Naturalists, 1209
Rocky Mountain Naturalists, 1235
Sargeant Bay Society, 1253
Shuswap Naturalists, 1297
Sydenham Field Naturalists, 1359
Thunder Bay Field Naturalists, 1377
Toronto Entomologists Association, 1384
Toronto Field Naturalists, 1384
Toronto Ornithological Club, 1386
White Rock & Surrey Naturalists, 1452
Williams Lake Field Naturalists, 1455
Willow Beach Field Naturalists, 1455

Naval Art & Science
Canadian Nautical Research Society, 440

Navigation
Canadian Navigation Society, 440

Needlework
Embroiderers' Association of Canada, Inc., 685

Netball
Netball Alberta, 1003

Networks of Centres of Excellence
Sustainable Forestry Initiative Inc., 1597

Neurofibromatosis
AboutFace, 3
L'Association de la Neurofibromatose du Québec, 101
British Columbia Neurofibromatosis Foundation, 247
Children's Tumor Foundation, 1516
Neurofibromatosis Association of Saskatchewan, 1003
Neurofibromatosis Society of Ontario, 1003

Neurology
British Columbia Centre for Ability, 235
Neurological Health Charities Canada, 1004

Neuropathology
Canadian Association of Neuropathologists, 322
Edmonton (Alberta) Nerve Pain Association, 675

Neuroscience
Headache Network Canada, 805

Newspapers
Association des médias écrits communautaires du Québec, 120

Northern Canada
Association of Canadian Universities for Northern Studies, 144

Nuclear Energy
World Nuclear Association, 1606

Nuclear Weapons
Physicians for Global Survival (Canada), 1158

Numismatics
Apprenp'tits Numismates, 75
Société d'archéologie et de numismatique de Montréal, 1309

Nurses
Association des professionnels en santé du travail, 126
Association québécoise des infirmières et intervenants en recherche clinique, 173
Canadian Association for the History of Nursing, 305
Canadian Association of Nurses in HIV/AIDS Care, 323
Canadian Association of Schools of Nursing, 332
Canadian Gerontological Nursing Association, 397
Canadian Indigenous Nurses Association, 411
Canadian Nurses Foundation, 443
Fédération de la santé du Québec - CSQ, 709
Fondation de l'Ordre des infirmières et infirmiers du Québec, 744

Gerontological Nursing Association of Ontario, 772
Victorian Order of Nurses for Canada, 1434

Nursing Homes
AdvantAge Ontario, 10

Nutrition
American Vegan Society, 1504
Canadian Foundation for Dietetic Research, 393
Helderleigh Foundation, 811

Obesity
Active Healthy Kids Canada, 7
Childhood Obesity Foundation, 560
ÉquiLibre - Groupe d'action sur le poids, 694

Occupational Health & Safety
Association des professionnels en santé du travail, 126
Association paritaire pour la santé et la sécurité du travail - Imprimerie et activités connexes, 164
Association québécoise pour l'hygiène, la santé et la sécurité du travail, 176
Association sectorielle: Fabrication d'équipement de transport et de machines, 178
Canadian Centre for Occupational Health & Safety, 353
Canadian Council on Rehabilitation & Work, 371
Centre patronal de santé et sécurité du travail du Québec, 536
Industrial Accident Victims Group of Ontario, 835
MultiPrévention, 980
National Institute of Disability Management & Research, 994
Occupational First Aid Attendants Association of British Columbia, 1054

Occupational Therapy
Canadian Occupational Therapy Foundation, 444
Ordre des ergothérapeutes du Québec, 1121

Oceanography
Canadian Meteorological & Oceanographic Society, 435

Oceans
Oceana Canada, 1054

Offenders (Criminal) & Ex-Offenders
Canadian Association of Elizabeth Fry Societies, 312
Canadian Training Institute, 496
The John Howard Society of British Columbia, 874
The John Howard Society of Canada, 874
The John Howard Society of Newfoundland & Labrador, 874
The John Howard Society of Northwest Territories, 874
The John Howard Society of Ontario, 874
The John Howard Society of Prince Edward Island, 875
The John Howard Society of Saskatchewan, 875
M2/W2 Association - Restorative Christian Ministries, 923
Operation Springboard, 1116
St. Leonard's Society of Canada, 1250

Oil
Enform, 688
Petroleum Tank Management Association of Alberta, 1154
Petrolia Discovery, 1155

Olympic Games
B2ten, 192
Canadian Olympic Committee, 445

Oncology
Canadian Association of Psychosocial Oncology, 330

Opera
Canadian Children's Opera Company, 356

Canadian Opera Company, 446
Edmonton Opera Association, 678
Manitoba Opera Association Inc., 941
Opéra Atelier, 1114
The Queen of Puddings Music Theatre Company, 1199
Soundstreams Canada, 1333
Vancouver Opera, 1428
Western Canadian Opera Society, 1449

Ophthalmology
Association des médecins ophtalmologistes du Québec, 120
International Council of Ophthalmology, 1545

Orchestras
Brantford Symphony Orchestra Association Inc., 227
Calgary Philharmonic Society, 273
Canadian Sinfonietta Youth Orchestra, 470
Cathedral Bluffs Symphony Orchestra, 517
Chebucto Symphony Orchestra, 555
Chilliwack Symphony Orchestra & Chorus, 563
Counterpoint Community Orchestra, 636
Dundas Valley Orchestra, 664
Durham Youth Orchestra, 665
Edmonton Symphony Orchestra, 679
Edmonton Youth Orchestra Association, 679
Ensemble contemporain de Montréal, 690
Esprit Orchestra, 695
Etobicoke Philharmonic Orchestra, 697
Georgian Bay Symphony, 771
Greater Victoria Youth Orchestra, 787
Guelph Symphony Orchestra, 793
Halton Mississauga Youth Orchestra, 800
Hamilton Philharmonic Orchestra, 801
Hamilton Philharmonic Youth Orchestra, 801
Huronia Symphony Orchestra, 828
International Symphony Orchestra of Sarnia, Ontario & Port Huron, Michigan, 861
La Jeunesse Youth Orchestra, 870
Kamloops Symphony, 880
Kingston Symphony Association, 889
Kitchener-Waterloo Chamber Orchestra, 890
Kitchener-Waterloo Symphony Orchestra Association Inc., 891
Kitchener-Waterloo Symphony Youth Orchestra, 891
Korean-Canadian Symphony Orchestra, 894
Lethbridge Symphony Orchestra, 908
London Community Orchestra, 918
National Arts Centre Orchestra of Canada, 989
National Youth Orchestra Canada, 997
Newfoundland Symphony Orchestra Association, 1023
Newfoundland Symphony Youth Orchestra, 1023
Niagara Youth Orchestra Association, 1026
Northumberland Orchestra Society, 1036
Nova Scotia Youth Orchestra, 1050
Oakville Symphony Orchestra, 1053
Okanagan Symphony Society, 1056
Ontario Philharmonic, 1095
Orchestra Toronto, 1117
Orchestras Canada, 1117
Orchestras Mississauga, 1117
Orchestre de chambre de Montréal, 1117
Orchestre Métropolitain, 1118
Orchestre symphonique de Laval, 1118
Orchestre symphonique de Longueuil, 1118
Orchestre symphonique de Québec, 1118
Orchestre symphonique de Sherbrooke, 1118
Orchestre symphonique de Trois-Rivières, 1118
Orchestre symphonique des jeunes de Montréal, 1118
Orchestre symphonique des jeunes de Sherbrooke, 1118
Orchestre symphonique des jeunes du West Island, 1118
Orchestre symphonique du Saguenay-Lac-St-Jean, 1119
Orchestre symphonique régional Abitibi-Témiscamingue, 1119
Orillia Youth Symphony Orchestra, 1126
Ottawa Chamber Orchestra, 1129
Ottawa Symphony Orchestra Inc., 1132

Ottawa Youth Orchestra Academy, 1132
Pembroke Symphony Orchestra, 1149
Peterborough Symphony Orchestra, 1154
Prince Edward Island Symphony Society, 1178
Prince George Symphony Orchestra Society, 1179
Quinte Symphony, 1201
Red Deer Symphony Orchestra, 1209
Regina Symphony Orchestra, 1212
Richmond Delta Youth Orchestra, 1230
Royal Conservatory Orchestra, 1242
Saskatoon Symphony Society, 1280
Saskatoon Youth Orchestra, 1280
Sault Symphony Association, 1281
Scarborough Philharmonic Orchestra, 1282
Sooke Philharmonic Society, 1333
Soundstreams Canada, 1333
South Saskatchewan Youth Orchestra, 1336
Sudbury Symphony Orchestra Association Inc., 1353
Sudbury Youth Orchestra Inc., 1353
Surrey Symphony Society, 1357
Symphony New Brunswick, 1360
Symphony Nova Scotia, 1360
Symphony on the Bay, 1360
Tafelmusik Baroque Orchestra & Chamber Choir, 1366
Thunder Bay Symphony Orchestra Association, 1378
Timmins Symphony Orchestra, 1380
Toronto Sinfonietta, 1387
Toronto Symphony Orchestra, 1387
Toronto Symphony Youth Orchestra, 1387
Vancouver Island Symphony, 1427
Vancouver Philharmonic Orchestra, 1428
Vancouver Symphony Society, 1429
Vancouver Youth Symphony Orchestra Society, 1429
Victoria Symphony Society, 1433
Windsor Symphony Orchestra, 1457
Winnipeg Symphony Orchestra Inc., 1459
Winnipeg Youth Orchestras, 1459
York Symphony Orchestra Inc., 1474

Organ Retrieval & Donation
Canadian Liver Foundation, 427
Canadian Transplant Association, 496
David Foster Foundation, 651
Fondation Diane Hébert Inc, 745

Organic Farming & Gardening
Canadian Organic Growers Inc., 446
Ecological Farmers of Ontario, 672
International Federation of Organic Agriculture Movements, 1548
Northeast Organic Farming Association, 1580
Wallace Center, Winrock International, 1601

Orienteering
Orienteering Québec, 1126

Orthodox Church
British Israel World Federation (Canada) Inc., 259
Serbian Orthodox Church - Orthodox Diocese of Canada, 1290

Orthopaedics
Canadian Orthopaedic Foundation, 448

Osteoporosis
Osteoporosis Canada, 1128

Otolaryngology
Canadian Society of Otolaryngology - Head & Neck Surgery, 485

Ozone Layer Depletion
Climate Institute, 1517

Pain
Canadian Institute for the Relief of Pain & Disability, 413
Chronic Pain Association of Canada, 568
Institute for the Study & Treatment of Pain, 844
International Association for the Study of Pain, 1537

Painting & Decorating
Association nationale des peintres - locale 99, 138

Palliative Care
Alberta Hospice Palliative Care Association, 38
Canadian Hospice Palliative Care Association, 409
Hospice of Waterloo Region, 822
Hospice Palliative Care Ontario, 823
Newfoundland & Labrador Palliative Care Association, 1020
North Shore Hospice Society, 1032
Nova Scotia Hospice Palliative Care Association, 1046
Saskatchewan Palliative Care Association, 1271

Parachuting
Canadian Sport Parachuting Association, 490

Paralysis
Association canadienne des ataxies familiales, 92

Paraplegia
Spinal Cord Injury Canada, 1343

Parents
Association Carrefour Famille Montcalm, 96
Association de Parents de Jumeaux et de Triplés de la région de Montréal, 103
Association des parents catholiques du Québec, 121
Association des parents et amis de la personne atteinte de maladie mentale Rive-Sud, 122
Association francophone des parents du Nouveau-Brunswick, 135
Association of Parent Support Groups in Ontario Inc., 155
Block Parent Program of Canada, 214
Block Watch Society of British Columbia, 215
Bridges Family Programs Association, 228
British Columbia Federation of Foster Parent Associations, 240
Canadian Parents for French, 450
Fédération des parents acadiens de la Nouvelle-Écosse, 716
Fédération des parents du Manitoba, 716
Fédération des parents francophones de Colombie-Britannique, 716
Fédération des parents francophones de l'Alberta, 717
Foster Parent Support Services Society, 755
Kids First Parent Association of Canada, 886
Multiple Birth Families Association, 979
Parent Action on Drugs, 1139
Parent Support Services Society of BC, 1139
People for Education, 1151
Pilot Parents, 1160
Regroupement de parents de personnes ayant une déficience intellectuelle de Montréal, 1214

Parkinson's
Parkinson Alberta Society, 1141
Parkinson Society Maritime Region, 1141
Parkinson Society Saskatchewan, 1141
Société Parkinson du Québec, 1322
Victoria Epilepsy & Parkinson's Centre Society, 1432

Parks
Alberta Recreation & Parks Association, 44
British Columbia Recreation & Parks Association, 250
Canada's Accredited Zoos & Aquariums, 281
Canadian Parks & Recreation Association, 450
Canadian Parks & Wilderness Society, 450
The Friends of Algonquin Park, 760
The Friends of Bon Echo Park, 760
The Friends of Charleston Lake Park, 760
Okanagan Similkameen Parks Society, 1056
Ontario Parks Association, 1095
Park People, 1140
Protected Areas Association of Newfoundland & Labrador, 1190
Quetico Foundation, 1201
Saskatchewan Parks & Recreation Association, 1271

Parliament
Commonwealth Parliamentary Association, 1518
Parliamentary Centre, 1142

Pathology
Canadian Association of Pathologists, 325

Patient Care
Kidney Cancer Canada Association, 884
Patients Canada, 1145

Patient Safety
Kidney Cancer Canada Association, 884
Patients Canada, 1145

Patients' Rights
Concerned Friends of Ontario Citizens in Care Facilities, 609
Kidney Cancer Canada Association, 884
Patients Canada, 1145

Pay Equity
Nova Scotia League for Equal Opportunities, 1046

Peace
Canadian Friends of Peace Now (Shalom Achshav), 395
Development & Peace, 654
Group of 78, 791
Mahatma Gandhi Canadian Foundation for World Peace, 925
The Marquis Project, Inc., 952
Mosaic Institute, 975
Peace & Environment Resource Centre, 1146
Peace Brigades International (Canada), 1146
Physicians for Global Survival (Canada), 1158
Project Peacemakers, 1187
Science for Peace, 1285

Pelvic Inflammatory Disease
Endometriosis Association, Inc., 1523

Pentathlon
Pentathlon Canada, 1150

Pentecostal Assemblies
Independent Assemblies of God International - Canada, 832
Pentecostal Assemblies of Canada, 1150
The Pentecostal Assemblies of Newfoundland & Labrador, 1150

Performing Arts
Associated Manitoba Arts Festivals, Inc., 89
Bowen Island Arts Council, 219
British Columbia Drama Association, 239
Canadian Arts Presenting Association, 296
Children's Arts Umbrella Association, 561
Community Folk Art Council of Toronto, 597
Dance Nova Scotia, 649
Dancemakers, 649
EDAM Performing Arts Society, 674
Governor General's Performing Arts Awards Foundation, 778
The Guild Society, 794
Intrepid Theatre Co. Society, 862
Kingston Kiwanis Music Festival, 889
National Arts Centre Foundation, 989
New Brunswick Arts Board, 1004
O Vertigo Danse, 1052
Prologue to the Performing Arts, 1188
Saskatchewan Music Festival Association Inc., 1270
Theatre Nova Scotia, 1374

Periodicals & Magazines
Association québécoise des éditeurs de magazines, 172

Personal Development
Heartwood Centre for Community Youth Development, 810
Society for Personal Growth, 1326

Pest Management
Croplife International, 1520
Northwest Coalition for Alternatives to Pesticides, 1580
Pesticide Action Network North America, 1583

Pets
Animal Aid Foundation, 70
Greyhound Pets of Atlantic Canada Society, 790

Pharmacy
Association des conseils des médecins, dentistes et pharmaciens du Québec, 109
Association of Faculties of Pharmacy of Canada, 148
Canadian Foundation for Pharmacy, 393

Philanthropy
Asper Foundation, 87
Association des professionnels en gestion philanthropique, 126
Azrieli Foundation, 191
Imagine Canada, 829
Toronto Community Foundation, 1383

Philately
British North America Philatelic Society Ltd., 259

Philosophy
Canadian Philosophical Association, 454

Photography
Fédération Internationale de l'Art Photographique, 1525
PAVED Arts, 1146
Photographic Historical Society of Canada, 1157

Physical Education & Training
Fédération des éducateurs et éducatrices physiques enseignants du Québec, 714
Physical & Health Education Canada, 1158

Physical Fitness
Active Healthy Kids Canada, 7
Canadian Fitness & Lifestyle Research Institute, 390
Physical & Health Education Canada, 1158
Randonneurs du Saguenay, 1204

Physical Therapy
World Confederation for Physical Therapy, 1604

Physicians
Canadian Physicians for Life, 454
Canadian Post-MD Education Registry, 458
Collège des médecins du Québec, 582
Doctors without Borders Canada, 660
Foundation for Advancing Family Medicine of the College of Family Physicians of Canada, 755
Israel Medical Association-Canadian Chapter, 866
Physicians Services Inc. Foundation, 1158
The Royal College of Physicians & Surgeons of Canada, 1241

Physiology
Canadian Physiological Society, 454

Pilots
Association des Aviateurs et Pilotes de Brousse du Québec, 106
Canadian Owners & Pilots Association, 448
The Ninety-Nines Inc., 1578

Pipes
Corporation des maîtres mécaniciens en tuyauterie du Québec, 630

Planetariums
H.R. MacMillan Space Centre Society, 824

Playwriting
Alberta Playwrights' Network, 42
Centre des auteurs dramatiques, 530
Manitoba Association of Playwrights, 931

Plowing
Canadian Plowing Organization, 456
World Ploughing Organization, 1607

Plumbing
Corporation des maîtres mécaniciens en tuyauterie du Québec, 630

Poetry
La Fondation Émile-Nelligan, 746
The Ontario Poetry Society, 1096

Police
Association des policières et policiers provinciaux du Québec, 123
Blue Line Racing Association, 215
Canadian Search Dog Association, 469

Poliomyelitis
Barrie Post Polio Association, 197
Post-Polio Awareness & Support Society of BC, 1168
Post-Polio Network Manitoba Inc., 1168

Polish Canadians
Canadian Polish Congress, 456
Polish Combatants Association, 1164
Toronto Sinfonietta, 1387

Political Organizations
Green Party Political Association of British Columbia, 789

Political Prisoners
Amnesty International - Canadian Section (English Speaking), 68
The Canadian Centre/International P.E.N., 354
PEN International, 1583

Political Science
Canadian Political Science Association, 457
International Political Science Association, 859
The Mackenzie Institute, 924

Pollution
Green Calgary, 788
The Pollution Probe Foundation, 1164

Polo
Canadian Polo Association, 457

Portuguese Canadians
Casa dos Acores do Ontário, 516
Portuguese Interagency Network, 1167

Poultry
Éleveurs de volailles du Québec, 684

Poultry Science
Rare Breeds Canada, 1204

Poverty
Active Support Against Poverty, 7
Blankets for Canada Society Inc., 214
Canada Without Poverty, 281
Canadian Physicians for Aid & Relief, 454
Change for Children Association, 551
Emmanuel International Canada, 686
Evangel Hall Mission, 698
Fredericton Anti-Poverty Association, 758
Frontiers Foundation, 763
HelpAge Canada, 812
Humanity First Canada, 827
Lookout Emergency Aid Society, 919
Mooreland Community Services, 973
Port Colborne Community Association for Research Extension, 1165
Réseau d'action et de communication pour le développement international, 1218
La rue des femmes, 1243
Society of St. Vincent de Paul - Toronto Central Council, 1330
The World Job & Food Bank Inc., 1466
World Vision Canada, 1467
Youth Empowerment & Support Services, 1475

Pregnancy
Birthright International, 212
International Confederation of Midwives, 1543

Preschools
Association d'éducation préscolaire du Québec, 99

Primates
International Primate Protection League, 1556
The Jane Goodall Institute of Canada, 868

Principals & Vice-Principals
Canadian Association of Principals, 328

Printing Industries
Association des enseignants en infographie et en imprimerie du Québec, 112

Registered Charitable Organizations Index / Prisons

Association paritaire pour la santé et la sécurité du travail - Imprimerie et activités connexes, 164

Prisons
Canadian Families & Corrections Network, 383
Church Council on Justice & Corrections, 569
Syndicat des agents de la paix en services correctionnels du Québec, 1362

Private Schools
Centre d'animation de développement et de recherche en éducation, 528
Fédération des établissements d'enseignement privés, 714
Fédération du personnel de l'enseignement privé, 720

Pro-Life Movement
Action Life (Ottawa) Inc., 6
Canadian Physicians for Life, 454
Hamilton Right to Life, 802
Lethbridge & District Pro-Life Association, 907
Life's Vision, 911
Prince Edward Island Right to Life Association, 1176
The Right to Life Association of Toronto & Area, 1232
Saskatchewan Pro Life Association, 1272

Prospecting
Mineralogical Association of Canada, 966

Prosthetics
The War Amputations of Canada, 1440

Prostitution
Maggie's: The Toronto Sex Workers Action Project, 925

Protestants
Operation Mobilization Canada, 1116
The Wesleyan Church of Canada - Central Canada District, 1447

Psoriasis
National Psoriasis Foundation - USA, 1577
Psoriasis Society of Canada, 1191

Psychiatric Patients
Psychosocial Rehabilitation Canada, 1192

Psychiatry
Canadian Academy of Child & Adolescent Psychiatry, 285

Psychology
Adlerian Psychology Association of British Columbia, 8
C.G. Jung Foundation of Ontario, 539
International Society for Affective Disorders, 1557
John E. Mack Institute, 1568

Public Administration
CPJ Corp., 638
Institute of Public Administration of Canada, 847

Public Health
Alberta Public Health Association, 43
Association pour la santé publique du Québec, 166
Canadian Association of Medical Teams Abroad, 321
Canadian Public Health Association, 462
Environmental Health Foundation of Canada, 692
International Institute of Concern for Public Health, 858
Ontario Public Health Association, 1098
Public Health Association of Nova Scotia, 1192

Public Libraries
Les bibliothèques publiques des régions de la Capitale-Nationale et Chaudière-Appalaches, 208

Public Policy
Atlantic Institute for Market Studies, 184
Caledon Institute of Social Policy, 270
Canada West Foundation, 281
Cardus Institute, 511
Couchiching Institute on Public Affairs, 632
CPJ Corp., 638
The Fraser Institute, 757
Institute On Governance, 848

Publishing
Association québécoise des éditeurs de magazines, 172
Canadian Centre for Studies in Publishing, 354
The Champlain Society, 551
Regroupement des éditeurs canadiens-français, 1215
Salon du livre de Toronto et Festival des écrivains, 1252
Société du droit de reproduction des auteurs, compositeurs et éditeurs au Canada (SODRAC 2003) inc., 1318

Puppetry
Ontario Puppetry Association, 1100

Purchasing
Corporation des approvisionneurs du Québec, 629

Québec
Association des employées et employés du gouvernement du Québec, 112
Association France-Québec, 1509
La cinémathèque québécoise, 569
Québec dans le monde, 1196
Société des attractions touristiques du Québec, 1317
Société historique de Québec, 1320

Rabbis
Kosher Check, 894

Race Relations
Arusha Centre Society, 86
B'nai Brith Canada, 192
League for Human Rights of B'nai Brith Canada, 903
Urban Alliance on Race Relations, 1422

Racquetball
British Columbia Racquetball Association, 250
Racquetball Canada, 1202

Radiation
International Commission on Radiological Protection, 855
Radiation Safety Institute of Canada, 1202

Radio Broadcasting
Association des radiodiffuseurs communautaires du Québec, 127
Catholic Youth Studio - KSM Inc., 521
Farm Radio International, 705
Fondation fransaskoise, 746
HMWN (Holy Mother World Networks) Radio Maria, 817
Parlimage CCF, 1143

Radiography
International Society of Radiographers & Radiological Technologists, 1561

Radiology
International Society of Radiographers & Radiological Technologists, 1561
Société canadienne-française de radiologie, 1309

Railroads & Railways
Alberta Pioneer Railway Association, 42
British Columbia Railway Historical Association, 250
Bytown Railway Society, 267
Canadian Northern Society, 441
Canadian Railroad Historical Association, 465
Central British Columbia Railway & Forest Industry Museum Society, 524
Chatham Railroad Museum Society, 555
Edmonton Radial Railway Society, 679
Huntsville & Lake of Bays Railway Society, 828
National Association of Railroad Passengers, 1573
North America Railway Hall of Fame, 1029
Toronto Railway Historical Association, 1386
Vintage Locomotive Society Inc., 1435
West Coast Railway Association, 1445

Rainforests
Conservation International, 1519
Friends of Clayoquot Sound, 760
Rainforest Alliance, 1586

Rape
Canadian Association of Sexual Assault Centres, 333
Ontario Coalition of Rape Crisis Centres, 1072
Oshawa-Durham Rape Crisis Centre, 1128
Ottawa Rape Crisis Centre, 1131
Prince Edward Island Rape & Sexual Assault Centre, 1176
Timmins & Area Women in Crisis Support & Information Centre on Violence Against Women, 1379
Vancouver Rape Relief & Women's Shelter, 1428

Reading
Reading Council for Literacy Advance in Montréal, 1205

Real Estate
Chambre immobilière de la Mauricie Inc., 550
Chambre immobilière des Laurentides, 551
Chambre immobilière du Saguenay-Lac St-Jean Inc., 551
Fédération des Chambres immobilières du Québec, 713
Fédération internationale des professions immobilières, 1526

Real Estate Boards
Chambre immobilière de l'Abitibi-Témiscamingue Inc., 550
Fédération des Chambres immobilières du Québec, 713

Recording Industry
Canadian Academy of Recording Arts & Sciences, 286
Musicaction, 984

Records Management
AIM Global, 1486

Recreation
Abbotsford Social Activity Association, 1
Alberta Recreation & Parks Association, 44
Association québécoise du loisir municipal, 175
British Columbia Recreation & Parks Association, 250
Canadian Owners & Pilots Association, 448
Canadian Parks & Recreation Association, 450
Fédération québécoise de la marche, 727
Fédération québécoise de la montagne et de l'escalade, 727
Fédération québécoise des centres communautaires de loisir inc., 728
Girl Guides of Canada, 773
Kids Up Front, 886
Ontario Trails Council, 1111
Outdoor Recreation Council of British Columbia, 1133
Outward Bound Canada, 1133
ParaSport & Recreation PEI, 1138
Physical & Health Education Canada, 1158
Recreation Nova Scotia, 1207
Right to Play, 1232
Road Scholar, 1586
Saskatchewan Parks & Recreation Association, 1271
Scouts Canada, 1286
Sunrise Therapeutic Riding & Learning Centre, 1354
Trans Canada Trail Foundation, 1394
Vecova Centre for Disability Services & Research, 1430
World Leisure & Recreation Association, 1606
YMCA Canada, 1471
YWCA Canada, 1481

Recreational Vehicles
Bikes Without Borders, 211

Recycling
Center for Health, Environment & Justice, 1516
Clean Nova Scotia Foundation, 573
Conserver Society of Hamilton & District Inc., 623
Environmental Education Ontario, 691
Pitch-In Canada, 1160
Recycling Council of Alberta, 1208
Recycling Council of British Columbia, 1208
Recycling Council of Ontario, 1208
Saskatchewan Waste Reduction Council, 1277
Société québécoise de récupération et de recyclage, 1323
Thames Region Ecological Association, 1373

Red Cross
Canadian Red Cross, 465

Refrigeration
Corporation des entreprises de traitement de l'air et du froid, 630

Refugees
Dejinta Beesha Multi-Service Centre, 652
Folk Arts Council of St Catharines, 742
Newcomer Women's Services Toronto, 1015
Programme Action Réfugiés Montréal, 1187
Saskatoon Open Door Society Inc., 1279
Sojourn House, 1332
World Vision Canada, 1467

Regional Development
Réseau des SADC et CAE, 1219

Regional Planning
Association des Aménagistes Régionaux du Québec, 105

Rehabilitation
Ability Society of Alberta, 2
Association des services de réhabilitation sociale du Québec inc., 128
British Columbia Centre for Ability Association, 235
Calgary Association of Self Help, 271
Canadian Association of Elizabeth Fry Societies, 312
Canadian Council on Rehabilitation & Work, 371
Easter Seals Canada, 669
Easter Seals New Brunswick, 669
The John Howard Society of British Columbia, 874
The John Howard Society of Canada, 874
The John Howard Society of Newfoundland & Labrador, 874
The John Howard Society of Northwest Territories, 874
The John Howard Society of Ontario, 874
The John Howard Society of Prince Edward Island, 875
The John Howard Society of Saskatchewan, 875
National Institute of Disability Management & Research, 994
Ontario Association of Children's Rehabilitation Services, 1062
Operation Springboard, 1116
The Renascent Centres for Alcoholism & Drug Addiction, 1217
Saskatchewan Abilities Council, 1255
Saskatchewan Association of Rehabilitation Centres, 1258
Starbright Children's Development Centre, 1348
Vecova Centre for Disability Services & Research, 1430

Religion
Africa Inland Mission International (Canada), 12
American Academy of Religion, 1488
Association des intervenantes et des intervenants en soins spirituels du Québec, 117
L'Association Zoroastrianne du Québec, 179
Back to the Bible Canada, 193
Block Rosary Group of Ontario, 215
Bukas Loob sa Diyos Covenant Community, 264
Canadian Christian Relief & Development Association, 356
Catholic Association of Religious & Family Life Educators of Ontario, 517

Catholic Youth Studio - KSM Inc., 521
Congregation of Missionaries of the Precious Blood, Atlantic Province, 613
Couples For Christ Foundation for Family & Life, 636
Couples For Christ, 636
Cursillo Movement of the Archdiocese of Toronto, 646
Daughters of Isabella, 651
Focolare Movement - Canada, 741
HMWN (Holy Mother World Networks) Radio Maria, 817
Holy Face Association, 819
International Community for Relief of Suffering & Starvation Canada, 855
Jews for Jesus, 873
Madonna House Apostolate, 925
Marguerite Bourgeoys Family Centre Fertility Care Programme, 949
Metropolitan Community Church of Toronto, 964
Multifaith Action Society, 979
The Neocatechumenal Way, 1003
Regnum Christi Movement, 1214
The Rosary Apostolate, Inc., 1236
Società Unita, 1307
Society of St. Vincent de Paul - Toronto Central Council, 1330
Toronto's Hare Krishna Centre, 1388
VISION TV, 1436
Yasodhara Ashram Society, 1470
Zoroastrian Society of Ontario, 1482

Religious Orders of Brothers
The Brothers of the Good Shepherd, 260
Frères de Notre-Dame de la Miséricorde, 760
Messagères de Notre-Dame de l'Assomption, 962
Sisters Adorers of the Precious Blood, 1300
Sisters of Saint Joseph of Peterborough, 1301
Sisters of the Child Jesus, 1301
Sisters of the Sacred Heart of Ragusa, 1301
Soeurs de Sainte-Marie de Namur, 1331

Religious Society of Friends
Canadian Friends Service Committee, 395
Friends Historical Association, 1527

Renewable Energy Resources
International Solar Energy Society, 1561
Marine Renewables Canada, 950
Renewable Natural Resources Foundation, 1586

Research
Association de la recherche industrielle du Québec, 102
The Canadian Association for HIV Research, 301
Canadian Association of Research Libraries, 331
Canadian Association on Water Quality, 337
Canadian Centre on Disability Studies, 354
Canadian Education & Research Institute for Counselling, 379
Canadian Fitness & Lifestyle Research Institute, 390
Canadian Institute for Jewish Research, 412
Canadian Nautical Research Society, 440
Canadian Transportation Research Forum, 497
Centre d'animation de développement et de recherche en éducation, 528
Centre for Addiction & Mental Health, 531
Earthwatch Institute, 1522
Fondation Les oiseleurs du Québec inc., 747
Foundation for Legal Research, 755
Genesis Research Foundation, 769
George Morris Centre, 770
Grand Manan Whale & Seabird Research Station, 780
Groupe de recherche en écologie sociale, 791
Harrow Early Immigrant Research Society, 804
Heiser Program for Research in Leprosy & Tuberculosis, 1529
Hope Studies Central, 821
International Association for Bear Research & Management, 1535

The Jane Goodall Institute of Canada, 868
The North-South Institute, 1036
Quesnel & District Child Development Centre Association, 1200
Société historique Alphonse-Desjardins, 1319
Tellus Institute, 1597
The Terry Fox Foundation, 1372
Traffic Injury Research Foundation, 1394
Ukrainian Canadian Research & Documentation Centre, 1402
Vecova Centre for Disability Services & Research, 1430

Respiratory Disorders
Canadian Network for Respiratory Care, 441
Canadian Thoracic Society, 494
Ontario Lung Association, 1089
Ontario Respiratory Care Society, 1101
TB Vets, 1367

Respiratory Therapy
Ontario Lung Association, 1089
Ontario Respiratory Care Society, 1101
Ordre professionnel des inhalothérapeutes du Québec, 1124

Restaurants
Association des restaurateurs du Québec, 127
International Hotel & Restaurant Association, 1550

Retail Trade
Association québécoise de la quincaillerie et des matériaux de construction, 170
Conseil québécois du commerce de détail, 620

Retinitis Pigmentosa
The Foundation Fighting Blindness, 755

Retirement
Seniors Association of Greater Edmonton, 1290
The Shepherds' Trust, 1295

Rett Syndrome
Ontario Rett Syndrome Association, 1102

Rifles
Dominion of Canada Rifle Association, 660
Fédération québécoise de tir, 728
Shooting Federation of Canada, 1297

Rivers & Streams
Grand River Conservation Foundation, 780
Partners FOR the Saskatchewan River Basin, 1144
St Mary's River Association, 1250

Roads & Roadbuilding
Association des constructeurs de routes et grands travaux du Québec, 110

Rodeos
Canadian Girls Rodeo Association, 398

Romanian Canadians & Romania
Fondation roumaine de Montréal, 748

Roofing Trade
Association des maîtres couvreurs du Québec, 118

Roses
Canadian Rose Society, 468

Royal Canadian Mounted Police
Royal Canadian Mounted Police Veterans' Association, 1240

Rugby
Saskatchewan Rugby Union, 1274

Rural Living
British Columbia Women's Institutes, 258
Cole Harbour Rural Heritage Society, 581
Federated Women's Institutes of Canada, 706
Federated Women's Institutes of Ontario, 706
Fédération des agricultrices du Québec, 711
Manitoba Women's Institutes, 947
National Farmers Foundation, 993
New Brunswick Women's Institute, 1013

Safety
Block Parent Program of Canada, 214
Block Watch Society of British Columbia, 215
Canada Safety Council, 280

Canadian Centre for Occupational Health & Safety, 353
Canadian Ski Patrol, 471
Enform, 688
Fire Prevention Canada, 738
Infant & Toddler Safety Association, 836
International Federation of Airworthiness, 1547
Ontario Safety League, 1103
Ottawa Safety Council, 1131
Parachute, 1138
Radiation Safety Institute of Canada, 1202
Safety Services Manitoba, 1245
Safety Services New Brunswick, 1245
Saskatchewan Prevention Institute, 1272

Sailing
Association maritime du Québec, 137
Canadian Power & Sail Squadrons (Canadian Headquarters), 459
Disabled Sailing Association of B.C., 658
Sail Canada, 1245
S.A.L.T.S. Sail & Life Training Society, 1252

Salmon
Atlantic Salmon Federation, 186
Nova Scotia Salmon Association, 1048
Salmon Preservation Association for the Waters of Newfoundland, 1252

Salvation Army
The Salvation Army in Canada, 1252

Scandinavian Canadians
Canadian-Scandinavian Foundation, 507

Schizophrenia
British Columbia Schizophrenia Society, 252
International Schizophrenia Foundation, 860
Manitoba Schizophrenia Society, Inc., 943
Schizophrenia Society of Alberta, 1283
Schizophrenia Society of Canada, 1283
Schizophrenia Society of New Brunswick, 1283
Schizophrenia Society of Newfoundland & Labrador, 1284
Schizophrenia Society of Nova Scotia, 1284
Schizophrenia Society of Ontario, 1284
Schizophrenia Society of Prince Edward Island, 1284
Schizophrenia Society of Saskatchewan, 1284
Société québécoise de la schizophrénie, 1323

Scholarships & Bursaries
Black Academic Scholarship Fund, 212
Canadian Scholarship Trust Foundation, 468
Horatio Alger Association of Canada, 821
The Latvian Relief Society of Canada, 900

School Libraries
Canadian Association of Professional Academic Librarians, 328

Schools
Association of Administrators of English Schools of Québec, 139
BC School Sports, 202
Canadian Association of Schools of Nursing, 332
Fédération québécoise des directions d'établissements d'enseignement, 728
Ontario Federation of School Athletic Associations, 1079
Société des écoles du monde du BI du Québec et de la francophonie, 1317

Science
Boîte à science - Conseil du loisir scientifique du Québec, 217
The Canadian Association for HIV Research, 301
Canadian Science & Technology Historical Association, 468
The Canadian Society for the Weizmann Institute of Science, 478
Centre de caractérisation microscopique des matériaux, 528
Centre for Inquiry Canada, 533
Earthwatch Institute, 1522
International Union of Biological Sciences, 1564
Réseau Technoscience, 1226
Science for Peace, 1285

Société Québécoise de Psilogie inc, 1323
Society for Canadian Women in Science & Technology, 1325
Visions of Science Network for Learning, 1436
Youth Science Canada, 1476

Scleroderma
Scleroderma Association of British Columbia, 1285
Scleroderma Canada, 1285
The Scleroderma Society of Ontario, 1285

Scottish Canadians
Clans & Scottish Societies of Canada, 572
Québec Thistle Council Inc., 1199
St. Andrew's Society of Toronto, 1248

Scottish Clans
Clan Lamont Society of Canada, 571
Clan Mackenzie Society of Canada, 571
Clans & Scottish Societies of Canada, 572

Scottish Studies
Scottish Studies Foundation Inc., 1286

Scouts
Association des Scouts du Canada, 127
Fédération des scouts de l'Atlantique, 718
Scouts Canada, 1286

Sculpture
Sculptors Society of Canada, 1287

Seafood
International Institute of Fisheries Economics & Trade, 1551

Search & Rescue
Canadian Lifeboat Institution, 427
Canadian Search Dog Association, 469
Northwestern Ontario Air Search & Rescue Association, 1039
Search & Rescue Volunteer Association of Canada, 1288

Securities
Chambre de la sécurité financière, 550

Senior Citizens
Abbeyfield Houses Society of Canada, 1
Abbotsford Social Activity Association, 1
AdvantAge Ontario, 10
Advocacy Centre for the Elderly, 10
Alberta Council on Aging, 31
Association pour aînés résidant à Laval, 165
Calgary Meals on Wheels, 273
Calgary Seniors' Resource Society, 274
Carefirst Seniors & Community Services Association, 511
LA Centre for Active Living, 531
Community Care for South Hastings, 596
Community Care Peterborough, 596
Conseil régional des personnes âgées italo-canadiennes de Montréal, 621
The Council on Aging of Ottawa, 635
Council on Aging, Windsor - Essex County, 636
Crossreach Adult Day Centre, 644
Drummond Foundation, 663
Elder Abuse Ontario, 681
Fédération des aînés et des retraités francophones de l'Ontario, 711
Fédération des aînés franco-manitobains inc., 711
Fédération des aînés fransaskois, 711
HelpAge Canada, 812
HelpAge International, 1529
Kerby Centre for the 55 Plus, 884
Korean Senior Citizens Society of Toronto, 893
Mid-Toronto Community Services, 965
Older Adult Centres' Association of Ontario, 1056
The Older Women's Network, 1056
Ontario Society of Senior Citizens' Organizations, 1108
Réseau FADOQ, 1223
Road Scholar, 1586
Saskatoon Senior Citizens Action Now Inc., 1280
Senior Link, 1290
Seniors in Need, 1290
SPRINT Senior Care, 1346

Registered Charitable Organizations Index / Seniors Centres

United Generations Ontario, 1411

Seniors Centres
Bernard Betel Centre for Creative Living, 205
Carrefour 50+ du Québec, 515
Centre de services Guigues, 530
Edmonton Aboriginal Senior Centre, 675
The Olde Forge Community Resource Centre, 1056

Separate Schools
Québec English School Boards Association, 1197

Sephardic Jews
Communauté sépharade unifiée du Québec, 594

Serbian Canadians
Serbian Orthodox Church - Orthodox Diocese of Canada, 1290

Service Organizations
Association des Grands Frères et Grandes Soeurs du Québec, 115
Big Brothers Big Sisters of Alberta, 209
Big Brothers Big Sisters of British Columbia, 209
Big Brothers Big Sisters of Canada, 209
Big Brothers Big Sisters of Eastern Newfoundland, 209
Big Brothers Big Sisters of Manitoba, 209
Big Brothers Big Sisters of New Brunswick, 209
Big Brothers Big Sisters of Nova Scotia, 210
Big Brothers Big Sisters of Ontario, 210
Big Brothers Big Sisters of Saskatchewan, 210
Canadian Children's Optimist Foundation, 356
Canadian Progress Club, 460
IODE Canada, 863
Junior League of Calgary, 878
Junior League of Edmonton, 878
Junior League of Halifax, 878
Junior League of Hamilton-Burlington, Inc., 878
Junior League of Toronto, 878
Kin Canada Foundation, 887
Lions Foundation of Canada, 913
The Municipal Chapter of Toronto IODE, 980
Rotary Club of Stratford Charitable Foundation, 1236
The Rotary Club of Toronto, 1236
Soroptimist Foundation of Canada, 1333
Soroptimist International of the Americas, 1595
Variety - The Children's Charity of BC, 1429
Variety - The Children's Charity of Manitoba, Tent 58 Inc., 1430
Variety Club of Southern Alberta, 1430
Western Regional Advocacy Group Society, 1450
World ORT Union, 1607

Sewing
Embroiderers' Association of Canada, Inc., 685

Sex Education
Action Canada for Sexual Health & Rights, 6
Health Initiatives for Youth Hamilton, 806
P.E.E.R.S. Alliance, 1148
Planned Parenthood Ottawa, 1161
Sex Information & Education Council of Canada, 1292
Sexual Health Centre Lunenburg County, 1293
Sexual Health Centre Saskatoon, 1293

Sexual Abuse
Amelia Rising Sexual Assault Centre of Nipissing, 66
British Columbia Society for Male Survivors of Sexual Abuse, 254
Centre d'aide et de lutte contre les agressions à caractère sexuel de Châteauguay, 527
Centre d'aide et de lutte contre les agressions à caractère sexuel de Granby, 527
EMPHASE Mauricie-Centre-du-Québec, 686
Fredericton Sexual Assault Crisis Centre, 759
Groupe d'aide et d'information sur le harcèlement sexuel au travail de la province de Québec, 791
Mouvement contre le viol et l'inceste, 976
Niagara Region Sexual Assault Centre, 1025
Ontario Coalition of Rape Crisis Centres, 1072
Oshawa-Durham Rape Crisis Centre, 1128
Ottawa Rape Crisis Centre, 1131
Parents-Unis Lanaudière, 1140
Sexual Assault Centre Kingston Inc., 1292
Sexual Assault Centre London, 1292
Sexual Assault Centre of Edmonton, 1292
Sexual Assault Crisis Centre of Essex County Inc., 1293
Sexual Assault Support Centre Ottawa, 1293
Timmins & Area Women in Crisis Support & Information Centre on Violence Against Women, 1379
Vancouver Rape Relief & Women's Shelter, 1428
Women's Support Network of York Region, 1463

Shakespeare, William
Bard on the Beach Theatre Society, 196

Ships
Armateurs du Saint-Laurent, 82

Shooting Sports
Alberta Metallic Silhouette Association, 40
Biathlon Canada, 207
Dominion of Canada Rifle Association, 660
Fédération québécoise de tir, 728
Shooting Federation of Canada, 1297

Sickle Cell Anemia
Sickle Cell Association of Ontario, 1297

Signs
Alberta Sign Association, 46

Single Parent Families
Entre Nous Femmes Housing Society, 690
Fédération des associations de familles monoparentales et recomposées du Québec, 711
Massey Centre for Women, 953
One Parent Families Association of Canada, 1058
Single Parent Association of Newfoundland, 1300
Single Persons Association of Montréal, 1300

Skating
Skate Canada, 1301

Skiing
Alberta Freestyle Ski Association, 36
Association des stations de ski du Québec, 128
BC Adaptive Snowsports, 200
Biathlon Canada, 207
Canadian Association for Disabled Skiing, 299
Canadian Association for Disabled Skiing - Alberta, 299
Canadian Association for Disabled Skiing - National Capital Division, 299
Canadian Association for Disabled Skiing - New Brunswick, 299
Canadian Ski Marathon, 471
Canadian Ski Patrol, 471
Cross Country Canada, 643
Ontario Track 3 Ski Association for the Disabled, 1110
Ski Hawks Ottawa, 1302

Skills Education
Community Microskills Development Centre, 606
Niagara West Employment & Learning Resource Centres, 1026
Ontario Network of Employment Skills Training Projects, 1093
Skills for Change, 1302

Skin, Diseases & Disorders
Association Québécoise du Lymphoedème, 176
DEBRA Canada, 652
Eczema Society of Canada, 674
Heiser Program for Research in Leprosy & Tuberculosis, 1529
The Scleroderma Society of Ontario, 1285
Secours aux lépreux (Canada) inc., 1288

Sleep Disorders
Canadian Sleep Society, 472
Fondation Sommeil: Association de personnes atteintes de déficiences reliées au sommeil, 748

Small Business
Fondation de l'entrepreneurship, 743

Smoking
Action on Smoking & Health, 6
Canadian Council for Tobacco Control, 367
Conseil québécois sur le tabac et la santé, 620

Snowboarding
Canadian Association for Disabled Skiing, 299

Snowmobiles
Fédération des clubs de motoneigistes du Québec, 713

Soaring
Association de vol à voile Champlain, 104

Social Assistance (International)
CAUSE Canada, 521
Fondation Jules et Paul-Émile Léger, 746
Oxfam Canada, 1134
Save the Children Canada, 1281
Sleeping Children Around the World, 1303
World University Service of Canada, 1467

Social Development
Bikes Without Borders, 211
Canadian Council on Social Development, 371
Réseau d'action et de communication pour le développement international, 1218

Social Housing
Active Support Against Poverty, 7
Christie-Ossington Neighbourhood Centre, 568
Nellie's Shelter, 1003
Our Harbour, 1132

Social Planning Councils
Community Development Council Durham, 596
Community Development Council of Quinte, 596
Community Development Halton, 596
Edmonton Social Planning Council, 679
Lakehead Social Planning Council, 896
Social Planning & Research Council of BC, 1306
Social Planning Council for the North Okanagan, 1306
Social Planning Council of Cambridge & North Dumfries, 1306
Social Planning Council of Kitchener-Waterloo, 1306
Social Planning Council of Ottawa, 1306
Social Planning Council of Peel, 1306
United Way of Guelph, Wellington & Dufferin, 1414

Social Policy
Caledon Institute of Social Policy, 270
Canada West Foundation, 281
Catherine Donnelly Foundation, 517
Community Sector Council, Newfoundland & Labrador, 607
The Fraser Institute, 757
Maytree Foundation, 954
Social Justice Committee, 1305
Social Planning Council of Kitchener-Waterloo, 1306

Social Services
Catholic Family Services of Peel Dufferin,
Family & Children's Services of the District of Rainy River,
United Way of Burlington & Greater Hamilton,
Abbotsford Community Services, 1
Access Counselling & Family Services, 5
Acclaim Health, 5
Les Amis de la déficience intellectuelle Rive-Nord, 67
Association des services de réhabilitation sociale du Québec inc., 128
Association of Neighbourhood Houses BC, 153
Battlefords United Way Inc., 200
Brant United Way, 226
BullyingCanada Inc., 264
Calgary Urban Project Society, 275
Canadian Training Institute, 496
Carefirst Seniors & Community Services Association, 511
Carrefour d'entraide de Drummond, 515
Catholic Children's Aid Society of Hamilton, 518
Catholic Children's Aid Society of Toronto, 518
Catholic Family Services of Peel Dufferin, 519
Catholic Family Services of Saskatoon, 519
Centraide Abitibi Témiscamingue et Nord-du-Québec, 522
Centraide Bas St-Laurent, 522
Centraide Centre du Québec, 522
Centraide Estrie, 522
Centraide Haute-Côte-Nord/Manicouagan, 522
Centraide Lanaudière, 522
Centraide Laurentides, 522
Centraide Mauricie, 522
Centraide Outaouais, 523
Centraide Québec, 523
Centraide Saguenay-Lac St-Jean, 523
Centraide sud-ouest du Québec, 523
Les Centres jeunesse de l'Outaouais, 537
Chez Doris, 557
Child & Family Services of Western Manitoba, 558
Children's Aid Society of Ottawa, 561
Children's Aid Society of the District of Nipissing & Parry Sound, 561
Children's Aid Society of the Districts of Sudbury & Manitoulin, 561
Children's Health Foundation of Vancouver Island, 561
Chinese Family Services of Ontario, 565
Chipman Community Care Inc., 565
Community Action Resource Centre, 595
Community Care for South Hastings, 596
Community Counselling Centre of Nipissing, 596
Community Living Walkerton & District, 606
Conseil national Société de Saint-Vincent de Paul, 619
Counselling Services of Belleville & District, 636
Covenant House Toronto, 637
Cowichan United Way, 637
East Wellington Community Services, 669
Entraide familiale de l'Outaouais inc., 690
Evangel Hall Mission, 698
Family & Children's Services Niagara, 701
Family & Children's Services of Frontenac, Lennox & Addington, 701
Family & Children's Services of Guelph & Wellington County, 702
Family & Children's Services of Renfrew County, 702
Family & Children's Services of the District of Rainy River, 702
Family Counselling & Support Services for Guelph-Wellington, 702
Family Counselling Centre of Cambridge & North Dumfries, 703
Family Day Care Services (Toronto), 703
Family Mediation Canada, 703
Family Service Kent, 704
Family Service Ontario, 704
Family Service Toronto, 704
Family Services of Greater Vancouver, 704
Family Services Perth-Huron, 705
Family Services Windsor-Essex Counselling & Advocacy Centre, 705
Family Services York Region (Georgina), 705
Fraserside Community Services Society, 758
Frontiers Foundation, 763
Good Shepherd Refuge Social Ministries, 777
Habitat for Humanity Canada, 796
Halton Children's Aid Society, 800
Halton Family Services, 800
HelpAge Canada, 812
Highland Shores Children's Aid, 814
Independent Living Canada, 833
India Rainbow Community Services of Peel, 834
Inn From the Cold Society, 838
Inner City Home of Sudbury, 839
International Social Service Canada, 860

Jessie's - The June Callwood Centre for Young Women, 870
Jewish Child & Family Services, 871
Jewish Family Services - Calgary, 871
Jewish Family Services of Ottawa-Carleton, 872
Kenora Fellowship Centre, 883
Kids Now, 886
Kiwassa Neighbourhood Services Association, 892
Lakeland United Way, 896
La Maison Benoit Labre, 926
Many Rivers Counselling & Support Services, 948
Mid-Toronto Community Services, 965
Mission Bon Accueil, 969
Mission Old Brewery, 969
New Circles Community Services, 1014
North Renfrew Family Services Inc., 1032
Northwood Neighbourhood Services, 1040
Ontario Association of Credit Counselling Services, 1063
Ontario Association of Residences Treating Youth, 1065
Ontario Society of Senior Citizens' Organizations, 1108
Operation Come Home, 1115
Peel Family Services, 1147
PLEA Community Services Society of BC, 1162
Portage Plains United Way, 1167
Powell River & District United Way, 1168
Renfrew County United Way, 1217
Rexdale Women's Centre, 1229
St. Christopher House, 1248
The Scott Mission, 1286
Second Harvest, 1288
Service à la famille chinoise du Grand Montréal, 1291
Service familial de Sudbury, 1291
ShareLife, 1294
Smithers Community Services Association, 1304
South Peace Community Resources Society, 1335
Sudbury Community Service Centre Inc., 1353
Support Enhance Access Service Centre, 1356
Timmins Family Counselling Centre, Inc., 1380
Ukrainian Canadian Social Services (Toronto) Inc, 1403
United Way Central & Northern Vancouver Island, 1413
United Way Elgin-St. Thomas, 1413
United Way for the City of Kawartha Lakes, 1413
United Way of Durham Region,
United Way of Burlington & Greater Hamilton, 1413
United Way of Cambridge & North Dumfries, 1413
United Way of Canada - Centraide Canada, 1413
United Way of Central Alberta, 1413
United Way of Chatham-Kent County, 1413
United Way of Cochrane-Timiskaming, 1413
United Way of East Kootenay, 1414
United Way of Fort McMurray, 1414
United Way of Greater Moncton & Southeastern New Brunswick, 1414
United Way of Greater Saint John Inc., 1414
United Way of Greater Simcoe County, 1414
United Way of Guelph, Wellington & Dufferin, 1414
United Way of Haldimand-Norfolk, 1414
United Way of Halifax Region, 1414
United Way of Halton Hills, 1414
United Way of Kingston, Frontenac, Lennox & Addington, 1414
United Way of Kitchener-Waterloo & Area, 1415
United Way of Leeds & Grenville, 1415
United Way of Lethbridge & South Western Alberta, 1415
United Way of London & Middlesex, 1415
United Way of Milton, 1415
United Way of North Okanagan Columbia Shuswap, 1415
United Way of Northern BC, 1415

United Way of Oakville, 1415
United Way of Peel Region, 1416
United Way of Perth-Huron, 1416
United Way of Peterborough & District, 1416
United Way of Pictou County, 1416
United Way of Prince Edward Island, 1416
United Way of Quinte, 1416
United Way of Regina, 1416
United Way of St Catharines & District, 1416
United Way of Sarnia-Lambton, 1416
United Way of Stormont, Dundas & Glengarry, 1417
United Way of the Alberta Capital Region, 1417
United Way of the Central Okanagan & South Okanagan/Similkameen, 1417
United Way of the Fraser Valley, 1417
United Way of Trail & District, 1417
United Way of Windsor-Essex County, 1417
United Way South Niagara, 1417
United Way/Centraide (Central NB) Inc., 1418
United Way/Centraide Ottawa, 1418
United Way/Centraide Sudbury & District, 1418
Victoria Youth Empowerment Society, 1434
Wellspring Cancer Support Foundation, 1444
Weyburn & District United Way, 1451
Woodstock & District Developmental Services, 1464
YMCA Canada, 1471
York Region Children's Aid Society, 1473
Yorkton & District United Way Inc., 1474
Youth Assisting Youth, 1475
Youth in Care Canada, 1475
YOUTHLINK, 1476
YWCA Canada, 1481

Social Work
Canadian Association for Social Work Education, 304
Canadian Social Work Foundation, 472

Socialism
Society for Socialist Studies, 1326

Sociology
Association internationale des sociologues de langue française, 1510

Softball
Softball Québec, 1332

Soil Science
Canadian Society of Soil Science, 488
International Union of Soil Sciences, 1565
Saskatchewan Soil Conservation Association, 1275
Soil Conservation Council of Canada, 1332

Solar Energy
International Solar Energy Society, 1561

Somalis & Somalia
Dejinta Beesha Multi-Service Centre, 652

Southeast Asia
Alliance for South Asian AIDS Prevention, 57

Space Sciences
H.R. MacMillan Space Centre Society, 824

Special Olympics
Special Olympics Alberta, 1339
Special Olympics BC, 1339
Special Olympics Manitoba, 1339
Special Olympics New Brunswick, 1339
Special Olympics Newfoundland & Labrador, 1340
Special Olympics Nova Scotia, 1340
Special Olympics Ontario, 1340
Special Olympics Prince Edward Island, 1340
Special Olympics Yukon, 1340

Speech Disorders
Association des jeunes bègues de Québec, 117
Canadian Stuttering Association, 491
The Hanen Centre, 803
International Society for Augmentative & Alternative Communication, 860
Speech & Hearing Association of Nova Scotia, 1340
The Speech & Stuttering Institute, 1340

Speech Therapy
Institute for Stuttering Treatment & Research & the Communication Improvement Program, 844

Speech-Language Pathologists & Audiologists
Alberta College of Speech-Language Pathologists & Audiologists, 30
British Columbia Association of Speech-Language Pathologists & Audiologists, 233
Speech-Language & Audiology Canada, 1341

Speleology
Société québécoise de spéléologie, 1324

Spina Bifida
L'Association de spina-bifida et d'hydrocéphalie du Québec, 104
Spina Bifida & Hydrocephalus Association of British Columbia, 1341
Spina Bifida & Hydrocephalus Association of Canada, 1341
Spina Bifida & Hydrocephalus Association of Northern Alberta, 1342
Spina Bifida & Hydrocephalus Association of Nova Scotia, 1342
Spina Bifida & Hydrocephalus Association of Ontario, 1342
Spina Bifida & Hydrocephalus Association of Prince Edward Island, 1342
Spina Bifida & Hydrocephalus Association of Southern Alberta, 1342
Spina Bifida Association of Manitoba, 1342

Spinal Cord
Rick Hansen Foundation, 1231
Spinal Cord Injury Canada, 1343

Sport Medicine
Canadian Academy of Sport Medicine, 287
Corporation des thérapeutes du sport du Québec, 631

Sports
Alberta Colleges Athletic Conference, 30
Alberta Sports Hall of Fame & Museum, 48
B2ten, 192
BC School Sports, 202
British Columbia Sports Hall of Fame & Museum, 255
Canadian Paralympic Committee, 449
Fédération québécoise des sports cyclistes, 730
Judo Canada, 876
Manitoba High Schools Athletic Association, 938
Manitoba Sports Hall of Fame & Museum, 945
New Brunswick Sports Hall of Fame, 1013
Northwestern Ontario Sports Hall of Fame & Museum, 1039
Ontario Colleges Athletic Association, 1073
Ontario Federation of School Athletic Associations, 1079
Prince Edward Island Sports Hall of Fame & Museum Inc., 1177
Réseau du sport étudiant du Québec, 1222
Réseau du sport étudiant du Québec Montréal, 1223
Saskatchewan Sports Hall of Fame & Museum, 1275
School Sports Newfoundland & Labrador, 1284
Société des Jeux de l'Acadie inc., 1318
Sport New Brunswick, 1344
Sports-Québec, 1346
True Sport Foundation, 1399
Ultimate Canada, 1404

Sports Cars
Sports Car Club of British Columbia, 1345

Sports for the Disabled
Achilles Canada, 5
Alberta Amputee Sports & Recreation Association, 22
Alberta Cerebral Palsy Sport Association, 27
Alberta Deaf Sports Association, 32
Alberta Northern Lights Wheelchair Basketball Society, 41
BC Adaptive Snowsports, 200

British Columbia Blind Sports & Recreation Association, 234
British Columbia Deaf Sports Federation, 238
British Columbia Wheelchair Sports Association, 258
Calgary Sledge Hockey Association, 274
Canadian Amputee Sports Association, 292
Canadian Association for Disabled Skiing, 299
Canadian Association for Disabled Skiing - Alberta, 299
Canadian Association for Disabled Skiing - National Capital Division, 299
Canadian Association for Disabled Skiing - New Brunswick, 299
Canadian Blind Sports Association Inc., 344
Canadian Cerebral Palsy Sports Association, 354
Canadian Deaf Ice Hockey Federation, 376
Canadian Electric Wheelchair Hockey Association, 380
Canadian Paralympic Committee, 449
Canadian Wheelchair Basketball Association, 503
Canadian Wheelchair Sports Association, 503
Disabled Sailing Association of B.C., 658
Ontario Blind Sports Association, 1068
Paralympic Sports Association (Alberta), 1138
ParaSport & Recreation PEI, 1138
ParaSport Ontario, 1139
Parasports Québec, 1139
Saskatchewan Deaf Sports Association, 1263
Ski Hawks Ottawa, 1302
Special Olympics BC, 1339
Special Olympics Yukon, 1340
SportAbility BC, 1345

Sports, Amateur
Canadian Athletes Now Fund, 337
Diving Plongeon Canada, 659
Hockey Canada Foundation, 817
Netball Alberta, 1003
Saint John Jeux Canada Games Foundation Inc., 1247

Squash
Squash Alberta, 1347
Squash Canada, 1347

Staff Training & Development
Open Door Group, 1114

Standards
Association pour la protection des intérêts des consommateurs de la Côte-Nord, 166

Statistics
International Statistical Institute, 1562

Streetcars
Ontario Electric Railway Historical Association, 1077

Stroke
Fondation des maladies du coeur du Québec, 745
Heart & Stroke Foundation of Alberta, NWT & Nunavut, 808
Heart & Stroke Foundation of British Columbia & Yukon, 808
Heart & Stroke Foundation of Canada, 808
Heart & Stroke Foundation of Manitoba, 808
Heart & Stroke Foundation of Nova Scotia, 809
Heart & Stroke Foundation of Ontario, 809
Heart & Stroke Foundation of Prince Edward Island Inc., 809
Heart & Stroke Foundation of Saskatchewan, 809
Stroke Recovery Association of BC, 1352

Student Exchanges
AFS Interculture Canada, 13
Experiences Canada, 699
Foundation for Educational Exchange Between Canada & the United States of America, 755

Students
Canadian Catholic Campus Ministry, 351
Canadian Friends of Yeshiva University, 395
Canadian Student Leadership Association, 491
Greater Montreal Athletic Association, 784

Réseau du sport étudiant du Québec Abitibi-Témiscamingue, 1222
Réseau du sport étudiant du Québec Laurentides-Lanaudière, 1223
Réseau du sport étudiant du Québec Saguenay-Lac St-Jean, 1223
Student Christian Movement of Canada, 1352

Stuttering
Association des jeunes bègues de Québec, 117
Canadian Stuttering Association, 491
Institute for Stuttering Treatment & Research & the Communication Improvement Program, 844

Suicide Prevention
Canadian Association for Suicide Prevention, 304
Centre for Suicide Prevention, 534
Suicide Action Montréal, 1353
Vancouver Island Crisis Society, 1426
Your Life Counts, 1475

Support Groups
Alcoholics Anonymous (GTA Intergroup), 52
Association of Parent Support Groups in Ontario Inc., 155
Association québécoise des troubles d'apprentissage - section Outaouais, 175
BC Hands & Voices, 201
Burn Survivors Association, 265
Chronic Pain Association of Canada, 568
From Grief To Action, 763
Mood Disorders Association of Ontario, 973
PeerNetBC, 1148
PFLAG Canada Inc., 1155
Projet d'intervention auprès des mineurs-res prostitués-ées, 1188
Self-Help Connection Clearinghouse Association, 1289
Self-Help Resource Centre, 1289
Suicide Action Montréal, 1353
Support Organization for Trisomy 18, 13 & Related Disorders, 1356
Vasculitis Foundation Canada, 1430

Surgeons
Canadian Association of General Surgeons, 316
The Royal College of Physicians & Surgeons of Canada, 1241

Surgery
Association d'oto-rhino-laryngologie et de chirurgie cervico-faciale du Québec, 99
Canadian Society of Otolaryngology - Head & Neck Surgery, 485
Ostomy Canada Society, 1129

Sustainable Cities
EcoSource Mississauga, 673
FutureWatch Environment & Development Education Partners, 765
International Centre for Sustainable Cities, 855

Sustainable Development
Alliance for Sustainability, 1487
American Farmland Trust, 1492
Community Energy Association, 597
David Suzuki Foundation, 651
Evergreen, 699
Friends of the Earth Canada, 762
Groupe de recherche en écologie sociale, 791
International Institute of Fisheries Economics & Trade, 1551
Marine Renewables Canada, 950
The Natural Step Canada, 999
The Pembina Institute, 1149
Physicians for Global Survival (Canada), 1158
Resource Efficient Agricultural Production, 1227
Saskatchewan Soil Conservation Association, 1275
UNEP - World Conservation Monitoring Centre, 1598
USC Canada, 1423
Wallace Center, Winrock International, 1601

Swimming
Swim Nova Scotia, 1358
Swimming Prince Edward Island, 1359

Synchro Canada, 1360
Synchro-Québec, 1361

Synagogues
Shaare Zion Congregation, 1293

Taiwanese Canadians & Taiwan
Taiwanese Canadian Cultural Society, 1366

Taxation
Canadian Tax Foundation, 492

Teaching
Alliance canadienne des responsables et enseignants en français (langue maternelle), 55
Alliance Française de Calgary, 57
Association canadienne des professeurs d'immersion, 94
Association des enseignantes et des enseignants franco-ontariens, 112
Association des enseignants en infographie et en imprimerie du Québec, 112
Association des ingénieurs-professeurs des sciences appliquées, 116
Association of British Columbia Teachers of English as an Additional Language, 140
Association québécoise de pédagogie collégiale, 170
Association québécoise des professeurs de français, 174
Black Educators Association of Nova Scotia, 213
Fédération des professionnelles et professionnels de l'éducation du Québec, 718
Fédération des Syndicats de l'Enseignement, 719

Technicians & Technologists
Association des technologues en agroalimentaire, 129
International Society of Radiographers & Radiological Technologists, 1561

Technology
Ability Society of Alberta, 2
BC Association for Individualized Technology and Supports, 201
Canadian Science & Technology Historical Association, 468
College of Medical Laboratory Technologists of Alberta, 586
Shad Valley International, 1293
Society for Canadian Women in Science & Technology, 1325
Visions of Science Network for Learning, 1436

Telecommunications
Canadian Overseas Telecommunications Union, 448
Canadian Wireless Telecommunications Association, 504

Telephones
Telephone Historical Centre, 1369

Television Broadcasting
Academy of Canadian Cinema & Television, 3
The Actors' Fund of Canada, 7
The Atlantic Film Festival Association, 184
Banff World Television Festival Foundation, 196
Independent Production Fund, 833
National Screen Institute - Canada, 996
Parlimage CCF, 1143
VISION TV, 1436
Women in Film & Television - Toronto, 1461

Tennis
Alberta Tennis Association, 49
Tennis Québec, 1371

Testing
Association des consultants et laboratoires experts, 110
Canadian Toy Testing Council, 496

Textiles
Canadian Textile Association, 494
Groupe CTT Group, 791
William Morris Society of Canada, 1455

Thalidomide
Thalidomide Victims Association of Canada, 1373

The Arts
Camrose Arts Society, 277
Canadian Arts Presenting Association, 296
Canadian Conference of the Arts, 363
Children's Arts Umbrella Association, 561
Emil Skarin Fund, 686
Hamber Foundation, 800
Manitoba Holiday Festival of the Arts Inc., 938
Ontario Society of Artists, 1107
Royal Canadian Academy of Arts, 1239
The Royal Society for the Encouragement of Arts, Manufactures & Commerce, 1587
Segal Centre for the Performing Arts at the Saidye, 1289
Station Arts Centre Cooperative, 1348
Tiger Hills Arts Association Inc., 1379
University of Saskatchewan Arts Council, 1420
Vancouver International Children's Festival, 1426
Volunteer Circle of the National Gallery of Canada, 1438
Western Front Society, 1449

The Middle East
Canadian Friends of Peace Now (Shalom Achshav), 395
Middle East Studies Association of North America, 1571

Theatre
The Actors' Fund of Canada, 7
Association des professionnels des arts de la scène du Québec, 125
Bard on the Beach Theatre Society, 196
Black Theatre Workshop, 213
British Columbia Drama Association, 239
The Canadian Stage Company, 490
Carousel Players, 514
Catalyst Theatre Society of Alberta, 517
Centre des auteurs dramatiques, 530
Le Cercle Molière, 537
Compagnie vox théâtre, 608
Evergreen Theatre Society, 699
Fédération québécoise du théâtre amateur, 731
First Pacific Theatre Society, 739
Globe Theatre Society, 775
Green Kids Inc., 788
The Guild Society, 794
Harbourfront Centre, 803
Intrepid Theatre Co. Society, 862
Kaleidoscope Theatre Productions Society, 880
Mulgrave Road Theatre Foundation, 978
Native Earth Performing Arts Inc., 998
Neptune Theatre Foundation, 1003
New West Theatre Society, 1014
Newfoundland & Labrador Drama Society, 1018
Ontario Ballet Theatre, 1067
Opéra Atelier, 1114
Playwrights' Workshop Montréal, 1162
Prairie Theatre Exchange, 1170
Pumphouse Theatres Society, 1194
Royal Manitoba Theatre Centre, 1242
Rumble Productions Society, 1244
Segal Centre for the Performing Arts at the Saidye, 1289
Shaw Festival, 1294
Sun Ergos, A Company of Theatre & Dance, 1354
Tarragon Theatre, 1367
Théâtre français de Toronto, 1374
Theatre Network (1975) Society, 1374
Theatre New Brunswick, 1374
Theatre Ontario, 1374
Théâtre populaire d'Acadie, 1375
Theatre Terrific Society, 1375
Vancouver Moving Theatre, 1427
Western Canada Theatre Company Society, 1448
Young People's Theatre, 1474

Theatres
Professional Association of Canadian Theatres, 1181

Théâtres associés inc., 1375

Theology
Student Christian Movement of Canada, 1352

Therapeutic Riding
Antigonish Therapeutic Riding Association, 72
British Columbia Therapeutic Riding Association, 257
Canadian Therapeutic Riding Association, 494
Central Ontario Developmental Riding Program, 525
Community Association for Riding for the Disabled, 596
Comox Valley Therapeutic Riding Society, 608
Cowichan Therapeutic Riding Association, 637
Equestrian Association for the Disabled, 694
Halifax Area Leisure & Therapeutic Riding Association, 798
Lanark County Therapeutic Riding Program, 897
Lethbridge Therapeutic Riding Association, 908
Little Bits Therapeutic Riding Association, 915
Manitoba Riding for the Disabled Association Inc., 943
Mount View Special Riding Association, 976
Ontario Therapeutic Riding Association, 1110
Pacific Riding for Developing Abilities, 1136
PARD Therapeutic Riding, 1139
Peace Area Riding for the Disabled, 1146
Quinte Therapeutic Riding Association, 1202
Regina Therapeutic Riding Association, 1212
SARI Therapeutic Riding, 1254
Sunrise Therapeutic Riding & Learning Centre, 1354
Victoria Therapeutic Riding Association, 1434
Windsor-Essex Therapeutic Riding Association, 1457

Therapy
Catholic Family Services of Toronto, 519
The Trident Mediation Counselling & Support Foundation, 1398

Thyroid Diseases
Thyroid Foundation of Canada, 1378

Tobacco Industry
Association nationale des distributeurs aux petites surfaces alimentaires, 138

Torture
Action des Chrétiens pour l'abolition de la torture, 6
Amnesty International - Canadian Section (English Speaking), 68
Canadian Centre for Victims of Torture, 354
Vancouver Association for the Survivors of Torture, 1425

Tourette Syndrome
Tourette Syndrome Foundation of Canada, 1388

Tourism
Association touristique régionale de Charlevoix, 178
Association touristique régionale du Saguenay-Lac-Saint-Jean, 179
Associations touristiques régionales associées du Québec, 179
Cambridge Tourism, 275
East Coast Trail Association, 668
Fondation Tourisme Jeunesse, 748
Hostelling International - Canada, 823
Office de Tourisme du Rocher-Percé, 1055
Tourisme Abitibi-Témiscamingue, 1392
Tourisme Baie-James, 1392
Tourisme Bas-Saint-Laurent, 1392
Tourisme Chaudière-Appalaches, 1392
Tourisme Côte-Nord, 1392
Tourisme Lanaudière, 1392
Tourisme Laurentides, 1392
Tourisme Mauricie, 1393
Tourisme Montréal/Office des congrès et du tourisme du Grand Montréal, 1393
World Leisure & Recreation Association, 1606

Toxicology
Association des intervenants en toxicomanie du Québec inc., 117

Toys
Canadian Toy Testing Council, 496

Track & Field Sports
Achilles Canada, 5

Trade
International Institute of Fisheries Economics & Trade, 1551

Traffic Injury
Traffic Injury Research Foundation, 1394

Translation
Canadian Translators, Terminologists & Interpreters Council, 496
Corporation des traducteurs, traductrices, terminologues et interprètes du Nouveau-Brunswick, 631
Fédération Internationale des Traducteurs, 1526
Lutheran Bible Translators of Canada Inc., 922
Ordre des traducteurs, terminologues et interprètes agréés du Québec, 1124
Wycliffe Bible Translators of Canada, Inc., 1470

Transportation
Association du camionnage du Québec inc., 130
Canadian Council of Motor Transport Administrators, 369
Canadian Transportation Research Forum, 497
Carefree Society, 511
Club de trafic de Québec, 575
National Association of Railroad Passengers, 1573
Teamsters Canada (CLC), 1368
Transport Action Canada, 1395
Vintage Locomotive Society Inc., 1435
West Coast Railway Association, 1445

Travel Industry
Association of Canadian Travel Agents - Manitoba & Nunavut, 144
Hostelling International - Canada, 823
International Association for Medical Assistance to Travellers, 853
Maison du Tourisme, 927
Travellers' Aid Society of Toronto, 1396

Trout
Trout Unlimited Canada, 1399

Trucks & Trucking
Association du camionnage du Québec inc., 130
Ontario Trucking Association,

Trust Companies
National Aboriginal Trust Officers Association, 989

Tuberculosis
Heiser Program for Research in Leprosy & Tuberculosis, 1529
TB Vets, 1367

Turkish Canadians
Turkish Community Heritage Centre of Canada, 1400

Turner's Syndrome
Association du Syndrome de Turner du Québec, 132
Turner's Syndrome Society, 1400

Ukrainian Canadians
Canadian Foundation for Ukrainian Studies, 394
Plast Ukrainian Youth Association of Canada, 1162
SUS Foundation of Canada, 1357
Ukrainian Canadian Congress, 1402
Ukrainian Canadian Foundation of Taras Shevchenko, 1402
Ukrainian Canadian Research & Documentation Centre, 1402
Ukrainian Canadian Social Services (Toronto) Inc, 1403

Ukrainian Genealogical & Historical Society of Canada, 1403
Ukrainian National Federation of Canada, 1403
Ukrainian Youth Association of Canada, 1404
United Ukrainian Charitable Trust, 1412
World Federation of Ukrainian Women's Organizations, 1466

Ukrainian Studies
Ukrainian National Federation of Canada, 1403
Ukrainian Youth Association of Canada, 1404

Underwater Archaeology
Underwater Archaeological Society of British Columbia, 1404

Unitarians
Canadian Unitarian Council, 499
First Unitarian Congregation of Toronto, 739

United Church of Canada
United Church of Canada, 1409
United Church of Canada Foundation, 1409

United Empire Loyalists
Missisquoi Historical Society, 969
United Empire Loyalists' Association of Canada, 1410

United Nations
United Nations Association in Canada, 1411

United States of America
Association Canado-Américaine, 1507

Universities & Colleges
Agence universitaire de la Francophonie, 14
AIESEC, 18
Alberta Colleges Athletic Conference, 30
Association des collèges privés du Québec, 109
Association des universités de la francophonie canadienne, 130
Association of Canadian Universities for Northern Studies, 144
Association of Faculties of Medicine of Canada, 148
Association of Faculties of Pharmacy of Canada, 148
Association québécoise de pédagogie collégiale, 170
Canadian Associates of Ben-Gurion University of the Negev, 297
Canadian Association for University Continuing Education, 306
Canadian Association of Schools of Nursing, 332
Canadian Association of University Business Officers, 334
Canadian Society for the Study of Higher Education, 478
Canadian University Music Society, 499
Council of Ontario Universities, 635
Ontario Colleges Athletic Association, 1073
United World Colleges, 1418
World University Service of Canada, 1467

University & College Libraries
Ontario College & University Library Association, 1072

Uranium
World Nuclear Association, 1606

Urban Planning
Association québécoise d'urbanisme, 168
International Centre for Sustainable Cities, 855

Urology
The Canadian Continence Foundation, 364

Vacation Industry
Mouvement québécois des vacances familiales inc., 978

Vegans
American Vegan Society, 1504

Vegetables
Association québécoise de la distribution de fruits et légumes, 170

Vegetarians
Earthsave Canada, 667
Toronto Vegetarian Association, 1388

Veterans
Association of Veterans & Friends of the Mackenzie-Papineau Battalion, International Brigades in Spain, 164
Canadian Battlefields Foundation, 342
Korea Veterans Association of Canada Inc., Heritage Unit, 893
Last Post Fund, 899
Polish Combatants Association, 1164
The War Amputations of Canada, 1440

Veterinary Medicine
Association des médecins vétérinaires praticiens du Québec, 120
Canadian Chihuahua Rescue & Transport, 355
Ordre des médecins vétérinaires du Québec, 1123

Video
Film & Video Arts Society Alberta, 735
Groupe intervention vidéo, 792
MuchFACT, 978
Parlimage CCF, 1143
Yorkton Film Festival, 1474

Vietnamese Canadians
Association des vietnamiens de Sherbrooke, 130
Vietnamese Association, Toronto, 1434
Vietnamese Canadian Federation, 1434

Violence
Association québécoise Plaidoyer-Victimes, 176
Centre des ressources sur la non-violence inc, 530
EMPHASE Mauricie-Centre-du-Québec, 686
The Mackenzie Institute, 924
Metropolitan Action Committee on Violence Against Women & Children, 964
Prairieaction Foundation, 1170
Sexual Assault Centre of Edmonton, 1292
Victims of Violence, 1432
Viol-secours inc., 1435

Violence Against Women
The Barbra Schlifer Commemorative Clinic, 196
Canadian Association of Sexual Assault Centres, 333
Fredericton Sexual Assault Crisis Centre, 759
Kawartha Sexual Assault Centre, 882
Metropolitan Action Committee on Violence Against Women & Children, 964
Niagara Region Sexual Assault Centre, 1025
Ontario Coalition of Rape Crisis Centres, 1072
Oshawa-Durham Rape Crisis Centre, 1128
Ottawa Rape Crisis Centre, 1131
Prince Edward Island Rape & Sexual Assault Centre, 1176
Sexual Assault Centre Kingston Inc., 1292
Springtide Resources, 1346
Stop Abuse in Families Society, 1350
Timmins & Area Women in Crisis Support & Information Centre on Violence Against Women, 1379
Vancouver & Lower Mainland Multicultural Family Support Services Society, 1424
Vancouver Rape Relief & Women's Shelter, 1428
Viol-secours inc., 1435
The White Ribbon Campaign, 1452

Violence Against the Elderly
Elder Abuse Ontario, 681
Stop Abuse in Families Society, 1350

Visual Arts
Association des artistes en arts visuels de Saint-Jérôme, 106
La Fondation Émile-Nelligan, 746
Fusion: The Ontario Clay & Glass Association, 765
Haliburton Highlands Guild of Fine Arts, 798
Harbourfront Centre, 803
Malaspina Printmakers Society, 927
Visual Arts Nova Scotia, 1436

Vocational & Technical Education
Canadian Training Institute, 496
JVS of Greater Toronto, 879

Niagara West Employment & Learning Resource Centres, 1026
Skills for Change, 1302
Skills Unlimited, 1302

Vocational Rehabilitation
Canadian Council on Rehabilitation & Work, 371
Flowercart, 741
Goodwill Industries of Alberta, 778
Horizon Achievement Centre, 821
National Institute of Disability Management & Research, 994
Regional Occupation Centre Foundation, 1212
Saskatchewan Abilities Council, 1255
Shelburne Association Supporting Inclusion, 1295
Vecova Centre for Disability Services & Research, 1430
The War Amputations of Canada, 1440

Volleyball
Fédération de volleyball du Québec, 710
Volleyball Alberta, 1437
Volleyball Canada, 1437

Volunteers
Association des bénévoles du don de sang, 107
Associés bénévoles qualifiés au service des jeunes, 179
Bathurst Volunteer Centre de Bénévolat Inc., 199
Canadian Children's Optimist Foundation, 356
Canadian Crossroads International, 373
CODA International Training, 1518
Fédération des centres d'action bénévole du Québec, 712
Junior League of Edmonton, 878
Nanaimo Volunteer and Information Centre Society, 988
Newcomer Women's Services Toronto, 1015
Pillar Nonprofit Network, 1160
Search & Rescue Volunteer Association of Canada, 1288
Volunteer Central Society, 1438
Volunteer Grandparents, 1438

Walking
Volkssport Association of Alberta, 1437

Waste Management
Center for Health, Environment & Justice, 1516
Clean Nova Scotia Foundation, 573
Environmental Action Barrie - Living Green, 691
Environmental Education Ontario, 691
Pitch-In Canada, 1160
Recycling Council of Alberta, 1208
Recycling Council of British Columbia, 1208
Société québécoise de récupération et de recyclage, 1323

Water & Wastewater
Gordon Foundation, 778

Water Pollution
Canadian Association on Water Quality, 337
WaterCan, 1442

Water Polo
Fédération de Water-Polo du Québec, 711

Water Resources
Alberta Lake Management Society, 39
Canadian Water Resources Association, 503
Elora Environment Centre, 685
FogQuest, 742
WaterCan, 1442

Water Safety
Canadian Lifeboat Institution, 427

Water Skiing
Water Ski & Wakeboard British Columbia, 1441
Water Ski & Wakeboard Canada, 1441

Water Supply
Christian Children's Fund of Canada, 567
FogQuest, 742

Wilderness
Alberta Wilderness Association, 52
Canadian Parks & Wilderness Society, 450

Registered Charitable Organizations Index / Wildlife

Conservation International, 1519
Outward Bound Canada, 1133
Quetico Foundation, 1201
Sierra Club of Canada, 1298
Valhalla Wilderness Society, 1424
Wilderness Committee, 1454

Wildlife

British Columbia Waterfowl Society, 258
Canadian Association for Humane Trapping, 301
Canadian Wildlife Federation, 504
Ducks Unlimited Canada, 663
Fondation de la faune du Québec, 744
Fur-Bearer Defenders, 765
Halifax Wildlife Association, 799
Lambton Wildlife Inc., 897
Manitoba Wildlife Federation, 947
North Island Wildlife Recovery Association, 1031
Saskatchewan Wildlife Federation, 1278
Wildlife Rescue Association of British Columbia, 1455

Wildlife Conservation

Conservation Enforcement Officers Association of Nova Scotia, 622
Ducks Unlimited Canada, 663
Elsa Wild Animal Appeal of Canada, 685
Friends of Ecological Reserves, 761
International Association for Bear Research & Management, 1535
International Primate Protection League, 1556
International Wildlife Rehabilitation Council, 1566
The Jane Goodall Institute of Canada, 868
Sea Shepherd Conservation Society - USA, 1588
Sierra Club of Canada, 1298
Société québécoise pour la défense des animaux, 1324
Valhalla Wilderness Society, 1424
Wildlife Preservation Canada, 1455
Wildlife Rescue Association of British Columbia, 1455
World Animal Protection, 1465
World Wildlife Fund - Canada, 1468
WWF International, 1608
ZOOCHECK Canada Inc., 1482

Women

Afghan Women's Counselling & Integration Community Support Organization, 12
Alliance des femmes de la francophonie canadienne, 55
Almas Jiwani Foundation, 59
Association des fermières de l'Ontario, 114
Breast Cancer Action, 227
Calgary Immigrant Women's Association, 272
Canadian Association of Elizabeth Fry Societies, 312
Canadian Hadassah WIZO, 399
Canadian Women Voters Congress, 505
Central Alberta Women's Outreach Society, 524
Central Nova Women's Resource Centre, 524
Cercles de fermières du Québec, 537
Coalition des femmes de l'Alberta, 577
Collectif des femmes immigrantes du Québec, 581
Dress for Success, 662
Emunah Women of Canada, 687
Federated Women's Institutes of Canada, 706
Fédération des agricultrices du Québec, 711
La Fédération des femmes acadiennes de la Nouvelle-Écosse, 715
Girl Guides of Canada, 773
Golden Women's Resource Centre Society, 776
Groupe intervention vidéo, 792
Immigrant Women's Health Centre, 831
Inter Pares, 851
Jean Tweed Treatment Centre, 869
Junior League of Edmonton, 878
Ladies' Morning Musical Club, 895
Malton Neighbourhood Services, 928
Massey Centre for Women, 953
MATCH International Women's Fund, 954
Na'amat Canada Inc., 987

National Association of Women & the Law, 990
Newcomer Women's Services Toronto, 1015
The Older Women's Network, 1056
Planned Parenthood Ottawa, 1161
Positive Women's Network, 1168
Rexdale Women's Centre, 1229
Soroptimist Foundation of Canada, 1333
Syndicat des agricultrices de la Côte-du-Sud, 1362
Syndicat des agricultrices du Centre du Québec, 1362
L'Union culturelle des Franco-Ontariennes, 1406
Windsor Women Working with Immigrant Women, 1457
Women's Centre of Montréal, 1462
Working Women Community Centre, 1464
World Federation of Ukrainian Women's Organizations, 1466
YWCA Canada, 1481

Women & Health

Advanced Coronary Treatment (ACT) Foundation of Canada, 10
British Columbia Centre of Excellence for Women's Health, 235
Endometriosis Association, Inc., 1523
Genesis Research Foundation, 769
Marguerite Bourgeoys Family Centre Fertility Care Programme, 949
Options for Sexual Health, 1117
Ovarian Cancer Canada, 1133
Simcoe Women's Wellness Centre Corporation, 1300
Vancouver Women's Health Collective, 1429

Women & Religion

Congrégation des Soeurs de Sainte-Anne, 612
Mouvement des femmes Chrétiennes, 977
National Council of Jewish Women of Canada, 992

Women & the Arts

Women's Art Association of Canada, 1461
Women's Musical Club of Toronto, 1463

Women & the Environment

British Columbia Women's Institutes, 258
Federated Women's Institutes of Ontario, 706
Manitoba Women's Institutes, 947
New Brunswick Women's Institute, 1013
Women's Healthy Environments Network, 1462

Women in Business, Industry & Trade

Conseil d'intervention pour l'accès des femmes au travail, 615
Soroptimist International of the Americas, 1595

Women in Crisis

Adsum for Women & Children, 9
Assaulted Women's Helpline, 87
Association d'entraide Le Chaînon inc., 99
Aurora House, 187
The Barbra Schlifer Commemorative Clinic, 196
Battlefords Interval House Society, 200
Calgary Women's Emergency Shelter Association, 275
Canadian Association of Sexual Assault Centres, 333
Centre d'aide et de lutte contre les agressions à caractère sexuel de la Rive-Sud, 527
Chez Doris, 557
Crossroads for Women Inc., 644
Fédération des maisons d'hébergement pour femmes, 715
Fredericton Sexual Assault Crisis Centre, 759
Halifax Transition House Association - Bryony House, 799
Interval House, 861
Maison des femmes de Québec inc., 926
Nellie's Shelter, 1003
Oasis Centre des femmes, 1054
La rue des femmes, 1243
Sexual Assault Centre Kingston Inc., 1292
Sexual Assault Centre London, 1292
Sexual Assault Crisis Centre of Essex County Inc., 1293
Sexual Assault Support Centre Ottawa, 1293

Society of St. Vincent de Paul - Toronto Central Council, 1330
South Central Committee on Family Violence, Inc., 1334
South Okanagan Women in Need Society, 1335
Springtide Resources, 1346
Street Haven at the Crossroads, 1352
Timmins & Area Women in Crisis Support & Information Centre on Violence Against Women, 1379
Vancouver Rape Relief & Women's Shelter, 1428
West Niagara Second Stage Housing & Counselling, 1446

Women in Professions

Canadian Indigenous Nurses Association, 411
The Ninety-Nines Inc., 1578
Society for Canadian Women in Science & Technology, 1325
Soroptimist International of the Americas, 1595
Women's Legal Education & Action Fund, 1462

Women in the Mass Media

Centre femmes de Rimouski, 531
Women in Film & Television - Toronto, 1461

Wood

British Columbia Wood Specialities Group Association, 258

Woodworking

Architectural Woodwork Manufacturers Association of British Columbia, 79

Workers' Compensation

Industrial Accident Victims Group of Ontario, 835

World Wars

Canadian Battlefields Foundation, 342

Writers

Alexandra Writers' Centre Society, 53
Association des auteures et des auteurs de l'Ontario français, 106
Association professionnelle des écrivains de la Sagamie-Côte-Nord, 167
Burnaby Writers' Society, 266
Canadian Authors Association, 338
The Canadian Centre/International P.E.N., 354
Canadian Journalism Foundation, 423
Canadian Writers' Foundation Inc., 506
Federation of British Columbia Writers, 722
Manitoba Writers' Guild Inc., 947
PEN International, 1583
Professional Writers Association of Canada, 1187
Saskatchewan Writers Guild, 1278
Société du droit de reproduction des auteurs, compositeurs et éditeurs au Canada (SODRAC 2003) inc., 1318
Société professionnelle des auteurs et des compositeurs du Québec, 1322
Writers' Federation of Nova Scotia, 1468
The Writers' Guild of Alberta, 1469

Yoga

Sivananda Ashram Yoga Camp, 1301
Yasodhara Ashram Society, 1470
Yoga Association of Alberta, 1473

Young Men's Christian Association

YMCA Canada, 1471

Young Offenders

The John Howard Society of Ontario, 874
St. Leonard's Society of Canada, 1250

Young Women's Christian Association

YWCA Canada, 1481

Youth

Active Healthy Kids Canada, 7
Association des Grands Frères et Grandes Soeurs du Québec, 115
Association des jeunes bègues de Québec, 117
Association des jeunes travailleurs et travailleuses de Montréal inc, 117
Association jeunesse fransaskoise, 137
Associés bénévoles qualifiés au service des jeunes, 179

The Atlantic Film Festival Association, 184
Big Brothers Big Sisters of Alberta, 209
Big Brothers Big Sisters of British Columbia, 209
Big Brothers Big Sisters of Canada, 209
Big Brothers Big Sisters of Eastern Newfoundland, 209
Big Brothers Big Sisters of Manitoba, 209
Big Brothers Big Sisters of New Brunswick, 209
Big Brothers Big Sisters of Nova Scotia, 210
Big Brothers Big Sisters of Ontario, 210
Big Brothers Big Sisters of Saskatchewan, 210
Boost Child & Youth Advocacy Centre, 218
Boundless Adventures Association, 219
Canada World Youth, 281
Canadian 4-H Council, 284
Canadian Children's Optimist Foundation, 356
Canadian Sinfonietta Youth Orchestra, 470
Carthy Foundation, 516
Catholic Youth Studio - KSM Inc., 521
Cercles des jeunes naturalistes, 537
Chantiers jeunesse, 551
Conseil jeunesse francophone de la Colombie-Britannique, 618
Conseil jeunesse provincial (Manitoba), 619
Covenant House Toronto, 637
Durham Youth Orchestra, 665
Edmonton Youth Orchestra Association, 679
ERS Training & Development Corporation, 695
Fédération de la jeunesse canadienne-française inc., 709
Fédération de la jeunesse franco-ontarienne, 709
Fédération des jeunes francophones du Nouveau-Brunswick Inc., 715
Federation of North American Explorers, 725
Fondation Dufresne et Gauthier, 746
Fondation Tourisme Jeunesse, 748
Francophonie jeunesse de l'Alberta, 757
Gainey Foundation, 766
Girl Guides of Canada, 773
Greater Victoria Youth Orchestra, 787
Guid'amies franco-manitobaines, 793
Halton Mississauga Youth Orchestra, 800
Hamilton Philharmonic Youth Orchestra, 801
Hashomer Hatzair Canada, 804
Heartwood Centre for Community Youth Development, 810
Horatio Alger Association of Canada, 821
Hostelling International - Canada, 823
Impact Society, 831
Jeunesse Acadienne et Francophone de l'Île-du-prince-Édouard, 870
Jeunesse du Monde, 870
La Jeunesse Youth Orchestra, 870
Jeunesses Musicales du Canada, 871
Junior Achievement Canada, 877
Justice for Children & Youth, 878
Kids Help Phone, 886
Kitchener-Waterloo Symphony Youth Orchestra, 891
Living Bible Explorers, 915
Maison Kekpart, 927
Malton Neighbourhood Services, 928
The Marquis Project, Inc., 952
McCreary Centre Society, 955
McMan Youth, Family & Community Services Association, 955
Moorelands Community Services, 973
National Youth Orchestra Canada, 997
Newfoundland Symphony Youth Orchestra, 1023
Niagara Youth Orchestra Association, 1026
Northern Youth Abroad Program, 1035
Nova Scotia Youth Orchestra, 1050
Ontario Association of Residences Treating Youth, 1065
Operation Come Home, 1115
Orchestre symphonique des jeunes de Montréal, 1118
Orchestre symphonique des jeunes de Sherbrooke, 1118
Orchestre symphonique des jeunes du West Island, 1118
Orillia Youth Symphony Orchestra, 1126

Ottawa Youth Orchestra Academy, 1132
Our Place (Peel), 1133
Oxford Child & Youth Centre, 1134
Pathways to Education Canada, 1145
Pioneer Clubs Canada Inc., 1160
Planned Parenthood Ottawa, 1161
Plast Ukrainian Youth Association of Canada, 1162
Ranch Ehrlo Society, 1204
Réseau Technoscience, 1226
Richmond Delta Youth Orchestra, 1230
St. Leonard's Youth & Family Services Society, 1250
Saskatoon Youth Orchestra, 1280
Scouts Canada, 1286
Société d'investissement jeunesse, 1314
South Saskatchewan Youth Orchestra, 1336
Sudbury Youth Orchestra Inc., 1353
Toronto Symphony Youth Orchestra, 1387
T.R.E.E. Foundation for Youth Development, 1397
Ukrainian Youth Association of Canada, 1404
United Generations Ontario, 1411
Vancouver Youth Symphony Orchestra Society, 1429
Victoria Youth Empowerment Society, 1434
Visions of Science Network for Learning, 1436
Voices for Children, 1437
Winnipeg Youth Orchestras, 1459
Young Alberta Book Society, 1474
Young People's Theatre, 1474
Youth Assisting Youth, 1475
Youth Ballet & Contemporary Dance of Saskatchewan Inc., 1475
Youth Challenge International, 1475
Youth Empowerment & Support Services, 1475
Youth Flight Canada, 1475
Youth in Care Canada, 1475
Youth Science Canada, 1476
YOUTHLINK, 1476

Zionism
Hashomer Hatzair Canada, 804
Mizrachi Organization of Canada, 970

Zoology
International Council for Archaeozoology, 1544

Zoos
Assiniboine Park Conservancy, 88
Calgary Zoological Society, 275
Canada's Accredited Zoos & Aquariums, 281
ZOOCHECK Canada Inc., 1482

Zoroastrianism
L'Association Zoroastrianne du Québec, 179
Ontario Zoroastrian Community Foundation, 1114
Zoroastrian Society of Ontario, 1482

CANADA'S INFORMATION RESOURCE CENTRE (CIRC)

Access all these great resources online, all the time, at Canada's Information Resource Centre (CIRC)
http://circ.greyhouse.ca

Canada's Information Resource Centre (CIRC) integrates all of Grey House Canada's award-winning reference content into one easy-to-use online resource. With **over 100,000 Canadian organizations** and **over 140,600 contacts**, plus thousands of additional facts and figures, CIRC is the most comprehensive resource for specialized database content in Canada! Access all 19 databases, including six recently added, with Canada Info Desk Complete - it's the total package!

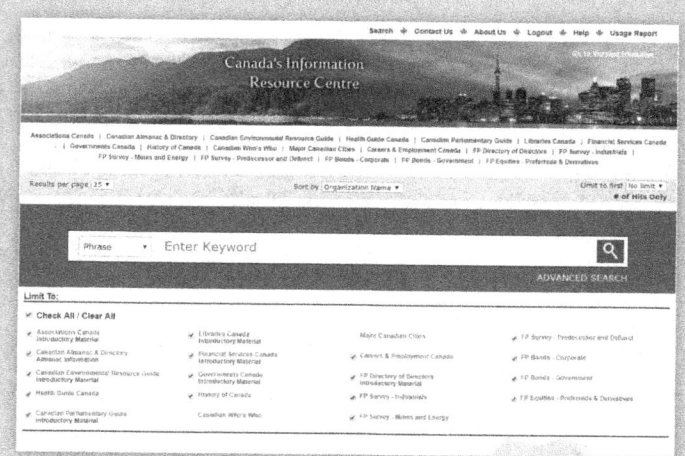

KEY ADVANTAGES OF CIRC:

- Seamlessly cross-database search content from select databases
- Save search results for future reference
- Link directly to websites or email addresses
- Clear display of your results makes compiling and adding to your research easier than ever before

DESIGN YOUR OWN CUSTOM CONTACT LISTS!

CIRC gives you the option to define and extract your own lists in seconds. Find new business leads, do keyword searches, locate upcoming conference attendees; all the information you want is right at your fingertips.

New FP Bonds and Surveys

CHOOSE BETWEEN KEYWORD AND ADVANCED SEARCH!

With CIRC, you can choose between Keyword and Advanced search to pinpoint information. Designed for both beginner and advanced researchers, you can conduct simple text searches as well as powerful Boolean searches.

PROFILES IN CIRC INCLUDE:

- Phone numbers, email addresses, fax numbers and full addresses for all branches of the organization
- Social media accounts, such as Twitter and Facebook
- Key contacts based on job titles
- Budgets, membership fees, staff sizes and more!

Search CIRC using common or unique fields, customized to your needs!

ONLY GREY HOUSE DIRECTORIES PROVIDE SPECIAL CONTENT YOU WON'T FIND ANYWHERE ELSE!

- **Associations Canada:** finances/funding sources, activities, publications, conferences, membership, awards, member profile
- **Canadian Parliamentary Guide:** private and political careers of elected members, complete list of constituencies and representatives
- **Canadian Environmental Resouce Guide:** products/services/areas of expertise, working languages, domestic markets, type of ownership, revenue sources
- **Financial Services:** type of ownership, number of employees, year founded, assets, revenue, ticker symbol
- **Libraries Canada:** staffing, special collections, services, year founded, national library symbol, regional system
- **Governments Canada:** municipal population
- **Canadian Who's Who:** birth city, publications, education (degrees, alma mater), career/occupation and employer
- **Major Canadian Cities:** demographics, ethnicity, immigration, language, education, housing, income, labour and transportation
- **Health Guide Canada:** chronic and mental illnesses, general resources, appendices and statistics
- **Careers & Employment Canada:** career associations, career employment websites, employers, industry directories, recruiters, scholarships, sector councils and summer jobs
- **FP Directory of Directors:** names, directorships, educational and professional backgrounds and email addresses of top Canadian directors; list of major companies and complete company contact information
- **FPbonds:** bond information in PDF form and with sortable tables
- **FPsurvey:** detailed profiles of current publicly traded companies, as well as past corporate changes

The new CIRC provides easier searching and faster, more pinpointed results of all of our great resources in Canada, from Associations and Government to Major Companies to Zoos and everything in between. Whether you need fully detailed information on your contact or just an email address, you can customize your search query to meet your needs.

Contact us now for a **free trial** subscription or visit http://circ.greyhouse.ca

For more information please contact Grey House Publishing Canada
Tel.: (866) 433-4739 or (416) 644-6479 Fax: (416) 644-1904 | info@greyhouse.ca | www.greyhouse.ca

CENTRE DE DOCUMENTATION DU CANADA (CDC)

Consultez en tout temps toutes ces excellentes ressources en ligne grâce au Centre de documentation du Canada (CDC) à http://circ.greyhouse.ca

Le Centre de documentation du Canada (CDC) regroupe sous une seule ressource en ligne conviviale tout le contenu des ouvrages de référence primés de Grey House Canada. Répertoriant plus de **100 000 entreprises canadiennes, et plus de 140 600 personnes-ressources**, faits et chiffres, il s'agit de la ressource la plus complète en matière de bases de données spécialisées au Canada! Grâce à l'ajout de trois bases de données, le Canada Info Desk Complete est plus avantageux que jamais alors qu'il coûte 50 % que l'abonnement aux ouvrages individuels. Accédez aux 19 bases de données dès maintenant – le Canadian Info Desk Complete vous offre un ensemble complet!

Nouveau FP Bonds et Surveys

PRINCIPAUX AVANTAGES DU CDC

- Recherche transversale efficace dans le contenu des bases de données
- Sauvegarde des résultats de recherche pour consultation future
- Lien direct aux sites Web et aux adresses électroniques
- Grâce à l'affichage lisible de vos résultats, il est dorénavant plus facile de compiler les résultats ou d'ajouter des critères à vos recherches

CONCEPTION PERSONNALISÉE DE VOS LISTES DE PERSONNES-RESSOURCES!

Le CDC vous permet de définir et d'extraire vos propres listes, et ce, en quelques secondes. Découvrez des clients potentiels, effectuez des recherches par mot-clé, trouvez les participants à une conférence à venir : l'information dont vous avez besoin, au bout de vos doigts.

CHOISISSEZ ENTRE RECHERCHES MOT-CLÉ ET AVANCÉE!

Grâce au CDC, vous pouvez choisir entre une recherche Mot-clé ou Avancée pour localiser l'information avec précision. Vous avez la possibilité d'effectuer des recherches en texte simple ou booléennes puissantes – les recherches sont conçues à l'intention des chercheurs débutants et avancés.

LES PROFILS DU CDC COMPRENNENT :

- Numéros de téléphone, adresses électroniques, numéros de télécopieur et adresses complètes pour toutes les succursales d'un organisme
- Comptes de médias sociaux, comme Twitter et Facebook
- Personnes-ressources clés en fonction des appellations d'emploi
- Budgets, frais d'adhésion, tailles du personnel et plus!

Effectuez des recherches dans le CDC à l'aide de champs uniques ou communs, personnalisés selon vos besoins!

SEULS LES RÉPERTOIRES DE GREY HOUSE VOUS OFFRENT UN CONTENU PARTICULIER QUE VOUS NE TROUVEREZ NULLE PART AILLEURS!

- **Le répertoire des associations du Canada** : sources de financement, activités, publications, congrès, membres, prix, profil de membre
- **Guide parlementaire canadien** : carrières privées et politiques des membres élus, liste complète des comtés et des représentants
- **Guide des ressources environnementales canadiennes** : produits/services/domaines d'expertise, langues de travail, marchés nationaux, type de propriétaire, sources de revenus
- **Services financiers** : type de propriétaire, nombre d'employés, année de la fondation, immobilisations, revenus, symbole au téléscripteur
- **Bibliothèques Canada** : personnel, collections particulières, services, année de la fondation, symbole de bibliothèque national, système régional
- **Gouvernements du Canada** : population municipale
- **Canadian Who's Who** : ville d'origine, publication, formation (diplômes et alma mater), carrière/emploi et employeur
- **Principales villes canadiennes** : données démographiques, ethnicité, immigration, langue, éducation, logement, revenu, main-d'œuvre et transport
- **Guide canadien de la santé** : maladies chroniques et mentales, ressources generales, annexes et statistiques.
- **Carrières et emplois Canada** : associations professionnelles, sites Web d'emplois, employeurs, répertoires par industrie, recruteurs, bourses, conseils sectoriels et emplois d'été
- **Répertoire des administrateurs** : prénom, nom de famille, poste de cadre et d'administrateur, parcours scolaire et professionnel et adresse électronique des cadres supérieurs canadiens; liste des sociétés les plus importantes au Canada et l'information complète des compagnies
- **FPbonds** : information sur les obligations en format PDF, avec tableaux à trier
- **FPsurvey** : profils détaillés de sociétés cotées en bourse et changements organisationnels antérieurs

Le nouveau CDC facilite la recherche au sein de toutes nos ressources au Canada et procure plus rapidement des résultats plus poussés – des associations au gouvernement en passant par les principales entreprises et les zoos, sans oublier tout un éventail d'organisations! Que vous ayez besoin d'information très détaillée au sujet de votre personne-ressource ou d'une simple adresse électronique, vous pouvez personnaliser votre requête afin qu'elle réponde à vos besoins. Contactez-nous sans tarder pour obtenir un **essai gratuit** ou visitez http://circ.greyhouse.ca

Pour obtenir plus d'information, veuillez contacter **Grey House Publishing Canada**
par tél. : 1 866 433-4739 ou 416 644-6479 par téléc. : 416 644-1904 | info@greyhouse.ca | www.greyhouse.ca

Canadian Almanac & Directory
The Definitive Resource for Facts & Figures About Canada

The *Canadian Almanac & Directory* has been Canada's most authoritative sourcebook for 171 years. Published annually since 1847, it continues to be widely used by publishers, business professionals, government offices, researchers, information specialists and anyone needing current, accessible information on every imaginable topic relevant to those who live and work in Canada.

A directory and a guide, the *Canadian Almanac & Directory* provides the most comprehensive picture of Canada, from physical attributes to economic and business summaries, leisure and recreation. It combines textual materials, charts, colour photographs and directory listings with detailed profiles, all verified and organized for easy retrieval. The *Canadian Almanac & Directory* is a wealth of general information, displaying national statistics on population, employment, CPI, imports and exports, as well as images of national awards, Canadian symbols, flags, emblems and Canadian parliamentary leaders.

For important contacts throughout Canada, for any number of business projects or for that once-in-a-while critical fact, the *Canadian Almanac & Directory* will help you find the leads you didn't even know existed—quickly and easily!

ALL THE INFORMATION YOU'LL EVER NEED, ORGANIZED INTO 17 DISTINCT CATEGORIES FOR EASY NAVIGATION!

Almanac—a fact-filled snapshot of Canada, including History, Geography, Economics and Vital Statistics.

Arts & Culture—includes 9 topics from Galleries to Zoos.

Associations—thousands of organizations arranged in 143 different topics, from Accounting to Writers.

Broadcasting—Canada's major Broadcasting Companies, Provincial Radio and Television Stations, Cable Companies, and Specialty Broadcasters.

Business & Finance—Accounting, Banking, Insurance, Canada's Major Companies and Stock Exchanges.

Education—arranged by Province and includes Districts, Government Agencies, Specialized and Independent Schools, Universities and Technical facilities.

Government—spread over three sections, with a Quick Reference Guide, Federal and Provincial listings, County and Municipal Districts and coverage of Courts in Canada.

Health—Government agencies, hospitals, community health centres, retirement care and mental health facilities.

Law Firms—all Major Law Firms, followed by smaller firms organized by Province and listed alphabetically.

Libraries—Canada's main Library/Archive and Government Departments for Libraries, followed by Provincial listings and Regional Systems.

Publishing—Books, Magazines and Newspapers organized by Province, including frequency and circulation figures.

Religion—broad information about religious groups and associations from 37 different denominations.

Sports—Associations in 110 categories, with detailed League and Team listings.

Transportation—complete listings for all major modes.

Utilities—Associations, Government Agencies and Provincial Utility Companies.

PRINT OR ONLINE—QUICK AND EASY ACCESS TO ALL THE INFORMATION YOU NEED!

Available in hardcover print or electronically via the web, the *Canadian Almanac & Directory* provides instant access to the people you need and the facts you want every time.

Canadian Almanac & Directory print edition is verified and updated annually. Ongoing changes are added to the web version on a regular basis. The web version allows you to narrow your search by using index fields such as name or type of organization, subject, location, contact name or title and postal code.

Online subscribers have the option to instantly generate their own contact lists and export them into spreadsheets for further use—a great alternative to high cost list broker services.

GREY HOUSE PUBLISHING CANADA
For more information please contact Grey House Publishing Canada
Tel.: (866)-433-4739 or (416) 644-6479 Fax: (416) 644-1904 | info@greyhouse.ca | www.greyhouse.ca

Répertoire et almanach canadien
La ressource de référence au sujet des données et des faits relatifs au Canada

Le *Répertoire et almanach canadien* constitue le guide canadien le plus rigoureux depuis 171 ans. Publié annuellement depuis 1847, il est toujours grandement utilisé dans le monde des affaires, les bureaux gouvernementaux, par les spécialistes de l'information, les chercheurs, les éditeurs ou quiconque est à la recherche d'information actuelle et accessible sur tous les sujets imaginables à propos des gens qui vivent et travaillent au Canada.

À la fois répertoire et guide, le *Répertoire et almanach canadien* dresse le tableau le plus complet du Canada, des caractéristiques physiques jusqu'aux revues économique et commerciale, en passant par les loisirs et les activités récréatives. Il combine des documents textuels, des représentations graphiques, des photographies en couleurs et des listes de répertoires accompagnées de profils détaillés. Autant d'information pointue et organisée de manière à ce qu'elle soit facile à obtenir. Le *Répertoire et almanach canadien* foisonne de renseignements généraux. Il présente des statistiques nationales sur la population, l'emploi, l'IPC, l'importation et l'exportation ainsi que des images des prix nationaux, des symboles canadiens, des drapeaux, des emblèmes et des leaders parlementaires canadiens.

Si vous cherchez des personnes-ressources essentielles un peu partout au Canada, peu importe qu'il s'agisse de projets d'affaires ou d'une question factuelle anecdotique, le Répertoire et almanach canadien vous fournira les pistes dont vous ignoriez l'existence – rapidement et facilement!

TOUTE L'INFORMATION DONT VOUS AUREZ BESOIN, ORGANISÉE EN 17 CATÉGORIES DISTINCTES POUR UNE CONSULTATION FACILE!

Almanach—un aperçu informatif du Canada, notamment l'histoire, la géographie, l'économie et les statistiques essentielles.

Arts et culture—comprends 9 sujets, des galeries aux zoos.

Associations—des milliers d'organisations classées selon 143 sujets différents, de l'actuariat au zoo.

Radiodiffusion—les principales sociétés de radiodiffusion au Canada, les stations radiophoniques et de télévision ainsi que les entreprises de câblodistribution et les diffuseurs thématiques.

Commerce et finance—comptabilité, services bancaires, assurances, principales entreprises et bourses canadiennes.

Éducation—organisé par province et comprend les arrondissements scolaires, les organismes gouvernementaux, les écoles spécialisées et indépendantes, les universités et les établissements techniques.

Gouvernement—s'étend sur trois sections et comprend un guide de référence, des listes fédérales et provinciales, les comtés et arrondissements municipaux ainsi que les cours canadiennes.

Santé—organismes gouvernementaux, hôpitaux, centres de santé communautaires, établissements de soins pour personnes retraitées et de soins de santé mentale.

Sociétés d'avocats—toutes les principales sociétés d'avocats, suivies des sociétés plus petites, classées par province et en ordre alphabétique.

Bibliothèques—la bibliothèque et les archives principales du Canada ainsi que les bibliothèques des ministères, suivis des listes provinciales et des systèmes régionaux.

Édition—livres, magazines et journaux classés par province, y compris leur fréquence et les données relatives à leur diffusion.

Religion—information générale au sujet des groupes religieux et des associations religieuses de 37 dénominations.

Sports—associations de 110 sports distincts; comprend des listes de ligues et d'équipes.

Transport—des listes complètes des principaux modes de transport.

Services publics—associations, organismes gouvernementaux et entreprises de services publics provinciales.

FORMAT PAPIER OU EN LIGNE— ACCÈS RAPIDE À TOUS LES RENSEIGNEMENTS DONT VOUS AVEZ BESOIN!

Offert sous couverture rigide ou en format électronique grâce au web, le *Répertoire et almanach canadien* offre invariablement un accès instantané aux représentants du gouvernement et aux faits qui font l'objet de vos recherches.

La version imprimée du Répertoire et almanach canadien est vérifiée et mise à jour annuellement. La version en ligne est mise à jour mensuellement. Cette version vous permet de circonscrire la recherche grâce aux champs de l'index comme le nom ou le type d'organisme, le sujet, l'emplacement, le nom ou le titre de la personne-ressource et le code postal.

Les abonnés au service en ligne peuvent générer instantanément leurs propres listes de contacts et les exporter en format feuille de calcul pour une utilisation approfondie – une solution de rechange géniale aux services dispendieux d'un commissionnaire en publipostage.

 Pour obtenir plus d'information, veuillez contacter Grey House Publishing Canada
par tél. : 1 866 433-4739 ou 416 644-6479 par téléc. : 416 644-1904 | info@greyhouse.ca | www.greyhouse.ca

Canadian Who's Who

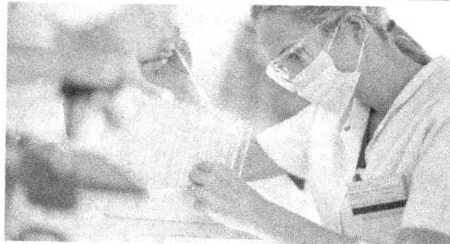

Canadian Who's Who is the only authoritative publication of its kind in Canada, offering access to the top 10 000 notable Canadians in all walks of life. Published annually to provide current and accurate information, the familiar bright-red volume is recognized as the standard reference source of contemporary Canadian biography.

Documenting the achievement of Canadians from a wide variety of occupations and professions, *Canadian Who's Who* records the diversity of culture in Canada. These biographies are organized alphabetically and provide detailed information on the accomplishments of notable Canadians, from coast to coast. All who are interested in the achievements of Canada's most influential citizens and their significant contributions to the country and the world beyond should acquire this reference title.

Detailed entries give date and place of birth, education, family details, career information, memberships, creative works, honours, languages, and awards, together with full addresses. Included are outstanding Canadians from business, academia, politics, sports, the arts and sciences, etc.

Every year the publisher invites new individuals to complete questionnaires from which new biographies are compiled. The publisher also gives those already listed in earlier editions an opportunity to update their biographies. Those listed are selected because of the positions they hold in Canadian society, or because of the contributions they have made to Canada.

AVAILABLE ONLINE!

Canadian Who's Who is also available online, through Canada's Information Resource Centre (CIRC). Readers can access this title's in-depth and vital networking content in the format that best suits their needs—in print, by subscription or online.

The print edition of *Canadian Who's Who 2018* contains 10,000 entries, while the online edition gives users access to 24,000 biographies, including all current listings and nearly 13,000 archived biographies dating back to 1999.

GREY HOUSE PUBLISHING CANADA

For more information please contact Grey House Publishing Canada
Tel.: (866)-433-4739 or (416) 644-6479 Fax: (416) 644-1904 | info@greyhouse.ca | www.greyhouse.ca

Canadian Who's Who

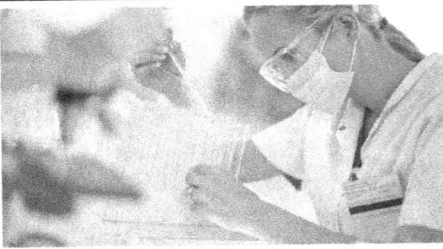

Canadian Who's Who est la seule publication digne de foi de son genre au Canada. Elle donne accès 10 000 dignitaires canadiens de tous les horizons. L'ouvrage annuel rouge vif bien connu, rempli d'information à jour et exacte, est la référence standard en matière de biographies canadiennes contemporaines.

Canadian Who's Who, qui porte sur les réalisations de Canadiens occupant une vaste gamme de postes et de professions, illustre la diversité de la culture canadienne. Ces biographies sont classées en ordre alphabétique et donnent de l'information détaillée sur les réalisations de Canadiens éminents, d'un océan à l'autre. Tous ceux qui s'intéressent aux réalisations des citoyens les plus influents au Canada et à leurs contributions importantes au pays et partout dans le monde doivent se procurer cet ouvrage de référence.

Les entrées détaillées indiquent la date et le lieu de la naissance, traitent de l'éducation, de la famille, de la carrière, des adhésions, des œuvres de création, des distinctions, des langues et des prix - en plus des adresses complètes. Elles comprennent des Canadiens exceptionnels du monde des affaires, des universités, de la politique, des sports, des arts, des sciences et plus encore!

Chaque année, l'éditeur invite de nouvelles personnes à remplir les questionnaires à partir desquels il prépare les nouvelles biographies. Il le remet également aux personnes qui font partie de numéros antérieurs afin de leur permettre d'effectuer une mise à jour. Les personnes retenues le sont en raison des postes qu'elles occupent dans la société canadienne ou de leurs contributions au Canada.

OFFERT EN FORMAT ÉLECTRONIQUE!

Canadian Who's Who est également offert en ligne par l'entremise du Centre de documentation du Canada (CDC). Les lecteurs peuvent accéder au contenu approfondi et essentiel au réseautage de cet ouvrage dans le format qui leur convient le mieux - version imprimée, en ligne ou par abonnement.

L'édition imprimée de *Canadian Who's Who 2018* compte 10 000 entrées tandis qu'en consultant la version en ligne, les utilisateurs ont accès à 24 000 biographies, dont fi ches d'actualité et 13 000 biographies archives qui remontent jusqu'à 1999.

GREY HOUSE PUBLISHING CANADA

Pour obtenir plus d'information, veuillez contacter Grey House Publishing Canada
par tél. : 1 866 433-4739 ou 416 644-6479 par téléc. : 416 644-1904 | info@greyhouse.ca | www.greyhouse.ca

Canadian Parliamentary Guide
Your Number One Source for All General Federal Elections Results!

Published annually since before Confederation, the *Canadian Parliamentary Guide* is an indispensable directory, providing biographical information on elected and appointed members in federal and provincial government. Featuring government institutions such as the Governor General's Household, Privy Council and Canadian legislature, this comprehensive collection provides historical and current election results with statistical, provincial and political data.

THE CANADIAN PARLIAMENTARY GUIDE IS BROKEN DOWN INTO FIVE COMPREHENSIVE CATEGORIES

Monarchy—biographical information on Her Majesty Queen Elizabeth II, The Royal Family and the Governor General

Federal Government—a separate chapter for each of the Privy Council, Senate and House of Commons (including a brief description of the institution, its history in both text and chart format and a list of current members), followed by unparalleled biographical sketches*

General Elections

1867–2011

- information is listed alphabetically by province then by riding name
- notes on each riding include: date of establishment, date of abolition, former division and later divisions, followed by election year and successful candidate's name and party
- by-election information follows

2015

- information for the 2015 election is organized in the same manner but also includes information on all the candidates who ran in each riding, their party affiliation and the number of votes won

Provincial and Territorial Governments—Each provincial chapter includes:

- statistical information
- description of Legislative Assembly
- biographical sketch of the Lieutenant Governor or Commissioner
- list of current Cabinet Members
- dates of legislatures since confederation
- current Members and Constituencies
- biographical sketches*
- general election and by-election results, including 2015 general elections in Alberta, Prince Edward Island, Newfoundland & Labrador, and the Northwest Territories.

Courts: Federal—each court chapter includes a description of the court (Supreme, Federal, Federal Court of Appeal, Court Martial Appeal and Tax Court), its history and a list of its judges followed by biographical sketches*

* Biographical sketches follow a concise yet in-depth format:

Personal Data—place of birth, education, family information

Political Career—political career path and services

Private Career—work history, organization memberships, military history

AVAILABLE IN PRINT AND NOW ONLINE!

Available in hardcover print, the *Canadian Parliamentary Guide* is also available electronically via the Web, providing instant access to the government officials you need and the facts you want every time. Use the web version to narrow your search with index fields such as institution, province and name.

Create your own contact lists! Online subscribers can instantly generate their own contact lists and export information into spreadsheets for further use. A great alternative to high cost list broker services!

Photo of the Rt. Hon. Justin Trudeau by Adam Scotti, provided by the Office of the Prime Minister © Her Majesty the Queen in Right of Canada, 2017.

GREY HOUSE PUBLISHING CANADA
For more information please contact Grey House Publishing Canada
Tel.: (866) 433-4739 or (416) 644-6479 Fax: (416) 644-1904 | info@greyhouse.ca | www.greyhouse.ca

Guide parlementaire canadien
Votre principale source d'information en matière de résultats d'élections fédérales!

Publié annuellement depuis avant la Confédération, le *Guide parlementaire canadien* est une source fondamentale de notices biographiques des membres élus et nommés aux gouvernements fédéral et provinciaux. Il y est question, notamment, d'établissements gouvernementaux comme la résidence du gouverneur général, le Conseil privé et la législature canadienne. Ce recueil exhaustif présente les résultats historiques et actuels accompagnés de données statistiques, provinciales et politiques.

OFFERT EN FORMAT PAPIER ET DÉSORMAIS ÉLECTRONIQUE!

LE GUIDE PARLEMENTAIRE CANADIEN EST DIVISÉ EN CINQ CATÉGORIES EXHAUSTIVES:

La monarchie—des renseignements biographiques sur Sa Majesté la reine Elizabeth II, la famille royale et le gouverneur général.

Le gouvernement fédéral—un chapitre distinct pour chacun des sujets suivants: Conseil privé, sénat, Chambre des communes (y compris une brève description de l'institution, son historique sous forme de textes et de graphiques et une liste des membres actuels) suivi de notes biographiques sans pareil.*

Les élections fédérales

1867–2011

- Les renseignements sont présentés en ordre alphabétique par province puis par circonscription.
- Les notes de chaque circonscription comprennent : La date d'établissement, la date d'abolition, l'ancienne circonscription, les circonscriptions ultérieures, etc. puis l'année d'élection ainsi que le nom et le parti des candidats élus.
- Viennent ensuite des renseignements sur l'élection partielle.

2015

- Les renseignements de l'élection 2015 sont organisés de la même manière, mais comprennent également de l'information sur tous les candidats qui se sont présentés dans chaque circonscription, leur appartenance politique et le nombre de voix récoltées.

Gouvernements provinciaux et territoriaux—Chaque chapitre portant sur le gouvernement provincial comprend :

- des renseignements statistiques
- une description de l'Assemblée législative
- des notes biographiques sur le lieutenant-gouverneur ou le commissaire
- une liste des ministres actuels
- les dates de périodes législatives depuis la Confédération
- une liste des membres et des circonscriptions
- des notes biographiques*
- les résultats des élections générales et partielles les résultats d'élections générales et partielles, y compris les élections générales de 2015 en Alberta, à l'Île-du-Prince-Édouard, à Terre-Neuve-et-Labrador et aux Territoires du Nord-Ouest.

Cours : fédérale—chaque chapitre comprend : une description de la cour (suprême, fédérale, cour d'appel fédérale, cour d'appel de la cour martiale et cour de l'impôt), son histoire, une liste des juges qui y siègent ainsi que des notes biographiques.*

* Les notes biographiques respectent un format concis, bien qu'approfondi :

Renseignements personnels—lieu de naissance, formation, renseignements familiaux

Carrière politique—cheminement politique et service public

Carrière privée—antécédents professionnels, membre d'organisations, antécédents militaires

Offert sous couverture rigide ou en format électronique grâce au web, le *Guide parlementaire canadien* donne invariablement un accès instantané aux représentants du gouvernement et aux faits qui font l'objet de vos recherches. Servez-vous de la version en ligne afin de circonscrire vos recherches grâce aux champs spéciaux de l'index comme l'institution, la province et le nom.

Créez vos propres listes! Les abonnés au service en ligne peuvent générer instantanément leurs propres listes de contacts et les exporter en format feuille de calcul pour une utilisation approfondie – une solution de rechange géniale aux services dispendieux d'un commissionnaire en publipostage!

Photo de le très honorable Justin Trudeau par Adam Scotti. Photo fournie par le Bureau du Premier ministre © Sa Majesté la Reine du Chef du Canada, 2017.

Pour obtenir plus d'information, veuillez contacter **Grey House Publishing Canada**
par tél. : 1 866 433-4739 ou 416 644-6479 par téléc. : 416 644-1904 | info@greyhouse.ca | www.greyhouse.ca

Directory of Directors
Your Best Source for Hard-to-Find Business Information

Since 1931, the *Financial Post Directory of Directors* has been recognizing leading Canadian companies and their execs. Today, this title is one of the most comprehensive resources for hard-to-find Canadian business information, allowing readers to access roughly 16,200 executive contacts from Canada's top 1,400 corporations. This prestigious title offers a definitive list of directorships and offices held by noteworthy Canadian business people. It also provides details on leading Canadian companies—publicly traded and privately-owned, including company name, contact information and the names of their executive officers and directors.

ACCESS THE COMPANIES & DIRECTORS YOU NEED IN NO TIME!

The updated 2018 edition of the *Directory of Directors* is jam-packed with information, including:

- **ALL-NEW front matter**: An infographic drawn from data in the book, an excerpt from the Canadian Board Diversity Council's latest Annual Report Card on gender diversity on corporate boards, an excerpt from *The Corporate Governance Review, Seventh Edition: Canada (2017)* by Law Business Research Ltd., which details the corporate governance regime in Canada, and rankings from the FP500.

- **Personal listings**: First name, last name, gender, birth date, degrees, schools attended, executive positions and directorships, previous positions held, main business address and more.

- **Company listings**: Boards of directors and executive officers, head office address, phone and fax numbers, toll-free number, web and email addresses.

Powerful indexes enabling researchers to target just the information they need include:

- An **industrial classification index**: List of key Canadian companies, sorted by industry type according to the Global Industry Classification Standard (GICS®).

- A **geographic location index** grouping all companies in the Company Listings section according to the city and province/state of the head office; and

- An **alphabetical list of abbreviations** providing definitions of common abbreviations used for terms, titles, organizations, honours/fellowships and degrees throughout the Directory.

AVAILABLE ONLINE!

The Directory is also available online, through Canada's Information Resource Centre. Readers can access this title's in-depth and vital networking content in the format that best suits their needs—in print, by subscription or online.

Create your own contact lists! Online subscribers can instantly generate their own contact lists and export information into spreadsheets for further use. A great alternative to high cost list broker services!

GREY HOUSE PUBLISHING CANADA

For more information please contact Grey House Publishing Canada
Tel.: (866)-433-4739 or (416) 644-6479 Fax: (416) 644-1904 | info@greyhouse.ca | www.greyhouse.ca

Répertoire des administrateurs
Votre source par excellence de renseignements professionnels difficiles à trouver

Depuis 1931, le Financial Post Directory of Directors (Répertoire des administrateurs du Financial Post) reconnaît les sociétés canadiennes importantes et leur haute direction. De nos jours, cet ouvrage compte parmi certaines des ressources les plus exhaustives lorsqu'il est question des renseignements d'affaires canadiens difficiles à trouver. Il permet aux lecteurs d'accéder à environ 16 200 coordonnées d'administrateurs provenant des 1 400 sociétés les plus importantes au Canada. Ce document prestigieux comprend une liste définitive des postes d'administrateurs et des fonctions que ces gens d'affaires canadiens remarquables occupent. Il offre également des détails sur des sociétés canadiennes importantes – privées ou négociées sur le marché – y compris le nom de l'entreprise, ses coordonnées et le nombre des membres de sa haute direction et de ses administrateurs.

UN ACCÈS RAPIDE ET FACILE À TOUS LES ENTREPRISES ET DIRECTEURS DONT VOUS AVEZ BESOIN!

La version mise à jour de 2018 du Répertoire des administrateurs du Financial Post est remplie d'information, notamment:

- **NOUVELLE section de textes préliminaires** – une infographie inspirée des données de l'ouvrage; un extrait du bulletin de rendement de 2016 de l'Institut des administrateurs de sociétés sur la mixité au sein des conseils d'administration; un extrait de *The Corporate Governance Review, Seventh Edition: Canada (2017)* par Law Business Research Ltd., qui explique en détail le régime de gouvernance d'entreprise au Canada; le classement le plus récent au FP500.

- **Données personnelles** – prénom, nom de famille, sexe, date de naissance, diplômes, écoles fréquentées, poste de cadre et d'administrateur, postes occupés préalablement, adresse professionnelle principale et plus encore.

- **Listes de sociétés** – conseils d'administration et cadres supérieurs, adresse du siège social, numéros de téléphone et de télécopieur, numéro sans frais, adresse électronique et site Web.

Des index puissants permettent aux utilisateurs de cibler l'information dont ils ont besoin, notamment:

- **Index de classement industriel** - énumère les sociétés classées par type d'industrie général selon le Global Industry Classification Standard (GICS[MD]).

- **l'Index des emplacements géographiques** qui comprend toutes les sociétés de la section Liste des sociétés en fonction de la ville et de la province/de l'état où se trouve le siège social;

- une **liste des abréviations en ordre alphabétique** définit les abréviations courantes pour la terminologie, les titres, les organisations, les distinctions/fellowships et les diplômes mentionnés dans le Répertoire.

OFFERT EN FORMAT ÉLECTRONIQUE!

Le Répertoire est également accessible en ligne par l'entremise du Centre de documentation du Canada. Les lecteurs peuvent accéder au contenu approfondi et essentiel au réseautage de cet ouvrage dans le format qui leur convient le mieux - version imprimée, en ligne ou par abonnement.

Créez vos propres listes! Les abonnés au service en ligne peuvent générer instantanément leurs propres listes de contacts et les exporter en format feuille de calcul pour une utilisation approfondie – une solution de rechange géniale aux services dispendieux d'un commissionnaire en publipostage.

Pour obtenir plus d'information, veuillez contacter Grey House Publishing Canada
par tél.: 1 866 433-4739 ou 416 644-6479 par téléc.: 416 644-1904 | info@greyhouse.ca | www.greyhouse.ca

Governments Canada

The Most Complete and Comprehensive Guide to Locating People and Programs in Canada

Governments Canada provides regularly updated listings on federal, provincial/territorial and municipal government departments, offices and agencies across Canada. Branch and regional offices are also included, along with all associated agencies, boards, commissions and Crown corporations.

Listings include contact name, full address, telephone and fax numbers, as well as e-mail addresses. You can be sure of our commitment to superior indexing and accuracy.

ACCESS IS PROVIDED TO THE KEY DECISION-MAKERS IN ALL LEVELS OF THE GOVERNMENT INCLUDING:

- Cabinets/ Executive Councils
- Elected Officials
- Governors General/ Lieutenant Governors/ Territorial Commissioners
- Prime Ministers/ Premiers/ Government Leaders
- Auditor General/ Provincial Auditors
- Electoral Officers
- Departments/ Agencies and Administration

THESE POWERFUL AND EASY-TO-USE INDEXES WERE DESIGNED TO HELP FIND QUICK AND AUTHORITATIVE RESULTS FOR ANY RESEARCH QUERY.

- **Topical Table of Contents**—a single unified index to all jurisdictions
- **Quick Reference Topics**—a detailed list with references to over 170 topics of interest
- **Highlights of Significant Changes**—a list of highlights of major changes that have recently occurred in government.
- **Contacts**—an invaluable networking and sales tool with over 300 pages of full contact information
- **Website/ Email listings**—organized by government and department or ministry
- **Acronyms**—an alphabetical list of the most commonly used acronyms

GOVERNMENTS CANADA IS AN ESSENTIAL FINDING TOOL FOR:

Lobbyists—Locate the right person for productive conversation on key issues

Lawyers, Accountants and Consultants—Access the most current names and addresses of key contacts in every government office

Librarians—Reduce research time with this all-in-one reference tool

Embassies & Consulates—Find the right referral contact or official from across Canada

Government Employees—Peruse the easy-to-find facts and information on all levels of government

Suppliers to Government—Locate the decision-makers to target your products or services

---

GREY HOUSE PUBLISHING CANADA For more information please contact Grey House Publishing Canada
Tel.: (866)-433-4739 or (416) 644-6479 Fax: (416) 644-1904 | info@greyhouse.ca | www.greyhouse.ca

Gouvernements du Canada

Le guide le plus complet et exhaustif pour trouver des personnes et des programmes au Canada

Ce répertoire offre des fiches descriptives mises à jour régulièrement au sujet des ministères fédéraux, provinciaux et territoriaux, des bureaux et des agences du gouvernement de partout au pays. Les directions générales et les bureaux régionaux en font également partie, tout comme les organismes associés, les conseils, les commissions et les sociétés de la Couronne.

Les fiches descriptives comprennent les noms de personnes-ressources, l'adresse complète, les numéros de téléphone et de télécopieur de même que les courriels. Vous pouvez compter sur notre engagement envers la précision et l'indexation de qualité supérieure.

VOUS AVEZ AINSI ACCÈS AUX DÉCIDEURS CLÉS À TOUS LES PALIERS DE GOUVERNEMENT, NOTAMMENT :

- Conseils des ministres/conseils exécutifs
- Représentants élus
- Gouverneur général/lieutenants gouverneurs/commissaires territoriaux
- Premiers ministres/premiers ministres provinciaux/leaders du gouvernement
- Vérificateur général du Canada/vérificateurs provinciaux
- Fonctionnaires électoraux
- Ministères/organismes et administration publique

CES INDEX PUISSANTS ET FACILES D'UTILISATION SONT CONÇUS POUR VOUS AIDER À OBTENIR DES RÉSULTATS RAPIDES ET DIGNES DE FOI, PEU IMPORTE VOTRE RECHERCHE.

- **Table des matières de noms communs**—un seul index unifié pour toutes les juridictions.
- **Guide éclair des sujets**—une liste détaillée accompagnée de références sur plus de 170 sujets d'intérêt.
- **Faits saillants des changements importants**—une liste des principaux changements importants récemment apportés au sein du gouvernement.
- **Personnes-ressources**—un outil irremplaçable de réseautage et de ventes grâce à plus de 300 pages de coordonnées complètes.
- **Listes de sites Web et de courriels**—classées par gouvernement et ministère.
- **Acronymes**—une liste alphabétique des acronymes les plus utilisés.

GOUVERNEMENTS DU CANADA EST L'OUTIL ESSENTIEL DES PROFESSIONNELS POUR TROUVER:

Des groupes de revendication—trouvez les bonnes personnes pour avoir une conversation productive sur des questions-clés.

Des avocats, des comptables et des conseillers—obtenez les noms et les adresses les plus courants des personnes-ressources clés de chaque bureau gouvernemental.

Des bibliothécaires—épargnez du temps de recherche grâce à cet outil de référence complet.

Des ambassades et des consulats—trouvez la bonne personne-ressource ou le bon fonctionnaire en matière de présentation partout au Canada.

Des employés du gouvernement—consultez les faits et renseignements faciles à obtenir à tous les paliers gouvernementaux.

Des fournisseurs du gouvernement—trouvez les décideurs afin de cibler vos produits et services.

 Pour obtenir plus d'information, veuillez contacter Grey House Publishing Canada
par tél. : 1 866 433-4739 ou 416 644-6479 par téléc. : 416 644-1904 | info@greyhouse.ca | www.greyhouse.ca

Health Guide Canada
An Informative Handbook on Health Services in Canada

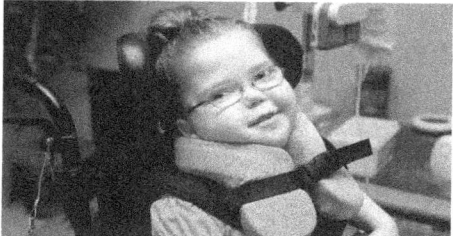  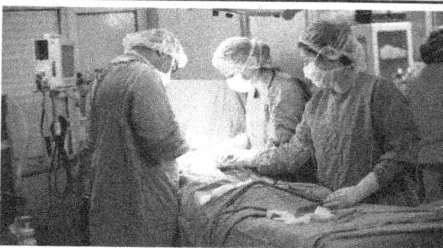

Health Guide Canada: An informative handbook on chronic and mental illnesses and health services in Canada offers a comprehensive overview of 107 chronic and mental illnesses, from Addison's to Wilson's disease. Each chapter includes an easy-to-understand medical description, plus a wide range of condition-specific support services and information resources that deal with the variety of issues concerning those with a chronic or mental illness, as well as those who support the illness community.

Health Guide Canada contains thousands of ways to deal with the many aspects of chronic or mental health disorder. It includes associations, government agencies, libraries and resource centres, educational facilities, hospitals and publications. In addition to chapters dealing with specific chronic or mental conditions, there is a chapter relevant to the health industry in general, as well as others dealing with charitable foundations, death and bereavement groups, homeopathic medicine, indigenous issues and sports for the disabled.

Specific sections include:

- Educational Material
- Section I: Chronic & Mental Illnesses
- Section II: General Resources
- Section III: Appendices
- Section IV: Statistics

Each listing will provide a description, address (including website, email address and social media links, if possible) and executives' names and titles, as well as a number of details specific to that type of organization.

In addition to patients and families, hospital and medical centre personnel can find the support they need in their work or study. *Health Guide Canada* is full of resources crucial for people with chronic illness as they transition from diagnosis to home, home to work, and work to community life.

PRINT OR ONLINE—QUICK AND EASY ACCESS TO ALL THE INFORMATION YOU NEED!

Available in softcover print or electronically via the web, *Health Guide Canada* provides instant access to the people you need and the facts you want every time. Whereas the print edition is verified and updated annually, ongoing changes are added to the web version on a regular basis. The web version allows you to narrow your search by using index fields such as name or type of organization, subject, location, contact name or title and postal code.

HEALTH GUIDE CANADA HELPS YOU FIND WHAT YOU NEED WITH THESE VALUABLE SOURCING TOOLS!

Entry Name Index—An alphabetical list of all entries, providing a quick and easy way to access any listing in this edition.

Tabs—Main sections are tabbed for easy look-up. Headers on each page make it easy to locate the data you need.

Create your own contact lists! Online subscribers have the option to instantly generate their own contact lists and export them into spreadsheets for further use—a great alternative to high cost list broker services.

GREY HOUSE PUBLISHING CANADA

For more information please contact Grey House Publishing Canada
Tel.: (866)-433-4739 or (416) 644-6479 Fax: (416) 644-1904 | info@greyhouse.ca | www.greyhouse.ca

Guide canadien de la santé
Un manuel informatif au sujet des services en santé au Canada

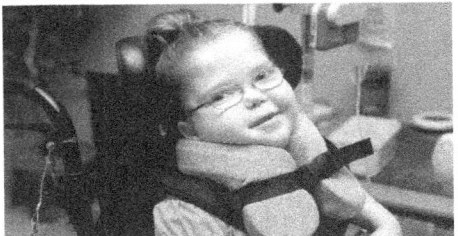  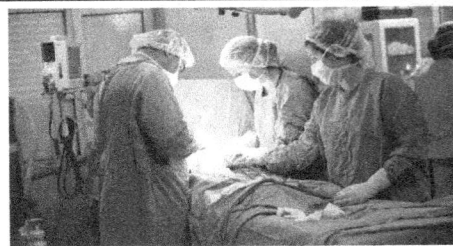

Le *Guide canadien de la santé : un manuel informatif au sujet des maladies chroniques et mentales de même que des services en santé au Canada* donne un aperçu exhaustif de 107 maladies chroniques et mentales, de la maladie d'Addison à celle de Wilson. Chaque chapitre comprend une description médicale facile à comprendre, une vaste gamme de services de soutien particuliers à l'état et des ressources documentaires qui portent sur diverses questions relatives aux personnes qui sont aux prises avec une maladie chronique ou mentale et à ceux qui soutiennent la communauté liée à cette maladie.

Le *Guide canadien de la santé* contient des milliers de moyens pour composer avec divers aspects d'une maladie chronique ou d'un problème de santé mentale. Il comprend des associations, des organismes gouvernementaux, des bibliothèques et des centres de documentation, des services d'éducation, des hôpitaux et des publications. En plus des chapitres qui portent sur des états chroniques ou mentaux, un chapitre traite de l'industrie de la santé en général; d'autres abordent les fondations qui réalisent des rêves, les groupes de soutien axés sur le décès et le deuil, la médecine homéopathique, les questions autochtones et les sports pour les personnes handicapées. Les sections incluent

- Matériel didactique
- Section I : Les maladies chroniques ou mentales
- Section II : Les ressources génériques
- Section III : Les annexes
- Section IV : Les statistiques

Chaque entrée comprend une description, une adresse (y compris le site Web, le courriel et les liens des médias sociaux, lorsque possible), les noms et titres des directeurs de même que plusieurs détails particuliers à ce type d'organisme.

Les membres du personnel des hôpitaux et des centres médicaux peuvent trouver, au même titre que parents et familles, le soutien dont ils ont besoin dans le cadre de leur travail ou de leurs études. Le *Guide canadien de la santé* est rempli de ressources capitales pour les personnes qui souffrent d'une maladie chronique alors qu'elles passent du diagnostic au retour à la maison, de la maison au travail et du travail à la vie au sein de la communauté.

OFFERT EN FORMAT PAPIER OU EN LIGNE—UN ACCÈS RAPIDE ET FACILE À TOUS LES RENSEIGNEMENTS DONT VOUS AVEZ BESOIN!

Offert sous couverture souple ou en format électronique grâce au web, le *Guide canadien de la santé* donne invariablement un accès instantané aux personnes et aux faits dont vous avez besoin. Si la version imprimée est vérifiée et mise à jour annuellement, des changements continus sont apportés mensuellement à la base de données en ligne. Servez-vous de la version en ligne afin de circonscrire vos recherches grâce à des champs spéciaux de l'index comme le nom de l'organisation ou son type, le sujet, l'emplacement, le nom de la personne-ressource ou son titre et le code postal.

LE GUIDE CANADIEN DE LA SANTÉ VOUS AIDERA À TROUVER CE DONT VOUS AVEZ BESOIN GRÂCE À CES OUTILS DE REPÉRAGE PRÉCIEUX!

Répertoire nominatif—une list alphabétique offrant un moyen rapide et facile d'accéder à toute liste de cette edition.

Onglets—les sections principals possèdent un onglet pour une consultation facile. Les notes en tête de chaque page vous aident à trouver les données voulues.

Créez vos propres listes! Les abonnés au service en ligne peuvent générer instantanément leurs propres listes de contacts et les exporter en format feuille de calcul pour une utilisation approfondie – une solution de rechange géniale aux services dispendieux d'un commissionnaire en publipostage.

 Pour obtenir plus d'information, veuillez contacter Grey House Publishing Canada par tél. : 1 866 433-4739 ou 416 644-6479 par téléc. : 416 644-1904 | info@greyhouse.ca | www.greyhouse.ca

Canadian Environmental Resource Guide
The Only Complete Guide to the Business of Environmental Management

The *Canadian Environmental Resource Guide* provides data on every aspect of the environment industry in unprecedented detail. It's one-stop searching for details on government offices and programs, information sources, product and service firms and trade fairs that pertain to the business of environmental management. All information is fully indexed and cross-referenced for easy use. The directory features current information and key contacts in Canada's environmental industry including:

ENVIRONMENTAL UP-DATE

- Information on prominent environmentalists, environmental abbreviations and a summary of recent environmental events
- Updated articles, rankings, statistics and charts on all aspects of the environmental industry
- Trade shows, conferences and seminars for the current year and beyond

ENVIRONMENTAL INDUSTRY RESOURCES

- Comprehensive listings for companies and firms producing and selling products and services in the environmental sector, including markets served, working language and percentage of revenue sources: public and private
- Environmental law firms, with lawyers' areas of speciality
- Detailed indexes by subject, geography and ISO

ENVIRONMENTAL GOVERNMENT LISTINGS

- Information on important intergovernmental offices and councils, and listings of environmental trade representatives abroad
- In-depth listings of environmental information at the municipal level, including population and number of households, water and waste treatment, landfill statistics and special by-laws and bans, as well as key environmental contacts for each municipality

Available in softcover print or electronically via the web, the *Canadian Environmental Resource Guide* provides instant access to the people you need and the facts you want every time. The *Canadian Environmental Resource Guide* is verified and updated annually. Ongoing changes are added to the web version on a regular basis.

CANADIAN ENVIRONMENTAL RESOURCE GUIDE OFFERS EVEN MORE CONTENT ONLINE!

Environmental Information Resources—Extensive listings of special libraries and thousands of environmental associations, with information on membership, environmental activities, key contacts and more.

Government Listings—Every federal and provincial department and agency influencing environmental initiatives and purchasing policies.

The web version allows you to narrow your search by using index fields such as name or type of organization, subject, location, contact name or title and postal code.

Create your own contact lists! Online subscribers have the option to instantly generate their own contact lists and export them into spreadsheets for further use—a great alternative to high cost list broker services.

GREY HOUSE PUBLISHING CANADA For more information please contact Grey House Publishing Canada
Tel.: (866) 433-4739 or (416) 644-6479 Fax: (416) 644-1904 | info@greyhouse.ca | www.greyhouse.ca

Guide des ressources environnementales canadiennes
Le seul guide complet dédié à la gestion de l'environnement

Le *Guide des ressources environnementales canadiennes* offre de l'information relative à tous les aspects de l'industrie de l'environnement dans les moindres détails. Il permet d'effectuer une recherche de données complètes sur les bureaux et programmes gouvernementaux, les sources de renseignements, les entreprises de produits et de services et les foires commerciales qui portent sur les activités de la gestion de l'environnement. Toute l'information est entièrement indexée et effectue un double renvoi pour une consultation facile. Le répertoire présente des renseignements actualisés et les personnes-ressources clés de l'industrie de l'environnement au Canada, y compris les suivants.

MISE À JOUR SUR L'INDUSTRIE DE L'ENVIRONNEMENT

- De l'information sur d'éminents environnementalistes, les abréviations utilisées dans le domaine de l'environnement et un résumé des événements environnementaux récents
- Des articles, des classements, des statistiques et des graphiques mis à jour sur tous les aspects de l'industrie verte
- Les salons professionnels, conférences et séminaires qui ont lieu cette année et ceux qui sont prévus

RESSOURCES DE L'INDUSTRIE ENVIRONNEMENTALE

- Des listes exhaustives des entreprises et des cabinets qui fabriquent ou offrent des produits et des services dans le domaine de l'environnement, y compris les marchés desservis, la langue de travail et la ventilation des sources de revenus – publics et privés
- Une liste complète des cabinets spécialisés en droit environnemental
- Des index selon le sujet, la géographie et la certification ISO

LISTES GOUVERNEMENTALES RELATIVES À L'ENVIRONNEMENT

- De l'information sur les bureaux et conseils intergouvernementaux importants ainsi que des listes des représentants de l'éco-commerce à l'extérieur du pays
- Des listes approfondies portant sur de l'information environnementale au palier municipal, notamment la population et le nombre de ménages, le traitement de l'eau et des déchets, des statistiques sur les décharges, des règlements et des interdictions spéciaux ainsi que des personnes-ressources clés en environnement pour chaque municipalité

Offert sous couverture rigide ou en format électronique grâce au Web, le *Guide des ressources environnementales canadiennes* offre invariablement un accès instantané aux représentants du gouvernement et aux faits qui font l'objet de vos recherches. Il est vérifié et mis à jour annuellement. La version en ligne est mise à jour mensuellement.

LE GUIDE DES RESSOURCES ENVIRONNEMENTALES CANADIENNES DONNE ACCÈS À PLUS DE CONTENU EN LIGNE!

Des ressources informationnelles sur l'environnement—Des bibliothèques et des centres de resources spécialisés, et des milliers d'associations environnementales, avec de l'information sur l'adhésion, les activités environnementales, les personnes-ressources principales et plus encore.

Listes gourvenementales—Toutes les agences et tous les services gouvernementaux fédéraux et provinciaux qui exercent une influence sur les initiatives en matière d'environnement et de politiques d'achat.

Servez-vous de la version en ligne afin de circonscrire vos recherches grâce à des champs spéciaux de l'index comme le nom de l'organisation ou son type, le sujet, l'emplacement, le nom de la personne-ressource ou son titre et le code postal.

Créez vos propres listes! Les abonnés au service en ligne peuvent générer instantanément leurs propres listes de contacts et les exporter en format feuille de calcul pour une utilisation approfondie—une solution de rechange géniale aux services dispendieux d'un commissionnaire en publipostage.

GREY HOUSE PUBLISHING CANADA Pour obtenir plus d'information, veuillez contacter Grey House Publishing Canada
par tél. : 1 866 433-4739 ou 416 644-6479 par téléc. : 416 644-1904 | info@greyhouse.ca | www.greyhouse.ca

Libraries Canada

Gain Access to Complete and Detailed Information on Canadian Libraries

Libraries Canada brings together the most current information from across the entire Canadian library sector, including libraries and branch libraries, educational libraries, regional systems, resource centres, archives, related periodicals, library schools and programs, provincial and governmental agencies and associations.

As the nation's leading library directory for over 30 years, *Libraries Canada* gives you access to almost 10,000 names and addresses of contacts in these institutions. Also included are valuable details such as library symbol, number of staff, operating systems, library type and acquisitions budget, hours of operation—all thoroughly indexed and easy to find.

INSTANT ACCESS TO CANADIAN LIBRARY SECTOR INFORMATION

Developed for publishers, advocacy groups, computer hardware suppliers, internet service providers and other diverse groups which provide products and services to the library community; associations that need to maintain a current list of library resources in Canada; and research departments, students and government agencies which require information about the types of services and programs available at various research institutions, *Libraries Canada* will help you find the information you need—quickly and easily.

EXPERT SEARCH OPTIONS AVAILABLE WITH ONLINE VERSION...

Available in print and online, *Libraries Canada* delivers easily accessible, quality information that has been verified and organized for easy retrieval. Five easy-to-use indexes assist you in navigating the print edition while the online version utilizes multiple index fields that help you get results.

Available on Grey House Publishing Canada's CIRC interface, you can choose between Keyword and Advanced search to pinpoint information. Designed for both novice and advanced researchers, you can conduct simple text searches as well as powerful Boolean searches, plus you can narrow your search by using index fields such as name or type of institution, headquarters, location, area code, contact name or title and postal code. Save your searches to build on at a later date or use the mark record function to view, print, e-mail or export your selected records.

Online subscribers have the option to instantly generate their own contact lists and export them into spreadsheets for further use. A great alternative to high cost list broker services.

LIBRARIES CANADA GIVES YOU ALL THE ESSENTIALS FOR EACH INSTITUTION:

Name, address, contact information, key personnel, number of staff

Collection information, type of library, acquisitions budget, subject area, special collection

User services, number of branches, hours of operation, ILL information, photocopy and microform facilities, for-fee research, Internet access

Systems information, details on electronic access, operating and online systems, Internet and e-mail software, Internet connectivity, access to electronic resources

Additional information including associations, publications and regional systems

With almost 60% of the data changing annually it has never been more important to have the latest version of *Libraries Canada*.

GREY HOUSE PUBLISHING CANADA
For more information please contact Grey House Publishing Canada
Tel.: (866) 433-4739 or (416) 644-6479 Fax: (416) 644-1904 | info@greyhouse.ca | www.greyhouse.ca

Bibliothèques Canada

Accédez aux renseignements complets et détaillés au sujet des bibliothèques canadiennes

Bibliothèques Canada combine les renseignements les plus à jour provenant du secteur des bibliothèques de partout au Canada, y compris les bibliothèques et leurs succursales, les bibliothèques éducatives, les systèmes régionaux, les centres de ressources, les archives, les périodiques pertinents, les écoles de bibliothéconomie et leurs programmes, les organismes provinciaux et gouvernementaux ainsi que les associations.

Principal répertoire des bibliothèques depuis plus de 30 ans, *Bibliothèques Canada* vous donne accès à près de 10 000 noms et adresses de personnes-ressources pour ces établissements. Il comprend également des détails précieux comme le symbole d'identification de bibliothèque, le nombre de membres du personnel, les systèmes d'exploitation, le type de bibliothèque et le budget attribué aux acquisitions, les heures d'ouverture – autant d'information minutieusement indexée et facile à trouver.

Offert en version imprimée et en ligne, *Bibliothèques Canada* offre des renseignements de qualité, facile d'accès, qui ont été vérifiés et organisés afin de les obtenir facilement. Cinq index conviviaux vous aident dans la navigation du numéro imprimé tandis que la version en ligne vous permet de saisir plusieurs champs d'index pour vous aider à découvrir l'information voulue.

ACCÈS INSTANTANÉ AUX RENSEIGNEMENTS DU DOMAINE DES BIBLIOTHÈQUES CANADIENNES

Conçu pour les éditeurs, les groupes de revendication, les fournisseurs de matériel informatique, les fournisseurs de services Internet et autres groupes qui offrent produits et services aux bibliothèques; les associations qui ont besoin de conserver une liste à jour des ressources bibliothécaires au Canada; les services de recherche, les organismes étudiants et gouvernementaux qui ont besoin d'information au sujet des types de services et de programmes offerts par divers établissements de recherche, *Bibliothèques Canada* vous aide à trouver l'information nécessaire – rapidement et simplement.

LA VERSION EN LIGNE COMPREND DES OPTIONS DE RECHERCHE POUSSÉES…

À partir de l'interface du Centre de documentation du Canada de Grey House Publishing Canada, vous pouvez choisir entre la recherche poussée et rapide pour cibler votre information. Vous pouvez effectuer des recherches par texte simple, conçues à la fois pour les chercheurs débutants et chevronnés, ainsi que des recherches booléennes puissantes. Vous pouvez également restreindre votre recherche à l'aide des champs d'index, comme le nom ou le type d'établissement, le siège social, l'emplacement, l'indicatif régional, le nom de la personne-ressource ou son titre et le code postal. Enregistrez vos recherches pour vous en servir plus tard ou utilisez la fonction de marquage pour afficher, imprimer, envoyer par courriel ou exporter les dossiers sélectionnés.

Les abonnés au service en ligne peuvent générer instantanément leurs propres listes de contacts et les exporter en format feuille de calcul pour une utilisation approfondie – une solution de rechange géniale aux services dispendieux d'un commissionnaire en publipostage.

BIBLIOTHÈQUES CANADA VOUS DONNE TOUS LES RENSEIGNEMENTS ESSENTIELS RELATIFS À CHAQUE ÉTABLISSEMENT :

Leurs nom et adresse, les coordonnées de la personne-ressource, les membres clés du personnel, le nombre de membres du personnel

L'information relative aux collections, le type de bibliothèque, le budget attribué aux acquisitions, le domaine, les collections particulières

Les services aux utilisateurs, le nombre de succursales, les heures d'ouverture, les renseignements relatifs au PEB, les services de photocopie et de microforme, la recherche rémunérée, l'accès à Internet

L'information relative aux systèmes, des détails sur l'accès électronique, les systèmes d'exploitation et ceux en ligne, Internet et le logiciel de messagerie électronique, la connectivité à Internet, l'accès aux ressources électroniques

L'information supplémentaire, y compris les associations, les publications et les systèmes régionaux

Alors que près de 60 % des données sont modifiées annuellement, il est plus important que jamais de posséder la plus récente version de *Bibliothèques Canada*.

 Pour obtenir plus d'information, veuillez contacter Grey House Publishing Canada
par tél. : 1 866 433-4739 ou 416 644-6479 par téléc. : 416 644-1904 | info@greyhouse.ca | www.greyhouse.ca

Financial Services Canada

Unparalleled Coverage of the Canadian Financial Service Industry

With corporate listings for over 30,000 organizations and hard-to-find business information, *Financial Services Canada* is the most up-to-date source for names and contact numbers of industry professionals, senior executives, portfolio managers, financial advisors, agency bureaucrats and elected representatives.

Financial Services Canada is the definitive resource for detailed listings—providing valuable contact information including: name, title, organization, profile, associated companies, telephone and fax numbers, e-mail and website addresses. Use our online database and refine your search by stock symbol, revenue, year founded, assets, ownership type or number of employees.

POWERFUL INDEXES HELP YOU LOCATE THE CRUCIAL FINANCIAL INFORMATION YOU NEED.

Organized with the user in mind, *Financial Services Canada* contains categorized listings and 4 easy-to-use indexes:

Alphabetic—financial organizations listed in alphabetical sequence by company name

Geographic—financial institutions broken down by town or city

Executive Name—all officers, directors and senior personnel in alphabetical order by surname

Insurance class—lists all companies by insurance type

Reduce the time you spend compiling lists, researching company information and searching for e-mail addresses. Whether you are interested in contacting a finance lawyer regarding international and domestic joint ventures, need to generate a list of foreign banks in Canada or want to contact the Toronto Stock Exchange—*Financial Services Canada* gives you the power to find all the data you need.

PRINT OR ONLINE—QUICK AND EASY ACCESS TO ALL THE INFORMATION YOU NEED!

Available in softcover print or electronically via the web, *Financial Services Canada* provides instant access to the people you need and the facts you want every time.

Financial Services Canada print edition is verified and updated annually. Ongoing changes are added to the web version on a regular basis. The web version allows you to narrow your search by using index fields such as name or type of organization, subject, location, contact name or title and postal code.

Create your own contact lists! Online subscribers have the option to instantly generate their own contact lists and export them into spreadsheets for further use—a great alternative to high cost list broker services.

ACCESS TO CURRENT LISTINGS FOR...

Banks and Depository Institutions
- Domestic and savings banks
- Foreign banks and branches
- Foreign bank representative offices
- Trust companies
- Credit unions

Non-Depository Institutions
- Bond rating companies
- Collection agencies
- Credit card companies
- Financing and loan companies
- Trustees in bankruptcy

Investment Management Firms, including securities and commodities
- Financial planning / investment management companies
- Investment dealers
- Investment fund companies
- Pension/money management companies
- Stock exchanges
- Holding companies

Insurance Companies, including federal and provincial
- Reinsurance companies
- Fraternal benefit societies
- Mutual benefit companies
- Reciprocal exchanges

Accounting and Law
- Accountants
- Actuary consulting firms
- Law firms (specializing in finance)

Major Canadian Companies
- Key financial contacts for public, private and Crown corporations

Associations
- Associations and institutes serving the financial services sector

Financial Technology & Services
- Companies involved in financial software and other technical areas.

Access even more content online:
Government and Publications
- Federal, provincial and territorial contacts
- Leading publications serving the financial services industry

---

GREY HOUSE PUBLISHING CANADA

For more information please contact Grey House Publishing Canada
Tel.: (866)-433-4739 or (416) 644-6479 Fax: (416) 644-1904 | info@greyhouse.ca | www.greyhouse.ca

Services financiers au Canada

Une couverture sans pareille de l'industrie des services financiers canadiens

Grâce à plus de 30 000 organisations et renseignements commerciaux rares, *Services financiers du Canada* est la source la plus à jour de noms et de coordonnées de professionnels, de membres de la haute direction, de gestionnaires de portefeuille, de conseillers financiers, de fonctionnaires et de représentants élus de l'industrie.

Services financiers du Canada intègre les plus récentes modifications à l'industrie afin de vous offrir les détails les plus à jour au sujet de chaque entreprise, notamment le nom, le titre, l'organisation, les numéros de téléphone et de télécopieur, le courriel et l'adresse du site Web. Servez-vous de la base de données en ligne et raffinez votre recherche selon le symbole, le revenu, l'année de création, les immobilisations, le type de propriété ou le nombre d'employés.

DES INDEX PUISSANTS VOUS AIDENT À TROUVER LES RENSEIGNEMENTS FINANCIERS ESSENTIELS DONT VOUS AVEZ BESOIN.

C'est avec l'utilisateur en tête que Services financiers au Canada a été conçu; il contient des listes catégorisées et quatre index faciles d'utilisation :

Alphabétique—les organisations financières apparaissent en ordre alphabétique, selon le nom de l'entreprise.

Géographique—les institutions financières sont détaillées par ville.

Nom de directeur—tous les agents, directeurs et cadres supérieurs sont classés en ordre alphabétique, selon leur nom de famille.

Classe d'assurance—toutes les entreprises selon leur type d'assurance.

Passez moins de temps à préparer des listes, à faire des recherches ou à chercher des contacts et des courriels. Que vous soyez intéressé à contacter un avocat en droit des affaires au sujet de projets conjoints internationaux et nationaux, que vous ayez besoin de générer une liste des banques étrangères au Canada ou que vous souhaitiez communiquer avec la Bourse de Toronto, *Services financiers au Canada* vous permet de trouver toutes les données dont vous avez besoin.

OFFERT EN FORMAT PAPIER OU EN LIGNE – UN ACCÈS RAPIDE ET FACILE À TOUS LES RENSEIGNEMENTS DONT VOUS AVEZ BESOIN!

Offert sous couverture rigide ou en format électronique grâce au Web, Services financiers du Canada donne invariablement un accès instantané aux personnes et aux faits dont vous avez besoin. Si la version imprimée est vérifiée et mise à jour annuellement, des changements continus sont apportés mensuellement à la base de données en ligne. Servez-vous de la version en ligne afin de circonscrire vos recherches grâce à des champs spéciaux de l'index comme le nom de l'organisation ou son type, le sujet, l'emplacement, le nom de la personne-ressource ou son titre et le code postal.

Créez vos propres listes! Les abonnés au service en ligne peuvent générer instantanément leurs propres listes de contacts et les exporter en format feuille de calcul pour une utilisation approfondie – une solution de rechange géniale aux services dispendieux d'un commissionnaire en publipostage.

ACCÉDEZ AUX LISTES ACTUELLES...

Banques et institutions de dépôt
- Banques nationales et d'épargne
- Banques étrangères et leurs succursales
- Bureaux des représentants de banques étrangères
- Sociétés de fiducie
- Coopératives d'épargne et de crédit

Établissements financiers
- Entreprises de notation des obligations
- Agences de placement
- Compagnies de carte de crédit
- Sociétés de financement et de prêt
- Syndics de faillite

Sociétés de gestion de placements, y compris les valeurs et marchandises
- Entreprises de planification financière et de gestion des investissements
- Maisons de courtage de valeurs
- Courtiers en épargne collective
- Entreprises de gestion de la pension/de trésorerie
- Bourses
- Sociétés de portefeuille

Compagnies d'assurance, fédérales et provinciales
- Compagnies de réassurance
- Sociétés fraternelles
- Sociétés de secours mutuel
- Échanges selon la formule de réciprocité

Comptabilité et droit
- Comptables
- Cabinets d'actuaires-conseils
- Cabinets d'avocats (spécialisés en finance)

Principales entreprises canadiennes
- Principaux contacts financiers pour les sociétés de capitaux publiques, privées et de la Couronne

Les associations et Technologie et services financiers

Accès à plus de contenu en ligne: Gouvernement et Publications
- Personnes-ressources aux paliers fédéral, provinciaux et territoriaux
- Principales publications qui desservent l'industrie des services financiers

---

 Pour obtenir plus d'information, veuillez contacter Grey House Publishing Canada
par tél. : 1 866 433-4739 ou 416 644-6479 par téléc. : 416 644-1904 | info@greyhouse.ca | www.greyhouse.ca

Major Canadian Cities
Compared & Ranked

Major Canadian Cities provides the user with numerous ways to rank and compare 50 major cities across Canada. All statistical information is at your fingertips; you can access details about the cities, each with a population of 100,000 or more. On Canada's Information Resource Centre (CIRC), you can instantly rank cities according to your preferences and make your own analytical tables with the data provided. There are hundreds of questions that these ranking tables will answer: Which cities have the youngest population? Where is the economic growth the strongest? Which cities have the best labour statistics?

A city profile for each location offers additional insights into the city to provide a sense of the location, its history, its recreational and cultural activities. Following the profile are rankings showing its uniqueness in the spectrum of cities across Canada: interesting notes about the city and how it ranks amongst the top 50 in different ways, such as most liveable, wealthiest and coldest! These reports are available only from Grey House Publishing Canada and only with your subscription to this exciting new product!

MAJOR CANADIAN CITIES SHOWS YOU THESE STATISTICAL TABLES:

Demographics
- Population Growth
- Age Characteristics
- Male/Female Ratio
- Marital Status

Housing
- Household Type & Size
- Housing Age & Value

Labour
- Labour Force
- Occupation
- Industry
- Place of Work

Ethnicity, Immigration & Language
- Mother Tongue
- Knowledge of Official Languages
- Language Spoken at Home
- Minority Populations
- Education
- Education Attainment

Income
- Median Income
- Median Income After Taxes
- Median Income by Family Type
- Median Income After Taxes by Family Type

Transportation
- Mode of Transportation to Work

AVAILABLE ONLINE!

Major Canadian Cities is available electronically via the Web, providing instant access to the facts you want about each city, as well as some interesting points showing how the city scores compared with others.

Use the online version to search statistics and create your own tables, or view pre-prepared tables in pdf form. This can help with research for academic work, infrastructure development or pure interest, with all the data you need in one, modifiable source.

GREY HOUSE PUBLISHING CANADA For more information please contact Grey House Publishing Canada
Tel.: (866) 433-4739 or (416) 644-6479 Fax: (416) 644-1904 | info@greyhouse.ca | www.greyhouse.ca

Principales villes canadiennes
Comparaison et classement

Principales villes canadiennes offre à l'utilisateur de nombreuses manières de classer et de comparer 50 villes principales du Canada. Toute l'information statistique se trouve au bout de vos doigts : vous pouvez obtenir des détails sur les villes, chacune comptant 100 000 habitants ou plus. Dans le Centre de documentation du Canada (CDC), vous pouvez classer instantanément les villes selon vos préférences et créer vos propres tableaux analytiques à l'aide des données fournies. Ces tableaux de classement répondent à des centaines de questions, notamment : quelles villes comptent la population la plus jeune? À quel endroit la croissance économique est-elle la plus forte? Quelles villes présentent les meilleures statistiques en matière de main-d'œuvre?

Un profil de ville offre des renseignements supplémentaires afin de vous donner une idée de son emplacement, de son histoire, de ses activités récréatives et culturelles. Suivent des classements qui démontrent l'unicité de la ville dans un spectre de villes qui se trouvent partout au Canada. Vous trouverez également des remarques intéressantes au sujet de la ville et de son classement parmi les 50 principales villes, par exemple selon celle où il fait le mieux vivre, où se trouvent les plus riches et où il fait le plus froid. Ces rapports sont disponibles uniquement auprès de Grey House Publishing Canada et dans le cadre de votre abonnement à ce nouveau produit emballant!

PRINCIPALES VILLES CANADIENNES COMPREND CES TABLEAUX STATISTIQUES :

Données démographiques
- Croissance de la population
- Caractéristiques relatives à l'âge
- Ratio homme/femme
- État matrimonial

Logement
- Type et taille du logement
- Âge et valeur du logement

Main-d'œuvre
- Population active
- Emploi
- Industrie
- Lieu de travail

Ethnicité, immigration et langue
- Langue maternelle
- Connaissance des langues officielles
- Langue parlée à la maison
- Populations minoritaires
- Formation
- Niveau scolaire

Revenu
- Revenu médian
- Revenu médian après impôts
- Revenu médian par type de famille
- Revenu médian après impôts par type de famille

Transport
- Moyen de transport vers le travail

OFFERT EN VERSION ÉLECTRONIQUE!

Principales villes canadiennes est offert en version électronique sur le Web. Vous accédez donc instantanément aux faits dont vous avez besoin pour chaque ville, de même que des éléments intéressants qui illustrent la comparaison entre les villes.

Servez-vous de la version en ligne pour effectuer des recherches parmi les statistiques et créer vos propres tableaux, ou consulter les tableaux déjà prêts en format PDF. Elle peut vous aider dans le cadre de recherches pour des travaux universitaires, pour le développement d'infrastructures ou consultez-la par simple curiosité – autant de données réunies en une source modifiable.

 Pour obtenir plus d'information, veuillez contacter Grey House Publishing Canada
par tél. : 1 866 433-4739 ou 416 644-6479 par téléc. : 416 644-1904 | info@greyhouse.ca | www.greyhouse.ca

WHEN SECURITIES AREN'T SOLID,
MAKE SURE YOUR INFORMATION IS

As the golden standard of publications for the Canadian financial services industry, the FP Bond books continue to be an indispensable source of must have information relating to companies operating in Canadian Capital Markets.

For all the information you need on Canadian Corporate & Government Debt Issues, Preferred Shares and Securities, Trust Units and Warrants – **ORDER YOUR COPY TODAY!**

ALL THE IN-DEPTH INFORMATION THAT YOU NEED – ALL IN ONE PLACE

FP Equities -
Preferreds
& Derivatives

Only $150.00*

FP Bonds -
Corporate

Only $180.00*

FP Bonds -
Government

Only $150.00*

Order all three books and SAVE over $70

*Plus shipping and applicable taxes

3 Easy Ways to Order

Phone: 1.866.433.4739 • Fax: 416.644.1904 • Email: info@greyhouse.ca

To Order: Toll Free Tel 1.866.433.4739 • Fax 416.644.1904

Financial Post Fixed Income Books are owned by Financial Post Data, a division of Postmedia Network Inc., and are exclusively printed and distributed by Grey House Publishing Canada.

THE FACTS FOUND FAST!

Tap into FP Corporate Surveys and access all the facts and figures you need to make better informed decisions.

Covering over 6,300 publicly traded Canadian companies, FP Survey - Industrials and FP Survey - Mines & Energy are loaded with financial and operational information. Discover companies' financial results, capital and debt structure, key corporate developments, major shareholders, directors and executive officers, subsidiaries and more!

The ideal complement, FP Survey - Predecessor & Defunct, provides a comprehensive record of changes to Canadian public corporations dating back over 80 years.

FP Corporate Surveys are completely unbiased, current and credible - make your investment decisions based on the facts.

ALL THE IN-DEPTH INFORMATION THAT YOU NEED – ALL IN ONE PLACE

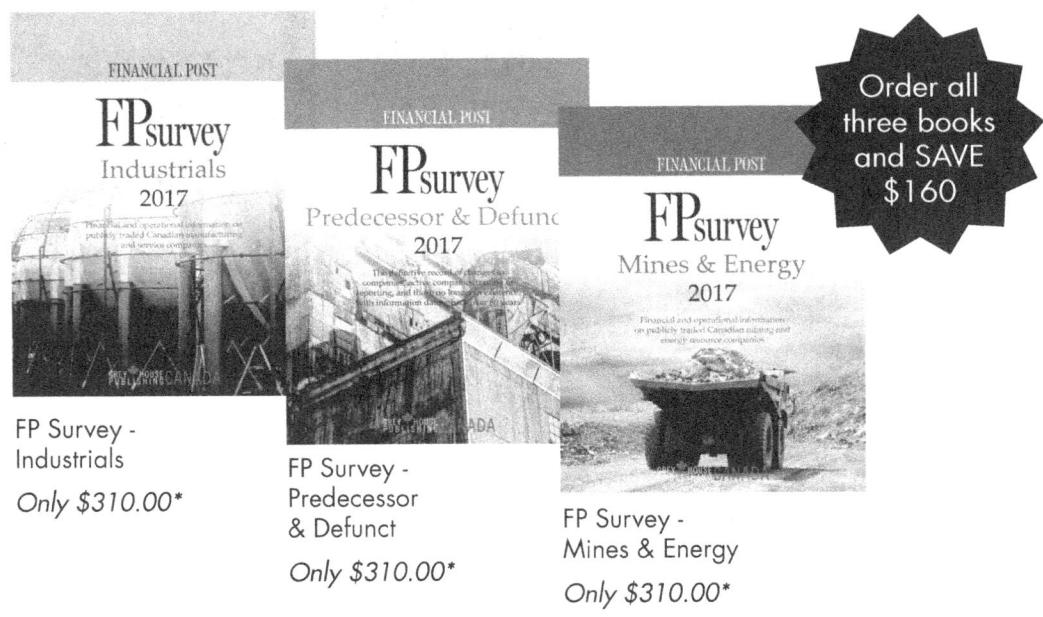

FP Survey - Industrials
Only $310.00*

FP Survey - Predecessor & Defunct
Only $310.00*

FP Survey - Mines & Energy
Only $310.00*

Order all three books and SAVE $160

*Plus shipping and applicable taxes

3 Easy Ways to Order

Phone: 1.866.433.4739 • Fax: 416.644.1904 • Email: info@greyhouse.ca

To Order: Toll Free Tel 1.866.433.4739 • Fax 416.644.1904

Financial Post Fixed Income Books are owned by Financial Post Data, a division of Postmedia Network Inc., and are exclusively printed and distributed by Grey House Publishing Canada.

ASSOCIATIONS CANADA

Grey House Publishing Canada
555 Richmond Street West, Suite 512
Toronto, Ontario M5V 3B1
Fax completed forms to: (416) 644-1904

FREE LISTING & UPDATE
Be sure your organization appears in Associations Canada

Associations Canada is Canada's complete directory to Canadian organizations and international groups including industry, commercial and professional associations, registered charities, special interest and common interest organizations.

This listing is **FREE**. To ensure a complete and accurate listing in the upcoming edition, simply complete this questionnaire and return it by **fax or by mail**. Include any relevant information such as phone, fax or toll free numbers, website and email addresses, and official translations (if applicable).

If you have any questions, please call Stuart Paterson at (416) 644-6478 or 1-866-433-4739, ext. 302. You can return this form either by **fax**: (416) 644-1904, by **mail** to the address above, or **email** to info@greyhouse.ca

Is your organization already listed in this publication? Yes, we're updating existing information_____ No, we're new_____
Completed by: _____ Phone: _____ Email: _____

ORGANIZATION
Name: _____

Street Address: _____

Phone: _____

Toll Free: _____

Fax: _____

Email: _____

Website: _____

Translated Name: _____

Also known as: _____

Acronym: _____

Founded: _____

CHIEF OFFICERS/STAFF
President _____

Secretary _____

Treasurer _____

Vice-President _____

Other Staff: please see following page

Number of staff: _____; Volunteers: _____

OTHER STAFF: (attach list if necessary)
Name: _____ Title: _____

Telephone: _____ Email: _____

Name: _____ Title: _____

Telephone: _____ Email: _____

Name: _____ Title: _____

Telephone: _____ Email: _____

MEMBERSHIP
Member of: _____

Number of members: _____

Membership profile: _____

Membership fee: _____

Membership in/ Affiliations with other organizations: _____

ADDITIONAL INFORMATION

_T FOCUS:

i. _____ ii. _____

iii. _____ iv. _____

SCOPE OF ACTIVITY:
International
National
Provincial/Territorial
Local
Regional

ORGANIZATION TYPE:
Professional
Trade/Industry/Business
Other (special/common interest)

Please indicate if you are a: Licensing Body   Registered Charity

MISSION STATEMENT/GOALS/MANDATE:
_____
_____
_____
_____

ANNUAL OPERATING BUDGET:

Less than $50,000	$50,000 - $99,999	$100,000 - $249,999
$250,000 - $499,999	$500,000 - $1,499,999	$1,500,000 - $2,999,999
$3,000,000 - $4,999,999	Over $5,000,000	

DO YOU:
Rent your Mailing Lists?   Yes   No
Have a Speakers Service?   Yes   No
Have an Internship Program?   Yes   No

SERIAL PUBLICATIONS:
Type: (eg. newsletter, journal, magazine) _____ Title: _____

Frequency: _____ Price: _____ Editor: _____

ISBN: _____ ISSN: _____ Accept advertising?   Yes   No

Description of contents:
_____
_____
_____

LIBRARY/RESOURCE CENTRE:
Does your organization have a library, resource centre or documentation centre?   Yes   No

Library/Resource/Documentation Centre Name: _____
Open to the Public: Yes   No   By Appointment Only

Library Contact Person: _____ Title: _____

Telephone: _____ Fax: _____ Email: _____

CONFERENCE/CONVENTIONS:
Please submit any literature pertaining to future conferences as it becomes available.

2019   2020   2021   2022

Name of Meeting: _____

Location: (City/Province/Country) _____

Facility: _____

Date: _____

Number of Attendees: _____

OTHER:
Awards: Please attach a list

Awareness Events (Please include the date): _____

Activities: _____

Committees: _____

Sources of funding: _____

WE THANK YOU FOR TAKING THE TIME TO PROVIDE YOUR VALUABLE INFORMATION.

By submitting this form you are granting Grey House Publishing express consent to reproduce this information in our publications, in electronic and/or print formats, where it is relevant and is intended to be used for research and/or commercial purposes. Additional editorial research may be undertaken to enhance the listing.